Profiles
of
New York

2006

Profiles of New York

A UNIVERSAL REFERENCE BOOK

Grey House Publishing

PUBLISHER: Leslie Mackenzie
EDITOR: David Garoogian
EDITORIAL DIRECTOR: Laura Mars-Proietti
RESEARCH ASSISTANTS: Stephanie Capozzi, Karynn Ketiinq, Michael Marturana

MARKETING DIRECTOR: Jessica Moody

Grey House Publishing, Inc.
185 Millerton Road
Millerton, NY 12546
518.789.8700
FAX 518.789.0545
www.greyhouse.com
e-mail: books @greyhouse.com

While every effort has been made to ensure the reliability of the information presented in this publication, Grey House Publishing neither guarantees the accuracy of the data contained herein nor assumes any responsibility for errors, omissions or discrepancies. Grey House accepts no payment for listing; inclusion in the publication of any organization, agency, institution, publication, service or individual does not imply endorsement of the editors or publisher.

Errors brought to the attention of the publisher and verified to the satisfaction of the publisher will be corrected in future editions.

Except by express prior written permission of the Copyright Proprietor no part of this work may be copied by any means of publication or communication now known or developed hereafter including, but not limited to, use in any directory or compilation or other print publication, in any information storage and retrieval system, in any other electronic device, or in any visual or audio-visual device or product.

This publication is an original and creative work, copyrighted by Grey House Publishing, Inc. and is fully protected by all applicable copyright laws, as well as by laws covering misappropriation, trade secrets and unfair competition.

Grey House has added value to the underlying factual material through one or more of the following efforts: unique and original selection; expression; arrangement; coordination; and classification.

Grey House Publishing, Inc. will defend its rights in this publication.

Copyright©2006 Grey House Publishing, Inc
All rights reserved

First edition published 2005
Printed in the USA

Profiles of New York   ISBN   1-59237-161-2
2-Volume Set (*Directory* and *Profiles of New York*)   ISBN   1-59237-162-0

Table of Contents

Introduction

User's Guide

Profiles
    Alphabetical by County/Place... 1
    Alphabetical Place Index 569
    Comparative Statistics.. 583

Education
    State Public School Profile 616
    School District Rankings 618
    NAEP: Public School Snapshot 641
    New York State Report Card: Overview of Performance.................... 647

Ancestry
    Ancestry Rankings 655

Hispanic Population
    Hispanic Rankings 701

Asian Population
    Asian Rankings... 735

Climate
    State Summary 757
    Weather Stations Map.. 759
    Weather Stations by County 760
    Weather Stations by City 761
    Weather Stations by Elevation 762
    National Weather Service Stations 763
    Cooperative Weather Stations... 772
    Weather Station Rankings.. 789
    Storm Events... 796

Maps
    Congressional Districts... 799
    Counties and Metro Areas.. 800
    Population... 801
    Household Size 806
    Median Age.. 807
    Income and Poverty 808
    Median Home Value... 810
    Homeownership Rate 811
    Educational Attainment... 812
    2004 Presidential Election 814

Introduction

Welcome to the second edition of *Profiles of New York State – Facts, Figures & Statistics for all 2,365 Populated Places in New York.* Significantly improved from the first edition, which was based solely on the content from Grey House Publishing's award-winning *Profiles of America,* this edition is 250 pages longer, and includes additional chapters of current demographic information and ranking sections, so that *Profiles of New York State* is the most comprehensive portrait of New York ever published.

First and foremost, you will find data on all populated communities and counties in the state of New York, from bustling urban centers to the hard-to-find outposts. New to this edition are detailed chapters on **Education, Ancestry, Hispanic Population, Asian Population**, and **Climate**. All chapters include **Comparative Statistics** or **Rankings**, and **4-color Maps** at the back of the book provide valuable information in a quickly processed, visual format. Here's an overview of each chapter:

1. Profiles
This chapter, organized by county, gives detailed profiles of 2,365 places plus 62 counties, and is based on the 2000 Census. This core Census data has been so extensively updated, however, that nearly 80% of this chapter has 2005 numbers. In addition, we have added current government statistics and original research, so that these profiles pull together statistical and descriptive information on every Census-recognized place in the state. Major fields of information include:

Geography	*Housing*	*Education*	*Religion*
Ancestry	*Transportation*	*Population*	*Climate*
Economy	*Industry*	*Health*	

In addition to place profiles, this chapter includes **Comparative Statistics** that compare New York's 100 largest communities by dozens of data points, and an **Alphabetical Place Index.**

2. Education
This chapter begins with an *Educational State Profile*, summarizing number of schools, students, diplomas granted and educational dollars spent, followed by a summary of *National Assessment of Educational Progress (NAEP)* 2005 test scores. Next are School District Rankings on 16 topics ranging from *Teacher/Student Ratios* to *High School Drop-Out Rates.* Following these rankings is detailed data for both NAEP scores and the *New York State Report Card* – an overview of student performance by subject, including easy-to-read charts and graphs.

3. Ancestry
This chapter provides a detailed look at the ancestral and racial makeup of New York. 217 ethnic categories are ranked three ways: 1) by number, based on all places regardless of population; 2) by percent, based on all places regardless of population; 3) by percent, based on places with populations of 10,000 or more. You will discover, for example, that there are 298 reported Afghans in Schenectady, representing .05% of that city's population, and that Newfield Hamlet in Tompkins County has the highest percentage residents who reported British ancestry – 51 people, or 6.4%.

4. Hispanic Population
This chapter defines New York's Hispanic population by 23 Hispanic backgrounds from *Argentinian* to *Venezuelan.* It ranks each of 15 categories, from Median Age to Median Home Value, by each Hispanic background. For example, you'll see that Ossining village in Westchester County has the highest

5. Asian Population
Similar in format to the chapter on Hispanic Population, this chapter defines Illinois' Asian population by 23 Asian backgrounds from *Bangladeshi* to *Vietnamese*. It ranks each of 14 categories, from *Median Age* to *Median Home Value*, by each Asian background. You will learn that Lincolnwood has the greatest number of *Koreans* as a percentage of the total population and Wilmette has the highest median household income of all *Japanese* in Illinois.

6. Weather
This important topic is explored in detail in this chapter, which includes a *State Summary*, and profiles of both *National and Cooperative Weather Stations*. In addition, you'll find *Weather Station Rankings*, where you'll see that, over the 30-year recorded period, Waukegan has had the lowest annual precipitation and Paw Paw 2 NW in Lee County the lowest recorded temperature (-33 degrees Fahrenheit).

This chapter also includes current *Storm* data. You'll see, at a glance, the most destructive ranked by both the most fatalities and the most property damage, from 1995 to 2005.

7. Maps
For a more visual point of view, there are 16 color maps of Illinois at the back of the book. They provide information on topics such as Core-Based Statistical Areas and Counties, Population Demographics, Household Size, Median Age, Male/Female Ratio, Income, Median Home Values, Educational Attainment, and another look at who voted for George Bush in 2004.

Note: The extensive **User's Guide** that follows this Introduction is segmented into six sections and examines, in some detail, each data field in the individual profiles and comparative sections for all chapters. It provides sources for all data points and statistical definitions as necessary.

User's Guide: Profiles

PLACES COVERED

All 62 counties.

616 incorporated municipalities. Municipalities are incorporated as either cities or villages.

936 minor civil divisions (called towns and reservations) for the states where the Census Bureau has determined that they serve as general-purpose governments. Those states are Connecticut, Maine, Massachusetts, Michigan, Minnesota, New Hampshire, New Jersey, New York, Pennsylvania, Rhode Island, Vermont, and Wisconsin. In some states incorporated municipalities are part of minor civil divisions and in some states they are independent of them.

434 census designated places (CDP). The U.S. Bureau of the Census defines a CDP as "a statistical entity, defined for each decennial census according to Census Bureau guidelines, comprising a densely settled concentration of population that is not within an incorporated place, but is locally identified by a name. CDPs are delineated cooperatively by state and local officials and the Census Bureau, following Census Bureau guidelines. Beginning with Census 2000 there are no size limits."

379 unincorporated communities. The communities included have both their own zip code and statistics for their ZIP Code Tabulation Area (ZCTA) available from the Census Bureau. They are referred to as "postal areas." A ZCTA is a statistical entity developed by the Census Bureau to approximate the delivery area for a US Postal Service 5-digit or 3-digit ZIP Code in the US and Puerto Rico. A ZCTA is an aggregation of census blocks that have the same predominant ZIP Code associated with the mailing addresses in the Census Bureau's Master Address File. Thus, the Postal Service's delivery areas have been adjusted to encompass whole census blocks so that the Census Bureau can tabulate census data for the ZCTAs. ZCTAs do not include all ZIP Codes used for mail delivery and therefore do not precisely depict the area within which mail deliveries associated with that ZIP Code occur. Additionally, some areas that are known by a unique name, although they are part of a larger incorporated place, are also included as "postal areas."

Important Notes

- *Profiles of New York* uses the term "community" to refer to all places except counties. The term "county" is used to refer to counties and county-equivalents. All places are defined as of the 2000 Census.
- Several states, including New York, have incorporated municipalities and minor civil divisions in the same county with the same name. Those communities are given separate entries (e.g. Adams, New York, in Jefferson County will be listed under both the village and town of Adams).
- The city of New York (composed of five coextensive counties/boroughs) has a unique format. Statistical information for the individual counties/boroughs can be found within the New York City entry. The five counties/boroughs are: Bronx County and Borough, Kings County and Brooklyn Borough, New York County and Manhattan Borough, Queens County and Borough, and Richmond County and Staten Island Borough.
- In each community profile, only school districts that have schools that are physically located within the community are shown. In addition, statistics for each school district cover the entire district, regardless of the physical location of the schools within the district.
- Special care should be taken when interpreting certain statistics for communities containing large colleges or universities. College students were counted as residents of the area in which they were living while attending college (as they have been since the 1950 census). One effect this may have is skewing the figures for population, income, housing, and educational attainment.
- Some information (e.g. unemployment rates) is available for both counties and individual communities. Other information is available for just counties (e.g. election results), or just individual communities (e.g. local newspapers).
- Some statistical information is available only for larger communities. In addition, the larger places are more apt to have services such as newspapers, airports, school districts, etc.
- For the most complete information on any community, you should also check the entry for the county in which the community is located. In addition, more information and services will be listed under the larger places in the county.
- For a more in-depth discussion of geographic areas, please refer to the Census Bureau's Geographic Areas Reference Manual at http://www.census.gov/geo/www/garm.html.

DATA SOURCES

CENSUS 2000

The parts of the data which are from the 2000 Decennial Census are from the following sources: *U.S. Bureau of the Census, Census of Population and Housing, 2000: Summary Files 1 and 3.* Summary File 3 (SF 3) consists of 813 detailed tables of Census 2000 social, economic and housing characteristics compiled from a sample of approximately 19 million housing units (about 1 in 6 households) that received the Census 2000 long-form questionnaire. Summary File 1 (SF 1) contains 286 tables focusing on age, sex, households, families, and housing units. This file presents 100-percent population and housing figures for the total population, for 63 race categories, and for many other race and Hispanic or Latino categories.

Comparing SF 3 Estimates with Corresponding Values in SF 1

As in earlier censuses, the responses from the sample of households reporting on long forms must be weighted to reflect the entire population. Specifically, each responding household represents, on average, six or seven other households who reported using short forms.

One consequence of the weighting procedures is that each estimate based on the long form responses has an associated confidence interval. These confidence intervals are wider (as a percentage of the estimate) for geographic areas with smaller populations and for characteristics that occur less frequently in the area being examined (such as the proportion of people in poverty in a middle-income neighborhood).

In order to release as much useful information as possible, statisticians must balance a number of factors. In particular, for Census 2000, the Bureau of the Census created weighting areas—geographic areas from which about two hundred or more long forms were completed—which are large enough to produce good quality estimates. If smaller weighting areas had been used, the confidence intervals around the estimates would have been significantly wider, rendering many estimates less useful due to their lower reliability.

The disadvantage of using weighting areas this large is that, for smaller geographic areas within them, the estimates of characteristics that are also reported on the short form will not match the counts reported in SF 1. Examples of these characteristics are the total number of people, the number of people reporting specific racial categories, and the number of housing units. The official values for items reported on the short form come from SF 1 and SF 2.

The differences between the long form estimates in SF 3 and values in SF 1 are particularly noticeable for the smallest places, tracts, and block groups. The long form estimates of total population and total housing units in SF 3 will, however, match the SF 1 counts for larger geographic areas such as counties and states, and will be essentially the same for medium and large cities.

SF 1 gives exact numbers even for very small groups and areas, whereas SF 3 gives estimates for small groups and areas such as tracts and small places that are less exact. The goal of SF 3 is to identify large differences among areas or large changes over time. Estimates for small areas and small population groups often do exhibit large changes from one census to the next, so having the capability to measure them is worthwhile.

2005 Estimates and 2010 Projections

Some 2000 Census data has been updated with data provided by Claritas. Founded in 1971, Claritas is the industry leader in applied demography and the preeminent provider of small-area demographic estimates.

INFORMATION FOR COMMUNITIES

PHYSICAL CHARACTERISTICS

Place Type: Lists the type of place (city, town, village, borough, special city, CDP, township, plantation, gore, district, grant, location, reservation, or postal area). *Source: U.S. Bureau of the Census, Census of Population and Housing, 2000: Summary File 1 and U.S. Postal Service, City State File.*

Land and Water Area: Land and water area in square miles. *Source: U.S. Bureau of the Census, Census of Population and Housing, 2000: Summary File 1.*

Latitude and Longitude: Latitude and longitude in degrees. *Source: U.S. Bureau of the Census, Census of Population and Housing, 2000: Summary File 1.*

Elevation: Elevation in feet. *Source: U.S. Geological Survey, Geographic Names Information System (GNIS).*

HISTORY

History: Historical information. *Source: Columbia University Press, The Columbia Gazetteer of North America; Original research.*

POPULATION

Population: 1990 and 2000 figures are a 100% count of population. 2005 estimates and 2010 projections were provided by Claritas. *Source: Claritas; U.S. Bureau of the Census, Census of Population and Housing, 2000: Summary File 1.*

Population by Race: 2005 estimates includes the U.S. Bureau of the Census categories of White alone; Black alone; Asian alone; and Hispanic of any race. Alone refers to the fact that these figures are not in combination with any other race.

The concept of race, as used by the Census Bureau, reflects self-identification by people according to the race or races with which they most closely identify. These categories are socio-political constructs and should not be interpreted as being scientific or anthropological in nature. Furthermore, the race categories include both racial and national-origin groups.

- **White.** A person having origins in any of the original peoples of Europe, the Middle East, or North Africa. It includes people who indicate their race as "White" or report entries such as Irish, German, Italian, Lebanese, Near Easterner, Arab, or Polish.
- **Black or African American.** A person having origins in any of the Black racial groups of Africa. It includes people who indicate their race as "Black, African American, or Negro," or provide written entries such as African American, Afro-American, Kenyan, Nigerian, or Haitian.
- **Asian.** A person having origins in any of the original peoples of the Far East, Southeast Asia, or the Indian subcontinent including, for example, Cambodia, China, India, Japan, Korea, Malaysia, Pakistan, the Philippine Islands, Thailand, and Vietnam. It includes "Asian Indian," "Chinese," "Filipino," "Korean," "Japanese," "Vietnamese," and "Other Asian."
- **Hispanic.** The data on the Hispanic or Latino population, which was asked of all people, were derived from answers to long-form questionnaire Item 5, and short-form questionnaire Item 7. The terms "Spanish," "Hispanic origin," and "Latino" are used interchangeably. Some respondents identify with all three terms, while others may identify with only one of these three specific terms. Hispanics or Latinos who identify with the terms "Spanish," "Hispanic," or "Latino" are those who classify themselves in one of the specific Hispanic or Latino categories listed on the questionnaire — "Mexican," "Puerto Rican," or "Cuban" — as well as those who indicate that they are "other Spanish, Hispanic, or Latino." People who do not identify with one of the specific origins listed on the questionnaire but indicate that they are "other Spanish, Hispanic, or Latino" are those whose origins are from Spain, the Spanish-speaking countries of Central or South America, the Dominican Republic, or people identifying themselves generally as Spanish, Spanish-American, Hispanic, Hispano, Latino, and so on. All write-in responses to the "other Spanish/Hispanic/Latino" category were coded. Origin can be viewed as the heritage, nationality group, lineage, or country of birth of the person or the person's parents or ancestors before their arrival in the United States. People who identify their origin as Spanish, Hispanic, or Latino may be of any race.

Population Density: 2005 population divided by the land area in square miles. *Source: Claritas; U.S. Bureau of the Census, Census of Population and Housing, 2000: Summary File 1.*

Average Household Size: Average household size was calculated by dividing the total population by the total number of households. Figures are 2005 estimates. *Source: Claritas.*

Median Age: Figures are 2005 estimates. *Source: Claritas.*

Male/Female Ratio: Number of males per 100 females. Figures are 2005 estimates. *Source: Claritas.*

Marital Status: Percentage of population never married, now married, widowed, or divorced. *Source: U.S. Bureau of the Census, Census of Population and Housing, 2000: Summary File 3.*

The marital status classification refers to the status at the time of enumeration. Data on marital status are tabulated only for the population 15 years old and over. Each person was asked whether they were "Now married," "Widowed," "Divorced," or "Never married." Couples who live together (for example, people in common-law marriages) were able to report the marital status they considered to be the most appropriate.

- **Never married.** Never married includes all people who have never been married, including people whose only marriage(s) was annulled.
- **Now married.** All people whose current marriage has not ended by widowhood or divorce. This category includes people defined as "separated."
- **Widowed.** This category includes widows and widowers who have not remarried.
- **Divorced.** This category includes people who are legally divorced and who have not remarried.

Foreign Born: Percentage of population who were not U.S. citizens at birth. Foreign-born people are those who indicated they were either a U.S. citizen by naturalization or they were not a citizen of the United States. *Source: U.S. Bureau of the Census, Census of Population and Housing, 2000: Summary File 3.*

Ancestry: Largest ancestry groups reported (up to five). Includes multiple ancestries. *Source: U.S. Bureau of the Census, Census of Population and Housing, 2000: Summary File 3.*

The data represent self-classification by people according to the ancestry group or groups with which they most closely identify. Ancestry refers to a person's ethnic origin or descent, "roots," heritage, or the place of birth of the person, the person's parents, or their ancestors before their arrival in the United States. Some ethnic identities, such as Egyptian or Polish, can be traced to geographic areas outside the United States, while other ethnicities such as Pennsylvania German or Cajun evolved in the United States.

The ancestry question was intended to provide data for groups that were not included in the Hispanic origin and race questions. Therefore, although data on all groups are collected, the ancestry data shown in these tabulations are for non-Hispanic and non-race groups. Hispanic and race groups are included in the "Other groups" category for the ancestry tables in these tabulations.

The ancestry question allowed respondents to report one or more ancestry groups, although only the first two were coded. If a response was in terms of a dual ancestry, for example, "Irish English," the person was assigned two codes, in this case one for Irish and another for English. However, in certain cases, multiple responses such as "French Canadian," "Greek Cypriote," and "Scotch Irish" were assigned a single code reflecting their status as unique groups. If a person reported one of these unique groups in addition to another group, for example, "Scotch Irish English," resulting in three terms, that person received one code for the unique group (Scotch-Irish) and another one for the remaining group (English). If a person reported "English Irish French," only English and Irish were coded. Certain combinations of ancestries where the ancestry group is a part of another, such as "German-Bavarian," were coded as a single ancestry using the more specific group (Bavarian). Also, responses such as "Polish-American" or "Italian-American" were coded and tabulated as a single entry (Polish or Italian).

The Census Bureau accepted "American" as a unique ethnicity if it was given alone, with an ambiguous response, or with state names. If the respondent listed any other ethnic identity such as "Italian-American," generally the "American" portion of the response was not coded. However, distinct groups such as "American Indian," "Mexican American," and "African American" were coded and identified separately because they represented groups who considered themselves different from those who reported as "Indian," "Mexican," or "African," respectively.

The data is based on the total number of ancestries reported and coded. Thus, the sum of the counts in this type of presentation is not the total population but the total of all responses.

ECONOMY

Unemployment Rate: 2005 annual average. Includes all civilians age 16 or over who were unemployed and looking for work. *Source: U.S. Department of Labor, Bureau of Labor Statistics, Local Area Unemployment Statistics (http://www.bls.gov/lau/home.htm).*

Total Civilian Labor Force: 2005 annual average. Includes all civilians age 16 or over who were either employed, or unemployed and looking for work. *Source: U.S. Department of Labor, Bureau of Labor Statistics, Local Area Unemployment Statistics (http://www.bls.gov/lau/home.htm).*

Single-Family Building Permits Issued: Building permits issued for new single-family housing units in 2005. *Source: U.S. Census Bureau, Manufacturing and Construction Division (http://www.census.gov/const/www/permitsindex.html).*

Multi-Family Building Permits Issued: Building permits issued for new multi-family housing units in 2005. *Source: U.S. Census Bureau, Manufacturing and Construction Division (http://www.census.gov/const/www/permitsindex.html).*

Statistics on housing units authorized by building permits include housing units issued in local permit-issuing jurisdictions by a building or zoning permit. Not all areas of the country require a building or zoning permit. The statistics only represent those areas that do require a permit. Current surveys indicate that construction is undertaken for all but a very small percentage of housing units authorized by building permits. A major portion typically get under way during the month of permit issuance and most of the remainder begin within the three following months. Because of this lag, the housing unit authorization statistics do not represent the number of units actually put into construction for the period shown, and should therefore not be directly interpreted as "housing starts."

Statistics are based upon reports submitted by local building permit officials in response to a mail survey. They are obtained using Form C-404 const/www/c404.pdf, "Report of New Privately-Owned Residential Building or Zoning Permits Issued." When a report is not received, missing data are either (1) obtained from the Survey of Use of Permits (SUP) which is used to collect information on housing starts, or (2) imputed based on the assumption that the ratio of current month authorizations to those of a year ago should be the same for reporting and non-reporting places.

Employment by Occupation: Percentage of the employed civilian population 16 years and over in management, professional, service, sales, farming, construction, and production occupations. *Source: U.S. Bureau of the Census, Census of Population and Housing, 2000: Summary File 3.*

- **Management** includes management, business, and financial operations occupations:
    Management occupations, except farmers and farm managers
    Farmers and farm managers
    Business and financial operations occupations:
        Business operations specialists
        Financial specialists

- **Professional** includes professional and related occupations:
    Computer and mathematical occupations
    Architecture and engineering occupations:
        Architects, surveyors, cartographers, and engineers
        Drafters, engineering, and mapping technicians
    Life, physical, and social science occupations
    Community and social services occupations
    Legal occupations
    Education, training, and library occupations
    Arts, design, entertainment, sports, and media occupations
    Healthcare practitioners and technical occupations:
        Health diagnosing and treating practitioners and technical occupations
        Health technologists and technicians

- **Service** occupations include:
    Healthcare support occupations
    Protective service occupations:
        Fire fighting, prevention, and law enforcement workers, including supervisors

vi User's Guide: Profiles

        Other protective service workers, including supervisors
        Food preparation and serving related occupations
        Building and grounds cleaning and maintenance occupations
        Personal care and service occupations

- **Sales** and office occupations include:
  Sales and related occupations
  Office and administrative support occupations

- **Farming,** fishing, and forestry occupations

- **Construction,** extraction, and maintenance occupations include:
  Construction and extraction occupations:
      Supervisors, construction, and extraction workers
      Construction trades workers
      Extraction workers
  Installation, maintenance, and repair occupations

- **Production,** transportation, and material moving occupations include:
  Production occupations
  Transportation and material moving occupations:
      Supervisors, transportation, and material moving workers
      Aircraft and traffic control occupations
      Motor vehicle operators
      Rail, water, and other transportation occupations
      Material moving workers

INCOME

Per Capita Income: Per capita income is the mean income computed for every man, woman, and child in a particular group. It is derived by dividing the total income of a particular group by the total population in that group. Per capita income is rounded to the nearest whole dollar. Figures shown are 2005 estimates. *Source: Claritas.*

Median Household Income: Includes the income of the householder and all other individuals 15 years old and over in the household, whether they are related to the householder or not. The median divides the income distribution into two equal parts: one-half of the cases falling below the median income and one-half above the median. For households, the median income is based on the distribution of the total number of households including those with no income. Median income for households is computed on the basis of a standard distribution and is rounded to the nearest whole dollar. Figures shown are 2005 estimates. *Source: Claritas.*

Average Household Income: Average household income is obtained by dividing total household income by the total number of households. Figures shown are 2005 estimates. *Source: Claritas.*

Percent of Households with Income of $100,000 or more: Figures shown are 2005 estimates. *Source: Claritas.*

Poverty Rate: Percentage of population with income in 1999 below the poverty level. Based on individuals for whom poverty status is determined. Poverty status was determined for all people except institutionalized people, people in military group quarters, people in college dormitories, and unrelated individuals under 15 years old. *Source: U.S. Bureau of the Census, Census of Population and Housing, 2000: Summary File 3.*

The poverty status of families and unrelated individuals in 1999 was determined using 48 thresholds (income cutoffs) arranged in a two-dimensional matrix. The matrix consists of family size (from 1 person to 9 or more people) cross-classified by presence and number of family members under 18 years old (from no children present to 8 or more children present). Unrelated individuals and 2-person families were further differentiated by the age of the reference person (RP) (under 65 years old and 65 years old and over).

To determine a person's poverty status, one compares the person's total family income with the poverty threshold appropriate for that person's family size and composition. If the total income of that person's family is less than the threshold appropriate for that family, then the person is considered poor, together with every member of his or her family. If a person is not living with anyone related by birth, marriage, or adoption, then the person's own income is compared with his or her poverty threshold.

TAXES

Total City Taxes Per Capita: Total city taxes collected divided by the population of the city. *Source: U.S. Bureau of the Census, State and Local Government Finances, 2002 (http://www.census.gov/govs/www/estimate.html).*

Taxes include:
- Property Taxes
- Sales and Gross Receipts Taxes
- Federal Customs Duties
- General Sales and Gross Receipts Taxes
- Selective Sales Taxes (alcoholic beverages; amusements; insurance premiums; motor fuels; pari-mutuels; public utilities; tobacco products; other)
- License Taxes (alcoholic beverages; amusements; corporations in general; hunting and fishing; motor vehicles motor vehicle operators; public utilities; occupation and business, NEC; other)
- Income Taxes (individual income; corporation net income; other)
- Death and Gift
- Documentary & Stock Transfer
- Severance
- Taxes, NEC

Total City Property Taxes Per Capita: Total city property taxes collected divided by the population of the city. *Source: U.S. Bureau of the Census, State and Local Government Finances, 2002 (http://www.census.gov/govs/www/estimate.html).*

Property Taxes include general property taxes, relating to property as a whole, taxed at a single rate or at classified rates according to the class of property. Property refers to real property (e.g. land and structures) as well as personal property; personal property can be either tangible (e.g. automobiles and boats) or intangible (e.g. bank accounts and stocks and bonds). Special property taxes, levied on selected types of property (e.g. oil and gas properties, house trailers, motor vehicles, and intangibles) and subject to rates not directly related to general property tax rates. Taxes based on income produced by property as a measure of its value on the assessment date.

EDUCATION

Educational Attainment: Figures shown are 2005 estimates and show the percent of population age 25 and over with a:

- **High school diploma (including GED) or higher:** includes people whose highest degree was a high school diploma or its equivalent, people who attended college but did not receive a degree, and people who received a college, university, or professional degree. People who reported completing the 12th grade but not receiving a diploma are not high school graduates.
- **Bachelor's degree or higher**
- **Master's degree or higher:** Master's degrees include the traditional MA and MS degrees and field-specific degrees, such as MSW, MEd, MBA, MLS, and Meng. *Source: Claritas.*

School Districts: Lists the name of each school district, the grade range (PK=pre-kindergarten; KG=kindergarten), the student enrollment, and the district headquarters' phone number. In each community profile, only school districts that have schools that are physically located within the community are shown. In addition, statistics for each school district cover the entire district, regardless of the physical location of the schools within the district. *Source: U.S. Department of Education, National Center for Educational Statistics, Directory of Public Elementary and Secondary Education Agencies, 2003-04.*

Four-year Colleges: Lists the name of each four-year college, the type of institution (private or public; for-profit or non-profit; religious affiliation; historically black college), the student enrollment, the phone number, and the annual tuition (including fees) for full-time, first-time undergraduate students (in-state and out-of-state). *Source: U.S. Department of Education, National Center for Educational Statistics, Directory of Postsecondary Institutions, 2004-05.*

Two-year Colleges: Lists the name of each two-year college, the type of institution (private or public; for-profit or non-profit; religious affiliation; historically black college), the student enrollment, the phone number, and the annual tuition (including fees) for full-time, first-time undergraduate students (in-state and out-of-state). *Source: U.S. Department of Education, National Center for Educational Statistics, Directory of Postsecondary Institutions, 2004-05.*

HOUSING

Homeownership Rate: Percentage of housing units that are owner-occupied. Figures shown are 2005 estimates. *Source: Claritas.*

Median Home Value: Median value of all owner-occupied housing units as reported by the owner. Figures shown are 2005 estimates. *Source: Claritas.*

Median Rent: Median monthly contract rent on specified renter-occupied and specified vacant-for-rent units. Specified renter-occupied and specified vacant-for-rent units exclude 1-family houses on 10 acres or more. Contract rent is the monthly rent agreed to or contracted for, regardless of any furnishings, utilities, fees, meals, or services that may be included. For vacant units, it is the monthly rent asked for the rental unit at the time of enumeration. *Source: U.S. Bureau of the Census, Census of Population and Housing, 2000: Summary File 3.*

Median Age of Housing: Median age of housing was calculated by subtracting median year structure built from 2000 (e.g. if the median year structure built is 1967, the median age of housing in that area is 33 years—2000 minus 1967). Year structure built refers to when the building was first constructed, not when it was remodeled, added to, or converted. For housing units under construction that met the housing unit definition—that is, all exterior windows, doors, and final usable floors were in place—the category "1999 or 2000" was used for tabulations. For mobile homes, houseboats, RVs, etc, the manufacturer's model year was assumed to be the year built. The data relate to the number of units built during the specified periods that were still in existence at the time of enumeration. *Source: U.S. Bureau of the Census, Census of Population and Housing, 2000: Summary File 3.*

HOSPITALS

Lists the hospital name and the number of licensed beds. *Source: Grey House Publishing, Directory of Hospital Personnel, 2005.*

SAFETY

Violent Crime Rate: Number of violent crimes reported per 10,000 population. Violent crimes include murder, forcible rape, robbery, and aggravated assault. *Source: Federal Bureau of Investigation, Uniform Crime Reports 2004 (http://www.fbi.gov/ucr/ucr.htm).*

Property Crime Rate: Number of property crimes reported per 10,000 population. Property crimes include burglary, larceny-theft, and motor vehicle theft. *Source: Federal Bureau of Investigation, Uniform Crime Reports 2004 (http://www.fbi.gov/ucr/ucr.htm).*

NEWSPAPERS

Lists the names of daily and weekly newspapers. Also includes the newspaper type and circulation, if available. *Source: BurrellesLuce MediaContacts 2005 (http://www.burrellesluce.com/MediaConnect).*

TRANSPORTATION

Commute to Work: Percentage of workers 16 years old and over that use the following means of transportation to commute to work: car; public transportation; walk; work from home. *Source: U.S. Bureau of the Census, Census of Population and Housing, 2000: Summary File 3.*

The means of transportation data for some areas may show workers using modes of public transportation that are not available in those areas (e.g. subway or elevated riders in a metropolitan area where there actually is no subway or elevated service). This result is largely due to people who worked during the reference week at a location that was different from their usual place of work (such as people away from home on business in an area where subway service was available) and people who used more than one means of transportation each day but whose principal means was unavailable where they lived (e.g. residents of non-metropolitan areas who drove to the fringe of a metropolitan area and took the commuter railroad most of the distance to work).

Travel Time to Work: Travel time to work for workers 16 years old and over. Reported for the following intervals: less than 15 minutes; 15 to 30 minutes; 30 to 45 minutes; 45 to 60 minutes; 60 minutes or more. *Source: U.S. Bureau of the Census, Census of Population and Housing, 2000: Summary File 3.*

Travel time to work refers to the total number of minutes that it usually took the person to get from home to work each day during the reference week. The elapsed time includes time spent waiting for public transportation, picking up passengers in carpools, and time spent in other activities related to getting to work.

Amtrak: Indicates if Amtrak service is available. Please note that the cities being served continually change. *Source: National Railroad Passenger Corporation, Amtrak National Timetable, 2005 (www.amtrak.com).*

AIRPORTS

Lists the local airport(s) along with type of service and hub size. *Source: U.S. Department of Transportation, Bureau of Transportation Statistics (http://www.bts.gov).*

ADDITIONAL INFORMATION CONTACTS

The following phone numbers are provided as sources of additional information: Chambers of Commerce; Economic Development Agencies; Boards of Realtors; Convention & Visitors Bureaus. Efforts have been made to provide the most recent area codes. However, area code changes may have occurred in listed numbers. *Source: Original research.*

INFORMATION FOR COUNTIES

PHYSICAL CHARACTERISTICS

Physical Location: Describes the physical location of the county. *Source: Columbia University Press, The Columbia Gazetteer of North America and original research.*

Land and Water Area: Land and water area in square miles. *Source: U.S. Bureau of the Census, Census of Population and Housing, 2000: Summary File 1.*

Time Zone: Lists the time zone. *Source: Original research.*

Year Organized: Year the county government was organized. *Source: National Association of Counties (www.naco.org).*

County Seat: Lists the county seat. If a county has more than one seat, then both are listed. *Source: National Association of Counties (www.naco.org).*

Metropolitan Area: Indicates the metropolitan area the county is located in. Also lists all the component counties of that metropolitan area. The Office of Management and Budget (OMB) defines metropolitan and micropolitan statistical areas. The current definitions are as of November 2004. *Source: U.S. Bureau of the Census (http://www.census.gov/population/www/estimates/metrodef.html).*

Climate: Includes all weather stations located within the county. Indicates the station name and elevation as well as the monthly average high and low temperatures, average precipitation, and average snowfall. The period of record is generally 1970-1999, however, certain weather stations contain averages going back as far as 1900. *Source: Grey House Publishing, Weather America: A Thirty-Year Summary of Statistical Weather Data and Rankings, 2001.*

POPULATION

Population: 1990 and 2000 figures are a 100% count of population. 2005 estimates and 2010 projections were provided by Claritas. *Source: Claritas; U.S. Bureau of the Census, Census of Population and Housing, 2000: Summary File 1.*

Population by Race: 2005 estimates includes the U.S. Bureau of the Census categories of White alone; Black alone; Asian alone; and Hispanic of any race. Alone refers to the fact that these figures are not in combination with any other race.

The concept of race, as used by the Census Bureau, reflects self-identification by people according to the race or races with which they most closely identify. These categories are socio-political constructs and should not be interpreted as being scientific or anthropological in nature. Furthermore, the race categories include both racial and national-origin groups.

- **White.** A person having origins in any of the original peoples of Europe, the Middle East, or North Africa. It includes people who indicate their race as "White" or report entries such as Irish, German, Italian, Lebanese, Near Easterner, Arab, or Polish.
- **Black or African American.** A person having origins in any of the Black racial groups of Africa. It includes people who indicate their race as "Black, African American, or Negro," or provide written entries such as African American, Afro-American, Kenyan, Nigerian, or Haitian.
- **Asian.** A person having origins in any of the original peoples of the Far East, Southeast Asia, or the Indian subcontinent including, for example, Cambodia, China, India, Japan, Korea, Malaysia, Pakistan, the Philippine Islands, Thailand, and Vietnam. It includes "Asian Indian," "Chinese," "Filipino," "Korean," "Japanese," "Vietnamese," and "Other Asian."
- **Hispanic.** The data on the Hispanic or Latino population, which was asked of all people, were derived from answers to long-form questionnaire Item 5, and short-form questionnaire Item 7. The terms "Spanish," "Hispanic origin," and "Latino" are used interchangeably. Some respondents identify with all three terms, while others may identify with only one of these three specific terms. Hispanics or Latinos who identify with the terms "Spanish," "Hispanic," or "Latino" are those who classify themselves in one of the specific Hispanic or Latino categories listed on the questionnaire — "Mexican," "Puerto Rican," or "Cuban" — as well as those who indicate that they are "other Spanish, Hispanic, or Latino." People who do not identify with one of the specific origins listed on the questionnaire but indicate that they are "other

Spanish, Hispanic, or Latino" are those whose origins are from Spain, the Spanish-speaking countries of Central or South America, the Dominican Republic, or people identifying themselves generally as Spanish, Spanish-American, Hispanic, Hispano, Latino, and so on. All write-in responses to the "other Spanish/Hispanic/Latino" category were coded. Origin can be viewed as the heritage, nationality group, lineage, or country of birth of the person or the person's parents or ancestors before their arrival in the United States. People who identify their origin as Spanish, Hispanic, or Latino may be of any race.

Population Density: 2005 population divided by the land area in square miles. *Source: Claritas; U.S. Bureau of the Census, Census of Population and Housing, 2000: Summary File 1.*

Average Household Size: Average household size was calculated by dividing the total population by the total number of households. Figures are 2005 estimates. *Source: Claritas.*

Median Age: Figures are 2005 estimates. *Source: Claritas.*

Male/Female Ratio: Number of males per 100 females. Figures are 2005 estimates. *Source: Claritas.*

RELIGION

Religion: Lists the largest religious groups (up to five) based on the number of adherents divided by the population of the county. Adherents are defined as "all members, including full members, their children and the estimated number of other regular participants who are not considered as communicant, confirmed or full members." The data is based on a study of 149 religious bodies sponsored by the Association of Statisticians of American Religious Bodies. The 149 bodies reported 268,254 congregations and 141,371,963 adherents. *Source: Glenmary Research Center, Religious Congregations & Membership in the United States 2000.*

ECONOMY

Unemployment Rate: 2005 annual average. Includes all civilians age 16 or over who were unemployed and looking for work. *Source: U.S. Department of Labor, Bureau of Labor Statistics, Local Area Unemployment Statistics (http://www.bls.gov/lau/home.htm).*

Total Civilian Labor Force: 2005 annual average. Includes all civilians age 16 or over who were either employed, or unemployed and looking for work. *Source: U.S. Department of Labor, Bureau of Labor Statistics, Local Area Unemployment Statistics (http://www.bls.gov/lau/home.htm).*

Leading Industries: Lists the three largest industries (excluding government) based on the number of employees. *Source: U.S. Bureau of the Census, County Business Patterns 2003 (http://www.census.gov/epcd/cbp/view/cbpview.html).*

Farms: The total number of farms and the total acreage they occupy. *Source: U.S. Department of Agriculture, National Agricultural Statistics Service, 2002 Census of Agriculture (http://www.nass.usda.gov/census).*

Companies that Employ 500 or more persons: The numbers of companies that employ 500 or more persons. Includes private employers only. *Source: U.S. Bureau of the Census, County Business Patterns 2003 (http://www.census.gov/epcd/cbp/view/cbpview.html).*

Companies that Employ 100 - 499 persons: The numbers of companies that employ 100 - 499 persons. Includes private employers only. *Source: U.S. Bureau of the Census, County Business Patterns 2003 (http://www.census.gov/epcd/cbp/view/cbpview.html).*

Companies that Employ 1 - 99 persons: The numbers of companies that employ 1 - 99 persons. Includes private employers only. *Source: U.S. Bureau of the Census, County Business Patterns 2003 (http://www.census.gov/epcd/cbp/view/cbpview.html)*

Black-Owned Businesses: Number of businesses that are majority-owned by a Black or African-American person(s). Majority ownership is defined as having 51 percent or more of the stock or equity in the business. Black or African American is defined as a person having origins in any of the black racial groups of Africa, including those who consider themselves to be "Haitian." *Source: U.S. Bureau of the Census, 2002 Economic Census, Survey of Business Owners: Black-Owned Firms, 2002 (http://www.census.gov/csd/sbo/index.html).*

Hispanic-Owned Businesses: Number of businesses that are majority-owned by a person(s) of Hispanic or Latino origin. Majority ownership is defined as having 51 percent or more of the stock or equity in the business. Hispanic or

Latino origin is defined as a person of Cuban, Mexican, Puerto Rican, South or Central American, or other Spanish culture or origin, regardless of race. *Source: U.S. Bureau of the Census, 2002 Economic Census, Survey of Business Owners: Hispanic-Owned Firms, 2002 (http://www.census.gov/csd/sbo/index.html).*

Women-Owned Businesses: Number of businesses that are majority-owned by a woman. Majority ownership is defined as having 51 percent or more of the stock or equity in the business. *Source: U.S. Bureau of the Census, 2002 Economic Census, Survey of Business Owners: Women-Owned Firms, 2002 (http://www.census.gov/csd/sbo/index.html).*

The Survey of Business Owners (SBO), formerly known as the Surveys of Minority- and Women-Owned Business Enterprises (SMOBE/SWOBE), provides statistics that describe the composition of U.S. businesses by gender, Hispanic or Latino origin, and race. Additional statistics include owner's age, education level, veteran status, and primary function in the business; family- and home-based businesses; types of customers and workers; and sources of financing for expansion, capital improvements, or start-up. Economic policymakers in federal, state and local governments use the SBO data to understand conditions of business success and failure by comparing census-to-census changes in business performances and by comparing minority-/nonminority- and women-/men-owned businesses.

Retail Sales per Capita: Total dollar amount of estimated retail sales divided by the estimated population of the county in 2006. *Source: Editor & Publisher Market Guide 2006*

Single-Family Building Permits Issued: Building permits issued for new, single-family housing units in 2005. *Source: U.S. Census Bureau, Manufacturing and Construction Division (http://www.census.gov/const/www/permitsindex.html).*

Multi-Family Building Permits Issued: Building permits issued for new, multi-family housing units in 2005. *Source: U.S. Census Bureau, Manufacturing and Construction Division (http://www.census.gov/const/www/permitsindex.html).*

Statistics on housing units authorized by building permits include housing units issued in local permit-issuing jurisdictions by a building or zoning permit. Not all areas of the country require a building or zoning permit. The statistics only represent those areas that do require a permit. Current surveys indicate that construction is undertaken for all but a very small percentage of housing units authorized by building permits. A major portion typically get under way during the month of permit issuance and most of the remainder begin within the three following months. Because of this lag, the housing unit authorization statistics do not represent the number of units actually put into construction for the period shown, and should therefore not be directly interpreted as "housing starts."

Statistics are based upon reports submitted by local building permit officials in response to a mail survey. They are obtained using Form C-404 const/www/c404.pdf, "Report of New Privately-Owned Residential Building or Zoning Permits Issued." When a report is not received, missing data are either (1) obtained from the Survey of Use of Permits (SUP) which is used to collect information on housing starts, or (2) imputed based on the assumption that the ratio of current month authorizations to those of a year ago should be the same for reporting and non-reporting places.

INCOME

Per Capita Income: Per capita income is the mean income computed for every man, woman, and child in a particular group. It is derived by dividing the total income of a particular group by the total population in that group. Per capita income is rounded to the nearest whole dollar. Figures shown are 2005 estimates. *Source: Claritas.*

Median Household Income: Includes the income of the householder and all other individuals 15 years old and over in the household, whether they are related to the householder or not. The median divides the income distribution into two equal parts: one-half of the cases falling below the median income and one-half above the median. For households, the median income is based on the distribution of the total number of households including those with no income. Median income for households is computed on the basis of a standard distribution and is rounded to the nearest whole dollar. Figures shown are 2005 estimates. *Source: Claritas.*

Average Household Income: Average household income is obtained by dividing total household income by the total number of households. Figures shown are 2005 estimates. *Source: Claritas.*

Percent of Households with Income of $100,000 or more: Figures shown are 2005 estimates. *Source: Claritas.*

Poverty Rate: Estimated percentage of population with income in 2003 below the poverty level. *Source: U.S. Bureau of the Census, Small Area Income & Poverty Estimates.*

Bankruptcy Rate: The personal bankruptcy filing rate is the number of bankruptcies per thousand residents in 2005. Personal bankruptcy filings include both Chapter 7 (liquidations) and Chapter 13 (reorganizations) based on the county of residence of the filer. *Source: Federal Deposit Insurance Corporation, Regional Economic Conditions (http://www2.fdic.gov/recon/index.html).*

TAXES

Total County Taxes Per Capita: Total county taxes collected divided by the population of the county. *Source: U.S. Bureau of the Census, State and Local Government Finances, 2002 (http://www.census.gov/govs/www/estimate.html).*

Taxes include:
- Property Taxes
- Sales and Gross Receipts Taxes
- Federal Customs Duties
- General Sales and Gross Receipts Taxes
- Selective Sales Taxes (alcoholic beverages; amusements; insurance premiums; motor fuels; pari-mutuels; public utilities; tobacco products; other)
- License Taxes (alcoholic beverages; amusements; corporations in general; hunting and fishing; motor vehicles motor vehicle operators; public utilities; occupation and business, NEC; other)
- Income Taxes (individual income; corporation net income; other)
- Death and Gift
- Documentary & Stock Transfer
- Severance
- Taxes, NEC

Total County Property Taxes Per Capita: Total county property taxes collected divided by the population of the county. *Source: U.S. Bureau of the Census, State and Local Government Finances, 2002 (http://www.census.gov/govs/www/estimate.html).*

Property Taxes include general property taxes, relating to property as a whole, taxed at a single rate or at classified rates according to the class of property. Property refers to real property (e.g. land and structures) as well as personal property; personal property can be either tangible (e.g. automobiles and boats) or intangible (e.g. bank accounts and stocks and bonds). Special property taxes, levied on selected types of property (e.g. oil and gas properties, house trailers, motor vehicles, and intangibles) and subject to rates not directly related to general property tax rates. Taxes based on income produced by property as a measure of its value on the assessment date.

EDUCATION

Educational Attainment: Figures shown are 2005 estimates and show the percent of population age 25 and over with a:

- **High school diploma (including GED) or higher:** includes people whose highest degree was a high school diploma or its equivalent, people who attended college but did not receive a degree, and people who received a college, university, or professional degree. People who reported completing the 12th grade but not receiving a diploma are not high school graduates.
- **Bachelor's degree or higher**
- **Master's degree or higher:** Master's degrees include the traditional MA and MS degrees and field-specific degrees, such as MSW, MEd, MBA, MLS, and Meng. *Source: Claritas.*

HOUSING

Homeownership Rate: Percentage of housing units that are owner-occupied. Figures shown are 2005 estimates. *Source: Claritas.*

Median Home Value: Median value of all owner-occupied housing units as reported by the owner. Figures shown are 2005 estimates. *Source: Claritas.*

Median Rent: Median monthly contract rent on specified renter-occupied and specified vacant-for-rent units. Specified renter-occupied and specified vacant-for-rent units exclude 1-family houses on 10 acres or more. Contract rent is the monthly rent agreed to or contracted for, regardless of any furnishings, utilities, fees, meals, or services that may be included. For vacant units, it is the monthly rent asked for the rental unit at the time of enumeration. *Source: U.S. Bureau of the Census, Census of Population and Housing, 2000: Summary File 3.*

Median Age of Housing: Median age of housing was calculated by subtracting median year structure built from 2000 (e.g. if the median year structure built is 1967, the median age of housing in that area is 33 years — 2000 minus 1967). Year structure built refers to when the building was first constructed, not when it was remodeled, added to, or converted. For housing units under construction that met the housing unit definition—that is, all exterior windows, doors, and final usable floors were in place—the category "1999 or 2000" was used for tabulations. For mobile homes, houseboats, RVs, etc, the manufacturer's model year was assumed to be the year built. The data relate to the number of units built during the specified periods that were still in existence at the time of enumeration. *Source: U.S. Bureau of the Census, Census of Population and Housing, 2000: Summary File 3.*

HEALTH AND VITAL STATISTICS

Birth Rate: Estimated number of births per 10,000 population in 2004. *Source: U.S. Census Bureau, Population Estimates, July 1, 2003 - July 1, 2004 (http://www.census.gov/popest/births.html).*

Death Rate: Estimated number of deaths per 10,000 population in 2004. *Source: U.S. Census Bureau, Population Estimates, July 1, 2003 - July 1, 2004 (http://www.census.gov/popest/births.html).*

Age-adjusted Cancer Mortality Rate: Number of age-adjusted deaths from cancer per 100,000 population in 2002. Cancer is defined as International Classification of Disease (ICD) codes C00 - D48.9 Neoplasms. *Source: Centers for Disease Control, CDC Wonder (http://wonder.cdc.gov).*

Age-adjusted death rates are weighted averages of the age-specific death rates, where the weights represent a fixed population by age. They are used because the rates of almost all causes of death vary by age. Age adjustment is a technique for "removing" the effects of age from crude rates, so as to allow meaningful comparisons across populations with different underlying age structures. For example, comparing the crude rate of heart disease in New York to that of California is misleading, because the relatively older population in New York will lead to a higher crude death rate, even if the age-specific rates of heart disease in New York and California are the same. For such a comparison, age-adjusted rates would be preferable. Age-adjusted rates should be viewed as relative indexes rather than as direct or actual measures of mortality risk.

Death rates based on counts of twenty or less (<=20) are flagged as "Unreliable". Death rates based on fewer than three years of data for counties with populations of less than 100,000 in the 1990 Census counts, are also flagged as "Unreliable" if the number of deaths is five or less (<=5).

Air Quality Index: The percentage of days in 2005 the AQI fell into the Good (0-50), Moderate (51-100), Unhealthy for Sensitive Groups (101-150), and Unhealthy (151+) ranges. *Source: Air Quality Index Report, 2005, U.S. Environmental Protection Agency, Office of Air and Radiation (http://www.epa.gov/oar).*

The AQI is an index for reporting daily air quality. It tells you how clean or polluted your air is, and what associated health concerns you should be aware of. The AQI focuses on health effects that can happen within a few hours or days after breathing polluted air. EPA uses the AQI for five major air pollutants regulated by the Clean Air Act: ground-level ozone, particulate matter, carbon monoxide, sulfur dioxide, and nitrogen dioxide. For each of these pollutants, EPA has established national air quality standards to protect against harmful health effects.

The AQI runs from 0 to 500. The higher the AQI value, the greater the level of air pollution and the greater the health danger. For example, an AQI value of 50 represents good air quality and little potential to affect public health, while an AQI value over 300 represents hazardous air quality. An AQI value of 100 generally corresponds to the national air quality standard for the pollutant, which is the level EPA has set to protect public health. So, AQI values below 100 are generally thought of as satisfactory. When AQI values are above 100, air quality is considered to be unhealthy—at first for certain sensitive groups of people, then for everyone as AQI values get higher. Each category corresponds to a different level of health concern. For example, when the AQI for a pollutant is between 51 and 100, the health concern is "Moderate." Here are the six levels of health concern and what they mean:

- "Good" The AQI value for your community is between 0 and 50. Air quality is considered satisfactory and air pollution poses little or no risk.
- "Moderate" The AQI for your community is between 51 and 100. Air quality is acceptable; however, for some pollutants there may be a moderate health concern for a very small number of individuals. For example, people who are unusually sensitive to ozone may experience respiratory symptoms.
- "Unhealthy for Sensitive Groups" Certain groups of people are particularly sensitive to the harmful effects of certain air pollutants. This means they are likely to be affected at lower levels than the general public. For example, children and adults who are active outdoors and people with respiratory disease are at greater risk from exposure to ozone, while people with heart disease are at greater risk from carbon monoxide. Some people may be sensitive to more than one pollutant. When AQI values are between 101 and 150, members of sensitive groups may experience health effects. The general public is not likely to be affected when the AQI is in this range.
- "Unhealthy" AQI values are between 151 and 200. Everyone may begin to experience health effects. Members of sensitive groups may experience more serious health effects.
- "Very Unhealthy" AQI values between 201 and 300 trigger a health alert, meaning everyone may experience more serious health effects.
- "Hazardous" AQI values over 300 trigger health warnings of emergency conditions. The entire population is more likely to be affected.

Number of Physicians: The number of active, non-federal physicians per 10,000 population in 2004. *Source: Area Resource File (ARF). February 2005. U.S. Department of Health and Human Services, Health Resources and Services Administration, Bureau of Health Professions, Rockville, MD.*

Number of Hospital Beds: The number of hospital beds per 10,000 population in 2003. *Source: Area Resource File (ARF). February 2005. U.S. Department of Health and Human Services, Health Resources and Services Administration, Bureau of Health Professions, Rockville, MD.*

Number of Hospital Admissions: The number of hospital admissions per 10,000 population in 2003. *Source: Area Resource File (ARF). February 2005. U.S. Department of Health and Human Services, Health Resources and Services Administration, Bureau of Health Professions, Rockville, MD.*

ELECTIONS

Elections: 2004 Presidential election results. *Source: Dave Leip's Atlas of U.S. Presidential Elections (http://www.uselectionatlas.org).*

NATIONAL AND STATE PARKS

Lists National and State parks located in the area. *Source: U.S. Geological Survey, Geographic Names Information System.*

ADDITIONAL INFORMATION CONTACTS

The following phone numbers are provided as sources of additional information: Chambers of Commerce; Economic Development Agencies; Boards of Realtors; Convention & Visitors Bureaus. Efforts have been made to provide the most recent area codes. However, area code changes may have occurred in listed numbers. *Source: Original research.*

User's Guide: Education

School District Rankings

Number of Schools: Total number of schools in the district. *Source: U.S. Department of Education, National Center for Education Statistics, Common Core of Data, Public Elementary/Secondary School Universe Survey: School Year 2003-2004.*

Number of Teachers: Teachers are defined as individuals who provide instruction to pre-kindergarten, kindergarten, grades 1 through 12, or ungraded classes, or individuals who teach in an environment other than a classroom setting, and who maintain daily student attendance records. Numbers reported are full-time equivalents (FTE). *Source: U.S. Department of Education, National Center for Education Statistics, Common Core of Data, Local Education Agency (School District) Universe Survey: School Year 2003-2004.*

Number of Students: A student is an individual for whom instruction is provided in an elementary or secondary education program that is not an adult education program and is under the jurisdiction of a school, school system, or other education institution. *Sources: U.S. Department of Education, National Center for Education Statistics, Common Core of Data, Local Education Agency (School District) Universe Survey: School Year 2003-2004 and Public Elementary/Secondary School Universe Survey: School Year 2003-2004*

Individual Education Program (IEP) Students: A written instructional plan for students with disabilities designated as special education students under IDEA-Part B. The written instructional plan includes a statement of present levels of educational performance of a child; statement of annual goals, including short-term instructional objectives; statement of specific educational services to be provided and the extent to which the child will be able to participate in regular educational programs; the projected date for initiation and anticipated duration of services; the appropriate objectives, criteria and evaluation procedures; and the schedules for determining, on at least an annual basis, whether instructional objectives are being achieved. *Source: U.S. Department of Education, National Center for Education Statistics, Common Core of Data, Local Education Agency (School District) Universe Survey: School Year 2003-2004*

English Language Learner (ELL) Students: Formerly referred to as Limited English Proficient (LEP). Students being served in appropriate programs of language assistance (e.g., English as a Second Language, High Intensity Language Training, bilingual education). Does not include pupils enrolled in a class to learn a language other than English. Also Limited-English-Proficient students are individuals who were not born in the United States or whose native language is a language other than English; or individuals who come from environments where a language other than English is dominant; or individuals who are American Indians and Alaskan Natives and who come from environments where a language other than English has had a significant impact on their level of English language proficiency; and who, by reason thereof, have sufficient difficulty speaking, reading, writing, or understanding the English language, to deny such individuals the opportunity to learn successfully in classrooms where the language of instruction is English or to participate fully in our society. *Source: U.S. Department of Education, National Center for Education Statistics, Common Core of Data, Local Education Agency (School District) Universe Survey: School Year 2003-2004*

Migrant Students: A migrant student as defined under federal regulation 34 CFR 200.40: 1) (a) Is younger than 22 (and has not graduated from high school or does not hold a high school equivalency certificate), but (b), if the child is too young to attend school-sponsored educational programs, is old enough to benefit from an organized instructional program; and 2) A migrant agricultural worker or a migrant fisher or has a parent, spouse, or guardian who is a migrant agricultural worker or a migrant fisher; and 3) Performs, or has a parent, spouse, or guardian who performs qualifying agricultural or fishing employment as a principal means of livelihood; and 4) Has moved within the preceding 36 months to obtain or to accompany or join a parent, spouse, or guardian to obtain, temporary or seasonal employment in agricultural or fishing work; and 5) Has moved from one school district to another; or in a state that is comprised of a single school district, has moved from one administrative area to another within such district; or resides in a school district of more than 15,000 square miles, and migrates a distance of 20 miles or more to a temporary residence to engage in a fishing activity. Provision 5 currently applies only to Alaska. *Source: U.S. Department of Education, National Center for Education Statistics, Common Core of Data, Public Elementary/Secondary School Universe Survey: School Year 2003-2004*

Students Eligible for Free Lunch Program: The free lunch program is defined as a program under the National School Lunch Act that provides cash subsidies for free lunches to students based on family size and income criteria. *Source: U.S. Department of Education, National Center for Education Statistics, Common Core of Data, Public Elementary/Secondary School Universe Survey: School Year 2003-2004*

Students Eligible for Reduced-Price Lunch Program: A student who is eligible to participate in the Reduced-Price Lunch Program under the National School Lunch Act. *Source: U.S. Department of Education, National Center for Education Statistics, Common Core of Data, Public Elementary/Secondary School Universe Survey: School Year 2003-2004*

Student/Teacher Ratio: The number of students divided by the number of teachers (FTE). See Number of Students and Number of Teachers above for for information.

Student/Librarian Ratio: The number of students divided by the number of library and media support staff. Library and media support staff are defined as staff members who render other professional library and media services; also includes library aides and those involved in library/media support. Their duties include selecting, preparing, caring for, and making available to instructional staff, equipment, films, filmstrips, transparencies, tapes, TV programs, and similar materials maintained separately or as part of an instructional materials center. Also included are activities in the audio-visual center, TV studio, related-work-study areas, and services provided by audio-visual personnel. Numbers are based on full-time equivalents. *Source: U.S. Department of Education, National Center for Education Statistics, Common Core of Data, Local Education Agency (School District) Universe Survey: School Year 2003-2004.*

Student/Counselor Ratio: The number of students divided by the number of guidance counselors. Guidance counselors are professional staff assigned specific duties and school time for any of the following activities in an elementary or secondary setting: counseling with students and parents; consulting with other staff members on learning problems; evaluating student abilities; assisting students in making educational and career choices; assisting students in personal and social development; providing referral assistance; and/or working with other staff members in planning and conducting guidance programs for students. The state applies its own standards in apportioning the aggregate of guidance counselors/directors into the elementary and secondary level components. Numbers reported are full-time equivalents. *Source: U.S. Department of Education, National Center for Education Statistics, Common Core of Data, Local Education Agency (School District) Universe Survey: School Year 2003-2004.*

Current Spending per Student: Expenditure for Instruction, Support Services, and Other Elementary/Secondary Programs. Includes salaries, employee benefits, purchased services, and supplies, as well as payments made by states on behalf of school districts. Also includes transfers made by school districts into their own retirement system. Excludes expenditure for Non-Elementary/Secondary Programs, debt service, capital outlay, and transfers to other governments or school districts. This item is formally called "Current Expenditures for Public Elementary/Secondary Education."

Instruction: Includes payments from all funds for salaries, employee benefits, supplies, materials, and contractual services for elementary/secondary instruction. It excludes capital outlay, debt service, and interfund transfers for elementary/secondary instruction. Instruction covers regular, special, and vocational programs offered in both the regular school year and summer school. It excludes instructional support activities as well as adult education and community services. Instruction salaries includes salaries for teachers and teacher aides and assistants.

Support Services: Relates to support services functions (series 2000) defined in Financial Accounting for Local and State School Systems (National Center for Education Statistics 2000). Includes payments from all funds for salaries, employee benefits, supplies, materials, and contractual services. It excludes capital outlay, debt service, and interfund transfers. It includes expenditure for the following functions:

- Business/Central/Other Support Services
- General Administration
- Instructional Staff Support
- Operation and Maintenance
- Pupil Support Services
- Pupil Transportation Services
- School Administration
- Nonspecified Support Services

Values shown are dollars per pupil per year. They were calculated by dividing the total dollar amounts by the fall membership. Fall membership is comprised of the total student enrollment on October 1 (or the closest school day to October 1) for all grade levels (including prekindergarten and kindergarten) and ungraded pupils. Membership includes students both present and absent on the measurement day. *Source: U.S. Department of Education, National Center for Education Statistics, Common Core of Data, School District Finance Survey (F-33), Fiscal Year 2001.*

Number of Diploma Recipients: A student who has received a diploma during the previous school year or subsequent summer school. This category includes regular diploma recipients and other diploma recipients. A High School Diploma is a formal document certifying the successful completion of a secondary school program prescribed by the state education agency or other appropriate body. *Source: U.S. Department of Education, National Center for Education Statistics, Common Core of Data, Local Education Agency (School District) Universe Survey: School Year 2003-2004.*

High School Drop-out Rate: A dropout is a student who was enrolled in school at some time during the previous school year; was not enrolled at the beginning of the current school year; has not graduated from high school or completed a state or district approved educational program; and does not meet any of the following exclusionary conditions: has transferred to another public school district, private school, or state- or district-approved educational program; is temporarily absent due to suspension or school-approved illness; or has died. The values shown cover grades 9 through 12. *Source: U.S. Department of Education, National Center for Education Statistics, Common Core of Data, Local Education Agency Universe Dropout File: School Year 2000-2001*

Note: n/a indicates data not available.

New York Educational Profile

Please refer to the District Rankings section in the front of this User's Guide for an explanation of data for all items except for the following:

Average Salary: The average teacher salary in 2003-2004. *Source: American Federation of Teachers, Survey & Analysis of Teacher Salary Trends 2004*

College Entrance Exam Scores:

Scholastic Aptitude Test (SAT). *Note: The College Board strongly discourages the comparison or ranking of states on the basis of SAT scores alone. Source: The College Board, Mean SAT Reasoning Test™ Verbal and Math Scores by State, with Changes for Selected Years, 2005*

American College Testing Program (ACT). *ACT, 2005 ACT National and State Scores*

National Assessment of Educational Progress (NAEP)

The National Assessment of Educational Progress (NAEP), also known as "the Nation's Report Card," is the only nationally representative and continuing assessment of what America's students know and can do in various subject areas. As a result of the "No Child Left Behind" legislation, all states are required to participate in NAEP. Beginning with the 2003-2004 school year, all schools in New York that are part of the sample drawn by the National Center for Education Statistics shall administer the biennial State academic assessments of 4th and 8th grade reading and mathematics under the National Assessment of Educational Progress. For more information please visit the U.S. Department of Education, National Center for Education Statistics at http://nces.ed.gov/nationsreportcard or the New York State Board of Education at http://www.isbe.state.il.us/assessment/naep.htm

User's Guide: Ancestry

Places Covered

The ranking tables are based on 1,977 places and 9 reservations in New York (except where noted). Places covered fall into one of the following categories:

1,552 incorporated municipalities. Municipalities are incorporated as either cities, towns, or villages.

434 census designated places (CDP). The U.S. Bureau of the Census defines a CDP as "a statistical entity, defined for each decennial census according to Census Bureau guidelines, comprising a densely settled concentration of population that is not within an incorporated place, but is locally identified by a name. CDPs are delineated cooperatively by state and local officials and the Census Bureau, following Census Bureau guidelines. Beginning with Census 2000 there are no size limits."

Source of Data

The ancestries shown in this chapter were compiled from three different sections of the 2000 Census: Race; Hispanic Origin; and Ancestry. While the ancestries are sorted alphabetically for ease-of-use, it's important to note the origin of each piece of data. Data for Race and Hispanic Origin was taken from Summary File 1 (SF1) while Ancestry data was taken from Summary File 3 (SF3). The distinction is important because SF1 contains the 100-percent data, which is the information compiled from the questions asked of all people and about every housing unit. SF3 was compiled from a sample of approximately 19 million housing units (about 1 in 6 households) that received the Census 2000 long-form questionnaire.

Ancestries Based on Race

The data on race were derived from answers to the question on race that was asked of all people. The concept of race, as used by the Census Bureau, reflects self-identification by people according to the race or races with which they most closely identify. These categories are sociopolitical constructs and should not be interpreted as being scientific or anthropological in nature. Furthermore, the race categories include both racial and national-origin groups.

If an individual did not provide a race response, the race or races of the householder or other household members were assigned using specific rules of precedence of household relationship. For example, if race was missing for a natural-born child in the household, then either the race or races of the householder, another natural-born child, or the spouse of the householder were assigned. If race was not reported for anyone in the household, the race or races of a householder in a previously processed household were assigned.

- African-American/Black:
    - Not Hispanic
    - Hispanic
- Alaska Native tribes, specified:
    - Alaska Athabascan
    - Aleut
    - Eskimo
    - Tlingit-Haida
    - All other tribes
- Alaska Native tribes, not specified
- American Indian or Alaska Native tribes, not specified
- American Indian tribes, specified:
    - Apache
    - Blackfeet
    - Cherokee
    - Cheyenne
    - Chickasaw
    - Chippewa
    - Choctaw
    - Colville
    - Comanche
    - Cree
    - Creek
    - Crow
    - Delaware
    - Houma
    - Iroquois
    - Kiowa
    - Latin American Indians
    - Lumbee
    - Menominee
    - Navajo
    - Osage
    - Ottawa
    - Paiute
    - Pima
    - Potawatomi
    - Pueblo
    - Puget Sound Salish
    - Seminole
    - Shoshone
    - Sioux
    - Tohono O'Odham
    - Ute
    - Yakama
    - Yaqui
    - Yuman
    - All other tribes
- American Indian tribes, not specified
- Asian:
    - Bangladeshi
    - Cambodian
    - Chinese, except Taiwanese
    - Filipino
    - Hmong
    - Indian
    - Indonesian
    - Japanese
    - Korean
    - Laotian
    - Malaysian
    - Pakistani
    - Sri Lankan
    - Taiwanese
    - Thai
    - Vietnamese
    - Other Asian, specified
    - Other Asian, not specified
- Hawaii Native/Pacific Islander:
    - Melanesian:
        - Fijian
        - Other Melanesian
    - Micronesian:
        - Guamanian/Chamorro
        - Other Micronesian
    - Polynesian:
        - Native Hawaiian
        - Samoan
        - Tongan
        - Other Polynesian
    - Other Pacific Islander, specified
    - Other Pacific Islander, not specified
- White:
    - Not Hispanic
    - Hispanic

African American or Black: A person having origins in any of the Black racial groups of Africa. It includes people who indicate their race as "Black, African Am., or Negro," or provide written entries such as African American, Afro American, Kenyan, Nigerian, or Haitian.

American Indian or Alaska Native: A person having origins in any of the original peoples of North and South America (including Central America) and who maintain tribal affiliation or community attachment. It includes people who classified themselves as described below.

American Indian - Includes people who indicated their race as "American Indian," entered the name of an Indian tribe, or reported such entries as Canadian Indian, French American Indian, or Spanish-American Indian.

Respondents who identified themselves as American Indian were asked to report their enrolled or principal tribe. Therefore, tribal data in tabulations reflect the written entries reported on the questionnaires. Some of the entries (for example, Iroquois, Sioux, Colorado River, and Flathead) represent nations or reservations. The information on tribe is based on self identification and therefore does not reflect any designation of federally or state-recognized tribe. Information on American Indian tribes is presented in summary files. The information for Census 2000 is derived from the American Indian Tribal Classification List for the 1990 census that was updated based on a December 1997 Federal Register Notice, entitled "Indian Entities Recognized and Eligible to Receive Service From the United States Bureau of Indian Affairs," Department of the Interior, Bureau of Indian Affairs, issued by the Office of Management and Budget.

Alaska Native - Includes written responses of Eskimos, Aleuts, and Alaska Indians, as well as entries such as Arctic Slope, Inupiat, Yupik, Alutiiq, Egegik, and Pribilovian. The Alaska tribes are the Alaskan Athabascan, Tlingit, and Haida. The information for Census 2000 is based on the American Indian Tribal Classification List for the 1990 census, which was expanded to list the individual Alaska Native Villages when provided as a written response for race.

Asian: A person having origins in any of the original peoples of the Far East, Southeast Asia, or the Indian subcontinent including, for example, Cambodia, China, India, Japan, Korea, Malaysia, Pakistan, the Philippine Islands, Thailand, and Vietnam. It includes "Asian Indian," "Chinese," "Filipino," "Korean," "Japanese," "Vietnamese," and "Other Asian."

Asian Indian - Includes people who indicated their race as "Asian Indian" or identified themselves as Bengalese, Bharat, Dravidian, East Indian, or Goanese.

Chinese - Includes people who indicate their race as "Chinese" or who identify themselves as Cantonese, or Chinese American.

Filipino - Includes people who indicate their race as "Filipino" or who report entries such as Philipino, Philipine, or Filipino American.

Japanese - Includes people who indicate their race as "Japanese" or who report entries such as Nipponese or Japanese American.

Korean - Includes people who indicate their race as "Korean" or who provide a response of Korean American.

Vietnamese - Includes people who indicate their race as "Vietnamese" or who provide a response of Vietnamese American.

Cambodian - Includes people who provide a response such as Cambodian or Cambodia.

Hmong - Includes people who provide a response such as Hmong, Laohmong, or Mong.

Laotian - Includes people who provide a response such as Laotian, Laos, or Lao.

Thai - Includes people who provide a response such as Thai, Thailand, or Siamese.

Other Asian - Includes people who provide a response of Bangladeshi; Bhutanese; Burmese; Indochinese; Indonesian; Iwo Jiman; Madagascar; Malaysian; Maldivian; Nepalese; Okinawan; Pakistani; Singaporean; Sri Lankan; or Other Asian, specified and Other Asian, not specified.

Native Hawaiian or Other Pacific Islander: A person having origins in any of the original peoples of Hawaii, Guam, Samoa, or other Pacific Islands. It includes people who indicate their race as "Native Hawaiian," "Guamanian or Chamorro," "Samoan," and "Other Pacific Islander."

Native Hawaiian - Includes people who indicate their race as "Native Hawaiian" or who identify themselves as "Part Hawaiian" or "Hawaiian."

Guamanian or Chamorro - Includes people who indicate their race as such, including written entries of Chamorro or Guam.

Samoan - Includes people who indicate their race as "Samoan" or who identify themselves as American Samoan or Western Samoan.

Other Pacific Islander - Includes people who provide a write-in response of a Pacific Islander group, such as Carolinian, Chuukese (Trukese), Fijian, Kosraean, Melanesian, Micronesian, Northern Mariana Islander, Palauan, Papua New Guinean, Pohnpeian, Polynesian, Solomon Islander, Tahitian, Tokelauan, Tongan, Yapese, or Pacific Islander, not specified.

White: A person having origins in any of the original peoples of Europe, the Middle East, or North Africa. It includes people who indicate their race as "White" or report entries such as Irish, German, Italian, Lebanese, Near Easterner, Arab, or Polish.

Ancestries Based on Hispanic Origin

Hispanic or Latino:	Salvadoran	Argentinean	Uruguayan
Central American:	Other Central American	Bolivian	Venezuelan
Costa Rican	Cuban	Chilean	Other South American
Guatemalan	Dominican Republic	Colombian	Other Hispanic/Latino
Honduran	Mexican	Ecuadorian	
Nicaraguan	Puerto Rican	Paraguayan	
Panamanian	South American:	Peruvian	

The data on the Hispanic or Latino population were derived from answers to a question that was asked of all people. The terms "Spanish," "Hispanic origin," and "Latino" are used interchangeably. Some respondents identify with all three terms while others may identify with only one of these three specific terms. Hispanics or Latinos who identify with the terms "Spanish," "Hispanic," or "Latino" are those who classify themselves in one of the specific Spanish, Hispanic, or Latino categories listed on the questionnaire ("Mexican," "Puerto Rican," or "Cuban") as well as those who indicate that they are "other Spanish/Hispanic/Latino." People who do not identify with one of the specific origins listed on the questionnaire but indicate that they are "other Spanish, Hispanic, or Latino" are those whose origins are from Spain, the Spanish-speaking countries of Central or South America, the Dominican Republic, or people identifying themselves generally as Spanish, Spanish-American, Hispanic, Hispano, Latino, and so on. All write-in responses to the "other Spanish/Hispanic/Latino" category were coded.

Origin can be viewed as the heritage, nationality group, lineage, or country of birth of the person or the person's parents or ancestors before their arrival in the United States. People who identify their origin as Spanish, Hispanic, or Latino may be of any race.

In all cases where the origin of households, families, or occupied housing units is classified as Spanish, Hispanic, or Latino, the origin of the householder is used. If an individual could not provide a Hispanic origin response, their origin was assigned using specific rules of precedence of household relationship. For example, if origin was missing for a natural-born daughter in the household, then either the origin of the householder, another natural-born child, or spouse of the householder was assigned. If Hispanic origin was not reported for anyone in the household, the Hispanic origin of a householder in a previously processed household with the same race was assigned.

Other Ancestries

Acadian/Cajun	Moroccan	French, except Basque	Scottish
Afghan	Palestinian	French Canadian	Serbian
African, Subsaharan:	Syrian	German	Slavic
African	Other Arab	German Russian	Slovak
Cape Verdean	Armenian	Greek	Slovene
Ethiopian	Assyrian/Chaldean/Syriac	Guyanese	Soviet Union
Ghanian	Australian	Hungarian	Swedish
Kenyan	Austrian	Icelander	Swiss
Liberian	Basque	Iranian	Turkish
Nigerian	Belgian	Irish	Ukrainian
Senegalese	Brazilian	Israeli	United States or American
Sierra Leonean	British	Italian	Welsh
Somalian	Bulgarian	Latvian	West Indian, excluding Hispanic:
South African	Canadian	Lithuanian	Bahamian
Sudanese	Carpatho Rusyn	Luxemburger	Barbadian
Ugandan	Celtic	Macedonian	Belizean
Zairian	Croatian	Maltese	Bermudan
Zimbabwean	Cypriot	New Zealander	British West Indian
Other Subsaharan African	Czech	Northern European	Dutch West Indian
Albanian	Czechoslovakian	Norwegian	Haitian
Alsatian	Danish	Pennsylvania German	Jamaican
Arab:	Dutch	Polish	Trinidadian and
Arab/Arabic	Eastern European	Portuguese	Tobagonian
Egyptian	English	Romanian	U.S. Virgin Islander
Iraqi	Estonian	Russian	West Indian
Jordanian	European	Scandinavian	Other West Indian
Lebanese	Finnish	Scotch-Irish	Yugoslavian

The data on ancestry were derived from answers to long-form questionnaire Item 10, which was asked of a sample of the population. The data represent self-classification by people according to the ancestry group or groups with which they most closely identify. Ancestry refers to a person's ethnic origin or descent, "roots," heritage, or the place of birth of the person, the person's parents, or their ancestors before their arrival in the United States. Some ethnic identities, such as Egyptian or Polish, can be traced to geographic areas outside the United States, while other ethnicities, such as Pennsylvania German or Cajun, evolved in the United States.

The intent of the ancestry question was not to measure the degree of attachment the respondent had to a particular ethnicity. For example, a response of "Irish" might reflect total involvement in an Irish community or only a memory of ancestors several generations removed from the individual. Also, the question was intended to provide data for groups that were not included in the Hispanic origin and race questions. Official Hispanic origin data come from long-form questionnaire Item 5, and official race data come from long-form questionnaire Item 6. Therefore, although data on all groups are collected, the ancestry data shown in these tabulations are for non-Hispanic and non-race groups.

The ancestry question allowed respondents to report one or more ancestry groups, although only the first two were coded. If a response was in terms of a dual ancestry, for example, "Irish English," the person was assigned two codes, in this case one for Irish and another for English. However, in certain cases, multiple responses such as "French Canadian," "Greek Cypriote," and "Scotch Irish" were assigned a single code reflecting their status as unique groups. If a person reported one of these unique groups in addition to another group, for example, "Scotch Irish English," resulting in three terms, that person received one code for the unique group (Scotch-Irish) and another one for the remaining group (English). If a person reported "English Irish French," only English and Irish were coded. Certain combinations of ancestries where the ancestry group is a part of another, such as "German-Bavarian," were coded as a single ancestry using the more specific group (Bavarian). Also, responses such as "Polish-American" or "Italian-American" were coded and tabulated as a single entry (Polish or Italian).

The Census Bureau accepted "American" as a unique ethnicity if it was given alone, with an ambiguous response, or with state names. If the respondent listed any other ethnic identity such as "Italian-American," generally the "American" portion of the response was not coded. However, distinct groups such as "American Indian," "Mexican American," and "African American" were coded and identified separately because they represented groups who considered themselves different from those who reported as "Indian," "Mexican," or "African," respectively.

Census 2000 tabulations on ancestry are presented using two types of data presentations — one using total people as the base, and the other using total responses as the base. This chapter uses total responses as the base and includes the total number of ancestries reported and coded. If a person reported a multiple ancestry such as "French Danish," that response was counted twice in the tabulations — once in the French category and again in the Danish category. Thus, the sum of the counts in this type of presentation is not the total population but the total of all responses.

An automated coding system was used for coding ancestry in Census 2000. This greatly reduced the potential for error associated with a clerical review. Specialists with knowledge of the subject matter reviewed, edited, coded, and resolved inconsistent or incomplete responses. The code list used in Census 2000, containing over 1,000 categories, reflects the results of the Census Bureau's experience with the 1990 ancestry question, research, and consultation with many ethnic experts. Many decisions were made to determine the classification of responses. These decisions affected the grouping of the tabulated data. For example, the Italian category includes the responses of Sicilian and Tuscan, as well as a number of other responses.

Although some people consider religious affiliation a component of ethnic identity, the ancestry question was not designed to collect any information concerning religion. Thus, if a religion was given as an answer to the ancestry question, it was listed in the "Other groups" category which is not shown in this chapter.

Ancestry should not be confused with a person's place of birth, although a person's place of birth and ancestry may be the same.

Ranking Section

In the ranking section of this chapter, each ancestry has three tables. The first table shows the top 10 places sorted by number (based on all places, regardless of population), the second table shows the top 10 places sorted by percent (based on all places, regardless of population), the third table shows the top 10 places sorted by percent (based on places with populations of 10,000 or more).

Within each table, column one displays the place name, the state, and the county (if a place spans more than one county, the county that holds the majority of the population is shown). Column two displays the number of people reporting each ancestry, and column three is the percent of the total population reporting each ancestry. For tables representing ancestries based on race or Hispanic origin, the 100-percent population figure from SF1 is used to calculate the value in the "%" column. For all other ancestries the sample population figure from SF3 is used to calculate the value in the "%" column.

Alphabetical Ancestry Cross-Reference Guide

Acadian/Cajun
Afghan
African *See African, sub-Saharan: African*
African American/Black
African American/Black: Hispanic
African American/Black: Not Hispanic
African, sub-Saharan
African, sub-Saharan: African
African, sub-Saharan: Cape Verdean
African, sub-Saharan: Ethiopian
African, sub-Saharan: Ghanian
African, sub-Saharan: Kenyan
African, sub-Saharan: Liberian
African, sub-Saharan: Nigerian
African, sub-Saharan: Other
African, sub-Saharan: Senegalese
African, sub-Saharan: Sierra Leonean
African, sub-Saharan: Somalian
African, sub-Saharan: South African
African, sub-Saharan: Sudanese
African, sub-Saharan: Ugandan
African, sub-Saharan: Zairian
African, sub-Saharan: Zimbabwean
Alaska Athabascan *See Alaska Native: Alaska Athabascan*
Alaska Native tribes, not specified
Alaska Native tribes, specified
Alaska Native: Alaska Athabascan
Alaska Native: Aleut
Alaska Native: All other tribes
Alaska Native: Eskimo
Alaska Native: Tlingit-Haida
Albanian
Aleut *See Alaska Native: Aleut*
Alsatian
American *See United States or American*
American Indian or Alaska Native tribes, not specified
American Indian tribes, not specified
American Indian tribes, specified
American Indian: All other tribes
American Indian: Apache
American Indian: Blackfeet
American Indian: Cherokee
American Indian: Cheyenne
American Indian: Chickasaw
American Indian: Chippewa
American Indian: Choctaw
American Indian: Colville
American Indian: Comanche
American Indian: Cree
American Indian: Creek
American Indian: Crow
American Indian: Delaware
American Indian: Houma
American Indian: Iroquois
American Indian: Kiowa
American Indian: Latin American Indians
American Indian: Lumbee
American Indian: Menominee
American Indian: Navajo
American Indian: Osage
American Indian: Ottawa
American Indian: Paiute
American Indian: Pima
American Indian: Potawatomi
American Indian: Pueblo
American Indian: Puget Sound Salish
American Indian: Seminole
American Indian: Shoshone
American Indian: Sioux
American Indian: Tohono O'Odham
American Indian: Ute
American Indian: Yakama
American Indian: Yaqui
American Indian: Yuman
Apache *See American Indian: Apache*
Arab
Arab/Arabic *See Arab: Arab/Arabic*
Arab: Arab/Arabic
Arab: Egyptian
Arab: Iraqi
Arab: Jordanian
Arab: Lebanese
Arab: Moroccan
Arab: Other
Arab: Palestinian
Arab: Syrian
Argentinean *See Hispanic: Argentinean*
Armenian
Asian
Asian: Bangladeshi
Asian: Cambodian
Asian: Chinese, except Taiwanese
Asian: Filipino
Asian: Hmong
Asian: Indian
Asian: Indonesian
Asian: Japanese
Asian: Korean
Asian: Laotian
Asian: Malaysian
Asian: Other Asian, not specified
Asian: Other Asian, specified
Asian: Pakistani
Asian: Sri Lankan
Asian: Taiwanese
Asian: Thai
Asian: Vietnamese
Assyrian/Chaldean/Syriac
Australian
Austrian
Bahamian *See West Indian: Bahamian, excluding Hispanic*
Bangladeshi *See Asian: Bangladeshi*
Barbadian *See West Indian: Barbadian, excluding Hispanic*
Basque
Belgian
Belizean *See West Indian: Belizean, excluding Hispanic*
Bermudan *See West Indian: Bermudan, excluding Hispanic*
Blackfeet *See American Indian: Blackfeet*
Bolivian *See Hispanic: Bolivian*
Brazilian
British
British West Indian *See West Indian: British West Indian, excluding Hispanic*
Bulgarian
Cambodian *See Asian: Cambodian*
Canadian
Cape Verdean *See African, sub-Saharan: Cape Verdean*
Carpatho Rusyn
Celtic
Central American: *See Hispanic: Central American*
Cherokee *See American Indian: Cherokee*
Cheyenne *See American Indian: Cheyenne*
Chickasaw *See American Indian: Chickasaw*
Chilean *See Hispanic: Chilean*
Chinese, except Taiwanese *See Asian: Chinese, except Taiwanese*
Chippewa *See American Indian: Chippewa*
Choctaw *See American Indian: Choctaw*
Colombian *See Hispanic: Colombian*
Colville *See American Indian: Colville*
Comanche *See American Indian: Comanche*
Costa Rican *See Hispanic: Costa Rican*
Cree *See American Indian: Cree*
Creek *See American Indian: Creek*
Croatian
Crow *See American Indian: Crow*
Cuban *See Hispanic: Cuban*
Cypriot
Czech
Czechoslovakian
Danish
Delaware *See American Indian: Delaware*
Dominican Republic *See Hispanic: Dominican Republic*
Dutch
Dutch West Indian *See West Indian: Dutch West Indian, excluding Hispanic*
Eastern European
Ecuadorian *See Hispanic: Ecuadorian*
Egyptian *See Arab: Egyptian*
English
Eskimo *See Alaska Native: Eskimo*
Estonian
Ethiopian *See African, sub-Saharan: Ethiopian*
European
Fijian *See Hawaii Native/Pacific Islander: Fijian*
Filipino *See Asian: Filipino*
Finnish
French Canadian
French, except Basque
German
German Russian
Ghanian *See African, sub-Saharan: Ghanian*
Greek
Guamanian or Chamorro *See Hawaii Native/Pacific Islander: Guamanian or Chamorro*
Guatemalan *See Hispanic: Guatemalan*
Guyanese
Haitian *See West Indian: Haitian, excluding Hispanic*
Hawaii Native/Pacific Islander
Hawaii Native/Pacific Islander: Fijian
Hawaii Native/Pacific Islander: Guamanian or Chamorro
Hawaii Native/Pacific Islander: Melanesian
Hawaii Native/Pacific Islander: Micronesian
Hawaii Native/Pacific Islander: Native Hawaiian
Hawaii Native/Pacific Islander: Other Melanesian
Hawaii Native/Pacific Islander: Other Micronesian

User's Guide: Ancestry xxv

Hawaii Native/Pacific Islander: Other Pacific Islander, not specified
Hawaii Native/Pacific Islander: Other Pacific Islander, specified
Hawaii Native/Pacific Islander: Other Polynesian
Hawaii Native/Pacific Islander: Polynesian
Hawaii Native/Pacific Islander: Samoan
Hawaii Native/Pacific Islander: Tongan
Hispanic or Latino
Hispanic: Argentinean
Hispanic: Bolivian
Hispanic: Central American
Hispanic: Chilean
Hispanic: Colombian
Hispanic: Costa Rican
Hispanic: Cuban
Hispanic: Dominican Republic
Hispanic: Ecuadorian
Hispanic: Guatemalan
Hispanic: Honduran
Hispanic: Mexican
Hispanic: Nicaraguan
Hispanic: Other
Hispanic: Other Central American
Hispanic: Other South American
Hispanic: Panamanian
Hispanic: Paraguayan
Hispanic: Peruvian
Hispanic: Puerto Rican
Hispanic: Salvadoran
Hispanic: South American
Hispanic: Uruguayan
Hispanic: Venezuelan
Hmong *See Asian: Hmong*
Honduran *See Hispanic: Honduran*
Houma *See American Indian: Houma*
Hungarian
Icelander
Indian, American *See American Indian*
Indian, Asian *See Asian: Indian*
Indonesian *See Asian: Indonesian*
Iranian
Iraqi *See Arab: Iraqi*
Irish
Iroquois *See American Indian: Iroquois*
Israeli
Italian
Jamaican *See West Indian: Jamaican, excluding Hispanic*
Japanese *See Asian: Japanese*
Jordanian *See Arab: Jordanian*
Kenyan *See African, sub-Saharan: Kenyan*
Kiowa *See American Indian: Kiowa*
Korean *See Asian: Korean*
Laotian *See Asian: Laotian*
Latin American Indians *See American Indian: Latin American Indians*
Latino *See Hispanic or Latino*
Latvian
Lebanese *See Arab: Lebanese*
Liberian *See African, sub-Saharan: Liberian*
Lithuanian
Lumbee *See American Indian: Lumbee*
Luxemburger
Macedonian
Malaysian *See Asian: Malaysian*
Maltese
Melanesian: *See Hawaii Native/Pacific Islander: Melanesian*
Menominee *See American Indian: Menominee*
Mexican *See Hispanic: Mexican*
Micronesian: *See Hawaii Native/Pacific Islander: Micronesian*
Moroccan *See Arab: Moroccan*
Native Hawaiian *See Hawaii Native/Pacific Islander: Native Hawaiian*
Navajo *See American Indian: Navajo*
New Zealander
Nicaraguan *See Hispanic: Nicaraguan*
Nigerian *See African, sub-Saharan: Nigerian*
Northern European
Norwegian
Osage *See American Indian: Osage*
Ottawa *See American Indian: Ottawa*
Paiute *See American Indian: Paiute*
Pakistani *See Asian: Pakistani*
Palestinian *See Arab: Palestinian*
Panamanian *See Hispanic: Panamanian*
Paraguayan *See Hispanic: Paraguayan*
Pennsylvania German
Peruvian *See Hispanic: Peruvian*
Pima *See American Indian: Pima*
Polish
Polynesian: *See Hawaii Native/Pacific Islander: Polynesian*
Portuguese
Potawatomi *See American Indian: Potawatomi*
Pueblo *See American Indian: Pueblo*
Puerto Rican *See Hispanic: Puerto Rican*
Puget Sound Salish *See American Indian: Puget Sound Salish*
Romanian
Russian
Salvadoran *See Hispanic: Salvadoran*
Samoan *See Hawaii Native/Pacific Islander: Samoan*
Scandinavian
Scotch-Irish
Scottish
Seminole *See American Indian: Seminole*
Senegalese *See African, sub-Saharan: Senegalese*
Serbian
Shoshone *See American Indian: Shoshone*
Sierra Leonean *See African, sub-Saharan: Sierra Leonean*
Sioux *See American Indian: Sioux*
Slavic
Slovak
Slovene
Somalian *See African, sub-Saharan: Somalian*
South African *See African, sub-Saharan: South African*
South American: *See Hispanic: South American*
Soviet Union
Sri Lankan *See Asian: Sri Lankan*
sub-Saharan African *See African, sub-Saharan*
Sudanese *See African, sub-Saharan: Sudanese*
Swedish
Swiss
Syrian *See Arab: Syrian*
Taiwanese *See Asian: Taiwanese*
Thai *See Asian: Thai*
Tlingit-Haida *See Alaska Native: Tlingit-Haida*
Tohono O'Odham *See American Indian: Tohono O'Odham*
Tongan *See Hawaii Native/Pacific Islander: Tongan*
Trinidadian and Tobagonian *See West Indian: Trinidadian and Tobagonian, excluding Hispanic*
Turkish
U.S. Virgin Islander *See West Indian: U.S. Virgin Islander, excluding Hispanic*
Ugandan *See African, sub-Saharan: Ugandan*
Ukrainian
United States or American
Uruguayan *See Hispanic: Uruguayan*
Ute *See American Indian: Ute*
Venezuelan *See Hispanic: Venezuelan*
Vietnamese *See Asian: Vietnamese*
Welsh
West Indian, excluding Hispanic
West Indian: Bahamian, excluding Hispanic
West Indian: Barbadian, excluding Hispanic
West Indian: Belizean, excluding Hispanic
West Indian: Bermudan, excluding Hispanic
West Indian: British West Indian, excluding Hispanic
West Indian: Dutch West Indian, excluding Hispanic
West Indian: Haitian, excluding Hispanic
West Indian: Jamaican, excluding Hispanic
West Indian: Other, excluding Hispanic
West Indian: Trinidadian and Tobagonian, excluding Hispanic
West Indian: U.S. Virgin Islanders, excluding Hispanic
West Indian: West Indian, excluding Hispanic
White
White: Hispanic
White: Not Hispanic
Yakama *See American Indian: Yakama*
Yaqui *See American Indian: Yaqui*
Yugoslavian
Yuman *See American Indian: Yuman*
Zairian *See African, sub-Saharan: Zairian*
Zimbabwean *See African, sub-Saharan: Zimbabwean*

User's Guide: Hispanic Population

Places Covered

Ranking tables cover all counties and all places in New York with populations of 10,000 or more.

Source of Data

CENSUS 2000

Data for this chapter was derived from following source: *U.S. Bureau of the Census, Census of Population and Housing, 2000: Summary File 4.* Summary File 4 (SF 4) contains sample data, which is the information compiled from the questions asked of a sample (generally 1-in-6) of all people and housing units. Summary File 4 is repeated or iterated for the total population and 335 additional population groups. This chapter focuses on the following 24 population groups:

Hispanic or Latino (of any race)
    Central American
        Costa Rican
        Guatemalan
        Honduran
        Nicaraguan
        Panamanian
        Salvadoran
    Cuban
    Dominican (Dominican Republic)
    Mexican
    Puerto Rican
    South American
        Argentinian
        Bolivian
        Chilean
        Colombian
        Ecuadorian
        Paraguayan
        Peruvian
        Uruguayan
        Venezuelan
    Spaniard
    Other Hispanic or Latino

Please note that the above list only includes Spanish-speaking population groups. Groups such as Brazilian are not classified as Hispanic by the Bureau of the Census because they primarily speak Portugese.

In order for any of the tables for a specific group to be shown in Summary File 4, the data must meet a minimum population threshold. For Summary File 4, all tables are repeated for each race group, American Indian and Alaska Native tribe, and Hispanic or Latino group if the 100-percent count of people of that specific group in a particular geographic area is 100 or more. There also must be 50 or more unweighted people of that specific group in a particular geographic area. For example, if there are 100 or more 100-percent people tabulated as Chilean in County A, and there are 50 or more unweighted people, then all matrices for Chilean are shown in SF 4 for County A.

To maintain confidentiality, the Census Bureau applies statistical procedures that introduce some uncertainty into data for small geographic areas with small population groups. Therefore, tables may contain both sampling and nonsampling error.

In an iterated file such as SF 4, the universes *households, families,* and *occupied housing units* are classified by the race or ethnic group of the householder. In any population table where there is no note, the universe classification is always based on the race or ethnicity of the person. In all housing tables, the universe classification is based on the race or ethnicity of the householder.

Comparing SF 4 Estimates with Corresponding Values in SF 1 and SF 2

As in earlier censuses, the responses from the sample of households reporting on long forms must be weighted to reflect the entire population. Specifically, each responding household represents, on average, six or seven other households who reported using short forms. One consequence of the weighting procedures is that each estimate based on the long form responses has an associated confidence interval. These confidence intervals are wider (as a percentage of the estimate) for geographic areas with smaller populations and for characteristics that occur less frequently in the area being examined (such as the proportion of people in poverty in a middle-income neighborhood). In order to release as much useful information as possible, statisticians must balance a number of factors. In particular, for Census 2000, the Bureau of the Census created weighting areas—geographic areas from which about two hundred or more long forms were completed—which are large enough to produce good quality estimates. If smaller weighting areas had been used, the confidence intervals around the estimates would have been significantly wider, rendering many estimates less useful due to their lower reliability. The disadvantage of using weighting areas this large is that, for smaller geographic areas within them, the estimates of characteristics that are also reported on the short form will not match the counts reported in SF 1 or SF 2. Examples of these characteristics are the total number of people, the number of people reporting specific racial categories, and the number of housing units. The official values for items reported on the short form come from SF 1 and SF 2. The differences between the long form estimates in SF 4 and values in SF 1 or SF 2 are particularly noticeable for the smallest places, tracts, and block groups. The long form estimates of total population and total housing units in SF 4 will, however, match the SF 1 and SF 2 counts for larger geographic areas such as counties and states, and will be essentially the same for medium and large cities. This phenomenon also occurred for the 1990 Census, although in that case, the weighting areas included relatively small places. As a result, the long form estimates matched the short form counts for those places, but the confidence intervals around the estimates of characteristics collected only on the long form were often significantly wider (as a percentage of the estimate). SF 1 gives exact numbers even for very small groups and areas; whereas, SF 4 gives estimates for small groups and areas such as tracts and small places that are less exact. The goal of SF 4 is to identify large differences among areas or large changes over time. Estimates for small areas and small population groups often do exhibit large changes from one census to the next, so having the capability to measure them is worthwhile.

Topics

POPULATION

Total Population: Sample count of total population.

Hispanic Population: The data on the Hispanic or Latino population, which was asked of all people, were derived from answers to long-form questionnaire Item 5, and short-form questionnaire Item 7. The terms "Spanish," "Hispanic origin," and "Latino" are used interchangeably. Some respondents identify with all three terms, while others may identify with only one of these three specific terms. Hispanics or Latinos who identify with the terms "Spanish," "Hispanic," or "Latino" are those who classify themselves in one of the specific Hispanic or Latino categories listed on the questionnaire — "Mexican," "Puerto Rican," or "Cuban" — as well as those who indicate that they are "other Spanish, Hispanic, or Latino." People who do not identify with one of the specific origins listed on the questionnaire but indicate that they are "other Spanish, Hispanic, or Latino" are those whose origins are from Spain, the Spanish-speaking countries of Central or South America, the Dominican Republic, or people identifying themselves generally as Spanish, Spanish-American, Hispanic, Hispano, Latino, and so on. All write-in responses to the "other Spanish/Hispanic/Latino" category were coded. Origin can be viewed as the heritage, nationality group, lineage, or country of birth of the person or the person's parents or ancestors before their arrival in the United States. People who identify their origin as Spanish, Hispanic, or Latino may be of any race.

Population groups whose primary language is not Spanish are not classified as Hispanic by the Bureau of the Census and are not included in this chapter (eg. Brazilian).

AGE

Median Age: Divides the age distribution into two equal parts: one-half of the cases falling below the median age and one-half above the median. Median age is computed on the basis of a single year of age standard distribution.

The data on age, which was asked of all people, were derived from answers to the long-form questionnaire Item 4 and short-form questionnaire Item 6. The age classification is based on the age of the person in complete years as of April 1, 2000. The age of the person usually was derived from their date of birth information. Their reported age was used only when date of birth information was unavailable.

HOUSEHOLD SIZE

Average Household Size: A measure obtained by dividing the number of people in households by the total number of households (or householders). In cases where household members are tabulated by race or Hispanic origin, household members are classified by the race or Hispanic origin of the householder rather than the race or Hispanic origin of each individual. Average household size is rounded to the nearest hundredth.

LANGUAGE SPOKEN AT HOME

English Only: Number and percentage of population 5 years and over who report speaking English-only at home.

Spanish: Number and percentage of population 5 years and over who report speaking Spanish at home.

Language spoken at home data were derived from answers to long-form questionnaire Items 11a and 11b, which were asked of a sample of the population. Data were edited to include in tabulations only the population 5 years old and over. Questions 11a and 11b referred to languages spoken at home in an effort to measure the current use of languages other than English. People who knew languages other than English but did not use them at home or who only used them elsewhere were excluded. Most people who reported speaking a language other than English at home also speak English. The questions did not permit determination of the primary or dominant language of people who spoke both English and another language.

FOREIGN-BORN

Foreign Born: Number and percentage of population who were not U.S. citizens at birth. Foreign-born people are those who indicated they were either a U.S. citizen by naturalization or they were not a citizen of the United States.

Foreign-Born Naturalized Citizens: Number and percentage of population who were not U.S. citizens at birth but became U.S. citizens by naturalization.

The data on place of birth were derived from answers to long-form questionnaire Item 12 which was asked of a sample of the population. Respondents were asked to report the U.S. state, Puerto Rico, U.S. Island Area, or foreign country where they were born. People not reporting a place of birth were assigned the state or country of birth of another family member or their residence 5 years earlier, or were imputed the response of another person with similar characteristics. People born outside the United States were asked to report their place of birth according to current international boundaries. Since numerous changes in boundaries of foreign countries have occurred in the last century, some people may have reported their place of birth in terms of boundaries that existed at the time of their birth or emigration, or in accordance with their own national preference.

EDUCATIONAL ATTAINMENT

High School Graduates: Number and percentage of the population age 25 and over who have a high school diploma or higher. This category includes people whose highest degree was a high school diploma or its equivalent, people who attended college but did not receive a degree, and people who received a college, university, or professional degree. People who reported completing the 12th grade but not receiving a diploma are not high school graduates.

4-Years College Graduates: Number and percentage of the population age 25 and over who have a 4-year college, university, or professional degree.

Data on educational attainment were derived from answers to long-form questionnaire Item 9, which was asked of a sample of the population. Data on attainment are tabulated for the population 25 years old and over.

The order in which degrees were listed on the questionnaire suggested that doctorate degrees were "higher" than professional school degrees, which were "higher" than master's degrees. The question included instructions for people currently enrolled in school to report the level of the previous grade attended or the highest degree received. Respondents who did not report educational attainment or enrollment level were assigned the attainment of a person of the same age, race, Hispanic or Latino origin, occupation and sex, where possible, who resided in the same or a nearby area. Respondents who filled more than one box were edited to the highest level or degree reported.

The question included a response category that allowed respondents to report completing the 12th grade without receiving a high school diploma. It allowed people who received either a high school diploma or the equivalent (Test of General Educational Development—G.E.D.) and did not attend college, to be reported as "high school graduate(s)." The category "Associate degree" included people whose highest degree is an associate degree, which generally requires 2 years of college level work and is either in an occupational program that prepares them for a specific occupation, or an academic program primarily in the arts and sciences. The course work may or may not be transferable to a bachelor's degree. Master's degrees include the traditional MA and MS degrees and field-specific degrees, such as MSW, MEd, MBA, MLS, and MEng. Some examples of professional degrees include medicine, dentistry, chiropractic, optometry, osteopathic medicine, pharmacy, podiatry, veterinary medicine, law, and theology. Vocational and technical training such as barber school training; business, trade, technical, and vocational schools; or other training for a specific trade, are specifically excluded.

INCOME AND POVERTY

Median Household Income (in dollars): Includes the income of the householder and all other individuals 15 years old and over in the household, whether they are related to the householder or not. The median divides the income distribution into two equal parts: one-half of the cases falling below the median income and one-half above the median. For households, the median income is based on the distribution of the total number of households including those with no income. Median income for households is computed on the basis of a standard distribution and is rounded to the nearest whole dollar.

Per Capita Income (in dollars): Per capita income is the mean income computed for every man, woman, and child in a particular group. It is derived by dividing the total income of a particular group by the total population in that group. Per capita income is rounded to the nearest whole dollar.

The data on income in 1999 were derived from answers to long-form questionnaire Items 31 and 32, which were asked of a sample of the population 15 years old and over. "Total income" is the sum of the amounts reported separately for wage or salary income; net self-employment income; interest, dividends, or net rental or royalty income or income from estates and trusts; social security or railroad retirement income; Supplemental Security Income (SSI); public assistance or welfare payments; retirement, survivor, or disability pensions; and all other income.

Receipts from the following sources are not included as income: capital gains, money received from the sale of property (unless the recipient was engaged in the business of selling such property); the value of income "in kind" from food stamps, public housing subsidies, medical care, employer contributions for individuals, etc.; withdrawal of bank deposits; money borrowed; tax refunds; exchange of money between relatives living in the same household; and gifts and lump-sum inheritances, insurance payments, and other types of lump-sum receipts.

The eight types of income reported in the census are defined as follows:

Wage or salary income. Wage or salary income includes total money earnings received for work performed as an employee during the calendar year 1999. It includes wages, salary, armed forces pay, commissions, tips, piece-rate payments, and cash bonuses earned before deductions were made for taxes, bonds, pensions, union dues, etc.

Self-employment income. Self-employment income includes both farm and nonfarm self-employment income. Nonfarm self-employment income includes net money income (gross receipts minus expenses) from one's own business, professional enterprise, or partnership. Gross receipts include the value of all goods sold and services rendered. Expenses include costs of goods purchased, rent, heat, light, power, depreciation charges, wages and salaries paid, business taxes (not personal income taxes), etc. Farm self-employment income includes net money income (gross receipts minus operating expenses) from the operation of a farm by a person on his or her own account, as an owner, renter, or sharecropper. Gross receipts include the value of all products sold, government farm programs, money received from the rental of farm equipment to others, and incidental receipts from the sale of wood, sand, gravel, etc. Operating expenses include cost of feed, fertilizer, seed, and other farming supplies, cash wages paid to farmhands, depreciation charges, cash rent, interest on farm mortgages, farm building repairs, farm taxes (not state and federal personal income taxes), etc. The value of fuel, food, or other farm products used for family living is not included as part of net income.

Interest, dividends, or net rental income. Interest, dividends, or net rental income includes interest on savings or bonds, dividends from stockholdings or membership in associations, net income from rental of property to others and receipts from boarders or lodgers, net royalties, and periodic payments from an estate or trust fund.

Social Security income. Social security income includes social security pensions and survivors benefits, permanent disability insurance payments made by the Social Security Administration prior to deductions for medical insurance, and railroad retirement insurance checks from the U.S. government. Medicare reimbursements are not included.

Supplemental Security Income (SSI). Supplemental Security Income (SSI) is a nationwide U.S. assistance program administered by the Social Security Administration that guarantees a minimum level of income for needy aged, blind, or disabled individuals. The census questionnaire for Puerto Rico asked about the receipt of SSI; however, SSI is not a federally administered program in Puerto Rico. Therefore, it is probably not being interpreted by most respondents as the same as SSI in the United States. The only way a resident of Puerto Rico could have appropriately reported SSI would have been if they lived in the United States at any time during calendar year 1999 and received SSI.

Public assistance income. Public assistance income includes general assistance and Temporary Assistance to Needy Families (TANF). Separate payments received for hospital or other medical care (vendor payments) are excluded. This does not include Supplemental Security Income (SSI).

Retirement income. Retirement income includes: (1) retirement pensions and survivor benefits from a former employer; labor union; or federal, state, or local government; and the U.S. military; (2) income from workers' compensation; disability income from companies or unions; federal, state, or local government; and the U.S. military; (3) periodic receipts from annuities and insurance; and (4) regular income from IRA and KEOGH plans. This does not include social security income.

All other income. All other income includes unemployment compensation, Veterans' Administration (VA) payments, alimony and child support, contributions received periodically from people not living in the household, military family allotments, and other kinds of periodic income other than earnings.

Poverty Status: Number and percentage of population with income in 1999 below the poverty level. Based on individuals for whom poverty status is determined. Poverty status was determined for all people except institutionalized people, people in military group quarters, people in college dormitories, and unrelated individuals under 15 years old.

The poverty status of families and unrelated individuals in 1999 was determined using 48 thresholds (income cutoffs) arranged in a two dimensional matrix. The matrix consists of family size (from 1 person to 9 or more people) cross-classified by presence and number of family members under 18 years old (from no children present to 8 or more children present). Unrelated individuals and 2-person families were further differentiated by the age of the reference person (RP) (under 65 years old and 65 years old and over).

To determine a person's poverty status, one compares the person's total family income with the poverty threshold appropriate for that person's family size and composition. If the total income of that person's family is less than the threshold appropriate for that family, then the person is considered poor, together with every member of his or her family. If a person is not living with anyone related by birth, marriage, or adoption, then the person's own income is compared with his or her poverty threshold.

HOUSING

Homeownership: Number and percentage of housing units that are owner-occupied.

The data on tenure, which was asked at all occupied housing units, were obtained from answers to long-form questionnaire Item 33, and short-form questionnaire Item 2. All occupied housing units are classified as either owner occupied or renter occupied.

A housing unit is owner occupied if the owner or co-owner lives in the unit even if it is mortgaged or not fully paid for. The owner or co-owner must live in the unit and usually is Person 1 on the questionnaire. The unit is "Owned by you or someone in this household with a mortgage or loan" if it is being purchased with a mortgage or some other debt arrangement, such as a deed of trust, trust deed, contract to purchase, land contract, or purchase agreement. The unit is also considered owned with a mortgage if it is built on leased land and there is a mortgage on the unit. Mobile homes occupied by owners with installment loans balances are also included in this category.

Median Gross Rent (in dollars): Median monthly gross rent on specified renter-occupied and specified vacant-for-rent units. Specified renter-occupied and specified vacant-for-rent units exclude 1-family houses on 10 acres or more.

The data on gross rent were obtained from answers to long-form questionnaire Items 45a-d, which were asked on a sample basis. Gross rent is the contract rent plus the estimated average monthly cost of utilities (electricity, gas, water and sewer) and fuels (oil, coal, kerosene, wood, etc.) if these are paid by the renter (or paid for the renter by someone else). Gross rent is intended to eliminate differentials that result from varying practices with respect to the inclusion of utilities and fuels as part of the rental payment. The estimated costs of utilities and fuels are reported on an annual basis but are converted to monthly figures for the tabulations. Renter units occupied without payment of cash rent are shown separately as "No cash rent" in the tabulations.

Housing units that are renter occupied without payment of cash rent are shown separately as "No cash rent" in census data products. The unit may be owned by friends or relatives who live elsewhere and who allow occupancy without charge. Rent-free houses or apartments may be provided to compensate caretakers, ministers, tenant farmers, sharecroppers, or others.

Contract rent is the monthly rent agreed to or contracted for, regardless of any furnishings, utilities, fees, meals, or services that may be included. For vacant units, it is the monthly rent asked for the rental unit at the time of enumeration.

If the contract rent includes rent for a business unit or for living quarters occupied by another household, only that part of the rent estimated to be for the respondent's unit was included. Excluded was any rent paid for additional units or for business premises.

If a renter pays rent to the owner of a condominium or cooperative, and the condominium fee or cooperative carrying charge also is paid by the renter to the owner, the condominium fee or carrying charge was included as rent.

If a renter receives payments from lodgers or roomers who are listed as members of the household, the rent without deduction for any payments received from the lodgers or roomers was to be reported. The respondent was to report the rent agreed to or contracted for even if paid by someone else such as friends or relatives living elsewhere, a church or welfare agency, or the government through subsidies or vouchers.

The median divides the rent distribution into two equal parts: one-half of the cases falling below the median contract rent and one-half above the median. Median contract rents are computed on the basis of a standard distribution and are rounded to the nearest whole dollar. Units reported as "No cash rent" are excluded.

Median Home Value (in dollars): Reported by the owner of specified owner-occupied or specified vacant-for-sale housing units. Specified owner-occupied and specified vacant-for-sale housing units include only 1-family houses on less than 10 acres without a business or medical office on the property. The data for "specified units" exclude mobile homes, houses with a business or medical office, houses on 10 or more acres, and housing units in multi-unit buildings.

The data on value (also referred to as "price asked" for vacant units) were obtained from answers to long-form questionnaire Item 51, which was asked on a sample basis at owner-occupied housing units and units that were being bought, or vacant for sale at the time of enumeration. Value is the respondent's estimate of how much the property (house and lot, mobile home and lot, or condominium unit) would sell for if it were for sale. If the house or mobile home was owned or being bought, but the land on which it sits was not, the respondent was asked to estimate the combined value of the house or mobile home and the land. For vacant units, value was the price asked for the property. Value was tabulated separately for all owner-occupied and vacant-for-sale housing units, owner-occupied and vacant-for-sale mobile homes, and specified owner-occupied and specified vacant-for-sale housing units.

The median divides the value distribution into two equal parts: one-half of the cases falling below the median value of the property (house and lot, mobile home and lot, or condominium unit) and one-half above the median. Median values are computed on the basis of a standard distribution and are rounded to the nearest hundred dollars.

User's Guide: Asian Population

Places Covered

Ranking tables cover all counties and places in New York with Asian and/or Native Hawaiian and other Pacific Islander residents.

Source of Data

CENSUS 2000

Data for this chapter was derived from following source: *U.S. Bureau of the Census, Census of Population and Housing, 2000: Summary File 4.* Summary File 4 (SF 4) contains sample data, which is the information compiled from the questions asked of a sample (generally 1-in-6) of all people and housing units. Summary File 4 is repeated or iterated for the total population and 335 additional population groups. This chapter focuses on the following 23 population groups:

Asian
    Asian Indian
    Bangladeshi
    Cambodian
    Chinese (except Taiwanese)
    Filipino
    Hmong
    Indonesian
    Japanese
    Korean
    Laotian
    Malaysian
    Pakistani
    Sri Lankan
    Taiwanese
    Thai
    Vietnamese
Native Hawaiian and Other Pacific Islander
    Fijian
    Guamanian or Chamorro
    Hawaiian, Native
    Samoan
    Tongan

Please note that this chapter only includes people who responded to the question on race by indicating only one race. These people are classified by the Census Bureau as the race *alone* population. For example, respondents reporting a single detailed Asian group, such as Korean or Filipino, would be included in the Asian *alone* population. Respondents reporting more than one detailed Asian group, such as Chinese and Japanese or Asian Indian and Chinese and Vietnamese would also be included in the Asian *alone* population. This is because all of the detailed groups in these example combinations are part of the larger Asian race category. The same criteria apply to the Native Hawaiian and Other Pacific Islander groups.

In order for any of the tables for a specific group to be shown in Summary File 4, the data must meet a minimum population threshold. For Summary File 4, all tables are repeated for each race group, American Indian and Alaska Native tribe, and Hispanic or Latino group if the 100-percent count of people of that specific group in a particular geographic area is 100 or more. There also must be 50 or more unweighted people of that specific group in a particular geographic area. For example, if there are 100 or more 100-percent people tabulated as Korean in County A, and there are 50 or more unweighted people, then all matrices for Korean are shown in SF 4 for County A.

To maintain confidentiality, the Census Bureau applies statistical procedures that introduce some uncertainty into data for small geographic areas with small population groups. Therefore, tables may contain both sampling and nonsampling error.

In an iterated file such as SF 4, the universes *households, families,* and *occupied housing units* are classified by the race or ethnic group of the householder. In any population table where there is no note, the universe classification is always based on the race or ethnicity of the person. In all housing tables, the universe classification is based on the race or ethnicity of the householder.

Comparing SF 4 Estimates with Corresponding Values in SF 1 and SF 2

As in earlier censuses, the responses from the sample of households reporting on long forms must be weighted to reflect the entire population. Specifically, each responding household represents, on average, six or seven other households who reported using short forms. One consequence of the weighting procedures is that each estimate based on the long form responses has an associated confidence interval. These confidence intervals are wider (as a percentage of the estimate) for geographic areas with smaller populations and for characteristics that occur less frequently in the area being examined (such as the proportion of people in poverty in a middle-income neighborhood). In order to release as much useful information as possible, statisticians must balance a number of factors. In particular, for Census 2000, the Bureau of the Census created weighting areas—geographic areas from which about two hundred or more long forms were completed—which are large enough to produce good quality estimates. If smaller weighting areas had been used, the confidence intervals around the estimates would have been significantly wider, rendering many estimates less useful due to their lower reliability. The disadvantage of using weighting areas this large is that, for smaller geographic areas within them, the estimates of characteristics that are also reported on the short form will not match the counts reported in SF 1 or SF 2. Examples of these characteristics are the total number of people, the number of people reporting specific racial categories, and the number of housing units. The official values for items reported on the short form come from SF 1 and SF 2. The differences between the long form estimates in SF 4 and values in SF 1 or SF 2 are particularly noticeable for the smallest places, tracts, and block groups. The long form estimates of total population and total housing units in SF 4 will, however, match the SF 1 and SF 2 counts for larger geographic areas such as counties and states, and will be essentially the same for medium and large cities. This phenomenon also occurred for the 1990 Census, although in that case, the weighting areas included relatively small places. As a result, the long form estimates matched the short form counts for those places, but the confidence intervals around the estimates of characteristics collected only on the long form were often significantly wider (as a percentage of the estimate). SF 1 gives exact numbers even for very small groups and areas; whereas, SF 4 gives estimates for small groups and areas such as tracts and small places that are less exact. The goal of SF 4 is to identify large differences among areas or large changes over time. Estimates for small areas and small population groups often do exhibit large changes from one census to the next, so having the capability to measure them is worthwhile.

Topics

POPULATION

Total Population: Sample count of total population of all races.

Asian Population: A person having origins in any of the original peoples of the Far East, Southeast Asia, or the Indian subcontinent including, for example, Cambodia, China, India, Japan, Korea, Malaysia, Pakistan, the Philippine Islands, Thailand, and Vietnam. It includes Asian Indian, Bangladeshi, Cambodian, Chinese (except Taiwanese), Filipino, Hmong, Indonesian, Japanese, Korean, Laotian, Malaysian, Pakistani, Sri Lankan, Taiwanese, Thai, and Vietnamese.

Native Hawaiian or Other Pacific Islander (NHPI) Population: A person having origins in any of the original peoples of Hawaii, Guam, Samoa, or other Pacific Islands. It includes people who indicate their race as Fijian, Guamanian or Chamorro, Native Hawaiian, Samoan, and Tongan.

The data on race, which was asked of all people, were derived from answers to long-form questionnaire Item 6 and short-form questionnaire Item 8. The concept of race, as used by the Census Bureau, reflects self-identification by people according to the race or races with which they most closely identify. These categories are socio-political constructs and should not be interpreted as being scientific or anthropological in nature. Furthermore, the race categories include both racial and national-origin groups.

If an individual did not provide a race response, the race or races of the householder or other household members were assigned using specific rules of precedence of household relationship. For example, if race was missing for a natural-born child in the household, then either the race or races of the householder, another natural-born child, or the spouse of the householder were assigned. If race was not reported for anyone in the household, the race or races of a householder in a previously processed household were assigned.

AGE

Median Age: Divides the age distribution into two equal parts: one-half of the cases falling below the median age and one-half above the median. Median age is computed on the basis of a single year of age standard distribution.

The data on age, which was asked of all people, were derived from answers to the long-form questionnaire Item 4 and short-form questionnaire Item 6. The age classification is based on the age of the person in complete years as of April 1, 2000. The age of the person usually was derived from their date of birth information. Their reported age was used only when date of birth information was unavailable.

HOUSEHOLD SIZE

Average Household Size: A measure obtained by dividing the number of people in households by the total number of households (or householders). In cases where household members are tabulated by race or Hispanic origin, household members are classified by the race or Hispanic origin of the householder rather than the race or Hispanic origin of each individual. Average household size is rounded to the nearest hundredth.

LANGUAGE SPOKEN AT HOME

English Only: Number and percentage of population 5 years and over who report speaking English-only at home.

Language spoken at home data were derived from answers to long-form questionnaire Items 11a and 11b, which were asked of a sample of the population. Data were edited to include in tabulations only the population 5 years old and over. Questions 11a and 11b referred to languages spoken at home in an effort to measure the current use of languages other than English. People who knew languages other than English but did not use them at home or who only used them elsewhere were excluded. Most people who reported speaking a language other than English at home also speak English. The questions did not permit determination of the primary or dominant language of people who spoke both English and another language.

FOREIGN-BORN

Foreign Born: Number and percentage of population who were not U.S. citizens at birth. Foreign-born people are those who indicated they were either a U.S. citizen by naturalization or they were not a citizen of the United States.

Foreign-Born Naturalized Citizens: Number and percentage of population who were not U.S. citizens at birth but became U.S. citizens by naturalization.

The data on place of birth were derived from answers to long-form questionnaire Item 12 which was asked of a sample of the population. Respondents were asked to report the U.S. state, Puerto Rico, U.S. Island Area, or foreign country where they were born. People not reporting a place of birth were assigned the state or country of birth of another family member or their residence 5 years earlier, or were imputed the response of another person with similar characteristics. People born outside the United States were asked to report their place of birth according to current international boundaries. Since numerous changes in boundaries of foreign countries have occurred in the last century, some people may have reported their place of birth in terms of boundaries that existed at the time of their birth or emigration, or in accordance with their own national preference.

EDUCATIONAL ATTAINMENT

High School Graduates: Number and percentage of the population age 25 and over who have a high school diploma or higher. This category includes people whose highest degree was a high school diploma or its equivalent, people who attended college but did not receive a degree, and people who received a college, university, or professional degree. People who reported completing the 12th grade but not receiving a diploma are not high school graduates.

Four-Year College Graduates: Number and percentage of the population age 25 and over who have a 4-year college, university, or professional degree.

Data on educational attainment were derived from answers to long-form questionnaire Item 9, which was asked of a sample of the population. Data on attainment are tabulated for the population 25 years old and over.

The order in which degrees were listed on the questionnaire suggested that doctorate degrees were "higher" than professional school degrees, which were "higher" than master's degrees. The question included instructions for people currently enrolled in school to report the level of the previous grade attended or the highest degree received. Respondents who did not report educational attainment or enrollment level were assigned the attainment of a person of the same age, race, Hispanic or Latino origin, occupation and sex, where possible, who resided in the same or a nearby area. Respondents who filled more than one box were edited to the highest level or degree reported.

The question included a response category that allowed respondents to report completing the 12th grade without receiving a high school diploma. It allowed people who received either a high school diploma or the equivalent (Test of General Educational Development—G.E.D.) and did not attend college, to be reported as "high school graduate(s)." The category "Associate degree" included people whose highest degree is an associate degree, which generally requires 2 years of college level work and is either in an occupational program that prepares them for a specific occupation, or an academic program primarily in the arts and sciences. The course work may or may not be transferable to a bachelor's degree. Master's degrees include the traditional MA and MS degrees and field-specific degrees, such as MSW, MEd, MBA, MLS, and MEng. Some examples of professional degrees include medicine, dentistry, chiropractic, optometry, osteopathic medicine, pharmacy, podiatry, veterinary medicine, law, and theology. Vocational and technical training such as barber school training; business, trade, technical, and vocational schools; or other training for a specific trade, are specifically excluded.

INCOME AND POVERTY

Median Household Income (in dollars): Includes the income of the householder and all other individuals 15 years old and over in the household, whether they are related to the householder or not. The median divides the income distribution into two equal parts: one-half of the cases falling below the median income and one-half above the median. For households, the median income is based on the distribution of the total number of households including those with no income. Median income for households is computed on the basis of a standard distribution and is rounded to the nearest whole dollar.

Per Capita Income (in dollars): Per capita income is the mean income computed for every man, woman, and child in a particular group. It is derived by dividing the total income of a particular group by the total population in that group. Per capita income is rounded to the nearest whole dollar.

The data on income in 1999 were derived from answers to long-form questionnaire Items 31 and 32, which were asked of a sample of the population 15 years old and over. "Total income" is the sum of the amounts reported separately for wage or salary income; net self-employment income; interest, dividends, or net rental or royalty income or income from estates and trusts; social security or railroad retirement income; Supplemental Security Income (SSI); public assistance or welfare payments; retirement, survivor, or disability pensions; and all other income.

Receipts from the following sources are not included as income: capital gains, money received from the sale of property (unless the recipient was engaged in the business of selling such property); the value of income "in kind" from food stamps, public housing subsidies, medical care, employer contributions for individuals, etc.; withdrawal of bank deposits; money borrowed; tax refunds; exchange of money between relatives living in the same household; and gifts and lump-sum inheritances, insurance payments, and other types of lump-sum receipts.

The eight types of income reported in the census are defined as follows:

Wage or salary income. Wage or salary income includes total money earnings received for work performed as an employee during the calendar year 1999. It includes wages, salary, armed forces pay, commissions, tips, piece-rate payments, and cash bonuses earned before deductions were made for taxes, bonds, pensions, union dues, etc.

Self-employment income. Self-employment income includes both farm and nonfarm self-employment income. Nonfarm self-employment income includes net money income (gross receipts minus expenses) from one's own business, professional enterprise, or partnership. Gross receipts include the value of all goods sold and services rendered. Expenses include costs of goods purchased, rent, heat, light, power, depreciation charges, wages and salaries paid, business taxes (not personal income taxes), etc. Farm self-employment income includes net money income (gross receipts minus operating expenses) from the operation of a farm by a person on his or her own account, as an owner, renter, or sharecropper. Gross receipts include the value of all products sold, government farm programs, money received from the rental of farm equipment to others, and incidental receipts from the sale of wood, sand, gravel, etc. Operating expenses include cost of feed, fertilizer, seed, and other farming supplies, cash wages paid to farmhands, depreciation charges, cash rent, interest on farm mortgages, farm building repairs, farm taxes (not state and federal personal income taxes), etc. The value of fuel, food, or other farm products used for family living is not included as part of net income.

Interest, dividends, or net rental income. Interest, dividends, or net rental income includes interest on savings or bonds, dividends from stockholdings or membership in associations, net income from rental of property to others and receipts from boarders or lodgers, net royalties, and periodic payments from an estate or trust fund.

Social Security income. Social security income includes social security pensions and survivors benefits, permanent disability insurance payments made by the Social Security Administration prior to deductions for medical insurance, and railroad retirement insurance checks from the U.S. government. Medicare reimbursements are not included.

Supplemental Security Income (SSI). Supplemental Security Income (SSI) is a nationwide U.S. assistance program administered by the Social Security Administration that guarantees a minimum level of income for needy aged, blind, or disabled individuals. The census questionnaire for Puerto Rico asked about the receipt of SSI; however, SSI is not a federally administered program in Puerto Rico. Therefore, it is probably not being interpreted by most respondents as the same as SSI in the United States. The only way a resident of Puerto Rico could have appropriately reported SSI would have been if they lived in the United States at any time during calendar year 1999 and received SSI.

Public assistance income. Public assistance income includes general assistance and Temporary Assistance to Needy Families (TANF). Separate payments received for hospital or other medical care (vendor payments) are excluded. This does not include Supplemental Security Income (SSI).

Retirement income. Retirement income includes: (1) retirement pensions and survivor benefits from a former employer; labor union; or federal, state, or local government; and the U.S. military; (2) income from workers' compensation; disability income from companies or unions; federal, state, or local government; and the U.S. military; (3) periodic receipts from annuities and insurance; and (4) regular income from IRA and KEOGH plans. This does not include social security income.

All other income. All other income includes unemployment compensation, Veterans' Administration (VA) payments, alimony and child support, contributions received periodically from people not living in the household, military family allotments, and other kinds of periodic income other than earnings.

Poverty Status: Number and percentage of population with income in 1999 below the poverty level. Based on individuals for whom poverty status is determined. Poverty status was determined for all people except institutionalized people, people in military group quarters, people in college dormitories, and unrelated individuals under 15 years old.

The poverty status of families and unrelated individuals in 1999 was determined using 48 thresholds (income cutoffs) arranged in a two dimensional matrix. The matrix consists of family size (from 1 person to 9 or more people) cross-classified by presence and number of family members under 18 years old (from no children present to 8 or more children present). Unrelated individuals and 2-person families were further differentiated by the age of the reference person (RP) (under 65 years old and 65 years old and over).

To determine a person's poverty status, one compares the person's total family income with the poverty threshold appropriate for that person's family size and composition. If the total income of that person's family is less than the threshold appropriate for that family, then the person is considered poor, together with every member of his or her family. If a person is not living with anyone related by birth, marriage, or adoption, then the person's own income is compared with his or her poverty threshold.

HOUSING

Homeownership: Number and percentage of housing units that are owner-occupied.

The data on tenure, which was asked at all occupied housing units, were obtained from answers to long-form questionnaire Item 33, and short-form questionnaire Item 2. All occupied housing units are classified as either owner occupied or renter occupied.

A housing unit is owner occupied if the owner or co-owner lives in the unit even if it is mortgaged or not fully paid for. The owner or co-owner must live in the unit and usually is Person 1 on the questionnaire. The unit is "Owned by you or someone in this household with a mortgage or loan" if it is being purchased with a mortgage or some other debt arrangement, such as a deed of trust, trust deed, contract to purchase, land contract, or purchase agreement. The unit is also considered owned with a mortgage if it is built on leased land and there is a mortgage on the unit. Mobile homes occupied by owners with installment loans balances are also included in this category.

Median Gross Rent (in dollars): Median monthly gross rent on specified renter-occupied and specified vacant-for-rent units. Specified renter-occupied and specified vacant-for-rent units exclude 1-family houses on 10 acres or more.

The data on gross rent were obtained from answers to long-form questionnaire Items 45a-d, which were asked on a sample basis. Gross rent is the contract rent plus the estimated average monthly cost of utilities (electricity, gas, water and sewer) and fuels (oil, coal, kerosene, wood, etc.) if these are paid by the renter (or paid for the renter by someone else). Gross rent is intended to eliminate differentials that result from varying practices with respect to the inclusion of utilities and fuels as part of the rental payment. The estimated costs of utilities and fuels are reported on an annual basis but are converted to monthly figures for the tabulations. Renter units occupied without payment of cash rent are shown separately as "No cash rent" in the tabulations.

Housing units that are renter occupied without payment of cash rent are shown separately as "No cash rent" in census data products. The unit may be owned by friends or relatives who live elsewhere and who allow occupancy without charge. Rent-free houses or apartments may be provided to compensate caretakers, ministers, tenant farmers, sharecroppers, or others.

Contract rent is the monthly rent agreed to or contracted for, regardless of any furnishings, utilities, fees, meals, or services that may be included. For vacant units, it is the monthly rent asked for the rental unit at the time of enumeration.

If the contract rent includes rent for a business unit or for living quarters occupied by another household, only that part of the rent estimated to be for the respondent's unit was included. Excluded was any rent paid for additional units or for business premises.

If a renter pays rent to the owner of a condominium or cooperative, and the condominium fee or cooperative carrying charge also is paid by the renter to the owner, the condominium fee or carrying charge was included as rent.

If a renter receives payments from lodgers or roomers who are listed as members of the household, the rent without deduction for any payments received from the lodgers or roomers was to be reported. The respondent was to report the rent agreed to or contracted for even if paid by someone else such as friends or relatives living elsewhere, a church or welfare agency, or the government through subsidies or vouchers.

The median divides the rent distribution into two equal parts: one-half of the cases falling below the median contract rent and one-half above the median. Median contract rents are computed on the basis of a standard distribution and are rounded to the nearest whole dollar. Units reported as "No cash rent" are excluded.

Median Home Value (in dollars): Reported by the owner of specified owner-occupied or specified vacant-for-sale housing units. Specified owner-occupied and specified vacant-for-sale housing units include only 1-family houses on less than 10 acres without a business or medical office on the property. The data for "specified units" exclude mobile homes, houses with a business or medical office, houses on 10 or more acres, and housing units in multi-unit buildings.

The data on value (also referred to as "price asked" for vacant units) were obtained from answers to long-form questionnaire Item 51, which was asked on a sample basis at owner-occupied housing units and units that were being bought, or vacant for sale at the time of enumeration. Value is the respondent's estimate of how much the property (house and lot, mobile home and lot, or condominium unit) would sell for if it were for sale. If the house or mobile home was owned or being bought, but the land on which it sits was not, the respondent was asked to estimate the combined value of the house or mobile home and the land. For vacant units, value was the price asked for the property. Value was tabulated separately for all owner-occupied and vacant-for-sale housing units, owner-occupied and vacant-for-sale mobile homes, and specified owner-occupied and specified vacant-for-sale housing units.

The median divides the value distribution into two equal parts: one-half of the cases falling below the median value of the property (house and lot, mobile home and lot, or condominium unit) and one-half above the median. Median values are computed on the basis of a standard distribution and are rounded to the nearest hundred dollars.

User's Guide: Weather

Inclusion Criteria — How the Data and Stations Were Selected

There were two central goals in the preparation of the weather chapter. The first was to select those data elements which would have the broadest possible use by the greatest range of potential users. For most of the National Weather Service stations there is a substantial quantity and variety of climatological data that is collected, however for the majority of stations the data is more limited. After evaluating the available data set, the editors chose nine temperature measures, five precipitation measures, and heating and cooling degree days — sixteen key data elements that are widely requested and are believed to be of the greatest general interest.

The second goal was to provide data for as many weather stations as possible. Although there are over 10,000 stations in the United States, not every station collects data for both precipitation and temperature, and even among those that do, the data is not always complete for the last thirty years. As the editors used a different methodology than that of NCDC to compute data, a formal data sufficiency criteria was devised and applied to the source tapes in order to select stations for inclusion.

Sources of the Data

The data in the weather chapter is compiled from several sources. The majority comes from the original National Climactic Data Center computer tapes (TD-3220 Summary of Month Co-Operative). This data was used to create the entire table for each Cooperative station and part of each National Weather Service station. The remainder of the data for each NWS station comes from the International Station Meteorological Climate Summary, Version 4.0, September 1996, which is also available from the NCDC.

NCDC has two main classes or types of weather stations; first order stations which are staffed by professional meteorologists and cooperative stations which are staffed by volunteers. In the weather chapter all first order stations operated by the National Weather Service are included, as well as every cooperative station that met our selection criteria.

Potential cautions in using *Weather America*

First, as with any statistical reference work of this type, users need to be aware of the source of the data. The information here comes from NOAA, and it is the most comprehensive and reliable core data available. Although it is the best, it is not perfect. Most weather stations are staffed by volunteers, times of observation sometimes vary, stations occasionally are moved (especially over a thirty year period), equipment is changed or upgraded, and all of these factors affect the uniformity of the data. the weather chapter does not attempt to correct for these factors, and is not intended for either climatologists or atmospheric scientists. Users with concerns about data collection and reporting protocols are both referred to NCDC technical documentation, and also, they are perhaps better served by using the original computer tapes themselves as well.

Second, users need to be aware of the methodology used, which is described later in this User's Guide. Although this methodology has produced fully satisfactory results, it is not directly compatible with other methodologies, hence variances in the results published here and those which appear in other publications will doubtlessly arise.

Third, is the trap of that informal logical fallacy known as "hasty generalization," and its corollaries. This may involve presuming the future will be like the past (specifically, next year will be an average year), or it may involve misunderstanding the limitations of an arithmetic average, but more interestingly, it may involve those mistakes made most innocently by generalizing informally on too broad a basis. As weather is highly localized, the data should be taken in that context. A weather station collects data about climatic conditions at that spot, and that spot may or may not be an effective paradigm for an entire town or area. For example, the weather station in Burlington, Vermont is located at the airport about 3 miles east of the center of town. Most of Burlington is a lot closer to Lake Champlain, and that should mean to a careful user that there could be a significant difference between the temperature readings gathered at the weather station and readings that might be gathered at City Hall downtown. How much would this difference be? How could it be estimated? There are no answers here for these sorts of questions, but it is important for users of this book to raise them for themselves. (It is interesting to note that similar situations abound across the country. For example, compare different readings for the multiple stations in San Francisco, CA or for those around New York City.)

Our source of data has been consistent, so has our methodology. The data has been computed and reported consistently as well. As a result, the the weather chapter should prove valuable to the careful and informed reader.

Weather Station Tables

The weather station tables are grouped by type (National Weather Service and Cooperative) and then arranged alphabetically. The station name is almost always a place name, and is shown here just as it appears in NCDC data. The station name is followed by the county in which the station is located, the elevation of the station (at the time beginning of the thirty year period) and the latitude and longitude.

The National Weather Service Station tables contain 30 data elements which were compiled from two different sources, the International Station Meteorological Climate Summary (ISMCS) and NCDC TD-3220 data tapes. The following 14 elements are from the ISMCS: maximum precipitation, minimum precipitation, maximum 24-hour precipitation, maximum snowfall, maximum 24-hour snowfall, thunderstorm days, foggy days, predominant sky cover, relative humidity (morning and afternoon), dewpoint, wind speed and direction, and maximum wind gust. The remaining 16 elements come from the TD-3220 data tapes. The period of record (POR) for data from the TD-3220 data tapes is 1970-1999. The POR for ISMCS data varies from station to station.

Weather Elements (National Weather Service and Cooperative Stations)

The following elements were compiled by the editor from the NCDC TD-3220 data tapes using a period of record of 1970-1999.

The average temperatures (maximum, minimum, and mean) are the average (see Methodology below) of those temperatures for all available values for a given month. For example, for a given station the average maximum temperature for July is the arithmetic average of all available maximum July temperatures for that station. (Maximum means the highest recorded temperature, minimum means the lowest recorded temperature, and mean means an arithmetic average temperature.)

The extreme maximum temperature is the highest temperature recorded in each month over the period 1970-1999. The extreme minimum temperature is the lowest temperature recorded in each month over the same time period.

The days for maximum temperature and minimum temperature are the average number of days those criteria were met for all available instances. The symbol >= means greater than or equal to, the symbol <= means less than or equal to. For example, for a given station, the number of days the maximum temperature was greater than or equal to 90°F in July, is just an arithmetic average of the number of days in all the available Julys for that station.

Heating and cooling degree days are based on the median temperature for a given day and its variance from 65°F. For example, for a given station if the day's high temperature was 50°F and the day's low temperature was 30°F, the median (midpoint) temperature was 40°F. 40°F is 25 degrees below 65°F, hence on this day there would be 25 heating degree days. The also applies for cooling degree days. For example, for a given station if the day's high temperature was 80°F and the day's low temperature was 70°F, the median (midpoint) temperature was 75°F. 75°F is 10 degrees above 65°F, hence on this day there would be 10 cooling degree days. All heating and/or cooling degree days in a month are summed for the month giving respective totals for each element for that month. These sums for a given month for a given station over the past thirty years are again summed and then arithmetically averaged. It should be noted that the heating and cooling degree days do not cancel each other out. It is possible to have both for a given station in the same month.

Precipitation data is computed the same as heating and cooling degree days. Mean precipitation and mean snowfall are arithmetic averages of cumulative totals for the month. All available values for the thirty year period for a given month for a given station are summed and then divided by the number of values. The same is true for days of greater than or equal to 0.1" and 1.0" of precipitation, and days of greater than or equal to 1.0" of snow depth on the ground. The word trace appears for precipitation and snowfall amounts that are too small to measure.

Finally, remember that all values presented in the tables and the rankings are averages of available data (see Methodology below) for that specific data element for the last thirty years (1970-1999).

Weather Elements (National Weather Service Stations Only)

The following elements were taken directly from the International Station Meteorological Climate Summary. The periods of records vary per station.

Maximum precipitation, minimum precipitation, maximum 24-hour precipitation, maximum snowfall, maximum 24-hour snowfall, thunderstorm days, foggy days, relative humidity (morning and afternoon), dewpoint, prevailing wind speed and direction, and maximum wind gust are all self-explanatory.

The word trace appears for precipitation and snowfall amounts that are too small to measure.

Predominant sky cover contains four possible entries: CLR (clear); SCT (scattered); BRK (broken); and OVR (overcast).

How Cooperative Stations Were Selected

The basic criteria is that a station must have data for temperature, precipitation, heating and cooling degree days of sufficient quantity in order to create a meaningful average. More specifically, the definition of sufficiency here has two parts. First, there must be 22 values for a given data element (with the exception of cooling degree days which required only 14 values in order to be considered sufficient- more about this later), and second, eight of the sixteen elements included in the table must pass this sufficiency test. For example, in regard to average maximum temperature (the first element on every data table), a given station needs to have a value for every month of at least 22 of the last thirty years in order to meet the criteria, and, in addition, every station included must have at least eight of the sixteen elements at least this minimal level of completeness in order to fulfill the criteria. By using this procedure, 3,933 stations met these requirements and are included here.

Methodology

The following discussion applies only to data compiled from the NCDC TD-3220 data tapes.

the weather chapter is based on an arithmetic average of all available data for a specific data element at a given station. For example, the average maximum daily high temperature during July for Pontiac, New York was abstracted from NCDC source tapes for the thirty Julys, starting in July, 1970 and ending in July, 1999. These thirty figures were then summed and divided by thirty to produce an arithmetic average. As might be expected, there were not thirty values for every data element on every table. For a variety of reasons, NCDC data is sometimes incomplete. Thus the following standards were established.

For those data elements where there were 26-30 values, the data was taken to be essentially complete and an average was computed. For data elements where there were 22-25 values, the data was taken as being partly complete but still valid enough to use to compute an average. Such averages are shown in ***bold italic*** type to indicate that there was less than 26 values. For the few data elements where there were not even 22 values, no average was computed and 'na' appears in the space. If any of the twelve months for a given data element reported a value of 'na', no annual average was computed and the annual average was reported as 'na' as well.

This procedure was followed for 15 of the 16 data elements. The one exception is cooling degree days. The collection of this data began in 1980 so the following standards were adopted: for those data elements where there were 17-20 values, the data was taken to be essentially complete and an average was computed. For data elements where there were 14-16 values, the data was taken as being partly complete but still valid enough to use to compute an average. Such averages are shown in ***bold italic*** type to indicate that there was 14-16 values. For the few data elements where there were not even 14 values, no average was computed and 'na' appears in the space. If any of the twelve months for a given data element reported a value of 'na', no annual average was computed and the annual average was reported as 'na' as well.

Thus the basic computational methodology of the weather chapter is to provide an arithmetic average. Because of this, such a pure arithmetic average is somewhat different from the special type of average (called a "normal") which NCDC procedures produces and appears in federal publications.

Perhaps the best outline of the contrasting normalization methodology is found in the following paragraph (which appears as part of an NCDC technical document titled, CLIM81 1961-1990 NORMALS TD-9641 prepared by Lewis France of NCDC in May, 1992):

Normals have been defined as the arithmetic mean of a climatological element computed over a long time period. International agreements eventually led to the decision that the appropriate time period would be three consecutive decades (Guttman, 1989). The data record should be consistent (have no changes in location, instruments, observation practices, etc.; these are identified here as "exposure changes") and have no missing values so a normal will reflect the actual average climatic conditions. If any significant exposure changes have occurred, the data record is said to be "inhomogeneous," and the normal may not reflect a true climatic average. Such data need to be adjusted to remove the nonclimatic inhomogeneities. The resulting (adjusted) record is then said to be "homogeneous." If no exposure changes have occurred at a station, the normal is calculated simply by averaging the appropriate 30 values from the 1961-1990 record.

In the main, there are two "inhomogeneities" that NCDC is correcting for with normalization: adjusting for variances in time of day of observation (at the so-called First Order stations data is based on midnight to midnight observation times and this practice is not necessarily followed at cooperative stations which are staffed by volunteers), and second, estimating data that is either missing or incongruent.

A long discussion of the normalization process is not required here but a short note concerning comparative results of the two methodologies is appropriate.

When the editors first started compiling the weather chapter a concern arose because the normalization process would not be replicated: would our methodology produce strikingly different results than NCDC's? To allay concerns, results of the two processes were compared for the time period normalized results are available (1961-1990). In short, what was found was that the answer to this question is no. Never-the-less, users should be aware that because of both the time period covered (1970-1999) and the methodology used, data in the weather chapter is not compatible with data from other sources.

Albany County

Located in eastern New York; bounded on the east by the Hudson River; includes the Helderbergs and part of the Catskills. Covers a land area of 523.45 square miles, a water area of 9.76 square miles, and is located in the Eastern Time Zone. The county government was organized in 1683. County seat is Albany.

Albany County is part of the Albany-Schenectady-Troy, NY Metropolitan Statistical Area. The entire metro area includes: Albany County, NY; Rensselaer County, NY; Saratoga County, NY; Schenectady County, NY; Schoharie County, NY

Weather Station: Albany County Airport   Elevation: 272 feet

	Jan	Feb	Mar	Apr	May	Jun	Jul	Aug	Sep	Oct	Nov	Dec
High	31	34	44	58	70	78	83	80	72	60	48	36
Low	13	15	25	36	46	55	60	58	50	39	31	20
Precip	2.6	2.2	3.1	3.2	3.6	3.6	3.4	3.6	3.3	3.2	3.3	2.8
Snow	17.2	12.5	11.1	2.5	tr	tr	tr	0.0	tr	0.2	5.0	13.6

High and Low temperatures in degrees Fahrenheit; Precipitation and Snow in inches

Population: 292,577 (1990); 294,565 (2000); 299,833 (2005); 305,162 (2010 projected); Race: 80.1% White, 12.4% Black, 3.9% Asian, 4.0% Hispanic of any race (2005); Density: 572.8 persons per square mile (2005); Average household size: 2.43 (2005); Median age: 37.9 (2005); Males per 100 females: 92.4 (2005).
Religion: Five largest groups: 47.0% Catholic Church, 4.1% Jewish Estimate, 2.6% The United Methodist Church, 1.8% Reformed Church in America, 1.3% Episcopal Church (2000).
Economy: Unemployment rate: 3.9% (2005); Total civilian labor force: 161,359 (2005); Leading industries: 16.9% health care and social assistance; 13.6% retail trade; 9.3% finance and insurance (2003); Farms: 484 totaling 69,063 acres (2002); Companies that employ 500 or more persons: 27 (2003); Companies that employ 100 to 499 persons: 255 (2003); Companies that employ less than 100 persons: 8,815 (2003); Black-owned businesses: n/a (2002); Hispanic-owned businesses: n/a (2002); Women-owned businesses: 5,383 (2002); Retail sales per capita: $18,071 (2006). Single-family building permits issued: 493 (2005); Multi-family building permits issued: 357 (2005).
Income: Per capita income: $27,368 (2005); Median household income: $49,362 (2005); Average household income: $65,259 (2005); Percent of households with income of $100,000 or more: 17.9% (2005); Poverty rate: 10.8% (2003); Bankruptcy rate: 6.06% (2005).
Taxes: Total county taxes per capita: $864 (2004); County property taxes per capita: $161 (2004).
Education: Percent of population age 25 and over with: High school diploma (including GED) or higher: 86.4% (2005); Bachelor's degree or higher: 33.4% (2005); Master's degree or higher: 15.7% (2005).
Housing: Homeownership rate: 58.3% (2005); Median home value: $163,737 (2005); Median rent: $509 per month (2000); Median age of housing: 44 years (2000).
Health: Birth rate: 109.2 per 10,000 population (2004); Death rate: 91.8 per 10,000 population (2004); Age-adjusted cancer mortality rate: 216.3 deaths per 100,000 population (2002); Air Quality Index: 72.6% good, 25.8% moderate, 1.6% unhealthy for sensitive individuals, 0.0% unhealthy (percent of days in 2005); Number of physicians: 53.0 per 10,000 population (2004); Hospital beds: 51.3 per 10,000 population (2003); Hospital admissions: 2,050.9 per 10,000 population (2003).
Elections: 2004 Presidential election results: 37.3% Bush, 60.7% Kerry, 1.8% Nader, 0.2% Badnarik
National and State Parks: Delmar State Game Farm; Thacher State Park
Additional Information Contacts
Albany County Government . . . . (518) 447-7300
   http://www.albanycounty.com/
City of Albany . . . . (518) 434-5090
   http://www.albanyny.org
City of Cohoes . . . . (518) 233-2119
   http://www.cohoes.com/
City of Watervliet . . . . (518) 270-3810
   http://www.watervliet.com/
Town of Bethlehem . . . . (518) 439-4955
   http://www.townofbethlehem.org/
Town of Coeymans . . . . (518) 756-6006
   http://www.coeymans.org/
Town of Colonie . . . . (518) 783-2700
   http://www.colonie.org/
Town of Guilderland . . . . (518) 356-1980
   http://www.townofguilderland.org/
Town of Knox . . . . (518) 872-2551
   http://www.helderweb.com/knox/
Town of New Scotland . . . . (518) 439-4889
   http://www.townofnewscotland.com/
Village of Colonie . . . . (518) 783-2700
   http://www.colonie.org/
Village of Menands . . . . (518) 434-2922
   http://www.villageofmenands.com/Home/

Albany County Communities

ALBANY (city). Covers a land area of 21.378 square miles and a water area of 0.465 square miles. Located at 42.66° N. Lat.; 73.78° W. Long. Elevation is 127 feet.
History: Native American trails running in all directions crossed at the site of Albany. Several ship captains, including Henry Hudson, dropped anchor in the shallows near the present city, and made friends with the inhabitants. The next settlers, who came in 1624, were mostly Walloons from Holland. They built a fort and called it Fort Orange. Dutch, Norwegians, Danes, Germans, and Scots all settled on this land. In 1652, Peter Stuyvesant was sent out by the West India Company to set up a court and he laid out space around Fort Orange for a new village called Beverwyck. In 1685, control was relinquished to the English. The town became a mixture of Dutch and British people and cultures. It was chartered as Albany in 1686. Early fur trade made Albany residents wealthy, but wars plagued the area for almost a century. At the end of the wars, Albany found itself at the crossroad of a developing nation, with travelers coming by land, water, and rail. Lumbering and manufacturing also became important in the 19th century.
Population: 100,756 (1990); 95,658 (2000); 95,781 (2005); 95,990 (2010 projected); Race: 57.5% White, 31.6% Black, 4.5% Asian, 7.2% Hispanic of any race (2005); Density: 4,480.3 persons per square mile (2005); Average household size: 2.35 (2005); Median age: 33.1 (2005); Males per 100 females: 91.4 (2005); Marriage status: 45.5% never married, 37.8% now married, 8.5% widowed, 8.2% divorced (2000); Foreign born: 8.6% (2000); Ancestry (includes multiple ancestries): 29.8% Other groups, 18.0% Irish, 12.4% Italian, 10.4% German, 5.2% English (2000).
Economy: Unemployment rate: 4.5% (2005); Total civilian labor force: 47,692 (2005); Single-family building permits issued: 3 (2005); Multi-family building permits issued: 182 (2005); Employment by occupation: 12.8% management, 28.2% professional, 18.3% services, 28.7% sales, 0.0% farming, 4.6% construction, 7.4% production (2000).
Income: Per capita income: $20,375 (2005); Median household income: $33,375 (2005); Average household income: $46,324 (2005); Percent of households with income of $100,000 or more: 9.5% (2005); Poverty rate: 21.7% (2000).
Taxes: Total city taxes per capita: $488 (2004); City property taxes per capita: $419 (2004).
Education: Percent of population age 25 and over with: High school diploma (including GED) or higher: 81.3% (2005); Bachelor's degree or higher: 32.7% (2005); Master's degree or higher: 15.4% (2005).

School District(s)
Albany City School District (PK-12)
   2003-04 Enrollment: 9,919 . . . . (518) 462-7200
Boces Albany-Schoh-Schenectady-Sarat (PK-PK)
   2003-04 Enrollment: 819 . . . . (518) 456-9215
Brighter Choice Charter Sch-Boys (KG-02)
   2003-04 Enrollment: 71 . . . . (518) 383-2877
Brighter Choice Charter Sch-Girls (KG-02)
   2003-04 Enrollment: 73 . . . . (518) 383-2877
Guilderland Central School District (KG-12)
   2003-04 Enrollment: 5,664 . . . . (518) 456-6200
New Covenant Charter School (KG-08)
   2003-04 Enrollment: 858 . . . . (518) 463-3912
New Paltz CSD (KG-12)
   2003-04 Enrollment: 2,376 . . . . (845) 256-4020
South Colonie Central School District (KG-12)
   2003-04 Enrollment: 5,745 . . . . (518) 869-3576

Four-year College(s)
Albany College of Pharmacy
   Fall 2004 Enrollment: 970 . . . . (518) 694-7200
   2005-06 Tuition: In-state $18,770; Out-of-state $18,770
Albany Law School
   Fall 2004 Enrollment: 770 . . . . (518) 445-2311

Albany Medical College
    Fall 2004 Enrollment: 683 . . . . (518) 262-5582
Excelsior College
    Fall 2004 Enrollment: 26,974. (518) 464-8500
SUNY at Albany (Public)
    Fall 2004 Enrollment: 16,293. (518) 442-3300
    2005-06 Tuition: In-state $5,887; Out-of-state $12,147
Sage College of Albany
    Fall 2004 Enrollment: 2,047. . . . . (518) 292-1717
    2005-06 Tuition: In-state $16,870; Out-of-state $16,870
The College of Saint Rose
    Fall 2004 Enrollment: 4,980. . . . . (518) 454-5111
    2005-06 Tuition: In-state $17,386; Out-of-state $17,386
Two-year College(s)
Albany BOCES-Adult Practical Nursing Program (Public)
    Fall 2004 Enrollment: 99 . . . . (518) 862-4800
Austin's School of Spa Technology
    Fall 2004 Enrollment: 71 . . . . (518) 438-7879
Bryant and Stratton College-Albany
    Fall 2004 Enrollment: 391 . . . . (518) 437-1802
    2005-06 Tuition: In-state $11,820; Out-of-state $11,820
ITT Technical Institute
    Fall 2004 Enrollment: 436 . . . . (518) 452-9300
    2005-06 Tuition: In-state $14,196; Out-of-state $14,196
Maria College of Albany
    Fall 2004 Enrollment: 787 . . . . (518) 438-3111
    2005-06 Tuition: In-state $7,560; Out-of-state $7,560
Memorial Hospital School of Nursing
    Fall 2004 Enrollment: 112 . . . . (518) 471-3260
    2005-06 Tuition: In-state $6,388; Out-of-state $9,477
Orlo School of Hair Design and Cosmetology
    Fall 2004 Enrollment: 71 . . . . (518) 459-7832
Housing: Homeownership rate: 38.1% (2005); Median home value: $137,999 (2005); Median rent: $479 per month (2000); Median age of housing: 60 years (2000).
Hospitals: Albany Medical Center Hospital (631 beds); Albany Memorial Hospital (165 beds); Capital District Psychiatric Center (165 beds); Saint Peter's Hospital (447 beds); Veterans Affairs Medical Center
Safety: Violent crime rate: 120.2 per 10,000 population; Property crime rate: 593.6 per 10,000 population (2004).
Newspapers: Metroland (Alternative, General - Circulation 37,000); The Evangelist (Catholic, Religious - Circulation 56,500); The Jewish World (Jewish, Religious - Circulation 3,800); The Legislative Gazette (General - Circulation 19,100); Times Union (Circulation 101,292)
Transportation: Commute to work: 73.0% car, 13.1% public transportation, 10.8% walk, 2.4% work from home (2000); Travel time to work: 37.7% less than 15 minutes, 43.9% 15 to 30 minutes, 12.2% 30 to 45 minutes, 2.5% 45 to 60 minutes, 3.6% 60 minutes or more (2000); Amtrak: Service available.
Additional Information Contacts
Albany-Colonie Regional Chamber . . . . (518) 458-9851
    http://www.ac-chamber.org/
City of Albany. . . . . (518) 434-5090
    http://www.albanyny.org
Guilderland Chamber of Commerce . . . . (518) 456-6611
    http://www.guilderlandchamber.com

ALTAMONT
(village). Covers a land area of 1.197 square miles and a water area of 0 square miles. Located at 42.70° N. Lat.; 74.03° W. Long. Elevation is 451 feet.
Population: 1,638 (1990); 1,737 (2000); 1,711 (2005); 1,684 (2010 projected); Race: 96.8% White, 1.5% Black, 0.1% Asian, 1.3% Hispanic of any race (2005); Density: 1,429.8 persons per square mile (2005); Average household size: 2.67 (2005); Median age: 38.4 (2005); Males per 100 females: 88.2 (2005); Marriage status: 25.8% never married, 61.4% now married, 7.2% widowed, 5.7% divorced (2000); Foreign born: 1.3% (2000); Ancestry (includes multiple ancestries): 22.6% Irish, 20.8% German, 18.7% Italian, 16.7% English, 11.0% Dutch (2000).
Economy: Dairying; vegetable, apple, and grain area. Single-family building permits issued: 0 (2005); Multi-family building permits issued: 0 (2005); Employment by occupation: 15.0% management, 31.1% professional, 10.8% services, 28.7% sales, 0.4% farming, 7.4% construction, 6.6% production (2000).
Income: Per capita income: $28,526 (2005); Median household income: $61,957 (2005); Average household income: $75,744 (2005); Percent of households with income of $100,000 or more: 25.5% (2005); Poverty rate: 4.0% (2000).
Education: Percent of population age 25 and over with: High school diploma (including GED) or higher: 89.9% (2005); Bachelor's degree or higher: 40.1% (2005); Master's degree or higher: 18.6% (2005).
School District(s)
Guilderland Central School District (KG-12)
    2003-04 Enrollment: 5,664 . . . . (518) 456-6200
Housing: Homeownership rate: 68.7% (2005); Median home value: $185,090 (2005); Median rent: $467 per month (2000); Median age of housing: 44 years (2000).
Safety: Violent crime rate: 0.0 per 10,000 population; Property crime rate: 0.0 per 10,000 population (2004).
Newspapers: The Altamont Enterprise (General - Circulation 7,250)
Transportation: Commute to work: 92.4% car, 1.3% public transportation, 2.6% walk, 3.2% work from home (2000); Travel time to work: 17.5% less than 15 minutes, 34.4% 15 to 30 minutes, 39.9% 30 to 45 minutes, 4.2% 45 to 60 minutes, 4.0% 60 minutes or more (2000)

BERNE
(town). Covers a land area of 64.120 square miles and a water area of 0.636 square miles. Located at 42.59° N. Lat.; 74.12° W. Long.
Population: 3,045 (1990); 2,846 (2000); 2,893 (2005); 2,944 (2010 projected); Race: 97.3% White, 0.4% Black, 0.6% Asian, 1.0% Hispanic of any race (2005); Density: 45.1 persons per square mile (2005); Average household size: 2.54 (2005); Median age: 40.9 (2005); Males per 100 females: 97.9 (2005); Marriage status: 25.9% never married, 59.9% now married, 6.5% widowed, 7.8% divorced (2000); Foreign born: 2.2% (2000); Ancestry (includes multiple ancestries): 24.6% German, 18.1% Irish, 10.6% Italian, 10.2% English, 9.3% Dutch (2000).
Economy: Small lakes nearby with summer residences. Single-family building permits issued: 21 (2005); Multi-family building permits issued: 0 (2005); Employment by occupation: 9.0% management, 20.4% professional, 14.1% services, 27.5% sales, 0.4% farming, 14.5% construction, 14.2% production (2000).
Income: Per capita income: $26,553 (2005); Median household income: $54,972 (2005); Average household income: $67,443 (2005); Percent of households with income of $100,000 or more: 16.6% (2005); Poverty rate: 5.4% (2000).
Taxes: Total city taxes per capita: $233 (2004); City property taxes per capita: $211 (2004).
Education: Percent of population age 25 and over with: High school diploma (including GED) or higher: 86.7% (2005); Bachelor's degree or higher: 19.4% (2005); Master's degree or higher: 10.3% (2005).
School District(s)
Berne-Knox-Westerlo Central School District (KG-12)
    2003-04 Enrollment: 1,100 . . . . (518) 872-1293
Housing: Homeownership rate: 84.7% (2005); Median home value: $142,507 (2005); Median rent: $413 per month (2000); Median age of housing: 39 years (2000).
Transportation: Commute to work: 93.4% car, 0.6% public transportation, 0.7% walk, 5.3% work from home (2000); Travel time to work: 16.6% less than 15 minutes, 22.9% 15 to 30 minutes, 38.6% 30 to 45 minutes, 15.3% 45 to 60 minutes, 6.5% 60 minutes or more (2000)

BETHLEHEM
(town). Covers a land area of 48.812 square miles and a water area of 0.771 square miles. Located at 42.60° N. Lat.; 73.82° W. Long.
Population: 27,552 (1990); 31,304 (2000); 32,969 (2005); 34,583 (2010 projected); Race: 93.4% White, 2.7% Black, 2.2% Asian, 2.4% Hispanic of any race (2005); Density: 675.4 persons per square mile (2005); Average household size: 2.56 (2005); Median age: 40.5 (2005); Males per 100 females: 91.8 (2005); Marriage status: 19.8% never married, 66.0% now married, 7.0% widowed, 7.2% divorced (2000); Foreign born: 4.8% (2000); Ancestry (includes multiple ancestries): 24.2% Irish, 21.5% German, 16.0% Italian, 13.7% English, 8.2% Other groups (2000).
Economy: Unemployment rate: 3.0% (2005); Total civilian labor force: 17,941 (2005); Single-family building permits issued: 95 (2005); Multi-family building permits issued: 0 (2005); Employment by occupation: 18.6% management, 36.7% professional, 9.9% services, 24.3% sales, 0.1% farming, 4.5% construction, 5.8% production (2000).
Income: Per capita income: $37,564 (2005); Median household income: $73,848 (2005); Average household income: $95,264 (2005); Percent of households with income of $100,000 or more: 34.2% (2005); Poverty rate: 3.1% (2000).

Taxes: Total city taxes per capita: $360 (2004); City property taxes per capita: $292 (2004).
Education: Percent of population age 25 and over with: High school diploma (including GED) or higher: 93.1% (2005); Bachelor's degree or higher: 49.8% (2005); Master's degree or higher: 27.1% (2005).
Housing: Homeownership rate: 75.8% (2005); Median home value: $204,840 (2005); Median rent: $653 per month (2000); Median age of housing: 34 years (2000).
Safety: Violent crime rate: 6.8 per 10,000 population; Property crime rate: 155.5 per 10,000 population (2004).
Transportation: Commute to work: 92.6% car, 2.0% public transportation, 1.4% walk, 3.5% work from home (2000); Travel time to work: 28.1% less than 15 minutes, 52.5% 15 to 30 minutes, 14.6% 30 to 45 minutes, 1.7% 45 to 60 minutes, 3.1% 60 minutes or more (2000)
Additional Information Contacts
Town of Bethlehem .... (518) 439-4955
http://www.townofbethlehem.org/

CLARKSVILLE (unincorporated postal area, zip code 12041). Covers a land area of 0.119 square miles and a water area of 0 square miles. Located at 42.54° N. Lat.; 73.97° W. Long.
Population: 0 (2000); Race: 100.0% White, 0.0% Black, 0.0% Asian, 0.0% Hispanic of any race (2000); Density: 0.0 persons per square mile (2000); Age: 0.0% under 18, 0.0% over 64 (2000); Marriage status: 53.3% never married, 46.7% now married, 0.0% widowed, 0.0% divorced (2000); Foreign born: 0.0% (2000); Ancestry (includes multiple ancestries): 20.0% Finnish, 20.0% Irish (2000).
Economy: Employment by occupation: 0.0% management, 0.0% professional, 43.5% services, 0.0% sales, 0.0% farming, 56.5% construction, 0.0% production (2000).
Income: Per capita income: $10,900 (2000); Median household income: $42,679 (2000); Poverty rate: 20.0% (2000).
Education: Percent of population age 25 and over with: High school diploma (including GED) or higher: 100.0% (2000); Bachelor's degree or higher: 0.0% (2000).

School District(s)
Bethlehem Central School District (KG-12)
    2003-04 Enrollment: 5,022 .... (518) 439-7098
Housing: Homeownership rate: 50.0% (2000); Median home value: $85,000 (2000); Median rent: $n/a per month (2000); Median age of housing: 45 years (2000).
Transportation: Commute to work: 73.9% car, 0.0% public transportation, 26.1% walk, 0.0% work from home (2000); Travel time to work: 26.1% less than 15 minutes, 43.5% 15 to 30 minutes, 30.4% 30 to 45 minutes, 0.0% 45 to 60 minutes, 0.0% 60 minutes or more (2000)

COEYMANS (town). Covers a land area of 50.173 square miles and a water area of 2.916 square miles. Located at 42.49° N. Lat.; 73.84° W. Long. Elevation is 50 feet.
Population: 8,158 (1990); 8,151 (2000); 8,149 (2005); 8,169 (2010 projected); Race: 93.3% White, 2.5% Black, 0.6% Asian, 4.4% Hispanic of any race (2005); Density: 162.4 persons per square mile (2005); Average household size: 2.58 (2005); Median age: 36.9 (2005); Males per 100 females: 95.7 (2005); Marriage status: 25.3% never married, 60.4% now married, 5.5% widowed, 8.8% divorced (2000); Foreign born: 1.8% (2000); Ancestry (includes multiple ancestries): 23.5% Irish, 19.7% German, 17.2% Italian, 9.3% English, 8.2% Dutch (2000).
Economy: Single-family building permits issued: 9 (2005); Multi-family building permits issued: 2 (2005); Employment by occupation: 10.8% management, 20.4% professional, 14.8% services, 28.6% sales, 0.2% farming, 0.3% construction, 16.8% production (2000).
Income: Per capita income: $25,749 (2005); Median household income: $54,847 (2005); Average household income: $66,357 (2005); Percent of households with income of $100,000 or more: 17.3% (2005); Poverty rate: 6.9% (2000).
Education: Percent of population age 25 and over with: High school diploma (including GED) or higher: 83.2% (2005); Bachelor's degree or higher: 16.4% (2005); Master's degree or higher: 6.6% (2005).

School District(s)
Ravena-Coeymans-Selkirk Central School District (PK-12)
    2003-04 Enrollment: 2,385 .... (518) 756-5201
Housing: Homeownership rate: 68.1% (2005); Median home value: $134,890 (2005); Median rent: $466 per month (2000); Median age of housing: 42 years (2000).
Transportation: Commute to work: 93.0% car, 1.4% public transportation, 2.8% walk, 1.8% work from home (2000); Travel time to work: 28.8% less than 15 minutes, 31.8% 15 to 30 minutes, 29.5% 30 to 45 minutes, 4.9% 45 to 60 minutes, 4.9% 60 minutes or more (2000)
Additional Information Contacts
Town of Coeymans .... (518) 756-6006
http://www.coeymans.org/

COEYMANS (CDP). Covers a land area of 1.092 square miles and a water area of 0.129 square miles. Located at 42.47° N. Lat.; 73.79° W. Long.
Population: 817 (1990); 835 (2000); 848 (2005); 858 (2010 projected); Race: 88.8% White, 5.4% Black, 0.5% Asian, 8.7% Hispanic of any race (2005); Density: 776.2 persons per square mile (2005); Average household size: 2.65 (2005); Median age: 34.4 (2005); Males per 100 females: 93.2 (2005); Marriage status: 28.5% never married, 55.3% now married, 8.2% widowed, 8.0% divorced (2000); Foreign born: 1.7% (2000); Ancestry (includes multiple ancestries): 30.1% Irish, 18.5% Italian, 10.7% German, 9.3% Other groups, 8.1% French (except Basque) (2000).
Economy: Employment by occupation: 12.9% management, 15.8% professional, 12.4% services, 35.4% sales, 0.0% farming, 4.0% construction, 19.6% production (2000).
Income: Per capita income: $19,695 (2005); Median household income: $44,630 (2005); Average household income: $51,180 (2005); Percent of households with income of $100,000 or more: 12.8% (2005); Poverty rate: 9.0% (2000).
Education: Percent of population age 25 and over with: High school diploma (including GED) or higher: 76.1% (2005); Bachelor's degree or higher: 16.4% (2005); Master's degree or higher: 3.8% (2005).
Housing: Homeownership rate: 50.3% (2005); Median home value: $123,246 (2005); Median rent: $443 per month (2000); Median age of housing: 60+ years (2000).
Transportation: Commute to work: 95.1% car, 2.7% public transportation, 1.0% walk, 0.0% work from home (2000); Travel time to work: 33.4% less than 15 minutes, 35.1% 15 to 30 minutes, 19.6% 30 to 45 minutes, 7.4% 45 to 60 minutes, 4.5% 60 minutes or more (2000)

COEYMANS HOLLOW (unincorporated postal area, zip code 12046). Covers a land area of 15.933 square miles and a water area of 0.034 square miles. Located at 42.47° N. Lat.; 73.92° W. Long.
Population: 0 (2000); Race: 100.0% White, 0.0% Black, 0.0% Asian, 0.0% Hispanic of any race (2000); Density: 0.0 persons per square mile (2000); Age: 26.0% under 18, 12.3% over 64 (2000); Marriage status: 17.3% never married, 67.8% now married, 5.4% widowed, 9.6% divorced (2000); Foreign born: 0.0% (2000); Ancestry (includes multiple ancestries): 29.2% German, 23.7% Irish, 15.8% United States or American, 12.2% English, 11.1% Italian (2000).
Economy: Employment by occupation: 7.0% management, 31.0% professional, 11.8% services, 21.5% sales, 0.0% farming, 7.9% construction, 20.8% production (2000).
Income: Per capita income: $27,496 (2000); Median household income: $60,313 (2000); Poverty rate: 3.6% (2000).
Education: Percent of population age 25 and over with: High school diploma (including GED) or higher: 83.1% (2000); Bachelor's degree or higher: 17.6% (2000).
Housing: Homeownership rate: 88.1% (2000); Median home value: $97,800 (2000); Median rent: $300 per month (2000); Median age of housing: 60 years (2000).
Transportation: Commute to work: 96.6% car, 0.0% public transportation, 1.8% walk, 1.6% work from home (2000); Travel time to work: 11.5% less than 15 minutes, 47.1% 15 to 30 minutes, 24.6% 30 to 45 minutes, 10.1% 45 to 60 minutes, 6.7% 60 minutes or more (2000)

COHOES (city). Covers a land area of 3.744 square miles and a water area of 0.499 square miles. Located at 42.77° N. Lat.; 73.70° W. Long. Elevation is 95 feet.
History: The world's first power-operated knitting mill was opened here in 1832. Van Schaick Mansion (1735), now a Museum, was used as headquarters by General Horatio Gates during the American Revolution. Settled by Dutch 1665, Incorporated 1869.
Population: 16,825 (1990); 15,521 (2000); 15,201 (2005); 14,925 (2010 projected); Race: 93.4% White, 3.0% Black, 1.1% Asian, 3.0% Hispanic of any race (2005); Density: 4,060.3 persons per square mile (2005); Average household size: 2.20 (2005); Median age: 38.7 (2005); Males per 100 females: 87.3 (2005); Marriage status: 32.6% never married, 47.4% now

married, 10.2% widowed, 9.8% divorced (2000); Foreign born: 5.3% (2000); Ancestry (includes multiple ancestries): 25.5% Irish, 19.2% French (except Basque), 13.9% Italian, 11.2% German, 10.3% Polish (2000).
Economy: Retailing and outlet center. Its manufacturing includes textiles, cabinetry, meat-packing, plastic products, paper products, machinery and consumer goods. Single-family building permits issued: 34 (2005); Multi-family building permits issued: 0 (2005); Employment by occupation: 12.7% management, 15.2% professional, 15.0% services, 33.9% sales, 0.2% farming, 7.4% construction, 15.6% production (2000).
Income: Per capita income: $21,778 (2005); Median household income: $37,089 (2005); Average household income: $47,353 (2005); Percent of households with income of $100,000 or more: 8.7% (2005); Poverty rate: 13.3% (2000).
Education: Percent of population age 25 and over with: High school diploma (including GED) or higher: 75.3% (2005); Bachelor's degree or higher: 15.5% (2005); Master's degree or higher: 4.7% (2005).

School District(s)
Cohoes City School District (KG-12)
  2003-04 Enrollment: 2,202 . . . . (518) 237-0100
North Colonie Central School District (KG-12)
  2003-04 Enrollment: 5,631 . . . . (518) 785-8591

Housing: Homeownership rate: 45.0% (2005); Median home value: $122,991 (2005); Median rent: $414 per month (2000); Median age of housing: 60+ years (2000).
Safety: Violent crime rate: 33.9 per 10,000 population; Property crime rate: 117.4 per 10,000 population (2004).
Transportation: Commute to work: 91.2% car, 2.0% public transportation, 4.4% walk, 2.1% work from home (2000); Travel time to work: 30.9% less than 15 minutes, 48.9% 15 to 30 minutes, 14.9% 30 to 45 minutes, 2.0% 45 to 60 minutes, 3.3% 60 minutes or more (2000)
Additional Information Contacts
City of Cohoes . . . . (518) 233-2119
  http://www.cohoes.com/
Cohoes Chamber of Commerce . . . . (518) 237-1766
  http://www.cohoeschamber.com

COLONIE (village).
Covers a land area of 3.303 square miles and a water area of 0.007 square miles. Located at 42.72° N. Lat.; 73.83° W. Long.
Population: 7,989 (1990); 7,916 (2000); 8,151 (2005); 8,390 (2010 projected); Race: 89.9% White, 4.0% Black, 4.1% Asian, 2.0% Hispanic of any race (2005); Density: 2,467.9 persons per square mile (2005); Average household size: 2.44 (2005); Median age: 42.7 (2005); Males per 100 females: 94.1 (2005); Marriage status: 23.5% never married, 58.2% now married, 7.5% widowed, 10.9% divorced (2000); Foreign born: 5.8% (2000); Ancestry (includes multiple ancestries): 26.5% Irish, 21.7% German, 20.4% Italian, 14.4% English, 11.1% Other groups (2000).
Economy: Single-family building permits issued: 80 (2005); Multi-family building permits issued: 0 (2005); Employment by occupation: 14.4% management, 20.2% professional, 13.1% services, 34.4% sales, 0.0% farming, 6.6% construction, 11.2% production (2000).
Income: Per capita income: $28,841 (2005); Median household income: $64,751 (2005); Average household income: $70,063 (2005); Percent of households with income of $100,000 or more: 19.6% (2005); Poverty rate: 3.9% (2000).
Education: Percent of population age 25 and over with: High school diploma (including GED) or higher: 89.6% (2005); Bachelor's degree or higher: 26.3% (2005); Master's degree or higher: 10.4% (2005).
Housing: Homeownership rate: 83.0% (2005); Median home value: $149,599 (2005); Median rent: $695 per month (2000); Median age of housing: 38 years (2000).
Transportation: Commute to work: 95.8% car, 2.7% public transportation, 0.6% walk, 0.6% work from home (2000); Travel time to work: 41.6% less than 15 minutes, 44.2% 15 to 30 minutes, 11.0% 30 to 45 minutes, 1.3% 45 to 60 minutes, 2.0% 60 minutes or more (2000)
Additional Information Contacts
Village of Colonie . . . . (518) 783-2700
  http://www.colonie.org/

COLONIE (town).
Covers a land area of 56.069 square miles and a water area of 1.796 square miles. Located at 42.72° N. Lat.; 73.78° W. Long.
History: Incorporated 1921.
Population: 76,536 (1990); 79,258 (2000); 81,465 (2005); 83,696 (2010 projected); Race: 87.8% White, 4.7% Black, 5.1% Asian, 2.4% Hispanic of any race (2005); Density: 1,452.9 persons per square mile (2005); Average household size: 2.53 (2005); Median age: 40.9 (2005); Males per 100 females: 93.5 (2005); Marriage status: 26.1% never married, 58.7% now married, 7.3% widowed, 7.9% divorced (2000); Foreign born: 6.8% (2000); Ancestry (includes multiple ancestries): 28.0% Irish, 20.3% Italian, 17.6% German, 10.4% Other groups, 9.7% English (2000).
Economy: The growth and configuration of major highways, the flat, well-drained topography, and favorable economic-political climate make Colonie more than just a suburb of Albany, but rather a significant community in its own right. The area North and West of Albany in general is experiencing both retail and residential growth. Unemployment rate: 3.5% (2005); Total civilian labor force: 44,939 (2005); Single-family building permits issued: 94 (2005); Multi-family building permits issued: 171 (2005); Employment by occupation: 16.4% management, 24.7% professional, 12.4% services, 31.1% sales, 0.1% farming, 6.5% construction, 8.8% production (2000).
Income: Per capita income: $30,057 (2005); Median household income: $60,079 (2005); Average household income: $74,475 (2005); Percent of households with income of $100,000 or more: 21.5% (2005); Poverty rate: 4.7% (2000).
Taxes: Total city taxes per capita: $248 (2004); City property taxes per capita: $205 (2004).
Education: Percent of population age 25 and over with: High school diploma (including GED) or higher: 89.1% (2005); Bachelor's degree or higher: 32.7% (2005); Master's degree or higher: 14.7% (2005).
Housing: Homeownership rate: 71.8% (2005); Median home value: $172,677 (2005); Median rent: $596 per month (2000); Median age of housing: 35 years (2000).
Safety: Violent crime rate: 12.0 per 10,000 population; Property crime rate: 367.3 per 10,000 population (2004).
Transportation: Commute to work: 92.8% car, 2.6% public transportation, 2.2% walk, 2.1% work from home (2000); Travel time to work: 35.8% less than 15 minutes, 49.5% 15 to 30 minutes, 10.4% 30 to 45 minutes, 1.9% 45 to 60 minutes, 2.4% 60 minutes or more (2000)
Additional Information Contacts
Town of Colonie . . . . (518) 783-2700
  http://www.colonie.org/

DELMAR (CDP).
Covers a land area of 4.382 square miles and a water area of 0 square miles. Located at 42.61° N. Lat.; 73.83° W. Long.
Population: 8,360 (1990); 8,292 (2000); 8,144 (2005); 8,091 (2010 projected); Race: 95.7% White, 1.5% Black, 1.6% Asian, 1.7% Hispanic of any race (2005); Density: 1,858.6 persons per square mile (2005); Average household size: 2.39 (2005); Median age: 44.3 (2005); Males per 100 females: 91.0 (2005); Marriage status: 18.6% never married, 66.5% now married, 7.6% widowed, 7.4% divorced (2000); Foreign born: 6.9% (2000); Ancestry (includes multiple ancestries): 26.8% Irish, 20.9% German, 17.0% English, 13.4% Italian, 7.9% Other groups (2000).
Economy: Manufacturing of construction materials. Employment by occupation: 19.6% management, 42.5% professional, 9.3% services, 22.9% sales, 0.2% farming, 2.8% construction, 2.7% production (2000).
Income: Per capita income: $43,048 (2005); Median household income: $76,298 (2005); Average household income: $101,777 (2005); Percent of households with income of $100,000 or more: 35.5% (2005); Poverty rate: 2.4% (2000).
Education: Percent of population age 25 and over with: High school diploma (including GED) or higher: 96.5% (2005); Bachelor's degree or higher: 60.6% (2005); Master's degree or higher: 34.8% (2005).

School District(s)
Bethlehem Central School District (KG-12)
  2003-04 Enrollment: 5,022 . . . . (518) 439-7098

Housing: Homeownership rate: 77.8% (2005); Median home value: $212,273 (2005); Median rent: $612 per month (2000); Median age of housing: 45 years (2000).
Newspapers: Clifton Park Spotlight (General - Circulation 2,500); Colonie Spotlight (General - Circulation 4,000); Loudonville Weekly (General - Circulation 5,000); Niskayuna Journal (General - Circulation 4,000); Rotterdam Journal (General - Circulation 4,000); Scotia Glenville Journal (General - Circulation 4,000); The Spotlight (General - Circulation 7,000)
Transportation: Commute to work: 88.7% car, 3.0% public transportation, 2.8% walk, 5.1% work from home (2000); Travel time to work: 30.2% less than 15 minutes, 51.6% 15 to 30 minutes, 14.1% 30 to 45 minutes, 1.3% 45 to 60 minutes, 2.8% 60 minutes or more (2000)
Additional Information Contacts

Delmar-Bethlehem Chamber of Commerce............(518) 439-0512
http://www.bethlehemchamber.com

EAST BERNE (unincorporated postal area, zip code 12059). Covers a land area of 28.253 square miles and a water area of 0.627 square miles. Located at 42.62° N. Lat.; 74.05° W. Long.
Population: 0 (2000); Race: 98.8% White, 0.0% Black, 0.0% Asian, 0.7% Hispanic of any race (2000); Density: 0.0 persons per square mile (2000); Age: 27.7% under 18, 10.7% over 64 (2000); Marriage status: 24.1% never married, 60.1% now married, 5.2% widowed, 10.6% divorced (2000); Foreign born: 1.3% (2000); Ancestry (includes multiple ancestries): 21.6% German, 20.6% Irish, 11.9% Italian, 9.2% English, 9.0% United States or American (2000).
Economy: Employment by occupation: 11.6% management, 23.4% professional, 13.8% services, 24.5% sales, 0.0% farming, 14.9% construction, 11.7% production (2000).
Income: Per capita income: $23,839 (2000); Median household income: $52,566 (2000); Poverty rate: 6.0% (2000).
Education: Percent of population age 25 and over with: High school diploma (including GED) or higher: 85.8% (2000); Bachelor's degree or higher: 24.4% (2000).
Housing: Homeownership rate: 84.7% (2000); Median home value: $108,200 (2000); Median rent: $430 per month (2000); Median age of housing: 33 years (2000).
Transportation: Commute to work: 93.1% car, 1.7% public transportation, 0.0% walk, 5.2% work from home (2000); Travel time to work: 10.9% less than 15 minutes, 28.4% 15 to 30 minutes, 43.3% 30 to 45 minutes, 10.8% 45 to 60 minutes, 6.5% 60 minutes or more (2000).

FEURA BUSH (unincorporated postal area, zip code 12067). Covers a land area of 21.972 square miles and a water area of 0.107 square miles. Located at 42.56° N. Lat.; 73.92° W. Long.
Population: 0 (2000); Race: 99.0% White, 0.4% Black, 0.0% Asian, 3.0% Hispanic of any race (2000); Density: 0.0 persons per square mile (2000); Age: 26.1% under 18, 11.6% over 64 (2000); Marriage status: 25.5% never married, 63.3% now married, 6.9% widowed, 4.3% divorced (2000); Foreign born: 1.4% (2000); Ancestry (includes multiple ancestries): 22.0% German, 19.8% Irish, 11.4% Dutch, 9.4% English, 8.8% French (except Basque) (2000).
Economy: Employment by occupation: 8.7% management, 20.9% professional, 12.9% services, 21.8% sales, 0.8% farming, 18.5% construction, 16.3% production (2000).
Income: Per capita income: $24,875 (2000); Median household income: $61,645 (2000); Poverty rate: 4.1% (2000).
Education: Percent of population age 25 and over with: High school diploma (including GED) or higher: 86.9% (2000); Bachelor's degree or higher: 21.1% (2000).
Housing: Homeownership rate: 79.9% (2000); Median home value: $98,900 (2000); Median rent: $449 per month (2000); Median age of housing: 42 years (2000).
Transportation: Commute to work: 94.6% car, 0.0% public transportation, 0.5% walk, 4.4% work from home (2000); Travel time to work: 16.1% less than 15 minutes, 48.2% 15 to 30 minutes, 30.4% 30 to 45 minutes, 4.3% 45 to 60 minutes, 1.1% 60 minutes or more (2000).

GLENMONT (unincorporated postal area, zip code 12077). Covers a land area of 9.573 square miles and a water area of 0 square miles. Located at 42.60° N. Lat.; 73.79° W. Long.
Population: 0 (2000); Race: 92.9% White, 4.6% Black, 1.0% Asian, 1.8% Hispanic of any race (2000); Density: 0.0 persons per square mile (2000); Age: 30.5% under 18, 10.4% over 64 (2000); Marriage status: 18.6% never married, 71.2% now married, 4.4% widowed, 5.8% divorced (2000); Foreign born: 4.0% (2000); Ancestry (includes multiple ancestries): 24.0% German, 21.8% Italian, 21.3% Irish, 15.5% English, 6.8% French (except Basque) (2000).
Economy: Employment by occupation: 22.4% management, 31.1% professional, 10.1% services, 27.2% sales, 0.0% farming, 3.4% construction, 5.8% production (2000).
Income: Per capita income: $28,160 (2000); Median household income: $66,270 (2000); Poverty rate: 3.2% (2000).
Education: Percent of population age 25 and over with: High school diploma (including GED) or higher: 92.4% (2000); Bachelor's degree or higher: 46.3% (2000).

School District(s)
Bethlehem Central School District (KG-12)
    2003-04 Enrollment: 5,022......................(518) 439-7098
Housing: Homeownership rate: 83.6% (2000); Median home value: $155,500 (2000); Median rent: $634 per month (2000); Median age of housing: 19 years (2000).
Transportation: Commute to work: 93.8% car, 1.2% public transportation, 1.9% walk, 2.7% work from home (2000); Travel time to work: 29.1% less than 15 minutes, 51.8% 15 to 30 minutes, 14.5% 30 to 45 minutes, 2.7% 45 to 60 minutes, 1.9% 60 minutes or more (2000).

GREEN ISLAND (town and village). Covers a land area of 0.698 square miles and a water area of 0.222 square miles. Located at 42.74° N. Lat.; 73.69° W. Long.
History: Incorporated 1869.
Population: 2,490 (1990); 2,278 (2000); 2,648 (2005); 2,989 (2010 projected); Race: 95.9% White, 2.0% Black, 0.5% Asian, 0.9% Hispanic of any race (2005); Density: 3,791.9 persons per square mile (2005); Average household size: 2.08 (2005); Median age: 37.7 (2005); Males per 100 females: 94.6 (2005); Marriage status: 37.1% never married, 43.9% now married, 10.6% widowed, 8.3% divorced (2000); Foreign born: 1.8% (2000); Ancestry (includes multiple ancestries): 34.2% Irish, 19.4% French (except Basque), 17.4% German, 17.0% Italian, 8.8% English (2000).
Economy: Food products, machinery. Single-family building permits issued: 0 (2005); Multi-family building permits issued: 0 (2005); Employment by occupation: 11.5% management, 15.1% professional, 16.9% services, 35.6% sales, 0.0% farming, 10.1% construction, 10.9% production (2000).
Income: Per capita income: $19,191 (2005); Median household income: $35,479 (2005); Average household income: $39,888 (2005); Percent of households with income of $100,000 or more: 1.5% (2005); Poverty rate: 10.0% (2000).
Education: Percent of population age 25 and over with: High school diploma (including GED) or higher: 86.9% (2005); Bachelor's degree or higher: 11.4% (2005); Master's degree or higher: 4.0% (2005).
School District(s)
Green Island Union Free School District (KG-12)
    2003-04 Enrollment: 316......................(518) 273-1422
Housing: Homeownership rate: 43.6% (2005); Median home value: $120,909 (2005); Median rent: $432 per month (2000); Median age of housing: 60+ years (2000).
Safety: Violent crime rate: 7.6 per 10,000 population; Property crime rate: 87.9 per 10,000 population (2004).
Transportation: Commute to work: 90.7% car, 3.8% public transportation, 3.2% walk, 1.8% work from home (2000); Travel time to work: 40.7% less than 15 minutes, 46.7% 15 to 30 minutes, 6.0% 30 to 45 minutes, 1.8% 45 to 60 minutes, 4.8% 60 minutes or more (2000).

GUILDERLAND (town). Covers a land area of 57.924 square miles and a water area of 0.770 square miles. Located at 42.70° N. Lat.; 73.92° W. Long. Elevation is 215 feet.
Population: 28,877 (1990); 32,688 (2000); 33,581 (2005); 34,440 (2010 projected); Race: 89.5% White, 2.8% Black, 5.7% Asian, 2.3% Hispanic of any race (2005); Density: 579.7 persons per square mile (2005); Average household size: 2.41 (2005); Median age: 40.4 (2005); Males per 100 females: 92.9 (2005); Marriage status: 24.1% never married, 60.8% now married, 6.6% widowed, 8.4% divorced (2000); Foreign born: 6.8% (2000); Ancestry (includes multiple ancestries): 24.1% Irish, 20.5% Italian, 20.4% German, 11.7% English, 10.8% Other groups (2000).
Economy: Unemployment rate: 2.8% (2005); Total civilian labor force: 20,201 (2005); Single-family building permits issued: 83 (2005); Multi-family building permits issued: 0 (2005); Employment by occupation: 20.3% management, 32.9% professional, 9.1% services, 26.3% sales, 0.2% farming, 5.4% construction, 5.8% production (2000).
Income: Per capita income: $34,979 (2005); Median household income: $67,556 (2005); Average household income: $83,721 (2005); Percent of households with income of $100,000 or more: 27.3% (2005); Poverty rate: 4.1% (2000).
Taxes: Total city taxes per capita: $266 (2004); City property taxes per capita: $207 (2004).
Education: Percent of population age 25 and over with: High school diploma (including GED) or higher: 92.5% (2005); Bachelor's degree or higher: 44.9% (2005); Master's degree or higher: 21.6% (2005).

School District(s)
Guilderland Central School District (KG-12)
   2003-04 Enrollment: 5,664 . . . . (518) 456-6200
Housing: Homeownership rate: 67.0% (2005); Median home value: $194,218 (2005); Median rent: $673 per month (2000); Median age of housing: 27 years (2000).
Safety: Violent crime rate: 9.1 per 10,000 population; Property crime rate: 307.0 per 10,000 population (2004).
Transportation: Commute to work: 93.6% car, 1.8% public transportation, 0.9% walk, 3.3% work from home (2000); Travel time to work: 26.4% less than 15 minutes, 51.0% 15 to 30 minutes, 16.6% 30 to 45 minutes, 2.3% 45 to 60 minutes, 3.6% 60 minutes or more (2000)
Additional Information Contacts
Town of Guilderland. . . . . (518) 356-1980
   http://www.townofguilderland.org/

KNOX (town). Covers a land area of 41.776 square miles and a water area of 0.140 square miles. Located at 42.68° N. Lat.; 74.10° W. Long.
Population: 2,655 (1990); 2,647 (2000); 2,721 (2005); 2,795 (2010 projected); Race: 96.8% White, 0.9% Black, 0.7% Asian, 0.3% Hispanic of any race (2005); Density: 65.1 persons per square mile (2005); Average household size: 2.72 (2005); Median age: 40.0 (2005); Males per 100 females: 100.7 (2005); Marriage status: 23.4% never married, 62.6% now married, 6.4% widowed, 7.6% divorced (2000); Foreign born: 1.1% (2000); Ancestry (includes multiple ancestries): 24.1% German, 23.7% Irish, 15.2% English, 10.9% Dutch, 9.1% Italian (2000).
Economy: Single-family building permits issued: 7 (2005); Multi-family building permits issued: 0 (2005); Employment by occupation: 11.0% management, 26.0% professional, 8.6% services, 26.3% sales, 0.9% farming, 13.9% construction, 13.3% production (2000).
Income: Per capita income: $27,780 (2005); Median household income: $69,006 (2005); Average household income: $75,666 (2005); Percent of households with income of $100,000 or more: 23.1% (2005); Poverty rate: 5.4% (2000).
Education: Percent of population age 25 and over with: High school diploma (including GED) or higher: 90.2% (2005); Bachelor's degree or higher: 23.4% (2005); Master's degree or higher: 11.1% (2005).
Housing: Homeownership rate: 90.2% (2005); Median home value: $167,030 (2005); Median rent: $367 per month (2000); Median age of housing: 28 years (2000).
Transportation: Commute to work: 93.2% car, 0.5% public transportation, 1.0% walk, 5.0% work from home (2000); Travel time to work: 12.4% less than 15 minutes, 25.3% 15 to 30 minutes, 37.3% 30 to 45 minutes, 14.9% 45 to 60 minutes, 10.1% 60 minutes or more (2000)
Additional Information Contacts
Town of Knox. . . . . (518) 872-2551
   http://www.helderweb.com/knox/

MEDUSA (CDP). Covers a land area of 6.786 square miles and a water area of 0.074 square miles. Located at 42.43° N. Lat.; 74.12° W. Long.
Population: 369 (1990); 376 (2000); 410 (2005); 436 (2010 projected); Race: 98.8% White, 0.0% Black, 0.2% Asian, 0.2% Hispanic of any race (2005); Density: 60.4 persons per square mile (2005); Average household size: 2.50 (2005); Median age: 41.5 (2005); Males per 100 females: 106.0 (2005); Marriage status: 19.3% never married, 62.6% now married, 8.5% widowed, 9.5% divorced (2000); Foreign born: 3.4% (2000); Ancestry (includes multiple ancestries): 26.7% Irish, 14.7% German, 13.7% English, 12.0% Italian, 10.0% United States or American (2000).
Economy: Employment by occupation: 11.7% management, 21.8% professional, 15.4% services, 17.6% sales, 1.1% farming, 16.0% construction, 16.5% production (2000).
Income: Per capita income: $27,006 (2005); Median household income: $52,439 (2005); Average household income: $67,515 (2005); Percent of households with income of $100,000 or more: 14.0% (2005); Poverty rate: 6.7% (2000).
Education: Percent of population age 25 and over with: High school diploma (including GED) or higher: 86.0% (2005); Bachelor's degree or higher: 19.4% (2005); Master's degree or higher: 9.4% (2005).
Housing: Homeownership rate: 79.3% (2005); Median home value: $147,273 (2005); Median rent: $450 per month (2000); Median age of housing: 39 years (2000).
Transportation: Commute to work: 93.5% car, 1.1% public transportation, 2.2% walk, 2.2% work from home (2000); Travel time to work: 22.5% less than 15 minutes, 27.5% 15 to 30 minutes, 22.0% 30 to 45 minutes, 13.7% 45 to 60 minutes, 14.3% 60 minutes or more (2000)

MENANDS (village). Covers a land area of 3.192 square miles and a water area of 0.216 square miles. Located at 42.69° N. Lat.; 73.72° W. Long.
History: Incorporated 1924.
Population: 4,326 (1990); 3,910 (2000); 3,871 (2005); 3,839 (2010 projected); Race: 78.7% White, 11.1% Black, 6.6% Asian, 3.5% Hispanic of any race (2005); Density: 1,212.9 persons per square mile (2005); Average household size: 2.08 (2005); Median age: 44.9 (2005); Males per 100 females: 87.5 (2005); Marriage status: 30.0% never married, 52.0% now married, 9.4% widowed, 8.5% divorced (2000); Foreign born: 10.7% (2000); Ancestry (includes multiple ancestries): 28.0% Irish, 15.8% Italian, 15.4% Other groups, 12.8% German, 8.5% English (2000).
Economy: Regional wholesale produce center. Single-family building permits issued: 3 (2005); Multi-family building permits issued: 0 (2005); Employment by occupation: 19.0% management, 31.8% professional, 11.5% services, 28.7% sales, 0.0% farming, 2.2% construction, 6.8% production (2000).
Income: Per capita income: $42,925 (2005); Median household income: $55,572 (2005); Average household income: $87,245 (2005); Percent of households with income of $100,000 or more: 21.7% (2005); Poverty rate: 5.4% (2000).
Education: Percent of population age 25 and over with: High school diploma (including GED) or higher: 92.7% (2005); Bachelor's degree or higher: 45.8% (2005); Master's degree or higher: 22.2% (2005).
School District(s)
Menands Union Free School District (KG-08)
   2003-04 Enrollment: 235 . . . . (518) 465-4561
Housing: Homeownership rate: 38.6% (2005); Median home value: $184,491 (2005); Median rent: $667 per month (2000); Median age of housing: 35 years (2000).
Safety: Violent crime rate: 20.6 per 10,000 population; Property crime rate: 403.9 per 10,000 population (2004).
Transportation: Commute to work: 87.9% car, 8.9% public transportation, 1.4% walk, 1.8% work from home (2000); Travel time to work: 45.6% less than 15 minutes, 39.0% 15 to 30 minutes, 10.2% 30 to 45 minutes, 2.8% 45 to 60 minutes, 2.4% 60 minutes or more (2000)
Additional Information Contacts
Village of Menands . . . . (518) 434-2922
   http://www.villageofmenands.com/Home/

NEW SCOTLAND (town). Covers a land area of 58.067 square miles and a water area of 0.331 square miles. Located at 42.62° N. Lat.; 73.93° W. Long.
Population: 9,102 (1990); 8,626 (2000); 8,952 (2005); 9,244 (2010 projected); Race: 97.8% White, 0.3% Black, 0.6% Asian, 1.1% Hispanic of any race (2005); Density: 154.2 persons per square mile (2005); Average household size: 2.53 (2005); Median age: 42.5 (2005); Males per 100 females: 95.2 (2005); Marriage status: 20.9% never married, 66.5% now married, 5.3% widowed, 7.3% divorced (2000); Foreign born: 2.5% (2000); Ancestry (includes multiple ancestries): 25.4% Irish, 25.4% German, 16.5% English, 11.6% Italian, 8.1% Dutch (2000).
Economy: Single-family building permits issued: 24 (2005); Multi-family building permits issued: 0 (2005); Employment by occupation: 16.2% management, 28.3% professional, 9.9% services, 24.0% sales, 0.5% farming, 12.3% construction, 8.9% production (2000).
Income: Per capita income: $34,292 (2005); Median household income: $69,107 (2005); Average household income: $86,669 (2005); Percent of households with income of $100,000 or more: 28.4% (2005); Poverty rate: 4.1% (2000).
Education: Percent of population age 25 and over with: High school diploma (including GED) or higher: 91.5% (2005); Bachelor's degree or higher: 35.1% (2005); Master's degree or higher: 15.9% (2005).
Housing: Homeownership rate: 81.7% (2005); Median home value: $180,565 (2005); Median rent: $495 per month (2000); Median age of housing: 37 years (2000).
Transportation: Commute to work: 96.0% car, 0.4% public transportation, 1.2% walk, 2.3% work from home (2000); Travel time to work: 19.6% less than 15 minutes, 52.2% 15 to 30 minutes, 22.7% 30 to 45 minutes, 3.4% 45 to 60 minutes, 2.1% 60 minutes or more (2000)
Additional Information Contacts
Town of New Scotland . . . . (518) 439-4889
   http://www.townofnewscotland.com/

PRESTON HOLLOW (unincorporated postal area, zip code 12469). Covers a land area of 41.556 square miles and a water area of 0.037 square miles. Located at 42.44° N. Lat.; 74.24° W. Long.
Population: 0 (2000); Race: 96.9% White, 0.0% Black, 0.0% Asian, 3.3% Hispanic of any race (2000); Density: 0.0 persons per square mile (2000); Age: 22.3% under 18, 16.2% over 64 (2000); Marriage status: 20.4% never married, 62.3% now married, 7.7% widowed, 9.6% divorced (2000); Foreign born: 3.8% (2000); Ancestry (includes multiple ancestries): 19.7% German, 18.3% Irish, 14.3% Italian, 10.2% English, 9.0% Other groups (2000).
Economy: Employment by occupation: 11.9% management, 13.6% professional, 11.3% services, 29.7% sales, 1.5% farming, 10.7% construction, 21.4% production (2000).
Income: Per capita income: $19,372 (2000); Median household income: $35,741 (2000); Poverty rate: 6.4% (2000).
Education: Percent of population age 25 and over with: High school diploma (including GED) or higher: 81.9% (2000); Bachelor's degree or higher: 10.7% (2000).
Housing: Homeownership rate: 85.5% (2000); Median home value: $78,700 (2000); Median rent: $400 per month (2000); Median age of housing: 33 years (2000).
Transportation: Commute to work: 87.5% car, 2.7% public transportation, 0.6% walk, 7.9% work from home (2000); Travel time to work: 22.8% less than 15 minutes, 29.1% 15 to 30 minutes, 12.3% 30 to 45 minutes, 22.8% 45 to 60 minutes, 12.9% 60 minutes or more (2000)

PRESTON-POTTER HOLLOW (CDP). Covers a land area of 10.109 square miles and a water area of 0 square miles. Located at 42.43° N. Lat.; 74.22° W. Long.
Population: 407 (1990); 374 (2000); 402 (2005); 421 (2010 projected); Race: 93.0% White, 5.0% Black, 0.2% Asian, 0.2% Hispanic of any race (2005); Density: 39.8 persons per square mile (2005); Average household size: 2.41 (2005); Median age: 43.3 (2005); Males per 100 females: 90.5 (2005); Marriage status: 22.2% never married, 60.9% now married, 8.5% widowed, 8.5% divorced (2000); Foreign born: 3.6% (2000); Ancestry (includes multiple ancestries): 19.5% German, 18.4% Irish, 13.9% English, 12.3% Dutch, 10.0% Italian (2000).
Economy: Employment by occupation: 15.7% management, 18.9% professional, 17.3% services, 13.4% sales, 1.6% farming, 12.6% construction, 20.5% production (2000).
Income: Per capita income: $19,963 (2005); Median household income: $38,250 (2005); Average household income: $48,054 (2005); Percent of households with income of $100,000 or more: 8.4% (2005); Poverty rate: 10.2% (2000).
Education: Percent of population age 25 and over with: High school diploma (including GED) or higher: 81.8% (2005); Bachelor's degree or higher: 9.9% (2005); Master's degree or higher: 4.7% (2005).
Housing: Homeownership rate: 83.8% (2005); Median home value: $113,462 (2005); Median rent: $343 per month (2000); Median age of housing: 60+ years (2000).
Transportation: Commute to work: 81.7% car, 5.6% public transportation, 0.0% walk, 12.7% work from home (2000); Travel time to work: 40.0% less than 15 minutes, 20.9% 15 to 30 minutes, 8.2% 30 to 45 minutes, 19.1% 45 to 60 minutes, 11.8% 60 minutes or more (2000)

RAVENA (village). Covers a land area of 1.339 square miles and a water area of 0 square miles. Located at 42.47° N. Lat.; 73.81° W. Long. Elevation is 182 feet.
History: Incorporated 1914.
Population: 3,497 (1990); 3,369 (2000); 3,344 (2005); 3,329 (2010 projected); Race: 90.8% White, 3.4% Black, 1.0% Asian, 5.8% Hispanic of any race (2005); Density: 2,497.0 persons per square mile (2005); Average household size: 2.40 (2005); Median age: 36.8 (2005); Males per 100 females: 90.5 (2005); Marriage status: 26.0% never married, 58.6% now married, 7.3% widowed, 8.1% divorced (2000); Foreign born: 3.2% (2000); Ancestry (includes multiple ancestries): 24.0% Irish, 21.7% Italian, 18.2% German, 11.5% Other groups, 7.4% English (2000).
Economy: Manufacturing of cement. Single-family building permits issued: 11 (2005); Multi-family building permits issued: 0 (2005); Employment by occupation: 9.9% management, 19.4% professional, 17.1% services, 31.1% sales, 0.0% farming, 9.3% construction, 13.2% production (2000).
Income: Per capita income: $23,612 (2005); Median household income: $47,783 (2005); Average household income: $56,545 (2005); Percent of households with income of $100,000 or more: 13.3% (2005); Poverty rate: 8.9% (2000).
Education: Percent of population age 25 and over with: High school diploma (including GED) or higher: 80.8% (2005); Bachelor's degree or higher: 17.8% (2005); Master's degree or higher: 8.0% (2005).
School District(s)
Ravena-Coeymans-Selkirk Central School District (PK-12)
    2003-04 Enrollment: 2,385 . . . . (518) 756-5201
Housing: Homeownership rate: 58.0% (2005); Median home value: $127,963 (2005); Median rent: $483 per month (2000); Median age of housing: 43 years (2000).
Newspapers: Greenville Local (General - Circulation 1,050); News-Herald (General - Circulation 3,250)
Transportation: Commute to work: 90.9% car, 2.6% public transportation, 4.6% walk, 1.4% work from home (2000); Travel time to work: 27.6% less than 15 minutes, 29.4% 15 to 30 minutes, 34.0% 30 to 45 minutes, 4.5% 45 to 60 minutes, 4.4% 60 minutes or more (2000)

RENSSELAERVILLE (town). Covers a land area of 61.463 square miles and a water area of 0.394 square miles. Located at 42.48° N. Lat.; 74.17° W. Long.
Population: 1,981 (1990); 1,915 (2000); 1,953 (2005); 1,997 (2010 projected); Race: 95.4% White, 2.0% Black, 0.3% Asian, 1.2% Hispanic of any race (2005); Density: 31.8 persons per square mile (2005); Average household size: 2.41 (2005); Median age: 44.0 (2005); Males per 100 females: 103.2 (2005); Marriage status: 21.9% never married, 60.8% now married, 7.9% widowed, 9.4% divorced (2000); Foreign born: 2.9% (2000); Ancestry (includes multiple ancestries): 21.1% German, 20.7% Irish, 11.6% English, 10.4% Italian, 9.6% Dutch (2000).
Economy: Single-family building permits issued: 9 (2005); Multi-family building permits issued: 0 (2005); Employment by occupation: 14.9% management, 21.2% professional, 12.0% services, 22.6% sales, 1.0% farming, 13.9% construction, 14.3% production (2000).
Income: Per capita income: $26,270 (2005); Median household income: $49,469 (2005); Average household income: $63,009 (2005); Percent of households with income of $100,000 or more: 13.8% (2005); Poverty rate: 5.3% (2000).
Education: Percent of population age 25 and over with: High school diploma (including GED) or higher: 86.5% (2005); Bachelor's degree or higher: 20.3% (2005); Master's degree or higher: 8.5% (2005).
School District(s)
Middleburgh Central School District (PK-12)
    2003-04 Enrollment: 1,061 . . . . (518) 827-5567
Housing: Homeownership rate: 83.7% (2005); Median home value: $144,614 (2005); Median rent: $463 per month (2000); Median age of housing: 44 years (2000).
Transportation: Commute to work: 90.8% car, 1.3% public transportation, 2.0% walk, 5.2% work from home (2000); Travel time to work: 19.0% less than 15 minutes, 23.7% 15 to 30 minutes, 21.0% 30 to 45 minutes, 22.4% 45 to 60 minutes, 13.7% 60 minutes or more (2000)

SELKIRK (unincorporated postal area, zip code 12158). Covers a land area of 29.141 square miles and a water area of 0.008 square miles. Located at 42.54° N. Lat.; 73.81° W. Long.
Population: 0 (2000); Race: 93.3% White, 3.6% Black, 2.0% Asian, 0.5% Hispanic of any race (2000); Density: 0.0 persons per square mile (2000); Age: 28.2% under 18, 10.9% over 64 (2000); Marriage status: 25.3% never married, 60.1% now married, 5.2% widowed, 9.4% divorced (2000); Foreign born: 3.0% (2000); Ancestry (includes multiple ancestries): 22.7% Irish, 21.1% German, 13.2% Italian, 10.4% Other groups, 8.7% English (2000).
Economy: Employment by occupation: 11.9% management, 20.6% professional, 12.6% services, 27.6% sales, 0.3% farming, 11.6% construction, 15.5% production (2000).
Income: Per capita income: $22,506 (2000); Median household income: $49,476 (2000); Poverty rate: 7.1% (2000).
Education: Percent of population age 25 and over with: High school diploma (including GED) or higher: 84.9% (2000); Bachelor's degree or higher: 19.0% (2000).
School District(s)
Ravena-Coeymans-Selkirk Central School District (PK-12)
    2003-04 Enrollment: 2,385 . . . . (518) 756-5201
Housing: Homeownership rate: 75.2% (2000); Median home value: $102,500 (2000); Median rent: $628 per month (2000); Median age of housing: 30 years (2000).

SLINGERLANDS (unincorporated postal area, zip code 12159). Covers a land area of 13.507 square miles and a water area of 0.012 square miles. Located at 42.64° N. Lat.; 73.87° W. Long.
Population: 0 (2000); Race: 92.3% White, 2.6% Black, 3.7% Asian, 1.5% Hispanic of any race (2000); Density: 0.0 persons per square mile (2000); Age: 27.2% under 18, 14.1% over 64 (2000); Marriage status: 19.8% never married, 66.6% now married, 6.8% widowed, 6.8% divorced (2000); Foreign born: 6.1% (2000); Ancestry (includes multiple ancestries): 22.3% Irish, 19.0% German, 14.8% Italian, 12.3% English, 11.9% Other groups (2000).
Economy: Employment by occupation: 22.8% management, 40.5% professional, 7.5% services, 22.2% sales, 0.0% farming, 2.6% construction, 4.3% production (2000).
Income: Per capita income: $36,728 (2000); Median household income: $65,227 (2000); Poverty rate: 4.0% (2000).
Education: Percent of population age 25 and over with: High school diploma (including GED) or higher: 94.9% (2000); Bachelor's degree or higher: 58.7% (2000).
Housing: Homeownership rate: 69.5% (2000); Median home value: $195,400 (2000); Median rent: $648 per month (2000); Median age of housing: 18 years (2000).
Transportation: Commute to work: 93.7% car, 0.9% public transportation, 1.3% walk, 4.2% work from home (2000); Travel time to work: 25.3% less than 15 minutes, 60.1% 15 to 30 minutes, 11.5% 30 to 45 minutes, 0.7% 45 to 60 minutes, 2.3% 60 minutes or more (2000)

VOORHEESVILLE (village). Covers a land area of 2.134 square miles and a water area of 0 square miles. Located at 42.65° N. Lat.; 73.92° W. Long. Elevation is 332 feet.
Population: 3,090 (1990); 2,705 (2000); 2,837 (2005); 2,962 (2010 projected); Race: 98.0% White, 0.4% Black, 0.6% Asian, 1.2% Hispanic of any race (2005); Density: 1,329.4 persons per square mile (2005); Average household size: 2.54 (2005); Median age: 43.5 (2005); Males per 100 females: 91.4 (2005); Marriage status: 23.0% never married, 66.1% now married, 2.9% widowed, 8.0% divorced (2000); Foreign born: 3.4% (2000); Ancestry (includes multiple ancestries): 31.8% Irish, 28.4% German, 18.7% English, 13.2% Italian, 7.8% Polish (2000).
Economy: Manufacturing of machinery. Single-family building permits issued: 3 (2005); Multi-family building permits issued: 0 (2005); Employment by occupation: 17.5% management, 31.6% professional, 9.0% services, 27.4% sales, 0.0% farming, 7.9% construction, 6.7% production (2000).
Income: Per capita income: $30,859 (2005); Median household income: $70,094 (2005); Average household income: $78,518 (2005); Percent of households with income of $100,000 or more: 26.6% (2005); Poverty rate: 1.3% (2000).
Education: Percent of population age 25 and over with: High school diploma (including GED) or higher: 94.7% (2005); Bachelor's degree or higher: 40.1% (2005); Master's degree or higher: 14.9% (2005).
School District(s)
Voorheesville Central School District (KG-12)
    2003-04 Enrollment: 1,268 . . . . (518) 765-3313
Housing: Homeownership rate: 80.0% (2005); Median home value: $175,858 (2005); Median rent: $567 per month (2000); Median age of housing: 35 years (2000).
Transportation: Commute to work: 97.0% car, 0.5% public transportation, 1.3% walk, 1.2% work from home (2000); Travel time to work: 19.6% less than 15 minutes, 56.2% 15 to 30 minutes, 20.2% 30 to 45 minutes, 1.9% 45 to 60 minutes, 2.0% 60 minutes or more (2000)

WATERVLIET (city). Covers a land area of 1.342 square miles and a water area of 0.152 square miles. Located at 42.72° N. Lat.; 73.70° W. Long. Elevation is 50 feet.
History: The U.S. Watervliet Arsenal here, which specializes in the production of heavy ordnance, was established 1813. In 1776, Ann Lee founded the first American community of Shakers (United Society of Believers) in Watervliet. Founded by the Dutch 1735, Incorporated as a city 1896.
Population: 11,275 (1990); 10,207 (2000); 9,966 (2005); 9,745 (2010 projected); Race: 89.2% White, 5.1% Black, 2.1% Asian, 5.4% Hispanic of any race (2005); Density: 7,428.4 persons per square mile (2005); Average household size: 2.15 (2005); Median age: 36.2 (2005); Males per 100 females: 89.3 (2005); Marriage status: 36.3% never married, 41.6% now married, 10.1% widowed, 12.0% divorced (2000); Foreign born: 4.2% (2000); Ancestry (includes multiple ancestries): 30.5% Irish, 19.1% Italian, 14.5% German, 12.4% French (except Basque), 10.5% Other groups (2000).
Economy: The U.S. Watervliet Arsenal here, which specializes in the production of heavy ordnance, was established 1813. Steel products and water and pressure-sensitive tapes are also made. Single-family building permits issued: 4 (2005); Multi-family building permits issued: 2 (2005); Employment by occupation: 10.7% management, 15.7% professional, 17.9% services, 34.8% sales, 0.0% farming, 7.9% construction, 13.0% production (2000).
Income: Per capita income: $20,097 (2005); Median household income: $35,801 (2005); Average household income: $43,186 (2005); Percent of households with income of $100,000 or more: 5.9% (2005); Poverty rate: 13.3% (2000).
Education: Percent of population age 25 and over with: High school diploma (including GED) or higher: 81.2% (2005); Bachelor's degree or higher: 14.7% (2005); Master's degree or higher: 5.2% (2005).
School District(s)
Maplewood Common School District (KG-08)
    2003-04 Enrollment: 185 . . . . (518) 273-1512
Watervliet City School District (KG-12)
    2003-04 Enrollment: 1,403 . . . . (518) 629-3200
Housing: Homeownership rate: 41.3% (2005); Median home value: $122,288 (2005); Median rent: $433 per month (2000); Median age of housing: 60+ years (2000).
Safety: Violent crime rate: 38.7 per 10,000 population; Property crime rate: 229.4 per 10,000 population (2004).
Transportation: Commute to work: 83.1% car, 8.5% public transportation, 4.3% walk, 3.1% work from home (2000); Travel time to work: 36.1% less than 15 minutes, 45.8% 15 to 30 minutes, 11.7% 30 to 45 minutes, 2.9% 45 to 60 minutes, 3.6% 60 minutes or more (2000)
Additional Information Contacts
City of Watervliet . . . . (518) 270-3810
    http://www.watervliet.com/

WESTERLO (town). Covers a land area of 57.881 square miles and a water area of 0.671 square miles. Located at 42.51° N. Lat.; 74.04° W. Long. Elevation is 1,144 feet.
Population: 3,325 (1990); 3,466 (2000); 3,554 (2005); 3,645 (2010 projected); Race: 97.7% White, 0.8% Black, 0.3% Asian, 1.2% Hispanic of any race (2005); Density: 61.4 persons per square mile (2005); Average household size: 2.56 (2005); Median age: 40.3 (2005); Males per 100 females: 96.1 (2005); Marriage status: 20.1% never married, 64.6% now married, 10.3% widowed, 5.1% divorced (2000); Foreign born: 1.8% (2000); Ancestry (includes multiple ancestries): 23.2% German, 20.8% Irish, 15.9% Italian, 10.2% English, 10.0% Dutch (2000).
Economy: Resort village. Single-family building permits issued: 13 (2005); Multi-family building permits issued: 0 (2005); Employment by occupation: 15.3% management, 19.6% professional, 16.7% services, 22.1% sales, 0.0% farming, 13.6% construction, 12.6% production (2000).
Income: Per capita income: $25,293 (2005); Median household income: $56,806 (2005); Average household income: $64,762 (2005); Percent of households with income of $100,000 or more: 13.9% (2005); Poverty rate: 5.4% (2000).
Education: Percent of population age 25 and over with: High school diploma (including GED) or higher: 86.1% (2005); Bachelor's degree or higher: 20.4% (2005); Master's degree or higher: 9.8% (2005).
Housing: Homeownership rate: 83.3% (2005); Median home value: $145,958 (2005); Median rent: $448 per month (2000); Median age of housing: 29 years (2000).
Transportation: Commute to work: 92.9% car, 1.1% public transportation, 2.6% walk, 3.4% work from home (2000); Travel time to work: 23.5% less than 15 minutes, 19.6% 15 to 30 minutes, 29.5% 30 to 45 minutes, 17.9% 45 to 60 minutes, 9.5% 60 minutes or more (2000)

WESTMERE (CDP). Covers a land area of 3.181 square miles and a water area of 0 square miles. Located at 42.69° N. Lat.; 73.87° W. Long.
Population: 6,750 (1990); 7,188 (2000); 7,475 (2005); 7,663 (2010 projected); Race: 84.7% White, 4.0% Black, 9.7% Asian, 2.8% Hispanic of any race (2005); Density: 2,350.0 persons per square mile (2005); Average household size: 2.26 (2005); Median age: 40.7 (2005); Males per 100

females: 91.3 (2005); Marriage status: 28.1% never married, 55.8% now married, 6.3% widowed, 9.8% divorced (2000); Foreign born: 10.6% (2000); Ancestry (includes multiple ancestries): 24.6% Irish, 20.2% Italian, 17.0% German, 15.6% Other groups, 9.4% English (2000).
Economy: Employment by occupation: 19.8% management, 37.2% professional, 10.4% services, 25.0% sales, 0.0% farming, 4.2% construction, 3.3% production (2000).
Income: Per capita income: $33,695 (2005); Median household income: $61,545 (2005); Average household income: $75,082 (2005); Percent of households with income of $100,000 or more: 23.2% (2005); Poverty rate: 4.1% (2000).
Education: Percent of population age 25 and over with: High school diploma (including GED) or higher: 91.4% (2005); Bachelor's degree or higher: 43.5% (2005); Master's degree or higher: 24.5% (2005).
Housing: Homeownership rate: 55.8% (2005); Median home value: $179,658 (2005); Median rent: $725 per month (2000); Median age of housing: 31 years (2000).
Transportation: Commute to work: 95.5% car, 1.9% public transportation, 0.5% walk, 2.2% work from home (2000); Travel time to work: 31.6% less than 15 minutes, 56.2% 15 to 30 minutes, 8.8% 30 to 45 minutes, 1.1% 45 to 60 minutes, 2.2% 60 minutes or more (2000)

Allegany County

Located in western New York; bounded on the south by Pennsylvania. Covers a land area of 1,030.22 square miles, a water area of 4.20 square miles, and is located in the Eastern Time Zone. The county government was organized in 1806. County seat is Belmont.

Weather Station: Alfred | | | | | | | | | | | Elevation: 1,768 feet
	Jan	Feb	Mar	Apr	May	Jun	Jul	Aug	Sep	Oct	Nov	Dec
High	31	34	44	56	68	76	80	78	70	59	46	36
Low	12	13	21	31	41	50	55	53	47	36	28	19
Precip	2.1	2.0	2.7	3.0	3.4	4.5	3.7	3.3	4.0	3.3	3.3	2.8
Snow	20.2	16.7	14.5	4.2	0.4	0.0	0.0	0.0	0.0	0.5	8.6	18.3

High and Low temperatures in degrees Fahrenheit; Precipitation and Snow in inches

Weather Station: Angelica | | | | | | | | | | | Elevation: 1,443 feet
	Jan	Feb	Mar	Apr	May	Jun	Jul	Aug	Sep	Oct	Nov	Dec
High	31	34	43	56	68	75	80	78	71	60	47	36
Low	13	13	21	31	41	49	54	53	46	36	29	19
Precip	2.0	2.0	2.4	2.9	3.2	4.6	3.7	3.8	3.8	3.2	3.0	2.5
Snow	15.1	11.3	10.1	3.0	0.2	0.0	0.0	0.0	0.0	0.3	5.7	13.4

High and Low temperatures in degrees Fahrenheit; Precipitation and Snow in inches

Weather Station: Bolivar | | | | | | | | | | | Elevation: 1,578 feet
	Jan	Feb	Mar	Apr	May	Jun	Jul	Aug	Sep	Oct	Nov	Dec
High	30	33	42	55	67	75	79	77	69	59	46	35
Low	11	12	21	31	40	49	54	53	46	35	28	18
Precip	2.3	1.9	2.7	3.1	3.4	5.0	4.4	3.8	4.2	3.2	3.2	2.8
Snow	19.3	14.7	12.4	2.9	0.2	tr	0.0	0.0	0.0	0.5	7.5	18.9

High and Low temperatures in degrees Fahrenheit; Precipitation and Snow in inches

Population: 50,470 (1990); 49,927 (2000); 50,801 (2005); 51,684 (2010 projected); Race: 96.3% White, 1.1% Black, 1.0% Asian, 1.3% Hispanic of any race (2005); Density: 49.3 persons per square mile (2005); Average household size: 2.73 (2005); Median age: 35.5 (2005); Males per 100 females: 99.7 (2005).
Religion: Five largest groups: 12.9% Catholic Church, 6.8% The United Methodist Church, 5.6% The Wesleyan Church, 1.6% American Baptist Churches in the USA, 1.4% Assemblies of God (2000).
Economy: Unemployment rate: 5.6% (2005); Total civilian labor force: 23,623 (2005); Leading industries: 22.3% manufacturing; 20.7% educational services; 16.9% health care and social assistance (2003); Farms: 867 totaling 180,169 acres (2002); Companies that employ 500 or more persons: 4 (2003); Companies that employ 100 to 499 persons: 16 (2003); Companies that employ less than 100 persons: 801 (2003); Black-owned businesses: n/a (2002); Hispanic-owned businesses: n/a (2002); Women-owned businesses: n/a (2002); Retail sales per capita: $7,164 (2006). Single-family building permits issued: 91 (2005); Multi-family building permits issued: 0 (2005).
Income: Per capita income: $17,065 (2005); Median household income: $36,249 (2005); Average household income: $45,473 (2005); Percent of households with income of $100,000 or more: 7.0% (2005); Poverty rate: 14.8% (2003); Bankruptcy rate: 6.74% (2005).
Education: Percent of population age 25 and over with: High school diploma (including GED) or higher: 83.4% (2005); Bachelor's degree or higher: 17.7% (2005); Master's degree or higher: 8.8% (2005).
Housing: Homeownership rate: 73.9% (2005); Median home value: $78,272 (2005); Median rent: $330 per month (2000); Median age of housing: 41 years (2000).
Health: Birth rate: 106.2 per 10,000 population (2004); Death rate: 104.0 per 10,000 population (2004); Age-adjusted cancer mortality rate: 243.3 deaths per 100,000 population (2002); Number of physicians: 9.6 per 10,000 population (2004); Hospital beds: 29.9 per 10,000 population (2003); Hospital admissions: 663.6 per 10,000 population (2003).
Elections: 2004 Presidential election results: 63.9% Bush, 34.1% Kerry, 1.7% Nader, 0.3% Badnarik
Additional Information Contacts
Allegany County Government . . . . (585) 268-7612
  http://www.alleganyco.com/
Town of Hume . . . . (585) 567-2666
  http://www.humetown.org/
Village of Alfred . . . . (607) 587-9188
  http://www.alfredny.org/

Allegany County Communities

ALFRED (village). Covers a land area of 1.179 square miles and a water area of 0 square miles. Located at 42.25° N. Lat.; 77.78° W. Long. Elevation is 1,762 feet.
Population: 4,559 (1990); 3,954 (2000); 4,318 (2005); 4,543 (2010 projected); Race: 87.3% White, 6.2% Black, 3.5% Asian, 3.3% Hispanic of any race (2005); Density: 3,661.1 persons per square mile (2005); Average household size: 7.00 (2005); Median age: 20.5 (2005); Males per 100 females: 143.0 (2005); Marriage status: 76.9% never married, 19.2% now married, 2.0% widowed, 1.8% divorced (2000); Foreign born: 5.9% (2000); Ancestry (includes multiple ancestries): 19.9% Irish, 19.6% German, 11.7% Italian, 11.5% Other groups, 11.5% English (2000).
Economy: Single-family building permits issued: 0 (2005); Multi-family building permits issued: 0 (2005); Employment by occupation: 5.9% management, 29.1% professional, 22.8% services, 29.1% sales, 1.8% farming, 5.0% construction, 6.4% production (2000).
Income: Per capita income: $8,728 (2005); Median household income: $24,012 (2005); Average household income: $44,494 (2005); Percent of households with income of $100,000 or more: 11.3% (2005); Poverty rate: 37.7% (2000).
Education: Percent of population age 25 and over with: High school diploma (including GED) or higher: 95.3% (2005); Bachelor's degree or higher: 70.7% (2005); Master's degree or higher: 50.7% (2005).
Four-year College(s)
Alfred University
  Fall 2004 Enrollment: 2,355 . . . . (607) 871-2111
  2005-06 Tuition: In-state $20,960; Out-of-state $20,960
SUNY College of Technology at Alfred (Public)
  Fall 2004 Enrollment: 3,597 . . . . (607) 587-4111
  2005-06 Tuition: In-state $5,348; Out-of-state $8,208
Housing: Homeownership rate: 34.5% (2005); Median home value: $132,798 (2005); Median rent: $339 per month (2000); Median age of housing: 56 years (2000).
Safety: Violent crime rate: 17.6 per 10,000 population; Property crime rate: 147.6 per 10,000 population (2004).
Transportation: Commute to work: 36.4% car, 0.8% public transportation, 60.2% walk, 1.3% work from home (2000); Travel time to work: 77.9% less than 15 minutes, 15.2% 15 to 30 minutes, 3.8% 30 to 45 minutes, 2.1% 45 to 60 minutes, 1.1% 60 minutes or more (2000)
Additional Information Contacts
Village of Alfred . . . . (607) 587-9188
  http://www.alfredny.org/

ALFRED (town). Covers a land area of 31.532 square miles and a water area of 0.055 square miles. Located at 42.24° N. Lat.; 77.78° W. Long. Elevation is 1,762 feet.
Population: 5,791 (1990); 5,140 (2000); 5,590 (2005); 5,909 (2010 projected); Race: 89.4% White, 4.9% Black, 3.3% Asian, 2.8% Hispanic of any race (2005); Density: 177.3 persons per square mile (2005); Average household size: 4.96 (2005); Median age: 20.9 (2005); Males per 100 females: 134.7 (2005); Marriage status: 67.7% never married, 27.8% now married, 2.1% widowed, 2.3% divorced (2000); Foreign born: 5.3% (2000);

Ancestry (includes multiple ancestries): 20.1% German, 19.0% Irish, 13.8% English, 11.2% Italian, 9.8% Other groups (2000).
Economy: Agriculture: dairy products; beef cattle; grain, potatoes. Manufactuers ceramics. Single-family building permits issued: 1 (2005); Multi-family building permits issued: 0 (2005); Employment by occupation: 8.3% management, 31.1% professional, 19.9% services, 26.0% sales, 1.7% farming, 5.5% construction, 7.4% production (2000).
Income: Per capita income: $12,110 (2005); Median household income: $36,053 (2005); Average household income: $51,028 (2005); Percent of households with income of $100,000 or more: 13.8% (2005); Poverty rate: 22.5% (2000).
Education: Percent of population age 25 and over with: High school diploma (including GED) or higher: 96.3% (2005); Bachelor's degree or higher: 60.4% (2005); Master's degree or higher: 40.7% (2005).
Housing: Homeownership rate: 51.8% (2005); Median home value: $136,033 (2005); Median rent: $360 per month (2000); Median age of housing: 40 years (2000).
Transportation: Commute to work: 49.8% car, 0.6% public transportation, 46.5% walk, 1.6% work from home (2000); Travel time to work: 74.0% less than 15 minutes, 16.9% 15 to 30 minutes, 4.8% 30 to 45 minutes, 1.7% 45 to 60 minutes, 2.6% 60 minutes or more (2000)

ALFRED STATION (unincorporated postal area, zip code 14803).
Aka Alfred. Covers a land area of 24.504 square miles and a water area of 0.017 square miles. Located at 42.25° N. Lat.; 77.77° W. Long.
Population: 0 (2000); Race: 96.9% White, 0.3% Black, 2.4% Asian, 0.4% Hispanic of any race (2000); Density: 0.0 persons per square mile (2000); Age: 26.9% under 18, 11.3% over 64 (2000); Marriage status: 28.6% never married, 63.0% now married, 4.1% widowed, 4.2% divorced (2000); Foreign born: 2.8% (2000); Ancestry (includes multiple ancestries): 22.3% German, 21.8% English, 13.5% Irish, 9.8% Italian, 7.9% United States or American (2000).
Economy: Employment by occupation: 14.5% management, 36.2% professional, 13.7% services, 17.1% sales, 1.3% farming, 8.0% construction, 9.3% production (2000).
Income: Per capita income: $19,183 (2000); Median household income: $40,208 (2000); Poverty rate: 11.9% (2000).
Education: Percent of population age 25 and over with: High school diploma (including GED) or higher: 94.6% (2000); Bachelor's degree or higher: 46.3% (2000).
Housing: Homeownership rate: 73.3% (2000); Median home value: $80,900 (2000); Median rent: $433 per month (2000); Median age of housing: 32 years (2000).
Newspapers: Moonlighter (General - Circulation 1,300); The Alfred Sun (General - Circulation 1,600)
Transportation: Commute to work: 90.3% car, 0.0% public transportation, 5.1% walk, 2.6% work from home (2000); Travel time to work: 60.8% less than 15 minutes, 22.9% 15 to 30 minutes, 7.9% 30 to 45 minutes, 1.0% 45 to 60 minutes, 7.4% 60 minutes or more (2000)

ALLEN (town).
Covers a land area of 36.378 square miles and a water area of 0.225 square miles. Located at 42.40° N. Lat.; 78.02° W. Long.
Population: 406 (1990); 462 (2000); 470 (2005); 479 (2010 projected); Race: 98.5% White, 0.0% Black, 0.0% Asian, 0.4% Hispanic of any race (2005); Density: 12.9 persons per square mile (2005); Average household size: 2.54 (2005); Median age: 39.6 (2005); Males per 100 females: 124.9 (2005); Marriage status: 22.6% never married, 63.9% now married, 5.2% widowed, 8.4% divorced (2000); Foreign born: 0.0% (2000); Ancestry (includes multiple ancestries): 35.9% German, 15.1% United States or American, 13.8% English, 11.7% Irish, 7.3% Polish (2000).
Economy: Single-family building permits issued: 7 (2005); Multi-family building permits issued: 0 (2005); Employment by occupation: 11.4% management, 14.4% professional, 15.0% services, 19.8% sales, 1.8% farming, 10.8% construction, 26.9% production (2000).
Income: Per capita income: $16,000 (2005); Median household income: $31,413 (2005); Average household income: $40,649 (2005); Percent of households with income of $100,000 or more: 4.9% (2005); Poverty rate: 18.7% (2000).
Education: Percent of population age 25 and over with: High school diploma (including GED) or higher: 76.3% (2005); Bachelor's degree or higher: 8.2% (2005); Master's degree or higher: 1.6% (2005).
Housing: Homeownership rate: 88.1% (2005); Median home value: $82,647 (2005); Median rent: $285 per month (2000); Median age of housing: 25 years (2000).
Transportation: Commute to work: 88.5% car, 1.2% public transportation, 3.0% walk, 6.1% work from home (2000); Travel time to work: 16.8% less than 15 minutes, 27.7% 15 to 30 minutes, 25.8% 30 to 45 minutes, 12.3% 45 to 60 minutes, 17.4% 60 minutes or more (2000)

ALMA (town).
Covers a land area of 36.461 square miles and a water area of 0.092 square miles. Located at 42.05° N. Lat.; 78.02° W. Long. Elevation is 1,552 feet.
Population: 846 (1990); 847 (2000); 865 (2005); 870 (2010 projected); Race: 97.9% White, 0.3% Black, 0.3% Asian, 0.0% Hispanic of any race (2005); Density: 23.7 persons per square mile (2005); Average household size: 2.57 (2005); Median age: 38.3 (2005); Males per 100 females: 105.5 (2005); Marriage status: 18.6% never married, 67.8% now married, 5.5% widowed, 8.1% divorced (2000); Foreign born: 0.9% (2000); Ancestry (includes multiple ancestries): 27.3% German, 22.6% English, 21.8% Irish, 8.9% Other groups, 4.9% United States or American (2000).
Economy: Single-family building permits issued: 4 (2005); Multi-family building permits issued: 0 (2005); Employment by occupation: 9.9% management, 20.7% professional, 11.4% services, 20.2% sales, 0.6% farming, 13.6% construction, 23.6% production (2000).
Income: Per capita income: $15,983 (2005); Median household income: $37,158 (2005); Average household income: $41,024 (2005); Percent of households with income of $100,000 or more: 3.3% (2005); Poverty rate: 12.0% (2000).
Education: Percent of population age 25 and over with: High school diploma (including GED) or higher: 83.7% (2005); Bachelor's degree or higher: 8.0% (2005); Master's degree or higher: 3.8% (2005).
Housing: Homeownership rate: 86.6% (2005); Median home value: $63,265 (2005); Median rent: $333 per month (2000); Median age of housing: 31 years (2000).
Transportation: Commute to work: 96.2% car, 0.0% public transportation, 0.3% walk, 3.5% work from home (2000); Travel time to work: 30.5% less than 15 minutes, 46.4% 15 to 30 minutes, 14.1% 30 to 45 minutes, 4.2% 45 to 60 minutes, 4.8% 60 minutes or more (2000)

ALMOND (village).
Covers a land area of 0.565 square miles and a water area of 0 square miles. Located at 42.32° N. Lat.; 77.73° W. Long.
Population: 458 (1990); 461 (2000); 522 (2005); 582 (2010 projected); Race: 97.3% White, 0.0% Black, 0.8% Asian, 1.7% Hispanic of any race (2005); Density: 924.3 persons per square mile (2005); Average household size: 2.33 (2005); Median age: 39.4 (2005); Males per 100 females: 87.8 (2005); Marriage status: 25.4% never married, 59.6% now married, 7.9% widowed, 7.0% divorced (2000); Foreign born: 1.8% (2000); Ancestry (includes multiple ancestries): 23.3% German, 18.2% English, 11.5% Irish, 6.7% Italian, 6.0% Other groups (2000).
Economy: Single-family building permits issued: 0 (2005); Multi-family building permits issued: 0 (2005); Employment by occupation: 3.8% management, 28.6% professional, 16.5% services, 26.4% sales, 1.1% farming, 8.8% construction, 14.8% production (2000).
Income: Per capita income: $21,001 (2005); Median household income: $35,385 (2005); Average household income: $48,940 (2005); Percent of households with income of $100,000 or more: 9.4% (2005); Poverty rate: 16.6% (2000).
Education: Percent of population age 25 and over with: High school diploma (including GED) or higher: 82.8% (2005); Bachelor's degree or higher: 25.8% (2005); Master's degree or higher: 12.2% (2005).
School District(s)
Alfred-Almond Central School District (KG-12)
    2003-04 Enrollment: 735 . . . . (607) 276-2981
Housing: Homeownership rate: 65.2% (2005); Median home value: $87,826 (2005); Median rent: $340 per month (2000); Median age of housing: 60+ years (2000).
Transportation: Commute to work: 90.4% car, 0.0% public transportation, 3.4% walk, 4.5% work from home (2000); Travel time to work: 62.9% less than 15 minutes, 24.7% 15 to 30 minutes, 10.0% 30 to 45 minutes, 1.2% 45 to 60 minutes, 1.2% 60 minutes or more (2000)

ALMOND (town).
Covers a land area of 45.811 square miles and a water area of 0.012 square miles. Located at 42.33° N. Lat.; 77.76° W. Long.
Population: 1,640 (1990); 1,604 (2000); 1,699 (2005); 1,820 (2010 projected); Race: 95.6% White, 0.1% Black, 3.4% Asian, 0.8% Hispanic of any race (2005); Density: 37.1 persons per square mile (2005); Average household size: 2.48 (2005); Median age: 42.1 (2005); Males per 100 females: 97.8 (2005); Marriage status: 25.9% never married, 60.5% now

married, 6.2% widowed, 7.4% divorced (2000); Foreign born: 3.0% (2000); Ancestry (includes multiple ancestries): 25.0% German, 20.0% English, 14.7% Irish, 9.0% United States or American, 7.2% Other groups (2000).
Economy: Single-family building permits issued: 2 (2005); Multi-family building permits issued: 0 (2005); Employment by occupation: 11.2% management, 22.5% professional, 17.7% services, 23.9% sales, 1.1% farming, 9.8% construction, 13.8% production (2000).
Income: Per capita income: $23,807 (2005); Median household income: $45,135 (2005); Average household income: $59,134 (2005); Percent of households with income of $100,000 or more: 12.1% (2005); Poverty rate: 11.0% (2000).
Education: Percent of population age 25 and over with: High school diploma (including GED) or higher: 88.6% (2005); Bachelor's degree or higher: 26.4% (2005); Master's degree or higher: 13.1% (2005).
Housing: Homeownership rate: 80.4% (2005); Median home value: $104,595 (2005); Median rent: $329 per month (2000); Median age of housing: 34 years (2000).
Transportation: Commute to work: 94.8% car, 0.4% public transportation, 1.9% walk, 2.5% work from home (2000); Travel time to work: 46.0% less than 15 minutes, 37.2% 15 to 30 minutes, 10.8% 30 to 45 minutes, 2.1% 45 to 60 minutes, 4.0% 60 minutes or more (2000)

AMITY (town). Covers a land area of 34.536 square miles and a water area of 0.082 square miles. Located at 42.22° N. Lat.; 78.02° W. Long.
Population: 2,255 (1990); 2,245 (2000); 2,211 (2005); 2,155 (2010 projected); Race: 97.5% White, 1.3% Black, 0.1% Asian, 0.9% Hispanic of any race (2005); Density: 64.0 persons per square mile (2005); Average household size: 2.50 (2005); Median age: 39.6 (2005); Males per 100 females: 100.8 (2005); Marriage status: 23.6% never married, 57.8% now married, 9.1% widowed, 9.5% divorced (2000); Foreign born: 0.9% (2000); Ancestry (includes multiple ancestries): 23.8% German, 17.1% English, 13.3% Irish, 9.1% Other groups, 8.5% Italian (2000).
Economy: Single-family building permits issued: 0 (2005); Multi-family building permits issued: 0 (2005); Employment by occupation: 7.3% management, 25.1% professional, 22.2% services, 21.3% sales, 1.7% farming, 9.6% construction, 12.7% production (2000).
Income: Per capita income: $16,947 (2005); Median household income: $37,008 (2005); Average household income: $42,090 (2005); Percent of households with income of $100,000 or more: 3.6% (2005); Poverty rate: 11.6% (2000).
Taxes: Total city taxes per capita: $198 (2004); City property taxes per capita: $183 (2004).
Education: Percent of population age 25 and over with: High school diploma (including GED) or higher: 83.4% (2005); Bachelor's degree or higher: 13.3% (2005); Master's degree or higher: 6.4% (2005).
Housing: Homeownership rate: 73.9% (2005); Median home value: $74,522 (2005); Median rent: $310 per month (2000); Median age of housing: 48 years (2000).
Safety: Violent crime rate: 0.0 per 10,000 population; Property crime rate: 0.0 per 10,000 population (2004).
Transportation: Commute to work: 88.5% car, 0.6% public transportation, 5.8% walk, 3.9% work from home (2000); Travel time to work: 40.9% less than 15 minutes, 38.9% 15 to 30 minutes, 11.7% 30 to 45 minutes, 4.2% 45 to 60 minutes, 4.2% 60 minutes or more (2000)

ANDOVER (village). Covers a land area of 0.997 square miles and a water area of 0.012 square miles. Located at 42.15° N. Lat.; 77.79° W. Long. Elevation is 1,665 feet.
Population: 1,125 (1990); 1,073 (2000); 1,094 (2005); 1,098 (2010 projected); Race: 96.4% White, 0.2% Black, 0.9% Asian, 1.5% Hispanic of any race (2005); Density: 1,097.7 persons per square mile (2005); Average household size: 2.44 (2005); Median age: 37.4 (2005); Males per 100 females: 92.9 (2005); Marriage status: 22.8% never married, 58.6% now married, 9.9% widowed, 8.7% divorced (2000); Foreign born: 1.3% (2000); Ancestry (includes multiple ancestries): 27.7% German, 23.5% English, 22.6% Irish, 7.1% United States or American, 5.4% Other groups (2000).
Economy: Single-family building permits issued: 0 (2005); Multi-family building permits issued: 0 (2005); Employment by occupation: 7.6% management, 23.7% professional, 22.2% services, 16.7% sales, 1.6% farming, 12.0% construction, 16.3% production (2000).
Income: Per capita income: $20,471 (2005); Median household income: $36,856 (2005); Average household income: $49,878 (2005); Percent of households with income of $100,000 or more: 8.7% (2005); Poverty rate: 12.0% (2000).
Education: Percent of population age 25 and over with: High school diploma (including GED) or higher: 86.1% (2005); Bachelor's degree or higher: 15.5% (2005); Master's degree or higher: 7.8% (2005).
School District(s)
Andover Central School District (KG-12)
    2003-04 Enrollment: 400 . . . . (607) 478-8491
Housing: Homeownership rate: 70.2% (2005); Median home value: $69,310 (2005); Median rent: $325 per month (2000); Median age of housing: 60+ years (2000).
Transportation: Commute to work: 87.6% car, 0.8% public transportation, 6.1% walk, 4.9% work from home (2000); Travel time to work: 34.5% less than 15 minutes, 44.6% 15 to 30 minutes, 8.1% 30 to 45 minutes, 4.3% 45 to 60 minutes, 8.5% 60 minutes or more (2000)

ANDOVER (town). Covers a land area of 39.466 square miles and a water area of 0.043 square miles. Located at 42.15° N. Lat.; 77.80° W. Long. Elevation is 1,665 feet.
History: Incorporated 1892.
Population: 1,981 (1990); 1,945 (2000); 2,008 (2005); 2,022 (2010 projected); Race: 97.4% White, 0.2% Black, 0.9% Asian, 1.5% Hispanic of any race (2005); Density: 50.9 persons per square mile (2005); Average household size: 2.57 (2005); Median age: 36.6 (2005); Males per 100 females: 92.7 (2005); Marriage status: 23.0% never married, 60.5% now married, 8.5% widowed, 8.0% divorced (2000); Foreign born: 0.9% (2000); Ancestry (includes multiple ancestries): 23.6% German, 20.7% English, 18.7% Irish, 10.7% United States or American, 5.7% Other groups (2000).
Economy: Oil wells; dairy products; field corn, hay. Single-family building permits issued: 1 (2005); Multi-family building permits issued: 0 (2005); Employment by occupation: 9.1% management, 18.3% professional, 20.1% services, 16.5% sales, 1.2% farming, 16.3% construction, 18.5% production (2000).
Income: Per capita income: $21,190 (2005); Median household income: $40,311 (2005); Average household income: $54,412 (2005); Percent of households with income of $100,000 or more: 10.1% (2005); Poverty rate: 10.4% (2000).
Education: Percent of population age 25 and over with: High school diploma (including GED) or higher: 84.7% (2005); Bachelor's degree or higher: 12.5% (2005); Master's degree or higher: 6.0% (2005).
Housing: Homeownership rate: 74.8% (2005); Median home value: $72,556 (2005); Median rent: $329 per month (2000); Median age of housing: 60+ years (2000).
Transportation: Commute to work: 88.4% car, 0.5% public transportation, 4.9% walk, 5.2% work from home (2000); Travel time to work: 33.4% less than 15 minutes, 42.5% 15 to 30 minutes, 9.3% 30 to 45 minutes, 6.5% 45 to 60 minutes, 8.3% 60 minutes or more (2000)

ANGELICA (village). Covers a land area of 2.148 square miles and a water area of 0 square miles. Located at 42.30° N. Lat.; 78.01° W. Long.
Population: 963 (1990); 903 (2000); 913 (2005); 924 (2010 projected); Race: 98.0% White, 0.0% Black, 0.0% Asian, 0.5% Hispanic of any race (2005); Density: 425.1 persons per square mile (2005); Average household size: 2.42 (2005); Median age: 36.6 (2005); Males per 100 females: 87.9 (2005); Marriage status: 19.7% never married, 62.2% now married, 10.2% widowed, 7.9% divorced (2000); Foreign born: 0.6% (2000); Ancestry (includes multiple ancestries): 28.9% German, 18.6% Irish, 16.3% English, 8.7% United States or American, 7.8% Other groups (2000).
Economy: Single-family building permits issued: 0 (2005); Multi-family building permits issued: 0 (2005); Employment by occupation: 6.7% management, 18.8% professional, 19.1% services, 24.0% sales, 1.5% farming, 9.8% construction, 20.1% production (2000).
Income: Per capita income: $17,708 (2005); Median household income: $37,038 (2005); Average household income: $42,885 (2005); Percent of households with income of $100,000 or more: 5.3% (2005); Poverty rate: 12.5% (2000).
Education: Percent of population age 25 and over with: High school diploma (including GED) or higher: 86.6% (2005); Bachelor's degree or higher: 14.7% (2005); Master's degree or higher: 6.6% (2005).
Housing: Homeownership rate: 73.2% (2005); Median home value: $71,111 (2005); Median rent: $334 per month (2000); Median age of housing: 60+ years (2000).
Transportation: Commute to work: 85.6% car, 0.8% public transportation, 5.0% walk, 7.6% work from home (2000); Travel time to work: 34.9% less than 15 minutes, 31.8% 15 to 30 minutes, 20.2% 30 to 45 minutes, 3.7% 45 to 60 minutes, 9.4% 60 minutes or more (2000)

ANGELICA (town). Covers a land area of 36.447 square miles and a water area of 0.022 square miles. Located at 42.30° N. Lat.; 78.02° W. Long.
History: Oldest village in the county; founded in 1800 by Captain Philip Church, nephew of Alexander Hamilton. Church is buried with his wife at Until the Day Dawns Cemetery. Contingent of French royalists settled here in 1806; one of them became the French ambassador to U.S.; another was Victor Marie du Pont de Nemours.
Population: 1,446 (1990); 1,411 (2000); 1,429 (2005); 1,445 (2010 projected); Race: 98.0% White, 0.3% Black, 0.0% Asian, 0.4% Hispanic of any race (2005); Density: 39.2 persons per square mile (2005); Average household size: 2.45 (2005); Median age: 38.2 (2005); Males per 100 females: 93.4 (2005); Marriage status: 22.1% never married, 61.1% now married, 8.2% widowed, 8.7% divorced (2000); Foreign born: 0.6% (2000); Ancestry (includes multiple ancestries): 24.6% German, 19.0% English, 16.2% Irish, 9.9% United States or American, 6.9% Other groups (2000).
Economy: Single-family building permits issued: 2 (2005); Multi-family building permits issued: 0 (2005); Employment by occupation: 9.0% management, 18.4% professional, 17.3% services, 21.9% sales, 1.6% farming, 10.2% construction, 21.6% production (2000).
Income: Per capita income: $18,688 (2005); Median household income: $38,222 (2005); Average household income: $45,806 (2005); Percent of households with income of $100,000 or more: 6.5% (2005); Poverty rate: 11.8% (2000).
Education: Percent of population age 25 and over with: High school diploma (including GED) or higher: 85.7% (2005); Bachelor's degree or higher: 15.9% (2005); Master's degree or higher: 6.9% (2005).
Housing: Homeownership rate: 77.4% (2005); Median home value: $76,489 (2005); Median rent: $326 per month (2000); Median age of housing: 56 years (2000).
Transportation: Commute to work: 86.5% car, 0.8% public transportation, 5.3% walk, 6.1% work from home (2000); Travel time to work: 32.7% less than 15 minutes, 31.5% 15 to 30 minutes, 22.0% 30 to 45 minutes, 4.9% 45 to 60 minutes, 8.9% 60 minutes or more (2000)

BELFAST (town). Covers a land area of 36.245 square miles and a water area of 0.282 square miles. Located at 42.31° N. Lat.; 78.11° W. Long. Elevation is 1,329 feet.
Population: 1,539 (1990); 1,714 (2000); 1,809 (2005); 1,903 (2010 projected); Race: 98.5% White, 0.0% Black, 0.1% Asian, 0.6% Hispanic of any race (2005); Density: 49.9 persons per square mile (2005); Average household size: 2.58 (2005); Median age: 35.5 (2005); Males per 100 females: 100.1 (2005); Marriage status: 22.6% never married, 58.5% now married, 9.2% widowed, 9.8% divorced (2000); Foreign born: 1.8% (2000); Ancestry (includes multiple ancestries): 25.7% German, 17.3% English, 15.0% Irish, 11.5% United States or American, 7.3% Italian (2000).
Economy: In dairying and poultry area. Single-family building permits issued: 5 (2005); Multi-family building permits issued: 0 (2005); Employment by occupation: 8.9% management, 23.6% professional, 16.1% services, 15.9% sales, 3.0% farming, 12.5% construction, 20.0% production (2000).
Income: Per capita income: $17,254 (2005); Median household income: $35,068 (2005); Average household income: $44,526 (2005); Percent of households with income of $100,000 or more: 5.8% (2005); Poverty rate: 19.4% (2000).
Education: Percent of population age 25 and over with: High school diploma (including GED) or higher: 80.0% (2005); Bachelor's degree or higher: 12.8% (2005); Master's degree or higher: 6.9% (2005).

School District(s)
Belfast Central School District (PK-12)
    2003-04 Enrollment: 463 . . . . (585) 365-9940

Housing: Homeownership rate: 73.8% (2005); Median home value: $79,912 (2005); Median rent: $301 per month (2000); Median age of housing: 41 years (2000).
Transportation: Commute to work: 86.5% car, 0.4% public transportation, 5.6% walk, 6.5% work from home (2000); Travel time to work: 28.9% less than 15 minutes, 27.9% 15 to 30 minutes, 24.5% 30 to 45 minutes, 8.0% 45 to 60 minutes, 10.7% 60 minutes or more (2000)

BELMONT (village). Covers a land area of 0.999 square miles and a water area of 0 square miles. Located at 42.22° N. Lat.; 78.03° W. Long. Elevation is 1,418 feet.
History: Inc. 1871.
Population: 1,006 (1990); 952 (2000); 925 (2005); 895 (2010 projected); Race: 96.2% White, 1.4% Black, 0.0% Asian, 1.3% Hispanic of any race (2005); Density: 925.9 persons per square mile (2005); Average household size: 2.40 (2005); Median age: 39.1 (2005); Males per 100 females: 105.6 (2005); Marriage status: 22.9% never married, 53.6% now married, 11.4% widowed, 12.1% divorced (2000); Foreign born: 1.4% (2000); Ancestry (includes multiple ancestries): 24.9% German, 16.5% Irish, 14.7% English, 14.3% Italian, 13.0% Other groups (2000).
Economy: In dairying area; metal fabrication, machinery. Single-family building permits issued: 0 (2005); Multi-family building permits issued: 0 (2005); Employment by occupation: 10.0% management, 25.2% professional, 26.0% services, 18.8% sales, 1.9% farming, 6.4% construction, 11.6% production (2000).
Income: Per capita income: $15,572 (2005); Median household income: $31,071 (2005); Average household income: $36,781 (2005); Percent of households with income of $100,000 or more: 2.3% (2005); Poverty rate: 12.7% (2000).
Education: Percent of population age 25 and over with: High school diploma (including GED) or higher: 82.5% (2005); Bachelor's degree or higher: 16.5% (2005); Master's degree or higher: 6.5% (2005).

School District(s)
Genesee Valley Central School District At Angelica-Belmont (PK-12)
    2003-04 Enrollment: 770 . . . . (585) 268-7900

Housing: Homeownership rate: 63.7% (2005); Median home value: $75,625 (2005); Median rent: $337 per month (2000); Median age of housing: 60+ years (2000).
Transportation: Commute to work: 82.5% car, 0.8% public transportation, 8.2% walk, 5.4% work from home (2000); Travel time to work: 38.7% less than 15 minutes, 40.5% 15 to 30 minutes, 8.9% 30 to 45 minutes, 3.6% 45 to 60 minutes, 8.3% 60 minutes or more (2000)

BIRDSALL (town). Covers a land area of 35.954 square miles and a water area of 0.091 square miles. Located at 42.39° N. Lat.; 77.90° W. Long. Elevation is 1,695 feet.
Population: 232 (1990); 268 (2000); 283 (2005); 295 (2010 projected); Race: 96.1% White, 2.5% Black, 0.0% Asian, 0.7% Hispanic of any race (2005); Density: 7.9 persons per square mile (2005); Average household size: 2.36 (2005); Median age: 45.5 (2005); Males per 100 females: 93.8 (2005); Marriage status: 16.8% never married, 59.4% now married, 12.7% widowed, 11.2% divorced (2000); Foreign born: 0.8% (2000); Ancestry (includes multiple ancestries): 21.7% German, 21.3% Irish, 20.8% United States or American, 8.3% Dutch, 7.9% Italian (2000).
Economy: Single-family building permits issued: 0 (2005); Multi-family building permits issued: 0 (2005); Employment by occupation: 15.2% management, 14.1% professional, 28.3% services, 9.8% sales, 0.0% farming, 19.6% construction, 13.0% production (2000).
Income: Per capita income: $13,993 (2005); Median household income: $29,545 (2005); Average household income: $33,000 (2005); Percent of households with income of $100,000 or more: 0.8% (2005); Poverty rate: 28.7% (2000).
Taxes: Total city taxes per capita: $599 (2004); City property taxes per capita: $596 (2004).
Education: Percent of population age 25 and over with: High school diploma (including GED) or higher: 72.8% (2005); Bachelor's degree or higher: 7.9% (2005); Master's degree or higher: 1.5% (2005).
Housing: Homeownership rate: 77.5% (2005); Median home value: $66,471 (2005); Median rent: $268 per month (2000); Median age of housing: 28 years (2000).
Transportation: Commute to work: 86.2% car, 0.0% public transportation, 5.7% walk, 8.0% work from home (2000); Travel time to work: 20.0% less than 15 minutes, 31.3% 15 to 30 minutes, 31.3% 30 to 45 minutes, 12.5% 45 to 60 minutes, 5.0% 60 minutes or more (2000)

BLACK CREEK (unincorporated postal area, zip code 14714). Covers a land area of 11.970 square miles and a water area of 0.036 square miles. Located at 42.28° N. Lat.; 78.23° W. Long. Elevation is 1,518 feet.
Population: 0 (2000); Race: 98.8% White, 0.0% Black, 0.0% Asian, 0.0% Hispanic of any race (2000); Density: 0.0 persons per square mile (2000); Age: 32.3% under 18, 11.9% over 64 (2000); Marriage status: 22.1% never married, 67.9% now married, 3.8% widowed, 6.3% divorced (2000); Foreign born: 0.3% (2000); Ancestry (includes multiple ancestries): 24.1% German, 15.2% English, 10.4% Irish, 9.8% Other groups, 8.5% United States or American (2000).

Economy: Employment by occupation: 13.5% management, 7.9% professional, 15.1% services, 18.3% sales, 3.2% farming, 15.1% construction, 27.0% production (2000).
Income: Per capita income: $12,474 (2000); Median household income: $34,688 (2000); Poverty rate: 16.2% (2000).
Education: Percent of population age 25 and over with: High school diploma (including GED) or higher: 75.5% (2000); Bachelor's degree or higher: 10.5% (2000).
Housing: Homeownership rate: 86.4% (2000); Median home value: $57,300 (2000); Median rent: $330 per month (2000); Median age of housing: 23 years (2000).
Transportation: Commute to work: 91.1% car, 0.0% public transportation, 0.0% walk, 8.9% work from home (2000); Travel time to work: 27.4% less than 15 minutes, 46.9% 15 to 30 minutes, 13.3% 30 to 45 minutes, 4.4% 45 to 60 minutes, 8.0% 60 minutes or more (2000)

BOLIVAR (village).
Covers a land area of 0.752 square miles and a water area of 0 square miles. Located at 42.06° N. Lat.; 78.16° W. Long. Elevation is 1,588 feet.
Population: 1,261 (1990); 1,173 (2000); 1,109 (2005); 1,074 (2010 projected); Race: 98.6% White, 0.8% Black, 0.1% Asian, 0.4% Hispanic of any race (2005); Density: 1,475.2 persons per square mile (2005); Average household size: 2.56 (2005); Median age: 34.0 (2005); Males per 100 females: 97.7 (2005); Marriage status: 32.1% never married, 49.0% now married, 7.6% widowed, 11.4% divorced (2000); Foreign born: 0.7% (2000); Ancestry (includes multiple ancestries): 21.4% German, 16.5% English, 15.9% Irish, 8.8% Other groups, 7.4% Italian (2000).
Economy: Single-family building permits issued: 1 (2005); Multi-family building permits issued: 0 (2005); Employment by occupation: 7.8% management, 19.7% professional, 15.7% services, 26.4% sales, 0.4% farming, 6.5% construction, 23.5% production (2000).
Income: Per capita income: $15,142 (2005); Median household income: $32,589 (2005); Average household income: $38,782 (2005); Percent of households with income of $100,000 or more: 4.6% (2005); Poverty rate: 20.0% (2000).
Education: Percent of population age 25 and over with: High school diploma (including GED) or higher: 85.7% (2005); Bachelor's degree or higher: 15.1% (2005); Master's degree or higher: 6.5% (2005).
School District(s)
Bolivar-Richburg Central School District (PK-12)
    2003-04 Enrollment: 1,008 . . . . (585) 928-2561
Housing: Homeownership rate: 64.2% (2005); Median home value: $64,000 (2005); Median rent: $305 per month (2000); Median age of housing: 60+ years (2000).
Safety: Violent crime rate: 0.0 per 10,000 population; Property crime rate: 138.4 per 10,000 population (2004).
Transportation: Commute to work: 88.1% car, 0.2% public transportation, 8.2% walk, 3.0% work from home (2000); Travel time to work: 32.5% less than 15 minutes, 35.5% 15 to 30 minutes, 24.5% 30 to 45 minutes, 2.8% 45 to 60 minutes, 4.7% 60 minutes or more (2000)

BOLIVAR (town).
Covers a land area of 35.869 square miles and a water area of 0.008 square miles. Located at 42.06° N. Lat.; 78.14° W. Long. Elevation is 1,588 feet.
History: Surrounding region was prominent early petroleum-producing area from late 19th to early 20th century. Incorporated 1882.
Population: 2,361 (1990); 2,223 (2000); 2,113 (2005); 2,054 (2010 projected); Race: 98.9% White, 0.4% Black, 0.0% Asian, 0.3% Hispanic of any race (2005); Density: 58.9 persons per square mile (2005); Average household size: 2.59 (2005); Median age: 35.9 (2005); Males per 100 females: 97.3 (2005); Marriage status: 24.7% never married, 60.1% now married, 6.3% widowed, 9.0% divorced (2000); Foreign born: 0.8% (2000); Ancestry (includes multiple ancestries): 19.4% German, 16.9% English, 11.4% Irish, 8.9% United States or American, 7.1% Other groups (2000).
Economy: Manufacturing of barber and industrial scissors; dairy farming. Single-family building permits issued: 0 (2005); Multi-family building permits issued: 0 (2005); Employment by occupation: 6.0% management, 16.6% professional, 15.3% services, 24.4% sales, 0.7% farming, 8.9% construction, 28.1% production (2000).
Income: Per capita income: $16,201 (2005); Median household income: $36,387 (2005); Average household income: $41,952 (2005); Percent of households with income of $100,000 or more: 5.5% (2005); Poverty rate: 16.0% (2000).
Education: Percent of population age 25 and over with: High school diploma (including GED) or higher: 82.4% (2005); Bachelor's degree or higher: 11.2% (2005); Master's degree or higher: 4.5% (2005).
Housing: Homeownership rate: 74.1% (2005); Median home value: $63,033 (2005); Median rent: $313 per month (2000); Median age of housing: 60+ years (2000).
Transportation: Commute to work: 90.2% car, 0.6% public transportation, 5.2% walk, 3.2% work from home (2000); Travel time to work: 33.8% less than 15 minutes, 38.7% 15 to 30 minutes, 19.6% 30 to 45 minutes, 1.6% 45 to 60 minutes, 6.3% 60 minutes or more (2000)

BURNS (town).
Covers a land area of 27.193 square miles and a water area of 0.011 square miles. Located at 42.44° N. Lat.; 77.77° W. Long. Elevation is 1,198 feet.
Population: 1,299 (1990); 1,248 (2000); 1,324 (2005); 1,378 (2010 projected); Race: 97.4% White, 0.0% Black, 0.2% Asian, 1.4% Hispanic of any race (2005); Density: 48.7 persons per square mile (2005); Average household size: 2.69 (2005); Median age: 38.1 (2005); Males per 100 females: 102.4 (2005); Marriage status: 22.5% never married, 61.9% now married, 5.9% widowed, 9.7% divorced (2000); Foreign born: 0.6% (2000); Ancestry (includes multiple ancestries): 25.2% German, 21.4% English, 20.2% Irish, 12.5% United States or American, 5.6% Other groups (2000).
Economy: Single-family building permits issued: 1 (2005); Multi-family building permits issued: 0 (2005); Employment by occupation: 9.6% management, 16.6% professional, 21.0% services, 16.6% sales, 2.8% farming, 11.2% construction, 22.1% production (2000).
Income: Per capita income: $17,173 (2005); Median household income: $37,308 (2005); Average household income: $46,214 (2005); Percent of households with income of $100,000 or more: 6.3% (2005); Poverty rate: 12.3% (2000).
Education: Percent of population age 25 and over with: High school diploma (including GED) or higher: 82.9% (2005); Bachelor's degree or higher: 11.6% (2005); Master's degree or higher: 5.2% (2005).
Housing: Homeownership rate: 79.5% (2005); Median home value: $78,673 (2005); Median rent: $357 per month (2000); Median age of housing: 60+ years (2000).
Transportation: Commute to work: 91.8% car, 0.6% public transportation, 5.3% walk, 2.3% work from home (2000); Travel time to work: 27.7% less than 15 minutes, 35.3% 15 to 30 minutes, 15.2% 30 to 45 minutes, 6.8% 45 to 60 minutes, 15.0% 60 minutes or more (2000)

CANASERAGA (village).
Covers a land area of 1.276 square miles and a water area of 0 square miles. Located at 42.46° N. Lat.; 77.77° W. Long. Elevation is 1,257 feet.
Population: 684 (1990); 594 (2000); 631 (2005); 659 (2010 projected); Race: 98.7% White, 0.0% Black, 0.3% Asian, 0.2% Hispanic of any race (2005); Density: 494.5 persons per square mile (2005); Average household size: 2.65 (2005); Median age: 37.4 (2005); Males per 100 females: 103.5 (2005); Marriage status: 25.5% never married, 61.1% now married, 5.9% widowed, 7.5% divorced (2000); Foreign born: 0.5% (2000); Ancestry (includes multiple ancestries): 25.9% German, 25.6% English, 23.7% Irish, 9.5% United States or American, 6.8% Italian (2000).
Economy: Single-family building permits issued: 0 (2005); Multi-family building permits issued: 0 (2005); Employment by occupation: 6.8% management, 16.1% professional, 24.1% services, 15.3% sales, 1.6% farming, 10.8% construction, 25.3% production (2000).
Income: Per capita income: $18,170 (2005); Median household income: $39,412 (2005); Average household income: $48,172 (2005); Percent of households with income of $100,000 or more: 5.5% (2005); Poverty rate: 12.8% (2000).
Education: Percent of population age 25 and over with: High school diploma (including GED) or higher: 81.7% (2005); Bachelor's degree or higher: 9.1% (2005); Master's degree or higher: 4.3% (2005).
School District(s)
Canaseraga Central School District (PK-12)
    2003-04 Enrollment: 349 . . . . (607) 545-6421
Housing: Homeownership rate: 75.2% (2005); Median home value: $65,636 (2005); Median rent: $335 per month (2000); Median age of housing: 60+ years (2000).
Transportation: Commute to work: 88.6% car, 1.2% public transportation, 8.2% walk, 2.0% work from home (2000); Travel time to work: 26.3% less than 15 minutes, 42.5% 15 to 30 minutes, 12.9% 30 to 45 minutes, 6.3% 45 to 60 minutes, 12.1% 60 minutes or more (2000)

CANEADEA (town). Covers a land area of 35.528 square miles and a water area of 0.809 square miles. Located at 42.40° N. Lat.; 78.16° W. Long.
Population: 2,551 (1990); 2,694 (2000); 2,776 (2005); 2,892 (2010 projected); Race: 95.7% White, 1.5% Black, 0.9% Asian, 3.4% Hispanic of any race (2005); Density: 78.1 persons per square mile (2005); Average household size: 3.91 (2005); Median age: 23.6 (2005); Males per 100 females: 81.9 (2005); Marriage status: 52.8% never married, 41.3% now married, 3.5% widowed, 2.4% divorced (2000); Foreign born: 4.6% (2000); Ancestry (includes multiple ancestries): 27.7% German, 17.7% English, 12.1% Irish, 8.8% United States or American, 7.3% Other groups (2000).
Economy: Resort village. Single-family building permits issued: 5 (2005); Multi-family building permits issued: 0 (2005); Employment by occupation: 6.9% management, 29.9% professional, 25.5% services, 23.1% sales, 1.7% farming, 7.1% construction, 5.7% production (2000).
Income: Per capita income: $11,432 (2005); Median household income: $34,100 (2005); Average household income: $39,894 (2005); Percent of households with income of $100,000 or more: 4.6% (2005); Poverty rate: 21.3% (2000).
Education: Percent of population age 25 and over with: High school diploma (including GED) or higher: 86.2% (2005); Bachelor's degree or higher: 37.1% (2005); Master's degree or higher: 20.1% (2005).
Housing: Homeownership rate: 64.6% (2005); Median home value: $92,586 (2005); Median rent: $310 per month (2000); Median age of housing: 34 years (2000).
Transportation: Commute to work: 47.3% car, 0.0% public transportation, 48.9% walk, 2.6% work from home (2000); Travel time to work: 74.4% less than 15 minutes, 8.9% 15 to 30 minutes, 7.1% 30 to 45 minutes, 4.7% 45 to 60 minutes, 4.9% 60 minutes or more (2000)

CENTERVILLE (town). Covers a land area of 35.413 square miles and a water area of 0.006 square miles. Located at 42.48° N. Lat.; 78.24° W. Long. Elevation is 1,150 feet.
Population: 678 (1990); 762 (2000); 786 (2005); 818 (2010 projected); Race: 93.8% White, 0.4% Black, 1.8% Asian, 3.6% Hispanic of any race (2005); Density: 22.2 persons per square mile (2005); Average household size: 2.94 (2005); Median age: 33.4 (2005); Males per 100 females: 98.0 (2005); Marriage status: 25.9% never married, 58.4% now married, 6.5% widowed, 9.2% divorced (2000); Foreign born: 0.6% (2000); Ancestry (includes multiple ancestries): 28.2% German, 11.1% United States or American, 9.7% Irish, 9.7% English, 7.5% Polish (2000).
Economy: Single-family building permits issued: 2 (2005); Multi-family building permits issued: 0 (2005); Employment by occupation: 12.7% management, 12.3% professional, 15.8% services, 19.7% sales, 4.6% farming, 6.7% construction, 28.2% production (2000).
Income: Per capita income: $14,052 (2005); Median household income: $31,967 (2005); Average household income: $41,367 (2005); Percent of households with income of $100,000 or more: 6.0% (2005); Poverty rate: 32.8% (2000).
Education: Percent of population age 25 and over with: High school diploma (including GED) or higher: 68.5% (2005); Bachelor's degree or higher: 7.7% (2005); Master's degree or higher: 2.3% (2005).
Housing: Homeownership rate: 80.9% (2005); Median home value: $88,718 (2005); Median rent: $284 per month (2000); Median age of housing: 30 years (2000).
Transportation: Commute to work: 83.6% car, 0.0% public transportation, 6.4% walk, 10.0% work from home (2000); Travel time to work: 22.2% less than 15 minutes, 38.9% 15 to 30 minutes, 15.1% 30 to 45 minutes, 12.7% 45 to 60 minutes, 11.1% 60 minutes or more (2000)

CERES (unincorporated postal area, zip code 14721). Covers a land area of 0.214 square miles and a water area of 0 square miles. Located at 41.99° N. Lat.; 78.27° W. Long.
Population: 0 (2000); Race: 96.7% White, 0.0% Black, 0.0% Asian, 0.0% Hispanic of any race (2000); Density: 0.0 persons per square mile (2000); Age: 28.9% under 18, 8.9% over 64 (2000); Marriage status: 13.6% never married, 80.3% now married, 0.0% widowed, 6.1% divorced (2000); Foreign born: 4.4% (2000); Ancestry (includes multiple ancestries): 34.4% German, 32.2% Irish, 17.8% English, 11.1% Scottish, 10.0% Dutch (2000).
Economy: Employment by occupation: 6.1% management, 36.4% professional, 12.1% services, 9.1% sales, 0.0% farming, 9.1% construction, 27.3% production (2000).
Income: Per capita income: $11,112 (2000); Median household income: $30,750 (2000); Poverty rate: 10.0% (2000).
Education: Percent of population age 25 and over with: High school diploma (including GED) or higher: 75.4% (2000); Bachelor's degree or higher: 9.8% (2000).
Housing: Homeownership rate: 87.5% (2000); Median home value: $34,000 (2000); Median rent: $325 per month (2000); Median age of housing: 55 years (2000).
Transportation: Commute to work: 93.5% car, 0.0% public transportation, 6.5% walk, 0.0% work from home (2000); Travel time to work: 12.9% less than 15 minutes, 22.6% 15 to 30 minutes, 45.2% 30 to 45 minutes, 0.0% 45 to 60 minutes, 19.4% 60 minutes or more (2000)

CLARKSVILLE (town). Covers a land area of 36.260 square miles and a water area of 0.011 square miles. Located at 42.13° N. Lat.; 78.24° W. Long.
Population: 1,041 (1990); 1,146 (2000); 1,284 (2005); 1,378 (2010 projected); Race: 98.2% White, 0.3% Black, 0.5% Asian, 0.2% Hispanic of any race (2005); Density: 35.4 persons per square mile (2005); Average household size: 2.52 (2005); Median age: 40.0 (2005); Males per 100 females: 98.5 (2005); Marriage status: 18.9% never married, 64.1% now married, 6.0% widowed, 10.9% divorced (2000); Foreign born: 0.2% (2000); Ancestry (includes multiple ancestries): 23.3% German, 17.0% English, 15.3% Irish, 8.2% United States or American, 7.0% Other groups (2000).
Economy: Single-family building permits issued: 10 (2005); Multi-family building permits issued: 0 (2005); Employment by occupation: 6.4% management, 17.1% professional, 13.5% services, 22.9% sales, 2.8% farming, 11.3% construction, 26.1% production (2000).
Income: Per capita income: $15,602 (2005); Median household income: $33,556 (2005); Average household income: $39,279 (2005); Percent of households with income of $100,000 or more: 3.9% (2005); Poverty rate: 14.4% (2000).
Education: Percent of population age 25 and over with: High school diploma (including GED) or higher: 81.4% (2005); Bachelor's degree or higher: 9.4% (2005); Master's degree or higher: 4.1% (2005).
Housing: Homeownership rate: 87.1% (2005); Median home value: $70,476 (2005); Median rent: $289 per month (2000); Median age of housing: 26 years (2000).
Transportation: Commute to work: 92.6% car, 0.4% public transportation, 0.2% walk, 6.8% work from home (2000); Travel time to work: 14.0% less than 15 minutes, 47.0% 15 to 30 minutes, 24.3% 30 to 45 minutes, 6.5% 45 to 60 minutes, 8.2% 60 minutes or more (2000)

CUBA (village). Covers a land area of 1.193 square miles and a water area of 0 square miles. Located at 42.21° N. Lat.; 78.27° W. Long. Elevation is 1,500 feet.
Population: 1,677 (1990); 1,633 (2000); 1,552 (2005); 1,519 (2010 projected); Race: 96.3% White, 1.0% Black, 0.8% Asian, 3.1% Hispanic of any race (2005); Density: 1,301.1 persons per square mile (2005); Average household size: 2.51 (2005); Median age: 38.5 (2005); Males per 100 females: 83.2 (2005); Marriage status: 27.5% never married, 54.2% now married, 8.6% widowed, 9.7% divorced (2000); Foreign born: 1.8% (2000); Ancestry (includes multiple ancestries): 20.6% German, 17.7% Irish, 17.7% English, 7.6% United States or American, 7.1% Polish (2000).
Economy: Single-family building permits issued: 0 (2005); Multi-family building permits issued: 0 (2005); Employment by occupation: 8.4% management, 23.0% professional, 17.1% services, 23.6% sales, 0.7% farming, 10.9% construction, 16.3% production (2000).
Income: Per capita income: $17,053 (2005); Median household income: $34,598 (2005); Average household income: $42,330 (2005); Percent of households with income of $100,000 or more: 5.7% (2005); Poverty rate: 12.9% (2000).
Education: Percent of population age 25 and over with: High school diploma (including GED) or higher: 84.6% (2005); Bachelor's degree or higher: 19.6% (2005); Master's degree or higher: 10.4% (2005).
School District(s)
Cuba-Rushford Central School District (PK-12)
   2003-04 Enrollment: 1,092 . . . . (585) 968-1556
Housing: Homeownership rate: 61.1% (2005); Median home value: $75,966 (2005); Median rent: $297 per month (2000); Median age of housing: 60+ years (2000).
Hospitals: Cuba Memorial Hospital (80 beds)
Newspapers: Patriot and Free Press (General - Circulation 6,000)
Transportation: Commute to work: 89.2% car, 0.0% public transportation, 7.5% walk, 2.4% work from home (2000); Travel time to work: 46.8% less

than 15 minutes, 34.3% 15 to 30 minutes, 11.7% 30 to 45 minutes, 1.2% 45 to 60 minutes, 6.0% 60 minutes or more (2000)

CUBA (town).
Covers a land area of 35.128 square miles and a water area of 0.700 square miles. Located at 42.21° N. Lat.; 78.26° W. Long. Elevation is 1,500 feet.
History: Seneca Oil Spring, where oil was first noted by Jesuit missionaries in early 17th century, is nearby; the spring was the precursor of the "Pennsylvania field," the first oil field in the U.S. Incorporated 1850.
Population: 3,401 (1990); 3,392 (2000); 3,281 (2005); 3,220 (2010 projected); Race: 97.4% White, 0.5% Black, 0.6% Asian, 1.8% Hispanic of any race (2005); Density: 93.4 persons per square mile (2005); Average household size: 2.49 (2005); Median age: 40.8 (2005); Males per 100 females: 91.9 (2005); Marriage status: 22.6% never married, 60.1% now married, 7.6% widowed, 9.6% divorced (2000); Foreign born: 1.8% (2000); Ancestry (includes multiple ancestries): 20.0% German, 19.8% English, 13.9% Irish, 7.7% United States or American, 6.7% Polish (2000).
Economy: Manufacturing: cheese, machinery, feed. Single-family building permits issued: 7 (2005); Multi-family building permits issued: 0 (2005); Employment by occupation: 10.5% management, 23.2% professional, 16.2% services, 21.9% sales, 1.1% farming, 9.3% construction, 17.8% production (2000).
Income: Per capita income: $19,214 (2005); Median household income: $38,283 (2005); Average household income: $47,595 (2005); Percent of households with income of $100,000 or more: 6.8% (2005); Poverty rate: 9.4% (2000).
Education: Percent of population age 25 and over with: High school diploma (including GED) or higher: 85.7% (2005); Bachelor's degree or higher: 19.0% (2005); Master's degree or higher: 7.8% (2005).
Housing: Homeownership rate: 73.9% (2005); Median home value: $81,024 (2005); Median rent: $313 per month (2000); Median age of housing: 44 years (2000).
Safety: Violent crime rate: 5.9 per 10,000 population; Property crime rate: 185.1 per 10,000 population (2004).
Transportation: Commute to work: 93.4% car, 0.0% public transportation, 4.3% walk, 1.5% work from home (2000); Travel time to work: 40.0% less than 15 minutes, 38.3% 15 to 30 minutes, 12.3% 30 to 45 minutes, 3.0% 45 to 60 minutes, 6.4% 60 minutes or more (2000)

FILLMORE (unincorporated postal area, zip code 14735).
Covers a land area of 79.733 square miles and a water area of 0.316 square miles. Located at 42.45° N. Lat.; 78.10° W. Long. Elevation is 1,213 feet.
Population: 0 (2000); Race: 97.8% White, 0.2% Black, 0.0% Asian, 0.8% Hispanic of any race (2000); Density: 0.0 persons per square mile (2000); Age: 28.5% under 18, 13.6% over 64 (2000); Marriage status: 22.9% never married, 61.8% now married, 7.2% widowed, 8.2% divorced (2000); Foreign born: 1.3% (2000); Ancestry (includes multiple ancestries): 31.6% German, 19.7% English, 14.3% Irish, 7.5% United States or American, 6.2% Other groups (2000).
Economy: In agricultural and timber area; fish traps and netting. Employment by occupation: 8.0% management, 17.6% professional, 14.5% services, 18.7% sales, 5.3% farming, 16.2% construction, 19.9% production (2000).
Income: Per capita income: $13,733 (2000); Median household income: $30,080 (2000); Poverty rate: 20.2% (2000).
Education: Percent of population age 25 and over with: High school diploma (including GED) or higher: 76.6% (2000); Bachelor's degree or higher: 12.9% (2000).

School District(s)
Fillmore Central School District (PK-12)
    2003-04 Enrollment: 761 . . . . (585) 567-2251

Housing: Homeownership rate: 74.5% (2000); Median home value: $53,000 (2000); Median rent: $306 per month (2000); Median age of housing: 39 years (2000).
Transportation: Commute to work: 83.3% car, 1.4% public transportation, 6.4% walk, 6.8% work from home (2000); Travel time to work: 34.9% less than 15 minutes, 19.4% 15 to 30 minutes, 21.9% 30 to 45 minutes, 7.9% 45 to 60 minutes, 15.9% 60 minutes or more (2000)

FRIENDSHIP (town).
Covers a land area of 36.219 square miles and a water area of 0.006 square miles. Located at 42.21° N. Lat.; 78.13° W. Long. Elevation is 1,514 feet.
History: Incorporated 1898.
Population: 2,185 (1990); 1,927 (2000); 1,865 (2005); 1,807 (2010 projected); Race: 95.8% White, 2.6% Black, 0.2% Asian, 0.7% Hispanic of any race (2005); Density: 51.5 persons per square mile (2005); Average household size: 2.46 (2005); Median age: 37.0 (2005); Males per 100 females: 99.0 (2005); Marriage status: 24.6% never married, 58.7% now married, 7.3% widowed, 9.4% divorced (2000); Foreign born: 0.5% (2000); Ancestry (includes multiple ancestries): 19.2% German, 13.4% United States or American, 12.0% Irish, 11.9% English, 7.5% Other groups (2000).
Economy: Agriculture. Manufacturing: hosiery, textiles, auto bodies, metal and wood products; timber. Single-family building permits issued: 1 (2005); Multi-family building permits issued: 0 (2005); Employment by occupation: 5.3% management, 20.1% professional, 16.4% services, 16.9% sales, 1.3% farming, 11.7% construction, 28.1% production (2000).
Income: Per capita income: $14,351 (2005); Median household income: $29,542 (2005); Average household income: $35,264 (2005); Percent of households with income of $100,000 or more: 2.8% (2005); Poverty rate: 21.5% (2000).
Taxes: Total city taxes per capita: $357 (2004); City property taxes per capita: $340 (2004).
Education: Percent of population age 25 and over with: High school diploma (including GED) or higher: 80.2% (2005); Bachelor's degree or higher: 11.8% (2005); Master's degree or higher: 4.2% (2005).

School District(s)
Friendship Central School District (PK-12)
    2003-04 Enrollment: 376 . . . . (716) 973-3534

Housing: Homeownership rate: 71.4% (2005); Median home value: $56,667 (2005); Median rent: $322 per month (2000); Median age of housing: 50 years (2000).
Safety: Violent crime rate: 41.8 per 10,000 population; Property crime rate: 198.3 per 10,000 population (2004).
Transportation: Commute to work: 90.6% car, 0.0% public transportation, 4.0% walk, 5.0% work from home (2000); Travel time to work: 38.9% less than 15 minutes, 31.3% 15 to 30 minutes, 20.4% 30 to 45 minutes, 4.4% 45 to 60 minutes, 5.0% 60 minutes or more (2000)

FRIENDSHIP (CDP).
Covers a land area of 2.752 square miles and a water area of 0 square miles. Located at 42.20° N. Lat.; 78.14° W. Long.
Population: 1,413 (1990); 1,176 (2000); 1,125 (2005); 1,084 (2010 projected); Race: 93.8% White, 4.1% Black, 0.1% Asian, 1.1% Hispanic of any race (2005); Density: 408.8 persons per square mile (2005); Average household size: 2.49 (2005); Median age: 34.7 (2005); Males per 100 females: 95.0 (2005); Marriage status: 26.8% never married, 56.6% now married, 7.5% widowed, 9.0% divorced (2000); Foreign born: 0.9% (2000); Ancestry (includes multiple ancestries): 20.5% German, 15.1% English, 11.5% United States or American, 10.5% Irish, 7.5% Other groups (2000).
Economy: Employment by occupation: 3.2% management, 17.6% professional, 17.6% services, 20.1% sales, 0.9% farming, 14.6% construction, 25.9% production (2000).
Income: Per capita income: $12,447 (2005); Median household income: $27,558 (2005); Average household income: $30,979 (2005); Percent of households with income of $100,000 or more: 0.7% (2005); Poverty rate: 25.7% (2000).
Education: Percent of population age 25 and over with: High school diploma (including GED) or higher: 83.1% (2005); Bachelor's degree or higher: 13.3% (2005); Master's degree or higher: 4.0% (2005).
Housing: Homeownership rate: 61.9% (2005); Median home value: $57,600 (2005); Median rent: $331 per month (2000); Median age of housing: 60+ years (2000).
Transportation: Commute to work: 90.0% car, 0.0% public transportation, 5.8% walk, 3.5% work from home (2000); Travel time to work: 39.0% less than 15 minutes, 32.2% 15 to 30 minutes, 18.6% 30 to 45 minutes, 4.8% 45 to 60 minutes, 5.3% 60 minutes or more (2000)

GENESEE (town).
Covers a land area of 36.292 square miles and a water area of 0.024 square miles. Located at 42.05° N. Lat.; 78.25° W. Long.
Population: 1,672 (1990); 1,803 (2000); 1,997 (2005); 2,151 (2010 projected); Race: 98.9% White, 0.1% Black, 0.0% Asian, 1.7% Hispanic of any race (2005); Density: 55.0 persons per square mile (2005); Average household size: 2.67 (2005); Median age: 38.1 (2005); Males per 100 females: 100.7 (2005); Marriage status: 17.5% never married, 67.7% now married, 5.5% widowed, 9.4% divorced (2000); Foreign born: 0.6% (2000); Ancestry (includes multiple ancestries): 26.5% German, 19.1% English, 15.8% Irish, 7.5% Italian, 7.1% Other groups (2000).
Economy: Single-family building permits issued: 8 (2005); Multi-family building permits issued: 0 (2005); Employment by occupation: 10.8%

management, 16.6% professional, 13.4% services, 22.4% sales, 0.8% farming, 12.1% construction, 23.9% production (2000).
Income: Per capita income: $18,046 (2005); Median household income: $42,206 (2005); Average household income: $48,114 (2005); Percent of households with income of $100,000 or more: 5.6% (2005); Poverty rate: 11.8% (2000).
Education: Percent of population age 25 and over with: High school diploma (including GED) or higher: 85.4% (2005); Bachelor's degree or higher: 9.8% (2005); Master's degree or higher: 5.2% (2005).
Housing: Homeownership rate: 87.7% (2005); Median home value: $75,175 (2005); Median rent: $330 per month (2000); Median age of housing: 28 years (2000).
Transportation: Commute to work: 93.5% car, 0.2% public transportation, 2.2% walk, 3.4% work from home (2000); Travel time to work: 18.6% less than 15 minutes, 50.2% 15 to 30 minutes, 23.3% 30 to 45 minutes, 2.6% 45 to 60 minutes, 5.4% 60 minutes or more (2000)

GRANGER (town). Covers a land area of 31.988 square miles and a water area of 0.046 square miles. Located at 42.47° N. Lat.; 78.01° W. Long.
Population: 515 (1990); 577 (2000); 589 (2005); 600 (2010 projected); Race: 94.9% White, 0.8% Black, 0.0% Asian, 0.0% Hispanic of any race (2005); Density: 18.4 persons per square mile (2005); Average household size: 2.64 (2005); Median age: 39.7 (2005); Males per 100 females: 118.1 (2005); Marriage status: 21.0% never married, 65.9% now married, 4.9% widowed, 8.3% divorced (2000); Foreign born: 1.1% (2000); Ancestry (includes multiple ancestries): 31.0% German, 22.3% English, 14.1% Irish, 12.4% Other groups, 10.5% United States or American (2000).
Economy: Single-family building permits issued: 1 (2005); Multi-family building permits issued: 0 (2005); Employment by occupation: 8.7% management, 19.9% professional, 6.1% services, 17.7% sales, 5.2% farming, 23.4% construction, 19.0% production (2000).
Income: Per capita income: $14,580 (2005); Median household income: $29,756 (2005); Average household income: $38,509 (2005); Percent of households with income of $100,000 or more: 5.4% (2005); Poverty rate: 31.2% (2000).
Education: Percent of population age 25 and over with: High school diploma (including GED) or higher: 71.3% (2005); Bachelor's degree or higher: 12.3% (2005); Master's degree or higher: 7.2% (2005).
Housing: Homeownership rate: 84.8% (2005); Median home value: $76,207 (2005); Median rent: $310 per month (2000); Median age of housing: 27 years (2000).
Transportation: Commute to work: 78.0% car, 3.1% public transportation, 4.5% walk, 10.8% work from home (2000); Travel time to work: 30.2% less than 15 minutes, 11.6% 15 to 30 minutes, 25.6% 30 to 45 minutes, 11.1% 45 to 60 minutes, 21.6% 60 minutes or more (2000)

GROVE (town). Covers a land area of 33.507 square miles and a water area of 0.223 square miles. Located at 42.47° N. Lat.; 77.89° W. Long.
Population: 479 (1990); 533 (2000); 567 (2005); 590 (2010 projected); Race: 96.1% White, 0.0% Black, 0.4% Asian, 1.4% Hispanic of any race (2005); Density: 16.9 persons per square mile (2005); Average household size: 2.47 (2005); Median age: 43.8 (2005); Males per 100 females: 98.3 (2005); Marriage status: 19.9% never married, 67.1% now married, 6.3% widowed, 6.7% divorced (2000); Foreign born: 1.3% (2000); Ancestry (includes multiple ancestries): 27.9% German, 17.4% Irish, 16.5% English, 9.1% Italian, 7.6% United States or American (2000).
Economy: Single-family building permits issued: 3 (2005); Multi-family building permits issued: 0 (2005); Employment by occupation: 10.8% management, 17.1% professional, 16.3% services, 15.1% sales, 2.0% farming, 17.9% construction, 20.7% production (2000).
Income: Per capita income: $20,547 (2005); Median household income: $45,500 (2005); Average household income: $50,652 (2005); Percent of households with income of $100,000 or more: 5.7% (2005); Poverty rate: 5.3% (2000).
Education: Percent of population age 25 and over with: High school diploma (including GED) or higher: 84.3% (2005); Bachelor's degree or higher: 10.1% (2005); Master's degree or higher: 4.2% (2005).
Housing: Homeownership rate: 87.8% (2005); Median home value: $88,235 (2005); Median rent: $300 per month (2000); Median age of housing: 27 years (2000).
Transportation: Commute to work: 89.2% car, 0.0% public transportation, 5.0% walk, 4.6% work from home (2000); Travel time to work: 30.6% less than 15 minutes, 16.2% 15 to 30 minutes, 20.5% 30 to 45 minutes, 11.4% 45 to 60 minutes, 21.4% 60 minutes or more (2000)

HOUGHTON (CDP). Covers a land area of 2.443 square miles and a water area of 0.018 square miles. Located at 42.42° N. Lat.; 78.15° W. Long. Elevation is 1,217 feet.
History: Seat of Houghton College (1923).
Population: 1,740 (1990); 1,748 (2000); 1,764 (2005); 1,814 (2010 projected); Race: 94.6% White, 2.3% Black, 1.0% Asian, 3.4% Hispanic of any race (2005); Density: 722.0 persons per square mile (2005); Average household size: 5.13 (2005); Median age: 22.1 (2005); Males per 100 females: 70.9 (2005); Marriage status: 63.5% never married, 33.1% now married, 2.1% widowed, 1.3% divorced (2000); Foreign born: 6.3% (2000); Ancestry (includes multiple ancestries): 28.6% German, 18.9% English, 12.7% Irish, 8.2% Other groups, 6.4% Italian (2000).
Economy: Agriculture: dairy products, fruit, grain. Employment by occupation: 5.7% management, 34.8% professional, 27.8% services, 25.9% sales, 0.9% farming, 3.8% construction, 1.2% production (2000).
Income: Per capita income: $10,321 (2005); Median household income: $37,951 (2005); Average household income: $43,009 (2005); Percent of households with income of $100,000 or more: 5.8% (2005); Poverty rate: 25.0% (2000).
Education: Percent of population age 25 and over with: High school diploma (including GED) or higher: 89.4% (2005); Bachelor's degree or higher: 62.8% (2005); Master's degree or higher: 35.7% (2005).
Four-year College(s)
Houghton College
   Fall 2004 Enrollment: 1,468. . . . . (585) 567-9200
   2005-06 Tuition: In-state $19,420; Out-of-state $19,420
Housing: Homeownership rate: 49.1% (2005); Median home value: $132,042 (2005); Median rent: $306 per month (2000); Median age of housing: 38 years (2000).
Transportation: Commute to work: 30.0% car, 0.0% public transportation, 66.2% walk, 2.4% work from home (2000); Travel time to work: 90.7% less than 15 minutes, 3.7% 15 to 30 minutes, 1.9% 30 to 45 minutes, 1.3% 45 to 60 minutes, 2.3% 60 minutes or more (2000)

HUME (town). Covers a land area of 37.937 square miles and a water area of 0.414 square miles. Located at 42.48° N. Lat.; 78.12° W. Long.
Population: 1,970 (1990); 1,987 (2000); 2,038 (2005); 2,110 (2010 projected); Race: 98.7% White, 0.2% Black, 0.3% Asian, 0.4% Hispanic of any race (2005); Density: 53.7 persons per square mile (2005); Average household size: 2.55 (2005); Median age: 37.9 (2005); Males per 100 females: 96.7 (2005); Marriage status: 23.4% never married, 60.3% now married, 7.1% widowed, 9.1% divorced (2000); Foreign born: 1.6% (2000); Ancestry (includes multiple ancestries): 31.0% German, 20.0% English, 14.9% Irish, 7.2% United States or American, 5.9% Polish (2000).
Economy: Single-family building permits issued: 1 (2005); Multi-family building permits issued: 0 (2005); Employment by occupation: 8.8% management, 17.6% professional, 14.7% services, 18.4% sales, 6.0% farming, 14.6% construction, 19.8% production (2000).
Income: Per capita income: $16,960 (2005); Median household income: $36,579 (2005); Average household income: $43,206 (2005); Percent of households with income of $100,000 or more: 5.8% (2005); Poverty rate: 17.2% (2000).
Taxes: Total city taxes per capita: $345 (2004); City property taxes per capita: $312 (2004).
Education: Percent of population age 25 and over with: High school diploma (including GED) or higher: 78.3% (2005); Bachelor's degree or higher: 13.4% (2005); Master's degree or higher: 5.6% (2005).
Housing: Homeownership rate: 74.0% (2005); Median home value: $84,733 (2005); Median rent: $315 per month (2000); Median age of housing: 60+ years (2000).
Transportation: Commute to work: 85.1% car, 1.3% public transportation, 6.5% walk, 5.4% work from home (2000); Travel time to work: 37.3% less than 15 minutes, 21.4% 15 to 30 minutes, 20.5% 30 to 45 minutes, 6.7% 45 to 60 minutes, 14.1% 60 minutes or more (2000)
Additional Information Contacts
Town of Hume . . . . (585) 567-2666
   http://www.humetown.org/

INDEPENDENCE (town). Covers a land area of 34.474 square miles and a water area of 0 square miles. Located at 42.05° N. Lat.; 77.78° W. Long.
Population: 1,026 (1990); 1,074 (2000); 1,135 (2005); 1,156 (2010 projected); Race: 98.8% White, 0.6% Black, 0.2% Asian, 0.5% Hispanic of any race (2005); Density: 32.9 persons per square mile (2005); Average

household size: 2.62 (2005); Median age: 38.5 (2005); Males per 100 females: 102.7 (2005); Marriage status: 25.0% never married, 59.6% now married, 7.4% widowed, 8.1% divorced (2000); Foreign born: 0.2% (2000); Ancestry (includes multiple ancestries): 18.7% English, 15.8% German, 13.6% Irish, 9.9% United States or American, 6.3% Other groups (2000).
Economy: Single-family building permits issued: 1 (2005); Multi-family building permits issued: 0 (2005); Employment by occupation: 10.0% management, 17.3% professional, 14.2% services, 16.2% sales, 4.4% farming, 13.3% construction, 24.8% production (2000).
Income: Per capita income: $15,751 (2005); Median household income: $38,227 (2005); Average household income: $41,288 (2005); Percent of households with income of $100,000 or more: 1.2% (2005); Poverty rate: 13.3% (2000).
Education: Percent of population age 25 and over with: High school diploma (including GED) or higher: 77.5% (2005); Bachelor's degree or higher: 10.4% (2005); Master's degree or higher: 4.7% (2005).
Housing: Homeownership rate: 81.5% (2005); Median home value: $61,765 (2005); Median rent: $314 per month (2000); Median age of housing: 60 years (2000).
Transportation: Commute to work: 83.9% car, 2.9% public transportation, 5.1% walk, 8.0% work from home (2000); Travel time to work: 24.3% less than 15 minutes, 40.0% 15 to 30 minutes, 22.3% 30 to 45 minutes, 6.3% 45 to 60 minutes, 7.0% 60 minutes or more (2000)

LITTLE GENESEE (unincorporated postal area, zip code 14754). Covers a land area of 12.860 square miles and a water area of 0.007 square miles. Located at 42.02° N. Lat.; 78.20° W. Long.
Population: 0 (2000); Race: 98.4% White, 0.0% Black, 0.0% Asian, 1.8% Hispanic of any race (2000); Density: 0.0 persons per square mile (2000); Age: 29.9% under 18, 8.0% over 64 (2000); Marriage status: 17.3% never married, 68.6% now married, 4.4% widowed, 9.7% divorced (2000); Foreign born: 0.0% (2000); Ancestry (includes multiple ancestries): 17.7% German, 14.2% English, 10.6% United States or American, 9.3% Irish, 8.9% Other groups (2000).
Economy: Employment by occupation: 6.0% management, 14.8% professional, 16.8% services, 19.6% sales, 1.2% farming, 16.0% construction, 25.6% production (2000).
Income: Per capita income: $11,529 (2000); Median household income: $30,417 (2000); Poverty rate: 20.0% (2000).
Education: Percent of population age 25 and over with: High school diploma (including GED) or higher: 85.0% (2000); Bachelor's degree or higher: 7.5% (2000).
Housing: Homeownership rate: 84.9% (2000); Median home value: $45,500 (2000); Median rent: $330 per month (2000); Median age of housing: 27 years (2000).
Transportation: Commute to work: 93.1% car, 0.8% public transportation, 2.8% walk, 3.3% work from home (2000); Travel time to work: 24.4% less than 15 minutes, 33.2% 15 to 30 minutes, 33.2% 30 to 45 minutes, 3.8% 45 to 60 minutes, 5.5% 60 minutes or more (2000)

NEW HUDSON (town). Covers a land area of 36.331 square miles and a water area of 0.107 square miles. Located at 42.31° N. Lat.; 78.24° W. Long.
Population: 715 (1990); 736 (2000); 740 (2005); 742 (2010 projected); Race: 98.1% White, 0.4% Black, 0.0% Asian, 1.2% Hispanic of any race (2005); Density: 20.4 persons per square mile (2005); Average household size: 2.69 (2005); Median age: 38.8 (2005); Males per 100 females: 97.3 (2005); Marriage status: 27.3% never married, 59.2% now married, 4.2% widowed, 9.2% divorced (2000); Foreign born: 0.5% (2000); Ancestry (includes multiple ancestries): 24.8% German, 16.1% Irish, 14.4% English, 8.4% European, 6.5% United States or American (2000).
Economy: Single-family building permits issued: 1 (2005); Multi-family building permits issued: 0 (2005); Employment by occupation: 15.7% management, 12.6% professional, 13.3% services, 24.8% sales, 2.4% farming, 12.6% construction, 18.5% production (2000).
Income: Per capita income: $16,696 (2005); Median household income: $38,348 (2005); Average household income: $44,927 (2005); Percent of households with income of $100,000 or more: 5.5% (2005); Poverty rate: 13.1% (2000).
Education: Percent of population age 25 and over with: High school diploma (including GED) or higher: 81.4% (2005); Bachelor's degree or higher: 11.9% (2005); Master's degree or higher: 2.8% (2005).
Housing: Homeownership rate: 85.8% (2005); Median home value: $88,500 (2005); Median rent: $322 per month (2000); Median age of housing: 26 years (2000).
Transportation: Commute to work: 85.6% car, 0.0% public transportation, 2.2% walk, 12.2% work from home (2000); Travel time to work: 28.7% less than 15 minutes, 43.0% 15 to 30 minutes, 15.2% 30 to 45 minutes, 3.7% 45 to 60 minutes, 9.4% 60 minutes or more (2000)

RICHBURG (village). Covers a land area of 0.925 square miles and a water area of 0 square miles. Located at 42.08° N. Lat.; 78.15° W. Long. Elevation is 1,655 feet.
Population: 494 (1990); 448 (2000); 421 (2005); 406 (2010 projected); Race: 98.3% White, 0.7% Black, 0.2% Asian, 0.0% Hispanic of any race (2005); Density: 455.3 persons per square mile (2005); Average household size: 2.72 (2005); Median age: 34.7 (2005); Males per 100 females: 90.5 (2005); Marriage status: 24.3% never married, 56.2% now married, 9.9% widowed, 9.6% divorced (2000); Foreign born: 0.0% (2000); Ancestry (includes multiple ancestries): 19.2% United States or American, 16.5% English, 12.7% Irish, 10.5% German, 8.9% Other groups (2000).
Economy: Single-family building permits issued: 1 (2005); Multi-family building permits issued: 0 (2005); Employment by occupation: 3.0% management, 9.8% professional, 21.3% services, 25.6% sales, 0.0% farming, 14.6% construction, 25.6% production (2000).
Income: Per capita income: $11,686 (2005); Median household income: $25,192 (2005); Average household income: $31,742 (2005); Percent of households with income of $100,000 or more: 1.3% (2005); Poverty rate: 16.6% (2000).
Education: Percent of population age 25 and over with: High school diploma (including GED) or higher: 78.2% (2005); Bachelor's degree or higher: 10.3% (2005); Master's degree or higher: 4.6% (2005).
School District(s)
Bolivar-Richburg Central School District (PK-12)
    2003-04 Enrollment: 1,008 . . . . (585) 928-2561
Housing: Homeownership rate: 74.8% (2005); Median home value: $55,122 (2005); Median rent: $329 per month (2000); Median age of housing: 60 years (2000).
Transportation: Commute to work: 95.4% car, 0.0% public transportation, 1.3% walk, 3.3% work from home (2000); Travel time to work: 25.0% less than 15 minutes, 33.8% 15 to 30 minutes, 31.1% 30 to 45 minutes, 2.7% 45 to 60 minutes, 7.4% 60 minutes or more (2000)

RUSHFORD (town). Covers a land area of 35.351 square miles and a water area of 0.756 square miles. Located at 42.38° N. Lat.; 78.23° W. Long.
Population: 1,176 (1990); 1,259 (2000); 1,292 (2005); 1,337 (2010 projected); Race: 98.9% White, 0.0% Black, 0.2% Asian, 1.3% Hispanic of any race (2005); Density: 36.5 persons per square mile (2005); Average household size: 2.59 (2005); Median age: 39.8 (2005); Males per 100 females: 99.1 (2005); Marriage status: 20.4% never married, 62.3% now married, 8.1% widowed, 9.3% divorced (2000); Foreign born: 0.9% (2000); Ancestry (includes multiple ancestries): 28.7% German, 19.1% English, 15.6% Irish, 10.4% United States or American, 9.6% Polish (2000).
Economy: Maple syrup, dairy products, apples. Single-family building permits issued: 6 (2005); Multi-family building permits issued: 0 (2005); Employment by occupation: 11.1% management, 17.2% professional, 17.9% services, 14.0% sales, 3.1% farming, 8.9% construction, 27.9% production (2000).
Income: Per capita income: $14,588 (2005); Median household income: $30,938 (2005); Average household income: $37,771 (2005); Percent of households with income of $100,000 or more: 4.6% (2005); Poverty rate: 16.1% (2000).
Education: Percent of population age 25 and over with: High school diploma (including GED) or higher: 81.3% (2005); Bachelor's degree or higher: 13.9% (2005); Master's degree or higher: 6.8% (2005).
School District(s)
Cuba-Rushford Central School District (PK-12)
    2003-04 Enrollment: 1,092 . . . . (585) 968-1556
Housing: Homeownership rate: 82.4% (2005); Median home value: $86,613 (2005); Median rent: $313 per month (2000); Median age of housing: 34 years (2000).
Safety: Violent crime rate: 0.0 per 10,000 population; Property crime rate: 0.0 per 10,000 population (2004).
Transportation: Commute to work: 83.7% car, 1.1% public transportation, 3.0% walk, 11.0% work from home (2000); Travel time to work: 27.8% less than 15 minutes, 33.3% 15 to 30 minutes, 18.3% 30 to 45 minutes, 7.9% 45 to 60 minutes, 12.7% 60 minutes or more (2000)

SCIO (town). Covers a land area of 35.243 square miles and a water area of 0.029 square miles. Located at 42.14° N. Lat.; 78.00° W. Long.
Population: 1,965 (1990); 1,914 (2000); 2,047 (2005); 2,094 (2010 projected); Race: 97.3% White, 0.3% Black, 0.4% Asian, 0.5% Hispanic of any race (2005); Density: 58.1 persons per square mile (2005); Average household size: 2.57 (2005); Median age: 39.5 (2005); Males per 100 females: 95.5 (2005); Marriage status: 20.4% never married, 64.6% now married, 6.7% widowed, 8.2% divorced (2000); Foreign born: 0.5% (2000); Ancestry (includes multiple ancestries): 22.4% German, 14.0% Irish, 12.2% English, 9.9% United States or American, 5.9% Italian (2000).
Economy: Single-family building permits issued: 5 (2005); Multi-family building permits issued: 0 (2005); Employment by occupation: 13.7% management, 16.3% professional, 16.3% services, 22.0% sales, 2.5% farming, 9.5% construction, 19.8% production (2000).
Income: Per capita income: $16,628 (2005); Median household income: $36,624 (2005); Average household income: $42,547 (2005); Percent of households with income of $100,000 or more: 5.1% (2005); Poverty rate: 14.6% (2000).
Education: Percent of population age 25 and over with: High school diploma (including GED) or higher: 82.1% (2005); Bachelor's degree or higher: 13.6% (2005); Master's degree or higher: 5.7% (2005).
School District(s)
Scio Central School District (KG-12)
    2003-04 Enrollment: 467 . . . . (716) 593-5510
Housing: Homeownership rate: 76.8% (2005); Median home value: $69,937 (2005); Median rent: $345 per month (2000); Median age of housing: 39 years (2000).
Transportation: Commute to work: 92.2% car, 0.5% public transportation, 3.5% walk, 3.0% work from home (2000); Travel time to work: 44.0% less than 15 minutes, 39.3% 15 to 30 minutes, 5.7% 30 to 45 minutes, 3.9% 45 to 60 minutes, 7.1% 60 minutes or more (2000)

STANNARDS (CDP). Covers a land area of 2.845 square miles and a water area of 0 square miles. Located at 42.08° N. Lat.; 77.92° W. Long.
Population: 1,028 (1990); 868 (2000); 883 (2005); 900 (2010 projected); Race: 98.0% White, 0.0% Black, 0.6% Asian, 0.5% Hispanic of any race (2005); Density: 310.4 persons per square mile (2005); Average household size: 2.28 (2005); Median age: 42.6 (2005); Males per 100 females: 98.9 (2005); Marriage status: 26.3% never married, 58.5% now married, 7.5% widowed, 7.7% divorced (2000); Foreign born: 1.2% (2000); Ancestry (includes multiple ancestries): 23.4% English, 18.8% German, 14.4% Irish, 10.8% United States or American, 7.8% Other groups (2000).
Economy: Employment by occupation: 12.4% management, 25.3% professional, 19.8% services, 20.9% sales, 0.0% farming, 6.6% construction, 15.1% production (2000).
Income: Per capita income: $23,024 (2005); Median household income: $42,721 (2005); Average household income: $52,397 (2005); Percent of households with income of $100,000 or more: 11.9% (2005); Poverty rate: 10.7% (2000).
Education: Percent of population age 25 and over with: High school diploma (including GED) or higher: 87.6% (2005); Bachelor's degree or higher: 23.3% (2005); Master's degree or higher: 9.7% (2005).
Housing: Homeownership rate: 70.1% (2005); Median home value: $86,857 (2005); Median rent: $333 per month (2000); Median age of housing: 32 years (2000).
Transportation: Commute to work: 90.9% car, 0.0% public transportation, 3.3% walk, 3.3% work from home (2000); Travel time to work: 44.9% less than 15 minutes, 29.4% 15 to 30 minutes, 15.1% 30 to 45 minutes, 5.1% 45 to 60 minutes, 5.4% 60 minutes or more (2000)

SWAIN (unincorporated postal area, zip code 14884). Aka Swains. Covers a land area of 22.216 square miles and a water area of 0.226 square miles. Located at 42.47° N. Lat.; 77.89° W. Long. Elevation is 1,309 feet.
Population: 0 (2000); Race: 100.0% White, 0.0% Black, 0.0% Asian, 0.0% Hispanic of any race (2000); Density: 0.0 persons per square mile (2000); Age: 21.4% under 18, 20.4% over 64 (2000); Marriage status: 17.3% never married, 68.5% now married, 6.5% widowed, 7.7% divorced (2000); Foreign born: 1.5% (2000); Ancestry (includes multiple ancestries): 21.4% German, 16.7% English, 13.6% Irish, 10.2% United States or American, 8.7% Scottish (2000).
Economy: Employment by occupation: 14.7% management, 21.7% professional, 18.6% services, 14.7% sales, 1.6% farming, 17.1% construction, 11.6% production (2000).

Income: Per capita income: $16,810 (2000); Median household income: $38,000 (2000); Poverty rate: 5.6% (2000).
Education: Percent of population age 25 and over with: High school diploma (including GED) or higher: 81.0% (2000); Bachelor's degree or higher: 12.1% (2000).
Housing: Homeownership rate: 85.2% (2000); Median home value: $60,400 (2000); Median rent: $296 per month (2000); Median age of housing: 28 years (2000).
Transportation: Commute to work: 85.6% car, 0.0% public transportation, 7.2% walk, 7.2% work from home (2000); Travel time to work: 33.6% less than 15 minutes, 21.6% 15 to 30 minutes, 17.2% 30 to 45 minutes, 8.6% 45 to 60 minutes, 19.0% 60 minutes or more (2000)

WARD (town). Covers a land area of 29.188 square miles and a water area of 0.006 square miles. Located at 42.22° N. Lat.; 77.90° W. Long.
Population: 334 (1990); 390 (2000); 421 (2005); 444 (2010 projected); Race: 95.7% White, 2.1% Black, 2.1% Asian, 0.0% Hispanic of any race (2005); Density: 14.4 persons per square mile (2005); Average household size: 2.86 (2005); Median age: 39.1 (2005); Males per 100 females: 94.0 (2005); Marriage status: 23.4% never married, 65.3% now married, 2.1% widowed, 9.1% divorced (2000); Foreign born: 1.7% (2000); Ancestry (includes multiple ancestries): 22.9% German, 14.9% Irish, 13.0% English, 7.2% Italian, 7.0% Other groups (2000).
Economy: Single-family building permits issued: 4 (2005); Multi-family building permits issued: 0 (2005); Employment by occupation: 14.8% management, 27.8% professional, 10.5% services, 23.5% sales, 1.2% farming, 9.9% construction, 12.3% production (2000).
Income: Per capita income: $16,422 (2005); Median household income: $45,086 (2005); Average household income: $46,224 (2005); Percent of households with income of $100,000 or more: 3.4% (2005); Poverty rate: 14.9% (2000).
Education: Percent of population age 25 and over with: High school diploma (including GED) or higher: 88.9% (2005); Bachelor's degree or higher: 17.3% (2005); Master's degree or higher: 11.4% (2005).
Housing: Homeownership rate: 93.2% (2005); Median home value: $77,407 (2005); Median rent: $225 per month (2000); Median age of housing: 26 years (2000).
Transportation: Commute to work: 92.4% car, 0.0% public transportation, 0.0% walk, 6.3% work from home (2000); Travel time to work: 23.6% less than 15 minutes, 41.2% 15 to 30 minutes, 27.0% 30 to 45 minutes, 5.4% 45 to 60 minutes, 2.7% 60 minutes or more (2000)

WELLSVILLE (village). Covers a land area of 2.384 square miles and a water area of 0 square miles. Located at 42.12° N. Lat.; 77.94° W. Long. Elevation is 1,517 feet.
Population: 5,423 (1990); 5,171 (2000); 4,896 (2005); 4,768 (2010 projected); Race: 94.6% White, 1.0% Black, 2.5% Asian, 1.2% Hispanic of any race (2005); Density: 2,053.3 persons per square mile (2005); Average household size: 2.36 (2005); Median age: 41.3 (2005); Males per 100 females: 88.3 (2005); Marriage status: 26.4% never married, 49.8% now married, 11.4% widowed, 12.4% divorced (2000); Foreign born: 2.1% (2000); Ancestry (includes multiple ancestries): 22.0% German, 19.5% Irish, 17.9% English, 7.7% United States or American, 6.6% Italian (2000).
Economy: Single-family building permits issued: 1 (2005); Multi-family building permits issued: 0 (2005); Employment by occupation: 12.4% management, 23.1% professional, 18.7% services, 23.9% sales, 0.3% farming, 6.2% construction, 15.3% production (2000).
Income: Per capita income: $18,658 (2005); Median household income: $27,795 (2005); Average household income: $41,667 (2005); Percent of households with income of $100,000 or more: 8.1% (2005); Poverty rate: 18.9% (2000).
Education: Percent of population age 25 and over with: High school diploma (including GED) or higher: 82.4% (2005); Bachelor's degree or higher: 20.1% (2005); Master's degree or higher: 10.4% (2005).
School District(s)
Wellsville Central School District (KG-12)
    2003-04 Enrollment: 1,390 . . . . (585) 593-4200
Housing: Homeownership rate: 55.6% (2005); Median home value: $78,846 (2005); Median rent: $356 per month (2000); Median age of housing: 60+ years (2000).
Hospitals: Jones Memorial Hospital (70 beds)
Safety: Violent crime rate: 16.5 per 10,000 population; Property crime rate: 299.5 per 10,000 population (2004).
Newspapers: Wellsville Daily Reporter (Circulation 1,000)

PROFILES OF NEW YORK / Allegany County

Transportation: Commute to work: 85.3% car, 3.3% public transportation, 7.8% walk, 2.7% work from home (2000); Travel time to work: 61.5% less than 15 minutes, 17.8% 15 to 30 minutes, 10.6% 30 to 45 minutes, 6.1% 45 to 60 minutes, 4.0% 60 minutes or more (2000)
Additional Information Contacts
Wellsville Area Chamber of Commerce . . . . (585) 593-5080
  http://www.wellsvilleareachamber.com

WELLSVILLE (town).
Covers a land area of 36.659 square miles and a water area of 0.028 square miles. Located at 42.12° N. Lat.; 77.93° W. Long. Elevation is 1,517 feet.
History: Wellsville was settled in 1795 and named for Gardiner Wells, early settler and chief landowner. Site of David A. Howe Library (1937), with museum and theater. Special museum, Mather Homestead, for visually impaired. Incorporated in 1871.
Population: 8,116 (1990); 7,678 (2000); 7,288 (2005); 7,131 (2010 projected); Race: 95.5% White, 0.8% Black, 2.1% Asian, 1.0% Hispanic of any race (2005); Density: 198.8 persons per square mile (2005); Average household size: 2.36 (2005); Median age: 42.0 (2005); Males per 100 females: 90.9 (2005); Marriage status: 23.9% never married, 55.6% now married, 10.3% widowed, 10.3% divorced (2000); Foreign born: 2.3% (2000); Ancestry (includes multiple ancestries): 22.2% German, 19.5% English, 19.4% Irish, 8.8% United States or American, 6.0% Italian (2000).
Economy: Manufacturing of oil-well supplies, turbines, advanced technology industrial systems, industrial heat exchangers, wooden furniture and wood items; in farming and dairying area. Single-family building permits issued: 2 (2005); Multi-family building permits issued: 0 (2005); Employment by occupation: 13.5% management, 22.4% professional, 17.2% services, 23.7% sales, 0.4% farming, 6.1% construction, 16.6% production (2000).
Income: Per capita income: $21,069 (2005); Median household income: $34,017 (2005); Average household income: $48,083 (2005); Percent of households with income of $100,000 or more: 10.2% (2005); Poverty rate: 16.0% (2000).
Education: Percent of population age 25 and over with: High school diploma (including GED) or higher: 83.5% (2005); Bachelor's degree or higher: 19.8% (2005); Master's degree or higher: 9.4% (2005).
Housing: Homeownership rate: 62.8% (2005); Median home value: $79,035 (2005); Median rent: $351 per month (2000); Median age of housing: 58 years (2000).
Transportation: Commute to work: 88.2% car, 2.1% public transportation, 5.7% walk, 2.7% work from home (2000); Travel time to work: 61.4% less than 15 minutes, 18.0% 15 to 30 minutes, 10.8% 30 to 45 minutes, 4.8% 45 to 60 minutes, 5.0% 60 minutes or more (2000)

WEST ALMOND (town).
Covers a land area of 36.043 square miles and a water area of 0.033 square miles. Located at 42.30° N. Lat.; 77.88° W. Long. Elevation is 1,857 feet.
Population: 277 (1990); 353 (2000); 355 (2005); 367 (2010 projected); Race: 96.3% White, 0.0% Black, 0.6% Asian, 2.3% Hispanic of any race (2005); Density: 9.8 persons per square mile (2005); Average household size: 2.63 (2005); Median age: 40.9 (2005); Males per 100 females: 106.4 (2005); Marriage status: 20.3% never married, 72.7% now married, 2.2% widowed, 4.8% divorced (2000); Foreign born: 2.3% (2000); Ancestry (includes multiple ancestries): 26.7% German, 18.6% Irish, 15.6% English, 9.1% United States or American, 7.2% Other groups (2000).
Economy: Employment by occupation: 9.5% management, 23.1% professional, 26.5% services, 12.2% sales, 4.1% farming, 13.6% construction, 10.9% production (2000).
Income: Per capita income: $21,458 (2005); Median household income: $50,379 (2005); Average household income: $56,426 (2005); Percent of households with income of $100,000 or more: 13.3% (2005); Poverty rate: 6.6% (2000).
Education: Percent of population age 25 and over with: High school diploma (including GED) or higher: 84.8% (2005); Bachelor's degree or higher: 18.4% (2005); Master's degree or higher: 5.7% (2005).
Housing: Homeownership rate: 85.2% (2005); Median home value: $82,000 (2005); Median rent: $288 per month (2000); Median age of housing: 26 years (2000).
Transportation: Commute to work: 93.8% car, 1.4% public transportation, 1.4% walk, 3.4% work from home (2000); Travel time to work: 11.4% less than 15 minutes, 51.4% 15 to 30 minutes, 24.3% 30 to 45 minutes, 5.0% 45 to 60 minutes, 7.9% 60 minutes or more (2000)

WHITESVILLE (unincorporated postal area, zip code 14897).
Covers a land area of 24.097 square miles and a water area of 0.007 square miles. Located at 42.03° N. Lat.; 77.79° W. Long. Elevation is 1,700 feet.
Population: 0 (2000); Race: 99.1% White, 0.0% Black, 0.0% Asian, 0.0% Hispanic of any race (2000); Density: 0.0 persons per square mile (2000); Age: 27.0% under 18, 14.3% over 64 (2000); Marriage status: 24.0% never married, 60.5% now married, 7.6% widowed, 7.9% divorced (2000); Foreign born: 0.2% (2000); Ancestry (includes multiple ancestries): 18.1% English, 15.7% Irish, 12.8% German, 8.9% United States or American, 5.5% Other groups (2000).
Economy: Manufacturing of dairy products wood products; timber. Employment by occupation: 9.6% management, 18.6% professional, 15.4% services, 15.7% sales, 2.9% farming, 13.6% construction, 24.2% production (2000).
Income: Per capita income: $13,066 (2000); Median household income: $33,750 (2000); Poverty rate: 13.3% (2000).
Education: Percent of population age 25 and over with: High school diploma (including GED) or higher: 76.5% (2000); Bachelor's degree or higher: 11.7% (2000).
School District(s)
Whitesville Central School District (KG-12)
  2003-04 Enrollment: 313 . . . . (607) 356-3301
Housing: Homeownership rate: 78.8% (2000); Median home value: $38,200 (2000); Median rent: $309 per month (2000); Median age of housing: 60+ years (2000).
Transportation: Commute to work: 85.8% car, 3.5% public transportation, 5.4% walk, 5.4% work from home (2000); Travel time to work: 24.7% less than 15 minutes, 41.5% 15 to 30 minutes, 21.0% 30 to 45 minutes, 6.3% 45 to 60 minutes, 6.5% 60 minutes or more (2000)

WILLING (town).
Covers a land area of 36.273 square miles and a water area of 0.007 square miles. Located at 42.05° N. Lat.; 77.89° W. Long.
Population: 1,428 (1990); 1,371 (2000); 1,324 (2005); 1,302 (2010 projected); Race: 97.7% White, 0.2% Black, 1.0% Asian, 0.8% Hispanic of any race (2005); Density: 36.5 persons per square mile (2005); Average household size: 2.51 (2005); Median age: 43.4 (2005); Males per 100 females: 99.1 (2005); Marriage status: 24.2% never married, 60.0% now married, 7.1% widowed, 8.7% divorced (2000); Foreign born: 0.9% (2000); Ancestry (includes multiple ancestries): 25.8% German, 24.9% English, 16.5% Irish, 8.8% United States or American, 6.9% Other groups (2000).
Economy: Single-family building permits issued: 3 (2005); Multi-family building permits issued: 0 (2005); Employment by occupation: 13.8% management, 18.3% professional, 17.3% services, 20.1% sales, 3.1% farming, 8.1% construction, 19.3% production (2000).
Income: Per capita income: $19,294 (2005); Median household income: $40,881 (2005); Average household income: $48,472 (2005); Percent of households with income of $100,000 or more: 8.0% (2005); Poverty rate: 14.9% (2000).
Education: Percent of population age 25 and over with: High school diploma (including GED) or higher: 84.7% (2005); Bachelor's degree or higher: 14.9% (2005); Master's degree or higher: 7.7% (2005).
Housing: Homeownership rate: 82.7% (2005); Median home value: $81,739 (2005); Median rent: $329 per month (2000); Median age of housing: 46 years (2000).
Transportation: Commute to work: 92.3% car, 0.0% public transportation, 1.2% walk, 6.4% work from home (2000); Travel time to work: 44.7% less than 15 minutes, 39.4% 15 to 30 minutes, 9.8% 30 to 45 minutes, 3.6% 45 to 60 minutes, 2.5% 60 minutes or more (2000)

WIRT (town).
Covers a land area of 35.898 square miles and a water area of 0.062 square miles. Located at 42.12° N. Lat.; 78.13° W. Long. Elevation is 1,893 feet.
Population: 1,143 (1990); 1,215 (2000); 1,196 (2005); 1,187 (2010 projected); Race: 97.7% White, 0.5% Black, 0.3% Asian, 0.0% Hispanic of any race (2005); Density: 33.3 persons per square mile (2005); Average household size: 2.68 (2005); Median age: 36.5 (2005); Males per 100 females: 100.3 (2005); Marriage status: 23.0% never married, 59.0% now married, 8.4% widowed, 9.6% divorced (2000); Foreign born: 0.3% (2000); Ancestry (includes multiple ancestries): 19.5% German, 18.2% English, 13.1% Irish, 12.8% United States or American, 5.3% Other groups (2000).
Economy: Single-family building permits issued: 5 (2005); Multi-family building permits issued: 0 (2005); Employment by occupation: 5.7%

management, 8.2% professional, 17.2% services, 21.0% sales, 4.0% farming, 16.3% construction, 27.5% production (2000).
Income: Per capita income: $15,100 (2005); Median household income: $31,929 (2005); Average household income: $39,838 (2005); Percent of households with income of $100,000 or more: 4.9% (2005); Poverty rate: 14.8% (2000).
Education: Percent of population age 25 and over with: High school diploma (including GED) or higher: 80.7% (2005); Bachelor's degree or higher: 8.1% (2005); Master's degree or higher: 3.3% (2005).
Housing: Homeownership rate: 82.8% (2005); Median home value: $63,158 (2005); Median rent: $299 per month (2000); Median age of housing: 36 years (2000).
Transportation: Commute to work: 94.9% car, 0.0% public transportation, 1.0% walk, 4.1% work from home (2000); Travel time to work: 19.8% less than 15 minutes, 32.1% 15 to 30 minutes, 27.0% 30 to 45 minutes, 12.6% 45 to 60 minutes, 8.6% 60 minutes or more (2000)

Bronx County and Borough

See New York City

Brooklyn Borough

See New York City

Broome County

Located in southern New York; bounded on the south by Pennsylvania. Covers a land area of 706.82 square miles, a water area of 8.64 square miles, and is located in the Eastern Time Zone. The county government was organized in 1806. County seat is Binghamton.

Broome County is part of the Binghamton, NY Metropolitan Statistical Area. The entire metro area includes: Broome County, NY; Tioga County, NY

Weather Station: Binghamton Edwin A. Link Field Elevation: 1,597 feet

	Jan	Feb	Mar	Apr	May	Jun	Jul	Aug	Sep	Oct	Nov	Dec
High	29	32	41	54	66	74	79	77	68	57	45	34
Low	15	17	25	35	47	55	60	58	50	40	31	21
Precip	2.5	2.4	2.9	3.4	3.4	3.7	3.5	3.4	3.6	3.0	3.3	3.1
Snow	19.8	15.7	14.5	4.5	0.2	tr	0.0	0.0	tr	0.8	7.8	17.5

High and Low temperatures in degrees Fahrenheit; Precipitation and Snow in inches

Population: 212,160 (1990); 200,536 (2000); 198,698 (2005); 196,704 (2010 projected); Race: 89.5% White, 4.1% Black, 3.4% Asian, 2.6% Hispanic of any race (2005); Density: 281.1 persons per square mile (2005); Average household size: 2.45 (2005); Median age: 39.1 (2005); Males per 100 females: 93.7 (2005).
Religion: Five largest groups: 33.1% Catholic Church, 8.4% The United Methodist Church, 1.9% Presbyterian Church (U.S.A.), 1.8% Episcopal Church, 1.5% Evangelical Lutheran Church in America (2000).
Economy: Unemployment rate: 4.9% (2005); Total civilian labor force: 96,597 (2005); Leading industries: 20.6% manufacturing; 17.0% health care and social assistance; 15.3% retail trade (2003); Farms: 588 totaling 98,276 acres (2002); Companies that employ 500 or more persons: 17 (2003); Companies that employ 100 to 499 persons: 108 (2003); Companies that employ less than 100 persons: 4,199 (2003); Black-owned businesses: n/a (2002); Hispanic-owned businesses: n/a (2002); Women-owned businesses: 3,798 (2002); Retail sales per capita: $13,148 (2006). Single-family building permits issued: 194 (2005); Multi-family building permits issued: 16 (2005).
Income: Per capita income: $21,617 (2005); Median household income: $39,507 (2005); Average household income: $52,115 (2005); Percent of households with income of $100,000 or more: 10.9% (2005); Poverty rate: 12.9% (2003); Bankruptcy rate: 6.36% (2005).
Taxes: Total county taxes per capita: $719 (2004); County property taxes per capita: $247 (2004).
Education: Percent of population age 25 and over with: High school diploma (including GED) or higher: 83.8% (2005); Bachelor's degree or higher: 22.8% (2005); Master's degree or higher: 10.2% (2005).
Housing: Homeownership rate: 65.7% (2005); Median home value: $94,260 (2005); Median rent: $393 per month (2000); Median age of housing: 47 years (2000).
Health: Birth rate: 103.7 per 10,000 population (2004); Death rate: 110.3 per 10,000 population (2004); Age-adjusted cancer mortality rate: 218.8 deaths per 100,000 population (2002); Number of physicians: 31.1 per 10,000 population (2004); Hospital beds: 41.2 per 10,000 population (2003); Hospital admissions: 1,377.7 per 10,000 population (2003).
Elections: 2004 Presidential election results: 47.4% Bush, 50.4% Kerry, 1.9% Nader, 0.3% Badnarik
National and State Parks: Broome State Forest; Chenango Valley State Park; Tracy Creek State Forest
Additional Information Contacts

Broome County Government	(607) 778-2109
http://www.gobroomecounty.com/	
City of Binghamton	(607) 772-7005
http://www.cityofbinghamton.com/	
Town of Union	(607) 786-2900
http://www.townofunion.com/	
Town of Vestal	(607) 748-1514
http://www.vestalny.com/content/	
Village of Johnson City	(607) 798-7861
http://www.johnsoncityny.org/	

Broome County Communities

BARKER (town). Covers a land area of 41.380 square miles and a water area of 0.406 square miles. Located at 42.28° N. Lat.; 75.91° W. Long.
Population: 2,714 (1990); 2,738 (2000); 2,722 (2005); 2,705 (2010 projected); Race: 97.4% White, 0.9% Black, 0.5% Asian, 0.8% Hispanic of any race (2005); Density: 65.8 persons per square mile (2005); Average household size: 2.70 (2005); Median age: 38.3 (2005); Males per 100 females: 107.5 (2005); Marriage status: 23.2% never married, 62.3% now married, 4.7% widowed, 9.8% divorced (2000); Foreign born: 2.0% (2000); Ancestry (includes multiple ancestries): 17.9% English, 17.4% German, 15.3% Irish, 8.9% Italian, 8.7% United States or American (2000).
Economy: Single-family building permits issued: 5 (2005); Multi-family building permits issued: 0 (2005); Employment by occupation: 13.6% management, 18.1% professional, 11.6% services, 26.6% sales, 0.0% farming, 13.0% construction, 17.0% production (2000).
Income: Per capita income: $18,470 (2005); Median household income: $42,430 (2005); Average household income: $49,926 (2005); Percent of households with income of $100,000 or more: 7.9% (2005); Poverty rate: 10.9% (2000).
Education: Percent of population age 25 and over with: High school diploma (including GED) or higher: 82.8% (2005); Bachelor's degree or higher: 14.7% (2005); Master's degree or higher: 6.9% (2005).
Housing: Homeownership rate: 87.0% (2005); Median home value: $84,898 (2005); Median rent: $358 per month (2000); Median age of housing: 32 years (2000).
Transportation: Commute to work: 94.6% car, 0.6% public transportation, 0.9% walk, 2.9% work from home (2000); Travel time to work: 15.3% less than 15 minutes, 49.9% 15 to 30 minutes, 27.0% 30 to 45 minutes, 3.1% 45 to 60 minutes, 4.8% 60 minutes or more (2000)

BINGHAMTON (city). Covers a land area of 10.438 square miles and a water area of 0.601 square miles. Located at 42.10° N. Lat.; 75.91° W. Long. Elevation is 863 feet.
History: Little is known of the Binghamton area before the Revolution. The site was purchased in 1786 by William Bingham, a Philadelphia merchant. Joseph Leonard, first permanent settler, built his log cabin nearby in 1787 and was soon joined by other pioneers, who called the new settlement Chenango. It was later renamed in honor of Bingham, who made liberal donations of land to the settlement. It was incorporated as a village in 1834 and as a city in 1867.
Population: 53,017 (1990); 47,380 (2000); 45,839 (2005); 44,233 (2010 projected); Race: 79.2% White, 10.9% Black, 4.0% Asian, 5.2% Hispanic of any race (2005); Density: 4,391.6 persons per square mile (2005); Average household size: 2.22 (2005); Median age: 37.5 (2005); Males per 100 females: 90.9 (2005); Marriage status: 37.0% never married, 41.9% now married, 9.9% widowed, 11.3% divorced (2000); Foreign born: 8.5% (2000); Ancestry (includes multiple ancestries): 19.7% Irish, 16.3% Other groups, 12.8% Italian, 12.0% German, 11.1% English (2000).
Economy: Unemployment rate: 5.5% (2005); Total civilian labor force: 20,896 (2005); Single-family building permits issued: 5 (2005); Multi-family building permits issued: 2 (2005); Employment by occupation: 9.5% management, 21.7% professional, 21.1% services, 27.0% sales, 0.1% farming, 5.5% construction, 15.1% production (2000).

Income: Per capita income: $18,616 (2005); Median household income: $28,299 (2005); Average household income: $40,708 (2005); Percent of households with income of $100,000 or more: 6.8% (2005); Poverty rate: 23.7% (2000).
Education: Percent of population age 25 and over with: High school diploma (including GED) or higher: 77.9% (2005); Bachelor's degree or higher: 21.3% (2005); Master's degree or higher: 10.3% (2005).

School District(s)
Binghamton City School District (PK-12)
    2003-04 Enrollment: 6,249 .... (607) 762-8100
Boces Broome-Delaware-Tioga (PK-PK)
    2003-04 Enrollment: 729 .... (607) 763-3309
Chenango Forks Central School District (PK-12)
    2003-04 Enrollment: 1,874 .... (607) 648-7543
Chenango Valley Central School District (PK-12)
    2003-04 Enrollment: 2,032 .... (607) 779-4710
Johnson City Central School District (KG-12)
    2003-04 Enrollment: 2,597 .... (607) 763-1230
Susquehanna Valley Central School District (KG-12)
    2003-04 Enrollment: 2,135 .... (607) 775-9100

Four-year College(s)
SUNY at Binghamton (Public)
    Fall 2004 Enrollment: 13,860 .... (607) 777-2000
    2005-06 Tuition: In-state $5,838; Out-of-state $12,098

Two-year College(s)
Broome Community College (Public)
    Fall 2004 Enrollment: 6,590 .... (607) 778-5000
    2005-06 Tuition: In-state $3,081; Out-of-state $5,895
Broome Delaware Tioga BOCES-Practical Nursing Program (Public)
    Fall 2004 Enrollment: 60 .... (607) 763-3212
Ridley-Lowell School of Business
    Fall 2004 Enrollment: 89 .... (607) 724-2941
Triple Cities School of Beauty Culture
    Fall 2004 Enrollment: 32 .... (518) 273-7741

Housing: Homeownership rate: 43.4% (2005); Median home value: $84,027 (2005); Median rent: $372 per month (2000); Median age of housing: 60+ years (2000).
Hospitals: Binghamton Psychiatric Center (387 beds); Lourdes Hospital (267 beds)
Safety: Violent crime rate: 33.4 per 10,000 population; Property crime rate: 423.9 per 10,000 population (2004).
Transportation: Commute to work: 83.1% car, 7.9% public transportation, 5.8% walk, 2.0% work from home (2000); Travel time to work: 51.0% less than 15 minutes, 37.2% 15 to 30 minutes, 6.3% 30 to 45 minutes, 2.0% 45 to 60 minutes, 3.5% 60 minutes or more (2000)

Additional Information Contacts
City of Binghamton .... (607) 772-7005
    http://www.cityofbinghamton.com/
Greater Binghamton Chamber of Commerce .... (607) 772-8860
    http://www.greaterbinghamtonchamber.com

BINGHAMTON
(town). Covers a land area of 25.427 square miles and a water area of 0.039 square miles. Located at 42.06° N. Lat.; 75.90° W. Long. Elevation is 863 feet.
History: Grew mainly after the Chenango Canal connected it with Utica in 1837. First railroad service began in 1869. State University of N.Y. at Binghamton in the vicinity. Settled 1787, Incorporated as a city 1867.
Population: 4,997 (1990); 4,969 (2000); 5,001 (2005); 5,032 (2010 projected); Race: 95.9% White, 1.3% Black, 0.9% Asian, 1.4% Hispanic of any race (2005); Density: 196.7 persons per square mile (2005); Average household size: 2.69 (2005); Median age: 40.7 (2005); Males per 100 females: 95.5 (2005); Marriage status: 19.4% never married, 67.0% now married, 6.8% widowed, 6.9% divorced (2000); Foreign born: 3.4% (2000); Ancestry (includes multiple ancestries): 21.4% Irish, 18.3% German, 14.5% English, 13.9% Italian, 7.5% Polish (2000).
Economy: Industrial city. Diverse industries include marking devices, foods, fabricated metal products, machinery, aerospace control systems, electronic equipment, photographic materials, and computers; precision machining. State University of N.Y. at Binghamton is in the vicinity. Single-family building permits issued: 10 (2005); Multi-family building permits issued: 0 (2005); Employment by occupation: 11.5% management, 28.7% professional, 16.6% services, 25.2% sales, 0.5% farming, 8.9% construction, 8.6% production (2000).
Income: Per capita income: $26,849 (2005); Median household income: $57,598 (2005); Average household income: $72,188 (2005); Percent of households with income of $100,000 or more: 18.6% (2005); Poverty rate: 5.3% (2000).
Education: Percent of population age 25 and over with: High school diploma (including GED) or higher: 91.2% (2005); Bachelor's degree or higher: 30.2% (2005); Master's degree or higher: 14.2% (2005).
Housing: Homeownership rate: 89.2% (2005); Median home value: $111,219 (2005); Median rent: $519 per month (2000); Median age of housing: 35 years (2000).
Transportation: Commute to work: 95.8% car, 0.8% public transportation, 0.3% walk, 2.8% work from home (2000); Travel time to work: 33.4% less than 15 minutes, 55.7% 15 to 30 minutes, 5.3% 30 to 45 minutes, 1.6% 45 to 60 minutes, 4.1% 60 minutes or more (2000)

CASTLE CREEK
(unincorporated postal area, zip code 13744). Covers a land area of 12.241 square miles and a water area of 0 square miles. Located at 42.25° N. Lat.; 75.91° W. Long.
Population: 0 (2000); Race: 98.4% White, 0.3% Black, 1.0% Asian, 0.0% Hispanic of any race (2000); Density: 0.0 persons per square mile (2000); Age: 27.6% under 18, 12.1% over 64 (2000); Marriage status: 23.9% never married, 59.8% now married, 3.9% widowed, 12.4% divorced (2000); Foreign born: 1.6% (2000); Ancestry (includes multiple ancestries): 18.9% Irish, 18.5% German, 18.2% English, 10.8% United States or American, 10.2% Italian (2000).
Economy: Employment by occupation: 10.6% management, 27.7% professional, 7.8% services, 23.5% sales, 0.8% farming, 11.3% construction, 18.2% production (2000).
Income: Per capita income: $19,114 (2000); Median household income: $38,813 (2000); Poverty rate: 11.1% (2000).
Education: Percent of population age 25 and over with: High school diploma (including GED) or higher: 86.7% (2000); Bachelor's degree or higher: 16.9% (2000).
Housing: Homeownership rate: 88.3% (2000); Median home value: $77,200 (2000); Median rent: $363 per month (2000); Median age of housing: 40 years (2000).
Transportation: Commute to work: 95.5% car, 0.0% public transportation, 1.9% walk, 0.3% work from home (2000); Travel time to work: 19.0% less than 15 minutes, 63.0% 15 to 30 minutes, 13.1% 30 to 45 minutes, 1.9% 45 to 60 minutes, 2.9% 60 minutes or more (2000)

CHENANGO
(town). Covers a land area of 33.922 square miles and a water area of 0.337 square miles. Located at 42.18° N. Lat.; 75.88° W. Long.
Population: 12,280 (1990); 11,454 (2000); 11,396 (2005); 11,313 (2010 projected); Race: 97.0% White, 0.7% Black, 0.6% Asian, 1.1% Hispanic of any race (2005); Density: 335.9 persons per square mile (2005); Average household size: 2.49 (2005); Median age: 42.0 (2005); Males per 100 females: 97.9 (2005); Marriage status: 20.2% never married, 62.3% now married, 7.0% widowed, 10.5% divorced (2000); Foreign born: 1.8% (2000); Ancestry (includes multiple ancestries): 23.2% Irish, 19.8% German, 17.1% English, 10.7% Italian, 6.6% Polish (2000).
Economy: Single-family building permits issued: 16 (2005); Multi-family building permits issued: 0 (2005); Employment by occupation: 12.8% management, 28.0% professional, 13.7% services, 26.2% sales, 0.3% farming, 7.3% construction, 11.7% production (2000).
Income: Per capita income: $26,680 (2005); Median household income: $54,202 (2005); Average household income: $66,327 (2005); Percent of households with income of $100,000 or more: 17.7% (2005); Poverty rate: 6.2% (2000).
Taxes: Total city taxes per capita: $233 (2004); City property taxes per capita: $201 (2004).
Education: Percent of population age 25 and over with: High school diploma (including GED) or higher: 89.6% (2005); Bachelor's degree or higher: 27.3% (2005); Master's degree or higher: 12.6% (2005).
Housing: Homeownership rate: 83.4% (2005); Median home value: $112,425 (2005); Median rent: $422 per month (2000); Median age of housing: 39 years (2000).
Transportation: Commute to work: 95.9% car, 0.1% public transportation, 1.2% walk, 2.4% work from home (2000); Travel time to work: 29.7% less than 15 minutes, 58.8% 15 to 30 minutes, 6.4% 30 to 45 minutes, 1.3% 45 to 60 minutes, 3.7% 60 minutes or more (2000)

CHENANGO FORKS
(unincorporated postal area, zip code 13746). Covers a land area of 23.135 square miles and a water area of 0.104 square miles. Located at 42.26° N. Lat.; 75.84° W. Long.

Population: 0 (2000); Race: 96.1% White, 0.2% Black, 0.5% Asian, 1.4% Hispanic of any race (2000); Density: 0.0 persons per square mile (2000); Age: 27.3% under 18, 14.5% over 64 (2000); Marriage status: 19.5% never married, 64.3% now married, 6.1% widowed, 10.1% divorced (2000); Foreign born: 1.0% (2000); Ancestry (includes multiple ancestries): 20.5% English, 18.7% Irish, 17.8% German, 8.9% Other groups, 8.4% Italian (2000).
Economy: Eleven miles North of Binghamton. Employment by occupation: 12.6% management, 17.4% professional, 16.3% services, 22.1% sales, 0.6% farming, 10.2% construction, 20.8% production (2000).
Income: Per capita income: $17,044 (2000); Median household income: $37,446 (2000); Poverty rate: 7.5% (2000).
Education: Percent of population age 25 and over with: High school diploma (including GED) or higher: 82.7% (2000); Bachelor's degree or higher: 12.5% (2000).
Housing: Homeownership rate: 87.3% (2000); Median home value: $69,300 (2000); Median rent: $298 per month (2000); Median age of housing: 29 years (2000).
Transportation: Commute to work: 98.0% car, 0.0% public transportation, 0.4% walk, 1.2% work from home (2000); Travel time to work: 20.0% less than 15 minutes, 49.1% 15 to 30 minutes, 22.0% 30 to 45 minutes, 4.3% 45 to 60 minutes, 4.5% 60 minutes or more (2000)

COLESVILLE (town). Covers a land area of 78.522 square miles and a water area of 0.691 square miles. Located at 42.17° N. Lat.; 75.66° W. Long.
Population: 5,590 (1990); 5,441 (2000); 5,562 (2005); 5,671 (2010 projected); Race: 97.6% White, 0.4% Black, 0.4% Asian, 1.0% Hispanic of any race (2005); Density: 70.8 persons per square mile (2005); Average household size: 2.74 (2005); Median age: 37.8 (2005); Males per 100 females: 99.6 (2005); Marriage status: 21.2% never married, 59.7% now married, 5.1% widowed, 14.0% divorced (2000); Foreign born: 1.2% (2000); Ancestry (includes multiple ancestries): 18.4% English, 17.4% German, 16.2% Irish, 9.9% Other groups, 9.8% United States or American (2000).
Economy: Single-family building permits issued: 11 (2005); Multi-family building permits issued: 0 (2005); Employment by occupation: 8.1% management, 12.9% professional, 15.6% services, 24.7% sales, 1.6% farming, 12.2% construction, 24.9% production (2000).
Income: Per capita income: $18,612 (2005); Median household income: $43,101 (2005); Average household income: $50,889 (2005); Percent of households with income of $100,000 or more: 7.7% (2005); Poverty rate: 10.3% (2000).
Education: Percent of population age 25 and over with: High school diploma (including GED) or higher: 76.2% (2005); Bachelor's degree or higher: 7.8% (2005); Master's degree or higher: 2.9% (2005).
Housing: Homeownership rate: 85.6% (2005); Median home value: $77,572 (2005); Median rent: $372 per month (2000); Median age of housing: 33 years (2000).
Transportation: Commute to work: 95.0% car, 0.5% public transportation, 2.0% walk, 2.0% work from home (2000); Travel time to work: 16.9% less than 15 minutes, 42.6% 15 to 30 minutes, 29.1% 30 to 45 minutes, 5.8% 45 to 60 minutes, 5.6% 60 minutes or more (2000)

CONKLIN (town). Covers a land area of 24.511 square miles and a water area of 0.420 square miles. Located at 42.05° N. Lat.; 75.82° W. Long. Elevation is 867 feet.
Population: 6,265 (1990); 5,940 (2000); 5,976 (2005); 6,011 (2010 projected); Race: 97.5% White, 1.0% Black, 0.2% Asian, 1.0% Hispanic of any race (2005); Density: 243.8 persons per square mile (2005); Average household size: 2.59 (2005); Median age: 39.8 (2005); Males per 100 females: 97.3 (2005); Marriage status: 23.7% never married, 63.7% now married, 5.3% widowed, 7.3% divorced (2000); Foreign born: 1.3% (2000); Ancestry (includes multiple ancestries): 20.6% Irish, 18.6% German, 15.7% English, 11.4% Italian, 5.3% Other groups (2000).
Economy: Single-family building permits issued: 4 (2005); Multi-family building permits issued: 0 (2005); Employment by occupation: 10.7% management, 18.8% professional, 15.4% services, 25.6% sales, 0.3% farming, 7.2% construction, 22.1% production (2000).
Income: Per capita income: $19,951 (2005); Median household income: $43,305 (2005); Average household income: $51,659 (2005); Percent of households with income of $100,000 or more: 11.2% (2005); Poverty rate: 10.5% (2000).
Education: Percent of population age 25 and over with: High school diploma (including GED) or higher: 83.8% (2005); Bachelor's degree or higher: 15.5% (2005); Master's degree or higher: 6.5% (2005).
School District(s)
Susquehanna Valley Central School District (KG-12)
   2003-04 Enrollment: 2,135 . . . . (607) 775-9100
Housing: Homeownership rate: 84.9% (2005); Median home value: $87,000 (2005); Median rent: $405 per month (2000); Median age of housing: 37 years (2000).
Newspapers: The Country Courier (General - Circulation 1,500); The Vestal Town Crier (General - Circulation 1,400); Windsor Standard (General - Circulation 1,400)
Transportation: Commute to work: 94.0% car, 0.3% public transportation, 2.7% walk, 1.6% work from home (2000); Travel time to work: 30.1% less than 15 minutes, 50.1% 15 to 30 minutes, 8.9% 30 to 45 minutes, 4.4% 45 to 60 minutes, 6.5% 60 minutes or more (2000)

DICKINSON (town). Covers a land area of 4.786 square miles and a water area of 0.075 square miles. Located at 42.12° N. Lat.; 75.91° W. Long.
History: Incorporated 1876.
Population: 5,486 (1990); 5,335 (2000); 5,310 (2005); 5,310 (2010 projected); Race: 90.9% White, 5.9% Black, 0.8% Asian, 2.4% Hispanic of any race (2005); Density: 1,109.6 persons per square mile (2005); Average household size: 2.65 (2005); Median age: 42.4 (2005); Males per 100 females: 103.4 (2005); Marriage status: 27.8% never married, 52.4% now married, 10.7% widowed, 9.1% divorced (2000); Foreign born: 4.6% (2000); Ancestry (includes multiple ancestries): 17.3% Irish, 15.3% German, 12.7% English, 9.7% Italian, 6.4% Slovak (2000).
Economy: Single-family building permits issued: 0 (2005); Multi-family building permits issued: 0 (2005); Employment by occupation: 9.8% management, 25.7% professional, 16.6% services, 30.4% sales, 0.0% farming, 6.4% construction, 11.2% production (2000).
Income: Per capita income: $21,908 (2005); Median household income: $42,723 (2005); Average household income: $53,982 (2005); Percent of households with income of $100,000 or more: 9.8% (2005); Poverty rate: 7.2% (2000).
Education: Percent of population age 25 and over with: High school diploma (including GED) or higher: 77.9% (2005); Bachelor's degree or higher: 19.7% (2005); Master's degree or higher: 7.5% (2005).
Housing: Homeownership rate: 68.4% (2005); Median home value: $92,632 (2005); Median rent: $397 per month (2000); Median age of housing: 55 years (2000).
Transportation: Commute to work: 95.6% car, 2.0% public transportation, 0.1% walk, 2.3% work from home (2000); Travel time to work: 53.4% less than 15 minutes, 35.2% 15 to 30 minutes, 7.8% 30 to 45 minutes, 0.3% 45 to 60 minutes, 3.2% 60 minutes or more (2000)

ENDICOTT (village). Covers a land area of 3.137 square miles and a water area of 0 square miles. Located at 42.10° N. Lat.; 76.05° W. Long. Elevation is 800 feet.
History: Settled c.1795; incorporated 1906.
Population: 13,531 (1990); 13,038 (2000); 12,852 (2005); 12,644 (2010 projected); Race: 89.5% White, 5.0% Black, 2.4% Asian, 2.1% Hispanic of any race (2005); Density: 4,096.8 persons per square mile (2005); Average household size: 2.15 (2005); Median age: 38.5 (2005); Males per 100 females: 90.6 (2005); Marriage status: 32.2% never married, 44.4% now married, 10.6% widowed, 12.9% divorced (2000); Foreign born: 4.9% (2000); Ancestry (includes multiple ancestries): 20.9% Italian, 19.1% Irish, 13.3% German, 12.5% English, 9.6% Other groups (2000).
Economy: Manufacturing: shoes, leather. Single-family building permits issued: 0 (2005); Multi-family building permits issued: 0 (2005); Employment by occupation: 9.0% management, 18.4% professional, 19.0% services, 29.3% sales, 0.3% farming, 5.6% construction, 18.4% production (2000).
Income: Per capita income: $18,515 (2005); Median household income: $28,591 (2005); Average household income: $38,740 (2005); Percent of households with income of $100,000 or more: 4.8% (2005); Poverty rate: 18.7% (2000).
Education: Percent of population age 25 and over with: High school diploma (including GED) or higher: 79.9% (2005); Bachelor's degree or higher: 17.1% (2005); Master's degree or higher: 7.0% (2005).
School District(s)
Union-Endicott Central School District (KG-12)
   2003-04 Enrollment: 4,536 . . . . (607) 757-2112

Housing: Homeownership rate: 41.4% (2005); Median home value: $85,321 (2005); Median rent: $402 per month (2000); Median age of housing: 59 years (2000).
Safety: Violent crime rate: 31.0 per 10,000 population; Property crime rate: 417.0 per 10,000 population (2004).
Transportation: Commute to work: 86.6% car, 2.6% public transportation, 7.3% walk, 2.9% work from home (2000); Travel time to work: 45.6% less than 15 minutes, 43.7% 15 to 30 minutes, 7.3% 30 to 45 minutes, 0.9% 45 to 60 minutes, 2.6% 60 minutes or more (2000).

ENDWELL (CDP).
Aka Hooper. Covers a land area of 3.682 square miles and a water area of 0.061 square miles. Located at 42.11° N. Lat.; 76.02° W. Long. Elevation is 1,000 feet.
History: Also called Hooper.
Population: 12,602 (1990); 11,706 (2000); 11,739 (2005); 11,766 (2010 projected); Race: 94.9% White, 1.6% Black, 1.8% Asian, 1.7% Hispanic of any race (2005); Density: 3,188.4 persons per square mile (2005); Average household size: 2.21 (2005); Median age: 44.1 (2005); Males per 100 females: 91.1 (2005); Marriage status: 20.2% never married, 61.8% now married, 8.0% widowed, 10.0% divorced (2000); Foreign born: 4.4% (2000); Ancestry (includes multiple ancestries): 20.1% Italian, 18.9% Irish, 15.2% German, 13.3% English, 8.4% Polish (2000).
Economy: Manufacturing of electronic parts and components. Employment by occupation: 16.7% management, 25.1% professional, 10.8% services, 31.9% sales, 0.0% farming, 5.2% construction, 10.4% production (2000).
Income: Per capita income: $26,249 (2005); Median household income: $44,775 (2005); Average household income: $57,923 (2005); Percent of households with income of $100,000 or more: 13.0% (2005); Poverty rate: 5.0% (2000).
Education: Percent of population age 25 and over with: High school diploma (including GED) or higher: 91.3% (2005); Bachelor's degree or higher: 31.9% (2005); Master's degree or higher: 13.4% (2005).
School District(s)
Maine-Endwell Central School District (KG-12)
    2003-04 Enrollment: 2,675 . . . . (607) 754-1400
Housing: Homeownership rate: 73.1% (2005); Median home value: $110,121 (2005); Median rent: $384 per month (2000); Median age of housing: 43 years (2000).
Transportation: Commute to work: 94.5% car, 1.0% public transportation, 2.6% walk, 1.7% work from home (2000); Travel time to work: 44.3% less than 15 minutes, 46.5% 15 to 30 minutes, 4.1% 30 to 45 minutes, 1.0% 45 to 60 minutes, 4.1% 60 minutes or more (2000).

FENTON (town).
Covers a land area of 32.887 square miles and a water area of 0.486 square miles. Located at 42.18° N. Lat.; 75.82° W. Long.
Population: 7,236 (1990); 6,909 (2000); 6,909 (2005); 6,910 (2010 projected); Race: 96.9% White, 1.2% Black, 0.3% Asian, 1.1% Hispanic of any race (2005); Density: 210.1 persons per square mile (2005); Average household size: 2.45 (2005); Median age: 42.8 (2005); Males per 100 females: 96.6 (2005); Marriage status: 20.7% never married, 62.5% now married, 6.6% widowed, 10.2% divorced (2000); Foreign born: 1.5% (2000); Ancestry (includes multiple ancestries): 17.8% English, 17.6% German, 16.6% Irish, 9.4% Italian, 7.9% Other groups (2000).
Economy: Single-family building permits issued: 8 (2005); Multi-family building permits issued: 0 (2005); Employment by occupation: 12.9% management, 19.6% professional, 17.3% services, 26.7% sales, 0.2% farming, 8.0% construction, 15.4% production (2000).
Income: Per capita income: $22,895 (2005); Median household income: $44,594 (2005); Average household income: $55,977 (2005); Percent of households with income of $100,000 or more: 12.4% (2005); Poverty rate: 6.8% (2000).
Education: Percent of population age 25 and over with: High school diploma (including GED) or higher: 86.1% (2005); Bachelor's degree or higher: 16.7% (2005); Master's degree or higher: 7.0% (2005).
Housing: Homeownership rate: 87.1% (2005); Median home value: $89,044 (2005); Median rent: $348 per month (2000); Median age of housing: 38 years (2000).
Transportation: Commute to work: 96.2% car, 0.8% public transportation, 0.5% walk, 2.4% work from home (2000); Travel time to work: 24.6% less than 15 minutes, 58.5% 15 to 30 minutes, 11.6% 30 to 45 minutes, 2.4% 45 to 60 minutes, 2.8% 60 minutes or more (2000).

GLEN AUBREY (unincorporated postal area, zip code 13777).
Covers a land area of 10.189 square miles and a water area of 0.006 square miles. Located at 42.25° N. Lat.; 76.01° W. Long.
Population: 0 (2000); Race: 97.8% White, 0.6% Black, 0.0% Asian, 0.0% Hispanic of any race (2000); Density: 0.0 persons per square mile (2000); Age: 30.9% under 18, 8.5% over 64 (2000); Marriage status: 19.8% never married, 67.1% now married, 5.4% widowed, 7.6% divorced (2000); Foreign born: 0.5% (2000); Ancestry (includes multiple ancestries): 17.7% United States or American, 15.6% German, 13.3% English, 11.8% Irish, 7.0% Other groups (2000).
Economy: Employment by occupation: 11.3% management, 13.0% professional, 18.6% services, 20.7% sales, 0.0% farming, 14.7% construction, 21.6% production (2000).
Income: Per capita income: $16,120 (2000); Median household income: $36,713 (2000); Poverty rate: 8.5% (2000).
Education: Percent of population age 25 and over with: High school diploma (including GED) or higher: 82.6% (2000); Bachelor's degree or higher: 9.6% (2000).
Housing: Homeownership rate: 90.9% (2000); Median home value: $73,000 (2000); Median rent: $331 per month (2000); Median age of housing: 17 years (2000).
Transportation: Commute to work: 93.5% car, 0.4% public transportation, 0.9% walk, 4.4% work from home (2000); Travel time to work: 8.0% less than 15 minutes, 44.2% 15 to 30 minutes, 38.5% 30 to 45 minutes, 1.8% 45 to 60 minutes, 7.5% 60 minutes or more (2000).

HARPURSVILLE (unincorporated postal area, zip code 13787).
Covers a land area of 59.355 square miles and a water area of 0.068 square miles. Located at 42.19° N. Lat.; 75.65° W. Long.
Population: 0 (2000); Race: 97.9% White, 1.0% Black, 0.1% Asian, 0.2% Hispanic of any race (2000); Density: 0.0 persons per square mile (2000); Age: 29.4% under 18, 10.9% over 64 (2000); Marriage status: 21.4% never married, 60.7% now married, 5.0% widowed, 12.9% divorced (2000); Foreign born: 2.2% (2000); Ancestry (includes multiple ancestries): 18.1% German, 17.5% Irish, 14.9% English, 10.1% United States or American, 7.9% Other groups (2000).
Economy: Employment by occupation: 9.5% management, 12.2% professional, 13.8% services, 26.0% sales, 1.5% farming, 13.9% construction, 23.0% production (2000).
Income: Per capita income: $16,430 (2000); Median household income: $39,056 (2000); Poverty rate: 7.3% (2000).
Education: Percent of population age 25 and over with: High school diploma (including GED) or higher: 73.8% (2000); Bachelor's degree or higher: 7.7% (2000).
School District(s)
Harpursville Central School District (PK-12)
    2003-04 Enrollment: 1,095 . . . . (607) 693-8101
Housing: Homeownership rate: 87.9% (2000); Median home value: $62,500 (2000); Median rent: $336 per month (2000); Median age of housing: 29 years (2000).
Transportation: Commute to work: 94.7% car, 0.5% public transportation, 0.9% walk, 3.3% work from home (2000); Travel time to work: 12.2% less than 15 minutes, 34.7% 15 to 30 minutes, 40.3% 30 to 45 minutes, 5.1% 45 to 60 minutes, 7.6% 60 minutes or more (2000).

JOHNSON CITY (village).
Covers a land area of 4.442 square miles and a water area of 0.135 square miles. Located at 42.11° N. Lat.; 75.95° W. Long. Elevation is 840 feet.
History: Originally called Lestershire, the area remained rural until a shoe company built a factory here in 1890. The name was changed in 1916. Incorporated 1892.
Population: 16,890 (1990); 15,535 (2000); 15,148 (2005); 14,749 (2010 projected); Race: 86.2% White, 4.1% Black, 6.1% Asian, 2.9% Hispanic of any race (2005); Density: 3,409.9 persons per square mile (2005); Average household size: 2.19 (2005); Median age: 40.3 (2005); Males per 100 females: 86.7 (2005); Marriage status: 31.0% never married, 47.4% now married, 12.3% widowed, 9.3% divorced (2000); Foreign born: 7.0% (2000); Ancestry (includes multiple ancestries): 17.2% Irish, 14.5% English, 14.3% German, 14.3% Other groups, 9.1% Italian (2000).
Economy: Noted for its Endicott-Johnson shoes. Manufacturing also includes computer equipment, electrical equipment, fabricated metal products, and photographic equipment. Single-family building permits issued: 4 (2005); Multi-family building permits issued: 0 (2005); Employment by occupation: 11.0% management, 21.5% professional,

18.9% services, 26.2% sales, 0.0% farming, 7.2% construction, 15.2% production (2000).
Income: Per capita income: $19,524 (2005); Median household income: $30,447 (2005); Average household income: $41,122 (2005); Percent of households with income of $100,000 or more: 6.9% (2005); Poverty rate: 16.0% (2000).
Education: Percent of population age 25 and over with: High school diploma (including GED) or higher: 81.7% (2005); Bachelor's degree or higher: 20.4% (2005); Master's degree or higher: 8.7% (2005).

School District(s)
Johnson City Central School District (KG-12)
    2003-04 Enrollment: 2,597 . . . . (607) 763-1230

Four-year College(s)
Davis College
    Fall 2004 Enrollment: 294 . . . . (607) 729-1581
    2005-06 Tuition: In-state $8,380; Out-of-state $8,380

Housing: Homeownership rate: 51.7% (2005); Median home value: $79,810 (2005); Median rent: $406 per month (2000); Median age of housing: 56 years (2000).
Hospitals: United Health Services Hospitals (516 beds)
Transportation: Commute to work: 84.0% car, 5.6% public transportation, 6.2% walk, 3.5% work from home (2000); Travel time to work: 52.7% less than 15 minutes, 37.5% 15 to 30 minutes, 5.6% 30 to 45 minutes, 1.7% 45 to 60 minutes, 2.4% 60 minutes or more (2000)
Additional Information Contacts
Village of Johnson City . . . . (607) 798-7861
    http://www.johnsoncityny.org/

KIRKWOOD (town). Covers a land area of 30.963 square miles and a water area of 0.427 square miles. Located at 42.08° N. Lat.; 75.81° W. Long.
Population: 6,096 (1990); 5,651 (2000); 5,670 (2005); 5,691 (2010 projected); Race: 97.5% White, 0.7% Black, 0.4% Asian, 0.8% Hispanic of any race (2005); Density: 183.1 persons per square mile (2005); Average household size: 2.47 (2005); Median age: 40.8 (2005); Males per 100 females: 99.4 (2005); Marriage status: 19.7% never married, 63.8% now married, 7.9% widowed, 8.5% divorced (2000); Foreign born: 1.4% (2000); Ancestry (includes multiple ancestries): 23.0% Irish, 17.4% English, 17.3% German, 11.7% Italian, 6.7% United States or American (2000).
Economy: Single-family building permits issued: 5 (2005); Multi-family building permits issued: 0 (2005); Employment by occupation: 11.6% management, 18.2% professional, 15.6% services, 25.7% sales, 0.9% farming, 9.2% construction, 18.8% production (2000).
Income: Per capita income: $22,139 (2005); Median household income: $44,326 (2005); Average household income: $54,577 (2005); Percent of households with income of $100,000 or more: 10.2% (2005); Poverty rate: 5.9% (2000).
Taxes: Total city taxes per capita: $146 (2004); City property taxes per capita: $116 (2004).
Education: Percent of population age 25 and over with: High school diploma (including GED) or higher: 84.5% (2005); Bachelor's degree or higher: 11.6% (2005); Master's degree or higher: 3.2% (2005).

School District(s)
Susquehanna Valley Central School District (KG-12)
    2003-04 Enrollment: 2,135 . . . . (607) 775-9100
Windsor Central School District (KG-12)
    2003-04 Enrollment: 2,045 . . . . (607) 655-8216

Housing: Homeownership rate: 76.4% (2005); Median home value: $93,504 (2005); Median rent: $422 per month (2000); Median age of housing: 36 years (2000).
Transportation: Commute to work: 93.8% car, 1.0% public transportation, 2.3% walk, 2.5% work from home (2000); Travel time to work: 37.2% less than 15 minutes, 45.3% 15 to 30 minutes, 9.6% 30 to 45 minutes, 2.3% 45 to 60 minutes, 5.5% 60 minutes or more (2000)

LISLE (village). Covers a land area of 0.928 square miles and a water area of 0 square miles. Located at 42.35° N. Lat.; 76.00° W. Long. Elevation is 975 feet.
Population: 361 (1990); 302 (2000); 307 (2005); 311 (2010 projected); Race: 97.4% White, 1.0% Black, 0.0% Asian, 1.6% Hispanic of any race (2005); Density: 330.9 persons per square mile (2005); Average household size: 2.56 (2005); Median age: 37.6 (2005); Males per 100 females: 93.1 (2005); Marriage status: 27.1% never married, 52.8% now married, 13.8% widowed, 6.4% divorced (2000); Foreign born: 1.3% (2000); Ancestry (includes multiple ancestries): 29.2% English, 19.9% Irish, 13.3% German, 8.0% Polish, 6.6% Slovak (2000).
Economy: Single-family building permits issued: 0 (2005); Multi-family building permits issued: 0 (2005); Employment by occupation: 9.5% management, 10.2% professional, 19.0% services, 29.9% sales, 0.0% farming, 10.2% construction, 21.2% production (2000).
Income: Per capita income: $18,974 (2005); Median household income: $42,105 (2005); Average household income: $48,542 (2005); Percent of households with income of $100,000 or more: 5.8% (2005); Poverty rate: 12.6% (2000).
Education: Percent of population age 25 and over with: High school diploma (including GED) or higher: 91.3% (2005); Bachelor's degree or higher: 11.1% (2005); Master's degree or higher: 4.8% (2005).
Housing: Homeownership rate: 74.2% (2005); Median home value: $86,552 (2005); Median rent: $327 per month (2000); Median age of housing: 60+ years (2000).
Transportation: Commute to work: 90.5% car, 0.0% public transportation, 5.1% walk, 4.4% work from home (2000); Travel time to work: 26.7% less than 15 minutes, 16.8% 15 to 30 minutes, 40.5% 30 to 45 minutes, 13.0% 45 to 60 minutes, 3.1% 60 minutes or more (2000)

LISLE (town). Covers a land area of 46.930 square miles and a water area of 0.055 square miles. Located at 42.36° N. Lat.; 76.04° W. Long. Elevation is 975 feet.
Population: 2,486 (1990); 2,707 (2000); 2,755 (2005); 2,799 (2010 projected); Race: 98.1% White, 0.7% Black, 0.0% Asian, 0.5% Hispanic of any race (2005); Density: 58.7 persons per square mile (2005); Average household size: 2.74 (2005); Median age: 36.0 (2005); Males per 100 females: 101.4 (2005); Marriage status: 23.8% never married, 61.4% now married, 6.8% widowed, 8.0% divorced (2000); Foreign born: 1.8% (2000); Ancestry (includes multiple ancestries): 18.1% Irish, 16.6% English, 16.3% German, 12.2% United States or American, 9.2% Other groups (2000).
Economy: In dairying area. Single-family building permits issued: 7 (2005); Multi-family building permits issued: 0 (2005); Employment by occupation: 8.8% management, 14.7% professional, 13.0% services, 25.4% sales, 3.1% farming, 11.9% construction, 23.1% production (2000).
Income: Per capita income: $16,779 (2005); Median household income: $39,319 (2005); Average household income: $45,998 (2005); Percent of households with income of $100,000 or more: 5.2% (2005); Poverty rate: 15.0% (2000).
Education: Percent of population age 25 and over with: High school diploma (including GED) or higher: 78.7% (2005); Bachelor's degree or higher: 11.0% (2005); Master's degree or higher: 4.6% (2005).
Housing: Homeownership rate: 82.8% (2005); Median home value: $79,145 (2005); Median rent: $327 per month (2000); Median age of housing: 31 years (2000).
Transportation: Commute to work: 91.6% car, 0.0% public transportation, 3.8% walk, 4.1% work from home (2000); Travel time to work: 30.8% less than 15 minutes, 20.2% 15 to 30 minutes, 32.3% 30 to 45 minutes, 11.9% 45 to 60 minutes, 4.8% 60 minutes or more (2000)

MAINE (town). Covers a land area of 45.738 square miles and a water area of 0.028 square miles. Located at 42.20° N. Lat.; 76.02° W. Long. Elevation is 919 feet.
Population: 5,606 (1990); 5,459 (2000); 5,487 (2005); 5,514 (2010 projected); Race: 97.5% White, 0.6% Black, 0.6% Asian, 0.7% Hispanic of any race (2005); Density: 120.0 persons per square mile (2005); Average household size: 2.63 (2005); Median age: 40.5 (2005); Males per 100 females: 100.6 (2005); Marriage status: 21.4% never married, 63.3% now married, 7.2% widowed, 8.1% divorced (2000); Foreign born: 1.5% (2000); Ancestry (includes multiple ancestries): 19.0% English, 18.0% Irish, 16.6% German, 10.7% Italian, 8.6% Polish (2000).
Economy: Single-family building permits issued: 10 (2005); Multi-family building permits issued: 0 (2005); Employment by occupation: 7.3% management, 21.5% professional, 20.4% services, 25.9% sales, 0.3% farming, 11.2% construction, 13.5% production (2000).
Income: Per capita income: $20,629 (2005); Median household income: $44,514 (2005); Average household income: $54,151 (2005); Percent of households with income of $100,000 or more: 9.8% (2005); Poverty rate: 5.9% (2000).
Education: Percent of population age 25 and over with: High school diploma (including GED) or higher: 82.4% (2005); Bachelor's degree or higher: 18.3% (2005); Master's degree or higher: 5.9% (2005).

School District(s)
Maine-Endwell Central School District (KG-12)
   2003-04 Enrollment: 2,675 . . . . (607) 754-1400
Housing: Homeownership rate: 87.4% (2005); Median home value: $94,184 (2005); Median rent: $442 per month (2000); Median age of housing: 35 years (2000).
Transportation: Commute to work: 97.5% car, 0.0% public transportation, 0.2% walk, 2.0% work from home (2000); Travel time to work: 24.1% less than 15 minutes, 60.6% 15 to 30 minutes, 10.6% 30 to 45 minutes, 1.0% 45 to 60 minutes, 3.7% 60 minutes or more (2000)

NANTICOKE (town). Covers a land area of 24.313 square miles and a water area of 0.035 square miles. Located at 42.28° N. Lat.; 76.02° W. Long. Elevation is 1,101 feet.
Population: 1,846 (1990); 1,790 (2000); 1,819 (2005); 1,846 (2010 projected); Race: 97.4% White, 0.3% Black, 0.4% Asian, 1.0% Hispanic of any race (2005); Density: 74.8 persons per square mile (2005); Average household size: 2.79 (2005); Median age: 36.0 (2005); Males per 100 females: 98.4 (2005); Marriage status: 22.6% never married, 63.6% now married, 4.9% widowed, 8.8% divorced (2000); Foreign born: 1.1% (2000); Ancestry (includes multiple ancestries): 18.7% German, 15.8% English, 14.8% Irish, 12.0% United States or American, 6.6% Other groups (2000).
Economy: Single-family building permits issued: 3 (2005); Multi-family building permits issued: 0 (2005); Employment by occupation: 9.0% management, 16.9% professional, 15.1% services, 22.3% sales, 0.0% farming, 12.6% construction, 24.0% production (2000).
Income: Per capita income: $17,391 (2005); Median household income: $40,977 (2005); Average household income: $48,520 (2005); Percent of households with income of $100,000 or more: 6.4% (2005); Poverty rate: 11.2% (2000).
Education: Percent of population age 25 and over with: High school diploma (including GED) or higher: 81.0% (2005); Bachelor's degree or higher: 8.6% (2005); Master's degree or higher: 3.9% (2005).
Housing: Homeownership rate: 89.3% (2005); Median home value: $75,000 (2005); Median rent: $375 per month (2000); Median age of housing: 23 years (2000).
Transportation: Commute to work: 94.7% car, 0.5% public transportation, 2.0% walk, 2.3% work from home (2000); Travel time to work: 10.9% less than 15 minutes, 45.1% 15 to 30 minutes, 34.7% 30 to 45 minutes, 2.9% 45 to 60 minutes, 6.4% 60 minutes or more (2000)

NINEVEH (unincorporated postal area, zip code 13813). Covers a land area of 35.441 square miles and a water area of 0.108 square miles. Located at 42.16° N. Lat.; 75.55° W. Long.
Population: 0 (2000); Race: 98.5% White, 1.5% Black, 0.0% Asian, 0.3% Hispanic of any race (2000); Density: 0.0 persons per square mile (2000); Age: 29.5% under 18, 12.5% over 64 (2000); Marriage status: 24.6% never married, 56.3% now married, 6.3% widowed, 12.8% divorced (2000); Foreign born: 1.7% (2000); Ancestry (includes multiple ancestries): 24.9% German, 24.3% English, 18.6% Irish, 15.8% Dutch, 7.7% Italian (2000).
Economy: Employment by occupation: 11.4% management, 15.1% professional, 16.2% services, 17.3% sales, 4.2% farming, 20.4% construction, 15.4% production (2000).
Income: Per capita income: $14,713 (2000); Median household income: $32,336 (2000); Poverty rate: 15.8% (2000).
Education: Percent of population age 25 and over with: High school diploma (including GED) or higher: 77.2% (2000); Bachelor's degree or higher: 11.3% (2000).
Housing: Homeownership rate: 85.6% (2000); Median home value: $68,100 (2000); Median rent: $401 per month (2000); Median age of housing: 31 years (2000).
Transportation: Commute to work: 91.1% car, 2.1% public transportation, 2.1% walk, 4.8% work from home (2000); Travel time to work: 27.8% less than 15 minutes, 31.3% 15 to 30 minutes, 24.4% 30 to 45 minutes, 9.1% 45 to 60 minutes, 7.4% 60 minutes or more (2000)

PORT CRANE (unincorporated postal area, zip code 13833). Covers a land area of 36.001 square miles and a water area of 0.052 square miles. Located at 42.18° N. Lat.; 75.77° W. Long.
Population: 0 (2000); Race: 97.7% White, 0.4% Black, 0.0% Asian, 1.3% Hispanic of any race (2000); Density: 0.0 persons per square mile (2000); Age: 28.2% under 18, 10.4% over 64 (2000); Marriage status: 23.4% never married, 61.1% now married, 4.1% widowed, 11.4% divorced (2000); Foreign born: 1.1% (2000); Ancestry (includes multiple ancestries): 17.4% English, 17.0% German, 12.5% Irish, 9.4% Other groups, 8.4% United States or American (2000).
Economy: Employment by occupation: 9.8% management, 15.0% professional, 20.3% services, 26.3% sales, 0.2% farming, 11.0% construction, 17.3% production (2000).
Income: Per capita income: $16,875 (2000); Median household income: $38,097 (2000); Poverty rate: 11.1% (2000).
Education: Percent of population age 25 and over with: High school diploma (including GED) or higher: 81.3% (2000); Bachelor's degree or higher: 11.4% (2000).
Housing: Homeownership rate: 85.4% (2000); Median home value: $78,400 (2000); Median rent: $381 per month (2000); Median age of housing: 29 years (2000).
Transportation: Commute to work: 97.3% car, 0.2% public transportation, 0.4% walk, 2.0% work from home (2000); Travel time to work: 19.4% less than 15 minutes, 61.2% 15 to 30 minutes, 15.9% 30 to 45 minutes, 2.6% 45 to 60 minutes, 0.9% 60 minutes or more (2000)

PORT DICKINSON (village). Covers a land area of 0.632 square miles and a water area of 0.052 square miles. Located at 42.13° N. Lat.; 75.89° W. Long.
Population: 1,785 (1990); 1,697 (2000); 1,753 (2005); 1,758 (2010 projected); Race: 95.8% White, 1.5% Black, 0.5% Asian, 0.7% Hispanic of any race (2005); Density: 2,775.6 persons per square mile (2005); Average household size: 2.26 (2005); Median age: 38.1 (2005); Males per 100 females: 87.5 (2005); Marriage status: 28.0% never married, 50.6% now married, 8.9% widowed, 12.6% divorced (2000); Foreign born: 1.8% (2000); Ancestry (includes multiple ancestries): 27.8% Irish, 17.6% German, 15.7% Italian, 14.5% English, 7.3% Other groups (2000).
Economy: Single-family building permits issued: 0 (2005); Multi-family building permits issued: 0 (2005); Employment by occupation: 11.5% management, 25.0% professional, 17.8% services, 30.6% sales, 0.0% farming, 5.7% construction, 9.4% production (2000).
Income: Per capita income: $22,233 (2005); Median household income: $41,189 (2005); Average household income: $50,290 (2005); Percent of households with income of $100,000 or more: 7.2% (2005); Poverty rate: 5.7% (2000).
Education: Percent of population age 25 and over with: High school diploma (including GED) or higher: 91.4% (2005); Bachelor's degree or higher: 24.6% (2005); Master's degree or higher: 9.9% (2005).
Housing: Homeownership rate: 57.8% (2005); Median home value: $92,701 (2005); Median rent: $419 per month (2000); Median age of housing: 60+ years (2000).
Safety: Violent crime rate: 18.1 per 10,000 population; Property crime rate: 234.8 per 10,000 population (2004).
Transportation: Commute to work: 95.3% car, 2.7% public transportation, 0.2% walk, 1.8% work from home (2000); Travel time to work: 47.4% less than 15 minutes, 42.1% 15 to 30 minutes, 5.6% 30 to 45 minutes, 0.9% 45 to 60 minutes, 4.1% 60 minutes or more (2000)

SANFORD (town). Covers a land area of 90.075 square miles and a water area of 0.928 square miles. Located at 42.08° N. Lat.; 75.48° W. Long.
Population: 2,576 (1990); 2,477 (2000); 2,470 (2005); 2,464 (2010 projected); Race: 97.7% White, 0.6% Black, 0.3% Asian, 3.0% Hispanic of any race (2005); Density: 27.4 persons per square mile (2005); Average household size: 2.47 (2005); Median age: 41.2 (2005); Males per 100 females: 100.6 (2005); Marriage status: 21.1% never married, 61.6% now married, 9.3% widowed, 7.9% divorced (2000); Foreign born: 2.2% (2000); Ancestry (includes multiple ancestries): 21.2% German, 16.6% English, 15.7% Irish, 12.6% Italian, 12.0% United States or American (2000).
Economy: Single-family building permits issued: 15 (2005); Multi-family building permits issued: 0 (2005); Employment by occupation: 10.9% management, 11.9% professional, 14.4% services, 20.3% sales, 3.8% farming, 10.8% construction, 27.9% production (2000).
Income: Per capita income: $20,864 (2005); Median household income: $39,422 (2005); Average household income: $51,535 (2005); Percent of households with income of $100,000 or more: 10.7% (2005); Poverty rate: 15.6% (2000).
Education: Percent of population age 25 and over with: High school diploma (including GED) or higher: 80.0% (2005); Bachelor's degree or higher: 12.6% (2005); Master's degree or higher: 5.4% (2005).
Housing: Homeownership rate: 80.4% (2005); Median home value: $91,489 (2005); Median rent: $372 per month (2000); Median age of housing: 45 years (2000).
Transportation: Commute to work: 89.1% car, 1.2% public transportation, 4.3% walk, 5.1% work from home (2000); Travel time to work: 42.4% less

than 15 minutes, 17.5% 15 to 30 minutes, 24.5% 30 to 45 minutes, 9.5% 45 to 60 minutes, 6.1% 60 minutes or more (2000)

TRIANGLE (town). Covers a land area of 38.087 square miles and a water area of 1.690 square miles. Located at 42.34° N. Lat.; 75.93° W. Long.
Population: 3,006 (1990); 3,032 (2000); 3,093 (2005); 3,148 (2010 projected); Race: 97.3% White, 0.3% Black, 0.4% Asian, 1.3% Hispanic of any race (2005); Density: 81.2 persons per square mile (2005); Average household size: 2.63 (2005); Median age: 37.5 (2005); Males per 100 females: 97.6 (2005); Marriage status: 25.2% never married, 59.1% now married, 5.9% widowed, 9.8% divorced (2000); Foreign born: 0.6% (2000); Ancestry (includes multiple ancestries): 17.9% German, 17.6% English, 16.2% Irish, 9.9% United States or American, 7.2% Polish (2000).
Economy: Single-family building permits issued: 5 (2005); Multi-family building permits issued: 0 (2005); Employment by occupation: 9.2% management, 18.3% professional, 13.9% services, 26.4% sales, 0.6% farming, 8.7% construction, 22.8% production (2000).
Income: Per capita income: $18,716 (2005); Median household income: $40,719 (2005); Average household income: $49,021 (2005); Percent of households with income of $100,000 or more: 7.3% (2005); Poverty rate: 11.4% (2000).
Education: Percent of population age 25 and over with: High school diploma (including GED) or higher: 81.9% (2005); Bachelor's degree or higher: 15.2% (2005); Master's degree or higher: 6.0% (2005).
Housing: Homeownership rate: 78.2% (2005); Median home value: $79,769 (2005); Median rent: $359 per month (2000); Median age of housing: 33 years (2000).
Transportation: Commute to work: 94.4% car, 0.0% public transportation, 2.4% walk, 2.7% work from home (2000); Travel time to work: 27.4% less than 15 minutes, 24.6% 15 to 30 minutes, 33.6% 30 to 45 minutes, 8.3% 45 to 60 minutes, 6.1% 60 minutes or more (2000)

UNION (town). Covers a land area of 35.168 square miles and a water area of 0.666 square miles. Located at 42.11° N. Lat.; 76.02° W. Long.
Population: 59,786 (1990); 56,298 (2000); 55,318 (2005); 54,270 (2010 projected); Race: 91.2% White, 3.2% Black, 3.2% Asian, 1.9% Hispanic of any race (2005); Density: 1,572.9 persons per square mile (2005); Average household size: 2.26 (2005); Median age: 40.7 (2005); Males per 100 females: 90.9 (2005); Marriage status: 26.6% never married, 53.9% now married, 9.5% widowed, 10.1% divorced (2000); Foreign born: 4.8% (2000); Ancestry (includes multiple ancestries): 19.1% Irish, 17.2% Italian, 15.0% German, 14.5% English, 9.5% Other groups (2000).
Economy: Unemployment rate: 4.6% (2005); Total civilian labor force: 28,209 (2005); Single-family building permits issued: 38 (2005); Multi-family building permits issued: 14 (2005); Employment by occupation: 12.2% management, 23.1% professional, 14.8% services, 28.9% sales, 0.1% farming, 6.4% construction, 14.4% production (2000).
Income: Per capita income: $22,169 (2005); Median household income: $37,214 (2005); Average household income: $49,261 (2005); Percent of households with income of $100,000 or more: 9.8% (2005); Poverty rate: 11.3% (2000).
Taxes: Total city taxes per capita: $133 (2004); City property taxes per capita: $117 (2004).
Education: Percent of population age 25 and over with: High school diploma (including GED) or higher: 84.9% (2005); Bachelor's degree or higher: 23.9% (2005); Master's degree or higher: 10.0% (2005).
Housing: Homeownership rate: 60.5% (2005); Median home value: $95,159 (2005); Median rent: $408 per month (2000); Median age of housing: 48 years (2000).
Transportation: Commute to work: 89.9% car, 2.4% public transportation, 4.4% walk, 2.6% work from home (2000); Travel time to work: 45.8% less than 15 minutes, 43.5% 15 to 30 minutes, 6.3% 30 to 45 minutes, 1.5% 45 to 60 minutes, 3.0% 60 minutes or more (2000)
Additional Information Contacts
Town of Union . . . . (607) 786-2900
http://www.townofunion.com/

VESTAL (town). Covers a land area of 52.180 square miles and a water area of 0.496 square miles. Located at 42.07° N. Lat.; 76.02° W. Long. Elevation is 829 feet.
Population: 26,733 (1990); 26,535 (2000); 26,947 (2005); 27,357 (2010 projected); Race: 84.3% White, 2.6% Black, 10.4% Asian, 3.0% Hispanic of any race (2005); Density: 516.4 persons per square mile (2005); Average household size: 3.06 (2005); Median age: 34.5 (2005); Males per 100 females: 90.4 (2005); Marriage status: 36.4% never married, 51.4% now married, 6.6% widowed, 5.5% divorced (2000); Foreign born: 9.7% (2000); Ancestry (includes multiple ancestries): 18.3% Irish, 17.8% German, 13.8% English, 13.7% Other groups, 12.9% Italian (2000).
Economy: Prominent retailing here and East to Johnson City-Binghamton area. Unemployment rate: 4.4% (2005); Total civilian labor force: 12,382 (2005); Single-family building permits issued: 30 (2005); Multi-family building permits issued: 0 (2005); Employment by occupation: 16.0% management, 31.6% professional, 13.7% services, 25.8% sales, 0.1% farming, 4.1% construction, 8.8% production (2000).
Income: Per capita income: $25,218 (2005); Median household income: $56,547 (2005); Average household income: $74,580 (2005); Percent of households with income of $100,000 or more: 21.8% (2005); Poverty rate: 7.1% (2000).
Taxes: Total city taxes per capita: $261 (2004); City property taxes per capita: $229 (2004).
Education: Percent of population age 25 and over with: High school diploma (including GED) or higher: 92.6% (2005); Bachelor's degree or higher: 39.1% (2005); Master's degree or higher: 19.3% (2005).

School District(s)
Vestal Central School District (KG-12)
    2003-04 Enrollment: 4,266 . . . . (607) 757-2241
Housing: Homeownership rate: 78.8% (2005); Median home value: $119,497 (2005); Median rent: $487 per month (2000); Median age of housing: 38 years (2000).
Safety: Violent crime rate: 3.3 per 10,000 population; Property crime rate: 195.8 per 10,000 population (2004).
Newspapers: Press & Sun-Bulletin (Circulation 56,244); The Jewish Observer of Central New York (Jewish - Circulation 5,000); The New Jewish Voice (Jewish - Circulation 4,200); The Reporter (Religious - Circulation 3,000)
Transportation: Commute to work: 85.4% car, 1.1% public transportation, 9.8% walk, 3.3% work from home (2000); Travel time to work: 45.7% less than 15 minutes, 44.4% 15 to 30 minutes, 6.0% 30 to 45 minutes, 1.0% 45 to 60 minutes, 3.0% 60 minutes or more (2000)
Additional Information Contacts
Town of Vestal . . . . (607) 748-1514
http://www.vestalny.com/content/

WHITNEY POINT (village). Covers a land area of 0.999 square miles and a water area of 0.088 square miles. Located at 42.33° N. Lat.; 75.97° W. Long. Elevation is 998 feet.
Population: 1,007 (1990); 965 (2000); 1,003 (2005); 1,034 (2010 projected); Race: 96.1% White, 0.2% Black, 0.3% Asian, 2.4% Hispanic of any race (2005); Density: 1,004.3 persons per square mile (2005); Average household size: 2.38 (2005); Median age: 38.3 (2005); Males per 100 females: 88.9 (2005); Marriage status: 28.2% never married, 53.7% now married, 7.9% widowed, 10.1% divorced (2000); Foreign born: 0.8% (2000); Ancestry (includes multiple ancestries): 25.6% English, 24.6% German, 18.7% Irish, 7.7% Other groups, 7.2% Italian (2000).
Economy: In farming and dairying area. Whitney Point flood-control reservoir for Binghamton located here. Single-family building permits issued: 1 (2005); Multi-family building permits issued: 0 (2005); Employment by occupation: 6.3% management, 24.8% professional, 16.2% services, 24.8% sales, 0.0% farming, 8.9% construction, 19.0% production (2000).
Income: Per capita income: $20,738 (2005); Median household income: $39,966 (2005); Average household income: $49,406 (2005); Percent of households with income of $100,000 or more: 6.9% (2005); Poverty rate: 13.2% (2000).
Education: Percent of population age 25 and over with: High school diploma (including GED) or higher: 83.6% (2005); Bachelor's degree or higher: 19.6% (2005); Master's degree or higher: 8.8% (2005).

School District(s)
Whitney Point Central School District (PK-12)
    2003-04 Enrollment: 1,858 . . . . (607) 692-8202
Housing: Homeownership rate: 68.4% (2005); Median home value: $73,077 (2005); Median rent: $376 per month (2000); Median age of housing: 58 years (2000).
Transportation: Commute to work: 87.6% car, 0.0% public transportation, 6.1% walk, 5.9% work from home (2000); Travel time to work: 30.2% less than 15 minutes, 23.3% 15 to 30 minutes, 30.9% 30 to 45 minutes, 10.1% 45 to 60 minutes, 5.5% 60 minutes or more (2000)

WINDSOR (village). Covers a land area of 1.081 square miles and a water area of 0.077 square miles. Located at 42.07° N. Lat.; 75.63° W. Long.
Population: 1,051 (1990); 901 (2000); 922 (2005); 940 (2010 projected); Race: 94.7% White, 1.8% Black, 0.4% Asian, 0.7% Hispanic of any race (2005); Density: 853.0 persons per square mile (2005); Average household size: 2.39 (2005); Median age: 39.3 (2005); Males per 100 females: 90.9 (2005); Marriage status: 25.9% never married, 58.6% now married, 8.0% widowed, 7.5% divorced (2000); Foreign born: 1.2% (2000); Ancestry (includes multiple ancestries): 22.1% English, 20.0% Irish, 19.5% German, 9.4% Italian, 8.9% Other groups (2000).
Economy: Employment by occupation: 8.2% management, 24.2% professional, 10.0% services, 30.8% sales, 1.4% farming, 7.0% construction, 18.4% production (2000).
Income: Per capita income: $20,908 (2005); Median household income: $41,250 (2005); Average household income: $49,942 (2005); Percent of households with income of $100,000 or more: 8.8% (2005); Poverty rate: 10.0% (2000).
Education: Percent of population age 25 and over with: High school diploma (including GED) or higher: 90.5% (2005); Bachelor's degree or higher: 17.3% (2005); Master's degree or higher: 8.5% (2005).

School District(s)
Windsor Central School District (KG-12)
   2003-04 Enrollment: 2,045 . . . . (607) 655-8216

Housing: Homeownership rate: 63.5% (2005); Median home value: $93,452 (2005); Median rent: $358 per month (2000); Median age of housing: 59 years (2000).
Transportation: Commute to work: 94.6% car, 0.7% public transportation, 1.9% walk, 2.3% work from home (2000); Travel time to work: 27.3% less than 15 minutes, 38.1% 15 to 30 minutes, 29.0% 30 to 45 minutes, 1.9% 45 to 60 minutes, 3.6% 60 minutes or more (2000)

WINDSOR (town). Covers a land area of 91.495 square miles and a water area of 1.262 square miles. Located at 42.07° N. Lat.; 75.66° W. Long.
Population: 6,440 (1990); 6,421 (2000); 6,424 (2005); 6,430 (2010 projected); Race: 97.5% White, 0.8% Black, 0.2% Asian, 1.0% Hispanic of any race (2005); Density: 70.2 persons per square mile (2005); Average household size: 2.69 (2005); Median age: 38.5 (2005); Males per 100 females: 99.1 (2005); Marriage status: 21.2% never married, 64.3% now married, 6.3% widowed, 8.2% divorced (2000); Foreign born: 0.3% (2000); Ancestry (includes multiple ancestries): 20.3% German, 19.5% Irish, 17.5% English, 7.8% Other groups, 6.4% Italian (2000).
Economy: In dairying area; summer resort. Single-family building permits issued: 17 (2005); Multi-family building permits issued: 0 (2005); Employment by occupation: 10.0% management, 17.3% professional, 10.7% services, 29.8% sales, 0.7% farming, 11.2% construction, 20.3% production (2000).
Income: Per capita income: $19,328 (2005); Median household income: $43,540 (2005); Average household income: $51,611 (2005); Percent of households with income of $100,000 or more: 8.2% (2005); Poverty rate: 10.4% (2000).
Education: Percent of population age 25 and over with: High school diploma (including GED) or higher: 83.2% (2005); Bachelor's degree or higher: 14.7% (2005); Master's degree or higher: 5.4% (2005).
Housing: Homeownership rate: 82.2% (2005); Median home value: $86,194 (2005); Median rent: $358 per month (2000); Median age of housing: 34 years (2000).
Transportation: Commute to work: 96.3% car, 0.3% public transportation, 0.5% walk, 2.3% work from home (2000); Travel time to work: 19.2% less than 15 minutes, 49.2% 15 to 30 minutes, 22.8% 30 to 45 minutes, 3.6% 45 to 60 minutes, 5.2% 60 minutes or more (2000)

Cattaraugus County

Located in western New York; bounded on the south by Pennsylvania; crossed by the Allegheny River. Covers a land area of 1,309.85 square miles, a water area of 12.40 square miles, and is located in the Eastern Time Zone. The county government was organized in 1808. County seat is Little Valley.

Cattaraugus County is part of the Olean, NY Micropolitan Statistical Area. The entire metro area includes: Cattaraugus County, NY

Weather Station: Allegany State Park   Elevation: 1,499 feet

	Jan	Feb	Mar	Apr	May	Jun	Jul	Aug	Sep	Oct	Nov	Dec
High	30	33	42	54	67	75	78	77	69	58	46	35
Low	12	13	20	31	40	49	54	53	46	36	29	20
Precip	3.0	2.5	3.3	3.5	3.9	4.9	4.3	4.1	4.5	3.8	4.1	3.7
Snow	na	na	na	na	tr	0.0	0.0	0.0	0.0	0.1	na	na

High and Low temperatures in degrees Fahrenheit; Precipitation and Snow in inches

Weather Station: Franklinville   Elevation: 1,548 feet

	Jan	Feb	Mar	Apr	May	Jun	Jul	Aug	Sep	Oct	Nov	Dec
High	29	31	40	53	66	74	78	76	69	58	45	34
Low	10	11	19	30	39	49	53	52	45	35	28	18
Precip	2.5	2.0	2.8	3.2	3.6	4.3	4.0	3.8	4.3	3.7	3.6	3.1
Snow	28.0	16.5	14.6	4.2	0.2	0.0	0.0	0.0	0.0	0.6	11.5	25.5

High and Low temperatures in degrees Fahrenheit; Precipitation and Snow in inches

Weather Station: Little Valley   Elevation: 1,624 feet

	Jan	Feb	Mar	Apr	May	Jun	Jul	Aug	Sep	Oct	Nov	Dec
High	30	32	41	54	66	74	79	77	69	58	46	35
Low	12	13	20	31	41	50	55	54	47	37	29	20
Precip	3.7	3.0	3.6	3.6	3.8	4.8	4.3	4.4	4.9	4.2	4.8	4.3
Snow	31.5	22.3	18.1	6.3	0.4	0.0	0.0	0.0	0.0	1.0	14.9	33.4

High and Low temperatures in degrees Fahrenheit; Precipitation and Snow in inches

Population: 84,234 (1990); 83,955 (2000); 83,266 (2005); 82,511 (2010 projected); Race: 94.4% White, 1.3% Black, 0.6% Asian, 1.5% Hispanic of any race (2005); Density: 63.6 persons per square mile (2005); Average household size: 2.58 (2005); Median age: 38.5 (2005); Males per 100 females: 96.3 (2005).
Religion: Five largest groups: 21.7% Catholic Church, 5.8% The United Methodist Church, 2.2% Lutheran Church-Missouri Synod, 1.6% Presbyterian Church (U.S.A.), 1.4% American Baptist Churches in the USA (2000).
Economy: Unemployment rate: 5.5% (2005); Total civilian labor force: 42,579 (2005); Leading industries: 22.4% manufacturing; 18.1% retail trade; 14.2% health care and social assistance (2003); Farms: 1,157 totaling 201,913 acres (2002); Companies that employ 500 or more persons: 5 (2003); Companies that employ 100 to 499 persons: 30 (2003); Companies that employ less than 100 persons: 1,746 (2003); Black-owned businesses: n/a (2002); Hispanic-owned businesses: n/a (2002); Women-owned businesses: 1,501 (2002); Retail sales per capita: $11,942 (2006). Single-family building permits issued: 198 (2005); Multi-family building permits issued: 6 (2005).
Income: Per capita income: $18,671 (2005); Median household income: $38,233 (2005); Average household income: $47,432 (2005); Percent of households with income of $100,000 or more: 7.6% (2005); Poverty rate: 13.6% (2003); Bankruptcy rate: 7.76% (2005).
Education: Percent of population age 25 and over with: High school diploma (including GED) or higher: 81.2% (2005); Bachelor's degree or higher: 14.9% (2005); Master's degree or higher: 6.6% (2005).
Housing: Homeownership rate: 74.8% (2005); Median home value: $91,041 (2005); Median rent: $328 per month (2000); Median age of housing: 46 years (2000).
Health: Birth rate: 126.0 per 10,000 population (2004); Death rate: 101.2 per 10,000 population (2004); Age-adjusted cancer mortality rate: 230.9 deaths per 100,000 population (2002); Number of physicians: 13.8 per 10,000 population (2004); Hospital beds: 24.7 per 10,000 population (2003); Hospital admissions: 1,062.7 per 10,000 population (2003).
Elections: 2004 Presidential election results: 58.5% Bush, 39.4% Kerry, 1.8% Nader, 0.2% Badnarik
National and State Parks: Allegany State Park; Harry E Dobbins Memorial State Forest
Additional Information Contacts
Cattaraugus County Government . . . . (716) 938-9111
   http://www.cattco.org/
City of Olean . . . . (716) 376-5604
   http://www.cityofolean.com/
Town of Allegany . . . . (716) 373-0120
   http://www.allegany.org/
Town of Franklinville . . . . (716) 676-3077
   http://www.franklinvilleny.org/
Village of Allegany . . . . (716) 373-0120
   http://www.allegany.org/
Village of Franklinville . . . . (716) 676-3010
   http://village.franklinvilleny.org/

Cattaraugus County Communities

ALLEGANY (village). Covers a land area of 0.700 square miles and a water area of 0.008 square miles. Located at 42.09° N. Lat.; 78.49° W. Long. Elevation is 1,420 feet.
Population: 2,104 (1990); 1,883 (2000); 1,902 (2005); 1,876 (2010 projected); Race: 95.6% White, 0.7% Black, 2.7% Asian, 1.2% Hispanic of any race (2005); Density: 2,717.3 persons per square mile (2005); Average household size: 2.45 (2005); Median age: 41.3 (2005); Males per 100 females: 86.1 (2005); Marriage status: 36.9% never married, 47.5% now married, 8.5% widowed, 7.0% divorced (2000); Foreign born: 3.7% (2000); Ancestry (includes multiple ancestries): 26.6% Irish, 26.0% German, 16.8% Italian, 11.5% English, 8.9% Polish (2000).
Economy: Single-family building permits issued: 1 (2005); Multi-family building permits issued: 0 (2005); Employment by occupation: 13.7% management, 27.2% professional, 16.3% services, 25.7% sales, 0.0% farming, 6.4% construction, 10.7% production (2000).
Income: Per capita income: $20,760 (2005); Median household income: $39,924 (2005); Average household income: $50,139 (2005); Percent of households with income of $100,000 or more: 11.1% (2005); Poverty rate: 18.8% (2000).
Education: Percent of population age 25 and over with: High school diploma (including GED) or higher: 92.6% (2005); Bachelor's degree or higher: 32.7% (2005); Master's degree or higher: 12.9% (2005).
School District(s)
Allegany - Limestone Central School District (PK-12)
    2003-04 Enrollment: 1,492 . . . . (716) 375-6600
Housing: Homeownership rate: 64.6% (2005); Median home value: $124,107 (2005); Median rent: $351 per month (2000); Median age of housing: 52 years (2000).
Safety: Violent crime rate: 70.5 per 10,000 population; Property crime rate: 1,226.3 per 10,000 population (2004).
Transportation: Commute to work: 89.3% car, 0.0% public transportation, 6.1% walk, 3.9% work from home (2000); Travel time to work: 64.1% less than 15 minutes, 23.6% 15 to 30 minutes, 5.6% 30 to 45 minutes, 3.9% 45 to 60 minutes, 2.7% 60 minutes or more (2000)
Additional Information Contacts
Village of Allegany . . . . (716) 373-0120
    http://www.allegany.org/

ALLEGANY (town). Covers a land area of 71.175 square miles and a water area of 0.485 square miles. Located at 42.08° N. Lat.; 78.49° W. Long. Elevation is 1,420 feet.
History: Incorporated 1906.
Population: 8,327 (1990); 8,230 (2000); 8,489 (2005); 8,657 (2010 projected); Race: 95.8% White, 1.0% Black, 1.7% Asian, 1.4% Hispanic of any race (2005); Density: 119.3 persons per square mile (2005); Average household size: 3.10 (2005); Median age: 31.0 (2005); Males per 100 females: 91.0 (2005); Marriage status: 36.6% never married, 50.5% now married, 6.4% widowed, 6.5% divorced (2000); Foreign born: 2.4% (2000); Ancestry (includes multiple ancestries): 32.0% German, 26.7% Irish, 14.7% Italian, 11.2% English, 9.0% Polish (2000).
Economy: Manufactures dairy products, cutlery, lumber; sand and gravel pits. Agriculture: hay, wheat, corn. Single-family building permits issued: 12 (2005); Multi-family building permits issued: 0 (2005); Employment by occupation: 10.8% management, 24.3% professional, 13.9% services, 30.8% sales, 0.5% farming, 8.1% construction, 11.5% production (2000).
Income: Per capita income: $18,353 (2005); Median household income: $43,363 (2005); Average household income: $53,560 (2005); Percent of households with income of $100,000 or more: 10.9% (2005); Poverty rate: 8.6% (2000).
Education: Percent of population age 25 and over with: High school diploma (including GED) or higher: 91.0% (2005); Bachelor's degree or higher: 25.5% (2005); Master's degree or higher: 12.3% (2005).
Housing: Homeownership rate: 80.2% (2005); Median home value: $115,229 (2005); Median rent: $364 per month (2000); Median age of housing: 36 years (2000).
Transportation: Commute to work: 83.5% car, 0.0% public transportation, 13.0% walk, 2.6% work from home (2000); Travel time to work: 57.3% less than 15 minutes, 29.8% 15 to 30 minutes, 6.7% 30 to 45 minutes, 2.1% 45 to 60 minutes, 4.2% 60 minutes or more (2000)
Additional Information Contacts
Town of Allegany . . . . (716) 373-0120
    http://www.allegany.org/

ALLEGANY RESERVATION (reservation). Covers a land area of 36.385 square miles and a water area of 7.272 square miles. Located at 42.11° N. Lat.; 78.76° W. Long.
Population: 1,143 (1990); 1,099 (2000); 1,038 (2005); 997 (2010 projected); Race: 43.0% White, 1.2% Black, 0.8% Asian, 3.2% Hispanic of any race (2005); Density: 28.5 persons per square mile (2005); Average household size: 2.69 (2005); Median age: 35.1 (2005); Males per 100 females: 103.5 (2005); Marriage status: 32.1% never married, 47.2% now married, 7.8% widowed, 12.9% divorced (2000); Foreign born: 0.2% (2000); Ancestry (includes multiple ancestries): 57.9% Other groups, 12.8% German, 8.4% Irish, 7.8% English, 3.0% Dutch (2000).
Economy: Employment by occupation: 7.0% management, 10.1% professional, 18.3% services, 24.8% sales, 1.9% farming, 12.5% construction, 25.3% production (2000).
Income: Per capita income: $15,160 (2005); Median household income: $33,182 (2005); Average household income: $40,110 (2005); Percent of households with income of $100,000 or more: 6.0% (2005); Poverty rate: 22.6% (2000).
Education: Percent of population age 25 and over with: High school diploma (including GED) or higher: 73.5% (2005); Bachelor's degree or higher: 6.6% (2005); Master's degree or higher: 3.4% (2005).
Housing: Homeownership rate: 69.7% (2005); Median home value: $69,200 (2005); Median rent: $250 per month (2000); Median age of housing: 31 years (2000).
Transportation: Commute to work: 89.1% car, 0.5% public transportation, 7.3% walk, 2.3% work from home (2000); Travel time to work: 51.1% less than 15 minutes, 35.1% 15 to 30 minutes, 2.9% 30 to 45 minutes, 4.3% 45 to 60 minutes, 6.6% 60 minutes or more (2000)

ASHFORD (town). Covers a land area of 51.297 square miles and a water area of 0.061 square miles. Located at 42.44° N. Lat.; 78.65° W. Long.
Population: 2,162 (1990); 2,223 (2000); 2,235 (2005); 2,251 (2010 projected); Race: 96.9% White, 1.7% Black, 0.2% Asian, 0.9% Hispanic of any race (2005); Density: 43.6 persons per square mile (2005); Average household size: 2.54 (2005); Median age: 40.1 (2005); Males per 100 females: 98.1 (2005); Marriage status: 19.3% never married, 66.9% now married, 3.6% widowed, 10.1% divorced (2000); Foreign born: 1.4% (2000); Ancestry (includes multiple ancestries): 40.9% German, 17.0% Irish, 14.6% English, 12.7% Polish, 4.4% United States or American (2000).
Economy: Single-family building permits issued: 7 (2005); Multi-family building permits issued: 0 (2005); Employment by occupation: 11.2% management, 12.4% professional, 19.9% services, 20.7% sales, 0.7% farming, 10.6% construction, 24.6% production (2000).
Income: Per capita income: $22,215 (2005); Median household income: $47,536 (2005); Average household income: $56,485 (2005); Percent of households with income of $100,000 or more: 8.9% (2005); Poverty rate: 6.3% (2000).
Education: Percent of population age 25 and over with: High school diploma (including GED) or higher: 87.5% (2005); Bachelor's degree or higher: 13.4% (2005); Master's degree or higher: 3.9% (2005).
Housing: Homeownership rate: 84.5% (2005); Median home value: $113,300 (2005); Median rent: $327 per month (2000); Median age of housing: 31 years (2000).
Transportation: Commute to work: 94.8% car, 0.5% public transportation, 1.6% walk, 2.7% work from home (2000); Travel time to work: 34.6% less than 15 minutes, 26.2% 15 to 30 minutes, 13.7% 30 to 45 minutes, 15.9% 45 to 60 minutes, 9.6% 60 minutes or more (2000)

CARROLLTON (town). Covers a land area of 42.289 square miles and a water area of 0.014 square miles. Located at 42.04° N. Lat.; 78.63° W. Long.
Population: 1,555 (1990); 1,410 (2000); 1,415 (2005); 1,428 (2010 projected); Race: 93.9% White, 2.3% Black, 0.2% Asian, 1.6% Hispanic of any race (2005); Density: 33.5 persons per square mile (2005); Average household size: 2.50 (2005); Median age: 40.8 (2005); Males per 100 females: 101.3 (2005); Marriage status: 22.8% never married, 62.4% now married, 7.6% widowed, 7.2% divorced (2000); Foreign born: 0.1% (2000); Ancestry (includes multiple ancestries): 24.9% German, 19.9% Irish, 15.1% Italian, 14.0% English, 7.8% Polish (2000).
Economy: Single-family building permits issued: 0 (2005); Multi-family building permits issued: 0 (2005); Employment by occupation: 8.8%

management, 10.8% professional, 15.0% services, 22.5% sales, 0.0% farming, 10.8% construction, 32.1% production (2000).
Income: Per capita income: $18,066 (2005); Median household income: $36,111 (2005); Average household income: $44,859 (2005); Percent of households with income of $100,000 or more: 5.8% (2005); Poverty rate: 14.4% (2000).
Taxes: Total city taxes per capita: $214 (2004); City property taxes per capita: $200 (2004).
Education: Percent of population age 25 and over with: High school diploma (including GED) or higher: 80.4% (2005); Bachelor's degree or higher: 11.0% (2005); Master's degree or higher: 3.5% (2005).
Housing: Homeownership rate: 81.3% (2005); Median home value: $70,444 (2005); Median rent: $309 per month (2000); Median age of housing: 37 years (2000).
Transportation: Commute to work: 93.4% car, 0.0% public transportation, 1.3% walk, 4.6% work from home (2000); Travel time to work: 37.0% less than 15 minutes, 39.6% 15 to 30 minutes, 13.9% 30 to 45 minutes, 2.8% 45 to 60 minutes, 6.6% 60 minutes or more (2000)

CATTARAUGUS (village).
Covers a land area of 1.120 square miles and a water area of 0 square miles. Located at 42.33° N. Lat.; 78.86° W. Long. Elevation is 1,383 feet.
History: Settled 1851 during construction of Erie Railroad; incorporated 1882.
Population: 1,100 (1990); 1,075 (2000); 1,049 (2005); 1,031 (2010 projected); Race: 98.7% White, 0.0% Black, 0.0% Asian, 2.5% Hispanic of any race (2005); Density: 936.3 persons per square mile (2005); Average household size: 2.42 (2005); Median age: 38.4 (2005); Males per 100 females: 101.3 (2005); Marriage status: 24.1% never married, 56.0% now married, 7.9% widowed, 12.0% divorced (2000); Foreign born: 1.1% (2000); Ancestry (includes multiple ancestries): 41.5% German, 20.3% English, 14.5% Irish, 7.0% United States or American, 6.2% Polish (2000).
Economy: Manufacturing of wood products, custom laminates, Railroad car and trailer-truck interiors; lumber milling. Agriculture: dairy products; poultry; hay; sweet corn, potatoes. Single-family building permits issued: 0 (2005); Multi-family building permits issued: 0 (2005); Employment by occupation: 5.5% management, 20.6% professional, 19.5% services, 21.8% sales, 1.3% farming, 8.8% construction, 22.5% production (2000).
Income: Per capita income: $20,048 (2005); Median household income: $35,690 (2005); Average household income: $47,696 (2005); Percent of households with income of $100,000 or more: 8.3% (2005); Poverty rate: 11.0% (2000).
Education: Percent of population age 25 and over with: High school diploma (including GED) or higher: 81.4% (2005); Bachelor's degree or higher: 18.8% (2005); Master's degree or higher: 8.0% (2005).

School District(s)
Cattaraugus-Little Valley Central School District (KG-12)
    2003-04 Enrollment: 1,143 . . . . (716) 938-9155

Housing: Homeownership rate: 66.4% (2005); Median home value: $83,462 (2005); Median rent: $307 per month (2000); Median age of housing: 60+ years (2000).
Safety: Violent crime rate: 0.0 per 10,000 population; Property crime rate: 38.2 per 10,000 population (2004).
Transportation: Commute to work: 88.2% car, 0.0% public transportation, 6.8% walk, 5.0% work from home (2000); Travel time to work: 35.8% less than 15 minutes, 32.2% 15 to 30 minutes, 18.1% 30 to 45 minutes, 6.1% 45 to 60 minutes, 7.7% 60 minutes or more (2000)

CATTARAUGUS RESERVATION (reservation).
Covers a land area of 5.760 square miles and a water area of 0.221 square miles. Located at 42.52° N. Lat.; 78.99° W. Long.
Population: 359 (1990); 388 (2000); 394 (2005); 401 (2010 projected); Race: 6.6% White, 0.0% Black, 0.0% Asian, 7.1% Hispanic of any race (2005); Density: 68.4 persons per square mile (2005); Average household size: 2.98 (2005); Median age: 30.0 (2005); Males per 100 females: 90.3 (2005); Marriage status: 53.3% never married, 27.2% now married, 8.6% widowed, 10.9% divorced (2000); Foreign born: 1.0% (2000); Ancestry (includes multiple ancestries): 72.3% Other groups, 1.6% Norwegian, 0.8% Senegalese (2000).
Economy: Employment by occupation: 0.0% management, 19.7% professional, 25.0% services, 24.3% sales, 0.0% farming, 13.8% construction, 17.1% production (2000).
Income: Per capita income: $13,147 (2005); Median household income: $32,778 (2005); Average household income: $39,242 (2005); Percent of households with income of $100,000 or more: 4.5% (2005); Poverty rate: 24.5% (2000).
Education: Percent of population age 25 and over with: High school diploma (including GED) or higher: 81.9% (2005); Bachelor's degree or higher: 14.5% (2005); Master's degree or higher: 3.1% (2005).
Housing: Homeownership rate: 72.0% (2005); Median home value: $59,333 (2005); Median rent: $134 per month (2000); Median age of housing: 23 years (2000).
Transportation: Commute to work: 100.0% car, 0.0% public transportation, 0.0% walk, 0.0% work from home (2000); Travel time to work: 56.2% less than 15 minutes, 17.1% 15 to 30 minutes, 16.4% 30 to 45 minutes, 0.0% 45 to 60 minutes, 10.3% 60 minutes or more (2000)

COLDSPRING (town).
Covers a land area of 51.471 square miles and a water area of 0.542 square miles. Located at 42.11° N. Lat.; 78.90° W. Long.
Population: 732 (1990); 751 (2000); 740 (2005); 723 (2010 projected); Race: 97.6% White, 0.4% Black, 0.0% Asian, 0.7% Hispanic of any race (2005); Density: 14.4 persons per square mile (2005); Average household size: 2.66 (2005); Median age: 40.3 (2005); Males per 100 females: 103.9 (2005); Marriage status: 28.2% never married, 56.4% now married, 4.5% widowed, 10.8% divorced (2000); Foreign born: 1.0% (2000); Ancestry (includes multiple ancestries): 23.8% German, 19.8% Irish, 18.5% English, 9.8% United States or American, 6.7% Other groups (2000).
Economy: Single-family building permits issued: 6 (2005); Multi-family building permits issued: 0 (2005); Employment by occupation: 8.1% management, 17.8% professional, 18.1% services, 14.6% sales, 4.0% farming, 14.6% construction, 22.7% production (2000).
Income: Per capita income: $17,372 (2005); Median household income: $36,875 (2005); Average household income: $46,241 (2005); Percent of households with income of $100,000 or more: 6.1% (2005); Poverty rate: 15.0% (2000).
Education: Percent of population age 25 and over with: High school diploma (including GED) or higher: 81.6% (2005); Bachelor's degree or higher: 8.5% (2005); Master's degree or higher: 2.8% (2005).
Housing: Homeownership rate: 82.4% (2005); Median home value: $82,571 (2005); Median rent: $313 per month (2000); Median age of housing: 37 years (2000).
Transportation: Commute to work: 92.2% car, 0.6% public transportation, 1.9% walk, 4.5% work from home (2000); Travel time to work: 28.5% less than 15 minutes, 32.5% 15 to 30 minutes, 22.4% 30 to 45 minutes, 8.8% 45 to 60 minutes, 7.8% 60 minutes or more (2000)

CONEWANGO (town).
Covers a land area of 36.155 square miles and a water area of 0.014 square miles. Located at 42.22° N. Lat.; 78.99° W. Long. Elevation is 1,294 feet.
Population: 1,702 (1990); 1,732 (2000); 1,603 (2005); 1,553 (2010 projected); Race: 98.1% White, 0.2% Black, 0.0% Asian, 0.7% Hispanic of any race (2005); Density: 44.3 persons per square mile (2005); Average household size: 3.37 (2005); Median age: 27.1 (2005); Males per 100 females: 106.8 (2005); Marriage status: 22.6% never married, 63.6% now married, 5.8% widowed, 8.0% divorced (2000); Foreign born: 1.0% (2000); Ancestry (includes multiple ancestries): 20.1% German, 11.4% English, 9.8% Irish, 5.9% United States or American, 5.8% Pennsylvania German (2000).
Economy: Single-family building permits issued: 2 (2005); Multi-family building permits issued: 0 (2005); Employment by occupation: 12.4% management, 12.4% professional, 16.3% services, 19.1% sales, 5.3% farming, 12.3% construction, 22.2% production (2000).
Income: Per capita income: $16,101 (2005); Median household income: $40,076 (2005); Average household income: $54,337 (2005); Percent of households with income of $100,000 or more: 9.5% (2005); Poverty rate: 23.6% (2000).
Education: Percent of population age 25 and over with: High school diploma (including GED) or higher: 66.9% (2005); Bachelor's degree or higher: 10.4% (2005); Master's degree or higher: 3.5% (2005).
Housing: Homeownership rate: 83.6% (2005); Median home value: $88,182 (2005); Median rent: $316 per month (2000); Median age of housing: 40 years (2000).
Transportation: Commute to work: 76.5% car, 0.9% public transportation, 5.1% walk, 15.3% work from home (2000); Travel time to work: 26.8% less than 15 minutes, 34.2% 15 to 30 minutes, 25.9% 30 to 45 minutes, 6.4% 45 to 60 minutes, 6.7% 60 minutes or more (2000)

CONEWANGO VALLEY (unincorporated postal area, zip code 14726). Aka Conewango. Covers a land area of 40.737 square miles and a water area of 0.003 square miles. Located at 42.25° N. Lat.; 79.03° W. Long.
Population: 0 (2000); Race: 98.6% White, 0.1% Black, 0.5% Asian, 0.4% Hispanic of any race (2000); Density: 0.0 persons per square mile (2000); Age: 42.8% under 18, 9.2% over 64 (2000); Marriage status: 26.7% never married, 60.2% now married, 6.1% widowed, 6.9% divorced (2000); Foreign born: 1.3% (2000); Ancestry (includes multiple ancestries): 22.2% German, 10.1% English, 9.3% Irish, 7.6% Pennsylvania German, 6.5% United States or American (2000).
Economy: Employment by occupation: 10.1% management, 10.1% professional, 17.1% services, 16.7% sales, 5.9% farming, 10.5% construction, 29.6% production (2000).
Income: Per capita income: $11,832 (2000); Median household income: $29,537 (2000); Poverty rate: 32.0% (2000).
Education: Percent of population age 25 and over with: High school diploma (including GED) or higher: 53.1% (2000); Bachelor's degree or higher: 6.7% (2000).
Housing: Homeownership rate: 83.0% (2000); Median home value: $46,200 (2000); Median rent: $338 per month (2000); Median age of housing: 43 years (2000).
Transportation: Commute to work: 62.8% car, 0.9% public transportation, 10.9% walk, 18.3% work from home (2000); Travel time to work: 25.8% less than 15 minutes, 31.8% 15 to 30 minutes, 27.4% 30 to 45 minutes, 7.7% 45 to 60 minutes, 7.4% 60 minutes or more (2000)

DAYTON (town). Covers a land area of 35.764 square miles and a water area of 0.279 square miles. Located at 42.39° N. Lat.; 79.00° W. Long.
Population: 1,915 (1990); 1,945 (2000); 1,827 (2005); 1,769 (2010 projected); Race: 97.1% White, 0.5% Black, 0.1% Asian, 1.3% Hispanic of any race (2005); Density: 51.1 persons per square mile (2005); Average household size: 2.56 (2005); Median age: 37.8 (2005); Males per 100 females: 97.1 (2005); Marriage status: 23.2% never married, 56.4% now married, 7.8% widowed, 12.6% divorced (2000); Foreign born: 1.4% (2000); Ancestry (includes multiple ancestries): 35.7% German, 19.6% English, 11.3% Irish, 7.8% Polish, 6.9% United States or American (2000).
Economy: Single-family building permits issued: 0 (2005); Multi-family building permits issued: 0 (2005); Employment by occupation: 6.6% management, 15.9% professional, 23.8% services, 19.1% sales, 2.5% farming, 13.1% construction, 19.1% production (2000).
Income: Per capita income: $17,563 (2005); Median household income: $36,534 (2005); Average household income: $44,752 (2005); Percent of households with income of $100,000 or more: 6.3% (2005); Poverty rate: 12.8% (2000).
Education: Percent of population age 25 and over with: High school diploma (including GED) or higher: 79.7% (2005); Bachelor's degree or higher: 11.3% (2005); Master's degree or higher: 4.4% (2005).
Housing: Homeownership rate: 79.0% (2005); Median home value: $82,870 (2005); Median rent: $302 per month (2000); Median age of housing: 60+ years (2000).
Transportation: Commute to work: 89.7% car, 1.3% public transportation, 3.8% walk, 4.3% work from home (2000); Travel time to work: 32.9% less than 15 minutes, 28.1% 15 to 30 minutes, 16.1% 30 to 45 minutes, 11.5% 45 to 60 minutes, 11.4% 60 minutes or more (2000)

DELEVAN (village). Covers a land area of 0.978 square miles and a water area of 0 square miles. Located at 42.49° N. Lat.; 78.48° W. Long. Elevation is 1,450 feet.
Population: 1,214 (1990); 1,089 (2000); 1,075 (2005); 1,054 (2010 projected); Race: 98.1% White, 0.1% Black, 0.7% Asian, 0.9% Hispanic of any race (2005); Density: 1,098.7 persons per square mile (2005); Average household size: 2.45 (2005); Median age: 35.1 (2005); Males per 100 females: 104.4 (2005); Marriage status: 27.2% never married, 56.9% now married, 5.4% widowed, 10.4% divorced (2000); Foreign born: 0.9% (2000); Ancestry (includes multiple ancestries): 36.5% German, 17.3% English, 14.7% Irish, 11.2% Polish, 8.7% Other groups (2000).
Economy: Single-family building permits issued: 0 (2005); Multi-family building permits issued: 0 (2005); Employment by occupation: 5.4% management, 17.0% professional, 13.8% services, 23.3% sales, 0.9% farming, 12.9% construction, 26.7% production (2000).
Income: Per capita income: $19,805 (2005); Median household income: $39,476 (2005); Average household income: $48,497 (2005); Percent of households with income of $100,000 or more: 7.1% (2005); Poverty rate: 14.8% (2000).
Education: Percent of population age 25 and over with: High school diploma (including GED) or higher: 87.0% (2005); Bachelor's degree or higher: 14.1% (2005); Master's degree or higher: 4.8% (2005).
School District(s)
Yorkshire-Pioneer Central School District (KG-12)
    2003-04 Enrollment: 2,928 . . . . (716) 492-9304
Housing: Homeownership rate: 61.3% (2005); Median home value: $104,449 (2005); Median rent: $279 per month (2000); Median age of housing: 46 years (2000).
Transportation: Commute to work: 94.1% car, 0.4% public transportation, 3.5% walk, 1.7% work from home (2000); Travel time to work: 42.0% less than 15 minutes, 17.3% 15 to 30 minutes, 18.8% 30 to 45 minutes, 14.7% 45 to 60 minutes, 7.2% 60 minutes or more (2000)

EAST OTTO (town). Covers a land area of 41.169 square miles and a water area of 0.204 square miles. Located at 42.38° N. Lat.; 78.74° W. Long.
Population: 1,003 (1990); 1,105 (2000); 1,164 (2005); 1,217 (2010 projected); Race: 98.2% White, 0.3% Black, 0.3% Asian, 1.2% Hispanic of any race (2005); Density: 28.3 persons per square mile (2005); Average household size: 2.63 (2005); Median age: 38.2 (2005); Males per 100 females: 104.9 (2005); Marriage status: 25.2% never married, 60.3% now married, 4.8% widowed, 9.7% divorced (2000); Foreign born: 1.2% (2000); Ancestry (includes multiple ancestries): 40.7% German, 16.7% Irish, 12.5% Polish, 11.0% English, 6.3% Italian (2000).
Economy: Single-family building permits issued: 4 (2005); Multi-family building permits issued: 0 (2005); Employment by occupation: 10.2% management, 11.7% professional, 18.4% services, 20.9% sales, 2.5% farming, 15.1% construction, 21.1% production (2000).
Income: Per capita income: $19,605 (2005); Median household income: $43,077 (2005); Average household income: $51,629 (2005); Percent of households with income of $100,000 or more: 8.1% (2005); Poverty rate: 12.2% (2000).
Taxes: Total city taxes per capita: $0 (2004); City property taxes per capita: $0 (2004).
Education: Percent of population age 25 and over with: High school diploma (including GED) or higher: 81.4% (2005); Bachelor's degree or higher: 9.6% (2005); Master's degree or higher: 3.3% (2005).
Housing: Homeownership rate: 84.6% (2005); Median home value: $108,824 (2005); Median rent: $345 per month (2000); Median age of housing: 32 years (2000).
Transportation: Commute to work: 90.3% car, 0.0% public transportation, 4.0% walk, 4.4% work from home (2000); Travel time to work: 18.5% less than 15 minutes, 34.9% 15 to 30 minutes, 16.4% 30 to 45 minutes, 16.6% 45 to 60 minutes, 13.7% 60 minutes or more (2000)

EAST RANDOLPH (village). Covers a land area of 1.090 square miles and a water area of 0 square miles. Located at 42.17° N. Lat.; 78.94° W. Long.
Population: 629 (1990); 630 (2000); 616 (2005); 611 (2010 projected); Race: 90.1% White, 5.5% Black, 1.3% Asian, 2.6% Hispanic of any race (2005); Density: 565.0 persons per square mile (2005); Average household size: 3.14 (2005); Median age: 29.2 (2005); Males per 100 females: 102.6 (2005); Marriage status: 32.3% never married, 53.5% now married, 7.6% widowed, 6.7% divorced (2000); Foreign born: 0.9% (2000); Ancestry (includes multiple ancestries): 19.5% Irish, 18.2% German, 18.1% English, 9.4% Other groups, 7.9% Swedish (2000).
Economy: Single-family building permits issued: 0 (2005); Multi-family building permits issued: 0 (2005); Employment by occupation: 4.4% management, 21.1% professional, 19.7% services, 18.7% sales, 2.7% farming, 8.5% construction, 24.8% production (2000).
Income: Per capita income: $17,261 (2005); Median household income: $46,818 (2005); Average household income: $53,865 (2005); Percent of households with income of $100,000 or more: 7.1% (2005); Poverty rate: 10.8% (2000).
Education: Percent of population age 25 and over with: High school diploma (including GED) or higher: 83.6% (2005); Bachelor's degree or higher: 14.6% (2005); Master's degree or higher: 6.1% (2005).
Housing: Homeownership rate: 73.0% (2005); Median home value: $90,313 (2005); Median rent: $351 per month (2000); Median age of housing: 60+ years (2000).
Transportation: Commute to work: 93.1% car, 0.0% public transportation, 4.8% walk, 1.4% work from home (2000); Travel time to work: 35.1% less

than 15 minutes, 33.7% 15 to 30 minutes, 22.1% 30 to 45 minutes, 6.3% 45 to 60 minutes, 2.8% 60 minutes or more (2000)

ELLICOTTVILLE (village).
Covers a land area of 0.835 square miles and a water area of 0.014 square miles. Located at 42.27° N. Lat.; 78.67° W. Long. Elevation is 1,549 feet.
Population: 513 (1990); 472 (2000); 496 (2005); 517 (2010 projected); Race: 99.6% White, 0.0% Black, 0.0% Asian, 1.2% Hispanic of any race (2005); Density: 593.9 persons per square mile (2005); Average household size: 1.92 (2005); Median age: 50.2 (2005); Males per 100 females: 100.0 (2005); Marriage status: 27.4% never married, 53.1% now married, 6.0% widowed, 13.5% divorced (2000); Foreign born: 5.0% (2000); Ancestry (includes multiple ancestries): 36.3% German, 28.4% Irish, 16.4% Polish, 14.1% English, 12.0% Italian (2000).
Economy: Single-family building permits issued: 7 (2005); Multi-family building permits issued: 0 (2005); Employment by occupation: 24.1% management, 18.0% professional, 21.6% services, 18.0% sales, 0.0% farming, 10.8% construction, 7.6% production (2000).
Income: Per capita income: $29,506 (2005); Median household income: $45,435 (2005); Average household income: $56,725 (2005); Percent of households with income of $100,000 or more: 12.0% (2005); Poverty rate: 12.3% (2000).
Education: Percent of population age 25 and over with: High school diploma (including GED) or higher: 91.4% (2005); Bachelor's degree or higher: 33.3% (2005); Master's degree or higher: 14.2% (2005).
School District(s)
Ellicottville Central School District (PK-12)
    2003-04 Enrollment: 702 . . . . (716) 699-2368
Housing: Homeownership rate: 64.0% (2005); Median home value: $183,065 (2005); Median rent: $380 per month (2000); Median age of housing: 60+ years (2000).
Transportation: Commute to work: 72.6% car, 0.0% public transportation, 19.7% walk, 7.7% work from home (2000); Travel time to work: 60.1% less than 15 minutes, 19.0% 15 to 30 minutes, 6.3% 30 to 45 minutes, 7.9% 45 to 60 minutes, 6.7% 60 minutes or more (2000)
Additional Information Contacts
Ellicottville Chamber of Commerce . . . . (800) 349-9099
    http://www.ellicottvilleny.com

ELLICOTTVILLE (town).
Covers a land area of 45.124 square miles and a water area of 0.097 square miles. Located at 42.29° N. Lat.; 78.64° W. Long. Elevation is 1,549 feet.
History: Incorporated 1881.
Population: 1,607 (1990); 1,738 (2000); 1,825 (2005); 1,894 (2010 projected); Race: 97.8% White, 0.2% Black, 0.4% Asian, 1.8% Hispanic of any race (2005); Density: 40.4 persons per square mile (2005); Average household size: 2.22 (2005); Median age: 46.0 (2005); Males per 100 females: 97.5 (2005); Marriage status: 22.8% never married, 60.0% now married, 6.1% widowed, 11.1% divorced (2000); Foreign born: 4.4% (2000); Ancestry (includes multiple ancestries): 39.1% German, 19.2% Irish, 12.8% English, 10.1% Polish, 5.8% Italian (2000).
Economy: In dairying and poultry area. Some manufacturing: lumber, furniture, sporting goods, automotive and industrial hand tools, cutlery. Single-family building permits issued: 49 (2005); Multi-family building permits issued: 4 (2005); Employment by occupation: 20.3% management, 18.0% professional, 15.2% services, 21.7% sales, 1.3% farming, 10.3% construction, 13.2% production (2000).
Income: Per capita income: $29,835 (2005); Median household income: $51,974 (2005); Average household income: $66,012 (2005); Percent of households with income of $100,000 or more: 16.9% (2005); Poverty rate: 7.7% (2000).
Education: Percent of population age 25 and over with: High school diploma (including GED) or higher: 87.7% (2005); Bachelor's degree or higher: 27.2% (2005); Master's degree or higher: 12.2% (2005).
Housing: Homeownership rate: 74.0% (2005); Median home value: $167,661 (2005); Median rent: $369 per month (2000); Median age of housing: 22 years (2000).
Safety: Violent crime rate: 5.6 per 10,000 population; Property crime rate: 570.8 per 10,000 population (2004).
Transportation: Commute to work: 87.7% car, 0.0% public transportation, 6.5% walk, 5.8% work from home (2000); Travel time to work: 50.6% less than 15 minutes, 20.8% 15 to 30 minutes, 11.0% 30 to 45 minutes, 8.6% 45 to 60 minutes, 8.9% 60 minutes or more (2000)

FARMERSVILLE (town).
Covers a land area of 47.771 square miles and a water area of 0.150 square miles. Located at 42.40° N. Lat.; 78.39° W. Long. Elevation is 1,840 feet.
Population: 869 (1990); 1,028 (2000); 1,051 (2005); 1,058 (2010 projected); Race: 99.0% White, 0.2% Black, 0.0% Asian, 1.0% Hispanic of any race (2005); Density: 22.0 persons per square mile (2005); Average household size: 2.59 (2005); Median age: 38.7 (2005); Males per 100 females: 98.7 (2005); Marriage status: 19.9% never married, 63.5% now married, 7.0% widowed, 9.6% divorced (2000); Foreign born: 1.2% (2000); Ancestry (includes multiple ancestries): 28.4% German, 19.2% English, 12.7% Polish, 12.4% Irish, 7.6% Welsh (2000).
Economy: Single-family building permits issued: 3 (2005); Multi-family building permits issued: 0 (2005); Employment by occupation: 7.9% management, 14.6% professional, 19.3% services, 14.6% sales, 1.1% farming, 7.5% construction, 35.0% production (2000).
Income: Per capita income: $19,275 (2005); Median household income: $44,716 (2005); Average household income: $49,895 (2005); Percent of households with income of $100,000 or more: 7.6% (2005); Poverty rate: 11.1% (2000).
Education: Percent of population age 25 and over with: High school diploma (including GED) or higher: 78.2% (2005); Bachelor's degree or higher: 8.7% (2005); Master's degree or higher: 2.7% (2005).
Housing: Homeownership rate: 86.9% (2005); Median home value: $91,618 (2005); Median rent: $356 per month (2000); Median age of housing: 32 years (2000).
Transportation: Commute to work: 91.3% car, 1.8% public transportation, 2.7% walk, 2.2% work from home (2000); Travel time to work: 24.3% less than 15 minutes, 27.5% 15 to 30 minutes, 16.6% 30 to 45 minutes, 12.5% 45 to 60 minutes, 19.1% 60 minutes or more (2000)

FARMERSVILLE STATION (unincorporated postal area, zip code 14060).
Aka Farmersville. Covers a land area of 15.659 square miles and a water area of 0.061 square miles. Located at 42.44° N. Lat.; 78.32° W. Long. Elevation is 1,730 feet.
Population: 0 (2000); Race: 96.6% White, 0.9% Black, 0.0% Asian, 0.0% Hispanic of any race (2000); Density: 0.0 persons per square mile (2000); Age: 23.8% under 18, 10.6% over 64 (2000); Marriage status: 24.6% never married, 58.8% now married, 7.0% widowed, 9.6% divorced (2000); Foreign born: 0.9% (2000); Ancestry (includes multiple ancestries): 27.7% German, 19.1% English, 17.7% Welsh, 13.4% Irish, 9.4% Polish (2000).
Economy: Employment by occupation: 9.4% management, 15.2% professional, 21.9% services, 16.5% sales, 2.2% farming, 3.1% construction, 31.7% production (2000).
Income: Per capita income: $13,546 (2000); Median household income: $32,232 (2000); Poverty rate: 14.0% (2000).
Education: Percent of population age 25 and over with: High school diploma (including GED) or higher: 80.1% (2000); Bachelor's degree or higher: 5.0% (2000).
Housing: Homeownership rate: 86.5% (2000); Median home value: $52,800 (2000); Median rent: $375 per month (2000); Median age of housing: 57 years (2000).
Transportation: Commute to work: 89.2% car, 0.0% public transportation, 3.8% walk, 4.7% work from home (2000); Travel time to work: 14.9% less than 15 minutes, 42.6% 15 to 30 minutes, 12.9% 30 to 45 minutes, 12.9% 45 to 60 minutes, 16.8% 60 minutes or more (2000)

FRANKLINVILLE (village).
Covers a land area of 1.069 square miles and a water area of 0 square miles. Located at 42.33° N. Lat.; 78.45° W. Long. Elevation is 1,589 feet.
Population: 1,739 (1990); 1,855 (2000); 1,732 (2005); 1,667 (2010 projected); Race: 98.6% White, 0.0% Black, 0.3% Asian, 1.0% Hispanic of any race (2005); Density: 1,620.5 persons per square mile (2005); Average household size: 2.62 (2005); Median age: 35.8 (2005); Males per 100 females: 92.0 (2005); Marriage status: 26.7% never married, 57.6% now married, 7.0% widowed, 8.6% divorced (2000); Foreign born: 0.6% (2000); Ancestry (includes multiple ancestries): 26.6% German, 17.7% English, 15.4% Irish, 10.8% Polish, 9.4% United States or American (2000).
Economy: Single-family building permits issued: 2 (2005); Multi-family building permits issued: 0 (2005); Employment by occupation: 6.8% management, 20.0% professional, 17.0% services, 22.1% sales, 2.7% farming, 7.2% construction, 24.1% production (2000).
Income: Per capita income: $16,656 (2005); Median household income: $36,184 (2005); Average household income: $43,338 (2005); Percent of

households with income of $100,000 or more: 6.6% (2005); Poverty rate: 11.4% (2000).
Education: Percent of population age 25 and over with: High school diploma (including GED) or higher: 79.6% (2005); Bachelor's degree or higher: 11.5% (2005); Master's degree or higher: 6.0% (2005).
School District(s)
Franklinville Central School District (PK-12)
    2003-04 Enrollment: 1,010 . . . . (716) 676-8029
Housing: Homeownership rate: 68.9% (2005); Median home value: $74,519 (2005); Median rent: $283 per month (2000); Median age of housing: 60+ years (2000).
Transportation: Commute to work: 84.6% car, 1.1% public transportation, 12.5% walk, 1.9% work from home (2000); Travel time to work: 35.5% less than 15 minutes, 24.5% 15 to 30 minutes, 22.8% 30 to 45 minutes, 6.5% 45 to 60 minutes, 10.7% 60 minutes or more (2000)
Additional Information Contacts
Village of Franklinville . . . . (716) 676-3010
    http://village.franklinvilleny.org/

FRANKLINVILLE (town). Covers a land area of 51.801 square miles and a water area of 0.179 square miles. Located at 42.31° N. Lat.; 78.47° W. Long. Elevation is 1,589 feet.
History: Settled 1806, incorporated 1874.
Population: 2,968 (1990); 3,128 (2000); 2,977 (2005); 2,879 (2010 projected); Race: 98.4% White, 0.1% Black, 0.2% Asian, 0.7% Hispanic of any race (2005); Density: 57.5 persons per square mile (2005); Average household size: 2.55 (2005); Median age: 38.4 (2005); Males per 100 females: 95.2 (2005); Marriage status: 25.1% never married, 56.7% now married, 7.8% widowed, 10.3% divorced (2000); Foreign born: 1.1% (2000); Ancestry (includes multiple ancestries): 25.3% German, 15.2% English, 14.0% Irish, 10.5% United States or American, 8.5% Polish (2000).
Economy: Manufacturing of dairy products, cutlery; lumber milling. Agriculture includes field corn, hay, and dairy farming. Single-family building permits issued: 7 (2005); Multi-family building permits issued: 0 (2005); Employment by occupation: 8.2% management, 15.4% professional, 20.3% services, 19.6% sales, 2.3% farming, 7.2% construction, 26.9% production (2000).
Income: Per capita income: $17,354 (2005); Median household income: $37,417 (2005); Average household income: $43,885 (2005); Percent of households with income of $100,000 or more: 6.5% (2005); Poverty rate: 13.6% (2000).
Education: Percent of population age 25 and over with: High school diploma (including GED) or higher: 77.4% (2005); Bachelor's degree or higher: 10.6% (2005); Master's degree or higher: 4.9% (2005).
Housing: Homeownership rate: 77.3% (2005); Median home value: $78,314 (2005); Median rent: $298 per month (2000); Median age of housing: 54 years (2000).
Transportation: Commute to work: 88.9% car, 0.6% public transportation, 7.6% walk, 2.2% work from home (2000); Travel time to work: 32.5% less than 15 minutes, 23.3% 15 to 30 minutes, 20.7% 30 to 45 minutes, 10.3% 45 to 60 minutes, 13.2% 60 minutes or more (2000)
Additional Information Contacts
Town of Franklinville . . . . (716) 676-3077
    http://www.franklinvilleny.org/

FREEDOM (town). Covers a land area of 40.318 square miles and a water area of 0.263 square miles. Located at 42.47° N. Lat.; 78.36° W. Long.
Population: 2,018 (1990); 2,493 (2000); 2,651 (2005); 2,793 (2010 projected); Race: 98.8% White, 0.2% Black, 0.2% Asian, 1.0% Hispanic of any race (2005); Density: 65.8 persons per square mile (2005); Average household size: 2.81 (2005); Median age: 36.8 (2005); Males per 100 females: 102.1 (2005); Marriage status: 26.7% never married, 58.7% now married, 4.2% widowed, 10.3% divorced (2000); Foreign born: 0.8% (2000); Ancestry (includes multiple ancestries): 34.8% German, 15.8% English, 13.6% Irish, 10.5% Polish, 7.5% United States or American (2000).
Economy: Single-family building permits issued: 3 (2005); Multi-family building permits issued: 0 (2005); Employment by occupation: 7.3% management, 9.3% professional, 15.2% services, 19.2% sales, 2.5% farming, 17.7% construction, 28.8% production (2000).
Income: Per capita income: $17,888 (2005); Median household income: $42,314 (2005); Average household income: $50,074 (2005); Percent of households with income of $100,000 or more: 8.1% (2005); Poverty rate: 11.3% (2000).
Education: Percent of population age 25 and over with: High school diploma (including GED) or higher: 75.5% (2005); Bachelor's degree or higher: 5.9% (2005); Master's degree or higher: 2.2% (2005).
Housing: Homeownership rate: 85.5% (2005); Median home value: $103,219 (2005); Median rent: $361 per month (2000); Median age of housing: 29 years (2000).
Transportation: Commute to work: 89.5% car, 0.0% public transportation, 2.3% walk, 7.4% work from home (2000); Travel time to work: 33.6% less than 15 minutes, 25.9% 15 to 30 minutes, 10.6% 30 to 45 minutes, 15.8% 45 to 60 minutes, 14.2% 60 minutes or more (2000)

GOWANDA (village). Covers a land area of 1.604 square miles and a water area of 0.011 square miles. Located at 42.46° N. Lat.; 78.93° W. Long. Elevation is 777 feet.
Population: 2,901 (1990); 2,842 (2000); 2,711 (2005); 2,620 (2010 projected); Race: 93.7% White, 0.6% Black, 0.4% Asian, 1.9% Hispanic of any race (2005); Density: 1,690.6 persons per square mile (2005); Average household size: 2.42 (2005); Median age: 42.7 (2005); Males per 100 females: 90.9 (2005); Marriage status: 27.9% never married, 49.6% now married, 10.5% widowed, 12.0% divorced (2000); Foreign born: 1.1% (2000); Ancestry (includes multiple ancestries): 30.5% German, 15.4% English, 14.3% Irish, 10.2% Polish, 6.7% Other groups (2000).
Economy: Single-family building permits issued: 0 (2005); Multi-family building permits issued: 0 (2005); Employment by occupation: 7.1% management, 27.3% professional, 21.3% services, 22.5% sales, 0.7% farming, 7.4% construction, 13.7% production (2000).
Income: Per capita income: $17,877 (2005); Median household income: $33,012 (2005); Average household income: $42,184 (2005); Percent of households with income of $100,000 or more: 7.9% (2005); Poverty rate: 14.4% (2000).
Education: Percent of population age 25 and over with: High school diploma (including GED) or higher: 75.3% (2005); Bachelor's degree or higher: 17.4% (2005); Master's degree or higher: 8.7% (2005).
School District(s)
Gowanda Central School District (PK-12)
    2003-04 Enrollment: 1,532 . . . . (716) 532-3325
Housing: Homeownership rate: 63.9% (2005); Median home value: $76,114 (2005); Median rent: $324 per month (2000); Median age of housing: 60+ years (2000).
Hospitals: Tri-County Memorial Hospital (65 beds)
Transportation: Commute to work: 88.7% car, 0.0% public transportation, 8.7% walk, 1.1% work from home (2000); Travel time to work: 54.5% less than 15 minutes, 16.2% 15 to 30 minutes, 8.1% 30 to 45 minutes, 14.2% 45 to 60 minutes, 6.9% 60 minutes or more (2000)
Additional Information Contacts
Gowanda Area Chamber of Commerce . . . . (716) 532-2834
    http://www.gowandachamber.org

GREAT VALLEY (town). Covers a land area of 50.169 square miles and a water area of 0.032 square miles. Located at 42.19° N. Lat.; 78.64° W. Long. Elevation is 1,464 feet.
Population: 2,090 (1990); 2,145 (2000); 2,078 (2005); 2,075 (2010 projected); Race: 95.8% White, 0.6% Black, 1.1% Asian, 1.3% Hispanic of any race (2005); Density: 41.4 persons per square mile (2005); Average household size: 2.50 (2005); Median age: 41.8 (2005); Males per 100 females: 108.6 (2005); Marriage status: 20.3% never married, 62.8% now married, 9.0% widowed, 7.9% divorced (2000); Foreign born: 0.7% (2000); Ancestry (includes multiple ancestries): 31.3% German, 25.8% Irish, 17.7% English, 9.6% Polish, 7.2% Italian (2000).
Economy: Wood products, lumber. Single-family building permits issued: 16 (2005); Multi-family building permits issued: 0 (2005); Employment by occupation: 7.0% management, 15.0% professional, 17.6% services, 25.5% sales, 0.3% farming, 11.2% construction, 23.3% production (2000).
Income: Per capita income: $20,103 (2005); Median household income: $42,615 (2005); Average household income: $50,120 (2005); Percent of households with income of $100,000 or more: 8.4% (2005); Poverty rate: 6.7% (2000).
Education: Percent of population age 25 and over with: High school diploma (including GED) or higher: 81.9% (2005); Bachelor's degree or higher: 11.1% (2005); Master's degree or higher: 3.8% (2005).
School District(s)
Ellicottville Central School District (PK-12)
    2003-04 Enrollment: 702 . . . . (716) 699-2368

Housing: Homeownership rate: 87.0% (2005); Median home value: $101,648 (2005); Median rent: $341 per month (2000); Median age of housing: 26 years (2000).
Transportation: Commute to work: 93.1% car, 0.6% public transportation, 0.8% walk, 4.9% work from home (2000); Travel time to work: 36.6% less than 15 minutes, 36.8% 15 to 30 minutes, 14.0% 30 to 45 minutes, 6.5% 45 to 60 minutes, 6.0% 60 minutes or more (2000)

HINSDALE (town).
Covers a land area of 38.757 square miles and a water area of 0.014 square miles. Located at 42.16° N. Lat.; 78.38° W. Long. Elevation is 1,489 feet.
Population: 2,095 (1990); 2,270 (2000); 2,418 (2005); 2,518 (2010 projected); Race: 96.8% White, 0.7% Black, 0.3% Asian, 1.2% Hispanic of any race (2005); Density: 62.4 persons per square mile (2005); Average household size: 2.58 (2005); Median age: 40.8 (2005); Males per 100 females: 97.4 (2005); Marriage status: 20.9% never married, 62.6% now married, 6.2% widowed, 10.3% divorced (2000); Foreign born: 0.6% (2000); Ancestry (includes multiple ancestries): 28.9% German, 15.9% English, 14.4% Irish, 10.2% United States or American, 6.8% Polish (2000).
Economy: Single-family building permits issued: 4 (2005); Multi-family building permits issued: 0 (2005); Employment by occupation: 9.2% management, 16.0% professional, 16.1% services, 25.0% sales, 1.9% farming, 7.9% construction, 23.8% production (2000).
Income: Per capita income: $17,797 (2005); Median household income: $36,671 (2005); Average household income: $44,565 (2005); Percent of households with income of $100,000 or more: 5.8% (2005); Poverty rate: 14.9% (2000).
Education: Percent of population age 25 and over with: High school diploma (including GED) or higher: 82.0% (2005); Bachelor's degree or higher: 11.5% (2005); Master's degree or higher: 4.9% (2005).

School District(s)
Hinsdale Central School District (KG-12)
    2003-04 Enrollment: 488 . . . . (716) 557-2227

Housing: Homeownership rate: 86.4% (2005); Median home value: $87,517 (2005); Median rent: $336 per month (2000); Median age of housing: 28 years (2000).
Transportation: Commute to work: 93.7% car, 1.2% public transportation, 2.2% walk, 2.9% work from home (2000); Travel time to work: 32.0% less than 15 minutes, 44.8% 15 to 30 minutes, 14.3% 30 to 45 minutes, 3.8% 45 to 60 minutes, 5.1% 60 minutes or more (2000)

HUMPHREY (town).
Covers a land area of 36.569 square miles and a water area of 0.020 square miles. Located at 42.21° N. Lat.; 78.52° W. Long.
Population: 580 (1990); 721 (2000); 723 (2005); 730 (2010 projected); Race: 96.1% White, 1.4% Black, 0.0% Asian, 1.7% Hispanic of any race (2005); Density: 19.8 persons per square mile (2005); Average household size: 2.68 (2005); Median age: 37.5 (2005); Males per 100 females: 104.2 (2005); Marriage status: 28.2% never married, 55.8% now married, 6.4% widowed, 9.7% divorced (2000); Foreign born: 0.3% (2000); Ancestry (includes multiple ancestries): 32.8% German, 19.0% Irish, 12.8% English, 8.0% Polish, 6.6% French (except Basque) (2000).
Economy: Single-family building permits issued: 3 (2005); Multi-family building permits issued: 0 (2005); Employment by occupation: 3.8% management, 18.9% professional, 18.5% services, 15.7% sales, 1.4% farming, 11.9% construction, 29.7% production (2000).
Income: Per capita income: $20,315 (2005); Median household income: $40,323 (2005); Average household income: $54,398 (2005); Percent of households with income of $100,000 or more: 10.4% (2005); Poverty rate: 11.3% (2000).
Education: Percent of population age 25 and over with: High school diploma (including GED) or higher: 69.6% (2005); Bachelor's degree or higher: 13.4% (2005); Master's degree or higher: 4.4% (2005).
Housing: Homeownership rate: 83.7% (2005); Median home value: $82,069 (2005); Median rent: $248 per month (2000); Median age of housing: 23 years (2000).
Transportation: Commute to work: 94.3% car, 0.7% public transportation, 1.8% walk, 1.8% work from home (2000); Travel time to work: 18.3% less than 15 minutes, 45.3% 15 to 30 minutes, 21.2% 30 to 45 minutes, 7.9% 45 to 60 minutes, 7.2% 60 minutes or more (2000)

ISCHUA (town).
Covers a land area of 32.376 square miles and a water area of 0.018 square miles. Located at 42.23° N. Lat.; 78.38° W. Long.
Population: 847 (1990); 895 (2000); 931 (2005); 965 (2010 projected); Race: 97.9% White, 0.0% Black, 0.2% Asian, 0.8% Hispanic of any race (2005); Density: 28.8 persons per square mile (2005); Average household size: 2.54 (2005); Median age: 41.4 (2005); Males per 100 females: 115.0 (2005); Marriage status: 18.7% never married, 68.0% now married, 5.2% widowed, 8.1% divorced (2000); Foreign born: 0.4% (2000); Ancestry (includes multiple ancestries): 30.8% German, 16.8% Irish, 11.1% English, 8.7% Polish, 7.7% United States or American (2000).
Economy: Single-family building permits issued: 4 (2005); Multi-family building permits issued: 0 (2005); Employment by occupation: 8.0% management, 12.3% professional, 11.6% services, 25.1% sales, 1.7% farming, 11.3% construction, 30.1% production (2000).
Income: Per capita income: $17,164 (2005); Median household income: $38,793 (2005); Average household income: $43,661 (2005); Percent of households with income of $100,000 or more: 4.6% (2005); Poverty rate: 14.0% (2000).
Education: Percent of population age 25 and over with: High school diploma (including GED) or higher: 78.0% (2005); Bachelor's degree or higher: 13.7% (2005); Master's degree or higher: 5.3% (2005).
Housing: Homeownership rate: 84.7% (2005); Median home value: $83,673 (2005); Median rent: $300 per month (2000); Median age of housing: 27 years (2000).
Transportation: Commute to work: 92.9% car, 0.0% public transportation, 3.4% walk, 3.7% work from home (2000); Travel time to work: 17.5% less than 15 minutes, 54.9% 15 to 30 minutes, 17.0% 30 to 45 minutes, 5.8% 45 to 60 minutes, 4.8% 60 minutes or more (2000)

KILL BUCK (unincorporated postal area, zip code 14748).
Covers a land area of 16.528 square miles and a water area of 0.019 square miles. Located at 42.13° N. Lat.; 78.64° W. Long.
Population: 0 (2000); Race: 88.2% White, 0.0% Black, 0.0% Asian, 1.9% Hispanic of any race (2000); Density: 0.0 persons per square mile (2000); Age: 22.6% under 18, 17.6% over 64 (2000); Marriage status: 23.3% never married, 59.6% now married, 7.5% widowed, 9.6% divorced (2000); Foreign born: 0.3% (2000); Ancestry (includes multiple ancestries): 24.9% German, 18.6% English, 18.0% Irish, 14.6% Other groups, 11.8% Polish (2000).
Economy: Employment by occupation: 7.8% management, 11.9% professional, 14.4% services, 15.6% sales, 1.1% farming, 10.7% construction, 38.5% production (2000).
Income: Per capita income: $14,226 (2000); Median household income: $31,364 (2000); Poverty rate: 18.6% (2000).
Education: Percent of population age 25 and over with: High school diploma (including GED) or higher: 72.3% (2000); Bachelor's degree or higher: 6.1% (2000).
Housing: Homeownership rate: 81.6% (2000); Median home value: $63,400 (2000); Median rent: $374 per month (2000); Median age of housing: 26 years (2000).
Transportation: Commute to work: 91.0% car, 0.8% public transportation, 3.5% walk, 4.7% work from home (2000); Travel time to work: 38.5% less than 15 minutes, 35.2% 15 to 30 minutes, 11.5% 30 to 45 minutes, 10.2% 45 to 60 minutes, 4.5% 60 minutes or more (2000)

LEON (town).
Covers a land area of 36.266 square miles and a water area of 0.014 square miles. Located at 42.30° N. Lat.; 79.00° W. Long. Elevation is 1,378 feet.
Population: 1,245 (1990); 1,380 (2000); 1,383 (2005); 1,341 (2010 projected); Race: 99.1% White, 0.0% Black, 0.1% Asian, 0.5% Hispanic of any race (2005); Density: 38.1 persons per square mile (2005); Average household size: 3.61 (2005); Median age: 24.6 (2005); Males per 100 females: 97.9 (2005); Marriage status: 30.5% never married, 59.2% now married, 4.7% widowed, 5.7% divorced (2000); Foreign born: 0.8% (2000); Ancestry (includes multiple ancestries): 26.7% German, 8.7% Pennsylvania German, 8.5% English, 7.0% Irish, 6.3% United States or American (2000).
Economy: Dairy products. Single-family building permits issued: 3 (2005); Multi-family building permits issued: 0 (2005); Employment by occupation: 9.8% management, 11.6% professional, 22.3% services, 14.9% sales, 4.4% farming, 8.8% construction, 28.1% production (2000).
Income: Per capita income: $13,085 (2005); Median household income: $36,213 (2005); Average household income: $46,123 (2005); Percent of households with income of $100,000 or more: 6.5% (2005); Poverty rate: 35.1% (2000).

Education: Percent of population age 25 and over with: High school diploma (including GED) or higher: 56.9% (2005); Bachelor's degree or higher: 7.0% (2005); Master's degree or higher: 2.2% (2005).
Housing: Homeownership rate: 82.2% (2005); Median home value: $86,056 (2005); Median rent: $334 per month (2000); Median age of housing: 33 years (2000).
Transportation: Commute to work: 65.2% car, 0.0% public transportation, 9.6% walk, 17.3% work from home (2000); Travel time to work: 33.3% less than 15 minutes, 20.2% 15 to 30 minutes, 20.7% 30 to 45 minutes, 10.8% 45 to 60 minutes, 15.0% 60 minutes or more (2000)

LIME LAKE-MACHIAS (CDP). Covers a land area of 3.300 square miles and a water area of 0.374 square miles. Located at 42.42° N. Lat.; 78.48° W. Long.
Population: 1,269 (1990); 1,422 (2000); 1,368 (2005); 1,335 (2010 projected); Race: 97.9% White, 0.1% Black, 0.0% Asian, 1.5% Hispanic of any race (2005); Density: 414.6 persons per square mile (2005); Average household size: 2.66 (2005); Median age: 43.5 (2005); Males per 100 females: 94.6 (2005); Marriage status: 17.9% never married, 60.6% now married, 13.3% widowed, 8.2% divorced (2000); Foreign born: 1.2% (2000); Ancestry (includes multiple ancestries): 26.9% German, 16.1% English, 12.4% Polish, 10.9% Irish, 8.8% United States or American (2000).
Economy: Employment by occupation: 11.2% management, 14.4% professional, 15.4% services, 21.7% sales, 1.9% farming, 10.0% construction, 25.4% production (2000).
Income: Per capita income: $16,652 (2005); Median household income: $31,600 (2005); Average household income: $43,670 (2005); Percent of households with income of $100,000 or more: 9.5% (2005); Poverty rate: 15.5% (2000).
Education: Percent of population age 25 and over with: High school diploma (including GED) or higher: 71.6% (2005); Bachelor's degree or higher: 10.2% (2005); Master's degree or higher: 4.9% (2005).
Housing: Homeownership rate: 74.0% (2005); Median home value: $95,233 (2005); Median rent: $335 per month (2000); Median age of housing: 45 years (2000).
Transportation: Commute to work: 93.0% car, 0.0% public transportation, 2.3% walk, 1.8% work from home (2000); Travel time to work: 29.2% less than 15 minutes, 35.4% 15 to 30 minutes, 13.0% 30 to 45 minutes, 12.3% 45 to 60 minutes, 10.1% 60 minutes or more (2000)

LIMESTONE (village). Covers a land area of 1.629 square miles and a water area of 0.014 square miles. Located at 42.02° N. Lat.; 78.63° W. Long. Elevation is 1,407 feet.
History: The field was the first major oil-producing region in the U.S. When the first well was successfully drilled near Titusville, Pennsylvania, in 1859, Allegany, Cattaraugus, and Chautaugua counties all shared in the prosperity.
Population: 459 (1990); 411 (2000); 413 (2005); 412 (2010 projected); Race: 97.1% White, 0.2% Black, 0.0% Asian, 0.7% Hispanic of any race (2005); Density: 253.5 persons per square mile (2005); Average household size: 2.36 (2005); Median age: 41.8 (2005); Males per 100 females: 91.2 (2005); Marriage status: 20.6% never married, 58.5% now married, 11.7% widowed, 9.2% divorced (2000); Foreign born: 0.0% (2000); Ancestry (includes multiple ancestries): 22.9% Irish, 22.1% German, 20.9% Italian, 11.3% English, 8.1% Other groups (2000).
Economy: Small amounts of oil and natural gas are extracted. Single-family building permits issued: 0 (2005); Multi-family building permits issued: 0 (2005); Employment by occupation: 4.0% management, 8.1% professional, 18.5% services, 15.6% sales, 0.0% farming, 11.0% construction, 42.8% production (2000).
Income: Per capita income: $17,433 (2005); Median household income: $31,406 (2005); Average household income: $41,143 (2005); Percent of households with income of $100,000 or more: 6.9% (2005); Poverty rate: 8.8% (2000).
Education: Percent of population age 25 and over with: High school diploma (including GED) or higher: 73.4% (2005); Bachelor's degree or higher: 5.8% (2005); Master's degree or higher: 2.4% (2005).
School District(s)
Allegany - Limestone Central School District (PK-12)
    2003-04 Enrollment: 1,492 . . . . (716) 375-6600
Housing: Homeownership rate: 73.7% (2005); Median home value: $60,417 (2005); Median rent: $317 per month (2000); Median age of housing: 42 years (2000).
Transportation: Commute to work: 94.2% car, 0.0% public transportation, 4.7% walk, 1.2% work from home (2000); Travel time to work: 52.1% less than 15 minutes, 33.7% 15 to 30 minutes, 7.7% 30 to 45 minutes, 3.0% 45 to 60 minutes, 3.6% 60 minutes or more (2000)

LITTLE VALLEY (village). Covers a land area of 1.002 square miles and a water area of 0 square miles. Located at 42.25° N. Lat.; 78.80° W. Long. Elevation is 1,594 feet.
Population: 1,188 (1990); 1,130 (2000); 1,042 (2005); 1,002 (2010 projected); Race: 95.2% White, 2.7% Black, 0.0% Asian, 3.4% Hispanic of any race (2005); Density: 1,039.5 persons per square mile (2005); Average household size: 2.60 (2005); Median age: 35.7 (2005); Males per 100 females: 115.3 (2005); Marriage status: 22.7% never married, 59.4% now married, 8.7% widowed, 9.2% divorced (2000); Foreign born: 0.0% (2000); Ancestry (includes multiple ancestries): 31.0% German, 13.4% English, 11.6% Irish, 8.5% Polish, 6.7% Other groups (2000).
Economy: Employment by occupation: 8.9% management, 11.1% professional, 18.7% services, 17.6% sales, 1.5% farming, 13.7% construction, 28.5% production (2000).
Income: Per capita income: $17,756 (2005); Median household income: $31,953 (2005); Average household income: $41,714 (2005); Percent of households with income of $100,000 or more: 4.2% (2005); Poverty rate: 15.5% (2000).
Education: Percent of population age 25 and over with: High school diploma (including GED) or higher: 73.0% (2005); Bachelor's degree or higher: 7.7% (2005); Master's degree or higher: 2.1% (2005).
School District(s)
Cattaraugus-Little Valley Central School District (KG-12)
    2003-04 Enrollment: 1,143 . . . . (716) 938-9155
Housing: Homeownership rate: 60.3% (2005); Median home value: $72,000 (2005); Median rent: $288 per month (2000); Median age of housing: 60+ years (2000).
Transportation: Commute to work: 84.0% car, 0.4% public transportation, 10.5% walk, 3.1% work from home (2000); Travel time to work: 44.2% less than 15 minutes, 30.9% 15 to 30 minutes, 11.1% 30 to 45 minutes, 4.3% 45 to 60 minutes, 9.5% 60 minutes or more (2000)

LITTLE VALLEY (town). Covers a land area of 29.927 square miles and a water area of 0.006 square miles. Located at 42.24° N. Lat.; 78.78° W. Long. Elevation is 1,594 feet.
History: Incorporated 1876.
Population: 1,881 (1990); 1,788 (2000); 1,656 (2005); 1,593 (2010 projected); Race: 95.5% White, 1.8% Black, 0.0% Asian, 2.3% Hispanic of any race (2005); Density: 55.3 persons per square mile (2005); Average household size: 2.54 (2005); Median age: 39.2 (2005); Males per 100 females: 111.5 (2005); Marriage status: 22.3% never married, 61.2% now married, 7.5% widowed, 9.0% divorced (2000); Foreign born: 0.4% (2000); Ancestry (includes multiple ancestries): 29.2% German, 15.3% English, 11.5% Irish, 10.0% Polish, 6.5% Italian (2000).
Economy: Manufacturing: feed; printing, lumber milling. Agriculture: grain, hay, fruit; livestock, poultry. Single-family building permits issued: 0 (2005); Multi-family building permits issued: 0 (2005); Employment by occupation: 10.5% management, 15.7% professional, 17.9% services, 18.5% sales, 1.9% farming, 12.4% construction, 23.2% production (2000).
Income: Per capita income: $19,233 (2005); Median household income: $35,804 (2005); Average household income: $46,097 (2005); Percent of households with income of $100,000 or more: 7.7% (2005); Poverty rate: 14.0% (2000).
Education: Percent of population age 25 and over with: High school diploma (including GED) or higher: 78.4% (2005); Bachelor's degree or higher: 11.7% (2005); Master's degree or higher: 4.4% (2005).
Housing: Homeownership rate: 69.9% (2005); Median home value: $82,299 (2005); Median rent: $286 per month (2000); Median age of housing: 60+ years (2000).
Transportation: Commute to work: 87.2% car, 0.3% public transportation, 7.5% walk, 3.9% work from home (2000); Travel time to work: 44.7% less than 15 minutes, 27.8% 15 to 30 minutes, 15.9% 30 to 45 minutes, 4.3% 45 to 60 minutes, 7.2% 60 minutes or more (2000)

LYNDON (town). Covers a land area of 33.210 square miles and a water area of 0.052 square miles. Located at 42.30° N. Lat.; 78.36° W. Long.
Population: 503 (1990); 661 (2000); 685 (2005); 706 (2010 projected); Race: 96.9% White, 0.7% Black, 0.0% Asian, 0.9% Hispanic of any race (2005); Density: 20.6 persons per square mile (2005); Average household

size: 2.58 (2005); Median age: 39.5 (2005); Males per 100 females: 101.5 (2005); Marriage status: 21.4% never married, 63.4% now married, 5.1% widowed, 10.1% divorced (2000); Foreign born: 2.3% (2000); Ancestry (includes multiple ancestries): 28.6% German, 14.0% Polish, 13.5% Irish, 12.4% English, 6.2% Other groups (2000).
Economy: Single-family building permits issued: 3 (2005); Multi-family building permits issued: 0 (2005); Employment by occupation: 7.9% management, 11.1% professional, 19.0% services, 14.7% sales, 2.4% farming, 17.5% construction, 27.4% production (2000).
Income: Per capita income: $16,369 (2005); Median household income: $37,125 (2005); Average household income: $42,311 (2005); Percent of households with income of $100,000 or more: 2.3% (2005); Poverty rate: 12.6% (2000).
Education: Percent of population age 25 and over with: High school diploma (including GED) or higher: 69.9% (2005); Bachelor's degree or higher: 8.0% (2005); Master's degree or higher: 2.7% (2005).
Housing: Homeownership rate: 90.9% (2005); Median home value: $84,667 (2005); Median rent: $375 per month (2000); Median age of housing: 22 years (2000).
Transportation: Commute to work: 84.2% car, 3.2% public transportation, 6.5% walk, 4.9% work from home (2000); Travel time to work: 24.3% less than 15 minutes, 33.6% 15 to 30 minutes, 21.7% 30 to 45 minutes, 6.0% 45 to 60 minutes, 14.5% 60 minutes or more (2000)

MACHIAS (town). Covers a land area of 40.602 square miles and a water area of 0.509 square miles. Located at 42.40° N. Lat.; 78.49° W. Long.
Population: 2,338 (1990); 2,482 (2000); 2,409 (2005); 2,348 (2010 projected); Race: 97.8% White, 0.2% Black, 0.1% Asian, 1.5% Hispanic of any race (2005); Density: 59.3 persons per square mile (2005); Average household size: 2.69 (2005); Median age: 41.6 (2005); Males per 100 females: 98.3 (2005); Marriage status: 20.3% never married, 61.3% now married, 9.8% widowed, 8.5% divorced (2000); Foreign born: 1.4% (2000); Ancestry (includes multiple ancestries): 35.1% German, 12.4% English, 12.4% Irish, 10.6% Polish, 8.0% United States or American (2000).
Economy: Resort. Dairy and maple-sugar products; poultry. Lumber, wood products. Single-family building permits issued: 7 (2005); Multi-family building permits issued: 0 (2005); Employment by occupation: 9.5% management, 15.1% professional, 14.8% services, 19.0% sales, 1.4% farming, 12.9% construction, 27.3% production (2000).
Income: Per capita income: $17,485 (2005); Median household income: $38,447 (2005); Average household income: $46,688 (2005); Percent of households with income of $100,000 or more: 9.3% (2005); Poverty rate: 12.8% (2000).
Education: Percent of population age 25 and over with: High school diploma (including GED) or higher: 73.9% (2005); Bachelor's degree or higher: 9.8% (2005); Master's degree or higher: 4.9% (2005).
Housing: Homeownership rate: 78.9% (2005); Median home value: $98,790 (2005); Median rent: $334 per month (2000); Median age of housing: 34 years (2000).
Transportation: Commute to work: 93.1% car, 0.0% public transportation, 2.1% walk, 3.0% work from home (2000); Travel time to work: 25.7% less than 15 minutes, 35.1% 15 to 30 minutes, 14.2% 30 to 45 minutes, 13.7% 45 to 60 minutes, 11.3% 60 minutes or more (2000)

MANSFIELD (town). Covers a land area of 39.574 square miles and a water area of 0.013 square miles. Located at 42.31° N. Lat.; 78.75° W. Long.
Population: 724 (1990); 800 (2000); 792 (2005); 776 (2010 projected); Race: 99.1% White, 0.1% Black, 0.3% Asian, 0.5% Hispanic of any race (2005); Density: 20.0 persons per square mile (2005); Average household size: 2.57 (2005); Median age: 39.6 (2005); Males per 100 females: 108.4 (2005); Marriage status: 22.3% never married, 64.8% now married, 6.5% widowed, 6.5% divorced (2000); Foreign born: 2.1% (2000); Ancestry (includes multiple ancestries): 39.2% German, 14.0% Irish, 13.6% English, 9.9% Polish, 7.6% United States or American (2000).
Economy: Single-family building permits issued: 12 (2005); Multi-family building permits issued: 0 (2005); Employment by occupation: 13.2% management, 14.4% professional, 16.6% services, 16.8% sales, 0.5% farming, 11.2% construction, 27.3% production (2000).
Income: Per capita income: $21,760 (2005); Median household income: $41,273 (2005); Average household income: $55,901 (2005); Percent of households with income of $100,000 or more: 7.5% (2005); Poverty rate: 8.0% (2000).
Education: Percent of population age 25 and over with: High school diploma (including GED) or higher: 82.6% (2005); Bachelor's degree or higher: 18.2% (2005); Master's degree or higher: 5.1% (2005).
Housing: Homeownership rate: 87.3% (2005); Median home value: $116,118 (2005); Median rent: $405 per month (2000); Median age of housing: 27 years (2000).
Transportation: Commute to work: 88.4% car, 0.0% public transportation, 4.4% walk, 6.2% work from home (2000); Travel time to work: 36.2% less than 15 minutes, 31.8% 15 to 30 minutes, 18.4% 30 to 45 minutes, 6.0% 45 to 60 minutes, 7.6% 60 minutes or more (2000)

NAPOLI (town). Covers a land area of 36.400 square miles and a water area of 0.144 square miles. Located at 42.21° N. Lat.; 78.89° W. Long. Elevation is 1,735 feet.
Population: 1,102 (1990); 1,159 (2000); 1,215 (2005); 1,232 (2010 projected); Race: 96.2% White, 0.6% Black, 1.2% Asian, 0.4% Hispanic of any race (2005); Density: 33.4 persons per square mile (2005); Average household size: 3.03 (2005); Median age: 35.3 (2005); Males per 100 females: 103.9 (2005); Marriage status: 21.9% never married, 65.3% now married, 4.6% widowed, 8.2% divorced (2000); Foreign born: 0.8% (2000); Ancestry (includes multiple ancestries): 26.9% German, 17.7% English, 15.7% Irish, 7.1% United States or American, 4.8% Pennsylvania German (2000).
Economy: Single-family building permits issued: 8 (2005); Multi-family building permits issued: 0 (2005); Employment by occupation: 6.6% management, 15.1% professional, 19.7% services, 14.6% sales, 5.1% farming, 10.6% construction, 28.4% production (2000).
Income: Per capita income: $15,442 (2005); Median household income: $37,979 (2005); Average household income: $46,247 (2005); Percent of households with income of $100,000 or more: 7.0% (2005); Poverty rate: 20.1% (2000).
Education: Percent of population age 25 and over with: High school diploma (including GED) or higher: 74.0% (2005); Bachelor's degree or higher: 8.4% (2005); Master's degree or higher: 3.2% (2005).
Housing: Homeownership rate: 87.0% (2005); Median home value: $80,175 (2005); Median rent: $259 per month (2000); Median age of housing: 29 years (2000).
Transportation: Commute to work: 85.6% car, 0.0% public transportation, 3.5% walk, 8.9% work from home (2000); Travel time to work: 23.9% less than 15 minutes, 32.2% 15 to 30 minutes, 30.1% 30 to 45 minutes, 7.2% 45 to 60 minutes, 6.6% 60 minutes or more (2000)

NEW ALBION (town). Covers a land area of 36.349 square miles and a water area of 0.077 square miles. Located at 42.31° N. Lat.; 78.87° W. Long.
Population: 1,978 (1990); 2,068 (2000); 2,059 (2005); 2,024 (2010 projected); Race: 98.7% White, 0.2% Black, 0.0% Asian, 2.4% Hispanic of any race (2005); Density: 56.6 persons per square mile (2005); Average household size: 2.52 (2005); Median age: 38.5 (2005); Males per 100 females: 101.1 (2005); Marriage status: 21.9% never married, 60.3% now married, 7.1% widowed, 10.7% divorced (2000); Foreign born: 1.2% (2000); Ancestry (includes multiple ancestries): 42.1% German, 18.6% English, 14.7% Irish, 7.2% Polish, 6.3% United States or American (2000).
Economy: Single-family building permits issued: 0 (2005); Multi-family building permits issued: 0 (2005); Employment by occupation: 5.8% management, 20.0% professional, 19.6% services, 20.6% sales, 0.7% farming, 13.0% construction, 20.3% production (2000).
Income: Per capita income: $19,283 (2005); Median household income: $39,207 (2005); Average household income: $48,133 (2005); Percent of households with income of $100,000 or more: 7.0% (2005); Poverty rate: 10.3% (2000).
Education: Percent of population age 25 and over with: High school diploma (including GED) or higher: 81.2% (2005); Bachelor's degree or higher: 13.3% (2005); Master's degree or higher: 6.2% (2005).
Housing: Homeownership rate: 78.0% (2005); Median home value: $85,962 (2005); Median rent: $313 per month (2000); Median age of housing: 60+ years (2000).
Transportation: Commute to work: 91.5% car, 0.0% public transportation, 3.6% walk, 4.0% work from home (2000); Travel time to work: 28.4% less than 15 minutes, 34.0% 15 to 30 minutes, 19.0% 30 to 45 minutes, 8.7% 45 to 60 minutes, 9.9% 60 minutes or more (2000)

OLEAN (city). Covers a land area of 5.930 square miles and a water area of 0.231 square miles. Located at 42.08° N. Lat.; 78.43° W. Long. Elevation is 1,451 feet.

History: Olean came to life as a lumber camp. From their lumber, settlers built rafts to sell to emigrants who gathered to await the spring flood which would float them down the Allegheny and Ohio Rivers to the western frontier.
Population: 16,946 (1990); 15,347 (2000); 14,891 (2005); 14,424 (2010 projected); Race: 92.3% White, 4.2% Black, 1.2% Asian, 1.9% Hispanic of any race (2005); Density: 2,511.1 persons per square mile (2005); Average household size: 2.35 (2005); Median age: 39.5 (2005); Males per 100 females: 88.8 (2005); Marriage status: 26.5% never married, 54.0% now married, 9.1% widowed, 10.4% divorced (2000); Foreign born: 1.8% (2000); Ancestry (includes multiple ancestries): 27.6% German, 21.2% Irish, 12.6% Italian, 12.0% English, 10.9% Polish (2000).
Economy: Single-family building permits issued: 5 (2005); Multi-family building permits issued: 2 (2005); Employment by occupation: 9.3% management, 25.1% professional, 18.9% services, 26.2% sales, 0.2% farming, 5.9% construction, 14.3% production (2000).
Income: Per capita income: $19,101 (2005); Median household income: $33,513 (2005); Average household income: $43,827 (2005); Percent of households with income of $100,000 or more: 6.4% (2005); Poverty rate: 15.9% (2000).
Education: Percent of population age 25 and over with: High school diploma (including GED) or higher: 83.8% (2005); Bachelor's degree or higher: 21.0% (2005); Master's degree or higher: 10.4% (2005).

School District(s)
Boces Cattar-Allegany-Erie-Wyoming (PK-PK)
   2003-04 Enrollment: 419 . . . . (716) 376-8246
Olean City School District (PK-12)
   2003-04 Enrollment: 2,541 . . . . (716) 375-8018

Two-year College(s)
Cattaraugus Allegany BOCES-Practical Nursing Program (Public)
   Fall 2004 Enrollment: 98 . . . . (716) 376-8200
Continental School of Beauty Culture
   Fall 2004 Enrollment: 67 . . . . (716) 372-5095
Olean Business Institute
   Fall 2004 Enrollment: 114 . . . . (716) 372-7978
   2005-06 Tuition: In-state $9,100; Out-of-state $9,100

Housing: Homeownership rate: 59.7% (2005); Median home value: $90,014 (2005); Median rent: $349 per month (2000); Median age of housing: 60+ years (2000).
Hospitals: Olean General Hospital (209 beds)
Safety: Violent crime rate: 11.3 per 10,000 population; Property crime rate: 451.5 per 10,000 population (2004).
Newspapers: Olean Times Herald (Circulation 16,619)
Transportation: Commute to work: 86.5% car, 2.2% public transportation, 8.2% walk, 1.9% work from home (2000); Travel time to work: 68.6% less than 15 minutes, 17.8% 15 to 30 minutes, 7.0% 30 to 45 minutes, 2.9% 45 to 60 minutes, 3.8% 60 minutes or more (2000)
Additional Information Contacts
Chamber of Commerce of Olean & Vicinity . . . . (716) 373-4230
   http://oleanny.org/ccov
City of Olean . . . . (716) 376-5604
   http://www.cityofolean.com/
Greater Olean Area Chamber of Commerce . . . . (716) 372-4433
   http://www.oleanny.com

OLEAN (town). Covers a land area of 29.641 square miles and a water area of 0.079 square miles. Located at 42.06° N. Lat.; 78.41° W. Long. Elevation is 1,451 feet.
History: Once an oil-based economy emanating from nearby Pennsylvania oil fields. St. Bonaventure University nearby. Major outfitting post for settlers moving west down the Allegheny and Ohio rivers in early 1800s. In 1972 a severe flood associated with Hurricane Agnes flooded large areas and damaged more than 2,900 homes. Settled 1804, Incorporated 1893.
Population: 1,999 (1990); 2,029 (2000); 1,880 (2005); 1,859 (2010 projected); Race: 98.0% White, 0.3% Black, 0.9% Asian, 0.6% Hispanic of any race (2005); Density: 63.4 persons per square mile (2005); Average household size: 2.40 (2005); Median age: 42.0 (2005); Males per 100 females: 100.9 (2005); Marriage status: 22.7% never married, 62.6% now married, 6.5% widowed, 8.2% divorced (2000); Foreign born: 0.9% (2000); Ancestry (includes multiple ancestries): 23.9% German, 21.3% Irish, 15.0% Italian, 14.9% English, 10.2% Polish (2000).
Economy: An important commercial center of the region. Manufacturing includes turbines and compressors for the oil industry, electrical items, cutlery and dairy products. St. Bonaventure University nearby.
Single-family building permits issued: 5 (2005); Multi-family building permits issued: 0 (2005); Employment by occupation: 9.2% management, 19.4% professional, 13.5% services, 30.3% sales, 0.0% farming, 10.4% construction, 17.2% production (2000).
Income: Per capita income: $23,254 (2005); Median household income: $44,545 (2005); Average household income: $55,879 (2005); Percent of households with income of $100,000 or more: 12.7% (2005); Poverty rate: 10.2% (2000).
Education: Percent of population age 25 and over with: High school diploma (including GED) or higher: 84.6% (2005); Bachelor's degree or higher: 19.3% (2005); Master's degree or higher: 7.8% (2005).
Housing: Homeownership rate: 81.7% (2005); Median home value: $105,625 (2005); Median rent: $340 per month (2000); Median age of housing: 45 years (2000).
Transportation: Commute to work: 94.7% car, 0.5% public transportation, 1.5% walk, 2.8% work from home (2000); Travel time to work: 57.8% less than 15 minutes, 27.4% 15 to 30 minutes, 7.0% 30 to 45 minutes, 3.7% 45 to 60 minutes, 4.2% 60 minutes or more (2000)

OTTO (town). Covers a land area of 32.179 square miles and a water area of 0.110 square miles. Located at 42.38° N. Lat.; 78.81° W. Long. Elevation is 1,266 feet.
Population: 777 (1990); 831 (2000); 842 (2005); 851 (2010 projected); Race: 98.5% White, 0.0% Black, 0.0% Asian, 0.6% Hispanic of any race (2005); Density: 26.2 persons per square mile (2005); Average household size: 2.64 (2005); Median age: 41.8 (2005); Males per 100 females: 99.1 (2005); Marriage status: 22.3% never married, 61.8% now married, 6.9% widowed, 9.0% divorced (2000); Foreign born: 0.9% (2000); Ancestry (includes multiple ancestries): 46.0% German, 17.2% English, 15.0% Irish, 8.6% Polish, 5.5% French (except Basque) (2000).
Economy: Single-family building permits issued: 2 (2005); Multi-family building permits issued: 0 (2005); Employment by occupation: 8.0% management, 16.8% professional, 15.2% services, 21.2% sales, 3.0% farming, 14.9% construction, 20.9% production (2000).
Income: Per capita income: $19,564 (2005); Median household income: $44,467 (2005); Average household income: $51,638 (2005); Percent of households with income of $100,000 or more: 8.5% (2005); Poverty rate: 9.4% (2000).
Taxes: Total city taxes per capita: $342 (2004); City property taxes per capita: $322 (2004).
Education: Percent of population age 25 and over with: High school diploma (including GED) or higher: 82.6% (2005); Bachelor's degree or higher: 8.3% (2005); Master's degree or higher: 4.1% (2005).
Housing: Homeownership rate: 93.1% (2005); Median home value: $85,897 (2005); Median rent: $383 per month (2000); Median age of housing: 39 years (2000).
Transportation: Commute to work: 89.3% car, 0.6% public transportation, 5.9% walk, 2.5% work from home (2000); Travel time to work: 20.6% less than 15 minutes, 36.5% 15 to 30 minutes, 15.1% 30 to 45 minutes, 11.0% 45 to 60 minutes, 16.8% 60 minutes or more (2000)

PERRYSBURG (village). Covers a land area of 0.987 square miles and a water area of 0 square miles. Located at 42.45° N. Lat.; 79.00° W. Long.
Population: 404 (1990); 408 (2000); 407 (2005); 400 (2010 projected); Race: 93.1% White, 0.7% Black, 0.0% Asian, 1.5% Hispanic of any race (2005); Density: 412.5 persons per square mile (2005); Average household size: 2.71 (2005); Median age: 45.4 (2005); Males per 100 females: 99.5 (2005); Marriage status: 37.3% never married, 47.1% now married, 5.2% widowed, 10.4% divorced (2000); Foreign born: 1.6% (2000); Ancestry (includes multiple ancestries): 32.0% German, 17.4% English, 16.4% Irish, 7.8% Italian, 7.8% Polish (2000).
Economy: Single-family building permits issued: 0 (2005); Multi-family building permits issued: 0 (2005); Employment by occupation: 3.7% management, 14.1% professional, 19.0% services, 28.2% sales, 1.2% farming, 9.2% construction, 24.5% production (2000).
Income: Per capita income: $22,239 (2005); Median household income: $43,824 (2005); Average household income: $59,283 (2005); Percent of households with income of $100,000 or more: 16.0% (2005); Poverty rate: 24.0% (2000).
Education: Percent of population age 25 and over with: High school diploma (including GED) or higher: 70.9% (2005); Bachelor's degree or higher: 8.9% (2005); Master's degree or higher: 2.8% (2005).
Housing: Homeownership rate: 74.0% (2005); Median home value: $98,333 (2005); Median rent: $308 per month (2000); Median age of housing: 60+ years (2000).

Transportation: Commute to work: 95.7% car, 0.0% public transportation, 1.2% walk, 3.1% work from home (2000); Travel time to work: 26.3% less than 15 minutes, 26.9% 15 to 30 minutes, 20.5% 30 to 45 minutes, 17.9% 45 to 60 minutes, 8.3% 60 minutes or more (2000)

PERRYSBURG (town). Covers a land area of 28.500 square miles and a water area of 0.038 square miles. Located at 42.46° N. Lat.; 79.01° W. Long.
Population: 1,838 (1990); 1,771 (2000); 1,776 (2005); 1,739 (2010 projected); Race: 94.8% White, 0.4% Black, 0.1% Asian, 0.8% Hispanic of any race (2005); Density: 62.3 persons per square mile (2005); Average household size: 2.54 (2005); Median age: 42.1 (2005); Males per 100 females: 100.0 (2005); Marriage status: 25.6% never married, 57.4% now married, 7.9% widowed, 9.2% divorced (2000); Foreign born: 2.7% (2000); Ancestry (includes multiple ancestries): 41.5% German, 17.3% Irish, 17.0% English, 10.8% Polish, 9.1% Italian (2000).
Economy: Manufacturing of wood products, furniture. Single-family building permits issued: 2 (2005); Multi-family building permits issued: 0 (2005); Employment by occupation: 8.1% management, 15.6% professional, 20.4% services, 24.0% sales, 2.2% farming, 10.6% construction, 19.2% production (2000).
Income: Per capita income: $20,417 (2005); Median household income: $41,679 (2005); Average household income: $51,246 (2005); Percent of households with income of $100,000 or more: 9.6% (2005); Poverty rate: 13.4% (2000).
Education: Percent of population age 25 and over with: High school diploma (including GED) or higher: 83.9% (2005); Bachelor's degree or higher: 12.3% (2005); Master's degree or higher: 5.3% (2005).
Housing: Homeownership rate: 81.1% (2005); Median home value: $103,553 (2005); Median rent: $298 per month (2000); Median age of housing: 50 years (2000).
Transportation: Commute to work: 93.6% car, 0.0% public transportation, 2.4% walk, 3.2% work from home (2000); Travel time to work: 35.7% less than 15 minutes, 25.0% 15 to 30 minutes, 17.3% 30 to 45 minutes, 14.5% 45 to 60 minutes, 7.6% 60 minutes or more (2000)

PERSIA (town). Covers a land area of 20.928 square miles and a water area of 0.063 square miles. Located at 42.43° N. Lat.; 78.94° W. Long.
Population: 2,530 (1990); 2,512 (2000); 2,396 (2005); 2,322 (2010 projected); Race: 96.5% White, 0.3% Black, 0.4% Asian, 1.1% Hispanic of any race (2005); Density: 114.5 persons per square mile (2005); Average household size: 2.58 (2005); Median age: 42.3 (2005); Males per 100 females: 90.0 (2005); Marriage status: 26.7% never married, 53.2% now married, 10.2% widowed, 9.9% divorced (2000); Foreign born: 1.0% (2000); Ancestry (includes multiple ancestries): 27.9% German, 17.5% Irish, 15.6% English, 13.1% Polish, 6.5% Italian (2000).
Economy: Single-family building permits issued: 0 (2005); Multi-family building permits issued: 0 (2005); Employment by occupation: 6.7% management, 23.8% professional, 23.4% services, 22.3% sales, 2.3% farming, 7.7% construction, 13.8% production (2000).
Income: Per capita income: $18,201 (2005); Median household income: $38,890 (2005); Average household income: $46,300 (2005); Percent of households with income of $100,000 or more: 8.2% (2005); Poverty rate: 13.1% (2000).
Education: Percent of population age 25 and over with: High school diploma (including GED) or higher: 76.7% (2005); Bachelor's degree or higher: 15.9% (2005); Master's degree or higher: 7.0% (2005).
Housing: Homeownership rate: 71.1% (2005); Median home value: $84,599 (2005); Median rent: $329 per month (2000); Median age of housing: 60+ years (2000).
Transportation: Commute to work: 90.9% car, 0.0% public transportation, 6.8% walk, 1.1% work from home (2000); Travel time to work: 52.6% less than 15 minutes, 19.5% 15 to 30 minutes, 9.7% 30 to 45 minutes, 12.2% 45 to 60 minutes, 6.1% 60 minutes or more (2000)

PORTVILLE (village). Covers a land area of 0.812 square miles and a water area of 0 square miles. Located at 42.03° N. Lat.; 78.33° W. Long. Elevation is 1,424 feet.
Population: 1,233 (1990); 1,024 (2000); 1,015 (2005); 986 (2010 projected); Race: 98.5% White, 0.6% Black, 0.0% Asian, 0.7% Hispanic of any race (2005); Density: 1,250.7 persons per square mile (2005); Average household size: 2.42 (2005); Median age: 38.0 (2005); Males per 100 females: 81.6 (2005); Marriage status: 24.1% never married, 54.9% now married, 10.2% widowed, 10.8% divorced (2000); Foreign born: 0.9% (2000); Ancestry (includes multiple ancestries): 28.0% German, 17.8% English, 15.3% Irish, 11.7% Polish, 9.6% Italian (2000).
Economy: Employment by occupation: 8.2% management, 17.2% professional, 19.7% services, 22.6% sales, 1.3% farming, 5.9% construction, 25.3% production (2000).
Income: Per capita income: $19,296 (2005); Median household income: $36,988 (2005); Average household income: $46,631 (2005); Percent of households with income of $100,000 or more: 8.1% (2005); Poverty rate: 14.8% (2000).
Education: Percent of population age 25 and over with: High school diploma (including GED) or higher: 87.1% (2005); Bachelor's degree or higher: 16.9% (2005); Master's degree or higher: 6.7% (2005).

School District(s)
Portville Central School District (PK-12)
 2003-04 Enrollment: 1,066 . . . . (716) 933-7141

Housing: Homeownership rate: 66.0% (2005); Median home value: $86,456 (2005); Median rent: $309 per month (2000); Median age of housing: 60+ years (2000).
Safety: Violent crime rate: 9.9 per 10,000 population; Property crime rate: 356.8 per 10,000 population (2004).
Transportation: Commute to work: 90.5% car, 0.2% public transportation, 4.8% walk, 2.8% work from home (2000); Travel time to work: 34.5% less than 15 minutes, 46.1% 15 to 30 minutes, 10.9% 30 to 45 minutes, 1.1% 45 to 60 minutes, 7.3% 60 minutes or more (2000)

PORTVILLE (town). Covers a land area of 35.637 square miles and a water area of 0.413 square miles. Located at 42.05° N. Lat.; 78.34° W. Long. Elevation is 1,424 feet.
History: Incorporated 1895.
Population: 4,397 (1990); 3,952 (2000); 3,951 (2005); 3,866 (2010 projected); Race: 97.6% White, 0.9% Black, 0.4% Asian, 1.0% Hispanic of any race (2005); Density: 110.9 persons per square mile (2005); Average household size: 2.51 (2005); Median age: 40.7 (2005); Males per 100 females: 94.0 (2005); Marriage status: 20.9% never married, 59.8% now married, 8.6% widowed, 10.8% divorced (2000); Foreign born: 1.5% (2000); Ancestry (includes multiple ancestries): 30.0% German, 16.4% English, 13.0% Irish, 8.7% United States or American, 8.0% Italian (2000).
Economy: Dairy products; grain, potatoes. Single-family building permits issued: 1 (2005); Multi-family building permits issued: 0 (2005); Employment by occupation: 12.4% management, 18.6% professional, 12.8% services, 25.5% sales, 0.4% farming, 7.4% construction, 23.0% production (2000).
Income: Per capita income: $21,322 (2005); Median household income: $44,010 (2005); Average household income: $53,521 (2005); Percent of households with income of $100,000 or more: 10.3% (2005); Poverty rate: 10.4% (2000).
Education: Percent of population age 25 and over with: High school diploma (including GED) or higher: 84.5% (2005); Bachelor's degree or higher: 17.6% (2005); Master's degree or higher: 8.4% (2005).
Housing: Homeownership rate: 79.7% (2005); Median home value: $93,450 (2005); Median rent: $328 per month (2000); Median age of housing: 45 years (2000).
Transportation: Commute to work: 93.3% car, 0.1% public transportation, 2.3% walk, 3.9% work from home (2000); Travel time to work: 36.1% less than 15 minutes, 43.5% 15 to 30 minutes, 10.4% 30 to 45 minutes, 4.3% 45 to 60 minutes, 5.6% 60 minutes or more (2000)

RANDOLPH (village). Covers a land area of 3.250 square miles and a water area of 0.007 square miles. Located at 42.16° N. Lat.; 78.98° W. Long. Elevation is 1,278 feet.
Population: 1,298 (1990); 1,316 (2000); 1,367 (2005); 1,375 (2010 projected); Race: 98.8% White, 0.1% Black, 0.0% Asian, 0.1% Hispanic of any race (2005); Density: 420.6 persons per square mile (2005); Average household size: 2.36 (2005); Median age: 39.3 (2005); Males per 100 females: 87.3 (2005); Marriage status: 22.7% never married, 54.6% now married, 12.0% widowed, 10.7% divorced (2000); Foreign born: 1.1% (2000); Ancestry (includes multiple ancestries): 30.5% German, 18.9% Irish, 18.2% English, 7.9% Swedish, 6.5% United States or American (2000).
Economy: Single-family building permits issued: 1 (2005); Multi-family building permits issued: 0 (2005); Employment by occupation: 13.0% management, 22.6% professional, 14.3% services, 19.7% sales, 2.4% farming, 6.9% construction, 21.1% production (2000).
Income: Per capita income: $21,592 (2005); Median household income: $36,910 (2005); Average household income: $50,350 (2005); Percent of

households with income of $100,000 or more: 9.0% (2005); Poverty rate: 6.0% (2000).
Education: Percent of population age 25 and over with: High school diploma (including GED) or higher: 81.9% (2005); Bachelor's degree or higher: 17.8% (2005); Master's degree or higher: 7.8% (2005).

School District(s)
Randolph Academy Union Free School District (07-12)
    2003-04 Enrollment: 187 . . . . (716) 358-6866
Randolph Central School District (PK-12)
    2003-04 Enrollment: 1,012 . . . . (716) 358-7005

Housing: Homeownership rate: 64.4% (2005); Median home value: $87,024 (2005); Median rent: $297 per month (2000); Median age of housing: 60+ years (2000).
Newspapers: Randolph Register (General - Circulation 1,500)
Transportation: Commute to work: 92.7% car, 0.0% public transportation, 3.8% walk, 3.5% work from home (2000); Travel time to work: 41.6% less than 15 minutes, 34.4% 15 to 30 minutes, 17.9% 30 to 45 minutes, 2.5% 45 to 60 minutes, 3.6% 60 minutes or more (2000)

RANDOLPH (town).
Covers a land area of 36.159 square miles and a water area of 0.141 square miles. Located at 42.15° N. Lat.; 78.99° W. Long. Elevation is 1,278 feet.
Population: 2,613 (1990); 2,681 (2000); 2,790 (2005); 2,815 (2010 projected); Race: 96.8% White, 1.2% Black, 0.3% Asian, 0.9% Hispanic of any race (2005); Density: 77.2 persons per square mile (2005); Average household size: 2.62 (2005); Median age: 38.0 (2005); Males per 100 females: 96.8 (2005); Marriage status: 24.3% never married, 57.7% now married, 9.6% widowed, 8.4% divorced (2000); Foreign born: 1.1% (2000); Ancestry (includes multiple ancestries): 23.2% German, 16.9% Irish, 16.7% English, 8.6% United States or American, 8.2% Swedish (2000).
Economy: State trout hatchery 2 miles Southeast of village. Single-family building permits issued: 6 (2005); Multi-family building permits issued: 0 (2005); Employment by occupation: 11.3% management, 18.7% professional, 15.8% services, 19.2% sales, 3.0% farming, 7.2% construction, 24.8% production (2000).
Income: Per capita income: $19,269 (2005); Median household income: $39,902 (2005); Average household income: $50,115 (2005); Percent of households with income of $100,000 or more: 8.2% (2005); Poverty rate: 6.6% (2000).
Education: Percent of population age 25 and over with: High school diploma (including GED) or higher: 79.0% (2005); Bachelor's degree or higher: 13.4% (2005); Master's degree or higher: 5.5% (2005).
Housing: Homeownership rate: 74.1% (2005); Median home value: $88,428 (2005); Median rent: $310 per month (2000); Median age of housing: 60+ years (2000).
Transportation: Commute to work: 93.5% car, 0.0% public transportation, 3.7% walk, 2.8% work from home (2000); Travel time to work: 41.1% less than 15 minutes, 34.6% 15 to 30 minutes, 18.5% 30 to 45 minutes, 3.0% 45 to 60 minutes, 2.8% 60 minutes or more (2000)

RED HOUSE (town).
Covers a land area of 55.687 square miles and a water area of 0.170 square miles. Located at 42.04° N. Lat.; 78.80° W. Long.
Population: 159 (1990); 38 (2000); 37 (2005); 35 (2010 projected); Race: 97.3% White, 0.0% Black, 0.0% Asian, 0.0% Hispanic of any race (2005); Density: 0.7 persons per square mile (2005); Average household size: 2.64 (2005); Median age: 48.1 (2005); Males per 100 females: 60.9 (2005); Marriage status: 22.9% never married, 68.6% now married, 5.7% widowed, 2.9% divorced (2000); Foreign born: 0.0% (2000); Ancestry (includes multiple ancestries): 33.3% German, 26.2% English, 26.2% Polish, 21.4% United States or American, 11.9% Italian (2000).
Economy: In Allegany Indian Reservation. Main entrance to Allegany State Park is here. Employment by occupation: 26.3% management, 26.3% professional, 15.8% services, 21.1% sales, 0.0% farming, 10.5% construction, 0.0% production (2000).
Income: Per capita income: $28,514 (2005); Median household income: $83,333 (2005); Average household income: $75,357 (2005); Percent of households with income of $100,000 or more: 35.7% (2005); Poverty rate: 4.8% (2000).
Education: Percent of population age 25 and over with: High school diploma (including GED) or higher: 88.5% (2005); Bachelor's degree or higher: 11.5% (2005); Master's degree or higher: 0.0% (2005).
Housing: Homeownership rate: 64.3% (2005); Median home value: $210,000 (2005); Median rent: $325 per month (2000); Median age of housing: 50 years (2000).
Transportation: Commute to work: 68.4% car, 0.0% public transportation, 10.5% walk, 21.1% work from home (2000); Travel time to work: 60.0% less than 15 minutes, 20.0% 15 to 30 minutes, 0.0% 30 to 45 minutes, 0.0% 45 to 60 minutes, 20.0% 60 minutes or more (2000)

SAINT BONAVENTURE (CDP).
Covers a land area of 2.030 square miles and a water area of 0.088 square miles. Located at 42.08° N. Lat.; 78.47° W. Long.
Population: 2,306 (1990); 2,127 (2000); 2,152 (2005); 2,200 (2010 projected); Race: 95.8% White, 2.4% Black, 0.7% Asian, 2.0% Hispanic of any race (2005); Density: 1,060.3 persons per square mile (2005); Average household size: 8.54 (2005); Median age: 20.6 (2005); Males per 100 females: 90.9 (2005); Marriage status: 62.9% never married, 31.5% now married, 4.4% widowed, 1.3% divorced (2000); Foreign born: 1.5% (2000); Ancestry (includes multiple ancestries): 36.8% Irish, 26.4% German, 25.5% Italian, 10.4% Polish, 6.6% English (2000).
Economy: Employment by occupation: 5.8% management, 19.0% professional, 19.4% services, 45.0% sales, 0.0% farming, 4.0% construction, 6.8% production (2000).
Income: Per capita income: $8,488 (2005); Median household income: $38,980 (2005); Average household income: $44,266 (2005); Percent of households with income of $100,000 or more: 5.2% (2005); Poverty rate: 9.0% (2000).
Education: Percent of population age 25 and over with: High school diploma (including GED) or higher: 91.6% (2005); Bachelor's degree or higher: 17.5% (2005); Master's degree or higher: 6.3% (2005).

Four-year College(s)
Saint Bonaventure University
    Fall 2004 Enrollment: 2,720 . . . . (716) 375-2000
    2005-06 Tuition: In-state $21,450; Out-of-state $21,450

Housing: Homeownership rate: 81.0% (2005); Median home value: $110,606 (2005); Median rent: $340 per month (2000); Median age of housing: 48 years (2000).
Transportation: Commute to work: 53.2% car, 0.0% public transportation, 43.1% walk, 1.0% work from home (2000); Travel time to work: 73.3% less than 15 minutes, 19.5% 15 to 30 minutes, 1.5% 30 to 45 minutes, 2.8% 45 to 60 minutes, 2.9% 60 minutes or more (2000)

SALAMANCA (city).
Covers a land area of 6.004 square miles and a water area of 0.232 square miles. Located at 42.15° N. Lat.; 78.71° W. Long. Elevation is 1,392 feet.
Population: 6,566 (1990); 6,097 (2000); 5,918 (2005); 5,701 (2010 projected); Race: 85.3% White, 1.0% Black, 0.5% Asian, 3.2% Hispanic of any race (2005); Density: 985.8 persons per square mile (2005); Average household size: 2.47 (2005); Median age: 37.8 (2005); Males per 100 females: 90.0 (2005); Marriage status: 27.7% never married, 50.1% now married, 11.6% widowed, 10.6% divorced (2000); Foreign born: 0.9% (2000); Ancestry (includes multiple ancestries): 25.6% German, 21.3% Irish, 16.0% Other groups, 13.8% Polish, 13.6% English (2000).
Economy: Single-family building permits issued: 3 (2005); Multi-family building permits issued: 0 (2005); Employment by occupation: 8.0% management, 15.5% professional, 20.1% services, 23.2% sales, 1.1% farming, 6.4% construction, 25.7% production (2000).
Income: Per capita income: $14,487 (2005); Median household income: $26,961 (2005); Average household income: $34,425 (2005); Percent of households with income of $100,000 or more: 2.8% (2005); Poverty rate: 22.2% (2000).
Education: Percent of population age 25 and over with: High school diploma (including GED) or higher: 77.4% (2005); Bachelor's degree or higher: 10.6% (2005); Master's degree or higher: 4.4% (2005).

School District(s)
Salamanca City School District (PK-12)
    2003-04 Enrollment: 1,513 . . . . (716) 945-2403

Housing: Homeownership rate: 61.0% (2005); Median home value: $63,862 (2005); Median rent: $296 per month (2000); Median age of housing: 60+ years (2000).
Safety: Violent crime rate: 166.3 per 10,000 population; Property crime rate: 477.1 per 10,000 population (2004).
Newspapers: Salamanca Press (Circulation 2,300)
Transportation: Commute to work: 89.6% car, 0.9% public transportation, 5.9% walk, 2.4% work from home (2000); Travel time to work: 50.8% less than 15 minutes, 32.1% 15 to 30 minutes, 11.1% 30 to 45 minutes, 2.3% 45 to 60 minutes, 3.7% 60 minutes or more (2000)
Additional Information Contacts

Salamanca Chamber of Commerce.................... (716) 945-2034
http://www.salamancachamber.com

SALAMANCA (town). Covers a land area of 18.248 square miles and a water area of 0 square miles. Located at 42.16° N. Lat.; 78.77° W. Long. Elevation is 1,392 feet.
History: In Allegany Indian Reservation. Allegany State Park is just S. Furniture, plastic and wood prods.; printing. Most of the city is built on land that is leased from the Seneca Nation's Allegany Indian Reservation. Settled in 1860s; inc. as city 1913.
Population: 477 (1990); 544 (2000); 512 (2005); 496 (2010 projected); Race: 96.7% White, 0.6% Black, 0.0% Asian, 0.8% Hispanic of any race (2005); Density: 28.1 persons per square mile (2005); Average household size: 2.56 (2005); Median age: 44.7 (2005); Males per 100 females: 109.8 (2005); Marriage status: 18.3% never married, 67.9% now married, 7.6% widowed, 6.2% divorced (2000); Foreign born: 0.0% (2000); Ancestry (includes multiple ancestries): 30.6% German, 20.0% Irish, 18.0% Polish, 16.3% English, 8.9% Italian (2000).
Economy: In Allegany Indian Reservation. Allegany State Park is just S. Furniture, plastic and wood prods.; printing. Most of the city is built on land that is leased from the Seneca Nation's Allegany Indian Reservation. Settled in 1860s; inc. as city 1913. Single-family building permits issued: 0 (2005); Multi-family building permits issued: 0 (2005); Employment by occupation: 10.2% management, 13.3% professional, 24.8% services, 22.4% sales, 2.0% farming, 12.6% construction, 14.6% production (2000).
Income: Per capita income: $19,219 (2005); Median household income: $42,941 (2005); Average household income: $49,200 (2005); Percent of households with income of $100,000 or more: 6.0% (2005); Poverty rate: 4.2% (2000).
Education: Percent of population age 25 and over with: High school diploma (including GED) or higher: 81.0% (2005); Bachelor's degree or higher: 12.9% (2005); Master's degree or higher: 7.2% (2005).
Housing: Homeownership rate: 89.0% (2005); Median home value: $88,571 (2005); Median rent: $325 per month (2000); Median age of housing: 41 years (2000).
Transportation: Commute to work: 94.9% car, 0.0% public transportation, 2.9% walk, 2.2% work from home (2000); Travel time to work: 38.9% less than 15 minutes, 31.9% 15 to 30 minutes, 17.0% 30 to 45 minutes, 7.4% 45 to 60 minutes, 4.8% 60 minutes or more (2000)

SOUTH DAYTON (village). Covers a land area of 1.006 square miles and a water area of 0 square miles. Located at 42.36° N. Lat.; 79.05° W. Long. Elevation is 1,303 feet.
Population: 601 (1990); 662 (2000); 630 (2005); 611 (2010 projected); Race: 97.9% White, 0.2% Black, 0.0% Asian, 2.5% Hispanic of any race (2005); Density: 626.4 persons per square mile (2005); Average household size: 2.64 (2005); Median age: 33.8 (2005); Males per 100 females: 86.9 (2005); Marriage status: 27.2% never married, 48.3% now married, 10.1% widowed, 14.4% divorced (2000); Foreign born: 1.2% (2000); Ancestry (includes multiple ancestries): 30.3% German, 24.7% English, 11.1% Irish, 7.6% Polish, 7.3% Other groups (2000).
Economy: Single-family building permits issued: 1 (2005); Multi-family building permits issued: 0 (2005); Employment by occupation: 5.0% management, 15.4% professional, 15.8% services, 21.9% sales, 3.8% farming, 9.2% construction, 28.8% production (2000).
Income: Per capita income: $15,131 (2005); Median household income: $33,556 (2005); Average household income: $39,885 (2005); Percent of households with income of $100,000 or more: 5.0% (2005); Poverty rate: 17.3% (2000).
Education: Percent of population age 25 and over with: High school diploma (including GED) or higher: 80.6% (2005); Bachelor's degree or higher: 12.6% (2005); Master's degree or higher: 5.6% (2005).
Housing: Homeownership rate: 70.3% (2005); Median home value: $72,414 (2005); Median rent: $304 per month (2000); Median age of housing: 60+ years (2000).
Transportation: Commute to work: 86.7% car, 2.0% public transportation, 4.4% walk, 5.2% work from home (2000); Travel time to work: 35.2% less than 15 minutes, 30.1% 15 to 30 minutes, 19.5% 30 to 45 minutes, 10.6% 45 to 60 minutes, 4.7% 60 minutes or more (2000)

SOUTH VALLEY (town). Covers a land area of 36.934 square miles and a water area of 0.167 square miles. Located at 42.03° N. Lat.; 78.99° W. Long.
Population: 281 (1990); 302 (2000); 318 (2005); 323 (2010 projected); Race: 98.1% White, 0.3% Black, 0.6% Asian, 0.0% Hispanic of any race (2005); Density: 8.6 persons per square mile (2005); Average household size: 2.37 (2005); Median age: 44.6 (2005); Males per 100 females: 120.8 (2005); Marriage status: 18.1% never married, 65.2% now married, 7.7% widowed, 9.0% divorced (2000); Foreign born: 0.0% (2000); Ancestry (includes multiple ancestries): 29.5% German, 25.9% Irish, 16.3% Swedish, 14.3% English, 6.0% Italian (2000).
Economy: Single-family building permits issued: 6 (2005); Multi-family building permits issued: 0 (2005); Employment by occupation: 10.2% management, 8.7% professional, 25.2% services, 17.3% sales, 0.0% farming, 15.7% construction, 22.8% production (2000).
Income: Per capita income: $23,223 (2005); Median household income: $49,063 (2005); Average household income: $55,112 (2005); Percent of households with income of $100,000 or more: 5.2% (2005); Poverty rate: 6.4% (2000).
Education: Percent of population age 25 and over with: High school diploma (including GED) or higher: 78.7% (2005); Bachelor's degree or higher: 3.0% (2005); Master's degree or higher: 0.9% (2005).
Housing: Homeownership rate: 91.0% (2005); Median home value: $104,167 (2005); Median rent: $250 per month (2000); Median age of housing: 22 years (2000).
Transportation: Commute to work: 92.6% car, 0.0% public transportation, 7.4% walk, 0.0% work from home (2000); Travel time to work: 9.8% less than 15 minutes, 27.9% 15 to 30 minutes, 48.4% 30 to 45 minutes, 8.2% 45 to 60 minutes, 5.7% 60 minutes or more (2000)

WEST VALLEY (unincorporated postal area, zip code 14171). Covers a land area of 51.540 square miles and a water area of 0.088 square miles. Located at 42.42° N. Lat.; 78.64° W. Long. Elevation is 1,522 feet.
History: In 1966, a private company opened a plant here to recycle uranium and plutonium, the idea being that nuclear power plants would deplete these materials if they were not conserved. This was incorrect, and by 1972 the plant had closed. In 1980 legislation was approved for an 8-year, $400-million cleanup of the plant. Relying on robotic labor to handle the radioactive waste, it still continues, and the cost has already reached $1.1 billion with the final cost estimated at $1.5 billion.
Population: 0 (2000); Race: 98.0% White, 0.3% Black, 0.2% Asian, 0.1% Hispanic of any race (2000); Density: 0.0 persons per square mile (2000); Age: 27.7% under 18, 10.3% over 64 (2000); Marriage status: 18.8% never married, 67.0% now married, 4.0% widowed, 10.1% divorced (2000); Foreign born: 1.8% (2000); Ancestry (includes multiple ancestries): 41.8% German, 17.2% Irish, 12.7% English, 11.9% Polish, 4.1% French (except Basque) (2000).
Economy: Employment by occupation: 10.6% management, 14.2% professional, 18.0% services, 20.5% sales, 0.7% farming, 11.2% construction, 24.9% production (2000).
Income: Per capita income: $19,169 (2000); Median household income: $42,727 (2000); Poverty rate: 6.2% (2000).
Education: Percent of population age 25 and over with: High school diploma (including GED) or higher: 87.4% (2000); Bachelor's degree or higher: 15.0% (2000).
School District(s)
West Valley Central School District (PK-12)
    2003-04 Enrollment: 492 .... (716) 942-3293
Housing: Homeownership rate: 86.5% (2000); Median home value: $75,100 (2000); Median rent: $328 per month (2000); Median age of housing: 28 years (2000).
Transportation: Commute to work: 94.4% car, 0.5% public transportation, 1.6% walk, 3.1% work from home (2000); Travel time to work: 35.1% less than 15 minutes, 26.0% 15 to 30 minutes, 13.1% 30 to 45 minutes, 17.4% 45 to 60 minutes, 8.4% 60 minutes or more (2000)

WESTON MILLS (CDP). Covers a land area of 6.657 square miles and a water area of 0.091 square miles. Located at 42.07° N. Lat.; 78.37° W. Long.
Population: 1,750 (1990); 1,608 (2000); 1,563 (2005); 1,542 (2010 projected); Race: 97.4% White, 1.0% Black, 0.4% Asian, 0.8% Hispanic of any race (2005); Density: 234.8 persons per square mile (2005); Average household size: 2.40 (2005); Median age: 41.5 (2005); Males per 100 females: 101.2 (2005); Marriage status: 19.4% never married, 59.1% now married, 7.8% widowed, 13.7% divorced (2000); Foreign born: 2.0% (2000); Ancestry (includes multiple ancestries): 26.1% German, 18.1% Irish, 16.7% English, 11.5% Italian, 10.0% Polish (2000).

Economy: Employment by occupation: 11.6% management, 18.4% professional, 12.3% services, 31.8% sales, 0.0% farming, 8.2% construction, 17.7% production (2000).
Income: Per capita income: $22,086 (2005); Median household income: $41,061 (2005); Average household income: $53,108 (2005); Percent of households with income of $100,000 or more: 10.6% (2005); Poverty rate: 5.1% (2000).
Education: Percent of population age 25 and over with: High school diploma (including GED) or higher: 83.6% (2005); Bachelor's degree or higher: 20.7% (2005); Master's degree or higher: 8.9% (2005).
Housing: Homeownership rate: 79.2% (2005); Median home value: $102,964 (2005); Median rent: $344 per month (2000); Median age of housing: 44 years (2000).
Transportation: Commute to work: 92.2% car, 0.0% public transportation, 2.9% walk, 4.3% work from home (2000); Travel time to work: 48.5% less than 15 minutes, 36.3% 15 to 30 minutes, 7.3% 30 to 45 minutes, 2.7% 45 to 60 minutes, 5.1% 60 minutes or more (2000)

YORKSHIRE (town). Covers a land area of 36.958 square miles and a water area of 0.071 square miles. Located at 42.49° N. Lat.; 78.48° W. Long. Elevation is 1,438 feet.
Population: 3,905 (1990); 4,210 (2000); 4,195 (2005); 4,150 (2010 projected); Race: 98.7% White, 0.0% Black, 0.4% Asian, 1.0% Hispanic of any race (2005); Density: 113.5 persons per square mile (2005); Average household size: 2.47 (2005); Median age: 37.2 (2005); Males per 100 females: 102.5 (2005); Marriage status: 22.8% never married, 59.0% now married, 6.9% widowed, 11.3% divorced (2000); Foreign born: 1.4% (2000); Ancestry (includes multiple ancestries): 35.5% German, 13.0% English, 11.2% Polish, 10.8% Irish, 9.0% United States or American (2000).
Economy: Single-family building permits issued: 3 (2005); Multi-family building permits issued: 0 (2005); Employment by occupation: 5.1% management, 12.1% professional, 13.6% services, 22.1% sales, 1.9% farming, 13.7% construction, 31.6% production (2000).
Income: Per capita income: $17,736 (2005); Median household income: $35,825 (2005); Average household income: $43,895 (2005); Percent of households with income of $100,000 or more: 5.3% (2005); Poverty rate: 13.7% (2000).
Education: Percent of population age 25 and over with: High school diploma (including GED) or higher: 82.2% (2005); Bachelor's degree or higher: 7.2% (2005); Master's degree or higher: 2.1% (2005).

School District(s)
Yorkshire-Pioneer Central School District (KG-12)
    2003-04 Enrollment: 2,928 . . . . (716) 492-9304
Housing: Homeownership rate: 76.7% (2005); Median home value: $87,650 (2005); Median rent: $323 per month (2000); Median age of housing: 26 years (2000).
Transportation: Commute to work: 94.5% car, 0.1% public transportation, 3.3% walk, 1.6% work from home (2000); Travel time to work: 39.6% less than 15 minutes, 21.6% 15 to 30 minutes, 18.1% 30 to 45 minutes, 11.7% 45 to 60 minutes, 9.0% 60 minutes or more (2000)

YORKSHIRE (CDP). Covers a land area of 1.847 square miles and a water area of 0.008 square miles. Located at 42.52° N. Lat.; 78.47° W. Long.
Population: 1,340 (1990); 1,403 (2000); 1,410 (2005); 1,400 (2010 projected); Race: 99.1% White, 0.1% Black, 0.4% Asian, 1.1% Hispanic of any race (2005); Density: 763.4 persons per square mile (2005); Average household size: 2.26 (2005); Median age: 38.1 (2005); Males per 100 females: 96.7 (2005); Marriage status: 17.7% never married, 57.8% now married, 10.6% widowed, 13.9% divorced (2000); Foreign born: 0.9% (2000); Ancestry (includes multiple ancestries): 31.6% German, 15.2% United States or American, 11.9% Irish, 11.8% English, 10.1% Polish (2000).
Economy: Employment by occupation: 2.4% management, 6.2% professional, 14.2% services, 25.5% sales, 1.2% farming, 9.6% construction, 41.0% production (2000).
Income: Per capita income: $16,991 (2005); Median household income: $32,061 (2005); Average household income: $38,332 (2005); Percent of households with income of $100,000 or more: 4.5% (2005); Poverty rate: 16.3% (2000).
Education: Percent of population age 25 and over with: High school diploma (including GED) or higher: 81.0% (2005); Bachelor's degree or higher: 2.1% (2005); Master's degree or higher: 0.7% (2005).
Housing: Homeownership rate: 77.8% (2005); Median home value: $52,778 (2005); Median rent: $346 per month (2000); Median age of housing: 21 years (2000).
Transportation: Commute to work: 95.4% car, 0.0% public transportation, 3.6% walk, 1.0% work from home (2000); Travel time to work: 36.7% less than 15 minutes, 15.5% 15 to 30 minutes, 28.0% 30 to 45 minutes, 9.3% 45 to 60 minutes, 10.5% 60 minutes or more (2000)

Cayuga County

Located in west central New York; bounded on the north by Lake Ontario; drained by the Seneca River. Covers a land area of 693.18 square miles, a water area of 170.46 square miles, and is located in the Eastern Time Zone. The county government was organized in 1799. County seat is Auburn.

Cayuga County is part of the Auburn, NY Micropolitan Statistical Area. The entire metro area includes: Cayuga County, NY

Weather Station: Aurora Research Farm   Elevation: 830 feet

	Jan	Feb	Mar	Apr	May	Jun	Jul	Aug	Sep	Oct	Nov	Dec
High	31	33	42	55	67	76	81	80	72	60	48	37
Low	16	17	25	36	46	56	60	58	51	41	33	23
Precip	1.9	1.9	2.5	3.2	3.2	4.2	3.4	3.7	4.3	3.3	3.4	2.5
Snow	14.0	12.1	11.3	4.3	0.4	0.0	0.0	0.0	0.0	0.4	5.9	13.4

High and Low temperatures in degrees Fahrenheit; Precipitation and Snow in inches

Population: 82,313 (1990); 81,963 (2000); 81,918 (2005); 81,819 (2010 projected); Race: 93.2% White, 4.2% Black, 0.4% Asian, 2.4% Hispanic of any race (2005); Density: 118.2 persons per square mile (2005); Average household size: 2.64 (2005); Median age: 38.8 (2005); Males per 100 females: 101.8 (2005).
Religion: Five largest groups: 33.1% Catholic Church, 4.9% The United Methodist Church, 1.8% American Baptist Churches in the USA, 1.7% Presbyterian Church (U.S.A.), 1.0% Conservative Baptist Association of America (2000).
Economy: Unemployment rate: 4.8% (2005); Total civilian labor force: 42,098 (2005); Leading industries: 20.7% manufacturing; 19.4% health care and social assistance; 18.4% retail trade (2003); Farms: 881 totaling 238,129 acres (2002); Companies that employ 500 or more persons: 1 (2003); Companies that employ 100 to 499 persons: 26 (2003); Companies that employ less than 100 persons: 1,561 (2003); Black-owned businesses: n/a (2002); Hispanic-owned businesses: n/a (2002); Women-owned businesses: 1,335 (2002); Retail sales per capita: $10,214 (2006). Single-family building permits issued: 161 (2005); Multi-family building permits issued: 0 (2005).
Income: Per capita income: $20,842 (2005); Median household income: $43,183 (2005); Average household income: $52,668 (2005); Percent of households with income of $100,000 or more: 10.1% (2005); Poverty rate: 11.6% (2003); Bankruptcy rate: 8.64% (2005).
Education: Percent of population age 25 and over with: High school diploma (including GED) or higher: 79.2% (2005); Bachelor's degree or higher: 15.5% (2005); Master's degree or higher: 6.2% (2005).
Housing: Homeownership rate: 72.7% (2005); Median home value: $102,637 (2005); Median rent: $392 per month (2000); Median age of housing: 51 years (2000).
Health: Birth rate: 90.2 per 10,000 population (2004); Death rate: 83.0 per 10,000 population (2004); Age-adjusted cancer mortality rate: 199.6 deaths per 100,000 population (2002); Number of physicians: 10.3 per 10,000 population (2004); Hospital beds: 29.8 per 10,000 population (2003); Hospital admissions: 738.0 per 10,000 population (2003).
Elections: 2004 Presidential election results: 49.2% Bush, 48.6% Kerry, 1.9% Nader, 0.2% Badnarik
National and State Parks: Bear Swamp State Forest; Fair Haven Beach State Park; Fillmore Glen State Park; Long Point State Park; Summer Hill State Forest

Additional Information Contacts
Cayuga County Government . . . . (315) 253-1308
    http://www.co.cayuga.ny.us/
City of Auburn . . . . (315) 255-4100
    http://www.ci.auburn.ny.us
Town of Aurelius . . . . (315) 255-1894
    http://co.cayuga.ny.us/aurelius/index.html
Town of Brutus . . . . (315) 834-9398
    http://co.cayuga.ny.us/brutus/

Town of Conquest . . . . (315) 776-4539
 http://co.cayuga.ny.us/conquest/
Town of Fleming . . . . (315) 292-8988
 http://co.cayuga.ny.us/fleming/
Town of Genoa . . . . (315) 364-5505
 http://co.cayuga.ny.us/genoa/
Town of Ira . . . . (315) 626-6905
 http://co.cayuga.ny.us/ira/
Town of Ledyard . . . . (315) 364-5707
 http://co.cayuga.ny.us/ledyard/
Town of Locke . . . . (315) 497-9338
 http://co.cayuga.ny.us/locke/
Town of Mentz . . . . (315) 776-8692
 http://co.cayuga.ny.us/mentz/
Town of Montezuma . . . . (315) 776-8844
 http://co.cayuga.ny.us/montezuma/
Town of Moravia . . . . (315) 497-1972
 http://co.cayuga.ny.us/townofmoravia/
Town of Niles . . . . (315) 497-0066
 http://co.cayuga.ny.us/niles/
Town of Owasco . . . . (315) 253-9021
 http://co.cayuga.ny.us/owasco/
Town of Scipio . . . . (315) 364-5740
 http://co.cayuga.ny.us/scipio/
Town of Sempronius . . . . (315) 496-2060
 http://co.cayuga.ny.us/sempronius/
Town of Sennett . . . . (315) 253-3712
 http://co.cayuga.ny.us/sennett/
Town of Springport . . . . (315) 889-7717
 http://co.cayuga.ny.us/springport/
Town of Sterling . . . . (315) 947-5666
 http://co.cayuga.ny.us/sterling/
Town of Throop . . . . (315) 252-7373
 http://co.cayuga.ny.us/throop/
Town of Venice . . . . (315) 497-1898
 http://co.cayuga.ny.us/venice/
Village of Cayuga . . . . (315) 252-1707
 http://co.cayuga.ny.us/cayugavil/
Village of Fair Haven . . . . (315) 947-5112
 http://co.cayuga.ny.us/fairhaven/
Village of Moravia . . . . (315) 497-1820
 http://co.cayuga.ny.us/villageofmoravia/
Village of Port Byron . . . . (315) 776-4321
 http://co.cayuga.ny.us/portbyron/
Village of Union Springs . . . . (315) 889-7341
 http://co.cayuga.ny.us/unionsprings/
Village of Weedsport . . . . (315) 834-6634
 http://co.cayuga.ny.us/weedsport/

Cayuga County Communities

AUBURN (city). Covers a land area of 8.391 square miles and a water area of 0.038 square miles. Located at 42.93° N. Lat.; 76.56° W. Long. Elevation is 677 feet.
History: In 1793, Colonel John Hardenbergh, surveyor and Revolutionary veteran, built the first cabin on the present site of Auburn and a year later erected the first gristmill on the Owasco Outlet. At a meeting in 1805 the present name was taken from Goldsmith's "The Deserted Village." Transportation facilities and abundant water power attracted industry. A scythe factory, a carpet factory, and the D. M. Osborne Company, which was later absorbed by International Harvester, were among its industries. The Auburn Theological Seminary, chartered by the Presbyterian General Assembly in 1819, was merged with the Union Theological Seminary in New York City 120 years later.
Population: 31,258 (1990); 28,574 (2000); 28,044 (2005); 27,396 (2010 projected); Race: 87.7% White, 8.2% Black, 0.6% Asian, 3.6% Hispanic of any race (2005); Density: 3,342.1 persons per square mile (2005); Average household size: 2.48 (2005); Median age: 38.1 (2005); Males per 100 females: 100.0 (2005); Marriage status: 30.3% never married, 48.7% now married, 11.2% widowed, 9.8% divorced (2000); Foreign born: 3.3% (2000); Ancestry (includes multiple ancestries): 22.1% Italian, 20.2% Irish, 14.6% English, 12.4% German, 9.5% Other groups (2000).
Economy: Unemployment rate: 5.1% (2005); Total civilian labor force: 13,367 (2005); Single-family building permits issued: 8 (2005); Multi-family building permits issued: 0 (2005); Employment by occupation: 7.0% management, 19.1% professional, 23.3% services, 24.5% sales, 0.4% farming, 6.9% construction, 18.7% production (2000).
Income: Per capita income: $19,434 (2005); Median household income: $34,529 (2005); Average household income: $44,505 (2005); Percent of households with income of $100,000 or more: 7.4% (2005); Poverty rate: 16.5% (2000).
Education: Percent of population age 25 and over with: High school diploma (including GED) or higher: 74.6% (2005); Bachelor's degree or higher: 13.8% (2005); Master's degree or higher: 5.6% (2005).
School District(s)
Auburn City School District (KG-12)
 2003-04 Enrollment: 4,993 . . . . (315) 255-8835
Boces Cayuga-Onondaga (UG-UG)
 2003-04 Enrollment: 256 . . . . (315) 253-0361
Two-year College(s)
Cayuga County Community College (Public)
 Fall 2004 Enrollment: 3,896 . . . . (315) 255-1743
 2005-06 Tuition: In-state $3,327; Out-of-state $6,227
Cayuga Onondaga BOCES-Practical Nursing Program (Public)
 Fall 2004 Enrollment: 37 . . . . (315) 253-0361
 2005-06 Tuition: In-state $5,430; Out-of-state $5,430
Housing: Homeownership rate: 52.6% (2005); Median home value: $91,457 (2005); Median rent: $393 per month (2000); Median age of housing: 60+ years (2000).
Hospitals: Auburn Memorial Hospital (226 beds)
Safety: Violent crime rate: 27.7 per 10,000 population; Property crime rate: 386.2 per 10,000 population (2004).
Newspapers: The Citizen (Circulation 13,075)
Transportation: Commute to work: 90.5% car, 2.1% public transportation, 4.6% walk, 1.8% work from home (2000); Travel time to work: 59.4% less than 15 minutes, 22.8% 15 to 30 minutes, 7.6% 30 to 45 minutes, 6.0% 45 to 60 minutes, 4.2% 60 minutes or more (2000)
Additional Information Contacts
Cayuga County Chamber of Commerce . . . . (315) 252-7291
 http://www.cayugacountychamber.org
City of Auburn . . . . (315) 255-4100
 http://www.ci.auburn.ny.us

AURELIUS (town). Covers a land area of 30.281 square miles and a water area of 1.652 square miles. Located at 42.92° N. Lat.; 76.66° W. Long.
Population: 2,913 (1990); 2,936 (2000); 2,964 (2005); 2,974 (2010 projected); Race: 98.7% White, 0.4% Black, 0.0% Asian, 1.3% Hispanic of any race (2005); Density: 97.9 persons per square mile (2005); Average household size: 2.56 (2005); Median age: 42.0 (2005); Males per 100 females: 96.7 (2005); Marriage status: 20.6% never married, 64.0% now married, 7.2% widowed, 8.1% divorced (2000); Foreign born: 1.8% (2000); Ancestry (includes multiple ancestries): 18.3% English, 16.3% Irish, 15.9% German, 14.9% United States or American, 12.2% Italian (2000).
Economy: Single-family building permits issued: 6 (2005); Multi-family building permits issued: 0 (2005); Employment by occupation: 10.8% management, 15.1% professional, 14.8% services, 26.1% sales, 2.2% farming, 11.4% construction, 19.6% production (2000).
Income: Per capita income: $22,470 (2005); Median household income: $46,684 (2005); Average household income: $56,267 (2005); Percent of households with income of $100,000 or more: 9.7% (2005); Poverty rate: 8.3% (2000).
Education: Percent of population age 25 and over with: High school diploma (including GED) or higher: 79.4% (2005); Bachelor's degree or higher: 13.9% (2005); Master's degree or higher: 5.6% (2005).
Housing: Homeownership rate: 84.1% (2005); Median home value: $102,690 (2005); Median rent: $382 per month (2000); Median age of housing: 47 years (2000).
Transportation: Commute to work: 94.0% car, 1.0% public transportation, 0.8% walk, 3.5% work from home (2000); Travel time to work: 44.2% less than 15 minutes, 35.5% 15 to 30 minutes, 9.0% 30 to 45 minutes, 6.9% 45 to 60 minutes, 4.5% 60 minutes or more (2000)
Additional Information Contacts
Town of Aurelius . . . . (315) 255-1894
 http://co.cayuga.ny.us/aurelius/index.html

AURORA (village). Covers a land area of 0.960 square miles and a water area of 0 square miles. Located at 42.74° N. Lat.; 76.69° W. Long. Elevation is 392 feet.
History: Seat of Wells College (1869).

Population: 687 (1990); 720 (2000); 705 (2005); 709 (2010 projected); Race: 91.5% White, 1.6% Black, 3.8% Asian, 2.3% Hispanic of any race (2005); Density: 734.7 persons per square mile (2005); Average household size: 3.79 (2005); Median age: 22.6 (2005); Males per 100 females: 39.3 (2005); Marriage status: 59.6% never married, 32.9% now married, 3.4% widowed, 4.1% divorced (2000); Foreign born: 4.5% (2000); Ancestry (includes multiple ancestries): 26.0% English, 22.9% Irish, 18.3% German, 11.3% Italian, 7.8% Other groups (2000).
Economy: Agriculture: grain; dairy products, poultry. Manufacturing: toys. Summer residences and recreation on Cayuga Lake. Single-family building permits issued: 0 (2005); Multi-family building permits issued: 0 (2005); Employment by occupation: 8.9% management, 31.2% professional, 22.1% services, 27.1% sales, 0.0% farming, 5.1% construction, 5.7% production (2000).
Income: Per capita income: $22,170 (2005); Median household income: $65,000 (2005); Average household income: $79,395 (2005); Percent of households with income of $100,000 or more: 24.2% (2005); Poverty rate: 4.8% (2000).
Education: Percent of population age 25 and over with: High school diploma (including GED) or higher: 94.6% (2005); Bachelor's degree or higher: 60.9% (2005); Master's degree or higher: 33.7% (2005).
School District(s)
Southern Cayuga Central School District (PK-12)
   2003-04 Enrollment: 1,010 . . . . (315) 364-7211
Four-year College(s)
Wells College
   Fall 2004 Enrollment: 390 . . . . (315) 364-3266
   2005-06 Tuition: In-state $15,790; Out-of-state $15,790
Housing: Homeownership rate: 67.2% (2005); Median home value: $144,388 (2005); Median rent: $454 per month (2000); Median age of housing: 60+ years (2000).
Transportation: Commute to work: 41.2% car, 0.0% public transportation, 51.1% walk, 7.2% work from home (2000); Travel time to work: 78.4% less than 15 minutes, 6.4% 15 to 30 minutes, 9.8% 30 to 45 minutes, 3.1% 45 to 60 minutes, 2.2% 60 minutes or more (2000)

BRUTUS (town). Covers a land area of 22.141 square miles and a water area of 0.358 square miles. Located at 43.04° N. Lat.; 76.54° W. Long.
Population: 5,013 (1990); 4,777 (2000); 4,837 (2005); 4,896 (2010 projected); Race: 98.0% White, 0.4% Black, 0.5% Asian, 1.1% Hispanic of any race (2005); Density: 218.5 persons per square mile (2005); Average household size: 2.61 (2005); Median age: 38.1 (2005); Males per 100 females: 93.2 (2005); Marriage status: 23.7% never married, 60.5% now married, 5.2% widowed, 10.5% divorced (2000); Foreign born: 0.7% (2000); Ancestry (includes multiple ancestries): 24.5% English, 20.3% Irish, 18.2% German, 10.6% Italian, 9.6% United States or American (2000).
Economy: Single-family building permits issued: 11 (2005); Multi-family building permits issued: 0 (2005); Employment by occupation: 10.4% management, 14.8% professional, 20.4% services, 20.8% sales, 2.2% farming, 12.8% construction, 18.6% production (2000).
Income: Per capita income: $21,032 (2005); Median household income: $44,638 (2005); Average household income: $54,438 (2005); Percent of households with income of $100,000 or more: 10.6% (2005); Poverty rate: 9.1% (2000).
Education: Percent of population age 25 and over with: High school diploma (including GED) or higher: 85.2% (2005); Bachelor's degree or higher: 15.4% (2005); Master's degree or higher: 5.6% (2005).
Housing: Homeownership rate: 79.2% (2005); Median home value: $92,115 (2005); Median rent: $400 per month (2000); Median age of housing: 29 years (2000).
Transportation: Commute to work: 91.6% car, 0.6% public transportation, 3.5% walk, 3.7% work from home (2000); Travel time to work: 35.1% less than 15 minutes, 31.5% 15 to 30 minutes, 23.2% 30 to 45 minutes, 6.2% 45 to 60 minutes, 4.0% 60 minutes or more (2000)
Additional Information Contacts
Town of Brutus. . . . . (315) 834-9398
   http://co.cayuga.ny.us/brutus/

CATO (village). Covers a land area of 0.988 square miles and a water area of 0.026 square miles. Located at 43.16° N. Lat.; 76.57° W. Long.
Population: 581 (1990); 601 (2000); 606 (2005); 612 (2010 projected); Race: 97.9% White, 0.7% Black, 0.0% Asian, 0.3% Hispanic of any race (2005); Density: 613.3 persons per square mile (2005); Average household size: 2.45 (2005); Median age: 38.0 (2005); Males per 100 females: 91.2 (2005); Marriage status: 20.0% never married, 66.4% now married, 8.2% widowed, 5.5% divorced (2000); Foreign born: 0.0% (2000); Ancestry (includes multiple ancestries): 24.0% English, 15.8% Irish, 14.1% United States or American, 11.2% German, 8.2% Polish (2000).
Economy: Single-family building permits issued: 0 (2005); Multi-family building permits issued: 0 (2005); Employment by occupation: 10.0% management, 16.7% professional, 17.0% services, 23.7% sales, 0.7% farming, 7.4% construction, 24.4% production (2000).
Income: Per capita income: $22,677 (2005); Median household income: $44,423 (2005); Average household income: $55,638 (2005); Percent of households with income of $100,000 or more: 12.6% (2005); Poverty rate: 6.9% (2000).
Education: Percent of population age 25 and over with: High school diploma (including GED) or higher: 81.6% (2005); Bachelor's degree or higher: 10.1% (2005); Master's degree or higher: 5.8% (2005).
School District(s)
Cato-Meridian Central School District (PK-12)
   2003-04 Enrollment: 1,267 . . . . (315) 626-3439
Housing: Homeownership rate: 57.5% (2005); Median home value: $96,889 (2005); Median rent: $359 per month (2000); Median age of housing: 60+ years (2000).
Transportation: Commute to work: 92.7% car, 0.0% public transportation, 3.5% walk, 3.8% work from home (2000); Travel time to work: 26.0% less than 15 minutes, 32.8% 15 to 30 minutes, 23.2% 30 to 45 minutes, 12.0% 45 to 60 minutes, 6.0% 60 minutes or more (2000)

CATO (town). Covers a land area of 33.632 square miles and a water area of 2.557 square miles. Located at 43.12° N. Lat.; 76.53° W. Long.
Population: 2,452 (1990); 2,744 (2000); 2,774 (2005); 2,797 (2010 projected); Race: 98.0% White, 0.4% Black, 0.3% Asian, 0.4% Hispanic of any race (2005); Density: 82.5 persons per square mile (2005); Average household size: 2.70 (2005); Median age: 38.8 (2005); Males per 100 females: 100.0 (2005); Marriage status: 23.7% never married, 64.0% now married, 6.4% widowed, 5.9% divorced (2000); Foreign born: 1.2% (2000); Ancestry (includes multiple ancestries): 16.8% German, 16.4% English, 15.9% Irish, 13.5% United States or American, 8.1% Italian (2000).
Economy: Single-family building permits issued: 14 (2005); Multi-family building permits issued: 0 (2005); Employment by occupation: 11.7% management, 11.2% professional, 16.2% services, 22.1% sales, 0.3% farming, 15.6% construction, 22.9% production (2000).
Income: Per capita income: $23,985 (2005); Median household income: $54,136 (2005); Average household income: $64,660 (2005); Percent of households with income of $100,000 or more: 14.7% (2005); Poverty rate: 8.3% (2000).
Education: Percent of population age 25 and over with: High school diploma (including GED) or higher: 86.1% (2005); Bachelor's degree or higher: 10.4% (2005); Master's degree or higher: 3.2% (2005).
Housing: Homeownership rate: 84.2% (2005); Median home value: $115,123 (2005); Median rent: $400 per month (2000); Median age of housing: 34 years (2000).
Transportation: Commute to work: 92.8% car, 0.2% public transportation, 1.5% walk, 5.0% work from home (2000); Travel time to work: 17.8% less than 15 minutes, 32.4% 15 to 30 minutes, 32.5% 30 to 45 minutes, 9.7% 45 to 60 minutes, 7.5% 60 minutes or more (2000)

CAYUGA (village). Covers a land area of 0.918 square miles and a water area of 0.427 square miles. Located at 42.91° N. Lat.; 76.72° W. Long.
Population: 677 (1990); 509 (2000); 514 (2005); 517 (2010 projected); Race: 99.2% White, 0.4% Black, 0.0% Asian, 0.6% Hispanic of any race (2005); Density: 559.9 persons per square mile (2005); Average household size: 2.46 (2005); Median age: 40.4 (2005); Males per 100 females: 94.0 (2005); Marriage status: 19.7% never married, 64.4% now married, 8.5% widowed, 7.5% divorced (2000); Foreign born: 1.4% (2000); Ancestry (includes multiple ancestries): 28.9% English, 22.1% Irish, 15.1% German, 9.1% Italian, 7.2% French (except Basque) (2000).
Economy: Single-family building permits issued: 0 (2005); Multi-family building permits issued: 0 (2005); Employment by occupation: 9.7% management, 16.4% professional, 21.4% services, 23.5% sales, 1.7% farming, 9.2% construction, 18.1% production (2000).
Income: Per capita income: $20,958 (2005); Median household income: $44,609 (2005); Average household income: $51,543 (2005); Percent of households with income of $100,000 or more: 7.7% (2005); Poverty rate: 3.1% (2000).

Education: Percent of population age 25 and over with: High school diploma (including GED) or higher: 87.4% (2005); Bachelor's degree or higher: 16.1% (2005); Master's degree or higher: 7.0% (2005).

School District(s)
Union Springs Central School District (KG-12)
 2003-04 Enrollment: 1,066 . . . . (315) 889-4101

Housing: Homeownership rate: 78.0% (2005); Median home value: $101,923 (2005); Median rent: $332 per month (2000); Median age of housing: 57 years (2000).

Transportation: Commute to work: 94.2% car, 2.5% public transportation, 1.3% walk, 2.1% work from home (2000); Travel time to work: 23.4% less than 15 minutes, 51.1% 15 to 30 minutes, 10.2% 30 to 45 minutes, 6.0% 45 to 60 minutes, 9.4% 60 minutes or more (2000)

Additional Information Contacts
Village of Cayuga. . . . . (315) 252-1707
 http://co.cayuga.ny.us/cayugavil/

CONQUEST
(town). Covers a land area of 35.192 square miles and a water area of 1.119 square miles. Located at 43.10° N. Lat.; 76.65° W. Long. Elevation is 441 feet.

Population: 1,859 (1990); 1,925 (2000); 1,990 (2005); 2,026 (2010 projected); Race: 98.4% White, 0.2% Black, 0.1% Asian, 0.6% Hispanic of any race (2005); Density: 56.5 persons per square mile (2005); Average household size: 2.83 (2005); Median age: 36.9 (2005); Males per 100 females: 100.4 (2005); Marriage status: 24.2% never married, 61.3% now married, 4.3% widowed, 10.2% divorced (2000); Foreign born: 0.5% (2000); Ancestry (includes multiple ancestries): 18.4% English, 16.6% United States or American, 15.6% Irish, 13.1% German, 9.0% Other groups (2000).

Economy: Single-family building permits issued: 1 (2005); Multi-family building permits issued: 0 (2005); Employment by occupation: 9.0% management, 9.2% professional, 13.4% services, 22.1% sales, 1.0% farming, 13.1% construction, 32.2% production (2000).

Income: Per capita income: $17,750 (2005); Median household income: $43,920 (2005); Average household income: $50,245 (2005); Percent of households with income of $100,000 or more: 7.5% (2005); Poverty rate: 12.4% (2000).

Education: Percent of population age 25 and over with: High school diploma (including GED) or higher: 74.5% (2005); Bachelor's degree or higher: 7.5% (2005); Master's degree or higher: 2.8% (2005).

Housing: Homeownership rate: 87.2% (2005); Median home value: $89,898 (2005); Median rent: $375 per month (2000); Median age of housing: 26 years (2000).

Transportation: Commute to work: 94.0% car, 0.2% public transportation, 1.4% walk, 3.9% work from home (2000); Travel time to work: 17.5% less than 15 minutes, 33.3% 15 to 30 minutes, 31.2% 30 to 45 minutes, 12.2% 45 to 60 minutes, 5.8% 60 minutes or more (2000)

Additional Information Contacts
Town of Conquest . . . . (315) 776-4539
 http://co.cayuga.ny.us/conquest/

FAIR HAVEN
(village). Covers a land area of 1.757 square miles and a water area of 1.162 square miles. Located at 43.32° N. Lat.; 76.70° W. Long.

Population: 895 (1990); 884 (2000); 845 (2005); 850 (2010 projected); Race: 98.0% White, 0.0% Black, 0.1% Asian, 0.9% Hispanic of any race (2005); Density: 481.1 persons per square mile (2005); Average household size: 2.19 (2005); Median age: 47.9 (2005); Males per 100 females: 96.1 (2005); Marriage status: 14.3% never married, 61.9% now married, 11.9% widowed, 11.9% divorced (2000); Foreign born: 2.1% (2000); Ancestry (includes multiple ancestries): 26.9% English, 21.1% German, 13.3% Irish, 9.2% French (except Basque), 7.0% United States or American (2000).

Economy: Resort village. Nearby is Fair Haven Beach State Park. Single-family building permits issued: 0 (2005); Multi-family building permits issued: 0 (2005); Employment by occupation: 16.2% management, 17.3% professional, 12.8% services, 24.2% sales, 0.3% farming, 13.6% construction, 15.6% production (2000).

Income: Per capita income: $21,955 (2005); Median household income: $40,526 (2005); Average household income: $47,953 (2005); Percent of households with income of $100,000 or more: 7.3% (2005); Poverty rate: 8.4% (2000).

Education: Percent of population age 25 and over with: High school diploma (including GED) or higher: 80.0% (2005); Bachelor's degree or higher: 21.6% (2005); Master's degree or higher: 7.5% (2005).

Housing: Homeownership rate: 75.4% (2005); Median home value: $97,679 (2005); Median rent: $339 per month (2000); Median age of housing: 50 years (2000).

Transportation: Commute to work: 93.0% car, 1.2% public transportation, 1.7% walk, 3.2% work from home (2000); Travel time to work: 27.7% less than 15 minutes, 31.9% 15 to 30 minutes, 20.2% 30 to 45 minutes, 13.3% 45 to 60 minutes, 6.9% 60 minutes or more (2000)

Additional Information Contacts
Fair Haven Area Chamber of Commerce . . . . (315) 947-6037
 http://www.fairhavenny.com
Village of Fair Haven . . . . (315) 947-5112
 http://co.cayuga.ny.us/fairhaven/

FLEMING
(town). Covers a land area of 21.828 square miles and a water area of 2.438 square miles. Located at 42.87° N. Lat.; 76.57° W. Long. Elevation is 908 feet.

Population: 2,644 (1990); 2,647 (2000); 2,577 (2005); 2,535 (2010 projected); Race: 98.8% White, 0.1% Black, 0.6% Asian, 0.9% Hispanic of any race (2005); Density: 118.1 persons per square mile (2005); Average household size: 2.49 (2005); Median age: 43.9 (2005); Males per 100 females: 101.2 (2005); Marriage status: 23.7% never married, 61.4% now married, 7.7% widowed, 7.2% divorced (2000); Foreign born: 2.5% (2000); Ancestry (includes multiple ancestries): 30.0% Irish, 18.7% Italian, 16.4% English, 12.5% German, 9.5% Polish (2000).

Economy: Single-family building permits issued: 14 (2005); Multi-family building permits issued: 0 (2005); Employment by occupation: 10.6% management, 29.0% professional, 16.5% services, 20.7% sales, 1.2% farming, 7.4% construction, 14.6% production (2000).

Income: Per capita income: $26,579 (2005); Median household income: $54,167 (2005); Average household income: $66,051 (2005); Percent of households with income of $100,000 or more: 14.7% (2005); Poverty rate: 5.7% (2000).

Education: Percent of population age 25 and over with: High school diploma (including GED) or higher: 88.6% (2005); Bachelor's degree or higher: 23.6% (2005); Master's degree or higher: 10.1% (2005).

Housing: Homeownership rate: 89.4% (2005); Median home value: $138,847 (2005); Median rent: $535 per month (2000); Median age of housing: 37 years (2000).

Transportation: Commute to work: 95.7% car, 0.0% public transportation, 1.8% walk, 2.5% work from home (2000); Travel time to work: 34.4% less than 15 minutes, 42.1% 15 to 30 minutes, 8.8% 30 to 45 minutes, 8.4% 45 to 60 minutes, 6.4% 60 minutes or more (2000)

Additional Information Contacts
Town of Fleming . . . . (315) 292-8988
 http://co.cayuga.ny.us/fleming/

GENOA
(town). Covers a land area of 39.656 square miles and a water area of 3.450 square miles. Located at 42.65° N. Lat.; 76.57° W. Long.

Population: 1,868 (1990); 1,914 (2000); 1,840 (2005); 1,811 (2010 projected); Race: 96.6% White, 0.5% Black, 0.2% Asian, 3.3% Hispanic of any race (2005); Density: 46.4 persons per square mile (2005); Average household size: 2.61 (2005); Median age: 40.0 (2005); Males per 100 females: 104.2 (2005); Marriage status: 24.1% never married, 62.7% now married, 5.1% widowed, 8.1% divorced (2000); Foreign born: 2.5% (2000); Ancestry (includes multiple ancestries): 20.1% English, 17.9% Irish, 15.7% German, 9.7% United States or American, 6.5% Other groups (2000).

Economy: Single-family building permits issued: 5 (2005); Multi-family building permits issued: 0 (2005); Employment by occupation: 12.3% management, 16.2% professional, 10.9% services, 22.4% sales, 7.2% farming, 11.9% construction, 19.2% production (2000).

Income: Per capita income: $23,720 (2005); Median household income: $50,802 (2005); Average household income: $61,820 (2005); Percent of households with income of $100,000 or more: 11.9% (2005); Poverty rate: 8.2% (2000).

Education: Percent of population age 25 and over with: High school diploma (including GED) or higher: 82.9% (2005); Bachelor's degree or higher: 17.9% (2005); Master's degree or higher: 8.3% (2005).

Housing: Homeownership rate: 81.4% (2005); Median home value: $105,189 (2005); Median rent: $355 per month (2000); Median age of housing: 43 years (2000).

Transportation: Commute to work: 89.9% car, 1.0% public transportation, 3.0% walk, 5.4% work from home (2000); Travel time to work: 26.2% less than 15 minutes, 37.7% 15 to 30 minutes, 26.3% 30 to 45 minutes, 3.1% 45 to 60 minutes, 6.8% 60 minutes or more (2000)

Additional Information Contacts

Town of Genoa .... (315) 364-5505
http://co.cayuga.ny.us/genoa/

IRA (town). Covers a land area of 34.843 square miles and a water area of 0.086 square miles. Located at 43.20° N. Lat.; 76.53° W. Long.
Population: 1,990 (1990); 2,426 (2000); 2,548 (2005); 2,665 (2010 projected); Race: 97.2% White, 0.5% Black, 0.0% Asian, 1.3% Hispanic of any race (2005); Density: 73.1 persons per square mile (2005); Average household size: 2.90 (2005); Median age: 37.1 (2005); Males per 100 females: 100.3 (2005); Marriage status: 23.7% never married, 63.9% now married, 4.9% widowed, 7.5% divorced (2000); Foreign born: 1.3% (2000); Ancestry (includes multiple ancestries): 19.6% Irish, 18.9% English, 17.4% German, 13.9% United States or American, 9.2% French (except Basque) (2000).
Economy: Single-family building permits issued: 10 (2005); Multi-family building permits issued: 0 (2005); Employment by occupation: 11.7% management, 14.2% professional, 15.5% services, 21.9% sales, 1.3% farming, 10.9% construction, 24.5% production (2000).
Income: Per capita income: $21,653 (2005); Median household income: $57,174 (2005); Average household income: $62,696 (2005); Percent of households with income of $100,000 or more: 14.1% (2005); Poverty rate: 7.0% (2000).
Education: Percent of population age 25 and over with: High school diploma (including GED) or higher: 85.9% (2005); Bachelor's degree or higher: 11.8% (2005); Master's degree or higher: 5.1% (2005).
Housing: Homeownership rate: 86.3% (2005); Median home value: $111,451 (2005); Median rent: $398 per month (2000); Median age of housing: 41 years (2000).
Transportation: Commute to work: 91.3% car, 0.1% public transportation, 2.5% walk, 5.6% work from home (2000); Travel time to work: 14.3% less than 15 minutes, 31.9% 15 to 30 minutes, 35.9% 30 to 45 minutes, 13.5% 45 to 60 minutes, 4.3% 60 minutes or more (2000)
Additional Information Contacts
Town of Ira.. (315) 626-6905
http://co.cayuga.ny.us/ira/

KING FERRY (unincorporated postal area, zip code 13081). Covers a land area of 30.280 square miles and a water area of 0 square miles. Located at 42.66° N. Lat.; 76.62° W. Long. Elevation is 958 feet.
Population: 0 (2000); Race: 96.5% White, 0.7% Black, 1.6% Asian, 0.2% Hispanic of any race (2000); Density: 0.0 persons per square mile (2000); Age: 26.3% under 18, 14.0% over 64 (2000); Marriage status: 21.7% never married, 63.9% now married, 6.2% widowed, 8.3% divorced (2000); Foreign born: 3.7% (2000); Ancestry (includes multiple ancestries): 26.1% English, 19.2% Irish, 17.9% German, 8.1% United States or American, 5.3% Other groups (2000).
Economy: Employment by occupation: 15.6% management, 20.9% professional, 10.4% services, 20.1% sales, 6.0% farming, 10.2% construction, 16.7% production (2000).
Income: Per capita income: $21,972 (2000); Median household income: $44,286 (2000); Poverty rate: 5.7% (2000).
Education: Percent of population age 25 and over with: High school diploma (including GED) or higher: 86.8% (2000); Bachelor's degree or higher: 26.1% (2000).
Housing: Homeownership rate: 82.7% (2000); Median home value: $92,500 (2000); Median rent: $343 per month (2000); Median age of housing: 41 years (2000).
Transportation: Commute to work: 92.2% car, 0.0% public transportation, 2.6% walk, 4.7% work from home (2000); Travel time to work: 28.6% less than 15 minutes, 31.7% 15 to 30 minutes, 26.2% 30 to 45 minutes, 5.1% 45 to 60 minutes, 8.2% 60 minutes or more (2000)

LEDYARD (town). Covers a land area of 36.325 square miles and a water area of 12.294 square miles. Located at 42.75° N. Lat.; 76.66° W. Long.
Population: 1,737 (1990); 1,832 (2000); 1,811 (2005); 1,798 (2010 projected); Race: 96.0% White, 0.6% Black, 1.6% Asian, 1.3% Hispanic of any race (2005); Density: 49.9 persons per square mile (2005); Average household size: 2.93 (2005); Median age: 35.5 (2005); Males per 100 females: 72.1 (2005); Marriage status: 37.1% never married, 51.5% now married, 5.5% widowed, 5.9% divorced (2000); Foreign born: 2.8% (2000); Ancestry (includes multiple ancestries): 27.2% English, 18.7% Irish, 16.8% German, 8.2% United States or American, 7.6% Italian (2000).
Economy: Single-family building permits issued: 5 (2005); Multi-family building permits issued: 0 (2005); Employment by occupation: 13.0% management, 25.0% professional, 19.3% services, 20.7% sales, 3.0% farming, 6.9% construction, 12.1% production (2000).
Income: Per capita income: $22,707 (2005); Median household income: $51,332 (2005); Average household income: $65,040 (2005); Percent of households with income of $100,000 or more: 15.8% (2005); Poverty rate: 3.4% (2000).
Education: Percent of population age 25 and over with: High school diploma (including GED) or higher: 87.5% (2005); Bachelor's degree or higher: 36.1% (2005); Master's degree or higher: 17.8% (2005).
Housing: Homeownership rate: 77.9% (2005); Median home value: $134,539 (2005); Median rent: $433 per month (2000); Median age of housing: 38 years (2000).
Transportation: Commute to work: 68.4% car, 0.0% public transportation, 24.8% walk, 6.6% work from home (2000); Travel time to work: 54.2% less than 15 minutes, 18.1% 15 to 30 minutes, 18.2% 30 to 45 minutes, 5.4% 45 to 60 minutes, 4.1% 60 minutes or more (2000)
Additional Information Contacts
Town of Ledyard .... (315) 364-5707
http://co.cayuga.ny.us/ledyard/

LOCKE (town). Covers a land area of 24.403 square miles and a water area of 0.015 square miles. Located at 42.64° N. Lat.; 76.42° W. Long. Elevation is 800 feet.
History: President Millard Fillmore born here.
Population: 1,917 (1990); 1,900 (2000); 1,808 (2005); 1,783 (2010 projected); Race: 98.3% White, 0.3% Black, 0.4% Asian, 0.5% Hispanic of any race (2005); Density: 74.1 persons per square mile (2005); Average household size: 2.63 (2005); Median age: 37.9 (2005); Males per 100 females: 98.7 (2005); Marriage status: 24.2% never married, 61.0% now married, 5.0% widowed, 9.7% divorced (2000); Foreign born: 1.6% (2000); Ancestry (includes multiple ancestries): 20.2% English, 16.1% Irish, 14.4% German, 10.2% United States or American, 5.8% Other groups (2000).
Economy: Single-family building permits issued: 3 (2005); Multi-family building permits issued: 0 (2005); Employment by occupation: 6.3% management, 15.2% professional, 15.3% services, 23.7% sales, 2.9% farming, 12.0% construction, 24.6% production (2000).
Income: Per capita income: $20,051 (2005); Median household income: $43,186 (2005); Average household income: $52,769 (2005); Percent of households with income of $100,000 or more: 9.2% (2005); Poverty rate: 8.9% (2000).
Education: Percent of population age 25 and over with: High school diploma (including GED) or higher: 77.8% (2005); Bachelor's degree or higher: 11.6% (2005); Master's degree or higher: 5.6% (2005).
Housing: Homeownership rate: 84.6% (2005); Median home value: $90,000 (2005); Median rent: $363 per month (2000); Median age of housing: 25 years (2000).
Transportation: Commute to work: 94.2% car, 0.3% public transportation, 1.6% walk, 3.6% work from home (2000); Travel time to work: 21.7% less than 15 minutes, 34.4% 15 to 30 minutes, 29.6% 30 to 45 minutes, 7.3% 45 to 60 minutes, 7.1% 60 minutes or more (2000)
Additional Information Contacts
Town of Locke .... (315) 497-9338
http://co.cayuga.ny.us/locke/

MARTVILLE (unincorporated postal area, zip code 13111). Covers a land area of 27.968 square miles and a water area of 0.037 square miles. Located at 43.25° N. Lat.; 76.61° W. Long.
Population: 0 (2000); Race: 97.2% White, 0.8% Black, 0.3% Asian, 1.7% Hispanic of any race (2000); Density: 0.0 persons per square mile (2000); Age: 32.1% under 18, 9.7% over 64 (2000); Marriage status: 24.4% never married, 65.9% now married, 3.8% widowed, 5.9% divorced (2000); Foreign born: 0.9% (2000); Ancestry (includes multiple ancestries): 16.2% Irish, 16.0% German, 14.7% English, 8.9% French (except Basque), 8.5% Other groups (2000).
Economy: Employment by occupation: 4.5% management, 14.6% professional, 13.1% services, 23.2% sales, 0.3% farming, 13.1% construction, 31.3% production (2000).
Income: Per capita income: $14,215 (2000); Median household income: $35,313 (2000); Poverty rate: 20.2% (2000).
Education: Percent of population age 25 and over with: High school diploma (including GED) or higher: 81.6% (2000); Bachelor's degree or higher: 10.2% (2000).
Housing: Homeownership rate: 82.0% (2000); Median home value: $59,200 (2000); Median rent: $390 per month (2000); Median age of housing: 22 years (2000).

Transportation: Commute to work: 94.7% car, 0.1% public transportation, 1.0% walk, 4.2% work from home (2000); Travel time to work: 19.3% less than 15 minutes, 29.6% 15 to 30 minutes, 23.1% 30 to 45 minutes, 15.2% 45 to 60 minutes, 12.8% 60 minutes or more (2000)

MELROSE PARK
(CDP). Aka Auburn Southeast. Covers a land area of 3.744 square miles and a water area of 0.554 square miles. Located at 42.91° N. Lat.; 76.53° W. Long.
Population: 2,091 (1990); 2,359 (2000); 2,306 (2005); 2,285 (2010 projected); Race: 98.7% White, 0.1% Black, 0.7% Asian, 0.4% Hispanic of any race (2005); Density: 616.0 persons per square mile (2005); Average household size: 2.56 (2005); Median age: 42.7 (2005); Males per 100 females: 95.9 (2005); Marriage status: 20.9% never married, 65.6% now married, 6.4% widowed, 7.1% divorced (2000); Foreign born: 2.4% (2000); Ancestry (includes multiple ancestries): 30.3% Irish, 23.5% Italian, 18.2% German, 17.8% English, 8.5% Polish (2000).
Economy: Employment by occupation: 10.4% management, 29.1% professional, 17.4% services, 26.2% sales, 0.8% farming, 7.9% construction, 8.3% production (2000).
Income: Per capita income: $28,046 (2005); Median household income: $58,295 (2005); Average household income: $71,628 (2005); Percent of households with income of $100,000 or more: 20.6% (2005); Poverty rate: 3.4% (2000).
Education: Percent of population age 25 and over with: High school diploma (including GED) or higher: 93.4% (2005); Bachelor's degree or higher: 34.5% (2005); Master's degree or higher: 11.3% (2005).
Housing: Homeownership rate: 92.1% (2005); Median home value: $130,807 (2005); Median rent: $485 per month (2000); Median age of housing: 48 years (2000).
Transportation: Commute to work: 92.4% car, 1.6% public transportation, 1.3% walk, 1.1% work from home (2000); Travel time to work: 49.2% less than 15 minutes, 29.0% 15 to 30 minutes, 8.2% 30 to 45 minutes, 7.8% 45 to 60 minutes, 5.8% 60 minutes or more (2000)

MENTZ
(town). Covers a land area of 17.049 square miles and a water area of 0.139 square miles. Located at 43.04° N. Lat.; 76.62° W. Long.
Population: 2,453 (1990); 2,446 (2000); 2,385 (2005); 2,359 (2010 projected); Race: 96.5% White, 1.0% Black, 0.2% Asian, 2.3% Hispanic of any race (2005); Density: 139.9 persons per square mile (2005); Average household size: 2.56 (2005); Median age: 38.8 (2005); Males per 100 females: 93.7 (2005); Marriage status: 27.6% never married, 57.9% now married, 7.7% widowed, 6.9% divorced (2000); Foreign born: 2.2% (2000); Ancestry (includes multiple ancestries): 23.5% English, 16.9% Irish, 13.1% German, 10.9% Italian, 9.1% Dutch (2000).
Economy: Single-family building permits issued: 0 (2005); Multi-family building permits issued: 0 (2005); Employment by occupation: 7.5% management, 14.0% professional, 18.3% services, 23.4% sales, 0.5% farming, 12.5% construction, 23.6% production (2000).
Income: Per capita income: $17,666 (2005); Median household income: $37,317 (2005); Average household income: $44,680 (2005); Percent of households with income of $100,000 or more: 5.9% (2005); Poverty rate: 11.8% (2000).
Education: Percent of population age 25 and over with: High school diploma (including GED) or higher: 76.4% (2005); Bachelor's degree or higher: 12.0% (2005); Master's degree or higher: 3.5% (2005).
Housing: Homeownership rate: 79.7% (2005); Median home value: $86,994 (2005); Median rent: $380 per month (2000); Median age of housing: 47 years (2000).
Transportation: Commute to work: 89.0% car, 1.5% public transportation, 2.3% walk, 5.3% work from home (2000); Travel time to work: 26.8% less than 15 minutes, 46.7% 15 to 30 minutes, 12.4% 30 to 45 minutes, 8.8% 45 to 60 minutes, 5.2% 60 minutes or more (2000)
Additional Information Contacts
Town of Mentz . . . . (315) 776-8692
http://co.cayuga.ny.us/mentz/

MERIDIAN
(village). Covers a land area of 0.692 square miles and a water area of 0 square miles. Located at 43.16° N. Lat.; 76.53° W. Long. Elevation is 455 feet.
Population: 351 (1990); 350 (2000); 350 (2005); 347 (2010 projected); Race: 97.4% White, 0.0% Black, 0.0% Asian, 1.4% Hispanic of any race (2005); Density: 505.8 persons per square mile (2005); Average household size: 2.87 (2005); Median age: 35.4 (2005); Males per 100 females: 104.7 (2005); Marriage status: 23.6% never married, 64.8% now married, 4.8% widowed, 6.8% divorced (2000); Foreign born: 1.2% (2000); Ancestry (includes multiple ancestries): 25.9% English, 17.7% German, 12.5% French (except Basque), 11.3% Irish, 8.4% United States or American (2000).
Economy: In agricultural area. Single-family building permits issued: 0 (2005); Multi-family building permits issued: 0 (2005); Employment by occupation: 10.9% management, 6.4% professional, 16.7% services, 30.1% sales, 1.3% farming, 17.3% construction, 17.3% production (2000).
Income: Per capita income: $20,314 (2005); Median household income: $53,906 (2005); Average household income: $58,279 (2005); Percent of households with income of $100,000 or more: 10.7% (2005); Poverty rate: 9.4% (2000).
Education: Percent of population age 25 and over with: High school diploma (including GED) or higher: 87.6% (2005); Bachelor's degree or higher: 13.8% (2005); Master's degree or higher: 3.7% (2005).
Housing: Homeownership rate: 76.2% (2005); Median home value: $94,615 (2005); Median rent: $346 per month (2000); Median age of housing: 60+ years (2000).
Transportation: Commute to work: 97.4% car, 0.0% public transportation, 2.6% walk, 0.0% work from home (2000); Travel time to work: 17.5% less than 15 minutes, 33.8% 15 to 30 minutes, 42.2% 30 to 45 minutes, 4.5% 45 to 60 minutes, 1.9% 60 minutes or more (2000)

MONTEZUMA
(town). Covers a land area of 18.304 square miles and a water area of 0.407 square miles. Located at 43.01° N. Lat.; 76.69° W. Long.
Population: 1,280 (1990); 1,431 (2000); 1,481 (2005); 1,520 (2010 projected); Race: 98.6% White, 0.1% Black, 0.2% Asian, 0.3% Hispanic of any race (2005); Density: 80.9 persons per square mile (2005); Average household size: 2.81 (2005); Median age: 37.2 (2005); Males per 100 females: 91.6 (2005); Marriage status: 26.3% never married, 59.0% now married, 6.8% widowed, 7.8% divorced (2000); Foreign born: 0.8% (2000); Ancestry (includes multiple ancestries): 23.3% Irish, 18.4% English, 14.7% German, 9.1% Other groups, 7.6% Italian (2000).
Economy: Single-family building permits issued: 0 (2005); Multi-family building permits issued: 0 (2005); Employment by occupation: 7.8% management, 11.3% professional, 14.5% services, 20.0% sales, 1.3% farming, 15.2% construction, 30.0% production (2000).
Income: Per capita income: $18,569 (2005); Median household income: $46,213 (2005); Average household income: $52,182 (2005); Percent of households with income of $100,000 or more: 8.3% (2005); Poverty rate: 15.4% (2000).
Education: Percent of population age 25 and over with: High school diploma (including GED) or higher: 73.1% (2005); Bachelor's degree or higher: 8.0% (2005); Master's degree or higher: 4.0% (2005).
Housing: Homeownership rate: 83.7% (2005); Median home value: $92,159 (2005); Median rent: $347 per month (2000); Median age of housing: 23 years (2000).
Transportation: Commute to work: 95.5% car, 0.0% public transportation, 1.6% walk, 2.4% work from home (2000); Travel time to work: 17.0% less than 15 minutes, 49.3% 15 to 30 minutes, 17.8% 30 to 45 minutes, 6.1% 45 to 60 minutes, 9.7% 60 minutes or more (2000)
Additional Information Contacts
Town of Montezuma . . . . (315) 776-8844
http://co.cayuga.ny.us/montezuma/

MORAVIA
(village). Covers a land area of 1.719 square miles and a water area of 0.004 square miles. Located at 42.71° N. Lat.; 76.42° W. Long. Elevation is 745 feet.
Population: 1,559 (1990); 1,363 (2000); 1,167 (2005); 1,043 (2010 projected); Race: 98.6% White, 0.3% Black, 0.3% Asian, 0.4% Hispanic of any race (2005); Density: 679.0 persons per square mile (2005); Average household size: 2.46 (2005); Median age: 40.4 (2005); Males per 100 females: 84.7 (2005); Marriage status: 27.4% never married, 50.8% now married, 11.3% widowed, 10.4% divorced (2000); Foreign born: 1.2% (2000); Ancestry (includes multiple ancestries): 26.0% English, 16.5% Irish, 13.6% German, 11.0% United States or American, 6.8% French (except Basque) (2000).
Economy: Single-family building permits issued: 1 (2005); Multi-family building permits issued: 0 (2005); Employment by occupation: 5.0% management, 18.6% professional, 19.1% services, 26.1% sales, 0.3% farming, 10.4% construction, 20.5% production (2000).
Income: Per capita income: $18,155 (2005); Median household income: $36,371 (2005); Average household income: $43,868 (2005); Percent of households with income of $100,000 or more: 5.9% (2005); Poverty rate: 9.2% (2000).

Education: Percent of population age 25 and over with: High school diploma (including GED) or higher: 81.0% (2005); Bachelor's degree or higher: 12.7% (2005); Master's degree or higher: 3.8% (2005).

School District(s)

Moravia Central School District (KG-12)
    2003-04 Enrollment: 1,162 . . . . (315) 497-2670
Moriah Central School District (PK-12)
    2003-04 Enrollment: 831 . . . . (518) 546-3301

Housing: Homeownership rate: 65.7% (2005); Median home value: $89,487 (2005); Median rent: $332 per month (2000); Median age of housing: 60+ years (2000).
Safety: Violent crime rate: 7.4 per 10,000 population; Property crime rate: 118.3 per 10,000 population (2004).
Newspapers: Moravia Republican Register (General - Circulation 2,200)
Transportation: Commute to work: 80.4% car, 0.7% public transportation, 14.4% walk, 4.4% work from home (2000); Travel time to work: 46.6% less than 15 minutes, 18.5% 15 to 30 minutes, 26.5% 30 to 45 minutes, 5.0% 45 to 60 minutes, 3.4% 60 minutes or more (2000)

Additional Information Contacts
Moravia Chamber of Commerce . . . . (315) 497-1341
    http://chamber.moraviany.com/
Village of Moravia . . . . (315) 497-1820
    http://co.cayuga.ny.us/villageofmoravia/

MORAVIA (town).
Covers a land area of 28.998 square miles and a water area of 0.652 square miles. Located at 42.72° N. Lat.; 76.42° W. Long. Elevation is 745 feet.
History: Fillmore Glen State Park and the birthplace of President Millard Fillmore are nearby. Incorporated 1837.
Population: 3,871 (1990); 4,040 (2000); 3,683 (2005); 3,495 (2010 projected); Race: 70.4% White, 23.2% Black, 0.2% Asian, 11.8% Hispanic of any race (2005); Density: 127.0 persons per square mile (2005); Average household size: 4.19 (2005); Median age: 35.8 (2005); Males per 100 females: 217.0 (2005); Marriage status: 42.3% never married, 45.6% now married, 5.3% widowed, 6.8% divorced (2000); Foreign born: 2.8% (2000); Ancestry (includes multiple ancestries): 16.9% English, 11.7% Irish, 11.0% German, 6.1% United States or American, 3.9% Dutch (2000).
Economy: Agriculture: cabbage, field corn, hay; dairying; and beef cattle. Single-family building permits issued: 2 (2005); Multi-family building permits issued: 0 (2005); Employment by occupation: 9.1% management, 17.5% professional, 17.6% services, 24.7% sales, 1.6% farming, 10.5% construction, 19.0% production (2000).
Income: Per capita income: $18,079 (2005); Median household income: $41,462 (2005); Average household income: $47,716 (2005); Percent of households with income of $100,000 or more: 5.6% (2005); Poverty rate: 8.7% (2000).
Education: Percent of population age 25 and over with: High school diploma (including GED) or higher: 54.2% (2005); Bachelor's degree or higher: 7.1% (2005); Master's degree or higher: 3.1% (2005).
Housing: Homeownership rate: 75.3% (2005); Median home value: $97,055 (2005); Median rent: $333 per month (2000); Median age of housing: 60+ years (2000).
Transportation: Commute to work: 86.5% car, 0.7% public transportation, 8.2% walk, 4.1% work from home (2000); Travel time to work: 39.3% less than 15 minutes, 22.1% 15 to 30 minutes, 28.4% 30 to 45 minutes, 5.7% 45 to 60 minutes, 4.6% 60 minutes or more (2000)

Additional Information Contacts
Town of Moravia . . . . (315) 497-1972
    http://co.cayuga.ny.us/townofmoravia/

NILES (town).
Covers a land area of 39.105 square miles and a water area of 4.261 square miles. Located at 42.81° N. Lat.; 76.41° W. Long.
Population: 1,194 (1990); 1,208 (2000); 1,173 (2005); 1,043 (2010 projected); Race: 99.1% White, 0.5% Black, 0.0% Asian, 0.3% Hispanic of any race (2005); Density: 30.0 persons per square mile (2005); Average household size: 2.49 (2005); Median age: 44.1 (2005); Males per 100 females: 107.2 (2005); Marriage status: 21.5% never married, 67.5% now married, 4.7% widowed, 6.3% divorced (2000); Foreign born: 1.7% (2000); Ancestry (includes multiple ancestries): 23.6% English, 22.8% Irish, 18.1% German, 7.3% Dutch, 6.4% Italian (2000).
Economy: Single-family building permits issued: 9 (2005); Multi-family building permits issued: 0 (2005); Employment by occupation: 17.1% management, 20.3% professional, 8.9% services, 21.3% sales, 4.5% farming, 10.9% construction, 17.1% production (2000).
Income: Per capita income: $24,864 (2005); Median household income: $48,981 (2005); Average household income: $61,790 (2005); Percent of households with income of $100,000 or more: 13.6% (2005); Poverty rate: 7.5% (2000).
Education: Percent of population age 25 and over with: High school diploma (including GED) or higher: 85.9% (2005); Bachelor's degree or higher: 23.1% (2005); Master's degree or higher: 9.8% (2005).
Housing: Homeownership rate: 90.7% (2005); Median home value: $131,618 (2005); Median rent: $373 per month (2000); Median age of housing: 47 years (2000).
Transportation: Commute to work: 90.9% car, 0.0% public transportation, 1.2% walk, 7.9% work from home (2000); Travel time to work: 13.2% less than 15 minutes, 42.4% 15 to 30 minutes, 27.5% 30 to 45 minutes, 12.3% 45 to 60 minutes, 4.6% 60 minutes or more (2000)

Additional Information Contacts
Town of Niles . . . . (315) 497-0066
    http://co.cayuga.ny.us/niles/

OWASCO (town).
Covers a land area of 20.932 square miles and a water area of 2.539 square miles. Located at 42.89° N. Lat.; 76.50° W. Long.
Population: 3,490 (1990); 3,755 (2000); 3,797 (2005); 3,838 (2010 projected); Race: 98.9% White, 0.1% Black, 0.6% Asian, 0.3% Hispanic of any race (2005); Density: 181.4 persons per square mile (2005); Average household size: 2.60 (2005); Median age: 42.9 (2005); Males per 100 females: 96.3 (2005); Marriage status: 18.9% never married, 67.8% now married, 6.1% widowed, 7.1% divorced (2000); Foreign born: 2.3% (2000); Ancestry (includes multiple ancestries): 29.0% Irish, 20.6% Italian, 17.8% English, 17.1% German, 8.6% Polish (2000).
Economy: Resort village. Single-family building permits issued: 12 (2005); Multi-family building permits issued: 0 (2005); Employment by occupation: 12.8% management, 29.6% professional, 14.6% services, 23.8% sales, 2.4% farming, 7.6% construction, 9.2% production (2000).
Income: Per capita income: $28,062 (2005); Median household income: $59,115 (2005); Average household income: $72,787 (2005); Percent of households with income of $100,000 or more: 22.5% (2005); Poverty rate: 4.5% (2000).
Education: Percent of population age 25 and over with: High school diploma (including GED) or higher: 90.6% (2005); Bachelor's degree or higher: 31.7% (2005); Master's degree or higher: 11.1% (2005).
Housing: Homeownership rate: 91.9% (2005); Median home value: $140,101 (2005); Median rent: $446 per month (2000); Median age of housing: 47 years (2000).
Transportation: Commute to work: 91.5% car, 1.0% public transportation, 2.2% walk, 3.1% work from home (2000); Travel time to work: 43.6% less than 15 minutes, 36.7% 15 to 30 minutes, 7.7% 30 to 45 minutes, 7.2% 45 to 60 minutes, 4.8% 60 minutes or more (2000)

Additional Information Contacts
Town of Owasco . . . . (315) 253-9021
    http://co.cayuga.ny.us/owasco/

PORT BYRON (village).
Covers a land area of 1.007 square miles and a water area of 0 square miles. Located at 43.03° N. Lat.; 76.62° W. Long.
Population: 1,359 (1990); 1,297 (2000); 1,275 (2005); 1,262 (2010 projected); Race: 94.7% White, 1.9% Black, 0.2% Asian, 3.0% Hispanic of any race (2005); Density: 1,265.9 persons per square mile (2005); Average household size: 2.53 (2005); Median age: 38.7 (2005); Males per 100 females: 90.6 (2005); Marriage status: 30.9% never married, 54.4% now married, 7.9% widowed, 6.8% divorced (2000); Foreign born: 1.3% (2000); Ancestry (includes multiple ancestries): 21.0% English, 18.2% Irish, 12.2% German, 12.2% Other groups, 12.0% Italian (2000).
Economy: Manufacturing of plastic products. Single-family building permits issued: 1 (2005); Multi-family building permits issued: 0 (2005); Employment by occupation: 5.8% management, 15.9% professional, 18.1% services, 24.6% sales, 0.3% farming, 11.8% construction, 23.4% production (2000).
Income: Per capita income: $18,196 (2005); Median household income: $38,853 (2005); Average household income: $44,970 (2005); Percent of households with income of $100,000 or more: 6.0% (2005); Poverty rate: 12.9% (2000).
Education: Percent of population age 25 and over with: High school diploma (including GED) or higher: 77.2% (2005); Bachelor's degree or higher: 10.7% (2005); Master's degree or higher: 2.7% (2005).

School District(s)
Port Byron Central School District (PK-12)
   2003-04 Enrollment: 1,172 . . . . (315) 776-5728
Housing: Homeownership rate: 71.4% (2005); Median home value: $88,454 (2005); Median rent: $372 per month (2000); Median age of housing: 58 years (2000).
Transportation: Commute to work: 90.8% car, 1.7% public transportation, 3.7% walk, 1.9% work from home (2000); Travel time to work: 28.1% less than 15 minutes, 44.0% 15 to 30 minutes, 12.1% 30 to 45 minutes, 9.6% 45 to 60 minutes, 6.2% 60 minutes or more (2000)
Additional Information Contacts
Village of Port Byron . . . . (315) 776-4321
   http://co.cayuga.ny.us/portbyron/

SCIPIO
SCIPIO (town). Covers a land area of 36.668 square miles and a water area of 2.662 square miles. Located at 42.80° N. Lat.; 76.57° W. Long.
Population: 1,517 (1990); 1,537 (2000); 1,652 (2005); 1,739 (2010 projected); Race: 97.8% White, 0.2% Black, 0.7% Asian, 1.6% Hispanic of any race (2005); Density: 45.1 persons per square mile (2005); Average household size: 2.63 (2005); Median age: 38.8 (2005); Males per 100 females: 98.3 (2005); Marriage status: 23.9% never married, 59.4% now married, 7.4% widowed, 9.4% divorced (2000); Foreign born: 1.3% (2000); Ancestry (includes multiple ancestries): 28.3% English, 19.8% German, 19.5% Irish, 10.3% United States or American, 7.5% Italian (2000).
Economy: Single-family building permits issued: 3 (2005); Multi-family building permits issued: 0 (2005); Employment by occupation: 10.9% management, 20.6% professional, 18.7% services, 19.4% sales, 6.8% farming, 7.5% construction, 16.1% production (2000).
Income: Per capita income: $20,064 (2005); Median household income: $48,886 (2005); Average household income: $52,863 (2005); Percent of households with income of $100,000 or more: 8.1% (2005); Poverty rate: 6.7% (2000).
Education: Percent of population age 25 and over with: High school diploma (including GED) or higher: 90.0% (2005); Bachelor's degree or higher: 19.2% (2005); Master's degree or higher: 7.2% (2005).
Housing: Homeownership rate: 85.0% (2005); Median home value: $110,503 (2005); Median rent: $385 per month (2000); Median age of housing: 45 years (2000).
Transportation: Commute to work: 90.2% car, 0.3% public transportation, 3.6% walk, 5.3% work from home (2000); Travel time to work: 20.7% less than 15 minutes, 45.9% 15 to 30 minutes, 17.1% 30 to 45 minutes, 9.9% 45 to 60 minutes, 6.4% 60 minutes or more (2000)
Additional Information Contacts
Town of Scipio . . . . (315) 364-5740
   http://co.cayuga.ny.us/scipio/

SCIPIO CENTER
SCIPIO CENTER (unincorporated postal area, zip code 13147). Aka Scipio. Covers a land area of 36.378 square miles and a water area of 0.004 square miles. Located at 42.77° N. Lat.; 76.57° W. Long. Elevation is 1,191 feet.
Population: 0 (2000); Race: 97.9% White, 0.0% Black, 0.0% Asian, 2.2% Hispanic of any race (2000); Density: 0.0 persons per square mile (2000); Age: 27.3% under 18, 13.5% over 64 (2000); Marriage status: 27.2% never married, 56.5% now married, 8.2% widowed, 8.2% divorced (2000); Foreign born: 1.4% (2000); Ancestry (includes multiple ancestries): 28.4% English, 20.7% Irish, 20.6% German, 8.0% United States or American, 6.1% Italian (2000).
Economy: Employment by occupation: 13.6% management, 19.4% professional, 14.7% services, 17.0% sales, 8.7% farming, 8.8% construction, 17.8% production (2000).
Income: Per capita income: $16,803 (2000); Median household income: $40,556 (2000); Poverty rate: 8.7% (2000).
Education: Percent of population age 25 and over with: High school diploma (including GED) or higher: 84.3% (2000); Bachelor's degree or higher: 16.1% (2000).
Housing: Homeownership rate: 84.2% (2000); Median home value: $72,400 (2000); Median rent: $443 per month (2000); Median age of housing: 60+ years (2000).
Transportation: Commute to work: 85.0% car, 0.0% public transportation, 7.0% walk, 7.6% work from home (2000); Travel time to work: 25.6% less than 15 minutes, 40.8% 15 to 30 minutes, 17.0% 30 to 45 minutes, 8.6% 45 to 60 minutes, 8.1% 60 minutes or more (2000)

SEMPRONIUS
SEMPRONIUS (town). Covers a land area of 29.377 square miles and a water area of 0.336 square miles. Located at 42.72° N. Lat.; 76.33° W. Long.
Population: 802 (1990); 893 (2000); 930 (2005); 936 (2010 projected); Race: 96.7% White, 0.9% Black, 1.3% Asian, 0.6% Hispanic of any race (2005); Density: 31.7 persons per square mile (2005); Average household size: 2.81 (2005); Median age: 35.4 (2005); Males per 100 females: 109.9 (2005); Marriage status: 24.5% never married, 62.0% now married, 3.4% widowed, 10.0% divorced (2000); Foreign born: 1.0% (2000); Ancestry (includes multiple ancestries): 19.9% English, 17.1% German, 16.0% Irish, 7.2% United States or American, 6.0% French (except Basque) (2000).
Economy: Single-family building permits issued: 4 (2005); Multi-family building permits issued: 0 (2005); Employment by occupation: 11.4% management, 14.2% professional, 17.4% services, 18.1% sales, 6.0% farming, 10.0% construction, 23.0% production (2000).
Income: Per capita income: $17,672 (2005); Median household income: $43,229 (2005); Average household income: $49,653 (2005); Percent of households with income of $100,000 or more: 6.6% (2005); Poverty rate: 8.9% (2000).
Education: Percent of population age 25 and over with: High school diploma (including GED) or higher: 84.1% (2005); Bachelor's degree or higher: 11.1% (2005); Master's degree or higher: 4.5% (2005).
Housing: Homeownership rate: 85.5% (2005); Median home value: $77,458 (2005); Median rent: $358 per month (2000); Median age of housing: 33 years (2000).
Transportation: Commute to work: 88.0% car, 0.5% public transportation, 4.5% walk, 5.2% work from home (2000); Travel time to work: 25.2% less than 15 minutes, 36.4% 15 to 30 minutes, 22.5% 30 to 45 minutes, 11.6% 45 to 60 minutes, 4.2% 60 minutes or more (2000)
Additional Information Contacts
Town of Sempronius . . . . (315) 496-2060
   http://co.cayuga.ny.us/sempronius/

SENNETT
SENNETT (town). Covers a land area of 28.818 square miles and a water area of 0.021 square miles. Located at 42.97° N. Lat.; 76.52° W. Long. Elevation is 598 feet.
Population: 2,913 (1990); 3,244 (2000); 3,461 (2005); 3,670 (2010 projected); Race: 95.7% White, 3.0% Black, 0.8% Asian, 0.9% Hispanic of any race (2005); Density: 120.1 persons per square mile (2005); Average household size: 2.90 (2005); Median age: 40.8 (2005); Males per 100 females: 96.4 (2005); Marriage status: 24.6% never married, 63.0% now married, 6.9% widowed, 5.6% divorced (2000); Foreign born: 3.2% (2000); Ancestry (includes multiple ancestries): 20.7% Irish, 20.2% English, 17.0% German, 14.7% Italian, 8.0% Polish (2000).
Economy: Single-family building permits issued: 21 (2005); Multi-family building permits issued: 0 (2005); Employment by occupation: 11.8% management, 23.7% professional, 14.1% services, 25.0% sales, 0.5% farming, 10.1% construction, 14.8% production (2000).
Income: Per capita income: $22,378 (2005); Median household income: $54,808 (2005); Average household income: $63,012 (2005); Percent of households with income of $100,000 or more: 16.3% (2005); Poverty rate: 4.9% (2000).
Education: Percent of population age 25 and over with: High school diploma (including GED) or higher: 88.4% (2005); Bachelor's degree or higher: 24.6% (2005); Master's degree or higher: 11.0% (2005).
Housing: Homeownership rate: 90.5% (2005); Median home value: $145,423 (2005); Median rent: $467 per month (2000); Median age of housing: 42 years (2000).
Transportation: Commute to work: 95.6% car, 0.2% public transportation, 0.7% walk, 3.2% work from home (2000); Travel time to work: 50.3% less than 15 minutes, 26.0% 15 to 30 minutes, 15.0% 30 to 45 minutes, 5.5% 45 to 60 minutes, 3.2% 60 minutes or more (2000)
Additional Information Contacts
Town of Sennett . . . . (315) 253-3712
   http://co.cayuga.ny.us/sennett/

SPRINGPORT
SPRINGPORT (town). Covers a land area of 21.535 square miles and a water area of 5.279 square miles. Located at 42.85° N. Lat.; 76.68° W. Long.
Population: 2,198 (1990); 2,256 (2000); 2,326 (2005); 2,408 (2010 projected); Race: 98.0% White, 0.8% Black, 0.2% Asian, 0.9% Hispanic of any race (2005); Density: 108.0 persons per square mile (2005); Average household size: 2.56 (2005); Median age: 40.5 (2005); Males per 100 females: 96.3 (2005); Marriage status: 23.0% never married, 61.3% now married, 6.1% widowed, 9.5% divorced (2000); Foreign born: 2.1% (2000); Ancestry (includes multiple ancestries): 22.0% Irish, 21.2% English, 19.8% German, 10.6% Italian, 8.7% United States or American (2000).

Economy: Single-family building permits issued: 8 (2005); Multi-family building permits issued: 0 (2005); Employment by occupation: 13.0% management, 17.5% professional, 12.9% services, 19.7% sales, 2.5% farming, 12.5% construction, 22.0% production (2000).
Income: Per capita income: $24,528 (2005); Median household income: $50,871 (2005); Average household income: $62,618 (2005); Percent of households with income of $100,000 or more: 14.1% (2005); Poverty rate: 8.6% (2000).
Education: Percent of population age 25 and over with: High school diploma (including GED) or higher: 87.6% (2005); Bachelor's degree or higher: 23.8% (2005); Master's degree or higher: 10.3% (2005).
Housing: Homeownership rate: 77.7% (2005); Median home value: $118,498 (2005); Median rent: $399 per month (2000); Median age of housing: 40 years (2000).
Transportation: Commute to work: 95.5% car, 0.0% public transportation, 1.4% walk, 2.8% work from home (2000); Travel time to work: 33.8% less than 15 minutes, 42.4% 15 to 30 minutes, 8.9% 30 to 45 minutes, 7.0% 45 to 60 minutes, 8.0% 60 minutes or more (2000)
Additional Information Contacts
Town of Springport . . . . (315) 889-7717
http://co.cayuga.ny.us/springport/

STERLING (town). Aka Sterling Station. Covers a land area of 45.647 square miles and a water area of 1.490 square miles. Located at 43.32° N. Lat.; 76.66° W. Long.
Population: 3,285 (1990); 3,432 (2000); 3,524 (2005); 3,644 (2010 projected); Race: 98.6% White, 0.0% Black, 0.1% Asian, 0.7% Hispanic of any race (2005); Density: 77.2 persons per square mile (2005); Average household size: 2.52 (2005); Median age: 40.3 (2005); Males per 100 females: 102.2 (2005); Marriage status: 20.8% never married, 64.0% now married, 5.8% widowed, 9.5% divorced (2000); Foreign born: 1.0% (2000); Ancestry (includes multiple ancestries): 21.4% English, 14.7% German, 12.5% Irish, 7.3% United States or American, 7.1% French (except Basque) (2000).
Economy: Single-family building permits issued: 5 (2005); Multi-family building permits issued: 0 (2005); Employment by occupation: 9.6% management, 14.5% professional, 12.1% services, 26.0% sales, 0.1% farming, 14.1% construction, 23.7% production (2000).
Income: Per capita income: $18,965 (2005); Median household income: $41,477 (2005); Average household income: $47,777 (2005); Percent of households with income of $100,000 or more: 7.7% (2005); Poverty rate: 11.7% (2000).
Education: Percent of population age 25 and over with: High school diploma (including GED) or higher: 83.1% (2005); Bachelor's degree or higher: 14.6% (2005); Master's degree or higher: 5.3% (2005).
Housing: Homeownership rate: 81.6% (2005); Median home value: $88,827 (2005); Median rent: $383 per month (2000); Median age of housing: 38 years (2000).
Transportation: Commute to work: 94.7% car, 0.3% public transportation, 1.2% walk, 3.1% work from home (2000); Travel time to work: 24.9% less than 15 minutes, 29.9% 15 to 30 minutes, 23.0% 30 to 45 minutes, 13.2% 45 to 60 minutes, 8.9% 60 minutes or more (2000)
Additional Information Contacts
Town of Sterling . . . . (315) 947-5666
http://co.cayuga.ny.us/sterling/

SUMMERHILL (town). Aka Summer Hill. Covers a land area of 25.884 square miles and a water area of 0.112 square miles. Located at 42.65° N. Lat.; 76.30° W. Long.
Population: 1,017 (1990); 1,098 (2000); 1,224 (2005); 1,308 (2010 projected); Race: 99.4% White, 0.2% Black, 0.0% Asian, 1.0% Hispanic of any race (2005); Density: 47.3 persons per square mile (2005); Average household size: 2.74 (2005); Median age: 36.8 (2005); Males per 100 females: 103.0 (2005); Marriage status: 25.4% never married, 62.1% now married, 3.9% widowed, 8.6% divorced (2000); Foreign born: 0.2% (2000); Ancestry (includes multiple ancestries): 17.6% English, 14.0% United States or American, 13.5% German, 12.1% Irish, 8.2% Dutch (2000).
Economy: Single-family building permits issued: 3 (2005); Multi-family building permits issued: 0 (2005); Employment by occupation: 8.4% management, 12.2% professional, 15.2% services, 21.6% sales, 3.0% farming, 12.0% construction, 27.6% production (2000).
Income: Per capita income: $17,388 (2005); Median household income: $43,989 (2005); Average household income: $47,612 (2005); Percent of households with income of $100,000 or more: 4.7% (2005); Poverty rate: 12.1% (2000).
Education: Percent of population age 25 and over with: High school diploma (including GED) or higher: 80.4% (2005); Bachelor's degree or higher: 10.5% (2005); Master's degree or higher: 3.9% (2005).
Housing: Homeownership rate: 87.0% (2005); Median home value: $89,326 (2005); Median rent: $404 per month (2000); Median age of housing: 28 years (2000).
Transportation: Commute to work: 92.4% car, 0.0% public transportation, 1.9% walk, 5.6% work from home (2000); Travel time to work: 17.1% less than 15 minutes, 50.3% 15 to 30 minutes, 21.2% 30 to 45 minutes, 7.6% 45 to 60 minutes, 3.7% 60 minutes or more (2000)
Additional Information Contacts
Town of Summerhill . . . . (315) 497-3494
http://co.cayuga.ny.us/summerhill/

THROOP (town). Covers a land area of 18.652 square miles and a water area of 0.048 square miles. Located at 42.98° N. Lat.; 76.61° W. Long.
Population: 1,792 (1990); 1,824 (2000); 1,827 (2005); 1,838 (2010 projected); Race: 98.8% White, 0.2% Black, 0.2% Asian, 1.4% Hispanic of any race (2005); Density: 98.0 persons per square mile (2005); Average household size: 2.55 (2005); Median age: 42.3 (2005); Males per 100 females: 101.4 (2005); Marriage status: 18.8% never married, 66.5% now married, 6.6% widowed, 8.1% divorced (2000); Foreign born: 1.9% (2000); Ancestry (includes multiple ancestries): 23.4% English, 20.7% Italian, 18.0% Irish, 16.5% German, 11.2% Polish (2000).
Economy: Single-family building permits issued: 8 (2005); Multi-family building permits issued: 0 (2005); Employment by occupation: 12.5% management, 16.4% professional, 13.9% services, 23.3% sales, 0.4% farming, 13.7% construction, 19.8% production (2000).
Income: Per capita income: $23,421 (2005); Median household income: $52,132 (2005); Average household income: $59,679 (2005); Percent of households with income of $100,000 or more: 13.0% (2005); Poverty rate: 3.2% (2000).
Education: Percent of population age 25 and over with: High school diploma (including GED) or higher: 82.7% (2005); Bachelor's degree or higher: 13.2% (2005); Master's degree or higher: 5.1% (2005).
Housing: Homeownership rate: 90.7% (2005); Median home value: $125,725 (2005); Median rent: $447 per month (2000); Median age of housing: 41 years (2000).
Transportation: Commute to work: 94.7% car, 0.4% public transportation, 1.1% walk, 3.1% work from home (2000); Travel time to work: 46.6% less than 15 minutes, 33.6% 15 to 30 minutes, 9.1% 30 to 45 minutes, 6.4% 45 to 60 minutes, 4.4% 60 minutes or more (2000)
Additional Information Contacts
Town of Throop . . . . (315) 252-7373
http://co.cayuga.ny.us/throop/

UNION SPRINGS (village). Covers a land area of 1.799 square miles and a water area of 0.010 square miles. Located at 42.84° N. Lat.; 76.69° W. Long. Elevation is 392 feet.
Population: 1,118 (1990); 1,074 (2000); 1,050 (2005); 1,041 (2010 projected); Race: 97.8% White, 1.5% Black, 0.1% Asian, 0.8% Hispanic of any race (2005); Density: 583.6 persons per square mile (2005); Average household size: 2.44 (2005); Median age: 40.7 (2005); Males per 100 females: 93.4 (2005); Marriage status: 19.4% never married, 62.0% now married, 8.0% widowed, 10.7% divorced (2000); Foreign born: 0.6% (2000); Ancestry (includes multiple ancestries): 20.8% English, 20.0% Irish, 17.4% German, 10.8% Italian, 8.7% French (except Basque) (2000).
Economy: Summer resort. Some manufacturing: transportation equipment, plastic products; dairy products; farming. Single-family building permits issued: 0 (2005); Multi-family building permits issued: 0 (2005); Employment by occupation: 12.7% management, 20.7% professional, 14.3% services, 19.0% sales, 1.8% farming, 11.4% construction, 20.2% production (2000).
Income: Per capita income: $22,512 (2005); Median household income: $48,433 (2005); Average household income: $54,971 (2005); Percent of households with income of $100,000 or more: 9.5% (2005); Poverty rate: 6.8% (2000).
Education: Percent of population age 25 and over with: High school diploma (including GED) or higher: 87.6% (2005); Bachelor's degree or higher: 23.6% (2005); Master's degree or higher: 11.5% (2005).
School District(s)
Union Springs Central School District (KG-12)
   2003-04 Enrollment: 1,066 . . . . (315) 889-4101

Housing: Homeownership rate: 72.6% (2005); Median home value: $103,500 (2005); Median rent: $371 per month (2000); Median age of housing: 60+ years (2000).
Transportation: Commute to work: 95.4% car, 0.0% public transportation, 2.6% walk, 1.8% work from home (2000); Travel time to work: 30.2% less than 15 minutes, 45.4% 15 to 30 minutes, 7.3% 30 to 45 minutes, 6.5% 45 to 60 minutes, 10.5% 60 minutes or more (2000)
Additional Information Contacts
Village of Union Springs. . . . . (315) 889-7341
  http://co.cayuga.ny.us/unionsprings/

VENICE
(town). Aka Stewart Corners. Covers a land area of 41.140 square miles and a water area of 0.179 square miles. Located at 42.72° N. Lat.; 76.53° W. Long.
Population: 1,315 (1990); 1,286 (2000); 1,417 (2005); 1,521 (2010 projected); Race: 97.2% White, 0.2% Black, 0.6% Asian, 2.3% Hispanic of any race (2005); Density: 34.4 persons per square mile (2005); Average household size: 2.70 (2005); Median age: 38.9 (2005); Males per 100 females: 99.3 (2005); Marriage status: 22.4% never married, 65.3% now married, 5.8% widowed, 6.6% divorced (2000); Foreign born: 0.8% (2000); Ancestry (includes multiple ancestries): 24.8% English, 19.9% Irish, 18.0% German, 5.6% United States or American, 5.6% French (except Basque) (2000).
Economy: Single-family building permits issued: 2 (2005); Multi-family building permits issued: 0 (2005); Employment by occupation: 16.4% management, 16.7% professional, 11.7% services, 16.0% sales, 9.1% farming, 9.1% construction, 20.9% production (2000).
Income: Per capita income: $18,426 (2005); Median household income: $43,188 (2005); Average household income: $49,733 (2005); Percent of households with income of $100,000 or more: 7.4% (2005); Poverty rate: 7.6% (2000).
Education: Percent of population age 25 and over with: High school diploma (including GED) or higher: 82.8% (2005); Bachelor's degree or higher: 15.1% (2005); Master's degree or higher: 4.9% (2005).
Housing: Homeownership rate: 81.9% (2005); Median home value: $100,413 (2005); Median rent: $425 per month (2000); Median age of housing: 60+ years (2000).
Transportation: Commute to work: 82.2% car, 0.3% public transportation, 6.2% walk, 9.5% work from home (2000); Travel time to work: 31.5% less than 15 minutes, 29.1% 15 to 30 minutes, 26.5% 30 to 45 minutes, 5.6% 45 to 60 minutes, 7.3% 60 minutes or more (2000)
Additional Information Contacts
Town of Venice . . . . (315) 497-1898
  http://co.cayuga.ny.us/venice/

VICTORY
(town). Covers a land area of 34.384 square miles and a water area of 0.044 square miles. Located at 43.21° N. Lat.; 76.64° W. Long. Elevation is 431 feet.
Population: 1,535 (1990); 1,838 (2000); 1,845 (2005); 1,819 (2010 projected); Race: 97.4% White, 0.3% Black, 0.3% Asian, 0.4% Hispanic of any race (2005); Density: 53.7 persons per square mile (2005); Average household size: 2.90 (2005); Median age: 36.3 (2005); Males per 100 females: 103.4 (2005); Marriage status: 24.4% never married, 63.8% now married, 3.3% widowed, 8.4% divorced (2000); Foreign born: 1.3% (2000); Ancestry (includes multiple ancestries): 18.0% German, 17.8% English, 15.1% Irish, 12.7% United States or American, 7.1% Polish (2000).
Economy: Single-family building permits issued: 5 (2005); Multi-family building permits issued: 0 (2005); Employment by occupation: 6.4% management, 14.0% professional, 11.2% services, 22.1% sales, 1.2% farming, 15.3% construction, 29.9% production (2000).
Income: Per capita income: $18,645 (2005); Median household income: $44,419 (2005); Average household income: $54,088 (2005); Percent of households with income of $100,000 or more: 10.4% (2005); Poverty rate: 10.6% (2000).
Education: Percent of population age 25 and over with: High school diploma (including GED) or higher: 80.7% (2005); Bachelor's degree or higher: 7.7% (2005); Master's degree or higher: 2.5% (2005).
Housing: Homeownership rate: 85.7% (2005); Median home value: $94,646 (2005); Median rent: $411 per month (2000); Median age of housing: 30 years (2000).
Transportation: Commute to work: 94.0% car, 0.4% public transportation, 0.9% walk, 3.7% work from home (2000); Travel time to work: 19.3% less than 15 minutes, 23.4% 15 to 30 minutes, 27.2% 30 to 45 minutes, 20.4% 45 to 60 minutes, 9.8% 60 minutes or more (2000)

WEEDSPORT
(village). Covers a land area of 0.974 square miles and a water area of 0 square miles. Located at 43.04° N. Lat.; 76.56° W. Long.
History: Incorporated 1831.
Population: 1,996 (1990); 2,017 (2000); 1,998 (2005); 1,995 (2010 projected); Race: 98.9% White, 0.3% Black, 0.4% Asian, 0.8% Hispanic of any race (2005); Density: 2,050.4 persons per square mile (2005); Average household size: 2.57 (2005); Median age: 39.3 (2005); Males per 100 females: 84.8 (2005); Marriage status: 28.0% never married, 55.3% now married, 7.1% widowed, 9.6% divorced (2000); Foreign born: 0.6% (2000); Ancestry (includes multiple ancestries): 25.9% English, 21.1% Irish, 17.5% German, 11.9% Italian, 7.8% Polish (2000).
Economy: Manufacturing of feed, flour, furniture; lumber milling; agriculture includes dairy products; poultry; fruit. Single-family building permits issued: 0 (2005); Multi-family building permits issued: 0 (2005); Employment by occupation: 11.7% management, 18.2% professional, 19.2% services, 25.6% sales, 0.3% farming, 8.0% construction, 16.9% production (2000).
Income: Per capita income: $22,755 (2005); Median household income: $46,959 (2005); Average household income: $57,552 (2005); Percent of households with income of $100,000 or more: 11.9% (2005); Poverty rate: 7.1% (2000).
Education: Percent of population age 25 and over with: High school diploma (including GED) or higher: 86.7% (2005); Bachelor's degree or higher: 19.5% (2005); Master's degree or higher: 6.9% (2005).
School District(s)
Weedsport Central School District (KG-12)
  2003-04 Enrollment: 1,031 . . . . (315) 834-6637
Housing: Homeownership rate: 67.1% (2005); Median home value: $106,189 (2005); Median rent: $402 per month (2000); Median age of housing: 60+ years (2000).
Safety: Violent crime rate: 0.0 per 10,000 population; Property crime rate: 120.7 per 10,000 population (2004).
Transportation: Commute to work: 90.3% car, 0.5% public transportation, 5.6% walk, 3.2% work from home (2000); Travel time to work: 37.8% less than 15 minutes, 34.8% 15 to 30 minutes, 19.1% 30 to 45 minutes, 5.3% 45 to 60 minutes, 3.0% 60 minutes or more (2000)
Additional Information Contacts
Village of Weedsport . . . . (315) 834-6634
  http://co.cayuga.ny.us/weedsport/
Weedsport Area Chamber of Commerce. . . . . (315) 834-2280
  http://www.chamber.weedsport.com

Chautauqua County

Located in western New York; bounded on the northwest by Lake Erie, and on the west and south by Pennsylvania. Covers a land area of 1,062.05 square miles, a water area of 437.97 square miles, and is located in the Eastern Time Zone. The county government was organized in 1808. County seat is Mayville.

Chautauqua County is part of the Jamestown-Dunkirk-Fredonia, NY Micropolitan Statistical Area. The entire metro area includes: Chautauqua County, NY

Weather Station: Fredonia   Elevation: 757 feet

	Jan	Feb	Mar	Apr	May	Jun	Jul	Aug	Sep	Oct	Nov	Dec
High	32	35	44	56	68	77	80	79	72	61	49	38
Low	19	19	27	37	48	57	62	61	54	44	36	26
Precip	2.6	2.1	2.7	3.2	3.3	3.9	3.9	3.8	5.0	4.1	4.2	3.4
Snow	27.0	16.6	10.5	2.5	0.3	0.0	0.0	0.0	0.0	0.3	7.6	21.2

High and Low temperatures in degrees Fahrenheit; Precipitation and Snow in inches

Weather Station: Westfield 2 SSE   Elevation: 705 feet

	Jan	Feb	Mar	Apr	May	Jun	Jul	Aug	Sep	Oct	Nov	Dec
High	32	34	43	55	67	75	80	77	70	59	48	37
Low	18	19	27	37	49	58	63	62	55	45	35	25
Precip	2.5	2.2	3.0	3.4	3.7	4.3	4.2	4.6	5.6	4.8	4.5	3.5
Snow	22.5	16.0	11.1	2.9	0.3	0.0	0.0	0.0	tr	0.6	8.7	24.0

High and Low temperatures in degrees Fahrenheit; Precipitation and Snow in inches

Population: 141,845 (1990); 139,750 (2000); 136,803 (2005); 133,763 (2010 projected); Race: 93.1% White, 2.5% Black, 0.6% Asian, 5.3% Hispanic of any race (2005); Density: 128.8 persons per square mile (2005); Average household size: 2.54 (2005); Median age: 38.7 (2005); Males per 100 females: 95.4 (2005).

Religion: Five largest groups: 24.9% Catholic Church, 7.9% The United Methodist Church, 4.0% Evangelical Lutheran Church in America, 1.5% Presbyterian Church (U.S.A.), 1.1% Episcopal Church (2000).
Economy: Unemployment rate: 4.9% (2005); Total civilian labor force: 67,420 (2005); Leading industries: 28.7% manufacturing; 17.1% health care and social assistance; 14.2% retail trade (2003); Farms: 1,734 totaling 255,896 acres (2002); Companies that employ 500 or more persons: 10 (2003); Companies that employ 100 to 499 persons: 59 (2003); Companies that employ less than 100 persons: 3,048 (2003); Black-owned businesses: n/a (2002); Hispanic-owned businesses: n/a (2002); Women-owned businesses: 2,290 (2002); Retail sales per capita: $11,205 (2006). Single-family building permits issued: 206 (2005); Multi-family building permits issued: 240 (2005).
Income: Per capita income: $19,212 (2005); Median household income: $37,383 (2005); Average household income: $47,741 (2005); Percent of households with income of $100,000 or more: 8.1% (2005); Poverty rate: 14.9% (2003); Bankruptcy rate: 8.87% (2005).
Taxes: Total county taxes per capita: $649 (2004); County property taxes per capita: $335 (2004).
Education: Percent of population age 25 and over with: High school diploma (including GED) or higher: 81.2% (2005); Bachelor's degree or higher: 17.0% (2005); Master's degree or higher: 7.2% (2005).
Housing: Homeownership rate: 69.6% (2005); Median home value: $95,284 (2005); Median rent: $339 per month (2000); Median age of housing: 57 years (2000).
Health: Birth rate: 106.7 per 10,000 population (2004); Death rate: 109.3 per 10,000 population (2004); Age-adjusted cancer mortality rate: 210.1 deaths per 100,000 population (2002); Air Quality Index: 83.6% good, 14.8% moderate, 1.6% unhealthy for sensitive individuals, 0.0% unhealthy (percent of days in 2005); Number of physicians: 14.1 per 10,000 population (2004); Hospital beds: 42.6 per 10,000 population (2003); Hospital admissions: 1,119.1 per 10,000 population (2003).
Elections: 2004 Presidential election results: 53.2% Bush, 44.7% Kerry, 1.8% Nader, 0.2% Badnarik
National and State Parks: Lake Erie State Park
Additional Information Contacts
Chautauqua County Government . . . . (716) 753-7111
  http://www.co.chautauqua.ny.us/
Town of Busti . . . . (716) 763-8561
  http://www.townofbusti.com/
Town of Ellicott . . . . (716) 665-5317
  http://www.townofellicott.com/
Town of Portland . . . . (716) 792-9614
  http://www.town.portland.ny.us/

Chautauqua County Communities

ARKWRIGHT (town). Covers a land area of 35.709 square miles and a water area of 0.057 square miles. Located at 42.39° N. Lat.; 79.24° W. Long. Elevation is 1,634 feet.
Population: 1,040 (1990); 1,126 (2000); 1,179 (2005); 1,225 (2010 projected); Race: 98.6% White, 0.3% Black, 0.1% Asian, 1.6% Hispanic of any race (2005); Density: 33.0 persons per square mile (2005); Average household size: 2.63 (2005); Median age: 40.1 (2005); Males per 100 females: 105.8 (2005); Marriage status: 20.2% never married, 67.0% now married, 3.1% widowed, 9.7% divorced (2000); Foreign born: 2.1% (2000); Ancestry (includes multiple ancestries): 29.9% German, 20.4% English, 18.3% Polish, 17.1% Irish, 9.3% Italian (2000).
Economy: Single-family building permits issued: 5 (2005); Multi-family building permits issued: 0 (2005); Employment by occupation: 7.7% management, 25.8% professional, 14.5% services, 19.5% sales, 1.0% farming, 11.8% construction, 19.8% production (2000).
Income: Per capita income: $22,583 (2005); Median household income: $48,939 (2005); Average household income: $59,431 (2005); Percent of households with income of $100,000 or more: 10.7% (2005); Poverty rate: 8.8% (2000).
Education: Percent of population age 25 and over with: High school diploma (including GED) or higher: 87.2% (2005); Bachelor's degree or higher: 21.3% (2005); Master's degree or higher: 10.5% (2005).
Housing: Homeownership rate: 90.0% (2005); Median home value: $99,857 (2005); Median rent: $371 per month (2000); Median age of housing: 26 years (2000).
Transportation: Commute to work: 95.5% car, 0.9% public transportation, 1.0% walk, 2.6% work from home (2000); Travel time to work: 26.7% less than 15 minutes, 48.4% 15 to 30 minutes, 14.9% 30 to 45 minutes, 3.8% 45 to 60 minutes, 6.3% 60 minutes or more (2000)

ASHVILLE (unincorporated postal area, zip code 14710). Covers a land area of 53.279 square miles and a water area of 0.019 square miles. Located at 42.09° N. Lat.; 79.40° W. Long.
Population: 0 (2000); Race: 98.4% White, 0.5% Black, 0.1% Asian, 0.2% Hispanic of any race (2000); Density: 0.0 persons per square mile (2000); Age: 26.8% under 18, 13.4% over 64 (2000); Marriage status: 20.5% never married, 66.7% now married, 4.9% widowed, 7.9% divorced (2000); Foreign born: 0.7% (2000); Ancestry (includes multiple ancestries): 19.6% English, 17.6% German, 16.8% Swedish, 12.4% Irish, 6.6% Italian (2000).
Economy: Employment by occupation: 9.1% management, 19.5% professional, 16.3% services, 22.4% sales, 1.0% farming, 10.9% construction, 20.9% production (2000).
Income: Per capita income: $17,128 (2000); Median household income: $39,113 (2000); Poverty rate: 9.3% (2000).
Education: Percent of population age 25 and over with: High school diploma (including GED) or higher: 84.3% (2000); Bachelor's degree or higher: 20.5% (2000).
Housing: Homeownership rate: 87.1% (2000); Median home value: $66,100 (2000); Median rent: $391 per month (2000); Median age of housing: 45 years (2000).
Transportation: Commute to work: 93.4% car, 0.5% public transportation, 0.2% walk, 5.7% work from home (2000); Travel time to work: 34.2% less than 15 minutes, 48.0% 15 to 30 minutes, 10.5% 30 to 45 minutes, 2.9% 45 to 60 minutes, 4.4% 60 minutes or more (2000)

BEMUS POINT (village). Covers a land area of 0.434 square miles and a water area of 0 square miles. Located at 42.16° N. Lat.; 79.39° W. Long.
Population: 383 (1990); 340 (2000); 355 (2005); 361 (2010 projected); Race: 96.9% White, 0.0% Black, 1.1% Asian, 1.4% Hispanic of any race (2005); Density: 817.3 persons per square mile (2005); Average household size: 1.97 (2005); Median age: 48.0 (2005); Males per 100 females: 83.9 (2005); Marriage status: 16.5% never married, 60.6% now married, 13.0% widowed, 9.9% divorced (2000); Foreign born: 1.2% (2000); Ancestry (includes multiple ancestries): 27.8% Swedish, 26.0% German, 22.8% English, 11.7% Irish, 9.4% Italian (2000).
Economy: Single-family building permits issued: 3 (2005); Multi-family building permits issued: 0 (2005); Employment by occupation: 11.8% management, 31.2% professional, 9.4% services, 24.1% sales, 0.0% farming, 12.4% construction, 11.2% production (2000).
Income: Per capita income: $25,056 (2005); Median household income: $35,652 (2005); Average household income: $49,417 (2005); Percent of households with income of $100,000 or more: 8.3% (2005); Poverty rate: 7.6% (2000).
Education: Percent of population age 25 and over with: High school diploma (including GED) or higher: 90.9% (2005); Bachelor's degree or higher: 33.7% (2005); Master's degree or higher: 15.6% (2005).
School District(s)
Bemus Point Central School District (PK-12)
  2003-04 Enrollment: 910 . . . . (716) 386-2375
Housing: Homeownership rate: 63.3% (2005); Median home value: $175,000 (2005); Median rent: $317 per month (2000); Median age of housing: 60+ years (2000).
Transportation: Commute to work: 84.0% car, 0.0% public transportation, 13.6% walk, 2.5% work from home (2000); Travel time to work: 39.2% less than 15 minutes, 38.6% 15 to 30 minutes, 18.4% 30 to 45 minutes, 0.0% 45 to 60 minutes, 3.8% 60 minutes or more (2000)

BROCTON (village). Covers a land area of 1.732 square miles and a water area of 0 square miles. Located at 42.39° N. Lat.; 79.44° W. Long. Elevation is 675 feet.
History: A short-lived community of the Brotherhood of the New Life was founded here in 1867 by Thomas L. Harris. Incorporated 1894.
Population: 1,387 (1990); 1,547 (2000); 1,505 (2005); 1,470 (2010 projected); Race: 95.7% White, 0.9% Black, 0.0% Asian, 2.5% Hispanic of any race (2005); Density: 868.9 persons per square mile (2005); Average household size: 2.44 (2005); Median age: 39.6 (2005); Males per 100 females: 88.6 (2005); Marriage status: 27.4% never married, 56.6% now married, 7.7% widowed, 8.2% divorced (2000); Foreign born: 1.1% (2000); Ancestry (includes multiple ancestries): 30.0% German, 19.2% Italian, 14.3% English, 12.0% Polish, 11.2% Irish (2000).

Economy: In grape-growing area. Manufacturing: machinery for ceramic and woodworking industries. Agriculture: poultry. Employment by occupation: 5.7% management, 14.3% professional, 21.0% services, 20.8% sales, 1.4% farming, 9.8% construction, 27.0% production (2000).
Income: Per capita income: $15,161 (2005); Median household income: $30,253 (2005); Average household income: $36,981 (2005); Percent of households with income of $100,000 or more: 2.8% (2005); Poverty rate: 13.2% (2000).
Education: Percent of population age 25 and over with: High school diploma (including GED) or higher: 79.8% (2005); Bachelor's degree or higher: 8.8% (2005); Master's degree or higher: 2.9% (2005).

School District(s)
Brocton Central School District (PK-12)
   2003-04 Enrollment: 933 . . . . (716) 792-2131

Housing: Homeownership rate: 68.2% (2005); Median home value: $83,587 (2005); Median rent: $331 per month (2000); Median age of housing: 59 years (2000).
Transportation: Commute to work: 93.9% car, 0.4% public transportation, 3.1% walk, 1.2% work from home (2000); Travel time to work: 36.0% less than 15 minutes, 51.9% 15 to 30 minutes, 6.0% 30 to 45 minutes, 1.6% 45 to 60 minutes, 4.4% 60 minutes or more (2000)

BUSTI (town). Covers a land area of 47.769 square miles and a water area of 0.015 square miles. Located at 42.08° N. Lat.; 79.32° W. Long. Elevation is 1,368 feet.
Population: 8,050 (1990); 7,760 (2000); 7,595 (2005); 7,423 (2010 projected); Race: 97.7% White, 0.6% Black, 0.5% Asian, 0.9% Hispanic of any race (2005); Density: 159.0 persons per square mile (2005); Average household size: 2.38 (2005); Median age: 43.7 (2005); Males per 100 females: 96.9 (2005); Marriage status: 20.2% never married, 62.4% now married, 7.3% widowed, 10.1% divorced (2000); Foreign born: 1.1% (2000); Ancestry (includes multiple ancestries): 25.5% Swedish, 22.3% German, 17.4% English, 14.1% Irish, 11.3% Italian (2000).
Economy: Single-family building permits issued: 11 (2005); Multi-family building permits issued: 0 (2005); Employment by occupation: 12.6% management, 20.6% professional, 13.3% services, 25.2% sales, 1.4% farming, 7.9% construction, 19.1% production (2000).
Income: Per capita income: $26,035 (2005); Median household income: $46,836 (2005); Average household income: $62,044 (2005); Percent of households with income of $100,000 or more: 14.6% (2005); Poverty rate: 6.2% (2000).
Taxes: Total city taxes per capita: $175 (2004); City property taxes per capita: $148 (2004).
Education: Percent of population age 25 and over with: High school diploma (including GED) or higher: 87.5% (2005); Bachelor's degree or higher: 25.1% (2005); Master's degree or higher: 10.1% (2005).
Housing: Homeownership rate: 79.7% (2005); Median home value: $116,761 (2005); Median rent: $370 per month (2000); Median age of housing: 44 years (2000).
Safety: Violent crime rate: 2.6 per 10,000 population; Property crime rate: 113.4 per 10,000 population (2004).
Transportation: Commute to work: 95.7% car, 0.5% public transportation, 0.6% walk, 3.2% work from home (2000); Travel time to work: 44.8% less than 15 minutes, 42.2% 15 to 30 minutes, 6.5% 30 to 45 minutes, 2.0% 45 to 60 minutes, 4.5% 60 minutes or more (2000)
Additional Information Contacts
Town of Busti . . . . (716) 763-8561
  http://www.townofbusti.com/

CARROLL (town). Covers a land area of 33.365 square miles and a water area of 0.001 square miles. Located at 42.04° N. Lat.; 79.12° W. Long.
Population: 3,504 (1990); 3,635 (2000); 3,572 (2005); 3,514 (2010 projected); Race: 98.9% White, 0.2% Black, 0.3% Asian, 0.6% Hispanic of any race (2005); Density: 107.1 persons per square mile (2005); Average household size: 2.62 (2005); Median age: 41.6 (2005); Males per 100 females: 94.3 (2005); Marriage status: 17.9% never married, 62.1% now married, 10.6% widowed, 9.4% divorced (2000); Foreign born: 0.4% (2000); Ancestry (includes multiple ancestries): 25.8% Swedish, 24.5% German, 19.1% English, 15.1% Irish, 8.9% Italian (2000).
Economy: Single-family building permits issued: 3 (2005); Multi-family building permits issued: 0 (2005); Employment by occupation: 8.2% management, 18.9% professional, 12.0% services, 29.9% sales, 1.1% farming, 6.7% construction, 23.0% production (2000).

Income: Per capita income: $18,852 (2005); Median household income: $42,359 (2005); Average household income: $48,255 (2005); Percent of households with income of $100,000 or more: 7.1% (2005); Poverty rate: 3.4% (2000).
Taxes: Total city taxes per capita: $317 (2004); City property taxes per capita: $296 (2004).
Education: Percent of population age 25 and over with: High school diploma (including GED) or higher: 83.1% (2005); Bachelor's degree or higher: 12.6% (2005); Master's degree or higher: 5.8% (2005).
Housing: Homeownership rate: 79.9% (2005); Median home value: $103,200 (2005); Median rent: $318 per month (2000); Median age of housing: 42 years (2000).
Safety: Violent crime rate: 11.1 per 10,000 population; Property crime rate: 22.3 per 10,000 population (2004).
Transportation: Commute to work: 93.0% car, 0.0% public transportation, 3.4% walk, 3.0% work from home (2000); Travel time to work: 39.7% less than 15 minutes, 47.7% 15 to 30 minutes, 7.9% 30 to 45 minutes, 0.4% 45 to 60 minutes, 4.2% 60 minutes or more (2000)

CASSADAGA (village). Covers a land area of 0.882 square miles and a water area of 0.175 square miles. Located at 42.34° N. Lat.; 79.31° W. Long. Elevation is 1,316 feet.
Population: 768 (1990); 676 (2000); 581 (2005); 559 (2010 projected); Race: 95.4% White, 0.0% Black, 1.2% Asian, 3.4% Hispanic of any race (2005); Density: 658.6 persons per square mile (2005); Average household size: 2.41 (2005); Median age: 44.0 (2005); Males per 100 females: 109.0 (2005); Marriage status: 20.4% never married, 63.2% now married, 11.0% widowed, 5.3% divorced (2000); Foreign born: 2.5% (2000); Ancestry (includes multiple ancestries): 29.4% German, 25.1% English, 19.9% Irish, 11.9% Polish, 9.9% Italian (2000).
Economy: Manufacturing: wood products. Single-family building permits issued: 1 (2005); Multi-family building permits issued: 0 (2005); Employment by occupation: 9.9% management, 24.8% professional, 10.8% services, 24.2% sales, 1.5% farming, 14.3% construction, 14.6% production (2000).
Income: Per capita income: $21,360 (2005); Median household income: $46,159 (2005); Average household income: $51,494 (2005); Percent of households with income of $100,000 or more: 8.7% (2005); Poverty rate: 2.4% (2000).
Education: Percent of population age 25 and over with: High school diploma (including GED) or higher: 95.0% (2005); Bachelor's degree or higher: 19.9% (2005); Master's degree or higher: 10.1% (2005).

School District(s)
Cassadaga Valley Central School District (PK-12)
   2003-04 Enrollment: 1,373 . . . . (716) 962-5155

Housing: Homeownership rate: 86.7% (2005); Median home value: $107,328 (2005); Median rent: $345 per month (2000); Median age of housing: 57 years (2000).
Transportation: Commute to work: 91.4% car, 0.0% public transportation, 3.9% walk, 4.2% work from home (2000); Travel time to work: 35.7% less than 15 minutes, 45.0% 15 to 30 minutes, 11.5% 30 to 45 minutes, 2.8% 45 to 60 minutes, 5.0% 60 minutes or more (2000)

CELORON (village). Covers a land area of 0.744 square miles and a water area of 0 square miles. Located at 42.10° N. Lat.; 79.28° W. Long.
History: Incorporated 1896.
Population: 1,232 (1990); 1,295 (2000); 1,260 (2005); 1,242 (2010 projected); Race: 93.0% White, 0.7% Black, 3.3% Asian, 3.2% Hispanic of any race (2005); Density: 1,694.0 persons per square mile (2005); Average household size: 2.47 (2005); Median age: 39.8 (2005); Males per 100 females: 96.9 (2005); Marriage status: 27.1% never married, 53.6% now married, 7.9% widowed, 11.4% divorced (2000); Foreign born: 1.7% (2000); Ancestry (includes multiple ancestries): 28.6% German, 19.2% Swedish, 16.8% English, 14.4% Irish, 10.1% Other groups (2000).
Economy: Summer recreational area. Single-family building permits issued: 0 (2005); Multi-family building permits issued: 0 (2005); Employment by occupation: 4.2% management, 12.2% professional, 19.9% services, 29.4% sales, 0.0% farming, 9.0% construction, 25.2% production (2000).
Income: Per capita income: $17,595 (2005); Median household income: $34,148 (2005); Average household income: $42,740 (2005); Percent of households with income of $100,000 or more: 5.3% (2005); Poverty rate: 13.2% (2000).

Education: Percent of population age 25 and over with: High school diploma (including GED) or higher: 79.1% (2005); Bachelor's degree or higher: 8.0% (2005); Master's degree or higher: 2.8% (2005).
Housing: Homeownership rate: 67.5% (2005); Median home value: $71,310 (2005); Median rent: $433 per month (2000); Median age of housing: 60+ years (2000).
Transportation: Commute to work: 94.6% car, 0.5% public transportation, 2.4% walk, 1.2% work from home (2000); Travel time to work: 53.9% less than 15 minutes, 37.6% 15 to 30 minutes, 4.1% 30 to 45 minutes, 2.7% 45 to 60 minutes, 1.7% 60 minutes or more (2000)

CHARLOTTE (town). Covers a land area of 36.501 square miles and a water area of 0 square miles. Located at 42.29° N. Lat.; 79.24° W. Long.
Population: 1,528 (1990); 1,713 (2000); 1,751 (2005); 1,781 (2010 projected); Race: 98.0% White, 0.0% Black, 0.7% Asian, 1.8% Hispanic of any race (2005); Density: 48.0 persons per square mile (2005); Average household size: 2.76 (2005); Median age: 36.8 (2005); Males per 100 females: 98.8 (2005); Marriage status: 23.1% never married, 60.9% now married, 6.7% widowed, 9.4% divorced (2000); Foreign born: 0.7% (2000); Ancestry (includes multiple ancestries): 24.0% German, 21.5% English, 12.6% Irish, 10.4% Swedish, 8.6% Polish (2000).
Economy: Single-family building permits issued: 8 (2005); Multi-family building permits issued: 0 (2005); Employment by occupation: 10.5% management, 14.9% professional, 17.5% services, 15.6% sales, 2.5% farming, 10.9% construction, 28.1% production (2000).
Income: Per capita income: $17,521 (2005); Median household income: $41,029 (2005); Average household income: $48,391 (2005); Percent of households with income of $100,000 or more: 6.6% (2005); Poverty rate: 11.7% (2000).
Education: Percent of population age 25 and over with: High school diploma (including GED) or higher: 79.3% (2005); Bachelor's degree or higher: 9.4% (2005); Master's degree or higher: 4.5% (2005).
Housing: Homeownership rate: 79.0% (2005); Median home value: $85,444 (2005); Median rent: $305 per month (2000); Median age of housing: 35 years (2000).
Transportation: Commute to work: 89.6% car, 0.0% public transportation, 2.7% walk, 6.4% work from home (2000); Travel time to work: 25.9% less than 15 minutes, 46.7% 15 to 30 minutes, 17.5% 30 to 45 minutes, 1.8% 45 to 60 minutes, 8.1% 60 minutes or more (2000)

CHAUTAUQUA (town). Covers a land area of 67.242 square miles and a water area of 0.067 square miles. Located at 42.22° N. Lat.; 79.48° W. Long.
History: Founded as meeting place for Methodist ministers and laity. Chautauqua Institute, founded in 1864, is located here. Famous people connected with the school include U.S. Presidents Garfield, Grant, McKinley, Harding, and both Roosevelts; explorers Admiral Richard Byrd and Amelia Earhart; inventors Henry Ford and Thomas Edison; Senator Robert Kennedy, William Jennings Bryan, Jane Addams, Ida Tarbell and N.Y. governor Al Smith. Village formerly known as Fair Point.
Population: 4,554 (1990); 4,666 (2000); 4,766 (2005); 4,732 (2010 projected); Race: 95.3% White, 2.1% Black, 0.6% Asian, 1.3% Hispanic of any race (2005); Density: 70.9 persons per square mile (2005); Average household size: 2.45 (2005); Median age: 42.8 (2005); Males per 100 females: 105.4 (2005); Marriage status: 21.0% never married, 63.9% now married, 6.5% widowed, 8.7% divorced (2000); Foreign born: 2.1% (2000); Ancestry (includes multiple ancestries): 24.1% German, 18.6% English, 13.2% Irish, 9.5% Swedish, 6.9% Italian (2000).
Economy: Resort village. Summer center for arts, education, religion, and recreation. Single-family building permits issued: 16 (2005); Multi-family building permits issued: 6 (2005); Employment by occupation: 11.5% management, 18.8% professional, 14.6% services, 23.2% sales, 1.9% farming, 10.8% construction, 19.2% production (2000).
Income: Per capita income: $22,330 (2005); Median household income: $41,558 (2005); Average household income: $54,078 (2005); Percent of households with income of $100,000 or more: 11.4% (2005); Poverty rate: 12.0% (2000).
Education: Percent of population age 25 and over with: High school diploma (including GED) or higher: 83.4% (2005); Bachelor's degree or higher: 24.9% (2005); Master's degree or higher: 9.8% (2005).
Housing: Homeownership rate: 78.7% (2005); Median home value: $121,320 (2005); Median rent: $329 per month (2000); Median age of housing: 49 years (2000).
Transportation: Commute to work: 90.1% car, 0.8% public transportation, 3.4% walk, 4.8% work from home (2000); Travel time to work: 47.5% less than 15 minutes, 29.5% 15 to 30 minutes, 16.1% 30 to 45 minutes, 2.5% 45 to 60 minutes, 4.5% 60 minutes or more (2000)
Additional Information Contacts
Chautauqua Chamber of Commerce . . . . (716) 366-6200
http://www.chautauquachamber.org

CHERRY CREEK (village). Covers a land area of 1.361 square miles and a water area of 0 square miles. Located at 42.29° N. Lat.; 79.09° W. Long. Elevation is 1,306 feet.
Population: 523 (1990); 551 (2000); 544 (2005); 541 (2010 projected); Race: 96.0% White, 0.2% Black, 0.4% Asian, 1.8% Hispanic of any race (2005); Density: 399.6 persons per square mile (2005); Average household size: 2.75 (2005); Median age: 38.5 (2005); Males per 100 females: 93.6 (2005); Marriage status: 22.4% never married, 60.2% now married, 5.8% widowed, 11.6% divorced (2000); Foreign born: 2.1% (2000); Ancestry (includes multiple ancestries): 33.5% German, 18.8% English, 11.4% United States or American, 7.2% Irish, 6.1% Other groups (2000).
Economy: Employment by occupation: 6.3% management, 17.3% professional, 20.5% services, 18.1% sales, 1.2% farming, 8.7% construction, 28.0% production (2000).
Income: Per capita income: $17,109 (2005); Median household income: $36,406 (2005); Average household income: $47,008 (2005); Percent of households with income of $100,000 or more: 7.6% (2005); Poverty rate: 18.3% (2000).
Education: Percent of population age 25 and over with: High school diploma (including GED) or higher: 84.7% (2005); Bachelor's degree or higher: 17.0% (2005); Master's degree or higher: 7.2% (2005).
Housing: Homeownership rate: 77.3% (2005); Median home value: $64,839 (2005); Median rent: $335 per month (2000); Median age of housing: 60+ years (2000).
Transportation: Commute to work: 92.9% car, 0.0% public transportation, 4.6% walk, 2.5% work from home (2000); Travel time to work: 33.8% less than 15 minutes, 15.8% 15 to 30 minutes, 35.0% 30 to 45 minutes, 9.0% 45 to 60 minutes, 6.4% 60 minutes or more (2000)

CHERRY CREEK (town). Covers a land area of 36.624 square miles and a water area of 0.013 square miles. Located at 42.29° N. Lat.; 79.11° W. Long. Elevation is 1,306 feet.
Population: 1,064 (1990); 1,152 (2000); 1,142 (2005); 1,138 (2010 projected); Race: 95.8% White, 0.1% Black, 0.2% Asian, 3.2% Hispanic of any race (2005); Density: 31.2 persons per square mile (2005); Average household size: 2.75 (2005); Median age: 37.7 (2005); Males per 100 females: 101.4 (2005); Marriage status: 24.3% never married, 60.4% now married, 4.2% widowed, 11.1% divorced (2000); Foreign born: 1.5% (2000); Ancestry (includes multiple ancestries): 31.4% German, 20.4% English, 11.5% Irish, 8.2% United States or American, 6.4% Polish (2000).
Economy: Agriculture: fruit and vineyards; dairy products; timber. Single-family building permits issued: 1 (2005); Multi-family building permits issued: 0 (2005); Employment by occupation: 4.9% management, 13.1% professional, 21.9% services, 18.2% sales, 4.0% farming, 10.7% construction, 27.1% production (2000).
Income: Per capita income: $18,937 (2005); Median household income: $42,390 (2005); Average household income: $50,964 (2005); Percent of households with income of $100,000 or more: 8.0% (2005); Poverty rate: 14.0% (2000).
Taxes: Total city taxes per capita: $278 (2004); City property taxes per capita: $264 (2004).
Education: Percent of population age 25 and over with: High school diploma (including GED) or higher: 78.6% (2005); Bachelor's degree or higher: 15.0% (2005); Master's degree or higher: 6.0% (2005).
Housing: Homeownership rate: 82.7% (2005); Median home value: $80,435 (2005); Median rent: $345 per month (2000); Median age of housing: 56 years (2000).
Transportation: Commute to work: 88.4% car, 0.0% public transportation, 5.2% walk, 5.6% work from home (2000); Travel time to work: 32.5% less than 15 minutes, 19.4% 15 to 30 minutes, 30.9% 30 to 45 minutes, 9.0% 45 to 60 minutes, 8.2% 60 minutes or more (2000)

CLYMER (town). Covers a land area of 36.061 square miles and a water area of 0.051 square miles. Located at 42.03° N. Lat.; 79.58° W. Long. Elevation is 1,468 feet.
Population: 1,445 (1990); 1,501 (2000); 1,635 (2005); 1,741 (2010 projected); Race: 98.8% White, 0.1% Black, 0.4% Asian, 0.6% Hispanic of any race (2005); Density: 45.3 persons per square mile (2005); Average household size: 2.96 (2005); Median age: 33.4 (2005); Males per 100

females: 100.1 (2005); Marriage status: 20.2% never married, 69.9% now married, 5.1% widowed, 4.8% divorced (2000); Foreign born: 0.9% (2000); Ancestry (includes multiple ancestries): 25.0% Dutch, 16.9% German, 11.0% English, 9.0% Irish, 4.1% Swedish (2000).
Economy: Single-family building permits issued: 3 (2005); Multi-family building permits issued: 0 (2005); Employment by occupation: 15.0% management, 16.0% professional, 15.1% services, 18.7% sales, 5.2% farming, 7.6% construction, 22.4% production (2000).
Income: Per capita income: $16,807 (2005); Median household income: $39,670 (2005); Average household income: $49,783 (2005); Percent of households with income of $100,000 or more: 7.4% (2005); Poverty rate: 12.1% (2000).
Education: Percent of population age 25 and over with: High school diploma (including GED) or higher: 75.6% (2005); Bachelor's degree or higher: 13.8% (2005); Master's degree or higher: 5.4% (2005).

School District(s)
Clymer Central School District (PK-12)
   2003-04 Enrollment: 514 . . . . (716) 355-4444
Housing: Homeownership rate: 81.2% (2005); Median home value: $88,000 (2005); Median rent: $273 per month (2000); Median age of housing: 60+ years (2000).
Transportation: Commute to work: 80.1% car, 1.0% public transportation, 7.6% walk, 10.0% work from home (2000); Travel time to work: 43.3% less than 15 minutes, 26.3% 15 to 30 minutes, 19.9% 30 to 45 minutes, 7.5% 45 to 60 minutes, 3.0% 60 minutes or more (2000)

DEWITTVILLE (unincorporated postal area, zip code 14728).
Covers a land area of 26.042 square miles and a water area of 0.010 square miles. Located at 42.25° N. Lat.; 79.43° W. Long. Elevation is 1,328 feet.
Population: 0 (2000); Race: 100.0% White, 0.0% Black, 0.0% Asian, 0.0% Hispanic of any race (2000); Density: 0.0 persons per square mile (2000); Age: 24.9% under 18, 23.5% over 64 (2000); Marriage status: 15.9% never married, 74.0% now married, 5.9% widowed, 4.3% divorced (2000); Foreign born: 2.1% (2000); Ancestry (includes multiple ancestries): 19.2% German, 15.4% Irish, 15.2% English, 10.1% United States or American, 8.4% Italian (2000).
Economy: Employment by occupation: 15.7% management, 24.8% professional, 10.0% services, 20.5% sales, 4.1% farming, 8.6% construction, 16.4% production (2000).
Income: Per capita income: $20,981 (2000); Median household income: $36,121 (2000); Poverty rate: 9.2% (2000).
Education: Percent of population age 25 and over with: High school diploma (including GED) or higher: 87.7% (2000); Bachelor's degree or higher: 23.7% (2000).
Housing: Homeownership rate: 88.8% (2000); Median home value: $96,500 (2000); Median rent: $347 per month (2000); Median age of housing: 46 years (2000).
Transportation: Commute to work: 93.5% car, 0.0% public transportation, 0.0% walk, 4.7% work from home (2000); Travel time to work: 36.3% less than 15 minutes, 37.3% 15 to 30 minutes, 20.8% 30 to 45 minutes, 2.5% 45 to 60 minutes, 3.2% 60 minutes or more (2000)

DUNKIRK (city).
Covers a land area of 4.529 square miles and a water area of 0.043 square miles. Located at 42.48° N. Lat.; 79.33° W. Long. Elevation is 598 feet.
History: In 1946, it developed a program to help Dunkerque, France (for which it was named), recover from World War II. Other U.S. cities followed, and established a program, called the One World Plan, to aid war-damaged European cities. Founded c.1800, Incorporated as city 1880.
Population: 13,989 (1990); 13,131 (2000); 12,511 (2005); 11,883 (2010 projected); Race: 79.6% White, 5.7% Black, 0.3% Asian, 24.5% Hispanic of any race (2005); Density: 2,762.7 persons per square mile (2005); Average household size: 2.37 (2005); Median age: 38.2 (2005); Males per 100 females: 91.6 (2005); Marriage status: 30.4% never married, 48.4% now married, 10.9% widowed, 10.4% divorced (2000); Foreign born: 2.1% (2000); Ancestry (includes multiple ancestries): 27.7% Polish, 22.1% Other groups, 19.4% German, 15.1% Italian, 10.9% Irish (2000).
Economy: It is a port of entry and trades extensively with other Great Lakes ports. Located in the grape belt, the city produces wines and other grape products. Manufacturing includes steel, food products and apparel. Single-family building permits issued: 0 (2005); Multi-family building permits issued: 0 (2005); Employment by occupation: 6.1% management, 15.3% professional, 21.6% services, 23.1% sales, 1.6% farming, 6.1% construction, 26.2% production (2000).
Income: Per capita income: $17,663 (2005); Median household income: $31,118 (2005); Average household income: $41,272 (2005); Percent of households with income of $100,000 or more: 4.9% (2005); Poverty rate: 22.3% (2000).
Education: Percent of population age 25 and over with: High school diploma (including GED) or higher: 75.3% (2005); Bachelor's degree or higher: 13.1% (2005); Master's degree or higher: 5.5% (2005).

School District(s)
Dunkirk City School District (KG-12)
   2003-04 Enrollment: 2,101 . . . . (716) 366-9300
Housing: Homeownership rate: 61.2% (2005); Median home value: $78,449 (2005); Median rent: $341 per month (2000); Median age of housing: 60+ years (2000).
Hospitals: Brooks Memorial Hospital (99 beds)
Safety: Violent crime rate: 52.6 per 10,000 population; Property crime rate: 263.0 per 10,000 population (2004).
Newspapers: Observer (Circulation 15,000)
Transportation: Commute to work: 89.9% car, 1.3% public transportation, 5.4% walk, 2.6% work from home (2000); Travel time to work: 66.4% less than 15 minutes, 18.6% 15 to 30 minutes, 7.1% 30 to 45 minutes, 3.3% 45 to 60 minutes, 4.6% 60 minutes or more (2000); Amtrak: Service available.

DUNKIRK (town).
Covers a land area of 6.244 square miles and a water area of 0.052 square miles. Located at 42.46° N. Lat.; 79.34° W. Long. Elevation is 598 feet.
Population: 1,482 (1990); 1,387 (2000); 1,364 (2005); 1,348 (2010 projected); Race: 93.5% White, 2.6% Black, 0.1% Asian, 4.8% Hispanic of any race (2005); Density: 218.4 persons per square mile (2005); Average household size: 2.66 (2005); Median age: 52.1 (2005); Males per 100 females: 87.9 (2005); Marriage status: 22.2% never married, 53.8% now married, 14.8% widowed, 9.1% divorced (2000); Foreign born: 2.2% (2000); Ancestry (includes multiple ancestries): 36.3% Polish, 26.1% German, 13.1% Italian, 11.0% Irish, 9.2% English (2000).
Economy: Single-family building permits issued: 0 (2005); Multi-family building permits issued: 0 (2005); Employment by occupation: 8.6% management, 17.2% professional, 22.3% services, 22.4% sales, 1.6% farming, 8.1% construction, 19.7% production (2000).
Income: Per capita income: $24,043 (2005); Median household income: $40,128 (2005); Average household income: $57,827 (2005); Percent of households with income of $100,000 or more: 10.9% (2005); Poverty rate: 11.7% (2000).
Education: Percent of population age 25 and over with: High school diploma (including GED) or higher: 73.6% (2005); Bachelor's degree or higher: 16.0% (2005); Master's degree or higher: 7.3% (2005).
Housing: Homeownership rate: 81.5% (2005); Median home value: $117,424 (2005); Median rent: $387 per month (2000); Median age of housing: 44 years (2000).
Transportation: Commute to work: 91.8% car, 1.4% public transportation, 2.4% walk, 3.8% work from home (2000); Travel time to work: 71.9% less than 15 minutes, 17.3% 15 to 30 minutes, 4.9% 30 to 45 minutes, 2.3% 45 to 60 minutes, 3.6% 60 minutes or more (2000); Amtrak: Service available.

ELLERY (town).
Covers a land area of 47.579 square miles and a water area of 0.023 square miles. Located at 42.17° N. Lat.; 79.37° W. Long.
Population: 4,534 (1990); 4,576 (2000); 4,571 (2005); 4,563 (2010 projected); Race: 98.1% White, 0.2% Black, 0.3% Asian, 1.2% Hispanic of any race (2005); Density: 96.1 persons per square mile (2005); Average household size: 2.44 (2005); Median age: 45.3 (2005); Males per 100 females: 95.5 (2005); Marriage status: 15.8% never married, 66.1% now married, 9.9% widowed, 8.3% divorced (2000); Foreign born: 1.5% (2000); Ancestry (includes multiple ancestries): 22.6% English, 21.8% German, 21.5% Swedish, 15.5% Irish, 9.5% Italian (2000).
Economy: Single-family building permits issued: 13 (2005); Multi-family building permits issued: 0 (2005); Employment by occupation: 15.1% management, 17.7% professional, 12.9% services, 25.9% sales, 0.0% farming, 15.5% construction, 12.8% production (2000).
Income: Per capita income: $24,726 (2005); Median household income: $46,909 (2005); Average household income: $59,543 (2005); Percent of households with income of $100,000 or more: 13.0% (2005); Poverty rate: 8.3% (2000).
Education: Percent of population age 25 and over with: High school diploma (including GED) or higher: 87.2% (2005); Bachelor's degree or higher: 23.9% (2005); Master's degree or higher: 9.2% (2005).

Housing: Homeownership rate: 83.0% (2005); Median home value: $129,545 (2005); Median rent: $341 per month (2000); Median age of housing: 38 years (2000).
Transportation: Commute to work: 94.3% car, 0.4% public transportation, 2.5% walk, 2.3% work from home (2000); Travel time to work: 30.3% less than 15 minutes, 50.6% 15 to 30 minutes, 13.4% 30 to 45 minutes, 2.0% 45 to 60 minutes, 3.6% 60 minutes or more (2000)

ELLICOTT (town).
Covers a land area of 30.490 square miles and a water area of 0.029 square miles. Located at 42.12° N. Lat.; 79.24° W. Long.
Population: 9,447 (1990); 9,280 (2000); 9,069 (2005); 8,847 (2010 projected); Race: 96.9% White, 0.6% Black, 1.1% Asian, 1.4% Hispanic of any race (2005); Density: 297.4 persons per square mile (2005); Average household size: 2.42 (2005); Median age: 43.9 (2005); Males per 100 females: 92.3 (2005); Marriage status: 21.4% never married, 59.5% now married, 9.5% widowed, 9.6% divorced (2000); Foreign born: 2.5% (2000); Ancestry (includes multiple ancestries): 22.0% Swedish, 18.4% Italian, 16.9% German, 15.9% English, 12.6% Irish (2000).
Economy: Single-family building permits issued: 8 (2005); Multi-family building permits issued: 0 (2005); Employment by occupation: 10.7% management, 16.0% professional, 16.1% services, 26.5% sales, 0.2% farming, 7.8% construction, 22.6% production (2000).
Income: Per capita income: $21,903 (2005); Median household income: $41,983 (2005); Average household income: $52,160 (2005); Percent of households with income of $100,000 or more: 9.7% (2005); Poverty rate: 8.8% (2000).
Education: Percent of population age 25 and over with: High school diploma (including GED) or higher: 82.4% (2005); Bachelor's degree or higher: 16.7% (2005); Master's degree or higher: 8.0% (2005).
Housing: Homeownership rate: 74.7% (2005); Median home value: $98,377 (2005); Median rent: $372 per month (2000); Median age of housing: 58 years (2000).
Safety: Violent crime rate: 12.9 per 10,000 population; Property crime rate: 520.9 per 10,000 population (2004).
Transportation: Commute to work: 93.0% car, 0.6% public transportation, 3.6% walk, 2.7% work from home (2000); Travel time to work: 60.7% less than 15 minutes, 29.2% 15 to 30 minutes, 5.8% 30 to 45 minutes, 1.7% 45 to 60 minutes, 2.7% 60 minutes or more (2000)
Additional Information Contacts
Town of Ellicott. . . . . (716) 665-5317
http://www.townofellicott.com/

ELLINGTON (town).
Covers a land area of 36.559 square miles and a water area of 0.008 square miles. Located at 42.22° N. Lat.; 79.11° W. Long. Elevation is 1,400 feet.
Population: 1,615 (1990); 1,639 (2000); 1,765 (2005); 1,804 (2010 projected); Race: 98.2% White, 0.2% Black, 0.2% Asian, 0.6% Hispanic of any race (2005); Density: 48.3 persons per square mile (2005); Average household size: 2.83 (2005); Median age: 38.5 (2005); Males per 100 females: 100.1 (2005); Marriage status: 23.4% never married, 62.4% now married, 4.7% widowed, 9.5% divorced (2000); Foreign born: 1.0% (2000); Ancestry (includes multiple ancestries): 25.9% German, 19.5% English, 14.0% Irish, 13.6% Swedish, 10.7% United States or American (2000).
Economy: In dairying and fruit-growing area. Single-family building permits issued: 8 (2005); Multi-family building permits issued: 0 (2005); Employment by occupation: 8.2% management, 15.8% professional, 14.7% services, 22.2% sales, 2.0% farming, 8.1% construction, 29.0% production (2000).
Income: Per capita income: $18,240 (2005); Median household income: $42,846 (2005); Average household income: $51,162 (2005); Percent of households with income of $100,000 or more: 7.2% (2005); Poverty rate: 12.2% (2000).
Education: Percent of population age 25 and over with: High school diploma (including GED) or higher: 79.9% (2005); Bachelor's degree or higher: 9.2% (2005); Master's degree or higher: 3.6% (2005).
Housing: Homeownership rate: 87.3% (2005); Median home value: $73,564 (2005); Median rent: $321 per month (2000); Median age of housing: 38 years (2000).
Transportation: Commute to work: 88.2% car, 1.1% public transportation, 4.6% walk, 5.2% work from home (2000); Travel time to work: 22.9% less than 15 minutes, 49.5% 15 to 30 minutes, 20.5% 30 to 45 minutes, 3.5% 45 to 60 minutes, 3.6% 60 minutes or more (2000)

FALCONER (village).
Covers a land area of 1.082 square miles and a water area of 0 square miles. Located at 42.11° N. Lat.; 79.20° W. Long. Elevation is 1,262 feet.
History: Settled 1807, incorporated 1891.
Population: 2,623 (1990); 2,540 (2000); 2,400 (2005); 2,293 (2010 projected); Race: 97.2% White, 0.7% Black, 0.5% Asian, 1.5% Hispanic of any race (2005); Density: 2,217.4 persons per square mile (2005); Average household size: 2.27 (2005); Median age: 41.3 (2005); Males per 100 females: 93.4 (2005); Marriage status: 27.4% never married, 51.8% now married, 9.6% widowed, 11.3% divorced (2000); Foreign born: 0.7% (2000); Ancestry (includes multiple ancestries): 23.4% Italian, 20.3% Swedish, 13.6% German, 12.5% English, 11.7% Irish (2000).
Economy: Manufacturing: furniture, machinery, transportation equipment, wood products. Single-family building permits issued: 0 (2005); Multi-family building permits issued: 0 (2005); Employment by occupation: 8.3% management, 12.2% professional, 19.7% services, 25.0% sales, 0.3% farming, 6.5% construction, 28.0% production (2000).
Income: Per capita income: $18,556 (2005); Median household income: $34,611 (2005); Average household income: $42,054 (2005); Percent of households with income of $100,000 or more: 4.8% (2005); Poverty rate: 10.1% (2000).
Education: Percent of population age 25 and over with: High school diploma (including GED) or higher: 79.2% (2005); Bachelor's degree or higher: 11.0% (2005); Master's degree or higher: 3.4% (2005).
School District(s)
Falconer Central School District (KG-12)
    2003-04 Enrollment: 1,420 . . . . (716) 665-6624
Housing: Homeownership rate: 62.4% (2005); Median home value: $79,347 (2005); Median rent: $322 per month (2000); Median age of housing: 60+ years (2000).
Transportation: Commute to work: 91.8% car, 1.2% public transportation, 6.1% walk, 0.9% work from home (2000); Travel time to work: 65.3% less than 15 minutes, 25.8% 15 to 30 minutes, 4.4% 30 to 45 minutes, 2.3% 45 to 60 minutes, 2.3% 60 minutes or more (2000)

FINDLEY LAKE (unincorporated postal area, zip code 14736).
Covers a land area of 5.032 square miles and a water area of 0 square miles. Located at 42.13° N. Lat.; 79.74° W. Long.
Population: 0 (2000); Race: 99.0% White, 0.0% Black, 0.0% Asian, 0.0% Hispanic of any race (2000); Density: 0.0 persons per square mile (2000); Age: 27.4% under 18, 8.3% over 64 (2000); Marriage status: 26.4% never married, 60.2% now married, 5.7% widowed, 7.7% divorced (2000); Foreign born: 1.6% (2000); Ancestry (includes multiple ancestries): 34.4% German, 18.2% English, 13.7% Irish, 10.8% Polish, 8.0% Italian (2000).
Economy: In dairying area. Employment by occupation: 12.3% management, 7.8% professional, 12.3% services, 32.5% sales, 0.0% farming, 7.1% construction, 27.9% production (2000).
Income: Per capita income: $16,303 (2000); Median household income: $41,500 (2000); Poverty rate: 9.7% (2000).
Education: Percent of population age 25 and over with: High school diploma (including GED) or higher: 84.6% (2000); Bachelor's degree or higher: 14.4% (2000).
Housing: Homeownership rate: 87.7% (2000); Median home value: $71,300 (2000); Median rent: $233 per month (2000); Median age of housing: 60+ years (2000).
Transportation: Commute to work: 96.7% car, 0.0% public transportation, 0.0% walk, 3.3% work from home (2000); Travel time to work: 18.6% less than 15 minutes, 52.4% 15 to 30 minutes, 23.4% 30 to 45 minutes, 5.5% 45 to 60 minutes, 0.0% 60 minutes or more (2000)
Additional Information Contacts
Findley Lake Chamber of Commerce . . . . (716) 769-7609
    http://www.findleylakeinfo.org

FORESTVILLE (village).
Covers a land area of 0.977 square miles and a water area of 0 square miles. Located at 42.47° N. Lat.; 79.17° W. Long. Elevation is 928 feet.
Population: 738 (1990); 770 (2000); 781 (2005); 791 (2010 projected); Race: 94.1% White, 0.4% Black, 0.0% Asian, 3.6% Hispanic of any race (2005); Density: 799.1 persons per square mile (2005); Average household size: 2.51 (2005); Median age: 39.1 (2005); Males per 100 females: 103.4 (2005); Marriage status: 22.2% never married, 55.8% now married, 9.7% widowed, 12.2% divorced (2000); Foreign born: 1.1% (2000); Ancestry (includes multiple ancestries): 28.8% German, 22.8% English, 17.8% Polish, 14.6% Irish, 11.8% Italian (2000).

Economy: Single-family building permits issued: 0 (2005); Multi-family building permits issued: 0 (2005); Employment by occupation: 8.2% management, 15.2% professional, 22.2% services, 21.8% sales, 0.0% farming, 8.9% construction, 23.7% production (2000).
Income: Per capita income: $16,610 (2005); Median household income: $35,326 (2005); Average household income: $41,568 (2005); Percent of households with income of $100,000 or more: 4.8% (2005); Poverty rate: 10.2% (2000).
Education: Percent of population age 25 and over with: High school diploma (including GED) or higher: 85.5% (2005); Bachelor's degree or higher: 13.6% (2005); Master's degree or higher: 4.3% (2005).

School District(s)
Forestville Central School District (KG-12)
   2003-04 Enrollment: 610 . . . . (716) 965-2742

Housing: Homeownership rate: 67.8% (2005); Median home value: $89,322 (2005); Median rent: $360 per month (2000); Median age of housing: 60+ years (2000).
Transportation: Commute to work: 88.9% car, 0.7% public transportation, 4.6% walk, 5.9% work from home (2000); Travel time to work: 25.0% less than 15 minutes, 53.5% 15 to 30 minutes, 10.1% 30 to 45 minutes, 4.5% 45 to 60 minutes, 6.9% 60 minutes or more (2000)

FREDONIA (village).
Covers a land area of 5.193 square miles and a water area of 0 square miles. Located at 42.44° N. Lat.; 79.33° W. Long. Elevation is 728 feet.
History: Incorporated 1829. Was the site of the first gas well in the U.S. The first local unit of the Natioanl Grange (Patrons of Husbandry) Movement was also founded here. State University of N.Y. at Fredonia here.
Population: 10,436 (1990); 10,706 (2000); 10,568 (2005); 10,415 (2010 projected); Race: 95.8% White, 1.0% Black, 1.6% Asian, 1.8% Hispanic of any race (2005); Density: 2,035.2 persons per square mile (2005); Average household size: 2.94 (2005); Median age: 25.0 (2005); Males per 100 females: 83.7 (2005); Marriage status: 47.4% never married, 41.6% now married, 6.0% widowed, 5.0% divorced (2000); Foreign born: 2.6% (2000); Ancestry (includes multiple ancestries): 25.8% German, 22.5% Italian, 17.5% Polish, 16.9% Irish, 13.6% English (2000).
Economy: Grape juice, wine, and canned foods are produced. Single-family building permits issued: 1 (2005); Multi-family building permits issued: 222 (2005); Employment by occupation: 7.7% management, 25.8% professional, 23.0% services, 25.5% sales, 0.4% farming, 4.6% construction, 13.1% production (2000).
Income: Per capita income: $18,174 (2005); Median household income: $39,902 (2005); Average household income: $50,760 (2005); Percent of households with income of $100,000 or more: 10.7% (2005); Poverty rate: 19.0% (2000).
Education: Percent of population age 25 and over with: High school diploma (including GED) or higher: 88.9% (2005); Bachelor's degree or higher: 33.0% (2005); Master's degree or higher: 17.1% (2005).

School District(s)
Fredonia Central School District (PK-12)
   2003-04 Enrollment: 1,857 . . . . (716) 679-1581

Four-year College(s)
SUNY at Fredonia (Public)
   Fall 2004 Enrollment: 5,359. . . . . (716) 673-3111
   2005-06 Tuition: In-state $5,441; Out-of-state $11,622

Housing: Homeownership rate: 54.3% (2005); Median home value: $132,902 (2005); Median rent: $393 per month (2000); Median age of housing: 52 years (2000).
Safety: Violent crime rate: 13.2 per 10,000 population; Property crime rate: 260.6 per 10,000 population (2004).
Transportation: Commute to work: 78.1% car, 0.5% public transportation, 16.3% walk, 3.6% work from home (2000); Travel time to work: 71.2% less than 15 minutes, 16.6% 15 to 30 minutes, 4.8% 30 to 45 minutes, 3.2% 45 to 60 minutes, 4.3% 60 minutes or more (2000)
Additional Information Contacts
Fredonia Chamber of Commerce . . . . (716) 679-1565
   http://www.fredoniachamber.org

FRENCH CREEK (town).
Covers a land area of 36.213 square miles and a water area of 0 square miles. Located at 42.04° N. Lat.; 79.69° W. Long.
Population: 916 (1990); 935 (2000); 1,018 (2005); 1,085 (2010 projected); Race: 98.8% White, 0.0% Black, 0.2% Asian, 0.0% Hispanic of any race (2005); Density: 28.1 persons per square mile (2005); Average household size: 2.80 (2005); Median age: 35.6 (2005); Males per 100 females: 110.3 (2005); Marriage status: 21.3% never married, 68.3% now married, 3.3% widowed, 7.1% divorced (2000); Foreign born: 1.0% (2000); Ancestry (includes multiple ancestries): 20.9% German, 16.6% Irish, 14.3% Dutch, 11.6% English, 7.4% Polish (2000).
Economy: Single-family building permits issued: 3 (2005); Multi-family building permits issued: 12 (2005); Employment by occupation: 15.0% management, 11.2% professional, 17.5% services, 19.1% sales, 6.1% farming, 11.2% construction, 20.0% production (2000).
Income: Per capita income: $16,933 (2005); Median household income: $39,947 (2005); Average household income: $47,356 (2005); Percent of households with income of $100,000 or more: 5.2% (2005); Poverty rate: 12.4% (2000).
Education: Percent of population age 25 and over with: High school diploma (including GED) or higher: 84.4% (2005); Bachelor's degree or higher: 11.2% (2005); Master's degree or higher: 1.3% (2005).
Housing: Homeownership rate: 79.7% (2005); Median home value: $89,333 (2005); Median rent: $313 per month (2000); Median age of housing: 25 years (2000).
Transportation: Commute to work: 87.1% car, 0.0% public transportation, 6.1% walk, 5.6% work from home (2000); Travel time to work: 46.0% less than 15 minutes, 22.0% 15 to 30 minutes, 15.3% 30 to 45 minutes, 9.7% 45 to 60 minutes, 6.9% 60 minutes or more (2000)

FREWSBURG (CDP).
Covers a land area of 3.363 square miles and a water area of 0 square miles. Located at 42.05° N. Lat.; 79.16° W. Long. Elevation is 1,261 feet.
Population: 1,958 (1990); 1,965 (2000); 1,968 (2005); 1,946 (2010 projected); Race: 99.2% White, 0.2% Black, 0.2% Asian, 0.3% Hispanic of any race (2005); Density: 585.2 persons per square mile (2005); Average household size: 2.60 (2005); Median age: 43.5 (2005); Males per 100 females: 88.9 (2005); Marriage status: 19.8% never married, 53.9% now married, 15.5% widowed, 10.7% divorced (2000); Foreign born: 0.8% (2000); Ancestry (includes multiple ancestries): 26.8% Swedish, 24.3% German, 23.8% English, 15.1% Irish, 7.2% Italian (2000).
Economy: Injection plastic molders, wood products; dairying. Employment by occupation: 5.4% management, 20.0% professional, 10.7% services, 30.2% sales, 0.7% farming, 3.1% construction, 29.8% production (2000).
Income: Per capita income: $18,983 (2005); Median household income: $41,513 (2005); Average household income: $47,153 (2005); Percent of households with income of $100,000 or more: 7.4% (2005); Poverty rate: 4.7% (2000).
Education: Percent of population age 25 and over with: High school diploma (including GED) or higher: 85.5% (2005); Bachelor's degree or higher: 14.3% (2005); Master's degree or higher: 7.9% (2005).

School District(s)
Frewsburg Central School District (KG-12)
   2003-04 Enrollment: 1,013 . . . . (716) 569-9241

Housing: Homeownership rate: 72.1% (2005); Median home value: $102,991 (2005); Median rent: $313 per month (2000); Median age of housing: 51 years (2000).
Transportation: Commute to work: 93.0% car, 0.0% public transportation, 4.1% walk, 2.3% work from home (2000); Travel time to work: 41.2% less than 15 minutes, 47.5% 15 to 30 minutes, 5.6% 30 to 45 minutes, 0.7% 45 to 60 minutes, 5.1% 60 minutes or more (2000)

GERRY (town).
Covers a land area of 36.163 square miles and a water area of 0 square miles. Located at 42.22° N. Lat.; 79.23° W. Long. Elevation is 1,302 feet.
Population: 2,147 (1990); 2,054 (2000); 2,021 (2005); 2,026 (2010 projected); Race: 98.2% White, 0.4% Black, 0.0% Asian, 1.0% Hispanic of any race (2005); Density: 55.9 persons per square mile (2005); Average household size: 3.05 (2005); Median age: 45.7 (2005); Males per 100 females: 88.7 (2005); Marriage status: 18.4% never married, 61.2% now married, 10.3% widowed, 10.0% divorced (2000); Foreign born: 1.5% (2000); Ancestry (includes multiple ancestries): 20.8% Swedish, 20.1% German, 18.4% English, 10.6% Irish, 8.4% Italian (2000).
Economy: Resort village. Single-family building permits issued: 4 (2005); Multi-family building permits issued: 0 (2005); Employment by occupation: 8.4% management, 15.9% professional, 15.5% services, 19.2% sales, 1.9% farming, 13.1% construction, 26.1% production (2000).
Income: Per capita income: $17,298 (2005); Median household income: $39,983 (2005); Average household income: $46,738 (2005); Percent of households with income of $100,000 or more: 6.2% (2005); Poverty rate: 12.8% (2000).

Education: Percent of population age 25 and over with: High school diploma (including GED) or higher: 81.0% (2005); Bachelor's degree or higher: 14.9% (2005); Master's degree or higher: 5.6% (2005).
Housing: Homeownership rate: 85.2% (2005); Median home value: $94,466 (2005); Median rent: $337 per month (2000); Median age of housing: 36 years (2000).
Transportation: Commute to work: 92.0% car, 0.3% public transportation, 3.2% walk, 4.1% work from home (2000); Travel time to work: 30.1% less than 15 minutes, 49.1% 15 to 30 minutes, 14.1% 30 to 45 minutes, 2.5% 45 to 60 minutes, 4.1% 60 minutes or more (2000)

HANOVER (town). Covers a land area of 49.298 square miles and a water area of 0.166 square miles. Located at 42.51° N. Lat.; 79.14° W. Long.
Population: 7,380 (1990); 7,638 (2000); 7,514 (2005); 7,366 (2010 projected); Race: 96.5% White, 0.5% Black, 0.2% Asian, 2.4% Hispanic of any race (2005); Density: 152.4 persons per square mile (2005); Average household size: 2.56 (2005); Median age: 40.8 (2005); Males per 100 females: 95.0 (2005); Marriage status: 22.0% never married, 60.6% now married, 7.6% widowed, 9.8% divorced (2000); Foreign born: 1.3% (2000); Ancestry (includes multiple ancestries): 31.2% German, 21.9% Italian, 16.2% Irish, 14.3% English, 14.1% Polish (2000).
Economy: Single-family building permits issued: 10 (2005); Multi-family building permits issued: 0 (2005); Employment by occupation: 8.4% management, 14.6% professional, 21.6% services, 21.7% sales, 0.8% farming, 10.2% construction, 22.7% production (2000).
Income: Per capita income: $20,493 (2005); Median household income: $43,091 (2005); Average household income: $51,065 (2005); Percent of households with income of $100,000 or more: 9.4% (2005); Poverty rate: 10.6% (2000).
Education: Percent of population age 25 and over with: High school diploma (including GED) or higher: 81.6% (2005); Bachelor's degree or higher: 14.4% (2005); Master's degree or higher: 6.7% (2005).
Housing: Homeownership rate: 77.6% (2005); Median home value: $106,212 (2005); Median rent: $363 per month (2000); Median age of housing: 57 years (2000).
Transportation: Commute to work: 89.4% car, 1.7% public transportation, 3.4% walk, 4.8% work from home (2000); Travel time to work: 30.2% less than 15 minutes, 37.0% 15 to 30 minutes, 10.5% 30 to 45 minutes, 13.6% 45 to 60 minutes, 8.7% 60 minutes or more (2000)

HARMONY (town). Covers a land area of 45.509 square miles and a water area of 0.108 square miles. Located at 42.05° N. Lat.; 79.44° W. Long.
Population: 2,177 (1990); 2,339 (2000); 2,429 (2005); 2,435 (2010 projected); Race: 97.8% White, 0.5% Black, 0.1% Asian, 0.7% Hispanic of any race (2005); Density: 53.4 persons per square mile (2005); Average household size: 2.75 (2005); Median age: 38.4 (2005); Males per 100 females: 98.3 (2005); Marriage status: 26.5% never married, 61.9% now married, 5.1% widowed, 6.6% divorced (2000); Foreign born: 0.3% (2000); Ancestry (includes multiple ancestries): 18.8% English, 17.6% German, 14.6% Swedish, 13.2% Irish, 6.8% Italian (2000).
Economy: Single-family building permits issued: 5 (2005); Multi-family building permits issued: 0 (2005); Employment by occupation: 5.4% management, 16.9% professional, 16.1% services, 24.7% sales, 1.3% farming, 14.0% construction, 21.6% production (2000).
Income: Per capita income: $17,375 (2005); Median household income: $38,624 (2005); Average household income: $47,743 (2005); Percent of households with income of $100,000 or more: 6.4% (2005); Poverty rate: 10.6% (2000).
Education: Percent of population age 25 and over with: High school diploma (including GED) or higher: 81.8% (2005); Bachelor's degree or higher: 10.5% (2005); Master's degree or higher: 3.4% (2005).
Housing: Homeownership rate: 84.6% (2005); Median home value: $85,362 (2005); Median rent: $341 per month (2000); Median age of housing: 46 years (2000).
Transportation: Commute to work: 92.4% car, 0.0% public transportation, 2.8% walk, 4.5% work from home (2000); Travel time to work: 22.0% less than 15 minutes, 50.8% 15 to 30 minutes, 18.6% 30 to 45 minutes, 5.6% 45 to 60 minutes, 3.0% 60 minutes or more (2000)

IRVING (unincorporated postal area, zip code 14081). Covers a land area of 36.435 square miles and a water area of 0.045 square miles. Located at 42.57° N. Lat.; 79.09° W. Long.
Population: 0 (2000); Race: 67.9% White, 0.8% Black, 0.7% Asian, 1.1% Hispanic of any race (2000); Density: 0.0 persons per square mile (2000); Age: 25.8% under 18, 16.7% over 64 (2000); Marriage status: 29.5% never married, 49.5% now married, 10.0% widowed, 11.1% divorced (2000); Foreign born: 2.0% (2000); Ancestry (includes multiple ancestries): 23.8% German, 16.2% Italian, 15.1% Irish, 14.7% Other groups, 11.6% Polish (2000).
Economy: Employment by occupation: 8.8% management, 11.7% professional, 20.9% services, 23.3% sales, 1.0% farming, 13.3% construction, 21.1% production (2000).
Income: Per capita income: $17,937 (2000); Median household income: $35,946 (2000); Poverty rate: 14.3% (2000).
Education: Percent of population age 25 and over with: High school diploma (including GED) or higher: 76.3% (2000); Bachelor's degree or higher: 14.5% (2000).
Housing: Homeownership rate: 81.5% (2000); Median home value: $67,800 (2000); Median rent: $339 per month (2000); Median age of housing: 44 years (2000).
Hospitals: TLC Health Network
Transportation: Commute to work: 96.6% car, 0.3% public transportation, 1.4% walk, 1.6% work from home (2000); Travel time to work: 29.7% less than 15 minutes, 30.9% 15 to 30 minutes, 15.3% 30 to 45 minutes, 17.5% 45 to 60 minutes, 6.7% 60 minutes or more (2000)

JAMESTOWN (city). Covers a land area of 8.977 square miles and a water area of 0.084 square miles. Located at 42.09° N. Lat.; 79.23° W. Long. Elevation is 1,317 feet.
History: The founder of the Jamestown settlement was James Prendergast, who purchased 1,000 acres of land his brother had earlier bought from the Holland Land Company. Among the early settlers were a number of skilled woodworkers, who began to make furniture to supply the needs of the pioneers of the region. In 1849, some Swedish immigrants appeared. After the close of the Civil War, many others joined them. Most of them were cabinet makers attracted by the furniture factories. In 1888, two years after Jamestown had become officially a city, construction of metal furniture was begun.
Population: 34,689 (1990); 31,730 (2000); 30,261 (2005); 28,753 (2010 projected); Race: 90.1% White, 3.9% Black, 0.7% Asian, 6.4% Hispanic of any race (2005); Density: 3,370.9 persons per square mile (2005); Average household size: 2.32 (2005); Median age: 36.8 (2005); Males per 100 females: 91.5 (2005); Marriage status: 29.3% never married, 49.5% now married, 8.9% widowed, 12.3% divorced (2000); Foreign born: 2.2% (2000); Ancestry (includes multiple ancestries): 19.1% Swedish, 18.4% Italian, 17.4% German, 14.1% Irish, 13.1% English (2000).
Economy: Unemployment rate: 5.3% (2005); Total civilian labor force: 14,751 (2005); Single-family building permits issued: 5 (2005); Multi-family building permits issued: 0 (2005); Employment by occupation: 8.2% management, 18.5% professional, 20.0% services, 23.4% sales, 0.1% farming, 6.5% construction, 23.3% production (2000).
Income: Per capita income: $16,474 (2005); Median household income: $27,792 (2005); Average household income: $37,340 (2005); Percent of households with income of $100,000 or more: 4.6% (2005); Poverty rate: 19.5% (2000).
Education: Percent of population age 25 and over with: High school diploma (including GED) or higher: 79.3% (2005); Bachelor's degree or higher: 14.7% (2005); Master's degree or higher: 6.2% (2005).

School District(s)
Jamestown City School District (PK-12)
    2003-04 Enrollment: 5,289 . . . . (716) 483-4420
Southwestern Central School District At Jamestown (KG-12)
    2003-04 Enrollment: 1,752 . . . . (716) 484-1136

Two-year College(s)
Jamestown Business College
    Fall 2004 Enrollment: 284 . . . . (716) 664-5100
    2005-06 Tuition: In-state $8,850; Out-of-state $8,850
Jamestown Community College (Public)
    Fall 2004 Enrollment: 3,819 . . . . (716) 665-5220
    2005-06 Tuition: In-state $3,680; Out-of-state $6,830

Housing: Homeownership rate: 51.6% (2005); Median home value: $75,211 (2005); Median rent: $320 per month (2000); Median age of housing: 60+ years (2000).
Hospitals: WCA Hospital (342 beds)
Safety: Violent crime rate: 54.2 per 10,000 population; Property crime rate: 340.8 per 10,000 population (2004).
Newspapers: Post-Journal (Circulation 20,150)

Transportation: Commute to work: 89.0% car, 2.7% public transportation, 5.8% walk, 1.3% work from home (2000); Travel time to work: 62.7% less than 15 minutes, 25.5% 15 to 30 minutes, 5.8% 30 to 45 minutes, 3.1% 45 to 60 minutes, 2.9% 60 minutes or more (2000); Amtrak: Service available.
Additional Information Contacts
Jamestown Chamber of Commerce . . . . (716) 484-1101
   http://www.chautauquachamber.org/

JAMESTOWN WEST
(CDP). Aka West Ellicott. Covers a land area of 2.511 square miles and a water area of 0 square miles. Located at 42.09° N. Lat.; 79.27° W. Long.
Population: 2,625 (1990); 2,535 (2000); 2,585 (2005); 2,622 (2010 projected); Race: 98.1% White, 0.2% Black, 0.9% Asian, 1.0% Hispanic of any race (2005); Density: 1,029.4 persons per square mile (2005); Average household size: 2.49 (2005); Median age: 48.2 (2005); Males per 100 females: 88.1 (2005); Marriage status: 18.3% never married, 58.9% now married, 12.8% widowed, 9.9% divorced (2000); Foreign born: 4.4% (2000); Ancestry (includes multiple ancestries): 21.9% Italian, 21.5% Swedish, 17.4% German, 14.8% English, 12.8% Irish (2000).
Economy: Employment by occupation: 14.5% management, 20.3% professional, 15.1% services, 28.6% sales, 0.0% farming, 5.4% construction, 16.2% production (2000).
Income: Per capita income: $22,964 (2005); Median household income: $42,714 (2005); Average household income: $54,858 (2005); Percent of households with income of $100,000 or more: 9.7% (2005); Poverty rate: 7.2% (2000).
Education: Percent of population age 25 and over with: High school diploma (including GED) or higher: 85.4% (2005); Bachelor's degree or higher: 25.9% (2005); Master's degree or higher: 15.2% (2005).
Housing: Homeownership rate: 81.3% (2005); Median home value: $120,584 (2005); Median rent: $466 per month (2000); Median age of housing: 47 years (2000).
Transportation: Commute to work: 94.1% car, 0.0% public transportation, 3.4% walk, 2.5% work from home (2000); Travel time to work: 65.4% less than 15 minutes, 26.4% 15 to 30 minutes, 7.0% 30 to 45 minutes, 0.8% 45 to 60 minutes, 0.4% 60 minutes or more (2000)

KENNEDY
(unincorporated postal area, zip code 14747). Covers a land area of 44.987 square miles and a water area of 0.032 square miles. Located at 42.15° N. Lat.; 79.08° W. Long.
Population: 0 (2000); Race: 98.1% White, 0.4% Black, 0.1% Asian, 0.4% Hispanic of any race (2000); Density: 0.0 persons per square mile (2000); Age: 27.0% under 18, 12.9% over 64 (2000); Marriage status: 17.5% never married, 66.3% now married, 6.5% widowed, 9.6% divorced (2000); Foreign born: 0.8% (2000); Ancestry (includes multiple ancestries): 24.9% German, 22.8% English, 16.8% Swedish, 14.1% Irish, 7.5% Italian (2000).
Economy: In agricultural area. Employment by occupation: 11.1% management, 15.3% professional, 15.2% services, 21.5% sales, 1.5% farming, 8.2% construction, 27.2% production (2000).
Income: Per capita income: $15,941 (2000); Median household income: $34,353 (2000); Poverty rate: 11.0% (2000).
Education: Percent of population age 25 and over with: High school diploma (including GED) or higher: 80.8% (2000); Bachelor's degree or higher: 11.9% (2000).
School District(s)
Falconer Central School District (KG-12)
   2003-04 Enrollment: 1,420 . . . . (716) 665-6624
Housing: Homeownership rate: 83.6% (2000); Median home value: $56,800 (2000); Median rent: $297 per month (2000); Median age of housing: 39 years (2000).
Transportation: Commute to work: 91.0% car, 0.6% public transportation, 3.5% walk, 3.6% work from home (2000); Travel time to work: 30.1% less than 15 minutes, 48.4% 15 to 30 minutes, 15.6% 30 to 45 minutes, 2.7% 45 to 60 minutes, 3.2% 60 minutes or more (2000)

KIANTONE
(town). Covers a land area of 18.471 square miles and a water area of 0.066 square miles. Located at 42.04° N. Lat.; 79.19° W. Long. Elevation is 1,505 feet.
Population: 1,301 (1990); 1,385 (2000); 1,369 (2005); 1,346 (2010 projected); Race: 98.6% White, 0.4% Black, 0.0% Asian, 0.2% Hispanic of any race (2005); Density: 74.1 persons per square mile (2005); Average household size: 2.58 (2005); Median age: 44.5 (2005); Males per 100 females: 98.4 (2005); Marriage status: 21.9% never married, 67.1% now married, 4.4% widowed, 6.6% divorced (2000); Foreign born: 1.7% (2000); Ancestry (includes multiple ancestries): 24.7% Swedish, 20.9% German, 18.2% Italian, 12.9% English, 8.6% Irish (2000).
Economy: Single-family building permits issued: 10 (2005); Multi-family building permits issued: 0 (2005); Employment by occupation: 10.0% management, 18.8% professional, 15.1% services, 27.8% sales, 1.2% farming, 10.1% construction, 17.0% production (2000).
Income: Per capita income: $24,790 (2005); Median household income: $49,782 (2005); Average household income: $63,912 (2005); Percent of households with income of $100,000 or more: 16.6% (2005); Poverty rate: 6.9% (2000).
Education: Percent of population age 25 and over with: High school diploma (including GED) or higher: 89.4% (2005); Bachelor's degree or higher: 21.1% (2005); Master's degree or higher: 10.6% (2005).
Housing: Homeownership rate: 89.3% (2005); Median home value: $128,344 (2005); Median rent: $339 per month (2000); Median age of housing: 47 years (2000).
Transportation: Commute to work: 95.8% car, 0.0% public transportation, 0.7% walk, 3.4% work from home (2000); Travel time to work: 41.8% less than 15 minutes, 43.3% 15 to 30 minutes, 6.8% 30 to 45 minutes, 2.2% 45 to 60 minutes, 6.0% 60 minutes or more (2000)

LAKEWOOD
(village). Covers a land area of 1.966 square miles and a water area of 0 square miles. Located at 42.10° N. Lat.; 79.32° W. Long. Elevation is 1,329 feet.
History: Settled 1809, incorporated 1893.
Population: 3,564 (1990); 3,258 (2000); 3,136 (2005); 3,005 (2010 projected); Race: 97.2% White, 0.8% Black, 0.8% Asian, 0.9% Hispanic of any race (2005); Density: 1,594.8 persons per square mile (2005); Average household size: 2.17 (2005); Median age: 44.8 (2005); Males per 100 females: 88.8 (2005); Marriage status: 20.6% never married, 56.5% now married, 9.2% widowed, 13.7% divorced (2000); Foreign born: 1.3% (2000); Ancestry (includes multiple ancestries): 26.2% German, 24.6% Swedish, 17.9% English, 17.6% Irish, 12.6% Italian (2000).
Economy: Resort village. Truck and bus engines. Single-family building permits issued: 4 (2005); Multi-family building permits issued: 0 (2005); Employment by occupation: 12.0% management, 25.5% professional, 15.1% services, 25.3% sales, 0.0% farming, 4.9% construction, 17.2% production (2000).
Income: Per capita income: $27,730 (2005); Median household income: $44,792 (2005); Average household income: $60,305 (2005); Percent of households with income of $100,000 or more: 14.2% (2005); Poverty rate: 5.5% (2000).
Education: Percent of population age 25 and over with: High school diploma (including GED) or higher: 90.4% (2005); Bachelor's degree or higher: 34.4% (2005); Master's degree or higher: 11.4% (2005).
Housing: Homeownership rate: 72.0% (2005); Median home value: $112,046 (2005); Median rent: $397 per month (2000); Median age of housing: 46 years (2000).
Transportation: Commute to work: 95.9% car, 1.1% public transportation, 0.4% walk, 2.5% work from home (2000); Travel time to work: 46.9% less than 15 minutes, 41.0% 15 to 30 minutes, 7.6% 30 to 45 minutes, 0.8% 45 to 60 minutes, 3.7% 60 minutes or more (2000)

MAYVILLE
(village). Covers a land area of 2.007 square miles and a water area of 0 square miles. Located at 42.25° N. Lat.; 79.50° W. Long. Elevation is 1,468 feet.
History: Incorporated 1830.
Population: 1,663 (1990); 1,756 (2000); 1,747 (2005); 1,708 (2010 projected); Race: 92.2% White, 4.9% Black, 0.9% Asian, 2.0% Hispanic of any race (2005); Density: 870.5 persons per square mile (2005); Average household size: 2.56 (2005); Median age: 37.6 (2005); Males per 100 females: 118.1 (2005); Marriage status: 22.9% never married, 61.2% now married, 6.7% widowed, 9.2% divorced (2000); Foreign born: 3.0% (2000); Ancestry (includes multiple ancestries): 22.1% German, 18.2% English, 12.9% Irish, 10.4% Swedish, 7.7% Italian (2000).
Economy: Resort village. Manufacturing of furniture and lights. Single-family building permits issued: 2 (2005); Multi-family building permits issued: 0 (2005); Employment by occupation: 9.0% management, 23.3% professional, 15.5% services, 23.3% sales, 0.1% farming, 8.1% construction, 20.7% production (2000).
Income: Per capita income: $18,268 (2005); Median household income: $36,370 (2005); Average household income: $44,887 (2005); Percent of households with income of $100,000 or more: 8.1% (2005); Poverty rate: 10.2% (2000).

Education: Percent of population age 25 and over with: High school diploma (including GED) or higher: 82.0% (2005); Bachelor's degree or higher: 20.1% (2005); Master's degree or higher: 8.9% (2005).

School District(s)
Chautauqua Lake Central School District (PK-12)
    2003-04 Enrollment: 976 . . . . (716) 753-5808
Housing: Homeownership rate: 63.7% (2005); Median home value: $113,571 (2005); Median rent: $310 per month (2000); Median age of housing: 56 years (2000).
Transportation: Commute to work: 87.3% car, 1.0% public transportation, 6.8% walk, 4.2% work from home (2000); Travel time to work: 55.5% less than 15 minutes, 21.4% 15 to 30 minutes, 15.9% 30 to 45 minutes, 2.6% 45 to 60 minutes, 4.7% 60 minutes or more (2000)

MINA (town). Covers a land area of 35.861 square miles and a water area of 0.440 square miles. Located at 42.13° N. Lat.; 79.70° W. Long. Elevation is 1,598 feet.
Population: 1,129 (1990); 1,176 (2000); 1,195 (2005); 1,205 (2010 projected); Race: 97.8% White, 0.3% Black, 0.2% Asian, 1.3% Hispanic of any race (2005); Density: 33.3 persons per square mile (2005); Average household size: 2.53 (2005); Median age: 42.4 (2005); Males per 100 females: 100.8 (2005); Marriage status: 20.3% never married, 67.2% now married, 5.4% widowed, 7.1% divorced (2000); Foreign born: 0.6% (2000); Ancestry (includes multiple ancestries): 26.0% German, 18.1% English, 13.6% Irish, 8.5% Polish, 8.0% United States or American (2000).
Economy: Single-family building permits issued: 5 (2005); Multi-family building permits issued: 0 (2005); Employment by occupation: 16.7% management, 11.7% professional, 14.8% services, 22.9% sales, 1.4% farming, 10.0% construction, 22.4% production (2000).
Income: Per capita income: $22,331 (2005); Median household income: $46,550 (2005); Average household income: $56,536 (2005); Percent of households with income of $100,000 or more: 11.7% (2005); Poverty rate: 9.3% (2000).
Education: Percent of population age 25 and over with: High school diploma (including GED) or higher: 82.1% (2005); Bachelor's degree or higher: 17.2% (2005); Master's degree or higher: 5.4% (2005).
Housing: Homeownership rate: 85.0% (2005); Median home value: $120,946 (2005); Median rent: $375 per month (2000); Median age of housing: 42 years (2000).
Transportation: Commute to work: 88.5% car, 0.0% public transportation, 3.9% walk, 6.9% work from home (2000); Travel time to work: 27.8% less than 15 minutes, 41.7% 15 to 30 minutes, 26.7% 30 to 45 minutes, 3.4% 45 to 60 minutes, 0.4% 60 minutes or more (2000)

NORTH HARMONY (town). Covers a land area of 42.186 square miles and a water area of 0.001 square miles. Located at 42.13° N. Lat.; 79.43° W. Long.
Population: 2,301 (1990); 2,521 (2000); 2,366 (2005); 2,288 (2010 projected); Race: 98.9% White, 0.2% Black, 0.0% Asian, 1.1% Hispanic of any race (2005); Density: 56.1 persons per square mile (2005); Average household size: 2.68 (2005); Median age: 40.6 (2005); Males per 100 females: 102.2 (2005); Marriage status: 18.1% never married, 70.3% now married, 4.8% widowed, 6.8% divorced (2000); Foreign born: 1.7% (2000); Ancestry (includes multiple ancestries): 22.6% English, 21.2% German, 16.8% Swedish, 12.8% Irish, 7.8% Dutch (2000).
Economy: Single-family building permits issued: 10 (2005); Multi-family building permits issued: 0 (2005); Employment by occupation: 11.9% management, 21.7% professional, 16.7% services, 22.6% sales, 1.4% farming, 8.9% construction, 16.7% production (2000).
Income: Per capita income: $22,530 (2005); Median household income: $48,115 (2005); Average household income: $60,300 (2005); Percent of households with income of $100,000 or more: 14.6% (2005); Poverty rate: 9.7% (2000).
Education: Percent of population age 25 and over with: High school diploma (including GED) or higher: 90.9% (2005); Bachelor's degree or higher: 26.9% (2005); Master's degree or higher: 11.8% (2005).
Housing: Homeownership rate: 87.3% (2005); Median home value: $107,653 (2005); Median rent: $430 per month (2000); Median age of housing: 46 years (2000).
Transportation: Commute to work: 92.7% car, 0.8% public transportation, 0.0% walk, 5.4% work from home (2000); Travel time to work: 33.6% less than 15 minutes, 45.8% 15 to 30 minutes, 12.7% 30 to 45 minutes, 4.0% 45 to 60 minutes, 3.9% 60 minutes or more (2000)

PANAMA (village). Covers a land area of 2.168 square miles and a water area of 0.024 square miles. Located at 42.07° N. Lat.; 79.48° W. Long. Elevation is 1,550 feet.
History: Panama Rocks, a 25-acre park with a 60-foot high rock outcropping containing abundant early Paleozoic marine fossils, is 1 mile West Southwest.
Population: 468 (1990); 491 (2000); 492 (2005); 481 (2010 projected); Race: 96.3% White, 1.4% Black, 0.2% Asian, 1.2% Hispanic of any race (2005); Density: 226.9 persons per square mile (2005); Average household size: 2.52 (2005); Median age: 41.7 (2005); Males per 100 females: 98.4 (2005); Marriage status: 17.0% never married, 64.1% now married, 8.2% widowed, 10.6% divorced (2000); Foreign born: 1.4% (2000); Ancestry (includes multiple ancestries): 24.1% German, 22.9% English, 13.5% Irish, 12.5% Swedish, 12.3% United States or American (2000).
Economy: Lumber. Single-family building permits issued: 0 (2005); Multi-family building permits issued: 0 (2005); Employment by occupation: 7.2% management, 28.1% professional, 15.3% services, 20.0% sales, 0.0% farming, 11.1% construction, 18.3% production (2000).
Income: Per capita income: $18,877 (2005); Median household income: $34,891 (2005); Average household income: $47,628 (2005); Percent of households with income of $100,000 or more: 9.2% (2005); Poverty rate: 11.7% (2000).
Education: Percent of population age 25 and over with: High school diploma (including GED) or higher: 84.5% (2005); Bachelor's degree or higher: 18.8% (2005); Master's degree or higher: 7.2% (2005).

School District(s)
Panama Central School District (KG-12)
    2003-04 Enrollment: 759 . . . . (716) 782-2455
Housing: Homeownership rate: 72.8% (2005); Median home value: $88,485 (2005); Median rent: $342 per month (2000); Median age of housing: 53 years (2000).
Transportation: Commute to work: 88.7% car, 0.0% public transportation, 8.3% walk, 1.3% work from home (2000); Travel time to work: 25.6% less than 15 minutes, 52.4% 15 to 30 minutes, 18.9% 30 to 45 minutes, 2.2% 45 to 60 minutes, 0.9% 60 minutes or more (2000)

POLAND (town). Covers a land area of 36.771 square miles and a water area of 0.095 square miles. Located at 42.14° N. Lat.; 79.11° W. Long.
Population: 2,639 (1990); 2,467 (2000); 2,277 (2005); 2,170 (2010 projected); Race: 97.8% White, 1.1% Black, 0.0% Asian, 1.8% Hispanic of any race (2005); Density: 61.9 persons per square mile (2005); Average household size: 2.58 (2005); Median age: 40.9 (2005); Males per 100 females: 101.7 (2005); Marriage status: 19.5% never married, 66.8% now married, 6.8% widowed, 7.0% divorced (2000); Foreign born: 1.0% (2000); Ancestry (includes multiple ancestries): 23.4% German, 22.3% English, 19.0% Swedish, 14.9% Irish, 8.2% Italian (2000).
Economy: Single-family building permits issued: 5 (2005); Multi-family building permits issued: 0 (2005); Employment by occupation: 10.9% management, 13.4% professional, 15.7% services, 22.4% sales, 1.1% farming, 8.5% construction, 27.9% production (2000).
Income: Per capita income: $20,808 (2005); Median household income: $43,005 (2005); Average household income: $53,597 (2005); Percent of households with income of $100,000 or more: 8.1% (2005); Poverty rate: 10.9% (2000).
Education: Percent of population age 25 and over with: High school diploma (including GED) or higher: 83.5% (2005); Bachelor's degree or higher: 11.4% (2005); Master's degree or higher: 2.7% (2005).
Housing: Homeownership rate: 84.2% (2005); Median home value: $84,605 (2005); Median rent: $297 per month (2000); Median age of housing: 44 years (2000).
Transportation: Commute to work: 92.8% car, 0.4% public transportation, 2.7% walk, 2.3% work from home (2000); Travel time to work: 37.1% less than 15 minutes, 44.7% 15 to 30 minutes, 12.4% 30 to 45 minutes, 4.1% 45 to 60 minutes, 1.7% 60 minutes or more (2000)

POMFRET (town). Covers a land area of 43.895 square miles and a water area of 0.281 square miles. Located at 42.41° N. Lat.; 79.35° W. Long.
Population: 14,224 (1990); 14,703 (2000); 14,560 (2005); 14,369 (2010 projected); Race: 94.6% White, 2.1% Black, 1.3% Asian, 2.8% Hispanic of any race (2005); Density: 331.7 persons per square mile (2005); Average household size: 2.87 (2005); Median age: 28.5 (2005); Males per 100 females: 88.1 (2005); Marriage status: 42.5% never married, 45.7% now

married, 5.4% widowed, 6.4% divorced (2000); Foreign born: 2.4% (2000); Ancestry (includes multiple ancestries): 26.0% German, 19.5% Italian, 19.2% Polish, 15.6% Irish, 14.1% English (2000).
Economy: Single-family building permits issued: 8 (2005); Multi-family building permits issued: 0 (2005); Employment by occupation: 8.5% management, 25.1% professional, 20.6% services, 24.6% sales, 0.9% farming, 5.7% construction, 14.6% production (2000).
Income: Per capita income: $19,293 (2005); Median household income: $41,778 (2005); Average household income: $52,906 (2005); Percent of households with income of $100,000 or more: 10.7% (2005); Poverty rate: 15.9% (2000).
Education: Percent of population age 25 and over with: High school diploma (including GED) or higher: 88.0% (2005); Bachelor's degree or higher: 29.1% (2005); Master's degree or higher: 14.1% (2005).
Housing: Homeownership rate: 63.1% (2005); Median home value: $128,890 (2005); Median rent: $393 per month (2000); Median age of housing: 50 years (2000).
Transportation: Commute to work: 79.8% car, 0.9% public transportation, 13.7% walk, 4.0% work from home (2000); Travel time to work: 65.4% less than 15 minutes, 20.3% 15 to 30 minutes, 6.2% 30 to 45 minutes, 3.8% 45 to 60 minutes, 4.3% 60 minutes or more (2000)

PORTLAND (town). Covers a land area of 34.256 square miles and a water area of 0.032 square miles. Located at 42.38° N. Lat.; 79.46° W. Long. Elevation is 760 feet.
Population: 4,832 (1990); 5,502 (2000); 5,368 (2005); 5,309 (2010 projected); Race: 80.5% White, 14.1% Black, 0.0% Asian, 10.7% Hispanic of any race (2005); Density: 156.7 persons per square mile (2005); Average household size: 3.26 (2005); Median age: 32.8 (2005); Males per 100 females: 140.2 (2005); Marriage status: 34.8% never married, 52.5% now married, 5.5% widowed, 7.2% divorced (2000); Foreign born: 5.3% (2000); Ancestry (includes multiple ancestries): 23.1% German, 11.7% English, 11.6% Italian, 11.0% Irish, 8.5% Polish (2000).
Economy: Single-family building permits issued: 3 (2005); Multi-family building permits issued: 0 (2005); Employment by occupation: 6.3% management, 15.5% professional, 21.7% services, 22.4% sales, 2.4% farming, 8.3% construction, 23.3% production (2000).
Income: Per capita income: $13,948 (2005); Median household income: $33,695 (2005); Average household income: $40,323 (2005); Percent of households with income of $100,000 or more: 5.2% (2005); Poverty rate: 11.2% (2000).
Education: Percent of population age 25 and over with: High school diploma (including GED) or higher: 66.8% (2005); Bachelor's degree or higher: 9.3% (2005); Master's degree or higher: 2.6% (2005).
Housing: Homeownership rate: 78.1% (2005); Median home value: $83,713 (2005); Median rent: $355 per month (2000); Median age of housing: 49 years (2000).
Transportation: Commute to work: 91.9% car, 0.2% public transportation, 2.4% walk, 3.6% work from home (2000); Travel time to work: 34.2% less than 15 minutes, 44.9% 15 to 30 minutes, 14.5% 30 to 45 minutes, 3.4% 45 to 60 minutes, 3.0% 60 minutes or more (2000)
Additional Information Contacts
Town of Portland . . . . (716) 792-9614
http://www.town.portland.ny.us/

RIPLEY (town). Aka Ripley Center. Covers a land area of 48.930 square miles and a water area of 0.088 square miles. Located at 42.26° N. Lat.; 79.69° W. Long. Elevation is 750 feet.
Population: 2,967 (1990); 2,636 (2000); 2,663 (2005); 2,700 (2010 projected); Race: 98.0% White, 0.3% Black, 0.2% Asian, 2.1% Hispanic of any race (2005); Density: 54.4 persons per square mile (2005); Average household size: 2.59 (2005); Median age: 37.6 (2005); Males per 100 females: 103.0 (2005); Marriage status: 20.0% never married, 61.8% now married, 9.0% widowed, 9.3% divorced (2000); Foreign born: 0.9% (2000); Ancestry (includes multiple ancestries): 33.7% German, 14.0% Irish, 13.0% English, 9.3% Italian, 8.8% Polish (2000).
Economy: Manufacturing: wood products, soft drinks. Agriculture: produce. Summer resort. Single-family building permits issued: 12 (2005); Multi-family building permits issued: 0 (2005); Employment by occupation: 9.0% management, 12.8% professional, 17.9% services, 17.0% sales, 1.5% farming, 14.1% construction, 27.7% production (2000).
Income: Per capita income: $17,464 (2005); Median household income: $37,275 (2005); Average household income: $45,153 (2005); Percent of households with income of $100,000 or more: 5.4% (2005); Poverty rate: 10.3% (2000).
Education: Percent of population age 25 and over with: High school diploma (including GED) or higher: 79.6% (2005); Bachelor's degree or higher: 8.4% (2005); Master's degree or higher: 1.1% (2005).
School District(s)
Ripley Central School District (PK-12)
   2003-04 Enrollment: 448 . . . . (716) 736-6201
Housing: Homeownership rate: 78.4% (2005); Median home value: $73,333 (2005); Median rent: $301 per month (2000); Median age of housing: 60 years (2000).
Transportation: Commute to work: 91.0% car, 1.3% public transportation, 3.6% walk, 3.7% work from home (2000); Travel time to work: 39.0% less than 15 minutes, 30.4% 15 to 30 minutes, 20.8% 30 to 45 minutes, 7.4% 45 to 60 minutes, 2.5% 60 minutes or more (2000)

RIPLEY (CDP). Covers a land area of 5.336 square miles and a water area of 0.232 square miles. Located at 42.21° N. Lat.; 88.16° W. Long.
Population: 1,189 (1990); 1,030 (2000); 1,009 (2005); 1,006 (2010 projected); Race: 98.2% White, 0.4% Black, 0.0% Asian, 2.3% Hispanic of any race (2005); Density: 189.1 persons per square mile (2005); Average household size: 2.43 (2005); Median age: 37.5 (2005); Males per 100 females: 99.4 (2005); Marriage status: 20.0% never married, 64.7% now married, 8.6% widowed, 6.8% divorced (2000); Foreign born: 1.8% (2000); Ancestry (includes multiple ancestries): 40.7% German, 15.8% Irish, 11.3% English, 10.1% Italian, 8.1% Polish (2000).
Economy: Employment by occupation: 5.3% management, 17.0% professional, 20.1% services, 22.1% sales, 0.8% farming, 11.8% construction, 22.9% production (2000).
Income: Per capita income: $18,927 (2005); Median household income: $37,927 (2005); Average household income: $45,907 (2005); Percent of households with income of $100,000 or more: 5.3% (2005); Poverty rate: 10.9% (2000).
Education: Percent of population age 25 and over with: High school diploma (including GED) or higher: 77.4% (2005); Bachelor's degree or higher: 9.6% (2005); Master's degree or higher: 1.8% (2005).
Housing: Homeownership rate: 71.2% (2005); Median home value: $55,876 (2005); Median rent: $249 per month (2000); Median age of housing: 60+ years (2000).
Transportation: Commute to work: 94.8% car, 0.8% public transportation, 4.3% walk, 0.0% work from home (2000); Travel time to work: 41.6% less than 15 minutes, 29.8% 15 to 30 minutes, 22.8% 30 to 45 minutes, 5.8% 45 to 60 minutes, 0.0% 60 minutes or more (2000)

SHERIDAN (town). Covers a land area of 37.294 square miles and a water area of 0.010 square miles. Located at 42.48° N. Lat.; 79.24° W. Long.
Population: 2,582 (1990); 2,838 (2000); 2,791 (2005); 2,728 (2010 projected); Race: 95.5% White, 0.7% Black, 0.3% Asian, 3.4% Hispanic of any race (2005); Density: 74.8 persons per square mile (2005); Average household size: 2.84 (2005); Median age: 45.5 (2005); Males per 100 females: 82.2 (2005); Marriage status: 18.4% never married, 59.9% now married, 14.5% widowed, 7.1% divorced (2000); Foreign born: 1.2% (2000); Ancestry (includes multiple ancestries): 29.2% German, 24.4% Polish, 16.5% Italian, 13.5% English, 11.9% Irish (2000).
Economy: Canned foods, paving material. Single-family building permits issued: 4 (2005); Multi-family building permits issued: 0 (2005); Employment by occupation: 12.0% management, 15.4% professional, 15.1% services, 20.8% sales, 2.5% farming, 12.0% construction, 22.2% production (2000).
Income: Per capita income: $23,019 (2005); Median household income: $47,618 (2005); Average household income: $63,438 (2005); Percent of households with income of $100,000 or more: 14.3% (2005); Poverty rate: 7.1% (2000).
Education: Percent of population age 25 and over with: High school diploma (including GED) or higher: 76.7% (2005); Bachelor's degree or higher: 10.9% (2005); Master's degree or higher: 4.6% (2005).
Housing: Homeownership rate: 88.1% (2005); Median home value: $125,205 (2005); Median rent: $380 per month (2000); Median age of housing: 47 years (2000).
Transportation: Commute to work: 93.7% car, 0.5% public transportation, 1.7% walk, 3.9% work from home (2000); Travel time to work: 42.1% less than 15 minutes, 39.7% 15 to 30 minutes, 7.8% 30 to 45 minutes, 6.8% 45 to 60 minutes, 3.5% 60 minutes or more (2000)

PROFILES OF NEW YORK / Chautauqua County

SHERMAN (village). Covers a land area of 0.830 square miles and a water area of 0 square miles. Located at 42.16° N. Lat.; 79.59° W. Long. Elevation is 1,539 feet.
Population: 694 (1990); 714 (2000); 687 (2005); 680 (2010 projected); Race: 97.8% White, 0.0% Black, 0.4% Asian, 0.6% Hispanic of any race (2005); Density: 827.9 persons per square mile (2005); Average household size: 2.46 (2005); Median age: 37.8 (2005); Males per 100 females: 93.5 (2005); Marriage status: 20.7% never married, 60.0% now married, 10.2% widowed, 9.1% divorced (2000); Foreign born: 1.3% (2000); Ancestry (includes multiple ancestries): 24.1% German, 18.0% English, 15.6% Dutch, 12.2% Irish, 9.5% Swedish (2000).
Economy: Single-family building permits issued: 0 (2005); Multi-family building permits issued: 0 (2005); Employment by occupation: 8.3% management, 16.2% professional, 21.4% services, 18.2% sales, 2.3% farming, 14.5% construction, 19.1% production (2000).
Income: Per capita income: $17,742 (2005); Median household income: $34,706 (2005); Average household income: $43,665 (2005); Percent of households with income of $100,000 or more: 6.8% (2005); Poverty rate: 10.6% (2000).
Education: Percent of population age 25 and over with: High school diploma (including GED) or higher: 85.0% (2005); Bachelor's degree or higher: 14.4% (2005); Master's degree or higher: 8.0% (2005).
School District(s)
Sherman Central School District (PK-12)
  2003-04 Enrollment: 567 . . . . (716) 761-6122
Housing: Homeownership rate: 67.4% (2005); Median home value: $70,357 (2005); Median rent: $266 per month (2000); Median age of housing: 60+ years (2000).
Transportation: Commute to work: 79.6% car, 1.2% public transportation, 12.5% walk, 6.1% work from home (2000); Travel time to work: 36.3% less than 15 minutes, 37.0% 15 to 30 minutes, 20.2% 30 to 45 minutes, 4.3% 45 to 60 minutes, 2.2% 60 minutes or more (2000)

SHERMAN (town). Covers a land area of 36.299 square miles and a water area of 0.094 square miles. Located at 42.13° N. Lat.; 79.59° W. Long. Elevation is 1,539 feet.
Population: 1,505 (1990); 1,553 (2000); 1,531 (2005); 1,536 (2010 projected); Race: 97.3% White, 0.4% Black, 0.6% Asian, 0.3% Hispanic of any race (2005); Density: 42.2 persons per square mile (2005); Average household size: 2.83 (2005); Median age: 33.4 (2005); Males per 100 females: 99.3 (2005); Marriage status: 23.9% never married, 60.7% now married, 6.9% widowed, 8.5% divorced (2000); Foreign born: 0.7% (2000); Ancestry (includes multiple ancestries): 27.0% German, 15.4% English, 14.2% Dutch, 12.8% Irish, 10.2% Swedish (2000).
Economy: Single-family building permits issued: 4 (2005); Multi-family building permits issued: 0 (2005); Employment by occupation: 13.2% management, 13.5% professional, 15.0% services, 15.3% sales, 7.6% farming, 16.5% construction, 19.0% production (2000).
Income: Per capita income: $15,624 (2005); Median household income: $37,097 (2005); Average household income: $44,205 (2005); Percent of households with income of $100,000 or more: 6.3% (2005); Poverty rate: 11.9% (2000).
Education: Percent of population age 25 and over with: High school diploma (including GED) or higher: 79.0% (2005); Bachelor's degree or higher: 13.3% (2005); Master's degree or higher: 6.3% (2005).
Housing: Homeownership rate: 73.4% (2005); Median home value: $79,884 (2005); Median rent: $272 per month (2000); Median age of housing: 60+ years (2000).
Transportation: Commute to work: 79.3% car, 2.9% public transportation, 8.7% walk, 8.4% work from home (2000); Travel time to work: 31.8% less than 15 minutes, 36.9% 15 to 30 minutes, 19.7% 30 to 45 minutes, 5.3% 45 to 60 minutes, 6.3% 60 minutes or more (2000)

SILVER CREEK (village). Covers a land area of 1.169 square miles and a water area of 0 square miles. Located at 42.54° N. Lat.; 79.16° W. Long. Elevation is 626 feet.
History: Annual grape festival held here in October. Incorporated 1848.
Population: 3,032 (1990); 2,896 (2000); 2,761 (2005); 2,635 (2010 projected); Race: 96.2% White, 0.2% Black, 0.2% Asian, 2.6% Hispanic of any race (2005); Density: 2,362.4 persons per square mile (2005); Average household size: 2.50 (2005); Median age: 37.5 (2005); Males per 100 females: 91.9 (2005); Marriage status: 21.1% never married, 58.4% now married, 9.2% widowed, 11.3% divorced (2000); Foreign born: 1.6% (2000); Ancestry (includes multiple ancestries): 31.9% Italian, 29.6% German, 13.9% Irish, 12.9% Polish, 9.4% English (2000).
Economy: Light manufacturing. In agricultural area: grapes, cherries, tomatoes. Summer resort. Single-family building permits issued: 15 (2005); Multi-family building permits issued: 0 (2005); Employment by occupation: 7.3% management, 17.9% professional, 25.0% services, 22.0% sales, 0.0% farming, 8.1% construction, 19.7% production (2000).
Income: Per capita income: $18,115 (2005); Median household income: $37,790 (2005); Average household income: $44,816 (2005); Percent of households with income of $100,000 or more: 8.4% (2005); Poverty rate: 12.9% (2000).
Education: Percent of population age 25 and over with: High school diploma (including GED) or higher: 81.0% (2005); Bachelor's degree or higher: 14.4% (2005); Master's degree or higher: 5.9% (2005).
School District(s)
Silver Creek Central School District (KG-12)
  2003-04 Enrollment: 1,254 . . . . (716) 934-2603
Housing: Homeownership rate: 70.9% (2005); Median home value: $95,490 (2005); Median rent: $377 per month (2000); Median age of housing: 60+ years (2000).
Safety: Violent crime rate: 27.9 per 10,000 population; Property crime rate: 153.7 per 10,000 population (2004).
Transportation: Commute to work: 91.4% car, 2.2% public transportation, 4.1% walk, 2.2% work from home (2000); Travel time to work: 36.2% less than 15 minutes, 26.8% 15 to 30 minutes, 10.8% 30 to 45 minutes, 17.9% 45 to 60 minutes, 8.3% 60 minutes or more (2000)

SINCLAIRVILLE (village). Covers a land area of 1.614 square miles and a water area of 0 square miles. Located at 42.26° N. Lat.; 79.26° W. Long. Elevation is 1,330 feet.
Population: 708 (1990); 665 (2000); 672 (2005); 681 (2010 projected); Race: 97.3% White, 0.3% Black, 1.0% Asian, 1.2% Hispanic of any race (2005); Density: 416.4 persons per square mile (2005); Average household size: 2.45 (2005); Median age: 37.7 (2005); Males per 100 females: 93.1 (2005); Marriage status: 21.2% never married, 57.6% now married, 11.2% widowed, 10.0% divorced (2000); Foreign born: 1.2% (2000); Ancestry (includes multiple ancestries): 25.1% English, 22.2% German, 13.5% Irish, 11.5% Swedish, 9.6% Polish (2000).
Economy: Canned foods; dairy products; lumbering. Single-family building permits issued: 1 (2005); Multi-family building permits issued: 0 (2005); Employment by occupation: 8.1% management, 20.8% professional, 17.3% services, 13.1% sales, 1.1% farming, 8.8% construction, 30.7% production (2000).
Income: Per capita income: $16,064 (2005); Median household income: $31,341 (2005); Average household income: $39,398 (2005); Percent of households with income of $100,000 or more: 5.1% (2005); Poverty rate: 22.6% (2000).
Education: Percent of population age 25 and over with: High school diploma (including GED) or higher: 78.4% (2005); Bachelor's degree or higher: 12.2% (2005); Master's degree or higher: 6.0% (2005).
School District(s)
Cassadaga Valley Central School District (PK-12)
  2003-04 Enrollment: 1,373 . . . . (716) 962-5155
Housing: Homeownership rate: 69.3% (2005); Median home value: $72,727 (2005); Median rent: $288 per month (2000); Median age of housing: 60+ years (2000).
Transportation: Commute to work: 90.2% car, 0.0% public transportation, 3.6% walk, 4.3% work from home (2000); Travel time to work: 23.9% less than 15 minutes, 50.8% 15 to 30 minutes, 20.5% 30 to 45 minutes, 1.5% 45 to 60 minutes, 3.4% 60 minutes or more (2000)

STOCKTON (town). Covers a land area of 47.314 square miles and a water area of 0.310 square miles. Located at 42.30° N. Lat.; 79.35° W. Long. Elevation is 1,328 feet.
Population: 2,515 (1990); 2,331 (2000); 2,130 (2005); 2,045 (2010 projected); Race: 96.8% White, 0.1% Black, 0.7% Asian, 2.0% Hispanic of any race (2005); Density: 45.0 persons per square mile (2005); Average household size: 2.69 (2005); Median age: 39.1 (2005); Males per 100 females: 98.1 (2005); Marriage status: 19.8% never married, 67.1% now married, 6.3% widowed, 6.8% divorced (2000); Foreign born: 0.9% (2000); Ancestry (includes multiple ancestries): 24.8% German, 19.3% English, 18.1% Irish, 8.2% Swedish, 8.1% Italian (2000).
Economy: Single-family building permits issued: 3 (2005); Multi-family building permits issued: 0 (2005); Employment by occupation: 8.0%

management, 17.0% professional, 18.6% services, 20.1% sales, 0.8% farming, 12.6% construction, 22.9% production (2000).
Income: Per capita income: $19,403 (2005); Median household income: $43,662 (2005); Average household income: $52,181 (2005); Percent of households with income of $100,000 or more: 9.1% (2005); Poverty rate: 9.9% (2000).
Education: Percent of population age 25 and over with: High school diploma (including GED) or higher: 84.5% (2005); Bachelor's degree or higher: 12.4% (2005); Master's degree or higher: 5.1% (2005).
Housing: Homeownership rate: 84.5% (2005); Median home value: $93,826 (2005); Median rent: $318 per month (2000); Median age of housing: 46 years (2000).
Transportation: Commute to work: 92.0% car, 0.0% public transportation, 2.5% walk, 5.0% work from home (2000); Travel time to work: 27.2% less than 15 minutes, 40.9% 15 to 30 minutes, 21.3% 30 to 45 minutes, 2.1% 45 to 60 minutes, 8.5% 60 minutes or more (2000)

VILLENOVA (town). Covers a land area of 36.122 square miles and a water area of 0.076 square miles. Located at 42.38° N. Lat.; 79.11° W. Long.
Population: 1,065 (1990); 1,121 (2000); 1,147 (2005); 1,174 (2010 projected); Race: 97.1% White, 0.2% Black, 0.6% Asian, 1.2% Hispanic of any race (2005); Density: 31.8 persons per square mile (2005); Average household size: 2.66 (2005); Median age: 39.2 (2005); Males per 100 females: 99.8 (2005); Marriage status: 25.2% never married, 62.7% now married, 4.8% widowed, 7.3% divorced (2000); Foreign born: 0.8% (2000); Ancestry (includes multiple ancestries): 35.3% German, 19.0% English, 14.9% Polish, 14.1% Irish, 10.3% Italian (2000).
Economy: Single-family building permits issued: 8 (2005); Multi-family building permits issued: 0 (2005); Employment by occupation: 10.4% management, 12.9% professional, 20.3% services, 14.1% sales, 6.0% farming, 14.5% construction, 21.8% production (2000).
Income: Per capita income: $17,125 (2005); Median household income: $41,585 (2005); Average household income: $45,469 (2005); Percent of households with income of $100,000 or more: 4.9% (2005); Poverty rate: 11.8% (2000).
Education: Percent of population age 25 and over with: High school diploma (including GED) or higher: 79.7% (2005); Bachelor's degree or higher: 10.4% (2005); Master's degree or higher: 3.1% (2005).
Housing: Homeownership rate: 86.8% (2005); Median home value: $99,123 (2005); Median rent: $366 per month (2000); Median age of housing: 41 years (2000).
Transportation: Commute to work: 90.0% car, 0.0% public transportation, 1.6% walk, 7.7% work from home (2000); Travel time to work: 30.0% less than 15 minutes, 33.2% 15 to 30 minutes, 19.4% 30 to 45 minutes, 11.3% 45 to 60 minutes, 6.2% 60 minutes or more (2000)

WESTFIELD (village). Covers a land area of 3.808 square miles and a water area of 0 square miles. Located at 42.32° N. Lat.; 79.57° W. Long. Elevation is 754 feet.
Population: 3,451 (1990); 3,481 (2000); 3,443 (2005); 3,411 (2010 projected); Race: 94.7% White, 0.4% Black, 0.9% Asian, 4.4% Hispanic of any race (2005); Density: 904.1 persons per square mile (2005); Average household size: 2.53 (2005); Median age: 40.7 (2005); Males per 100 females: 90.9 (2005); Marriage status: 21.7% never married, 57.7% now married, 9.1% widowed, 11.5% divorced (2000); Foreign born: 1.4% (2000); Ancestry (includes multiple ancestries): 23.1% German, 21.1% English, 17.3% Irish, 15.6% Italian, 9.7% Other groups (2000).
Economy: Single-family building permits issued: 1 (2005); Multi-family building permits issued: 0 (2005); Employment by occupation: 8.8% management, 19.5% professional, 18.7% services, 27.6% sales, 0.8% farming, 10.2% construction, 14.5% production (2000).
Income: Per capita income: $17,689 (2005); Median household income: $35,281 (2005); Average household income: $43,898 (2005); Percent of households with income of $100,000 or more: 6.5% (2005); Poverty rate: 17.4% (2000).
Education: Percent of population age 25 and over with: High school diploma (including GED) or higher: 82.7% (2005); Bachelor's degree or higher: 23.2% (2005); Master's degree or higher: 10.3% (2005).
School District(s)
Westfield Central School District (KG-12)
    2003-04 Enrollment: 897 . . . . (716) 326-2151
Housing: Homeownership rate: 66.9% (2005); Median home value: $108,488 (2005); Median rent: $359 per month (2000); Median age of housing: 60+ years (2000).

Hospitals: Westfield Memorial Hospital (32 beds)
Newspapers: Mayville Sentinel (General - Circulation 500); West County Quality Guide (General - Circulation 10,100); Westfield Republican (General - Circulation 1,455)
Transportation: Commute to work: 88.9% car, 0.3% public transportation, 6.8% walk, 2.4% work from home (2000); Travel time to work: 49.5% less than 15 minutes, 22.6% 15 to 30 minutes, 17.8% 30 to 45 minutes, 6.3% 45 to 60 minutes, 3.8% 60 minutes or more (2000)
Additional Information Contacts
Westfield & Barcelona Chamber of Commerce . . . . (716) 326-4000
   http://www.w-bcc.com

WESTFIELD (town). Covers a land area of 47.205 square miles and a water area of 0.060 square miles. Located at 42.31° N. Lat.; 79.58° W. Long. Elevation is 754 feet.
History: In 1873 Thomas and Charles Bradwell Welch, ardent Prohibitionists, devised method of pressing Concord grapes into unfermented wine. Settled 1800, incorporated 1833.
Population: 5,194 (1990); 5,232 (2000); 5,220 (2005); 5,206 (2010 projected); Race: 95.8% White, 0.3% Black, 1.0% Asian, 3.5% Hispanic of any race (2005); Density: 110.6 persons per square mile (2005); Average household size: 2.51 (2005); Median age: 41.3 (2005); Males per 100 females: 93.4 (2005); Marriage status: 21.0% never married, 59.3% now married, 9.1% widowed, 10.7% divorced (2000); Foreign born: 1.3% (2000); Ancestry (includes multiple ancestries): 25.4% German, 21.3% English, 15.9% Irish, 12.7% Italian, 8.6% United States or American (2000).
Economy: Manufacturing of paper goods; large grape-juice and grape-concentrate industry (since 1896); in grape-growing area. Single-family building permits issued: 3 (2005); Multi-family building permits issued: 0 (2005); Employment by occupation: 8.8% management, 17.3% professional, 16.8% services, 26.7% sales, 2.7% farming, 11.2% construction, 16.5% production (2000).
Income: Per capita income: $17,779 (2005); Median household income: $35,993 (2005); Average household income: $43,998 (2005); Percent of households with income of $100,000 or more: 6.9% (2005); Poverty rate: 13.8% (2000).
Education: Percent of population age 25 and over with: High school diploma (including GED) or higher: 82.0% (2005); Bachelor's degree or higher: 20.6% (2005); Master's degree or higher: 9.9% (2005).
Housing: Homeownership rate: 70.7% (2005); Median home value: $112,318 (2005); Median rent: $364 per month (2000); Median age of housing: 60+ years (2000).
Transportation: Commute to work: 89.3% car, 0.2% public transportation, 5.9% walk, 3.3% work from home (2000); Travel time to work: 48.7% less than 15 minutes, 24.6% 15 to 30 minutes, 18.0% 30 to 45 minutes, 6.2% 45 to 60 minutes, 2.5% 60 minutes or more (2000)

Chemung County

Located in southern New York; hilly area bounded on the south by Pennsylvania; cut by the Chemung River Valley. Covers a land area of 408.17 square miles, a water area of 2.62 square miles, and is located in the Eastern Time Zone. The county government was organized in 1836. County seat is Elmira.

Chemung County is part of the Elmira, NY Metropolitan Statistical Area. The entire metro area includes: Chemung County, NY

Weather Station: Elmira   Elevation: 843 feet

	Jan	Feb	Mar	Apr	May	Jun	Jul	Aug	Sep	Oct	Nov	Dec
High	33	35	44	57	70	78	83	81	73	61	49	37
Low	15	16	23	34	44	53	58	56	49	38	31	21
Precip	1.9	2.0	2.6	2.9	3.0	3.8	3.5	3.3	3.5	2.9	3.1	2.4
Snow	10.2	9.9	8.8	1.7	0.1	0.0	0.0	0.0	0.0	0.2	2.9	8.9

High and Low temperatures in degrees Fahrenheit; Precipitation and Snow in inches

Population: 95,195 (1990); 91,070 (2000); 90,057 (2005); 88,976 (2010 projected); Race: 89.7% White, 6.6% Black, 1.1% Asian, 2.4% Hispanic of any race (2005); Density: 220.6 persons per square mile (2005); Average household size: 2.57 (2005); Median age: 38.9 (2005); Males per 100 females: 97.6 (2005).
Religion: Five largest groups: 24.9% Catholic Church, 6.3% The United Methodist Church, 2.3% American Baptist Churches in the USA, 2.1% Presbyterian Church (U.S.A.), 1.8% Assemblies of God (2000).

PROFILES OF NEW YORK / Chemung County

Economy: Unemployment rate: 5.4% (2005); Total civilian labor force: 40,803 (2005); Leading industries: 20.0% health care and social assistance; 19.9% manufacturing; 16.9% retail trade (2003); Farms: 427 totaling 69,183 acres (2002); Companies that employ 500 or more persons: 5 (2003); Companies that employ 100 to 499 persons: 46 (2003); Companies that employ less than 100 persons: 1,878 (2003); Black-owned businesses: 113 (2002); Hispanic-owned businesses: n/a (2002); Women-owned businesses: 1,581 (2002); Retail sales per capita: $14,400 (2006). Single-family building permits issued: 107 (2005); Multi-family building permits issued: 0 (2005).
Income: Per capita income: $20,953 (2005); Median household income: $40,842 (2005); Average household income: $51,765 (2005); Percent of households with income of $100,000 or more: 9.9% (2005); Poverty rate: 13.5% (2003); Bankruptcy rate: 6.08% (2005).
Taxes: Total county taxes per capita: $756 (2004); County property taxes per capita: $256 (2004).
Education: Percent of population age 25 and over with: High school diploma (including GED) or higher: 82.1% (2005); Bachelor's degree or higher: 18.6% (2005); Master's degree or higher: 8.2% (2005).
Housing: Homeownership rate: 69.6% (2005); Median home value: $81,865 (2005); Median rent: $400 per month (2000); Median age of housing: 49 years (2000).
Health: Birth rate: 115.1 per 10,000 population (2004); Death rate: 106.1 per 10,000 population (2004); Age-adjusted cancer mortality rate: 236.1 deaths per 100,000 population (2002); Air Quality Index: 96.7% good, 3.3% moderate, 0.0% unhealthy for sensitive individuals, 0.0% unhealthy (percent of days in 2005); Number of physicians: 26.3 per 10,000 population (2004); Hospital beds: 64.5 per 10,000 population (2003); Hospital admissions: 1,743.4 per 10,000 population (2003).
Elections: 2004 Presidential election results: 54.6% Bush, 43.7% Kerry, 1.5% Nader, 0.2% Badnarik

Additional Information Contacts
Chemung County Government .... (607) 737-2912
  http://www.chemungcounty.com/
City of Elmira .... (607) 737-5673
  http://www.ci.elmira.ny.us/index.html
Town of Big Flats .... (607) 562-8443
  http://www.bigflatsny.gov/index/index.html
Town of Chemung .... (607) 529-3532
  http://www.townofchemung.com/
Town of Southport .... (607) 734-1548
  http://www.townofsouthport.com/
Village of Horseheads .... (607) 739-5691
  http://www.horseheads.org/

Chemung County Communities

ASHLAND (town). Covers a land area of 14.141 square miles and a water area of 0.367 square miles. Located at 42.02° N. Lat.; 76.73° W. Long.
Population: 1,948 (1990); 1,951 (2000); 1,943 (2005); 1,966 (2010 projected); Race: 96.5% White, 2.0% Black, 0.2% Asian, 2.6% Hispanic of any race (2005); Density: 137.4 persons per square mile (2005); Average household size: 2.43 (2005); Median age: 40.9 (2005); Males per 100 females: 102.4 (2005); Marriage status: 22.7% never married, 58.0% now married, 6.4% widowed, 12.9% divorced (2000); Foreign born: 1.2% (2000); Ancestry (includes multiple ancestries): 15.7% Irish, 15.3% German, 14.5% English, 7.7% United States or American, 5.9% Italian (2000).
Economy: Single-family building permits issued: 1 (2005); Multi-family building permits issued: 0 (2005); Employment by occupation: 8.9% management, 14.6% professional, 20.9% services, 24.2% sales, 0.1% farming, 12.4% construction, 18.9% production (2000).
Income: Per capita income: $20,181 (2005); Median household income: $39,261 (2005); Average household income: $48,758 (2005); Percent of households with income of $100,000 or more: 6.5% (2005); Poverty rate: 11.2% (2000).
Education: Percent of population age 25 and over with: High school diploma (including GED) or higher: 76.7% (2005); Bachelor's degree or higher: 8.6% (2005); Master's degree or higher: 4.5% (2005).
Housing: Homeownership rate: 84.8% (2005); Median home value: $55,732 (2005); Median rent: $318 per month (2000); Median age of housing: 29 years (2000).
Transportation: Commute to work: 95.8% car, 0.4% public transportation, 2.3% walk, 1.0% work from home (2000); Travel time to work: 21.5% less than 15 minutes, 57.9% 15 to 30 minutes, 13.4% 30 to 45 minutes, 2.6% 45 to 60 minutes, 4.6% 60 minutes or more (2000)

BALDWIN (town). Covers a land area of 25.765 square miles and a water area of 0.010 square miles. Located at 42.09° N. Lat.; 76.66° W. Long.
Population: 829 (1990); 853 (2000); 923 (2005); 972 (2010 projected); Race: 97.2% White, 1.0% Black, 0.2% Asian, 0.4% Hispanic of any race (2005); Density: 35.8 persons per square mile (2005); Average household size: 2.50 (2005); Median age: 41.9 (2005); Males per 100 females: 108.8 (2005); Marriage status: 17.0% never married, 69.8% now married, 6.3% widowed, 6.9% divorced (2000); Foreign born: 0.2% (2000); Ancestry (includes multiple ancestries): 17.7% German, 14.7% United States or American, 12.8% Irish, 9.6% English, 8.2% Polish (2000).
Economy: Single-family building permits issued: 6 (2005); Multi-family building permits issued: 0 (2005); Employment by occupation: 8.4% management, 11.4% professional, 14.5% services, 24.4% sales, 0.5% farming, 14.5% construction, 26.4% production (2000).
Income: Per capita income: $20,523 (2005); Median household income: $42,969 (2005); Average household income: $51,335 (2005); Percent of households with income of $100,000 or more: 5.7% (2005); Poverty rate: 9.2% (2000).
Education: Percent of population age 25 and over with: High school diploma (including GED) or higher: 78.4% (2005); Bachelor's degree or higher: 8.2% (2005); Master's degree or higher: 1.7% (2005).
Housing: Homeownership rate: 86.7% (2005); Median home value: $73,548 (2005); Median rent: $321 per month (2000); Median age of housing: 33 years (2000).
Transportation: Commute to work: 96.7% car, 0.0% public transportation, 0.8% walk, 1.3% work from home (2000); Travel time to work: 4.2% less than 15 minutes, 61.6% 15 to 30 minutes, 20.5% 30 to 45 minutes, 6.5% 45 to 60 minutes, 7.3% 60 minutes or more (2000)

BIG FLATS (town). Covers a land area of 44.492 square miles and a water area of 0.564 square miles. Located at 42.14° N. Lat.; 76.91° W. Long. Elevation is 910 feet.
Population: 7,596 (1990); 7,224 (2000); 7,590 (2005); 7,925 (2010 projected); Race: 95.5% White, 1.4% Black, 2.1% Asian, 0.9% Hispanic of any race (2005); Density: 170.6 persons per square mile (2005); Average household size: 2.60 (2005); Median age: 42.5 (2005); Males per 100 females: 96.8 (2005); Marriage status: 18.6% never married, 69.5% now married, 5.5% widowed, 6.4% divorced (2000); Foreign born: 3.1% (2000); Ancestry (includes multiple ancestries): 25.6% German, 17.9% Irish, 17.3% English, 11.4% Italian, 7.5% Polish (2000).
Economy: Single-family building permits issued: 36 (2005); Multi-family building permits issued: 0 (2005); Employment by occupation: 15.3% management, 31.0% professional, 12.6% services, 23.3% sales, 0.0% farming, 6.0% construction, 11.9% production (2000).
Income: Per capita income: $26,807 (2005); Median household income: $58,620 (2005); Average household income: $69,638 (2005); Percent of households with income of $100,000 or more: 18.8% (2005); Poverty rate: 2.6% (2000).
Education: Percent of population age 25 and over with: High school diploma (including GED) or higher: 93.5% (2005); Bachelor's degree or higher: 32.8% (2005); Master's degree or higher: 16.5% (2005).

School District(s)
Horseheads Central School District (KG-12)
  2003-04 Enrollment: 4,378 .... (607) 739-5601
Housing: Homeownership rate: 88.8% (2005); Median home value: $119,181 (2005); Median rent: $501 per month (2000); Median age of housing: 33 years (2000).
Transportation: Commute to work: 94.5% car, 0.6% public transportation, 1.1% walk, 3.4% work from home (2000); Travel time to work: 34.0% less than 15 minutes, 54.2% 15 to 30 minutes, 5.9% 30 to 45 minutes, 2.3% 45 to 60 minutes, 3.6% 60 minutes or more (2000)

Additional Information Contacts
Town of Big Flats .... (607) 562-8443
  http://www.bigflatsny.gov/index/index.html

BIG FLATS (CDP). Covers a land area of 3.909 square miles and a water area of 0.018 square miles. Located at 42.14° N. Lat.; 76.93° W. Long.
Population: 2,658 (1990); 2,482 (2000); 2,660 (2005); 2,855 (2010 projected); Race: 94.4% White, 1.8% Black, 2.5% Asian, 1.3% Hispanic of any race (2005); Density: 680.4 persons per square mile (2005); Average

household size: 2.58 (2005); Median age: 42.3 (2005); Males per 100 females: 94.3 (2005); Marriage status: 18.5% never married, 73.5% now married, 4.2% widowed, 3.8% divorced (2000); Foreign born: 3.4% (2000); Ancestry (includes multiple ancestries): 22.7% English, 22.1% Irish, 19.9% German, 9.4% Italian, 9.2% Polish (2000).
Economy: Employment by occupation: 15.3% management, 37.9% professional, 9.8% services, 19.7% sales, 0.0% farming, 3.2% construction, 14.0% production (2000).
Income: Per capita income: $27,155 (2005); Median household income: $59,709 (2005); Average household income: $69,925 (2005); Percent of households with income of $100,000 or more: 17.3% (2005); Poverty rate: 1.5% (2000).
Education: Percent of population age 25 and over with: High school diploma (including GED) or higher: 94.1% (2005); Bachelor's degree or higher: 38.7% (2005); Master's degree or higher: 18.6% (2005).
Housing: Homeownership rate: 85.9% (2005); Median home value: $127,461 (2005); Median rent: $492 per month (2000); Median age of housing: 37 years (2000).
Transportation: Commute to work: 95.6% car, 0.0% public transportation, 2.8% walk, 1.6% work from home (2000); Travel time to work: 33.6% less than 15 minutes, 52.1% 15 to 30 minutes, 9.0% 30 to 45 minutes, 3.1% 45 to 60 minutes, 2.1% 60 minutes or more (2000)

BIG FLATS AIRPORT (CDP). Covers a land area of 11.716 square miles and a water area of 0.036 square miles. Located at 42.16° N. Lat.; 76.88° W. Long.
Population: 2,248 (1990); 2,184 (2000); 2,285 (2005); 2,346 (2010 projected); Race: 95.7% White, 1.6% Black, 1.9% Asian, 0.4% Hispanic of any race (2005); Density: 195.0 persons per square mile (2005); Average household size: 2.61 (2005); Median age: 43.8 (2005); Males per 100 females: 94.0 (2005); Marriage status: 18.1% never married, 67.7% now married, 7.9% widowed, 6.4% divorced (2000); Foreign born: 3.3% (2000); Ancestry (includes multiple ancestries): 26.3% German, 19.1% Irish, 12.1% English, 11.2% Other groups, 10.9% Italian (2000).
Economy: Employment by occupation: 16.3% management, 26.1% professional, 17.9% services, 26.6% sales, 0.0% farming, 4.7% construction, 8.5% production (2000).
Income: Per capita income: $28,312 (2005); Median household income: $63,560 (2005); Average household income: $73,934 (2005); Percent of households with income of $100,000 or more: 20.2% (2005); Poverty rate: 3.7% (2000).
Education: Percent of population age 25 and over with: High school diploma (including GED) or higher: 93.3% (2005); Bachelor's degree or higher: 26.1% (2005); Master's degree or higher: 12.6% (2005).
Housing: Homeownership rate: 93.1% (2005); Median home value: $116,463 (2005); Median rent: $577 per month (2000); Median age of housing: 27 years (2000).
Transportation: Commute to work: 96.1% car, 1.3% public transportation, 0.0% walk, 2.6% work from home (2000); Travel time to work: 31.1% less than 15 minutes, 59.7% 15 to 30 minutes, 5.7% 30 to 45 minutes, 1.0% 45 to 60 minutes, 2.5% 60 minutes or more (2000)

BREESPORT (unincorporated postal area, zip code 14816). Covers a land area of 5.400 square miles and a water area of 0.017 square miles. Located at 42.17° N. Lat.; 76.73° W. Long.
Population: 0 (2000); Race: 98.8% White, 1.2% Black, 0.0% Asian, 0.3% Hispanic of any race (2000); Density: 0.0 persons per square mile (2000); Age: 33.0% under 18, 5.3% over 64 (2000); Marriage status: 19.0% never married, 69.7% now married, 0.7% widowed, 10.7% divorced (2000); Foreign born: 0.0% (2000); Ancestry (includes multiple ancestries): 38.0% English, 28.2% Irish, 11.7% German, 7.9% Other groups, 5.0% Dutch (2000).
Economy: Employment by occupation: 2.4% management, 15.7% professional, 32.8% services, 21.5% sales, 0.0% farming, 3.8% construction, 23.9% production (2000).
Income: Per capita income: $16,695 (2000); Median household income: $44,375 (2000); Poverty rate: 11.7% (2000).
Education: Percent of population age 25 and over with: High school diploma (including GED) or higher: 88.3% (2000); Bachelor's degree or higher: 8.8% (2000).
Housing: Homeownership rate: 72.8% (2000); Median home value: $64,400 (2000); Median rent: $376 per month (2000); Median age of housing: 38 years (2000).
Transportation: Commute to work: 96.2% car, 0.0% public transportation, 3.8% walk, 0.0% work from home (2000); Travel time to work: 21.2% less than 15 minutes, 62.8% 15 to 30 minutes, 13.0% 30 to 45 minutes, 0.0% 45 to 60 minutes, 3.1% 60 minutes or more (2000)

CATLIN (town). Covers a land area of 38.018 square miles and a water area of 0.001 square miles. Located at 42.25° N. Lat.; 76.91° W. Long.
Population: 2,626 (1990); 2,649 (2000); 2,873 (2005); 3,026 (2010 projected); Race: 98.3% White, 0.6% Black, 0.2% Asian, 0.4% Hispanic of any race (2005); Density: 75.6 persons per square mile (2005); Average household size: 2.64 (2005); Median age: 38.2 (2005); Males per 100 females: 97.2 (2005); Marriage status: 23.0% never married, 63.7% now married, 3.7% widowed, 9.5% divorced (2000); Foreign born: 0.8% (2000); Ancestry (includes multiple ancestries): 21.9% English, 18.9% Irish, 17.9% German, 8.6% United States or American, 8.2% Italian (2000).
Economy: Single-family building permits issued: 6 (2005); Multi-family building permits issued: 0 (2005); Employment by occupation: 6.8% management, 15.3% professional, 14.2% services, 32.2% sales, 0.3% farming, 10.1% construction, 21.0% production (2000).
Income: Per capita income: $21,984 (2005); Median household income: $45,176 (2005); Average household income: $57,945 (2005); Percent of households with income of $100,000 or more: 11.5% (2005); Poverty rate: 6.5% (2000).
Education: Percent of population age 25 and over with: High school diploma (including GED) or higher: 81.6% (2005); Bachelor's degree or higher: 10.3% (2005); Master's degree or higher: 3.1% (2005).
Housing: Homeownership rate: 86.6% (2005); Median home value: $82,416 (2005); Median rent: $363 per month (2000); Median age of housing: 34 years (2000).
Transportation: Commute to work: 96.9% car, 0.2% public transportation, 0.6% walk, 1.8% work from home (2000); Travel time to work: 17.8% less than 15 minutes, 59.3% 15 to 30 minutes, 17.1% 30 to 45 minutes, 1.1% 45 to 60 minutes, 4.7% 60 minutes or more (2000)

CHEMUNG (town). Covers a land area of 49.461 square miles and a water area of 0.564 square miles. Located at 42.03° N. Lat.; 76.62° W. Long. Elevation is 847 feet.
Population: 2,558 (1990); 2,665 (2000); 2,619 (2005); 2,615 (2010 projected); Race: 97.6% White, 0.5% Black, 0.3% Asian, 1.0% Hispanic of any race (2005); Density: 53.0 persons per square mile (2005); Average household size: 2.70 (2005); Median age: 37.4 (2005); Males per 100 females: 99.5 (2005); Marriage status: 17.2% never married, 69.3% now married, 5.0% widowed, 8.5% divorced (2000); Foreign born: 1.0% (2000); Ancestry (includes multiple ancestries): 20.1% German, 16.7% Irish, 13.4% English, 8.1% Italian, 7.4% Other groups (2000).
Economy: Single-family building permits issued: 5 (2005); Multi-family building permits issued: 0 (2005); Employment by occupation: 9.5% management, 21.0% professional, 14.2% services, 19.9% sales, 0.7% farming, 12.3% construction, 22.4% production (2000).
Income: Per capita income: $17,505 (2005); Median household income: $40,854 (2005); Average household income: $46,460 (2005); Percent of households with income of $100,000 or more: 6.1% (2005); Poverty rate: 11.7% (2000).
Education: Percent of population age 25 and over with: High school diploma (including GED) or higher: 76.5% (2005); Bachelor's degree or higher: 12.1% (2005); Master's degree or higher: 2.7% (2005).
School District(s)
Waverly Central School District (KG-12)
   2003-04 Enrollment: 1,786 . . . . (607) 565-2841
Housing: Homeownership rate: 86.9% (2005); Median home value: $72,584 (2005); Median rent: $384 per month (2000); Median age of housing: 36 years (2000).
Transportation: Commute to work: 93.3% car, 0.4% public transportation, 0.4% walk, 4.8% work from home (2000); Travel time to work: 18.8% less than 15 minutes, 51.2% 15 to 30 minutes, 21.2% 30 to 45 minutes, 4.1% 45 to 60 minutes, 4.7% 60 minutes or more (2000)
Additional Information Contacts
Town of Chemung . . . . (607) 529-3532
   http://www.townofchemung.com/

ELMIRA (city). Covers a land area of 7.315 square miles and a water area of 0.269 square miles. Located at 42.09° N. Lat.; 76.81° W. Long. Elevation is 873 feet.
History: The Sullivan-Clinton Expedition entered the region of Elmira in 1779. Most of the early settlers were emigrants from Wyoming and Wilkes-Barre, Pennsylvania. In 1789 a famine struck the valley as the result of a frost. The only deaths that occurred resulted not from starvation

but from overeating when food was finally obtained. The present name was adopted in 1828. According to local tradition, Nathan Teall, an early settler, had a daughter named Elmira, for whom her mother called in a shrill, far-reaching voice. When it was decided to adopt a new name, several people suggested the one they had heard so often when Elmira was a child.
Population: 33,719 (1990); 30,940 (2000); 30,115 (2005); 29,227 (2010 projected); Race: 79.9% White, 14.8% Black, 0.7% Asian, 4.3% Hispanic of any race (2005); Density: 4,116.7 persons per square mile (2005); Average household size: 2.69 (2005); Median age: 33.8 (2005); Males per 100 females: 101.8 (2005); Marriage status: 35.8% never married, 44.6% now married, 7.7% widowed, 11.9% divorced (2000); Foreign born: 2.2% (2000); Ancestry (includes multiple ancestries): 17.4% Irish, 16.5% German, 14.3% Other groups, 11.0% Italian, 9.6% English (2000).
Economy: Unemployment rate: 6.1% (2005); Total civilian labor force: 11,938 (2005); Single-family building permits issued: 6 (2005); Multi-family building permits issued: 0 (2005); Employment by occupation: 8.3% management, 19.0% professional, 24.3% services, 26.2% sales, 0.2% farming, 5.8% construction, 16.2% production (2000).
Income: Per capita income: $15,988 (2005); Median household income: $29,897 (2005); Average household income: $38,874 (2005); Percent of households with income of $100,000 or more: 5.0% (2005); Poverty rate: 23.1% (2000).
Education: Percent of population age 25 and over with: High school diploma (including GED) or higher: 74.1% (2005); Bachelor's degree or higher: 14.3% (2005); Master's degree or higher: 5.7% (2005).

School District(s)
Boces Schuyler-Chemung-Tioga (PK-PK)
   2003-04 Enrollment: 358 . . . . (607) 739-3581
Elmira City School District (PK-12)
   2003-04 Enrollment: 7,613 . . . . (607) 735-3010

Four-year College(s)
Elmira College
   Fall 2004 Enrollment: 1,853 . . . . (607) 735-1800
   2005-06 Tuition: In-state $28,500; Out-of-state $28,500

Two-year College(s)
Arnot Ogden Medical Center
   Fall 2004 Enrollment: 53 . . . . (607) 737-4153
Elmira Business Institute
   Fall 2004 Enrollment: 557 . . . . (607) 733-7177
   2005-06 Tuition: In-state $8,670; Out-of-state $8,670
Schuyler-Chemung-Tioga BOCES (Public)
   Fall 2004 Enrollment: 94 . . . . (607) 739-3581
   2005-06 Tuition: In-state $6,500; Out-of-state $6,500

Housing: Homeownership rate: 48.7% (2005); Median home value: $63,687 (2005); Median rent: $381 per month (2000); Median age of housing: 60+ years (2000).
Hospitals: ArnotOgden Medical Center (256 beds); St. Joseph's Hospital (251 beds)
Newspapers: Star-Gazette (Circulation 28,740)
Transportation: Commute to work: 84.1% car, 2.7% public transportation, 9.6% walk, 2.3% work from home (2000); Travel time to work: 53.4% less than 15 minutes, 31.6% 15 to 30 minutes, 8.4% 30 to 45 minutes, 2.8% 45 to 60 minutes, 3.7% 60 minutes or more (2000)

Additional Information Contacts
Chemung County Chamber of Commerce . . . . (607) 734-5137
   http://www.chemungchamber.org
City of Elmira . . . . (607) 737-5673
   http://www.ci.elmira.ny.us/index.html

ELMIRA (town).
Covers a land area of 22.287 square miles and a water area of 0.283 square miles. Located at 42.09° N. Lat.; 76.83° W. Long. Elevation is 873 feet.
History: Formerly Newtown, renamed for Elmira Teall, an innkeeper's daughter. The Treaty of Painted Post, ending warfare between settlers and the Iroquois confederation, was signed here in 1791. Site of a Confederate prison camp in 1864-1865 and 3,000 Confederate prisoners are buried here. The well-known Elmira Correctional Facility (est. 1876) led the way in prison reform. Mark Twain spent many summers in Elmira and is buried here. Settled 1788, Incorporated 1864.
Population: 7,445 (1990); 7,199 (2000); 7,018 (2005); 6,800 (2010 projected); Race: 95.6% White, 1.9% Black, 1.4% Asian, 0.6% Hispanic of any race (2005); Density: 314.9 persons per square mile (2005); Average household size: 2.34 (2005); Median age: 44.8 (2005); Males per 100 females: 89.7 (2005); Marriage status: 21.0% never married, 61.1% now married, 9.4% widowed, 8.5% divorced (2000); Foreign born: 3.0% (2000); Ancestry (includes multiple ancestries): 24.4% Irish, 22.2% German, 15.3% English, 11.2% Italian, 9.0% Polish (2000).
Economy: It is a distributing and manufacturing center with plants that make electronic and fire-fighting equipment, automotive parts and iron and steel products. Single-family building permits issued: 1 (2005); Multi-family building permits issued: 0 (2005); Employment by occupation: 12.1% management, 34.1% professional, 13.8% services, 25.3% sales, 0.4% farming, 7.0% construction, 7.2% production (2000).
Income: Per capita income: $31,634 (2005); Median household income: $53,413 (2005); Average household income: $73,727 (2005); Percent of households with income of $100,000 or more: 19.4% (2005); Poverty rate: 5.5% (2000).
Taxes: Total city taxes per capita: $225 (2004); City property taxes per capita: $189 (2004).
Education: Percent of population age 25 and over with: High school diploma (including GED) or higher: 95.0% (2005); Bachelor's degree or higher: 36.9% (2005); Master's degree or higher: 18.1% (2005).
Housing: Homeownership rate: 84.1% (2005); Median home value: $103,104 (2005); Median rent: $521 per month (2000); Median age of housing: 51 years (2000).
Safety: Violent crime rate: 0.0 per 10,000 population; Property crime rate: 52.5 per 10,000 population (2004).
Transportation: Commute to work: 95.8% car, 0.2% public transportation, 1.2% walk, 2.5% work from home (2000); Travel time to work: 50.7% less than 15 minutes, 34.4% 15 to 30 minutes, 8.2% 30 to 45 minutes, 2.7% 45 to 60 minutes, 4.1% 60 minutes or more (2000)

ELMIRA HEIGHTS (village).
Covers a land area of 1.138 square miles and a water area of 0 square miles. Located at 42.12° N. Lat.; 76.82° W. Long. Elevation is 867 feet.
Population: 4,359 (1990); 4,170 (2000); 4,047 (2005); 3,867 (2010 projected); Race: 96.8% White, 1.2% Black, 0.5% Asian, 1.2% Hispanic of any race (2005); Density: 3,556.4 persons per square mile (2005); Average household size: 2.18 (2005); Median age: 39.5 (2005); Males per 100 females: 87.5 (2005); Marriage status: 26.4% never married, 49.6% now married, 10.9% widowed, 13.1% divorced (2000); Foreign born: 3.2% (2000); Ancestry (includes multiple ancestries): 18.1% German, 17.6% Irish, 13.6% English, 11.7% Polish, 10.6% Italian (2000).
Economy: Single-family building permits issued: 0 (2005); Multi-family building permits issued: 0 (2005); Employment by occupation: 8.0% management, 21.1% professional, 16.4% services, 26.4% sales, 0.0% farming, 10.8% construction, 17.2% production (2000).
Income: Per capita income: $18,059 (2005); Median household income: $31,813 (2005); Average household income: $39,321 (2005); Percent of households with income of $100,000 or more: 4.6% (2005); Poverty rate: 9.8% (2000).
Education: Percent of population age 25 and over with: High school diploma (including GED) or higher: 81.8% (2005); Bachelor's degree or higher: 12.4% (2005); Master's degree or higher: 6.1% (2005).

School District(s)
Elmira Heights Central School District (KG-12)
   2003-04 Enrollment: 1,109 . . . . (607) 734-7114

Housing: Homeownership rate: 53.6% (2005); Median home value: $69,112 (2005); Median rent: $377 per month (2000); Median age of housing: 60+ years (2000).
Safety: Violent crime rate: 14.7 per 10,000 population; Property crime rate: 345.6 per 10,000 population (2004).
Transportation: Commute to work: 90.4% car, 1.2% public transportation, 6.8% walk, 1.1% work from home (2000); Travel time to work: 59.5% less than 15 minutes, 26.7% 15 to 30 minutes, 8.6% 30 to 45 minutes, 2.5% 45 to 60 minutes, 2.7% 60 minutes or more (2000)

ERIN (town).
Covers a land area of 44.319 square miles and a water area of 0.153 square miles. Located at 42.18° N. Lat.; 76.67° W. Long.
Population: 2,002 (1990); 2,054 (2000); 2,131 (2005); 2,187 (2010 projected); Race: 98.7% White, 0.1% Black, 0.5% Asian, 0.6% Hispanic of any race (2005); Density: 48.1 persons per square mile (2005); Average household size: 2.68 (2005); Median age: 38.5 (2005); Males per 100 females: 103.7 (2005); Marriage status: 23.3% never married, 64.3% now married, 4.3% widowed, 8.2% divorced (2000); Foreign born: 1.3% (2000); Ancestry (includes multiple ancestries): 19.1% German, 14.4% Irish, 13.5% English, 12.7% United States or American, 8.1% Italian (2000).
Economy: Single-family building permits issued: 6 (2005); Multi-family building permits issued: 0 (2005); Employment by occupation: 9.1%

management, 14.8% professional, 15.4% services, 27.5% sales, 0.8% farming, 9.8% construction, 22.5% production (2000).
Income: Per capita income: $19,765 (2005); Median household income: $47,460 (2005); Average household income: $53,048 (2005); Percent of households with income of $100,000 or more: 7.4% (2005); Poverty rate: 7.5% (2000).
Education: Percent of population age 25 and over with: High school diploma (including GED) or higher: 84.9% (2005); Bachelor's degree or higher: 10.5% (2005); Master's degree or higher: 3.7% (2005).
Housing: Homeownership rate: 91.8% (2005); Median home value: $74,190 (2005); Median rent: $325 per month (2000); Median age of housing: 28 years (2000).
Transportation: Commute to work: 96.5% car, 0.3% public transportation, 1.6% walk, 1.4% work from home (2000); Travel time to work: 8.2% less than 15 minutes, 60.4% 15 to 30 minutes, 20.7% 30 to 45 minutes, 4.8% 45 to 60 minutes, 5.9% 60 minutes or more (2000)

HORSEHEADS (village). Covers a land area of 3.872 square miles and a water area of 0 square miles. Located at 42.16° N. Lat.; 76.82° W. Long. Elevation is 898 feet.
Population: 6,802 (1990); 6,452 (2000); 6,311 (2005); 6,169 (2010 projected); Race: 94.2% White, 1.6% Black, 2.9% Asian, 1.3% Hispanic of any race (2005); Density: 1,630.0 persons per square mile (2005); Average household size: 2.22 (2005); Median age: 42.7 (2005); Males per 100 females: 86.9 (2005); Marriage status: 21.6% never married, 57.5% now married, 9.2% widowed, 11.6% divorced (2000); Foreign born: 1.9% (2000); Ancestry (includes multiple ancestries): 20.0% German, 19.1% Irish, 16.1% English, 11.4% Italian, 8.1% Polish (2000).
Economy: Single-family building permits issued: 0 (2005); Multi-family building permits issued: 0 (2005); Employment by occupation: 10.5% management, 23.2% professional, 18.8% services, 26.8% sales, 0.0% farming, 4.9% construction, 15.7% production (2000).
Income: Per capita income: $23,541 (2005); Median household income: $39,781 (2005); Average household income: $51,969 (2005); Percent of households with income of $100,000 or more: 9.3% (2005); Poverty rate: 8.8% (2000).
Education: Percent of population age 25 and over with: High school diploma (including GED) or higher: 87.4% (2005); Bachelor's degree or higher: 19.9% (2005); Master's degree or higher: 8.7% (2005).

School District(s)
Horseheads Central School District (KG-12)
    2003-04 Enrollment: 4,378 . . . . (607) 739-5601
Housing: Homeownership rate: 66.7% (2005); Median home value: $86,248 (2005); Median rent: $446 per month (2000); Median age of housing: 46 years (2000).
Transportation: Commute to work: 92.7% car, 0.9% public transportation, 3.3% walk, 2.4% work from home (2000); Travel time to work: 56.2% less than 15 minutes, 33.0% 15 to 30 minutes, 5.5% 30 to 45 minutes, 2.6% 45 to 60 minutes, 2.7% 60 minutes or more (2000)
Additional Information Contacts
Village of Horseheads . . . . (607) 739-5691
    http://www.horseheads.org/

HORSEHEADS (town). Covers a land area of 35.862 square miles and a water area of 0.052 square miles. Located at 42.15° N. Lat.; 76.81° W. Long. Elevation is 898 feet.
History: Settled 1789, incorporated 1837.
Population: 19,926 (1990); 19,561 (2000); 19,364 (2005); 19,174 (2010 projected); Race: 94.9% White, 1.5% Black, 2.3% Asian, 1.0% Hispanic of any race (2005); Density: 540.0 persons per square mile (2005); Average household size: 2.42 (2005); Median age: 42.2 (2005); Males per 100 females: 87.0 (2005); Marriage status: 21.3% never married, 59.7% now married, 8.4% widowed, 10.6% divorced (2000); Foreign born: 2.5% (2000); Ancestry (includes multiple ancestries): 19.9% German, 17.8% Irish, 16.6% English, 11.9% Italian, 9.0% Other groups (2000).
Economy: Manufacturing: coil and precision springs, cable TV connectors, plastic products, electronic tubes, power amplifiers, TV camera systems, image and storage tubes; sand, gravel pits. Agriculture: dairy products; poultry, apples. Single-family building permits issued: 25 (2005); Multi-family building permits issued: 0 (2005); Employment by occupation: 10.6% management, 23.1% professional, 18.8% services, 25.1% sales, 0.0% farming, 7.1% construction, 15.3% production (2000).
Income: Per capita income: $22,675 (2005); Median household income: $42,714 (2005); Average household income: $53,640 (2005); Percent of households with income of $100,000 or more: 11.1% (2005); Poverty rate: 8.3% (2000).
Education: Percent of population age 25 and over with: High school diploma (including GED) or higher: 85.5% (2005); Bachelor's degree or higher: 20.0% (2005); Master's degree or higher: 8.3% (2005).
Housing: Homeownership rate: 69.1% (2005); Median home value: $92,906 (2005); Median rent: $438 per month (2000); Median age of housing: 43 years (2000).
Transportation: Commute to work: 94.3% car, 0.5% public transportation, 2.7% walk, 1.8% work from home (2000); Travel time to work: 49.7% less than 15 minutes, 37.0% 15 to 30 minutes, 7.1% 30 to 45 minutes, 2.8% 45 to 60 minutes, 3.4% 60 minutes or more (2000)

HORSEHEADS NORTH (CDP). Covers a land area of 2.302 square miles and a water area of 0 square miles. Located at 42.19° N. Lat.; 76.80° W. Long.
Population: 3,003 (1990); 2,852 (2000); 2,861 (2005); 2,916 (2010 projected); Race: 96.6% White, 0.7% Black, 1.7% Asian, 0.5% Hispanic of any race (2005); Density: 1,243.0 persons per square mile (2005); Average household size: 2.56 (2005); Median age: 39.5 (2005); Males per 100 females: 90.6 (2005); Marriage status: 15.7% never married, 67.1% now married, 6.5% widowed, 10.7% divorced (2000); Foreign born: 1.0% (2000); Ancestry (includes multiple ancestries): 20.4% German, 19.4% English, 14.9% Irish, 13.4% Italian, 9.4% Other groups (2000).
Economy: Employment by occupation: 10.8% management, 30.9% professional, 12.2% services, 23.5% sales, 0.0% farming, 6.7% construction, 15.9% production (2000).
Income: Per capita income: $23,453 (2005); Median household income: $54,340 (2005); Average household income: $60,018 (2005); Percent of households with income of $100,000 or more: 13.9% (2005); Poverty rate: 4.8% (2000).
Education: Percent of population age 25 and over with: High school diploma (including GED) or higher: 92.9% (2005); Bachelor's degree or higher: 23.7% (2005); Master's degree or higher: 7.4% (2005).
Housing: Homeownership rate: 76.9% (2005); Median home value: $123,034 (2005); Median rent: $450 per month (2000); Median age of housing: 35 years (2000).
Transportation: Commute to work: 100.0% car, 0.0% public transportation, 0.0% walk, 0.0% work from home (2000); Travel time to work: 42.3% less than 15 minutes, 41.8% 15 to 30 minutes, 8.8% 30 to 45 minutes, 3.7% 45 to 60 minutes, 3.5% 60 minutes or more (2000)

LOWMAN (unincorporated postal area, zip code 14861). Covers a land area of 32.604 square miles and a water area of 0.024 square miles. Located at 42.07° N. Lat.; 76.69° W. Long.
Population: 0 (2000); Race: 97.1% White, 0.0% Black, 0.0% Asian, 0.0% Hispanic of any race (2000); Density: 0.0 persons per square mile (2000); Age: 23.9% under 18, 15.3% over 64 (2000); Marriage status: 14.7% never married, 72.7% now married, 5.8% widowed, 6.8% divorced (2000); Foreign born: 0.6% (2000); Ancestry (includes multiple ancestries): 19.8% German, 15.5% Irish, 13.2% United States or American, 8.9% English, 7.8% Polish (2000).
Economy: Employment by occupation: 12.0% management, 8.1% professional, 15.0% services, 24.9% sales, 0.3% farming, 13.6% construction, 26.1% production (2000).
Income: Per capita income: $16,186 (2000); Median household income: $34,464 (2000); Poverty rate: 13.7% (2000).
Education: Percent of population age 25 and over with: High school diploma (including GED) or higher: 71.3% (2000); Bachelor's degree or higher: 5.2% (2000).
Housing: Homeownership rate: 86.2% (2000); Median home value: $58,300 (2000); Median rent: $370 per month (2000); Median age of housing: 29 years (2000).
Transportation: Commute to work: 97.3% car, 0.0% public transportation, 0.5% walk, 1.9% work from home (2000); Travel time to work: 8.0% less than 15 minutes, 60.0% 15 to 30 minutes, 21.1% 30 to 45 minutes, 5.4% 45 to 60 minutes, 5.5% 60 minutes or more (2000)

MILLPORT (village). Covers a land area of 0.362 square miles and a water area of 0 square miles. Located at 42.26° N. Lat.; 76.83° W. Long.
Population: 342 (1990); 297 (2000); 268 (2005); 256 (2010 projected); Race: 96.6% White, 0.0% Black, 0.0% Asian, 2.2% Hispanic of any race (2005); Density: 740.8 persons per square mile (2005); Average household size: 2.46 (2005); Median age: 39.9 (2005); Males per 100 females: 101.5 (2005); Marriage status: 25.0% never married, 43.6% now married, 12.7%

widowed, 18.6% divorced (2000); Foreign born: 3.0% (2000); Ancestry (includes multiple ancestries): 28.6% English, 24.6% German, 20.9% Irish, 12.1% Italian, 11.8% French (except Basque) (2000).
Economy: In agricultural area. Single-family building permits issued: 0 (2005); Multi-family building permits issued: 0 (2005); Employment by occupation: 2.3% management, 6.0% professional, 25.6% services, 21.1% sales, 0.0% farming, 15.0% construction, 30.1% production (2000).
Income: Per capita income: $19,076 (2005); Median household income: $37,206 (2005); Average household income: $46,904 (2005); Percent of households with income of $100,000 or more: 11.9% (2005); Poverty rate: 12.8% (2000).
Education: Percent of population age 25 and over with: High school diploma (including GED) or higher: 75.8% (2005); Bachelor's degree or higher: 5.9% (2005); Master's degree or higher: 0.5% (2005).
Housing: Homeownership rate: 77.1% (2005); Median home value: $48,889 (2005); Median rent: $381 per month (2000); Median age of housing: 60+ years (2000).
Transportation: Commute to work: 98.4% car, 0.0% public transportation, 1.6% walk, 0.0% work from home (2000); Travel time to work: 10.9% less than 15 minutes, 71.9% 15 to 30 minutes, 7.0% 30 to 45 minutes, 6.3% 45 to 60 minutes, 3.9% 60 minutes or more (2000)

PINE CITY (unincorporated postal area, zip code 14871). Covers a land area of 56.540 square miles and a water area of 0.261 square miles. Located at 42.04° N. Lat.; 76.90° W. Long. Elevation is 1,002 feet.
Population: 0 (2000); Race: 98.6% White, 0.2% Black, 0.8% Asian, 0.6% Hispanic of any race (2000); Density: 0.0 persons per square mile (2000); Age: 22.3% under 18, 16.0% over 64 (2000); Marriage status: 18.2% never married, 67.0% now married, 5.1% widowed, 9.7% divorced (2000); Foreign born: 1.8% (2000); Ancestry (includes multiple ancestries): 25.1% German, 23.9% English, 16.1% Irish, 8.7% Italian, 6.1% Other groups (2000).
Economy: Employment by occupation: 9.8% management, 24.8% professional, 18.3% services, 24.5% sales, 0.5% farming, 9.6% construction, 12.4% production (2000).
Income: Per capita income: $22,023 (2000); Median household income: $45,284 (2000); Poverty rate: 4.8% (2000).
Education: Percent of population age 25 and over with: High school diploma (including GED) or higher: 89.4% (2000); Bachelor's degree or higher: 20.8% (2000).

School District(s)
Elmira City School District (PK-12)
   2003-04 Enrollment: 7,613 . . . . (607) 735-3010
Housing: Homeownership rate: 89.0% (2000); Median home value: $76,200 (2000); Median rent: $367 per month (2000); Median age of housing: 43 years (2000).
Transportation: Commute to work: 96.4% car, 0.3% public transportation, 1.0% walk, 2.3% work from home (2000); Travel time to work: 29.9% less than 15 minutes, 48.7% 15 to 30 minutes, 16.4% 30 to 45 minutes, 2.2% 45 to 60 minutes, 2.8% 60 minutes or more (2000)

PINE VALLEY (unincorporated postal area, zip code 14872). Covers a land area of 3.293 square miles and a water area of 0.009 square miles. Located at 42.21° N. Lat.; 76.84° W. Long. Elevation is 890 feet.
Population: 0 (2000); Race: 94.7% White, 0.0% Black, 0.0% Asian, 0.0% Hispanic of any race (2000); Density: 0.0 persons per square mile (2000); Age: 36.8% under 18, 14.1% over 64 (2000); Marriage status: 27.4% never married, 53.7% now married, 6.0% widowed, 12.9% divorced (2000); Foreign born: 0.7% (2000); Ancestry (includes multiple ancestries): 25.3% English, 22.7% German, 17.6% Irish, 15.8% Other groups, 9.0% Italian (2000).
Economy: Employment by occupation: 9.7% management, 13.3% professional, 19.9% services, 14.8% sales, 2.0% farming, 11.7% construction, 28.6% production (2000).
Income: Per capita income: $11,894 (2000); Median household income: $26,786 (2000); Poverty rate: 20.7% (2000).
Education: Percent of population age 25 and over with: High school diploma (including GED) or higher: 78.9% (2000); Bachelor's degree or higher: 12.9% (2000).
Housing: Homeownership rate: 66.2% (2000); Median home value: $58,300 (2000); Median rent: $365 per month (2000); Median age of housing: 36 years (2000).
Transportation: Commute to work: 90.9% car, 0.0% public transportation, 0.0% walk, 9.1% work from home (2000); Travel time to work: 29.6% less than 15 minutes, 37.3% 15 to 30 minutes, 30.2% 30 to 45 minutes, 3.0% 45 to 60 minutes, 0.0% 60 minutes or more (2000)

SOUTHPORT (town). Covers a land area of 46.522 square miles and a water area of 0.293 square miles. Located at 42.05° N. Lat.; 76.84° W. Long. Elevation is 889 feet.
Population: 11,571 (1990); 11,185 (2000); 10,855 (2005); 10,528 (2010 projected); Race: 88.7% White, 8.0% Black, 0.3% Asian, 3.8% Hispanic of any race (2005); Density: 233.3 persons per square mile (2005); Average household size: 2.63 (2005); Median age: 40.8 (2005); Males per 100 females: 109.5 (2005); Marriage status: 26.3% never married, 56.2% now married, 7.1% widowed, 10.3% divorced (2000); Foreign born: 2.0% (2000); Ancestry (includes multiple ancestries): 19.7% German, 17.0% English, 16.3% Irish, 9.0% Italian, 6.2% United States or American (2000).
Economy: Single-family building permits issued: 6 (2005); Multi-family building permits issued: 0 (2005); Employment by occupation: 6.9% management, 21.1% professional, 21.4% services, 25.4% sales, 0.2% farming, 7.0% construction, 18.0% production (2000).
Income: Per capita income: $20,858 (2005); Median household income: $43,044 (2005); Average household income: $51,940 (2005); Percent of households with income of $100,000 or more: 9.2% (2005); Poverty rate: 11.7% (2000).
Education: Percent of population age 25 and over with: High school diploma (including GED) or higher: 80.8% (2005); Bachelor's degree or higher: 14.2% (2005); Master's degree or higher: 7.1% (2005).
Housing: Homeownership rate: 78.8% (2005); Median home value: $74,933 (2005); Median rent: $414 per month (2000); Median age of housing: 49 years (2000).
Safety: Violent crime rate: 3.7 per 10,000 population; Property crime rate: 38.4 per 10,000 population (2004).
Transportation: Commute to work: 95.3% car, 0.5% public transportation, 1.1% walk, 1.9% work from home (2000); Travel time to work: 39.3% less than 15 minutes, 40.4% 15 to 30 minutes, 14.0% 30 to 45 minutes, 2.1% 45 to 60 minutes, 4.1% 60 minutes or more (2000)
Additional Information Contacts
Town of Southport . . . . (607) 734-1548
   http://www.townofsouthport.com/

SOUTHPORT (CDP). Covers a land area of 6.575 square miles and a water area of 0.165 square miles. Located at 42.06° N. Lat.; 76.80° W. Long.
Population: 7,857 (1990); 7,396 (2000); 6,914 (2005); 6,433 (2010 projected); Race: 95.3% White, 2.4% Black, 0.5% Asian, 1.1% Hispanic of any race (2005); Density: 1,051.5 persons per square mile (2005); Average household size: 2.31 (2005); Median age: 43.1 (2005); Males per 100 females: 89.4 (2005); Marriage status: 23.5% never married, 55.7% now married, 9.0% widowed, 11.8% divorced (2000); Foreign born: 1.2% (2000); Ancestry (includes multiple ancestries): 19.0% Irish, 18.8% German, 15.4% English, 11.5% Italian, 7.8% United States or American (2000).
Economy: Employment by occupation: 5.1% management, 18.8% professional, 23.1% services, 26.1% sales, 0.2% farming, 6.5% construction, 20.1% production (2000).
Income: Per capita income: $19,448 (2005); Median household income: $38,419 (2005); Average household income: $44,114 (2005); Percent of households with income of $100,000 or more: 4.9% (2005); Poverty rate: 14.2% (2000).
Education: Percent of population age 25 and over with: High school diploma (including GED) or higher: 85.7% (2005); Bachelor's degree or higher: 12.3% (2005); Master's degree or higher: 5.5% (2005).
Housing: Homeownership rate: 74.5% (2005); Median home value: $60,761 (2005); Median rent: $423 per month (2000); Median age of housing: 50 years (2000).
Transportation: Commute to work: 94.6% car, 0.8% public transportation, 1.3% walk, 1.9% work from home (2000); Travel time to work: 46.4% less than 15 minutes, 34.7% 15 to 30 minutes, 11.7% 30 to 45 minutes, 2.8% 45 to 60 minutes, 4.5% 60 minutes or more (2000)

VAN ETTEN (village). Covers a land area of 0.869 square miles and a water area of 0 square miles. Located at 42.19° N. Lat.; 76.55° W. Long.
Population: 552 (1990); 581 (2000); 562 (2005); 551 (2010 projected); Race: 98.2% White, 0.2% Black, 0.4% Asian, 0.0% Hispanic of any race (2005); Density: 646.7 persons per square mile (2005); Average household size: 2.48 (2005); Median age: 33.4 (2005); Males per 100 females: 89.2 (2005); Marriage status: 25.7% never married, 54.2% now married, 8.6%

widowed, 11.4% divorced (2000); Foreign born: 0.5% (2000); Ancestry (includes multiple ancestries): 19.8% Irish, 18.5% German, 15.4% English, 8.9% Other groups, 7.7% Finnish (2000).
Economy: Employment by occupation: 10.0% management, 20.1% professional, 14.6% services, 27.6% sales, 2.1% farming, 10.9% construction, 14.6% production (2000).
Income: Per capita income: $14,969 (2005); Median household income: $31,622 (2005); Average household income: $37,059 (2005); Percent of households with income of $100,000 or more: 2.6% (2005); Poverty rate: 15.0% (2000).
Education: Percent of population age 25 and over with: High school diploma (including GED) or higher: 78.9% (2005); Bachelor's degree or higher: 11.1% (2005); Master's degree or higher: 4.6% (2005).

School District(s)
Spencer-Van Etten Central School District (PK-12)
   2003-04 Enrollment: 1,147 . . . . (607) 589-7100
Housing: Homeownership rate: 69.6% (2005); Median home value: $68,667 (2005); Median rent: $325 per month (2000); Median age of housing: 59 years (2000).
Transportation: Commute to work: 88.3% car, 1.3% public transportation, 4.2% walk, 5.0% work from home (2000); Travel time to work: 22.5% less than 15 minutes, 16.3% 15 to 30 minutes, 43.2% 30 to 45 minutes, 13.7% 45 to 60 minutes, 4.4% 60 minutes or more (2000)

VAN ETTEN (town). Covers a land area of 41.563 square miles and a water area of 0.006 square miles. Located at 42.20° N. Lat.; 76.57° W. Long.
Population: 1,507 (1990); 1,518 (2000); 1,465 (2005); 1,436 (2010 projected); Race: 98.2% White, 0.5% Black, 0.3% Asian, 0.8% Hispanic of any race (2005); Density: 35.2 persons per square mile (2005); Average household size: 2.49 (2005); Median age: 36.8 (2005); Males per 100 females: 98.0 (2005); Marriage status: 23.1% never married, 60.3% now married, 6.7% widowed, 9.8% divorced (2000); Foreign born: 2.0% (2000); Ancestry (includes multiple ancestries): 17.6% German, 14.4% Irish, 13.1% English, 10.3% United States or American, 7.7% Italian (2000).
Economy: In agricultural area. Single-family building permits issued: 2 (2005); Multi-family building permits issued: 0 (2005); Employment by occupation: 9.3% management, 16.4% professional, 15.1% services, 22.7% sales, 1.0% farming, 13.6% construction, 22.0% production (2000).
Income: Per capita income: $17,555 (2005); Median household income: $36,857 (2005); Average household income: $43,737 (2005); Percent of households with income of $100,000 or more: 4.8% (2005); Poverty rate: 12.5% (2000).
Education: Percent of population age 25 and over with: High school diploma (including GED) or higher: 83.2% (2005); Bachelor's degree or higher: 11.7% (2005); Master's degree or higher: 5.5% (2005).
Housing: Homeownership rate: 77.6% (2005); Median home value: $75,435 (2005); Median rent: $339 per month (2000); Median age of housing: 40 years (2000).
Transportation: Commute to work: 93.5% car, 0.6% public transportation, 2.6% walk, 2.6% work from home (2000); Travel time to work: 17.2% less than 15 minutes, 22.8% 15 to 30 minutes, 41.7% 30 to 45 minutes, 13.0% 45 to 60 minutes, 5.3% 60 minutes or more (2000)

VETERAN (town). Covers a land area of 38.426 square miles and a water area of 0.055 square miles. Located at 42.25° N. Lat.; 76.80° W. Long.
Population: 3,468 (1990); 3,271 (2000); 3,161 (2005); 3,120 (2010 projected); Race: 97.9% White, 0.4% Black, 0.3% Asian, 1.0% Hispanic of any race (2005); Density: 82.3 persons per square mile (2005); Average household size: 2.54 (2005); Median age: 43.2 (2005); Males per 100 females: 97.4 (2005); Marriage status: 22.2% never married, 59.9% now married, 7.7% widowed, 10.1% divorced (2000); Foreign born: 0.7% (2000); Ancestry (includes multiple ancestries): 21.6% German, 21.4% English, 18.5% Irish, 10.0% Other groups, 6.5% Italian (2000).
Economy: Single-family building permits issued: 4 (2005); Multi-family building permits issued: 0 (2005); Employment by occupation: 14.9% management, 18.3% professional, 15.8% services, 21.4% sales, 1.7% farming, 10.9% construction, 16.9% production (2000).
Income: Per capita income: $25,154 (2005); Median household income: $51,092 (2005); Average household income: $63,853 (2005); Percent of households with income of $100,000 or more: 12.6% (2005); Poverty rate: 10.6% (2000).
Education: Percent of population age 25 and over with: High school diploma (including GED) or higher: 85.9% (2005); Bachelor's degree or higher: 17.6% (2005); Master's degree or higher: 7.3% (2005).
Housing: Homeownership rate: 89.3% (2005); Median home value: $112,083 (2005); Median rent: $372 per month (2000); Median age of housing: 34 years (2000).
Transportation: Commute to work: 93.4% car, 0.7% public transportation, 2.8% walk, 3.1% work from home (2000); Travel time to work: 22.4% less than 15 minutes, 50.7% 15 to 30 minutes, 21.4% 30 to 45 minutes, 1.8% 45 to 60 minutes, 3.7% 60 minutes or more (2000)

WELLSBURG (village). Covers a land area of 0.570 square miles and a water area of 0 square miles. Located at 42.01° N. Lat.; 76.72° W. Long. Elevation is 824 feet.
Population: 617 (1990); 631 (2000); 653 (2005); 670 (2010 projected); Race: 96.8% White, 2.3% Black, 0.0% Asian, 2.5% Hispanic of any race (2005); Density: 1,145.6 persons per square mile (2005); Average household size: 2.56 (2005); Median age: 37.9 (2005); Males per 100 females: 100.9 (2005); Marriage status: 26.0% never married, 54.6% now married, 7.4% widowed, 12.1% divorced (2000); Foreign born: 1.6% (2000); Ancestry (includes multiple ancestries): 20.4% Irish, 17.5% German, 17.0% English, 7.8% United States or American, 5.2% Dutch (2000).
Economy: Single-family building permits issued: 3 (2005); Multi-family building permits issued: 0 (2005); Employment by occupation: 7.0% management, 14.1% professional, 23.8% services, 25.0% sales, 0.0% farming, 14.1% construction, 16.0% production (2000).
Income: Per capita income: $19,306 (2005); Median household income: $38,654 (2005); Average household income: $48,824 (2005); Percent of households with income of $100,000 or more: 5.5% (2005); Poverty rate: 13.7% (2000).
Education: Percent of population age 25 and over with: High school diploma (including GED) or higher: 76.0% (2005); Bachelor's degree or higher: 6.2% (2005); Master's degree or higher: 3.7% (2005).
Housing: Homeownership rate: 79.6% (2005); Median home value: $64,154 (2005); Median rent: $302 per month (2000); Median age of housing: 55 years (2000).
Transportation: Commute to work: 96.0% car, 0.4% public transportation, 2.8% walk, 0.8% work from home (2000); Travel time to work: 21.5% less than 15 minutes, 58.6% 15 to 30 minutes, 8.8% 30 to 45 minutes, 4.8% 45 to 60 minutes, 6.4% 60 minutes or more (2000)

WEST ELMIRA (CDP). Covers a land area of 3.012 square miles and a water area of 0.094 square miles. Located at 42.08° N. Lat.; 76.84° W. Long. Elevation is 888 feet.
Population: 5,218 (1990); 5,136 (2000); 4,996 (2005); 4,845 (2010 projected); Race: 95.1% White, 2.4% Black, 1.6% Asian, 0.7% Hispanic of any race (2005); Density: 1,658.9 persons per square mile (2005); Average household size: 2.33 (2005); Median age: 45.6 (2005); Males per 100 females: 87.8 (2005); Marriage status: 20.4% never married, 62.8% now married, 9.9% widowed, 6.9% divorced (2000); Foreign born: 3.1% (2000); Ancestry (includes multiple ancestries): 26.5% Irish, 22.5% German, 17.5% English, 12.9% Italian, 7.4% Polish (2000).
Economy: Employment by occupation: 14.0% management, 40.5% professional, 13.6% services, 24.8% sales, 0.0% farming, 4.9% construction, 2.2% production (2000).
Income: Per capita income: $35,170 (2005); Median household income: $61,029 (2005); Average household income: $81,670 (2005); Percent of households with income of $100,000 or more: 23.4% (2005); Poverty rate: 5.7% (2000).
Education: Percent of population age 25 and over with: High school diploma (including GED) or higher: 97.2% (2005); Bachelor's degree or higher: 45.1% (2005); Master's degree or higher: 21.7% (2005).
Housing: Homeownership rate: 86.6% (2005); Median home value: $115,576 (2005); Median rent: $646 per month (2000); Median age of housing: 50 years (2000).
Transportation: Commute to work: 97.5% car, 0.0% public transportation, 0.0% walk, 2.1% work from home (2000); Travel time to work: 50.2% less than 15 minutes, 36.0% 15 to 30 minutes, 7.2% 30 to 45 minutes, 2.8% 45 to 60 minutes, 3.7% 60 minutes or more (2000)

Chenango County

Located in central New York; bounded on the east by the Unadilla River; drained by the Susquehanna, Otselic, and Chenango Rivers. Covers a land area of 894.36 square miles, a water area of 4.34 square miles, and is located in the Eastern Time Zone. The county government was organized in 1798. County seat is Norwich.

Weather Station: Norwich Elevation: 1,017 feet

	Jan	Feb	Mar	Apr	May	Jun	Jul	Aug	Sep	Oct	Nov	Dec
High	31	34	44	56	69	76	81	79	71	60	47	36
Low	12	12	22	32	43	51	56	55	47	36	29	19
Precip	2.8	2.4	3.0	3.4	3.7	4.1	3.6	3.5	4.2	3.3	3.7	3.3
Snow	18.0	14.0	11.4	3.3	0.1	0.0	0.0	0.0	0.0	0.3	6.0	15.8

High and Low temperatures in degrees Fahrenheit; Precipitation and Snow in inches

Population: 51,768 (1990); 51,401 (2000); 51,946 (2005); 52,483 (2010 projected); Race: 97.0% White, 1.2% Black, 0.4% Asian, 2.0% Hispanic of any race (2005); Density: 58.1 persons per square mile (2005); Average household size: 2.54 (2005); Median age: 39.7 (2005); Males per 100 females: 97.3 (2005).
Religion: Five largest groups: 15.5% Catholic Church, 8.2% The United Methodist Church, 3.0% Episcopal Church, 2.2% United Church of Christ, 1.7% General Association of Regular Baptist Churches (2000).
Economy: Unemployment rate: 5.0% (2005); Total civilian labor force: 24,358 (2005); Leading industries: 24.1% manufacturing; 16.1% retail trade; 14.5% health care and social assistance (2003); Farms: 960 totaling 189,980 acres (2002); Companies that employ 500 or more persons: 2 (2003); Companies that employ 100 to 499 persons: 16 (2003); Companies that employ less than 100 persons: 970 (2003); Black-owned businesses: n/a (2002); Hispanic-owned businesses: n/a (2002); Women-owned businesses: n/a (2002); Retail sales per capita: $9,612 (2006). Single-family building permits issued: 84 (2005); Multi-family building permits issued: 40 (2005).
Income: Per capita income: $18,873 (2005); Median household income: $37,568 (2005); Average household income: $47,024 (2005); Percent of households with income of $100,000 or more: 7.9% (2005); Poverty rate: 13.5% (2003); Bankruptcy rate: 7.07% (2005).
Education: Percent of population age 25 and over with: High school diploma (including GED) or higher: 80.5% (2005); Bachelor's degree or higher: 14.2% (2005); Master's degree or higher: 5.9% (2005).
Housing: Homeownership rate: 75.7% (2005); Median home value: $86,086 (2005); Median rent: $352 per month (2000); Median age of housing: 40 years (2000).
Health: Birth rate: 108.2 per 10,000 population (2004); Death rate: 114.7 per 10,000 population (2004); Age-adjusted cancer mortality rate: 215.7 deaths per 100,000 population (2002); Number of physicians: 11.0 per 10,000 population (2004); Hospital beds: 26.7 per 10,000 population (2003); Hospital admissions: 337.4 per 10,000 population (2003).
Elections: 2004 Presidential election results: 54.3% Bush, 43.5% Kerry, 2.0% Nader, 0.2% Badnarik
National and State Parks: Chenango State Forest
Additional Information Contacts
Chenango County Government . . . . (607) 337-1430
http://www.co.chenango.ny.us/
City of Norwich . . . . (607) 334-1230
http://www.norwichnewyork.net/

Chenango County Communities

AFTON (village). Covers a land area of 1.519 square miles and a water area of 0.078 square miles. Located at 42.22° N. Lat.; 75.52° W. Long. Elevation is 981 feet.
Population: 838 (1990); 836 (2000); 809 (2005); 797 (2010 projected); Race: 98.3% White, 0.0% Black, 0.2% Asian, 2.6% Hispanic of any race (2005); Density: 532.6 persons per square mile (2005); Average household size: 2.24 (2005); Median age: 41.6 (2005); Males per 100 females: 94.0 (2005); Marriage status: 20.7% never married, 60.5% now married, 9.8% widowed, 9.0% divorced (2000); Foreign born: 1.7% (2000); Ancestry (includes multiple ancestries): 22.9% English, 16.2% German, 14.3% Irish, 10.6% United States or American, 7.7% Italian (2000).
Economy: Employment by occupation: 5.4% management, 25.1% professional, 20.7% services, 24.3% sales, 0.6% farming, 9.0% construction, 15.0% production (2000).
Income: Per capita income: $21,826 (2005); Median household income: $37,540 (2005); Average household income: $48,643 (2005); Percent of households with income of $100,000 or more: 9.4% (2005); Poverty rate: 9.8% (2000).
Education: Percent of population age 25 and over with: High school diploma (including GED) or higher: 81.8% (2005); Bachelor's degree or higher: 15.4% (2005); Master's degree or higher: 6.8% (2005).
School District(s)
Afton Central School District (KG-12)
    2003-04 Enrollment: 718 . . . . (607) 639-8229
Housing: Homeownership rate: 65.4% (2005); Median home value: $89,474 (2005); Median rent: $315 per month (2000); Median age of housing: 60+ years (2000).
Transportation: Commute to work: 80.3% car, 0.9% public transportation, 11.8% walk, 7.0% work from home (2000); Travel time to work: 38.1% less than 15 minutes, 25.7% 15 to 30 minutes, 20.2% 30 to 45 minutes, 11.1% 45 to 60 minutes, 4.9% 60 minutes or more (2000)

AFTON (town). Covers a land area of 45.922 square miles and a water area of 0.600 square miles. Located at 42.22° N. Lat.; 75.52° W. Long. Elevation is 981 feet.
Population: 2,972 (1990); 2,977 (2000); 2,982 (2005); 2,997 (2010 projected); Race: 98.6% White, 0.3% Black, 0.2% Asian, 1.3% Hispanic of any race (2005); Density: 64.9 persons per square mile (2005); Average household size: 2.46 (2005); Median age: 40.6 (2005); Males per 100 females: 99.6 (2005); Marriage status: 21.0% never married, 58.9% now married, 9.2% widowed, 10.9% divorced (2000); Foreign born: 1.8% (2000); Ancestry (includes multiple ancestries): 19.6% German, 16.7% English, 15.3% United States or American, 13.6% Irish, 6.4% Italian (2000).
Economy: In agricultural area. Lumber, wood products, livestock feed. Employment by occupation: 9.3% management, 16.9% professional, 16.9% services, 20.5% sales, 2.2% farming, 13.3% construction, 20.9% production (2000).
Income: Per capita income: $18,039 (2005); Median household income: $37,088 (2005); Average household income: $44,168 (2005); Percent of households with income of $100,000 or more: 6.3% (2005); Poverty rate: 11.9% (2000).
Education: Percent of population age 25 and over with: High school diploma (including GED) or higher: 78.7% (2005); Bachelor's degree or higher: 12.4% (2005); Master's degree or higher: 5.0% (2005).
Housing: Homeownership rate: 81.8% (2005); Median home value: $89,716 (2005); Median rent: $329 per month (2000); Median age of housing: 31 years (2000).
Transportation: Commute to work: 89.3% car, 1.0% public transportation, 4.5% walk, 5.2% work from home (2000); Travel time to work: 24.3% less than 15 minutes, 26.7% 15 to 30 minutes, 29.2% 30 to 45 minutes, 14.8% 45 to 60 minutes, 5.0% 60 minutes or more (2000)

BAINBRIDGE (village). Covers a land area of 1.283 square miles and a water area of 0.040 square miles. Located at 42.29° N. Lat.; 75.48° W. Long. Elevation is 1,006 feet.
Population: 1,574 (1990); 1,365 (2000); 1,441 (2005); 1,507 (2010 projected); Race: 98.1% White, 0.4% Black, 0.3% Asian, 1.9% Hispanic of any race (2005); Density: 1,123.5 persons per square mile (2005); Average household size: 2.31 (2005); Median age: 38.4 (2005); Males per 100 females: 96.1 (2005); Marriage status: 25.5% never married, 57.4% now married, 7.3% widowed, 9.8% divorced (2000); Foreign born: 1.3% (2000); Ancestry (includes multiple ancestries): 22.7% English, 20.2% German, 14.6% Irish, 7.7% Italian, 4.8% United States or American (2000).
Economy: Employment by occupation: 9.2% management, 21.9% professional, 15.2% services, 20.7% sales, 0.3% farming, 7.8% construction, 25.0% production (2000).
Income: Per capita income: $21,785 (2005); Median household income: $39,286 (2005); Average household income: $50,308 (2005); Percent of households with income of $100,000 or more: 8.8% (2005); Poverty rate: 12.0% (2000).
Education: Percent of population age 25 and over with: High school diploma (including GED) or higher: 86.7% (2005); Bachelor's degree or higher: 18.0% (2005); Master's degree or higher: 9.5% (2005).
School District(s)
Bainbridge-Guilford Central School District (PK-12)
    2003-04 Enrollment: 1,041 . . . . (607) 967-6321
Housing: Homeownership rate: 62.0% (2005); Median home value: $91,441 (2005); Median rent: $336 per month (2000); Median age of housing: 60+ years (2000).
Transportation: Commute to work: 90.1% car, 0.0% public transportation, 7.3% walk, 1.8% work from home (2000); Travel time to work: 55.1% less

than 15 minutes, 18.9% 15 to 30 minutes, 10.9% 30 to 45 minutes, 8.9% 45 to 60 minutes, 6.3% 60 minutes or more (2000)

Additional Information Contacts
Bainbridge Chamber of Commerce . . . . (607) 967-8700
  http://www.bainbridgeny.org

BAINBRIDGE (town).
Covers a land area of 34.303 square miles and a water area of 0.439 square miles. Located at 42.29° N. Lat.; 75.47° W. Long. Elevation is 1,006 feet.
History: Settled before 1790, incorporated 1829.
Population: 3,445 (1990); 3,401 (2000); 3,549 (2005); 3,674 (2010 projected); Race: 98.0% White, 0.5% Black, 0.3% Asian, 2.2% Hispanic of any race (2005); Density: 103.5 persons per square mile (2005); Average household size: 2.44 (2005); Median age: 39.8 (2005); Males per 100 females: 102.0 (2005); Marriage status: 22.6% never married, 62.8% now married, 5.5% widowed, 9.0% divorced (2000); Foreign born: 2.3% (2000); Ancestry (includes multiple ancestries): 18.3% English, 16.9% German, 14.7% Irish, 8.1% Dutch, 6.1% United States or American (2000).
Economy: Dairying and farming area. Manufacturing: resin glues, sealants, adhesives. Employment by occupation: 9.4% management, 17.7% professional, 13.5% services, 18.3% sales, 1.7% farming, 9.9% construction, 29.5% production (2000).
Income: Per capita income: $21,081 (2005); Median household income: $42,301 (2005); Average household income: $51,350 (2005); Percent of households with income of $100,000 or more: 8.6% (2005); Poverty rate: 10.9% (2000).
Education: Percent of population age 25 and over with: High school diploma (including GED) or higher: 85.5% (2005); Bachelor's degree or higher: 14.1% (2005); Master's degree or higher: 7.3% (2005).
Housing: Homeownership rate: 75.6% (2005); Median home value: $94,523 (2005); Median rent: $352 per month (2000); Median age of housing: 55 years (2000).
Transportation: Commute to work: 89.2% car, 1.5% public transportation, 3.5% walk, 5.0% work from home (2000); Travel time to work: 48.3% less than 15 minutes, 27.8% 15 to 30 minutes, 11.5% 30 to 45 minutes, 5.5% 45 to 60 minutes, 6.9% 60 minutes or more (2000)

COLUMBUS (town).
Covers a land area of 37.429 square miles and a water area of 0.078 square miles. Located at 42.69° N. Lat.; 75.36° W. Long.
Population: 869 (1990); 931 (2000); 1,075 (2005); 1,176 (2010 projected); Race: 97.1% White, 0.4% Black, 0.2% Asian, 2.2% Hispanic of any race (2005); Density: 28.7 persons per square mile (2005); Average household size: 2.67 (2005); Median age: 40.0 (2005); Males per 100 females: 99.8 (2005); Marriage status: 23.9% never married, 62.6% now married, 5.4% widowed, 8.1% divorced (2000); Foreign born: 1.4% (2000); Ancestry (includes multiple ancestries): 20.8% English, 17.4% Irish, 17.1% German, 8.4% Other groups, 6.1% Dutch (2000).
Economy: Single-family building permits issued: 9 (2005); Multi-family building permits issued: 0 (2005); Employment by occupation: 16.0% management, 13.1% professional, 14.0% services, 24.0% sales, 3.3% farming, 10.0% construction, 19.5% production (2000).
Income: Per capita income: $16,908 (2005); Median household income: $33,030 (2005); Average household income: $44,552 (2005); Percent of households with income of $100,000 or more: 7.2% (2005); Poverty rate: 21.3% (2000).
Education: Percent of population age 25 and over with: High school diploma (including GED) or higher: 76.1% (2005); Bachelor's degree or higher: 9.3% (2005); Master's degree or higher: 4.7% (2005).
Housing: Homeownership rate: 87.6% (2005); Median home value: $85,818 (2005); Median rent: $288 per month (2000); Median age of housing: 31 years (2000).
Transportation: Commute to work: 86.5% car, 0.0% public transportation, 8.1% walk, 4.7% work from home (2000); Travel time to work: 32.3% less than 15 minutes, 31.3% 15 to 30 minutes, 18.3% 30 to 45 minutes, 9.0% 45 to 60 minutes, 9.0% 60 minutes or more (2000)

COVENTRY (town).
Covers a land area of 48.745 square miles and a water area of 0.134 square miles. Located at 42.29° N. Lat.; 75.62° W. Long. Elevation is 1,665 feet.
Population: 1,517 (1990); 1,589 (2000); 1,576 (2005); 1,566 (2010 projected); Race: 99.0% White, 0.3% Black, 0.1% Asian, 1.9% Hispanic of any race (2005); Density: 32.3 persons per square mile (2005); Average household size: 2.70 (2005); Median age: 38.5 (2005); Males per 100 females: 103.1 (2005); Marriage status: 22.3% never married, 61.9% now married, 4.4% widowed, 11.4% divorced (2000); Foreign born: 4.4% (2000); Ancestry (includes multiple ancestries): 23.1% German, 14.0% English, 11.3% Irish, 10.5% United States or American, 9.2% Italian (2000).
Economy: Employment by occupation: 10.3% management, 13.8% professional, 15.8% services, 18.9% sales, 2.3% farming, 14.1% construction, 24.8% production (2000).
Income: Per capita income: $17,968 (2005); Median household income: $38,988 (2005); Average household income: $48,572 (2005); Percent of households with income of $100,000 or more: 7.4% (2005); Poverty rate: 14.9% (2000).
Education: Percent of population age 25 and over with: High school diploma (including GED) or higher: 79.1% (2005); Bachelor's degree or higher: 9.1% (2005); Master's degree or higher: 4.2% (2005).
Housing: Homeownership rate: 87.7% (2005); Median home value: $81,406 (2005); Median rent: $314 per month (2000); Median age of housing: 23 years (2000).
Transportation: Commute to work: 89.4% car, 0.7% public transportation, 2.9% walk, 6.9% work from home (2000); Travel time to work: 22.4% less than 15 minutes, 33.7% 15 to 30 minutes, 24.7% 30 to 45 minutes, 10.1% 45 to 60 minutes, 9.0% 60 minutes or more (2000)

GERMAN (town).
Covers a land area of 28.396 square miles and a water area of 0.036 square miles. Located at 42.48° N. Lat.; 75.82° W. Long.
Population: 311 (1990); 378 (2000); 387 (2005); 391 (2010 projected); Race: 96.6% White, 1.0% Black, 0.0% Asian, 2.6% Hispanic of any race (2005); Density: 13.6 persons per square mile (2005); Average household size: 2.74 (2005); Median age: 35.5 (2005); Males per 100 females: 110.3 (2005); Marriage status: 26.6% never married, 61.4% now married, 4.4% widowed, 7.6% divorced (2000); Foreign born: 3.8% (2000); Ancestry (includes multiple ancestries): 24.9% English, 19.3% Irish, 13.4% United States or American, 13.4% German, 8.0% Italian (2000).
Economy: Employment by occupation: 9.0% management, 12.0% professional, 22.2% services, 18.0% sales, 1.8% farming, 16.8% construction, 20.4% production (2000).
Income: Per capita income: $15,090 (2005); Median household income: $39,464 (2005); Average household income: $41,418 (2005); Percent of households with income of $100,000 or more: 2.1% (2005); Poverty rate: 21.2% (2000).
Education: Percent of population age 25 and over with: High school diploma (including GED) or higher: 81.0% (2005); Bachelor's degree or higher: 11.0% (2005); Master's degree or higher: 5.5% (2005).
Housing: Homeownership rate: 88.7% (2005); Median home value: $79,444 (2005); Median rent: $275 per month (2000); Median age of housing: 21 years (2000).
Transportation: Commute to work: 89.5% car, 0.0% public transportation, 1.9% walk, 8.0% work from home (2000); Travel time to work: 14.8% less than 15 minutes, 25.5% 15 to 30 minutes, 8.7% 30 to 45 minutes, 22.1% 45 to 60 minutes, 28.9% 60 minutes or more (2000)

GREENE (village).
Covers a land area of 1.069 square miles and a water area of 0.040 square miles. Located at 42.33° N. Lat.; 75.77° W. Long. Elevation is 924 feet.
Population: 1,819 (1990); 1,701 (2000); 1,704 (2005); 1,708 (2010 projected); Race: 97.9% White, 0.4% Black, 0.5% Asian, 1.3% Hispanic of any race (2005); Density: 1,593.7 persons per square mile (2005); Average household size: 2.26 (2005); Median age: 39.6 (2005); Males per 100 females: 91.0 (2005); Marriage status: 28.0% never married, 49.4% now married, 10.1% widowed, 12.6% divorced (2000); Foreign born: 1.0% (2000); Ancestry (includes multiple ancestries): 25.3% English, 23.0% Irish, 19.2% German, 8.9% Italian, 8.5% French (except Basque) (2000).
Economy: Employment by occupation: 11.2% management, 26.5% professional, 15.1% services, 24.8% sales, 1.3% farming, 8.3% construction, 12.7% production (2000).
Income: Per capita income: $20,478 (2005); Median household income: $34,764 (2005); Average household income: $46,169 (2005); Percent of households with income of $100,000 or more: 9.7% (2005); Poverty rate: 11.8% (2000).
Education: Percent of population age 25 and over with: High school diploma (including GED) or higher: 86.9% (2005); Bachelor's degree or higher: 19.7% (2005); Master's degree or higher: 10.8% (2005).

School District(s)
Greene Central School District (KG-12)
  2003-04 Enrollment: 1,359 . . . . (607) 656-4161

Housing: Homeownership rate: 51.7% (2005); Median home value: $113,966 (2005); Median rent: $372 per month (2000); Median age of housing: 60+ years (2000).
Safety: Violent crime rate: 5.9 per 10,000 population; Property crime rate: 0.0 per 10,000 population (2004).
Newspapers: Chenango American (General - Circulation 2,350); Oxford Review Times (General - Circulation 625); Whitney Point Reporter (General - Circulation 575)
Transportation: Commute to work: 86.2% car, 0.1% public transportation, 10.3% walk, 3.1% work from home (2000); Travel time to work: 43.8% less than 15 minutes, 18.9% 15 to 30 minutes, 27.6% 30 to 45 minutes, 7.3% 45 to 60 minutes, 2.5% 60 minutes or more (2000)
Additional Information Contacts
Greene Chamber of Commerce . . . . (607) 656-8225
http://www.greenenys.com

GREENE (town).
Covers a land area of 75.136 square miles and a water area of 0.483 square miles. Located at 42.32° N. Lat.; 75.76° W. Long. Elevation is 924 feet.
History: Settled 1792, incorporated 1842.
Population: 6,053 (1990); 5,729 (2000); 5,682 (2005); 5,646 (2010 projected); Race: 98.2% White, 0.4% Black, 0.3% Asian, 1.1% Hispanic of any race (2005); Density: 75.6 persons per square mile (2005); Average household size: 2.47 (2005); Median age: 40.0 (2005); Males per 100 females: 97.3 (2005); Marriage status: 22.8% never married, 57.9% now married, 6.1% widowed, 13.2% divorced (2000); Foreign born: 0.8% (2000); Ancestry (includes multiple ancestries): 25.8% English, 20.6% Irish, 17.7% German, 7.8% United States or American, 6.0% Italian (2000).
Economy: In dairying area. Manufacturing: fabricated metal products, construction equipment, electronic equipment, wire. Employment by occupation: 11.7% management, 20.4% professional, 12.3% services, 24.5% sales, 1.0% farming, 11.5% construction, 18.6% production (2000).
Income: Per capita income: $20,758 (2005); Median household income: $41,851 (2005); Average household income: $51,095 (2005); Percent of households with income of $100,000 or more: 10.7% (2005); Poverty rate: 10.1% (2000).
Education: Percent of population age 25 and over with: High school diploma (including GED) or higher: 87.0% (2005); Bachelor's degree or higher: 16.8% (2005); Master's degree or higher: 7.9% (2005).
Housing: Homeownership rate: 74.4% (2005); Median home value: $107,692 (2005); Median rent: $367 per month (2000); Median age of housing: 38 years (2000).
Transportation: Commute to work: 91.2% car, 0.0% public transportation, 4.9% walk, 3.6% work from home (2000); Travel time to work: 37.6% less than 15 minutes, 23.5% 15 to 30 minutes, 28.1% 30 to 45 minutes, 5.9% 45 to 60 minutes, 4.9% 60 minutes or more (2000)

GUILFORD (town).
Covers a land area of 61.664 square miles and a water area of 0.225 square miles. Located at 42.40° N. Lat.; 75.45° W. Long.
Population: 2,875 (1990); 3,046 (2000); 3,183 (2005); 3,279 (2010 projected); Race: 96.8% White, 1.0% Black, 0.3% Asian, 1.6% Hispanic of any race (2005); Density: 51.6 persons per square mile (2005); Average household size: 2.53 (2005); Median age: 39.6 (2005); Males per 100 females: 102.4 (2005); Marriage status: 20.8% never married, 61.3% now married, 6.3% widowed, 11.5% divorced (2000); Foreign born: 1.1% (2000); Ancestry (includes multiple ancestries): 19.3% English, 18.9% German, 12.5% Irish, 9.8% United States or American, 8.5% Other groups (2000).
Economy: Employment by occupation: 8.4% management, 15.6% professional, 10.5% services, 22.3% sales, 1.5% farming, 14.3% construction, 27.4% production (2000).
Income: Per capita income: $17,211 (2005); Median household income: $38,176 (2005); Average household income: $43,582 (2005); Percent of households with income of $100,000 or more: 5.2% (2005); Poverty rate: 12.0% (2000).
Education: Percent of population age 25 and over with: High school diploma (including GED) or higher: 81.0% (2005); Bachelor's degree or higher: 11.7% (2005); Master's degree or higher: 4.4% (2005).
School District(s)
Bainbridge-Guilford Central School District (PK-12)
    2003-04 Enrollment: 1,041 . . . . (607) 967-6321
Housing: Homeownership rate: 86.1% (2005); Median home value: $76,111 (2005); Median rent: $330 per month (2000); Median age of housing: 30 years (2000).
Transportation: Commute to work: 95.0% car, 0.6% public transportation, 2.8% walk, 0.9% work from home (2000); Travel time to work: 20.3% less than 15 minutes, 50.4% 15 to 30 minutes, 14.7% 30 to 45 minutes, 6.0% 45 to 60 minutes, 8.6% 60 minutes or more (2000)

LINCKLAEN (town).
Covers a land area of 26.272 square miles and a water area of 0 square miles. Located at 42.68° N. Lat.; 75.84° W. Long.
Population: 486 (1990); 416 (2000); 419 (2005); 424 (2010 projected); Race: 96.4% White, 1.2% Black, 0.2% Asian, 1.4% Hispanic of any race (2005); Density: 15.9 persons per square mile (2005); Average household size: 2.65 (2005); Median age: 39.2 (2005); Males per 100 females: 105.4 (2005); Marriage status: 29.0% never married, 55.0% now married, 6.3% widowed, 9.7% divorced (2000); Foreign born: 0.0% (2000); Ancestry (includes multiple ancestries): 22.1% English, 18.2% German, 14.9% United States or American, 11.0% Irish, 8.3% Other groups (2000).
Economy: Employment by occupation: 8.6% management, 10.3% professional, 14.6% services, 14.6% sales, 5.4% farming, 19.5% construction, 27.0% production (2000).
Income: Per capita income: $17,894 (2005); Median household income: $34,565 (2005); Average household income: $47,453 (2005); Percent of households with income of $100,000 or more: 7.6% (2005); Poverty rate: 17.0% (2000).
Education: Percent of population age 25 and over with: High school diploma (including GED) or higher: 78.0% (2005); Bachelor's degree or higher: 5.1% (2005); Master's degree or higher: 2.2% (2005).
Housing: Homeownership rate: 77.8% (2005); Median home value: $78,636 (2005); Median rent: $329 per month (2000); Median age of housing: 29 years (2000).
Transportation: Commute to work: 92.3% car, 0.0% public transportation, 6.1% walk, 0.0% work from home (2000); Travel time to work: 29.8% less than 15 minutes, 7.2% 15 to 30 minutes, 34.8% 30 to 45 minutes, 11.0% 45 to 60 minutes, 17.1% 60 minutes or more (2000)

MCDONOUGH (town).
Covers a land area of 39.111 square miles and a water area of 0.520 square miles. Located at 42.50° N. Lat.; 75.72° W. Long.
Population: 809 (1990); 870 (2000); 909 (2005); 933 (2010 projected); Race: 95.9% White, 1.4% Black, 0.3% Asian, 5.2% Hispanic of any race (2005); Density: 23.2 persons per square mile (2005); Average household size: 2.44 (2005); Median age: 42.6 (2005); Males per 100 females: 106.1 (2005); Marriage status: 21.7% never married, 64.0% now married, 7.9% widowed, 6.4% divorced (2000); Foreign born: 2.7% (2000); Ancestry (includes multiple ancestries): 18.4% English, 16.4% Irish, 13.2% United States or American, 10.1% Other groups, 9.5% German (2000).
Economy: Employment by occupation: 10.4% management, 13.8% professional, 14.8% services, 24.2% sales, 2.1% farming, 13.0% construction, 21.8% production (2000).
Income: Per capita income: $18,694 (2005); Median household income: $35,012 (2005); Average household income: $45,679 (2005); Percent of households with income of $100,000 or more: 7.3% (2005); Poverty rate: 9.8% (2000).
Education: Percent of population age 25 and over with: High school diploma (including GED) or higher: 75.3% (2005); Bachelor's degree or higher: 8.9% (2005); Master's degree or higher: 3.1% (2005).
Housing: Homeownership rate: 89.0% (2005); Median home value: $61,148 (2005); Median rent: $300 per month (2000); Median age of housing: 36 years (2000).
Transportation: Commute to work: 84.8% car, 2.1% public transportation, 5.3% walk, 7.7% work from home (2000); Travel time to work: 13.9% less than 15 minutes, 38.2% 15 to 30 minutes, 26.6% 30 to 45 minutes, 10.7% 45 to 60 minutes, 10.7% 60 minutes or more (2000)

MOUNT UPTON (unincorporated postal area, zip code 13809).
Covers a land area of 21.757 square miles and a water area of 0 square miles. Located at 42.39° N. Lat.; 75.41° W. Long. Elevation is 1,036 feet.
Population: 0 (2000); Race: 94.9% White, 1.6% Black, 0.2% Asian, 2.5% Hispanic of any race (2000); Density: 0.0 persons per square mile (2000); Age: 23.8% under 18, 10.8% over 64 (2000); Marriage status: 21.5% never married, 62.8% now married, 4.8% widowed, 10.9% divorced (2000); Foreign born: 0.8% (2000); Ancestry (includes multiple ancestries): 18.9% German, 16.2% English, 14.4% Irish, 13.3% United States or American, 9.5% Other groups (2000).
Economy: Employment by occupation: 7.5% management, 10.8% professional, 12.1% services, 22.1% sales, 0.8% farming, 17.1% construction, 29.7% production (2000).

Income: Per capita income: $15,080 (2000); Median household income: $36,574 (2000); Poverty rate: 10.7% (2000).
Education: Percent of population age 25 and over with: High school diploma (including GED) or higher: 81.5% (2000); Bachelor's degree or higher: 8.6% (2000).
Housing: Homeownership rate: 86.3% (2000); Median home value: $54,100 (2000); Median rent: $329 per month (2000); Median age of housing: 33 years (2000).
Transportation: Commute to work: 96.7% car, 0.7% public transportation, 1.0% walk, 0.5% work from home (2000); Travel time to work: 13.6% less than 15 minutes, 52.7% 15 to 30 minutes, 18.0% 30 to 45 minutes, 5.2% 45 to 60 minutes, 10.5% 60 minutes or more (2000)

NEW BERLIN (village). Covers a land area of 1.078 square miles and a water area of 0 square miles. Located at 42.62° N. Lat.; 75.33° W. Long. Elevation is 1,093 feet.
Population: 1,220 (1990); 1,129 (2000); 1,032 (2005); 1,004 (2010 projected); Race: 97.7% White, 0.5% Black, 0.4% Asian, 1.2% Hispanic of any race (2005); Density: 957.1 persons per square mile (2005); Average household size: 2.63 (2005); Median age: 44.3 (2005); Males per 100 females: 81.4 (2005); Marriage status: 23.3% never married, 55.4% now married, 11.6% widowed, 9.7% divorced (2000); Foreign born: 1.0% (2000); Ancestry (includes multiple ancestries): 18.7% English, 16.8% German, 15.5% Irish, 12.4% United States or American, 8.3% Dutch (2000).
Economy: Employment by occupation: 12.3% management, 16.3% professional, 18.4% services, 27.8% sales, 1.9% farming, 5.7% construction, 17.6% production (2000).
Income: Per capita income: $17,526 (2005); Median household income: $31,288 (2005); Average household income: $42,290 (2005); Percent of households with income of $100,000 or more: 6.6% (2005); Poverty rate: 18.5% (2000).
Education: Percent of population age 25 and over with: High school diploma (including GED) or higher: 76.1% (2005); Bachelor's degree or higher: 16.8% (2005); Master's degree or higher: 4.1% (2005).

School District(s)
Unadilla Valley Central School District (PK-12)
    2003-04 Enrollment: 1,096 . . . . (607) 847-7500

Housing: Homeownership rate: 61.6% (2005); Median home value: $70,811 (2005); Median rent: $327 per month (2000); Median age of housing: 60+ years (2000).
Transportation: Commute to work: 81.7% car, 2.1% public transportation, 9.4% walk, 5.3% work from home (2000); Travel time to work: 32.4% less than 15 minutes, 29.1% 15 to 30 minutes, 19.4% 30 to 45 minutes, 10.8% 45 to 60 minutes, 8.3% 60 minutes or more (2000)

NEW BERLIN (town). Covers a land area of 46.377 square miles and a water area of 0.309 square miles. Located at 42.60° N. Lat.; 75.39° W. Long. Elevation is 1,093 feet.
History: Incorporated 1819.
Population: 3,046 (1990); 2,803 (2000); 2,743 (2005); 2,724 (2010 projected); Race: 97.9% White, 0.5% Black, 0.2% Asian, 2.3% Hispanic of any race (2005); Density: 59.1 persons per square mile (2005); Average household size: 2.54 (2005); Median age: 41.4 (2005); Males per 100 females: 90.5 (2005); Marriage status: 21.5% never married, 59.8% now married, 8.7% widowed, 10.0% divorced (2000); Foreign born: 0.8% (2000); Ancestry (includes multiple ancestries): 22.0% English, 14.5% German, 13.6% Irish, 11.9% United States or American, 7.5% Other groups (2000).
Economy: In dairying and farming area. Agriculture: feed, lumber, wood products. Single-family building permits issued: 10 (2005); Multi-family building permits issued: 0 (2005); Employment by occupation: 12.1% management, 17.1% professional, 16.4% services, 23.7% sales, 2.4% farming, 8.2% construction, 20.2% production (2000).
Income: Per capita income: $18,954 (2005); Median household income: $36,218 (2005); Average household income: $46,782 (2005); Percent of households with income of $100,000 or more: 7.4% (2005); Poverty rate: 16.1% (2000).
Education: Percent of population age 25 and over with: High school diploma (including GED) or higher: 80.6% (2005); Bachelor's degree or higher: 15.9% (2005); Master's degree or higher: 5.7% (2005).
Housing: Homeownership rate: 75.6% (2005); Median home value: $82,033 (2005); Median rent: $326 per month (2000); Median age of housing: 49 years (2000).
Transportation: Commute to work: 87.5% car, 1.2% public transportation, 5.5% walk, 4.8% work from home (2000); Travel time to work: 29.7% less than 15 minutes, 36.1% 15 to 30 minutes, 16.5% 30 to 45 minutes, 6.8% 45 to 60 minutes, 10.9% 60 minutes or more (2000)

NORTH NORWICH (town). Aka Galena. Covers a land area of 28.216 square miles and a water area of 0.031 square miles. Located at 42.60° N. Lat.; 75.50° W. Long.
Population: 1,998 (1990); 1,966 (2000); 2,064 (2005); 2,093 (2010 projected); Race: 98.2% White, 0.4% Black, 0.9% Asian, 0.8% Hispanic of any race (2005); Density: 73.1 persons per square mile (2005); Average household size: 2.65 (2005); Median age: 38.2 (2005); Males per 100 females: 95.6 (2005); Marriage status: 23.9% never married, 60.8% now married, 6.4% widowed, 8.9% divorced (2000); Foreign born: 2.5% (2000); Ancestry (includes multiple ancestries): 20.3% English, 19.7% German, 16.0% Irish, 9.0% Italian, 8.2% United States or American (2000).
Economy: Employment by occupation: 15.3% management, 16.1% professional, 16.6% services, 22.3% sales, 1.9% farming, 10.1% construction, 17.7% production (2000).
Income: Per capita income: $20,574 (2005); Median household income: $41,387 (2005); Average household income: $54,582 (2005); Percent of households with income of $100,000 or more: 11.1% (2005); Poverty rate: 16.1% (2000).
Education: Percent of population age 25 and over with: High school diploma (including GED) or higher: 80.6% (2005); Bachelor's degree or higher: 13.8% (2005); Master's degree or higher: 6.1% (2005).
Housing: Homeownership rate: 85.6% (2005); Median home value: $88,810 (2005); Median rent: $348 per month (2000); Median age of housing: 28 years (2000).
Transportation: Commute to work: 92.3% car, 0.9% public transportation, 2.6% walk, 3.8% work from home (2000); Travel time to work: 47.9% less than 15 minutes, 31.3% 15 to 30 minutes, 5.4% 30 to 45 minutes, 6.7% 45 to 60 minutes, 8.7% 60 minutes or more (2000)

NORTH PITCHER (unincorporated postal area, zip code 13124). Covers a land area of 5.128 square miles and a water area of 0 square miles. Located at 42.63° N. Lat.; 75.82° W. Long.
Population: 0 (2000); Race: 97.7% White, 0.0% Black, 0.0% Asian, 5.2% Hispanic of any race (2000); Density: 0.0 persons per square mile (2000); Age: 29.3% under 18, 3.4% over 64 (2000); Marriage status: 33.6% never married, 58.7% now married, 1.4% widowed, 6.3% divorced (2000); Foreign born: 0.0% (2000); Ancestry (includes multiple ancestries): 25.3% German, 20.7% English, 16.1% Polish, 9.8% Irish, 8.6% Other groups (2000).
Economy: Employment by occupation: 4.2% management, 16.8% professional, 23.2% services, 21.1% sales, 0.0% farming, 17.9% construction, 16.8% production (2000).
Income: Per capita income: $12,761 (2000); Median household income: $35,938 (2000); Poverty rate: 6.4% (2000).
Education: Percent of population age 25 and over with: High school diploma (including GED) or higher: 88.2% (2000); Bachelor's degree or higher: 12.7% (2000).
Housing: Homeownership rate: 85.5% (2000); Median home value: $50,000 (2000); Median rent: $325 per month (2000); Median age of housing: 40 years (2000).
Transportation: Commute to work: 92.6% car, 0.0% public transportation, 5.3% walk, 2.1% work from home (2000); Travel time to work: 19.4% less than 15 minutes, 11.8% 15 to 30 minutes, 41.9% 30 to 45 minutes, 7.5% 45 to 60 minutes, 19.4% 60 minutes or more (2000)

NORWICH (city). Covers a land area of 2.038 square miles and a water area of 0 square miles. Located at 42.53° N. Lat.; 75.52° W. Long. Elevation is 1,015 feet.
Population: 7,753 (1990); 7,355 (2000); 7,246 (2005); 7,136 (2010 projected); Race: 95.6% White, 2.0% Black, 0.8% Asian, 1.0% Hispanic of any race (2005); Density: 3,555.5 persons per square mile (2005); Average household size: 2.33 (2005); Median age: 39.5 (2005); Males per 100 females: 80.6 (2005); Marriage status: 28.0% never married, 46.1% now married, 13.3% widowed, 12.6% divorced (2000); Foreign born: 3.2% (2000); Ancestry (includes multiple ancestries): 18.5% English, 18.4% Irish, 15.6% Italian, 14.9% German, 6.0% United States or American (2000).
Economy: Single-family building permits issued: 1 (2005); Multi-family building permits issued: 0 (2005); Employment by occupation: 15.1% management, 23.0% professional, 17.1% services, 24.1% sales, 0.5% farming, 8.8% construction, 11.3% production (2000).

Income: Per capita income: $18,706 (2005); Median household income: $29,891 (2005); Average household income: $41,107 (2005); Percent of households with income of $100,000 or more: 5.9% (2005); Poverty rate: 18.7% (2000).
Education: Percent of population age 25 and over with: High school diploma (including GED) or higher: 81.4% (2005); Bachelor's degree or higher: 20.8% (2005); Master's degree or higher: 8.3% (2005).

School District(s)
Boces Delaw-Chenango-Madison-Otsego (PK-PK)
   2003-04 Enrollment: 278 . . . . (607) 335-1233
Norwich City School District (PK-12)
   2003-04 Enrollment: 2,247 . . . . (607) 334-1600

Two-year College(s)
Delaware Chenango Madison Ostego BOCES-Practical Nursing (Public)
   Fall 2004 Enrollment: 53 . . . . (607) 337-4299
Housing: Homeownership rate: 48.3% (2005); Median home value: $87,230 (2005); Median rent: $372 per month (2000); Median age of housing: 60+ years (2000).
Hospitals: Chenango Memorial Hospital (139 beds)
Safety: Violent crime rate: 19.3 per 10,000 population; Property crime rate: 406.1 per 10,000 population (2004).
Newspapers: Gazette (General - Circulation 2,500); The Evening Sun (Circulation 5,800)
Transportation: Commute to work: 85.9% car, 0.2% public transportation, 9.9% walk, 3.2% work from home (2000); Travel time to work: 63.1% less than 15 minutes, 20.6% 15 to 30 minutes, 6.2% 30 to 45 minutes, 1.5% 45 to 60 minutes, 8.6% 60 minutes or more (2000)
Additional Information Contacts
Chenango County Chamber of Commerce . . . . (607) 334-1400
   http://www.chenangony.org
City of Norwich . . . . (607) 334-1230
   http://www.norwichnewyork.net/

NORWICH (town).
Covers a land area of 42.044 square miles and a water area of 0.055 square miles. Located at 42.51° N. Lat.; 75.49° W. Long. Elevation is 1,015 feet.
History: Gail Borden born here. Settled 1788. Incorporated 1915.
Population: 3,944 (1990); 3,836 (2000); 3,860 (2005); 3,895 (2010 projected); Race: 96.5% White, 0.7% Black, 0.6% Asian, 2.7% Hispanic of any race (2005); Density: 91.8 persons per square mile (2005); Average household size: 2.48 (2005); Median age: 41.1 (2005); Males per 100 females: 93.1 (2005); Marriage status: 17.5% never married, 65.8% now married, 8.0% widowed, 8.6% divorced (2000); Foreign born: 1.1% (2000); Ancestry (includes multiple ancestries): 20.5% German, 17.3% English, 17.1% Irish, 8.7% United States or American, 7.1% Other groups (2000).
Economy: Manufacturing: pharmaceuticals, aerospace electrical systems, wood and metal products, apparel. In dairying and farming area. Single-family building permits issued: 0 (2005); Multi-family building permits issued: 0 (2005); Employment by occupation: 11.6% management, 19.3% professional, 14.5% services, 30.4% sales, 0.3% farming, 8.0% construction, 16.0% production (2000).
Income: Per capita income: $20,756 (2005); Median household income: $40,752 (2005); Average household income: $51,524 (2005); Percent of households with income of $100,000 or more: 13.1% (2005); Poverty rate: 13.1% (2000).
Education: Percent of population age 25 and over with: High school diploma (including GED) or higher: 81.0% (2005); Bachelor's degree or higher: 15.1% (2005); Master's degree or higher: 6.6% (2005).
Housing: Homeownership rate: 85.5% (2005); Median home value: $88,895 (2005); Median rent: $361 per month (2000); Median age of housing: 28 years (2000).
Transportation: Commute to work: 94.8% car, 0.3% public transportation, 0.6% walk, 3.8% work from home (2000); Travel time to work: 48.3% less than 15 minutes, 28.9% 15 to 30 minutes, 8.5% 30 to 45 minutes, 5.1% 45 to 60 minutes, 9.2% 60 minutes or more (2000)

OTSELIC (town).
Covers a land area of 38.001 square miles and a water area of 0.040 square miles. Located at 42.69° N. Lat.; 75.73° W. Long.
Population: 990 (1990); 1,001 (2000); 1,022 (2005); 1,041 (2010 projected); Race: 98.3% White, 0.0% Black, 0.1% Asian, 2.3% Hispanic of any race (2005); Density: 26.9 persons per square mile (2005); Average household size: 2.75 (2005); Median age: 34.1 (2005); Males per 100 females: 100.4 (2005); Marriage status: 23.4% never married, 61.7% now married, 5.9% widowed, 9.0% divorced (2000); Foreign born: 1.3% (2000); Ancestry (includes multiple ancestries): 23.1% English, 17.0% Irish, 16.7% German, 9.6% Other groups, 6.6% French (except Basque) (2000).
Economy: Employment by occupation: 11.2% management, 15.0% professional, 15.2% services, 12.8% sales, 4.8% farming, 16.9% construction, 24.2% production (2000).
Income: Per capita income: $16,749 (2005); Median household income: $37,736 (2005); Average household income: $46,139 (2005); Percent of households with income of $100,000 or more: 6.5% (2005); Poverty rate: 16.0% (2000).
Education: Percent of population age 25 and over with: High school diploma (including GED) or higher: 79.4% (2005); Bachelor's degree or higher: 11.2% (2005); Master's degree or higher: 3.8% (2005).
Housing: Homeownership rate: 84.6% (2005); Median home value: $63,529 (2005); Median rent: $345 per month (2000); Median age of housing: 45 years (2000).
Transportation: Commute to work: 87.5% car, 0.5% public transportation, 5.5% walk, 6.5% work from home (2000); Travel time to work: 25.6% less than 15 minutes, 17.2% 15 to 30 minutes, 31.3% 30 to 45 minutes, 9.7% 45 to 60 minutes, 16.2% 60 minutes or more (2000)

OXFORD (village).
Covers a land area of 1.778 square miles and a water area of 0 square miles. Located at 42.44° N. Lat.; 75.59° W. Long. Elevation is 973 feet.
Population: 1,738 (1990); 1,584 (2000); 1,465 (2005); 1,429 (2010 projected); Race: 96.9% White, 1.6% Black, 0.8% Asian, 2.3% Hispanic of any race (2005); Density: 823.9 persons per square mile (2005); Average household size: 2.57 (2005); Median age: 40.2 (2005); Males per 100 females: 95.1 (2005); Marriage status: 26.2% never married, 52.7% now married, 8.1% widowed, 13.0% divorced (2000); Foreign born: 0.6% (2000); Ancestry (includes multiple ancestries): 25.9% English, 16.9% German, 16.7% Irish, 11.2% United States or American, 11.0% Other groups (2000).
Economy: Employment by occupation: 10.4% management, 25.1% professional, 16.8% services, 24.3% sales, 1.6% farming, 8.8% construction, 12.9% production (2000).
Income: Per capita income: $19,469 (2005); Median household income: $41,530 (2005); Average household income: $48,323 (2005); Percent of households with income of $100,000 or more: 6.7% (2005); Poverty rate: 14.3% (2000).
Education: Percent of population age 25 and over with: High school diploma (including GED) or higher: 84.4% (2005); Bachelor's degree or higher: 20.6% (2005); Master's degree or higher: 8.9% (2005).

School District(s)
Oxford Academy And Central School District (PK-12)
   2003-04 Enrollment: 955 . . . . (607) 843-2025
Housing: Homeownership rate: 67.6% (2005); Median home value: $84,667 (2005); Median rent: $308 per month (2000); Median age of housing: 60+ years (2000).
Safety: Violent crime rate: 6.4 per 10,000 population; Property crime rate: 267.9 per 10,000 population (2004).
Transportation: Commute to work: 88.3% car, 2.9% public transportation, 5.7% walk, 2.8% work from home (2000); Travel time to work: 39.2% less than 15 minutes, 38.9% 15 to 30 minutes, 9.5% 30 to 45 minutes, 6.0% 45 to 60 minutes, 6.5% 60 minutes or more (2000)

OXFORD (town).
Covers a land area of 60.090 square miles and a water area of 0.326 square miles. Located at 42.40° N. Lat.; 75.59° W. Long. Elevation is 973 feet.
History: Site of N.Y. State Women's Relief Corps Home built in 1896 and now operated as the N.Y. State Veterans' Home. Settled 1788; incorporated 1808.
Population: 4,075 (1990); 3,992 (2000); 3,887 (2005); 3,881 (2010 projected); Race: 96.8% White, 1.4% Black, 0.3% Asian, 1.9% Hispanic of any race (2005); Density: 64.7 persons per square mile (2005); Average household size: 2.73 (2005); Median age: 44.3 (2005); Males per 100 females: 101.1 (2005); Marriage status: 21.9% never married, 58.2% now married, 8.4% widowed, 11.5% divorced (2000); Foreign born: 1.9% (2000); Ancestry (includes multiple ancestries): 20.6% English, 16.7% Irish, 15.0% German, 8.5% Other groups, 7.8% United States or American (2000).
Economy: In agricultural area: poultry; dairy products. Employment by occupation: 12.2% management, 19.1% professional, 13.6% services, 22.5% sales, 2.6% farming, 9.4% construction, 20.6% production (2000).
Income: Per capita income: $17,777 (2005); Median household income: $36,548 (2005); Average household income: $44,967 (2005); Percent of

households with income of $100,000 or more: 6.8% (2005); Poverty rate: 13.6% (2000).
Education: Percent of population age 25 and over with: High school diploma (including GED) or higher: 81.3% (2005); Bachelor's degree or higher: 14.1% (2005); Master's degree or higher: 5.4% (2005).
Housing: Homeownership rate: 79.7% (2005); Median home value: $94,917 (2005); Median rent: $319 per month (2000); Median age of housing: 45 years (2000).
Transportation: Commute to work: 85.1% car, 1.3% public transportation, 3.4% walk, 9.1% work from home (2000); Travel time to work: 29.5% less than 15 minutes, 43.6% 15 to 30 minutes, 11.2% 30 to 45 minutes, 6.1% 45 to 60 minutes, 9.6% 60 minutes or more (2000)

PHARSALIA (town). Covers a land area of 38.841 square miles and a water area of 0.287 square miles. Located at 42.59° N. Lat.; 75.73° W. Long. Elevation is 1,562 feet.
Population: 735 (1990); 542 (2000); 554 (2005); 564 (2010 projected); Race: 98.4% White, 0.5% Black, 0.0% Asian, 0.9% Hispanic of any race (2005); Density: 14.3 persons per square mile (2005); Average household size: 2.68 (2005); Median age: 38.1 (2005); Males per 100 females: 101.5 (2005); Marriage status: 19.4% never married, 63.1% now married, 6.1% widowed, 11.4% divorced (2000); Foreign born: 2.6% (2000); Ancestry (includes multiple ancestries): 18.1% English, 11.6% Irish, 10.0% Other groups, 9.8% German, 7.3% Italian (2000).
Economy: Employment by occupation: 14.9% management, 11.8% professional, 19.0% services, 18.1% sales, 1.8% farming, 14.9% construction, 19.5% production (2000).
Income: Per capita income: $19,991 (2005); Median household income: $40,735 (2005); Average household income: $53,502 (2005); Percent of households with income of $100,000 or more: 8.7% (2005); Poverty rate: 22.1% (2000).
Education: Percent of population age 25 and over with: High school diploma (including GED) or higher: 80.1% (2005); Bachelor's degree or higher: 11.4% (2005); Master's degree or higher: 2.3% (2005).
Housing: Homeownership rate: 86.5% (2005); Median home value: $82,571 (2005); Median rent: $238 per month (2000); Median age of housing: 24 years (2000).
Transportation: Commute to work: 90.8% car, 0.9% public transportation, 0.9% walk, 7.4% work from home (2000); Travel time to work: 17.9% less than 15 minutes, 36.8% 15 to 30 minutes, 21.9% 30 to 45 minutes, 9.0% 45 to 60 minutes, 14.4% 60 minutes or more (2000)

PITCHER (town). Covers a land area of 28.479 square miles and a water area of 0 square miles. Located at 42.60° N. Lat.; 75.83° W. Long.
Population: 751 (1990); 848 (2000); 873 (2005); 895 (2010 projected); Race: 99.5% White, 0.3% Black, 0.0% Asian, 2.9% Hispanic of any race (2005); Density: 30.7 persons per square mile (2005); Average household size: 2.85 (2005); Median age: 35.6 (2005); Males per 100 females: 102.6 (2005); Marriage status: 30.5% never married, 56.8% now married, 3.2% widowed, 9.4% divorced (2000); Foreign born: 1.1% (2000); Ancestry (includes multiple ancestries): 17.5% German, 12.8% English, 11.7% Other groups, 9.5% Irish, 8.9% Dutch (2000).
Economy: Employment by occupation: 7.6% management, 11.3% professional, 18.0% services, 15.5% sales, 3.7% farming, 18.9% construction, 25.1% production (2000).
Income: Per capita income: $17,385 (2005); Median household income: $39,701 (2005); Average household income: $49,600 (2005); Percent of households with income of $100,000 or more: 8.2% (2005); Poverty rate: 17.0% (2000).
Education: Percent of population age 25 and over with: High school diploma (including GED) or higher: 76.1% (2005); Bachelor's degree or higher: 8.5% (2005); Master's degree or higher: 2.4% (2005).
Housing: Homeownership rate: 82.7% (2005); Median home value: $60,698 (2005); Median rent: $328 per month (2000); Median age of housing: 35 years (2000).
Transportation: Commute to work: 89.4% car, 0.0% public transportation, 2.6% walk, 8.0% work from home (2000); Travel time to work: 13.7% less than 15 minutes, 25.5% 15 to 30 minutes, 33.3% 30 to 45 minutes, 15.0% 45 to 60 minutes, 12.5% 60 minutes or more (2000)

PLYMOUTH (town). Covers a land area of 42.185 square miles and a water area of 0.151 square miles. Located at 42.60° N. Lat.; 75.60° W. Long.
Population: 1,704 (1990); 2,049 (2000); 2,067 (2005); 2,060 (2010 projected); Race: 88.1% White, 9.5% Black, 0.0% Asian, 8.6% Hispanic of any race (2005); Density: 49.0 persons per square mile (2005); Average household size: 2.96 (2005); Median age: 36.2 (2005); Males per 100 females: 134.4 (2005); Marriage status: 20.4% never married, 66.7% now married, 4.0% widowed, 9.0% divorced (2000); Foreign born: 1.4% (2000); Ancestry (includes multiple ancestries): 16.4% Irish, 14.0% German, 12.3% English, 9.0% United States or American, 8.6% Other groups (2000).
Economy: Employment by occupation: 10.8% management, 17.4% professional, 18.9% services, 20.6% sales, 1.9% farming, 11.8% construction, 18.6% production (2000).
Income: Per capita income: $17,052 (2005); Median household income: $39,662 (2005); Average household income: $47,930 (2005); Percent of households with income of $100,000 or more: 6.3% (2005); Poverty rate: 14.3% (2000).
Education: Percent of population age 25 and over with: High school diploma (including GED) or higher: 66.5% (2005); Bachelor's degree or higher: 9.6% (2005); Master's degree or higher: 3.5% (2005).
Housing: Homeownership rate: 84.5% (2005); Median home value: $75,217 (2005); Median rent: $363 per month (2000); Median age of housing: 27 years (2000).
Transportation: Commute to work: 95.5% car, 0.3% public transportation, 2.1% walk, 1.7% work from home (2000); Travel time to work: 27.2% less than 15 minutes, 48.3% 15 to 30 minutes, 10.2% 30 to 45 minutes, 5.2% 45 to 60 minutes, 9.1% 60 minutes or more (2000)

PRESTON (town). Covers a land area of 34.896 square miles and a water area of 0.150 square miles. Located at 42.51° N. Lat.; 75.61° W. Long.
Population: 1,100 (1990); 928 (2000); 946 (2005); 965 (2010 projected); Race: 96.7% White, 1.2% Black, 0.6% Asian, 1.1% Hispanic of any race (2005); Density: 27.1 persons per square mile (2005); Average household size: 2.65 (2005); Median age: 42.5 (2005); Males per 100 females: 110.2 (2005); Marriage status: 20.5% never married, 61.8% now married, 6.5% widowed, 11.2% divorced (2000); Foreign born: 1.4% (2000); Ancestry (includes multiple ancestries): 14.9% German, 13.6% English, 11.7% Irish, 11.7% United States or American, 8.6% Italian (2000).
Economy: Employment by occupation: 14.3% management, 13.2% professional, 17.9% services, 21.4% sales, 2.2% farming, 11.7% construction, 19.2% production (2000).
Income: Per capita income: $18,282 (2005); Median household income: $38,419 (2005); Average household income: $47,052 (2005); Percent of households with income of $100,000 or more: 8.1% (2005); Poverty rate: 11.5% (2000).
Education: Percent of population age 25 and over with: High school diploma (including GED) or higher: 71.8% (2005); Bachelor's degree or higher: 10.4% (2005); Master's degree or higher: 4.1% (2005).
Housing: Homeownership rate: 91.0% (2005); Median home value: $69,245 (2005); Median rent: $408 per month (2000); Median age of housing: 27 years (2000).
Transportation: Commute to work: 88.5% car, 1.4% public transportation, 3.2% walk, 7.0% work from home (2000); Travel time to work: 32.8% less than 15 minutes, 36.7% 15 to 30 minutes, 17.3% 30 to 45 minutes, 4.1% 45 to 60 minutes, 9.0% 60 minutes or more (2000)

SHERBURNE (village). Covers a land area of 1.520 square miles and a water area of 0 square miles. Located at 42.67° N. Lat.; 75.49° W. Long. Elevation is 1,055 feet.
Population: 1,531 (1990); 1,455 (2000); 1,320 (2005); 1,279 (2010 projected); Race: 98.6% White, 0.8% Black, 0.0% Asian, 2.0% Hispanic of any race (2005); Density: 868.2 persons per square mile (2005); Average household size: 2.19 (2005); Median age: 39.9 (2005); Males per 100 females: 87.8 (2005); Marriage status: 27.8% never married, 50.2% now married, 11.1% widowed, 10.9% divorced (2000); Foreign born: 1.0% (2000); Ancestry (includes multiple ancestries): 18.3% English, 17.5% Irish, 16.6% German, 10.2% Italian, 9.4% Other groups (2000).
Economy: Employment by occupation: 7.7% management, 20.2% professional, 18.3% services, 27.9% sales, 0.9% farming, 7.6% construction, 17.4% production (2000).
Income: Per capita income: $21,659 (2005); Median household income: $33,333 (2005); Average household income: $46,962 (2005); Percent of households with income of $100,000 or more: 7.5% (2005); Poverty rate: 18.6% (2000).
Taxes: Total city taxes per capita: $206 (2004); City property taxes per capita: $189 (2004).

Education: Percent of population age 25 and over with: High school diploma (including GED) or higher: 79.6% (2005); Bachelor's degree or higher: 21.6% (2005); Master's degree or higher: 7.3% (2005).

School District(s)
Sherburne-Earlville Central School District (KG-12)
   2003-04 Enrollment: 1,758 . . . . (607) 674-7300
Housing: Homeownership rate: 50.8% (2005); Median home value: $85,750 (2005); Median rent: $324 per month (2000); Median age of housing: 60+ years (2000).
Safety: Violent crime rate: 13.8 per 10,000 population; Property crime rate: 283.3 per 10,000 population (2004).
Newspapers: Sherburne News (General - Circulation 2,000)
Transportation: Commute to work: 86.9% car, 0.8% public transportation, 9.6% walk, 2.4% work from home (2000); Travel time to work: 37.8% less than 15 minutes, 38.6% 15 to 30 minutes, 6.7% 30 to 45 minutes, 2.6% 45 to 60 minutes, 14.3% 60 minutes or more (2000)

SHERBURNE (town). Covers a land area of 43.566 square miles and a water area of 0.011 square miles. Located at 42.68° N. Lat.; 75.49° W. Long. Elevation is 1,055 feet.
History: Former summer resort. Settled 1793, incorporated 1830.
Population: 3,903 (1990); 3,979 (2000); 4,064 (2005); 4,189 (2010 projected); Race: 98.4% White, 0.3% Black, 0.1% Asian, 1.5% Hispanic of any race (2005); Density: 93.3 persons per square mile (2005); Average household size: 2.42 (2005); Median age: 39.3 (2005); Males per 100 females: 93.4 (2005); Marriage status: 23.4% never married, 59.9% now married, 7.6% widowed, 9.1% divorced (2000); Foreign born: 0.5% (2000); Ancestry (includes multiple ancestries): 23.3% English, 13.5% Irish, 12.1% German, 11.5% United States or American, 10.0% Other groups (2000).
Economy: Manufacturing: pet foods, metalworking, hospital supplies, computer circuit boards, art supplies. In dairying area. Rogers Environmental Education Center. Employment by occupation: 11.4% management, 17.9% professional, 14.8% services, 25.5% sales, 2.6% farming, 9.8% construction, 18.0% production (2000).
Income: Per capita income: $20,028 (2005); Median household income: $36,654 (2005); Average household income: $48,314 (2005); Percent of households with income of $100,000 or more: 8.4% (2005); Poverty rate: 16.4% (2000).
Education: Percent of population age 25 and over with: High school diploma (including GED) or higher: 80.4% (2005); Bachelor's degree or higher: 14.4% (2005); Master's degree or higher: 6.3% (2005).
Housing: Homeownership rate: 71.5% (2005); Median home value: $85,464 (2005); Median rent: $346 per month (2000); Median age of housing: 49 years (2000).
Transportation: Commute to work: 89.0% car, 1.0% public transportation, 6.1% walk, 3.8% work from home (2000); Travel time to work: 38.8% less than 15 minutes, 36.9% 15 to 30 minutes, 10.0% 30 to 45 minutes, 4.5% 45 to 60 minutes, 9.8% 60 minutes or more (2000)

SMITHVILLE (town). Covers a land area of 50.542 square miles and a water area of 0.398 square miles. Located at 42.42° N. Lat.; 75.75° W. Long.
Population: 1,167 (1990); 1,347 (2000); 1,447 (2005); 1,533 (2010 projected); Race: 97.3% White, 0.8% Black, 0.5% Asian, 1.7% Hispanic of any race (2005); Density: 28.6 persons per square mile (2005); Average household size: 2.69 (2005); Median age: 39.8 (2005); Males per 100 females: 108.5 (2005); Marriage status: 24.3% never married, 61.3% now married, 6.5% widowed, 8.0% divorced (2000); Foreign born: 1.2% (2000); Ancestry (includes multiple ancestries): 20.1% German, 17.4% English, 14.2% Irish, 7.4% Dutch, 6.3% Other groups (2000).
Economy: Employment by occupation: 10.1% management, 16.4% professional, 14.4% services, 22.9% sales, 1.6% farming, 9.6% construction, 24.9% production (2000).
Income: Per capita income: $17,806 (2005); Median household income: $40,192 (2005); Average household income: $47,356 (2005); Percent of households with income of $100,000 or more: 5.9% (2005); Poverty rate: 9.7% (2000).
Education: Percent of population age 25 and over with: High school diploma (including GED) or higher: 80.5% (2005); Bachelor's degree or higher: 12.1% (2005); Master's degree or higher: 5.3% (2005).
Housing: Homeownership rate: 87.2% (2005); Median home value: $84,306 (2005); Median rent: $359 per month (2000); Median age of housing: 29 years (2000).
Transportation: Commute to work: 93.4% car, 0.2% public transportation, 0.6% walk, 3.7% work from home (2000); Travel time to work: 20.9% less than 15 minutes, 29.7% 15 to 30 minutes, 28.7% 30 to 45 minutes, 11.5% 45 to 60 minutes, 9.2% 60 minutes or more (2000)

SMITHVILLE FLATS (unincorporated postal area, zip code 13841). Covers a land area of 8.789 square miles and a water area of 0.289 square miles. Located at 42.42° N. Lat.; 75.83° W. Long. Elevation is 1,024 feet.
Population: 0 (2000); Race: 100.0% White, 0.0% Black, 0.0% Asian, 0.0% Hispanic of any race (2000); Density: 0.0 persons per square mile (2000); Age: 36.3% under 18, 10.0% over 64 (2000); Marriage status: 18.1% never married, 69.6% now married, 6.4% widowed, 6.0% divorced (2000); Foreign born: 1.4% (2000); Ancestry (includes multiple ancestries): 13.5% German, 11.9% English, 10.7% Irish, 9.4% Dutch, 6.6% French (except Basque) (2000).
Economy: Employment by occupation: 11.0% management, 12.3% professional, 14.7% services, 24.5% sales, 0.0% farming, 12.3% construction, 25.2% production (2000).
Income: Per capita income: $12,965 (2000); Median household income: $35,167 (2000); Poverty rate: 5.3% (2000).
Education: Percent of population age 25 and over with: High school diploma (including GED) or higher: 79.8% (2000); Bachelor's degree or higher: 5.4% (2000).
Housing: Homeownership rate: 84.2% (2000); Median home value: $52,200 (2000); Median rent: $325 per month (2000); Median age of housing: 36 years (2000).
Transportation: Commute to work: 95.0% car, 0.6% public transportation, 1.9% walk, 0.0% work from home (2000); Travel time to work: 28.6% less than 15 minutes, 26.1% 15 to 30 minutes, 35.4% 30 to 45 minutes, 6.8% 45 to 60 minutes, 3.1% 60 minutes or more (2000)

SMYRNA (village). Covers a land area of 0.246 square miles and a water area of 0 square miles. Located at 42.68° N. Lat.; 75.57° W. Long.
Population: 211 (1990); 241 (2000); 218 (2005); 210 (2010 projected); Race: 98.6% White, 0.0% Black, 0.0% Asian, 0.0% Hispanic of any race (2005); Density: 888.0 persons per square mile (2005); Average household size: 2.99 (2005); Median age: 31.8 (2005); Males per 100 females: 84.7 (2005); Marriage status: 33.3% never married, 57.8% now married, 3.3% widowed, 5.6% divorced (2000); Foreign born: 0.0% (2000); Ancestry (includes multiple ancestries): 22.6% English, 15.3% German, 12.8% United States or American, 6.4% Irish, 5.5% French Canadian (2000).
Economy: Employment by occupation: 2.6% management, 10.3% professional, 23.1% services, 14.5% sales, 3.4% farming, 17.1% construction, 29.1% production (2000).
Income: Per capita income: $12,156 (2005); Median household income: $37,946 (2005); Average household income: $36,301 (2005); Percent of households with income of $100,000 or more: 0.0% (2005); Poverty rate: 12.0% (2000).
Education: Percent of population age 25 and over with: High school diploma (including GED) or higher: 84.4% (2005); Bachelor's degree or higher: 13.3% (2005); Master's degree or higher: 2.3% (2005).
Housing: Homeownership rate: 61.6% (2005); Median home value: $53,571 (2005); Median rent: $302 per month (2000); Median age of housing: 60+ years (2000).
Transportation: Commute to work: 79.1% car, 4.3% public transportation, 8.7% walk, 7.8% work from home (2000); Travel time to work: 34.9% less than 15 minutes, 33.0% 15 to 30 minutes, 20.8% 30 to 45 minutes, 0.0% 45 to 60 minutes, 11.3% 60 minutes or more (2000)

SMYRNA (town). Covers a land area of 42.105 square miles and a water area of 0.071 square miles. Located at 42.68° N. Lat.; 75.62° W. Long.
Population: 1,265 (1990); 1,418 (2000); 1,411 (2005); 1,421 (2010 projected); Race: 98.3% White, 0.0% Black, 0.1% Asian, 0.7% Hispanic of any race (2005); Density: 33.5 persons per square mile (2005); Average household size: 2.95 (2005); Median age: 35.7 (2005); Males per 100 females: 103.6 (2005); Marriage status: 27.8% never married, 59.9% now married, 4.3% widowed, 8.0% divorced (2000); Foreign born: 1.2% (2000); Ancestry (includes multiple ancestries): 18.6% English, 13.5% United States or American, 12.8% German, 10.5% Irish, 6.0% Other groups (2000).
Economy: In dairying and lumbering area. Employment by occupation: 9.8% management, 11.3% professional, 17.1% services, 16.3% sales, 5.0% farming, 14.8% construction, 25.6% production (2000).
Income: Per capita income: $14,109 (2005); Median household income: $34,938 (2005); Average household income: $41,561 (2005); Percent of

households with income of $100,000 or more: 4.8% (2005); Poverty rate: 17.8% (2000).
Education: Percent of population age 25 and over with: High school diploma (including GED) or higher: 76.0% (2005); Bachelor's degree or higher: 8.0% (2005); Master's degree or higher: 2.9% (2005).
Housing: Homeownership rate: 81.6% (2005); Median home value: $65,890 (2005); Median rent: $311 per month (2000); Median age of housing: 29 years (2000).
Transportation: Commute to work: 86.8% car, 0.8% public transportation, 4.1% walk, 7.5% work from home (2000); Travel time to work: 34.5% less than 15 minutes, 36.0% 15 to 30 minutes, 15.6% 30 to 45 minutes, 3.0% 45 to 60 minutes, 10.9% 60 minutes or more (2000)

SOUTH NEW BERLIN (unincorporated postal area, zip code 13843). Covers a land area of 43.818 square miles and a water area of 0.242 square miles. Located at 42.53° N. Lat.; 75.38° W. Long. Elevation is 1,058 feet.
Population: 0 (2000); Race: 96.7% White, 0.4% Black, 0.0% Asian, 0.5% Hispanic of any race (2000); Density: 0.0 persons per square mile (2000); Age: 28.0% under 18, 10.2% over 64 (2000); Marriage status: 23.3% never married, 60.1% now married, 7.0% widowed, 9.5% divorced (2000); Foreign born: 1.3% (2000); Ancestry (includes multiple ancestries): 19.2% English, 17.3% German, 15.2% Irish, 10.4% Other groups, 7.8% United States or American (2000).
Economy: Employment by occupation: 14.7% management, 16.3% professional, 15.2% services, 18.0% sales, 2.2% farming, 9.7% construction, 23.8% production (2000).
Income: Per capita income: $17,751 (2000); Median household income: $34,522 (2000); Poverty rate: 13.3% (2000).
Education: Percent of population age 25 and over with: High school diploma (including GED) or higher: 84.9% (2000); Bachelor's degree or higher: 16.6% (2000).
School District(s)
Unadilla Valley Central School District (PK-12)
   2003-04 Enrollment: 1,096 . . . . (607) 847-7500
Housing: Homeownership rate: 83.5% (2000); Median home value: $56,800 (2000); Median rent: $351 per month (2000); Median age of housing: 37 years (2000).
Transportation: Commute to work: 92.1% car, 0.2% public transportation, 2.4% walk, 4.6% work from home (2000); Travel time to work: 20.0% less than 15 minutes, 45.5% 15 to 30 minutes, 14.5% 30 to 45 minutes, 5.4% 45 to 60 minutes, 14.6% 60 minutes or more (2000)

SOUTH OTSELIC (unincorporated postal area, zip code 13155). Covers a land area of 26.735 square miles and a water area of 0.051 square miles. Located at 42.66° N. Lat.; 75.76° W. Long. Elevation is 1,226 feet.
Population: 0 (2000); Race: 96.7% White, 1.2% Black, 0.0% Asian, 0.9% Hispanic of any race (2000); Density: 0.0 persons per square mile (2000); Age: 29.4% under 18, 13.0% over 64 (2000); Marriage status: 23.2% never married, 59.7% now married, 6.2% widowed, 10.9% divorced (2000); Foreign born: 1.3% (2000); Ancestry (includes multiple ancestries): 24.1% English, 16.1% Irish, 15.5% German, 12.4% Other groups, 9.5% United States or American (2000).
Economy: Employment by occupation: 10.5% management, 15.3% professional, 13.6% services, 14.6% sales, 3.4% farming, 20.0% construction, 22.7% production (2000).
Income: Per capita income: $15,938 (2000); Median household income: $34,167 (2000); Poverty rate: 13.3% (2000).
Education: Percent of population age 25 and over with: High school diploma (including GED) or higher: 81.1% (2000); Bachelor's degree or higher: 12.8% (2000).
School District(s)
Georgetown-South Otselic Central School District (KG-12)
   2003-04 Enrollment: 456 . . . . (315) 653-7591
Housing: Homeownership rate: 80.3% (2000); Median home value: $43,600 (2000); Median rent: $339 per month (2000); Median age of housing: 48 years (2000).
Transportation: Commute to work: 89.3% car, 1.4% public transportation, 4.5% walk, 4.8% work from home (2000); Travel time to work: 28.2% less than 15 minutes, 8.3% 15 to 30 minutes, 37.5% 30 to 45 minutes, 8.7% 45 to 60 minutes, 17.3% 60 minutes or more (2000)

SOUTH PLYMOUTH (unincorporated postal area, zip code 13844). Covers a land area of 31.688 square miles and a water area of 0.042 square miles. Located at 42.60° N. Lat.; 75.67° W. Long.
Population: 0 (2000); Race: 83.6% White, 13.5% Black, 0.8% Asian, 8.5% Hispanic of any race (2000); Density: 0.0 persons per square mile (2000); Age: 20.0% under 18, 9.5% over 64 (2000); Marriage status: 22.1% never married, 70.0% now married, 2.4% widowed, 5.5% divorced (2000); Foreign born: 1.4% (2000); Ancestry (includes multiple ancestries): 13.0% English, 9.7% German, 9.5% Irish, 7.4% United States or American, 6.9% Other groups (2000).
Economy: Employment by occupation: 9.7% management, 15.2% professional, 16.9% services, 21.6% sales, 1.4% farming, 15.0% construction, 20.2% production (2000).
Income: Per capita income: $12,964 (2000); Median household income: $33,309 (2000); Poverty rate: 18.3% (2000).
Education: Percent of population age 25 and over with: High school diploma (including GED) or higher: 60.2% (2000); Bachelor's degree or higher: 7.2% (2000).
School District(s)
Unadilla Valley Central School District (PK-12)
   2003-04 Enrollment: 1,096 . . . . (607) 847-7500
Housing: Homeownership rate: 86.9% (2000); Median home value: $51,000 (2000); Median rent: $328 per month (2000); Median age of housing: 25 years (2000).
Transportation: Commute to work: 96.3% car, 0.6% public transportation, 0.6% walk, 2.5% work from home (2000); Travel time to work: 16.2% less than 15 minutes, 51.4% 15 to 30 minutes, 16.2% 30 to 45 minutes, 4.3% 45 to 60 minutes, 11.8% 60 minutes or more (2000)

Clinton County

Located in northeastern New York; bounded on the north by the Canadian province of Quebec, and on the east by Lake Champlain and the Vermont border; includes the North Adirondacks. Covers a land area of 1,038.95 square miles, a water area of 78.67 square miles, and is located in the Eastern Time Zone. The county government was organized in 1788. County seat is Plattsburgh.

Clinton County is part of the Plattsburgh, NY Micropolitan Statistical Area. The entire metro area includes: Clinton County, NY

Weather Station: Chazy   Elevation: 167 feet

	Jan	Feb	Mar	Apr	May	Jun	Jul	Aug	Sep	Oct	Nov	Dec
High	27	30	40	55	68	76	81	78	69	57	45	32
Low	6	9	20	33	44	53	58	56	48	37	28	14
Precip	1.1	na	1.4	2.4	2.9	3.2	3.6	3.9	3.5	3.0	2.6	1.5
Snow	14.0	11.0	9.1	2.9	0.1	0.0	0.0	0.0	0.0	0.3	5.8	12.8

High and Low temperatures in degrees Fahrenheit; Precipitation and Snow in inches

Weather Station: Dannemora   Elevation: 1,338 feet

	Jan	Feb	Mar	Apr	May	Jun	Jul	Aug	Sep	Oct	Nov	Dec
High	26	29	39	52	66	75	79	76	68	56	42	31
Low	7	10	20	33	45	54	58	56	48	38	27	14
Precip	2.3	2.0	2.3	2.9	3.2	3.6	3.8	4.4	4.0	3.4	3.3	2.8
Snow	na	na	na	3.6	tr	0.0	0.0	0.0	tr	0.2	na	na

High and Low temperatures in degrees Fahrenheit; Precipitation and Snow in inches

Weather Station: Peru 2 WSW   Elevation: 508 feet

	Jan	Feb	Mar	Apr	May	Jun	Jul	Aug	Sep	Oct	Nov	Dec
High	28	31	41	55	69	77	82	79	70	58	45	33
Low	8	11	21	33	44	54	59	56	48	37	28	16
Precip	1.6	1.5	1.8	2.6	2.6	3.3	3.4	3.4	3.1	2.8	2.7	2.0
Snow	13.5	12.1	11.1	4.0	0.0	0.0	0.0	0.0	0.0	0.5	4.3	12.9

High and Low temperatures in degrees Fahrenheit; Precipitation and Snow in Inches

Population: 85,969 (1990); 79,894 (2000); 82,084 (2005); 84,330 (2010 projected); Race: 93.0% White, 3.6% Black, 0.9% Asian, 2.9% Hispanic of any race (2005); Density: 79.0 persons per square mile (2005); Average household size: 2.66 (2005); Median age: 37.0 (2005); Males per 100 females: 104.3 (2005).
Religion: Five largest groups: 60.9% Catholic Church, 2.8% The United Methodist Church, 1.4% The Wesleyan Church, 1.0% Presbyterian Church (U.S.A.), 0.6% Episcopal Church (2000).
Economy: Unemployment rate: 5.3% (2005); Total civilian labor force: 39,892 (2005); Leading industries: 18.5% manufacturing; 18.5% health care and social assistance; 17.0% retail trade (2003); Farms: 604 totaling

168,536 acres (2002); Companies that employ 500 or more persons: 3 (2003); Companies that employ 100 to 499 persons: 36 (2003); Companies that employ less than 100 persons: 1,864 (2003); Black-owned businesses: n/a (2002); Hispanic-owned businesses: n/a (2002); Women-owned businesses: 1,246 (2002); Retail sales per capita: $13,417 (2006). Single-family building permits issued: 263 (2005); Multi-family building permits issued: 62 (2005).
Income: Per capita income: $21,031 (2005); Median household income: $42,442 (2005); Average household income: $52,477 (2005); Percent of households with income of $100,000 or more: 10.5% (2005); Poverty rate: 12.6% (2003); Bankruptcy rate: 5.42% (2005).
Taxes: Total county taxes per capita: $603 (2004); County property taxes per capita: $170 (2004).
Education: Percent of population age 25 and over with: High school diploma (including GED) or higher: 76.6% (2005); Bachelor's degree or higher: 18.0% (2005); Master's degree or higher: 8.1% (2005).
Housing: Homeownership rate: 68.3% (2005); Median home value: $117,072 (2005); Median rent: $395 per month (2000); Median age of housing: 34 years (2000).
Health: Birth rate: 94.4 per 10,000 population (2004); Death rate: 87.8 per 10,000 population (2004); Age-adjusted cancer mortality rate: 224.1 deaths per 100,000 population (2002); Number of physicians: 23.0 per 10,000 population (2000); Hospital beds: 48.5 per 10,000 population (2003); Hospital admissions: 1,230.0 per 10,000 population (2003).
Elections: 2004 Presidential election results: 45.4% Bush, 52.2% Kerry, 2.0% Nader, 0.2% Badnarik
National and State Parks: Ausable Marsh State Game Management Area; Clinton State Forest; Clinton State Forest Number Eight; Cumberland Bay State Park; King Bay State Wetlands Game Management Area; Lake Alice State Game Management Area; Miner Lake State Park; New York State Game Management Area
Additional Information Contacts
Clinton County Government . . . . (518) 565-4600
    http://www.co.clinton.ny.us/
Town of Clinton . . . . (845) 266-5853
    http://www.townofclinton.com/

Clinton County Communities

ALTONA (town). Covers a land area of 101.061 square miles and a water area of 0.278 square miles. Located at 44.87° N. Lat.; 73.65° W. Long.
Population: 2,775 (1990); 3,160 (2000); 3,184 (2005); 3,216 (2010 projected); Race: 82.6% White, 11.6% Black, 0.1% Asian, 9.1% Hispanic of any race (2005); Density: 31.5 persons per square mile (2005); Average household size: 3.43 (2005); Median age: 36.2 (2005); Males per 100 females: 156.4 (2005); Marriage status: 34.7% never married, 51.3% now married, 5.3% widowed, 8.6% divorced (2000); Foreign born: 5.1% (2000); Ancestry (includes multiple ancestries): 15.5% French (except Basque), 13.7% French Canadian, 12.4% United States or American, 6.8% English, 6.0% Other groups (2000).
Economy: Single-family building permits issued: 11 (2005); Multi-family building permits issued: 0 (2005); Employment by occupation: 6.5% management, 13.7% professional, 19.4% services, 18.7% sales, 1.1% farming, 12.3% construction, 28.3% production (2000).
Income: Per capita income: $17,612 (2005); Median household income: $42,240 (2005); Average household income: $47,433 (2005); Percent of households with income of $100,000 or more: 6.7% (2005); Poverty rate: 12.6% (2000).
Education: Percent of population age 25 and over with: High school diploma (including GED) or higher: 59.1% (2005); Bachelor's degree or higher: 7.2% (2005); Master's degree or higher: 2.9% (2005).
School District(s)
Chazy Union Free School District (KG-12)
    2003-04 Enrollment: 611 . . . . (518) 846-7135
Housing: Homeownership rate: 82.7% (2005); Median home value: $89,516 (2005); Median rent: $303 per month (2000); Median age of housing: 26 years (2000).
Transportation: Commute to work: 92.9% car, 1.9% public transportation, 1.9% walk, 2.7% work from home (2000); Travel time to work: 10.2% less than 15 minutes, 42.0% 15 to 30 minutes, 34.5% 30 to 45 minutes, 6.8% 45 to 60 minutes, 6.5% 60 minutes or more (2000)

ALTONA (CDP). Covers a land area of 1.680 square miles and a water area of 0 square miles. Located at 44.89° N. Lat.; 73.65° W. Long.
Population: 1,018 (1990); 1,056 (2000); 1,014 (2005); 1,030 (2010 projected); Race: 47.3% White, 36.0% Black, 0.1% Asian, 27.4% Hispanic of any race (2005); Density: 603.6 persons per square mile (2005); Average household size: 7.40 (2005); Median age: 34.8 (2005); Males per 100 females: 541.8 (2005); Marriage status: 52.8% never married, 36.4% now married, 4.4% widowed, 6.5% divorced (2000); Foreign born: 10.2% (2000); Ancestry (includes multiple ancestries): 9.5% French Canadian, 6.5% French (except Basque), 3.9% English, 2.6% United States or American, 1.7% Irish (2000).
Economy: Employment by occupation: 5.9% management, 12.5% professional, 15.8% services, 23.0% sales, 0.0% farming, 12.5% construction, 30.3% production (2000).
Income: Per capita income: $18,392 (2005); Median household income: $49,559 (2005); Average household income: $48,449 (2005); Percent of households with income of $100,000 or more: 6.6% (2005); Poverty rate: 14.8% (2000).
Education: Percent of population age 25 and over with: High school diploma (including GED) or higher: 35.1% (2005); Bachelor's degree or higher: 3.2% (2005); Master's degree or higher: 1.5% (2005).
Housing: Homeownership rate: 65.0% (2005); Median home value: $75,217 (2005); Median rent: $240 per month (2000); Median age of housing: 48 years (2000).
Transportation: Commute to work: 93.3% car, 4.0% public transportation, 2.7% walk, 0.0% work from home (2000); Travel time to work: 24.2% less than 15 minutes, 30.2% 15 to 30 minutes, 28.9% 30 to 45 minutes, 6.7% 45 to 60 minutes, 10.1% 60 minutes or more (2000)

AU SABLE (town). Covers a land area of 39.119 square miles and a water area of 4.759 square miles. Located at 44.51° N. Lat.; 73.51° W. Long.
Population: 2,870 (1990); 3,015 (2000); 3,032 (2005); 3,060 (2010 projected); Race: 97.5% White, 1.0% Black, 0.4% Asian, 1.6% Hispanic of any race (2005); Density: 77.5 persons per square mile (2005); Average household size: 2.50 (2005); Median age: 38.9 (2005); Males per 100 females: 96.8 (2005); Marriage status: 20.1% never married, 63.1% now married, 8.1% widowed, 8.8% divorced (2000); Foreign born: 2.4% (2000); Ancestry (includes multiple ancestries): 23.4% French (except Basque), 13.9% English, 13.2% Irish, 9.6% French Canadian, 8.6% United States or American (2000).
Economy: Single-family building permits issued: 10 (2005); Multi-family building permits issued: 0 (2005); Employment by occupation: 8.7% management, 16.4% professional, 24.0% services, 21.8% sales, 1.4% farming, 11.1% construction, 16.7% production (2000).
Income: Per capita income: $18,234 (2005); Median household income: $37,480 (2005); Average household income: $45,120 (2005); Percent of households with income of $100,000 or more: 6.6% (2005); Poverty rate: 12.0% (2000).
Education: Percent of population age 25 and over with: High school diploma (including GED) or higher: 75.9% (2005); Bachelor's degree or higher: 12.5% (2005); Master's degree or higher: 5.6% (2005).
Housing: Homeownership rate: 73.9% (2005); Median home value: $96,623 (2005); Median rent: $376 per month (2000); Median age of housing: 33 years (2000).
Transportation: Commute to work: 93.1% car, 0.0% public transportation, 2.3% walk, 4.4% work from home (2000); Travel time to work: 22.9% less than 15 minutes, 44.4% 15 to 30 minutes, 21.4% 30 to 45 minutes, 6.9% 45 to 60 minutes, 4.5% 60 minutes or more (2000)

AU SABLE FORKS (CDP). Covers a land area of 2.495 square miles and a water area of 0.009 square miles. Located at 44.44° N. Lat.; 73.67° W. Long.
Population: 668 (1990); 670 (2000); 672 (2005); 676 (2010 projected); Race: 98.8% White, 0.4% Black, 0.0% Asian, 0.3% Hispanic of any race (2005); Density: 269.3 persons per square mile (2005); Average household size: 2.46 (2005); Median age: 38.0 (2005); Males per 100 females: 99.4 (2005); Marriage status: 18.1% never married, 62.3% now married, 10.1% widowed, 9.5% divorced (2000); Foreign born: 0.0% (2000); Ancestry (includes multiple ancestries): 29.4% French (except Basque), 15.8% United States or American, 13.7% Irish, 13.2% English, 10.2% French Canadian (2000).
Economy: Employment by occupation: 6.8% management, 12.1% professional, 33.5% services, 21.4% sales, 0.4% farming, 17.4% construction, 8.5% production (2000).
Income: Per capita income: $18,750 (2005); Median household income: $37,974 (2005); Average household income: $46,154 (2005); Percent of

households with income of $100,000 or more: 9.2% (2005); Poverty rate: 13.5% (2000).
Education: Percent of population age 25 and over with: High school diploma (including GED) or higher: 74.9% (2005); Bachelor's degree or higher: 7.5% (2005); Master's degree or higher: 3.6% (2005).
Housing: Homeownership rate: 69.2% (2005); Median home value: $96,765 (2005); Median rent: $317 per month (2000); Median age of housing: 53 years (2000).
Transportation: Commute to work: 89.2% car, 1.1% public transportation, 7.9% walk, 1.8% work from home (2000); Travel time to work: 31.4% less than 15 minutes, 13.5% 15 to 30 minutes, 38.7% 30 to 45 minutes, 12.0% 45 to 60 minutes, 4.4% 60 minutes or more (2000)

BEEKMANTOWN (town). Covers a land area of 60.473 square miles and a water area of 9.126 square miles. Located at 44.77° N. Lat.; 73.50° W. Long.
Population: 5,108 (1990); 5,326 (2000); 5,525 (2005); 5,726 (2010 projected); Race: 97.5% White, 0.8% Black, 0.5% Asian, 1.3% Hispanic of any race (2005); Density: 91.4 persons per square mile (2005); Average household size: 2.60 (2005); Median age: 38.9 (2005); Males per 100 females: 99.1 (2005); Marriage status: 23.0% never married, 63.3% now married, 4.6% widowed, 9.0% divorced (2000); Foreign born: 2.0% (2000); Ancestry (includes multiple ancestries): 24.8% French (except Basque), 12.8% French Canadian, 12.5% Irish, 11.3% United States or American, 8.9% English (2000).
Economy: Single-family building permits issued: 22 (2005); Multi-family building permits issued: 0 (2005); Employment by occupation: 9.6% management, 19.6% professional, 19.6% services, 23.7% sales, 1.7% farming, 9.1% construction, 16.6% production (2000).
Income: Per capita income: $23,256 (2005); Median household income: $48,785 (2005); Average household income: $60,189 (2005); Percent of households with income of $100,000 or more: 12.7% (2005); Poverty rate: 12.9% (2000).
Education: Percent of population age 25 and over with: High school diploma (including GED) or higher: 79.9% (2005); Bachelor's degree or higher: 19.9% (2005); Master's degree or higher: 8.4% (2005).
Housing: Homeownership rate: 82.1% (2005); Median home value: $121,005 (2005); Median rent: $389 per month (2000); Median age of housing: 23 years (2000).
Transportation: Commute to work: 93.5% car, 0.3% public transportation, 1.9% walk, 4.3% work from home (2000); Travel time to work: 33.5% less than 15 minutes, 51.8% 15 to 30 minutes, 6.7% 30 to 45 minutes, 2.8% 45 to 60 minutes, 5.3% 60 minutes or more (2000)

BLACK BROOK (town). Covers a land area of 130.203 square miles and a water area of 4.145 square miles. Located at 44.50° N. Lat.; 73.78° W. Long. Elevation is 966 feet.
Population: 1,556 (1990); 1,660 (2000); 1,752 (2005); 1,845 (2010 projected); Race: 98.3% White, 0.2% Black, 0.2% Asian, 0.8% Hispanic of any race (2005); Density: 13.5 persons per square mile (2005); Average household size: 2.49 (2005); Median age: 40.0 (2005); Males per 100 females: 102.8 (2005); Marriage status: 23.8% never married, 60.2% now married, 8.2% widowed, 7.8% divorced (2000); Foreign born: 0.5% (2000); Ancestry (includes multiple ancestries): 31.2% French (except Basque), 15.8% Irish, 12.0% United States or American, 11.0% French Canadian, 9.3% English (2000).
Economy: Single-family building permits issued: 7 (2005); Multi-family building permits issued: 0 (2005); Employment by occupation: 7.0% management, 11.3% professional, 33.1% services, 19.8% sales, 2.3% farming, 14.1% construction, 12.4% production (2000).
Income: Per capita income: $21,978 (2005); Median household income: $40,712 (2005); Average household income: $54,772 (2005); Percent of households with income of $100,000 or more: 10.8% (2005); Poverty rate: 14.0% (2000).
Education: Percent of population age 25 and over with: High school diploma (including GED) or higher: 76.7% (2005); Bachelor's degree or higher: 9.6% (2005); Master's degree or higher: 4.0% (2005).
Housing: Homeownership rate: 80.8% (2005); Median home value: $98,750 (2005); Median rent: $323 per month (2000); Median age of housing: 40 years (2000).
Transportation: Commute to work: 90.4% car, 0.9% public transportation, 6.7% walk, 2.1% work from home (2000); Travel time to work: 20.9% less than 15 minutes, 18.2% 15 to 30 minutes, 41.8% 30 to 45 minutes, 12.1% 45 to 60 minutes, 7.1% 60 minutes or more (2000)

CADYVILLE (unincorporated postal area, zip code 12918). Covers a land area of 36.924 square miles and a water area of 0.015 square miles. Located at 44.69° N. Lat.; 73.66° W. Long. Elevation is 747 feet.
Population: 0 (2000); Race: 99.1% White, 0.4% Black, 0.0% Asian, 0.0% Hispanic of any race (2000); Density: 0.0 persons per square mile (2000); Age: 26.1% under 18, 12.3% over 64 (2000); Marriage status: 23.3% never married, 66.5% now married, 4.4% widowed, 5.8% divorced (2000); Foreign born: 2.2% (2000); Ancestry (includes multiple ancestries): 25.1% French (except Basque), 15.1% Irish, 14.6% French Canadian, 12.5% English, 12.1% United States or American (2000).
Economy: In Adirondack Park. Employment by occupation: 6.7% management, 19.1% professional, 27.5% services, 25.5% sales, 0.0% farming, 5.2% construction, 16.1% production (2000).
Income: Per capita income: $19,438 (2000); Median household income: $47,057 (2000); Poverty rate: 6.8% (2000).
Education: Percent of population age 25 and over with: High school diploma (including GED) or higher: 83.3% (2000); Bachelor's degree or higher: 16.1% (2000).
School District(s)
Saranac Central School District (KG-12)
    2003-04 Enrollment: 1,968 . . . . (518) 565-5600
Housing: Homeownership rate: 87.0% (2000); Median home value: $78,400 (2000); Median rent: $390 per month (2000); Median age of housing: 40 years (2000).
Transportation: Commute to work: 94.3% car, 0.6% public transportation, 1.3% walk, 3.1% work from home (2000); Travel time to work: 25.5% less than 15 minutes, 47.9% 15 to 30 minutes, 16.7% 30 to 45 minutes, 6.5% 45 to 60 minutes, 3.5% 60 minutes or more (2000)

CHAMPLAIN (village). Covers a land area of 1.402 square miles and a water area of 0.048 square miles. Located at 44.98° N. Lat.; 73.44° W. Long. Elevation is 152 feet.
Population: 1,326 (1990); 1,173 (2000); 1,086 (2005); 1,071 (2010 projected); Race: 96.8% White, 0.9% Black, 0.8% Asian, 1.1% Hispanic of any race (2005); Density: 774.6 persons per square mile (2005); Average household size: 2.19 (2005); Median age: 40.9 (2005); Males per 100 females: 86.6 (2005); Marriage status: 24.6% never married, 54.2% now married, 10.5% widowed, 10.7% divorced (2000); Foreign born: 6.5% (2000); Ancestry (includes multiple ancestries): 21.5% French (except Basque), 18.1% French Canadian, 12.5% United States or American, 10.1% Other groups, 10.1% Irish (2000).
Economy: Single-family building permits issued: 1 (2005); Multi-family building permits issued: 0 (2005); Employment by occupation: 10.0% management, 17.5% professional, 15.2% services, 31.0% sales, 0.4% farming, 4.6% construction, 21.2% production (2000).
Income: Per capita income: $20,510 (2005); Median household income: $34,407 (2005); Average household income: $44,909 (2005); Percent of households with income of $100,000 or more: 8.3% (2005); Poverty rate: 10.7% (2000).
Education: Percent of population age 25 and over with: High school diploma (including GED) or higher: 69.1% (2005); Bachelor's degree or higher: 14.7% (2005); Master's degree or higher: 6.9% (2005).
School District(s)
Northeastern Clinton Central School District (KG-12)
    2003-04 Enrollment: 1,657 . . . . (518) 298-8242
Housing: Homeownership rate: 59.8% (2005); Median home value: $91,714 (2005); Median rent: $352 per month (2000); Median age of housing: 60+ years (2000).
Transportation: Commute to work: 88.4% car, 2.3% public transportation, 7.5% walk, 0.9% work from home (2000); Travel time to work: 64.6% less than 15 minutes, 17.0% 15 to 30 minutes, 11.0% 30 to 45 minutes, 2.1% 45 to 60 minutes, 5.3% 60 minutes or more (2000)

CHAMPLAIN (town). Covers a land area of 51.211 square miles and a water area of 7.622 square miles. Located at 44.96° N. Lat.; 73.41° W. Long. Elevation is 152 feet.
History: Settled 1789, incorporated 1873.
Population: 5,796 (1990); 5,791 (2000); 5,980 (2005); 6,176 (2010 projected); Race: 97.4% White, 0.7% Black, 0.5% Asian, 1.3% Hispanic of any race (2005); Density: 116.8 persons per square mile (2005); Average household size: 2.37 (2005); Median age: 40.1 (2005); Males per 100 females: 95.4 (2005); Marriage status: 23.4% never married, 58.1% now married, 7.6% widowed, 10.9% divorced (2000); Foreign born: 6.5% (2000); Ancestry (includes multiple ancestries): 20.5% French (except

Basque), 19.6% French Canadian, 14.9% United States or American, 10.4% Irish, 9.0% English (2000).
Economy: Port of entry. Manufacturing: knitting mills, textiles. Single-family building permits issued: 11 (2005); Multi-family building permits issued: 0 (2005); Employment by occupation: 11.7% management, 13.8% professional, 16.0% services, 26.3% sales, 1.1% farming, 6.9% construction, 24.3% production (2000).
Income: Per capita income: $22,489 (2005); Median household income: $43,118 (2005); Average household income: $52,807 (2005); Percent of households with income of $100,000 or more: 11.0% (2005); Poverty rate: 9.2% (2000).
Education: Percent of population age 25 and over with: High school diploma (including GED) or higher: 77.4% (2005); Bachelor's degree or higher: 15.2% (2005); Master's degree or higher: 4.5% (2005).
Housing: Homeownership rate: 68.9% (2005); Median home value: $110,458 (2005); Median rent: $363 per month (2000); Median age of housing: 42 years (2000).
Transportation: Commute to work: 85.8% car, 1.0% public transportation, 9.1% walk, 2.8% work from home (2000); Travel time to work: 60.8% less than 15 minutes, 19.4% 15 to 30 minutes, 10.2% 30 to 45 minutes, 2.7% 45 to 60 minutes, 7.0% 60 minutes or more (2000)

CHAZY (town). Covers a land area of 54.174 square miles and a water area of 7.116 square miles. Located at 44.85° N. Lat.; 73.46° W. Long. Elevation is 151 feet.
History: Miner Institute, agricultural and environmental research center, founded by William Miner, Railroad industrialist and philanthropist, in the 19th century.
Population: 3,890 (1990); 4,181 (2000); 4,278 (2005); 4,385 (2010 projected); Race: 97.7% White, 0.4% Black, 0.8% Asian, 0.9% Hispanic of any race (2005); Density: 79.0 persons per square mile (2005); Average household size: 2.61 (2005); Median age: 38.8 (2005); Males per 100 females: 96.4 (2005); Marriage status: 21.2% never married, 66.3% now married, 5.7% widowed, 6.9% divorced (2000); Foreign born: 5.2% (2000); Ancestry (includes multiple ancestries): 22.7% French (except Basque), 16.7% United States or American, 14.4% French Canadian, 11.8% Irish, 10.8% English (2000).
Economy: In agricultural area. Single-family building permits issued: 18 (2005); Multi-family building permits issued: 0 (2005); Employment by occupation: 9.5% management, 18.5% professional, 17.7% services, 22.3% sales, 1.5% farming, 9.9% construction, 20.5% production (2000).
Income: Per capita income: $21,888 (2005); Median household income: $48,442 (2005); Average household income: $56,666 (2005); Percent of households with income of $100,000 or more: 11.8% (2005); Poverty rate: 10.0% (2000).
Education: Percent of population age 25 and over with: High school diploma (including GED) or higher: 80.3% (2005); Bachelor's degree or higher: 20.2% (2005); Master's degree or higher: 6.7% (2005).
School District(s)
Chazy Union Free School District (KG-12)
   2003-04 Enrollment: 611 . . . . (518) 846-7135
Housing: Homeownership rate: 80.5% (2005); Median home value: $125,969 (2005); Median rent: $394 per month (2000); Median age of housing: 33 years (2000).
Transportation: Commute to work: 93.3% car, 0.8% public transportation, 1.4% walk, 4.1% work from home (2000); Travel time to work: 24.5% less than 15 minutes, 55.9% 15 to 30 minutes, 13.2% 30 to 45 minutes, 1.8% 45 to 60 minutes, 4.6% 60 minutes or more (2000)

CHURUBUSCO (unincorporated postal area, zip code 12923). Covers a land area of 57.245 square miles and a water area of 0.023 square miles. Located at 44.94° N. Lat.; 73.96° W. Long. Elevation is 1,194 feet.
Population: 0 (2000); Race: 99.1% White, 0.0% Black, 0.0% Asian, 0.9% Hispanic of any race (2000); Density: 0.0 persons per square mile (2000); Age: 25.8% under 18, 13.6% over 64 (2000); Marriage status: 21.5% never married, 63.7% now married, 7.7% widowed, 7.1% divorced (2000); Foreign born: 1.9% (2000); Ancestry (includes multiple ancestries): 29.8% French (except Basque), 17.4% French Canadian, 11.1% Other groups, 9.1% Irish, 8.5% United States or American (2000).
Economy: Employment by occupation: 16.9% management, 13.2% professional, 18.4% services, 14.3% sales, 9.2% farming, 6.6% construction, 21.3% production (2000).
Income: Per capita income: $12,166 (2000); Median household income: $28,015 (2000); Poverty rate: 19.9% (2000).

Education: Percent of population age 25 and over with: High school diploma (including GED) or higher: 65.1% (2000); Bachelor's degree or higher: 7.6% (2000).
Housing: Homeownership rate: 79.9% (2000); Median home value: $42,900 (2000); Median rent: $250 per month (2000); Median age of housing: 60+ years (2000).
Transportation: Commute to work: 82.8% car, 0.7% public transportation, 5.2% walk, 10.1% work from home (2000); Travel time to work: 35.7% less than 15 minutes, 18.7% 15 to 30 minutes, 24.5% 30 to 45 minutes, 10.4% 45 to 60 minutes, 10.8% 60 minutes or more (2000)

CLINTON (town). Covers a land area of 67.113 square miles and a water area of 0.029 square miles. Located at 44.94° N. Lat.; 73.94° W. Long.
Population: 663 (1990); 727 (2000); 769 (2005); 790 (2010 projected); Race: 98.3% White, 0.1% Black, 0.4% Asian, 0.5% Hispanic of any race (2005); Density: 11.5 persons per square mile (2005); Average household size: 2.62 (2005); Median age: 40.3 (2005); Males per 100 females: 109.0 (2005); Marriage status: 23.1% never married, 63.5% now married, 7.0% widowed, 6.4% divorced (2000); Foreign born: 1.7% (2000); Ancestry (includes multiple ancestries): 32.9% French (except Basque), 16.5% French Canadian, 11.2% Irish, 10.1% Other groups, 8.5% United States or American (2000).
Economy: Single-family building permits issued: 2 (2005); Multi-family building permits issued: 0 (2005); Employment by occupation: 16.8% management, 13.4% professional, 18.5% services, 15.8% sales, 8.4% farming, 6.0% construction, 21.1% production (2000).
Income: Per capita income: $14,659 (2005); Median household income: $32,439 (2005); Average household income: $38,473 (2005); Percent of households with income of $100,000 or more: 3.8% (2005); Poverty rate: 17.9% (2000).
Education: Percent of population age 25 and over with: High school diploma (including GED) or higher: 66.8% (2005); Bachelor's degree or higher: 7.0% (2005); Master's degree or higher: 2.3% (2005).
Housing: Homeownership rate: 83.3% (2005); Median home value: $68,696 (2005); Median rent: $250 per month (2000); Median age of housing: 60+ years (2000).
Transportation: Commute to work: 82.9% car, 0.7% public transportation, 4.8% walk, 10.6% work from home (2000); Travel time to work: 35.2% less than 15 minutes, 18.4% 15 to 30 minutes, 24.1% 30 to 45 minutes, 12.3% 45 to 60 minutes, 10.0% 60 minutes or more (2000)
Additional Information Contacts
Town of Clinton . . . . (845) 266-5853
   http://www.townofclinton.com/

CUMBERLAND HEAD (CDP). Covers a land area of 3.701 square miles and a water area of 0 square miles. Located at 44.71° N. Lat.; 73.40° W. Long.
Population: 1,698 (1990); 1,532 (2000); 1,605 (2005); 1,649 (2010 projected); Race: 96.0% White, 1.6% Black, 0.3% Asian, 1.1% Hispanic of any race (2005); Density: 433.6 persons per square mile (2005); Average household size: 2.38 (2005); Median age: 43.1 (2005); Males per 100 females: 98.4 (2005); Marriage status: 18.4% never married, 63.1% now married, 8.7% widowed, 9.7% divorced (2000); Foreign born: 6.3% (2000); Ancestry (includes multiple ancestries): 19.3% English, 18.0% French (except Basque), 16.0% Irish, 13.2% French Canadian, 12.9% German (2000).
Economy: Employment by occupation: 14.2% management, 34.2% professional, 11.4% services, 24.9% sales, 0.0% farming, 6.4% construction, 8.9% production (2000).
Income: Per capita income: $34,849 (2005); Median household income: $63,183 (2005); Average household income: $83,109 (2005); Percent of households with income of $100,000 or more: 24.2% (2005); Poverty rate: 3.5% (2000).
Education: Percent of population age 25 and over with: High school diploma (including GED) or higher: 92.2% (2005); Bachelor's degree or higher: 42.3% (2005); Master's degree or higher: 26.5% (2005).
Housing: Homeownership rate: 85.6% (2005); Median home value: $144,444 (2005); Median rent: $579 per month (2000); Median age of housing: 40 years (2000).
Transportation: Commute to work: 92.4% car, 1.5% public transportation, 4.3% walk, 1.8% work from home (2000); Travel time to work: 37.1% less than 15 minutes, 37.3% 15 to 30 minutes, 11.7% 30 to 45 minutes, 7.3% 45 to 60 minutes, 6.6% 60 minutes or more (2000)

PROFILES OF NEW YORK / Clinton County 79

DANNEMORA (village). Covers a land area of 1.206 square miles and a water area of 0 square miles. Located at 44.72° N. Lat.; 73.71° W. Long. Elevation is 1,439 feet.
Population: 4,005 (1990); 4,129 (2000); 4,306 (2005); 4,453 (2010 projected); Race: 47.6% White, 37.7% Black, 1.3% Asian, 21.1% Hispanic of any race (2005); Density: 3,570.0 persons per square mile (2005); Average household size: 8.84 (2005); Median age: 33.9 (2005); Males per 100 females: 555.4 (2005); Marriage status: 42.7% never married, 50.2% now married, 2.8% widowed, 4.4% divorced (2000); Foreign born: 12.4% (2000); Ancestry (includes multiple ancestries): 8.1% French (except Basque), 6.9% Irish, 4.1% French Canadian, 3.0% Other groups, 2.9% United States or American (2000).
Economy: Single-family building permits issued: 2 (2005); Multi-family building permits issued: 0 (2005); Employment by occupation: 9.1% management, 19.7% professional, 28.1% services, 28.3% sales, 0.0% farming, 5.0% construction, 9.7% production (2000).
Income: Per capita income: $20,493 (2005); Median household income: $52,738 (2005); Average household income: $61,915 (2005); Percent of households with income of $100,000 or more: 15.8% (2005); Poverty rate: 14.5% (2000).
Education: Percent of population age 25 and over with: High school diploma (including GED) or higher: 39.8% (2005); Bachelor's degree or higher: 5.4% (2005); Master's degree or higher: 1.7% (2005).

School District(s)
Saranac Central School District (KG-12)
    2003-04 Enrollment: 1,968 . . . . (518) 565-5600
Housing: Homeownership rate: 65.3% (2005); Median home value: $102,837 (2005); Median rent: $347 per month (2000); Median age of housing: 58 years (2000).
Transportation: Commute to work: 88.3% car, 0.4% public transportation, 6.9% walk, 2.9% work from home (2000); Travel time to work: 35.8% less than 15 minutes, 45.4% 15 to 30 minutes, 13.5% 30 to 45 minutes, 3.8% 45 to 60 minutes, 1.5% 60 minutes or more (2000)

DANNEMORA (town). Covers a land area of 59.188 square miles and a water area of 6.624 square miles. Located at 44.73° N. Lat.; 73.83° W. Long. Elevation is 1,439 feet.
History: Incorporated 1881.
Population: 5,232 (1990); 5,149 (2000); 5,291 (2005); 5,392 (2010 projected); Race: 54.1% White, 32.9% Black, 1.2% Asian, 18.3% Hispanic of any race (2005); Density: 89.4 persons per square mile (2005); Average household size: 6.16 (2005); Median age: 34.9 (2005); Males per 100 females: 390.8 (2005); Marriage status: 38.8% never married, 51.9% now married, 4.2% widowed, 5.2% divorced (2000); Foreign born: 10.7% (2000); Ancestry (includes multiple ancestries): 12.3% French (except Basque), 7.9% Irish, 5.5% French Canadian, 4.3% Other groups, 3.7% English (2000).
Economy: Site of Clinton Correctional Facility. Single-family building permits issued: 5 (2005); Multi-family building permits issued: 0 (2005); Employment by occupation: 8.0% management, 17.3% professional, 29.0% services, 26.5% sales, 0.0% farming, 7.2% construction, 12.0% production (2000).
Income: Per capita income: $20,078 (2005); Median household income: $44,339 (2005); Average household income: $52,098 (2005); Percent of households with income of $100,000 or more: 9.9% (2005); Poverty rate: 14.2% (2000).
Education: Percent of population age 25 and over with: High school diploma (including GED) or higher: 45.3% (2005); Bachelor's degree or higher: 5.5% (2005); Master's degree or higher: 2.2% (2005).
Housing: Homeownership rate: 73.9% (2005); Median home value: $85,810 (2005); Median rent: $344 per month (2000); Median age of housing: 48 years (2000).
Transportation: Commute to work: 91.6% car, 0.2% public transportation, 4.0% walk, 2.9% work from home (2000); Travel time to work: 22.6% less than 15 minutes, 35.4% 15 to 30 minutes, 30.7% 30 to 45 minutes, 6.3% 45 to 60 minutes, 5.1% 60 minutes or more (2000)

ELLENBURG (town). Covers a land area of 106.433 square miles and a water area of 0.966 square miles. Located at 44.84° N. Lat.; 73.91° W. Long.
Population: 1,847 (1990); 1,812 (2000); 1,787 (2005); 1,787 (2010 projected); Race: 98.9% White, 0.0% Black, 0.3% Asian, 1.1% Hispanic of any race (2005); Density: 16.8 persons per square mile (2005); Average household size: 2.52 (2005); Median age: 39.5 (2005); Males per 100 females: 97.2 (2005); Marriage status: 25.6% never married, 59.9% now married, 8.5% widowed, 6.0% divorced (2000); Foreign born: 3.0% (2000); Ancestry (includes multiple ancestries): 32.4% French (except Basque), 15.2% Irish, 12.0% French Canadian, 10.6% English, 8.8% United States or American (2000).
Economy: Single-family building permits issued: 11 (2005); Multi-family building permits issued: 0 (2005); Employment by occupation: 16.0% management, 12.3% professional, 21.0% services, 20.2% sales, 2.1% farming, 7.2% construction, 21.2% production (2000).
Income: Per capita income: $20,130 (2005); Median household income: $40,079 (2005); Average household income: $50,648 (2005); Percent of households with income of $100,000 or more: 10.3% (2005); Poverty rate: 13.4% (2000).
Taxes: Total city taxes per capita: $432 (2004); City property taxes per capita: $424 (2004).
Education: Percent of population age 25 and over with: High school diploma (including GED) or higher: 74.1% (2005); Bachelor's degree or higher: 10.9% (2005); Master's degree or higher: 5.3% (2005).
Housing: Homeownership rate: 80.6% (2005); Median home value: $84,954 (2005); Median rent: $312 per month (2000); Median age of housing: 47 years (2000).
Transportation: Commute to work: 83.3% car, 0.9% public transportation, 3.1% walk, 11.7% work from home (2000); Travel time to work: 28.0% less than 15 minutes, 15.3% 15 to 30 minutes, 36.2% 30 to 45 minutes, 12.6% 45 to 60 minutes, 7.9% 60 minutes or more (2000)

ELLENBURG CENTER (unincorporated postal area, zip code 12934). Covers a land area of 76.185 square miles and a water area of 0.040 square miles. Located at 44.86° N. Lat.; 73.89° W. Long. Elevation is 1,203 feet.
Population: 0 (2000); Race: 95.7% White, 0.3% Black, 0.5% Asian, 0.0% Hispanic of any race (2000); Density: 0.0 persons per square mile (2000); Age: 26.1% under 18, 13.2% over 64 (2000); Marriage status: 28.1% never married, 58.0% now married, 8.4% widowed, 5.5% divorced (2000); Foreign born: 2.2% (2000); Ancestry (includes multiple ancestries): 37.7% French (except Basque), 15.0% Irish, 11.0% English, 10.6% French Canadian, 8.4% United States or American (2000).
Economy: Employment by occupation: 15.1% management, 9.9% professional, 18.7% services, 20.2% sales, 2.9% farming, 7.8% construction, 25.4% production (2000).
Income: Per capita income: $15,355 (2000); Median household income: $33,603 (2000); Poverty rate: 12.9% (2000).
Education: Percent of population age 25 and over with: High school diploma (including GED) or higher: 72.8% (2000); Bachelor's degree or higher: 6.9% (2000).
Housing: Homeownership rate: 78.2% (2000); Median home value: $56,400 (2000); Median rent: $271 per month (2000); Median age of housing: 49 years (2000).
Transportation: Commute to work: 82.4% car, 0.0% public transportation, 2.9% walk, 13.5% work from home (2000); Travel time to work: 29.5% less than 15 minutes, 10.7% 15 to 30 minutes, 32.2% 30 to 45 minutes, 16.1% 45 to 60 minutes, 11.4% 60 minutes or more (2000)

ELLENBURG DEPOT (unincorporated postal area, zip code 12935). Aka Ellenburg. Covers a land area of 86.867 square miles and a water area of 3.451 square miles. Located at 44.83° N. Lat.; 73.80° W. Long. Elevation is 900 feet.
Population: 0 (2000); Race: 58.3% White, 30.9% Black, 0.9% Asian, 15.1% Hispanic of any race (2000); Density: 0.0 persons per square mile (2000); Age: 11.7% under 18, 5.1% over 64 (2000); Marriage status: 38.6% never married, 53.0% now married, 3.2% widowed, 5.2% divorced (2000); Foreign born: 9.8% (2000); Ancestry (includes multiple ancestries): 12.6% French (except Basque), 7.3% Irish, 6.1% French Canadian, 4.5% Other groups, 3.9% English (2000).
Economy: Employment by occupation: 9.5% management, 14.1% professional, 24.7% services, 24.5% sales, 0.2% farming, 10.1% construction, 16.9% production (2000).
Income: Per capita income: $17,955 (2000); Median household income: $38,311 (2000); Poverty rate: 14.5% (2000).
Education: Percent of population age 25 and over with: High school diploma (including GED) or higher: 45.9% (2000); Bachelor's degree or higher: 5.1% (2000).

School District(s)
Northern Adirondack Central School District (KG-12)
    2003-04 Enrollment: 1,128 . . . . (518) 594-7060

Housing: Homeownership rate: 77.0% (2000); Median home value: $60,600 (2000); Median rent: $357 per month (2000); Median age of housing: 44 years (2000).
Transportation: Commute to work: 90.5% car, 0.8% public transportation, 3.8% walk, 3.6% work from home (2000); Travel time to work: 22.7% less than 15 minutes, 29.6% 15 to 30 minutes, 37.6% 30 to 45 minutes, 4.5% 45 to 60 minutes, 5.6% 60 minutes or more (2000)

KEESEVILLE (village).
Covers a land area of 1.168 square miles and a water area of 0.053 square miles. Located at 44.50° N. Lat.; 73.48° W. Long.
Population: 1,854 (1990); 1,850 (2000); 1,821 (2005); 1,813 (2010 projected); Race: 96.3% White, 1.2% Black, 0.3% Asian, 1.6% Hispanic of any race (2005); Density: 1,559.6 persons per square mile (2005); Average household size: 2.57 (2005); Median age: 37.9 (2005); Males per 100 females: 95.2 (2005); Marriage status: 27.3% never married, 57.0% now married, 7.0% widowed, 8.7% divorced (2000); Foreign born: 2.4% (2000); Ancestry (includes multiple ancestries): 30.6% French (except Basque), 14.3% Irish, 13.6% Other groups, 10.3% English, 7.1% United States or American (2000).
Economy: Single-family building permits issued: 0 (2005); Multi-family building permits issued: 0 (2005); Employment by occupation: 8.9% management, 16.7% professional, 24.6% services, 22.5% sales, 0.4% farming, 9.5% construction, 17.4% production (2000).
Income: Per capita income: $17,065 (2005); Median household income: $35,455 (2005); Average household income: $43,054 (2005); Percent of households with income of $100,000 or more: 5.6% (2005); Poverty rate: 15.3% (2000).
Education: Percent of population age 25 and over with: High school diploma (including GED) or higher: 73.3% (2005); Bachelor's degree or higher: 12.7% (2005); Master's degree or higher: 6.3% (2005).
School District(s)
Ausable Valley Central School District (KG-12)
    2003-04 Enrollment: 1,377 . . . . (518) 834-2845
Housing: Homeownership rate: 66.9% (2005); Median home value: $91,887 (2005); Median rent: $391 per month (2000); Median age of housing: 60+ years (2000).
Transportation: Commute to work: 92.2% car, 0.0% public transportation, 4.8% walk, 2.7% work from home (2000); Travel time to work: 29.1% less than 15 minutes, 47.4% 15 to 30 minutes, 15.5% 30 to 45 minutes, 2.9% 45 to 60 minutes, 5.1% 60 minutes or more (2000); Amtrak: Service available.

LYON MOUNTAIN (CDP).
Covers a land area of 10.178 square miles and a water area of 0 square miles. Located at 44.72° N. Lat.; 73.90° W. Long. Elevation is 1,768 feet.
Population: 508 (1990); 458 (2000); 447 (2005); 438 (2010 projected); Race: 96.4% White, 0.2% Black, 0.0% Asian, 0.0% Hispanic of any race (2005); Density: 43.9 persons per square mile (2005); Average household size: 2.09 (2005); Median age: 50.6 (2005); Males per 100 females: 92.7 (2005); Marriage status: 19.8% never married, 56.3% now married, 18.8% widowed, 5.3% divorced (2000); Foreign born: 3.9% (2000); Ancestry (includes multiple ancestries): 32.8% French (except Basque), 22.2% Irish, 11.4% Polish, 10.2% English, 8.9% Other groups (2000).
Economy: Employment by occupation: 2.6% management, 23.2% professional, 34.2% services, 20.6% sales, 0.0% farming, 8.4% construction, 11.0% production (2000).
Income: Per capita income: $20,039 (2005); Median household income: $30,000 (2005); Average household income: $41,857 (2005); Percent of households with income of $100,000 or more: 6.1% (2005); Poverty rate: 14.1% (2000).
Education: Percent of population age 25 and over with: High school diploma (including GED) or higher: 80.6% (2005); Bachelor's degree or higher: 7.1% (2005); Master's degree or higher: 7.1% (2005).
School District(s)
Chazy Union Free School District (KG-12)
    2003-04 Enrollment: 611 . . . . (518) 846-7135
Housing: Homeownership rate: 84.1% (2005); Median home value: $40,043 (2005); Median rent: $183 per month (2000); Median age of housing: 60+ years (2000).
Transportation: Commute to work: 91.0% car, 0.0% public transportation, 4.5% walk, 2.6% work from home (2000); Travel time to work: 12.6% less than 15 minutes, 27.8% 15 to 30 minutes, 44.4% 30 to 45 minutes, 15.2% 45 to 60 minutes, 0.0% 60 minutes or more (2000)

MOOERS (CDP).
Covers a land area of 1.186 square miles and a water area of 0.058 square miles. Located at 44.96° N. Lat.; 73.58° W. Long. Elevation is 265 feet.
Population: 481 (1990); 440 (2000); 419 (2005); 405 (2010 projected); Race: 97.6% White, 0.2% Black, 0.5% Asian, 2.1% Hispanic of any race (2005); Density: 353.2 persons per square mile (2005); Average household size: 2.34 (2005); Median age: 41.7 (2005); Males per 100 females: 97.6 (2005); Marriage status: 15.5% never married, 72.8% now married, 11.7% widowed, 0.0% divorced (2000); Foreign born: 10.4% (2000); Ancestry (includes multiple ancestries): 27.4% French (except Basque), 22.9% Other groups, 14.7% Irish, 13.9% French Canadian, 10.4% United States or American (2000).
Economy: Employment by occupation: 18.9% management, 8.1% professional, 28.1% services, 15.1% sales, 0.0% farming, 10.3% construction, 19.5% production (2000).
Income: Per capita income: $16,689 (2005); Median household income: $31,905 (2005); Average household income: $39,064 (2005); Percent of households with income of $100,000 or more: 7.8% (2005); Poverty rate: 19.2% (2000).
Education: Percent of population age 25 and over with: High school diploma (including GED) or higher: 78.4% (2005); Bachelor's degree or higher: 11.8% (2005); Master's degree or higher: 3.4% (2005).
School District(s)
Northeastern Clinton Central School District (KG-12)
    2003-04 Enrollment: 1,657 . . . . (518) 298-8242
Housing: Homeownership rate: 73.7% (2005); Median home value: $87,027 (2005); Median rent: $394 per month (2000); Median age of housing: 60+ years (2000).
Transportation: Commute to work: 92.4% car, 0.0% public transportation, 7.6% walk, 0.0% work from home (2000); Travel time to work: 25.9% less than 15 minutes, 55.1% 15 to 30 minutes, 13.5% 30 to 45 minutes, 0.0% 45 to 60 minutes, 5.4% 60 minutes or more (2000)

MOOERS (town).
Covers a land area of 87.661 square miles and a water area of 0.335 square miles. Located at 44.95° N. Lat.; 73.64° W. Long. Elevation is 265 feet.
Population: 2,995 (1990); 3,404 (2000); 3,253 (2005); 3,155 (2010 projected); Race: 98.0% White, 0.3% Black, 0.3% Asian, 1.1% Hispanic of any race (2005); Density: 37.1 persons per square mile (2005); Average household size: 2.63 (2005); Median age: 37.8 (2005); Males per 100 females: 103.2 (2005); Marriage status: 26.5% never married, 59.3% now married, 7.6% widowed, 6.5% divorced (2000); Foreign born: 3.4% (2000); Ancestry (includes multiple ancestries): 21.8% French (except Basque), 21.1% French Canadian, 13.4% Irish, 13.0% Other groups, 11.7% United States or American (2000).
Economy: Port of entry, at Quebec border 3.3 miles North Northwest. Single-family building permits issued: 7 (2005); Multi-family building permits issued: 0 (2005); Employment by occupation: 9.7% management, 12.3% professional, 21.4% services, 17.1% sales, 3.8% farming, 15.3% construction, 20.4% production (2000).
Income: Per capita income: $18,888 (2005); Median household income: $43,903 (2005); Average household income: $49,711 (2005); Percent of households with income of $100,000 or more: 8.4% (2005); Poverty rate: 10.9% (2000).
Education: Percent of population age 25 and over with: High school diploma (including GED) or higher: 77.3% (2005); Bachelor's degree or higher: 12.5% (2005); Master's degree or higher: 3.5% (2005).
Housing: Homeownership rate: 85.2% (2005); Median home value: $92,111 (2005); Median rent: $393 per month (2000); Median age of housing: 27 years (2000).
Transportation: Commute to work: 94.3% car, 0.3% public transportation, 2.5% walk, 2.9% work from home (2000); Travel time to work: 21.0% less than 15 minutes, 42.1% 15 to 30 minutes, 25.4% 30 to 45 minutes, 3.6% 45 to 60 minutes, 7.9% 60 minutes or more (2000)

MOOERS FORKS (unincorporated postal area, zip code 12959).
Covers a land area of 42.095 square miles and a water area of 0.058 square miles. Located at 44.95° N. Lat.; 73.68° W. Long. Elevation is 379 feet.
Population: 0 (2000); Race: 99.3% White, 0.0% Black, 0.0% Asian, 0.0% Hispanic of any race (2000); Density: 0.0 persons per square mile (2000); Age: 24.1% under 18, 10.2% over 64 (2000); Marriage status: 24.0% never married, 58.0% now married, 8.5% widowed, 9.5% divorced (2000); Foreign born: 2.9% (2000); Ancestry (includes multiple ancestries): 25.7%

French (except Basque), 23.6% French Canadian, 15.0% Irish, 13.6% United States or American, 9.2% Other groups (2000).
Economy: Employment by occupation: 4.9% management, 13.2% professional, 20.7% services, 14.3% sales, 3.7% farming, 20.7% construction, 22.5% production (2000).
Income: Per capita income: $15,528 (2000); Median household income: $38,924 (2000); Poverty rate: 16.6% (2000).
Education: Percent of population age 25 and over with: High school diploma (including GED) or higher: 69.3% (2000); Bachelor's degree or higher: 11.8% (2000).
Housing: Homeownership rate: 84.6% (2000); Median home value: $67,900 (2000); Median rent: $392 per month (2000); Median age of housing: 24 years (2000).
Transportation: Commute to work: 96.0% car, 0.0% public transportation, 1.3% walk, 2.7% work from home (2000); Travel time to work: 17.3% less than 15 minutes, 35.8% 15 to 30 minutes, 39.1% 30 to 45 minutes, 3.8% 45 to 60 minutes, 4.0% 60 minutes or more (2000)

MORRISONVILLE (CDP).
Covers a land area of 2.586 square miles and a water area of 0.094 square miles. Located at 44.69° N. Lat.; 73.55° W. Long.
Population: 1,742 (1990); 1,702 (2000); 1,776 (2005); 1,846 (2010 projected); Race: 97.5% White, 0.8% Black, 0.5% Asian, 1.3% Hispanic of any race (2005); Density: 686.9 persons per square mile (2005); Average household size: 2.56 (2005); Median age: 39.5 (2005); Males per 100 females: 97.8 (2005); Marriage status: 29.8% never married, 54.8% now married, 7.6% widowed, 7.9% divorced (2000); Foreign born: 2.7% (2000); Ancestry (includes multiple ancestries): 25.1% French (except Basque), 15.4% Irish, 14.5% English, 10.6% French Canadian, 9.9% Other groups (2000).
Economy: Employment by occupation: 8.5% management, 23.8% professional, 26.5% services, 19.0% sales, 1.0% farming, 3.4% construction, 17.9% production (2000).
Income: Per capita income: $22,682 (2005); Median household income: $55,069 (2005); Average household income: $56,760 (2005); Percent of households with income of $100,000 or more: 13.1% (2005); Poverty rate: 15.2% (2000).
Education: Percent of population age 25 and over with: High school diploma (including GED) or higher: 81.9% (2005); Bachelor's degree or higher: 20.9% (2005); Master's degree or higher: 11.3% (2005).
School District(s)
Saranac Central School District (KG-12)
    2003-04 Enrollment: 1,968 . . . . (518) 565-5600
Housing: Homeownership rate: 74.2% (2005); Median home value: $129,756 (2005); Median rent: $363 per month (2000); Median age of housing: 29 years (2000).
Transportation: Commute to work: 98.3% car, 0.0% public transportation, 0.0% walk, 1.7% work from home (2000); Travel time to work: 47.6% less than 15 minutes, 39.4% 15 to 30 minutes, 3.4% 30 to 45 minutes, 3.1% 45 to 60 minutes, 6.5% 60 minutes or more (2000)

PARC (CDP).
Covers a land area of 1.395 square miles and a water area of 0 square miles. Located at 44.66° N. Lat.; 73.45° W. Long.
Population: 5,560 (1990); 54 (2000); 56 (2005); 59 (2010 projected); Race: 96.4% White, 0.0% Black, 0.0% Asian, 0.0% Hispanic of any race (2005); Density: 40.1 persons per square mile (2005); Average household size: 1.93 (2005); Median age: 35.2 (2005); Males per 100 females: 75.0 (2005); Marriage status: 0.0% never married, 86.4% now married, 0.0% widowed, 13.6% divorced (2000); Foreign born: 22.4% (2000); Ancestry (includes multiple ancestries): 34.7% French Canadian, 30.6% German, 26.5% Irish, 22.4% Canadian, 12.2% Welsh (2000).
Economy: Employment by occupation: 18.2% management, 0.0% professional, 0.0% services, 42.4% sales, 0.0% farming, 18.2% construction, 21.2% production (2000).
Income: Per capita income: $20,491 (2005); Median household income: $39,500 (2005); Average household income: $39,569 (2005); Percent of households with income of $100,000 or more: 0.0% (2005); Poverty rate: 34.7% (2000).
Education: Percent of population age 25 and over with: High school diploma (including GED) or higher: 72.9% (2005); Bachelor's degree or higher: 31.3% (2005); Master's degree or higher: 18.8% (2005).
Housing: Homeownership rate: 27.6% (2005); Median home value: $91,250 (2005); Median rent: $677 per month (2000); Median age of housing: 54 years (2000).
Transportation: Commute to work: 81.8% car, 0.0% public transportation, 18.2% walk, 0.0% work from home (2000); Travel time to work: 81.8% less than 15 minutes, 18.2% 15 to 30 minutes, 0.0% 30 to 45 minutes, 0.0% 45 to 60 minutes, 0.0% 60 minutes or more (2000)

PERU (town).
Covers a land area of 79.352 square miles and a water area of 13.054 square miles. Located at 44.58° N. Lat.; 73.52° W. Long. Elevation is 355 feet.
Population: 6,254 (1990); 6,370 (2000); 6,743 (2005); 7,103 (2010 projected); Race: 97.3% White, 0.9% Black, 0.8% Asian, 1.0% Hispanic of any race (2005); Density: 85.0 persons per square mile (2005); Average household size: 2.69 (2005); Median age: 38.8 (2005); Males per 100 females: 93.7 (2005); Marriage status: 21.3% never married, 63.3% now married, 5.5% widowed, 9.9% divorced (2000); Foreign born: 2.7% (2000); Ancestry (includes multiple ancestries): 21.2% French (except Basque), 19.3% Irish, 11.4% Other groups, 10.8% German, 10.2% United States or American (2000).
Economy: Lumber, wood products. Single-family building permits issued: 48 (2005); Multi-family building permits issued: 0 (2005); Employment by occupation: 13.0% management, 23.5% professional, 16.7% services, 23.1% sales, 1.4% farming, 9.6% construction, 12.6% production (2000).
Income: Per capita income: $23,548 (2005); Median household income: $46,441 (2005); Average household income: $61,630 (2005); Percent of households with income of $100,000 or more: 13.2% (2005); Poverty rate: 11.1% (2000).
Education: Percent of population age 25 and over with: High school diploma (including GED) or higher: 82.9% (2005); Bachelor's degree or higher: 21.3% (2005); Master's degree or higher: 11.4% (2005).
School District(s)
Peru Central School District (KG-12)
    2003-04 Enrollment: 2,303 . . . . (518) 643-6000
Housing: Homeownership rate: 82.1% (2005); Median home value: $128,935 (2005); Median rent: $416 per month (2000); Median age of housing: 26 years (2000).
Transportation: Commute to work: 95.5% car, 0.4% public transportation, 0.9% walk, 3.0% work from home (2000); Travel time to work: 26.2% less than 15 minutes, 57.9% 15 to 30 minutes, 8.2% 30 to 45 minutes, 2.8% 45 to 60 minutes, 4.9% 60 minutes or more (2000)

PERU (CDP).
Covers a land area of 1.602 square miles and a water area of 0 square miles. Located at 44.58° N. Lat.; 73.53° W. Long.
Population: 1,565 (1990); 1,514 (2000); 1,537 (2005); 1,587 (2010 projected); Race: 97.7% White, 0.8% Black, 0.9% Asian, 0.6% Hispanic of any race (2005); Density: 959.2 persons per square mile (2005); Average household size: 2.73 (2005); Median age: 39.6 (2005); Males per 100 females: 86.5 (2005); Marriage status: 17.8% never married, 63.4% now married, 8.8% widowed, 9.9% divorced (2000); Foreign born: 0.9% (2000); Ancestry (includes multiple ancestries): 19.1% Irish, 15.3% French (except Basque), 12.6% German, 12.4% French Canadian, 9.9% English (2000).
Economy: Employment by occupation: 18.1% management, 22.9% professional, 15.2% services, 28.9% sales, 0.0% farming, 6.5% construction, 8.5% production (2000).
Income: Per capita income: $20,325 (2005); Median household income: $43,371 (2005); Average household income: $52,815 (2005); Percent of households with income of $100,000 or more: 9.6% (2005); Poverty rate: 14.6% (2000).
Education: Percent of population age 25 and over with: High school diploma (including GED) or higher: 89.7% (2005); Bachelor's degree or higher: 24.4% (2005); Master's degree or higher: 9.3% (2005).
Housing: Homeownership rate: 80.1% (2005); Median home value: $123,283 (2005); Median rent: $488 per month (2000); Median age of housing: 43 years (2000).
Transportation: Commute to work: 95.0% car, 0.0% public transportation, 1.1% walk, 3.8% work from home (2000); Travel time to work: 13.5% less than 15 minutes, 73.3% 15 to 30 minutes, 7.4% 30 to 45 minutes, 3.8% 45 to 60 minutes, 1.9% 60 minutes or more (2000)

PLATTSBURGH (city).
Covers a land area of 5.047 square miles and a water area of 1.537 square miles. Located at 44.69° N. Lat.; 73.45° W. Long. Elevation is 135 feet.
History: Plattsburg was established at the mouth of the Saranac River, which began to provide water power for manufacturing in 1785. The first mills ground corn and cut lumber for the settlers.
Population: 21,242 (1990); 18,816 (2000); 19,311 (2005); 19,811 (2010 projected); Race: 92.9% White, 2.5% Black, 2.1% Asian, 2.7% Hispanic of

any race (2005); Density: 3,826.3 persons per square mile (2005); Average household size: 2.42 (2005); Median age: 32.0 (2005); Males per 100 females: 86.1 (2005); Marriage status: 45.5% never married, 36.8% now married, 9.1% widowed, 8.5% divorced (2000); Foreign born: 5.8% (2000); Ancestry (includes multiple ancestries): 20.5% French (except Basque), 16.5% Irish, 10.3% Other groups, 10.1% English, 8.7% German (2000).
Economy: Single-family building permits issued: 13 (2005); Multi-family building permits issued: 62 (2005); Employment by occupation: 8.4% management, 23.8% professional, 22.4% services, 28.3% sales, 0.2% farming, 5.2% construction, 11.7% production (2000).
Income: Per capita income: $19,213 (2005); Median household income: $31,380 (2005); Average household income: $44,004 (2005); Percent of households with income of $100,000 or more: 8.7% (2005); Poverty rate: 23.1% (2000).
Education: Percent of population age 25 and over with: High school diploma (including GED) or higher: 82.4% (2005); Bachelor's degree or higher: 26.8% (2005); Master's degree or higher: 13.6% (2005).

School District(s)
Beekmantown Central School District (PK-12)
   2003-04 Enrollment: 2,179 . . . . (518) 563-8250
Boces Clinton-Essex-Warren-Washing (UG-UG)
   2003-04 Enrollment: 393 . . . . (518) 561-0100
Plattsburgh City School District (PK-12)
   2003-04 Enrollment: 2,055 . . . . (518) 957-6002

Four-year College(s)
SUNY College at Plattsburgh (Public)
   Fall 2004 Enrollment: 5,909. . . . . (518) 564-2000
   2005-06 Tuition: In-state $5,296; Out-of-state $11,556

Two-year College(s)
CVPH Medical Center School of Radiologic Technology
   Fall 2004 Enrollment: 25 . . . . (518) 562-7510
Clinton Community College (Public)
   Fall 2004 Enrollment: 2,288. . . . . (518) 562-4200
   2005-06 Tuition: In-state $3,040; Out-of-state $7,550
Clinton Essex Warren Washington BOCES-Practical Nursing Program (Public)
   Fall 2004 Enrollment: 24 . . . . (518) 561-0100

Housing: Homeownership rate: 36.6% (2005); Median home value: $143,620 (2005); Median rent: $418 per month (2000); Median age of housing: 44 years (2000).
Hospitals: Champlain Valley Physicians Hospital (405 beds)
Safety: Violent crime rate: 12.0 per 10,000 population; Property crime rate: 343.2 per 10,000 population (2004).
Newspapers: Press Republican (Circulation 20,270)
Transportation: Commute to work: 81.2% car, 3.3% public transportation, 12.0% walk, 2.1% work from home (2000); Travel time to work: 70.8% less than 15 minutes, 18.6% 15 to 30 minutes, 6.1% 30 to 45 minutes, 1.2% 45 to 60 minutes, 3.4% 60 minutes or more (2000); Amtrak: Service available.
Additional Information Contacts
Plattsburgh North Country Chamber of Commerce . . . . (518) 563-1000
http://www.northcountrychamber.com

PLATTSBURGH (town). Covers a land area of 45.687 square miles and a water area of 22.115 square miles. Located at 44.68° N. Lat.; 73.49° W. Long. Elevation is 135 feet.
History: During the War of 1812 a makeshift American fleet under Thomas Macdonough defeated the British in a pitched battle on Lake Champlain near Plattsburgh, compelling an accompanying land-invasion force under Sir George Prevost to return to Canada. Seat of the State University of N.Y. College at Plattsburgh. Settled 1767, Incorporated 1902.
Population: 17,166 (1990); 11,190 (2000); 11,588 (2005); 11,991 (2010 projected); Race: 96.6% White, 1.1% Black, 0.6% Asian, 1.1% Hispanic of any race (2005); Density: 253.6 persons per square mile (2005); Average household size: 2.50 (2005); Median age: 38.9 (2005); Males per 100 females: 97.2 (2005); Marriage status: 22.5% never married, 62.3% now married, 6.3% widowed, 8.9% divorced (2000); Foreign born: 3.9% (2000); Ancestry (includes multiple ancestries): 24.3% French (except Basque), 17.8% Irish, 14.0% French Canadian, 10.6% English, 9.2% United States or American (2000).
Economy: Trade and distribution point, with plants making paper and plastics. A major source of employment was the adjoining Plattsburgh Air Force Base, a Strategic Air Command installation, which was closed in 1993. The city is also a summer vacation center, attracting Canadians as well as Americans. Single-family building permits issued: 39 (2005); Multi-family building permits issued: 0 (2005); Employment by occupation: 9.9% management, 20.0% professional, 21.2% services, 25.4% sales, 0.3% farming, 8.1% construction, 15.2% production (2000).
Income: Per capita income: $23,209 (2005); Median household income: $47,860 (2005); Average household income: $57,705 (2005); Percent of households with income of $100,000 or more: 12.0% (2005); Poverty rate: 11.9% (2000).
Education: Percent of population age 25 and over with: High school diploma (including GED) or higher: 79.8% (2005); Bachelor's degree or higher: 20.8% (2005); Master's degree or higher: 10.1% (2005).
Housing: Homeownership rate: 78.3% (2005); Median home value: $118,393 (2005); Median rent: $412 per month (2000); Median age of housing: 28 years (2000).
Transportation: Commute to work: 94.2% car, 1.5% public transportation, 1.4% walk, 2.7% work from home (2000); Travel time to work: 51.9% less than 15 minutes, 31.8% 15 to 30 minutes, 7.2% 30 to 45 minutes, 3.4% 45 to 60 minutes, 5.7% 60 minutes or more (2000); Amtrak: Service available.

PLATTSBURGH WEST (CDP). Covers a land area of 1.756 square miles and a water area of 0.086 square miles. Located at 44.68° N. Lat.; 73.50° W. Long.
Population: 1,274 (1990); 1,289 (2000); 1,377 (2005); 1,460 (2010 projected); Race: 95.1% White, 1.7% Black, 0.9% Asian, 1.2% Hispanic of any race (2005); Density: 784.0 persons per square mile (2005); Average household size: 2.53 (2005); Median age: 35.2 (2005); Males per 100 females: 90.2 (2005); Marriage status: 30.3% never married, 54.7% now married, 5.7% widowed, 9.3% divorced (2000); Foreign born: 1.8% (2000); Ancestry (includes multiple ancestries): 26.3% French (except Basque), 24.1% United States or American, 14.1% Other groups, 12.5% Irish, 10.7% French Canadian (2000).
Economy: Employment by occupation: 9.3% management, 5.7% professional, 35.5% services, 22.8% sales, 0.0% farming, 8.9% construction, 17.8% production (2000).
Income: Per capita income: $12,687 (2005); Median household income: $27,206 (2005); Average household income: $32,055 (2005); Percent of households with income of $100,000 or more: 0.6% (2005); Poverty rate: 25.9% (2000).
Education: Percent of population age 25 and over with: High school diploma (including GED) or higher: 53.5% (2005); Bachelor's degree or higher: 3.7% (2005); Master's degree or higher: 0.0% (2005).
Housing: Homeownership rate: 81.7% (2005); Median home value: $49,048 (2005); Median rent: $415 per month (2000); Median age of housing: 13 years (2000).
Transportation: Commute to work: 95.9% car, 2.6% public transportation, 1.5% walk, 0.0% work from home (2000); Travel time to work: 65.4% less than 15 minutes, 27.1% 15 to 30 minutes, 3.2% 30 to 45 minutes, 3.2% 45 to 60 minutes, 1.1% 60 minutes or more (2000)

REDFORD (CDP). Covers a land area of 1.368 square miles and a water area of 0.107 square miles. Located at 44.60° N. Lat.; 73.80° W. Long. Elevation is 1,119 feet.
Population: 463 (1990); 512 (2000); 530 (2005); 546 (2010 projected); Race: 99.1% White, 0.0% Black, 0.4% Asian, 0.4% Hispanic of any race (2005); Density: 387.4 persons per square mile (2005); Average household size: 2.80 (2005); Median age: 35.6 (2005); Males per 100 females: 96.3 (2005); Marriage status: 19.6% never married, 69.6% now married, 1.7% widowed, 9.2% divorced (2000); Foreign born: 0.0% (2000); Ancestry (includes multiple ancestries): 24.6% French (except Basque), 18.0% United States or American, 17.5% Irish, 12.3% Other groups, 10.9% French Canadian (2000).
Economy: Employment by occupation: 5.2% management, 14.5% professional, 37.3% services, 24.9% sales, 4.0% farming, 5.6% construction, 8.4% production (2000).
Income: Per capita income: $22,783 (2005); Median household income: $55,398 (2005); Average household income: $63,889 (2005); Percent of households with income of $100,000 or more: 16.4% (2005); Poverty rate: 2.7% (2000).
Education: Percent of population age 25 and over with: High school diploma (including GED) or higher: 83.9% (2005); Bachelor's degree or higher: 7.3% (2005); Master's degree or higher: 4.1% (2005).
Housing: Homeownership rate: 84.7% (2005); Median home value: $99,946 (2005); Median rent: $247 per month (2000); Median age of housing: 31 years (2000).
Transportation: Commute to work: 96.3% car, 0.0% public transportation, 0.0% walk, 3.7% work from home (2000); Travel time to work: 14.6% less

than 15 minutes, 21.0% 15 to 30 minutes, 44.6% 30 to 45 minutes, 6.9% 45 to 60 minutes, 12.9% 60 minutes or more (2000)

ROUSES POINT (village). Covers a land area of 1.776 square miles and a water area of 0.424 square miles. Located at 44.98° N. Lat.; 73.36° W. Long. Elevation is 116 feet.
History: Incorporated 1877.
Population: 2,377 (1990); 2,277 (2000); 2,469 (2005); 2,618 (2010 projected); Race: 97.1% White, 0.9% Black, 0.5% Asian, 1.6% Hispanic of any race (2005); Density: 1,389.9 persons per square mile (2005); Average household size: 2.27 (2005); Median age: 40.6 (2005); Males per 100 females: 90.8 (2005); Marriage status: 23.8% never married, 55.9% now married, 9.2% widowed, 11.0% divorced (2000); Foreign born: 8.3% (2000); Ancestry (includes multiple ancestries): 22.0% French (except Basque), 21.0% French Canadian, 13.5% Irish, 12.5% English, 8.0% German (2000).
Economy: Paper-packaging manufacturing and pharmaceuticals. In agricultural area. Single-family building permits issued: 13 (2005); Multi-family building permits issued: 0 (2005); Employment by occupation: 12.4% management, 14.2% professional, 15.6% services, 27.4% sales, 0.4% farming, 5.8% construction, 24.3% production (2000).
Income: Per capita income: $25,098 (2005); Median household income: $44,437 (2005); Average household income: $55,798 (2005); Percent of households with income of $100,000 or more: 12.2% (2005); Poverty rate: 9.9% (2000).
Education: Percent of population age 25 and over with: High school diploma (including GED) or higher: 83.8% (2005); Bachelor's degree or higher: 18.6% (2005); Master's degree or higher: 5.6% (2005).
School District(s)
Northeastern Clinton Central School District (KG-12)
    2003-04 Enrollment: 1,657 . . . . (518) 298-8242
Housing: Homeownership rate: 57.5% (2005); Median home value: $121,726 (2005); Median rent: $376 per month (2000); Median age of housing: 46 years (2000).
Safety: Violent crime rate: 16.9 per 10,000 population; Property crime rate: 67.6 per 10,000 population (2004).
Transportation: Commute to work: 80.9% car, 0.6% public transportation, 14.9% walk, 1.7% work from home (2000); Travel time to work: 66.7% less than 15 minutes, 14.5% 15 to 30 minutes, 10.6% 30 to 45 minutes, 2.7% 45 to 60 minutes, 5.5% 60 minutes or more (2000); Amtrak: Service available.
Additional Information Contacts
Northern Tier Chamber of Commerce . . . . (518) 297-3040

SARANAC (town). Covers a land area of 115.737 square miles and a water area of 0.641 square miles. Located at 44.65° N. Lat.; 73.77° W. Long. Elevation is 800 feet.
Population: 3,801 (1990); 4,165 (2000); 4,308 (2005); 4,447 (2010 projected); Race: 98.4% White, 0.2% Black, 0.3% Asian, 1.2% Hispanic of any race (2005); Density: 37.2 persons per square mile (2005); Average household size: 2.68 (2005); Median age: 38.5 (2005); Males per 100 females: 95.7 (2005); Marriage status: 21.4% never married, 66.1% now married, 4.4% widowed, 8.1% divorced (2000); Foreign born: 1.5% (2000); Ancestry (includes multiple ancestries): 25.3% French (except Basque), 16.7% Irish, 14.9% French Canadian, 10.6% United States or American, 8.5% English (2000).
Economy: Single-family building permits issued: 24 (2005); Multi-family building permits issued: 0 (2005); Employment by occupation: 9.1% management, 19.3% professional, 33.1% services, 21.1% sales, 1.1% farming, 6.5% construction, 9.8% production (2000).
Income: Per capita income: $22,231 (2005); Median household income: $55,816 (2005); Average household income: $59,670 (2005); Percent of households with income of $100,000 or more: 13.7% (2005); Poverty rate: 9.8% (2000).
Education: Percent of population age 25 and over with: High school diploma (including GED) or higher: 85.8% (2005); Bachelor's degree or higher: 17.0% (2005); Master's degree or higher: 7.2% (2005).
School District(s)
Saranac Central School District (KG-12)
    2003-04 Enrollment: 1,968 . . . . (518) 565-5600
Housing: Homeownership rate: 85.7% (2005); Median home value: $120,019 (2005); Median rent: $351 per month (2000); Median age of housing: 37 years (2000).
Transportation: Commute to work: 93.6% car, 0.0% public transportation, 3.1% walk, 3.3% work from home (2000); Travel time to work: 20.7% less than 15 minutes, 38.4% 15 to 30 minutes, 24.8% 30 to 45 minutes, 10.8% 45 to 60 minutes, 5.3% 60 minutes or more (2000)

SCHUYLER FALLS (town). Covers a land area of 36.490 square miles and a water area of 0.316 square miles. Located at 44.66° N. Lat.; 73.56° W. Long. Elevation is 429 feet.
Population: 4,774 (1990); 5,128 (2000); 5,283 (2005); 5,446 (2010 projected); Race: 97.2% White, 1.1% Black, 0.4% Asian, 1.0% Hispanic of any race (2005); Density: 144.8 persons per square mile (2005); Average household size: 2.68 (2005); Median age: 37.8 (2005); Males per 100 females: 100.7 (2005); Marriage status: 24.9% never married, 60.7% now married, 4.3% widowed, 10.0% divorced (2000); Foreign born: 3.7% (2000); Ancestry (includes multiple ancestries): 24.7% French (except Basque), 13.7% Irish, 12.3% United States or American, 10.4% English, 9.9% French Canadian (2000).
Economy: Single-family building permits issued: 19 (2005); Multi-family building permits issued: 0 (2005); Employment by occupation: 9.8% management, 15.3% professional, 23.6% services, 23.3% sales, 0.5% farming, 11.9% construction, 15.7% production (2000).
Income: Per capita income: $20,893 (2005); Median household income: $47,147 (2005); Average household income: $55,471 (2005); Percent of households with income of $100,000 or more: 10.5% (2005); Poverty rate: 9.6% (2000).
Education: Percent of population age 25 and over with: High school diploma (including GED) or higher: 77.6% (2005); Bachelor's degree or higher: 13.5% (2005); Master's degree or higher: 5.2% (2005).
School District(s)
Peru Central School District (KG-12)
    2003-04 Enrollment: 2,303 . . . . (518) 643-6000
Housing: Homeownership rate: 81.6% (2005); Median home value: $111,762 (2005); Median rent: $397 per month (2000); Median age of housing: 22 years (2000).
Transportation: Commute to work: 95.8% car, 0.3% public transportation, 0.9% walk, 3.0% work from home (2000); Travel time to work: 40.6% less than 15 minutes, 47.7% 15 to 30 minutes, 3.6% 30 to 45 minutes, 1.7% 45 to 60 minutes, 6.4% 60 minutes or more (2000)

WEST CHAZY (unincorporated postal area, zip code 12992). Covers a land area of 72.805 square miles and a water area of 0.107 square miles. Located at 44.82° N. Lat.; 73.51° W. Long. Elevation is 265 feet.
Population: 0 (2000); Race: 98.3% White, 0.2% Black, 0.9% Asian, 0.3% Hispanic of any race (2000); Density: 0.0 persons per square mile (2000); Age: 27.4% under 18, 8.9% over 64 (2000); Marriage status: 19.4% never married, 64.9% now married, 5.1% widowed, 10.6% divorced (2000); Foreign born: 3.5% (2000); Ancestry (includes multiple ancestries): 21.1% French (except Basque), 15.6% French Canadian, 15.2% United States or American, 9.6% Irish, 7.6% English (2000).
Economy: Employment by occupation: 8.6% management, 12.5% professional, 19.8% services, 22.1% sales, 0.9% farming, 12.2% construction, 23.9% production (2000).
Income: Per capita income: $15,316 (2000); Median household income: $36,979 (2000); Poverty rate: 17.1% (2000).
Education: Percent of population age 25 and over with: High school diploma (including GED) or higher: 75.1% (2000); Bachelor's degree or higher: 12.4% (2000).
Housing: Homeownership rate: 84.4% (2000); Median home value: $81,100 (2000); Median rent: $401 per month (2000); Median age of housing: 22 years (2000).
Transportation: Commute to work: 94.0% car, 0.5% public transportation, 1.5% walk, 4.1% work from home (2000); Travel time to work: 24.2% less than 15 minutes, 57.1% 15 to 30 minutes, 13.4% 30 to 45 minutes, 2.3% 45 to 60 minutes, 3.0% 60 minutes or more (2000)

Columbia County

Located in southeastern New York; bounded on the east by Massachusetts, and on the west by the Hudson River. Covers a land area of 635.73 square miles, a water area of 12.54 square miles, and is located in the Eastern Time Zone. The county government was organized in 1786. County seat is Hudson.

Columbia County is part of the Hudson, NY Micropolitan Statistical Area. The entire metro area includes: Columbia County, NY

Weather Station: Hudson Correctionl Facility Elevation: 59 feet

	Jan	Feb	Mar	Apr	May	Jun	Jul	Aug	Sep	Oct	Nov	Dec
High	34	37	47	61	73	81	85	82	74	63	50	38
Low	15	17	26	36	47	56	60	59	52	40	32	22
Precip	3.0	2.5	3.2	3.6	4.3	3.6	3.8	3.8	3.9	3.5	3.4	3.0
Snow	na	na	4.4	1.5	0.0	0.0	0.0	0.0	0.0	0.1	1.1	na

High and Low temperatures in degrees Fahrenheit; Precipitation and Snow in inches

Population: 62,982 (1990); 63,094 (2000); 63,662 (2005); 64,214 (2010 projected); Race: 91.2% White, 4.8% Black, 1.2% Asian, 3.4% Hispanic of any race (2005); Density: 100.1 persons per square mile (2005); Average household size: 2.51 (2005); Median age: 41.7 (2005); Males per 100 females: 99.4 (2005).
Religion: Five largest groups: 27.4% Catholic Church, 4.4% The United Methodist Church, 4.1% Reformed Church in America, 3.9% Evangelical Lutheran Church in America, 2.0% Episcopal Church (2000).
Economy: Unemployment rate: 3.9% (2005); Total civilian labor force: 32,092 (2005); Leading industries: 24.8% health care and social assistance; 18.7% retail trade; 11.4% manufacturing (2003); Farms: 498 totaling 119,718 acres (2002); Companies that employ 500 or more persons: 1 (2003); Companies that employ 100 to 499 persons: 22 (2003); Companies that employ less than 100 persons: 1,686 (2003); Black-owned businesses: n/a (2002); Hispanic-owned businesses: n/a (2002); Women-owned businesses: 1,923 (2002); Retail sales per capita: $10,386 (2006). Single-family building permits issued: 323 (2005); Multi-family building permits issued: 12 (2005).
Income: Per capita income: $25,711 (2005); Median household income: $47,840 (2005); Average household income: $63,105 (2005); Percent of households with income of $100,000 or more: 15.0% (2005); Poverty rate: 9.8% (2003); Bankruptcy rate: 4.50% (2005).
Education: Percent of population age 25 and over with: High school diploma (including GED) or higher: 81.0% (2005); Bachelor's degree or higher: 22.8% (2005); Master's degree or higher: 10.5% (2005).
Housing: Homeownership rate: 71.0% (2005); Median home value: $164,364 (2005); Median rent: $446 per month (2000); Median age of housing: 42 years (2000).
Health: Birth rate: 98.2 per 10,000 population (2004); Death rate: 110.9 per 10,000 population (2004); Age-adjusted cancer mortality rate: 212.1 deaths per 100,000 population (2002); Number of physicians: 16.2 per 10,000 population (2004); Hospital beds: 41.4 per 10,000 population (2003); Hospital admissions: 979.8 per 10,000 population (2003).
Elections: 2004 Presidential election results: 46.5% Bush, 51.2% Kerry, 2.0% Nader, 0.2% Badnarik
National and State Parks: Beebe Hill State Forest; Clermont State Park; Lake Taghkanic State Park; Martin Van Buren National Historic Site; Taconic State Park
Additional Information Contacts
Columbia County Government. . . . . (518) 828-7858
  http://www.govt.co.columbia.ny.us/

Columbia County Communities

ANCRAM (town). Covers a land area of 42.573 square miles and a water area of 0.188 square miles. Located at 42.03° N. Lat.; 73.58° W. Long.
Population: 1,510 (1990); 1,513 (2000); 1,635 (2005); 1,745 (2010 projected); Race: 98.0% White, 0.9% Black, 0.2% Asian, 1.3% Hispanic of any race (2005); Density: 38.4 persons per square mile (2005); Average household size: 2.49 (2005); Median age: 44.7 (2005); Males per 100 females: 105.1 (2005); Marriage status: 23.7% never married, 60.5% now married, 6.0% widowed, 9.8% divorced (2000); Foreign born: 4.2% (2000); Ancestry (includes multiple ancestries): 21.8% German, 18.3% Irish, 10.6% English, 7.9% United States or American, 7.1% Dutch (2000).
Economy: Single-family building permits issued: 24 (2005); Multi-family building permits issued: 0 (2005); Employment by occupation: 15.3% management, 17.0% professional, 15.7% services, 15.9% sales, 3.3% farming, 13.1% construction, 19.7% production (2000).
Income: Per capita income: $27,170 (2005); Median household income: $52,544 (2005); Average household income: $67,614 (2005); Percent of households with income of $100,000 or more: 15.7% (2005); Poverty rate: 7.4% (2000).
Education: Percent of population age 25 and over with: High school diploma (including GED) or higher: 79.3% (2005); Bachelor's degree or higher: 19.3% (2005); Master's degree or higher: 9.1% (2005).
Housing: Homeownership rate: 80.5% (2005); Median home value: $161,316 (2005); Median rent: $523 per month (2000); Median age of housing: 35 years (2000).
Transportation: Commute to work: 85.7% car, 1.8% public transportation, 4.5% walk, 8.1% work from home (2000); Travel time to work: 34.7% less than 15 minutes, 25.6% 15 to 30 minutes, 23.9% 30 to 45 minutes, 6.0% 45 to 60 minutes, 9.8% 60 minutes or more (2000)

ANCRAMDALE (unincorporated postal area, zip code 12503). Covers a land area of 27.515 square miles and a water area of 0.213 square miles. Located at 42.04° N. Lat.; 73.57° W. Long.
Population: 0 (2000); Race: 96.6% White, 2.6% Black, 0.0% Asian, 0.9% Hispanic of any race (2000); Density: 0.0 persons per square mile (2000); Age: 20.4% under 18, 18.9% over 64 (2000); Marriage status: 24.5% never married, 59.0% now married, 7.0% widowed, 9.6% divorced (2000); Foreign born: 4.8% (2000); Ancestry (includes multiple ancestries): 23.8% German, 15.7% Irish, 12.3% English, 8.9% Italian, 6.0% United States or American (2000).
Economy: Employment by occupation: 15.4% management, 17.8% professional, 18.0% services, 13.8% sales, 3.7% farming, 11.9% construction, 19.4% production (2000).
Income: Per capita income: $21,114 (2000); Median household income: $45,417 (2000); Poverty rate: 7.5% (2000).
Education: Percent of population age 25 and over with: High school diploma (including GED) or higher: 76.0% (2000); Bachelor's degree or higher: 19.6% (2000).
Housing: Homeownership rate: 83.6% (2000); Median home value: $119,500 (2000); Median rent: $543 per month (2000); Median age of housing: 35 years (2000).
Transportation: Commute to work: 85.8% car, 1.6% public transportation, 5.6% walk, 7.0% work from home (2000); Travel time to work: 37.8% less than 15 minutes, 26.8% 15 to 30 minutes, 19.6% 30 to 45 minutes, 5.5% 45 to 60 minutes, 10.4% 60 minutes or more (2000)

AUSTERLITZ (town). Covers a land area of 48.737 square miles and a water area of 0.098 square miles. Located at 42.32° N. Lat.; 73.52° W. Long.
Population: 1,456 (1990); 1,453 (2000); 1,494 (2005); 1,532 (2010 projected); Race: 96.5% White, 1.1% Black, 1.0% Asian, 1.0% Hispanic of any race (2005); Density: 30.7 persons per square mile (2005); Average household size: 2.29 (2005); Median age: 48.0 (2005); Males per 100 females: 104.1 (2005); Marriage status: 19.8% never married, 66.6% now married, 5.7% widowed, 7.9% divorced (2000); Foreign born: 4.4% (2000); Ancestry (includes multiple ancestries): 22.9% German, 20.6% Irish, 19.9% English, 9.9% Italian, 9.3% United States or American (2000).
Economy: Single-family building permits issued: 26 (2005); Multi-family building permits issued: 0 (2005); Employment by occupation: 14.6% management, 28.8% professional, 13.4% services, 23.4% sales, 0.9% farming, 10.5% construction, 8.4% production (2000).
Income: Per capita income: $41,976 (2005); Median household income: $65,083 (2005); Average household income: $96,333 (2005); Percent of households with income of $100,000 or more: 28.4% (2005); Poverty rate: 5.6% (2000).
Education: Percent of population age 25 and over with: High school diploma (including GED) or higher: 91.1% (2005); Bachelor's degree or higher: 41.8% (2005); Master's degree or higher: 20.3% (2005).
Housing: Homeownership rate: 84.3% (2005); Median home value: $243,000 (2005); Median rent: $490 per month (2000); Median age of housing: 27 years (2000).
Transportation: Commute to work: 75.4% car, 3.5% public transportation, 6.6% walk, 14.0% work from home (2000); Travel time to work: 31.1% less than 15 minutes, 29.7% 15 to 30 minutes, 21.0% 30 to 45 minutes, 9.8% 45 to 60 minutes, 8.5% 60 minutes or more (2000)

CANAAN (town). Covers a land area of 36.718 square miles and a water area of 0.241 square miles. Located at 42.40° N. Lat.; 73.44° W. Long. Elevation is 847 feet.
Population: 1,773 (1990); 1,820 (2000); 1,878 (2005); 1,926 (2010 projected); Race: 85.8% White, 10.0% Black, 0.9% Asian, 2.9% Hispanic of any race (2005); Density: 51.1 persons per square mile (2005); Average household size: 2.81 (2005); Median age: 38.5 (2005); Males per 100 females: 136.5 (2005); Marriage status: 30.0% never married, 56.4% now married, 6.4% widowed, 7.1% divorced (2000); Foreign born: 2.3% (2000); Ancestry (includes multiple ancestries): 18.6% German, 15.5% English, 13.0% Irish, 10.1% Italian, 7.3% Other groups (2000).

Economy: Commercial activities include pet food processing. Berkshire Industrial School for boys is nearby. Single-family building permits issued: 16 (2005); Multi-family building permits issued: 0 (2005); Employment by occupation: 19.7% management, 27.2% professional, 12.8% services, 20.5% sales, 0.8% farming, 10.6% construction, 8.5% production (2000).
Income: Per capita income: $32,193 (2005); Median household income: $63,942 (2005); Average household income: $89,327 (2005); Percent of households with income of $100,000 or more: 29.1% (2005); Poverty rate: 5.1% (2000).
Education: Percent of population age 25 and over with: High school diploma (including GED) or higher: 90.9% (2005); Bachelor's degree or higher: 44.5% (2005); Master's degree or higher: 22.4% (2005).

School District(s)
Berkshire Union Free School District (07-12)
    2003-04 Enrollment: 238 . . . . (518) 781-3500

Housing: Homeownership rate: 83.0% (2005); Median home value: $234,314 (2005); Median rent: $522 per month (2000); Median age of housing: 42 years (2000).
Transportation: Commute to work: 84.8% car, 6.5% public transportation, 2.3% walk, 6.1% work from home (2000); Travel time to work: 19.7% less than 15 minutes, 38.5% 15 to 30 minutes, 19.5% 30 to 45 minutes, 10.2% 45 to 60 minutes, 12.2% 60 minutes or more (2000)

CHATHAM (village).
Covers a land area of 1.178 square miles and a water area of 0.004 square miles. Located at 42.36° N. Lat.; 73.60° W. Long. Elevation is 473 feet.
Population: 1,920 (1990); 1,758 (2000); 1,831 (2005); 1,897 (2010 projected); Race: 94.0% White, 3.0% Black, 0.7% Asian, 2.2% Hispanic of any race (2005); Density: 1,554.0 persons per square mile (2005); Average household size: 2.33 (2005); Median age: 39.3 (2005); Males per 100 females: 91.3 (2005); Marriage status: 28.8% never married, 52.4% now married, 8.5% widowed, 10.2% divorced (2000); Foreign born: 3.6% (2000); Ancestry (includes multiple ancestries): 21.3% German, 19.2% Irish, 12.7% English, 9.1% Italian, 8.6% Other groups (2000).
Economy: Single-family building permits issued: 0 (2005); Multi-family building permits issued: 2 (2005); Employment by occupation: 11.3% management, 20.9% professional, 18.5% services, 24.4% sales, 0.7% farming, 13.3% construction, 10.9% production (2000).
Income: Per capita income: $25,083 (2005); Median household income: $44,268 (2005); Average household income: $58,215 (2005); Percent of households with income of $100,000 or more: 13.2% (2005); Poverty rate: 8.4% (2000).
Education: Percent of population age 25 and over with: High school diploma (including GED) or higher: 82.7% (2005); Bachelor's degree or higher: 26.0% (2005); Master's degree or higher: 12.0% (2005).

School District(s)
Chatham Central School District (KG-12)
    2003-04 Enrollment: 1,501 . . . . (518) 392-1501

Housing: Homeownership rate: 54.3% (2005); Median home value: $149,849 (2005); Median rent: $449 per month (2000); Median age of housing: 60+ years (2000).
Safety: Violent crime rate: 44.7 per 10,000 population; Property crime rate: 497.2 per 10,000 population (2004).
Transportation: Commute to work: 83.6% car, 0.2% public transportation, 7.6% walk, 7.5% work from home (2000); Travel time to work: 33.6% less than 15 minutes, 29.0% 15 to 30 minutes, 19.2% 30 to 45 minutes, 10.5% 45 to 60 minutes, 7.7% 60 minutes or more (2000)

CHATHAM (town).
Covers a land area of 53.266 square miles and a water area of 0.272 square miles. Located at 42.41° N. Lat.; 73.58° W. Long. Elevation is 473 feet.
History: Incorporated 1869.
Population: 4,413 (1990); 4,249 (2000); 4,276 (2005); 4,308 (2010 projected); Race: 95.6% White, 1.7% Black, 1.1% Asian, 0.8% Hispanic of any race (2005); Density: 80.3 persons per square mile (2005); Average household size: 2.36 (2005); Median age: 44.5 (2005); Males per 100 females: 95.6 (2005); Marriage status: 21.2% never married, 64.9% now married, 6.6% widowed, 7.3% divorced (2000); Foreign born: 3.3% (2000); Ancestry (includes multiple ancestries): 20.6% Irish, 19.9% German, 17.1% English, 10.4% Italian, 8.2% Polish (2000).
Economy: Railroad junction in diversified farm area. Manufacturing: boxboard, plastic moldings. Summer residences and recreation on small lakes nearby. Single-family building permits issued: 14 (2005); Multi-family building permits issued: 0 (2005); Employment by occupation: 14.7% management, 24.2% professional, 13.5% services, 26.3% sales, 0.4% farming, 10.6% construction, 10.3% production (2000).
Income: Per capita income: $35,906 (2005); Median household income: $58,824 (2005); Average household income: $84,804 (2005); Percent of households with income of $100,000 or more: 23.3% (2005); Poverty rate: 6.6% (2000).
Education: Percent of population age 25 and over with: High school diploma (including GED) or higher: 88.1% (2005); Bachelor's degree or higher: 31.3% (2005); Master's degree or higher: 17.0% (2005).
Housing: Homeownership rate: 77.0% (2005); Median home value: $194,238 (2005); Median rent: $508 per month (2000); Median age of housing: 52 years (2000).
Transportation: Commute to work: 85.0% car, 2.4% public transportation, 4.3% walk, 7.0% work from home (2000); Travel time to work: 26.9% less than 15 minutes, 30.8% 15 to 30 minutes, 27.5% 30 to 45 minutes, 7.3% 45 to 60 minutes, 7.4% 60 minutes or more (2000)

CLAVERACK (town).
Covers a land area of 47.655 square miles and a water area of 0.300 square miles. Located at 42.23° N. Lat.; 73.69° W. Long.
History: Fine old buildings include Van Rensselaer manor house; former county courthouse (built 1786).
Population: 6,414 (1990); 6,401 (2000); 6,430 (2005); 6,462 (2010 projected); Race: 92.6% White, 4.4% Black, 0.4% Asian, 3.7% Hispanic of any race (2005); Density: 134.9 persons per square mile (2005); Average household size: 2.53 (2005); Median age: 42.0 (2005); Males per 100 females: 100.8 (2005); Marriage status: 23.8% never married, 58.7% now married, 9.4% widowed, 8.1% divorced (2000); Foreign born: 3.4% (2000); Ancestry (includes multiple ancestries): 22.1% German, 19.6% Irish, 15.5% Italian, 12.1% English, 9.7% Dutch (2000).
Economy: Single-family building permits issued: 20 (2005); Multi-family building permits issued: 0 (2005); Employment by occupation: 10.7% management, 20.5% professional, 17.0% services, 21.4% sales, 2.1% farming, 10.7% construction, 17.6% production (2000).
Income: Per capita income: $23,019 (2005); Median household income: $46,950 (2005); Average household income: $57,256 (2005); Percent of households with income of $100,000 or more: 11.4% (2005); Poverty rate: 6.7% (2000).
Education: Percent of population age 25 and over with: High school diploma (including GED) or higher: 79.6% (2005); Bachelor's degree or higher: 17.8% (2005); Master's degree or higher: 7.6% (2005).

School District(s)
Hudson City School District (PK-12)
    2003-04 Enrollment: 2,417 . . . . (518) 828-4360

Housing: Homeownership rate: 73.6% (2005); Median home value: $143,986 (2005); Median rent: $447 per month (2000); Median age of housing: 46 years (2000).
Transportation: Commute to work: 91.5% car, 1.4% public transportation, 2.2% walk, 3.9% work from home (2000); Travel time to work: 34.8% less than 15 minutes, 43.2% 15 to 30 minutes, 10.2% 30 to 45 minutes, 6.8% 45 to 60 minutes, 4.9% 60 minutes or more (2000)

CLAVERACK-RED MILLS (CDP).
Covers a land area of 2.931 square miles and a water area of 0.014 square miles. Located at 42.22° N. Lat.; 73.72° W. Long.
Population: 1,152 (1990); 1,061 (2000); 1,044 (2005); 1,035 (2010 projected); Race: 97.0% White, 1.0% Black, 0.0% Asian, 1.2% Hispanic of any race (2005); Density: 356.2 persons per square mile (2005); Average household size: 2.21 (2005); Median age: 48.6 (2005); Males per 100 females: 99.2 (2005); Marriage status: 20.9% never married, 57.1% now married, 13.0% widowed, 9.0% divorced (2000); Foreign born: 0.0% (2000); Ancestry (includes multiple ancestries): 24.5% Irish, 21.9% German, 15.5% English, 15.4% Italian, 14.0% Dutch (2000).
Economy: Employment by occupation: 14.9% management, 25.7% professional, 15.3% services, 19.2% sales, 0.0% farming, 8.6% construction, 16.3% production (2000).
Income: Per capita income: $33,676 (2005); Median household income: $58,333 (2005); Average household income: $74,486 (2005); Percent of households with income of $100,000 or more: 16.9% (2005); Poverty rate: 3.1% (2000).
Education: Percent of population age 25 and over with: High school diploma (including GED) or higher: 87.5% (2005); Bachelor's degree or higher: 29.7% (2005); Master's degree or higher: 11.0% (2005).

Housing: Homeownership rate: 78.6% (2005); Median home value: $174,185 (2005); Median rent: $545 per month (2000); Median age of housing: 47 years (2000).
Transportation: Commute to work: 91.7% car, 0.0% public transportation, 3.9% walk, 4.4% work from home (2000); Travel time to work: 53.0% less than 15 minutes, 34.4% 15 to 30 minutes, 6.5% 30 to 45 minutes, 2.8% 45 to 60 minutes, 3.3% 60 minutes or more (2000)

CLERMONT (town). Covers a land area of 17.988 square miles and a water area of 1.212 square miles. Located at 42.08° N. Lat.; 73.85° W. Long. Elevation is 228 feet.
Population: 1,443 (1990); 1,726 (2000); 1,826 (2005); 1,919 (2010 projected); Race: 95.9% White, 1.5% Black, 0.5% Asian, 3.7% Hispanic of any race (2005); Density: 101.5 persons per square mile (2005); Average household size: 2.96 (2005); Median age: 37.7 (2005); Males per 100 females: 96.1 (2005); Marriage status: 27.8% never married, 55.3% now married, 6.4% widowed, 10.4% divorced (2000); Foreign born: 4.1% (2000); Ancestry (includes multiple ancestries): 31.5% German, 24.0% Irish, 14.4% Italian, 9.6% English, 8.7% Other groups (2000).
Economy: Single-family building permits issued: 13 (2005); Multi-family building permits issued: 0 (2005); Employment by occupation: 11.5% management, 24.0% professional, 18.9% services, 20.2% sales, 2.6% farming, 11.6% construction, 11.2% production (2000).
Income: Per capita income: $26,041 (2005); Median household income: $59,138 (2005); Average household income: $76,254 (2005); Percent of households with income of $100,000 or more: 20.9% (2005); Poverty rate: 9.4% (2000).
Education: Percent of population age 25 and over with: High school diploma (including GED) or higher: 85.8% (2005); Bachelor's degree or higher: 23.1% (2005); Master's degree or higher: 10.8% (2005).
Housing: Homeownership rate: 76.1% (2005); Median home value: $191,667 (2005); Median rent: $528 per month (2000); Median age of housing: 37 years (2000).
Transportation: Commute to work: 87.5% car, 2.0% public transportation, 2.1% walk, 7.5% work from home (2000); Travel time to work: 24.3% less than 15 minutes, 37.7% 15 to 30 minutes, 14.1% 30 to 45 minutes, 7.6% 45 to 60 minutes, 16.3% 60 minutes or more (2000)

COPAKE (town). Covers a land area of 40.959 square miles and a water area of 1.155 square miles. Located at 42.13° N. Lat.; 73.56° W. Long. Elevation is 550 feet.
Population: 3,118 (1990); 3,278 (2000); 3,325 (2005); 3,377 (2010 projected); Race: 96.5% White, 0.8% Black, 0.2% Asian, 3.4% Hispanic of any race (2005); Density: 81.2 persons per square mile (2005); Average household size: 2.51 (2005); Median age: 43.1 (2005); Males per 100 females: 105.2 (2005); Marriage status: 23.9% never married, 60.6% now married, 8.1% widowed, 7.4% divorced (2000); Foreign born: 4.0% (2000); Ancestry (includes multiple ancestries): 21.0% Irish, 20.2% German, 15.2% Italian, 10.2% English, 6.0% Dutch (2000).
Economy: In summer recreational area. Single-family building permits issued: 29 (2005); Multi-family building permits issued: 0 (2005); Employment by occupation: 10.3% management, 17.8% professional, 23.9% services, 24.5% sales, 2.4% farming, 12.2% construction, 9.0% production (2000).
Income: Per capita income: $27,368 (2005); Median household income: $49,400 (2005); Average household income: $66,429 (2005); Percent of households with income of $100,000 or more: 15.9% (2005); Poverty rate: 8.1% (2000).
Education: Percent of population age 25 and over with: High school diploma (including GED) or higher: 81.1% (2005); Bachelor's degree or higher: 20.4% (2005); Master's degree or higher: 11.3% (2005).
Housing: Homeownership rate: 75.1% (2005); Median home value: $151,238 (2005); Median rent: $491 per month (2000); Median age of housing: 32 years (2000).
Safety: Violent crime rate: 9.1 per 10,000 population; Property crime rate: 39.2 per 10,000 population (2004).
Transportation: Commute to work: 87.6% car, 2.5% public transportation, 2.1% walk, 6.5% work from home (2000); Travel time to work: 24.3% less than 15 minutes, 30.4% 15 to 30 minutes, 29.1% 30 to 45 minutes, 8.4% 45 to 60 minutes, 7.8% 60 minutes or more (2000)

COPAKE FALLS (unincorporated postal area, zip code 12517). Covers a land area of 5.252 square miles and a water area of 0 square miles. Located at 42.14° N. Lat.; 73.51° W. Long.
Population: 0 (2000); Race: 93.8% White, 0.0% Black, 0.0% Asian, 5.5% Hispanic of any race (2000); Density: 0.0 persons per square mile (2000); Age: 25.8% under 18, 9.1% over 64 (2000); Marriage status: 32.5% never married, 47.8% now married, 15.8% widowed, 3.8% divorced (2000); Foreign born: 2.5% (2000); Ancestry (includes multiple ancestries): 40.7% German, 28.0% Irish, 19.3% Italian, 18.9% English, 10.9% Other groups (2000).
Economy: Employment by occupation: 13.1% management, 19.3% professional, 20.0% services, 24.1% sales, 8.3% farming, 9.0% construction, 6.2% production (2000).
Income: Per capita income: $22,089 (2000); Median household income: $26,389 (2000); Poverty rate: 8.4% (2000).
Education: Percent of population age 25 and over with: High school diploma (including GED) or higher: 79.0% (2000); Bachelor's degree or higher: 28.7% (2000).
Housing: Homeownership rate: 71.3% (2000); Median home value: $120,500 (2000); Median rent: $492 per month (2000); Median age of housing: 44 years (2000).
Transportation: Commute to work: 72.7% car, 0.0% public transportation, 7.9% walk, 15.1% work from home (2000); Travel time to work: 37.3% less than 15 minutes, 22.9% 15 to 30 minutes, 15.3% 30 to 45 minutes, 20.3% 45 to 60 minutes, 4.2% 60 minutes or more (2000)

COPAKE LAKE (CDP). Covers a land area of 9.592 square miles and a water area of 0.734 square miles. Located at 42.14° N. Lat.; 73.59° W. Long.
Population: 606 (1990); 762 (2000); 757 (2005); 757 (2010 projected); Race: 96.3% White, 0.3% Black, 0.0% Asian, 2.5% Hispanic of any race (2005); Density: 78.9 persons per square mile (2005); Average household size: 2.47 (2005); Median age: 40.9 (2005); Males per 100 females: 105.1 (2005); Marriage status: 23.2% never married, 59.9% now married, 6.7% widowed, 10.2% divorced (2000); Foreign born: 7.1% (2000); Ancestry (includes multiple ancestries): 23.3% Irish, 21.3% Italian, 14.2% German, 10.9% Dutch, 10.6% United States or American (2000).
Economy: Employment by occupation: 13.3% management, 15.8% professional, 33.4% services, 16.4% sales, 3.1% farming, 13.0% construction, 5.0% production (2000).
Income: Per capita income: $25,281 (2005); Median household income: $48,784 (2005); Average household income: $62,541 (2005); Percent of households with income of $100,000 or more: 18.6% (2005); Poverty rate: 13.5% (2000).
Education: Percent of population age 25 and over with: High school diploma (including GED) or higher: 80.9% (2005); Bachelor's degree or higher: 19.1% (2005); Master's degree or higher: 7.7% (2005).
Housing: Homeownership rate: 78.1% (2005); Median home value: $165,000 (2005); Median rent: $488 per month (2000); Median age of housing: 31 years (2000).
Transportation: Commute to work: 88.9% car, 2.2% public transportation, 0.0% walk, 7.4% work from home (2000); Travel time to work: 31.8% less than 15 minutes, 25.1% 15 to 30 minutes, 33.4% 30 to 45 minutes, 3.3% 45 to 60 minutes, 6.4% 60 minutes or more (2000)

CRARYVILLE (unincorporated postal area, zip code 12521). Covers a land area of 32.988 square miles and a water area of 0.184 square miles. Located at 42.17° N. Lat.; 73.65° W. Long. Elevation is 635 feet.
Population: 0 (2000); Race: 94.5% White, 0.7% Black, 0.1% Asian, 1.4% Hispanic of any race (2000); Density: 0.0 persons per square mile (2000); Age: 23.1% under 18, 16.2% over 64 (2000); Marriage status: 21.2% never married, 60.4% now married, 6.8% widowed, 11.6% divorced (2000); Foreign born: 8.2% (2000); Ancestry (includes multiple ancestries): 15.1% Italian, 14.1% German, 13.8% Irish, 8.8% Other groups, 8.4% English (2000).
Economy: Employment by occupation: 16.4% management, 23.8% professional, 17.2% services, 21.7% sales, 1.4% farming, 9.5% construction, 10.0% production (2000).
Income: Per capita income: $24,321 (2000); Median household income: $36,490 (2000); Poverty rate: 11.8% (2000).
Education: Percent of population age 25 and over with: High school diploma (including GED) or higher: 87.0% (2000); Bachelor's degree or higher: 27.6% (2000).

School District(s)
Taconic Hills Central School District (KG-12)
    2003-04 Enrollment: 1,871 . . . . (518) 325-0313

Housing: Homeownership rate: 78.9% (2000); Median home value: $118,200 (2000); Median rent: $461 per month (2000); Median age of housing: 33 years (2000).
Transportation: Commute to work: 86.5% car, 3.8% public transportation, 1.7% walk, 7.2% work from home (2000); Travel time to work: 18.0% less than 15 minutes, 48.3% 15 to 30 minutes, 18.1% 30 to 45 minutes, 6.8% 45 to 60 minutes, 8.9% 60 minutes or more (2000)

EAST CHATHAM (unincorporated postal area, zip code 12060).
Covers a land area of 36.946 square miles and a water area of 0.103 square miles. Located at 42.42° N. Lat.; 73.50° W. Long.
Population: 0 (2000); Race: 96.0% White, 1.9% Black, 0.5% Asian, 0.5% Hispanic of any race (2000); Density: 0.0 persons per square mile (2000); Age: 22.4% under 18, 14.9% over 64 (2000); Marriage status: 22.6% never married, 63.7% now married, 9.2% widowed, 4.5% divorced (2000); Foreign born: 3.8% (2000); Ancestry (includes multiple ancestries): 19.3% German, 17.7% English, 17.1% Irish, 10.8% Italian, 8.1% Other groups (2000).
Economy: Employment by occupation: 12.5% management, 29.4% professional, 14.6% services, 25.6% sales, 0.7% farming, 6.9% construction, 10.3% production (2000).
Income: Per capita income: $27,648 (2000); Median household income: $46,319 (2000); Poverty rate: 5.6% (2000).
Education: Percent of population age 25 and over with: High school diploma (including GED) or higher: 90.8% (2000); Bachelor's degree or higher: 37.9% (2000).
Housing: Homeownership rate: 81.1% (2000); Median home value: $129,400 (2000); Median rent: $440 per month (2000); Median age of housing: 34 years (2000).
Transportation: Commute to work: 85.4% car, 6.0% public transportation, 0.9% walk, 7.7% work from home (2000); Travel time to work: 18.1% less than 15 minutes, 35.2% 15 to 30 minutes, 30.8% 30 to 45 minutes, 8.5% 45 to 60 minutes, 7.4% 60 minutes or more (2000)

ELIZAVILLE (unincorporated postal area, zip code 12523).
Covers a land area of 24.847 square miles and a water area of 0.126 square miles. Located at 42.08° N. Lat.; 73.77° W. Long. Elevation is 284 feet.
Population: 0 (2000); Race: 99.2% White, 0.5% Black, 0.0% Asian, 1.9% Hispanic of any race (2000); Density: 0.0 persons per square mile (2000); Age: 23.4% under 18, 16.5% over 64 (2000); Marriage status: 21.6% never married, 59.2% now married, 9.5% widowed, 9.7% divorced (2000); Foreign born: 4.9% (2000); Ancestry (includes multiple ancestries): 26.1% German, 16.9% Italian, 13.7% Irish, 11.3% English, 8.4% United States or American (2000).
Economy: Employment by occupation: 14.2% management, 15.0% professional, 19.8% services, 18.3% sales, 1.2% farming, 15.2% construction, 16.3% production (2000).
Income: Per capita income: $18,792 (2000); Median household income: $40,385 (2000); Poverty rate: 7.8% (2000).
Education: Percent of population age 25 and over with: High school diploma (including GED) or higher: 80.7% (2000); Bachelor's degree or higher: 15.0% (2000).
Housing: Homeownership rate: 82.3% (2000); Median home value: $116,200 (2000); Median rent: $515 per month (2000); Median age of housing: 34 years (2000).
Transportation: Commute to work: 92.4% car, 2.8% public transportation, 0.9% walk, 3.2% work from home (2000); Travel time to work: 16.9% less than 15 minutes, 42.9% 15 to 30 minutes, 20.9% 30 to 45 minutes, 7.2% 45 to 60 minutes, 12.1% 60 minutes or more (2000)

GALLATIN (town). Aka Gallatinville.
Covers a land area of 39.250 square miles and a water area of 0.361 square miles. Located at 42.06° N. Lat.; 73.71° W. Long.
Population: 1,658 (1990); 1,499 (2000); 1,454 (2005); 1,405 (2010 projected); Race: 97.0% White, 0.6% Black, 1.2% Asian, 3.2% Hispanic of any race (2005); Density: 37.0 persons per square mile (2005); Average household size: 2.41 (2005); Median age: 43.6 (2005); Males per 100 females: 104.5 (2005); Marriage status: 25.4% never married, 61.3% now married, 6.3% widowed, 7.0% divorced (2000); Foreign born: 3.7% (2000); Ancestry (includes multiple ancestries): 24.9% German, 20.1% Italian, 14.7% Irish, 9.1% English, 6.1% Dutch (2000).
Economy: Employment by occupation: 12.0% management, 20.5% professional, 14.5% services, 21.6% sales, 1.8% farming, 17.9% construction, 11.6% production (2000).

Income: Per capita income: $24,574 (2005); Median household income: $47,929 (2005); Average household income: $59,038 (2005); Percent of households with income of $100,000 or more: 11.9% (2005); Poverty rate: 5.6% (2000).
Taxes: Total city taxes per capita: $375 (2004); City property taxes per capita: $310 (2004).
Education: Percent of population age 25 and over with: High school diploma (including GED) or higher: 84.7% (2005); Bachelor's degree or higher: 24.7% (2005); Master's degree or higher: 12.6% (2005).
Housing: Homeownership rate: 81.9% (2005); Median home value: $184,553 (2005); Median rent: $482 per month (2000); Median age of housing: 38 years (2000).
Transportation: Commute to work: 86.1% car, 4.4% public transportation, 2.2% walk, 5.9% work from home (2000); Travel time to work: 17.3% less than 15 minutes, 34.5% 15 to 30 minutes, 24.5% 30 to 45 minutes, 10.3% 45 to 60 minutes, 13.4% 60 minutes or more (2000)

GERMANTOWN (town).
Covers a land area of 12.153 square miles and a water area of 1.759 square miles. Located at 42.13° N. Lat.; 73.87° W. Long. Elevation is 138 feet.
Population: 2,010 (1990); 2,018 (2000); 2,013 (2005); 2,012 (2010 projected); Race: 96.5% White, 1.5% Black, 0.5% Asian, 1.9% Hispanic of any race (2005); Density: 165.6 persons per square mile (2005); Average household size: 2.38 (2005); Median age: 43.6 (2005); Males per 100 females: 95.1 (2005); Marriage status: 22.5% never married, 60.5% now married, 8.4% widowed, 8.6% divorced (2000); Foreign born: 5.0% (2000); Ancestry (includes multiple ancestries): 31.2% German, 22.4% Irish, 15.3% Italian, 11.8% English, 6.4% Dutch (2000).
Economy: Single-family building permits issued: 11 (2005); Multi-family building permits issued: 0 (2005); Employment by occupation: 8.8% management, 21.2% professional, 18.7% services, 21.6% sales, 3.1% farming, 13.8% construction, 12.7% production (2000).
Income: Per capita income: $25,924 (2005); Median household income: $46,582 (2005); Average household income: $61,507 (2005); Percent of households with income of $100,000 or more: 16.2% (2005); Poverty rate: 7.9% (2000).
Education: Percent of population age 25 and over with: High school diploma (including GED) or higher: 81.5% (2005); Bachelor's degree or higher: 22.8% (2005); Master's degree or higher: 8.8% (2005).

School District(s)
Germantown Central School District (KG-12)
 2003-04 Enrollment: 713 . . . . (518) 537-6280

Housing: Homeownership rate: 72.8% (2005); Median home value: $191,429 (2005); Median rent: $441 per month (2000); Median age of housing: 56 years (2000).
Safety: Violent crime rate: 0.0 per 10,000 population; Property crime rate: 19.8 per 10,000 population (2004).
Transportation: Commute to work: 91.1% car, 2.3% public transportation, 1.8% walk, 4.0% work from home (2000); Travel time to work: 32.0% less than 15 minutes, 32.5% 15 to 30 minutes, 16.2% 30 to 45 minutes, 8.7% 45 to 60 minutes, 10.7% 60 minutes or more (2000)

GERMANTOWN (CDP).
Covers a land area of 2.674 square miles and a water area of 0.016 square miles. Located at 42.13° N. Lat.; 73.88° W. Long.
Population: 820 (1990); 862 (2000); 860 (2005); 858 (2010 projected); Race: 96.2% White, 1.2% Black, 0.6% Asian, 2.2% Hispanic of any race (2005); Density: 321.6 persons per square mile (2005); Average household size: 2.41 (2005); Median age: 41.1 (2005); Males per 100 females: 91.1 (2005); Marriage status: 24.9% never married, 62.0% now married, 6.4% widowed, 6.6% divorced (2000); Foreign born: 3.2% (2000); Ancestry (includes multiple ancestries): 34.8% German, 24.2% Irish, 13.0% English, 7.8% Other groups, 7.5% Italian (2000).
Economy: Employment by occupation: 8.1% management, 18.9% professional, 20.0% services, 25.6% sales, 2.3% farming, 13.1% construction, 12.0% production (2000).
Income: Per capita income: $25,348 (2005); Median household income: $48,627 (2005); Average household income: $60,868 (2005); Percent of households with income of $100,000 or more: 15.1% (2005); Poverty rate: 7.2% (2000).
Education: Percent of population age 25 and over with: High school diploma (including GED) or higher: 84.5% (2005); Bachelor's degree or higher: 21.8% (2005); Master's degree or higher: 7.5% (2005).

Housing: Homeownership rate: 75.1% (2005); Median home value: $184,127 (2005); Median rent: $491 per month (2000); Median age of housing: 60+ years (2000).
Transportation: Commute to work: 91.5% car, 2.6% public transportation, 1.7% walk, 2.6% work from home (2000); Travel time to work: 32.8% less than 15 minutes, 35.2% 15 to 30 minutes, 11.9% 30 to 45 minutes, 10.4% 45 to 60 minutes, 9.7% 60 minutes or more (2000)

GHENT (town). Covers a land area of 45.176 square miles and a water area of 0.221 square miles. Located at 42.31° N. Lat.; 73.64° W. Long.
Population: 4,812 (1990); 5,276 (2000); 5,400 (2005); 5,530 (2010 projected); Race: 96.9% White, 1.1% Black, 0.2% Asian, 1.8% Hispanic of any race (2005); Density: 119.5 persons per square mile (2005); Average household size: 2.57 (2005); Median age: 42.0 (2005); Males per 100 females: 94.8 (2005); Marriage status: 19.5% never married, 62.8% now married, 9.8% widowed, 7.9% divorced (2000); Foreign born: 3.2% (2000); Ancestry (includes multiple ancestries): 24.5% German, 18.5% Irish, 14.5% English, 11.9% Italian, 11.1% Polish (2000).
Economy: Single-family building permits issued: 20 (2005); Multi-family building permits issued: 0 (2005); Employment by occupation: 14.1% management, 22.3% professional, 14.3% services, 23.1% sales, 0.5% farming, 11.5% construction, 14.2% production (2000).
Income: Per capita income: $25,951 (2005); Median household income: $50,445 (2005); Average household income: $66,090 (2005); Percent of households with income of $100,000 or more: 15.1% (2005); Poverty rate: 4.6% (2000).
Education: Percent of population age 25 and over with: High school diploma (including GED) or higher: 80.0% (2005); Bachelor's degree or higher: 24.9% (2005); Master's degree or higher: 11.9% (2005).
Housing: Homeownership rate: 74.6% (2005); Median home value: $164,751 (2005); Median rent: $451 per month (2000); Median age of housing: 34 years (2000).
Transportation: Commute to work: 90.5% car, 0.5% public transportation, 2.9% walk, 5.3% work from home (2000); Travel time to work: 33.6% less than 15 minutes, 35.2% 15 to 30 minutes, 14.2% 30 to 45 minutes, 7.9% 45 to 60 minutes, 9.0% 60 minutes or more (2000)

GHENT (CDP). Covers a land area of 1.540 square miles and a water area of 0.004 square miles. Located at 42.32° N. Lat.; 73.61° W. Long.
Population: 549 (1990); 586 (2000); 601 (2005); 616 (2010 projected); Race: 97.7% White, 0.8% Black, 0.3% Asian, 1.2% Hispanic of any race (2005); Density: 390.3 persons per square mile (2005); Average household size: 2.43 (2005); Median age: 40.2 (2005); Males per 100 females: 99.7 (2005); Marriage status: 26.6% never married, 56.5% now married, 9.1% widowed, 7.8% divorced (2000); Foreign born: 3.0% (2000); Ancestry (includes multiple ancestries): 20.6% German, 14.3% Italian, 14.0% Irish, 14.0% Polish, 10.4% Dutch (2000).
Economy: Employment by occupation: 10.5% management, 20.7% professional, 6.1% services, 30.3% sales, 0.0% farming, 12.1% construction, 20.4% production (2000).
Income: Per capita income: $27,749 (2005); Median household income: $58,717 (2005); Average household income: $67,490 (2005); Percent of households with income of $100,000 or more: 13.0% (2005); Poverty rate: 3.5% (2000).
Education: Percent of population age 25 and over with: High school diploma (including GED) or higher: 79.4% (2005); Bachelor's degree or higher: 23.4% (2005); Master's degree or higher: 16.4% (2005).
Housing: Homeownership rate: 73.7% (2005); Median home value: $146,203 (2005); Median rent: $490 per month (2000); Median age of housing: 52 years (2000).
Transportation: Commute to work: 91.3% car, 0.0% public transportation, 6.8% walk, 1.9% work from home (2000); Travel time to work: 36.4% less than 15 minutes, 26.2% 15 to 30 minutes, 17.7% 30 to 45 minutes, 6.9% 45 to 60 minutes, 12.8% 60 minutes or more (2000)

GREENPORT (town). Covers a land area of 18.766 square miles and a water area of 1.719 square miles. Located at 42.24° N. Lat.; 73.78° W. Long.
Population: 4,101 (1990); 4,180 (2000); 4,148 (2005); 4,111 (2010 projected); Race: 89.4% White, 6.3% Black, 1.2% Asian, 4.8% Hispanic of any race (2005); Density: 221.0 persons per square mile (2005); Average household size: 2.31 (2005); Median age: 43.1 (2005); Males per 100 females: 94.4 (2005); Marriage status: 21.0% never married, 56.8% now married, 12.0% widowed, 10.1% divorced (2000); Foreign born: 3.0% (2000); Ancestry (includes multiple ancestries): 19.6% German, 18.3% Italian, 17.8% Irish, 11.5% Other groups, 9.2% Polish (2000).
Economy: Single-family building permits issued: 9 (2005); Multi-family building permits issued: 0 (2005); Employment by occupation: 12.3% management, 18.0% professional, 20.5% services, 24.7% sales, 1.3% farming, 8.8% construction, 14.3% production (2000).
Income: Per capita income: $22,844 (2005); Median household income: $40,836 (2005); Average household income: $51,712 (2005); Percent of households with income of $100,000 or more: 10.9% (2005); Poverty rate: 10.3% (2000).
Education: Percent of population age 25 and over with: High school diploma (including GED) or higher: 79.0% (2005); Bachelor's degree or higher: 16.6% (2005); Master's degree or higher: 9.6% (2005).
Housing: Homeownership rate: 67.2% (2005); Median home value: $137,605 (2005); Median rent: $443 per month (2000); Median age of housing: 40 years (2000).
Transportation: Commute to work: 89.5% car, 1.7% public transportation, 4.3% walk, 2.7% work from home (2000); Travel time to work: 51.0% less than 15 minutes, 24.9% 15 to 30 minutes, 5.9% 30 to 45 minutes, 6.3% 45 to 60 minutes, 11.9% 60 minutes or more (2000)

HILLSDALE (town). Covers a land area of 47.638 square miles and a water area of 0.134 square miles. Located at 42.22° N. Lat.; 73.53° W. Long. Elevation is 678 feet.
Population: 1,793 (1990); 1,744 (2000); 1,772 (2005); 1,801 (2010 projected); Race: 97.8% White, 0.5% Black, 0.6% Asian, 2.3% Hispanic of any race (2005); Density: 37.2 persons per square mile (2005); Average household size: 2.37 (2005); Median age: 44.2 (2005); Males per 100 females: 98.7 (2005); Marriage status: 21.1% never married, 60.2% now married, 6.7% widowed, 12.0% divorced (2000); Foreign born: 6.7% (2000); Ancestry (includes multiple ancestries): 19.4% German, 17.4% Irish, 15.3% Italian, 14.5% English, 7.9% Polish (2000).
Economy: Skiing at nearby Catamount Mt. in the Berkshires. Single-family building permits issued: 15 (2005); Multi-family building permits issued: 0 (2005); Employment by occupation: 13.1% management, 23.7% professional, 15.6% services, 20.0% sales, 3.2% farming, 15.0% construction, 9.3% production (2000).
Income: Per capita income: $30,007 (2005); Median household income: $47,634 (2005); Average household income: $71,181 (2005); Percent of households with income of $100,000 or more: 18.5% (2005); Poverty rate: 8.3% (2000).
Education: Percent of population age 25 and over with: High school diploma (including GED) or higher: 87.1% (2005); Bachelor's degree or higher: 33.1% (2005); Master's degree or higher: 18.0% (2005).
Housing: Homeownership rate: 72.6% (2005); Median home value: $201,538 (2005); Median rent: $544 per month (2000); Median age of housing: 43 years (2000).
Newspapers: The Columbia County Independent (General - Circulation 10,100); The Paper (General - Circulation 20,000); The Rensselaer County Independent (General - Circulation 10,100)
Transportation: Commute to work: 80.0% car, 2.5% public transportation, 6.9% walk, 10.1% work from home (2000); Travel time to work: 32.4% less than 15 minutes, 31.1% 15 to 30 minutes, 22.1% 30 to 45 minutes, 5.4% 45 to 60 minutes, 9.0% 60 minutes or more (2000)

HUDSON (city). Covers a land area of 2.169 square miles and a water area of 0.154 square miles. Located at 42.25° N. Lat.; 73.78° W. Long. Elevation is 10 feet.
History: The city was a whaling and trading port until 1812. Its industries included textiles, furniture, cement, and metal products, but these are largely gone. Many colonial and Revolutionary era homes are in the area. Olana, estate of Frederic E. Church, 2.5 miles South of city. Settled c.1622 by the Dutch and later in 1783 by English whalers; incorporated 1785.
Population: 8,034 (1990); 7,524 (2000); 7,223 (2005); 6,915 (2010 projected); Race: 59.8% White, 25.4% Black, 4.6% Asian, 11.2% Hispanic of any race (2005); Density: 3,329.4 persons per square mile (2005); Average household size: 2.56 (2005); Median age: 36.2 (2005); Males per 100 females: 109.2 (2005); Marriage status: 36.8% never married, 42.4% now married, 11.2% widowed, 9.6% divorced (2000); Foreign born: 10.5% (2000); Ancestry (includes multiple ancestries): 27.8% Other groups, 13.7% Italian, 12.1% Irish, 10.6% German, 8.3% Polish (2000).
Economy: Single-family building permits issued: 1 (2005); Multi-family building permits issued: 10 (2005); Employment by occupation: 4.6% management, 16.6% professional, 24.1% services, 24.2% sales, 1.1% farming, 5.4% construction, 24.0% production (2000).

Income: Per capita income: $15,712 (2005); Median household income: $26,361 (2005); Average household income: $35,613 (2005); Percent of households with income of $100,000 or more: 3.7% (2005); Poverty rate: 25.6% (2000).
Education: Percent of population age 25 and over with: High school diploma (including GED) or higher: 60.6% (2005); Bachelor's degree or higher: 8.8% (2005); Master's degree or higher: 2.8% (2005).

School District(s)
Austin L. Carr Charter School
   2003-04 Enrollment: n/a .... (518) 822-8540
Hudson City School District (PK-12)
   2003-04 Enrollment: 2,417 .... (518) 828-4360

Two-year College(s)
Columbia-Greene Community College (Public)
   Fall 2004 Enrollment: 1,753 .... (518) 828-4181
   2005-06 Tuition: In-state $2,832; Out-of-state $5,664

Housing: Homeownership rate: 33.7% (2005); Median home value: $110,662 (2005); Median rent: $390 per month (2000); Median age of housing: 60+ years (2000).
Hospitals: Columbia Memorial Hospital (194 beds)
Newspapers: Register-Star (Circulation 7,000)
Transportation: Commute to work: 75.6% car, 6.2% public transportation, 12.7% walk, 2.8% work from home (2000); Travel time to work: 54.4% less than 15 minutes, 27.6% 15 to 30 minutes, 8.5% 30 to 45 minutes, 3.7% 45 to 60 minutes, 5.9% 60 minutes or more (2000); Amtrak: Service available.

Additional Information Contacts
Columbia County Chamber of Commerce............. (518) 828-4417
   http://www.columbiachamber-ny.com

KINDERHOOK (village).
Covers a land area of 1.909 square miles and a water area of 0 square miles. Located at 42.39° N. Lat.; 73.70° W. Long. Elevation is 256 feet.
Population: 1,293 (1990); 1,275 (2000); 1,295 (2005); 1,303 (2010 projected); Race: 98.0% White, 0.8% Black, 0.0% Asian, 2.0% Hispanic of any race (2005); Density: 678.2 persons per square mile (2005); Average household size: 2.29 (2005); Median age: 45.2 (2005); Males per 100 females: 92.1 (2005); Marriage status: 26.2% never married, 58.4% now married, 7.0% widowed, 8.4% divorced (2000); Foreign born: 3.6% (2000); Ancestry (includes multiple ancestries): 27.2% Irish, 21.9% German, 15.3% English, 14.9% Italian, 8.0% Dutch (2000).
Economy: Single-family building permits issued: 12 (2005); Multi-family building permits issued: 0 (2005); Employment by occupation: 17.1% management, 33.6% professional, 12.1% services, 23.4% sales, 0.3% farming, 7.2% construction, 6.3% production (2000).
Income: Per capita income: $31,902 (2005); Median household income: $63,086 (2005); Average household income: $72,990 (2005); Percent of households with income of $100,000 or more: 22.4% (2005); Poverty rate: 2.3% (2000).
Education: Percent of population age 25 and over with: High school diploma (including GED) or higher: 94.2% (2005); Bachelor's degree or higher: 47.3% (2005); Master's degree or higher: 20.2% (2005).

School District(s)
Kinderhook Central School District (KG-12)
   2003-04 Enrollment: 2,285 .... (518) 758-7575

Housing: Homeownership rate: 80.7% (2005); Median home value: $217,196 (2005); Median rent: $525 per month (2000); Median age of housing: 48 years (2000).
Transportation: Commute to work: 90.2% car, 0.7% public transportation, 4.7% walk, 4.0% work from home (2000); Travel time to work: 31.2% less than 15 minutes, 24.4% 15 to 30 minutes, 32.6% 30 to 45 minutes, 5.4% 45 to 60 minutes, 6.4% 60 minutes or more (2000)

KINDERHOOK (town).
Covers a land area of 31.835 square miles and a water area of 0.589 square miles. Located at 42.41° N. Lat.; 73.67° W. Long. Elevation is 256 feet.
History: Kinderhook (Dutch for "children's corner") was named by its Dutch settlers. President Martin Van Buren was born and buried in Kinderhook. Settled before the American Revolution. Richard Upjohn designed St. Paul's Church (1851) here. The Van Buren homestead, "Lindenwald," is South of the village. The House of History, maintained by the county historical society, occupies an early-19th-century mansion. Incorporated 1838.
Population: 8,112 (1990); 8,296 (2000); 8,586 (2005); 8,863 (2010 projected); Race: 96.7% White, 0.8% Black, 1.2% Asian, 1.9% Hispanic of any race (2005); Density: 269.7 persons per square mile (2005); Average household size: 2.57 (2005); Median age: 42.2 (2005); Males per 100 females: 93.7 (2005); Marriage status: 21.7% never married, 63.0% now married, 7.1% widowed, 8.2% divorced (2000); Foreign born: 2.4% (2000); Ancestry (includes multiple ancestries): 24.3% Irish, 23.6% German, 16.4% Italian, 13.5% English, 7.4% Polish (2000).
Economy: Manufacturing of mechanical and hydraulic presses. Single-family building permits issued: 36 (2005); Multi-family building permits issued: 0 (2005); Employment by occupation: 15.0% management, 24.8% professional, 11.3% services, 26.7% sales, 1.0% farming, 11.1% construction, 10.1% production (2000).
Income: Per capita income: $27,684 (2005); Median household income: $58,742 (2005); Average household income: $69,298 (2005); Percent of households with income of $100,000 or more: 19.7% (2005); Poverty rate: 4.6% (2000).
Education: Percent of population age 25 and over with: High school diploma (including GED) or higher: 87.1% (2005); Bachelor's degree or higher: 29.2% (2005); Master's degree or higher: 11.2% (2005).
Housing: Homeownership rate: 77.4% (2005); Median home value: $184,895 (2005); Median rent: $481 per month (2000); Median age of housing: 32 years (2000).
Transportation: Commute to work: 91.7% car, 1.3% public transportation, 2.4% walk, 4.2% work from home (2000); Travel time to work: 26.4% less than 15 minutes, 29.3% 15 to 30 minutes, 34.0% 30 to 45 minutes, 4.9% 45 to 60 minutes, 5.5% 60 minutes or more (2000)

LIVINGSTON (town).
Covers a land area of 38.228 square miles and a water area of 0.722 square miles. Located at 42.12° N. Lat.; 73.79° W. Long.
Population: 3,582 (1990); 3,424 (2000); 3,445 (2005); 3,483 (2010 projected); Race: 97.0% White, 1.5% Black, 0.5% Asian, 2.1% Hispanic of any race (2005); Density: 90.1 persons per square mile (2005); Average household size: 2.51 (2005); Median age: 43.7 (2005); Males per 100 females: 92.0 (2005); Marriage status: 22.2% never married, 57.7% now married, 10.7% widowed, 9.4% divorced (2000); Foreign born: 4.8% (2000); Ancestry (includes multiple ancestries): 27.1% German, 18.3% Italian, 12.9% Irish, 12.4% English, 5.8% United States or American (2000).
Economy: Single-family building permits issued: 18 (2005); Multi-family building permits issued: 0 (2005); Employment by occupation: 14.3% management, 17.3% professional, 19.1% services, 19.3% sales, 2.7% farming, 11.0% construction, 16.3% production (2000).
Income: Per capita income: $25,725 (2005); Median household income: $45,032 (2005); Average household income: $62,383 (2005); Percent of households with income of $100,000 or more: 14.6% (2005); Poverty rate: 5.9% (2000).
Education: Percent of population age 25 and over with: High school diploma (including GED) or higher: 79.0% (2005); Bachelor's degree or higher: 18.0% (2005); Master's degree or higher: 7.3% (2005).
Housing: Homeownership rate: 74.7% (2005); Median home value: $145,114 (2005); Median rent: $500 per month (2000); Median age of housing: 31 years (2000).
Transportation: Commute to work: 87.8% car, 2.7% public transportation, 5.4% walk, 2.9% work from home (2000); Travel time to work: 36.0% less than 15 minutes, 34.6% 15 to 30 minutes, 14.4% 30 to 45 minutes, 4.9% 45 to 60 minutes, 10.2% 60 minutes or more (2000)

LORENZ PARK (CDP).
Covers a land area of 1.844 square miles and a water area of 0.126 square miles. Located at 42.26° N. Lat.; 73.76° W. Long.
Population: 1,804 (1990); 1,981 (2000); 1,921 (2005); 1,869 (2010 projected); Race: 89.7% White, 5.9% Black, 0.9% Asian, 5.9% Hispanic of any race (2005); Density: 1,041.7 persons per square mile (2005); Average household size: 2.23 (2005); Median age: 42.3 (2005); Males per 100 females: 87.2 (2005); Marriage status: 18.2% never married, 57.7% now married, 14.7% widowed, 9.5% divorced (2000); Foreign born: 3.7% (2000); Ancestry (includes multiple ancestries): 19.7% Italian, 18.5% Irish, 15.2% Other groups, 14.3% German, 10.7% Polish (2000).
Economy: Employment by occupation: 8.0% management, 14.8% professional, 23.0% services, 30.8% sales, 0.0% farming, 7.8% construction, 15.6% production (2000).
Income: Per capita income: $19,546 (2005); Median household income: $37,930 (2005); Average household income: $43,560 (2005); Percent of households with income of $100,000 or more: 4.3% (2005); Poverty rate: 9.1% (2000).

Education: Percent of population age 25 and over with: High school diploma (including GED) or higher: 77.9% (2005); Bachelor's degree or higher: 10.6% (2005); Master's degree or higher: 4.9% (2005).
Housing: Homeownership rate: 68.2% (2005); Median home value: $125,534 (2005); Median rent: $408 per month (2000); Median age of housing: 34 years (2000).
Transportation: Commute to work: 91.8% car, 2.0% public transportation, 2.2% walk, 3.4% work from home (2000); Travel time to work: 54.7% less than 15 minutes, 22.9% 15 to 30 minutes, 4.0% 30 to 45 minutes, 5.8% 45 to 60 minutes, 12.6% 60 minutes or more (2000)

MALDEN BRIDGE (unincorporated postal area, zip code 12115). Covers a land area of 5.619 square miles and a water area of 0.024 square miles. Located at 42.47° N. Lat.; 73.58° W. Long.
Population: 0 (2000); Race: 92.8% White, 0.0% Black, 1.8% Asian, 2.2% Hispanic of any race (2000); Density: 0.0 persons per square mile (2000); Age: 26.0% under 18, 3.1% over 64 (2000); Marriage status: 14.7% never married, 76.5% now married, 0.0% widowed, 8.8% divorced (2000); Foreign born: 0.0% (2000); Ancestry (includes multiple ancestries): 42.2% Irish, 23.8% German, 21.1% English, 17.5% Other groups, 16.6% Italian (2000).
Economy: Employment by occupation: 6.5% management, 22.8% professional, 16.3% services, 26.8% sales, 0.0% farming, 24.4% construction, 3.3% production (2000).
Income: Per capita income: $24,779 (2000); Median household income: $52,083 (2000); Poverty rate: 0.0% (2000).
Education: Percent of population age 25 and over with: High school diploma (including GED) or higher: 92.1% (2000); Bachelor's degree or higher: 37.5% (2000).
Housing: Homeownership rate: 80.2% (2000); Median home value: $117,000 (2000); Median rent: $475 per month (2000); Median age of housing: 43 years (2000).
Transportation: Commute to work: 82.9% car, 11.1% public transportation, 0.0% walk, 6.0% work from home (2000); Travel time to work: 18.2% less than 15 minutes, 34.5% 15 to 30 minutes, 27.3% 30 to 45 minutes, 15.5% 45 to 60 minutes, 4.5% 60 minutes or more (2000)

NEW LEBANON (town). Covers a land area of 35.896 square miles and a water area of 0.078 square miles. Located at 42.46° N. Lat.; 73.44° W. Long.
History: Samuel Tilden was born here. Site of Roman Catholic Shrine of Our Lady of Lourdes.
Population: 2,379 (1990); 2,454 (2000); 2,467 (2005); 2,487 (2010 projected); Race: 94.4% White, 1.5% Black, 2.1% Asian, 1.3% Hispanic of any race (2005); Density: 68.7 persons per square mile (2005); Average household size: 2.44 (2005); Median age: 41.1 (2005); Males per 100 females: 95.8 (2005); Marriage status: 23.0% never married, 60.0% now married, 6.3% widowed, 10.8% divorced (2000); Foreign born: 4.2% (2000); Ancestry (includes multiple ancestries): 19.8% German, 19.1% Irish, 16.9% English, 12.4% Italian, 9.3% French (except Basque) (2000).
Economy: Single-family building permits issued: 5 (2005); Multi-family building permits issued: 0 (2005); Employment by occupation: 12.3% management, 26.3% professional, 13.9% services, 22.8% sales, 1.3% farming, 11.3% construction, 12.0% production (2000).
Income: Per capita income: $24,243 (2005); Median household income: $49,797 (2005); Average household income: $58,806 (2005); Percent of households with income of $100,000 or more: 12.0% (2005); Poverty rate: 9.0% (2000).
Education: Percent of population age 25 and over with: High school diploma (including GED) or higher: 86.5% (2005); Bachelor's degree or higher: 28.5% (2005); Master's degree or higher: 13.3% (2005).

School District(s)
New Lebanon Central School District (KG-12)
    2003-04 Enrollment: 625 . . . . (518) 794-9016
Housing: Homeownership rate: 74.8% (2005); Median home value: $184,280 (2005); Median rent: $482 per month (2000); Median age of housing: 38 years (2000).
Transportation: Commute to work: 87.9% car, 1.3% public transportation, 3.7% walk, 6.0% work from home (2000); Travel time to work: 36.6% less than 15 minutes, 26.7% 15 to 30 minutes, 20.3% 30 to 45 minutes, 11.2% 45 to 60 minutes, 5.3% 60 minutes or more (2000)

NIVERVILLE (CDP). Covers a land area of 2.886 square miles and a water area of 0.523 square miles. Located at 42.44° N. Lat.; 73.65° W. Long.
Population: 1,809 (1990); 1,737 (2000); 1,704 (2005); 1,684 (2010 projected); Race: 97.8% White, 0.6% Black, 0.4% Asian, 0.2% Hispanic of any race (2005); Density: 590.4 persons per square mile (2005); Average household size: 2.49 (2005); Median age: 40.0 (2005); Males per 100 females: 100.9 (2005); Marriage status: 24.1% never married, 63.4% now married, 6.2% widowed, 6.3% divorced (2000); Foreign born: 0.7% (2000); Ancestry (includes multiple ancestries): 22.6% Irish, 21.2% German, 17.3% Italian, 13.6% English, 10.2% Polish (2000).
Economy: Employment by occupation: 10.3% management, 20.5% professional, 9.4% services, 25.4% sales, 0.0% farming, 19.8% construction, 14.7% production (2000).
Income: Per capita income: $25,791 (2005); Median household income: $52,769 (2005); Average household income: $63,997 (2005); Percent of households with income of $100,000 or more: 14.9% (2005); Poverty rate: 8.2% (2000).
Education: Percent of population age 25 and over with: High school diploma (including GED) or higher: 87.9% (2005); Bachelor's degree or higher: 20.1% (2005); Master's degree or higher: 8.5% (2005).
Housing: Homeownership rate: 82.7% (2005); Median home value: $141,500 (2005); Median rent: $546 per month (2000); Median age of housing: 40 years (2000).
Transportation: Commute to work: 96.6% car, 0.7% public transportation, 0.6% walk, 2.1% work from home (2000); Travel time to work: 23.1% less than 15 minutes, 28.9% 15 to 30 minutes, 37.2% 30 to 45 minutes, 4.7% 45 to 60 minutes, 6.1% 60 minutes or more (2000)

OLD CHATHAM (unincorporated postal area, zip code 12136). Covers a land area of 19.049 square miles and a water area of 0.016 square miles. Located at 42.43° N. Lat.; 73.55° W. Long.
Population: 0 (2000); Race: 98.0% White, 0.0% Black, 0.4% Asian, 1.0% Hispanic of any race (2000); Density: 0.0 persons per square mile (2000); Age: 22.4% under 18, 18.8% over 64 (2000); Marriage status: 21.9% never married, 64.3% now married, 6.9% widowed, 6.9% divorced (2000); Foreign born: 4.0% (2000); Ancestry (includes multiple ancestries): 28.0% Irish, 22.0% German, 14.1% English, 11.0% Italian, 9.4% Polish (2000).
Economy: Employment by occupation: 19.4% management, 29.5% professional, 12.2% services, 24.1% sales, 1.2% farming, 5.6% construction, 8.0% production (2000).
Income: Per capita income: $38,045 (2000); Median household income: $52,083 (2000); Poverty rate: 4.2% (2000).
Education: Percent of population age 25 and over with: High school diploma (including GED) or higher: 89.2% (2000); Bachelor's degree or higher: 40.3% (2000).
Housing: Homeownership rate: 75.8% (2000); Median home value: $150,000 (2000); Median rent: $558 per month (2000); Median age of housing: 51 years (2000).
Transportation: Commute to work: 84.0% car, 0.0% public transportation, 5.6% walk, 10.5% work from home (2000); Travel time to work: 24.6% less than 15 minutes, 18.6% 15 to 30 minutes, 39.5% 30 to 45 minutes, 9.9% 45 to 60 minutes, 7.4% 60 minutes or more (2000)

PHILMONT (village). Covers a land area of 1.177 square miles and a water area of 0.031 square miles. Located at 42.24° N. Lat.; 73.64° W. Long.
Population: 1,623 (1990); 1,480 (2000); 1,508 (2005); 1,527 (2010 projected); Race: 93.2% White, 2.2% Black, 0.1% Asian, 5.4% Hispanic of any race (2005); Density: 1,280.7 persons per square mile (2005); Average household size: 2.50 (2005); Median age: 35.9 (2005); Males per 100 females: 99.2 (2005); Marriage status: 34.3% never married, 48.4% now married, 7.3% widowed, 10.1% divorced (2000); Foreign born: 2.4% (2000); Ancestry (includes multiple ancestries): 20.4% Irish, 20.4% German, 12.5% Other groups, 11.3% English, 9.8% Italian (2000).
Economy: Single-family building permits issued: 4 (2005); Multi-family building permits issued: 0 (2005); Employment by occupation: 7.3% management, 17.8% professional, 20.5% services, 23.9% sales, 1.4% farming, 9.5% construction, 19.6% production (2000).
Income: Per capita income: $18,535 (2005); Median household income: $34,464 (2005); Average household income: $45,991 (2005); Percent of households with income of $100,000 or more: 7.0% (2005); Poverty rate: 13.7% (2000).
Education: Percent of population age 25 and over with: High school diploma (including GED) or higher: 75.9% (2005); Bachelor's degree or higher: 14.7% (2005); Master's degree or higher: 6.6% (2005).

Housing: Homeownership rate: 50.6% (2005); Median home value: $121,837 (2005); Median rent: $426 per month (2000); Median age of housing: 60+ years (2000).
Transportation: Commute to work: 92.4% car, 2.5% public transportation, 2.8% walk, 2.3% work from home (2000); Travel time to work: 31.3% less than 15 minutes, 45.0% 15 to 30 minutes, 12.3% 30 to 45 minutes, 8.1% 45 to 60 minutes, 3.3% 60 minutes or more (2000)

SPENCERTOWN (unincorporated postal area, zip code 12165). Covers a land area of 4.452 square miles and a water area of 0.016 square miles. Located at 42.31° N. Lat.; 73.51° W. Long. Elevation is 690 feet.
Population: 0 (2000); Race: 100.0% White, 0.0% Black, 0.0% Asian, 0.0% Hispanic of any race (2000); Density: 0.0 persons per square mile (2000); Age: 24.0% under 18, 19.2% over 64 (2000); Marriage status: 15.9% never married, 75.7% now married, 1.6% widowed, 6.9% divorced (2000); Foreign born: 1.3% (2000); Ancestry (includes multiple ancestries): 24.9% English, 19.2% Irish, 18.3% United States or American, 10.9% German, 8.7% Italian (2000).
Economy: Employment by occupation: 20.6% management, 22.5% professional, 11.8% services, 23.5% sales, 0.0% farming, 11.8% construction, 9.8% production (2000).
Income: Per capita income: $26,431 (2000); Median household income: $45,972 (2000); Poverty rate: 1.7% (2000).
Education: Percent of population age 25 and over with: High school diploma (including GED) or higher: 95.9% (2000); Bachelor's degree or higher: 36.3% (2000).
Housing: Homeownership rate: 80.2% (2000); Median home value: $128,800 (2000); Median rent: $483 per month (2000); Median age of housing: 28 years (2000).
Transportation: Commute to work: 79.0% car, 2.0% public transportation, 4.0% walk, 15.0% work from home (2000); Travel time to work: 9.4% less than 15 minutes, 32.9% 15 to 30 minutes, 30.6% 30 to 45 minutes, 11.8% 45 to 60 minutes, 15.3% 60 minutes or more (2000)

STOCKPORT (town). Covers a land area of 11.641 square miles and a water area of 1.511 square miles. Located at 42.31° N. Lat.; 73.75° W. Long.
Population: 3,085 (1990); 2,933 (2000); 2,994 (2005); 3,053 (2010 projected); Race: 96.7% White, 1.3% Black, 0.1% Asian, 2.4% Hispanic of any race (2005); Density: 257.2 persons per square mile (2005); Average household size: 2.58 (2005); Median age: 38.4 (2005); Males per 100 females: 95.9 (2005); Marriage status: 23.7% never married, 59.0% now married, 6.8% widowed, 10.5% divorced (2000); Foreign born: 3.0% (2000); Ancestry (includes multiple ancestries): 23.2% German, 19.1% Irish, 18.1% Italian, 12.2% English, 9.9% Dutch (2000).
Economy: Single-family building permits issued: 3 (2005); Multi-family building permits issued: 0 (2005); Employment by occupation: 8.7% management, 15.5% professional, 19.0% services, 26.3% sales, 1.1% farming, 13.8% construction, 15.5% production (2000).
Income: Per capita income: $21,559 (2005); Median household income: $47,403 (2005); Average household income: $55,273 (2005); Percent of households with income of $100,000 or more: 10.7% (2005); Poverty rate: 12.5% (2000).
Education: Percent of population age 25 and over with: High school diploma (including GED) or higher: 83.1% (2005); Bachelor's degree or higher: 11.1% (2005); Master's degree or higher: 4.2% (2005).
Housing: Homeownership rate: 74.0% (2005); Median home value: $127,791 (2005); Median rent: $445 per month (2000); Median age of housing: 45 years (2000).
Safety: Violent crime rate: 0.0 per 10,000 population; Property crime rate: 0.0 per 10,000 population (2004).
Transportation: Commute to work: 92.8% car, 0.3% public transportation, 1.8% walk, 4.5% work from home (2000); Travel time to work: 33.8% less than 15 minutes, 41.5% 15 to 30 minutes, 11.6% 30 to 45 minutes, 8.9% 45 to 60 minutes, 4.2% 60 minutes or more (2000)

STOTTVILLE (CDP). Covers a land area of 4.118 square miles and a water area of 0.022 square miles. Located at 42.28° N. Lat.; 73.74° W. Long.
Population: 1,360 (1990); 1,355 (2000); 1,381 (2005); 1,407 (2010 projected); Race: 94.4% White, 1.4% Black, 0.9% Asian, 2.9% Hispanic of any race (2005); Density: 335.3 persons per square mile (2005); Average household size: 2.45 (2005); Median age: 39.7 (2005); Males per 100 females: 91.0 (2005); Marriage status: 25.2% never married, 56.8% now married, 7.6% widowed, 10.5% divorced (2000); Foreign born: 3.1% (2000); Ancestry (includes multiple ancestries): 21.7% Irish, 18.4% German, 15.7% English, 14.0% Italian, 7.9% United States or American (2000).
Economy: Employment by occupation: 7.3% management, 18.3% professional, 19.5% services, 21.7% sales, 0.0% farming, 16.3% construction, 16.9% production (2000).
Income: Per capita income: $20,874 (2005); Median household income: $40,114 (2005); Average household income: $50,635 (2005); Percent of households with income of $100,000 or more: 10.3% (2005); Poverty rate: 19.7% (2000).
Education: Percent of population age 25 and over with: High school diploma (including GED) or higher: 79.9% (2005); Bachelor's degree or higher: 8.5% (2005); Master's degree or higher: 4.3% (2005).
Housing: Homeownership rate: 65.7% (2005); Median home value: $129,891 (2005); Median rent: $407 per month (2000); Median age of housing: 57 years (2000).
Transportation: Commute to work: 91.7% car, 0.0% public transportation, 2.2% walk, 5.6% work from home (2000); Travel time to work: 44.0% less than 15 minutes, 33.8% 15 to 30 minutes, 9.9% 30 to 45 minutes, 9.3% 45 to 60 minutes, 3.0% 60 minutes or more (2000)

STUYVESANT (town). Covers a land area of 25.051 square miles and a water area of 1.694 square miles. Located at 42.40° N. Lat.; 73.75° W. Long.
Population: 2,178 (1990); 2,188 (2000); 2,166 (2005); 2,144 (2010 projected); Race: 97.4% White, 1.0% Black, 0.7% Asian, 1.2% Hispanic of any race (2005); Density: 86.5 persons per square mile (2005); Average household size: 2.52 (2005); Median age: 39.1 (2005); Males per 100 females: 95.8 (2005); Marriage status: 21.2% never married, 64.8% now married, 5.6% widowed, 8.5% divorced (2000); Foreign born: 2.8% (2000); Ancestry (includes multiple ancestries): 25.4% German, 16.8% Italian, 15.2% Irish, 12.7% English, 11.9% Polish (2000).
Economy: Single-family building permits issued: 8 (2005); Multi-family building permits issued: 0 (2005); Employment by occupation: 14.4% management, 25.0% professional, 15.8% services, 24.8% sales, 2.1% farming, 7.1% construction, 10.7% production (2000).
Income: Per capita income: $25,233 (2005); Median household income: $55,295 (2005); Average household income: $63,386 (2005); Percent of households with income of $100,000 or more: 15.8% (2005); Poverty rate: 4.3% (2000).
Taxes: Total city taxes per capita: $146 (2004); City property taxes per capita: $109 (2004).
Education: Percent of population age 25 and over with: High school diploma (including GED) or higher: 86.5% (2005); Bachelor's degree or higher: 27.6% (2005); Master's degree or higher: 12.0% (2005).
Housing: Homeownership rate: 78.2% (2005); Median home value: $168,886 (2005); Median rent: $518 per month (2000); Median age of housing: 48 years (2000).
Transportation: Commute to work: 90.3% car, 1.5% public transportation, 2.4% walk, 4.0% work from home (2000); Travel time to work: 21.9% less than 15 minutes, 33.3% 15 to 30 minutes, 30.7% 30 to 45 minutes, 8.4% 45 to 60 minutes, 5.7% 60 minutes or more (2000)

TAGHKANIC (town). Covers a land area of 40.032 square miles and a water area of 0.130 square miles. Located at 42.13° N. Lat.; 73.67° W. Long.
Population: 1,111 (1990); 1,118 (2000); 1,130 (2005); 1,141 (2010 projected); Race: 98.3% White, 0.7% Black, 0.1% Asian, 1.6% Hispanic of any race (2005); Density: 28.2 persons per square mile (2005); Average household size: 2.38 (2005); Median age: 47.4 (2005); Males per 100 females: 103.2 (2005); Marriage status: 21.7% never married, 62.7% now married, 7.3% widowed, 8.3% divorced (2000); Foreign born: 6.8% (2000); Ancestry (includes multiple ancestries): 20.1% German, 17.8% Irish, 14.3% Italian, 10.4% English, 8.1% Dutch (2000).
Economy: Single-family building permits issued: 13 (2005); Multi-family building permits issued: 0 (2005); Employment by occupation: 13.7% management, 21.6% professional, 15.5% services, 23.5% sales, 1.4% farming, 10.2% construction, 14.1% production (2000).
Income: Per capita income: $30,402 (2005); Median household income: $51,519 (2005); Average household income: $71,663 (2005); Percent of households with income of $100,000 or more: 17.5% (2005); Poverty rate: 9.1% (2000).
Education: Percent of population age 25 and over with: High school diploma (including GED) or higher: 83.4% (2005); Bachelor's degree or higher: 26.5% (2005); Master's degree or higher: 13.2% (2005).

Housing: Homeownership rate: 84.4% (2005); Median home value: $211,468 (2005); Median rent: $520 per month (2000); Median age of housing: 33 years (2000).
Transportation: Commute to work: 84.2% car, 5.3% public transportation, 4.3% walk, 6.1% work from home (2000); Travel time to work: 18.5% less than 15 minutes, 40.4% 15 to 30 minutes, 20.0% 30 to 45 minutes, 10.7% 45 to 60 minutes, 10.3% 60 minutes or more (2000)

VALATIE (village). Covers a land area of 1.233 square miles and a water area of 0.036 square miles. Located at 42.41° N. Lat.; 73.67° W. Long.
History: Incorporated 1856.
Population: 1,467 (1990); 1,712 (2000); 1,756 (2005); 1,799 (2010 projected); Race: 96.0% White, 1.0% Black, 0.8% Asian, 4.9% Hispanic of any race (2005); Density: 1,423.9 persons per square mile (2005); Average household size: 2.87 (2005); Median age: 43.7 (2005); Males per 100 females: 82.2 (2005); Marriage status: 22.9% never married, 57.2% now married, 10.1% widowed, 9.7% divorced (2000); Foreign born: 2.6% (2000); Ancestry (includes multiple ancestries): 23.9% Irish, 22.2% German, 15.4% Italian, 11.4% Other groups, 11.1% English (2000).
Economy: In dairying, poultry-raising and apple-growing region. Single-family building permits issued: 26 (2005); Multi-family building permits issued: 0 (2005); Employment by occupation: 15.0% management, 20.3% professional, 16.2% services, 25.3% sales, 2.1% farming, 12.2% construction, 9.1% production (2000).
Income: Per capita income: $21,658 (2005); Median household income: $50,347 (2005); Average household income: $59,301 (2005); Percent of households with income of $100,000 or more: 14.7% (2005); Poverty rate: 10.5% (2000).
Education: Percent of population age 25 and over with: High school diploma (including GED) or higher: 73.2% (2005); Bachelor's degree or higher: 19.0% (2005); Master's degree or higher: 7.7% (2005).

School District(s)
Kinderhook Central School District (KG-12)
    2003-04 Enrollment: 2,285 . . . . (518) 758-7575

Housing: Homeownership rate: 59.5% (2005); Median home value: $160,246 (2005); Median rent: $425 per month (2000); Median age of housing: 51 years (2000).
Transportation: Commute to work: 89.4% car, 0.7% public transportation, 4.3% walk, 3.6% work from home (2000); Travel time to work: 30.2% less than 15 minutes, 31.5% 15 to 30 minutes, 32.1% 30 to 45 minutes, 3.1% 45 to 60 minutes, 3.1% 60 minutes or more (2000)

Cortland County

Located in central New York; drained by the Tioughnioga River. Covers a land area of 499.65 square miles, a water area of 1.87 square miles, and is located in the Eastern Time Zone. The county government was organized in 1808. County seat is Cortland.

Cortland County is part of the Cortland, NY Micropolitan Statistical Area. The entire metro area includes: Cortland County, NY

Weather Station: Cortland — Elevation: 1,128 feet

	Jan	Feb	Mar	Apr	May	Jun	Jul	Aug	Sep	Oct	Nov	Dec
High	30	32	41	54	67	76	81	79	70	59	46	35
Low	15	16	24	34	45	54	59	57	49	40	32	22
Precip	2.7	2.5	3.1	3.2	3.2	4.0	3.5	3.0	4.0	3.2	3.5	3.5
Snow	22.4	19.1	15.1	4.0	tr	0.0	0.0	0.0	0.0	0.4	8.3	22.0

High and Low temperatures in degrees Fahrenheit; Precipitation and Snow in inches

Weather Station: Tully Heiberg Forest — Elevation: 1,896 feet

	Jan	Feb	Mar	Apr	May	Jun	Jul	Aug	Sep	Oct	Nov	Dec
High	26	29	37	50	63	71	76	74	66	55	43	32
Low	11	12	21	32	43	52	57	55	48	37	28	18
Precip	2.9	2.9	3.4	3.8	4.0	4.6	4.0	3.8	4.9	3.8	3.9	3.6
Snow	27.5	24.4	22.8	8.7	0.7	tr	0.0	0.0	tr	1.6	12.5	27.0

High and Low temperatures in degrees Fahrenheit; Precipitation and Snow in inches

Population: 48,963 (1990); 48,599 (2000); 48,832 (2005); 49,043 (2010 projected); Race: 96.1% White, 1.5% Black, 0.7% Asian, 1.7% Hispanic of any race (2005); Density: 97.7 persons per square mile (2005); Average household size: 2.63 (2005); Median age: 35.3 (2005); Males per 100 females: 93.6 (2005).
Religion: Five largest groups: 13.8% Catholic Church, 6.4% The United Methodist Church, 2.6% American Baptist Churches in the USA, 1.9% United Church of Christ, 1.8% General Association of Regular Baptist Churches (2000).
Economy: Unemployment rate: 5.4% (2005); Total civilian labor force: 24,113 (2005); Leading industries: 22.5% manufacturing; 21.6% health care and social assistance; 15.4% retail trade (2003); Farms: 569 totaling 127,052 acres (2002); Companies that employ 500 or more persons: 4 (2003); Companies that employ 100 to 499 persons: 22 (2003); Companies that employ less than 100 persons: 1,071 (2003); Black-owned businesses: n/a (2002); Hispanic-owned businesses: n/a (2002); Women-owned businesses: n/a (2002); Retail sales per capita: $13,099 (2006); Single-family building permits issued: 57 (2005); Multi-family building permits issued: 0 (2005).
Income: Per capita income: $19,060 (2005); Median household income: $38,712 (2005); Average household income: $49,149 (2005); Percent of households with income of $100,000 or more: 8.8% (2005); Poverty rate: 13.4% (2003); Bankruptcy rate: 8.54% (2005).
Taxes: Total county taxes per capita: $819 (2004); County property taxes per capita: $377 (2004).
Education: Percent of population age 25 and over with: High school diploma (including GED) or higher: 82.8% (2005); Bachelor's degree or higher: 18.7% (2005); Master's degree or higher: 8.1% (2005).
Housing: Homeownership rate: 64.9% (2005); Median home value: $112,309 (2005); Median rent: $393 per month (2000); Median age of housing: 48 years (2000).
Health: Birth rate: 117.5 per 10,000 population (2004); Death rate: 85.1 per 10,000 population (2004); Age-adjusted cancer mortality rate: 222.6 deaths per 100,000 population (2002); Number of physicians: 13.7 per 10,000 population (2004); Hospital beds: 41.3 per 10,000 population (2003); Hospital admissions: 1,044.1 per 10,000 population (2003).
Elections: 2004 Presidential election results: 51.0% Bush, 46.9% Kerry, 1.8% Nader, 0.2% Badnarik

Additional Information Contacts
Cortland County Government . . . . (607) 753-5052
    http://www2.cortland-co.org/
City of Cortland . . . . (518) 233-2119
    http://www.cortland.org/
Town of Preble . . . . (607) 749-3199
    http://www.preble-ny.org/

Cortland County Communities

CINCINNATUS (town). Covers a land area of 25.443 square miles and a water area of 0.050 square miles. Located at 42.53° N. Lat.; 75.92° W. Long. Elevation is 1,046 feet.
Population: 1,122 (1990); 1,051 (2000); 1,026 (2005); 989 (2010 projected); Race: 98.1% White, 0.4% Black, 0.0% Asian, 3.2% Hispanic of any race (2005); Density: 40.3 persons per square mile (2005); Average household size: 2.47 (2005); Median age: 40.7 (2005); Males per 100 females: 91.4 (2005); Marriage status: 21.7% never married, 58.7% now married, 10.4% widowed, 9.2% divorced (2000); Foreign born: 0.2% (2000); Ancestry (includes multiple ancestries): 18.8% English, 14.4% German, 10.9% Irish, 8.8% Other groups, 6.2% Italian (2000).
Economy: Single-family building permits issued: 1 (2005); Multi-family building permits issued: 0 (2005); Employment by occupation: 9.7% management, 18.3% professional, 16.6% services, 22.5% sales, 3.4% farming, 11.6% construction, 18.1% production (2000).
Income: Per capita income: $21,690 (2005); Median household income: $45,068 (2005); Average household income: $53,245 (2005); Percent of households with income of $100,000 or more: 7.9% (2005); Poverty rate: 7.3% (2000).
Taxes: Total city taxes per capita: $85 (2004); City property taxes per capita: $72 (2004).
Education: Percent of population age 25 and over with: High school diploma (including GED) or higher: 83.9% (2005); Bachelor's degree or higher: 12.3% (2005); Master's degree or higher: 5.9% (2005).

School District(s)
Cincinnatus Central School District (PK-12)
    2003-04 Enrollment: 734 . . . . (607) 863-3200

Housing: Homeownership rate: 78.8% (2005); Median home value: $89,688 (2005); Median rent: $381 per month (2000); Median age of housing: 58 years (2000).
Transportation: Commute to work: 80.7% car, 1.9% public transportation, 6.3% walk, 8.4% work from home (2000); Travel time to work: 26.1% less than 15 minutes, 31.9% 15 to 30 minutes, 25.5% 30 to 45 minutes, 6.9% 45 to 60 minutes, 9.6% 60 minutes or more (2000)

CORTLAND (city). Covers a land area of 3.922 square miles and a water area of 0.015 square miles. Located at 42.60° N. Lat.; 76.18° W. Long. Elevation is 1,130 feet.
History: Elmer Ambrose Sperry (1860-1030), inventor, was born in Cortland. Sperry is credited with 400 patents.
Population: 19,801 (1990); 18,740 (2000); 18,449 (2005); 18,162 (2010 projected); Race: 94.3% White, 2.6% Black, 0.9% Asian, 2.5% Hispanic of any race (2005); Density: 4,704.4 persons per square mile (2005); Average household size: 2.68 (2005); Median age: 30.0 (2005); Males per 100 females: 88.9 (2005); Marriage status: 43.4% never married, 40.0% now married, 7.7% widowed, 8.9% divorced (2000); Foreign born: 3.5% (2000); Ancestry (includes multiple ancestries): 21.2% Irish, 18.4% Italian, 17.0% German, 16.5% English, 7.6% Other groups (2000).
Economy: Single-family building permits issued: 3 (2005); Multi-family building permits issued: 0 (2005); Employment by occupation: 9.5% management, 19.5% professional, 21.5% services, 26.8% sales, 0.1% farming, 6.8% construction, 15.7% production (2000).
Income: Per capita income: $15,247 (2005); Median household income: $29,280 (2005); Average household income: $38,922 (2005); Percent of households with income of $100,000 or more: 5.0% (2005); Poverty rate: 24.7% (2000).
Education: Percent of population age 25 and over with: High school diploma (including GED) or higher: 79.7% (2005); Bachelor's degree or higher: 19.0% (2005); Master's degree or higher: 8.0% (2005).

School District(s)
Cortland City School District (KG-12)
 2003-04 Enrollment: 2,847 . . . . (607) 758-4100

Four-year College(s)
SUNY College at Cortland (Public)
 Fall 2004 Enrollment: 7,350. . . . . (607) 753-2011
 2005-06 Tuition: In-state $5,344; Out-of-state $11,294

Housing: Homeownership rate: 43.6% (2005); Median home value: $107,671 (2005); Median rent: $387 per month (2000); Median age of housing: 60+ years (2000).
Hospitals: Cortland Memorial Hospital (181 beds)
Safety: Violent crime rate: 40.0 per 10,000 population; Property crime rate: 271.4 per 10,000 population (2004).
Newspapers: Consumer News (General - Circulation 11,337); Cortland Standard (Circulation 11,500)
Transportation: Commute to work: 78.9% car, 3.9% public transportation, 12.5% walk, 3.1% work from home (2000); Travel time to work: 63.0% less than 15 minutes, 18.3% 15 to 30 minutes, 10.8% 30 to 45 minutes, 5.4% 45 to 60 minutes, 2.4% 60 minutes or more (2000)
Additional Information Contacts
City of Cortland . . . . (518) 233-2119
 http://www.cortland.org/
Cortland County Chamber of Commerce. . . . . (607) 756-2814
 http://www.cortlandchamber.com

CORTLAND WEST (CDP). Covers a land area of 5.208 square miles and a water area of 0. Located at 42.59° N. Lat.; 76.22° W. Long.
Population: 1,073 (1990); 1,345 (2000); 1,400 (2005); 1,418 (2010 projected); Race: 94.9% White, 1.5% Black, 1.6% Asian, 1.4% Hispanic of any race (2005); Density: 268.8 persons per square mile (2005); Average household size: 2.68 (2005); Median age: 44.9 (2005); Males per 100 females: 89.7 (2005); Marriage status: 17.9% never married, 70.8% now married, 2.7% widowed, 8.7% divorced (2000); Foreign born: 3.7% (2000); Ancestry (includes multiple ancestries): 21.5% English, 20.1% Italian, 17.9% Irish, 16.9% German, 8.0% United States or American (2000).
Economy: Employment by occupation: 14.1% management, 26.2% professional, 11.7% services, 27.6% sales, 0.0% farming, 8.8% construction, 11.5% production (2000).
Income: Per capita income: $26,170 (2005); Median household income: $54,592 (2005); Average household income: $69,057 (2005); Percent of households with income of $100,000 or more: 19.9% (2005); Poverty rate: 7.1% (2000).
Education: Percent of population age 25 and over with: High school diploma (including GED) or higher: 89.0% (2005); Bachelor's degree or higher: 32.2% (2005); Master's degree or higher: 18.5% (2005).
Housing: Homeownership rate: 91.0% (2005); Median home value: $169,318 (2005); Median rent: $428 per month (2000); Median age of housing: 31 years (2000).
Transportation: Commute to work: 92.2% car, 3.8% public transportation, 0.9% walk, 3.1% work from home (2000); Travel time to work: 61.7% less than 15 minutes, 14.0% 15 to 30 minutes, 14.0% 30 to 45 minutes, 9.4% 45 to 60 minutes, 1.0% 60 minutes or more (2000)

CORTLANDVILLE (town). Covers a land area of 49.803 square miles and a water area of 0.084 square miles. Located at 42.58° N. Lat.; 76.17° W. Long.
Population: 8,054 (1990); 7,919 (2000); 8,020 (2005); 8,128 (2010 projected); Race: 96.2% White, 0.7% Black, 1.1% Asian, 1.6% Hispanic of any race (2005); Density: 161.0 persons per square mile (2005); Average household size: 2.45 (2005); Median age: 39.9 (2005); Males per 100 females: 92.4 (2005); Marriage status: 25.9% never married, 59.0% now married, 7.1% widowed, 8.0% divorced (2000); Foreign born: 2.0% (2000); Ancestry (includes multiple ancestries): 19.0% English, 18.6% Irish, 15.9% German, 12.1% Italian, 8.6% United States or American (2000).
Economy: Single-family building permits issued: 14 (2005); Multi-family building permits issued: 0 (2005); Employment by occupation: 12.8% management, 18.2% professional, 17.6% services, 25.7% sales, 0.7% farming, 9.4% construction, 15.5% production (2000).
Income: Per capita income: $22,917 (2005); Median household income: $41,691 (2005); Average household income: $55,744 (2005); Percent of households with income of $100,000 or more: 12.0% (2005); Poverty rate: 12.6% (2000).
Education: Percent of population age 25 and over with: High school diploma (including GED) or higher: 84.4% (2005); Bachelor's degree or higher: 19.5% (2005); Master's degree or higher: 9.3% (2005).
Housing: Homeownership rate: 71.1% (2005); Median home value: $128,521 (2005); Median rent: $442 per month (2000); Median age of housing: 37 years (2000).
Transportation: Commute to work: 89.8% car, 2.2% public transportation, 3.1% walk, 4.1% work from home (2000); Travel time to work: 53.3% less than 15 minutes, 25.7% 15 to 30 minutes, 10.0% 30 to 45 minutes, 6.9% 45 to 60 minutes, 4.1% 60 minutes or more (2000)

CUYLER (town). Covers a land area of 43.516 square miles and a water area of 0. Located at 42.72° N. Lat.; 75.93° W. Long.
Population: 850 (1990); 1,036 (2000); 1,227 (2005); 1,370 (2010 projected); Race: 97.7% White, 0.0% Black, 0.4% Asian, 1.0% Hispanic of any race (2005); Density: 28.2 persons per square mile (2005); Average household size: 2.82 (2005); Median age: 35.4 (2005); Males per 100 females: 100.8 (2005); Marriage status: 20.3% never married, 62.2% now married, 6.5% widowed, 11.0% divorced (2000); Foreign born: 1.0% (2000); Ancestry (includes multiple ancestries): 17.9% English, 15.9% Irish, 15.3% German, 11.0% United States or American, 8.3% Other groups (2000).
Economy: Single-family building permits issued: 1 (2005); Multi-family building permits issued: 0 (2005); Employment by occupation: 10.7% management, 13.3% professional, 16.4% services, 12.9% sales, 7.1% farming, 11.3% construction, 28.2% production (2000).
Income: Per capita income: $15,261 (2005); Median household income: $40,199 (2005); Average household income: $43,046 (2005); Percent of households with income of $100,000 or more: 2.8% (2005); Poverty rate: 16.8% (2000).
Education: Percent of population age 25 and over with: High school diploma (including GED) or higher: 73.2% (2005); Bachelor's degree or higher: 9.5% (2005); Master's degree or higher: 5.1% (2005).
Housing: Homeownership rate: 83.0% (2005); Median home value: $90,517 (2005); Median rent: $344 per month (2000); Median age of housing: 29 years (2000).
Transportation: Commute to work: 86.6% car, 1.6% public transportation, 4.9% walk, 6.8% work from home (2000); Travel time to work: 15.9% less than 15 minutes, 28.7% 15 to 30 minutes, 27.0% 30 to 45 minutes, 15.6% 45 to 60 minutes, 12.8% 60 minutes or more (2000)

FREETOWN (town). Covers a land area of 25.549 square miles and a water area of 0.075 square miles. Located at 42.53° N. Lat.; 76.01° W. Long.
Population: 688 (1990); 789 (2000); 883 (2005); 934 (2010 projected); Race: 98.5% White, 0.3% Black, 0.0% Asian, 0.0% Hispanic of any race (2005); Density: 34.6 persons per square mile (2005); Average household size: 2.89 (2005); Median age: 36.0 (2005); Males per 100 females: 113.3 (2005); Marriage status: 22.0% never married, 64.0% now married, 3.7% widowed, 10.3% divorced (2000); Foreign born: 1.3% (2000); Ancestry

(includes multiple ancestries): 22.1% English, 16.6% German, 14.4% Irish, 9.3% Other groups, 7.5% United States or American (2000).
Economy: Single-family building permits issued: 1 (2005); Multi-family building permits issued: 0 (2005); Employment by occupation: 14.0% management, 11.4% professional, 20.6% services, 13.5% sales, 2.4% farming, 8.5% construction, 29.6% production (2000).
Income: Per capita income: $15,835 (2005); Median household income: $39,225 (2005); Average household income: $45,694 (2005); Percent of households with income of $100,000 or more: 5.2% (2005); Poverty rate: 13.3% (2000).
Education: Percent of population age 25 and over with: High school diploma (including GED) or higher: 77.1% (2005); Bachelor's degree or higher: 12.8% (2005); Master's degree or higher: 4.3% (2005).
Housing: Homeownership rate: 85.3% (2005); Median home value: $86,271 (2005); Median rent: $425 per month (2000); Median age of housing: 23 years (2000).
Transportation: Commute to work: 86.0% car, 0.8% public transportation, 3.0% walk, 9.1% work from home (2000); Travel time to work: 13.3% less than 15 minutes, 46.7% 15 to 30 minutes, 23.9% 30 to 45 minutes, 10.3% 45 to 60 minutes, 5.8% 60 minutes or more (2000)

HARFORD (town). Covers a land area of 24.175 square miles and a water area of 0.003 square miles. Located at 42.43° N. Lat.; 76.20° W. Long.
Population: 886 (1990); 920 (2000); 969 (2005); 1,009 (2010 projected); Race: 96.8% White, 2.4% Black, 0.2% Asian, 0.4% Hispanic of any race (2005); Density: 40.1 persons per square mile (2005); Average household size: 2.65 (2005); Median age: 36.5 (2005); Males per 100 females: 99.4 (2005); Marriage status: 20.1% never married, 64.4% now married, 6.3% widowed, 9.2% divorced (2000); Foreign born: 0.9% (2000); Ancestry (includes multiple ancestries): 22.4% English, 14.1% German, 12.3% Irish, 7.5% United States or American, 6.7% Dutch (2000).
Economy: Single-family building permits issued: 4 (2005); Multi-family building permits issued: 0 (2005); Employment by occupation: 10.2% management, 20.0% professional, 16.9% services, 19.6% sales, 6.9% farming, 9.1% construction, 17.3% production (2000).
Income: Per capita income: $16,950 (2005); Median household income: $38,145 (2005); Average household income: $44,877 (2005); Percent of households with income of $100,000 or more: 4.4% (2005); Poverty rate: 8.3% (2000).
Education: Percent of population age 25 and over with: High school diploma (including GED) or higher: 82.1% (2005); Bachelor's degree or higher: 13.2% (2005); Master's degree or higher: 3.9% (2005).
Housing: Homeownership rate: 82.2% (2005); Median home value: $90,755 (2005); Median rent: $425 per month (2000); Median age of housing: 31 years (2000).
Transportation: Commute to work: 93.5% car, 0.9% public transportation, 1.8% walk, 3.4% work from home (2000); Travel time to work: 17.9% less than 15 minutes, 37.5% 15 to 30 minutes, 31.7% 30 to 45 minutes, 5.6% 45 to 60 minutes, 7.2% 60 minutes or more (2000)

HOMER (village). Covers a land area of 1.669 square miles and a water area of 0 square miles. Located at 42.63° N. Lat.; 76.18° W. Long. Elevation is 1,133 feet.
Population: 3,635 (1990); 3,368 (2000); 3,329 (2005); 3,279 (2010 projected); Race: 97.1% White, 1.1% Black, 0.7% Asian, 1.2% Hispanic of any race (2005); Density: 1,995.0 persons per square mile (2005); Average household size: 2.41 (2005); Median age: 40.7 (2005); Males per 100 females: 85.8 (2005); Marriage status: 23.6% never married, 57.5% now married, 9.1% widowed, 9.8% divorced (2000); Foreign born: 1.7% (2000); Ancestry (includes multiple ancestries): 25.9% English, 20.7% German, 20.4% Irish, 9.7% Italian, 5.9% Scottish (2000).
Economy: Single-family building permits issued: 0 (2005); Multi-family building permits issued: 0 (2005); Employment by occupation: 15.2% management, 28.4% professional, 14.3% services, 20.6% sales, 1.5% farming, 6.1% construction, 14.0% production (2000).
Income: Per capita income: $24,461 (2005); Median household income: $43,319 (2005); Average household income: $57,910 (2005); Percent of households with income of $100,000 or more: 14.0% (2005); Poverty rate: 9.7% (2000).
Education: Percent of population age 25 and over with: High school diploma (including GED) or higher: 90.9% (2005); Bachelor's degree or higher: 27.8% (2005); Master's degree or higher: 12.4% (2005).

School District(s)
Homer Central School District (KG-12)
    2003-04 Enrollment: 2,367 . . . . (607) 749-7241
Housing: Homeownership rate: 69.6% (2005); Median home value: $119,796 (2005); Median rent: $377 per month (2000); Median age of housing: 58 years (2000).
Transportation: Commute to work: 87.7% car, 2.2% public transportation, 2.7% walk, 6.3% work from home (2000); Travel time to work: 52.7% less than 15 minutes, 21.3% 15 to 30 minutes, 13.4% 30 to 45 minutes, 7.1% 45 to 60 minutes, 5.6% 60 minutes or more (2000)

HOMER (town). Covers a land area of 50.361 square miles and a water area of 0.304 square miles. Located at 42.65° N. Lat.; 76.17° W. Long. Elevation is 1,133 feet.
History: Old Homer Village Historic District here. Settled 1791, incorporated 1835.
Population: 6,508 (1990); 6,363 (2000); 6,531 (2005); 6,600 (2010 projected); Race: 97.5% White, 0.8% Black, 0.4% Asian, 1.2% Hispanic of any race (2005); Density: 129.7 persons per square mile (2005); Average household size: 2.56 (2005); Median age: 39.6 (2005); Males per 100 females: 92.7 (2005); Marriage status: 23.5% never married, 60.3% now married, 7.5% widowed, 8.7% divorced (2000); Foreign born: 1.8% (2000); Ancestry (includes multiple ancestries): 26.7% English, 19.0% Irish, 18.2% German, 9.2% Italian, 6.9% United States or American (2000).
Economy: Farm trade center, with manufacturing of industrial filament; prefabricated houses, metalworking compounds, wood handles and spindles, specialized production and automation equipment, sand and gravel pits. Single-family building permits issued: 6 (2005); Multi-family building permits issued: 0 (2005); Employment by occupation: 13.7% management, 24.5% professional, 13.1% services, 21.3% sales, 2.9% farming, 8.4% construction, 16.1% production (2000).
Income: Per capita income: $24,288 (2005); Median household income: $47,559 (2005); Average household income: $61,534 (2005); Percent of households with income of $100,000 or more: 14.4% (2005); Poverty rate: 9.4% (2000).
Taxes: Total city taxes per capita: $93 (2004); City property taxes per capita: $69 (2004).
Education: Percent of population age 25 and over with: High school diploma (including GED) or higher: 89.7% (2005); Bachelor's degree or higher: 26.1% (2005); Master's degree or higher: 10.9% (2005).
Housing: Homeownership rate: 76.0% (2005); Median home value: $125,848 (2005); Median rent: $385 per month (2000); Median age of housing: 50 years (2000).
Transportation: Commute to work: 89.8% car, 1.8% public transportation, 2.5% walk, 5.3% work from home (2000); Travel time to work: 44.2% less than 15 minutes, 26.9% 15 to 30 minutes, 15.0% 30 to 45 minutes, 6.1% 45 to 60 minutes, 7.8% 60 minutes or more (2000)

LAPEER (town). Covers a land area of 25.075 square miles and a water area of 0.101 square miles. Located at 42.44° N. Lat.; 76.10° W. Long. Elevation is 1,326 feet.
Population: 613 (1990); 686 (2000); 745 (2005); 796 (2010 projected); Race: 98.1% White, 0.0% Black, 0.8% Asian, 0.3% Hispanic of any race (2005); Density: 29.7 persons per square mile (2005); Average household size: 2.75 (2005); Median age: 36.0 (2005); Males per 100 females: 100.3 (2005); Marriage status: 20.0% never married, 67.7% now married, 3.1% widowed, 9.2% divorced (2000); Foreign born: 0.3% (2000); Ancestry (includes multiple ancestries): 22.6% Irish, 20.4% German, 17.9% English, 9.8% United States or American, 5.7% Other groups (2000).
Economy: Single-family building permits issued: 1 (2005); Multi-family building permits issued: 0 (2005); Employment by occupation: 17.4% management, 15.2% professional, 16.0% services, 20.7% sales, 2.7% farming, 9.5% construction, 18.5% production (2000).
Income: Per capita income: $18,168 (2005); Median household income: $39,773 (2005); Average household income: $49,945 (2005); Percent of households with income of $100,000 or more: 8.9% (2005); Poverty rate: 10.7% (2000).
Taxes: Total city taxes per capita: $366 (2004); City property taxes per capita: $352 (2004).
Education: Percent of population age 25 and over with: High school diploma (including GED) or higher: 88.8% (2005); Bachelor's degree or higher: 8.7% (2005); Master's degree or higher: 3.5% (2005).
Housing: Homeownership rate: 79.7% (2005); Median home value: $105,357 (2005); Median rent: $338 per month (2000); Median age of housing: 32 years (2000).

PROFILES OF NEW YORK / Cortland County

Transportation: Commute to work: 91.8% car, 0.0% public transportation, 2.7% walk, 5.5% work from home (2000); Travel time to work: 20.6% less than 15 minutes, 37.7% 15 to 30 minutes, 24.6% 30 to 45 minutes, 15.1% 45 to 60 minutes, 2.0% 60 minutes or more (2000)

MARATHON (village). Covers a land area of 1.129 square miles and a water area of 0 square miles. Located at 42.44° N. Lat.; 76.03° W. Long. Elevation is 1,020 feet.
Population: 1,171 (1990); 1,063 (2000); 957 (2005); 941 (2010 projected); Race: 98.7% White, 0.6% Black, 0.0% Asian, 0.5% Hispanic of any race (2005); Density: 847.5 persons per square mile (2005); Average household size: 2.45 (2005); Median age: 37.2 (2005); Males per 100 females: 81.9 (2005); Marriage status: 24.5% never married, 56.8% now married, 9.4% widowed, 9.2% divorced (2000); Foreign born: 2.3% (2000); Ancestry (includes multiple ancestries): 16.7% English, 16.6% German, 9.7% Irish, 9.0% United States or American, 7.3% Other groups (2000).
Economy: Single-family building permits issued: 0 (2005); Multi-family building permits issued: 0 (2005); Employment by occupation: 10.6% management, 21.0% professional, 18.7% services, 18.7% sales, 1.6% farming, 10.6% construction, 18.9% production (2000).
Income: Per capita income: $20,136 (2005); Median household income: $37,941 (2005); Average household income: $49,410 (2005); Percent of households with income of $100,000 or more: 9.5% (2005); Poverty rate: 12.4% (2000).
Education: Percent of population age 25 and over with: High school diploma (including GED) or higher: 80.5% (2005); Bachelor's degree or higher: 14.4% (2005); Master's degree or higher: 6.6% (2005).
School District(s)
Marathon Central School District (KG-12)
    2003-04 Enrollment: 1,010 . . . . (607) 849-3251
Housing: Homeownership rate: 57.7% (2005); Median home value: $92,388 (2005); Median rent: $361 per month (2000); Median age of housing: 60+ years (2000).
Newspapers: The Cortland Sunday Democrat (General - Circulation 11,000)
Transportation: Commute to work: 87.9% car, 0.0% public transportation, 8.2% walk, 3.4% work from home (2000); Travel time to work: 31.3% less than 15 minutes, 38.1% 15 to 30 minutes, 19.4% 30 to 45 minutes, 7.9% 45 to 60 minutes, 3.3% 60 minutes or more (2000)

MARATHON (town). Covers a land area of 24.974 square miles and a water area of 0.094 square miles. Located at 42.44° N. Lat.; 76.02° W. Long. Elevation is 1,020 feet.
Population: 2,019 (1990); 2,189 (2000); 2,096 (2005); 2,107 (2010 projected); Race: 97.6% White, 1.5% Black, 0.0% Asian, 0.7% Hispanic of any race (2005); Density: 83.9 persons per square mile (2005); Average household size: 2.62 (2005); Median age: 37.4 (2005); Males per 100 females: 94.3 (2005); Marriage status: 21.9% never married, 61.4% now married, 7.2% widowed, 9.6% divorced (2000); Foreign born: 1.5% (2000); Ancestry (includes multiple ancestries): 21.2% English, 17.4% German, 11.5% Irish, 9.3% United States or American, 6.7% Dutch (2000).
Economy: Manufacturing: boats, transportation equipment. Agriculture: dairy products; poultry; field corn and hay. Single-family building permits issued: 3 (2005); Multi-family building permits issued: 0 (2005); Employment by occupation: 13.3% management, 19.9% professional, 17.3% services, 18.6% sales, 1.7% farming, 9.2% construction, 20.0% production (2000).
Income: Per capita income: $18,374 (2005); Median household income: $40,414 (2005); Average household income: $48,201 (2005); Percent of households with income of $100,000 or more: 7.3% (2005); Poverty rate: 10.9% (2000).
Education: Percent of population age 25 and over with: High school diploma (including GED) or higher: 84.2% (2005); Bachelor's degree or higher: 12.1% (2005); Master's degree or higher: 5.1% (2005).
Housing: Homeownership rate: 72.1% (2005); Median home value: $96,260 (2005); Median rent: $362 per month (2000); Median age of housing: 54 years (2000).
Transportation: Commute to work: 89.5% car, 0.0% public transportation, 5.2% walk, 5.1% work from home (2000); Travel time to work: 27.1% less than 15 minutes, 39.6% 15 to 30 minutes, 21.6% 30 to 45 minutes, 7.6% 45 to 60 minutes, 4.1% 60 minutes or more (2000)

MCGRAW (village). Covers a land area of 0.985 square miles and a water area of 0 square miles. Located at 42.59° N. Lat.; 76.09° W. Long. Elevation is 1,180 feet.
History: Incorporated 1869.
Population: 1,058 (1990); 1,000 (2000); 1,057 (2005); 1,095 (2010 projected); Race: 96.8% White, 0.2% Black, 0.0% Asian, 1.3% Hispanic of any race (2005); Density: 1,073.6 persons per square mile (2005); Average household size: 2.57 (2005); Median age: 36.8 (2005); Males per 100 females: 93.9 (2005); Marriage status: 25.0% never married, 56.8% now married, 11.7% widowed, 6.5% divorced (2000); Foreign born: 0.7% (2000); Ancestry (includes multiple ancestries): 32.0% English, 13.5% German, 12.9% Irish, 7.4% Dutch, 6.9% Other groups (2000).
Economy: Manufacturing of jewelry, silverware, apparel. Single-family building permits issued: 0 (2005); Multi-family building permits issued: 0 (2005); Employment by occupation: 9.0% management, 11.5% professional, 18.7% services, 25.8% sales, 0.0% farming, 9.4% construction, 25.6% production (2000).
Income: Per capita income: $19,303 (2005); Median household income: $38,929 (2005); Average household income: $49,179 (2005); Percent of households with income of $100,000 or more: 8.8% (2005); Poverty rate: 9.9% (2000).
Education: Percent of population age 25 and over with: High school diploma (including GED) or higher: 81.0% (2005); Bachelor's degree or higher: 6.2% (2005); Master's degree or higher: 3.1% (2005).
School District(s)
Mcgraw Central School District (KG-12)
    2003-04 Enrollment: 618 . . . . (607) 836-3636
Housing: Homeownership rate: 65.9% (2005); Median home value: $95,542 (2005); Median rent: $367 per month (2000); Median age of housing: 60+ years (2000).
Safety: Violent crime rate: 0.0 per 10,000 population; Property crime rate: 121.0 per 10,000 population (2004).
Transportation: Commute to work: 86.0% car, 1.7% public transportation, 9.9% walk, 2.2% work from home (2000); Travel time to work: 53.6% less than 15 minutes, 31.2% 15 to 30 minutes, 7.3% 30 to 45 minutes, 3.5% 45 to 60 minutes, 4.4% 60 minutes or more (2000)

MUNSONS CORNERS (CDP). Covers a land area of 2.248 square miles and a water area of 0.005 square miles. Located at 42.58° N. Lat.; 76.20° W. Long.
Population: 2,576 (1990); 2,426 (2000); 2,300 (2005); 2,257 (2010 projected); Race: 95.0% White, 1.0% Black, 1.8% Asian, 2.0% Hispanic of any race (2005); Density: 1,023.1 persons per square mile (2005); Average household size: 2.19 (2005); Median age: 35.5 (2005); Males per 100 females: 87.3 (2005); Marriage status: 33.2% never married, 50.6% now married, 10.6% widowed, 5.6% divorced (2000); Foreign born: 3.3% (2000); Ancestry (includes multiple ancestries): 17.4% Irish, 16.9% German, 11.8% Italian, 10.7% English, 10.3% United States or American (2000).
Economy: Employment by occupation: 12.5% management, 20.1% professional, 14.8% services, 29.3% sales, 1.4% farming, 6.9% construction, 15.0% production (2000).
Income: Per capita income: $19,070 (2005); Median household income: $30,000 (2005); Average household income: $41,189 (2005); Percent of households with income of $100,000 or more: 6.4% (2005); Poverty rate: 21.6% (2000).
Education: Percent of population age 25 and over with: High school diploma (including GED) or higher: 79.7% (2005); Bachelor's degree or higher: 19.6% (2005); Master's degree or higher: 7.7% (2005).
Housing: Homeownership rate: 48.9% (2005); Median home value: $123,917 (2005); Median rent: $469 per month (2000); Median age of housing: 31 years (2000).
Transportation: Commute to work: 86.8% car, 5.3% public transportation, 2.8% walk, 3.8% work from home (2000); Travel time to work: 63.2% less than 15 minutes, 22.0% 15 to 30 minutes, 10.2% 30 to 45 minutes, 2.6% 45 to 60 minutes, 2.0% 60 minutes or more (2000)

PREBLE (town). Covers a land area of 26.954 square miles and a water area of 0.595 square miles. Located at 42.74° N. Lat.; 76.13° W. Long. Elevation is 1,188 feet.
Population: 1,577 (1990); 1,582 (2000); 1,423 (2005); 1,387 (2010 projected); Race: 97.3% White, 1.5% Black, 0.1% Asian, 0.6% Hispanic of any race (2005); Density: 52.8 persons per square mile (2005); Average household size: 2.51 (2005); Median age: 38.7 (2005); Males per 100 females: 104.5 (2005); Marriage status: 23.3% never married, 62.7% now married, 3.2% widowed, 10.8% divorced (2000); Foreign born: 1.0% (2000); Ancestry (includes multiple ancestries): 20.7% Irish, 19.9% English, 19.0% German, 10.7% United States or American, 8.0% Italian (2000).

Economy: Single-family building permits issued: 1 (2005); Multi-family building permits issued: 0 (2005); Employment by occupation: 11.0% management, 26.9% professional, 9.8% services, 21.6% sales, 1.5% farming, 12.8% construction, 16.4% production (2000).
Income: Per capita income: $23,134 (2005); Median household income: $48,957 (2005); Average household income: $58,163 (2005); Percent of households with income of $100,000 or more: 13.3% (2005); Poverty rate: 7.7% (2000).
Education: Percent of population age 25 and over with: High school diploma (including GED) or higher: 87.1% (2005); Bachelor's degree or higher: 25.5% (2005); Master's degree or higher: 11.3% (2005).
Housing: Homeownership rate: 83.6% (2005); Median home value: $121,721 (2005); Median rent: $429 per month (2000); Median age of housing: 33 years (2000).
Transportation: Commute to work: 94.0% car, 0.0% public transportation, 2.2% walk, 3.3% work from home (2000); Travel time to work: 25.4% less than 15 minutes, 35.3% 15 to 30 minutes, 28.8% 30 to 45 minutes, 6.3% 45 to 60 minutes, 4.3% 60 minutes or more (2000)

Additional Information Contacts
Town of Preble.................................... (607) 749-3199
http://www.preble-ny.org/

SCOTT (town). Covers a land area of 22.261 square miles and a water area of 0.150 square miles. Located at 42.73° N. Lat.; 76.23° W. Long. Elevation is 1,403 feet.
Population: 1,167 (1990); 1,193 (2000); 1,248 (2005); 1,269 (2010 projected); Race: 98.4% White, 0.1% Black, 0.6% Asian, 0.2% Hispanic of any race (2005); Density: 56.1 persons per square mile (2005); Average household size: 2.79 (2005); Median age: 37.3 (2005); Males per 100 females: 102.3 (2005); Marriage status: 26.2% never married, 61.7% now married, 3.8% widowed, 8.4% divorced (2000); Foreign born: 1.0% (2000); Ancestry (includes multiple ancestries): 20.7% English, 19.6% Irish, 19.2% German, 9.6% United States or American, 6.8% French (except Basque) (2000).
Economy: Single-family building permits issued: 2 (2005); Multi-family building permits issued: 0 (2005); Employment by occupation: 11.6% management, 16.8% professional, 17.1% services, 23.4% sales, 1.7% farming, 13.8% construction, 15.6% production (2000).
Income: Per capita income: $18,594 (2005); Median household income: $45,516 (2005); Average household income: $51,913 (2005); Percent of households with income of $100,000 or more: 10.1% (2005); Poverty rate: 9.9% (2000).
Education: Percent of population age 25 and over with: High school diploma (including GED) or higher: 80.0% (2005); Bachelor's degree or higher: 13.7% (2005); Master's degree or higher: 5.3% (2005).
Housing: Homeownership rate: 89.9% (2005); Median home value: $105,986 (2005); Median rent: $428 per month (2000); Median age of housing: 29 years (2000).
Transportation: Commute to work: 95.7% car, 0.0% public transportation, 1.4% walk, 1.9% work from home (2000); Travel time to work: 13.0% less than 15 minutes, 50.1% 15 to 30 minutes, 17.0% 30 to 45 minutes, 10.8% 45 to 60 minutes, 9.0% 60 minutes or more (2000)

SOLON (town). Covers a land area of 29.716 square miles and a water area of 0.019 square miles. Located at 42.59° N. Lat.; 76.02° W. Long. Elevation is 1,307 feet.
Population: 1,008 (1990); 1,108 (2000); 1,171 (2005); 1,191 (2010 projected); Race: 97.9% White, 0.2% Black, 0.2% Asian, 1.0% Hispanic of any race (2005); Density: 39.4 persons per square mile (2005); Average household size: 2.85 (2005); Median age: 36.6 (2005); Males per 100 females: 98.1 (2005); Marriage status: 24.0% never married, 63.3% now married, 2.6% widowed, 10.1% divorced (2000); Foreign born: 0.3% (2000); Ancestry (includes multiple ancestries): 19.9% Irish, 16.4% German, 15.9% English, 11.9% Other groups, 10.6% United States or American (2000).
Economy: Single-family building permits issued: 3 (2005); Multi-family building permits issued: 0 (2005); Employment by occupation: 11.4% management, 12.7% professional, 20.4% services, 13.6% sales, 2.2% farming, 13.4% construction, 26.3% production (2000).
Income: Per capita income: $18,023 (2005); Median household income: $45,513 (2005); Average household income: $51,350 (2005); Percent of households with income of $100,000 or more: 7.1% (2005); Poverty rate: 9.1% (2000).
Education: Percent of population age 25 and over with: High school diploma (including GED) or higher: 76.3% (2005); Bachelor's degree or higher: 9.3% (2005); Master's degree or higher: 4.9% (2005).
Housing: Homeownership rate: 87.8% (2005); Median home value: $87,627 (2005); Median rent: $389 per month (2000); Median age of housing: 25 years (2000).
Transportation: Commute to work: 92.4% car, 0.7% public transportation, 2.4% walk, 3.7% work from home (2000); Travel time to work: 14.9% less than 15 minutes, 56.9% 15 to 30 minutes, 14.9% 30 to 45 minutes, 8.9% 45 to 60 minutes, 4.4% 60 minutes or more (2000)

TAYLOR (town). Covers a land area of 30.048 square miles and a water area of 0.057 square miles. Located at 42.60° N. Lat.; 75.91° W. Long.
Population: 542 (1990); 500 (2000); 468 (2005); 451 (2010 projected); Race: 97.9% White, 0.4% Black, 0.2% Asian, 1.7% Hispanic of any race (2005); Density: 15.6 persons per square mile (2005); Average household size: 2.75 (2005); Median age: 39.1 (2005); Males per 100 females: 108.0 (2005); Marriage status: 23.3% never married, 66.6% now married, 6.6% widowed, 3.4% divorced (2000); Foreign born: 1.9% (2000); Ancestry (includes multiple ancestries): 17.5% English, 14.8% German, 13.1% United States or American, 10.0% Other groups, 8.1% Irish (2000).
Economy: Single-family building permits issued: 0 (2005); Multi-family building permits issued: 0 (2005); Employment by occupation: 13.2% management, 19.2% professional, 7.3% services, 15.0% sales, 7.3% farming, 12.4% construction, 25.6% production (2000).
Income: Per capita income: $20,726 (2005); Median household income: $43,100 (2005); Average household income: $57,059 (2005); Percent of households with income of $100,000 or more: 10.0% (2005); Poverty rate: 11.4% (2000).
Education: Percent of population age 25 and over with: High school diploma (including GED) or higher: 74.4% (2005); Bachelor's degree or higher: 11.3% (2005); Master's degree or higher: 3.9% (2005).
Housing: Homeownership rate: 80.6% (2005); Median home value: $92,500 (2005); Median rent: $388 per month (2000); Median age of housing: 44 years (2000).
Transportation: Commute to work: 84.6% car, 0.9% public transportation, 0.0% walk, 14.5% work from home (2000); Travel time to work: 17.4% less than 15 minutes, 26.2% 15 to 30 minutes, 39.5% 30 to 45 minutes, 9.2% 45 to 60 minutes, 7.7% 60 minutes or more (2000)

TRUXTON (town). Covers a land area of 44.691 square miles and a water area of 0.037 square miles. Located at 42.70° N. Lat.; 76.02° W. Long.
Population: 1,064 (1990); 1,225 (2000); 1,120 (2005); 1,083 (2010 projected); Race: 96.7% White, 1.3% Black, 0.2% Asian, 0.7% Hispanic of any race (2005); Density: 25.1 persons per square mile (2005); Average household size: 2.72 (2005); Median age: 37.8 (2005); Males per 100 females: 98.6 (2005); Marriage status: 20.4% never married, 65.1% now married, 6.1% widowed, 8.5% divorced (2000); Foreign born: 1.9% (2000); Ancestry (includes multiple ancestries): 20.1% Irish, 18.3% English, 15.5% German, 8.4% Other groups, 7.7% French (except Basque) (2000).
Economy: Single-family building permits issued: 3 (2005); Multi-family building permits issued: 0 (2005); Employment by occupation: 14.9% management, 17.9% professional, 14.6% services, 19.5% sales, 4.8% farming, 9.8% construction, 18.5% production (2000).
Income: Per capita income: $20,712 (2005); Median household income: $46,205 (2005); Average household income: $56,238 (2005); Percent of households with income of $100,000 or more: 9.0% (2005); Poverty rate: 11.6% (2000).
Education: Percent of population age 25 and over with: High school diploma (including GED) or higher: 81.5% (2005); Bachelor's degree or higher: 14.4% (2005); Master's degree or higher: 5.2% (2005).

School District(s)
Homer Central School District (KG-12)
    2003-04 Enrollment: 2,367 .... (607) 749-7241
Housing: Homeownership rate: 78.4% (2005); Median home value: $104,423 (2005); Median rent: $344 per month (2000); Median age of housing: 29 years (2000).
Transportation: Commute to work: 89.7% car, 0.7% public transportation, 4.0% walk, 4.9% work from home (2000); Travel time to work: 14.9% less than 15 minutes, 49.2% 15 to 30 minutes, 20.0% 30 to 45 minutes, 9.9% 45 to 60 minutes, 6.0% 60 minutes or more (2000)

VIRGIL (town). Covers a land area of 47.327 square miles and a water area of 0.042 square miles. Located at 42.51° N. Lat.; 76.15° W. Long.
Population: 2,172 (1990); 2,287 (2000); 2,353 (2005); 2,421 (2010 projected); Race: 97.0% White, 0.9% Black, 0.4% Asian, 1.5% Hispanic of any race (2005); Density: 49.7 persons per square mile (2005); Average household size: 2.69 (2005); Median age: 39.1 (2005); Males per 100 females: 100.6 (2005); Marriage status: 19.6% never married, 64.6% now married, 6.0% widowed, 9.8% divorced (2000); Foreign born: 1.2% (2000); Ancestry (includes multiple ancestries): 21.4% English, 17.1% German, 15.0% Irish, 9.6% United States or American, 8.7% Italian (2000).
Economy: Single-family building permits issued: 11 (2005); Multi-family building permits issued: 0 (2005); Employment by occupation: 17.3% management, 22.1% professional, 13.8% services, 22.1% sales, 2.1% farming, 9.7% construction, 12.9% production (2000).
Income: Per capita income: $22,217 (2005); Median household income: $48,168 (2005); Average household income: $59,134 (2005); Percent of households with income of $100,000 or more: 14.6% (2005); Poverty rate: 6.7% (2000).
Education: Percent of population age 25 and over with: High school diploma (including GED) or higher: 85.8% (2005); Bachelor's degree or higher: 24.6% (2005); Master's degree or higher: 10.4% (2005).
Housing: Homeownership rate: 83.4% (2005); Median home value: $120,165 (2005); Median rent: $454 per month (2000); Median age of housing: 27 years (2000).
Transportation: Commute to work: 90.3% car, 0.3% public transportation, 0.7% walk, 8.2% work from home (2000); Travel time to work: 30.2% less than 15 minutes, 43.2% 15 to 30 minutes, 17.8% 30 to 45 minutes, 4.9% 45 to 60 minutes, 3.8% 60 minutes or more (2000)

WILLET (town). Covers a land area of 25.835 square miles and a water area of 0.242 square miles. Located at 42.45° N. Lat.; 75.92° W. Long. Elevation is 1,039 feet.
Population: 892 (1990); 1,011 (2000); 1,103 (2005); 1,146 (2010 projected); Race: 98.6% White, 0.0% Black, 0.1% Asian, 0.0% Hispanic of any race (2005); Density: 42.7 persons per square mile (2005); Average household size: 2.69 (2005); Median age: 36.2 (2005); Males per 100 females: 104.3 (2005); Marriage status: 22.8% never married, 64.2% now married, 4.5% widowed, 8.6% divorced (2000); Foreign born: 0.5% (2000); Ancestry (includes multiple ancestries): 19.8% German, 15.9% Irish, 14.8% English, 9.3% Other groups, 8.9% United States or American (2000).
Economy: Single-family building permits issued: 3 (2005); Multi-family building permits issued: 0 (2005); Employment by occupation: 12.8% management, 11.0% professional, 14.8% services, 23.2% sales, 3.3% farming, 14.3% construction, 20.5% production (2000).
Income: Per capita income: $19,225 (2005); Median household income: $42,027 (2005); Average household income: $51,720 (2005); Percent of households with income of $100,000 or more: 8.3% (2005); Poverty rate: 12.9% (2000).
Education: Percent of population age 25 and over with: High school diploma (including GED) or higher: 82.7% (2005); Bachelor's degree or higher: 7.4% (2005); Master's degree or higher: 3.5% (2005).
Housing: Homeownership rate: 81.0% (2005); Median home value: $84,054 (2005); Median rent: $375 per month (2000); Median age of housing: 29 years (2000).
Transportation: Commute to work: 89.0% car, 0.0% public transportation, 2.5% walk, 7.6% work from home (2000); Travel time to work: 13.3% less than 15 minutes, 20.4% 15 to 30 minutes, 46.4% 30 to 45 minutes, 10.4% 45 to 60 minutes, 9.5% 60 minutes or more (2000)

Delaware County

Located in southern New York, in the west Catskills; bounded on the northwest by the Susquehanna River, and on the southwest by the Delaware River and the Pennsylvania border. Covers a land area of 1,446.37 square miles, a water area of 21.67 square miles, and is located in the Eastern Time Zone. The county government was organized in 1797. County seat is Delhi.

Weather Station: Deposit   Elevation: 997 feet

	Jan	Feb	Mar	Apr	May	Jun	Jul	Aug	Sep	Oct	Nov	Dec
High	32	35	45	58	70	77	81	79	71	61	48	36
Low	13	14	23	33	43	52	57	56	49	38	30	20
Precip	2.9	2.7	3.4	3.8	3.9	3.9	4.0	4.1	3.8	3.6	4.0	3.4
Snow	17.0	11.4	na	3.2	tr	0.0	0.0	0.0	0.0	tr	4.2	na

High and Low temperatures in degrees Fahrenheit; Precipitation and Snow in inches

Weather Station: Walton   Elevation: 1,240 feet

	Jan	Feb	Mar	Apr	May	Jun	Jul	Aug	Sep	Oct	Nov	Dec
High	31	34	44	57	69	77	81	79	71	60	47	35
Low	12	13	23	33	43	51	56	55	48	37	29	19
Precip	3.0	2.8	3.6	4.0	4.3	4.2	4.5	4.1	4.0	4.0	4.3	3.7
Snow	23.4	19.0	16.9	6.4	0.4	tr	0.0	0.0	tr	0.5	9.0	20.3

High and Low temperatures in degrees Fahrenheit; Precipitation and Snow in inches

Population: 47,263 (1990); 48,055 (2000); 46,970 (2005); 45,854 (2010 projected); Race: 95.5% White, 2.0% Black, 0.8% Asian, 2.7% Hispanic of any race (2005); Density: 32.5 persons per square mile (2005); Average household size: 2.45 (2005); Median age: 42.7 (2005); Males per 100 females: 97.3 (2005).
Religion: Five largest groups: 16.1% Catholic Church, 9.9% The United Methodist Church, 4.3% Presbyterian Church (U.S.A.), 4.1% The Salvation Army, 1.5% American Baptist Churches in the USA (2000).
Economy: Unemployment rate: 4.2% (2005); Total civilian labor force: 23,594 (2005); Leading industries: 32.1% manufacturing; 19.4% health care and social assistance; 13.0% retail trade (2003); Farms: 788 totaling 191,537 acres (2002); Companies that employ 500 or more persons: 3 (2003); Companies that employ 100 to 499 persons: 14 (2003); Companies that employ less than 100 persons: 1,170 (2003); Black-owned businesses: n/a (2002); Hispanic-owned businesses: n/a (2002); Women-owned businesses: 1,317 (2002); Retail sales per capita: $9,897 (2006). Single-family building permits issued: 165 (2005); Multi-family building permits issued: 3 (2005).
Income: Per capita income: $20,184 (2005); Median household income: $37,695 (2005); Average household income: $48,572 (2005); Percent of households with income of $100,000 or more: 8.6% (2005); Poverty rate: 12.6% (2003); Bankruptcy rate: 5.53% (2005).
Education: Percent of population age 25 and over with: High school diploma (including GED) or higher: 79.8% (2005); Bachelor's degree or higher: 16.7% (2005); Master's degree or higher: 7.2% (2005).
Housing: Homeownership rate: 76.2% (2005); Median home value: $111,760 (2005); Median rent: $358 per month (2000); Median age of housing: 36 years (2000).
Health: Birth rate: 90.0 per 10,000 population (2004); Death rate: 120.4 per 10,000 population (2004); Age-adjusted cancer mortality rate: 212.7 deaths per 100,000 population (2002); Number of physicians: 11.6 per 10,000 population (2004); Hospital beds: 28.8 per 10,000 population (2003); Hospital admissions: 690.0 per 10,000 population (2003).
Elections: 2004 Presidential election results: 56.5% Bush, 41.2% Kerry, 2.0% Nader, 0.2% Badnarik
National and State Parks: Delaware State Forest
Additional Information Contacts
Delaware County Government......................(607) 746-6691
    http://www.co.delaware.ny.us/
Town of Franklin................................(518) 891-2189
    http://townoffranklin.com/
Village of Stamford..............................(607) 652-6671
    http://www.stamfordny.com/

Delaware County Communities

ANDES (village). Covers a land area of 1.142 square miles and a water area of 0 square miles. Located at 42.18° N. Lat.; 74.78° W. Long. Elevation is 1,621 feet.
Population: 292 (1990); 289 (2000); 283 (2005); 277 (2010 projected); Race: 96.1% White, 0.7% Black, 1.1% Asian, 4.6% Hispanic of any race (2005); Density: 247.8 persons per square mile (2005); Average household size: 2.14 (2005); Median age: 44.2 (2005); Males per 100 females: 114.4 (2005); Marriage status: 24.5% never married, 59.2% now married, 7.6% widowed, 8.7% divorced (2000); Foreign born: 3.2% (2000); Ancestry (includes multiple ancestries): 24.8% German, 12.4% Scottish, 12.4% English, 11.1% Irish, 11.1% Italian (2000).
Economy: Employment by occupation: 16.8% management, 16.8% professional, 24.5% services, 23.1% sales, 0.0% farming, 8.4% construction, 10.5% production (2000).
Income: Per capita income: $28,445 (2005); Median household income: $39,500 (2005); Average household income: $60,985 (2005); Percent of households with income of $100,000 or more: 16.7% (2005); Poverty rate: 7.6% (2000).

Education: Percent of population age 25 and over with: High school diploma (including GED) or higher: 83.9% (2005); Bachelor's degree or higher: 24.2% (2005); Master's degree or higher: 14.2% (2005).

School District(s)
Andes Central School District (KG-12)
    2003-04 Enrollment: 143 . . . . (845) 676-3167
Housing: Homeownership rate: 69.7% (2005); Median home value: $132,000 (2005); Median rent: $356 per month (2000); Median age of housing: 60+ years (2000).
Transportation: Commute to work: 71.5% car, 0.0% public transportation, 20.8% walk, 7.6% work from home (2000); Travel time to work: 41.4% less than 15 minutes, 37.6% 15 to 30 minutes, 12.0% 30 to 45 minutes, 0.0% 45 to 60 minutes, 9.0% 60 minutes or more (2000)

ANDES (town). Covers a land area of 109.067 square miles and a water area of 3.464 square miles. Located at 42.14° N. Lat.; 74.79° W. Long. Elevation is 1,621 feet.
Population: 1,292 (1990); 1,356 (2000); 1,311 (2005); 1,287 (2010 projected); Race: 96.3% White, 0.8% Black, 0.9% Asian, 2.5% Hispanic of any race (2005); Density: 12.0 persons per square mile (2005); Average household size: 2.20 (2005); Median age: 49.5 (2005); Males per 100 females: 103.9 (2005); Marriage status: 20.1% never married, 62.6% now married, 8.7% widowed, 8.6% divorced (2000); Foreign born: 5.5% (2000); Ancestry (includes multiple ancestries): 24.3% German, 12.5% Irish, 11.5% English, 10.8% United States or American, 10.3% Italian (2000).
Economy: Single-family building permits issued: 8 (2005); Multi-family building permits issued: 0 (2005); Employment by occupation: 13.5% management, 17.9% professional, 18.2% services, 25.5% sales, 0.5% farming, 14.9% construction, 9.6% production (2000).
Income: Per capita income: $25,873 (2005); Median household income: $39,474 (2005); Average household income: $56,913 (2005); Percent of households with income of $100,000 or more: 12.2% (2005); Poverty rate: 9.4% (2000).
Education: Percent of population age 25 and over with: High school diploma (including GED) or higher: 84.7% (2005); Bachelor's degree or higher: 19.4% (2005); Master's degree or higher: 8.4% (2005).
Housing: Homeownership rate: 84.9% (2005); Median home value: $143,411 (2005); Median rent: $381 per month (2000); Median age of housing: 30 years (2000).
Transportation: Commute to work: 76.7% car, 3.3% public transportation, 10.3% walk, 9.4% work from home (2000); Travel time to work: 32.5% less than 15 minutes, 31.7% 15 to 30 minutes, 17.2% 30 to 45 minutes, 8.4% 45 to 60 minutes, 10.2% 60 minutes or more (2000)

ARKVILLE (unincorporated postal area, zip code 12406). Covers a land area of 37.597 square miles and a water area of 0.006 square miles. Located at 42.13° N. Lat.; 74.57° W. Long. Elevation is 1,373 feet.
Population: 0 (2000); Race: 99.1% White, 0.0% Black, 0.9% Asian, 0.9% Hispanic of any race (2000); Density: 0.0 persons per square mile (2000); Age: 23.6% under 18, 21.6% over 64 (2000); Marriage status: 21.9% never married, 54.9% now married, 9.5% widowed, 13.6% divorced (2000); Foreign born: 5.3% (2000); Ancestry (includes multiple ancestries): 22.9% German, 22.2% Irish, 12.6% United States or American, 12.0% English, 10.4% Italian (2000).
Economy: Employment by occupation: 8.2% management, 20.9% professional, 19.8% services, 28.0% sales, 1.9% farming, 10.6% construction, 10.6% production (2000).
Income: Per capita income: $17,402 (2000); Median household income: $27,054 (2000); Poverty rate: 19.5% (2000).
Education: Percent of population age 25 and over with: High school diploma (including GED) or higher: 78.5% (2000); Bachelor's degree or higher: 13.7% (2000).
Housing: Homeownership rate: 71.2% (2000); Median home value: $69,900 (2000); Median rent: $373 per month (2000); Median age of housing: 35 years (2000).
Newspapers: Catskill Mountain News (General - Circulation 4,100)
Transportation: Commute to work: 86.6% car, 1.6% public transportation, 8.5% walk, 3.3% work from home (2000); Travel time to work: 44.9% less than 15 minutes, 18.6% 15 to 30 minutes, 11.9% 30 to 45 minutes, 16.1% 45 to 60 minutes, 8.5% 60 minutes or more (2000)

BLOOMVILLE (unincorporated postal area, zip code 13739). Covers a land area of 42.466 square miles and a water area of 0.012 square miles. Located at 42.36° N. Lat.; 74.78° W. Long. Elevation is 1,455 feet.
Population: 0 (2000); Race: 97.5% White, 1.1% Black, 0.6% Asian, 1.4% Hispanic of any race (2000); Density: 0.0 persons per square mile (2000); Age: 25.9% under 18, 19.1% over 64 (2000); Marriage status: 27.0% never married, 58.5% now married, 8.1% widowed, 6.5% divorced (2000); Foreign born: 3.9% (2000); Ancestry (includes multiple ancestries): 18.3% German, 11.3% Irish, 8.7% Polish, 8.5% English, 7.5% Italian (2000).
Economy: Employment by occupation: 13.5% management, 14.0% professional, 14.5% services, 20.2% sales, 6.2% farming, 10.7% construction, 20.9% production (2000).
Income: Per capita income: $16,172 (2000); Median household income: $31,875 (2000); Poverty rate: 17.4% (2000).
Education: Percent of population age 25 and over with: High school diploma (including GED) or higher: 75.9% (2000); Bachelor's degree or higher: 10.7% (2000).
Housing: Homeownership rate: 80.8% (2000); Median home value: $71,900 (2000); Median rent: $380 per month (2000); Median age of housing: 25 years (2000).
Transportation: Commute to work: 92.6% car, 0.5% public transportation, 2.1% walk, 4.9% work from home (2000); Travel time to work: 27.0% less than 15 minutes, 50.9% 15 to 30 minutes, 12.9% 30 to 45 minutes, 4.6% 45 to 60 minutes, 4.6% 60 minutes or more (2000)

BOVINA (town). Covers a land area of 44.384 square miles and a water area of 0.160 square miles. Located at 42.26° N. Lat.; 74.78° W. Long.
Population: 549 (1990); 664 (2000); 673 (2005); 646 (2010 projected); Race: 98.2% White, 0.1% Black, 0.4% Asian, 4.0% Hispanic of any race (2005); Density: 15.2 persons per square mile (2005); Average household size: 2.34 (2005); Median age: 46.2 (2005); Males per 100 females: 101.5 (2005); Marriage status: 21.5% never married, 62.5% now married, 10.0% widowed, 6.1% divorced (2000); Foreign born: 4.4% (2000); Ancestry (includes multiple ancestries): 20.1% Irish, 17.5% German, 17.4% English, 12.5% Scottish, 8.2% Italian (2000).
Economy: Single-family building permits issued: 2 (2005); Multi-family building permits issued: 0 (2005); Employment by occupation: 14.1% management, 30.6% professional, 10.0% services, 19.2% sales, 5.8% farming, 12.7% construction, 7.6% production (2000).
Income: Per capita income: $25,431 (2005); Median household income: $48,854 (2005); Average household income: $59,634 (2005); Percent of households with income of $100,000 or more: 12.9% (2005); Poverty rate: 5.7% (2000).
Education: Percent of population age 25 and over with: High school diploma (including GED) or higher: 90.2% (2005); Bachelor's degree or higher: 29.7% (2005); Master's degree or higher: 13.5% (2005).
Housing: Homeownership rate: 82.9% (2005); Median home value: $135,955 (2005); Median rent: $314 per month (2000); Median age of housing: 25 years (2000).
Transportation: Commute to work: 84.0% car, 0.7% public transportation, 7.6% walk, 7.3% work from home (2000); Travel time to work: 35.6% less than 15 minutes, 33.0% 15 to 30 minutes, 19.5% 30 to 45 minutes, 2.2% 45 to 60 minutes, 9.7% 60 minutes or more (2000)

BOVINA CENTER (unincorporated postal area, zip code 13740). Covers a land area of 36.842 square miles and a water area of 0.008 square miles. Located at 42.27° N. Lat.; 74.75° W. Long.
Population: 0 (2000); Race: 99.3% White, 0.0% Black, 0.0% Asian, 1.1% Hispanic of any race (2000); Density: 0.0 persons per square mile (2000); Age: 26.8% under 18, 17.3% over 64 (2000); Marriage status: 22.5% never married, 61.6% now married, 10.9% widowed, 5.0% divorced (2000); Foreign born: 4.0% (2000); Ancestry (includes multiple ancestries): 18.7% Irish, 18.2% German, 16.8% English, 15.0% Scottish, 8.8% Italian (2000).
Economy: Employment by occupation: 15.9% management, 32.2% professional, 9.4% services, 15.9% sales, 4.9% farming, 13.5% construction, 8.2% production (2000).
Income: Per capita income: $18,818 (2000); Median household income: $43,750 (2000); Poverty rate: 6.5% (2000).
Education: Percent of population age 25 and over with: High school diploma (including GED) or higher: 91.6% (2000); Bachelor's degree or higher: 31.9% (2000).
Housing: Homeownership rate: 86.0% (2000); Median home value: $91,300 (2000); Median rent: $311 per month (2000); Median age of housing: 24 years (2000).
Transportation: Commute to work: 81.0% car, 0.8% public transportation, 9.1% walk, 8.7% work from home (2000); Travel time to work: 34.8% less than 15 minutes, 33.5% 15 to 30 minutes, 19.9% 30 to 45 minutes, 2.7% 45 to 60 minutes, 9.0% 60 minutes or more (2000)

COLCHESTER (town). Covers a land area of 137.434 square miles and a water area of 4.766 square miles. Located at 42.02° N. Lat.; 74.96° W. Long.
Population: 1,928 (1990); 2,042 (2000); 2,026 (2005); 2,013 (2010 projected); Race: 98.6% White, 0.4% Black, 0.1% Asian, 1.0% Hispanic of any race (2005); Density: 14.7 persons per square mile (2005); Average household size: 2.39 (2005); Median age: 46.1 (2005); Males per 100 females: 94.4 (2005); Marriage status: 19.0% never married, 61.3% now married, 11.1% widowed, 8.6% divorced (2000); Foreign born: 2.1% (2000); Ancestry (includes multiple ancestries): 21.0% German, 17.2% Irish, 13.6% Italian, 12.2% English, 6.1% United States or American (2000).
Economy: Single-family building permits issued: 19 (2005); Multi-family building permits issued: 0 (2005); Employment by occupation: 8.4% management, 19.6% professional, 16.3% services, 19.3% sales, 1.3% farming, 14.8% construction, 20.3% production (2000).
Income: Per capita income: $16,977 (2005); Median household income: $33,986 (2005); Average household income: $39,923 (2005); Percent of households with income of $100,000 or more: 3.8% (2005); Poverty rate: 12.7% (2000).
Taxes: Total city taxes per capita: $700 (2004); City property taxes per capita: $681 (2004).
Education: Percent of population age 25 and over with: High school diploma (including GED) or higher: 77.1% (2005); Bachelor's degree or higher: 10.1% (2005); Master's degree or higher: 5.1% (2005).
Housing: Homeownership rate: 80.4% (2005); Median home value: $98,241 (2005); Median rent: $338 per month (2000); Median age of housing: 33 years (2000).
Safety: Violent crime rate: 4.9 per 10,000 population; Property crime rate: 34.5 per 10,000 population (2004).
Transportation: Commute to work: 88.5% car, 1.0% public transportation, 4.7% walk, 5.3% work from home (2000); Travel time to work: 30.8% less than 15 minutes, 29.7% 15 to 30 minutes, 17.7% 30 to 45 minutes, 8.3% 45 to 60 minutes, 13.4% 60 minutes or more (2000)

DAVENPORT (town). Covers a land area of 52.353 square miles and a water area of 0.130 square miles. Located at 42.44° N. Lat.; 74.92° W. Long. Elevation is 1,309 feet.
Population: 2,476 (1990); 2,774 (2000); 2,785 (2005); 2,773 (2010 projected); Race: 97.7% White, 0.8% Black, 0.4% Asian, 1.3% Hispanic of any race (2005); Density: 53.2 persons per square mile (2005); Average household size: 2.40 (2005); Median age: 40.4 (2005); Males per 100 females: 100.2 (2005); Marriage status: 22.4% never married, 59.0% now married, 8.1% widowed, 10.5% divorced (2000); Foreign born: 1.7% (2000); Ancestry (includes multiple ancestries): 21.7% German, 16.1% Irish, 14.6% English, 10.5% Italian, 10.2% United States or American (2000).
Economy: Single-family building permits issued: 5 (2005); Multi-family building permits issued: 0 (2005); Employment by occupation: 11.4% management, 19.6% professional, 17.3% services, 21.3% sales, 1.3% farming, 9.4% construction, 19.6% production (2000).
Income: Per capita income: $22,654 (2005); Median household income: $39,763 (2005); Average household income: $54,296 (2005); Percent of households with income of $100,000 or more: 10.6% (2005); Poverty rate: 10.1% (2000).
Education: Percent of population age 25 and over with: High school diploma (including GED) or higher: 79.2% (2005); Bachelor's degree or higher: 15.9% (2005); Master's degree or higher: 6.3% (2005).
School District(s)
Charlotte Valley Central School District (KG-12)
    2003-04 Enrollment: 427 . . . . (607) 278-5511
Housing: Homeownership rate: 78.5% (2005); Median home value: $104,167 (2005); Median rent: $389 per month (2000); Median age of housing: 23 years (2000).
Transportation: Commute to work: 92.1% car, 0.5% public transportation, 2.3% walk, 4.1% work from home (2000); Travel time to work: 36.0% less than 15 minutes, 43.8% 15 to 30 minutes, 7.8% 30 to 45 minutes, 4.7% 45 to 60 minutes, 7.7% 60 minutes or more (2000)

DE LANCEY (unincorporated postal area, zip code 13752). Covers a land area of 45.179 square miles and a water area of 0.065 square miles. Located at 42.18° N. Lat.; 74.89° W. Long.
Population: 0 (2000); Race: 99.4% White, 0.3% Black, 0.3% Asian, 0.7% Hispanic of any race (2000); Density: 0.0 persons per square mile (2000); Age: 21.1% under 18, 21.0% over 64 (2000); Marriage status: 21.4% never married, 64.1% now married, 7.4% widowed, 7.1% divorced (2000); Foreign born: 6.2% (2000); Ancestry (includes multiple ancestries): 20.1% German, 18.9% Irish, 13.1% Scottish, 11.7% English, 10.8% United States or American (2000).
Economy: Employment by occupation: 7.9% management, 28.7% professional, 12.0% services, 20.8% sales, 3.8% farming, 14.5% construction, 12.3% production (2000).
Income: Per capita income: $24,689 (2000); Median household income: $41,964 (2000); Poverty rate: 9.8% (2000).
Education: Percent of population age 25 and over with: High school diploma (including GED) or higher: 86.1% (2000); Bachelor's degree or higher: 21.2% (2000).
Housing: Homeownership rate: 85.4% (2000); Median home value: $86,500 (2000); Median rent: $453 per month (2000); Median age of housing: 30 years (2000).
Transportation: Commute to work: 87.2% car, 0.0% public transportation, 2.2% walk, 9.6% work from home (2000); Travel time to work: 29.3% less than 15 minutes, 35.3% 15 to 30 minutes, 15.9% 30 to 45 minutes, 10.2% 45 to 60 minutes, 9.2% 60 minutes or more (2000)

DELHI (village). Covers a land area of 3.180 square miles and a water area of 0 square miles. Located at 42.27° N. Lat.; 74.91° W. Long. Elevation is 1,370 feet.
Population: 3,064 (1990); 2,583 (2000); 2,608 (2005); 2,616 (2010 projected); Race: 80.8% White, 12.9% Black, 2.6% Asian, 5.8% Hispanic of any race (2005); Density: 820.0 persons per square mile (2005); Average household size: 3.65 (2005); Median age: 22.1 (2005); Males per 100 females: 104.9 (2005); Marriage status: 61.1% never married, 28.1% now married, 6.1% widowed, 4.8% divorced (2000); Foreign born: 7.6% (2000); Ancestry (includes multiple ancestries): 19.3% German, 18.7% Irish, 18.6% Italian, 15.5% Other groups, 12.6% English (2000).
Economy: Single-family building permits issued: 1 (2005); Multi-family building permits issued: 0 (2005); Employment by occupation: 8.3% management, 24.9% professional, 29.4% services, 14.2% sales, 7.5% farming, 6.1% construction, 9.6% production (2000).
Income: Per capita income: $15,014 (2005); Median household income: $37,078 (2005); Average household income: $48,556 (2005); Percent of households with income of $100,000 or more: 10.3% (2005); Poverty rate: 14.1% (2000).
Education: Percent of population age 25 and over with: High school diploma (including GED) or higher: 82.7% (2005); Bachelor's degree or higher: 28.0% (2005); Master's degree or higher: 14.4% (2005).
School District(s)
Delhi Central School District (KG-12)
    2003-04 Enrollment: 1,003 . . . . (607) 746-1300
Four-year College(s)
SUNY College of Technology at Delhi (Public)
    Fall 2004 Enrollment: 2,483. . . . . (607) 746-4000
    2005-06 Tuition: In-state $5,329; Out-of-state $8,189
Housing: Homeownership rate: 56.5% (2005); Median home value: $127,746 (2005); Median rent: $402 per month (2000); Median age of housing: 60+ years (2000).
Hospitals: O'Connor Hospital (28 beds)
Safety: Violent crime rate: 7.8 per 10,000 population; Property crime rate: 35.2 per 10,000 population (2004).
Newspapers: Delaware County Times (General - Circulation 1,500)
Transportation: Commute to work: 73.7% car, 1.0% public transportation, 15.6% walk, 8.1% work from home (2000); Travel time to work: 68.7% less than 15 minutes, 14.1% 15 to 30 minutes, 11.9% 30 to 45 minutes, 1.2% 45 to 60 minutes, 4.2% 60 minutes or more (2000)
Additional Information Contacts
Delaware County Chamber of Commerce . . . . (607) 746-2281
   http://www.delawarecounty.org

DELHI (town). Covers a land area of 64.566 square miles and a water area of 0.042 square miles. Located at 42.27° N. Lat.; 74.91° W. Long. Elevation is 1,370 feet.
History: Shortly after the Revolutionary War, Ebenezer Foote was so influential locally and as a member of the state legislature that he was nicknamed "the Great Mogul." At the suggestions of facetious citizens the community was named for Delhi, India, the capital city of the real Great Mogul.
Population: 5,015 (1990); 4,629 (2000); 4,638 (2005); 4,630 (2010 projected); Race: 87.7% White, 7.9% Black, 1.8% Asian, 3.6% Hispanic of

any race (2005); Density: 71.8 persons per square mile (2005); Average household size: 3.09 (2005); Median age: 33.8 (2005); Males per 100 females: 102.6 (2005); Marriage status: 41.7% never married, 46.6% now married, 6.4% widowed, 5.4% divorced (2000); Foreign born: 5.1% (2000); Ancestry (includes multiple ancestries): 18.3% German, 15.9% Irish, 15.0% Italian, 14.7% English, 12.3% Other groups (2000).
Economy: Single-family building permits issued: 6 (2005); Multi-family building permits issued: 0 (2005); Employment by occupation: 11.1% management, 29.3% professional, 23.8% services, 13.4% sales, 4.7% farming, 8.0% construction, 9.7% production (2000).
Income: Per capita income: $18,488 (2005); Median household income: $41,903 (2005); Average household income: $52,986 (2005); Percent of households with income of $100,000 or more: 10.2% (2005); Poverty rate: 9.8% (2000).
Education: Percent of population age 25 and over with: High school diploma (including GED) or higher: 82.4% (2005); Bachelor's degree or higher: 27.3% (2005); Master's degree or higher: 15.0% (2005).
Housing: Homeownership rate: 69.9% (2005); Median home value: $132,673 (2005); Median rent: $399 per month (2000); Median age of housing: 43 years (2000).
Transportation: Commute to work: 81.6% car, 0.9% public transportation, 10.2% walk, 6.2% work from home (2000); Travel time to work: 60.3% less than 15 minutes, 19.8% 15 to 30 minutes, 12.8% 30 to 45 minutes, 2.6% 45 to 60 minutes, 4.6% 60 minutes or more (2000)

DENVER (unincorporated postal area, zip code 12421). Covers a land area of 36.590 square miles and a water area of 0.008 square miles. Located at 42.25° N. Lat.; 74.54° W. Long.
Population: 0 (2000); Race: 95.1% White, 0.0% Black, 3.2% Asian, 3.7% Hispanic of any race (2000); Density: 0.0 persons per square mile (2000); Age: 15.3% under 18, 25.9% over 64 (2000); Marriage status: 27.4% never married, 53.0% now married, 6.6% widowed, 13.0% divorced (2000); Foreign born: 7.1% (2000); Ancestry (includes multiple ancestries): 19.6% German, 17.8% Irish, 17.1% Italian, 12.3% English, 12.1% Other groups (2000).
Economy: Employment by occupation: 4.3% management, 14.6% professional, 12.7% services, 31.7% sales, 0.0% farming, 19.6% construction, 17.1% production (2000).
Income: Per capita income: $23,714 (2000); Median household income: $31,250 (2000); Poverty rate: 7.9% (2000).
Education: Percent of population age 25 and over with: High school diploma (including GED) or higher: 79.3% (2000); Bachelor's degree or higher: 23.3% (2000).
Housing: Homeownership rate: 84.6% (2000); Median home value: $78,600 (2000); Median rent: $380 per month (2000); Median age of housing: 27 years (2000).
Transportation: Commute to work: 85.5% car, 4.8% public transportation, 0.0% walk, 8.4% work from home (2000); Travel time to work: 17.3% less than 15 minutes, 37.0% 15 to 30 minutes, 10.2% 30 to 45 minutes, 8.5% 45 to 60 minutes, 27.1% 60 minutes or more (2000)

DEPOSIT (village). Covers a land area of 1.258 square miles and a water area of 0.060 square miles. Located at 42.06° N. Lat.; 75.42° W. Long. Elevation is 991 feet.
Population: 1,936 (1990); 1,699 (2000); 1,579 (2005); 1,534 (2010 projected); Race: 95.6% White, 1.1% Black, 1.3% Asian, 4.0% Hispanic of any race (2005); Density: 1,255.5 persons per square mile (2005); Average household size: 2.32 (2005); Median age: 36.3 (2005); Males per 100 females: 88.6 (2005); Marriage status: 26.1% never married, 53.2% now married, 12.2% widowed, 8.5% divorced (2000); Foreign born: 1.1% (2000); Ancestry (includes multiple ancestries): 21.6% German, 14.6% English, 14.3% Irish, 11.5% Italian, 11.0% United States or American (2000).
Economy: Single-family building permits issued: 0 (2005); Multi-family building permits issued: 0 (2005); Employment by occupation: 7.7% management, 14.3% professional, 15.8% services, 23.4% sales, 1.4% farming, 12.1% construction, 25.3% production (2000).
Income: Per capita income: $16,417 (2005); Median household income: $28,404 (2005); Average household income: $38,121 (2005); Percent of households with income of $100,000 or more: 4.3% (2005); Poverty rate: 17.6% (2000).
Education: Percent of population age 25 and over with: High school diploma (including GED) or higher: 80.4% (2005); Bachelor's degree or higher: 11.4% (2005); Master's degree or higher: 4.4% (2005).

School District(s)
Deposit Central School District (KG-12)
   2003-04 Enrollment: 692 . . . . (607) 467-5380
Housing: Homeownership rate: 60.0% (2005); Median home value: $77,982 (2005); Median rent: $335 per month (2000); Median age of housing: 60+ years (2000).
Newspapers: Deposit Courier (General - Circulation 2,200); Towne Crier (General - Circulation 7,500)
Transportation: Commute to work: 86.9% car, 1.2% public transportation, 9.2% walk, 2.0% work from home (2000); Travel time to work: 53.8% less than 15 minutes, 11.4% 15 to 30 minutes, 17.2% 30 to 45 minutes, 9.2% 45 to 60 minutes, 8.4% 60 minutes or more (2000)

DEPOSIT (town). Covers a land area of 43.011 square miles and a water area of 1.581 square miles. Located at 42.07° N. Lat.; 75.39° W. Long.
Population: 1,824 (1990); 1,687 (2000); 1,606 (2005); 1,581 (2010 projected); Race: 96.9% White, 1.7% Black, 0.7% Asian, 1.6% Hispanic of any race (2005); Density: 37.3 persons per square mile (2005); Average household size: 2.35 (2005); Median age: 38.6 (2005); Males per 100 females: 92.6 (2005); Marriage status: 24.0% never married, 54.7% now married, 10.8% widowed, 10.5% divorced (2000); Foreign born: 0.8% (2000); Ancestry (includes multiple ancestries): 20.4% German, 15.4% Irish, 14.6% English, 9.6% Italian, 9.6% United States or American (2000).
Economy: Single-family building permits issued: 11 (2005); Multi-family building permits issued: 0 (2005); Employment by occupation: 7.2% management, 13.8% professional, 12.7% services, 26.4% sales, 1.7% farming, 11.7% construction, 26.5% production (2000).
Income: Per capita income: $17,159 (2005); Median household income: $32,340 (2005); Average household income: $40,407 (2005); Percent of households with income of $100,000 or more: 5.0% (2005); Poverty rate: 15.8% (2000).
Education: Percent of population age 25 and over with: High school diploma (including GED) or higher: 83.8% (2005); Bachelor's degree or higher: 10.4% (2005); Master's degree or higher: 3.9% (2005).
Housing: Homeownership rate: 68.9% (2005); Median home value: $93,000 (2005); Median rent: $315 per month (2000); Median age of housing: 46 years (2000).
Transportation: Commute to work: 90.8% car, 0.9% public transportation, 5.7% walk, 2.3% work from home (2000); Travel time to work: 46.8% less than 15 minutes, 16.4% 15 to 30 minutes, 17.9% 30 to 45 minutes, 10.9% 45 to 60 minutes, 7.9% 60 minutes or more (2000)
Additional Information Contacts
Deposit Chamber of Commerce . . . . (607) 467-2556
   http://www.depositchamber.com/

DOWNSVILLE (unincorporated postal area, zip code 13755). Covers a land area of 45.298 square miles and a water area of 0 square miles. Located at 42.08° N. Lat.; 75.00° W. Long.
Population: 0 (2000); Race: 98.8% White, 0.0% Black, 0.0% Asian, 1.5% Hispanic of any race (2000); Density: 0.0 persons per square mile (2000); Age: 21.4% under 18, 18.6% over 64 (2000); Marriage status: 18.3% never married, 62.9% now married, 10.3% widowed, 8.5% divorced (2000); Foreign born: 1.7% (2000); Ancestry (includes multiple ancestries): 18.1% German, 16.7% Irish, 11.4% English, 11.1% Italian, 8.6% Polish (2000).
Economy: Employment by occupation: 8.2% management, 19.5% professional, 17.8% services, 20.7% sales, 0.4% farming, 13.4% construction, 20.1% production (2000).
Income: Per capita income: $15,424 (2000); Median household income: $31,121 (2000); Poverty rate: 11.7% (2000).
Education: Percent of population age 25 and over with: High school diploma (including GED) or higher: 80.8% (2000); Bachelor's degree or higher: 10.4% (2000).

School District(s)
Downsville Central School District (PK-12)
   2003-04 Enrollment: 373 . . . . (607) 363-2101
Housing: Homeownership rate: 75.4% (2000); Median home value: $68,000 (2000); Median rent: $346 per month (2000); Median age of housing: 37 years (2000).
Transportation: Commute to work: 87.3% car, 0.6% public transportation, 6.8% walk, 4.9% work from home (2000); Travel time to work: 33.7% less than 15 minutes, 33.3% 15 to 30 minutes, 18.3% 30 to 45 minutes, 6.3% 45 to 60 minutes, 8.5% 60 minutes or more (2000)

EAST BRANCH (unincorporated postal area, zip code 13756). Covers a land area of 29.390 square miles and a water area of 0.009 square miles. Located at 42.01° N. Lat.; 75.11° W. Long. Elevation is 1,007 feet.
Population: 0 (2000); Race: 93.2% White, 0.0% Black, 0.0% Asian, 1.2% Hispanic of any race (2000); Density: 0.0 persons per square mile (2000); Age: 23.2% under 18, 20.7% over 64 (2000); Marriage status: 21.7% never married, 70.2% now married, 6.7% widowed, 1.3% divorced (2000); Foreign born: 5.2% (2000); Ancestry (includes multiple ancestries): 30.3% Irish, 18.0% German, 15.2% United States or American, 10.3% Italian, 9.1% English (2000).
Economy: Employment by occupation: 4.7% management, 8.2% professional, 20.6% services, 21.8% sales, 2.4% farming, 7.1% construction, 35.3% production (2000).
Income: Per capita income: $14,461 (2000); Median household income: $34,583 (2000); Poverty rate: 17.5% (2000).
Education: Percent of population age 25 and over with: High school diploma (including GED) or higher: 75.9% (2000); Bachelor's degree or higher: 10.3% (2000).
Housing: Homeownership rate: 81.9% (2000); Median home value: $67,000 (2000); Median rent: $331 per month (2000); Median age of housing: 19 years (2000).
Transportation: Commute to work: 91.2% car, 0.0% public transportation, 4.1% walk, 4.7% work from home (2000); Travel time to work: 21.0% less than 15 minutes, 28.4% 15 to 30 minutes, 28.4% 30 to 45 minutes, 8.0% 45 to 60 minutes, 14.2% 60 minutes or more (2000)

EAST MEREDITH (unincorporated postal area, zip code 13757). Covers a land area of 38.067 square miles and a water area of 0.042 square miles. Located at 42.41° N. Lat.; 74.91° W. Long.
Population: 0 (2000); Race: 98.5% White, 0.0% Black, 0.2% Asian, 1.4% Hispanic of any race (2000); Density: 0.0 persons per square mile (2000); Age: 23.9% under 18, 12.9% over 64 (2000); Marriage status: 20.8% never married, 62.9% now married, 6.5% widowed, 9.9% divorced (2000); Foreign born: 3.3% (2000); Ancestry (includes multiple ancestries): 26.3% German, 17.5% Irish, 14.2% English, 7.9% Italian, 7.5% United States or American (2000).
Economy: Employment by occupation: 19.3% management, 20.3% professional, 17.7% services, 14.0% sales, 2.7% farming, 10.5% construction, 15.6% production (2000).
Income: Per capita income: $17,134 (2000); Median household income: $34,632 (2000); Poverty rate: 15.0% (2000).
Education: Percent of population age 25 and over with: High school diploma (including GED) or higher: 77.9% (2000); Bachelor's degree or higher: 18.9% (2000).
Housing: Homeownership rate: 82.5% (2000); Median home value: $68,000 (2000); Median rent: $341 per month (2000); Median age of housing: 27 years (2000).
Transportation: Commute to work: 88.2% car, 0.6% public transportation, 2.7% walk, 8.4% work from home (2000); Travel time to work: 17.5% less than 15 minutes, 56.7% 15 to 30 minutes, 19.6% 30 to 45 minutes, 1.8% 45 to 60 minutes, 4.4% 60 minutes or more (2000)

FLEISCHMANNS (village). Covers a land area of 0.668 square miles and a water area of 0.012 square miles. Located at 42.15° N. Lat.; 74.53° W. Long. Elevation is 1,520 feet.
Population: 351 (1990); 351 (2000); 354 (2005); 354 (2010 projected); Race: 92.1% White, 2.3% Black, 2.5% Asian, 27.4% Hispanic of any race (2005); Density: 529.6 persons per square mile (2005); Average household size: 2.44 (2005); Median age: 38.6 (2005); Males per 100 females: 87.3 (2005); Marriage status: 22.5% never married, 49.5% now married, 14.9% widowed, 13.1% divorced (2000); Foreign born: 22.7% (2000); Ancestry (includes multiple ancestries): 22.7% Other groups, 21.5% German, 17.0% Irish, 10.5% Italian, 7.1% Dutch (2000).
Economy: Single-family building permits issued: 1 (2005); Multi-family building permits issued: 3 (2005); Employment by occupation: 12.2% management, 8.4% professional, 19.8% services, 30.5% sales, 0.0% farming, 8.4% construction, 20.6% production (2000).
Income: Per capita income: $17,987 (2005); Median household income: $34,211 (2005); Average household income: $43,914 (2005); Percent of households with income of $100,000 or more: 5.5% (2005); Poverty rate: 21.7% (2000).
Education: Percent of population age 25 and over with: High school diploma (including GED) or higher: 71.7% (2005); Bachelor's degree or higher: 9.3% (2005); Master's degree or higher: 6.1% (2005).
Housing: Homeownership rate: 55.9% (2005); Median home value: $117,000 (2005); Median rent: $350 per month (2000); Median age of housing: 60+ years (2000).
Transportation: Commute to work: 74.8% car, 3.9% public transportation, 18.9% walk, 2.4% work from home (2000); Travel time to work: 51.6% less than 15 minutes, 25.0% 15 to 30 minutes, 4.0% 30 to 45 minutes, 9.7% 45 to 60 minutes, 9.7% 60 minutes or more (2000)
Additional Information Contacts
Fleishmanns Chamber of Commerce .... (845) 254-5514
http://www.delawarecounty.org

FRANKLIN (village). Covers a land area of 0.345 square miles and a water area of 0 square miles. Located at 42.34° N. Lat.; 75.16° W. Long. Elevation is 1,582 feet.
Population: 409 (1990); 402 (2000); 373 (2005); 355 (2010 projected); Race: 98.4% White, 0.3% Black, 0.0% Asian, 1.1% Hispanic of any race (2005); Density: 1,081.8 persons per square mile (2005); Average household size: 2.39 (2005); Median age: 40.1 (2005); Males per 100 females: 86.5 (2005); Marriage status: 25.9% never married, 51.2% now married, 15.1% widowed, 7.8% divorced (2000); Foreign born: 1.7% (2000); Ancestry (includes multiple ancestries): 32.7% German, 20.5% Irish, 17.8% English, 11.4% Italian, 6.2% Polish (2000).
Economy: Single-family building permits issued: 0 (2005); Multi-family building permits issued: 0 (2005); Employment by occupation: 9.2% management, 23.6% professional, 11.3% services, 27.2% sales, 1.5% farming, 14.9% construction, 12.3% production (2000).
Income: Per capita income: $16,723 (2005); Median household income: $31,857 (2005); Average household income: $39,984 (2005); Percent of households with income of $100,000 or more: 6.4% (2005); Poverty rate: 13.1% (2000).
Education: Percent of population age 25 and over with: High school diploma (including GED) or higher: 88.9% (2005); Bachelor's degree or higher: 26.6% (2005); Master's degree or higher: 12.3% (2005).
School District(s)
Franklin Central School District (PK-12)
    2003-04 Enrollment: 335 .... (607) 829-3551
Housing: Homeownership rate: 65.4% (2005); Median home value: $118,085 (2005); Median rent: $343 per month (2000); Median age of housing: 60+ years (2000).
Transportation: Commute to work: 84.2% car, 0.0% public transportation, 13.2% walk, 2.6% work from home (2000); Travel time to work: 25.4% less than 15 minutes, 50.3% 15 to 30 minutes, 15.7% 30 to 45 minutes, 6.5% 45 to 60 minutes, 2.2% 60 minutes or more (2000)

FRANKLIN (town). Covers a land area of 81.448 square miles and a water area of 0.110 square miles. Located at 42.32° N. Lat.; 75.10° W. Long. Elevation is 1,582 feet.
Population: 2,471 (1990); 2,621 (2000); 2,503 (2005); 2,379 (2010 projected); Race: 97.8% White, 1.2% Black, 0.2% Asian, 0.8% Hispanic of any race (2005); Density: 30.7 persons per square mile (2005); Average household size: 2.50 (2005); Median age: 42.5 (2005); Males per 100 females: 100.2 (2005); Marriage status: 20.8% never married, 63.5% now married, 8.5% widowed, 7.1% divorced (2000); Foreign born: 1.7% (2000); Ancestry (includes multiple ancestries): 26.2% German, 17.6% Irish, 16.2% English, 12.9% Italian, 7.2% United States or American (2000).
Economy: Employment by occupation: 14.1% management, 24.1% professional, 12.2% services, 20.7% sales, 3.6% farming, 12.9% construction, 12.4% production (2000).
Income: Per capita income: $20,256 (2005); Median household income: $41,324 (2005); Average household income: $50,564 (2005); Percent of households with income of $100,000 or more: 9.5% (2005); Poverty rate: 10.4% (2000).
Education: Percent of population age 25 and over with: High school diploma (including GED) or higher: 82.5% (2005); Bachelor's degree or higher: 18.0% (2005); Master's degree or higher: 6.8% (2005).
Housing: Homeownership rate: 82.6% (2005); Median home value: $124,359 (2005); Median rent: $365 per month (2000); Median age of housing: 44 years (2000).
Transportation: Commute to work: 86.0% car, 1.0% public transportation, 6.2% walk, 6.8% work from home (2000); Travel time to work: 23.4% less than 15 minutes, 46.2% 15 to 30 minutes, 17.3% 30 to 45 minutes, 3.9% 45 to 60 minutes, 9.2% 60 minutes or more (2000)

Additional Information Contacts
Town of Franklin .... (518) 891-2189
  http://townoffranklin.com/

GRAND GORGE (unincorporated postal area, zip code 12434).
Covers a land area of 9.652 square miles and a water area of 0 square miles. Located at 42.36° N. Lat.; 74.50° W. Long. Elevation is 1,411 feet.
Population: 0 (2000); Race: 96.5% White, 0.0% Black, 0.0% Asian, 0.6% Hispanic of any race (2000); Density: 0.0 persons per square mile (2000); Age: 22.7% under 18, 16.8% over 64 (2000); Marriage status: 28.6% never married, 60.2% now married, 4.5% widowed, 6.7% divorced (2000); Foreign born: 0.4% (2000); Ancestry (includes multiple ancestries): 18.2% Irish, 17.4% German, 10.8% English, 9.3% Dutch, 8.4% Other groups (2000).
Economy: Employment by occupation: 17.3% management, 15.7% professional, 19.3% services, 16.0% sales, 1.7% farming, 15.3% construction, 14.7% production (2000).
Income: Per capita income: $18,138 (2000); Median household income: $31,250 (2000); Poverty rate: 21.0% (2000).
Education: Percent of population age 25 and over with: High school diploma (including GED) or higher: 87.5% (2000); Bachelor's degree or higher: 13.7% (2000).
Housing: Homeownership rate: 73.6% (2000); Median home value: $70,900 (2000); Median rent: $332 per month (2000); Median age of housing: 42 years (2000).
Transportation: Commute to work: 94.5% car, 2.1% public transportation, 2.1% walk, 1.4% work from home (2000); Travel time to work: 42.5% less than 15 minutes, 31.9% 15 to 30 minutes, 15.1% 30 to 45 minutes, 4.2% 45 to 60 minutes, 6.3% 60 minutes or more (2000)

HAMDEN (town).
Covers a land area of 59.833 square miles and a water area of 0.031 square miles. Located at 42.21° N. Lat.; 75.00° W. Long.
Population: 1,144 (1990); 1,280 (2000); 1,274 (2005); 1,248 (2010 projected); Race: 97.5% White, 0.2% Black, 0.0% Asian, 1.6% Hispanic of any race (2005); Density: 21.3 persons per square mile (2005); Average household size: 2.31 (2005); Median age: 45.1 (2005); Males per 100 females: 99.1 (2005); Marriage status: 22.3% never married, 60.1% now married, 8.9% widowed, 8.7% divorced (2000); Foreign born: 2.8% (2000); Ancestry (includes multiple ancestries): 22.6% Irish, 16.6% English, 16.6% German, 10.9% Italian, 8.5% Scottish (2000).
Economy: Single-family building permits issued: 8 (2005); Multi-family building permits issued: 0 (2005); Employment by occupation: 12.3% management, 18.0% professional, 15.6% services, 23.2% sales, 5.3% farming, 12.7% construction, 12.9% production (2000).
Income: Per capita income: $24,257 (2005); Median household income: $44,138 (2005); Average household income: $55,566 (2005); Percent of households with income of $100,000 or more: 10.1% (2005); Poverty rate: 10.4% (2000).
Education: Percent of population age 25 and over with: High school diploma (including GED) or higher: 78.5% (2005); Bachelor's degree or higher: 14.7% (2005); Master's degree or higher: 6.6% (2005).
Housing: Homeownership rate: 81.2% (2005); Median home value: $117,931 (2005); Median rent: $375 per month (2000); Median age of housing: 37 years (2000).
Transportation: Commute to work: 88.2% car, 1.7% public transportation, 1.0% walk, 8.7% work from home (2000); Travel time to work: 31.6% less than 15 minutes, 36.1% 15 to 30 minutes, 13.9% 30 to 45 minutes, 6.9% 45 to 60 minutes, 11.5% 60 minutes or more (2000)

HANCOCK (village).
Covers a land area of 1.574 square miles and a water area of 0.127 square miles. Located at 41.95° N. Lat.; 75.28° W. Long. Elevation is 924 feet.
Population: 1,330 (1990); 1,189 (2000); 1,112 (2005); 1,080 (2010 projected); Race: 97.1% White, 0.3% Black, 0.4% Asian, 4.5% Hispanic of any race (2005); Density: 706.4 persons per square mile (2005); Average household size: 2.30 (2005); Median age: 45.7 (2005); Males per 100 females: 88.2 (2005); Marriage status: 24.8% never married, 57.5% now married, 10.5% widowed, 7.2% divorced (2000); Foreign born: 4.2% (2000); Ancestry (includes multiple ancestries): 19.5% English, 18.0% German, 16.4% Irish, 11.8% Italian, 8.5% Other groups (2000).
Economy: Single-family building permits issued: 0 (2005); Multi-family building permits issued: 0 (2005); Employment by occupation: 7.3% management, 23.0% professional, 16.1% services, 21.0% sales, 1.8% farming, 8.2% construction, 22.7% production (2000).
Income: Per capita income: $18,362 (2005); Median household income: $31,554 (2005); Average household income: $41,822 (2005); Percent of households with income of $100,000 or more: 7.9% (2005); Poverty rate: 15.6% (2000).
Education: Percent of population age 25 and over with: High school diploma (including GED) or higher: 73.0% (2005); Bachelor's degree or higher: 13.9% (2005); Master's degree or higher: 6.2% (2005).
School District(s)
Hancock Central School District (PK-12)
  2003-04 Enrollment: 490 .... (607) 637-1301
Housing: Homeownership rate: 60.7% (2005); Median home value: $90,488 (2005); Median rent: $329 per month (2000); Median age of housing: 60+ years (2000).
Safety: Violent crime rate: 60.9 per 10,000 population; Property crime rate: 174.1 per 10,000 population (2004).
Newspapers: Hancock Herald (General - Circulation 2,300)
Transportation: Commute to work: 73.7% car, 1.8% public transportation, 13.5% walk, 9.2% work from home (2000); Travel time to work: 58.9% less than 15 minutes, 19.1% 15 to 30 minutes, 7.8% 30 to 45 minutes, 5.8% 45 to 60 minutes, 8.3% 60 minutes or more (2000)
Additional Information Contacts
Hancock Chamber of Commerce..................... (607) 637-4756
  http://www.hancockareachamber.com

HANCOCK (town).
Covers a land area of 159.330 square miles and a water area of 2.500 square miles. Located at 41.96° N. Lat.; 75.17° W. Long. Elevation is 924 feet.
Population: 3,384 (1990); 3,449 (2000); 3,362 (2005); 3,270 (2010 projected); Race: 96.4% White, 0.8% Black, 1.1% Asian, 3.2% Hispanic of any race (2005); Density: 21.1 persons per square mile (2005); Average household size: 2.43 (2005); Median age: 43.3 (2005); Males per 100 females: 98.5 (2005); Marriage status: 22.4% never married, 61.4% now married, 9.4% widowed, 6.8% divorced (2000); Foreign born: 3.6% (2000); Ancestry (includes multiple ancestries): 20.8% German, 16.1% Irish, 15.3% English, 9.5% United States or American, 9.3% Italian (2000).
Economy: Single-family building permits issued: 9 (2005); Multi-family building permits issued: 0 (2005); Employment by occupation: 8.5% management, 18.5% professional, 15.8% services, 17.6% sales, 2.2% farming, 9.9% construction, 27.5% production (2000).
Income: Per capita income: $18,537 (2005); Median household income: $34,260 (2005); Average household income: $44,489 (2005); Percent of households with income of $100,000 or more: 7.2% (2005); Poverty rate: 14.3% (2000).
Taxes: Total city taxes per capita: $423 (2004); City property taxes per capita: $406 (2004).
Education: Percent of population age 25 and over with: High school diploma (including GED) or higher: 74.5% (2005); Bachelor's degree or higher: 12.5% (2005); Master's degree or higher: 5.4% (2005).
Housing: Homeownership rate: 76.2% (2005); Median home value: $92,117 (2005); Median rent: $339 per month (2000); Median age of housing: 35 years (2000).
Transportation: Commute to work: 83.5% car, 1.0% public transportation, 8.0% walk, 6.9% work from home (2000); Travel time to work: 40.7% less than 15 minutes, 22.8% 15 to 30 minutes, 17.8% 30 to 45 minutes, 7.6% 45 to 60 minutes, 11.3% 60 minutes or more (2000)

HARPERSFIELD (town).
Covers a land area of 42.143 square miles and a water area of 0.213 square miles. Located at 42.43° N. Lat.; 74.67° W. Long.
Population: 1,450 (1990); 1,603 (2000); 1,566 (2005); 1,562 (2010 projected); Race: 97.8% White, 0.8% Black, 0.3% Asian, 4.1% Hispanic of any race (2005); Density: 37.2 persons per square mile (2005); Average household size: 2.66 (2005); Median age: 48.0 (2005); Males per 100 females: 90.3 (2005); Marriage status: 20.2% never married, 66.6% now married, 9.1% widowed, 4.2% divorced (2000); Foreign born: 3.9% (2000); Ancestry (includes multiple ancestries): 17.8% German, 16.6% Italian, 15.3% Irish, 10.9% English, 8.8% Other groups (2000).
Economy: Single-family building permits issued: 2 (2005); Multi-family building permits issued: 0 (2005); Employment by occupation: 12.0% management, 19.6% professional, 18.9% services, 23.0% sales, 1.8% farming, 9.9% construction, 14.9% production (2000).
Income: Per capita income: $21,517 (2005); Median household income: $39,438 (2005); Average household income: $53,892 (2005); Percent of households with income of $100,000 or more: 9.5% (2005); Poverty rate: 18.3% (2000).

Education: Percent of population age 25 and over with: High school diploma (including GED) or higher: 76.1% (2005); Bachelor's degree or higher: 16.9% (2005); Master's degree or higher: 8.9% (2005).
Housing: Homeownership rate: 79.5% (2005); Median home value: $112,016 (2005); Median rent: $377 per month (2000); Median age of housing: 34 years (2000).
Transportation: Commute to work: 84.4% car, 1.0% public transportation, 9.0% walk, 5.3% work from home (2000); Travel time to work: 43.8% less than 15 minutes, 19.4% 15 to 30 minutes, 21.4% 30 to 45 minutes, 6.1% 45 to 60 minutes, 9.3% 60 minutes or more (2000)

HOBART (village).
Covers a land area of 0.511 square miles and a water area of 0 square miles. Located at 42.37° N. Lat.; 74.66° W. Long. Elevation is 1,636 feet.
Population: 385 (1990); 390 (2000); 364 (2005); 344 (2010 projected); Race: 90.4% White, 8.0% Black, 0.5% Asian, 0.5% Hispanic of any race (2005); Density: 712.9 persons per square mile (2005); Average household size: 2.55 (2005); Median age: 43.0 (2005); Males per 100 females: 94.7 (2005); Marriage status: 28.8% never married, 54.4% now married, 10.4% widowed, 6.3% divorced (2000); Foreign born: 0.0% (2000); Ancestry (includes multiple ancestries): 13.8% Irish, 13.8% Italian, 13.5% English, 13.2% Other groups, 13.0% German (2000).
Economy: Single-family building permits issued: 1 (2005); Multi-family building permits issued: 0 (2005); Employment by occupation: 7.5% management, 22.0% professional, 11.6% services, 25.4% sales, 4.6% farming, 11.6% construction, 17.3% production (2000).
Income: Per capita income: $20,107 (2005); Median household income: $45,761 (2005); Average household income: $48,374 (2005); Percent of households with income of $100,000 or more: 8.4% (2005); Poverty rate: 17.6% (2000).
Education: Percent of population age 25 and over with: High school diploma (including GED) or higher: 70.3% (2005); Bachelor's degree or higher: 22.9% (2005); Master's degree or higher: 6.8% (2005).
Housing: Homeownership rate: 65.7% (2005); Median home value: $110,256 (2005); Median rent: $393 per month (2000); Median age of housing: 60+ years (2000).
Transportation: Commute to work: 90.2% car, 4.3% public transportation, 1.8% walk, 0.6% work from home (2000); Travel time to work: 54.0% less than 15 minutes, 23.3% 15 to 30 minutes, 10.4% 30 to 45 minutes, 6.1% 45 to 60 minutes, 6.1% 60 minutes or more (2000)

KORTRIGHT (town).
Covers a land area of 62.615 square miles and a water area of 0.095 square miles. Located at 42.40° N. Lat.; 74.79° W. Long.
Population: 1,410 (1990); 1,633 (2000); 1,597 (2005); 1,566 (2010 projected); Race: 85.9% White, 10.8% Black, 0.6% Asian, 4.8% Hispanic of any race (2005); Density: 25.5 persons per square mile (2005); Average household size: 2.68 (2005); Median age: 37.6 (2005); Males per 100 females: 109.9 (2005); Marriage status: 29.1% never married, 57.4% now married, 7.8% widowed, 5.8% divorced (2000); Foreign born: 3.0% (2000); Ancestry (includes multiple ancestries): 15.3% German, 13.4% Irish, 10.7% English, 9.6% Polish, 7.4% Italian (2000).
Economy: Single-family building permits issued: 5 (2005); Multi-family building permits issued: 0 (2005); Employment by occupation: 19.0% management, 13.8% professional, 16.6% services, 14.5% sales, 6.6% farming, 10.9% construction, 18.7% production (2000).
Income: Per capita income: $18,433 (2005); Median household income: $37,167 (2005); Average household income: $47,404 (2005); Percent of households with income of $100,000 or more: 5.2% (2005); Poverty rate: 12.6% (2000).
Education: Percent of population age 25 and over with: High school diploma (including GED) or higher: 77.7% (2005); Bachelor's degree or higher: 9.6% (2005); Master's degree or higher: 3.4% (2005).
Housing: Homeownership rate: 84.4% (2005); Median home value: $102,593 (2005); Median rent: $381 per month (2000); Median age of housing: 26 years (2000).
Transportation: Commute to work: 86.8% car, 0.6% public transportation, 3.8% walk, 8.4% work from home (2000); Travel time to work: 31.7% less than 15 minutes, 41.1% 15 to 30 minutes, 18.8% 30 to 45 minutes, 3.2% 45 to 60 minutes, 5.2% 60 minutes or more (2000)

MARGARETVILLE (village).
Covers a land area of 0.701 square miles and a water area of 0 square miles. Located at 42.14° N. Lat.; 74.65° W. Long. Elevation is 1,320 feet.
Population: 639 (1990); 643 (2000); 578 (2005); 565 (2010 projected); Race: 97.9% White, 0.2% Black, 1.4% Asian, 0.7% Hispanic of any race (2005); Density: 824.2 persons per square mile (2005); Average household size: 2.29 (2005); Median age: 52.3 (2005); Males per 100 females: 72.5 (2005); Marriage status: 11.1% never married, 64.6% now married, 15.7% widowed, 8.5% divorced (2000); Foreign born: 3.9% (2000); Ancestry (includes multiple ancestries): 17.1% Irish, 14.7% German, 11.0% Italian, 9.3% English, 5.2% Dutch (2000).
Economy: Single-family building permits issued: 1 (2005); Multi-family building permits issued: 0 (2005); Employment by occupation: 13.8% management, 25.9% professional, 14.7% services, 31.3% sales, 1.8% farming, 8.0% construction, 4.5% production (2000).
Income: Per capita income: $23,339 (2005); Median household income: $32,838 (2005); Average household income: $44,841 (2005); Percent of households with income of $100,000 or more: 8.3% (2005); Poverty rate: 16.5% (2000).
Education: Percent of population age 25 and over with: High school diploma (including GED) or higher: 77.1% (2005); Bachelor's degree or higher: 13.6% (2005); Master's degree or higher: 7.7% (2005).
School District(s)
Margaretville Central School District (KG-12)
    2003-04 Enrollment: 546 . . . . (845) 586-2647
Housing: Homeownership rate: 62.3% (2005); Median home value: $129,688 (2005); Median rent: $357 per month (2000); Median age of housing: 60+ years (2000).
Hospitals: Margaretville Memorial Hospital (15 beds)
Transportation: Commute to work: 72.0% car, 1.4% public transportation, 22.4% walk, 4.2% work from home (2000); Travel time to work: 62.9% less than 15 minutes, 9.8% 15 to 30 minutes, 10.7% 30 to 45 minutes, 4.9% 45 to 60 minutes, 11.7% 60 minutes or more (2000)
Additional Information Contacts
Margaretville Chamber of Commerce . . . . (845) 586-3300
    http://www.margaretville.org

MASONVILLE (town).
Covers a land area of 54.205 square miles and a water area of 0.119 square miles. Located at 42.23° N. Lat.; 75.33° W. Long. Elevation is 1,294 feet.
Population: 1,389 (1990); 1,405 (2000); 1,409 (2005); 1,382 (2010 projected); Race: 95.5% White, 2.3% Black, 0.3% Asian, 2.1% Hispanic of any race (2005); Density: 26.0 persons per square mile (2005); Average household size: 2.61 (2005); Median age: 39.7 (2005); Males per 100 females: 114.5 (2005); Marriage status: 20.5% never married, 65.8% now married, 5.9% widowed, 7.9% divorced (2000); Foreign born: 2.4% (2000); Ancestry (includes multiple ancestries): 19.8% German, 16.6% Irish, 15.5% English, 9.5% United States or American, 8.5% Italian (2000).
Economy: Single-family building permits issued: 6 (2005); Multi-family building permits issued: 0 (2005); Employment by occupation: 9.3% management, 11.2% professional, 16.6% services, 20.7% sales, 3.2% farming, 12.3% construction, 26.7% production (2000).
Income: Per capita income: $17,724 (2005); Median household income: $37,472 (2005); Average household income: $46,011 (2005); Percent of households with income of $100,000 or more: 6.9% (2005); Poverty rate: 14.4% (2000).
Education: Percent of population age 25 and over with: High school diploma (including GED) or higher: 80.5% (2005); Bachelor's degree or higher: 9.8% (2005); Master's degree or higher: 3.2% (2005).
School District(s)
Sidney Central School District (KG-12)
    2003-04 Enrollment: 1,381 . . . . (607) 563-2135
Housing: Homeownership rate: 88.7% (2005); Median home value: $110,843 (2005); Median rent: $332 per month (2000); Median age of housing: 30 years (2000).
Transportation: Commute to work: 92.6% car, 1.1% public transportation, 1.0% walk, 4.7% work from home (2000); Travel time to work: 32.4% less than 15 minutes, 37.2% 15 to 30 minutes, 19.1% 30 to 45 minutes, 4.6% 45 to 60 minutes, 6.8% 60 minutes or more (2000)

MEREDITH (town).
Covers a land area of 58.214 square miles and a water area of 0.114 square miles. Located at 42.37° N. Lat.; 74.94° W. Long.
Population: 1,513 (1990); 1,588 (2000); 1,549 (2005); 1,507 (2010 projected); Race: 97.9% White, 0.3% Black, 0.6% Asian, 1.5% Hispanic of any race (2005); Density: 26.6 persons per square mile (2005); Average household size: 2.54 (2005); Median age: 41.9 (2005); Males per 100 females: 99.1 (2005); Marriage status: 22.6% never married, 61.1% now

married, 6.9% widowed, 9.4% divorced (2000); Foreign born: 3.7% (2000); Ancestry (includes multiple ancestries): 23.8% German, 18.5% Irish, 13.6% English, 9.2% Dutch, 8.4% United States or American (2000).
Economy: Single-family building permits issued: 4 (2005); Multi-family building permits issued: 0 (2005); Employment by occupation: 14.7% management, 25.7% professional, 17.2% services, 17.7% sales, 1.2% farming, 11.5% construction, 12.1% production (2000).
Income: Per capita income: $22,703 (2005); Median household income: $46,250 (2005); Average household income: $57,504 (2005); Percent of households with income of $100,000 or more: 11.3% (2005); Poverty rate: 14.2% (2000).
Education: Percent of population age 25 and over with: High school diploma (including GED) or higher: 80.1% (2005); Bachelor's degree or higher: 21.0% (2005); Master's degree or higher: 8.2% (2005).
Housing: Homeownership rate: 83.3% (2005); Median home value: $127,878 (2005); Median rent: $339 per month (2000); Median age of housing: 29 years (2000).
Transportation: Commute to work: 88.6% car, 0.6% public transportation, 3.7% walk, 5.8% work from home (2000); Travel time to work: 24.0% less than 15 minutes, 51.4% 15 to 30 minutes, 14.3% 30 to 45 minutes, 2.7% 45 to 60 minutes, 7.7% 60 minutes or more (2000)

MIDDLETOWN (town). Covers a land area of 96.401 square miles and a water area of 0.865 square miles. Located at 42.16° N. Lat.; 74.61° W. Long.
Population: 3,406 (1990); 4,051 (2000); 3,971 (2005); 3,898 (2010 projected); Race: 93.6% White, 1.1% Black, 1.1% Asian, 8.4% Hispanic of any race (2005); Density: 41.2 persons per square mile (2005); Average household size: 2.40 (2005); Median age: 47.7 (2005); Males per 100 females: 94.8 (2005); Marriage status: 18.7% never married, 62.4% now married, 8.8% widowed, 10.1% divorced (2000); Foreign born: 10.2% (2000); Ancestry (includes multiple ancestries): 17.4% German, 15.4% Irish, 12.4% Other groups, 11.9% Italian, 10.2% English (2000).
Economy: Single-family building permits issued: 21 (2005); Multi-family building permits issued: 0 (2005); Employment by occupation: 12.4% management, 17.0% professional, 18.1% services, 26.0% sales, 2.4% farming, 11.6% construction, 12.4% production (2000).
Income: Per capita income: $21,359 (2005); Median household income: $39,138 (2005); Average household income: $49,739 (2005); Percent of households with income of $100,000 or more: 10.8% (2005); Poverty rate: 16.8% (2000).
Education: Percent of population age 25 and over with: High school diploma (including GED) or higher: 78.2% (2005); Bachelor's degree or higher: 16.0% (2005); Master's degree or higher: 8.1% (2005).
Housing: Homeownership rate: 77.6% (2005); Median home value: $132,234 (2005); Median rent: $367 per month (2000); Median age of housing: 34 years (2000).
Transportation: Commute to work: 84.3% car, 1.4% public transportation, 8.6% walk, 5.7% work from home (2000); Travel time to work: 46.5% less than 15 minutes, 21.1% 15 to 30 minutes, 12.2% 30 to 45 minutes, 8.6% 45 to 60 minutes, 11.6% 60 minutes or more (2000)

ROXBURY (town). Covers a land area of 87.159 square miles and a water area of 0.457 square miles. Located at 42.30° N. Lat.; 74.55° W. Long. Elevation is 1,495 feet.
Population: 2,388 (1990); 2,509 (2000); 2,416 (2005); 2,320 (2010 projected); Race: 96.6% White, 0.9% Black, 0.8% Asian, 1.4% Hispanic of any race (2005); Density: 27.7 persons per square mile (2005); Average household size: 2.28 (2005); Median age: 46.4 (2005); Males per 100 females: 96.7 (2005); Marriage status: 25.5% never married, 59.4% now married, 6.1% widowed, 9.1% divorced (2000); Foreign born: 3.4% (2000); Ancestry (includes multiple ancestries): 21.2% German, 19.1% Irish, 12.5% Italian, 10.0% English, 8.8% Other groups (2000).
Economy: Single-family building permits issued: 16 (2005); Multi-family building permits issued: 0 (2005); Employment by occupation: 12.4% management, 21.8% professional, 12.8% services, 25.8% sales, 0.9% farming, 13.9% construction, 12.4% production (2000).
Income: Per capita income: $25,373 (2005); Median household income: $40,337 (2005); Average household income: $57,323 (2005); Percent of households with income of $100,000 or more: 16.3% (2005); Poverty rate: 13.4% (2000).
Education: Percent of population age 25 and over with: High school diploma (including GED) or higher: 83.4% (2005); Bachelor's degree or higher: 20.3% (2005); Master's degree or higher: 8.3% (2005).

School District(s)
Roxbury Central School District (KG-12)
   2003-04 Enrollment: 357 . . . . (607) 326-4151
Housing: Homeownership rate: 80.5% (2005); Median home value: $129,681 (2005); Median rent: $350 per month (2000); Median age of housing: 30 years (2000).
Transportation: Commute to work: 87.6% car, 2.7% public transportation, 3.1% walk, 6.1% work from home (2000); Travel time to work: 35.7% less than 15 minutes, 33.0% 15 to 30 minutes, 12.2% 30 to 45 minutes, 6.2% 45 to 60 minutes, 12.9% 60 minutes or more (2000)

SIDNEY (village). Covers a land area of 2.361 square miles and a water area of 0.009 square miles. Located at 42.30° N. Lat.; 75.39° W. Long. Elevation is 992 feet.
Population: 4,720 (1990); 4,068 (2000); 3,737 (2005); 3,532 (2010 projected); Race: 95.4% White, 1.3% Black, 1.4% Asian, 2.1% Hispanic of any race (2005); Density: 1,582.6 persons per square mile (2005); Average household size: 2.27 (2005); Median age: 40.3 (2005); Males per 100 females: 86.9 (2005); Marriage status: 25.9% never married, 51.5% now married, 12.8% widowed, 9.9% divorced (2000); Foreign born: 2.1% (2000); Ancestry (includes multiple ancestries): 19.6% German, 17.6% English, 12.3% Irish, 11.8% Italian, 11.0% United States or American (2000).
Economy: Single-family building permits issued: 1 (2005); Multi-family building permits issued: 0 (2005); Employment by occupation: 10.0% management, 19.2% professional, 15.5% services, 23.6% sales, 0.0% farming, 9.2% construction, 22.4% production (2000).
Income: Per capita income: $15,675 (2005); Median household income: $29,460 (2005); Average household income: $35,064 (2005); Percent of households with income of $100,000 or more: 3.0% (2005); Poverty rate: 18.5% (2000).
Education: Percent of population age 25 and over with: High school diploma (including GED) or higher: 82.1% (2005); Bachelor's degree or higher: 15.7% (2005); Master's degree or higher: 5.1% (2005).

School District(s)
Sidney Central School District (KG-12)
   2003-04 Enrollment: 1,381 . . . . (607) 563-2135
Housing: Homeownership rate: 59.0% (2005); Median home value: $82,978 (2005); Median rent: $333 per month (2000); Median age of housing: 56 years (2000).
Safety: Violent crime rate: 12.7 per 10,000 population; Property crime rate: 527.4 per 10,000 population (2004).
Newspapers: Tri-Town News (General - Circulation 5,000)
Transportation: Commute to work: 86.9% car, 1.4% public transportation, 7.5% walk, 2.9% work from home (2000); Travel time to work: 67.4% less than 15 minutes, 11.1% 15 to 30 minutes, 7.0% 30 to 45 minutes, 6.5% 45 to 60 minutes, 8.0% 60 minutes or more (2000)
Additional Information Contacts
Sidney Chamber of Commerce . . . . (607) 561-2642
   http://www.sidneychamber.org

SIDNEY (town). Covers a land area of 50.288 square miles and a water area of 0.378 square miles. Located at 42.30° N. Lat.; 75.32° W. Long. Elevation is 992 feet.
Population: 6,630 (1990); 6,109 (2000); 5,950 (2005); 5,780 (2010 projected); Race: 95.9% White, 1.2% Black, 1.1% Asian, 2.0% Hispanic of any race (2005); Density: 118.3 persons per square mile (2005); Average household size: 2.33 (2005); Median age: 41.2 (2005); Males per 100 females: 91.3 (2005); Marriage status: 24.3% never married, 53.8% now married, 11.7% widowed, 10.3% divorced (2000); Foreign born: 2.0% (2000); Ancestry (includes multiple ancestries): 21.8% German, 17.6% English, 13.1% Irish, 12.1% United States or American, 9.7% Italian (2000).
Economy: Single-family building permits issued: 7 (2005); Multi-family building permits issued: 0 (2005); Employment by occupation: 11.4% management, 20.2% professional, 14.7% services, 20.5% sales, 0.3% farming, 10.1% construction, 22.8% production (2000).
Income: Per capita income: $17,580 (2005); Median household income: $32,192 (2005); Average household income: $40,563 (2005); Percent of households with income of $100,000 or more: 5.4% (2005); Poverty rate: 14.3% (2000).
Education: Percent of population age 25 and over with: High school diploma (including GED) or higher: 80.0% (2005); Bachelor's degree or higher: 16.0% (2005); Master's degree or higher: 5.2% (2005).

Housing: Homeownership rate: 68.8% (2005); Median home value: $86,612 (2005); Median rent: $330 per month (2000); Median age of housing: 50 years (2000).
Transportation: Commute to work: 87.9% car, 1.3% public transportation, 5.6% walk, 4.3% work from home (2000); Travel time to work: 57.5% less than 15 minutes, 18.4% 15 to 30 minutes, 11.8% 30 to 45 minutes, 5.4% 45 to 60 minutes, 6.9% 60 minutes or more (2000)

SIDNEY CENTER (unincorporated postal area, zip code 13839).
Covers a land area of 44.890 square miles and a water area of 0.092 square miles. Located at 42.23° N. Lat.; 75.25° W. Long. Elevation is 1,290 feet.
Population: 0 (2000); Race: 98.5% White, 0.6% Black, 0.0% Asian, 0.2% Hispanic of any race (2000); Density: 0.0 persons per square mile (2000); Age: 30.0% under 18, 12.9% over 64 (2000); Marriage status: 21.9% never married, 60.2% now married, 7.4% widowed, 10.5% divorced (2000); Foreign born: 1.5% (2000); Ancestry (includes multiple ancestries): 20.9% United States or American, 19.9% German, 13.1% English, 10.0% Irish, 6.3% Italian (2000).
Economy: Employment by occupation: 12.4% management, 9.9% professional, 13.3% services, 20.5% sales, 0.4% farming, 11.8% construction, 31.5% production (2000).
Income: Per capita income: $14,622 (2000); Median household income: $30,042 (2000); Poverty rate: 10.1% (2000).
Education: Percent of population age 25 and over with: High school diploma (including GED) or higher: 74.3% (2000); Bachelor's degree or higher: 5.7% (2000).

School District(s)
Sidney Central School District (KG-12)
    2003-04 Enrollment: 1,381 . . . . (607) 563-2135
Housing: Homeownership rate: 80.5% (2000); Median home value: $59,800 (2000); Median rent: $290 per month (2000); Median age of housing: 33 years (2000).
Transportation: Commute to work: 89.8% car, 0.0% public transportation, 3.8% walk, 5.6% work from home (2000); Travel time to work: 24.3% less than 15 minutes, 45.0% 15 to 30 minutes, 18.4% 30 to 45 minutes, 4.2% 45 to 60 minutes, 8.1% 60 minutes or more (2000)

SOUTH KORTRIGHT (unincorporated postal area, zip code 13842).
Covers a land area of 14.397 square miles and a water area of 0.076 square miles. Located at 42.37° N. Lat.; 74.72° W. Long.
Population: 0 (2000); Race: 77.2% White, 20.4% Black, 0.0% Asian, 0.0% Hispanic of any race (2000); Density: 0.0 persons per square mile (2000); Age: 36.7% under 18, 15.4% over 64 (2000); Marriage status: 35.3% never married, 55.0% now married, 5.5% widowed, 4.2% divorced (2000); Foreign born: 1.1% (2000); Ancestry (includes multiple ancestries): 18.0% Irish, 15.0% German, 12.2% Polish, 11.5% English, 8.7% United States or American (2000).
Economy: Employment by occupation: 15.2% management, 31.3% professional, 19.4% services, 16.6% sales, 2.3% farming, 3.2% construction, 12.0% production (2000).
Income: Per capita income: $15,096 (2000); Median household income: $42,500 (2000); Poverty rate: 3.7% (2000).
Education: Percent of population age 25 and over with: High school diploma (including GED) or higher: 82.1% (2000); Bachelor's degree or higher: 16.9% (2000).

School District(s)
South Kortright Central School District (KG-12)
    2003-04 Enrollment: 469 . . . . (607) 538-9111
Housing: Homeownership rate: 88.4% (2000); Median home value: $79,000 (2000); Median rent: $408 per month (2000); Median age of housing: 50 years (2000).
Transportation: Commute to work: 77.5% car, 0.9% public transportation, 15.5% walk, 5.2% work from home (2000); Travel time to work: 57.9% less than 15 minutes, 21.8% 15 to 30 minutes, 14.4% 30 to 45 minutes, 4.5% 45 to 60 minutes, 1.5% 60 minutes or more (2000)

STAMFORD (village).
Covers a land area of 1.326 square miles and a water area of <.001 square miles. Located at 42.41° N. Lat.; 74.61° W. Long. Elevation is 1,827 feet.
Population: 1,211 (1990); 1,265 (2000); 1,201 (2005); 1,170 (2010 projected); Race: 97.8% White, 0.4% Black, 0.7% Asian, 5.2% Hispanic of any race (2005); Density: 906.0 persons per square mile (2005); Average household size: 2.51 (2005); Median age: 47.4 (2005); Males per 100 females: 86.8 (2005); Marriage status: 21.1% never married, 59.5% now married, 10.6% widowed, 8.7% divorced (2000); Foreign born: 5.3% (2000); Ancestry (includes multiple ancestries): 19.2% German, 17.3% Irish, 13.7% Italian, 13.0% English, 6.8% United States or American (2000).
Economy: Single-family building permits issued: 2 (2005); Multi-family building permits issued: 0 (2005); Employment by occupation: 8.8% management, 25.1% professional, 20.4% services, 20.4% sales, 0.8% farming, 6.1% construction, 18.4% production (2000).
Income: Per capita income: $20,000 (2005); Median household income: $34,741 (2005); Average household income: $46,070 (2005); Percent of households with income of $100,000 or more: 6.1% (2005); Poverty rate: 15.2% (2000).
Education: Percent of population age 25 and over with: High school diploma (including GED) or higher: 75.1% (2005); Bachelor's degree or higher: 21.2% (2005); Master's degree or higher: 11.6% (2005).

School District(s)
Boces Otsego-Delaw-Schoharie-Greene (UG-UG)
    2003-04 Enrollment: 170 . . . . (607) 652-1209
Stamford Central School District (KG-12)
    2003-04 Enrollment: 453 . . . . (607) 652-7301
Housing: Homeownership rate: 57.2% (2005); Median home value: $102,809 (2005); Median rent: $374 per month (2000); Median age of housing: 60+ years (2000).
Newspapers: The Mountain Eagle (Stamford) (General - Circulation 5,000)
Transportation: Commute to work: 79.8% car, 0.6% public transportation, 14.0% walk, 4.6% work from home (2000); Travel time to work: 59.2% less than 15 minutes, 13.3% 15 to 30 minutes, 20.5% 30 to 45 minutes, 2.6% 45 to 60 minutes, 4.4% 60 minutes or more (2000)
Additional Information Contacts
Village of Stamford. . . . . (607) 652-6671
    http://www.stamfordny.com/

STAMFORD (town).
Covers a land area of 48.477 square miles and a water area of 0 square miles. Located at 42.37° N. Lat.; 74.64° W. Long. Elevation is 1,827 feet.
Population: 2,047 (1990); 1,943 (2000); 1,817 (2005); 1,724 (2010 projected); Race: 96.0% White, 1.9% Black, 0.5% Asian, 2.7% Hispanic of any race (2005); Density: 37.5 persons per square mile (2005); Average household size: 2.40 (2005); Median age: 42.9 (2005); Males per 100 females: 95.4 (2005); Marriage status: 27.7% never married, 55.6% now married, 9.5% widowed, 7.3% divorced (2000); Foreign born: 4.1% (2000); Ancestry (includes multiple ancestries): 20.5% German, 15.8% Irish, 13.4% English, 12.7% Italian, 11.0% United States or American (2000).
Economy: Employment by occupation: 9.4% management, 22.2% professional, 16.2% services, 22.5% sales, 3.3% farming, 7.2% construction, 19.1% production (2000).
Income: Per capita income: $20,355 (2005); Median household income: $41,141 (2005); Average household income: $48,229 (2005); Percent of households with income of $100,000 or more: 8.2% (2005); Poverty rate: 12.0% (2000).
Taxes: Total city taxes per capita: $300 (2004); City property taxes per capita: $281 (2004).
Education: Percent of population age 25 and over with: High school diploma (including GED) or higher: 75.6% (2005); Bachelor's degree or higher: 19.7% (2005); Master's degree or higher: 7.2% (2005).
Housing: Homeownership rate: 68.5% (2005); Median home value: $114,947 (2005); Median rent: $379 per month (2000); Median age of housing: 53 years (2000).
Newspapers: The Mountain Eagle (Stamford) (General - Circulation 5,000)
Transportation: Commute to work: 84.1% car, 1.1% public transportation, 8.9% walk, 4.9% work from home (2000); Travel time to work: 53.5% less than 15 minutes, 21.8% 15 to 30 minutes, 15.1% 30 to 45 minutes, 3.7% 45 to 60 minutes, 5.9% 60 minutes or more (2000)

TOMPKINS (town).
Covers a land area of 98.244 square miles and a water area of 6.216 square miles. Located at 42.11° N. Lat.; 75.25° W. Long.
Population: 994 (1990); 1,105 (2000); 1,111 (2005); 1,092 (2010 projected); Race: 98.4% White, 1.0% Black, 0.0% Asian, 1.5% Hispanic of any race (2005); Density: 11.3 persons per square mile (2005); Average household size: 2.43 (2005); Median age: 43.3 (2005); Males per 100 females: 102.4 (2005); Marriage status: 19.5% never married, 65.1% now married, 6.4% widowed, 9.0% divorced (2000); Foreign born: 2.9% (2000); Ancestry (includes multiple ancestries): 15.7% German, 13.2% English, 13.0% Irish, 12.5% United States or American, 7.8% Italian (2000).

Economy: Single-family building permits issued: 17 (2005); Multi-family building permits issued: 0 (2005); Employment by occupation: 7.5% management, 9.9% professional, 14.8% services, 23.9% sales, 4.0% farming, 12.1% construction, 27.9% production (2000).
Income: Per capita income: $19,310 (2005); Median household income: $40,000 (2005); Average household income: $46,392 (2005); Percent of households with income of $100,000 or more: 6.6% (2005); Poverty rate: 8.9% (2000).
Education: Percent of population age 25 and over with: High school diploma (including GED) or higher: 74.7% (2005); Bachelor's degree or higher: 6.8% (2005); Master's degree or higher: 1.8% (2005).
Housing: Homeownership rate: 86.7% (2005); Median home value: $112,292 (2005); Median rent: $329 per month (2000); Median age of housing: 23 years (2000).
Transportation: Commute to work: 88.1% car, 1.0% public transportation, 2.8% walk, 3.8% work from home (2000); Travel time to work: 27.9% less than 15 minutes, 34.7% 15 to 30 minutes, 21.6% 30 to 45 minutes, 5.3% 45 to 60 minutes, 10.5% 60 minutes or more (2000)

TREADWELL (unincorporated postal area, zip code 13846).
Covers a land area of 11.350 square miles and a water area of 0 square miles. Located at 42.34° N. Lat.; 75.05° W. Long. Elevation is 1,530 feet.
Population: 0 (2000); Race: 95.3% White, 0.0% Black, 0.0% Asian, 0.0% Hispanic of any race (2000); Density: 0.0 persons per square mile (2000); Age: 21.5% under 18, 24.5% over 64 (2000); Marriage status: 20.7% never married, 60.5% now married, 5.5% widowed, 13.3% divorced (2000); Foreign born: 4.7% (2000); Ancestry (includes multiple ancestries): 30.9% German, 17.1% Irish, 13.4% English, 9.1% Scottish, 8.4% United States or American (2000).
Economy: Employment by occupation: 13.1% management, 21.3% professional, 14.4% services, 31.9% sales, 8.1% farming, 5.6% construction, 5.6% production (2000).
Income: Per capita income: $18,217 (2000); Median household income: $31,979 (2000); Poverty rate: 10.2% (2000).
Education: Percent of population age 25 and over with: High school diploma (including GED) or higher: 85.8% (2000); Bachelor's degree or higher: 22.5% (2000).

School District(s)
Delhi Central School District (KG-12)
    2003-04 Enrollment: 1,003 .... (607) 746-1300

Housing: Homeownership rate: 85.7% (2000); Median home value: $83,600 (2000); Median rent: $275 per month (2000); Median age of housing: 57 years (2000).
Transportation: Commute to work: 73.7% car, 0.0% public transportation, 12.2% walk, 14.1% work from home (2000); Travel time to work: 31.3% less than 15 minutes, 53.7% 15 to 30 minutes, 12.7% 30 to 45 minutes, 0.0% 45 to 60 minutes, 2.2% 60 minutes or more (2000)

WALTON (village).
Covers a land area of 1.578 square miles and a water area of 0.018 square miles. Located at 42.17° N. Lat.; 75.13° W. Long. Elevation is 1,226 feet.
Population: 3,418 (1990); 3,070 (2000); 2,840 (2005); 2,734 (2010 projected); Race: 97.7% White, 0.5% Black, 0.4% Asian, 2.0% Hispanic of any race (2005); Density: 1,799.5 persons per square mile (2005); Average household size: 2.20 (2005); Median age: 41.7 (2005); Males per 100 females: 88.2 (2005); Marriage status: 28.6% never married, 47.4% now married, 10.5% widowed, 13.5% divorced (2000); Foreign born: 1.6% (2000); Ancestry (includes multiple ancestries): 21.5% Irish, 16.2% English, 13.5% German, 9.7% Italian, 7.7% Scottish (2000).
Economy: Single-family building permits issued: 1 (2005); Multi-family building permits issued: 0 (2005); Employment by occupation: 10.5% management, 20.1% professional, 26.3% services, 16.5% sales, 0.5% farming, 6.4% construction, 19.6% production (2000).
Income: Per capita income: $18,492 (2005); Median household income: $30,777 (2005); Average household income: $40,540 (2005); Percent of households with income of $100,000 or more: 4.5% (2005); Poverty rate: 12.4% (2000).
Education: Percent of population age 25 and over with: High school diploma (including GED) or higher: 80.1% (2005); Bachelor's degree or higher: 17.4% (2005); Master's degree or higher: 6.1% (2005).

School District(s)
Walton Central School District (KG-12)
    2003-04 Enrollment: 1,148 .... (607) 865-4116

Housing: Homeownership rate: 57.6% (2005); Median home value: $96,545 (2005); Median rent: $360 per month (2000); Median age of housing: 60+ years (2000).
Hospitals: Delaware Valley Hospital (42 beds)
Safety: Violent crime rate: 50.7 per 10,000 population; Property crime rate: 287.3 per 10,000 population (2004).
Newspapers: The Walton Reporter (General - Circulation 7,100)
Transportation: Commute to work: 81.6% car, 0.0% public transportation, 11.8% walk, 4.0% work from home (2000); Travel time to work: 61.3% less than 15 minutes, 16.7% 15 to 30 minutes, 15.7% 30 to 45 minutes, 2.4% 45 to 60 minutes, 3.8% 60 minutes or more (2000)

Additional Information Contacts
Walton Chamber of Commerce .... (800) 639-4296
    http://www.waltonchamber.com

WALTON (town).
Covers a land area of 97.199 square miles and a water area of 0.427 square miles. Located at 42.17° N. Lat.; 75.13° W. Long. Elevation is 1,226 feet.
Population: 5,953 (1990); 5,607 (2000); 5,406 (2005); 5,196 (2010 projected); Race: 97.6% White, 0.4% Black, 0.7% Asian, 1.4% Hispanic of any race (2005); Density: 55.6 persons per square mile (2005); Average household size: 2.29 (2005); Median age: 43.2 (2005); Males per 100 females: 92.3 (2005); Marriage status: 23.5% never married, 58.4% now married, 8.2% widowed, 9.8% divorced (2000); Foreign born: 1.2% (2000); Ancestry (includes multiple ancestries): 18.8% Irish, 17.0% German, 15.8% English, 8.0% United States or American, 7.7% Italian (2000).
Economy: Single-family building permits issued: 11 (2005); Multi-family building permits issued: 0 (2005); Employment by occupation: 10.5% management, 19.0% professional, 19.6% services, 17.9% sales, 1.5% farming, 10.2% construction, 21.3% production (2000).
Income: Per capita income: $20,320 (2005); Median household income: $35,630 (2005); Average household income: $46,550 (2005); Percent of households with income of $100,000 or more: 7.0% (2005); Poverty rate: 12.1% (2000).
Education: Percent of population age 25 and over with: High school diploma (including GED) or higher: 81.6% (2005); Bachelor's degree or higher: 16.9% (2005); Master's degree or higher: 7.3% (2005).
Housing: Homeownership rate: 70.8% (2005); Median home value: $105,059 (2005); Median rent: $369 per month (2000); Median age of housing: 45 years (2000).
Transportation: Commute to work: 85.6% car, 0.5% public transportation, 6.7% walk, 5.7% work from home (2000); Travel time to work: 52.0% less than 15 minutes, 23.9% 15 to 30 minutes, 16.7% 30 to 45 minutes, 2.5% 45 to 60 minutes, 4.9% 60 minutes or more (2000)

Dutchess County

Located in southeastern New York; bounded on the west by the Hudson River, and on the east by Connecticut; includes part of the Taconic Mountains. Covers a land area of 801.59 square miles, a water area of 23.78 square miles, and is located in the Eastern Time Zone. The county government was organized in 1683. County seat is Poughkeepsie.

Dutchess County is part of the Poughkeepsie-Newburgh-Middletown, NY Metropolitan Statistical Area. The entire metro area includes: Dutchess County, NY; Orange County, NY

Weather Station: Glenham   Elevation: 272 feet

	Jan	Feb	Mar	Apr	May	Jun	Jul	Aug	Sep	Oct	Nov	Dec
High	36	39	48	60	72	81	86	84	76	65	53	40
Low	16	18	28	39	49	58	63	62	53	42	33	23
Precip	3.3	2.9	3.4	4.0	4.4	4.1	4.8	4.0	4.0	3.7	3.8	3.3
Snow	11.7	9.5	5.8	1.1	tr	0.0	0.0	0.0	0.0	0.1	1.9	6.6

High and Low temperatures in degrees Fahrenheit; Precipitation and Snow in inches

Weather Station: Poughkeepsie Dutchess Co. Arpt.   Elevation: 154 feet

	Jan	Feb	Mar	Apr	May	Jun	Jul	Aug	Sep	Oct	Nov	Dec
High	34	38	48	60	71	79	84	82	74	62	51	39
Low	15	18	27	36	47	56	61	60	51	39	31	22
Precip	3.0	2.6	3.5	3.8	4.8	3.7	4.8	3.9	3.6	3.6	3.5	3.1
Snow	10.6	8.2	5.5	1.6	0.0	0.0	0.0	0.0	0.0	tr	2.2	6.4

High and Low temperatures in degrees Fahrenheit; Precipitation and Snow in inches

Population: 259,462 (1990); 280,150 (2000); 295,585 (2005); 311,612 (2010 projected); Race: 81.1% White, 10.1% Black, 3.4% Asian, 8.4% Hispanic of any race (2005); Density: 368.7 persons per square mile

(2005); Average household size: 2.79 (2005); Median age: 37.7 (2005); Males per 100 females: 99.5 (2005).
Religion: Five largest groups: 43.0% Catholic Church, 2.4% The United Methodist Church, 1.8% Reformed Church in America, 1.6% Episcopal Church, 1.3% Assemblies of God (2000).
Economy: Unemployment rate: 3.9% (2005); Total civilian labor force: 147,881 (2005); Leading industries: 17.9% health care and social assistance; 17.7% manufacturing; 14.7% retail trade (2003); Farms: 667 totaling 112,339 acres (2002); Companies that employ 500 or more persons: 17 (2003); Companies that employ 100 to 499 persons: 109 (2003); Companies that employ less than 100 persons: 7,091 (2003); Black-owned businesses: 923 (2002); Hispanic-owned businesses: 874 (2002); Women-owned businesses: 7,197 (2002); Retail sales per capita: $13,998 (2006). Single-family building permits issued: 858 (2005); Multi-family building permits issued: 154 (2005).
Income: Per capita income: $27,385 (2005); Median household income: $61,077 (2005); Average household income: $74,799 (2005); Percent of households with income of $100,000 or more: 23.7% (2005); Poverty rate: 8.0% (2003); Bankruptcy rate: 4.45% (2005).
Taxes: Total county taxes per capita: $678 (2004); County property taxes per capita: $196 (2004).
Education: Percent of population age 25 and over with: High school diploma (including GED) or higher: 84.1% (2005); Bachelor's degree or higher: 27.7% (2005); Master's degree or higher: 11.9% (2005).
Housing: Homeownership rate: 69.5% (2005); Median home value: $239,293 (2005); Median rent: $630 per month (2000); Median age of housing: 35 years (2000).
Health: Birth rate: 111.0 per 10,000 population (2004); Death rate: 77.2 per 10,000 population (2004); Age-adjusted cancer mortality rate: 217.3 deaths per 100,000 population (2002); Air Quality Index: 96.2% good, 3.0% moderate, 0.8% unhealthy for sensitive individuals, 0.0% unhealthy (percent of days in 2005); Number of physicians: 25.7 per 10,000 population (2004); Hospital beds: 38.1 per 10,000 population (2003); Hospital admissions: 1,029.4 per 10,000 population (2003).
Elections: 2004 Presidential election results: 51.2% Bush, 47.0% Kerry, 1.6% Nader, 0.2% Badnarik
National and State Parks: Eleanor Roosevelt National Historic Site; Home of Franklin D Roosevelt National Historic Site; James Baird State Park; Mills Memorial State Park; Norrie State Park; Vanderbilt Mansion National Historic Site

Additional Information Contacts
Dutchess County Government . . . . (845) 486-2020
  http://www.dutchessny.gov/
City of Beacon . . . . (845) 838-5000
  http://www.cityofbeacon.org/
City of Poughkeepsie . . . . (845) 451-4200
  http://www.cityofpoughkeepsie.com/
Town of Beekman . . . . (845) 724-5300
  http://www.townofbeekman.com/
Town of East Fishkill . . . . (845) 221-4303
  http://www.eastfishkillny.org/
Town of Hyde Park . . . . (845) 229-5111
  http://www.hydeparkny.us/
Town of La Grange . . . . (845) 452-1830
  http://www.lagrangeny.org/
Town of Pine Plains . . . . (518) 398-7155
  http://pineplains-ny.gov/content
Town of Pleasant Valley . . . . (845) 635-3274
  http://www.ci.pleasant-valley.ny.us/site/pages/home.html
Town of Red Hook . . . . (845) 758-4600
  http://www.redhook.org/
Town of Union Vale . . . . (845) 724-5600
  http://www2.marist.edu/unionvale

Dutchess County Communities

AMENIA (town). Covers a land area of 43.316 square miles and a water area of 0.248 square miles. Located at 41.81° N. Lat.; 73.55° W. Long. Elevation is 573 feet.
History: Thomas L. Harris had his Brotherhood of the New Life sect here, 1863-1867.
Population: 5,195 (1990); 4,048 (2000); 4,238 (2005); 4,447 (2010 projected); Race: 93.3% White, 2.4% Black, 0.6% Asian, 4.7% Hispanic of any race (2005); Density: 97.8 persons per square mile (2005); Average household size: 2.45 (2005); Median age: 41.2 (2005); Males per 100 females: 95.7 (2005); Marriage status: 24.2% never married, 55.8% now married, 10.7% widowed, 9.3% divorced (2000); Foreign born: 5.1% (2000); Ancestry (includes multiple ancestries): 27.3% Irish, 13.2% German, 11.0% Italian, 8.6% United States or American, 8.6% Other groups (2000).
Economy: Dairying area. Single-family building permits issued: 12 (2005); Multi-family building permits issued: 6 (2005); Employment by occupation: 5.4% management, 18.3% professional, 25.4% services, 22.2% sales, 3.3% farming, 12.0% construction, 13.4% production (2000).
Income: Per capita income: $26,693 (2005); Median household income: $48,396 (2005); Average household income: $64,582 (2005); Percent of households with income of $100,000 or more: 14.9% (2005); Poverty rate: 8.1% (2000).
Education: Percent of population age 25 and over with: High school diploma (including GED) or higher: 72.6% (2005); Bachelor's degree or higher: 14.1% (2005); Master's degree or higher: 8.1% (2005).

School District(s)
Northeast Central School District (KG-12)
    2003-04 Enrollment: 890 . . . . (845) 373-4100
Housing: Homeownership rate: 68.7% (2005); Median home value: $187,255 (2005); Median rent: $495 per month (2000); Median age of housing: 39 years (2000).
Newspapers: Harlem Valley Times (General - Circulation 5,050)
Transportation: Commute to work: 92.3% car, 1.3% public transportation, 3.1% walk, 2.8% work from home (2000); Travel time to work: 41.4% less than 15 minutes, 30.4% 15 to 30 minutes, 13.0% 30 to 45 minutes, 5.8% 45 to 60 minutes, 9.5% 60 minutes or more (2000)

AMENIA (CDP). Covers a land area of 2.017 square miles and a water area of 0.013 square miles. Located at 41.84° N. Lat.; 73.55° W. Long.
Population: 1,057 (1990); 1,115 (2000); 1,102 (2005); 1,100 (2010 projected); Race: 89.7% White, 3.4% Black, 0.6% Asian, 5.1% Hispanic of any race (2005); Density: 546.4 persons per square mile (2005); Average household size: 2.49 (2005); Median age: 39.0 (2005); Males per 100 females: 95.4 (2005); Marriage status: 26.8% never married, 57.7% now married, 4.9% widowed, 10.7% divorced (2000); Foreign born: 6.1% (2000); Ancestry (includes multiple ancestries): 32.6% Irish, 14.3% Italian, 11.6% French (except Basque), 9.9% United States or American, 9.7% English (2000).
Economy: Employment by occupation: 4.8% management, 21.4% professional, 26.8% services, 21.4% sales, 0.0% farming, 18.8% construction, 6.9% production (2000).
Income: Per capita income: $27,612 (2005); Median household income: $57,902 (2005); Average household income: $68,533 (2005); Percent of households with income of $100,000 or more: 17.6% (2005); Poverty rate: 6.5% (2000).
Education: Percent of population age 25 and over with: High school diploma (including GED) or higher: 77.5% (2005); Bachelor's degree or higher: 17.3% (2005); Master's degree or higher: 9.8% (2005).
Housing: Homeownership rate: 62.8% (2005); Median home value: $197,647 (2005); Median rent: $556 per month (2000); Median age of housing: 54 years (2000).
Transportation: Commute to work: 94.3% car, 0.9% public transportation, 3.6% walk, 1.2% work from home (2000); Travel time to work: 49.7% less than 15 minutes, 25.7% 15 to 30 minutes, 10.9% 30 to 45 minutes, 5.9% 45 to 60 minutes, 7.9% 60 minutes or more (2000)

ARLINGTON (CDP). Covers a land area of 4.890 square miles and a water area of 0.011 square miles. Located at 41.69° N. Lat.; 73.89° W. Long. Elevation is 200 feet.
History: Seat of Vassar College.
Population: 11,948 (1990); 12,481 (2000); 12,974 (2005); 13,426 (2010 projected); Race: 70.8% White, 14.8% Black, 9.2% Asian, 7.0% Hispanic of any race (2005); Density: 2,653.4 persons per square mile (2005); Average household size: 2.88 (2005); Median age: 31.4 (2005); Males per 100 females: 85.1 (2005); Marriage status: 39.3% never married, 45.0% now married, 8.0% widowed, 7.6% divorced (2000); Foreign born: 12.8% (2000); Ancestry (includes multiple ancestries): 21.3% Other groups, 17.6% Italian, 16.0% Irish, 13.2% German, 10.3% English (2000).
Economy: Employment by occupation: 8.5% management, 30.2% professional, 15.1% services, 31.0% sales, 0.2% farming, 4.8% construction, 10.2% production (2000).
Income: Per capita income: $21,567 (2005); Median household income: $48,721 (2005); Average household income: $60,009 (2005); Percent of

households with income of $100,000 or more: 13.5% (2005); Poverty rate: 10.3% (2000).
Education: Percent of population age 25 and over with: High school diploma (including GED) or higher: 83.7% (2005); Bachelor's degree or higher: 28.5% (2005); Master's degree or higher: 14.2% (2005).
Housing: Homeownership rate: 45.8% (2005); Median home value: $195,234 (2005); Median rent: $669 per month (2000); Median age of housing: 39 years (2000).
Transportation: Commute to work: 73.2% car, 2.4% public transportation, 21.3% walk, 1.4% work from home (2000); Travel time to work: 49.3% less than 15 minutes, 26.9% 15 to 30 minutes, 10.5% 30 to 45 minutes, 5.9% 45 to 60 minutes, 7.4% 60 minutes or more (2000)

BARRYTOWN
(unincorporated postal area, zip code 12507). Covers a land area of 0.869 square miles and a water area of 0 square miles. Located at 42.00° N. Lat.; 73.92° W. Long.
Population: 0 (2000); Race: 50.2% White, 0.0% Black, 32.9% Asian, 0.0% Hispanic of any race (2000); Density: 0.0 persons per square mile (2000); Age: 17.9% under 18, 0.0% over 64 (2000); Marriage status: 43.4% never married, 56.6% now married, 0.0% widowed, 0.0% divorced (2000); Foreign born: 41.1% (2000); Ancestry (includes multiple ancestries): 38.2% Other groups, 17.9% German, 15.5% Irish, 8.7% Russian, 8.2% United States or American (2000).
Economy: Employment by occupation: 39.3% management, 32.8% professional, 18.0% services, 9.8% sales, 0.0% farming, 0.0% construction, 0.0% production (2000).
Income: Per capita income: $12,624 (2000); Median household income: $53,750 (2000); Poverty rate: 15.5% (2000).
Education: Percent of population age 25 and over with: High school diploma (including GED) or higher: 78.2% (2000); Bachelor's degree or higher: 68.8% (2000).

Four-year College(s)
Unification Theological Seminary
    Fall 2004 Enrollment: 119 . . . . (845) 752-3000

Housing: Homeownership rate: 66.7% (2000); Median home value: $625,000 (2000); Median rent: $325 per month (2000); Median age of housing: 60+ years (2000).
Transportation: Commute to work: 82.0% car, 0.0% public transportation, 18.0% walk, 0.0% work from home (2000); Travel time to work: 80.3% less than 15 minutes, 0.0% 15 to 30 minutes, 0.0% 30 to 45 minutes, 19.7% 45 to 60 minutes, 0.0% 60 minutes or more (2000)

BEACON
(city). Covers a land area of 4.775 square miles and a water area of 0.114 square miles. Located at 41.50° N. Lat.; 73.96° W. Long. Elevation is 150 feet.
History: An incline railroad ascends Mt. Beacon, site of a towering monument to American Revolutionary soldiers who built signal fires there to warn of the coming of the British. Beacon's historic buildings include the Madam Brett homestead (1709) and the Van Wyck homestead (1732). Settled 1663, Incorporated as a city in 1913.
Population: 13,256 (1990); 13,808 (2000); 13,877 (2005); 14,047 (2010 projected); Race: 63.1% White, 22.6% Black, 2.0% Asian, 19.8% Hispanic of any race (2005); Density: 2,906.1 persons per square mile (2005); Average household size: 2.70 (2005); Median age: 37.3 (2005); Males per 100 females: 90.7 (2005); Marriage status: 30.2% never married, 53.3% now married, 6.9% widowed, 9.6% divorced (2000); Foreign born: 8.5% (2000); Ancestry (includes multiple ancestries): 32.4% Other groups, 17.5% Italian, 16.1% Irish, 13.2% German, 6.6% English (2000).
Economy: Has textile and related industries, other varied manufacturing and a large industrial research firm. Beacon Correctional Facility is in the city. Single-family building permits issued: 21 (2005); Multi-family building permits issued: 52 (2005); Employment by occupation: 11.3% management, 20.4% professional, 17.6% services, 26.9% sales, 0.2% farming, 9.7% construction, 13.9% production (2000).
Income: Per capita income: $23,950 (2005); Median household income: $50,821 (2005); Average household income: $61,921 (2005); Percent of households with income of $100,000 or more: 15.2% (2005); Poverty rate: 11.0% (2000).
Education: Percent of population age 25 and over with: High school diploma (including GED) or higher: 77.6% (2005); Bachelor's degree or higher: 18.9% (2005); Master's degree or higher: 7.4% (2005).

School District(s)
Beacon City School District (PK-12)
    2003-04 Enrollment: 3,613 . . . . (845) 838-6900

Housing: Homeownership rate: 56.8% (2005); Median home value: $185,939 (2005); Median rent: $579 per month (2000); Median age of housing: 49 years (2000).
Hospitals: St. Francis Hospital (100 beds)
Transportation: Commute to work: 88.2% car, 6.5% public transportation, 3.6% walk, 1.0% work from home (2000); Travel time to work: 26.8% less than 15 minutes, 24.4% 15 to 30 minutes, 21.2% 30 to 45 minutes, 10.8% 45 to 60 minutes, 16.8% 60 minutes or more (2000)
Additional Information Contacts
City of Beacon . . . . (845) 838-5000
    http://www.cityofbeacon.org/

BEEKMAN
(town). Covers a land area of 30.003 square miles and a water area of 0.265 square miles. Located at 41.60° N. Lat.; 73.70° W. Long.
Population: 10,447 (1990); 11,452 (2000); 12,664 (2005); 13,855 (2010 projected); Race: 91.6% White, 2.9% Black, 2.4% Asian, 7.5% Hispanic of any race (2005); Density: 422.1 persons per square mile (2005); Average household size: 3.04 (2005); Median age: 36.8 (2005); Males per 100 females: 99.7 (2005); Marriage status: 20.5% never married, 69.1% now married, 4.6% widowed, 5.8% divorced (2000); Foreign born: 4.7% (2000); Ancestry (includes multiple ancestries): 32.9% Italian, 25.9% Irish, 13.9% German, 11.9% Other groups, 8.6% English (2000).
Economy: Single-family building permits issued: 39 (2005); Multi-family building permits issued: 0 (2005); Employment by occupation: 14.5% management, 21.3% professional, 12.3% services, 27.3% sales, 0.3% farming, 13.0% construction, 11.4% production (2000).
Income: Per capita income: $29,472 (2005); Median household income: $76,884 (2005); Average household income: $88,825 (2005); Percent of households with income of $100,000 or more: 30.7% (2005); Poverty rate: 4.7% (2000).
Education: Percent of population age 25 and over with: High school diploma (including GED) or higher: 91.5% (2005); Bachelor's degree or higher: 26.9% (2005); Master's degree or higher: 9.9% (2005).
Housing: Homeownership rate: 86.3% (2005); Median home value: $280,510 (2005); Median rent: $733 per month (2000); Median age of housing: 20 years (2000).
Transportation: Commute to work: 93.7% car, 2.5% public transportation, 0.3% walk, 3.3% work from home (2000); Travel time to work: 13.4% less than 15 minutes, 26.3% 15 to 30 minutes, 24.3% 30 to 45 minutes, 17.2% 45 to 60 minutes, 18.9% 60 minutes or more (2000)
Additional Information Contacts
Town of Beekman . . . . (845) 724-5300
    http://www.townofbeekman.com/

BRINCKERHOFF
(CDP). Covers a land area of 1.086 square miles and a water area of 0.027 square miles. Located at 41.55° N. Lat.; 73.87° W. Long.
Population: 2,756 (1990); 2,734 (2000); 2,553 (2005); 2,516 (2010 projected); Race: 88.4% White, 4.6% Black, 5.6% Asian, 7.8% Hispanic of any race (2005); Density: 2,351.7 persons per square mile (2005); Average household size: 2.66 (2005); Median age: 40.3 (2005); Males per 100 females: 95.5 (2005); Marriage status: 24.0% never married, 67.1% now married, 4.8% widowed, 4.1% divorced (2000); Foreign born: 7.4% (2000); Ancestry (includes multiple ancestries): 38.4% Italian, 20.1% German, 19.7% Irish, 11.0% Other groups, 9.6% English (2000).
Economy: Employment by occupation: 13.1% management, 26.9% professional, 14.4% services, 32.6% sales, 0.0% farming, 3.6% construction, 9.3% production (2000).
Income: Per capita income: $29,363 (2005); Median household income: $71,908 (2005); Average household income: $78,005 (2005); Percent of households with income of $100,000 or more: 18.2% (2005); Poverty rate: 3.0% (2000).
Education: Percent of population age 25 and over with: High school diploma (including GED) or higher: 90.5% (2005); Bachelor's degree or higher: 32.5% (2005); Master's degree or higher: 16.9% (2005).
Housing: Homeownership rate: 86.1% (2005); Median home value: $248,574 (2005); Median rent: $811 per month (2000); Median age of housing: 29 years (2000).
Transportation: Commute to work: 89.1% car, 3.1% public transportation, 4.3% walk, 1.5% work from home (2000); Travel time to work: 31.3% less than 15 minutes, 26.6% 15 to 30 minutes, 15.7% 30 to 45 minutes, 10.5% 45 to 60 minutes, 15.9% 60 minutes or more (2000)

CLINTON (town). Covers a land area of 38.458 square miles and a water area of 0.368 square miles. Located at 41.85° N. Lat.; 73.81° W. Long.
Population: 3,760 (1990); 4,010 (2000); 4,231 (2005); 4,475 (2010 projected); Race: 95.2% White, 1.8% Black, 1.5% Asian, 1.9% Hispanic of any race (2005); Density: 110.0 persons per square mile (2005); Average household size: 2.61 (2005); Median age: 42.4 (2005); Males per 100 females: 99.6 (2005); Marriage status: 18.0% never married, 68.1% now married, 5.9% widowed, 8.0% divorced (2000); Foreign born: 4.3% (2000); Ancestry (includes multiple ancestries): 22.7% German, 20.9% Irish, 20.7% Italian, 13.9% English, 6.6% Other groups (2000).
Economy: Single-family building permits issued: 25 (2005); Multi-family building permits issued: 0 (2005); Employment by occupation: 19.7% management, 28.2% professional, 11.1% services, 22.6% sales, 0.5% farming, 8.5% construction, 9.3% production (2000).
Income: Per capita income: $33,436 (2005); Median household income: $74,325 (2005); Average household income: $85,841 (2005); Percent of households with income of $100,000 or more: 30.7% (2005); Poverty rate: 3.7% (2000).
Education: Percent of population age 25 and over with: High school diploma (including GED) or higher: 91.0% (2005); Bachelor's degree or higher: 35.4% (2005); Master's degree or higher: 13.9% (2005).
Housing: Homeownership rate: 85.3% (2005); Median home value: $265,203 (2005); Median rent: $648 per month (2000); Median age of housing: 32 years (2000).
Transportation: Commute to work: 87.0% car, 3.5% public transportation, 2.8% walk, 6.0% work from home (2000); Travel time to work: 13.5% less than 15 minutes, 36.0% 15 to 30 minutes, 28.6% 30 to 45 minutes, 7.8% 45 to 60 minutes, 14.1% 60 minutes or more (2000)

CLINTON CORNERS (unincorporated postal area, zip code 12514). Covers a land area of 27.763 square miles and a water area of 0.070 square miles. Located at 41.87° N. Lat.; 73.76° W. Long. Elevation is 304 feet.
Population: 0 (2000); Race: 97.1% White, 0.9% Black, 0.0% Asian, 1.3% Hispanic of any race (2000); Density: 0.0 persons per square mile (2000); Age: 27.8% under 18, 11.9% over 64 (2000); Marriage status: 14.8% never married, 73.5% now married, 4.7% widowed, 7.0% divorced (2000); Foreign born: 3.7% (2000); Ancestry (includes multiple ancestries): 28.1% Italian, 24.5% Irish, 22.6% German, 14.1% English, 5.7% Other groups (2000).
Economy: Resort village. Small lakes nearby. Employment by occupation: 17.7% management, 30.5% professional, 14.4% services, 21.5% sales, 0.7% farming, 7.0% construction, 8.0% production (2000).
Income: Per capita income: $28,361 (2000); Median household income: $62,553 (2000); Poverty rate: 2.2% (2000).
Education: Percent of population age 25 and over with: High school diploma (including GED) or higher: 91.4% (2000); Bachelor's degree or higher: 34.3% (2000).
Housing: Homeownership rate: 90.3% (2000); Median home value: $163,100 (2000); Median rent: $648 per month (2000); Median age of housing: 28 years (2000).
Transportation: Commute to work: 88.5% car, 1.8% public transportation, 3.2% walk, 6.4% work from home (2000); Travel time to work: 12.0% less than 15 minutes, 33.6% 15 to 30 minutes, 33.7% 30 to 45 minutes, 8.0% 45 to 60 minutes, 12.8% 60 minutes or more (2000)

CROWN HEIGHTS (CDP). Covers a land area of 2.140 square miles and a water area of 0.551 square miles. Located at 41.64° N. Lat.; 73.93° W. Long.
Population: 3,200 (1990); 2,992 (2000); 3,328 (2005); 3,654 (2010 projected); Race: 81.6% White, 8.7% Black, 5.5% Asian, 8.6% Hispanic of any race (2005); Density: 1,555.3 persons per square mile (2005); Average household size: 2.90 (2005); Median age: 37.8 (2005); Males per 100 females: 95.8 (2005); Marriage status: 25.7% never married, 63.0% now married, 7.2% widowed, 4.0% divorced (2000); Foreign born: 9.5% (2000); Ancestry (includes multiple ancestries): 30.1% Italian, 23.0% Irish, 16.5% Other groups, 12.9% German, 7.1% United States or American (2000).
Economy: Employment by occupation: 13.5% management, 23.6% professional, 16.5% services, 27.2% sales, 0.0% farming, 9.4% construction, 9.8% production (2000).
Income: Per capita income: $24,099 (2005); Median household income: $62,935 (2005); Average household income: $69,832 (2005); Percent of households with income of $100,000 or more: 19.9% (2005); Poverty rate: 2.0% (2000).
Education: Percent of population age 25 and over with: High school diploma (including GED) or higher: 88.8% (2005); Bachelor's degree or higher: 20.6% (2005); Master's degree or higher: 6.3% (2005).
Housing: Homeownership rate: 83.3% (2005); Median home value: $219,774 (2005); Median rent: $630 per month (2000); Median age of housing: 36 years (2000).
Transportation: Commute to work: 88.5% car, 5.7% public transportation, 3.1% walk, 1.8% work from home (2000); Travel time to work: 39.5% less than 15 minutes, 28.0% 15 to 30 minutes, 13.0% 30 to 45 minutes, 6.1% 45 to 60 minutes, 13.4% 60 minutes or more (2000)

DOVER (town). Covers a land area of 55.697 square miles and a water area of 0.643 square miles. Located at 41.68° N. Lat.; 73.58° W. Long.
Population: 7,778 (1990); 8,565 (2000); 9,089 (2005); 9,596 (2010 projected); Race: 88.0% White, 5.9% Black, 1.4% Asian, 8.2% Hispanic of any race (2005); Density: 163.2 persons per square mile (2005); Average household size: 2.81 (2005); Median age: 36.7 (2005); Males per 100 females: 105.8 (2005); Marriage status: 25.6% never married, 58.8% now married, 5.9% widowed, 9.7% divorced (2000); Foreign born: 5.7% (2000); Ancestry (includes multiple ancestries): 28.3% Irish, 18.3% Italian, 14.4% German, 10.3% Other groups, 9.9% English (2000).
Economy: Dairy products; vegetables. Terminus of Harlem line of Metro-North commuter Railroad. Single-family building permits issued: 43 (2005); Multi-family building permits issued: 0 (2005); Employment by occupation: 8.8% management, 17.8% professional, 19.9% services, 21.0% sales, 0.8% farming, 17.1% construction, 14.6% production (2000).
Income: Per capita income: $23,871 (2005); Median household income: $58,828 (2005); Average household income: $65,906 (2005); Percent of households with income of $100,000 or more: 15.9% (2005); Poverty rate: 8.4% (2000).
Education: Percent of population age 25 and over with: High school diploma (including GED) or higher: 81.2% (2005); Bachelor's degree or higher: 15.1% (2005); Master's degree or higher: 5.8% (2005).
Housing: Homeownership rate: 73.9% (2005); Median home value: $201,759 (2005); Median rent: $561 per month (2000); Median age of housing: 29 years (2000).
Transportation: Commute to work: 94.0% car, 3.0% public transportation, 1.3% walk, 1.7% work from home (2000); Travel time to work: 20.8% less than 15 minutes, 29.5% 15 to 30 minutes, 17.8% 30 to 45 minutes, 13.5% 45 to 60 minutes, 18.4% 60 minutes or more (2000)

DOVER PLAINS (CDP). Covers a land area of 1.217 square miles and a water area of 0.014 square miles. Located at 41.74° N. Lat.; 73.58° W. Long.
Population: 1,847 (1990); 1,996 (2000); 1,871 (2005); 1,814 (2010 projected); Race: 92.9% White, 2.7% Black, 1.6% Asian, 6.5% Hispanic of any race (2005); Density: 1,537.1 persons per square mile (2005); Average household size: 2.37 (2005); Median age: 41.6 (2005); Males per 100 females: 100.5 (2005); Marriage status: 28.3% never married, 50.4% now married, 12.2% widowed, 9.2% divorced (2000); Foreign born: 5.0% (2000); Ancestry (includes multiple ancestries): 29.3% Irish, 18.7% Italian, 13.9% German, 10.7% English, 10.5% Other groups (2000).
Economy: Employment by occupation: 5.2% management, 20.8% professional, 21.2% services, 24.4% sales, 1.4% farming, 14.7% construction, 12.2% production (2000).
Income: Per capita income: $22,825 (2005); Median household income: $38,474 (2005); Average household income: $52,560 (2005); Percent of households with income of $100,000 or more: 11.8% (2005); Poverty rate: 13.4% (2000).
Education: Percent of population age 25 and over with: High school diploma (including GED) or higher: 70.2% (2005); Bachelor's degree or higher: 9.2% (2005); Master's degree or higher: 6.2% (2005).
School District(s)
Dover Union Free School District (KG-12)
    2003-04 Enrollment: 1,757 . . . . (845) 832-4500
Housing: Homeownership rate: 64.6% (2005); Median home value: $154,717 (2005); Median rent: $575 per month (2000); Median age of housing: 36 years (2000).
Transportation: Commute to work: 90.8% car, 0.0% public transportation, 2.6% walk, 6.6% work from home (2000); Travel time to work: 27.0% less than 15 minutes, 36.3% 15 to 30 minutes, 13.1% 30 to 45 minutes, 10.6% 45 to 60 minutes, 13.1% 60 minutes or more (2000)
Additional Information Contacts

Dover-Wingdale Chamber of Commerce............... (845) 877-9800
http://www.members.aol.com/dwcoc/

EAST FISHKILL (town).
Covers a land area of 56.905 square miles and a water area of 0.448 square miles. Located at 41.57° N. Lat.; 73.79° W. Long.
Population: 22,101 (1990); 25,589 (2000); 28,506 (2005); 31,320 (2010 projected); Race: 91.6% White, 2.4% Black, 3.3% Asian, 5.2% Hispanic of any race (2005); Density: 500.9 persons per square mile (2005); Average household size: 3.06 (2005); Median age: 37.6 (2005); Males per 100 females: 98.1 (2005); Marriage status: 20.2% never married, 71.0% now married, 3.9% widowed, 4.9% divorced (2000); Foreign born: 7.1% (2000); Ancestry (includes multiple ancestries): 30.0% Italian, 25.9% Irish, 19.4% German, 10.7% Other groups, 9.6% English (2000).
Economy: Unemployment rate: 3.7% (2005); Total civilian labor force: 15,229 (2005); Single-family building permits issued: 186 (2005); Multi-family building permits issued: 0 (2005); Employment by occupation: 15.3% management, 26.6% professional, 10.3% services, 26.3% sales, 0.2% farming, 11.6% construction, 9.7% production (2000).
Income: Per capita income: $34,237 (2005); Median household income: $91,553 (2005); Average household income: $104,289 (2005); Percent of households with income of $100,000 or more: 44.0% (2005); Poverty rate: 2.8% (2000).
Education: Percent of population age 25 and over with: High school diploma (including GED) or higher: 91.5% (2005); Bachelor's degree or higher: 35.5% (2005); Master's degree or higher: 15.5% (2005).
Housing: Homeownership rate: 89.9% (2005); Median home value: $309,197 (2005); Median rent: $639 per month (2000); Median age of housing: 26 years 2000.
Safety: Violent crime rate: 30.3 per 10,000 population; Property crime rate: 113.4 per 10,000 population (2004).
Transportation: Commute to work: 91.8% car, 3.9% public transportation, 0.5% walk, 3.5% work from home (2000); Travel time to work: 16.5% less than 15 minutes, 30.5% 15 to 30 minutes, 18.8% 30 to 45 minutes, 13.8% 45 to 60 minutes, 20.5% 60 minutes or more (2000)
Additional Information Contacts
Town of East Fishkill .... (845) 221-4303
http://www.eastfishkillny.org/

FAIRVIEW (CDP).
Covers a land area of 3.481 square miles and a water area of 0.054 square miles. Located at 41.72° N. Lat.; 73.91° W. Long.
Population: 4,811 (1990); 5,421 (2000); 5,453 (2005); 5,493 (2010 projected); Race: 76.0% White, 14.1% Black, 3.3% Asian, 7.1% Hispanic of any race (2005); Density: 1,566.4 persons per square mile (2005); Average household size: 2.79 (2005); Median age: 37.8 (2005); Males per 100 females: 101.0 (2005); Marriage status: 34.8% never married, 51.8% now married, 6.6% widowed, 6.8% divorced (2000); Foreign born: 8.3% (2000); Ancestry (includes multiple ancestries): 25.9% Irish, 19.4% Italian, 15.8% Other groups, 15.7% German, 10.3% English (2000).
Economy: Employment by occupation: 9.8% management, 22.9% professional, 18.0% services, 25.7% sales, 0.0% farming, 12.2% construction, 11.4% production (2000).
Income: Per capita income: $22,618 (2005); Median household income: $51,844 (2005); Average household income: $58,189 (2005); Percent of households with income of $100,000 or more: 14.2% (2005); Poverty rate: 8.5% (2000).
Education: Percent of population age 25 and over with: High school diploma (including GED) or higher: 78.9% (2005); Bachelor's degree or higher: 15.7% (2005); Master's degree or higher: 4.8% (2005).
Housing: Homeownership rate: 71.6% (2005); Median home value: $161,028 (2005); Median rent: $685 per month (2000); Median age of housing: 44 years (2000).
Transportation: Commute to work: 89.6% car, 5.6% public transportation, 1.7% walk, 1.7% work from home (2000); Travel time to work: 36.9% less than 15 minutes, 31.3% 15 to 30 minutes, 13.9% 30 to 45 minutes, 5.8% 45 to 60 minutes, 12.1% 60 minutes or more (2000)

FISHKILL (village).
Covers a land area of 0.877 square miles and a water area of 0 square miles. Located at 41.53° N. Lat.; 73.89° W. Long.
Population: 1,957 (1990); 1,735 (2000); 1,744 (2005); 1,749 (2010 projected); Race: 92.7% White, 2.9% Black, 1.6% Asian, 8.4% Hispanic of any race (2005); Density: 1,989.0 persons per square mile (2005); Average household size: 1.78 (2005); Median age: 48.5 (2005); Males per 100 females: 76.5 (2005); Marriage status: 24.8% never married, 44.1% now married, 20.3% widowed, 10.8% divorced (2000); Foreign born: 9.0% (2000); Ancestry (includes multiple ancestries): 24.0% Italian, 22.7% Irish, 14.4% German, 12.6% Other groups, 8.6% English (2000).
Economy: Single-family building permits issued: 0 (2005); Multi-family building permits issued: 0 (2005); Employment by occupation: 12.4% management, 16.7% professional, 14.9% services, 32.7% sales, 0.0% farming, 13.6% construction, 9.7% production (2000).
Income: Per capita income: $30,962 (2005); Median household income: $43,016 (2005); Average household income: $55,043 (2005); Percent of households with income of $100,000 or more: 13.1% (2005); Poverty rate: 8.4% (2000).
Education: Percent of population age 25 and over with: High school diploma (including GED) or higher: 79.0% (2005); Bachelor's degree or higher: 23.7% (2005); Master's degree or higher: 10.5% (2005).
School District(s)
Beacon City School District (PK-12)
    2003-04 Enrollment: 3,613 .... (845) 838-6900
Wappingers Central School District (KG-12)
    2003-04 Enrollment: 12,146 .... (845) 298-5000
Housing: Homeownership rate: 42.8% (2005); Median home value: $209,827 (2005); Median rent: $670 per month (2000); Median age of housing: 29 years (2000).
Safety: Violent crime rate: 79.7 per 10,000 population; Property crime rate: 369.9 per 10,000 population (2004).
Transportation: Commute to work: 84.6% car, 5.6% public transportation, 5.6% walk, 3.1% work from home (2000); Travel time to work: 31.8% less than 15 minutes, 18.6% 15 to 30 minutes, 17.3% 30 to 45 minutes, 12.0% 45 to 60 minutes, 20.2% 60 minutes or more (2000)
Additional Information Contacts
Greater Southern Dutchess Chamber of Commerce...... (845) 897-2067
http://www.gsdcc.org

FISHKILL (town).
Covers a land area of 27.417 square miles and a water area of 4.565 square miles. Located at 41.52° N. Lat.; 73.91° W. Long.
History: Nearby village of Fishkill Landing joined Matteawan (1913) to form Beacon city.
Population: 17,642 (1990); 20,258 (2000); 20,855 (2005); 21,568 (2010 projected); Race: 74.9% White, 14.1% Black, 4.2% Asian, 12.4% Hispanic of any race (2005); Density: 760.6 persons per square mile (2005); Average household size: 2.90 (2005); Median age: 39.0 (2005); Males per 100 females: 135.1 (2005); Marriage status: 29.4% never married, 58.1% now married, 7.0% widowed, 5.5% divorced (2000); Foreign born: 10.3% (2000); Ancestry (includes multiple ancestries): 23.1% Italian, 17.3% Irish, 13.4% German, 12.0% Other groups, 6.9% English (2000).
Economy: Manufacturing of concrete building material, computer equipment. Fishkill Correctional Facility. Single-family building permits issued: 163 (2005); Multi-family building permits issued: 0 (2005); Employment by occupation: 14.0% management, 25.7% professional, 13.9% services, 27.4% sales, 0.0% farming, 8.3% construction, 10.7% production (2000).
Income: Per capita income: $25,942 (2005); Median household income: $59,392 (2005); Average household income: $70,574 (2005); Percent of households with income of $100,000 or more: 19.7% (2005); Poverty rate: 5.4% (2000).
Education: Percent of population age 25 and over with: High school diploma (including GED) or higher: 72.9% (2005); Bachelor's degree or higher: 24.8% (2005); Master's degree or higher: 10.5% (2005).
Housing: Homeownership rate: 65.5% (2005); Median home value: $226,183 (2005); Median rent: $743 per month (2000); Median age of housing: 28 years (2000).
Transportation: Commute to work: 88.4% car, 6.5% public transportation, 2.4% walk, 2.0% work from home (2000); Travel time to work: 28.2% less than 15 minutes, 24.8% 15 to 30 minutes, 20.4% 30 to 45 minutes, 9.4% 45 to 60 minutes, 17.3% 60 minutes or more (2000)

HAVILAND (CDP).
Covers a land area of 3.871 square miles and a water area of 0.020 square miles. Located at 41.76° N. Lat.; 73.90° W. Long.
Population: 3,605 (1990); 3,710 (2000); 3,976 (2005); 4,219 (2010 projected); Race: 91.8% White, 3.4% Black, 2.4% Asian, 2.9% Hispanic of any race (2005); Density: 1,027.2 persons per square mile (2005); Average household size: 2.59 (2005); Median age: 40.0 (2005); Males per 100 females: 90.6 (2005); Marriage status: 18.5% never married, 66.3% now married, 7.1% widowed, 8.0% divorced (2000); Foreign born: 3.9% (2000);

Ancestry (includes multiple ancestries): 28.4% Irish, 25.1% Italian, 19.3% German, 12.0% English, 6.7% Other groups (2000).
Economy: Employment by occupation: 11.9% management, 29.4% professional, 11.9% services, 28.2% sales, 0.0% farming, 10.3% construction, 8.3% production (2000).
Income: Per capita income: $23,837 (2005); Median household income: $51,885 (2005); Average household income: $61,711 (2005); Percent of households with income of $100,000 or more: 16.2% (2005); Poverty rate: 7.4% (2000).
Education: Percent of population age 25 and over with: High school diploma (including GED) or higher: 87.5% (2005); Bachelor's degree or higher: 25.2% (2005); Master's degree or higher: 11.3% (2005).
Housing: Homeownership rate: 80.9% (2005); Median home value: $186,250 (2005); Median rent: $623 per month (2000); Median age of housing: 35 years (2000).
Transportation: Commute to work: 94.5% car, 1.6% public transportation, 0.0% walk, 3.3% work from home (2000); Travel time to work: 33.6% less than 15 minutes, 35.6% 15 to 30 minutes, 14.7% 30 to 45 minutes, 5.5% 45 to 60 minutes, 10.5% 60 minutes or more (2000)

HILLSIDE LAKE (CDP). Covers a land area of 1.519 square miles and a water area of 0.040 square miles. Located at 41.62° N. Lat.; 73.79° W. Long.
Population: 1,692 (1990); 2,022 (2000); 2,345 (2005); 2,653 (2010 projected); Race: 93.8% White, 2.0% Black, 1.3% Asian, 3.8% Hispanic of any race (2005); Density: 1,543.6 persons per square mile (2005); Average household size: 3.15 (2005); Median age: 36.0 (2005); Males per 100 females: 97.7 (2005); Marriage status: 14.7% never married, 76.3% now married, 5.3% widowed, 3.7% divorced (2000); Foreign born: 3.6% (2000); Ancestry (includes multiple ancestries): 35.6% Italian, 29.8% Irish, 16.6% German, 12.2% English, 7.2% Polish (2000).
Economy: Employment by occupation: 14.2% management, 23.7% professional, 8.6% services, 28.2% sales, 0.0% farming, 14.8% construction, 10.5% production (2000).
Income: Per capita income: $29,648 (2005); Median household income: $82,976 (2005); Average household income: $93,322 (2005); Percent of households with income of $100,000 or more: 40.4% (2005); Poverty rate: 0.9% (2000).
Education: Percent of population age 25 and over with: High school diploma (including GED) or higher: 90.2% (2005); Bachelor's degree or higher: 35.4% (2005); Master's degree or higher: 19.4% (2005).
Housing: Homeownership rate: 93.2% (2005); Median home value: $238,421 (2005); Median rent: $1,125 per month (2000); Median age of housing: 32 years (2000).
Transportation: Commute to work: 96.4% car, 0.7% public transportation, 0.0% walk, 2.9% work from home (2000); Travel time to work: 18.3% less than 15 minutes, 25.2% 15 to 30 minutes, 23.1% 30 to 45 minutes, 15.8% 45 to 60 minutes, 17.6% 60 minutes or more (2000)

HOLMES (unincorporated postal area, zip code 12531). Covers a land area of 13.939 square miles and a water area of 0.674 square miles. Located at 41.51° N. Lat.; 73.67° W. Long.
Population: 0 (2000); Race: 95.3% White, 1.0% Black, 0.3% Asian, 5.8% Hispanic of any race (2000); Density: 0.0 persons per square mile (2000); Age: 29.2% under 18, 12.8% over 64 (2000); Marriage status: 25.2% never married, 57.8% now married, 8.8% widowed, 8.2% divorced (2000); Foreign born: 3.7% (2000); Ancestry (includes multiple ancestries): 33.6% Italian, 26.8% Irish, 12.9% German, 8.6% English, 8.4% Other groups (2000).
Economy: Employment by occupation: 15.8% management, 19.5% professional, 10.9% services, 32.7% sales, 0.0% farming, 14.0% construction, 7.0% production (2000).
Income: Per capita income: $24,943 (2000); Median household income: $65,272 (2000); Poverty rate: 0.8% (2000).
Education: Percent of population age 25 and over with: High school diploma (including GED) or higher: 88.6% (2000); Bachelor's degree or higher: 25.7% (2000).
Housing: Homeownership rate: 85.7% (2000); Median home value: $184,600 (2000); Median rent: $787 per month (2000); Median age of housing: 36 years (2000).
Transportation: Commute to work: 92.0% car, 2.7% public transportation, 0.6% walk, 4.7% work from home (2000); Travel time to work: 11.4% less than 15 minutes, 26.8% 15 to 30 minutes, 27.0% 30 to 45 minutes, 14.2% 45 to 60 minutes, 20.6% 60 minutes or more (2000)

HOPEWELL JUNCTION (CDP). Aka Hopewell. Covers a land area of 2.827 square miles and a water area of 0 square miles. Located at 41.58° N. Lat.; 73.80° W. Long. Elevation is 257 feet.
Population: 1,786 (1990); 2,610 (2000); 2,830 (2005); 3,042 (2010 projected); Race: 91.1% White, 1.5% Black, 5.4% Asian, 5.3% Hispanic of any race (2005); Density: 1,001.2 persons per square mile (2005); Average household size: 2.87 (2005); Median age: 37.2 (2005); Males per 100 females: 96.8 (2005); Marriage status: 20.9% never married, 67.3% now married, 3.0% widowed, 8.8% divorced (2000); Foreign born: 11.1% (2000); Ancestry (includes multiple ancestries): 26.4% Italian, 24.0% Irish, 16.2% Other groups, 14.7% English, 14.0% German (2000).
Economy: Employment by occupation: 12.4% management, 25.7% professional, 12.4% services, 26.4% sales, 0.0% farming, 12.5% construction, 10.6% production (2000).
Income: Per capita income: $32,825 (2005); Median household income: $74,799 (2005); Average household income: $94,143 (2005); Percent of households with income of $100,000 or more: 35.6% (2005); Poverty rate: 4.3% (2000).
Education: Percent of population age 25 and over with: High school diploma (including GED) or higher: 89.6% (2005); Bachelor's degree or higher: 29.9% (2005); Master's degree or higher: 15.6% (2005).
School District(s)
Wappingers Central School District (KG-12)
    2003-04 Enrollment: 12,146 . . . . (845) 298-5000
Housing: Homeownership rate: 77.3% (2005); Median home value: $284,354 (2005); Median rent: $634 per month (2000); Median age of housing: 34 years (2000).
Transportation: Commute to work: 95.8% car, 1.8% public transportation, 0.0% walk, 1.7% work from home (2000); Travel time to work: 18.2% less than 15 minutes, 36.4% 15 to 30 minutes, 22.1% 30 to 45 minutes, 14.2% 45 to 60 minutes, 9.1% 60 minutes or more (2000)

HYDE PARK (town). Covers a land area of 36.958 square miles and a water area of 2.894 square miles. Located at 41.79° N. Lat.; 73.90° W. Long. Elevation is 184 feet.
History: Site of Roosevelt estate, part of FDR National Historic Site where President Franklin D. Roosevelt was born and is buried. Roosevelt Library contains historical material dating from 1910 until Roosevelt's death. Adjacent is the Eleanor Roosevelt National Historic Site (Val-Kill), an estate built for Mrs. Roosevelt by her husband. Frederick W. Vanderbilt mansion also here. All three homes are national historic sites. Seat of Culinary Institute of America. Settled c.1740.
Population: 21,230 (1990); 20,851 (2000); 21,119 (2005); 21,550 (2010 projected); Race: 89.7% White, 4.6% Black, 1.7% Asian, 4.3% Hispanic of any race (2005); Density: 571.4 persons per square mile (2005); Average household size: 2.79 (2005); Median age: 37.2 (2005); Males per 100 females: 99.6 (2005); Marriage status: 22.4% never married, 63.4% now married, 6.6% widowed, 7.6% divorced (2000); Foreign born: 4.9% (2000); Ancestry (includes multiple ancestries): 21.9% Irish, 19.6% Italian, 18.3% German, 11.2% English, 9.1% Other groups (2000).
Economy: Single-family building permits issued: 0 (2005); Multi-family building permits issued: 0 (2005); Employment by occupation: 11.9% management, 25.1% professional, 15.5% services, 27.1% sales, 0.1% farming, 10.9% construction, 9.5% production (2000).
Income: Per capita income: $23,889 (2005); Median household income: $55,855 (2005); Average household income: $65,055 (2005); Percent of households with income of $100,000 or more: 17.2% (2005); Poverty rate: 5.7% (2000).
Education: Percent of population age 25 and over with: High school diploma (including GED) or higher: 86.9% (2005); Bachelor's degree or higher: 24.6% (2005); Master's degree or higher: 10.5% (2005).
School District(s)
Hyde Park Central School District (KG-12)
    2003-04 Enrollment: 4,682 . . . . (845) 483-3600
Four-year College(s)
Culinary Institute of America
    Fall 2004 Enrollment: 2,453. (845) 452-9600
    2005-06 Tuition: In-state $19,180; Out-of-state $19,180
Two-year College(s)
Beauty School of Middletown
    Fall 2004 Enrollment: 46 . . . . (845) 229-6541
Housing: Homeownership rate: 74.3% (2005); Median home value: $190,191 (2005); Median rent: $604 per month (2000); Median age of housing: 35 years (2000).

Transportation: Commute to work: 93.0% car, 2.2% public transportation, 2.2% walk, 1.9% work from home (2000); Travel time to work: 29.2% less than 15 minutes, 39.0% 15 to 30 minutes, 17.3% 30 to 45 minutes, 6.5% 45 to 60 minutes, 8.1% 60 minutes or more (2000)

Additional Information Contacts
Hyde Park Chamber of Commerce .... (845) 229-8612
http://www.hydeparkchamber.org/
Town of Hyde Park .... (845) 229-5111
http://www.hydeparkny.us/

LA GRANGE (town). Covers a land area of 39.700 square miles and a water area of 0.165 square miles. Located at 41.67° N. Lat.; 73.80° W. Long.
Population: 13,274 (1990); 14,928 (2000); 16,095 (2005); 17,274 (2010 projected); Race: 90.5% White, 2.7% Black, 3.8% Asian, 5.8% Hispanic of any race (2005); Density: 405.4 persons per square mile (2005); Average household size: 2.90 (2005); Median age: 38.7 (2005); Males per 100 females: 96.9 (2005); Marriage status: 20.7% never married, 68.3% now married, 5.4% widowed, 5.6% divorced (2000); Foreign born: 7.5% (2000); Ancestry (includes multiple ancestries): 29.3% Irish, 24.2% Italian, 20.5% German, 12.0% English, 10.9% Other groups (2000).
Economy: Single-family building permits issued: 41 (2005); Multi-family building permits issued: 0 (2005); Employment by occupation: 15.8% management, 32.0% professional, 12.0% services, 21.1% sales, 0.1% farming, 11.0% construction, 7.9% production (2000).
Income: Per capita income: $32,899 (2005); Median household income: $85,055 (2005); Average household income: $95,138 (2005); Percent of households with income of $100,000 or more: 38.3% (2005); Poverty rate: 3.7% (2000).
Taxes: Total city taxes per capita: $273 (2004); City property taxes per capita: $190 (2004).
Education: Percent of population age 25 and over with: High school diploma (including GED) or higher: 93.5% (2005); Bachelor's degree or higher: 36.5% (2005); Master's degree or higher: 15.3% (2005).
Housing: Homeownership rate: 90.2% (2005); Median home value: $277,018 (2005); Median rent: $804 per month (2000); Median age of housing: 32 years (2000).
Transportation: Commute to work: 93.2% car, 2.0% public transportation, 1.0% walk, 3.6% work from home (2000); Travel time to work: 22.5% less than 15 minutes, 38.7% 15 to 30 minutes, 13.4% 30 to 45 minutes, 8.8% 45 to 60 minutes, 16.6% 60 minutes or more (2000)

Additional Information Contacts
Town of La Grange .... (845) 452-1830
http://www.lagrangeny.org/

LAGRANGEVILLE (unincorporated postal area, zip code 12540). Aka La Grange. Covers a land area of 33.023 square miles and a water area of 0.070 square miles. Located at 41.65° N. Lat.; 73.74° W. Long.
Population: 0 (2000); Race: 92.3% White, 1.3% Black, 4.0% Asian, 1.9% Hispanic of any race (2000); Density: 0.0 persons per square mile (2000); Age: 29.2% under 18, 11.0% over 64 (2000); Marriage status: 21.0% never married, 67.1% now married, 6.1% widowed, 5.8% divorced (2000); Foreign born: 9.1% (2000); Ancestry (includes multiple ancestries): 28.3% Irish, 26.3% Italian, 17.0% German, 11.0% English, 7.9% Other groups (2000).
Economy: Employment by occupation: 15.8% management, 26.5% professional, 10.7% services, 26.4% sales, 0.2% farming, 12.7% construction, 7.7% production (2000).
Income: Per capita income: $25,647 (2000); Median household income: $69,420 (2000); Poverty rate: 2.3% (2000).
Education: Percent of population age 25 and over with: High school diploma (including GED) or higher: 92.5% (2000); Bachelor's degree or higher: 32.6% (2000).

School District(s)
Arlington Central School District (KG-12)
    2003-04 Enrollment: 10,102 .... (845) 486-4460
Housing: Homeownership rate: 86.8% (2000); Median home value: $186,100 (2000); Median rent: $728 per month (2000); Median age of housing: 24 years (2000).
Transportation: Commute to work: 93.4% car, 1.0% public transportation, 1.2% walk, 3.8% work from home (2000); Travel time to work: 18.6% less than 15 minutes, 36.9% 15 to 30 minutes, 15.4% 30 to 45 minutes, 12.8% 45 to 60 minutes, 16.3% 60 minutes or more (2000)

MILAN (town). Covers a land area of 36.100 square miles and a water area of 0.188 square miles. Located at 41.97° N. Lat.; 73.78° W. Long. Elevation is 433 feet.
Population: 1,895 (1990); 4,559 (2000); 5,022 (2005); 5,517 (2010 projected); Race: 45.5% White, 37.7% Black, 1.2% Asian, 22.2% Hispanic of any race (2005); Density: 139.1 persons per square mile (2005); Average household size: 4.72 (2005); Median age: 36.9 (2005); Males per 100 females: 261.8 (2005); Marriage status: 45.7% never married, 44.2% now married, 3.1% widowed, 7.0% divorced (2000); Foreign born: 10.7% (2000); Ancestry (includes multiple ancestries): 12.6% German, 10.5% Irish, 10.1% Italian, 6.3% English, 3.7% Other groups (2000).
Economy: Single-family building permits issued: 29 (2005); Multi-family building permits issued: 0 (2005); Employment by occupation: 10.6% management, 30.0% professional, 17.5% services, 21.7% sales, 1.1% farming, 8.5% construction, 10.5% production (2000).
Income: Per capita income: $21,698 (2005); Median household income: $63,246 (2005); Average household income: $83,617 (2005); Percent of households with income of $100,000 or more: 24.2% (2005); Poverty rate: 4.6% (2000).
Education: Percent of population age 25 and over with: High school diploma (including GED) or higher: 48.1% (2005); Bachelor's degree or higher: 14.9% (2005); Master's degree or higher: 7.5% (2005).
Housing: Homeownership rate: 79.1% (2005); Median home value: $239,271 (2005); Median rent: $549 per month (2000); Median age of housing: 38 years (2000).
Transportation: Commute to work: 85.8% car, 3.1% public transportation, 5.8% walk, 5.3% work from home (2000); Travel time to work: 28.1% less than 15 minutes, 29.0% 15 to 30 minutes, 21.5% 30 to 45 minutes, 11.0% 45 to 60 minutes, 10.4% 60 minutes or more (2000)

MILLBROOK (village). Covers a land area of 1.870 square miles and a water area of 0.050 square miles. Located at 41.78° N. Lat.; 73.69° W. Long. Elevation is 569 feet.
History: Seat of Institute of Ecosystem Studies- N.Y. Botanical Gardens; Millbrook Preparatory School. Many estates and second homes for New Yorkers. Noted for polo playing. Incorporated 1896.
Population: 1,339 (1990); 1,429 (2000); 1,522 (2005); 1,621 (2010 projected); Race: 95.3% White, 2.9% Black, 0.3% Asian, 4.3% Hispanic of any race (2005); Density: 814.0 persons per square mile (2005); Average household size: 2.07 (2005); Median age: 44.8 (2005); Males per 100 females: 86.5 (2005); Marriage status: 24.4% never married, 51.1% now married, 11.6% widowed, 12.9% divorced (2000); Foreign born: 6.5% (2000); Ancestry (includes multiple ancestries): 27.0% Italian, 24.3% Irish, 17.0% English, 16.7% German, 5.1% Polish (2000).
Economy: In dairying and limited stock-raising area. Single-family building permits issued: 0 (2005); Multi-family building permits issued: 0 (2005); Employment by occupation: 14.2% management, 25.9% professional, 17.9% services, 26.4% sales, 0.6% farming, 9.5% construction, 5.6% production (2000).
Income: Per capita income: $31,405 (2005); Median household income: $42,099 (2005); Average household income: $65,027 (2005); Percent of households with income of $100,000 or more: 16.9% (2005); Poverty rate: 5.7% (2000).
Education: Percent of population age 25 and over with: High school diploma (including GED) or higher: 89.9% (2005); Bachelor's degree or higher: 33.5% (2005); Master's degree or higher: 16.2% (2005).

School District(s)
Millbrook Central School District (KG-12)
    2003-04 Enrollment: 1,198 .... (845) 677-4200
Housing: Homeownership rate: 51.2% (2005); Median home value: $281,879 (2005); Median rent: $589 per month (2000); Median age of housing: 60+ years (2000).
Newspapers: Millbrook Round Table (General - Circulation 2,500); Register Herald (General - Circulation 2,000); The Voice-Ledger (General - Circulation 2,580)
Transportation: Commute to work: 78.9% car, 4.2% public transportation, 10.8% walk, 5.5% work from home (2000); Travel time to work: 38.1% less than 15 minutes, 24.1% 15 to 30 minutes, 26.8% 30 to 45 minutes, 3.9% 45 to 60 minutes, 7.1% 60 minutes or more (2000)

MILLERTON (village). Covers a land area of 0.629 square miles and a water area of 0 square miles. Located at 41.95° N. Lat.; 73.50° W. Long. Elevation is 701 feet.

Population: 884 (1990); 925 (2000); 947 (2005); 975 (2010 projected); Race: 91.3% White, 3.1% Black, 1.8% Asian, 6.0% Hispanic of any race (2005); Density: 1,505.4 persons per square mile (2005); Average household size: 2.42 (2005); Median age: 41.5 (2005); Males per 100 females: 90.9 (2005); Marriage status: 29.6% never married, 49.9% now married, 8.4% widowed, 12.2% divorced (2000); Foreign born: 4.7% (2000); Ancestry (includes multiple ancestries): 25.1% Irish, 17.1% German, 16.1% English, 13.1% Other groups, 12.6% Italian (2000).
Economy: In dairying area. Working-class population. Single-family building permits issued: 0 (2005); Multi-family building permits issued: 0 (2005); Employment by occupation: 10.9% management, 15.2% professional, 19.0% services, 26.8% sales, 0.9% farming, 11.6% construction, 15.6% production (2000).
Income: Per capita income: $23,777 (2005); Median household income: $46,314 (2005); Average household income: $56,976 (2005); Percent of households with income of $100,000 or more: 14.6% (2005); Poverty rate: 14.3% (2000).
Education: Percent of population age 25 and over with: High school diploma (including GED) or higher: 76.0% (2005); Bachelor's degree or higher: 13.8% (2005); Master's degree or higher: 4.7% (2005).
Housing: Homeownership rate: 55.8% (2005); Median home value: $178,652 (2005); Median rent: $538 per month (2000); Median age of housing: 60+ years (2000).
Newspapers: The Millerton News (General - Circulation 2,500)
Transportation: Commute to work: 88.0% car, 2.8% public transportation, 5.9% walk, 2.3% work from home (2000); Travel time to work: 42.1% less than 15 minutes, 35.3% 15 to 30 minutes, 7.2% 30 to 45 minutes, 4.3% 45 to 60 minutes, 11.1% 60 minutes or more (2000)

MYERS CORNER (CDP).
Covers a land area of 4.262 square miles and a water area of 0.015 square miles. Located at 41.59° N. Lat.; 73.87° W. Long. Elevation is 216 feet.
Population: 5,599 (1990); 5,546 (2000); 5,730 (2005); 5,911 (2010 projected); Race: 83.8% White, 4.7% Black, 7.0% Asian, 8.2% Hispanic of any race (2005); Density: 1,344.4 persons per square mile (2005); Average household size: 3.01 (2005); Median age: 39.9 (2005); Males per 100 females: 95.4 (2005); Marriage status: 20.1% never married, 72.0% now married, 3.4% widowed, 4.5% divorced (2000); Foreign born: 9.3% (2000); Ancestry (includes multiple ancestries): 32.8% Italian, 24.7% Irish, 18.4% Other groups, 15.6% German, 8.3% English (2000).
Economy: Employment by occupation: 15.2% management, 28.5% professional, 11.5% services, 26.5% sales, 0.0% farming, 7.0% construction, 11.2% production (2000).
Income: Per capita income: $32,344 (2005); Median household income: $87,462 (2005); Average household income: $96,885 (2005); Percent of households with income of $100,000 or more: 41.4% (2005); Poverty rate: 3.3% (2000).
Education: Percent of population age 25 and over with: High school diploma (including GED) or higher: 92.6% (2005); Bachelor's degree or higher: 36.4% (2005); Master's degree or higher: 14.9% (2005).
Housing: Homeownership rate: 93.6% (2005); Median home value: $263,378 (2005); Median rent: $678 per month (2000); Median age of housing: 29 years (2000).
Transportation: Commute to work: 91.1% car, 3.2% public transportation, 1.2% walk, 4.2% work from home (2000); Travel time to work: 23.1% less than 15 minutes, 38.1% 15 to 30 minutes, 12.7% 30 to 45 minutes, 9.5% 45 to 60 minutes, 16.7% 60 minutes or more (2000)

NORTH EAST (town).
Covers a land area of 43.376 square miles and a water area of 0.327 square miles. Located at 41.94° N. Lat.; 73.52° W. Long.
Population: 2,918 (1990); 3,002 (2000); 3,125 (2005); 3,256 (2010 projected); Race: 94.8% White, 2.3% Black, 0.7% Asian, 4.9% Hispanic of any race (2005); Density: 72.0 persons per square mile (2005); Average household size: 2.58 (2005); Median age: 41.3 (2005); Males per 100 females: 97.7 (2005); Marriage status: 28.2% never married, 56.2% now married, 7.9% widowed, 7.8% divorced (2000); Foreign born: 4.7% (2000); Ancestry (includes multiple ancestries): 19.4% German, 19.0% Irish, 14.3% Italian, 13.4% English, 8.4% Other groups (2000).
Economy: Single-family building permits issued: 24 (2005); Multi-family building permits issued: 0 (2005); Employment by occupation: 11.9% management, 22.9% professional, 16.6% services, 20.9% sales, 4.3% farming, 9.4% construction, 13.9% production (2000).
Income: Per capita income: $27,649 (2005); Median household income: $55,704 (2005); Average household income: $68,337 (2005); Percent of households with income of $100,000 or more: 16.8% (2005); Poverty rate: 12.3% (2000).
Education: Percent of population age 25 and over with: High school diploma (including GED) or higher: 77.0% (2005); Bachelor's degree or higher: 20.5% (2005); Master's degree or higher: 9.4% (2005).
Housing: Homeownership rate: 68.5% (2005); Median home value: $195,056 (2005); Median rent: $573 per month (2000); Median age of housing: 43 years (2000).
Transportation: Commute to work: 82.0% car, 1.4% public transportation, 9.1% walk, 6.7% work from home (2000); Travel time to work: 46.0% less than 15 minutes, 30.6% 15 to 30 minutes, 7.4% 30 to 45 minutes, 6.0% 45 to 60 minutes, 9.9% 60 minutes or more (2000)

PAWLING (village).
Aka Stonehouse. Covers a land area of 2.037 square miles and a water area of 0 square miles. Located at 41.56° N. Lat.; 73.59° W. Long. Elevation is 465 feet.
Population: 1,974 (1990); 2,233 (2000); 2,256 (2005); 2,316 (2010 projected); Race: 87.8% White, 2.5% Black, 2.9% Asian, 9.8% Hispanic of any race (2005); Density: 1,107.7 persons per square mile (2005); Average household size: 2.37 (2005); Median age: 43.2 (2005); Males per 100 females: 91.2 (2005); Marriage status: 26.1% never married, 57.2% now married, 8.9% widowed, 7.9% divorced (2000); Foreign born: 8.0% (2000); Ancestry (includes multiple ancestries): 28.4% Irish, 26.3% Italian, 13.3% German, 8.5% Other groups, 8.3% English (2000).
Economy: Single-family building permits issued: 1 (2005); Multi-family building permits issued: 0 (2005); Employment by occupation: 11.1% management, 25.6% professional, 15.8% services, 23.0% sales, 0.0% farming, 12.4% construction, 12.2% production (2000).
Income: Per capita income: $28,297 (2005); Median household income: $55,435 (2005); Average household income: $66,242 (2005); Percent of households with income of $100,000 or more: 18.3% (2005); Poverty rate: 7.3% (2000).
Education: Percent of population age 25 and over with: High school diploma (including GED) or higher: 87.7% (2005); Bachelor's degree or higher: 25.0% (2005); Master's degree or higher: 8.2% (2005).
School District(s)
Pawling Central School District (KG-12)
    2003-04 Enrollment: 1,422 . . . . (845) 855-4600
Housing: Homeownership rate: 54.0% (2005); Median home value: $246,375 (2005); Median rent: $590 per month (2000); Median age of housing: 47 years (2000).
Newspapers: Pawling News Chronicle (General - Circulation 2,100)
Transportation: Commute to work: 81.3% car, 6.2% public transportation, 7.1% walk, 4.6% work from home (2000); Travel time to work: 34.7% less than 15 minutes, 9.3% 15 to 30 minutes, 23.6% 30 to 45 minutes, 14.7% 45 to 60 minutes, 17.6% 60 minutes or more (2000)
Additional Information Contacts
Pawling Chamber of Commerce Ch . . . . (845) 855-0500
   http://www.pawling.org/chamber/

PAWLING (town).
Aka Stonehouse. Covers a land area of 44.180 square miles and a water area of 0.805 square miles. Located at 41.56° N. Lat.; 73.60° W. Long. Elevation is 465 feet.
History: In 1937, Thomas E. Dewey, three-term governor and two-time nominee for U.S. president, purchased a 486-acre farm here, although his legal address was the Roosevelt Hotel in N.Y. city. When he returned to legal practice after being governor, he resided at the World Trade Center. He and his wife are buried in Pawling Cemetery. Settled by Quakers c.1740; Incorporated 1893.
Population: 5,947 (1990); 7,521 (2000); 8,407 (2005); 9,274 (2010 projected); Race: 93.0% White, 1.6% Black, 1.9% Asian, 6.7% Hispanic of any race (2005); Density: 190.3 persons per square mile (2005); Average household size: 2.63 (2005); Median age: 40.6 (2005); Males per 100 females: 95.6 (2005); Marriage status: 22.1% never married, 63.4% now married, 6.0% widowed, 8.4% divorced (2000); Foreign born: 7.4% (2000); Ancestry (includes multiple ancestries): 26.7% Irish, 26.7% Italian, 15.0% German, 10.5% English, 8.0% Other groups (2000).
Economy: Manufacturing of plastics, rubber products and tiles. In resort and diversified-farming area. Single-family building permits issued: 24 (2005); Multi-family building permits issued: 0 (2005); Employment by occupation: 15.8% management, 21.1% professional, 13.9% services, 25.8% sales, 1.0% farming, 13.0% construction, 9.4% production (2000).
Income: Per capita income: $34,167 (2005); Median household income: $70,969 (2005); Average household income: $89,609 (2005); Percent of

households with income of $100,000 or more: 29.6% (2005); Poverty rate: 3.3% (2000).
Education: Percent of population age 25 and over with: High school diploma (including GED) or higher: 90.4% (2005); Bachelor's degree or higher: 28.4% (2005); Master's degree or higher: 11.3% (2005).
Housing: Homeownership rate: 75.8% (2005); Median home value: $276,600 (2005); Median rent: $649 per month (2000); Median age of housing: 38 years (2000).
Transportation: Commute to work: 83.2% car, 6.1% public transportation, 3.0% walk, 7.3% work from home (2000); Travel time to work: 24.2% less than 15 minutes, 16.7% 15 to 30 minutes, 20.6% 30 to 45 minutes, 15.5% 45 to 60 minutes, 23.0% 60 minutes or more (2000)

PINE PLAINS (town). Covers a land area of 30.892 square miles and a water area of 0.458 square miles. Located at 41.97° N. Lat.; 73.65° W. Long. Elevation is 474 feet.
Population: 2,287 (1990); 2,569 (2000); 2,728 (2005); 2,894 (2010 projected); Race: 95.5% White, 0.8% Black, 1.1% Asian, 1.4% Hispanic of any race (2005); Density: 88.3 persons per square mile (2005); Average household size: 2.55 (2005); Median age: 41.3 (2005); Males per 100 females: 92.8 (2005); Marriage status: 27.4% never married, 56.5% now married, 7.0% widowed, 9.1% divorced (2000); Foreign born: 5.8% (2000); Ancestry (includes multiple ancestries): 21.4% Irish, 19.6% German, 18.0% Italian, 13.2% English, 8.6% Other groups (2000).
Economy: In diversified agricultural area. Single-family building permits issued: 15 (2005); Multi-family building permits issued: 6 (2005); Employment by occupation: 11.5% management, 19.2% professional, 16.4% services, 24.4% sales, 2.1% farming, 12.2% construction, 14.2% production (2000).
Income: Per capita income: $29,654 (2005); Median household income: $54,566 (2005); Average household income: $75,596 (2005); Percent of households with income of $100,000 or more: 20.7% (2005); Poverty rate: 9.2% (2000).
Education: Percent of population age 25 and over with: High school diploma (including GED) or higher: 81.7% (2005); Bachelor's degree or higher: 22.8% (2005); Master's degree or higher: 11.6% (2005).
School District(s)
Pine Plains Central School District (KG-12)
    2003-04 Enrollment: 1,420 . . . . (518) 398-7181
Housing: Homeownership rate: 70.4% (2005); Median home value: $186,326 (2005); Median rent: $529 per month (2000); Median age of housing: 44 years (2000).
Safety: Violent crime rate: 0.0 per 10,000 population; Property crime rate: 41.1 per 10,000 population (2004).
Transportation: Commute to work: 85.2% car, 3.3% public transportation, 6.5% walk, 4.3% work from home (2000); Travel time to work: 31.9% less than 15 minutes, 24.1% 15 to 30 minutes, 21.8% 30 to 45 minutes, 9.0% 45 to 60 minutes, 13.3% 60 minutes or more (2000)
Additional Information Contacts
Town of Pine Plains . . . . (518) 398-7155
    http://pineplains-ny.gov/content

PINE PLAINS (CDP). Covers a land area of 2.093 square miles and a water area of 0.200 square miles. Located at 41.97° N. Lat.; 73.66° W. Long.
Population: 1,312 (1990); 1,412 (2000); 1,422 (2005); 1,467 (2010 projected); Race: 95.9% White, 0.4% Black, 0.7% Asian, 1.7% Hispanic of any race (2005); Density: 679.3 persons per square mile (2005); Average household size: 2.55 (2005); Median age: 41.0 (2005); Males per 100 females: 89.9 (2005); Marriage status: 29.0% never married, 54.9% now married, 8.6% widowed, 7.4% divorced (2000); Foreign born: 3.7% (2000); Ancestry (includes multiple ancestries): 21.5% Irish, 21.3% German, 16.9% Italian, 12.7% English, 8.2% French (except Basque) (2000).
Economy: Employment by occupation: 12.8% management, 20.4% professional, 18.8% services, 26.1% sales, 0.6% farming, 8.9% construction, 12.5% production (2000).
Income: Per capita income: $28,431 (2005); Median household income: $56,858 (2005); Average household income: $72,437 (2005); Percent of households with income of $100,000 or more: 19.9% (2005); Poverty rate: 13.3% (2000).
Education: Percent of population age 25 and over with: High school diploma (including GED) or higher: 77.5% (2005); Bachelor's degree or higher: 21.4% (2005); Master's degree or higher: 12.6% (2005).

Housing: Homeownership rate: 67.7% (2005); Median home value: $166,216 (2005); Median rent: $511 per month (2000); Median age of housing: 51 years (2000).
Transportation: Commute to work: 83.8% car, 3.2% public transportation, 9.2% walk, 3.4% work from home (2000); Travel time to work: 36.5% less than 15 minutes, 20.3% 15 to 30 minutes, 22.4% 30 to 45 minutes, 9.2% 45 to 60 minutes, 11.6% 60 minutes or more (2000)

PLEASANT VALLEY (town). Covers a land area of 32.920 square miles and a water area of 0.316 square miles. Located at 41.77° N. Lat.; 73.80° W. Long.
Population: 8,063 (1990); 9,066 (2000); 9,547 (2005); 10,063 (2010 projected); Race: 94.8% White, 2.2% Black, 0.7% Asian, 3.6% Hispanic of any race (2005); Density: 290.0 persons per square mile (2005); Average household size: 2.59 (2005); Median age: 39.4 (2005); Males per 100 females: 97.4 (2005); Marriage status: 22.8% never married, 62.5% now married, 5.7% widowed, 9.0% divorced (2000); Foreign born: 3.9% (2000); Ancestry (includes multiple ancestries): 23.7% German, 22.8% Irish, 21.0% Italian, 11.6% English, 7.6% Other groups (2000).
Economy: Light manufacturing. Single-family building permits issued: 47 (2005); Multi-family building permits issued: 42 (2005); Employment by occupation: 11.6% management, 28.5% professional, 12.8% services, 21.6% sales, 0.8% farming, 13.7% construction, 10.9% production (2000).
Income: Per capita income: $29,300 (2005); Median household income: $61,626 (2005); Average household income: $75,880 (2005); Percent of households with income of $100,000 or more: 23.6% (2005); Poverty rate: 5.6% (2000).
Taxes: Total city taxes per capita: $230 (2004); City property taxes per capita: $169 (2004).
Education: Percent of population age 25 and over with: High school diploma (including GED) or higher: 89.9% (2005); Bachelor's degree or higher: 25.9% (2005); Master's degree or higher: 12.2% (2005).
School District(s)
Arlington Central School District (KG-12)
    2003-04 Enrollment: 10,102 . . . . (845) 486-4460
Housing: Homeownership rate: 72.9% (2005); Median home value: $241,487 (2005); Median rent: $669 per month (2000); Median age of housing: 29 years (2000).
Transportation: Commute to work: 92.6% car, 1.2% public transportation, 1.2% walk, 4.7% work from home (2000); Travel time to work: 18.5% less than 15 minutes, 43.9% 15 to 30 minutes, 21.1% 30 to 45 minutes, 6.0% 45 to 60 minutes, 10.5% 60 minutes or more (2000)
Additional Information Contacts
Town of Pleasant Valley . . . . (845) 635-3274
    http://www.ci.pleasant-valley.ny.us/site/pages/home.html

PLEASANT VALLEY (CDP). Covers a land area of 1.568 square miles and a water area of 0.037 square miles. Located at 41.74° N. Lat.; 73.82° W. Long.
Population: 1,688 (1990); 1,839 (2000); 1,884 (2005); 1,942 (2010 projected); Race: 94.3% White, 3.1% Black, 0.9% Asian, 3.6% Hispanic of any race (2005); Density: 1,201.4 persons per square mile (2005); Average household size: 2.41 (2005); Median age: 38.8 (2005); Males per 100 females: 94.6 (2005); Marriage status: 26.8% never married, 54.6% now married, 9.7% widowed, 8.8% divorced (2000); Foreign born: 4.5% (2000); Ancestry (includes multiple ancestries): 30.5% Irish, 25.3% German, 23.0% Italian, 10.8% English, 7.6% Dutch (2000).
Economy: Employment by occupation: 9.4% management, 25.0% professional, 15.5% services, 20.7% sales, 1.7% farming, 13.4% construction, 14.3% production (2000).
Income: Per capita income: $26,572 (2005); Median household income: $52,459 (2005); Average household income: $64,019 (2005); Percent of households with income of $100,000 or more: 17.3% (2005); Poverty rate: 2.7% (2000).
Education: Percent of population age 25 and over with: High school diploma (including GED) or higher: 91.0% (2005); Bachelor's degree or higher: 23.9% (2005); Master's degree or higher: 11.4% (2005).
Housing: Homeownership rate: 51.0% (2005); Median home value: $234,390 (2005); Median rent: $755 per month (2000); Median age of housing: 32 years (2000).
Transportation: Commute to work: 91.8% car, 1.6% public transportation, 2.1% walk, 3.2% work from home (2000); Travel time to work: 16.9% less than 15 minutes, 44.6% 15 to 30 minutes, 22.0% 30 to 45 minutes, 5.6% 45 to 60 minutes, 10.8% 60 minutes or more (2000)

POUGHKEEPSIE (city). Covers a land area of 5.145 square miles and a water area of 0.553 square miles. Located at 41.70° N. Lat.; 73.92° W. Long. Elevation is 209 feet.
History: It became the temporary state capital in 1777, and the U.S. Constitution was ratified (1788) here. Seat of Vassar and Marist Colleges and a community college. Several historic 18th-century buildings still stand. Hyde Park lies just north. Settled 1687 by the Dutch, Incorporated as a city 1854.
Population: 28,844 (1990); 29,871 (2000); 30,318 (2005); 30,934 (2010 projected); Race: 47.3% White, 38.6% Black, 2.1% Asian, 14.6% Hispanic of any race (2005); Density: 5,893.1 persons per square mile (2005); Average household size: 2.49 (2005); Median age: 33.9 (2005); Males per 100 females: 92.2 (2005); Marriage status: 40.5% never married, 41.5% now married, 8.5% widowed, 9.5% divorced (2000); Foreign born: 13.9% (2000); Ancestry (includes multiple ancestries): 39.4% Other groups, 12.4% Italian, 11.9% Irish, 8.6% German, 5.1% Jamaican (2000).
Economy: A trade center with industries such as printing, lithography, computer assembly and electronics research. Manufacturing includes machinery, precision instruments, dairy equipment, clothing and chemicals. Seat of Vassar and Marist colleges and a community college. At north end of the Hudson branch of Metro-North commuter railroad. Unemployment rate: 4.7% (2005); Total civilian labor force: 13,803 (2005); Single-family building permits issued: 18 (2005); Multi-family building permits issued: 0 (2005); Employment by occupation: 9.8% management, 20.5% professional, 26.9% services, 23.7% sales, 0.4% farming, 7.2% construction, 11.6% production (2000).
Income: Per capita income: $17,792 (2005); Median household income: $30,591 (2005); Average household income: $43,492 (2005); Percent of households with income of $100,000 or more: 9.2% (2005); Poverty rate: 22.7% (2000).
Education: Percent of population age 25 and over with: High school diploma (including GED) or higher: 72.2% (2005); Bachelor's degree or higher: 19.3% (2005); Master's degree or higher: 8.6% (2005).

School District(s)
Arlington Central School District (KG-12)
    2003-04 Enrollment: 10,102 . . . . (845) 486-4460
Boces Dutchess (UG-UG)
    2003-04 Enrollment: 412 . . . . (845) 486-4800
Hyde Park Central School District (KG-12)
    2003-04 Enrollment: 4,682 . . . . (845) 483-3600
Poughkeepsie City School District (PK-12)
    2003-04 Enrollment: 4,880 . . . . (845) 451-4950
Spackenkill Union Free School District (KG-12)
    2003-04 Enrollment: 1,835 . . . . (845) 463-7800
Wappingers Central School District (KG-12)
    2003-04 Enrollment: 12,146 . . . . (845) 298-5000

Four-year College(s)
Marist College
    Fall 2004 Enrollment: 5,646 . . . . (845) 575-3000
    2005-06 Tuition: In-state $21,202; Out-of-state $21,202
Vassar College
    Fall 2004 Enrollment: 2,475 . . . . (845) 437-7000
    2005-06 Tuition: In-state $33,800; Out-of-state $33,800

Two-year College(s)
Dutchess BOCES-School of Practical Nursing (Public)
    Fall 2004 Enrollment: 145 . . . . (845) 486-8001
Dutchess Community College (Public)
    Fall 2004 Enrollment: 7,790 . . . . (845) 431-8000
    2005-06 Tuition: In-state $2,977; Out-of-state $5,577
Ridley-Lowell School of Business
    Fall 2004 Enrollment: 159 . . . . (845) 471-0330

Housing: Homeownership rate: 37.0% (2005); Median home value: $164,051 (2005); Median rent: $543 per month (2000); Median age of housing: 55 years (2000).
Hospitals: Hudson River Psychiatric Center (125 beds); St. Francis Hospital (400 beds); Vassar Brothers Hospital (365 beds)
Safety: Violent crime rate: 118.1 per 10,000 population; Property crime rate: 398.3 per 10,000 population (2004).
Newspapers: Poughkeepsie Journal (Circulation 40,036)
Transportation: Commute to work: 79.3% car, 9.9% public transportation, 7.0% walk, 3.1% work from home (2000); Travel time to work: 43.5% less than 15 minutes, 27.9% 15 to 30 minutes, 15.0% 30 to 45 minutes, 5.0% 45 to 60 minutes, 8.6% 60 minutes or more (2000); Amtrak: Service available.

Additional Information Contacts
City of Poughkeepsie . . . . (845) 451-4200
    http://www.cityofpoughkeepsie.com/
Poughkeepsie Chamber Commerce . . . . (845) 454-1700
    http://www.pokchamb.org

POUGHKEEPSIE (town). Covers a land area of 28.758 square miles and a water area of 2.434 square miles. Located at 41.67° N. Lat.; 73.90° W. Long. Elevation is 209 feet.
History: The name of Poughkeepsie had its origins in a Native American name, the original probably meaning "reed-covered lodge by the little water place." The first record of European settlement dates from 1683. Growth at first was slow, but in 1777 Poughkeepsie was made the capital of the state. The chief event in the history of the town was the ratification of the Federal Constitution by the State on July 26, 1788. Early in the 19th century, Poughkeepsie became prominent as a river port. With the opening of the Erie Canal in 1825, however, competition caused a decline in the value of Dutchess County produce. Poughkeepsie turned to industry and trade. It also acquired a reputation as an educational center, with the most important advance being the founding of Vassar College in 1861.
Population: 40,143 (1990); 42,777 (2000); 45,291 (2005); 47,694 (2010 projected); Race: 78.9% White, 9.5% Black, 7.2% Asian, 7.1% Hispanic of any race (2005); Density: 1,574.9 persons per square mile (2005); Average household size: 2.91 (2005); Median age: 35.5 (2005); Males per 100 females: 90.9 (2005); Marriage status: 29.7% never married, 57.8% now married, 6.2% widowed, 6.2% divorced (2000); Foreign born: 10.6% (2000); Ancestry (includes multiple ancestries): 20.5% Italian, 19.5% Irish, 16.3% Other groups, 14.3% German, 10.6% English (2000).
Economy: Unemployment rate: 3.8% (2005); Total civilian labor force: 22,682 (2005); Single-family building permits issued: 43 (2005); Multi-family building permits issued: 0 (2005); Employment by occupation: 11.0% management, 28.6% professional, 14.8% services, 28.1% sales, 0.2% farming, 7.3% construction, 10.0% production (2000).
Income: Per capita income: $26,616 (2005); Median household income: $62,694 (2005); Average household income: $75,453 (2005); Percent of households with income of $100,000 or more: 23.1% (2005); Poverty rate: 5.7% (2000).
Taxes: Total city taxes per capita: $414 (2004); City property taxes per capita: $361 (2004).
Education: Percent of population age 25 and over with: High school diploma (including GED) or higher: 87.4% (2005); Bachelor's degree or higher: 30.8% (2005); Master's degree or higher: 14.2% (2005).
Housing: Homeownership rate: 69.9% (2005); Median home value: $220,331 (2005); Median rent: $677 per month (2000); Median age of housing: 38 years (2000).
Safety: Violent crime rate: 18.3 per 10,000 population; Property crime rate: 247.0 per 10,000 population (2004).
Transportation: Commute to work: 84.8% car, 3.7% public transportation, 8.7% walk, 1.9% work from home (2000); Travel time to work: 39.1% less than 15 minutes, 32.1% 15 to 30 minutes, 12.4% 30 to 45 minutes, 5.9% 45 to 60 minutes, 10.6% 60 minutes or more (2000); Amtrak: Service available.

POUGHQUAG (unincorporated postal area, zip code 12570). Covers a land area of 16.307 square miles and a water area of 0.029 square miles. Located at 41.61° N. Lat.; 73.67° W. Long. Elevation is 429 feet.
Population: 0 (2000); Race: 94.9% White, 0.6% Black, 1.2% Asian, 5.9% Hispanic of any race (2000); Density: 0.0 persons per square mile (2000); Age: 30.4% under 18, 7.3% over 64 (2000); Marriage status: 20.5% never married, 71.1% now married, 3.6% widowed, 4.8% divorced (2000); Foreign born: 4.7% (2000); Ancestry (includes multiple ancestries): 31.5% Italian, 25.4% Irish, 13.1% German, 10.8% Other groups, 10.2% English (2000).
Economy: Employment by occupation: 16.7% management, 21.7% professional, 12.6% services, 25.8% sales, 0.2% farming, 12.8% construction, 10.2% production (2000).
Income: Per capita income: $28,029 (2000); Median household income: $74,877 (2000); Poverty rate: 1.7% (2000).
Education: Percent of population age 25 and over with: High school diploma (including GED) or higher: 92.8% (2000); Bachelor's degree or higher: 31.4% (2000).

School District(s)
Arlington Central School District (KG-12)
    2003-04 Enrollment: 10,102 . . . . (845) 486-4460

Housing: Homeownership rate: 89.3% (2000); Median home value: $195,200 (2000); Median rent: $736 per month (2000); Median age of housing: 17 years (2000).
Transportation: Commute to work: 93.7% car, 2.8% public transportation, 0.6% walk, 2.6% work from home (2000); Travel time to work: 14.7% less than 15 minutes, 25.5% 15 to 30 minutes, 22.6% 30 to 45 minutes, 15.8% 45 to 60 minutes, 21.3% 60 minutes or more (2000)

RED HOOK (village).
Covers a land area of 1.084 square miles and a water area of 0 square miles. Located at 41.99° N. Lat.; 73.87° W. Long. Elevation is 218 feet.
Population: 1,794 (1990); 1,805 (2000); 1,872 (2005); 1,975 (2010 projected); Race: 93.6% White, 0.7% Black, 2.7% Asian, 5.5% Hispanic of any race (2005); Density: 1,726.7 persons per square mile (2005); Average household size: 2.31 (2005); Median age: 40.7 (2005); Males per 100 females: 97.7 (2005); Marriage status: 27.0% never married, 54.9% now married, 8.5% widowed, 9.6% divorced (2000); Foreign born: 6.5% (2000); Ancestry (includes multiple ancestries): 22.9% German, 21.2% Irish, 13.3% Italian, 12.9% English, 9.0% Other groups (2000).
Economy: Single-family building permits issued: 0 (2005); Multi-family building permits issued: 0 (2005); Employment by occupation: 9.3% management, 28.1% professional, 16.1% services, 27.8% sales, 0.1% farming, 11.5% construction, 7.0% production (2000).
Income: Per capita income: $23,780 (2005); Median household income: $41,964 (2005); Average household income: $54,295 (2005); Percent of households with income of $100,000 or more: 13.4% (2005); Poverty rate: 8.6% (2000).
Education: Percent of population age 25 and over with: High school diploma (including GED) or higher: 84.5% (2005); Bachelor's degree or higher: 29.0% (2005); Master's degree or higher: 14.7% (2005).
School District(s)
Red Hook Central School District (KG-12)
    2003-04 Enrollment: 2,381 . . . . (845) 758-2241
Housing: Homeownership rate: 61.9% (2005); Median home value: $207,178 (2005); Median rent: $528 per month (2000); Median age of housing: 54 years (2000).
Transportation: Commute to work: 89.1% car, 0.9% public transportation, 6.0% walk, 3.4% work from home (2000); Travel time to work: 42.2% less than 15 minutes, 29.2% 15 to 30 minutes, 16.0% 30 to 45 minutes, 6.2% 45 to 60 minutes, 6.4% 60 minutes or more (2000)
Additional Information Contacts
Red Hook Chamber of Commerce. . . . . (845) 758-0824
    http://www.redhookchamber.org

RED HOOK (town).
Covers a land area of 36.706 square miles and a water area of 3.397 square miles. Located at 42.01° N. Lat.; 73.88° W. Long. Elevation is 218 feet.
Population: 9,565 (1990); 10,408 (2000); 11,252 (2005); 12,144 (2010 projected); Race: 93.1% White, 1.6% Black, 2.8% Asian, 3.5% Hispanic of any race (2005); Density: 306.5 persons per square mile (2005); Average household size: 2.84 (2005); Median age: 36.2 (2005); Males per 100 females: 93.2 (2005); Marriage status: 33.3% never married, 53.5% now married, 5.9% widowed, 7.3% divorced (2000); Foreign born: 6.4% (2000); Ancestry (includes multiple ancestries): 22.4% German, 21.1% Irish, 16.9% Italian, 15.7% English, 10.2% Other groups (2000).
Economy: Manufacturing: paper products, soap, and soap-dispensing machines; in dairying and fruit-growing area. Single-family building permits issued: 19 (2005); Multi-family building permits issued: 0 (2005); Employment by occupation: 9.4% management, 31.3% professional, 15.3% services, 27.5% sales, 0.1% farming, 9.0% construction, 7.3% production (2000).
Income: Per capita income: $23,686 (2005); Median household income: $52,888 (2005); Average household income: $66,049 (2005); Percent of households with income of $100,000 or more: 19.7% (2005); Poverty rate: 8.7% (2000).
Education: Percent of population age 25 and over with: High school diploma (including GED) or higher: 89.1% (2005); Bachelor's degree or higher: 36.0% (2005); Master's degree or higher: 15.8% (2005).
Housing: Homeownership rate: 73.1% (2005); Median home value: $232,081 (2005); Median rent: $547 per month (2000); Median age of housing: 40 years (2000).
Transportation: Commute to work: 82.9% car, 1.5% public transportation, 9.4% walk, 5.0% work from home (2000); Travel time to work: 38.4% less than 15 minutes, 28.9% 15 to 30 minutes, 18.6% 30 to 45 minutes, 8.4% 45 to 60 minutes, 5.8% 60 minutes or more (2000)

Additional Information Contacts
Town of Red Hook . . . . (845) 758-4600
    http://www.redhook.org/

RED OAKS MILL (CDP).
Covers a land area of 3.518 square miles and a water area of 0.080 square miles. Located at 41.65° N. Lat.; 73.87° W. Long.
Population: 4,906 (1990); 4,930 (2000); 4,980 (2005); 5,078 (2010 projected); Race: 87.8% White, 5.6% Black, 3.2% Asian, 7.4% Hispanic of any race (2005); Density: 1,415.7 persons per square mile (2005); Average household size: 2.82 (2005); Median age: 40.7 (2005); Males per 100 females: 95.0 (2005); Marriage status: 19.9% never married, 70.5% now married, 4.9% widowed, 4.7% divorced (2000); Foreign born: 8.0% (2000); Ancestry (includes multiple ancestries): 26.1% Irish, 22.3% German, 22.2% Italian, 13.1% Other groups, 12.7% English (2000).
Economy: Employment by occupation: 12.8% management, 29.9% professional, 12.8% services, 23.8% sales, 0.0% farming, 10.6% construction, 10.1% production (2000).
Income: Per capita income: $34,180 (2005); Median household income: $85,598 (2005); Average household income: $96,022 (2005); Percent of households with income of $100,000 or more: 39.5% (2005); Poverty rate: 2.8% (2000).
Education: Percent of population age 25 and over with: High school diploma (including GED) or higher: 93.1% (2005); Bachelor's degree or higher: 35.3% (2005); Master's degree or higher: 17.8% (2005).
Housing: Homeownership rate: 93.7% (2005); Median home value: $250,163 (2005); Median rent: $665 per month (2000); Median age of housing: 38 years (2000).
Transportation: Commute to work: 91.6% car, 4.6% public transportation, 1.1% walk, 2.8% work from home (2000); Travel time to work: 27.3% less than 15 minutes, 39.5% 15 to 30 minutes, 12.0% 30 to 45 minutes, 6.5% 45 to 60 minutes, 14.7% 60 minutes or more (2000)

RHINEBECK (village).
Covers a land area of 1.618 square miles and a water area of 0.012 square miles. Located at 41.92° N. Lat.; 73.90° W. Long. Elevation is 200 feet.
Population: 3,038 (1990); 3,077 (2000); 3,332 (2005); 3,588 (2010 projected); Race: 93.5% White, 1.9% Black, 1.7% Asian, 5.5% Hispanic of any race (2005); Density: 2,059.8 persons per square mile (2005); Average household size: 2.19 (2005); Median age: 47.2 (2005); Males per 100 females: 82.2 (2005); Marriage status: 23.8% never married, 52.8% now married, 12.4% widowed, 11.1% divorced (2000); Foreign born: 4.1% (2000); Ancestry (includes multiple ancestries): 24.0% Irish, 17.9% German, 17.1% Italian, 14.9% English, 7.7% Other groups (2000).
Economy: Single-family building permits issued: 5 (2005); Multi-family building permits issued: 0 (2005); Employment by occupation: 17.3% management, 34.0% professional, 16.4% services, 22.8% sales, 0.0% farming, 6.8% construction, 2.7% production (2000).
Income: Per capita income: $35,306 (2005); Median household income: $48,954 (2005); Average household income: $74,590 (2005); Percent of households with income of $100,000 or more: 21.3% (2005); Poverty rate: 9.2% (2000).
Education: Percent of population age 25 and over with: High school diploma (including GED) or higher: 87.1% (2005); Bachelor's degree or higher: 40.8% (2005); Master's degree or higher: 20.6% (2005).
School District(s)
Rhinebeck Central School District (KG-12)
    2003-04 Enrollment: 1,284 . . . . (845) 871-5520
Housing: Homeownership rate: 58.2% (2005); Median home value: $255,251 (2005); Median rent: $705 per month (2000); Median age of housing: 42 years (2000).
Hospitals: Cornerstone of Rhinebeck (76 beds); Northern Dutchess Hospital (68 beds)
Safety: Violent crime rate: 3.2 per 10,000 population; Property crime rate: 92.9 per 10,000 population (2004).
Newspapers: Hyde Park Townsman (General - Circulation 2,550)
Transportation: Commute to work: 82.9% car, 4.4% public transportation, 5.5% walk, 5.5% work from home (2000); Travel time to work: 37.0% less than 15 minutes, 26.4% 15 to 30 minutes, 23.0% 30 to 45 minutes, 4.5% 45 to 60 minutes, 9.1% 60 minutes or more (2000); Amtrak: Service available.
Additional Information Contacts
Rhinebeck Chamber of Commerce . . . . (845) 876-5904
    http://www.rhinebeckchamber.com

RHINEBECK (town). Covers a land area of 36.259 square miles and a water area of 3.570 square miles. Located at 41.92° N. Lat.; 73.90° W. Long. Elevation is 200 feet.
History: It is the site of Beekman Arms, said to be the oldest hotel in the U.S., and of a pre-Revolutionary Dutch Reformed church and cemetery. Unique collection of aircraft from before and during World War I at Old Rhinebeck Aerodrome. Settled before 1700, incorporated 1834.
Population: 7,558 (1990); 7,762 (2000); 8,322 (2005); 8,854 (2010 projected); Race: 90.7% White, 4.1% Black, 2.1% Asian, 5.4% Hispanic of any race (2005); Density: 229.5 persons per square mile (2005); Average household size: 2.53 (2005); Median age: 45.6 (2005); Males per 100 females: 92.4 (2005); Marriage status: 23.1% never married, 58.6% now married, 8.8% widowed, 9.5% divorced (2000); Foreign born: 6.3% (2000); Ancestry (includes multiple ancestries): 21.2% Irish, 18.1% German, 16.1% Italian, 13.3% English, 8.7% Other groups (2000).
Economy: Tourism center. Single-family building permits issued: 14 (2005); Multi-family building permits issued: 0 (2005); Employment by occupation: 16.8% management, 33.0% professional, 13.4% services, 22.5% sales, 0.1% farming, 8.9% construction, 5.3% production (2000).
Income: Per capita income: $33,673 (2005); Median household income: $59,317 (2005); Average household income: $81,274 (2005); Percent of households with income of $100,000 or more: 24.9% (2005); Poverty rate: 9.7% (2000).
Education: Percent of population age 25 and over with: High school diploma (including GED) or higher: 86.4% (2005); Bachelor's degree or higher: 38.6% (2005); Master's degree or higher: 18.8% (2005).
Housing: Homeownership rate: 67.3% (2005); Median home value: $264,536 (2005); Median rent: $697 per month (2000); Median age of housing: 41 years (2000).
Transportation: Commute to work: 83.7% car, 3.1% public transportation, 2.8% walk, 8.7% work from home (2000); Travel time to work: 37.0% less than 15 minutes, 25.4% 15 to 30 minutes, 20.5% 30 to 45 minutes, 7.0% 45 to 60 minutes, 10.2% 60 minutes or more (2000); Amtrak: Service available.

SALT POINT (unincorporated postal area, zip code 12578). Covers a land area of 15.976 square miles and a water area of 0.028 square miles. Located at 41.80° N. Lat.; 73.78° W. Long. Elevation is 260 feet.
Population: 0 (2000); Race: 94.3% White, 2.4% Black, 0.0% Asian, 1.4% Hispanic of any race (2000); Density: 0.0 persons per square mile (2000); Age: 26.6% under 18, 8.9% over 64 (2000); Marriage status: 20.2% never married, 70.7% now married, 4.5% widowed, 4.6% divorced (2000); Foreign born: 3.0% (2000); Ancestry (includes multiple ancestries): 24.4% German, 23.6% Italian, 21.5% Irish, 11.1% English, 8.5% Other groups (2000).
Economy: Employment by occupation: 14.1% management, 33.2% professional, 9.0% services, 22.6% sales, 0.6% farming, 12.7% construction, 7.7% production (2000).
Income: Per capita income: $26,042 (2000); Median household income: $60,650 (2000); Poverty rate: 7.3% (2000).
Education: Percent of population age 25 and over with: High school diploma (including GED) or higher: 92.2% (2000); Bachelor's degree or higher: 28.5% (2000).
Housing: Homeownership rate: 82.1% (2000); Median home value: $170,500 (2000); Median rent: $627 per month (2000); Median age of housing: 32 years (2000).
Transportation: Commute to work: 91.7% car, 2.7% public transportation, 1.4% walk, 4.1% work from home (2000); Travel time to work: 12.3% less than 15 minutes, 35.2% 15 to 30 minutes, 28.3% 30 to 45 minutes, 6.3% 45 to 60 minutes, 18.0% 60 minutes or more (2000).

SPACKENKILL (CDP). Covers a land area of 2.911 square miles and a water area of 0 square miles. Located at 41.65° N. Lat.; 73.90° W. Long.
Population: 4,660 (1990); 4,756 (2000); 4,772 (2005); 4,841 (2010 projected); Race: 84.4% White, 4.4% Black, 8.1% Asian, 6.8% Hispanic of any race (2005); Density: 1,639.2 persons per square mile (2005); Average household size: 2.81 (2005); Median age: 44.3 (2005); Males per 100 females: 96.4 (2005); Marriage status: 17.3% never married, 74.8% now married, 4.2% widowed, 3.8% divorced (2000); Foreign born: 15.5% (2000); Ancestry (includes multiple ancestries): 17.9% Irish, 16.1% Other groups, 13.2% German, 13.1% Italian, 12.1% English (2000).
Economy: Employment by occupation: 16.5% management, 34.9% professional, 9.6% services, 26.5% sales, 0.3% farming, 4.3% construction, 7.7% production (2000).
Income: Per capita income: $38,825 (2005); Median household income: $89,685 (2005); Average household income: $109,058 (2005); Percent of households with income of $100,000 or more: 43.0% (2005); Poverty rate: 1.5% (2000).
Education: Percent of population age 25 and over with: High school diploma (including GED) or higher: 92.9% (2005); Bachelor's degree or higher: 49.5% (2005); Master's degree or higher: 26.5% (2005).
Housing: Homeownership rate: 94.5% (2005); Median home value: $264,011 (2005); Median rent: $1,159 per month (2000); Median age of housing: 36 years (2000).
Transportation: Commute to work: 91.0% car, 3.9% public transportation, 0.4% walk, 4.6% work from home (2000); Travel time to work: 40.7% less than 15 minutes, 33.5% 15 to 30 minutes, 8.7% 30 to 45 minutes, 6.9% 45 to 60 minutes, 10.2% 60 minutes or more (2000)

STAATSBURG (CDP). Covers a land area of 1.978 square miles and a water area of 0 square miles. Located at 41.85° N. Lat.; 73.92° W. Long. Elevation is 30 feet.
Population: 975 (1990); 911 (2000); 932 (2005); 949 (2010 projected); Race: 88.5% White, 6.0% Black, 1.7% Asian, 2.7% Hispanic of any race (2005); Density: 471.2 persons per square mile (2005); Average household size: 2.60 (2005); Median age: 41.0 (2005); Males per 100 females: 93.0 (2005); Marriage status: 21.7% never married, 65.5% now married, 8.5% widowed, 4.3% divorced (2000); Foreign born: 5.1% (2000); Ancestry (includes multiple ancestries): 24.5% English, 23.3% German, 17.8% Irish, 14.4% Italian, 8.8% Dutch (2000).
Economy: Employment by occupation: 15.3% management, 23.6% professional, 17.3% services, 23.0% sales, 0.0% farming, 11.4% construction, 9.4% production (2000).
Income: Per capita income: $28,815 (2005); Median household income: $65,064 (2005); Average household income: $74,804 (2005); Percent of households with income of $100,000 or more: 21.8% (2005); Poverty rate: 9.2% (2000).
Education: Percent of population age 25 and over with: High school diploma (including GED) or higher: 85.7% (2005); Bachelor's degree or higher: 24.1% (2005); Master's degree or higher: 15.9% (2005).
Housing: Homeownership rate: 79.9% (2005); Median home value: $178,626 (2005); Median rent: $763 per month (2000); Median age of housing: 52 years (2000).
Transportation: Commute to work: 87.9% car, 3.6% public transportation, 6.7% walk, 1.8% work from home (2000); Travel time to work: 32.2% less than 15 minutes, 36.1% 15 to 30 minutes, 14.8% 30 to 45 minutes, 9.6% 45 to 60 minutes, 7.3% 60 minutes or more (2000)

STANFORD (town). Covers a land area of 49.989 square miles and a water area of 0.287 square miles. Located at 41.88° N. Lat.; 73.70° W. Long.
Population: 3,495 (1990); 3,544 (2000); 3,788 (2005); 4,049 (2010 projected); Race: 93.7% White, 1.7% Black, 1.9% Asian, 3.7% Hispanic of any race (2005); Density: 75.8 persons per square mile (2005); Average household size: 2.48 (2005); Median age: 42.9 (2005); Males per 100 females: 101.9 (2005); Marriage status: 22.5% never married, 65.5% now married, 4.9% widowed, 7.2% divorced (2000); Foreign born: 5.0% (2000); Ancestry (includes multiple ancestries): 23.5% Irish, 22.1% German, 19.9% Italian, 14.4% English, 8.5% Other groups (2000).
Economy: Single-family building permits issued: 17 (2005); Multi-family building permits issued: 0 (2005); Employment by occupation: 13.9% management, 32.9% professional, 16.9% services, 20.4% sales, 1.0% farming, 10.1% construction, 4.9% production (2000).
Income: Per capita income: $34,210 (2005); Median household income: $60,897 (2005); Average household income: $83,750 (2005); Percent of households with income of $100,000 or more: 24.3% (2005); Poverty rate: 4.3% (2000).
Education: Percent of population age 25 and over with: High school diploma (including GED) or higher: 87.7% (2005); Bachelor's degree or higher: 31.4% (2005); Master's degree or higher: 15.9% (2005).
Housing: Homeownership rate: 72.0% (2005); Median home value: $287,500 (2005); Median rent: $621 per month (2000); Median age of housing: 34 years (2000).
Transportation: Commute to work: 82.4% car, 2.1% public transportation, 7.6% walk, 5.6% work from home (2000); Travel time to work: 24.1% less than 15 minutes, 30.8% 15 to 30 minutes, 27.1% 30 to 45 minutes, 7.7% 45 to 60 minutes, 10.3% 60 minutes or more (2000)

STANFORDVILLE (unincorporated postal area, zip code 12581). Aka Stanford. Covers a land area of 39.117 square miles and a water area of 0.126 square miles. Located at 41.89° N. Lat.; 73.69° W. Long. Elevation is 360 feet.
Population: 0 (2000); Race: 92.6% White, 1.9% Black, 0.0% Asian, 3.1% Hispanic of any race (2000); Density: 0.0 persons per square mile (2000); Age: 20.8% under 18, 13.3% over 64 (2000); Marriage status: 25.2% never married, 62.9% now married, 5.1% widowed, 6.8% divorced (2000); Foreign born: 5.5% (2000); Ancestry (includes multiple ancestries): 24.1% German, 22.4% Irish, 19.0% Italian, 13.7% English, 10.7% Other groups (2000).
Economy: Employment by occupation: 11.1% management, 27.4% professional, 20.5% services, 21.3% sales, 1.6% farming, 12.1% construction, 5.9% production (2000).
Income: Per capita income: $30,191 (2000); Median household income: $50,306 (2000); Poverty rate: 6.0% (2000).
Education: Percent of population age 25 and over with: High school diploma (including GED) or higher: 84.1% (2000); Bachelor's degree or higher: 26.1% (2000).

School District(s)
Pine Plains Central School District (KG-12)
    2003-04 Enrollment: 1,420 . . . . (518) 398-7181
Housing: Homeownership rate: 65.2% (2000); Median home value: $173,700 (2000); Median rent: $613 per month (2000); Median age of housing: 38 years (2000).
Transportation: Commute to work: 83.3% car, 1.6% public transportation, 5.9% walk, 5.5% work from home (2000); Travel time to work: 25.8% less than 15 minutes, 34.1% 15 to 30 minutes, 21.7% 30 to 45 minutes, 8.4% 45 to 60 minutes, 10.0% 60 minutes or more (2000)

STORMVILLE (unincorporated postal area, zip code 12582). Covers a land area of 16.176 square miles and a water area of 0.256 square miles. Located at 41.55° N. Lat.; 73.72° W. Long. Elevation is 317 feet.
Population: 0 (2000); Race: 95.0% White, 0.5% Black, 2.4% Asian, 0.5% Hispanic of any race (2000); Density: 0.0 persons per square mile (2000); Age: 30.8% under 18, 5.8% over 64 (2000); Marriage status: 18.7% never married, 73.8% now married, 3.4% widowed, 4.1% divorced (2000); Foreign born: 6.3% (2000); Ancestry (includes multiple ancestries): 32.2% Italian, 22.7% Irish, 20.0% German, 10.1% English, 7.6% Other groups (2000).
Economy: Employment by occupation: 16.0% management, 26.2% professional, 8.2% services, 26.1% sales, 0.4% farming, 14.1% construction, 9.0% production (2000).
Income: Per capita income: $27,596 (2000); Median household income: $79,776 (2000); Poverty rate: 3.0% (2000).
Education: Percent of population age 25 and over with: High school diploma (including GED) or higher: 93.2% (2000); Bachelor's degree or higher: 33.9% (2000).

School District(s)
Pawling Central School District (KG-12)
    2003-04 Enrollment: 1,422 . . . . (845) 855-4600
Housing: Homeownership rate: 93.0% (2000); Median home value: $199,300 (2000); Median rent: $730 per month (2000); Median age of housing: 23 years (2000).
Transportation: Commute to work: 92.6% car, 3.6% public transportation, 0.0% walk, 3.4% work from home (2000); Travel time to work: 6.4% less than 15 minutes, 35.1% 15 to 30 minutes, 23.3% 30 to 45 minutes, 16.4% 45 to 60 minutes, 18.9% 60 minutes or more (2000)

TIVOLI (village). Covers a land area of 1.756 square miles and a water area of 0.031 square miles. Located at 42.05° N. Lat.; 73.91° W. Long.
Population: 1,035 (1990); 1,163 (2000); 1,315 (2005); 1,467 (2010 projected); Race: 94.5% White, 0.5% Black, 1.5% Asian, 4.1% Hispanic of any race (2005); Density: 748.7 persons per square mile (2005); Average household size: 2.34 (2005); Median age: 35.7 (2005); Males per 100 females: 84.7 (2005); Marriage status: 38.5% never married, 45.9% now married, 5.1% widowed, 10.6% divorced (2000); Foreign born: 3.4% (2000); Ancestry (includes multiple ancestries): 24.1% Irish, 21.3% German, 20.8% Italian, 16.4% English, 7.9% Other groups (2000).
Economy: Single-family building permits issued: 2 (2005); Multi-family building permits issued: 0 (2005); Employment by occupation: 9.6% management, 30.4% professional, 15.3% services, 24.2% sales, 0.3% farming, 12.3% construction, 8.0% production (2000).

Income: Per capita income: $24,746 (2005); Median household income: $46,848 (2005); Average household income: $57,977 (2005); Percent of households with income of $100,000 or more: 15.5% (2005); Poverty rate: 17.5% (2000).
Education: Percent of population age 25 and over with: High school diploma (including GED) or higher: 90.2% (2005); Bachelor's degree or higher: 35.2% (2005); Master's degree or higher: 15.4% (2005).
Housing: Homeownership rate: 48.8% (2005); Median home value: $194,643 (2005); Median rent: $629 per month (2000); Median age of housing: 50 years (2000).
Transportation: Commute to work: 86.5% car, 3.4% public transportation, 3.7% walk, 4.5% work from home (2000); Travel time to work: 32.1% less than 15 minutes, 28.9% 15 to 30 minutes, 19.7% 30 to 45 minutes, 11.4% 45 to 60 minutes, 7.9% 60 minutes or more (2000)

UNION VALE (town). Covers a land area of 37.694 square miles and a water area of 0.125 square miles. Located at 41.69° N. Lat.; 73.69° W. Long.
Population: 3,577 (1990); 4,546 (2000); 5,237 (2005); 5,898 (2010 projected); Race: 93.0% White, 2.6% Black, 1.7% Asian, 4.9% Hispanic of any race (2005); Density: 138.9 persons per square mile (2005); Average household size: 3.36 (2005); Median age: 39.1 (2005); Males per 100 females: 98.9 (2005); Marriage status: 20.9% never married, 68.2% now married, 3.7% widowed, 7.2% divorced (2000); Foreign born: 5.8% (2000); Ancestry (includes multiple ancestries): 32.0% Italian, 31.1% Irish, 20.8% German, 9.0% English, 5.2% Polish (2000).
Economy: Single-family building permits issued: 18 (2005); Multi-family building permits issued: 0 (2005); Employment by occupation: 15.9% management, 27.5% professional, 12.7% services, 22.4% sales, 0.6% farming, 11.5% construction, 9.4% production (2000).
Income: Per capita income: $28,796 (2005); Median household income: $81,402 (2005); Average household income: $96,714 (2005); Percent of households with income of $100,000 or more: 36.3% (2005); Poverty rate: 2.9% (2000).
Education: Percent of population age 25 and over with: High school diploma (including GED) or higher: 83.1% (2005); Bachelor's degree or higher: 29.7% (2005); Master's degree or higher: 13.2% (2005).
Housing: Homeownership rate: 87.9% (2005); Median home value: $300,639 (2005); Median rent: $692 per month (2000); Median age of housing: 24 years (2000).
Transportation: Commute to work: 92.9% car, 0.7% public transportation, 0.6% walk, 5.4% work from home (2000); Travel time to work: 16.8% less than 15 minutes, 36.2% 15 to 30 minutes, 20.7% 30 to 45 minutes, 10.1% 45 to 60 minutes, 16.2% 60 minutes or more (2000)
Additional Information Contacts
Town of Union Vale . . . . (845) 724-5600
    http://www2.marist.edu/unionvale/

VERBANK (unincorporated postal area, zip code 12585). Covers a land area of 5.993 square miles and a water area of 0.065 square miles. Located at 41.72° N. Lat.; 73.71° W. Long.
Population: 0 (2000); Race: 92.0% White, 3.9% Black, 4.0% Asian, 1.9% Hispanic of any race (2000); Density: 0.0 persons per square mile (2000); Age: 28.6% under 18, 13.9% over 64 (2000); Marriage status: 18.7% never married, 61.3% now married, 4.1% widowed, 15.9% divorced (2000); Foreign born: 5.8% (2000); Ancestry (includes multiple ancestries): 39.8% Irish, 30.8% Italian, 18.4% German, 8.8% English, 5.0% Other groups (2000).
Economy: Employment by occupation: 12.0% management, 48.4% professional, 14.8% services, 10.7% sales, 0.0% farming, 6.0% construction, 8.2% production (2000).
Income: Per capita income: $25,022 (2000); Median household income: $50,673 (2000); Poverty rate: 0.0% (2000).
Education: Percent of population age 25 and over with: High school diploma (including GED) or higher: 86.3% (2000); Bachelor's degree or higher: 30.8% (2000).
Housing: Homeownership rate: 79.5% (2000); Median home value: $165,200 (2000); Median rent: $673 per month (2000); Median age of housing: 38 years (2000).
Transportation: Commute to work: 90.6% car, 0.0% public transportation, 0.0% walk, 8.0% work from home (2000); Travel time to work: 23.3% less than 15 minutes, 34.5% 15 to 30 minutes, 26.1% 30 to 45 minutes, 8.4% 45 to 60 minutes, 7.8% 60 minutes or more (2000)

WAPPINGER (town). Covers a land area of 27.275 square miles and a water area of 1.319 square miles. Located at 41.58° N. Lat.; 73.90° W. Long.
History: Society of the Cincinnati founded here in 1783. Incorporated 1871.
Population: 26,008 (1990); 26,274 (2000); 26,837 (2005); 27,553 (2010 projected); Race: 82.9% White, 5.6% Black, 5.8% Asian, 10.7% Hispanic of any race (2005); Density: 983.9 persons per square mile (2005); Average household size: 2.66 (2005); Median age: 37.6 (2005); Males per 100 females: 98.3 (2005); Marriage status: 25.3% never married, 61.9% now married, 5.1% widowed, 7.8% divorced (2000); Foreign born: 10.4% (2000); Ancestry (includes multiple ancestries): 28.5% Italian, 24.5% Irish, 18.3% Other groups, 16.5% German, 7.8% English (2000).
Economy: Manufacturing includes lighting equipment, commercial woodworking, cabinets. Unemployment rate: 4.1% (2005); Total civilian labor force: 14,937 (2005); Single-family building permits issued: 37 (2005); Multi-family building permits issued: 0 (2005); Employment by occupation: 11.7% management, 27.4% professional, 15.4% services, 24.2% sales, 0.2% farming, 10.6% construction, 10.4% production (2000).
Income: Per capita income: $29,443 (2005); Median household income: $65,680 (2005); Average household income: $77,933 (2005); Percent of households with income of $100,000 or more: 26.2% (2005); Poverty rate: 4.1% (2000).
Taxes: Total city taxes per capita: $276 (2004); City property taxes per capita: $216 (2004).
Education: Percent of population age 25 and over with: High school diploma (including GED) or higher: 88.6% (2005); Bachelor's degree or higher: 29.2% (2005); Master's degree or higher: 10.9% (2005).
Housing: Homeownership rate: 66.5% (2005); Median home value: $240,449 (2005); Median rent: $724 per month (2000); Median age of housing: 32 years (2000).
Transportation: Commute to work: 91.5% car, 4.9% public transportation, 0.9% walk, 1.9% work from home (2000); Travel time to work: 23.9% less than 15 minutes, 36.0% 15 to 30 minutes, 13.4% 30 to 45 minutes, 10.0% 45 to 60 minutes, 16.6% 60 minutes or more (2000)

WAPPINGERS FALLS (village). Covers a land area of 1.141 square miles and a water area of 0.065 square miles. Located at 41.59° N. Lat.; 73.91° W. Long. Elevation is 150 feet.
Population: 4,605 (1990); 4,929 (2000); 5,011 (2005); 5,138 (2010 projected); Race: 77.5% White, 7.2% Black, 3.5% Asian, 21.4% Hispanic of any race (2005); Density: 4,393.2 persons per square mile (2005); Average household size: 2.50 (2005); Median age: 34.7 (2005); Males per 100 females: 93.5 (2005); Marriage status: 33.3% never married, 47.6% now married, 8.9% widowed, 10.2% divorced (2000); Foreign born: 16.7% (2000); Ancestry (includes multiple ancestries): 27.2% Italian, 24.6% Other groups, 20.4% Irish, 14.9% German, 5.6% English (2000).
Economy: Single-family building permits issued: 1 (2005); Multi-family building permits issued: 48 (2005); Employment by occupation: 7.6% management, 22.4% professional, 24.0% services, 26.8% sales, 0.2% farming, 9.3% construction, 9.7% production (2000).
Income: Per capita income: $20,869 (2005); Median household income: $41,839 (2005); Average household income: $51,750 (2005); Percent of households with income of $100,000 or more: 11.3% (2005); Poverty rate: 12.3% (2000).
Education: Percent of population age 25 and over with: High school diploma (including GED) or higher: 79.8% (2005); Bachelor's degree or higher: 19.3% (2005); Master's degree or higher: 6.3% (2005).

School District(s)
Wappingers Central School District (KG-12)
    2003-04 Enrollment: 12,146 . . . . (845) 298-5000

Housing: Homeownership rate: 39.7% (2005); Median home value: $190,143 (2005); Median rent: $636 per month (2000); Median age of housing: 48 years (2000).
Safety: Violent crime rate: 42.0 per 10,000 population; Property crime rate: 277.9 per 10,000 population (2004).
Newspapers: Beacon Free Press (General - Circulation 8,300); Southern Dutchess News (General - Circulation 12,000)
Transportation: Commute to work: 91.0% car, 3.7% public transportation, 2.8% walk, 0.5% work from home (2000); Travel time to work: 34.6% less than 15 minutes, 31.1% 15 to 30 minutes, 14.1% 30 to 45 minutes, 9.4% 45 to 60 minutes, 10.9% 60 minutes or more (2000)

WASHINGTON (town). Covers a land area of 59.072 square miles and a water area of 0.293 square miles. Located at 41.78° N. Lat.; 73.68° W. Long.
Population: 4,479 (1990); 4,742 (2000); 5,037 (2005); 5,350 (2010 projected); Race: 94.0% White, 2.8% Black, 1.1% Asian, 5.1% Hispanic of any race (2005); Density: 85.3 persons per square mile (2005); Average household size: 2.43 (2005); Median age: 42.3 (2005); Males per 100 females: 93.6 (2005); Marriage status: 23.1% never married, 60.7% now married, 7.1% widowed, 9.2% divorced (2000); Foreign born: 6.7% (2000); Ancestry (includes multiple ancestries): 26.0% Irish, 24.9% Italian, 16.8% German, 15.9% English, 7.7% Other groups (2000).
Economy: Single-family building permits issued: 14 (2005); Multi-family building permits issued: 0 (2005); Employment by occupation: 14.0% management, 23.8% professional, 14.6% services, 27.4% sales, 2.9% farming, 12.9% construction, 4.4% production (2000).
Income: Per capita income: $31,965 (2005); Median household income: $54,428 (2005); Average household income: $76,998 (2005); Percent of households with income of $100,000 or more: 21.2% (2005); Poverty rate: 7.2% (2000).
Education: Percent of population age 25 and over with: High school diploma (including GED) or higher: 91.2% (2005); Bachelor's degree or higher: 34.2% (2005); Master's degree or higher: 13.3% (2005).
Housing: Homeownership rate: 62.8% (2005); Median home value: $315,000 (2005); Median rent: $621 per month (2000); Median age of housing: 46 years (2000).
Transportation: Commute to work: 81.9% car, 3.3% public transportation, 6.8% walk, 6.9% work from home (2000); Travel time to work: 33.4% less than 15 minutes, 26.3% 15 to 30 minutes, 25.0% 30 to 45 minutes, 5.0% 45 to 60 minutes, 10.3% 60 minutes or more (2000)

WASSAIC (unincorporated postal area, zip code 12592). Covers a land area of 14.364 square miles and a water area of 0.181 square miles. Located at 41.78° N. Lat.; 73.55° W. Long.
Population: 0 (2000); Race: 89.9% White, 3.8% Black, 0.0% Asian, 4.6% Hispanic of any race (2000); Density: 0.0 persons per square mile (2000); Age: 24.0% under 18, 14.7% over 64 (2000); Marriage status: 31.0% never married, 48.8% now married, 8.1% widowed, 12.0% divorced (2000); Foreign born: 2.2% (2000); Ancestry (includes multiple ancestries): 28.0% Irish, 14.5% German, 10.6% Other groups, 10.0% United States or American, 8.9% Italian (2000).
Economy: Employment by occupation: 3.4% management, 16.7% professional, 26.6% services, 23.9% sales, 0.0% farming, 9.5% construction, 19.9% production (2000).
Income: Per capita income: $17,925 (2000); Median household income: $32,426 (2000); Poverty rate: 7.0% (2000).
Education: Percent of population age 25 and over with: High school diploma (including GED) or higher: 67.9% (2000); Bachelor's degree or higher: 11.2% (2000).

School District(s)
Northeast Central School District (KG-12)
    2003-04 Enrollment: 890 . . . . (845) 373-4100

Housing: Homeownership rate: 69.4% (2000); Median home value: $115,900 (2000); Median rent: $463 per month (2000); Median age of housing: 38 years (2000).
Transportation: Commute to work: 93.9% car, 3.6% public transportation, 0.0% walk, 2.5% work from home (2000); Travel time to work: 38.1% less than 15 minutes, 24.7% 15 to 30 minutes, 17.9% 30 to 45 minutes, 5.9% 45 to 60 minutes, 13.4% 60 minutes or more (2000)

WINGDALE (unincorporated postal area, zip code 12594). Covers a land area of 14.777 square miles and a water area of 0.096 square miles. Located at 41.64° N. Lat.; 73.56° W. Long.
Population: 0 (2000); Race: 84.1% White, 8.2% Black, 0.0% Asian, 7.6% Hispanic of any race (2000); Density: 0.0 persons per square mile (2000); Age: 29.8% under 18, 8.9% over 64 (2000); Marriage status: 22.3% never married, 61.2% now married, 6.4% widowed, 10.1% divorced (2000); Foreign born: 8.1% (2000); Ancestry (includes multiple ancestries): 25.9% Irish, 16.8% Italian, 15.3% German, 10.4% Other groups, 8.4% United States or American (2000).
Economy: Magnesium plant. Employment by occupation: 11.7% management, 14.5% professional, 21.5% services, 21.8% sales, 0.0% farming, 15.6% construction, 14.8% production (2000).
Income: Per capita income: $19,496 (2000); Median household income: $52,338 (2000); Poverty rate: 5.6% (2000).

Education: Percent of population age 25 and over with: High school diploma (including GED) or higher: 81.2% (2000); Bachelor's degree or higher: 15.6% (2000).

School District(s)
Dover Union Free School District (KG-12)
   2003-04 Enrollment: 1,757 . . . . (845) 832-4500

Housing: Homeownership rate: 76.6% (2000); Median home value: $154,100 (2000); Median rent: $556 per month (2000); Median age of housing: 24 years (2000).

Transportation: Commute to work: 93.6% car, 4.8% public transportation, 0.0% walk, 1.6% work from home (2000); Travel time to work: 23.3% less than 15 minutes, 25.3% 15 to 30 minutes, 17.5% 30 to 45 minutes, 11.4% 45 to 60 minutes, 22.4% 60 minutes or more (2000)

Erie County

Located in western New York; bounded on the west by Lake Erie; drained by the Cattaraugus and Tonawanda Creeks. Covers a land area of 1,044.21 square miles, a water area of 182.68 square miles, and is located in the Eastern Time Zone. The county government was organized in 1821. County seat is Buffalo.

Erie County is part of the Buffalo-Niagara Falls, NY Metropolitan Statistical Area. The entire metro area includes: Erie County, NY; Niagara County, NY

Weather Station: Buffalo Int'l Airport   Elevation: 702 feet

	Jan	Feb	Mar	Apr	May	Jun	Jul	Aug	Sep	Oct	Nov	Dec
High	31	33	42	54	67	75	80	78	71	59	47	36
Low	18	18	26	36	48	57	62	61	53	43	34	24
Precip	3.1	2.4	3.0	3.0	3.3	3.7	3.2	3.8	3.9	3.3	3.8	3.8
Snow	26.7	18.0	12.5	3.5	0.3	tr	tr	tr	tr	0.3	9.6	24.8

High and Low temperatures in degrees Fahrenheit; Precipitation and Snow in inches

Weather Station: Colden 1 N   Elevation: 1,023 feet

	Jan	Feb	Mar	Apr	May	Jun	Jul	Aug	Sep	Oct	Nov	Dec
High	30	32	41	54	67	75	79	77	70	59	46	35
Low	13	13	21	32	42	51	56	55	48	38	30	21
Precip	3.7	2.8	3.6	3.7	3.6	4.2	4.1	4.2	4.9	4.0	4.8	4.5
Snow	47.2	28.6	18.7	6.3	0.3	0.0	0.0	0.0	0.0	0.7	17.8	37.9

High and Low temperatures in degrees Fahrenheit; Precipitation and Snow in inches

Population: 968,532 (1990); 950,265 (2000); 938,438 (2005); 925,932 (2010 projected); Race: 80.5% White, 13.9% Black, 1.9% Asian, 3.9% Hispanic of any race (2005); Density: 898.7 persons per square mile (2005); Average household size: 2.47 (2005); Median age: 39.3 (2005); Males per 100 females: 92.3 (2005).

Religion: Five largest groups: 57.3% Catholic Church, 2.1% Jewish Estimate, 2.0% Evangelical Lutheran Church in America, 2.0% The United Methodist Church, 1.5% The Wesleyan Church (2000).

Economy: Unemployment rate: 5.3% (2005); Total civilian labor force: 474,620 (2005); Leading industries: 16.9% health care and social assistance; 13.4% manufacturing; 13.1% retail trade (2003); Farms: 1,289 totaling 161,747 acres (2002); Companies that employ 500 or more persons: 73 (2003); Companies that employ 100 to 499 persons: 603 (2003); Companies that employ less than 100 persons: 22,008 (2003); Black-owned businesses: 2,305 (2002); Hispanic-owned businesses: 784 (2002); Women-owned businesses: 15,569 (2002); Retail sales per capita: $13,048 (2006). Single-family building permits issued: 1,304 (2005); Multi-family building permits issued: 319 (2005).

Income: Per capita income: $23,427 (2005); Median household income: $43,767 (2005); Average household income: $57,163 (2005); Percent of households with income of $100,000 or more: 13.7% (2005); Poverty rate: 13.0% (2003); Bankruptcy rate: 9.12% (2005).

Taxes: Total county taxes per capita: $593 (2004); County property taxes per capita: $161 (2004).

Education: Percent of population age 25 and over with: High school diploma (including GED) or higher: 83.1% (2005); Bachelor's degree or higher: 24.9% (2005); Master's degree or higher: 10.3% (2005).

Housing: Homeownership rate: 65.9% (2005); Median home value: $115,121 (2005); Median rent: $411 per month (2000); Median age of housing: 47 years (2000).

Health: Birth rate: 114.9 per 10,000 population (2004); Death rate: 105.4 per 10,000 population (2004); Age-adjusted cancer mortality rate: 219.2 deaths per 100,000 population (2002); Air Quality Index: 66.8% good, 30.1% moderate, 3.0% unhealthy for sensitive individuals, 0.0% unhealthy (percent of days in 2005); Number of physicians: 37.7 per 10,000 population (2004); Hospital beds: 55.4 per 10,000 population (2003); Hospital admissions: 1,588.3 per 10,000 population (2003).

Elections: 2004 Presidential election results: 41.4% Bush, 56.4% Kerry, 1.9% Nader, 0.2% Badnarik.

National and State Parks: Beaver Island State Park; Buckhorn Island State Park; Evangola State Park

Additional Information Contacts

Erie County Government . . . . (716) 858-7500
   http://www.erie.gov/
City of Buffalo. . . . . (716) 851-4200
   http://www.ci.buffalo.ny.us/
City of Lackawanna . . . . (716) 827-6452
   http://www.ci.lackawanna.ny.us/
City of Tonawanda . . . . (716) 695-1800
   http://www.ci.tonawanda.ny.us/
Town of Amherst . . . . (716) 631-7000
   http://www.amherst.ny.us/
Town of Cheektowaga . . . . (716) 686-3434
   http://tocny.org/
Town of Eden . . . . (716) 992-3408
   http://www.edenny.org/
Town of Evans . . . . (716) 549-5754
   http://www.townofevans.org/
Town of Grand Island. . . . . (716) 773-9600
   http://www.grand-island.ny.us/
Town of Hamburg . . . . (716) 649-6111
   http://www.townofhamburgny.com/
Town of Orchard Park . . . . (716) 662-6400
   http://www.orchardparkny.org/
Town of Tonawanda . . . . (716) 877-8800
   http://www.tonawanda.ny.us/
Town of West Seneca . . . . (716) 674-5600
   http://www.westseneca.net/
Village of Akron . . . . (716) 542-9636
   http://www.erie.gov/AKRON/
Village of Depew . . . . (716) 683-1400
   http://www.villageofdepew.org/
Village of East Aurora . . . . (716) 652-3280
   http://www.east-aurora.ny.us/
Village of Hamburg . . . . (716) 649-0200
   http://www.villagehamburg.com/
Village of Kenmore. . . . . (716) 873-5700
   http://www.vi.kenmore.ny.us/
Village of Lancaster . . . . (716) 683-2105
   http://www.lancastervillage.org/framework.php?module=home
Village of Williamsville . . . . (716) 632-4120
   http://village.williamsville.ny.us/

Erie County Communities

AKRON (village). Covers a land area of 1.963 square miles and a water area of 0 square miles. Located at 43.01° N. Lat.; 78.49° W. Long. Elevation is 679 feet.

History: Nearby is Tonawanda Indian Reservation. Incorporated 1849.

Population: 2,942 (1990); 3,085 (2000); 2,990 (2005); 2,893 (2010 projected); Race: 97.3% White, 0.6% Black, 0.0% Asian, 0.9% Hispanic of any race (2005); Density: 1,522.9 persons per square mile (2005); Average household size: 2.31 (2005); Median age: 40.1 (2005); Males per 100 females: 88.6 (2005); Marriage status: 23.4% never married, 54.4% now married, 10.2% widowed, 12.0% divorced (2000); Foreign born: 0.8% (2000); Ancestry (includes multiple ancestries): 39.5% German, 21.6% Irish, 19.2% English, 17.0% Polish, 10.1% Italian (2000).

Economy: Shipping center for dairying and farming region. Manufactures metal fabricated and wood products, transportation equipment, food, computer parts. Agriculture: wheat, hay, potatoes, cabbage, mushrooms. Single-family building permits issued: 1 (2005); Multi-family building permits issued: 0 (2005); Employment by occupation: 7.3% management, 13.6% professional, 20.9% services, 30.0% sales, 0.4% farming, 10.7% construction, 17.0% production (2000).

Income: Per capita income: $20,178 (2005); Median household income: $39,718 (2005); Average household income: $46,330 (2005); Percent of households with income of $100,000 or more: 5.1% (2005); Poverty rate: 8.2% (2000).

Education: Percent of population age 25 and over with: High school diploma (including GED) or higher: 83.3% (2005); Bachelor's degree or higher: 17.2% (2005); Master's degree or higher: 8.0% (2005).

School District(s)
Akron Central School District (PK-12)
    2003-04 Enrollment: 1,699 . . . . (716) 542-5101

Housing: Homeownership rate: 63.3% (2005); Median home value: $119,318 (2005); Median rent: $372 per month (2000); Median age of housing: 51 years (2000).
Safety: Violent crime rate: 29.5 per 10,000 population; Property crime rate: 95.0 per 10,000 population (2004).
Newspapers: Akron Bugle (General - Circulation 1,800)
Transportation: Commute to work: 96.1% car, 0.6% public transportation, 1.6% walk, 1.7% work from home (2000); Travel time to work: 37.9% less than 15 minutes, 30.2% 15 to 30 minutes, 18.0% 30 to 45 minutes, 8.5% 45 to 60 minutes, 5.4% 60 minutes or more (2000)

Additional Information Contacts
Akron Chamber of Commerce . . . . (716) 542-9636
    http://www.erie.gov/akron
Village of Akron . . . . (716) 542-9636
    http://www.erie.gov/AKRON/

ALDEN (village). Covers a land area of 2.720 square miles and a water area of 0 square miles. Located at 42.90° N. Lat.; 78.49° W. Long. Elevation is 866 feet.
Population: 2,457 (1990); 2,666 (2000); 2,689 (2005); 2,715 (2010 projected); Race: 98.2% White, 0.4% Black, 0.9% Asian, 0.1% Hispanic of any race (2005); Density: 988.6 persons per square mile (2005); Average household size: 2.41 (2005); Median age: 38.7 (2005); Males per 100 females: 99.0 (2005); Marriage status: 25.4% never married, 55.8% now married, 7.4% widowed, 11.5% divorced (2000); Foreign born: 3.0% (2000); Ancestry (includes multiple ancestries): 41.7% German, 26.0% Polish, 17.0% Irish, 14.1% Italian, 10.7% English (2000).
Economy: Single-family building permits issued: 3 (2005); Multi-family building permits issued: 0 (2005); Employment by occupation: 9.7% management, 15.2% professional, 16.8% services, 31.3% sales, 0.7% farming, 8.5% construction, 17.8% production (2000).
Income: Per capita income: $25,456 (2005); Median household income: $48,578 (2005); Average household income: $61,196 (2005); Percent of households with income of $100,000 or more: 10.3% (2005); Poverty rate: 7.6% (2000).
Education: Percent of population age 25 and over with: High school diploma (including GED) or higher: 85.4% (2005); Bachelor's degree or higher: 16.4% (2005); Master's degree or higher: 7.1% (2005).

School District(s)
Alden Central School District (PK-12)
    2003-04 Enrollment: 2,072 . . . . (716) 937-9116

Housing: Homeownership rate: 70.3% (2005); Median home value: $112,713 (2005); Median rent: $438 per month (2000); Median age of housing: 39 years (2000).
Transportation: Commute to work: 92.9% car, 0.0% public transportation, 5.6% walk, 1.1% work from home (2000); Travel time to work: 28.1% less than 15 minutes, 34.8% 15 to 30 minutes, 22.4% 30 to 45 minutes, 10.2% 45 to 60 minutes, 4.5% 60 minutes or more (2000)

Additional Information Contacts
Alden Chamber of Commerce . . . . (716) 937-6177
    http://www.aldenny.org

ALDEN (town). Covers a land area of 34.456 square miles and a water area of 0.059 square miles. Located at 42.90° N. Lat.; 78.51° W. Long. Elevation is 866 feet.
History: Incorporated 1869.
Population: 10,372 (1990); 10,470 (2000); 10,881 (2005); 11,235 (2010 projected); Race: 89.3% White, 7.6% Black, 0.3% Asian, 3.8% Hispanic of any race (2005); Density: 315.8 persons per square mile (2005); Average household size: 3.18 (2005); Median age: 41.4 (2005); Males per 100 females: 120.2 (2005); Marriage status: 25.3% never married, 61.8% now married, 6.8% widowed, 6.2% divorced (2000); Foreign born: 2.8% (2000); Ancestry (includes multiple ancestries): 37.9% German, 24.6% Polish, 13.9% Irish, 10.3% Italian, 7.2% English (2000).
Economy: Manufactures machinery, fabricated metal products, electronic goods. Agricultural region. Single-family building permits issued: 11 (2005); Multi-family building permits issued: 0 (2005); Employment by occupation: 12.1% management, 14.6% professional, 14.1% services, 28.7% sales, 0.5% farming, 11.4% construction, 18.5% production (2000).
Income: Per capita income: $21,889 (2005); Median household income: $55,207 (2005); Average household income: $64,455 (2005); Percent of households with income of $100,000 or more: 14.3% (2005); Poverty rate: 5.9% (2000).
Education: Percent of population age 25 and over with: High school diploma (including GED) or higher: 71.6% (2005); Bachelor's degree or higher: 13.0% (2005); Master's degree or higher: 5.1% (2005).
Housing: Homeownership rate: 83.1% (2005); Median home value: $131,072 (2005); Median rent: $438 per month (2000); Median age of housing: 39 years (2000).
Transportation: Commute to work: 91.6% car, 0.5% public transportation, 2.6% walk, 4.7% work from home (2000); Travel time to work: 25.3% less than 15 minutes, 36.1% 15 to 30 minutes, 26.9% 30 to 45 minutes, 6.7% 45 to 60 minutes, 5.0% 60 minutes or more (2000)

AMHERST (town). Covers a land area of 53.247 square miles and a water area of 0.274 square miles. Located at 42.99° N. Lat.; 78.76° W. Long. Elevation is 600 feet.
Population: 111,711 (1990); 116,510 (2000); 118,014 (2005); 119,112 (2010 projected); Race: 87.0% White, 4.7% Black, 6.6% Asian, 1.6% Hispanic of any race (2005); Density: 2,216.3 persons per square mile (2005); Average household size: 2.56 (2005); Median age: 40.7 (2005); Males per 100 females: 89.8 (2005); Marriage status: 23.6% never married, 62.1% now married, 7.7% widowed, 6.6% divorced (2000); Foreign born: 9.0% (2000); Ancestry (includes multiple ancestries): 25.6% German, 17.8% Italian, 16.5% Irish, 13.0% Polish, 10.9% Other groups (2000).
Economy: Manufacturing: environmental pollution controls, sheet metal, plastic molding, industrial rubber supplies. Unemployment rate: 4.1% (2005); Total civilian labor force: 61,038 (2005); Single-family building permits issued: 229 (2005); Multi-family building permits issued: 234 (2005); Employment by occupation: 19.2% management, 32.9% professional, 10.7% services, 26.7% sales, 0.0% farming, 3.9% construction, 6.6% production (2000).
Income: Per capita income: $31,726 (2005); Median household income: $62,294 (2005); Average household income: $80,299 (2005); Percent of households with income of $100,000 or more: 25.7% (2005); Poverty rate: 6.4% (2000).
Taxes: Total city taxes per capita: $573 (2004); City property taxes per capita: $520 (2004).
Education: Percent of population age 25 and over with: High school diploma (including GED) or higher: 91.9% (2005); Bachelor's degree or higher: 47.5% (2005); Master's degree or higher: 22.7% (2005).

School District(s)
Amherst Central School District (KG-12)
    2003-04 Enrollment: 3,125 . . . . (716) 362-3051
Sweet Home Central School District (KG-12)
    2003-04 Enrollment: 3,867 . . . . (716) 250-1402

Four-year College(s)
Bryant and Stratton College-Amherst Campus
    Fall 2004 Enrollment: 299 . . . . (716) 691-0012
    2005-06 Tuition: In-state $11,820; Out-of-state $11,820
Daemen College
    Fall 2004 Enrollment: 2,186 . . . . (716) 839-3600
    2005-06 Tuition: In-state $16,800; Out-of-state $16,800

Housing: Homeownership rate: 74.3% (2005); Median home value: $142,166 (2005); Median rent: $598 per month (2000); Median age of housing: 33 years (2000).
Safety: Violent crime rate: 9.9 per 10,000 population; Property crime rate: 160.1 per 10,000 population (2004).
Transportation: Commute to work: 92.6% car, 1.2% public transportation, 2.2% walk, 3.5% work from home (2000); Travel time to work: 32.2% less than 15 minutes, 48.0% 15 to 30 minutes, 16.0% 30 to 45 minutes, 1.7% 45 to 60 minutes, 2.0% 60 minutes or more (2000)

Additional Information Contacts
Town of Amherst . . . . (716) 631-7000
    http://www.amherst.ny.us/

ANGOLA (village). Covers a land area of 1.426 square miles and a water area of 0 square miles. Located at 42.63° N. Lat.; 79.03° W. Long. Elevation is 689 feet.
History: Incorporated 1873.
Population: 2,231 (1990); 2,266 (2000); 2,203 (2005); 2,136 (2010 projected); Race: 95.8% White, 0.7% Black, 0.5% Asian, 1.8% Hispanic of any race (2005); Density: 1,545.3 persons per square mile (2005); Average household size: 2.67 (2005); Median age: 36.6 (2005); Males per 100

females: 93.6 (2005); Marriage status: 24.6% never married, 57.8% now married, 8.0% widowed, 9.7% divorced (2000); Foreign born: 2.3% (2000); Ancestry (includes multiple ancestries): 31.6% German, 25.4% Italian, 19.9% Irish, 13.0% Polish, 6.1% English (2000).
Economy: Summer resort. Manufacturing: water treatment and filtration equipment. Employment by occupation: 8.4% management, 20.9% professional, 20.9% services, 22.8% sales, 0.8% farming, 10.0% construction, 16.1% production (2000).
Income: Per capita income: $20,414 (2005); Median household income: $47,080 (2005); Average household income: $54,578 (2005); Percent of households with income of $100,000 or more: 12.1% (2005); Poverty rate: 11.2% (2000).
Education: Percent of population age 25 and over with: High school diploma (including GED) or higher: 85.8% (2005); Bachelor's degree or higher: 19.3% (2005); Master's degree or higher: 8.2% (2005).

School District(s)
Boces Erie 2-Chautauqua-Cattaraugus (UG-UG)
  2003-04 Enrollment: 602 . . . . (716) 549-4454
Evans-Brant Central School District (Lake Shore) (KG-12)
  2003-04 Enrollment: 3,230 . . . . (716) 926-2201

Two-year College(s)
Erie 2 Chautauqua Cattaraugus BOCES-Practical Nursing Program (Public)
  Fall 2004 Enrollment: 185 . . . . (716) 549-4454

Housing: Homeownership rate: 71.5% (2005); Median home value: $110,336 (2005); Median rent: $382 per month (2000); Median age of housing: 58 years (2000).
Safety: Violent crime rate: 31.4 per 10,000 population; Property crime rate: 237.6 per 10,000 population (2004).
Transportation: Commute to work: 97.7% car, 0.8% public transportation, 0.8% walk, 0.3% work from home (2000); Travel time to work: 39.8% less than 15 minutes, 22.0% 15 to 30 minutes, 24.2% 30 to 45 minutes, 11.4% 45 to 60 minutes, 2.6% 60 minutes or more (2000).

ANGOLA ON THE LAKE (CDP). Covers a land area of 2.525 square miles and a water area of 0 square miles. Located at 42.65° N. Lat.; 79.04° W. Long.
Population: 1,719 (1990); 1,771 (2000); 1,795 (2005); 1,746 (2010 projected); Race: 98.8% White, 0.4% Black, 0.0% Asian, 1.0% Hispanic of any race (2005); Density: 711.0 persons per square mile (2005); Average household size: 2.30 (2005); Median age: 41.8 (2005); Males per 100 females: 92.8 (2005); Marriage status: 29.6% never married, 50.6% now married, 9.5% widowed, 10.4% divorced (2000); Foreign born: 3.8% (2000); Ancestry (includes multiple ancestries): 30.1% German, 21.3% Italian, 18.2% Polish, 16.6% Irish, 12.8% English (2000).
Economy: Employment by occupation: 10.4% management, 17.0% professional, 17.6% services, 23.6% sales, 0.0% farming, 4.3% construction, 27.0% production (2000).
Income: Per capita income: $21,075 (2005); Median household income: $33,245 (2005); Average household income: $48,438 (2005); Percent of households with income of $100,000 or more: 9.6% (2005); Poverty rate: 13.0% (2000).
Education: Percent of population age 25 and over with: High school diploma (including GED) or higher: 74.6% (2005); Bachelor's degree or higher: 11.7% (2005); Master's degree or higher: 4.7% (2005).
Housing: Homeownership rate: 78.4% (2005); Median home value: $99,535 (2005); Median rent: $391 per month (2000); Median age of housing: 47 years (2000).
Transportation: Commute to work: 99.1% car, 0.9% public transportation, 0.0% walk, 0.0% work from home (2000); Travel time to work: 26.2% less than 15 minutes, 32.8% 15 to 30 minutes, 23.8% 30 to 45 minutes, 12.6% 45 to 60 minutes, 4.5% 60 minutes or more (2000).

AURORA (town). Covers a land area of 36.393 square miles and a water area of 0 square miles. Located at 42.75° N. Lat.; 78.62° W. Long.
History: Seat of Christ the King Seminary. Site (1895-1939) of the Roycroft Shops, founded by Elbert Hubbard. Restored home of Millard and Abigail Fillmore as a National Historic Landmark. Incorporated 1874.
Population: 13,433 (1990); 13,996 (2000); 13,882 (2005); 13,759 (2010 projected); Race: 98.5% White, 0.2% Black, 0.5% Asian, 0.7% Hispanic of any race (2005); Density: 381.4 persons per square mile (2005); Average household size: 2.54 (2005); Median age: 42.5 (2005); Males per 100 females: 94.2 (2005); Marriage status: 20.7% never married, 64.3% now married, 8.0% widowed, 7.0% divorced (2000); Foreign born: 2.5% (2000);

Ancestry (includes multiple ancestries): 39.3% German, 21.2% Irish, 18.1% English, 15.1% Polish, 11.4% Italian (2000).
Economy: Manufacturing: industrial equipment, electrical and electronic equipment, consumer goods, metal fabrication. Single-family building permits issued: 33 (2005); Multi-family building permits issued: 0 (2005); Employment by occupation: 15.1% management, 30.2% professional, 10.7% services, 23.5% sales, 0.3% farming, 9.5% construction, 10.7% production (2000).
Income: Per capita income: $29,243 (2005); Median household income: $61,625 (2005); Average household income: $73,386 (2005); Percent of households with income of $100,000 or more: 22.9% (2005); Poverty rate: 3.6% (2000).
Taxes: Total city taxes per capita: $243 (2004); City property taxes per capita: $203 (2004).
Education: Percent of population age 25 and over with: High school diploma (including GED) or higher: 90.7% (2005); Bachelor's degree or higher: 36.5% (2005); Master's degree or higher: 13.9% (2005).
Housing: Homeownership rate: 79.5% (2005); Median home value: $148,648 (2005); Median rent: $456 per month (2000); Median age of housing: 48 years (2000).
Safety: Violent crime rate: 4.3 per 10,000 population; Property crime rate: 129.9 per 10,000 population (2004).
Transportation: Commute to work: 91.6% car, 0.6% public transportation, 4.2% walk, 2.8% work from home (2000); Travel time to work: 32.0% less than 15 minutes, 29.3% 15 to 30 minutes, 29.0% 30 to 45 minutes, 6.6% 45 to 60 minutes, 3.1% 60 minutes or more (2000).

BILLINGTON HEIGHTS (CDP). Covers a land area of 3.127 square miles and a water area of 0 square miles. Located at 42.78° N. Lat.; 78.61° W. Long.
Population: 1,729 (1990); 1,691 (2000); 1,816 (2005); 1,925 (2010 projected); Race: 98.1% White, 0.6% Black, 0.8% Asian, 1.0% Hispanic of any race (2005); Density: 580.7 persons per square mile (2005); Average household size: 2.49 (2005); Median age: 47.8 (2005); Males per 100 females: 95.7 (2005); Marriage status: 16.6% never married, 71.4% now married, 3.9% widowed, 8.1% divorced (2000); Foreign born: 1.1% (2000); Ancestry (includes multiple ancestries): 33.9% German, 18.4% English, 18.4% Polish, 16.4% Irish, 10.3% Italian (2000).
Economy: Employment by occupation: 14.0% management, 26.5% professional, 15.7% services, 24.3% sales, 0.0% farming, 4.4% construction, 15.0% production (2000).
Income: Per capita income: $34,987 (2005); Median household income: $66,204 (2005); Average household income: $86,884 (2005); Percent of households with income of $100,000 or more: 28.2% (2005); Poverty rate: 2.0% (2000).
Education: Percent of population age 25 and over with: High school diploma (including GED) or higher: 92.3% (2005); Bachelor's degree or higher: 39.5% (2005); Master's degree or higher: 15.5% (2005).
Housing: Homeownership rate: 90.4% (2005); Median home value: $182,115 (2005); Median rent: $178 per month (2000); Median age of housing: 40 years (2000).
Transportation: Commute to work: 93.4% car, 3.2% public transportation, 0.9% walk, 2.5% work from home (2000); Travel time to work: 22.3% less than 15 minutes, 43.6% 15 to 30 minutes, 27.0% 30 to 45 minutes, 7.1% 45 to 60 minutes, 0.0% 60 minutes or more (2000).

BLASDELL (village). Covers a land area of 1.151 square miles and a water area of 0 square miles. Located at 42.79° N. Lat.; 78.82° W. Long. Elevation is 600 feet.
History: Incorporated 1898.
Population: 2,900 (1990); 2,718 (2000); 2,598 (2005); 2,474 (2010 projected); Race: 95.9% White, 0.2% Black, 0.1% Asian, 4.3% Hispanic of any race (2005); Density: 2,257.6 persons per square mile (2005); Average household size: 2.22 (2005); Median age: 38.2 (2005); Males per 100 females: 91.0 (2005); Marriage status: 29.4% never married, 48.8% now married, 11.0% widowed, 10.8% divorced (2000); Foreign born: 1.8% (2000); Ancestry (includes multiple ancestries): 35.8% German, 25.5% Irish, 25.1% Polish, 13.3% Italian, 6.5% English (2000).
Economy: Metal products, abrasives, chemicals; farming. Single-family building permits issued: 1 (2005); Multi-family building permits issued: 0 (2005); Employment by occupation: 8.5% management, 14.5% professional, 18.8% services, 27.3% sales, 0.0% farming, 8.0% construction, 22.9% production (2000).
Income: Per capita income: $20,818 (2005); Median household income: $38,781 (2005); Average household income: $46,055 (2005); Percent of

households with income of $100,000 or more: 7.4% (2005); Poverty rate: 6.4% (2000).
Education: Percent of population age 25 and over with: High school diploma (including GED) or higher: 80.3% (2005); Bachelor's degree or higher: 11.9% (2005); Master's degree or higher: 3.7% (2005).

School District(s)
Frontier Central School District (KG-12)
   2003-04 Enrollment: 5,622 . . . . (716) 926-1711
Housing: Homeownership rate: 55.7% (2005); Median home value: $94,060 (2005); Median rent: $414 per month (2000); Median age of housing: 53 years (2000).
Transportation: Commute to work: 91.7% car, 0.5% public transportation, 2.8% walk, 3.6% work from home (2000); Travel time to work: 36.9% less than 15 minutes, 43.2% 15 to 30 minutes, 14.3% 30 to 45 minutes, 1.2% 45 to 60 minutes, 4.4% 60 minutes or more (2000)

BOSTON (town). Covers a land area of 35.830 square miles and a water area of 0 square miles. Located at 42.65° N. Lat.; 78.76° W. Long.
Population: 7,445 (1990); 7,897 (2000); 7,985 (2005); 8,074 (2010 projected); Race: 98.7% White, 0.2% Black, 0.3% Asian, 0.9% Hispanic of any race (2005); Density: 222.9 persons per square mile (2005); Average household size: 2.58 (2005); Median age: 41.2 (2005); Males per 100 females: 100.8 (2005); Marriage status: 20.8% never married, 66.2% now married, 5.4% widowed, 7.6% divorced (2000); Foreign born: 3.2% (2000); Ancestry (includes multiple ancestries): 41.3% German, 23.3% Irish, 22.7% Polish, 13.0% English, 9.9% Italian (2000).
Economy: Single-family building permits issued: 17 (2005); Multi-family building permits issued: 2 (2005); Employment by occupation: 12.9% management, 20.6% professional, 12.3% services, 27.5% sales, 0.4% farming, 11.3% construction, 15.1% production (2000).
Income: Per capita income: $24,110 (2005); Median household income: $52,802 (2005); Average household income: $62,088 (2005); Percent of households with income of $100,000 or more: 15.4% (2005); Poverty rate: 5.9% (2000).
Education: Percent of population age 25 and over with: High school diploma (including GED) or higher: 87.5% (2005); Bachelor's degree or higher: 22.3% (2005); Master's degree or higher: 8.3% (2005).
Housing: Homeownership rate: 83.4% (2005); Median home value: $139,215 (2005); Median rent: $447 per month (2000); Median age of housing: 39 years (2000).
Transportation: Commute to work: 96.7% car, 0.0% public transportation, 1.0% walk, 2.2% work from home (2000); Travel time to work: 18.0% less than 15 minutes, 44.3% 15 to 30 minutes, 27.8% 30 to 45 minutes, 6.4% 45 to 60 minutes, 3.5% 60 minutes or more (2000)

BOWMANSVILLE (unincorporated postal area, zip code 14026). Covers a land area of 0.851 square miles and a water area of 0 square miles. Located at 42.94° N. Lat.; 78.68° W. Long. Elevation is 701 feet.
Population: 0 (2000); Race: 100.0% White, 0.0% Black, 0.0% Asian, 0.0% Hispanic of any race (2000); Density: 0.0 persons per square mile (2000); Age: 24.1% under 18, 20.0% over 64 (2000); Marriage status: 26.1% never married, 65.0% now married, 2.6% widowed, 6.2% divorced (2000); Foreign born: 2.6% (2000); Ancestry (includes multiple ancestries): 34.7% German, 29.4% Polish, 22.5% Italian, 9.2% Russian, 4.9% Swedish (2000).
Economy: Stone quarrying. Employment by occupation: 11.6% management, 29.5% professional, 13.3% services, 25.5% sales, 0.0% farming, 13.9% construction, 6.2% production (2000).
Income: Per capita income: $17,301 (2000); Median household income: $50,357 (2000); Poverty rate: 2.4% (2000).
Education: Percent of population age 25 and over with: High school diploma (including GED) or higher: 82.2% (2000); Bachelor's degree or higher: 17.2% (2000).
Housing: Homeownership rate: 81.1% (2000); Median home value: $106,600 (2000); Median rent: $394 per month (2000); Median age of housing: 47 years (2000).
Transportation: Commute to work: 100.0% car, 0.0% public transportation, 0.0% walk, 0.0% work from home (2000); Travel time to work: 32.5% less than 15 minutes, 59.4% 15 to 30 minutes, 4.9% 30 to 45 minutes, 0.0% 45 to 60 minutes, 3.2% 60 minutes or more (2000)

BRANT (town). Covers a land area of 24.308 square miles and a water area of 0.441 square miles. Located at 42.59° N. Lat.; 79.04° W. Long. Elevation is 756 feet.
Population: 2,119 (1990); 1,906 (2000); 1,891 (2005); 1,877 (2010 projected); Race: 93.9% White, 1.0% Black, 0.0% Asian, 1.4% Hispanic of any race (2005); Density: 77.8 persons per square mile (2005); Average household size: 2.66 (2005); Median age: 40.6 (2005); Males per 100 females: 92.2 (2005); Marriage status: 24.5% never married, 58.4% now married, 9.3% widowed, 7.8% divorced (2000); Foreign born: 1.8% (2000); Ancestry (includes multiple ancestries): 32.6% German, 29.3% Italian, 18.6% Irish, 14.8% Polish, 7.8% Other groups (2000).
Economy: Single-family building permits issued: 6 (2005); Multi-family building permits issued: 0 (2005); Employment by occupation: 9.4% management, 14.6% professional, 19.8% services, 23.1% sales, 0.7% farming, 11.6% construction, 20.8% production (2000).
Income: Per capita income: $22,792 (2005); Median household income: $51,006 (2005); Average household income: $60,415 (2005); Percent of households with income of $100,000 or more: 14.1% (2005); Poverty rate: 6.4% (2000).
Education: Percent of population age 25 and over with: High school diploma (including GED) or higher: 81.1% (2005); Bachelor's degree or higher: 15.0% (2005); Master's degree or higher: 4.9% (2005).

School District(s)
Evans-Brant Central School District (Lake Shore) (KG-12)
   2003-04 Enrollment: 3,230 . . . . (716) 926-2201
Housing: Homeownership rate: 81.1% (2005); Median home value: $113,707 (2005); Median rent: $375 per month (2000); Median age of housing: 57 years (2000).
Safety: Violent crime rate: 0.0 per 10,000 population; Property crime rate: 52.4 per 10,000 population (2004).
Transportation: Commute to work: 93.5% car, 0.2% public transportation, 2.7% walk, 2.7% work from home (2000); Travel time to work: 26.2% less than 15 minutes, 27.6% 15 to 30 minutes, 22.6% 30 to 45 minutes, 16.4% 45 to 60 minutes, 7.2% 60 minutes or more (2000)

BUFFALO (city). Covers a land area of 40.613 square miles and a water area of 11.900 square miles. Located at 42.90° N. Lat.; 78.84° W. Long. Elevation is 583 feet.
History: Although Joseph Ellicott chose and mapped the site of Buffalo for the Holland Land Company in 1799, it was not until 1804 that he divided the land into lots and offered them for sale. He modeled the city plan after that of Washington, D.C. He called the place New Amsterdam, but settlers preferred to name it after Buffalo Creek. Buffalo was incorporated as a village in 1816. The early welfare of the settlement depended on its function as a trading center. The Erie Canal, opened in 1825, brought trade and prosperity. Buffalo stood at the transportation break in the great east-west route. In 1832, Buffalo was incorporated into a city. Steam engine manufacturers and other industries sprang up. After the Civil War, Buffalo became a railroad center.
Population: 328,123 (1990); 292,648 (2000); 282,089 (2005); 271,548 (2010 projected); Race: 50.7% White, 39.8% Black, 1.8% Asian, 9.1% Hispanic of any race (2005); Density: 6,945.8 persons per square mile (2005); Average household size: 2.38 (2005); Median age: 34.8 (2005); Males per 100 females: 89.6 (2005); Marriage status: 40.0% never married, 40.5% now married, 9.1% widowed, 10.4% divorced (2000); Foreign born: 4.4% (2000); Ancestry (includes multiple ancestries): 39.5% Other groups, 13.6% German, 12.2% Irish, 11.7% Italian, 11.7% Polish (2000).
Economy: Unemployment rate: 6.6% (2005); Total civilian labor force: 124,741 (2005); Single-family building permits issued: 97 (2005); Multi-family building permits issued: 13 (2005); Employment by occupation: 8.4% management, 20.8% professional, 21.1% services, 27.0% sales, 0.1% farming, 5.5% construction, 17.2% production (2000).
Income: Per capita income: $16,431 (2005); Median household income: $26,877 (2005); Average household income: $38,195 (2005); Percent of households with income of $100,000 or more: 5.6% (2005); Poverty rate: 26.6% (2000).
Taxes: Total city taxes per capita: $533 (2004); City property taxes per capita: $456 (2004).
Education: Percent of population age 25 and over with: High school diploma (including GED) or higher: 75.0% (2005); Bachelor's degree or higher: 18.8% (2005); Master's degree or higher: 8.0% (2005).

School District(s)
Buffalo City School District (PK-12)
   2003-04 Enrollment: 41,089 . . . . (716) 851-3575
Buffalo United Charter Sch (KG-04)
   2003-04 Enrollment: 237 . . . . (716) 835-9862
Charter School For Applied Technology (KG-08)
   2003-04 Enrollment: 934 . . . . (716) 876-7505

Cheektowaga Central School District (KG-12)
  2003-04 Enrollment: 2,416 . . . . (716) 686-3606
Comm Charter School (KG-04)
  2003-04 Enrollment: 246 . . . . (716) 832-2551
Enterprise Charter School (KG-08)
  2003-04 Enrollment: 421 . . . . (716) 873-2962
Kenmore-Tonawanda Union Free School District (PK-12)
  2003-04 Enrollment: 9,033 . . . . (716) 874-8400
King Ctr Charter School (KG-04)
  2003-04 Enrollment: 105 . . . . (716) 891-7912
Kipp Sankofa Charter School (05-05)
  2003-04 Enrollment: 84 . . . . (716) 446-5708
Pinnacle Charter School (KG-03)
  2003-04 Enrollment: 147 . . . . (716) 633-8146
South Buffalo Charter School (KG-07)
  2003-04 Enrollment: 469 . . . . (716) 826-7213
Stepping Stone Acad Charter School (KG-07)
  2003-04 Enrollment: 505 . . . . (716) 895-5766
Tapestry Charter School (KG-06)
  2003-04 Enrollment: 162 . . . . (716) 332-0754

Four-year College(s)
Canisius College
  Fall 2004 Enrollment: 5,018 . . . . (716) 883-7000
  2005-06 Tuition: In-state $23,297; Out-of-state $23,297
D'Youville College
  Fall 2004 Enrollment: 2,728 . . . . (716) 829-8000
  2005-06 Tuition: In-state $15,800; Out-of-state $15,800
Medaille College
  Fall 2004 Enrollment: 2,526 . . . . (716) 880-2000
  2005-06 Tuition: In-state $15,030; Out-of-state $15,030
SUNY College at Buffalo (Public)
  Fall 2004 Enrollment: 11,072 . . . . (716) 878-4000
  2005-06 Tuition: In-state $5,231; Out-of-state $11,491
SUNY at Buffalo (Public)
  Fall 2004 Enrollment: 27,276 . . . . (716) 645-2000
  2005-06 Tuition: In-state $6,068; Out-of-state $12,328
Villa Maria College Buffalo
  Fall 2004 Enrollment: 504 . . . . (716) 896-0700
  2005-06 Tuition: In-state $11,060; Out-of-state $11,060

Two-year College(s)
Bryant and Stratton College-Buffalo
  Fall 2004 Enrollment: 625 . . . . (716) 884-9120
  2005-06 Tuition: In-state $11,820; Out-of-state $11,820
Continental School of Beauty Culture
  Fall 2004 Enrollment: 109 . . . . (716) 833-5016
Erie Community College (Public)
  Fall 2004 Enrollment: 12,833 . . . . (716) 842-2770
  2005-06 Tuition: In-state $3,200; Out-of-state $6,100
National Tractor Trailer School Inc
  Fall 2004 Enrollment: 28 . . . . (716) 849-6887
Trocaire College
  Fall 2004 Enrollment: 1,009 . . . . (716) 826-1200
  2005-06 Tuition: In-state $10,170; Out-of-state $10,170

Housing: Homeownership rate: 43.6% (2005); Median home value: $72,589 (2005); Median rent: $364 per month (2000); Median age of housing: 60+ years (2000).
Hospitals: Bry Lin Hospitals (88 beds); Buffalo General Hospital (511 beds); Buffalo Psychiatric Center (240 beds); Children's Hospital of Buffalo (313 beds); Department of Veterans Affairs Western New York Healthcare; Erie County Medical Center (550 beds); Mercy Hospital of Buffalo (349 beds); Millard Fillmore Health System (189 beds); Millard Fillmore Suburban Hospital (189 beds); Roswell Park Cancer Institute (133 beds); Sheehan Memorial Hospital (109 beds); Sisters of Charity Hospital (413 beds)
Safety: Violent crime rate: 133.2 per 10,000 population; Property crime rate: 569.1 per 10,000 population (2004).
Newspapers: Buffalo Criterion (Black, General - Circulation 10,000); Buffalo Jewish Review (Jewish, Religious - Circulation 4,800); Buffalo Rocket (General - Circulation 16,500); Fine Print News (General - Circulation 32,000); Riverside Review (General - Circulation 14,300); Riverside Times (General - Circulation 12,000); The Buffalo News (Circulation 225,000); The Challenger (Black - Circulation 10,000); West Side Times (General - Circulation 13,000)
Transportation: Commute to work: 79.8% car, 12.3% public transportation, 5.3% walk, 1.7% work from home (2000); Travel time to work: 32.2% less than 15 minutes, 46.4% 15 to 30 minutes, 13.4% 30 to 45 minutes, 3.5% 45 to 60 minutes, 4.6% 60 minutes or more (2000); Amtrak: Service available.
Additional Information Contacts
Buffalo Niagara Partnership . . . . (716) 852-7100
  http://www.thepartnership.org
City of Buffalo . . . . (716) 851-4200
  http://www.ci.buffalo.ny.us/

CATTARAUGUS RESERVATION (reservation). Covers a land area of 34.941 square miles and a water area of 0.236 square miles. Located at 42.68° N. Lat.; 94.13° W. Long.
Population: 1,789 (1990); 2,001 (2000); 1,994 (2005); 1,990 (2010 projected); Race: 16.2% White, 0.0% Black, 0.0% Asian, 1.1% Hispanic of any race (2005); Density: 57.1 persons per square mile (2005); Average household size: 2.79 (2005); Median age: 30.6 (2005); Males per 100 females: 91.5 (2005); Marriage status: 40.3% never married, 38.5% now married, 8.3% widowed, 12.9% divorced (2000); Foreign born: 4.3% (2000); Ancestry (includes multiple ancestries): 38.0% Other groups, 3.0% German, 2.8% Irish, 1.8% French (except Basque), 1.5% Polish (2000).
Economy: Employment by occupation: 8.1% management, 11.6% professional, 28.4% services, 25.0% sales, 2.2% farming, 11.4% construction, 13.4% production (2000).
Income: Per capita income: $14,457 (2005); Median household income: $31,818 (2005); Average household income: $40,318 (2005); Percent of households with income of $100,000 or more: 6.0% (2005); Poverty rate: 30.6% (2000).
Education: Percent of population age 25 and over with: High school diploma (including GED) or higher: 73.9% (2005); Bachelor's degree or higher: 17.4% (2005); Master's degree or higher: 7.0% (2005).
Housing: Homeownership rate: 72.3% (2005); Median home value: $59,938 (2005); Median rent: $260 per month (2000); Median age of housing: 28 years (2000).
Transportation: Commute to work: 95.0% car, 0.0% public transportation, 4.0% walk, 1.0% work from home (2000); Travel time to work: 46.0% less than 15 minutes, 29.0% 15 to 30 minutes, 15.0% 30 to 45 minutes, 5.6% 45 to 60 minutes, 4.5% 60 minutes or more (2000)

CHAFFEE (unincorporated postal area, zip code 14030). Covers a land area of 22.240 square miles and a water area of 0.140 square miles. Located at 42.56° N. Lat.; 78.49° W. Long.
Population: 0 (2000); Race: 96.8% White, 0.0% Black, 0.4% Asian, 0.0% Hispanic of any race (2000); Density: 0.0 persons per square mile (2000); Age: 23.9% under 18, 11.6% over 64 (2000); Marriage status: 26.6% never married, 59.5% now married, 5.4% widowed, 8.6% divorced (2000); Foreign born: 0.3% (2000); Ancestry (includes multiple ancestries): 37.5% German, 22.9% Polish, 14.2% English, 10.8% Irish, 9.5% Italian (2000).
Economy: Employment by occupation: 7.9% management, 17.2% professional, 14.2% services, 26.1% sales, 2.2% farming, 12.8% construction, 19.6% production (2000).
Income: Per capita income: $17,147 (2000); Median household income: $35,938 (2000); Poverty rate: 7.4% (2000).
Education: Percent of population age 25 and over with: High school diploma (including GED) or higher: 80.9% (2000); Bachelor's degree or higher: 10.6% (2000).
Housing: Homeownership rate: 78.9% (2000); Median home value: $86,200 (2000); Median rent: $381 per month (2000); Median age of housing: 46 years (2000).
Transportation: Commute to work: 88.2% car, 0.6% public transportation, 3.2% walk, 6.4% work from home (2000); Travel time to work: 33.5% less than 15 minutes, 23.1% 15 to 30 minutes, 21.4% 30 to 45 minutes, 15.2% 45 to 60 minutes, 6.9% 60 minutes or more (2000)

CHEEKTOWAGA (town). Covers a land area of 29.531 square miles and a water area of 0 square miles. Located at 42.91° N. Lat.; 78.75° W. Long. Elevation is 659 feet.
History: Named for the Indian translation of "place of the crab apple tree". Population grew significantly after World War II. Settled 1809. Incorporated 1834.
Population: 99,314 (1990); 94,019 (2000); 91,201 (2005); 88,303 (2010 projected); Race: 93.2% White, 4.0% Black, 1.3% Asian, 1.3% Hispanic of any race (2005); Density: 3,088.3 persons per square mile (2005); Average household size: 2.32 (2005); Median age: 42.6 (2005); Males per 100 females: 89.0 (2005); Marriage status: 25.1% never married, 55.6% now married, 10.9% widowed, 8.4% divorced (2000); Foreign born: 4.3%

(2000); Ancestry (includes multiple ancestries): 39.9% Polish, 29.9% German, 16.0% Italian, 14.1% Irish, 5.8% English (2000).
Economy: Buffalo International Airport nearby. Unemployment rate: 5.3% (2005); Total civilian labor force: 49,421 (2005); Single-family building permits issued: 31 (2005); Multi-family building permits issued: 36 (2005); Employment by occupation: 10.5% management, 16.8% professional, 14.8% services, 31.9% sales, 0.1% farming, 7.5% construction, 18.3% production (2000).
Income: Per capita income: $22,304 (2005); Median household income: $42,649 (2005); Average household income: $51,364 (2005); Percent of households with income of $100,000 or more: 8.9% (2005); Poverty rate: 6.5% (2000).
Taxes: Total city taxes per capita: $476 (2004); City property taxes per capita: $445 (2004).
Education: Percent of population age 25 and over with: High school diploma (including GED) or higher: 80.5% (2005); Bachelor's degree or higher: 15.2% (2005); Master's degree or higher: 4.8% (2005).

School District(s)
Cheektowaga Central School District (KG-12)
    2003-04 Enrollment: 2,416 . . . . (716) 686-3606
Cheektowaga-Maryvale Union Free School District (KG-12)
    2003-04 Enrollment: 2,478 . . . . (716) 631-7407
Cheektowaga-Sloan Union Free School District (PK-12)
    2003-04 Enrollment: 1,531 . . . . (716) 891-6402
Cleveland Hill Union Free School District (KG-12)
    2003-04 Enrollment: 1,587 . . . . (716) 836-7200

Housing: Homeownership rate: 71.9% (2005); Median home value: $100,045 (2005); Median rent: $468 per month (2000); Median age of housing: 41 years (2000).
Hospitals: St. Joseph Hospital (208 beds)
Safety: Violent crime rate: 20.5 per 10,000 population; Property crime rate: 327.7 per 10,000 population (2004).
Newspapers: Am-Pol Eagle (Ethnic, General - Circulation 2,400); Cheektowaga Times (General - Circulation 5,600); Metro Community News Alden (General - Circulation 5,846); Metro Community News Am-ton (General - Circulation 15,493); Metro Community News Amherst/Getzville (General - Circulation 17,542); Metro Community News Cheektowaga/Harlem/Genesee (General - Circulation 11,396); Metro Community News Cheektowaga/Union/Genesee (General - Circulation 9,623); Metro Community News Clarence (General - Circulation 8,705); Metro Community News Eggertsville (General - Circulation 12,917); Metro Community News Grand Island (General - Circulation 6,439); Metro Community News Kenmore/Tonawanda (General - Circulation 14,251); Metro Community News Lancaster (General - Circulation 11,661); Metro Community News Lewiston/Youngstown (General - Circulation 11,614); Metro Community News Lockport City (General - Circulation 10,223); Metro Community News Lockport Town (General - Circulation 10,395); Metro Community News Newfane/Gasport (General - Circulation 8,680); Metro Community News Niagara Falls North (General - Circulation 8,811); Metro Community News Niagara Falls South (General - Circulation 11,680); Metro Community News Niagara Falls/La Salle (General - Circulation 11,178); Metro Community News North Tonawanda (General - Circulation 14,495); Metro Community News South Buffalo (General - Circulation 17,325); Metro Community News South Cheektowaga (General - Circulation 17,537); Metro Community News Tonawanda (General - Circulation 11,751); Metro Community News Wheatfield (General - Circulation 4,486); Metro Community News Williamsville (General - Circulation 12,500).
Transportation: Commute to work: 95.5% car, 1.3% public transportation, 1.4% walk, 1.4% work from home (2000); Travel time to work: 32.2% less than 15 minutes, 51.7% 15 to 30 minutes, 11.5% 30 to 45 minutes, 2.0% 45 to 60 minutes, 2.7% 60 minutes or more (2000)

Additional Information Contacts
Cheektowaga Chamber of Commerce. . . . . (716) 684-5838
    http://www.cheektowaga.org
Town of Cheektowaga . . . . (716) 686-3434
    http://tocny.org/

CHEEKTOWAGA
(CDP). Covers a land area of 25.450 square miles and a water area of 0 square miles. Located at 42.91° N. Lat.; 78.76° W. Long.
Population: 84,387 (1990); 79,988 (2000); 77,745 (2005); 75,424 (2010 projected); Race: 92.5% White, 4.6% Black, 1.5% Asian, 1.3% Hispanic of any race (2005); Density: 3,054.8 persons per square mile (2005); Average household size: 2.31 (2005); Median age: 42.5 (2005); Males per 100 females: 88.6 (2005); Marriage status: 25.3% never married, 55.6% now married, 10.9% widowed, 8.2% divorced (2000); Foreign born: 4.4% (2000); Ancestry (includes multiple ancestries): 39.4% Polish, 30.0% German, 15.7% Italian, 14.0% Irish, 6.0% Other groups (2000).
Economy: Employment by occupation: 10.9% management, 17.3% professional, 14.5% services, 32.2% sales, 0.1% farming, 7.1% construction, 18.0% production (2000).
Income: Per capita income: $22,440 (2005); Median household income: $42,540 (2005); Average household income: $51,534 (2005); Percent of households with income of $100,000 or more: 9.1% (2005); Poverty rate: 6.5% (2000).
Education: Percent of population age 25 and over with: High school diploma (including GED) or higher: 81.1% (2005); Bachelor's degree or higher: 16.0% (2005); Master's degree or higher: 5.2% (2005).
Housing: Homeownership rate: 71.1% (2005); Median home value: $100,421 (2005); Median rent: $467 per month (2000); Median age of housing: 41 years (2000).
Transportation: Commute to work: 95.3% car, 1.4% public transportation, 1.4% walk, 1.5% work from home (2000); Travel time to work: 31.7% less than 15 minutes, 52.0% 15 to 30 minutes, 11.5% 30 to 45 minutes, 2.1% 45 to 60 minutes, 2.8% 60 minutes or more (2000)

CLARENCE
(town). Covers a land area of 53.404 square miles and a water area of 0.057 square miles. Located at 43.00° N. Lat.; 78.64° W. Long.
Population: 20,041 (1990); 26,123 (2000); 28,462 (2005); 30,575 (2010 projected); Race: 96.1% White, 0.8% Black, 2.0% Asian, 1.1% Hispanic of any race (2005); Density: 533.0 persons per square mile (2005); Average household size: 2.84 (2005); Median age: 40.9 (2005); Males per 100 females: 94.4 (2005); Marriage status: 19.7% never married, 67.5% now married, 7.1% widowed, 5.7% divorced (2000); Foreign born: 4.6% (2000); Ancestry (includes multiple ancestries): 35.6% German, 22.1% Italian, 19.3% Irish, 15.0% Polish, 12.2% English (2000).
Economy: Manufacturing: machinery. Single-family building permits issued: 123 (2005); Multi-family building permits issued: 8 (2005); Employment by occupation: 19.3% management, 28.2% professional, 10.4% services, 27.2% sales, 0.1% farming, 6.4% construction, 8.3% production (2000).
Income: Per capita income: $39,903 (2005); Median household income: $82,781 (2005); Average household income: $112,343 (2005); Percent of households with income of $100,000 or more: 39.2% (2005); Poverty rate: 1.9% (2000).
Education: Percent of population age 25 and over with: High school diploma (including GED) or higher: 94.4% (2005); Bachelor's degree or higher: 42.3% (2005); Master's degree or higher: 18.9% (2005).

School District(s)
Clarence Central School District (KG-12)
    2003-04 Enrollment: 4,920 . . . . (716) 407-9102

Housing: Homeownership rate: 88.3% (2005); Median home value: $199,393 (2005); Median rent: $480 per month (2000); Median age of housing: 31 years (2000).
Transportation: Commute to work: 94.6% car, 0.5% public transportation, 0.9% walk, 3.7% work from home (2000); Travel time to work: 27.5% less than 15 minutes, 41.1% 15 to 30 minutes, 24.5% 30 to 45 minutes, 3.8% 45 to 60 minutes, 3.1% 60 minutes or more (2000)

Additional Information Contacts
Clarence Chamber of Commerce . . . . (716) 631-3888
    http://www.clarence.org

CLARENCE CENTER
(CDP). Covers a land area of 2.124 square miles and a water area of 0 square miles. Located at 43.01° N. Lat.; 78.63° W. Long. Elevation is 635 feet.
Population: 1,376 (1990); 1,747 (2000); 1,979 (2005); 2,192 (2010 projected); Race: 97.7% White, 0.7% Black, 0.2% Asian, 1.3% Hispanic of any race (2005); Density: 931.7 persons per square mile (2005); Average household size: 2.81 (2005); Median age: 37.7 (2005); Males per 100 females: 95.7 (2005); Marriage status: 19.7% never married, 69.5% now married, 3.5% widowed, 7.3% divorced (2000); Foreign born: 4.8% (2000); Ancestry (includes multiple ancestries): 41.3% German, 27.7% Italian, 17.9% Irish, 15.3% English, 8.1% Polish (2000).
Economy: Employment by occupation: 9.8% management, 26.9% professional, 19.2% services, 30.9% sales, 1.0% farming, 5.5% construction, 6.7% production (2000).
Income: Per capita income: $31,997 (2005); Median household income: $80,147 (2005); Average household income: $89,819 (2005); Percent of

households with income of $100,000 or more: 32.8% (2005); Poverty rate: 1.0% (2000).
Education: Percent of population age 25 and over with: High school diploma (including GED) or higher: 95.1% (2005); Bachelor's degree or higher: 41.5% (2005); Master's degree or higher: 14.0% (2005).
School District(s)
Clarence Central School District (KG-12)
    2003-04 Enrollment: 4,920 . . . . (716) 407-9102
Housing: Homeownership rate: 89.9% (2005); Median home value: $164,080 (2005); Median rent: $714 per month (2000); Median age of housing: 37 years (2000).
Transportation: Commute to work: 94.2% car, 2.4% public transportation, 0.9% walk, 1.7% work from home (2000); Travel time to work: 26.6% less than 15 minutes, 44.6% 15 to 30 minutes, 19.0% 30 to 45 minutes, 3.6% 45 to 60 minutes, 6.2% 60 minutes or more (2000)

COLDEN (town). Covers a land area of 35.648 square miles and a water area of 0.085 square miles. Located at 42.65° N. Lat.; 78.65° W. Long. Elevation is 1,100 feet.
Population: 2,899 (1990); 3,323 (2000); 3,371 (2005); 3,420 (2010 projected); Race: 98.6% White, 0.0% Black, 0.2% Asian, 0.5% Hispanic of any race (2005); Density: 94.6 persons per square mile (2005); Average household size: 2.58 (2005); Median age: 41.1 (2005); Males per 100 females: 101.6 (2005); Marriage status: 20.9% never married, 64.6% now married, 4.3% widowed, 10.2% divorced (2000); Foreign born: 3.8% (2000); Ancestry (includes multiple ancestries): 42.6% German, 21.3% Polish, 17.2% Irish, 13.1% English, 10.3% Italian (2000).
Economy: Single-family building permits issued: 9 (2005); Multi-family building permits issued: 0 (2005); Employment by occupation: 11.1% management, 18.7% professional, 15.0% services, 22.8% sales, 0.3% farming, 16.1% construction, 16.0% production (2000).
Income: Per capita income: $27,060 (2005); Median household income: $56,632 (2005); Average household income: $69,900 (2005); Percent of households with income of $100,000 or more: 16.6% (2005); Poverty rate: 3.4% (2000).
Education: Percent of population age 25 and over with: High school diploma (including GED) or higher: 93.0% (2005); Bachelor's degree or higher: 22.6% (2005); Master's degree or higher: 11.8% (2005).
School District(s)
Springville-Griffith Institute Central School District (KG-12)
    2003-04 Enrollment: 2,385 . . . . (716) 592-3230
Housing: Homeownership rate: 86.2% (2005); Median home value: $145,163 (2005); Median rent: $414 per month (2000); Median age of housing: 42 years (2000).
Transportation: Commute to work: 94.7% car, 0.5% public transportation, 1.0% walk, 3.6% work from home (2000); Travel time to work: 18.7% less than 15 minutes, 37.0% 15 to 30 minutes, 25.4% 30 to 45 minutes, 13.2% 45 to 60 minutes, 5.6% 60 minutes or more (2000)

COLLINS (town). Covers a land area of 48.122 square miles and a water area of 0.044 square miles. Located at 42.49° N. Lat.; 78.90° W. Long. Elevation is 883 feet.
Population: 6,020 (1990); 8,307 (2000); 7,765 (2005); 7,822 (2010 projected); Race: 53.5% White, 32.7% Black, 0.2% Asian, 17.4% Hispanic of any race (2005); Density: 161.4 persons per square mile (2005); Average household size: 4.60 (2005); Median age: 36.4 (2005); Males per 100 females: 268.7 (2005); Marriage status: 37.0% never married, 52.4% now married, 3.1% widowed, 7.6% divorced (2000); Foreign born: 6.7% (2000); Ancestry (includes multiple ancestries): 21.5% German, 8.8% English, 7.4% Irish, 5.9% Polish, 5.8% Italian (2000).
Economy: Single-family building permits issued: 7 (2005); Multi-family building permits issued: 0 (2005); Employment by occupation: 8.9% management, 20.2% professional, 20.4% services, 19.7% sales, 2.1% farming, 14.0% construction, 14.6% production (2000).
Income: Per capita income: $15,841 (2005); Median household income: $39,307 (2005); Average household income: $50,335 (2005); Percent of households with income of $100,000 or more: 9.9% (2005); Poverty rate: 8.5% (2000).
Education: Percent of population age 25 and over with: High school diploma (including GED) or higher: 48.9% (2005); Bachelor's degree or higher: 6.6% (2005); Master's degree or higher: 2.3% (2005).
School District(s)
Gowanda Central School District (PK-12)
    2003-04 Enrollment: 1,532 . . . . (716) 532-3325
Housing: Homeownership rate: 76.1% (2005); Median home value: $83,593 (2005); Median rent: $315 per month (2000); Median age of housing: 49 years (2000).
Transportation: Commute to work: 90.1% car, 0.4% public transportation, 3.4% walk, 3.9% work from home (2000); Travel time to work: 41.9% less than 15 minutes, 23.8% 15 to 30 minutes, 12.4% 30 to 45 minutes, 12.9% 45 to 60 minutes, 8.9% 60 minutes or more (2000)

CONCORD (town). Covers a land area of 70.094 square miles and a water area of 0.067 square miles. Located at 42.53° N. Lat.; 78.68° W. Long. Elevation is 1,342 feet.
Population: 8,387 (1990); 8,526 (2000); 8,664 (2005); 8,795 (2010 projected); Race: 98.1% White, 0.7% Black, 0.3% Asian, 1.8% Hispanic of any race (2005); Density: 123.6 persons per square mile (2005); Average household size: 2.57 (2005); Median age: 40.2 (2005); Males per 100 females: 95.3 (2005); Marriage status: 21.4% never married, 62.6% now married, 8.4% widowed, 7.6% divorced (2000); Foreign born: 1.2% (2000); Ancestry (includes multiple ancestries): 44.6% German, 14.8% Irish, 14.7% Polish, 13.0% English, 10.9% Italian (2000).
Economy: Single-family building permits issued: 14 (2005); Multi-family building permits issued: 0 (2005); Employment by occupation: 10.2% management, 19.0% professional, 16.9% services, 24.4% sales, 0.7% farming, 11.2% construction, 17.6% production (2000).
Income: Per capita income: $22,776 (2005); Median household income: $46,595 (2005); Average household income: $57,483 (2005); Percent of households with income of $100,000 or more: 12.6% (2005); Poverty rate: 6.6% (2000).
Education: Percent of population age 25 and over with: High school diploma (including GED) or higher: 83.8% (2005); Bachelor's degree or higher: 17.8% (2005); Master's degree or higher: 7.0% (2005).
Housing: Homeownership rate: 73.8% (2005); Median home value: $120,121 (2005); Median rent: $378 per month (2000); Median age of housing: 40 years (2000).
Transportation: Commute to work: 92.1% car, 0.0% public transportation, 3.4% walk, 3.7% work from home (2000); Travel time to work: 40.7% less than 15 minutes, 22.1% 15 to 30 minutes, 21.2% 30 to 45 minutes, 11.4% 45 to 60 minutes, 4.5% 60 minutes or more (2000)

DEPEW (village). Covers a land area of 5.067 square miles and a water area of 0 square miles. Located at 42.91° N. Lat.; 78.70° W. Long. Elevation is 685 feet.
History: Founded in 1892 as a village, it was named for Chauncey M. Depew (1834-1928), a Railroad executive and later a U.S. senator. Incorporated 1894.
Population: 17,673 (1990); 16,629 (2000); 15,960 (2005); 15,281 (2010 projected); Race: 97.4% White, 0.8% Black, 0.6% Asian, 1.0% Hispanic of any race (2005); Density: 3,150.0 persons per square mile (2005); Average household size: 2.39 (2005); Median age: 41.4 (2005); Males per 100 females: 93.2 (2005); Marriage status: 25.2% never married, 56.0% now married, 9.8% widowed, 9.1% divorced (2000); Foreign born: 3.5% (2000); Ancestry (includes multiple ancestries): 40.2% Polish, 33.5% German, 17.3% Italian, 15.1% Irish, 6.8% English (2000).
Economy: Diverse manufacturing includes plastics, food, machinery, apparel, furniture, transportation equipment. Single-family building permits issued: 15 (2005); Multi-family building permits issued: 0 (2005); Employment by occupation: 9.6% management, 15.4% professional, 17.5% services, 30.2% sales, 0.1% farming, 9.1% construction, 18.1% production (2000).
Income: Per capita income: $23,027 (2005); Median household income: $46,633 (2005); Average household income: $54,745 (2005); Percent of households with income of $100,000 or more: 10.1% (2005); Poverty rate: 5.4% (2000).
Education: Percent of population age 25 and over with: High school diploma (including GED) or higher: 80.9% (2005); Bachelor's degree or higher: 12.7% (2005); Master's degree or higher: 3.1% (2005).
School District(s)
Depew Union Free School District (KG-12)
    2003-04 Enrollment: 2,378 . . . . (716) 686-2251
Lancaster Central School District (KG-12)
    2003-04 Enrollment: 6,204 . . . . (716) 686-3200
Housing: Homeownership rate: 73.2% (2005); Median home value: $110,148 (2005); Median rent: $463 per month (2000); Median age of housing: 41 years (2000).
Safety: Violent crime rate: 14.8 per 10,000 population; Property crime rate: 218.2 per 10,000 population (2004).

Transportation: Commute to work: 96.3% car, 0.6% public transportation, 1.4% walk, 0.8% work from home (2000); Travel time to work: 36.8% less than 15 minutes, 46.8% 15 to 30 minutes, 12.4% 30 to 45 minutes, 1.8% 45 to 60 minutes, 2.3% 60 minutes or more (2000); Amtrak: Service available.

Additional Information Contacts
Village of Depew .... (716) 683-1400
http://www.villageofdepew.org/

DERBY (unincorporated postal area, zip code 14047).
Covers a land area of 12.353 square miles and a water area of 0.008 square miles. Located at 42.69° N. Lat.; 78.98° W. Long. Elevation is 707 feet.
Population: 0 (2000); Race: 98.5% White, 0.4% Black, 0.2% Asian, 2.4% Hispanic of any race (2000); Density: 0.0 persons per square mile (2000); Age: 25.7% under 18, 10.8% over 64 (2000); Marriage status: 24.5% never married, 60.1% now married, 7.3% widowed, 8.2% divorced (2000); Foreign born: 2.2% (2000); Ancestry (includes multiple ancestries): 34.4% German, 24.5% Irish, 19.9% Polish, 14.5% Italian, 8.9% English (2000).
Economy: In grape-growing region. Light manufacturing. Employment by occupation: 12.3% management, 20.3% professional, 16.2% services, 25.5% sales, 0.0% farming, 9.5% construction, 16.2% production (2000).
Income: Per capita income: $21,432 (2000); Median household income: $52,445 (2000); Poverty rate: 3.9% (2000).
Education: Percent of population age 25 and over with: High school diploma (including GED) or higher: 86.1% (2000); Bachelor's degree or higher: 21.9% (2000).

School District(s)
Evans-Brant Central School District (Lake Shore) (KG-12)
   2003-04 Enrollment: 3,230 .... (716) 926-2201
Housing: Homeownership rate: 85.9% (2000); Median home value: $87,600 (2000); Median rent: $513 per month (2000); Median age of housing: 30 years (2000).
Transportation: Commute to work: 94.7% car, 0.7% public transportation, 2.7% walk, 1.9% work from home (2000); Travel time to work: 18.8% less than 15 minutes, 32.5% 15 to 30 minutes, 36.9% 30 to 45 minutes, 9.0% 45 to 60 minutes, 2.9% 60 minutes or more (2000)

Additional Information Contacts
Evans-Brant Chamber of Commerce .... (716) 947-4225
http://www.ebccny.org

EAST AMHERST (unincorporated postal area, zip code 14051).
Aka Transit. Covers a land area of 14.889 square miles and a water area of 0.021 square miles. Located at 43.02° N. Lat.; 78.70° W. Long.
Population: 0 (2000); Race: 92.8% White, 1.2% Black, 4.4% Asian, 0.8% Hispanic of any race (2000); Density: 0.0 persons per square mile (2000); Age: 30.1% under 18, 7.8% over 64 (2000); Marriage status: 20.5% never married, 72.1% now married, 3.6% widowed, 3.8% divorced (2000); Foreign born: 9.4% (2000); Ancestry (includes multiple ancestries): 27.1% German, 23.4% Italian, 17.3% Irish, 13.6% Polish, 11.2% English (2000).
Economy: Employment by occupation: 24.6% management, 34.5% professional, 9.1% services, 24.9% sales, 0.1% farming, 2.4% construction, 4.4% production (2000).
Income: Per capita income: $39,841 (2000); Median household income: $88,317 (2000); Poverty rate: 2.3% (2000).
Education: Percent of population age 25 and over with: High school diploma (including GED) or higher: 96.0% (2000); Bachelor's degree or higher: 59.8% (2000).

School District(s)
Williamsville Central School District (KG-12)
   2003-04 Enrollment: 10,760 .... (716) 626-8005
Housing: Homeownership rate: 94.2% (2000); Median home value: $172,200 (2000); Median rent: $742 per month (2000); Median age of housing: 17 years (2000).
Transportation: Commute to work: 94.9% car, 0.3% public transportation, 0.9% walk, 3.3% work from home (2000); Travel time to work: 25.2% less than 15 minutes, 43.6% 15 to 30 minutes, 25.5% 30 to 45 minutes, 3.3% 45 to 60 minutes, 2.4% 60 minutes or more (2000)

EAST AURORA (village).
Covers a land area of 2.515 square miles and a water area of 0 square miles. Located at 42.76° N. Lat.; 78.61° W. Long. Elevation is 917 feet.
Population: 6,764 (1990); 6,673 (2000); 6,398 (2005); 6,142 (2010 projected); Race: 98.6% White, 0.2% Black, 0.5% Asian, 0.9% Hispanic of any race (2005); Density: 2,544.4 persons per square mile (2005); Average household size: 2.54 (2005); Median age: 41.6 (2005); Males per 100 females: 88.6 (2005); Marriage status: 21.9% never married, 59.1% now married, 11.1% widowed, 7.8% divorced (2000); Foreign born: 2.6% (2000); Ancestry (includes multiple ancestries): 36.9% German, 18.4% Irish, 18.1% English, 13.9% Polish, 13.0% Italian (2000).
Economy: Single-family building permits issued: 0 (2005); Multi-family building permits issued: 0 (2005); Employment by occupation: 13.2% management, 32.4% professional, 11.5% services, 24.4% sales, 0.7% farming, 8.3% construction, 9.6% production (2000).
Income: Per capita income: $26,565 (2005); Median household income: $56,375 (2005); Average household income: $65,705 (2005); Percent of households with income of $100,000 or more: 18.6% (2005); Poverty rate: 3.7% (2000).
Education: Percent of population age 25 and over with: High school diploma (including GED) or higher: 86.3% (2005); Bachelor's degree or higher: 38.6% (2005); Master's degree or higher: 15.3% (2005).

School District(s)
East Aurora Union Free School District (KG-12)
   2003-04 Enrollment: 2,091 .... (716) 687-2302
Iroquois Central School District (KG-12)
   2003-04 Enrollment: 2,905 .... (716) 652-3000

Four-year College(s)
Christ the King Seminary
   Fall 2004 Enrollment: 103 .... (716) 652-8900
Housing: Homeownership rate: 69.9% (2005); Median home value: $137,950 (2005); Median rent: $466 per month (2000); Median age of housing: 60+ years (2000).
Newspapers: Elma Review (General - Circulation 1,200)
Transportation: Commute to work: 86.9% car, 1.0% public transportation, 6.9% walk, 3.4% work from home (2000); Travel time to work: 36.5% less than 15 minutes, 25.8% 15 to 30 minutes, 28.6% 30 to 45 minutes, 5.1% 45 to 60 minutes, 3.9% 60 minutes or more (2000)

Additional Information Contacts
Greater East Aurora Chamber of Commerce .... (716) 652-8444
http://www.eanycc.com
Village of East Aurora .... (716) 652-3280
http://www.east-aurora.ny.us/

EAST CONCORD (unincorporated postal area, zip code 14055).
Covers a land area of 26.627 square miles and a water area of 0.040 square miles. Located at 42.55° N. Lat.; 78.61° W. Long. Elevation is 1,456 feet.
Population: 0 (2000); Race: 99.1% White, 0.0% Black, 0.2% Asian, 0.0% Hispanic of any race (2000); Density: 0.0 persons per square mile (2000); Age: 25.3% under 18, 10.1% over 64 (2000); Marriage status: 24.3% never married, 59.2% now married, 4.8% widowed, 11.6% divorced (2000); Foreign born: 0.2% (2000); Ancestry (includes multiple ancestries): 43.3% German, 15.2% Irish, 11.2% Italian, 9.1% French (except Basque), 8.9% Polish (2000).
Economy: Employment by occupation: 11.5% management, 14.8% professional, 19.4% services, 27.6% sales, 0.0% farming, 8.8% construction, 17.8% production (2000).
Income: Per capita income: $17,802 (2000); Median household income: $39,500 (2000); Poverty rate: 8.2% (2000).
Education: Percent of population age 25 and over with: High school diploma (including GED) or higher: 81.5% (2000); Bachelor's degree or higher: 11.3% (2000).
Housing: Homeownership rate: 81.0% (2000); Median home value: $94,500 (2000); Median rent: $386 per month (2000); Median age of housing: 32 years (2000).
Transportation: Commute to work: 93.9% car, 0.4% public transportation, 1.2% walk, 4.5% work from home (2000); Travel time to work: 34.5% less than 15 minutes, 31.9% 15 to 30 minutes, 21.3% 30 to 45 minutes, 7.9% 45 to 60 minutes, 4.4% 60 minutes or more (2000)

EDEN (town).
Aka Eden Center. Covers a land area of 39.821 square miles and a water area of 0.030 square miles. Located at 42.65° N. Lat.; 78.88° W. Long. Elevation is 797 feet.
History: The "Original American Kazoo" is still made here, and though the factory itself may no longer be toured, there is still a visitors center that explains modern production methods as well as West African origins of the instrument. Established in 1916, this is now the world's only metal kazoo factory.
Population: 7,416 (1990); 8,076 (2000); 7,994 (2005); 7,912 (2010 projected); Race: 98.1% White, 0.6% Black, 0.2% Asian, 1.3% Hispanic of any race (2005); Density: 200.7 persons per square mile (2005); Average

household size: 2.78 (2005); Median age: 40.6 (2005); Males per 100 females: 98.7 (2005); Marriage status: 22.1% never married, 65.3% now married, 6.0% widowed, 6.7% divorced (2000); Foreign born: 1.6% (2000); Ancestry (includes multiple ancestries): 40.8% German, 21.4% Irish, 18.2% Polish, 12.0% Italian, 11.5% English (2000).
Economy: Manufacturing: various brass manufacturing, tools and dies, electronic measuring devices. Single-family building permits issued: 8 (2005); Multi-family building permits issued: 0 (2005); Employment by occupation: 11.3% management, 20.3% professional, 12.9% services, 28.9% sales, 1.2% farming, 10.6% construction, 14.9% production (2000).
Income: Per capita income: $27,322 (2005); Median household income: $62,840 (2005); Average household income: $75,049 (2005); Percent of households with income of $100,000 or more: 20.9% (2005); Poverty rate: 2.4% (2000).
Education: Percent of population age 25 and over with: High school diploma (including GED) or higher: 85.4% (2005); Bachelor's degree or higher: 23.3% (2005); Master's degree or higher: 8.6% (2005).

School District(s)
Eden Central School District (PK-12)
   2003-04 Enrollment: 1,844 .... (716) 992-3629

Housing: Homeownership rate: 87.2% (2005); Median home value: $142,860 (2005); Median rent: $448 per month (2000); Median age of housing: 44 years (2000).
Safety: Violent crime rate: 3.7 per 10,000 population; Property crime rate: 94.6 per 10,000 population (2004).
Transportation: Commute to work: 93.8% car, 0.5% public transportation, 1.5% walk, 3.8% work from home (2000); Travel time to work: 21.8% less than 15 minutes, 31.3% 15 to 30 minutes, 32.0% 30 to 45 minutes, 9.8% 45 to 60 minutes, 5.2% 60 minutes or more (2000)

Additional Information Contacts
Eden Chamber of Commerce .... (716) 992-4799
   http://www.edenny.org/chamber.html
Town of Eden .... (716) 992-3408
   http://www.edenny.org/

EDEN (CDP). Covers a land area of 5.639 square miles and a water area of 0 square miles. Located at 42.64° N. Lat.; 78.89° W. Long.
Population: 3,250 (1990); 3,579 (2000); 3,622 (2005); 3,662 (2010 projected); Race: 97.6% White, 0.9% Black, 0.4% Asian, 0.5% Hispanic of any race (2005); Density: 642.3 persons per square mile (2005); Average household size: 2.84 (2005); Median age: 39.8 (2005); Males per 100 females: 102.3 (2005); Marriage status: 21.6% never married, 65.7% now married, 5.9% widowed, 6.8% divorced (2000); Foreign born: 1.2% (2000); Ancestry (includes multiple ancestries): 38.5% German, 22.3% Irish, 20.5% Polish, 15.9% English, 11.6% Italian (2000).
Economy: Employment by occupation: 10.5% management, 18.7% professional, 10.8% services, 35.8% sales, 0.3% farming, 10.2% construction, 13.5% production (2000).
Income: Per capita income: $26,423 (2005); Median household income: $62,883 (2005); Average household income: $74,013 (2005); Percent of households with income of $100,000 or more: 19.9% (2005); Poverty rate: 3.1% (2000).
Education: Percent of population age 25 and over with: High school diploma (including GED) or higher: 88.1% (2005); Bachelor's degree or higher: 22.7% (2005); Master's degree or higher: 7.6% (2005).
Housing: Homeownership rate: 85.3% (2005); Median home value: $138,339 (2005); Median rent: $439 per month (2000); Median age of housing: 43 years (2000).
Transportation: Commute to work: 93.2% car, 0.8% public transportation, 1.5% walk, 4.4% work from home (2000); Travel time to work: 21.6% less than 15 minutes, 27.4% 15 to 30 minutes, 36.0% 30 to 45 minutes, 8.6% 45 to 60 minutes, 6.5% 60 minutes or more (2000)

ELMA (town). Covers a land area of 34.494 square miles and a water area of 0 square miles. Located at 42.82° N. Lat.; 78.63° W. Long. Elevation is 700 feet.
Population: 10,355 (1990); 11,304 (2000); 11,334 (2005); 11,355 (2010 projected); Race: 99.0% White, 0.1% Black, 0.4% Asian, 0.7% Hispanic of any race (2005); Density: 328.6 persons per square mile (2005); Average household size: 2.67 (2005); Median age: 43.9 (2005); Males per 100 females: 97.7 (2005); Marriage status: 19.7% never married, 67.5% now married, 6.3% widowed, 6.6% divorced (2000); Foreign born: 2.7% (2000); Ancestry (includes multiple ancestries): 34.4% German, 29.1% Polish, 14.4% Italian, 14.2% Irish, 9.2% English (2000).
Economy: Single-family building permits issued: 31 (2005); Multi-family building permits issued: 2 (2005); Employment by occupation: 15.9% management, 24.8% professional, 11.8% services, 24.6% sales, 0.2% farming, 9.5% construction, 13.1% production (2000).
Income: Per capita income: $29,358 (2005); Median household income: $63,199 (2005); Average household income: $77,888 (2005); Percent of households with income of $100,000 or more: 24.1% (2005); Poverty rate: 3.4% (2000).
Education: Percent of population age 25 and over with: High school diploma (including GED) or higher: 90.0% (2005); Bachelor's degree or higher: 29.4% (2005); Master's degree or higher: 12.5% (2005).

School District(s)
Iroquois Central School District (KG-12)
   2003-04 Enrollment: 2,905 .... (716) 652-3000

Housing: Homeownership rate: 89.0% (2005); Median home value: $178,851 (2005); Median rent: $514 per month (2000); Median age of housing: 37 years (2000).
Transportation: Commute to work: 94.7% car, 1.0% public transportation, 1.6% walk, 2.6% work from home (2000); Travel time to work: 25.4% less than 15 minutes, 42.5% 15 to 30 minutes, 25.9% 30 to 45 minutes, 4.9% 45 to 60 minutes, 1.4% 60 minutes or more (2000)

ELMA CENTER (CDP). Aka Elma. Covers a land area of 6.243 square miles and a water area of 0 square miles. Located at 42.83° N. Lat.; 78.63° W. Long. Elevation is 801 feet.
Population: 2,354 (1990); 2,491 (2000); 2,389 (2005); 2,369 (2010 projected); Race: 98.8% White, 0.0% Black, 0.5% Asian, 0.8% Hispanic of any race (2005); Density: 382.7 persons per square mile (2005); Average household size: 2.53 (2005); Median age: 46.2 (2005); Males per 100 females: 95.5 (2005); Marriage status: 19.4% never married, 67.8% now married, 8.0% widowed, 4.8% divorced (2000); Foreign born: 4.3% (2000); Ancestry (includes multiple ancestries): 34.5% German, 26.9% Polish, 12.9% English, 11.3% Italian, 10.7% Irish (2000).
Economy: Employment by occupation: 19.5% management, 27.1% professional, 10.5% services, 20.2% sales, 0.5% farming, 6.9% construction, 15.3% production (2000).
Income: Per capita income: $29,577 (2005); Median household income: $59,223 (2005); Average household income: $74,852 (2005); Percent of households with income of $100,000 or more: 25.8% (2005); Poverty rate: 3.4% (2000).
Education: Percent of population age 25 and over with: High school diploma (including GED) or higher: 91.8% (2005); Bachelor's degree or higher: 34.0% (2005); Master's degree or higher: 16.1% (2005).
Housing: Homeownership rate: 89.6% (2005); Median home value: $181,891 (2005); Median rent: $505 per month (2000); Median age of housing: 37 years (2000).
Transportation: Commute to work: 98.4% car, 0.0% public transportation, 0.0% walk, 1.6% work from home (2000); Travel time to work: 22.1% less than 15 minutes, 46.4% 15 to 30 minutes, 24.9% 30 to 45 minutes, 3.8% 45 to 60 minutes, 2.7% 60 minutes or more (2000)

EVANS (town). Covers a land area of 41.845 square miles and a water area of 0.008 square miles. Located at 42.64° N. Lat.; 79.03° W. Long.
Population: 17,478 (1990); 17,594 (2000); 17,402 (2005); 17,167 (2010 projected); Race: 97.6% White, 0.4% Black, 0.3% Asian, 1.5% Hispanic of any race (2005); Density: 415.9 persons per square mile (2005); Average household size: 2.60 (2005); Median age: 39.6 (2005); Males per 100 females: 95.8 (2005); Marriage status: 24.2% never married, 58.6% now married, 7.8% widowed, 9.4% divorced (2000); Foreign born: 2.3% (2000); Ancestry (includes multiple ancestries): 35.1% German, 21.8% Irish, 20.5% Polish, 17.3% Italian, 8.3% English (2000).
Economy: Single-family building permits issued: 22 (2005); Multi-family building permits issued: 20 (2005); Employment by occupation: 10.1% management, 18.9% professional, 15.7% services, 27.0% sales, 0.1% farming, 9.5% construction, 18.8% production (2000).
Income: Per capita income: $22,801 (2005); Median household income: $49,693 (2005); Average household income: $59,051 (2005); Percent of households with income of $100,000 or more: 14.8% (2005); Poverty rate: 7.0% (2000).
Taxes: Total city taxes per capita: $399 (2004); City property taxes per capita: $374 (2004).
Education: Percent of population age 25 and over with: High school diploma (including GED) or higher: 84.4% (2005); Bachelor's degree or higher: 18.8% (2005); Master's degree or higher: 7.7% (2005).

Housing: Homeownership rate: 81.1% (2005); Median home value: $111,872 (2005); Median rent: $434 per month (2000); Median age of housing: 45 years (2000).
Safety: Violent crime rate: 4.6 per 10,000 population; Property crime rate: 169.5 per 10,000 population (2004).
Transportation: Commute to work: 96.7% car, 0.8% public transportation, 1.4% walk, 1.0% work from home (2000); Travel time to work: 24.4% less than 15 minutes, 26.0% 15 to 30 minutes, 32.1% 30 to 45 minutes, 14.0% 45 to 60 minutes, 3.5% 60 minutes or more (2000)
Additional Information Contacts
Town of Evans . . . . (716) 549-5754
http://www.townofevans.org/

FARNHAM (village).
Covers a land area of 1.208 square miles and a water area of 0 square miles. Located at 42.59° N. Lat.; 79.08° W. Long. Elevation is 631 feet.
Population: 427 (1990); 322 (2000); 316 (2005); 314 (2010 projected); Race: 95.3% White, 0.9% Black, 0.0% Asian, 0.9% Hispanic of any race (2005); Density: 261.7 persons per square mile (2005); Average household size: 2.82 (2005); Median age: 38.3 (2005); Males per 100 females: 90.4 (2005); Marriage status: 27.8% never married, 54.0% now married, 8.1% widowed, 10.1% divorced (2000); Foreign born: 1.2% (2000); Ancestry (includes multiple ancestries): 40.2% German, 24.5% Italian, 18.9% Irish, 7.1% Polish, 4.0% United States or American (2000).
Economy: Manufacturing: canned foods, textiles. Single-family building permits issued: 0 (2005); Multi-family building permits issued: 0 (2005); Employment by occupation: 2.9% management, 4.3% professional, 31.9% services, 23.9% sales, 0.0% farming, 14.5% construction, 22.5% production (2000).
Income: Per capita income: $18,663 (2005); Median household income: $42,826 (2005); Average household income: $50,826 (2005); Percent of households with income of $100,000 or more: 11.6% (2005); Poverty rate: 7.7% (2000).
Education: Percent of population age 25 and over with: High school diploma (including GED) or higher: 81.0% (2005); Bachelor's degree or higher: 8.1% (2005); Master's degree or higher: 1.9% (2005).
Housing: Homeownership rate: 72.3% (2005); Median home value: $93,500 (2005); Median rent: $380 per month (2000); Median age of housing: 60+ years (2000).
Transportation: Commute to work: 96.9% car, 0.0% public transportation, 0.0% walk, 3.1% work from home (2000); Travel time to work: 33.1% less than 15 minutes, 29.0% 15 to 30 minutes, 13.7% 30 to 45 minutes, 16.9% 45 to 60 minutes, 7.3% 60 minutes or more (2000)

GETZVILLE (unincorporated postal area, zip code 14068).
Covers a land area of 3.832 square miles and a water area of 0 square miles. Located at 43.02° N. Lat.; 78.76° W. Long. Elevation is 582 feet.
Population: 0 (2000); Race: 87.9% White, 3.5% Black, 6.4% Asian, 2.3% Hispanic of any race (2000); Density: 0.0 persons per square mile (2000); Age: 19.9% under 18, 12.9% over 64 (2000); Marriage status: 12.1% never married, 79.4% now married, 4.8% widowed, 3.7% divorced (2000); Foreign born: 5.9% (2000); Ancestry (includes multiple ancestries): 16.7% German, 14.9% Italian, 9.8% Polish, 9.6% Irish, 8.0% Other groups (2000).
Economy: Employment by occupation: 16.5% management, 26.8% professional, 13.5% services, 33.0% sales, 0.0% farming, 3.7% construction, 6.6% production (2000).
Income: Per capita income: $17,663 (2000); Median household income: $68,559 (2000); Poverty rate: 5.6% (2000).
Education: Percent of population age 25 and over with: High school diploma (including GED) or higher: 89.0% (2000); Bachelor's degree or higher: 43.0% (2000).
Two-year College(s)
ITT Technical Institute
    Fall 2004 Enrollment: 719 . . . . (716) 689-2200
    2005-06 Tuition: In-state $14,196; Out-of-state $14,196
Housing: Homeownership rate: 79.5% (2000); Median home value: $154,600 (2000); Median rent: $657 per month (2000); Median age of housing: 17 years (2000).
Transportation: Commute to work: 86.9% car, 0.3% public transportation, 9.9% walk, 2.9% work from home (2000); Travel time to work: 33.8% less than 15 minutes, 46.0% 15 to 30 minutes, 16.7% 30 to 45 minutes, 1.4% 45 to 60 minutes, 2.1% 60 minutes or more (2000)

GLENWOOD (unincorporated postal area, zip code 14069).
Covers a land area of 5.437 square miles and a water area of 0 square miles. Located at 42.60° N. Lat.; 78.64° W. Long. Elevation is 1,195 feet.
Population: 0 (2000); Race: 100.0% White, 0.0% Black, 0.0% Asian, 1.0% Hispanic of any race (2000); Density: 0.0 persons per square mile (2000); Age: 16.5% under 18, 11.1% over 64 (2000); Marriage status: 21.3% never married, 66.9% now married, 3.8% widowed, 8.0% divorced (2000); Foreign born: 3.7% (2000); Ancestry (includes multiple ancestries): 45.4% German, 19.7% English, 18.5% Irish, 11.1% Polish, 11.0% Italian (2000).
Economy: Employment by occupation: 16.2% management, 22.3% professional, 6.6% services, 31.2% sales, 0.0% farming, 8.9% construction, 14.8% production (2000).
Income: Per capita income: $30,286 (2000); Median household income: $51,094 (2000); Poverty rate: 5.6% (2000).
Education: Percent of population age 25 and over with: High school diploma (including GED) or higher: 94.3% (2000); Bachelor's degree or higher: 24.2% (2000).
Housing: Homeownership rate: 70.8% (2000); Median home value: $95,000 (2000); Median rent: $367 per month (2000); Median age of housing: 32 years (2000).
Transportation: Commute to work: 99.3% car, 0.0% public transportation, 0.0% walk, 0.0% work from home (2000); Travel time to work: 13.6% less than 15 minutes, 31.1% 15 to 30 minutes, 33.1% 30 to 45 minutes, 19.2% 45 to 60 minutes, 2.9% 60 minutes or more (2000)

GRAND ISLAND (town).
Covers a land area of 28.514 square miles and a water area of 4.785 square miles. Located at 43.01° N. Lat.; 78.95° W. Long.
Population: 17,561 (1990); 18,621 (2000); 18,765 (2005); 18,884 (2010 projected); Race: 95.4% White, 1.9% Black, 1.2% Asian, 1.3% Hispanic of any race (2005); Density: 658.1 persons per square mile (2005); Average household size: 2.67 (2005); Median age: 40.4 (2005); Males per 100 females: 96.9 (2005); Marriage status: 21.7% never married, 65.6% now married, 5.3% widowed, 7.4% divorced (2000); Foreign born: 4.2% (2000); Ancestry (includes multiple ancestries): 30.3% German, 21.4% Irish, 20.1% Italian, 15.1% Polish, 13.4% English (2000).
Economy: Single-family building permits issued: 86 (2005); Multi-family building permits issued: 0 (2005); Employment by occupation: 15.5% management, 26.1% professional, 11.3% services, 26.4% sales, 0.1% farming, 7.3% construction, 13.3% production (2000).
Income: Per capita income: $29,826 (2005); Median household income: $68,105 (2005); Average household income: $79,166 (2005); Percent of households with income of $100,000 or more: 26.4% (2005); Poverty rate: 3.0% (2000).
Education: Percent of population age 25 and over with: High school diploma (including GED) or higher: 92.7% (2005); Bachelor's degree or higher: 32.6% (2005); Master's degree or higher: 13.1% (2005).
School District(s)
Grand Island Central School District (KG-12)
    2003-04 Enrollment: 3,190 . . . . (716) 773-8801
Housing: Homeownership rate: 84.0% (2005); Median home value: $146,672 (2005); Median rent: $530 per month (2000); Median age of housing: 31 years (2000).
Newspapers: Island Dispatch (General - Circulation 3,106); Lewiston/Porter Sentinel (General - Circulation 10,792); Niagara/Wheatfield Tribune (General - Circulation 11,900)
Transportation: Commute to work: 95.4% car, 0.5% public transportation, 0.5% walk, 2.8% work from home (2000); Travel time to work: 28.6% less than 15 minutes, 54.2% 15 to 30 minutes, 12.7% 30 to 45 minutes, 2.3% 45 to 60 minutes, 2.2% 60 minutes or more (2000)
Additional Information Contacts
Grand Island Chamber of Commerce . . . . (716) 773-3651
    http://www.gichamber.org
Town of Grand Island. . . . . (716) 773-9600
    http://www.grand-island.ny.us/

HAMBURG (village).
Covers a land area of 2.513 square miles and a water area of 0 square miles. Located at 42.72° N. Lat.; 78.83° W. Long. Elevation is 825 feet.
Population: 10,442 (1990); 10,116 (2000); 9,715 (2005); 9,312 (2010 projected); Race: 98.5% White, 0.2% Black, 0.4% Asian, 0.8% Hispanic of any race (2005); Density: 3,865.7 persons per square mile (2005); Average household size: 2.48 (2005); Median age: 39.9 (2005); Males per 100 females: 88.2 (2005); Marriage status: 20.8% never married, 61.6% now

married, 8.6% widowed, 8.9% divorced (2000); Foreign born: 2.0% (2000); Ancestry (includes multiple ancestries): 36.1% German, 27.0% Irish, 18.7% Italian, 15.4% English, 14.0% Polish (2000).
Economy: Single-family building permits issued: 0 (2005); Multi-family building permits issued: 0 (2005); Employment by occupation: 14.4% management, 26.7% professional, 14.7% services, 28.1% sales, 0.3% farming, 4.7% construction, 11.1% production (2000).
Income: Per capita income: $26,619 (2005); Median household income: $57,621 (2005); Average household income: $65,745 (2005); Percent of households with income of $100,000 or more: 18.7% (2005); Poverty rate: 3.0% (2000).
Education: Percent of population age 25 and over with: High school diploma (including GED) or higher: 90.7% (2005); Bachelor's degree or higher: 38.1% (2005); Master's degree or higher: 13.6% (2005).

School District(s)
Frontier Central School District (KG-12)
    2003-04 Enrollment: 5,622 .... (716) 926-1711
Hamburg Central School District (PK-12)
    2003-04 Enrollment: 4,153 .... (716) 646-3220
Hopevale Union Free School District At Hamburg (07-12)
    2003-04 Enrollment: 119 .... (716) 648-1930

Four-year College(s)
Hilbert College
    Fall 2004 Enrollment: 1,107 .... (716) 649-7900
    2005-06 Tuition: In-state $14,930; Out-of-state $14,930

Housing: Homeownership rate: 71.8% (2005); Median home value: $129,102 (2005); Median rent: $489 per month (2000); Median age of housing: 48 years (2000).
Safety: Violent crime rate: 12.2 per 10,000 population; Property crime rate: 198.8 per 10,000 population (2004).
Newspapers: The Sun & Erie County Independent (General - Circulation 10,202)
Transportation: Commute to work: 91.8% car, 0.3% public transportation, 3.3% walk, 3.8% work from home (2000); Travel time to work: 38.2% less than 15 minutes, 33.3% 15 to 30 minutes, 22.6% 30 to 45 minutes, 2.4% 45 to 60 minutes, 3.4% 60 minutes or more (2000)

Additional Information Contacts
Hamburg Chamber of Commerce .... (716) 649-7917
    http://www.hamburg-chamber.org
Village of Hamburg .... (716) 649-0200
    http://www.villagehamburg.com/

HAMBURG (town). Covers a land area of 41.285 square miles and a water area of 0.021 square miles. Located at 42.74° N. Lat.; 78.84° W. Long. Elevation is 825 feet.
History: Seat of Hilbert College. Settled c.1808, incorporated 1874.
Population: 53,735 (1990); 56,259 (2000); 56,898 (2005); 57,407 (2010 projected); Race: 97.5% White, 0.6% Black, 0.5% Asian, 1.8% Hispanic of any race (2005); Density: 1,378.2 persons per square mile (2005); Average household size: 2.52 (2005); Median age: 40.4 (2005); Males per 100 females: 91.3 (2005); Marriage status: 23.8% never married, 58.9% now married, 8.6% widowed, 8.8% divorced (2000); Foreign born: 2.9% (2000); Ancestry (includes multiple ancestries): 33.9% German, 24.2% Irish, 22.7% Polish, 17.9% Italian, 10.2% English (2000).
Economy: Residential and industrial suburb of Buffalo. Its manufacturing includes rubber goods and optical products. Unemployment rate: 4.9% (2005); Total civilian labor force: 31,567 (2005); Single-family building permits issued: 201 (2005); Multi-family building permits issued: 0 (2005); Employment by occupation: 12.2% management, 22.3% professional, 14.8% services, 28.6% sales, 0.1% farming, 7.1% construction, 14.8% production (2000).
Income: Per capita income: $25,510 (2005); Median household income: $54,429 (2005); Average household income: $63,844 (2005); Percent of households with income of $100,000 or more: 17.2% (2005); Poverty rate: 4.5% (2000).
Taxes: Total city taxes per capita: $423 (2004); City property taxes per capita: $377 (2004).
Education: Percent of population age 25 and over with: High school diploma (including GED) or higher: 87.1% (2005); Bachelor's degree or higher: 26.2% (2005); Master's degree or higher: 10.0% (2005).
Housing: Homeownership rate: 74.5% (2005); Median home value: $126,749 (2005); Median rent: $508 per month (2000); Median age of housing: 38 years (2000).
Safety: Violent crime rate: 1.1 per 10,000 population; Property crime rate: 79.6 per 10,000 population (2004).
Transportation: Commute to work: 94.8% car, 0.5% public transportation, 1.8% walk, 2.4% work from home (2000); Travel time to work: 31.8% less than 15 minutes, 39.6% 15 to 30 minutes, 22.1% 30 to 45 minutes, 3.4% 45 to 60 minutes, 3.1% 60 minutes or more (2000)

Additional Information Contacts
Town of Hamburg .... (716) 649-6111
    http://www.townofhamburgny.com/

HARRIS HILL (CDP). Covers a land area of 4.044 square miles and a water area of 0 square miles. Located at 42.96° N. Lat.; 78.67° W. Long. Elevation is 727 feet.
Population: 4,577 (1990); 4,881 (2000); 5,096 (2005); 5,224 (2010 projected); Race: 96.5% White, 0.6% Black, 1.8% Asian, 1.1% Hispanic of any race (2005); Density: 1,260.2 persons per square mile (2005); Average household size: 2.58 (2005); Median age: 43.5 (2005); Males per 100 females: 94.3 (2005); Marriage status: 18.3% never married, 68.8% now married, 7.5% widowed, 5.4% divorced (2000); Foreign born: 4.5% (2000); Ancestry (includes multiple ancestries): 33.8% German, 23.5% Irish, 20.8% Italian, 15.6% Polish, 11.9% English (2000).
Economy: Employment by occupation: 21.8% management, 29.6% professional, 8.8% services, 27.1% sales, 0.0% farming, 5.3% construction, 7.4% production (2000).
Income: Per capita income: $34,428 (2005); Median household income: $71,830 (2005); Average household income: $88,567 (2005); Percent of households with income of $100,000 or more: 29.9% (2005); Poverty rate: 1.5% (2000).
Education: Percent of population age 25 and over with: High school diploma (including GED) or higher: 96.1% (2005); Bachelor's degree or higher: 42.2% (2005); Master's degree or higher: 19.8% (2005).
Housing: Homeownership rate: 92.5% (2005); Median home value: $158,512 (2005); Median rent: $590 per month (2000); Median age of housing: 43 years (2000).
Transportation: Commute to work: 95.8% car, 0.3% public transportation, 0.0% walk, 3.9% work from home (2000); Travel time to work: 32.2% less than 15 minutes, 42.7% 15 to 30 minutes, 20.4% 30 to 45 minutes, 3.1% 45 to 60 minutes, 1.7% 60 minutes or more (2000)

HOLLAND (town). Covers a land area of 35.796 square miles and a water area of 0.031 square miles. Located at 42.64° N. Lat.; 78.51° W. Long. Elevation is 1,111 feet.
Population: 3,604 (1990); 3,603 (2000); 3,591 (2005); 3,583 (2010 projected); Race: 97.6% White, 0.7% Black, 0.6% Asian, 0.5% Hispanic of any race (2005); Density: 100.3 persons per square mile (2005); Average household size: 2.65 (2005); Median age: 38.0 (2005); Males per 100 females: 98.8 (2005); Marriage status: 24.0% never married, 63.1% now married, 4.8% widowed, 8.0% divorced (2000); Foreign born: 0.7% (2000); Ancestry (includes multiple ancestries): 39.6% German, 19.1% Polish, 17.6% Irish, 12.6% English, 9.4% Italian (2000).
Economy: Farm community - dairy products, vegetables, field corn, hay. Single-family building permits issued: 6 (2005); Multi-family building permits issued: 0 (2005); Employment by occupation: 16.0% management, 15.1% professional, 12.6% services, 24.9% sales, 1.6% farming, 13.8% construction, 16.0% production (2000).
Income: Per capita income: $23,388 (2005); Median household income: $53,997 (2005); Average household income: $62,027 (2005); Percent of households with income of $100,000 or more: 16.0% (2005); Poverty rate: 9.7% (2000).
Education: Percent of population age 25 and over with: High school diploma (including GED) or higher: 89.2% (2005); Bachelor's degree or higher: 15.5% (2005); Master's degree or higher: 6.7% (2005).

School District(s)
Holland Central School District (PK-12)
    2003-04 Enrollment: 1,336 .... (716) 537-8222

Housing: Homeownership rate: 79.8% (2005); Median home value: $133,540 (2005); Median rent: $424 per month (2000); Median age of housing: 37 years (2000).
Transportation: Commute to work: 95.2% car, 0.0% public transportation, 2.8% walk, 1.6% work from home (2000); Travel time to work: 21.9% less than 15 minutes, 28.1% 15 to 30 minutes, 30.3% 30 to 45 minutes, 16.8% 45 to 60 minutes, 2.9% 60 minutes or more (2000)

HOLLAND (CDP). Covers a land area of 3.555 square miles and a water area of 0 square miles. Located at 42.64° N. Lat.; 78.54° W. Long.
Population: 1,288 (1990); 1,261 (2000); 1,145 (2005); 1,111 (2010 projected); Race: 97.5% White, 1.0% Black, 0.6% Asian, 0.5% Hispanic of

any race (2005); Density: 322.1 persons per square mile (2005); Average household size: 2.52 (2005); Median age: 38.3 (2005); Males per 100 females: 96.7 (2005); Marriage status: 25.9% never married, 56.7% now married, 8.8% widowed, 8.6% divorced (2000); Foreign born: 0.4% (2000); Ancestry (includes multiple ancestries): 33.4% German, 18.6% Polish, 14.1% Irish, 11.9% English, 10.9% Italian (2000).
Economy: Employment by occupation: 13.0% management, 14.7% professional, 12.0% services, 26.2% sales, 2.9% farming, 17.6% construction, 13.6% production (2000).
Income: Per capita income: $22,487 (2005); Median household income: $49,051 (2005); Average household income: $56,713 (2005); Percent of households with income of $100,000 or more: 14.8% (2005); Poverty rate: 10.2% (2000).
Education: Percent of population age 25 and over with: High school diploma (including GED) or higher: 80.2% (2005); Bachelor's degree or higher: 19.1% (2005); Master's degree or higher: 8.0% (2005).
Housing: Homeownership rate: 64.3% (2005); Median home value: $125,000 (2005); Median rent: $439 per month (2000); Median age of housing: 55 years (2000).
Transportation: Commute to work: 89.2% car, 0.0% public transportation, 6.7% walk, 2.9% work from home (2000); Travel time to work: 25.2% less than 15 minutes, 35.1% 15 to 30 minutes, 24.2% 30 to 45 minutes, 10.3% 45 to 60 minutes, 5.3% 60 minutes or more (2000)

KENMORE (village).
Covers a land area of 1.436 square miles and a water area of 0 square miles. Located at 42.96° N. Lat.; 78.87° W. Long. Elevation is 612 feet.
History: Named for a prominent citizen. Incorporated 1899.
Population: 17,180 (1990); 16,426 (2000); 15,694 (2005); 14,963 (2010 projected); Race: 96.0% White, 1.4% Black, 0.8% Asian, 1.7% Hispanic of any race (2005); Density: 10,927.5 persons per square mile (2005); Average household size: 2.28 (2005); Median age: 40.0 (2005); Males per 100 females: 87.1 (2005); Marriage status: 29.5% never married, 52.1% now married, 9.6% widowed, 8.8% divorced (2000); Foreign born: 2.9% (2000); Ancestry (includes multiple ancestries): 30.8% German, 26.8% Italian, 22.5% Irish, 11.9% Polish, 10.2% English (2000).
Economy: Single-family building permits issued: 0 (2005); Multi-family building permits issued: 0 (2005); Employment by occupation: 12.6% management, 25.8% professional, 14.1% services, 28.5% sales, 0.0% farming, 6.1% construction, 12.9% production (2000).
Income: Per capita income: $24,961 (2005); Median household income: $47,694 (2005); Average household income: $56,568 (2005); Percent of households with income of $100,000 or more: 11.9% (2005); Poverty rate: 5.2% (2000).
Education: Percent of population age 25 and over with: High school diploma (including GED) or higher: 89.2% (2005); Bachelor's degree or higher: 28.9% (2005); Master's degree or higher: 10.9% (2005).
School District(s)
Kenmore-Tonawanda Union Free School District (PK-12)
    2003-04 Enrollment: 9,033 . . . . (716) 874-8400
Housing: Homeownership rate: 66.7% (2005); Median home value: $98,451 (2005); Median rent: $450 per month (2000); Median age of housing: 60+ years (2000).
Hospitals: Kenmore Mercy Hospital (184 beds)
Safety: Violent crime rate: 11.9 per 10,000 population; Property crime rate: 162.2 per 10,000 population (2004).
Transportation: Commute to work: 92.5% car, 3.9% public transportation, 1.5% walk, 1.2% work from home (2000); Travel time to work: 29.0% less than 15 minutes, 53.7% 15 to 30 minutes, 13.2% 30 to 45 minutes, 2.2% 45 to 60 minutes, 1.9% 60 minutes or more (2000)
Additional Information Contacts
Kenmore-Town of Tonawanda Chamber of Commerce . . . (716) 874-1202
    http://www.ken-ton.org
Village of Kenmore . . . . (716) 873-5700
    http://www.vi.kenmore.ny.us/

LACKAWANNA (city).
Covers a land area of 6.122 square miles and a water area of 0 square miles. Located at 42.81° N. Lat.; 78.82° W. Long. Elevation is 592 feet.
History: Named for the Lackawanna Steel Company. Formerly a major steel-making center, Lackawanna experienced the total decline of its foremost industry in the 1970s and 1980s. A distinguished city landmark is the elaborate Basilica of Our Lady of Victory, a Roman Catholic shrine. Incorporated 1909.
Population: 20,585 (1990); 19,064 (2000); 18,400 (2005); 17,755 (2010 projected); Race: 83.0% White, 9.9% Black, 0.4% Asian, 5.4% Hispanic of any race (2005); Density: 3,005.5 persons per square mile (2005); Average household size: 2.29 (2005); Median age: 38.6 (2005); Males per 100 females: 93.4 (2005); Marriage status: 30.2% never married, 48.1% now married, 11.0% widowed, 10.8% divorced (2000); Foreign born: 6.2% (2000); Ancestry (includes multiple ancestries): 29.7% Polish, 17.0% Italian, 16.0% German, 14.9% Other groups, 14.5% Irish (2000).
Economy: Manufacturing: abrasives, chemicals, concrete. Single-family building permits issued: 1 (2005); Multi-family building permits issued: 0 (2005); Employment by occupation: 6.9% management, 15.5% professional, 18.0% services, 31.8% sales, 0.0% farming, 7.2% construction, 20.5% production (2000).
Income: Per capita income: $19,031 (2005); Median household income: $33,715 (2005); Average household income: $43,234 (2005); Percent of households with income of $100,000 or more: 5.8% (2005); Poverty rate: 16.7% (2000).
Education: Percent of population age 25 and over with: High school diploma (including GED) or higher: 75.9% (2005); Bachelor's degree or higher: 11.8% (2005); Master's degree or higher: 4.4% (2005).
School District(s)
Global Concepts Charter School (KG-04)
    2003-04 Enrollment: 239 . . . . (716) 824-4912
Lackawanna City School District (PK-12)
    2003-04 Enrollment: 2,041 . . . . (716) 827-6767
Housing: Homeownership rate: 57.6% (2005); Median home value: $87,628 (2005); Median rent: $350 per month (2000); Median age of housing: 50 years (2000).
Hospitals: Our Lady of Victory Hospital (74 beds)
Safety: Violent crime rate: 60.0 per 10,000 population; Property crime rate: 238.5 per 10,000 population (2004).
Newspapers: Front Page (General - Circulation 5,500); South Buffalo News (General - Circulation 5,000)
Transportation: Commute to work: 91.3% car, 4.5% public transportation, 2.6% walk, 1.1% work from home (2000); Travel time to work: 31.6% less than 15 minutes, 48.1% 15 to 30 minutes, 12.7% 30 to 45 minutes, 3.9% 45 to 60 minutes, 3.7% 60 minutes or more (2000)
Additional Information Contacts
City of Lackawanna . . . . (716) 827-6452
    http://www.ci.lackawanna.ny.us/
Lackawanna Chamber of Commerce . . . . (716) 823-8841
    http://www.lackawannachamber.com/

LAKE ERIE BEACH (CDP).
Covers a land area of 3.850 square miles and a water area of 0 square miles. Located at 42.62° N. Lat.; 79.08° W. Long.
Population: 4,509 (1990); 4,499 (2000); 4,188 (2005); 3,951 (2010 projected); Race: 97.3% White, 0.2% Black, 0.0% Asian, 1.0% Hispanic of any race (2005); Density: 1,087.9 persons per square mile (2005); Average household size: 2.58 (2005); Median age: 39.1 (2005); Males per 100 females: 99.6 (2005); Marriage status: 23.0% never married, 58.9% now married, 7.4% widowed, 10.7% divorced (2000); Foreign born: 2.5% (2000); Ancestry (includes multiple ancestries): 39.2% German, 26.1% Polish, 20.5% Irish, 17.2% Italian, 8.1% English (2000).
Economy: Employment by occupation: 6.5% management, 18.8% professional, 13.3% services, 28.8% sales, 0.0% farming, 9.4% construction, 23.2% production (2000).
Income: Per capita income: $19,182 (2005); Median household income: $42,676 (2005); Average household income: $49,557 (2005); Percent of households with income of $100,000 or more: 10.5% (2005); Poverty rate: 8.1% (2000).
Education: Percent of population age 25 and over with: High school diploma (including GED) or higher: 85.2% (2005); Bachelor's degree or higher: 18.0% (2005); Master's degree or higher: 8.0% (2005).
Housing: Homeownership rate: 83.7% (2005); Median home value: $96,788 (2005); Median rent: $479 per month (2000); Median age of housing: 49 years (2000).
Transportation: Commute to work: 98.6% car, 0.8% public transportation, 0.0% walk, 0.6% work from home (2000); Travel time to work: 22.2% less than 15 minutes, 18.2% 15 to 30 minutes, 30.4% 30 to 45 minutes, 23.6% 45 to 60 minutes, 5.5% 60 minutes or more (2000)

LAKE VIEW (unincorporated postal area, zip code 14085).
Aka Lakeview. Covers a land area of 6.173 square miles and a water area of 0

square miles. Located at 42.71° N. Lat.; 78.93° W. Long. Elevation is 722 feet.
Population: 0 (2000); Race: 99.1% White, 0.2% Black, 0.0% Asian, 1.3% Hispanic of any race (2000); Density: 0.0 persons per square mile (2000); Age: 28.9% under 18, 9.6% over 64 (2000); Marriage status: 22.1% never married, 65.1% now married, 6.0% widowed, 6.8% divorced (2000); Foreign born: 1.9% (2000); Ancestry (includes multiple ancestries): 33.5% German, 24.8% Irish, 24.5% Polish, 21.0% Italian, 9.8% English (2000).
Economy: Employment by occupation: 11.9% management, 22.8% professional, 16.1% services, 25.9% sales, 0.0% farming, 9.3% construction, 13.9% production (2000).
Income: Per capita income: $24,242 (2000); Median household income: $58,438 (2000); Poverty rate: 1.8% (2000).
Education: Percent of population age 25 and over with: High school diploma (including GED) or higher: 89.3% (2000); Bachelor's degree or higher: 25.5% (2000).

School District(s)
Frontier Central School District (KG-12)
    2003-04 Enrollment: 5,622 . . . . (716) 926-1711
Housing: Homeownership rate: 93.1% (2000); Median home value: $104,100 (2000); Median rent: $607 per month (2000); Median age of housing: 34 years (2000).
Transportation: Commute to work: 95.2% car, 0.3% public transportation, 2.1% walk, 2.1% work from home (2000); Travel time to work: 21.1% less than 15 minutes, 35.5% 15 to 30 minutes, 33.5% 30 to 45 minutes, 5.1% 45 to 60 minutes, 4.8% 60 minutes or more (2000)

LANCASTER (village). Covers a land area of 2.693 square miles and a water area of 0.029 square miles. Located at 42.90° N. Lat.; 78.67° W. Long. Elevation is 696 feet.
Population: 11,940 (1990); 11,188 (2000); 11,688 (2005); 12,147 (2010 projected); Race: 98.3% White, 0.4% Black, 0.2% Asian, 1.1% Hispanic of any race (2005); Density: 4,340.7 persons per square mile (2005); Average household size: 2.33 (2005); Median age: 40.5 (2005); Males per 100 females: 91.9 (2005); Marriage status: 24.4% never married, 56.4% now married, 10.6% widowed, 8.6% divorced (2000); Foreign born: 1.5% (2000); Ancestry (includes multiple ancestries): 38.3% German, 29.6% Polish, 14.9% Italian, 14.9% Irish, 7.7% English (2000).
Economy: Single-family building permits issued: 1 (2005); Multi-family building permits issued: 2 (2005); Employment by occupation: 10.1% management, 18.3% professional, 18.0% services, 27.9% sales, 0.3% farming, 9.8% construction, 15.6% production (2000).
Income: Per capita income: $23,588 (2005); Median household income: $45,487 (2005); Average household income: $54,451 (2005); Percent of households with income of $100,000 or more: 11.1% (2005); Poverty rate: 5.1% (2000).
Education: Percent of population age 25 and over with: High school diploma (including GED) or higher: 84.5% (2005); Bachelor's degree or higher: 17.5% (2005); Master's degree or higher: 5.1% (2005).

School District(s)
Lancaster Central School District (KG-12)
    2003-04 Enrollment: 6,204 . . . . (716) 686-3200
Housing: Homeownership rate: 69.1% (2005); Median home value: $110,923 (2005); Median rent: $420 per month (2000); Median age of housing: 47 years (2000).
Transportation: Commute to work: 95.1% car, 0.4% public transportation, 2.4% walk, 0.8% work from home (2000); Travel time to work: 31.8% less than 15 minutes, 42.9% 15 to 30 minutes, 21.3% 30 to 45 minutes, 1.8% 45 to 60 minutes, 2.2% 60 minutes or more (2000)
Additional Information Contacts
Lancaster Area Chamber of Commerce . . . . (716) 681-9755
    http://www.coloniechamber.org
Village of Lancaster . . . . (716) 683-2105
    http://www.lancastervillage.org/framework.php?module=home

LANCASTER (town). Covers a land area of 37.841 square miles and a water area of 0.056 square miles. Located at 42.90° N. Lat.; 78.66° W. Long. Elevation is 696 feet.
History: Incorporated 1849.
Population: 32,181 (1990); 39,019 (2000); 41,273 (2005); 43,300 (2010 projected); Race: 97.6% White, 1.0% Black, 0.5% Asian, 0.8% Hispanic of any race (2005); Density: 1,090.7 persons per square mile (2005); Average household size: 2.57 (2005); Median age: 39.5 (2005); Males per 100 females: 94.1 (2005); Marriage status: 23.2% never married, 61.3% now married, 8.3% widowed, 7.2% divorced (2000); Foreign born: 2.6% (2000); Ancestry (includes multiple ancestries): 35.6% Polish, 35.4% German, 18.0% Italian, 13.9% Irish, 7.1% English (2000).
Economy: Its industries include lumber mills, dairy farms, and stone quarries. Unemployment rate: 4.4% (2005); Total civilian labor force: 23,493 (2005); Single-family building permits issued: 110 (2005); Multi-family building permits issued: 0 (2005); Employment by occupation: 14.0% management, 19.6% professional, 15.4% services, 29.7% sales, 0.1% farming, 7.9% construction, 13.3% production (2000).
Income: Per capita income: $25,582 (2005); Median household income: $57,006 (2005); Average household income: $65,101 (2005); Percent of households with income of $100,000 or more: 18.2% (2005); Poverty rate: 3.9% (2000).
Taxes: Total city taxes per capita: $351 (2004); City property taxes per capita: $309 (2004).
Education: Percent of population age 25 and over with: High school diploma (including GED) or higher: 85.8% (2005); Bachelor's degree or higher: 22.2% (2005); Master's degree or higher: 7.0% (2005).
Housing: Homeownership rate: 77.5% (2005); Median home value: $134,217 (2005); Median rent: $431 per month (2000); Median age of housing: 36 years (2000).
Transportation: Commute to work: 96.6% car, 0.3% public transportation, 1.0% walk, 1.4% work from home (2000); Travel time to work: 27.8% less than 15 minutes, 47.4% 15 to 30 minutes, 19.7% 30 to 45 minutes, 2.6% 45 to 60 minutes, 2.5% 60 minutes or more (2000)

LAWTONS (unincorporated postal area, zip code 14091). Covers a land area of 21.698 square miles and a water area of 0.008 square miles. Located at 42.53° N. Lat.; 78.88° W. Long. Elevation is 849 feet.
Population: 0 (2000); Race: 71.8% White, 0.3% Black, 3.6% Asian, 1.6% Hispanic of any race (2000); Density: 0.0 persons per square mile (2000); Age: 27.3% under 18, 10.7% over 64 (2000); Marriage status: 30.6% never married, 52.3% now married, 4.5% widowed, 12.6% divorced (2000); Foreign born: 4.5% (2000); Ancestry (includes multiple ancestries): 38.8% German, 20.2% Other groups, 16.0% Irish, 7.9% Polish, 5.5% Italian (2000).
Economy: Employment by occupation: 14.3% management, 17.6% professional, 20.4% services, 13.9% sales, 4.6% farming, 14.9% construction, 14.3% production (2000).
Income: Per capita income: $16,724 (2000); Median household income: $36,528 (2000); Poverty rate: 16.8% (2000).
Education: Percent of population age 25 and over with: High school diploma (including GED) or higher: 80.9% (2000); Bachelor's degree or higher: 15.7% (2000).
Housing: Homeownership rate: 75.8% (2000); Median home value: $80,300 (2000); Median rent: $403 per month (2000); Median age of housing: 43 years (2000).
Transportation: Commute to work: 84.6% car, 0.0% public transportation, 1.3% walk, 11.4% work from home (2000); Travel time to work: 27.1% less than 15 minutes, 32.3% 15 to 30 minutes, 29.7% 30 to 45 minutes, 4.0% 45 to 60 minutes, 6.9% 60 minutes or more (2000)

MARILLA (town). Covers a land area of 27.559 square miles and a water area of 0 square miles. Located at 42.82° N. Lat.; 78.53° W. Long. Elevation is 840 feet.
Population: 5,250 (1990); 5,709 (2000); 5,724 (2005); 5,745 (2010 projected); Race: 99.0% White, 0.2% Black, 0.2% Asian, 0.6% Hispanic of any race (2005); Density: 207.7 persons per square mile (2005); Average household size: 2.77 (2005); Median age: 40.0 (2005); Males per 100 females: 98.7 (2005); Marriage status: 21.3% never married, 66.9% now married, 5.2% widowed, 6.5% divorced (2000); Foreign born: 2.0% (2000); Ancestry (includes multiple ancestries): 42.8% German, 23.9% Polish, 15.7% Irish, 15.4% Italian, 7.7% English (2000).
Economy: Single-family building permits issued: 18 (2005); Multi-family building permits issued: 0 (2005); Employment by occupation: 16.3% management, 18.9% professional, 11.9% services, 23.7% sales, 0.2% farming, 10.6% construction, 18.4% production (2000).
Income: Per capita income: $25,851 (2005); Median household income: $62,157 (2005); Average household income: $71,623 (2005); Percent of households with income of $100,000 or more: 19.7% (2005); Poverty rate: 3.7% (2000).
Taxes: Total city taxes per capita: $220 (2004); City property taxes per capita: $179 (2004).
Education: Percent of population age 25 and over with: High school diploma (including GED) or higher: 89.3% (2005); Bachelor's degree or higher: 17.1% (2005); Master's degree or higher: 5.3% (2005).

School District(s)
Iroquois Central School District (KG-12)
   2003-04 Enrollment: 2,905 . . . . (716) 652-3000
Housing: Homeownership rate: 92.3% (2005); Median home value: $149,351 (2005); Median rent: $492 per month (2000); Median age of housing: 27 years (2000).
Transportation: Commute to work: 96.0% car, 0.4% public transportation, 0.5% walk, 3.1% work from home (2000); Travel time to work: 21.1% less than 15 minutes, 34.9% 15 to 30 minutes, 34.2% 30 to 45 minutes, 4.9% 45 to 60 minutes, 4.8% 60 minutes or more (2000)

NEWSTEAD (town). Covers a land area of 50.963 square miles and a water area of 0.137 square miles. Located at 43.01° N. Lat.; 78.51° W. Long.
Population: 7,440 (1990); 8,404 (2000); 8,488 (2005); 8,558 (2010 projected); Race: 98.0% White, 0.6% Black, 0.2% Asian, 0.6% Hispanic of any race (2005); Density: 166.6 persons per square mile (2005); Average household size: 2.45 (2005); Median age: 40.8 (2005); Males per 100 females: 96.3 (2005); Marriage status: 23.0% never married, 60.6% now married, 9.0% widowed, 7.3% divorced (2000); Foreign born: 1.7% (2000); Ancestry (includes multiple ancestries): 41.4% German, 18.0% Irish, 16.6% Polish, 13.0% English, 10.8% Italian (2000).
Economy: Single-family building permits issued: 24 (2005); Multi-family building permits issued: 0 (2005); Employment by occupation: 9.9% management, 13.5% professional, 17.5% services, 25.9% sales, 0.1% farming, 12.3% construction, 20.8% production (2000).
Income: Per capita income: $21,534 (2005); Median household income: $46,018 (2005); Average household income: $52,548 (2005); Percent of households with income of $100,000 or more: 8.7% (2005); Poverty rate: 4.2% (2000).
Education: Percent of population age 25 and over with: High school diploma (including GED) or higher: 85.1% (2005); Bachelor's degree or higher: 13.5% (2005); Master's degree or higher: 5.4% (2005).
Housing: Homeownership rate: 77.7% (2005); Median home value: $121,898 (2005); Median rent: $384 per month (2000); Median age of housing: 37 years (2000).
Transportation: Commute to work: 96.1% car, 0.7% public transportation, 1.4% walk, 1.8% work from home (2000); Travel time to work: 36.1% less than 15 minutes, 24.6% 15 to 30 minutes, 24.7% 30 to 45 minutes, 9.5% 45 to 60 minutes, 5.1% 60 minutes or more (2000)

NORTH BOSTON (CDP). Covers a land area of 4.105 square miles and a water area of 0 square miles. Located at 42.68° N. Lat.; 78.78° W. Long.
Population: 2,581 (1990); 2,680 (2000); 2,607 (2005); 2,588 (2010 projected); Race: 98.9% White, 0.2% Black, 0.0% Asian, 1.2% Hispanic of any race (2005); Density: 635.1 persons per square mile (2005); Average household size: 2.51 (2005); Median age: 41.6 (2005); Males per 100 females: 100.2 (2005); Marriage status: 19.3% never married, 65.7% now married, 7.7% widowed, 7.4% divorced (2000); Foreign born: 2.5% (2000); Ancestry (includes multiple ancestries): 41.5% German, 23.4% Polish, 22.3% Irish, 14.4% English, 13.0% Italian (2000).
Economy: Employment by occupation: 11.1% management, 22.1% professional, 12.8% services, 29.1% sales, 0.0% farming, 12.3% construction, 12.6% production (2000).
Income: Per capita income: $24,347 (2005); Median household income: $50,437 (2005); Average household income: $61,031 (2005); Percent of households with income of $100,000 or more: 14.7% (2005); Poverty rate: 1.8% (2000).
Education: Percent of population age 25 and over with: High school diploma (including GED) or higher: 88.9% (2005); Bachelor's degree or higher: 18.7% (2005); Master's degree or higher: 5.4% (2005).
Housing: Homeownership rate: 81.9% (2005); Median home value: $129,135 (2005); Median rent: $455 per month (2000); Median age of housing: 36 years (2000).
Transportation: Commute to work: 97.1% car, 0.0% public transportation, 0.4% walk, 2.5% work from home (2000); Travel time to work: 19.8% less than 15 minutes, 43.1% 15 to 30 minutes, 28.9% 30 to 45 minutes, 5.9% 45 to 60 minutes, 2.4% 60 minutes or more (2000)

NORTH COLLINS (village). Covers a land area of 0.801 square miles and a water area of 0 square miles. Located at 42.59° N. Lat.; 78.93° W. Long. Elevation is 847 feet.
Population: 1,335 (1990); 1,079 (2000); 1,037 (2005); 1,017 (2010 projected); Race: 87.8% White, 1.6% Black, 1.7% Asian, 6.3% Hispanic of any race (2005); Density: 1,295.4 persons per square mile (2005); Average household size: 2.55 (2005); Median age: 37.8 (2005); Males per 100 females: 101.4 (2005); Marriage status: 24.0% never married, 56.6% now married, 11.8% widowed, 7.6% divorced (2000); Foreign born: 2.6% (2000); Ancestry (includes multiple ancestries): 34.7% German, 20.5% Italian, 16.8% Polish, 13.7% English, 12.3% Irish (2000).
Economy: Single-family building permits issued: 1 (2005); Multi-family building permits issued: 0 (2005); Employment by occupation: 11.4% management, 13.4% professional, 15.8% services, 22.4% sales, 1.0% farming, 11.6% construction, 24.2% production (2000).
Income: Per capita income: $19,532 (2005); Median household income: $42,700 (2005); Average household income: $49,748 (2005); Percent of households with income of $100,000 or more: 8.1% (2005); Poverty rate: 9.3% (2000).
Taxes: Total city taxes per capita: $275 (2004); City property taxes per capita: $242 (2004).
Education: Percent of population age 25 and over with: High school diploma (including GED) or higher: 81.4% (2005); Bachelor's degree or higher: 12.5% (2005); Master's degree or higher: 4.7% (2005).
School District(s)
North Collins Central School District (PK-12)
   2003-04 Enrollment: 723 . . . . (716) 337-0101
Housing: Homeownership rate: 75.2% (2005); Median home value: $97,805 (2005); Median rent: $414 per month (2000); Median age of housing: 60+ years (2000).
Transportation: Commute to work: 93.0% car, 0.0% public transportation, 4.0% walk, 3.0% work from home (2000); Travel time to work: 21.9% less than 15 minutes, 42.8% 15 to 30 minutes, 15.6% 30 to 45 minutes, 16.7% 45 to 60 minutes, 3.1% 60 minutes or more (2000)

NORTH COLLINS (town). Covers a land area of 42.862 square miles and a water area of 0.160 square miles. Located at 42.58° N. Lat.; 78.88° W. Long. Elevation is 847 feet.
History: Settled c.1810, incorporated 1911.
Population: 3,502 (1990); 3,376 (2000); 3,330 (2005); 3,283 (2010 projected); Race: 94.6% White, 0.5% Black, 1.0% Asian, 3.0% Hispanic of any race (2005); Density: 77.7 persons per square mile (2005); Average household size: 2.64 (2005); Median age: 39.4 (2005); Males per 100 females: 98.9 (2005); Marriage status: 21.3% never married, 61.4% now married, 8.9% widowed, 8.4% divorced (2000); Foreign born: 3.0% (2000); Ancestry (includes multiple ancestries): 43.4% German, 16.0% Polish, 14.7% Italian, 14.3% Irish, 10.0% English (2000).
Economy: In fruit-growing region. Manufacturing: farm machinery, wire. Natural-gas wells. Single-family building permits issued: 6 (2005); Multi-family building permits issued: 0 (2005); Employment by occupation: 13.9% management, 17.5% professional, 13.9% services, 18.2% sales, 1.8% farming, 15.3% construction, 19.5% production (2000).
Income: Per capita income: $23,881 (2005); Median household income: $52,019 (2005); Average household income: $61,917 (2005); Percent of households with income of $100,000 or more: 15.4% (2005); Poverty rate: 7.7% (2000).
Education: Percent of population age 25 and over with: High school diploma (including GED) or higher: 84.0% (2005); Bachelor's degree or higher: 17.0% (2005); Master's degree or higher: 7.2% (2005).
Housing: Homeownership rate: 82.9% (2005); Median home value: $114,370 (2005); Median rent: $406 per month (2000); Median age of housing: 50 years (2000).
Transportation: Commute to work: 90.4% car, 0.7% public transportation, 1.6% walk, 6.6% work from home (2000); Travel time to work: 19.6% less than 15 minutes, 38.0% 15 to 30 minutes, 22.2% 30 to 45 minutes, 14.9% 45 to 60 minutes, 5.3% 60 minutes or more (2000)

ORCHARD PARK (village). Covers a land area of 1.344 square miles and a water area of 0.041 square miles. Located at 42.76° N. Lat.; 78.74° W. Long. Elevation is 886 feet.
Population: 3,280 (1990); 3,294 (2000); 3,211 (2005); 3,120 (2010 projected); Race: 97.1% White, 0.7% Black, 1.2% Asian, 0.9% Hispanic of any race (2005); Density: 2,388.7 persons per square mile (2005); Average household size: 2.30 (2005); Median age: 43.7 (2005); Males per 100 females: 92.3 (2005); Marriage status: 22.1% never married, 59.5% now married, 7.4% widowed, 11.0% divorced (2000); Foreign born: 3.1% (2000); Ancestry (includes multiple ancestries): 30.2% German, 27.9% Irish, 17.1% English, 15.5% Italian, 11.3% Polish (2000).
Economy: Single-family building permits issued: 0 (2005); Multi-family building permits issued: 0 (2005); Employment by occupation: 13.7%

management, 31.7% professional, 10.8% services, 34.3% sales, 0.0% farming, 2.0% construction, 7.6% production (2000).
Income: Per capita income: $34,077 (2005); Median household income: $58,854 (2005); Average household income: $78,242 (2005); Percent of households with income of $100,000 or more: 26.2% (2005); Poverty rate: 4.3% (2000).
Education: Percent of population age 25 and over with: High school diploma (including GED) or higher: 94.7% (2005); Bachelor's degree or higher: 49.7% (2005); Master's degree or higher: 23.2% (2005).

School District(s)
Orchard Park Central School District (KG-12)
    2003-04 Enrollment: 5,186 . . . . (716) 209-6280

Two-year College(s)
Bryant and Stratton College-Lackawanna
    Fall 2004 Enrollment: 505 . . . . (716) 677-9500
    2005-06 Tuition: In-state $11,820; Out-of-state $11,820

Housing: Homeownership rate: 64.7% (2005); Median home value: $184,161 (2005); Median rent: $565 per month (2000); Median age of housing: 43 years (2000).
Newspapers: The Southtowns Citizen (General - Circulation 5,990)
Transportation: Commute to work: 94.5% car, 0.4% public transportation, 0.7% walk, 3.8% work from home (2000); Travel time to work: 35.4% less than 15 minutes, 42.5% 15 to 30 minutes, 17.1% 30 to 45 minutes, 1.7% 45 to 60 minutes, 3.3% 60 minutes or more (2000)

Additional Information Contacts
Orchard Park Chamber of Commerce . . . . (716) 662-3366
    http://www.orchardparkchamber.com

ORCHARD PARK (town).
Covers a land area of 38.508 square miles and a water area of 0.074 square miles. Located at 42.76° N. Lat.; 78.75° W. Long. Elevation is 886 feet.
History: Until 1934, called East Hamburg. Incorporated 1921.
Population: 24,632 (1990); 27,637 (2000); 27,936 (2005); 28,168 (2010 projected); Race: 97.1% White, 0.6% Black, 1.3% Asian, 1.1% Hispanic of any race (2005); Density: 725.5 persons per square mile (2005); Average household size: 2.64 (2005); Median age: 43.0 (2005); Males per 100 females: 92.4 (2005); Marriage status: 21.4% never married, 63.5% now married, 7.6% widowed, 7.5% divorced (2000); Foreign born: 4.0% (2000); Ancestry (includes multiple ancestries): 32.0% German, 25.3% Irish, 18.7% Polish, 17.4% Italian, 10.9% English (2000).
Economy: Some manufacturing. NFL franchise at Rich Stadium (capacity 80,926), 2.5 miles to Northwest. Unemployment rate: 4.2% (2005); Total civilian labor force: 14,953 (2005); Single-family building permits issued: 104 (2005); Multi-family building permits issued: 2 (2005); Employment by occupation: 17.6% management, 28.4% professional, 12.3% services, 26.2% sales, 0.1% farming, 5.6% construction, 9.8% production (2000).
Income: Per capita income: $33,108 (2005); Median household income: $69,324 (2005); Average household income: $86,696 (2005); Percent of households with income of $100,000 or more: 30.5% (2005); Poverty rate: 3.2% (2000).
Education: Percent of population age 25 and over with: High school diploma (including GED) or higher: 89.8% (2005); Bachelor's degree or higher: 38.7% (2005); Master's degree or higher: 17.2% (2005).
Housing: Homeownership rate: 78.6% (2005); Median home value: $173,157 (2005); Median rent: $598 per month (2000); Median age of housing: 30 years (2000).
Safety: Violent crime rate: 3.9 per 10,000 population; Property crime rate: 184.3 per 10,000 population (2004).
Transportation: Commute to work: 95.8% car, 0.3% public transportation, 0.9% walk, 2.3% work from home (2000); Travel time to work: 28.5% less than 15 minutes, 41.8% 15 to 30 minutes, 23.2% 30 to 45 minutes, 3.7% 45 to 60 minutes, 2.8% 60 minutes or more (2000)

Additional Information Contacts
Town of Orchard Park . . . . (716) 662-6400
    http://www.orchardparkny.org/

SARDINIA (town).
Covers a land area of 50.213 square miles and a water area of 0.168 square miles. Located at 42.55° N. Lat.; 78.53° W. Long. Elevation is 1,398 feet.
Population: 2,635 (1990); 2,692 (2000); 2,729 (2005); 2,766 (2010 projected); Race: 96.9% White, 0.5% Black, 0.5% Asian, 0.7% Hispanic of any race (2005); Density: 54.3 persons per square mile (2005); Average household size: 2.81 (2005); Median age: 39.5 (2005); Males per 100 females: 100.4 (2005); Marriage status: 24.7% never married, 61.8% now married, 4.5% widowed, 9.0% divorced (2000); Foreign born: 0.4% (2000);
Ancestry (includes multiple ancestries): 41.0% German, 18.9% Polish, 15.8% Irish, 12.8% English, 11.4% Italian (2000).
Economy: Single-family building permits issued: 12 (2005); Multi-family building permits issued: 0 (2005); Employment by occupation: 8.7% management, 14.9% professional, 15.3% services, 26.0% sales, 1.2% farming, 11.7% construction, 22.2% production (2000).
Income: Per capita income: $20,346 (2005); Median household income: $46,806 (2005); Average household income: $57,242 (2005); Percent of households with income of $100,000 or more: 12.7% (2005); Poverty rate: 7.8% (2000).
Education: Percent of population age 25 and over with: High school diploma (including GED) or higher: 79.9% (2005); Bachelor's degree or higher: 10.3% (2005); Master's degree or higher: 5.1% (2005).
Housing: Homeownership rate: 84.7% (2005); Median home value: $121,204 (2005); Median rent: $406 per month (2000); Median age of housing: 44 years (2000).
Transportation: Commute to work: 90.1% car, 0.7% public transportation, 2.3% walk, 6.4% work from home (2000); Travel time to work: 29.0% less than 15 minutes, 23.5% 15 to 30 minutes, 23.2% 30 to 45 minutes, 17.5% 45 to 60 minutes, 6.8% 60 minutes or more (2000)

SLOAN (village).
Covers a land area of 0.794 square miles and a water area of 0 square miles. Located at 42.89° N. Lat.; 78.79° W. Long.
History: Incorporated 1896.
Population: 3,830 (1990); 3,775 (2000); 3,615 (2005); 3,450 (2010 projected); Race: 98.8% White, 0.3% Black, 0.1% Asian, 0.9% Hispanic of any race (2005); Density: 4,554.0 persons per square mile (2005); Average household size: 2.20 (2005); Median age: 43.4 (2005); Males per 100 females: 89.6 (2005); Marriage status: 24.9% never married, 51.1% now married, 14.1% widowed, 9.8% divorced (2000); Foreign born: 3.7% (2000); Ancestry (includes multiple ancestries): 55.8% Polish, 20.7% German, 12.5% Italian, 11.1% Irish, 3.4% English (2000).
Economy: Railroad shops. Commercial-residential community. Single-family building permits issued: 0 (2005); Multi-family building permits issued: 0 (2005); Employment by occupation: 6.6% management, 16.9% professional, 16.0% services, 29.4% sales, 0.4% farming, 10.6% construction, 20.0% production (2000).
Income: Per capita income: $17,311 (2005); Median household income: $32,432 (2005); Average household income: $38,112 (2005); Percent of households with income of $100,000 or more: 2.7% (2005); Poverty rate: 11.5% (2000).
Education: Percent of population age 25 and over with: High school diploma (including GED) or higher: 67.3% (2005); Bachelor's degree or higher: 8.4% (2005); Master's degree or higher: 2.7% (2005).

School District(s)
Cheektowaga-Sloan Union Free School District (PK-12)
    2003-04 Enrollment: 1,531 . . . . (716) 891-6402

Housing: Homeownership rate: 72.8% (2005); Median home value: $85,325 (2005); Median rent: $384 per month (2000); Median age of housing: 54 years (2000).
Transportation: Commute to work: 94.7% car, 1.1% public transportation, 2.6% walk, 0.8% work from home (2000); Travel time to work: 34.3% less than 15 minutes, 50.0% 15 to 30 minutes, 11.6% 30 to 45 minutes, 0.9% 45 to 60 minutes, 3.2% 60 minutes or more (2000)

SOUTH WALES (unincorporated postal area, zip code 14139).
Covers a land area of 23.139 square miles and a water area of 0.038 square miles. Located at 42.71° N. Lat.; 78.53° W. Long.
Population: 0 (2000); Race: 98.8% White, 0.0% Black, 0.2% Asian, 0.6% Hispanic of any race (2000); Density: 0.0 persons per square mile (2000); Age: 23.4% under 18, 11.8% over 64 (2000); Marriage status: 19.0% never married, 61.5% now married, 8.3% widowed, 11.3% divorced (2000); Foreign born: 2.5% (2000); Ancestry (includes multiple ancestries): 41.3% German, 20.4% Polish, 19.1% Irish, 13.9% English, 9.6% Italian (2000).
Economy: Employment by occupation: 13.7% management, 28.2% professional, 12.1% services, 18.9% sales, 0.5% farming, 11.7% construction, 14.9% production (2000).
Income: Per capita income: $22,283 (2000); Median household income: $49,886 (2000); Poverty rate: 2.9% (2000).
Education: Percent of population age 25 and over with: High school diploma (including GED) or higher: 90.8% (2000); Bachelor's degree or higher: 24.1% (2000).
Housing: Homeownership rate: 86.5% (2000); Median home value: $101,800 (2000); Median rent: $408 per month (2000); Median age of housing: 42 years (2000).

Transportation: Commute to work: 90.3% car, 0.3% public transportation, 7.1% walk, 2.4% work from home (2000); Travel time to work: 24.5% less than 15 minutes, 38.2% 15 to 30 minutes, 24.7% 30 to 45 minutes, 10.1% 45 to 60 minutes, 2.4% 60 minutes or more (2000)

SPRINGVILLE (village).
Covers a land area of 3.652 square miles and a water area of 0.009 square miles. Located at 42.50° N. Lat.; 78.67° W. Long. Elevation is 1,341 feet.
History: Settled 1807, incorporated 1834.
Population: 4,330 (1990); 4,252 (2000); 4,368 (2005); 4,473 (2010 projected); Race: 98.0% White, 0.6% Black, 0.5% Asian, 0.8% Hispanic of any race (2005); Density: 1,196.1 persons per square mile (2005); Average household size: 2.46 (2005); Median age: 40.7 (2005); Males per 100 females: 86.5 (2005); Marriage status: 23.7% never married, 55.7% now married, 11.4% widowed, 9.2% divorced (2000); Foreign born: 1.0% (2000); Ancestry (includes multiple ancestries): 44.7% German, 16.1% Irish, 12.7% English, 12.6% Polish, 8.4% Italian (2000).
Economy: Manufacturing: lightning protection devices, plastic products, machine parts, machinery; lumbering. Dairy and poultry farms. Single-family building permits issued: 0 (2005); Multi-family building permits issued: 0 (2005); Employment by occupation: 9.9% management, 18.4% professional, 19.9% services, 26.8% sales, 0.3% farming, 9.4% construction, 15.2% production (2000).
Income: Per capita income: $22,053 (2005); Median household income: $41,538 (2005); Average household income: $52,990 (2005); Percent of households with income of $100,000 or more: 10.7% (2005); Poverty rate: 7.4% (2000).
Education: Percent of population age 25 and over with: High school diploma (including GED) or higher: 85.3% (2005); Bachelor's degree or higher: 21.3% (2005); Master's degree or higher: 8.0% (2005).

School District(s)
Springville-Griffith Institute Central School District (KG-12)
    2003-04 Enrollment: 2,385 . . . . (716) 592-3230

Housing: Homeownership rate: 61.9% (2005); Median home value: $116,446 (2005); Median rent: $380 per month (2000); Median age of housing: 53 years (2000).
Hospitals: Bertrand Chaffee Hospital (49 beds)
Newspapers: Springville Journal (General - Circulation 4,512)
Transportation: Commute to work: 89.0% car, 0.0% public transportation, 6.1% walk, 3.4% work from home (2000); Travel time to work: 50.7% less than 15 minutes, 18.4% 15 to 30 minutes, 14.4% 30 to 45 minutes, 12.2% 45 to 60 minutes, 4.3% 60 minutes or more (2000)
Additional Information Contacts
Springville Chamber of Commerce . . . . (716) 592-4746
    http://www.springvillechamber.com

TONAWANDA (city).
Covers a land area of 3.794 square miles and a water area of 0.299 square miles. Located at 43.01° N. Lat.; 78.87° W. Long. Elevation is 572 feet.
Population: 17,284 (1990); 16,136 (2000); 15,467 (2005); 14,775 (2010 projected); Race: 97.8% White, 0.6% Black, 0.5% Asian, 1.1% Hispanic of any race (2005); Density: 4,076.6 persons per square mile (2005); Average household size: 2.35 (2005); Median age: 40.4 (2005); Males per 100 females: 95.0 (2005); Marriage status: 23.1% never married, 57.5% now married, 8.6% widowed, 10.8% divorced (2000); Foreign born: 3.4% (2000); Ancestry (includes multiple ancestries): 37.7% German, 19.7% Irish, 17.5% Italian, 13.1% Polish, 8.6% English (2000).
Economy: Single-family building permits issued: 2 (2005); Multi-family building permits issued: 0 (2005); Employment by occupation: 9.7% management, 16.1% professional, 14.7% services, 32.7% sales, 0.0% farming, 8.5% construction, 18.3% production (2000).
Income: Per capita income: $21,205 (2005); Median household income: $41,398 (2005); Average household income: $49,716 (2005); Percent of households with income of $100,000 or more: 8.0% (2005); Poverty rate: 7.1% (2000).
Education: Percent of population age 25 and over with: High school diploma (including GED) or higher: 85.3% (2005); Bachelor's degree or higher: 13.7% (2005); Master's degree or higher: 4.0% (2005).

School District(s)
Kenmore-Tonawanda Union Free School District (PK-12)
    2003-04 Enrollment: 9,033 . . . . (716) 874-8400
Sweet Home Central School District (KG-12)
    2003-04 Enrollment: 3,867 . . . . (716) 250-1402
Tonawanda City School District (PK-12)
    2003-04 Enrollment: 2,343 . . . . (716) 694-7784

Two-year College(s)
MarJon School of Beauty Culture Ltd
    Fall 2004 Enrollment: 79 . . . . (716) 836-6240

Housing: Homeownership rate: 72.8% (2005); Median home value: $89,293 (2005); Median rent: $390 per month (2000); Median age of housing: 52 years (2000).
Safety: Violent crime rate: 21.6 per 10,000 population; Property crime rate: 218.1 per 10,000 population (2004).
Transportation: Commute to work: 94.5% car, 1.0% public transportation, 2.3% walk, 1.3% work from home (2000); Travel time to work: 36.2% less than 15 minutes, 47.6% 15 to 30 minutes, 11.2% 30 to 45 minutes, 2.2% 45 to 60 minutes, 2.7% 60 minutes or more (2000)
Additional Information Contacts
City of Tonawanda . . . . (716) 695-1800
    http://www.ci.tonawanda.ny.us/

TONAWANDA (town).
Covers a land area of 18.804 square miles and a water area of 1.560 square miles. Located at 42.98° N. Lat.; 78.85° W. Long. Elevation is 572 feet.
History: Named for the Iroquois translation of "swift water". Incorporated as a village 1854, and as a city in 1903.
Population: 82,464 (1990); 78,155 (2000); 75,017 (2005); 71,903 (2010 projected); Race: 95.0% White, 1.9% Black, 1.5% Asian, 1.7% Hispanic of any race (2005); Density: 3,989.4 persons per square mile (2005); Average household size: 2.31 (2005); Median age: 42.7 (2005); Males per 100 females: 88.6 (2005); Marriage status: 25.1% never married, 56.4% now married, 10.2% widowed, 8.3% divorced (2000); Foreign born: 4.5% (2000); Ancestry (includes multiple ancestries): 32.7% German, 24.2% Italian, 21.5% Irish, 14.0% Polish, 10.6% English (2000).
Economy: An industrial suburb of Buffalo and a lake port, it is a commercial center and transshipment point. Manufacturing: steel, office equipment, chemicals, paint, plastics. Unemployment rate: 4.8% (2005); Total civilian labor force: 40,121 (2005); Single-family building permits issued: 15 (2005); Multi-family building permits issued: 0 (2005); Employment by occupation: 11.7% management, 23.3% professional, 13.5% services, 30.6% sales, 0.1% farming, 6.9% construction, 13.9% production (2000).
Income: Per capita income: $23,870 (2005); Median household income: $45,990 (2005); Average household income: $54,790 (2005); Percent of households with income of $100,000 or more: 10.8% (2005); Poverty rate: 6.9% (2000).
Taxes: Total city taxes per capita: $328 (2004); City property taxes per capita: $294 (2004).
Education: Percent of population age 25 and over with: High school diploma (including GED) or higher: 87.6% (2005); Bachelor's degree or higher: 26.9% (2005); Master's degree or higher: 9.9% (2005).
Housing: Homeownership rate: 73.3% (2005); Median home value: $108,394 (2005); Median rent: $467 per month (2000); Median age of housing: 48 years (2000).
Safety: Violent crime rate: 13.4 per 10,000 population; Property crime rate: 169.5 per 10,000 population (2004).
Transportation: Commute to work: 93.4% car, 2.9% public transportation, 1.7% walk, 1.4% work from home (2000); Travel time to work: 33.1% less than 15 minutes, 50.3% 15 to 30 minutes, 12.1% 30 to 45 minutes, 1.9% 45 to 60 minutes, 2.5% 60 minutes or more (2000)
Additional Information Contacts
Town of Tonawanda . . . . (716) 877-8800
    http://www.tonawanda.ny.us/

TONAWANDA (CDP).
Covers a land area of 17.368 square miles and a water area of 1.560 square miles. Located at 42.98° N. Lat.; 78.85° W. Long.
Population: 65,284 (1990); 61,729 (2000); 59,323 (2005); 56,940 (2010 projected); Race: 94.7% White, 2.0% Black, 1.7% Asian, 1.7% Hispanic of any race (2005); Density: 3,415.7 persons per square mile (2005); Average household size: 2.32 (2005); Median age: 43.5 (2005); Males per 100 females: 89.1 (2005); Marriage status: 23.9% never married, 57.6% now married, 10.3% widowed, 8.2% divorced (2000); Foreign born: 4.9% (2000); Ancestry (includes multiple ancestries): 33.2% German, 23.5% Italian, 21.3% Irish, 14.6% Polish, 10.8% English (2000).
Economy: Employment by occupation: 11.4% management, 22.6% professional, 13.4% services, 31.2% sales, 0.2% farming, 7.1% construction, 14.2% production (2000).
Income: Per capita income: $23,581 (2005); Median household income: $45,597 (2005); Average household income: $54,311 (2005); Percent of

households with income of $100,000 or more: 10.5% (2005); Poverty rate: 7.3% (2000).
Education: Percent of population age 25 and over with: High school diploma (including GED) or higher: 87.1% (2005); Bachelor's degree or higher: 26.3% (2005); Master's degree or higher: 9.7% (2005).
Housing: Homeownership rate: 75.1% (2005); Median home value: $110,664 (2005); Median rent: $476 per month (2000); Median age of housing: 46 years (2000).
Transportation: Commute to work: 93.6% car, 2.6% public transportation, 1.8% walk, 1.4% work from home (2000); Travel time to work: 34.3% less than 15 minutes, 49.3% 15 to 30 minutes, 11.8% 30 to 45 minutes, 1.9% 45 to 60 minutes, 2.7% 60 minutes or more (2000)

TOWN LINE (CDP). Covers a land area of 4.638 square miles and a water area of 0 square miles. Located at 42.88° N. Lat.; 78.55° W. Long.
Population: 2,721 (1990); 2,521 (2000); 2,658 (2005); 2,742 (2010 projected); Race: 99.2% White, 0.0% Black, 0.2% Asian, 0.3% Hispanic of any race (2005); Density: 573.1 persons per square mile (2005); Average household size: 2.73 (2005); Median age: 43.6 (2005); Males per 100 females: 101.8 (2005); Marriage status: 20.2% never married, 71.2% now married, 4.1% widowed, 4.5% divorced (2000); Foreign born: 2.0% (2000); Ancestry (includes multiple ancestries): 41.6% German, 28.8% Polish, 11.0% Irish, 9.9% English, 7.3% Italian (2000).
Economy: Employment by occupation: 17.1% management, 17.3% professional, 11.1% services, 27.4% sales, 1.2% farming, 8.3% construction, 17.7% production (2000).
Income: Per capita income: $25,452 (2005); Median household income: $60,668 (2005); Average household income: $69,458 (2005); Percent of households with income of $100,000 or more: 21.0% (2005); Poverty rate: 3.8% (2000).
Education: Percent of population age 25 and over with: High school diploma (including GED) or higher: 81.4% (2005); Bachelor's degree or higher: 17.1% (2005); Master's degree or higher: 7.0% (2005).
Housing: Homeownership rate: 92.0% (2005); Median home value: $137,666 (2005); Median rent: $448 per month (2000); Median age of housing: 37 years (2000).
Transportation: Commute to work: 94.6% car, 0.0% public transportation, 0.0% walk, 5.4% work from home (2000); Travel time to work: 27.4% less than 15 minutes, 42.2% 15 to 30 minutes, 23.4% 30 to 45 minutes, 3.2% 45 to 60 minutes, 3.7% 60 minutes or more (2000)

WALES (town). Covers a land area of 35.604 square miles and a water area of 0.039 square miles. Located at 42.73° N. Lat.; 78.52° W. Long.
Population: 2,917 (1990); 2,960 (2000); 2,990 (2005); 3,022 (2010 projected); Race: 98.3% White, 0.1% Black, 0.5% Asian, 1.0% Hispanic of any race (2005); Density: 84.0 persons per square mile (2005); Average household size: 2.60 (2005); Median age: 40.9 (2005); Males per 100 females: 97.6 (2005); Marriage status: 21.1% never married, 63.2% now married, 6.9% widowed, 8.8% divorced (2000); Foreign born: 2.2% (2000); Ancestry (includes multiple ancestries): 44.1% German, 18.5% Polish, 14.6% Irish, 11.8% English, 11.5% Italian (2000).
Economy: Single-family building permits issued: 4 (2005); Multi-family building permits issued: 0 (2005); Employment by occupation: 15.8% management, 23.3% professional, 12.4% services, 23.0% sales, 1.1% farming, 11.5% construction, 13.0% production (2000).
Income: Per capita income: $25,403 (2005); Median household income: $56,956 (2005); Average household income: $66,048 (2005); Percent of households with income of $100,000 or more: 17.8% (2005); Poverty rate: 3.6% (2000).
Education: Percent of population age 25 and over with: High school diploma (including GED) or higher: 90.7% (2005); Bachelor's degree or higher: 22.7% (2005); Master's degree or higher: 10.1% (2005).
Housing: Homeownership rate: 86.8% (2005); Median home value: $157,885 (2005); Median rent: $417 per month (2000); Median age of housing: 37 years (2000).
Transportation: Commute to work: 95.2% car, 0.2% public transportation, 1.6% walk, 3.0% work from home (2000); Travel time to work: 20.3% less than 15 minutes, 36.5% 15 to 30 minutes, 32.4% 30 to 45 minutes, 7.7% 45 to 60 minutes, 3.1% 60 minutes or more (2000)

WEST FALLS (unincorporated postal area, zip code 14170). Covers a land area of 15.087 square miles and a water area of 0.055 square miles. Located at 42.69° N. Lat.; 78.67° W. Long. Elevation is 942 feet.
Population: 0 (2000); Race: 99.6% White, 0.0% Black, 0.0% Asian, 0.5% Hispanic of any race (2000); Density: 0.0 persons per square mile (2000);

Age: 27.0% under 18, 12.1% over 64 (2000); Marriage status: 21.3% never married, 66.4% now married, 4.5% widowed, 7.8% divorced (2000); Foreign born: 3.6% (2000); Ancestry (includes multiple ancestries): 47.0% German, 23.8% Irish, 21.6% Polish, 17.3% English, 11.8% Italian (2000).
Economy: Employment by occupation: 15.1% management, 19.5% professional, 14.1% services, 23.9% sales, 0.0% farming, 12.8% construction, 14.7% production (2000).
Income: Per capita income: $22,209 (2000); Median household income: $50,741 (2000); Poverty rate: 6.3% (2000).
Education: Percent of population age 25 and over with: High school diploma (including GED) or higher: 93.2% (2000); Bachelor's degree or higher: 27.4% (2000).
Housing: Homeownership rate: 88.9% (2000); Median home value: $106,500 (2000); Median rent: $450 per month (2000); Median age of housing: 44 years (2000).
Transportation: Commute to work: 97.3% car, 0.2% public transportation, 0.0% walk, 2.0% work from home (2000); Travel time to work: 25.1% less than 15 minutes, 35.8% 15 to 30 minutes, 27.6% 30 to 45 minutes, 8.5% 45 to 60 minutes, 3.1% 60 minutes or more (2000)

WEST SENECA (town). Covers a land area of 21.370 square miles and a water area of 0.022 square miles. Located at 42.83° N. Lat.; 78.76° W. Long. Elevation is 600 feet.
Population: 47,830 (1990); 45,920 (2000); 44,892 (2005); 43,832 (2010 projected); Race: 97.7% White, 0.6% Black, 0.7% Asian, 1.1% Hispanic of any race (2005); Density: 2,100.7 persons per square mile (2005); Average household size: 2.47 (2005); Median age: 42.8 (2005); Males per 100 females: 91.6 (2005); Marriage status: 24.4% never married, 59.3% now married, 8.9% widowed, 7.4% divorced (2000); Foreign born: 3.1% (2000); Ancestry (includes multiple ancestries): 32.8% German, 30.9% Polish, 22.9% Irish, 17.9% Italian, 6.7% English (2000).
Economy: Unemployment rate: 4.7% (2005); Total civilian labor force: 24,635 (2005); Single-family building permits issued: 54 (2005); Multi-family building permits issued: 0 (2005); Employment by occupation: 12.9% management, 19.5% professional, 15.5% services, 30.2% sales, 0.2% farming, 7.4% construction, 14.4% production (2000).
Income: Per capita income: $24,081 (2005); Median household income: $52,095 (2005); Average household income: $58,952 (2005); Percent of households with income of $100,000 or more: 12.9% (2005); Poverty rate: 4.6% (2000).
Taxes: Total city taxes per capita: $499 (2004); City property taxes per capita: $466 (2004).
Education: Percent of population age 25 and over with: High school diploma (including GED) or higher: 86.1% (2005); Bachelor's degree or higher: 20.4% (2005); Master's degree or higher: 7.2% (2005).

School District(s)
Boces Erie 1 (PK-PK)
   2003-04 Enrollment: 726 . . . . (716) 821-7001
West Seneca Central School District (KG-12)
   2003-04 Enrollment: 7,697 . . . . (716) 677-3101

Two-year College(s)
Continental School of Beauty Culture
   Fall 2004 Enrollment: 118 . . . . (716) 675-8205
Erie 1 BOCES-Practical Nursing Program
   Fall 2004 Enrollment: 89 . . . . (716) 822-3333

Housing: Homeownership rate: 78.7% (2005); Median home value: $122,671 (2005); Median rent: $483 per month (2000); Median age of housing: 39 years (2000).
Hospitals: Western New York Children's Psychiatric Center (46 beds)
Safety: Violent crime rate: 13.7 per 10,000 population; Property crime rate: 230.6 per 10,000 population (2004).
Transportation: Commute to work: 95.4% car, 1.0% public transportation, 1.8% walk, 1.5% work from home (2000); Travel time to work: 32.3% less than 15 minutes, 46.5% 15 to 30 minutes, 14.8% 30 to 45 minutes, 3.1% 45 to 60 minutes, 3.3% 60 minutes or more (2000)
Additional Information Contacts
Town of West Seneca . . . . (716) 674-5600
   http://www.westseneca.net/
West Seneca Chamber of Commerce . . . . (716) 674-4900
   http://www.westseneca.com

WEST SENECA (CDP). Covers a land area of 21.383 square miles and a water area of 0.022 square miles. Located at 42.83° N. Lat.; 78.76° W. Long.

Population: 47,866 (1990); 45,943 (2000); 44,917 (2005); 43,859 (2010 projected); Race: 97.7% White, 0.6% Black, 0.7% Asian, 1.1% Hispanic of any race (2005); Density: 2,100.6 persons per square mile (2005); Average household size: 2.47 (2005); Median age: 42.8 (2005); Males per 100 females: 91.6 (2005); Marriage status: 24.4% never married, 59.3% now married, 8.9% widowed, 7.4% divorced (2000); Foreign born: 3.1% (2000); Ancestry (includes multiple ancestries): 32.8% German, 30.9% Polish, 22.9% Irish, 17.9% Italian, 6.7% English (2000).
Economy: Employment by occupation: 12.9% management, 19.5% professional, 15.5% services, 30.1% sales, 0.2% farming, 7.4% construction, 14.4% production (2000).
Income: Per capita income: $24,077 (2005); Median household income: $52,067 (2005); Average household income: $58,944 (2005); Percent of households with income of $100,000 or more: 12.9% (2005); Poverty rate: 4.6% (2000).
Education: Percent of population age 25 and over with: High school diploma (including GED) or higher: 86.2% (2005); Bachelor's degree or higher: 20.4% (2005); Master's degree or higher: 7.2% (2005).
Housing: Homeownership rate: 78.7% (2005); Median home value: $122,645 (2005); Median rent: $483 per month (2000); Median age of housing: 39 years (2000).
Transportation: Commute to work: 95.4% car, 1.0% public transportation, 1.8% walk, 1.5% work from home (2000); Travel time to work: 32.3% less than 15 minutes, 46.5% 15 to 30 minutes, 14.8% 30 to 45 minutes, 3.1% 45 to 60 minutes, 3.3% 60 minutes or more (2000)

WILLIAMSVILLE (village).
Covers a land area of 1.253 square miles and a water area of 0 square miles. Located at 42.96° N. Lat.; 78.74° W. Long. Elevation is 672 feet.
History: Settled c.1800, incorporated 1869.
Population: 5,583 (1990); 5,573 (2000); 5,384 (2005); 5,239 (2010 projected); Race: 96.6% White, 0.8% Black, 1.3% Asian, 1.6% Hispanic of any race (2005); Density: 4,297.0 persons per square mile (2005); Average household size: 2.17 (2005); Median age: 45.8 (2005); Males per 100 females: 76.5 (2005); Marriage status: 27.3% never married, 50.8% now married, 12.2% widowed, 9.7% divorced (2000); Foreign born: 3.3% (2000); Ancestry (includes multiple ancestries): 33.4% German, 21.8% Irish, 15.1% Italian, 11.6% English, 11.0% Polish (2000).
Economy: Manufacturing: machinery. Single-family building permits issued: 1 (2005); Multi-family building permits issued: 0 (2005); Employment by occupation: 21.9% management, 27.8% professional, 13.1% services, 24.4% sales, 0.0% farming, 5.2% construction, 7.6% production (2000).
Income: Per capita income: $30,874 (2005); Median household income: $53,491 (2005); Average household income: $65,906 (2005); Percent of households with income of $100,000 or more: 18.5% (2005); Poverty rate: 4.5% (2000).
Education: Percent of population age 25 and over with: High school diploma (including GED) or higher: 92.0% (2005); Bachelor's degree or higher: 45.2% (2005); Master's degree or higher: 16.9% (2005).

School District(s)
Clarence Central School District (KG-12)
   2003-04 Enrollment: 4,920 . . . . (716) 407-9102
Williamsville Central School District (KG-12)
   2003-04 Enrollment: 10,760 . . . . (716) 626-8005

Two-year College(s)
Leon Studio 1 School of Hair Design & Career Training Center
   Fall 2004 Enrollment: 134 . . . . (716) 631-3878
New York Institute of Massage Inc
   Fall 2004 Enrollment: 65 . . . . (716) 633-0355

Housing: Homeownership rate: 59.5% (2005); Median home value: $129,353 (2005); Median rent: $601 per month (2000); Median age of housing: 48 years (2000).
Newspapers: Amherst Bee (General - Circulation 11,774); Cheektowaga Bee (General - Circulation 1,425); Clarence Bee (General - Circulation 4,595); Depew Bee (General - Circulation 1,450); East Aurora/Elma Bee (General - Circulation 1,656); Ken-Ton Bee (General - Circulation 1,554); Lancaster Bee (General - Circulation 3,547); Orchard Park Bee (General - Circulation 2,598); West Seneca Bee (General - Circulation 5,962)
Transportation: Commute to work: 87.0% car, 2.7% public transportation, 4.3% walk, 5.0% work from home (2000); Travel time to work: 42.4% less than 15 minutes, 48.7% 15 to 30 minutes, 7.4% 30 to 45 minutes, 0.0% 45 to 60 minutes, 1.6% 60 minutes or more (2000)
Additional Information Contacts

Amherst Chamber of Commerce . . . . (716) 632-6905
   http://www.amherst.org
Village of Williamsville . . . . (716) 632-4120
   http://village.williamsville.ny.us/

Essex County

Located in northeastern New York, in the Adirondacks; bounded on the east by Lake Champlain; drained by the Hudson and Ausable Rivers; includes Lake Placid and Saranac Lake, and Mt. Marcy, the highest point in the state (5,344 ft). Covers a land area of 1,796.80 square miles, a water area of 119.70 square miles, and is located in the Eastern Time Zone. The county government was organized in 1799. County seat is Elizabethtown.

Weather Station: Lake Placid 2 S   Elevation: 1,938 feet

	Jan	Feb	Mar	Apr	May	Jun	Jul	Aug	Sep	Oct	Nov	Dec
High	26	29	39	51	65	73	77	74	66	55	42	31
Low	4	6	16	28	39	47	52	51	43	33	24	11
Precip	2.6	2.0	2.7	2.7	3.2	4.0	4.0	4.3	4.3	3.6	3.4	2.6
Snow	na	na	na	na	0.3	0.0	0.0	0.0	tr	1.1	na	na

High and Low temperatures in degrees Fahrenheit; Precipitation and Snow in inches

Weather Station: Ray Brook   Elevation: 1,617 feet

	Jan	Feb	Mar	Apr	May	Jun	Jul	Aug	Sep	Oct	Nov	Dec
High	26	29	38	50	64	72	77	75	67	55	41	30
Low	4	5	14	27	39	48	52	50	43	33	24	11
Precip	2.7	2.1	2.7	2.9	3.2	3.9	3.9	4.2	4.2	3.5	3.6	3.0
Snow	27.7	21.6	21.3	11.0	1.2	tr	0.0	tr	tr	2.0	14.8	24.9

High and Low temperatures in degrees Fahrenheit; Precipitation and Snow in inches

Population: 37,152 (1990); 38,851 (2000); 39,165 (2005); 39,468 (2010 projected); Race: 94.2% White, 3.5% Black, 0.6% Asian, 2.6% Hispanic of any race (2005); Density: 21.8 persons per square mile (2005); Average household size: 2.54 (2005); Median age: 40.7 (2005); Males per 100 females: 107.8 (2005).
Religion: Five largest groups: 36.5% Catholic Church, 7.3% The United Methodist Church, 1.9% Episcopal Church, 1.3% United Church of Christ, 1.2% American Baptist Churches in the USA (2000).
Economy: Unemployment rate: 5.3% (2005); Total civilian labor force: 18,747 (2005); Leading industries: 21.6% accommodation and food services; 18.8% retail trade; 17.9% health care and social assistance (2003); Farms: 236 totaling 55,022 acres (2002); Companies that employ 500 or more persons: 1 (2003); Companies that employ 100 to 499 persons: 11 (2003); Companies that employ less than 100 persons: 1,153 (2003); Black-owned businesses: n/a (2002); Hispanic-owned businesses: n/a (2002); Women-owned businesses: 960 (2002); Retail sales per capita: $11,137 (2006). Single-family building permits issued: 292 (2005); Multi-family building permits issued: 0 (2005).
Income: Per capita income: $21,177 (2005); Median household income: $40,153 (2005); Average household income: $50,539 (2005); Percent of households with income of $100,000 or more: 9.0% (2005); Poverty rate: 11.5% (2003); Bankruptcy rate: 4.55% (2005).
Education: Percent of population age 25 and over with: High school diploma (including GED) or higher: 80.4% (2005); Bachelor's degree or higher: 18.5% (2005); Master's degree or higher: 8.1% (2005).
Housing: Homeownership rate: 73.7% (2005); Median home value: $118,240 (2005); Median rent: $385 per month (2000); Median age of housing: 45 years (2000).
Health: Birth rate: 89.2 per 10,000 population (2004); Death rate: 105.7 per 10,000 population (2004); Age-adjusted cancer mortality rate: 224.7 deaths per 100,000 population (2002); Air Quality Index: 85.8% good, 14.0% moderate, 0.3% unhealthy for sensitive individuals, 0.0% unhealthy (percent of days in 2005); Number of physicians: 10.8 per 10,000 population (2004); Hospital beds: 10.3 per 10,000 population (2003); Hospital admissions: 200.2 per 10,000 population (2003).
Elections: 2004 Presidential election results: 51.7% Bush, 45.9% Kerry, 2.1% Nader, 0.2% Badnarik
National and State Parks: Wickham Marsh State Game Management Area
Additional Information Contacts

Essex County Government . . . . (518) 873-3700
   http://www.co.essex.ny.us/
Town of Newcomb . . . . (518) 582-3211
   http://www.newcombny,.com/
Town of North Elba . . . . (518) 523-2162
   http://www.townofnorthelba.org

Town of Westport................................ (518) 962-4419
http://www.westportny.net/

Essex County Communities

BLOOMINGDALE (unincorporated postal area, zip code 12913). Covers a land area of 59.488 square miles and a water area of 0.524 square miles. Located at 44.42° N. Lat.; 73.99° W. Long. Elevation is 1,535 feet.
Population: 0 (2000); Race: 98.1% White, 0.0% Black, 0.0% Asian, 0.2% Hispanic of any race (2000); Density: 0.0 persons per square mile (2000); Age: 27.7% under 18, 13.2% over 64 (2000); Marriage status: 21.5% never married, 61.0% now married, 7.9% widowed, 9.6% divorced (2000); Foreign born: 1.4% (2000); Ancestry (includes multiple ancestries): 21.9% French (except Basque), 21.0% Irish, 16.0% German, 12.1% English, 11.6% United States or American (2000).
Economy: Employment by occupation: 8.0% management, 20.5% professional, 20.6% services, 25.8% sales, 0.9% farming, 13.3% construction, 10.9% production (2000).
Income: Per capita income: $17,133 (2000); Median household income: $37,847 (2000); Poverty rate: 8.3% (2000).
Education: Percent of population age 25 and over with: High school diploma (including GED) or higher: 84.7% (2000); Bachelor's degree or higher: 17.7% (2000).
Housing: Homeownership rate: 78.9% (2000); Median home value: $79,500 (2000); Median rent: $404 per month (2000); Median age of housing: 26 years (2000).
Transportation: Commute to work: 96.1% car, 0.4% public transportation, 0.7% walk, 2.8% work from home (2000); Travel time to work: 26.9% less than 15 minutes, 47.7% 15 to 30 minutes, 17.1% 30 to 45 minutes, 5.8% 45 to 60 minutes, 2.5% 60 minutes or more (2000)

CHESTERFIELD (town). Covers a land area of 78.841 square miles and a water area of 26.399 square miles. Located at 44.47° N. Lat.; 73.47° W. Long.
Population: 2,250 (1990); 2,409 (2000); 2,371 (2005); 2,333 (2010 projected); Race: 97.7% White, 0.3% Black, 0.3% Asian, 1.2% Hispanic of any race (2005); Density: 30.1 persons per square mile (2005); Average household size: 2.50 (2005); Median age: 41.8 (2005); Males per 100 females: 96.1 (2005); Marriage status: 26.4% never married, 59.6% now married, 5.6% widowed, 8.4% divorced (2000); Foreign born: 2.7% (2000); Ancestry (includes multiple ancestries): 41.9% French (except Basque), 19.4% Irish, 13.6% Other groups, 12.4% English, 8.7% German (2000).
Economy: Single-family building permits issued: 8 (2005); Multi-family building permits issued: 0 (2005); Employment by occupation: 11.7% management, 18.7% professional, 21.5% services, 20.9% sales, 0.9% farming, 10.0% construction, 16.5% production (2000).
Income: Per capita income: $23,446 (2005); Median household income: $46,337 (2005); Average household income: $58,332 (2005); Percent of households with income of $100,000 or more: 14.3% (2005); Poverty rate: 12.8% (2000).
Education: Percent of population age 25 and over with: High school diploma (including GED) or higher: 81.9% (2005); Bachelor's degree or higher: 20.6% (2005); Master's degree or higher: 10.2% (2005).
Housing: Homeownership rate: 81.5% (2005); Median home value: $118,027 (2005); Median rent: $397 per month (2000); Median age of housing: 43 years (2000).
Transportation: Commute to work: 92.9% car, 0.0% public transportation, 3.6% walk, 3.1% work from home (2000); Travel time to work: 28.9% less than 15 minutes, 43.4% 15 to 30 minutes, 18.4% 30 to 45 minutes, 4.0% 45 to 60 minutes, 5.3% 60 minutes or more (2000)

CROWN POINT (town). Covers a land area of 76.266 square miles and a water area of 5.638 square miles. Located at 43.95° N. Lat.; 73.48° W. Long. Elevation is 214 feet.
History: The French began building Fort St. Frederic in 1731. In the French and Indian Wars the fort resisted early English attacks but was demolished (1759) before the advance of Jeffrey Amherst. The British began building a new fort, Fort Amherst (renamed Crown Point), in 1759. Early in the Revolution, Crown Point was captured by Seth Warner and the Green Mt. Boys. Abandoned (1777) to Gen. John Burgoyne. Crown Point Reservation, with bathing and fishing, a Museum and ruins of colonial forts, is nearby.
Population: 2,048 (1990); 2,119 (2000); 2,046 (2005); 1,970 (2010 projected); Race: 97.6% White, 0.0% Black, 0.7% Asian, 0.2% Hispanic of any race (2005); Density: 26.8 persons per square mile (2005); Average household size: 2.61 (2005); Median age: 38.4 (2005); Males per 100 females: 102.0 (2005); Marriage status: 22.6% never married, 62.0% now married, 6.6% widowed, 8.8% divorced (2000); Foreign born: 1.2% (2000); Ancestry (includes multiple ancestries): 20.7% French (except Basque), 17.6% English, 15.7% Irish, 13.7% Other groups, 10.5% United States or American (2000).
Economy: Summer resort on historic site. Single-family building permits issued: 0 (2005); Multi-family building permits issued: 0 (2005); Employment by occupation: 9.8% management, 15.9% professional, 17.1% services, 18.8% sales, 2.2% farming, 14.1% construction, 22.1% production (2000).
Income: Per capita income: $20,723 (2005); Median household income: $43,061 (2005); Average household income: $53,737 (2005); Percent of households with income of $100,000 or more: 8.8% (2005); Poverty rate: 14.6% (2000).
Education: Percent of population age 25 and over with: High school diploma (including GED) or higher: 79.0% (2005); Bachelor's degree or higher: 12.7% (2005); Master's degree or higher: 5.9% (2005).
School District(s)
Crown Point Central School District (KG-12)
    2003-04 Enrollment: 324....................... (518) 597-4200
Housing: Homeownership rate: 77.7% (2005); Median home value: $100,359 (2005); Median rent: $396 per month (2000); Median age of housing: 35 years (2000).
Transportation: Commute to work: 91.9% car, 0.2% public transportation, 2.0% walk, 4.9% work from home (2000); Travel time to work: 30.8% less than 15 minutes, 32.0% 15 to 30 minutes, 18.9% 30 to 45 minutes, 9.2% 45 to 60 minutes, 9.1% 60 minutes or more (2000)

ELIZABETHTOWN (town). Covers a land area of 81.681 square miles and a water area of 1.405 square miles. Located at 44.19° N. Lat.; 73.59° W. Long. Elevation is 591 feet.
Population: 1,324 (1990); 1,315 (2000); 1,290 (2005); 1,272 (2010 projected); Race: 96.8% White, 1.1% Black, 0.9% Asian, 0.5% Hispanic of any race (2005); Density: 15.8 persons per square mile (2005); Average household size: 2.63 (2005); Median age: 48.5 (2005); Males per 100 females: 94.0 (2005); Marriage status: 20.0% never married, 56.0% now married, 14.3% widowed, 9.7% divorced (2000); Foreign born: 1.4% (2000); Ancestry (includes multiple ancestries): 25.7% French (except Basque), 22.9% Irish, 16.6% English, 15.0% German, 8.6% Other groups (2000).
Economy: Resort village. Single-family building permits issued: 8 (2005); Multi-family building permits issued: 0 (2005); Employment by occupation: 6.7% management, 25.3% professional, 24.7% services, 18.1% sales, 1.4% farming, 12.3% construction, 11.6% production (2000).
Income: Per capita income: $19,438 (2005); Median household income: $38,750 (2005); Average household income: $47,714 (2005); Percent of households with income of $100,000 or more: 8.2% (2005); Poverty rate: 15.7% (2000).
Education: Percent of population age 25 and over with: High school diploma (including GED) or higher: 80.2% (2005); Bachelor's degree or higher: 18.5% (2005); Master's degree or higher: 7.4% (2005).
School District(s)
Elizabethtown-Lewis Central School District (KG-12)
    2003-04 Enrollment: 386....................... (518) 873-6371
Housing: Homeownership rate: 68.6% (2005); Median home value: $112,917 (2005); Median rent: $370 per month (2000); Median age of housing: 60+ years (2000).
Hospitals: Elizabethtown Community Hospital (25 beds)
Newspapers: North Countryman (General - Circulation 3,500); Valley News (General - Circulation 3,058)
Transportation: Commute to work: 89.0% car, 1.8% public transportation, 4.2% walk, 3.3% work from home (2000); Travel time to work: 60.4% less than 15 minutes, 21.0% 15 to 30 minutes, 7.4% 30 to 45 minutes, 5.3% 45 to 60 minutes, 5.9% 60 minutes or more (2000)

ESSEX (town). Covers a land area of 31.707 square miles and a water area of 5.872 square miles. Located at 44.27° N. Lat.; 73.41° W. Long. Elevation is 268 feet.
Population: 702 (1990); 713 (2000); 669 (2005); 655 (2010 projected); Race: 99.9% White, 0.0% Black, 0.0% Asian, 0.1% Hispanic of any race (2005); Density: 21.1 persons per square mile (2005); Average household size: 2.31 (2005); Median age: 46.4 (2005); Males per 100 females: 102.7 (2005); Marriage status: 25.1% never married, 55.9% now married, 7.7%

widowed, 11.3% divorced (2000); Foreign born: 2.3% (2000); Ancestry (includes multiple ancestries): 14.2% English, 13.6% Irish, 12.9% French (except Basque), 11.0% German, 9.1% United States or American (2000).
Economy: Ferry to Charlotte, Vt. Single-family building permits issued: 4 (2005); Multi-family building permits issued: 0 (2005); Employment by occupation: 12.3% management, 16.5% professional, 17.9% services, 16.8% sales, 3.9% farming, 18.4% construction, 14.2% production (2000).
Income: Per capita income: $23,601 (2005); Median household income: $42,500 (2005); Average household income: $53,633 (2005); Percent of households with income of $100,000 or more: 12.8% (2005); Poverty rate: 11.0% (2000).
Education: Percent of population age 25 and over with: High school diploma (including GED) or higher: 76.3% (2005); Bachelor's degree or higher: 25.1% (2005); Master's degree or higher: 12.2% (2005).
Housing: Homeownership rate: 84.8% (2005); Median home value: $125,000 (2005); Median rent: $409 per month (2000); Median age of housing: 60+ years (2000).
Transportation: Commute to work: 93.8% car, 0.0% public transportation, 1.1% walk, 5.1% work from home (2000); Travel time to work: 39.5% less than 15 minutes, 34.1% 15 to 30 minutes, 11.1% 30 to 45 minutes, 8.1% 45 to 60 minutes, 7.2% 60 minutes or more (2000)

JAY (town). Covers a land area of 67.737 square miles and a water area of 0.522 square miles. Located at 44.38° N. Lat.; 73.71° W. Long.
Population: 2,276 (1990); 2,306 (2000); 2,306 (2005); 2,310 (2010 projected); Race: 98.3% White, 0.4% Black, 0.3% Asian, 0.9% Hispanic of any race (2005); Density: 34.0 persons per square mile (2005); Average household size: 2.47 (2005); Median age: 41.8 (2005); Males per 100 females: 94.9 (2005); Marriage status: 22.6% never married, 61.5% now married, 7.9% widowed, 8.0% divorced (2000); Foreign born: 1.9% (2000); Ancestry (includes multiple ancestries): 33.8% French (except Basque), 20.2% English, 19.0% Irish, 11.0% Other groups, 9.9% German (2000).
Economy: Resort village in Adirondack Mountains. Single-family building permits issued: 31 (2005); Multi-family building permits issued: 0 (2005); Employment by occupation: 8.6% management, 20.0% professional, 28.0% services, 20.1% sales, 0.8% farming, 12.0% construction, 10.5% production (2000).
Income: Per capita income: $19,340 (2005); Median household income: $39,158 (2005); Average household income: $47,535 (2005); Percent of households with income of $100,000 or more: 7.3% (2005); Poverty rate: 8.7% (2000).
Taxes: Total city taxes per capita: $558 (2004); City property taxes per capita: $525 (2004).
Education: Percent of population age 25 and over with: High school diploma (including GED) or higher: 83.5% (2005); Bachelor's degree or higher: 19.6% (2005); Master's degree or higher: 7.3% (2005).
Housing: Homeownership rate: 78.7% (2005); Median home value: $113,254 (2005); Median rent: $383 per month (2000); Median age of housing: 37 years (2000).
Transportation: Commute to work: 90.3% car, 0.9% public transportation, 3.5% walk, 4.7% work from home (2000); Travel time to work: 27.0% less than 15 minutes, 23.9% 15 to 30 minutes, 34.4% 30 to 45 minutes, 10.5% 45 to 60 minutes, 4.2% 60 minutes or more (2000)

KEENE (town). Covers a land area of 156.046 square miles and a water area of 0.578 square miles. Located at 44.21° N. Lat.; 73.78° W. Long. Elevation is 834 feet.
Population: 908 (1990); 1,063 (2000); 1,096 (2005); 1,110 (2010 projected); Race: 98.6% White, 0.0% Black, 0.8% Asian, 0.5% Hispanic of any race (2005); Density: 7.0 persons per square mile (2005); Average household size: 2.37 (2005); Median age: 47.6 (2005); Males per 100 females: 86.7 (2005); Marriage status: 20.7% never married, 60.6% now married, 9.7% widowed, 9.0% divorced (2000); Foreign born: 0.8% (2000); Ancestry (includes multiple ancestries): 32.9% Irish, 28.2% English, 16.2% French (except Basque), 14.2% German, 7.1% Other groups (2000).
Economy: Resort village. Single-family building permits issued: 11 (2005); Multi-family building permits issued: 0 (2005); Employment by occupation: 14.8% management, 24.3% professional, 22.3% services, 21.9% sales, 0.8% farming, 14.4% construction, 1.4% production (2000).
Income: Per capita income: $19,657 (2005); Median household income: $39,082 (2005); Average household income: $45,848 (2005); Percent of households with income of $100,000 or more: 5.6% (2005); Poverty rate: 4.7% (2000).
Education: Percent of population age 25 and over with: High school diploma (including GED) or higher: 87.1% (2005); Bachelor's degree or higher: 36.6% (2005); Master's degree or higher: 17.8% (2005).
Housing: Homeownership rate: 79.9% (2005); Median home value: $179,545 (2005); Median rent: $371 per month (2000); Median age of housing: 53 years (2000).
Transportation: Commute to work: 85.7% car, 0.0% public transportation, 5.7% walk, 8.1% work from home (2000); Travel time to work: 47.0% less than 15 minutes, 30.3% 15 to 30 minutes, 15.0% 30 to 45 minutes, 3.7% 45 to 60 minutes, 3.9% 60 minutes or more (2000)

KEENE VALLEY (unincorporated postal area, zip code 12943). Covers a land area of 105.681 square miles and a water area of 0.559 square miles. Located at 44.17° N. Lat.; 73.78° W. Long.
Population: 0 (2000); Race: 100.0% White, 0.0% Black, 0.0% Asian, 0.0% Hispanic of any race (2000); Density: 0.0 persons per square mile (2000); Age: 18.5% under 18, 34.9% over 64 (2000); Marriage status: 21.3% never married, 55.4% now married, 13.2% widowed, 10.2% divorced (2000); Foreign born: 0.5% (2000); Ancestry (includes multiple ancestries): 29.5% English, 25.6% Irish, 19.2% French (except Basque), 13.8% German, 6.9% United States or American (2000).
Economy: Resort village in Adirondack Mountains. Employment by occupation: 13.3% management, 31.0% professional, 18.4% services, 25.3% sales, 1.3% farming, 10.8% construction, 0.0% production (2000).
Income: Per capita income: $18,678 (2000); Median household income: $32,813 (2000); Poverty rate: 5.9% (2000).
Education: Percent of population age 25 and over with: High school diploma (including GED) or higher: 90.5% (2000); Bachelor's degree or higher: 48.7% (2000).

School District(s)
Keene Central School District (KG-12)
 2003-04 Enrollment: 183 . . . . (518) 576-4555

Housing: Homeownership rate: 77.6% (2000); Median home value: $119,400 (2000); Median rent: $370 per month (2000); Median age of housing: 60+ years (2000).
Transportation: Commute to work: 82.5% car, 0.0% public transportation, 12.3% walk, 3.9% work from home (2000); Travel time to work: 60.1% less than 15 minutes, 18.9% 15 to 30 minutes, 12.2% 30 to 45 minutes, 3.4% 45 to 60 minutes, 5.4% 60 minutes or more (2000)

LAKE PLACID (village). Covers a land area of 1.379 square miles and a water area of 0.146 square miles. Located at 44.28° N. Lat.; 73.98° W. Long. Elevation is 1,882 feet.
History: Winter Olympics (1932, 1980) and the World Bobsled Championships (1969) were held here. The farm and burial place of the abolitionist John Brown are nearby. Terminus of 133-mile Northville-Lake Placid trail connecting Adirondack foothills and High Peaks region. Settled 1850, Incorporated 1900.
Population: 2,485 (1990); 2,638 (2000); 2,822 (2005); 2,998 (2010 projected); Race: 95.7% White, 1.1% Black, 1.1% Asian, 1.4% Hispanic of any race (2005); Density: 2,046.7 persons per square mile (2005); Average household size: 1.99 (2005); Median age: 38.1 (2005); Males per 100 females: 91.8 (2005); Marriage status: 35.9% never married, 46.3% now married, 9.9% widowed, 7.8% divorced (2000); Foreign born: 7.1% (2000); Ancestry (includes multiple ancestries): 24.5% Irish, 21.0% French (except Basque), 16.5% English, 12.5% German, 9.8% Other groups (2000).
Economy: Manufacturing of foot supports and transportation equipment. Famous resort and sports center; Winter Olympics (1932, 1980) and the World Bobsled Championships (1969) were held here. Lake Placid has a summer theater and music festival, a figure-skating school and annual winter sports competitions. Single-family building permits issued: 55 (2005); Multi-family building permits issued: 0 (2005); Employment by occupation: 16.1% management, 16.9% professional, 30.6% services, 22.1% sales, 0.0% farming, 9.8% construction, 4.7% production (2000).
Income: Per capita income: $21,189 (2005); Median household income: $31,233 (2005); Average household income: $42,198 (2005); Percent of households with income of $100,000 or more: 6.1% (2005); Poverty rate: 13.2% (2000).
Education: Percent of population age 25 and over with: High school diploma (including GED) or higher: 88.6% (2005); Bachelor's degree or higher: 29.5% (2005); Master's degree or higher: 10.1% (2005).

School District(s)
Lake Placid Central School District (KG-12)
 2003-04 Enrollment: 903 . . . . (518) 523-2475

Housing: Homeownership rate: 44.2% (2005); Median home value: $155,612 (2005); Median rent: $396 per month (2000); Median age of housing: 60+ years (2000).
Safety: Violent crime rate: 18.3 per 10,000 population; Property crime rate: 230.1 per 10,000 population (2004).
Newspapers: Lake Placid News (General - Circulation 4,500)
Transportation: Commute to work: 77.1% car, 2.2% public transportation, 13.4% walk, 5.9% work from home (2000); Travel time to work: 78.1% less than 15 minutes, 14.1% 15 to 30 minutes, 4.4% 30 to 45 minutes, 0.9% 45 to 60 minutes, 2.5% 60 minutes or more (2000); Amtrak: Service available.
Additional Information Contacts
Lake Placid Chamber of Commerce . . . . (518) 523-2445
  http://www.lakeplacid.com/

LEWIS
(town). Covers a land area of 84.782 square miles and a water area of 0.200 square miles. Located at 44.28° N. Lat.; 73.54° W. Long.
Population: 1,009 (1990); 1,200 (2000); 1,232 (2005); 1,237 (2010 projected); Race: 99.4% White, 0.2% Black, 0.0% Asian, 0.2% Hispanic of any race (2005); Density: 14.5 persons per square mile (2005); Average household size: 2.48 (2005); Median age: 40.0 (2005); Males per 100 females: 108.5 (2005); Marriage status: 21.1% never married, 59.1% now married, 7.4% widowed, 12.5% divorced (2000); Foreign born: 1.5% (2000); Ancestry (includes multiple ancestries): 32.0% French (except Basque), 20.8% Irish, 18.5% English, 13.4% Other groups, 11.6% United States or American (2000).
Economy: Single-family building permits issued: 3 (2005); Multi-family building permits issued: 0 (2005); Employment by occupation: 10.7% management, 19.5% professional, 22.6% services, 15.8% sales, 3.9% farming, 11.3% construction, 16.2% production (2000).
Income: Per capita income: $20,298 (2005); Median household income: $41,614 (2005); Average household income: $50,317 (2005); Percent of households with income of $100,000 or more: 6.6% (2005); Poverty rate: 8.1% (2000).
Education: Percent of population age 25 and over with: High school diploma (including GED) or higher: 76.6% (2005); Bachelor's degree or higher: 15.4% (2005); Master's degree or higher: 7.9% (2005).
Housing: Homeownership rate: 82.7% (2005); Median home value: $98,750 (2005); Median rent: $387 per month (2000); Median age of housing: 32 years (2000).
Transportation: Commute to work: 93.9% car, 0.0% public transportation, 2.3% walk, 3.8% work from home (2000); Travel time to work: 43.6% less than 15 minutes, 28.3% 15 to 30 minutes, 16.7% 30 to 45 minutes, 8.4% 45 to 60 minutes, 3.0% 60 minutes or more (2000)

MINERVA
(town). Covers a land area of 158.647 square miles and a water area of 3.487 square miles. Located at 43.84° N. Lat.; 74.03° W. Long. Elevation is 1,388 feet.
Population: 779 (1990); 796 (2000); 802 (2005); 804 (2010 projected); Race: 97.4% White, 0.4% Black, 0.1% Asian, 0.1% Hispanic of any race (2005); Density: 5.1 persons per square mile (2005); Average household size: 2.44 (2005); Median age: 43.6 (2005); Males per 100 females: 111.6 (2005); Marriage status: 20.2% never married, 62.0% now married, 6.9% widowed, 11.0% divorced (2000); Foreign born: 1.6% (2000); Ancestry (includes multiple ancestries): 36.4% Irish, 21.7% French (except Basque), 16.1% English, 11.8% German, 10.3% Other groups (2000).
Economy: Resort village. Hunting nearby. Single-family building permits issued: 10 (2005); Multi-family building permits issued: 0 (2005); Employment by occupation: 6.5% management, 17.0% professional, 22.0% services, 17.9% sales, 4.8% farming, 20.2% construction, 11.6% production (2000).
Income: Per capita income: $17,662 (2005); Median household income: $33,208 (2005); Average household income: $43,055 (2005); Percent of households with income of $100,000 or more: 7.3% (2005); Poverty rate: 13.6% (2000).
Education: Percent of population age 25 and over with: High school diploma (including GED) or higher: 83.9% (2005); Bachelor's degree or higher: 17.4% (2005); Master's degree or higher: 7.2% (2005).
Housing: Homeownership rate: 86.0% (2005); Median home value: $112,864 (2005); Median rent: $338 per month (2000); Median age of housing: 40 years (2000).
Transportation: Commute to work: 96.3% car, 0.0% public transportation, 0.9% walk, 2.8% work from home (2000); Travel time to work: 36.3% less than 15 minutes, 29.3% 15 to 30 minutes, 15.6% 30 to 45 minutes, 8.6% 45 to 60 minutes, 10.2% 60 minutes or more (2000)

MINEVILLE-WITHERBEE
(CDP). Covers a land area of 4.445 square miles and a water area of 0.007 square miles. Located at 44.08° N. Lat.; 73.52° W. Long.
Population: 1,745 (1990); 1,747 (2000); 1,729 (2005); 1,706 (2010 projected); Race: 87.4% White, 9.4% Black, 0.2% Asian, 8.7% Hispanic of any race (2005); Density: 389.0 persons per square mile (2005); Average household size: 2.86 (2005); Median age: 34.8 (2005); Males per 100 females: 139.8 (2005); Marriage status: 33.8% never married, 53.0% now married, 9.0% widowed, 4.2% divorced (2000); Foreign born: 2.5% (2000); Ancestry (includes multiple ancestries): 26.6% French (except Basque), 13.5% Other groups, 10.6% Irish, 8.8% French Canadian, 8.1% Polish (2000).
Economy: Employment by occupation: 4.8% management, 15.8% professional, 17.2% services, 15.5% sales, 0.0% farming, 18.4% construction, 28.3% production (2000).
Income: Per capita income: $25,417 (2005); Median household income: $48,551 (2005); Average household income: $64,236 (2005); Percent of households with income of $100,000 or more: 16.2% (2005); Poverty rate: 10.4% (2000).
Education: Percent of population age 25 and over with: High school diploma (including GED) or higher: 69.5% (2005); Bachelor's degree or higher: 6.4% (2005); Master's degree or higher: 4.2% (2005).
School District(s)
Moriah Central School District (PK-12)
  2003-04 Enrollment: 831 . . . . (518) 546-3301
Housing: Homeownership rate: 76.0% (2005); Median home value: $84,719 (2005); Median rent: $360 per month (2000); Median age of housing: 60+ years (2000).
Transportation: Commute to work: 96.7% car, 0.8% public transportation, 1.0% walk, 1.5% work from home (2000); Travel time to work: 28.1% less than 15 minutes, 25.5% 15 to 30 minutes, 24.7% 30 to 45 minutes, 12.2% 45 to 60 minutes, 9.5% 60 minutes or more (2000)

MORIAH
(town). Covers a land area of 64.685 square miles and a water area of 6.466 square miles. Located at 44.05° N. Lat.; 73.49° W. Long. Elevation is 950 feet.
Population: 4,808 (1990); 4,879 (2000); 4,791 (2005); 4,697 (2010 projected); Race: 93.4% White, 3.8% Black, 0.8% Asian, 4.3% Hispanic of any race (2005); Density: 74.1 persons per square mile (2005); Average household size: 2.54 (2005); Median age: 38.6 (2005); Males per 100 females: 111.3 (2005); Marriage status: 26.3% never married, 54.9% now married, 10.4% widowed, 8.4% divorced (2000); Foreign born: 1.3% (2000); Ancestry (includes multiple ancestries): 26.5% French (except Basque), 16.1% Irish, 11.5% English, 11.5% Other groups, 8.7% Italian (2000).
Economy: In former iron-mining area. Single-family building permits issued: 13 (2005); Multi-family building permits issued: 0 (2005); Employment by occupation: 5.0% management, 14.7% professional, 18.6% services, 23.2% sales, 0.7% farming, 14.5% construction, 23.4% production (2000).
Income: Per capita income: $22,802 (2005); Median household income: $41,923 (2005); Average household income: $54,834 (2005); Percent of households with income of $100,000 or more: 10.6% (2005); Poverty rate: 12.8% (2000).
Education: Percent of population age 25 and over with: High school diploma (including GED) or higher: 75.8% (2005); Bachelor's degree or higher: 7.8% (2005); Master's degree or higher: 4.3% (2005).
Housing: Homeownership rate: 76.4% (2005); Median home value: $93,088 (2005); Median rent: $345 per month (2000); Median age of housing: 59 years (2000).
Safety: Violent crime rate: 0.0 per 10,000 population; Property crime rate: 0.0 per 10,000 population (2004).
Transportation: Commute to work: 93.6% car, 0.5% public transportation, 1.6% walk, 3.6% work from home (2000); Travel time to work: 27.9% less than 15 minutes, 24.9% 15 to 30 minutes, 26.1% 30 to 45 minutes, 9.2% 45 to 60 minutes, 11.9% 60 minutes or more (2000)

MORIAH CENTER
(unincorporated postal area, zip code 12961). Covers a land area of 15.944 square miles and a water area of 0.168 square miles. Located at 44.06° N. Lat.; 73.58° W. Long. Elevation is 796 feet.
Population: 0 (2000); Race: 100.0% White, 0.0% Black, 0.0% Asian, 0.0% Hispanic of any race (2000); Density: 0.0 persons per square mile (2000); Age: 37.1% under 18, 7.1% over 64 (2000); Marriage status: 10.1% never

married, 76.1% now married, 6.4% widowed, 7.3% divorced (2000); Foreign born: 1.2% (2000); Ancestry (includes multiple ancestries): 62.9% French (except Basque), 31.8% Irish, 15.3% Italian, 8.2% English, 8.2% Other groups (2000).
Economy: Employment by occupation: 11.4% management, 8.9% professional, 2.5% services, 19.0% sales, 1.3% farming, 26.6% construction, 30.4% production (2000).
Income: Per capita income: $17,343 (2000); Median household income: $48,125 (2000); Poverty rate: 20.0% (2000).
Education: Percent of population age 25 and over with: High school diploma (including GED) or higher: 94.3% (2000); Bachelor's degree or higher: 9.5% (2000).
Housing: Homeownership rate: 96.4% (2000); Median home value: $82,200 (2000); Median rent: $375 per month (2000); Median age of housing: 30 years (2000).
Transportation: Commute to work: 90.4% car, 0.0% public transportation, 8.2% walk, 1.4% work from home (2000); Travel time to work: 33.3% less than 15 minutes, 20.8% 15 to 30 minutes, 26.4% 30 to 45 minutes, 11.1% 45 to 60 minutes, 8.3% 60 minutes or more (2000)

NEW RUSSIA (unincorporated postal area, zip code 12964). Covers a land area of 27.775 square miles and a water area of 0.289 square miles. Located at 44.12° N. Lat.; 73.64° W. Long. Elevation is 628 feet.
Population: 0 (2000); Race: 100.0% White, 0.0% Black, 0.0% Asian, 0.0% Hispanic of any race (2000); Density: 0.0 persons per square mile (2000); Age: 23.3% under 18, 10.7% over 64 (2000); Marriage status: 22.8% never married, 65.4% now married, 3.1% widowed, 8.7% divorced (2000); Foreign born: 4.4% (2000); Ancestry (includes multiple ancestries): 32.1% Irish, 25.8% English, 12.6% French (except Basque), 9.4% Italian, 7.5% European (2000).
Economy: Employment by occupation: 5.3% management, 30.3% professional, 15.8% services, 27.6% sales, 0.0% farming, 14.5% construction, 6.6% production (2000).
Income: Per capita income: $19,183 (2000); Median household income: $47,000 (2000); Poverty rate: 11.3% (2000).
Education: Percent of population age 25 and over with: High school diploma (including GED) or higher: 90.9% (2000); Bachelor's degree or higher: 25.5% (2000).
Housing: Homeownership rate: 82.3% (2000); Median home value: $58,900 (2000); Median rent: $438 per month (2000); Median age of housing: 60+ years (2000).
Transportation: Commute to work: 92.1% car, 5.3% public transportation, 0.0% walk, 2.6% work from home (2000); Travel time to work: 63.5% less than 15 minutes, 14.9% 15 to 30 minutes, 0.0% 30 to 45 minutes, 9.5% 45 to 60 minutes, 12.2% 60 minutes or more (2000)

NEWCOMB (town). Covers a land area of 226.582 square miles and a water area of 6.600 square miles. Located at 43.97° N. Lat.; 74.16° W. Long. Elevation is 1,571 feet.
Population: 544 (1990); 481 (2000); 471 (2005); 468 (2010 projected); Race: 96.0% White, 0.0% Black, 0.0% Asian, 0.4% Hispanic of any race (2005); Density: 2.1 persons per square mile (2005); Average household size: 2.24 (2005); Median age: 53.4 (2005); Males per 100 females: 96.3 (2005); Marriage status: 14.7% never married, 69.2% now married, 13.2% widowed, 2.9% divorced (2000); Foreign born: 6.8% (2000); Ancestry (includes multiple ancestries): 22.2% French (except Basque), 20.6% Irish, 18.3% English, 11.3% German, 10.1% Other groups (2000).
Economy: Ilmenite, magnetite. Single-family building permits issued: 5 (2005); Multi-family building permits issued: 0 (2005); Employment by occupation: 4.1% management, 18.8% professional, 28.4% services, 19.8% sales, 2.0% farming, 7.6% construction, 19.3% production (2000).
Income: Per capita income: $17,431 (2005); Median household income: $32,857 (2005); Average household income: $38,845 (2005); Percent of households with income of $100,000 or more: 2.9% (2005); Poverty rate: 9.1% (2000).
Education: Percent of population age 25 and over with: High school diploma (including GED) or higher: 78.9% (2005); Bachelor's degree or higher: 20.5% (2005); Master's degree or higher: 9.7% (2005).
School District(s)
Newcomb Central School District (PK-12)
    2003-04 Enrollment: 76 . . . . (518) 582-3341
Housing: Homeownership rate: 89.5% (2005); Median home value: $122,523 (2005); Median rent: $325 per month (2000); Median age of housing: 41 years (2000).
Transportation: Commute to work: 88.2% car, 0.0% public transportation, 5.1% walk, 6.7% work from home (2000); Travel time to work: 57.7% less than 15 minutes, 14.8% 15 to 30 minutes, 9.9% 30 to 45 minutes, 4.9% 45 to 60 minutes, 12.6% 60 minutes or more (2000)
Additional Information Contacts
Town of Newcomb . . . . (518) 582-3211
    http://www.newcombny,.com/

NORTH ELBA (town). Covers a land area of 151.882 square miles and a water area of 4.570 square miles. Located at 44.28° N. Lat.; 74.02° W. Long. Elevation is 1,955 feet.
History: Here are the farm, home (now a museum), and grave of John Brown.
Population: 7,871 (1990); 8,661 (2000); 9,206 (2005); 9,712 (2010 projected); Race: 84.3% White, 11.5% Black, 1.0% Asian, 7.1% Hispanic of any race (2005); Density: 60.6 persons per square mile (2005); Average household size: 2.87 (2005); Median age: 38.6 (2005); Males per 100 females: 144.5 (2005); Marriage status: 25.6% never married, 60.6% now married, 6.8% widowed, 7.0% divorced (2000); Foreign born: 8.1% (2000); Ancestry (includes multiple ancestries): 21.0% Irish, 19.0% French (except Basque), 15.2% English, 11.2% German, 10.2% Other groups (2000).
Economy: Single-family building permits issued: 55 (2005); Multi-family building permits issued: 0 (2005); Employment by occupation: 13.3% management, 20.1% professional, 28.0% services, 22.9% sales, 0.0% farming, 8.8% construction, 7.0% production (2000).
Income: Per capita income: $21,811 (2005); Median household income: $39,265 (2005); Average household income: $50,355 (2005); Percent of households with income of $100,000 or more: 8.5% (2005); Poverty rate: 10.9% (2000).
Education: Percent of population age 25 and over with: High school diploma (including GED) or higher: 82.0% (2005); Bachelor's degree or higher: 21.8% (2005); Master's degree or higher: 9.0% (2005).
Housing: Homeownership rate: 61.1% (2005); Median home value: $147,949 (2005); Median rent: $412 per month (2000); Median age of housing: 42 years (2000).
Transportation: Commute to work: 84.3% car, 1.2% public transportation, 8.3% walk, 5.5% work from home (2000); Travel time to work: 68.3% less than 15 minutes, 22.4% 15 to 30 minutes, 5.0% 30 to 45 minutes, 1.7% 45 to 60 minutes, 2.6% 60 minutes or more (2000)
Additional Information Contacts
Town of North Elba . . . . (518) 523-2162
    http://www.townofnorthelba.org

NORTH HUDSON (town). Covers a land area of 180.132 square miles and a water area of 3.070 square miles. Located at 43.99° N. Lat.; 73.72° W. Long. Elevation is 884 feet.
Population: 256 (1990); 266 (2000); 282 (2005); 295 (2010 projected); Race: 95.4% White, 0.0% Black, 0.7% Asian, 0.0% Hispanic of any race (2005); Density: 1.6 persons per square mile (2005); Average household size: 2.29 (2005); Median age: 42.4 (2005); Males per 100 females: 101.4 (2005); Marriage status: 18.0% never married, 63.6% now married, 9.7% widowed, 8.8% divorced (2000); Foreign born: 0.0% (2000); Ancestry (includes multiple ancestries): 32.5% French (except Basque), 27.6% Irish, 24.3% Other groups, 17.2% English, 14.6% German (2000).
Economy: Single-family building permits issued: 7 (2005); Multi-family building permits issued: 0 (2005); Employment by occupation: 4.4% management, 6.1% professional, 30.7% services, 25.4% sales, 0.0% farming, 23.7% construction, 9.6% production (2000).
Income: Per capita income: $18,511 (2005); Median household income: $33,036 (2005); Average household income: $42,439 (2005); Percent of households with income of $100,000 or more: 5.7% (2005); Poverty rate: 10.1% (2000).
Education: Percent of population age 25 and over with: High school diploma (including GED) or higher: 74.2% (2005); Bachelor's degree or higher: 11.3% (2005); Master's degree or higher: 0.0% (2005).
Housing: Homeownership rate: 84.6% (2005); Median home value: $88,696 (2005); Median rent: $406 per month (2000); Median age of housing: 50 years (2000).
Transportation: Commute to work: 94.7% car, 0.0% public transportation, 2.6% walk, 2.6% work from home (2000); Travel time to work: 23.4% less than 15 minutes, 37.8% 15 to 30 minutes, 15.3% 30 to 45 minutes, 0.0% 45 to 60 minutes, 23.4% 60 minutes or more (2000)

OLMSTEDVILLE (unincorporated postal area, zip code 12857). Covers a land area of 66.647 square miles and a water area of 0.921 square miles. Located at 43.79° N. Lat.; 73.94° W. Long.
Population: 0 (2000); Race: 98.9% White, 0.0% Black, 0.0% Asian, 0.8% Hispanic of any race (2000); Density: 0.0 persons per square mile (2000); Age: 27.3% under 18, 16.5% over 64 (2000); Marriage status: 24.0% never married, 63.0% now married, 4.2% widowed, 8.8% divorced (2000); Foreign born: 2.1% (2000); Ancestry (includes multiple ancestries): 35.9% Irish, 20.3% French (except Basque), 15.0% English, 13.7% German, 8.9% Other groups (2000).
Economy: Resort village. Employment by occupation: 9.0% management, 19.4% professional, 18.5% services, 15.8% sales, 5.9% farming, 20.7% construction, 10.8% production (2000).
Income: Per capita income: $14,686 (2000); Median household income: $32,411 (2000); Poverty rate: 13.2% (2000).
Education: Percent of population age 25 and over with: High school diploma (including GED) or higher: 86.1% (2000); Bachelor's degree or higher: 15.9% (2000).

School District(s)
Minerva Central School District (KG-12)
    2003-04 Enrollment: 143 . . . . (518) 251-2000
Housing: Homeownership rate: 83.2% (2000); Median home value: $88,600 (2000); Median rent: $333 per month (2000); Median age of housing: 35 years (2000).
Transportation: Commute to work: 95.8% car, 0.0% public transportation, 3.3% walk, 0.9% work from home (2000); Travel time to work: 34.0% less than 15 minutes, 25.5% 15 to 30 minutes, 17.9% 30 to 45 minutes, 10.8% 45 to 60 minutes, 11.8% 60 minutes or more (2000)

PARADOX (unincorporated postal area, zip code 12858). Covers a land area of 12.934 square miles and a water area of 0.105 square miles. Located at 43.88° N. Lat.; 73.65° W. Long. Elevation is 875 feet.
Population: 0 (2000); Race: 100.0% White, 0.0% Black, 0.0% Asian, 0.0% Hispanic of any race (2000); Density: 0.0 persons per square mile (2000); Age: 14.0% under 18, 21.1% over 64 (2000); Marriage status: 21.6% never married, 62.7% now married, 5.9% widowed, 9.8% divorced (2000); Foreign born: 5.3% (2000); Ancestry (includes multiple ancestries): 35.1% German, 28.1% English, 22.8% French (except Basque), 14.0% Other groups, 12.3% Italian (2000).
Economy: Employment by occupation: 0.0% management, 27.8% professional, 27.8% services, 16.7% sales, 11.1% farming, 16.7% construction, 0.0% production (2000).
Income: Per capita income: $8,663 (2000); Median household income: $16,094 (2000); Poverty rate: 17.5% (2000).
Education: Percent of population age 25 and over with: High school diploma (including GED) or higher: 66.7% (2000); Bachelor's degree or higher: 13.3% (2000).
Housing: Homeownership rate: 90.5% (2000); Median home value: $59,200 (2000); Median rent: $n/a per month (2000); Median age of housing: 34 years (2000).
Transportation: Commute to work: 100.0% car, 0.0% public transportation, 0.0% walk, 0.0% work from home (2000); Travel time to work: 16.7% less than 15 minutes, 55.6% 15 to 30 minutes, 16.7% 30 to 45 minutes, 11.1% 45 to 60 minutes, 0.0% 60 minutes or more (2000)

PORT HENRY (village). Covers a land area of 1.202 square miles and a water area of 0.281 square miles. Located at 44.04° N. Lat.; 73.46° W. Long. Elevation is 108 feet.
History: Incorporated 1869.
Population: 1,263 (1990); 1,152 (2000); 1,123 (2005); 1,098 (2010 projected); Race: 97.1% White, 1.0% Black, 0.7% Asian, 2.0% Hispanic of any race (2005); Density: 934.6 persons per square mile (2005); Average household size: 2.31 (2005); Median age: 40.0 (2005); Males per 100 females: 94.6 (2005); Marriage status: 24.5% never married, 49.6% now married, 14.0% widowed, 11.9% divorced (2000); Foreign born: 1.6% (2000); Ancestry (includes multiple ancestries): 25.2% French (except Basque), 19.0% Irish, 14.4% Italian, 13.3% English, 12.0% Other groups (2000).
Economy: Resort village. In dairying area. Single-family building permits issued: 0 (2005); Multi-family building permits issued: 0 (2005); Employment by occupation: 9.0% management, 12.1% professional, 22.4% services, 23.1% sales, 0.7% farming, 7.6% construction, 25.1% production (2000).
Income: Per capita income: $21,837 (2005); Median household income: $36,759 (2005); Average household income: $48,701 (2005); Percent of households with income of $100,000 or more: 6.8% (2005); Poverty rate: 19.2% (2000).
Education: Percent of population age 25 and over with: High school diploma (including GED) or higher: 77.5% (2005); Bachelor's degree or higher: 10.4% (2005); Master's degree or higher: 5.1% (2005).

School District(s)
Moriah Central School District (PK-12)
    2003-04 Enrollment: 831 . . . . (518) 546-3301
Housing: Homeownership rate: 64.5% (2005); Median home value: $90,462 (2005); Median rent: $341 per month (2000); Median age of housing: 60+ years (2000).
Transportation: Commute to work: 91.5% car, 0.9% public transportation, 3.9% walk, 3.2% work from home (2000); Travel time to work: 32.4% less than 15 minutes, 25.5% 15 to 30 minutes, 24.1% 30 to 45 minutes, 8.7% 45 to 60 minutes, 9.2% 60 minutes or more (2000); Amtrak: Service available.

SAINT ARMAND (town). Covers a land area of 56.543 square miles and a water area of 0.900 square miles. Located at 44.39° N. Lat.; 74.05° W. Long.
Population: 1,317 (1990); 1,321 (2000); 1,302 (2005); 1,295 (2010 projected); Race: 97.8% White, 0.3% Black, 0.2% Asian, 1.4% Hispanic of any race (2005); Density: 23.0 persons per square mile (2005); Average household size: 2.41 (2005); Median age: 40.7 (2005); Males per 100 females: 98.2 (2005); Marriage status: 24.3% never married, 61.4% now married, 6.1% widowed, 8.1% divorced (2000); Foreign born: 2.0% (2000); Ancestry (includes multiple ancestries): 24.5% Irish, 24.5% French (except Basque), 14.5% German, 13.9% English, 8.9% Other groups (2000).
Economy: Single-family building permits issued: 8 (2005); Multi-family building permits issued: 0 (2005); Employment by occupation: 7.1% management, 26.5% professional, 21.1% services, 24.2% sales, 0.5% farming, 11.6% construction, 9.0% production (2000).
Income: Per capita income: $23,391 (2005); Median household income: $47,266 (2005); Average household income: $56,294 (2005); Percent of households with income of $100,000 or more: 12.4% (2005); Poverty rate: 8.1% (2000).
Taxes: Total city taxes per capita: $373 (2004); City property taxes per capita: $340 (2004).
Education: Percent of population age 25 and over with: High school diploma (including GED) or higher: 85.7% (2005); Bachelor's degree or higher: 21.9% (2005); Master's degree or higher: 9.7% (2005).
Housing: Homeownership rate: 74.5% (2005); Median home value: $119,275 (2005); Median rent: $426 per month (2000); Median age of housing: 43 years (2000).
Transportation: Commute to work: 93.0% car, 0.3% public transportation, 1.2% walk, 5.0% work from home (2000); Travel time to work: 43.1% less than 15 minutes, 39.5% 15 to 30 minutes, 10.8% 30 to 45 minutes, 2.5% 45 to 60 minutes, 4.1% 60 minutes or more (2000)

SCHROON (town). Covers a land area of 133.196 square miles and a water area of 8.045 square miles. Located at 43.84° N. Lat.; 73.75° W. Long.
Population: 1,695 (1990); 1,759 (2000); 1,775 (2005); 1,794 (2010 projected); Race: 97.7% White, 1.2% Black, 0.3% Asian, 0.5% Hispanic of any race (2005); Density: 13.3 persons per square mile (2005); Average household size: 2.35 (2005); Median age: 43.6 (2005); Males per 100 females: 88.0 (2005); Marriage status: 25.2% never married, 59.6% now married, 9.9% widowed, 5.3% divorced (2000); Foreign born: 2.7% (2000); Ancestry (includes multiple ancestries): 24.5% English, 23.8% Irish, 22.9% German, 18.9% French (except Basque), 6.6% Italian (2000).
Economy: Single-family building permits issued: 26 (2005); Multi-family building permits issued: 0 (2005); Employment by occupation: 7.0% management, 17.1% professional, 23.4% services, 24.9% sales, 2.6% farming, 12.8% construction, 12.1% production (2000).
Income: Per capita income: $17,091 (2005); Median household income: $30,794 (2005); Average household income: $39,616 (2005); Percent of households with income of $100,000 or more: 5.3% (2005); Poverty rate: 11.0% (2000).
Education: Percent of population age 25 and over with: High school diploma (including GED) or higher: 83.2% (2005); Bachelor's degree or higher: 17.2% (2005); Master's degree or higher: 6.5% (2005).

Housing: Homeownership rate: 69.4% (2005); Median home value: $126,881 (2005); Median rent: $328 per month (2000); Median age of housing: 34 years (2000).
Transportation: Commute to work: 83.4% car, 0.0% public transportation, 9.8% walk, 6.1% work from home (2000); Travel time to work: 57.1% less than 15 minutes, 16.0% 15 to 30 minutes, 14.7% 30 to 45 minutes, 7.3% 45 to 60 minutes, 5.0% 60 minutes or more (2000)

SCHROON LAKE (unincorporated postal area, zip code 12870).
Covers a land area of 108.823 square miles and a water area of 6.238 square miles. Located at 43.83° N. Lat.; 73.75° W. Long. Elevation is 867 feet.
Population: 0 (2000); Race: 98.1% White, 0.4% Black, 0.1% Asian, 0.3% Hispanic of any race (2000); Density: 0.0 persons per square mile (2000); Age: 23.1% under 18, 18.4% over 64 (2000); Marriage status: 25.1% never married, 59.7% now married, 10.0% widowed, 5.2% divorced (2000); Foreign born: 2.6% (2000); Ancestry (includes multiple ancestries): 24.4% Irish, 24.3% English, 22.8% German, 18.6% French (except Basque), 6.2% Dutch (2000).
Economy: Resort village. Employment by occupation: 6.8% management, 17.0% professional, 23.3% services, 25.6% sales, 2.0% farming, 12.5% construction, 12.7% production (2000).
Income: Per capita income: $15,603 (2000); Median household income: $29,865 (2000); Poverty rate: 10.7% (2000).
Education: Percent of population age 25 and over with: High school diploma (including GED) or higher: 84.3% (2000); Bachelor's degree or higher: 17.4% (2000).

School District(s)
Schroon Lake Central School District (KG-12)
    2003-04 Enrollment: 306 . . . . (518) 532-7164
Housing: Homeownership rate: 68.9% (2000); Median home value: $85,700 (2000); Median rent: $330 per month (2000); Median age of housing: 34 years (2000).
Transportation: Commute to work: 83.1% car, 0.0% public transportation, 9.8% walk, 6.4% work from home (2000); Travel time to work: 58.1% less than 15 minutes, 14.9% 15 to 30 minutes, 14.9% 30 to 45 minutes, 6.9% 45 to 60 minutes, 5.2% 60 minutes or more (2000)
Additional Information Contacts
Schroon Lake Chamber of Commerce . . . . (518) 532-7675
http://www.schroonlake.org

TICONDEROGA (town). Covers a land area of 81.777 square miles and a water area of 6.502 square miles. Located at 43.85° N. Lat.; 73.45° W. Long. Elevation is 154 feet.
History: Ticonderoga is a variation of the Native American "Cheonderoga," meaning "between two waters." The French built a military road at the site and in 1755 they constructed Fort Carillon, later called Fort Ticonderoga.
Population: 5,145 (1990); 5,167 (2000); 5,160 (2005); 5,177 (2010 projected); Race: 97.9% White, 0.7% Black, 0.4% Asian, 0.6% Hispanic of any race (2005); Density: 63.1 persons per square mile (2005); Average household size: 2.50 (2005); Median age: 39.5 (2005); Males per 100 females: 94.1 (2005); Marriage status: 24.2% never married, 57.0% now married, 8.4% widowed, 10.5% divorced (2000); Foreign born: 2.4% (2000); Ancestry (includes multiple ancestries): 20.0% Irish, 18.8% French (except Basque), 13.0% English, 12.0% Other groups, 9.9% Italian (2000).
Economy: Single-family building permits issued: 18 (2005); Multi-family building permits issued: 0 (2005); Employment by occupation: 9.8% management, 17.2% professional, 24.7% services, 18.5% sales, 0.6% farming, 11.9% construction, 17.4% production (2000).
Income: Per capita income: $18,499 (2005); Median household income: $36,860 (2005); Average household income: $45,080 (2005); Percent of households with income of $100,000 or more: 6.1% (2005); Poverty rate: 15.5% (2000).
Education: Percent of population age 25 and over with: High school diploma (including GED) or higher: 77.8% (2005); Bachelor's degree or higher: 13.5% (2005); Master's degree or higher: 5.1% (2005).

School District(s)
Ticonderoga Central School District (KG-12)
    2003-04 Enrollment: 1,075 . . . . (518) 585-6674
Housing: Homeownership rate: 73.4% (2005); Median home value: $111,047 (2005); Median rent: $391 per month (2000); Median age of housing: 52 years (2000).
Hospitals: Moses-Ludington Hospital (15 beds)
Safety: Violent crime rate: 7.7 per 10,000 population; Property crime rate: 145.0 per 10,000 population (2004).

Newspapers: Times of Ti (General - Circulation 11,300)
Transportation: Commute to work: 89.2% car, 0.6% public transportation, 6.1% walk, 3.2% work from home (2000); Travel time to work: 69.0% less than 15 minutes, 12.8% 15 to 30 minutes, 6.8% 30 to 45 minutes, 7.0% 45 to 60 minutes, 4.3% 60 minutes or more (2000); Amtrak: Service available.
Additional Information Contacts
Ticonderoga Area Chamber of Commerce . . . . (518) 585-6619
http://www.ticonderogany.com

UPPER JAY (unincorporated postal area, zip code 12987). Covers a land area of 27.742 square miles and a water area of 0.107 square miles. Located at 44.32° N. Lat.; 73.79° W. Long. Elevation is 686 feet.
Population: 0 (2000); Race: 97.0% White, 0.0% Black, 0.0% Asian, 2.3% Hispanic of any race (2000); Density: 0.0 persons per square mile (2000); Age: 17.8% under 18, 20.8% over 64 (2000); Marriage status: 18.1% never married, 62.4% now married, 11.5% widowed, 8.0% divorced (2000); Foreign born: 6.4% (2000); Ancestry (includes multiple ancestries): 25.8% French (except Basque), 21.2% Irish, 20.8% English, 8.7% German, 6.8% Scottish (2000).
Economy: Resort village. Employment by occupation: 8.8% management, 22.8% professional, 30.9% services, 14.0% sales, 0.0% farming, 14.0% construction, 9.6% production (2000).
Income: Per capita income: $20,601 (2000); Median household income: $33,125 (2000); Poverty rate: 3.8% (2000).
Education: Percent of population age 25 and over with: High school diploma (including GED) or higher: 88.1% (2000); Bachelor's degree or higher: 27.4% (2000).
Housing: Homeownership rate: 84.9% (2000); Median home value: $73,200 (2000); Median rent: $392 per month (2000); Median age of housing: 36 years (2000).
Transportation: Commute to work: 90.2% car, 0.0% public transportation, 0.0% walk, 9.8% work from home (2000); Travel time to work: 19.2% less than 15 minutes, 42.5% 15 to 30 minutes, 27.5% 30 to 45 minutes, 5.0% 45 to 60 minutes, 5.8% 60 minutes or more (2000)

WESTPORT (town). Covers a land area of 58.434 square miles and a water area of 8.455 square miles. Located at 44.18° N. Lat.; 73.45° W. Long. Elevation is 271 feet.
Population: 1,446 (1990); 1,362 (2000); 1,329 (2005); 1,304 (2010 projected); Race: 97.1% White, 0.2% Black, 1.3% Asian, 1.2% Hispanic of any race (2005); Density: 22.7 persons per square mile (2005); Average household size: 2.25 (2005); Median age: 46.3 (2005); Males per 100 females: 95.2 (2005); Marriage status: 18.6% never married, 62.1% now married, 9.9% widowed, 9.5% divorced (2000); Foreign born: 2.5% (2000); Ancestry (includes multiple ancestries): 24.3% English, 12.9% French (except Basque), 11.4% Irish, 10.0% German, 7.3% United States or American (2000).
Economy: Lumber. Annual county fair and a summer regatta held here. Single-family building permits issued: 2 (2005); Multi-family building permits issued: 0 (2005); Employment by occupation: 13.5% management, 32.1% professional, 13.4% services, 20.5% sales, 1.0% farming, 7.8% construction, 11.7% production (2000).
Income: Per capita income: $27,203 (2005); Median household income: $47,477 (2005); Average household income: $61,275 (2005); Percent of households with income of $100,000 or more: 14.6% (2005); Poverty rate: 7.7% (2000).
Education: Percent of population age 25 and over with: High school diploma (including GED) or higher: 84.8% (2005); Bachelor's degree or higher: 31.9% (2005); Master's degree or higher: 17.3% (2005).

School District(s)
Westport Central School District (KG-12)
    2003-04 Enrollment: 251 . . . . (518) 962-8244
Housing: Homeownership rate: 75.3% (2005); Median home value: $138,768 (2005); Median rent: $374 per month (2000); Median age of housing: 60+ years (2000).
Transportation: Commute to work: 90.2% car, 0.0% public transportation, 3.6% walk, 5.7% work from home (2000); Travel time to work: 40.3% less than 15 minutes, 36.5% 15 to 30 minutes, 10.8% 30 to 45 minutes, 5.5% 45 to 60 minutes, 6.9% 60 minutes or more (2000); Amtrak: Service available.
Additional Information Contacts
Town of Westport . . . . (518) 962-4419
http://www.westportny.net/
Westport Chamber of Commerce . . . . (518) 962-8383
http://www.westportny.com

WILLSBORO (town). Covers a land area of 42.704 square miles and a water area of 30.694 square miles. Located at 44.37° N. Lat.; 73.40° W. Long. Elevation is 215 feet.
Population: 1,754 (1990); 1,903 (2000); 1,893 (2005); 1,885 (2010 projected); Race: 98.3% White, 0.3% Black, 0.0% Asian, 0.5% Hispanic of any race (2005); Density: 44.3 persons per square mile (2005); Average household size: 2.33 (2005); Median age: 43.6 (2005); Males per 100 females: 98.2 (2005); Marriage status: 22.3% never married, 59.8% now married, 9.6% widowed, 8.2% divorced (2000); Foreign born: 1.6% (2000); Ancestry (includes multiple ancestries): 20.3% French (except Basque), 17.4% English, 15.4% Irish, 8.3% German, 6.9% United States or American (2000).
Economy: Manufacturing of consumer goods, chemicals, plastic products, textiles. Single-family building permits issued: 8 (2005); Multi-family building permits issued: 0 (2005); Employment by occupation: 11.1% management, 16.4% professional, 17.5% services, 21.3% sales, 3.7% farming, 12.2% construction, 18.0% production (2000).
Income: Per capita income: $23,446 (2005); Median household income: $43,405 (2005); Average household income: $54,240 (2005); Percent of households with income of $100,000 or more: 11.1% (2005); Poverty rate: 9.5% (2000).
Education: Percent of population age 25 and over with: High school diploma (including GED) or higher: 77.3% (2005); Bachelor's degree or higher: 18.1% (2005); Master's degree or higher: 8.0% (2005).
School District(s)
Willsboro Central School District (PK-12)
    2003-04 Enrollment: 378 . . . . (518) 963-4456
Housing: Homeownership rate: 81.4% (2005); Median home value: $101,955 (2005); Median rent: $378 per month (2000); Median age of housing: 42 years (2000).
Transportation: Commute to work: 89.1% car, 0.3% public transportation, 2.3% walk, 7.7% work from home (2000); Travel time to work: 49.0% less than 15 minutes, 23.9% 15 to 30 minutes, 17.7% 30 to 45 minutes, 3.5% 45 to 60 minutes, 5.9% 60 minutes or more (2000)

WILMINGTON (town). Covers a land area of 65.158 square miles and a water area of 0.295 square miles. Located at 44.39° N. Lat.; 73.80° W. Long.
Population: 1,020 (1990); 1,131 (2000); 1,144 (2005); 1,150 (2010 projected); Race: 98.6% White, 0.2% Black, 0.3% Asian, 0.8% Hispanic of any race (2005); Density: 17.6 persons per square mile (2005); Average household size: 2.43 (2005); Median age: 37.9 (2005); Males per 100 females: 96.6 (2005); Marriage status: 23.1% never married, 60.0% now married, 8.5% widowed, 8.4% divorced (2000); Foreign born: 3.6% (2000); Ancestry (includes multiple ancestries): 23.9% French (except Basque), 22.9% Irish, 14.1% English, 13.4% German, 9.0% Other groups (2000).
Economy: Resort village. Road to Whiteface Mt. Ski Center starts here. Single-family building permits issued: 20 (2005); Multi-family building permits issued: 0 (2005); Employment by occupation: 8.0% management, 21.1% professional, 28.3% services, 21.3% sales, 0.4% farming, 13.3% construction, 7.6% production (2000).
Income: Per capita income: $21,818 (2005); Median household income: $41,825 (2005); Average household income: $52,994 (2005); Percent of households with income of $100,000 or more: 11.7% (2005); Poverty rate: 10.0% (2000).
Education: Percent of population age 25 and over with: High school diploma (including GED) or higher: 79.9% (2005); Bachelor's degree or higher: 23.6% (2005); Master's degree or higher: 10.7% (2005).
Housing: Homeownership rate: 72.4% (2005); Median home value: $129,040 (2005); Median rent: $367 per month (2000); Median age of housing: 40 years (2000).
Transportation: Commute to work: 89.6% car, 1.0% public transportation, 2.7% walk, 6.2% work from home (2000); Travel time to work: 24.6% less than 15 minutes, 34.0% 15 to 30 minutes, 16.8% 30 to 45 minutes, 7.4% 45 to 60 minutes, 17.2% 60 minutes or more (2000)

Franklin County

Located in northeastern New York, partly in the Adirondacks; bounded on the north by the Canadian province of Quebec; drained by the Saranac, St. Regis, Salmon, Little Salmon, Chateaugay, and Raquette Rivers; includes many lakes, including Saranac Lake and Tupper Lake. Covers a land area of 1,631.49 square miles, a water area of 65.95 square miles, and is located in the Eastern Time Zone. The county government was organized in 1808. County seat is Malone.

Franklin County is part of the Malone, NY Micropolitan Statistical Area. The entire metro area includes: Franklin County, NY

Weather Station: Chasm Falls   Elevation: 1,059 feet

	Jan	Feb	Mar	Apr	May	Jun	Jul	Aug	Sep	Oct	Nov	Dec
High	26	29	39	52	67	75	79	76	67	56	43	30
Low	5	6	17	30	42	50	55	53	46	36	26	12
Precip	2.7	2.5	2.9	3.0	3.3	4.0	4.3	5.6	4.4	3.6	3.8	3.5
Snow	27.3	26.1	20.3	8.3	0.4	tr	0.0	0.0	0.0	0.8	11.9	26.1

High and Low temperatures in degrees Fahrenheit; Precipitation and Snow in inches

Population: 46,540 (1990); 51,134 (2000); 51,230 (2005); 51,299 (2010 projected); Race: 84.4% White, 7.0% Black, 0.5% Asian, 4.1% Hispanic of any race (2005); Density: 31.4 persons per square mile (2005); Average household size: 2.81 (2005); Median age: 37.8 (2005); Males per 100 females: 121.2 (2005).
Religion: Five largest groups: 53.7% Catholic Church, 4.5% The United Methodist Church, 1.3% Southern Baptist Convention, 0.9% Episcopal Church, 0.8% Presbyterian Church (U.S.A.) (2000).
Economy: Unemployment rate: 6.0% (2005); Total civilian labor force: 22,298 (2005); Leading industries: 28.5% health care and social assistance; 17.1% retail trade; 10.4% accommodation and food services (2003); Farms: 532 totaling 138,236 acres (2002); Companies that employ 500 or more persons: 1 (2003); Companies that employ 100 to 499 persons: 11 (2003); Companies that employ less than 100 persons: 1,064 (2003); Black-owned businesses: n/a (2002); Hispanic-owned businesses: n/a (2002); Women-owned businesses: 789 (2002); Retail sales per capita: $7,823 (2006). Single-family building permits issued: 165 (2005); Multi-family building permits issued: 0 (2005).
Income: Per capita income: $18,720 (2005); Median household income: $36,436 (2005); Average household income: $46,312 (2005); Percent of households with income of $100,000 or more: 7.4% (2005); Poverty rate: 14.6% (2003); Bankruptcy rate: 4.45% (2005).
Taxes: Total county taxes per capita: $482 (2004); County property taxes per capita: $240 (2004).
Education: Percent of population age 25 and over with: High school diploma (including GED) or higher: 69.7% (2005); Bachelor's degree or higher: 13.0% (2005); Master's degree or higher: 5.8% (2005).
Housing: Homeownership rate: 70.8% (2005); Median home value: $91,081 (2005); Median rent: $340 per month (2000); Median age of housing: 45 years (2000).
Health: Birth rate: 96.5 per 10,000 population (2004); Death rate: 85.9 per 10,000 population (2004); Age-adjusted cancer mortality rate: 218.9 deaths per 100,000 population (2002); Air Quality Index: 94.2% good, 5.2% moderate, 0.6% unhealthy for sensitive individuals, 0.0% unhealthy (percent of days in 2005); Number of physicians: 17.7 per 10,000 population (2004); Hospital beds: 44.7 per 10,000 population (2003); Hospital admissions: 1,340.9 per 10,000 population (2003).
Elections: 2004 Presidential election results: 45.8% Bush, 52.1% Kerry, 1.9% Nader, 0.1% Badnarik
National and State Parks: Franklin State Forest; Franklin State Forest Number Four; Franklin State Forest Number Nine; Franklin State Forest Number One; Franklin State Forest Number Six; Franklin State Forest Number Three; Franklin State Forest Number Two
Additional Information Contacts
Franklin County Government . . . . (518) 483-6767
    http://www.franklincony.org/
Town of Brighton . . . . (585) 784-5251
    http://www.townofbrighton.org/

Franklin County Communities

ALTAMONT (town). Covers a land area of 117.621 square miles and a water area of 12.489 square miles. Located at 44.23° N. Lat.; 74.47° W. Long.
Population: 6,199 (1990); 6,137 (2000); 6,066 (2005); 6,003 (2010 projected); Race: 98.1% White, 1.1% Black, 0.1% Asian, 0.5% Hispanic of any race (2005); Density: 51.6 persons per square mile (2005); Average household size: 2.49 (2005); Median age: 40.1 (2005); Males per 100 females: 100.9 (2005); Marriage status: 28.5% never married, 49.9% now married, 9.3% widowed, 12.3% divorced (2000); Foreign born: 3.2% (2000); Ancestry (includes multiple ancestries): 45.4% French (except

Basque), 21.0% Irish, 10.4% French Canadian, 9.3% English, 7.5% Other groups (2000).
Economy: Employment by occupation: 7.9% management, 19.4% professional, 33.3% services, 18.6% sales, 1.5% farming, 10.9% construction, 8.4% production (2000).
Income: Per capita income: $18,848 (2005); Median household income: $40,441 (2005); Average household income: $46,586 (2005); Percent of households with income of $100,000 or more: 5.7% (2005); Poverty rate: 13.4% (2000).
Education: Percent of population age 25 and over with: High school diploma (including GED) or higher: 76.6% (2005); Bachelor's degree or higher: 13.3% (2005); Master's degree or higher: 5.0% (2005).
Housing: Homeownership rate: 69.4% (2005); Median home value: $112,481 (2005); Median rent: $330 per month (2000); Median age of housing: 46 years (2000).
Transportation: Commute to work: 92.3% car, 0.8% public transportation, 4.6% walk, 1.6% work from home (2000); Travel time to work: 71.8% less than 15 minutes, 9.1% 15 to 30 minutes, 11.4% 30 to 45 minutes, 4.1% 45 to 60 minutes, 3.6% 60 minutes or more (2000)

BANGOR (town). Covers a land area of 43.107 square miles and a water area of 0 square miles. Located at 44.84° N. Lat.; 74.44° W. Long.
Population: 2,080 (1990); 2,147 (2000); 2,166 (2005); 2,179 (2010 projected); Race: 98.4% White, 0.0% Black, 0.1% Asian, 1.2% Hispanic of any race (2005); Density: 50.2 persons per square mile (2005); Average household size: 2.71 (2005); Median age: 37.7 (2005); Males per 100 females: 97.4 (2005); Marriage status: 24.7% never married, 61.2% now married, 6.6% widowed, 7.4% divorced (2000); Foreign born: 2.1% (2000); Ancestry (includes multiple ancestries): 28.2% French (except Basque), 15.3% Irish, 11.9% English, 10.8% French Canadian, 10.2% United States or American (2000).
Economy: Single-family building permits issued: 17 (2005); Multi-family building permits issued: 0 (2005); Employment by occupation: 12.0% management, 16.0% professional, 24.7% services, 18.2% sales, 5.1% farming, 9.9% construction, 14.1% production (2000).
Income: Per capita income: $16,064 (2005); Median household income: $35,357 (2005); Average household income: $42,722 (2005); Percent of households with income of $100,000 or more: 5.4% (2005); Poverty rate: 18.2% (2000).
Education: Percent of population age 25 and over with: High school diploma (including GED) or higher: 78.5% (2005); Bachelor's degree or higher: 9.9% (2005); Master's degree or higher: 4.0% (2005).
Housing: Homeownership rate: 81.0% (2005); Median home value: $76,316 (2005); Median rent: $286 per month (2000); Median age of housing: 43 years (2000).
Transportation: Commute to work: 88.0% car, 0.0% public transportation, 4.4% walk, 6.7% work from home (2000); Travel time to work: 41.0% less than 15 minutes, 38.6% 15 to 30 minutes, 8.4% 30 to 45 minutes, 4.2% 45 to 60 minutes, 7.9% 60 minutes or more (2000)

BELLMONT (town). Covers a land area of 164.434 square miles and a water area of 2.812 square miles. Located at 44.74° N. Lat.; 74.10° W. Long.
Population: 1,246 (1990); 1,423 (2000); 1,416 (2005); 1,412 (2010 projected); Race: 98.0% White, 0.1% Black, 0.8% Asian, 0.3% Hispanic of any race (2005); Density: 8.6 persons per square mile (2005); Average household size: 2.43 (2005); Median age: 42.0 (2005); Males per 100 females: 101.4 (2005); Marriage status: 25.7% never married, 57.4% now married, 6.1% widowed, 10.8% divorced (2000); Foreign born: 2.8% (2000); Ancestry (includes multiple ancestries): 54.2% French (except Basque), 20.4% Irish, 18.8% English, 10.7% Other groups, 5.7% German (2000).
Economy: Single-family building permits issued: 8 (2005); Multi-family building permits issued: 0 (2005); Employment by occupation: 10.8% management, 18.6% professional, 28.0% services, 20.0% sales, 2.2% farming, 9.4% construction, 11.0% production (2000).
Income: Per capita income: $20,296 (2005); Median household income: $39,236 (2005); Average household income: $48,971 (2005); Percent of households with income of $100,000 or more: 7.7% (2005); Poverty rate: 9.8% (2000).
Education: Percent of population age 25 and over with: High school diploma (including GED) or higher: 76.4% (2005); Bachelor's degree or higher: 13.7% (2005); Master's degree or higher: 8.3% (2005).

Housing: Homeownership rate: 87.8% (2005); Median home value: $88,571 (2005); Median rent: $313 per month (2000); Median age of housing: 39 years (2000).
Transportation: Commute to work: 90.2% car, 0.0% public transportation, 5.1% walk, 4.2% work from home (2000); Travel time to work: 21.9% less than 15 minutes, 52.3% 15 to 30 minutes, 13.6% 30 to 45 minutes, 8.2% 45 to 60 minutes, 4.0% 60 minutes or more (2000)

BOMBAY (town). Covers a land area of 35.783 square miles and a water area of 0.104 square miles. Located at 44.94° N. Lat.; 74.59° W. Long. Elevation is 189 feet.
Population: 1,158 (1990); 1,192 (2000); 1,237 (2005); 1,274 (2010 projected); Race: 90.2% White, 0.3% Black, 0.2% Asian, 0.9% Hispanic of any race (2005); Density: 34.6 persons per square mile (2005); Average household size: 2.42 (2005); Median age: 38.8 (2005); Males per 100 females: 89.1 (2005); Marriage status: 22.4% never married, 59.3% now married, 7.5% widowed, 10.8% divorced (2000); Foreign born: 3.6% (2000); Ancestry (includes multiple ancestries): 24.0% French (except Basque), 17.2% Irish, 16.0% Other groups, 11.6% French Canadian, 8.5% United States or American (2000).
Economy: Single-family building permits issued: 0 (2005); Multi-family building permits issued: 0 (2005); Employment by occupation: 9.4% management, 12.8% professional, 22.1% services, 18.0% sales, 2.6% farming, 13.1% construction, 22.1% production (2000).
Income: Per capita income: $16,035 (2005); Median household income: $31,364 (2005); Average household income: $38,740 (2005); Percent of households with income of $100,000 or more: 4.1% (2005); Poverty rate: 20.9% (2000).
Education: Percent of population age 25 and over with: High school diploma (including GED) or higher: 77.6% (2005); Bachelor's degree or higher: 8.2% (2005); Master's degree or higher: 4.8% (2005).
Housing: Homeownership rate: 78.3% (2005); Median home value: $67,746 (2005); Median rent: $330 per month (2000); Median age of housing: 35 years (2000).
Transportation: Commute to work: 89.2% car, 0.0% public transportation, 4.6% walk, 5.3% work from home (2000); Travel time to work: 30.7% less than 15 minutes, 42.3% 15 to 30 minutes, 19.8% 30 to 45 minutes, 3.5% 45 to 60 minutes, 3.7% 60 minutes or more (2000)

BRANDON (town). Covers a land area of 41.305 square miles and a water area of 0.024 square miles. Located at 44.75° N. Lat.; 74.42° W. Long.
Population: 394 (1990); 542 (2000); 598 (2005); 651 (2010 projected); Race: 96.7% White, 0.2% Black, 0.7% Asian, 1.3% Hispanic of any race (2005); Density: 14.5 persons per square mile (2005); Average household size: 2.73 (2005); Median age: 38.5 (2005); Males per 100 females: 106.2 (2005); Marriage status: 19.1% never married, 69.7% now married, 2.1% widowed, 9.1% divorced (2000); Foreign born: 1.3% (2000); Ancestry (includes multiple ancestries): 41.7% French (except Basque), 16.4% Irish, 16.1% English, 10.8% United States or American, 9.9% Other groups (2000).
Economy: Single-family building permits issued: 0 (2005); Multi-family building permits issued: 0 (2005); Employment by occupation: 7.5% management, 17.5% professional, 25.0% services, 16.2% sales, 0.0% farming, 8.8% construction, 25.0% production (2000).
Income: Per capita income: $16,838 (2005); Median household income: $34,490 (2005); Average household income: $45,594 (2005); Percent of households with income of $100,000 or more: 8.2% (2005); Poverty rate: 22.7% (2000).
Education: Percent of population age 25 and over with: High school diploma (including GED) or higher: 62.9% (2005); Bachelor's degree or higher: 12.9% (2005); Master's degree or higher: 5.3% (2005).
Housing: Homeownership rate: 89.0% (2005); Median home value: $57,400 (2005); Median rent: $247 per month (2000); Median age of housing: 30 years (2000).
Transportation: Commute to work: 96.3% car, 0.0% public transportation, 0.9% walk, 2.7% work from home (2000); Travel time to work: 14.6% less than 15 minutes, 63.4% 15 to 30 minutes, 6.6% 30 to 45 minutes, 7.5% 45 to 60 minutes, 8.0% 60 minutes or more (2000)

BRIGHTON (town). Covers a land area of 78.029 square miles and a water area of 4.974 square miles. Located at 44.44° N. Lat.; 74.23° W. Long.
Population: 1,511 (1990); 1,682 (2000); 1,669 (2005); 1,699 (2010 projected); Race: 79.0% White, 19.1% Black, 1.4% Asian, 0.4% Hispanic of

any race (2005); Density: 21.4 persons per square mile (2005); Average household size: 5.18 (2005); Median age: 25.5 (2005); Males per 100 females: 202.4 (2005); Marriage status: 10.7% never married, 76.9% now married, 8.9% widowed, 3.5% divorced (2000); Foreign born: 0.8% (2000); Ancestry (includes multiple ancestries): 10.1% French (except Basque), 9.3% Irish, 8.9% English, 8.3% German, 4.2% Italian (2000).
Economy: Unemployment rate: 3.5% (2005); Total civilian labor force: 18,270 (2005); Single-family building permits issued: 12 (2005); Multi-family building permits issued: 0 (2005); Employment by occupation: 11.9% management, 29.8% professional, 19.0% services, 17.8% sales, 0.0% farming, 17.0% construction, 4.5% production (2000).
Income: Per capita income: $12,945 (2005); Median household income: $52,108 (2005); Average household income: $56,592 (2005); Percent of households with income of $100,000 or more: 11.8% (2005); Poverty rate: 6.2% (2000).
Education: Percent of population age 25 and over with: High school diploma (including GED) or higher: 79.4% (2005); Bachelor's degree or higher: 27.7% (2005); Master's degree or higher: 16.3% (2005).
Housing: Homeownership rate: 78.9% (2005); Median home value: $118,824 (2005); Median rent: $441 per month (2000); Median age of housing: 51 years (2000).
Transportation: Commute to work: 85.0% car, 0.0% public transportation, 6.7% walk, 6.5% work from home (2000); Travel time to work: 39.8% less than 15 minutes, 35.7% 15 to 30 minutes, 14.1% 30 to 45 minutes, 6.5% 45 to 60 minutes, 3.9% 60 minutes or more (2000)
Additional Information Contacts
Town of Brighton . . . . (585) 784-5251
http://www.townofbrighton.org/

BRUSHTON (village). Covers a land area of 0.277 square miles and a water area of 0 square miles. Located at 44.83° N. Lat.; 74.51° W. Long. Elevation is 477 feet.
Population: 522 (1990); 479 (2000); 492 (2005); 507 (2010 projected); Race: 98.4% White, 0.4% Black, 0.6% Asian, 1.4% Hispanic of any race (2005); Density: 1,774.0 persons per square mile (2005); Average household size: 2.21 (2005); Median age: 40.8 (2005); Males per 100 females: 85.7 (2005); Marriage status: 25.3% never married, 47.5% now married, 12.7% widowed, 14.5% divorced (2000); Foreign born: 1.3% (2000); Ancestry (includes multiple ancestries): 35.6% French (except Basque), 14.8% Irish, 13.3% English, 7.1% German, 5.6% United States or American (2000).
Economy: In farming and dairying area. Single-family building permits issued: 2 (2005); Multi-family building permits issued: 0 (2005); Employment by occupation: 1.8% management, 19.3% professional, 28.1% services, 18.1% sales, 0.0% farming, 10.5% construction, 22.2% production (2000).
Income: Per capita income: $16,275 (2005); Median household income: $22,889 (2005); Average household income: $35,908 (2005); Percent of households with income of $100,000 or more: 5.4% (2005); Poverty rate: 19.4% (2000).
Education: Percent of population age 25 and over with: High school diploma (including GED) or higher: 76.7% (2005); Bachelor's degree or higher: 6.5% (2005); Master's degree or higher: 4.4% (2005).
School District(s)
Brushton-Moira Central School District (KG-12)
    2003-04 Enrollment: 862 . . . . (518) 529-8948
Housing: Homeownership rate: 56.5% (2005); Median home value: $65,161 (2005); Median rent: $314 per month (2000); Median age of housing: 59 years (2000).
Transportation: Commute to work: 90.2% car, 0.0% public transportation, 8.7% walk, 1.2% work from home (2000); Travel time to work: 31.0% less than 15 minutes, 41.5% 15 to 30 minutes, 21.1% 30 to 45 minutes, 4.7% 45 to 60 minutes, 1.8% 60 minutes or more (2000)

BURKE (village). Covers a land area of 0.292 square miles and a water area of 0 square miles. Located at 44.90° N. Lat.; 74.17° W. Long.
Population: 209 (1990); 213 (2000); 217 (2005); 221 (2010 projected); Race: 98.6% White, 0.0% Black, 0.0% Asian, 0.9% Hispanic of any race (2005); Density: 742.7 persons per square mile (2005); Average household size: 2.47 (2005); Median age: 46.6 (2005); Males per 100 females: 97.3 (2005); Marriage status: 20.0% never married, 61.2% now married, 14.7% widowed, 4.1% divorced (2000); Foreign born: 1.4% (2000); Ancestry (includes multiple ancestries): 26.6% French (except Basque), 20.2% Irish, 17.0% English, 11.0% German, 8.7% United States or American (2000).
Economy: Single-family building permits issued: 0 (2005); Multi-family building permits issued: 0 (2005); Employment by occupation: 9.5% management, 25.3% professional, 27.4% services, 12.6% sales, 4.2% farming, 12.6% construction, 8.4% production (2000).
Income: Per capita income: $20,366 (2005); Median household income: $40,000 (2005); Average household income: $45,824 (2005); Percent of households with income of $100,000 or more: 8.0% (2005); Poverty rate: 10.1% (2000).
Education: Percent of population age 25 and over with: High school diploma (including GED) or higher: 83.5% (2005); Bachelor's degree or higher: 21.5% (2005); Master's degree or higher: 9.5% (2005).
Housing: Homeownership rate: 64.8% (2005); Median home value: $66,800 (2005); Median rent: $263 per month (2000); Median age of housing: 60+ years (2000).
Transportation: Commute to work: 96.8% car, 2.1% public transportation, 0.0% walk, 1.1% work from home (2000); Travel time to work: 37.2% less than 15 minutes, 46.8% 15 to 30 minutes, 4.3% 30 to 45 minutes, 4.3% 45 to 60 minutes, 7.4% 60 minutes or more (2000)

BURKE (town). Covers a land area of 44.379 square miles and a water area of 0 square miles. Located at 44.91° N. Lat.; 74.17° W. Long.
Population: 1,231 (1990); 1,359 (2000); 1,398 (2005); 1,429 (2010 projected); Race: 97.8% White, 0.4% Black, 0.0% Asian, 0.5% Hispanic of any race (2005); Density: 31.5 persons per square mile (2005); Average household size: 2.76 (2005); Median age: 38.1 (2005); Males per 100 females: 102.9 (2005); Marriage status: 22.8% never married, 63.1% now married, 7.4% widowed, 6.7% divorced (2000); Foreign born: 4.0% (2000); Ancestry (includes multiple ancestries): 24.9% French (except Basque), 15.1% English, 13.2% Irish, 12.7% United States or American, 8.2% French Canadian (2000).
Economy: In dairying area. Single-family building permits issued: 8 (2005); Multi-family building permits issued: 0 (2005); Employment by occupation: 16.8% management, 15.3% professional, 21.2% services, 19.2% sales, 3.5% farming, 11.7% construction, 12.3% production (2000).
Income: Per capita income: $16,927 (2005); Median household income: $38,750 (2005); Average household income: $45,894 (2005); Percent of households with income of $100,000 or more: 6.5% (2005); Poverty rate: 16.4% (2000).
Education: Percent of population age 25 and over with: High school diploma (including GED) or higher: 82.3% (2005); Bachelor's degree or higher: 9.9% (2005); Master's degree or higher: 3.1% (2005).
Housing: Homeownership rate: 82.6% (2005); Median home value: $80,909 (2005); Median rent: $331 per month (2000); Median age of housing: 32 years (2000).
Transportation: Commute to work: 85.6% car, 0.3% public transportation, 2.5% walk, 11.6% work from home (2000); Travel time to work: 28.8% less than 15 minutes, 52.1% 15 to 30 minutes, 4.5% 30 to 45 minutes, 6.2% 45 to 60 minutes, 8.4% 60 minutes or more (2000)

CHATEAUGAY (village). Covers a land area of 1.078 square miles and a water area of 0 square miles. Located at 44.92° N. Lat.; 74.07° W. Long. Elevation is 972 feet.
Population: 862 (1990); 798 (2000); 805 (2005); 818 (2010 projected); Race: 98.8% White, 0.5% Black, 0.0% Asian, 0.7% Hispanic of any race (2005); Density: 746.7 persons per square mile (2005); Average household size: 2.31 (2005); Median age: 41.3 (2005); Males per 100 females: 89.0 (2005); Marriage status: 27.8% never married, 50.5% now married, 9.8% widowed, 11.9% divorced (2000); Foreign born: 2.3% (2000); Ancestry (includes multiple ancestries): 25.7% French (except Basque), 25.5% Irish, 10.8% English, 9.7% United States or American, 7.6% French Canadian (2000).
Economy: Employment by occupation: 11.4% management, 30.0% professional, 22.6% services, 19.1% sales, 2.0% farming, 6.9% construction, 8.0% production (2000).
Income: Per capita income: $19,588 (2005); Median household income: $37,423 (2005); Average household income: $44,914 (2005); Percent of households with income of $100,000 or more: 4.9% (2005); Poverty rate: 16.3% (2000).
Education: Percent of population age 25 and over with: High school diploma (including GED) or higher: 79.2% (2005); Bachelor's degree or higher: 16.2% (2005); Master's degree or higher: 8.3% (2005).
School District(s)
Chateaugay Central School District (KG-12)
    2003-04 Enrollment: 630 . . . . (518) 497-6420

Housing: Homeownership rate: 72.5% (2005); Median home value: $63,433 (2005); Median rent: $281 per month (2000); Median age of housing: 60+ years (2000).
Transportation: Commute to work: 88.7% car, 0.0% public transportation, 5.8% walk, 5.2% work from home (2000); Travel time to work: 42.6% less than 15 minutes, 42.3% 15 to 30 minutes, 3.7% 30 to 45 minutes, 4.6% 45 to 60 minutes, 6.7% 60 minutes or more (2000)

CHATEAUGAY
(town). Covers a land area of 49.748 square miles and a water area of 0 square miles. Located at 44.93° N. Lat.; 74.07° W. Long. Elevation is 972 feet.
History: Settled 1796, incorporated 1869.
Population: 1,659 (1990); 2,036 (2000); 2,058 (2005); 2,088 (2010 projected); Race: 88.3% White, 7.9% Black, 0.0% Asian, 7.4% Hispanic of any race (2005); Density: 41.4 persons per square mile (2005); Average household size: 2.79 (2005); Median age: 38.0 (2005); Males per 100 females: 125.7 (2005); Marriage status: 32.1% never married, 52.2% now married, 7.4% widowed, 8.3% divorced (2000); Foreign born: 2.5% (2000); Ancestry (includes multiple ancestries): 22.9% French (except Basque), 17.6% Irish, 11.3% English, 8.0% United States or American, 6.2% French Canadian (2000).
Economy: Port of entry. Manufacturing: cheese. State trout hatchery. Single-family building permits issued: 4 (2005); Multi-family building permits issued: 0 (2005); Employment by occupation: 11.9% management, 22.7% professional, 25.5% services, 18.3% sales, 3.3% farming, 6.8% construction, 11.5% production (2000).
Income: Per capita income: $17,292 (2005); Median household income: $36,200 (2005); Average household income: $41,582 (2005); Percent of households with income of $100,000 or more: 3.7% (2005); Poverty rate: 17.5% (2000).
Education: Percent of population age 25 and over with: High school diploma (including GED) or higher: 69.1% (2005); Bachelor's degree or higher: 10.3% (2005); Master's degree or higher: 5.3% (2005).
Housing: Homeownership rate: 77.8% (2005); Median home value: $69,612 (2005); Median rent: $288 per month (2000); Median age of housing: 60+ years (2000).
Transportation: Commute to work: 87.2% car, 0.0% public transportation, 5.4% walk, 6.5% work from home (2000); Travel time to work: 42.7% less than 15 minutes, 37.6% 15 to 30 minutes, 7.9% 30 to 45 minutes, 5.1% 45 to 60 minutes, 6.7% 60 minutes or more (2000)

CONSTABLE
(town). Covers a land area of 32.820 square miles and a water area of 0 square miles. Located at 44.94° N. Lat.; 74.29° W. Long.
Population: 1,203 (1990); 1,428 (2000); 1,529 (2005); 1,622 (2010 projected); Race: 98.4% White, 0.0% Black, 0.1% Asian, 0.1% Hispanic of any race (2005); Density: 46.6 persons per square mile (2005); Average household size: 2.62 (2005); Median age: 39.0 (2005); Males per 100 females: 102.5 (2005); Marriage status: 24.5% never married, 59.8% now married, 7.5% widowed, 8.2% divorced (2000); Foreign born: 2.9% (2000); Ancestry (includes multiple ancestries): 30.3% French (except Basque), 15.8% Irish, 11.2% English, 9.0% French Canadian, 7.5% Other groups (2000).
Economy: Single-family building permits issued: 7 (2005); Multi-family building permits issued: 0 (2005); Employment by occupation: 8.6% management, 10.8% professional, 25.4% services, 22.3% sales, 1.3% farming, 11.8% construction, 19.7% production (2000).
Income: Per capita income: $17,702 (2005); Median household income: $36,995 (2005); Average household income: $46,196 (2005); Percent of households with income of $100,000 or more: 7.4% (2005); Poverty rate: 16.4% (2000).
Education: Percent of population age 25 and over with: High school diploma (including GED) or higher: 77.2% (2005); Bachelor's degree or higher: 6.9% (2005); Master's degree or higher: 2.8% (2005).
Housing: Homeownership rate: 80.6% (2005); Median home value: $75,955 (2005); Median rent: $310 per month (2000); Median age of housing: 35 years (2000).
Transportation: Commute to work: 90.4% car, 0.5% public transportation, 4.5% walk, 4.3% work from home (2000); Travel time to work: 42.8% less than 15 minutes, 35.9% 15 to 30 minutes, 6.9% 30 to 45 minutes, 5.9% 45 to 60 minutes, 8.6% 60 minutes or more (2000)

DICKINSON
(town). Covers a land area of 44.258 square miles and a water area of 0.046 square miles. Located at 44.73° N. Lat.; 74.53° W. Long. Elevation is 730 feet.
Population: 751 (1990); 739 (2000); 739 (2005); 739 (2010 projected); Race: 98.1% White, 0.4% Black, 0.3% Asian, 0.4% Hispanic of any race (2005); Density: 16.7 persons per square mile (2005); Average household size: 2.47 (2005); Median age: 41.6 (2005); Males per 100 females: 104.1 (2005); Marriage status: 21.5% never married, 61.8% now married, 8.1% widowed, 8.6% divorced (2000); Foreign born: 1.2% (2000); Ancestry (includes multiple ancestries): 36.2% French (except Basque), 22.0% English, 14.9% Irish, 6.0% Other groups, 4.7% French Canadian (2000).
Economy: Single-family building permits issued: 2 (2005); Multi-family building permits issued: 0 (2005); Employment by occupation: 10.3% management, 15.2% professional, 26.5% services, 15.5% sales, 6.1% farming, 10.6% construction, 15.8% production (2000).
Income: Per capita income: $19,327 (2005); Median household income: $37,828 (2005); Average household income: $47,768 (2005); Percent of households with income of $100,000 or more: 6.0% (2005); Poverty rate: 16.5% (2000).
Education: Percent of population age 25 and over with: High school diploma (including GED) or higher: 74.0% (2005); Bachelor's degree or higher: 9.4% (2005); Master's degree or higher: 3.4% (2005).
Housing: Homeownership rate: 87.3% (2005); Median home value: $74,167 (2005); Median rent: $281 per month (2000); Median age of housing: 33 years (2000).
Transportation: Commute to work: 82.5% car, 0.0% public transportation, 4.0% walk, 11.6% work from home (2000); Travel time to work: 23.2% less than 15 minutes, 33.3% 15 to 30 minutes, 23.2% 30 to 45 minutes, 9.0% 45 to 60 minutes, 11.2% 60 minutes or more (2000)

DICKINSON CENTER
(unincorporated postal area, zip code 12930). Aka Dickinson. Covers a land area of 31.229 square miles and a water area of 0.046 square miles. Located at 44.73° N. Lat.; 74.53° W. Long. Elevation is 938 feet.
Population: 0 (2000); Race: 97.0% White, 0.0% Black, 0.0% Asian, 0.0% Hispanic of any race (2000); Density: 0.0 persons per square mile (2000); Age: 26.2% under 18, 12.0% over 64 (2000); Marriage status: 20.7% never married, 60.2% now married, 7.4% widowed, 11.7% divorced (2000); Foreign born: 1.6% (2000); Ancestry (includes multiple ancestries): 31.3% French (except Basque), 15.5% English, 14.6% Irish, 5.7% Other groups, 5.2% United States or American (2000).
Economy: Employment by occupation: 6.8% management, 17.1% professional, 29.9% services, 12.4% sales, 6.8% farming, 8.8% construction, 18.3% production (2000).
Income: Per capita income: $15,135 (2000); Median household income: $34,063 (2000); Poverty rate: 18.4% (2000).
Education: Percent of population age 25 and over with: High school diploma (including GED) or higher: 69.9% (2000); Bachelor's degree or higher: 12.4% (2000).
Housing: Homeownership rate: 86.2% (2000); Median home value: $41,000 (2000); Median rent: $272 per month (2000); Median age of housing: 35 years (2000).
Transportation: Commute to work: 85.9% car, 0.0% public transportation, 1.6% walk, 10.0% work from home (2000); Travel time to work: 21.9% less than 15 minutes, 34.8% 15 to 30 minutes, 25.0% 30 to 45 minutes, 9.4% 45 to 60 minutes, 8.9% 60 minutes or more (2000)

DUANE
(town). Covers a land area of 75.054 square miles and a water area of 2.923 square miles. Located at 44.63° N. Lat.; 74.27° W. Long.
Population: 152 (1990); 159 (2000); 162 (2005); 164 (2010 projected); Race: 98.1% White, 0.0% Black, 0.0% Asian, 1.2% Hispanic of any race (2005); Density: 2.2 persons per square mile (2005); Average household size: 2.19 (2005); Median age: 50.7 (2005); Males per 100 females: 97.6 (2005); Marriage status: 17.3% never married, 66.1% now married, 10.2% widowed, 6.3% divorced (2000); Foreign born: 5.1% (2000); Ancestry (includes multiple ancestries): 47.1% French (except Basque), 21.0% English, 18.1% Irish, 15.9% German, 9.4% Other groups (2000).
Economy: Single-family building permits issued: 0 (2005); Multi-family building permits issued: 0 (2005); Employment by occupation: 15.9% management, 25.4% professional, 17.5% services, 15.9% sales, 4.8% farming, 6.3% construction, 14.3% production (2000).
Income: Per capita income: $21,682 (2005); Median household income: $45,000 (2005); Average household income: $47,466 (2005); Percent of households with income of $100,000 or more: 2.7% (2005); Poverty rate: 14.5% (2000).
Education: Percent of population age 25 and over with: High school diploma (including GED) or higher: 85.7% (2005); Bachelor's degree or higher: 18.8% (2005); Master's degree or higher: 10.5% (2005).

Housing: Homeownership rate: 90.5% (2005); Median home value: $98,571 (2005); Median rent: $n/a per month (2000); Median age of housing: 39 years (2000).
Transportation: Commute to work: 71.4% car, 0.0% public transportation, 3.2% walk, 25.4% work from home (2000); Travel time to work: 8.5% less than 15 minutes, 83.0% 15 to 30 minutes, 8.5% 30 to 45 minutes, 0.0% 45 to 60 minutes, 0.0% 60 minutes or more (2000)

FORT COVINGTON (town). Covers a land area of 36.750 square miles and a water area of 0 square miles. Located at 44.96° N. Lat.; 74.50° W. Long. Elevation is 181 feet.
Population: 1,676 (1990); 1,645 (2000); 1,623 (2005); 1,625 (2010 projected); Race: 94.7% White, 0.4% Black, 0.8% Asian, 1.2% Hispanic of any race (2005); Density: 44.2 persons per square mile (2005); Average household size: 2.60 (2005); Median age: 40.3 (2005); Males per 100 females: 90.0 (2005); Marriage status: 24.3% never married, 60.3% now married, 8.0% widowed, 7.4% divorced (2000); Foreign born: 4.2% (2000); Ancestry (includes multiple ancestries): 23.3% French (except Basque), 17.3% French Canadian, 15.8% Irish, 10.5% English, 10.5% Other groups (2000).
Economy: Port of entry. Single-family building permits issued: 0 (2005); Multi-family building permits issued: 0 (2005); Employment by occupation: 7.7% management, 20.4% professional, 20.1% services, 16.0% sales, 2.1% farming, 13.6% construction, 20.1% production (2000).
Income: Per capita income: $17,620 (2005); Median household income: $35,647 (2005); Average household income: $45,805 (2005); Percent of households with income of $100,000 or more: 6.9% (2005); Poverty rate: 14.7% (2000).
Education: Percent of population age 25 and over with: High school diploma (including GED) or higher: 79.5% (2005); Bachelor's degree or higher: 12.8% (2005); Master's degree or higher: 7.0% (2005).

School District(s)
Salmon River Central School District (PK-12)
    2003-04 Enrollment: 1,604 . . . . (518) 358-6610

Housing: Homeownership rate: 80.4% (2005); Median home value: $69,550 (2005); Median rent: $288 per month (2000); Median age of housing: 57 years (2000).
Transportation: Commute to work: 88.8% car, 0.0% public transportation, 2.2% walk, 7.2% work from home (2000); Travel time to work: 38.0% less than 15 minutes, 37.6% 15 to 30 minutes, 17.9% 30 to 45 minutes, 2.0% 45 to 60 minutes, 4.5% 60 minutes or more (2000)

FRANKLIN (town). Covers a land area of 170.230 square miles and a water area of 4.979 square miles. Located at 44.51° N. Lat.; 74.06° W. Long.
Population: 1,016 (1990); 1,197 (2000); 1,240 (2005); 1,276 (2010 projected); Race: 98.0% White, 0.6% Black, 0.2% Asian, 0.2% Hispanic of any race (2005); Density: 7.3 persons per square mile (2005); Average household size: 2.48 (2005); Median age: 42.9 (2005); Males per 100 females: 99.7 (2005); Marriage status: 24.6% never married, 61.5% now married, 7.5% widowed, 6.4% divorced (2000); Foreign born: 1.0% (2000); Ancestry (includes multiple ancestries): 19.8% French (except Basque), 17.1% United States or American, 17.0% Irish, 15.1% German, 13.8% English (2000).
Economy: Single-family building permits issued: 14 (2005); Multi-family building permits issued: 0 (2005); Employment by occupation: 12.5% management, 26.6% professional, 17.1% services, 24.4% sales, 0.7% farming, 12.8% construction, 5.9% production (2000).
Income: Per capita income: $21,577 (2005); Median household income: $46,489 (2005); Average household income: $52,590 (2005); Percent of households with income of $100,000 or more: 7.6% (2005); Poverty rate: 7.3% (2000).
Education: Percent of population age 25 and over with: High school diploma (including GED) or higher: 86.1% (2005); Bachelor's degree or higher: 24.0% (2005); Master's degree or higher: 10.0% (2005).
Housing: Homeownership rate: 89.6% (2005); Median home value: $117,754 (2005); Median rent: $460 per month (2000); Median age of housing: 28 years (2000).
Transportation: Commute to work: 96.7% car, 0.0% public transportation, 1.9% walk, 1.1% work from home (2000); Travel time to work: 13.3% less than 15 minutes, 50.7% 15 to 30 minutes, 25.1% 30 to 45 minutes, 7.7% 45 to 60 minutes, 3.2% 60 minutes or more (2000)

HARRIETSTOWN (town). Covers a land area of 196.808 square miles and a water area of 16.840 square miles. Located at 44.30° N. Lat.; 74.19° W. Long.
Population: 5,621 (1990); 5,575 (2000); 5,550 (2005); 5,530 (2010 projected); Race: 97.7% White, 0.4% Black, 0.8% Asian, 1.0% Hispanic of any race (2005); Density: 28.2 persons per square mile (2005); Average household size: 2.15 (2005); Median age: 40.2 (2005); Males per 100 females: 93.3 (2005); Marriage status: 32.1% never married, 49.8% now married, 8.5% widowed, 9.5% divorced (2000); Foreign born: 2.9% (2000); Ancestry (includes multiple ancestries): 26.6% Irish, 25.1% French (except Basque), 13.8% English, 13.1% German, 9.6% Other groups (2000).
Economy: Single-family building permits issued: 21 (2005); Multi-family building permits issued: 0 (2005); Employment by occupation: 9.4% management, 25.5% professional, 23.5% services, 24.4% sales, 1.0% farming, 9.0% construction, 7.2% production (2000).
Income: Per capita income: $23,318 (2005); Median household income: $37,449 (2005); Average household income: $49,497 (2005); Percent of households with income of $100,000 or more: 11.7% (2005); Poverty rate: 12.6% (2000).
Education: Percent of population age 25 and over with: High school diploma (including GED) or higher: 85.1% (2005); Bachelor's degree or higher: 28.2% (2005); Master's degree or higher: 11.0% (2005).
Housing: Homeownership rate: 52.1% (2005); Median home value: $127,241 (2005); Median rent: $348 per month (2000); Median age of housing: 60+ years (2000).
Transportation: Commute to work: 88.6% car, 1.8% public transportation, 6.7% walk, 1.7% work from home (2000); Travel time to work: 58.6% less than 15 minutes, 28.9% 15 to 30 minutes, 6.1% 30 to 45 minutes, 2.4% 45 to 60 minutes, 3.9% 60 minutes or more (2000)

HOGANSBURG (unincorporated postal area, zip code 13655). Covers a land area of 16.811 square miles and a water area of 1.683 square miles. Located at 44.98° N. Lat.; 74.67° W. Long. Elevation is 181 feet.
History: Awakesasne (Mohawk Indian) Museum here.
Population: 0 (2000); Race: 3.5% White, 0.0% Black, 0.3% Asian, 0.3% Hispanic of any race (2000); Density: 0.0 persons per square mile (2000); Age: 35.0% under 18, 7.7% over 64 (2000); Marriage status: 31.1% never married, 47.3% now married, 7.5% widowed, 14.2% divorced (2000); Foreign born: 5.1% (2000); Ancestry (includes multiple ancestries): 3.9% Other groups, 0.3% Irish, 0.3% French (except Basque), 0.2% Scottish, 0.2% English (2000).
Economy: Employment by occupation: 8.4% management, 14.6% professional, 21.5% services, 20.8% sales, 1.6% farming, 12.4% construction, 20.6% production (2000).
Income: Per capita income: $11,981 (2000); Median household income: $32,500 (2000); Poverty rate: 22.4% (2000).
Education: Percent of population age 25 and over with: High school diploma (including GED) or higher: 68.1% (2000); Bachelor's degree or higher: 8.3% (2000).

School District(s)
Salmon River Central School District (PK-12)
    2003-04 Enrollment: 1,604 . . . . (518) 358-6610

Housing: Homeownership rate: 63.6% (2000); Median home value: $90,200 (2000); Median rent: $404 per month (2000); Median age of housing: 49 years (2000).
Transportation: Commute to work: 89.2% car, 4.2% public transportation, 0.6% walk, 0.2% work from home (2000); Travel time to work: 85.3% less than 15 minutes, 3.6% 15 to 30 minutes, 6.7% 30 to 45 minutes, 1.4% 45 to 60 minutes, 3.0% 60 minutes or more (2000)

LAKE CLEAR (unincorporated postal area, zip code 12945). Covers a land area of 35.311 square miles and a water area of 0.238 square miles. Located at 44.36° N. Lat.; 74.25° W. Long. Elevation is 1,611 feet.
Population: 0 (2000); Race: 96.1% White, 0.0% Black, 0.0% Asian, 0.0% Hispanic of any race (2000); Density: 0.0 persons per square mile (2000); Age: 14.0% under 18, 14.2% over 64 (2000); Marriage status: 30.6% never married, 59.8% now married, 5.5% widowed, 4.0% divorced (2000); Foreign born: 2.8% (2000); Ancestry (includes multiple ancestries): 24.1% United States or American, 15.3% French (except Basque), 11.5% Irish, 10.7% English, 8.6% German (2000).
Economy: Resort village. Employment by occupation: 20.7% management, 10.2% professional, 17.1% services, 21.3% sales, 0.0% farming, 14.7% construction, 16.0% production (2000).

Income: Per capita income: $18,830 (2000); Median household income: $49,833 (2000); Poverty rate: 8.9% (2000).
Education: Percent of population age 25 and over with: High school diploma (including GED) or higher: 83.6% (2000); Bachelor's degree or higher: 16.8% (2000).
Housing: Homeownership rate: 85.3% (2000); Median home value: $84,100 (2000); Median rent: $533 per month (2000); Median age of housing: 50 years (2000).
Transportation: Commute to work: 97.4% car, 1.8% public transportation, 0.0% walk, 0.8% work from home (2000); Travel time to work: 33.6% less than 15 minutes, 41.5% 15 to 30 minutes, 14.6% 30 to 45 minutes, 2.4% 45 to 60 minutes, 7.9% 60 minutes or more (2000)

MALONE (village).
Covers a land area of 3.164 square miles and a water area of 0.031 square miles. Located at 44.85° N. Lat.; 74.28° W. Long. Elevation is 722 feet.
History: Was gathering point for the Fenians, who raided Canada in 1866. Settled c.1800, Incorporated 1833.
Population: 6,778 (1990); 6,075 (2000); 5,752 (2005); 5,520 (2010 projected); Race: 97.7% White, 0.5% Black, 0.7% Asian, 1.1% Hispanic of any race (2005); Density: 1,817.9 persons per square mile (2005); Average household size: 2.31 (2005); Median age: 42.1 (2005); Males per 100 females: 80.8 (2005); Marriage status: 26.5% never married, 51.1% now married, 12.8% widowed, 9.6% divorced (2000); Foreign born: 2.3% (2000); Ancestry (includes multiple ancestries): 25.5% French (except Basque), 15.3% Irish, 14.3% United States or American, 11.1% French Canadian, 10.4% English (2000).
Economy: Manufacturing of aluminum and bronze powder, footwear, building materials, paper, clothing, cheese, lumber, furniture and machinery. Railroad shops. In agricultural area: dairy products, potatoes and grain. Summer resort. Single-family building permits issued: 0 (2005); Multi-family building permits issued: 0 (2005); Employment by occupation: 8.3% management, 22.1% professional, 20.0% services, 24.9% sales, 1.0% farming, 9.2% construction, 14.5% production (2000).
Income: Per capita income: $18,871 (2005); Median household income: $29,009 (2005); Average household income: $42,629 (2005); Percent of households with income of $100,000 or more: 6.7% (2005); Poverty rate: 16.4% (2000).
Education: Percent of population age 25 and over with: High school diploma (including GED) or higher: 72.8% (2005); Bachelor's degree or higher: 16.2% (2005); Master's degree or higher: 9.2% (2005).

School District(s)
Boces Franklin-Essex-Hamilton (PK-PK)
    2003-04 Enrollment: 451 . . . . (518) 483-6420
Malone Central School District (PK-12)
    2003-04 Enrollment: 2,499 . . . . (518) 483-7800
Housing: Homeownership rate: 51.4% (2005); Median home value: $78,670 (2005); Median rent: $359 per month (2000); Median age of housing: 60+ years (2000).
Hospitals: Alice Hyde Medical Center (76 beds)
Safety: Violent crime rate: 36.6 per 10,000 population; Property crime rate: 440.9 per 10,000 population (2004).
Newspapers: The Malone Telegram (Circulation 6,500)
Transportation: Commute to work: 86.2% car, 1.1% public transportation, 7.6% walk, 4.1% work from home (2000); Travel time to work: 72.8% less than 15 minutes, 13.2% 15 to 30 minutes, 3.3% 30 to 45 minutes, 3.6% 45 to 60 minutes, 7.1% 60 minutes or more (2000)
Additional Information Contacts
Malone Chamber of Commerce. . . . . (518) 483-3760
    http://www.malonenychamber.com/

MALONE (town).
Covers a land area of 101.862 square miles and a water area of 0.926 square miles. Located at 44.82° N. Lat.; 74.28° W. Long. Elevation is 722 feet.
History: Malone was settled by Vermonters in 1802. The name was bestowed by William Constable, an early landowner, in honor of his friend, Edmund Malone, Shakespearian scholar.
Population: 12,982 (1990); 14,981 (2000); 14,813 (2005); 14,584 (2010 projected); Race: 72.0% White, 19.9% Black, 0.9% Asian, 11.5% Hispanic of any race (2005); Density: 145.4 persons per square mile (2005); Average household size: 3.68 (2005); Median age: 36.4 (2005); Males per 100 females: 185.9 (2005); Marriage status: 39.8% never married, 46.4% now married, 7.0% widowed, 6.8% divorced (2000); Foreign born: 6.1% (2000); Ancestry (includes multiple ancestries): 17.5% French (except Basque), 10.9% Irish, 8.6% French Canadian, 8.0% United States or American, 5.6% English (2000).
Economy: Single-family building permits issued: 30 (2005); Multi-family building permits issued: 0 (2005); Employment by occupation: 9.6% management, 20.6% professional, 19.4% services, 26.4% sales, 1.5% farming, 8.5% construction, 13.9% production (2000).
Income: Per capita income: $19,488 (2005); Median household income: $33,032 (2005); Average household income: $46,243 (2005); Percent of households with income of $100,000 or more: 7.6% (2005); Poverty rate: 12.7% (2000).
Education: Percent of population age 25 and over with: High school diploma (including GED) or higher: 52.6% (2005); Bachelor's degree or higher: 9.9% (2005); Master's degree or higher: 4.7% (2005).
Housing: Homeownership rate: 63.5% (2005); Median home value: $86,907 (2005); Median rent: $353 per month (2000); Median age of housing: 53 years (2000).
Transportation: Commute to work: 86.9% car, 0.9% public transportation, 5.4% walk, 5.8% work from home (2000); Travel time to work: 63.8% less than 15 minutes, 18.7% 15 to 30 minutes, 5.1% 30 to 45 minutes, 4.2% 45 to 60 minutes, 8.2% 60 minutes or more (2000)

MOIRA (town).
Covers a land area of 45.232 square miles and a water area of 0 square miles. Located at 44.83° N. Lat.; 74.54° W. Long.
Population: 2,684 (1990); 2,857 (2000); 2,938 (2005); 3,017 (2010 projected); Race: 98.4% White, 0.5% Black, 0.3% Asian, 0.7% Hispanic of any race (2005); Density: 65.0 persons per square mile (2005); Average household size: 2.48 (2005); Median age: 38.9 (2005); Males per 100 females: 96.1 (2005); Marriage status: 26.5% never married, 56.7% now married, 7.0% widowed, 9.8% divorced (2000); Foreign born: 1.8% (2000); Ancestry (includes multiple ancestries): 26.0% French (except Basque), 15.9% Irish, 15.0% United States or American, 13.7% English, 7.4% French Canadian (2000).
Economy: Employment by occupation: 9.0% management, 14.2% professional, 26.7% services, 18.0% sales, 1.3% farming, 9.3% construction, 21.6% production (2000).
Income: Per capita income: $15,534 (2005); Median household income: $30,421 (2005); Average household income: $38,339 (2005); Percent of households with income of $100,000 or more: 4.7% (2005); Poverty rate: 18.4% (2000).
Education: Percent of population age 25 and over with: High school diploma (including GED) or higher: 74.6% (2005); Bachelor's degree or higher: 7.2% (2005); Master's degree or higher: 3.1% (2005).
Housing: Homeownership rate: 73.7% (2005); Median home value: $67,949 (2005); Median rent: $313 per month (2000); Median age of housing: 33 years (2000).
Transportation: Commute to work: 87.4% car, 0.0% public transportation, 5.6% walk, 6.1% work from home (2000); Travel time to work: 25.4% less than 15 minutes, 45.4% 15 to 30 minutes, 16.6% 30 to 45 minutes, 5.0% 45 to 60 minutes, 7.5% 60 minutes or more (2000)

NORTH BANGOR (unincorporated postal area, zip code 12966).
Covers a land area of 86.191 square miles and a water area of 0.006 square miles. Located at 44.81° N. Lat.; 74.40° W. Long.
Population: 0 (2000); Race: 97.7% White, 0.0% Black, 0.1% Asian, 0.9% Hispanic of any race (2000); Density: 0.0 persons per square mile (2000); Age: 29.5% under 18, 11.7% over 64 (2000); Marriage status: 23.6% never married, 63.0% now married, 5.8% widowed, 7.6% divorced (2000); Foreign born: 2.0% (2000); Ancestry (includes multiple ancestries): 30.1% French (except Basque), 14.1% Irish, 12.3% English, 11.3% French Canadian, 9.6% United States or American (2000).
Economy: Employment by occupation: 11.6% management, 16.2% professional, 25.1% services, 17.7% sales, 4.3% farming, 9.5% construction, 15.6% production (2000).
Income: Per capita income: $13,882 (2000); Median household income: $31,458 (2000); Poverty rate: 18.3% (2000).
Education: Percent of population age 25 and over with: High school diploma (including GED) or higher: 75.8% (2000); Bachelor's degree or higher: 9.8% (2000).
Housing: Homeownership rate: 83.4% (2000); Median home value: $54,400 (2000); Median rent: $286 per month (2000); Median age of housing: 35 years (2000).
Transportation: Commute to work: 88.8% car, 0.0% public transportation, 3.6% walk, 5.6% work from home (2000); Travel time to work: 37.1% less than 15 minutes, 42.1% 15 to 30 minutes, 7.8% 30 to 45 minutes, 5.5% 45 to 60 minutes, 7.5% 60 minutes or more (2000)

OWLS HEAD (unincorporated postal area, zip code 12969). Covers a land area of 113.992 square miles and a water area of 0.517 square miles. Located at 44.71° N. Lat.; 74.09° W. Long. Elevation is 1,526 feet.
Population: 0 (2000); Race: 97.9% White, 0.4% Black, 0.0% Asian, 0.0% Hispanic of any race (2000); Density: 0.0 persons per square mile (2000); Age: 25.9% under 18, 13.3% over 64 (2000); Marriage status: 26.7% never married, 56.4% now married, 6.9% widowed, 10.0% divorced (2000); Foreign born: 3.4% (2000); Ancestry (includes multiple ancestries): 51.3% French (except Basque), 20.6% Irish, 16.7% English, 12.1% Other groups, 8.5% German (2000).
Economy: Employment by occupation: 9.2% management, 20.8% professional, 29.6% services, 23.3% sales, 0.0% farming, 7.5% construction, 9.6% production (2000).
Income: Per capita income: $14,705 (2000); Median household income: $31,406 (2000); Poverty rate: 10.1% (2000).
Education: Percent of population age 25 and over with: High school diploma (including GED) or higher: 80.2% (2000); Bachelor's degree or higher: 15.2% (2000).
Housing: Homeownership rate: 89.2% (2000); Median home value: $46,000 (2000); Median rent: $350 per month (2000); Median age of housing: 47 years (2000).
Transportation: Commute to work: 89.7% car, 0.0% public transportation, 6.9% walk, 2.1% work from home (2000); Travel time to work: 14.9% less than 15 minutes, 55.3% 15 to 30 minutes, 14.5% 30 to 45 minutes, 8.3% 45 to 60 minutes, 7.0% 60 minutes or more (2000)

PAUL SMITHS (unincorporated postal area, zip code 12970). Covers a land area of 91.745 square miles and a water area of 2.107 square miles. Located at 44.45° N. Lat.; 74.28° W. Long.
History: Founded 1859 as one of the first wilderness resorts in region, it got its present name from successful entrepreneur Apollos ('Pol, then Paul) Smith, who had established himself by the time he died in 1912 at age 87 as the Adirondacks' most famous historical figure. Site of Paul Smith's College of Arts and Sciences, which was funded by the estate of Smith's son Phelps, who died in 1937.
Population: 0 (2000); Race: 99.0% White, 0.8% Black, 0.1% Asian, 0.0% Hispanic of any race (2000); Density: 0.0 persons per square mile (2000); Age: 8.6% under 18, 4.0% over 64 (2000); Marriage status: 10.5% never married, 78.3% now married, 8.5% widowed, 2.6% divorced (2000); Foreign born: 0.3% (2000); Ancestry (includes multiple ancestries): 8.1% English, 7.9% German, 7.8% Irish, 7.0% French (except Basque), 4.1% United States or American (2000).
Economy: Employment by occupation: 14.1% management, 29.2% professional, 17.8% services, 17.5% sales, 0.0% farming, 17.2% construction, 4.2% production (2000).
Income: Per capita income: $10,373 (2000); Median household income: $44,306 (2000); Poverty rate: 5.8% (2000).
Education: Percent of population age 25 and over with: High school diploma (including GED) or higher: 79.3% (2000); Bachelor's degree or higher: 33.0% (2000).

Four-year College(s)
Paul Smiths College of Arts and Science
  Fall 2004 Enrollment: 818 . . . . (518) 327-6000
  2005-06 Tuition: In-state $18,470; Out-of-state $18,470
Housing: Homeownership rate: 72.6% (2000); Median home value: $79,300 (2000); Median rent: $493 per month (2000); Median age of housing: 41 years (2000).
Transportation: Commute to work: 85.8% car, 0.0% public transportation, 7.7% walk, 4.7% work from home (2000); Travel time to work: 42.0% less than 15 minutes, 31.9% 15 to 30 minutes, 14.7% 30 to 45 minutes, 8.0% 45 to 60 minutes, 3.4% 60 minutes or more (2000)

SAINT REGIS FALLS (unincorporated postal area, zip code 12980). Covers a land area of 191.864 square miles and a water area of 1.668 square miles. Located at 44.63° N. Lat.; 74.53° W. Long. Elevation is 1,291 feet.
Population: 0 (2000); Race: 98.2% White, 0.6% Black, 0.0% Asian, 0.0% Hispanic of any race (2000); Density: 0.0 persons per square mile (2000); Age: 26.6% under 18, 15.2% over 64 (2000); Marriage status: 27.0% never married, 51.7% now married, 11.7% widowed, 9.7% divorced (2000); Foreign born: 1.4% (2000); Ancestry (includes multiple ancestries): 40.3% French (except Basque), 20.2% Irish, 14.0% English, 9.5% Other groups, 6.4% German (2000).
Economy: Employment by occupation: 6.4% management, 13.8% professional, 23.1% services, 19.3% sales, 2.8% farming, 16.6% construction, 18.0% production (2000).
Income: Per capita income: $13,633 (2000); Median household income: $26,979 (2000); Poverty rate: 16.7% (2000).
Education: Percent of population age 25 and over with: High school diploma (including GED) or higher: 70.1% (2000); Bachelor's degree or higher: 6.9% (2000).
Housing: Homeownership rate: 78.6% (2000); Median home value: $35,200 (2000); Median rent: $316 per month (2000); Median age of housing: 37 years (2000).
Transportation: Commute to work: 93.9% car, 1.5% public transportation, 3.7% walk, 0.9% work from home (2000); Travel time to work: 29.7% less than 15 minutes, 12.5% 15 to 30 minutes, 30.8% 30 to 45 minutes, 17.8% 45 to 60 minutes, 9.2% 60 minutes or more (2000)

SAINT REGIS MOHAWK RESERVATION (reservation). Covers a land area of 18.982 square miles and a water area of 1.979 square miles. Located at 44.98° N. Lat.; 74.67° W. Long.
Population: 1,978 (1990); 2,699 (2000); 2,652 (2005); 2,603 (2010 projected); Race: 4.3% White, 0.0% Black, 0.0% Asian, 1.2% Hispanic of any race (2005); Density: 139.7 persons per square mile (2005); Average household size: 2.93 (2005); Median age: 32.3 (2005); Males per 100 females: 97.5 (2005); Marriage status: 32.9% never married, 45.1% now married, 7.8% widowed, 14.2% divorced (2000); Foreign born: 5.0% (2000); Ancestry (includes multiple ancestries): 1.7% Other groups, 0.1% French (except Basque), 0.1% United States or American, 0.1% Irish, 0.1% Scottish (2000).
Economy: Employment by occupation: 8.0% management, 14.3% professional, 20.8% services, 22.5% sales, 1.7% farming, 12.6% construction, 20.1% production (2000).
Income: Per capita income: $15,577 (2005); Median household income: $38,841 (2005); Average household income: $45,408 (2005); Percent of households with income of $100,000 or more: 6.8% (2005); Poverty rate: 22.4% (2000).
Education: Percent of population age 25 and over with: High school diploma (including GED) or higher: 67.5% (2005); Bachelor's degree or higher: 7.6% (2005); Master's degree or higher: 4.4% (2005).
Housing: Homeownership rate: 64.7% (2005); Median home value: $139,645 (2005); Median rent: $410 per month (2000); Median age of housing: 48 years (2000).
Transportation: Commute to work: 86.1% car, 5.2% public transportation, 0.0% walk, 0.0% work from home (2000); Travel time to work: 84.9% less than 15 minutes, 3.8% 15 to 30 minutes, 7.0% 30 to 45 minutes, 1.4% 45 to 60 minutes, 2.9% 60 minutes or more (2000)

SANTA CLARA (town). Covers a land area of 175.022 square miles and a water area of 16.695 square miles. Located at 44.41° N. Lat.; 74.36° W. Long. Elevation is 1,339 feet.
Population: 311 (1990); 395 (2000); 394 (2005); 394 (2010 projected); Race: 97.2% White, 0.3% Black, 0.3% Asian, 0.0% Hispanic of any race (2005); Density: 2.3 persons per square mile (2005); Average household size: 2.49 (2005); Median age: 47.0 (2005); Males per 100 females: 108.5 (2005); Marriage status: 17.4% never married, 68.9% now married, 6.2% widowed, 7.5% divorced (2000); Foreign born: 1.0% (2000); Ancestry (includes multiple ancestries): 22.1% English, 20.6% Irish, 18.4% French (except Basque), 16.9% German, 10.3% Other groups (2000).
Economy: Single-family building permits issued: 9 (2005); Multi-family building permits issued: 0 (2005); Employment by occupation: 11.2% management, 20.9% professional, 18.2% services, 20.9% sales, 2.1% farming, 12.8% construction, 13.9% production (2000).
Income: Per capita income: $26,060 (2005); Median household income: $51,351 (2005); Average household income: $64,984 (2005); Percent of households with income of $100,000 or more: 13.3% (2005); Poverty rate: 7.4% (2000).
Education: Percent of population age 25 and over with: High school diploma (including GED) or higher: 89.9% (2005); Bachelor's degree or higher: 32.9% (2005); Master's degree or higher: 13.6% (2005).
Housing: Homeownership rate: 75.3% (2005); Median home value: $176,250 (2005); Median rent: $342 per month (2000); Median age of housing: 24 years (2000).
Transportation: Commute to work: 90.8% car, 1.1% public transportation, 6.5% walk, 1.6% work from home (2000); Travel time to work: 26.5% less than 15 minutes, 40.3% 15 to 30 minutes, 20.4% 30 to 45 minutes, 6.6% 45 to 60 minutes, 6.1% 60 minutes or more (2000)

SARANAC LAKE (village). Covers a land area of 2.782 square miles and a water area of 0.220 square miles. Located at 44.32° N. Lat.; 74.13° W. Long. Elevation is 1,547 feet.
Population: 5,377 (1990); 5,041 (2000); 5,149 (2005); 5,259 (2010 projected); Race: 97.3% White, 0.8% Black, 0.5% Asian, 1.0% Hispanic of any race (2005); Density: 1,850.8 persons per square mile (2005); Average household size: 2.09 (2005); Median age: 38.5 (2005); Males per 100 females: 93.1 (2005); Marriage status: 35.2% never married, 45.1% now married, 9.0% widowed, 10.7% divorced (2000); Foreign born: 2.5% (2000); Ancestry (includes multiple ancestries): 30.1% Irish, 29.4% French (except Basque), 14.0% German, 13.8% English, 11.7% Other groups (2000).
Economy: Single-family building permits issued: 6 (2005); Multi-family building permits issued: 0 (2005); Employment by occupation: 7.6% management, 25.2% professional, 26.2% services, 26.8% sales, 0.2% farming, 7.7% construction, 6.3% production (2000).
Income: Per capita income: $21,231 (2005); Median household income: $33,829 (2005); Average household income: $43,891 (2005); Percent of households with income of $100,000 or more: 8.4% (2005); Poverty rate: 13.8% (2000).
Education: Percent of population age 25 and over with: High school diploma (including GED) or higher: 86.5% (2005); Bachelor's degree or higher: 26.9% (2005); Master's degree or higher: 10.8% (2005).
School District(s)
Saranac Lake Central School District (KG-12)
    2003-04 Enrollment: 1,625 . . . . (518) 891-5460
Two-year College(s)
North Country Community College (Public)
    Fall 2004 Enrollment: 1,407. (518) 891-2915
    2005-06 Tuition: In-state $3,690; Out-of-state $8,640
Housing: Homeownership rate: 46.5% (2005); Median home value: $120,594 (2005); Median rent: $353 per month (2000); Median age of housing: 60+ years (2000).
Hospitals: Adirondack Medical Center (97 beds)
Safety: Violent crime rate: 42.1 per 10,000 population; Property crime rate: 208.7 per 10,000 population (2004).
Newspapers: Adirondack Daily Enterprise (Circulation 4,000)
Transportation: Commute to work: 87.2% car, 2.0% public transportation, 8.2% walk, 1.6% work from home (2000); Travel time to work: 61.4% less than 15 minutes, 26.7% 15 to 30 minutes, 5.7% 30 to 45 minutes, 2.9% 45 to 60 minutes, 3.3% 60 minutes or more (2000)
Additional Information Contacts
Saranac Lake Chamber of Commerce . . . . (518) 891-1990
    http://www.saranaclake.com

TUPPER LAKE (village). Covers a land area of 1.778 square miles and a water area of 0.003 square miles. Located at 44.23° N. Lat.; 74.46° W. Long. Elevation is 560 feet.
History: Settled 1890, incorporated 1902.
Population: 4,087 (1990); 3,935 (2000); 3,870 (2005); 3,818 (2010 projected); Race: 98.4% White, 0.7% Black, 0.0% Asian, 0.4% Hispanic of any race (2005); Density: 2,176.1 persons per square mile (2005); Average household size: 2.30 (2005); Median age: 37.9 (2005); Males per 100 females: 94.4 (2005); Marriage status: 27.7% never married, 49.4% now married, 7.8% widowed, 15.1% divorced (2000); Foreign born: 2.5% (2000); Ancestry (includes multiple ancestries): 50.1% French (except Basque), 21.1% Irish, 9.7% French Canadian, 9.3% English, 9.0% Other groups (2000).
Economy: Woodworking. Single-family building permits issued: 15 (2005); Multi-family building permits issued: 0 (2005); Employment by occupation: 7.8% management, 16.4% professional, 37.7% services, 15.8% sales, 1.2% farming, 10.5% construction, 10.6% production (2000).
Income: Per capita income: $19,210 (2005); Median household income: $37,310 (2005); Average household income: $44,136 (2005); Percent of households with income of $100,000 or more: 4.3% (2005); Poverty rate: 11.7% (2000).
Education: Percent of population age 25 and over with: High school diploma (including GED) or higher: 77.8% (2005); Bachelor's degree or higher: 9.7% (2005); Master's degree or higher: 2.5% (2005).
School District(s)
Tupper Lake Central School District (PK-12)
    2003-04 Enrollment: 1,164 . . . . (518) 359-3371
Housing: Homeownership rate: 63.3% (2005); Median home value: $98,008 (2005); Median rent: $324 per month (2000); Median age of housing: 54 years (2000).
Safety: Violent crime rate: 30.7 per 10,000 population; Property crime rate: 204.7 per 10,000 population (2004).
Newspapers: Tupper Lake Free Press (General - Circulation 3,700)
Transportation: Commute to work: 91.3% car, 0.6% public transportation, 6.0% walk, 1.1% work from home (2000); Travel time to work: 72.2% less than 15 minutes, 9.3% 15 to 30 minutes, 11.4% 30 to 45 minutes, 4.1% 45 to 60 minutes, 3.0% 60 minutes or more (2000)
Additional Information Contacts
Tupper Lake Chamber Commerce . . . . (518) 572-6984
    http://www.tupperlakeinfo.com

VERMONTVILLE (unincorporated postal area, zip code 12989). Covers a land area of 101.969 square miles and a water area of 0.526 square miles. Located at 44.51° N. Lat.; 74.06° W. Long.
Population: 0 (2000); Race: 97.2% White, 0.0% Black, 0.2% Asian, 0.0% Hispanic of any race (2000); Density: 0.0 persons per square mile (2000); Age: 25.9% under 18, 14.0% over 64 (2000); Marriage status: 23.3% never married, 63.0% now married, 7.8% widowed, 5.9% divorced (2000); Foreign born: 1.2% (2000); Ancestry (includes multiple ancestries): 21.9% French (except Basque), 20.6% Irish, 15.2% English, 13.5% German, 13.2% United States or American (2000).
Economy: Employment by occupation: 10.3% management, 27.4% professional, 16.3% services, 25.0% sales, 0.5% farming, 13.4% construction, 7.1% production (2000).
Income: Per capita income: $18,377 (2000); Median household income: $41,382 (2000); Poverty rate: 5.8% (2000).
Education: Percent of population age 25 and over with: High school diploma (including GED) or higher: 85.2% (2000); Bachelor's degree or higher: 23.0% (2000).
Housing: Homeownership rate: 89.2% (2000); Median home value: $71,800 (2000); Median rent: $453 per month (2000); Median age of housing: 38 years (2000).
Transportation: Commute to work: 95.2% car, 0.0% public transportation, 2.7% walk, 1.6% work from home (2000); Travel time to work: 14.8% less than 15 minutes, 52.0% 15 to 30 minutes, 24.0% 30 to 45 minutes, 5.4% 45 to 60 minutes, 3.8% 60 minutes or more (2000)

WAVERLY (town). Covers a land area of 125.240 square miles and a water area of 1.158 square miles. Located at 44.56° N. Lat.; 74.53° W. Long.
Population: 1,068 (1990); 1,118 (2000); 1,116 (2005); 1,118 (2010 projected); Race: 99.5% White, 0.0% Black, 0.0% Asian, 0.3% Hispanic of any race (2005); Density: 8.9 persons per square mile (2005); Average household size: 2.44 (2005); Median age: 39.2 (2005); Males per 100 females: 101.1 (2005); Marriage status: 28.6% never married, 51.9% now married, 11.0% widowed, 8.5% divorced (2000); Foreign born: 1.2% (2000); Ancestry (includes multiple ancestries): 41.5% French (except Basque), 22.7% Irish, 13.3% English, 9.2% Other groups, 5.9% German (2000).
Economy: Single-family building permits issued: 2 (2005); Multi-family building permits issued: 0 (2005); Employment by occupation: 6.0% management, 13.0% professional, 24.2% services, 20.5% sales, 1.8% farming, 17.9% construction, 16.6% production (2000).
Income: Per capita income: $17,399 (2005); Median household income: $33,443 (2005); Average household income: $42,489 (2005); Percent of households with income of $100,000 or more: 8.3% (2005); Poverty rate: 15.6% (2000).
Education: Percent of population age 25 and over with: High school diploma (including GED) or higher: 68.4% (2005); Bachelor's degree or higher: 6.7% (2005); Master's degree or higher: 2.1% (2005).
Housing: Homeownership rate: 79.9% (2005); Median home value: $58,675 (2005); Median rent: $313 per month (2000); Median age of housing: 39 years (2000).
Transportation: Commute to work: 93.1% car, 1.3% public transportation, 4.5% walk, 1.1% work from home (2000); Travel time to work: 31.2% less than 15 minutes, 11.6% 15 to 30 minutes, 29.3% 30 to 45 minutes, 18.5% 45 to 60 minutes, 9.4% 60 minutes or more (2000)

WESTVILLE (town). Aka West Constable. Covers a land area of 34.822 square miles and a water area of 0 square miles. Located at 44.93° N. Lat.; 74.38° W. Long. Elevation is 205 feet.

Population: 1,620 (1990); 1,823 (2000); 1,866 (2005); 1,892 (2010 projected); Race: 97.5% White, 0.8% Black, 0.2% Asian, 0.8% Hispanic of any race (2005); Density: 53.6 persons per square mile (2005); Average household size: 2.66 (2005); Median age: 38.2 (2005); Males per 100 females: 99.4 (2005); Marriage status: 24.6% never married, 60.8% now married, 7.1% widowed, 7.4% divorced (2000); Foreign born: 1.7% (2000); Ancestry (includes multiple ancestries): 26.9% French (except Basque), 13.0% Irish, 11.1% English, 10.7% French Canadian, 10.5% United States or American (2000).
Economy: Single-family building permits issued: 8 (2005); Multi-family building permits issued: 0 (2005); Employment by occupation: 8.7% management, 14.1% professional, 24.1% services, 23.6% sales, 2.5% farming, 12.0% construction, 15.1% production (2000).
Income: Per capita income: $19,006 (2005); Median household income: $39,254 (2005); Average household income: $50,477 (2005); Percent of households with income of $100,000 or more: 7.4% (2005); Poverty rate: 12.8% (2000).
Education: Percent of population age 25 and over with: High school diploma (including GED) or higher: 74.1% (2005); Bachelor's degree or higher: 6.3% (2005); Master's degree or higher: 2.4% (2005).
Housing: Homeownership rate: 86.6% (2005); Median home value: $73,846 (2005); Median rent: $332 per month (2000); Median age of housing: 25 years (2000).
Transportation: Commute to work: 89.9% car, 0.0% public transportation, 3.6% walk, 5.6% work from home (2000); Travel time to work: 34.9% less than 15 minutes, 41.6% 15 to 30 minutes, 10.7% 30 to 45 minutes, 6.5% 45 to 60 minutes, 6.3% 60 minutes or more (2000)

Fulton County

Located in east central New York, in the Adirondacks; drained by East Canada Creek and the Sacandaga River; includes several lakes. Covers a land area of 496.17 square miles, a water area of 36.73 square miles, and is located in the Eastern Time Zone. The county government was organized in 1838. County seat is Johnstown.

Fulton County is part of the Gloversville, NY Micropolitan Statistical Area. The entire metro area includes: Fulton County, NY

Weather Station: Gloversville — Elevation: 898 feet

	Jan	Feb	Mar	Apr	May	Jun	Jul	Aug	Sep	Oct	Nov	Dec
High	28	32	41	56	68	76	81	78	70	59	45	33
Low	10	12	22	33	45	54	59	57	49	37	29	17
Precip	3.1	2.7	3.5	3.7	4.0	4.2	4.0	4.1	4.1	3.6	3.8	3.5
Snow	20.9	15.6	14.1	3.0	tr	0.0	0.0	0.0	0.0	tr	5.1	17.5

High and Low temperatures in degrees Fahrenheit; Precipitation and Snow in inches

Population: 54,191 (1990); 55,073 (2000); 55,365 (2005); 55,633 (2010 projected); Race: 95.1% White, 2.2% Black, 0.9% Asian, 2.1% Hispanic of any race (2005); Density: 111.6 persons per square mile (2005); Average household size: 2.49 (2005); Median age: 39.8 (2005); Males per 100 females: 96.7 (2005).
Religion: Five largest groups: 24.2% Catholic Church, 8.1% The United Methodist Church, 2.2% Evangelical Lutheran Church in America, 1.8% Presbyterian Church (U.S.A.), 1.1% Independent, Non-Charismatic Churches (2000).
Economy: Unemployment rate: 5.5% (2005); Total civilian labor force: 27,105 (2005); Leading industries: 30.8% health care and social assistance; 18.0% manufacturing; 13.1% retail trade (2003); Farms: 246 totaling 37,652 acres (2002); Companies that employ 500 or more persons: 3 (2003); Companies that employ 100 to 499 persons: 23 (2003); Companies that employ less than 100 persons: 1,152 (2003); Black-owned businesses: n/a (2002); Hispanic-owned businesses: n/a (2002); Women-owned businesses: 707 (2002); Retail sales per capita: $11,581 (2006). Single-family building permits issued: 110 (2005); Multi-family building permits issued: 0 (2005).
Income: Per capita income: $19,680 (2005); Median household income: $38,238 (2005); Average household income: $47,434 (2005); Percent of households with income of $100,000 or more: 8.0% (2005); Poverty rate: 12.7% (2003); Bankruptcy rate: 9.65% (2005).
Taxes: Total county taxes per capita: $665 (2004); County property taxes per capita: $429 (2004).
Education: Percent of population age 25 and over with: High school diploma (including GED) or higher: 77.8% (2005); Bachelor's degree or higher: 13.5% (2005); Master's degree or higher: 5.6% (2005).
Housing: Homeownership rate: 72.6% (2005); Median home value: $94,674 (2005); Median rent: $360 per month (2000); Median age of housing: 52 years (2000).
Health: Birth rate: 100.1 per 10,000 population (2004); Death rate: 106.7 per 10,000 population (2004); Age-adjusted cancer mortality rate: 227.7 deaths per 100,000 population (2002); Number of physicians: 12.1 per 10,000 population (2004); Hospital beds: 31.9 per 10,000 population (2003); Hospital admissions: 735.2 per 10,000 population (2003).
Elections: 2004 Presidential election results: 56.6% Bush, 41.4% Kerry, 1.8% Nader, 0.2% Badnarik
National and State Parks: Adirondack State Park; Sir William Johnson State Park
Additional Information Contacts

Fulton County Government	(518) 736-5555
http://www.fulton.ny.us/	
City of Gloversville	(518) 773-4542
http://www.cityofgloversville.com/	
City of Johnstown	(518) 736-4011
http://www.cityofjohnstown-ny.com/	

Fulton County Communities

BLEECKER (town). Covers a land area of 57.211 square miles and a water area of 2.252 square miles. Located at 43.15° N. Lat.; 74.38° W. Long.
Population: 515 (1990); 573 (2000); 604 (2005); 622 (2010 projected); Race: 97.4% White, 0.0% Black, 1.5% Asian, 0.5% Hispanic of any race (2005); Density: 10.6 persons per square mile (2005); Average household size: 2.42 (2005); Median age: 47.7 (2005); Males per 100 females: 98.7 (2005); Marriage status: 18.3% never married, 73.1% now married, 2.0% widowed, 6.6% divorced (2000); Foreign born: 0.3% (2000); Ancestry (includes multiple ancestries): 22.8% German, 19.1% English, 14.3% Irish, 11.7% Italian, 8.6% Dutch (2000).
Economy: Single-family building permits issued: 2 (2005); Multi-family building permits issued: 0 (2005); Employment by occupation: 13.0% management, 13.7% professional, 14.8% services, 23.7% sales, 0.7% farming, 17.0% construction, 17.0% production (2000).
Income: Per capita income: $25,137 (2005); Median household income: $48,019 (2005); Average household income: $60,730 (2005); Percent of households with income of $100,000 or more: 15.6% (2005); Poverty rate: 4.2% (2000).
Education: Percent of population age 25 and over with: High school diploma (including GED) or higher: 78.2% (2005); Bachelor's degree or higher: 22.7% (2005); Master's degree or higher: 8.7% (2005).
Housing: Homeownership rate: 95.2% (2005); Median home value: $112,838 (2005); Median rent: $325 per month (2000); Median age of housing: 28 years (2000).
Transportation: Commute to work: 93.9% car, 3.1% public transportation, 0.0% walk, 3.1% work from home (2000); Travel time to work: 12.6% less than 15 minutes, 43.7% 15 to 30 minutes, 21.7% 30 to 45 minutes, 10.2% 45 to 60 minutes, 11.8% 60 minutes or more (2000)

BROADALBIN (village). Covers a land area of 1.013 square miles and a water area of 0 square miles. Located at 43.05° N. Lat.; 74.19° W. Long. Elevation is 820 feet.
Population: 1,397 (1990); 1,411 (2000); 1,365 (2005); 1,363 (2010 projected); Race: 98.4% White, 0.5% Black, 0.0% Asian, 0.4% Hispanic of any race (2005); Density: 1,347.3 persons per square mile (2005); Average household size: 2.52 (2005); Median age: 38.3 (2005); Males per 100 females: 91.4 (2005); Marriage status: 20.1% never married, 62.6% now married, 8.2% widowed, 9.1% divorced (2000); Foreign born: 0.6% (2000); Ancestry (includes multiple ancestries): 23.6% German, 22.5% Irish, 15.8% Italian, 14.5% Polish, 11.0% English (2000).
Economy: Single-family building permits issued: 4 (2005); Multi-family building permits issued: 0 (2005); Employment by occupation: 12.7% management, 20.4% professional, 15.2% services, 31.2% sales, 0.0% farming, 9.6% construction, 10.8% production (2000).
Income: Per capita income: $22,735 (2005); Median household income: $39,324 (2005); Average household income: $57,130 (2005); Percent of households with income of $100,000 or more: 9.4% (2005); Poverty rate: 5.3% (2000).
Education: Percent of population age 25 and over with: High school diploma (including GED) or higher: 87.8% (2005); Bachelor's degree or higher: 17.1% (2005); Master's degree or higher: 5.7% (2005).

School District(s)
Broadalbin-Perth Central School District (PK-12)
   2003-04 Enrollment: 2,208 . . . . (518) 954-2500
Housing: Homeownership rate: 75.8% (2005); Median home value: $108,589 (2005); Median rent: $427 per month (2000); Median age of housing: 60+ years (2000).
Transportation: Commute to work: 94.7% car, 0.3% public transportation, 3.1% walk, 1.3% work from home (2000); Travel time to work: 28.2% less than 15 minutes, 38.2% 15 to 30 minutes, 13.9% 30 to 45 minutes, 12.1% 45 to 60 minutes, 7.7% 60 minutes or more (2000)

BROADALBIN (town).
Covers a land area of 31.725 square miles and a water area of 8.052 square miles. Located at 43.07° N. Lat.; 74.16° W. Long. Elevation is 820 feet.
History: Settled 1770, incorporated 1924.
Population: 4,397 (1990); 5,066 (2000); 5,198 (2005); 5,323 (2010 projected); Race: 98.1% White, 0.7% Black, 0.1% Asian, 1.4% Hispanic of any race (2005); Density: 163.8 persons per square mile (2005); Average household size: 2.57 (2005); Median age: 39.2 (2005); Males per 100 females: 98.2 (2005); Marriage status: 18.6% never married, 64.2% now married, 6.1% widowed, 11.0% divorced (2000); Foreign born: 1.6% (2000); Ancestry (includes multiple ancestries): 21.6% German, 20.2% Irish, 14.0% Italian, 13.1% English, 10.3% Polish (2000).
Economy: Summer recreational area. Fiber conversion; spray cleaners and soaps; furniture. Single-family building permits issued: 13 (2005); Multi-family building permits issued: 0 (2005); Employment by occupation: 10.8% management, 18.3% professional, 16.5% services, 26.3% sales, 0.2% farming, 11.1% construction, 16.9% production (2000).
Income: Per capita income: $22,081 (2005); Median household income: $45,149 (2005); Average household income: $55,589 (2005); Percent of households with income of $100,000 or more: 9.8% (2005); Poverty rate: 5.2% (2000).
Education: Percent of population age 25 and over with: High school diploma (including GED) or higher: 84.2% (2005); Bachelor's degree or higher: 13.0% (2005); Master's degree or higher: 4.1% (2005).
Housing: Homeownership rate: 84.2% (2005); Median home value: $109,538 (2005); Median rent: $410 per month (2000); Median age of housing: 36 years (2000).
Transportation: Commute to work: 94.5% car, 0.6% public transportation, 1.5% walk, 2.9% work from home (2000); Travel time to work: 20.3% less than 15 minutes, 39.2% 15 to 30 minutes, 20.6% 30 to 45 minutes, 10.5% 45 to 60 minutes, 9.5% 60 minutes or more (2000)

CAROGA (town).
Covers a land area of 50.848 square miles and a water area of 3.388 square miles. Located at 43.14° N. Lat.; 74.49° W. Long.
Population: 1,337 (1990); 1,407 (2000); 1,381 (2005); 1,370 (2010 projected); Race: 99.0% White, 0.0% Black, 0.3% Asian, 0.4% Hispanic of any race (2005); Density: 27.2 persons per square mile (2005); Average household size: 2.35 (2005); Median age: 44.0 (2005); Males per 100 females: 102.8 (2005); Marriage status: 20.4% never married, 58.3% now married, 7.5% widowed, 13.8% divorced (2000); Foreign born: 1.2% (2000); Ancestry (includes multiple ancestries): 20.2% German, 16.8% English, 15.0% Irish, 9.7% Italian, 7.9% Dutch (2000).
Economy: Single-family building permits issued: 6 (2005); Multi-family building permits issued: 0 (2005); Employment by occupation: 8.0% management, 17.0% professional, 15.9% services, 21.3% sales, 0.3% farming, 14.2% construction, 23.2% production (2000).
Income: Per capita income: $20,811 (2005); Median household income: $39,500 (2005); Average household income: $48,520 (2005); Percent of households with income of $100,000 or more: 7.0% (2005); Poverty rate: 9.0% (2000).
Education: Percent of population age 25 and over with: High school diploma (including GED) or higher: 81.2% (2005); Bachelor's degree or higher: 13.5% (2005); Master's degree or higher: 6.5% (2005).
Housing: Homeownership rate: 90.6% (2005); Median home value: $93,288 (2005); Median rent: $382 per month (2000); Median age of housing: 49 years (2000).
Transportation: Commute to work: 94.6% car, 1.4% public transportation, 1.1% walk, 2.9% work from home (2000); Travel time to work: 11.6% less than 15 minutes, 49.7% 15 to 30 minutes, 18.9% 30 to 45 minutes, 4.9% 45 to 60 minutes, 14.9% 60 minutes or more (2000)

CAROGA LAKE (unincorporated postal area, zip code 12032).
Covers a land area of 46.354 square miles and a water area of 1.419 square miles. Located at 43.15° N. Lat.; 74.49° W. Long. Elevation is 1,500 feet.
Population: 0 (2000); Race: 98.0% White, 0.0% Black, 1.1% Asian, 0.0% Hispanic of any race (2000); Density: 0.0 persons per square mile (2000); Age: 18.6% under 18, 19.9% over 64 (2000); Marriage status: 21.2% never married, 57.2% now married, 8.6% widowed, 13.0% divorced (2000); Foreign born: 1.6% (2000); Ancestry (includes multiple ancestries): 22.2% German, 16.8% English, 15.9% Irish, 9.2% Italian, 7.7% Dutch (2000).
Economy: Resort village in the Adirondack Mountains. Employment by occupation: 9.9% management, 17.4% professional, 15.2% services, 22.0% sales, 0.6% farming, 12.9% construction, 22.0% production (2000).
Income: Per capita income: $19,672 (2000); Median household income: $35,263 (2000); Poverty rate: 9.0% (2000).
Education: Percent of population age 25 and over with: High school diploma (including GED) or higher: 78.4% (2000); Bachelor's degree or higher: 14.6% (2000).
School District(s)
Wheelerville Union Free School District (KG-08)
   2003-04 Enrollment: 156 . . . . (518) 835-2171
Housing: Homeownership rate: 90.6% (2000); Median home value: $59,200 (2000); Median rent: $361 per month (2000); Median age of housing: 48 years (2000).
Transportation: Commute to work: 93.5% car, 0.0% public transportation, 1.4% walk, 5.1% work from home (2000); Travel time to work: 11.9% less than 15 minutes, 48.1% 15 to 30 minutes, 18.1% 30 to 45 minutes, 6.8% 45 to 60 minutes, 15.1% 60 minutes or more (2000)

EPHRATAH (town).
Covers a land area of 39.219 square miles and a water area of 0.223 square miles. Located at 43.02° N. Lat.; 74.55° W. Long. Elevation is 666 feet.
Population: 1,556 (1990); 1,693 (2000); 1,631 (2005); 1,602 (2010 projected); Race: 99.0% White, 0.4% Black, 0.1% Asian, 0.2% Hispanic of any race (2005); Density: 41.6 persons per square mile (2005); Average household size: 2.65 (2005); Median age: 38.1 (2005); Males per 100 females: 99.9 (2005); Marriage status: 22.8% never married, 60.3% now married, 7.2% widowed, 9.8% divorced (2000); Foreign born: 0.9% (2000); Ancestry (includes multiple ancestries): 20.7% German, 14.1% Irish, 9.4% English, 9.3% Dutch, 8.1% Italian (2000).
Economy: Single-family building permits issued: 0 (2005); Multi-family building permits issued: 0 (2005); Employment by occupation: 5.0% management, 13.5% professional, 18.4% services, 17.6% sales, 1.5% farming, 15.4% construction, 28.6% production (2000).
Income: Per capita income: $17,421 (2005); Median household income: $39,357 (2005); Average household income: $45,862 (2005); Percent of households with income of $100,000 or more: 5.2% (2005); Poverty rate: 15.3% (2000).
Taxes: Total city taxes per capita: $298 (2004); City property taxes per capita: $287 (2004).
Education: Percent of population age 25 and over with: High school diploma (including GED) or higher: 67.8% (2005); Bachelor's degree or higher: 6.7% (2005); Master's degree or higher: 1.9% (2005).
Housing: Homeownership rate: 90.1% (2005); Median home value: $81,944 (2005); Median rent: $307 per month (2000); Median age of housing: 34 years (2000).
Transportation: Commute to work: 93.9% car, 0.0% public transportation, 0.8% walk, 4.4% work from home (2000); Travel time to work: 14.5% less than 15 minutes, 49.6% 15 to 30 minutes, 20.9% 30 to 45 minutes, 5.8% 45 to 60 minutes, 9.2% 60 minutes or more (2000)

GLOVERSVILLE (city).
Covers a land area of 5.092 square miles and a water area of 0.005 square miles. Located at 43.05° N. Lat.; 74.34° W. Long. Elevation is 796 feet.
History: Gloversville was named for its outstanding industry. The making of fine kid gloves became a Fulton County specialty. The beginnings of the industry in the county have been traced back to the 1760's when Sir William Johnson brought over as settlers a group of glovers from Perthshire, Scotland, who made gloves for local sale.
Population: 16,656 (1990); 15,413 (2000); 15,166 (2005); 14,914 (2010 projected); Race: 94.6% White, 2.1% Black, 1.1% Asian, 2.2% Hispanic of any race (2005); Density: 2,978.5 persons per square mile (2005); Average household size: 2.36 (2005); Median age: 38.1 (2005); Males per 100 females: 88.8 (2005); Marriage status: 27.0% never married, 50.7% now married, 10.0% widowed, 12.3% divorced (2000); Foreign born: 2.9% (2000); Ancestry (includes multiple ancestries): 21.8% Italian, 16.2% Irish, 15.9% German, 12.3% English, 9.4% Other groups (2000).

Economy: Single-family building permits issued: 2 (2005); Multi-family building permits issued: 0 (2005); Employment by occupation: 8.9% management, 14.7% professional, 17.9% services, 23.7% sales, 0.2% farming, 7.6% construction, 27.1% production (2000).
Income: Per capita income: $17,144 (2005); Median household income: $29,704 (2005); Average household income: $39,191 (2005); Percent of households with income of $100,000 or more: 5.2% (2005); Poverty rate: 19.3% (2000).
Education: Percent of population age 25 and over with: High school diploma (including GED) or higher: 74.4% (2005); Bachelor's degree or higher: 12.0% (2005); Master's degree or higher: 5.4% (2005).

School District(s)
Gloversville City School District (PK-12)
    2003-04 Enrollment: 3,226 .... (518) 775-5600

Housing: Homeownership rate: 54.6% (2005); Median home value: $78,264 (2005); Median rent: $348 per month (2000); Median age of housing: 60+ years (2000).
Hospitals: Nathan Littauer Hospital and Nursing Home (208 beds)
Safety: Violent crime rate: 36.1 per 10,000 population; Property crime rate: 408.4 per 10,000 population (2004).
Newspapers: Leader-Herald (Circulation 10,906)
Transportation: Commute to work: 88.3% car, 2.6% public transportation, 5.7% walk, 2.3% work from home (2000); Travel time to work: 55.1% less than 15 minutes, 26.5% 15 to 30 minutes, 5.8% 30 to 45 minutes, 4.6% 45 to 60 minutes, 8.0% 60 minutes or more (2000)

Additional Information Contacts
City of Gloversville .... (518) 773-4542
    http://www.cityofgloversville.com/
Fulton County Regional Chamber .... (518) 725-0641
    http://www.fultoncountyny.org

JOHNSTOWN (city). Covers a land area of 4.860 square miles and a water area of 0.006 square miles. Located at 43.00° N. Lat.; 74.37° W. Long. Elevation is 650 feet.
History: Its leather-glove industry dates back to 1800. Notable buildings include the county courthouse (1774) and Fort Johnstown (1771) and the county jail. The last American Revolutionary battle in N.Y. state was fought in Johnstown on Oct. 25, 1781. Elizabeth Cady Stanton born here. Founded 1772, Incorporated 1895.
Population: 9,059 (1990); 8,511 (2000); 8,404 (2005); 8,285 (2010 projected); Race: 95.9% White, 0.6% Black, 1.7% Asian, 1.3% Hispanic of any race (2005); Density: 1,729.1 persons per square mile (2005); Average household size: 2.35 (2005); Median age: 39.9 (2005); Males per 100 females: 87.8 (2005); Marriage status: 24.2% never married, 56.6% now married, 10.2% widowed, 8.9% divorced (2000); Foreign born: 1.9% (2000); Ancestry (includes multiple ancestries): 24.1% German, 16.7% Irish, 15.5% Italian, 12.8% English, 8.3% French (except Basque) (2000).
Economy: Leather-glove industry dates back to 1800. Knitted goods, a variety of other leather goods, molded plastics, glue and chemicals are also made. Single-family building permits issued: 2 (2005); Multi-family building permits issued: 0 (2005); Employment by occupation: 10.7% management, 16.8% professional, 14.7% services, 27.2% sales, 0.2% farming, 8.8% construction, 21.6% production (2000).
Income: Per capita income: $19,596 (2005); Median household income: $35,378 (2005); Average household income: $44,630 (2005); Percent of households with income of $100,000 or more: 7.5% (2005); Poverty rate: 13.2% (2000).
Education: Percent of population age 25 and over with: High school diploma (including GED) or higher: 82.2% (2005); Bachelor's degree or higher: 17.9% (2005); Master's degree or higher: 6.0% (2005).

School District(s)
Boces Hamilton-Fulton-Montgomery (UG-UG)
    2003-04 Enrollment: 275 .... (518) 762-4634
Broadalbin-Perth Central School District (PK-12)
    2003-04 Enrollment: 2,208 .... (518) 954-2500
Johnstown City School District (PK-12)
    2003-04 Enrollment: 2,168 .... (518) 762-4611

Two-year College(s)
Fulton-Montgomery Community College (Public)
    Fall 2004 Enrollment: 2,071 .... (518) 762-4651
    2005-06 Tuition: In-state $3,240; Out-of-state $6,190

Housing: Homeownership rate: 59.6% (2005); Median home value: $92,500 (2005); Median rent: $375 per month (2000); Median age of housing: 60+ years (2000).
Safety: Violent crime rate: 8.2 per 10,000 population; Property crime rate: 344.6 per 10,000 population (2004).
Transportation: Commute to work: 92.6% car, 1.6% public transportation, 3.4% walk, 2.2% work from home (2000); Travel time to work: 53.7% less than 15 minutes, 27.7% 15 to 30 minutes, 6.9% 30 to 45 minutes, 4.4% 45 to 60 minutes, 7.4% 60 minutes or more (2000)

Additional Information Contacts
City of Johnstown .... (518) 736-4011
    http://www.cityofjohnstown-ny.com/

JOHNSTOWN (town). Covers a land area of 70.214 square miles and a water area of 1.162 square miles. Located at 43.04° N. Lat.; 74.38° W. Long. Elevation is 650 feet.
Population: 6,417 (1990); 7,166 (2000); 7,186 (2005); 7,233 (2010 projected); Race: 89.4% White, 6.4% Black, 1.4% Asian, 4.6% Hispanic of any race (2005); Density: 102.3 persons per square mile (2005); Average household size: 2.85 (2005); Median age: 41.3 (2005); Males per 100 females: 113.2 (2005); Marriage status: 29.3% never married, 58.9% now married, 6.9% widowed, 4.9% divorced (2000); Foreign born: 1.7% (2000); Ancestry (includes multiple ancestries): 15.4% German, 14.0% Italian, 12.9% Irish, 11.5% English, 7.3% United States or American (2000).
Economy: Single-family building permits issued: 18 (2005); Multi-family building permits issued: 0 (2005); Employment by occupation: 9.2% management, 19.1% professional, 15.6% services, 23.3% sales, 0.3% farming, 11.5% construction, 20.9% production (2000).
Income: Per capita income: $20,855 (2005); Median household income: $45,933 (2005); Average household income: $53,589 (2005); Percent of households with income of $100,000 or more: 11.0% (2005); Poverty rate: 9.1% (2000).
Education: Percent of population age 25 and over with: High school diploma (including GED) or higher: 69.9% (2005); Bachelor's degree or higher: 12.4% (2005); Master's degree or higher: 6.5% (2005).
Housing: Homeownership rate: 89.4% (2005); Median home value: $99,008 (2005); Median rent: $408 per month (2000); Median age of housing: 38 years (2000).
Transportation: Commute to work: 94.7% car, 1.0% public transportation, 1.4% walk, 2.2% work from home (2000); Travel time to work: 55.1% less than 15 minutes, 27.3% 15 to 30 minutes, 5.9% 30 to 45 minutes, 5.5% 45 to 60 minutes, 6.1% 60 minutes or more (2000)

MAYFIELD (village). Covers a land area of 0.892 square miles and a water area of 0.187 square miles. Located at 43.10° N. Lat.; 74.26° W. Long.
Population: 815 (1990); 800 (2000); 782 (2005); 778 (2010 projected); Race: 98.0% White, 0.5% Black, 0.0% Asian, 1.2% Hispanic of any race (2005); Density: 876.7 persons per square mile (2005); Average household size: 2.53 (2005); Median age: 36.4 (2005); Males per 100 females: 86.6 (2005); Marriage status: 25.7% never married, 59.4% now married, 5.5% widowed, 9.4% divorced (2000); Foreign born: 1.6% (2000); Ancestry (includes multiple ancestries): 16.6% Irish, 16.5% German, 11.8% Italian, 11.7% English, 10.9% Dutch (2000).
Economy: Single-family building permits issued: 1 (2005); Multi-family building permits issued: 0 (2005); Employment by occupation: 9.7% management, 16.2% professional, 16.4% services, 28.0% sales, 0.7% farming, 12.4% construction, 16.6% production (2000).
Income: Per capita income: $18,926 (2005); Median household income: $41,914 (2005); Average household income: $47,896 (2005); Percent of households with income of $100,000 or more: 7.4% (2005); Poverty rate: 10.8% (2000).
Education: Percent of population age 25 and over with: High school diploma (including GED) or higher: 81.0% (2005); Bachelor's degree or higher: 8.9% (2005); Master's degree or higher: 2.6% (2005).

School District(s)
Mayfield Central School District (PK-12)
    2003-04 Enrollment: 1,201 .... (518) 661-8207

Housing: Homeownership rate: 76.4% (2005); Median home value: $90,566 (2005); Median rent: $370 per month (2000); Median age of housing: 59 years (2000).
Transportation: Commute to work: 93.9% car, 2.0% public transportation, 0.7% walk, 2.2% work from home (2000); Travel time to work: 32.5% less than 15 minutes, 36.8% 15 to 30 minutes, 11.5% 30 to 45 minutes, 11.5% 45 to 60 minutes, 7.8% 60 minutes or more (2000)

MAYFIELD (town). Covers a land area of 58.434 square miles and a water area of 6.260 square miles. Located at 43.10° N. Lat.; 74.25° W. Long.
Population: 5,738 (1990); 6,432 (2000); 6,624 (2005); 6,808 (2010 projected); Race: 97.3% White, 0.5% Black, 0.8% Asian, 1.1% Hispanic of any race (2005); Density: 113.4 persons per square mile (2005); Average household size: 2.49 (2005); Median age: 40.5 (2005); Males per 100 females: 97.1 (2005); Marriage status: 22.3% never married, 60.6% now married, 7.4% widowed, 9.7% divorced (2000); Foreign born: 1.7% (2000); Ancestry (includes multiple ancestries): 19.7% German, 14.3% Irish, 12.5% English, 10.8% Italian, 9.6% Dutch (2000).
Economy: Single-family building permits issued: 21 (2005); Multi-family building permits issued: 0 (2005); Employment by occupation: 10.2% management, 19.2% professional, 14.0% services, 23.7% sales, 0.9% farming, 11.9% construction, 20.1% production (2000).
Income: Per capita income: $21,794 (2005); Median household income: $44,190 (2005); Average household income: $53,997 (2005); Percent of households with income of $100,000 or more: 9.9% (2005); Poverty rate: 8.6% (2000).
Education: Percent of population age 25 and over with: High school diploma (including GED) or higher: 80.5% (2005); Bachelor's degree or higher: 13.3% (2005); Master's degree or higher: 6.1% (2005).
Housing: Homeownership rate: 83.8% (2005); Median home value: $97,994 (2005); Median rent: $315 per month (2000); Median age of housing: 31 years (2000).
Transportation: Commute to work: 95.8% car, 0.5% public transportation, 1.7% walk, 1.6% work from home (2000); Travel time to work: 34.5% less than 15 minutes, 42.5% 15 to 30 minutes, 8.1% 30 to 45 minutes, 7.5% 45 to 60 minutes, 7.4% 60 minutes or more (2000)

NORTHAMPTON (town). Covers a land area of 21.049 square miles and a water area of 13.674 square miles. Located at 43.20° N. Lat.; 74.17° W. Long.
Population: 2,705 (1990); 2,760 (2000); 2,797 (2005); 2,835 (2010 projected); Race: 97.9% White, 0.4% Black, 0.6% Asian, 1.5% Hispanic of any race (2005); Density: 132.9 persons per square mile (2005); Average household size: 2.33 (2005); Median age: 43.0 (2005); Males per 100 females: 99.1 (2005); Marriage status: 20.7% never married, 61.8% now married, 7.9% widowed, 9.6% divorced (2000); Foreign born: 1.1% (2000); Ancestry (includes multiple ancestries): 20.0% German, 17.5% Irish, 15.4% English, 8.3% Other groups, 7.6% Dutch (2000).
Economy: Single-family building permits issued: 18 (2005); Multi-family building permits issued: 0 (2005); Employment by occupation: 11.0% management, 18.4% professional, 18.1% services, 23.4% sales, 1.2% farming, 10.5% construction, 17.5% production (2000).
Income: Per capita income: $23,807 (2005); Median household income: $44,926 (2005); Average household income: $54,969 (2005); Percent of households with income of $100,000 or more: 11.1% (2005); Poverty rate: 11.0% (2000).
Education: Percent of population age 25 and over with: High school diploma (including GED) or higher: 83.2% (2005); Bachelor's degree or higher: 16.8% (2005); Master's degree or higher: 6.7% (2005).
Housing: Homeownership rate: 75.8% (2005); Median home value: $129,787 (2005); Median rent: $391 per month (2000); Median age of housing: 39 years (2000).
Transportation: Commute to work: 90.0% car, 0.6% public transportation, 5.8% walk, 3.4% work from home (2000); Travel time to work: 33.2% less than 15 minutes, 20.6% 15 to 30 minutes, 25.5% 30 to 45 minutes, 9.7% 45 to 60 minutes, 11.1% 60 minutes or more (2000)

NORTHVILLE (village). Covers a land area of 1.064 square miles and a water area of 0.353 square miles. Located at 43.22° N. Lat.; 74.17° W. Long. Elevation is 764 feet.
History: Incorporated 1873.
Population: 1,180 (1990); 1,139 (2000); 1,115 (2005); 1,105 (2010 projected); Race: 97.0% White, 0.6% Black, 1.4% Asian, 2.1% Hispanic of any race (2005); Density: 1,048.3 persons per square mile (2005); Average household size: 2.26 (2005); Median age: 40.5 (2005); Males per 100 females: 90.6 (2005); Marriage status: 27.7% never married, 55.6% now married, 8.4% widowed, 8.4% divorced (2000); Foreign born: 0.9% (2000); Ancestry (includes multiple ancestries): 19.5% German, 17.5% Irish, 14.6% English, 7.8% Dutch, 7.2% Other groups (2000).
Economy: South terminus of Lake Placid Trail. Single-family building permits issued: 4 (2005); Multi-family building permits issued: 0 (2005); Employment by occupation: 8.6% management, 25.6% professional, 14.3% services, 24.6% sales, 2.8% farming, 8.3% construction, 15.8% production (2000).
Income: Per capita income: $23,870 (2005); Median household income: $43,780 (2005); Average household income: $53,877 (2005); Percent of households with income of $100,000 or more: 10.5% (2005); Poverty rate: 13.4% (2000).
Education: Percent of population age 25 and over with: High school diploma (including GED) or higher: 85.0% (2005); Bachelor's degree or higher: 20.1% (2005); Master's degree or higher: 8.3% (2005).

School District(s)
Northville Central School District (PK-12)
    2003-04 Enrollment: 549 . . . . (518) 863-7000

Housing: Homeownership rate: 64.2% (2005); Median home value: $116,458 (2005); Median rent: $392 per month (2000); Median age of housing: 60+ years (2000).
Safety: Violent crime rate: 0.0 per 10,000 population; Property crime rate: 17.5 per 10,000 population (2004).
Transportation: Commute to work: 81.8% car, 1.3% public transportation, 11.6% walk, 4.9% work from home (2000); Travel time to work: 37.7% less than 15 minutes, 21.3% 15 to 30 minutes, 24.3% 30 to 45 minutes, 6.3% 45 to 60 minutes, 10.5% 60 minutes or more (2000)

OPPENHEIM (town). Covers a land area of 56.273 square miles and a water area of 0.185 square miles. Located at 43.08° N. Lat.; 74.70° W. Long.
Population: 1,848 (1990); 1,774 (2000); 1,820 (2005); 1,858 (2010 projected); Race: 98.0% White, 0.9% Black, 0.4% Asian, 0.7% Hispanic of any race (2005); Density: 32.3 persons per square mile (2005); Average household size: 2.53 (2005); Median age: 39.7 (2005); Males per 100 females: 104.5 (2005); Marriage status: 25.3% never married, 61.7% now married, 5.7% widowed, 7.3% divorced (2000); Foreign born: 1.8% (2000); Ancestry (includes multiple ancestries): 26.0% German, 12.5% Irish, 9.0% Dutch, 7.7% English, 7.1% Other groups (2000).
Economy: Single-family building permits issued: 4 (2005); Multi-family building permits issued: 0 (2005); Employment by occupation: 6.3% management, 14.7% professional, 15.2% services, 21.4% sales, 2.5% farming, 13.4% construction, 26.6% production (2000).
Income: Per capita income: $16,075 (2005); Median household income: $35,864 (2005); Average household income: $40,449 (2005); Percent of households with income of $100,000 or more: 3.3% (2005); Poverty rate: 12.4% (2000).
Education: Percent of population age 25 and over with: High school diploma (including GED) or higher: 71.5% (2005); Bachelor's degree or higher: 5.8% (2005); Master's degree or higher: 2.6% (2005).
Housing: Homeownership rate: 86.9% (2005); Median home value: $74,083 (2005); Median rent: $318 per month (2000); Median age of housing: 35 years (2000).
Transportation: Commute to work: 93.3% car, 0.0% public transportation, 1.0% walk, 5.1% work from home (2000); Travel time to work: 29.0% less than 15 minutes, 30.6% 15 to 30 minutes, 23.3% 30 to 45 minutes, 10.5% 45 to 60 minutes, 6.6% 60 minutes or more (2000)

PERTH (town). Covers a land area of 26.061 square miles and a water area of 0.021 square miles. Located at 43.00° N. Lat.; 74.18° W. Long.
Population: 3,377 (1990); 3,638 (2000); 3,844 (2005); 4,016 (2010 projected); Race: 90.9% White, 6.8% Black, 0.2% Asian, 4.0% Hispanic of any race (2005); Density: 147.5 persons per square mile (2005); Average household size: 2.72 (2005); Median age: 37.9 (2005); Males per 100 females: 107.1 (2005); Marriage status: 20.7% never married, 65.0% now married, 5.0% widowed, 9.3% divorced (2000); Foreign born: 1.5% (2000); Ancestry (includes multiple ancestries): 19.7% Italian, 17.0% Polish, 15.8% German, 14.2% Irish, 10.0% English (2000).
Economy: Single-family building permits issued: 8 (2005); Multi-family building permits issued: 0 (2005); Employment by occupation: 10.1% management, 17.5% professional, 13.2% services, 29.7% sales, 0.6% farming, 13.6% construction, 15.4% production (2000).
Income: Per capita income: $20,029 (2005); Median household income: $46,171 (2005); Average household income: $53,675 (2005); Percent of households with income of $100,000 or more: 11.1% (2005); Poverty rate: 6.1% (2000).
Education: Percent of population age 25 and over with: High school diploma (including GED) or higher: 86.5% (2005); Bachelor's degree or higher: 15.6% (2005); Master's degree or higher: 6.7% (2005).

Housing: Homeownership rate: 88.0% (2005); Median home value: $128,210 (2005); Median rent: $405 per month (2000); Median age of housing: 28 years (2000).
Transportation: Commute to work: 90.4% car, 1.2% public transportation, 1.9% walk, 6.6% work from home (2000); Travel time to work: 28.4% less than 15 minutes, 37.2% 15 to 30 minutes, 19.3% 30 to 45 minutes, 5.9% 45 to 60 minutes, 9.2% 60 minutes or more (2000)

STRATFORD (town). Covers a land area of 75.181 square miles and a water area of 1.505 square miles. Located at 43.17° N. Lat.; 74.65° W. Long. Elevation is 1,075 feet.
Population: 586 (1990); 640 (2000); 710 (2005); 767 (2010 projected); Race: 96.5% White, 1.4% Black, 0.0% Asian, 1.3% Hispanic of any race (2005); Density: 9.4 persons per square mile (2005); Average household size: 2.64 (2005); Median age: 42.6 (2005); Males per 100 females: 113.2 (2005); Marriage status: 29.8% never married, 53.0% now married, 7.4% widowed, 9.8% divorced (2000); Foreign born: 0.3% (2000); Ancestry (includes multiple ancestries): 17.4% German, 14.1% Irish, 13.3% English, 9.4% Other groups, 6.8% French (except Basque) (2000).
Economy: Single-family building permits issued: 7 (2005); Multi-family building permits issued: 0 (2005); Employment by occupation: 11.3% management, 10.0% professional, 15.9% services, 20.9% sales, 2.9% farming, 14.6% construction, 24.3% production (2000).
Income: Per capita income: $15,133 (2005); Median household income: $31,786 (2005); Average household income: $39,238 (2005); Percent of households with income of $100,000 or more: 4.1% (2005); Poverty rate: 24.4% (2000).
Education: Percent of population age 25 and over with: High school diploma (including GED) or higher: 71.8% (2005); Bachelor's degree or higher: 8.3% (2005); Master's degree or higher: 1.6% (2005).
Housing: Homeownership rate: 85.9% (2005); Median home value: $74,800 (2005); Median rent: $288 per month (2000); Median age of housing: 43 years (2000).
Transportation: Commute to work: 93.3% car, 0.8% public transportation, 1.7% walk, 4.2% work from home (2000); Travel time to work: 11.0% less than 15 minutes, 34.6% 15 to 30 minutes, 26.3% 30 to 45 minutes, 11.8% 45 to 60 minutes, 16.2% 60 minutes or more (2000)

Genesee County

Located in western New York; drained by Tonawanda and Oak Orchard Creeks. Covers a land area of 494.11 square miles, a water area of 1.22 square miles, and is located in the Eastern Time Zone. The county government was organized in 1802. County seat is Batavia.

Genesee County is part of the Batavia, NY Micropolitan Statistical Area. The entire metro area includes: Genesee County, NY

Weather Station: Batavia Elevation: 898 feet

	Jan	Feb	Mar	Apr	May	Jun	Jul	Aug	Sep	Oct	Nov	Dec
High	32	34	44	57	69	78	82	79	72	61	48	37
Low	16	17	25	36	47	56	61	59	52	41	32	22
Precip	1.9	1.9	2.3	3.0	3.3	3.9	3.3	3.6	4.0	3.1	2.8	2.4
Snow	21.3	17.1	12.6	3.9	0.4	0.0	0.0	0.0	0.0	0.2	6.8	20.0

High and Low temperatures in degrees Fahrenheit; Precipitation and Snow in inches

Population: 60,060 (1990); 60,370 (2000); 60,044 (2005); 59,671 (2010 projected); Race: 94.1% White, 2.6% Black, 0.6% Asian, 2.1% Hispanic of any race (2005); Density: 121.5 persons per square mile (2005); Average household size: 2.61 (2005); Median age: 39.2 (2005); Males per 100 females: 96.5 (2005).
Religion: Five largest groups: 40.2% Catholic Church, 5.4% The United Methodist Church, 4.6% Presbyterian Church (U.S.A.), 2.1% Episcopal Church, 1.6% American Baptist Churches in the USA (2000).
Economy: Unemployment rate: 4.9% (2005); Total civilian labor force: 33,242 (2005); Leading industries: 19.2% manufacturing; 16.1% retail trade; 14.8% health care and social assistance (2003); Farms: 580 totaling 177,370 acres (2002); Companies that employ 500 or more persons: 2 (2003); Companies that employ 100 to 499 persons: 26 (2003); Companies that employ less than 100 persons: 1,311 (2003); Black-owned businesses: n/a (2002); Hispanic-owned businesses: n/a (2002); Women-owned businesses: 826 (2002); Retail sales per capita: $9,735 (2006). Single-family building permits issued: 84 (2005); Multi-family building permits issued: 8 (2005).
Income: Per capita income: $20,917 (2005); Median household income: $45,113 (2005); Average household income: $53,773 (2005); Percent of households with income of $100,000 or more: 9.5% (2005); Poverty rate: 9.1% (2003); Bankruptcy rate: 7.19% (2005).
Education: Percent of population age 25 and over with: High school diploma (including GED) or higher: 84.5% (2005); Bachelor's degree or higher: 16.2% (2005); Master's degree or higher: 6.1% (2005).
Housing: Homeownership rate: 73.5% (2005); Median home value: $117,595 (2005); Median rent: $434 per month (2000); Median age of housing: 49 years (2000).
Health: Birth rate: 116.9 per 10,000 population (2004); Death rate: 99.7 per 10,000 population (2004); Age-adjusted cancer mortality rate: 211.7 deaths per 100,000 population (2002); Number of physicians: 11.7 per 10,000 population (2004); Hospital beds: 47.4 per 10,000 population (2003); Hospital admissions: 1,501.6 per 10,000 population (2003).
Elections: 2004 Presidential election results: 60.6% Bush, 37.5% Kerry, 1.6% Nader, 0.2% Badnarik
National and State Parks: Iroquois National Wildlife Refuge; Oak Orchard Creek State Game Refuge; White Memorial State Game Farm
Additional Information Contacts
Genesee County Government . . . . (585) 344-2550
http://www.co.genesee.ny.us/
City of Batavia . . . . (585) 345-6330
http://www.batavianewyork.com/
Town of Batavia . . . . (585) 343-1729
http://www.townofbatavia.com/
Village of Oakfield . . . . (585) 948-5862
http://www.oakfield.govoffice.com/

Genesee County Communities

ALABAMA (town). Covers a land area of 42.550 square miles and a water area of 0.211 square miles. Located at 43.08° N. Lat.; 78.39° W. Long.
Population: 1,998 (1990); 1,881 (2000); 1,917 (2005); 1,897 (2010 projected); Race: 94.9% White, 1.0% Black, 0.3% Asian, 1.5% Hispanic of any race (2005); Density: 45.1 persons per square mile (2005); Average household size: 2.77 (2005); Median age: 37.2 (2005); Males per 100 females: 100.3 (2005); Marriage status: 26.5% never married, 60.9% now married, 6.3% widowed, 6.2% divorced (2000); Foreign born: 0.5% (2000); Ancestry (includes multiple ancestries): 44.7% German, 14.7% English, 13.7% Irish, 13.2% Polish, 8.2% Italian (2000).
Economy: Single-family building permits issued: 2 (2005); Multi-family building permits issued: 2 (2005); Employment by occupation: 9.1% management, 13.7% professional, 14.6% services, 24.5% sales, 2.4% farming, 14.9% construction, 20.8% production (2000).
Income: Per capita income: $17,879 (2005); Median household income: $45,061 (2005); Average household income: $49,602 (2005); Percent of households with income of $100,000 or more: 7.2% (2005); Poverty rate: 6.3% (2000).
Education: Percent of population age 25 and over with: High school diploma (including GED) or higher: 82.1% (2005); Bachelor's degree or higher: 9.3% (2005); Master's degree or higher: 3.3% (2005).
Housing: Homeownership rate: 80.5% (2005); Median home value: $108,578 (2005); Median rent: $368 per month (2000); Median age of housing: 49 years (2000).
Transportation: Commute to work: 94.1% car, 0.0% public transportation, 2.2% walk, 3.2% work from home (2000); Travel time to work: 21.8% less than 15 minutes, 44.0% 15 to 30 minutes, 18.4% 30 to 45 minutes, 8.0% 45 to 60 minutes, 7.7% 60 minutes or more (2000)

ALEXANDER (village). Covers a land area of 0.438 square miles and a water area of 0 square miles. Located at 42.90° N. Lat.; 78.25° W. Long. Elevation is 940 feet.
Population: 445 (1990); 481 (2000); 474 (2005); 464 (2010 projected); Race: 98.1% White, 0.0% Black, 1.5% Asian, 0.4% Hispanic of any race (2005); Density: 1,083.4 persons per square mile (2005); Average household size: 2.74 (2005); Median age: 34.6 (2005); Males per 100 females: 107.0 (2005); Marriage status: 19.7% never married, 62.3% now married, 5.2% widowed, 12.8% divorced (2000); Foreign born: 0.4% (2000); Ancestry (includes multiple ancestries): 44.7% German, 24.2% English, 20.3% Polish, 15.3% Irish, 11.2% Italian (2000).
Economy: Single-family building permits issued: 0 (2005); Multi-family building permits issued: 0 (2005); Employment by occupation: 11.0% management, 16.7% professional, 24.8% services, 22.0% sales, 0.7% farming, 9.2% construction, 15.6% production (2000).

Income: Per capita income: $22,410 (2005); Median household income: $57,181 (2005); Average household income: $61,402 (2005); Percent of households with income of $100,000 or more: 10.4% (2005); Poverty rate: 0.8% (2000).
Education: Percent of population age 25 and over with: High school diploma (including GED) or higher: 95.4% (2005); Bachelor's degree or higher: 18.7% (2005); Master's degree or higher: 5.3% (2005).

School District(s)
Alexander Central School District (KG-12)
    2003-04 Enrollment: 1,027 . . . . (585) 591-1551

Housing: Homeownership rate: 78.0% (2005); Median home value: $120,890 (2005); Median rent: $395 per month (2000); Median age of housing: 54 years (2000).
Transportation: Commute to work: 91.5% car, 0.0% public transportation, 6.3% walk, 2.2% work from home (2000); Travel time to work: 32.5% less than 15 minutes, 38.9% 15 to 30 minutes, 9.1% 30 to 45 minutes, 13.6% 45 to 60 minutes, 6.0% 60 minutes or more (2000)

ALEXANDER (town).
Covers a land area of 35.514 square miles and a water area of 0.030 square miles. Located at 42.90° N. Lat.; 78.25° W. Long. Elevation is 940 feet.
Population: 2,233 (1990); 2,451 (2000); 2,471 (2005); 2,455 (2010 projected); Race: 98.1% White, 0.4% Black, 0.5% Asian, 0.6% Hispanic of any race (2005); Density: 69.6 persons per square mile (2005); Average household size: 2.79 (2005); Median age: 37.4 (2005); Males per 100 females: 96.7 (2005); Marriage status: 20.0% never married, 62.9% now married, 7.2% widowed, 9.9% divorced (2000); Foreign born: 2.6% (2000); Ancestry (includes multiple ancestries): 41.6% German, 20.9% English, 16.9% Irish, 13.0% Italian, 12.4% Polish (2000).
Economy: Single-family building permits issued: 3 (2005); Multi-family building permits issued: 0 (2005); Employment by occupation: 10.9% management, 16.1% professional, 18.1% services, 22.4% sales, 2.7% farming, 10.8% construction, 19.1% production (2000).
Income: Per capita income: $20,883 (2005); Median household income: $50,256 (2005); Average household income: $58,308 (2005); Percent of households with income of $100,000 or more: 8.7% (2005); Poverty rate: 6.9% (2000).
Education: Percent of population age 25 and over with: High school diploma (including GED) or higher: 91.1% (2005); Bachelor's degree or higher: 13.4% (2005); Master's degree or higher: 4.4% (2005).
Housing: Homeownership rate: 82.1% (2005); Median home value: $120,543 (2005); Median rent: $399 per month (2000); Median age of housing: 40 years (2000).
Transportation: Commute to work: 93.5% car, 0.4% public transportation, 3.2% walk, 1.2% work from home (2000); Travel time to work: 31.1% less than 15 minutes, 42.5% 15 to 30 minutes, 7.9% 30 to 45 minutes, 13.6% 45 to 60 minutes, 4.9% 60 minutes or more (2000)

BASOM (unincorporated postal area, zip code 14013).
Covers a land area of 38.955 square miles and a water area of 0.210 square miles. Located at 43.07° N. Lat.; 78.40° W. Long. Elevation is 716 feet.
Population: 0 (2000); Race: 79.7% White, 0.2% Black, 0.2% Asian, 0.4% Hispanic of any race (2000); Density: 0.0 persons per square mile (2000); Age: 26.5% under 18, 15.5% over 64 (2000); Marriage status: 29.2% never married, 55.7% now married, 8.1% widowed, 6.9% divorced (2000); Foreign born: 0.4% (2000); Ancestry (includes multiple ancestries): 37.3% German, 17.3% Other groups, 13.8% Irish, 12.8% English, 10.4% Polish (2000).
Economy: Employment by occupation: 7.8% management, 13.4% professional, 14.4% services, 24.3% sales, 1.9% farming, 14.3% construction, 23.9% production (2000).
Income: Per capita income: $14,955 (2000); Median household income: $35,926 (2000); Poverty rate: 8.8% (2000).
Education: Percent of population age 25 and over with: High school diploma (including GED) or higher: 79.2% (2000); Bachelor's degree or higher: 9.8% (2000).
Housing: Homeownership rate: 83.7% (2000); Median home value: $74,200 (2000); Median rent: $404 per month (2000); Median age of housing: 49 years (2000).
Transportation: Commute to work: 93.9% car, 0.0% public transportation, 3.2% walk, 2.5% work from home (2000); Travel time to work: 25.5% less than 15 minutes, 40.0% 15 to 30 minutes, 18.7% 30 to 45 minutes, 7.7% 45 to 60 minutes, 8.1% 60 minutes or more (2000)

BATAVIA (city).
Covers a land area of 5.187 square miles and a water area of 0.065 square miles. Located at 42.99° N. Lat.; 78.18° W. Long. Elevation is 895 feet.
History: Batavia is noteworthy as the "capital" of the Holland Land Purchase. In 1801, Joseph Ellicott, surveyor and subagent for the company, built a land office on the site. Ellicott proposed naming the place Bustia or Bustiville, for Paul Busti, the company's general agent. The latter objected and proposed Batavia, the name of the Dutch republic to which the proprietors belonged.
Population: 16,310 (1990); 16,256 (2000); 15,876 (2005); 15,482 (2010 projected); Race: 88.2% White, 7.0% Black, 1.2% Asian, 3.6% Hispanic of any race (2005); Density: 3,060.7 persons per square mile (2005); Average household size: 2.49 (2005); Median age: 39.3 (2005); Males per 100 females: 93.3 (2005); Marriage status: 28.2% never married, 48.9% now married, 11.8% widowed, 11.0% divorced (2000); Foreign born: 4.0% (2000); Ancestry (includes multiple ancestries): 23.5% German, 21.5% Italian, 17.1% Irish, 15.3% English, 11.2% Polish (2000).
Economy: Single-family building permits issued: 2 (2005); Multi-family building permits issued: 0 (2005); Employment by occupation: 9.2% management, 22.9% professional, 21.5% services, 23.3% sales, 0.2% farming, 6.6% construction, 16.3% production (2000).
Income: Per capita income: $19,529 (2005); Median household income: $35,435 (2005); Average household income: $46,146 (2005); Percent of households with income of $100,000 or more: 6.7% (2005); Poverty rate: 12.3% (2000).
Education: Percent of population age 25 and over with: High school diploma (including GED) or higher: 80.0% (2005); Bachelor's degree or higher: 18.5% (2005); Master's degree or higher: 7.2% (2005).

School District(s)
Batavia City School District (KG-12)
    2003-04 Enrollment: 2,682 . . . . (585) 343-2480

Two-year College(s)
Continental School of Beauty Culture
    Fall 2004 Enrollment: 48 . . . . (585) 272-8060
Genesee Community College (Public)
    Fall 2004 Enrollment: 6,106. . . . . (585) 343-0055
    2005-06 Tuition: In-state $3,380; Out-of-state $3,730
Genesee Valley BOCES-Practical Nursing Program (Public)
    Fall 2004 Enrollment: 84 . . . . (585) 344-7704

Housing: Homeownership rate: 55.7% (2005); Median home value: $108,322 (2005); Median rent: $438 per month (2000); Median age of housing: 60+ years (2000).
Hospitals: United Memorial Medical Center (126 beds)
Safety: Violent crime rate: 29.4 per 10,000 population; Property crime rate: 460.2 per 10,000 population (2004).
Newspapers: The Daily News (Circulation 15,000); The Drummer (General - Circulation 23,000)
Transportation: Commute to work: 89.3% car, 0.3% public transportation, 6.9% walk, 1.4% work from home (2000); Travel time to work: 57.8% less than 15 minutes, 15.5% 15 to 30 minutes, 13.4% 30 to 45 minutes, 11.0% 45 to 60 minutes, 2.3% 60 minutes or more (2000)

Additional Information Contacts
Batavia Chamber of Commerce. . . . . (518) 343-7440
    http://www.geneseeny.com
City of Batavia . . . . (585) 345-6330
    http://www.batavianewyork.com/

BATAVIA (town).
Covers a land area of 48.432 square miles and a water area of 0.035 square miles. Located at 42.99° N. Lat.; 78.21° W. Long. Elevation is 895 feet.
History: Laid out in 1801 by Joseph Ellicott, agent for the Holland Land Company, the city was a center of the Anti-Masonic movement in the 19th century. Attica prison, site of the 1971 riots, is nearby. Incorporated 1915.
Population: 6,055 (1990); 5,915 (2000); 6,125 (2005); 6,318 (2010 projected); Race: 96.5% White, 1.0% Black, 1.0% Asian, 0.8% Hispanic of any race (2005); Density: 126.5 persons per square mile (2005); Average household size: 2.49 (2005); Median age: 41.3 (2005); Males per 100 females: 92.8 (2005); Marriage status: 21.9% never married, 61.0% now married, 8.7% widowed, 8.5% divorced (2000); Foreign born: 2.0% (2000); Ancestry (includes multiple ancestries): 35.8% German, 20.2% Irish, 19.0% English, 12.4% Italian, 10.3% Polish (2000).
Economy: Produces a variety of light manufacturing. Single-family building permits issued: 11 (2005); Multi-family building permits issued: 0 (2005); Employment by occupation: 8.5% management, 20.2% professional,

20.0% services, 23.0% sales, 2.4% farming, 8.3% construction, 17.6% production (2000).
Income: Per capita income: $21,985 (2005); Median household income: $43,371 (2005); Average household income: $54,573 (2005); Percent of households with income of $100,000 or more: 9.5% (2005); Poverty rate: 9.6% (2000).
Education: Percent of population age 25 and over with: High school diploma (including GED) or higher: 82.1% (2005); Bachelor's degree or higher: 12.8% (2005); Master's degree or higher: 4.4% (2005).
Housing: Homeownership rate: 83.1% (2005); Median home value: $115,308 (2005); Median rent: $416 per month (2000); Median age of housing: 34 years (2000).
Transportation: Commute to work: 92.4% car, 0.0% public transportation, 1.6% walk, 5.7% work from home (2000); Travel time to work: 49.3% less than 15 minutes, 26.1% 15 to 30 minutes, 11.1% 30 to 45 minutes, 8.1% 45 to 60 minutes, 5.4% 60 minutes or more (2000)
Additional Information Contacts
Town of Batavia . . . . (585) 343-1729
http://www.townofbatavia.com/

BERGEN (village). Covers a land area of 0.619 square miles and a water area of 0 square miles. Located at 43.08° N. Lat.; 77.94° W. Long. Elevation is 606 feet.
Population: 1,111 (1990); 1,240 (2000); 1,175 (2005); 1,146 (2010 projected); Race: 94.6% White, 0.5% Black, 1.2% Asian, 2.1% Hispanic of any race (2005); Density: 1,897.3 persons per square mile (2005); Average household size: 2.61 (2005); Median age: 36.0 (2005); Males per 100 females: 102.2 (2005); Marriage status: 23.2% never married, 65.8% now married, 4.1% widowed, 7.0% divorced (2000); Foreign born: 2.0% (2000); Ancestry (includes multiple ancestries): 34.3% German, 19.1% Irish, 17.0% English, 12.8% Italian, 7.4% United States or American (2000).
Economy: Single-family building permits issued: 0 (2005); Multi-family building permits issued: 0 (2005); Employment by occupation: 9.7% management, 19.9% professional, 12.6% services, 22.3% sales, 1.8% farming, 10.3% construction, 23.5% production (2000).
Income: Per capita income: $23,600 (2005); Median household income: $55,225 (2005); Average household income: $61,486 (2005); Percent of households with income of $100,000 or more: 13.7% (2005); Poverty rate: 3.6% (2000).
Education: Percent of population age 25 and over with: High school diploma (including GED) or higher: 89.9% (2005); Bachelor's degree or higher: 23.0% (2005); Master's degree or higher: 7.2% (2005).
School District(s)
Byron-Bergen Central School District (KG-12)
　　2003-04 Enrollment: 1,255 . . . . (585) 494-1220
Housing: Homeownership rate: 72.9% (2005); Median home value: $119,131 (2005); Median rent: $458 per month (2000); Median age of housing: 60+ years (2000).
Transportation: Commute to work: 94.0% car, 0.2% public transportation, 3.2% walk, 2.3% work from home (2000); Travel time to work: 32.5% less than 15 minutes, 39.4% 15 to 30 minutes, 21.8% 30 to 45 minutes, 4.9% 45 to 60 minutes, 1.4% 60 minutes or more (2000)

BERGEN (town). Covers a land area of 27.633 square miles and a water area of 0.006 square miles. Located at 43.08° N. Lat.; 77.96° W. Long. Elevation is 606 feet.
Population: 2,794 (1990); 3,182 (2000); 3,155 (2005); 3,126 (2010 projected); Race: 97.0% White, 0.3% Black, 0.7% Asian, 1.5% Hispanic of any race (2005); Density: 114.2 persons per square mile (2005); Average household size: 2.61 (2005); Median age: 38.4 (2005); Males per 100 females: 102.1 (2005); Marriage status: 22.7% never married, 64.1% now married, 6.5% widowed, 6.6% divorced (2000); Foreign born: 2.3% (2000); Ancestry (includes multiple ancestries): 33.3% German, 19.6% Irish, 18.7% English, 10.2% Italian, 8.3% Polish (2000).
Economy: Single-family building permits issued: 8 (2005); Multi-family building permits issued: 0 (2005); Employment by occupation: 9.5% management, 18.8% professional, 13.2% services, 22.2% sales, 0.7% farming, 12.8% construction, 22.8% production (2000).
Income: Per capita income: $23,639 (2005); Median household income: $53,632 (2005); Average household income: $61,740 (2005); Percent of households with income of $100,000 or more: 13.2% (2005); Poverty rate: 4.1% (2000).
Education: Percent of population age 25 and over with: High school diploma (including GED) or higher: 89.7% (2005); Bachelor's degree or higher: 19.5% (2005); Master's degree or higher: 6.8% (2005).
Housing: Homeownership rate: 80.7% (2005); Median home value: $120,709 (2005); Median rent: $457 per month (2000); Median age of housing: 38 years (2000).
Transportation: Commute to work: 94.9% car, 0.3% public transportation, 1.8% walk, 2.3% work from home (2000); Travel time to work: 24.0% less than 15 minutes, 40.2% 15 to 30 minutes, 24.6% 30 to 45 minutes, 6.9% 45 to 60 minutes, 4.3% 60 minutes or more (2000)

BETHANY (town). Aka Bethany Center. Covers a land area of 36.087 square miles and a water area of 0 square miles. Located at 42.92° N. Lat.; 78.14° W. Long.
Population: 1,808 (1990); 1,760 (2000); 1,737 (2005); 1,727 (2010 projected); Race: 97.2% White, 0.9% Black, 0.3% Asian, 0.6% Hispanic of any race (2005); Density: 48.1 persons per square mile (2005); Average household size: 2.72 (2005); Median age: 39.5 (2005); Males per 100 females: 104.6 (2005); Marriage status: 24.8% never married, 62.3% now married, 4.5% widowed, 8.4% divorced (2000); Foreign born: 1.0% (2000); Ancestry (includes multiple ancestries): 33.5% German, 21.9% English, 21.0% Irish, 13.0% Italian, 8.0% Polish (2000).
Economy: Single-family building permits issued: 10 (2005); Multi-family building permits issued: 0 (2005); Employment by occupation: 10.5% management, 15.9% professional, 14.5% services, 24.6% sales, 4.8% farming, 8.8% construction, 20.9% production (2000).
Income: Per capita income: $21,547 (2005); Median household income: $50,370 (2005); Average household income: $58,549 (2005); Percent of households with income of $100,000 or more: 11.7% (2005); Poverty rate: 5.1% (2000).
Taxes: Total city taxes per capita: $147 (2004); City property taxes per capita: $119 (2004).
Education: Percent of population age 25 and over with: High school diploma (including GED) or higher: 89.2% (2005); Bachelor's degree or higher: 15.2% (2005); Master's degree or higher: 7.2% (2005).
Housing: Homeownership rate: 82.0% (2005); Median home value: $118,564 (2005); Median rent: $400 per month (2000); Median age of housing: 46 years (2000).
Transportation: Commute to work: 90.9% car, 0.2% public transportation, 2.7% walk, 4.6% work from home (2000); Travel time to work: 33.0% less than 15 minutes, 39.3% 15 to 30 minutes, 11.9% 30 to 45 minutes, 8.1% 45 to 60 minutes, 7.8% 60 minutes or more (2000)

BYRON (town). Covers a land area of 32.197 square miles and a water area of 0.057 square miles. Located at 43.08° N. Lat.; 78.06° W. Long. Elevation is 616 feet.
Population: 2,345 (1990); 2,493 (2000); 2,493 (2005); 2,495 (2010 projected); Race: 94.7% White, 0.2% Black, 0.5% Asian, 5.4% Hispanic of any race (2005); Density: 77.4 persons per square mile (2005); Average household size: 2.79 (2005); Median age: 37.0 (2005); Males per 100 females: 99.4 (2005); Marriage status: 20.9% never married, 66.9% now married, 3.8% widowed, 8.4% divorced (2000); Foreign born: 1.3% (2000); Ancestry (includes multiple ancestries): 32.2% German, 27.3% English, 21.4% Irish, 10.5% Italian, 9.1% United States or American (2000).
Economy: Single-family building permits issued: 0 (2005); Multi-family building permits issued: 0 (2005); Employment by occupation: 8.8% management, 19.3% professional, 12.1% services, 25.5% sales, 2.5% farming, 13.3% construction, 18.4% production (2000).
Income: Per capita income: $23,589 (2005); Median household income: $57,165 (2005); Average household income: $65,854 (2005); Percent of households with income of $100,000 or more: 14.2% (2005); Poverty rate: 5.0% (2000).
Education: Percent of population age 25 and over with: High school diploma (including GED) or higher: 89.6% (2005); Bachelor's degree or higher: 14.8% (2005); Master's degree or higher: 4.2% (2005).
Housing: Homeownership rate: 86.1% (2005); Median home value: $118,163 (2005); Median rent: $465 per month (2000); Median age of housing: 30 years (2000).
Transportation: Commute to work: 93.8% car, 0.0% public transportation, 1.4% walk, 4.1% work from home (2000); Travel time to work: 25.3% less than 15 minutes, 33.3% 15 to 30 minutes, 24.1% 30 to 45 minutes, 13.9% 45 to 60 minutes, 3.5% 60 minutes or more (2000)

CORFU (village). Covers a land area of 0.989 square miles and a water area of 0 square miles. Located at 42.95° N. Lat.; 78.40° W. Long. Elevation is 861 feet.
Population: 835 (1990); 795 (2000); 682 (2005); 651 (2010 projected); Race: 96.6% White, 0.9% Black, 0.0% Asian, 2.2% Hispanic of any race

(2005); Density: 689.9 persons per square mile (2005); Average household size: 2.52 (2005); Median age: 37.1 (2005); Males per 100 females: 91.0 (2005); Marriage status: 22.8% never married, 61.6% now married, 9.8% widowed, 5.7% divorced (2000); Foreign born: 1.4% (2000); Ancestry (includes multiple ancestries): 44.6% German, 17.6% Irish, 16.8% Polish, 15.6% English, 13.6% Italian (2000).
Economy: Single-family building permits issued: 0 (2005); Multi-family building permits issued: 0 (2005); Employment by occupation: 7.5% management, 17.6% professional, 14.6% services, 28.6% sales, 0.5% farming, 12.1% construction, 19.1% production (2000).
Income: Per capita income: $19,538 (2005); Median household income: $43,418 (2005); Average household income: $49,170 (2005); Percent of households with income of $100,000 or more: 7.0% (2005); Poverty rate: 4.2% (2000).
Education: Percent of population age 25 and over with: High school diploma (including GED) or higher: 87.8% (2005); Bachelor's degree or higher: 15.6% (2005); Master's degree or higher: 6.4% (2005).
School District(s)
Pembroke Central School District (PK-12)
    2003-04 Enrollment: 1,407 . . . . (585) 599-4525
Housing: Homeownership rate: 68.6% (2005); Median home value: $122,500 (2005); Median rent: $428 per month (2000); Median age of housing: 56 years (2000).
Transportation: Commute to work: 93.0% car, 0.0% public transportation, 5.4% walk, 0.5% work from home (2000); Travel time to work: 21.2% less than 15 minutes, 47.2% 15 to 30 minutes, 18.1% 30 to 45 minutes, 10.4% 45 to 60 minutes, 3.1% 60 minutes or more (2000)

DARIEN (town). Covers a land area of 47.532 square miles and a water area of 0.062 square miles. Located at 42.90° N. Lat.; 78.38° W. Long. Elevation is 1,001 feet.
Population: 2,979 (1990); 3,061 (2000); 3,133 (2005); 3,235 (2010 projected); Race: 99.1% White, 0.1% Black, 0.1% Asian, 0.2% Hispanic of any race (2005); Density: 65.9 persons per square mile (2005); Average household size: 2.83 (2005); Median age: 38.7 (2005); Males per 100 females: 108.0 (2005); Marriage status: 20.4% never married, 69.7% now married, 4.6% widowed, 5.3% divorced (2000); Foreign born: 1.0% (2000); Ancestry (includes multiple ancestries): 46.0% German, 21.9% Polish, 16.6% Irish, 14.2% English, 6.4% Italian (2000).
Economy: Single-family building permits issued: 13 (2005); Multi-family building permits issued: 0 (2005); Employment by occupation: 12.0% management, 18.1% professional, 13.6% services, 20.6% sales, 1.2% farming, 14.7% construction, 19.8% production (2000).
Income: Per capita income: $20,850 (2005); Median household income: $53,451 (2005); Average household income: $58,425 (2005); Percent of households with income of $100,000 or more: 10.9% (2005); Poverty rate: 3.2% (2000).
Education: Percent of population age 25 and over with: High school diploma (including GED) or higher: 85.8% (2005); Bachelor's degree or higher: 13.6% (2005); Master's degree or higher: 6.1% (2005).
Housing: Homeownership rate: 86.0% (2005); Median home value: $139,938 (2005); Median rent: $441 per month (2000); Median age of housing: 43 years (2000).
Transportation: Commute to work: 94.0% car, 0.3% public transportation, 0.9% walk, 4.2% work from home (2000); Travel time to work: 20.8% less than 15 minutes, 38.1% 15 to 30 minutes, 22.9% 30 to 45 minutes, 12.6% 45 to 60 minutes, 5.6% 60 minutes or more (2000)

DARIEN CENTER (unincorporated postal area, zip code 14040). Covers a land area of 32.956 square miles and a water area of 0.132 square miles. Located at 42.89° N. Lat.; 78.37° W. Long. Elevation is 1,019 feet.
Population: 0 (2000); Race: 98.0% White, 0.0% Black, 0.0% Asian, 0.4% Hispanic of any race (2000); Density: 0.0 persons per square mile (2000); Age: 25.8% under 18, 11.0% over 64 (2000); Marriage status: 19.3% never married, 70.7% now married, 3.9% widowed, 6.1% divorced (2000); Foreign born: 1.1% (2000); Ancestry (includes multiple ancestries): 43.9% German, 20.2% Polish, 17.1% Irish, 11.3% English, 5.7% Italian (2000).
Economy: Employment by occupation: 12.4% management, 15.8% professional, 13.9% services, 23.2% sales, 1.2% farming, 14.1% construction, 19.3% production (2000).
Income: Per capita income: $19,473 (2000); Median household income: $49,549 (2000); Poverty rate: 2.9% (2000).
Education: Percent of population age 25 and over with: High school diploma (including GED) or higher: 82.5% (2000); Bachelor's degree or higher: 11.6% (2000).
Housing: Homeownership rate: 86.4% (2000); Median home value: $87,300 (2000); Median rent: $442 per month (2000); Median age of housing: 39 years (2000).
Transportation: Commute to work: 93.7% car, 0.5% public transportation, 0.9% walk, 4.2% work from home (2000); Travel time to work: 19.6% less than 15 minutes, 36.7% 15 to 30 minutes, 26.1% 30 to 45 minutes, 12.8% 45 to 60 minutes, 4.8% 60 minutes or more (2000)

EAST BETHANY (unincorporated postal area, zip code 14054). Covers a land area of 29.288 square miles and a water area of 0 square miles. Located at 42.90° N. Lat.; 78.13° W. Long. Elevation is 1,006 feet.
Population: 0 (2000); Race: 97.9% White, 1.3% Black, 0.1% Asian, 0.9% Hispanic of any race (2000); Density: 0.0 persons per square mile (2000); Age: 25.8% under 18, 10.9% over 64 (2000); Marriage status: 24.2% never married, 62.2% now married, 4.9% widowed, 8.7% divorced (2000); Foreign born: 1.1% (2000); Ancestry (includes multiple ancestries): 33.9% German, 22.4% English, 19.9% Irish, 11.0% Italian, 7.5% Polish (2000).
Economy: Employment by occupation: 10.5% management, 16.4% professional, 13.8% services, 25.2% sales, 5.3% farming, 7.9% construction, 20.8% production (2000).
Income: Per capita income: $18,977 (2000); Median household income: $45,400 (2000); Poverty rate: 2.8% (2000).
Education: Percent of population age 25 and over with: High school diploma (including GED) or higher: 89.8% (2000); Bachelor's degree or higher: 15.4% (2000).
Housing: Homeownership rate: 83.3% (2000); Median home value: $80,700 (2000); Median rent: $382 per month (2000); Median age of housing: 48 years (2000).
Transportation: Commute to work: 92.8% car, 0.3% public transportation, 1.6% walk, 4.0% work from home (2000); Travel time to work: 33.3% less than 15 minutes, 39.6% 15 to 30 minutes, 12.8% 30 to 45 minutes, 7.7% 45 to 60 minutes, 6.5% 60 minutes or more (2000)

ELBA (village). Covers a land area of 1.017 square miles and a water area of 0 square miles. Located at 43.07° N. Lat.; 78.18° W. Long. Elevation is 761 feet.
Population: 703 (1990); 696 (2000); 630 (2005); 605 (2010 projected); Race: 95.1% White, 1.7% Black, 0.2% Asian, 5.2% Hispanic of any race (2005); Density: 619.3 persons per square mile (2005); Average household size: 2.83 (2005); Median age: 38.2 (2005); Males per 100 females: 99.4 (2005); Marriage status: 23.7% never married, 65.2% now married, 6.3% widowed, 4.9% divorced (2000); Foreign born: 2.4% (2000); Ancestry (includes multiple ancestries): 29.6% German, 24.0% English, 19.5% Italian, 17.2% Irish, 9.8% Polish (2000).
Economy: Single-family building permits issued: 1 (2005); Multi-family building permits issued: 0 (2005); Employment by occupation: 8.9% management, 20.4% professional, 14.2% services, 23.7% sales, 2.7% farming, 12.4% construction, 17.8% production (2000).
Income: Per capita income: $20,841 (2005); Median household income: $52,885 (2005); Average household income: $58,879 (2005); Percent of households with income of $100,000 or more: 10.8% (2005); Poverty rate: 5.7% (2000).
Education: Percent of population age 25 and over with: High school diploma (including GED) or higher: 90.3% (2005); Bachelor's degree or higher: 22.3% (2005); Master's degree or higher: 7.7% (2005).
School District(s)
Elba Central School District (KG-12)
    2003-04 Enrollment: 585 . . . . (585) 757-9967
Housing: Homeownership rate: 83.9% (2005); Median home value: $119,248 (2005); Median rent: $468 per month (2000); Median age of housing: 60+ years (2000).
Transportation: Commute to work: 96.3% car, 0.0% public transportation, 2.5% walk, 0.6% work from home (2000); Travel time to work: 35.7% less than 15 minutes, 32.9% 15 to 30 minutes, 12.7% 30 to 45 minutes, 8.4% 45 to 60 minutes, 10.2% 60 minutes or more (2000)

ELBA (town). Covers a land area of 35.700 square miles and a water area of 0 square miles. Located at 43.08° N. Lat.; 78.16° W. Long. Elevation is 761 feet.
Population: 2,407 (1990); 2,439 (2000); 2,414 (2005); 2,408 (2010 projected); Race: 91.1% White, 1.6% Black, 0.0% Asian, 7.8% Hispanic of any race (2005); Density: 67.6 persons per square mile (2005); Average

household size: 2.83 (2005); Median age: 38.1 (2005); Males per 100 females: 100.8 (2005); Marriage status: 22.0% never married, 66.8% now married, 5.5% widowed, 5.8% divorced (2000); Foreign born: 2.1% (2000); Ancestry (includes multiple ancestries): 30.7% German, 19.9% English, 16.8% Irish, 13.4% Italian, 12.8% Polish (2000).
Economy: In agricultural area. Single-family building permits issued: 2 (2005); Multi-family building permits issued: 0 (2005); Employment by occupation: 9.8% management, 19.4% professional, 13.0% services, 22.2% sales, 3.0% farming, 13.1% construction, 19.4% production (2000).
Income: Per capita income: $20,574 (2005); Median household income: $50,991 (2005); Average household income: $57,535 (2005); Percent of households with income of $100,000 or more: 11.2% (2005); Poverty rate: 6.5% (2000).
Education: Percent of population age 25 and over with: High school diploma (including GED) or higher: 85.4% (2005); Bachelor's degree or higher: 17.4% (2005); Master's degree or higher: 6.4% (2005).
Housing: Homeownership rate: 83.6% (2005); Median home value: $113,714 (2005); Median rent: $458 per month (2000); Median age of housing: 54 years (2000).
Transportation: Commute to work: 93.7% car, 0.0% public transportation, 2.5% walk, 3.7% work from home (2000); Travel time to work: 36.4% less than 15 minutes, 34.0% 15 to 30 minutes, 10.6% 30 to 45 minutes, 12.5% 45 to 60 minutes, 6.5% 60 minutes or more (2000)

LE ROY (village). Covers a land area of 2.696 square miles and a water area of 0 square miles. Located at 42.97° N. Lat.; 77.99° W. Long. Elevation is 869 feet.
Population: 4,974 (1990); 4,462 (2000); 4,319 (2005); 4,193 (2010 projected); Race: 94.7% White, 2.6% Black, 0.6% Asian, 1.2% Hispanic of any race (2005); Density: 1,601.8 persons per square mile (2005); Average household size: 2.38 (2005); Median age: 39.4 (2005); Males per 100 females: 87.5 (2005); Marriage status: 28.6% never married, 52.6% now married, 8.3% widowed, 10.4% divorced (2000); Foreign born: 1.2% (2000); Ancestry (includes multiple ancestries): 22.9% German, 21.2% English, 21.2% Italian, 20.1% Irish, 7.0% Other groups (2000).
Economy: Single-family building permits issued: 2 (2005); Multi-family building permits issued: 0 (2005); Employment by occupation: 8.8% management, 15.2% professional, 19.8% services, 26.6% sales, 0.4% farming, 7.7% construction, 21.5% production (2000).
Income: Per capita income: $20,729 (2005); Median household income: $39,084 (2005); Average household income: $48,438 (2005); Percent of households with income of $100,000 or more: 7.8% (2005); Poverty rate: 7.3% (2000).
Education: Percent of population age 25 and over with: High school diploma (including GED) or higher: 84.9% (2005); Bachelor's degree or higher: 15.1% (2005); Master's degree or higher: 5.6% (2005).

School District(s)
Boces Genesee Valley (PK-PK)
   2003-04 Enrollment: 398 . . . . (585) 658-7905
Le Roy Central School District (KG-12)
   2003-04 Enrollment: 1,410 . . . . (585) 768-8133

Housing: Homeownership rate: 59.7% (2005); Median home value: $116,205 (2005); Median rent: $430 per month (2000); Median age of housing: 60+ years (2000).
Safety: Violent crime rate: 13.7 per 10,000 population; Property crime rate: 308.1 per 10,000 population (2004).
Transportation: Commute to work: 92.7% car, 0.4% public transportation, 5.1% walk, 0.3% work from home (2000); Travel time to work: 35.6% less than 15 minutes, 26.2% 15 to 30 minutes, 27.9% 30 to 45 minutes, 9.0% 45 to 60 minutes, 1.2% 60 minutes or more (2000)

LE ROY (town). Covers a land area of 42.171 square miles and a water area of 0 square miles. Located at 42.98° N. Lat.; 77.97° W. Long. Elevation is 869 feet.
History: In 1897, Pearl Bixby Wait, a local carpenter, perfected the formula for Jello gelatin dessert, then sold it for $450. Until 1964, General Foods had a plant that produced Jello in the village. Jello Museum is housed in the Historical Society Building. Settled 1793, Incorporated 1834.
Population: 8,176 (1990); 7,790 (2000); 7,451 (2005); 7,215 (2010 projected); Race: 95.9% White, 2.0% Black, 0.5% Asian, 1.2% Hispanic of any race (2005); Density: 176.7 persons per square mile (2005); Average household size: 2.52 (2005); Median age: 40.1 (2005); Males per 100 females: 92.6 (2005); Marriage status: 25.7% never married, 56.7% now married, 6.8% widowed, 10.9% divorced (2000); Foreign born: 1.3%

(2000); Ancestry (includes multiple ancestries): 28.3% German, 22.2% Irish, 20.3% English, 19.7% Italian, 5.7% Other groups (2000).
Economy: Manufacturing includes porcelain and polymer insulators, motor vehicle parts, dairy products, office supplies, machinery and canning. In rich agricultural area: poultry, fruit. Single-family building permits issued: 12 (2005); Multi-family building permits issued: 0 (2005); Employment by occupation: 9.0% management, 18.1% professional, 16.6% services, 24.4% sales, 0.7% farming, 7.4% construction, 23.8% production (2000).
Income: Per capita income: $21,620 (2005); Median household income: $45,216 (2005); Average household income: $53,725 (2005); Percent of households with income of $100,000 or more: 10.2% (2005); Poverty rate: 5.6% (2000).
Education: Percent of population age 25 and over with: High school diploma (including GED) or higher: 86.5% (2005); Bachelor's degree or higher: 16.7% (2005); Master's degree or higher: 6.1% (2005).
Housing: Homeownership rate: 69.3% (2005); Median home value: $119,717 (2005); Median rent: $438 per month (2000); Median age of housing: 50 years (2000).
Transportation: Commute to work: 94.0% car, 0.2% public transportation, 3.6% walk, 1.1% work from home (2000); Travel time to work: 36.1% less than 15 minutes, 26.5% 15 to 30 minutes, 27.1% 30 to 45 minutes, 8.0% 45 to 60 minutes, 2.3% 60 minutes or more (2000)

OAKFIELD (village). Covers a land area of 0.663 square miles and a water area of 0 square miles. Located at 43.06° N. Lat.; 78.27° W. Long. Elevation is 753 feet.
Population: 1,880 (1990); 1,805 (2000); 1,720 (2005); 1,662 (2010 projected); Race: 96.6% White, 1.2% Black, 0.3% Asian, 1.3% Hispanic of any race (2005); Density: 2,593.2 persons per square mile (2005); Average household size: 2.75 (2005); Median age: 36.7 (2005); Males per 100 females: 93.3 (2005); Marriage status: 26.7% never married, 57.8% now married, 6.9% widowed, 8.6% divorced (2000); Foreign born: 1.3% (2000); Ancestry (includes multiple ancestries): 28.0% German, 22.2% Italian, 19.3% English, 18.2% Irish, 9.5% Polish (2000).
Economy: Single-family building permits issued: 0 (2005); Multi-family building permits issued: 0 (2005); Employment by occupation: 8.1% management, 16.0% professional, 15.3% services, 27.3% sales, 2.9% farming, 12.6% construction, 17.8% production (2000).
Income: Per capita income: $17,713 (2005); Median household income: $43,946 (2005); Average household income: $48,636 (2005); Percent of households with income of $100,000 or more: 6.6% (2005); Poverty rate: 11.6% (2000).
Education: Percent of population age 25 and over with: High school diploma (including GED) or higher: 82.6% (2005); Bachelor's degree or higher: 13.1% (2005); Master's degree or higher: 5.4% (2005).

School District(s)
Oakfield-Alabama Central School District (KG-12)
   2003-04 Enrollment: 1,107 . . . . (585) 948-5211

Housing: Homeownership rate: 69.9% (2005); Median home value: $94,885 (2005); Median rent: $381 per month (2000); Median age of housing: 60+ years (2000).
Transportation: Commute to work: 89.2% car, 2.3% public transportation, 4.2% walk, 3.4% work from home (2000); Travel time to work: 36.8% less than 15 minutes, 37.1% 15 to 30 minutes, 13.5% 30 to 45 minutes, 9.3% 45 to 60 minutes, 3.4% 60 minutes or more (2000)

Additional Information Contacts
Village of Oakfield . . . . (585) 948-5862
   http://www.oakfield.govoffice.com/

OAKFIELD (town). Covers a land area of 23.452 square miles and a water area of 0.466 square miles. Located at 43.07° N. Lat.; 78.27° W. Long. Elevation is 753 feet.
History: Settled 1850, incorporated 1858.
Population: 3,312 (1990); 3,203 (2000); 3,151 (2005); 3,074 (2010 projected); Race: 97.1% White, 1.0% Black, 0.3% Asian, 1.5% Hispanic of any race (2005); Density: 134.4 persons per square mile (2005); Average household size: 2.75 (2005); Median age: 37.8 (2005); Males per 100 females: 95.2 (2005); Marriage status: 26.4% never married, 58.2% now married, 7.1% widowed, 8.3% divorced (2000); Foreign born: 0.9% (2000); Ancestry (includes multiple ancestries): 31.8% German, 17.1% Italian, 16.6% English, 16.1% Irish, 12.6% Polish (2000).
Economy: In wheat area. Food canning. Gypsum quarrying and processing. Iroquois National Wildlife Refuge, featuring migratory waterfowl of Eastern North America, occupies much of Orchard Swamp. Single-family building permits issued: 1 (2005); Multi-family building permits issued: 6

(2005); Employment by occupation: 8.4% management, 15.9% professional, 14.6% services, 25.4% sales, 3.6% farming, 14.0% construction, 18.0% production (2000).
Income: Per capita income: $19,421 (2005); Median household income: $45,894 (2005); Average household income: $53,386 (2005); Percent of households with income of $100,000 or more: 10.7% (2005); Poverty rate: 7.8% (2000).
Education: Percent of population age 25 and over with: High school diploma (including GED) or higher: 83.3% (2005); Bachelor's degree or higher: 12.6% (2005); Master's degree or higher: 5.3% (2005).
Housing: Homeownership rate: 78.3% (2005); Median home value: $99,857 (2005); Median rent: $394 per month (2000); Median age of housing: 60+ years (2000).
Transportation: Commute to work: 91.8% car, 1.3% public transportation, 3.1% walk, 2.8% work from home (2000); Travel time to work: 42.4% less than 15 minutes, 33.3% 15 to 30 minutes, 12.2% 30 to 45 minutes, 9.5% 45 to 60 minutes, 2.5% 60 minutes or more (2000)

PAVILION (town). Covers a land area of 35.626 square miles and a water area of 0.101 square miles. Located at 42.90° N. Lat.; 78.00° W. Long. Elevation is 932 feet.
Population: 2,327 (1990); 2,467 (2000); 2,546 (2005); 2,611 (2010 projected); Race: 97.7% White, 0.5% Black, 0.2% Asian, 0.6% Hispanic of any race (2005); Density: 71.5 persons per square mile (2005); Average household size: 2.73 (2005); Median age: 39.1 (2005); Males per 100 females: 101.9 (2005); Marriage status: 21.5% never married, 65.8% now married, 5.7% widowed, 7.0% divorced (2000); Foreign born: 1.8% (2000); Ancestry (includes multiple ancestries): 27.4% English, 25.0% Irish, 23.6% German, 13.4% Italian, 7.7% Other groups (2000).
Economy: Single-family building permits issued: 2 (2005); Multi-family building permits issued: 0 (2005); Employment by occupation: 12.4% management, 15.7% professional, 12.4% services, 24.4% sales, 1.8% farming, 10.7% construction, 22.6% production (2000).
Income: Per capita income: $24,109 (2005); Median household income: $57,824 (2005); Average household income: $65,861 (2005); Percent of households with income of $100,000 or more: 14.9% (2005); Poverty rate: 5.4% (2000).
Education: Percent of population age 25 and over with: High school diploma (including GED) or higher: 88.8% (2005); Bachelor's degree or higher: 19.5% (2005); Master's degree or higher: 7.2% (2005).

School District(s)
Pavilion Central School District (KG-12)
    2003-04 Enrollment: 927 . . . . (585) 584-3115
Housing: Homeownership rate: 85.9% (2005); Median home value: $119,769 (2005); Median rent: $391 per month (2000); Median age of housing: 42 years (2000).
Transportation: Commute to work: 93.3% car, 1.1% public transportation, 2.5% walk, 2.5% work from home (2000); Travel time to work: 28.6% less than 15 minutes, 32.6% 15 to 30 minutes, 23.0% 30 to 45 minutes, 12.4% 45 to 60 minutes, 3.4% 60 minutes or more (2000)

PEMBROKE (town). Covers a land area of 41.706 square miles and a water area of 0.014 square miles. Located at 42.98° N. Lat.; 78.39° W. Long. Elevation is 845 feet.
Population: 4,232 (1990); 4,530 (2000); 4,415 (2005); 4,352 (2010 projected); Race: 98.1% White, 0.4% Black, 0.2% Asian, 1.0% Hispanic of any race (2005); Density: 105.9 persons per square mile (2005); Average household size: 2.68 (2005); Median age: 39.3 (2005); Males per 100 females: 96.0 (2005); Marriage status: 21.3% never married, 63.0% now married, 7.9% widowed, 7.8% divorced (2000); Foreign born: 1.5% (2000); Ancestry (includes multiple ancestries): 42.9% German, 19.5% Polish, 18.4% Irish, 16.0% English, 10.0% Italian (2000).
Economy: Single-family building permits issued: 8 (2005); Multi-family building permits issued: 0 (2005); Employment by occupation: 9.6% management, 15.4% professional, 15.2% services, 25.9% sales, 1.6% farming, 9.7% construction, 22.6% production (2000).
Income: Per capita income: $19,812 (2005); Median household income: $46,574 (2005); Average household income: $53,141 (2005); Percent of households with income of $100,000 or more: 8.1% (2005); Poverty rate: 4.8% (2000).
Taxes: Total city taxes per capita: $41 (2004); City property taxes per capita: $15 (2004).
Education: Percent of population age 25 and over with: High school diploma (including GED) or higher: 84.5% (2005); Bachelor's degree or higher: 15.3% (2005); Master's degree or higher: 5.6% (2005).

Housing: Homeownership rate: 79.4% (2005); Median home value: $132,485 (2005); Median rent: $444 per month (2000); Median age of housing: 48 years (2000).
Transportation: Commute to work: 94.2% car, 0.0% public transportation, 2.0% walk, 3.0% work from home (2000); Travel time to work: 23.7% less than 15 minutes, 38.7% 15 to 30 minutes, 18.2% 30 to 45 minutes, 13.2% 45 to 60 minutes, 6.1% 60 minutes or more (2000)

STAFFORD (town). Covers a land area of 31.130 square miles and a water area of 0.111 square miles. Located at 42.99° N. Lat.; 78.08° W. Long. Elevation is 996 feet.
Population: 2,593 (1990); 2,409 (2000); 2,625 (2005); 2,739 (2010 projected); Race: 97.6% White, 1.4% Black, 0.3% Asian, 0.2% Hispanic of any race (2005); Density: 84.3 persons per square mile (2005); Average household size: 2.60 (2005); Median age: 41.5 (2005); Males per 100 females: 99.6 (2005); Marriage status: 20.1% never married, 69.0% now married, 5.0% widowed, 6.0% divorced (2000); Foreign born: 0.5% (2000); Ancestry (includes multiple ancestries): 27.1% English, 26.8% German, 20.0% Irish, 16.4% Italian, 7.8% Polish (2000).
Economy: Single-family building permits issued: 7 (2005); Multi-family building permits issued: 0 (2005); Employment by occupation: 12.1% management, 20.6% professional, 11.9% services, 27.2% sales, 2.7% farming, 9.2% construction, 16.3% production (2000).
Income: Per capita income: $23,844 (2005); Median household income: $55,596 (2005); Average household income: $62,032 (2005); Percent of households with income of $100,000 or more: 13.3% (2005); Poverty rate: 3.7% (2000).
Education: Percent of population age 25 and over with: High school diploma (including GED) or higher: 90.5% (2005); Bachelor's degree or higher: 19.2% (2005); Master's degree or higher: 7.4% (2005).
Housing: Homeownership rate: 85.2% (2005); Median home value: $123,098 (2005); Median rent: $405 per month (2000); Median age of housing: 47 years (2000).
Transportation: Commute to work: 95.9% car, 0.2% public transportation, 1.3% walk, 1.8% work from home (2000); Travel time to work: 40.9% less than 15 minutes, 28.0% 15 to 30 minutes, 17.6% 30 to 45 minutes, 8.7% 45 to 60 minutes, 4.7% 60 minutes or more (2000)

TONAWANDA RESERVATION (reservation). Covers a land area of 9.192 square miles and a water area of 0.067 square miles. Located at 43.06° N. Lat.; 78.43° W. Long.
Population: 491 (1990); 533 (2000); 535 (2005); 537 (2010 projected); Race: 61.9% White, 4.1% Black, 0.0% Asian, 7.1% Hispanic of any race (2005); Density: 58.2 persons per square mile (2005); Average household size: 2.82 (2005); Median age: 34.7 (2005); Males per 100 females: 98.1 (2005); Marriage status: 41.9% never married, 41.9% now married, 9.7% widowed, 6.6% divorced (2000); Foreign born: 0.0% (2000); Ancestry (includes multiple ancestries): 65.9% Other groups, 6.9% Irish, 6.1% German, 5.5% English, 2.9% Dutch (2000).
Economy: Employment by occupation: 3.1% management, 10.2% professional, 22.8% services, 17.3% sales, 0.0% farming, 7.1% construction, 39.4% production (2000).
Income: Per capita income: $10,958 (2005); Median household income: $26,818 (2005); Average household income: $30,855 (2005); Percent of households with income of $100,000 or more: 0.0% (2005); Poverty rate: 16.1% (2000).
Education: Percent of population age 25 and over with: High school diploma (including GED) or higher: 78.4% (2005); Bachelor's degree or higher: 8.3% (2005); Master's degree or higher: 3.0% (2005).
Housing: Homeownership rate: 87.4% (2005); Median home value: $49,600 (2005); Median rent: $225 per month (2000); Median age of housing: 30 years (2000).
Transportation: Commute to work: 94.4% car, 0.0% public transportation, 5.5% walk, 0.0% work from home (2000); Travel time to work: 10.9% less than 15 minutes, 28.3% 15 to 30 minutes, 18.1% 30 to 45 minutes, 7.9% 45 to 60 minutes, 4.7% 60 minutes or more (2000)

Greene County

Located in southeastern New York, mainly in the Catskills; bounded on the east by the Hudson River; includes many small lakes. Covers a land area of 647.75 square miles, a water area of 10.38 square miles, and is located in the Eastern Time Zone. The county government was organized in 1800. County seat is Catskill.

Population: 44,739 (1990); 48,195 (2000); 49,314 (2005); 50,456 (2010 projected); Race: 90.1% White, 5.9% Black, 0.8% Asian, 5.1% Hispanic of any race (2005); Density: 76.1 persons per square mile (2005); Average household size: 2.61 (2005); Median age: 40.0 (2005); Males per 100 females: 105.6 (2005).
Religion: Five largest groups: 19.5% Catholic Church, 7.1% The United Methodist Church, 2.7% Reformed Church in America, 1.1% Lutheran Church-Missouri Synod, 1.0% Evangelical Lutheran Church in America (2000).
Economy: Unemployment rate: 4.8% (2005); Total civilian labor force: 23,605 (2005); Leading industries: 23.3% retail trade; 20.6% accommodation and food services; 9.6% health care and social assistance (2003); Farms: 342 totaling 57,898 acres (2002); Companies that employ 500 or more persons: 2 (2003); Companies that employ 100 to 499 persons: 15 (2003); Companies that employ less than 100 persons: 1,129 (2003); Black-owned businesses: n/a (2002); Hispanic-owned businesses: n/a (2002); Women-owned businesses: 1,120 (2002); Retail sales per capita: $9,801 (2006). Single-family building permits issued: 337 (2005); Multi-family building permits issued: 38 (2005).
Income: Per capita income: $22,229 (2005); Median household income: $42,332 (2005); Average household income: $54,901 (2005); Percent of households with income of $100,000 or more: 11.7% (2005); Poverty rate: 12.9% (2003); Bankruptcy rate: 5.70% (2005).
Taxes: Total county taxes per capita: $756 (2004); County property taxes per capita: $314 (2004).
Education: Percent of population age 25 and over with: High school diploma (including GED) or higher: 78.9% (2005); Bachelor's degree or higher: 16.6% (2005); Master's degree or higher: 7.5% (2005).
Housing: Homeownership rate: 72.4% (2005); Median home value: $135,341 (2005); Median rent: $429 per month (2000); Median age of housing: 36 years (2000).
Health: Birth rate: 89.8 per 10,000 population (2004); Death rate: 107.3 per 10,000 population (2004); Age-adjusted cancer mortality rate: 254.4 deaths per 100,000 population (2002); Number of physicians: 6.7 per 10,000 population (2004); Hospital beds: 0.0 per 10,000 population (2003); Hospital admissions: 0.0 per 10,000 population (2003).
Elections: 2004 Presidential election results: 58.0% Bush, 39.9% Kerry, 1.7% Nader, 0.2% Badnarik
National and State Parks: Catskill State Park
Additional Information Contacts
Greene County Government . . . . (518) 943-2050
   http://www.greenegovernment.com/
Town of Catskill . . . . (518) 943-2141
   http://www.townofcatskillny.gov/Public_Documents/index
Town of Coxsackie . . . . (518) 731-2727
   http://www.coxsackie.org/
Town of Halcott . . . . (845) 254-9920
   http://www.townofhalcott.com/
Village of Catskill . . . . (518) 943-2141
   http://www.townofcatskill.com/

Greene County Communities

ACRA (unincorporated postal area, zip code 12405). Covers a land area of 3.908 square miles and a water area of 0 square miles. Located at 42.32° N. Lat.; 74.07° W. Long. Elevation is 546 feet.
Population: 0 (2000); Race: 96.0% White, 1.5% Black, 0.0% Asian, 2.6% Hispanic of any race (2000); Density: 0.0 persons per square mile (2000); Age: 36.0% under 18, 7.9% over 64 (2000); Marriage status: 26.9% never married, 55.1% now married, 7.2% widowed, 10.9% divorced (2000); Foreign born: 9.4% (2000); Ancestry (includes multiple ancestries): 28.1% German, 23.7% Irish, 15.4% Other groups, 13.6% Italian, 7.2% United States or American (2000).
Economy: Resort village. Employment by occupation: 5.2% management, 16.0% professional, 29.3% services, 22.6% sales, 0.0% farming, 18.1% construction, 8.7% production (2000).
Income: Per capita income: $21,149 (2000); Median household income: $48,846 (2000); Poverty rate: 17.2% (2000).
Education: Percent of population age 25 and over with: High school diploma (including GED) or higher: 86.9% (2000); Bachelor's degree or higher: 19.0% (2000).
Housing: Homeownership rate: 85.2% (2000); Median home value: $87,500 (2000); Median rent: $425 per month (2000); Median age of housing: 32 years (2000).
Transportation: Commute to work: 100.0% car, 0.0% public transportation, 0.0% walk, 0.0% work from home (2000); Travel time to work: 23.1% less than 15 minutes, 18.5% 15 to 30 minutes, 17.3% 30 to 45 minutes, 8.1% 45 to 60 minutes, 33.1% 60 minutes or more (2000)

ASHLAND (town). Covers a land area of 25.971 square miles and a water area of 0 square miles. Located at 42.32° N. Lat.; 74.33° W. Long. Elevation is 1,423 feet.
Population: 803 (1990); 752 (2000); 711 (2005); 673 (2010 projected); Race: 97.2% White, 0.6% Black, 1.1% Asian, 3.1% Hispanic of any race (2005); Density: 27.4 persons per square mile (2005); Average household size: 2.43 (2005); Median age: 42.2 (2005); Males per 100 females: 99.2 (2005); Marriage status: 19.1% never married, 64.7% now married, 9.6% widowed, 6.5% divorced (2000); Foreign born: 4.6% (2000); Ancestry (includes multiple ancestries): 19.7% German, 16.6% Irish, 15.6% English, 12.2% Italian, 11.9% Other groups (2000).
Economy: Employment by occupation: 11.0% management, 15.9% professional, 14.2% services, 26.6% sales, 0.9% farming, 15.3% construction, 16.2% production (2000).
Income: Per capita income: $24,068 (2005); Median household income: $43,421 (2005); Average household income: $58,604 (2005); Percent of households with income of $100,000 or more: 13.0% (2005); Poverty rate: 15.8% (2000).
Taxes: Total city taxes per capita: $617 (2004); City property taxes per capita: $581 (2004).
Education: Percent of population age 25 and over with: High school diploma (including GED) or higher: 85.2% (2005); Bachelor's degree or higher: 13.3% (2005); Master's degree or higher: 7.0% (2005).
Housing: Homeownership rate: 79.5% (2005); Median home value: $129,167 (2005); Median rent: $475 per month (2000); Median age of housing: 31 years (2000).
Transportation: Commute to work: 88.0% car, 3.9% public transportation, 1.5% walk, 6.0% work from home (2000); Travel time to work: 32.8% less than 15 minutes, 24.2% 15 to 30 minutes, 20.1% 30 to 45 minutes, 6.7% 45 to 60 minutes, 16.2% 60 minutes or more (2000)

ATHENS (village). Covers a land area of 3.370 square miles and a water area of 1.231 square miles. Located at 42.26° N. Lat.; 73.81° W. Long. Elevation is 50 feet.
Population: 1,708 (1990); 1,695 (2000); 1,687 (2005); 1,753 (2010 projected); Race: 94.8% White, 1.3% Black, 1.1% Asian, 1.1% Hispanic of any race (2005); Density: 500.6 persons per square mile (2005); Average household size: 2.41 (2005); Median age: 42.5 (2005); Males per 100 females: 86.2 (2005); Marriage status: 25.5% never married, 54.0% now married, 9.4% widowed, 11.1% divorced (2000); Foreign born: 2.8% (2000); Ancestry (includes multiple ancestries): 23.2% Irish, 22.9% Italian, 19.5% German, 10.2% English, 7.7% Dutch (2000).
Economy: Single-family building permits issued: 12 (2005); Multi-family building permits issued: 0 (2005); Employment by occupation: 9.4% management, 18.2% professional, 21.2% services, 26.0% sales, 0.7% farming, 9.4% construction, 15.0% production (2000).
Income: Per capita income: $23,893 (2005); Median household income: $44,526 (2005); Average household income: $57,218 (2005); Percent of households with income of $100,000 or more: 12.1% (2005); Poverty rate: 10.8% (2000).
Education: Percent of population age 25 and over with: High school diploma (including GED) or higher: 71.8% (2005); Bachelor's degree or higher: 15.0% (2005); Master's degree or higher: 5.9% (2005).
####School District(s)
Coxsackie-Athens Central School District (KG-12)
   2003-04 Enrollment: 2,506 . . . . (518) 731-1710
Housing: Homeownership rate: 69.6% (2005); Median home value: $121,412 (2005); Median rent: $420 per month (2000); Median age of housing: 60+ years (2000).
Transportation: Commute to work: 90.3% car, 1.9% public transportation, 4.3% walk, 2.5% work from home (2000); Travel time to work: 36.0% less than 15 minutes, 27.2% 15 to 30 minutes, 15.8% 30 to 45 minutes, 11.1% 45 to 60 minutes, 10.0% 60 minutes or more (2000)

ATHENS (town). Covers a land area of 26.177 square miles and a water area of 2.662 square miles. Located at 42.27° N. Lat.; 73.84° W. Long. Elevation is 50 feet.
History: Settled 1686, incorporated 1805.
Population: 3,561 (1990); 3,991 (2000); 4,357 (2005); 4,697 (2010 projected); Race: 95.6% White, 1.0% Black, 1.1% Asian, 2.0% Hispanic of

any race (2005); Density: 166.4 persons per square mile (2005); Average household size: 2.45 (2005); Median age: 42.4 (2005); Males per 100 females: 93.2 (2005); Marriage status: 21.8% never married, 61.2% now married, 8.2% widowed, 8.7% divorced (2000); Foreign born: 5.6% (2000); Ancestry (includes multiple ancestries): 22.7% Italian, 21.9% Irish, 18.4% German, 10.9% English, 6.7% Polish (2000).
Economy: Summer resort. Single-family building permits issued: 26 (2005); Multi-family building permits issued: 0 (2005); Employment by occupation: 10.4% management, 18.4% professional, 19.2% services, 26.4% sales, 0.7% farming, 11.3% construction, 13.5% production (2000).
Income: Per capita income: $25,377 (2005); Median household income: $47,209 (2005); Average household income: $61,807 (2005); Percent of households with income of $100,000 or more: 15.4% (2005); Poverty rate: 8.7% (2000).
Education: Percent of population age 25 and over with: High school diploma (including GED) or higher: 79.6% (2005); Bachelor's degree or higher: 18.9% (2005); Master's degree or higher: 9.3% (2005).
Housing: Homeownership rate: 75.0% (2005); Median home value: $133,707 (2005); Median rent: $445 per month (2000); Median age of housing: 37 years (2000).
Transportation: Commute to work: 94.3% car, 0.9% public transportation, 2.2% walk, 1.8% work from home (2000); Travel time to work: 34.7% less than 15 minutes, 26.0% 15 to 30 minutes, 17.4% 30 to 45 minutes, 13.7% 45 to 60 minutes, 8.2% 60 minutes or more (2000)

CAIRO (town). Covers a land area of 59.974 square miles and a water area of 0.162 square miles. Located at 42.30° N. Lat.; 74.00° W. Long. Elevation is 343 feet.
Population: 5,418 (1990); 6,355 (2000); 6,606 (2005); 6,857 (2010 projected); Race: 97.0% White, 0.6% Black, 0.3% Asian, 4.3% Hispanic of any race (2005); Density: 110.1 persons per square mile (2005); Average household size: 2.44 (2005); Median age: 41.4 (2005); Males per 100 females: 92.5 (2005); Marriage status: 22.5% never married, 57.7% now married, 7.2% widowed, 12.6% divorced (2000); Foreign born: 7.5% (2000); Ancestry (includes multiple ancestries): 27.1% German, 21.8% Irish, 19.1% Italian, 7.9% Other groups, 6.4% English (2000).
Economy: Single-family building permits issued: 36 (2005); Multi-family building permits issued: 2 (2005); Employment by occupation: 9.2% management, 17.1% professional, 18.1% services, 25.8% sales, 1.0% farming, 15.0% construction, 13.8% production (2000).
Income: Per capita income: $23,489 (2005); Median household income: $45,069 (2005); Average household income: $57,261 (2005); Percent of households with income of $100,000 or more: 13.8% (2005); Poverty rate: 10.4% (2000).
Education: Percent of population age 25 and over with: High school diploma (including GED) or higher: 76.4% (2005); Bachelor's degree or higher: 12.1% (2005); Master's degree or higher: 5.4% (2005).
School District(s)
Cairo-Durham Central School District (KG-12)
    2003-04 Enrollment: 1,813 . . . . (518) 622-8534
Housing: Homeownership rate: 72.8% (2005); Median home value: $124,713 (2005); Median rent: $414 per month (2000); Median age of housing: 32 years (2000).
Safety: Violent crime rate: 6.1 per 10,000 population; Property crime rate: 41.3 per 10,000 population (2004).
Transportation: Commute to work: 93.4% car, 0.2% public transportation, 2.7% walk, 3.2% work from home (2000); Travel time to work: 29.8% less than 15 minutes, 35.0% 15 to 30 minutes, 15.2% 30 to 45 minutes, 8.1% 45 to 60 minutes, 11.9% 60 minutes or more (2000)

CAIRO (CDP). Covers a land area of 4.250 square miles and a water area of 0.010 square miles. Located at 42.30° N. Lat.; 74.00° W. Long.
Population: 1,273 (1990); 1,390 (2000); 1,392 (2005); 1,395 (2010 projected); Race: 94.6% White, 1.2% Black, 0.2% Asian, 7.8% Hispanic of any race (2005); Density: 327.5 persons per square mile (2005); Average household size: 2.29 (2005); Median age: 41.1 (2005); Males per 100 females: 84.6 (2005); Marriage status: 25.1% never married, 53.9% now married, 8.6% widowed, 12.5% divorced (2000); Foreign born: 5.8% (2000); Ancestry (includes multiple ancestries): 28.4% Italian, 27.2% German, 19.9% Irish, 9.1% Other groups, 7.8% French Canadian (2000).
Economy: Employment by occupation: 10.3% management, 18.3% professional, 10.1% services, 27.9% sales, 0.0% farming, 16.8% construction, 16.6% production (2000).
Income: Per capita income: $20,792 (2005); Median household income: $34,722 (2005); Average household income: $47,299 (2005); Percent of households with income of $100,000 or more: 9.2% (2005); Poverty rate: 13.2% (2000).
Education: Percent of population age 25 and over with: High school diploma (including GED) or higher: 65.2% (2005); Bachelor's degree or higher: 14.9% (2005); Master's degree or higher: 5.3% (2005).
Housing: Homeownership rate: 58.9% (2005); Median home value: $126,033 (2005); Median rent: $387 per month (2000); Median age of housing: 41 years (2000).
Transportation: Commute to work: 89.8% car, 1.0% public transportation, 4.3% walk, 3.9% work from home (2000); Travel time to work: 31.6% less than 15 minutes, 34.0% 15 to 30 minutes, 11.9% 30 to 45 minutes, 5.5% 45 to 60 minutes, 17.0% 60 minutes or more (2000)

CATSKILL (village). Covers a land area of 2.238 square miles and a water area of 0.592 square miles. Located at 42.21° N. Lat.; 73.86° W. Long. Elevation is 47 feet.
Population: 4,690 (1990); 4,392 (2000); 4,347 (2005); 4,331 (2010 projected); Race: 81.4% White, 12.8% Black, 0.9% Asian, 7.0% Hispanic of any race (2005); Density: 1,941.9 persons per square mile (2005); Average household size: 2.45 (2005); Median age: 37.4 (2005); Males per 100 females: 89.4 (2005); Marriage status: 32.1% never married, 48.8% now married, 10.8% widowed, 8.4% divorced (2000); Foreign born: 4.3% (2000); Ancestry (includes multiple ancestries): 21.3% Irish, 20.4% Other groups, 18.7% German, 14.7% Italian, 7.4% United States or American (2000).
Economy: Single-family building permits issued: 7 (2005); Multi-family building permits issued: 0 (2005); Employment by occupation: 8.3% management, 10.3% professional, 28.8% services, 30.3% sales, 0.0% farming, 8.9% construction, 13.4% production (2000).
Income: Per capita income: $17,009 (2005); Median household income: $30,748 (2005); Average household income: $41,184 (2005); Percent of households with income of $100,000 or more: 8.1% (2005); Poverty rate: 19.0% (2000).
Education: Percent of population age 25 and over with: High school diploma (including GED) or higher: 77.8% (2005); Bachelor's degree or higher: 13.5% (2005); Master's degree or higher: 7.1% (2005).
School District(s)
Catskill Central School District (KG-12)
    2003-04 Enrollment: 1,817 . . . . (518) 943-4696
Two-year College(s)
Columbia Green Beauty School
    Fall 2004 Enrollment: 26 . . . . (518) 943-2224
Housing: Homeownership rate: 52.5% (2005); Median home value: $113,951 (2005); Median rent: $435 per month (2000); Median age of housing: 60+ years (2000).
Safety: Violent crime rate: 36.6 per 10,000 population; Property crime rate: 462.5 per 10,000 population (2004).
Newspapers: Daily Mail (Circulation 33,789)
Transportation: Commute to work: 85.5% car, 1.1% public transportation, 11.0% walk, 1.3% work from home (2000); Travel time to work: 44.6% less than 15 minutes, 26.6% 15 to 30 minutes, 9.3% 30 to 45 minutes, 10.0% 45 to 60 minutes, 9.5% 60 minutes or more (2000)
Additional Information Contacts
Greene County Chamber of Commerce . . . . (518) 943-4222
    http://www.greenecounty-chamber.com
Village of Catskill . . . . (518) 943-2141
    http://www.townofcatskill.com/

CATSKILL (town). Covers a land area of 60.530 square miles and a water area of 3.649 square miles. Located at 42.21° N. Lat.; 73.92° W. Long. Elevation is 47 feet.
History: Originally known as Catskill Landing, the settlement of Catskill was subsidiary to the old Dutch hamlet of Kaatskill, in the hills to the west. Mountains, creeks, and village were named by the Dutch for the wildcats that occasionally came down from the hills, where they roamed in large numbers. In the heyday of turnpike and river transportation, the place bustled with prosperity. Thomas Cole lived and painted in the village. Settled 17th, incorporated in 1806.
Population: 11,965 (1990); 11,849 (2000); 11,995 (2005); 12,154 (2010 projected); Race: 89.6% White, 6.2% Black, 0.9% Asian, 4.7% Hispanic of any race (2005); Density: 198.2 persons per square mile (2005); Average household size: 2.44 (2005); Median age: 40.8 (2005); Males per 100 females: 90.0 (2005); Marriage status: 25.5% never married, 54.6% now married, 9.2% widowed, 10.7% divorced (2000); Foreign born: 4.6%

(2000); Ancestry (includes multiple ancestries): 22.2% Irish, 20.6% German, 18.2% Italian, 12.4% Other groups, 7.5% English (2000).
Economy: Connected with the manufacturing town of Hudson, N.Y. by the Rip Van Winkle Bridge (completed 1935), it is a gateway to resorts in the Catskill Mts. The Catskill Game Farm is nearby. Single-family building permits issued: 44 (2005); Multi-family building permits issued: 8 (2005); Employment by occupation: 11.9% management, 17.5% professional, 19.5% services, 26.8% sales, 1.0% farming, 10.2% construction, 13.2% production (2000).
Income: Per capita income: $22,030 (2005); Median household income: $38,484 (2005); Average household income: $52,884 (2005); Percent of households with income of $100,000 or more: 11.6% (2005); Poverty rate: 14.9% (2000).
Education: Percent of population age 25 and over with: High school diploma (including GED) or higher: 79.2% (2005); Bachelor's degree or higher: 14.0% (2005); Master's degree or higher: 6.0% (2005).
Housing: Homeownership rate: 64.6% (2005); Median home value: $133,943 (2005); Median rent: $442 per month (2000); Median age of housing: 46 years (2000).
Transportation: Commute to work: 87.8% car, 1.2% public transportation, 5.1% walk, 4.9% work from home (2000); Travel time to work: 33.9% less than 15 minutes, 30.7% 15 to 30 minutes, 13.4% 30 to 45 minutes, 8.1% 45 to 60 minutes, 14.0% 60 minutes or more (2000)
Additional Information Contacts
Town of Catskill . . . . (518) 943-2141
http://www.townofcatskillny.gov/Public_Documents/index

CLIMAX (unincorporated postal area, zip code 12042). Covers a land area of 14.618 square miles and a water area of 0.147 square miles. Located at 42.40° N. Lat.; 73.90° W. Long. Elevation is 254 feet.
Population: 0 (2000); Race: 98.9% White, 0.0% Black, 0.0% Asian, 1.8% Hispanic of any race (2000); Density: 0.0 persons per square mile (2000); Age: 23.0% under 18, 13.3% over 64 (2000); Marriage status: 21.8% never married, 69.3% now married, 4.3% widowed, 4.6% divorced (2000); Foreign born: 5.2% (2000); Ancestry (includes multiple ancestries): 28.1% German, 27.9% Irish, 21.6% Italian, 20.5% English, 7.5% French (except Basque) (2000).
Economy: Employment by occupation: 5.5% management, 22.7% professional, 9.9% services, 37.2% sales, 0.0% farming, 14.0% construction, 10.8% production (2000).
Income: Per capita income: $15,764 (2000); Median household income: $41,313 (2000); Poverty rate: 8.4% (2000).
Education: Percent of population age 25 and over with: High school diploma (including GED) or higher: 92.4% (2000); Bachelor's degree or higher: 14.5% (2000).
Housing: Homeownership rate: 85.9% (2000); Median home value: $107,100 (2000); Median rent: $470 per month (2000); Median age of housing: 33 years (2000).
Transportation: Commute to work: 86.6% car, 6.7% public transportation, 2.0% walk, 4.7% work from home (2000); Travel time to work: 22.0% less than 15 minutes, 31.7% 15 to 30 minutes, 25.6% 30 to 45 minutes, 11.6% 45 to 60 minutes, 9.1% 60 minutes or more (2000)

CORNWALLVILLE (unincorporated postal area, zip code 12418). Covers a land area of 17.772 square miles and a water area of 0 square miles. Located at 42.35° N. Lat.; 74.15° W. Long.
Population: 0 (2000); Race: 98.7% White, 0.0% Black, 0.0% Asian, 0.0% Hispanic of any race (2000); Density: 0.0 persons per square mile (2000); Age: 22.9% under 18, 20.5% over 64 (2000); Marriage status: 12.4% never married, 72.3% now married, 10.8% widowed, 4.5% divorced (2000); Foreign born: 14.5% (2000); Ancestry (includes multiple ancestries): 26.3% Irish, 14.5% United States or American, 11.1% German, 9.8% Other groups, 9.8% Italian (2000).
Economy: Employment by occupation: 12.9% management, 18.0% professional, 16.5% services, 35.6% sales, 0.0% farming, 2.1% construction, 14.9% production (2000).
Income: Per capita income: $18,408 (2000); Median household income: $35,750 (2000); Poverty rate: 10.3% (2000).
Education: Percent of population age 25 and over with: High school diploma (including GED) or higher: 80.1% (2000); Bachelor's degree or higher: 20.4% (2000).
Housing: Homeownership rate: 89.1% (2000); Median home value: $69,000 (2000); Median rent: $325 per month (2000); Median age of housing: 28 years (2000).

Transportation: Commute to work: 91.3% car, 4.9% public transportation, 2.2% walk, 0.0% work from home (2000); Travel time to work: 24.0% less than 15 minutes, 31.7% 15 to 30 minutes, 20.2% 30 to 45 minutes, 9.8% 45 to 60 minutes, 14.2% 60 minutes or more (2000)

COXSACKIE (village). Covers a land area of 2.173 square miles and a water area of 0.430 square miles. Located at 42.35° N. Lat.; 73.80° W. Long. Elevation is 139 feet.
Population: 2,789 (1990); 2,895 (2000); 2,872 (2005); 2,849 (2010 projected); Race: 96.5% White, 1.7% Black, 0.7% Asian, 2.6% Hispanic of any race (2005); Density: 1,321.5 persons per square mile (2005); Average household size: 2.43 (2005); Median age: 37.6 (2005); Males per 100 females: 88.6 (2005); Marriage status: 28.3% never married, 51.6% now married, 9.7% widowed, 10.5% divorced (2000); Foreign born: 3.2% (2000); Ancestry (includes multiple ancestries): 20.6% Irish, 19.3% German, 15.7% Italian, 10.9% English, 10.7% United States or American (2000).
Economy: Single-family building permits issued: 6 (2005); Multi-family building permits issued: 0 (2005); Employment by occupation: 11.1% management, 19.9% professional, 18.1% services, 26.9% sales, 0.4% farming, 9.2% construction, 14.5% production (2000).
Income: Per capita income: $20,651 (2005); Median household income: $41,567 (2005); Average household income: $49,336 (2005); Percent of households with income of $100,000 or more: 8.8% (2005); Poverty rate: 12.7% (2000).
Education: Percent of population age 25 and over with: High school diploma (including GED) or higher: 81.0% (2005); Bachelor's degree or higher: 16.0% (2005); Master's degree or higher: 9.0% (2005).
School District(s)
Coxsackie-Athens Central School District (KG-12)
    2003-04 Enrollment: 2,506 . . . . (518) 731-1710
Housing: Homeownership rate: 60.0% (2005); Median home value: $132,022 (2005); Median rent: $403 per month (2000); Median age of housing: 59 years (2000).
Safety: Violent crime rate: 31.2 per 10,000 population; Property crime rate: 83.3 per 10,000 population (2004).
Transportation: Commute to work: 94.0% car, 0.9% public transportation, 3.1% walk, 2.0% work from home (2000); Travel time to work: 34.6% less than 15 minutes, 24.2% 15 to 30 minutes, 27.6% 30 to 45 minutes, 8.1% 45 to 60 minutes, 5.4% 60 minutes or more (2000)
Additional Information Contacts
Coxsackie Chamber of Commerce . . . . (518) 731-7300
http://www.coxsackieareachamber.com

COXSACKIE (town). Covers a land area of 36.897 square miles and a water area of 1.479 square miles. Located at 42.34° N. Lat.; 73.84° W. Long. Elevation is 139 feet.
History: Franklin air-cooled automobile engine invented here. Settled by the Dutch before 1700; incorporated 1867.
Population: 7,633 (1990); 8,884 (2000); 8,970 (2005); 9,074 (2010 projected); Race: 68.8% White, 22.4% Black, 0.9% Asian, 13.5% Hispanic of any race (2005); Density: 243.1 persons per square mile (2005); Average household size: 3.67 (2005); Median age: 29.5 (2005); Males per 100 females: 187.8 (2005); Marriage status: 46.8% never married, 41.7% now married, 5.6% widowed, 5.9% divorced (2000); Foreign born: 6.8% (2000); Ancestry (includes multiple ancestries): 14.8% Irish, 13.6% German, 12.6% Italian, 7.8% United States or American, 5.8% English (2000).
Economy: In diversified-farming area. Manufacturing of sheet metal goods. Single-family building permits issued: 60 (2005); Multi-family building permits issued: 16 (2005); Employment by occupation: 11.8% management, 17.5% professional, 17.4% services, 26.5% sales, 0.9% farming, 10.8% construction, 15.1% production (2000).
Income: Per capita income: $18,351 (2005); Median household income: $41,618 (2005); Average household income: $50,585 (2005); Percent of households with income of $100,000 or more: 8.7% (2005); Poverty rate: 12.9% (2000).
Education: Percent of population age 25 and over with: High school diploma (including GED) or higher: 69.7% (2005); Bachelor's degree or higher: 12.9% (2005); Master's degree or higher: 5.4% (2005).
Housing: Homeownership rate: 68.9% (2005); Median home value: $133,406 (2005); Median rent: $411 per month (2000); Median age of housing: 38 years (2000).
Transportation: Commute to work: 92.5% car, 1.6% public transportation, 2.8% walk, 2.4% work from home (2000); Travel time to work: 31.8% less

than 15 minutes, 24.9% 15 to 30 minutes, 26.5% 30 to 45 minutes, 9.3% 45 to 60 minutes, 7.5% 60 minutes or more (2000)

Additional Information Contacts
Town of Coxsackie................................(518) 731-2727
http://www.coxsackie.org/

DURHAM (town). Covers a land area of 49.250 square miles and a water area of 0.020 square miles. Located at 42.38° N. Lat.; 74.14° W. Long.

Population: 2,324 (1990); 2,592 (2000); 2,755 (2005); 2,912 (2010 projected); Race: 98.4% White, 0.1% Black, 0.5% Asian, 1.4% Hispanic of any race (2005); Density: 55.9 persons per square mile (2005); Average household size: 2.43 (2005); Median age: 44.0 (2005); Males per 100 females: 99.2 (2005); Marriage status: 19.6% never married, 62.7% now married, 8.3% widowed, 9.4% divorced (2000); Foreign born: 10.3% (2000); Ancestry (includes multiple ancestries): 30.4% Irish, 16.8% German, 11.4% Italian, 11.3% United States or American, 6.6% Other groups (2000).

Economy: Single-family building permits issued: 5 (2005); Multi-family building permits issued: 0 (2005); Employment by occupation: 12.1% management, 19.6% professional, 14.9% services, 23.7% sales, 1.0% farming, 10.9% construction, 17.7% production (2000).

Income: Per capita income: $20,706 (2005); Median household income: $38,824 (2005); Average household income: $49,698 (2005); Percent of households with income of $100,000 or more: 9.2% (2005); Poverty rate: 11.5% (2000).

Education: Percent of population age 25 and over with: High school diploma (including GED) or higher: 79.1% (2005); Bachelor's degree or higher: 17.9% (2005); Master's degree or higher: 8.3% (2005).

School District(s)
Cairo-Durham Central School District (KG-12)
2003-04 Enrollment: 1,813 ....(518) 622-8534

Housing: Homeownership rate: 80.8% (2005); Median home value: $132,549 (2005); Median rent: $361 per month (2000); Median age of housing: 31 years (2000).

Safety: Violent crime rate: 0.0 per 10,000 population; Property crime rate: 11.3 per 10,000 population (2004).

Transportation: Commute to work: 90.2% car, 3.0% public transportation, 1.6% walk, 4.5% work from home (2000); Travel time to work: 25.9% less than 15 minutes, 24.6% 15 to 30 minutes, 24.6% 30 to 45 minutes, 11.5% 45 to 60 minutes, 13.4% 60 minutes or more (2000)

EARLTON (unincorporated postal area, zip code 12058). Covers a land area of 18.339 square miles and a water area of 0.276 square miles. Located at 42.35° N. Lat.; 73.92° W. Long.

Population: 0 (2000); Race: 95.1% White, 0.3% Black, 1.0% Asian, 2.6% Hispanic of any race (2000); Density: 0.0 persons per square mile (2000); Age: 21.6% under 18, 12.8% over 64 (2000); Marriage status: 24.9% never married, 60.3% now married, 5.6% widowed, 9.1% divorced (2000); Foreign born: 6.1% (2000); Ancestry (includes multiple ancestries): 22.3% German, 18.4% Italian, 17.3% Irish, 11.6% United States or American, 9.1% Other groups (2000).

Economy: Employment by occupation: 10.0% management, 20.6% professional, 15.7% services, 26.6% sales, 2.0% farming, 11.1% construction, 14.0% production (2000).

Income: Per capita income: $17,136 (2000); Median household income: $42,898 (2000); Poverty rate: 7.3% (2000).

Education: Percent of population age 25 and over with: High school diploma (including GED) or higher: 81.5% (2000); Bachelor's degree or higher: 10.9% (2000).

Housing: Homeownership rate: 76.4% (2000); Median home value: $93,100 (2000); Median rent: $447 per month (2000); Median age of housing: 24 years (2000).

Transportation: Commute to work: 91.3% car, 0.0% public transportation, 3.4% walk, 4.3% work from home (2000); Travel time to work: 18.7% less than 15 minutes, 40.9% 15 to 30 minutes, 18.3% 30 to 45 minutes, 15.2% 45 to 60 minutes, 6.9% 60 minutes or more (2000)

EAST DURHAM (unincorporated postal area, zip code 12423). Covers a land area of 13.691 square miles and a water area of 0 square miles. Located at 42.37° N. Lat.; 74.10° W. Long.

Population: 0 (2000); Race: 99.6% White, 0.0% Black, 0.0% Asian, 4.6% Hispanic of any race (2000); Density: 0.0 persons per square mile (2000); Age: 20.1% under 18, 20.0% over 64 (2000); Marriage status: 20.8% never married, 61.8% now married, 9.2% widowed, 8.2% divorced (2000); Foreign born: 12.3% (2000); Ancestry (includes multiple ancestries): 34.9% Irish, 22.9% German, 12.9% Italian, 10.1% United States or American, 6.8% Other groups (2000).

Economy: Employment by occupation: 11.4% management, 18.0% professional, 12.9% services, 25.5% sales, 1.7% farming, 13.1% construction, 17.3% production (2000).

Income: Per capita income: $16,113 (2000); Median household income: $29,402 (2000); Poverty rate: 14.4% (2000).

Education: Percent of population age 25 and over with: High school diploma (including GED) or higher: 78.8% (2000); Bachelor's degree or higher: 14.9% (2000).

Housing: Homeownership rate: 73.8% (2000); Median home value: $100,300 (2000); Median rent: $350 per month (2000); Median age of housing: 28 years (2000).

Transportation: Commute to work: 92.0% car, 2.4% public transportation, 0.7% walk, 3.6% work from home (2000); Travel time to work: 30.3% less than 15 minutes, 22.8% 15 to 30 minutes, 20.3% 30 to 45 minutes, 16.3% 45 to 60 minutes, 10.3% 60 minutes or more (2000)

EAST JEWETT (unincorporated postal area, zip code 12424). Covers a land area of 21.290 square miles and a water area of 0.120 square miles. Located at 42.24° N. Lat.; 74.15° W. Long.

Population: 0 (2000); Race: 99.4% White, 0.0% Black, 0.6% Asian, 2.1% Hispanic of any race (2000); Density: 0.0 persons per square mile (2000); Age: 21.6% under 18, 20.4% over 64 (2000); Marriage status: 16.2% never married, 68.3% now married, 7.0% widowed, 8.5% divorced (2000); Foreign born: 10.5% (2000); Ancestry (includes multiple ancestries): 22.2% Irish, 17.1% Italian, 15.6% English, 15.0% German, 8.4% United States or American (2000).

Economy: Resort village. Employment by occupation: 20.4% management, 31.4% professional, 12.4% services, 13.9% sales, 1.5% farming, 15.3% construction, 5.1% production (2000).

Income: Per capita income: $21,215 (2000); Median household income: $40,972 (2000); Poverty rate: 11.7% (2000).

Education: Percent of population age 25 and over with: High school diploma (including GED) or higher: 85.4% (2000); Bachelor's degree or higher: 45.5% (2000).

Housing: Homeownership rate: 77.5% (2000); Median home value: $113,500 (2000); Median rent: $475 per month (2000); Median age of housing: 24 years (2000).

Transportation: Commute to work: 83.5% car, 3.0% public transportation, 5.3% walk, 4.5% work from home (2000); Travel time to work: 22.8% less than 15 minutes, 31.5% 15 to 30 minutes, 15.7% 30 to 45 minutes, 7.1% 45 to 60 minutes, 22.8% 60 minutes or more (2000)

ELKA PARK (unincorporated postal area, zip code 12427). Covers a land area of 46.252 square miles and a water area of 0.018 square miles. Located at 42.16° N. Lat.; 74.15° W. Long.

Population: 0 (2000); Race: 100.0% White, 0.0% Black, 0.0% Asian, 1.4% Hispanic of any race (2000); Density: 0.0 persons per square mile (2000); Age: 27.9% under 18, 13.2% over 64 (2000); Marriage status: 30.8% never married, 52.5% now married, 5.0% widowed, 11.6% divorced (2000); Foreign born: 1.9% (2000); Ancestry (includes multiple ancestries): 52.2% Irish, 25.0% German, 16.1% Italian, 15.4% French (except Basque), 4.8% United States or American (2000).

Economy: Employment by occupation: 14.1% management, 8.9% professional, 15.2% services, 34.6% sales, 0.0% farming, 24.6% construction, 2.6% production (2000).

Income: Per capita income: $21,376 (2000); Median household income: $47,375 (2000); Poverty rate: 17.5% (2000).

Education: Percent of population age 25 and over with: High school diploma (including GED) or higher: 88.2% (2000); Bachelor's degree or higher: 30.2% (2000).

Housing: Homeownership rate: 88.4% (2000); Median home value: $98,300 (2000); Median rent: $479 per month (2000); Median age of housing: 60+ years (2000).

Transportation: Commute to work: 94.2% car, 3.1% public transportation, 2.6% walk, 0.0% work from home (2000); Travel time to work: 40.3% less than 15 minutes, 16.2% 15 to 30 minutes, 2.6% 30 to 45 minutes, 12.0% 45 to 60 minutes, 28.8% 60 minutes or more (2000)

FREEHOLD (unincorporated postal area, zip code 12431). Covers a land area of 16.561 square miles and a water area of 0 square miles. Located at 42.36° N. Lat.; 74.02° W. Long. Elevation is 428 feet.

Population: 0 (2000); Race: 96.2% White, 0.0% Black, 0.0% Asian, 5.1% Hispanic of any race (2000); Density: 0.0 persons per square mile (2000); Age: 29.1% under 18, 10.4% over 64 (2000); Marriage status: 9.6% never married, 73.2% now married, 7.9% widowed, 9.3% divorced (2000); Foreign born: 2.6% (2000); Ancestry (includes multiple ancestries): 24.9% Irish, 22.7% German, 19.3% Italian, 10.3% Dutch, 8.0% English (2000).
Economy: Employment by occupation: 11.3% management, 24.0% professional, 15.0% services, 25.7% sales, 3.1% farming, 9.1% construction, 11.8% production (2000).
Income: Per capita income: $19,959 (2000); Median household income: $45,862 (2000); Poverty rate: 6.0% (2000).
Education: Percent of population age 25 and over with: High school diploma (including GED) or higher: 78.2% (2000); Bachelor's degree or higher: 19.8% (2000).
Housing: Homeownership rate: 85.3% (2000); Median home value: $103,000 (2000); Median rent: $375 per month (2000); Median age of housing: 26 years (2000).
Transportation: Commute to work: 92.6% car, 1.6% public transportation, 3.2% walk, 2.6% work from home (2000); Travel time to work: 30.7% less than 15 minutes, 27.2% 15 to 30 minutes, 17.2% 30 to 45 minutes, 13.4% 45 to 60 minutes, 11.6% 60 minutes or more (2000)

GREENVILLE (town).
Covers a land area of 38.927 square miles and a water area of 0.194 square miles. Located at 42.39° N. Lat.; 74.01° W. Long. Elevation is 708 feet.
Population: 3,135 (1990); 3,316 (2000); 3,386 (2005); 3,460 (2010 projected); Race: 96.1% White, 0.4% Black, 2.0% Asian, 1.9% Hispanic of any race (2005); Density: 87.0 persons per square mile (2005); Average household size: 2.43 (2005); Median age: 42.5 (2005); Males per 100 females: 93.8 (2005); Marriage status: 16.5% never married, 65.5% now married, 9.8% widowed, 8.2% divorced (2000); Foreign born: 7.6% (2000); Ancestry (includes multiple ancestries): 28.6% Irish, 23.3% German, 19.2% Italian, 14.2% English, 7.4% Dutch (2000).
Economy: Resort village. Single-family building permits issued: 40 (2005); Multi-family building permits issued: 0 (2005); Employment by occupation: 12.9% management, 21.5% professional, 14.0% services, 24.9% sales, 2.5% farming, 8.4% construction, 15.8% production (2000).
Income: Per capita income: $22,109 (2005); Median household income: $43,011 (2005); Average household income: $53,663 (2005); Percent of households with income of $100,000 or more: 10.0% (2005); Poverty rate: 8.7% (2000).
Education: Percent of population age 25 and over with: High school diploma (including GED) or higher: 83.9% (2005); Bachelor's degree or higher: 21.5% (2005); Master's degree or higher: 8.0% (2005).

School District(s)
Greenville Central School District (KG-12)
    2003-04 Enrollment: 1,376 . . . . (518) 966-5070
Housing: Homeownership rate: 79.3% (2005); Median home value: $142,980 (2005); Median rent: $423 per month (2000); Median age of housing: 33 years (2000).
Transportation: Commute to work: 87.1% car, 1.8% public transportation, 7.8% walk, 3.3% work from home (2000); Travel time to work: 33.3% less than 15 minutes, 24.7% 15 to 30 minutes, 19.3% 30 to 45 minutes, 10.9% 45 to 60 minutes, 11.8% 60 minutes or more (2000)
Additional Information Contacts
Greenville Chamber of Commerce . . . . (518) 966-5050
   http://www.greenecounty-chamber.com

GREENVILLE (CDP).
Covers a land area of 3.449 square miles and a water area of 0.027 square miles. Located at 42.40° N. Lat.; 74.01° W. Long.
Population: 508 (1990); 493 (2000); 492 (2005); 492 (2010 projected); Race: 99.0% White, 0.2% Black, 0.0% Asian, 0.8% Hispanic of any race (2005); Density: 142.6 persons per square mile (2005); Average household size: 2.11 (2005); Median age: 48.9 (2005); Males per 100 females: 87.1 (2005); Marriage status: 27.1% never married, 53.4% now married, 11.5% widowed, 8.0% divorced (2000); Foreign born: 24.0% (2000); Ancestry (includes multiple ancestries): 28.2% English, 26.7% Irish, 19.8% Italian, 16.8% German, 7.6% Dutch (2000).
Economy: Employment by occupation: 24.3% management, 18.0% professional, 18.0% services, 22.8% sales, 0.0% farming, 3.9% construction, 13.1% production (2000).
Income: Per capita income: $22,835 (2005); Median household income: $38,214 (2005); Average household income: $48,219 (2005); Percent of households with income of $100,000 or more: 12.0% (2005); Poverty rate: 21.7% (2000).
Education: Percent of population age 25 and over with: High school diploma (including GED) or higher: 87.6% (2005); Bachelor's degree or higher: 34.7% (2005); Master's degree or higher: 10.8% (2005).
Housing: Homeownership rate: 70.0% (2005); Median home value: $144,817 (2005); Median rent: $522 per month (2000); Median age of housing: 48 years (2000).
Transportation: Commute to work: 83.0% car, 0.0% public transportation, 13.1% walk, 3.9% work from home (2000); Travel time to work: 33.3% less than 15 minutes, 25.3% 15 to 30 minutes, 23.7% 30 to 45 minutes, 10.6% 45 to 60 minutes, 7.1% 60 minutes or more (2000)

HALCOTT (town).
Covers a land area of 23.040 square miles and a water area of 0 square miles. Located at 42.20° N. Lat.; 74.48° W. Long.
Population: 189 (1990); 193 (2000); 194 (2005); 197 (2010 projected); Race: 99.0% White, 0.0% Black, 0.0% Asian, 1.5% Hispanic of any race (2005); Density: 8.4 persons per square mile (2005); Average household size: 2.28 (2005); Median age: 48.3 (2005); Males per 100 females: 106.4 (2005); Marriage status: 25.0% never married, 63.6% now married, 4.5% widowed, 6.8% divorced (2000); Foreign born: 9.8% (2000); Ancestry (includes multiple ancestries): 22.0% German, 21.5% English, 20.6% Italian, 8.4% Greek, 8.4% Irish (2000).
Economy: Single-family building permits issued: 3 (2005); Multi-family building permits issued: 0 (2005); Employment by occupation: 20.0% management, 17.9% professional, 17.9% services, 16.8% sales, 0.0% farming, 20.0% construction, 7.4% production (2000).
Income: Per capita income: $27,835 (2005); Median household income: $36,607 (2005); Average household income: $63,529 (2005); Percent of households with income of $100,000 or more: 16.5% (2005); Poverty rate: 20.8% (2000).
Education: Percent of population age 25 and over with: High school diploma (including GED) or higher: 85.1% (2005); Bachelor's degree or higher: 18.2% (2005); Master's degree or higher: 10.4% (2005).
Housing: Homeownership rate: 82.4% (2005); Median home value: $160,000 (2005); Median rent: $463 per month (2000); Median age of housing: 31 years (2000).
Transportation: Commute to work: 82.6% car, 3.3% public transportation, 3.3% walk, 10.9% work from home (2000); Travel time to work: 14.6% less than 15 minutes, 29.3% 15 to 30 minutes, 18.3% 30 to 45 minutes, 13.4% 45 to 60 minutes, 24.4% 60 minutes or more (2000)
Additional Information Contacts
Town of Halcott . . . . (845) 254-9920
   http://www.townofhalcott.com/

HANNACROIX (unincorporated postal area, zip code 12087).
Covers a land area of 13.021 square miles and a water area of 0.183 square miles. Located at 42.43° N. Lat.; 73.89° W. Long.
Population: 0 (2000); Race: 100.0% White, 0.0% Black, 0.0% Asian, 0.0% Hispanic of any race (2000); Density: 0.0 persons per square mile (2000); Age: 33.4% under 18, 6.1% over 64 (2000); Marriage status: 32.9% never married, 62.7% now married, 3.1% widowed, 1.2% divorced (2000); Foreign born: 1.7% (2000); Ancestry (includes multiple ancestries): 33.3% German, 18.1% Irish, 12.9% Italian, 11.3% Dutch, 9.5% English (2000).
Economy: Employment by occupation: 20.3% management, 9.7% professional, 15.2% services, 20.3% sales, 12.2% farming, 17.3% construction, 5.1% production (2000).
Income: Per capita income: $17,260 (2000); Median household income: $49,135 (2000); Poverty rate: 15.3% (2000).
Education: Percent of population age 25 and over with: High school diploma (including GED) or higher: 78.3% (2000); Bachelor's degree or higher: 23.0% (2000).
Housing: Homeownership rate: 67.9% (2000); Median home value: $124,300 (2000); Median rent: $471 per month (2000); Median age of housing: 34 years (2000).
Transportation: Commute to work: 87.8% car, 0.0% public transportation, 0.0% walk, 12.2% work from home (2000); Travel time to work: 10.6% less than 15 minutes, 27.4% 15 to 30 minutes, 35.6% 30 to 45 minutes, 21.6% 45 to 60 minutes, 4.8% 60 minutes or more (2000)

HENSONVILLE (unincorporated postal area, zip code 12439).
Covers a land area of 0.445 square miles and a water area of 0 square miles. Located at 42.30° N. Lat.; 74.22° W. Long.
Population: 0 (2000); Race: 100.0% White, 0.0% Black, 0.0% Asian, 0.0% Hispanic of any race (2000); Density: 0.0 persons per square mile (2000);

Age: 28.7% under 18, 13.9% over 64 (2000); Marriage status: 31.8% never married, 47.1% now married, 4.7% widowed, 16.5% divorced (2000); Foreign born: 4.3% (2000); Ancestry (includes multiple ancestries): 31.3% German, 17.4% Irish, 15.7% Norwegian, 11.3% Greek, 11.3% Italian (2000).
Economy: Employment by occupation: 24.1% management, 6.9% professional, 25.9% services, 6.9% sales, 0.0% farming, 20.7% construction, 15.5% production (2000).
Income: Per capita income: $18,852 (2000); Median household income: $29,167 (2000); Poverty rate: 6.3% (2000).
Education: Percent of population age 25 and over with: High school diploma (including GED) or higher: 87.8% (2000); Bachelor's degree or higher: 23.0% (2000).
Housing: Homeownership rate: 38.0% (2000); Median home value: $110,400 (2000); Median rent: $400 per month (2000); Median age of housing: 22 years (2000).
Transportation: Commute to work: 75.9% car, 0.0% public transportation, 24.1% walk, 0.0% work from home (2000); Travel time to work: 63.8% less than 15 minutes, 13.8% 15 to 30 minutes, 8.6% 30 to 45 minutes, 6.9% 45 to 60 minutes, 6.9% 60 minutes or more (2000)

HUNTER (village). Covers a land area of 1.617 square miles and a water area of 0.035 square miles. Located at 42.20° N. Lat.; 74.21° W. Long. Elevation is 1,603 feet.
Population: 458 (1990); 490 (2000); 514 (2005); 539 (2010 projected); Race: 98.4% White, 0.4% Black, 0.2% Asian, 1.6% Hispanic of any race (2005); Density: 317.8 persons per square mile (2005); Average household size: 2.04 (2005); Median age: 46.6 (2005); Males per 100 females: 104.8 (2005); Marriage status: 25.1% never married, 54.1% now married, 5.3% widowed, 15.5% divorced (2000); Foreign born: 10.8% (2000); Ancestry (includes multiple ancestries): 22.9% Italian, 13.6% German, 13.3% Irish, 12.5% English, 10.2% Polish (2000).
Economy: Single-family building permits issued: 4 (2005); Multi-family building permits issued: 0 (2005); Employment by occupation: 11.2% management, 20.2% professional, 25.5% services, 18.6% sales, 1.6% farming, 12.2% construction, 10.6% production (2000).
Income: Per capita income: $26,522 (2005); Median household income: $38,103 (2005); Average household income: $54,097 (2005); Percent of households with income of $100,000 or more: 10.7% (2005); Poverty rate: 15.5% (2000).
Education: Percent of population age 25 and over with: High school diploma (including GED) or higher: 89.1% (2005); Bachelor's degree or higher: 20.7% (2005); Master's degree or higher: 6.6% (2005).

School District(s)
Hunter-Tannersville Central School District (KG-12)
    2003-04 Enrollment: 522 . . . . (518) 589-5400
Housing: Homeownership rate: 58.7% (2005); Median home value: $161,111 (2005); Median rent: $363 per month (2000); Median age of housing: 32 years (2000).
Transportation: Commute to work: 78.6% car, 3.2% public transportation, 12.3% walk, 4.3% work from home (2000); Travel time to work: 46.9% less than 15 minutes, 21.8% 15 to 30 minutes, 12.8% 30 to 45 minutes, 10.1% 45 to 60 minutes, 8.4% 60 minutes or more (2000)

Additional Information Contacts
Hunter Chamber of Commerce . . . . (518) 263-4900
    http://www.hunterchamber.org/

HUNTER (town). Covers a land area of 90.455 square miles and a water area of 0.281 square miles. Located at 42.18° N. Lat.; 74.16° W. Long. Elevation is 1,603 feet.
Population: 2,116 (1990); 2,721 (2000); 2,798 (2005); 2,888 (2010 projected); Race: 97.0% White, 0.6% Black, 0.1% Asian, 2.4% Hispanic of any race (2005); Density: 30.9 persons per square mile (2005); Average household size: 2.50 (2005); Median age: 41.4 (2005); Males per 100 females: 102.5 (2005); Marriage status: 32.2% never married, 47.8% now married, 8.8% widowed, 11.2% divorced (2000); Foreign born: 6.2% (2000); Ancestry (includes multiple ancestries): 22.7% Irish, 18.0% Italian, 14.0% German, 7.5% English, 6.8% Other groups (2000).
Economy: Resort village. Single-family building permits issued: 16 (2005); Multi-family building permits issued: 0 (2005); Employment by occupation: 9.9% management, 21.5% professional, 20.6% services, 23.8% sales, 4.7% farming, 12.8% construction, 6.7% production (2000).
Income: Per capita income: $22,724 (2005); Median household income: $38,520 (2005); Average household income: $50,413 (2005); Percent of households with income of $100,000 or more: 8.9% (2005); Poverty rate: 19.5% (2000).
Taxes: Total city taxes per capita: $504 (2004); City property taxes per capita: $446 (2004).
Education: Percent of population age 25 and over with: High school diploma (including GED) or higher: 80.7% (2005); Bachelor's degree or higher: 19.0% (2005); Master's degree or higher: 8.6% (2005).
Housing: Homeownership rate: 66.3% (2005); Median home value: $145,664 (2005); Median rent: $407 per month (2000); Median age of housing: 37 years (2000).
Transportation: Commute to work: 85.7% car, 1.7% public transportation, 6.8% walk, 4.8% work from home (2000); Travel time to work: 55.8% less than 15 minutes, 18.0% 15 to 30 minutes, 7.0% 30 to 45 minutes, 6.9% 45 to 60 minutes, 12.3% 60 minutes or more (2000)

JEFFERSON HEIGHTS (CDP). Aka Jefferson. Covers a land area of 1.468 square miles and a water area of 0.021 square miles. Located at 42.23° N. Lat.; 73.87° W. Long.
Population: 1,055 (1990); 1,104 (2000); 1,053 (2005); 1,043 (2010 projected); Race: 94.9% White, 2.8% Black, 1.6% Asian, 1.2% Hispanic of any race (2005); Density: 717.5 persons per square mile (2005); Average household size: 2.95 (2005); Median age: 60.4 (2005); Males per 100 females: 68.2 (2005); Marriage status: 14.7% never married, 54.4% now married, 16.9% widowed, 14.0% divorced (2000); Foreign born: 2.5% (2000); Ancestry (includes multiple ancestries): 27.1% German, 21.2% Italian, 18.7% Irish, 7.4% French (except Basque), 7.3% Dutch (2000).
Economy: Employment by occupation: 7.0% management, 22.8% professional, 14.3% services, 34.8% sales, 0.0% farming, 10.5% construction, 10.5% production (2000).
Income: Per capita income: $20,625 (2005); Median household income: $47,643 (2005); Average household income: $52,304 (2005); Percent of households with income of $100,000 or more: 8.1% (2005); Poverty rate: 7.5% (2000).
Education: Percent of population age 25 and over with: High school diploma (including GED) or higher: 83.3% (2005); Bachelor's degree or higher: 11.5% (2005); Master's degree or higher: 4.8% (2005).
Housing: Homeownership rate: 65.0% (2005); Median home value: $155,696 (2005); Median rent: $492 per month (2000); Median age of housing: 44 years (2000).
Transportation: Commute to work: 93.7% car, 0.0% public transportation, 3.9% walk, 2.4% work from home (2000); Travel time to work: 42.8% less than 15 minutes, 24.9% 15 to 30 minutes, 6.8% 30 to 45 minutes, 10.2% 45 to 60 minutes, 15.4% 60 minutes or more (2000)

JEWETT (town). Covers a land area of 50.334 square miles and a water area of 0.173 square miles. Located at 42.24° N. Lat.; 74.24° W. Long.
Population: 923 (1990); 970 (2000); 988 (2005); 1,006 (2010 projected); Race: 97.4% White, 0.0% Black, 1.5% Asian, 3.7% Hispanic of any race (2005); Density: 19.6 persons per square mile (2005); Average household size: 2.37 (2005); Median age: 47.4 (2005); Males per 100 females: 98.8 (2005); Marriage status: 14.8% never married, 68.2% now married, 7.7% widowed, 9.3% divorced (2000); Foreign born: 11.0% (2000); Ancestry (includes multiple ancestries): 23.9% Irish, 19.7% German, 16.8% Italian, 14.9% English, 5.5% Polish (2000).
Economy: Single-family building permits issued: 19 (2005); Multi-family building permits issued: 0 (2005); Employment by occupation: 17.6% management, 21.3% professional, 18.1% services, 19.5% sales, 1.1% farming, 12.1% construction, 10.3% production (2000).
Income: Per capita income: $27,831 (2005); Median household income: $47,019 (2005); Average household income: $65,941 (2005); Percent of households with income of $100,000 or more: 18.0% (2005); Poverty rate: 12.0% (2000).
Education: Percent of population age 25 and over with: High school diploma (including GED) or higher: 86.8% (2005); Bachelor's degree or higher: 31.0% (2005); Master's degree or higher: 14.0% (2005).
Housing: Homeownership rate: 78.9% (2005); Median home value: $169,886 (2005); Median rent: $477 per month (2000); Median age of housing: 28 years (2000).
Transportation: Commute to work: 84.1% car, 1.4% public transportation, 4.2% walk, 8.4% work from home (2000); Travel time to work: 31.6% less than 15 minutes, 34.9% 15 to 30 minutes, 12.2% 30 to 45 minutes, 5.4% 45 to 60 minutes, 15.8% 60 minutes or more (2000)

LANESVILLE (unincorporated postal area, zip code 12450). Covers a land area of 19.327 square miles and a water area of 0.004 square miles. Located at 42.15° N. Lat.; 74.23° W. Long.
Population: 0 (2000); Race: 95.2% White, 0.5% Black, 1.1% Asian, 5.3% Hispanic of any race (2000); Density: 0.0 persons per square mile (2000); Age: 27.4% under 18, 12.6% over 64 (2000); Marriage status: 25.1% never married, 50.9% now married, 13.5% widowed, 10.5% divorced (2000); Foreign born: 13.6% (2000); Ancestry (includes multiple ancestries): 20.5% Other groups, 16.8% German, 14.0% Irish, 10.6% Italian, 10.3% English (2000).
Economy: Resort village. Employment by occupation: 7.2% management, 23.3% professional, 15.0% services, 32.8% sales, 4.4% farming, 5.6% construction, 11.7% production (2000).
Income: Per capita income: $22,447 (2000); Median household income: $36,875 (2000); Poverty rate: 20.5% (2000).
Education: Percent of population age 25 and over with: High school diploma (including GED) or higher: 73.4% (2000); Bachelor's degree or higher: 14.7% (2000).
Housing: Homeownership rate: 63.5% (2000); Median home value: $84,200 (2000); Median rent: $306 per month (2000); Median age of housing: 25 years (2000).
Transportation: Commute to work: 88.0% car, 3.0% public transportation, 1.8% walk, 7.2% work from home (2000); Travel time to work: 45.5% less than 15 minutes, 29.2% 15 to 30 minutes, 7.8% 30 to 45 minutes, 10.4% 45 to 60 minutes, 7.1% 60 minutes or more (2000)

LEEDS (CDP). Covers a land area of 0.520 square miles and a water area of 0.012 square miles. Located at 42.25° N. Lat.; 73.89° W. Long.
Population: 377 (1990); 369 (2000); 391 (2005); 403 (2010 projected); Race: 90.8% White, 6.1% Black, 0.0% Asian, 9.5% Hispanic of any race (2005); Density: 751.4 persons per square mile (2005); Average household size: 2.09 (2005); Median age: 38.9 (2005); Males per 100 females: 81.9 (2005); Marriage status: 32.8% never married, 43.8% now married, 5.2% widowed, 18.3% divorced (2000); Foreign born: 5.5% (2000); Ancestry (includes multiple ancestries): 29.9% German, 28.7% Italian, 26.8% Irish, 16.5% Other groups, 10.4% Dutch (2000).
Economy: Employment by occupation: 7.8% management, 24.0% professional, 20.8% services, 19.8% sales, 0.0% farming, 6.8% construction, 20.8% production (2000).
Income: Per capita income: $36,208 (2005); Median household income: $52,557 (2005); Average household income: $75,709 (2005); Percent of households with income of $100,000 or more: 25.7% (2005); Poverty rate: 7.7% (2000).
Education: Percent of population age 25 and over with: High school diploma (including GED) or higher: 79.0% (2005); Bachelor's degree or higher: 17.5% (2005); Master's degree or higher: 2.7% (2005).
Housing: Homeownership rate: 61.0% (2005); Median home value: $155,769 (2005); Median rent: $424 per month (2000); Median age of housing: 57 years (2000).
Transportation: Commute to work: 100.0% car, 0.0% public transportation, 0.0% walk, 0.0% work from home (2000); Travel time to work: 39.8% less than 15 minutes, 29.6% 15 to 30 minutes, 16.1% 30 to 45 minutes, 12.9% 45 to 60 minutes, 1.6% 60 minutes or more (2000)

LEXINGTON (town). Covers a land area of 79.707 square miles and a water area of 0.031 square miles. Located at 42.21° N. Lat.; 74.38° W. Long. Elevation is 1,331 feet.
Population: 845 (1990); 830 (2000); 838 (2005); 847 (2010 projected); Race: 96.9% White, 0.0% Black, 0.8% Asian, 1.4% Hispanic of any race (2005); Density: 10.5 persons per square mile (2005); Average household size: 2.19 (2005); Median age: 49.2 (2005); Males per 100 females: 87.1 (2005); Marriage status: 20.0% never married, 58.4% now married, 10.0% widowed, 11.6% divorced (2000); Foreign born: 9.0% (2000); Ancestry (includes multiple ancestries): 18.0% Irish, 17.3% German, 15.8% Italian, 13.7% English, 10.0% United States or American (2000).
Economy: Resort village. Single-family building permits issued: 10 (2005); Multi-family building permits issued: 0 (2005); Employment by occupation: 14.3% management, 21.0% professional, 17.6% services, 21.6% sales, 1.1% farming, 17.1% construction, 7.3% production (2000).
Income: Per capita income: $24,069 (2005); Median household income: $33,917 (2005); Average household income: $52,663 (2005); Percent of households with income of $100,000 or more: 13.3% (2005); Poverty rate: 12.9% (2000).
Education: Percent of population age 25 and over with: High school diploma (including GED) or higher: 81.5% (2005); Bachelor's degree or higher: 22.2% (2005); Master's degree or higher: 12.9% (2005).
Housing: Homeownership rate: 82.0% (2005); Median home value: $138,144 (2005); Median rent: $342 per month (2000); Median age of housing: 39 years (2000).
Transportation: Commute to work: 85.8% car, 2.8% public transportation, 3.1% walk, 7.4% work from home (2000); Travel time to work: 23.9% less than 15 minutes, 34.4% 15 to 30 minutes, 12.9% 30 to 45 minutes, 6.7% 45 to 60 minutes, 22.1% 60 minutes or more (2000)

MAPLECREST (unincorporated postal area, zip code 12454). Covers a land area of 18.754 square miles and a water area of 0.034 square miles. Located at 42.28° N. Lat.; 74.18° W. Long.
Population: 0 (2000); Race: 99.0% White, 0.0% Black, 0.0% Asian, 1.9% Hispanic of any race (2000); Density: 0.0 persons per square mile (2000); Age: 25.6% under 18, 10.2% over 64 (2000); Marriage status: 24.6% never married, 63.7% now married, 4.4% widowed, 7.2% divorced (2000); Foreign born: 4.8% (2000); Ancestry (includes multiple ancestries): 25.1% Irish, 21.9% Italian, 17.6% German, 10.6% English, 7.5% Dutch (2000).
Economy: Resort village. Employment by occupation: 14.2% management, 22.8% professional, 24.3% services, 17.2% sales, 2.6% farming, 11.6% construction, 7.1% production (2000).
Income: Per capita income: $20,637 (2000); Median household income: $39,821 (2000); Poverty rate: 9.7% (2000).
Education: Percent of population age 25 and over with: High school diploma (including GED) or higher: 83.3% (2000); Bachelor's degree or higher: 22.9% (2000).
Housing: Homeownership rate: 73.5% (2000); Median home value: $97,800 (2000); Median rent: $422 per month (2000); Median age of housing: 32 years (2000).
Transportation: Commute to work: 88.8% car, 1.9% public transportation, 5.6% walk, 3.0% work from home (2000); Travel time to work: 44.4% less than 15 minutes, 30.1% 15 to 30 minutes, 11.2% 30 to 45 minutes, 5.0% 45 to 60 minutes, 9.3% 60 minutes or more (2000)

NEW BALTIMORE (town). Covers a land area of 41.578 square miles and a water area of 1.530 square miles. Located at 42.41° N. Lat.; 73.84° W. Long.
Population: 3,371 (1990); 3,417 (2000); 3,500 (2005); 3,587 (2010 projected); Race: 97.2% White, 0.7% Black, 0.6% Asian, 1.8% Hispanic of any race (2005); Density: 84.2 persons per square mile (2005); Average household size: 2.65 (2005); Median age: 43.2 (2005); Males per 100 females: 95.3 (2005); Marriage status: 19.5% never married, 67.4% now married, 5.4% widowed, 7.8% divorced (2000); Foreign born: 3.0% (2000); Ancestry (includes multiple ancestries): 28.6% German, 23.3% Irish, 15.5% Italian, 13.0% English, 10.8% Dutch (2000).
Economy: Single-family building permits issued: 12 (2005); Multi-family building permits issued: 0 (2005); Employment by occupation: 15.9% management, 21.4% professional, 11.6% services, 25.0% sales, 1.9% farming, 12.0% construction, 12.2% production (2000).
Income: Per capita income: $23,102 (2005); Median household income: $52,244 (2005); Average household income: $59,093 (2005); Percent of households with income of $100,000 or more: 11.0% (2005); Poverty rate: 7.2% (2000).
Education: Percent of population age 25 and over with: High school diploma (including GED) or higher: 85.2% (2005); Bachelor's degree or higher: 22.0% (2005); Master's degree or higher: 11.2% (2005).
Housing: Homeownership rate: 85.2% (2005); Median home value: $141,924 (2005); Median rent: $483 per month (2000); Median age of housing: 36 years (2000).
Transportation: Commute to work: 91.3% car, 1.8% public transportation, 0.0% walk, 6.9% work from home (2000); Travel time to work: 19.3% less than 15 minutes, 28.6% 15 to 30 minutes, 34.3% 30 to 45 minutes, 11.7% 45 to 60 minutes, 6.1% 60 minutes or more (2000)

OAK HILL (unincorporated postal area, zip code 12460). Covers a land area of 3.227 square miles and a water area of 0 square miles. Located at 42.40° N. Lat.; 74.15° W. Long.
Population: 0 (2000); Race: 100.0% White, 0.0% Black, 0.0% Asian, 0.0% Hispanic of any race (2000); Density: 0.0 persons per square mile (2000); Age: 27.0% under 18, 10.2% over 64 (2000); Marriage status: 19.1% never married, 57.3% now married, 2.9% widowed, 20.7% divorced (2000); Foreign born: 2.1% (2000); Ancestry (includes multiple ancestries): 18.0%

United States or American, 16.8% German, 16.1% Irish, 11.1% French (except Basque), 8.0% Other groups (2000).
Economy: Employment by occupation: 11.0% management, 7.3% professional, 20.9% services, 17.8% sales, 2.1% farming, 11.5% construction, 29.3% production (2000).
Income: Per capita income: $14,212 (2000); Median household income: $34,844 (2000); Poverty rate: 17.9% (2000).
Education: Percent of population age 25 and over with: High school diploma (including GED) or higher: 76.0% (2000); Bachelor's degree or higher: 15.0% (2000).
Housing: Homeownership rate: 85.0% (2000); Median home value: $93,000 (2000); Median rent: $425 per month (2000); Median age of housing: 60+ years (2000).
Transportation: Commute to work: 88.2% car, 0.0% public transportation, 4.8% walk, 7.0% work from home (2000); Travel time to work: 35.1% less than 15 minutes, 13.2% 15 to 30 minutes, 31.6% 30 to 45 minutes, 0.0% 45 to 60 minutes, 20.1% 60 minutes or more (2000)

PALENVILLE (CDP).
Covers a land area of 3.322 square miles and a water area of 0 square miles. Located at 42.17° N. Lat.; 74.01° W. Long. Elevation is 470 feet.
History: Legendary home of Rip Van Winkle; Sleepy Hollow, where he reputedly slept for 20 years, is nearby.
Population: 1,096 (1990); 1,120 (2000); 1,043 (2005); 1,024 (2010 projected); Race: 95.6% White, 0.5% Black, 1.9% Asian, 2.1% Hispanic of any race (2005); Density: 314.0 persons per square mile (2005); Average household size: 2.58 (2005); Median age: 39.7 (2005); Males per 100 females: 96.4 (2005); Marriage status: 21.4% never married, 67.1% now married, 5.2% widowed, 6.3% divorced (2000); Foreign born: 4.5% (2000); Ancestry (includes multiple ancestries): 25.5% German, 19.7% Irish, 18.1% English, 13.3% United States or American, 12.3% Italian (2000).
Economy: Resort village. Employment by occupation: 13.2% management, 12.9% professional, 19.3% services, 28.6% sales, 1.7% farming, 13.2% construction, 11.2% production (2000).
Income: Per capita income: $25,149 (2005); Median household income: $49,390 (2005); Average household income: $63,568 (2005); Percent of households with income of $100,000 or more: 17.0% (2005); Poverty rate: 7.4% (2000).
Education: Percent of population age 25 and over with: High school diploma (including GED) or higher: 86.8% (2005); Bachelor's degree or higher: 12.3% (2005); Master's degree or higher: 4.4% (2005).
Housing: Homeownership rate: 71.9% (2005); Median home value: $139,961 (2005); Median rent: $450 per month (2000); Median age of housing: 34 years (2000).
Transportation: Commute to work: 82.8% car, 0.0% public transportation, 1.0% walk, 12.6% work from home (2000); Travel time to work: 20.9% less than 15 minutes, 29.4% 15 to 30 minutes, 26.0% 30 to 45 minutes, 4.7% 45 to 60 minutes, 18.9% 60 minutes or more (2000)

PRATTSVILLE (town).
Covers a land area of 19.616 square miles and a water area of 0.103 square miles. Located at 42.31° N. Lat.; 74.41° W. Long. Elevation is 1,165 feet.
Population: 774 (1990); 665 (2000); 587 (2005); 558 (2010 projected); Race: 99.3% White, 0.0% Black, 0.0% Asian, 1.7% Hispanic of any race (2005); Density: 29.9 persons per square mile (2005); Average household size: 2.60 (2005); Median age: 37.3 (2005); Males per 100 females: 90.6 (2005); Marriage status: 18.9% never married, 59.1% now married, 9.8% widowed, 12.2% divorced (2000); Foreign born: 5.7% (2000); Ancestry (includes multiple ancestries): 17.7% German, 15.4% Irish, 10.6% Italian, 9.8% United States or American, 8.8% English (2000).
Economy: Resort village. Single-family building permits issued: 5 (2005); Multi-family building permits issued: 0 (2005); Employment by occupation: 6.5% management, 15.3% professional, 29.5% services, 27.6% sales, 1.1% farming, 8.8% construction, 11.1% production (2000).
Income: Per capita income: $16,253 (2005); Median household income: $34,688 (2005); Average household income: $42,212 (2005); Percent of households with income of $100,000 or more: 4.0% (2005); Poverty rate: 11.5% (2000).
Education: Percent of population age 25 and over with: High school diploma (including GED) or higher: 79.6% (2005); Bachelor's degree or higher: 13.4% (2005); Master's degree or higher: 5.0% (2005).
Housing: Homeownership rate: 83.2% (2005); Median home value: $118,421 (2005); Median rent: $283 per month (2000); Median age of housing: 38 years (2000).
Transportation: Commute to work: 87.3% car, 1.9% public transportation, 6.2% walk, 3.5% work from home (2000); Travel time to work: 40.8% less than 15 minutes, 38.4% 15 to 30 minutes, 12.4% 30 to 45 minutes, 1.2% 45 to 60 minutes, 7.2% 60 minutes or more (2000)

PURLING
(unincorporated postal area, zip code 12470). Covers a land area of 4.703 square miles and a water area of 0.033 square miles. Located at 42.28° N. Lat.; 74.02° W. Long. Elevation is 489 feet.
Population: 0 (2000); Race: 91.2% White, 5.1% Black, 0.0% Asian, 8.9% Hispanic of any race (2000); Density: 0.0 persons per square mile (2000); Age: 25.5% under 18, 18.7% over 64 (2000); Marriage status: 23.0% never married, 55.2% now married, 11.6% widowed, 10.2% divorced (2000); Foreign born: 6.5% (2000); Ancestry (includes multiple ancestries): 26.5% German, 19.0% Irish, 15.0% Italian, 12.8% Other groups, 4.2% Albanian (2000).
Economy: Employment by occupation: 4.2% management, 7.2% professional, 18.1% services, 19.8% sales, 2.2% farming, 21.4% construction, 27.0% production (2000).
Income: Per capita income: $16,093 (2000); Median household income: $43,333 (2000); Poverty rate: 1.3% (2000).
Education: Percent of population age 25 and over with: High school diploma (including GED) or higher: 73.2% (2000); Bachelor's degree or higher: 8.5% (2000).
Housing: Homeownership rate: 77.2% (2000); Median home value: $93,900 (2000); Median rent: $425 per month (2000); Median age of housing: 35 years (2000).
Transportation: Commute to work: 96.1% car, 0.0% public transportation, 0.0% walk, 3.9% work from home (2000); Travel time to work: 22.4% less than 15 minutes, 48.1% 15 to 30 minutes, 21.1% 30 to 45 minutes, 4.0% 45 to 60 minutes, 4.3% 60 minutes or more (2000)

ROUND TOP
(unincorporated postal area, zip code 12473). Covers a land area of 21.900 square miles and a water area of 0.026 square miles. Located at 42.26° N. Lat.; 74.03° W. Long.
Population: 0 (2000); Race: 97.6% White, 0.0% Black, 0.0% Asian, 4.4% Hispanic of any race (2000); Density: 0.0 persons per square mile (2000); Age: 16.3% under 18, 19.7% over 64 (2000); Marriage status: 20.7% never married, 48.7% now married, 2.8% widowed, 27.9% divorced (2000); Foreign born: 15.8% (2000); Ancestry (includes multiple ancestries): 43.9% German, 23.4% Irish, 17.7% Italian, 8.9% Other groups, 7.9% French (except Basque) (2000).
Economy: Resort village. Round Top Mt. is nearby. Employment by occupation: 6.8% management, 29.1% professional, 24.3% services, 21.6% sales, 0.0% farming, 9.2% construction, 8.9% production (2000).
Income: Per capita income: $18,037 (2000); Median household income: $34,844 (2000); Poverty rate: 10.3% (2000).
Education: Percent of population age 25 and over with: High school diploma (including GED) or higher: 76.0% (2000); Bachelor's degree or higher: 15.9% (2000).
Housing: Homeownership rate: 72.3% (2000); Median home value: $82,800 (2000); Median rent: $419 per month (2000); Median age of housing: 33 years (2000).
Transportation: Commute to work: 97.9% car, 0.0% public transportation, 2.1% walk, 0.0% work from home (2000); Travel time to work: 33.9% less than 15 minutes, 22.6% 15 to 30 minutes, 23.6% 30 to 45 minutes, 6.2% 45 to 60 minutes, 13.7% 60 minutes or more (2000)

SOUTH CAIRO
(unincorporated postal area, zip code 12482). Covers a land area of 0.664 square miles and a water area of 0 square miles. Located at 42.27° N. Lat.; 73.95° W. Long.
Population: 0 (2000); Race: 95.0% White, 0.0% Black, 0.0% Asian, 5.0% Hispanic of any race (2000); Density: 0.0 persons per square mile (2000); Age: 26.1% under 18, 35.2% over 64 (2000); Marriage status: 12.1% never married, 59.9% now married, 14.9% widowed, 13.0% divorced (2000); Foreign born: 6.9% (2000); Ancestry (includes multiple ancestries): 19.1% Italian, 18.9% German, 11.7% Other groups, 11.7% Norwegian, 8.4% Irish (2000).
Economy: Resort village. Employment by occupation: 0.0% management, 8.8% professional, 10.1% services, 23.6% sales, 4.7% farming, 17.6% construction, 35.1% production (2000).
Income: Per capita income: $17,810 (2000); Median household income: $28,036 (2000); Poverty rate: 2.2% (2000).
Education: Percent of population age 25 and over with: High school diploma (including GED) or higher: 67.4% (2000); Bachelor's degree or higher: 2.7% (2000).

Housing: Homeownership rate: 76.5% (2000); Median home value: $98,100 (2000); Median rent: $413 per month (2000); Median age of housing: 19 years (2000).
Transportation: Commute to work: 86.5% car, 0.0% public transportation, 0.0% walk, 13.5% work from home (2000); Travel time to work: 9.4% less than 15 minutes, 85.2% 15 to 30 minutes, 5.5% 30 to 45 minutes, 0.0% 45 to 60 minutes, 0.0% 60 minutes or more (2000)

SURPRISE (unincorporated postal area, zip code 12176). Covers a land area of 3.589 square miles and a water area of 0.031 square miles. Located at 42.39° N. Lat.; 73.96° W. Long.
Population: 0 (2000); Race: 100.0% White, 0.0% Black, 0.0% Asian, 0.0% Hispanic of any race (2000); Density: 0.0 persons per square mile (2000); Age: 24.8% under 18, 25.5% over 64 (2000); Marriage status: 13.6% never married, 57.6% now married, 14.4% widowed, 14.4% divorced (2000); Foreign born: 0.0% (2000); Ancestry (includes multiple ancestries): 39.3% German, 33.8% English, 20.0% Dutch, 19.3% Italian, 11.0% Norwegian (2000).
Economy: Employment by occupation: 7.3% management, 26.8% professional, 8.5% services, 26.8% sales, 0.0% farming, 8.5% construction, 22.0% production (2000).
Income: Per capita income: $25,610 (2000); Median household income: $47,321 (2000); Poverty rate: 4.8% (2000).
Education: Percent of population age 25 and over with: High school diploma (including GED) or higher: 58.4% (2000); Bachelor's degree or higher: 8.9% (2000).
Housing: Homeownership rate: 85.5% (2000); Median home value: $112,500 (2000); Median rent: $525 per month (2000); Median age of housing: 30 years (2000).
Transportation: Commute to work: 100.0% car, 0.0% public transportation, 0.0% walk, 0.0% work from home (2000); Travel time to work: 38.9% less than 15 minutes, 50.0% 15 to 30 minutes, 0.0% 30 to 45 minutes, 0.0% 45 to 60 minutes, 11.1% 60 minutes or more (2000)

TANNERSVILLE (village). Covers a land area of 1.113 square miles and a water area of 0.032 square miles. Located at 42.19° N. Lat.; 74.13° W. Long.
Population: 471 (1990); 448 (2000); 463 (2005); 480 (2010 projected); Race: 95.0% White, 1.1% Black, 0.2% Asian, 3.7% Hispanic of any race (2005); Density: 415.9 persons per square mile (2005); Average household size: 2.05 (2005); Median age: 47.5 (2005); Males per 100 females: 97.9 (2005); Marriage status: 35.1% never married, 43.7% now married, 8.9% widowed, 12.3% divorced (2000); Foreign born: 7.8% (2000); Ancestry (includes multiple ancestries): 21.1% Italian, 19.6% Irish, 10.0% United States or American, 8.7% German, 7.4% English (2000).
Economy: Resort village. Single-family building permits issued: 3 (2005); Multi-family building permits issued: 0 (2005); Employment by occupation: 12.5% management, 12.0% professional, 32.1% services, 21.2% sales, 0.0% farming, 12.0% construction, 10.3% production (2000).
Income: Per capita income: $19,519 (2005); Median household income: $32,333 (2005); Average household income: $39,989 (2005); Percent of households with income of $100,000 or more: 5.8% (2005); Poverty rate: 18.5% (2000).
Education: Percent of population age 25 and over with: High school diploma (including GED) or higher: 89.2% (2005); Bachelor's degree or higher: 23.5% (2005); Master's degree or higher: 11.9% (2005).
School District(s)
Hunter-Tannersville Central School District (KG-12)
   2003-04 Enrollment: 522 . . . . (518) 589-5400
Housing: Homeownership rate: 61.1% (2005); Median home value: $156,061 (2005); Median rent: $408 per month (2000); Median age of housing: 60+ years (2000).
Transportation: Commute to work: 77.7% car, 1.1% public transportation, 8.7% walk, 9.2% work from home (2000); Travel time to work: 52.1% less than 15 minutes, 15.0% 15 to 30 minutes, 4.2% 30 to 45 minutes, 8.4% 45 to 60 minutes, 20.4% 60 minutes or more (2000)

WEST COXSACKIE (unincorporated postal area, zip code 12192). Covers a land area of 17.671 square miles and a water area of 0.053 square miles. Located at 42.39° N. Lat.; 73.83° W. Long.
Population: 0 (2000); Race: 98.0% White, 0.0% Black, 0.4% Asian, 1.8% Hispanic of any race (2000); Density: 0.0 persons per square mile (2000); Age: 18.5% under 18, 14.5% over 64 (2000); Marriage status: 18.5% never married, 65.8% now married, 6.3% widowed, 9.4% divorced (2000); Foreign born: 3.6% (2000); Ancestry (includes multiple ancestries): 27.6% German, 25.2% Irish, 15.2% Italian, 10.8% Dutch, 9.8% English (2000).
Economy: Employment by occupation: 15.8% management, 21.8% professional, 13.3% services, 21.2% sales, 0.6% farming, 11.2% construction, 16.1% production (2000).
Income: Per capita income: $21,600 (2000); Median household income: $44,250 (2000); Poverty rate: 9.1% (2000).
Education: Percent of population age 25 and over with: High school diploma (including GED) or higher: 82.3% (2000); Bachelor's degree or higher: 21.0% (2000).
Housing: Homeownership rate: 90.1% (2000); Median home value: $97,200 (2000); Median rent: $525 per month (2000); Median age of housing: 36 years (2000).
Transportation: Commute to work: 91.1% car, 1.9% public transportation, 1.5% walk, 5.5% work from home (2000); Travel time to work: 25.0% less than 15 minutes, 25.8% 15 to 30 minutes, 32.2% 30 to 45 minutes, 9.6% 45 to 60 minutes, 7.4% 60 minutes or more (2000)

WEST KILL (unincorporated postal area, zip code 12492). Covers a land area of 17.698 square miles and a water area of 0 square miles. Located at 42.20° N. Lat.; 74.34° W. Long.
Population: 0 (2000); Race: 96.6% White, 0.0% Black, 0.0% Asian, 1.4% Hispanic of any race (2000); Density: 0.0 persons per square mile (2000); Age: 19.2% under 18, 23.4% over 64 (2000); Marriage status: 20.9% never married, 54.1% now married, 11.9% widowed, 13.1% divorced (2000); Foreign born: 6.9% (2000); Ancestry (includes multiple ancestries): 26.8% Irish, 21.3% German, 19.2% Italian, 16.5% English, 11.3% United States or American (2000).
Economy: Employment by occupation: 10.9% management, 23.4% professional, 19.5% services, 18.0% sales, 0.0% farming, 19.5% construction, 8.6% production (2000).
Income: Per capita income: $22,125 (2000); Median household income: $33,750 (2000); Poverty rate: 13.4% (2000).
Education: Percent of population age 25 and over with: High school diploma (including GED) or higher: 91.6% (2000); Bachelor's degree or higher: 28.6% (2000).
Housing: Homeownership rate: 78.3% (2000); Median home value: $79,300 (2000); Median rent: $375 per month (2000); Median age of housing: 37 years (2000).
Transportation: Commute to work: 85.7% car, 4.8% public transportation, 3.2% walk, 6.3% work from home (2000); Travel time to work: 33.1% less than 15 minutes, 26.3% 15 to 30 minutes, 15.3% 30 to 45 minutes, 6.8% 45 to 60 minutes, 18.6% 60 minutes or more (2000)

WINDHAM (town). Covers a land area of 45.289 square miles and a water area of 0.099 square miles. Located at 42.31° N. Lat.; 74.22° W. Long.
Population: 1,682 (1990); 1,660 (2000); 1,629 (2005); 1,546 (2010 projected); Race: 98.4% White, 0.3% Black, 0.1% Asian, 2.0% Hispanic of any race (2005); Density: 36.0 persons per square mile (2005); Average household size: 2.27 (2005); Median age: 46.4 (2005); Males per 100 females: 90.3 (2005); Marriage status: 20.0% never married, 60.7% now married, 9.0% widowed, 10.3% divorced (2000); Foreign born: 9.1% (2000); Ancestry (includes multiple ancestries): 25.6% Irish, 20.8% German, 17.5% Italian, 12.6% English, 6.6% Dutch (2000).
Economy: Resort village. Single-family building permits issued: 29 (2005); Multi-family building permits issued: 12 (2005); Employment by occupation: 16.7% management, 16.2% professional, 22.2% services, 19.8% sales, 1.6% farming, 12.0% construction, 11.5% production (2000).
Income: Per capita income: $27,974 (2005); Median household income: $43,022 (2005); Average household income: $63,556 (2005); Percent of households with income of $100,000 or more: 15.8% (2005); Poverty rate: 9.3% (2000).
Education: Percent of population age 25 and over with: High school diploma (including GED) or higher: 85.6% (2005); Bachelor's degree or higher: 24.2% (2005); Master's degree or higher: 11.3% (2005).
School District(s)
Windham-Ashland-Jewett Central School District (KG-12)
   2003-04 Enrollment: 512 . . . . (518) 734-3403
Housing: Homeownership rate: 71.1% (2005); Median home value: $164,414 (2005); Median rent: $426 per month (2000); Median age of housing: 23 years (2000).
Safety: Violent crime rate: 0.0 per 10,000 population; Property crime rate: 170.0 per 10,000 population (2004).
Newspapers: Windham Journal (General - Circulation 2,000)

Transportation: Commute to work: 84.7% car, 2.1% public transportation, 8.4% walk, 4.1% work from home (2000); Travel time to work: 54.4% less than 15 minutes, 20.1% 15 to 30 minutes, 10.5% 30 to 45 minutes, 4.3% 45 to 60 minutes, 10.7% 60 minutes or more (2000)

WINDHAM

WINDHAM (CDP). Covers a land area of 1.875 square miles and a water area of 0 square miles. Located at 42.31° N. Lat.; 74.24° W. Long.
Population: 367 (1990); 359 (2000); 352 (2005); 334 (2010 projected); Race: 99.1% White, 0.0% Black, 0.0% Asian, 1.1% Hispanic of any race (2005); Density: 187.7 persons per square mile (2005); Average household size: 2.06 (2005); Median age: 48.9 (2005); Males per 100 females: 98.9 (2005); Marriage status: 16.2% never married, 62.5% now married, 11.3% widowed, 10.0% divorced (2000); Foreign born: 15.0% (2000); Ancestry (includes multiple ancestries): 29.1% Irish, 18.6% English, 18.4% German, 8.5% Polish, 7.3% Italian (2000).
Economy: Employment by occupation: 12.7% management, 17.6% professional, 19.0% services, 16.2% sales, 0.0% farming, 12.0% construction, 22.5% production (2000).
Income: Per capita income: $26,612 (2005); Median household income: $39,597 (2005); Average household income: $54,781 (2005); Percent of households with income of $100,000 or more: 15.8% (2005); Poverty rate: 10.5% (2000).
Education: Percent of population age 25 and over with: High school diploma (including GED) or higher: 79.5% (2005); Bachelor's degree or higher: 22.0% (2005); Master's degree or higher: 9.3% (2005).
Housing: Homeownership rate: 57.3% (2005); Median home value: $175,000 (2005); Median rent: $422 per month (2000); Median age of housing: 26 years (2000).
Transportation: Commute to work: 83.8% car, 2.1% public transportation, 10.6% walk, 3.5% work from home (2000); Travel time to work: 45.3% less than 15 minutes, 20.4% 15 to 30 minutes, 11.7% 30 to 45 minutes, 2.9% 45 to 60 minutes, 19.7% 60 minutes or more (2000)

Hamilton County

Located in north central New York, in the Adirondacks; drained by tributaries of the Hudson, and by the Raquette, Black, and Sacandaga Rivers; includes many lakes. Covers a land area of 1,720.39 square miles, a water area of 87.41 square miles, and is located in the Eastern Time Zone. The county government was organized in 1816. County seat is Lake Pleasant.

Weather Station: Indian Lake 2 SW   Elevation: 1,660 feet

	Jan	Feb	Mar	Apr	May	Jun	Jul	Aug	Sep	Oct	Nov	Dec
High	25	28	37	49	63	71	75	73	65	54	41	30
Low	3	4	14	27	39	48	52	51	44	33	25	11
Precip	3.1	2.3	3.1	2.8	3.5	3.7	3.5	3.9	4.3	3.8	3.5	2.7
Snow	na	na	na	na	0.0	0.0	0.0	0.0	0.0	0.2	na	na

High and Low temperatures in degrees Fahrenheit; Precipitation and Snow in inches

Population: 5,279 (1990); 5,379 (2000); 5,252 (2005); 5,121 (2010 projected); Race: 97.0% White, 1.4% Black, 0.2% Asian, 1.1% Hispanic of any race (2005); Density: 3.1 persons per square mile (2005); Average household size: 2.23 (2005); Median age: 46.6 (2005); Males per 100 females: 98.1 (2005).
Religion: Five largest groups: 49.4% Catholic Church, 11.1% The United Methodist Church, 6.3% The Wesleyan Church, 2.6% The Evangelical Free Church of America, 1.9% Conservative Baptist Association of America (2000).
Economy: Unemployment rate: 5.2% (2005); Total civilian labor force: 3,186 (2005); Leading industries: 22.6% accommodation and food services; 21.3% retail trade; 13.5% arts (2003); Farms: 24 totaling 1,410 acres (2002); Companies that employ 500 or more persons: 0 (2003); Companies that employ 100 to 499 persons: 0 (2003); Companies that employ less than 100 persons: 205 (2003); Black-owned businesses: n/a (2002); Hispanic-owned businesses: n/a (2002); Women-owned businesses: n/a (2002); Retail sales per capita: $7,415 (2006). Single-family building permits issued: 73 (2005); Multi-family building permits issued: 0 (2005).
Income: Per capita income: $22,386 (2005); Median household income: $37,319 (2005); Average household income: $49,582 (2005); Percent of households with income of $100,000 or more: 9.2% (2005); Poverty rate: 9.5% (2003); Bankruptcy rate: 4.02% (2005).
Taxes: Total county taxes per capita: $1,234 (2004); County property taxes per capita: $745 (2004).

Education: Percent of population age 25 and over with: High school diploma (including GED) or higher: 83.5% (2005); Bachelor's degree or higher: 18.4% (2005); Master's degree or higher: 7.8% (2005).
Housing: Homeownership rate: 79.2% (2005); Median home value: $132,731 (2005); Median rent: $362 per month (2000); Median age of housing: 39 years (2000).
Health: Birth rate: 76.5 per 10,000 population (2004); Death rate: 162.6 per 10,000 population (2004); Age-adjusted cancer mortality rate: 257.3 deaths per 100,000 population (2002); Air Quality Index: 96.4% good, 3.3% moderate, 0.3% unhealthy for sensitive individuals, 0.0% unhealthy (percent of days in 2005); Number of physicians: 5.7 per 10,000 population (2004); Hospital beds: 0.0 per 10,000 population (2003); Hospital admissions: 0.0 per 10,000 population (2003).
Elections: 2004 Presidential election results: 67.0% Bush, 31.0% Kerry, 1.6% Nader, 0.4% Badnarik
Additional Information Contacts
Hamilton County Government . . . . (518) 548-6651
  http://www.hamiltoncounty.com/

Hamilton County Communities

ARIETTA (town). Covers a land area of 317.596 square miles and a water area of 11.808 square miles. Located at 43.51° N. Lat.; 74.57° W. Long.
Population: 300 (1990); 293 (2000); 283 (2005); 272 (2010 projected); Race: 100.0% White, 0.0% Black, 0.0% Asian, 0.0% Hispanic of any race (2005); Density: 0.9 persons per square mile (2005); Average household size: 2.28 (2005); Median age: 46.1 (2005); Males per 100 females: 97.9 (2005); Marriage status: 18.1% never married, 59.1% now married, 10.4% widowed, 12.4% divorced (2000); Foreign born: 0.9% (2000); Ancestry (includes multiple ancestries): 25.8% German, 20.6% Irish, 18.7% English, 11.3% United States or American, 9.2% Other groups.
Economy: Single-family building permits issued: 4 (2005); Multi-family building permits issued: 0 (2005); Employment by occupation: 17.6% management, 22.1% professional, 9.6% services, 22.8% sales, 0.0% farming, 14.0% construction, 14.0% production (2000).
Income: Per capita income: $32,032 (2005); Median household income: $47,656 (2005); Average household income: $73,105 (2005); Percent of households with income of $100,000 or more: 20.2% (2005); Poverty rate: 2.8% (2000).
Education: Percent of population age 25 and over with: High school diploma (including GED) or higher: 86.3% (2005); Bachelor's degree or higher: 24.5% (2005); Master's degree or higher: 9.8% (2005).
Housing: Homeownership rate: 92.7% (2005); Median home value: $145,395 (2005); Median rent: $425 per month (2000); Median age of housing: 40 years (2000).
Transportation: Commute to work: 94.3% car, 2.1% public transportation, 1.4% walk, 2.1% work from home (2000); Travel time to work: 43.5% less than 15 minutes, 15.2% 15 to 30 minutes, 8.7% 30 to 45 minutes, 9.4% 45 to 60 minutes, 23.2% 60 minutes or more (2000)

BENSON (town). Covers a land area of 82.663 square miles and a water area of 0.507 square miles. Located at 43.25° N. Lat.; 74.27° W. Long. Elevation is 1,156 feet.
Population: 168 (1990); 201 (2000); 195 (2005); 187 (2010 projected); Race: 99.5% White, 0.0% Black, 0.0% Asian, 2.1% Hispanic of any race (2005); Density: 2.4 persons per square mile (2005); Average household size: 2.47 (2005); Median age: 43.6 (2005); Males per 100 females: 99.0 (2005); Marriage status: 22.2% never married, 66.1% now married, 7.0% widowed, 4.7% divorced (2000); Foreign born: 1.9% (2000); Ancestry (includes multiple ancestries): 30.5% Irish, 24.8% German, 16.7% Italian, 7.1% Dutch, 6.7% Polish (2000).
Economy: Employment by occupation: 17.6% management, 24.1% professional, 9.3% services, 28.7% sales, 1.9% farming, 8.3% construction, 10.2% production (2000).
Income: Per capita income: $24,859 (2005); Median household income: $55,603 (2005); Average household income: $61,361 (2005); Percent of households with income of $100,000 or more: 16.5% (2005); Poverty rate: 2.4% (2000).
Education: Percent of population age 25 and over with: High school diploma (including GED) or higher: 86.2% (2005); Bachelor's degree or higher: 24.8% (2005); Master's degree or higher: 6.2% (2005).
Housing: Homeownership rate: 78.5% (2005); Median home value: $112,500 (2005); Median rent: $467 per month (2000); Median age of housing: 41 years (2000).

Transportation: Commute to work: 84.6% car, 0.0% public transportation, 0.0% walk, 15.4% work from home (2000); Travel time to work: 19.3% less than 15 minutes, 26.1% 15 to 30 minutes, 20.5% 30 to 45 minutes, 21.6% 45 to 60 minutes, 12.5% 60 minutes or more (2000)

BLUE MOUNTAIN LAKE (unincorporated postal area, zip code 12812). Covers a land area of 47.337 square miles and a water area of 0.759 square miles. Located at 43.86° N. Lat.; 74.43° W. Long. Elevation is 1,829 feet.

History: Comprehensive Adirondack Museum.
Population: 0 (2000); Race: 100.0% White, 0.0% Black, 0.0% Asian, 0.0% Hispanic of any race (2000); Density: 0.0 persons per square mile (2000); Age: 24.7% under 18, 18.7% over 64 (2000); Marriage status: 12.2% never married, 65.2% now married, 7.8% widowed, 14.8% divorced (2000); Foreign born: 0.0% (2000); Ancestry (includes multiple ancestries): 18.7% French (except Basque), 18.0% Irish, 18.0% English, 8.7% United States or American, 8.0% Italian (2000).
Economy: In summer and winter resort area. Employment by occupation: 18.4% management, 28.9% professional, 18.4% services, 17.1% sales, 0.0% farming, 17.1% construction, 0.0% production (2000).
Income: Per capita income: $15,795 (2000); Median household income: $30,208 (2000); Poverty rate: 6.7% (2000).
Education: Percent of population age 25 and over with: High school diploma (including GED) or higher: 93.3% (2000); Bachelor's degree or higher: 24.8% (2000).
Housing: Homeownership rate: 79.4% (2000); Median home value: $82,800 (2000); Median rent: $267 per month (2000); Median age of housing: 60+ years (2000).
Transportation: Commute to work: 84.2% car, 0.0% public transportation, 11.8% walk, 3.9% work from home (2000); Travel time to work: 39.7% less than 15 minutes, 27.4% 15 to 30 minutes, 21.9% 30 to 45 minutes, 5.5% 45 to 60 minutes, 5.5% 60 minutes or more (2000)

HOFFMEISTER (unincorporated postal area, zip code 13353). Covers a land area of 163.245 square miles and a water area of 2.967 square miles. Located at 43.39° N. Lat.; 74.72° W. Long. Elevation is 1,857 feet.

Population: 0 (2000); Race: 98.4% White, 0.0% Black, 0.0% Asian, 0.0% Hispanic of any race (2000); Density: 0.0 persons per square mile (2000); Age: 10.2% under 18, 25.0% over 64 (2000); Marriage status: 12.8% never married, 79.5% now married, 2.6% widowed, 5.1% divorced (2000); Foreign born: 0.0% (2000); Ancestry (includes multiple ancestries): 33.6% Dutch, 30.5% German, 21.1% Irish, 14.8% English, 10.9% Polish (2000).
Economy: Employment by occupation: 29.4% management, 5.9% professional, 0.0% services, 29.4% sales, 0.0% farming, 3.9% construction, 31.4% production (2000).
Income: Per capita income: $12,864 (2000); Median household income: $25,417 (2000); Poverty rate: 7.3% (2000).
Education: Percent of population age 25 and over with: High school diploma (including GED) or higher: 68.5% (2000); Bachelor's degree or higher: 9.3% (2000).
Housing: Homeownership rate: 90.7% (2000); Median home value: $67,000 (2000); Median rent: $n/a per month (2000); Median age of housing: 47 years (2000).
Transportation: Commute to work: 84.3% car, 0.0% public transportation, 0.0% walk, 15.7% work from home (2000); Travel time to work: 20.9% less than 15 minutes, 0.0% 15 to 30 minutes, 51.2% 30 to 45 minutes, 0.0% 45 to 60 minutes, 27.9% 60 minutes or more (2000)

HOPE (town). Covers a land area of 40.739 square miles and a water area of 0.873 square miles. Located at 43.30° N. Lat.; 74.20° W. Long.

Population: 358 (1990); 392 (2000); 377 (2005); 363 (2010 projected); Race: 98.7% White, 0.8% Black, 0.0% Asian, 1.3% Hispanic of any race (2005); Density: 9.3 persons per square mile (2005); Average household size: 2.48 (2005); Median age: 40.7 (2005); Males per 100 females: 87.6 (2005); Marriage status: 21.8% never married, 58.4% now married, 6.9% widowed, 12.9% divorced (2000); Foreign born: 1.3% (2000); Ancestry (includes multiple ancestries): 31.3% Irish, 25.4% German, 17.4% Dutch, 15.3% English, 11.9% Other groups (2000).
Economy: Single-family building permits issued: 2 (2005); Multi-family building permits issued: 0 (2005); Employment by occupation: 4.0% management, 12.7% professional, 17.9% services, 24.9% sales, 1.2% farming, 12.1% construction, 27.2% production (2000).
Income: Per capita income: $19,934 (2005); Median household income: $37,903 (2005); Average household income: $49,441 (2005); Percent of households with income of $100,000 or more: 7.2% (2005); Poverty rate: 12.4% (2000).
Education: Percent of population age 25 and over with: High school diploma (including GED) or higher: 75.0% (2005); Bachelor's degree or higher: 6.7% (2005); Master's degree or higher: 2.2% (2005).
Housing: Homeownership rate: 83.6% (2005); Median home value: $91,500 (2005); Median rent: $306 per month (2000); Median age of housing: 36 years (2000).
Transportation: Commute to work: 92.3% car, 0.0% public transportation, 3.6% walk, 4.1% work from home (2000); Travel time to work: 27.8% less than 15 minutes, 17.9% 15 to 30 minutes, 34.0% 30 to 45 minutes, 3.1% 45 to 60 minutes, 17.3% 60 minutes or more (2000)

INDIAN LAKE (town). Covers a land area of 252.831 square miles and a water area of 13.404 square miles. Located at 43.78° N. Lat.; 74.29° W. Long. Elevation is 1,752 feet.

History: Dr. Thomas Durant and William West Durant, father and son, were early promoters of the Indian Lake section of the Adirondacks. The father, financier and railroad builder, constructed a railroad from Saratoga to Blue Mountain Lake, and the son expanded his father's promotional activities by building elaborate camps and selling them to the wealthy.
Population: 1,481 (1990); 1,471 (2000); 1,461 (2005); 1,452 (2010 projected); Race: 97.6% White, 1.1% Black, 0.0% Asian, 1.3% Hispanic of any race (2005); Density: 5.8 persons per square mile (2005); Average household size: 2.21 (2005); Median age: 46.8 (2005); Males per 100 females: 93.8 (2005); Marriage status: 18.9% never married, 62.5% now married, 10.5% widowed, 8.1% divorced (2000); Foreign born: 2.0% (2000); Ancestry (includes multiple ancestries): 27.5% Irish, 27.5% English, 21.2% French (except Basque), 14.8% German, 5.4% Other groups (2000).
Economy: Single-family building permits issued: 24 (2005); Multi-family building permits issued: 0 (2005); Employment by occupation: 10.4% management, 16.8% professional, 18.6% services, 21.3% sales, 1.8% farming, 22.5% construction, 8.8% production (2000).
Income: Per capita income: $22,037 (2005); Median household income: $37,461 (2005); Average household income: $48,462 (2005); Percent of households with income of $100,000 or more: 8.0% (2005); Poverty rate: 8.5% (2000).
Education: Percent of population age 25 and over with: High school diploma (including GED) or higher: 86.4% (2005); Bachelor's degree or higher: 19.0% (2005); Master's degree or higher: 9.6% (2005).

School District(s)
Indian Lake Central School District (KG-12)
    2003-04 Enrollment: 206 . . . . (518) 648-5024

Housing: Homeownership rate: 77.3% (2005); Median home value: $129,343 (2005); Median rent: $353 per month (2000); Median age of housing: 34 years (2000).
Transportation: Commute to work: 91.3% car, 0.7% public transportation, 4.1% walk, 3.1% work from home (2000); Travel time to work: 52.9% less than 15 minutes, 22.1% 15 to 30 minutes, 11.6% 30 to 45 minutes, 4.2% 45 to 60 minutes, 9.2% 60 minutes or more (2000)
Additional Information Contacts
Indian Lake Chamber of Commerce . . . . (518) 648-5112
    http://www.indian-lake.com

INLET (town). Covers a land area of 62.289 square miles and a water area of 4.107 square miles. Located at 43.74° N. Lat.; 74.76° W. Long.

Population: 343 (1990); 406 (2000); 423 (2005); 424 (2010 projected); Race: 96.7% White, 0.0% Black, 0.0% Asian, 2.8% Hispanic of any race (2005); Density: 6.8 persons per square mile (2005); Average household size: 2.13 (2005); Median age: 44.9 (2005); Males per 100 females: 104.3 (2005); Marriage status: 17.3% never married, 64.8% now married, 8.5% widowed, 9.4% divorced (2000); Foreign born: 0.7% (2000); Ancestry (includes multiple ancestries): 22.6% German, 19.4% Irish, 18.1% English, 10.4% Italian, 6.2% Dutch (2000).
Economy: Resort village. Single-family building permits issued: 3 (2005); Multi-family building permits issued: 0 (2005); Employment by occupation: 14.4% management, 11.0% professional, 25.8% services, 30.6% sales, 3.8% farming, 8.1% construction, 6.2% production (2000).
Income: Per capita income: $24,590 (2005); Median household income: $35,500 (2005); Average household income: $51,960 (2005); Percent of households with income of $100,000 or more: 11.6% (2005); Poverty rate: 13.2% (2000).
Taxes: Total city taxes per capita: $2,594 (2004); City property taxes per capita: $2,469 (2004).

Education: Percent of population age 25 and over with: High school diploma (including GED) or higher: 92.4% (2005); Bachelor's degree or higher: 16.5% (2005); Master's degree or higher: 2.2% (2005).

School District(s)
Inlet Common School District (PK-06)
    2003-04 Enrollment: 33 .... (315) 369-3222

Housing: Homeownership rate: 79.4% (2005); Median home value: $185,417 (2005); Median rent: $317 per month (2000); Median age of housing: 46 years (2000).

Transportation: Commute to work: 82.9% car, 0.0% public transportation, 17.1% walk, 0.0% work from home (2000); Travel time to work: 67.8% less than 15 minutes, 20.1% 15 to 30 minutes, 5.0% 30 to 45 minutes, 1.0% 45 to 60 minutes, 6.0% 60 minutes or more (2000)

Additional Information Contacts
Inlet Chamber of Commerce .... (315) 357-5501
    http://www.inletny.com

LAKE PLEASANT
(town). Covers a land area of 188.082 square miles and a water area of 9.893 square miles. Located at 43.54° N. Lat.; 74.40° W. Long. Elevation is 1,791 feet.

Population: 887 (1990); 876 (2000); 850 (2005); 823 (2010 projected); Race: 95.2% White, 3.2% Black, 0.5% Asian, 0.8% Hispanic of any race (2005); Density: 4.5 persons per square mile (2005); Average household size: 2.21 (2005); Median age: 46.2 (2005); Males per 100 females: 106.3 (2005); Marriage status: 20.2% never married, 66.2% now married, 7.5% widowed, 6.0% divorced (2000); Foreign born: 1.0% (2000); Ancestry (includes multiple ancestries): 28.4% English, 23.6% German, 17.8% Irish, 12.5% Dutch, 8.7% French (except Basque) (2000).

Economy: In Adirondack Mountains. Summer and winter recreation; summer residences. Single-family building permits issued: 7 (2005); Multi-family building permits issued: 0 (2005); Employment by occupation: 19.3% management, 16.1% professional, 24.0% services, 20.5% sales, 1.2% farming, 12.5% construction, 6.4% production (2000).

Income: Per capita income: $23,666 (2005); Median household income: $39,390 (2005); Average household income: $51,504 (2005); Percent of households with income of $100,000 or more: 11.2% (2005); Poverty rate: 7.1% (2000).

Education: Percent of population age 25 and over with: High school diploma (including GED) or higher: 81.2% (2005); Bachelor's degree or higher: 19.7% (2005); Master's degree or higher: 10.2% (2005).

Housing: Homeownership rate: 77.6% (2005); Median home value: $141,667 (2005); Median rent: $366 per month (2000); Median age of housing: 38 years (2000).

Transportation: Commute to work: 80.7% car, 0.0% public transportation, 11.7% walk, 3.3% work from home (2000); Travel time to work: 68.2% less than 15 minutes, 10.5% 15 to 30 minutes, 8.9% 30 to 45 minutes, 2.1% 45 to 60 minutes, 10.2% 60 minutes or more (2000)

LONG LAKE
(town). Covers a land area of 407.874 square miles and a water area of 42.027 square miles. Located at 43.95° N. Lat.; 74.56° W. Long. Elevation is 1,683 feet.

Population: 930 (1990); 852 (2000); 807 (2005); 776 (2010 projected); Race: 96.7% White, 1.6% Black, 0.2% Asian, 1.2% Hispanic of any race (2005); Density: 2.0 persons per square mile (2005); Average household size: 2.15 (2005); Median age: 49.0 (2005); Males per 100 females: 98.3 (2005); Marriage status: 22.9% never married, 57.6% now married, 10.2% widowed, 9.4% divorced (2000); Foreign born: 1.2% (2000); Ancestry (includes multiple ancestries): 21.1% French (except Basque), 19.4% Irish, 16.7% English, 15.2% German, 14.5% United States or American (2000).

Economy: Resort village. Single-family building permits issued: 20 (2005); Multi-family building permits issued: 0 (2005); Employment by occupation: 12.2% management, 20.7% professional, 20.4% services, 19.1% sales, 1.9% farming, 14.6% construction, 11.1% production (2000).

Income: Per capita income: $22,292 (2005); Median household income: $33,190 (2005); Average household income: $47,727 (2005); Percent of households with income of $100,000 or more: 6.9% (2005); Poverty rate: 15.6% (2000).

Education: Percent of population age 25 and over with: High school diploma (including GED) or higher: 82.6% (2005); Bachelor's degree or higher: 25.4% (2005); Master's degree or higher: 11.1% (2005).

School District(s)
Long Lake Central School District (PK-12)
    2003-04 Enrollment: 84 .... (518) 624-2147

Housing: Homeownership rate: 76.0% (2005); Median home value: $151,531 (2005); Median rent: $400 per month (2000); Median age of housing: 40 years (2000).

Transportation: Commute to work: 80.5% car, 0.0% public transportation, 14.9% walk, 4.1% work from home (2000); Travel time to work: 65.3% less than 15 minutes, 16.1% 15 to 30 minutes, 13.0% 30 to 45 minutes, 0.6% 45 to 60 minutes, 5.1% 60 minutes or more (2000)

MOREHOUSE
(town). Covers a land area of 191.108 square miles and a water area of 3.625 square miles. Located at 43.43° N. Lat.; 74.72° W. Long.

Population: 106 (1990); 151 (2000); 145 (2005); 139 (2010 projected); Race: 97.9% White, 0.0% Black, 0.0% Asian, 0.7% Hispanic of any race (2005); Density: 0.8 persons per square mile (2005); Average household size: 2.27 (2005); Median age: 51.9 (2005); Males per 100 females: 123.1 (2005); Marriage status: 12.8% never married, 79.5% now married, 2.6% widowed, 5.1% divorced (2000); Foreign born: 0.0% (2000); Ancestry (includes multiple ancestries): 33.6% Dutch, 30.5% German, 21.1% Irish, 14.8% English, 10.9% Polish (2000).

Economy: Single-family building permits issued: 3 (2005); Multi-family building permits issued: 0 (2005); Employment by occupation: 29.4% management, 5.9% professional, 0.0% services, 29.4% sales, 0.0% farming, 3.9% construction, 31.4% production (2000).

Income: Per capita income: $16,500 (2005); Median household income: $32,273 (2005); Average household income: $37,383 (2005); Percent of households with income of $100,000 or more: 0.0% (2005); Poverty rate: 7.3% (2000).

Education: Percent of population age 25 and over with: High school diploma (including GED) or higher: 67.3% (2005); Bachelor's degree or higher: 8.8% (2005); Master's degree or higher: 2.7% (2005).

Housing: Homeownership rate: 87.5% (2005); Median home value: $107,500 (2005); Median rent: $n/a per month (2000); Median age of housing: 47 years (2000).

Transportation: Commute to work: 84.3% car, 0.0% public transportation, 0.0% walk, 15.7% work from home (2000); Travel time to work: 20.9% less than 15 minutes, 0.0% 15 to 30 minutes, 51.2% 30 to 45 minutes, 0.0% 45 to 60 minutes, 27.9% 60 minutes or more (2000)

PISECO
(unincorporated postal area, zip code 12139). Covers a land area of 180.076 square miles and a water area of 3.377 square miles. Located at 43.40° N. Lat.; 74.57° W. Long.

Population: 0 (2000); Race: 96.2% White, 0.0% Black, 0.0% Asian, 0.0% Hispanic of any race (2000); Density: 0.0 persons per square mile (2000); Age: 27.2% under 18, 15.4% over 64 (2000); Marriage status: 19.2% never married, 60.4% now married, 8.6% widowed, 11.8% divorced (2000); Foreign born: 1.0% (2000); Ancestry (includes multiple ancestries): 24.0% German, 19.6% Irish, 19.6% English, 11.9% United States or American, 9.6% Other groups (2000).

Economy: Has airport. Employment by occupation: 18.0% management, 22.6% professional, 9.8% services, 21.1% sales, 0.0% farming, 14.3% construction, 14.3% production (2000).

Income: Per capita income: $24,669 (2000); Median household income: $36,375 (2000); Poverty rate: 2.9% (2000).

Education: Percent of population age 25 and over with: High school diploma (including GED) or higher: 85.4% (2000); Bachelor's degree or higher: 25.4% (2000).

School District(s)
Piseco Common School District (PK-06)
    2003-04 Enrollment: 15 .... (518) 548-7555

Housing: Homeownership rate: 96.0% (2000); Median home value: $103,100 (2000); Median rent: $425 per month (2000); Median age of housing: 40 years (2000).

Transportation: Commute to work: 94.2% car, 2.2% public transportation, 1.4% walk, 2.2% work from home (2000); Travel time to work: 42.2% less than 15 minutes, 15.6% 15 to 30 minutes, 8.9% 30 to 45 minutes, 9.6% 45 to 60 minutes, 23.7% 60 minutes or more (2000)

RAQUETTE LAKE
(unincorporated postal area, zip code 13436). Covers a land area of 29.602 square miles and a water area of 0.888 square miles. Located at 43.80° N. Lat.; 74.66° W. Long.

History: Located 4 miles South is Great Camp Sagamore- Adirondack Great Camp, former summer home of Vanderbilt family (built in 1897 by William West Durant), featuring 29 buildings.

Population: 0 (2000); Race: 96.9% White, 0.0% Black, 0.0% Asian, 0.0% Hispanic of any race (2000); Density: 0.0 persons per square mile (2000);

Age: 17.6% under 18, 26.0% over 64 (2000); Marriage status: 22.3% never married, 50.0% now married, 17.9% widowed, 9.8% divorced (2000); Foreign born: 0.0% (2000); Ancestry (includes multiple ancestries): 24.4% English, 16.8% Irish, 13.7% French (except Basque), 13.0% United States or American, 11.5% German (2000).
Economy: Employment by occupation: 23.3% management, 9.3% professional, 11.6% services, 23.3% sales, 0.0% farming, 9.3% construction, 23.3% production (2000).
Income: Per capita income: $14,571 (2000); Median household income: $22,813 (2000); Poverty rate: 12.6% (2000).
Education: Percent of population age 25 and over with: High school diploma (including GED) or higher: 87.3% (2000); Bachelor's degree or higher: 18.6% (2000).

School District(s)
Raquette Lake Union Free School District (02-06)
  2003-04 Enrollment: 6 . . . . (315) 354-4733
Housing: Homeownership rate: 81.8% (2000); Median home value: $95,000 (2000); Median rent: $325 per month (2000); Median age of housing: 36 years (2000).
Transportation: Commute to work: 69.0% car, 0.0% public transportation, 31.0% walk, 0.0% work from home (2000); Travel time to work: 83.3% less than 15 minutes, 9.5% 15 to 30 minutes, 7.1% 30 to 45 minutes, 0.0% 45 to 60 minutes, 0.0% 60 minutes or more (2000)

SPECULATOR (village). Covers a land area of 44.645 square miles and a water area of 2.581 square miles. Located at 43.52° N. Lat.; 74.36° W. Long. Elevation is 1,739 feet.
Population: 400 (1990); 348 (2000); 337 (2005); 328 (2010 projected); Race: 92.6% White, 4.7% Black, 0.9% Asian, 1.5% Hispanic of any race (2005); Density: 7.5 persons per square mile (2005); Average household size: 2.11 (2005); Median age: 49.2 (2005); Males per 100 females: 110.6 (2005); Marriage status: 21.5% never married, 61.3% now married, 8.0% widowed, 9.1% divorced (2000); Foreign born: 2.0% (2000); Ancestry (includes multiple ancestries): 35.1% English, 16.4% German, 15.4% Irish, 13.1% Dutch, 8.5% French (except Basque) (2000).
Economy: In winter (skiing) and summer-resort area; lumbering. Single-family building permits issued: 5 (2005); Multi-family building permits issued: 0 (2005); Employment by occupation: 16.9% management, 16.3% professional, 24.1% services, 27.1% sales, 1.2% farming, 9.0% construction, 5.4% production (2000).
Income: Per capita income: $27,349 (2005); Median household income: $40,909 (2005); Average household income: $56,438 (2005); Percent of households with income of $100,000 or more: 14.4% (2005); Poverty rate: 4.3% (2000).
Education: Percent of population age 25 and over with: High school diploma (including GED) or higher: 84.1% (2005); Bachelor's degree or higher: 23.5% (2005); Master's degree or higher: 12.3% (2005).

School District(s)
Lake Pleasant Central School District (PK-09)
  2003-04 Enrollment: 99 . . . . (518) 548-7571
Housing: Homeownership rate: 70.6% (2005); Median home value: $147,656 (2005); Median rent: $358 per month (2000); Median age of housing: 45 years (2000).
Newspapers: Hamilton County News (General - Circulation 3,699)
Transportation: Commute to work: 64.3% car, 0.0% public transportation, 24.0% walk, 5.8% work from home (2000); Travel time to work: 69.7% less than 15 minutes, 7.6% 15 to 30 minutes, 13.8% 30 to 45 minutes, 1.4% 45 to 60 minutes, 7.6% 60 minutes or more (2000)
Additional Information Contacts
Adirondacks Speculator Region Chamber of Commerce . . (518) 548-4521
  http://www.adrkmts.com

WELLS (town). Covers a land area of 177.211 square miles and a water area of 1.170 square miles. Located at 43.43° N. Lat.; 74.29° W. Long. Elevation is 1,021 feet.
Population: 706 (1990); 737 (2000); 711 (2005); 685 (2010 projected); Race: 95.8% White, 1.8% Black, 0.3% Asian, 0.1% Hispanic of any race (2005); Density: 4.0 persons per square mile (2005); Average household size: 2.24 (2005); Median age: 47.3 (2005); Males per 100 females: 95.3 (2005); Marriage status: 16.4% never married, 58.8% now married, 11.5% widowed, 13.2% divorced (2000); Foreign born: 2.5% (2000); Ancestry (includes multiple ancestries): 20.2% Irish, 18.5% German, 18.4% English, 11.7% Dutch, 11.4% French (except Basque) (2000).
Economy: Logging. Single-family building permits issued: 5 (2005); Multi-family building permits issued: 0 (2005); Employment by occupation: 7.0% management, 19.9% professional, 22.3% services, 24.6% sales, 2.3% farming, 12.3% construction, 11.6% production (2000).
Income: Per capita income: $18,348 (2005); Median household income: $32,600 (2005); Average household income: $40,708 (2005); Percent of households with income of $100,000 or more: 6.9% (2005); Poverty rate: 15.7% (2000).
Education: Percent of population age 25 and over with: High school diploma (including GED) or higher: 81.7% (2005); Bachelor's degree or higher: 12.6% (2005); Master's degree or higher: 4.1% (2005).

School District(s)
Wells Central School District (PK-12)
  2003-04 Enrollment: 180 . . . . (518) 924-6000
Housing: Homeownership rate: 79.9% (2005); Median home value: $113,571 (2005); Median rent: $371 per month (2000); Median age of housing: 42 years (2000).
Transportation: Commute to work: 88.4% car, 0.7% public transportation, 6.2% walk, 4.1% work from home (2000); Travel time to work: 33.6% less than 15 minutes, 27.1% 15 to 30 minutes, 11.8% 30 to 45 minutes, 13.9% 45 to 60 minutes, 13.6% 60 minutes or more (2000)

Herkimer County

Located in central and north central New York, extending north into the Adirondacks and south into the Mohawk Valley; drained by the Mohawk, Unadilla, Black, and Moose Rivers. Covers a land area of 1,411.25 square miles, a water area of 47.10 square miles, and is located in the Eastern Time Zone. The county government was organized in 1791. County seat is Herkimer.

Herkimer County is part of the Utica-Rome, NY Metropolitan Statistical Area. The entire metro area includes: Herkimer County, NY; Oneida County, NY

Weather Station: Old Forge   Elevation: 1,719 feet

	Jan	Feb	Mar	Apr	May	Jun	Jul	Aug	Sep	Oct	Nov	Dec
High	25	28	37	50	64	72	76	74	65	54	41	30
Low	1	3	14	26	38	47	52	50	43	32	23	10
Precip	4.2	2.9	3.7	3.7	4.0	4.2	4.5	4.4	5.3	4.5	4.9	4.3
Snow	58.9	39.1	38.1	13.4	2.2	tr	0.0	0.0	tr	3.4	24.5	47.1

High and Low temperatures in degrees Fahrenheit; Precipitation and Snow in inches

Weather Station: Stillwater Reservoir   Elevation: 1,689 feet

	Jan	Feb	Mar	Apr	May	Jun	Jul	Aug	Sep	Oct	Nov	Dec
High	25	27	36	49	63	71	75	73	65	54	41	30
Low	2	3	13	28	41	50	55	54	46	35	26	11
Precip	3.7	2.7	3.3	3.6	3.9	4.3	4.6	4.8	5.1	4.2	4.6	4.2
Snow	51.7	35.4	29.8	10.4	1.1	0.0	0.0	0.0	tr	2.2	19.1	41.1

High and Low temperatures in degrees Fahrenheit; Precipitation and Snow in inches

Population: 65,797 (1990); 64,427 (2000); 63,519 (2005); 62,558 (2010 projected); Race: 97.3% White, 0.8% Black, 0.6% Asian, 1.2% Hispanic of any race (2005); Density: 45.0 persons per square mile (2005); Average household size: 2.47 (2005); Median age: 40.4 (2005); Males per 100 females: 94.4 (2005).
Religion: Five largest groups: 36.5% Catholic Church, 6.7% The United Methodist Church, 2.5% Evangelical Lutheran Church in America, 2.4% American Baptist Churches in the USA, 1.1% Presbyterian Church (U.S.A.) (2000).
Economy: Unemployment rate: 5.2% (2005); Total civilian labor force: 31,721 (2005); Leading industries: 30.2% manufacturing; 19.4% health care and social assistance; 15.6% retail trade (2003); Farms: 690 totaling 159,258 acres (2002); Companies that employ 500 or more persons: 1 (2003); Companies that employ 100 to 499 persons: 17 (2003); Companies that employ less than 100 persons: 1,168 (2003); Black-owned businesses: n/a (2002); Hispanic-owned businesses: n/a (2002); Women-owned businesses: 1,072 (2002); Retail sales per capita: $7,487 (2006). Single-family building permits issued: 162 (2005); Multi-family building permits issued: 0 (2005).
Income: Per capita income: $18,748 (2005); Median household income: $37,583 (2005); Average household income: $45,605 (2005); Percent of households with income of $100,000 or more: 6.9% (2005); Poverty rate: 12.4% (2003); Bankruptcy rate: 11.16% (2005).
Taxes: Total county taxes per capita: $595 (2004); County property taxes per capita: $247 (2004).

Education: Percent of population age 25 and over with: High school diploma (including GED) or higher: 79.4% (2005); Bachelor's degree or higher: 15.7% (2005); Master's degree or higher: 5.8% (2005).
Housing: Homeownership rate: 71.7% (2005); Median home value: $88,383 (2005); Median rent: $346 per month (2000); Median age of housing: 50 years (2000).
Health: Birth rate: 111.5 per 10,000 population (2004); Death rate: 117.3 per 10,000 population (2004); Age-adjusted cancer mortality rate: 219.1 deaths per 100,000 population (2002); Air Quality Index: 97.5% good, 2.5% moderate, 0.0% unhealthy for sensitive individuals, 0.0% unhealthy (percent of days in 2005); Number of physicians: 8.0 per 10,000 population (2004); Hospital beds: 54.6 per 10,000 population (2003); Hospital admissions: 779.2 per 10,000 population (2003).
Elections: 2004 Presidential election results: 56.6% Bush, 41.2% Kerry, 2.0% Nader, 0.2% Badnarik
National and State Parks: Black Creek State Forest
Additional Information Contacts
Herkimer County Government . . . . (315) 867-1002
  http://www.herkimercounty.org/
Town of Danube. . . . . (315) 823-3400
  http://town.danube.ny.us/content?module=DTP_Home_Page_Info
Town of Schuyler . . . . (315) 733-7458
  http://www.geocities.com/townofschuyler/
Village of Ilion . . . . (315) 895-7449
  http://www.ilionny.com/

Herkimer County Communities

COLD BROOK (village). Covers a land area of 0.441 square miles and a water area of 0 square miles. Located at 43.24° N. Lat.; 75.03° W. Long.
Population: 310 (1990); 336 (2000); 347 (2005); 352 (2010 projected); Race: 99.7% White, 0.0% Black, 0.3% Asian, 0.0% Hispanic of any race (2005); Density: 786.1 persons per square mile (2005); Average household size: 2.67 (2005); Median age: 35.1 (2005); Males per 100 females: 105.3 (2005); Marriage status: 25.6% never married, 55.7% now married, 5.7% widowed, 13.0% divorced (2000); Foreign born: 0.0% (2000); Ancestry (includes multiple ancestries): 21.1% Irish, 17.7% English, 14.6% German, 13.4% United States or American, 12.3% French (except Basque) (2000).
Economy: Single-family building permits issued: 0 (2005); Multi-family building permits issued: 0 (2005); Employment by occupation: 6.1% management, 16.5% professional, 18.9% services, 28.7% sales, 3.0% farming, 7.3% construction, 19.5% production (2000).
Income: Per capita income: $15,937 (2005); Median household income: $34,310 (2005); Average household income: $42,538 (2005); Percent of households with income of $100,000 or more: 5.4% (2005); Poverty rate: 10.9% (2000).
Education: Percent of population age 25 and over with: High school diploma (including GED) or higher: 83.3% (2005); Bachelor's degree or higher: 5.1% (2005); Master's degree or higher: 2.3% (2005).
Housing: Homeownership rate: 76.9% (2005); Median home value: $70,968 (2005); Median rent: $370 per month (2000); Median age of housing: 60+ years (2000).
Transportation: Commute to work: 98.8% car, 0.0% public transportation, 0.0% walk, 1.2% work from home (2000); Travel time to work: 8.8% less than 15 minutes, 28.7% 15 to 30 minutes, 52.5% 30 to 45 minutes, 8.8% 45 to 60 minutes, 1.3% 60 minutes or more (2000)

COLUMBIA (town). Covers a land area of 34.997 square miles and a water area of 0.023 square miles. Located at 42.92° N. Lat.; 75.04° W. Long.
Population: 1,587 (1990); 1,630 (2000); 1,592 (2005); 1,599 (2010 projected); Race: 98.5% White, 0.0% Black, 0.3% Asian, 0.6% Hispanic of any race (2005); Density: 45.5 persons per square mile (2005); Average household size: 2.74 (2005); Median age: 38.4 (2005); Males per 100 females: 109.5 (2005); Marriage status: 23.7% never married, 64.2% now married, 5.5% widowed, 6.6% divorced (2000); Foreign born: 0.9% (2000); Ancestry (includes multiple ancestries): 24.8% German, 17.6% Irish, 13.8% English, 10.3% Polish, 8.6% French (except Basque) (2000).
Economy: Single-family building permits issued: 10 (2005); Multi-family building permits issued: 0 (2005); Employment by occupation: 14.7% management, 17.9% professional, 11.8% services, 23.5% sales, 1.4% farming, 8.8% construction, 21.8% production (2000).
Income: Per capita income: $19,094 (2005); Median household income: $44,429 (2005); Average household income: $52,409 (2005); Percent of households with income of $100,000 or more: 9.0% (2005); Poverty rate: 14.5% (2000).
Education: Percent of population age 25 and over with: High school diploma (including GED) or higher: 83.1% (2005); Bachelor's degree or higher: 12.7% (2005); Master's degree or higher: 4.5% (2005).
Housing: Homeownership rate: 85.9% (2005); Median home value: $89,111 (2005); Median rent: $349 per month (2000); Median age of housing: 30 years (2000).
Transportation: Commute to work: 88.5% car, 0.3% public transportation, 3.3% walk, 7.0% work from home (2000); Travel time to work: 15.8% less than 15 minutes, 42.3% 15 to 30 minutes, 29.3% 30 to 45 minutes, 6.8% 45 to 60 minutes, 5.8% 60 minutes or more (2000)

DANUBE (town). Covers a land area of 29.375 square miles and a water area of 0.271 square miles. Located at 42.98° N. Lat.; 74.80° W. Long.
Population: 1,099 (1990); 1,098 (2000); 1,082 (2005); 1,066 (2010 projected); Race: 95.5% White, 1.2% Black, 1.7% Asian, 1.3% Hispanic of any race (2005); Density: 36.8 persons per square mile (2005); Average household size: 2.71 (2005); Median age: 36.8 (2005); Males per 100 females: 110.1 (2005); Marriage status: 30.2% never married, 55.9% now married, 6.1% widowed, 7.8% divorced (2000); Foreign born: 2.3% (2000); Ancestry (includes multiple ancestries): 22.4% German, 10.2% Irish, 9.1% Italian, 9.0% French (except Basque), 8.2% Polish (2000).
Economy: Single-family building permits issued: 10 (2005); Multi-family building permits issued: 0 (2005); Employment by occupation: 10.9% management, 12.6% professional, 12.6% services, 17.7% sales, 4.7% farming, 9.7% construction, 31.9% production (2000).
Income: Per capita income: $16,758 (2005); Median household income: $38,833 (2005); Average household income: $45,331 (2005); Percent of households with income of $100,000 or more: 6.3% (2005); Poverty rate: 18.4% (2000).
Education: Percent of population age 25 and over with: High school diploma (including GED) or higher: 70.2% (2005); Bachelor's degree or higher: 8.3% (2005); Master's degree or higher: 2.2% (2005).
Housing: Homeownership rate: 86.5% (2005); Median home value: $68,372 (2005); Median rent: $318 per month (2000); Median age of housing: 29 years (2000).
Transportation: Commute to work: 87.6% car, 1.0% public transportation, 2.5% walk, 8.1% work from home (2000); Travel time to work: 30.0% less than 15 minutes, 42.2% 15 to 30 minutes, 16.5% 30 to 45 minutes, 7.0% 45 to 60 minutes, 4.3% 60 minutes or more (2000)
Additional Information Contacts
Town of Danube. . . . . (315) 823-3400
  http://town.danube.ny.us/content?module=DTP_Home_Page_Info

DOLGEVILLE (village). Covers a land area of 1.832 square miles and a water area of 0.034 square miles. Located at 43.10° N. Lat.; 74.77° W. Long. Elevation is 802 feet.
History: Incorporated 1891.
Population: 2,452 (1990); 2,166 (2000); 2,091 (2005); 2,011 (2010 projected); Race: 96.7% White, 0.4% Black, 0.7% Asian, 1.2% Hispanic of any race (2005); Density: 1,141.5 persons per square mile (2005); Average household size: 2.32 (2005); Median age: 41.0 (2005); Males per 100 females: 88.2 (2005); Marriage status: 23.1% never married, 56.6% now married, 12.4% widowed, 7.9% divorced (2000); Foreign born: 1.4% (2000); Ancestry (includes multiple ancestries): 26.3% German, 15.7% Irish, 14.5% Italian, 10.9% English, 7.6% French (except Basque) (2000).
Economy: Manufacturing: textiles, wood products, sporting goods, apparel, piano parts. Single-family building permits issued: 0 (2005); Multi-family building permits issued: 0 (2005); Employment by occupation: 8.2% management, 17.9% professional, 14.2% services, 25.8% sales, 0.9% farming, 9.2% construction, 23.8% production (2000).
Income: Per capita income: $17,497 (2005); Median household income: $35,471 (2005); Average household income: $40,389 (2005); Percent of households with income of $100,000 or more: 4.1% (2005); Poverty rate: 10.9% (2000).
Education: Percent of population age 25 and over with: High school diploma (including GED) or higher: 79.6% (2005); Bachelor's degree or higher: 17.0% (2005); Master's degree or higher: 7.4% (2005).
School District(s)
Dolgeville Central School District (PK-12)
  2003-04 Enrollment: 963 . . . . (315) 429-3155

Housing: Homeownership rate: 62.7% (2005); Median home value: $67,692 (2005); Median rent: $281 per month (2000); Median age of housing: 60+ years (2000).
Transportation: Commute to work: 92.8% car, 0.0% public transportation, 6.0% walk, 0.8% work from home (2000); Travel time to work: 45.1% less than 15 minutes, 31.3% 15 to 30 minutes, 12.6% 30 to 45 minutes, 7.6% 45 to 60 minutes, 3.4% 60 minutes or more (2000)

EAGLE BAY (unincorporated postal area, zip code 13331). Covers a land area of 72.504 square miles and a water area of 4.343 square miles. Located at 43.82° N. Lat.; 74.87° W. Long.
Population: 0 (2000); Race: 100.0% White, 0.0% Black, 0.0% Asian, 0.0% Hispanic of any race (2000); Density: 0.0 persons per square mile (2000); Age: 25.5% under 18, 23.0% over 64 (2000); Marriage status: 21.2% never married, 65.8% now married, 7.7% widowed, 5.4% divorced (2000); Foreign born: 1.4% (2000); Ancestry (includes multiple ancestries): 29.9% English, 24.5% German, 20.1% Irish, 15.8% French (except Basque), 6.1% Dutch (2000).
Economy: Resort village in the Adirondack Mountains. Employment by occupation: 10.8% management, 6.9% professional, 31.4% services, 24.5% sales, 3.9% farming, 7.8% construction, 14.7% production (2000).
Income: Per capita income: $15,459 (2000); Median household income: $28,750 (2000); Poverty rate: 12.2% (2000).
Education: Percent of population age 25 and over with: High school diploma (including GED) or higher: 89.9% (2000); Bachelor's degree or higher: 15.2% (2000).
Housing: Homeownership rate: 88.1% (2000); Median home value: $108,300 (2000); Median rent: $400 per month (2000); Median age of housing: 47 years (2000).
Transportation: Commute to work: 64.1% car, 0.0% public transportation, 33.3% walk, 0.0% work from home (2000); Travel time to work: 52.6% less than 15 minutes, 34.6% 15 to 30 minutes, 10.3% 30 to 45 minutes, 0.0% 45 to 60 minutes, 2.6% 60 minutes or more (2000)

FAIRFIELD (town). Covers a land area of 41.136 square miles and a water area of 0.190 square miles. Located at 43.12° N. Lat.; 74.93° W. Long.
Population: 1,442 (1990); 1,607 (2000); 1,639 (2005); 1,656 (2010 projected); Race: 98.3% White, 0.6% Black, 0.0% Asian, 0.3% Hispanic of any race (2005); Density: 39.8 persons per square mile (2005); Average household size: 2.81 (2005); Median age: 40.1 (2005); Males per 100 females: 101.6 (2005); Marriage status: 26.6% never married, 61.2% now married, 5.7% widowed, 6.5% divorced (2000); Foreign born: 1.5% (2000); Ancestry (includes multiple ancestries): 24.0% German, 20.0% Irish, 13.0% English, 9.9% Italian, 7.9% French (except Basque) (2000).
Economy: Single-family building permits issued: 0 (2005); Multi-family building permits issued: 0 (2005); Employment by occupation: 11.5% management, 17.5% professional, 13.8% services, 26.1% sales, 2.6% farming, 12.4% construction, 16.1% production (2000).
Income: Per capita income: $18,956 (2005); Median household income: $46,103 (2005); Average household income: $52,509 (2005); Percent of households with income of $100,000 or more: 7.7% (2005); Poverty rate: 11.6% (2000).
Education: Percent of population age 25 and over with: High school diploma (including GED) or higher: 74.4% (2005); Bachelor's degree or higher: 12.6% (2005); Master's degree or higher: 5.1% (2005).
Housing: Homeownership rate: 85.6% (2005); Median home value: $94,274 (2005); Median rent: $368 per month (2000); Median age of housing: 46 years (2000).
Transportation: Commute to work: 90.4% car, 0.0% public transportation, 3.4% walk, 5.9% work from home (2000); Travel time to work: 26.8% less than 15 minutes, 40.1% 15 to 30 minutes, 23.6% 30 to 45 minutes, 5.3% 45 to 60 minutes, 4.2% 60 minutes or more (2000)

FRANKFORT (village). Covers a land area of 1.003 square miles and a water area of 0.015 square miles. Located at 43.03° N. Lat.; 75.07° W. Long.
Population: 2,693 (1990); 2,537 (2000); 2,360 (2005); 2,211 (2010 projected); Race: 97.5% White, 0.0% Black, 0.3% Asian, 1.4% Hispanic of any race (2005); Density: 2,352.0 persons per square mile (2005); Average household size: 2.29 (2005); Median age: 40.5 (2005); Males per 100 females: 84.5 (2005); Marriage status: 28.2% never married, 51.4% now married, 10.3% widowed, 10.1% divorced (2000); Foreign born: 3.5% (2000); Ancestry (includes multiple ancestries): 48.9% Italian, 12.0% Irish, 11.1% German, 10.2% English, 5.3% Polish (2000).
Economy: Single-family building permits issued: 0 (2005); Multi-family building permits issued: 0 (2005); Employment by occupation: 13.1% management, 14.3% professional, 19.6% services, 30.7% sales, 0.0% farming, 7.4% construction, 14.9% production (2000).
Income: Per capita income: $16,618 (2005); Median household income: $30,494 (2005); Average household income: $38,038 (2005); Percent of households with income of $100,000 or more: 3.0% (2005); Poverty rate: 15.5% (2000).
Education: Percent of population age 25 and over with: High school diploma (including GED) or higher: 72.7% (2005); Bachelor's degree or higher: 9.7% (2005); Master's degree or higher: 2.9% (2005).

School District(s)
Frankfort-Schuyler Central School District (KG-12)
    2003-04 Enrollment: 1,166 . . . . (315) 894-5083

Housing: Homeownership rate: 59.9% (2005); Median home value: $85,957 (2005); Median rent: $363 per month (2000); Median age of housing: 60+ years (2000).
Safety: Violent crime rate: 28.4 per 10,000 population; Property crime rate: 137.8 per 10,000 population (2004).
Transportation: Commute to work: 92.4% car, 1.0% public transportation, 4.7% walk, 1.3% work from home (2000); Travel time to work: 42.8% less than 15 minutes, 40.3% 15 to 30 minutes, 10.1% 30 to 45 minutes, 2.7% 45 to 60 minutes, 4.1% 60 minutes or more (2000)

FRANKFORT (town). Covers a land area of 37.216 square miles and a water area of 0.113 square miles. Located at 43.04° N. Lat.; 75.11° W. Long.
History: Settled 1723, incorporated 1863.
Population: 7,494 (1990); 7,478 (2000); 7,394 (2005); 7,296 (2010 projected); Race: 97.5% White, 0.9% Black, 0.2% Asian, 1.4% Hispanic of any race (2005); Density: 198.7 persons per square mile (2005); Average household size: 2.45 (2005); Median age: 41.3 (2005); Males per 100 females: 91.4 (2005); Marriage status: 24.7% never married, 58.0% now married, 8.3% widowed, 9.1% divorced (2000); Foreign born: 2.1% (2000); Ancestry (includes multiple ancestries): 44.8% Italian, 14.1% Irish, 13.4% German, 9.6% English, 7.7% Polish (2000).
Economy: Office and library equipment, threaded fittings, agriculture and industrial hand tools. Single-family building permits issued: 13 (2005); Multi-family building permits issued: 0 (2005); Employment by occupation: 13.1% management, 15.1% professional, 19.8% services, 27.1% sales, 0.0% farming, 8.6% construction, 16.3% production (2000).
Income: Per capita income: $19,886 (2005); Median household income: $43,644 (2005); Average household income: $48,586 (2005); Percent of households with income of $100,000 or more: 6.7% (2005); Poverty rate: 9.2% (2000).
Education: Percent of population age 25 and over with: High school diploma (including GED) or higher: 78.6% (2005); Bachelor's degree or higher: 13.7% (2005); Master's degree or higher: 4.5% (2005).
Housing: Homeownership rate: 75.1% (2005); Median home value: $98,372 (2005); Median rent: $395 per month (2000); Median age of housing: 47 years (2000).
Transportation: Commute to work: 94.5% car, 0.6% public transportation, 2.1% walk, 2.4% work from home (2000); Travel time to work: 36.3% less than 15 minutes, 45.5% 15 to 30 minutes, 11.4% 30 to 45 minutes, 2.4% 45 to 60 minutes, 4.3% 60 minutes or more (2000)

GERMAN FLATTS (town). Covers a land area of 33.742 square miles and a water area of 0.519 square miles. Located at 43.00° N. Lat.; 75.01° W. Long.
Population: 14,345 (1990); 13,629 (2000); 13,221 (2005); 12,790 (2010 projected); Race: 97.5% White, 0.9% Black, 0.2% Asian, 2.1% Hispanic of any race (2005); Density: 391.8 persons per square mile (2005); Average household size: 2.45 (2005); Median age: 39.3 (2005); Males per 100 females: 89.1 (2005); Marriage status: 25.5% never married, 54.6% now married, 9.6% widowed, 10.2% divorced (2000); Foreign born: 0.8% (2000); Ancestry (includes multiple ancestries): 22.8% German, 19.6% Irish, 16.4% Italian, 13.2% English, 8.5% French (except Basque) (2000).
Economy: Single-family building permits issued: 3 (2005); Multi-family building permits issued: 0 (2005); Employment by occupation: 8.9% management, 17.4% professional, 17.6% services, 30.1% sales, 0.2% farming, 8.7% construction, 17.1% production (2000).
Income: Per capita income: $16,954 (2005); Median household income: $35,919 (2005); Average household income: $40,898 (2005); Percent of households with income of $100,000 or more: 4.6% (2005); Poverty rate: 13.7% (2000).

Education: Percent of population age 25 and over with: High school diploma (including GED) or higher: 79.7% (2005); Bachelor's degree or higher: 16.4% (2005); Master's degree or higher: 5.4% (2005).
Housing: Homeownership rate: 65.8% (2005); Median home value: $84,535 (2005); Median rent: $355 per month (2000); Median age of housing: 60+ years (2000).
Transportation: Commute to work: 91.0% car, 1.2% public transportation, 5.6% walk, 1.8% work from home (2000); Travel time to work: 42.7% less than 15 minutes, 35.1% 15 to 30 minutes, 14.6% 30 to 45 minutes, 3.4% 45 to 60 minutes, 4.2% 60 minutes or more (2000)

HERKIMER (village). Covers a land area of 2.413 square miles and a water area of 0.124 square miles. Located at 43.02° N. Lat.; 74.99° W. Long. Elevation is 407 feet.
History: Formerly shipping, commercial and trade center for surrounding Mohawk valley Agriculture and industrial area that stretched west through village of Mohawk to Ilion and Frankfort. Herkimer County Historical Society has important documents and exhibits here. World-renowned Herkimer diamonds (actually a clear quartz) are to be found along West Canada Creek Valley north of the village. Settled c.1725, Incorporated 1807.
Population: 7,945 (1990); 7,498 (2000); 7,240 (2005); 6,999 (2010 projected); Race: 94.3% White, 2.0% Black, 2.1% Asian, 1.9% Hispanic of any race (2005); Density: 3,000.2 persons per square mile (2005); Average household size: 2.33 (2005); Median age: 40.3 (2005); Males per 100 females: 89.2 (2005); Marriage status: 30.1% never married, 49.9% now married, 11.8% widowed, 8.1% divorced (2000); Foreign born: 4.7% (2000); Ancestry (includes multiple ancestries): 25.4% Italian, 15.9% Irish, 15.4% German, 7.4% English, 7.3% Other groups (2000).
Economy: Manufacturing includes machinery, consumer goods, wood products and firearms. Single-family building permits issued: 0 (2005); Multi-family building permits issued: 0 (2005); Employment by occupation: 8.4% management, 16.6% professional, 22.5% services, 32.7% sales, 0.0% farming, 5.0% construction, 14.9% production (2000).
Income: Per capita income: $18,602 (2005); Median household income: $28,655 (2005); Average household income: $41,132 (2005); Percent of households with income of $100,000 or more: 6.7% (2005); Poverty rate: 14.8% (2000).
Education: Percent of population age 25 and over with: High school diploma (including GED) or higher: 76.0% (2005); Bachelor's degree or higher: 15.1% (2005); Master's degree or higher: 6.8% (2005).

School District(s)
Boces Herk-Fulton-Hamilton-Otsego
   2003-04 Enrollment: n/a . . . . (315) 867-2023
Herkimer Central School District (KG-12)
   2003-04 Enrollment: 1,302 . . . . (315) 866-2230

Two-year College(s)
Herkimer County Community College (Public)
   Fall 2004 Enrollment: 3,472. (315) 866-0300
   2005-06 Tuition: In-state $3,130; Out-of-state $5,330

Housing: Homeownership rate: 49.6% (2005); Median home value: $86,187 (2005); Median rent: $356 per month (2000); Median age of housing: 60+ years (2000).
Newspapers: Images (General - Circulation 8,500); The Evening Telegram (Circulation 7,000)
Transportation: Commute to work: 86.2% car, 1.8% public transportation, 9.5% walk, 1.6% work from home (2000); Travel time to work: 53.2% less than 15 minutes, 26.5% 15 to 30 minutes, 12.1% 30 to 45 minutes, 2.7% 45 to 60 minutes, 5.5% 60 minutes or more (2000)

HERKIMER (town). Covers a land area of 31.562 square miles and a water area of 0.561 square miles. Located at 43.03° N. Lat.; 74.98° W. Long. Elevation is 407 feet.
History: Herkimer was settled by a group of Palatines in 1725 and was long known as German Flats. In 1776 Fort Dayton, a wooden structure surrounded by a stockade, was built on a plot now at the center of town. From that fort on August 4, 1777, General Nicholas Herkimer marched to the Battle of Oriskany. The town was named for him.
Population: 10,401 (1990); 9,962 (2000); 9,713 (2005); 9,461 (2010 projected); Race: 95.4% White, 1.6% Black, 1.7% Asian, 1.6% Hispanic of any race (2005); Density: 307.7 persons per square mile (2005); Average household size: 2.39 (2005); Median age: 41.3 (2005); Males per 100 females: 90.4 (2005); Marriage status: 27.1% never married, 53.9% now married, 11.2% widowed, 7.8% divorced (2000); Foreign born: 4.2% (2000); Ancestry (includes multiple ancestries): 23.3% Italian, 17.8% German, 15.3% Irish, 8.0% English, 7.5% Polish (2000).
Economy: Single-family building permits issued: 4 (2005); Multi-family building permits issued: 0 (2005); Employment by occupation: 8.4% management, 18.1% professional, 20.7% services, 31.4% sales, 0.0% farming, 5.6% construction, 15.8% production (2000).
Income: Per capita income: $19,325 (2005); Median household income: $32,535 (2005); Average household income: $44,400 (2005); Percent of households with income of $100,000 or more: 8.0% (2005); Poverty rate: 13.3% (2000).
Education: Percent of population age 25 and over with: High school diploma (including GED) or higher: 77.4% (2005); Bachelor's degree or higher: 16.6% (2005); Master's degree or higher: 7.2% (2005).
Housing: Homeownership rate: 58.8% (2005); Median home value: $89,625 (2005); Median rent: $355 per month (2000); Median age of housing: 60+ years (2000).
Transportation: Commute to work: 88.6% car, 1.6% public transportation, 7.2% walk, 1.8% work from home (2000); Travel time to work: 51.4% less than 15 minutes, 26.9% 15 to 30 minutes, 13.0% 30 to 45 minutes, 3.0% 45 to 60 minutes, 5.7% 60 minutes or more (2000)

ILION (village). Covers a land area of 2.477 square miles and a water area of 0.046 square miles. Located at 43.01° N. Lat.; 75.04° W. Long. Elevation is 410 feet.
History: Part of the former Herkimer (village). Remington Arms Museum. Incorporated 1852.
Population: 8,911 (1990); 8,610 (2000); 8,263 (2005); 7,913 (2010 projected); Race: 96.9% White, 1.0% Black, 0.3% Asian, 2.2% Hispanic of any race (2005); Density: 3,336.5 persons per square mile (2005); Average household size: 2.48 (2005); Median age: 37.7 (2005); Males per 100 females: 86.1 (2005); Marriage status: 25.8% never married, 52.8% now married, 10.0% widowed, 11.4% divorced (2000); Foreign born: 0.8% (2000); Ancestry (includes multiple ancestries): 22.8% German, 20.6% Irish, 13.2% English, 12.2% Italian, 8.8% French (except Basque) (2000).
Economy: Manufacturing: consumer goods, powder, metal products, lumber. In dairying area. Single-family building permits issued: 1 (2005); Multi-family building permits issued: 0 (2005); Employment by occupation: 8.5% management, 18.1% professional, 17.9% services, 31.5% sales, 0.2% farming, 8.8% construction, 15.1% production (2000).
Income: Per capita income: $16,012 (2005); Median household income: $34,159 (2005); Average household income: $38,878 (2005); Percent of households with income of $100,000 or more: 3.8% (2005); Poverty rate: 17.1% (2000).
Education: Percent of population age 25 and over with: High school diploma (including GED) or higher: 79.7% (2005); Bachelor's degree or higher: 18.6% (2005); Master's degree or higher: 6.4% (2005).

School District(s)
Ilion Central School District (PK-12)
   2003-04 Enrollment: 1,794 . . . . (315) 894-9934

Two-year College(s)
Herkimer County BOCES-Practical Nursing Program (Public)
   Fall 2004 Enrollment: 49 . . . . (315) 895-2210

Housing: Homeownership rate: 60.0% (2005); Median home value: $82,510 (2005); Median rent: $357 per month (2000); Median age of housing: 60+ years (2000).
Safety: Violent crime rate: 11.9 per 10,000 population; Property crime rate: 134.7 per 10,000 population (2004).
Transportation: Commute to work: 90.3% car, 0.9% public transportation, 6.9% walk, 1.3% work from home (2000); Travel time to work: 38.8% less than 15 minutes, 38.4% 15 to 30 minutes, 14.6% 30 to 45 minutes, 3.1% 45 to 60 minutes, 5.1% 60 minutes or more (2000)
Additional Information Contacts
Village of Ilion. . . . . (315) 895-7449
   http://www.ilionny.com/

JORDANVILLE (unincorporated postal area, zip code 13361). Covers a land area of 26.577 square miles and a water area of 0.027 square miles. Located at 42.90° N. Lat.; 74.89° W. Long.
History: Site of Holy Trinity Russian Orthodox Seminary (largest Eastern Orthodox monastery in North America), with traditional Russian architecture and gold-clad Byzantine domes that are visible for miles.
Population: 0 (2000); Race: 97.6% White, 0.8% Black, 0.4% Asian, 0.6% Hispanic of any race (2000); Density: 0.0 persons per square mile (2000); Age: 25.9% under 18, 13.2% over 64 (2000); Marriage status: 20.5% never married, 64.1% now married, 6.0% widowed, 9.5% divorced (2000);

Foreign born: 4.6% (2000); Ancestry (includes multiple ancestries): 26.8% German, 15.5% Irish, 12.4% Polish, 12.1% English, 7.1% United States or American (2000).
Economy: Agriculture: dairying; field corn, hay. Employment by occupation: 9.8% management, 19.6% professional, 17.6% services, 16.7% sales, 3.9% farming, 16.3% construction, 16.0% production (2000).
Income: Per capita income: $14,979 (2000); Median household income: $33,125 (2000); Poverty rate: 16.4% (2000).
Education: Percent of population age 25 and over with: High school diploma (including GED) or higher: 82.8% (2000); Bachelor's degree or higher: 13.9% (2000).
Housing: Homeownership rate: 82.0% (2000); Median home value: $58,200 (2000); Median rent: $380 per month (2000); Median age of housing: 47 years (2000).
Transportation: Commute to work: 85.6% car, 0.0% public transportation, 6.4% walk, 7.4% work from home (2000); Travel time to work: 22.0% less than 15 minutes, 33.6% 15 to 30 minutes, 34.7% 30 to 45 minutes, 5.1% 45 to 60 minutes, 4.7% 60 minutes or more (2000).

LITCHFIELD (town). Covers a land area of 29.606 square miles and a water area of 0.051 square miles. Located at 42.97° N. Lat.; 75.14° W. Long.
Population: 1,414 (1990); 1,453 (2000); 1,573 (2005); 1,667 (2010 projected); Race: 98.5% White, 0.1% Black, 0.3% Asian, 0.8% Hispanic of any race (2005); Density: 53.1 persons per square mile (2005); Average household size: 2.77 (2005); Median age: 38.0 (2005); Males per 100 females: 103.5 (2005); Marriage status: 22.8% never married, 65.3% now married, 4.5% widowed, 7.4% divorced (2000); Foreign born: 0.6% (2000); Ancestry (includes multiple ancestries): 22.1% Irish, 18.5% English, 17.1% German, 13.3% French (except Basque), 12.9% Italian (2000).
Economy: Single-family building permits issued: 11 (2005); Multi-family building permits issued: 0 (2005); Employment by occupation: 16.0% management, 17.1% professional, 11.4% services, 24.4% sales, 2.1% farming, 9.7% construction, 19.1% production (2000).
Income: Per capita income: $20,880 (2005); Median household income: $50,560 (2005); Average household income: $57,826 (2005); Percent of households with income of $100,000 or more: 11.6% (2005); Poverty rate: 9.7% (2000).
Education: Percent of population age 25 and over with: High school diploma (including GED) or higher: 86.4% (2005); Bachelor's degree or higher: 13.5% (2005); Master's degree or higher: 4.3% (2005).
Housing: Homeownership rate: 85.7% (2005); Median home value: $97,328 (2005); Median rent: $321 per month (2000); Median age of housing: 28 years (2000).
Transportation: Commute to work: 89.5% car, 0.7% public transportation, 2.2% walk, 6.5% work from home (2000); Travel time to work: 21.6% less than 15 minutes, 48.4% 15 to 30 minutes, 20.6% 30 to 45 minutes, 5.1% 45 to 60 minutes, 4.3% 60 minutes or more (2000).

LITTLE FALLS (city). Covers a land area of 3.795 square miles and a water area of 0.169 square miles. Located at 43.04° N. Lat.; 74.85° W. Long. Elevation is 375 feet.
Population: 5,829 (1990); 5,188 (2000); 5,005 (2005); 4,811 (2010 projected); Race: 97.1% White, 0.5% Black, 0.9% Asian, 0.7% Hispanic of any race (2005); Density: 1,318.8 persons per square mile (2005); Average household size: 2.19 (2005); Median age: 43.0 (2005); Males per 100 females: 85.4 (2005); Marriage status: 28.4% never married, 49.2% now married, 11.8% widowed, 10.7% divorced (2000); Foreign born: 1.9% (2000); Ancestry (includes multiple ancestries): 23.6% German, 21.1% Irish, 19.3% Italian, 11.6% English, 8.4% Polish (2000).
Economy: Single-family building permits issued: 4 (2005); Multi-family building permits issued: 0 (2005); Employment by occupation: 8.6% management, 20.1% professional, 17.3% services, 27.3% sales, 0.7% farming, 7.2% construction, 18.9% production (2000).
Income: Per capita income: $17,069 (2005); Median household income: $27,241 (2005); Average household income: $36,372 (2005); Percent of households with income of $100,000 or more: 5.1% (2005); Poverty rate: 16.6% (2000).
Education: Percent of population age 25 and over with: High school diploma (including GED) or higher: 78.1% (2005); Bachelor's degree or higher: 16.6% (2005); Master's degree or higher: 5.5% (2005).
School District(s)
Little Falls City School District (KG-12)
    2003-04 Enrollment: 1,165 . . . . (315) 823-1470

Housing: Homeownership rate: 52.6% (2005); Median home value: $76,351 (2005); Median rent: $314 per month (2000); Median age of housing: 60+ years (2000).
Hospitals: Little Falls Hospital (25 beds)
Newspapers: The Evening Times (Circulation 5,023)
Transportation: Commute to work: 82.0% car, 3.9% public transportation, 11.8% walk, 1.9% work from home (2000); Travel time to work: 51.7% less than 15 minutes, 29.9% 15 to 30 minutes, 10.3% 30 to 45 minutes, 3.4% 45 to 60 minutes, 4.6% 60 minutes or more (2000).

LITTLE FALLS (town). Covers a land area of 22.406 square miles and a water area of 0.167 square miles. Located at 43.01° N. Lat.; 74.89° W. Long. Elevation is 375 feet.
History: Home of Gen. Nicholas Herkimer, hero of Battle of Oriskany. Settled c.1725; incorporated as city 1895.
Population: 1,642 (1990); 1,544 (2000); 1,473 (2005); 1,427 (2010 projected); Race: 98.2% White, 0.3% Black, 1.1% Asian, 0.3% Hispanic of any race (2005); Density: 65.7 persons per square mile (2005); Average household size: 2.61 (2005); Median age: 40.7 (2005); Males per 100 females: 100.7 (2005); Marriage status: 22.1% never married, 64.2% now married, 6.9% widowed, 6.8% divorced (2000); Foreign born: 1.4% (2000); Ancestry (includes multiple ancestries): 23.6% German, 20.6% Irish, 16.2% Italian, 12.1% Polish, 11.1% English (2000).
Economy: At falls of Mohawk River (water power) and on N.Y. State Barge Canal (locks here). Manufacturing: paper, fiberglass products and fabrication, printed packaging materials, consumer goods, apparel. Single-family building permits issued: 0 (2005); Multi-family building permits issued: 0 (2005); Employment by occupation: 14.8% management, 15.9% professional, 19.9% services, 19.4% sales, 1.3% farming, 10.0% construction, 18.7% production (2000).
Income: Per capita income: $21,881 (2005); Median household income: $46,124 (2005); Average household income: $57,145 (2005); Percent of households with income of $100,000 or more: 8.2% (2005); Poverty rate: 10.7% (2000).
Education: Percent of population age 25 and over with: High school diploma (including GED) or higher: 83.0% (2005); Bachelor's degree or higher: 13.2% (2005); Master's degree or higher: 5.3% (2005).
Housing: Homeownership rate: 91.3% (2005); Median home value: $93,434 (2005); Median rent: $410 per month (2000); Median age of housing: 33 years (2000).
Transportation: Commute to work: 91.8% car, 0.3% public transportation, 2.2% walk, 5.4% work from home (2000); Travel time to work: 49.9% less than 15 minutes, 29.6% 15 to 30 minutes, 8.6% 30 to 45 minutes, 5.3% 45 to 60 minutes, 6.5% 60 minutes or more (2000).

MANHEIM (town). Covers a land area of 29.033 square miles and a water area of 0.624 square miles. Located at 43.06° N. Lat.; 74.79° W. Long.
Population: 3,527 (1990); 3,171 (2000); 3,056 (2005); 2,950 (2010 projected); Race: 97.3% White, 0.5% Black, 0.6% Asian, 0.9% Hispanic of any race (2005); Density: 105.3 persons per square mile (2005); Average household size: 2.40 (2005); Median age: 40.5 (2005); Males per 100 females: 94.0 (2005); Marriage status: 24.6% never married, 56.7% now married, 10.8% widowed, 7.9% divorced (2000); Foreign born: 0.8% (2000); Ancestry (includes multiple ancestries): 27.6% German, 15.5% Irish, 12.9% Italian, 10.4% English, 8.6% Polish (2000).
Economy: Single-family building permits issued: 4 (2005); Multi-family building permits issued: 0 (2005); Employment by occupation: 12.6% management, 14.7% professional, 17.0% services, 23.3% sales, 2.5% farming, 6.9% construction, 22.9% production (2000).
Income: Per capita income: $17,806 (2005); Median household income: $36,327 (2005); Average household income: $42,594 (2005); Percent of households with income of $100,000 or more: 6.0% (2005); Poverty rate: 12.7% (2000).
Education: Percent of population age 25 and over with: High school diploma (including GED) or higher: 76.6% (2005); Bachelor's degree or higher: 16.3% (2005); Master's degree or higher: 6.2% (2005).
Housing: Homeownership rate: 69.8% (2005); Median home value: $72,647 (2005); Median rent: $274 per month (2000); Median age of housing: 60+ years (2000).
Transportation: Commute to work: 91.4% car, 0.0% public transportation, 5.1% walk, 3.0% work from home (2000); Travel time to work: 44.5% less than 15 minutes, 30.6% 15 to 30 minutes, 14.1% 30 to 45 minutes, 7.7% 45 to 60 minutes, 3.0% 60 minutes or more (2000).

MIDDLEVILLE (village). Covers a land area of 0.744 square miles and a water area of 0.047 square miles. Located at 43.13° N. Lat.; 74.96° W. Long. Elevation is 600 feet.
Population: 624 (1990); 550 (2000); 553 (2005); 557 (2010 projected); Race: 96.7% White, 2.0% Black, 0.0% Asian, 0.9% Hispanic of any race (2005); Density: 743.2 persons per square mile (2005); Average household size: 2.68 (2005); Median age: 47.0 (2005); Males per 100 females: 85.6 (2005); Marriage status: 28.5% never married, 54.9% now married, 5.7% widowed, 10.8% divorced (2000); Foreign born: 0.9% (2000); Ancestry (includes multiple ancestries): 20.3% English, 20.1% German, 17.6% Irish, 12.0% Polish, 9.9% French (except Basque) (2000).
Economy: In dairying area. Single-family building permits issued: 0 (2005); Multi-family building permits issued: 0 (2005); Employment by occupation: 6.7% management, 22.2% professional, 15.1% services, 30.1% sales, 0.4% farming, 8.4% construction, 17.2% production (2000).
Income: Per capita income: $19,491 (2005); Median household income: $43,182 (2005); Average household income: $50,109 (2005); Percent of households with income of $100,000 or more: 5.3% (2005); Poverty rate: 8.0% (2000).
Education: Percent of population age 25 and over with: High school diploma (including GED) or higher: 74.3% (2005); Bachelor's degree or higher: 10.9% (2005); Master's degree or higher: 4.1% (2005).
Housing: Homeownership rate: 73.3% (2005); Median home value: $86,000 (2005); Median rent: $375 per month (2000); Median age of housing: 60+ years (2000).
Transportation: Commute to work: 94.1% car, 0.0% public transportation, 2.5% walk, 2.5% work from home (2000); Travel time to work: 26.1% less than 15 minutes, 45.7% 15 to 30 minutes, 21.3% 30 to 45 minutes, 2.6% 45 to 60 minutes, 4.3% 60 minutes or more (2000)

MOHAWK (village). Covers a land area of 0.884 square miles and a water area of 0.025 square miles. Located at 43.01° N. Lat.; 75.00° W. Long. Elevation is 407 feet.
History: Settled 1826, incorporated 1844.
Population: 2,986 (1990); 2,660 (2000); 2,563 (2005); 2,457 (2010 projected); Race: 98.0% White, 0.7% Black, 0.3% Asian, 3.0% Hispanic of any race (2005); Density: 2,900.0 persons per square mile (2005); Average household size: 2.28 (2005); Median age: 41.2 (2005); Males per 100 females: 93.1 (2005); Marriage status: 29.9% never married, 52.8% now married, 8.3% widowed, 9.1% divorced (2000); Foreign born: 0.2% (2000); Ancestry (includes multiple ancestries): 24.6% Italian, 22.5% German, 19.9% Irish, 10.4% English, 7.3% Polish (2000).
Economy: Manufacturing: measuring tapes, fishing reels; metal fabrication. Single-family building permits issued: 0 (2005); Multi-family building permits issued: 0 (2005); Employment by occupation: 7.9% management, 16.1% professional, 18.3% services, 31.0% sales, 0.4% farming, 7.0% construction, 19.3% production (2000).
Income: Per capita income: $18,442 (2005); Median household income: $34,935 (2005); Average household income: $41,517 (2005); Percent of households with income of $100,000 or more: 5.3% (2005); Poverty rate: 8.5% (2000).
Education: Percent of population age 25 and over with: High school diploma (including GED) or higher: 81.6% (2005); Bachelor's degree or higher: 15.9% (2005); Master's degree or higher: 4.1% (2005).
School District(s)
Mohawk Central School District (KG-12)
    2003-04 Enrollment: 988 . . . . (315) 867-2904
Housing: Homeownership rate: 64.6% (2005); Median home value: $83,775 (2005); Median rent: $344 per month (2000); Median age of housing: 60+ years (2000).
Safety: Violent crime rate: 15.4 per 10,000 population; Property crime rate: 92.6 per 10,000 population (2004).
Transportation: Commute to work: 91.8% car, 1.8% public transportation, 4.8% walk, 1.6% work from home (2000); Travel time to work: 52.2% less than 15 minutes, 28.9% 15 to 30 minutes, 12.9% 30 to 45 minutes, 2.5% 45 to 60 minutes, 3.4% 60 minutes or more (2000)
Additional Information Contacts
Herkimer County Chamber of Commerce . . . . (315) 866-7820
    http://www.herkimercountychamber.com

NEWPORT (village). Covers a land area of 0.510 square miles and a water area of 0.060 square miles. Located at 43.18° N. Lat.; 75.01° W. Long. Elevation is 412 feet.
Population: 676 (1990); 640 (2000); 624 (2005); 620 (2010 projected); Race: 98.9% White, 1.0% Black, 0.0% Asian, 0.3% Hispanic of any race (2005); Density: 1,224.7 persons per square mile (2005); Average household size: 2.38 (2005); Median age: 39.3 (2005); Males per 100 females: 86.8 (2005); Marriage status: 22.2% never married, 50.9% now married, 11.2% widowed, 15.7% divorced (2000); Foreign born: 1.2% (2000); Ancestry (includes multiple ancestries): 22.3% Irish, 15.7% German, 14.5% English, 11.9% Italian, 7.0% United States or American (2000).
Economy: Single-family building permits issued: 0 (2005); Multi-family building permits issued: 0 (2005); Employment by occupation: 12.2% management, 33.6% professional, 15.9% services, 17.3% sales, 0.7% farming, 6.8% construction, 13.6% production (2000).
Income: Per capita income: $21,458 (2005); Median household income: $37,700 (2005); Average household income: $51,107 (2005); Percent of households with income of $100,000 or more: 15.3% (2005); Poverty rate: 7.8% (2000).
Education: Percent of population age 25 and over with: High school diploma (including GED) or higher: 85.2% (2005); Bachelor's degree or higher: 25.1% (2005); Master's degree or higher: 7.4% (2005).
School District(s)
West Canada Valley Central School District (PK-12)
    2003-04 Enrollment: 945 . . . . (315) 845-6800
Housing: Homeownership rate: 65.6% (2005); Median home value: $97,778 (2005); Median rent: $328 per month (2000); Median age of housing: 60+ years (2000).
Transportation: Commute to work: 91.0% car, 0.0% public transportation, 3.1% walk, 5.9% work from home (2000); Travel time to work: 22.7% less than 15 minutes, 37.0% 15 to 30 minutes, 30.8% 30 to 45 minutes, 5.1% 45 to 60 minutes, 4.4% 60 minutes or more (2000)

NEWPORT (town). Covers a land area of 32.035 square miles and a water area of 0.472 square miles. Located at 43.18° N. Lat.; 75.02° W. Long. Elevation is 412 feet.
Population: 2,148 (1990); 2,192 (2000); 2,153 (2005); 2,141 (2010 projected); Race: 98.5% White, 0.7% Black, 0.0% Asian, 1.1% Hispanic of any race (2005); Density: 67.2 persons per square mile (2005); Average household size: 2.59 (2005); Median age: 40.2 (2005); Males per 100 females: 89.4 (2005); Marriage status: 21.2% never married, 59.1% now married, 7.8% widowed, 11.9% divorced (2000); Foreign born: 1.8% (2000); Ancestry (includes multiple ancestries): 20.5% Irish, 19.2% German, 14.1% Polish, 12.9% English, 9.8% Italian (2000).
Economy: Single-family building permits issued: 6 (2005); Multi-family building permits issued: 0 (2005); Employment by occupation: 13.0% management, 22.6% professional, 16.7% services, 23.3% sales, 2.0% farming, 7.5% construction, 15.0% production (2000).
Income: Per capita income: $19,680 (2005); Median household income: $42,500 (2005); Average household income: $50,925 (2005); Percent of households with income of $100,000 or more: 9.3% (2005); Poverty rate: 8.2% (2000).
Education: Percent of population age 25 and over with: High school diploma (including GED) or higher: 79.9% (2005); Bachelor's degree or higher: 16.6% (2005); Master's degree or higher: 6.5% (2005).
Housing: Homeownership rate: 80.4% (2005); Median home value: $104,051 (2005); Median rent: $356 per month (2000); Median age of housing: 46 years (2000).
Transportation: Commute to work: 93.4% car, 0.0% public transportation, 1.3% walk, 5.4% work from home (2000); Travel time to work: 21.6% less than 15 minutes, 38.9% 15 to 30 minutes, 26.1% 30 to 45 minutes, 6.3% 45 to 60 minutes, 7.0% 60 minutes or more (2000)

NORWAY (town). Covers a land area of 35.618 square miles and a water area of 0.264 square miles. Located at 43.21° N. Lat.; 74.95° W. Long.
Population: 663 (1990); 711 (2000); 751 (2005); 784 (2010 projected); Race: 99.2% White, 0.0% Black, 0.0% Asian, 0.5% Hispanic of any race (2005); Density: 21.1 persons per square mile (2005); Average household size: 2.81 (2005); Median age: 37.4 (2005); Males per 100 females: 115.8 (2005); Marriage status: 28.8% never married, 56.3% now married, 5.7% widowed, 9.2% divorced (2000); Foreign born: 1.0% (2000); Ancestry (includes multiple ancestries): 25.3% German, 19.1% English, 15.8% French (except Basque), 14.6% Irish, 12.1% Other groups (2000).
Economy: Single-family building permits issued: 12 (2005); Multi-family building permits issued: 0 (2005); Employment by occupation: 8.0%

management, 13.3% professional, 14.4% services, 22.2% sales, 1.1% farming, 13.3% construction, 27.7% production (2000).
Income: Per capita income: $17,420 (2005); Median household income: $42,008 (2005); Average household income: $48,998 (2005); Percent of households with income of $100,000 or more: 7.5% (2005); Poverty rate: 10.1% (2000).
Education: Percent of population age 25 and over with: High school diploma (including GED) or higher: 72.6% (2005); Bachelor's degree or higher: 12.1% (2005); Master's degree or higher: 5.2% (2005).
Housing: Homeownership rate: 90.3% (2005); Median home value: $86,410 (2005); Median rent: $404 per month (2000); Median age of housing: 30 years (2000).
Transportation: Commute to work: 88.7% car, 2.8% public transportation, 2.3% walk, 6.2% work from home (2000); Travel time to work: 13.0% less than 15 minutes, 20.2% 15 to 30 minutes, 46.1% 30 to 45 minutes, 12.0% 45 to 60 minutes, 8.7% 60 minutes or more (2000)

OHIO (town). Covers a land area of 302.573 square miles and a water area of 6.401 square miles. Located at 43.42° N. Lat.; 74.94° W. Long. Elevation is 1,374 feet.
Population: 880 (1990); 922 (2000); 909 (2005); 906 (2010 projected); Race: 96.3% White, 1.0% Black, 0.2% Asian, 0.8% Hispanic of any race (2005); Density: 3.0 persons per square mile (2005); Average household size: 2.58 (2005); Median age: 39.9 (2005); Males per 100 females: 102.4 (2005); Marriage status: 24.7% never married, 62.0% now married, 5.0% widowed, 8.4% divorced (2000); Foreign born: 1.0% (2000); Ancestry (includes multiple ancestries): 28.2% Irish, 20.4% German, 11.6% French (except Basque), 11.3% Polish, 10.0% Other groups (2000).
Economy: Single-family building permits issued: 8 (2005); Multi-family building permits issued: 0 (2005); Employment by occupation: 6.6% management, 15.6% professional, 12.8% services, 23.7% sales, 1.3% farming, 18.4% construction, 21.7% production (2000).
Income: Per capita income: $16,031 (2005); Median household income: $33,545 (2005); Average household income: $41,399 (2005); Percent of households with income of $100,000 or more: 5.1% (2005); Poverty rate: 20.9% (2000).
Education: Percent of population age 25 and over with: High school diploma (including GED) or higher: 75.1% (2005); Bachelor's degree or higher: 10.3% (2005); Master's degree or higher: 7.2% (2005).
Housing: Homeownership rate: 88.6% (2005); Median home value: $81,944 (2005); Median rent: $360 per month (2000); Median age of housing: 29 years (2000).
Transportation: Commute to work: 95.9% car, 0.0% public transportation, 2.6% walk, 0.5% work from home (2000); Travel time to work: 13.1% less than 15 minutes, 13.4% 15 to 30 minutes, 35.1% 30 to 45 minutes, 32.7% 45 to 60 minutes, 5.7% 60 minutes or more (2000)

OLD FORGE (unincorporated postal area, zip code 13420). Covers a land area of 123.605 square miles and a water area of 4.140 square miles. Located at 43.70° N. Lat.; 74.94° W. Long. Elevation is 1,740 feet.
Population: 0 (2000); Race: 98.8% White, 0.0% Black, 0.6% Asian, 1.1% Hispanic of any race (2000); Density: 0.0 persons per square mile (2000); Age: 18.3% under 18, 17.9% over 64 (2000); Marriage status: 24.7% never married, 58.8% now married, 7.8% widowed, 8.7% divorced (2000); Foreign born: 2.1% (2000); Ancestry (includes multiple ancestries): 28.0% Irish, 25.3% German, 17.8% English, 11.0% French (except Basque), 9.3% Italian (2000).
Economy: Popular winter-sports (snowmobiling) and summer-resort area; logging; hunting, fishing. Employment by occupation: 14.8% management, 18.2% professional, 20.8% services, 24.2% sales, 2.1% farming, 11.9% construction, 8.0% production (2000).
Income: Per capita income: $20,645 (2000); Median household income: $36,000 (2000); Poverty rate: 8.2% (2000).
Education: Percent of population age 25 and over with: High school diploma (including GED) or higher: 91.1% (2000); Bachelor's degree or higher: 28.7% (2000).

School District(s)
Town Of Webb Union Free School District (KG-12)
　　2003-04 Enrollment: 377 . . . . (315) 369-3222
Housing: Homeownership rate: 74.5% (2000); Median home value: $116,900 (2000); Median rent: $370 per month (2000); Median age of housing: 37 years (2000).
Transportation: Commute to work: 72.1% car, 2.8% public transportation, 18.5% walk, 5.9% work from home (2000); Travel time to work: 73.8% less than 15 minutes, 13.2% 15 to 30 minutes, 2.5% 30 to 45 minutes, 1.3% 45 to 60 minutes, 9.2% 60 minutes or more (2000)

POLAND (village). Covers a land area of 0.535 square miles and a water area of 0.006 square miles. Located at 43.22° N. Lat.; 75.06° W. Long. Elevation is 707 feet.
Population: 420 (1990); 451 (2000); 459 (2005); 464 (2010 projected); Race: 95.6% White, 0.4% Black, 3.5% Asian, 2.6% Hispanic of any race (2005); Density: 857.2 persons per square mile (2005); Average household size: 2.31 (2005); Median age: 40.8 (2005); Males per 100 females: 93.7 (2005); Marriage status: 25.1% never married, 60.2% now married, 6.7% widowed, 7.9% divorced (2000); Foreign born: 0.5% (2000); Ancestry (includes multiple ancestries): 26.1% German, 23.2% English, 16.8% Irish, 6.9% Dutch, 6.6% French (except Basque) (2000).
Economy: Single-family building permits issued: 0 (2005); Multi-family building permits issued: 0 (2005); Employment by occupation: 11.2% management, 19.6% professional, 22.9% services, 20.1% sales, 2.3% farming, 7.5% construction, 16.4% production (2000).
Income: Per capita income: $22,369 (2005); Median household income: $42,500 (2005); Average household income: $51,595 (2005); Percent of households with income of $100,000 or more: 7.5% (2005); Poverty rate: 11.1% (2000).
Education: Percent of population age 25 and over with: High school diploma (including GED) or higher: 90.7% (2005); Bachelor's degree or higher: 17.4% (2005); Master's degree or higher: 5.0% (2005).

School District(s)
Poland Central School District (PK-12)
　　2003-04 Enrollment: 758 . . . . (315) 826-0203
Housing: Homeownership rate: 76.9% (2005); Median home value: $97,105 (2005); Median rent: $377 per month (2000); Median age of housing: 60+ years (2000).
Transportation: Commute to work: 95.1% car, 0.0% public transportation, 3.4% walk, 1.5% work from home (2000); Travel time to work: 19.8% less than 15 minutes, 42.1% 15 to 30 minutes, 21.3% 30 to 45 minutes, 10.4% 45 to 60 minutes, 6.4% 60 minutes or more (2000)

RUSSIA (town). Covers a land area of 56.576 square miles and a water area of 3.825 square miles. Located at 43.29° N. Lat.; 75.07° W. Long.
Population: 2,294 (1990); 2,487 (2000); 2,543 (2005); 2,557 (2010 projected); Race: 97.2% White, 0.6% Black, 1.0% Asian, 0.4% Hispanic of any race (2005); Density: 44.9 persons per square mile (2005); Average household size: 2.46 (2005); Median age: 41.1 (2005); Males per 100 females: 108.8 (2005); Marriage status: 19.9% never married, 65.3% now married, 4.8% widowed, 9.9% divorced (2000); Foreign born: 0.5% (2000); Ancestry (includes multiple ancestries): 21.4% English, 20.7% German, 18.2% Irish, 11.1% Polish, 8.8% Welsh (2000).
Economy: Single-family building permits issued: 12 (2005); Multi-family building permits issued: 0 (2005); Employment by occupation: 12.9% management, 19.7% professional, 15.8% services, 24.1% sales, 1.4% farming, 9.6% construction, 16.5% production (2000).
Income: Per capita income: $20,819 (2005); Median household income: $39,150 (2005); Average household income: $51,251 (2005); Percent of households with income of $100,000 or more: 10.4% (2005); Poverty rate: 14.9% (2000).
Education: Percent of population age 25 and over with: High school diploma (including GED) or higher: 89.0% (2005); Bachelor's degree or higher: 19.8% (2005); Master's degree or higher: 7.4% (2005).
Housing: Homeownership rate: 83.3% (2005); Median home value: $89,939 (2005); Median rent: $366 per month (2000); Median age of housing: 39 years (2000).
Transportation: Commute to work: 94.7% car, 0.0% public transportation, 2.2% walk, 2.8% work from home (2000); Travel time to work: 17.9% less than 15 minutes, 29.6% 15 to 30 minutes, 37.2% 30 to 45 minutes, 9.3% 45 to 60 minutes, 6.0% 60 minutes or more (2000)

SALISBURY (town). Covers a land area of 107.413 square miles and a water area of 0.783 square miles. Located at 43.19° N. Lat.; 74.81° W. Long. Elevation is 1,221 feet.
Population: 1,934 (1990); 1,953 (2000); 1,934 (2005); 1,896 (2010 projected); Race: 98.2% White, 0.1% Black, 0.7% Asian, 0.2% Hispanic of any race (2005); Density: 18.0 persons per square mile (2005); Average household size: 2.78 (2005); Median age: 37.5 (2005); Males per 100 females: 104.0 (2005); Marriage status: 24.5% never married, 60.0% now married, 6.6% widowed, 8.9% divorced (2000); Foreign born: 1.8% (2000);

Ancestry (includes multiple ancestries): 25.5% German, 20.1% Irish, 16.7% English, 10.7% Dutch, 9.4% French (except Basque) (2000).
Economy: Single-family building permits issued: 3 (2005); Multi-family building permits issued: 0 (2005); Employment by occupation: 7.7% management, 12.6% professional, 17.5% services, 17.4% sales, 2.7% farming, 12.9% construction, 29.2% production (2000).
Income: Per capita income: $14,712 (2005); Median household income: $36,875 (2005); Average household income: $40,880 (2005); Percent of households with income of $100,000 or more: 3.3% (2005); Poverty rate: 12.3% (2000).
Education: Percent of population age 25 and over with: High school diploma (including GED) or higher: 70.7% (2005); Bachelor's degree or higher: 8.4% (2005); Master's degree or higher: 2.5% (2005).
Housing: Homeownership rate: 86.1% (2005); Median home value: $79,015 (2005); Median rent: $309 per month (2000); Median age of housing: 32 years (2000).
Transportation: Commute to work: 93.3% car, 0.0% public transportation, 1.7% walk, 4.1% work from home (2000); Travel time to work: 28.9% less than 15 minutes, 36.7% 15 to 30 minutes, 13.1% 30 to 45 minutes, 11.9% 45 to 60 minutes, 9.4% 60 minutes or more (2000)

SALISBURY CENTER (unincorporated postal area, zip code 13454). Covers a land area of 78.783 square miles and a water area of 0.628 square miles. Located at 43.22° N. Lat.; 74.80° W. Long.
Population: 0 (2000); Race: 96.6% White, 2.1% Black, 0.0% Asian, 0.0% Hispanic of any race (2000); Density: 0.0 persons per square mile (2000); Age: 28.7% under 18, 13.5% over 64 (2000); Marriage status: 21.2% never married, 64.8% now married, 5.2% widowed, 8.8% divorced (2000); Foreign born: 2.3% (2000); Ancestry (includes multiple ancestries): 22.7% Irish, 22.3% German, 19.4% English, 10.9% Other groups, 8.5% French (except Basque) (2000).
Economy: Employment by occupation: 10.1% management, 13.4% professional, 14.2% services, 14.6% sales, 0.7% farming, 15.3% construction, 31.7% production (2000).
Income: Per capita income: $13,689 (2000); Median household income: $34,625 (2000); Poverty rate: 12.7% (2000).
Education: Percent of population age 25 and over with: High school diploma (including GED) or higher: 71.3% (2000); Bachelor's degree or higher: 8.0% (2000).
Housing: Homeownership rate: 85.2% (2000); Median home value: $56,700 (2000); Median rent: $325 per month (2000); Median age of housing: 34 years (2000).
Transportation: Commute to work: 96.3% car, 0.0% public transportation, 1.5% walk, 2.2% work from home (2000); Travel time to work: 29.9% less than 15 minutes, 34.1% 15 to 30 minutes, 13.4% 30 to 45 minutes, 10.0% 45 to 60 minutes, 12.6% 60 minutes or more (2000)

SCHUYLER (town). Covers a land area of 39.835 square miles and a water area of 0.451 square miles. Located at 43.09° N. Lat.; 75.09° W. Long.
Population: 3,508 (1990); 3,385 (2000); 3,435 (2005); 3,485 (2010 projected); Race: 97.2% White, 1.0% Black, 0.8% Asian, 0.8% Hispanic of any race (2005); Density: 86.2 persons per square mile (2005); Average household size: 2.34 (2005); Median age: 41.4 (2005); Males per 100 females: 95.2 (2005); Marriage status: 23.6% never married, 58.3% now married, 5.8% widowed, 12.3% divorced (2000); Foreign born: 4.1% (2000); Ancestry (includes multiple ancestries): 25.4% Italian, 19.3% Irish, 16.9% German, 11.6% Polish, 9.3% English (2000).
Economy: Single-family building permits issued: 17 (2005); Multi-family building permits issued: 0 (2005); Employment by occupation: 12.7% management, 16.0% professional, 16.7% services, 27.8% sales, 0.7% farming, 10.6% construction, 15.4% production (2000).
Income: Per capita income: $21,945 (2005); Median household income: $39,471 (2005); Average household income: $51,046 (2005); Percent of households with income of $100,000 or more: 9.4% (2005); Poverty rate: 9.4% (2000).
Education: Percent of population age 25 and over with: High school diploma (including GED) or higher: 79.6% (2005); Bachelor's degree or higher: 14.1% (2005); Master's degree or higher: 3.7% (2005).
Housing: Homeownership rate: 85.3% (2005); Median home value: $71,513 (2005); Median rent: $323 per month (2000); Median age of housing: 24 years (2000).
Transportation: Commute to work: 94.1% car, 0.4% public transportation, 1.4% walk, 3.7% work from home (2000); Travel time to work: 26.2% less than 15 minutes, 50.6% 15 to 30 minutes, 14.9% 30 to 45 minutes, 4.2% 45 to 60 minutes, 4.1% 60 minutes or more (2000)
Additional Information Contacts
Town of Schuyler . . . . (315) 733-7458
http://www.geocities.com/townofschuyler/

STARK (town). Covers a land area of 31.515 square miles and a water area of 0.007 square miles. Located at 42.91° N. Lat.; 74.81° W. Long.
Population: 730 (1990); 767 (2000); 807 (2005); 819 (2010 projected); Race: 99.4% White, 0.4% Black, 0.0% Asian, 0.2% Hispanic of any race (2005); Density: 25.6 persons per square mile (2005); Average household size: 2.63 (2005); Median age: 39.2 (2005); Males per 100 females: 108.5 (2005); Marriage status: 19.4% never married, 63.5% now married, 5.7% widowed, 11.3% divorced (2000); Foreign born: 1.2% (2000); Ancestry (includes multiple ancestries): 22.9% German, 11.3% Irish, 10.6% English, 9.0% Polish, 8.6% United States or American (2000).
Economy: Single-family building permits issued: 0 (2005); Multi-family building permits issued: 0 (2005); Employment by occupation: 14.2% management, 16.0% professional, 14.2% services, 15.7% sales, 4.6% farming, 15.7% construction, 19.4% production (2000).
Income: Per capita income: $16,834 (2005); Median household income: $37,540 (2005); Average household income: $44,251 (2005); Percent of households with income of $100,000 or more: 5.5% (2005); Poverty rate: 19.9% (2000).
Education: Percent of population age 25 and over with: High school diploma (including GED) or higher: 80.2% (2005); Bachelor's degree or higher: 15.4% (2005); Master's degree or higher: 9.5% (2005).
Housing: Homeownership rate: 83.4% (2005); Median home value: $79,524 (2005); Median rent: $375 per month (2000); Median age of housing: 54 years (2000).
Transportation: Commute to work: 82.2% car, 0.0% public transportation, 4.7% walk, 12.5% work from home (2000); Travel time to work: 18.9% less than 15 minutes, 42.5% 15 to 30 minutes, 24.6% 30 to 45 minutes, 5.7% 45 to 60 minutes, 8.2% 60 minutes or more (2000)

VAN HORNESVILLE (unincorporated postal area, zip code 13475). Covers a land area of 0.691 square miles and a water area of 0 square miles. Located at 42.87° N. Lat.; 74.84° W. Long.
Population: 0 (2000); Race: 100.0% White, 0.0% Black, 0.0% Asian, 0.0% Hispanic of any race (2000); Density: 0.0 persons per square mile (2000); Age: 22.2% under 18, 0.0% over 64 (2000); Marriage status: 28.6% never married, 71.4% now married, 0.0% widowed, 0.0% divorced (2000); Foreign born: 0.0% (2000); Ancestry (includes multiple ancestries): 77.8% Other groups, 22.2% United States or American (2000).
Economy: Employment by occupation: 60.0% management, 40.0% professional, 0.0% services, 0.0% sales, 0.0% farming, 0.0% construction, 0.0% production (2000).
Income: Per capita income: $44,889 (2000); Median household income: $152,338 (2000); Poverty rate: 0.0% (2000).
Education: Percent of population age 25 and over with: High school diploma (including GED) or higher: 100.0% (2000); Bachelor's degree or higher: 100.0% (2000).
School District(s)
Van Hornesville-Owen D. Young Central School District (KG-12)
    2003-04 Enrollment: 231 . . . . (315) 858-0729
Housing: Homeownership rate: 100.0% (2000); Median home value: $137,500 (2000); Median rent: $n/a per month (2000); Median age of housing: 60+ years (2000).
Transportation: Commute to work: 100.0% car, 0.0% public transportation, 0.0% walk, 0.0% work from home (2000); Travel time to work: 0.0% less than 15 minutes, 100.0% 15 to 30 minutes, 0.0% 30 to 45 minutes, 0.0% 45 to 60 minutes, 0.0% 60 minutes or more (2000)

WARREN (town). Covers a land area of 38.184 square miles and a water area of 0.275 square miles. Located at 42.88° N. Lat.; 74.93° W. Long.
Population: 1,077 (1990); 1,136 (2000); 1,138 (2005); 1,130 (2010 projected); Race: 96.5% White, 1.1% Black, 0.4% Asian, 1.5% Hispanic of any race (2005); Density: 29.8 persons per square mile (2005); Average household size: 2.86 (2005); Median age: 38.9 (2005); Males per 100 females: 126.7 (2005); Marriage status: 22.0% never married, 64.9% now married, 8.6% widowed, 4.5% divorced (2000); Foreign born: 6.1% (2000); Ancestry (includes multiple ancestries): 22.3% German, 17.0% Irish, 13.0% English, 10.8% Italian, 10.4% Polish (2000).

Economy: Single-family building permits issued: 4 (2005); Multi-family building permits issued: 0 (2005); Employment by occupation: 16.2% management, 18.3% professional, 16.6% services, 20.1% sales, 2.5% farming, 11.4% construction, 14.9% production (2000).
Income: Per capita income: $17,655 (2005); Median household income: $43,242 (2005); Average household income: $48,989 (2005); Percent of households with income of $100,000 or more: 4.3% (2005); Poverty rate: 12.3% (2000).
Education: Percent of population age 25 and over with: High school diploma (including GED) or higher: 79.6% (2005); Bachelor's degree or higher: 13.2% (2005); Master's degree or higher: 5.6% (2005).
Housing: Homeownership rate: 82.7% (2005); Median home value: $82,308 (2005); Median rent: $313 per month (2000); Median age of housing: 42 years (2000).
Transportation: Commute to work: 83.2% car, 0.0% public transportation, 4.7% walk, 10.8% work from home (2000); Travel time to work: 27.9% less than 15 minutes, 26.7% 15 to 30 minutes, 33.3% 30 to 45 minutes, 6.4% 45 to 60 minutes, 5.7% 60 minutes or more (2000)

WEBB (town). Covers a land area of 450.989 square miles and a water area of 31.929 square miles. Located at 43.76° N. Lat.; 74.94° W. Long.
Population: 1,637 (1990); 1,912 (2000); 1,922 (2005); 1,967 (2010 projected); Race: 97.0% White, 1.2% Black, 0.5% Asian, 1.2% Hispanic of any race (2005); Density: 4.3 persons per square mile (2005); Average household size: 2.22 (2005); Median age: 44.9 (2005); Males per 100 females: 97.3 (2005); Marriage status: 24.2% never married, 60.0% now married, 7.7% widowed, 8.1% divorced (2000); Foreign born: 2.0% (2000); Ancestry (includes multiple ancestries): 27.1% Irish, 25.1% German, 19.7% English, 12.0% French (except Basque), 8.4% Italian (2000).
Economy: Single-family building permits issued: 38 (2005); Multi-family building permits issued: 0 (2005); Employment by occupation: 14.2% management, 17.0% professional, 21.9% services, 24.0% sales, 2.3% farming, 12.0% construction, 8.7% production (2000).
Income: Per capita income: $21,707 (2005); Median household income: $38,441 (2005); Average household income: $47,962 (2005); Percent of households with income of $100,000 or more: 8.2% (2005); Poverty rate: 8.8% (2000).
Education: Percent of population age 25 and over with: High school diploma (including GED) or higher: 90.8% (2005); Bachelor's degree or higher: 26.6% (2005); Master's degree or higher: 10.6% (2005).
Housing: Homeownership rate: 76.4% (2005); Median home value: $154,167 (2005); Median rent: $373 per month (2000); Median age of housing: 40 years (2000).
Transportation: Commute to work: 71.7% car, 2.5% public transportation, 19.7% walk, 5.3% work from home (2000); Travel time to work: 70.7% less than 15 minutes, 15.2% 15 to 30 minutes, 3.3% 30 to 45 minutes, 1.2% 45 to 60 minutes, 9.6% 60 minutes or more (2000)

WEST WINFIELD (village). Covers a land area of 0.899 square miles and a water area of 0 square miles. Located at 42.88° N. Lat.; 75.19° W. Long. Elevation is 1,220 feet.
Population: 871 (1990); 862 (2000); 851 (2005); 841 (2010 projected); Race: 99.5% White, 0.0% Black, 0.4% Asian, 0.0% Hispanic of any race (2005); Density: 947.0 persons per square mile (2005); Average household size: 2.40 (2005); Median age: 41.7 (2005); Males per 100 females: 90.0 (2005); Marriage status: 21.4% never married, 64.0% now married, 9.0% widowed, 5.5% divorced (2000); Foreign born: 2.6% (2000); Ancestry (includes multiple ancestries): 21.4% Irish, 19.0% English, 18.0% German, 9.7% Italian, 7.8% Welsh (2000).
Economy: Single-family building permits issued: 0 (2005); Multi-family building permits issued: 0 (2005); Employment by occupation: 6.1% management, 27.8% professional, 16.8% services, 30.6% sales, 1.0% farming, 5.4% construction, 12.2% production (2000).
Income: Per capita income: $20,197 (2005); Median household income: $41,979 (2005); Average household income: $48,415 (2005); Percent of households with income of $100,000 or more: 7.6% (2005); Poverty rate: 9.1% (2000).
Education: Percent of population age 25 and over with: High school diploma (including GED) or higher: 84.8% (2005); Bachelor's degree or higher: 23.2% (2005); Master's degree or higher: 9.7% (2005).

School District(s)
Bridgewater-West Winfield Central School District (KG-12)
    2003-04 Enrollment: 1,448 . . . . (315) 822-6161

Housing: Homeownership rate: 69.6% (2005); Median home value: $91,194 (2005); Median rent: $302 per month (2000); Median age of housing: 60+ years (2000).
Newspapers: West Winfield Star (General - Circulation 1,100)
Transportation: Commute to work: 84.8% car, 0.0% public transportation, 12.4% walk, 2.8% work from home (2000); Travel time to work: 33.4% less than 15 minutes, 25.3% 15 to 30 minutes, 35.0% 30 to 45 minutes, 3.4% 45 to 60 minutes, 2.9% 60 minutes or more (2000)

WINFIELD (town). Covers a land area of 23.645 square miles and a water area of 0.006 square miles. Located at 42.89° N. Lat.; 75.16° W. Long.
Population: 2,146 (1990); 2,202 (2000); 2,179 (2005); 2,150 (2010 projected); Race: 98.8% White, 0.0% Black, 0.4% Asian, 0.6% Hispanic of any race (2005); Density: 92.2 persons per square mile (2005); Average household size: 2.63 (2005); Median age: 38.3 (2005); Males per 100 females: 94.6 (2005); Marriage status: 23.5% never married, 62.4% now married, 6.6% widowed, 7.5% divorced (2000); Foreign born: 1.7% (2000); Ancestry (includes multiple ancestries): 20.3% German, 19.7% Irish, 15.9% English, 11.8% Italian, 8.6% Welsh (2000).
Economy: In agricultural area; summer resort. Single-family building permits issued: 2 (2005); Multi-family building permits issued: 0 (2005); Employment by occupation: 10.0% management, 20.1% professional, 18.1% services, 26.0% sales, 0.7% farming, 7.2% construction, 17.9% production (2000).
Income: Per capita income: $20,765 (2005); Median household income: $43,935 (2005); Average household income: $54,713 (2005); Percent of households with income of $100,000 or more: 10.2% (2005); Poverty rate: 8.0% (2000).
Education: Percent of population age 25 and over with: High school diploma (including GED) or higher: 83.1% (2005); Bachelor's degree or higher: 19.0% (2005); Master's degree or higher: 9.0% (2005).
Housing: Homeownership rate: 78.5% (2005); Median home value: $91,269 (2005); Median rent: $308 per month (2000); Median age of housing: 39 years (2000).
Transportation: Commute to work: 86.5% car, 0.9% public transportation, 7.1% walk, 5.5% work from home (2000); Travel time to work: 26.7% less than 15 minutes, 32.0% 15 to 30 minutes, 34.1% 30 to 45 minutes, 2.2% 45 to 60 minutes, 4.9% 60 minutes or more (2000)

Jefferson County

Located in northern New York; bounded on the west by Lake Ontario, and on the northwest by the St. Lawrence River; drained by the Black and Indian Rivers. Covers a land area of 1,272.20 square miles, a water area of 584.88 square miles, and is located in the Eastern Time Zone. The county government was organized in 1805. County seat is Watertown.

Jefferson County is part of the Watertown-Fort Drum, NY Micropolitan Statistical Area. The entire metro area includes: Jefferson County, NY

Weather Station: Watertown   Elevation: 495 feet

	Jan	Feb	Mar	Apr	May	Jun	Jul	Aug	Sep	Oct	Nov	Dec
High	28	31	40	53	66	75	80	78	70	58	46	34
Low	9	11	22	35	47	56	61	59	51	40	31	17
Precip	3.6	2.5	2.8	3.0	3.3	3.5	3.2	3.8	4.6	3.8	4.5	3.7
Snow	35.0	22.4	14.5	3.3	tr	0.0	0.0	0.0	0.0	0.3	7.8	27.5

High and Low temperatures in degrees Fahrenheit; Precipitation and Snow in inches

Weather Station: Watertown Airport   Elevation: 314 feet

	Jan	Feb	Mar	Apr	May	Jun	Jul	Aug	Sep	Oct	Nov	Dec
High	29	31	40	54	66	74	79	78	70	58	46	34
Low	9	11	21	33	44	53	58	56	48	38	30	17
Precip	2.7	2.3	2.4	2.8	2.8	2.9	2.5	3.0	3.8	3.1	3.4	2.8
Snow	27.8	19.3	12.1	2.5	tr	tr	tr	tr	tr	0.2	6.5	22.7

High and Low temperatures in degrees Fahrenheit; Precipitation and Snow in inches

Population: 110,943 (1990); 111,738 (2000); 115,901 (2005); 120,198 (2010 projected); Race: 81.2% White, 10.6% Black, 1.1% Asian, 8.5% Hispanic of any race (2005); Density: 91.1 persons per square mile (2005); Average household size: 2.74 (2005); Median age: 33.6 (2005); Males per 100 females: 107.8 (2005).
Religion: Five largest groups: 27.7% Catholic Church, 6.0% The United Methodist Church, 1.9% Episcopal Church, 1.4% Presbyterian Church (U.S.A.), 1.2% American Baptist Churches in the USA (2000).

Economy: Unemployment rate: 6.2% (2005); Total civilian labor force: 47,360 (2005); Leading industries: 21.7% health care and social assistance; 21.2% retail trade; 11.4% accommodation and food services (2003); Farms: 1,028 totaling 330,561 acres (2002); Companies that employ 500 or more persons: 2 (2003); Companies that employ 100 to 499 persons: 25 (2003); Companies that employ less than 100 persons: 2,340 (2003); Black-owned businesses: n/a (2002); Hispanic-owned businesses: n/a (2002); Women-owned businesses: 1,746 (2002); Retail sales per capita: $13,467 (2006). Single-family building permits issued: 369 (2005); Multi-family building permits issued: 26 (2005).
Income: Per capita income: $18,494 (2005); Median household income: $38,185 (2005); Average household income: $47,515 (2005); Percent of households with income of $100,000 or more: 7.7% (2005); Poverty rate: 14.5% (2003); Bankruptcy rate: 5.47% (2005).
Taxes: Total county taxes per capita: $707 (2004); County property taxes per capita: $351 (2004).
Education: Percent of population age 25 and over with: High school diploma (including GED) or higher: 83.1% (2005); Bachelor's degree or higher: 16.1% (2005); Master's degree or higher: 6.3% (2005).
Housing: Homeownership rate: 59.4% (2005); Median home value: $98,045 (2005); Median rent: $388 per month (2000); Median age of housing: 40 years (2000).
Health: Birth rate: 132.1 per 10,000 population (2004); Death rate: 77.1 per 10,000 population (2004); Age-adjusted cancer mortality rate: 229.1 deaths per 100,000 population (2002); Air Quality Index: 86.5% good, 12.2% moderate, 1.4% unhealthy for sensitive individuals, 0.0% unhealthy (percent of days in 2005); Number of physicians: 18.2 per 10,000 population (2004); Hospital beds: 32.9 per 10,000 population (2003); Hospital admissions: 978.7 per 10,000 population (2003).
Elections: 2004 Presidential election results: 54.7% Bush, 43.5% Kerry, 1.7% Nader, 0.1% Badnarik
National and State Parks: Brownville State Game Farm; Burnham Point State Park; Canoe Point And Picnic Point State Park; Cedar Point State Park; Grass Point State Park; Keewaydin Point State Park; Kring Point State Park; Long Point State Park; Mary Island State Park; Perch River State Game Management Area; Sackets Harbor Battlefield State Park; Southwich Beach State Park; Wellesley Island State Park; Westcott Beach State Park

Additional Information Contacts
Jefferson County Government . . . . (315) 785-3000
  http://www.co.jefferson.ny.us/
City of Watertown . . . . (315) 785-7780
  http://www.citywatertown.org/
Town of Champion . . . . (315) 493-3240
  http://www.racog.org/Champion/Championhomepage.asp
Village of West Carthage . . . . (315) 493-2552
  http://www.racog.org/West%20Carthage/WestCarthageHomePage.asp

Jefferson County Communities

ADAMS (village). Covers a land area of 1.541 square miles and a water area of 0 square miles. Located at 43.80° N. Lat.; 76.02° W. Long. Elevation is 597 feet.
Population: 1,931 (1990); 1,624 (2000); 1,602 (2005); 1,599 (2010 projected); Race: 96.1% White, 1.9% Black, 0.2% Asian, 2.5% Hispanic of any race (2005); Density: 1,039.7 persons per square mile (2005); Average household size: 2.25 (2005); Median age: 37.7 (2005); Males per 100 females: 89.4 (2005); Marriage status: 22.8% never married, 51.1% now married, 13.8% widowed, 12.3% divorced (2000); Foreign born: 2.1% (2000); Ancestry (includes multiple ancestries): 23.8% English, 16.2% Irish, 14.7% German, 11.6% French (except Basque), 10.0% United States or American (2000).
Economy: Employment by occupation: 9.2% management, 20.9% professional, 19.7% services, 24.3% sales, 0.8% farming, 11.4% construction, 13.7% production (2000).
Income: Per capita income: $20,135 (2005); Median household income: $34,241 (2005); Average household income: $45,281 (2005); Percent of households with income of $100,000 or more: 7.7% (2005); Poverty rate: 15.3% (2000).
Education: Percent of population age 25 and over with: High school diploma (including GED) or higher: 83.1% (2005); Bachelor's degree or higher: 18.8% (2005); Master's degree or higher: 6.6% (2005).
School District(s)
South Jefferson Central School District (PK-12)
  2003-04 Enrollment: 2,044 . . . . (315) 583-6104
Housing: Homeownership rate: 58.3% (2005); Median home value: $95,313 (2005); Median rent: $317 per month (2000); Median age of housing: 60+ years (2000).
Safety: Violent crime rate: 0.0 per 10,000 population; Property crime rate: 36.7 per 10,000 population (2004).
Newspapers: Lure of the Lake (General - Circulation 5,000)
Transportation: Commute to work: 94.0% car, 0.5% public transportation, 1.6% walk, 3.4% work from home (2000); Travel time to work: 32.6% less than 15 minutes, 44.3% 15 to 30 minutes, 12.3% 30 to 45 minutes, 4.2% 45 to 60 minutes, 6.5% 60 minutes or more (2000)

Additional Information Contacts
South Jefferson Chamber of Commerce . . . . (315) 232-4215
  http://www.1000islands.com

ADAMS (town). Covers a land area of 42.401 square miles and a water area of 0.024 square miles. Located at 43.84° N. Lat.; 76.02° W. Long. Elevation is 597 feet.
History: Incorporated 1851.
Population: 5,006 (1990); 4,782 (2000); 4,734 (2005); 4,720 (2010 projected); Race: 96.9% White, 0.7% Black, 0.5% Asian, 1.5% Hispanic of any race (2005); Density: 111.6 persons per square mile (2005); Average household size: 2.50 (2005); Median age: 38.0 (2005); Males per 100 females: 94.9 (2005); Marriage status: 20.3% never married, 61.1% now married, 7.5% widowed, 11.0% divorced (2000); Foreign born: 1.2% (2000); Ancestry (includes multiple ancestries): 16.7% English, 16.6% German, 12.8% United States or American, 12.3% Irish, 11.8% French (except Basque) (2000).
Economy: In dairy region. Manufactures surgical equipment, wood products. Employment by occupation: 10.3% management, 22.6% professional, 18.7% services, 21.7% sales, 1.1% farming, 10.7% construction, 15.0% production (2000).
Income: Per capita income: $21,702 (2005); Median household income: $45,909 (2005); Average household income: $54,286 (2005); Percent of households with income of $100,000 or more: 11.1% (2005); Poverty rate: 9.6% (2000).
Education: Percent of population age 25 and over with: High school diploma (including GED) or higher: 88.3% (2005); Bachelor's degree or higher: 17.6% (2005); Master's degree or higher: 6.9% (2005).
Housing: Homeownership rate: 74.3% (2005); Median home value: $102,604 (2005); Median rent: $348 per month (2000); Median age of housing: 55 years (2000).
Transportation: Commute to work: 93.9% car, 0.2% public transportation, 1.5% walk, 4.2% work from home (2000); Travel time to work: 34.1% less than 15 minutes, 43.2% 15 to 30 minutes, 12.6% 30 to 45 minutes, 4.6% 45 to 60 minutes, 5.6% 60 minutes or more (2000)

ADAMS CENTER (CDP). Covers a land area of 4.956 square miles and a water area of 0.008 square miles. Located at 43.86° N. Lat.; 76.00° W. Long. Elevation is 610 feet.
Population: 1,675 (1990); 1,500 (2000); 1,478 (2005); 1,468 (2010 projected); Race: 98.3% White, 0.1% Black, 0.4% Asian, 0.9% Hispanic of any race (2005); Density: 298.2 persons per square mile (2005); Average household size: 2.62 (2005); Median age: 37.1 (2005); Males per 100 females: 97.9 (2005); Marriage status: 16.2% never married, 64.0% now married, 5.3% widowed, 14.5% divorced (2000); Foreign born: 0.0% (2000); Ancestry (includes multiple ancestries): 19.9% English, 18.6% German, 12.9% Irish, 12.4% French (except Basque), 10.8% Italian (2000).
Economy: Nine miles South Southwest of Watertown. Employment by occupation: 7.0% management, 24.1% professional, 16.6% services, 22.5% sales, 1.3% farming, 6.9% construction, 21.5% production (2000).
Income: Per capita income: $21,360 (2005); Median household income: $51,359 (2005); Average household income: $55,876 (2005); Percent of households with income of $100,000 or more: 9.2% (2005); Poverty rate: 6.9% (2000).
Education: Percent of population age 25 and over with: High school diploma (including GED) or higher: 92.2% (2005); Bachelor's degree or higher: 16.6% (2005); Master's degree or higher: 9.3% (2005).
School District(s)
South Jefferson Central School District (PK-12)
  2003-04 Enrollment: 2,044 . . . . (315) 583-6104
Housing: Homeownership rate: 80.5% (2005); Median home value: $101,541 (2005); Median rent: $416 per month (2000); Median age of housing: 42 years (2000).
Transportation: Commute to work: 95.3% car, 0.0% public transportation, 1.1% walk, 3.5% work from home (2000); Travel time to work: 36.3% less

than 15 minutes, 43.5% 15 to 30 minutes, 14.0% 30 to 45 minutes, 2.5% 45 to 60 minutes, 3.8% 60 minutes or more (2000)

ALEXANDRIA (town). Covers a land area of 72.969 square miles and a water area of 11.551 square miles. Located at 44.31° N. Lat.; 75.89° W. Long.
History: Incorporated 1878.
Population: 3,956 (1990); 4,097 (2000); 4,225 (2005); 4,373 (2010 projected); Race: 97.3% White, 1.1% Black, 0.0% Asian, 1.6% Hispanic of any race (2005); Density: 57.9 persons per square mile (2005); Average household size: 2.42 (2005); Median age: 42.0 (2005); Males per 100 females: 96.2 (2005); Marriage status: 19.5% never married, 62.2% now married, 10.0% widowed, 8.3% divorced (2000); Foreign born: 2.0% (2000); Ancestry (includes multiple ancestries): 21.8% German, 14.5% English, 13.7% Irish, 11.5% French (except Basque), 9.7% United States or American (2000).
Economy: Manufactures clothing, wood products, machinery, boats. Dairying. Resort village. Employment by occupation: 10.6% management, 20.1% professional, 16.8% services, 24.0% sales, 2.2% farming, 15.3% construction, 11.0% production (2000).
Income: Per capita income: $20,068 (2005); Median household income: $38,050 (2005); Average household income: $48,018 (2005); Percent of households with income of $100,000 or more: 9.5% (2005); Poverty rate: 13.6% (2000).
Education: Percent of population age 25 and over with: High school diploma (including GED) or higher: 85.7% (2005); Bachelor's degree or higher: 16.8% (2005); Master's degree or higher: 6.2% (2005).
Housing: Homeownership rate: 75.8% (2005); Median home value: $98,995 (2005); Median rent: $389 per month (2000); Median age of housing: 35 years (2000).
Transportation: Commute to work: 86.0% car, 0.9% public transportation, 6.3% walk, 6.0% work from home (2000); Travel time to work: 41.1% less than 15 minutes, 28.5% 15 to 30 minutes, 25.4% 30 to 45 minutes, 2.6% 45 to 60 minutes, 2.5% 60 minutes or more (2000)

ALEXANDRIA BAY (village). Covers a land area of 0.738 square miles and a water area of 0.791 square miles. Located at 44.33° N. Lat.; 75.91° W. Long. Elevation is 284 feet.
Population: 1,194 (1990); 1,088 (2000); 1,100 (2005); 1,128 (2010 projected); Race: 98.7% White, 0.3% Black, 0.0% Asian, 0.9% Hispanic of any race (2005); Density: 1,490.2 persons per square mile (2005); Average household size: 2.21 (2005); Median age: 45.8 (2005); Males per 100 females: 82.4 (2005); Marriage status: 28.8% never married, 45.7% now married, 14.4% widowed, 11.1% divorced (2000); Foreign born: 1.9% (2000); Ancestry (includes multiple ancestries): 18.2% German, 18.0% Irish, 15.4% English, 11.2% United States or American, 8.7% French (except Basque) (2000).
Economy: Employment by occupation: 14.3% management, 20.1% professional, 18.2% services, 26.8% sales, 0.6% farming, 11.9% construction, 8.0% production (2000).
Income: Per capita income: $20,668 (2005); Median household income: $33,973 (2005); Average household income: $43,843 (2005); Percent of households with income of $100,000 or more: 7.8% (2005); Poverty rate: 13.5% (2000).
Education: Percent of population age 25 and over with: High school diploma (including GED) or higher: 87.2% (2005); Bachelor's degree or higher: 18.5% (2005); Master's degree or higher: 6.6% (2005).
School District(s)
Alexandria Central School District (KG-12)
    2003-04 Enrollment: 666 . . . . (315) 482-9971
Housing: Homeownership rate: 56.9% (2005); Median home value: $97,222 (2005); Median rent: $383 per month (2000); Median age of housing: 60+ years (2000).
Hospitals: EJ Noble Hospital/Samaritan (52 beds)
Safety: Violent crime rate: 0.0 per 10,000 population; Property crime rate: 155.3 per 10,000 population (2004).
Newspapers: Thousand Islands Sun (General - Circulation 6,379)
Transportation: Commute to work: 79.8% car, 0.4% public transportation, 12.6% walk, 6.5% work from home (2000); Travel time to work: 51.3% less than 15 minutes, 21.3% 15 to 30 minutes, 22.7% 30 to 45 minutes, 2.3% 45 to 60 minutes, 2.3% 60 minutes or more (2000)
Additional Information Contacts
Alexandria Bay Chamber of Commerce . . . . (315) 482-9531
    http://www.alexbay.org

ANTWERP (village). Covers a land area of 1.049 square miles and a water area of 0.030 square miles. Located at 44.20° N. Lat.; 75.60° W. Long. Elevation is 545 feet.
Population: 739 (1990); 716 (2000); 717 (2005); 733 (2010 projected); Race: 93.9% White, 0.6% Black, 1.1% Asian, 7.4% Hispanic of any race (2005); Density: 683.3 persons per square mile (2005); Average household size: 2.67 (2005); Median age: 36.7 (2005); Males per 100 females: 95.4 (2005); Marriage status: 28.5% never married, 52.8% now married, 10.0% widowed, 8.7% divorced (2000); Foreign born: 0.5% (2000); Ancestry (includes multiple ancestries): 20.0% English, 13.7% Other groups, 12.1% French (except Basque), 11.8% Irish, 10.0% German (2000).
Economy: Single-family building permits issued: 0 (2005); Multi-family building permits issued: 0 (2005); Employment by occupation: 9.4% management, 10.6% professional, 26.0% services, 21.7% sales, 0.8% farming, 16.5% construction, 15.0% production (2000).
Income: Per capita income: $16,621 (2005); Median household income: $38,606 (2005); Average household income: $44,303 (2005); Percent of households with income of $100,000 or more: 4.5% (2005); Poverty rate: 19.2% (2000).
Education: Percent of population age 25 and over with: High school diploma (including GED) or higher: 81.6% (2005); Bachelor's degree or higher: 10.6% (2005); Master's degree or higher: 4.5% (2005).
School District(s)
Indian River Central School District (KG-12)
    2003-04 Enrollment: 3,377 . . . . (315) 642-3481
Housing: Homeownership rate: 69.9% (2005); Median home value: $66,809 (2005); Median rent: $293 per month (2000); Median age of housing: 60+ years (2000).
Transportation: Commute to work: 94.1% car, 0.0% public transportation, 4.3% walk, 0.8% work from home (2000); Travel time to work: 34.3% less than 15 minutes, 24.0% 15 to 30 minutes, 27.2% 30 to 45 minutes, 7.5% 45 to 60 minutes, 7.1% 60 minutes or more (2000)

ANTWERP (town). Covers a land area of 106.901 square miles and a water area of 1.544 square miles. Located at 44.22° N. Lat.; 75.62° W. Long. Elevation is 545 feet.
Population: 1,856 (1990); 1,793 (2000); 1,822 (2005); 1,870 (2010 projected); Race: 96.3% White, 1.0% Black, 0.4% Asian, 4.0% Hispanic of any race (2005); Density: 17.0 persons per square mile (2005); Average household size: 2.81 (2005); Median age: 35.6 (2005); Males per 100 females: 102.4 (2005); Marriage status: 27.7% never married, 57.7% now married, 6.9% widowed, 7.7% divorced (2000); Foreign born: 0.6% (2000); Ancestry (includes multiple ancestries): 15.3% English, 13.7% German, 13.0% Irish, 12.7% United States or American, 11.3% French (except Basque) (2000).
Economy: Twenty-two miles Northeast of Watertown. Employment by occupation: 14.9% management, 13.8% professional, 17.7% services, 18.3% sales, 1.3% farming, 16.3% construction, 17.7% production (2000).
Income: Per capita income: $17,234 (2005); Median household income: $38,559 (2005); Average household income: $48,457 (2005); Percent of households with income of $100,000 or more: 6.5% (2005); Poverty rate: 17.6% (2000).
Education: Percent of population age 25 and over with: High school diploma (including GED) or higher: 79.1% (2005); Bachelor's degree or higher: 9.3% (2005); Master's degree or higher: 3.9% (2005).
Housing: Homeownership rate: 76.5% (2005); Median home value: $78,925 (2005); Median rent: $335 per month (2000); Median age of housing: 60+ years (2000).
Transportation: Commute to work: 90.4% car, 0.0% public transportation, 4.2% walk, 4.6% work from home (2000); Travel time to work: 33.2% less than 15 minutes, 26.9% 15 to 30 minutes, 23.4% 30 to 45 minutes, 8.8% 45 to 60 minutes, 7.6% 60 minutes or more (2000)

BLACK RIVER (village). Covers a land area of 1.810 square miles and a water area of 0.040 square miles. Located at 44.01° N. Lat.; 75.79° W. Long. Elevation is 570 feet.
Population: 1,349 (1990); 1,285 (2000); 1,360 (2005); 1,433 (2010 projected); Race: 86.6% White, 6.0% Black, 3.6% Asian, 2.8% Hispanic of any race (2005); Density: 751.2 persons per square mile (2005); Average household size: 2.39 (2005); Median age: 38.3 (2005); Males per 100 females: 92.6 (2005); Marriage status: 21.2% never married, 65.5% now married, 5.9% widowed, 7.4% divorced (2000); Foreign born: 4.1% (2000); Ancestry (includes multiple ancestries): 21.1% Irish, 17.0% English, 14.4% German, 12.3% French (except Basque), 10.3% Other groups (2000).

Economy: Single-family building permits issued: 5 (2005); Multi-family building permits issued: 0 (2005); Employment by occupation: 14.9% management, 24.0% professional, 20.3% services, 18.7% sales, 0.9% farming, 5.8% construction, 15.4% production (2000).
Income: Per capita income: $23,805 (2005); Median household income: $49,489 (2005); Average household income: $56,998 (2005); Percent of households with income of $100,000 or more: 11.1% (2005); Poverty rate: 6.1% (2000).
Education: Percent of population age 25 and over with: High school diploma (including GED) or higher: 88.9% (2005); Bachelor's degree or higher: 20.8% (2005); Master's degree or higher: 8.1% (2005).
School District(s)
Carthage Central School District (KG-12)
  2003-04 Enrollment: 2,937 . . . . (315) 493-5000
Housing: Homeownership rate: 65.0% (2005); Median home value: $109,964 (2005); Median rent: $373 per month (2000); Median age of housing: 53 years (2000).
Transportation: Commute to work: 94.6% car, 0.3% public transportation, 2.5% walk, 2.1% work from home (2000); Travel time to work: 41.9% less than 15 minutes, 49.2% 15 to 30 minutes, 5.2% 30 to 45 minutes, 1.5% 45 to 60 minutes, 2.3% 60 minutes or more (2000)

BROWNVILLE (village).
Covers a land area of 0.648 square miles and a water area of 0.005 square miles. Located at 44.00° N. Lat.; 75.98° W. Long. Elevation is 354 feet.
Population: 1,138 (1990); 1,022 (2000); 1,195 (2005); 1,341 (2010 projected); Race: 96.8% White, 1.0% Black, 0.2% Asian, 1.9% Hispanic of any race (2005); Density: 1,843.6 persons per square mile (2005); Average household size: 2.39 (2005); Median age: 40.8 (2005); Males per 100 females: 89.4 (2005); Marriage status: 22.4% never married, 56.1% now married, 8.1% widowed, 13.3% divorced (2000); Foreign born: 2.6% (2000); Ancestry (includes multiple ancestries): 23.3% Irish, 16.3% German, 13.6% English, 13.0% French (except Basque), 9.3% United States or American (2000).
Economy: Employment by occupation: 10.4% management, 17.3% professional, 15.1% services, 32.2% sales, 0.6% farming, 8.6% construction, 15.7% production (2000).
Income: Per capita income: $20,254 (2005); Median household income: $39,194 (2005); Average household income: $48,110 (2005); Percent of households with income of $100,000 or more: 8.6% (2005); Poverty rate: 8.4% (2000).
Education: Percent of population age 25 and over with: High school diploma (including GED) or higher: 85.5% (2005); Bachelor's degree or higher: 17.7% (2005); Master's degree or higher: 4.9% (2005).
School District(s)
General Brown Central School District (PK-12)
  2003-04 Enrollment: 1,572 . . . . (315) 639-4711
Housing: Homeownership rate: 68.4% (2005); Median home value: $108,633 (2005); Median rent: $348 per month (2000); Median age of housing: 60+ years (2000).
Transportation: Commute to work: 89.1% car, 0.0% public transportation, 3.9% walk, 6.2% work from home (2000); Travel time to work: 51.9% less than 15 minutes, 35.8% 15 to 30 minutes, 5.9% 30 to 45 minutes, 0.0% 45 to 60 minutes, 6.4% 60 minutes or more (2000)

BROWNVILLE (town).
Covers a land area of 59.302 square miles and a water area of 7.317 square miles. Located at 44.03° N. Lat.; 76.02° W. Long. Elevation is 354 feet.
Population: 5,604 (1990); 5,843 (2000); 6,133 (2005); 6,424 (2010 projected); Race: 96.6% White, 0.7% Black, 0.4% Asian, 1.4% Hispanic of any race (2005); Density: 103.4 persons per square mile (2005); Average household size: 2.62 (2005); Median age: 39.0 (2005); Males per 100 females: 93.9 (2005); Marriage status: 21.9% never married, 62.4% now married, 6.5% widowed, 9.3% divorced (2000); Foreign born: 2.1% (2000); Ancestry (includes multiple ancestries): 23.6% Irish, 16.2% German, 14.4% English, 14.1% French (except Basque), 7.8% United States or American (2000).
Economy: Employment by occupation: 9.6% management, 17.3% professional, 20.1% services, 25.4% sales, 0.5% farming, 9.8% construction, 17.2% production (2000).
Income: Per capita income: $18,744 (2005); Median household income: $42,048 (2005); Average household income: $48,724 (2005); Percent of households with income of $100,000 or more: 8.1% (2005); Poverty rate: 8.2% (2000).
Education: Percent of population age 25 and over with: High school diploma (including GED) or higher: 82.7% (2005); Bachelor's degree or higher: 13.7% (2005); Master's degree or higher: 4.1% (2005).
Housing: Homeownership rate: 78.3% (2005); Median home value: $107,340 (2005); Median rent: $344 per month (2000); Median age of housing: 39 years (2000).
Transportation: Commute to work: 95.2% car, 0.1% public transportation, 1.5% walk, 3.0% work from home (2000); Travel time to work: 31.7% less than 15 minutes, 49.1% 15 to 30 minutes, 13.8% 30 to 45 minutes, 0.6% 45 to 60 minutes, 4.9% 60 minutes or more (2000)

CALCIUM (CDP).
Covers a land area of 5.587 square miles and a water area of 0 square miles. Located at 44.03° N. Lat.; 75.84° W. Long. Elevation is 472 feet.
Population: 2,465 (1990); 3,346 (2000); 3,462 (2005); 3,561 (2010 projected); Race: 47.8% White, 33.1% Black, 1.2% Asian, 24.4% Hispanic of any race (2005); Density: 619.7 persons per square mile (2005); Average household size: 3.10 (2005); Median age: 24.7 (2005); Males per 100 females: 101.2 (2005); Marriage status: 12.2% never married, 81.6% now married, 1.2% widowed, 5.0% divorced (2000); Foreign born: 4.4% (2000); Ancestry (includes multiple ancestries): 42.2% Other groups, 12.2% Irish, 11.6% German, 6.6% Italian, 6.3% French (except Basque) (2000).
Economy: Employment by occupation: 7.2% management, 14.8% professional, 22.8% services, 37.0% sales, 1.3% farming, 5.6% construction, 11.3% production (2000).
Income: Per capita income: $12,299 (2005); Median household income: $32,557 (2005); Average household income: $38,188 (2005); Percent of households with income of $100,000 or more: 2.2% (2005); Poverty rate: 15.4% (2000).
Education: Percent of population age 25 and over with: High school diploma (including GED) or higher: 88.9% (2005); Bachelor's degree or higher: 10.5% (2005); Master's degree or higher: 2.7% (2005).
School District(s)
Indian River Central School District (KG-12)
  2003-04 Enrollment: 3,377 . . . . (315) 642-3481
Housing: Homeownership rate: 22.2% (2005); Median home value: $82,468 (2005); Median rent: $399 per month (2000); Median age of housing: 14 years (2000).
Transportation: Commute to work: 93.3% car, 0.4% public transportation, 0.5% walk, 4.0% work from home (2000); Travel time to work: 60.2% less than 15 minutes, 37.3% 15 to 30 minutes, 0.0% 30 to 45 minutes, 1.3% 45 to 60 minutes, 1.3% 60 minutes or more (2000)

CAPE VINCENT (village).
Covers a land area of 0.733 square miles and a water area of 0.020 square miles. Located at 44.12° N. Lat.; 76.33° W. Long. Elevation is 253 feet.
Population: 700 (1990); 760 (2000); 743 (2005); 739 (2010 projected); Race: 98.4% White, 0.1% Black, 0.3% Asian, 1.1% Hispanic of any race (2005); Density: 1,014.3 persons per square mile (2005); Average household size: 2.14 (2005); Median age: 44.5 (2005); Males per 100 females: 83.9 (2005); Marriage status: 21.9% never married, 54.0% now married, 12.6% widowed, 11.6% divorced (2000); Foreign born: 3.0% (2000); Ancestry (includes multiple ancestries): 20.0% German, 18.8% Irish, 16.8% English, 14.9% French (except Basque), 9.5% United States or American (2000).
Economy: Employment by occupation: 11.5% management, 24.8% professional, 22.7% services, 23.6% sales, 0.0% farming, 6.2% construction, 11.2% production (2000).
Income: Per capita income: $21,040 (2005); Median household income: $34,250 (2005); Average household income: $44,684 (2005); Percent of households with income of $100,000 or more: 8.6% (2005); Poverty rate: 16.4% (2000).
Education: Percent of population age 25 and over with: High school diploma (including GED) or higher: 86.2% (2005); Bachelor's degree or higher: 22.1% (2005); Master's degree or higher: 9.7% (2005).
School District(s)
Thousand Islands Central School District (KG-12)
  2003-04 Enrollment: 1,179 . . . . (315) 686-5594
Housing: Homeownership rate: 65.8% (2005); Median home value: $103,082 (2005); Median rent: $333 per month (2000); Median age of housing: 60+ years (2000).
Safety: Violent crime rate: 0.0 per 10,000 population; Property crime rate: 65.3 per 10,000 population (2004).

Transportation: Commute to work: 82.3% car, 0.0% public transportation, 13.0% walk, 4.7% work from home (2000); Travel time to work: 41.5% less than 15 minutes, 20.6% 15 to 30 minutes, 21.6% 30 to 45 minutes, 9.6% 45 to 60 minutes, 6.6% 60 minutes or more (2000)
Additional Information Contacts
Cape Vincent Chamber of Commerce . . . . (315) 654-2481
http://www.capevincent.org

CAPE VINCENT (town).
Covers a land area of 56.475 square miles and a water area of 33.387 square miles. Located at 44.13° N. Lat.; 76.26° W. Long. Elevation is 253 feet.
Population: 2,768 (1990); 3,345 (2000); 3,286 (2005); 3,321 (2010 projected); Race: 59.6% White, 33.4% Black, 0.4% Asian, 16.5% Hispanic of any race (2005); Density: 58.2 persons per square mile (2005); Average household size: 3.76 (2005); Median age: 38.2 (2005); Males per 100 females: 218.7 (2005); Marriage status: 42.7% never married, 43.1% now married, 5.2% widowed, 9.0% divorced (2000); Foreign born: 8.6% (2000); Ancestry (includes multiple ancestries): 13.0% Irish, 11.7% German, 9.6% French (except Basque), 9.3% English, 4.8% United States or American (2000).
Economy: A center for the Thousand Islands resort, tourism, and recreation area. Has ferry connections to Wolfe Island, Ontario, and thence to Kingston, Ontario. Port of entry. US fish hatchery. Employment by occupation: 17.3% management, 17.2% professional, 19.6% services, 23.8% sales, 0.6% farming, 10.7% construction, 10.8% production (2000).
Income: Per capita income: $18,321 (2005); Median household income: $40,808 (2005); Average household income: $51,188 (2005); Percent of households with income of $100,000 or more: 9.3% (2005); Poverty rate: 12.3% (2000).
Taxes: Total city taxes per capita: $106 (2004); City property taxes per capita: $81 (2004).
Education: Percent of population age 25 and over with: High school diploma (including GED) or higher: 51.9% (2005); Bachelor's degree or higher: 10.2% (2005); Master's degree or higher: 4.0% (2005).
Housing: Homeownership rate: 81.0% (2005); Median home value: $111,996 (2005); Median rent: $348 per month (2000); Median age of housing: 26 years (2000).
Transportation: Commute to work: 89.1% car, 0.0% public transportation, 5.8% walk, 4.9% work from home (2000); Travel time to work: 38.2% less than 15 minutes, 23.6% 15 to 30 minutes, 23.1% 30 to 45 minutes, 9.7% 45 to 60 minutes, 5.4% 60 minutes or more (2000)

CARTHAGE (village).
Covers a land area of 2.513 square miles and a water area of 0.169 square miles. Located at 43.98° N. Lat.; 75.60° W. Long. Elevation is 743 feet.
History: Settled before 1801, incorporated 1841.
Population: 4,344 (1990); 3,721 (2000); 3,937 (2005); 4,119 (2010 projected); Race: 85.6% White, 8.6% Black, 1.0% Asian, 5.2% Hispanic of any race (2005); Density: 1,566.4 persons per square mile (2005); Average household size: 2.57 (2005); Median age: 35.4 (2005); Males per 100 females: 92.0 (2005); Marriage status: 22.6% never married, 59.7% now married, 10.5% widowed, 7.2% divorced (2000); Foreign born: 4.0% (2000); Ancestry (includes multiple ancestries): 19.0% German, 18.5% Irish, 15.2% Other groups, 12.1% English, 11.5% French (except Basque) (2000).
Economy: In agricultural area. Manufacturing: paper, machinery, concrete, tile, cheese. Small lakes (with summer residences and winter sports) nearby. As with the rest of the greater Watertown region, village has economically benefited from the rapid growth of nearby Fort Drum, although the social impact has been mixed. Single-family building permits issued: 1 (2005); Multi-family building permits issued: 0 (2005); Employment by occupation: 7.5% management, 20.0% professional, 25.0% services, 24.9% sales, 0.8% farming, 9.2% construction, 12.5% production (2000).
Income: Per capita income: $15,034 (2005); Median household income: $26,584 (2005); Average household income: $37,704 (2005); Percent of households with income of $100,000 or more: 6.7% (2005); Poverty rate: 23.5% (2000).
Education: Percent of population age 25 and over with: High school diploma (including GED) or higher: 81.0% (2005); Bachelor's degree or higher: 14.3% (2005); Master's degree or higher: 5.3% (2005).
School District(s)
Carthage Central School District (KG-12)
    2003-04 Enrollment: 2,937 . . . . (315) 493-5000
Housing: Homeownership rate: 44.7% (2005); Median home value: $90,180 (2005); Median rent: $344 per month (2000); Median age of housing: 60+ years (2000).
Hospitals: Carthage Area Hospital (78 beds)
Safety: Violent crime rate: 13.4 per 10,000 population; Property crime rate: 221.9 per 10,000 population (2004).
Newspapers: Carthage Republican Tribune (General - Circulation 3,000)
Transportation: Commute to work: 89.6% car, 0.6% public transportation, 4.6% walk, 2.5% work from home (2000); Travel time to work: 46.0% less than 15 minutes, 35.9% 15 to 30 minutes, 15.5% 30 to 45 minutes, 1.3% 45 to 60 minutes, 1.3% 60 minutes or more (2000)
Additional Information Contacts
Carthage Chamber of Commerce . . . . (315) 493-3590
http://www.carthageny.com

CHAMPION (town).
Covers a land area of 44.302 square miles and a water area of 0.770 square miles. Located at 43.97° N. Lat.; 75.67° W. Long.
Population: 4,574 (1990); 4,361 (2000); 4,405 (2005); 4,467 (2010 projected); Race: 87.9% White, 5.3% Black, 1.4% Asian, 6.1% Hispanic of any race (2005); Density: 99.4 persons per square mile (2005); Average household size: 2.54 (2005); Median age: 35.7 (2005); Males per 100 females: 94.0 (2005); Marriage status: 20.8% never married, 64.3% now married, 6.4% widowed, 8.5% divorced (2000); Foreign born: 3.1% (2000); Ancestry (includes multiple ancestries): 16.4% Irish, 15.9% German, 11.6% Other groups, 10.8% English, 10.1% French (except Basque) (2000).
Economy: Employment by occupation: 11.0% management, 16.7% professional, 16.3% services, 26.1% sales, 0.4% farming, 9.4% construction, 20.1% production (2000).
Income: Per capita income: $19,189 (2005); Median household income: $40,930 (2005); Average household income: $48,775 (2005); Percent of households with income of $100,000 or more: 8.3% (2005); Poverty rate: 10.5% (2000).
Taxes: Total city taxes per capita: $105 (2004); City property taxes per capita: $94 (2004).
Education: Percent of population age 25 and over with: High school diploma (including GED) or higher: 84.4% (2005); Bachelor's degree or higher: 14.5% (2005); Master's degree or higher: 5.3% (2005).
Housing: Homeownership rate: 64.6% (2005); Median home value: $91,869 (2005); Median rent: $387 per month (2000); Median age of housing: 37 years (2000).
Transportation: Commute to work: 90.1% car, 2.4% public transportation, 3.6% walk, 3.5% work from home (2000); Travel time to work: 38.2% less than 15 minutes, 41.8% 15 to 30 minutes, 14.0% 30 to 45 minutes, 2.6% 45 to 60 minutes, 3.3% 60 minutes or more (2000)
Additional Information Contacts
Town of Champion . . . . (315) 493-3240
http://www.racog.org/Champion/Championhomepage.asp

CHAUMONT (village).
Covers a land area of 1.024 square miles and a water area of 0.076 square miles. Located at 44.06° N. Lat.; 76.13° W. Long. Elevation is 293 feet.
Population: 613 (1990); 592 (2000); 608 (2005); 620 (2010 projected); Race: 92.9% White, 4.8% Black, 0.0% Asian, 2.6% Hispanic of any race (2005); Density: 593.8 persons per square mile (2005); Average household size: 2.47 (2005); Median age: 40.3 (2005); Males per 100 females: 91.8 (2005); Marriage status: 24.9% never married, 53.5% now married, 10.0% widowed, 11.7% divorced (2000); Foreign born: 0.0% (2000); Ancestry (includes multiple ancestries): 22.4% German, 19.1% English, 18.4% Irish, 14.6% French (except Basque), 9.2% United States or American (2000).
Economy: Regional recreation center. Single-family building permits issued: 2 (2005); Multi-family building permits issued: 0 (2005); Employment by occupation: 12.5% management, 19.7% professional, 18.2% services, 30.3% sales, 0.0% farming, 8.7% construction, 10.6% production (2000).
Income: Per capita income: $18,732 (2005); Median household income: $40,625 (2005); Average household income: $45,102 (2005); Percent of households with income of $100,000 or more: 4.9% (2005); Poverty rate: 8.4% (2000).
Education: Percent of population age 25 and over with: High school diploma (including GED) or higher: 87.8% (2005); Bachelor's degree or higher: 14.1% (2005); Master's degree or higher: 8.1% (2005).
School District(s)
Lyme Central School District (KG-12)
    2003-04 Enrollment: 361 . . . . (315) 649-2417

Housing: Homeownership rate: 70.7% (2005); Median home value: $84,444 (2005); Median rent: $336 per month (2000); Median age of housing: 60+ years (2000).
Transportation: Commute to work: 89.4% car, 0.0% public transportation, 8.2% walk, 1.6% work from home (2000); Travel time to work: 30.7% less than 15 minutes, 47.8% 15 to 30 minutes, 13.9% 30 to 45 minutes, 1.6% 45 to 60 minutes, 6.0% 60 minutes or more (2000)
Additional Information Contacts
Chaumont-Three Mile Bay . . . . (315) 649-3404

CLAYTON
(village). Covers a land area of 1.620 square miles and a water area of 0.944 square miles. Located at 44.23° N. Lat.; 76.08° W. Long. Elevation is 222 feet.
Population: 2,160 (1990); 1,821 (2000); 1,901 (2005); 1,993 (2010 projected); Race: 87.3% White, 7.0% Black, 0.6% Asian, 8.2% Hispanic of any race (2005); Density: 1,173.2 persons per square mile (2005); Average household size: 2.15 (2005); Median age: 43.0 (2005); Males per 100 females: 83.3 (2005); Marriage status: 17.6% never married, 57.1% now married, 13.7% widowed, 11.6% divorced (2000); Foreign born: 1.7% (2000); Ancestry (includes multiple ancestries): 19.7% Irish, 18.0% German, 14.5% English, 13.2% French (except Basque), 8.6% United States or American (2000).
Economy: Employment by occupation: 8.2% management, 23.3% professional, 18.2% services, 28.3% sales, 0.0% farming, 11.9% construction, 10.1% production (2000).
Income: Per capita income: $21,515 (2005); Median household income: $35,625 (2005); Average household income: $46,140 (2005); Percent of households with income of $100,000 or more: 8.1% (2005); Poverty rate: 11.7% (2000).
Education: Percent of population age 25 and over with: High school diploma (including GED) or higher: 87.5% (2005); Bachelor's degree or higher: 28.1% (2005); Master's degree or higher: 9.0% (2005).
School District(s)
Thousand Islands Central School District (KG-12)
    2003-04 Enrollment: 1,179 . . . . (315) 686-5594
Housing: Homeownership rate: 57.8% (2005); Median home value: $111,167 (2005); Median rent: $416 per month (2000); Median age of housing: 58 years (2000).
Safety: Violent crime rate: 10.9 per 10,000 population; Property crime rate: 185.4 per 10,000 population (2004).
Transportation: Commute to work: 84.7% car, 1.9% public transportation, 7.4% walk, 5.0% work from home (2000); Travel time to work: 47.4% less than 15 minutes, 18.1% 15 to 30 minutes, 27.6% 30 to 45 minutes, 3.6% 45 to 60 minutes, 3.2% 60 minutes or more (2000)
Additional Information Contacts
Clayton Chamber of Commerce . . . . (315) 686-3771
    http://www.1000islands-clayton.com/

CLAYTON
(town). Covers a land area of 82.564 square miles and a water area of 21.469 square miles. Located at 44.20° N. Lat.; 76.08° W. Long. Elevation is 222 feet.
History: North American freshwater craft at Antique Boat Museum, similar to one at Mystic, Connecticut; Thousand Islands Museum; Clayton Historic District. Incorporated 1872.
Population: 4,629 (1990); 4,817 (2000); 4,949 (2005); 5,088 (2010 projected); Race: 90.1% White, 5.7% Black, 0.3% Asian, 8.3% Hispanic of any race (2005); Density: 59.9 persons per square mile (2005); Average household size: 2.46 (2005); Median age: 39.1 (2005); Males per 100 females: 93.2 (2005); Marriage status: 19.4% never married, 63.8% now married, 7.5% widowed, 9.3% divorced (2000); Foreign born: 2.7% (2000); Ancestry (includes multiple ancestries): 18.2% German, 17.7% Irish, 15.9% English, 12.3% French (except Basque), 7.6% United States or American (2000).
Economy: Manufacturing: snowplows, graphic-meter charts; boat repairing. Employment by occupation: 9.9% management, 19.2% professional, 20.7% services, 27.5% sales, 0.5% farming, 12.0% construction, 10.2% production (2000).
Income: Per capita income: $19,633 (2005); Median household income: $40,518 (2005); Average household income: $48,123 (2005); Percent of households with income of $100,000 or more: 6.8% (2005); Poverty rate: 8.0% (2000).
Education: Percent of population age 25 and over with: High school diploma (including GED) or higher: 87.7% (2005); Bachelor's degree or higher: 20.0% (2005); Master's degree or higher: 8.5% (2005).

Housing: Homeownership rate: 73.0% (2005); Median home value: $113,668 (2005); Median rent: $428 per month (2000); Median age of housing: 35 years (2000).
Transportation: Commute to work: 87.8% car, 1.2% public transportation, 5.6% walk, 5.0% work from home (2000); Travel time to work: 38.2% less than 15 minutes, 28.7% 15 to 30 minutes, 26.4% 30 to 45 minutes, 3.3% 45 to 60 minutes, 3.4% 60 minutes or more (2000)

DEFERIET
(village). Covers a land area of 0.711 square miles and a water area of 0.036 square miles. Located at 44.03° N. Lat.; 75.68° W. Long.
Population: 293 (1990); 309 (2000); 303 (2005); 301 (2010 projected); Race: 88.4% White, 4.0% Black, 2.0% Asian, 3.3% Hispanic of any race (2005); Density: 426.4 persons per square mile (2005); Average household size: 2.53 (2005); Median age: 39.1 (2005); Males per 100 females: 96.8 (2005); Marriage status: 19.2% never married, 68.0% now married, 9.2% widowed, 3.6% divorced (2000); Foreign born: 1.2% (2000); Ancestry (includes multiple ancestries): 26.1% United States or American, 13.3% Irish, 11.0% Italian, 8.7% German, 7.0% Other groups (2000).
Economy: Employment by occupation: 13.7% management, 6.5% professional, 19.4% services, 29.0% sales, 0.0% farming, 16.9% construction, 14.5% production (2000).
Income: Per capita income: $19,332 (2005); Median household income: $39,355 (2005); Average household income: $48,813 (2005); Percent of households with income of $100,000 or more: 10.0% (2005); Poverty rate: 13.3% (2000).
Education: Percent of population age 25 and over with: High school diploma (including GED) or higher: 82.6% (2005); Bachelor's degree or higher: 6.5% (2005); Master's degree or higher: 2.0% (2005).
Housing: Homeownership rate: 80.8% (2005); Median home value: $74,848 (2005); Median rent: $385 per month (2000); Median age of housing: 60+ years (2000).
Transportation: Commute to work: 81.4% car, 0.0% public transportation, 12.4% walk, 6.2% work from home (2000); Travel time to work: 51.2% less than 15 minutes, 34.7% 15 to 30 minutes, 14.0% 30 to 45 minutes, 0.0% 45 to 60 minutes, 0.0% 60 minutes or more (2000)

DEPAUVILLE
(CDP). Covers a land area of 9.789 square miles and a water area of 0 square miles. Located at 44.14° N. Lat.; 76.05° W. Long. Elevation is 298 feet.
Population: 474 (1990); 512 (2000); 533 (2005); 549 (2010 projected); Race: 95.7% White, 0.0% Black, 0.0% Asian, 4.3% Hispanic of any race (2005); Density: 54.4 persons per square mile (2005); Average household size: 2.79 (2005); Median age: 31.9 (2005); Males per 100 females: 101.1 (2005); Marriage status: 19.9% never married, 73.9% now married, 0.8% widowed, 5.4% divorced (2000); Foreign born: 0.8% (2000); Ancestry (includes multiple ancestries): 22.6% Irish, 17.0% French Canadian, 16.6% German, 9.9% Other groups, 6.1% French (except Basque) (2000).
Economy: Employment by occupation: 12.9% management, 14.1% professional, 22.0% services, 27.5% sales, 0.0% farming, 9.8% construction, 13.7% production (2000).
Income: Per capita income: $17,678 (2005); Median household income: $43,152 (2005); Average household income: $49,332 (2005); Percent of households with income of $100,000 or more: 5.8% (2005); Poverty rate: 1.6% (2000).
Education: Percent of population age 25 and over with: High school diploma (including GED) or higher: 89.3% (2005); Bachelor's degree or higher: 7.2% (2005); Master's degree or higher: 6.3% (2005).
Housing: Homeownership rate: 83.8% (2005); Median home value: $88,485 (2005); Median rent: $473 per month (2000); Median age of housing: 59 years (2000).
Transportation: Commute to work: 91.8% car, 0.0% public transportation, 0.0% walk, 8.2% work from home (2000); Travel time to work: 15.2% less than 15 minutes, 51.8% 15 to 30 minutes, 28.0% 30 to 45 minutes, 0.0% 45 to 60 minutes, 5.1% 60 minutes or more (2000)

DEXTER
(village). Covers a land area of 0.414 square miles and a water area of 0.072 square miles. Located at 44.00° N. Lat.; 76.04° W. Long. Elevation is 325 feet.
History: Incorporated 1855.
Population: 1,101 (1990); 1,120 (2000); 1,111 (2005); 1,120 (2010 projected); Race: 96.3% White, 0.6% Black, 0.6% Asian, 1.5% Hispanic of any race (2005); Density: 2,683.0 persons per square mile (2005); Average household size: 2.60 (2005); Median age: 37.9 (2005); Males per 100 females: 79.2 (2005); Marriage status: 31.7% never married, 49.5% now

married, 8.0% widowed, 10.8% divorced (2000); Foreign born: 0.6% (2000); Ancestry (includes multiple ancestries): 26.0% Irish, 17.4% French (except Basque), 17.1% English, 14.9% German, 7.1% Italian (2000).
Economy: Single-family building permits issued: 0 (2005); Multi-family building permits issued: 0 (2005); Employment by occupation: 8.0% management, 15.7% professional, 21.3% services, 30.6% sales, 0.6% farming, 6.9% construction, 17.0% production (2000).
Income: Per capita income: $18,719 (2005); Median household income: $37,404 (2005); Average household income: $47,541 (2005); Percent of households with income of $100,000 or more: 7.7% (2005); Poverty rate: 14.1% (2000).
Education: Percent of population age 25 and over with: High school diploma (including GED) or higher: 81.0% (2005); Bachelor's degree or higher: 8.3% (2005); Master's degree or higher: 3.5% (2005).

School District(s)
General Brown Central School District (PK-12)
    2003-04 Enrollment: 1,572 . . . . (315) 639-4711
Housing: Homeownership rate: 60.9% (2005); Median home value: $90,133 (2005); Median rent: $314 per month (2000); Median age of housing: 60+ years (2000).
Safety: Violent crime rate: 0.0 per 10,000 population; Property crime rate: 17.8 per 10,000 population (2004).
Transportation: Commute to work: 93.8% car, 0.4% public transportation, 2.8% walk, 3.0% work from home (2000); Travel time to work: 32.1% less than 15 minutes, 55.1% 15 to 30 minutes, 6.0% 30 to 45 minutes, 1.2% 45 to 60 minutes, 5.6% 60 minutes or more (2000)

ELLISBURG (village). Covers a land area of 1.011 square miles and a water area of 0 square miles. Located at 43.73° N. Lat.; 76.13° W. Long.
Population: 246 (1990); 269 (2000); 281 (2005); 294 (2010 projected); Race: 98.6% White, 0.0% Black, 0.0% Asian, 0.7% Hispanic of any race (2005); Density: 278.0 persons per square mile (2005); Average household size: 2.87 (2005); Median age: 35.1 (2005); Males per 100 females: 89.9 (2005); Marriage status: 24.4% never married, 61.9% now married, 4.5% widowed, 9.1% divorced (2000); Foreign born: 0.0% (2000); Ancestry (includes multiple ancestries): 25.5% English, 20.0% German, 19.1% Irish, 12.8% United States or American, 8.5% French (except Basque) (2000).
Economy: Employment by occupation: 12.0% management, 9.0% professional, 16.0% services, 30.0% sales, 12.0% farming, 5.0% construction, 16.0% production (2000).
Income: Per capita income: $19,262 (2005); Median household income: $50,833 (2005); Average household income: $55,230 (2005); Percent of households with income of $100,000 or more: 10.2% (2005); Poverty rate: 21.6% (2000).
Education: Percent of population age 25 and over with: High school diploma (including GED) or higher: 84.0% (2005); Bachelor's degree or higher: 13.0% (2005); Master's degree or higher: 7.1% (2005).
Housing: Homeownership rate: 71.4% (2005); Median home value: $69,091 (2005); Median rent: $331 per month (2000); Median age of housing: 60+ years (2000).
Transportation: Commute to work: 81.4% car, 3.1% public transportation, 4.1% walk, 11.3% work from home (2000); Travel time to work: 12.8% less than 15 minutes, 37.2% 15 to 30 minutes, 24.4% 30 to 45 minutes, 4.7% 45 to 60 minutes, 20.9% 60 minutes or more (2000)

ELLISBURG (town). Covers a land area of 85.256 square miles and a water area of 1.337 square miles. Located at 43.74° N. Lat.; 76.11° W. Long.
Population: 3,386 (1990); 3,541 (2000); 3,682 (2005); 3,827 (2010 projected); Race: 95.9% White, 1.2% Black, 0.5% Asian, 2.7% Hispanic of any race (2005); Density: 43.2 persons per square mile (2005); Average household size: 2.73 (2005); Median age: 36.9 (2005); Males per 100 females: 98.4 (2005); Marriage status: 21.1% never married, 65.5% now married, 6.3% widowed, 7.1% divorced (2000); Foreign born: 0.6% (2000); Ancestry (includes multiple ancestries): 21.4% English, 15.9% Irish, 14.0% German, 11.5% French (except Basque), 10.1% United States or American (2000).
Economy: Employment by occupation: 13.8% management, 17.8% professional, 14.3% services, 21.0% sales, 7.3% farming, 11.5% construction, 14.2% production (2000).
Income: Per capita income: $21,719 (2005); Median household income: $45,900 (2005); Average household income: $59,104 (2005); Percent of households with income of $100,000 or more: 14.3% (2005); Poverty rate: 13.6% (2000).
Education: Percent of population age 25 and over with: High school diploma (including GED) or higher: 78.3% (2005); Bachelor's degree or higher: 12.9% (2005); Master's degree or higher: 5.7% (2005).
Housing: Homeownership rate: 81.6% (2005); Median home value: $90,172 (2005); Median rent: $365 per month (2000); Median age of housing: 44 years (2000).
Transportation: Commute to work: 89.0% car, 0.2% public transportation, 4.5% walk, 6.2% work from home (2000); Travel time to work: 34.1% less than 15 minutes, 29.8% 15 to 30 minutes, 17.0% 30 to 45 minutes, 9.3% 45 to 60 minutes, 9.8% 60 minutes or more (2000)

EVANS MILLS (village). Covers a land area of 0.787 square miles and a water area of 0 square miles. Located at 44.08° N. Lat.; 75.80° W. Long. Elevation is 430 feet.
Population: 661 (1990); 605 (2000); 624 (2005); 642 (2010 projected); Race: 86.9% White, 8.5% Black, 2.1% Asian, 1.8% Hispanic of any race (2005); Density: 792.9 persons per square mile (2005); Average household size: 2.35 (2005); Median age: 37.3 (2005); Males per 100 females: 98.7 (2005); Marriage status: 23.4% never married, 56.2% now married, 10.4% widowed, 10.0% divorced (2000); Foreign born: 2.6% (2000); Ancestry (includes multiple ancestries): 19.9% Irish, 16.6% German, 15.7% English, 10.1% French (except Basque), 8.6% Other groups (2000).
Economy: Single-family building permits issued: 0 (2005); Multi-family building permits issued: 0 (2005); Employment by occupation: 11.3% management, 26.4% professional, 17.4% services, 29.1% sales, 0.8% farming, 7.9% construction, 7.2% production (2000).
Income: Per capita income: $20,970 (2005); Median household income: $43,136 (2005); Average household income: $49,192 (2005); Percent of households with income of $100,000 or more: 9.4% (2005); Poverty rate: 13.4% (2000).
Education: Percent of population age 25 and over with: High school diploma (including GED) or higher: 86.3% (2005); Bachelor's degree or higher: 19.5% (2005); Master's degree or higher: 7.7% (2005).

School District(s)
Indian River Central School District (KG-12)
    2003-04 Enrollment: 3,377 . . . . (315) 642-3481
Housing: Homeownership rate: 59.0% (2005); Median home value: $102,536 (2005); Median rent: $292 per month (2000); Median age of housing: 55 years (2000).
Transportation: Commute to work: 94.3% car, 0.0% public transportation, 1.8% walk, 3.9% work from home (2000); Travel time to work: 33.1% less than 15 minutes, 53.2% 15 to 30 minutes, 9.3% 30 to 45 minutes, 0.7% 45 to 60 minutes, 3.7% 60 minutes or more (2000)

FELTS MILLS (unincorporated postal area, zip code 13638). Covers a land area of 0.978 square miles and a water area of 0 square miles. Located at 44.02° N. Lat.; 75.76° W. Long.
Population: 0 (2000); Race: 88.4% White, 1.0% Black, 1.0% Asian, 6.2% Hispanic of any race (2000); Density: 0.0 persons per square mile (2000); Age: 30.0% under 18, 13.7% over 64 (2000); Marriage status: 21.2% never married, 67.1% now married, 2.5% widowed, 9.2% divorced (2000); Foreign born: 1.0% (2000); Ancestry (includes multiple ancestries): 25.1% Irish, 23.0% English, 17.1% Other groups, 16.3% German, 14.0% French (except Basque) (2000).
Economy: Employment by occupation: 11.6% management, 17.9% professional, 18.8% services, 7.1% sales, 4.5% farming, 10.7% construction, 29.5% production (2000).
Income: Per capita income: $14,964 (2000); Median household income: $36,111 (2000); Poverty rate: 13.8% (2000).
Education: Percent of population age 25 and over with: High school diploma (including GED) or higher: 82.5% (2000); Bachelor's degree or higher: 12.6% (2000).
Housing: Homeownership rate: 68.0% (2005); Median home value: $61,500 (2005); Median rent: $465 per month (2000); Median age of housing: 48 years (2000).
Transportation: Commute to work: 91.7% car, 3.8% public transportation, 0.0% walk, 4.5% work from home (2000); Travel time to work: 56.7% less than 15 minutes, 40.2% 15 to 30 minutes, 3.1% 30 to 45 minutes, 0.0% 45 to 60 minutes, 0.0% 60 minutes or more (2000)

FORT DRUM (CDP). Covers a land area of 25.265 square miles and a water area of 0.085 square miles. Located at 44.03° N. Lat.; 75.75° W. Long.
Population: 11,586 (1990); 12,123 (2000); 14,031 (2005); 15,773 (2010 projected); Race: 50.5% White, 27.7% Black, 2.3% Asian, 22.8% Hispanic

of any race (2005); Density: 555.3 persons per square mile (2005); Average household size: 5.11 (2005); Median age: 23.3 (2005); Males per 100 females: 177.7 (2005); Marriage status: 42.7% never married, 53.5% now married, 0.1% widowed, 3.7% divorced (2000); Foreign born: 8.6% (2000); Ancestry (includes multiple ancestries): 38.6% Other groups, 15.4% German, 11.1% Irish, 7.2% Italian, 5.3% English (2000).
Economy: Employment by occupation: 12.9% management, 20.0% professional, 28.4% services, 28.3% sales, 2.3% farming, 4.5% construction, 3.6% production (2000).
Income: Per capita income: $14,477 (2005); Median household income: $37,673 (2005); Average household income: $44,817 (2005); Percent of households with income of $100,000 or more: 3.3% (2005); Poverty rate: 6.2% (2000).
Education: Percent of population age 25 and over with: High school diploma (including GED) or higher: 96.8% (2005); Bachelor's degree or higher: 20.8% (2005); Master's degree or higher: 4.8% (2005).
Housing: Homeownership rate: 0.5% (2005); Median home value: $64,286 (2005); Median rent: $608 per month (2000); Median age of housing: 12 years (2000).
Hospitals: Guthrie Ambulatory Health Care Clinic
Transportation: Commute to work: 58.0% car, 0.8% public transportation, 33.2% walk, 6.8% work from home (2000); Travel time to work: 80.1% less than 15 minutes, 14.9% 15 to 30 minutes, 1.8% 30 to 45 minutes, 1.1% 45 to 60 minutes, 2.2% 60 minutes or more (2000)

GLEN PARK (village).
Covers a land area of 0.702 square miles and a water area of 0.027 square miles. Located at 43.99° N. Lat.; 75.95° W. Long. Elevation is 347 feet.
Population: 527 (1990); 487 (2000); 539 (2005); 579 (2010 projected); Race: 95.4% White, 0.4% Black, 0.9% Asian, 2.8% Hispanic of any race (2005); Density: 767.5 persons per square mile (2005); Average household size: 2.72 (2005); Median age: 33.6 (2005); Males per 100 females: 84.0 (2005); Marriage status: 23.0% never married, 60.9% now married, 7.0% widowed, 9.0% divorced (2000); Foreign born: 1.0% (2000); Ancestry (includes multiple ancestries): 22.2% French (except Basque), 20.9% Irish, 17.8% German, 14.9% English, 11.1% Other groups (2000).
Economy: Employment by occupation: 9.5% management, 15.8% professional, 20.5% services, 27.4% sales, 1.1% farming, 10.0% construction, 15.8% production (2000).
Income: Per capita income: $15,951 (2005); Median household income: $33,947 (2005); Average household income: $43,422 (2005); Percent of households with income of $100,000 or more: 7.6% (2005); Poverty rate: 14.3% (2000).
Education: Percent of population age 25 and over with: High school diploma (including GED) or higher: 79.8% (2005); Bachelor's degree or higher: 6.3% (2005); Master's degree or higher: 0.3% (2005).
Housing: Homeownership rate: 71.2% (2005); Median home value: $82,500 (2005); Median rent: $406 per month (2000); Median age of housing: 60+ years (2000).
Safety: Violent crime rate: 0.0 per 10,000 population; Property crime rate: 0.0 per 10,000 population (2004).
Transportation: Commute to work: 99.0% car, 0.0% public transportation, 0.0% walk, 1.0% work from home (2000); Travel time to work: 62.1% less than 15 minutes, 27.9% 15 to 30 minutes, 6.8% 30 to 45 minutes, 2.1% 45 to 60 minutes, 1.1% 60 minutes or more (2000)

GREAT BEND (CDP).
Covers a land area of 5.874 square miles and a water area of 0.018 square miles. Located at 44.03° N. Lat.; 75.70° W. Long.
Population: 829 (1990); 801 (2000); 826 (2005); 845 (2010 projected); Race: 88.7% White, 4.4% Black, 0.7% Asian, 2.2% Hispanic of any race (2005); Density: 140.6 persons per square mile (2005); Average household size: 2.51 (2005); Median age: 36.3 (2005); Males per 100 females: 102.0 (2005); Marriage status: 22.0% never married, 63.9% now married, 4.4% widowed, 9.7% divorced (2000); Foreign born: 3.5% (2000); Ancestry (includes multiple ancestries): 14.4% United States or American, 12.2% Irish, 10.4% French (except Basque), 10.3% German, 8.5% English (2000).
Economy: Employment by occupation: 8.6% management, 17.8% professional, 16.2% services, 28.3% sales, 0.0% farming, 3.2% construction, 26.0% production (2000).
Income: Per capita income: $16,780 (2005); Median household income: $38,651 (2005); Average household income: $42,128 (2005); Percent of households with income of $100,000 or more: 4.0% (2005); Poverty rate: 13.2% (2000).
Education: Percent of population age 25 and over with: High school diploma (including GED) or higher: 81.7% (2005); Bachelor's degree or higher: 10.4% (2005); Master's degree or higher: 4.1% (2005).
Housing: Homeownership rate: 72.3% (2005); Median home value: $88,696 (2005); Median rent: $373 per month (2000); Median age of housing: 35 years (2000).
Transportation: Commute to work: 86.8% car, 8.7% public transportation, 3.0% walk, 1.5% work from home (2000); Travel time to work: 30.7% less than 15 minutes, 44.1% 15 to 30 minutes, 17.9% 30 to 45 minutes, 7.3% 45 to 60 minutes, 0.0% 60 minutes or more (2000)

HENDERSON (town).
Covers a land area of 41.315 square miles and a water area of 11.652 square miles. Located at 43.84° N. Lat.; 76.18° W. Long.
Population: 1,268 (1990); 1,377 (2000); 1,421 (2005); 1,470 (2010 projected); Race: 98.0% White, 0.0% Black, 0.0% Asian, 1.3% Hispanic of any race (2005); Density: 34.4 persons per square mile (2005); Average household size: 2.33 (2005); Median age: 46.2 (2005); Males per 100 females: 100.1 (2005); Marriage status: 21.6% never married, 61.2% now married, 8.3% widowed, 8.9% divorced (2000); Foreign born: 1.5% (2000); Ancestry (includes multiple ancestries): 22.9% English, 17.1% Irish, 14.3% German, 10.5% United States or American, 6.5% French (except Basque) (2000).
Economy: Employment by occupation: 14.5% management, 18.0% professional, 15.8% services, 24.2% sales, 2.1% farming, 15.1% construction, 10.3% production (2000).
Income: Per capita income: $22,796 (2005); Median household income: $42,634 (2005); Average household income: $53,102 (2005); Percent of households with income of $100,000 or more: 10.7% (2005); Poverty rate: 11.1% (2000).
Education: Percent of population age 25 and over with: High school diploma (including GED) or higher: 86.0% (2005); Bachelor's degree or higher: 18.4% (2005); Master's degree or higher: 7.5% (2005).
Housing: Homeownership rate: 82.8% (2005); Median home value: $117,177 (2005); Median rent: $333 per month (2000); Median age of housing: 42 years (2000).
Transportation: Commute to work: 89.3% car, 0.4% public transportation, 2.8% walk, 7.2% work from home (2000); Travel time to work: 26.3% less than 15 minutes, 37.5% 15 to 30 minutes, 23.7% 30 to 45 minutes, 4.7% 45 to 60 minutes, 7.8% 60 minutes or more (2000)
Additional Information Contacts
Henderson Harbor Chamber of Commerce . . . . (315) 938-5568

http://www.thousandislands.com/tsite/communities/HENDERSON+HARBOR

HERRINGS (village).
Covers a land area of 0.289 square miles and a water area of 0.046 square miles. Located at 44.02° N. Lat.; 75.66° W. Long.
Population: 140 (1990); 129 (2000); 127 (2005); 125 (2010 projected); Race: 77.2% White, 11.8% Black, 0.0% Asian, 7.1% Hispanic of any race (2005); Density: 439.7 persons per square mile (2005); Average household size: 3.02 (2005); Median age: 33.3 (2005); Males per 100 females: 95.4 (2005); Marriage status: 27.3% never married, 65.7% now married, 1.0% widowed, 6.1% divorced (2000); Foreign born: 3.5% (2000); Ancestry (includes multiple ancestries): 14.9% United States or American, 12.1% Irish, 11.3% Italian, 9.2% Other groups, 5.0% German (2000).
Economy: Employment by occupation: 5.9% management, 7.8% professional, 19.6% services, 27.5% sales, 0.0% farming, 19.6% construction, 19.6% production (2000).
Income: Per capita income: $13,295 (2005); Median household income: $40,000 (2005); Average household income: $39,940 (2005); Percent of households with income of $100,000 or more: 0.0% (2005); Poverty rate: 18.8% (2000).
Education: Percent of population age 25 and over with: High school diploma (including GED) or higher: 84.2% (2005); Bachelor's degree or higher: 3.9% (2005); Master's degree or higher: 1.3% (2005).
Housing: Homeownership rate: 78.6% (2005); Median home value: $63,333 (2005); Median rent: $364 per month (2000); Median age of housing: 60+ years (2000).
Transportation: Commute to work: 100.0% car, 0.0% public transportation, 0.0% walk, 0.0% work from home (2000); Travel time to work: 34.5% less than 15 minutes, 40.0% 15 to 30 minutes, 20.0% 30 to 45 minutes, 5.5% 45 to 60 minutes, 0.0% 60 minutes or more (2000)

HOUNSFIELD (town). Covers a land area of 49.262 square miles and a water area of 71.156 square miles. Located at 43.94° N. Lat.; 76.07° W. Long.
Population: 3,089 (1990); 3,323 (2000); 3,359 (2005); 3,419 (2010 projected); Race: 95.9% White, 1.4% Black, 0.4% Asian, 3.1% Hispanic of any race (2005); Density: 68.2 persons per square mile (2005); Average household size: 2.40 (2005); Median age: 37.9 (2005); Males per 100 females: 106.5 (2005); Marriage status: 25.8% never married, 60.4% now married, 6.4% widowed, 7.5% divorced (2000); Foreign born: 2.5% (2000); Ancestry (includes multiple ancestries): 21.8% Irish, 19.0% English, 16.4% German, 10.0% French (except Basque), 8.6% Italian (2000).
Economy: Employment by occupation: 13.1% management, 21.7% professional, 17.4% services, 24.0% sales, 1.7% farming, 10.5% construction, 11.5% production (2000).
Income: Per capita income: $23,352 (2005); Median household income: $47,155 (2005); Average household income: $55,914 (2005); Percent of households with income of $100,000 or more: 9.5% (2005); Poverty rate: 10.6% (2000).
Education: Percent of population age 25 and over with: High school diploma (including GED) or higher: 86.6% (2005); Bachelor's degree or higher: 25.5% (2005); Master's degree or higher: 9.3% (2005).
Housing: Homeownership rate: 65.8% (2005); Median home value: $110,887 (2005); Median rent: $483 per month (2000); Median age of housing: 49 years (2000).
Transportation: Commute to work: 87.9% car, 0.0% public transportation, 5.6% walk, 5.5% work from home (2000); Travel time to work: 35.2% less than 15 minutes, 42.9% 15 to 30 minutes, 15.4% 30 to 45 minutes, 2.7% 45 to 60 minutes, 3.7% 60 minutes or more (2000)

LA FARGEVILLE (CDP). Covers a land area of 3.476 square miles and a water area of 0.038 square miles. Located at 44.19° N. Lat.; 75.96° W. Long. Elevation is 381 feet.
Population: 490 (1990); 588 (2000); 589 (2005); 593 (2010 projected); Race: 80.6% White, 16.5% Black, 0.7% Asian, 0.7% Hispanic of any race (2005); Density: 169.4 persons per square mile (2005); Average household size: 2.63 (2005); Median age: 35.9 (2005); Males per 100 females: 82.9 (2005); Marriage status: 22.0% never married, 63.2% now married, 11.5% widowed, 3.3% divorced (2000); Foreign born: 4.9% (2000); Ancestry (includes multiple ancestries): 16.3% English, 15.5% Irish, 15.0% German, 8.9% United States or American, 8.7% Other groups (2000).
Economy: In timber and lumbering area. Employment by occupation: 9.0% management, 16.3% professional, 8.6% services, 27.3% sales, 1.2% farming, 10.6% construction, 26.9% production (2000).
Income: Per capita income: $16,787 (2005); Median household income: $33,696 (2005); Average household income: $43,973 (2005); Percent of households with income of $100,000 or more: 6.3% (2005); Poverty rate: 28.1% (2000).
Education: Percent of population age 25 and over with: High school diploma (including GED) or higher: 82.9% (2005); Bachelor's degree or higher: 14.1% (2005); Master's degree or higher: 3.5% (2005).

School District(s)
La Fargeville Central School District (KG-12)
    2003-04 Enrollment: 571 . . . . (315) 658-2241

Housing: Homeownership rate: 63.4% (2005); Median home value: $80,870 (2005); Median rent: $228 per month (2000); Median age of housing: 60+ years (2000).
Transportation: Commute to work: 89.4% car, 0.0% public transportation, 7.2% walk, 1.7% work from home (2000); Travel time to work: 42.0% less than 15 minutes, 33.3% 15 to 30 minutes, 17.3% 30 to 45 minutes, 3.5% 45 to 60 minutes, 3.9% 60 minutes or more (2000)

LE RAY (town). Covers a land area of 73.709 square miles and a water area of 0.322 square miles. Located at 44.07° N. Lat.; 75.80° W. Long.
Population: 17,973 (1990); 19,836 (2000); 22,049 (2005); 24,065 (2010 projected); Race: 56.0% White, 25.3% Black, 2.0% Asian, 20.0% Hispanic of any race (2005); Density: 299.1 persons per square mile (2005); Average household size: 3.88 (2005); Median age: 24.4 (2005); Males per 100 females: 144.0 (2005); Marriage status: 33.6% never married, 59.5% now married, 1.6% widowed, 5.3% divorced (2000); Foreign born: 6.6% (2000); Ancestry (includes multiple ancestries): 32.8% Other groups, 14.7% German, 13.4% Irish, 7.5% English, 6.8% Italian (2000).
Economy: Employment by occupation: 11.9% management, 19.9% professional, 22.1% services, 28.3% sales, 1.1% farming, 7.6% construction, 9.1% production (2000).

Income: Per capita income: $15,645 (2005); Median household income: $38,549 (2005); Average household income: $46,546 (2005); Percent of households with income of $100,000 or more: 5.4% (2005); Poverty rate: 9.1% (2000).
Education: Percent of population age 25 and over with: High school diploma (including GED) or higher: 92.3% (2005); Bachelor's degree or higher: 18.5% (2005); Master's degree or higher: 5.9% (2005).
Housing: Homeownership rate: 25.3% (2005); Median home value: $99,007 (2005); Median rent: $481 per month (2000); Median age of housing: 15 years (2000).
Transportation: Commute to work: 69.7% car, 0.6% public transportation, 23.0% walk, 5.5% work from home (2000); Travel time to work: 68.7% less than 15 minutes, 24.5% 15 to 30 minutes, 2.9% 30 to 45 minutes, 1.2% 45 to 60 minutes, 2.6% 60 minutes or more (2000)

LORRAINE (town). Covers a land area of 39.006 square miles and a water area of 0.007 square miles. Located at 43.75° N. Lat.; 75.97° W. Long. Elevation is 998 feet.
Population: 737 (1990); 930 (2000); 941 (2005); 948 (2010 projected); Race: 99.6% White, 0.0% Black, 0.0% Asian, 1.1% Hispanic of any race (2005); Density: 24.1 persons per square mile (2005); Average household size: 2.78 (2005); Median age: 35.1 (2005); Males per 100 females: 99.4 (2005); Marriage status: 22.6% never married, 59.7% now married, 7.3% widowed, 10.4% divorced (2000); Foreign born: 0.8% (2000); Ancestry (includes multiple ancestries): 17.2% English, 12.8% Irish, 11.1% Other groups, 10.6% United States or American, 9.9% French (except Basque) (2000).
Economy: Employment by occupation: 10.8% management, 13.6% professional, 21.6% services, 19.2% sales, 2.6% farming, 12.2% construction, 20.0% production (2000).
Income: Per capita income: $18,297 (2005); Median household income: $43,913 (2005); Average household income: $50,939 (2005); Percent of households with income of $100,000 or more: 9.5% (2005); Poverty rate: 15.5% (2000).
Education: Percent of population age 25 and over with: High school diploma (including GED) or higher: 78.6% (2005); Bachelor's degree or higher: 9.2% (2005); Master's degree or higher: 2.8% (2005).
Housing: Homeownership rate: 88.8% (2005); Median home value: $81,905 (2005); Median rent: $338 per month (2000); Median age of housing: 25 years (2000).
Transportation: Commute to work: 91.1% car, 1.0% public transportation, 1.5% walk, 5.7% work from home (2000); Travel time to work: 20.1% less than 15 minutes, 40.2% 15 to 30 minutes, 23.5% 30 to 45 minutes, 7.8% 45 to 60 minutes, 8.4% 60 minutes or more (2000)

LYME (town). Covers a land area of 56.111 square miles and a water area of 50.810 square miles. Located at 44.06° N. Lat.; 76.17° W. Long.
Population: 1,701 (1990); 2,015 (2000); 2,048 (2005); 2,076 (2010 projected); Race: 94.5% White, 3.2% Black, 0.1% Asian, 1.9% Hispanic of any race (2005); Density: 36.5 persons per square mile (2005); Average household size: 2.42 (2005); Median age: 45.2 (2005); Males per 100 females: 100.2 (2005); Marriage status: 19.1% never married, 63.4% now married, 7.1% widowed, 10.4% divorced (2000); Foreign born: 1.1% (2000); Ancestry (includes multiple ancestries): 20.0% German, 19.7% English, 16.4% Irish, 12.5% French (except Basque), 8.6% United States or American (2000).
Economy: Employment by occupation: 12.9% management, 19.1% professional, 13.2% services, 26.5% sales, 0.2% farming, 11.9% construction, 16.1% production (2000).
Income: Per capita income: $21,384 (2005); Median household income: $42,056 (2005); Average household income: $51,358 (2005); Percent of households with income of $100,000 or more: 8.4% (2005); Poverty rate: 10.2% (2000).
Education: Percent of population age 25 and over with: High school diploma (including GED) or higher: 86.1% (2005); Bachelor's degree or higher: 16.8% (2005); Master's degree or higher: 6.6% (2005).
Housing: Homeownership rate: 84.8% (2005); Median home value: $109,296 (2005); Median rent: $352 per month (2000); Median age of housing: 35 years (2000).
Transportation: Commute to work: 93.6% car, 0.0% public transportation, 3.7% walk, 2.1% work from home (2000); Travel time to work: 23.0% less than 15 minutes, 41.3% 15 to 30 minutes, 24.1% 30 to 45 minutes, 4.6% 45 to 60 minutes, 7.0% 60 minutes or more (2000)

MANNSVILLE (village). Covers a land area of 0.920 square miles and a water area of 0.009 square miles. Located at 43.71° N. Lat.; 76.06° W. Long.
Population: 444 (1990); 400 (2000); 409 (2005); 419 (2010 projected); Race: 98.5% White, 0.0% Black, 1.0% Asian, 1.7% Hispanic of any race (2005); Density: 444.3 persons per square mile (2005); Average household size: 2.74 (2005); Median age: 36.5 (2005); Males per 100 females: 89.4 (2005); Marriage status: 24.2% never married, 61.0% now married, 8.2% widowed, 6.6% divorced (2000); Foreign born: 0.7% (2000); Ancestry (includes multiple ancestries): 25.4% English, 22.0% German, 15.2% Irish, 13.4% United States or American, 8.6% French (except Basque) (2000).
Economy: Employment by occupation: 2.4% management, 12.1% professional, 12.6% services, 37.9% sales, 3.4% farming, 16.0% construction, 15.5% production (2000).
Income: Per capita income: $22,886 (2005); Median household income: $56,389 (2005); Average household income: $62,399 (2005); Percent of households with income of $100,000 or more: 14.8% (2005); Poverty rate: 15.7% (2000).
Taxes: Total city taxes per capita: $106 (2004); City property taxes per capita: $101 (2004).
Education: Percent of population age 25 and over with: High school diploma (including GED) or higher: 86.1% (2005); Bachelor's degree or higher: 11.6% (2005); Master's degree or higher: 7.3% (2005).

School District(s)
South Jefferson Central School District (PK-12)
    2003-04 Enrollment: 2,044 . . . . (315) 583-6104

Housing: Homeownership rate: 75.8% (2005); Median home value: $92,353 (2005); Median rent: $338 per month (2000); Median age of housing: 60+ years (2000).
Transportation: Commute to work: 95.6% car, 0.0% public transportation, 0.5% walk, 3.0% work from home (2000); Travel time to work: 32.5% less than 15 minutes, 23.4% 15 to 30 minutes, 15.2% 30 to 45 minutes, 14.2% 45 to 60 minutes, 14.7% 60 minutes or more (2000)

NATURAL BRIDGE (CDP). Covers a land area of 1.390 square miles and a water area of 0 square miles. Located at 44.06° N. Lat.; 75.49° W. Long. Elevation is 800 feet.
Population: 425 (1990); 392 (2000); 370 (2005); 366 (2010 projected); Race: 93.5% White, 0.8% Black, 0.3% Asian, 6.2% Hispanic of any race (2005); Density: 266.1 persons per square mile (2005); Average household size: 2.62 (2005); Median age: 35.2 (2005); Males per 100 females: 109.0 (2005); Marriage status: 28.8% never married, 55.5% now married, 2.1% widowed, 13.5% divorced (2000); Foreign born: 0.0% (2000); Ancestry (includes multiple ancestries): 25.5% English, 18.4% French (except Basque), 12.2% United States or American, 6.5% Irish, 3.6% Polish (2000).
Economy: Indian River has cut through limestone here to form a bridge and caverns that are a popular tourist attraction. Employment by occupation: 12.5% management, 0.0% professional, 44.2% services, 5.8% sales, 0.0% farming, 0.0% construction, 37.5% production (2000).
Income: Per capita income: $13,068 (2005); Median household income: $30,875 (2005); Average household income: $34,291 (2005); Percent of households with income of $100,000 or more: 0.0% (2005); Poverty rate: 26.4% (2000).
Education: Percent of population age 25 and over with: High school diploma (including GED) or higher: 63.6% (2005); Bachelor's degree or higher: 0.0% (2005); Master's degree or higher: 0.0% (2005).
Housing: Homeownership rate: 68.8% (2005); Median home value: $38,571 (2005); Median rent: $386 per month (2000); Median age of housing: 60+ years (2000).
Transportation: Commute to work: 93.3% car, 0.0% public transportation, 0.0% walk, 6.7% work from home (2000); Travel time to work: 6.3% less than 15 minutes, 40.2% 15 to 30 minutes, 30.4% 30 to 45 minutes, 17.0% 45 to 60 minutes, 6.3% 60 minutes or more (2000)

ORLEANS (town). Covers a land area of 71.114 square miles and a water area of 6.672 square miles. Located at 44.24° N. Lat.; 75.97° W. Long.
Population: 2,248 (1990); 2,465 (2000); 2,503 (2005); 2,546 (2010 projected); Race: 91.5% White, 5.4% Black, 0.3% Asian, 2.0% Hispanic of any race (2005); Density: 35.2 persons per square mile (2005); Average household size: 2.59 (2005); Median age: 38.2 (2005); Males per 100 females: 102.7 (2005); Marriage status: 21.9% never married, 66.3% now married, 6.3% widowed, 5.5% divorced (2000); Foreign born: 2.7% (2000); Ancestry (includes multiple ancestries): 16.1% German, 15.6% Irish, 14.1% English, 10.8% French (except Basque), 8.0% United States or American (2000).
Economy: Employment by occupation: 12.8% management, 15.1% professional, 13.0% services, 25.8% sales, 2.2% farming, 13.0% construction, 18.1% production (2000).
Income: Per capita income: $18,915 (2005); Median household income: $40,604 (2005); Average household income: $48,922 (2005); Percent of households with income of $100,000 or more: 7.5% (2005); Poverty rate: 12.2% (2000).
Education: Percent of population age 25 and over with: High school diploma (including GED) or higher: 84.4% (2005); Bachelor's degree or higher: 15.4% (2005); Master's degree or higher: 7.3% (2005).
Housing: Homeownership rate: 79.8% (2005); Median home value: $99,370 (2005); Median rent: $333 per month (2000); Median age of housing: 36 years (2000).
Transportation: Commute to work: 90.3% car, 0.0% public transportation, 3.8% walk, 4.8% work from home (2000); Travel time to work: 35.4% less than 15 minutes, 38.0% 15 to 30 minutes, 20.5% 30 to 45 minutes, 2.1% 45 to 60 minutes, 4.0% 60 minutes or more (2000)

PAMELIA (town). Covers a land area of 33.962 square miles and a water area of 1.438 square miles. Located at 44.04° N. Lat.; 75.89° W. Long.
Population: 2,811 (1990); 2,897 (2000); 3,080 (2005); 3,252 (2010 projected); Race: 90.4% White, 3.1% Black, 1.6% Asian, 4.7% Hispanic of any race (2005); Density: 90.7 persons per square mile (2005); Average household size: 2.72 (2005); Median age: 36.5 (2005); Males per 100 females: 102.6 (2005); Marriage status: 27.1% never married, 61.0% now married, 3.0% widowed, 9.0% divorced (2000); Foreign born: 2.5% (2000); Ancestry (includes multiple ancestries): 19.4% French (except Basque), 18.8% Irish, 18.4% German, 14.3% English, 10.8% Other groups (2000).
Economy: Single-family building permits issued: 4 (2005); Multi-family building permits issued: 0 (2005); Employment by occupation: 10.3% management, 14.7% professional, 18.9% services, 30.1% sales, 0.5% farming, 9.6% construction, 16.0% production (2000).
Income: Per capita income: $19,561 (2005); Median household income: $44,689 (2005); Average household income: $52,875 (2005); Percent of households with income of $100,000 or more: 10.3% (2005); Poverty rate: 11.9% (2000).
Taxes: Total city taxes per capita: $148 (2004); City property taxes per capita: $117 (2004).
Education: Percent of population age 25 and over with: High school diploma (including GED) or higher: 86.8% (2005); Bachelor's degree or higher: 14.3% (2005); Master's degree or higher: 4.8% (2005).
Housing: Homeownership rate: 78.5% (2005); Median home value: $115,994 (2005); Median rent: $412 per month (2000); Median age of housing: 25 years (2000).
Transportation: Commute to work: 91.4% car, 0.5% public transportation, 2.0% walk, 5.8% work from home (2000); Travel time to work: 48.5% less than 15 minutes, 40.4% 15 to 30 minutes, 7.3% 30 to 45 minutes, 0.4% 45 to 60 minutes, 3.3% 60 minutes or more (2000)

PHILADELPHIA (village). Covers a land area of 0.898 square miles and a water area of 0 square miles. Located at 44.15° N. Lat.; 75.70° W. Long. Elevation is 490 feet.
Population: 1,478 (1990); 1,519 (2000); 1,600 (2005); 1,710 (2010 projected); Race: 74.1% White, 12.2% Black, 1.8% Asian, 13.8% Hispanic of any race (2005); Density: 1,782.4 persons per square mile (2005); Average household size: 2.74 (2005); Median age: 28.3 (2005); Males per 100 females: 95.6 (2005); Marriage status: 18.8% never married, 65.2% now married, 6.9% widowed, 9.2% divorced (2000); Foreign born: 3.3% (2000); Ancestry (includes multiple ancestries): 20.1% Other groups, 14.4% German, 13.6% Irish, 10.9% United States or American, 10.9% English (2000).
Economy: Single-family building permits issued: 0 (2005); Multi-family building permits issued: 0 (2005); Employment by occupation: 7.9% management, 19.0% professional, 21.1% services, 26.9% sales, 1.2% farming, 11.3% construction, 12.7% production (2000).
Income: Per capita income: $14,408 (2005); Median household income: $31,755 (2005); Average household income: $39,406 (2005); Percent of households with income of $100,000 or more: 3.9% (2005); Poverty rate: 17.4% (2000).
Education: Percent of population age 25 and over with: High school diploma (including GED) or higher: 84.9% (2005); Bachelor's degree or higher: 15.4% (2005); Master's degree or higher: 4.4% (2005).

School District(s)
Indian River Central School District (KG-12)
   2003-04 Enrollment: 3,377 . . . . (315) 642-3481
Housing: Homeownership rate: 33.7% (2005); Median home value: $82,708 (2005); Median rent: $325 per month (2000); Median age of housing: 20 years (2000).
Transportation: Commute to work: 91.5% car, 2.4% public transportation, 4.3% walk, 1.4% work from home (2000); Travel time to work: 24.1% less than 15 minutes, 51.9% 15 to 30 minutes, 17.1% 30 to 45 minutes, 1.8% 45 to 60 minutes, 5.1% 60 minutes or more (2000)

PHILADELPHIA (town). Covers a land area of 37.600 square miles and a water area of 0 square miles. Located at 44.15° N. Lat.; 75.71° W. Long. Elevation is 490 feet.
Population: 2,136 (1990); 2,140 (2000); 2,250 (2005); 2,403 (2010 projected); Race: 78.6% White, 9.3% Black, 1.4% Asian, 11.6% Hispanic of any race (2005); Density: 59.8 persons per square mile (2005); Average household size: 2.77 (2005); Median age: 30.1 (2005); Males per 100 females: 97.9 (2005); Marriage status: 19.3% never married, 66.8% now married, 5.7% widowed, 8.2% divorced (2000); Foreign born: 3.4% (2000); Ancestry (includes multiple ancestries): 16.3% Other groups, 15.4% German, 14.8% Irish, 13.1% English, 11.6% United States or American (2000).
Economy: Single-family building permits issued: 16 (2005); Multi-family building permits issued: 0 (2005); Employment by occupation: 9.5% management, 20.1% professional, 19.9% services, 23.3% sales, 2.5% farming, 10.5% construction, 14.1% production (2000).
Income: Per capita income: $16,340 (2005); Median household income: $37,051 (2005); Average household income: $45,221 (2005); Percent of households with income of $100,000 or more: 6.2% (2005); Poverty rate: 13.8% (2000).
Education: Percent of population age 25 and over with: High school diploma (including GED) or higher: 85.8% (2005); Bachelor's degree or higher: 15.4% (2005); Master's degree or higher: 5.4% (2005).
Housing: Homeownership rate: 48.1% (2005); Median home value: $88,313 (2005); Median rent: $333 per month (2000); Median age of housing: 25 years (2000).
Transportation: Commute to work: 89.3% car, 1.7% public transportation, 3.3% walk, 5.0% work from home (2000); Travel time to work: 27.0% less than 15 minutes, 48.2% 15 to 30 minutes, 17.9% 30 to 45 minutes, 1.8% 45 to 60 minutes, 5.0% 60 minutes or more (2000)

PLESSIS (unincorporated postal area, zip code 13675). Covers a land area of 1.527 square miles and a water area of 0 square miles. Located at 44.27° N. Lat.; 75.84° W. Long. Elevation is 405 feet.
Population: 0 (2000); Race: 100.0% White, 0.0% Black, 0.0% Asian, 0.0% Hispanic of any race (2000); Density: 0.0 persons per square mile (2000); Age: 27.3% under 18, 10.1% over 64 (2000); Marriage status: 23.6% never married, 56.9% now married, 0.0% widowed, 19.4% divorced (2000); Foreign born: 0.0% (2000); Ancestry (includes multiple ancestries): 39.4% German, 30.3% Irish, 22.2% United States or American, 9.1% Other groups (2000).
Economy: Resort village. Lakes nearby. Employment by occupation: 37.8% management, 31.1% professional, 0.0% services, 15.6% sales, 15.6% farming, 0.0% construction, 0.0% production (2000).
Income: Per capita income: $13,739 (2000); Median household income: $23,875 (2000); Poverty rate: 22.2% (2000).
Education: Percent of population age 25 and over with: High school diploma (including GED) or higher: 88.9% (2000); Bachelor's degree or higher: 9.5% (2000).
Housing: Homeownership rate: 61.3% (2000); Median home value: $162,500 (2000); Median rent: $375 per month (2000); Median age of housing: 7 years (2000).
Transportation: Commute to work: 100.0% car, 0.0% public transportation, 0.0% walk, 0.0% work from home (2000); Travel time to work: 78.4% less than 15 minutes, 21.6% 15 to 30 minutes, 0.0% 30 to 45 minutes, 0.0% 45 to 60 minutes, 0.0% 60 minutes or more (2000)

REDWOOD (CDP). Covers a land area of 2.036 square miles and a water area of 0.515 square miles. Located at 44.30° N. Lat.; 75.80° W. Long. Elevation is 382 feet.
Population: 530 (1990); 584 (2000); 610 (2005); 634 (2010 projected); Race: 97.0% White, 2.0% Black, 0.0% Asian, 0.0% Hispanic of any race (2005); Density: 299.6 persons per square mile (2005); Average household size: 2.79 (2005); Median age: 35.8 (2005); Males per 100 females: 96.1 (2005); Marriage status: 20.0% never married, 68.9% now married, 7.2% widowed, 3.9% divorced (2000); Foreign born: 2.9% (2000); Ancestry (includes multiple ancestries): 15.4% French (except Basque), 14.7% Irish, 14.7% German, 9.4% French Canadian, 9.3% English (2000).
Economy: Resort village. Employment by occupation: 4.8% management, 24.4% professional, 34.0% services, 14.0% sales, 2.8% farming, 6.8% construction, 13.2% production (2000).
Income: Per capita income: $18,148 (2005); Median household income: $43,116 (2005); Average household income: $50,548 (2005); Percent of households with income of $100,000 or more: 6.8% (2005); Poverty rate: 12.1% (2000).
Education: Percent of population age 25 and over with: High school diploma (including GED) or higher: 86.8% (2005); Bachelor's degree or higher: 11.1% (2005); Master's degree or higher: 6.7% (2005).
Housing: Homeownership rate: 77.2% (2005); Median home value: $93,824 (2005); Median rent: $433 per month (2000); Median age of housing: 60+ years (2000).
Transportation: Commute to work: 88.8% car, 0.0% public transportation, 3.6% walk, 5.6% work from home (2000); Travel time to work: 43.6% less than 15 minutes, 38.6% 15 to 30 minutes, 9.3% 30 to 45 minutes, 3.4% 45 to 60 minutes, 5.1% 60 minutes or more (2000)

RODMAN (town). Covers a land area of 42.243 square miles and a water area of 0.012 square miles. Located at 43.85° N. Lat.; 75.91° W. Long. Elevation is 724 feet.
Population: 1,016 (1990); 1,147 (2000); 1,118 (2005); 1,085 (2010 projected); Race: 97.9% White, 0.7% Black, 0.0% Asian, 5.3% Hispanic of any race (2005); Density: 26.5 persons per square mile (2005); Average household size: 2.90 (2005); Median age: 36.2 (2005); Males per 100 females: 107.0 (2005); Marriage status: 26.6% never married, 64.1% now married, 4.4% widowed, 5.0% divorced (2000); Foreign born: 2.8% (2000); Ancestry (includes multiple ancestries): 21.7% English, 19.4% Irish, 16.7% German, 9.2% French (except Basque), 7.3% Italian (2000).
Economy: Employment by occupation: 12.7% management, 19.3% professional, 16.9% services, 21.3% sales, 3.7% farming, 12.3% construction, 13.9% production (2000).
Income: Per capita income: $18,645 (2005); Median household income: $43,843 (2005); Average household income: $54,143 (2005); Percent of households with income of $100,000 or more: 10.4% (2005); Poverty rate: 9.5% (2000).
Education: Percent of population age 25 and over with: High school diploma (including GED) or higher: 85.8% (2005); Bachelor's degree or higher: 14.2% (2005); Master's degree or higher: 7.0% (2005).
Housing: Homeownership rate: 87.3% (2005); Median home value: $111,165 (2005); Median rent: $323 per month (2000); Median age of housing: 25 years (2000).
Transportation: Commute to work: 87.9% car, 0.7% public transportation, 3.7% walk, 5.9% work from home (2000); Travel time to work: 27.9% less than 15 minutes, 45.0% 15 to 30 minutes, 17.5% 30 to 45 minutes, 3.1% 45 to 60 minutes, 6.4% 60 minutes or more (2000)

RUTLAND (town). Covers a land area of 45.190 square miles and a water area of 0.196 square miles. Located at 43.96° N. Lat.; 75.79° W. Long.
Population: 3,023 (1990); 2,959 (2000); 3,146 (2005); 3,323 (2010 projected); Race: 90.8% White, 3.8% Black, 1.0% Asian, 4.9% Hispanic of any race (2005); Density: 69.6 persons per square mile (2005); Average household size: 2.63 (2005); Median age: 37.3 (2005); Males per 100 females: 101.8 (2005); Marriage status: 23.5% never married, 63.2% now married, 4.2% widowed, 9.1% divorced (2000); Foreign born: 1.8% (2000); Ancestry (includes multiple ancestries): 17.3% Irish, 15.6% German, 14.9% English, 10.3% French (except Basque), 9.5% Other groups (2000).
Economy: Employment by occupation: 10.4% management, 16.1% professional, 19.3% services, 21.1% sales, 3.6% farming, 8.7% construction, 20.8% production (2000).
Income: Per capita income: $17,497 (2005); Median household income: $38,955 (2005); Average household income: $45,986 (2005); Percent of households with income of $100,000 or more: 6.1% (2005); Poverty rate: 12.1% (2000).
Education: Percent of population age 25 and over with: High school diploma (including GED) or higher: 83.9% (2005); Bachelor's degree or higher: 10.3% (2005); Master's degree or higher: 4.2% (2005).
Housing: Homeownership rate: 72.4% (2005); Median home value: $91,215 (2005); Median rent: $402 per month (2000); Median age of housing: 34 years (2000).

Transportation: Commute to work: 92.0% car, 0.5% public transportation, 1.9% walk, 5.3% work from home (2000); Travel time to work: 34.0% less than 15 minutes, 55.1% 15 to 30 minutes, 6.9% 30 to 45 minutes, 1.4% 45 to 60 minutes, 2.6% 60 minutes or more (2000)

SACKETS HARBOR (village).
Covers a land area of 2.275 square miles and a water area of 0.004 square miles. Located at 43.94° N. Lat.; 76.11° W. Long. Elevation is 278 feet.
History: In 1809 infantry was stationed here to enforce the Embargo Act and control smuggling. Following the outbreak of the War of 1812, it became the center of U.S. naval and military activity for Upper St. Lawrence Valley and Lake Ontario. Further expansion occurred during the 1830s and 1840s due to the Patriots War in Canada. Its growth led to the development of Pine Camp (Fort Drum) near Watertown. Zebulon Pike is buried here. Settled c.1801, Incorporated 1814.
Population: 1,313 (1990); 1,386 (2000); 1,420 (2005); 1,446 (2010 projected); Race: 95.6% White, 0.8% Black, 0.4% Asian, 4.4% Hispanic of any race (2005); Density: 624.1 persons per square mile (2005); Average household size: 2.07 (2005); Median age: 36.0 (2005); Males per 100 females: 112.9 (2005); Marriage status: 29.7% never married, 54.9% now married, 6.3% widowed, 9.1% divorced (2000); Foreign born: 4.4% (2000); Ancestry (includes multiple ancestries): 23.8% Irish, 20.4% English, 18.1% German, 9.3% Other groups, 9.0% French (except Basque) (2000).
Economy: Summer resort. Employment by occupation: 12.4% management, 29.2% professional, 20.0% services, 24.8% sales, 0.6% farming, 6.7% construction, 6.2% production (2000).
Income: Per capita income: $27,468 (2005); Median household income: $47,739 (2005); Average household income: $56,543 (2005); Percent of households with income of $100,000 or more: 8.7% (2005); Poverty rate: 7.8% (2000).
Education: Percent of population age 25 and over with: High school diploma (including GED) or higher: 92.3% (2005); Bachelor's degree or higher: 38.4% (2005); Master's degree or higher: 14.8% (2005).

School District(s)
Sackets Harbor Central School District (KG-12)
    2003-04 Enrollment: 473 . . . . (315) 646-3575

Housing: Homeownership rate: 43.1% (2005); Median home value: $119,919 (2005); Median rent: $501 per month (2000); Median age of housing: 60+ years (2000).
Safety: Violent crime rate: 14.3 per 10,000 population; Property crime rate: 57.3 per 10,000 population (2004).
Transportation: Commute to work: 89.7% car, 0.0% public transportation, 5.4% walk, 3.8% work from home (2000); Travel time to work: 26.2% less than 15 minutes, 45.0% 15 to 30 minutes, 21.9% 30 to 45 minutes, 4.1% 45 to 60 minutes, 2.9% 60 minutes or more (2000)

Additional Information Contacts
Sackets Harbor Chamber of Commerce . . . . (315) 646-1700
    http://www.sacketsharborchamberofcommerce.com

THERESA (village).
Covers a land area of 1.264 square miles and a water area of 0.051 square miles. Located at 44.21° N. Lat.; 75.79° W. Long. Elevation is 391 feet.
Population: 889 (1990); 812 (2000); 875 (2005); 931 (2010 projected); Race: 90.4% White, 6.3% Black, 0.8% Asian, 2.1% Hispanic of any race (2005); Density: 692.3 persons per square mile (2005); Average household size: 2.57 (2005); Median age: 37.1 (2005); Males per 100 females: 109.8 (2005); Marriage status: 25.4% never married, 59.8% now married, 5.5% widowed, 9.2% divorced (2000); Foreign born: 1.0% (2000); Ancestry (includes multiple ancestries): 15.4% German, 14.9% Irish, 14.8% English, 12.5% United States or American, 9.0% French (except Basque) (2000).
Economy: Single-family building permits issued: 0 (2005); Multi-family building permits issued: 0 (2005); Employment by occupation: 10.3% management, 17.0% professional, 17.3% services, 27.3% sales, 0.6% farming, 12.7% construction, 14.8% production (2000).
Income: Per capita income: $20,517 (2005); Median household income: $43,125 (2005); Average household income: $52,801 (2005); Percent of households with income of $100,000 or more: 9.7% (2005); Poverty rate: 14.3% (2000).
Education: Percent of population age 25 and over with: High school diploma (including GED) or higher: 85.5% (2005); Bachelor's degree or higher: 15.0% (2005); Master's degree or higher: 7.1% (2005).

School District(s)
Indian River Central School District (KG-12)
    2003-04 Enrollment: 3,377 . . . . (315) 642-3481

Housing: Homeownership rate: 73.8% (2005); Median home value: $80,556 (2005); Median rent: $348 per month (2000); Median age of housing: 60+ years (2000).
Transportation: Commute to work: 92.2% car, 0.3% public transportation, 4.5% walk, 2.4% work from home (2000); Travel time to work: 28.4% less than 15 minutes, 31.5% 15 to 30 minutes, 31.8% 30 to 45 minutes, 3.4% 45 to 60 minutes, 4.9% 60 minutes or more (2000)

THERESA (town).
Covers a land area of 65.440 square miles and a water area of 4.277 square miles. Located at 44.24° N. Lat.; 75.79° W. Long. Elevation is 391 feet.
Population: 2,274 (1990); 2,414 (2000); 2,612 (2005); 2,794 (2010 projected); Race: 93.8% White, 4.6% Black, 0.3% Asian, 1.4% Hispanic of any race (2005); Density: 39.9 persons per square mile (2005); Average household size: 2.72 (2005); Median age: 36.4 (2005); Males per 100 females: 107.0 (2005); Marriage status: 25.1% never married, 61.8% now married, 4.2% widowed, 8.9% divorced (2000); Foreign born: 1.4% (2000); Ancestry (includes multiple ancestries): 15.7% German, 14.9% United States or American, 14.9% Irish, 13.5% English, 8.0% French (except Basque) (2000).
Economy: Lakes (resorts) nearby. Single-family building permits issued: 24 (2005); Multi-family building permits issued: 0 (2005); Employment by occupation: 8.4% management, 15.1% professional, 21.5% services, 19.7% sales, 1.6% farming, 17.2% construction, 16.5% production (2000).
Income: Per capita income: $18,764 (2005); Median household income: $41,487 (2005); Average household income: $51,002 (2005); Percent of households with income of $100,000 or more: 8.5% (2005); Poverty rate: 15.3% (2000).
Education: Percent of population age 25 and over with: High school diploma (including GED) or higher: 79.1% (2005); Bachelor's degree or higher: 11.3% (2005); Master's degree or higher: 5.7% (2005).
Housing: Homeownership rate: 80.3% (2005); Median home value: $77,165 (2005); Median rent: $373 per month (2000); Median age of housing: 37 years (2000).
Transportation: Commute to work: 92.5% car, 0.1% public transportation, 3.2% walk, 4.0% work from home (2000); Travel time to work: 20.2% less than 15 minutes, 39.4% 15 to 30 minutes, 30.1% 30 to 45 minutes, 3.6% 45 to 60 minutes, 6.7% 60 minutes or more (2000)

THREE MILE BAY (unincorporated postal area, zip code 13693).
Covers a land area of 22.009 square miles and a water area of 0 square miles. Located at 44.06° N. Lat.; 76.24° W. Long. Elevation is 265 feet.
Population: 0 (2000); Race: 98.0% White, 0.0% Black, 1.0% Asian, 0.6% Hispanic of any race (2000); Density: 0.0 persons per square mile (2000); Age: 19.2% under 18, 21.4% over 64 (2000); Marriage status: 12.9% never married, 72.9% now married, 6.9% widowed, 7.4% divorced (2000); Foreign born: 2.8% (2000); Ancestry (includes multiple ancestries): 23.4% English, 22.2% German, 16.0% Irish, 9.3% French (except Basque), 7.7% United States or American (2000).
Economy: Employment by occupation: 5.4% management, 22.7% professional, 8.6% services, 33.0% sales, 1.1% farming, 8.6% construction, 20.5% production (2000).
Income: Per capita income: $18,704 (2000); Median household income: $37,143 (2000); Poverty rate: 10.3% (2000).
Education: Percent of population age 25 and over with: High school diploma (including GED) or higher: 82.9% (2000); Bachelor's degree or higher: 16.0% (2000).
Housing: Homeownership rate: 90.8% (2000); Median home value: $69,800 (2000); Median rent: $325 per month (2000); Median age of housing: 31 years (2000).
Transportation: Commute to work: 92.1% car, 0.0% public transportation, 4.5% walk, 3.4% work from home (2000); Travel time to work: 20.9% less than 15 minutes, 27.3% 15 to 30 minutes, 30.8% 30 to 45 minutes, 11.0% 45 to 60 minutes, 9.9% 60 minutes or more (2000)

WATERTOWN (city).
Covers a land area of 8.957 square miles and a water area of 0.318 square miles. Located at 43.97° N. Lat.; 75.90° W. Long. Elevation is 478 feet.
History: In 1800, five New Englanders hacked their way up from the Mohawk Valley, stopped at the rocky Black River Falls, and named the site Watertown. They built sawmills and gristmills along the river, and burned piles of lumber for potash. The five and ten cent store originated in Watertown during county fair week in 1878. Frank W. Woolworth (1852-1910), a clerk in Moore & Smith's general store, piled leftover odds and ends on a table and put up a sign: "Any Article 5 cents." The entire

stock was sold out in a few hours. Inspired by this success, Woolworth opened his first store in Utica the following year.
Population: 29,437 (1990); 26,705 (2000); 26,800 (2005); 26,951 (2010 projected); Race: 80.5% White, 10.6% Black, 1.5% Asian, 7.9% Hispanic of any race (2005); Density: 2,991.9 persons per square mile (2005); Average household size: 2.37 (2005); Median age: 35.2 (2005); Males per 100 females: 91.7 (2005); Marriage status: 27.2% never married, 52.9% now married, 8.7% widowed, 11.2% divorced (2000); Foreign born: 4.0% (2000); Ancestry (includes multiple ancestries): 18.3% Irish, 14.6% Other groups, 12.6% German, 11.8% Italian, 10.4% English (2000).
Economy: Unemployment rate: 5.3% (2005); Total civilian labor force: 11,376 (2005); Single-family building permits issued: 12 (2005); Multi-family building permits issued: 4 (2005); Employment by occupation: 9.7% management, 20.0% professional, 21.2% services, 28.4% sales, 0.3% farming, 7.5% construction, 12.9% production (2000).
Income: Per capita income: $17,942 (2005); Median household income: $30,548 (2005); Average household income: $41,106 (2005); Percent of households with income of $100,000 or more: 6.0% (2005); Poverty rate: 19.3% (2000).
Taxes: Total city taxes per capita: $404 (2004); City property taxes per capita: $366 (2004).
Education: Percent of population age 25 and over with: High school diploma (including GED) or higher: 82.6% (2005); Bachelor's degree or higher: 17.5% (2005); Master's degree or higher: 7.5% (2005).

School District(s)
Boces Jeffer-Lewis-Hamil-Herk-Oneida (UG-UG)
   2003-04 Enrollment: 452 . . . . (315) 779-7010
Watertown City School District (PK-12)
   2003-04 Enrollment: 4,334 . . . . (315) 785-3700

Two-year College(s)
Jefferson Community College (Public)
   Fall 2004 Enrollment: 3,764 . . . . (315) 786-2200
   2005-06 Tuition: In-state $3,294; Out-of-state $4,724
Jefferson Lewis BOCES-Practical Nursing Program (Public)
   Fall 2004 Enrollment: 82 . . . . (315) 779-7200
   2005-06 Tuition: In-state $6,800; Out-of-state $6,800

Housing: Homeownership rate: 43.5% (2005); Median home value: $95,102 (2005); Median rent: $377 per month (2000); Median age of housing: 60+ years (2000).
Hospitals: Mercy Northern of New York (300 beds); Samaritan Medical Center (267 beds)
Safety: Violent crime rate: 24.2 per 10,000 population; Property crime rate: 328.7 per 10,000 population (2004).
Newspapers: Fort Drum Sentinel (General - Circulation 36,000); Watertown Daily Times (Circulation 31,610)
Transportation: Commute to work: 90.3% car, 1.8% public transportation, 5.1% walk, 1.7% work from home (2000); Travel time to work: 58.1% less than 15 minutes, 31.2% 15 to 30 minutes, 5.2% 30 to 45 minutes, 1.3% 45 to 60 minutes, 4.2% 60 minutes or more (2000)

Additional Information Contacts
City of Watertown . . . . (315) 785-7780
   http://www.citywatertown.org/
Watertown North Country Chamber of Commerce . . . . (315) 788-4400
   http://www.watertownny.com

WATERTOWN (town).
Covers a land area of 35.985 square miles and a water area of 0.073 square miles. Located at 43.93° N. Lat.; 75.92° W. Long. Elevation is 478 feet.
History: Public Square Historic District in the city. Settled c.1800,Incorporated as a city 1869.
Population: 4,333 (1990); 4,482 (2000); 4,706 (2005); 4,965 (2010 projected); Race: 73.5% White, 18.8% Black, 0.6% Asian, 11.8% Hispanic of any race (2005); Density: 130.8 persons per square mile (2005); Average household size: 3.09 (2005); Median age: 38.4 (2005); Males per 100 females: 142.3 (2005); Marriage status: 30.4% never married, 55.4% now married, 4.9% widowed, 9.3% divorced (2000); Foreign born: 5.4% (2000); Ancestry (includes multiple ancestries): 17.9% Irish, 15.8% English, 11.2% German, 11.2% French (except Basque), 8.8% Italian (2000).
Economy: Manufacturing includes papermaking machinery, foundry and die castings, irrigation equipment, electric motors, railroad equipment and high-pressure aircraft hydraulic systems. Dairy region. Resort area. Employment by occupation: 14.7% management, 22.3% professional, 18.7% services, 27.0% sales, 0.3% farming, 7.6% construction, 9.3% production (2000).

Income: Per capita income: $24,940 (2005); Median household income: $46,395 (2005); Average household income: $66,195 (2005); Percent of households with income of $100,000 or more: 15.9% (2005); Poverty rate: 4.7% (2000).
Education: Percent of population age 25 and over with: High school diploma (including GED) or higher: 72.3% (2005); Bachelor's degree or higher: 17.3% (2005); Master's degree or higher: 8.3% (2005).
Housing: Homeownership rate: 86.5% (2005); Median home value: $112,072 (2005); Median rent: $356 per month (2000); Median age of housing: 24 years (2000).
Transportation: Commute to work: 95.7% car, 0.0% public transportation, 1.6% walk, 2.4% work from home (2000); Travel time to work: 52.1% less than 15 minutes, 34.5% 15 to 30 minutes, 6.1% 30 to 45 minutes, 2.5% 45 to 60 minutes, 4.8% 60 minutes or more (2000)

WELLESLEY ISLAND (unincorporated postal area, zip code 13640).
Covers a land area of 13.111 square miles and a water area of 1.014 square miles. Located at 44.32° N. Lat.; 76.01° W. Long.
Population: 0 (2000); Race: 97.3% White, 2.7% Black, 0.0% Asian, 0.0% Hispanic of any race (2000); Density: 0.0 persons per square mile (2000); Age: 11.0% under 18, 19.6% over 64 (2000); Marriage status: 13.4% never married, 58.6% now married, 15.5% widowed, 12.5% divorced (2000); Foreign born: 6.7% (2000); Ancestry (includes multiple ancestries): 26.7% English, 26.7% Irish, 9.8% French (except Basque), 8.6% Other groups, 8.2% Hungarian (2000).
Economy: Employment by occupation: 6.7% management, 14.8% professional, 31.5% services, 18.8% sales, 0.0% farming, 16.8% construction, 11.4% production (2000).
Income: Per capita income: $26,242 (2000); Median household income: $43,750 (2000); Poverty rate: 3.1% (2000).
Education: Percent of population age 25 and over with: High school diploma (including GED) or higher: 89.0% (2000); Bachelor's degree or higher: 22.9% (2000).
Housing: Homeownership rate: 87.4% (2000); Median home value: $108,800 (2000); Median rent: $475 per month (2000); Median age of housing: 40 years (2000).
Transportation: Commute to work: 96.0% car, 0.0% public transportation, 4.0% walk, 0.0% work from home (2000); Travel time to work: 29.5% less than 15 minutes, 28.9% 15 to 30 minutes, 32.2% 30 to 45 minutes, 2.7% 45 to 60 minutes, 6.7% 60 minutes or more (2000)

WEST CARTHAGE (village).
Covers a land area of 1.195 square miles and a water area of 0.113 square miles. Located at 43.97° N. Lat.; 75.62° W. Long. Elevation is 821 feet.
History: Incorporated 1888.
Population: 2,185 (1990); 2,102 (2000); 2,102 (2005); 2,124 (2010 projected); Race: 81.8% White, 7.4% Black, 2.4% Asian, 11.3% Hispanic of any race (2005); Density: 1,758.3 persons per square mile (2005); Average household size: 2.46 (2005); Median age: 32.5 (2005); Males per 100 females: 87.0 (2005); Marriage status: 18.7% never married, 64.6% now married, 9.0% widowed, 7.7% divorced (2000); Foreign born: 4.9% (2000); Ancestry (includes multiple ancestries): 17.6% Irish, 17.6% Other groups, 15.5% German, 12.8% English, 8.8% French (except Basque) (2000).
Economy: Employment by occupation: 10.7% management, 17.7% professional, 17.7% services, 29.7% sales, 0.0% farming, 7.9% construction, 16.5% production (2000).
Income: Per capita income: $18,052 (2005); Median household income: $34,672 (2005); Average household income: $44,484 (2005); Percent of households with income of $100,000 or more: 7.4% (2005); Poverty rate: 10.6% (2000).
Education: Percent of population age 25 and over with: High school diploma (including GED) or higher: 83.8% (2005); Bachelor's degree or higher: 18.9% (2005); Master's degree or higher: 5.1% (2005).
Housing: Homeownership rate: 48.5% (2005); Median home value: $86,000 (2005); Median rent: $386 per month (2000); Median age of housing: 56 years (2000).
Transportation: Commute to work: 90.8% car, 1.8% public transportation, 4.1% walk, 2.3% work from home (2000); Travel time to work: 37.6% less than 15 minutes, 42.2% 15 to 30 minutes, 13.4% 30 to 45 minutes, 2.1% 45 to 60 minutes, 4.7% 60 minutes or more (2000)

Additional Information Contacts
Village of West Carthage . . . . (315) 493-2552
   http://www.racog.org/West%20Carthage/WestCarthageHomePage.asp

WILNA (town). Covers a land area of 78.917 square miles and a water area of 0.628 square miles. Located at 44.01° N. Lat.; 75.59° W. Long.
Population: 6,899 (1990); 6,235 (2000); 6,392 (2005); 6,565 (2010 projected); Race: 88.1% White, 6.2% Black, 0.9% Asian, 4.3% Hispanic of any race (2005); Density: 81.0 persons per square mile (2005); Average household size: 2.61 (2005); Median age: 36.3 (2005); Males per 100 females: 96.0 (2005); Marriage status: 23.3% never married, 60.2% now married, 8.8% widowed, 7.7% divorced (2000); Foreign born: 3.1% (2000); Ancestry (includes multiple ancestries): 16.8% Irish, 15.2% German, 13.0% Other groups, 12.2% English, 12.0% French (except Basque) (2000).
Economy: Single-family building permits issued: 4 (2005); Multi-family building permits issued: 0 (2005); Employment by occupation: 9.3% management, 17.5% professional, 20.8% services, 23.2% sales, 2.4% farming, 9.4% construction, 17.4% production (2000).
Income: Per capita income: $15,597 (2005); Median household income: $31,861 (2005); Average household income: $40,121 (2005); Percent of households with income of $100,000 or more: 5.6% (2005); Poverty rate: 20.4% (2000).
Education: Percent of population age 25 and over with: High school diploma (including GED) or higher: 79.7% (2005); Bachelor's degree or higher: 11.1% (2005); Master's degree or higher: 4.9% (2005).
Housing: Homeownership rate: 58.4% (2005); Median home value: $84,662 (2005); Median rent: $358 per month (2000); Median age of housing: 60+ years (2000).
Transportation: Commute to work: 90.2% car, 1.0% public transportation, 3.2% walk, 3.8% work from home (2000); Travel time to work: 38.4% less than 15 minutes, 35.4% 15 to 30 minutes, 20.0% 30 to 45 minutes, 3.4% 45 to 60 minutes, 2.8% 60 minutes or more (2000)

WORTH (town). Covers a land area of 43.219 square miles and a water area of 0.086 square miles. Located at 43.75° N. Lat.; 75.86° W. Long.
Population: 219 (1990); 234 (2000); 240 (2005); 246 (2010 projected); Race: 83.8% White, 12.1% Black, 0.0% Asian, 2.5% Hispanic of any race (2005); Density: 5.6 persons per square mile (2005); Average household size: 2.38 (2005); Median age: 40.9 (2005); Males per 100 females: 118.2 (2005); Marriage status: 27.0% never married, 64.0% now married, 3.2% widowed, 5.8% divorced (2000); Foreign born: 1.3% (2000); Ancestry (includes multiple ancestries): 21.9% German, 17.7% English, 17.3% French (except Basque), 11.4% United States or American, 8.9% Irish (2000).
Economy: Employment by occupation: 8.3% management, 12.0% professional, 21.3% services, 15.7% sales, 5.6% farming, 18.5% construction, 18.5% production (2000).
Income: Per capita income: $15,979 (2005); Median household income: $33,864 (2005); Average household income: $37,970 (2005); Percent of households with income of $100,000 or more: 1.0% (2005); Poverty rate: 13.9% (2000).
Education: Percent of population age 25 and over with: High school diploma (including GED) or higher: 75.7% (2005); Bachelor's degree or higher: 7.1% (2005); Master's degree or higher: 4.1% (2005).
Housing: Homeownership rate: 86.1% (2005); Median home value: $71,818 (2005); Median rent: $335 per month (2000); Median age of housing: 28 years (2000).
Transportation: Commute to work: 95.4% car, 0.0% public transportation, 2.8% walk, 1.9% work from home (2000); Travel time to work: 17.9% less than 15 minutes, 33.0% 15 to 30 minutes, 35.8% 30 to 45 minutes, 11.3% 45 to 60 minutes, 1.9% 60 minutes or more (2000)

Kings County

See New York City

Lewis County

Located in north central New York; includes the foothills of the Adirondacks in the east; drained by the Black River. Covers a land area of 1,275.42 square miles, a water area of 14.47 square miles, and is located in the Eastern Time Zone. The county government was organized in 1805. County seat is Lowville.

Weather Station: Lowville — Elevation: 859 feet

	Jan	Feb	Mar	Apr	May	Jun	Jul	Aug	Sep	Oct	Nov	Dec
High	26	29	38	52	66	74	79	77	68	56	44	32
Low	7	9	20	32	43	52	56	54	46	36	28	15
Precip	3.6	2.5	3.0	3.1	3.1	3.4	3.6	3.5	4.1	3.5	4.1	3.6
Snow	37.9	22.7	17.5	5.0	0.3	0.0	0.0	0.0	tr	0.7	10.3	30.7

High and Low temperatures in degrees Fahrenheit; Precipitation and Snow in inches

Population: 26,796 (1990); 26,944 (2000); 26,544 (2005); 26,121 (2010 projected); Race: 97.1% White, 1.3% Black, 0.2% Asian, 1.2% Hispanic of any race (2005); Density: 20.8 persons per square mile (2005); Average household size: 2.63 (2005); Median age: 38.5 (2005); Males per 100 females: 98.5 (2005).
Religion: Five largest groups: 43.8% Catholic Church, 6.7% The United Methodist Church, 5.4% Conservative Mennonite Conference, 1.6% Presbyterian Church (U.S.A.), 1.3% Mennonite Church USA (2000).
Economy: Unemployment rate: 6.2% (2005); Total civilian labor force: 12,737 (2005); Leading industries: 28.8% manufacturing; 20.7% health care and social assistance; 13.7% retail trade (2003); Farms: 721 totaling 196,774 acres (2002); Companies that employ 500 or more persons: 1 (2003); Companies that employ 100 to 499 persons: 3 (2003); Companies that employ less than 100 persons: 521 (2003); Black-owned businesses: n/a (2002); Hispanic-owned businesses: n/a (2002); Women-owned businesses: n/a (2002); Retail sales per capita: $8,743 (2006). Single-family building permits issued: 137 (2005); Multi-family building permits issued: 0 (2005).
Income: Per capita income: $17,393 (2005); Median household income: $37,971 (2005); Average household income: $45,201 (2005); Percent of households with income of $100,000 or more: 6.0% (2005); Poverty rate: 12.9% (2003); Bankruptcy rate: 4.59% (2005).
Education: Percent of population age 25 and over with: High school diploma (including GED) or higher: 80.9% (2005); Bachelor's degree or higher: 11.7% (2005); Master's degree or higher: 5.2% (2005).
Housing: Homeownership rate: 77.4% (2005); Median home value: $95,338 (2005); Median rent: $350 per month (2000); Median age of housing: 39 years (2000).
Health: Birth rate: 117.1 per 10,000 population (2004); Death rate: 79.4 per 10,000 population (2004); Age-adjusted cancer mortality rate: 227.4 deaths per 100,000 population (2002); Number of physicians: 9.8 per 10,000 population (2004); Hospital beds: 0.0 per 10,000 population (2003); Hospital admissions: 0.0 per 10,000 population (2003).
Elections: 2004 Presidential election results: 58.1% Bush, 39.9% Kerry, 1.9% Nader, 0.1% Badnarik
National and State Parks: Sand Flats State Park; Whetstone Gulf State Park
Additional Information Contacts
Lewis County Government. . . . . (315) 376-5355
  http://www.lewiscountyny.org/
Town of Harrisburg . . . . (315) 688-4193
  http://www.tughillcouncil.com/Harrisburg.htm

Lewis County Communities

CASTORLAND (village). Covers a land area of 0.282 square miles and a water area of 0 square miles. Located at 43.88° N. Lat.; 75.51° W. Long. Elevation is 739 feet.
Population: 292 (1990); 306 (2000); 287 (2005); 277 (2010 projected); Race: 94.4% White, 2.4% Black, 0.3% Asian, 2.4% Hispanic of any race (2005); Density: 1,017.1 persons per square mile (2005); Average household size: 2.61 (2005); Median age: 39.2 (2005); Males per 100 females: 88.8 (2005); Marriage status: 33.8% never married, 56.0% now married, 8.0% widowed, 2.2% divorced (2000); Foreign born: 1.7% (2000); Ancestry (includes multiple ancestries): 41.9% German, 15.9% French (except Basque), 10.0% Irish, 7.6% English, 5.0% Swiss (2000).
Economy: Employment by occupation: 8.8% management, 11.8% professional, 29.4% services, 18.4% sales, 0.0% farming, 9.6% construction, 22.1% production (2000).
Income: Per capita income: $15,686 (2005); Median household income: $35,833 (2005); Average household income: $40,568 (2005); Percent of households with income of $100,000 or more: 2.7% (2005); Poverty rate: 13.3% (2000).
Education: Percent of population age 25 and over with: High school diploma (including GED) or higher: 84.7% (2005); Bachelor's degree or higher: 14.3% (2005); Master's degree or higher: 3.1% (2005).

Housing: Homeownership rate: 59.1% (2005); Median home value: $87,333 (2005); Median rent: $368 per month (2000); Median age of housing: 60+ years (2000).
Transportation: Commute to work: 87.7% car, 2.9% public transportation, 5.1% walk, 4.3% work from home (2000); Travel time to work: 29.5% less than 15 minutes, 43.2% 15 to 30 minutes, 15.2% 30 to 45 minutes, 8.3% 45 to 60 minutes, 3.8% 60 minutes or more (2000)

CONSTABLEVILLE (village).
Covers a land area of 1.120 square miles and a water area of 0 square miles. Located at 43.56° N. Lat.; 75.42° W. Long.
Population: 307 (1990); 305 (2000); 305 (2005); 301 (2010 projected); Race: 100.0% White, 0.0% Black, 0.0% Asian, 0.7% Hispanic of any race (2005); Density: 272.4 persons per square mile (2005); Average household size: 2.38 (2005); Median age: 38.0 (2005); Males per 100 females: 95.5 (2005); Marriage status: 31.6% never married, 47.4% now married, 9.6% widowed, 11.4% divorced (2000); Foreign born: 0.0% (2000); Ancestry (includes multiple ancestries): 39.7% German, 29.5% Irish, 19.9% Polish, 17.6% English, 7.7% French (except Basque) (2000).
Economy: In timber and dairying area. Employment by occupation: 14.5% management, 9.4% professional, 7.7% services, 33.3% sales, 0.9% farming, 6.0% construction, 28.2% production (2000).
Income: Per capita income: $20,623 (2005); Median household income: $48,125 (2005); Average household income: $49,141 (2005); Percent of households with income of $100,000 or more: 6.3% (2005); Poverty rate: 16.5% (2000).
Education: Percent of population age 25 and over with: High school diploma (including GED) or higher: 83.4% (2005); Bachelor's degree or higher: 10.2% (2005); Master's degree or higher: 6.8% (2005).
School District(s)
South Lewis Central School District (KG-12)
  2003-04 Enrollment: 1,223 . . . . (315) 348-2500
Housing: Homeownership rate: 77.3% (2005); Median home value: $72,500 (2005); Median rent: $327 per month (2000); Median age of housing: 60+ years (2000).
Transportation: Commute to work: 89.5% car, 0.0% public transportation, 6.1% walk, 0.0% work from home (2000); Travel time to work: 36.0% less than 15 minutes, 19.3% 15 to 30 minutes, 11.4% 30 to 45 minutes, 17.5% 45 to 60 minutes, 15.8% 60 minutes or more (2000)

COPENHAGEN (village).
Covers a land area of 1.201 square miles and a water area of 0 square miles. Located at 43.89° N. Lat.; 75.67° W. Long. Elevation is 1,174 feet.
Population: 876 (1990); 865 (2000); 840 (2005); 807 (2010 projected); Race: 91.4% White, 3.3% Black, 0.0% Asian, 4.9% Hispanic of any race (2005); Density: 699.2 persons per square mile (2005); Average household size: 2.66 (2005); Median age: 29.3 (2005); Males per 100 females: 95.8 (2005); Marriage status: 24.1% never married, 63.6% now married, 6.2% widowed, 6.2% divorced (2000); Foreign born: 2.0% (2000); Ancestry (includes multiple ancestries): 23.1% French (except Basque), 21.0% German, 20.7% Irish, 15.3% English, 8.0% Other groups (2000).
Economy: In dairying, cheese-making, and timber area. Employment by occupation: 9.8% management, 11.0% professional, 19.3% services, 26.9% sales, 2.8% farming, 11.3% construction, 19.0% production (2000).
Income: Per capita income: $14,176 (2005); Median household income: $33,167 (2005); Average household income: $37,682 (2005); Percent of households with income of $100,000 or more: 1.3% (2005); Poverty rate: 13.4% (2000).
Education: Percent of population age 25 and over with: High school diploma (including GED) or higher: 84.3% (2005); Bachelor's degree or higher: 9.7% (2005); Master's degree or higher: 1.4% (2005).
School District(s)
Copenhagen Central School District (KG-12)
  2003-04 Enrollment: 604 . . . . (315) 688-4411
Housing: Homeownership rate: 48.1% (2005); Median home value: $86,977 (2005); Median rent: $379 per month (2000); Median age of housing: 60+ years (2000).
Transportation: Commute to work: 76.7% car, 3.5% public transportation, 8.5% walk, 10.8% work from home (2000); Travel time to work: 20.2% less than 15 minutes, 41.9% 15 to 30 minutes, 31.5% 30 to 45 minutes, 3.7% 45 to 60 minutes, 2.8% 60 minutes or more (2000)

CROGHAN (village).
Covers a land area of 0.436 square miles and a water area of 0 square miles. Located at 43.89° N. Lat.; 75.39° W. Long. Elevation is 847 feet.
Population: 664 (1990); 665 (2000); 657 (2005); 641 (2010 projected); Race: 97.0% White, 2.3% Black, 0.3% Asian, 1.1% Hispanic of any race (2005); Density: 1,507.4 persons per square mile (2005); Average household size: 2.29 (2005); Median age: 39.9 (2005); Males per 100 females: 87.7 (2005); Marriage status: 23.4% never married, 62.1% now married, 11.5% widowed, 2.9% divorced (2000); Foreign born: 3.4% (2000); Ancestry (includes multiple ancestries): 46.6% German, 24.8% French (except Basque), 9.8% Other groups, 7.0% English, 6.7% Irish (2000).
Economy: Employment by occupation: 5.4% management, 22.6% professional, 15.2% services, 21.9% sales, 2.4% farming, 13.1% construction, 19.5% production (2000).
Income: Per capita income: $16,884 (2005); Median household income: $31,705 (2005); Average household income: $38,650 (2005); Percent of households with income of $100,000 or more: 4.9% (2005); Poverty rate: 10.8% (2000).
Education: Percent of population age 25 and over with: High school diploma (including GED) or higher: 80.4% (2005); Bachelor's degree or higher: 18.0% (2005); Master's degree or higher: 7.8% (2005).
Housing: Homeownership rate: 62.4% (2005); Median home value: $98,478 (2005); Median rent: $313 per month (2000); Median age of housing: 60+ years (2000).
Transportation: Commute to work: 90.3% car, 0.0% public transportation, 8.0% walk, 1.0% work from home (2000); Travel time to work: 42.0% less than 15 minutes, 35.7% 15 to 30 minutes, 10.8% 30 to 45 minutes, 9.1% 45 to 60 minutes, 2.4% 60 minutes or more (2000)

CROGHAN (town).
Covers a land area of 179.419 square miles and a water area of 2.646 square miles. Located at 43.95° N. Lat.; 75.37° W. Long. Elevation is 847 feet.
History: American Maple Museum.
Population: 3,071 (1990); 3,161 (2000); 3,050 (2005); 2,943 (2010 projected); Race: 98.8% White, 0.4% Black, 0.1% Asian, 0.8% Hispanic of any race (2005); Density: 17.0 persons per square mile (2005); Average household size: 2.77 (2005); Median age: 38.3 (2005); Males per 100 females: 101.5 (2005); Marriage status: 25.4% never married, 62.7% now married, 6.5% widowed, 5.3% divorced (2000); Foreign born: 2.2% (2000); Ancestry (includes multiple ancestries): 51.5% German, 22.1% French (except Basque), 11.7% Irish, 7.9% Other groups, 6.8% English (2000).
Economy: Timber harvesting. Employment by occupation: 11.4% management, 15.0% professional, 14.8% services, 17.8% sales, 7.2% farming, 11.1% construction, 22.7% production (2000).
Income: Per capita income: $15,810 (2005); Median household income: $38,210 (2005); Average household income: $43,757 (2005); Percent of households with income of $100,000 or more: 4.4% (2005); Poverty rate: 12.1% (2000).
Taxes: Total city taxes per capita: $334 (2004); City property taxes per capita: $319 (2004).
Education: Percent of population age 25 and over with: High school diploma (including GED) or higher: 81.1% (2005); Bachelor's degree or higher: 9.5% (2005); Master's degree or higher: 4.2% (2005).
Housing: Homeownership rate: 81.0% (2005); Median home value: $106,083 (2005); Median rent: $342 per month (2000); Median age of housing: 37 years (2000).
Transportation: Commute to work: 83.7% car, 0.0% public transportation, 9.9% walk, 5.4% work from home (2000); Travel time to work: 42.5% less than 15 minutes, 37.8% 15 to 30 minutes, 10.7% 30 to 45 minutes, 5.8% 45 to 60 minutes, 3.2% 60 minutes or more (2000)

DENMARK (town).
Covers a land area of 50.603 square miles and a water area of 0.425 square miles. Located at 43.89° N. Lat.; 75.60° W. Long.
Population: 2,718 (1990); 2,747 (2000); 2,628 (2005); 2,522 (2010 projected); Race: 95.1% White, 1.4% Black, 0.2% Asian, 3.4% Hispanic of any race (2005); Density: 51.9 persons per square mile (2005); Average household size: 2.75 (2005); Median age: 34.8 (2005); Males per 100 females: 102.2 (2005); Marriage status: 22.4% never married, 67.6% now married, 4.7% widowed, 5.3% divorced (2000); Foreign born: 2.0% (2000); Ancestry (includes multiple ancestries): 24.6% German, 18.3% Irish, 17.8% French (except Basque), 11.6% English, 11.4% United States or American (2000).
Economy: Employment by occupation: 12.5% management, 13.5% professional, 16.7% services, 23.3% sales, 3.0% farming, 10.5% construction, 20.5% production (2000).

Income: Per capita income: $17,138 (2005); Median household income: $40,991 (2005); Average household income: $46,831 (2005); Percent of households with income of $100,000 or more: 6.9% (2005); Poverty rate: 12.4% (2000).
Education: Percent of population age 25 and over with: High school diploma (including GED) or higher: 84.9% (2005); Bachelor's degree or higher: 12.1% (2005); Master's degree or higher: 4.4% (2005).
Housing: Homeownership rate: 70.0% (2005); Median home value: $99,683 (2005); Median rent: $383 per month (2000); Median age of housing: 53 years (2000).
Transportation: Commute to work: 82.1% car, 1.4% public transportation, 6.3% walk, 8.8% work from home (2000); Travel time to work: 30.7% less than 15 minutes, 42.2% 15 to 30 minutes, 21.8% 30 to 45 minutes, 2.9% 45 to 60 minutes, 2.3% 60 minutes or more (2000)

DIANA (town). Covers a land area of 137.348 square miles and a water area of 3.491 square miles. Located at 44.10° N. Lat.; 75.35° W. Long.
Population: 1,743 (1990); 1,661 (2000); 1,599 (2005); 1,545 (2010 projected); Race: 96.9% White, 0.3% Black, 0.5% Asian, 0.9% Hispanic of any race (2005); Density: 11.6 persons per square mile (2005); Average household size: 2.54 (2005); Median age: 40.4 (2005); Males per 100 females: 96.7 (2005); Marriage status: 18.2% never married, 64.8% now married, 8.3% widowed, 8.6% divorced (2000); Foreign born: 1.2% (2000); Ancestry (includes multiple ancestries): 32.0% French (except Basque), 19.5% English, 16.4% Irish, 14.1% German, 11.7% Other groups (2000).
Economy: Employment by occupation: 8.0% management, 14.9% professional, 17.7% services, 23.5% sales, 1.5% farming, 13.8% construction, 20.5% production (2000).
Income: Per capita income: $18,099 (2005); Median household income: $37,405 (2005); Average household income: $45,937 (2005); Percent of households with income of $100,000 or more: 6.7% (2005); Poverty rate: 12.1% (2000).
Education: Percent of population age 25 and over with: High school diploma (including GED) or higher: 79.5% (2005); Bachelor's degree or higher: 10.4% (2005); Master's degree or higher: 4.5% (2005).
Housing: Homeownership rate: 81.1% (2005); Median home value: $71,978 (2005); Median rent: $317 per month (2000); Median age of housing: 42 years (2000).
Transportation: Commute to work: 89.5% car, 0.8% public transportation, 6.1% walk, 2.5% work from home (2000); Travel time to work: 33.0% less than 15 minutes, 21.9% 15 to 30 minutes, 23.0% 30 to 45 minutes, 12.2% 45 to 60 minutes, 10.0% 60 minutes or more (2000)

GLENFIELD (unincorporated postal area, zip code 13343). Covers a land area of 53.797 square miles and a water area of 0.486 square miles. Located at 43.74° N. Lat.; 75.35° W. Long. Elevation is 800 feet.
Population: 0 (2000); Race: 98.4% White, 0.2% Black, 0.0% Asian, 0.1% Hispanic of any race (2000); Density: 0.0 persons per square mile (2000); Age: 27.5% under 18, 12.2% over 64 (2000); Marriage status: 26.0% never married, 59.9% now married, 5.6% widowed, 8.4% divorced (2000); Foreign born: 0.1% (2000); Ancestry (includes multiple ancestries): 24.3% German, 17.2% Irish, 17.0% French (except Basque), 13.3% English, 10.9% United States or American (2000).
Economy: Employment by occupation: 7.5% management, 19.2% professional, 15.3% services, 17.6% sales, 3.3% farming, 11.8% construction, 25.4% production (2000).
Income: Per capita income: $15,291 (2000); Median household income: $34,091 (2000); Poverty rate: 11.8% (2000).
Education: Percent of population age 25 and over with: High school diploma (including GED) or higher: 80.4% (2000); Bachelor's degree or higher: 14.9% (2000).

School District(s)
South Lewis Central School District (KG-12)
  2003-04 Enrollment: 1,223 . . . . (315) 348-2500
Housing: Homeownership rate: 85.5% (2000); Median home value: $60,000 (2000); Median rent: $353 per month (2000); Median age of housing: 26 years (2000).
Transportation: Commute to work: 91.0% car, 0.0% public transportation, 3.4% walk, 4.3% work from home (2000); Travel time to work: 28.6% less than 15 minutes, 48.0% 15 to 30 minutes, 11.9% 30 to 45 minutes, 4.8% 45 to 60 minutes, 6.8% 60 minutes or more (2000)

GREIG (town). Covers a land area of 92.912 square miles and a water area of 1.416 square miles. Located at 43.69° N. Lat.; 75.31° W. Long.
Population: 1,323 (1990); 1,365 (2000); 1,365 (2005); 1,371 (2010 projected); Race: 99.1% White, 0.0% Black, 0.4% Asian, 1.2% Hispanic of any race (2005); Density: 14.7 persons per square mile (2005); Average household size: 2.50 (2005); Median age: 41.9 (2005); Males per 100 females: 99.3 (2005); Marriage status: 22.1% never married, 63.0% now married, 6.6% widowed, 8.3% divorced (2000); Foreign born: 0.8% (2000); Ancestry (includes multiple ancestries): 19.7% Irish, 16.0% German, 15.2% French (except Basque), 13.4% United States or American, 10.7% English (2000).
Economy: Employment by occupation: 11.6% management, 17.0% professional, 20.1% services, 13.6% sales, 4.7% farming, 11.8% construction, 21.2% production (2000).
Income: Per capita income: $18,806 (2005); Median household income: $39,357 (2005); Average household income: $46,904 (2005); Percent of households with income of $100,000 or more: 7.9% (2005); Poverty rate: 8.9% (2000).
Education: Percent of population age 25 and over with: High school diploma (including GED) or higher: 80.4% (2005); Bachelor's degree or higher: 12.9% (2005); Master's degree or higher: 6.4% (2005).
Housing: Homeownership rate: 86.8% (2005); Median home value: $106,530 (2005); Median rent: $370 per month (2000); Median age of housing: 25 years (2000).
Transportation: Commute to work: 89.0% car, 0.4% public transportation, 2.6% walk, 7.1% work from home (2000); Travel time to work: 20.3% less than 15 minutes, 51.3% 15 to 30 minutes, 12.9% 30 to 45 minutes, 4.8% 45 to 60 minutes, 10.7% 60 minutes or more (2000)

HARRISBURG (town). Covers a land area of 39.906 square miles and a water area of 0 square miles. Located at 43.81° N. Lat.; 75.65° W. Long. Elevation is 1,365 feet.
Population: 425 (1990); 423 (2000); 420 (2005); 404 (2010 projected); Race: 97.1% White, 1.0% Black, 0.5% Asian, 0.5% Hispanic of any race (2005); Density: 10.5 persons per square mile (2005); Average household size: 2.98 (2005); Median age: 36.4 (2005); Males per 100 females: 110.0 (2005); Marriage status: 26.4% never married, 66.3% now married, 2.0% widowed, 5.3% divorced (2000); Foreign born: 1.3% (2000); Ancestry (includes multiple ancestries): 28.8% Irish, 27.0% German, 22.1% French (except Basque), 16.2% English, 8.2% Other groups (2000).
Economy: Employment by occupation: 23.4% management, 14.1% professional, 16.1% services, 14.6% sales, 5.9% farming, 13.7% construction, 12.2% production (2000).
Income: Per capita income: $13,185 (2005); Median household income: $34,318 (2005); Average household income: $39,273 (2005); Percent of households with income of $100,000 or more: 3.5% (2005); Poverty rate: 13.6% (2000).
Education: Percent of population age 25 and over with: High school diploma (including GED) or higher: 69.0% (2005); Bachelor's degree or higher: 9.7% (2005); Master's degree or higher: 6.0% (2005).
Housing: Homeownership rate: 90.1% (2005); Median home value: $97,000 (2005); Median rent: $375 per month (2000); Median age of housing: 25 years (2000).
Transportation: Commute to work: 74.6% car, 1.0% public transportation, 7.3% walk, 16.1% work from home (2000); Travel time to work: 34.3% less than 15 minutes, 38.4% 15 to 30 minutes, 14.5% 30 to 45 minutes, 2.9% 45 to 60 minutes, 9.9% 60 minutes or more (2000)
Additional Information Contacts
Town of Harrisburg . . . . (315) 688-4193
  http://www.tughillcouncil.com/Harrisburg.htm

HARRISVILLE (village). Covers a land area of 0.769 square miles and a water area of 0.027 square miles. Located at 44.15° N. Lat.; 75.32° W. Long. Elevation is 777 feet.
Population: 703 (1990); 653 (2000); 627 (2005); 605 (2010 projected); Race: 99.0% White, 0.0% Black, 0.3% Asian, 0.0% Hispanic of any race (2005); Density: 815.8 persons per square mile (2005); Average household size: 2.41 (2005); Median age: 40.0 (2005); Males per 100 females: 88.3 (2005); Marriage status: 18.0% never married, 60.6% now married, 11.3% widowed, 10.1% divorced (2000); Foreign born: 0.5% (2000); Ancestry (includes multiple ancestries): 35.0% French (except Basque), 19.8% English, 19.3% Irish, 14.6% German, 8.1% Scottish (2000).
Economy: Employment by occupation: 7.5% management, 16.2% professional, 20.2% services, 19.8% sales, 1.6% farming, 16.6% construction, 18.2% production (2000).
Income: Per capita income: $17,460 (2005); Median household income: $33,542 (2005); Average household income: $42,106 (2005); Percent of

households with income of $100,000 or more: 6.5% (2005); Poverty rate: 16.1% (2000).
Education: Percent of population age 25 and over with: High school diploma (including GED) or higher: 83.4% (2005); Bachelor's degree or higher: 11.5% (2005); Master's degree or higher: 6.2% (2005).

School District(s)
Harrisville Central School District (KG-12)
   2003-04 Enrollment: 382 . . . . (315) 543-2707
Housing: Homeownership rate: 72.3% (2005); Median home value: $65,263 (2005); Median rent: $300 per month (2000); Median age of housing: 60+ years (2000).
Transportation: Commute to work: 88.7% car, 0.8% public transportation, 6.5% walk, 2.4% work from home (2000); Travel time to work: 38.4% less than 15 minutes, 18.6% 15 to 30 minutes, 19.4% 30 to 45 minutes, 14.0% 45 to 60 minutes, 9.5% 60 minutes or more (2000)

LEWIS (town).
Covers a land area of 64.695 square miles and a water area of 0.455 square miles. Located at 43.47° N. Lat.; 75.52° W. Long.
Population: 858 (1990); 857 (2000); 901 (2005); 927 (2010 projected); Race: 98.6% White, 1.2% Black, 0.0% Asian, 0.4% Hispanic of any race (2005); Density: 13.9 persons per square mile (2005); Average household size: 2.83 (2005); Median age: 36.1 (2005); Males per 100 females: 102.0 (2005); Marriage status: 31.8% never married, 58.1% now married, 3.3% widowed, 6.7% divorced (2000); Foreign born: 0.7% (2000); Ancestry (includes multiple ancestries): 38.1% German, 19.7% Irish, 15.8% Polish, 7.8% French (except Basque), 5.1% Swiss (2000).
Economy: Single-family building permits issued: 3 (2005); Multi-family building permits issued: 0 (2005); Employment by occupation: 8.9% management, 13.5% professional, 16.2% services, 20.8% sales, 3.6% farming, 11.4% construction, 25.6% production (2000).
Income: Per capita income: $16,706 (2005); Median household income: $42,250 (2005); Average household income: $47,335 (2005); Percent of households with income of $100,000 or more: 7.2% (2005); Poverty rate: 10.7% (2000).
Education: Percent of population age 25 and over with: High school diploma (including GED) or higher: 84.7% (2005); Bachelor's degree or higher: 9.2% (2005); Master's degree or higher: 3.6% (2005).
Housing: Homeownership rate: 84.6% (2005); Median home value: $87,708 (2005); Median rent: $344 per month (2000); Median age of housing: 32 years (2000).
Transportation: Commute to work: 85.6% car, 0.7% public transportation, 1.5% walk, 9.0% work from home (2000); Travel time to work: 24.4% less than 15 minutes, 30.6% 15 to 30 minutes, 23.9% 30 to 45 minutes, 12.3% 45 to 60 minutes, 8.8% 60 minutes or more (2000)

LEYDEN (town).
Covers a land area of 33.322 square miles and a water area of 0.224 square miles. Located at 43.54° N. Lat.; 75.36° W. Long.
History: Originally known as Kelsey's Mills, it was renamed in 1839 in anticipation of becoming a thriving port upon completion of the Black River Canal.
Population: 1,796 (1990); 1,792 (2000); 1,783 (2005); 1,779 (2010 projected); Race: 98.7% White, 0.8% Black, 0.0% Asian, 0.3% Hispanic of any race (2005); Density: 53.5 persons per square mile (2005); Average household size: 2.60 (2005); Median age: 37.6 (2005); Males per 100 females: 97.5 (2005); Marriage status: 28.4% never married, 57.5% now married, 6.2% widowed, 8.0% divorced (2000); Foreign born: 0.5% (2000); Ancestry (includes multiple ancestries): 27.0% German, 22.8% Irish, 19.1% French (except Basque), 10.3% English, 9.9% Polish (2000).
Economy: Single-family building permits issued: 11 (2005); Multi-family building permits issued: 0 (2005); Employment by occupation: 9.0% management, 9.0% professional, 19.0% services, 22.4% sales, 3.2% farming, 10.9% construction, 26.6% production (2000).
Income: Per capita income: $16,505 (2005); Median household income: $33,731 (2005); Average household income: $42,153 (2005); Percent of households with income of $100,000 or more: 5.8% (2005); Poverty rate: 19.0% (2000).
Education: Percent of population age 25 and over with: High school diploma (including GED) or higher: 76.5% (2005); Bachelor's degree or higher: 5.5% (2005); Master's degree or higher: 1.5% (2005).
Housing: Homeownership rate: 77.5% (2005); Median home value: $82,130 (2005); Median rent: $331 per month (2000); Median age of housing: 49 years (2000).
Transportation: Commute to work: 86.3% car, 0.0% public transportation, 3.9% walk, 6.3% work from home (2000); Travel time to work: 46.9% less than 15 minutes, 21.6% 15 to 30 minutes, 12.9% 30 to 45 minutes, 10.7% 45 to 60 minutes, 8.0% 60 minutes or more (2000)

LOWVILLE (village).
Covers a land area of 1.899 square miles and a water area of 0 square miles. Located at 43.78° N. Lat.; 75.48° W. Long. Elevation is 869 feet.
Population: 3,617 (1990); 3,476 (2000); 3,340 (2005); 3,237 (2010 projected); Race: 95.4% White, 1.6% Black, 0.8% Asian, 1.8% Hispanic of any race (2005); Density: 1,759.2 persons per square mile (2005); Average household size: 2.44 (2005); Median age: 41.5 (2005); Males per 100 females: 84.4 (2005); Marriage status: 21.1% never married, 56.8% now married, 13.1% widowed, 9.0% divorced (2000); Foreign born: 1.2% (2000); Ancestry (includes multiple ancestries): 34.4% German, 18.8% Irish, 15.0% English, 12.5% French (except Basque), 5.8% Other groups (2000).
Economy: Single-family building permits issued: 0 (2005); Multi-family building permits issued: 0 (2005); Employment by occupation: 9.0% management, 22.9% professional, 21.6% services, 21.9% sales, 0.8% farming, 9.9% construction, 13.9% production (2000).
Income: Per capita income: $19,015 (2005); Median household income: $35,298 (2005); Average household income: $43,644 (2005); Percent of households with income of $100,000 or more: 5.3% (2005); Poverty rate: 14.9% (2000).
Education: Percent of population age 25 and over with: High school diploma (including GED) or higher: 81.6% (2005); Bachelor's degree or higher: 19.5% (2005); Master's degree or higher: 10.9% (2005).

School District(s)
Lowville Academy & Central School District (KG-12)
   2003-04 Enrollment: 1,396 . . . . (315) 376-9000
Housing: Homeownership rate: 58.8% (2005); Median home value: $106,924 (2005); Median rent: $342 per month (2000); Median age of housing: 60+ years (2000).
Hospitals: Lewis County General Hospital (54 beds)
Safety: Violent crime rate: 20.9 per 10,000 population; Property crime rate: 263.0 per 10,000 population (2004).
Newspapers: Lowville Journal and Republican (General - Circulation 5,280)
Transportation: Commute to work: 82.9% car, 0.4% public transportation, 10.4% walk, 4.1% work from home (2000); Travel time to work: 74.3% less than 15 minutes, 6.2% 15 to 30 minutes, 10.6% 30 to 45 minutes, 4.4% 45 to 60 minutes, 4.4% 60 minutes or more (2000)
Additional Information Contacts
Lowville Chamber of Commerce . . . . (315) 376-2213
http://www.lewiscountychamber.org/

LOWVILLE (town).
Covers a land area of 37.797 square miles and a water area of 0.324 square miles. Located at 43.80° N. Lat.; 75.50° W. Long. Elevation is 869 feet.
History: Lowville was the home of Dr. Franklin B. Hough (1822-1885), called the "father of American forestry" for his conservation activities. Settled 1798, incorporated in 1854.
Population: 4,849 (1990); 4,548 (2000); 4,422 (2005); 4,303 (2010 projected); Race: 96.2% White, 1.3% Black, 0.7% Asian, 1.9% Hispanic of any race (2005); Density: 117.0 persons per square mile (2005); Average household size: 2.49 (2005); Median age: 41.2 (2005); Males per 100 females: 88.3 (2005); Marriage status: 20.4% never married, 59.2% now married, 12.7% widowed, 7.6% divorced (2000); Foreign born: 1.2% (2000); Ancestry (includes multiple ancestries): 36.1% German, 18.7% Irish, 14.5% English, 13.0% French (except Basque), 5.7% Other groups (2000).
Economy: Trade center in dairying area. Manufacturing of dairy products, sporting goods; timber. Single-family building permits issued: 9 (2005); Multi-family building permits issued: 0 (2005); Employment by occupation: 13.5% management, 20.2% professional, 19.9% services, 20.6% sales, 1.6% farming, 9.5% construction, 14.7% production (2000).
Income: Per capita income: $18,306 (2005); Median household income: $34,920 (2005); Average household income: $43,325 (2005); Percent of households with income of $100,000 or more: 5.8% (2005); Poverty rate: 13.9% (2000).
Education: Percent of population age 25 and over with: High school diploma (including GED) or higher: 81.6% (2005); Bachelor's degree or higher: 17.7% (2005); Master's degree or higher: 9.3% (2005).
Housing: Homeownership rate: 61.3% (2005); Median home value: $107,320 (2005); Median rent: $345 per month (2000); Median age of housing: 60+ years (2000).

Transportation: Commute to work: 81.4% car, 0.7% public transportation, 9.6% walk, 6.2% work from home (2000); Travel time to work: 71.3% less than 15 minutes, 10.1% 15 to 30 minutes, 9.7% 30 to 45 minutes, 3.9% 45 to 60 minutes, 5.0% 60 minutes or more (2000)

LYONS FALLS (village). Covers a land area of 0.982 square miles and a water area of 0.093 square miles. Located at 43.61° N. Lat.; 75.36° W. Long. Elevation is 844 feet.
History: Black River Canal, begun in 1838, completed in 1858, ceased operation in 1922. Never successfully competed with railroad. Completely abandoned in 1926 when its final function as a feeder of water to the New York State Barge Canal was assumed by Delta Lake (northeast of Rome) and Hinckley Reservoir, north of Utica.
Population: 698 (1990); 591 (2000); 554 (2005); 543 (2010 projected); Race: 98.4% White, 0.0% Black, 0.0% Asian, 0.5% Hispanic of any race (2005); Density: 564.4 persons per square mile (2005); Average household size: 2.43 (2005); Median age: 39.9 (2005); Males per 100 females: 106.7 (2005); Marriage status: 25.6% never married, 54.0% now married, 11.2% widowed, 9.3% divorced (2000); Foreign born: 0.7% (2000); Ancestry (includes multiple ancestries): 26.6% German, 18.8% Irish, 17.6% English, 12.6% French (except Basque), 8.5% Polish (2000).
Economy: Paper milling. Co-generation of electric power (hydro and burning of wood residue) here and at Lyonsdale, 2 miles east on Moose River. Paper milling also at Lyonsdale. Employment by occupation: 6.7% management, 23.5% professional, 19.2% services, 20.0% sales, 2.0% farming, 9.0% construction, 19.6% production (2000).
Income: Per capita income: $20,384 (2005); Median household income: $32,879 (2005); Average household income: $49,529 (2005); Percent of households with income of $100,000 or more: 10.5% (2005); Poverty rate: 16.7% (2000).
Education: Percent of population age 25 and over with: High school diploma (including GED) or higher: 86.6% (2005); Bachelor's degree or higher: 18.0% (2005); Master's degree or higher: 9.7% (2005).
Housing: Homeownership rate: 67.1% (2005); Median home value: $78,529 (2005); Median rent: $338 per month (2000); Median age of housing: 60+ years (2000).
Transportation: Commute to work: 77.5% car, 0.0% public transportation, 17.0% walk, 4.3% work from home (2000); Travel time to work: 43.8% less than 15 minutes, 29.8% 15 to 30 minutes, 8.3% 30 to 45 minutes, 7.9% 45 to 60 minutes, 10.3% 60 minutes or more (2000)

LYONSDALE (town). Covers a land area of 68.812 square miles and a water area of 1.292 square miles. Located at 43.60° N. Lat.; 75.30° W. Long. Elevation is 1,072 feet.
Population: 1,281 (1990); 1,273 (2000); 1,313 (2005); 1,351 (2010 projected); Race: 95.1% White, 3.7% Black, 0.0% Asian, 0.9% Hispanic of any race (2005); Density: 19.1 persons per square mile (2005); Average household size: 2.66 (2005); Median age: 36.2 (2005); Males per 100 females: 104.5 (2005); Marriage status: 27.1% never married, 58.1% now married, 7.3% widowed, 7.5% divorced (2000); Foreign born: 0.8% (2000); Ancestry (includes multiple ancestries): 23.8% German, 21.8% French (except Basque), 18.6% Irish, 12.9% English, 12.4% Other groups (2000).
Economy: Single-family building permits issued: 28 (2005); Multi-family building permits issued: 0 (2005); Employment by occupation: 3.7% management, 8.7% professional, 21.2% services, 16.2% sales, 1.8% farming, 16.9% construction, 31.5% production (2000).
Income: Per capita income: $16,045 (2005); Median household income: $38,233 (2005); Average household income: $42,647 (2005); Percent of households with income of $100,000 or more: 5.1% (2005); Poverty rate: 20.0% (2000).
Education: Percent of population age 25 and over with: High school diploma (including GED) or higher: 74.1% (2005); Bachelor's degree or higher: 4.4% (2005); Master's degree or higher: 1.5% (2005).
Housing: Homeownership rate: 81.8% (2005); Median home value: $65,067 (2005); Median rent: $306 per month (2000); Median age of housing: 31 years (2000).
Transportation: Commute to work: 94.2% car, 0.0% public transportation, 4.2% walk, 1.3% work from home (2000); Travel time to work: 32.1% less than 15 minutes, 33.2% 15 to 30 minutes, 11.8% 30 to 45 minutes, 13.1% 45 to 60 minutes, 9.8% 60 minutes or more (2000)

MARTINSBURG (town). Covers a land area of 75.791 square miles and a water area of 0.297 square miles. Located at 43.73° N. Lat.; 75.48° W. Long.
Population: 1,358 (1990); 1,249 (2000); 1,226 (2005); 1,193 (2010 projected); Race: 96.6% White, 2.1% Black, 0.0% Asian, 0.4% Hispanic of any race (2005); Density: 16.2 persons per square mile (2005); Average household size: 2.58 (2005); Median age: 37.4 (2005); Males per 100 females: 103.7 (2005); Marriage status: 27.2% never married, 60.5% now married, 5.8% widowed, 6.5% divorced (2000); Foreign born: 0.7% (2000); Ancestry (includes multiple ancestries): 27.8% German, 21.0% Irish, 17.3% French (except Basque), 14.0% English, 7.7% Other groups (2000).
Economy: Employment by occupation: 14.1% management, 16.6% professional, 14.3% services, 20.1% sales, 10.5% farming, 8.7% construction, 15.7% production (2000).
Income: Per capita income: $16,427 (2005); Median household income: $35,155 (2005); Average household income: $42,311 (2005); Percent of households with income of $100,000 or more: 4.2% (2005); Poverty rate: 11.9% (2000).
Education: Percent of population age 25 and over with: High school diploma (including GED) or higher: 86.4% (2005); Bachelor's degree or higher: 10.4% (2005); Master's degree or higher: 3.8% (2005).
Housing: Homeownership rate: 80.5% (2005); Median home value: $95,965 (2005); Median rent: $373 per month (2000); Median age of housing: 60+ years (2000).
Transportation: Commute to work: 83.1% car, 0.0% public transportation, 8.8% walk, 7.0% work from home (2000); Travel time to work: 59.8% less than 15 minutes, 21.9% 15 to 30 minutes, 9.9% 30 to 45 minutes, 2.5% 45 to 60 minutes, 6.0% 60 minutes or more (2000)

MONTAGUE (town). Covers a land area of 65.073 square miles and a water area of 0.214 square miles. Located at 43.73° N. Lat.; 75.71° W. Long.
Population: 47 (1990); 108 (2000); 102 (2005); 97 (2010 projected); Race: 100.0% White, 0.0% Black, 0.0% Asian, 0.0% Hispanic of any race (2005); Density: 1.6 persons per square mile (2005); Average household size: 2.32 (2005); Median age: 43.2 (2005); Males per 100 females: 85.5 (2005); Marriage status: 7.8% never married, 76.6% now married, 0.0% widowed, 15.6% divorced (2000); Foreign born: 0.0% (2000); Ancestry (includes multiple ancestries): 23.8% Other groups, 23.8% English, 22.8% Irish, 17.8% United States or American, 15.8% German (2000).
Economy: Employment by occupation: 14.3% management, 14.3% professional, 11.9% services, 26.2% sales, 0.0% farming, 11.9% construction, 21.4% production (2000).
Income: Per capita income: $19,559 (2005); Median household income: $36,875 (2005); Average household income: $45,341 (2005); Percent of households with income of $100,000 or more: 9.1% (2005); Poverty rate: 14.9% (2000).
Education: Percent of population age 25 and over with: High school diploma (including GED) or higher: 83.3% (2005); Bachelor's degree or higher: 9.7% (2005); Master's degree or higher: 6.9% (2005).
Housing: Homeownership rate: 88.6% (2005); Median home value: $91,818 (2005); Median rent: $n/a per month (2000); Median age of housing: 23 years (2000).
Transportation: Commute to work: 94.9% car, 0.0% public transportation, 0.0% walk, 5.1% work from home (2000); Travel time to work: 8.1% less than 15 minutes, 43.2% 15 to 30 minutes, 10.8% 30 to 45 minutes, 32.4% 45 to 60 minutes, 5.4% 60 minutes or more (2000)

NEW BREMEN (town). Covers a land area of 55.529 square miles and a water area of 0.219 square miles. Located at 43.85° N. Lat.; 75.37° W. Long.
Population: 2,526 (1990); 2,722 (2000); 2,695 (2005); 2,641 (2010 projected); Race: 95.6% White, 3.3% Black, 0.1% Asian, 0.7% Hispanic of any race (2005); Density: 48.5 persons per square mile (2005); Average household size: 2.82 (2005); Median age: 36.7 (2005); Males per 100 females: 95.0 (2005); Marriage status: 24.0% never married, 66.5% now married, 5.2% widowed, 4.3% divorced (2000); Foreign born: 1.0% (2000); Ancestry (includes multiple ancestries): 48.7% German, 19.6% French (except Basque), 12.5% Irish, 11.8% Other groups, 4.0% English (2000).
Economy: Employment by occupation: 7.5% management, 16.0% professional, 14.7% services, 20.2% sales, 4.3% farming, 13.9% construction, 23.4% production (2000).
Income: Per capita income: $16,359 (2005); Median household income: $39,593 (2005); Average household income: $46,117 (2005); Percent of households with income of $100,000 or more: 5.5% (2005); Poverty rate: 11.1% (2000).

Education: Percent of population age 25 and over with: High school diploma (including GED) or higher: 81.8% (2005); Bachelor's degree or higher: 10.5% (2005); Master's degree or higher: 4.3% (2005).
Housing: Homeownership rate: 84.9% (2005); Median home value: $100,746 (2005); Median rent: $370 per month (2000); Median age of housing: 34 years (2000).
Transportation: Commute to work: 89.9% car, 0.0% public transportation, 4.1% walk, 5.3% work from home (2000); Travel time to work: 44.0% less than 15 minutes, 35.0% 15 to 30 minutes, 9.6% 30 to 45 minutes, 7.5% 45 to 60 minutes, 3.8% 60 minutes or more (2000)

OSCEOLA (town). Covers a land area of 87.033 square miles and a water area of 0.010 square miles. Located at 43.53° N. Lat.; 75.70° W. Long.
Population: 239 (1990); 265 (2000); 275 (2005); 279 (2010 projected); Race: 99.3% White, 0.0% Black, 0.0% Asian, 0.7% Hispanic of any race (2005); Density: 3.2 persons per square mile (2005); Average household size: 2.33 (2005); Median age: 41.8 (2005); Males per 100 females: 97.8 (2005); Marriage status: 17.6% never married, 60.2% now married, 8.6% widowed, 13.6% divorced (2000); Foreign born: 2.2% (2000); Ancestry (includes multiple ancestries): 17.3% United States or American, 16.2% German, 16.2% Irish, 6.1% French (except Basque), 5.0% Swiss (2000).
Economy: Employment by occupation: 5.9% management, 14.4% professional, 11.0% services, 17.8% sales, 2.5% farming, 11.9% construction, 36.4% production (2000).
Income: Per capita income: $21,882 (2005); Median household income: $39,688 (2005); Average household income: $50,996 (2005); Percent of households with income of $100,000 or more: 4.2% (2005); Poverty rate: 12.2% (2000).
Education: Percent of population age 25 and over with: High school diploma (including GED) or higher: 83.3% (2005); Bachelor's degree or higher: 9.4% (2005); Master's degree or higher: 4.2% (2005).
Housing: Homeownership rate: 87.3% (2005); Median home value: $83,600 (2005); Median rent: $275 per month (2000); Median age of housing: 40 years (2000).
Transportation: Commute to work: 96.4% car, 0.0% public transportation, 0.0% walk, 3.6% work from home (2000); Travel time to work: 14.8% less than 15 minutes, 27.8% 15 to 30 minutes, 19.4% 30 to 45 minutes, 13.9% 45 to 60 minutes, 24.1% 60 minutes or more (2000)

PINCKNEY (town). Covers a land area of 41.063 square miles and a water area of 0.048 square miles. Located at 43.83° N. Lat.; 75.78° W. Long.
Population: 323 (1990); 319 (2000); 315 (2005); 306 (2010 projected); Race: 93.3% White, 4.8% Black, 0.3% Asian, 1.9% Hispanic of any race (2005); Density: 7.7 persons per square mile (2005); Average household size: 2.60 (2005); Median age: 40.4 (2005); Males per 100 females: 99.4 (2005); Marriage status: 25.4% never married, 57.3% now married, 5.4% widowed, 11.9% divorced (2000); Foreign born: 0.0% (2000); Ancestry (includes multiple ancestries): 28.6% English, 26.5% Irish, 16.6% German, 12.2% French (except Basque), 12.2% United States or American (2000).
Economy: Employment by occupation: 8.9% management, 8.9% professional, 25.5% services, 19.1% sales, 8.3% farming, 22.3% construction, 7.0% production (2000).
Income: Per capita income: $14,825 (2005); Median household income: $37,885 (2005); Average household income: $38,595 (2005); Percent of households with income of $100,000 or more: 0.0% (2005); Poverty rate: 14.0% (2000).
Education: Percent of population age 25 and over with: High school diploma (including GED) or higher: 84.2% (2005); Bachelor's degree or higher: 9.5% (2005); Master's degree or higher: 1.4% (2005).
Housing: Homeownership rate: 90.1% (2005); Median home value: $92,353 (2005); Median rent: $275 per month (2000); Median age of housing: 23 years (2000).
Transportation: Commute to work: 86.4% car, 0.0% public transportation, 9.1% walk, 4.5% work from home (2000); Travel time to work: 18.4% less than 15 minutes, 47.6% 15 to 30 minutes, 23.1% 30 to 45 minutes, 2.7% 45 to 60 minutes, 8.2% 60 minutes or more (2000)

PORT LEYDEN (village). Covers a land area of 0.605 square miles and a water area of 0.052 square miles. Located at 43.58° N. Lat.; 75.34° W. Long. Elevation is 897 feet.
Population: 723 (1990); 665 (2000); 656 (2005); 657 (2010 projected); Race: 98.5% White, 0.3% Black, 0.0% Asian, 0.3% Hispanic of any race (2005); Density: 1,084.6 persons per square mile (2005); Average household size: 2.55 (2005); Median age: 40.4 (2005); Males per 100 females: 94.1 (2005); Marriage status: 26.1% never married, 56.6% now married, 11.3% widowed, 6.0% divorced (2000); Foreign born: 0.0% (2000); Ancestry (includes multiple ancestries): 25.2% French (except Basque), 23.6% Irish, 21.2% German, 9.9% English, 8.7% Other groups (2000).
Economy: Employment by occupation: 4.9% management, 12.2% professional, 19.1% services, 22.8% sales, 5.3% farming, 7.3% construction, 28.5% production (2000).
Income: Per capita income: $13,767 (2005); Median household income: $27,778 (2005); Average household income: $32,986 (2005); Percent of households with income of $100,000 or more: 2.7% (2005); Poverty rate: 23.7% (2000).
Education: Percent of population age 25 and over with: High school diploma (including GED) or higher: 68.2% (2005); Bachelor's degree or higher: 7.1% (2005); Master's degree or higher: 2.0% (2005).
School District(s)
South Lewis Central School District (KG-12)
    2003-04 Enrollment: 1,223 . . . . (315) 348-2500
Housing: Homeownership rate: 63.0% (2005); Median home value: $67,500 (2005); Median rent: $300 per month (2000); Median age of housing: 60+ years (2000).
Transportation: Commute to work: 95.1% car, 0.0% public transportation, 0.0% walk, 2.5% work from home (2000); Travel time to work: 28.7% less than 15 minutes, 27.8% 15 to 30 minutes, 16.9% 30 to 45 minutes, 16.9% 45 to 60 minutes, 9.7% 60 minutes or more (2000)

TURIN (village). Covers a land area of 1.022 square miles and a water area of 0 square miles. Located at 43.62° N. Lat.; 75.40° W. Long. Elevation is 1,264 feet.
Population: 295 (1990); 263 (2000); 253 (2005); 245 (2010 projected); Race: 99.6% White, 0.0% Black, 0.0% Asian, 0.0% Hispanic of any race (2005); Density: 247.4 persons per square mile (2005); Average household size: 2.50 (2005); Median age: 44.8 (2005); Males per 100 females: 87.4 (2005); Marriage status: 31.3% never married, 57.9% now married, 7.2% widowed, 3.6% divorced (2000); Foreign born: 0.0% (2000); Ancestry (includes multiple ancestries): 31.0% Irish, 24.1% German, 13.8% English, 12.6% French (except Basque), 7.7% Italian (2000).
Economy: Employment by occupation: 12.8% management, 17.9% professional, 11.1% services, 20.5% sales, 0.0% farming, 17.1% construction, 20.5% production (2000).
Income: Per capita income: $19,615 (2005); Median household income: $39,853 (2005); Average household income: $49,134 (2005); Percent of households with income of $100,000 or more: 6.9% (2005); Poverty rate: 10.0% (2000).
Education: Percent of population age 25 and over with: High school diploma (including GED) or higher: 88.4% (2005); Bachelor's degree or higher: 17.4% (2005); Master's degree or higher: 8.7% (2005).
School District(s)
South Lewis Central School District (KG-12)
    2003-04 Enrollment: 1,223 . . . . (315) 348-2500
Housing: Homeownership rate: 83.2% (2005); Median home value: $77,143 (2005); Median rent: $380 per month (2000); Median age of housing: 60+ years (2000).
Transportation: Commute to work: 86.3% car, 1.7% public transportation, 6.0% walk, 6.0% work from home (2000); Travel time to work: 40.9% less than 15 minutes, 29.1% 15 to 30 minutes, 11.8% 30 to 45 minutes, 7.3% 45 to 60 minutes, 10.9% 60 minutes or more (2000)

TURIN (town). Covers a land area of 31.176 square miles and a water area of 0.206 square miles. Located at 43.66° N. Lat.; 75.42° W. Long. Elevation is 1,264 feet.
Population: 873 (1990); 793 (2000); 773 (2005); 754 (2010 projected); Race: 99.4% White, 0.4% Black, 0.0% Asian, 0.4% Hispanic of any race (2005); Density: 24.8 persons per square mile (2005); Average household size: 2.59 (2005); Median age: 41.4 (2005); Males per 100 females: 97.2 (2005); Marriage status: 26.3% never married, 63.3% now married, 5.5% widowed, 4.9% divorced (2000); Foreign born: 0.1% (2000); Ancestry (includes multiple ancestries): 30.8% German, 23.5% Irish, 16.1% English, 14.8% Polish, 11.5% French (except Basque) (2000).
Economy: In timber area. Winter recreation (downhill skiing and snowmobiling) center. Employment by occupation: 22.2% management, 15.2% professional, 9.5% services, 16.8% sales, 7.3% farming, 11.1% construction, 17.9% production (2000).

Income: Per capita income: $19,855 (2005); Median household income: $41,273 (2005); Average household income: $51,275 (2005); Percent of households with income of $100,000 or more: 9.7% (2005); Poverty rate: 10.5% (2000).
Education: Percent of population age 25 and over with: High school diploma (including GED) or higher: 82.7% (2005); Bachelor's degree or higher: 16.9% (2005); Master's degree or higher: 7.2% (2005).
Housing: Homeownership rate: 83.2% (2005); Median home value: $110,759 (2005); Median rent: $380 per month (2000); Median age of housing: 60+ years (2000).
Transportation: Commute to work: 77.1% car, 1.1% public transportation, 6.3% walk, 15.4% work from home (2000); Travel time to work: 46.3% less than 15 minutes, 29.3% 15 to 30 minutes, 12.1% 30 to 45 minutes, 7.8% 45 to 60 minutes, 4.6% 60 minutes or more (2000)

WATSON
(town). Covers a land area of 112.730 square miles and a water area of 3.022 square miles. Located at 43.80° N. Lat.; 75.29° W. Long. Elevation is 749 feet.
Population: 1,613 (1990); 1,987 (2000); 2,045 (2005); 2,100 (2010 projected); Race: 97.5% White, 1.6% Black, 0.1% Asian, 1.2% Hispanic of any race (2005); Density: 18.1 persons per square mile (2005); Average household size: 2.52 (2005); Median age: 40.1 (2005); Males per 100 females: 105.3 (2005); Marriage status: 23.9% never married, 62.5% now married, 6.2% widowed, 7.5% divorced (2000); Foreign born: 0.5% (2000); Ancestry (includes multiple ancestries): 32.2% German, 20.9% Irish, 19.1% French (except Basque), 11.7% English, 8.3% Other groups (2000).
Economy: Single-family building permits issued: 12 (2005); Multi-family building permits issued: 0 (2005); Employment by occupation: 8.3% management, 16.0% professional, 18.1% services, 18.9% sales, 2.9% farming, 10.1% construction, 25.7% production (2000).
Income: Per capita income: $18,965 (2005); Median household income: $39,780 (2005); Average household income: $47,880 (2005); Percent of households with income of $100,000 or more: 6.3% (2005); Poverty rate: 11.3% (2000).
Taxes: Total city taxes per capita: $346 (2004); City property taxes per capita: $334 (2004).
Education: Percent of population age 25 and over with: High school diploma (including GED) or higher: 78.8% (2005); Bachelor's degree or higher: 11.9% (2005); Master's degree or higher: 5.2% (2005).
Housing: Homeownership rate: 83.6% (2005); Median home value: $99,727 (2005); Median rent: $358 per month (2000); Median age of housing: 24 years (2000).
Transportation: Commute to work: 90.1% car, 0.2% public transportation, 3.6% walk, 4.9% work from home (2000); Travel time to work: 36.5% less than 15 minutes, 41.5% 15 to 30 minutes, 10.6% 30 to 45 minutes, 4.6% 45 to 60 minutes, 6.8% 60 minutes or more (2000)

WEST LEYDEN
(unincorporated postal area, zip code 13489). Covers a land area of 37.340 square miles and a water area of 0.088 square miles. Located at 43.45° N. Lat.; 75.52° W. Long. Elevation is 1,496 feet.
Population: 0 (2000); Race: 99.8% White, 0.0% Black, 0.0% Asian, 0.0% Hispanic of any race (2000); Density: 0.0 persons per square mile (2000); Age: 32.0% under 18, 7.9% over 64 (2000); Marriage status: 31.9% never married, 57.0% now married, 3.9% widowed, 7.2% divorced (2000); Foreign born: 0.5% (2000); Ancestry (includes multiple ancestries): 36.3% German, 18.0% Irish, 15.4% Polish, 6.7% French (except Basque), 5.1% Swiss (2000).
Economy: Employment by occupation: 9.8% management, 12.8% professional, 16.0% services, 21.5% sales, 3.3% farming, 10.3% construction, 26.5% production (2000).
Income: Per capita income: $13,398 (2000); Median household income: $36,429 (2000); Poverty rate: 10.6% (2000).
Education: Percent of population age 25 and over with: High school diploma (including GED) or higher: 85.7% (2000); Bachelor's degree or higher: 8.4% (2000).
Housing: Homeownership rate: 84.7% (2000); Median home value: $59,400 (2000); Median rent: $344 per month (2000); Median age of housing: 33 years (2000).
Transportation: Commute to work: 85.1% car, 0.8% public transportation, 2.0% walk, 9.3% work from home (2000); Travel time to work: 26.2% less than 15 minutes, 30.6% 15 to 30 minutes, 23.7% 30 to 45 minutes, 12.0% 45 to 60 minutes, 7.5% 60 minutes or more (2000)

WEST TURIN
(town). Covers a land area of 102.214 square miles and a water area of 0.178 square miles. Located at 43.58° N. Lat.; 75.46° W. Long.
Population: 1,753 (1990); 1,674 (2000); 1,632 (2005); 1,606 (2010 projected); Race: 99.1% White, 0.0% Black, 0.1% Asian, 0.3% Hispanic of any race (2005); Density: 16.0 persons per square mile (2005); Average household size: 2.58 (2005); Median age: 38.3 (2005); Males per 100 females: 104.3 (2005); Marriage status: 27.5% never married, 55.5% now married, 8.8% widowed, 8.2% divorced (2000); Foreign born: 0.7% (2000); Ancestry (includes multiple ancestries): 33.1% German, 18.9% Irish, 15.8% English, 13.9% Polish, 9.6% French (except Basque) (2000).
Economy: Employment by occupation: 12.5% management, 16.9% professional, 14.3% services, 20.4% sales, 7.5% farming, 8.3% construction, 20.1% production (2000).
Income: Per capita income: $18,825 (2005); Median household income: $39,023 (2005); Average household income: $48,535 (2005); Percent of households with income of $100,000 or more: 7.7% (2005); Poverty rate: 16.4% (2000).
Education: Percent of population age 25 and over with: High school diploma (including GED) or higher: 81.1% (2005); Bachelor's degree or higher: 13.1% (2005); Master's degree or higher: 6.5% (2005).
Housing: Homeownership rate: 76.9% (2005); Median home value: $87,067 (2005); Median rent: $348 per month (2000); Median age of housing: 60+ years (2000).
Transportation: Commute to work: 80.0% car, 0.3% public transportation, 13.7% walk, 4.3% work from home (2000); Travel time to work: 40.6% less than 15 minutes, 27.8% 15 to 30 minutes, 12.2% 30 to 45 minutes, 9.7% 45 to 60 minutes, 9.7% 60 minutes or more (2000)

Livingston County

Located in west central New York, in the Finger Lakes area; drained by the Genesee River; includes Conesus and Hemlock Lakes. Covers a land area of 632.13 square miles, a water area of 8.32 square miles, and is located in the Eastern Time Zone. The county government was organized in 1821. County seat is Geneseo.

Livingston County is part of the Rochester, NY Metropolitan Statistical Area. The entire metro area includes: Livingston County, NY; Monroe County, NY; Ontario County, NY; Orleans County, NY; Wayne County, NY

Weather Station: Dansville | | | | | | | | | | | Elevation: 659 feet

	Jan	Feb	Mar	Apr	May	Jun	Jul	Aug	Sep	Oct	Nov	Dec
High	33	35	44	57	69	78	83	81	73	62	49	38
Low	16	16	24	34	44	53	58	57	49	39	32	22
Precip	1.5	1.3	1.9	2.6	2.9	3.7	3.2	3.4	3.6	2.8	2.6	2.0
Snow	12.6	10.4	7.4	2.5	0.2	0.0	0.0	0.0	0.0	tr	3.6	10.5

High and Low temperatures in degrees Fahrenheit; Precipitation and Snow in inches

Population: 62,372 (1990); 64,328 (2000); 64,696 (2005); 65,037 (2010 projected); Race: 93.8% White, 3.1% Black, 1.0% Asian, 2.8% Hispanic of any race (2005); Density: 102.3 persons per square mile (2005); Average household size: 2.89 (2005); Median age: 36.5 (2005); Males per 100 females: 100.1 (2005).
Religion: Five largest groups: 22.2% Catholic Church, 4.6% The United Methodist Church, 3.7% Presbyterian Church (U.S.A.), 1.2% Evangelical Lutheran Church in America, 1.0% Episcopal Church (2000).
Economy: Unemployment rate: 5.1% (2005); Total civilian labor force: 33,102 (2005); Leading industries: 21.5% retail trade; 17.2% manufacturing; 15.2% accommodation and food services (2003); Farms: 801 totaling 209,496 acres (2002); Companies that employ 500 or more persons: 1 (2003); Companies that employ 100 to 499 persons: 12 (2003); Companies that employ less than 100 persons: 1,274 (2003); Black-owned businesses: n/a (2002); Hispanic-owned businesses: n/a (2002); Women-owned businesses: 1,072 (2002); Retail sales per capita: $9,847 (2006). Single-family building permits issued: 208 (2005); Multi-family building permits issued: 0 (2005).
Income: Per capita income: $20,101 (2005); Median household income: $46,345 (2005); Average household income: $55,469 (2005); Percent of households with income of $100,000 or more: 11.0% (2005); Poverty rate: 10.8% (2003); Bankruptcy rate: 5.16% (2005).
Education: Percent of population age 25 and over with: High school diploma (including GED) or higher: 82.3% (2005); Bachelor's degree or higher: 19.6% (2005); Master's degree or higher: 8.2% (2005).

Housing: Homeownership rate: 74.5% (2005); Median home value: $107,720 (2005); Median rent: $438 per month (2000); Median age of housing: 40 years (2000).
Health: Birth rate: 101.8 per 10,000 population (2004); Death rate: 75.3 per 10,000 population (2004); Age-adjusted cancer mortality rate: 242.3 deaths per 100,000 population (2002); Number of physicians: 9.3 per 10,000 population (2004); Hospital beds: 9.6 per 10,000 population (2003); Hospital admissions: 522.2 per 10,000 population (2003).
Elections: 2004 Presidential election results: 59.2% Bush, 38.4% Kerry, 2.1% Nader, 0.3% Badnarik
National and State Parks: Boyd-Parker State Park; Rattlesnake Hill State Wildlife Management Area
Additional Information Contacts
Livingston County Government . . . . (585) 243-7000
  http://www.co.livingston.state.ny.us/
Town of Geneseo . . . . (585) 243-1177
  http://www.geneseony.org/
Village of Dansville . . . . (716) 335-5330
  http://dansvilleny.org/
Village of Geneseo . . . . (585) 243-1177
  http://www.geneseony.org/
Village of Mount Morris . . . . (585) 658-4160
  http://www.villageofmountmorris.com/

Livingston County Communities

AVON (village). Covers a land area of 2.999 square miles and a water area of 0 square miles. Located at 42.91° N. Lat.; 77.74° W. Long. Elevation is 651 feet.
Population: 3,001 (1990); 2,977 (2000); 2,966 (2005); 2,961 (2010 projected); Race: 96.2% White, 1.7% Black, 0.9% Asian, 0.9% Hispanic of any race (2005); Density: 989.1 persons per square mile (2005); Average household size: 2.56 (2005); Median age: 38.5 (2005); Males per 100 females: 90.7 (2005); Marriage status: 26.2% never married, 57.0% now married, 8.5% widowed, 8.3% divorced (2000); Foreign born: 1.3% (2000); Ancestry (includes multiple ancestries): 33.6% German, 22.6% Irish, 17.6% English, 10.8% Italian, 7.5% Dutch (2000).
Economy: Single-family building permits issued: 6 (2005); Multi-family building permits issued: 0 (2005); Employment by occupation: 14.0% management, 26.7% professional, 11.2% services, 20.0% sales, 0.0% farming, 7.4% construction, 20.7% production (2000).
Income: Per capita income: $24,455 (2005); Median household income: $45,341 (2005); Average household income: $58,027 (2005); Percent of households with income of $100,000 or more: 11.7% (2005); Poverty rate: 7.5% (2000).
Education: Percent of population age 25 and over with: High school diploma (including GED) or higher: 91.2% (2005); Bachelor's degree or higher: 30.1% (2005); Master's degree or higher: 10.5% (2005).
School District(s)
Avon Central School District (KG-12)
  2003-04 Enrollment: 1,167 . . . . (585) 226-2455
Housing: Homeownership rate: 64.2% (2005); Median home value: $128,071 (2005); Median rent: $477 per month (2000); Median age of housing: 56 years (2000).
Safety: Violent crime rate: 3.4 per 10,000 population; Property crime rate: 194.4 per 10,000 population (2004).
Transportation: Commute to work: 90.2% car, 0.0% public transportation, 3.5% walk, 5.4% work from home (2000); Travel time to work: 37.3% less than 15 minutes, 28.2% 15 to 30 minutes, 30.5% 30 to 45 minutes, 2.5% 45 to 60 minutes, 1.6% 60 minutes or more (2000)

AVON (town). Covers a land area of 41.158 square miles and a water area of 0.063 square miles. Located at 42.89° N. Lat.; 77.73° W. Long. Elevation is 651 feet.
History: Incorporated 1867.
Population: 6,283 (1990); 6,443 (2000); 6,433 (2005); 6,414 (2010 projected); Race: 96.3% White, 1.2% Black, 0.9% Asian, 1.6% Hispanic of any race (2005); Density: 156.3 persons per square mile (2005); Average household size: 2.52 (2005); Median age: 39.4 (2005); Males per 100 females: 94.0 (2005); Marriage status: 22.5% never married, 61.9% now married, 6.2% widowed, 9.3% divorced (2000); Foreign born: 1.5% (2000); Ancestry (includes multiple ancestries): 26.6% German, 25.2% Irish, 17.7% English, 11.1% Italian, 5.8% Dutch (2000).
Economy: Manufacturing: frozen foods, fabricated metal products, thermoplastics, and injection moldings. Agriculture: oats, wheat; sheep, hogs; dairying. Single-family building permits issued: 22 (2005); Multi-family building permits issued: 0 (2005); Employment by occupation: 12.9% management, 25.6% professional, 10.7% services, 22.6% sales, 1.1% farming, 9.8% construction, 17.4% production (2000).
Income: Per capita income: $24,155 (2005); Median household income: $47,579 (2005); Average household income: $58,625 (2005); Percent of households with income of $100,000 or more: 11.1% (2005); Poverty rate: 6.7% (2000).
Education: Percent of population age 25 and over with: High school diploma (including GED) or higher: 88.8% (2005); Bachelor's degree or higher: 24.2% (2005); Master's degree or higher: 9.1% (2005).
Housing: Homeownership rate: 75.3% (2005); Median home value: $116,915 (2005); Median rent: $483 per month (2000); Median age of housing: 42 years (2000).
Transportation: Commute to work: 92.2% car, 0.2% public transportation, 2.8% walk, 3.5% work from home (2000); Travel time to work: 28.3% less than 15 minutes, 33.7% 15 to 30 minutes, 31.1% 30 to 45 minutes, 4.8% 45 to 60 minutes, 2.2% 60 minutes or more (2000)

CALEDONIA (village). Covers a land area of 2.135 square miles and a water area of 0 square miles. Located at 42.97° N. Lat.; 77.85° W. Long. Elevation is 666 feet.
Population: 2,262 (1990); 2,327 (2000); 2,287 (2005); 2,212 (2010 projected); Race: 94.2% White, 3.2% Black, 1.0% Asian, 1.1% Hispanic of any race (2005); Density: 1,071.0 persons per square mile (2005); Average household size: 2.58 (2005); Median age: 38.8 (2005); Males per 100 females: 95.5 (2005); Marriage status: 24.6% never married, 62.9% now married, 5.8% widowed, 6.7% divorced (2000); Foreign born: 1.1% (2000); Ancestry (includes multiple ancestries): 27.3% German, 22.3% Irish, 19.5% English, 15.6% Italian, 6.6% Other groups (2000).
Economy: Single-family building permits issued: 1 (2005); Multi-family building permits issued: 0 (2005); Employment by occupation: 13.7% management, 19.4% professional, 9.5% services, 31.3% sales, 0.6% farming, 6.9% construction, 18.5% production (2000).
Income: Per capita income: $22,436 (2005); Median household income: $48,161 (2005); Average household income: $57,021 (2005); Percent of households with income of $100,000 or more: 12.5% (2005); Poverty rate: 5.2% (2000).
Education: Percent of population age 25 and over with: High school diploma (including GED) or higher: 90.1% (2005); Bachelor's degree or higher: 20.3% (2005); Master's degree or higher: 6.9% (2005).
School District(s)
Caledonia-Mumford Central School District (KG-12)
  2003-04 Enrollment: 1,133 . . . . (585) 538-3400
Housing: Homeownership rate: 73.3% (2005); Median home value: $115,221 (2005); Median rent: $431 per month (2000); Median age of housing: 57 years (2000).
Safety: Violent crime rate: 31.0 per 10,000 population; Property crime rate: 261.1 per 10,000 population (2004).
Transportation: Commute to work: 93.6% car, 0.0% public transportation, 4.2% walk, 1.9% work from home (2000); Travel time to work: 27.2% less than 15 minutes, 30.0% 15 to 30 minutes, 33.0% 30 to 45 minutes, 5.9% 45 to 60 minutes, 3.9% 60 minutes or more (2000)

CALEDONIA (town). Covers a land area of 44.119 square miles and a water area of 0.186 square miles. Located at 42.96° N. Lat.; 77.83° W. Long. Elevation is 666 feet.
History: Incorporated 1887.
Population: 4,441 (1990); 4,567 (2000); 4,424 (2005); 4,274 (2010 projected); Race: 94.9% White, 2.8% Black, 0.7% Asian, 0.9% Hispanic of any race (2005); Density: 100.3 persons per square mile (2005); Average household size: 2.73 (2005); Median age: 38.3 (2005); Males per 100 females: 100.3 (2005); Marriage status: 23.6% never married, 65.2% now married, 3.9% widowed, 7.3% divorced (2000); Foreign born: 1.0% (2000); Ancestry (includes multiple ancestries): 26.0% German, 22.9% Irish, 17.1% English, 14.6% Italian, 7.0% Other groups (2000).
Economy: Manufacturing: electrical equipment; dairy and farm supplies; limestone quarries. Agriculture: dairy products; grain. Site of state trout hatchery. Single-family building permits issued: 3 (2005); Multi-family building permits issued: 0 (2005); Employment by occupation: 13.0% management, 17.3% professional, 8.9% services, 29.3% sales, 1.9% farming, 11.2% construction, 18.5% production (2000).
Income: Per capita income: $21,940 (2005); Median household income: $49,922 (2005); Average household income: $59,460 (2005); Percent of

households with income of $100,000 or more: 13.3% (2005); Poverty rate: 5.0% (2000).
Education: Percent of population age 25 and over with: High school diploma (including GED) or higher: 90.0% (2005); Bachelor's degree or higher: 17.3% (2005); Master's degree or higher: 5.8% (2005).
Housing: Homeownership rate: 80.4% (2005); Median home value: $119,402 (2005); Median rent: $436 per month (2000); Median age of housing: 36 years (2000).
Transportation: Commute to work: 95.1% car, 0.0% public transportation, 2.2% walk, 2.5% work from home (2000); Travel time to work: 26.6% less than 15 minutes, 32.1% 15 to 30 minutes, 31.7% 30 to 45 minutes, 7.3% 45 to 60 minutes, 2.3% 60 minutes or more (2000)

CONESUS (town). Covers a land area of 32.923 square miles and a water area of 2.902 square miles. Located at 42.71° N. Lat.; 77.67° W. Long. Elevation is 1,199 feet.
Population: 2,196 (1990); 2,353 (2000); 2,349 (2005); 2,346 (2010 projected); Race: 98.7% White, 0.1% Black, 0.0% Asian, 0.2% Hispanic of any race (2005); Density: 71.3 persons per square mile (2005); Average household size: 2.67 (2005); Median age: 39.4 (2005); Males per 100 females: 96.7 (2005); Marriage status: 22.0% never married, 63.9% now married, 6.6% widowed, 7.6% divorced (2000); Foreign born: 1.1% (2000); Ancestry (includes multiple ancestries): 29.2% German, 20.8% English, 18.2% Irish, 11.7% Italian, 6.1% Other groups (2000).
Economy: Single-family building permits issued: 10 (2005); Multi-family building permits issued: 0 (2005); Employment by occupation: 13.5% management, 15.8% professional, 16.1% services, 22.3% sales, 1.2% farming, 10.2% construction, 20.9% production (2000).
Income: Per capita income: $24,745 (2005); Median household income: $53,756 (2005); Average household income: $66,017 (2005); Percent of households with income of $100,000 or more: 15.8% (2005); Poverty rate: 5.3% (2000).
Taxes: Total city taxes per capita: $337 (2004); City property taxes per capita: $292 (2004).
Education: Percent of population age 25 and over with: High school diploma (including GED) or higher: 89.1% (2005); Bachelor's degree or higher: 16.5% (2005); Master's degree or higher: 4.8% (2005).
Housing: Homeownership rate: 89.3% (2005); Median home value: $124,237 (2005); Median rent: $478 per month (2000); Median age of housing: 26 years (2000).
Transportation: Commute to work: 93.0% car, 0.0% public transportation, 1.1% walk, 5.3% work from home (2000); Travel time to work: 11.2% less than 15 minutes, 31.5% 15 to 30 minutes, 22.8% 30 to 45 minutes, 22.9% 45 to 60 minutes, 11.6% 60 minutes or more (2000)

DALTON (unincorporated postal area, zip code 14836). Covers a land area of 35.294 square miles and a water area of 0.050 square miles. Located at 42.52° N. Lat.; 77.93° W. Long.
Population: 0 (2000); Race: 98.9% White, 0.0% Black, 0.0% Asian, 0.2% Hispanic of any race (2000); Density: 0.0 persons per square mile (2000); Age: 25.4% under 18, 9.2% over 64 (2000); Marriage status: 21.5% never married, 68.2% now married, 4.7% widowed, 5.6% divorced (2000); Foreign born: 0.6% (2000); Ancestry (includes multiple ancestries): 27.7% German, 17.1% English, 16.8% Irish, 11.4% Italian, 8.3% United States or American (2000).
Economy: Employment by occupation: 8.2% management, 12.6% professional, 21.0% services, 13.4% sales, 2.6% farming, 16.4% construction, 25.7% production (2000).
Income: Per capita income: $17,126 (2000); Median household income: $43,676 (2000); Poverty rate: 6.8% (2000).
Education: Percent of population age 25 and over with: High school diploma (including GED) or higher: 84.0% (2000); Bachelor's degree or higher: 13.1% (2000).
School District(s)
Dalton-Nunda Central School District (Keshequa) (KG-12)
    2003-04 Enrollment: 936 . . . . (585) 468-2541
Housing: Homeownership rate: 85.1% (2000); Median home value: $61,300 (2000); Median rent: $392 per month (2000); Median age of housing: 33 years (2000).
Transportation: Commute to work: 93.1% car, 0.6% public transportation, 1.6% walk, 4.1% work from home (2000); Travel time to work: 29.7% less than 15 minutes, 20.1% 15 to 30 minutes, 25.2% 30 to 45 minutes, 8.9% 45 to 60 minutes, 16.1% 60 minutes or more (2000)

DANSVILLE (village). Covers a land area of 2.366 square miles and a water area of 0 square miles. Located at 42.56° N. Lat.; 77.69° W. Long. Elevation is 1,025 feet.
History: Clara Barton founded (1881) first local chapter of the American Red Cross here. Settled 1795, incorporated 1845.
Population: 5,039 (1990); 4,832 (2000); 4,628 (2005); 4,415 (2010 projected); Race: 95.5% White, 1.3% Black, 0.7% Asian, 2.5% Hispanic of any race (2005); Density: 1,956.1 persons per square mile (2005); Average household size: 2.57 (2005); Median age: 37.6 (2005); Males per 100 females: 90.7 (2005); Marriage status: 28.0% never married, 52.2% now married, 9.3% widowed, 10.5% divorced (2000); Foreign born: 2.6% (2000); Ancestry (includes multiple ancestries): 35.9% German, 22.1% Irish, 16.8% English, 6.8% United States or American, 6.2% Other groups (2000).
Economy: Manufacturing: apparel, electronic equipment, fabricated metal products. Agriculture: beans, potatoes. Single-family building permits issued: 2 (2005); Multi-family building permits issued: 0 (2005); Employment by occupation: 8.9% management, 15.5% professional, 16.1% services, 26.5% sales, 1.1% farming, 10.4% construction, 21.6% production (2000).
Income: Per capita income: $15,918 (2005); Median household income: $32,857 (2005); Average household income: $39,671 (2005); Percent of households with income of $100,000 or more: 5.4% (2005); Poverty rate: 17.0% (2000).
Education: Percent of population age 25 and over with: High school diploma (including GED) or higher: 82.0% (2005); Bachelor's degree or higher: 13.0% (2005); Master's degree or higher: 4.7% (2005).
School District(s)
Dansville Central School District (PK-12)
    2003-04 Enrollment: 1,750 . . . . (585) 335-4000
Housing: Homeownership rate: 59.5% (2005); Median home value: $82,234 (2005); Median rent: $395 per month (2000); Median age of housing: 60+ years (2000).
Hospitals: Nicholas H. Noyes Memorial Hospital (72 beds)
Safety: Violent crime rate: 23.3 per 10,000 population; Property crime rate: 536.7 per 10,000 population (2004).
Newspapers: Genesee Country Express (General - Circulation 3,000)
Transportation: Commute to work: 86.8% car, 1.3% public transportation, 7.9% walk, 4.0% work from home (2000); Travel time to work: 47.6% less than 15 minutes, 23.5% 15 to 30 minutes, 10.2% 30 to 45 minutes, 11.4% 45 to 60 minutes, 7.2% 60 minutes or more (2000)
Additional Information Contacts
Village of Dansville. . . . . (716) 335-5330
    http://dansvilleny.org/

GENESEO (village). Covers a land area of 2.788 square miles and a water area of 0 square miles. Located at 42.79° N. Lat.; 77.81° W. Long. Elevation is 596 feet.
History: Major salt mine cave-in and diversion of surface drainage into subterranean channels occurred in 1995. Estates of the Wadsworth family, northeast and south of village. English-style Genesee Valley Hunt each fall. Seat of State University of N.Y. College at Geneseo. Settled c.1790, Incorporated 1832.
Population: 7,225 (1990); 7,579 (2000); 8,171 (2005); 8,655 (2010 projected); Race: 92.2% White, 1.4% Black, 4.5% Asian, 2.9% Hispanic of any race (2005); Density: 2,930.7 persons per square mile (2005); Average household size: 4.25 (2005); Median age: 22.0 (2005); Males per 100 females: 65.5 (2005); Marriage status: 68.3% never married, 25.2% now married, 3.7% widowed, 2.8% divorced (2000); Foreign born: 5.6% (2000); Ancestry (includes multiple ancestries): 25.9% Irish, 22.1% German, 21.3% Italian, 14.1% English, 8.8% Other groups (2000).
Economy: Trade center in agricultural area: peas, corn. Manufacturing of athletic clothing and sportswear. Salt deposits. Summer residence and recreation at Conegus Lake. Seat of State University of N.Y. College at Geneseo. Single-family building permits issued: 6 (2005); Multi-family building permits issued: 0 (2005); Employment by occupation: 10.0% management, 27.5% professional, 22.4% services, 27.1% sales, 0.0% farming, 4.3% construction, 8.7% production (2000).
Income: Per capita income: $13,493 (2005); Median household income: $33,995 (2005); Average household income: $49,349 (2005); Percent of households with income of $100,000 or more: 12.6% (2005); Poverty rate: 41.7% (2000).
Taxes: Total city taxes per capita: $158 (2004); City property taxes per capita: $138 (2004).

Education: Percent of population age 25 and over with: High school diploma (including GED) or higher: 82.6% (2005); Bachelor's degree or higher: 43.3% (2005); Master's degree or higher: 26.3% (2005).

School District(s)
Geneseo Central School District (KG-12)
    2003-04 Enrollment: 929 . . . . (585) 243-3450

Four-year College(s)
SUNY College at Geneseo (Public)
    Fall 2004 Enrollment: 5,573. . . . . (585) 245-5211
    2005-06 Tuition: In-state $5,520; Out-of-state $11,780

Housing: Homeownership rate: 39.8% (2005); Median home value: $140,427 (2005); Median rent: $449 per month (2000); Median age of housing: 36 years (2000).
Safety: Violent crime rate: 6.3 per 10,000 population; Property crime rate: 172.7 per 10,000 population (2004).
Newspapers: Livingston County News (General - Circulation 6,200); The Lake & Valley Clarion (General - Circulation 2,500)
Transportation: Commute to work: 61.7% car, 0.8% public transportation, 34.0% walk, 3.2% work from home (2000); Travel time to work: 66.5% less than 15 minutes, 12.9% 15 to 30 minutes, 12.2% 30 to 45 minutes, 6.0% 45 to 60 minutes, 2.3% 60 minutes or more (2000)

Additional Information Contacts
Livingston County Chamber of Commerce . . . . (585) 243-2222
    http://www.livingstoncountychamber.com
Village of Geneseo. . . . . (585) 243-1177
    http://www.geneseony.org/

GENESEO (town). Covers a land area of 43.959 square miles and a water area of 1.245 square miles. Located at 42.80° N. Lat.; 77.78° W. Long. Elevation is 596 feet.
History: Geneseo is best known for its association with the Wadsworth family. They became the squires of the middle Genesee in 1790. Members of the family served as legislators at the state and national levels.
Population: 9,178 (1990); 9,654 (2000); 10,635 (2005); 11,486 (2010 projected); Race: 93.6% White, 1.1% Black, 3.5% Asian, 2.4% Hispanic of any race (2005); Density: 241.9 persons per square mile (2005); Average household size: 3.68 (2005); Median age: 23.4 (2005); Males per 100 females: 72.4 (2005); Marriage status: 59.9% never married, 32.5% now married, 3.6% widowed, 4.0% divorced (2000); Foreign born: 4.8% (2000); Ancestry (includes multiple ancestries): 26.6% Irish, 22.7% German, 19.5% Italian, 16.9% English, 7.4% Other groups (2000).
Economy: Single-family building permits issued: 6 (2005); Multi-family building permits issued: 0 (2005); Employment by occupation: 10.7% management, 27.8% professional, 20.3% services, 27.1% sales, 0.4% farming, 6.0% construction, 7.7% production (2000).
Income: Per capita income: $17,763 (2005); Median household income: $44,701 (2005); Average household income: $59,802 (2005); Percent of households with income of $100,000 or more: 16.1% (2005); Poverty rate: 29.8% (2000).
Taxes: Total city taxes per capita: $102 (2004); City property taxes per capita: $85 (2004).
Education: Percent of population age 25 and over with: High school diploma (including GED) or higher: 86.3% (2005); Bachelor's degree or higher: 40.9% (2005); Master's degree or higher: 22.9% (2005).
Housing: Homeownership rate: 53.3% (2005); Median home value: $145,052 (2005); Median rent: $459 per month (2000); Median age of housing: 35 years (2000).
Transportation: Commute to work: 70.3% car, 0.7% public transportation, 25.0% walk, 3.8% work from home (2000); Travel time to work: 59.2% less than 15 minutes, 14.4% 15 to 30 minutes, 17.0% 30 to 45 minutes, 7.0% 45 to 60 minutes, 2.3% 60 minutes or more (2000)

Additional Information Contacts
Town of Geneseo. . . . . (585) 243-1177
    http://www.geneseony.org/

GROVELAND (town). Covers a land area of 39.166 square miles and a water area of 0.736 square miles. Located at 42.69° N. Lat.; 77.78° W. Long.
Population: 3,190 (1990); 3,853 (2000); 3,887 (2005); 3,943 (2010 projected); Race: 53.0% White, 37.3% Black, 0.1% Asian, 20.8% Hispanic of any race (2005); Density: 99.2 persons per square mile (2005); Average household size: 6.87 (2005); Median age: 36.7 (2005); Males per 100 females: 419.7 (2005); Marriage status: 50.0% never married, 37.7% now married, 2.2% widowed, 10.1% divorced (2000); Foreign born: 7.0% (2000); Ancestry (includes multiple ancestries): 11.8% German, 10.0% Irish, 7.8% English, 4.2% Italian, 2.3% United States or American (2000).
Economy: Single-family building permits issued: 6 (2005); Multi-family building permits issued: 0 (2005); Employment by occupation: 9.0% management, 28.7% professional, 14.4% services, 21.2% sales, 1.1% farming, 7.5% construction, 18.1% production (2000).
Income: Per capita income: $14,545 (2005); Median household income: $48,759 (2005); Average household income: $58,949 (2005); Percent of households with income of $100,000 or more: 12.7% (2005); Poverty rate: 8.8% (2000).
Education: Percent of population age 25 and over with: High school diploma (including GED) or higher: 45.5% (2005); Bachelor's degree or higher: 8.9% (2005); Master's degree or higher: 3.5% (2005).
Housing: Homeownership rate: 75.4% (2005); Median home value: $125,833 (2005); Median rent: $499 per month (2000); Median age of housing: 46 years (2000).
Transportation: Commute to work: 92.8% car, 0.0% public transportation, 1.8% walk, 4.3% work from home (2000); Travel time to work: 19.3% less than 15 minutes, 34.8% 15 to 30 minutes, 21.3% 30 to 45 minutes, 16.8% 45 to 60 minutes, 7.8% 60 minutes or more (2000)

HEMLOCK (unincorporated postal area, zip code 14466). Covers a land area of 16.347 square miles and a water area of 0 square miles. Located at 42.78° N. Lat.; 77.59° W. Long.
Population: 0 (2000); Race: 99.6% White, 0.3% Black, 0.0% Asian, 0.1% Hispanic of any race (2000); Density: 0.0 persons per square mile (2000); Age: 22.3% under 18, 8.2% over 64 (2000); Marriage status: 27.0% never married, 58.1% now married, 6.2% widowed, 8.7% divorced (2000); Foreign born: 0.8% (2000); Ancestry (includes multiple ancestries): 28.4% German, 21.0% Irish, 20.6% English, 11.5% Italian, 5.5% Polish (2000).
Economy: Employment by occupation: 8.9% management, 18.7% professional, 11.0% services, 19.2% sales, 0.2% farming, 11.6% construction, 30.5% production (2000).
Income: Per capita income: $18,248 (2000); Median household income: $42,434 (2000); Poverty rate: 3.3% (2000).
Education: Percent of population age 25 and over with: High school diploma (including GED) or higher: 87.9% (2000); Bachelor's degree or higher: 18.6% (2000).
Housing: Homeownership rate: 78.7% (2000); Median home value: $89,300 (2000); Median rent: $341 per month (2000); Median age of housing: 34 years (2000).
Transportation: Commute to work: 95.4% car, 1.6% public transportation, 0.0% walk, 1.1% work from home (2000); Travel time to work: 24.8% less than 15 minutes, 17.5% 15 to 30 minutes, 29.7% 30 to 45 minutes, 16.9% 45 to 60 minutes, 11.1% 60 minutes or more (2000)

HUNT (unincorporated postal area, zip code 14846). Aka Washington Hunt. Covers a land area of 33.305 square miles and a water area of 0.315 square miles. Located at 42.54° N. Lat.; 77.99° W. Long.
Population: 0 (2000); Race: 98.9% White, 0.1% Black, 0.0% Asian, 0.5% Hispanic of any race (2000); Density: 0.0 persons per square mile (2000); Age: 28.6% under 18, 9.2% over 64 (2000); Marriage status: 19.4% never married, 63.6% now married, 5.2% widowed, 11.8% divorced (2000); Foreign born: 1.1% (2000); Ancestry (includes multiple ancestries): 33.0% German, 19.4% English, 18.8% Irish, 9.6% Italian, 7.8% Other groups (2000).
Economy: Employment by occupation: 7.8% management, 14.3% professional, 20.0% services, 16.4% sales, 3.6% farming, 17.0% construction, 20.9% production (2000).
Income: Per capita income: $13,486 (2000); Median household income: $34,000 (2000); Poverty rate: 19.0% (2000).
Education: Percent of population age 25 and over with: High school diploma (including GED) or higher: 79.4% (2000); Bachelor's degree or higher: 8.1% (2000).
Housing: Homeownership rate: 87.1% (2000); Median home value: $59,100 (2000); Median rent: $317 per month (2000); Median age of housing: 32 years (2000).
Transportation: Commute to work: 92.5% car, 1.2% public transportation, 1.6% walk, 4.0% work from home (2000); Travel time to work: 27.8% less than 15 minutes, 20.4% 15 to 30 minutes, 22.3% 30 to 45 minutes, 15.5% 45 to 60 minutes, 13.9% 60 minutes or more (2000)

LAKEVILLE (unincorporated postal area, zip code 14480). Covers a land area of 1.426 square miles and a water area of 0 square miles. Located at 42.83° N. Lat.; 77.70° W. Long.

Population: 0 (2000); Race: 93.2% White, 0.0% Black, 0.0% Asian, 0.0% Hispanic of any race (2000); Density: 0.0 persons per square mile (2000); Age: 28.3% under 18, 10.5% over 64 (2000); Marriage status: 24.5% never married, 62.2% now married, 3.0% widowed, 10.3% divorced (2000); Foreign born: 1.2% (2000); Ancestry (includes multiple ancestries): 44.1% German, 29.0% Irish, 12.3% Italian, 11.1% English, 8.4% Other groups (2000).
Economy: Employment by occupation: 8.8% management, 17.8% professional, 15.0% services, 37.0% sales, 0.0% farming, 9.6% construction, 11.9% production (2000).
Income: Per capita income: $18,122 (2000); Median household income: $41,447 (2000); Poverty rate: 12.8% (2000).
Education: Percent of population age 25 and over with: High school diploma (including GED) or higher: 94.6% (2000); Bachelor's degree or higher: 17.5% (2000).
Housing: Homeownership rate: 64.2% (2000); Median home value: $91,100 (2000); Median rent: $551 per month (2000); Median age of housing: 36 years (2000).
Transportation: Commute to work: 88.1% car, 0.0% public transportation, 5.1% walk, 4.5% work from home (2000); Travel time to work: 24.6% less than 15 minutes, 34.6% 15 to 30 minutes, 26.0% 30 to 45 minutes, 10.4% 45 to 60 minutes, 4.4% 60 minutes or more (2000)
Additional Information Contacts
Lakeville Chamber of Commerce . . . . (716) 346-6440
http://www.laccny.org

LEICESTER (village).
Covers a land area of 0.356 square miles and a water area of 0 square miles. Located at 42.77° N. Lat.; 77.89° W. Long.
Population: 502 (1990); 469 (2000); 471 (2005); 462 (2010 projected); Race: 95.5% White, 0.2% Black, 0.0% Asian, 2.5% Hispanic of any race (2005); Density: 1,323.4 persons per square mile (2005); Average household size: 2.63 (2005); Median age: 41.3 (2005); Males per 100 females: 109.3 (2005); Marriage status: 22.8% never married, 63.0% now married, 9.2% widowed, 5.0% divorced (2000); Foreign born: 1.3% (2000); Ancestry (includes multiple ancestries): 28.3% German, 20.4% English, 20.2% Italian, 16.7% Irish, 9.8% Scottish (2000).
Economy: Single-family building permits issued: 0 (2005); Multi-family building permits issued: 0 (2005); Employment by occupation: 8.6% management, 23.6% professional, 13.6% services, 31.4% sales, 0.0% farming, 10.0% construction, 12.7% production (2000).
Income: Per capita income: $19,920 (2005); Median household income: $46,484 (2005); Average household income: $51,411 (2005); Percent of households with income of $100,000 or more: 5.0% (2005); Poverty rate: 13.1% (2000).
Education: Percent of population age 25 and over with: High school diploma (including GED) or higher: 83.4% (2005); Bachelor's degree or higher: 20.6% (2005); Master's degree or higher: 6.7% (2005).
Housing: Homeownership rate: 78.8% (2005); Median home value: $94,186 (2005); Median rent: $531 per month (2000); Median age of housing: 49 years (2000).
Transportation: Commute to work: 98.1% car, 0.0% public transportation, 0.9% walk, 0.9% work from home (2000); Travel time to work: 43.1% less than 15 minutes, 22.7% 15 to 30 minutes, 14.7% 30 to 45 minutes, 10.4% 45 to 60 minutes, 9.0% 60 minutes or more (2000)

LEICESTER (town).
Covers a land area of 33.524 square miles and a water area of 0.005 square miles. Located at 42.77° N. Lat.; 77.90° W. Long.
Population: 2,223 (1990); 2,287 (2000); 2,233 (2005); 2,183 (2010 projected); Race: 97.8% White, 0.8% Black, 0.0% Asian, 1.1% Hispanic of any race (2005); Density: 66.6 persons per square mile (2005); Average household size: 2.65 (2005); Median age: 38.1 (2005); Males per 100 females: 102.1 (2005); Marriage status: 22.1% never married, 62.9% now married, 6.6% widowed, 8.3% divorced (2000); Foreign born: 1.1% (2000); Ancestry (includes multiple ancestries): 31.6% German, 24.7% English, 20.1% Italian, 18.0% Irish, 8.8% Polish (2000).
Economy: Single-family building permits issued: 1 (2005); Multi-family building permits issued: 0 (2005); Employment by occupation: 13.3% management, 20.3% professional, 15.3% services, 20.3% sales, 3.0% farming, 12.3% construction, 15.4% production (2000).
Income: Per capita income: $19,093 (2005); Median household income: $43,768 (2005); Average household income: $50,422 (2005); Percent of households with income of $100,000 or more: 7.1% (2005); Poverty rate: 8.2% (2000).
Education: Percent of population age 25 and over with: High school diploma (including GED) or higher: 78.3% (2005); Bachelor's degree or higher: 15.7% (2005); Master's degree or higher: 5.6% (2005).
Housing: Homeownership rate: 81.8% (2005); Median home value: $90,671 (2005); Median rent: $462 per month (2000); Median age of housing: 38 years (2000).
Transportation: Commute to work: 94.5% car, 0.6% public transportation, 0.6% walk, 4.3% work from home (2000); Travel time to work: 37.7% less than 15 minutes, 21.7% 15 to 30 minutes, 18.7% 30 to 45 minutes, 14.2% 45 to 60 minutes, 7.7% 60 minutes or more (2000)

LIMA (village).
Covers a land area of 1.379 square miles and a water area of 0 square miles. Located at 42.90° N. Lat.; 77.61° W. Long. Elevation is 846 feet.
Population: 2,165 (1990); 2,459 (2000); 2,498 (2005); 2,513 (2010 projected); Race: 96.2% White, 1.4% Black, 0.7% Asian, 1.9% Hispanic of any race (2005); Density: 1,811.7 persons per square mile (2005); Average household size: 3.16 (2005); Median age: 33.0 (2005); Males per 100 females: 95.3 (2005); Marriage status: 31.9% never married, 56.7% now married, 4.6% widowed, 6.7% divorced (2000); Foreign born: 3.8% (2000); Ancestry (includes multiple ancestries): 26.6% German, 25.9% Irish, 19.0% English, 10.5% Italian, 7.9% Other groups (2000).
Economy: Single-family building permits issued: 3 (2005); Multi-family building permits issued: 0 (2005); Employment by occupation: 11.7% management, 25.1% professional, 17.1% services, 27.5% sales, 0.0% farming, 6.0% construction, 12.6% production (2000).
Income: Per capita income: $17,980 (2005); Median household income: $47,038 (2005); Average household income: $52,835 (2005); Percent of households with income of $100,000 or more: 8.1% (2005); Poverty rate: 5.3% (2000).
Education: Percent of population age 25 and over with: High school diploma (including GED) or higher: 91.8% (2005); Bachelor's degree or higher: 28.8% (2005); Master's degree or higher: 9.4% (2005).
School District(s)
Honeoye Falls-Lima Central School District (KG-12)
   2003-04 Enrollment: 2,601 . . . . (585) 624-7010
Housing: Homeownership rate: 65.9% (2005); Median home value: $123,990 (2005); Median rent: $455 per month (2000); Median age of housing: 34 years (2000).
Transportation: Commute to work: 83.0% car, 0.8% public transportation, 13.7% walk, 2.5% work from home (2000); Travel time to work: 39.9% less than 15 minutes, 29.0% 15 to 30 minutes, 26.1% 30 to 45 minutes, 4.3% 45 to 60 minutes, 0.6% 60 minutes or more (2000)

LIMA (town).
Covers a land area of 31.898 square miles and a water area of 0.043 square miles. Located at 42.89° N. Lat.; 77.61° W. Long. Elevation is 846 feet.
Population: 4,187 (1990); 4,541 (2000); 4,529 (2005); 4,528 (2010 projected); Race: 97.2% White, 1.0% Black, 0.4% Asian, 1.3% Hispanic of any race (2005); Density: 142.0 persons per square mile (2005); Average household size: 2.89 (2005); Median age: 37.7 (2005); Males per 100 females: 96.5 (2005); Marriage status: 27.1% never married, 60.0% now married, 5.8% widowed, 7.0% divorced (2000); Foreign born: 3.2% (2000); Ancestry (includes multiple ancestries): 24.9% German, 22.5% Irish, 21.9% English, 10.0% Italian, 6.8% United States or American (2000).
Economy: Makes concrete. Agriculture: wheat, vegetables, and fruits. Single-family building permits issued: 7 (2005); Multi-family building permits issued: 0 (2005); Employment by occupation: 13.6% management, 26.5% professional, 14.0% services, 24.8% sales, 0.4% farming, 6.8% construction, 14.0% production (2000).
Income: Per capita income: $22,040 (2005); Median household income: $53,546 (2005); Average household income: $61,019 (2005); Percent of households with income of $100,000 or more: 14.9% (2005); Poverty rate: 4.5% (2000).
Education: Percent of population age 25 and over with: High school diploma (including GED) or higher: 89.6% (2005); Bachelor's degree or higher: 27.5% (2005); Master's degree or higher: 10.9% (2005).
Housing: Homeownership rate: 76.0% (2005); Median home value: $127,427 (2005); Median rent: $468 per month (2000); Median age of housing: 31 years (2000).
Transportation: Commute to work: 89.5% car, 0.8% public transportation, 7.6% walk, 2.1% work from home (2000); Travel time to work: 33.5% less than 15 minutes, 27.4% 15 to 30 minutes, 30.6% 30 to 45 minutes, 5.9% 45 to 60 minutes, 2.5% 60 minutes or more (2000)

LIVONIA (village). Covers a land area of 1.022 square miles and a water area of 0 square miles. Located at 42.82° N. Lat.; 77.66° W. Long. Elevation is 1,047 feet.
Population: 1,434 (1990); 1,373 (2000); 1,353 (2005); 1,343 (2010 projected); Race: 97.3% White, 1.0% Black, 0.3% Asian, 1.3% Hispanic of any race (2005); Density: 1,323.9 persons per square mile (2005); Average household size: 2.55 (2005); Median age: 35.8 (2005); Males per 100 females: 94.7 (2005); Marriage status: 21.7% never married, 62.9% now married, 6.5% widowed, 8.9% divorced (2000); Foreign born: 1.5% (2000); Ancestry (includes multiple ancestries): 32.1% Irish, 29.3% German, 19.2% English, 12.1% Italian, 7.1% Other groups (2000).
Economy: Single-family building permits issued: 42 (2005); Multi-family building permits issued: 0 (2005); Employment by occupation: 11.0% management, 25.2% professional, 14.9% services, 27.2% sales, 0.3% farming, 10.6% construction, 10.7% production (2000).
Income: Per capita income: $24,085 (2005); Median household income: $51,471 (2005); Average household income: $61,476 (2005); Percent of households with income of $100,000 or more: 14.7% (2005); Poverty rate: 6.0% (2000).
Education: Percent of population age 25 and over with: High school diploma (including GED) or higher: 93.8% (2005); Bachelor's degree or higher: 26.1% (2005); Master's degree or higher: 9.8% (2005).
School District(s)
Livonia Central School District (KG-12)
    2003-04 Enrollment: 2,132 . . . . (585) 346-4000
Housing: Homeownership rate: 67.5% (2005); Median home value: $120,984 (2005); Median rent: $500 per month (2000); Median age of housing: 46 years (2000).
Transportation: Commute to work: 92.7% car, 0.1% public transportation, 3.5% walk, 3.2% work from home (2000); Travel time to work: 28.2% less than 15 minutes, 27.1% 15 to 30 minutes, 30.8% 30 to 45 minutes, 9.7% 45 to 60 minutes, 4.2% 60 minutes or more (2000)

LIVONIA (town). Covers a land area of 38.294 square miles and a water area of 2.708 square miles. Located at 42.81° N. Lat.; 77.65° W. Long. Elevation is 1,047 feet.
Population: 6,804 (1990); 7,286 (2000); 7,266 (2005); 7,265 (2010 projected); Race: 98.0% White, 0.5% Black, 0.3% Asian, 0.9% Hispanic of any race (2005); Density: 189.7 persons per square mile (2005); Average household size: 2.69 (2005); Median age: 38.4 (2005); Males per 100 females: 96.7 (2005); Marriage status: 20.9% never married, 63.0% now married, 6.4% widowed, 9.7% divorced (2000); Foreign born: 1.2% (2000); Ancestry (includes multiple ancestries): 34.7% German, 25.4% Irish, 20.5% English, 13.7% Italian, 6.2% Other groups (2000).
Economy: In agricultural area. Summer residences and recreation. Single-family building permits issued: 59 (2005); Multi-family building permits issued: 0 (2005); Employment by occupation: 10.7% management, 24.4% professional, 14.0% services, 25.4% sales, 0.2% farming, 11.9% construction, 13.3% production (2000).
Income: Per capita income: $22,556 (2005); Median household income: $56,281 (2005); Average household income: $60,328 (2005); Percent of households with income of $100,000 or more: 11.2% (2005); Poverty rate: 5.3% (2000).
Education: Percent of population age 25 and over with: High school diploma (including GED) or higher: 91.8% (2005); Bachelor's degree or higher: 25.9% (2005); Master's degree or higher: 9.7% (2005).
Housing: Homeownership rate: 81.8% (2005); Median home value: $117,949 (2005); Median rent: $479 per month (2000); Median age of housing: 35 years (2000).
Transportation: Commute to work: 95.7% car, 0.3% public transportation, 1.6% walk, 2.1% work from home (2000); Travel time to work: 20.2% less than 15 minutes, 26.6% 15 to 30 minutes, 37.6% 30 to 45 minutes, 11.6% 45 to 60 minutes, 4.0% 60 minutes or more (2000)

MOUNT MORRIS (village). Covers a land area of 2.034 square miles and a water area of 0 square miles. Located at 42.72° N. Lat.; 77.87° W. Long. Elevation is 626 feet.
Population: 3,102 (1990); 3,266 (2000); 3,159 (2005); 3,056 (2010 projected); Race: 94.4% White, 0.9% Black, 0.9% Asian, 6.5% Hispanic of any race (2005); Density: 1,553.3 persons per square mile (2005); Average household size: 2.54 (2005); Median age: 39.6 (2005); Males per 100 females: 88.0 (2005); Marriage status: 29.8% never married, 42.3% now married, 12.2% widowed, 15.8% divorced (2000); Foreign born: 5.2% (2000); Ancestry (includes multiple ancestries): 34.1% Italian, 18.8% German, 17.8% Irish, 11.8% Other groups, 9.9% English (2000).
Economy: Single-family building permits issued: 5 (2005); Multi-family building permits issued: 0 (2005); Employment by occupation: 9.2% management, 17.7% professional, 22.2% services, 23.2% sales, 4.5% farming, 10.7% construction, 12.5% production (2000).
Income: Per capita income: $15,848 (2005); Median household income: $33,200 (2005); Average household income: $39,147 (2005); Percent of households with income of $100,000 or more: 3.6% (2005); Poverty rate: 14.3% (2000).
Education: Percent of population age 25 and over with: High school diploma (including GED) or higher: 73.1% (2005); Bachelor's degree or higher: 13.8% (2005); Master's degree or higher: 5.5% (2005).
School District(s)
Mount Morris Central School District (KG-12)
    2003-04 Enrollment: 649 . . . . (585) 658-2568
Housing: Homeownership rate: 59.8% (2005); Median home value: $76,651 (2005); Median rent: $405 per month (2000); Median age of housing: 60+ years (2000).
Safety: Violent crime rate: 46.8 per 10,000 population; Property crime rate: 371.4 per 10,000 population (2004).
Transportation: Commute to work: 96.1% car, 0.4% public transportation, 0.8% walk, 2.3% work from home (2000); Travel time to work: 44.4% less than 15 minutes, 24.1% 15 to 30 minutes, 12.8% 30 to 45 minutes, 11.3% 45 to 60 minutes, 7.4% 60 minutes or more (2000)
Additional Information Contacts
Village of Mount Morris . . . . (585) 658-4160
    http://www.villageofmountmorris.com/

MOUNT MORRIS (town). Covers a land area of 50.677 square miles and a water area of 0.060 square miles. Located at 42.67° N. Lat.; 77.88° W. Long. Elevation is 626 feet.
Population: 4,633 (1990); 4,567 (2000); 4,406 (2005); 4,276 (2010 projected); Race: 95.3% White, 0.7% Black, 0.7% Asian, 5.0% Hispanic of any race (2005); Density: 86.9 persons per square mile (2005); Average household size: 2.58 (2005); Median age: 39.6 (2005); Males per 100 females: 93.5 (2005); Marriage status: 29.4% never married, 45.4% now married, 10.9% widowed, 14.3% divorced (2000); Foreign born: 3.9% (2000); Ancestry (includes multiple ancestries): 29.3% Italian, 19.8% German, 17.5% Irish, 10.1% Other groups, 9.1% English (2000).
Economy: Mt. Morris Dam for flood control is on the Genesee here. Single-family building permits issued: 2 (2005); Multi-family building permits issued: 0 (2005); Employment by occupation: 10.4% management, 17.0% professional, 19.9% services, 22.9% sales, 3.1% farming, 10.6% construction, 16.1% production (2000).
Income: Per capita income: $16,858 (2005); Median household income: $35,044 (2005); Average household income: $42,661 (2005); Percent of households with income of $100,000 or more: 4.9% (2005); Poverty rate: 13.1% (2000).
Education: Percent of population age 25 and over with: High school diploma (including GED) or higher: 73.3% (2005); Bachelor's degree or higher: 12.7% (2005); Master's degree or higher: 5.2% (2005).
Housing: Homeownership rate: 66.4% (2005); Median home value: $78,767 (2005); Median rent: $403 per month (2000); Median age of housing: 53 years (2000).
Transportation: Commute to work: 94.7% car, 0.5% public transportation, 1.0% walk, 3.6% work from home (2000); Travel time to work: 41.2% less than 15 minutes, 27.3% 15 to 30 minutes, 14.6% 30 to 45 minutes, 10.8% 45 to 60 minutes, 6.1% 60 minutes or more (2000)

NORTH DANSVILLE (town). Covers a land area of 9.827 square miles and a water area of 0 square miles. Located at 42.56° N. Lat.; 77.69° W. Long.
Population: 5,783 (1990); 5,738 (2000); 5,528 (2005); 5,310 (2010 projected); Race: 96.0% White, 1.0% Black, 0.7% Asian, 2.1% Hispanic of any race (2005); Density: 562.6 persons per square mile (2005); Average household size: 2.50 (2005); Median age: 39.5 (2005); Males per 100 females: 90.2 (2005); Marriage status: 26.9% never married, 53.2% now married, 9.6% widowed, 10.3% divorced (2000); Foreign born: 2.2% (2000); Ancestry (includes multiple ancestries): 34.7% German, 21.0% Irish, 16.1% English, 7.4% United States or American, 5.7% Italian (2000).
Economy: Single-family building permits issued: 3 (2005); Multi-family building permits issued: 0 (2005); Employment by occupation: 9.2% management, 14.6% professional, 16.2% services, 26.9% sales, 1.1% farming, 9.9% construction, 22.2% production (2000).

Income: Per capita income: $16,941 (2005); Median household income: $34,058 (2005); Average household income: $41,390 (2005); Percent of households with income of $100,000 or more: 6.3% (2005); Poverty rate: 15.4% (2000).
Education: Percent of population age 25 and over with: High school diploma (including GED) or higher: 81.7% (2005); Bachelor's degree or higher: 12.6% (2005); Master's degree or higher: 4.7% (2005).
Housing: Homeownership rate: 63.1% (2005); Median home value: $82,357 (2005); Median rent: $392 per month (2000); Median age of housing: 60+ years (2000).
Transportation: Commute to work: 87.6% car, 1.1% public transportation, 7.1% walk, 4.2% work from home (2000); Travel time to work: 48.5% less than 15 minutes, 22.3% 15 to 30 minutes, 10.3% 30 to 45 minutes, 10.8% 45 to 60 minutes, 8.2% 60 minutes or more (2000)

NUNDA (village).
Covers a land area of 0.985 square miles and a water area of 0 square miles. Located at 42.58° N. Lat.; 77.93° W. Long. Elevation is 944 feet.
Population: 1,379 (1990); 1,330 (2000); 1,312 (2005); 1,283 (2010 projected); Race: 97.8% White, 0.2% Black, 0.4% Asian, 0.8% Hispanic of any race (2005); Density: 1,331.6 persons per square mile (2005); Average household size: 2.60 (2005); Median age: 37.6 (2005); Males per 100 females: 90.7 (2005); Marriage status: 23.6% never married, 55.8% now married, 10.8% widowed, 9.9% divorced (2000); Foreign born: 0.5% (2000); Ancestry (includes multiple ancestries): 28.0% German, 25.3% Irish, 21.5% English, 9.0% Italian, 6.7% Other groups (2000).
Economy: Single-family building permits issued: 0 (2005); Multi-family building permits issued: 0 (2005); Employment by occupation: 9.3% management, 16.8% professional, 19.6% services, 22.0% sales, 2.7% farming, 14.1% construction, 15.5% production (2000).
Income: Per capita income: $20,689 (2005); Median household income: $44,353 (2005); Average household income: $51,429 (2005); Percent of households with income of $100,000 or more: 9.1% (2005); Poverty rate: 12.7% (2000).
Education: Percent of population age 25 and over with: High school diploma (including GED) or higher: 86.7% (2005); Bachelor's degree or higher: 11.2% (2005); Master's degree or higher: 4.5% (2005).

School District(s)
Dalton-Nunda Central School District (Keshequa) (KG-12)
    2003-04 Enrollment: 936 . . . . (585) 468-2541

Housing: Homeownership rate: 62.7% (2005); Median home value: $82,195 (2005); Median rent: $352 per month (2000); Median age of housing: 60+ years (2000).
Transportation: Commute to work: 88.2% car, 1.0% public transportation, 5.5% walk, 4.8% work from home (2000); Travel time to work: 32.3% less than 15 minutes, 30.0% 15 to 30 minutes, 16.5% 30 to 45 minutes, 8.4% 45 to 60 minutes, 12.7% 60 minutes or more (2000)

NUNDA (town).
Covers a land area of 37.061 square miles and a water area of 0.031 square miles. Located at 42.57° N. Lat.; 77.92° W. Long. Elevation is 944 feet.
History: Incorporated 1839.
Population: 2,931 (1990); 3,017 (2000); 2,978 (2005); 2,943 (2010 projected); Race: 98.1% White, 0.5% Black, 0.2% Asian, 0.8% Hispanic of any race (2005); Density: 80.4 persons per square mile (2005); Average household size: 2.63 (2005); Median age: 37.7 (2005); Males per 100 females: 97.6 (2005); Marriage status: 22.9% never married, 60.9% now married, 7.3% widowed, 9.0% divorced (2000); Foreign born: 0.6% (2000); Ancestry (includes multiple ancestries): 26.3% German, 20.7% Irish, 20.3% English, 10.1% Italian, 7.2% United States or American (2000).
Economy: Manufacturing: canned foods, dairy products, machinery. Agriculture: poultry; grain. Single-family building permits issued: 4 (2005); Multi-family building permits issued: 0 (2005); Employment by occupation: 9.7% management, 14.9% professional, 19.8% services, 17.3% sales, 2.2% farming, 18.1% construction, 18.0% production (2000).
Income: Per capita income: $19,777 (2005); Median household income: $43,787 (2005); Average household income: $50,945 (2005); Percent of households with income of $100,000 or more: 8.1% (2005); Poverty rate: 9.1% (2000).
Education: Percent of population age 25 and over with: High school diploma (including GED) or higher: 83.8% (2005); Bachelor's degree or higher: 12.1% (2005); Master's degree or higher: 5.1% (2005).
Housing: Homeownership rate: 77.3% (2005); Median home value: $79,440 (2005); Median rent: $368 per month (2000); Median age of housing: 58 years (2000).

Safety: Violent crime rate: 0.0 per 10,000 population; Property crime rate: 132.0 per 10,000 population (2004).
Transportation: Commute to work: 91.3% car, 0.7% public transportation, 3.6% walk, 4.2% work from home (2000); Travel time to work: 29.5% less than 15 minutes, 26.6% 15 to 30 minutes, 20.3% 30 to 45 minutes, 9.3% 45 to 60 minutes, 14.3% 60 minutes or more (2000)

OSSIAN (town).
Covers a land area of 39.635 square miles and a water area of 0.036 square miles. Located at 42.52° N. Lat.; 77.78° W. Long.
Population: 797 (1990); 751 (2000); 714 (2005); 696 (2010 projected); Race: 99.2% White, 0.3% Black, 0.0% Asian, 0.0% Hispanic of any race (2005); Density: 18.0 persons per square mile (2005); Average household size: 2.71 (2005); Median age: 39.9 (2005); Males per 100 females: 113.1 (2005); Marriage status: 19.4% never married, 69.6% now married, 4.4% widowed, 6.6% divorced (2000); Foreign born: 1.3% (2000); Ancestry (includes multiple ancestries): 35.2% German, 20.1% Irish, 16.5% English, 14.9% United States or American, 7.5% Italian (2000).
Economy: Single-family building permits issued: 2 (2005); Multi-family building permits issued: 0 (2005); Employment by occupation: 9.9% management, 19.1% professional, 13.6% services, 24.0% sales, 0.8% farming, 13.8% construction, 18.8% production (2000).
Income: Per capita income: $22,178 (2005); Median household income: $54,529 (2005); Average household income: $59,895 (2005); Percent of households with income of $100,000 or more: 12.2% (2005); Poverty rate: 6.5% (2000).
Education: Percent of population age 25 and over with: High school diploma (including GED) or higher: 84.9% (2005); Bachelor's degree or higher: 9.7% (2005); Master's degree or higher: 3.0% (2005).
Housing: Homeownership rate: 87.8% (2005); Median home value: $98,205 (2005); Median rent: $413 per month (2000); Median age of housing: 44 years (2000).
Transportation: Commute to work: 92.5% car, 0.0% public transportation, 1.9% walk, 5.1% work from home (2000); Travel time to work: 26.0% less than 15 minutes, 25.4% 15 to 30 minutes, 25.1% 30 to 45 minutes, 8.5% 45 to 60 minutes, 15.0% 60 minutes or more (2000)

PIFFARD (unincorporated postal area, zip code 14533).
Covers a land area of 30.243 square miles and a water area of 0.007 square miles. Located at 42.84° N. Lat.; 77.88° W. Long. Elevation is 569 feet.
Population: 0 (2000); Race: 96.3% White, 1.1% Black, 2.5% Asian, 0.0% Hispanic of any race (2000); Density: 0.0 persons per square mile (2000); Age: 25.2% under 18, 14.0% over 64 (2000); Marriage status: 23.5% never married, 64.3% now married, 5.4% widowed, 6.8% divorced (2000); Foreign born: 2.3% (2000); Ancestry (includes multiple ancestries): 27.3% German, 26.2% Irish, 17.7% Italian, 11.5% English, 10.0% United States or American (2000).
Economy: Employment by occupation: 8.7% management, 11.1% professional, 17.4% services, 28.8% sales, 1.1% farming, 12.0% construction, 20.9% production (2000).
Income: Per capita income: $20,713 (2000); Median household income: $43,897 (2000); Poverty rate: 2.3% (2000).
Education: Percent of population age 25 and over with: High school diploma (including GED) or higher: 85.6% (2000); Bachelor's degree or higher: 12.3% (2000).
Housing: Homeownership rate: 80.4% (2000); Median home value: $85,600 (2000); Median rent: $455 per month (2000); Median age of housing: 44 years (2000).
Transportation: Commute to work: 91.2% car, 0.0% public transportation, 3.8% walk, 5.0% work from home (2000); Travel time to work: 32.2% less than 15 minutes, 32.1% 15 to 30 minutes, 17.8% 30 to 45 minutes, 12.8% 45 to 60 minutes, 5.2% 60 minutes or more (2000)

PORTAGE (town).
Covers a land area of 26.372 square miles and a water area of 0.255 square miles. Located at 42.55° N. Lat.; 77.98° W. Long.
Population: 893 (1990); 859 (2000); 866 (2005); 875 (2010 projected); Race: 97.6% White, 0.1% Black, 0.5% Asian, 0.8% Hispanic of any race (2005); Density: 32.8 persons per square mile (2005); Average household size: 2.75 (2005); Median age: 36.5 (2005); Males per 100 females: 99.1 (2005); Marriage status: 23.3% never married, 59.3% now married, 6.3% widowed, 11.2% divorced (2000); Foreign born: 0.7% (2000); Ancestry (includes multiple ancestries): 31.2% German, 21.8% English, 18.9% Irish, 10.2% Other groups, 6.8% United States or American (2000).
Economy: Single-family building permits issued: 5 (2005); Multi-family building permits issued: 0 (2005); Employment by occupation: 7.0%

management, 8.8% professional, 21.2% services, 19.8% sales, 2.9% farming, 14.7% construction, 25.5% production (2000).
Income: Per capita income: $15,811 (2005); Median household income: $36,038 (2005); Average household income: $42,802 (2005); Percent of households with income of $100,000 or more: 4.8% (2005); Poverty rate: 14.0% (2000).
Education: Percent of population age 25 and over with: High school diploma (including GED) or higher: 81.0% (2005); Bachelor's degree or higher: 7.2% (2005); Master's degree or higher: 2.7% (2005).
Housing: Homeownership rate: 83.8% (2005); Median home value: $71,429 (2005); Median rent: $300 per month (2000); Median age of housing: 50 years (2000).
Transportation: Commute to work: 93.7% car, 0.0% public transportation, 1.1% walk, 4.7% work from home (2000); Travel time to work: 32.9% less than 15 minutes, 24.5% 15 to 30 minutes, 18.4% 30 to 45 minutes, 11.8% 45 to 60 minutes, 12.4% 60 minutes or more (2000)

SCOTTSBURG (unincorporated postal area, zip code 14545). Covers a land area of 2.060 square miles and a water area of 0 square miles. Located at 42.66° N. Lat.; 77.71° W. Long.
Population: 0 (2000); Race: 96.3% White, 0.0% Black, 0.0% Asian, 0.0% Hispanic of any race (2000); Density: 0.0 persons per square mile (2000); Age: 25.9% under 18, 11.1% over 64 (2000); Marriage status: 22.2% never married, 68.2% now married, 7.1% widowed, 2.5% divorced (2000); Foreign born: 1.2% (2000); Ancestry (includes multiple ancestries): 42.4% German, 25.9% Irish, 14.8% Dutch, 14.0% English, 10.7% United States or American (2000).
Economy: Employment by occupation: 2.5% management, 21.3% professional, 23.8% services, 10.7% sales, 0.0% farming, 4.1% construction, 37.7% production (2000).
Income: Per capita income: $17,090 (2000); Median household income: $47,083 (2000); Poverty rate: 5.1% (2000).
Education: Percent of population age 25 and over with: High school diploma (including GED) or higher: 80.5% (2000); Bachelor's degree or higher: 4.1% (2000).
Housing: Homeownership rate: 90.6% (2000); Median home value: $67,900 (2000); Median rent: $500 per month (2000); Median age of housing: 50 years (2000).
Transportation: Commute to work: 91.8% car, 0.0% public transportation, 3.3% walk, 3.3% work from home (2000); Travel time to work: 12.7% less than 15 minutes, 41.5% 15 to 30 minutes, 10.2% 30 to 45 minutes, 23.7% 45 to 60 minutes, 11.9% 60 minutes or more (2000)

SPARTA (town). Covers a land area of 27.743 square miles and a water area of 0 square miles. Located at 42.62° N. Lat.; 77.70° W. Long.
Population: 1,578 (1990); 1,627 (2000); 1,698 (2005); 1,726 (2010 projected); Race: 97.2% White, 0.4% Black, 0.9% Asian, 0.3% Hispanic of any race (2005); Density: 61.2 persons per square mile (2005); Average household size: 2.69 (2005); Median age: 41.9 (2005); Males per 100 females: 106.6 (2005); Marriage status: 18.4% never married, 69.9% now married, 4.2% widowed, 7.5% divorced (2000); Foreign born: 1.6% (2000); Ancestry (includes multiple ancestries): 32.1% German, 21.0% Irish, 13.9% English, 9.8% United States or American, 8.3% Dutch (2000).
Economy: Single-family building permits issued: 1 (2005); Multi-family building permits issued: 0 (2005); Employment by occupation: 6.0% management, 18.5% professional, 15.6% services, 22.5% sales, 2.2% farming, 10.4% construction, 24.7% production (2000).
Income: Per capita income: $20,638 (2005); Median household income: $47,898 (2005); Average household income: $55,535 (2005); Percent of households with income of $100,000 or more: 9.7% (2005); Poverty rate: 10.2% (2000).
Education: Percent of population age 25 and over with: High school diploma (including GED) or higher: 86.1% (2005); Bachelor's degree or higher: 12.7% (2005); Master's degree or higher: 5.7% (2005).
Housing: Homeownership rate: 91.8% (2005); Median home value: $96,486 (2005); Median rent: $379 per month (2000); Median age of housing: 32 years (2000).
Transportation: Commute to work: 95.2% car, 0.0% public transportation, 1.3% walk, 3.2% work from home (2000); Travel time to work: 22.7% less than 15 minutes, 30.3% 15 to 30 minutes, 17.9% 30 to 45 minutes, 16.5% 45 to 60 minutes, 12.6% 60 minutes or more (2000)

SPRINGWATER (town). Covers a land area of 53.272 square miles and a water area of 0.040 square miles. Located at 42.63° N. Lat.; 77.57° W. Long. Elevation is 970 feet.
Population: 2,407 (1990); 2,322 (2000); 2,330 (2005); 2,345 (2010 projected); Race: 96.8% White, 0.4% Black, 0.7% Asian, 0.4% Hispanic of any race (2005); Density: 43.7 persons per square mile (2005); Average household size: 2.62 (2005); Median age: 41.1 (2005); Males per 100 females: 107.9 (2005); Marriage status: 23.6% never married, 61.3% now married, 5.5% widowed, 9.5% divorced (2000); Foreign born: 0.9% (2000); Ancestry (includes multiple ancestries): 29.0% German, 19.3% Irish, 14.5% English, 9.6% Italian, 8.9% United States or American (2000).
Economy: Single-family building permits issued: 4 (2005); Multi-family building permits issued: 0 (2005); Employment by occupation: 9.5% management, 17.9% professional, 14.7% services, 17.9% sales, 0.4% farming, 14.9% construction, 24.8% production (2000).
Income: Per capita income: $20,572 (2005); Median household income: $46,318 (2005); Average household income: $52,548 (2005); Percent of households with income of $100,000 or more: 8.8% (2005); Poverty rate: 9.4% (2000).
Education: Percent of population age 25 and over with: High school diploma (including GED) or higher: 81.4% (2005); Bachelor's degree or higher: 12.9% (2005); Master's degree or higher: 4.3% (2005).
Housing: Homeownership rate: 87.6% (2005); Median home value: $82,216 (2005); Median rent: $348 per month (2000); Median age of housing: 27 years (2000).
Transportation: Commute to work: 94.6% car, 0.0% public transportation, 0.8% walk, 3.4% work from home (2000); Travel time to work: 15.4% less than 15 minutes, 23.9% 15 to 30 minutes, 18.6% 30 to 45 minutes, 20.9% 45 to 60 minutes, 21.2% 60 minutes or more (2000)

WEST SPARTA (town). Covers a land area of 33.443 square miles and a water area of 0 square miles. Located at 42.61° N. Lat.; 77.77° W. Long. Elevation is 1,613 feet.
Population: 1,335 (1990); 1,244 (2000); 1,188 (2005); 1,159 (2010 projected); Race: 98.6% White, 0.0% Black, 0.5% Asian, 0.3% Hispanic of any race (2005); Density: 35.5 persons per square mile (2005); Average household size: 2.71 (2005); Median age: 38.8 (2005); Males per 100 females: 101.0 (2005); Marriage status: 22.6% never married, 60.1% now married, 5.4% widowed, 11.9% divorced (2000); Foreign born: 0.7% (2000); Ancestry (includes multiple ancestries): 30.2% German, 19.7% Irish, 13.1% United States or American, 12.6% English, 7.6% Italian (2000).
Economy: Single-family building permits issued: 3 (2005); Multi-family building permits issued: 0 (2005); Employment by occupation: 9.5% management, 12.4% professional, 20.1% services, 21.6% sales, 1.8% farming, 15.6% construction, 19.0% production (2000).
Income: Per capita income: $19,277 (2005); Median household income: $46,443 (2005); Average household income: $52,277 (2005); Percent of households with income of $100,000 or more: 8.4% (2005); Poverty rate: 8.9% (2000).
Education: Percent of population age 25 and over with: High school diploma (including GED) or higher: 79.6% (2005); Bachelor's degree or higher: 9.2% (2005); Master's degree or higher: 4.3% (2005).
Housing: Homeownership rate: 87.2% (2005); Median home value: $73,333 (2005); Median rent: $427 per month (2000); Median age of housing: 25 years (2000).
Transportation: Commute to work: 93.9% car, 0.5% public transportation, 1.5% walk, 3.6% work from home (2000); Travel time to work: 24.1% less than 15 minutes, 31.0% 15 to 30 minutes, 18.2% 30 to 45 minutes, 15.9% 45 to 60 minutes, 10.8% 60 minutes or more (2000)

YORK (town). Covers a land area of 49.059 square miles and a water area of 0.007 square miles. Located at 42.85° N. Lat.; 77.89° W. Long. Elevation is 787 feet.
Population: 3,513 (1990); 3,219 (2000); 3,232 (2005); 3,268 (2010 projected); Race: 97.7% White, 0.7% Black, 0.8% Asian, 0.8% Hispanic of any race (2005); Density: 65.9 persons per square mile (2005); Average household size: 2.68 (2005); Median age: 39.4 (2005); Males per 100 females: 102.1 (2005); Marriage status: 24.3% never married, 61.9% now married, 6.4% widowed, 7.5% divorced (2000); Foreign born: 3.8% (2000); Ancestry (includes multiple ancestries): 30.7% Irish, 22.7% German, 16.1% English, 14.9% Italian, 7.4% French (except Basque) (2000).
Economy: Single-family building permits issued: 5 (2005); Multi-family building permits issued: 0 (2005); Employment by occupation: 11.5% management, 9.5% professional, 17.9% services, 26.5% sales, 2.7% farming, 10.6% construction, 21.4% production (2000).
Income: Per capita income: $23,472 (2005); Median household income: $51,111 (2005); Average household income: $62,888 (2005); Percent of

households with income of $100,000 or more: 12.3% (2005); Poverty rate: 1.8% (2000).
Education: Percent of population age 25 and over with: High school diploma (including GED) or higher: 84.2% (2005); Bachelor's degree or higher: 12.5% (2005); Master's degree or higher: 3.5% (2005).
Housing: Homeownership rate: 81.4% (2005); Median home value: $108,962 (2005); Median rent: $466 per month (2000); Median age of housing: 47 years (2000).
Transportation: Commute to work: 89.1% car, 0.0% public transportation, 5.0% walk, 5.9% work from home (2000); Travel time to work: 32.0% less than 15 minutes, 31.5% 15 to 30 minutes, 19.9% 30 to 45 minutes, 11.7% 45 to 60 minutes, 4.8% 60 minutes or more (2000)

Madison County

Located in central New York; drained by the Chenango and Unadilla Rivers; includes Cazenovia Lake, part of Oneida Lake, and other lakes. Covers a land area of 655.86 square miles, a water area of 5.69 square miles, and is located in the Eastern Time Zone. The county government was organized in 1806. County seat is Wampsville.

Madison County is part of the Syracuse, NY Metropolitan Statistical Area. The entire metro area includes: Madison County, NY; Onondaga County, NY; Oswego County, NY

Population: 69,120 (1990); 69,441 (2000); 70,631 (2005); 71,833 (2010 projected); Race: 96.0% White, 1.5% Black, 0.8% Asian, 1.5% Hispanic of any race (2005); Density: 107.7 persons per square mile (2005); Average household size: 2.69 (2005); Median age: 37.7 (2005); Males per 100 females: 96.3 (2005).
Religion: Five largest groups: 18.2% Catholic Church, 7.7% The United Methodist Church, 4.1% American Baptist Churches in the USA, 2.3% Presbyterian Church (U.S.A.), 1.3% Episcopal Church (2000).
Economy: Unemployment rate: 5.1% (2005); Total civilian labor force: 36,184 (2005); Leading industries: 13.9% health care and social assistance; 13.6% retail trade; 13.3% manufacturing (2003); Farms: 734 totaling 168,264 acres (2002); Companies that employ 500 or more persons: 4 (2003); Companies that employ 100 to 499 persons: 22 (2003); Companies that employ less than 100 persons: 1,416 (2003); Black-owned businesses: n/a (2002); Hispanic-owned businesses: n/a (2002); Women-owned businesses: 729 (2002); Retail sales per capita: $10,659 (2006); Single-family building permits issued: 186 (2005); Multi-family building permits issued: 28 (2005).
Income: Per capita income: $22,194 (2005); Median household income: $45,771 (2005); Average household income: $58,815 (2005); Percent of households with income of $100,000 or more: 13.2% (2005); Poverty rate: 10.4% (2003); Bankruptcy rate: 7.05% (2005).
Education: Percent of population age 25 and over with: High school diploma (including GED) or higher: 83.4% (2005); Bachelor's degree or higher: 21.8% (2005); Master's degree or higher: 8.8% (2005).
Housing: Homeownership rate: 75.5% (2005); Median home value: $105,023 (2005); Median rent: $422 per month (2000); Median age of housing: 43 years (2000).
Health: Birth rate: 94.3 per 10,000 population (2004); Death rate: 86.9 per 10,000 population (2004); Age-adjusted cancer mortality rate: 221.8 deaths per 100,000 population (2002); Air Quality Index: 94.5% good, 5.5% moderate, 0.0% unhealthy for sensitive individuals, 0.0% unhealthy (percent of days in 2005); Number of physicians: 15.1 per 10,000 population (2004); Hospital beds: 49.1 per 10,000 population (2003); Hospital admissions: 889.2 per 10,000 population (2003).
Elections: 2004 Presidential election results: 54.6% Bush, 43.3% Kerry, 1.8% Nader, 0.3% Badnarik
National and State Parks: Chittenango Falls State Park
Additional Information Contacts
Madison County Government . . . . (315) 366-2011
    http://www.madisoncounty.org/
City of Oneida . . . . (315) 363-4800
    http://www.ci.oneida.ny.us/
Village of Canastota . . . . (315) 697-7559
    http://www.village.canastota.ny.us/
Village of Chittenango . . . . (315) 687-3936
    http://chittenango.org/

Madison County Communities

BOUCKVILLE (unincorporated postal area, zip code 13310). Covers a land area of 7.360 square miles and a water area of 0.070 square miles. Located at 42.88° N. Lat.; 75.56° W. Long. Elevation is 1,150 feet.
Population: 0 (2000); Race: 100.0% White, 0.0% Black, 0.0% Asian, 0.0% Hispanic of any race (2000); Density: 0.0 persons per square mile (2000); Age: 19.1% under 18, 28.2% over 64 (2000); Marriage status: 20.2% never married, 46.3% now married, 9.0% widowed, 24.4% divorced (2000); Foreign born: 0.0% (2000); Ancestry (includes multiple ancestries): 22.8% English, 18.6% German, 18.3% Italian, 15.6% Irish, 7.9% French (except Basque) (2000).
Economy: Employment by occupation: 15.7% management, 18.2% professional, 16.7% services, 21.7% sales, 0.0% farming, 20.2% construction, 7.6% production (2000).
Income: Per capita income: $17,652 (2000); Median household income: $26,827 (2000); Poverty rate: 8.7% (2000).
Education: Percent of population age 25 and over with: High school diploma (including GED) or higher: 83.8% (2000); Bachelor's degree or higher: 22.2% (2000).
Housing: Homeownership rate: 77.0% (2000); Median home value: $84,100 (2000); Median rent: $225 per month (2000); Median age of housing: 37 years (2000).
Transportation: Commute to work: 85.9% car, 0.0% public transportation, 7.1% walk, 7.1% work from home (2000); Travel time to work: 45.1% less than 15 minutes, 22.3% 15 to 30 minutes, 13.0% 30 to 45 minutes, 7.1% 45 to 60 minutes, 12.5% 60 minutes or more (2000)

BROOKFIELD (town). Covers a land area of 77.947 square miles and a water area of 0.097 square miles. Located at 42.80° N. Lat.; 75.34° W. Long.
Population: 2,225 (1990); 2,403 (2000); 2,463 (2005); 2,525 (2010 projected); Race: 97.9% White, 0.7% Black, 0.6% Asian, 0.5% Hispanic of any race (2005); Density: 31.6 persons per square mile (2005); Average household size: 2.68 (2005); Median age: 36.9 (2005); Males per 100 females: 99.4 (2005); Marriage status: 21.4% never married, 61.0% now married, 7.4% widowed, 10.2% divorced (2000); Foreign born: 1.5% (2000); Ancestry (includes multiple ancestries): 23.1% English, 15.3% Irish, 13.7% United States or American, 11.2% German, 6.3% Welsh (2000).
Economy: Single-family building permits issued: 5 (2005); Multi-family building permits issued: 0 (2005); Employment by occupation: 11.4% management, 12.5% professional, 21.3% services, 20.0% sales, 3.9% farming, 13.4% construction, 17.6% production (2000).
Income: Per capita income: $14,880 (2005); Median household income: $33,735 (2005); Average household income: $39,880 (2005); Percent of households with income of $100,000 or more: 3.4% (2005); Poverty rate: 13.9% (2000).
Education: Percent of population age 25 and over with: High school diploma (including GED) or higher: 77.4% (2005); Bachelor's degree or higher: 9.2% (2005); Master's degree or higher: 4.2% (2005).
School District(s)
Brookfield Central School District (KG-12)
    2003-04 Enrollment: 255 . . . . (315) 899-3323
Housing: Homeownership rate: 85.6% (2005); Median home value: $60,724 (2005); Median rent: $348 per month (2000); Median age of housing: 37 years (2000).
Transportation: Commute to work: 87.7% car, 0.0% public transportation, 4.1% walk, 8.1% work from home (2000); Travel time to work: 18.7% less than 15 minutes, 31.4% 15 to 30 minutes, 33.7% 30 to 45 minutes, 10.4% 45 to 60 minutes, 5.7% 60 minutes or more (2000)

CANASTOTA (village). Covers a land area of 3.321 square miles and a water area of 0 square miles. Located at 43.08° N. Lat.; 75.75° W. Long.
History: International Boxing Hall of Fame is here. Incorporated 1835.
Population: 4,673 (1990); 4,425 (2000); 4,393 (2005); 4,389 (2010 projected); Race: 97.3% White, 0.8% Black, 0.4% Asian, 1.5% Hispanic of any race (2005); Density: 1,322.6 persons per square mile (2005); Average household size: 2.31 (2005); Median age: 38.5 (2005); Males per 100 females: 89.4 (2005); Marriage status: 23.0% never married, 53.6% now married, 11.5% widowed, 11.9% divorced (2000); Foreign born: 3.0% (2000); Ancestry (includes multiple ancestries): 30.5% Italian, 17.1% German, 15.7% Irish, 13.2% English, 9.5% United States or American (2000).
Economy: Manufacturing: medical products, plastic products, machinery, limestone products. In potato, bean, onion and sweet corn-growing area.

Single-family building permits issued: 2 (2005); Multi-family building permits issued: 0 (2005); Employment by occupation: 7.9% management, 13.9% professional, 15.9% services, 30.4% sales, 0.8% farming, 9.7% construction, 21.5% production (2000).
Income: Per capita income: $18,608 (2005); Median household income: $37,960 (2005); Average household income: $42,755 (2005); Percent of households with income of $100,000 or more: 5.0% (2005); Poverty rate: 14.8% (2000).
Education: Percent of population age 25 and over with: High school diploma (including GED) or higher: 75.6% (2005); Bachelor's degree or higher: 16.1% (2005); Master's degree or higher: 3.7% (2005).

School District(s)
Canastota Central School District (KG-12)
   2003-04 Enrollment: 1,547 . . . . (315) 697-2025

Housing: Homeownership rate: 58.6% (2005); Median home value: $91,216 (2005); Median rent: $380 per month (2000); Median age of housing: 52 years (2000).
Newspapers: Canastota Bee-Journal (General - Circulation 2,050); Indian Country Today (Canastota) (Native American - Circulation 17,000)
Transportation: Commute to work: 88.6% car, 0.4% public transportation, 7.0% walk, 3.1% work from home (2000); Travel time to work: 36.6% less than 15 minutes, 28.7% 15 to 30 minutes, 25.6% 30 to 45 minutes, 7.0% 45 to 60 minutes, 2.1% 60 minutes or more (2000)
Additional Information Contacts
Canastota Chamber of Commerce . . . . (315) 697-3677
   http://www.canastota.org
Village of Canastota . . . . (315) 697-7559
   http://www.village.canastota.ny.us/

CAZENOVIA (village). Covers a land area of 1.574 square miles and a water area of 0 square miles. Located at 42.93° N. Lat.; 75.85° W. Long. Elevation is 1,182 feet.
Population: 3,050 (1990); 2,614 (2000); 2,733 (2005); 2,837 (2010 projected); Race: 94.4% White, 2.9% Black, 0.7% Asian, 4.4% Hispanic of any race (2005); Density: 1,735.9 persons per square mile (2005); Average household size: 2.73 (2005); Median age: 32.6 (2005); Males per 100 females: 74.4 (2005); Marriage status: 31.0% never married, 55.5% now married, 8.5% widowed, 5.0% divorced (2000); Foreign born: 3.9% (2000); Ancestry (includes multiple ancestries): 20.9% Irish, 20.9% German, 17.1% English, 8.5% Italian, 5.4% Other groups (2000).
Economy: Single-family building permits issued: 11 (2005); Multi-family building permits issued: 0 (2005); Employment by occupation: 14.5% management, 31.4% professional, 13.2% services, 28.5% sales, 1.1% farming, 7.2% construction, 4.2% production (2000).
Income: Per capita income: $26,369 (2005); Median household income: $45,098 (2005); Average household income: $70,734 (2005); Percent of households with income of $100,000 or more: 21.7% (2005); Poverty rate: 7.0% (2000).
Education: Percent of population age 25 and over with: High school diploma (including GED) or higher: 92.0% (2005); Bachelor's degree or higher: 44.7% (2005); Master's degree or higher: 22.1% (2005).

School District(s)
Cazenovia Central School District (KG-12)
   2003-04 Enrollment: 1,804 . . . . (315) 655-1317

Four-year College(s)
Cazenovia College
   Fall 2004 Enrollment: 1,180 . . . . (800) 654-3210
   2005-06 Tuition: In-state $18,940; Out-of-state $18,940

Housing: Homeownership rate: 60.8% (2005); Median home value: $156,678 (2005); Median rent: $458 per month (2000); Median age of housing: 60+ years (2000).
Newspapers: Hi Neighbor (General - Circulation 9,500)
Transportation: Commute to work: 79.6% car, 0.3% public transportation, 14.5% walk, 4.9% work from home (2000); Travel time to work: 45.7% less than 15 minutes, 16.5% 15 to 30 minutes, 27.1% 30 to 45 minutes, 8.5% 45 to 60 minutes, 2.2% 60 minutes or more (2000)
Additional Information Contacts
Cazenovia Chamber of Commerce . . . . (315) 655-9243
   http://www.cazenovia.com

CAZENOVIA (town). Covers a land area of 49.893 square miles and a water area of 1.829 square miles. Located at 42.91° N. Lat.; 75.85° W. Long. Elevation is 1,182 feet.
History: Seat of Cazenovia College. Settled 1793, incorporated 1810.

Population: 6,514 (1990); 6,481 (2000); 6,831 (2005); 7,150 (2010 projected); Race: 96.7% White, 1.3% Black, 0.7% Asian, 2.2% Hispanic of any race (2005); Density: 136.9 persons per square mile (2005); Average household size: 2.71 (2005); Median age: 39.8 (2005); Males per 100 females: 89.0 (2005); Marriage status: 23.6% never married, 64.1% now married, 5.7% widowed, 6.6% divorced (2000); Foreign born: 2.7% (2000); Ancestry (includes multiple ancestries): 21.7% Irish, 20.7% German, 19.0% English, 10.3% Italian, 5.4% Polish (2000).
Economy: In dairy farming area; dielectrics, electronics circuitry. Single-family building permits issued: 14 (2005); Multi-family building permits issued: 0 (2005); Employment by occupation: 18.2% management, 32.9% professional, 10.1% services, 25.3% sales, 1.1% farming, 6.4% construction, 6.0% production (2000).
Income: Per capita income: $33,289 (2005); Median household income: $65,632 (2005); Average household income: $89,532 (2005); Percent of households with income of $100,000 or more: 30.3% (2005); Poverty rate: 4.3% (2000).
Education: Percent of population age 25 and over with: High school diploma (including GED) or higher: 94.8% (2005); Bachelor's degree or higher: 49.6% (2005); Master's degree or higher: 25.1% (2005).
Housing: Homeownership rate: 77.9% (2005); Median home value: $185,968 (2005); Median rent: $452 per month (2000); Median age of housing: 46 years (2000).
Transportation: Commute to work: 84.9% car, 0.3% public transportation, 7.4% walk, 6.4% work from home (2000); Travel time to work: 38.6% less than 15 minutes, 19.4% 15 to 30 minutes, 25.6% 30 to 45 minutes, 12.3% 45 to 60 minutes, 4.0% 60 minutes or more (2000)

CHITTENANGO (village). Covers a land area of 2.442 square miles and a water area of 0 square miles. Located at 43.04° N. Lat.; 75.87° W. Long. Elevation is 416 feet.
Population: 4,792 (1990); 4,855 (2000); 4,849 (2005); 4,857 (2010 projected); Race: 98.0% White, 0.5% Black, 0.3% Asian, 1.1% Hispanic of any race (2005); Density: 1,985.9 persons per square mile (2005); Average household size: 2.58 (2005); Median age: 38.0 (2005); Males per 100 females: 89.1 (2005); Marriage status: 25.0% never married, 59.9% now married, 6.7% widowed, 8.4% divorced (2000); Foreign born: 3.9% (2000); Ancestry (includes multiple ancestries): 22.4% English, 22.1% Irish, 21.1% German, 11.6% Italian, 7.3% French (except Basque) (2000).
Economy: Agricultural and dairying area. Summer resort with scenic Chittenango Falls on small Chittenango Creek to South. Single-family building permits issued: 22 (2005); Multi-family building permits issued: 0 (2005); Employment by occupation: 12.0% management, 20.4% professional, 14.2% services, 29.1% sales, 0.3% farming, 8.7% construction, 15.3% production (2000).
Income: Per capita income: $23,569 (2005); Median household income: $48,905 (2005); Average household income: $60,155 (2005); Percent of households with income of $100,000 or more: 13.9% (2005); Poverty rate: 6.2% (2000).
Taxes: Total city taxes per capita: $232 (2004); City property taxes per capita: $201 (2004).
Education: Percent of population age 25 and over with: High school diploma (including GED) or higher: 87.3% (2005); Bachelor's degree or higher: 21.2% (2005); Master's degree or higher: 8.7% (2005).

School District(s)
Chittenango Central School District (KG-12)
   2003-04 Enrollment: 2,565 . . . . (315) 687-2669

Housing: Homeownership rate: 71.8% (2005); Median home value: $98,841 (2005); Median rent: $469 per month (2000); Median age of housing: 35 years (2000).
Safety: Violent crime rate: 12.3 per 10,000 population; Property crime rate: 229.3 per 10,000 population (2004).
Newspapers: Chittenango/Bridgeport Times (General - Circulation 1,600)
Transportation: Commute to work: 94.6% car, 0.0% public transportation, 2.5% walk, 1.7% work from home (2000); Travel time to work: 23.8% less than 15 minutes, 46.3% 15 to 30 minutes, 23.3% 30 to 45 minutes, 4.3% 45 to 60 minutes, 2.2% 60 minutes or more (2000)
Additional Information Contacts
Village of Chittenango . . . . (315) 687-3936
   http://chittenango.org/

DE RUYTER (village). Covers a land area of 0.343 square miles and a water area of 0 square miles. Located at 42.75° N. Lat.; 75.88° W. Long.
Population: 568 (1990); 531 (2000); 542 (2005); 556 (2010 projected); Race: 96.3% White, 0.9% Black, 1.1% Asian, 0.6% Hispanic of any race

(2005); Density: 1,578.2 persons per square mile (2005); Average household size: 2.43 (2005); Median age: 39.3 (2005); Males per 100 females: 79.5 (2005); Marriage status: 29.8% never married, 45.8% now married, 11.3% widowed, 13.1% divorced (2000); Foreign born: 3.3% (2000); Ancestry (includes multiple ancestries): 26.6% German, 25.1% English, 13.5% Irish, 10.2% United States or American, 9.1% Italian (2000).
Economy: Single-family building permits issued: 0 (2005); Multi-family building permits issued: 0 (2005); Employment by occupation: 3.3% management, 25.8% professional, 18.2% services, 14.8% sales, 1.0% farming, 14.8% construction, 22.0% production (2000).
Income: Per capita income: $17,339 (2005); Median household income: $33,953 (2005); Average household income: $42,141 (2005); Percent of households with income of $100,000 or more: 4.5% (2005); Poverty rate: 11.8% (2000).
Education: Percent of population age 25 and over with: High school diploma (including GED) or higher: 88.3% (2005); Bachelor's degree or higher: 20.5% (2005); Master's degree or higher: 9.0% (2005).

School District(s)
De Ruyter Central School District (KG-12)
    2003-04 Enrollment: 508 . . . . (315) 852-3410

Housing: Homeownership rate: 61.4% (2005); Median home value: $97,097 (2005); Median rent: $270 per month (2000); Median age of housing: 60+ years (2000).
Transportation: Commute to work: 82.6% car, 0.0% public transportation, 12.3% walk, 4.1% work from home (2000); Travel time to work: 24.6% less than 15 minutes, 21.9% 15 to 30 minutes, 35.8% 30 to 45 minutes, 9.6% 45 to 60 minutes, 8.0% 60 minutes or more (2000)

DE RUYTER (town). Covers a land area of 30.503 square miles and a water area of 0.776 square miles. Located at 42.77° N. Lat.; 75.86° W. Long.
Population: 1,458 (1990); 1,532 (2000); 1,563 (2005); 1,598 (2010 projected); Race: 95.8% White, 2.1% Black, 0.6% Asian, 0.6% Hispanic of any race (2005); Density: 51.2 persons per square mile (2005); Average household size: 2.53 (2005); Median age: 39.1 (2005); Males per 100 females: 94.2 (2005); Marriage status: 25.2% never married, 56.9% now married, 7.3% widowed, 10.6% divorced (2000); Foreign born: 1.9% (2000); Ancestry (includes multiple ancestries): 22.1% English, 20.6% German, 16.3% Irish, 7.2% United States or American, 6.8% Italian (2000).
Economy: Single-family building permits issued: 3 (2005); Multi-family building permits issued: 0 (2005); Employment by occupation: 9.4% management, 20.6% professional, 16.2% services, 16.7% sales, 2.5% farming, 15.5% construction, 19.1% production (2000).
Income: Per capita income: $18,605 (2005); Median household income: $39,811 (2005); Average household income: $47,055 (2005); Percent of households with income of $100,000 or more: 6.1% (2005); Poverty rate: 11.8% (2000).
Education: Percent of population age 25 and over with: High school diploma (including GED) or higher: 85.1% (2005); Bachelor's degree or higher: 16.0% (2005); Master's degree or higher: 6.2% (2005).
Housing: Homeownership rate: 78.5% (2005); Median home value: $93,505 (2005); Median rent: $299 per month (2000); Median age of housing: 46 years (2000).
Transportation: Commute to work: 83.7% car, 0.3% public transportation, 7.3% walk, 8.1% work from home (2000); Travel time to work: 25.9% less than 15 minutes, 22.8% 15 to 30 minutes, 28.4% 30 to 45 minutes, 15.1% 45 to 60 minutes, 7.8% 60 minutes or more (2000)

EARLVILLE (village). Covers a land area of 1.084 square miles and a water area of 0 square miles. Located at 42.74° N. Lat.; 75.54° W. Long. Elevation is 1,100 feet.
Population: 883 (1990); 791 (2000); 737 (2005); 729 (2010 projected); Race: 99.1% White, 0.0% Black, 0.3% Asian, 1.2% Hispanic of any race (2005); Density: 679.6 persons per square mile (2005); Average household size: 2.60 (2005); Median age: 38.7 (2005); Males per 100 females: 89.9 (2005); Marriage status: 23.1% never married, 59.9% now married, 7.5% widowed, 9.4% divorced (2000); Foreign born: 1.1% (2000); Ancestry (includes multiple ancestries): 23.9% English, 22.1% German, 12.9% Irish, 12.9% United States or American, 6.0% Italian (2000).
Economy: Single-family building permits issued: 0 (2005); Multi-family building permits issued: 0 (2005); Employment by occupation: 9.0% management, 18.0% professional, 20.6% services, 19.2% sales, 1.4% farming, 10.4% construction, 21.4% production (2000).
Income: Per capita income: $16,849 (2005); Median household income: $37,375 (2005); Average household income: $43,878 (2005); Percent of households with income of $100,000 or more: 3.9% (2005); Poverty rate: 11.8% (2000).
Education: Percent of population age 25 and over with: High school diploma (including GED) or higher: 75.9% (2005); Bachelor's degree or higher: 11.0% (2005); Master's degree or higher: 3.7% (2005).
Housing: Homeownership rate: 78.1% (2005); Median home value: $72,206 (2005); Median rent: $391 per month (2000); Median age of housing: 60+ years (2000).
Transportation: Commute to work: 94.1% car, 1.1% public transportation, 2.0% walk, 2.8% work from home (2000); Travel time to work: 34.7% less than 15 minutes, 34.4% 15 to 30 minutes, 15.2% 30 to 45 minutes, 8.5% 45 to 60 minutes, 7.3% 60 minutes or more (2000)

EATON (town). Covers a land area of 44.745 square miles and a water area of 0.834 square miles. Located at 42.87° N. Lat.; 75.62° W. Long. Elevation is 1,200 feet.
Population: 5,362 (1990); 4,826 (2000); 4,871 (2005); 4,946 (2010 projected); Race: 87.7% White, 8.3% Black, 1.6% Asian, 2.9% Hispanic of any race (2005); Density: 108.9 persons per square mile (2005); Average household size: 3.53 (2005); Median age: 25.3 (2005); Males per 100 females: 103.6 (2005); Marriage status: 38.2% never married, 47.5% now married, 6.0% widowed, 8.3% divorced (2000); Foreign born: 3.2% (2000); Ancestry (includes multiple ancestries): 19.4% English, 15.9% Irish, 15.8% German, 8.0% Italian, 7.6% Other groups (2000).
Economy: Single-family building permits issued: 13 (2005); Multi-family building permits issued: 0 (2005); Employment by occupation: 12.6% management, 17.0% professional, 23.0% services, 19.4% sales, 4.1% farming, 11.5% construction, 12.4% production (2000).
Income: Per capita income: $17,004 (2005); Median household income: $43,682 (2005); Average household income: $56,496 (2005); Percent of households with income of $100,000 or more: 11.7% (2005); Poverty rate: 9.5% (2000).
Education: Percent of population age 25 and over with: High school diploma (including GED) or higher: 81.6% (2005); Bachelor's degree or higher: 21.9% (2005); Master's degree or higher: 7.8% (2005).
Housing: Homeownership rate: 72.3% (2005); Median home value: $93,049 (2005); Median rent: $432 per month (2000); Median age of housing: 43 years (2000).
Transportation: Commute to work: 80.1% car, 0.1% public transportation, 13.2% walk, 5.1% work from home (2000); Travel time to work: 44.5% less than 15 minutes, 28.4% 15 to 30 minutes, 12.6% 30 to 45 minutes, 9.2% 45 to 60 minutes, 5.3% 60 minutes or more (2000)

ERIEVILLE (unincorporated postal area, zip code 13061). Covers a land area of 21.450 square miles and a water area of 0.513 square miles. Located at 42.85° N. Lat.; 75.74° W. Long.
Population: 0 (2000); Race: 98.9% White, 0.0% Black, 0.0% Asian, 0.1% Hispanic of any race (2000); Density: 0.0 persons per square mile (2000); Age: 27.6% under 18, 10.1% over 64 (2000); Marriage status: 19.9% never married, 64.2% now married, 6.7% widowed, 9.1% divorced (2000); Foreign born: 1.2% (2000); Ancestry (includes multiple ancestries): 23.9% German, 19.9% Irish, 17.8% English, 7.9% United States or American, 7.2% Welsh (2000).
Economy: Lakes, reservoirs nearby. Employment by occupation: 10.2% management, 21.0% professional, 12.6% services, 26.0% sales, 0.0% farming, 13.2% construction, 16.9% production (2000).
Income: Per capita income: $19,326 (2000); Median household income: $47,014 (2000); Poverty rate: 5.9% (2000).
Education: Percent of population age 25 and over with: High school diploma (including GED) or higher: 88.2% (2000); Bachelor's degree or higher: 28.3% (2000).
Housing: Homeownership rate: 89.0% (2000); Median home value: $91,100 (2000); Median rent: $438 per month (2000); Median age of housing: 43 years (2000).
Transportation: Commute to work: 93.2% car, 0.0% public transportation, 1.3% walk, 5.0% work from home (2000); Travel time to work: 16.7% less than 15 minutes, 30.0% 15 to 30 minutes, 24.3% 30 to 45 minutes, 18.8% 45 to 60 minutes, 10.1% 60 minutes or more (2000)

FENNER (town). Covers a land area of 31.118 square miles and a water area of 0.028 square miles. Located at 42.97° N. Lat.; 75.78° W. Long.

Population: 1,694 (1990); 1,680 (2000); 1,596 (2005); 1,579 (2010 projected); Race: 98.9% White, 0.1% Black, 0.3% Asian, 0.4% Hispanic of any race (2005); Density: 51.3 persons per square mile (2005); Average household size: 2.71 (2005); Median age: 38.1 (2005); Males per 100 females: 98.3 (2005); Marriage status: 22.5% never married, 63.9% now married, 3.1% widowed, 10.4% divorced (2000); Foreign born: 1.8% (2000); Ancestry (includes multiple ancestries): 21.9% German, 18.9% English, 18.6% Irish, 9.5% United States or American, 8.0% Italian (2000).
Economy: Single-family building permits issued: 7 (2005); Multi-family building permits issued: 0 (2005); Employment by occupation: 15.8% management, 16.5% professional, 12.0% services, 22.8% sales, 3.4% farming, 10.5% construction, 18.9% production (2000).
Income: Per capita income: $22,561 (2005); Median household income: $49,821 (2005); Average household income: $61,133 (2005); Percent of households with income of $100,000 or more: 13.4% (2005); Poverty rate: 7.1% (2000).
Education: Percent of population age 25 and over with: High school diploma (including GED) or higher: 83.7% (2005); Bachelor's degree or higher: 19.1% (2005); Master's degree or higher: 6.1% (2005).
Housing: Homeownership rate: 83.9% (2005); Median home value: $111,688 (2005); Median rent: $429 per month (2000); Median age of housing: 24 years (2000).
Transportation: Commute to work: 92.2% car, 0.0% public transportation, 2.4% walk, 4.6% work from home (2000); Travel time to work: 27.2% less than 15 minutes, 31.2% 15 to 30 minutes, 28.5% 30 to 45 minutes, 10.0% 45 to 60 minutes, 3.2% 60 minutes or more (2000)

GEORGETOWN (town). Covers a land area of 40.090 square miles and a water area of 0.072 square miles. Located at 42.78° N. Lat.; 75.74° W. Long. Elevation is 1,413 feet.
Population: 932 (1990); 946 (2000); 959 (2005); 981 (2010 projected); Race: 78.9% White, 16.4% Black, 0.0% Asian, 9.6% Hispanic of any race (2005); Density: 23.9 persons per square mile (2005); Average household size: 3.69 (2005); Median age: 36.9 (2005); Males per 100 females: 168.6 (2005); Marriage status: 31.8% never married, 60.0% now married, 2.5% widowed, 5.7% divorced (2000); Foreign born: 0.4% (2000); Ancestry (includes multiple ancestries): 18.0% German, 17.8% English, 11.6% Irish, 5.3% United States or American, 3.9% French (except Basque) (2000).
Economy: Single-family building permits issued: 3 (2005); Multi-family building permits issued: 0 (2005); Employment by occupation: 9.8% management, 13.0% professional, 20.1% services, 20.1% sales, 3.3% farming, 12.2% construction, 21.7% production (2000).
Income: Per capita income: $13,745 (2005); Median household income: $42,303 (2005); Average household income: $45,038 (2005); Percent of households with income of $100,000 or more: 3.1% (2005); Poverty rate: 11.4% (2000).
Education: Percent of population age 25 and over with: High school diploma (including GED) or higher: 58.3% (2005); Bachelor's degree or higher: 7.0% (2005); Master's degree or higher: 2.2% (2005).
Housing: Homeownership rate: 87.7% (2005); Median home value: $75,789 (2005); Median rent: $283 per month (2000); Median age of housing: 60+ years (2000).
Transportation: Commute to work: 90.8% car, 1.4% public transportation, 3.8% walk, 4.1% work from home (2000); Travel time to work: 15.6% less than 15 minutes, 34.3% 15 to 30 minutes, 23.5% 30 to 45 minutes, 11.0% 45 to 60 minutes, 15.6% 60 minutes or more (2000)

HAMILTON (village). Covers a land area of 2.352 square miles and a water area of 0.156 square miles. Located at 42.82° N. Lat.; 75.54° W. Long. Elevation is 1,126 feet.
Population: 3,828 (1990); 3,509 (2000); 3,520 (2005); 3,527 (2010 projected); Race: 90.2% White, 2.9% Black, 4.7% Asian, 3.1% Hispanic of any race (2005); Density: 1,496.9 persons per square mile (2005); Average household size: 5.11 (2005); Median age: 20.8 (2005); Males per 100 females: 83.5 (2005); Marriage status: 68.8% never married, 23.2% now married, 4.5% widowed, 3.5% divorced (2000); Foreign born: 6.6% (2000); Ancestry (includes multiple ancestries): 18.8% English, 17.2% Irish, 14.4% German, 14.2% Other groups, 9.4% Italian (2000).
Economy: Single-family building permits issued: 3 (2005); Multi-family building permits issued: 20 (2005); Employment by occupation: 7.9% management, 43.6% professional, 13.6% services, 29.2% sales, 0.2% farming, 1.9% construction, 3.6% production (2000).
Income: Per capita income: $14,412 (2005); Median household income: $42,500 (2005); Average household income: $63,367 (2005); Percent of households with income of $100,000 or more: 19.6% (2005); Poverty rate: 18.5% (2000).
Education: Percent of population age 25 and over with: High school diploma (including GED) or higher: 93.8% (2005); Bachelor's degree or higher: 53.1% (2005); Master's degree or higher: 33.6% (2005).

School District(s)
Hamilton Central School District (KG-12)
    2003-04 Enrollment: 740 . . . . (315) 824-3721

Four-year College(s)
Colgate University
    Fall 2004 Enrollment: 2,831 . . . . (315) 228-1000
    2005-06 Tuition: In-state $32,885; Out-of-state $32,885

Housing: Homeownership rate: 52.7% (2005); Median home value: $134,961 (2005); Median rent: $423 per month (2000); Median age of housing: 60+ years (2000).
Hospitals: Community Memorial Hospital (88 beds)
Newspapers: Hamilton Tribune (General - Circulation 1,600); The Mid-York Weekly (General - Circulation 7,500)
Transportation: Commute to work: 39.2% car, 0.0% public transportation, 51.9% walk, 6.7% work from home (2000); Travel time to work: 77.6% less than 15 minutes, 14.0% 15 to 30 minutes, 5.6% 30 to 45 minutes, 1.5% 45 to 60 minutes, 1.4% 60 minutes or more (2000)
Additional Information Contacts
Southern Madison County Chamber of Commerce . . . . (315) 824-8213
    http://www.hamiltonny.com/chamber/

HAMILTON (town). Covers a land area of 41.362 square miles and a water area of 0.082 square miles. Located at 42.79° N. Lat.; 75.49° W. Long. Elevation is 1,126 feet.
History: Seat of Colgate University. Settled 1795, incorporated 1816.
Population: 6,221 (1990); 5,733 (2000); 5,646 (2005); 5,651 (2010 projected); Race: 92.9% White, 2.0% Black, 3.2% Asian, 2.7% Hispanic of any race (2005); Density: 136.5 persons per square mile (2005); Average household size: 3.74 (2005); Median age: 23.2 (2005); Males per 100 females: 88.8 (2005); Marriage status: 53.1% never married, 36.9% now married, 4.7% widowed, 5.2% divorced (2000); Foreign born: 4.2% (2000); Ancestry (includes multiple ancestries): 20.7% English, 16.0% Irish, 16.0% German, 11.5% Other groups, 8.4% Italian (2000).
Economy: In dairying and farming region. Single-family building permits issued: 8 (2005); Multi-family building permits issued: 0 (2005); Employment by occupation: 10.5% management, 35.1% professional, 14.1% services, 24.9% sales, 0.4% farming, 4.7% construction, 10.5% production (2000).
Income: Per capita income: $17,694 (2005); Median household income: $44,918 (2005); Average household income: $61,344 (2005); Percent of households with income of $100,000 or more: 15.6% (2005); Poverty rate: 14.4% (2000).
Taxes: Total city taxes per capita: $96 (2004); City property taxes per capita: $82 (2004).
Education: Percent of population age 25 and over with: High school diploma (including GED) or higher: 89.3% (2005); Bachelor's degree or higher: 35.7% (2005); Master's degree or higher: 19.5% (2005).
Housing: Homeownership rate: 68.2% (2005); Median home value: $105,855 (2005); Median rent: $403 per month (2000); Median age of housing: 60+ years (2000).
Transportation: Commute to work: 60.9% car, 0.2% public transportation, 31.6% walk, 5.8% work from home (2000); Travel time to work: 64.8% less than 15 minutes, 18.5% 15 to 30 minutes, 8.8% 30 to 45 minutes, 5.2% 45 to 60 minutes, 2.8% 60 minutes or more (2000)

HUBBARDSVILLE (unincorporated postal area, zip code 13355). Covers a land area of 24.447 square miles and a water area of 0.008 square miles. Located at 42.81° N. Lat.; 75.43° W. Long. Elevation is 1,218 feet.
Population: 0 (2000); Race: 96.2% White, 0.8% Black, 0.3% Asian, 2.2% Hispanic of any race (2000); Density: 0.0 persons per square mile (2000); Age: 31.2% under 18, 11.3% over 64 (2000); Marriage status: 20.9% never married, 62.7% now married, 4.5% widowed, 11.9% divorced (2000); Foreign born: 1.0% (2000); Ancestry (includes multiple ancestries): 19.0% English, 15.8% German, 13.6% Irish, 10.9% Other groups, 8.9% Italian (2000).
Economy: Employment by occupation: 10.1% management, 17.6% professional, 16.4% services, 20.4% sales, 1.9% farming, 13.8% construction, 19.8% production (2000).

Income: Per capita income: $14,938 (2000); Median household income: $39,408 (2000); Poverty rate: 12.9% (2000).
Education: Percent of population age 25 and over with: High school diploma (including GED) or higher: 81.1% (2000); Bachelor's degree or higher: 8.5% (2000).
Housing: Homeownership rate: 90.6% (2000); Median home value: $57,200 (2000); Median rent: $317 per month (2000); Median age of housing: 50 years (2000).
Transportation: Commute to work: 92.2% car, 0.0% public transportation, 0.3% walk, 7.5% work from home (2000); Travel time to work: 35.6% less than 15 minutes, 34.5% 15 to 30 minutes, 14.8% 30 to 45 minutes, 11.3% 45 to 60 minutes, 3.9% 60 minutes or more (2000)

LEBANON (town). Covers a land area of 43.432 square miles and a water area of 0.245 square miles. Located at 42.78° N. Lat.; 75.62° W. Long.
Population: 1,265 (1990); 1,329 (2000); 1,379 (2005); 1,430 (2010 projected); Race: 98.7% White, 0.0% Black, 0.4% Asian, 2.6% Hispanic of any race (2005); Density: 31.8 persons per square mile (2005); Average household size: 2.57 (2005); Median age: 39.3 (2005); Males per 100 females: 99.0 (2005); Marriage status: 22.2% never married, 60.9% now married, 6.1% widowed, 10.7% divorced (2000); Foreign born: 1.5% (2000); Ancestry (includes multiple ancestries): 21.7% English, 17.5% German, 12.7% Irish, 8.9% United States or American, 7.6% Italian (2000).
Economy: Single-family building permits issued: 4 (2005); Multi-family building permits issued: 0 (2005); Employment by occupation: 13.5% management, 17.8% professional, 17.0% services, 20.0% sales, 1.9% farming, 14.5% construction, 15.4% production (2000).
Income: Per capita income: $17,163 (2005); Median household income: $37,378 (2005); Average household income: $44,074 (2005); Percent of households with income of $100,000 or more: 5.4% (2005); Poverty rate: 13.9% (2000).
Education: Percent of population age 25 and over with: High school diploma (including GED) or higher: 81.7% (2005); Bachelor's degree or higher: 16.2% (2005); Master's degree or higher: 6.5% (2005).
Housing: Homeownership rate: 81.2% (2005); Median home value: $87,234 (2005); Median rent: $383 per month (2000); Median age of housing: 29 years (2000).
Transportation: Commute to work: 91.3% car, 0.0% public transportation, 3.9% walk, 4.4% work from home (2000); Travel time to work: 37.7% less than 15 minutes, 31.4% 15 to 30 minutes, 16.0% 30 to 45 minutes, 6.8% 45 to 60 minutes, 8.1% 60 minutes or more (2000)

LENOX (town). Covers a land area of 36.402 square miles and a water area of 0 square miles. Located at 43.09° N. Lat.; 75.75° W. Long.
Population: 8,621 (1990); 8,665 (2000); 8,850 (2005); 9,047 (2010 projected); Race: 97.5% White, 0.6% Black, 0.3% Asian, 1.2% Hispanic of any race (2005); Density: 243.1 persons per square mile (2005); Average household size: 2.44 (2005); Median age: 39.5 (2005); Males per 100 females: 94.3 (2005); Marriage status: 23.0% never married, 57.1% now married, 8.8% widowed, 11.1% divorced (2000); Foreign born: 1.8% (2000); Ancestry (includes multiple ancestries): 22.8% Italian, 21.9% German, 19.1% Irish, 14.3% English, 7.0% United States or American (2000).
Economy: Single-family building permits issued: 26 (2005); Multi-family building permits issued: 4 (2005); Employment by occupation: 8.4% management, 16.2% professional, 16.0% services, 27.7% sales, 0.8% farming, 10.0% construction, 20.9% production (2000).
Income: Per capita income: $19,990 (2005); Median household income: $42,986 (2005); Average household income: $48,490 (2005); Percent of households with income of $100,000 or more: 7.8% (2005); Poverty rate: 10.6% (2000).
Education: Percent of population age 25 and over with: High school diploma (including GED) or higher: 80.2% (2005); Bachelor's degree or higher: 18.3% (2005); Master's degree or higher: 5.3% (2005).
Housing: Homeownership rate: 70.9% (2005); Median home value: $102,174 (2005); Median rent: $407 per month (2000); Median age of housing: 45 years (2000).
Transportation: Commute to work: 92.6% car, 0.5% public transportation, 3.6% walk, 2.5% work from home (2000); Travel time to work: 32.0% less than 15 minutes, 33.1% 15 to 30 minutes, 25.4% 30 to 45 minutes, 7.0% 45 to 60 minutes, 2.5% 60 minutes or more (2000)

LINCOLN (town). Covers a land area of 24.972 square miles and a water area of 0.027 square miles. Located at 43.04° N. Lat.; 75.73° W. Long.
Population: 1,669 (1990); 1,818 (2000); 1,937 (2005); 2,028 (2010 projected); Race: 97.7% White, 0.2% Black, 0.7% Asian, 0.9% Hispanic of any race (2005); Density: 77.6 persons per square mile (2005); Average household size: 2.68 (2005); Median age: 39.5 (2005); Males per 100 females: 109.0 (2005); Marriage status: 23.1% never married, 65.6% now married, 3.9% widowed, 7.4% divorced (2000); Foreign born: 0.7% (2000); Ancestry (includes multiple ancestries): 21.6% German, 17.9% English, 17.3% Irish, 13.7% Italian, 8.1% United States or American (2000).
Economy: Single-family building permits issued: 5 (2005); Multi-family building permits issued: 0 (2005); Employment by occupation: 13.2% management, 16.0% professional, 12.9% services, 22.1% sales, 2.5% farming, 11.8% construction, 21.5% production (2000).
Income: Per capita income: $24,654 (2005); Median household income: $52,367 (2005); Average household income: $66,143 (2005); Percent of households with income of $100,000 or more: 15.8% (2005); Poverty rate: 5.1% (2000).
Education: Percent of population age 25 and over with: High school diploma (including GED) or higher: 81.5% (2005); Bachelor's degree or higher: 16.1% (2005); Master's degree or higher: 6.0% (2005).
Housing: Homeownership rate: 86.7% (2005); Median home value: $113,611 (2005); Median rent: $420 per month (2000); Median age of housing: 27 years (2000).
Transportation: Commute to work: 93.0% car, 0.0% public transportation, 3.1% walk, 3.3% work from home (2000); Travel time to work: 33.3% less than 15 minutes, 32.7% 15 to 30 minutes, 23.0% 30 to 45 minutes, 7.9% 45 to 60 minutes, 3.1% 60 minutes or more (2000)

MADISON (village). Covers a land area of 0.503 square miles and a water area of 0 square miles. Located at 42.90° N. Lat.; 75.51° W. Long.
Population: 316 (1990); 315 (2000); 328 (2005); 331 (2010 projected); Race: 99.7% White, 0.0% Black, 0.3% Asian, 1.2% Hispanic of any race (2005); Density: 652.3 persons per square mile (2005); Average household size: 2.25 (2005); Median age: 39.1 (2005); Males per 100 females: 86.4 (2005); Marriage status: 33.6% never married, 51.7% now married, 6.8% widowed, 7.9% divorced (2000); Foreign born: 0.3% (2000); Ancestry (includes multiple ancestries): 25.9% English, 14.8% German, 14.2% Irish, 11.7% Welsh, 6.9% Polish (2000).
Economy: Single-family building permits issued: 0 (2005); Multi-family building permits issued: 0 (2005); Employment by occupation: 8.0% management, 13.1% professional, 19.4% services, 27.4% sales, 6.9% farming, 13.1% construction, 12.0% production (2000).
Income: Per capita income: $17,546 (2005); Median household income: $31,000 (2005); Average household income: $39,418 (2005); Percent of households with income of $100,000 or more: 5.5% (2005); Poverty rate: 12.9% (2000).
Education: Percent of population age 25 and over with: High school diploma (including GED) or higher: 83.2% (2005); Bachelor's degree or higher: 6.0% (2005); Master's degree or higher: 4.3% (2005).
School District(s)
Madison Central School District (PK-12)
    2003-04 Enrollment: 482 . . . . (315) 893-1878
Housing: Homeownership rate: 65.8% (2005); Median home value: $92,174 (2005); Median rent: $390 per month (2000); Median age of housing: 60+ years (2000).
Transportation: Commute to work: 87.0% car, 2.4% public transportation, 5.3% walk, 5.3% work from home (2000); Travel time to work: 38.8% less than 15 minutes, 36.3% 15 to 30 minutes, 16.3% 30 to 45 minutes, 6.3% 45 to 60 minutes, 2.5% 60 minutes or more (2000)

MADISON (town). Covers a land area of 40.893 square miles and a water area of 0.510 square miles. Located at 42.87° N. Lat.; 75.50° W. Long.
Population: 2,774 (1990); 2,801 (2000); 3,008 (2005); 3,126 (2010 projected); Race: 97.5% White, 0.4% Black, 0.7% Asian, 1.1% Hispanic of any race (2005); Density: 73.6 persons per square mile (2005); Average household size: 2.43 (2005); Median age: 40.7 (2005); Males per 100 females: 98.3 (2005); Marriage status: 23.7% never married, 61.8% now married, 6.0% widowed, 8.5% divorced (2000); Foreign born: 1.9% (2000); Ancestry (includes multiple ancestries): 23.9% English, 17.4% Irish, 17.4% German, 7.3% United States or American, 7.1% Other groups (2000).

Economy: In dairying area. Single-family building permits issued: 3 (2005); Multi-family building permits issued: 0 (2005); Employment by occupation: 11.8% management, 23.3% professional, 20.1% services, 20.0% sales, 2.6% farming, 10.7% construction, 11.4% production (2000).
Income: Per capita income: $20,793 (2005); Median household income: $39,300 (2005); Average household income: $50,388 (2005); Percent of households with income of $100,000 or more: 10.6% (2005); Poverty rate: 13.0% (2000).
Education: Percent of population age 25 and over with: High school diploma (including GED) or higher: 84.8% (2005); Bachelor's degree or higher: 23.0% (2005); Master's degree or higher: 12.3% (2005).
Housing: Homeownership rate: 80.1% (2005); Median home value: $105,987 (2005); Median rent: $394 per month (2000); Median age of housing: 35 years (2000).
Transportation: Commute to work: 91.0% car, 0.7% public transportation, 3.8% walk, 4.5% work from home (2000); Travel time to work: 45.3% less than 15 minutes, 25.8% 15 to 30 minutes, 17.0% 30 to 45 minutes, 6.1% 45 to 60 minutes, 5.8% 60 minutes or more (2000)

MORRISVILLE
(village). Covers a land area of 1.153 square miles and a water area of 0 square miles. Located at 42.89° N. Lat.; 75.64° W. Long. Elevation is 1,226 feet.
Population: 2,732 (1990); 2,148 (2000); 2,179 (2005); 2,210 (2010 projected); Race: 74.3% White, 17.8% Black, 3.4% Asian, 6.0% Hispanic of any race (2005); Density: 1,890.3 persons per square mile (2005); Average household size: 6.12 (2005); Median age: 20.5 (2005); Males per 100 females: 109.5 (2005); Marriage status: 52.4% never married, 35.9% now married, 6.2% widowed, 5.6% divorced (2000); Foreign born: 7.1% (2000); Ancestry (includes multiple ancestries): 17.7% German, 15.0% Irish, 13.1% Other groups, 12.4% English, 8.5% Italian (2000).
Economy: The SUNY College of Agriculture and Technology at Morrisville is here. Single-family building permits issued: 0 (2005); Multi-family building permits issued: 0 (2005); Employment by occupation: 10.9% management, 15.4% professional, 31.0% services, 16.6% sales, 8.8% farming, 7.3% construction, 10.0% production (2000).
Income: Per capita income: $10,407 (2005); Median household income: $41,273 (2005); Average household income: $50,035 (2005); Percent of households with income of $100,000 or more: 12.9% (2005); Poverty rate: 19.7% (2000).
Education: Percent of population age 25 and over with: High school diploma (including GED) or higher: 83.8% (2005); Bachelor's degree or higher: 23.2% (2005); Master's degree or higher: 11.4% (2005).
School District(s)
Morrisville-Eaton Central School District (KG-12)
    2003-04 Enrollment: 877 . . . . (315) 684-9300
Four-year College(s)
Morrisville State College (Public)
    Fall 2004 Enrollment: 3,386. (315) 684-6000
    2005-06 Tuition: In-state $5,600; Out-of-state $8,460
Housing: Homeownership rate: 52.8% (2005); Median home value: $96,522 (2005); Median rent: $409 per month (2000); Median age of housing: 60+ years (2000).
Transportation: Commute to work: 64.1% car, 0.3% public transportation, 30.3% walk, 3.6% work from home (2000); Travel time to work: 66.1% less than 15 minutes, 20.5% 15 to 30 minutes, 4.1% 30 to 45 minutes, 5.3% 45 to 60 minutes, 4.0% 60 minutes or more (2000)

MUNNSVILLE
(village). Covers a land area of 0.863 square miles and a water area of 0 square miles. Located at 42.97° N. Lat.; 75.58° W. Long. Elevation is 679 feet.
Population: 438 (1990); 437 (2000); 454 (2005); 466 (2010 projected); Race: 98.5% White, 0.4% Black, 0.0% Asian, 1.1% Hispanic of any race (2005); Density: 526.3 persons per square mile (2005); Average household size: 2.58 (2005); Median age: 37.9 (2005); Males per 100 females: 94.0 (2005); Marriage status: 26.9% never married, 54.6% now married, 7.7% widowed, 10.8% divorced (2000); Foreign born: 1.4% (2000); Ancestry (includes multiple ancestries): 27.5% German, 18.6% Irish, 16.9% English, 16.0% French (except Basque), 6.8% Italian (2000).
Economy: Quarry. Single-family building permits issued: 0 (2005); Multi-family building permits issued: 0 (2005); Employment by occupation: 4.0% management, 12.0% professional, 21.1% services, 24.6% sales, 2.3% farming, 17.1% construction, 18.9% production (2000).
Income: Per capita income: $19,625 (2005); Median household income: $42,895 (2005); Average household income: $49,886 (2005); Percent of households with income of $100,000 or more: 6.8% (2005); Poverty rate: 14.8% (2000).
Education: Percent of population age 25 and over with: High school diploma (including GED) or higher: 75.2% (2005); Bachelor's degree or higher: 9.2% (2005); Master's degree or higher: 2.3% (2005).
School District(s)
Stockbridge Valley Central School District (PK-12)
    2003-04 Enrollment: 555 . . . . (315) 495-4400
Housing: Homeownership rate: 65.9% (2005); Median home value: $86,087 (2005); Median rent: $415 per month (2000); Median age of housing: 60+ years (2000).
Transportation: Commute to work: 90.3% car, 0.0% public transportation, 5.7% walk, 2.3% work from home (2000); Travel time to work: 29.2% less than 15 minutes, 40.4% 15 to 30 minutes, 18.1% 30 to 45 minutes, 7.6% 45 to 60 minutes, 4.7% 60 minutes or more (2000)

NELSON
(town). Covers a land area of 43.116 square miles and a water area of 0.932 square miles. Located at 42.87° N. Lat.; 75.74° W. Long.
Population: 1,892 (1990); 1,964 (2000); 1,921 (2005); 1,844 (2010 projected); Race: 98.3% White, 0.2% Black, 0.0% Asian, 1.6% Hispanic of any race (2005); Density: 44.6 persons per square mile (2005); Average household size: 2.63 (2005); Median age: 41.2 (2005); Males per 100 females: 102.4 (2005); Marriage status: 20.3% never married, 69.0% now married, 4.1% widowed, 6.6% divorced (2000); Foreign born: 0.9% (2000); Ancestry (includes multiple ancestries): 21.9% German, 21.2% Irish, 20.1% English, 8.6% Italian, 8.2% United States or American (2000).
Economy: Single-family building permits issued: 7 (2005); Multi-family building permits issued: 0 (2005); Employment by occupation: 10.6% management, 26.6% professional, 12.0% services, 23.6% sales, 0.6% farming, 11.4% construction, 15.3% production (2000).
Income: Per capita income: $25,357 (2005); Median household income: $58,439 (2005); Average household income: $66,635 (2005); Percent of households with income of $100,000 or more: 17.6% (2005); Poverty rate: 5.1% (2000).
Education: Percent of population age 25 and over with: High school diploma (including GED) or higher: 89.4% (2005); Bachelor's degree or higher: 28.7% (2005); Master's degree or higher: 13.0% (2005).
Housing: Homeownership rate: 87.6% (2005); Median home value: $125,676 (2005); Median rent: $521 per month (2000); Median age of housing: 39 years (2000).
Transportation: Commute to work: 91.7% car, 0.0% public transportation, 1.4% walk, 6.4% work from home (2000); Travel time to work: 27.5% less than 15 minutes, 22.9% 15 to 30 minutes, 26.0% 30 to 45 minutes, 15.6% 45 to 60 minutes, 7.9% 60 minutes or more (2000)

NEW WOODSTOCK
(unincorporated postal area, zip code 13122). Covers a land area of 19.665 square miles and a water area of 0 square miles. Located at 42.83° N. Lat.; 75.84° W. Long. Elevation is 1,303 feet.
Population: 0 (2000); Race: 97.3% White, 0.3% Black, 0.1% Asian, 3.3% Hispanic of any race (2000); Density: 0.0 persons per square mile (2000); Age: 27.9% under 18, 9.8% over 64 (2000); Marriage status: 22.4% never married, 65.9% now married, 3.3% widowed, 8.4% divorced (2000); Foreign born: 1.8% (2000); Ancestry (includes multiple ancestries): 17.5% English, 16.8% United States or American, 14.3% Irish, 11.6% German, 6.4% Italian (2000).
Economy: Employment by occupation: 16.4% management, 19.0% professional, 13.7% services, 23.3% sales, 1.9% farming, 13.3% construction, 12.3% production (2000).
Income: Per capita income: $23,704 (2000); Median household income: $51,923 (2000); Poverty rate: 4.1% (2000).
Education: Percent of population age 25 and over with: High school diploma (including GED) or higher: 87.3% (2000); Bachelor's degree or higher: 24.8% (2000).
Housing: Homeownership rate: 84.8% (2000); Median home value: $79,800 (2000); Median rent: $418 per month (2000); Median age of housing: 56 years (2000).
Transportation: Commute to work: 86.4% car, 0.0% public transportation, 3.9% walk, 9.7% work from home (2000); Travel time to work: 31.5% less than 15 minutes, 16.5% 15 to 30 minutes, 25.2% 30 to 45 minutes, 21.8% 45 to 60 minutes, 5.0% 60 minutes or more (2000)

NORTH BROOKFIELD
(unincorporated postal area, zip code 13418). Covers a land area of 6.749 square miles and a water area of <.001 square miles. Located at 42.85° N. Lat.; 75.39° W. Long.

Population: 0 (2000); Race: 100.0% White, 0.0% Black, 0.0% Asian, 0.0% Hispanic of any race (2000); Density: 0.0 persons per square mile (2000); Age: 32.3% under 18, 12.9% over 64 (2000); Marriage status: 22.8% never married, 58.0% now married, 11.9% widowed, 7.3% divorced (2000); Foreign born: 0.0% (2000); Ancestry (includes multiple ancestries): 28.1% English, 14.9% German, 10.9% Irish, 5.0% United States or American, 4.6% Dutch (2000).
Economy: Employment by occupation: 7.6% management, 12.2% professional, 15.3% services, 21.4% sales, 6.9% farming, 22.9% construction, 13.7% production (2000).
Income: Per capita income: $12,306 (2000); Median household income: $31,346 (2000); Poverty rate: 9.7% (2000).
Education: Percent of population age 25 and over with: High school diploma (including GED) or higher: 76.2% (2000); Bachelor's degree or higher: 9.9% (2000).
Housing: Homeownership rate: 92.2% (2000); Median home value: $49,500 (2000); Median rent: $n/a per month (2000); Median age of housing: 60+ years (2000).
Transportation: Commute to work: 85.0% car, 0.0% public transportation, 4.7% walk, 8.7% work from home (2000); Travel time to work: 18.1% less than 15 minutes, 53.4% 15 to 30 minutes, 20.7% 30 to 45 minutes, 5.2% 45 to 60 minutes, 2.6% 60 minutes or more (2000)

ONEIDA (city). Aka East. Covers a land area of 22.030 square miles and a water area of 0.047 square miles. Located at 43.08° N. Lat.; 75.65° W. Long. Elevation is 413 feet.
History: The establishment and early growth of Oneida resulted from a shrewd bargain made by Sands Higinbotham, owner of the city site, with the railroad. The railroad received free right of way across his land, plus ample ground for a station, on the condition that it stop every passenger train at the depot for ten minutes for refreshments. Higinbotham then built the Railroad House to serve meals to passengers.
Population: 10,850 (1990); 10,987 (2000); 10,952 (2005); 10,906 (2010 projected); Race: 95.8% White, 0.9% Black, 0.7% Asian, 1.2% Hispanic of any race (2005); Density: 497.1 persons per square mile (2005); Average household size: 2.44 (2005); Median age: 39.2 (2005); Males per 100 females: 93.5 (2005); Marriage status: 27.3% never married, 53.8% now married, 8.3% widowed, 10.6% divorced (2000); Foreign born: 1.8% (2000); Ancestry (includes multiple ancestries): 21.7% Irish, 20.4% German, 14.9% English, 12.2% Italian, 5.8% United States or American (2000).
Economy: Single-family building permits issued: 32 (2005); Multi-family building permits issued: 4 (2005); Employment by occupation: 10.6% management, 17.6% professional, 17.7% services, 28.1% sales, 0.4% farming, 6.7% construction, 18.8% production (2000).
Income: Per capita income: $23,035 (2005); Median household income: $40,718 (2005); Average household income: $55,162 (2005); Percent of households with income of $100,000 or more: 11.0% (2005); Poverty rate: 12.5% (2000).
Education: Percent of population age 25 and over with: High school diploma (including GED) or higher: 80.8% (2005); Bachelor's degree or higher: 18.6% (2005); Master's degree or higher: 6.7% (2005).
School District(s)
Oneida City School District (KG-12)
    2003-04 Enrollment: 2,550 . . . . (315) 363-2550
Housing: Homeownership rate: 60.6% (2005); Median home value: $98,555 (2005); Median rent: $410 per month (2000); Median age of housing: 60+ years (2000).
Hospitals: Oneida Healthcare Center (101 beds)
Safety: Violent crime rate: 27.3 per 10,000 population; Property crime rate: 497.4 per 10,000 population (2004).
Newspapers: Oneida Daily Dispatch (Circulation 6,775)
Transportation: Commute to work: 91.1% car, 1.7% public transportation, 4.0% walk, 2.2% work from home (2000); Travel time to work: 54.0% less than 15 minutes, 20.4% 15 to 30 minutes, 18.0% 30 to 45 minutes, 5.2% 45 to 60 minutes, 2.4% 60 minutes or more (2000)
Additional Information Contacts
City of Oneida . . . . (315) 363-4800
    http://www.ci.oneida.ny.us/
Greater Oneida Chamber of Commerce . . . . (315) 363-4300
    http://www.oneidachamber.com/business.htm

SMITHFIELD (town). Covers a land area of 24.328 square miles and a water area of 0.008 square miles. Located at 42.96° N. Lat.; 75.66° W. Long.

Population: 1,053 (1990); 1,205 (2000); 1,239 (2005); 1,270 (2010 projected); Race: 96.1% White, 1.3% Black, 0.4% Asian, 0.4% Hispanic of any race (2005); Density: 50.9 persons per square mile (2005); Average household size: 2.84 (2005); Median age: 36.8 (2005); Males per 100 females: 100.8 (2005); Marriage status: 27.7% never married, 55.8% now married, 5.5% widowed, 11.1% divorced (2000); Foreign born: 1.6% (2000); Ancestry (includes multiple ancestries): 20.9% English, 15.0% German, 11.3% Irish, 9.6% French (except Basque), 7.8% United States or American (2000).
Economy: Single-family building permits issued: 2 (2005); Multi-family building permits issued: 0 (2005); Employment by occupation: 16.0% management, 10.5% professional, 13.9% services, 19.4% sales, 2.3% farming, 12.6% construction, 25.4% production (2000).
Income: Per capita income: $17,643 (2005); Median household income: $38,063 (2005); Average household income: $50,023 (2005); Percent of households with income of $100,000 or more: 11.2% (2005); Poverty rate: 16.2% (2000).
Taxes: Total city taxes per capita: $282 (2004); City property taxes per capita: $269 (2004).
Education: Percent of population age 25 and over with: High school diploma (including GED) or higher: 72.6% (2005); Bachelor's degree or higher: 11.6% (2005); Master's degree or higher: 2.8% (2005).
Housing: Homeownership rate: 83.8% (2005); Median home value: $76,800 (2005); Median rent: $381 per month (2000); Median age of housing: 28 years (2000).
Transportation: Commute to work: 92.7% car, 0.8% public transportation, 3.8% walk, 2.7% work from home (2000); Travel time to work: 32.0% less than 15 minutes, 33.1% 15 to 30 minutes, 16.8% 30 to 45 minutes, 10.5% 45 to 60 minutes, 7.7% 60 minutes or more (2000)

STOCKBRIDGE (town). Covers a land area of 31.661 square miles and a water area of 0 square miles. Located at 42.98° N. Lat.; 75.58° W. Long.
Population: 1,968 (1990); 2,080 (2000); 2,168 (2005); 2,227 (2010 projected); Race: 96.3% White, 0.6% Black, 0.5% Asian, 1.3% Hispanic of any race (2005); Density: 68.5 persons per square mile (2005); Average household size: 2.76 (2005); Median age: 36.1 (2005); Males per 100 females: 100.9 (2005); Marriage status: 26.9% never married, 60.0% now married, 6.2% widowed, 6.8% divorced (2000); Foreign born: 1.4% (2000); Ancestry (includes multiple ancestries): 23.2% German, 18.4% Irish, 18.0% English, 9.9% French (except Basque), 6.5% United States or American (2000).
Economy: Single-family building permits issued: 2 (2005); Multi-family building permits issued: 0 (2005); Employment by occupation: 9.0% management, 12.0% professional, 16.2% services, 23.8% sales, 5.7% farming, 11.7% construction, 21.5% production (2000).
Income: Per capita income: $18,705 (2005); Median household income: $44,709 (2005); Average household income: $51,494 (2005); Percent of households with income of $100,000 or more: 7.3% (2005); Poverty rate: 12.9% (2000).
Education: Percent of population age 25 and over with: High school diploma (including GED) or higher: 80.4% (2005); Bachelor's degree or higher: 8.5% (2005); Master's degree or higher: 2.8% (2005).
Housing: Homeownership rate: 78.6% (2005); Median home value: $87,535 (2005); Median rent: $408 per month (2000); Median age of housing: 44 years (2000).
Transportation: Commute to work: 88.6% car, 0.6% public transportation, 5.0% walk, 5.0% work from home (2000); Travel time to work: 31.0% less than 15 minutes, 38.9% 15 to 30 minutes, 15.8% 30 to 45 minutes, 7.3% 45 to 60 minutes, 6.9% 60 minutes or more (2000)

SULLIVAN (town). Covers a land area of 73.362 square miles and a water area of 0.199 square miles. Located at 43.08° N. Lat.; 75.88° W. Long.
Population: 14,622 (1990); 14,991 (2000); 15,248 (2005); 15,525 (2010 projected); Race: 98.2% White, 0.4% Black, 0.3% Asian, 0.8% Hispanic of any race (2005); Density: 207.8 persons per square mile (2005); Average household size: 2.58 (2005); Median age: 39.8 (2005); Males per 100 females: 95.7 (2005); Marriage status: 23.0% never married, 61.9% now married, 5.2% widowed, 9.8% divorced (2000); Foreign born: 2.6% (2000); Ancestry (includes multiple ancestries): 22.0% German, 21.8% Irish, 19.9% English, 11.0% Italian, 7.6% French (except Basque) (2000).
Economy: Single-family building permits issued: 14 (2005); Multi-family building permits issued: 0 (2005); Employment by occupation: 10.6%

management, 18.1% professional, 13.3% services, 29.3% sales, 0.6% farming, 10.5% construction, 17.5% production (2000).
Income: Per capita income: $24,153 (2005); Median household income: $50,401 (2005); Average household income: $62,124 (2005); Percent of households with income of $100,000 or more: 14.9% (2005); Poverty rate: 7.0% (2000).
Education: Percent of population age 25 and over with: High school diploma (including GED) or higher: 84.3% (2005); Bachelor's degree or higher: 17.5% (2005); Master's degree or higher: 5.6% (2005).
Housing: Homeownership rate: 82.6% (2005); Median home value: $102,794 (2005); Median rent: $474 per month (2000); Median age of housing: 31 years (2000).
Transportation: Commute to work: 93.9% car, 0.5% public transportation, 1.8% walk, 2.7% work from home (2000); Travel time to work: 18.7% less than 15 minutes, 47.0% 15 to 30 minutes, 27.9% 30 to 45 minutes, 3.6% 45 to 60 minutes, 2.7% 60 minutes or more (2000)

WAMPSVILLE (village). Covers a land area of 1.012 square miles and a water area of 0 square miles. Located at 43.08° N. Lat.; 75.70° W. Long. Elevation is 450 feet.
Population: 501 (1990); 561 (2000); 590 (2005); 618 (2010 projected); Race: 95.8% White, 0.2% Black, 0.5% Asian, 2.5% Hispanic of any race (2005); Density: 583.0 persons per square mile (2005); Average household size: 2.69 (2005); Median age: 36.8 (2005); Males per 100 females: 102.1 (2005); Marriage status: 19.4% never married, 66.7% now married, 5.5% widowed, 8.5% divorced (2000); Foreign born: 2.0% (2000); Ancestry (includes multiple ancestries): 29.7% German, 27.4% Irish, 19.6% English, 10.0% Italian, 6.4% French (except Basque) (2000).
Economy: In dairying area. Single-family building permits issued: 0 (2005); Multi-family building permits issued: 0 (2005); Employment by occupation: 12.0% management, 13.8% professional, 15.9% services, 28.3% sales, 1.4% farming, 9.4% construction, 19.2% production (2000).
Income: Per capita income: $18,746 (2005); Median household income: $43,973 (2005); Average household income: $50,502 (2005); Percent of households with income of $100,000 or more: 7.3% (2005); Poverty rate: 4.3% (2000).
Education: Percent of population age 25 and over with: High school diploma (including GED) or higher: 89.0% (2005); Bachelor's degree or higher: 18.7% (2005); Master's degree or higher: 5.2% (2005).

School District(s)
Oneida City School District (KG-12)
    2003-04 Enrollment: 2,550 . . . . (315) 363-2550

Housing: Homeownership rate: 83.6% (2005); Median home value: $106,868 (2005); Median rent: $438 per month (2000); Median age of housing: 46 years (2000).
Transportation: Commute to work: 96.7% car, 0.0% public transportation, 1.9% walk, 1.5% work from home (2000); Travel time to work: 41.4% less than 15 minutes, 22.9% 15 to 30 minutes, 31.6% 30 to 45 minutes, 1.9% 45 to 60 minutes, 2.3% 60 minutes or more (2000)

Manhattan Borough
See New York City

Monroe County

Located in western New York; bounded on the north by Lake Ontario; drained by the Genesee River. Covers a land area of 659.29 square miles, a water area of 706.31 square miles, and is located in the Eastern Time Zone. The county government was organized in 1821. County seat is Rochester.

Monroe County is part of the Rochester, NY Metropolitan Statistical Area. The entire metro area includes: Livingston County, NY; Monroe County, NY; Ontario County, NY; Orleans County, NY; Wayne County, NY

Weather Station: Rochester Int'l Airport   Elevation: 597 feet

	Jan	Feb	Mar	Apr	May	Jun	Jul	Aug	Sep	Oct	Nov	Dec
High	31	33	43	56	68	77	82	80	72	60	48	37
Low	17	17	25	36	47	56	61	59	52	41	33	23
Precip	2.3	2.1	2.6	2.7	2.8	3.3	3.0	3.5	3.4	2.7	2.9	2.8
Snow	25.7	22.1	16.3	4.9	0.5	tr	tr	0.0	tr	0.1	8.0	21.9

High and Low temperatures in degrees Fahrenheit; Precipitation and Snow in inches

Population: 713,968 (1990); 735,343 (2000); 737,839 (2005); 739,943 (2010 projected); Race: 76.8% White, 14.9% Black, 2.9% Asian, 6.3% Hispanic of any race (2005); Density: 1,119.1 persons per square mile (2005); Average household size: 2.55 (2005); Median age: 37.6 (2005); Males per 100 females: 93.5 (2005).
Religion: Five largest groups: 35.7% Catholic Church, 3.1% Jewish Estimate, 2.0% The United Methodist Church, 1.9% Presbyterian Church (U.S.A.), 1.8% American Baptist Churches in the USA (2000).
Economy: Unemployment rate: 4.6% (2005); Total civilian labor force: 376,303 (2005); Leading industries: 17.0% manufacturing; 14.9% health care and social assistance; 11.7% retail trade (2003); Farms: 631 totaling 106,561 acres (2002); Companies that employ 500 or more persons: 54 (2003); Companies that employ 100 to 499 persons: 485 (2003); Companies that employ less than 100 persons: 16,425 (2003); Black-owned businesses: 2,844 (2002); Hispanic-owned businesses: 1,095 (2002); Women-owned businesses: 16,113 (2002); Retail sales per capita: $12,758 (2006); Single-family building permits issued: 1,395 (2005); Multi-family building permits issued: 348 (2005).
Income: Per capita income: $25,581 (2005); Median household income: $49,412 (2005); Average household income: $64,315 (2005); Percent of households with income of $100,000 or more: 17.3% (2005); Poverty rate: 12.7% (2003); Bankruptcy rate: 6.43% (2005).
Taxes: Total county taxes per capita: $681 (2004); County property taxes per capita: $282 (2004).
Education: Percent of population age 25 and over with: High school diploma (including GED) or higher: 85.0% (2005); Bachelor's degree or higher: 31.2% (2005); Master's degree or higher: 12.7% (2005).
Housing: Homeownership rate: 65.9% (2005); Median home value: $125,983 (2005); Median rent: $535 per month (2000); Median age of housing: 40 years (2000).
Health: Birth rate: 121.1 per 10,000 population (2004); Death rate: 83.7 per 10,000 population (2004); Age-adjusted cancer mortality rate: 209.9 deaths per 100,000 population (2002); Air Quality Index: 74.8% good, 24.7% moderate, 0.5% unhealthy for sensitive individuals, 0.0% unhealthy (percent of days in 2005); Number of physicians: 45.2 per 10,000 population (2004); Hospital beds: 28.7 per 10,000 population (2003); Hospital admissions: 1,228.4 per 10,000 population (2003).
Elections: 2004 Presidential election results: 47.7% Bush, 50.6% Kerry, 1.5% Nader, 0.2% Badnarik
National and State Parks: Braddock Bay State Park; Hamlin Beach State Park

Additional Information Contacts

Monroe County Government	(585) 428-5301
http://www.monroecounty.gov/	
City of Rochester	(585) 428-5990
http://www.ci.rochester.ny.us/	
Town of Chili	(585) 889-3550
http://www.townofchili.org/portal/	
Town of Clarkson	(585) 637-1131
http://www.clarksonny.org/	
Town of Gates	(585) 247-6100
http://www.townofgates.org/	
Town of Greece	(585) 225-2000
http://townofgreece.org/	
Town of Hamlin	(585) 964-2421
http://www.hamlinny.org/	
Town of Henrietta	(585) 334-7700
http://www.townofhenrietta.org/	
Town of Irondequoit	(585) 467-8840
http://www.irondequoit.org/	
Town of Mendon	(585) 624-6060
http://www.townofmendon.org/	
Town of Ogden	(585) 352-2100
http://www.ogdenny.com/	
Town of Parma	(585) 392-9461
http://www.parmany.org/	
Town of Penfield	(585) 340-8600
http://www.penfield.org/	
Town of Perinton	(585) 223-0770
http://www.perinton.org/	
Town of Pittsford	(585) 248-6220
http://www.townofpittsford.com/	
Town of Riga	(585) 293-3880
http://www.townofriga.org/	
Town of Rush	(585) 533-1312
http://www.townofrush.org/	
Town of Webster	(585) 872-1000
http://www.ci.webster.ny.us/	

Town of Wheatland .... (585) 889-1553
    http://www.townofwheatland.org/
Village of Brockport .... (585) 637-5300
    http://brockportny.org/
Village of Churchville .... (585) 293-3720
    http://www.churchville.net/
Village of Hilton .... (585) 392-4144
    http://www.hiltonny.org/
Village of Webster .... (585) 872-1000
    http://www.ci.webster.ny.us/

Monroe County Communities

BRIGHTON (town). Covers a land area of 15.456 square miles and a water area of 0.172 square miles. Located at 43.12° N. Lat.; 77.56° W. Long. Elevation is 458 feet.
Population: 34,458 (1990); 35,588 (2000); 34,859 (2005); 34,213 (2010 projected); Race: 83.0% White, 4.3% Black, 10.2% Asian, 2.9% Hispanic of any race (2005); Density: 2,255.3 persons per square mile (2005); Average household size: 2.24 (2005); Median age: 41.5 (2005); Males per 100 females: 89.4 (2005); Marriage status: 27.1% never married, 55.0% now married, 9.1% widowed, 8.7% divorced (2000); Foreign born: 15.4% (2000); Ancestry (includes multiple ancestries): 18.3% Other groups, 18.2% German, 16.9% Irish, 13.3% English, 11.7% Italian (2000).
Economy: Unemployment rate: 3.5% (2005); Total civilian labor force: 18,270 (2005); Single-family building permits issued: 24 (2005); Multi-family building permits issued: 182 (2005); Employment by occupation: 16.0% management, 45.1% professional, 8.8% services, 21.0% sales, 0.1% farming, 3.4% construction, 5.7% production (2000).
Income: Per capita income: $35,237 (2005); Median household income: $58,422 (2005); Average household income: $77,448 (2005); Percent of households with income of $100,000 or more: 23.9% (2005); Poverty rate: 6.1% (2000).
Taxes: Total city taxes per capita: $371 (2004); City property taxes per capita: $315 (2004).
Education: Percent of population age 25 and over with: High school diploma (including GED) or higher: 91.4% (2005); Bachelor's degree or higher: 57.2% (2005); Master's degree or higher: 30.9% (2005).
Housing: Homeownership rate: 57.7% (2005); Median home value: $149,818 (2005); Median rent: $668 per month (2000); Median age of housing: 39 years (2000).
Safety: Violent crime rate: 11.4 per 10,000 population; Property crime rate: 304.4 per 10,000 population (2004).
Transportation: Commute to work: 92.0% car, 1.9% public transportation, 1.5% walk, 3.9% work from home (2000); Travel time to work: 44.5% less than 15 minutes, 47.6% 15 to 30 minutes, 5.7% 30 to 45 minutes, 0.9% 45 to 60 minutes, 1.2% 60 minutes or more (2000)

BRIGHTON (CDP). Covers a land area of 15.447 square miles and a water area of 0.172 square miles. Located at 43.12° N. Lat.; 77.56° W. Long.
Population: 34,455 (1990); 35,584 (2000); 34,856 (2005); 34,210 (2010 projected); Race: 83.0% White, 4.3% Black, 10.2% Asian, 2.9% Hispanic of any race (2005); Density: 2,256.5 persons per square mile (2005); Average household size: 2.24 (2005); Median age: 41.5 (2005); Males per 100 females: 89.4 (2005); Marriage status: 27.1% never married, 55.0% now married, 9.1% widowed, 8.7% divorced (2000); Foreign born: 15.4% (2000); Ancestry (includes multiple ancestries): 18.3% Other groups, 18.2% German, 16.9% Irish, 13.3% English, 11.7% Italian (2000).
Economy: Employment by occupation: 16.0% management, 45.1% professional, 8.8% services, 21.0% sales, 0.1% farming, 3.4% construction, 5.7% production (2000).
Income: Per capita income: $35,239 (2005); Median household income: $58,421 (2005); Average household income: $77,450 (2005); Percent of households with income of $100,000 or more: 23.9% (2005); Poverty rate: 6.1% (2000).
Education: Percent of population age 25 and over with: High school diploma (including GED) or higher: 91.4% (2005); Bachelor's degree or higher: 57.2% (2005); Master's degree or higher: 30.9% (2005).
Housing: Homeownership rate: 57.7% (2005); Median home value: $149,818 (2005); Median rent: $668 per month (2000); Median age of housing: 39 years (2000).
Transportation: Commute to work: 91.9% car, 1.9% public transportation, 1.5% walk, 3.9% work from home (2000); Travel time to work: 44.5% less than 15 minutes, 47.6% 15 to 30 minutes, 5.7% 30 to 45 minutes, 0.9% 45 to 60 minutes, 1.2% 60 minutes or more (2000)

BROCKPORT (village). Covers a land area of 2.160 square miles and a water area of 0.047 square miles. Located at 43.21° N. Lat.; 77.93° W. Long. Elevation is 543 feet.
History: Seat of State University of N.Y. College at Brockport. Incorporated 1829.
Population: 8,799 (1990); 8,103 (2000); 8,013 (2005); 7,970 (2010 projected); Race: 90.9% White, 4.8% Black, 1.1% Asian, 3.6% Hispanic of any race (2005); Density: 3,710.4 persons per square mile (2005); Average household size: 3.42 (2005); Median age: 23.6 (2005); Males per 100 females: 91.1 (2005); Marriage status: 50.6% never married, 38.0% now married, 5.4% widowed, 6.0% divorced (2000); Foreign born: 2.6% (2000); Ancestry (includes multiple ancestries): 24.1% German, 18.9% Irish, 17.1% English, 12.0% Italian, 9.9% Other groups (2000).
Economy: In agricultural area. Manufacturing of glass containers, cleaning materials; nurseries. Single-family building permits issued: 4 (2005); Multi-family building permits issued: 0 (2005); Employment by occupation: 9.8% management, 22.8% professional, 23.2% services, 28.6% sales, 0.3% farming, 6.8% construction, 8.4% production (2000).
Income: Per capita income: $16,728 (2005); Median household income: $43,051 (2005); Average household income: $51,753 (2005); Percent of households with income of $100,000 or more: 10.3% (2005); Poverty rate: 19.2% (2000).
Education: Percent of population age 25 and over with: High school diploma (including GED) or higher: 87.6% (2005); Bachelor's degree or higher: 37.1% (2005); Master's degree or higher: 17.9% (2005).

School District(s)
Brockport Central School District (KG-12)
    2003-04 Enrollment: 4,480 .... (585) 637-1810

Four-year College(s)
SUNY College at Brockport (Public)
    Fall 2004 Enrollment: 8,595 .... (716) 395-2211
    2005-06 Tuition: In-state $4,350; Out-of-state $11,243

Housing: Homeownership rate: 45.0% (2005); Median home value: $104,603 (2005); Median rent: $516 per month (2000); Median age of housing: 46 years (2000).
Hospitals: Lakeside Memorial Hospital (61 beds)
Safety: Violent crime rate: 23.4 per 10,000 population; Property crime rate: 202.1 per 10,000 population (2004).
Newspapers: Brockport Post (General - Circulation 2,109)
Transportation: Commute to work: 73.4% car, 0.9% public transportation, 23.6% walk, 1.7% work from home (2000); Travel time to work: 51.5% less than 15 minutes, 23.6% 15 to 30 minutes, 19.3% 30 to 45 minutes, 3.4% 45 to 60 minutes, 2.1% 60 minutes or more (2000)
Additional Information Contacts
Brockport Chamber of Commerce .... (585) 637-8684
    http://www.brockport.net
Village of Brockport .... (585) 637-5300
    http://brockportny.org/

CHILI (town). Covers a land area of 39.747 square miles and a water area of 0.190 square miles. Located at 43.10° N. Lat.; 77.74° W. Long.
Population: 25,178 (1990); 27,638 (2000); 28,555 (2005); 29,429 (2010 projected); Race: 89.5% White, 6.8% Black, 1.3% Asian, 2.1% Hispanic of any race (2005); Density: 718.4 persons per square mile (2005); Average household size: 2.68 (2005); Median age: 38.8 (2005); Males per 100 females: 94.8 (2005); Marriage status: 25.1% never married, 62.7% now married, 5.6% widowed, 6.7% divorced (2000); Foreign born: 6.6% (2000); Ancestry (includes multiple ancestries): 27.2% German, 19.1% Italian, 18.8% Irish, 14.5% English, 9.3% Other groups (2000).
Economy: Unemployment rate: 4.3% (2005); Total civilian labor force: 15,608 (2005); Single-family building permits issued: 101 (2005); Multi-family building permits issued: 4 (2005); Employment by occupation: 13.8% management, 24.4% professional, 14.1% services, 28.4% sales, 0.1% farming, 5.0% construction, 14.1% production (2000).
Income: Per capita income: $25,946 (2005); Median household income: $59,978 (2005); Average household income: $68,859 (2005); Percent of households with income of $100,000 or more: 18.4% (2005); Poverty rate: 3.6% (2000).
Education: Percent of population age 25 and over with: High school diploma (including GED) or higher: 89.7% (2005); Bachelor's degree or higher: 28.8% (2005); Master's degree or higher: 10.2% (2005).

Housing: Homeownership rate: 80.1% (2005); Median home value: $129,555 (2005); Median rent: $579 per month (2000); Median age of housing: 30 years (2000).
Transportation: Commute to work: 94.6% car, 0.7% public transportation, 2.3% walk, 1.8% work from home (2000); Travel time to work: 28.9% less than 15 minutes, 53.9% 15 to 30 minutes, 12.3% 30 to 45 minutes, 2.1% 45 to 60 minutes, 2.9% 60 minutes or more (2000)
Additional Information Contacts
Town of Chili . . . . (585) 889-3550
http://www.townofchili.org/portal/

CHURCHVILLE (village).
Covers a land area of 1.135 square miles and a water area of 0.001 square miles. Located at 43.10° N. Lat.; 77.88° W. Long.
History: Frances E. Willard born here.
Population: 1,717 (1990); 1,887 (2000); 1,865 (2005); 1,885 (2010 projected); Race: 95.8% White, 0.6% Black, 1.1% Asian, 0.4% Hispanic of any race (2005); Density: 1,643.3 persons per square mile (2005); Average household size: 2.58 (2005); Median age: 38.2 (2005); Males per 100 females: 90.7 (2005); Marriage status: 25.1% never married, 59.8% now married, 5.8% widowed, 9.3% divorced (2000); Foreign born: 3.1% (2000); Ancestry (includes multiple ancestries): 29.3% German, 22.9% Irish, 19.4% English, 12.2% Italian, 7.2% Polish (2000).
Economy: Agricultural area. Manufacturing of vacuum pump fluids. Single-family building permits issued: 5 (2005); Multi-family building permits issued: 0 (2005); Employment by occupation: 11.9% management, 29.8% professional, 10.4% services, 26.4% sales, 0.4% farming, 7.1% construction, 14.1% production (2000).
Income: Per capita income: $26,007 (2005); Median household income: $61,719 (2005); Average household income: $66,894 (2005); Percent of households with income of $100,000 or more: 15.0% (2005); Poverty rate: 4.2% (2000).
Education: Percent of population age 25 and over with: High school diploma (including GED) or higher: 92.4% (2005); Bachelor's degree or higher: 33.3% (2005); Master's degree or higher: 13.1% (2005).
School District(s)
Churchville-Chili Central School District (KG-12)
 2003-04 Enrollment: 4,482 . . . . (585) 293-1800
Housing: Homeownership rate: 85.7% (2005); Median home value: $116,494 (2005); Median rent: $469 per month (2000); Median age of housing: 27 years (2000).
Transportation: Commute to work: 96.3% car, 0.0% public transportation, 1.0% walk, 2.2% work from home (2000); Travel time to work: 18.2% less than 15 minutes, 49.0% 15 to 30 minutes, 27.8% 30 to 45 minutes, 3.0% 45 to 60 minutes, 2.0% 60 minutes or more (2000)
Additional Information Contacts
Village of Churchville . . . . (585) 293-3720
http://www.churchville.net/

CLARKSON (town).
Covers a land area of 33.221 square miles and a water area of 0.005 square miles. Located at 43.24° N. Lat.; 77.93° W. Long. Elevation is 429 feet.
Population: 4,517 (1990); 6,072 (2000); 6,420 (2005); 6,759 (2010 projected); Race: 92.8% White, 2.4% Black, 0.5% Asian, 3.6% Hispanic of any race (2005); Density: 193.2 persons per square mile (2005); Average household size: 2.95 (2005); Median age: 37.6 (2005); Males per 100 females: 95.5 (2005); Marriage status: 18.2% never married, 65.2% now married, 9.3% widowed, 7.3% divorced (2000); Foreign born: 2.3% (2000); Ancestry (includes multiple ancestries): 28.6% German, 25.0% Irish, 20.5% English, 17.7% Italian, 9.6% Other groups (2000).
Economy: Single-family building permits issued: 17 (2005); Multi-family building permits issued: 0 (2005); Employment by occupation: 12.7% management, 22.3% professional, 13.3% services, 25.2% sales, 0.2% farming, 6.5% construction, 19.8% production (2000).
Income: Per capita income: $22,812 (2005); Median household income: $60,164 (2005); Average household income: $64,161 (2005); Percent of households with income of $100,000 or more: 14.7% (2005); Poverty rate: 4.9% (2000).
Taxes: Total city taxes per capita: $253 (2004); City property taxes per capita: $195 (2004).
Education: Percent of population age 25 and over with: High school diploma (including GED) or higher: 86.2% (2005); Bachelor's degree or higher: 27.6% (2005); Master's degree or higher: 11.6% (2005).

Housing: Homeownership rate: 81.5% (2005); Median home value: $129,304 (2005); Median rent: $434 per month (2000); Median age of housing: 24 years (2000).
Transportation: Commute to work: 95.7% car, 0.4% public transportation, 0.4% walk, 2.9% work from home (2000); Travel time to work: 25.4% less than 15 minutes, 33.2% 15 to 30 minutes, 32.3% 30 to 45 minutes, 5.0% 45 to 60 minutes, 4.2% 60 minutes or more (2000)
Additional Information Contacts
Town of Clarkson . . . . (585) 637-1131
http://www.clarksonny.org/

EAST ROCHESTER (town and village).
Covers a land area of 1.353 square miles and a water area of 0 square miles. Located at 43.11° N. Lat.; 77.48° W. Long.
Population: 6,932 (1990); 6,650 (2000); 6,449 (2005); 6,250 (2010 projected); Race: 94.8% White, 1.9% Black, 0.9% Asian, 3.3% Hispanic of any race (2005); Density: 4,766.8 persons per square mile (2005); Average household size: 2.37 (2005); Median age: 38.0 (2005); Males per 100 females: 88.8 (2005); Marriage status: 32.7% never married, 46.6% now married, 7.6% widowed, 13.0% divorced (2000); Foreign born: 5.2% (2000); Ancestry (includes multiple ancestries): 33.8% Italian, 21.7% German, 19.2% Irish, 16.0% English, 6.0% Other groups (2000).
Economy: Single-family building permits issued: 2 (2005); Multi-family building permits issued: 0 (2005); Employment by occupation: 10.8% management, 21.8% professional, 17.5% services, 29.7% sales, 0.0% farming, 6.6% construction, 13.6% production (2000).
Income: Per capita income: $20,633 (2005); Median household income: $41,668 (2005); Average household income: $48,169 (2005); Percent of households with income of $100,000 or more: 7.2% (2005); Poverty rate: 9.3% (2000).
Education: Percent of population age 25 and over with: High school diploma (including GED) or higher: 83.7% (2005); Bachelor's degree or higher: 22.3% (2005); Master's degree or higher: 7.8% (2005).
School District(s)
East Rochester Union Free School District (PK-12)
 2003-04 Enrollment: 1,294 . . . . (585) 248-6302
Housing: Homeownership rate: 63.5% (2005); Median home value: $93,599 (2005); Median rent: $530 per month (2000); Median age of housing: 55 years (2000).
Safety: Violent crime rate: 12.3 per 10,000 population; Property crime rate: 231.5 per 10,000 population (2004).
Transportation: Commute to work: 92.3% car, 1.5% public transportation, 2.9% walk, 3.3% work from home (2000); Travel time to work: 37.3% less than 15 minutes, 51.1% 15 to 30 minutes, 8.6% 30 to 45 minutes, 0.8% 45 to 60 minutes, 2.2% 60 minutes or more (2000)

FAIRPORT (village).
Covers a land area of 1.575 square miles and a water area of 0.049 square miles. Located at 43.09° N. Lat.; 77.44° W. Long.
History: Incorporated 1867.
Population: 5,943 (1990); 5,740 (2000); 5,691 (2005); 5,644 (2010 projected); Race: 96.5% White, 0.9% Black, 1.1% Asian, 2.0% Hispanic of any race (2005); Density: 3,613.9 persons per square mile (2005); Average household size: 2.37 (2005); Median age: 39.4 (2005); Males per 100 females: 92.5 (2005); Marriage status: 24.9% never married, 57.3% now married, 6.3% widowed, 11.5% divorced (2000); Foreign born: 3.4% (2000); Ancestry (includes multiple ancestries): 28.3% German, 21.7% Irish, 20.2% Italian, 15.0% English, 6.0% Polish (2000).
Economy: Manufacturing: electronic products, chemicals, plastics, transportation equipment, machinery. Nurseries; agriculture: apples, peaches, potatoes; honey. Single-family building permits issued: 1 (2005); Multi-family building permits issued: 0 (2005); Employment by occupation: 18.3% management, 31.9% professional, 13.1% services, 21.2% sales, 0.0% farming, 6.0% construction, 9.6% production (2000).
Income: Per capita income: $35,431 (2005); Median household income: $63,484 (2005); Average household income: $83,526 (2005); Percent of households with income of $100,000 or more: 25.5% (2005); Poverty rate: 3.3% (2000).
Education: Percent of population age 25 and over with: High school diploma (including GED) or higher: 91.6% (2005); Bachelor's degree or higher: 46.3% (2005); Master's degree or higher: 18.3% (2005).
School District(s)
Boces Monroe 1 (PK-PK)
 2003-04 Enrollment: 1,466 . . . . (585) 383-2200

Fairport Central School District (KG-12)
  2003-04 Enrollment: 7,115 . . . . (585) 421-2004
Housing: Homeownership rate: 69.1% (2005); Median home value: $153,691 (2005); Median rent: $560 per month (2000); Median age of housing: 59 years (2000).
Safety: Violent crime rate: 8.8 per 10,000 population; Property crime rate: 145.6 per 10,000 population (2004).
Transportation: Commute to work: 92.8% car, 0.2% public transportation, 3.2% walk, 3.3% work from home (2000); Travel time to work: 36.6% less than 15 minutes, 47.3% 15 to 30 minutes, 12.5% 30 to 45 minutes, 2.4% 45 to 60 minutes, 1.3% 60 minutes or more (2000)
Additional Information Contacts
Fairport Chamber of Commerce . . . . (716) 454-2220
  http://www.rochesterbusinessalliance.com

GATES (town). Covers a land area of 15.233 square miles and a water area of 0.075 square miles. Located at 43.15° N. Lat.; 77.70° W. Long.
Population: 28,583 (1990); 29,275 (2000); 28,827 (2005); 28,358 (2010 projected); Race: 86.0% White, 7.8% Black, 2.9% Asian, 3.8% Hispanic of any race (2005); Density: 1,892.4 persons per square mile (2005); Average household size: 2.46 (2005); Median age: 41.3 (2005); Males per 100 females: 92.9 (2005); Marriage status: 23.7% never married, 58.5% now married, 8.4% widowed, 9.4% divorced (2000); Foreign born: 9.4% (2000); Ancestry (includes multiple ancestries): 32.6% Italian, 20.1% German, 14.7% Irish, 10.3% Other groups, 9.6% English (2000).
Economy: Unemployment rate: 5.1% (2005); Total civilian labor force: 14,850 (2005); Single-family building permits issued: 40 (2005); Multi-family building permits issued: 56 (2005); Employment by occupation: 10.1% management, 17.8% professional, 13.2% services, 30.8% sales, 0.0% farming, 7.0% construction, 21.1% production (2000).
Income: Per capita income: $24,235 (2005); Median household income: $49,982 (2005); Average household income: $58,949 (2005); Percent of households with income of $100,000 or more: 12.4% (2005); Poverty rate: 5.6% (2000).
Education: Percent of population age 25 and over with: High school diploma (including GED) or higher: 80.8% (2005); Bachelor's degree or higher: 17.0% (2005); Master's degree or higher: 5.4% (2005).
Housing: Homeownership rate: 77.5% (2005); Median home value: $109,901 (2005); Median rent: $561 per month (2000); Median age of housing: 33 years (2000).
Safety: Violent crime rate: 9.3 per 10,000 population; Property crime rate: 399.0 per 10,000 population (2004).
Transportation: Commute to work: 95.9% car, 0.8% public transportation, 0.9% walk, 1.6% work from home (2000); Travel time to work: 41.3% less than 15 minutes, 47.3% 15 to 30 minutes, 6.7% 30 to 45 minutes, 1.4% 45 to 60 minutes, 3.3% 60 minutes or more (2000)
Additional Information Contacts
Town of Gates . . . . (585) 247-6100
  http://www.townofgates.org/

GATES-NORTH GATES (CDP). Covers a land area of 4.654 square miles and a water area of 0.041 square miles. Located at 43.16° N. Lat.; 77.69° W. Long.
Population: 14,995 (1990); 15,138 (2000); 14,621 (2005); 14,096 (2010 projected); Race: 85.0% White, 7.4% Black, 3.5% Asian, 4.3% Hispanic of any race (2005); Density: 3,141.4 persons per square mile (2005); Average household size: 2.39 (2005); Median age: 40.8 (2005); Males per 100 females: 91.8 (2005); Marriage status: 23.6% never married, 56.4% now married, 8.3% widowed, 11.7% divorced (2000); Foreign born: 11.4% (2000); Ancestry (includes multiple ancestries): 36.0% Italian, 17.0% German, 12.5% Irish, 11.9% Other groups, 7.3% English (2000).
Economy: Employment by occupation: 9.5% management, 15.9% professional, 13.9% services, 29.8% sales, 0.0% farming, 7.0% construction, 23.8% production (2000).
Income: Per capita income: $23,292 (2005); Median household income: $47,631 (2005); Average household income: $55,531 (2005); Percent of households with income of $100,000 or more: 11.4% (2005); Poverty rate: 6.8% (2000).
Education: Percent of population age 25 and over with: High school diploma (including GED) or higher: 77.4% (2005); Bachelor's degree or higher: 13.5% (2005); Master's degree or higher: 4.0% (2005).
Housing: Homeownership rate: 72.8% (2005); Median home value: $106,904 (2005); Median rent: $546 per month (2000); Median age of housing: 34 years (2000).

Transportation: Commute to work: 96.1% car, 1.0% public transportation, 0.9% walk, 1.5% work from home (2000); Travel time to work: 43.0% less than 15 minutes, 47.0% 15 to 30 minutes, 6.6% 30 to 45 minutes, 1.0% 45 to 60 minutes, 2.4% 60 minutes or more (2000)

GREECE (town). Covers a land area of 47.425 square miles and a water area of 3.931 square miles. Located at 43.23° N. Lat.; 77.68° W. Long. Elevation is 272 feet.
Population: 90,106 (1990); 94,141 (2000); 94,862 (2005); 95,464 (2010 projected); Race: 92.0% White, 3.5% Black, 1.7% Asian, 3.3% Hispanic of any race (2005); Density: 2,000.3 persons per square mile (2005); Average household size: 2.52 (2005); Median age: 40.3 (2005); Males per 100 females: 92.5 (2005); Marriage status: 23.9% never married, 59.7% now married, 7.7% widowed, 8.7% divorced (2000); Foreign born: 6.6% (2000); Ancestry (includes multiple ancestries): 27.9% Italian, 26.2% German, 18.5% Irish, 12.4% English, 7.8% Other groups (2000).
Economy: Unemployment rate: 4.6% (2005); Total civilian labor force: 50,399 (2005); Single-family building permits issued: 214 (2005); Multi-family building permits issued: 10 (2005); Employment by occupation: 12.3% management, 21.5% professional, 13.0% services, 29.2% sales, 0.1% farming, 6.5% construction, 17.5% production (2000).
Income: Per capita income: $25,558 (2005); Median household income: $53,210 (2005); Average household income: $63,839 (2005); Percent of households with income of $100,000 or more: 15.8% (2005); Poverty rate: 4.8% (2000).
Taxes: Total city taxes per capita: $330 (2004); City property taxes per capita: $284 (2004).
Education: Percent of population age 25 and over with: High school diploma (including GED) or higher: 87.8% (2005); Bachelor's degree or higher: 23.5% (2005); Master's degree or higher: 7.7% (2005).
Housing: Homeownership rate: 75.3% (2005); Median home value: $126,032 (2005); Median rent: $590 per month (2000); Median age of housing: 33 years (2000).
Safety: Violent crime rate: 7.9 per 10,000 population; Property crime rate: 247.4 per 10,000 population (2004).
Transportation: Commute to work: 96.0% car, 0.7% public transportation, 1.1% walk, 1.7% work from home (2000); Travel time to work: 30.4% less than 15 minutes, 53.5% 15 to 30 minutes, 12.3% 30 to 45 minutes, 1.6% 45 to 60 minutes, 2.2% 60 minutes or more (2000)
Additional Information Contacts
Greece Chamber of Commerce. . . . . (585) 227-7272
  http://www.greecechamber.org
Town of Greece . . . . (585) 225-2000
  http://townofgreece.org/

GREECE (CDP). Covers a land area of 4.331 square miles and a water area of 0 square miles. Located at 43.20° N. Lat.; 77.70° W. Long.
Population: 15,556 (1990); 14,614 (2000); 14,086 (2005); 13,576 (2010 projected); Race: 92.7% White, 3.1% Black, 1.9% Asian, 3.1% Hispanic of any race (2005); Density: 3,252.3 persons per square mile (2005); Average household size: 2.39 (2005); Median age: 44.1 (2005); Males per 100 females: 90.0 (2005); Marriage status: 23.2% never married, 57.5% now married, 8.6% widowed, 10.7% divorced (2000); Foreign born: 6.7% (2000); Ancestry (includes multiple ancestries): 27.3% Italian, 26.5% German, 17.3% Irish, 11.2% English, 7.8% Polish (2000).
Economy: Employment by occupation: 10.3% management, 22.0% professional, 13.1% services, 28.0% sales, 0.0% farming, 6.3% construction, 20.3% production (2000).
Income: Per capita income: $24,422 (2005); Median household income: $48,349 (2005); Average household income: $57,981 (2005); Percent of households with income of $100,000 or more: 12.6% (2005); Poverty rate: 4.3% (2000).
Education: Percent of population age 25 and over with: High school diploma (including GED) or higher: 85.7% (2005); Bachelor's degree or higher: 20.7% (2005); Master's degree or higher: 6.6% (2005).
Housing: Homeownership rate: 77.1% (2005); Median home value: $119,955 (2005); Median rent: $561 per month (2000); Median age of housing: 36 years (2000).
Transportation: Commute to work: 95.2% car, 1.2% public transportation, 1.5% walk, 1.5% work from home (2000); Travel time to work: 35.6% less than 15 minutes, 51.7% 15 to 30 minutes, 8.4% 30 to 45 minutes, 1.9% 45 to 60 minutes, 2.4% 60 minutes or more (2000)

HAMLIN (town). Covers a land area of 43.411 square miles and a water area of 1.101 square miles. Located at 43.31° N. Lat.; 77.92° W. Long.

Population: 9,203 (1990); 9,355 (2000); 9,305 (2005); 9,255 (2010 projected); Race: 96.1% White, 1.2% Black, 0.4% Asian, 2.2% Hispanic of any race (2005); Density: 214.3 persons per square mile (2005); Average household size: 2.82 (2005); Median age: 35.8 (2005); Males per 100 females: 98.3 (2005); Marriage status: 24.8% never married, 63.4% now married, 3.6% widowed, 8.2% divorced (2000); Foreign born: 2.1% (2000); Ancestry (includes multiple ancestries): 34.0% German, 20.1% Irish, 17.4% English, 15.6% Italian, 7.8% United States or American (2000).
Economy: Single-family building permits issued: 7 (2005); Multi-family building permits issued: 0 (2005); Employment by occupation: 11.3% management, 15.1% professional, 12.7% services, 28.7% sales, 0.1% farming, 10.0% construction, 22.0% production (2000).
Income: Per capita income: $22,139 (2005); Median household income: $55,109 (2005); Average household income: $61,975 (2005); Percent of households with income of $100,000 or more: 14.5% (2005); Poverty rate: 6.0% (2000).
Education: Percent of population age 25 and over with: High school diploma (including GED) or higher: 88.3% (2005); Bachelor's degree or higher: 15.4% (2005); Master's degree or higher: 5.1% (2005).
Housing: Homeownership rate: 84.8% (2005); Median home value: $115,804 (2005); Median rent: $479 per month (2000); Median age of housing: 27 years (2000).
Transportation: Commute to work: 96.3% car, 0.5% public transportation, 1.5% walk, 1.7% work from home (2000); Travel time to work: 15.2% less than 15 minutes, 27.9% 15 to 30 minutes, 38.9% 30 to 45 minutes, 12.8% 45 to 60 minutes, 5.3% 60 minutes or more (2000)
Additional Information Contacts
Town of Hamlin . . . . (585) 964-2421
http://www.hamlinny.org/

HENRIETTA (town).
Covers a land area of 35.409 square miles and a water area of 0.186 square miles. Located at 43.06° N. Lat.; 77.62° W. Long. Elevation is 596 feet.
Population: 36,376 (1990); 39,028 (2000); 40,727 (2005); 42,204 (2010 projected); Race: 81.5% White, 8.0% Black, 6.6% Asian, 3.8% Hispanic of any race (2005); Density: 1,150.2 persons per square mile (2005); Average household size: 3.01 (2005); Median age: 31.5 (2005); Males per 100 females: 111.6 (2005); Marriage status: 35.9% never married, 52.5% now married, 5.1% widowed, 6.6% divorced (2000); Foreign born: 8.4% (2000); Ancestry (includes multiple ancestries): 23.5% German, 17.0% Irish, 16.2% Italian, 14.8% Other groups, 13.0% English (2000).
Economy: Unemployment rate: 4.1% (2005); Total civilian labor force: 22,429 (2005); Single-family building permits issued: 171 (2005); Multi-family building permits issued: 0 (2005); Employment by occupation: 11.5% management, 27.1% professional, 13.9% services, 30.1% sales, 0.0% farming, 6.2% construction, 11.2% production (2000).
Income: Per capita income: $22,386 (2005); Median household income: $57,145 (2005); Average household income: $64,818 (2005); Percent of households with income of $100,000 or more: 16.2% (2005); Poverty rate: 9.1% (2000).
Taxes: Total city taxes per capita: $128 (2004); City property taxes per capita: $69 (2004).
Education: Percent of population age 25 and over with: High school diploma (including GED) or higher: 90.4% (2005); Bachelor's degree or higher: 30.5% (2005); Master's degree or higher: 11.3% (2005).
School District(s)
Rush-Henrietta Central School District (KG-12)
   2003-04 Enrollment: 5,859 . . . . (585) 359-5012
Housing: Homeownership rate: 72.8% (2005); Median home value: $126,686 (2005); Median rent: $643 per month (2000); Median age of housing: 31 years (2000).
Transportation: Commute to work: 89.4% car, 1.5% public transportation, 6.3% walk, 1.9% work from home (2000); Travel time to work: 38.3% less than 15 minutes, 46.8% 15 to 30 minutes, 11.3% 30 to 45 minutes, 1.6% 45 to 60 minutes, 1.9% 60 minutes or more (2000)
Additional Information Contacts
Town of Henrietta. . . . . (585) 334-7700
   http://www.townofhenrietta.org/

HILTON (village).
Covers a land area of 1.676 square miles and a water area of 0 square miles. Located at 43.29° N. Lat.; 77.79° W. Long. Elevation is 281 feet.
Population: 5,237 (1990); 5,856 (2000); 6,006 (2005); 6,162 (2010 projected); Race: 96.0% White, 2.1% Black, 0.6% Asian, 1.9% Hispanic of any race (2005); Density: 3,583.7 persons per square mile (2005); Average household size: 2.83 (2005); Median age: 35.6 (2005); Males per 100 females: 93.2 (2005); Marriage status: 24.6% never married, 59.0% now married, 7.5% widowed, 8.9% divorced (2000); Foreign born: 2.2% (2000); Ancestry (includes multiple ancestries): 39.2% German, 25.8% Irish, 19.5% English, 18.9% Italian, 7.2% Polish (2000).
Economy: Milling; metalworking fluids. Agriculture: fruit, wheat. Single-family building permits issued: 13 (2005); Multi-family building permits issued: 71 (2005); Employment by occupation: 8.8% management, 25.2% professional, 13.1% services, 29.5% sales, 0.0% farming, 8.8% construction, 14.5% production (2000).
Income: Per capita income: $21,789 (2005); Median household income: $55,519 (2005); Average household income: $60,957 (2005); Percent of households with income of $100,000 or more: 11.6% (2005); Poverty rate: 4.4% (2000).
Education: Percent of population age 25 and over with: High school diploma (including GED) or higher: 89.8% (2005); Bachelor's degree or higher: 20.8% (2005); Master's degree or higher: 6.3% (2005).
School District(s)
Hilton Central School District (KG-12)
   2003-04 Enrollment: 4,441 . . . . (585) 392-1000
Housing: Homeownership rate: 72.9% (2005); Median home value: $116,616 (2005); Median rent: $535 per month (2000); Median age of housing: 25 years (2000).
Transportation: Commute to work: 95.1% car, 1.4% public transportation, 1.4% walk, 1.1% work from home (2000); Travel time to work: 19.6% less than 15 minutes, 45.3% 15 to 30 minutes, 27.5% 30 to 45 minutes, 5.5% 45 to 60 minutes, 2.0% 60 minutes or more (2000)
Additional Information Contacts
Village of Hilton . . . . (585) 392-4144
   http://www.hiltonny.org/

HONEOYE FALLS (village).
Covers a land area of 2.594 square miles and a water area of 0 square miles. Located at 42.95° N. Lat.; 77.58° W. Long. Elevation is 668 feet.
History: Incorporated 1838.
Population: 2,340 (1990); 2,595 (2000); 2,631 (2005); 2,673 (2010 projected); Race: 96.3% White, 1.4% Black, 1.1% Asian, 1.3% Hispanic of any race (2005); Density: 1,014.2 persons per square mile (2005); Average household size: 2.30 (2005); Median age: 42.7 (2005); Males per 100 females: 82.2 (2005); Marriage status: 23.4% never married, 55.6% now married, 10.3% widowed, 10.6% divorced (2000); Foreign born: 2.2% (2000); Ancestry (includes multiple ancestries): 34.1% German, 25.5% English, 23.9% Irish, 13.9% Italian, 5.2% Polish (2000).
Economy: Manufacturing: air, gas, and liquid filtration equipment; safety flashers, railroad lanterns, reflectors, terminal boards and strips. Agriculture: grain, vegetables; dairying. Single-family building permits issued: 2 (2005); Multi-family building permits issued: 8 (2005); Employment by occupation: 18.3% management, 32.8% professional, 10.7% services, 23.5% sales, 0.0% farming, 7.8% construction, 6.9% production (2000).
Income: Per capita income: $31,882 (2005); Median household income: $56,584 (2005); Average household income: $72,620 (2005); Percent of households with income of $100,000 or more: 21.9% (2005); Poverty rate: 2.5% (2000).
Education: Percent of population age 25 and over with: High school diploma (including GED) or higher: 93.3% (2005); Bachelor's degree or higher: 43.5% (2005); Master's degree or higher: 16.4% (2005).
School District(s)
Honeoye Falls-Lima Central School District (KG-12)
   2003-04 Enrollment: 2,601 . . . . (585) 624-7010
Housing: Homeownership rate: 62.4% (2005); Median home value: $144,953 (2005); Median rent: $475 per month (2000); Median age of housing: 45 years (2000).
Transportation: Commute to work: 92.5% car, 0.0% public transportation, 4.1% walk, 3.1% work from home (2000); Travel time to work: 21.1% less than 15 minutes, 42.2% 15 to 30 minutes, 32.2% 30 to 45 minutes, 3.1% 45 to 60 minutes, 1.5% 60 minutes or more (2000)

IRONDEQUOIT (CDP and town).
Covers a land area of 15.186 square miles and a water area of 1.633 square miles. Located at 43.20° N. Lat.; 77.57° W. Long. Elevation is 385 feet.
History: Named for the Iroquoian translation of "bay". Settled 1791, organized 1839.
Population: 52,371 (1990); 52,354 (2000); 51,862 (2005); 51,388 (2010 projected); Race: 90.8% White, 4.8% Black, 1.2% Asian, 4.1% Hispanic of

any race (2005); Density: 3,415.0 persons per square mile (2005); Average household size: 2.32 (2005); Median age: 44.3 (2005); Males per 100 females: 86.3 (2005); Marriage status: 22.5% never married, 58.4% now married, 10.9% widowed, 8.3% divorced (2000); Foreign born: 8.1% (2000); Ancestry (includes multiple ancestries): 28.6% Italian, 22.7% German, 18.8% Irish, 11.5% English, 8.7% Other groups (2000).
Economy: Unemployment rate: 4.8% (2005); Total civilian labor force: 25,676 (2005); Single-family building permits issued: 13 (2005); Multi-family building permits issued: 0 (2005); Employment by occupation: 14.2% management, 27.3% professional, 11.7% services, 28.0% sales, 0.1% farming, 6.3% construction, 12.5% production (2000).
Income: Per capita income: $26,108 (2005); Median household income: $49,436 (2005); Average household income: $60,177 (2005); Percent of households with income of $100,000 or more: 14.2% (2005); Poverty rate: 5.4% (2000).
Taxes: Total city taxes per capita: $356 (2004); City property taxes per capita: $314 (2004).
Education: Percent of population age 25 and over with: High school diploma (including GED) or higher: 84.4% (2005); Bachelor's degree or higher: 27.9% (2005); Master's degree or higher: 10.5% (2005).
Housing: Homeownership rate: 79.7% (2005); Median home value: $113,136 (2005); Median rent: $587 per month (2000); Median age of housing: 46 years (2000).
Safety: Violent crime rate: 12.7 per 10,000 population; Property crime rate: 383.0 per 10,000 population (2004).
Transportation: Commute to work: 94.0% car, 1.6% public transportation, 1.4% walk, 2.6% work from home (2000); Travel time to work: 32.3% less than 15 minutes, 55.0% 15 to 30 minutes, 9.2% 30 to 45 minutes, 1.1% 45 to 60 minutes, 2.4% 60 minutes or more (2000)
Additional Information Contacts
Town of Irondequoit . . . . (585) 467-8840
http://www.irondequoit.org/

MENDON (town). Covers a land area of 39.804 square miles and a water area of 0.145 square miles. Located at 42.98° N. Lat.; 77.56° W. Long.
Population: 6,845 (1990); 8,370 (2000); 8,835 (2005); 9,269 (2010 projected); Race: 96.9% White, 0.9% Black, 1.4% Asian, 1.2% Hispanic of any race (2005); Density: 222.0 persons per square mile (2005); Average household size: 2.71 (2005); Median age: 41.1 (2005); Males per 100 females: 95.5 (2005); Marriage status: 18.8% never married, 69.2% now married, 4.8% widowed, 7.2% divorced (2000); Foreign born: 3.6% (2000); Ancestry (includes multiple ancestries): 32.4% German, 22.7% English, 21.4% Irish, 13.1% Italian, 5.4% United States or American (2000).
Economy: Single-family building permits issued: 26 (2005); Multi-family building permits issued: 0 (2005); Employment by occupation: 23.9% management, 34.2% professional, 7.8% services, 22.9% sales, 0.0% farming, 5.5% construction, 5.7% production (2000).
Income: Per capita income: $43,679 (2005); Median household income: $90,202 (2005); Average household income: $117,987 (2005); Percent of households with income of $100,000 or more: 44.5% (2005); Poverty rate: 3.0% (2000).
Education: Percent of population age 25 and over with: High school diploma (including GED) or higher: 94.6% (2005); Bachelor's degree or higher: 53.5% (2005); Master's degree or higher: 22.7% (2005).
Housing: Homeownership rate: 83.7% (2005); Median home value: $220,643 (2005); Median rent: $484 per month (2000); Median age of housing: 26 years (2000).
Transportation: Commute to work: 91.4% car, 0.0% public transportation, 2.0% walk, 5.6% work from home (2000); Travel time to work: 16.3% less than 15 minutes, 47.4% 15 to 30 minutes, 30.5% 30 to 45 minutes, 3.6% 45 to 60 minutes, 2.2% 60 minutes or more (2000)
Additional Information Contacts
Town of Mendon . . . . (585) 624-6060
http://www.townofmendon.org/

NORTH CHILI (unincorporated postal area, zip code 14514). Covers a land area of 2.803 square miles and a water area of 0 square miles. Located at 43.12° N. Lat.; 77.80° W. Long. Elevation is 582 feet.
History: Seat of Roberts Wesleyan College.
Population: 0 (2000); Race: 93.8% White, 2.4% Black, 0.7% Asian, 1.5% Hispanic of any race (2000); Density: 0.0 persons per square mile (2000); Age: 23.3% under 18, 15.5% over 64 (2000); Marriage status: 33.3% never married, 53.3% now married, 6.6% widowed, 6.7% divorced (2000); Foreign born: 4.3% (2000); Ancestry (includes multiple ancestries): 27.8% German, 16.9% Irish, 13.7% Italian, 13.5% English, 8.5% Other groups (2000).
Economy: Employment by occupation: 12.8% management, 23.9% professional, 20.4% services, 26.1% sales, 0.0% farming, 3.7% construction, 13.1% production (2000).
Income: Per capita income: $18,888 (2000); Median household income: $43,941 (2000); Poverty rate: 4.7% (2000).
Education: Percent of population age 25 and over with: High school diploma (including GED) or higher: 87.6% (2000); Bachelor's degree or higher: 26.8% (2000).
Housing: Homeownership rate: 63.9% (2000); Median home value: $99,300 (2000); Median rent: $545 per month (2000); Median age of housing: 31 years (2000).
Transportation: Commute to work: 85.8% car, 1.8% public transportation, 10.0% walk, 1.7% work from home (2000); Travel time to work: 29.0% less than 15 minutes, 48.0% 15 to 30 minutes, 19.4% 30 to 45 minutes, 0.5% 45 to 60 minutes, 3.1% 60 minutes or more (2000)

OGDEN (town). Covers a land area of 36.550 square miles and a water area of 0.244 square miles. Located at 43.17° N. Lat.; 77.81° W. Long.
Population: 16,912 (1990); 18,492 (2000); 19,339 (2005); 20,140 (2010 projected); Race: 96.2% White, 1.4% Black, 0.8% Asian, 1.6% Hispanic of any race (2005); Density: 529.1 persons per square mile (2005); Average household size: 2.79 (2005); Median age: 37.7 (2005); Males per 100 females: 95.9 (2005); Marriage status: 25.6% never married, 64.1% now married, 3.8% widowed, 6.5% divorced (2000); Foreign born: 4.5% (2000); Ancestry (includes multiple ancestries): 30.6% German, 24.4% Italian, 19.0% Irish, 16.3% English, 7.1% Polish (2000).
Economy: Single-family building permits issued: 56 (2005); Multi-family building permits issued: 13 (2005); Employment by occupation: 13.4% management, 28.5% professional, 10.6% services, 28.9% sales, 0.2% farming, 5.1% construction, 13.4% production (2000).
Income: Per capita income: $26,525 (2005); Median household income: $66,260 (2005); Average household income: $73,562 (2005); Percent of households with income of $100,000 or more: 21.7% (2005); Poverty rate: 2.7% (2000).
Taxes: Total city taxes per capita: $280 (2004); City property taxes per capita: $235 (2004).
Education: Percent of population age 25 and over with: High school diploma (including GED) or higher: 91.8% (2005); Bachelor's degree or higher: 33.4% (2005); Master's degree or higher: 11.4% (2005).
Housing: Homeownership rate: 80.1% (2005); Median home value: $142,742 (2005); Median rent: $622 per month (2000); Median age of housing: 29 years (2000).
Safety: Violent crime rate: 2.6 per 10,000 population; Property crime rate: 173.2 per 10,000 population (2004).
Transportation: Commute to work: 94.0% car, 0.8% public transportation, 2.8% walk, 2.2% work from home (2000); Travel time to work: 27.6% less than 15 minutes, 55.2% 15 to 30 minutes, 12.6% 30 to 45 minutes, 1.9% 45 to 60 minutes, 2.7% 60 minutes or more (2000)
Additional Information Contacts
Town of Ogden . . . . (585) 352-2100
http://www.ogdenny.com/

PARMA (town). Covers a land area of 41.960 square miles and a water area of 0.976 square miles. Located at 43.27° N. Lat.; 77.79° W. Long.
Population: 13,873 (1990); 14,822 (2000); 15,473 (2005); 16,091 (2010 projected); Race: 96.4% White, 1.6% Black, 0.6% Asian, 1.4% Hispanic of any race (2005); Density: 368.8 persons per square mile (2005); Average household size: 2.76 (2005); Median age: 38.8 (2005); Males per 100 females: 99.0 (2005); Marriage status: 23.0% never married, 63.5% now married, 5.8% widowed, 7.6% divorced (2000); Foreign born: 2.7% (2000); Ancestry (includes multiple ancestries): 33.9% German, 21.0% Irish, 20.4% English, 19.9% Italian, 6.2% Polish (2000).
Economy: Single-family building permits issued: 62 (2005); Multi-family building permits issued: 0 (2005); Employment by occupation: 11.7% management, 22.8% professional, 12.0% services, 26.3% sales, 0.3% farming, 9.7% construction, 17.0% production (2000).
Income: Per capita income: $25,006 (2005); Median household income: $59,511 (2005); Average household income: $68,486 (2005); Percent of households with income of $100,000 or more: 17.8% (2005); Poverty rate: 4.1% (2000).
Education: Percent of population age 25 and over with: High school diploma (including GED) or higher: 89.2% (2005); Bachelor's degree or higher: 21.7% (2005); Master's degree or higher: 7.5% (2005).

Housing: Homeownership rate: 83.8% (2005); Median home value: $129,807 (2005); Median rent: $530 per month (2000); Median age of housing: 31 years (2000).
Transportation: Commute to work: 95.9% car, 0.5% public transportation, 0.8% walk, 2.4% work from home (2000); Travel time to work: 18.8% less than 15 minutes, 49.0% 15 to 30 minutes, 26.2% 30 to 45 minutes, 4.0% 45 to 60 minutes, 1.9% 60 minutes or more (2000)
Additional Information Contacts
Town of Parma................................... (585) 392-9461
http://www.parmany.org/

PENFIELD (town). Covers a land area of 37.501 square miles and a water area of 0.416 square miles. Located at 43.15° N. Lat.; 77.46° W. Long.
Population: 30,216 (1990); 34,645 (2000); 36,106 (2005); 37,464 (2010 projected); Race: 92.4% White, 2.5% Black, 3.5% Asian, 1.9% Hispanic of any race (2005); Density: 962.8 persons per square mile (2005); Average household size: 2.63 (2005); Median age: 42.2 (2005); Males per 100 females: 92.3 (2005); Marriage status: 20.4% never married, 65.4% now married, 6.1% widowed, 8.1% divorced (2000); Foreign born: 8.8% (2000); Ancestry (includes multiple ancestries): 24.3% German, 23.5% Italian, 18.3% Irish, 16.2% English, 8.0% Other groups (2000).
Economy: Unemployment rate: 3.6% (2005); Total civilian labor force: 19,172 (2005); Single-family building permits issued: 136 (2005); Multi-family building permits issued: 0 (2005); Employment by occupation: 21.1% management, 30.2% professional, 9.9% services, 25.7% sales, 0.3% farming, 4.8% construction, 8.1% production (2000).
Income: Per capita income: $34,615 (2005); Median household income: $72,184 (2005); Average household income: $90,078 (2005); Percent of households with income of $100,000 or more: 32.3% (2005); Poverty rate: 3.7% (2000).
Taxes: Total city taxes per capita: $236 (2004); City property taxes per capita: $170 (2004).
Education: Percent of population age 25 and over with: High school diploma (including GED) or higher: 91.4% (2005); Bachelor's degree or higher: 46.2% (2005); Master's degree or higher: 19.3% (2005).
School District(s)
Penfield Central School District (KG-12)
    2003-04 Enrollment: 4,960 .... (585) 249-5700
Housing: Homeownership rate: 83.3% (2005); Median home value: $161,091 (2005); Median rent: $640 per month (2000); Median age of housing: 27 years (2000).
Transportation: Commute to work: 94.9% car, 0.3% public transportation, 1.1% walk, 3.3% work from home (2000); Travel time to work: 26.5% less than 15 minutes, 57.6% 15 to 30 minutes, 12.3% 30 to 45 minutes, 1.5% 45 to 60 minutes, 2.1% 60 minutes or more (2000)
Additional Information Contacts
Town of Penfield .... (585) 340-8600
http://www.penfield.org/

PERINTON (town). Covers a land area of 34.127 square miles and a water area of 0.314 square miles. Located at 43.08° N. Lat.; 77.44° W. Long.
Population: 43,015 (1990); 46,090 (2000); 46,600 (2005); 47,094 (2010 projected); Race: 92.8% White, 2.0% Black, 3.3% Asian, 1.9% Hispanic of any race (2005); Density: 1,365.5 persons per square mile (2005); Average household size: 2.57 (2005); Median age: 41.0 (2005); Males per 100 females: 93.2 (2005); Marriage status: 20.0% never married, 66.0% now married, 6.0% widowed, 8.1% divorced (2000); Foreign born: 6.6% (2000); Ancestry (includes multiple ancestries): 24.6% German, 20.6% Irish, 19.6% Italian, 16.1% English, 7.7% Other groups (2000).
Economy: Unemployment rate: 3.4% (2005); Total civilian labor force: 26,073 (2005); Single-family building permits issued: 66 (2005); Multi-family building permits issued: 4 (2005); Employment by occupation: 22.3% management, 32.8% professional, 10.0% services, 24.8% sales, 0.1% farming, 3.7% construction, 6.3% production (2000).
Income: Per capita income: $37,917 (2005); Median household income: $78,905 (2005); Average household income: $97,041 (2005); Percent of households with income of $100,000 or more: 35.1% (2005); Poverty rate: 2.9% (2000).
Education: Percent of population age 25 and over with: High school diploma (including GED) or higher: 94.3% (2005); Bachelor's degree or higher: 52.0% (2005); Master's degree or higher: 21.4% (2005).

Housing: Homeownership rate: 80.7% (2005); Median home value: $175,695 (2005); Median rent: $656 per month (2000); Median age of housing: 27 years (2000).
Transportation: Commute to work: 93.9% car, 0.3% public transportation, 0.9% walk, 4.4% work from home (2000); Travel time to work: 27.8% less than 15 minutes, 49.3% 15 to 30 minutes, 18.7% 30 to 45 minutes, 2.0% 45 to 60 minutes, 2.2% 60 minutes or more (2000)
Additional Information Contacts
Town of Perinton .... (585) 223-0770
http://www.perinton.org/

PITTSFORD (village). Covers a land area of 0.657 square miles and a water area of 0.029 square miles. Located at 43.08° N. Lat.; 77.51° W. Long.
Population: 1,488 (1990); 1,418 (2000); 1,358 (2005); 1,284 (2010 projected); Race: 97.5% White, 0.7% Black, 0.5% Asian, 1.1% Hispanic of any race (2005); Density: 2,065.6 persons per square mile (2005); Average household size: 2.19 (2005); Median age: 42.6 (2005); Males per 100 females: 93.2 (2005); Marriage status: 24.2% never married, 57.6% now married, 9.0% widowed, 9.2% divorced (2000); Foreign born: 3.9% (2000); Ancestry (includes multiple ancestries): 27.9% German, 24.5% Irish, 21.9% English, 10.9% Italian, 5.3% Other groups (2000).
Economy: Single-family building permits issued: 0 (2005); Multi-family building permits issued: 0 (2005); Employment by occupation: 24.1% management, 38.0% professional, 9.6% services, 22.3% sales, 0.3% farming, 3.8% construction, 2.1% production (2000).
Income: Per capita income: $40,253 (2005); Median household income: $67,463 (2005); Average household income: $87,492 (2005); Percent of households with income of $100,000 or more: 27.1% (2005); Poverty rate: 5.2% (2000).
Education: Percent of population age 25 and over with: High school diploma (including GED) or higher: 96.1% (2005); Bachelor's degree or higher: 63.4% (2005); Master's degree or higher: 27.7% (2005).
School District(s)
Pittsford Central School District (KG-12)
    2003-04 Enrollment: 6,022 .... (585) 218-1004
Housing: Homeownership rate: 72.6% (2005); Median home value: $178,994 (2005); Median rent: $681 per month (2000); Median age of housing: 60+ years (2000).
Newspapers: Brighton - Pittsford Post (General - Circulation 9,930); East Rochester Post (General - Circulation 1,319); Henrietta Post (General - Circulation 3,285); Penfield Post (General - Circulation 3,652); Perinton-Fairport Post (General - Circulation 5,164)
Transportation: Commute to work: 89.2% car, 0.7% public transportation, 2.3% walk, 7.3% work from home (2000); Travel time to work: 34.8% less than 15 minutes, 48.3% 15 to 30 minutes, 11.2% 30 to 45 minutes, 2.4% 45 to 60 minutes, 3.2% 60 minutes or more (2000)

PITTSFORD (town). Covers a land area of 23.191 square miles and a water area of 0.190 square miles. Located at 43.08° N. Lat.; 77.51° W. Long.
History: Incorporated 1827.
Population: 24,497 (1990); 27,219 (2000); 27,562 (2005); 27,965 (2010 projected); Race: 91.4% White, 1.7% Black, 5.5% Asian, 1.6% Hispanic of any race (2005); Density: 1,188.5 persons per square mile (2005); Average household size: 2.85 (2005); Median age: 42.2 (2005); Males per 100 females: 87.9 (2005); Marriage status: 21.9% never married, 67.5% now married, 6.0% widowed, 4.7% divorced (2000); Foreign born: 7.9% (2000); Ancestry (includes multiple ancestries): 23.7% German, 20.9% Irish, 17.2% English, 15.4% Italian, 9.5% Other groups (2000).
Economy: Manufacturing: filters, electrical equipment, safes, testing and measuring equipment. Farming. Unemployment rate: 3.3% (2005); Total civilian labor force: 14,228 (2005); Single-family building permits issued: 95 (2005); Multi-family building permits issued: 0 (2005); Employment by occupation: 25.4% management, 34.0% professional, 7.5% services, 26.6% sales, 0.1% farming, 2.1% construction, 4.4% production (2000).
Income: Per capita income: $46,881 (2005); Median household income: $98,607 (2005); Average household income: $130,489 (2005); Percent of households with income of $100,000 or more: 49.2% (2005); Poverty rate: 2.9% (2000).
Taxes: Total city taxes per capita: $351 (2004); City property taxes per capita: $267 (2004).
Education: Percent of population age 25 and over with: High school diploma (including GED) or higher: 96.2% (2005); Bachelor's degree or higher: 65.4% (2005); Master's degree or higher: 32.7% (2005).

PROFILES OF NEW YORK / Monroe County 223

Housing: Homeownership rate: 87.6% (2005); Median home value: $230,901 (2005); Median rent: $738 per month (2000); Median age of housing: 32 years (2000).
Transportation: Commute to work: 88.2% car, 0.7% public transportation, 5.3% walk, 5.1% work from home (2000); Travel time to work: 33.8% less than 15 minutes, 52.3% 15 to 30 minutes, 10.3% 30 to 45 minutes, 1.1% 45 to 60 minutes, 2.4% 60 minutes or more (2000)
Additional Information Contacts
Town of Pittsford .... (585) 248-6220
http://www.townofpittsford.com/

RIGA (town). Covers a land area of 35.170 square miles and a water area of 0.128 square miles. Located at 43.09° N. Lat.; 77.88° W. Long. Elevation is 640 feet.
Population: 5,114 (1990); 5,437 (2000); 5,506 (2005); 5,582 (2010 projected); Race: 96.9% White, 0.7% Black, 0.9% Asian, 1.1% Hispanic of any race (2005); Density: 156.6 persons per square mile (2005); Average household size: 2.74 (2005); Median age: 39.3 (2005); Males per 100 females: 99.1 (2005); Marriage status: 21.2% never married, 65.7% now married, 5.3% widowed, 7.8% divorced (2000); Foreign born: 3.4% (2000); Ancestry (includes multiple ancestries): 28.1% German, 22.0% English, 18.0% Irish, 13.9% Italian, 8.0% Polish (2000).
Economy: Single-family building permits issued: 12 (2005); Multi-family building permits issued: 0 (2005); Employment by occupation: 12.6% management, 25.0% professional, 9.8% services, 26.3% sales, 0.9% farming, 8.7% construction, 16.6% production (2000).
Income: Per capita income: $26,634 (2005); Median household income: $63,849 (2005); Average household income: $72,639 (2005); Percent of households with income of $100,000 or more: 19.6% (2005); Poverty rate: 3.8% (2000).
Education: Percent of population age 25 and over with: High school diploma (including GED) or higher: 92.3% (2005); Bachelor's degree or higher: 33.7% (2005); Master's degree or higher: 11.8% (2005).
Housing: Homeownership rate: 89.6% (2005); Median home value: $131,624 (2005); Median rent: $479 per month (2000); Median age of housing: 29 years (2000).
Transportation: Commute to work: 94.7% car, 0.0% public transportation, 0.9% walk, 4.2% work from home (2000); Travel time to work: 20.4% less than 15 minutes, 51.0% 15 to 30 minutes, 24.0% 30 to 45 minutes, 2.7% 45 to 60 minutes, 1.9% 60 minutes or more (2000)
Additional Information Contacts
Town of Riga .... (585) 293-3880
http://www.townofriga.org/

ROCHESTER (city). Covers a land area of 35.835 square miles and a water area of 1.266 square miles. Located at 43.16° N. Lat.; 77.61° W. Long. Elevation is 513 feet.
History: The first settler on the site of Rochester was Ebenezer "Indian" Allen, who was granted a 100-acre tract at the falls of the Genesee River on the condition that he erect a mill for use by the Native Americans. Allen built his mill in 1789. After changing hands several times, the area was finally purchased in 1803 by Colonel William Fitzhugh, Major Charles Carroll, and Colonel Nathaniel Rochester, all from Maryland. The village was incorporated as Rochesterville in 1817. The construction of the Erie Canal through Rochester assured the town supremacy over its neighbors. Rochester was the home of George Eastman, who invented and manufactured films for cameras. In 1888 the first Kodak camera was put on the market. The Eastman School of Music was later named for him. In 1840, the University of Rochester was founded by a convention of Baptists.
Population: 231,642 (1990); 219,773 (2000); 213,435 (2005); 207,450 (2010 projected); Race: 42.7% White, 42.3% Black, 2.6% Asian, 15.1% Hispanic of any race (2005); Density: 5,956.1 persons per square mile (2005); Average household size: 2.47 (2005); Median age: 32.6 (2005); Males per 100 females: 92.5 (2005); Marriage status: 43.7% never married, 38.1% now married, 7.0% widowed, 11.1% divorced (2000); Foreign born: 7.3% (2000); Ancestry (includes multiple ancestries): 45.5% Other groups, 10.9% German, 10.0% Italian, 9.6% Irish, 5.8% English (2000).
Economy: Manufacturing: leather handles, builders hardware, industrial ceramics, precision tool and die manufacturing machinery, filters, measuring devices, packing tools. Expanding suburban housing area. Unemployment rate: 6.1% (2005); Total civilian labor force: 96,446 (2005); Single-family building permits issued: 65 (2005); Multi-family building permits issued: 0 (2005); Employment by occupation: 8.9% management, 22.1% professional, 21.1% services, 23.8% sales, 0.1% farming, 6.3% construction, 17.7% production (2000).
Income: Per capita income: $16,385 (2005); Median household income: $28,896 (2005); Average household income: $39,569 (2005); Percent of households with income of $100,000 or more: 5.9% (2005); Poverty rate: 25.9% (2000).
Taxes: Total city taxes per capita: $848 (2004); City property taxes per capita: $763 (2004).
Education: Percent of population age 25 and over with: High school diploma (including GED) or higher: 73.2% (2005); Bachelor's degree or higher: 20.4% (2005); Master's degree or higher: 8.1% (2005).

School District(s)
Brighton Central School District (KG-12)
   2003-04 Enrollment: 3,582 .... (585) 242-5080
Charter School Of Sci & Tech (KG-08)
   2003-04 Enrollment: 1,044 .... (585) 454-0100
Churchville-Chili Central School District (KG-12)
   2003-04 Enrollment: 4,482 .... (585) 293-1800
East Irondequoit Central School District (KG-12)
   2003-04 Enrollment: 3,514 .... (585) 339-1210
Eugenio Maria De Hostos Charter School (KG-05)
   2003-04 Enrollment: 241 .... (585) 544-6170
Gates-Chili Central School District (KG-12)
   2003-04 Enrollment: 5,057 .... (585) 247-5050
Genesee Comm Charter School At The R (KG-04)
   2003-04 Enrollment: 159 .... (585) 271-4552
Greece Central School District (PK-12)
   2003-04 Enrollment: 13,799 .... (585) 621-1000
Penfield Central School District (KG-12)
   2003-04 Enrollment: 4,960 .... (585) 249-5700
Pittsford Central School District (KG-12)
   2003-04 Enrollment: 6,022 .... (585) 218-1004
Rochester City School District (PK-12)
   2003-04 Enrollment: 34,598 .... (585) 262-8378
Rochester Leadership Acad Charter School (KG-08)
   2003-04 Enrollment: 564 .... (585) 454-5000
Rush-Henrietta Central School District (KG-12)
   2003-04 Enrollment: 5,859 .... (585) 359-5012
West Irondequoit Central School District (KG-12)
   2003-04 Enrollment: 3,949 .... (585) 342-5500

Four-year College(s)
Bexley Hall Episcopal Seminary
   Fall 2004 Enrollment: 40 .... (585) 546-2160
Colgate Rochester Crozer Divinity School
   Fall 2004 Enrollment: 116 .... (585) 271-1320
Nazareth College of Rochester
   Fall 2004 Enrollment: 3,140 .... (585) 389-2525
   2005-06 Tuition: In-state $19,874; Out-of-state $19,874
Northeastern Seminary
   Fall 2004 Enrollment: 126 .... (585) 594-6000
Roberts Wesleyan College
   Fall 2004 Enrollment: 1,920 .... (585) 594-6000
   2005-06 Tuition: In-state $19,324; Out-of-state $19,324
Rochester General Hospital School of Medical Technology
   Fall 2004 Enrollment: 9 .... (585) 922-4274
Rochester Institute of Technology
   Fall 2004 Enrollment: 14,552 .... (585) 475-2411
   2005-06 Tuition: In-state $23,619; Out-of-state $23,619
Saint John Fisher College
   Fall 2004 Enrollment: 3,376 .... (585) 385-8000
   2005-06 Tuition: In-state $19,560; Out-of-state $19,560
St Bernard's School of Theology and Ministry
   Fall 2004 Enrollment: 152 .... (585) 271-3657
Talmudical Institute of Upstate New York
   Fall 2004 Enrollment: 16 .... (716) 473-2810
   2005-06 Tuition: In-state $4,500; Out-of-state $4,500
University of Rochester
   Fall 2004 Enrollment: 8,329 .... (585) 275-2121
   2005-06 Tuition: In-state $30,540; Out-of-state $30,540

Two-year College(s)
Bryant and Stratton College-Henrietta
   Fall 2004 Enrollment: 325 .... (585) 292-5627
   2005-06 Tuition: In-state $11,820; Out-of-state $11,820
Bryant and Stratton College-Rochester
   Fall 2004 Enrollment: 203 .... (716) 720-0660
   2005-06 Tuition: In-state $11,820; Out-of-state $11,820

Continental School of Beauty Culture
  Fall 2004 Enrollment: 166 . . . . (585) 272-8060
Isabella G Hart School of Practical Nursing
  Fall 2004 Enrollment: 99 . . . . (585) 922-1784
Monroe Community College (Public)
  Fall 2004 Enrollment: 17,502. . . . . (585) 292-2000
  2005-06 Tuition: In-state $2,915; Out-of-state $5,515
Rochester Business Institute
  Fall 2004 Enrollment: 1,091. . . . . (585) 266-0430
  2005-06 Tuition: In-state $12,550; Out-of-state $12,550
Shear Ego International School of Hair Design
  Fall 2004 Enrollment: 105 . . . . (585) 342-0070
Housing: Homeownership rate: 40.2% (2005); Median home value: $73,642 (2005); Median rent: $473 per month (2000); Median age of housing: 60+ years (2000).
Hospitals: Highland Hospital/University of Rochester Medical Center (272 beds); Monroe Community Hospital (566 beds); Rochester General Hospital (528 beds); Rochester Psychiatric Center (180 beds); Strong Memorial Hospital, University of Rochester (750 beds); Unity Health Systems St. Mary's Hospital (215 beds)
Safety: Violent crime rate: 82.7 per 10,000 population; Property crime rate: 717.3 per 10,000 population (2004).
Newspapers: Ad Net Community News - Gates/Chili Edition (General - Circulation 16,000); Ad Net Community News - Greece Edition (General - Circulation 30,000); Catholic Courier (Catholic - Circulation 46,147); City Newspaper (Alternative - Circulation 40,000); Daily Record (Circulation 15,000); Democrat and Chronicle (Circulation 166,727); Gates/Chili News (General - Circulation 9,800); Greece Post (General - Circulation 7,993); Irondequoit Post (General - Circulation 7,125); Jewish Ledger (Jewish - Circulation 8,000)
Transportation: Commute to work: 81.7% car, 8.1% public transportation, 6.5% walk, 2.3% work from home (2000); Travel time to work: 36.7% less than 15 minutes, 46.3% 15 to 30 minutes, 10.6% 30 to 45 minutes, 2.3% 45 to 60 minutes, 4.0% 60 minutes or more (2000); Amtrak: Service available.
Additional Information Contacts
City of Rochester . . . . (585) 428-5990
  http://www.ci.rochester.ny.us/
Rochester Business Alliance . . . . (585) 244-1800
  http://www.rochesterbusinessalliance.com

RUSH (town). Covers a land area of 30.508 square miles and a water area of 0.169 square miles. Located at 42.98° N. Lat.; 77.67° W. Long.
Population: 3,217 (1990); 3,603 (2000); 3,647 (2005); 3,706 (2010 projected); Race: 91.1% White, 6.0% Black, 0.9% Asian, 2.4% Hispanic of any race (2005); Density: 119.5 persons per square mile (2005); Average household size: 2.79 (2005); Median age: 41.1 (2005); Males per 100 females: 119.8 (2005); Marriage status: 22.8% never married, 66.6% now married, 6.0% widowed, 4.6% divorced (2000); Foreign born: 4.2% (2000); Ancestry (includes multiple ancestries): 35.8% German, 23.0% Irish, 17.0% English, 11.2% Italian, 7.2% Polish (2000).
Economy: Single-family building permits issued: 7 (2005); Multi-family building permits issued: 0 (2005); Employment by occupation: 14.3% management, 35.3% professional, 7.8% services, 26.1% sales, 0.0% farming, 6.4% construction, 9.9% production (2000).
Income: Per capita income: $31,360 (2005); Median household income: $76,066 (2005); Average household income: $86,938 (2005); Percent of households with income of $100,000 or more: 31.1% (2005); Poverty rate: 0.5% (2000).
Education: Percent of population age 25 and over with: High school diploma (including GED) or higher: 92.4% (2005); Bachelor's degree or higher: 44.4% (2005); Master's degree or higher: 16.8% (2005).
School District(s)
Rush-Henrietta Central School District (KG-12)
  2003-04 Enrollment: 5,859 . . . . (585) 359-5012
Housing: Homeownership rate: 89.5% (2005); Median home value: $170,577 (2005); Median rent: $470 per month (2000); Median age of housing: 35 years (2000).
Transportation: Commute to work: 94.3% car, 0.0% public transportation, 0.3% walk, 4.7% work from home (2000); Travel time to work: 19.3% less than 15 minutes, 53.5% 15 to 30 minutes, 24.6% 30 to 45 minutes, 2.2% 45 to 60 minutes, 0.3% 60 minutes or more (2000)
Additional Information Contacts
Town of Rush. . . . . (585) 533-1312
  http://www.townofrush.org/

SCOTTSVILLE (village). Covers a land area of 1.081 square miles and a water area of 0 square miles. Located at 43.02° N. Lat.; 77.75° W. Long.
Population: 1,912 (1990); 2,128 (2000); 2,128 (2005); 2,107 (2010 projected); Race: 88.9% White, 6.2% Black, 0.8% Asian, 4.1% Hispanic of any race (2005); Density: 1,968.1 persons per square mile (2005); Average household size: 2.50 (2005); Median age: 39.3 (2005); Males per 100 females: 94.3 (2005); Marriage status: 23.7% never married, 62.0% now married, 6.3% widowed, 8.0% divorced (2000); Foreign born: 2.8% (2000); Ancestry (includes multiple ancestries): 29.6% German, 20.7% Irish, 20.5% English, 11.8% Italian, 7.6% Other groups (2000).
Economy: Single-family building permits issued: 3 (2005); Multi-family building permits issued: 0 (2005); Employment by occupation: 10.4% management, 29.0% professional, 18.5% services, 23.4% sales, 0.4% farming, 7.7% construction, 10.7% production (2000).
Income: Per capita income: $29,417 (2005); Median household income: $61,015 (2005); Average household income: $73,512 (2005); Percent of households with income of $100,000 or more: 20.2% (2005); Poverty rate: 2.3% (2000).
Education: Percent of population age 25 and over with: High school diploma (including GED) or higher: 92.6% (2005); Bachelor's degree or higher: 38.9% (2005); Master's degree or higher: 17.0% (2005).
School District(s)
Wheatland-Chili Central School District (KG-12)
  2003-04 Enrollment: 905 . . . . (585) 889-6246
Housing: Homeownership rate: 74.2% (2005); Median home value: $119,901 (2005); Median rent: $528 per month (2000); Median age of housing: 41 years (2000).
Transportation: Commute to work: 90.4% car, 0.7% public transportation, 4.1% walk, 4.8% work from home (2000); Travel time to work: 28.6% less than 15 minutes, 47.6% 15 to 30 minutes, 18.4% 30 to 45 minutes, 2.5% 45 to 60 minutes, 2.9% 60 minutes or more (2000)

SPENCERPORT (village). Covers a land area of 1.364 square miles and a water area of 0.032 square miles. Located at 43.18° N. Lat.; 77.80° W. Long.
History: Site of John T. Trowbridge's boyhood home. Incorporated 1867.
Population: 3,622 (1990); 3,559 (2000); 3,615 (2005); 3,669 (2010 projected); Race: 96.9% White, 0.8% Black, 0.6% Asian, 2.5% Hispanic of any race (2005); Density: 2,650.8 persons per square mile (2005); Average household size: 2.48 (2005); Median age: 39.7 (2005); Males per 100 females: 90.8 (2005); Marriage status: 25.8% never married, 61.8% now married, 5.4% widowed, 7.0% divorced (2000); Foreign born: 5.2% (2000); Ancestry (includes multiple ancestries): 29.4% German, 25.0% Italian, 20.9% Irish, 20.3% English, 6.5% Polish (2000).
Economy: Single-family building permits issued: 1 (2005); Multi-family building permits issued: 0 (2005); Employment by occupation: 9.9% management, 30.8% professional, 10.5% services, 32.8% sales, 0.0% farming, 5.2% construction, 10.7% production (2000).
Income: Per capita income: $28,945 (2005); Median household income: $63,739 (2005); Average household income: $71,094 (2005); Percent of households with income of $100,000 or more: 20.8% (2005); Poverty rate: 1.5% (2000).
Education: Percent of population age 25 and over with: High school diploma (including GED) or higher: 89.4% (2005); Bachelor's degree or higher: 37.1% (2005); Master's degree or higher: 13.2% (2005).
School District(s)
Boces Monroe 2-Orleans (PK-PK)
  2003-04 Enrollment: 529 . . . . (585) 352-2410
Spencerport Central School District (KG-12)
  2003-04 Enrollment: 4,350 . . . . (585) 349-5102
Housing: Homeownership rate: 71.1% (2005); Median home value: $141,111 (2005); Median rent: $584 per month (2000); Median age of housing: 40 years (2000).
Newspapers: Hamlin/Clarkson Herald (General - Circulation 6,006); Suburban News (General - Circulation 32,000)
Transportation: Commute to work: 94.3% car, 2.1% public transportation, 2.1% walk, 1.5% work from home (2000); Travel time to work: 32.7% less than 15 minutes, 49.1% 15 to 30 minutes, 13.7% 30 to 45 minutes, 2.3% 45 to 60 minutes, 2.2% 60 minutes or more (2000)

SWEDEN (town). Covers a land area of 33.546 square miles and a water area of 0.159 square miles. Located at 43.20° N. Lat.; 77.93° W. Long.

Population: 14,181 (1990); 13,716 (2000); 13,838 (2005); 13,911 (2010 projected); Race: 91.6% White, 4.0% Black, 1.2% Asian, 3.7% Hispanic of any race (2005); Density: 412.5 persons per square mile (2005); Average household size: 2.98 (2005); Median age: 27.5 (2005); Males per 100 females: 94.9 (2005); Marriage status: 41.2% never married, 46.9% now married, 4.4% widowed, 7.4% divorced (2000); Foreign born: 3.2% (2000); Ancestry (includes multiple ancestries): 23.2% German, 17.8% Irish, 17.4% English, 14.1% Italian, 9.5% Other groups (2000).
Economy: Single-family building permits issued: 8 (2005); Multi-family building permits issued: 0 (2005); Employment by occupation: 11.7% management, 24.9% professional, 17.8% services, 27.4% sales, 0.5% farming, 7.4% construction, 10.4% production (2000).
Income: Per capita income: $20,965 (2005); Median household income: $50,174 (2005); Average household income: $60,207 (2005); Percent of households with income of $100,000 or more: 15.7% (2005); Poverty rate: 13.3% (2000).
Education: Percent of population age 25 and over with: High school diploma (including GED) or higher: 87.6% (2005); Bachelor's degree or higher: 34.2% (2005); Master's degree or higher: 14.9% (2005).
Housing: Homeownership rate: 57.9% (2005); Median home value: $125,803 (2005); Median rent: $520 per month (2000); Median age of housing: 35 years (2000).
Transportation: Commute to work: 82.3% car, 0.5% public transportation, 15.3% walk, 1.6% work from home (2000); Travel time to work: 43.5% less than 15 minutes, 27.9% 15 to 30 minutes, 21.0% 30 to 45 minutes, 5.2% 45 to 60 minutes, 2.3% 60 minutes or more (2000)

WEBSTER (village).
Covers a land area of 2.195 square miles and a water area of 0 square miles. Located at 43.21° N. Lat.; 77.42° W. Long. Elevation is 408 feet.
Population: 5,505 (1990); 5,216 (2000); 5,092 (2005); 4,978 (2010 projected); Race: 86.5% White, 5.2% Black, 4.5% Asian, 2.8% Hispanic of any race (2005); Density: 2,319.8 persons per square mile (2005); Average household size: 2.31 (2005); Median age: 36.7 (2005); Males per 100 females: 89.1 (2005); Marriage status: 28.6% never married, 52.8% now married, 7.7% widowed, 10.8% divorced (2000); Foreign born: 13.0% (2000); Ancestry (includes multiple ancestries): 24.3% German, 17.8% Italian, 16.2% English, 16.0% Irish, 10.2% Other groups (2000).
Economy: Single-family building permits issued: 0 (2005); Multi-family building permits issued: 0 (2005); Employment by occupation: 12.2% management, 28.9% professional, 19.1% services, 21.3% sales, 0.4% farming, 5.7% construction, 12.5% production (2000).
Income: Per capita income: $23,284 (2005); Median household income: $41,981 (2005); Average household income: $53,474 (2005); Percent of households with income of $100,000 or more: 12.9% (2005); Poverty rate: 11.9% (2000).
Education: Percent of population age 25 and over with: High school diploma (including GED) or higher: 86.9% (2005); Bachelor's degree or higher: 27.5% (2005); Master's degree or higher: 12.0% (2005).
School District(s)
Webster Central School District (KG-12)
    2003-04 Enrollment: 8,736 . . . . (585) 265-3600
Housing: Homeownership rate: 43.6% (2005); Median home value: $125,367 (2005); Median rent: $505 per month (2000); Median age of housing: 37 years (2000).
Newspapers: Wayne County Mail (General - Circulation 3,800); Webster Herald (General - Circulation 4,332); Webster Post (General - Circulation 4,025)
Transportation: Commute to work: 93.9% car, 0.3% public transportation, 2.5% walk, 3.0% work from home (2000); Travel time to work: 39.8% less than 15 minutes, 35.8% 15 to 30 minutes, 18.3% 30 to 45 minutes, 2.5% 45 to 60 minutes, 3.6% 60 minutes or more (2000)
Additional Information Contacts
Village of Webster . . . . (585) 872-1000
    http://www.ci.webster.ny.us/
Webster Chamber of Commerce . . . . (585) 265-3960
    http://www.websterchamber.com

WEBSTER (town).
Covers a land area of 34.040 square miles and a water area of 1.454 square miles. Located at 43.22° N. Lat.; 77.45° W. Long. Elevation is 408 feet.
History: Incorporated 1905.
Population: 31,639 (1990); 37,926 (2000); 40,571 (2005); 42,977 (2010 projected); Race: 94.0% White, 1.9% Black, 2.3% Asian, 2.1% Hispanic of any race (2005); Density: 1,191.9 persons per square mile (2005); Average household size: 2.54 (2005); Median age: 40.4 (2005); Males per 100 females: 95.0 (2005); Marriage status: 21.8% never married, 64.7% now married, 6.0% widowed, 7.6% divorced (2000); Foreign born: 6.7% (2000); Ancestry (includes multiple ancestries): 27.0% German, 23.7% Italian, 18.5% Irish, 14.6% English, 7.7% Polish (2000).
Economy: Manufacturing. In fruit-growing area. Unemployment rate: 3.7% (2005); Total civilian labor force: 22,063 (2005); Single-family building permits issued: 232 (2005); Multi-family building permits issued: 0 (2005); Employment by occupation: 17.4% management, 30.8% professional, 10.5% services, 24.4% sales, 0.1% farming, 5.8% construction, 11.0% production (2000).
Income: Per capita income: $30,659 (2005); Median household income: $66,917 (2005); Average household income: $77,623 (2005); Percent of households with income of $100,000 or more: 25.5% (2005); Poverty rate: 3.9% (2000).
Education: Percent of population age 25 and over with: High school diploma (including GED) or higher: 91.8% (2005); Bachelor's degree or higher: 37.4% (2005); Master's degree or higher: 14.9% (2005).
Housing: Homeownership rate: 77.8% (2005); Median home value: $150,548 (2005); Median rent: $609 per month (2000); Median age of housing: 27 years (2000).
Safety: Violent crime rate: 7.0 per 10,000 population; Property crime rate: 144.8 per 10,000 population (2004).
Transportation: Commute to work: 94.6% car, 0.6% public transportation, 0.8% walk, 3.8% work from home (2000); Travel time to work: 31.3% less than 15 minutes, 50.6% 15 to 30 minutes, 14.4% 30 to 45 minutes, 1.5% 45 to 60 minutes, 2.1% 60 minutes or more (2000)
Additional Information Contacts
Town of Webster . . . . (585) 872-1000
    http://www.ci.webster.ny.us/

WEST HENRIETTA (unincorporated postal area, zip code 14586).
Covers a land area of 10.709 square miles and a water area of 0 square miles. Located at 43.04° N. Lat.; 77.68° W. Long.
Population: 0 (2000); Race: 85.8% White, 7.3% Black, 5.1% Asian, 0.8% Hispanic of any race (2000); Density: 0.0 persons per square mile (2000); Age: 27.0% under 18, 7.9% over 64 (2000); Marriage status: 27.0% never married, 61.9% now married, 3.4% widowed, 7.7% divorced (2000); Foreign born: 5.8% (2000); Ancestry (includes multiple ancestries): 27.0% German, 22.7% Italian, 15.8% Irish, 14.9% English, 14.8% Other groups (2000).
Economy: Employment by occupation: 14.6% management, 27.9% professional, 9.8% services, 30.7% sales, 0.2% farming, 5.6% construction, 11.3% production (2000).
Income: Per capita income: $23,686 (2000); Median household income: $60,191 (2000); Poverty rate: 3.3% (2000).
Education: Percent of population age 25 and over with: High school diploma (including GED) or higher: 92.9% (2000); Bachelor's degree or higher: 34.3% (2000).
School District(s)
Rush-Henrietta Central School District (KG-12)
    2003-04 Enrollment: 5,859 . . . . (585) 359-5012
Housing: Homeownership rate: 76.1% (2000); Median home value: $101,600 (2000); Median rent: $737 per month (2000); Median age of housing: 20 years (2000).
Transportation: Commute to work: 95.9% car, 1.0% public transportation, 0.8% walk, 2.4% work from home (2000); Travel time to work: 26.2% less than 15 minutes, 53.3% 15 to 30 minutes, 16.5% 30 to 45 minutes, 2.1% 45 to 60 minutes, 1.9% 60 minutes or more (2000)

WHEATLAND (town).
Covers a land area of 30.622 square miles and a water area of 0.077 square miles. Located at 43.00° N. Lat.; 77.81° W. Long.
Population: 5,093 (1990); 5,149 (2000); 5,061 (2005); 4,974 (2010 projected); Race: 90.9% White, 5.4% Black, 0.9% Asian, 3.2% Hispanic of any race (2005); Density: 165.3 persons per square mile (2005); Average household size: 2.51 (2005); Median age: 38.5 (2005); Males per 100 females: 94.8 (2005); Marriage status: 24.2% never married, 62.9% now married, 5.2% widowed, 7.7% divorced (2000); Foreign born: 1.6% (2000); Ancestry (includes multiple ancestries): 26.2% German, 21.7% Irish, 19.4% English, 13.2% Italian, 9.8% United States or American (2000).
Economy: Single-family building permits issued: 12 (2005); Multi-family building permits issued: 0 (2005); Employment by occupation: 15.6% management, 25.0% professional, 13.7% services, 25.0% sales, 0.1% farming, 8.5% construction, 12.1% production (2000).

Income: Per capita income: $28,536 (2005); Median household income: $62,777 (2005); Average household income: $71,493 (2005); Percent of households with income of $100,000 or more: 21.2% (2005); Poverty rate: 3.5% (2000).
Education: Percent of population age 25 and over with: High school diploma (including GED) or higher: 91.1% (2005); Bachelor's degree or higher: 32.8% (2005); Master's degree or higher: 12.8% (2005).
Housing: Homeownership rate: 70.5% (2005); Median home value: $125,543 (2005); Median rent: $634 per month (2000); Median age of housing: 35 years (2000).
Transportation: Commute to work: 91.7% car, 0.3% public transportation, 2.2% walk, 5.1% work from home (2000); Travel time to work: 22.2% less than 15 minutes, 46.3% 15 to 30 minutes, 24.7% 30 to 45 minutes, 3.0% 45 to 60 minutes, 3.8% 60 minutes or more (2000)
Additional Information Contacts
Town of Wheatland . . . . (585) 889-1553
http://www.townofwheatland.org/

Montgomery County

Located in east central New York, in the Mohawk River Valley; crossed by the Barge Canal; drained by Schoharie Creek. Covers a land area of 404.82 square miles, a water area of 5.51 square miles, and is located in the Eastern Time Zone. The county government was organized in 1772. County seat is Fonda.

Montgomery County is part of the Amsterdam, NY Micropolitan Statistical Area. The entire metro area includes: Montgomery County, NY

Population: 51,981 (1990); 49,708 (2000); 49,364 (2005); 48,980 (2010 projected); Race: 93.1% White, 1.8% Black, 0.8% Asian, 9.6% Hispanic of any race (2005); Density: 121.9 persons per square mile (2005); Average household size: 2.45 (2005); Median age: 40.5 (2005); Males per 100 females: 92.5 (2005).
Religion: Five largest groups: 48.9% Catholic Church, 6.5% Evangelical Lutheran Church in America, 5.1% Reformed Church in America, 3.9% The United Methodist Church, 1.1% Independent, Non-Charismatic Churches (2000).
Economy: Unemployment rate: 5.6% (2005); Total civilian labor force: 24,786 (2005); Leading industries: 27.2% manufacturing; 22.8% health care and social assistance; 16.3% retail trade (2003); Farms: 624 totaling 151,977 acres (2002); Companies that employ 500 or more persons: 2 (2003); Companies that employ 100 to 499 persons: 24 (2003); Companies that employ less than 100 persons: 1,057 (2003); Black-owned businesses: n/a (2002); Hispanic-owned businesses: n/a (2002); Women-owned businesses: 1,146 (2002); Retail sales per capita: $13,292 (2006). Single-family building permits issued: 82 (2005); Multi-family building permits issued: 0 (2005).
Income: Per capita income: $19,770 (2005); Median household income: $36,781 (2005); Average household income: $47,326 (2005); Percent of households with income of $100,000 or more: 8.2% (2005); Poverty rate: 13.0% (2003); Bankruptcy rate: 9.07% (2005).
Education: Percent of population age 25 and over with: High school diploma (including GED) or higher: 78.2% (2005); Bachelor's degree or higher: 13.7% (2005); Master's degree or higher: 5.6% (2005).
Housing: Homeownership rate: 67.6% (2005); Median home value: $92,531 (2005); Median rent: $353 per month (2000); Median age of housing: 60+ years (2000).
Health: Birth rate: 123.6 per 10,000 population (2004); Death rate: 128.4 per 10,000 population (2004); Age-adjusted cancer mortality rate: 195.1 deaths per 100,000 population (2002); Number of physicians: 17.1 per 10,000 population (2004); Hospital beds: 69.4 per 10,000 population (2003); Hospital admissions: 1,327.1 per 10,000 population (2003).
Elections: 2004 Presidential election results: 53.4% Bush, 44.5% Kerry, 1.9% Nader, 0.2% Badnarik
Additional Information Contacts
Montgomery County Government . . . . (518) 853-3431
http://www.co.montgomery.ny.us/

Montgomery County Communities

AMES (village). Covers a land area of 0.132 square miles and a water area of 0 square miles. Located at 42.83° N. Lat.; 74.60° W. Long. Elevation is 713 feet.

Population: 166 (1990); 173 (2000); 189 (2005); 199 (2010 projected); Race: 98.9% White, 0.0% Black, 0.0% Asian, 0.0% Hispanic of any race (2005); Density: 1,426.5 persons per square mile (2005); Average household size: 2.52 (2005); Median age: 38.7 (2005); Males per 100 females: 101.1 (2005); Marriage status: 19.7% never married, 54.0% now married, 13.1% widowed, 13.1% divorced (2000); Foreign born: 1.2% (2000); Ancestry (includes multiple ancestries): 24.6% German, 12.9% English, 11.7% Irish, 11.1% French (except Basque), 9.4% Other groups (2000).
Economy: Single-family building permits issued: 0 (2005); Multi-family building permits issued: 0 (2005); Employment by occupation: 20.2% management, 14.6% professional, 16.9% services, 15.7% sales, 0.0% farming, 10.1% construction, 22.5% production (2000).
Income: Per capita income: $19,894 (2005); Median household income: $40,417 (2005); Average household income: $50,133 (2005); Percent of households with income of $100,000 or more: 13.3% (2005); Poverty rate: 8.8% (2000).
Education: Percent of population age 25 and over with: High school diploma (including GED) or higher: 85.8% (2005); Bachelor's degree or higher: 17.3% (2005); Master's degree or higher: 5.5% (2005).
Housing: Homeownership rate: 74.7% (2005); Median home value: $105,769 (2005); Median rent: $319 per month (2000); Median age of housing: 60+ years (2000).
Transportation: Commute to work: 85.4% car, 0.0% public transportation, 9.0% walk, 5.6% work from home (2000); Travel time to work: 46.4% less than 15 minutes, 31.0% 15 to 30 minutes, 20.2% 30 to 45 minutes, 2.4% 45 to 60 minutes, 0.0% 60 minutes or more (2000)

AMSTERDAM (city). Covers a land area of 5.947 square miles and a water area of 0.339 square miles. Located at 42.94° N. Lat.; 74.19° W. Long. Elevation is 264 feet.
History: Amsterdam was first settled by Albert Veeder, who came from Schenectady in 1783. The village of Amsterdam was so named in 1804. It began to grow in size and industrial importance after the Erie Canal was opened in 1825 and the Utica & Schenectady Railroad was constructed through it in 1836. The local carpet industry traces its beginnings to 1838, when William E. Greene established a carpet mill. The knitting industry was started by Greene in 1856.
Population: 20,693 (1990); 18,355 (2000); 17,858 (2005); 17,358 (2010 projected); Race: 86.3% White, 3.4% Black, 1.0% Asian, 22.3% Hispanic of any race (2005); Density: 3,002.9 persons per square mile (2005); Average household size: 2.28 (2005); Median age: 39.8 (2005); Males per 100 females: 86.3 (2005); Marriage status: 28.5% never married, 48.4% now married, 13.3% widowed, 9.8% divorced (2000); Foreign born: 4.9% (2000); Ancestry (includes multiple ancestries): 24.8% Italian, 20.0% Polish, 19.6% Other groups, 13.8% Irish, 12.0% German (2000).
Economy: Single-family building permits issued: 3 (2005); Multi-family building permits issued: 0 (2005); Employment by occupation: 9.6% management, 19.3% professional, 16.2% services, 27.7% sales, 0.4% farming, 7.1% construction, 19.8% production (2000).
Income: Per capita income: $18,681 (2005); Median household income: $30,583 (2005); Average household income: $41,345 (2005); Percent of households with income of $100,000 or more: 6.4% (2005); Poverty rate: 16.3% (2000).
Education: Percent of population age 25 and over with: High school diploma (including GED) or higher: 75.7% (2005); Bachelor's degree or higher: 15.0% (2005); Master's degree or higher: 6.0% (2005).
School District(s)
Amsterdam City School District (KG-12)
    2003-04 Enrollment: 3,782 . . . . (518) 843-5217
Broadalbin-Perth Central School District (PK-12)
    2003-04 Enrollment: 2,208 . . . . (518) 954-2500
Housing: Homeownership rate: 51.4% (2005); Median home value: $86,104 (2005); Median rent: $349 per month (2000); Median age of housing: 60+ years (2000).
Hospitals: Amsterdam Memorial Hospital (39 beds); St. Mary's Hospital (143 beds)
Safety: Violent crime rate: 16.1 per 10,000 population; Property crime rate: 118.8 per 10,000 population (2004).
Newspapers: The Recorder (Circulation 9,506)
Transportation: Commute to work: 87.8% car, 5.2% public transportation, 3.3% walk, 2.1% work from home (2000); Travel time to work: 47.9% less than 15 minutes, 23.0% 15 to 30 minutes, 16.2% 30 to 45 minutes, 9.5% 45 to 60 minutes, 3.4% 60 minutes or more (2000); Amtrak: Service available.

Additional Information Contacts
Montgomery County Chamber of Commerce . . . . (518) 842-8200
  http://www.montgomerycountyny.com

AMSTERDAM (town).
Covers a land area of 29.680 square miles and a water area of 0.651 square miles. Located at 42.95° N. Lat.; 74.18° W. Long. Elevation is 264 feet.
History: Historically famous for carpet manufacturing. The area was settled in 1783 and was named Amsterdam for its many early settlers from the Netherlands. Nearby stands Fort Johnson, home of the British colonial leader Sir William Johnson. Incorporated 1885.
Population: 5,983 (1990); 5,820 (2000); 5,806 (2005); 5,777 (2010 projected); Race: 97.2% White, 1.1% Black, 0.2% Asian, 3.5% Hispanic of any race (2005); Density: 195.6 persons per square mile (2005); Average household size: 2.56 (2005); Median age: 46.3 (2005); Males per 100 females: 91.6 (2005); Marriage status: 22.5% never married, 59.8% now married, 11.3% widowed, 6.4% divorced (2000); Foreign born: 3.3% (2000); Ancestry (includes multiple ancestries): 24.5% Polish, 22.5% Italian, 17.1% German, 16.3% Irish, 8.3% English (2000).
Economy: Manufacturing now includes machinery, apparel, leather goods, furniture, transportation equipment, consumer goods. Single-family building permits issued: 11 (2005); Multi-family building permits issued: 0 (2005); Employment by occupation: 8.5% management, 19.7% professional, 13.7% services, 28.1% sales, 0.1% farming, 11.0% construction, 19.0% production (2000).
Income: Per capita income: $21,735 (2005); Median household income: $42,295 (2005); Average household income: $52,927 (2005); Percent of households with income of $100,000 or more: 9.7% (2005); Poverty rate: 7.0% (2000).
Education: Percent of population age 25 and over with: High school diploma (including GED) or higher: 82.7% (2005); Bachelor's degree or higher: 13.9% (2005); Master's degree or higher: 6.4% (2005).
Housing: Homeownership rate: 83.2% (2005); Median home value: $118,945 (2005); Median rent: $394 per month (2000); Median age of housing: 50 years (2000).
Transportation: Commute to work: 93.4% car, 1.9% public transportation, 1.0% walk, 3.2% work from home (2000); Travel time to work: 40.3% less than 15 minutes, 27.9% 15 to 30 minutes, 15.9% 30 to 45 minutes, 10.8% 45 to 60 minutes, 5.1% 60 minutes or more (2000); Amtrak: Service available.

CANAJOHARIE (village).
Covers a land area of 1.296 square miles and a water area of 0.043 square miles. Located at 42.90° N. Lat.; 74.57° W. Long. Elevation is 311 feet.
Population: 2,364 (1990); 2,257 (2000); 2,193 (2005); 2,149 (2010 projected); Race: 94.9% White, 1.4% Black, 0.8% Asian, 2.3% Hispanic of any race (2005); Density: 1,692.1 persons per square mile (2005); Average household size: 2.40 (2005); Median age: 38.1 (2005); Males per 100 females: 91.2 (2005); Marriage status: 26.3% never married, 55.9% now married, 8.7% widowed, 9.1% divorced (2000); Foreign born: 3.2% (2000); Ancestry (includes multiple ancestries): 23.7% German, 12.7% Italian, 12.6% English, 11.7% Irish, 10.5% Other groups (2000).
Economy: Single-family building permits issued: 2 (2005); Multi-family building permits issued: 0 (2005); Employment by occupation: 15.6% management, 16.9% professional, 15.7% services, 24.7% sales, 0.5% farming, 7.0% construction, 19.7% production (2000).
Income: Per capita income: $21,182 (2005); Median household income: $36,420 (2005); Average household income: $49,710 (2005); Percent of households with income of $100,000 or more: 10.9% (2005); Poverty rate: 12.4% (2000).
Education: Percent of population age 25 and over with: High school diploma (including GED) or higher: 82.8% (2005); Bachelor's degree or higher: 19.4% (2005); Master's degree or higher: 8.9% (2005).

School District(s)
Canajoharie Central School District (PK-12)
  2003-04 Enrollment: 1,113 . . . . (518) 673-6302

Housing: Homeownership rate: 56.5% (2005); Median home value: $85,102 (2005); Median rent: $371 per month (2000); Median age of housing: 60+ years (2000).
Transportation: Commute to work: 81.6% car, 1.3% public transportation, 13.9% walk, 2.5% work from home (2000); Travel time to work: 49.9% less than 15 minutes, 15.1% 15 to 30 minutes, 14.2% 30 to 45 minutes, 13.2% 45 to 60 minutes, 7.6% 60 minutes or more (2000)

CANAJOHARIE (town).
Covers a land area of 42.906 square miles and a water area of 0.198 square miles. Located at 42.87° N. Lat.; 74.59° W. Long. Elevation is 311 feet.
History: Here are Van Alstyne House (1749), with historical collections, and a library and art gallery. Settled c.1730 by Dutch and Germans; incorporated 1829.
Population: 3,909 (1990); 3,797 (2000); 3,789 (2005); 3,781 (2010 projected); Race: 95.9% White, 1.0% Black, 0.8% Asian, 1.7% Hispanic of any race (2005); Density: 88.3 persons per square mile (2005); Average household size: 2.50 (2005); Median age: 39.2 (2005); Males per 100 females: 95.1 (2005); Marriage status: 23.7% never married, 61.4% now married, 7.6% widowed, 7.4% divorced (2000); Foreign born: 2.8% (2000); Ancestry (includes multiple ancestries): 25.3% German, 13.3% English, 12.2% Irish, 11.0% Italian, 8.8% Other groups (2000).
Economy: Electroplating, plastic products, food. Single-family building permits issued: 6 (2005); Multi-family building permits issued: 0 (2005); Employment by occupation: 14.7% management, 14.4% professional, 15.9% services, 21.5% sales, 2.4% farming, 8.5% construction, 22.7% production (2000).
Income: Per capita income: $19,770 (2005); Median household income: $36,469 (2005); Average household income: $48,871 (2005); Percent of households with income of $100,000 or more: 9.9% (2005); Poverty rate: 11.3% (2000).
Education: Percent of population age 25 and over with: High school diploma (including GED) or higher: 82.2% (2005); Bachelor's degree or higher: 16.5% (2005); Master's degree or higher: 6.7% (2005).
Housing: Homeownership rate: 68.3% (2005); Median home value: $89,327 (2005); Median rent: $367 per month (2000); Median age of housing: 60+ years (2000).
Transportation: Commute to work: 84.5% car, 1.3% public transportation, 10.5% walk, 3.4% work from home (2000); Travel time to work: 47.8% less than 15 minutes, 19.9% 15 to 30 minutes, 14.8% 30 to 45 minutes, 10.1% 45 to 60 minutes, 7.3% 60 minutes or more (2000)

CHARLESTON (town).
Covers a land area of 42.608 square miles and a water area of 0.228 square miles. Located at 42.81° N. Lat.; 74.34° W. Long. Elevation is 1,134 feet.
Population: 1,107 (1990); 1,292 (2000); 1,240 (2005); 1,207 (2010 projected); Race: 97.1% White, 1.0% Black, 0.3% Asian, 2.2% Hispanic of any race (2005); Density: 29.1 persons per square mile (2005); Average household size: 2.68 (2005); Median age: 38.2 (2005); Males per 100 females: 102.6 (2005); Marriage status: 23.1% never married, 64.6% now married, 4.5% widowed, 7.9% divorced (2000); Foreign born: 0.9% (2000); Ancestry (includes multiple ancestries): 25.2% German, 14.9% Irish, 12.7% Italian, 9.4% United States or American, 8.8% English (2000).
Economy: Single-family building permits issued: 6 (2005); Multi-family building permits issued: 0 (2005); Employment by occupation: 10.0% management, 15.9% professional, 15.9% services, 19.8% sales, 2.7% farming, 12.9% construction, 22.9% production (2000).
Income: Per capita income: $20,839 (2005); Median household income: $46,824 (2005); Average household income: $55,931 (2005); Percent of households with income of $100,000 or more: 10.8% (2005); Poverty rate: 10.1% (2000).
Education: Percent of population age 25 and over with: High school diploma (including GED) or higher: 80.6% (2005); Bachelor's degree or higher: 12.0% (2005); Master's degree or higher: 5.3% (2005).
Housing: Homeownership rate: 87.2% (2005); Median home value: $106,707 (2005); Median rent: $417 per month (2000); Median age of housing: 24 years (2000).
Transportation: Commute to work: 93.9% car, 0.0% public transportation, 2.0% walk, 4.1% work from home (2000); Travel time to work: 8.1% less than 15 minutes, 25.1% 15 to 30 minutes, 32.2% 30 to 45 minutes, 19.7% 45 to 60 minutes, 14.9% 60 minutes or more (2000)

FLORIDA (town).
Covers a land area of 50.356 square miles and a water area of 1.138 square miles. Located at 42.89° N. Lat.; 74.20° W. Long.
Population: 2,637 (1990); 2,731 (2000); 2,828 (2005); 2,903 (2010 projected); Race: 98.0% White, 0.3% Black, 0.2% Asian, 3.5% Hispanic of any race (2005); Density: 56.2 persons per square mile (2005); Average household size: 2.55 (2005); Median age: 41.8 (2005); Males per 100 females: 99.6 (2005); Marriage status: 22.0% never married, 62.2% now married, 7.4% widowed, 8.4% divorced (2000); Foreign born: 1.1% (2000);

Ancestry (includes multiple ancestries): 23.6% German, 16.6% Polish, 16.0% Italian, 13.4% Irish, 8.4% United States or American (2000).
Economy: Single-family building permits issued: 6 (2005); Multi-family building permits issued: 0 (2005); Employment by occupation: 12.1% management, 15.9% professional, 11.9% services, 25.0% sales, 1.1% farming, 15.3% construction, 18.6% production (2000).
Income: Per capita income: $21,952 (2005); Median household income: $50,366 (2005); Average household income: $55,437 (2005); Percent of households with income of $100,000 or more: 11.1% (2005); Poverty rate: 4.4% (2000).
Education: Percent of population age 25 and over with: High school diploma (including GED) or higher: 83.1% (2005); Bachelor's degree or higher: 13.0% (2005); Master's degree or higher: 4.2% (2005).
Housing: Homeownership rate: 86.6% (2005); Median home value: $121,471 (2005); Median rent: $343 per month (2000); Median age of housing: 38 years (2000).
Transportation: Commute to work: 91.8% car, 1.2% public transportation, 1.6% walk, 5.0% work from home (2000); Travel time to work: 25.9% less than 15 minutes, 35.7% 15 to 30 minutes, 22.8% 30 to 45 minutes, 9.7% 45 to 60 minutes, 5.8% 60 minutes or more (2000)

FONDA (village). Covers a land area of 0.533 square miles and a water area of 0.073 square miles. Located at 42.95° N. Lat.; 74.37° W. Long. Elevation is 294 feet.
History: Formally a freight transfer point on the N.Y. Central railroad. Incorporated 1850.
Population: 1,072 (1990); 810 (2000); 829 (2005); 834 (2010 projected); Race: 97.7% White, 0.2% Black, 0.8% Asian, 2.8% Hispanic of any race (2005); Density: 1,555.8 persons per square mile (2005); Average household size: 2.26 (2005); Median age: 36.9 (2005); Males per 100 females: 84.6 (2005); Marriage status: 24.1% never married, 52.9% now married, 10.2% widowed, 12.9% divorced (2000); Foreign born: 4.2% (2000); Ancestry (includes multiple ancestries): 19.4% Irish, 18.7% Italian, 18.7% German, 9.7% English, 9.7% Dutch (2000).
Economy: Manufacturing of aluminum products, apparel and textiles. Single-family building permits issued: 0 (2005); Multi-family building permits issued: 0 (2005); Employment by occupation: 8.7% management, 15.1% professional, 24.9% services, 17.4% sales, 0.5% farming, 6.4% construction, 26.9% production (2000).
Income: Per capita income: $17,702 (2005); Median household income: $31,300 (2005); Average household income: $39,550 (2005); Percent of households with income of $100,000 or more: 4.4% (2005); Poverty rate: 11.7% (2000).
Taxes: Total city taxes per capita: $264 (2004); City property taxes per capita: $232 (2004).
Education: Percent of population age 25 and over with: High school diploma (including GED) or higher: 72.8% (2005); Bachelor's degree or higher: 9.5% (2005); Master's degree or higher: 4.6% (2005).

School District(s)
Fonda-Fultonville Central School District (KG-12)
    2003-04 Enrollment: 1,606 . . . . (518) 853-4415

Housing: Homeownership rate: 55.0% (2005); Median home value: $68,800 (2005); Median rent: $318 per month (2000); Median age of housing: 60+ years (2000).
Transportation: Commute to work: 90.1% car, 1.6% public transportation, 7.0% walk, 1.3% work from home (2000); Travel time to work: 44.3% less than 15 minutes, 34.3% 15 to 30 minutes, 10.3% 30 to 45 minutes, 7.7% 45 to 60 minutes, 3.4% 60 minutes or more (2000)

FORT JOHNSON (village). Covers a land area of 0.744 square miles and a water area of 0.100 square miles. Located at 42.95° N. Lat.; 74.23° W. Long.
History: Fort Johnson (1749), once home of Sir William Johnson, is now a museum.
Population: 615 (1990); 491 (2000); 483 (2005); 464 (2010 projected); Race: 97.7% White, 1.0% Black, 0.0% Asian, 3.3% Hispanic of any race (2005); Density: 649.1 persons per square mile (2005); Average household size: 2.44 (2005); Median age: 41.0 (2005); Males per 100 females: 92.4 (2005); Marriage status: 24.9% never married, 60.0% now married, 8.6% widowed, 6.5% divorced (2000); Foreign born: 1.6% (2000); Ancestry (includes multiple ancestries): 28.7% German, 19.8% Irish, 17.6% Polish, 15.8% Italian, 9.6% United States or American (2000).
Economy: Single-family building permits issued: 0 (2005); Multi-family building permits issued: 0 (2005); Employment by occupation: 5.2% management, 17.5% professional, 15.9% services, 30.3% sales, 0.8% farming, 8.4% construction, 21.9% production (2000).
Income: Per capita income: $23,287 (2005); Median household income: $44,146 (2005); Average household income: $56,806 (2005); Percent of households with income of $100,000 or more: 13.1% (2005); Poverty rate: 7.1% (2000).
Education: Percent of population age 25 and over with: High school diploma (including GED) or higher: 85.3% (2005); Bachelor's degree or higher: 9.5% (2005); Master's degree or higher: 4.0% (2005).
Housing: Homeownership rate: 83.3% (2005); Median home value: $90,000 (2005); Median rent: $389 per month (2000); Median age of housing: 60+ years (2000).
Transportation: Commute to work: 97.2% car, 1.2% public transportation, 1.6% walk, 0.0% work from home (2000); Travel time to work: 48.2% less than 15 minutes, 24.7% 15 to 30 minutes, 14.2% 30 to 45 minutes, 11.3% 45 to 60 minutes, 1.6% 60 minutes or more (2000)

FORT PLAIN (village). Aka South Fort Plain. Covers a land area of 1.362 square miles and a water area of 0.051 square miles. Located at 42.93° N. Lat.; 74.62° W. Long. Elevation is 317 feet.
History: Settled 1723, incorporated 1832.
Population: 2,416 (1990); 2,288 (2000); 2,238 (2005); 2,192 (2010 projected); Race: 98.2% White, 0.1% Black, 0.4% Asian, 2.3% Hispanic of any race (2005); Density: 1,643.2 persons per square mile (2005); Average household size: 2.34 (2005); Median age: 38.6 (2005); Males per 100 females: 91.8 (2005); Marriage status: 28.3% never married, 47.7% now married, 13.0% widowed, 11.1% divorced (2000); Foreign born: 3.4% (2000); Ancestry (includes multiple ancestries): 26.7% German, 11.1% United States or American, 10.7% Italian, 9.9% Dutch, 9.4% Irish (2000).
Economy: In dairying and poultry area. Single-family building permits issued: 0 (2005); Multi-family building permits issued: 0 (2005); Employment by occupation: 7.7% management, 15.1% professional, 16.8% services, 28.5% sales, 0.3% farming, 6.6% construction, 25.0% production (2000).
Income: Per capita income: $19,951 (2005); Median household income: $32,756 (2005); Average household income: $45,630 (2005); Percent of households with income of $100,000 or more: 9.8% (2005); Poverty rate: 14.0% (2000).
Education: Percent of population age 25 and over with: High school diploma (including GED) or higher: 78.6% (2005); Bachelor's degree or higher: 12.8% (2005); Master's degree or higher: 6.7% (2005).

School District(s)
Fort Plain Central School District (PK-12)
    2003-04 Enrollment: 959 . . . . (518) 993-4000

Housing: Homeownership rate: 57.3% (2005); Median home value: $75,000 (2005); Median rent: $370 per month (2000); Median age of housing: 60+ years (2000).
Safety: Violent crime rate: 0.0 per 10,000 population; Property crime rate: 49.0 per 10,000 population (2004).
Newspapers: Courier-Standard-Enterprise (General - Circulation 5,000)
Transportation: Commute to work: 88.2% car, 2.4% public transportation, 6.3% walk, 2.8% work from home (2000); Travel time to work: 43.8% less than 15 minutes, 18.3% 15 to 30 minutes, 18.8% 30 to 45 minutes, 9.8% 45 to 60 minutes, 9.2% 60 minutes or more (2000)

FULTONVILLE (village). Covers a land area of 0.481 square miles and a water area of 0.037 square miles. Located at 42.94° N. Lat.; 74.36° W. Long.
Population: 748 (1990); 710 (2000); 724 (2005); 733 (2010 projected); Race: 97.4% White, 0.0% Black, 1.4% Asian, 3.0% Hispanic of any race (2005); Density: 1,506.1 persons per square mile (2005); Average household size: 2.50 (2005); Median age: 35.9 (2005); Males per 100 females: 88.5 (2005); Marriage status: 25.5% never married, 56.8% now married, 8.0% widowed, 9.6% divorced (2000); Foreign born: 1.5% (2000); Ancestry (includes multiple ancestries): 24.7% German, 16.9% Irish, 13.2% Dutch, 10.5% English, 9.6% Italian (2000).
Economy: Manufacturing: apparel, textiles. Employment by occupation: 8.1% management, 13.7% professional, 20.6% services, 24.5% sales, 3.6% farming, 6.3% construction, 23.3% production (2000).
Income: Per capita income: $19,496 (2005); Median household income: $38,947 (2005); Average household income: $47,828 (2005); Percent of households with income of $100,000 or more: 6.2% (2005); Poverty rate: 6.9% (2000).

Education: Percent of population age 25 and over with: High school diploma (including GED) or higher: 81.0% (2005); Bachelor's degree or higher: 9.5% (2005); Master's degree or higher: 2.5% (2005).

School District(s)

Fonda-Fultonville CSD (KG-12)
    2003-04 Enrollment: 1,606 . . . . (518) 853-4415
Johnstown City Sd (PK-12)
    2003-04 Enrollment: 2,168 . . . . (518) 762-4611

Housing: Homeownership rate: 69.0% (2005); Median home value: $80,784 (2005); Median rent: $385 per month (2000); Median age of housing: 60+ years (2000).

Transportation: Commute to work: 88.9% car, 0.9% public transportation, 4.5% walk, 4.5% work from home (2000); Travel time to work: 37.2% less than 15 minutes, 41.0% 15 to 30 minutes, 6.3% 30 to 45 minutes, 6.6% 45 to 60 minutes, 8.8% 60 minutes or more (2000)

GLEN (town). Covers a land area of 38.704 square miles and a water area of 0.586 square miles. Located at 42.91° N. Lat.; 74.35° W. Long.
Population: 1,950 (1990); 2,222 (2000); 2,198 (2005); 2,197 (2010 projected); Race: 92.9% White, 4.0% Black, 1.8% Asian, 3.8% Hispanic of any race (2005); Density: 56.8 persons per square mile (2005); Average household size: 2.79 (2005); Median age: 38.3 (2005); Males per 100 females: 109.1 (2005); Marriage status: 26.1% never married, 57.8% now married, 7.0% widowed, 9.0% divorced (2000); Foreign born: 0.5% (2000); Ancestry (includes multiple ancestries): 22.6% German, 16.2% Irish, 14.8% Italian, 10.5% Polish, 9.2% Other groups (2000).
Economy: Single-family building permits issued: 2 (2005); Multi-family building permits issued: 0 (2005); Employment by occupation: 11.9% management, 16.6% professional, 15.1% services, 23.7% sales, 4.8% farming, 11.0% construction, 17.0% production (2000).
Income: Per capita income: $20,934 (2005); Median household income: $48,446 (2005); Average household income: $55,756 (2005); Percent of households with income of $100,000 or more: 8.6% (2005); Poverty rate: 6.0% (2000).
Education: Percent of population age 25 and over with: High school diploma (including GED) or higher: 78.9% (2005); Bachelor's degree or higher: 15.8% (2005); Master's degree or higher: 6.0% (2005).
Housing: Homeownership rate: 81.3% (2005); Median home value: $100,016 (2005); Median rent: $392 per month (2000); Median age of housing: 51 years (2000).
Transportation: Commute to work: 90.8% car, 0.3% public transportation, 2.6% walk, 5.2% work from home (2000); Travel time to work: 32.7% less than 15 minutes, 36.4% 15 to 30 minutes, 14.7% 30 to 45 minutes, 7.9% 45 to 60 minutes, 8.4% 60 minutes or more (2000)

HAGAMAN (village). Covers a land area of 1.542 square miles and a water area of 0 square miles. Located at 42.97° N. Lat.; 74.15° W. Long.
Population: 1,377 (1990); 1,357 (2000); 1,289 (2005); 1,242 (2010 projected); Race: 97.3% White, 0.8% Black, 0.5% Asian, 3.6% Hispanic of any race (2005); Density: 836.2 persons per square mile (2005); Average household size: 2.39 (2005); Median age: 42.3 (2005); Males per 100 females: 99.2 (2005); Marriage status: 22.9% never married, 60.8% now married, 10.1% widowed, 6.2% divorced (2000); Foreign born: 3.5% (2000); Ancestry (includes multiple ancestries): 26.7% Polish, 22.2% Italian, 18.7% German, 18.4% Irish, 7.6% Other groups (2000).
Economy: Single-family building permits issued: 0 (2005); Multi-family building permits issued: 0 (2005); Employment by occupation: 10.4% management, 21.5% professional, 13.0% services, 31.4% sales, 0.0% farming, 9.0% construction, 14.7% production (2000).
Income: Per capita income: $23,496 (2005); Median household income: $47,266 (2005); Average household income: $53,613 (2005); Percent of households with income of $100,000 or more: 8.9% (2005); Poverty rate: 6.7% (2000).
Education: Percent of population age 25 and over with: High school diploma (including GED) or higher: 86.5% (2005); Bachelor's degree or higher: 17.9% (2005); Master's degree or higher: 7.3% (2005).
Housing: Homeownership rate: 80.5% (2005); Median home value: $117,602 (2005); Median rent: $385 per month (2000); Median age of housing: 52 years (2000).
Transportation: Commute to work: 95.4% car, 1.9% public transportation, 1.0% walk, 1.4% work from home (2000); Travel time to work: 37.6% less than 15 minutes, 26.7% 15 to 30 minutes, 19.4% 30 to 45 minutes, 11.2% 45 to 60 minutes, 5.2% 60 minutes or more (2000)

MINDEN (town). Covers a land area of 51.042 square miles and a water area of 0.416 square miles. Located at 42.93° N. Lat.; 74.67° W. Long.
Population: 4,474 (1990); 4,202 (2000); 4,149 (2005); 4,090 (2010 projected); Race: 98.1% White, 0.1% Black, 0.7% Asian, 2.0% Hispanic of any race (2005); Density: 81.3 persons per square mile (2005); Average household size: 2.45 (2005); Median age: 39.4 (2005); Males per 100 females: 96.4 (2005); Marriage status: 24.5% never married, 55.3% now married, 9.7% widowed, 10.5% divorced (2000); Foreign born: 3.0% (2000); Ancestry (includes multiple ancestries): 24.9% German, 10.8% United States or American, 10.8% English, 9.7% Italian, 8.0% Dutch (2000).
Economy: Single-family building permits issued: 5 (2005); Multi-family building permits issued: 0 (2005); Employment by occupation: 9.7% management, 13.2% professional, 14.7% services, 30.0% sales, 2.2% farming, 9.0% construction, 21.2% production (2000).
Income: Per capita income: $18,287 (2005); Median household income: $33,540 (2005); Average household income: $44,185 (2005); Percent of households with income of $100,000 or more: 7.2% (2005); Poverty rate: 12.0% (2000).
Education: Percent of population age 25 and over with: High school diploma (including GED) or higher: 76.3% (2005); Bachelor's degree or higher: 9.9% (2005); Master's degree or higher: 5.3% (2005).
Housing: Homeownership rate: 68.8% (2005); Median home value: $78,874 (2005); Median rent: $366 per month (2000); Median age of housing: 60+ years (2000).
Transportation: Commute to work: 86.6% car, 1.3% public transportation, 7.0% walk, 4.8% work from home (2000); Travel time to work: 38.1% less than 15 minutes, 23.4% 15 to 30 minutes, 22.7% 30 to 45 minutes, 7.1% 45 to 60 minutes, 8.8% 60 minutes or more (2000)

MOHAWK (town). Covers a land area of 34.724 square miles and a water area of 0.684 square miles. Located at 42.95° N. Lat.; 74.37° W. Long.
Population: 3,976 (1990); 3,902 (2000); 3,931 (2005); 3,958 (2010 projected); Race: 97.0% White, 0.5% Black, 1.0% Asian, 2.0% Hispanic of any race (2005); Density: 113.2 persons per square mile (2005); Average household size: 2.57 (2005); Median age: 39.5 (2005); Males per 100 females: 94.9 (2005); Marriage status: 21.4% never married, 61.5% now married, 6.9% widowed, 10.3% divorced (2000); Foreign born: 2.3% (2000); Ancestry (includes multiple ancestries): 24.2% German, 16.6% Italian, 15.8% Irish, 12.7% English, 8.6% United States or American (2000).
Economy: Single-family building permits issued: 14 (2005); Multi-family building permits issued: 0 (2005); Employment by occupation: 15.3% management, 19.1% professional, 17.6% services, 20.6% sales, 1.2% farming, 7.0% construction, 19.2% production (2000).
Income: Per capita income: $21,594 (2005); Median household income: $45,128 (2005); Average household income: $55,080 (2005); Percent of households with income of $100,000 or more: 11.8% (2005); Poverty rate: 9.6% (2000).
Taxes: Total city taxes per capita: $91 (2004); City property taxes per capita: $68 (2004).
Education: Percent of population age 25 and over with: High school diploma (including GED) or higher: 82.5% (2005); Bachelor's degree or higher: 14.5% (2005); Master's degree or higher: 5.6% (2005).
Housing: Homeownership rate: 80.2% (2005); Median home value: $110,260 (2005); Median rent: $319 per month (2000); Median age of housing: 45 years (2000).
Transportation: Commute to work: 94.4% car, 0.7% public transportation, 2.9% walk, 1.7% work from home (2000); Travel time to work: 39.8% less than 15 minutes, 38.9% 15 to 30 minutes, 10.3% 30 to 45 minutes, 7.0% 45 to 60 minutes, 4.1% 60 minutes or more (2000)

NELLISTON (village). Covers a land area of 1.101 square miles and a water area of 0.089 square miles. Located at 42.93° N. Lat.; 74.61° W. Long.
Population: 569 (1990); 622 (2000); 641 (2005); 658 (2010 projected); Race: 97.3% White, 0.0% Black, 0.2% Asian, 0.8% Hispanic of any race (2005); Density: 582.3 persons per square mile (2005); Average household size: 2.41 (2005); Median age: 40.9 (2005); Males per 100 females: 95.4 (2005); Marriage status: 21.4% never married, 57.5% now married, 10.9% widowed, 10.1% divorced (2000); Foreign born: 1.0% (2000); Ancestry (includes multiple ancestries): 30.1% German, 14.4% Irish, 12.3% Italian, 10.1% United States or American, 10.1% Dutch (2000).

Economy: Employment by occupation: 7.2% management, 13.5% professional, 15.1% services, 27.1% sales, 0.8% farming, 13.1% construction, 23.1% production (2000).
Income: Per capita income: $18,651 (2005); Median household income: $37,143 (2005); Average household income: $44,944 (2005); Percent of households with income of $100,000 or more: 4.9% (2005); Poverty rate: 9.8% (2000).
Education: Percent of population age 25 and over with: High school diploma (including GED) or higher: 66.4% (2005); Bachelor's degree or higher: 5.9% (2005); Master's degree or higher: 2.7% (2005).
Housing: Homeownership rate: 77.1% (2005); Median home value: $63,061 (2005); Median rent: $391 per month (2000); Median age of housing: 60+ years (2000).
Transportation: Commute to work: 89.8% car, 0.0% public transportation, 4.5% walk, 4.9% work from home (2000); Travel time to work: 45.1% less than 15 minutes, 24.5% 15 to 30 minutes, 21.0% 30 to 45 minutes, 3.9% 45 to 60 minutes, 5.6% 60 minutes or more (2000)

PALATINE (town). Covers a land area of 41.206 square miles and a water area of 0.518 square miles. Located at 42.95° N. Lat.; 74.56° W. Long.
Population: 2,787 (1990); 3,070 (2000); 3,208 (2005); 3,331 (2010 projected); Race: 97.0% White, 1.2% Black, 0.7% Asian, 0.8% Hispanic of any race (2005); Density: 77.9 persons per square mile (2005); Average household size: 2.69 (2005); Median age: 39.4 (2005); Males per 100 females: 94.0 (2005); Marriage status: 21.7% never married, 60.4% now married, 10.4% widowed, 7.5% divorced (2000); Foreign born: 1.4% (2000); Ancestry (includes multiple ancestries): 26.5% German, 10.4% United States or American, 10.4% Dutch, 10.1% Italian, 10.0% Irish (2000).
Economy: Single-family building permits issued: 7 (2005); Multi-family building permits issued: 0 (2005); Employment by occupation: 11.7% management, 15.7% professional, 15.4% services, 19.0% sales, 3.6% farming, 10.6% construction, 24.0% production (2000).
Income: Per capita income: $20,167 (2005); Median household income: $39,184 (2005); Average household income: $53,387 (2005); Percent of households with income of $100,000 or more: 9.6% (2005); Poverty rate: 11.5% (2000).
Education: Percent of population age 25 and over with: High school diploma (including GED) or higher: 72.9% (2005); Bachelor's degree or higher: 8.2% (2005); Master's degree or higher: 2.4% (2005).
Housing: Homeownership rate: 77.9% (2005); Median home value: $77,656 (2005); Median rent: $325 per month (2000); Median age of housing: 50 years (2000).
Transportation: Commute to work: 86.9% car, 0.1% public transportation, 4.0% walk, 8.1% work from home (2000); Travel time to work: 37.8% less than 15 minutes, 27.8% 15 to 30 minutes, 18.7% 30 to 45 minutes, 8.1% 45 to 60 minutes, 7.6% 60 minutes or more (2000)

PALATINE BRIDGE (village). Covers a land area of 0.888 square miles and a water area of 0.063 square miles. Located at 42.91° N. Lat.; 74.57° W. Long. Elevation is 337 feet.
Population: 668 (1990); 706 (2000); 733 (2005); 757 (2010 projected); Race: 97.5% White, 0.4% Black, 1.9% Asian, 1.0% Hispanic of any race (2005); Density: 825.6 persons per square mile (2005); Average household size: 2.54 (2005); Median age: 50.8 (2005); Males per 100 females: 88.4 (2005); Marriage status: 14.3% never married, 58.8% now married, 19.8% widowed, 7.2% divorced (2000); Foreign born: 1.6% (2000); Ancestry (includes multiple ancestries): 25.9% German, 15.1% Irish, 12.7% Italian, 11.2% English, 10.3% Dutch (2000).
Economy: Single-family building permits issued: 2 (2005); Multi-family building permits issued: 0 (2005); Employment by occupation: 11.8% management, 20.2% professional, 15.1% services, 22.1% sales, 0.0% farming, 9.6% construction, 21.3% production (2000).
Income: Per capita income: $23,675 (2005); Median household income: $38,643 (2005); Average household income: $56,384 (2005); Percent of households with income of $100,000 or more: 10.7% (2005); Poverty rate: 11.8% (2000).
Education: Percent of population age 25 and over with: High school diploma (including GED) or higher: 80.5% (2005); Bachelor's degree or higher: 13.0% (2005); Master's degree or higher: 5.0% (2005).
Housing: Homeownership rate: 64.4% (2005); Median home value: $90,980 (2005); Median rent: $318 per month (2000); Median age of housing: 60 years (2000).
Transportation: Commute to work: 94.8% car, 0.7% public transportation, 3.7% walk, 0.7% work from home (2000); Travel time to work: 45.1% less than 15 minutes, 19.2% 15 to 30 minutes, 22.9% 30 to 45 minutes, 6.8% 45 to 60 minutes, 6.0% 60 minutes or more (2000)

ROOT (town). Covers a land area of 50.807 square miles and a water area of 0.209 square miles. Located at 42.85° N. Lat.; 74.48° W. Long.
Population: 1,692 (1990); 1,752 (2000); 1,806 (2005); 1,843 (2010 projected); Race: 97.6% White, 0.7% Black, 0.6% Asian, 1.6% Hispanic of any race (2005); Density: 35.5 persons per square mile (2005); Average household size: 2.63 (2005); Median age: 40.8 (2005); Males per 100 females: 101.8 (2005); Marriage status: 20.8% never married, 64.5% now married, 6.1% widowed, 8.6% divorced (2000); Foreign born: 1.1% (2000); Ancestry (includes multiple ancestries): 24.0% German, 12.4% Irish, 12.0% United States or American, 11.8% English, 10.8% Dutch (2000).
Economy: Single-family building permits issued: 9 (2005); Multi-family building permits issued: 0 (2005); Employment by occupation: 8.3% management, 12.1% professional, 13.8% services, 27.8% sales, 2.3% farming, 13.7% construction, 22.0% production (2000).
Income: Per capita income: $19,474 (2005); Median household income: $43,702 (2005); Average household income: $51,119 (2005); Percent of households with income of $100,000 or more: 9.4% (2005); Poverty rate: 11.8% (2000).
Education: Percent of population age 25 and over with: High school diploma (including GED) or higher: 76.3% (2005); Bachelor's degree or higher: 12.2% (2005); Master's degree or higher: 3.3% (2005).
Housing: Homeownership rate: 88.5% (2005); Median home value: $90,610 (2005); Median rent: $396 per month (2000); Median age of housing: 30 years (2000).
Transportation: Commute to work: 89.8% car, 0.0% public transportation, 4.3% walk, 3.3% work from home (2000); Travel time to work: 19.5% less than 15 minutes, 36.6% 15 to 30 minutes, 22.2% 30 to 45 minutes, 11.8% 45 to 60 minutes, 9.9% 60 minutes or more (2000)

SAINT JOHNSVILLE (village). Covers a land area of 0.856 square miles and a water area of <.001 square miles. Located at 43.00° N. Lat.; 74.67° W. Long.
Population: 1,918 (1990); 1,685 (2000); 1,666 (2005); 1,650 (2010 projected); Race: 98.9% White, 0.1% Black, 0.2% Asian, 2.3% Hispanic of any race (2005); Density: 1,945.1 persons per square mile (2005); Average household size: 2.40 (2005); Median age: 43.6 (2005); Males per 100 females: 88.0 (2005); Marriage status: 27.5% never married, 49.8% now married, 14.4% widowed, 8.3% divorced (2000); Foreign born: 2.1% (2000); Ancestry (includes multiple ancestries): 19.8% German, 19.8% Italian, 11.2% English, 11.0% Irish, 8.2% Dutch (2000).
Economy: Single-family building permits issued: 0 (2005); Multi-family building permits issued: 0 (2005); Employment by occupation: 7.3% management, 17.3% professional, 20.4% services, 20.3% sales, 0.6% farming, 8.9% construction, 25.2% production (2000).
Income: Per capita income: $17,466 (2005); Median household income: $33,382 (2005); Average household income: $40,693 (2005); Percent of households with income of $100,000 or more: 4.6% (2005); Poverty rate: 14.4% (2000).
Education: Percent of population age 25 and over with: High school diploma (including GED) or higher: 73.7% (2005); Bachelor's degree or higher: 13.1% (2005); Master's degree or higher: 7.8% (2005).

School District(s)
Saint Johnsville Central School District (PK-12)
   2003-04 Enrollment: 492 . . . . (518) 568-7023

Housing: Homeownership rate: 61.6% (2005); Median home value: $75,684 (2005); Median rent: $317 per month (2000); Median age of housing: 60+ years (2000).
Transportation: Commute to work: 79.6% car, 0.4% public transportation, 15.5% walk, 3.7% work from home (2000); Travel time to work: 41.3% less than 15 minutes, 27.0% 15 to 30 minutes, 14.4% 30 to 45 minutes, 7.8% 45 to 60 minutes, 9.4% 60 minutes or more (2000)

SAINT JOHNSVILLE (town). Covers a land area of 16.835 square miles and a water area of 0.542 square miles. Located at 43.00° N. Lat.; 74.67° W. Long.
Population: 2,773 (1990); 2,565 (2000); 2,551 (2005); 2,535 (2010 projected); Race: 98.7% White, 0.1% Black, 0.2% Asian, 2.3% Hispanic of any race (2005); Density: 151.5 persons per square mile (2005); Average household size: 2.42 (2005); Median age: 41.6 (2005); Males per 100 females: 92.5 (2005); Marriage status: 25.5% never married, 54.8% now married, 12.2% widowed, 7.4% divorced (2000); Foreign born: 1.4%

(2000); Ancestry (includes multiple ancestries): 22.4% German, 19.5% Italian, 12.6% Irish, 9.9% English, 8.0% Dutch (2000).
Economy: Single-family building permits issued: 9 (2005); Multi-family building permits issued: 0 (2005); Employment by occupation: 11.7% management, 14.6% professional, 19.3% services, 17.6% sales, 1.3% farming, 9.6% construction, 26.0% production (2000).
Income: Per capita income: $18,283 (2005); Median household income: $36,083 (2005); Average household income: $43,397 (2005); Percent of households with income of $100,000 or more: 5.8% (2005); Poverty rate: 12.4% (2000).
Education: Percent of population age 25 and over with: High school diploma (including GED) or higher: 76.2% (2005); Bachelor's degree or higher: 12.6% (2005); Master's degree or higher: 6.9% (2005).
Housing: Homeownership rate: 68.4% (2005); Median home value: $78,966 (2005); Median rent: $313 per month (2000); Median age of housing: 60+ years (2000).
Transportation: Commute to work: 81.9% car, 0.3% public transportation, 11.4% walk, 5.2% work from home (2000); Travel time to work: 39.8% less than 15 minutes, 25.7% 15 to 30 minutes, 17.4% 30 to 45 minutes, 7.7% 45 to 60 minutes, 9.4% 60 minutes or more (2000)

SPRAKERS
(unincorporated postal area, zip code 12166). Covers a land area of 46.970 square miles and a water area of 0 square miles. Located at 42.83° N. Lat.; 74.45° W. Long.
Population: 0 (2000); Race: 98.8% White, 0.1% Black, 0.1% Asian, 1.1% Hispanic of any race (2000); Density: 0.0 persons per square mile (2000); Age: 25.8% under 18, 12.4% over 64 (2000); Marriage status: 23.3% never married, 63.6% now married, 4.9% widowed, 8.3% divorced (2000); Foreign born: 0.9% (2000); Ancestry (includes multiple ancestries): 21.5% German, 16.0% United States or American, 12.6% Irish, 11.2% English, 10.0% Italian (2000).
Economy: Employment by occupation: 9.6% management, 12.7% professional, 14.6% services, 24.2% sales, 2.4% farming, 11.3% construction, 25.2% production (2000).
Income: Per capita income: $16,574 (2000); Median household income: $39,737 (2000); Poverty rate: 12.6% (2000).
Education: Percent of population age 25 and over with: High school diploma (including GED) or higher: 78.8% (2000); Bachelor's degree or higher: 11.8% (2000).
Housing: Homeownership rate: 88.2% (2000); Median home value: $68,000 (2000); Median rent: $422 per month (2000); Median age of housing: 32 years (2000).
Transportation: Commute to work: 89.2% car, 0.0% public transportation, 5.3% walk, 3.7% work from home (2000); Travel time to work: 16.4% less than 15 minutes, 34.8% 15 to 30 minutes, 25.0% 30 to 45 minutes, 12.4% 45 to 60 minutes, 11.5% 60 minutes or more (2000)

TRIBES HILL
(CDP). Covers a land area of 2.279 square miles and a water area of 0.124 square miles. Located at 42.95° N. Lat.; 74.29° W. Long.
Population: 1,060 (1990); 1,024 (2000); 948 (2005); 929 (2010 projected); Race: 95.9% White, 1.2% Black, 0.7% Asian, 1.4% Hispanic of any race (2005); Density: 416.0 persons per square mile (2005); Average household size: 2.41 (2005); Median age: 45.4 (2005); Males per 100 females: 91.1 (2005); Marriage status: 19.4% never married, 58.0% now married, 9.8% widowed, 12.8% divorced (2000); Foreign born: 2.0% (2000); Ancestry (includes multiple ancestries): 23.4% Italian, 22.6% German, 18.7% Irish, 16.4% Polish, 10.6% United States or American (2000).
Economy: Employment by occupation: 15.8% management, 19.7% professional, 20.1% services, 21.6% sales, 1.9% farming, 8.4% construction, 12.4% production (2000).
Income: Per capita income: $20,459 (2005); Median household income: $39,200 (2005); Average household income: $49,226 (2005); Percent of households with income of $100,000 or more: 9.4% (2005); Poverty rate: 7.4% (2000).
Education: Percent of population age 25 and over with: High school diploma (including GED) or higher: 91.5% (2005); Bachelor's degree or higher: 12.2% (2005); Master's degree or higher: 4.7% (2005).
Housing: Homeownership rate: 87.8% (2005); Median home value: $112,338 (2005); Median rent: $303 per month (2000); Median age of housing: 52 years (2000).
Transportation: Commute to work: 96.5% car, 3.5% public transportation, 0.0% walk, 0.0% work from home (2000); Travel time to work: 31.1% less than 15 minutes, 40.2% 15 to 30 minutes, 22.0% 30 to 45 minutes, 3.0% 45 to 60 minutes, 3.7% 60 minutes or more (2000)

Nassau County

Located in southeastern New York, on western Long Island; bounded on the west by Queens borough of New York city, on the south by the Atlantic Ocean, and on the north by Long Island Sound. Covers a land area of 286.69 square miles, a water area of 166.39 square miles, and is located in the Eastern Time Zone. The county government was organized in 1899. County seat is Mineola.

Nassau County is part of the New York-Northern New Jersey-Long Island, NY-NJ-PA Metropolitan Statistical Area. The entire metro area includes: Edison, NJ Metropolitan Division (Middlesex County, NJ; Monmouth County, NJ; Ocean County, NJ; Somerset County, NJ); Nassau-Suffolk, NY Metropolitan Division (Nassau County, NY; Suffolk County, NY); New York-White Plains-Wayne, NY-NJ Metropolitan Division (Bergen County, NJ; Hudson County, NJ; Passaic County, NJ; Bronx County, NY; Kings County, NY; New York County, NY; Putnam County, NY; Queens County, NY; Richmond County, NY; Rockland County, NY; Westchester County, NY); Newark-Union, NJ-PA Metropolitan Division (Essex County, NJ; Hunterdon County, NJ; Morris County, NJ; Sussex County, NJ; Union County, NJ; Pike County, PA)

Population: 1,287,844 (1990); 1,334,544 (2000); 1,341,332 (2005); 1,347,523 (2010 projected); Race: 75.2% White, 11.4% Black, 6.3% Asian, 12.3% Hispanic of any race (2005); Density: 4,678.6 persons per square mile (2005); Average household size: 2.99 (2005); Median age: 40.0 (2005); Males per 100 females: 93.5 (2005).
Religion: Five largest groups: 52.0% Catholic Church, 15.5% Jewish Estimate, 1.5% Evangelical Lutheran Church in America, 1.3% The United Methodist Church, 1.2% Episcopal Church (2000).
Economy: Unemployment rate: 4.1% (2005); Total civilian labor force: 694,622 (2005); Leading industries: 16.4% health care and social assistance; 15.3% retail trade; 8.4% finance and insurance (2003); Farms: 65 totaling 1,118 acres (2002); Companies that employ 500 or more persons: 63 (2003); Companies that employ 100 to 499 persons: 697 (2003); Companies that employ less than 100 persons: 46,266 (2003); Black-owned businesses: 6,827 (2002); Hispanic-owned businesses: 9,151 (2002); Women-owned businesses: 37,932 (2002); Retail sales per capita: $19,159 (2006). Single-family building permits issued: 1,197 (2005); Multi-family building permits issued: 238 (2005).
Income: Per capita income: $36,221 (2005); Median household income: $81,998 (2005); Average household income: $107,239 (2005); Percent of households with income of $100,000 or more: 39.1% (2005); Poverty rate: 5.9% (2003); Bankruptcy rate: 3.08% (2005).
Taxes: Total county taxes per capita: $1,361 (2004); County property taxes per capita: $674 (2004).
Education: Percent of population age 25 and over with: High school diploma (including GED) or higher: 86.6% (2005); Bachelor's degree or higher: 35.2% (2005); Master's degree or higher: 15.5% (2005).
Housing: Homeownership rate: 80.5% (2005); Median home value: $400,532 (2005); Median rent: $898 per month (2000); Median age of housing: 47 years (2000).
Health: Birth rate: 122.0 per 10,000 population (2004); Death rate: 84.1 per 10,000 population (2004); Age-adjusted cancer mortality rate: 195.2 deaths per 100,000 population (2002); Air Quality Index: 69.2% good, 29.7% moderate, 1.1% unhealthy for sensitive individuals, 0.0% unhealthy (percent of days in 2005); Number of physicians: 66.0 per 10,000 population (2004); Hospital beds: 36.1 per 10,000 population (2003); Hospital admissions: 1,797.8 per 10,000 population (2003).
Elections: 2004 Presidential election results: 46.6% Bush, 52.2% Kerry, 1.0% Nader, 0.1% Badnarik
National and State Parks: Bethpage State Park; Hempstead Lake State Park; Jones Beach State Park; Oyster Bay National Wildlife Refuge; Sagamore Hill National Historical Site; Valley Stream State Park
Additional Information Contacts
Nassau County Government . . . . (516) 571-3000
 http://www.nassaucountyny.gov/
City of Glen Cove . . . . (516) 676-2000
 http://www.glencove-li.com/
City of Long Beach . . . . (516) 431-1000
 http://www.longbeachny.org/
Town of Hempstead . . . . (516) 489-5000
 http://www.townofhempstead.org/
Town of North Hempstead . . . . (516) 869-6311
 http://www.northhempstead.com/

Town of Oyster Bay . . . . (516) 624-6350
  http://www.oysterbaytown.com/
Village of Cedarhurst . . . . (516) 295-5770
  http://www.cedarhurst.gov/
Village of East Hills . . . . (516) 621-5600
  http://www.villageofeasthills.org/
Village of East Rockaway . . . . (516) 887-6300
  http://www.villageofeastrockaway.org/
Village of East Williston . . . . (516) 746-0782
  http://eastwilliston.org/
Village of Farmingdale . . . . (516) 249-0093
  http://www.farmingdalevillage.com/
Village of Floral Park . . . . (516) 326-6300
  http://www.fpvillage.org/
Village of Flower Hill . . . . (516) 627-5000
  http://www.villageflowerhill.com/
Village of Freeport . . . . (516) 377-2200
  http://www.freeportny.com/
Village of Garden City . . . . (516) 465-4000
  http://www.gardencityny.net/gcvillage.htm
Village of Great Neck . . . . (516) 482-0019
  http://www.greatneckvillage.org/
Village of Great Neck Plaza . . . . (516) 482-4500
  http://www.greatneckplaza.net/
Village of Hempstead . . . . (516) 489-3400
  http://www.villageofhempstead.org/
Village of Lawrence . . . . (516) 239-4600
  http://www.villageoflawrence.org/
Village of Massapequa Park . . . . (516) 798-0244
  http://www.ci.massapequa-park.ny.us/
Village of Matinecock . . . . (516) 671-7790
  http://www.matinecockvillage.org/
Village of New Hyde Park . . . . (516) 354-0022
  http://www.vnhp.org/
Village of Rockville Centre . . . . (516) 678-9300
  http://www.ci.rockville-centre.ny.us/
Village of Saddle Rock . . . . (516) 482-9400
  http://www.saddlerock.org/
Village of Sands Point . . . . (516) 883-3044
  http://www.sandspoint.org/
Village of Westbury . . . . (516) 334-1700
  http://www.villageofwestbury.org/

Nassau County Communities

ALBERTSON (CDP). Covers a land area of 0.661 square miles and a water area of 0 square miles. Located at 40.77° N. Lat.; 73.64° W. Long. Elevation is 140 feet.
Population: 5,166 (1990); 5,200 (2000); 5,209 (2005); 5,228 (2010 projected); Race: 75.1% White, 0.3% Black, 20.5% Asian, 7.8% Hispanic of any race (2005); Density: 7,880.4 persons per square mile (2005); Average household size: 2.88 (2005); Median age: 43.1 (2005); Males per 100 females: 94.4 (2005); Marriage status: 20.5% never married, 65.3% now married, 10.2% widowed, 4.0% divorced (2000); Foreign born: 20.3% (2000); Ancestry (includes multiple ancestries): 23.8% Italian, 21.5% Other groups, 17.5% Irish, 11.0% German, 7.9% Polish (2000).
Economy: Manufactures wire and cable. Employment by occupation: 18.4% management, 26.8% professional, 8.9% services, 32.8% sales, 0.0% farming, 7.9% construction, 5.1% production (2000).
Income: Per capita income: $35,458 (2005); Median household income: $78,178 (2005); Average household income: $102,270 (2005); Percent of households with income of $100,000 or more: 38.6% (2005); Poverty rate: 4.7% (2000).
Education: Percent of population age 25 and over with: High school diploma (including GED) or higher: 85.1% (2005); Bachelor's degree or higher: 39.0% (2005); Master's degree or higher: 16.5% (2005).
School District(s)
Herricks Union Free School District (KG-12)
  2003-04 Enrollment: 3,939 . . . . (516) 248-3105
Mineola Union Free School District (PK-12)
  2003-04 Enrollment: 2,903 . . . . (516) 741-5036
Housing: Homeownership rate: 91.4% (2005); Median home value: $452,143 (2005); Median rent: $1,150 per month (2000); Median age of housing: 46 years (2000).

Transportation: Commute to work: 87.6% car, 8.5% public transportation, 2.4% walk, 1.0% work from home (2000); Travel time to work: 19.5% less than 15 minutes, 34.8% 15 to 30 minutes, 19.4% 30 to 45 minutes, 11.1% 45 to 60 minutes, 15.2% 60 minutes or more (2000)

ATLANTIC BEACH (village). Covers a land area of 0.483 square miles and a water area of 0.520 square miles. Located at 40.59° N. Lat.; 73.73° W. Long. Elevation is 12 feet.
Population: 1,933 (1990); 1,986 (2000); 1,916 (2005); 1,859 (2010 projected); Race: 95.8% White, 1.0% Black, 1.1% Asian, 3.9% Hispanic of any race (2005); Density: 3,969.8 persons per square mile (2005); Average household size: 2.56 (2005); Median age: 49.5 (2005); Males per 100 females: 92.8 (2005); Marriage status: 16.9% never married, 67.6% now married, 9.0% widowed, 6.5% divorced (2000); Foreign born: 7.4% (2000); Ancestry (includes multiple ancestries): 19.2% Other groups, 17.5% Italian, 11.9% Irish, 11.8% Russian, 10.3% United States or American (2000).
Economy: Resort and residential village. Employment by occupation: 19.8% management, 33.4% professional, 7.6% services, 28.7% sales, 0.0% farming, 6.2% construction, 4.3% production (2000).
Income: Per capita income: $46,235 (2005); Median household income: $88,261 (2005); Average household income: $115,849 (2005); Percent of households with income of $100,000 or more: 42.8% (2005); Poverty rate: 5.6% (2000).
Education: Percent of population age 25 and over with: High school diploma (including GED) or higher: 94.9% (2005); Bachelor's degree or higher: 47.8% (2005); Master's degree or higher: 21.3% (2005).
Housing: Homeownership rate: 86.8% (2005); Median home value: $635,732 (2005); Median rent: $1,132 per month (2000); Median age of housing: 49 years (2000).
Transportation: Commute to work: 77.4% car, 15.0% public transportation, 1.5% walk, 4.6% work from home (2000); Travel time to work: 15.6% less than 15 minutes, 18.9% 15 to 30 minutes, 16.3% 30 to 45 minutes, 15.9% 45 to 60 minutes, 33.3% 60 minutes or more (2000)

BALDWIN (CDP). Covers a land area of 2.949 square miles and a water area of 0.011 square miles. Located at 40.66° N. Lat.; 73.61° W. Long. Elevation is 27 feet.
History: Named for F.W. Baldwin, an early settler. Settled 1640s.
Population: 22,719 (1990); 23,455 (2000); 23,169 (2005); 22,889 (2010 projected); Race: 54.5% White, 31.3% Black, 3.9% Asian, 15.0% Hispanic of any race (2005); Density: 7,857.5 persons per square mile (2005); Average household size: 3.01 (2005); Median age: 38.8 (2005); Males per 100 females: 91.0 (2005); Marriage status: 26.9% never married, 59.6% now married, 6.8% widowed, 6.7% divorced (2000); Foreign born: 21.5% (2000); Ancestry (includes multiple ancestries): 26.7% Other groups, 20.7% Italian, 20.0% Irish, 11.7% German, 4.7% Haitian (2000).
Economy: Commuter population. Varied manufacturing. Employment by occupation: 17.4% management, 25.6% professional, 13.7% services, 26.9% sales, 0.1% farming, 8.4% construction, 7.8% production (2000).
Income: Per capita income: $31,789 (2005); Median household income: $79,846 (2005); Average household income: $94,807 (2005); Percent of households with income of $100,000 or more: 36.2% (2005); Poverty rate: 5.4% (2000).
Education: Percent of population age 25 and over with: High school diploma (including GED) or higher: 87.3% (2005); Bachelor's degree or higher: 35.5% (2005); Master's degree or higher: 14.1% (2005).
School District(s)
Baldwin Union Free School District (KG-12)
  2003-04 Enrollment: 5,408 . . . . (516) 377-9271
Housing: Homeownership rate: 83.8% (2005); Median home value: $328,698 (2005); Median rent: $833 per month (2000); Median age of housing: 55 years (2000).
Newspapers: Polish American World (Catholic, General - Circulation 9,000)
Transportation: Commute to work: 75.9% car, 17.9% public transportation, 2.5% walk, 2.8% work from home (2000); Travel time to work: 19.2% less than 15 minutes, 26.9% 15 to 30 minutes, 18.8% 30 to 45 minutes, 10.4% 45 to 60 minutes, 24.7% 60 minutes or more (2000)
Additional Information Contacts
Baldwin Chamber of Commerce . . . . (516) 223-8080
  http://www.baldwinchamber.com

BALDWIN HARBOR (CDP). Covers a land area of 1.227 square miles and a water area of 0.477 square miles. Located at 40.63° N. Lat.; 73.60° W. Long.

Population: 7,899 (1990); 8,147 (2000); 8,154 (2005); 8,162 (2010 projected); Race: 73.7% White, 15.0% Black, 6.3% Asian, 9.6% Hispanic of any race (2005); Density: 6,647.8 persons per square mile (2005); Average household size: 2.94 (2005); Median age: 40.5 (2005); Males per 100 females: 94.6 (2005); Marriage status: 22.5% never married, 65.7% now married, 7.6% widowed, 4.2% divorced (2000); Foreign born: 15.3% (2000); Ancestry (includes multiple ancestries): 24.6% Italian, 18.4% Other groups, 16.1% Irish, 10.2% German, 8.1% Russian (2000).
Economy: Employment by occupation: 18.8% management, 28.1% professional, 10.3% services, 29.3% sales, 0.0% farming, 6.2% construction, 7.3% production (2000).
Income: Per capita income: $39,293 (2005); Median household income: $94,670 (2005); Average household income: $115,441 (2005); Percent of households with income of $100,000 or more: 46.9% (2005); Poverty rate: 2.8% (2000).
Education: Percent of population age 25 and over with: High school diploma (including GED) or higher: 89.6% (2005); Bachelor's degree or higher: 40.9% (2005); Master's degree or higher: 17.8% (2005).
Housing: Homeownership rate: 93.4% (2005); Median home value: $380,656 (2005); Median rent: $905 per month (2000); Median age of housing: 42 years (2000).
Transportation: Commute to work: 80.8% car, 13.6% public transportation, 0.9% walk, 3.6% work from home (2000); Travel time to work: 17.5% less than 15 minutes, 22.1% 15 to 30 minutes, 22.6% 30 to 45 minutes, 12.6% 45 to 60 minutes, 25.2% 60 minutes or more (2000)

BARNUM ISLAND (CDP). Aka North Long Beach. Covers a land area of 0.945 square miles and a water area of 0.368 square miles. Located at 40.60° N. Lat.; 73.64° W. Long.
Population: 2,624 (1990); 2,487 (2000); 2,401 (2005); 2,328 (2010 projected); Race: 88.1% White, 0.3% Black, 3.2% Asian, 14.2% Hispanic of any race (2005); Density: 2,540.8 persons per square mile (2005); Average household size: 2.94 (2005); Median age: 44.2 (2005); Males per 100 females: 97.8 (2005); Marriage status: 25.2% never married, 62.4% now married, 5.7% widowed, 6.7% divorced (2000); Foreign born: 11.3% (2000); Ancestry (includes multiple ancestries): 29.8% Italian, 18.9% Irish, 16.0% Other groups, 13.8% German, 6.2% Polish (2000).
Economy: Employment by occupation: 15.4% management, 22.6% professional, 15.0% services, 32.3% sales, 0.0% farming, 6.9% construction, 7.8% production (2000).
Income: Per capita income: $32,185 (2005); Median household income: $83,199 (2005); Average household income: $93,411 (2005); Percent of households with income of $100,000 or more: 34.7% (2005); Poverty rate: 10.8% (2000).
Education: Percent of population age 25 and over with: High school diploma (including GED) or higher: 85.6% (2005); Bachelor's degree or higher: 22.6% (2005); Master's degree or higher: 7.2% (2005).
Housing: Homeownership rate: 85.2% (2005); Median home value: $408,824 (2005); Median rent: $888 per month (2000); Median age of housing: 36 years (2000).
Transportation: Commute to work: 77.7% car, 18.4% public transportation, 1.3% walk, 1.7% work from home (2000); Travel time to work: 19.0% less than 15 minutes, 26.6% 15 to 30 minutes, 19.6% 30 to 45 minutes, 10.7% 45 to 60 minutes, 24.1% 60 minutes or more (2000)

BAXTER ESTATES (village). Covers a land area of 0.180 square miles and a water area of 0 square miles. Located at 40.83° N. Lat.; 73.69° W. Long.
Population: 1,113 (1990); 1,006 (2000); 899 (2005); 867 (2010 projected); Race: 78.5% White, 3.7% Black, 9.9% Asian, 19.2% Hispanic of any race (2005); Density: 4,981.5 persons per square mile (2005); Average household size: 2.68 (2005); Median age: 40.2 (2005); Males per 100 females: 100.2 (2005); Marriage status: 28.1% never married, 59.1% now married, 7.0% widowed, 5.8% divorced (2000); Foreign born: 30.1% (2000); Ancestry (includes multiple ancestries): 29.2% Other groups, 15.5% Irish, 15.4% Italian, 9.1% German, 7.0% Polish (2000).
Economy: Residential village overlooking Manhasset Bay. Single-family building permits issued: 0 (2005); Multi-family building permits issued: 0 (2005); Employment by occupation: 22.1% management, 29.8% professional, 14.5% services, 19.6% sales, 0.0% farming, 6.0% construction, 7.9% production (2000).
Income: Per capita income: $51,549 (2005); Median household income: $99,653 (2005); Average household income: $138,336 (2005); Percent of households with income of $100,000 or more: 49.9% (2005); Poverty rate: 4.7% (2000).
Education: Percent of population age 25 and over with: High school diploma (including GED) or higher: 88.8% (2005); Bachelor's degree or higher: 54.0% (2005); Master's degree or higher: 28.8% (2005).
Housing: Homeownership rate: 64.2% (2005); Median home value: $747,984 (2005); Median rent: $1,061 per month (2000); Median age of housing: 54 years (2000).
Transportation: Commute to work: 54.5% car, 24.3% public transportation, 9.3% walk, 7.1% work from home (2000); Travel time to work: 24.3% less than 15 minutes, 23.8% 15 to 30 minutes, 17.0% 30 to 45 minutes, 7.4% 45 to 60 minutes, 27.4% 60 minutes or more (2000)

BAY PARK (CDP). Covers a land area of 0.434 square miles and a water area of 0.119 square miles. Located at 40.63° N. Lat.; 73.66° W. Long.
Population: 2,280 (1990); 2,300 (2000); 2,288 (2005); 2,292 (2010 projected); Race: 95.1% White, 0.7% Black, 1.3% Asian, 6.0% Hispanic of any race (2005); Density: 5,277.7 persons per square mile (2005); Average household size: 2.59 (2005); Median age: 41.4 (2005); Males per 100 females: 97.4 (2005); Marriage status: 25.0% never married, 57.2% now married, 3.9% widowed, 14.0% divorced (2000); Foreign born: 11.1% (2000); Ancestry (includes multiple ancestries): 35.9% Italian, 30.7% Irish, 19.8% German, 9.1% Other groups, 6.3% Polish (2000).
Economy: Employment by occupation: 12.1% management, 16.0% professional, 16.1% services, 38.3% sales, 0.0% farming, 8.8% construction, 8.8% production (2000).
Income: Per capita income: $29,191 (2005); Median household income: $69,262 (2005); Average household income: $75,726 (2005); Percent of households with income of $100,000 or more: 26.1% (2005); Poverty rate: 2.4% (2000).
Education: Percent of population age 25 and over with: High school diploma (including GED) or higher: 86.7% (2005); Bachelor's degree or higher: 20.6% (2005); Master's degree or higher: 8.0% (2005).
Housing: Homeownership rate: 83.2% (2005); Median home value: $324,569 (2005); Median rent: $897 per month (2000); Median age of housing: 55 years (2000).
Transportation: Commute to work: 86.4% car, 10.0% public transportation, 1.1% walk, 2.4% work from home (2000); Travel time to work: 24.0% less than 15 minutes, 24.5% 15 to 30 minutes, 19.2% 30 to 45 minutes, 8.5% 45 to 60 minutes, 23.8% 60 minutes or more (2000)

BAYVILLE (village). Covers a land area of 1.409 square miles and a water area of 0.053 square miles. Located at 40.90° N. Lat.; 73.55° W. Long. Elevation is 40 feet.
History: Incorporated 1919.
Population: 7,193 (1990); 7,135 (2000); 7,137 (2005); 7,142 (2010 projected); Race: 94.5% White, 0.5% Black, 2.2% Asian, 6.1% Hispanic of any race (2005); Density: 5,067.1 persons per square mile (2005); Average household size: 2.74 (2005); Median age: 41.4 (2005); Males per 100 females: 96.3 (2005); Marriage status: 24.5% never married, 62.9% now married, 7.6% widowed, 5.0% divorced (2000); Foreign born: 11.4% (2000); Ancestry (includes multiple ancestries): 33.6% Italian, 25.6% Irish, 16.9% German, 10.2% English, 8.3% Other groups (2000).
Economy: Single-family building permits issued: 9 (2005); Multi-family building permits issued: 0 (2005); Employment by occupation: 19.3% management, 20.7% professional, 13.4% services, 29.8% sales, 0.3% farming, 7.5% construction, 9.0% production (2000).
Income: Per capita income: $41,065 (2005); Median household income: $80,986 (2005); Average household income: $111,680 (2005); Percent of households with income of $100,000 or more: 37.6% (2005); Poverty rate: 4.7% (2000).
Education: Percent of population age 25 and over with: High school diploma (including GED) or higher: 88.6% (2005); Bachelor's degree or higher: 34.4% (2005); Master's degree or higher: 14.9% (2005).
School District(s)
Locust Valley Central School District (KG-12)
    2003-04 Enrollment: 2,275 . . . . (516) 674-6310
Housing: Homeownership rate: 77.8% (2005); Median home value: $476,525 (2005); Median rent: $973 per month (2000); Median age of housing: 40 years (2000).
Transportation: Commute to work: 84.9% car, 5.6% public transportation, 3.1% walk, 5.1% work from home (2000); Travel time to work: 19.1% less than 15 minutes, 24.2% 15 to 30 minutes, 20.8% 30 to 45 minutes, 15.0% 45 to 60 minutes, 20.9% 60 minutes or more (2000)

BELLEROSE (village). Covers a land area of 0.096 square miles and a water area of 0 square miles. Located at 40.72° N. Lat.; 73.71° W. Long.
History: Settled 1908, incorporated 1924.
Population: 1,101 (1990); 1,173 (2000); 1,179 (2005); 1,174 (2010 projected); Race: 85.4% White, 0.8% Black, 10.9% Asian, 5.3% Hispanic of any race (2005); Density: 12,269.7 persons per square mile (2005); Average household size: 3.18 (2005); Median age: 40.2 (2005); Males per 100 females: 96.2 (2005); Marriage status: 22.9% never married, 67.4% now married, 6.0% widowed, 3.8% divorced (2000); Foreign born: 10.2% (2000); Ancestry (includes multiple ancestries): 34.8% Irish, 23.6% Italian, 19.9% German, 12.4% Other groups, 6.8% English (2000).
Economy: Manufacturing: machinery. Belmont Park Race Track is nearby. Single-family building permits issued: 0 (2005); Multi-family building permits issued: 0 (2005); Employment by occupation: 23.5% management, 31.8% professional, 4.1% services, 30.9% sales, 0.0% farming, 2.7% construction, 7.0% production (2000).
Income: Per capita income: $43,441 (2005); Median household income: $116,389 (2005); Average household income: $138,053 (2005); Percent of households with income of $100,000 or more: 58.0% (2005); Poverty rate: 0.9% (2000).
Education: Percent of population age 25 and over with: High school diploma (including GED) or higher: 94.5% (2005); Bachelor's degree or higher: 55.2% (2005); Master's degree or higher: 28.5% (2005).
Housing: Homeownership rate: 93.0% (2005); Median home value: $478,846 (2005); Median rent: $679 per month (2000); Median age of housing: 60+ years (2000).
Transportation: Commute to work: 59.8% car, 32.3% public transportation, 3.4% walk, 3.8% work from home (2000); Travel time to work: 18.0% less than 15 minutes, 22.8% 15 to 30 minutes, 19.1% 30 to 45 minutes, 10.3% 45 to 60 minutes, 29.8% 60 minutes or more (2000)

BELLEROSE TERRACE (CDP). Covers a land area of 0.097 square miles and a water area of 0 square miles. Located at 40.72° N. Lat.; 73.72° W. Long.
Population: 2,014 (1990); 2,157 (2000); 2,121 (2005); 2,098 (2010 projected); Race: 53.1% White, 10.2% Black, 21.2% Asian, 26.3% Hispanic of any race (2005); Density: 21,841.4 persons per square mile (2005); Average household size: 3.45 (2005); Median age: 36.6 (2005); Males per 100 females: 100.3 (2005); Marriage status: 31.5% never married, 57.8% now married, 6.2% widowed, 4.6% divorced (2000); Foreign born: 30.4% (2000); Ancestry (includes multiple ancestries): 37.2% Other groups, 21.6% Irish, 17.5% Italian, 5.8% German, 2.5% Guyanese (2000).
Economy: Employment by occupation: 9.3% management, 22.2% professional, 15.8% services, 34.4% sales, 0.7% farming, 7.5% construction, 10.2% production (2000).
Income: Per capita income: $26,498 (2005); Median household income: $85,333 (2005); Average household income: $91,535 (2005); Percent of households with income of $100,000 or more: 35.7% (2005); Poverty rate: 2.6% (2000).
Education: Percent of population age 25 and over with: High school diploma (including GED) or higher: 86.8% (2005); Bachelor's degree or higher: 26.8% (2005); Master's degree or higher: 7.6% (2005).
Housing: Homeownership rate: 86.0% (2005); Median home value: $299,612 (2005); Median rent: $805 per month (2000); Median age of housing: 60+ years (2000).
Transportation: Commute to work: 68.7% car, 27.2% public transportation, 1.2% walk, 1.8% work from home (2000); Travel time to work: 13.1% less than 15 minutes, 28.6% 15 to 30 minutes, 21.4% 30 to 45 minutes, 9.8% 45 to 60 minutes, 27.1% 60 minutes or more (2000)

BELLMORE (CDP). Covers a land area of 2.476 square miles and a water area of 0.525 square miles. Located at 40.66° N. Lat.; 73.52° W. Long. Elevation is 24 feet.
Population: 16,438 (1990); 16,441 (2000); 16,318 (2005); 16,208 (2010 projected); Race: 94.4% White, 0.7% Black, 2.8% Asian, 4.0% Hispanic of any race (2005); Density: 6,590.8 persons per square mile (2005); Average household size: 2.90 (2005); Median age: 40.5 (2005); Males per 100 females: 96.0 (2005); Marriage status: 21.3% never married, 66.9% now married, 7.2% widowed, 4.6% divorced (2000); Foreign born: 7.5% (2000); Ancestry (includes multiple ancestries): 26.2% Italian, 22.1% Irish, 17.4% German, 13.1% Other groups, 7.0% Polish (2000).
Economy: Residential village. Employment by occupation: 19.7% management, 23.4% professional, 10.1% services, 33.3% sales, 0.0% farming, 7.1% construction, 6.5% production (2000).
Income: Per capita income: $37,503 (2005); Median household income: $84,994 (2005); Average household income: $108,428 (2005); Percent of households with income of $100,000 or more: 40.9% (2005); Poverty rate: 2.4% (2000).
Education: Percent of population age 25 and over with: High school diploma (including GED) or higher: 91.3% (2005); Bachelor's degree or higher: 37.6% (2005); Master's degree or higher: 15.2% (2005).

School District(s)
Bellmore Union Free School District (PK-06)
    2003-04 Enrollment: 1,277 . . . . (516) 679-2909
Bellmore-Merrick Central High School District (07-12)
    2003-04 Enrollment: 5,832 . . . . (516) 992-1001
North Bellmore Union Free School District (KG-06)
    2003-04 Enrollment: 2,528 . . . . (516) 992-3000

Housing: Homeownership rate: 88.1% (2005); Median home value: $401,864 (2005); Median rent: $922 per month (2000); Median age of housing: 45 years (2000).
Newspapers: Bellmore/Merrick Observer (General - Circulation 4,900); Seaford/Wantagh Observer (General - Circulation 5,000)
Transportation: Commute to work: 77.9% car, 16.8% public transportation, 1.4% walk, 3.5% work from home (2000); Travel time to work: 19.4% less than 15 minutes, 28.7% 15 to 30 minutes, 19.5% 30 to 45 minutes, 10.6% 45 to 60 minutes, 21.7% 60 minutes or more (2000)

Additional Information Contacts
Bellmore Chamber of Commerce . . . . (516) 679-1875
   http://www.bellmorechamber.com

BETHPAGE (CDP). Covers a land area of 3.624 square miles and a water area of 0 square miles. Located at 40.74° N. Lat.; 73.48° W. Long. Elevation is 110 feet.
History: Named for the biblical village of Bethpage, between Bethany and the Mount of Olives. A village restoration in Old Bethpage features 20 pre-Civil War buildings.
Population: 15,761 (1990); 16,543 (2000); 17,002 (2005); 17,425 (2010 projected); Race: 91.9% White, 0.5% Black, 4.1% Asian, 6.4% Hispanic of any race (2005); Density: 4,691.2 persons per square mile (2005); Average household size: 2.85 (2005); Median age: 41.7 (2005); Males per 100 females: 93.8 (2005); Marriage status: 23.5% never married, 63.1% now married, 9.1% widowed, 4.3% divorced (2000); Foreign born: 10.8% (2000); Ancestry (includes multiple ancestries): 39.3% Italian, 26.3% Irish, 17.0% German, 10.7% Other groups, 6.6% Polish (2000).
Economy: Aerospace research. Manufacturing of upholstering fabrics here, as well. Employment by occupation: 16.8% management, 21.5% professional, 13.9% services, 32.4% sales, 0.2% farming, 8.0% construction, 7.1% production (2000).
Income: Per capita income: $33,543 (2005); Median household income: $79,805 (2005); Average household income: $95,015 (2005); Percent of households with income of $100,000 or more: 37.5% (2005); Poverty rate: 3.3% (2000).
Education: Percent of population age 25 and over with: High school diploma (including GED) or higher: 85.4% (2005); Bachelor's degree or higher: 25.9% (2005); Master's degree or higher: 9.2% (2005).

School District(s)
Bethpage Union Free School District (KG-12)
    2003-04 Enrollment: 3,006 . . . . (516) 644-4001
Plainedge Union Free School District (PK-12)
    2003-04 Enrollment: 3,606 . . . . (516) 992-7455

Four-year College(s)
Briarcliffe College
    Fall 2004 Enrollment: 1,478. . . . . (516) 918-3600
    2005-06 Tuition: In-state $15,096; Out-of-state $15,096

Housing: Homeownership rate: 88.0% (2005); Median home value: $378,609 (2005); Median rent: $908 per month (2000); Median age of housing: 44 years (2000).
Hospitals: New Island Hospital (223 beds)
Transportation: Commute to work: 85.3% car, 10.4% public transportation, 1.6% walk, 2.4% work from home (2000); Travel time to work: 25.2% less than 15 minutes, 32.5% 15 to 30 minutes, 18.1% 30 to 45 minutes, 7.3% 45 to 60 minutes, 17.0% 60 minutes or more (2000)

Additional Information Contacts
Bethpage Chamber of Commerce . . . . (516) 433-0010
   http://www.bethpagecommunity.com

BROOKVILLE (village). Covers a land area of 4.008 square miles and a water area of 0 square miles. Located at 40.81° N. Lat.; 73.57° W. Long. Elevation is 123 feet.
Population: 4,468 (1990); 2,126 (2000); 2,184 (2005); 2,241 (2010 projected); Race: 88.7% White, 1.8% Black, 8.1% Asian, 3.2% Hispanic of any race (2005); Density: 544.9 persons per square mile (2005); Average household size: 3.45 (2005); Median age: 38.9 (2005); Males per 100 females: 97.5 (2005); Marriage status: 18.6% never married, 76.0% now married, 3.5% widowed, 2.0% divorced (2000); Foreign born: 11.5% (2000); Ancestry (includes multiple ancestries): 19.6% Other groups, 16.8% Italian, 11.6% Russian, 9.2% German, 9.1% Polish (2000).
Economy: Single-family building permits issued: 14 (2005); Multi-family building permits issued: 0 (2005); Employment by occupation: 31.4% management, 32.3% professional, 7.9% services, 24.3% sales, 0.0% farming, 2.2% construction, 1.8% production (2000).
Income: Per capita income: $87,604 (2005); Median household income: $248,387 (2005); Average household income: $295,999 (2005); Percent of households with income of $100,000 or more: 78.2% (2005); Poverty rate: 2.9% (2000).
Education: Percent of population age 25 and over with: High school diploma (including GED) or higher: 95.6% (2005); Bachelor's degree or higher: 67.8% (2005); Master's degree or higher: 31.9% (2005).
Four-year College(s)
Long Island University-C W Post Campus
    Fall 2004 Enrollment: 9,941 . . . . (516) 299-2900
    2005-06 Tuition: In-state $22,100; Out-of-state $22,100
Housing: Homeownership rate: 93.8% (2005); Median home value: $1 million+ (2005); Median rent: $950 per month (2000); Median age of housing: 39 years (2000).
Transportation: Commute to work: 79.6% car, 7.7% public transportation, 2.5% walk, 9.9% work from home (2000); Travel time to work: 21.0% less than 15 minutes, 31.1% 15 to 30 minutes, 17.3% 30 to 45 minutes, 9.6% 45 to 60 minutes, 20.9% 60 minutes or more (2000)

CARLE PLACE (CDP). Covers a land area of 0.942 square miles and a water area of 0 square miles. Located at 40.75° N. Lat.; 73.61° W. Long.
Population: 5,107 (1990); 5,247 (2000); 5,174 (2005); 5,101 (2010 projected); Race: 86.1% White, 2.8% Black, 7.5% Asian, 10.0% Hispanic of any race (2005); Density: 5,495.4 persons per square mile (2005); Average household size: 2.76 (2005); Median age: 40.6 (2005); Males per 100 females: 92.3 (2005); Marriage status: 24.3% never married, 63.4% now married, 8.6% widowed, 3.7% divorced (2000); Foreign born: 13.5% (2000); Ancestry (includes multiple ancestries): 30.7% Italian, 21.9% Irish, 17.8% German, 13.5% Other groups, 5.9% English (2000).
Economy: Several shopping centers in the area. Employment by occupation: 18.6% management, 22.5% professional, 8.9% services, 31.7% sales, 0.0% farming, 9.7% construction, 8.5% production (2000).
Income: Per capita income: $36,962 (2005); Median household income: $84,637 (2005); Average household income: $100,128 (2005); Percent of households with income of $100,000 or more: 39.9% (2005); Poverty rate: 5.4% (2000).
Education: Percent of population age 25 and over with: High school diploma (including GED) or higher: 87.4% (2005); Bachelor's degree or higher: 34.4% (2005); Master's degree or higher: 10.4% (2005).
School District(s)
Carle Place Union Free School District (KG-12)
    2003-04 Enrollment: 1,500 . . . . (516) 622-6442
Housing: Homeownership rate: 73.1% (2005); Median home value: $406,627 (2005); Median rent: $921 per month (2000); Median age of housing: 49 years (2000).
Transportation: Commute to work: 82.6% car, 11.1% public transportation, 4.1% walk, 1.7% work from home (2000); Travel time to work: 33.2% less than 15 minutes, 25.8% 15 to 30 minutes, 17.0% 30 to 45 minutes, 6.2% 45 to 60 minutes, 17.8% 60 minutes or more (2000)
Additional Information Contacts
Carmel-Kent Chamber of Commerce . . . . (845) 225-7834
    http://www.carmelkentchamber.com

CEDARHURST (village). Covers a land area of 0.682 square miles and a water area of 0 square miles. Located at 40.62° N. Lat.; 73.72° W. Long.
History: Incorporated 1910.
Population: 5,716 (1990); 6,164 (2000); 6,098 (2005); 6,034 (2010 projected); Race: 87.8% White, 1.5% Black, 4.1% Asian, 11.6% Hispanic of any race (2005); Density: 8,945.2 persons per square mile (2005); Average household size: 2.72 (2005); Median age: 39.5 (2005); Males per 100 females: 92.1 (2005); Marriage status: 23.9% never married, 61.0% now married, 7.7% widowed, 7.4% divorced (2000); Foreign born: 17.2% (2000); Ancestry (includes multiple ancestries): 24.7% Other groups, 15.3% Italian, 12.2% United States or American, 10.5% Russian, 9.7% Polish (2000).
Economy: Manufacturing of tension meters, tachometers, and dental alloys. Single-family building permits issued: 0 (2005); Multi-family building permits issued: 0 (2005); Employment by occupation: 19.4% management, 28.1% professional, 7.8% services, 30.7% sales, 0.0% farming, 7.1% construction, 6.9% production (2000).
Income: Per capita income: $31,412 (2005); Median household income: $63,976 (2005); Average household income: $83,749 (2005); Percent of households with income of $100,000 or more: 29.7% (2005); Poverty rate: 5.3% (2000).
Education: Percent of population age 25 and over with: High school diploma (including GED) or higher: 88.8% (2005); Bachelor's degree or higher: 44.7% (2005); Master's degree or higher: 22.6% (2005).
School District(s)
Lawrence Union Free School District (PK-12)
    2003-04 Enrollment: 3,692 . . . . (516) 295-7030
Housing: Homeownership rate: 65.3% (2005); Median home value: $468,935 (2005); Median rent: $1,004 per month (2000); Median age of housing: 55 years (2000).
Transportation: Commute to work: 75.5% car, 13.3% public transportation, 6.2% walk, 5.0% work from home (2000); Travel time to work: 28.1% less than 15 minutes, 22.3% 15 to 30 minutes, 18.7% 30 to 45 minutes, 10.4% 45 to 60 minutes, 20.6% 60 minutes or more (2000)
Additional Information Contacts
Village of Cedarhurst . . . . (516) 295-5770
    http://www.cedarhurst.gov/

CENTRE ISLAND (village). Covers a land area of 1.118 square miles and a water area of 0.002 square miles. Located at 40.90° N. Lat.; 73.51° W. Long. Elevation is 35 feet.
Population: 439 (1990); 444 (2000); 450 (2005); 455 (2010 projected); Race: 96.0% White, 0.4% Black, 0.9% Asian, 4.0% Hispanic of any race (2005); Density: 402.6 persons per square mile (2005); Average household size: 2.51 (2005); Median age: 46.1 (2005); Males per 100 females: 97.4 (2005); Marriage status: 19.6% never married, 64.9% now married, 9.1% widowed, 6.4% divorced (2000); Foreign born: 14.8% (2000); Ancestry (includes multiple ancestries): 16.0% United States or American, 15.7% Irish, 14.4% Italian, 13.0% English, 12.6% German (2000).
Economy: Single-family building permits issued: 0 (2005); Multi-family building permits issued: 0 (2005); Employment by occupation: 35.7% management, 25.6% professional, 5.0% services, 21.6% sales, 0.0% farming, 10.1% construction, 2.0% production (2000).
Income: Per capita income: $91,967 (2005); Median household income: $144,318 (2005); Average household income: $231,201 (2005); Percent of households with income of $100,000 or more: 60.9% (2005); Poverty rate: 12.6% (2000).
Education: Percent of population age 25 and over with: High school diploma (including GED) or higher: 97.6% (2005); Bachelor's degree or higher: 58.1% (2005); Master's degree or higher: 20.4% (2005).
Housing: Homeownership rate: 78.2% (2005); Median home value: $1 million+ (2005); Median rent: $2,000+ per month (2000); Median age of housing: 55 years (2000).
Transportation: Commute to work: 67.5% car, 17.3% public transportation, 4.2% walk, 7.9% work from home (2000); Travel time to work: 15.9% less than 15 minutes, 23.9% 15 to 30 minutes, 11.9% 30 to 45 minutes, 13.1% 45 to 60 minutes, 35.2% 60 minutes or more (2000)

COVE NECK (village). Covers a land area of 1.285 square miles and a water area of 0.287 square miles. Located at 40.87° N. Lat.; 73.49° W. Long. Elevation is 22 feet.
History: "Sagamore Hill," home of Theodore Roosevelt, is here.
Population: 332 (1990); 300 (2000); 313 (2005); 327 (2010 projected); Race: 92.0% White, 0.0% Black, 6.1% Asian, 5.8% Hispanic of any race (2005); Density: 243.6 persons per square mile (2005); Average household size: 2.72 (2005); Median age: 45.1 (2005); Males per 100 females: 94.4 (2005); Marriage status: 13.3% never married, 70.9% now married, 11.3% widowed, 4.4% divorced (2000); Foreign born: 9.2% (2000); Ancestry (includes multiple ancestries): 23.7% German, 20.6% Italian, 17.7% Other groups, 14.9% English, 10.7% Irish (2000).

Economy: Single-family building permits issued: 0 (2005); Multi-family building permits issued: 0 (2005); Employment by occupation: 30.2% management, 34.5% professional, 7.8% services, 25.9% sales, 0.0% farming, 0.0% construction, 1.7% production (2000).
Income: Per capita income: $86,518 (2005); Median household income: $182,692 (2005); Average household income: $235,478 (2005); Percent of households with income of $100,000 or more: 72.2% (2005); Poverty rate: 0.0% (2000).
Education: Percent of population age 25 and over with: High school diploma (including GED) or higher: 95.2% (2005); Bachelor's degree or higher: 56.3% (2005); Master's degree or higher: 25.5% (2005).
Housing: Homeownership rate: 81.7% (2005); Median home value: $1 million+ (2005); Median rent: $775 per month (2000); Median age of housing: 50 years (2000).
Transportation: Commute to work: 73.3% car, 10.3% public transportation, 5.2% walk, 8.6% work from home (2000); Travel time to work: 17.9% less than 15 minutes, 26.4% 15 to 30 minutes, 23.6% 30 to 45 minutes, 12.3% 45 to 60 minutes, 19.8% 60 minutes or more (2000)

EAST ATLANTIC BEACH (CDP).
Covers a land area of 0.299 square miles and a water area of 0.381 square miles. Located at 40.58° N. Lat.; 73.70° W. Long.
Population: 2,168 (1990); 2,257 (2000); 2,203 (2005); 2,128 (2010 projected); Race: 96.5% White, 0.4% Black, 1.1% Asian, 4.1% Hispanic of any race (2005); Density: 7,363.9 persons per square mile (2005); Average household size: 2.50 (2005); Median age: 41.3 (2005); Males per 100 females: 99.5 (2005); Marriage status: 29.1% never married, 56.5% now married, 4.2% widowed, 10.3% divorced (2000); Foreign born: 6.3% (2000); Ancestry (includes multiple ancestries): 33.0% Irish, 25.2% Italian, 13.2% Other groups, 11.1% German, 8.3% Russian (2000).
Economy: Employment by occupation: 14.6% management, 27.0% professional, 14.4% services, 30.3% sales, 0.0% farming, 8.2% construction, 5.5% production (2000).
Income: Per capita income: $37,957 (2005); Median household income: $78,295 (2005); Average household income: $95,023 (2005); Percent of households with income of $100,000 or more: 37.3% (2005); Poverty rate: 1.6% (2000).
Education: Percent of population age 25 and over with: High school diploma (including GED) or higher: 94.6% (2005); Bachelor's degree or higher: 39.3% (2005); Master's degree or higher: 14.5% (2005).
Housing: Homeownership rate: 69.5% (2005); Median home value: $597,990 (2005); Median rent: $1,092 per month (2000); Median age of housing: 48 years (2000).
Transportation: Commute to work: 71.0% car, 20.4% public transportation, 2.1% walk, 5.1% work from home (2000); Travel time to work: 16.2% less than 15 minutes, 16.5% 15 to 30 minutes, 21.4% 30 to 45 minutes, 11.4% 45 to 60 minutes, 34.4% 60 minutes or more (2000)

EAST GARDEN CITY (CDP).
Covers a land area of 3.032 square miles and a water area of 0 square miles. Located at 40.73° N. Lat.; 73.59° W. Long.
Population: 1,098 (1990); 979 (2000); 913 (2005); 848 (2010 projected); Race: 32.1% White, 58.8% Black, 1.4% Asian, 17.4% Hispanic of any race (2005); Density: 301.1 persons per square mile (2005); Average household size: 3.51 (2005); Median age: 32.8 (2005); Males per 100 females: 98.0 (2005); Marriage status: 28.4% never married, 59.7% now married, 7.1% widowed, 4.7% divorced (2000); Foreign born: 25.3% (2000); Ancestry (includes multiple ancestries): 49.5% Other groups, 10.6% Irish, 7.0% German, 7.0% Jamaican, 6.4% United States or American (2000).
Economy: Employment by occupation: 22.1% management, 17.5% professional, 17.5% services, 24.6% sales, 0.0% farming, 2.3% construction, 15.9% production (2000).
Income: Per capita income: $22,093 (2005); Median household income: $65,549 (2005); Average household income: $74,481 (2005); Percent of households with income of $100,000 or more: 15.0% (2005); Poverty rate: 7.8% (2000).
Education: Percent of population age 25 and over with: High school diploma (including GED) or higher: 87.1% (2005); Bachelor's degree or higher: 38.4% (2005); Master's degree or higher: 18.5% (2005).
Housing: Homeownership rate: 55.0% (2005); Median home value: $261,413 (2005); Median rent: $944 per month (2000); Median age of housing: 54 years (2000).
Transportation: Commute to work: 83.5% car, 10.9% public transportation, 1.0% walk, 3.5% work from home (2000); Travel time to work: 26.5% less than 15 minutes, 35.3% 15 to 30 minutes, 16.7% 30 to 45 minutes, 5.3% 45 to 60 minutes, 16.2% 60 minutes or more (2000)

EAST HILLS (village).
Covers a land area of 2.287 square miles and a water area of 0 square miles. Located at 40.79° N. Lat.; 73.62° W. Long. Elevation is 2,300 feet.
History: Incorporated 1931.
Population: 6,746 (1990); 6,842 (2000); 6,878 (2005); 6,917 (2010 projected); Race: 90.8% White, 1.0% Black, 6.4% Asian, 1.9% Hispanic of any race (2005); Density: 3,007.3 persons per square mile (2005); Average household size: 3.09 (2005); Median age: 43.1 (2005); Males per 100 females: 96.2 (2005); Marriage status: 16.6% never married, 76.8% now married, 3.8% widowed, 2.7% divorced (2000); Foreign born: 11.2% (2000); Ancestry (includes multiple ancestries): 22.1% Other groups, 16.7% Russian, 11.7% United States or American, 9.0% Polish, 7.3% Italian (2000).
Economy: Single-family building permits issued: 0 (2005); Multi-family building permits issued: 0 (2005); Employment by occupation: 20.9% management, 43.2% professional, 3.1% services, 29.6% sales, 0.0% farming, 1.4% construction, 1.9% production (2000).
Income: Per capita income: $65,558 (2005); Median household income: $157,881 (2005); Average household income: $202,565 (2005); Percent of households with income of $100,000 or more: 70.1% (2005); Poverty rate: 1.6% (2000).
Education: Percent of population age 25 and over with: High school diploma (including GED) or higher: 97.8% (2005); Bachelor's degree or higher: 73.4% (2005); Master's degree or higher: 39.2% (2005).
Housing: Homeownership rate: 98.5% (2005); Median home value: $937,927 (2005); Median rent: $1,010 per month (2000); Median age of housing: 45 years (2000).
Transportation: Commute to work: 79.3% car, 13.3% public transportation, 0.3% walk, 6.9% work from home (2000); Travel time to work: 14.9% less than 15 minutes, 35.1% 15 to 30 minutes, 13.8% 30 to 45 minutes, 10.0% 45 to 60 minutes, 26.2% 60 minutes or more (2000)
Additional Information Contacts
Village of East Hills . . . . (516) 621-5600
http://www.villageofeasthills.org/

EAST MASSAPEQUA (CDP).
Covers a land area of 3.498 square miles and a water area of 0.089 square miles. Located at 40.67° N. Lat.; 73.43° W. Long.
Population: 19,782 (1990); 19,565 (2000); 19,084 (2005); 18,569 (2010 projected); Race: 77.6% White, 14.3% Black, 2.7% Asian, 8.7% Hispanic of any race (2005); Density: 5,455.3 persons per square mile (2005); Average household size: 3.00 (2005); Median age: 39.4 (2005); Males per 100 females: 94.2 (2005); Marriage status: 25.7% never married, 61.3% now married, 7.1% widowed, 5.9% divorced (2000); Foreign born: 12.3% (2000); Ancestry (includes multiple ancestries): 29.6% Italian, 23.4% Irish, 17.1% Other groups, 16.3% German, 5.0% Polish (2000).
Economy: Employment by occupation: 16.2% management, 22.8% professional, 14.5% services, 31.1% sales, 0.0% farming, 8.8% construction, 6.5% production (2000).
Income: Per capita income: $33,967 (2005); Median household income: $86,508 (2005); Average household income: $101,234 (2005); Percent of households with income of $100,000 or more: 40.8% (2005); Poverty rate: 3.4% (2000).
Education: Percent of population age 25 and over with: High school diploma (including GED) or higher: 88.3% (2005); Bachelor's degree or higher: 33.3% (2005); Master's degree or higher: 12.8% (2005).
Housing: Homeownership rate: 84.8% (2005); Median home value: $376,844 (2005); Median rent: $1,042 per month (2000); Median age of housing: 44 years (2000).
Transportation: Commute to work: 83.2% car, 12.7% public transportation, 1.4% walk, 2.3% work from home (2000); Travel time to work: 19.3% less than 15 minutes, 28.5% 15 to 30 minutes, 19.3% 30 to 45 minutes, 9.6% 45 to 60 minutes, 23.4% 60 minutes or more (2000)

EAST MEADOW (CDP).
Covers a land area of 6.291 square miles and a water area of 0.012 square miles. Located at 40.71° N. Lat.; 73.55° W. Long. Elevation is 40 feet.
Population: 36,909 (1990); 37,461 (2000); 38,751 (2005); 39,936 (2010 projected); Race: 80.3% White, 5.5% Black, 9.3% Asian, 9.6% Hispanic of any race (2005); Density: 6,160.1 persons per square mile (2005); Average household size: 3.03 (2005); Median age: 40.0 (2005); Males per 100 females: 99.1 (2005); Marriage status: 21.7% never married, 65.2% now

married, 7.9% widowed, 5.3% divorced (2000); Foreign born: 14.5% (2000); Ancestry (includes multiple ancestries): 28.4% Italian, 18.5% Other groups, 17.4% Irish, 11.8% German, 8.8% Polish (2000).
Economy: Employment by occupation: 14.8% management, 24.1% professional, 11.5% services, 33.3% sales, 0.1% farming, 8.6% construction, 7.7% production (2000).
Income: Per capita income: $30,876 (2005); Median household income: $74,633 (2005); Average household income: $91,906 (2005); Percent of households with income of $100,000 or more: 33.7% (2005); Poverty rate: 3.8% (2000).
Education: Percent of population age 25 and over with: High school diploma (including GED) or higher: 86.2% (2005); Bachelor's degree or higher: 28.9% (2005); Master's degree or higher: 12.8% (2005).

School District(s)
East Meadow Union Free School District (KG-12)
    2003-04 Enrollment: 8,094 . . . . (516) 478-5776

Housing: Homeownership rate: 87.1% (2005); Median home value: $351,861 (2005); Median rent: $859 per month (2000); Median age of housing: 45 years (2000).
Transportation: Commute to work: 86.5% car, 8.4% public transportation, 2.8% walk, 2.0% work from home (2000); Travel time to work: 24.2% less than 15 minutes, 32.7% 15 to 30 minutes, 19.7% 30 to 45 minutes, 7.7% 45 to 60 minutes, 15.8% 60 minutes or more (2000)

Additional Information Contacts
East Meadow Chamber of Commerce. . . . . (516) 796-0921
    http://www.emchamber.com
Nassau Council of Chambers . . . . (516) 396-0200

EAST NORWICH (CDP).
Covers a land area of 1.047 square miles and a water area of 0 square miles. Located at 40.84° N. Lat.; 73.53° W. Long. Elevation is 208 feet.
Population: 2,698 (1990); 2,675 (2000); 2,972 (2005); 3,240 (2010 projected); Race: 94.4% White, 1.0% Black, 3.0% Asian, 4.5% Hispanic of any race (2005); Density: 2,838.1 persons per square mile (2005); Average household size: 2.80 (2005); Median age: 42.8 (2005); Males per 100 females: 93.7 (2005); Marriage status: 18.0% never married, 69.6% now married, 6.6% widowed, 5.8% divorced (2000); Foreign born: 9.7% (2000); Ancestry (includes multiple ancestries): 29.5% Italian, 23.4% Irish, 17.0% German, 8.9% Other groups, 6.2% Polish (2000).
Economy: Employment by occupation: 21.4% management, 30.3% professional, 13.1% services, 29.0% sales, 0.0% farming, 3.7% construction, 2.5% production (2000).
Income: Per capita income: $43,579 (2005); Median household income: $101,009 (2005); Average household income: $121,039 (2005); Percent of households with income of $100,000 or more: 50.6% (2005); Poverty rate: 3.7% (2000).
Education: Percent of population age 25 and over with: High school diploma (including GED) or higher: 89.5% (2005); Bachelor's degree or higher: 45.2% (2005); Master's degree or higher: 20.1% (2005).

School District(s)
Oyster Bay-East Norwich Central School District (PK-12)
    2003-04 Enrollment: 1,569 . . . . (516) 624-6504

Housing: Homeownership rate: 94.0% (2005); Median home value: $543,320 (2005); Median rent: $645 per month (2000); Median age of housing: 45 years (2000).
Transportation: Commute to work: 83.9% car, 11.1% public transportation, 1.3% walk, 3.7% work from home (2000); Travel time to work: 22.9% less than 15 minutes, 36.0% 15 to 30 minutes, 15.2% 30 to 45 minutes, 4.7% 45 to 60 minutes, 21.2% 60 minutes or more (2000)

EAST ROCKAWAY (village).
Covers a land area of 1.022 square miles and a water area of 0.006 square miles. Located at 40.64° N. Lat.; 73.66° W. Long.
History: Named for the Algonquian translation of "sand place". Settled c.1688. Incorporated 1900.
Population: 10,152 (1990); 10,414 (2000); 10,329 (2005); 10,233 (2010 projected); Race: 94.1% White, 0.9% Black, 2.4% Asian, 8.1% Hispanic of any race (2005); Density: 10,104.4 persons per square mile (2005); Average household size: 2.62 (2005); Median age: 40.8 (2005); Males per 100 females: 91.2 (2005); Marriage status: 22.7% never married, 61.3% now married, 8.2% widowed, 7.9% divorced (2000); Foreign born: 10.4% (2000); Ancestry (includes multiple ancestries): 27.4% Italian, 25.6% Irish, 15.6% Other groups, 12.6% German, 6.2% Russian (2000).
Economy: Mostly residential with some light manufacturing. Single-family building permits issued: 3 (2005); Multi-family building permits issued: 2 (2005); Employment by occupation: 17.2% management, 26.1% professional, 13.9% services, 30.6% sales, 0.0% farming, 7.3% construction, 4.9% production (2000).
Income: Per capita income: $36,292 (2005); Median household income: $68,792 (2005); Average household income: $93,532 (2005); Percent of households with income of $100,000 or more: 33.4% (2005); Poverty rate: 3.5% (2000).
Education: Percent of population age 25 and over with: High school diploma (including GED) or higher: 88.8% (2005); Bachelor's degree or higher: 35.3% (2005); Master's degree or higher: 15.5% (2005).

School District(s)
East Rockaway Union Free School District (KG-12)
    2003-04 Enrollment: 1,245 . . . . (516) 887-8300
Lynbrook Union Free School District (KG-12)
    2003-04 Enrollment: 3,141 . . . . (516) 887-0253

Housing: Homeownership rate: 71.6% (2005); Median home value: $410,354 (2005); Median rent: $849 per month (2000); Median age of housing: 53 years (2000).
Transportation: Commute to work: 76.4% car, 18.0% public transportation, 3.5% walk, 1.5% work from home (2000); Travel time to work: 23.9% less than 15 minutes, 23.8% 15 to 30 minutes, 19.6% 30 to 45 minutes, 8.3% 45 to 60 minutes, 24.3% 60 minutes or more (2000)

Additional Information Contacts
Village of East Rockaway . . . . (516) 887-6300
    http://www.villageofeastrockaway.org/

EAST WILLISTON (village).
Covers a land area of 0.563 square miles and a water area of 0 square miles. Located at 40.76° N. Lat.; 73.63° W. Long. Elevation is 119 feet.
History: Incorporated 1926.
Population: 2,515 (1990); 2,503 (2000); 2,530 (2005); 2,559 (2010 projected); Race: 94.1% White, 0.4% Black, 4.1% Asian, 3.3% Hispanic of any race (2005); Density: 4,495.5 persons per square mile (2005); Average household size: 3.00 (2005); Median age: 42.4 (2005); Males per 100 females: 95.7 (2005); Marriage status: 22.2% never married, 67.9% now married, 6.6% widowed, 3.2% divorced (2000); Foreign born: 6.9% (2000); Ancestry (includes multiple ancestries): 33.5% Italian, 28.6% Irish, 15.9% German, 8.0% Other groups, 6.1% Polish (2000).
Economy: Single-family building permits issued: 5 (2005); Multi-family building permits issued: 0 (2005); Employment by occupation: 22.5% management, 35.4% professional, 5.9% services, 30.3% sales, 0.0% farming, 1.6% construction, 4.2% production (2000).
Income: Per capita income: $58,379 (2005); Median household income: $132,338 (2005); Average household income: $175,416 (2005); Percent of households with income of $100,000 or more: 65.4% (2005); Poverty rate: 1.7% (2000).
Education: Percent of population age 25 and over with: High school diploma (including GED) or higher: 95.3% (2005); Bachelor's degree or higher: 59.4% (2005); Master's degree or higher: 33.7% (2005).

School District(s)
East Williston Union Free School District (KG-12)
    2003-04 Enrollment: 1,812 . . . . (516) 333-3758

Housing: Homeownership rate: 96.8% (2005); Median home value: $737,928 (2005); Median rent: $1,063 per month (2000); Median age of housing: 51 years (2000).
Transportation: Commute to work: 76.1% car, 18.7% public transportation, 1.1% walk, 4.0% work from home (2000); Travel time to work: 26.6% less than 15 minutes, 27.8% 15 to 30 minutes, 13.0% 30 to 45 minutes, 7.2% 45 to 60 minutes, 25.4% 60 minutes or more (2000)

Additional Information Contacts
Village of East Williston . . . . (516) 746-0782
    http://eastwilliston.org/

ELMONT (CDP).
Covers a land area of 3.405 square miles and a water area of 0.003 square miles. Located at 40.70° N. Lat.; 73.70° W. Long. Elevation is 43 feet.
Population: 28,612 (1990); 32,657 (2000); 32,352 (2005); 32,031 (2010 projected); Race: 32.8% White, 45.4% Black, 9.9% Asian, 15.6% Hispanic of any race (2005); Density: 9,500.3 persons per square mile (2005); Average household size: 3.37 (2005); Median age: 37.4 (2005); Males per 100 females: 91.2 (2005); Marriage status: 29.7% never married, 56.2% now married, 7.6% widowed, 6.5% divorced (2000); Foreign born: 36.9% (2000); Ancestry (includes multiple ancestries): 33.0% Other groups, 18.4% Italian, 10.9% Haitian, 6.3% German, 6.0% Jamaican (2000).

Economy: Although chiefly residential, Elmont has some light industry. Belmont Park racetrack is nearby. Employment by occupation: 11.5% management, 18.8% professional, 18.9% services, 32.1% sales, 0.3% farming, 7.5% construction, 10.9% production (2000).
Income: Per capita income: $24,590 (2005); Median household income: $70,056 (2005); Average household income: $82,380 (2005); Percent of households with income of $100,000 or more: 28.9% (2005); Poverty rate: 7.5% (2000).
Education: Percent of population age 25 and over with: High school diploma (including GED) or higher: 80.0% (2005); Bachelor's degree or higher: 21.2% (2005); Master's degree or higher: 8.1% (2005).

School District(s)
Elmont Union Free School District (PK-06)
    2003-04 Enrollment: 4,248 . . . . (516) 326-5500
Sewanhaka Central High School District (07-12)
    2003-04 Enrollment: 8,435 . . . . (516) 488-9800

Housing: Homeownership rate: 78.1% (2005); Median home value: $326,282 (2005); Median rent: $791 per month (2000); Median age of housing: 49 years (2000).
Newspapers: Elmont Herald (General - Circulation 5,400)
Transportation: Commute to work: 78.5% car, 16.4% public transportation, 3.3% walk, 1.6% work from home (2000); Travel time to work: 14.5% less than 15 minutes, 27.2% 15 to 30 minutes, 22.8% 30 to 45 minutes, 9.8% 45 to 60 minutes, 25.7% 60 minutes or more (2000).

FARMINGDALE
(village). Covers a land area of 1.130 square miles and a water area of 0 square miles. Located at 40.73° N. Lat.; 73.44° W. Long. Elevation is 70 feet.
History: Seat of State University of N.Y. at Farmingdale Settled 1695, incorporated 1904.
Population: 8,134 (1990); 8,399 (2000); 8,432 (2005); 8,457 (2010 projected); Race: 81.6% White, 2.5% Black, 5.2% Asian, 16.7% Hispanic of any race (2005); Density: 7,461.4 persons per square mile (2005); Average household size: 2.64 (2005); Median age: 39.9 (2005); Males per 100 females: 96.4 (2005); Marriage status: 30.0% never married, 55.2% now married, 6.8% widowed, 8.0% divorced (2000); Foreign born: 17.1% (2000); Ancestry (includes multiple ancestries): 34.3% Italian, 24.6% Irish, 18.5% Other groups, 17.0% German, 5.7% Polish (2000).
Economy: Manufacturing: machinery, printing equipment, electrical equipment, ammunition, electronics; metal fabrication. Republic Airport is located just East of community. Single-family building permits issued: 21 (2005); Multi-family building permits issued: 0 (2005); Employment by occupation: 14.4% management, 21.8% professional, 13.8% services, 30.3% sales, 0.0% farming, 9.3% construction, 10.4% production (2000).
Income: Per capita income: $32,851 (2005); Median household income: $68,625 (2005); Average household income: $85,413 (2005); Percent of households with income of $100,000 or more: 29.5% (2005); Poverty rate: 5.6% (2000).
Education: Percent of population age 25 and over with: High school diploma (including GED) or higher: 84.4% (2005); Bachelor's degree or higher: 28.8% (2005); Master's degree or higher: 11.2% (2005).

Four-year College(s)
Farmingdale State University of New York (Public)
    Fall 2004 Enrollment: 6,250. . . . . (516) 420-2000
    2005-06 Tuition: In-state $5,267; Out-of-state $11,527

Housing: Homeownership rate: 61.0% (2005); Median home value: $331,481 (2005); Median rent: $868 per month (2000); Median age of housing: 43 years (2000).
Transportation: Commute to work: 74.6% car, 14.8% public transportation, 6.0% walk, 4.1% work from home (2000); Travel time to work: 28.7% less than 15 minutes, 32.3% 15 to 30 minutes, 15.6% 30 to 45 minutes, 5.5% 45 to 60 minutes, 17.8% 60 minutes or more (2000)
Additional Information Contacts
Village of Farmingdale. . . . . (516) 249-0093
    http://www.farmingdalevillage.com/

FLORAL PARK
(village). Covers a land area of 1.372 square miles and a water area of 0 square miles. Located at 40.72° N. Lat.; 73.70° W. Long. Elevation is 90 feet.
History: Named to promote the beauty of the town. Incorporated 1908.
Population: 15,947 (1990); 15,967 (2000); 15,809 (2005); 15,644 (2010 projected); Race: 90.9% White, 0.8% Black, 5.6% Asian, 7.3% Hispanic of any race (2005); Density: 11,520.7 persons per square mile (2005); Average household size: 2.76 (2005); Median age: 41.2 (2005); Males per 100 females: 90.6 (2005); Marriage status: 27.0% never married, 59.2% now married, 8.6% widowed, 5.2% divorced (2000); Foreign born: 11.6% (2000); Ancestry (includes multiple ancestries): 36.1% Irish, 30.6% Italian, 18.4% German, 10.0% Other groups, 6.2% Polish (2000).
Economy: Single-family building permits issued: 6 (2005); Multi-family building permits issued: 2 (2005); Employment by occupation: 17.1% management, 26.8% professional, 13.3% services, 29.3% sales, 0.0% farming, 7.9% construction, 5.6% production (2000).
Income: Per capita income: $38,113 (2005); Median household income: $86,906 (2005); Average household income: $104,574 (2005); Percent of households with income of $100,000 or more: 42.1% (2005); Poverty rate: 3.1% (2000).
Education: Percent of population age 25 and over with: High school diploma (including GED) or higher: 90.3% (2005); Bachelor's degree or higher: 37.1% (2005); Master's degree or higher: 15.2% (2005).

School District(s)
Floral Park-Bellerose Union Free School District (PK-06)
    2003-04 Enrollment: 1,668 . . . . (516) 327-9300
Sewanhaka Central High School District (07-12)
    2003-04 Enrollment: 8,435 . . . . (516) 488-9800

Housing: Homeownership rate: 79.2% (2005); Median home value: $437,834 (2005); Median rent: $829 per month (2000); Median age of housing: 60+ years (2000).
Safety: Violent crime rate: 8.8 per 10,000 population; Property crime rate: 39.6 per 10,000 population (2004).
Newspapers: Floral Park Bulletin (General - Circulation 8,000); The Gateway (General - Circulation 12,000)
Transportation: Commute to work: 74.1% car, 19.6% public transportation, 3.0% walk, 2.3% work from home (2000); Travel time to work: 17.8% less than 15 minutes, 28.5% 15 to 30 minutes, 20.5% 30 to 45 minutes, 11.1% 45 to 60 minutes, 22.1% 60 minutes or more (2000)
Additional Information Contacts
Village of Floral Park . . . . (516) 326-6300
    http://www.fpvillage.org/

FLOWER HILL
(village). Covers a land area of 1.616 square miles and a water area of 0 square miles. Located at 40.80° N. Lat.; 73.67° W. Long.
History: Incorporated 1931.
Population: 4,490 (1990); 4,508 (2000); 4,531 (2005); 4,562 (2010 projected); Race: 81.5% White, 1.4% Black, 13.4% Asian, 4.8% Hispanic of any race (2005); Density: 2,804.5 persons per square mile (2005); Average household size: 3.06 (2005); Median age: 43.7 (2005); Males per 100 females: 95.1 (2005); Marriage status: 21.0% never married, 71.1% now married, 5.2% widowed, 2.7% divorced (2000); Foreign born: 21.5% (2000); Ancestry (includes multiple ancestries): 21.7% Italian, 19.0% Other groups, 15.0% Irish, 8.3% German, 8.1% Iranian (2000).
Economy: In shore-resort area. Single-family building permits issued: 2 (2005); Multi-family building permits issued: 0 (2005); Employment by occupation: 24.6% management, 32.0% professional, 6.3% services, 32.0% sales, 0.0% farming, 2.1% construction, 3.0% production (2000).
Income: Per capita income: $63,978 (2005); Median household income: $135,392 (2005); Average household income: $194,087 (2005); Percent of households with income of $100,000 or more: 62.2% (2005); Poverty rate: 2.9% (2000).
Education: Percent of population age 25 and over with: High school diploma (including GED) or higher: 94.2% (2005); Bachelor's degree or higher: 61.3% (2005); Master's degree or higher: 31.1% (2005).
Housing: Homeownership rate: 92.4% (2005); Median home value: $1 million+ (2005); Median rent: $1,104 per month (2000); Median age of housing: 45 years (2000).
Transportation: Commute to work: 67.9% car, 23.6% public transportation, 0.4% walk, 8.0% work from home (2000); Travel time to work: 20.6% less than 15 minutes, 22.2% 15 to 30 minutes, 16.5% 30 to 45 minutes, 15.5% 45 to 60 minutes, 25.2% 60 minutes or more (2000)
Additional Information Contacts
Village of Flower Hill . . . . (516) 627-5000
    http://www.villageflowerhill.com/

FRANKLIN SQUARE
(CDP). Covers a land area of 2.885 square miles and a water area of 0 square miles. Located at 40.70° N. Lat.; 73.67° W. Long. Elevation is 68 feet.
Population: 28,205 (1990); 29,342 (2000); 29,772 (2005); 30,207 (2010 projected); Race: 88.5% White, 1.7% Black, 5.4% Asian, 9.6% Hispanic of any race (2005); Density: 10,318.2 persons per square mile (2005); Average household size: 2.91 (2005); Median age: 41.0 (2005); Males per

100 females: 91.0 (2005); Marriage status: 23.5% never married, 61.6% now married, 9.8% widowed, 5.1% divorced (2000); Foreign born: 16.5% (2000); Ancestry (includes multiple ancestries): 47.6% Italian, 19.1% Irish, 13.9% Other groups, 13.7% German, 3.8% Polish (2000).
Economy: Although chiefly residential, there is significant manufacturing, including fire extinguishers, partitions and laminates, wire products, adhesives, hair products, die castings, asphalt-block flooring and brick pavers, electrical machinery and equipment, furniture, lighting fixtures, foundation garments, and hydraulic systems. Employment by occupation: 15.4% management, 17.9% professional, 12.8% services, 34.5% sales, 0.1% farming, 10.4% construction, 8.9% production (2000).
Income: Per capita income: $27,874 (2005); Median household income: $69,468 (2005); Average household income: $80,918 (2005); Percent of households with income of $100,000 or more: 29.3% (2005); Poverty rate: 5.0% (2000).
Education: Percent of population age 25 and over with: High school diploma (including GED) or higher: 83.1% (2005); Bachelor's degree or higher: 22.3% (2005); Master's degree or higher: 8.0% (2005).

School District(s)
Franklin Square Union Free School District (KG-06)
   2003-04 Enrollment: 1,942 .... (516) 505-6975
Sewanhaka Central High School District (07-12)
   2003-04 Enrollment: 8,435 .... (516) 488-9800
Valley Stream 13 Union Free School District (KG-06)
   2003-04 Enrollment: 2,103 .... (516) 568-6100
Valley Stream Central High School District (07-12)
   2003-04 Enrollment: 4,566 .... (516) 872-5601

Housing: Homeownership rate: 81.3% (2005); Median home value: $378,261 (2005); Median rent: $821 per month (2000); Median age of housing: 48 years (2000).
Newspapers: Franklin Square Bulletin (General - Circulation 8,500)
Transportation: Commute to work: 84.2% car, 11.4% public transportation, 1.9% walk, 2.0% work from home (2000); Travel time to work: 18.7% less than 15 minutes, 32.1% 15 to 30 minutes, 23.3% 30 to 45 minutes, 8.8% 45 to 60 minutes, 17.0% 60 minutes or more (2000)
Additional Information Contacts
Franklin Square Chamber of Commerce .... (516) 775-0001
   http://www.franklinsquarechamber.org

FREEPORT (village).
Covers a land area of 4.594 square miles and a water area of 0.236 square miles. Located at 40.65° N. Lat.; 73.58° W. Long. Elevation is 23 feet.
History: Named for its port, used in colonial days by cargo ships to avoid British taxes. Settled as a village c.1650. Incorporated 1892.
Population: 39,894 (1990); 43,783 (2000); 43,710 (2005); 43,636 (2010 projected); Race: 36.0% White, 36.1% Black, 1.6% Asian, 38.3% Hispanic of any race (2005); Density: 9,515.4 persons per square mile (2005); Average household size: 3.30 (2005); Median age: 36.5 (2005); Males per 100 females: 93.5 (2005); Marriage status: 32.9% never married, 52.1% now married, 7.1% widowed, 7.9% divorced (2000); Foreign born: 29.9% (2000); Ancestry (includes multiple ancestries): 52.6% Other groups, 9.1% Italian, 8.8% Irish, 7.5% German, 3.1% United States or American (2000).
Economy: Resort and deep-sea fishing and oystering center, with access to the Atlantic Ocean through Jones Inlet. Jones Beach State Park is nearby. Unemployment rate: 5.0% (2005); Total civilian labor force: 22,717 (2005); Single-family building permits issued: 9 (2005); Multi-family building permits issued: 0 (2005); Employment by occupation: 10.4% management, 17.0% professional, 20.6% services, 28.0% sales, 0.1% farming, 8.2% construction, 15.7% production (2000).
Income: Per capita income: $23,384 (2005); Median household income: $62,490 (2005); Average household income: $75,446 (2005); Percent of households with income of $100,000 or more: 25.2% (2005); Poverty rate: 10.6% (2000).
Education: Percent of population age 25 and over with: High school diploma (including GED) or higher: 72.7% (2005); Bachelor's degree or higher: 20.3% (2005); Master's degree or higher: 8.8% (2005).

School District(s)
Freeport Union Free School District (PK-12)
   2003-04 Enrollment: 7,146 .... (516) 867-5205

Housing: Homeownership rate: 65.4% (2005); Median home value: $287,851 (2005); Median rent: $819 per month (2000); Median age of housing: 46 years (2000).
Safety: Violent crime rate: 41.3 per 10,000 population; Property crime rate: 199.5 per 10,000 population (2004).
Transportation: Commute to work: 76.2% car, 15.2% public transportation, 4.9% walk, 2.2% work from home (2000); Travel time to work: 23.1% less than 15 minutes, 32.4% 15 to 30 minutes, 19.1% 30 to 45 minutes, 9.0% 45 to 60 minutes, 16.3% 60 minutes or more (2000)
Additional Information Contacts
Village of Freeport .... (516) 377-2200
   http://www.freeportny.com/

GARDEN CITY (village).
Covers a land area of 5.339 square miles and a water area of 0.005 square miles. Located at 40.72° N. Lat.; 73.65° W. Long. Elevation is 88 feet.
History: Named to promote the city as a beautiful place. Was founded in 1869 and planned by the merchant Alexander Stewart. In 1927, Charles Lindbergh began his historic transatlantic flight from nearby Roosevelt Field. Adelphi University is here. Incorporated 1919.
Population: 21,674 (1990); 21,672 (2000); 21,879 (2005); 22,088 (2010 projected); Race: 92.0% White, 2.1% Black, 4.3% Asian, 3.6% Hispanic of any race (2005); Density: 4,098.3 persons per square mile (2005); Average household size: 2.94 (2005); Median age: 41.4 (2005); Males per 100 females: 91.2 (2005); Marriage status: 24.6% never married, 64.5% now married, 7.2% widowed, 3.7% divorced (2000); Foreign born: 8.5% (2000); Ancestry (includes multiple ancestries): 35.2% Irish, 30.2% Italian, 18.9% German, 8.0% Other groups, 7.0% English (2000).
Economy: Residential community, with printing, publishing and retailing as the major industries. Roosevelt Field Mall, one of the largest malls in the U.S. is here. Single-family building permits issued: 29 (2005); Multi-family building permits issued: 0 (2005); Employment by occupation: 23.7% management, 32.6% professional, 7.9% services, 31.2% sales, 0.0% farming, 1.6% construction, 3.1% production (2000).
Income: Per capita income: $57,152 (2005); Median household income: $121,647 (2005); Average household income: $166,981 (2005); Percent of households with income of $100,000 or more: 59.1% (2005); Poverty rate: 2.3% (2000).
Education: Percent of population age 25 and over with: High school diploma (including GED) or higher: 96.6% (2005); Bachelor's degree or higher: 61.6% (2005); Master's degree or higher: 29.9% (2005).

School District(s)
Boces Nassau (PK-PK)
   2003-04 Enrollment: 2,039 .... (516) 396-2200
Garden City Union Free School District (KG-12)
   2003-04 Enrollment: 4,150 .... (516) 478-1010

Four-year College(s)
Adelphi University
   Fall 2004 Enrollment: 7,592 .... (516) 877-3000
   2005-06 Tuition: In-state $19,960; Out-of-state $19,960

Two-year College(s)
Career Institute of Health & Technology
   Fall 2004 Enrollment: 744 .... (516) 877-1225
Nassau Community College (Public)
   Fall 2004 Enrollment: 21,446 .... (516) 222-7355
   2005-06 Tuition: In-state $3,140; Out-of-state $6,280
Sanford-Brown Institute
   Fall 2004 Enrollment: 785 .... (888) 781-3600

Housing: Homeownership rate: 93.2% (2005); Median home value: $752,116 (2005); Median rent: $1,561 per month (2000); Median age of housing: 52 years (2000).
Safety: Violent crime rate: 5.0 per 10,000 population; Property crime rate: 132.4 per 10,000 population (2004).
Transportation: Commute to work: 68.5% car, 23.0% public transportation, 3.6% walk, 4.7% work from home (2000); Travel time to work: 25.8% less than 15 minutes, 24.6% 15 to 30 minutes, 14.4% 30 to 45 minutes, 9.5% 45 to 60 minutes, 25.7% 60 minutes or more (2000)
Additional Information Contacts
Garden City Chamber of Commerce .... (516) 746-7724
   http://www.gardencitychamber.org
Village of Garden City .... (516) 465-4000
   http://www.gardencityny.net/gcvillage.htm

GARDEN CITY PARK (CDP).
Covers a land area of 0.974 square miles and a water area of 0 square miles. Located at 40.74° N. Lat.; 73.66° W. Long.
Population: 7,437 (1990); 7,554 (2000); 7,539 (2005); 7,524 (2010 projected); Race: 61.3% White, 4.6% Black, 27.7% Asian, 10.6% Hispanic of any race (2005); Density: 7,743.9 persons per square mile (2005); Average household size: 3.05 (2005); Median age: 42.6 (2005); Males per

100 females: 93.3 (2005); Marriage status: 24.2% never married, 62.3% now married, 9.3% widowed, 4.2% divorced (2000); Foreign born: 26.8% (2000); Ancestry (includes multiple ancestries): 31.1% Other groups, 23.2% Italian, 17.2% Irish, 10.8% German, 5.8% Polish (2000).
Economy: Employment by occupation: 14.2% management, 30.5% professional, 11.7% services, 30.8% sales, 0.0% farming, 6.5% construction, 6.3% production (2000).
Income: Per capita income: $34,619 (2005); Median household income: $88,872 (2005); Average household income: $105,451 (2005); Percent of households with income of $100,000 or more: 42.8% (2005); Poverty rate: 1.0% (2000).
Education: Percent of population age 25 and over with: High school diploma (including GED) or higher: 85.9% (2005); Bachelor's degree or higher: 36.9% (2005); Master's degree or higher: 17.9% (2005).
School District(s)
Mineola Union Free School District (PK-12)
   2003-04 Enrollment: 2,903 . . . . (516) 741-5036
New Hyde Park-Garden City Park Union Free School District (PK-06)
   2003-04 Enrollment: 1,823 . . . . (516) 352-6257
Housing: Homeownership rate: 84.6% (2005); Median home value: $443,661 (2005); Median rent: $769 per month (2000); Median age of housing: 47 years (2000).
Transportation: Commute to work: 81.6% car, 12.4% public transportation, 2.9% walk, 2.8% work from home (2000); Travel time to work: 24.3% less than 15 minutes, 30.9% 15 to 30 minutes, 20.9% 30 to 45 minutes, 9.3% 45 to 60 minutes, 14.5% 60 minutes or more (2000).

GARDEN CITY SOUTH (CDP). Covers a land area of 0.414 square miles and a water area of 0 square miles. Located at 40.71° N. Lat.; 73.66° W. Long.
Population: 4,073 (1990); 3,974 (2000); 3,831 (2005); 3,681 (2010 projected); Race: 93.3% White, 0.5% Black, 4.4% Asian, 8.2% Hispanic of any race (2005); Density: 9,260.2 persons per square mile (2005); Average household size: 2.84 (2005); Median age: 41.6 (2005); Males per 100 females: 91.4 (2005); Marriage status: 23.1% never married, 61.2% now married, 11.0% widowed, 4.7% divorced (2000); Foreign born: 12.9% (2000); Ancestry (includes multiple ancestries): 40.2% Italian, 23.2% Irish, 13.1% German, 11.1% Other groups, 4.6% Polish (2000).
Economy: Employment by occupation: 17.1% management, 25.3% professional, 11.2% services, 32.9% sales, 0.0% farming, 7.6% construction, 5.9% production (2000).
Income: Per capita income: $35,443 (2005); Median household income: $85,353 (2005); Average household income: $100,654 (2005); Percent of households with income of $100,000 or more: 42.9% (2005); Poverty rate: 6.0% (2000).
Education: Percent of population age 25 and over with: High school diploma (including GED) or higher: 88.0% (2005); Bachelor's degree or higher: 32.2% (2005); Master's degree or higher: 12.6% (2005).
Housing: Homeownership rate: 88.2% (2005); Median home value: $448,607 (2005); Median rent: $1,084 per month (2000); Median age of housing: 52 years (2000).
Transportation: Commute to work: 84.3% car, 12.5% public transportation, 0.9% walk, 1.9% work from home (2000); Travel time to work: 25.8% less than 15 minutes, 26.5% 15 to 30 minutes, 20.5% 30 to 45 minutes, 10.1% 45 to 60 minutes, 17.1% 60 minutes or more (2000).

GLEN COVE (city). Covers a land area of 6.646 square miles and a water area of 12.605 square miles. Located at 40.86° N. Lat.; 73.62° W. Long. Elevation is 115 feet.
History: Settled 1668, attracted affluent class after Civil War. In 1920s it became core of the Gold Coast as mansions were built, including waterfront community on East Island at north end (once known as Morgans Island when owned by J.P. Morgan). In 19th century it attracted industry, including one of the world's largest starch factories. Incorporated as a city 1918.
Population: 24,149 (1990); 26,622 (2000); 26,870 (2005); 27,136 (2010 projected); Race: 76.4% White, 6.9% Black, 5.2% Asian, 25.7% Hispanic of any race (2005); Density: 4,043.3 persons per square mile (2005); Average household size: 2.81 (2005); Median age: 40.3 (2005); Males per 100 females: 93.8 (2005); Marriage status: 28.1% never married, 55.2% now married, 9.6% widowed, 7.1% divorced (2000); Foreign born: 27.9% (2000); Ancestry (includes multiple ancestries): 31.8% Other groups, 26.7% Italian, 12.8% Irish, 7.4% German, 6.2% Polish (2000).
Economy: Chiefly residential, it has varied high-technology equipment and chemical industries. The Webb Institute of Naval Architecture is here. Unemployment rate: 4.4% (2005); Total civilian labor force: 13,392 (2005); Single-family building permits issued: 13 (2005); Multi-family building permits issued: 0 (2005); Employment by occupation: 15.2% management, 19.2% professional, 20.9% services, 26.8% sales, 0.0% farming, 9.1% construction, 8.9% production (2000).
Income: Per capita income: $30,667 (2005); Median household income: $63,338 (2005); Average household income: $83,894 (2005); Percent of households with income of $100,000 or more: 27.0% (2005); Poverty rate: 9.1% (2000).
Education: Percent of population age 25 and over with: High school diploma (including GED) or higher: 77.7% (2005); Bachelor's degree or higher: 27.8% (2005); Master's degree or higher: 11.4% (2005).
School District(s)
Glen Cove City School District (PK-12)
   2003-04 Enrollment: 3,188 . . . . (516) 759-7217
North Shore Csd (KG-12)
   2003-04 Enrollment: 2,652 . . . . (516) 705-0350
Four-year College(s)
Webb Institute
   Fall 2004 Enrollment: 76 . . . . (516) 671-2213
Housing: Homeownership rate: 58.7% (2005); Median home value: $429,123 (2005); Median rent: $907 per month (2000); Median age of housing: 45 years (2000).
Hospitals: North Shore University Hospital at Glen Cove (265 beds)
Safety: Violent crime rate: 13.4 per 10,000 population; Property crime rate: 89.1 per 10,000 population (2004).
Newspapers: Gold Coast Gazette (General - Circulation 4,000)
Transportation: Commute to work: 84.2% car, 7.5% public transportation, 4.2% walk, 2.8% work from home (2000); Travel time to work: 35.0% less than 15 minutes, 28.4% 15 to 30 minutes, 16.7% 30 to 45 minutes, 6.1% 45 to 60 minutes, 13.9% 60 minutes or more (2000)
Additional Information Contacts
City of Glen Cove. . . . . (516) 676-2000
   http://www.glencove-li.com/
Glen Cove Chamber of Commerce . . . . (516) 676-6666
   http://www.glencovechamber.org

GLEN HEAD (CDP). Covers a land area of 1.611 square miles and a water area of 0 square miles. Located at 40.84° N. Lat.; 73.61° W. Long. Elevation is 167 feet.
Population: 4,488 (1990); 4,625 (2000); 4,781 (2005); 4,930 (2010 projected); Race: 93.6% White, 0.8% Black, 2.8% Asian, 6.0% Hispanic of any race (2005); Density: 2,967.6 persons per square mile (2005); Average household size: 2.73 (2005); Median age: 43.0 (2005); Males per 100 females: 91.8 (2005); Marriage status: 22.6% never married, 65.1% now married, 7.3% widowed, 5.1% divorced (2000); Foreign born: 11.9% (2000); Ancestry (includes multiple ancestries): 36.7% Italian, 22.4% Irish, 12.2% German, 11.6% Other groups, 8.7% English (2000).
Economy: Employment by occupation: 16.3% management, 26.9% professional, 10.5% services, 31.9% sales, 0.0% farming, 5.9% construction, 8.4% production (2000).
Income: Per capita income: $40,578 (2005); Median household income: $83,955 (2005); Average household income: $110,627 (2005); Percent of households with income of $100,000 or more: 39.9% (2005); Poverty rate: 2.4% (2000).
Education: Percent of population age 25 and over with: High school diploma (including GED) or higher: 90.8% (2005); Bachelor's degree or higher: 39.7% (2005); Master's degree or higher: 18.2% (2005).
School District(s)
North Shore Central School District (KG-12)
   2003-04 Enrollment: 2,652 . . . . (516) 705-0350
Housing: Homeownership rate: 85.8% (2005); Median home value: $567,035 (2005); Median rent: $938 per month (2000); Median age of housing: 45 years (2000).
Transportation: Commute to work: 87.3% car, 9.2% public transportation, 0.8% walk, 2.6% work from home (2000); Travel time to work: 31.0% less than 15 minutes, 29.8% 15 to 30 minutes, 15.2% 30 to 45 minutes, 8.6% 45 to 60 minutes, 15.3% 60 minutes or more (2000)

GLENWOOD LANDING (CDP). Covers a land area of 0.985 square miles and a water area of 0 square miles. Located at 40.82° N. Lat.; 73.63° W. Long.
Population: 3,407 (1990); 3,541 (2000); 3,707 (2005); 3,866 (2010 projected); Race: 94.2% White, 0.4% Black, 3.3% Asian, 4.2% Hispanic of any race (2005); Density: 3,764.2 persons per square mile (2005); Average

household size: 2.84 (2005); Median age: 42.0 (2005); Males per 100 females: 88.8 (2005); Marriage status: 21.2% never married, 67.9% now married, 7.9% widowed, 3.0% divorced (2000); Foreign born: 10.7% (2000); Ancestry (includes multiple ancestries): 29.0% Irish, 26.8% Italian, 18.6% German, 9.9% English, 9.3% Other groups (2000).
Economy: In summer recreational and residential region, and agricultural area; boat repairing. Large power station. Employment by occupation: 18.7% management, 26.2% professional, 15.7% services, 26.1% sales, 0.4% farming, 7.2% construction, 5.6% production (2000).
Income: Per capita income: $37,819 (2005); Median household income: $89,724 (2005); Average household income: $107,429 (2005); Percent of households with income of $100,000 or more: 43.4% (2005); Poverty rate: 2.4% (2000).
Education: Percent of population age 25 and over with: High school diploma (including GED) or higher: 92.3% (2005); Bachelor's degree or higher: 42.0% (2005); Master's degree or higher: 19.0% (2005).
Housing: Homeownership rate: 88.6% (2005); Median home value: $567,663 (2005); Median rent: $1,073 per month (2000); Median age of housing: 49 years (2000).
Transportation: Commute to work: 81.3% car, 12.4% public transportation, 3.1% walk, 3.3% work from home (2000); Travel time to work: 29.1% less than 15 minutes, 23.8% 15 to 30 minutes, 20.8% 30 to 45 minutes, 7.9% 45 to 60 minutes, 18.5% 60 minutes or more (2000)

GREAT NECK
(village). Aka Great Neck Plaza. Covers a land area of 1.351 square miles and a water area of 0.019 square miles. Located at 40.80° N. Lat.; 73.73° W. Long. Elevation is 100 feet.
Population: 8,806 (1990); 9,538 (2000); 9,659 (2005); 9,786 (2010 projected); Race: 81.9% White, 2.8% Black, 6.7% Asian, 11.8% Hispanic of any race (2005); Density: 7,151.9 persons per square mile (2005); Average household size: 2.91 (2005); Median age: 40.8 (2005); Males per 100 females: 95.1 (2005); Marriage status: 24.7% never married, 62.0% now married, 8.5% widowed, 4.8% divorced (2000); Foreign born: 35.7% (2000); Ancestry (includes multiple ancestries): 24.5% Other groups, 21.6% Iranian, 8.2% Russian, 6.4% Polish, 6.4% United States or American (2000).
Economy: Single-family building permits issued: 9 (2005); Multi-family building permits issued: 67 (2005); Employment by occupation: 19.1% management, 33.3% professional, 9.1% services, 31.4% sales, 0.0% farming, 3.4% construction, 3.6% production (2000).
Income: Per capita income: $42,389 (2005); Median household income: $86,035 (2005); Average household income: $123,087 (2005); Percent of households with income of $100,000 or more: 43.2% (2005); Poverty rate: 7.8% (2000).
Education: Percent of population age 25 and over with: High school diploma (including GED) or higher: 88.2% (2005); Bachelor's degree or higher: 50.8% (2005); Master's degree or higher: 30.0% (2005).

School District(s)
Great Neck Union Free School District (PK-12)
    2003-04 Enrollment: 6,113 . . . . (516) 773-1405

Housing: Homeownership rate: 74.1% (2005); Median home value: $755,007 (2005); Median rent: $869 per month (2000); Median age of housing: 49 years (2000).
Newspapers: Jewish Tribune (Jewish, Religious - Circulation 10,000); Long Island Jewish World (Jewish, Religious - Circulation 26,000); Manhattan Jewish Sentinel (Jewish, Religious - Circulation 40,000)
Transportation: Commute to work: 61.5% car, 29.4% public transportation, 2.4% walk, 5.9% work from home (2000); Travel time to work: 21.0% less than 15 minutes, 14.8% 15 to 30 minutes, 21.1% 30 to 45 minutes, 12.7% 45 to 60 minutes, 30.4% 60 minutes or more (2000)
Additional Information Contacts
Great Neck Chamber of Commerce . . . . (516) 487-2000
   http://www.greatneckchamber.org
Village of Great Neck . . . . (516) 482-0019
   http://www.greatneckvillage.org/

GREAT NECK ESTATES
(village). Covers a land area of 0.770 square miles and a water area of 0.036 square miles. Located at 40.78° N. Lat.; 73.73° W. Long.
History: Incorporated 1911.
Population: 2,652 (1990); 2,756 (2000); 2,790 (2005); 2,841 (2010 projected); Race: 90.5% White, 1.0% Black, 6.7% Asian, 2.8% Hispanic of any race (2005); Density: 3,625.5 persons per square mile (2005); Average household size: 3.00 (2005); Median age: 44.1 (2005); Males per 100 females: 93.3 (2005); Marriage status: 18.2% never married, 72.0% now married, 6.5% widowed, 3.3% divorced (2000); Foreign born: 23.4% (2000); Ancestry (includes multiple ancestries): 21.0% Other groups, 14.9% Russian, 11.9% Polish, 10.8% Iranian, 9.8% United States or American (2000).
Economy: Single-family building permits issued: 2 (2005); Multi-family building permits issued: 0 (2005); Employment by occupation: 21.4% management, 47.6% professional, 5.4% services, 21.8% sales, 0.0% farming, 1.4% construction, 2.4% production (2000).
Income: Per capita income: $72,875 (2005); Median household income: $161,111 (2005); Average household income: $218,624 (2005); Percent of households with income of $100,000 or more: 70.9% (2005); Poverty rate: 2.3% (2000).
Education: Percent of population age 25 and over with: High school diploma (including GED) or higher: 93.9% (2005); Bachelor's degree or higher: 71.0% (2005); Master's degree or higher: 47.4% (2005).
Housing: Homeownership rate: 94.7% (2005); Median home value: $1 million+ (2005); Median rent: $2,000+ per month (2000); Median age of housing: 60+ years (2000).
Safety: Violent crime rate: 0.0 per 10,000 population; Property crime rate: 32.7 per 10,000 population (2004).
Transportation: Commute to work: 66.5% car, 22.0% public transportation, 1.4% walk, 9.4% work from home (2000); Travel time to work: 24.6% less than 15 minutes, 19.8% 15 to 30 minutes, 20.3% 30 to 45 minutes, 15.0% 45 to 60 minutes, 20.2% 60 minutes or more (2000)

GREAT NECK GARDENS
(CDP). Covers a land area of 0.168 square miles and a water area of 0 square miles. Located at 40.79° N. Lat.; 73.72° W. Long.
Population: 1,004 (1990); 1,089 (2000); 1,073 (2005); 1,066 (2010 projected); Race: 84.5% White, 0.7% Black, 11.6% Asian, 3.4% Hispanic of any race (2005); Density: 6,372.8 persons per square mile (2005); Average household size: 2.95 (2005); Median age: 43.9 (2005); Males per 100 females: 102.5 (2005); Marriage status: 17.4% never married, 76.4% now married, 3.0% widowed, 3.2% divorced (2000); Foreign born: 27.5% (2000); Ancestry (includes multiple ancestries): 19.5% Other groups, 14.1% Russian, 13.2% Iranian, 11.9% Polish, 7.8% United States or American (2000).
Economy: Employment by occupation: 14.6% management, 45.1% professional, 5.9% services, 33.1% sales, 0.0% farming, 0.0% construction, 1.3% production (2000).
Income: Per capita income: $67,989 (2005); Median household income: $142,857 (2005); Average household income: $200,419 (2005); Percent of households with income of $100,000 or more: 68.1% (2005); Poverty rate: 0.0% (2000).
Education: Percent of population age 25 and over with: High school diploma (including GED) or higher: 97.3% (2005); Bachelor's degree or higher: 80.5% (2005); Master's degree or higher: 52.8% (2005).
Housing: Homeownership rate: 98.1% (2005); Median home value: $837,230 (2005); Median rent: $2,000+ per month (2000); Median age of housing: 54 years (2000).
Transportation: Commute to work: 67.8% car, 24.0% public transportation, 2.2% walk, 6.0% work from home (2000); Travel time to work: 27.5% less than 15 minutes, 9.9% 15 to 30 minutes, 27.3% 30 to 45 minutes, 10.9% 45 to 60 minutes, 24.4% 60 minutes or more (2000)

GREAT NECK PLAZA
(village). Aka Great Neck. Covers a land area of 0.308 square miles and a water area of 0 square miles. Located at 40.78° N. Lat.; 73.72° W. Long.
Population: 6,053 (1990); 6,433 (2000); 7,067 (2005); 7,623 (2010 projected); Race: 89.0% White, 1.9% Black, 4.1% Asian, 7.9% Hispanic of any race (2005); Density: 22,908.6 persons per square mile (2005); Average household size: 1.77 (2005); Median age: 47.6 (2005); Males per 100 females: 77.4 (2005); Marriage status: 23.5% never married, 49.0% now married, 15.5% widowed, 12.1% divorced (2000); Foreign born: 26.3% (2000); Ancestry (includes multiple ancestries): 21.9% Other groups, 14.5% Russian, 9.1% Iranian, 8.7% United States or American, 7.6% Polish (2000).
Economy: Incorporated 1930. Single-family building permits issued: 0 (2005); Multi-family building permits issued: 0 (2005); Employment by occupation: 21.9% management, 34.2% professional, 8.5% services, 30.6% sales, 0.1% farming, 2.1% construction, 2.6% production (2000).
Income: Per capita income: $49,162 (2005); Median household income: $60,567 (2005); Average household income: $86,958 (2005); Percent of households with income of $100,000 or more: 27.7% (2005); Poverty rate: 7.1% (2000).

Education: Percent of population age 25 and over with: High school diploma (including GED) or higher: 89.9% (2005); Bachelor's degree or higher: 56.3% (2005); Master's degree or higher: 30.5% (2005).
Housing: Homeownership rate: 49.9% (2005); Median home value: $321,454 (2005); Median rent: $987 per month (2000); Median age of housing: 42 years (2000).
Transportation: Commute to work: 60.0% car, 28.8% public transportation, 5.7% walk, 4.8% work from home (2000); Travel time to work: 18.0% less than 15 minutes, 22.5% 15 to 30 minutes, 22.0% 30 to 45 minutes, 13.7% 45 to 60 minutes, 23.8% 60 minutes or more (2000)
Additional Information Contacts
Village of Great Neck Plaza . . . . (516) 482-4500
http://www.greatneckplaza.net/

GREENVALE
(CDP). Aka North Roslyn. Covers a land area of 0.257 square miles and a water area of 0 square miles. Located at 40.81° N. Lat.; 73.62° W. Long. Elevation is 200 feet.
History: C.W. Post campus of Long Island University.
Population: 965 (1990); 2,231 (2000); 2,258 (2005); 2,346 (2010 projected); Race: 50.5% White, 21.3% Black, 13.2% Asian, 17.9% Hispanic of any race (2005); Density: 8,779.3 persons per square mile (2005); Average household size: 6.19 (2005); Median age: 22.2 (2005); Males per 100 females: 79.2 (2005); Marriage status: 60.3% never married, 35.1% now married, 3.2% widowed, 1.4% divorced (2000); Foreign born: 21.3% (2000); Ancestry (includes multiple ancestries): 28.9% Other groups, 26.6% Italian, 18.1% Irish, 9.3% German, 8.3% Polish (2000).
Economy: Employment by occupation: 9.0% management, 20.1% professional, 23.2% services, 40.4% sales, 0.0% farming, 1.9% construction, 5.4% production (2000).
Income: Per capita income: $21,304 (2005); Median household income: $73,259 (2005); Average household income: $113,671 (2005); Percent of households with income of $100,000 or more: 37.3% (2005); Poverty rate: 4.4% (2000).
Education: Percent of population age 25 and over with: High school diploma (including GED) or higher: 88.4% (2005); Bachelor's degree or higher: 38.8% (2005); Master's degree or higher: 14.9% (2005).
School District(s)
Roslyn Union Free School District (PK-12)
   2003-04 Enrollment: 3,237 . . . . (516) 625-6303
Housing: Homeownership rate: 75.1% (2005); Median home value: $538,043 (2005); Median rent: $1,208 per month (2000); Median age of housing: 52 years (2000).
Transportation: Commute to work: 52.9% car, 7.7% public transportation, 35.3% walk, 3.6% work from home (2000); Travel time to work: 53.3% less than 15 minutes, 21.7% 15 to 30 minutes, 12.8% 30 to 45 minutes, 3.8% 45 to 60 minutes, 8.4% 60 minutes or more (2000)
Additional Information Contacts
Greenvale Chamber of Commerce . . . . (516) 621-8811
http://www.gvccc.com

HARBOR HILLS
(CDP). Covers a land area of 0.112 square miles and a water area of 0.063 square miles. Located at 40.78° N. Lat.; 73.74° W. Long.
Population: 568 (1990); 563 (2000); 588 (2005); 606 (2010 projected); Race: 94.9% White, 0.2% Black, 3.2% Asian, 1.2% Hispanic of any race (2005); Density: 5,267.1 persons per square mile (2005); Average household size: 3.13 (2005); Median age: 41.5 (2005); Males per 100 females: 100.0 (2005); Marriage status: 15.1% never married, 77.4% now married, 5.3% widowed, 2.2% divorced (2000); Foreign born: 29.0% (2000); Ancestry (includes multiple ancestries): 22.0% Other groups, 19.9% Russian, 19.7% Iranian, 6.6% Irish, 5.6% United States or American (2000).
Economy: Employment by occupation: 33.6% management, 43.6% professional, 6.0% services, 16.8% sales, 0.0% farming, 0.0% construction, 0.0% production (2000).
Income: Per capita income: $70,408 (2005); Median household income: $167,391 (2005); Average household income: $220,213 (2005); Percent of households with income of $100,000 or more: 73.4% (2005); Poverty rate: 4.4% (2000).
Education: Percent of population age 25 and over with: High school diploma (including GED) or higher: 95.8% (2005); Bachelor's degree or higher: 63.3% (2005); Master's degree or higher: 38.9% (2005).
Housing: Homeownership rate: 98.4% (2005); Median home value: $1 million+ (2005); Median rent: $n/a per month (2000); Median age of housing: 51 years (2000).
Transportation: Commute to work: 75.2% car, 18.8% public transportation, 0.0% walk, 6.0% work from home (2000); Travel time to work: 24.3% less than 15 minutes, 12.3% 15 to 30 minutes, 23.0% 30 to 45 minutes, 9.8% 45 to 60 minutes, 30.6% 60 minutes or more (2000)

HARBOR ISLE
(CDP). Covers a land area of 0.182 square miles and a water area of 0.051 square miles. Located at 40.60° N. Lat.; 73.66° W. Long.
Population: 1,373 (1990); 1,334 (2000); 1,291 (2005); 1,229 (2010 projected); Race: 96.3% White, 0.2% Black, 1.5% Asian, 4.6% Hispanic of any race (2005); Density: 7,089.9 persons per square mile (2005); Average household size: 2.68 (2005); Median age: 43.8 (2005); Males per 100 females: 92.4 (2005); Marriage status: 19.1% never married, 65.3% now married, 7.5% widowed, 8.1% divorced (2000); Foreign born: 8.8% (2000); Ancestry (includes multiple ancestries): 32.6% Italian, 20.5% Irish, 13.3% German, 9.6% Russian, 8.7% Polish (2000).
Economy: Employment by occupation: 18.2% management, 20.9% professional, 12.7% services, 26.6% sales, 0.0% farming, 11.6% construction, 10.0% production (2000).
Income: Per capita income: $39,210 (2005); Median household income: $91,414 (2005); Average household income: $105,021 (2005); Percent of households with income of $100,000 or more: 42.9% (2005); Poverty rate: 3.6% (2000).
Education: Percent of population age 25 and over with: High school diploma (including GED) or higher: 89.2% (2005); Bachelor's degree or higher: 26.4% (2005); Master's degree or higher: 10.8% (2005).
Housing: Homeownership rate: 95.4% (2005); Median home value: $414,110 (2005); Median rent: $708 per month (2000); Median age of housing: 43 years (2000).
Transportation: Commute to work: 89.6% car, 8.2% public transportation, 0.0% walk, 2.1% work from home (2000); Travel time to work: 25.3% less than 15 minutes, 18.2% 15 to 30 minutes, 21.3% 30 to 45 minutes, 10.6% 45 to 60 minutes, 24.6% 60 minutes or more (2000)

HEMPSTEAD
(village). Covers a land area of 3.680 square miles and a water area of 0.004 square miles. Located at 40.70° N. Lat.; 73.61° W. Long. Elevation is 54 feet.
History: The town grew significantly in the 1970s with the construction of nearby freeways, large retail outlets and the expansion of regional suburban industries. Settled in 1644 by English colonists who named it for their old home in England, Hemel-Hempstead. Seat of Hofstra University. Has many colonial houses and monuments. Founded as a village. Incorporated 1853.
Population: 49,435 (1990); 56,554 (2000); 56,773 (2005); 56,985 (2010 projected); Race: 22.1% White, 53.5% Black, 1.3% Asian, 35.6% Hispanic of any race (2005); Density: 15,425.6 persons per square mile (2005); Average household size: 3.83 (2005); Median age: 31.0 (2005); Males per 100 females: 92.3 (2005); Marriage status: 45.6% never married, 42.4% now married, 5.8% widowed, 6.2% divorced (2000); Foreign born: 33.2% (2000); Ancestry (includes multiple ancestries): 61.0% Other groups, 5.4% Jamaican, 2.8% Haitian, 2.7% Italian, 2.4% Irish (2000).
Economy: A retail center for the area. Electronic equipment, tools, chemicals and metal products are made here. Seat of Hofstra University. Unemployment rate: 6.2% (2005); Total civilian labor force: 25,900 (2005); Single-family building permits issued: 34 (2005); Multi-family building permits issued: 20 (2005); Employment by occupation: 7.3% management, 14.6% professional, 28.3% services, 27.9% sales, 0.3% farming, 6.7% construction, 14.9% production (2000).
Income: Per capita income: $16,307 (2005); Median household income: $47,936 (2005); Average household income: $60,374 (2005); Percent of households with income of $100,000 or more: 16.5% (2005); Poverty rate: 17.7% (2000).
Education: Percent of population age 25 and over with: High school diploma (including GED) or higher: 66.3% (2005); Bachelor's degree or higher: 15.8% (2005); Master's degree or higher: 6.3% (2005).
School District(s)
Hempstead Union Free School District (PK-12)
   2003-04 Enrollment: 7,128 . . . . (516) 292-7001
Uniondale Union Free School District (KG-12)
   2003-04 Enrollment: 6,411 . . . . (516) 560-8824
Four-year College(s)
Hofstra University
   Fall 2004 Enrollment: 12,999 . . . . (516) 463-6600
   2005-06 Tuition: In-state $23,130; Out-of-state $23,130

Two-year College(s)
Franklin Career Institute
   Fall 2004 Enrollment: 262 . . . . (516) 481-4444
Long Island Beauty School Inc
   Fall 2004 Enrollment: 149 . . . . (516) 483-6259
Suburban Technical School
   Fall 2004 Enrollment: 221 . . . . (516) 481-6660

Housing: Homeownership rate: 43.4% (2005); Median home value: $268,985 (2005); Median rent: $788 per month (2000); Median age of housing: 45 years (2000).
Hospitals: Nassau County Medical Center (631 beds)
Safety: Violent crime rate: 59.9 per 10,000 population; Property crime rate: 220.4 per 10,000 population (2004).
Newspapers: La Tribuna Hispana USA - Brooklyn/Queens Edition (Hispanic - Circulation 60,000); La Tribuna Hispana USA - Nassau County Edition (Hispanic - Circulation 15,000); La Tribuna Hispana USA - Suffolk County Edition (Hispanic - Circulation 15,000)
Transportation: Commute to work: 63.4% car, 24.3% public transportation, 8.8% walk, 1.5% work from home (2000); Travel time to work: 22.1% less than 15 minutes, 29.7% 15 to 30 minutes, 23.9% 30 to 45 minutes, 8.7% 45 to 60 minutes, 15.6% 60 minutes or more (2000)
Additional Information Contacts
Hempstead Chamber of Commerce . . . . (516) 483-2000
   http://www.hempsteadchamber.org
Village of Hempstead. . . . . (516) 489-3400
   http://www.villageofhempstead.org/

HEMPSTEAD (town). Covers a land area of 119.963 square miles and a water area of 71.372 square miles. Located at 40.67° N. Lat.; 73.62° W. Long. Elevation is 54 feet.
History: In 1644, the first settlers of Hempstead found a well-watered grassy plain on which their cattle grew fat. The virgin soil was excellent for timothy, rye, wheat, and maize. The score or more families who made up the settlement prospered. Not before 1801, however, did the village begin to grow appreciably.
Population: 725,630 (1990); 755,924 (2000); 757,215 (2005); 758,301 (2010 projected); Race: 70.2% White, 16.8% Black, 4.6% Asian, 14.0% Hispanic of any race (2005); Density: 6,312.1 persons per square mile (2005); Average household size: 3.07 (2005); Median age: 39.0 (2005); Males per 100 females: 93.1 (2005); Marriage status: 26.8% never married, 59.8% now married, 7.6% widowed, 5.7% divorced (2000); Foreign born: 17.8% (2000); Ancestry (includes multiple ancestries): 25.5% Other groups, 23.7% Italian, 17.6% Irish, 11.5% German, 5.1% Polish (2000).
Economy: Unemployment rate: 4.3% (2005); Total civilian labor force: 390,589 (2005); Single-family building permits issued: 638 (2005); Multi-family building permits issued: 0 (2005); Employment by occupation: 15.3% management, 22.8% professional, 14.8% services, 30.9% sales, 0.1% farming, 7.5% construction, 8.6% production (2000).
Income: Per capita income: $31,749 (2005); Median household income: $77,807 (2005); Average household income: $96,821 (2005); Percent of households with income of $100,000 or more: 35.9% (2005); Poverty rate: 5.8% (2000).
Taxes: Total city taxes per capita: $343 (2004); City property taxes per capita: $284 (2004).
Education: Percent of population age 25 and over with: High school diploma (including GED) or higher: 85.3% (2005); Bachelor's degree or higher: 31.2% (2005); Master's degree or higher: 13.3% (2005).
Housing: Homeownership rate: 80.9% (2005); Median home value: $370,027 (2005); Median rent: $847 per month (2000); Median age of housing: 48 years (2000).
Transportation: Commute to work: 77.7% car, 16.2% public transportation, 2.7% walk, 2.6% work from home (2000); Travel time to work: 20.7% less than 15 minutes, 29.1% 15 to 30 minutes, 20.1% 30 to 45 minutes, 9.4% 45 to 60 minutes, 20.7% 60 minutes or more (2000)
Additional Information Contacts
Town of Hempstead. . . . . (516) 489-5000
   http://www.townofhempstead.org/

HERRICKS (CDP). Covers a land area of 0.560 square miles and a water area of 0 square miles. Located at 40.75° N. Lat.; 73.66° W. Long.
Population: 4,097 (1990); 4,076 (2000); 4,004 (2005); 3,930 (2010 projected); Race: 62.3% White, 0.4% Black, 33.8% Asian, 5.2% Hispanic of any race (2005); Density: 7,155.7 persons per square mile (2005); Average household size: 3.07 (2005); Median age: 42.5 (2005); Males per 100 females: 91.9 (2005); Marriage status: 22.5% never married, 66.0% now married, 7.1% widowed, 4.4% divorced (2000); Foreign born: 27.0% (2000); Ancestry (includes multiple ancestries): 32.1% Other groups, 21.6% Italian, 16.6% Irish, 10.5% German, 8.3% Polish (2000).
Economy: Employment by occupation: 18.6% management, 29.6% professional, 8.1% services, 31.6% sales, 0.0% farming, 7.2% construction, 4.9% production (2000).
Income: Per capita income: $34,930 (2005); Median household income: $87,221 (2005); Average household income: $107,337 (2005); Percent of households with income of $100,000 or more: 41.2% (2005); Poverty rate: 4.5% (2000).
Education: Percent of population age 25 and over with: High school diploma (including GED) or higher: 91.7% (2005); Bachelor's degree or higher: 38.4% (2005); Master's degree or higher: 19.4% (2005).
Housing: Homeownership rate: 97.0% (2005); Median home value: $475,272 (2005); Median rent: $1,625 per month (2000); Median age of housing: 49 years (2000).
Transportation: Commute to work: 83.0% car, 13.0% public transportation, 0.8% walk, 3.2% work from home (2000); Travel time to work: 19.0% less than 15 minutes, 24.3% 15 to 30 minutes, 19.9% 30 to 45 minutes, 12.0% 45 to 60 minutes, 24.8% 60 minutes or more (2000)

HEWLETT (CDP). Covers a land area of 0.890 square miles and a water area of 0.006 square miles. Located at 40.64° N. Lat.; 73.69° W. Long.
Population: 6,620 (1990); 7,060 (2000); 7,125 (2005); 7,197 (2010 projected); Race: 87.1% White, 1.4% Black, 6.5% Asian, 11.6% Hispanic of any race (2005); Density: 8,009.1 persons per square mile (2005); Average household size: 2.65 (2005); Median age: 43.1 (2005); Males per 100 females: 91.0 (2005); Marriage status: 24.1% never married, 62.6% now married, 7.5% widowed, 5.8% divorced (2000); Foreign born: 17.0% (2000); Ancestry (includes multiple ancestries): 25.2% Italian, 21.4% Other groups, 12.9% Irish, 10.3% Russian, 9.3% United States or American (2000).
Economy: One of "Five Towns" of Long Island. Residential area, with small light industry. Employment by occupation: 19.6% management, 22.3% professional, 13.2% services, 31.3% sales, 0.0% farming, 6.9% construction, 6.7% production (2000).
Income: Per capita income: $40,919 (2005); Median household income: $74,572 (2005); Average household income: $108,507 (2005); Percent of households with income of $100,000 or more: 38.4% (2005); Poverty rate: 2.9% (2000).
Education: Percent of population age 25 and over with: High school diploma (including GED) or higher: 89.1% (2005); Bachelor's degree or higher: 39.8% (2005); Master's degree or higher: 16.6% (2005).
School District(s)
Hewlett-Woodmere Union Free School District (PK-12)
   2003-04 Enrollment: 3,327 . . . . (516) 374-8100
Housing: Homeownership rate: 77.6% (2005); Median home value: $399,719 (2005); Median rent: $920 per month (2000); Median age of housing: 51 years (2000).
Transportation: Commute to work: 74.7% car, 17.7% public transportation, 2.5% walk, 4.1% work from home (2000); Travel time to work: 25.9% less than 15 minutes, 23.6% 15 to 30 minutes, 21.4% 30 to 45 minutes, 9.8% 45 to 60 minutes, 19.3% 60 minutes or more (2000)

HEWLETT BAY PARK (village). Covers a land area of 0.350 square miles and a water area of 0.021 square miles. Located at 40.63° N. Lat.; 73.69° W. Long.
Population: 440 (1990); 484 (2000); 556 (2005); 599 (2010 projected); Race: 89.0% White, 1.6% Black, 4.9% Asian, 5.9% Hispanic of any race (2005); Density: 1,587.1 persons per square mile (2005); Average household size: 3.18 (2005); Median age: 47.2 (2005); Males per 100 females: 92.4 (2005); Marriage status: 19.5% never married, 71.1% now married, 5.7% widowed, 3.6% divorced (2000); Foreign born: 11.3% (2000); Ancestry (includes multiple ancestries): 27.8% Other groups, 23.3% Russian, 14.0% United States or American, 6.8% Polish, 4.5% Italian (2000).
Economy: Single-family building permits issued: 1 (2005); Multi-family building permits issued: 0 (2005); Employment by occupation: 30.1% management, 40.8% professional, 7.8% services, 18.9% sales, 0.0% farming, 1.5% construction, 1.0% production (2000).
Income: Per capita income: $93,687 (2005); Median household income: $245,588 (2005); Average household income: $297,657 (2005); Percent of households with income of $100,000 or more: 82.9% (2005); Poverty rate: 4.8% (2000).

Education: Percent of population age 25 and over with: High school diploma (including GED) or higher: 96.4% (2005); Bachelor's degree or higher: 66.8% (2005); Master's degree or higher: 37.6% (2005).
Housing: Homeownership rate: 95.4% (2005); Median home value: $1 million+ (2005); Median rent: $792 per month (2000); Median age of housing: 58 years (2000).
Transportation: Commute to work: 70.9% car, 11.3% public transportation, 4.4% walk, 12.8% work from home (2000); Travel time to work: 26.0% less than 15 minutes, 23.2% 15 to 30 minutes, 22.0% 30 to 45 minutes, 16.4% 45 to 60 minutes, 12.4% 60 minutes or more (2000)

HEWLETT HARBOR (village).
Covers a land area of 0.725 square miles and a water area of 0.092 square miles. Located at 40.63° N. Lat.; 73.68° W. Long.
Population: 1,193 (1990); 1,271 (2000); 1,384 (2005); 1,428 (2010 projected); Race: 94.6% White, 0.3% Black, 3.3% Asian, 1.3% Hispanic of any race (2005); Density: 1,910.2 persons per square mile (2005); Average household size: 3.04 (2005); Median age: 45.2 (2005); Males per 100 females: 91.4 (2005); Marriage status: 14.6% never married, 78.6% now married, 4.9% widowed, 2.0% divorced (2000); Foreign born: 7.2% (2000); Ancestry (includes multiple ancestries): 18.1% Other groups, 17.9% Russian, 16.2% United States or American, 8.2% Polish, 6.9% Italian (2000).
Economy: Single-family building permits issued: 1 (2005); Multi-family building permits issued: 0 (2005); Employment by occupation: 26.7% management, 33.8% professional, 2.9% services, 33.3% sales, 0.0% farming, 1.9% construction, 1.4% production (2000).
Income: Per capita income: $80,462 (2005); Median household income: $179,114 (2005); Average household income: $244,211 (2005); Percent of households with income of $100,000 or more: 70.0% (2005); Poverty rate: 0.7% (2000).
Education: Percent of population age 25 and over with: High school diploma (including GED) or higher: 97.3% (2005); Bachelor's degree or higher: 64.5% (2005); Master's degree or higher: 34.6% (2005).
Housing: Homeownership rate: 99.3% (2005); Median home value: $1 million+ (2005); Median rent: $n/a per month (2000); Median age of housing: 45 years (2000).
Transportation: Commute to work: 84.0% car, 9.2% public transportation, 0.0% walk, 6.0% work from home (2000); Travel time to work: 21.4% less than 15 minutes, 18.7% 15 to 30 minutes, 21.4% 30 to 45 minutes, 13.1% 45 to 60 minutes, 25.5% 60 minutes or more (2000)

HEWLETT NECK (village).
Covers a land area of 0.213 square miles and a water area of 0.014 square miles. Located at 40.62° N. Lat.; 73.69° W. Long.
Population: 547 (1990); 504 (2000); 493 (2005); 469 (2010 projected); Race: 99.0% White, 0.4% Black, 0.2% Asian, 1.2% Hispanic of any race (2005); Density: 2,317.4 persons per square mile (2005); Average household size: 3.33 (2005); Median age: 39.3 (2005); Males per 100 females: 99.6 (2005); Marriage status: 17.7% never married, 77.3% now married, 3.6% widowed, 1.4% divorced (2000); Foreign born: 3.4% (2000); Ancestry (includes multiple ancestries): 29.1% Russian, 19.2% United States or American, 19.0% Polish, 10.1% Other groups, 4.7% Austrian (2000).
Economy: Single-family building permits issued: 1 (2005); Multi-family building permits issued: 0 (2005); Employment by occupation: 24.0% management, 27.1% professional, 3.6% services, 39.6% sales, 0.0% farming, 2.7% construction, 3.1% production (2000).
Income: Per capita income: $70,355 (2005); Median household income: $196,154 (2005); Average household income: $234,358 (2005); Percent of households with income of $100,000 or more: 85.8% (2005); Poverty rate: 1.2% (2000).
Education: Percent of population age 25 and over with: High school diploma (including GED) or higher: 98.6% (2005); Bachelor's degree or higher: 74.2% (2005); Master's degree or higher: 34.2% (2005).
Housing: Homeownership rate: 98.6% (2005); Median home value: $1 million+ (2005); Median rent: $725 per month (2000); Median age of housing: 52 years (2000).
Transportation: Commute to work: 76.4% car, 13.8% public transportation, 0.0% walk, 9.8% work from home (2000); Travel time to work: 27.6% less than 15 minutes, 13.3% 15 to 30 minutes, 20.2% 30 to 45 minutes, 20.7% 45 to 60 minutes, 18.2% 60 minutes or more (2000)

HICKSVILLE (CDP).
Covers a land area of 6.812 square miles and a water area of 0.005 square miles. Located at 40.76° N. Lat.; 73.52° W. Long. Elevation is 149 feet.
History: Named for Charles Hicks, a Quaker reformer. Founded 1648.
Population: 40,174 (1990); 41,260 (2000); 41,339 (2005); 41,475 (2010 projected); Race: 78.5% White, 1.9% Black, 12.8% Asian, 12.4% Hispanic of any race (2005); Density: 6,068.8 persons per square mile (2005); Average household size: 3.00 (2005); Median age: 40.5 (2005); Males per 100 females: 96.2 (2005); Marriage status: 26.3% never married, 60.5% now married, 7.9% widowed, 5.3% divorced (2000); Foreign born: 18.0% (2000); Ancestry (includes multiple ancestries): 28.2% Italian, 23.4% Irish, 20.1% Other groups, 16.6% German, 6.2% Polish (2000).
Economy: Chiefly residential, with electronic and metal products manufacturing as well as some nearby vegetable farming. Site of the Broadway Mall, one of the largest shopping centers in U.S. Employment by occupation: 13.3% management, 19.9% professional, 14.8% services, 33.3% sales, 0.2% farming, 8.9% construction, 9.5% production (2000).
Income: Per capita income: $31,270 (2005); Median household income: $77,675 (2005); Average household income: $92,968 (2005); Percent of households with income of $100,000 or more: 34.6% (2005); Poverty rate: 3.7% (2000).
Education: Percent of population age 25 and over with: High school diploma (including GED) or higher: 86.5% (2005); Bachelor's degree or higher: 25.8% (2005); Master's degree or higher: 10.0% (2005).

School District(s)
Hicksville Union Free School District (PK-12)
    2003-04 Enrollment: 5,266 . . . . (516) 733-6600

Housing: Homeownership rate: 85.7% (2005); Median home value: $356,798 (2005); Median rent: $974 per month (2000); Median age of housing: 46 years (2000).
Newspapers: Bethpage Newsgram (General - Circulation 2,974); Jericho News Journal (General - Circulation 1,278); Mid Island Times (General - Circulation 5,685); Syosset Advance (General - Circulation 5,365); The East Meadow Beacon (General - Circulation 5,600); The Great Neck News (General - Circulation 5,500); The Hempstead Beacon (Black, General - Circulation 5,100); The Merrick Beacon (General - Circulation 4,100); The Uniondale Beacon (General - Circulation 5,300); The West Hempstead Beacon (General - Circulation 5,400); This Week - Babylon/West Islip Edition (General - Circulation 18,697); This Week - Bay Shore Edition (General - Circulation 18,185); This Week - Centereach Edition (General - Circulation 11,825); This Week - Deer Park Edition (General - Circulation 14,466); This Week - Farmingdale/Bethpage Edition (General - Circulation 16,862); This Week - Holbrook/Bohemia Edition (General - Circulation 16,911); This Week - Islip Edition (General - Circulation 14,864); This Week - Medford/Farmingville/Yaphank Edition (General - Circulation 14,423); This Week - Moriches/North Mastic/North Shirley Edition (General - Circulation 14,199); This Week - North Brentwood Edition (General - Circulation 13,031); This Week - Patchogue Edition (General - Circulation 19,549); This Week - Plainview/Old Bethpage Editiion (General - Circulation 11,699); This Week - Port Jefferson Edition (General - Circulation 19,036); This Week - Riverhead Edition (General - Circulation 11,166); This Week - Rocky Point Edition (General - Circulation 18,413); This Week - Ronkonkoma Edition (General - Circulation 15,956); This Week - Sayville/Oakdale Edition (General - Circulation 15,586); This Week - South Brentwood Edition (General - Circulation 12,964); This Week - South Shirley/South Mastic Edition (General - Circulation 15,023); This Week - Stony Brook/Setaullet Edition (General - Circulation 11,874); This Week - Syosset/Woodbury Edition (General - Circulation 12,373); This Week - West Babylon Edition (General - Circulation 15,386)
Transportation: Commute to work: 84.0% car, 12.0% public transportation, 1.9% walk, 1.6% work from home (2000); Travel time to work: 23.4% less than 15 minutes, 32.4% 15 to 30 minutes, 18.1% 30 to 45 minutes, 8.6% 45 to 60 minutes, 17.6% 60 minutes or more (2000)
Additional Information Contacts
Hicksville Chamber of Commerce . . . . (516) 931-7170
    http://www.hicksvillechamber.com

INWOOD (CDP).
Covers a land area of 1.699 square miles and a water area of 0.428 square miles. Located at 40.61° N. Lat.; 73.74° W. Long. Elevation is 10 feet.
Population: 7,767 (1990); 9,325 (2000); 9,317 (2005); 9,294 (2010 projected); Race: 44.0% White, 29.2% Black, 2.8% Asian, 33.6% Hispanic of any race (2005); Density: 5,483.7 persons per square mile (2005); Average household size: 3.13 (2005); Median age: 35.8 (2005); Males per

100 females: 89.8 (2005); Marriage status: 30.9% never married, 52.0% now married, 9.5% widowed, 7.6% divorced (2000); Foreign born: 28.1% (2000); Ancestry (includes multiple ancestries): 45.9% Other groups, 27.1% Italian, 8.2% Irish, 4.9% German, 3.8% Jamaican (2000).
Economy: Affluent residential area; some light manufacturing. Employment by occupation: 7.0% management, 14.6% professional, 26.7% services, 27.3% sales, 0.0% farming, 11.7% construction, 12.7% production (2000).
Income: Per capita income: $17,250 (2005); Median household income: $43,960 (2005); Average household income: $53,506 (2005); Percent of households with income of $100,000 or more: 11.7% (2005); Poverty rate: 14.6% (2000).
Education: Percent of population age 25 and over with: High school diploma (including GED) or higher: 68.6% (2005); Bachelor's degree or higher: 10.4% (2005); Master's degree or higher: 3.9% (2005).
School District(s)
Lawrence Union Free School District (PK-12)
  2003-04 Enrollment: 3,692 . . . . (516) 295-7030
Housing: Homeownership rate: 46.9% (2005); Median home value: $314,545 (2005); Median rent: $706 per month (2000); Median age of housing: 53 years (2000).
Transportation: Commute to work: 76.2% car, 14.1% public transportation, 7.9% walk, 1.5% work from home (2000); Travel time to work: 35.5% less than 15 minutes, 20.6% 15 to 30 minutes, 22.3% 30 to 45 minutes, 7.7% 45 to 60 minutes, 13.8% 60 minutes or more (2000)

ISLAND PARK (village). Covers a land area of 0.368 square miles and a water area of 0 square miles. Located at 40.60° N. Lat.; 73.65° W. Long. Elevation is 7 feet.
History: Incorporated 1926.
Population: 4,860 (1990); 4,732 (2000); 4,772 (2005); 4,813 (2010 projected); Race: 85.1% White, 2.1% Black, 1.2% Asian, 24.3% Hispanic of any race (2005); Density: 12,974.5 persons per square mile (2005); Average household size: 2.79 (2005); Median age: 39.7 (2005); Males per 100 females: 91.3 (2005); Marriage status: 29.8% never married, 55.0% now married, 7.3% widowed, 7.9% divorced (2000); Foreign born: 19.4% (2000); Ancestry (includes multiple ancestries): 37.1% Italian, 23.6% Irish, 23.5% Other groups, 11.0% German, 4.0% English (2000).
Economy: Single-family building permits issued: 3 (2005); Multi-family building permits issued: 0 (2005); Employment by occupation: 8.4% management, 16.6% professional, 22.0% services, 30.4% sales, 0.0% farming, 11.3% construction, 11.3% production (2000).
Income: Per capita income: $25,145 (2005); Median household income: $60,597 (2005); Average household income: $69,196 (2005); Percent of households with income of $100,000 or more: 19.6% (2005); Poverty rate: 8.1% (2000).
Education: Percent of population age 25 and over with: High school diploma (including GED) or higher: 80.3% (2005); Bachelor's degree or higher: 15.9% (2005); Master's degree or higher: 6.5% (2005).
School District(s)
Island Park Union Free School District (KG-08)
  2003-04 Enrollment: 795 . . . . (516) 431-7268
Housing: Homeownership rate: 58.4% (2005); Median home value: $329,504 (2005); Median rent: $922 per month (2000); Median age of housing: 45 years (2000).
Newspapers: Baldwin - Freeport Tribune (General - Circulation 9,700); Five Towns Tribune (General - Circulation 2,800); Freeport Tribune (General - Circulation 18,050); Garden City Tribune (General - Circulation 2,800); Hicksville-Levittown Tribune (General - Circulation 3,800); Island Park Tribune (General - Circulation 22,500); Long Beach Tribune (General - Circulation 17,500); Manhattan Tribune (General - Circulation 10,000); Merrick-Bellmore Tribune (General - Circulation 46,000); Oceanside-Rockville Center-East Rockaway Tribune (General - Circulation 26,059); Valley Stream-Lynbrook-Malverne Tribune (General - Circulation 36,500)
Transportation: Commute to work: 79.9% car, 15.4% public transportation, 2.8% walk, 1.7% work from home (2000); Travel time to work: 23.6% less than 15 minutes, 31.7% 15 to 30 minutes, 20.1% 30 to 45 minutes, 10.0% 45 to 60 minutes, 14.6% 60 minutes or more (2000)

JERICHO (CDP). Covers a land area of 4.059 square miles and a water area of 0 square miles. Located at 40.78° N. Lat.; 73.53° W. Long. Elevation is 194 feet.
Population: 13,141 (1990); 13,045 (2000); 13,319 (2005); 13,590 (2010 projected); Race: 80.9% White, 1.9% Black, 15.3% Asian, 2.6% Hispanic of any race (2005); Density: 3,281.6 persons per square mile (2005); Average household size: 2.86 (2005); Median age: 44.2 (2005); Males per 100 females: 94.2 (2005); Marriage status: 18.1% never married, 70.0% now married, 6.3% widowed, 5.5% divorced (2000); Foreign born: 13.9% (2000); Ancestry (includes multiple ancestries): 25.5% Other groups, 16.1% Russian, 11.7% Italian, 10.5% Polish, 7.1% United States or American (2000).
Economy: Chiefly residential; some light manufacturing. Employment by occupation: 25.3% management, 35.0% professional, 5.5% services, 27.0% sales, 0.0% farming, 2.1% construction, 5.0% production (2000).
Income: Per capita income: $55,957 (2005); Median household income: $119,146 (2005); Average household income: $158,204 (2005); Percent of households with income of $100,000 or more: 58.8% (2005); Poverty rate: 4.7% (2000).
Education: Percent of population age 25 and over with: High school diploma (including GED) or higher: 96.0% (2005); Bachelor's degree or higher: 60.2% (2005); Master's degree or higher: 29.9% (2005).
School District(s)
Jericho Union Free School District (KG-12)
  2003-04 Enrollment: 3,210 . . . . (516) 681-4100
Housing: Homeownership rate: 85.7% (2005); Median home value: $655,526 (2005); Median rent: $1,251 per month (2000); Median age of housing: 40 years (2000).
Transportation: Commute to work: 80.3% car, 14.2% public transportation, 0.8% walk, 4.4% work from home (2000); Travel time to work: 18.5% less than 15 minutes, 32.4% 15 to 30 minutes, 14.8% 30 to 45 minutes, 8.6% 45 to 60 minutes, 25.7% 60 minutes or more (2000)

KENSINGTON (village). Covers a land area of 0.254 square miles and a water area of 0 square miles. Located at 40.79° N. Lat.; 73.72° W. Long.
Population: 1,104 (1990); 1,209 (2000); 1,281 (2005); 1,340 (2010 projected); Race: 89.0% White, 0.5% Black, 7.2% Asian, 5.5% Hispanic of any race (2005); Density: 5,035.1 persons per square mile (2005); Average household size: 2.90 (2005); Median age: 46.6 (2005); Males per 100 females: 92.6 (2005); Marriage status: 18.3% never married, 70.6% now married, 8.8% widowed, 2.3% divorced (2000); Foreign born: 25.8% (2000); Ancestry (includes multiple ancestries): 16.9% Russian, 15.0% Iranian, 13.2% Polish, 12.9% Other groups, 8.7% United States or American (2000).
Economy: Single-family building permits issued: 0 (2005); Multi-family building permits issued: 0 (2005); Employment by occupation: 21.1% management, 44.6% professional, 2.0% services, 30.5% sales, 0.0% farming, 1.0% construction, 0.8% production (2000).
Income: Per capita income: $60,466 (2005); Median household income: $124,688 (2005); Average household income: $175,641 (2005); Percent of households with income of $100,000 or more: 59.0% (2005); Poverty rate: 1.2% (2000).
Education: Percent of population age 25 and over with: High school diploma (including GED) or higher: 93.0% (2005); Bachelor's degree or higher: 70.0% (2005); Master's degree or higher: 38.1% (2005).
Housing: Homeownership rate: 96.4% (2005); Median home value: $998,786 (2005); Median rent: $1,393 per month (2000); Median age of housing: 53 years (2000).
Safety: Violent crime rate: 0.0 per 10,000 population; Property crime rate: 24.9 per 10,000 population (2004).
Transportation: Commute to work: 56.5% car, 29.8% public transportation, 2.8% walk, 10.1% work from home (2000); Travel time to work: 17.3% less than 15 minutes, 17.9% 15 to 30 minutes, 18.8% 30 to 45 minutes, 15.3% 45 to 60 minutes, 30.8% 60 minutes or more (2000)

KINGS POINT (village). Covers a land area of 3.342 square miles and a water area of 0.639 square miles. Located at 40.81° N. Lat.; 73.73° W. Long. Elevation is 26 feet.
History: Seat of U.S. Merchant Marine Academy (established 1942). Incorporated 1924.
Population: 4,843 (1990); 5,076 (2000); 5,254 (2005); 5,420 (2010 projected); Race: 89.9% White, 0.8% Black, 4.6% Asian, 2.0% Hispanic of any race (2005); Density: 1,572.2 persons per square mile (2005); Average household size: 3.70 (2005); Median age: 35.2 (2005); Males per 100 females: 122.5 (2005); Marriage status: 29.0% never married, 64.0% now married, 4.9% widowed, 2.1% divorced (2000); Foreign born: 29.4% (2000); Ancestry (includes multiple ancestries): 29.3% Iranian, 13.8% Other groups, 10.2% United States or American, 8.7% Russian, 5.8% Polish (2000).

Economy: Single-family building permits issued: 9 (2005); Multi-family building permits issued: 0 (2005); Employment by occupation: 28.4% management, 27.2% professional, 7.0% services, 33.4% sales, 0.0% farming, 1.0% construction, 2.9% production (2000).
Income: Per capita income: $62,016 (2005); Median household income: $163,653 (2005); Average household income: $227,778 (2005); Percent of households with income of $100,000 or more: 68.4% (2005); Poverty rate: 6.5% (2000).
Education: Percent of population age 25 and over with: High school diploma (including GED) or higher: 94.3% (2005); Bachelor's degree or higher: 63.0% (2005); Master's degree or higher: 31.0% (2005).

Four-year College(s)
United States Merchant Marine Academy (Public)
    Fall 2004 Enrollment: 962 . . . . (516) 773-5000

Housing: Homeownership rate: 94.6% (2005); Median home value: $1 million+ (2005); Median rent: $979 per month (2000); Median age of housing: 45 years (2000).
Transportation: Commute to work: 65.8% car, 24.2% public transportation, 2.6% walk, 6.2% work from home (2000); Travel time to work: 17.6% less than 15 minutes, 14.2% 15 to 30 minutes, 18.0% 30 to 45 minutes, 15.0% 45 to 60 minutes, 35.3% 60 minutes or more (2000)

LAKE SUCCESS (village).
Covers a land area of 1.881 square miles and a water area of 0.036 square miles. Located at 40.77° N. Lat.; 73.71° W. Long. Elevation is 200 feet.
History: Lake Success was the temporary home of the UN from 1946 to 1950. Settled c.1730, incorporated 1926.
Population: 2,484 (1990); 2,797 (2000); 2,841 (2005); 2,903 (2010 projected); Race: 71.4% White, 6.8% Black, 20.5% Asian, 1.1% Hispanic of any race (2005); Density: 1,510.7 persons per square mile (2005); Average household size: 3.46 (2005); Median age: 55.2 (2005); Males per 100 females: 80.8 (2005); Marriage status: 14.5% never married, 74.8% now married, 8.8% widowed, 1.9% divorced (2000); Foreign born: 23.5% (2000); Ancestry (includes multiple ancestries): 24.4% Other groups, 14.2% Russian, 9.7% United States or American, 8.9% Polish, 7.5% Italian (2000).
Economy: Single-family building permits issued: 10 (2005); Multi-family building permits issued: 0 (2005); Employment by occupation: 26.0% management, 39.9% professional, 2.8% services, 24.4% sales, 0.0% farming, 1.7% construction, 5.1% production (2000).
Income: Per capita income: $62,074 (2005); Median household income: $148,939 (2005); Average household income: $205,122 (2005); Percent of households with income of $100,000 or more: 69.7% (2005); Poverty rate: 1.9% (2000).
Education: Percent of population age 25 and over with: High school diploma (including GED) or higher: 89.6% (2005); Bachelor's degree or higher: 56.6% (2005); Master's degree or higher: 32.7% (2005).
Housing: Homeownership rate: 97.3% (2005); Median home value: $1 million+ (2005); Median rent: $2,000+ per month (2000); Median age of housing: 47 years (2000).
Safety: Violent crime rate: 24.7 per 10,000 population; Property crime rate: 176.2 per 10,000 population (2004).
Transportation: Commute to work: 72.9% car, 18.5% public transportation, 1.1% walk, 7.6% work from home (2000); Travel time to work: 23.7% less than 15 minutes, 22.3% 15 to 30 minutes, 19.4% 30 to 45 minutes, 12.2% 45 to 60 minutes, 22.6% 60 minutes or more (2000)

LAKEVIEW (CDP).
Aka Lake View. Covers a land area of 0.958 square miles and a water area of 0.212 square miles. Located at 40.67° N. Lat.; 73.65° W. Long.
Population: 5,476 (1990); 5,607 (2000); 5,376 (2005); 5,134 (2010 projected); Race: 6.2% White, 85.6% Black, 0.3% Asian, 7.2% Hispanic of any race (2005); Density: 5,609.2 persons per square mile (2005); Average household size: 3.71 (2005); Median age: 37.4 (2005); Males per 100 females: 83.4 (2005); Marriage status: 34.3% never married, 48.9% now married, 8.5% widowed, 8.3% divorced (2000); Foreign born: 21.3% (2000); Ancestry (includes multiple ancestries): 58.4% Other groups, 11.9% Jamaican, 5.0% Haitian, 2.6% African, 2.6% Trinidadian and Tobagonian (2000).
Economy: Employment by occupation: 14.0% management, 21.3% professional, 18.6% services, 27.8% sales, 0.0% farming, 7.3% construction, 11.1% production (2000).
Income: Per capita income: $24,283 (2005); Median household income: $76,727 (2005); Average household income: $86,863 (2005); Percent of households with income of $100,000 or more: 32.3% (2005); Poverty rate: 6.3% (2000).
Education: Percent of population age 25 and over with: High school diploma (including GED) or higher: 83.3% (2005); Bachelor's degree or higher: 25.5% (2005); Master's degree or higher: 11.7% (2005).
Housing: Homeownership rate: 88.7% (2005); Median home value: $292,193 (2005); Median rent: $942 per month (2000); Median age of housing: 44 years (2000).
Transportation: Commute to work: 79.4% car, 18.4% public transportation, 1.3% walk, 0.4% work from home (2000); Travel time to work: 11.8% less than 15 minutes, 29.7% 15 to 30 minutes, 24.5% 30 to 45 minutes, 9.3% 45 to 60 minutes, 24.6% 60 minutes or more (2000)

LATTINGTOWN (village).
Covers a land area of 3.781 square miles and a water area of 0.036 square miles. Located at 40.89° N. Lat.; 73.59° W. Long. Elevation is 65 feet.
Population: 1,859 (1990); 1,860 (2000); 1,881 (2005); 1,903 (2010 projected); Race: 92.8% White, 0.7% Black, 4.7% Asian, 2.8% Hispanic of any race (2005); Density: 497.5 persons per square mile (2005); Average household size: 3.02 (2005); Median age: 44.0 (2005); Males per 100 females: 93.9 (2005); Marriage status: 20.8% never married, 69.8% now married, 6.1% widowed, 3.3% divorced (2000); Foreign born: 14.4% (2000); Ancestry (includes multiple ancestries): 24.3% Italian, 22.3% Irish, 12.0% German, 10.3% English, 9.7% Other groups (2000).
Economy: Single-family building permits issued: 1 (2005); Multi-family building permits issued: 0 (2005); Employment by occupation: 29.0% management, 28.3% professional, 7.7% services, 28.1% sales, 0.0% farming, 4.0% construction, 3.0% production (2000).
Income: Per capita income: $80,784 (2005); Median household income: $159,551 (2005); Average household income: $242,127 (2005); Percent of households with income of $100,000 or more: 66.8% (2005); Poverty rate: 4.5% (2000).
Education: Percent of population age 25 and over with: High school diploma (including GED) or higher: 93.4% (2005); Bachelor's degree or higher: 61.0% (2005); Master's degree or higher: 29.9% (2005).
Housing: Homeownership rate: 87.0% (2005); Median home value: $1 million+ (2005); Median rent: $1,208 per month (2000); Median age of housing: 43 years (2000).
Transportation: Commute to work: 79.8% car, 6.8% public transportation, 2.2% walk, 11.2% work from home (2000); Travel time to work: 22.6% less than 15 minutes, 21.5% 15 to 30 minutes, 25.8% 30 to 45 minutes, 8.9% 45 to 60 minutes, 21.3% 60 minutes or more (2000)

LAUREL HOLLOW (village).
Covers a land area of 2.924 square miles and a water area of 0.161 square miles. Located at 40.85° N. Lat.; 73.47° W. Long. Elevation is 91 feet.
History: Until 1935, called Laurelton.
Population: 1,748 (1990); 1,930 (2000); 1,965 (2005); 1,999 (2010 projected); Race: 88.5% White, 1.2% Black, 9.0% Asian, 2.6% Hispanic of any race (2005); Density: 672.0 persons per square mile (2005); Average household size: 3.24 (2005); Median age: 42.7 (2005); Males per 100 females: 89.3 (2005); Marriage status: 18.8% never married, 71.3% now married, 5.3% widowed, 4.7% divorced (2000); Foreign born: 12.2% (2000); Ancestry (includes multiple ancestries): 27.2% Italian, 15.0% Irish, 13.7% German, 12.0% Other groups, 8.4% English (2000).
Economy: In summer-resort area. JFK International Airport to the Southwest. Single-family building permits issued: 6 (2005); Multi-family building permits issued: 0 (2005); Employment by occupation: 30.3% management, 34.7% professional, 7.5% services, 22.5% sales, 0.0% farming, 1.5% construction, 3.5% production (2000).
Income: Per capita income: $89,330 (2005); Median household income: $230,603 (2005); Average household income: $286,573 (2005); Percent of households with income of $100,000 or more: 78.4% (2005); Poverty rate: 1.9% (2000).
Education: Percent of population age 25 and over with: High school diploma (including GED) or higher: 96.6% (2005); Bachelor's degree or higher: 69.2% (2005); Master's degree or higher: 38.1% (2005).
Housing: Homeownership rate: 93.6% (2005); Median home value: $1 million+ (2005); Median rent: $1,109 per month (2000); Median age of housing: 36 years (2000).
Transportation: Commute to work: 72.9% car, 18.3% public transportation, 1.1% walk, 7.4% work from home (2000); Travel time to work: 21.0% less than 15 minutes, 26.7% 15 to 30 minutes, 15.7% 30 to 45 minutes, 4.3% 45 to 60 minutes, 32.2% 60 minutes or more (2000)

LAWRENCE

LAWRENCE (village). Covers a land area of 3.849 square miles and a water area of 0.845 square miles. Located at 40.61° N. Lat.; 73.72° W. Long.
History: Incorporated 1897.
Population: 6,513 (1990); 6,522 (2000); 6,563 (2005); 6,613 (2010 projected); Race: 94.0% White, 1.2% Black, 2.4% Asian, 3.6% Hispanic of any race (2005); Density: 1,705.2 persons per square mile (2005); Average household size: 3.16 (2005); Median age: 35.7 (2005); Males per 100 females: 95.2 (2005); Marriage status: 21.0% never married, 67.4% now married, 7.3% widowed, 4.2% divorced (2000); Foreign born: 14.4% (2000); Ancestry (includes multiple ancestries): 27.3% Other groups, 14.6% United States or American, 9.7% Polish, 7.1% Russian, 5.5% Hungarian (2000).
Economy: A few light industries: machine parts, canvas. In resort area. Single-family building permits issued: 1 (2005); Multi-family building permits issued: 0 (2005); Employment by occupation: 19.4% management, 42.6% professional, 7.1% services, 27.2% sales, 0.0% farming, 1.5% construction, 2.2% production (2000).
Income: Per capita income: $49,284 (2005); Median household income: $114,087 (2005); Average household income: $155,654 (2005); Percent of households with income of $100,000 or more: 54.4% (2005); Poverty rate: 6.3% (2000).
Education: Percent of population age 25 and over with: High school diploma (including GED) or higher: 95.3% (2005); Bachelor's degree or higher: 64.0% (2005); Master's degree or higher: 34.6% (2005).

School District(s)
Lawrence Union Free School District (PK-12)
    2003-04 Enrollment: 3,692 . . . . (516) 295-7030

Four-year College(s)
Sh'or Yoshuv Rabbinical College
    Fall 2004 Enrollment: 126 . . . . (516) 239-9002
    2005-06 Tuition: In-state $8,000; Out-of-state $8,000

Housing: Homeownership rate: 79.8% (2005); Median home value: $872,543 (2005); Median rent: $1,035 per month (2000); Median age of housing: 49 years (2000).
Newspapers: Baldwin Herald (General - Circulation 3,500); Long Island Graphic (General - Circulation 1,300); Meadowbrook Times (General - Circulation 2,000); Nassau Herald (General - Circulation 12,650); Oceanside/Island Park Herald (General - Circulation 5,250); Rockaway Journal (General - Circulation 2,300); Rockville Centre Herald (General - Circulation 5,386); Valley Stream Herald (General - Circulation 9,000); Village Herald (General - Circulation 5,271)
Transportation: Commute to work: 75.2% car, 17.2% public transportation, 2.0% walk, 4.7% work from home (2000); Travel time to work: 21.3% less than 15 minutes, 12.9% 15 to 30 minutes, 17.7% 30 to 45 minutes, 19.6% 45 to 60 minutes, 28.5% 60 minutes or more (2000)
Additional Information Contacts
Village of Lawrence . . . . (516) 239-4600
    http://www.villageoflawrence.org/

LEVITTOWN

LEVITTOWN (CDP). Covers a land area of 6.876 square miles and a water area of 0 square miles. Located at 40.72° N. Lat.; 73.51° W. Long. Elevation is 75 feet.
History: Named for William Levitt, developer of model surburban communities. It was originally developed by Levitt and Sons, Inc. a as mass-produced area of private, low-cost housing, and became the propotype for many postwar housing developments throughout the country. Founded 1947.
Population: 53,296 (1990); 53,067 (2000); 52,983 (2005); 52,929 (2010 projected); Race: 91.9% White, 0.8% Black, 3.9% Asian, 9.2% Hispanic of any race (2005); Density: 7,705.3 persons per square mile (2005); Average household size: 3.06 (2005); Median age: 39.1 (2005); Males per 100 females: 95.1 (2005); Marriage status: 24.8% never married, 62.0% now married, 7.3% widowed, 5.9% divorced (2000); Foreign born: 8.5% (2000); Ancestry (includes multiple ancestries): 34.0% Italian, 30.4% Irish, 18.5% German, 12.1% Other groups, 5.5% Polish (2000).
Economy: Employment by occupation: 12.4% management, 19.7% professional, 15.0% services, 34.0% sales, 0.0% farming, 9.8% construction, 9.0% production (2000).
Income: Per capita income: $29,500 (2005); Median household income: $78,405 (2005); Average household income: $89,820 (2005); Percent of households with income of $100,000 or more: 33.4% (2005); Poverty rate: 2.9% (2000).
Education: Percent of population age 25 and over with: High school diploma (including GED) or higher: 88.9% (2005); Bachelor's degree or higher: 22.5% (2005); Master's degree or higher: 8.4% (2005).

School District(s)
Island Trees Union Free School District (KG-12)
    2003-04 Enrollment: 2,795 . . . . (516) 520-2100
Levittown Union Free School District (KG-12)
    2003-04 Enrollment: 8,027 . . . . (516) 520-8300

Two-year College(s)
Brittany Beauty School
    Fall 2004 Enrollment: 175 . . . . (516) 731-8300
Hunter Business School
    Fall 2004 Enrollment: 289 . . . . (516) 796-1000
    2005-06 Tuition: In-state $7,500; Out-of-state $7,500

Housing: Homeownership rate: 89.7% (2005); Median home value: $330,754 (2005); Median rent: $1,011 per month (2000); Median age of housing: 50 years (2000).
Transportation: Commute to work: 87.1% car, 9.5% public transportation, 1.2% walk, 1.6% work from home (2000); Travel time to work: 22.2% less than 15 minutes, 35.5% 15 to 30 minutes, 18.6% 30 to 45 minutes, 6.9% 45 to 60 minutes, 16.9% 60 minutes or more (2000)

LIDO BEACH

LIDO BEACH (CDP). Covers a land area of 1.717 square miles and a water area of 2.544 square miles. Located at 40.58° N. Lat.; 73.62° W. Long. Elevation is 8 feet.
Population: 2,795 (1990); 2,825 (2000); 2,695 (2005); 2,520 (2010 projected); Race: 94.9% White, 0.8% Black, 2.0% Asian, 4.0% Hispanic of any race (2005); Density: 1,569.2 persons per square mile (2005); Average household size: 2.44 (2005); Median age: 48.8 (2005); Males per 100 females: 97.1 (2005); Marriage status: 18.0% never married, 65.1% now married, 9.7% widowed, 7.2% divorced (2000); Foreign born: 11.5% (2000); Ancestry (includes multiple ancestries): 17.1% Italian, 16.9% Other groups, 15.4% Russian, 10.2% Irish, 8.6% Polish (2000).
Economy: Employment by occupation: 21.3% management, 36.6% professional, 4.0% services, 30.2% sales, 0.0% farming, 3.2% construction, 4.8% production (2000).
Income: Per capita income: $54,557 (2005); Median household income: $96,329 (2005); Average household income: $131,814 (2005); Percent of households with income of $100,000 or more: 48.3% (2005); Poverty rate: 2.9% (2000).
Education: Percent of population age 25 and over with: High school diploma (including GED) or higher: 94.5% (2005); Bachelor's degree or higher: 55.8% (2005); Master's degree or higher: 32.0% (2005).

School District(s)
Long Beach City School District (PK-12)
    2003-04 Enrollment: 4,458 . . . . (516) 897-2104

Housing: Homeownership rate: 91.5% (2005); Median home value: $597,782 (2005); Median rent: $1,179 per month (2000); Median age of housing: 40 years (2000).
Transportation: Commute to work: 74.0% car, 20.6% public transportation, 0.5% walk, 4.9% work from home (2000); Travel time to work: 18.3% less than 15 minutes, 19.5% 15 to 30 minutes, 20.7% 30 to 45 minutes, 12.3% 45 to 60 minutes, 29.2% 60 minutes or more (2000)

LOCUST VALLEY

LOCUST VALLEY (CDP). Covers a land area of 0.919 square miles and a water area of 0.019 square miles. Located at 40.87° N. Lat.; 73.59° W. Long. Elevation is 121 feet.
Population: 3,490 (1990); 3,521 (2000); 3,499 (2005); 3,479 (2010 projected); Race: 83.3% White, 4.3% Black, 2.5% Asian, 19.1% Hispanic of any race (2005); Density: 3,808.1 persons per square mile (2005); Average household size: 2.78 (2005); Median age: 39.7 (2005); Males per 100 females: 96.1 (2005); Marriage status: 29.9% never married, 55.0% now married, 6.8% widowed, 8.3% divorced (2000); Foreign born: 20.6% (2000); Ancestry (includes multiple ancestries): 25.0% Italian, 23.4% Other groups, 20.0% Irish, 11.6% Polish, 9.8% English (2000).
Economy: Affluent residential area. Some light manufacturing. Employment by occupation: 15.8% management, 16.4% professional, 19.7% services, 28.7% sales, 0.0% farming, 12.9% construction, 6.5% production (2000).
Income: Per capita income: $43,118 (2005); Median household income: $70,184 (2005); Average household income: $119,002 (2005); Percent of households with income of $100,000 or more: 35.9% (2005); Poverty rate: 6.4% (2000).

Education: Percent of population age 25 and over with: High school diploma (including GED) or higher: 86.7% (2005); Bachelor's degree or higher: 32.6% (2005); Master's degree or higher: 10.9% (2005).

School District(s)
Locust Valley Central School District (KG-12)
    2003-04 Enrollment: 2,275 . . . . (516) 674-6310

Housing: Homeownership rate: 73.4% (2005); Median home value: $505,192 (2005); Median rent: $858 per month (2000); Median age of housing: 56 years (2000).

Transportation: Commute to work: 82.8% car, 8.6% public transportation, 2.5% walk, 5.6% work from home (2000); Travel time to work: 34.0% less than 15 minutes, 24.8% 15 to 30 minutes, 19.7% 30 to 45 minutes, 6.9% 45 to 60 minutes, 14.5% 60 minutes or more (2000)

Additional Information Contacts
Locust Valley Chamber of Commerce . . . . (516) 676-9501
    http://www.locustvalley.com/chamber.html

LONG BEACH
(city). Covers a land area of 2.137 square miles and a water area of 1.757 square miles. Located at 40.58° N. Lat.; 73.66° W. Long. Elevation is 9 feet.

History: Named for its beach on the Atlantic shore of Long Island. Incorporated 1922.

Population: 33,510 (1990); 35,462 (2000); 35,480 (2005); 35,434 (2010 projected); Race: 81.8% White, 6.4% Black, 3.1% Asian, 15.1% Hispanic of any race (2005); Density: 16,603.4 persons per square mile (2005); Average household size: 2.36 (2005); Median age: 42.0 (2005); Males per 100 females: 93.7 (2005); Marriage status: 32.7% never married, 49.0% now married, 8.7% widowed, 9.5% divorced (2000); Foreign born: 15.3% (2000); Ancestry (includes multiple ancestries): 25.4% Other groups, 20.9% Irish, 16.3% Italian, 9.3% German, 6.7% Russian (2000).

Economy: Manufacturing: clothing, machinery, umbrellas. Railroad terminus. Former resort. Popular beach. Unemployment rate: 4.0% (2005); Total civilian labor force: 19,748 (2005); Single-family building permits issued: 7 (2005); Multi-family building permits issued: 20 (2005); Employment by occupation: 15.6% management, 26.7% professional, 14.5% services, 30.4% sales, 0.0% farming, 6.0% construction, 6.8% production (2000).

Income: Per capita income: $36,500 (2005); Median household income: $65,002 (2005); Average household income: $84,391 (2005); Percent of households with income of $100,000 or more: 28.0% (2005); Poverty rate: 9.4% (2000).

Education: Percent of population age 25 and over with: High school diploma (including GED) or higher: 88.7% (2005); Bachelor's degree or higher: 37.1% (2005); Master's degree or higher: 14.9% (2005).

School District(s)
Long Beach City School District (PK-12)
    2003-04 Enrollment: 4,458 . . . . (516) 897-2104

Four-year College(s)
Rabbinical College of Long Island
    Fall 2004 Enrollment: 117 . . . . (516) 431-7414
    2005-06 Tuition: In-state $7,400; Out-of-state $7,400

Housing: Homeownership rate: 53.5% (2005); Median home value: $357,377 (2005); Median rent: $962 per month (2000); Median age of housing: 43 years (2000).

Hospitals: Long Beach Medical Center (203 beds)

Safety: Violent crime rate: 29.3 per 10,000 population; Property crime rate: 122.0 per 10,000 population (2004).

Newspapers: Long Beach Herald (General - Circulation 6,210)

Transportation: Commute to work: 71.3% car, 20.7% public transportation, 4.0% walk, 2.7% work from home (2000); Travel time to work: 18.0% less than 15 minutes, 23.4% 15 to 30 minutes, 22.2% 30 to 45 minutes, 10.3% 45 to 60 minutes, 26.1% 60 minutes or more (2000)

Additional Information Contacts
City of Long Beach . . . . (516) 431-1000
    http://www.longbeachny.org/
Long Beach Chamber of Commerce . . . . (516) 432-6000
    http://www.longislandnet.com/longbeach

LYNBROOK
(village). Covers a land area of 1.999 square miles and a water area of 0 square miles. Located at 40.65° N. Lat.; 73.67° W. Long. Elevation is 21 feet.

History: Old Church dates from 1800. The area was settled in 1785 and was called Bloomfield. The name *Lynbrook* (formed by reversing the syllables in *Brooklyn*) was adopted in 1895. Incorporated 1911.

Population: 19,208 (1990); 19,911 (2000); 19,760 (2005); 19,596 (2010 projected); Race: 89.3% White, 1.4% Black, 4.0% Asian, 11.2% Hispanic of any race (2005); Density: 9,885.3 persons per square mile (2005); Average household size: 2.70 (2005); Median age: 41.5 (2005); Males per 100 females: 90.7 (2005); Marriage status: 23.8% never married, 60.1% now married, 10.0% widowed, 6.1% divorced (2000); Foreign born: 13.6% (2000); Ancestry (includes multiple ancestries): 35.9% Italian, 25.2% Irish, 16.7% German, 14.2% Other groups, 4.7% Polish (2000).

Economy: Sheet-metal and furniture manufacturing. Single-family building permits issued: 0 (2005); Multi-family building permits issued: 2 (2005); Employment by occupation: 16.6% management, 19.2% professional, 14.6% services, 33.9% sales, 0.2% farming, 7.3% construction, 8.2% production (2000).

Income: Per capita income: $31,446 (2005); Median household income: $71,300 (2005); Average household income: $83,864 (2005); Percent of households with income of $100,000 or more: 31.6% (2005); Poverty rate: 4.2% (2000).

Education: Percent of population age 25 and over with: High school diploma (including GED) or higher: 86.4% (2005); Bachelor's degree or higher: 29.6% (2005); Master's degree or higher: 10.8% (2005).

School District(s)
Lynbrook Union Free School District (KG-12)
    2003-04 Enrollment: 3,141 . . . . (516) 887-0253
Malverne Union Free School District (KG-12)
    2003-04 Enrollment: 1,826 . . . . (516) 887-6405

Housing: Homeownership rate: 72.6% (2005); Median home value: $364,042 (2005); Median rent: $857 per month (2000); Median age of housing: 57 years (2000).

Safety: Violent crime rate: 7.6 per 10,000 population; Property crime rate: 84.2 per 10,000 population (2004).

Transportation: Commute to work: 76.5% car, 19.0% public transportation, 2.3% walk, 1.7% work from home (2000); Travel time to work: 22.7% less than 15 minutes, 26.9% 15 to 30 minutes, 20.4% 30 to 45 minutes, 9.0% 45 to 60 minutes, 20.9% 60 minutes or more (2000)

Additional Information Contacts
Lynbrook Chamber of Commerce . . . . (516) 593-3436
    http://www.lynbrookusa.com

MALVERNE
(village). Covers a land area of 1.051 square miles and a water area of 0 square miles. Located at 40.67° N. Lat.; 73.67° W. Long. Elevation is 24 feet.

History: Settled in the early 1800s, incorporated 1921.

Population: 9,054 (1990); 8,934 (2000); 9,265 (2005); 9,579 (2010 projected); Race: 89.1% White, 2.5% Black, 4.1% Asian, 8.0% Hispanic of any race (2005); Density: 8,813.9 persons per square mile (2005); Average household size: 2.87 (2005); Median age: 42.6 (2005); Males per 100 females: 94.0 (2005); Marriage status: 23.0% never married, 65.0% now married, 7.7% widowed, 4.3% divorced (2000); Foreign born: 13.7% (2000); Ancestry (includes multiple ancestries): 38.0% Italian, 26.8% Irish, 15.0% German, 12.7% Other groups, 6.8% English (2000).

Economy: Single-family building permits issued: 2 (2005); Multi-family building permits issued: 0 (2005); Employment by occupation: 14.4% management, 25.4% professional, 14.8% services, 31.3% sales, 0.0% farming, 7.9% construction, 6.2% production (2000).

Income: Per capita income: $38,592 (2005); Median household income: $94,759 (2005); Average household income: $110,477 (2005); Percent of households with income of $100,000 or more: 46.0% (2005); Poverty rate: 1.6% (2000).

Education: Percent of population age 25 and over with: High school diploma (including GED) or higher: 92.2% (2005); Bachelor's degree or higher: 36.7% (2005); Master's degree or higher: 14.8% (2005).

School District(s)
Malverne Union Free School District (KG-12)
    2003-04 Enrollment: 1,826 . . . . (516) 887-6405

Housing: Homeownership rate: 94.1% (2005); Median home value: $404,022 (2005); Median rent: $1,050 per month (2000); Median age of housing: 55 years (2000).

Transportation: Commute to work: 78.7% car, 17.1% public transportation, 1.2% walk, 2.5% work from home (2000); Travel time to work: 19.6% less than 15 minutes, 27.6% 15 to 30 minutes, 22.0% 30 to 45 minutes, 11.0% 45 to 60 minutes, 19.8% 60 minutes or more (2000)

MALVERNE PARK OAKS
(CDP). Covers a land area of 0.117 square miles and a water area of 0 square miles. Located at 40.68° N. Lat.; 73.66° W. Long.

Population: 488 (1990); 470 (2000); 496 (2005); 521 (2010 projected); **Race:** 86.1% White, 6.0% Black, 5.6% Asian, 10.7% Hispanic of any race (2005); **Density:** 4,223.5 persons per square mile (2005); Average household size: 2.68 (2005); Median age: 45.0 (2005); Males per 100 females: 92.2 (2005); Marriage status: 14.7% never married, 78.7% now married, 4.6% widowed, 2.0% divorced (2000); Foreign born: 14.1% (2000); Ancestry (includes multiple ancestries): 52.0% Italian, 18.5% Irish, 12.9% Other groups, 12.9% English, 8.8% German (2000).
Economy: Employment by occupation: 22.7% management, 24.0% professional, 7.0% services, 36.0% sales, 0.0% farming, 6.2% construction, 4.1% production (2000).
Income: Per capita income: $41,850 (2005); Median household income: $96,458 (2005); Average household income: $112,203 (2005); Percent of households with income of $100,000 or more: 45.4% (2005); Poverty rate: 0.0% (2000).
Education: Percent of population age 25 and over with: High school diploma (including GED) or higher: 81.5% (2005); Bachelor's degree or higher: 42.9% (2005); Master's degree or higher: 20.2% (2005).
Housing: Homeownership rate: 96.8% (2005); Median home value: $450,000 (2005); Median rent: $n/a per month (2000); Median age of housing: 52 years (2000).
Transportation: Commute to work: 79.3% car, 12.8% public transportation, 0.0% walk, 7.9% work from home (2000); Travel time to work: 12.1% less than 15 minutes, 27.8% 15 to 30 minutes, 34.5% 30 to 45 minutes, 3.1% 45 to 60 minutes, 22.4% 60 minutes or more (2000)

MANHASSET (CDP).
Covers a land area of 2.385 square miles and a water area of 0.029 square miles. Located at 40.79° N. Lat.; 73.69° W. Long. Elevation is 100 feet.
Population: 7,718 (1990); 8,362 (2000); 8,464 (2005); 8,541 (2010 projected); **Race:** 74.1% White, 12.3% Black, 9.1% Asian, 9.1% Hispanic of any race (2005); **Density:** 3,548.5 persons per square mile (2005); Average household size: 2.98 (2005); Median age: 42.6 (2005); Males per 100 females: 88.8 (2005); Marriage status: 23.9% never married, 61.2% now married, 8.9% widowed, 6.1% divorced (2000); Foreign born: 19.4% (2000); Ancestry (includes multiple ancestries): 24.5% Other groups, 24.5% Italian, 18.2% Irish, 11.6% German, 4.9% Polish (2000).
Economy: In estates area. Some light manufacturing: electrical and electronic goods, consumer goods, textiles. Retailing center for area nicknamed "Miracle Mile." Employment by occupation: 21.4% management, 30.5% professional, 13.1% services, 27.1% sales, 0.1% farming, 3.9% construction, 4.0% production (2000).
Income: Per capita income: $48,599 (2005); Median household income: $101,496 (2005); Average household income: $143,003 (2005); Percent of households with income of $100,000 or more: 50.5% (2005); Poverty rate: 5.7% (2000).
Education: Percent of population age 25 and over with: High school diploma (including GED) or higher: 88.3% (2005); Bachelor's degree or higher: 51.0% (2005); Master's degree or higher: 26.5% (2005).
School District(s)
Manhasset Union Free School District (KG-12)
    2003-04 Enrollment: 2,700 . . . . (516) 627-4400
Housing: Homeownership rate: 77.2% (2005); Median home value: $852,253 (2005); Median rent: $731 per month (2000); Median age of housing: 58 years (2000).
Hospitals: North Shore University Hospital (731 beds)
Transportation: Commute to work: 61.8% car, 25.9% public transportation, 7.8% walk, 4.3% work from home (2000); Travel time to work: 26.3% less than 15 minutes, 25.9% 15 to 30 minutes, 15.2% 30 to 45 minutes, 10.3% 45 to 60 minutes, 22.3% 60 minutes or more (2000)
Additional Information Contacts
Manhasset Chamber of Commerce . . . . (516) 627-1098
  http://www.manhasset.org/chamber/

MANHASSET HILLS (CDP).
Covers a land area of 0.593 square miles and a water area of 0 square miles. Located at 40.75° N. Lat.; 73.68° W. Long.
Population: 3,722 (1990); 3,661 (2000); 3,482 (2005); 3,296 (2010 projected); **Race:** 61.9% White, 0.5% Black, 35.2% Asian, 4.5% Hispanic of any race (2005); **Density:** 5,873.2 persons per square mile (2005); Average household size: 2.97 (2005); Median age: 46.5 (2005); Males per 100 females: 92.1 (2005); Marriage status: 17.4% never married, 75.0% now married, 5.7% widowed, 1.9% divorced (2000); Foreign born: 26.8% (2000); Ancestry (includes multiple ancestries): 34.7% Other groups, 17.8% Italian, 8.1% German, 7.5% Irish, 6.5% United States or American (2000).
Economy: Employment by occupation: 17.5% management, 38.8% professional, 4.1% services, 32.1% sales, 0.0% farming, 4.9% construction, 2.5% production (2000).
Income: Per capita income: $50,072 (2005); Median household income: $114,516 (2005); Average household income: $148,763 (2005); Percent of households with income of $100,000 or more: 56.9% (2005); Poverty rate: 2.8% (2000).
Education: Percent of population age 25 and over with: High school diploma (including GED) or higher: 93.3% (2005); Bachelor's degree or higher: 56.6% (2005); Master's degree or higher: 26.6% (2005).
Housing: Homeownership rate: 98.4% (2005); Median home value: $715,956 (2005); Median rent: $2,000+ per month (2000); Median age of housing: 38 years (2000).
Transportation: Commute to work: 86.3% car, 11.0% public transportation, 0.4% walk, 2.2% work from home (2000); Travel time to work: 22.8% less than 15 minutes, 30.9% 15 to 30 minutes, 15.1% 30 to 45 minutes, 11.9% 45 to 60 minutes, 19.4% 60 minutes or more (2000)

MANORHAVEN (village).
Covers a land area of 0.470 square miles and a water area of 0.164 square miles. Located at 40.84° N. Lat.; 73.71° W. Long. Elevation is 40 feet.
History: Incorporated 1930.
Population: 5,672 (1990); 6,138 (2000); 6,336 (2005); 6,524 (2010 projected); **Race:** 70.9% White, 1.8% Black, 17.6% Asian, 22.9% Hispanic of any race (2005); **Density:** 13,476.7 persons per square mile (2005); Average household size: 2.55 (2005); Median age: 38.9 (2005); Males per 100 females: 98.4 (2005); Marriage status: 22.7% never married, 61.3% now married, 5.4% widowed, 10.6% divorced (2000); Foreign born: 35.6% (2000); Ancestry (includes multiple ancestries): 33.9% Other groups, 20.1% Italian, 9.1% Irish, 8.3% German, 4.4% Russian (2000).
Economy: In water recreation-oriented area. Single-family building permits issued: 2 (2005); Multi-family building permits issued: 12 (2005); Employment by occupation: 21.1% management, 21.3% professional, 16.7% services, 26.5% sales, 0.0% farming, 4.4% construction, 10.0% production (2000).
Income: Per capita income: $40,258 (2005); Median household income: $69,063 (2005); Average household income: $102,416 (2005); Percent of households with income of $100,000 or more: 35.8% (2005); Poverty rate: 8.9% (2000).
Education: Percent of population age 25 and over with: High school diploma (including GED) or higher: 87.0% (2005); Bachelor's degree or higher: 40.8% (2005); Master's degree or higher: 17.6% (2005).
Housing: Homeownership rate: 39.0% (2005); Median home value: $432,252 (2005); Median rent: $1,381 per month (2000); Median age of housing: 37 years (2000).
Transportation: Commute to work: 75.5% car, 15.9% public transportation, 3.4% walk, 4.3% work from home (2000); Travel time to work: 27.3% less than 15 minutes, 23.2% 15 to 30 minutes, 19.0% 30 to 45 minutes, 7.1% 45 to 60 minutes, 23.4% 60 minutes or more (2000)

MASSAPEQUA (CDP).
Covers a land area of 3.649 square miles and a water area of 0.368 square miles. Located at 40.67° N. Lat.; 73.47° W. Long. Elevation is 26 feet.
History: Named for the Masapequa Indians. It is chiefly residential. Pop. figure also includes Arlyn Oaks, Crown Village, and Nassau Shores.
Population: 22,018 (1990); 22,652 (2000); 22,962 (2005); 23,268 (2010 projected); **Race:** 96.6% White, 0.2% Black, 1.6% Asian, 3.4% Hispanic of any race (2005); **Density:** 6,292.4 persons per square mile (2005); Average household size: 3.03 (2005); Median age: 40.6 (2005); Males per 100 females: 95.6 (2005); Marriage status: 20.7% never married, 68.7% now married, 6.7% widowed, 3.9% divorced (2000); Foreign born: 4.8% (2000); Ancestry (includes multiple ancestries): 39.6% Italian, 28.8% Irish, 20.4% German, 6.4% English, 6.3% Other groups (2000).
Economy: Chiefly residential. Employment by occupation: 18.1% management, 23.0% professional, 13.4% services, 31.0% sales, 0.2% farming, 8.6% construction, 5.8% production (2000).
Income: Per capita income: $38,829 (2005); Median household income: $94,760 (2005); Average household income: $117,170 (2005); Percent of households with income of $100,000 or more: 46.3% (2005); Poverty rate: 2.3% (2000).
Education: Percent of population age 25 and over with: High school diploma (including GED) or higher: 92.8% (2005); Bachelor's degree or higher: 33.8% (2005); Master's degree or higher: 12.5% (2005).

School District(s)
Massapequa Union Free School District (KG-12)
  2003-04 Enrollment: 8,248 . . . . (516) 797-6160
Plainedge Union Free School District (PK-12)
  2003-04 Enrollment: 3,606 . . . . (516) 992-7455
Housing: Homeownership rate: 93.9% (2005); Median home value: $446,446 (2005); Median rent: $983 per month (2000); Median age of housing: 45 years (2000).
Transportation: Commute to work: 81.7% car, 15.2% public transportation, 0.4% walk, 2.5% work from home (2000); Travel time to work: 17.3% less than 15 minutes, 28.7% 15 to 30 minutes, 20.3% 30 to 45 minutes, 9.3% 45 to 60 minutes, 24.4% 60 minutes or more (2000)
Additional Information Contacts
Massapequa Chamber of Commerce . . . . (516) 541-1443
  http://www.massapequachamber.com

MASSAPEQUA PARK (village).
Covers a land area of 2.159 square miles and a water area of 0.045 square miles. Located at 40.68° N. Lat.; 73.44° W. Long. Elevation is 24 feet.
History: Named for the Masapequa Indians. Incorporated 1931.
Population: 18,044 (1990); 17,499 (2000); 17,422 (2005); 17,360 (2010 projected); Race: 96.5% White, 0.4% Black, 1.7% Asian, 4.1% Hispanic of any race (2005); Density: 8,068.8 persons per square mile (2005); Average household size: 2.99 (2005); Median age: 40.6 (2005); Males per 100 females: 95.5 (2005); Marriage status: 20.6% never married, 68.2% now married, 7.6% widowed, 3.6% divorced (2000); Foreign born: 5.6% (2000); Ancestry (includes multiple ancestries): 41.0% Italian, 31.2% Irish, 16.8% German, 6.0% Other groups, 4.3% English (2000).
Economy: Single-family building permits issued: 2 (2005); Multi-family building permits issued: 0 (2005); Employment by occupation: 15.7% management, 24.0% professional, 13.7% services, 31.3% sales, 0.0% farming, 7.8% construction, 7.5% production (2000).
Income: Per capita income: $34,944 (2005); Median household income: $90,746 (2005); Average household income: $104,355 (2005); Percent of households with income of $100,000 or more: 43.3% (2005); Poverty rate: 1.4% (2000).
Education: Percent of population age 25 and over with: High school diploma (including GED) or higher: 92.4% (2005); Bachelor's degree or higher: 31.5% (2005); Master's degree or higher: 11.3% (2005).
School District(s)
Massapequa Union Free School District (KG-12)
  2003-04 Enrollment: 8,248 . . . . (516) 797-6160
Housing: Homeownership rate: 96.6% (2005); Median home value: $400,914 (2005); Median rent: $790 per month (2000); Median age of housing: 45 years (2000).
Newspapers: Massapequa Post (General - Circulation 4,700)
Transportation: Commute to work: 80.6% car, 15.1% public transportation, 1.2% walk, 2.8% work from home (2000); Travel time to work: 21.3% less than 15 minutes, 25.5% 15 to 30 minutes, 20.4% 30 to 45 minutes, 8.9% 45 to 60 minutes, 23.9% 60 minutes or more (2000)
Additional Information Contacts
Village of Massapequa Park . . . . (516) 798-0244
  http://www.ci.massapequa-park.ny.us/

MATINECOCK (village).
Covers a land area of 2.649 square miles and a water area of 0.005 square miles. Located at 40.87° N. Lat.; 73.58° W. Long.
Population: 872 (1990); 836 (2000); 851 (2005); 867 (2010 projected); Race: 95.2% White, 0.9% Black, 2.2% Asian, 3.6% Hispanic of any race (2005); Density: 321.2 persons per square mile (2005); Average household size: 2.98 (2005); Median age: 41.2 (2005); Males per 100 females: 96.1 (2005); Marriage status: 18.3% never married, 72.8% now married, 4.2% widowed, 4.8% divorced (2000); Foreign born: 10.7% (2000); Ancestry (includes multiple ancestries): 20.2% English, 18.1% Italian, 16.0% Irish, 13.9% German, 8.3% United States or American (2000).
Economy: In water-oriented recreational area. Oyster Bay National Wildlife Refuge to East. Single-family building permits issued: 1 (2005); Multi-family building permits issued: 0 (2005); Employment by occupation: 33.4% management, 22.6% professional, 8.7% services, 27.1% sales, 0.0% farming, 4.7% construction, 3.4% production (2000).
Income: Per capita income: $78,773 (2005); Median household income: $163,043 (2005); Average household income: $234,292 (2005); Percent of households with income of $100,000 or more: 64.7% (2005); Poverty rate: 4.1% (2000).
Education: Percent of population age 25 and over with: High school diploma (including GED) or higher: 97.0% (2005); Bachelor's degree or higher: 65.7% (2005); Master's degree or higher: 25.5% (2005).
Housing: Homeownership rate: 79.4% (2005); Median home value: $1 million+ (2005); Median rent: $1,113 per month (2000); Median age of housing: 48 years (2000).
Transportation: Commute to work: 79.9% car, 11.5% public transportation, 4.6% walk, 4.0% work from home (2000); Travel time to work: 20.4% less than 15 minutes, 22.6% 15 to 30 minutes, 14.8% 30 to 45 minutes, 7.5% 45 to 60 minutes, 34.6% 60 minutes or more (2000)
Additional Information Contacts
Village of Matinecock . . . . (516) 671-7790
  http://www.matinecockvillage.org/

MERRICK (CDP).
Covers a land area of 4.197 square miles and a water area of 0.997 square miles. Located at 40.65° N. Lat.; 73.55° W. Long. Elevation is 23 feet.
Population: 23,042 (1990); 22,764 (2000); 22,335 (2005); 21,904 (2010 projected); Race: 93.5% White, 0.7% Black, 3.0% Asian, 5.2% Hispanic of any race (2005); Density: 5,321.1 persons per square mile (2005); Average household size: 3.00 (2005); Median age: 40.7 (2005); Males per 100 females: 93.4 (2005); Marriage status: 20.2% never married, 69.5% now married, 5.8% widowed, 4.6% divorced (2000); Foreign born: 7.9% (2000); Ancestry (includes multiple ancestries): 22.0% Italian, 16.6% Irish, 16.3% Other groups, 11.6% German, 11.0% Russian (2000).
Economy: Although chiefly residential, it has some light manufacturing. Employment by occupation: 21.4% management, 29.2% professional, 9.9% services, 27.8% sales, 0.1% farming, 5.6% construction, 5.9% production (2000).
Income: Per capita income: $42,048 (2005); Median household income: $104,200 (2005); Average household income: $126,150 (2005); Percent of households with income of $100,000 or more: 52.2% (2005); Poverty rate: 2.8% (2000).
Education: Percent of population age 25 and over with: High school diploma (including GED) or higher: 94.0% (2005); Bachelor's degree or higher: 47.1% (2005); Master's degree or higher: 22.6% (2005).
School District(s)
Bellmore-Merrick Central High School District (07-12)
  2003-04 Enrollment: 5,832 . . . . (516) 992-1001
Merrick Union Free School District (KG-06)
  2003-04 Enrollment: 1,970 . . . . (516) 992-7240
North Merrick Union Free School District (KG-06)
  2003-04 Enrollment: 1,311 . . . . (516) 292-3694
Housing: Homeownership rate: 94.2% (2005); Median home value: $481,441 (2005); Median rent: $968 per month (2000); Median age of housing: 44 years (2000).
Newspapers: Bellmore Life (General - Circulation 4,062); Freeport/Baldwin Leader (General - Circulation 1,903); Merrick Life (General - Circulation 6,252); Wantagh/Seaford Citizen (General - Circulation 2,850)
Transportation: Commute to work: 75.9% car, 18.3% public transportation, 1.2% walk, 4.3% work from home (2000); Travel time to work: 18.4% less than 15 minutes, 30.7% 15 to 30 minutes, 18.2% 30 to 45 minutes, 8.1% 45 to 60 minutes, 24.5% 60 minutes or more (2000)
Additional Information Contacts
Merrick Chamber of Commerce . . . . (516) 771-1171
  http://www.merrickchamber.com

MILL NECK (village).
Covers a land area of 2.579 square miles and a water area of 0.349 square miles. Located at 40.88° N. Lat.; 73.55° W. Long.
Population: 977 (1990); 825 (2000); 838 (2005); 850 (2010 projected); Race: 88.4% White, 0.2% Black, 7.4% Asian, 7.3% Hispanic of any race (2005); Density: 324.9 persons per square mile (2005); Average household size: 2.83 (2005); Median age: 46.5 (2005); Males per 100 females: 96.7 (2005); Marriage status: 18.8% never married, 70.5% now married, 7.5% widowed, 3.2% divorced (2000); Foreign born: 14.0% (2000); Ancestry (includes multiple ancestries): 20.9% Italian, 16.4% Irish, 14.8% German, 11.9% Other groups, 10.3% English (2000).
Economy: Single-family building permits issued: 5 (2005); Multi-family building permits issued: 0 (2005); Employment by occupation: 27.1% management, 32.3% professional, 4.9% services, 27.1% sales, 0.0% farming, 6.5% construction, 2.2% production (2000).
Income: Per capita income: $75,418 (2005); Median household income: $140,000 (2005); Average household income: $213,514 (2005); Percent of

households with income of $100,000 or more: 64.9% (2005); Poverty rate: 2.9% (2000).
Education: Percent of population age 25 and over with: High school diploma (including GED) or higher: 96.7% (2005); Bachelor's degree or higher: 52.5% (2005); Master's degree or higher: 26.1% (2005).
Housing: Homeownership rate: 86.8% (2005); Median home value: $1 million+ (2005); Median rent: $1,375 per month (2000); Median age of housing: 45 years (2000).
Transportation: Commute to work: 78.4% car, 9.9% public transportation, 2.5% walk, 9.3% work from home (2000); Travel time to work: 21.8% less than 15 minutes, 31.0% 15 to 30 minutes, 14.3% 30 to 45 minutes, 6.8% 45 to 60 minutes, 26.2% 60 minutes or more (2000)

MINEOLA
(village). Covers a land area of 1.861 square miles and a water area of 0 square miles. Located at 40.74° N. Lat.; 73.63° W. Long. Elevation is 107 feet.
History: Named for the Algonquian translation of "pleasant village". Incorporated 1906.
Population: 19,006 (1990); 19,234 (2000); 19,119 (2005); 19,000 (2010 projected); Race: 81.6% White, 1.3% Black, 6.3% Asian, 16.8% Hispanic of any race (2005); Density: 10,275.5 persons per square mile (2005); Average household size: 2.57 (2005); Median age: 40.2 (2005); Males per 100 females: 93.6 (2005); Marriage status: 27.2% never married, 58.2% now married, 7.8% widowed, 6.8% divorced (2000); Foreign born: 27.1% (2000); Ancestry (includes multiple ancestries): 24.0% Italian, 19.5% Irish, 19.3% Other groups, 14.2% German, 10.8% Portuguese (2000).
Economy: Chiefly residential, it is a commercial center, with some light industry. Single-family building permits issued: 5 (2005); Multi-family building permits issued: 0 (2005); Employment by occupation: 14.9% management, 23.5% professional, 14.1% services, 28.0% sales, 0.1% farming, 9.9% construction, 9.5% production (2000).
Income: Per capita income: $32,189 (2005); Median household income: $68,933 (2005); Average household income: $82,657 (2005); Percent of households with income of $100,000 or more: 28.3% (2005); Poverty rate: 4.2% (2000).
Education: Percent of population age 25 and over with: High school diploma (including GED) or higher: 81.9% (2005); Bachelor's degree or higher: 29.9% (2005); Master's degree or higher: 12.7% (2005).

School District(s)
Mineola Union Free School District (PK-12)
    2003-04 Enrollment: 2,903 . . . . (516) 741-5036

Four-year College(s)
New York College of Traditional Chinese Medicine
    Fall 2004 Enrollment: 166 . . . . (516) 739-1545

Housing: Homeownership rate: 63.1% (2005); Median home value: $393,702 (2005); Median rent: $913 per month (2000); Median age of housing: 49 years (2000).
Hospitals: Winthrop University Hospital (591 beds)
Newspapers: Farmingdale Observer (General - Circulation 3,120); Floral Park Dispatch (General - Circulation 1,320); Garden City Life (General - Circulation 2,922); Glen Cove Record Pilot (General - Circulation 5,673); Great Neck Record (General - Circulation 5,793); Hicksville Illustrated News (General - Circulation 5,162); Levittown Tribune (General - Circulation 3,864); Manhasset Press (General - Circulation 4,085); Massapequan Observer (General - Circulation 2,324); Mineola American (General - Circulation 4,007); New Hyde Park Illustrated (General - Circulation 3,345); Oyster Bay Enterprise Pilot (General - Circulation 2,200); Plainview/Old Bethpage Herald (General - Circulation 2,347); Port Washington News (General - Circulation 6,729); Roslyn News (General - Circulation 3,100); Syosset/Jericho Tribune (General - Circulation 3,233); Three Village Times (General - Circulation 2,048); Westbury Times (General - Circulation 3,148)
Transportation: Commute to work: 76.2% car, 15.5% public transportation, 5.2% walk, 2.6% work from home (2000); Travel time to work: 27.8% less than 15 minutes, 27.6% 15 to 30 minutes, 19.7% 30 to 45 minutes, 8.3% 45 to 60 minutes, 16.6% 60 minutes or more (2000)
Additional Information Contacts
Mineola Chamber of Commerce . . . . (516) 294-8822
    http://www.mineolachamber.com

MUNSEY PARK
(village). Covers a land area of 0.519 square miles and a water area of 0 square miles. Located at 40.80° N. Lat.; 73.68° W. Long.
Population: 2,692 (1990); 2,632 (2000); 2,610 (2005); 2,589 (2010 projected); Race: 91.1% White, 0.5% Black, 7.6% Asian, 1.5% Hispanic of any race (2005); Density: 5,031.0 persons per square mile (2005); Average household size: 3.19 (2005); Median age: 40.2 (2005); Males per 100 females: 98.5 (2005); Marriage status: 20.4% never married, 72.7% now married, 3.6% widowed, 3.3% divorced (2000); Foreign born: 11.8% (2000); Ancestry (includes multiple ancestries): 33.2% Irish, 27.7% Italian, 13.6% German, 10.0% Other groups, 9.0% English (2000).
Economy: Single-family building permits issued: 0 (2005); Multi-family building permits issued: 0 (2005); Employment by occupation: 31.7% management, 32.3% professional, 5.6% services, 26.5% sales, 0.0% farming, 2.0% construction, 1.9% production (2000).
Income: Per capita income: $68,206 (2005); Median household income: $176,271 (2005); Average household income: $217,625 (2005); Percent of households with income of $100,000 or more: 77.1% (2005); Poverty rate: 2.3% (2000).
Education: Percent of population age 25 and over with: High school diploma (including GED) or higher: 98.8% (2005); Bachelor's degree or higher: 74.2% (2005); Master's degree or higher: 38.1% (2005).
Housing: Homeownership rate: 97.9% (2005); Median home value: $1 million+ (2005); Median rent: $2,000+ per month (2000); Median age of housing: 59 years (2000).
Transportation: Commute to work: 60.0% car, 33.7% public transportation, 1.0% walk, 5.3% work from home (2000); Travel time to work: 16.7% less than 15 minutes, 21.3% 15 to 30 minutes, 13.7% 30 to 45 minutes, 11.9% 45 to 60 minutes, 36.3% 60 minutes or more (2000)

MUTTONTOWN
(village). Covers a land area of 6.088 square miles and a water area of 0 square miles. Located at 40.82° N. Lat.; 73.52° W. Long.
Population: 3,024 (1990); 3,412 (2000); 3,499 (2005); 3,575 (2010 projected); Race: 73.0% White, 2.7% Black, 21.7% Asian, 2.3% Hispanic of any race (2005); Density: 574.8 persons per square mile (2005); Average household size: 3.33 (2005); Median age: 41.2 (2005); Males per 100 females: 94.9 (2005); Marriage status: 20.2% never married, 73.1% now married, 3.1% widowed, 3.6% divorced (2000); Foreign born: 20.5% (2000); Ancestry (includes multiple ancestries): 28.1% Other groups, 17.7% Italian, 8.4% United States or American, 8.0% Russian, 7.9% German (2000).
Economy: Single-family building permits issued: 13 (2005); Multi-family building permits issued: 0 (2005); Employment by occupation: 28.5% management, 32.8% professional, 7.4% services, 26.8% sales, 0.3% farming, 1.2% construction, 3.1% production (2000).
Income: Per capita income: $83,164 (2005); Median household income: $210,938 (2005); Average household income: $267,001 (2005); Percent of households with income of $100,000 or more: 75.4% (2005); Poverty rate: 3.4% (2000).
Education: Percent of population age 25 and over with: High school diploma (including GED) or higher: 94.1% (2005); Bachelor's degree or higher: 63.0% (2005); Master's degree or higher: 35.6% (2005).
Housing: Homeownership rate: 94.7% (2005); Median home value: $1 million+ (2005); Median rent: $883 per month (2000); Median age of housing: 29 years (2000).
Transportation: Commute to work: 79.6% car, 13.0% public transportation, 2.0% walk, 4.7% work from home (2000); Travel time to work: 14.5% less than 15 minutes, 25.7% 15 to 30 minutes, 17.9% 30 to 45 minutes, 11.9% 45 to 60 minutes, 30.0% 60 minutes or more (2000)

NEW CASSEL
(CDP). Covers a land area of 1.466 square miles and a water area of 0 square miles. Located at 40.76° N. Lat.; 73.56° W. Long.
Population: 10,257 (1990); 13,298 (2000); 13,700 (2005); 14,059 (2010 projected); Race: 33.1% White, 42.9% Black, 1.5% Asian, 48.7% Hispanic of any race (2005); Density: 9,347.1 persons per square mile (2005); Average household size: 4.60 (2005); Median age: 31.6 (2005); Males per 100 females: 99.7 (2005); Marriage status: 40.7% never married, 49.1% now married, 5.5% widowed, 4.7% divorced (2000); Foreign born: 45.3% (2000); Ancestry (includes multiple ancestries): 52.7% Other groups, 9.5% Haitian, 4.4% Jamaican, 3.1% Italian, 2.8% African (2000).
Economy: Employment by occupation: 5.9% management, 11.4% professional, 28.1% services, 23.1% sales, 0.1% farming, 7.1% construction, 24.3% production (2000).
Income: Per capita income: $17,458 (2005); Median household income: $62,837 (2005); Average household income: $80,142 (2005); Percent of households with income of $100,000 or more: 26.1% (2005); Poverty rate: 14.8% (2000).

Education: Percent of population age 25 and over with: High school diploma (including GED) or higher: 54.6% (2005); Bachelor's degree or higher: 10.6% (2005); Master's degree or higher: 3.0% (2005).
Housing: Homeownership rate: 61.7% (2005); Median home value: $274,260 (2005); Median rent: $1,129 per month (2000); Median age of housing: 42 years (2000).
Transportation: Commute to work: 74.7% car, 16.3% public transportation, 4.8% walk, 1.5% work from home (2000); Travel time to work: 23.8% less than 15 minutes, 39.3% 15 to 30 minutes, 18.1% 30 to 45 minutes, 5.7% 45 to 60 minutes, 13.2% 60 minutes or more (2000)

NEW HYDE PARK (village).
Covers a land area of 0.844 square miles and a water area of 0 square miles. Located at 40.73° N. Lat.; 73.68° W. Long. Elevation is 125 feet.
History: Incorporated 1927.
Population: 9,728 (1990); 9,523 (2000); 9,444 (2005); 9,421 (2010 projected); Race: 73.9% White, 0.9% Black, 19.6% Asian, 11.1% Hispanic of any race (2005); Density: 11,188.2 persons per square mile (2005); Average household size: 2.89 (2005); Median age: 41.3 (2005); Males per 100 females: 91.8 (2005); Marriage status: 25.4% never married, 59.6% now married, 9.5% widowed, 5.5% divorced (2000); Foreign born: 21.2% (2000); Ancestry (includes multiple ancestries): 33.7% Italian, 22.4% Other groups, 20.0% Irish, 12.6% German, 9.5% Polish (2000).
Economy: Residential community with some manufacturing and a few farms. Single-family building permits issued: 3 (2005); Multi-family building permits issued: 0 (2005); Employment by occupation: 12.5% management, 25.0% professional, 10.2% services, 31.9% sales, 0.0% farming, 8.4% construction, 12.0% production (2000).
Income: Per capita income: $30,222 (2005); Median household income: $72,206 (2005); Average household income: $87,317 (2005); Percent of households with income of $100,000 or more: 32.5% (2005); Poverty rate: 3.3% (2000).
Education: Percent of population age 25 and over with: High school diploma (including GED) or higher: 80.8% (2005); Bachelor's degree or higher: 27.3% (2005); Master's degree or higher: 9.9% (2005).
School District(s)
Great Neck Union Free School District (PK-12)
    2003-04 Enrollment: 6,113 . . . . (516) 773-1405
Herricks Union Free School District (KG-12)
    2003-04 Enrollment: 3,939 . . . . (516) 248-3105
New Hyde Park-Garden City Park Union Free School District (PK-06)
    2003-04 Enrollment: 1,823 . . . . (516) 352-6257
Sewanhaka Central High School District (07-12)
    2003-04 Enrollment: 8,435 . . . . (516) 488-9800
Housing: Homeownership rate: 82.8% (2005); Median home value: $411,285 (2005); Median rent: $852 per month (2000); Median age of housing: 51 years (2000).
Hospitals: Long Island Jewish Hospital (827 beds); Schneider Children's Hospital (154 beds)
Transportation: Commute to work: 78.0% car, 16.3% public transportation, 3.1% walk, 2.2% work from home (2000); Travel time to work: 21.5% less than 15 minutes, 31.4% 15 to 30 minutes, 21.6% 30 to 45 minutes, 8.7% 45 to 60 minutes, 16.8% 60 minutes or more (2000)
Additional Information Contacts
New Hyde Park Chamber of Commerce . . . . (516) 437-2021
    http://www.nhpchamber.com/
Village of New Hyde Park . . . . (516) 354-0022
    http://www.vnhp.org/

NORTH BELLMORE (CDP).
Covers a land area of 2.609 square miles and a water area of 0 square miles. Located at 40.68° N. Lat.; 73.53° W. Long. Elevation is 52 feet.
Population: 19,713 (1990); 20,079 (2000); 20,219 (2005); 20,385 (2010 projected); Race: 89.3% White, 3.0% Black, 4.4% Asian, 6.1% Hispanic of any race (2005); Density: 7,750.2 persons per square mile (2005); Average household size: 3.04 (2005); Median age: 40.1 (2005); Males per 100 females: 94.8 (2005); Marriage status: 22.8% never married, 64.0% now married, 7.7% widowed, 5.5% divorced (2000); Foreign born: 9.3% (2000); Ancestry (includes multiple ancestries): 32.0% Italian, 23.7% Irish, 15.7% German, 14.2% Other groups, 6.4% Polish (2000).
Economy: Employment by occupation: 17.3% management, 20.4% professional, 13.1% services, 34.0% sales, 0.0% farming, 8.7% construction, 6.7% production (2000).
Income: Per capita income: $32,496 (2005); Median household income: $85,016 (2005); Average household income: $98,147 (2005); Percent of households with income of $100,000 or more: 39.9% (2005); Poverty rate: 4.0% (2000).
Education: Percent of population age 25 and over with: High school diploma (including GED) or higher: 88.0% (2005); Bachelor's degree or higher: 30.6% (2005); Master's degree or higher: 11.6% (2005).
School District(s)
North Bellmore Union Free School District (KG-06)
    2003-04 Enrollment: 2,528 . . . . (516) 992-3000
Housing: Homeownership rate: 89.5% (2005); Median home value: $370,459 (2005); Median rent: $929 per month (2000); Median age of housing: 45 years (2000).
Transportation: Commute to work: 80.3% car, 15.0% public transportation, 1.3% walk, 2.6% work from home (2000); Travel time to work: 18.0% less than 15 minutes, 35.4% 15 to 30 minutes, 18.3% 30 to 45 minutes, 7.9% 45 to 60 minutes, 20.4% 60 minutes or more (2000)

NORTH HEMPSTEAD (town).
Covers a land area of 53.578 square miles and a water area of 15.531 square miles. Located at 40.77° N. Lat.; 73.66° W. Long.
Population: 211,355 (1990); 222,611 (2000); 224,379 (2005); 226,048 (2010 projected); Race: 74.1% White, 6.9% Black, 12.2% Asian, 12.2% Hispanic of any race (2005); Density: 4,187.9 persons per square mile (2005); Average household size: 2.91 (2005); Median age: 41.2 (2005); Males per 100 females: 93.4 (2005); Marriage status: 24.6% never married, 63.0% now married, 7.4% widowed, 5.0% divorced (2000); Foreign born: 24.9% (2000); Ancestry (includes multiple ancestries): 25.2% Other groups, 17.9% Italian, 12.9% Irish, 8.9% German, 5.9% Polish (2000).
Economy: Unemployment rate: 3.8% (2005); Total civilian labor force: 114,315 (2005); Single-family building permits issued: 96 (2005); Multi-family building permits issued: 0 (2005); Employment by occupation: 19.0% management, 29.2% professional, 11.4% services, 28.4% sales, 0.0% farming, 5.3% construction, 6.8% production (2000).
Income: Per capita income: $45,366 (2005); Median household income: $92,179 (2005); Average household income: $131,337 (2005); Percent of households with income of $100,000 or more: 45.9% (2005); Poverty rate: 4.8% (2000).
Taxes: Total city taxes per capita: $486 (2004); City property taxes per capita: $397 (2004).
Education: Percent of population age 25 and over with: High school diploma (including GED) or higher: 86.9% (2005); Bachelor's degree or higher: 45.5% (2005); Master's degree or higher: 22.7% (2005).
Housing: Homeownership rate: 78.4% (2005); Median home value: $561,061 (2005); Median rent: $1,001 per month (2000); Median age of housing: 48 years (2000).
Transportation: Commute to work: 73.5% car, 18.3% public transportation, 3.6% walk, 3.9% work from home (2000); Travel time to work: 22.6% less than 15 minutes, 26.8% 15 to 30 minutes, 18.5% 30 to 45 minutes, 10.0% 45 to 60 minutes, 22.1% 60 minutes or more (2000)
Additional Information Contacts
Town of North Hempstead . . . . (516) 869-6311
    http://www.northhempstead.com/

NORTH HILLS (village).
Covers a land area of 2.788 square miles and a water area of 0 square miles. Located at 40.77° N. Lat.; 73.67° W. Long.
Population: 3,453 (1990); 4,301 (2000); 4,483 (2005); 4,663 (2010 projected); Race: 75.2% White, 1.2% Black, 21.3% Asian, 1.4% Hispanic of any race (2005); Density: 1,607.8 persons per square mile (2005); Average household size: 2.36 (2005); Median age: 54.6 (2005); Males per 100 females: 91.2 (2005); Marriage status: 11.7% never married, 76.2% now married, 7.6% widowed, 4.5% divorced (2000); Foreign born: 20.0% (2000); Ancestry (includes multiple ancestries): 24.7% Other groups, 15.1% United States or American, 11.5% Russian, 10.8% Italian, 9.5% Polish (2000).
Economy: Single-family building permits issued: 1 (2005); Multi-family building permits issued: 0 (2005); Employment by occupation: 28.1% management, 33.7% professional, 3.8% services, 32.3% sales, 0.0% farming, 0.2% construction, 1.9% production (2000).
Income: Per capita income: $98,182 (2005); Median household income: $173,086 (2005); Average household income: $230,472 (2005); Percent of households with income of $100,000 or more: 70.6% (2005); Poverty rate: 6.3% (2000).
Education: Percent of population age 25 and over with: High school diploma (including GED) or higher: 94.0% (2005); Bachelor's degree or higher: 61.3% (2005); Master's degree or higher: 31.1% (2005).

Housing: Homeownership rate: 95.2% (2005); Median home value: $1 million+ (2005); Median rent: $2,000+ per month (2000); Median age of housing: 15 years (2000).
Transportation: Commute to work: 77.8% car, 15.1% public transportation, 0.6% walk, 6.2% work from home (2000); Travel time to work: 11.9% less than 15 minutes, 24.4% 15 to 30 minutes, 18.1% 30 to 45 minutes, 18.3% 45 to 60 minutes, 27.3% 60 minutes or more (2000)

NORTH LYNBROOK (CDP).
Covers a land area of 0.093 square miles and a water area of 0 square miles. Located at 40.66° N. Lat.; 73.67° W. Long.
Population: 689 (1990); 742 (2000); 757 (2005); 770 (2010 projected); Race: 85.1% White, 4.4% Black, 4.2% Asian, 13.2% Hispanic of any race (2005); Density: 8,150.4 persons per square mile (2005); Average household size: 3.33 (2005); Median age: 48.2 (2005); Males per 100 females: 92.6 (2005); Marriage status: 33.1% never married, 51.2% now married, 13.2% widowed, 2.5% divorced (2000); Foreign born: 20.3% (2000); Ancestry (includes multiple ancestries): 43.8% Italian, 30.1% Irish, 13.1% German, 12.1% Other groups, 3.8% United States or American (2000).
Economy: Employment by occupation: 13.5% management, 23.9% professional, 10.4% services, 34.6% sales, 0.0% farming, 12.9% construction, 4.7% production (2000).
Income: Per capita income: $31,012 (2005); Median household income: $86,149 (2005); Average household income: $95,330 (2005); Percent of households with income of $100,000 or more: 41.0% (2005); Poverty rate: 2.9% (2000).
Education: Percent of population age 25 and over with: High school diploma (including GED) or higher: 75.4% (2005); Bachelor's degree or higher: 26.0% (2005); Master's degree or higher: 14.7% (2005).
Housing: Homeownership rate: 91.6% (2005); Median home value: $385,227 (2005); Median rent: $686 per month (2000); Median age of housing: 60+ years (2000).
Transportation: Commute to work: 78.8% car, 19.6% public transportation, 1.6% walk, 0.0% work from home (2000); Travel time to work: 24.4% less than 15 minutes, 29.5% 15 to 30 minutes, 14.1% 30 to 45 minutes, 4.5% 45 to 60 minutes, 27.6% 60 minutes or more (2000)

NORTH MASSAPEQUA (CDP).
Covers a land area of 3.024 square miles and a water area of 0 square miles. Located at 40.70° N. Lat.; 73.46° W. Long. Elevation is 52 feet.
Population: 19,397 (1990); 19,152 (2000); 19,112 (2005); 19,069 (2010 projected); Race: 96.5% White, 0.3% Black, 1.5% Asian, 4.3% Hispanic of any race (2005); Density: 6,319.8 persons per square mile (2005); Average household size: 3.00 (2005); Median age: 40.3 (2005); Males per 100 females: 93.7 (2005); Marriage status: 22.9% never married, 64.3% now married, 7.6% widowed, 5.3% divorced (2000); Foreign born: 5.4% (2000); Ancestry (includes multiple ancestries): 48.9% Italian, 23.5% Irish, 15.3% German, 7.2% Other groups, 6.6% Polish (2000).
Economy: Employment by occupation: 16.2% management, 18.8% professional, 14.5% services, 33.1% sales, 0.1% farming, 8.8% construction, 8.6% production (2000).
Income: Per capita income: $31,826 (2005); Median household income: $80,688 (2005); Average household income: $95,229 (2005); Percent of households with income of $100,000 or more: 37.3% (2005); Poverty rate: 2.9% (2000).
Education: Percent of population age 25 and over with: High school diploma (including GED) or higher: 88.5% (2005); Bachelor's degree or higher: 23.7% (2005); Master's degree or higher: 8.0% (2005).
School District(s)
Farmingdale Union Free School District (KG-12)
    2003-04 Enrollment: 6,472 . . . . (516) 752-6510
Plainedge Union Free School District (PK-12)
    2003-04 Enrollment: 3,606 . . . . (516) 992-7455
Housing: Homeownership rate: 91.6% (2005); Median home value: $386,101 (2005); Median rent: $993 per month (2000); Median age of housing: 44 years (2000).
Transportation: Commute to work: 85.2% car, 11.7% public transportation, 0.6% walk, 2.1% work from home (2000); Travel time to work: 23.7% less than 15 minutes, 31.4% 15 to 30 minutes, 19.7% 30 to 45 minutes, 6.3% 45 to 60 minutes, 18.9% 60 minutes or more (2000)

NORTH MERRICK (CDP).
Covers a land area of 1.770 square miles and a water area of 0.009 square miles. Located at 40.68° N. Lat.; 73.55° W. Long. Elevation is 48 feet.
Population: 12,107 (1990); 11,844 (2000); 11,754 (2005); 11,643 (2010 projected); Race: 91.3% White, 1.5% Black, 4.3% Asian, 4.9% Hispanic of any race (2005); Density: 6,639.1 persons per square mile (2005); Average household size: 2.94 (2005); Median age: 40.7 (2005); Males per 100 females: 95.6 (2005); Marriage status: 21.4% never married, 64.3% now married, 8.1% widowed, 6.2% divorced (2000); Foreign born: 7.9% (2000); Ancestry (includes multiple ancestries): 34.5% Italian, 25.2% Irish, 18.8% German, 11.4% Other groups, 7.4% Polish (2000).
Economy: Employment by occupation: 16.9% management, 24.6% professional, 11.5% services, 33.1% sales, 0.0% farming, 8.6% construction, 5.3% production (2000).
Income: Per capita income: $36,986 (2005); Median household income: $92,702 (2005); Average household income: $108,609 (2005); Percent of households with income of $100,000 or more: 44.3% (2005); Poverty rate: 3.5% (2000).
Education: Percent of population age 25 and over with: High school diploma (including GED) or higher: 92.8% (2005); Bachelor's degree or higher: 33.5% (2005); Master's degree or higher: 12.7% (2005).
School District(s)
North Bellmore Union Free School District (KG-06)
    2003-04 Enrollment: 2,528 . . . . (516) 992-3000
North Merrick Union Free School District (KG-06)
    2003-04 Enrollment: 1,311 . . . . (516) 292-3694
Housing: Homeownership rate: 93.1% (2005); Median home value: $395,055 (2005); Median rent: $1,040 per month (2000); Median age of housing: 47 years (2000).
Transportation: Commute to work: 80.6% car, 13.3% public transportation, 2.1% walk, 3.6% work from home (2000); Travel time to work: 19.8% less than 15 minutes, 32.8% 15 to 30 minutes, 18.4% 30 to 45 minutes, 8.0% 45 to 60 minutes, 21.0% 60 minutes or more (2000)

NORTH NEW HYDE PARK (CDP).
Covers a land area of 1.978 square miles and a water area of 0 square miles. Located at 40.74° N. Lat.; 73.68° W. Long. Elevation is 101 feet.
Population: 14,475 (1990); 14,542 (2000); 14,767 (2005); 14,997 (2010 projected); Race: 75.1% White, 0.5% Black, 21.0% Asian, 6.3% Hispanic of any race (2005); Density: 7,463.8 persons per square mile (2005); Average household size: 2.91 (2005); Median age: 44.3 (2005); Males per 100 females: 91.0 (2005); Marriage status: 22.6% never married, 64.3% now married, 9.0% widowed, 4.2% divorced (2000); Foreign born: 21.3% (2000); Ancestry (includes multiple ancestries): 28.0% Italian, 20.7% Irish, 20.3% Other groups, 12.3% German, 5.2% Polish (2000).
Economy: Employment by occupation: 17.5% management, 26.7% professional, 10.9% services, 29.4% sales, 0.0% farming, 8.0% construction, 7.6% production (2000).
Income: Per capita income: $37,431 (2005); Median household income: $83,607 (2005); Average household income: $108,338 (2005); Percent of households with income of $100,000 or more: 40.0% (2005); Poverty rate: 2.7% (2000).
Education: Percent of population age 25 and over with: High school diploma (including GED) or higher: 87.5% (2005); Bachelor's degree or higher: 34.0% (2005); Master's degree or higher: 16.4% (2005).
Housing: Homeownership rate: 93.7% (2005); Median home value: $441,346 (2005); Median rent: $994 per month (2000); Median age of housing: 53 years (2000).
Transportation: Commute to work: 81.0% car, 14.7% public transportation, 1.6% walk, 2.5% work from home (2000); Travel time to work: 20.1% less than 15 minutes, 29.7% 15 to 30 minutes, 21.2% 30 to 45 minutes, 8.5% 45 to 60 minutes, 20.5% 60 minutes or more (2000)

NORTH VALLEY STREAM (CDP).
Covers a land area of 1.883 square miles and a water area of 0.003 square miles. Located at 40.68° N. Lat.; 73.70° W. Long. Elevation is 40 feet.
Population: 14,574 (1990); 15,789 (2000); 15,456 (2005); 15,112 (2010 projected); Race: 31.6% White, 48.5% Black, 9.8% Asian, 12.0% Hispanic of any race (2005); Density: 8,206.1 persons per square mile (2005); Average household size: 3.33 (2005); Median age: 38.5 (2005); Males per 100 females: 87.6 (2005); Marriage status: 28.2% never married, 57.8% now married, 8.0% widowed, 6.0% divorced (2000); Foreign born: 34.3% (2000); Ancestry (includes multiple ancestries): 28.2% Other groups, 16.9% Italian, 11.3% Haitian, 8.6% Irish, 8.4% Jamaican (2000).
Economy: Employment by occupation: 15.5% management, 26.2% professional, 12.6% services, 29.3% sales, 0.0% farming, 6.9% construction, 9.5% production (2000).

Income: Per capita income: $27,105 (2005); Median household income: $80,734 (2005); Average household income: $90,107 (2005); Percent of households with income of $100,000 or more: 34.9% (2005); Poverty rate: 3.7% (2000).
Education: Percent of population age 25 and over with: High school diploma (including GED) or higher: 85.6% (2005); Bachelor's degree or higher: 28.0% (2005); Master's degree or higher: 10.6% (2005).
Housing: Homeownership rate: 89.6% (2005); Median home value: $339,545 (2005); Median rent: $923 per month (2000); Median age of housing: 48 years (2000).
Transportation: Commute to work: 76.4% car, 21.3% public transportation, 0.8% walk, 0.8% work from home (2000); Travel time to work: 10.8% less than 15 minutes, 25.2% 15 to 30 minutes, 24.3% 30 to 45 minutes, 10.8% 45 to 60 minutes, 28.8% 60 minutes or more (2000)

NORTH WANTAGH (CDP).
Covers a land area of 1.844 square miles and a water area of 0.006 square miles. Located at 40.69° N. Lat.; 73.50° W. Long.
Population: 12,261 (1990); 12,156 (2000); 12,425 (2005); 12,691 (2010 projected); Race: 94.6% White, 0.7% Black, 2.3% Asian, 6.2% Hispanic of any race (2005); Density: 6,737.8 persons per square mile (2005); Average household size: 2.78 (2005); Median age: 41.3 (2005); Males per 100 females: 92.2 (2005); Marriage status: 21.3% never married, 65.7% now married, 7.6% widowed, 5.4% divorced (2000); Foreign born: 7.1% (2000); Ancestry (includes multiple ancestries): 34.6% Italian, 27.9% Irish, 18.6% German, 11.8% Other groups, 6.7% Russian (2000).
Economy: Employment by occupation: 17.0% management, 25.0% professional, 12.8% services, 31.1% sales, 0.0% farming, 8.0% construction, 6.1% production (2000).
Income: Per capita income: $35,193 (2005); Median household income: $79,315 (2005); Average household income: $97,605 (2005); Percent of households with income of $100,000 or more: 34.5% (2005); Poverty rate: 2.9% (2000).
Education: Percent of population age 25 and over with: High school diploma (including GED) or higher: 93.3% (2005); Bachelor's degree or higher: 33.7% (2005); Master's degree or higher: 13.1% (2005).
Housing: Homeownership rate: 91.4% (2005); Median home value: $366,436 (2005); Median rent: $723 per month (2000); Median age of housing: 45 years (2000).
Transportation: Commute to work: 83.5% car, 12.0% public transportation, 1.1% walk, 3.0% work from home (2000); Travel time to work: 18.0% less than 15 minutes, 37.7% 15 to 30 minutes, 19.6% 30 to 45 minutes, 5.8% 45 to 60 minutes, 18.9% 60 minutes or more (2000)

OCEANSIDE (CDP).
Covers a land area of 5.018 square miles and a water area of 0.404 square miles. Located at 40.63° N. Lat.; 73.63° W. Long. Elevation is 10 feet.
Population: 32,423 (1990); 32,733 (2000); 33,500 (2005); 34,218 (2010 projected); Race: 93.2% White, 0.8% Black, 2.4% Asian, 7.9% Hispanic of any race (2005); Density: 6,676.4 persons per square mile (2005); Average household size: 2.90 (2005); Median age: 41.8 (2005); Males per 100 females: 94.1 (2005); Marriage status: 22.0% never married, 66.1% now married, 7.3% widowed, 4.7% divorced (2000); Foreign born: 10.6% (2000); Ancestry (includes multiple ancestries): 29.0% Italian, 17.9% Irish, 16.6% Other groups, 13.2% German, 7.4% Russian (2000).
Economy: Employment by occupation: 16.7% management, 26.1% professional, 12.0% services, 30.7% sales, 0.1% farming, 8.3% construction, 6.1% production (2000).
Income: Per capita income: $35,179 (2005); Median household income: $86,600 (2005); Average household income: $101,946 (2005); Percent of households with income of $100,000 or more: 41.9% (2005); Poverty rate: 3.5% (2000).
Education: Percent of population age 25 and over with: High school diploma (including GED) or higher: 90.2% (2005); Bachelor's degree or higher: 36.3% (2005); Master's degree or higher: 17.8% (2005).
School District(s)
Oceanside Union Free School District (KG-12)
    2003-04 Enrollment: 6,369 . . . . (516) 678-1215
Housing: Homeownership rate: 88.5% (2005); Median home value: $396,487 (2005); Median rent: $871 per month (2000); Median age of housing: 44 years (2000).
Hospitals: South Nassau Communities Hospital (435 beds)
Transportation: Commute to work: 78.1% car, 16.2% public transportation, 1.6% walk, 3.5% work from home (2000); Travel time to work: 20.1% less than 15 minutes, 24.2% 15 to 30 minutes, 20.0% 30 to 45 minutes, 11.1% 45 to 60 minutes, 24.5% 60 minutes or more (2000)
Additional Information Contacts
Oceanside Chamber of Commerce . . . . (516) 763-9177
    http://www.oceansidechamber.org

OLD BETHPAGE (CDP).
Covers a land area of 4.118 square miles and a water area of 0.003 square miles. Located at 40.76° N. Lat.; 73.45° W. Long.
Population: 5,610 (1990); 5,400 (2000); 5,529 (2005); 5,654 (2010 projected); Race: 93.1% White, 1.5% Black, 3.8% Asian, 2.6% Hispanic of any race (2005); Density: 1,342.7 persons per square mile (2005); Average household size: 2.92 (2005); Median age: 43.1 (2005); Males per 100 females: 92.4 (2005); Marriage status: 20.7% never married, 67.8% now married, 7.1% widowed, 4.3% divorced (2000); Foreign born: 8.5% (2000); Ancestry (includes multiple ancestries): 25.8% Italian, 17.4% Other groups, 11.7% German, 10.3% Irish, 9.2% Polish (2000).
Economy: Employment by occupation: 25.3% management, 27.0% professional, 7.5% services, 33.1% sales, 0.0% farming, 3.9% construction, 3.3% production (2000).
Income: Per capita income: $43,177 (2005); Median household income: $101,659 (2005); Average household income: $125,337 (2005); Percent of households with income of $100,000 or more: 50.8% (2005); Poverty rate: 4.3% (2000).
Education: Percent of population age 25 and over with: High school diploma (including GED) or higher: 93.0% (2005); Bachelor's degree or higher: 50.1% (2005); Master's degree or higher: 21.0% (2005).
School District(s)
Plainview-Old Bethpage Central School District (KG-12)
    2003-04 Enrollment: 4,970 . . . . (516) 937-6301
Housing: Homeownership rate: 90.6% (2005); Median home value: $486,194 (2005); Median rent: $319 per month (2000); Median age of housing: 40 years (2000).
Transportation: Commute to work: 81.8% car, 14.4% public transportation, 0.6% walk, 3.2% work from home (2000); Travel time to work: 22.9% less than 15 minutes, 29.1% 15 to 30 minutes, 14.4% 30 to 45 minutes, 9.6% 45 to 60 minutes, 23.9% 60 minutes or more (2000)

OLD BROOKVILLE (village).
Covers a land area of 3.975 square miles and a water area of 0.001 square miles. Located at 40.82° N. Lat.; 73.60° W. Long. Elevation is 92 feet.
Population: 1,823 (1990); 2,167 (2000); 2,273 (2005); 2,376 (2010 projected); Race: 86.2% White, 1.8% Black, 9.5% Asian, 1.8% Hispanic of any race (2005); Density: 571.8 persons per square mile (2005); Average household size: 2.99 (2005); Median age: 43.9 (2005); Males per 100 females: 97.1 (2005); Marriage status: 20.5% never married, 69.4% now married, 5.6% widowed, 4.5% divorced (2000); Foreign born: 14.6% (2000); Ancestry (includes multiple ancestries): 23.4% Italian, 14.6% Other groups, 12.6% Irish, 11.8% German, 8.9% English (2000).
Economy: Single-family building permits issued: 7 (2005); Multi-family building permits issued: 0 (2005); Employment by occupation: 28.9% management, 32.3% professional, 7.2% services, 24.0% sales, 0.0% farming, 2.8% construction, 4.8% production (2000).
Income: Per capita income: $76,171 (2005); Median household income: $152,049 (2005); Average household income: $227,513 (2005); Percent of households with income of $100,000 or more: 64.4% (2005); Poverty rate: 2.4% (2000).
Education: Percent of population age 25 and over with: High school diploma (including GED) or higher: 95.4% (2005); Bachelor's degree or higher: 59.3% (2005); Master's degree or higher: 28.3% (2005).
Housing: Homeownership rate: 89.5% (2005); Median home value: $1 million+ (2005); Median rent: $897 per month (2000); Median age of housing: 36 years (2000).
Safety: Violent crime rate: 4.5 per 10,000 population; Property crime rate: 262.9 per 10,000 population (2004).
Transportation: Commute to work: 82.3% car, 8.7% public transportation, 2.2% walk, 6.2% work from home (2000); Travel time to work: 13.5% less than 15 minutes, 29.6% 15 to 30 minutes, 22.0% 30 to 45 minutes, 10.8% 45 to 60 minutes, 24.0% 60 minutes or more (2000)

OLD WESTBURY (village).
Covers a land area of 8.561 square miles and a water area of 0 square miles. Located at 40.78° N. Lat.; 73.59° W. Long.
Population: 3,257 (1990); 4,228 (2000); 4,464 (2005); 4,667 (2010 projected); Race: 56.3% White, 22.0% Black, 13.9% Asian, 9.3% Hispanic

of any race (2005); Density: 521.4 persons per square mile (2005); Average household size: 4.06 (2005); Median age: 34.1 (2005); Males per 100 females: 85.9 (2005); Marriage status: 31.7% never married, 63.0% now married, 2.9% widowed, 2.4% divorced (2000); Foreign born: 19.5% (2000); Ancestry (includes multiple ancestries): 29.6% Other groups, 12.9% Italian, 8.0% United States or American, 7.8% Russian, 5.8% Polish (2000).
Economy: Single-family building permits issued: 7 (2005); Multi-family building permits issued: 0 (2005); Employment by occupation: 27.0% management, 33.3% professional, 8.3% services, 26.8% sales, 0.0% farming, 0.6% construction, 4.0% production (2000).
Income: Per capita income: $54,009 (2005); Median household income: $157,854 (2005); Average household income: $213,510 (2005); Percent of households with income of $100,000 or more: 70.2% (2005); Poverty rate: 3.5% (2000).
Education: Percent of population age 25 and over with: High school diploma (including GED) or higher: 94.0% (2005); Bachelor's degree or higher: 63.9% (2005); Master's degree or higher: 33.7% (2005).

School District(s)
East Williston Union Free School District (KG-12)
   2003-04 Enrollment: 1,812 . . . . (516) 333-3758
Westbury Union Free School District (PK-12)
   2003-04 Enrollment: 4,036 . . . . (516) 876-5016

Four-year College(s)
New York Institute of Technology-Old Westbury
   Fall 2004 Enrollment: 8,347. . . . . (516) 686-7516
   2005-06 Tuition: In-state $19,236; Out-of-state $19,236
SUNY College at Old Westbury (Public)
   Fall 2004 Enrollment: 3,359. . . . . (516) 876-3000
   2005-06 Tuition: In-state $4,350; Out-of-state $10,300

Housing: Homeownership rate: 91.1% (2005); Median home value: $1 million+ (2005); Median rent: $1,642 per month (2000); Median age of housing: 34 years (2000).
Safety: Violent crime rate: 9.1 per 10,000 population; Property crime rate: 127.5 per 10,000 population (2004).
Transportation: Commute to work: 74.0% car, 15.7% public transportation, 4.7% walk, 5.6% work from home (2000); Travel time to work: 17.4% less than 15 minutes, 27.8% 15 to 30 minutes, 18.3% 30 to 45 minutes, 8.8% 45 to 60 minutes, 27.8% 60 minutes or more (2000)

OYSTER BAY (town).
Covers a land area of 104.370 square miles and a water area of 65.127 square miles. Located at 40.75° N. Lat.; 73.50° W. Long. Elevation is 8 feet.
History: Nearby is Theodore Roosevelt's estate, Sagamore Hill, which was made a national shrine in 1953 and a National Historic Site in 1963. Also of interest in Oyster Bay are several 18th-century houses, the Theodore Roosevelt Memorial Bird Sanctuary, a 12-acre wildlife sanctuary owned by the National Audubon Society, which adjoins Roosevelt's grave and the Oyster Bay National Wildlife Refuge. Settled 1653.
Population: 293,200 (1990); 293,925 (2000); 297,388 (2005); 300,604 (2010 projected); Race: 87.8% White, 2.0% Black, 6.7% Asian, 6.6% Hispanic of any race (2005); Density: 2,849.4 persons per square mile (2005); Average household size: 2.94 (2005); Median age: 41.3 (2005); Males per 100 females: 94.7 (2005); Marriage status: 22.7% never married, 65.1% now married, 7.4% widowed, 4.8% divorced (2000); Foreign born: 12.1% (2000); Ancestry (includes multiple ancestries): 29.9% Italian, 20.6% Irish, 15.0% Other groups, 14.5% German, 6.7% Polish (2000).
Economy: In shore recreation area. Unemployment rate: 3.8% (2005); Total civilian labor force: 156,452 (2005); Single-family building permits issued: 166 (2005); Multi-family building permits issued: 4 (2005); Employment by occupation: 18.6% management, 24.7% professional, 11.9% services, 30.9% sales, 0.1% farming, 7.1% construction, 6.7% production (2000).
Income: Per capita income: $41,176 (2005); Median household income: $90,957 (2005); Average household income: $119,843 (2005); Percent of households with income of $100,000 or more: 44.5% (2005); Poverty rate: 3.3% (2000).
Taxes: Total city taxes per capita: $503 (2004); City property taxes per capita: $422 (2004).
Education: Percent of population age 25 and over with: High school diploma (including GED) or higher: 90.0% (2005); Bachelor's degree or higher: 38.0% (2005); Master's degree or higher: 16.0% (2005).

School District(s)
Oyster Bay-East Norwich Central School District (PK-12)
   2003-04 Enrollment: 1,569 . . . . (516) 624-6504

Housing: Homeownership rate: 87.1% (2005); Median home value: $439,051 (2005); Median rent: $973 per month (2000); Median age of housing: 44 years (2000).
Newspapers: Oyster Bay Guardian (General - Circulation 4,000)
Transportation: Commute to work: 82.1% car, 12.7% public transportation, 1.6% walk, 3.2% work from home (2000); Travel time to work: 22.8% less than 15 minutes, 29.5% 15 to 30 minutes, 18.3% 30 to 45 minutes, 8.1% 45 to 60 minutes, 21.3% 60 minutes or more (2000)
Additional Information Contacts
Oyster Bay Chamber of Commerce. . . . . (516) 922-6464
   http://www.oysterbay.org
Town of Oyster Bay . . . . (516) 624-6350
   http://www.oysterbaytown.com/

OYSTER BAY (CDP).
Covers a land area of 0.537 square miles and a water area of 0.004 square miles. Located at 40.42° N. Lat.; 89.41° W. Long.
Population: 6,687 (1990); 6,826 (2000); 6,758 (2005); 6,691 (2010 projected); Race: 88.4% White, 3.2% Black, 2.5% Asian, 17.2% Hispanic of any race (2005); Density: 12,583.1 persons per square mile (2005); Average household size: 2.41 (2005); Median age: 41.6 (2005); Males per 100 females: 93.5 (2005); Marriage status: 28.3% never married, 55.9% now married, 8.8% widowed, 7.0% divorced (2000); Foreign born: 15.3% (2000); Ancestry (includes multiple ancestries): 26.4% Italian, 20.1% Irish, 17.7% Other groups, 15.7% German, 7.5% Polish (2000).
Economy: Employment by occupation: 18.2% management, 26.0% professional, 13.3% services, 27.9% sales, 0.5% farming, 7.3% construction, 6.8% production (2000).
Income: Per capita income: $41,161 (2005); Median household income: $68,574 (2005); Average household income: $98,734 (2005); Percent of households with income of $100,000 or more: 31.2% (2005); Poverty rate: 7.8% (2000).
Education: Percent of population age 25 and over with: High school diploma (including GED) or higher: 88.1% (2005); Bachelor's degree or higher: 43.1% (2005); Master's degree or higher: 16.7% (2005).
Housing: Homeownership rate: 56.0% (2005); Median home value: $474,910 (2005); Median rent: $983 per month (2000); Median age of housing: 46 years (2000).
Transportation: Commute to work: 79.9% car, 9.0% public transportation, 6.1% walk, 3.3% work from home (2000); Travel time to work: 26.1% less than 15 minutes, 29.8% 15 to 30 minutes, 20.3% 30 to 45 minutes, 6.9% 45 to 60 minutes, 17.0% 60 minutes or more (2000)

OYSTER BAY COVE (village).
Covers a land area of 4.204 square miles and a water area of 0.060 square miles. Located at 40.86° N. Lat.; 73.49° W. Long.
Population: 2,109 (1990); 2,262 (2000); 2,298 (2005); 2,335 (2010 projected); Race: 86.3% White, 2.7% Black, 8.2% Asian, 2.0% Hispanic of any race (2005); Density: 546.7 persons per square mile (2005); Average household size: 3.13 (2005); Median age: 43.3 (2005); Males per 100 females: 94.3 (2005); Marriage status: 18.8% never married, 73.7% now married, 4.3% widowed, 3.1% divorced (2000); Foreign born: 10.9% (2000); Ancestry (includes multiple ancestries): 17.8% Italian, 15.0% Irish, 13.4% Other groups, 12.3% German, 7.6% Russian (2000).
Economy: Single-family building permits issued: 2 (2005); Multi-family building permits issued: 0 (2005); Employment by occupation: 30.7% management, 32.4% professional, 6.4% services, 27.1% sales, 0.0% farming, 1.4% construction, 1.9% production (2000).
Income: Per capita income: $88,202 (2005); Median household income: $224,590 (2005); Average household income: $276,141 (2005); Percent of households with income of $100,000 or more: 74.1% (2005); Poverty rate: 2.6% (2000).
Education: Percent of population age 25 and over with: High school diploma (including GED) or higher: 96.1% (2005); Bachelor's degree or higher: 69.0% (2005); Master's degree or higher: 31.9% (2005).
Housing: Homeownership rate: 93.9% (2005); Median home value: $1 million+ (2005); Median rent: $1,438 per month (2000); Median age of housing: 28 years (2000).
Safety: Violent crime rate: 0.0 per 10,000 population; Property crime rate: 26.4 per 10,000 population (2004).
Transportation: Commute to work: 78.7% car, 11.6% public transportation, 1.0% walk, 7.4% work from home (2000); Travel time to work: 15.4% less than 15 minutes, 31.6% 15 to 30 minutes, 19.3% 30 to 45 minutes, 6.7% 45 to 60 minutes, 27.0% 60 minutes or more (2000)

PLAINEDGE (CDP). Covers a land area of 1.431 square miles and a water area of 0 square miles. Located at 40.72° N. Lat.; 73.47° W. Long.
Population: 8,712 (1990); 9,195 (2000); 9,198 (2005); 9,210 (2010 projected); Race: 92.2% White, 0.8% Black, 3.3% Asian, 6.9% Hispanic of any race (2005); Density: 6,427.9 persons per square mile (2005); Average household size: 3.00 (2005); Median age: 39.7 (2005); Males per 100 females: 93.0 (2005); Marriage status: 23.2% never married, 64.3% now married, 7.7% widowed, 4.8% divorced (2000); Foreign born: 9.8% (2000); Ancestry (includes multiple ancestries): 37.5% Italian, 27.1% Irish, 18.3% German, 11.1% Other groups, 5.9% Polish (2000).
Economy: Employment by occupation: 16.5% management, 18.1% professional, 10.5% services, 34.4% sales, 0.2% farming, 10.7% construction, 9.6% production (2000).
Income: Per capita income: $29,611 (2005); Median household income: $73,140 (2005); Average household income: $88,634 (2005); Percent of households with income of $100,000 or more: 33.5% (2005); Poverty rate: 2.4% (2000).
Education: Percent of population age 25 and over with: High school diploma (including GED) or higher: 86.6% (2005); Bachelor's degree or higher: 23.5% (2005); Master's degree or higher: 7.1% (2005).
Housing: Homeownership rate: 90.6% (2005); Median home value: $358,988 (2005); Median rent: $725 per month (2000); Median age of housing: 45 years (2000).
Transportation: Commute to work: 88.6% car, 9.4% public transportation, 0.8% walk, 0.8% work from home (2000); Travel time to work: 24.7% less than 15 minutes, 36.0% 15 to 30 minutes, 14.9% 30 to 45 minutes, 7.2% 45 to 60 minutes, 17.3% 60 minutes or more (2000)

PLAINVIEW (CDP). Covers a land area of 5.725 square miles and a water area of 0 square miles. Located at 40.78° N. Lat.; 73.47° W. Long. Elevation is 151 feet.
Population: 26,207 (1990); 25,637 (2000); 26,589 (2005); 27,475 (2010 projected); Race: 91.2% White, 0.5% Black, 6.6% Asian, 3.3% Hispanic of any race (2005); Density: 4,644.5 persons per square mile (2005); Average household size: 2.96 (2005); Median age: 42.9 (2005); Males per 100 females: 94.6 (2005); Marriage status: 19.0% never married, 70.0% now married, 6.8% widowed, 4.2% divorced (2000); Foreign born: 12.0% (2000); Ancestry (includes multiple ancestries): 19.2% Other groups, 19.2% Italian, 10.9% Russian, 9.9% Irish, 9.3% Polish (2000).
Economy: Employment by occupation: 21.2% management, 29.6% professional, 8.2% services, 32.0% sales, 0.0% farming, 4.4% construction, 4.6% production (2000).
Income: Per capita income: $43,244 (2005); Median household income: $105,480 (2005); Average household income: $126,292 (2005); Percent of households with income of $100,000 or more: 52.9% (2005); Poverty rate: 3.0% (2000).
Education: Percent of population age 25 and over with: High school diploma (including GED) or higher: 92.2% (2005); Bachelor's degree or higher: 48.5% (2005); Master's degree or higher: 22.1% (2005).
School District(s)
Bethpage Union Free School District (KG-12)
    2003-04 Enrollment: 3,006 . . . . (516) 644-4001
Plainview-Old Bethpage Central School District (KG-12)
    2003-04 Enrollment: 4,970 . . . . (516) 937-6301
Syosset Central School District (KG-12)
    2003-04 Enrollment: 6,623 . . . . (516) 364-5605
Housing: Homeownership rate: 93.7% (2005); Median home value: $488,188 (2005); Median rent: $823 per month (2000); Median age of housing: 43 years (2000).
Hospitals: Plainview Hospital (239 beds)
Newspapers: Levittown Town Crier (General - Circulation 14,250)
Transportation: Commute to work: 81.0% car, 14.4% public transportation, 0.9% walk, 3.1% work from home (2000); Travel time to work: 26.9% less than 15 minutes, 24.9% 15 to 30 minutes, 16.5% 30 to 45 minutes, 8.5% 45 to 60 minutes, 23.3% 60 minutes or more (2000)

PLANDOME (village). Covers a land area of 0.492 square miles and a water area of 0.011 square miles. Located at 40.80° N. Lat.; 73.70° W. Long.
Population: 1,347 (1990); 1,272 (2000); 1,312 (2005); 1,339 (2010 projected); Race: 94.0% White, 0.2% Black, 4.7% Asian, 2.7% Hispanic of any race (2005); Density: 2,666.2 persons per square mile (2005); Average household size: 3.09 (2005); Median age: 42.1 (2005); Males per 100 females: 96.1 (2005); Marriage status: 22.3% never married, 70.9% now married, 4.6% widowed, 2.2% divorced (2000); Foreign born: 9.7% (2000); Ancestry (includes multiple ancestries): 40.3% Irish, 23.9% Italian, 16.6% German, 9.4% English, 7.6% Other groups (2000).
Economy: Single-family building permits issued: 0 (2005); Multi-family building permits issued: 0 (2005); Employment by occupation: 29.0% management, 35.4% professional, 6.5% services, 27.8% sales, 0.0% farming, 1.0% construction, 0.4% production (2000).
Income: Per capita income: $90,695 (2005); Median household income: $229,375 (2005); Average household income: $279,547 (2005); Percent of households with income of $100,000 or more: 76.2% (2005); Poverty rate: 4.5% (2000).
Education: Percent of population age 25 and over with: High school diploma (including GED) or higher: 98.5% (2005); Bachelor's degree or higher: 77.5% (2005); Master's degree or higher: 39.7% (2005).
Housing: Homeownership rate: 96.9% (2005); Median home value: $1 million+ (2005); Median rent: $1,625 per month (2000); Median age of housing: 60+ years (2000).
Transportation: Commute to work: 58.4% car, 32.1% public transportation, 0.6% walk, 8.9% work from home (2000); Travel time to work: 20.1% less than 15 minutes, 16.5% 15 to 30 minutes, 19.4% 30 to 45 minutes, 15.0% 45 to 60 minutes, 29.1% 60 minutes or more (2000)

PLANDOME HEIGHTS (village). Covers a land area of 0.181 square miles and a water area of 0.006 square miles. Located at 40.80° N. Lat.; 73.70° W. Long. Elevation is 90 feet.
Population: 852 (1990); 971 (2000); 949 (2005); 939 (2010 projected); Race: 91.3% White, 0.4% Black, 7.5% Asian, 4.4% Hispanic of any race (2005); Density: 5,229.4 persons per square mile (2005); Average household size: 2.97 (2005); Median age: 40.9 (2005); Males per 100 females: 92.5 (2005); Marriage status: 20.3% never married, 67.5% now married, 8.0% widowed, 4.2% divorced (2000); Foreign born: 12.8% (2000); Ancestry (includes multiple ancestries): 30.5% Italian, 25.3% Irish, 12.8% German, 9.6% Other groups, 7.2% English (2000).
Economy: Single-family building permits issued: 0 (2005); Multi-family building permits issued: 0 (2005); Employment by occupation: 23.2% management, 36.7% professional, 4.1% services, 32.9% sales, 0.0% farming, 2.2% construction, 1.0% production (2000).
Income: Per capita income: $67,674 (2005); Median household income: $141,667 (2005); Average household income: $201,324 (2005); Percent of households with income of $100,000 or more: 66.5% (2005); Poverty rate: 1.5% (2000).
Education: Percent of population age 25 and over with: High school diploma (including GED) or higher: 97.5% (2005); Bachelor's degree or higher: 71.0% (2005); Master's degree or higher: 38.8% (2005).
Housing: Homeownership rate: 95.6% (2005); Median home value: $985,227 (2005); Median rent: $2,000+ per month (2000); Median age of housing: 57 years (2000).
Transportation: Commute to work: 67.2% car, 26.2% public transportation, 4.6% walk, 2.0% work from home (2000); Travel time to work: 26.7% less than 15 minutes, 13.7% 15 to 30 minutes, 22.7% 30 to 45 minutes, 11.5% 45 to 60 minutes, 25.4% 60 minutes or more (2000)

PLANDOME MANOR (village). Covers a land area of 0.512 square miles and a water area of 0.082 square miles. Located at 40.81° N. Lat.; 73.69° W. Long.
Population: 790 (1990); 838 (2000); 821 (2005); 812 (2010 projected); Race: 89.8% White, 0.6% Black, 6.8% Asian, 2.8% Hispanic of any race (2005); Density: 1,604.4 persons per square mile (2005); Average household size: 2.96 (2005); Median age: 43.2 (2005); Males per 100 females: 92.3 (2005); Marriage status: 16.8% never married, 75.0% now married, 6.0% widowed, 2.2% divorced (2000); Foreign born: 14.8% (2000); Ancestry (includes multiple ancestries): 23.0% Irish, 19.8% Italian, 12.9% Other groups, 9.9% German, 9.4% Greek (2000).
Economy: Single-family building permits issued: 0 (2005); Multi-family building permits issued: 0 (2005); Employment by occupation: 27.7% management, 37.1% professional, 5.1% services, 27.2% sales, 0.0% farming, 1.5% construction, 1.5% production (2000).
Income: Per capita income: $84,790 (2005); Median household income: $199,219 (2005); Average household income: $251,309 (2005); Percent of households with income of $100,000 or more: 77.6% (2005); Poverty rate: 2.2% (2000).
Education: Percent of population age 25 and over with: High school diploma (including GED) or higher: 95.5% (2005); Bachelor's degree or higher: 68.4% (2005); Master's degree or higher: 36.1% (2005).

Housing: Homeownership rate: 94.2% (2005); Median home value: $1 million+ (2005); Median rent: $2,000+ per month (2000); Median age of housing: 47 years (2000).
Transportation: Commute to work: 59.6% car, 33.4% public transportation, 0.5% walk, 6.4% work from home (2000); Travel time to work: 17.9% less than 15 minutes, 16.5% 15 to 30 minutes, 22.0% 30 to 45 minutes, 16.5% 45 to 60 minutes, 27.2% 60 minutes or more (2000)

POINT LOOKOUT (CDP).
Covers a land area of 0.199 square miles and a water area of 0 square miles. Located at 40.59° N. Lat.; 73.58° W. Long.
Population: 1,510 (1990); 1,472 (2000); 1,343 (2005); 1,255 (2010 projected); Race: 96.2% White, 0.7% Black, 0.7% Asian, 2.8% Hispanic of any race (2005); Density: 6,733.0 persons per square mile (2005); Average household size: 2.37 (2005); Median age: 45.2 (2005); Males per 100 females: 95.5 (2005); Marriage status: 25.7% never married, 59.4% now married, 11.2% widowed, 3.6% divorced (2000); Foreign born: 6.2% (2000); Ancestry (includes multiple ancestries): 46.4% Irish, 24.3% Italian, 16.8% German, 9.7% English, 4.1% Polish (2000).
Economy: Employment by occupation: 21.6% management, 26.0% professional, 13.3% services, 23.9% sales, 0.0% farming, 8.8% construction, 6.3% production (2000).
Income: Per capita income: $51,500 (2005); Median household income: $78,596 (2005); Average household income: $121,984 (2005); Percent of households with income of $100,000 or more: 39.0% (2005); Poverty rate: 12.6% (2000).
Education: Percent of population age 25 and over with: High school diploma (including GED) or higher: 95.6% (2005); Bachelor's degree or higher: 49.5% (2005); Master's degree or higher: 22.6% (2005).
Housing: Homeownership rate: 80.2% (2005); Median home value: $640,441 (2005); Median rent: $1,040 per month (2000); Median age of housing: 56 years (2000).
Transportation: Commute to work: 70.8% car, 13.1% public transportation, 12.2% walk, 1.1% work from home (2000); Travel time to work: 25.7% less than 15 minutes, 23.2% 15 to 30 minutes, 16.7% 30 to 45 minutes, 12.6% 45 to 60 minutes, 21.8% 60 minutes or more (2000)

PORT WASHINGTON (CDP).
Covers a land area of 4.210 square miles and a water area of 1.421 square miles. Located at 40.82° N. Lat.; 73.68° W. Long. Elevation is 70 feet.
History: Named for George Washington, first President of the U.S. Initially important for extensive sand pits; center for seaplanes 1900-1920; early College of Long Island, 1920-1930s.
Population: 15,235 (1990); 15,215 (2000); 15,245 (2005); 15,120 (2010 projected); Race: 84.0% White, 3.4% Black, 6.9% Asian, 13.0% Hispanic of any race (2005); Density: 3,620.8 persons per square mile (2005); Average household size: 2.76 (2005); Median age: 41.4 (2005); Males per 100 females: 91.6 (2005); Marriage status: 21.4% never married, 65.6% now married, 7.4% widowed, 5.7% divorced (2000); Foreign born: 21.3% (2000); Ancestry (includes multiple ancestries): 22.7% Other groups, 19.8% Italian, 17.0% Irish, 10.7% German, 7.5% Polish (2000).
Economy: Extensive manufacturing, much of it reflecting its past association with the region's aircraft and aerospace industry, but also including machinery, electronic equipment, building materials. Employment by occupation: 22.7% management, 32.8% professional, 11.9% services, 24.6% sales, 0.1% farming, 3.9% construction, 3.9% production (2000).
Income: Per capita income: $50,573 (2005); Median household income: $99,348 (2005); Average household income: $139,348 (2005); Percent of households with income of $100,000 or more: 49.7% (2005); Poverty rate: 4.7% (2000).
Education: Percent of population age 25 and over with: High school diploma (including GED) or higher: 89.9% (2005); Bachelor's degree or higher: 53.6% (2005); Master's degree or higher: 26.3% (2005).
School District(s)
Port Washington Union Free School District (KG-12)
    2003-04 Enrollment: 4,740 . . . . (516) 767-5005
Housing: Homeownership rate: 74.0% (2005); Median home value: $689,177 (2005); Median rent: $1,087 per month (2000); Median age of housing: 54 years (2000).
Newspapers: Sports Eye (Circulation 7,416)
Transportation: Commute to work: 66.2% car, 24.6% public transportation, 4.4% walk, 4.0% work from home (2000); Travel time to work: 23.3% less than 15 minutes, 21.0% 15 to 30 minutes, 18.0% 30 to 45 minutes, 10.2% 45 to 60 minutes, 27.5% 60 minutes or more (2000)
Additional Information Contacts

Port Washington Chamber of Commerce . . . . (516) 883-6566
http://www.portwashington.com

PORT WASHINGTON NORTH (village).
Covers a land area of 0.480 square miles and a water area of 0.021 square miles. Located at 40.84° N. Lat.; 73.70° W. Long.
Population: 2,736 (1990); 2,700 (2000); 2,601 (2005); 2,531 (2010 projected); Race: 82.2% White, 1.3% Black, 12.8% Asian, 8.1% Hispanic of any race (2005); Density: 5,418.6 persons per square mile (2005); Average household size: 2.49 (2005); Median age: 43.2 (2005); Males per 100 females: 95.1 (2005); Marriage status: 23.7% never married, 64.8% now married, 6.5% widowed, 5.1% divorced (2000); Foreign born: 19.7% (2000); Ancestry (includes multiple ancestries): 26.7% Other groups, 15.2% Italian, 10.7% Russian, 9.5% Polish, 8.4% German (2000).
Economy: Single-family building permits issued: 2 (2005); Multi-family building permits issued: 0 (2005); Employment by occupation: 23.2% management, 36.7% professional, 7.2% services, 26.4% sales, 0.0% farming, 3.2% construction, 3.3% production (2000).
Income: Per capita income: $58,179 (2005); Median household income: $98,291 (2005); Average household income: $144,902 (2005); Percent of households with income of $100,000 or more: 49.1% (2005); Poverty rate: 5.5% (2000).
Education: Percent of population age 25 and over with: High school diploma (including GED) or higher: 93.1% (2005); Bachelor's degree or higher: 59.5% (2005); Master's degree or higher: 27.8% (2005).
Housing: Homeownership rate: 61.2% (2005); Median home value: $742,647 (2005); Median rent: $1,100 per month (2000); Median age of housing: 35 years (2000).
Transportation: Commute to work: 61.2% car, 28.4% public transportation, 3.2% walk, 6.5% work from home (2000); Travel time to work: 15.9% less than 15 minutes, 18.6% 15 to 30 minutes, 21.1% 30 to 45 minutes, 11.1% 45 to 60 minutes, 33.4% 60 minutes or more (2000)

ROCKVILLE CENTRE (village).
Covers a land area of 3.277 square miles and a water area of 0.083 square miles. Located at 40.66° N. Lat.; 73.63° W. Long. Elevation is 31 feet.
History: Named for Reverend Mordecai "Rock" Smith. Seat of Molloy Catholic College for Women. Incorporated 1893.
Population: 24,727 (1990); 24,568 (2000); 24,319 (2005); 24,081 (2010 projected); Race: 88.2% White, 4.7% Black, 1.8% Asian, 9.8% Hispanic of any race (2005); Density: 7,420.5 persons per square mile (2005); Average household size: 2.67 (2005); Median age: 41.5 (2005); Males per 100 females: 88.7 (2005); Marriage status: 24.8% never married, 60.6% now married, 9.4% widowed, 5.2% divorced (2000); Foreign born: 10.3% (2000); Ancestry (includes multiple ancestries): 33.4% Irish, 23.6% Italian, 15.5% German, 13.2% Other groups, 6.5% Russian (2000).
Economy: Unemployment rate: 3.5% (2005); Total civilian labor force: 13,054 (2005); Single-family building permits issued: 10 (2005); Multi-family building permits issued: 0 (2005); Employment by occupation: 20.2% management, 30.1% professional, 12.0% services, 28.2% sales, 0.1% farming, 4.3% construction, 5.1% production (2000).
Income: Per capita income: $47,106 (2005); Median household income: $92,150 (2005); Average household income: $125,373 (2005); Percent of households with income of $100,000 or more: 46.1% (2005); Poverty rate: 5.0% (2000).
Education: Percent of population age 25 and over with: High school diploma (including GED) or higher: 91.0% (2005); Bachelor's degree or higher: 49.8% (2005); Master's degree or higher: 24.1% (2005).
School District(s)
Rockville Centre Union Free School District (KG-12)
    2003-04 Enrollment: 3,606 . . . . (516) 255-8920
Four-year College(s)
Molloy College
    Fall 2004 Enrollment: 3,352. . . . . (516) 678-5000
    2005-06 Tuition: In-state $16,500; Out-of-state $16,500
Housing: Homeownership rate: 71.8% (2005); Median home value: $565,924 (2005); Median rent: $819 per month (2000); Median age of housing: 56 years (2000).
Hospitals: Mercy Medical Center (387 beds)
Safety: Violent crime rate: 5.3 per 10,000 population; Property crime rate: 115.4 per 10,000 population (2004).
Transportation: Commute to work: 70.3% car, 21.8% public transportation, 3.6% walk, 4.0% work from home (2000); Travel time to work: 23.6% less than 15 minutes, 25.2% 15 to 30 minutes, 16.9% 30 to 45 minutes, 10.5% 45 to 60 minutes, 23.7% 60 minutes or more (2000)

Additional Information Contacts
Rockville Centre Chamber of Commerce . . . . (516) 766-0666
  http://www.rvcchamber.com
Village of Rockville Centre . . . . (516) 678-9300
  http://www.ci.rockville-centre.ny.us/

ROOSEVELT (CDP).
Covers a land area of 1.778 square miles and a water area of 0.013 square miles. Located at 40.67° N. Lat.; 73.58° W. Long. Elevation is 40 feet.

History: Named for Franklin Delano Roosevelt, 32nd President of the U.S. Troubled school district was taken over by the State Department of Education in mid-1990s for restructuring and improvement.

Population: 15,030 (1990); 15,854 (2000); 15,337 (2005); 14,815 (2010 projected); Race: 7.6% White, 77.8% Black, 0.6% Asian, 18.3% Hispanic of any race (2005); Density: 8,626.0 persons per square mile (2005); Average household size: 3.91 (2005); Median age: 33.1 (2005); Males per 100 females: 89.6 (2005); Marriage status: 40.1% never married, 45.5% now married, 6.6% widowed, 7.8% divorced (2000); Foreign born: 24.6% (2000); Ancestry (includes multiple ancestries): 66.6% Other groups, 7.5% Jamaican, 3.8% Haitian, 3.5% United States or American, 1.9% African (2000).

Economy: A large retail business exists in Roosevelt, and the town has become the county's busiest economic area. Employment by occupation: 6.6% management, 17.5% professional, 24.2% services, 29.0% sales, 0.0% farming, 8.9% construction, 13.8% production (2000).

Income: Per capita income: $18,597 (2005); Median household income: $61,362 (2005); Average household income: $71,997 (2005); Percent of households with income of $100,000 or more: 22.6% (2005); Poverty rate: 15.0% (2000).

Education: Percent of population age 25 and over with: High school diploma (including GED) or higher: 70.6% (2005); Bachelor's degree or higher: 14.2% (2005); Master's degree or higher: 5.7% (2005).

School District(s)
Roosevelt Children's Acad Charter School (KG-05)
  2003-04 Enrollment: 298 . . . . (516) 867-6202
Roosevelt Union Free School District (PK-12)
  2003-04 Enrollment: 2,882 . . . . (516) 867-8616

Housing: Homeownership rate: 73.7% (2005); Median home value: $255,338 (2005); Median rent: $853 per month (2000); Median age of housing: 46 years (2000).

Newspapers: The Long Island Catholic (Catholic, Religious - Circulation 112,000)

Transportation: Commute to work: 75.6% car, 18.4% public transportation, 2.3% walk, 2.2% work from home (2000); Travel time to work: 17.1% less than 15 minutes, 35.2% 15 to 30 minutes, 21.3% 30 to 45 minutes, 10.2% 45 to 60 minutes, 16.2% 60 minutes or more (2000)

Additional Information Contacts
Roosevelt Chamber of Commerce. . . . . (516) 379-9787

ROSLYN (village).
Covers a land area of 0.630 square miles and a water area of 0.008 square miles. Located at 40.80° N. Lat.; 73.65° W. Long.

History: Cedarmere, home of William Cullen Bryant, is here. Incorporated 1932.

Population: 1,965 (1990); 2,570 (2000); 2,622 (2005); 2,678 (2010 projected); Race: 82.5% White, 2.8% Black, 8.3% Asian, 8.3% Hispanic of any race (2005); Density: 4,164.8 persons per square mile (2005); Average household size: 2.45 (2005); Median age: 46.9 (2005); Males per 100 females: 85.3 (2005); Marriage status: 21.6% never married, 61.1% now married, 8.2% widowed, 9.1% divorced (2000); Foreign born: 20.3% (2000); Ancestry (includes multiple ancestries): 22.8% Other groups, 16.1% Italian, 8.9% Irish, 7.2% United States or American, 6.9% Russian (2000).

Economy: Manufacturing of printing equipment, food products and fabricated steel products. Single-family building permits issued: 2 (2005); Multi-family building permits issued: 100 (2005); Employment by occupation: 22.0% management, 35.4% professional, 8.7% services, 27.9% sales, 0.0% farming, 2.4% construction, 3.7% production (2000).

Income: Per capita income: $51,837 (2005); Median household income: $80,587 (2005); Average household income: $125,297 (2005); Percent of households with income of $100,000 or more: 40.4% (2005); Poverty rate: 4.1% (2000).

Education: Percent of population age 25 and over with: High school diploma (including GED) or higher: 92.0% (2005); Bachelor's degree or higher: 54.7% (2005); Master's degree or higher: 27.1% (2005).

Housing: Homeownership rate: 66.8% (2005); Median home value: $280,000 (2005); Median rent: $1,549 per month (2000); Median age of housing: 45 years (2000).

Hospitals: St. Francis Hospital-Heart Center (279 beds)

Transportation: Commute to work: 77.9% car, 14.4% public transportation, 2.1% walk, 4.9% work from home (2000); Travel time to work: 16.7% less than 15 minutes, 35.4% 15 to 30 minutes, 14.4% 30 to 45 minutes, 8.8% 45 to 60 minutes, 24.7% 60 minutes or more (2000)

ROSLYN ESTATES (village).
Covers a land area of 0.444 square miles and a water area of 0 square miles. Located at 40.79° N. Lat.; 73.66° W. Long.

Population: 1,184 (1990); 1,210 (2000); 1,232 (2005); 1,247 (2010 projected); Race: 91.4% White, 0.2% Black, 6.1% Asian, 2.8% Hispanic of any race (2005); Density: 2,777.3 persons per square mile (2005); Average household size: 3.07 (2005); Median age: 40.8 (2005); Males per 100 females: 96.8 (2005); Marriage status: 14.5% never married, 77.8% now married, 4.2% widowed, 3.5% divorced (2000); Foreign born: 10.0% (2000); Ancestry (includes multiple ancestries): 18.0% Russian, 14.8% Other groups, 13.9% Polish, 10.2% United States or American, 5.4% German (2000).

Economy: Single-family building permits issued: 0 (2005); Multi-family building permits issued: 0 (2005); Employment by occupation: 23.3% management, 44.2% professional, 5.5% services, 22.9% sales, 0.0% farming, 1.1% construction, 3.1% production (2000).

Income: Per capita income: $72,766 (2005); Median household income: $175,500 (2005); Average household income: $223,560 (2005); Percent of households with income of $100,000 or more: 74.1% (2005); Poverty rate: 2.5% (2000).

Education: Percent of population age 25 and over with: High school diploma (including GED) or higher: 97.5% (2005); Bachelor's degree or higher: 81.0% (2005); Master's degree or higher: 42.6% (2005).

Housing: Homeownership rate: 98.5% (2005); Median home value: $1 million+ (2005); Median rent: $1,625 per month (2000); Median age of housing: 47 years (2000).

Transportation: Commute to work: 77.0% car, 14.7% public transportation, 1.1% walk, 7.2% work from home (2000); Travel time to work: 13.7% less than 15 minutes, 25.8% 15 to 30 minutes, 19.8% 30 to 45 minutes, 13.1% 45 to 60 minutes, 27.6% 60 minutes or more (2000)

ROSLYN HARBOR (village).
Covers a land area of 1.191 square miles and a water area of 0 square miles. Located at 40.81° N. Lat.; 73.63° W. Long.

Population: 1,114 (1990); 1,023 (2000); 1,018 (2005); 1,022 (2010 projected); Race: 88.9% White, 1.6% Black, 6.8% Asian, 3.9% Hispanic of any race (2005); Density: 854.7 persons per square mile (2005); Average household size: 2.93 (2005); Median age: 47.3 (2005); Males per 100 females: 95.4 (2005); Marriage status: 17.5% never married, 72.6% now married, 6.1% widowed, 3.9% divorced (2000); Foreign born: 16.5% (2000); Ancestry (includes multiple ancestries): 19.7% Italian, 14.7% Russian, 10.4% Other groups, 9.4% Polish, 6.6% German (2000).

Economy: Single-family building permits issued: 1 (2005); Multi-family building permits issued: 0 (2005); Employment by occupation: 26.2% management, 37.0% professional, 8.7% services, 21.7% sales, 0.0% farming, 2.7% construction, 3.6% production (2000).

Income: Per capita income: $65,661 (2005); Median household income: $144,167 (2005); Average household income: $192,076 (2005); Percent of households with income of $100,000 or more: 65.2% (2005); Poverty rate: 2.5% (2000).

Education: Percent of population age 25 and over with: High school diploma (including GED) or higher: 93.5% (2005); Bachelor's degree or higher: 63.8% (2005); Master's degree or higher: 35.3% (2005).

Housing: Homeownership rate: 95.7% (2005); Median home value: $1 million+ (2005); Median rent: $825 per month (2000); Median age of housing: 43 years (2000).

Transportation: Commute to work: 77.1% car, 16.8% public transportation, 1.8% walk, 4.3% work from home (2000); Travel time to work: 14.8% less than 15 minutes, 31.1% 15 to 30 minutes, 17.3% 30 to 45 minutes, 5.6% 45 to 60 minutes, 31.1% 60 minutes or more (2000)

ROSLYN HEIGHTS (CDP).
Covers a land area of 1.490 square miles and a water area of 0 square miles. Located at 40.78° N. Lat.; 73.64° W. Long. Elevation is 210 feet.

Population: 6,405 (1990); 6,295 (2000); 6,216 (2005); 6,142 (2010 projected); Race: 72.9% White, 7.0% Black, 14.3% Asian, 8.5% Hispanic of

any race (2005); Density: 4,170.6 persons per square mile (2005); Average household size: 2.93 (2005); Median age: 41.3 (2005); Males per 100 females: 94.7 (2005); Marriage status: 23.2% never married, 64.2% now married, 7.5% widowed, 5.1% divorced (2000); Foreign born: 24.0% (2000); Ancestry (includes multiple ancestries): 29.9% Other groups, 12.9% Italian, 7.8% United States or American, 7.4% Russian, 6.4% Polish (2000).
Economy: Employment by occupation: 18.7% management, 31.1% professional, 10.1% services, 30.9% sales, 0.0% farming, 4.1% construction, 5.1% production (2000).
Income: Per capita income: $44,399 (2005); Median household income: $97,184 (2005); Average household income: $130,000 (2005); Percent of households with income of $100,000 or more: 48.7% (2005); Poverty rate: 5.7% (2000).
Education: Percent of population age 25 and over with: High school diploma (including GED) or higher: 91.5% (2005); Bachelor's degree or higher: 50.3% (2005); Master's degree or higher: 25.4% (2005).

School District(s)

East Williston Union Free School District (KG-12)
    2003-04 Enrollment: 1,812 .... (516) 333-3758
Roslyn Union Free School District (PK-12)
    2003-04 Enrollment: 3,237 .... (516) 625-6303
Housing: Homeownership rate: 83.6% (2005); Median home value: $653,605 (2005); Median rent: $791 per month (2000); Median age of housing: 48 years (2000).
Transportation: Commute to work: 80.4% car, 11.9% public transportation, 2.1% walk, 4.8% work from home (2000); Travel time to work: 19.7% less than 15 minutes, 30.5% 15 to 30 minutes, 20.2% 30 to 45 minutes, 6.9% 45 to 60 minutes, 22.7% 60 minutes or more (2000)

RUSSELL GARDENS (village).
Covers a land area of 0.183 square miles and a water area of 0 square miles. Located at 40.78° N. Lat.; 73.72° W. Long.
Population: 1,027 (1990); 1,074 (2000); 1,085 (2005); 1,086 (2010 projected); Race: 80.6% White, 0.6% Black, 15.3% Asian, 5.1% Hispanic of any race (2005); Density: 5,925.0 persons per square mile (2005); Average household size: 2.72 (2005); Median age: 42.8 (2005); Males per 100 females: 105.1 (2005); Marriage status: 21.9% never married, 66.5% now married, 7.5% widowed, 4.1% divorced (2000); Foreign born: 22.3% (2000); Ancestry (includes multiple ancestries): 30.3% Other groups, 14.2% Russian, 11.7% Polish, 7.5% United States or American, 4.5% Eastern European (2000).
Economy: Single-family building permits issued: 0 (2005); Multi-family building permits issued: 0 (2005); Employment by occupation: 22.3% management, 44.1% professional, 4.0% services, 20.9% sales, 0.0% farming, 3.0% construction, 5.6% production (2000).
Income: Per capita income: $66,476 (2005); Median household income: $119,408 (2005); Average household income: $178,528 (2005); Percent of households with income of $100,000 or more: 57.4% (2005); Poverty rate: 3.7% (2000).
Education: Percent of population age 25 and over with: High school diploma (including GED) or higher: 92.8% (2005); Bachelor's degree or higher: 74.5% (2005); Master's degree or higher: 43.8% (2005).
Housing: Homeownership rate: 74.9% (2005); Median home value: $943,966 (2005); Median rent: $795 per month (2000); Median age of housing: 59 years (2000).
Transportation: Commute to work: 63.8% car, 27.4% public transportation, 3.2% walk, 4.0% work from home (2000); Travel time to work: 15.9% less than 15 minutes, 24.9% 15 to 30 minutes, 17.6% 30 to 45 minutes, 18.0% 45 to 60 minutes, 23.5% 60 minutes or more (2000)

SADDLE ROCK (village).
Covers a land area of 0.244 square miles and a water area of 0.015 square miles. Located at 40.79° N. Lat.; 73.74° W. Long.
Population: 832 (1990); 791 (2000); 840 (2005); 880 (2010 projected); Race: 87.0% White, 0.7% Black, 9.0% Asian, 1.4% Hispanic of any race (2005); Density: 3,440.5 persons per square mile (2005); Average household size: 2.99 (2005); Median age: 49.6 (2005); Males per 100 females: 94.0 (2005); Marriage status: 24.1% never married, 69.2% now married, 5.1% widowed, 1.7% divorced (2000); Foreign born: 40.1% (2000); Ancestry (includes multiple ancestries): 21.0% Other groups, 15.5% Iranian, 10.5% Russian, 9.7% United States or American, 5.8% Polish (2000).
Economy: Single-family building permits issued: 5 (2005); Multi-family building permits issued: 0 (2005); Employment by occupation: 24.6% management, 32.2% professional, 4.1% services, 34.5% sales, 0.0% farming, 0.6% construction, 4.1% production (2000).
Income: Per capita income: $65,667 (2005); Median household income: $147,500 (2005); Average household income: $196,299 (2005); Percent of households with income of $100,000 or more: 66.9% (2005); Poverty rate: 3.0% (2000).
Education: Percent of population age 25 and over with: High school diploma (including GED) or higher: 92.6% (2005); Bachelor's degree or higher: 59.5% (2005); Master's degree or higher: 30.9% (2005).
Housing: Homeownership rate: 97.5% (2005); Median home value: $1 million+ (2005); Median rent: $700 per month (2000); Median age of housing: 45 years (2000).
Transportation: Commute to work: 71.7% car, 20.8% public transportation, 0.9% walk, 5.1% work from home (2000); Travel time to work: 17.2% less than 15 minutes, 13.5% 15 to 30 minutes, 24.5% 30 to 45 minutes, 23.8% 45 to 60 minutes, 21.0% 60 minutes or more (2000)
Additional Information Contacts
Village of Saddle Rock .... (516) 482-9400
    http://www.saddlerock.org/

SADDLE ROCK ESTATES (CDP).
Covers a land area of 0.078 square miles and a water area of 0 square miles. Located at 40.79° N. Lat.; 73.74° W. Long.
Population: 420 (1990); 424 (2000); 446 (2005); 464 (2010 projected); Race: 93.7% White, 2.0% Black, 1.6% Asian, 1.3% Hispanic of any race (2005); Density: 5,745.0 persons per square mile (2005); Average household size: 3.19 (2005); Median age: 39.6 (2005); Males per 100 females: 99.1 (2005); Marriage status: 14.3% never married, 76.3% now married, 3.7% widowed, 5.7% divorced (2000); Foreign born: 18.9% (2000); Ancestry (includes multiple ancestries): 25.5% Russian, 19.1% United States or American, 16.6% Polish, 15.7% Other groups, 6.8% Romanian (2000).
Economy: Employment by occupation: 17.4% management, 55.6% professional, 7.3% services, 16.9% sales, 0.0% farming, 0.0% construction, 2.8% production (2000).
Income: Per capita income: $62,707 (2005); Median household income: $176,786 (2005); Average household income: $199,768 (2005); Percent of households with income of $100,000 or more: 73.6% (2005); Poverty rate: 0.0% (2000).
Education: Percent of population age 25 and over with: High school diploma (including GED) or higher: 100.0% (2005); Bachelor's degree or higher: 89.5% (2005); Master's degree or higher: 60.9% (2005).
Housing: Homeownership rate: 97.9% (2005); Median home value: $1 million+ (2005); Median rent: $n/a per month (2000); Median age of housing: 58 years (2000).
Transportation: Commute to work: 71.9% car, 24.7% public transportation, 0.0% walk, 3.4% work from home (2000); Travel time to work: 20.9% less than 15 minutes, 22.1% 15 to 30 minutes, 14.5% 30 to 45 minutes, 19.2% 45 to 60 minutes, 23.3% 60 minutes or more (2000)

SALISBURY (CDP).
Covers a land area of 1.723 square miles and a water area of 0.013 square miles. Located at 40.74° N. Lat.; 73.56° W. Long.
Population: 12,226 (1990); 12,341 (2000); 12,463 (2005); 12,593 (2010 projected); Race: 82.2% White, 1.6% Black, 12.2% Asian, 11.6% Hispanic of any race (2005); Density: 7,235.0 persons per square mile (2005); Average household size: 3.09 (2005); Median age: 40.8 (2005); Males per 100 females: 93.6 (2005); Marriage status: 22.5% never married, 66.3% now married, 6.1% widowed, 5.1% divorced (2000); Foreign born: 17.5% (2000); Ancestry (includes multiple ancestries): 28.1% Italian, 20.1% Irish, 19.7% Other groups, 13.7% German, 6.7% Polish (2000).
Economy: Employment by occupation: 16.4% management, 25.9% professional, 13.6% services, 30.0% sales, 0.0% farming, 6.7% construction, 7.4% production (2000).
Income: Per capita income: $31,726 (2005); Median household income: $84,136 (2005); Average household income: $97,839 (2005); Percent of households with income of $100,000 or more: 37.8% (2005); Poverty rate: 3.7% (2000).
Education: Percent of population age 25 and over with: High school diploma (including GED) or higher: 90.0% (2005); Bachelor's degree or higher: 34.9% (2005); Master's degree or higher: 14.3% (2005).
Housing: Homeownership rate: 92.3% (2005); Median home value: $368,487 (2005); Median rent: $940 per month (2000); Median age of housing: 46 years (2000).

Transportation: Commute to work: 84.5% car, 11.6% public transportation, 0.8% walk, 3.0% work from home (2000); Travel time to work: 24.4% less than 15 minutes, 32.2% 15 to 30 minutes, 18.7% 30 to 45 minutes, 8.5% 45 to 60 minutes, 16.2% 60 minutes or more (2000)

SANDS POINT (village).
Covers a land area of 4.237 square miles and a water area of 1.384 square miles. Located at 40.84° N. Lat.; 73.71° W. Long.

History: Sands Point promontory (lighthouse) is at tip of Manhasset Neck, Northwest of village.

Population: 2,477 (1990); 2,786 (2000); 2,798 (2005); 2,830 (2010 projected); Race: 85.6% White, 2.0% Black, 10.1% Asian, 5.1% Hispanic of any race (2005); Density: 660.3 persons per square mile (2005); Average household size: 3.21 (2005); Median age: 43.7 (2005); Males per 100 females: 92.6 (2005); Marriage status: 19.0% never married, 71.7% now married, 5.4% widowed, 3.9% divorced (2000); Foreign born: 16.5% (2000); Ancestry (includes multiple ancestries): 16.6% Other groups, 14.0% Italian, 11.7% Russian, 9.9% Irish, 9.7% German (2000).

Economy: Single-family building permits issued: 7 (2005); Multi-family building permits issued: 0 (2005); Employment by occupation: 24.5% management, 40.5% professional, 6.7% services, 25.7% sales, 0.0% farming, 0.8% construction, 1.9% production (2000).

Income: Per capita income: $94,150 (2005); Median household income: $271,341 (2005); Average household income: $301,131 (2005); Percent of households with income of $100,000 or more: 76.7% (2005); Poverty rate: 3.1% (2000).

Education: Percent of population age 25 and over with: High school diploma (including GED) or higher: 97.0% (2005); Bachelor's degree or higher: 71.7% (2005); Master's degree or higher: 42.6% (2005).

Housing: Homeownership rate: 94.3% (2005); Median home value: $1 million+ (2005); Median rent: $1,375 per month (2000); Median age of housing: 44 years (2000).

Transportation: Commute to work: 65.0% car, 22.7% public transportation, 2.6% walk, 9.7% work from home (2000); Travel time to work: 22.0% less than 15 minutes, 17.2% 15 to 30 minutes, 19.1% 30 to 45 minutes, 10.0% 45 to 60 minutes, 30.8% 60 minutes or more (2000)

Additional Information Contacts
Village of Sands Point . . . . (516) 883-3044
http://www.sandspoint.org/

SEA CLIFF (village).
Covers a land area of 1.088 square miles and a water area of 0.877 square miles. Located at 40.84° N. Lat.; 73.64° W. Long.

History: Incorporated 1883.

Population: 5,054 (1990); 5,066 (2000); 5,020 (2005); 4,976 (2010 projected); Race: 93.4% White, 2.1% Black, 1.6% Asian, 6.0% Hispanic of any race (2005); Density: 4,612.8 persons per square mile (2005); Average household size: 2.52 (2005); Median age: 43.6 (2005); Males per 100 females: 95.9 (2005); Marriage status: 27.1% never married, 60.5% now married, 7.1% widowed, 5.4% divorced (2000); Foreign born: 16.3% (2000); Ancestry (includes multiple ancestries): 20.3% Irish, 18.9% Italian, 13.1% German, 11.9% Other groups, 9.2% Russian (2000).

Economy: Single-family building permits issued: 2 (2005); Multi-family building permits issued: 3 (2005); Employment by occupation: 20.9% management, 32.4% professional, 11.2% services, 23.6% sales, 0.0% farming, 6.1% construction, 5.7% production (2000).

Income: Per capita income: $47,759 (2005); Median household income: $93,700 (2005); Average household income: $119,664 (2005); Percent of households with income of $100,000 or more: 46.9% (2005); Poverty rate: 2.8% (2000).

Education: Percent of population age 25 and over with: High school diploma (including GED) or higher: 94.6% (2005); Bachelor's degree or higher: 57.6% (2005); Master's degree or higher: 27.8% (2005).

School District(s)
North Shore Central School District (KG-12)
    2003-04 Enrollment: 2,652 . . . . (516) 705-0350

Housing: Homeownership rate: 74.2% (2005); Median home value: $637,066 (2005); Median rent: $988 per month (2000); Median age of housing: 60+ years (2000).

Transportation: Commute to work: 83.8% car, 9.4% public transportation, 2.6% walk, 4.1% work from home (2000); Travel time to work: 20.3% less than 15 minutes, 36.2% 15 to 30 minutes, 22.1% 30 to 45 minutes, 6.2% 45 to 60 minutes, 15.2% 60 minutes or more (2000)

SEAFORD (CDP).
Covers a land area of 2.600 square miles and a water area of 0.014 square miles. Located at 40.66° N. Lat.; 73.49° W. Long. Elevation is 9 feet.

History: The county Museum of Natural History is here. Settled 1643.

Population: 15,597 (1990); 15,791 (2000); 15,826 (2005); 15,877 (2010 projected); Race: 95.7% White, 0.5% Black, 2.2% Asian, 5.0% Hispanic of any race (2005); Density: 6,086.4 persons per square mile (2005); Average household size: 2.97 (2005); Median age: 39.8 (2005); Males per 100 females: 96.1 (2005); Marriage status: 24.9% never married, 63.2% now married, 7.2% widowed, 4.7% divorced (2000); Foreign born: 5.9% (2000); Ancestry (includes multiple ancestries): 37.7% Italian, 28.9% Irish, 19.1% German, 7.2% Other groups, 6.0% Polish (2000).

Economy: Resort village, with marinas and boatyards. Employment by occupation: 18.0% management, 20.7% professional, 14.0% services, 30.3% sales, 0.2% farming, 8.5% construction, 8.3% production (2000).

Income: Per capita income: $35,984 (2005); Median household income: $93,676 (2005); Average household income: $106,178 (2005); Percent of households with income of $100,000 or more: 45.6% (2005); Poverty rate: 3.6% (2000).

Education: Percent of population age 25 and over with: High school diploma (including GED) or higher: 92.2% (2005); Bachelor's degree or higher: 31.1% (2005); Master's degree or higher: 10.9% (2005).

School District(s)
Levittown Union Free School District (KG-12)
    2003-04 Enrollment: 8,027 . . . . (516) 520-8300
Seaford Union Free School District (KG-12)
    2003-04 Enrollment: 2,706 . . . . (516) 592-4001

Housing: Homeownership rate: 89.4% (2005); Median home value: $398,582 (2005); Median rent: $1,060 per month (2000); Median age of housing: 44 years (2000).

Transportation: Commute to work: 81.2% car, 14.8% public transportation, 1.2% walk, 2.3% work from home (2000); Travel time to work: 18.0% less than 15 minutes, 34.9% 15 to 30 minutes, 17.9% 30 to 45 minutes, 7.2% 45 to 60 minutes, 22.0% 60 minutes or more (2000)

Additional Information Contacts
Seaford Chamber of Commerce . . . . (516) 783-5544
http://www.seaford.li/chamber

SEARINGTOWN (CDP).
Covers a land area of 0.920 square miles and a water area of 0 square miles. Located at 40.77° N. Lat.; 73.65° W. Long.

Population: 5,020 (1990); 5,034 (2000); 5,081 (2005); 5,134 (2010 projected); Race: 60.2% White, 1.5% Black, 34.2% Asian, 3.5% Hispanic of any race (2005); Density: 5,524.5 persons per square mile (2005); Average household size: 3.20 (2005); Median age: 44.4 (2005); Males per 100 females: 94.3 (2005); Marriage status: 19.6% never married, 72.6% now married, 6.5% widowed, 1.3% divorced (2000); Foreign born: 28.6% (2000); Ancestry (includes multiple ancestries): 31.5% Other groups, 16.0% Italian, 8.7% Russian, 5.8% German, 5.7% Polish (2000).

Economy: Employment by occupation: 26.4% management, 36.6% professional, 4.3% services, 25.7% sales, 0.0% farming, 2.8% construction, 4.2% production (2000).

Income: Per capita income: $55,415 (2005); Median household income: $137,092 (2005); Average household income: $177,530 (2005); Percent of households with income of $100,000 or more: 67.2% (2005); Poverty rate: 1.1% (2000).

Education: Percent of population age 25 and over with: High school diploma (including GED) or higher: 93.0% (2005); Bachelor's degree or higher: 56.8% (2005); Master's degree or higher: 29.8% (2005).

Housing: Homeownership rate: 97.4% (2005); Median home value: $746,435 (2005); Median rent: $875 per month (2000); Median age of housing: 39 years (2000).

Transportation: Commute to work: 81.2% car, 14.4% public transportation, 0.3% walk, 4.1% work from home (2000); Travel time to work: 15.3% less than 15 minutes, 25.0% 15 to 30 minutes, 20.6% 30 to 45 minutes, 15.3% 45 to 60 minutes, 23.8% 60 minutes or more (2000)

SOUTH FARMINGDALE (CDP).
Covers a land area of 2.187 square miles and a water area of 0 square miles. Located at 40.71° N. Lat.; 73.44° W. Long. Elevation is 53 feet.

Population: 15,567 (1990); 15,061 (2000); 14,789 (2005); 14,511 (2010 projected); Race: 90.4% White, 1.1% Black, 4.4% Asian, 7.9% Hispanic of any race (2005); Density: 6,761.6 persons per square mile (2005); Average household size: 3.06 (2005); Median age: 39.8 (2005); Males per 100

females: 96.9 (2005); Marriage status: 23.1% never married, 64.5% now married, 7.5% widowed, 4.9% divorced (2000); Foreign born: 8.8% (2000); Ancestry (includes multiple ancestries): 37.8% Italian, 24.5% Irish, 20.6% German, 10.0% Other groups, 5.6% Polish (2000).
Economy: Employment by occupation: 15.1% management, 20.1% professional, 15.6% services, 30.8% sales, 0.0% farming, 10.8% construction, 7.5% production (2000).
Income: Per capita income: $30,149 (2005); Median household income: $80,912 (2005); Average household income: $91,522 (2005); Percent of households with income of $100,000 or more: 35.1% (2005); Poverty rate: 2.8% (2000).
Education: Percent of population age 25 and over with: High school diploma (including GED) or higher: 87.5% (2005); Bachelor's degree or higher: 22.5% (2005); Master's degree or higher: 7.2% (2005).
Housing: Homeownership rate: 90.7% (2005); Median home value: $352,423 (2005); Median rent: $1,091 per month (2000); Median age of housing: 44 years (2000).
Transportation: Commute to work: 84.5% car, 11.6% public transportation, 1.2% walk, 2.3% work from home (2000); Travel time to work: 21.6% less than 15 minutes, 30.6% 15 to 30 minutes, 20.2% 30 to 45 minutes, 8.1% 45 to 60 minutes, 19.4% 60 minutes or more (2000)

SOUTH FLORAL PARK (village). Aka Jamaica Square. Covers a land area of 0.100 square miles and a water area of 0 square miles. Located at 40.71° N. Lat.; 73.70° W. Long.
History: Until 1931 called Jamaica Square.
Population: 1,478 (1990); 1,578 (2000); 1,487 (2005); 1,429 (2010 projected); Race: 13.7% White, 66.2% Black, 4.4% Asian, 12.7% Hispanic of any race (2005); Density: 14,866.4 persons per square mile (2005); Average household size: 3.56 (2005); Median age: 37.6 (2005); Males per 100 females: 96.7 (2005); Marriage status: 33.5% never married, 51.9% now married, 7.1% widowed, 7.5% divorced (2000); Foreign born: 35.0% (2000); Ancestry (includes multiple ancestries): 47.5% Other groups, 16.4% Jamaican, 7.4% Italian, 5.7% Haitian, 4.7% Irish (2000).
Economy: Single-family building permits issued: 1 (2005); Multi-family building permits issued: 0 (2005); Employment by occupation: 11.9% management, 19.8% professional, 20.0% services, 27.7% sales, 0.3% farming, 9.4% construction, 11.0% production (2000).
Income: Per capita income: $22,882 (2005); Median household income: $69,626 (2005); Average household income: $81,400 (2005); Percent of households with income of $100,000 or more: 26.1% (2005); Poverty rate: 2.8% (2000).
Education: Percent of population age 25 and over with: High school diploma (including GED) or higher: 79.5% (2005); Bachelor's degree or higher: 22.6% (2005); Master's degree or higher: 9.5% (2005).
Housing: Homeownership rate: 85.2% (2005); Median home value: $330,435 (2005); Median rent: $926 per month (2000); Median age of housing: 43 years (2000).
Transportation: Commute to work: 76.3% car, 18.7% public transportation, 2.7% walk, 0.6% work from home (2000); Travel time to work: 13.9% less than 15 minutes, 29.0% 15 to 30 minutes, 24.4% 30 to 45 minutes, 10.5% 45 to 60 minutes, 22.2% 60 minutes or more (2000)

SOUTH HEMPSTEAD (CDP). Covers a land area of 0.586 square miles and a water area of 0 square miles. Located at 40.68° N. Lat.; 73.62° W. Long.
Population: 3,014 (1990); 3,188 (2000); 3,217 (2005); 3,249 (2010 projected); Race: 71.8% White, 18.3% Black, 2.7% Asian, 13.1% Hispanic of any race (2005); Density: 5,490.6 persons per square mile (2005); Average household size: 3.12 (2005); Median age: 38.9 (2005); Males per 100 females: 94.3 (2005); Marriage status: 24.4% never married, 62.1% now married, 7.9% widowed, 5.7% divorced (2000); Foreign born: 14.6% (2000); Ancestry (includes multiple ancestries): 24.2% Irish, 22.6% Italian, 19.9% German, 18.5% Other groups, 6.5% English (2000).
Economy: Employment by occupation: 14.4% management, 31.1% professional, 17.1% services, 25.5% sales, 0.0% farming, 6.3% construction, 5.6% production (2000).
Income: Per capita income: $34,325 (2005); Median household income: $89,449 (2005); Average household income: $107,105 (2005); Percent of households with income of $100,000 or more: 42.4% (2005); Poverty rate: 2.4% (2000).
Education: Percent of population age 25 and over with: High school diploma (including GED) or higher: 90.0% (2005); Bachelor's degree or higher: 36.8% (2005); Master's degree or higher: 16.3% (2005).

School District(s)
Rockville Centre Union Free School District (KG-12)
   2003-04 Enrollment: 3,606 . . . . (516) 255-8920
Housing: Homeownership rate: 89.5% (2005); Median home value: $322,774 (2005); Median rent: $647 per month (2000); Median age of housing: 50 years (2000).
Transportation: Commute to work: 79.6% car, 16.0% public transportation, 0.8% walk, 3.2% work from home (2000); Travel time to work: 15.8% less than 15 minutes, 34.3% 15 to 30 minutes, 19.7% 30 to 45 minutes, 7.9% 45 to 60 minutes, 22.3% 60 minutes or more (2000)

SOUTH VALLEY STREAM (CDP). Covers a land area of 0.879 square miles and a water area of 0 square miles. Located at 40.65° N. Lat.; 73.71° W. Long.
Population: 5,328 (1990); 5,638 (2000); 5,630 (2005); 5,633 (2010 projected); Race: 61.4% White, 13.4% Black, 19.3% Asian, 7.3% Hispanic of any race (2005); Density: 6,406.0 persons per square mile (2005); Average household size: 2.85 (2005); Median age: 44.3 (2005); Males per 100 females: 92.5 (2005); Marriage status: 18.1% never married, 65.1% now married, 11.6% widowed, 5.2% divorced (2000); Foreign born: 21.0% (2000); Ancestry (includes multiple ancestries): 34.0% Other groups, 11.0% United States or American, 10.4% Polish, 10.4% Russian, 10.1% Italian (2000).
Economy: Employment by occupation: 22.7% management, 26.9% professional, 6.9% services, 32.6% sales, 0.0% farming, 5.7% construction, 5.2% production (2000).
Income: Per capita income: $31,528 (2005); Median household income: $73,993 (2005); Average household income: $89,830 (2005); Percent of households with income of $100,000 or more: 37.4% (2005); Poverty rate: 5.3% (2000).
Education: Percent of population age 25 and over with: High school diploma (including GED) or higher: 92.0% (2005); Bachelor's degree or higher: 49.1% (2005); Master's degree or higher: 24.0% (2005).
Housing: Homeownership rate: 78.4% (2005); Median home value: $406,568 (2005); Median rent: $805 per month (2000); Median age of housing: 45 years (2000).
Transportation: Commute to work: 73.5% car, 19.3% public transportation, 1.9% walk, 4.4% work from home (2000); Travel time to work: 17.5% less than 15 minutes, 19.2% 15 to 30 minutes, 27.3% 30 to 45 minutes, 12.8% 45 to 60 minutes, 23.2% 60 minutes or more (2000)

STEWART MANOR (village). Covers a land area of 0.198 square miles and a water area of 0 square miles. Located at 40.72° N. Lat.; 73.68° W. Long.
History: Laid out 1926, incorporated 1927.
Population: 2,002 (1990); 1,935 (2000); 1,994 (2005); 2,018 (2010 projected); Race: 89.5% White, 3.0% Black, 2.9% Asian, 5.6% Hispanic of any race (2005); Density: 10,083.2 persons per square mile (2005); Average household size: 2.67 (2005); Median age: 41.1 (2005); Males per 100 females: 85.5 (2005); Marriage status: 25.2% never married, 62.8% now married, 7.3% widowed, 4.8% divorced (2000); Foreign born: 7.1% (2000); Ancestry (includes multiple ancestries): 39.2% Irish, 30.8% Italian, 16.9% German, 7.9% Other groups, 7.6% Polish (2000).
Economy: Single-family building permits issued: 0 (2005); Multi-family building permits issued: 0 (2005); Employment by occupation: 22.7% management, 28.5% professional, 8.8% services, 31.7% sales, 0.0% farming, 3.6% construction, 4.7% production (2000).
Income: Per capita income: $40,953 (2005); Median household income: $96,639 (2005); Average household income: $109,464 (2005); Percent of households with income of $100,000 or more: 47.9% (2005); Poverty rate: 2.6% (2000).
Education: Percent of population age 25 and over with: High school diploma (including GED) or higher: 95.5% (2005); Bachelor's degree or higher: 45.8% (2005); Master's degree or higher: 19.6% (2005).

School District(s)
Elmont Union Free School District (PK-06)
   2003-04 Enrollment: 4,248 . . . . (516) 326-5500
Housing: Homeownership rate: 87.0% (2005); Median home value: $467,092 (2005); Median rent: $1,111 per month (2000); Median age of housing: 60+ years (2000).
Transportation: Commute to work: 72.9% car, 19.4% public transportation, 3.6% walk, 2.9% work from home (2000); Travel time to work: 16.8% less than 15 minutes, 28.5% 15 to 30 minutes, 20.9% 30 to 45 minutes, 9.4% 45 to 60 minutes, 24.4% 60 minutes or more (2000)

SYOSSET (CDP). Covers a land area of 4.985 square miles and a water area of 0 square miles. Located at 40.81° N. Lat.; 73.50° W. Long. Elevation is 200 feet.
Population: 18,967 (1990); 18,544 (2000); 18,939 (2005); 19,305 (2010 projected); Race: 80.1% White, 0.6% Black, 17.3% Asian, 3.8% Hispanic of any race (2005); Density: 3,798.9 persons per square mile (2005); Average household size: 2.92 (2005); Median age: 42.0 (2005); Males per 100 females: 96.5 (2005); Marriage status: 19.9% never married, 70.3% now married, 6.4% widowed, 3.4% divorced (2000); Foreign born: 17.6% (2000); Ancestry (includes multiple ancestries): 23.8% Other groups, 21.2% Italian, 13.8% Irish, 11.9% German, 8.2% Polish (2000).
Economy: Extensive manufacturing: electronic equipment, pharmaceuticals, photographic equipment, building materials, plastic products. Employment by occupation: 21.9% management, 29.2% professional, 7.8% services, 30.9% sales, 0.1% farming, 4.5% construction, 5.6% production (2000).
Income: Per capita income: $45,564 (2005); Median household income: $104,156 (2005); Average household income: $131,984 (2005); Percent of households with income of $100,000 or more: 52.0% (2005); Poverty rate: 2.8% (2000).
Education: Percent of population age 25 and over with: High school diploma (including GED) or higher: 94.1% (2005); Bachelor's degree or higher: 54.0% (2005); Master's degree or higher: 24.2% (2005).
School District(s)
Cold Spring Harbor Central School District (KG-12)
    2003-04 Enrollment: 2,092 . . . . (631) 692-8036
New York City Public Schools (PK-12)
    2003-04 Enrollment: 1,023,674 . . . . (718) 935-2794
Syosset Central School District (KG-12)
    2003-04 Enrollment: 6,623 . . . . (516) 364-5605
Four-year College(s)
New York College of Health Professions
    Fall 2004 Enrollment: 889 . . . . (516) 364-0808
    2005-06 Tuition: In-state $10,084; Out-of-state $10,084
Two-year College(s)
Culinary Academy of Long Island
    Fall 2004 Enrollment: 111 . . . . (516) 364-4344
Housing: Homeownership rate: 92.6% (2005); Median home value: $554,343 (2005); Median rent: $880 per month (2000); Median age of housing: 44 years (2000).
Hospitals: Northshore University Hospital at Syosset (204 beds)
Transportation: Commute to work: 75.7% car, 16.9% public transportation, 1.8% walk, 4.9% work from home (2000); Travel time to work: 25.8% less than 15 minutes, 25.3% 15 to 30 minutes, 17.4% 30 to 45 minutes, 5.5% 45 to 60 minutes, 26.1% 60 minutes or more (2000)

THOMASTON (village). Covers a land area of 0.417 square miles and a water area of 0 square miles. Located at 40.78° N. Lat.; 73.71° W. Long.
Population: 2,594 (1990); 2,607 (2000); 2,560 (2005); 2,543 (2010 projected); Race: 74.6% White, 0.9% Black, 19.1% Asian, 8.6% Hispanic of any race (2005); Density: 6,135.3 persons per square mile (2005); Average household size: 2.72 (2005); Median age: 42.8 (2005); Males per 100 females: 92.3 (2005); Marriage status: 19.5% never married, 67.9% now married, 5.6% widowed, 7.1% divorced (2000); Foreign born: 27.2% (2000); Ancestry (includes multiple ancestries): 27.6% Other groups, 14.9% Russian, 8.4% Polish, 7.7% Italian, 6.4% United States or American (2000).
Economy: Single-family building permits issued: 3 (2005); Multi-family building permits issued: 0 (2005); Employment by occupation: 22.2% management, 34.4% professional, 7.2% services, 30.2% sales, 0.0% farming, 2.6% construction, 3.4% production (2000).
Income: Per capita income: $51,252 (2005); Median household income: $99,330 (2005); Average household income: $139,023 (2005); Percent of households with income of $100,000 or more: 49.7% (2005); Poverty rate: 4.4% (2000).
Education: Percent of population age 25 and over with: High school diploma (including GED) or higher: 91.7% (2005); Bachelor's degree or higher: 58.3% (2005); Master's degree or higher: 35.3% (2005).
Housing: Homeownership rate: 79.9% (2005); Median home value: $682,269 (2005); Median rent: $1,293 per month (2000); Median age of housing: 53 years (2000).
Transportation: Commute to work: 60.4% car, 27.5% public transportation, 3.1% walk, 8.7% work from home (2000); Travel time to work: 20.1% less than 15 minutes, 21.1% 15 to 30 minutes, 18.8% 30 to 45 minutes, 14.4% 45 to 60 minutes, 25.7% 60 minutes or more (2000)

UNIONDALE (CDP). Covers a land area of 2.652 square miles and a water area of 0 square miles. Located at 40.70° N. Lat.; 73.59° W. Long. Elevation is 57 feet.
History: Named for the American union of states. Downtown suburban growth since the 1970s.
Population: 20,328 (1990); 23,011 (2000); 23,073 (2005); 23,120 (2010 projected); Race: 20.9% White, 61.2% Black, 2.0% Asian, 24.8% Hispanic of any race (2005); Density: 8,699.8 persons per square mile (2005); Average household size: 3.92 (2005); Median age: 36.3 (2005); Males per 100 females: 91.3 (2005); Marriage status: 32.2% never married, 52.4% now married, 8.5% widowed, 6.9% divorced (2000); Foreign born: 34.1% (2000); Ancestry (includes multiple ancestries): 48.6% Other groups, 10.6% Jamaican, 8.2% Haitian, 4.3% Italian, 4.2% Irish (2000).
Economy: Large arena, new hotels and office and retail sites. Employment by occupation: 10.4% management, 19.2% professional, 19.2% services, 29.8% sales, 0.0% farming, 7.3% construction, 14.1% production (2000).
Income: Per capita income: $20,067 (2005); Median household income: $65,614 (2005); Average household income: $76,044 (2005); Percent of households with income of $100,000 or more: 25.8% (2005); Poverty rate: 8.8% (2000).
Education: Percent of population age 25 and over with: High school diploma (including GED) or higher: 72.9% (2005); Bachelor's degree or higher: 19.3% (2005); Master's degree or higher: 8.4% (2005).
School District(s)
Uniondale Union Free School District (KG-12)
    2003-04 Enrollment: 6,411 . . . . (516) 560-8824
Two-year College(s)
Veeb Nassau County School of Practical Nursing (Public)
    Fall 2004 Enrollment: 186 . . . . (516) 572-1704
    2005-06 Tuition: In-state $9,000; Out-of-state $9,000
Housing: Homeownership rate: 78.8% (2005); Median home value: $271,963 (2005); Median rent: $836 per month (2000); Median age of housing: 47 years (2000).
Transportation: Commute to work: 78.3% car, 17.1% public transportation, 2.0% walk, 2.4% work from home (2000); Travel time to work: 18.3% less than 15 minutes, 33.0% 15 to 30 minutes, 19.4% 30 to 45 minutes, 8.7% 45 to 60 minutes, 20.6% 60 minutes or more (2000)

UNIVERSITY GARDENS (CDP). Covers a land area of 0.591 square miles and a water area of 0 square miles. Located at 40.77° N. Lat.; 73.72° W. Long.
Population: 4,381 (1990); 4,138 (2000); 4,053 (2005); 3,964 (2010 projected); Race: 73.4% White, 3.0% Black, 19.0% Asian, 9.2% Hispanic of any race (2005); Density: 6,863.2 persons per square mile (2005); Average household size: 2.45 (2005); Median age: 43.6 (2005); Males per 100 females: 89.8 (2005); Marriage status: 19.1% never married, 66.1% now married, 6.5% widowed, 8.3% divorced (2000); Foreign born: 25.2% (2000); Ancestry (includes multiple ancestries): 27.3% Other groups, 13.1% Italian, 8.4% Irish, 8.3% United States or American, 7.1% Russian (2000).
Economy: Employment by occupation: 25.2% management, 29.9% professional, 7.3% services, 28.9% sales, 0.0% farming, 3.9% construction, 4.9% production (2000).
Income: Per capita income: $45,186 (2005); Median household income: $81,299 (2005); Average household income: $110,791 (2005); Percent of households with income of $100,000 or more: 38.4% (2005); Poverty rate: 2.4% (2000).
Education: Percent of population age 25 and over with: High school diploma (including GED) or higher: 90.4% (2005); Bachelor's degree or higher: 52.9% (2005); Master's degree or higher: 29.0% (2005).
Housing: Homeownership rate: 81.7% (2005); Median home value: $531,318 (2005); Median rent: $685 per month (2000); Median age of housing: 53 years (2000).
Transportation: Commute to work: 70.2% car, 21.8% public transportation, 2.6% walk, 5.0% work from home (2000); Travel time to work: 21.5% less than 15 minutes, 28.7% 15 to 30 minutes, 20.8% 30 to 45 minutes, 8.4% 45 to 60 minutes, 20.6% 60 minutes or more (2000)

UPPER BROOKVILLE (village). Covers a land area of 4.303 square miles and a water area of 0 square miles. Located at 40.84° N. Lat.; 73.56° W. Long. Elevation is 156 feet.

Population: 1,453 (1990); 1,801 (2000); 1,857 (2005); 1,911 (2010 projected); Race: 76.1% White, 8.9% Black, 10.1% Asian, 7.2% Hispanic of any race (2005); Density: 431.5 persons per square mile (2005); Average household size: 3.15 (2005); Median age: 41.9 (2005); Males per 100 females: 94.7 (2005); Marriage status: 23.7% never married, 66.9% now married, 5.2% widowed, 4.3% divorced (2000); Foreign born: 19.1% (2000); Ancestry (includes multiple ancestries): 22.4% Other groups, 16.1% Italian, 14.7% Irish, 8.9% German, 5.7% Russian (2000).
Economy: Single-family building permits issued: 5 (2005); Multi-family building permits issued: 0 (2005); Employment by occupation: 30.7% management, 35.4% professional, 8.6% services, 21.5% sales, 0.4% farming, 1.2% construction, 2.2% production (2000).
Income: Per capita income: $64,965 (2005); Median household income: $147,115 (2005); Average household income: $192,750 (2005); Percent of households with income of $100,000 or more: 62.5% (2005); Poverty rate: 2.5% (2000).
Education: Percent of population age 25 and over with: High school diploma (including GED) or higher: 93.8% (2005); Bachelor's degree or higher: 59.2% (2005); Master's degree or higher: 33.3% (2005).
Housing: Homeownership rate: 85.6% (2005); Median home value: $1 million+ (2005); Median rent: $486 per month (2000); Median age of housing: 35 years (2000).
Transportation: Commute to work: 82.7% car, 6.6% public transportation, 3.0% walk, 7.2% work from home (2000); Travel time to work: 13.2% less than 15 minutes, 28.8% 15 to 30 minutes, 24.2% 30 to 45 minutes, 10.8% 45 to 60 minutes, 23.0% 60 minutes or more (2000)

VALLEY STREAM (village).
Covers a land area of 3.441 square miles and a water area of 0.025 square miles. Located at 40.66° N. Lat.; 73.70° W. Long. Elevation is 18 feet.
Population: 33,962 (1990); 36,368 (2000); 36,133 (2005); 35,898 (2010 projected); Race: 69.7% White, 12.1% Black, 9.2% Asian, 16.8% Hispanic of any race (2005); Density: 10,501.2 persons per square mile (2005); Average household size: 2.94 (2005); Median age: 40.4 (2005); Males per 100 females: 92.2 (2005); Marriage status: 26.6% never married, 58.2% now married, 9.0% widowed, 6.1% divorced (2000); Foreign born: 19.6% (2000); Ancestry (includes multiple ancestries): 31.8% Italian, 23.9% Other groups, 17.2% Irish, 11.3% German, 4.6% Polish (2000).
Economy: Unemployment rate: 4.3% (2005); Total civilian labor force: 19,154 (2005); Single-family building permits issued: 9 (2005); Multi-family building permits issued: 0 (2005); Employment by occupation: 14.0% management, 19.5% professional, 13.9% services, 35.6% sales, 0.0% farming, 8.8% construction, 8.1% production (2000).
Income: Per capita income: $28,986 (2005); Median household income: $72,102 (2005); Average household income: $85,025 (2005); Percent of households with income of $100,000 or more: 31.1% (2005); Poverty rate: 3.5% (2000).
Education: Percent of population age 25 and over with: High school diploma (including GED) or higher: 86.2% (2005); Bachelor's degree or higher: 25.0% (2005); Master's degree or higher: 9.1% (2005).

School District(s)
Elmont Union Free School District (PK-06)
    2003-04 Enrollment: 4,248 .... (516) 326-5500
Hewlett-Woodmere Union Free School District (PK-12)
    2003-04 Enrollment: 3,327 .... (516) 374-8100
Valley Stream 13 Union Free School District (KG-06)
    2003-04 Enrollment: 2,103 .... (516) 568-6100
Valley Stream 24 Union Free School District (KG-06)
    2003-04 Enrollment: 1,070 .... (516) 256-0153
Valley Stream 30 Union Free School District (KG-06)
    2003-04 Enrollment: 1,502 .... (516) 285-9881
Valley Stream Central High School District (07-12)
    2003-04 Enrollment: 4,566 .... (516) 872-5601

Two-year College(s)
Business Informatics Center Inc
    Fall 2004 Enrollment: 101 .... (516) 561-0050
    2005-06 Tuition: In-state $9,675; Out-of-state $9,675

Housing: Homeownership rate: 80.5% (2005); Median home value: $346,240 (2005); Median rent: $895 per month (2000); Median age of housing: 52 years (2000).
Hospitals: Franklin Hospital Medical Center (305 beds)
Transportation: Commute to work: 77.3% car, 17.1% public transportation, 3.0% walk, 2.0% work from home (2000); Travel time to work: 20.8% less than 15 minutes, 28.1% 15 to 30 minutes, 20.3% 30 to 45 minutes, 11.7% 45 to 60 minutes, 19.1% 60 minutes or more (2000)

Additional Information Contacts
Valley Stream Chamber of Commerce .... (516) 825-1741
    http://www.valley-stream.com

WANTAGH (CDP).
Covers a land area of 3.843 square miles and a water area of 0.297 square miles. Located at 40.67° N. Lat.; 73.51° W. Long. Elevation is 21 feet.
Population: 18,567 (1990); 18,971 (2000); 18,973 (2005); 18,993 (2010 projected); Race: 95.7% White, 0.3% Black, 2.5% Asian, 4.5% Hispanic of any race (2005); Density: 4,936.8 persons per square mile (2005); Average household size: 3.05 (2005); Median age: 39.6 (2005); Males per 100 females: 95.4 (2005); Marriage status: 21.4% never married, 68.8% now married, 6.7% widowed, 3.2% divorced (2000); Foreign born: 5.7% (2000); Ancestry (includes multiple ancestries): 31.2% Italian, 27.5% Irish, 21.7% German, 8.1% Other groups, 6.0% Polish (2000).
Economy: A causeway leads to Jones Beach State Park. Employment by occupation: 22.6% management, 24.3% professional, 11.8% services, 28.2% sales, 0.0% farming, 7.6% construction, 5.5% production (2000).
Income: Per capita income: $37,497 (2005); Median household income: $95,638 (2005); Average household income: $113,862 (2005); Percent of households with income of $100,000 or more: 46.9% (2005); Poverty rate: 1.5% (2000).
Education: Percent of population age 25 and over with: High school diploma (including GED) or higher: 91.4% (2005); Bachelor's degree or higher: 38.0% (2005); Master's degree or higher: 15.4% (2005).

School District(s)
Levittown Union Free School District (KG-12)
    2003-04 Enrollment: 8,027 .... (516) 520-8300
Wantagh Union Free School District (KG-12)
    2003-04 Enrollment: 3,578 .... (516) 679-6300

Housing: Homeownership rate: 93.7% (2005); Median home value: $423,883 (2005); Median rent: $890 per month (2000); Median age of housing: 46 years (2000).
Transportation: Commute to work: 78.5% car, 16.8% public transportation, 1.3% walk, 2.9% work from home (2000); Travel time to work: 20.6% less than 15 minutes, 28.3% 15 to 30 minutes, 18.1% 30 to 45 minutes, 9.6% 45 to 60 minutes, 23.3% 60 minutes or more (2000)

Additional Information Contacts
Wantagh Chamber of Commerce .... (516) 679-0100
    http://www.wantaghmall.org

WEST HEMPSTEAD (CDP).
Covers a land area of 2.658 square miles and a water area of 0.095 square miles. Located at 40.69° N. Lat.; 73.65° W. Long. Elevation is 67 feet.
Population: 17,707 (1990); 18,713 (2000); 19,029 (2005); 19,339 (2010 projected); Race: 75.3% White, 9.3% Black, 6.9% Asian, 14.0% Hispanic of any race (2005); Density: 7,157.9 persons per square mile (2005); Average household size: 3.15 (2005); Median age: 38.7 (2005); Males per 100 females: 96.2 (2005); Marriage status: 25.0% never married, 62.7% now married, 7.5% widowed, 4.7% divorced (2000); Foreign born: 18.1% (2000); Ancestry (includes multiple ancestries): 27.9% Italian, 23.7% Other groups, 15.6% Irish, 12.5% German, 5.7% United States or American (2000).
Economy: Employment by occupation: 16.8% management, 24.5% professional, 12.8% services, 31.2% sales, 0.1% farming, 7.0% construction, 7.6% production (2000).
Income: Per capita income: $30,568 (2005); Median household income: $80,357 (2005); Average household income: $95,791 (2005); Percent of households with income of $100,000 or more: 37.2% (2005); Poverty rate: 4.7% (2000).
Education: Percent of population age 25 and over with: High school diploma (including GED) or higher: 88.1% (2005); Bachelor's degree or higher: 34.5% (2005); Master's degree or higher: 14.2% (2005).

School District(s)
West Hempstead Union Free School District (KG-12)
    2003-04 Enrollment: 2,349 .... (516) 390-3107

Housing: Homeownership rate: 88.0% (2005); Median home value: $362,104 (2005); Median rent: $898 per month (2000); Median age of housing: 51 years (2000).
Transportation: Commute to work: 83.7% car, 12.3% public transportation, 0.9% walk, 2.9% work from home (2000); Travel time to work: 21.2% less than 15 minutes, 29.9% 15 to 30 minutes, 19.6% 30 to 45 minutes, 9.6% 45 to 60 minutes, 19.6% 60 minutes or more (2000)

WESTBURY (village). Covers a land area of 2.386 square miles and a water area of 0 square miles. Located at 40.75° N. Lat.; 73.58° W. Long. Elevation is 107 feet.
History: Named for Westbury, England. Old Westbury Gardens and manor of former Phipps estate rivals formal gardens of Europe. Seat of N.Y. Institute of Technology's central campus; State University of N.Y. College at Old Westbury. Incorporated 1924.
Population: 12,948 (1990); 14,263 (2000); 14,269 (2005); 14,262 (2010 projected); Race: 56.0% White, 25.4% Black, 5.6% Asian, 23.5% Hispanic of any race (2005); Density: 5,981.5 persons per square mile (2005); Average household size: 3.10 (2005); Median age: 38.8 (2005); Males per 100 females: 98.5 (2005); Marriage status: 31.4% never married, 56.7% now married, 6.8% widowed, 5.1% divorced (2000); Foreign born: 31.3% (2000); Ancestry (includes multiple ancestries): 34.4% Other groups, 23.4% Italian, 12.0% Irish, 8.3% German, 3.9% Jamaican (2000).
Economy: Single-family building permits issued: 4 (2005); Multi-family building permits issued: 6 (2005); Employment by occupation: 15.9% management, 21.4% professional, 17.1% services, 27.6% sales, 0.1% farming, 7.6% construction, 10.3% production (2000).
Income: Per capita income: $31,151 (2005); Median household income: $81,107 (2005); Average household income: $96,163 (2005); Percent of households with income of $100,000 or more: 37.8% (2005); Poverty rate: 5.3% (2000).
Education: Percent of population age 25 and over with: High school diploma (including GED) or higher: 79.4% (2005); Bachelor's degree or higher: 31.2% (2005); Master's degree or higher: 12.9% (2005).

School District(s)
East Meadow Union Free School District (KG-12)
   2003-04 Enrollment: 8,094 .... (516) 478-5776
Westbury Union Free School District (PK-12)
   2003-04 Enrollment: 4,036 .... (516) 876-5016

Two-year College(s)
The Chubb Institute-Westbury
   Fall 2004 Enrollment: 254 .... (602) 328-2800

Housing: Homeownership rate: 77.0% (2005); Median home value: $368,577 (2005); Median rent: $973 per month (2000); Median age of housing: 47 years (2000).
Transportation: Commute to work: 77.7% car, 14.5% public transportation, 4.1% walk, 2.0% work from home (2000); Travel time to work: 26.8% less than 15 minutes, 29.3% 15 to 30 minutes, 15.4% 30 to 45 minutes, 8.0% 45 to 60 minutes, 20.5% 60 minutes or more (2000)

Additional Information Contacts
Village of Westbury .... (516) 334-1700
   http://www.villageofwestbury.org/
Westbury Chamber of Commerce .... (516) 997-3966
   http://www.westburychamber.com

WILLISTON PARK (village). Covers a land area of 0.628 square miles and a water area of 0 square miles. Located at 40.75° N. Lat.; 73.64° W. Long. Elevation is 127 feet.
History: Incorporated 1926.
Population: 7,516 (1990); 7,261 (2000); 7,182 (2005); 7,099 (2010 projected); Race: 86.0% White, 0.6% Black, 10.1% Asian, 5.6% Hispanic of any race (2005); Density: 11,439.0 persons per square mile (2005); Average household size: 2.75 (2005); Median age: 40.5 (2005); Males per 100 females: 90.0 (2005); Marriage status: 25.4% never married, 62.3% now married, 8.2% widowed, 4.0% divorced (2000); Foreign born: 14.8% (2000); Ancestry (includes multiple ancestries): 32.6% Irish, 27.0% Italian, 16.2% German, 14.8% Other groups, 6.2% Polish (2000).
Economy: Single-family building permits issued: 0 (2005); Multi-family building permits issued: 0 (2005); Employment by occupation: 14.7% management, 27.3% professional, 14.4% services, 28.3% sales, 0.0% farming, 8.5% construction, 6.7% production (2000).
Income: Per capita income: $35,874 (2005); Median household income: $84,905 (2005); Average household income: $98,323 (2005); Percent of households with income of $100,000 or more: 40.3% (2005); Poverty rate: 1.9% (2000).
Education: Percent of population age 25 and over with: High school diploma (including GED) or higher: 88.9% (2005); Bachelor's degree or higher: 33.0% (2005); Master's degree or higher: 15.7% (2005).

School District(s)
Herricks Union Free School District (KG-12)
   2003-04 Enrollment: 3,939 .... (516) 248-3105
Mineola Union Free School District (PK-12)
   2003-04 Enrollment: 2,903 .... (516) 741-5036

Housing: Homeownership rate: 76.0% (2005); Median home value: $428,662 (2005); Median rent: $1,028 per month (2000); Median age of housing: 60 years (2000).
Newspapers: New Hyde Park Herald Courier (General - Circulation 2,875); Williston Times (General - Circulation 4,200)
Transportation: Commute to work: 82.4% car, 11.5% public transportation, 4.5% walk, 0.9% work from home (2000); Travel time to work: 22.9% less than 15 minutes, 31.9% 15 to 30 minutes, 17.3% 30 to 45 minutes, 9.3% 45 to 60 minutes, 18.7% 60 minutes or more (2000)

Additional Information Contacts
Willistons Chamber of Commerce .... (516) 739-1943
   http://www.chamberofthewillistons.org

WOODBURY (CDP). Covers a land area of 5.056 square miles and a water area of 0.009 square miles. Located at 40.81° N. Lat.; 73.46° W. Long. Elevation is 186 feet.
Population: 8,008 (1990); 9,010 (2000); 9,743 (2005); 10,395 (2010 projected); Race: 87.8% White, 1.2% Black, 9.5% Asian, 1.8% Hispanic of any race (2005); Density: 1,926.9 persons per square mile (2005); Average household size: 3.14 (2005); Median age: 46.2 (2005); Males per 100 females: 88.0 (2005); Marriage status: 18.4% never married, 65.8% now married, 11.5% widowed, 4.3% divorced (2000); Foreign born: 13.3% (2000); Ancestry (includes multiple ancestries): 16.5% Other groups, 14.9% Russian, 12.6% United States or American, 11.4% Italian, 8.1% Polish (2000).
Economy: Employment by occupation: 26.3% management, 34.2% professional, 2.0% services, 33.0% sales, 0.0% farming, 2.3% construction, 2.2% production (2000).
Income: Per capita income: $61,617 (2005); Median household income: $138,921 (2005); Average household income: $190,119 (2005); Percent of households with income of $100,000 or more: 65.2% (2005); Poverty rate: 3.3% (2000).
Education: Percent of population age 25 and over with: High school diploma (including GED) or higher: 88.6% (2005); Bachelor's degree or higher: 58.7% (2005); Master's degree or higher: 28.1% (2005).

School District(s)
Syosset Central School District (KG-12)
   2003-04 Enrollment: 6,623 .... (516) 364-5605

Housing: Homeownership rate: 82.4% (2005); Median home value: $883,413 (2005); Median rent: $1,354 per month (2000); Median age of housing: 26 years (2000).
Transportation: Commute to work: 78.1% car, 16.3% public transportation, 0.4% walk, 5.2% work from home (2000); Travel time to work: 20.4% less than 15 minutes, 30.8% 15 to 30 minutes, 14.6% 30 to 45 minutes, 6.8% 45 to 60 minutes, 27.4% 60 minutes or more (2000)

WOODMERE (CDP). Covers a land area of 2.555 square miles and a water area of 0.141 square miles. Located at 40.63° N. Lat.; 73.72° W. Long. Elevation is 30 feet.
Population: 15,562 (1990); 16,447 (2000); 17,579 (2005); 18,616 (2010 projected); Race: 89.6% White, 2.4% Black, 5.2% Asian, 4.8% Hispanic of any race (2005); Density: 6,879.6 persons per square mile (2005); Average household size: 3.12 (2005); Median age: 41.0 (2005); Males per 100 females: 95.3 (2005); Marriage status: 19.8% never married, 70.0% now married, 6.7% widowed, 3.5% divorced (2000); Foreign born: 15.2% (2000); Ancestry (includes multiple ancestries): 26.0% Other groups, 14.5% Russian, 12.1% Polish, 11.1% United States or American, 7.0% Italian (2000).
Economy: Employment by occupation: 22.6% management, 35.7% professional, 4.7% services, 30.5% sales, 0.1% farming, 2.6% construction, 3.8% production (2000).
Income: Per capita income: $44,239 (2005); Median household income: $102,965 (2005); Average household income: $136,910 (2005); Percent of households with income of $100,000 or more: 51.3% (2005); Poverty rate: 4.3% (2000).
Education: Percent of population age 25 and over with: High school diploma (including GED) or higher: 93.9% (2005); Bachelor's degree or higher: 56.1% (2005); Master's degree or higher: 28.5% (2005).

School District(s)
Lawrence Union Free School District (PK-12)
   2003-04 Enrollment: 3,692 .... (516) 295-7030

Housing: Homeownership rate: 90.7% (2005); Median home value: $588,255 (2005); Median rent: $965 per month (2000); Median age of housing: 45 years (2000).
Transportation: Commute to work: 73.8% car, 17.4% public transportation, 1.5% walk, 7.0% work from home (2000); Travel time to work: 19.5% less than 15 minutes, 19.1% 15 to 30 minutes, 19.9% 30 to 45 minutes, 12.6% 45 to 60 minutes, 28.9% 60 minutes or more (2000)

WOODSBURGH (village). Covers a land area of 0.363 square miles and a water area of 0.030 square miles. Located at 40.62° N. Lat.; 73.70° W. Long. Elevation is 8 feet.
Population: 1,225 (1990); 831 (2000); 684 (2005); 652 (2010 projected); Race: 98.7% White, 0.4% Black, 0.4% Asian, 2.6% Hispanic of any race (2005); Density: 1,882.2 persons per square mile (2005); Average household size: 3.35 (2005); Median age: 40.2 (2005); Males per 100 females: 101.2 (2005); Marriage status: 21.5% never married, 72.4% now married, 3.7% widowed, 2.4% divorced (2000); Foreign born: 7.5% (2000); Ancestry (includes multiple ancestries): 30.6% United States or American, 18.6% Other groups, 10.3% Russian, 8.6% Polish, 5.2% Italian (2000).
Economy: In summer-resort area. Single-family building permits issued: 0 (2005); Multi-family building permits issued: 0 (2005); Employment by occupation: 29.5% management, 34.7% professional, 2.7% services, 29.5% sales, 0.0% farming, 1.4% construction, 2.2% production (2000).
Income: Per capita income: $76,681 (2005); Median household income: $207,407 (2005); Average household income: $257,108 (2005); Percent of households with income of $100,000 or more: 78.9% (2005); Poverty rate: 0.4% (2000).
Education: Percent of population age 25 and over with: High school diploma (including GED) or higher: 98.8% (2005); Bachelor's degree or higher: 73.1% (2005); Master's degree or higher: 43.3% (2005).
Housing: Homeownership rate: 97.1% (2005); Median home value: $1 million+ (2005); Median rent: $n/a per month (2000); Median age of housing: 47 years (2000).
Transportation: Commute to work: 88.3% car, 7.1% public transportation, 1.4% walk, 3.3% work from home (2000); Travel time to work: 29.0% less than 15 minutes, 13.2% 15 to 30 minutes, 19.7% 30 to 45 minutes, 14.6% 45 to 60 minutes, 23.4% 60 minutes or more (2000)

New York City

Covers a land area of 303.311 square miles and a water area of 165.564 square miles. Located at 40.70° N. Lat.; 73.91° W. Long.
History: Adrien Block erected four trading houses in New York in 1613, prompting permanent settlement. In 1633, the first church was built, and that was soon followed by the establishment of Fort Amsterdam. After the battle of Long Island in 1776, when Sir William Howe's British forces defeated the forces of General George Washington, the city passed into English hands and remained in their control until 1783. Congress met in New York from 1785-1790, and it was here that George Washington was inaugurated as president.
Population: 7,322,552 (1990); 8,008,278 (2000); 8,113,728 (2005); 8,219,118 (2010 projected); Race: 42.7% White, 26.1% Black, 10.9% Asian, 28.6% Hispanic of any race (2005); Density: 26,750.5 persons per square mile (2005); Average household size: 2.66 (2005); Median age: 35.8 (2005); Males per 100 females: 90.8 (2005); Marriage status: 37.6% never married, 47.7% now married, 7.0% widowed, 7.7% divorced (2000); Foreign born: 35.9% (2000); Ancestry (includes multiple ancestries): 48.1% Other groups, 8.7% Italian, 5.3% Irish, 3.2% German, 3.0% Russian (2000).
Economy: Unemployment rate: 5.8% (2005); Total civilian labor force: 3,733,908 (2005); Single-family building permits issued: 1,300 (2005); Multi-family building permits issued: 30,299 (2005); Employment by occupation: 13.5% management, 23.3% professional, 18.6% services, 27.4% sales, 0.0% farming, 6.4% construction, 10.9% production (2000).
Income: Per capita income: $24,898 (2005); Median household income: $43,515 (2005); Average household income: $65,503 (2005); Percent of households with income of $100,000 or more: 17.7% (2005); Poverty rate: 21.2% (2000).
Taxes: Total city taxes per capita: $3,548 (2004); City property taxes per capita: $1,463 (2004).
Education: Percent of population age 25 and over with: High school diploma (including GED) or higher: 72.1% (2005); Bachelor's degree or higher: 27.2% (2005); Master's degree or higher: 11.5% (2005).

Housing: Homeownership rate: 30.2% (2005); Median home value: $364,783 (2005); Median rent: $646 per month (2000); Median age of housing: 51 years (2000).
Safety: Violent crime rate: 68.7 per 10,000 population; Property crime rate: 211.3 per 10,000 population (2004).
Transportation: Commute to work: 32.9% car, 52.8% public transportation, 10.4% walk, 2.9% work from home (2000); Travel time to work: 11.6% less than 15 minutes, 22.9% 15 to 30 minutes, 25.3% 30 to 45 minutes, 15.7% 45 to 60 minutes, 24.5% 60 minutes or more (2000); Amtrak: Service available.
Airports: John F Kennedy International (primary service/large hub); LaGuardia International (primary service/large hub); Newark Liberty International (Newark, NJ) (primary service/large hub)
National and State Parks: Castle Clinton National Monument; Statue of Liberty National Monument; Gateway National Recreation Area
Additional Information Contacts
American Indonesia Chamber . . . . (212) 687-4505
Bronx Chamber of Commerce . . . . (718) 828-3900
  http://www.bronxmall.com/com/chamber/
Brooklyn Chamber of Commerce . . . . (718) 875-1000
  http://www.ibrooklyn.com
Brunei-American Chamber of Commerce . . . . (718) 794-9896
City of New York . . . . (212) 669-2400
  http://nyc.gov/
Coney Island Chamber of Commerce . . . . (718) 266-1234
  http://www.coneyislandchamberofcommerce.org
French-American Chamber of Commerce . . . . (212) 867-0123
Greater New York Chamber of Commerce . . . . (212) 686-7220
  http://nyc.chamber.com
Greenwich Village-Chelsea Chamber of Commerce . . . . . . (212) 255-5811
  http://www.gvccc.com
Harlem Chamber of Commerce . . . . (212) 862-7200
  http://www.chamber.harlemdiscover.com
Manhattan Chamber of Commerce . . . . (212) 479-7772
  http://www.manhattancc.org/
Nigerian American Chamber of Commerce . . . . (212) 791-4161
  http://www.nigeriabusinessinfo.com/bilateral-chambers.htm
Slovak American Chamber of Commerce . . . . (212) 679-7044
  http://www.amcham.sk/Contact
Staten Island Chamber of Commerce . . . . (718) 727-1900
  http://www.sichamber.com
Swiss-American Chamber of Commerce . . . . (212) 246-7789
West Side Chamber of Commerce . . . . (212) 541-8880
  http://www.westsidechamber.org
Women's International Chamber . . . . (212) 809-5121

Five Boroughs of New York City

BRONX (borough). Aka Bronx County. Located in southeastern New York State; the northernmost borough of New York city, situated between Manhattan and the Westchester County line; bounded on the west by the Hudson River, on the southwest by Spuyten Duyvil Creek and the Harlem River, on the south by the East River, and on the east by Long Island Sound. Covers a land area of 42.03 square miles, a water area of 15.40 square miles, and is located in the Eastern Time Zone.

Bronx County is part of the New York-Northern New Jersey-Long Island, NY-NJ-PA Metropolitan Statistical Area. The entire metro area includes: Edison, NJ Metropolitan Division (Middlesex County, NJ; Monmouth County, NJ; Ocean County, NJ; Somerset County, NJ); Nassau-Suffolk, NY Metropolitan Division (Nassau County, NY; Suffolk County, NY); New York-White Plains-Wayne, NY-NJ Metropolitan Division (Bergen County, NJ; Hudson County, NJ; Passaic County, NJ; Bronx County, NY; Kings County, NY; New York County, NY; Putnam County, NY; Queens County, NY; Richmond County, NY; Rockland County, NY; Westchester County, NY); Newark-Union, NJ-PA Metropolitan Division (Essex County, NJ; Hunterdon County, NJ; Morris County, NJ; Sussex County, NJ; Union County, NJ; Pike County, PA)

Population: 1,203,745 (1990); 1,332,650 (2000); 1,374,586 (2005); 1,417,726 (2010 projected); Race: 28.3% White, 34.6% Black, 2.9% Asian, 52.3% Hispanic of any race (2005); Density: 32,707.2 persons per square mile (2005); Average household size: 2.89 (2005); Median age: 32.1 (2005); Males per 100 females: 88.3 (2005).

Religion: Five largest groups: 43.7% Catholic Church, 6.3% Jewish Estimate, 0.9% Muslim Estimate, 0.9% American Baptist Churches in the USA, 0.8% Assemblies of God (2000).
Economy: Unemployment rate: 7.5% (2005); Total civilian labor force: 503,577 (2005); Leading industries: 53.8% health care and social assistance; 8.3% retail trade; 4.5% educational services (2003); Farms: 0 totaling 0 acres (2002); Companies that employ 500 or more persons: 44 (2003); Companies that employ 100 to 499 persons: 246 (2003); Companies that employ less than 100 persons: 14,963 (2003); Black-owned businesses: 23,624 (2002); Hispanic-owned businesses: 38,325 (2002); Women-owned businesses: 39,087 (2002); Retail sales per capita: $4,254 (2006). Single-family building permits issued: 29 (2005); Multi-family building permits issued: 4,908 (2005).
Income: Per capita income: $15,587 (2005); Median household income: $31,202 (2005); Average household income: $43,940 (2005); Percent of households with income of $100,000 or more: 8.8% (2005); Poverty rate: 26.8% (2003); Bankruptcy rate: 6.65% (2005).
Education: Percent of population age 25 and over with: High school diploma (including GED) or higher: 62.0% (2005); Bachelor's degree or higher: 14.4% (2005); Master's degree or higher: 5.7% (2005).
Housing: Homeownership rate: 19.7% (2005); Median home value: $298,199 (2005); Median rent: $560 per month (2000); Median age of housing: 47 years (2000).
Health: Birth rate: 181.0 per 10,000 population (2004); Death rate: 70.7 per 10,000 population (2004); Age-adjusted cancer mortality rate: 198.7 deaths per 100,000 population (2002); Air Quality Index: 54.8% good, 42.7% moderate, 2.5% unhealthy for sensitive individuals, 0.0% unhealthy (percent of days in 2005); Number of physicians: 25.0 per 10,000 population (2004); Hospital beds: 39.2 per 10,000 population (2003); Hospital admissions: 1,385.6 per 10,000 population (2003).
Elections: 2004 Presidential election results: 16.5% Bush, 82.8% Kerry, 0.6% Nader, 0.0% Badnarik.

School District(s)
Bronx Charter Sch Better Learning (01-01)
   2003-04 Enrollment: 50 .... (845) 753-2227
Bronx Charter School - Arts (KG-03)
   2003-04 Enrollment: 155 .... (212) 926-7549
Bronx Prep Charter School (05-09)
   2003-04 Enrollment: 249 .... (212) 307-3177
Carl C. Icahn Charter School, The (KG-04)
   2003-04 Enrollment: 176 .... (718) 716-8105
Family Life Acad Charter School (KG-03)
   2003-04 Enrollment: 183 .... (718) 410-8100
Harriet Tubman Charter School (KG-05)
   2003-04 Enrollment: 171 .... (718) 537-9912
Kipp Academy Charter School (05-08)
   2003-04 Enrollment: 247 .... (718) 665-3555
NYC Alternative HS District (10-12)
   2003-04 Enrollment: 1,828 .... (212) 374-5082
New York City Geographic District # 7 (PK-10)
   2003-04 Enrollment: 1,295 .... (718) 742-6482
New York City Geographic District # 8 (PK-09)
   2003-04 Enrollment: 146 .... (718) 409-8150
New York City Geographic District # 9 (KG-10)
   2003-04 Enrollment: 1,839 .... (718) 741-7030
New York City Geographic District #10 (KG-09)
   2003-04 Enrollment: 621 .... (718) 741-7030
New York City Geographic District #11 (KG-10)
   2003-04 Enrollment: 1,441 .... (718) 519-2614
New York City Geographic District #12 (PK-08)
   2003-04 Enrollment: 1,028 .... (718) 328-2310
New York City Public Schools (PK-12)
   2003-04 Enrollment: 1,023,674 .... (718) 935-2794
Readnet Bronx Charter School (KG-01)
   2003-04 Enrollment: 74 .... (212) 838-2344

Four-year College(s)
CUNY Lehman College (Public)
   Fall 2004 Enrollment: 10,281 .... (718) 960-8000
   2005-06 Tuition: In-state $4,290; Out-of-state $8,930
College of Mount Saint Vincent
   Fall 2004 Enrollment: 1,685 .... (718) 405-3200
   2005-06 Tuition: In-state $20,500; Out-of-state $20,500
Fordham University
   Fall 2004 Enrollment: 14,861 .... (718) 817-1000
   2005-06 Tuition: In-state $28,596; Out-of-state $28,596

Manhattan College
   Fall 2004 Enrollment: 3,299 .... (718) 862-8000
   2005-06 Tuition: In-state $20,600; Out-of-state $20,600
Monroe College-Main Campus
   Fall 2004 Enrollment: 4,284 .... (718) 933-6700
   2005-06 Tuition: In-state $14,640; Out-of-state $14,640
SUNY Maritime College (Public)
   Fall 2004 Enrollment: 1,201 .... (718) 409-7200
   2005-06 Tuition: In-state $9,826; Out-of-state $15,615

Two-year College(s)
CUNY Bronx Community College (Public)
   Fall 2004 Enrollment: 8,367 .... (718) 284-5100
   2005-06 Tuition: In-state $3,104; Out-of-state $4,864
CUNY Hostos Community College (Public)
   Fall 2004 Enrollment: 4,340 .... (718) 518-4444
   2005-06 Tuition: In-state $3,105; Out-of-state $4,865

Hospitals: Bronx Childrens Psychiatric Center (78 beds); Bronx Psychiatric Center (360 beds); Bronx-Lebanon Hospital Center (847 beds); Calvary Hospital (200 beds); Hebrew Hospital Home (480 beds); Jacobi Medical Center (527 beds); Lincoln Medical and Mental Health Center (418 beds); Montefiore Medical Center (1062 beds); Our Lady of Mercy Medical Center (612 beds); St. Barnabas Hospital (461 beds); Union Hospital of the Bronx (201 beds); Veterans Affairs Medical Center (459 beds); Weiler Hospital; Westchester Square Medical Center (205 beds)
Newspapers: Bronx Press Newspaper Group (General - Circulation 40,000); Bronx Times Reporter - Castle Hill Edition (General - Circulation 29,000); Co-Op City Times (General - Circulation 18,000); Riverdale Review (General - Circulation 20,000); The Riverdale Press (General - Circulation 14,500)

Additional Information Contacts
Bronx Borough President .... (718) 590-3500
   http://bronxboropres.nyc.gov/
Bronx Chamber of Commerce .... (718) 828-3900
   http://www.bronxmall.com/com/chamber/
Brunei-American Chamber of Commerce .... (718) 794-9896

BROOKLYN (borough).
Aka Kings County. Located in southeastern New York State. One of the five counties/boroughs of New York City. Covers a land area of 70.61 square miles, a water area of 26.29 square miles, and is located in the Eastern Time Zone.

Kings County is part of the New York-Northern New Jersey-Long Island, NY-NJ-PA Metropolitan Statistical Area. The entire metro area includes: Edison, NJ Metropolitan Division (Middlesex County, NJ; Monmouth County, NJ; Ocean County, NJ; Somerset County, NJ); Nassau-Suffolk, NY Metropolitan Division (Nassau County, NY; Suffolk County, NY); New York-White Plains-Wayne, NY-NJ Metropolitan Division (Bergen County, NJ; Hudson County, NJ; Passaic County, NJ; Bronx County, NY; Kings County, NY; New York County, NY; Putnam County, NY; Queens County, NY; Richmond County, NY; Rockland County, NY; Westchester County, NY); Newark-Union, NJ-PA Metropolitan Division (Essex County, NJ; Hunterdon County, NJ; Morris County, NJ; Sussex County, NJ; Union County, NJ; Pike County, PA)

Weather Station: New York Avenue V Brooklyn   Elevation: 19 feet

	Jan	Feb	Mar	Apr	May	Jun	Jul	Aug	Sep	Oct	Nov	Dec
High	39	42	50	60	71	79	85	83	76	65	54	44
Low	26	28	35	44	54	64	70	69	61	50	41	32
Precip	3.9	3.0	4.1	3.9	4.3	3.5	4.3	4.1	3.9	3.4	3.9	3.6
Snow	7.2	7.8	3.6	0.4	tr	0.0	0.0	0.0	0.0	tr	0.4	2.1

High and Low temperatures in degrees Fahrenheit; Precipitation and Snow in inches

Population: 2,300,664 (1990); 2,465,326 (2000); 2,472,995 (2005); 2,479,313 (2010 projected); Race: 39.4% White, 36.4% Black, 8.5% Asian, 20.5% Hispanic of any race (2005); Density: 35,025.3 persons per square mile (2005); Average household size: 2.81 (2005); Median age: 34.7 (2005); Males per 100 females: 89.1 (2005).
Religion: Five largest groups: 37.0% Catholic Church, 15.4% Jewish Estimate, 2.3% Muslim Estimate, 2.3% American Baptist Churches in the USA, 0.9% Seventh-day Adventist Church (2000).
Economy: Unemployment rate: 6.2% (2005); Total civilian labor force: 1,052,692 (2005); Leading industries: 32.1% health care and social assistance; 11.9% retail trade; 7.7% manufacturing (2003); Farms: 1 totaling n/a acres (2002); Companies that employ 500 or more persons: 80 (2003); Companies that employ 100 to 499 persons: 447 (2003); Companies that employ less than 100 persons: 40,714 (2003);

Black-owned businesses: 37,499 (2002); Hispanic-owned businesses: 22,373 (2002); Women-owned businesses: 62,500 (2002); Retail sales per capita: $5,424 (2006). Single-family building permits issued: 105 (2005); Multi-family building permits issued: 8,923 (2005).

Income: Per capita income: $18,843 (2005); Median household income: $36,405 (2005); Average household income: $52,329 (2005); Percent of households with income of $100,000 or more: 12.6% (2005); Poverty rate: 23.3% (2003); Bankruptcy rate: 4.95% (2005).

Education: Percent of population age 25 and over with: High school diploma (including GED) or higher: 68.7% (2005); Bachelor's degree or higher: 21.7% (2005); Master's degree or higher: 8.8% (2005).

Housing: Homeownership rate: 27.1% (2005); Median home value: $375,900 (2005); Median rent: $621 per month (2000); Median age of housing: 55 years (2000).

Health: Birth rate: 164.7 per 10,000 population (2004); Death rate: 74.3 per 10,000 population (2004); Age-adjusted cancer mortality rate: 184.3 deaths per 100,000 population (2002); Air Quality Index: 62.2% good, 36.7% moderate, 1.1% unhealthy for sensitive individuals, 0.0% unhealthy (percent of days in 2005); Number of physicians: 29.0 per 10,000 population (2004); Hospital beds: 32.9 per 10,000 population (2003); Hospital admissions: 1,152.6 per 10,000 population (2003).

Elections: 2004 Presidential election results: 24.3% Bush, 74.9% Kerry, 0.7% Nader, 0.1% Badnarik

School District(s)

Beginning With Children Charter School (KG-08)
   2003-04 Enrollment: 452 . . . . (718) 388-8847
Brooklyn Charter School (KG-04)
   2003-04 Enrollment: 120 . . . . (718) 452-3423
Brooklyn Excelsior Charter Sch (KG-04)
   2003-04 Enrollment: 206 . . . . (212) 431-4477
Comm Partnership Charter School (KG-04)
   2003-04 Enrollment: 250 . . . . (718) 330-0480
Explore Charter School (KG-04)
   2003-04 Enrollment: 239 . . . . (212) 678-3587
NYC Alternative HS District (10-12)
   2003-04 Enrollment: 1,828 . . . . (212) 374-5082
New York City Geographic District #13 (09-09)
   2003-04 Enrollment: 99 . . . . (718) 636-3204
New York City Geographic District #15 (06-11)
   2003-04 Enrollment: 2,011 . . . . (718) 330-9300
New York City Geographic District #16 (PK-08)
   2003-04 Enrollment: 418 . . . . (718) 574-2800
New York City Geographic District #17 (06-09)
   2003-04 Enrollment: 518 . . . . (718) 826-7950
New York City Geographic District #18 (PK-06)
   2003-04 Enrollment: 479 . . . . (718) 927-5170
New York City Geographic District #32 (06-09)
   2003-04 Enrollment: 677 . . . . (718) 574-1125
New York City Public Schools (PK-12)
   2003-04 Enrollment: 1,023,674 . . . . (718) 935-2794
New York City Public Schools (PK-12)
   2003-04 Enrollment: 1,023,674 . . . . (718) 935-2794

Four-year College(s)

Beth Hamedrash Shaarei Yosher Institute
   Fall 2004 Enrollment: 120 . . . . (718) 854-2290
   2005-06 Tuition: In-state $6,010; Out-of-state $6,010
Beth Hatalmud Rabbinical College
   Fall 2004 Enrollment: 61 . . . . (718) 259-2525
   2005-06 Tuition: In-state $5,000; Out-of-state $5,000
Brooklyn Law School
   Fall 2004 Enrollment: 1,518 . . . . (718) 625-2200
CUNY Brooklyn College (Public)
   Fall 2004 Enrollment: 15,384 . . . . (718) 951-5000
   2005-06 Tuition: In-state $4,377; Out-of-state $9,017
CUNY Medgar Evers College (Public)
   Fall 2004 Enrollment: 5,170 . . . . (718) 270-4900
   2005-06 Tuition: In-state $4,252; Out-of-state $8,892
CUNY New York City College of Technology (Public)
   Fall 2004 Enrollment: 11,772 . . . . (718) 260-5000
   2005-06 Tuition: In-state $4,289; Out-of-state $8,929
Central Yeshiva Tomchei Tmimim Lubavitz
   Fall 2004 Enrollment: 546 . . . . (718) 434-0784
   2005-06 Tuition: In-state $4,800; Out-of-state $4,800
Darkei Noam Rabbinical College
   Fall 2004 Enrollment: 41 . . . . (718) 338-9444
   2005-06 Tuition: In-state $5,000; Out-of-state $5,000
Long Island University-Brooklyn Campus
   Fall 2004 Enrollment: 8,003 . . . . (718) 488-1000
   2005-06 Tuition: In-state $23,212; Out-of-state $23,212
Machzikei Hadath Rabbinical College
   Fall 2004 Enrollment: 139 . . . . (718) 854-8791
   2005-06 Tuition: In-state $6,100; Out-of-state $6,100
Mesivta Torah Vodaath Rabbinical Seminary
   Fall 2004 Enrollment: 338 . . . . (718) 941-8000
   2005-06 Tuition: In-state $6,100; Out-of-state $6,100
Mesivta of Eastern Parkway-Yeshiva Zichron Meilech
   Fall 2004 Enrollment: 56 . . . . (718) 438-1002
   2005-06 Tuition: In-state $6,400; Out-of-state $6,400
Mirrer Yeshiva Cent Institute
   Fall 2004 Enrollment: 309 . . . . (718) 645-0536
   2005-06 Tuition: In-state $4,700; Out-of-state $4,700
Polytechnic University
   Fall 2004 Enrollment: 2,819 . . . . (718) 260-3100
   2005-06 Tuition: In-state $28,650; Out-of-state $28,650
Pratt Institute-Main
   Fall 2004 Enrollment: 4,540 . . . . (718) 636-3600
   2005-06 Tuition: In-state $27,580; Out-of-state $27,580
Rabbinical Academy Mesivta Rabbi Chaim Berlin
   Fall 2004 Enrollment: 314 . . . . (718) 377-0777
   2005-06 Tuition: In-state $7,300; Out-of-state $7,300
Rabbinical College Bobover Yeshiva Bnei Zion
   Fall 2004 Enrollment: 351 . . . . (718) 438-2018
   2005-06 Tuition: In-state $4,400; Out-of-state $4,400
Rabbinical College of Ch'san Sofer New York
   Fall 2004 Enrollment: 116 . . . . (718) 236-1171
   2005-06 Tuition: In-state $5,500; Out-of-state $5,500
Rabbinical College of Ohr Shimon Yisroel
   Fall 2004 Enrollment: 165 . . . . (718) 855-4092
   2005-06 Tuition: In-state $6,000; Out-of-state $6,000
Rabbinical Seminary M'kor Chaim
   Fall 2004 Enrollment: 45 . . . . (718) 851-0183
   2005-06 Tuition: In-state $5,000; Out-of-state $5,000
Rabbinical Seminary of Adas Yereim
   Fall 2004 Enrollment: 89 . . . . (212) 388-1751
SUNY Health Science Center at Brooklyn (Public)
   Fall 2004 Enrollment: 1,569 . . . . (718) 270-1000
Saint Josephs College-Main Campus
   Fall 2004 Enrollment: 1,336 . . . . (718) 636-6800
   2005-06 Tuition: In-state $12,374; Out-of-state $12,374
Talmudical Seminary Oholei Torah
   Fall 2004 Enrollment: 211 . . . . (718) 774-5050
   2005-06 Tuition: In-state $5,400; Out-of-state $5,400
Torah Temimah Talmudical Seminary
   Fall 2004 Enrollment: 216 . . . . (718) 853-8500
   2005-06 Tuition: In-state $7,800; Out-of-state $7,800
United Talmudical Seminary
   Fall 2004 Enrollment: 1,125 . . . . (718) 963-9770
   2005-06 Tuition: In-state $6,000; Out-of-state $6,000
Yeshiva Derech Chaim
   Fall 2004 Enrollment: 176 . . . . (718) 438-5476
   2005-06 Tuition: In-state $7,000; Out-of-state $7,000
Yeshiva Gedolah Imrei Yosef D'spinka
   Fall 2004 Enrollment: 202 . . . . (718) 851-1600
   2005-06 Tuition: In-state $4,400; Out-of-state $4,400
Yeshiva Karlin Stolin
   Fall 2004 Enrollment: 99 . . . . (718) 232-7800
   2005-06 Tuition: In-state $5,500; Out-of-state $5,500
Yeshiva and Kollel Harbotzas Torah
   Fall 2004 Enrollment: 33 . . . . (718) 692-0208
   2005-06 Tuition: In-state $4,600; Out-of-state $4,600
Yeshivas Novominsk
   Fall 2004 Enrollment: 142 . . . . (718) 438-2727
   2005-06 Tuition: In-state $6,500; Out-of-state $6,500
Yeshivat Mikdash Melech
   Fall 2004 Enrollment: 79 . . . . (718) 339-1090
   2005-06 Tuition: In-state $6,500; Out-of-state $6,500

Two-year College(s)

ASA Institute of Business and Computer Technology
   Fall 2004 Enrollment: 2,952 . . . . (718) 522-9073
   2005-06 Tuition: In-state $11,464; Out-of-state $11,464
Allen School-Brooklyn
   Fall 2004 Enrollment: 781 . . . . (718) 243-1700
Associated Beth Rivkah Schools
   Fall 2004 Enrollment: 76 . . . . (718) 735-0400
   2005-06 Tuition: In-state $5,000; Out-of-state $5,000
Berk Trade and Business School
   Fall 2004 Enrollment: 120 . . . . (718) 625-6037
Brooklyn Institute of Business Technology
   Fall 2004 Enrollment: 172 . . . . (718) 859-3900
   2005-06 Tuition: In-state $11,520; Out-of-state $11,520
CUNY Kingsborough Community College (Public)
   Fall 2004 Enrollment: 15,356 . . . . (718) 368-5000
   2005-06 Tuition: In-state $3,100; Out-of-state $4,860
Career Institute of Health and Technology
   Fall 2004 Enrollment: 879 . . . . (718) 422-1212
Centurion Professional Training
   Fall 2004 Enrollment: 40 . . . . (718) 646-4507
Charles Stuart School of Diamond Setting
   Fall 2004 Enrollment: 32 . . . . (718) 339-2640
Gamla College
   Fall 2004 Enrollment: 214 . . . . (718) 339-4747
Hair Design Institute at Fifth Avenue
   Fall 2004 Enrollment: 99 . . . . (718) 745-1000
Institute of Design and Construction
   Fall 2004 Enrollment: 224 . . . . (718) 855-3661
   2005-06 Tuition: In-state $6,480; Out-of-state $6,480
Learning Institute for Beauty Sciences-Brooklyn
   Fall 2004 Enrollment: 248 . . . . (800) 223-3271
Long Island College Hospital School of Nursing
   Fall 2004 Enrollment: 123 . . . . (718) 780-1953
   2005-06 Tuition: In-state $11,400; Out-of-state $11,400
Long Island College Hospital School of Radiologic Sciences
   Fall 2004 Enrollment: 34 . . . . (718) 780-4651
   2005-06 Tuition: In-state $10,150; Out-of-state $10,150
Merkaz Bnos-Business School
   Fall 2004 Enrollment: 182 . . . . (718) 234-4000
Seminar L'moros Bais Yaakov
   Fall 2004 Enrollment: 397 . . . . (718) 851-2900
   2005-06 Tuition: In-state $6,500; Out-of-state $6,500

Hospitals: Beth Israel Medical Center-Kings Highway Division (212 beds); Brookdale University Hospital and Medical Center (529 beds); Brooklyn Hospital Center (653 beds); Caledonian Hospital; Coney Island Hospital (433 beds); Interfaith Medical Center (287 beds); Kings County Hospital Center (1204 beds); Kingsboro Psychiatric Center (614 beds); Kingsbrook Jewish Medical Center (864 beds); Long Island College Hospital (506 beds); Lutheran Medical Center (476 beds); Maimonides Medical Center (705 beds); NY Community Hospital of Brooklyn (134 beds); New York Methodist Hospital (612 beds); St. Mary's Hospital (285 beds); University Hospital of Brooklyn (376 beds); Veterans Affairs Medical Center (942 beds); Victory Memorial Hospital (346 beds); Woodhull Medical & Mental Health Center; Wyckoff Heights Medical Center (305 beds)

Newspapers: Afro Times (Black, General - Circulation 55,502); Bay News (General - Circulation 21,420); Bay Ridge Courier (General - Circulation 42,000); Bay Ridge Paper (General - Circulation 27,300); Brooklyn Arts & Entertainment Journal (General - Circulation 50,000); Brooklyn Eagle (General - Circulation 100,000); Brooklyn Graphic (General - Circulation 9,350); Brooklyn Heights Courier (General - Circulation 7,000); Brooklyn Heights Paper (General - Circulation 7,100); Brooklyn Spectator (General - Circulation 8,950); Canarsie Courier (General - Circulation 10,000); Canarsie Digest (General - Circulation 10,135); Caribbean Life - Bronx Edition (Ethnic - Circulation 41,666); Caribbean Life - Brooklyn Edition (Ethnic - Circulation 41,666); Caribbean Life - Queens Edition (Ethnic - Circulation 41,666); Carroll Gardens-Cobble Hill Courier (General - Circulation 51,000); Darbininkas (General - Circulation 3,000); Der Yid (General, Jewish, Religious - Circulation 49,000); Downtown News (General - Circulation 7,100); Eltingville/Annadale American (General - Circulation 28,000); Flatbush Life (General - Circulation 12,350); Great Kills Village Reporter (General - Circulation 28,000); Greenpoint Gazette (General - Circulation 5,000); Haiti Observateur (French - Circulation 75,000); Hamodia (Jewish - Circulation 30,000); Harbor Watch (General - Circulation 24,000); Home Reporter & Sunset News (General - Circulation 9,850); Kensington Paper (General - Circulation 10,000); Kings Courier (General - Circulation 19,430); Kurier Russian American Weekly Newspaper (Ethnic - Circulation 40,000); Laiks (Ethnic - Circulation 9,500); New Dorp Star Reporter (General - Circulation 28,000); New York Daily Challenge (Circulation 79,540); North Shore Star (General - Circulation 28,000); Park Slope Courier (General - Circulation 27,000); South Shore Star (General - Circulation 28,000); Spring Creek Sun (General - Circulation 8,500); Staten Island Star (General - Circulation 28,000); The Bensonhurst Paper (General - Circulation 5,000); The Brooklyn Daily Eagle (Circulation 5,000); The Brooklyn Heights Press (General - Circulation 19,500); The Brooklyn Paper of Carroll Gardens & Cobble Hill (General - Circulation 7,100); The Business Journal (General - Circulation 60,000); The Fort Greene/Clinton Hill Paper (General - Circulation 3,000); The Haitian Times (Ethnic - Circulation 15,000); The Jewish Herald (Jewish - Circulation 312,000); The Jewish Press (Jewish - Circulation 85,000); The Midwood Paper (General - Circulation 2,000); The New American (Black, General - Circulation 54,355); The Park Slope Paper (General - Circulation 8,400); The Sunset Park Paper (General - Circulation 8,400); The Windsor Terrace Edition (General - Circulation 3,000)

Additional Information Contacts

Brooklyn Borough President . . . . (718) 802-3700
   http://www.brooklyn-usa.org/
Brooklyn Chamber of Commerce. (718) 875-1000
   http://www.ibrooklyn.com
Coney Island Chamber of Commerce . . . . (718) 266-1234
   http://www.coneyislandchamberofcommerce.org

MANHATTAN (borough). Aka New York County. Located in southeastern New York State. One of the five counties/boroughs New York City. Covers a land area of 22.96 square miles, a water area of 10.81 square miles, and is located in the Eastern Time Zone.

New York County is part of the New York-Northern New Jersey-Long Island, NY-NJ-PA Metropolitan Statistical Area. The entire metro area includes: Edison, NJ Metropolitan Division (Middlesex County, NJ; Monmouth County, NJ; Ocean County, NJ; Somerset County, NJ); Nassau-Suffolk, NY Metropolitan Division (Nassau County, NY; Suffolk County, NY); New York-White Plains-Wayne, NY-NJ Metropolitan Division (Bergen County, NJ; Hudson County, NJ; Passaic County, NJ; Bronx County, NY; Kings County, NY; New York County, NY; Putnam County, NY; Queens County, NY; Richmond County, NY; Rockland County, NY; Westchester County, NY); Newark-Union, NJ-PA Metropolitan Division (Essex County, NJ; Hunterdon County, NJ; Morris County, NJ; Sussex County, NJ; Union County, NJ; Pike County, PA)

Weather Station: New York Central Park Observatory   Elevation: 131 feet

	Jan	Feb	Mar	Apr	May	Jun	Jul	Aug	Sep	Oct	Nov	Dec
High	38	41	50	62	72	80	85	84	76	65	54	44
Low	26	28	35	44	54	63	69	68	60	50	41	32
Precip	4.1	3.3	4.3	4.1	4.6	3.8	4.5	4.2	4.2	3.9	4.4	3.9
Snow	7.3	7.5	3.4	0.4	tr	0.0	tr	0.0	0.0	tr	0.4	2.2

High and Low temperatures in degrees Fahrenheit; Precipitation and Snow in inches

Population: 1,487,530 (1990); 1,537,195 (2000); 1,576,353 (2005); 1,616,428 (2010 projected); Race: 53.8% White, 16.3% Black, 10.5% Asian, 27.4% Hispanic of any race (2005); Density: 68,645.3 persons per square mile (2005); Average household size: 2.08 (2005); Median age: 37.7 (2005); Males per 100 females: 91.1 (2005).
Religion: Five largest groups: 36.7% Catholic Church, 20.5% Jewish Estimate, 2.4% Muslim Estimate, 1.9% American Baptist Churches in the USA, 1.5% Episcopal Church (2000).
Economy: Unemployment rate: 5.1% (2005); Total civilian labor force: 875,298 (2005); Leading industries: 16.5% finance and insurance; 12.9% professional (2003); Farms: 4 totaling 4 acres (2002); Companies that employ 500 or more persons: 468 (2003); Companies that employ 100 to 499 persons: 2,501 (2003); Companies that employ less than 100 persons: 100,344 (2003); Black-owned businesses: 16,008 (2002); Hispanic-owned businesses: 31,850 (2002); Women-owned businesses: 86,364 (2002); Retail sales per capita: $20,174 (2006). Single-family building permits issued: 3 (2005); Multi-family building permits issued: 8,490 (2005).
Income: Per capita income: $46,545 (2005); Median household income: $54,955 (2005); Average household income: $95,849 (2005); Percent of households with income of $100,000 or more: 28.6% (2005); Poverty rate: 18.6% (2003); Bankruptcy rate: 5.11% (2005).
Education: Percent of population age 25 and over with: High school diploma (including GED) or higher: 78.2% (2005); Bachelor's degree or higher: 48.7% (2005); Master's degree or higher: 23.0% (2005).

Housing: Homeownership rate: 19.8% (2005); Median home value: $628,864 (2005); Median rent: $740 per month (2000); Median age of housing: 54 years (2000).
Health: Birth rate: 130.5 per 10,000 population (2004); Death rate: 70.1 per 10,000 population (2004); Age-adjusted cancer mortality rate: 197.3 deaths per 100,000 population (2002); Air Quality Index: 48.8% good, 49.9% moderate, 1.4% unhealthy for sensitive individuals, 0.0% unhealthy (percent of days in 2005); Number of physicians: 118.1 per 10,000 population (2004); Hospital beds: 82.2 per 10,000 population (2003); Hospital admissions: 2,962.7 per 10,000 population (2003).
Elections: 2004 Presidential election results: 16.7% Bush, 82.1% Kerry, 0.9% Nader, 0.2% Badnarik
National and State Parks: Castle Clinton National Monument; Statue of Liberty National Monument

School District(s)

Amber Charter School (KG-04)
  2003-04 Enrollment: 234 . . . . (212) 534-9667
East Harlem Vill Acad Charter Sch (05-05)
  2003-04 Enrollment: 76 . . . . (212) 410-5612
Harbor Sci & Arts Charter School (01-08)
  2003-04 Enrollment: 202 . . . . (212) 427-2244
Harlem Day Charter School (KG-03)
  2003-04 Enrollment: 159 . . . . (212) 876-9953
John A. Reisenbach Charter School (KG-08)
  2003-04 Enrollment: 447 . . . . (212) 666-3941
John V. Lindsay Wildcat Acad Charter (08-12)
  2003-04 Enrollment: 420 . . . . (212) 635-3800
Kipp S.T.A.R. Charter School (05-05)
  2003-04 Enrollment: 87 . . . . (917) 566-1273
NYC Alternative HS District (10-12)
  2003-04 Enrollment: 1,828 . . . . (212) 374-5082
New York City Geographic District # 1 (09-09)
  2003-04 Enrollment: 63 . . . . (212) 602-9701
New York City Geographic District # 2 (06-12)
  2003-04 Enrollment: 760 . . . . (212) 330-9400
New York City Geographic District # 3 (PK-09)
  2003-04 Enrollment: 510 . . . . (212) 678-2880
New York City Geographic District # 4 (KG-06)
  2003-04 Enrollment: 489 . . . . (212) 828-3590
New York City Public Schools (PK-12)
  2003-04 Enrollment: 1,023,674 . . . . (718) 935-2794
Reach Charter School
  2003-04 Enrollment: n/a . . . . (212) 349-8073
Sisulu Children's Charter School (KG-05)
  2003-04 Enrollment: 265 . . . . (212) 663-8216

Four-year College(s)

Bank Street College of Education
  Fall 2004 Enrollment: 1,086 . . . . (212) 875-4400
Barnard College
  Fall 2004 Enrollment: 2,287 . . . . (212) 854-5262
  2005-06 Tuition: In-state $30,676; Out-of-state $30,676
Berkeley College
  Fall 2004 Enrollment: 2,670 . . . . (212) 986-4343
  2005-06 Tuition: In-state $16,950; Out-of-state $16,950
Boricua College
  Fall 2004 Enrollment: 1,176 . . . . (212) 694-1000
  2005-06 Tuition: In-state $9,000; Out-of-state $9,000
CUNY Bernard M Baruch College (Public)
  Fall 2004 Enrollment: 15,537 . . . . (646) 312-2196
  2005-06 Tuition: In-state $4,320; Out-of-state $8,960
CUNY City College (Public)
  Fall 2004 Enrollment: 12,099 . . . . (212) 650-7000
  2005-06 Tuition: In-state $4,279; Out-of-state $8,919
CUNY Graduate School and University Center (Public)
  Fall 2004 Enrollment: 4,234 . . . . (212) 817-7000
CUNY Hunter College (Public)
  Fall 2004 Enrollment: 20,243 . . . . (212) 772-4000
  2005-06 Tuition: In-state $4,349; Out-of-state $8,989
CUNY John Jay College Criminal Justice (Public)
  Fall 2004 Enrollment: 14,080 . . . . (212) 237-8000
  2005-06 Tuition: In-state $4,279; Out-of-state $8,919
Columbia University in the City of New York
  Fall 2004 Enrollment: 21,648 . . . . (212) 854-1754
  2005-06 Tuition: In-state $33,246; Out-of-state $33,246
Cooper Union for the Advancement of Science and Art
  Fall 2004 Enrollment: 972 . . . . (212) 353-4000
  2005-06 Tuition: In-state $28,950; Out-of-state $28,950
Fashion Institute of Technology (Public)
  Fall 2004 Enrollment: 10,513 . . . . (212) 217-7999
  2005-06 Tuition: In-state $3,494; Out-of-state $9,642
Globe Institute of Technology
  Fall 2004 Enrollment: 1,229 . . . . (212) 349-4330
  2005-06 Tuition: In-state $9,136; Out-of-state $9,136
Hebrew Union College-Jewish Institute of Religion
  Fall 2004 Enrollment: 169 . . . . (212) 674-5300
Jewish Theological Seminary of America
  Fall 2004 Enrollment: 612 . . . . (212) 678-8000
  2005-06 Tuition: In-state $11,900; Out-of-state $11,900
Laboratory Institute of Merchandising
  Fall 2004 Enrollment: 608 . . . . (212) 752-1530
  2005-06 Tuition: In-state $17,050; Out-of-state $17,050
Manhattan School of Music
  Fall 2004 Enrollment: 906 . . . . (212) 749-2802
  2005-06 Tuition: In-state $26,460; Out-of-state $26,460
Marymount Manhattan College
  Fall 2004 Enrollment: 2,077 . . . . (212) 517-0400
  2005-06 Tuition: In-state $18,529; Out-of-state $18,529
Mesivtha Tifereth Jerusalem of America
  Fall 2004 Enrollment: 85 . . . . (212) 964-2830
  2005-06 Tuition: In-state $6,200; Out-of-state $6,200
Metropolitan College of New York
  Fall 2004 Enrollment: 1,589 . . . . (800) 338-4465
  2005-06 Tuition: In-state $13,088; Out-of-state $13,088
Metropolitan Institute for Training in Psychoanalytic Psychotherapy
  Fall 2004 Enrollment: -1 . . . . (212) 496-2858
Mount Sinai School of Medicine
  Fall 2004 Enrollment: 650 . . . . (212) 241-8716
New York Academy of Art
  Fall 2004 Enrollment: 119 . . . . (212) 966-0300
New York College of Podiatric Medicine
  Fall 2004 Enrollment: 283 . . . . (212) 410-8000
New York Institute of Technology-Manhattan Campus
  Fall 2004 Enrollment: 2,538 . . . . (212) 261-1500
  2005-06 Tuition: In-state $19,236; Out-of-state $19,236
New York Law School
  Fall 2004 Enrollment: 1,575 . . . . (212) 431-2100
New York School of Interior Design
  Fall 2004 Enrollment: 759 . . . . (212) 472-1500
  2005-06 Tuition: In-state $14,380; Out-of-state $14,380
New York Theological Seminary
  Fall 2004 Enrollment: -1 . . . . (212) 870-1211
New York University
  Fall 2004 Enrollment: 39,408 . . . . (212) 998-1212
  2005-06 Tuition: In-state $31,690; Out-of-state $31,690
Pace University-New York
  Fall 2004 Enrollment: 13,670 . . . . (212) 346-1200
  2005-06 Tuition: In-state $25,384; Out-of-state $25,384
Pacific College of Oriental Medicine-New York
  Fall 2004 Enrollment: 414 . . . . (212) 982-3456
Rockefeller University
  Fall 2004 Enrollment: 193 . . . . (212) 327-8000
SUNY College of Optometry (Public)
  Fall 2004 Enrollment: 296 . . . . (212) 938-4000
School of Visual Arts
  Fall 2004 Enrollment: 3,478 . . . . (212) 592-2000
  2005-06 Tuition: In-state $20,080; Out-of-state $20,080
Swedish Institute College of Health Sciences
  Fall 2004 Enrollment: 166 . . . . (212) 924-5900
  2005-06 Tuition: In-state $8,250; Out-of-state $8,250
Teachers College at Columbia University
  Fall 2004 Enrollment: 5,036 . . . . (212) 678-3000
The General Theological Seminary
  Fall 2004 Enrollment: 146 . . . . (212) 243-5150
The Juilliard School
  Fall 2004 Enrollment: 1,039 . . . . (212) 799-5000
  2005-06 Tuition: In-state $24,330; Out-of-state $24,330
The New School
  Fall 2004 Enrollment: 8,812 . . . . (212) 229-5600
  2005-06 Tuition: In-state $26,540; Out-of-state $26,540

Touro College
Fall 2004 Enrollment: 19,618 . . . . (212) 463-0400
2005-06 Tuition: In-state $10,900; Out-of-state $10,900
Tri-State College of Acupuncture
Fall 2004 Enrollment: 169 . . . . (212) 242-2255
Union Theological Seminary
Fall 2004 Enrollment: 200 . . . . (212) 662-7100
Weill Cornell Medical College
Fall 2004 Enrollment: 780 . . . . (212) 746-5454
Yeshiva University
Fall 2004 Enrollment: 6,129 . . . . (212) 960-5400
2005-06 Tuition: In-state $25,600; Out-of-state $25,600

Two-year College(s)

American Academy McAllister Institute of Funeral Services
Fall 2004 Enrollment: 132 . . . . (212) 757-1190
2005-06 Tuition: In-state $9,200; Out-of-state $9,200
American Academy of Dramatic Arts
Fall 2004 Enrollment: 267 . . . . (212) 686-9244
2005-06 Tuition: In-state $16,500; Out-of-state $16,500
American Barber Institute Inc
Fall 2004 Enrollment: 159 . . . . (212) 290-2289
American Musical and Dramatic Academy
Fall 2004 Enrollment: 758 . . . . (212) 787-5300
2005-06 Tuition: In-state $21,080; Out-of-state $21,080
Apex Technical School
Fall 2004 Enrollment: 1,248 . . . . (212) 645-3300
CUNY Borough of Manhattan Community College (Public)
Fall 2004 Enrollment: 18,854 . . . . (212) 220-8000
2005-06 Tuition: In-state $3,068; Out-of-state $4,828
Caliber Training Institute
Fall 2004 Enrollment: 860 . . . . (212) 564-0500
Career Blazers Learning Center
Fall 2004 Enrollment: 206 . . . . (212) 725-7900
Carsten Institute of New York
Fall 2004 Enrollment: -1 . . . . (212) 675-4884
Circle in the Square Theater School
Fall 2004 Enrollment: 96 . . . . (212) 307-0388
2005-06 Tuition: In-state $10,000; Out-of-state $10,000
Cope Institute
Fall 2004 Enrollment: 34 . . . . (212) 809-5935
Dance Theatre of Harlem Inc
Fall 2004 Enrollment: 13 . . . . (212) 690-2800
2005-06 Tuition: In-state $7,200; Out-of-state $7,200
FEGS Trades and Business School
Fall 2004 Enrollment: 15 . . . . (212) 366-8466
French Culinary Institute
Fall 2004 Enrollment: 372 . . . . (212) 219-8890
Gemological Institute of America-New York
Fall 2004 Enrollment: 129 . . . . (212) 944-5900
Global Business Institute
Fall 2004 Enrollment: 325 . . . . (212) 663-1500
2005-06 Tuition: In-state $12,600; Out-of-state $12,600
Harlem School of Technology
Fall 2004 Enrollment: 45 . . . . (212) 932-2849
Helene Fuld College of Nursing
Fall 2004 Enrollment: 391 . . . . (212) 423-2700
2005-06 Tuition: In-state $13,012; Out-of-state $13,012
Institute of Audio Research
Fall 2004 Enrollment: 939 . . . . (212) 677-7580
Interboro Institute
Fall 2004 Enrollment: 3,875 . . . . (212) 399-0093
2005-06 Tuition: In-state $8,620; Out-of-state $8,620
Joffrey Ballet School-American Ballet Center
Fall 2004 Enrollment: 56 . . . . (212) 254-8520
2005-06 Tuition: In-state $10,896; Out-of-state $10,896
Katharine Gibbs School-New York City
Fall 2004 Enrollment: 2,962 . . . . (212) 867-9300
2005-06 Tuition: In-state $15,017; Out-of-state $15,017
Learning Institute for Beauty Sciences-Manhattan
Fall 2004 Enrollment: 554 . . . . (800) 223-3271
Lia Schorr Institute of Cosmetic Skin Care Training
Fall 2004 Enrollment: 101 . . . . (212) 486-9541
Mandl School
Fall 2004 Enrollment: 867 . . . . (212) 247-3434

Manhattan School of Computer Technology
Fall 2004 Enrollment: 227 . . . . (212) 349-9768
Memorial Hospital School of Radiation Therapy Technology
Fall 2004 Enrollment: 20 . . . . (212) 639-6835
2005-06 Tuition: In-state $3,000; Out-of-state $3,000
Merce Cunningham Studio
Fall 2004 Enrollment: 37 . . . . (212) 255-8240
2005-06 Tuition: In-state $4,250; Out-of-state $4,250
Neighborhood Playhouse School of the Theater
Fall 2004 Enrollment: 87 . . . . (212) 688-3770
New York Career Institute
Fall 2004 Enrollment: 716 . . . . (212) 962-0002
2005-06 Tuition: In-state $9,600; Out-of-state $9,600
New York Institute of English and Business
Fall 2004 Enrollment: 503 . . . . (212) 725-9400
2005-06 Tuition: In-state $13,924; Out-of-state $13,924
New York International Beauty School Ltd
Fall 2004 Enrollment: 262 . . . . (212) 868-7171
New York Paralegal School
Fall 2004 Enrollment: 281 . . . . (212) 349-8800
Phillips Beth Israel School of Nursing
Fall 2004 Enrollment: 175 . . . . (212) 614-6110
2005-06 Tuition: In-state $13,985; Out-of-state $13,985
Professional Business College
Fall 2004 Enrollment: 560 . . . . (212) 226-7300
2005-06 Tuition: In-state $8,250; Out-of-state $8,250
Sanford-Brown Institute
Fall 2004 Enrollment: 568 . . . . (646) 313-4519
School for Film and Television
Fall 2004 Enrollment: 215 . . . . (212) 645-0030
2005-06 Tuition: In-state $19,650; Out-of-state $19,650
Spanish-American Institute
Fall 2004 Enrollment: 48 . . . . (212) 840-7111
Studio Jewelers
Fall 2004 Enrollment: 69 . . . . (212) 686-1944
Taylor Business Institute
Fall 2004 Enrollment: 832 . . . . (212) 229-1963
2005-06 Tuition: In-state $10,200; Out-of-state $10,200
Technical Career Institutes
Fall 2004 Enrollment: 3,040 . . . . (212) 594-4000
2005-06 Tuition: In-state $9,565; Out-of-state $9,565
The Ailey School
Fall 2004 Enrollment: 68 . . . . (212) 405-9008
2005-06 Tuition: In-state $8,870; Out-of-state $8,870
The Art Institute of New York City
Fall 2004 Enrollment: 1,662 . . . . (212) 226-5500
2005-06 Tuition: In-state $21,000; Out-of-state $21,000
The Chubb Institute-Manhattan
Fall 2004 Enrollment: 529 . . . . (212) 659-2116
Training Solutions Inc
Fall 2004 Enrollment: 17 . . . . (212) 947-3039
Wood Tobe-Coburn School
Fall 2004 Enrollment: 255 . . . . (212) 686-9040
2005-06 Tuition: In-state $14,450; Out-of-state $14,450

Hospitals: Bellevue Hospital Center (1232 beds); Beth Israel Health Care System (1368 beds); Cabrini Medical Center (493 beds); Cornerstone of Medical Arts Center Hospital (100 beds); Department of Veteran Affairs NY Harbor Health System (350 beds); Gracie Square Hospital (157 beds); Hospital for Joint Diseases Orthopaedic Institute (216 beds); Hospital for Special Surgery (160 beds); Lenox Hill Hospital (652 beds); Manhattan Eye, Ear & Throat Hospital (150 beds); Manhattan Psychiatric Center; Memorial Sloan-Kettering Cancer Center (437 beds); Metropolitan Hospital Center (597 beds); Mount Sinai Hospital (1171 beds); NYU Downtown Hospital (160 beds); NYU School of Medicine (878 beds); New York - Presbyterian Hospital (2344 beds); New York Eye and Ear Infirmary (103 beds); New York State Psychiatric Institute (70 beds); North General Hospital (200 beds); Rockefeller University Hospital (20 beds); St. Luke's Roosevelt Hospital Center (1046 beds); St. Vincent's Hospital & Medical Center of NY (891 beds); St. Vincent's Midtown Hospital (150 beds)

Newspapers: AM New York (Circulation 311,000); American Banker (Circulation 12,755); American Metal Market (Circulation 9,400); Amsterdam News (Black - Circulation 60,000); Carib News (Black, Ethnic - Circulation 67,000); Catholic New York (Catholic - Circulation 132,085); Chelsea Clinton News (General - Circulation 15,000); Daily Journal (Circulation 65,000); Daily Racing Form (Circulation 14,631); Daily Variety Gotham (Circulation 30,000); Downtown Express (General - Circulation

40,000); Downtown Resident (General - Circulation 50,000); El Diario la Prensa (Circulation 75,000); Financial Times - U.S. Edition (Circulation 133,000); Forward (Jewish - Circulation 30,000); Gay City News (Gay/Lesbian - Circulation 35,000); Greenwich Village Gazette (General - Circulation 40,000); Hellenic Times (Ethnic, General - Circulation 15,000); Hoy (Circulation 94,000); Hurriyet (Circulation 10,000); Impacto Latin News (Hispanic - Circulation 57,000); Irish Echo (Ethnic - Circulation 62,000); Irish Voice (Ethnic - Circulation 80,000); Jewish Post of New York (Jewish, Religious - Circulation 19,300); La Voz Hispana (General, Hispanic - Circulation 60,800); Midtown Resident (General - Circulation 40,000); New York Blade News (Gay/Lesbian - Circulation 50,000); New York Law Journal (Circulation 12,682); New York Observer (General - Circulation 55,000); New York Post (Circulation 620,080); New York Press (Alternative, General - Circulation 115,000); New York Resident (General - Circulation 165,000); Nordstjernan (Ethnic, Religious - Circulation 7,400); Novoye Russkoye Slovo (Circulation 55,000); Nowy Dziennik/Polish Daily News (Circulation 10,000); OCS News (Asian - Circulation 20,000); Our Town (General - Circulation 64,000); People's Weekly World (General - Circulation 50,000); Sing Tao Daily (Circulation 50,000); Standard & Poor's Daily News (Circulation 3,318); Standard & Poor's Dividend Record (Circulation 1,996); The Armenian Church (Religious - Circulation 48,000); The Bond Buyer (Circulation 3,800); The Daily Deal (Circulation 50,000); The Electricity Daily (Circulation 500); The Filipino Reporter (Asian, General - Circulation 50,000); The Jewish Week (Jewish - Circulation 97,600); The Main Street Wire (General - Circulation 9,500); The New York Beacon (Black - Circulation 53,000); The New York Daily News (Circulation 737,030); The New York Sun (Circulation 26,263); The New York Times (Circulation 1,133,763); The Trusted Professional (General - Circulation 34,000); The Village Voice (Circulation 250,000); The Wall Street Journal (Circulation 1,888,621); The Westsider (General - Circulation 15,000); Upper Westside Resident (General - Circulation 50,000); Vaba Eesti Sona-Free Estonian Word (Ethnic - Circulation 2,500); West Side Spirit (General - Circulation 76,000); Women's Wear Daily (Circulation 50,000)

Additional Information Contacts

American Indonesia Chamber	(212) 687-4505
City of New York	(212) 669-2400
http://nyc.gov/	
French-American Chamber of Commerce	(212) 867-0123
Greater New York Chamber of Commerce	(212) 686-7220
http://nyc.chamber.com	
Greenwich Village-Chelsea Chamber of Commerce	(212) 255-5811
http://www.gvccc.com	
Harlem Chamber of Commerce	(212) 862-7200
http://www.chamber.harlemdiscover.com	
Manhattan Borough President	(212) 669-8300
http://www.mbpo.org/	
Manhattan Chamber of Commerce	(212) 479-7772
http://www.manhattancc.org/	
Nigerian American Chamber of Commerce	(212) 791-4161
http://www.nigeriabusinessinfo.com/bilateral-chambers.htm	
Slovak American Chamber of Commerce	(212) 679-7044
http://www.amcham.sk/Contact	
Swiss-American Chamber of Commerce	(212) 246-7789
West Side Chamber of Commerce	(212) 541-8880
http://www.westsidechamber.org	
Women's International Chamber	(212) 809-5121

QUEENS (borough). Aka Queens County. Located in southeastern New York State, on Long Island; one of the five counties/boroughs New York City; bounded on the west and north by the East River. Covers a land area of 109.24 square miles, a water area of 69.04 square miles, and is located in the Eastern Time Zone. The county government was organized in 1683. County seat is Jamaica.

Queens County is part of the New York-Northern New Jersey-Long Island, NY-NJ-PA Metropolitan Statistical Area. The entire metro area includes: Edison, NJ Metropolitan Division (Middlesex County, NJ; Monmouth County, NJ; Ocean County, NJ; Somerset County, NJ); Nassau-Suffolk, NY Metropolitan Division (Nassau County, NY; Suffolk County, NY); New York-White Plains-Wayne, NY-NJ Metropolitan Division (Bergen County, NJ; Hudson County, NJ; Passaic County, NJ; Bronx County, NY; Kings County, NY; New York County, NY; Putnam County, NY; Queens County, NY; Richmond County, NY; Rockland County, NY; Westchester County, NY); Newark-Union, NJ-PA Metropolitan Division (Essex County, NJ; Hunterdon County, NJ; Morris County, NJ; Sussex County, NJ; Union County, NJ; Pike County, PA)

Weather Station: New York JFK Int'l Airport · Elevation: 13 feet

	Jan	Feb	Mar	Apr	May	Jun	Jul	Aug	Sep	Oct	Nov	Dec
High	39	41	49	59	68	77	83	82	75	64	54	44
Low	26	28	34	43	53	62	69	68	61	50	41	32
Precip	3.6	2.8	3.8	3.7	4.1	3.6	3.8	3.6	3.4	3.1	3.5	3.3
Snow	6.8	7.1	3.4	0.6	tr	0.0	tr	0.0	0.0	tr	0.3	2.3

High and Low temperatures in degrees Fahrenheit; Precipitation and Snow in inches

Weather Station: New York Laguardia Airport · Elevation: 9 feet

	Jan	Feb	Mar	Apr	May	Jun	Jul	Aug	Sep	Oct	Nov	Dec
High	38	41	49	60	70	79	85	83	75	64	54	44
Low	26	28	35	44	54	64	70	69	62	51	42	32
Precip	3.5	2.8	3.9	3.6	4.1	3.5	4.2	4.0	3.7	3.3	3.7	3.5
Snow	7.4	7.9	3.8	0.4	tr	0.0	tr	0.0	0.0	tr	0.4	2.7

High and Low temperatures in degrees Fahrenheit; Precipitation and Snow in inches

Population: 1,951,636 (1990); 2,229,379 (2000); 2,223,275 (2005); 2,215,488 (2010 projected); Race: 41.0% White, 19.8% Black, 19.8% Asian, 26.6% Hispanic of any race (2005); Density: 20,353.1 persons per square mile (2005); Average household size: 2.89 (2005); Median age: 37.4 (2005); Males per 100 females: 93.6 (2005).

Religion: Five largest groups: 28.9% Catholic Church, 10.7% Jewish Estimate, 2.3% Muslim Estimate, 0.8% Greek Orthodox Archdiocese of America, 0.7% American Baptist Churches in the USA (2000).

Economy: Unemployment rate: 5.2% (2005); Total civilian labor force: 1,074,559 (2005); Leading industries: 19.9% health care and social assistance; 12.5% transportation and warehousing; 11.1% retail trade (2003); Farms: 2 totaling n/a acres (2002); Companies that employ 500 or more persons: 87 (2003); Companies that employ 100 to 499 persons: 557 (2003); Companies that employ less than 100 persons: 38,774 (2003); Black-owned businesses: 18,687 (2002); Hispanic-owned businesses: 35,244 (2002); Women-owned businesses: 53,550 (2002); Retail sales per capita: $6,176 (2006). Single-family building permits issued: 334 (2005); Multi-family building permits issued: 6,935 (2005).

Income: Per capita income: $21,510 (2005); Median household income: $47,967 (2005); Average household income: $61,762 (2005); Percent of households with income of $100,000 or more: 16.6% (2005); Poverty rate: 15.4% (2003); Bankruptcy rate: 5.10% (2005).

Education: Percent of population age 25 and over with: High school diploma (including GED) or higher: 74.3% (2005); Bachelor's degree or higher: 24.3% (2005); Master's degree or higher: 9.2% (2005).

Housing: Homeownership rate: 43.1% (2005); Median home value: $342,258 (2005); Median rent: $721 per month (2000); Median age of housing: 50 years (2000).

Health: Birth rate: 137.5 per 10,000 population (2004); Death rate: 70.7 per 10,000 population (2004); Age-adjusted cancer mortality rate: 170.2 deaths per 100,000 population (2002); Air Quality Index: 55.9% good, 41.1% moderate, 3.0% unhealthy for sensitive individuals, 0.0% unhealthy (percent of days in 2005); Number of physicians: 26.6 per 10,000 population (2004); Hospital beds: 24.7 per 10,000 population (2003); Hospital admissions: 855.4 per 10,000 population (2003).

Elections: 2004 Presidential election results: 27.4% Bush, 71.7% Kerry, 0.7% Nader, 0.1% Badnarik

School District(s)

Merrick Academy-Queens Public Charter (KG-05)	
2003-04 Enrollment: 397	(718) 479-3753
NYC Alternative HS District (10-12)	
2003-04 Enrollment: 1,828	(212) 374-5082
New York City Geographic District #24 (PK-04)	
2003-04 Enrollment: 642	(718) 417-2602
New York City Geographic District #26 (KG-10)	
2003-04 Enrollment: 998	(718) 631-6900
New York City Geographic District #28 (PK-09)	
2003-04 Enrollment: 263	(718) 557-2611
New York City Geographic District #29 (PK-07)	
2003-04 Enrollment: 1,425	(718) 978-5900
New York City Geographic District #29 (PK-07)	
2003-04 Enrollment: 1,425	(718) 978-5900
New York City Geographic District #30 (PK-09)	
2003-04 Enrollment: 981	(718) 777-4700
New York City Geographic District #30 (PK-09)	
2003-04 Enrollment: 981	(718) 777-4700
New York City Public Schools (PK-12)	
2003-04 Enrollment: 1,023,674	(718) 935-2794
Our World Neighborhood Charter School (KG-06)	
2003-04 Enrollment: 501	(212) 237-7421

Four-year College(s)

Beis Medrash Heichal Dovid
   Fall 2004 Enrollment: 76 . . . . (718) 868-2300
   2005-06 Tuition: In-state $5,750; Out-of-state $5,750
CUNY Queens College (Public)
   Fall 2004 Enrollment: 17,395. . . . . (718) 997-5000
   2005-06 Tuition: In-state $4,377; Out-of-state $9,017
CUNY School of Law at Queens College (Public)
   Fall 2004 Enrollment: 447 . . . . (718) 340-4200
   2005-06 Tuition: In-state n/a; Out-of-state n/a
CUNY York College (Public)
   Fall 2004 Enrollment: 5,743. . . . . (718) 262-2000
   2005-06 Tuition: In-state $4,262; Out-of-state $8,902
DeVry Institute of Technology & Keller Graduate School of Management-New Yo
   Fall 2004 Enrollment: 1,806. . . . . (718) 472-2728
   2005-06 Tuition: In-state $13,370; Out-of-state $13,370
Rabbinical Seminary of America
   Fall 2004 Enrollment: 446 . . . . (718) 268-4700
   2005-06 Tuition: In-state $6,000; Out-of-state $6,000
St Vincent Catholic Medical Center New York-Brooklyn and Queens
   Fall 2004 Enrollment: 92 . . . . (718) 357-0500
   2005-06 Tuition: In-state n/a; Out-of-state n/a
St. John's University-New York
   Fall 2004 Enrollment: 19,813. . . . . (718) 990-6161
   2005-06 Tuition: In-state $23,370; Out-of-state $23,370
Vaughn College of Aeronautics and Technology
   Fall 2004 Enrollment: 1,258. . . . . (718) 429-6600
   2005-06 Tuition: In-state $13,820; Out-of-state $13,820

Two-year College(s)

Allen School-Jamaica
   Fall 2004 Enrollment: 940 . . . . (718) 291-2200
   2005-06 Tuition: In-state n/a; Out-of-state n/a
CUNY La Guardia Community College (Public)
   Fall 2004 Enrollment: 13,592. . . . . (718) 482-5000
   2005-06 Tuition: In-state $3,092; Out-of-state $4,852
CUNY Queensborough Community College (Public)
   Fall 2004 Enrollment: 12,798. . . . . (718) 631-6262
   2005-06 Tuition: In-state $3,086; Out-of-state $4,846
Global Business Institute
   Fall 2004 Enrollment: 170 . . . . (718) 327-2220
   2005-06 Tuition: In-state $12,600; Out-of-state $12,600
Learning Institute for Beauty Sciences-Queens
   Fall 2004 Enrollment: 241 . . . . (800) 223-3271
   2005-06 Tuition: In-state n/a; Out-of-state n/a
Midway Paris Beauty School
   Fall 2004 Enrollment: 114 . . . . (718) 418-2790
   2005-06 Tuition: In-state n/a; Out-of-state n/a
New York Automotive and Diesel Institute
   Fall 2004 Enrollment: 330 . . . . (718) 658-0006
   2005-06 Tuition: In-state n/a; Out-of-state n/a
New York School for Medical and Dental Assistants
   Fall 2004 Enrollment: 357 . . . . (718) 793-2330
   2005-06 Tuition: In-state n/a; Out-of-state n/a
St Vincent Catholic Medical Center School of Nursing-Brooklyn and Queens
   Fall 2004 Enrollment: 118 . . . . (718) 357-0500
   2005-06 Tuition: In-state $5,682; Out-of-state $5,682

Hospitals: Creedmoor Psychiatric Center (Queens Village) (450 beds); Elmhurst Hospital Center (Elmhurst) (513 beds); Flushing Hospital Medical Center (Flushing) (250 beds); Hillside Hospital (Glen Oaks) (223 beds); Holliswood Hospital (Holliswood) (100 beds); Jamaica Hospital Medical Center (Jamaica) (384 beds); New York Hospital Medical Center of Queens (Flushing) (439 beds); North Shore University Hospital (Flushing) (302 beds); Parkway Hospital (Flushing) (251 beds); Peninsula Hospital Center (Far Rockaway) (272 beds); Queens Childrens Psychiatric Center (Bellerose) (86 beds); Queens Hospital Center (Jamaica) (408 beds); Saint John's Episcopal Hospital, South Shore (Far Rockaway) (332 beds); Saint Mary's Hospital for Children (Bayside) (95 beds); Saint Vincents Catholic Medical Center of NY (Jamaica) (1,707 beds)

Newspapers: Bayside Times (Bayside) (General - Circulation 11,504); Brooklyn Downtown Star (Maspeth) (General - Circulation 15,000); Campana (Astoria) (Ethnic - Circulation 9,500); El Tiempo de Nueva York (Jackson Heights) (Hispanic - Circulation 50,000); Forest Hills Rego Park Times (Maspeth) (General - Circulation 30,000); Glendale Register (Maspeth) (General - Circulation 120,000); Greek News (Astoria) (Circulation 50,000); Greenpoint Star & Northside News (Maspeth) (General - Circulation 15,000); Howard Beach Times (Bayside) (General - Circulation 1,200); Jackson Heights News (Maspeth) (General - Circulation 50,000); Korea Central Daily News (Long Island City) (Circulation 10,000); Korea Times (Long Island City) (Circulation 40,000); Leader Observer (Maspeth) (General - Circulation 8,000); Long Island City Journal (Maspeth) (General - Circulation 50,000); Queens Chronicle (Rego Park) (General - Circulation 160,000); Queens Examiner (Maspeth) (General - Circulation 16,000); Queens Gazette (Long Island City) (General - Circulation 250,000); Queens Ledger (Maspeth) (General - Circulation 28,500); Queens Tribune (Fresh Meadows) (General - Circulation 146,000); Resumen Newspaper (Woodside) (Hispanic - Circulation 37,000); The Liberty Times, USA (Flushing) (Circulation 40,000); The National Herald (Long Island City) (Circulation 50,000); The Wave (Far Rockaway) (General - Circulation 12,300); Times Newsweekly (Ridgewood) (General - Circulation 23,075); Woodside Herald (Sunnyside) (General - Circulation 14,000); World Journal (Whitestone) (Circulation 80,000); World Journal - New York Edition (Circulation 100,000)

Airports: John F Kennedy International (primary service/large hub); LaGuardia International (primary service/large hub); Newark Liberty International (Newark, NJ) (primary service/large hub)

Additional Information Contacts
Queens Borough President . . . . (718) 286-3000
   http://www.queensbp.org/

Neighborhoods in Queens

ARVERNE (unincorporated postal area, zip code 11692). Covers a land area of 1.014 square miles and a water area of 0 square miles. Located at 40.59° N. Lat.; 73.79° W. Long.
Population: 0 (2000); Race: 15.6% White, 68.3% Black, 1.3% Asian, 17.3% Hispanic of any race (2000); Density: 0.0 persons per square mile (2000); Age: 31.2% under 18, 9.6% over 64 (2000); Marriage status: 42.0% never married, 43.9% now married, 7.0% widowed, 7.0% divorced (2000); Foreign born: 24.4% (2000); Ancestry (includes multiple ancestries): 54.9% Other groups, 8.1% Jamaican, 3.8% Guyanese, 2.6% United States or American, 2.6% Nigerian (2000).
Economy: Employment by occupation: 9.0% management, 15.7% professional, 22.8% services, 30.8% sales, 0.0% farming, 9.3% construction, 12.5% production (2000).
Income: Per capita income: $13,153 (2000); Median household income: $29,059 (2000); Poverty rate: 26.0% (2000).
Education: Percent of population age 25 and over with: High school diploma (including GED) or higher: 67.9% (2000); Bachelor's degree or higher: 13.6% (2000).

School District(s)
New York City Public Schools (PK-12)
   2003-04 Enrollment: 1,023,674 . . . . (718) 935-2794

Housing: Homeownership rate: 29.4% (2000); Median home value: $161,700 (2000); Median rent: $534 per month (2000); Median age of housing: 36 years (2000).
Transportation: Commute to work: 41.0% car, 50.2% public transportation, 6.5% walk, 1.7% work from home (2000); Travel time to work: 12.8% less than 15 minutes, 15.1% 15 to 30 minutes, 16.9% 30 to 45 minutes, 15.5% 45 to 60 minutes, 39.7% 60 minutes or more (2000)

BREEZY POINT (unincorporated postal area, zip code 11697). Covers a land area of 2.232 square miles and a water area of 0 square miles. Located at 40.55° N. Lat.; 73.90° W. Long.
Population: 0 (2000); Race: 99.3% White, 0.2% Black, 0.0% Asian, 0.9% Hispanic of any race (2000); Density: 0.0 persons per square mile (2000); Age: 20.5% under 18, 22.2% over 64 (2000); Marriage status: 25.8% never married, 57.0% now married, 14.2% widowed, 3.0% divorced (2000); Foreign born: 3.8% (2000); Ancestry (includes multiple ancestries): 60.3% Irish, 21.2% Italian, 16.4% German, 4.0% English, 3.2% Polish (2000).
Economy: Employment by occupation: 20.7% management, 25.3% professional, 15.3% services, 22.1% sales, 0.0% farming, 10.1% construction, 6.5% production (2000).
Income: Per capita income: $31,101 (2000); Median household income: $58,491 (2000); Poverty rate: 5.4% (2000).
Education: Percent of population age 25 and over with: High school diploma (including GED) or higher: 91.5% (2000); Bachelor's degree or higher: 32.8% (2000).

Housing: Homeownership rate: 96.0% (2000); Median home value: $249,500 (2000); Median rent: $246 per month (2000); Median age of housing: 45 years (2000).
Transportation: Commute to work: 76.5% car, 19.4% public transportation, 0.7% walk, 1.7% work from home (2000); Travel time to work: 9.4% less than 15 minutes, 21.2% 15 to 30 minutes, 20.5% 30 to 45 minutes, 14.0% 45 to 60 minutes, 34.8% 60 minutes or more (2000)

COLLEGE POINT (unincorporated postal area, zip code 11356).
Covers a land area of 1.540 square miles and a water area of 0 square miles. Located at 40.78° N. Lat.; 73.84° W. Long.
Population: 0 (2000); Race: 69.2% White, 1.1% Black, 15.8% Asian, 25.2% Hispanic of any race (2000); Density: 0.0 persons per square mile (2000); Age: 23.5% under 18, 10.9% over 64 (2000); Marriage status: 28.3% never married, 58.2% now married, 7.9% widowed, 5.6% divorced (2000); Foreign born: 33.9% (2000); Ancestry (includes multiple ancestries): 41.3% Other groups, 19.0% Italian, 13.4% Irish, 11.3% German, 5.6% United States or American (2000).
Economy: Employment by occupation: 13.0% management, 15.9% professional, 14.8% services, 35.5% sales, 0.2% farming, 8.5% construction, 12.1% production (2000).
Income: Per capita income: $21,406 (2000); Median household income: $48,738 (2000); Poverty rate: 9.3% (2000).
Education: Percent of population age 25 and over with: High school diploma (including GED) or higher: 80.7% (2000); Bachelor's degree or higher: 20.0% (2000).
School District(s)
New York City Public Schools (PK-12)
    2003-04 Enrollment: 1,023,674 . . . . (718) 935-2794
Housing: Homeownership rate: 51.7% (2000); Median home value: $220,500 (2000); Median rent: $771 per month (2000); Median age of housing: 49 years (2000).
Transportation: Commute to work: 66.2% car, 25.5% public transportation, 6.2% walk, 1.6% work from home (2000); Travel time to work: 16.0% less than 15 minutes, 25.1% 15 to 30 minutes, 20.5% 30 to 45 minutes, 10.1% 45 to 60 minutes, 28.2% 60 minutes or more (2000)

CORONA (unincorporated postal area, zip code 11368).
Covers a land area of 2.570 square miles and a water area of 0 square miles. Located at 40.74° N. Lat.; 73.85° W. Long.
Population: 0 (2000); Race: 35.9% White, 17.1% Black, 10.1% Asian, 65.0% Hispanic of any race (2000); Density: 0.0 persons per square mile (2000); Age: 26.7% under 18, 7.4% over 64 (2000); Marriage status: 35.6% never married, 52.9% now married, 4.7% widowed, 6.8% divorced (2000); Foreign born: 62.3% (2000); Ancestry (includes multiple ancestries): 74.2% Other groups, 2.4% Italian, 2.2% United States or American, 1.4% Jamaican, 1.0% Russian (2000).
Economy: Employment by occupation: 6.1% management, 9.2% professional, 28.5% services, 23.9% sales, 0.1% farming, 10.9% construction, 21.3% production (2000).
Income: Per capita income: $12,412 (2000); Median household income: $34,746 (2000); Poverty rate: 22.2% (2000).
Education: Percent of population age 25 and over with: High school diploma (including GED) or higher: 56.0% (2000); Bachelor's degree or higher: 11.5% (2000).
School District(s)
New York City Public Schools (PK-12)
    2003-04 Enrollment: 1,023,674 . . . . (718) 935-2794
Housing: Homeownership rate: 21.1% (2000); Median home value: $211,700 (2000); Median rent: $726 per month (2000); Median age of housing: 42 years (2000).
Transportation: Commute to work: 30.5% car, 58.9% public transportation, 8.1% walk, 1.6% work from home (2000); Travel time to work: 9.1% less than 15 minutes, 18.9% 15 to 30 minutes, 26.1% 30 to 45 minutes, 17.8% 45 to 60 minutes, 28.0% 60 minutes or more (2000)

FOREST HILLS (unincorporated postal area, zip code 11375).
Covers a land area of 2.434 square miles and a water area of 0.201 square miles. Located at 40.72° N. Lat.; 73.84° W. Long.
Population: 0 (2000); Race: 71.5% White, 2.3% Black, 20.1% Asian, 10.4% Hispanic of any race (2000); Density: 0.0 persons per square mile (2000); Age: 15.2% under 18, 19.0% over 64 (2000); Marriage status: 28.3% never married, 54.5% now married, 9.2% widowed, 8.0% divorced (2000); Foreign born: 47.4% (2000); Ancestry (includes multiple ancestries): 40.1% Other groups, 11.5% Russian, 6.2% Italian, 5.7% Polish, 5.4% Irish (2000).
Economy: Employment by occupation: 20.9% management, 32.3% professional, 10.2% services, 27.5% sales, 0.0% farming, 3.1% construction, 6.1% production (2000).
Income: Per capita income: $31,513 (2000); Median household income: $51,350 (2000); Poverty rate: 9.9% (2000).
Education: Percent of population age 25 and over with: High school diploma (including GED) or higher: 88.6% (2000); Bachelor's degree or higher: 48.9% (2000).
School District(s)
New York City Public Schools (PK-12)
    2003-04 Enrollment: 1,023,674 . . . . (718) 935-2794
Housing: Homeownership rate: 40.3% (2000); Median home value: $300,100 (2000); Median rent: $833 per month (2000); Median age of housing: 50 years (2000).
Transportation: Commute to work: 31.1% car, 60.2% public transportation, 4.7% walk, 3.4% work from home (2000); Travel time to work: 6.9% less than 15 minutes, 13.9% 15 to 30 minutes, 28.8% 30 to 45 minutes, 25.1% 45 to 60 minutes, 25.4% 60 minutes or more (2000)

HOLLIS (unincorporated postal area, zip code 11423).
Covers a land area of 1.623 square miles and a water area of 0 square miles. Located at 40.71° N. Lat.; 73.76° W. Long.
Population: 0 (2000); Race: 18.8% White, 44.9% Black, 17.5% Asian, 16.2% Hispanic of any race (2000); Density: 0.0 persons per square mile (2000); Age: 25.2% under 18, 12.1% over 64 (2000); Marriage status: 33.7% never married, 52.0% now married, 7.5% widowed, 6.8% divorced (2000); Foreign born: 47.0% (2000); Ancestry (includes multiple ancestries): 52.3% Other groups, 8.3% Guyanese, 8.0% Haitian, 4.8% United States or American, 4.8% Jamaican (2000).
Economy: Employment by occupation: 10.6% management, 18.7% professional, 19.3% services, 31.9% sales, 0.0% farming, 7.1% construction, 12.4% production (2000).
Income: Per capita income: $18,722 (2000); Median household income: $46,047 (2000); Poverty rate: 12.7% (2000).
Education: Percent of population age 25 and over with: High school diploma (including GED) or higher: 76.2% (2000); Bachelor's degree or higher: 24.0% (2000).
School District(s)
New York City Public Schools (PK-12)
    2003-04 Enrollment: 1,023,674 . . . . (718) 935-2794
Housing: Homeownership rate: 59.5% (2000); Median home value: $194,000 (2000); Median rent: $693 per month (2000); Median age of housing: 49 years (2000).
Transportation: Commute to work: 48.5% car, 46.2% public transportation, 3.5% walk, 1.4% work from home (2000); Travel time to work: 9.2% less than 15 minutes, 19.3% 15 to 30 minutes, 21.1% 30 to 45 minutes, 16.0% 45 to 60 minutes, 34.3% 60 minutes or more (2000)

HOWARD BEACH (unincorporated postal area, zip code 11414).
Covers a land area of 2.289 square miles and a water area of 0 square miles. Located at 40.65° N. Lat.; 73.84° W. Long.
Population: 0 (2000); Race: 92.2% White, 1.1% Black, 3.2% Asian, 9.4% Hispanic of any race (2000); Density: 0.0 persons per square mile (2000); Age: 18.0% under 18, 21.2% over 64 (2000); Marriage status: 27.0% never married, 55.4% now married, 10.4% widowed, 7.3% divorced (2000); Foreign born: 14.0% (2000); Ancestry (includes multiple ancestries): 47.6% Italian, 16.8% Other groups, 11.9% Irish, 7.9% German, 3.9% Polish (2000).
Economy: Employment by occupation: 14.3% management, 19.2% professional, 14.6% services, 31.1% sales, 0.0% farming, 10.5% construction, 10.4% production (2000).
Income: Per capita income: $25,535 (2000); Median household income: $51,175 (2000); Poverty rate: 6.7% (2000).
Education: Percent of population age 25 and over with: High school diploma (including GED) or higher: 78.8% (2000); Bachelor's degree or higher: 19.3% (2000).
School District(s)
New York City Public Schools (PK-12)
    2003-04 Enrollment: 1,023,674 . . . . (718) 935-2794
Housing: Homeownership rate: 69.7% (2000); Median home value: $339,500 (2000); Median rent: $769 per month (2000); Median age of housing: 37 years (2000).

Transportation: Commute to work: 69.9% car, 24.5% public transportation, 2.9% walk, 1.4% work from home (2000); Travel time to work: 17.7% less than 15 minutes, 26.5% 15 to 30 minutes, 19.7% 30 to 45 minutes, 14.1% 45 to 60 minutes, 22.0% 60 minutes or more (2000)

JACKSON HEIGHTS (unincorporated postal area, zip code 11372).
Covers a land area of 0.725 square miles and a water area of 0 square miles. Located at 40.75° N. Lat.; 73.88° W. Long.
Population: 0 (2000); Race: 50.8% White, 2.5% Black, 16.7% Asian, 56.6% Hispanic of any race (2000); Density: 0.0 persons per square mile (2000); Age: 20.6% under 18, 11.5% over 64 (2000); Marriage status: 34.0% never married, 51.4% now married, 6.1% widowed, 8.6% divorced (2000); Foreign born: 66.0% (2000); Ancestry (includes multiple ancestries): 66.9% Other groups, 3.5% Irish, 3.2% Italian, 2.0% German, 1.9% Polish (2000).
Economy: Employment by occupation: 9.1% management, 14.2% professional, 26.7% services, 25.0% sales, 0.0% farming, 8.1% construction, 16.9% production (2000).
Income: Per capita income: $17,054 (2000); Median household income: $39,084 (2000); Poverty rate: 18.8% (2000).
Education: Percent of population age 25 and over with: High school diploma (including GED) or higher: 69.8% (2000); Bachelor's degree or higher: 23.7% (2000).
School District(s)
New York City Public Schools (PK-12)
    2003-04 Enrollment: 1,023,674 . . . . (718) 935-2794
Renaissance Charter School, The (KG-12)
    2003-04 Enrollment: 486 . . . . (718) 803-0060
Housing: Homeownership rate: 26.7% (2000); Median home value: $244,700 (2000); Median rent: $716 per month (2000); Median age of housing: 55 years (2000).
Transportation: Commute to work: 22.5% car, 66.6% public transportation, 7.8% walk, 2.2% work from home (2000); Travel time to work: 7.7% less than 15 minutes, 16.5% 15 to 30 minutes, 30.0% 30 to 45 minutes, 22.6% 45 to 60 minutes, 23.3% 60 minutes or more (2000)

KEW GARDENS (unincorporated postal area, zip code 11415).
Covers a land area of 0.598 square miles and a water area of 0 square miles. Located at 40.70° N. Lat.; 73.82° W. Long.
Population: 0 (2000); Race: 64.4% White, 6.9% Black, 12.7% Asian, 20.1% Hispanic of any race (2000); Density: 0.0 persons per square mile (2000); Age: 18.9% under 18, 11.6% over 64 (2000); Marriage status: 34.7% never married, 51.2% now married, 6.1% widowed, 8.0% divorced (2000); Foreign born: 48.7% (2000); Ancestry (includes multiple ancestries): 38.7% Other groups, 9.8% Russian, 5.0% Polish, 4.9% Italian, 4.6% Irish (2000).
Economy: Employment by occupation: 13.1% management, 25.8% professional, 17.9% services, 28.3% sales, 0.0% farming, 5.8% construction, 9.0% production (2000).
Income: Per capita income: $23,809 (2000); Median household income: $45,344 (2000); Poverty rate: 13.2% (2000).
Education: Percent of population age 25 and over with: High school diploma (including GED) or higher: 82.5% (2000); Bachelor's degree or higher: 39.5% (2000).
School District(s)
New York City Public Schools (PK-12)
    2003-04 Enrollment: 1,023,674 . . . . (718) 935-2794
Housing: Homeownership rate: 24.4% (2000); Median home value: $283,700 (2000); Median rent: $766 per month (2000); Median age of housing: 53 years (2000).
Transportation: Commute to work: 37.9% car, 56.3% public transportation, 3.9% walk, 1.5% work from home (2000); Travel time to work: 7.8% less than 15 minutes, 17.5% 15 to 30 minutes, 27.8% 30 to 45 minutes, 23.5% 45 to 60 minutes, 23.4% 60 minutes or more (2000)

MASPETH (unincorporated postal area, zip code 11378).
Covers a land area of 2.588 square miles and a water area of 0 square miles. Located at 40.72° N. Lat.; 73.90° W. Long.
Population: 0 (2000); Race: 82.1% White, 0.6% Black, 5.8% Asian, 19.7% Hispanic of any race (2000); Density: 0.0 persons per square mile (2000); Age: 20.8% under 18, 15.6% over 64 (2000); Marriage status: 29.7% never married, 54.1% now married, 10.2% widowed, 6.1% divorced (2000); Foreign born: 31.0% (2000); Ancestry (includes multiple ancestries): 26.4% Other groups, 23.5% Italian, 17.2% Polish, 14.9% Irish, 10.3% German (2000).
Economy: Employment by occupation: 10.9% management, 13.5% professional, 16.8% services, 33.1% sales, 0.0% farming, 13.7% construction, 12.0% production (2000).
Income: Per capita income: $20,777 (2000); Median household income: $43,107 (2000); Poverty rate: 9.7% (2000).
Education: Percent of population age 25 and over with: High school diploma (including GED) or higher: 74.4% (2000); Bachelor's degree or higher: 15.5% (2000).
School District(s)
New York City Public Schools (PK-12)
    2003-04 Enrollment: 1,023,674 . . . . (718) 935-2794
Housing: Homeownership rate: 50.0% (2000); Median home value: $213,200 (2000); Median rent: $727 per month (2000); Median age of housing: 58 years (2000).
Transportation: Commute to work: 56.3% car, 34.4% public transportation, 7.4% walk, 1.3% work from home (2000); Travel time to work: 15.6% less than 15 minutes, 26.5% 15 to 30 minutes, 20.3% 30 to 45 minutes, 16.3% 45 to 60 minutes, 21.3% 60 minutes or more (2000)

MIDDLE VILLAGE (unincorporated postal area, zip code 11379).
Covers a land area of 1.893 square miles and a water area of 0 square miles. Located at 40.71° N. Lat.; 73.89° W. Long.
Population: 0 (2000); Race: 89.0% White, 0.5% Black, 4.4% Asian, 10.5% Hispanic of any race (2000); Density: 0.0 persons per square mile (2000); Age: 18.1% under 18, 19.4% over 64 (2000); Marriage status: 28.3% never married, 54.7% now married, 10.8% widowed, 6.3% divorced (2000); Foreign born: 27.1% (2000); Ancestry (includes multiple ancestries): 33.6% Italian, 17.3% Irish, 17.1% Other groups, 15.3% German, 7.7% Polish (2000).
Economy: Employment by occupation: 14.9% management, 17.2% professional, 14.4% services, 32.2% sales, 0.0% farming, 10.5% construction, 10.8% production (2000).
Income: Per capita income: $24,062 (2000); Median household income: $49,083 (2000); Poverty rate: 8.6% (2000).
Education: Percent of population age 25 and over with: High school diploma (including GED) or higher: 78.8% (2000); Bachelor's degree or higher: 20.1% (2000).
School District(s)
New York City Public Schools (PK-12)
    2003-04 Enrollment: 1,023,674 . . . . (718) 935-2794
Housing: Homeownership rate: 55.3% (2000); Median home value: $244,000 (2000); Median rent: $722 per month (2000); Median age of housing: 54 years (2000).
Transportation: Commute to work: 56.2% car, 36.9% public transportation, 4.3% walk, 2.1% work from home (2000); Travel time to work: 11.9% less than 15 minutes, 27.8% 15 to 30 minutes, 21.7% 30 to 45 minutes, 16.6% 45 to 60 minutes, 22.1% 60 minutes or more (2000)

OAKLAND GARDENS (unincorporated postal area, zip code 11364).
Covers a land area of 2.820 square miles and a water area of 0 square miles. Located at 40.74° N. Lat.; 73.75° W. Long.
Population: 0 (2000); Race: 60.1% White, 1.2% Black, 32.9% Asian, 7.3% Hispanic of any race (2000); Density: 0.0 persons per square mile (2000); Age: 19.6% under 18, 18.3% over 64 (2000); Marriage status: 24.6% never married, 60.9% now married, 7.9% widowed, 6.5% divorced (2000); Foreign born: 37.1% (2000); Ancestry (includes multiple ancestries): 46.1% Other groups, 13.7% Italian, 8.6% Irish, 5.9% German, 5.4% Polish (2000).
Economy: Employment by occupation: 18.1% management, 24.5% professional, 10.9% services, 32.0% sales, 0.1% farming, 4.9% construction, 9.5% production (2000).
Income: Per capita income: $26,651 (2000); Median household income: $54,031 (2000); Poverty rate: 6.1% (2000).
Education: Percent of population age 25 and over with: High school diploma (including GED) or higher: 86.6% (2000); Bachelor's degree or higher: 38.4% (2000).
Housing: Homeownership rate: 67.7% (2000); Median home value: $282,400 (2000); Median rent: $860 per month (2000); Median age of housing: 47 years (2000).
Transportation: Commute to work: 69.8% car, 25.0% public transportation, 1.9% walk, 2.9% work from home (2000); Travel time to work: 12.2% less than 15 minutes, 25.3% 15 to 30 minutes, 22.6% 30 to 45 minutes, 12.4% 45 to 60 minutes, 27.5% 60 minutes or more (2000)

REGO PARK (unincorporated postal area, zip code 11374). Covers a land area of 0.913 square miles and a water area of 0 square miles. Located at 40.72° N. Lat.; 73.86° W. Long.
Population: 0 (2000); Race: 66.3% White, 2.5% Black, 23.4% Asian, 12.6% Hispanic of any race (2000); Density: 0.0 persons per square mile (2000); Age: 16.9% under 18, 18.2% over 64 (2000); Marriage status: 28.9% never married, 54.8% now married, 9.2% widowed, 7.1% divorced (2000); Foreign born: 59.1% (2000); Ancestry (includes multiple ancestries): 45.0% Other groups, 15.6% Russian, 5.0% Italian, 4.1% Polish, 3.3% Irish (2000).
Economy: Employment by occupation: 15.9% management, 28.1% professional, 13.1% services, 29.1% sales, 0.0% farming, 4.4% construction, 9.4% production (2000).
Income: Per capita income: $23,176 (2000); Median household income: $40,998 (2000); Poverty rate: 13.3% (2000).
Education: Percent of population age 25 and over with: High school diploma (including GED) or higher: 84.5% (2000); Bachelor's degree or higher: 40.8% (2000).

School District(s)
New York City Public Schools (PK-12)
    2003-04 Enrollment: 1,023,674 . . . . (718) 935-2794
Housing: Homeownership rate: 34.8% (2000); Median home value: $264,600 (2000); Median rent: $771 per month (2000); Median age of housing: 49 years (2000).
Transportation: Commute to work: 34.1% car, 56.4% public transportation, 6.7% walk, 2.4% work from home (2000); Travel time to work: 8.4% less than 15 minutes, 14.6% 15 to 30 minutes, 25.4% 30 to 45 minutes, 26.0% 45 to 60 minutes, 25.5% 60 minutes or more (2000).

RICHMOND HILL (unincorporated postal area, zip code 11418). Covers a land area of 1.608 square miles and a water area of 0 square miles. Located at 40.69° N. Lat.; 73.83° W. Long.
Population: 0 (2000); Race: 40.6% White, 8.6% Black, 16.7% Asian, 37.3% Hispanic of any race (2000); Density: 0.0 persons per square mile (2000); Age: 26.6% under 18, 8.6% over 64 (2000); Marriage status: 34.0% never married, 54.0% now married, 5.8% widowed, 6.2% divorced (2000); Foreign born: 51.6% (2000); Ancestry (includes multiple ancestries): 56.5% Other groups, 9.1% Guyanese, 5.8% Italian, 4.6% Irish, 3.6% German (2000).
Economy: Employment by occupation: 9.2% management, 16.8% professional, 21.7% services, 27.6% sales, 0.0% farming, 9.2% construction, 15.5% production (2000).
Income: Per capita income: $15,708 (2000); Median household income: $40,924 (2000); Poverty rate: 16.4% (2000).
Education: Percent of population age 25 and over with: High school diploma (including GED) or higher: 68.8% (2000); Bachelor's degree or higher: 19.7% (2000).

School District(s)
New York City Public Schools (PK-12)
    2003-04 Enrollment: 1,023,674 . . . . (718) 935-2794
Housing: Homeownership rate: 39.0% (2000); Median home value: $209,600 (2000); Median rent: $726 per month (2000); Median age of housing: 60+ years (2000).
Transportation: Commute to work: 41.2% car, 51.4% public transportation, 5.3% walk, 1.6% work from home (2000); Travel time to work: 9.5% less than 15 minutes, 17.8% 15 to 30 minutes, 21.4% 30 to 45 minutes, 14.2% 45 to 60 minutes, 37.1% 60 minutes or more (2000).

ROCKAWAY PARK (unincorporated postal area, zip code 11694). Covers a land area of 1.519 square miles and a water area of 0 square miles. Located at 40.57° N. Lat.; 73.84° W. Long.
Population: 0 (2000); Race: 87.3% White, 6.3% Black, 2.1% Asian, 9.1% Hispanic of any race (2000); Density: 0.0 persons per square mile (2000); Age: 20.7% under 18, 20.2% over 64 (2000); Marriage status: 26.7% never married, 57.3% now married, 9.5% widowed, 6.6% divorced (2000); Foreign born: 13.5% (2000); Ancestry (includes multiple ancestries): 36.0% Irish, 17.8% Other groups, 12.7% Italian, 6.9% German, 5.3% Polish (2000).
Economy: Employment by occupation: 15.1% management, 29.9% professional, 15.3% services, 26.8% sales, 0.1% farming, 6.7% construction, 6.1% production (2000).
Income: Per capita income: $28,501 (2000); Median household income: $48,604 (2000); Poverty rate: 12.5% (2000).
Education: Percent of population age 25 and over with: High school diploma (including GED) or higher: 82.1% (2000); Bachelor's degree or higher: 34.8% (2000).

School District(s)
New York City Public Schools (PK-12)
    2003-04 Enrollment: 1,023,674 . . . . (718) 935-2794
Housing: Homeownership rate: 45.5% (2000); Median home value: $363,000 (2000); Median rent: $645 per month (2000); Median age of housing: 52 years (2000).
Transportation: Commute to work: 66.4% car, 24.5% public transportation, 5.9% walk, 2.7% work from home (2000); Travel time to work: 14.9% less than 15 minutes, 23.1% 15 to 30 minutes, 20.7% 30 to 45 minutes, 9.8% 45 to 60 minutes, 31.6% 60 minutes or more (2000).
Additional Information Contacts
Rockaways Chamber of Commerce . . . . (718) 634-1300
    http://www.rockawaychamberofcommerce.com

ROSEDALE (unincorporated postal area, zip code 11422). Covers a land area of 6.262 square miles and a water area of 0 square miles. Located at 40.65° N. Lat.; 73.73° W. Long.
Population: 0 (2000); Race: 12.7% White, 73.1% Black, 3.1% Asian, 9.0% Hispanic of any race (2000); Density: 0.0 persons per square mile (2000); Age: 27.8% under 18, 7.9% over 64 (2000); Marriage status: 34.7% never married, 50.9% now married, 6.4% widowed, 8.0% divorced (2000); Foreign born: 43.8% (2000); Ancestry (includes multiple ancestries): 35.7% Other groups, 17.1% Jamaican, 13.9% Haitian, 4.0% United States or American, 3.3% Italian (2000).
Economy: Employment by occupation: 11.5% management, 22.6% professional, 19.7% services, 28.8% sales, 0.0% farming, 6.6% construction, 10.7% production (2000).
Income: Per capita income: $20,232 (2000); Median household income: $58,396 (2000); Poverty rate: 7.2% (2000).
Education: Percent of population age 25 and over with: High school diploma (including GED) or higher: 82.6% (2000); Bachelor's degree or higher: 20.9% (2000).

School District(s)
New York City Public Schools (PK-12)
    2003-04 Enrollment: 1,023,674 . . . . (718) 935-2794
Housing: Homeownership rate: 69.5% (2000); Median home value: $186,600 (2000); Median rent: $872 per month (2000); Median age of housing: 43 years (2000).
Transportation: Commute to work: 61.8% car, 33.8% public transportation, 2.1% walk, 1.5% work from home (2000); Travel time to work: 7.2% less than 15 minutes, 18.0% 15 to 30 minutes, 22.2% 30 to 45 minutes, 13.1% 45 to 60 minutes, 39.4% 60 minutes or more (2000).

SAINT ALBANS (unincorporated postal area, zip code 11412). Covers a land area of 1.899 square miles and a water area of 0 square miles. Located at 40.69° N. Lat.; 73.76° W. Long.
Population: 0 (2000); Race: 1.6% White, 93.9% Black, 0.6% Asian, 3.4% Hispanic of any race (2000); Density: 0.0 persons per square mile (2000); Age: 25.6% under 18, 14.4% over 64 (2000); Marriage status: 38.8% never married, 41.7% now married, 10.1% widowed, 9.4% divorced (2000); Foreign born: 27.5% (2000); Ancestry (includes multiple ancestries): 54.2% Other groups, 13.3% Jamaican, 5.4% United States or American, 4.4% Haitian, 2.2% Trinidadian and Tobagonian (2000).
Economy: Employment by occupation: 11.6% management, 17.8% professional, 23.5% services, 29.7% sales, 0.0% farming, 7.1% construction, 10.2% production (2000).
Income: Per capita income: $18,686 (2000); Median household income: $48,536 (2000); Poverty rate: 11.7% (2000).
Education: Percent of population age 25 and over with: High school diploma (including GED) or higher: 77.8% (2000); Bachelor's degree or higher: 17.2% (2000).

School District(s)
New York City Geographic District #29 (PK-07)
    2003-04 Enrollment: 1,425 . . . . (718) 978-5900
New York City Public Schools (PK-12)
    2003-04 Enrollment: 1,023,674 . . . . (718) 935-2794
Housing: Homeownership rate: 71.7% (2000); Median home value: $169,400 (2000); Median rent: $707 per month (2000); Median age of housing: 53 years (2000).
Transportation: Commute to work: 52.4% car, 43.8% public transportation, 1.9% walk, 1.3% work from home (2000); Travel time to

work: 6.4% less than 15 minutes, 17.8% 15 to 30 minutes, 20.3% 30 to 45 minutes, 12.7% 45 to 60 minutes, 42.8% 60 minutes or more (2000)

SOUTH OZONE PARK (unincorporated postal area, zip code 11420). Covers a land area of 2.115 square miles and a water area of 0 square miles. Located at 40.67° N. Lat.; 73.81° W. Long.
Population: 0 (2000); Race: 21.2% White, 35.7% Black, 13.1% Asian, 22.9% Hispanic of any race (2000); Density: 0.0 persons per square mile (2000); Age: 27.2% under 18, 9.0% over 64 (2000); Marriage status: 32.9% never married, 54.3% now married, 6.2% widowed, 6.5% divorced (2000); Foreign born: 43.8% (2000); Ancestry (includes multiple ancestries): 48.6% Other groups, 10.2% Guyanese, 6.5% Italian, 4.2% Trinidadian and Tobagonian, 3.9% West Indian (2000).
Economy: Employment by occupation: 8.6% management, 14.6% professional, 21.1% services, 31.6% sales, 0.0% farming, 10.7% construction, 13.3% production (2000).
Income: Per capita income: $16,558 (2000); Median household income: $47,584 (2000); Poverty rate: 12.1% (2000).
Education: Percent of population age 25 and over with: High school diploma (including GED) or higher: 70.9% (2000); Bachelor's degree or higher: 12.8% (2000).

School District(s)
New York City Public Schools (PK-12)
    2003-04 Enrollment: 1,023,674 . . . . (718) 935-2794

Housing: Homeownership rate: 66.9% (2000); Median home value: $173,300 (2000); Median rent: $736 per month (2000); Median age of housing: 51 years (2000).
Transportation: Commute to work: 53.4% car, 41.6% public transportation, 2.4% walk, 1.5% work from home (2000); Travel time to work: 10.5% less than 15 minutes, 18.0% 15 to 30 minutes, 19.7% 30 to 45 minutes, 16.1% 45 to 60 minutes, 35.8% 60 minutes or more (2000)

SOUTH RICHMOND HILL (unincorporated postal area, zip code 11419). Covers a land area of 1.137 square miles and a water area of 0 square miles. Located at 40.68° N. Lat.; 73.82° W. Long.
Population: 0 (2000); Race: 18.2% White, 14.7% Black, 25.0% Asian, 23.9% Hispanic of any race (2000); Density: 0.0 persons per square mile (2000); Age: 27.1% under 18, 6.7% over 64 (2000); Marriage status: 30.8% never married, 58.4% now married, 4.6% widowed, 6.2% divorced (2000); Foreign born: 61.6% (2000); Ancestry (includes multiple ancestries): 51.1% Other groups, 18.0% Guyanese, 5.0% Trinidadian and Tobagonian, 4.5% West Indian, 3.3% Italian (2000).
Economy: Employment by occupation: 8.4% management, 11.4% professional, 20.4% services, 32.3% sales, 0.0% farming, 9.2% construction, 18.2% production (2000).
Income: Per capita income: $14,707 (2000); Median household income: $43,066 (2000); Poverty rate: 14.3% (2000).
Education: Percent of population age 25 and over with: High school diploma (including GED) or higher: 61.7% (2000); Bachelor's degree or higher: 11.2% (2000).
Housing: Homeownership rate: 54.0% (2000); Median home value: $181,500 (2000); Median rent: $706 per month (2000); Median age of housing: 57 years (2000).
Transportation: Commute to work: 42.0% car, 50.7% public transportation, 5.1% walk, 1.3% work from home (2000); Travel time to work: 8.5% less than 15 minutes, 16.4% 15 to 30 minutes, 21.2% 30 to 45 minutes, 17.2% 45 to 60 minutes, 36.7% 60 minutes or more (2000)

SPRINGFIELD GARDENS (unincorporated postal area, zip code 11413). Covers a land area of 3.071 square miles and a water area of 0 square miles. Located at 40.66° N. Lat.; 73.75° W. Long.
Population: 0 (2000); Race: 3.4% White, 89.6% Black, 0.9% Asian, 5.2% Hispanic of any race (2000); Density: 0.0 persons per square mile (2000); Age: 25.3% under 18, 10.9% over 64 (2000); Marriage status: 36.7% never married, 47.7% now married, 7.1% widowed, 8.5% divorced (2000); Foreign born: 33.2% (2000); Ancestry (includes multiple ancestries): 48.5% Other groups, 16.7% Jamaican, 7.0% Haitian, 4.5% United States or American, 3.0% Trinidadian and Tobagonian (2000).
Economy: Employment by occupation: 11.3% management, 20.8% professional, 20.3% services, 30.4% sales, 0.1% farming, 6.8% construction, 10.3% production (2000).
Income: Per capita income: $20,835 (2000); Median household income: $56,726 (2000); Poverty rate: 6.8% (2000).

Education: Percent of population age 25 and over with: High school diploma (including GED) or higher: 80.7% (2000); Bachelor's degree or higher: 22.3% (2000).
Housing: Homeownership rate: 74.2% (2000); Median home value: $181,500 (2000); Median rent: $803 per month (2000); Median age of housing: 47 years (2000).
Transportation: Commute to work: 57.5% car, 39.5% public transportation, 1.7% walk, 0.7% work from home (2000); Travel time to work: 6.7% less than 15 minutes, 19.4% 15 to 30 minutes, 21.1% 30 to 45 minutes, 13.8% 45 to 60 minutes, 39.0% 60 minutes or more (2000)

SUNNYSIDE (unincorporated postal area, zip code 11104). Covers a land area of 0.396 square miles and a water area of 0 square miles. Located at 40.74° N. Lat.; 73.91° W. Long.
Population: 0 (2000); Race: 57.2% White, 2.1% Black, 24.8% Asian, 28.7% Hispanic of any race (2000); Density: 0.0 persons per square mile (2000); Age: 17.8% under 18, 11.8% over 64 (2000); Marriage status: 35.3% never married, 49.6% now married, 7.4% widowed, 7.7% divorced (2000); Foreign born: 60.8% (2000); Ancestry (includes multiple ancestries): 54.2% Other groups, 8.7% Irish, 4.7% Italian, 3.7% Romanian, 3.5% German (2000).
Economy: Employment by occupation: 11.9% management, 16.3% professional, 20.6% services, 26.8% sales, 0.2% farming, 8.0% construction, 16.2% production (2000).
Income: Per capita income: $19,674 (2000); Median household income: $37,962 (2000); Poverty rate: 17.1% (2000).
Education: Percent of population age 25 and over with: High school diploma (including GED) or higher: 75.5% (2000); Bachelor's degree or higher: 28.6% (2000).
Housing: Homeownership rate: 14.1% (2000); Median home value: $233,400 (2000); Median rent: $705 per month (2000); Median age of housing: 60+ years (2000).
Transportation: Commute to work: 20.7% car, 66.9% public transportation, 8.9% walk, 2.1% work from home (2000); Travel time to work: 8.4% less than 15 minutes, 19.4% 15 to 30 minutes, 36.2% 30 to 45 minutes, 21.0% 45 to 60 minutes, 15.0% 60 minutes or more (2000)

WHITESTONE (unincorporated postal area, zip code 11357). Covers a land area of 2.770 square miles and a water area of 0 square miles. Located at 40.78° N. Lat.; 73.81° W. Long.
Population: 0 (2000); Race: 83.1% White, 0.6% Black, 12.1% Asian, 7.5% Hispanic of any race (2000); Density: 0.0 persons per square mile (2000); Age: 18.3% under 18, 20.9% over 64 (2000); Marriage status: 24.2% never married, 59.5% now married, 10.2% widowed, 6.1% divorced (2000); Foreign born: 28.5% (2000); Ancestry (includes multiple ancestries): 32.0% Italian, 22.7% Other groups, 12.6% Irish, 7.6% Greek, 6.2% German (2000).
Economy: Employment by occupation: 17.3% management, 22.0% professional, 13.3% services, 29.2% sales, 0.0% farming, 8.9% construction, 9.2% production (2000).
Income: Per capita income: $26,422 (2000); Median household income: $54,910 (2000); Poverty rate: 6.5% (2000).
Education: Percent of population age 25 and over with: High school diploma (including GED) or higher: 82.1% (2000); Bachelor's degree or higher: 27.4% (2000).

School District(s)
New York City Public Schools (PK-12)
    2003-04 Enrollment: 1,023,674 . . . . (718) 935-2794

Housing: Homeownership rate: 72.8% (2000); Median home value: $292,800 (2000); Median rent: $874 per month (2000); Median age of housing: 47 years (2000).
Transportation: Commute to work: 72.5% car, 23.0% public transportation, 1.9% walk, 2.3% work from home (2000); Travel time to work: 15.2% less than 15 minutes, 27.6% 15 to 30 minutes, 22.9% 30 to 45 minutes, 10.5% 45 to 60 minutes, 23.9% 60 minutes or more (2000)

WOODHAVEN (unincorporated postal area, zip code 11421). Aka Wood Haven. Covers a land area of 1.229 square miles and a water area of 0 square miles. Located at 40.69° N. Lat.; 73.85° W. Long.
Population: 0 (2000); Race: 48.3% White, 4.4% Black, 14.4% Asian, 43.5% Hispanic of any race (2000); Density: 0.0 persons per square mile (2000); Age: 26.2% under 18, 10.5% over 64 (2000); Marriage status: 30.5% never married, 57.0% now married, 6.1% widowed, 6.3% divorced (2000); Foreign born: 42.2% (2000); Ancestry (includes multiple

ancestries): 57.0% Other groups, 9.3% Italian, 7.8% Irish, 6.2% German, 3.6% Guyanese (2000).
Economy: Employment by occupation: 8.9% management, 15.6% professional, 18.5% services, 31.4% sales, 0.0% farming, 10.3% construction, 15.3% production (2000).
Income: Per capita income: $16,846 (2000); Median household income: $44,550 (2000); Poverty rate: 12.2% (2000).
Education: Percent of population age 25 and over with: High school diploma (including GED) or higher: 72.9% (2000); Bachelor's degree or higher: 17.3% (2000).

School District(s)
New York City Public Schools (PK-12)
   2003-04 Enrollment: 1,023,674 . . . . (718) 935-2794
Housing: Homeownership rate: 51.9% (2000); Median home value: $173,700 (2000); Median rent: $730 per month (2000); Median age of housing: 60+ years (2000).
Transportation: Commute to work: 45.1% car, 49.0% public transportation, 4.6% walk, 0.8% work from home (2000); Travel time to work: 8.3% less than 15 minutes, 16.4% 15 to 30 minutes, 20.2% 30 to 45 minutes, 18.6% 45 to 60 minutes, 36.5% 60 minutes or more (2000)

WOODSIDE (unincorporated postal area, zip code 11377). Covers a land area of 2.554 square miles and a water area of 0 square miles. Located at 40.74° N. Lat.; 73.90° W. Long.
Population: 0 (2000); Race: 42.2% White, 3.9% Black, 29.7% Asian, 38.1% Hispanic of any race (2000); Density: 0.0 persons per square mile (2000); Age: 20.3% under 18, 10.9% over 64 (2000); Marriage status: 34.3% never married, 52.7% now married, 5.7% widowed, 7.3% divorced (2000); Foreign born: 60.9% (2000); Ancestry (includes multiple ancestries): 66.2% Other groups, 8.1% Irish, 3.8% Italian, 2.4% German, 2.3% United States or American (2000).
Economy: Employment by occupation: 10.2% management, 14.4% professional, 23.1% services, 26.9% sales, 0.1% farming, 8.0% construction, 17.3% production (2000).
Income: Per capita income: $16,735 (2000); Median household income: $37,360 (2000); Poverty rate: 17.1% (2000).
Education: Percent of population age 25 and over with: High school diploma (including GED) or higher: 71.6% (2000); Bachelor's degree or higher: 23.0% (2000).

School District(s)
New York City Public Schools (PK-12)
   2003-04 Enrollment: 1,023,674 . . . . (718) 935-2794
Housing: Homeownership rate: 27.1% (2000); Median home value: $225,900 (2000); Median rent: $707 per month (2000); Median age of housing: 49 years (2000).
Transportation: Commute to work: 26.3% car, 65.2% public transportation, 6.2% walk, 1.4% work from home (2000); Travel time to work: 8.0% less than 15 minutes, 18.1% 15 to 30 minutes, 37.3% 30 to 45 minutes, 20.5% 45 to 60 minutes, 16.1% 60 minutes or more (2000)

End of Neighborhoods in Queens

STATEN ISLAND (borough). Aka Richmond County. Located in southeastern New York State. One of the five counties/boroughs of New York City. Covers a land area of 58.48 square miles, a water area of 44.02 square miles, and is located in the Eastern Time Zone. County seat is St. George.

Richmond County is part of the New York-Northern New Jersey-Long Island, NY-NJ-PA Metropolitan Statistical Area. The entire metro area includes: Edison, NJ Metropolitan Division (Middlesex County, NJ; Monmouth County, NJ; Ocean County, NJ; Somerset County, NJ); Nassau-Suffolk, NY Metropolitan Division (Nassau County, NY; Suffolk County, NY); New York-White Plains-Wayne, NY-NJ Metropolitan Division (Bergen County, NJ; Hudson County, NJ; Passaic County, NJ; Bronx County, NY; Kings County, NY; New York County, NY; Putnam County, NY; Queens County, NY; Richmond County, NY; Rockland County, NY; Westchester County, NY); Newark-Union, NJ-PA Metropolitan Division (Essex County, NJ; Hunterdon County, NJ; Morris County, NJ; Sussex County, NJ; Union County, NJ; Pike County, PA)

Population: 378,977 (1990); 443,728 (2000); 466,519 (2005); 490,163 (2010 projected); Race: 73.8% White, 10.5% Black, 6.9% Asian, 15.2% Hispanic of any race (2005); Density: 7,977.6 persons per square mile (2005); Average household size: 2.82 (2005); Median age: 37.3 (2005); Males per 100 females: 94.2 (2005).
Religion: Five largest groups: 59.7% Catholic Church, 7.6% Jewish Estimate, 1.8% Muslim Estimate, 0.9% Evangelical Lutheran Church in America, 0.8% Assemblies of God (2000).
Economy: Unemployment rate: 5.1% (2005); Total civilian labor force: 227,783 (2005); Leading industries: 27.0% health care and social assistance; 17.7% retail trade; 7.9% construction (2003); Farms: 16 totaling 44 acres (2002); Companies that employ 500 or more persons: 11 (2003); Companies that employ 100 to 499 persons: 102 (2003); Companies that employ less than 100 persons: 7,688 (2003); Black-owned businesses: 2,291 (2002); Hispanic-owned businesses: 1,688 (2002); Women-owned businesses: 9,615 (2002); Retail sales per capita: $8,535 (2006). Single-family building permits issued: 829 (2005); Multi-family building permits issued: 1,043 (2005).
Income: Per capita income: $27,427 (2005); Median household income: $62,131 (2005); Average household income: $76,357 (2005); Percent of households with income of $100,000 or more: 25.1% (2005); Poverty rate: 10.1% (2003); Bankruptcy rate: 4.21% (2005).
Education: Percent of population age 25 and over with: High school diploma (including GED) or higher: 82.5% (2005); Bachelor's degree or higher: 23.1% (2005); Master's degree or higher: 9.0% (2005).
Housing: Homeownership rate: 64.0% (2005); Median home value: $356,463 (2005); Median rent: $656 per month (2000); Median age of housing: 31 years (2000).
Health: Birth rate: 125.4 per 10,000 population (2004); Death rate: 75.1 per 10,000 population (2004); Age-adjusted cancer mortality rate: 208.1 deaths per 100,000 population (2002); Air Quality Index: 68.5% good, 28.8% moderate, 2.7% unhealthy for sensitive individuals, 0.0% unhealthy (percent of days in 2005); Number of physicians: 37.7 per 10,000 population (2004); Hospital beds: 34.0 per 10,000 population (2003); Hospital admissions: 1,530.9 per 10,000 population (2003).
Elections: 2004 Presidential election results: 56.4% Bush, 42.7% Kerry, 0.7% Nader, 0.1% Badnarik
National and State Parks: Gateway National Recreation Area

School District(s)
Hawthorne-Cedar Knolls Union Free School District (03-12)
   2003-04 Enrollment: 320 . . . . (914) 773-7345
New York City Geographic District #31 (PK-05)
   2003-04 Enrollment: 650 . . . . (718) 420-5673
New York City Public Schools (PK-12)
   2003-04 Enrollment: 1,023,674 . . . . (718) 935-2794

Four-year College(s)
CUNY College of Staten Island (Public)
   Fall 2004 Enrollment: 12,442 . . . . (718) 982-2000
   2005-06 Tuition: In-state $4,328; Out-of-state $8,968
Wagner College
   Fall 2004 Enrollment: 2,259 . . . . (718) 390-3100
   2005-06 Tuition: In-state $25,350; Out-of-state $25,350

Two-year College(s)
St Vincent Catholic Medical Center-Staten Island
   Fall 2004 Enrollment: 99 . . . . (718) 818-6470
   2005-06 Tuition: In-state $11,600; Out-of-state $11,600
Willsey Institute
   Fall 2004 Enrollment: 75 . . . . (718) 442-5706
Hospitals: South Beach Psychiatric Center (322 beds); St. Vincent's Staten Island/Bayley Seton Campuses (198 beds); Staten Island University Hospital (813 beds)
Newspapers: Staten Island Advance (Circulation 67,033); Staten Island Register (General - Circulation 20,000)
Additional Information Contacts
Staten Island Borough President . . . . (718) 816-2000
   http://statenislandusa.com/
Staten Island Chamber of Commerce . . . . (718) 727-1900
   http://www.sichamber.com

Niagara County

Located in western New York; bounded on the west by the Niagara River and Lake Erie, and on the north by Lake Ontario; drained by Tonawanda Creek; includes Niagara Falls. Covers a land area of 522.95 square miles, a water area of 616.89 square miles, and is located in the Eastern Time Zone. The county government was organized in 1808. County seat is Lockport.

PROFILES OF NEW YORK / Niagara County

Niagara County is part of the Buffalo-Niagara Falls, NY Metropolitan Statistical Area. The entire metro area includes: Erie County, NY; Niagara County, NY

Weather Station: Lockport 2 SE — Elevation: 603 feet

	Jan	Feb	Mar	Apr	May	Jun	Jul	Aug	Sep	Oct	Nov	Dec
High	32	34	43	57	69	77	82	79	71	60	48	37
Low	17	18	25	36	47	55	61	60	52	42	33	23
Precip	2.5	2.2	2.8	3.1	3.0	3.6	3.1	3.4	3.7	3.1	3.5	3.3
Snow	24.3	18.5	12.1	4.2	0.4	tr	0.0	0.0	tr	tr	7.5	19.1

High and Low temperatures in degrees Fahrenheit; Precipitation and Snow in inches

Weather Station: Lockport 4 NE — Elevation: 439 feet

	Jan	Feb	Mar	Apr	May	Jun	Jul	Aug	Sep	Oct	Nov	Dec
High	31	32	42	54	67	76	81	79	71	60	48	36
Low	16	17	25	36	46	55	60	59	51	41	33	23
Precip	2.1	2.2	2.8	3.2	2.9	3.6	3.1	3.6	3.9	2.9	3.2	3.3
Snow	15.2	15.6	8.8	2.9	0.3	0.0	0.0	0.0	0.0	tr	4.0	16.1

High and Low temperatures in degrees Fahrenheit; Precipitation and Snow in inches

Population: 220,756 (1990); 219,846 (2000); 217,848 (2005); 215,670 (2010 projected); Race: 89.4% White, 7.0% Black, 0.9% Asian, 1.8% Hispanic of any race (2005); Density: 416.6 persons per square mile (2005); Average household size: 2.47 (2005); Median age: 39.5 (2005); Males per 100 females: 93.7 (2005).
Religion: Five largest groups: 35.7% Catholic Church, 5.1% Lutheran Church-Missouri Synod, 3.5% The United Methodist Church, 2.4% Evangelical Lutheran Church in America, 2.0% Presbyterian Church (U.S.A.) (2000).
Economy: Unemployment rate: 5.6% (2005); Total civilian labor force: 112,152 (2005); Leading industries: 20.0% manufacturing; 16.1% health care and social assistance; 16.0% retail trade (2003); Farms: 801 totaling 148,041 acres (2002); Companies that employ 500 or more persons: 8 (2003); Companies that employ 100 to 499 persons: 84 (2003); Companies that employ less than 100 persons: 4,458 (2003); Black-owned businesses: n/a (2002); Hispanic-owned businesses: n/a (2002); Women-owned businesses: 4,210 (2002); Retail sales per capita: $11,321 (2006); Single-family building permits issued: 386 (2005); Multi-family building permits issued: 87 (2005).
Income: Per capita income: $21,880 (2005); Median household income: $42,970 (2005); Average household income: $53,594 (2005); Percent of households with income of $100,000 or more: 11.6% (2005); Poverty rate: 11.4% (2003); Bankruptcy rate: 10.18% (2005).
Taxes: Total county taxes per capita: $697 (2004); County property taxes per capita: $324 (2004).
Education: Percent of population age 25 and over with: High school diploma (including GED) or higher: 83.6% (2005); Bachelor's degree or higher: 17.7% (2005); Master's degree or higher: 6.8% (2005).
Housing: Homeownership rate: 70.8% (2005); Median home value: $100,954 (2005); Median rent: $385 per month (2000); Median age of housing: 46 years (2000).
Health: Birth rate: 109.8 per 10,000 population (2004); Death rate: 109.5 per 10,000 population (2004); Age-adjusted cancer mortality rate: 223.3 deaths per 100,000 population (2002); Air Quality Index: 65.8% good, 31.2% moderate, 3.0% unhealthy for sensitive individuals, 0.0% unhealthy (percent of days in 2005); Number of physicians: 12.0 per 10,000 population (2004); Hospital beds: 29.6 per 10,000 population (2003); Hospital admissions: 1,010.5 per 10,000 population (2003).
Elections: 2004 Presidential election results: 48.8% Bush, 49.3% Kerry, 1.7% Nader, 0.2% Badnarik
National and State Parks: Brydges State Park; Devils Hole State Park; Fort Niagara State Park; Fourmile Creek State Park; Joseph Davis State Park; Lower Niagara River State Park; New York State Reservation; Whirlpool State Park
Additional Information Contacts

Niagara County Government	(716) 439-7000
http://www.niagaracounty.com/	
City of Lockport	(716) 439-6676
http://www.elockport.com/	
City of Niagara Falls	(716) 286-4340
http://www.niagarafallsusa.org/	
City of North Tonawanda	(716) 695-8555
http://www.northtonawanda.org/	
Town of Cambria	(716) 433-7664
http://www.townofcambria.com/	
Town of Lockport	(716) 439-9520
http://www.elockport.com/	
Town of Niagara	(716) 297-2150
http://www.townofniagara.com/	
Town of Wheatfield	(716) 694-6440
http://wheatfield.ny.us/	
Town of Wilson	(716) 751-6704
http://www.wilsonnewyork.com/	
Village of Wilson	(716) 751-6704
http://www.wilsonnewyork.com/	

Niagara County Communities

APPLETON (unincorporated postal area, zip code 14008). Covers a land area of 24.984 square miles and a water area of 0 square miles. Located at 43.31° N. Lat.; 78.63° W. Long. Elevation is 339 feet.
Population: 0 (2000); Race: 93.4% White, 3.8% Black, 0.0% Asian, 1.6% Hispanic of any race (2000); Density: 0.0 persons per square mile (2000); Age: 25.9% under 18, 13.2% over 64 (2000); Marriage status: 23.3% never married, 60.7% now married, 7.8% widowed, 8.2% divorced (2000); Foreign born: 3.4% (2000); Ancestry (includes multiple ancestries): 40.5% German, 18.6% English, 16.6% Irish, 10.0% Polish, 9.0% Other groups (2000).
Economy: Employment by occupation: 14.2% management, 15.1% professional, 20.5% services, 12.6% sales, 2.8% farming, 9.7% construction, 25.1% production (2000).
Income: Per capita income: $18,484 (2000); Median household income: $41,563 (2000); Poverty rate: 6.5% (2000).
Education: Percent of population age 25 and over with: High school diploma (including GED) or higher: 84.8% (2000); Bachelor's degree or higher: 10.9% (2000).
Housing: Homeownership rate: 85.2% (2000); Median home value: $79,900 (2000); Median rent: $392 per month (2000); Median age of housing: 60+ years (2000).
Transportation: Commute to work: 94.6% car, 0.8% public transportation, 1.8% walk, 2.0% work from home (2000); Travel time to work: 37.1% less than 15 minutes, 37.8% 15 to 30 minutes, 11.6% 30 to 45 minutes, 9.1% 45 to 60 minutes, 4.5% 60 minutes or more (2000)

BARKER (village). Covers a land area of 0.420 square miles and a water area of 0 square miles. Located at 43.32° N. Lat.; 78.55° W. Long. Elevation is 331 feet.
Population: 569 (1990); 577 (2000); 554 (2005); 544 (2010 projected); Race: 98.0% White, 0.7% Black, 0.0% Asian, 1.6% Hispanic of any race (2005); Density: 1,317.6 persons per square mile (2005); Average household size: 2.73 (2005); Median age: 37.1 (2005); Males per 100 females: 100.0 (2005); Marriage status: 27.3% never married, 55.7% now married, 9.5% widowed, 7.5% divorced (2000); Foreign born: 0.7% (2000); Ancestry (includes multiple ancestries): 30.0% English, 27.2% German, 23.2% Irish, 10.1% Polish, 6.8% French (except Basque) (2000).
Economy: In fruit-growing area. Single-family building permits issued: 0 (2005); Multi-family building permits issued: 0 (2005); Employment by occupation: 4.1% management, 11.8% professional, 21.8% services, 16.8% sales, 1.8% farming, 13.6% construction, 30.0% production (2000).
Income: Per capita income: $16,828 (2005); Median household income: $40,966 (2005); Average household income: $45,924 (2005); Percent of households with income of $100,000 or more: 6.9% (2005); Poverty rate: 9.6% (2000).
Education: Percent of population age 25 and over with: High school diploma (including GED) or higher: 88.7% (2005); Bachelor's degree or higher: 9.6% (2005); Master's degree or higher: 4.1% (2005).

School District(s)
Barker Central School District (PK-12)
    2003-04 Enrollment: 1,139 . . . . (716) 795-3832

Housing: Homeownership rate: 65.0% (2005); Median home value: $94,091 (2005); Median rent: $363 per month (2000); Median age of housing: 60+ years (2000).
Transportation: Commute to work: 89.6% car, 0.5% public transportation, 5.0% walk, 5.0% work from home (2000); Travel time to work: 34.1% less than 15 minutes, 27.5% 15 to 30 minutes, 19.0% 30 to 45 minutes, 10.9% 45 to 60 minutes, 8.5% 60 minutes or more (2000)

BURT (unincorporated postal area, zip code 14028). Covers a land area of 11.241 square miles and a water area of 0 square miles. Located at 43.32° N. Lat.; 78.71° W. Long. Elevation is 320 feet.
Population: 0 (2000); Race: 97.4% White, 0.3% Black, 0.0% Asian, 0.0% Hispanic of any race (2000); Density: 0.0 persons per square mile (2000);

Age: 25.3% under 18, 14.8% over 64 (2000); Marriage status: 22.8% never married, 57.2% now married, 6.6% widowed, 13.4% divorced (2000); Foreign born: 2.5% (2000); Ancestry (includes multiple ancestries): 30.8% German, 21.5% English, 17.0% Irish, 8.2% Italian, 6.6% French (except Basque) (2000).
Economy: Manufacturing of chemicals, catalysts and additives; fruit and vegetables. Employment by occupation: 8.7% management, 17.3% professional, 12.1% services, 14.2% sales, 3.1% farming, 8.3% construction, 36.2% production (2000).
Income: Per capita income: $18,579 (2000); Median household income: $48,393 (2000); Poverty rate: 6.2% (2000).
Education: Percent of population age 25 and over with: High school diploma (including GED) or higher: 85.4% (2000); Bachelor's degree or higher: 10.1% (2000).
School District(s)
Newfane Central School District (PK-12)
　2003-04 Enrollment: 2,174 . . . . (716) 778-6850
Housing: Homeownership rate: 80.9% (2000); Median home value: $79,300 (2000); Median rent: $437 per month (2000); Median age of housing: 48 years (2000).
Transportation: Commute to work: 98.6% car, 0.0% public transportation, 0.0% walk, 1.4% work from home (2000); Travel time to work: 27.8% less than 15 minutes, 40.3% 15 to 30 minutes, 15.0% 30 to 45 minutes, 11.8% 45 to 60 minutes, 5.1% 60 minutes or more (2000)

CAMBRIA (town). Covers a land area of 39.872 square miles and a water area of 0 square miles. Located at 43.17° N. Lat.; 78.83° W. Long.
Population: 4,779 (1990); 5,393 (2000); 5,455 (2005); 5,518 (2010 projected); Race: 97.9% White, 0.3% Black, 0.7% Asian, 0.7% Hispanic of any race (2005); Density: 136.8 persons per square mile (2005); Average household size: 2.65 (2005); Median age: 40.6 (2005); Males per 100 females: 99.4 (2005); Marriage status: 22.7% never married, 65.2% now married, 7.5% widowed, 4.6% divorced (2000); Foreign born: 2.1% (2000); Ancestry (includes multiple ancestries): 33.4% German, 16.8% Irish, 15.7% Italian, 15.5% Polish, 13.6% English (2000).
Economy: Single-family building permits issued: 22 (2005); Multi-family building permits issued: 0 (2005); Employment by occupation: 12.7% management, 16.7% professional, 16.5% services, 21.2% sales, 1.1% farming, 11.1% construction, 20.8% production (2000).
Income: Per capita income: $23,588 (2005); Median household income: $52,398 (2005); Average household income: $62,119 (2005); Percent of households with income of $100,000 or more: 17.2% (2005); Poverty rate: 5.1% (2000).
Education: Percent of population age 25 and over with: High school diploma (including GED) or higher: 88.0% (2005); Bachelor's degree or higher: 16.8% (2005); Master's degree or higher: 4.8% (2005).
Housing: Homeownership rate: 82.1% (2005); Median home value: $140,555 (2005); Median rent: $428 per month (2000); Median age of housing: 35 years (2000).
Transportation: Commute to work: 96.6% car, 0.0% public transportation, 0.9% walk, 2.5% work from home (2000); Travel time to work: 28.3% less than 15 minutes, 43.5% 15 to 30 minutes, 20.9% 30 to 45 minutes, 4.7% 45 to 60 minutes, 2.6% 60 minutes or more (2000)
Additional Information Contacts
Town of Cambria . . . . (716) 433-7664
　http://www.townofcambria.com/

GASPORT (CDP). Covers a land area of 2.868 square miles and a water area of 0.057 square miles. Located at 43.19° N. Lat.; 78.57° W. Long.
Population: 1,336 (1990); 1,248 (2000); 1,226 (2005); 1,214 (2010 projected); Race: 95.3% White, 0.6% Black, 1.0% Asian, 0.6% Hispanic of any race (2005); Density: 427.5 persons per square mile (2005); Average household size: 2.69 (2005); Median age: 43.5 (2005); Males per 100 females: 93.4 (2005); Marriage status: 18.8% never married, 66.1% now married, 9.3% widowed, 5.8% divorced (2000); Foreign born: 1.8% (2000); Ancestry (includes multiple ancestries): 42.0% German, 18.1% English, 11.5% Irish, 10.6% Italian, 6.7% Polish (2000).
Economy: Manufacturing: vegetable and fruit-grading and handling equipment, computerized control systems, orchard-spray equipment, pallets, and boxes. Limestone quarry. Employment by occupation: 9.2% management, 24.5% professional, 12.6% services, 27.3% sales, 0.0% farming, 7.5% construction, 19.0% production (2000).
Income: Per capita income: $20,138 (2005); Median household income: $46,175 (2005); Average household income: $49,626 (2005); Percent of households with income of $100,000 or more: 5.5% (2005); Poverty rate: 6.4% (2000).
Education: Percent of population age 25 and over with: High school diploma (including GED) or higher: 87.0% (2005); Bachelor's degree or higher: 15.2% (2005); Master's degree or higher: 5.4% (2005).
School District(s)
Royalton-Hartland Central School District (KG-12)
　2003-04 Enrollment: 1,682 . . . . (716) 735-3031
Housing: Homeownership rate: 75.8% (2005); Median home value: $113,451 (2005); Median rent: $393 per month (2000); Median age of housing: 37 years (2000).
Transportation: Commute to work: 98.2% car, 0.0% public transportation, 0.0% walk, 1.8% work from home (2000); Travel time to work: 26.7% less than 15 minutes, 45.5% 15 to 30 minutes, 12.4% 30 to 45 minutes, 8.8% 45 to 60 minutes, 6.6% 60 minutes or more (2000)

HARTLAND (town). Covers a land area of 52.353 square miles and a water area of 0.039 square miles. Located at 43.24° N. Lat.; 78.53° W. Long.
Population: 3,911 (1990); 4,165 (2000); 4,129 (2005); 4,095 (2010 projected); Race: 97.4% White, 0.6% Black, 0.1% Asian, 1.1% Hispanic of any race (2005); Density: 78.9 persons per square mile (2005); Average household size: 2.68 (2005); Median age: 39.4 (2005); Males per 100 females: 100.4 (2005); Marriage status: 22.5% never married, 60.6% now married, 6.8% widowed, 10.1% divorced (2000); Foreign born: 1.7% (2000); Ancestry (includes multiple ancestries): 35.2% German, 21.6% English, 14.7% Irish, 9.2% Polish, 8.9% Italian (2000).
Economy: Single-family building permits issued: 4 (2005); Multi-family building permits issued: 0 (2005); Employment by occupation: 9.5% management, 13.7% professional, 17.4% services, 17.6% sales, 1.0% farming, 15.4% construction, 25.4% production (2000).
Income: Per capita income: $19,243 (2005); Median household income: $44,151 (2005); Average household income: $51,626 (2005); Percent of households with income of $100,000 or more: 8.3% (2005); Poverty rate: 9.3% (2000).
Education: Percent of population age 25 and over with: High school diploma (including GED) or higher: 82.9% (2005); Bachelor's degree or higher: 9.8% (2005); Master's degree or higher: 2.7% (2005).
Housing: Homeownership rate: 85.1% (2005); Median home value: $98,732 (2005); Median rent: $362 per month (2000); Median age of housing: 51 years (2000).
Transportation: Commute to work: 93.9% car, 0.3% public transportation, 0.3% walk, 5.2% work from home (2000); Travel time to work: 22.9% less than 15 minutes, 47.8% 15 to 30 minutes, 15.6% 30 to 45 minutes, 5.6% 45 to 60 minutes, 8.1% 60 minutes or more (2000)

LEWISTON (village). Covers a land area of 1.065 square miles and a water area of 0.111 square miles. Located at 43.17° N. Lat.; 79.04° W. Long. Elevation is 363 feet.
Population: 3,048 (1990); 2,781 (2000); 2,705 (2005); 2,621 (2010 projected); Race: 98.1% White, 0.1% Black, 0.6% Asian, 0.8% Hispanic of any race (2005); Density: 2,538.9 persons per square mile (2005); Average household size: 2.16 (2005); Median age: 47.7 (2005); Males per 100 females: 84.8 (2005); Marriage status: 27.5% never married, 48.9% now married, 15.7% widowed, 7.9% divorced (2000); Foreign born: 8.5% (2000); Ancestry (includes multiple ancestries): 24.0% Italian, 23.6% Irish, 20.6% German, 14.9% English, 9.5% Polish (2000).
Economy: Single-family building permits issued: 3 (2005); Multi-family building permits issued: 0 (2005); Employment by occupation: 13.4% management, 21.6% professional, 16.2% services, 28.4% sales, 0.0% farming, 8.9% construction, 11.4% production (2000).
Income: Per capita income: $23,315 (2005); Median household income: $39,442 (2005); Average household income: $48,345 (2005); Percent of households with income of $100,000 or more: 6.5% (2005); Poverty rate: 8.6% (2000).
Education: Percent of population age 25 and over with: High school diploma (including GED) or higher: 91.7% (2005); Bachelor's degree or higher: 24.5% (2005); Master's degree or higher: 8.8% (2005).
School District(s)
Niagara-Wheatfield Central School District (PK-12)
　2003-04 Enrollment: 4,060 . . . . (716) 215-3003
Housing: Homeownership rate: 62.8% (2005); Median home value: $117,927 (2005); Median rent: $511 per month (2000); Median age of housing: 45 years (2000).
Hospitals: Mount St. Mary's Hospital (179 beds)

Transportation: Commute to work: 94.3% car, 0.0% public transportation, 3.4% walk, 1.8% work from home (2000); Travel time to work: 48.3% less than 15 minutes, 36.2% 15 to 30 minutes, 9.4% 30 to 45 minutes, 3.5% 45 to 60 minutes, 2.5% 60 minutes or more (2000)

LEWISTON (town). Covers a land area of 37.266 square miles and a water area of 3.763 square miles. Located at 43.16° N. Lat.; 79.00° W. Long. Elevation is 363 feet.

History: As with Lewis county, named after Governor Morgan Lewis. Settled c.1796, incorporated 1822.

Population: 15,500 (1990); 16,257 (2000); 16,478 (2005); 16,702 (2010 projected); Race: 96.5% White, 1.1% Black, 0.8% Asian, 1.2% Hispanic of any race (2005); Density: 442.2 persons per square mile (2005); Average household size: 2.72 (2005); Median age: 41.4 (2005); Males per 100 females: 89.4 (2005); Marriage status: 30.7% never married, 54.9% now married, 8.3% widowed, 6.2% divorced (2000); Foreign born: 7.7% (2000); Ancestry (includes multiple ancestries): 26.9% Italian, 24.2% German, 18.5% Irish, 14.2% English, 13.4% Polish (2000).

Economy: Manufacturing of chemicals, construction materials. Massive 2.4-million kw hydroelectric pumped storage project South and East of village. Artpark, a 200-acre theater and arts complex here. Single-family building permits issued: 20 (2005); Multi-family building permits issued: 0 (2005); Employment by occupation: 13.0% management, 22.0% professional, 13.5% services, 31.7% sales, 0.3% farming, 8.1% construction, 11.4% production (2000).

Income: Per capita income: $26,616 (2005); Median household income: $56,531 (2005); Average household income: $70,630 (2005); Percent of households with income of $100,000 or more: 19.7% (2005); Poverty rate: 5.8% (2000).

Taxes: Total city taxes per capita: $221 (2004); City property taxes per capita: $111 (2004).

Education: Percent of population age 25 and over with: High school diploma (including GED) or higher: 88.9% (2005); Bachelor's degree or higher: 28.5% (2005); Master's degree or higher: 13.2% (2005).

Housing: Homeownership rate: 79.8% (2005); Median home value: $133,455 (2005); Median rent: $509 per month (2000); Median age of housing: 41 years (2000).

Safety: Violent crime rate: 3.1 per 10,000 population; Property crime rate: 113.5 per 10,000 population (2004).

Transportation: Commute to work: 89.6% car, 1.0% public transportation, 6.1% walk, 3.2% work from home (2000); Travel time to work: 39.8% less than 15 minutes, 37.2% 15 to 30 minutes, 16.1% 30 to 45 minutes, 3.9% 45 to 60 minutes, 3.1% 60 minutes or more (2000)

LOCKPORT (city). Covers a land area of 8.528 square miles and a water area of 0.120 square miles. Located at 43.17° N. Lat.; 78.69° W. Long. Elevation is 492 feet.

Population: 24,299 (1990); 22,279 (2000); 21,333 (2005); 20,459 (2010 projected); Race: 89.8% White, 6.5% Black, 0.6% Asian, 2.9% Hispanic of any race (2005); Density: 2,501.5 persons per square mile (2005); Average household size: 2.31 (2005); Median age: 37.5 (2005); Males per 100 females: 92.2 (2005); Marriage status: 28.4% never married, 50.9% now married, 9.0% widowed, 11.8% divorced (2000); Foreign born: 2.5% (2000); Ancestry (includes multiple ancestries): 31.8% German, 23.0% Irish, 15.7% Italian, 14.4% English, 9.8% Other groups (2000).

Economy: Unemployment rate: 5.9% (2005); Total civilian labor force: 11,029 (2005); Single-family building permits issued: 2 (2005); Multi-family building permits issued: 0 (2005); Employment by occupation: 10.0% management, 17.0% professional, 19.5% services, 24.3% sales, 0.6% farming, 8.3% construction, 20.3% production (2000).

Income: Per capita income: $21,387 (2005); Median household income: $38,038 (2005); Average household income: $49,089 (2005); Percent of households with income of $100,000 or more: 10.1% (2005); Poverty rate: 13.3% (2000).

Education: Percent of population age 25 and over with: High school diploma (including GED) or higher: 81.7% (2005); Bachelor's degree or higher: 18.1% (2005); Master's degree or higher: 7.3% (2005).

School District(s)
Lockport City School District (PK-12)
    2003-04 Enrollment: 5,703 . . . . (716) 478-4835
Starpoint Central School District (KG-12)
    2003-04 Enrollment: 2,848 . . . . (716) 210-2352

Housing: Homeownership rate: 57.3% (2005); Median home value: $86,868 (2005); Median rent: $397 per month (2000); Median age of housing: 60+ years (2000).

Hospitals: Lockport Memorial Hospital (134 beds)

Safety: Violent crime rate: 33.7 per 10,000 population; Property crime rate: 487.5 per 10,000 population (2004).

Newspapers: The Retailer (General - Circulation 28,400); Union-Sun & Journal (Circulation 17,500)

Transportation: Commute to work: 93.5% car, 1.1% public transportation, 3.4% walk, 1.4% work from home (2000); Travel time to work: 51.8% less than 15 minutes, 21.4% 15 to 30 minutes, 19.1% 30 to 45 minutes, 4.9% 45 to 60 minutes, 2.9% 60 minutes or more (2000)

Additional Information Contacts
City of Lockport . . . . (716) 439-6676
    http://www.elockport.com/
Lockport - Eastern Chamber of Commerce . . . . (716) 285-9141
    http://www.niagarachamber.org

LOCKPORT (town). Covers a land area of 44.632 square miles and a water area of 0.083 square miles. Located at 43.15° N. Lat.; 78.67° W. Long. Elevation is 492 feet.

History: Built around a series of locks on the old Erie Canal. Settled 1821, incorporated 1865.

Population: 16,723 (1990); 19,653 (2000); 20,479 (2005); 21,239 (2010 projected); Race: 90.7% White, 5.4% Black, 1.6% Asian, 1.7% Hispanic of any race (2005); Density: 458.8 persons per square mile (2005); Average household size: 2.58 (2005); Median age: 38.3 (2005); Males per 100 females: 97.1 (2005); Marriage status: 23.7% never married, 59.2% now married, 7.0% widowed, 10.0% divorced (2000); Foreign born: 3.0% (2000); Ancestry (includes multiple ancestries): 33.7% German, 17.2% Irish, 14.0% Italian, 13.7% English, 12.9% Polish (2000).

Economy: Manufacturing includes automotive radiators, metal and paper products, chemicals, plastics. In a rich fruit and dairy region. Single-family building permits issued: 118 (2005); Multi-family building permits issued: 4 (2005); Employment by occupation: 11.9% management, 18.7% professional, 14.6% services, 28.1% sales, 0.1% farming, 9.2% construction, 17.3% production (2000).

Income: Per capita income: $25,003 (2005); Median household income: $50,984 (2005); Average household income: $63,822 (2005); Percent of households with income of $100,000 or more: 16.2% (2005); Poverty rate: 7.7% (2000).

Taxes: Total city taxes per capita: $262 (2004); City property taxes per capita: $226 (2004).

Education: Percent of population age 25 and over with: High school diploma (including GED) or higher: 87.9% (2005); Bachelor's degree or higher: 20.2% (2005); Master's degree or higher: 7.8% (2005).

Housing: Homeownership rate: 78.0% (2005); Median home value: $107,392 (2005); Median rent: $364 per month (2000); Median age of housing: 20 years (2000).

Transportation: Commute to work: 97.1% car, 0.5% public transportation, 0.7% walk, 1.5% work from home (2000); Travel time to work: 34.7% less than 15 minutes, 33.9% 15 to 30 minutes, 23.3% 30 to 45 minutes, 4.9% 45 to 60 minutes, 3.3% 60 minutes or more (2000)

Additional Information Contacts
Town of Lockport . . . . (716) 439-9520
    http://www.elockport.com/

MIDDLEPORT (village). Covers a land area of 0.873 square miles and a water area of 0 square miles. Located at 43.21° N. Lat.; 78.47° W. Long. Elevation is 517 feet.

History: Grew after completion of Erie Canal (1825). Settled 1812, incorporated 1859.

Population: 1,876 (1990); 1,917 (2000); 1,821 (2005); 1,722 (2010 projected); Race: 96.8% White, 1.2% Black, 0.4% Asian, 3.2% Hispanic of any race (2005); Density: 2,085.9 persons per square mile (2005); Average household size: 2.55 (2005); Median age: 37.3 (2005); Males per 100 females: 90.9 (2005); Marriage status: 20.4% never married, 64.0% now married, 6.6% widowed, 9.1% divorced (2000); Foreign born: 3.7% (2000); Ancestry (includes multiple ancestries): 32.8% German, 19.2% English, 16.7% Irish, 11.3% Italian, 9.5% Polish (2000).

Economy: Manufacturing: water and groundwater metering equipment, agricultural chemicals, machinery. Single-family building permits issued: 0 (2005); Multi-family building permits issued: 4 (2005); Employment by occupation: 5.1% management, 12.4% professional, 22.2% services, 20.1% sales, 1.6% farming, 16.8% construction, 21.8% production (2000).

Income: Per capita income: $18,668 (2005); Median household income: $39,919 (2005); Average household income: $47,679 (2005); Percent of

households with income of $100,000 or more: 7.0% (2005); Poverty rate: 8.3% (2000).
Education: Percent of population age 25 and over with: High school diploma (including GED) or higher: 83.1% (2005); Bachelor's degree or higher: 10.2% (2005); Master's degree or higher: 3.4% (2005).
School District(s)
Royalton-Hartland Central School District (KG-12)
   2003-04 Enrollment: 1,682 . . . . (716) 735-3031
Housing: Homeownership rate: 66.3% (2005); Median home value: $88,140 (2005); Median rent: $339 per month (2000); Median age of housing: 60+ years (2000).
Safety: Violent crime rate: 5.4 per 10,000 population; Property crime rate: 300.4 per 10,000 population (2004).
Transportation: Commute to work: 91.9% car, 0.0% public transportation, 2.8% walk, 4.6% work from home (2000); Travel time to work: 33.9% less than 15 minutes, 38.0% 15 to 30 minutes, 12.4% 30 to 45 minutes, 8.0% 45 to 60 minutes, 7.7% 60 minutes or more (2000)

NEWFANE (town). Covers a land area of 51.847 square miles and a water area of 1.627 square miles. Located at 43.29° N. Lat.; 78.70° W. Long. Elevation is 317 feet.
Population: 8,996 (1990); 9,657 (2000); 9,631 (2005); 9,616 (2010 projected); Race: 96.7% White, 0.8% Black, 0.3% Asian, 1.5% Hispanic of any race (2005); Density: 185.8 persons per square mile (2005); Average household size: 2.65 (2005); Median age: 39.9 (2005); Males per 100 females: 97.5 (2005); Marriage status: 23.0% never married, 60.5% now married, 6.6% widowed, 9.8% divorced (2000); Foreign born: 1.7% (2000); Ancestry (includes multiple ancestries): 40.7% German, 19.6% English, 18.5% Irish, 7.3% Italian, 6.6% Polish (2000).
Economy: In fruit-growing area; nurseries. Single-family building permits issued: 15 (2005); Multi-family building permits issued: 0 (2005); Employment by occupation: 9.2% management, 15.5% professional, 18.0% services, 18.1% sales, 2.1% farming, 10.9% construction, 26.3% production (2000).
Income: Per capita income: $20,611 (2005); Median household income: $45,657 (2005); Average household income: $53,358 (2005); Percent of households with income of $100,000 or more: 9.2% (2005); Poverty rate: 6.8% (2000).
Education: Percent of population age 25 and over with: High school diploma (including GED) or higher: 86.6% (2005); Bachelor's degree or higher: 13.6% (2005); Master's degree or higher: 5.3% (2005).
School District(s)
Newfane Central School District (PK-12)
   2003-04 Enrollment: 2,174 . . . . (716) 778-6850
Housing: Homeownership rate: 82.8% (2005); Median home value: $100,201 (2005); Median rent: $398 per month (2000); Median age of housing: 43 years (2000).
Hospitals: Inter-Community Memorial Hospital (71 beds)
Transportation: Commute to work: 95.8% car, 0.2% public transportation, 1.8% walk, 1.9% work from home (2000); Travel time to work: 38.0% less than 15 minutes, 35.7% 15 to 30 minutes, 14.8% 30 to 45 minutes, 8.3% 45 to 60 minutes, 3.2% 60 minutes or more (2000)

NEWFANE (CDP). Covers a land area of 4.668 square miles and a water area of 0 square miles. Located at 43.28° N. Lat.; 78.70° W. Long.
Population: 3,001 (1990); 3,129 (2000); 2,994 (2005); 2,906 (2010 projected); Race: 97.3% White, 0.8% Black, 0.3% Asian, 0.6% Hispanic of any race (2005); Density: 641.4 persons per square mile (2005); Average household size: 2.74 (2005); Median age: 39.8 (2005); Males per 100 females: 91.2 (2005); Marriage status: 24.0% never married, 59.8% now married, 7.4% widowed, 8.8% divorced (2000); Foreign born: 1.2% (2000); Ancestry (includes multiple ancestries): 39.0% German, 19.5% Irish, 18.2% English, 8.3% French (except Basque), 8.0% Italian (2000).
Economy: Employment by occupation: 7.5% management, 13.1% professional, 20.0% services, 20.7% sales, 1.1% farming, 9.8% construction, 27.8% production (2000).
Income: Per capita income: $20,133 (2005); Median household income: $43,604 (2005); Average household income: $51,835 (2005); Percent of households with income of $100,000 or more: 8.4% (2005); Poverty rate: 9.3% (2000).
Education: Percent of population age 25 and over with: High school diploma (including GED) or higher: 85.4% (2005); Bachelor's degree or higher: 11.6% (2005); Master's degree or higher: 3.4% (2005).

Housing: Homeownership rate: 77.1% (2005); Median home value: $94,532 (2005); Median rent: $403 per month (2000); Median age of housing: 46 years (2000).
Transportation: Commute to work: 94.8% car, 0.0% public transportation, 3.1% walk, 2.2% work from home (2000); Travel time to work: 37.0% less than 15 minutes, 35.3% 15 to 30 minutes, 16.5% 30 to 45 minutes, 8.7% 45 to 60 minutes, 2.6% 60 minutes or more (2000)

NIAGARA (town). Covers a land area of 9.393 square miles and a water area of 0 square miles. Located at 43.11° N. Lat.; 78.98° W. Long.
Population: 9,880 (1990); 8,978 (2000); 8,810 (2005); 8,626 (2010 projected); Race: 91.8% White, 3.6% Black, 0.8% Asian, 1.6% Hispanic of any race (2005); Density: 937.9 persons per square mile (2005); Average household size: 2.45 (2005); Median age: 40.1 (2005); Males per 100 females: 95.2 (2005); Marriage status: 25.7% never married, 54.2% now married, 8.4% widowed, 11.7% divorced (2000); Foreign born: 3.6% (2000); Ancestry (includes multiple ancestries): 24.7% Italian, 22.2% German, 15.4% Irish, 11.5% English, 10.6% Polish (2000).
Economy: Single-family building permits issued: 3 (2005); Multi-family building permits issued: 0 (2005); Employment by occupation: 9.6% management, 12.8% professional, 17.5% services, 28.5% sales, 1.0% farming, 9.1% construction, 21.5% production (2000).
Income: Per capita income: $19,747 (2005); Median household income: $41,509 (2005); Average household income: $48,312 (2005); Percent of households with income of $100,000 or more: 6.1% (2005); Poverty rate: 9.3% (2000).
Education: Percent of population age 25 and over with: High school diploma (including GED) or higher: 79.4% (2005); Bachelor's degree or higher: 10.4% (2005); Master's degree or higher: 4.4% (2005).
Four-year College(s)
Niagara University
   Fall 2004 Enrollment: 3,689. . . . . (716) 285-1212
   2005-06 Tuition: In-state $19,800; Out-of-state $19,800
Housing: Homeownership rate: 76.3% (2005); Median home value: $90,658 (2005); Median rent: $499 per month (2000); Median age of housing: 36 years (2000).
Safety: Violent crime rate: 25.9 per 10,000 population; Property crime rate: 423.2 per 10,000 population (2004).
Transportation: Commute to work: 96.3% car, 0.3% public transportation, 2.1% walk, 0.8% work from home (2000); Travel time to work: 45.8% less than 15 minutes, 37.1% 15 to 30 minutes, 14.9% 30 to 45 minutes, 1.1% 45 to 60 minutes, 1.1% 60 minutes or more (2000)
Additional Information Contacts
Town of Niagara. . . . . (716) 297-2150
   http://www.townofniagara.com/

NIAGARA FALLS (city). Covers a land area of 14.054 square miles and a water area of 2.749 square miles. Located at 43.09° N. Lat.; 79.01° W. Long. Elevation is 618 feet.
History: Named for the Iroquois Indian translation of "at the neck". The first published view of Niagara Falls, reproduced in a volume in 1697, was a sketch made by Father Louis Hennepin, who visited the falls in 1678. In 1745 and 1750 the French built two forts near the falls to supplement Fort Niagara at the mouth of the river and to guard the upper end of the portage. Before the approach of the British in 1759, Chabert Joncaire, French master of the portage, burned the forts and retreated across the river. Under British occupation, Fort Schlosser was erected. Augustus Porter purchased the land immediately surrounding the falls in 1805 or 1806, and became master of the portage. Visioning a manufacturing center that would rival the English city, Porter named the settlement Manchester. The settlement and fort were burned in the War of 1812. The Niagara water power turned the first generator in 1881, and the falls continued to be a source of power for the surrounding area. The falls have been a tourist attraction since at least the early 19th century.
Population: 61,840 (1990); 55,593 (2000); 53,415 (2005); 51,242 (2010 projected); Race: 73.0% White, 21.2% Black, 1.2% Asian, 2.8% Hispanic of any race (2005); Density: 3,800.7 persons per square mile (2005); Average household size: 2.28 (2005); Median age: 39.1 (2005); Males per 100 females: 88.7 (2005); Marriage status: 31.7% never married, 46.8% now married, 10.2% widowed, 11.4% divorced (2000); Foreign born: 5.0% (2000); Ancestry (includes multiple ancestries): 23.1% Italian, 20.8% Other groups, 16.7% German, 13.7% Irish, 11.0% Polish (2000).
Economy: Unemployment rate: 7.0% (2005); Total civilian labor force: 24,433 (2005); Single-family building permits issued: 1 (2005); Multi-family building permits issued: 0 (2005); Employment by occupation: 9.2%

management, 15.1% professional, 20.0% services, 29.2% sales, 0.1% farming, 7.7% construction, 18.7% production (2000).
Income: Per capita income: $17,236 (2005); Median household income: $29,129 (2005); Average household income: $38,978 (2005); Percent of households with income of $100,000 or more: 5.5% (2005); Poverty rate: 19.5% (2000).
Education: Percent of population age 25 and over with: High school diploma (including GED) or higher: 77.1% (2005); Bachelor's degree or higher: 12.8% (2005); Master's degree or higher: 4.9% (2005).

School District(s)
Niagara Falls City School District (PK-12)
    2003-04 Enrollment: 8,736 . . . . (716) 286-4205
Niagara-Wheatfield Central School District (PK-12)
    2003-04 Enrollment: 4,060 . . . . (716) 215-3003

Two-year College(s)
Cheryl Fells School of Business
    Fall 2004 Enrollment: 23 . . . . (716) 297-2750

Housing: Homeownership rate: 58.5% (2005); Median home value: $73,110 (2005); Median rent: $342 per month (2000); Median age of housing: 54 years (2000).
Hospitals: Niagara Falls Memorial Medical Center
Safety: Violent crime rate: 117.4 per 10,000 population; Property crime rate: 549.2 per 10,000 population (2004).
Newspapers: Niagara Gazette (Circulation 23,687)
Transportation: Commute to work: 89.1% car, 3.1% public transportation, 5.2% walk, 1.7% work from home (2000); Travel time to work: 50.0% less than 15 minutes, 33.5% 15 to 30 minutes, 12.3% 30 to 45 minutes, 2.3% 45 to 60 minutes, 2.0% 60 minutes or more (2000); Amtrak: Service available.
Additional Information Contacts
City of Niagara Falls. . . . . (716) 286-4340
    http://www.niagarafallsusa.org/
Niagara Falls Chamber of Commerce . . . . (716) 285-9141
    http://www.niagarachamber.org

NORTH TONAWANDA (city).
Covers a land area of 10.100 square miles and a water area of 0.839 square miles. Located at 43.04° N. Lat.; 78.86° W. Long. Elevation is 575 feet.
History: Named for its location north of Tonawanda. Settled c.1802. Incorporated as a city 1897.
Population: 34,989 (1990); 33,262 (2000); 31,986 (2005); 30,712 (2010 projected); Race: 97.3% White, 0.4% Black, 0.8% Asian, 1.6% Hispanic of any race (2005); Density: 3,166.9 persons per square mile (2005); Average household size: 2.40 (2005); Median age: 39.9 (2005); Males per 100 females: 95.1 (2005); Marriage status: 26.6% never married, 57.2% now married, 7.8% widowed, 8.3% divorced (2000); Foreign born: 3.6% (2000); Ancestry (includes multiple ancestries): 35.3% German, 20.9% Polish, 17.0% Italian, 17.0% Irish, 10.2% English (2000).
Economy: It is a port of entry and has a variety of manufacturing, including furniture, chemicals, plastics, and castings. Unemployment rate: 5.0% (2005); Total civilian labor force: 17,863 (2005); Single-family building permits issued: 8 (2005); Multi-family building permits issued: 0 (2005); Employment by occupation: 10.4% management, 19.4% professional, 14.2% services, 28.6% sales, 0.2% farming, 7.3% construction, 19.8% production (2000).
Income: Per capita income: $22,458 (2005); Median household income: $44,619 (2005); Average household income: $53,705 (2005); Percent of households with income of $100,000 or more: 11.0% (2005); Poverty rate: 7.2% (2000).
Education: Percent of population age 25 and over with: High school diploma (including GED) or higher: 85.7% (2005); Bachelor's degree or higher: 19.8% (2005); Master's degree or higher: 7.2% (2005).

School District(s)
Niagara-Wheatfield Central School District (PK-12)
    2003-04 Enrollment: 4,060 . . . . (716) 215-3003
North Tonawanda City School District (PK-12)
    2003-04 Enrollment: 4,643 . . . . (716) 807-3500

Housing: Homeownership rate: 69.8% (2005); Median home value: $99,410 (2005); Median rent: $431 per month (2000); Median age of housing: 47 years (2000).
Hospitals: DeGraff Memorial Hospital (70 beds)
Safety: Violent crime rate: 10.8 per 10,000 population; Property crime rate: 178.0 per 10,000 population (2004).
Newspapers: Tonawanda News (Circulation 11,063); Tonawanda News Extra (General - Circulation 13,500)
Transportation: Commute to work: 95.2% car, 0.5% public transportation, 2.2% walk, 1.5% work from home (2000); Travel time to work: 31.5% less than 15 minutes, 49.0% 15 to 30 minutes, 16.1% 30 to 45 minutes, 1.8% 45 to 60 minutes, 1.6% 60 minutes or more (2000)
Additional Information Contacts
City of North Tonawanda . . . . (716) 695-8555
    http://www.northtonawanda.org/
North Tonawanda Chamber of Commerce . . . . (716) 692-5120
    http://www.the-tonawandas.com

OLCOTT (CDP).
Covers a land area of 4.592 square miles and a water area of 0.722 square miles. Located at 43.33° N. Lat.; 78.71° W. Long. Elevation is 277 feet.
Population: 1,432 (1990); 1,156 (2000); 1,049 (2005); 1,003 (2010 projected); Race: 96.1% White, 0.9% Black, 0.7% Asian, 2.8% Hispanic of any race (2005); Density: 228.4 persons per square mile (2005); Average household size: 2.38 (2005); Median age: 42.5 (2005); Males per 100 females: 101.0 (2005); Marriage status: 22.3% never married, 55.9% now married, 5.8% widowed, 16.0% divorced (2000); Foreign born: 2.4% (2000); Ancestry (includes multiple ancestries): 28.2% German, 27.1% English, 9.7% Irish, 8.2% Italian, 6.5% French (except Basque) (2000).
Economy: Manufacturing of industrial chemicals. Employment by occupation: 12.0% management, 15.1% professional, 15.1% services, 13.3% sales, 3.1% farming, 8.4% construction, 33.1% production (2000).
Income: Per capita income: $21,998 (2005); Median household income: $48,664 (2005); Average household income: $52,200 (2005); Percent of households with income of $100,000 or more: 5.0% (2005); Poverty rate: 8.4% (2000).
Education: Percent of population age 25 and over with: High school diploma (including GED) or higher: 84.8% (2005); Bachelor's degree or higher: 10.1% (2005); Master's degree or higher: 3.3% (2005).
Housing: Homeownership rate: 78.5% (2005); Median home value: $93,978 (2005); Median rent: $421 per month (2000); Median age of housing: 47 years (2000).
Transportation: Commute to work: 97.7% car, 0.0% public transportation, 0.0% walk, 2.3% work from home (2000); Travel time to work: 30.9% less than 15 minutes, 37.0% 15 to 30 minutes, 17.0% 30 to 45 minutes, 6.5% 45 to 60 minutes, 8.5% 60 minutes or more (2000)

PENDLETON (town).
Covers a land area of 27.178 square miles and a water area of 0.264 square miles. Located at 43.09° N. Lat.; 78.76° W. Long. Elevation is 580 feet.
Population: 5,010 (1990); 6,050 (2000); 6,294 (2005); 6,517 (2010 projected); Race: 98.2% White, 0.6% Black, 0.3% Asian, 0.8% Hispanic of any race (2005); Density: 231.6 persons per square mile (2005); Average household size: 2.81 (2005); Median age: 40.0 (2005); Males per 100 females: 100.1 (2005); Marriage status: 21.6% never married, 66.6% now married, 6.5% widowed, 5.3% divorced (2000); Foreign born: 2.3% (2000); Ancestry (includes multiple ancestries): 44.9% German, 16.7% Italian, 16.3% Irish, 15.9% Polish, 12.0% English (2000).
Economy: Single-family building permits issued: 20 (2005); Multi-family building permits issued: 0 (2005); Employment by occupation: 13.1% management, 25.8% professional, 11.0% services, 24.5% sales, 0.3% farming, 11.9% construction, 13.5% production (2000).
Income: Per capita income: $27,306 (2005); Median household income: $68,371 (2005); Average household income: $76,733 (2005); Percent of households with income of $100,000 or more: 25.4% (2005); Poverty rate: 4.7% (2000).
Education: Percent of population age 25 and over with: High school diploma (including GED) or higher: 90.6% (2005); Bachelor's degree or higher: 24.8% (2005); Master's degree or higher: 9.1% (2005).
Housing: Homeownership rate: 91.8% (2005); Median home value: $158,875 (2005); Median rent: $565 per month (2000); Median age of housing: 30 years (2000).
Transportation: Commute to work: 94.9% car, 0.0% public transportation, 0.4% walk, 4.6% work from home (2000); Travel time to work: 22.7% less than 15 minutes, 46.1% 15 to 30 minutes, 25.3% 30 to 45 minutes, 3.4% 45 to 60 minutes, 2.5% 60 minutes or more (2000)

PORTER (town).
Covers a land area of 33.213 square miles and a water area of 4.530 square miles. Located at 43.25° N. Lat.; 78.99° W. Long.
Population: 7,110 (1990); 6,920 (2000); 6,836 (2005); 6,740 (2010 projected); Race: 97.1% White, 0.7% Black, 0.6% Asian, 0.9% Hispanic of any race (2005); Density: 205.8 persons per square mile (2005); Average

household size: 2.60 (2005); Median age: 42.3 (2005); Males per 100 females: 98.3 (2005); Marriage status: 23.8% never married, 60.2% now married, 7.3% widowed, 8.7% divorced (2000); Foreign born: 5.7% (2000); Ancestry (includes multiple ancestries): 28.0% German, 21.4% Irish, 17.9% English, 17.8% Italian, 11.0% Polish (2000).
Economy: Single-family building permits issued: 11 (2005); Multi-family building permits issued: 0 (2005); Employment by occupation: 14.4% management, 22.2% professional, 14.1% services, 23.5% sales, 0.0% farming, 9.2% construction, 16.6% production (2000).
Income: Per capita income: $27,956 (2005); Median household income: $59,156 (2005); Average household income: $72,070 (2005); Percent of households with income of $100,000 or more: 21.2% (2005); Poverty rate: 4.1% (2000).
Education: Percent of population age 25 and over with: High school diploma (including GED) or higher: 89.6% (2005); Bachelor's degree or higher: 26.5% (2005); Master's degree or higher: 9.9% (2005).
Housing: Homeownership rate: 81.3% (2005); Median home value: $127,714 (2005); Median rent: $459 per month (2000); Median age of housing: 42 years (2000).
Transportation: Commute to work: 94.9% car, 0.1% public transportation, 1.2% walk, 3.1% work from home (2000); Travel time to work: 27.5% less than 15 minutes, 43.4% 15 to 30 minutes, 19.6% 30 to 45 minutes, 6.5% 45 to 60 minutes, 3.0% 60 minutes or more (2000)

RANSOMVILLE (CDP). Covers a land area of 6.199 square miles and a water area of 0 square miles. Located at 43.23° N. Lat.; 78.91° W. Long. Elevation is 327 feet.
Population: 1,542 (1990); 1,488 (2000); 1,500 (2005); 1,473 (2010 projected); Race: 96.4% White, 1.4% Black, 0.1% Asian, 0.9% Hispanic of any race (2005); Density: 242.0 persons per square mile (2005); Average household size: 3.01 (2005); Median age: 41.8 (2005); Males per 100 females: 100.3 (2005); Marriage status: 27.5% never married, 54.5% now married, 8.2% widowed, 9.8% divorced (2000); Foreign born: 2.8% (2000); Ancestry (includes multiple ancestries): 29.4% German, 18.3% English, 17.6% Irish, 12.3% Polish, 9.8% Italian (2000).
Economy: In fruit-growing area. Employment by occupation: 10.3% management, 22.4% professional, 16.0% services, 16.1% sales, 0.0% farming, 12.5% construction, 22.8% production (2000).
Income: Per capita income: $23,377 (2005); Median household income: $58,232 (2005); Average household income: $67,144 (2005); Percent of households with income of $100,000 or more: 19.2% (2005); Poverty rate: 2.8% (2000).
Education: Percent of population age 25 and over with: High school diploma (including GED) or higher: 77.5% (2005); Bachelor's degree or higher: 16.3% (2005); Master's degree or higher: 5.7% (2005).

School District(s)
Wilson Central School District (PK-12)
    2003-04 Enrollment: 1,504 . . . . (716) 751-9341

Housing: Homeownership rate: 80.8% (2005); Median home value: $110,260 (2005); Median rent: $379 per month (2000); Median age of housing: 49 years (2000).
Transportation: Commute to work: 93.2% car, 0.0% public transportation, 0.7% walk, 3.9% work from home (2000); Travel time to work: 23.5% less than 15 minutes, 54.2% 15 to 30 minutes, 12.2% 30 to 45 minutes, 7.2% 45 to 60 minutes, 2.8% 60 minutes or more (2000)

RAPIDS (CDP). Covers a land area of 3.667 square miles and a water area of 0 square miles. Located at 43.10° N. Lat.; 78.64° W. Long. Elevation is 591 feet.
Population: 1,152 (1990); 1,356 (2000); 1,433 (2005); 1,503 (2010 projected); Race: 96.4% White, 2.1% Black, 0.0% Asian, 0.6% Hispanic of any race (2005); Density: 390.8 persons per square mile (2005); Average household size: 2.52 (2005); Median age: 36.4 (2005); Males per 100 females: 99.6 (2005); Marriage status: 25.1% never married, 56.7% now married, 3.8% widowed, 14.4% divorced (2000); Foreign born: 1.1% (2000); Ancestry (includes multiple ancestries): 41.7% German, 30.9% Irish, 13.7% Polish, 10.5% English, 9.1% Italian (2000).
Economy: Employment by occupation: 5.3% management, 14.7% professional, 20.2% services, 25.0% sales, 0.0% farming, 14.7% construction, 20.1% production (2000).
Income: Per capita income: $22,741 (2005); Median household income: $44,388 (2005); Average household income: $57,372 (2005); Percent of households with income of $100,000 or more: 9.5% (2005); Poverty rate: 7.0% (2000).
Education: Percent of population age 25 and over with: High school diploma (including GED) or higher: 82.1% (2005); Bachelor's degree or higher: 13.0% (2005); Master's degree or higher: 6.6% (2005).
Housing: Homeownership rate: 92.1% (2005); Median home value: $82,941 (2005); Median rent: $388 per month (2000); Median age of housing: 18 years (2000).
Transportation: Commute to work: 100.0% car, 0.0% public transportation, 0.0% walk, 0.0% work from home (2000); Travel time to work: 18.5% less than 15 minutes, 49.7% 15 to 30 minutes, 23.0% 30 to 45 minutes, 3.2% 45 to 60 minutes, 5.5% 60 minutes or more (2000)

ROYALTON (town). Aka Royalton Center. Covers a land area of 69.825 square miles and a water area of 0.258 square miles. Located at 43.17° N. Lat.; 78.54° W. Long.
Population: 7,453 (1990); 7,710 (2000); 7,601 (2005); 7,491 (2010 projected); Race: 96.5% White, 0.7% Black, 0.8% Asian, 1.5% Hispanic of any race (2005); Density: 108.9 persons per square mile (2005); Average household size: 2.71 (2005); Median age: 39.2 (2005); Males per 100 females: 98.1 (2005); Marriage status: 20.0% never married, 66.4% now married, 5.8% widowed, 7.8% divorced (2000); Foreign born: 2.0% (2000); Ancestry (includes multiple ancestries): 43.3% German, 17.3% Irish, 15.8% English, 8.8% Italian, 8.1% Polish (2000).
Economy: Single-family building permits issued: 13 (2005); Multi-family building permits issued: 2 (2005); Employment by occupation: 9.4% management, 15.9% professional, 12.8% services, 25.7% sales, 1.1% farming, 14.1% construction, 21.0% production (2000).
Income: Per capita income: $20,365 (2005); Median household income: $47,774 (2005); Average household income: $54,511 (2005); Percent of households with income of $100,000 or more: 9.6% (2005); Poverty rate: 6.8% (2000).
Taxes: Total city taxes per capita: $124 (2004); City property taxes per capita: $103 (2004).
Education: Percent of population age 25 and over with: High school diploma (including GED) or higher: 83.5% (2005); Bachelor's degree or higher: 12.3% (2005); Master's degree or higher: 4.6% (2005).
Housing: Homeownership rate: 81.3% (2005); Median home value: $111,222 (2005); Median rent: $376 per month (2000); Median age of housing: 47 years (2000).
Transportation: Commute to work: 96.2% car, 0.0% public transportation, 1.4% walk, 2.4% work from home (2000); Travel time to work: 28.3% less than 15 minutes, 40.5% 15 to 30 minutes, 17.4% 30 to 45 minutes, 10.3% 45 to 60 minutes, 3.6% 60 minutes or more (2000)

SANBORN (unincorporated postal area, zip code 14132). Covers a land area of 24.681 square miles and a water area of 0.049 square miles. Located at 43.14° N. Lat.; 78.88° W. Long. Elevation is 638 feet.
Population: 0 (2000); Race: 94.0% White, 0.0% Black, 0.1% Asian, 0.9% Hispanic of any race (2000); Density: 0.0 persons per square mile (2000); Age: 26.7% under 18, 13.5% over 64 (2000); Marriage status: 23.1% never married, 64.6% now married, 7.0% widowed, 5.3% divorced (2000); Foreign born: 1.9% (2000); Ancestry (includes multiple ancestries): 35.0% German, 16.2% Italian, 13.1% Polish, 12.3% English, 11.8% Irish (2000).
Economy: Employment by occupation: 11.3% management, 16.9% professional, 14.8% services, 27.5% sales, 1.0% farming, 11.1% construction, 17.3% production (2000).
Income: Per capita income: $20,040 (2000); Median household income: $43,639 (2000); Poverty rate: 5.1% (2000).
Education: Percent of population age 25 and over with: High school diploma (including GED) or higher: 88.9% (2000); Bachelor's degree or higher: 17.7% (2000).

School District(s)
Niagara-Wheatfield Central School District (PK-12)
    2003-04 Enrollment: 4,060 . . . . (716) 215-3003

Two-year College(s)
Niagara County Community College (Public)
    Fall 2004 Enrollment: 5,546 . . . . (716) 614-6222
    2005-06 Tuition: In-state $3,096; Out-of-state $4,644
Orleans Niagara BOCES-Practical Nursing Program (Public)
    Fall 2004 Enrollment: n/a . . . . (800) 836-7510

Housing: Homeownership rate: 80.8% (2000); Median home value: $102,300 (2000); Median rent: $412 per month (2000); Median age of housing: 35 years (2000).
Transportation: Commute to work: 96.3% car, 0.5% public transportation, 1.0% walk, 1.9% work from home (2000); Travel time to work: 30.9% less

than 15 minutes, 42.9% 15 to 30 minutes, 19.0% 30 to 45 minutes, 5.2% 45 to 60 minutes, 2.1% 60 minutes or more (2000)

SOMERSET (town). Covers a land area of 37.174 square miles and a water area of 0.068 square miles. Located at 43.33° N. Lat.; 78.54° W. Long.
Population: 2,655 (1990); 2,865 (2000); 2,823 (2005); 2,780 (2010 projected); Race: 96.5% White, 0.7% Black, 0.9% Asian, 1.8% Hispanic of any race (2005); Density: 75.9 persons per square mile (2005); Average household size: 2.87 (2005); Median age: 37.6 (2005); Males per 100 females: 105.2 (2005); Marriage status: 23.6% never married, 63.3% now married, 5.9% widowed, 7.2% divorced (2000); Foreign born: 1.2% (2000); Ancestry (includes multiple ancestries): 33.3% German, 20.3% English, 16.4% Irish, 8.3% Polish, 7.5% Italian (2000).
Economy: Single-family building permits issued: 2 (2005); Multi-family building permits issued: 0 (2005); Employment by occupation: 8.6% management, 18.0% professional, 14.3% services, 17.9% sales, 2.2% farming, 14.0% construction, 25.1% production (2000).
Income: Per capita income: $19,728 (2005); Median household income: $47,873 (2005); Average household income: $56,294 (2005); Percent of households with income of $100,000 or more: 13.5% (2005); Poverty rate: 10.1% (2000).
Education: Percent of population age 25 and over with: High school diploma (including GED) or higher: 84.2% (2005); Bachelor's degree or higher: 12.6% (2005); Master's degree or higher: 5.3% (2005).
Housing: Homeownership rate: 80.1% (2005); Median home value: $99,124 (2005); Median rent: $383 per month (2000); Median age of housing: 60+ years (2000).
Transportation: Commute to work: 93.8% car, 0.1% public transportation, 1.9% walk, 4.1% work from home (2000); Travel time to work: 36.2% less than 15 minutes, 25.6% 15 to 30 minutes, 19.7% 30 to 45 minutes, 9.5% 45 to 60 minutes, 9.0% 60 minutes or more (2000)

SOUTH LOCKPORT (CDP). Covers a land area of 5.746 square miles and a water area of 0.023 square miles. Located at 43.13° N. Lat.; 78.68° W. Long. Elevation is 635 feet.
Population: 7,112 (1990); 8,552 (2000); 8,977 (2005); 9,367 (2010 projected); Race: 88.8% White, 6.4% Black, 1.6% Asian, 2.4% Hispanic of any race (2005); Density: 1,562.4 persons per square mile (2005); Average household size: 2.39 (2005); Median age: 36.3 (2005); Males per 100 females: 90.5 (2005); Marriage status: 24.5% never married, 56.7% now married, 7.0% widowed, 11.8% divorced (2000); Foreign born: 3.3% (2000); Ancestry (includes multiple ancestries): 31.8% German, 15.9% Irish, 15.0% Polish, 14.7% Italian, 10.2% Other groups (2000).
Economy: Employment by occupation: 10.7% management, 15.2% professional, 15.3% services, 32.9% sales, 0.0% farming, 8.2% construction, 17.8% production (2000).
Income: Per capita income: $20,837 (2005); Median household income: $40,980 (2005); Average household income: $49,829 (2005); Percent of households with income of $100,000 or more: 9.3% (2005); Poverty rate: 12.5% (2000).
Education: Percent of population age 25 and over with: High school diploma (including GED) or higher: 86.0% (2005); Bachelor's degree or higher: 16.2% (2005); Master's degree or higher: 5.2% (2005).
Housing: Homeownership rate: 69.8% (2005); Median home value: $77,135 (2005); Median rent: $351 per month (2000); Median age of housing: 17 years (2000).
Transportation: Commute to work: 96.7% car, 1.0% public transportation, 1.6% walk, 0.7% work from home (2000); Travel time to work: 36.0% less than 15 minutes, 33.3% 15 to 30 minutes, 22.3% 30 to 45 minutes, 5.3% 45 to 60 minutes, 3.1% 60 minutes or more (2000)

TUSCARORA RESERVATION (reservation). Covers a land area of 9.270 square miles and a water area of 0 square miles. Located at 43.16° N. Lat.; 78.95° W. Long.
Population: 725 (1990); 1,138 (2000); 1,119 (2005); 1,099 (2010 projected); Race: 58.6% White, 14.6% Black, 0.9% Asian, 2.3% Hispanic of any race (2005); Density: 120.7 persons per square mile (2005); Average household size: 2.83 (2005); Median age: 27.8 (2005); Males per 100 females: 104.9 (2005); Marriage status: 30.9% never married, 57.3% now married, 5.8% widowed, 6.0% divorced (2000); Foreign born: 1.1% (2000); Ancestry (includes multiple ancestries): 30.6% Other groups, 4.7% Polish, 2.4% German, 1.7% English, 0.9% Italian (2000).

Economy: Employment by occupation: 13.1% management, 14.3% professional, 15.2% services, 32.8% sales, 0.5% farming, 8.4% construction, 15.8% production (2000).
Income: Per capita income: $17,500 (2005); Median household income: $39,375 (2005); Average household income: $49,576 (2005); Percent of households with income of $100,000 or more: 11.9% (2005); Poverty rate: 13.0% (2000).
Education: Percent of population age 25 and over with: High school diploma (including GED) or higher: 86.1% (2005); Bachelor's degree or higher: 17.5% (2005); Master's degree or higher: 5.1% (2005).
Housing: Homeownership rate: 78.7% (2005); Median home value: $89,740 (2005); Median rent: $325 per month (2000); Median age of housing: 43 years (2000).
Transportation: Commute to work: 92.3% car, 3.7% public transportation, 1.4% walk, 2.6% work from home (2000); Travel time to work: 41.8% less than 15 minutes, 43.4% 15 to 30 minutes, 6.4% 30 to 45 minutes, 1.7% 45 to 60 minutes, 6.7% 60 minutes or more (2000)

WHEATFIELD (town). Covers a land area of 27.914 square miles and a water area of 0.694 square miles. Located at 43.09° N. Lat.; 78.89° W. Long.
Population: 11,125 (1990); 14,086 (2000); 15,614 (2005); 16,984 (2010 projected); Race: 96.7% White, 1.4% Black, 0.8% Asian, 0.9% Hispanic of any race (2005); Density: 559.4 persons per square mile (2005); Average household size: 2.61 (2005); Median age: 41.8 (2005); Males per 100 females: 93.3 (2005); Marriage status: 20.6% never married, 65.0% now married, 8.5% widowed, 5.8% divorced (2000); Foreign born: 3.9% (2000); Ancestry (includes multiple ancestries): 36.2% German, 25.0% Italian, 16.6% Polish, 14.0% Irish, 11.0% English (2000).
Economy: Single-family building permits issued: 126 (2005); Multi-family building permits issued: 77 (2005); Employment by occupation: 13.5% management, 19.6% professional, 12.2% services, 25.4% sales, 0.1% farming, 9.2% construction, 19.9% production (2000).
Income: Per capita income: $26,545 (2005); Median household income: $61,563 (2005); Average household income: $68,290 (2005); Percent of households with income of $100,000 or more: 19.3% (2005); Poverty rate: 4.2% (2000).
Taxes: Total city taxes per capita: $214 (2004); City property taxes per capita: $156 (2004).
Education: Percent of population age 25 and over with: High school diploma (including GED) or higher: 86.6% (2005); Bachelor's degree or higher: 21.5% (2005); Master's degree or higher: 7.9% (2005).
Housing: Homeownership rate: 79.8% (2005); Median home value: $145,618 (2005); Median rent: $459 per month (2000); Median age of housing: 24 years (2000).
Transportation: Commute to work: 97.3% car, 0.3% public transportation, 0.7% walk, 1.5% work from home (2000); Travel time to work: 31.0% less than 15 minutes, 45.8% 15 to 30 minutes, 17.2% 30 to 45 minutes, 3.1% 45 to 60 minutes, 2.9% 60 minutes or more (2000)
Additional Information Contacts
Town of Wheatfield . . . . (716) 694-6440
http://wheatfield.ny.us/

WILSON (village). Covers a land area of 0.823 square miles and a water area of 0.177 square miles. Located at 43.31° N. Lat.; 78.82° W. Long. Elevation is 290 feet.
Population: 1,307 (1990); 1,213 (2000); 1,174 (2005); 1,133 (2010 projected); Race: 98.7% White, 0.5% Black, 0.0% Asian, 0.9% Hispanic of any race (2005); Density: 1,427.1 persons per square mile (2005); Average household size: 2.35 (2005); Median age: 42.7 (2005); Males per 100 females: 94.4 (2005); Marriage status: 22.9% never married, 60.9% now married, 8.7% widowed, 7.5% divorced (2000); Foreign born: 2.7% (2000); Ancestry (includes multiple ancestries): 44.2% German, 21.9% English, 15.9% Irish, 10.2% Polish, 6.2% United States or American (2000).
Economy: Single-family building permits issued: 2 (2005); Multi-family building permits issued: 0 (2005); Employment by occupation: 9.1% management, 21.1% professional, 16.1% services, 29.1% sales, 0.3% farming, 9.1% construction, 15.2% production (2000).
Income: Per capita income: $20,756 (2005); Median household income: $40,250 (2005); Average household income: $48,833 (2005); Percent of households with income of $100,000 or more: 7.6% (2005); Poverty rate: 4.6% (2000).
Education: Percent of population age 25 and over with: High school diploma (including GED) or higher: 86.3% (2005); Bachelor's degree or higher: 17.6% (2005); Master's degree or higher: 9.4% (2005).

School District(s)
Wilson Central School District (PK-12)
   2003-04 Enrollment: 1,504 . . . . (716) 751-9341
Housing: Homeownership rate: 77.8% (2005); Median home value: $105,346 (2005); Median rent: $392 per month (2000); Median age of housing: 54 years (2000).
Transportation: Commute to work: 89.8% car, 0.0% public transportation, 5.1% walk, 4.0% work from home (2000); Travel time to work: 32.8% less than 15 minutes, 29.6% 15 to 30 minutes, 22.1% 30 to 45 minutes, 7.5% 45 to 60 minutes, 8.0% 60 minutes or more (2000)
Additional Information Contacts
Village of Wilson . . . . (716) 751-6704
   http://www.wilsonnewyork.com/

WILSON (town). Covers a land area of 49.526 square miles and a water area of 1.933 square miles. Located at 43.29° N. Lat.; 78.84° W. Long. Elevation is 290 feet.
History: Incorporated 1858.
Population: 5,761 (1990); 5,840 (2000); 5,845 (2005); 5,850 (2010 projected); Race: 97.2% White, 0.5% Black, 0.3% Asian, 1.1% Hispanic of any race (2005); Density: 118.0 persons per square mile (2005); Average household size: 2.58 (2005); Median age: 40.8 (2005); Males per 100 females: 97.5 (2005); Marriage status: 22.6% never married, 61.4% now married, 6.3% widowed, 9.8% divorced (2000); Foreign born: 2.4% (2000); Ancestry (includes multiple ancestries): 37.6% German, 15.9% Irish, 15.9% English, 12.3% Italian, 10.9% Polish (2000).
Economy: Summer resort; some manufacturing: foods. Single-family building permits issued: 12 (2005); Multi-family building permits issued: 0 (2005); Employment by occupation: 10.8% management, 16.7% professional, 14.5% services, 20.1% sales, 1.3% farming, 11.7% construction, 24.9% production (2000).
Income: Per capita income: $22,669 (2005); Median household income: $50,773 (2005); Average household income: $58,446 (2005); Percent of households with income of $100,000 or more: 11.6% (2005); Poverty rate: 5.2% (2000).
Education: Percent of population age 25 and over with: High school diploma (including GED) or higher: 83.0% (2005); Bachelor's degree or higher: 15.3% (2005); Master's degree or higher: 6.1% (2005).
Housing: Homeownership rate: 86.7% (2005); Median home value: $112,483 (2005); Median rent: $429 per month (2000); Median age of housing: 43 years (2000).
Transportation: Commute to work: 94.8% car, 0.2% public transportation, 2.9% walk, 1.6% work from home (2000); Travel time to work: 23.1% less than 15 minutes, 38.0% 15 to 30 minutes, 26.3% 30 to 45 minutes, 7.7% 45 to 60 minutes, 4.9% 60 minutes or more (2000)
Additional Information Contacts
Town of Wilson . . . . (716) 751-6704
   http://www.wilsonnewyork.com/

YOUNGSTOWN (village). Covers a land area of 1.160 square miles and a water area of 0.242 square miles. Located at 43.24° N. Lat.; 79.04° W. Long. Elevation is 301 feet.
History: Just North is Fort Niagara, which has been restored.
Population: 2,075 (1990); 1,957 (2000); 1,965 (2005); 1,981 (2010 projected); Race: 98.1% White, 0.0% Black, 0.0% Asian, 1.0% Hispanic of any race (2005); Density: 1,694.4 persons per square mile (2005); Average household size: 2.38 (2005); Median age: 42.5 (2005); Males per 100 females: 91.5 (2005); Marriage status: 22.0% never married, 60.2% now married, 10.4% widowed, 7.4% divorced (2000); Foreign born: 7.3% (2000); Ancestry (includes multiple ancestries): 25.4% Irish, 23.1% English, 22.6% German, 19.0% Italian, 11.5% Polish (2000).
Economy: Single-family building permits issued: 4 (2005); Multi-family building permits issued: 0 (2005); Employment by occupation: 13.0% management, 23.6% professional, 13.2% services, 27.9% sales, 0.0% farming, 9.3% construction, 12.9% production (2000).
Income: Per capita income: $27,975 (2005); Median household income: $56,383 (2005); Average household income: $66,550 (2005); Percent of households with income of $100,000 or more: 18.9% (2005); Poverty rate: 3.9% (2000).
Education: Percent of population age 25 and over with: High school diploma (including GED) or higher: 93.4% (2005); Bachelor's degree or higher: 27.3% (2005); Master's degree or higher: 9.6% (2005).
School District(s)
Lewiston-Porter Central School District (PK-12)
   2003-04 Enrollment: 2,402 . . . . (716) 286-7266

Housing: Homeownership rate: 74.2% (2005); Median home value: $129,886 (2005); Median rent: $463 per month (2000); Median age of housing: 42 years (2000).
Transportation: Commute to work: 96.3% car, 0.3% public transportation, 1.0% walk, 2.1% work from home (2000); Travel time to work: 30.7% less than 15 minutes, 42.9% 15 to 30 minutes, 16.6% 30 to 45 minutes, 7.1% 45 to 60 minutes, 2.7% 60 minutes or more (2000)

Oneida County

Located in central New York; bounded partly on the west by Oneida Lake, rising to the Adirondacks in the east and northeast; drained by the Mohawk and Black Rivers; includes several lakes. Covers a land area of 1,212.70 square miles, a water area of 44.41 square miles, and is located in the Eastern Time Zone. The county government was organized in 1798. County seat is Utica.

Oneida County is part of the Utica-Rome, NY Metropolitan Statistical Area. The entire metro area includes: Herkimer County, NY; Oneida County, NY

Weather Station: Boonville 2 SSW   Elevation: 1,578 feet

	Jan	Feb	Mar	Apr	May	Jun	Jul	Aug	Sep	Oct	Nov	Dec
High	24	27	36	50	64	72	76	74	66	54	41	30
Low	8	10	19	31	43	52	56	55	47	37	27	15
Precip	5.7	4.4	5.0	4.6	4.4	4.8	4.1	4.6	6.0	4.8	5.8	5.9
Snow	59.3	42.8	34.7	10.2	0.9	tr	0.0	0.0	tr	2.2	21.2	47.3

High and Low temperatures in degrees Fahrenheit; Precipitation and Snow in inches

Weather Station: Utica Oneida County Airport   Elevation: 711 feet

	Jan	Feb	Mar	Apr	May	Jun	Jul	Aug	Sep	Oct	Nov	Dec
High	29	31	41	54	68	76	81	78	70	58	45	34
Low	14	15	24	36	46	55	60	59	51	40	32	20
Precip	3.5	3.0	3.7	3.6	3.7	4.1	3.7	3.6	4.5	3.4	4.0	4.0
Snow	26.4	19.0	17.1	3.7	tr	0.0	tr	tr	tr	0.6	9.8	21.9

High and Low temperatures in degrees Fahrenheit; Precipitation and Snow in inches

Population: 250,836 (1990); 235,469 (2000); 234,415 (2005); 233,193 (2010 projected); Race: 89.0% White, 6.2% Black, 1.5% Asian, 4.1% Hispanic of any race (2005); Density: 193.3 persons per square mile (2005); Average household size: 2.57 (2005); Median age: 39.3 (2005); Males per 100 females: 99.2 (2005).
Religion: Five largest groups: 35.6% Catholic Church, 4.4% The United Methodist Church, 1.8% Presbyterian Church (U.S.A.), 1.6% Episcopal Church, 1.3% American Baptist Churches in the USA (2000).
Economy: Unemployment rate: 4.8% (2005); Total civilian labor force: 111,806 (2005); Leading industries: 21.6% health care and social assistance; 13.8% manufacturing; 13.7% retail trade (2003); Farms: 1,087 totaling 220,486 acres (2002); Companies that employ 500 or more persons: 25 (2003); Companies that employ 100 to 499 persons: 117 (2003); Companies that employ less than 100 persons: 4,894 (2003); Black-owned businesses: 246 (2002); Hispanic-owned businesses: n/a (2002); Women-owned businesses: 4,123 (2002); Retail sales per capita: $11,722 (2006). Single-family building permits issued: 401 (2005); Multi-family building permits issued: 33 (2005).
Income: Per capita income: $20,955 (2005); Median household income: $40,551 (2005); Average household income: $51,859 (2005); Percent of households with income of $100,000 or more: 10.2% (2005); Poverty rate: 12.8% (2003); Bankruptcy rate: 9.58% (2005).
Taxes: Total county taxes per capita: $594 (2004); County property taxes per capita: $243 (2004).
Education: Percent of population age 25 and over with: High school diploma (including GED) or higher: 79.2% (2005); Bachelor's degree or higher: 18.4% (2005); Master's degree or higher: 7.5% (2005).
Housing: Homeownership rate: 67.9% (2005); Median home value: $98,687 (2005); Median rent: $375 per month (2000); Median age of housing: 48 years (2000).
Health: Birth rate: 107.3 per 10,000 population (2004); Death rate: 102.4 per 10,000 population (2004); Age-adjusted cancer mortality rate: 212.3 deaths per 100,000 population (2002); Air Quality Index: 77.3% good, 22.5% moderate, 0.3% unhealthy for sensitive individuals, 0.0% unhealthy (percent of days in 2005); Number of physicians: 23.7 per 10,000 population (2004); Hospital beds: 68.7 per 10,000 population (2003); Hospital admissions: 1,451.9 per 10,000 population (2003).
Elections: 2004 Presidential election results: 54.9% Bush, 42.8% Kerry, 2.1% Nader, 0.2% Badnarik

National and State Parks: Boonville Gorge State Park; Fort Stanwix National Monument; Verona Beach State Park

Additional Information Contacts

Oneida County Government	(315) 798-5900
http://www.oneidacounty.org/	
City of Rome	(315) 336-6000
http://www.romenewyork.com/	
City of Sherrill	(315) 363-2440
http://www.sherrillny.org/	
City of Utica	(315) 792-0113
http://www.cityofutica.com/	
Town of Floyd	(315) 865-4256
http://town.floyd.ny.us/content	
Town of New Hartford	(315) 733-7500
http://www.town.new-hartford.ny.us/	
Town of Paris	(315) 839-5400
http://town.paris.ny.us/content	
Town of Westmoreland	(315) 853-8001
http://town.westmoreland.ny.us/content	
Town of Whitestown	(315) 736-1131
http://www.whitestown.ny.us/content	
Village of Boonville	(315) 943-2052
http://village.boonville.ny.us/content	
Village of Clinton	(845) 266-5853
http://www.townofclinton.com/	
Village of Holland Patent	(315) 865-4853
http://village.holland-patent.ny.us/content	
Village of New Hartford	(315) 733-7500
http://www.town.new-hartford.ny.us/	
Village of Whitesboro	(315) 736-1613
http://village.whitesboro.ny.us/content	

Oneida County Communities

ALDER CREEK (unincorporated postal area, zip code 13301). Covers a land area of 3.538 square miles and a water area of 0 square miles. Located at 43.41° N. Lat.; 75.21° W. Long. Elevation is 1,199 feet.
Population: 0 (2000); Race: 100.0% White, 0.0% Black, 0.0% Asian, 0.0% Hispanic of any race (2000); Density: 0.0 persons per square mile (2000); Age: 13.1% under 18, 24.1% over 64 (2000); Marriage status: 25.8% never married, 61.3% now married, 12.9% widowed, 0.0% divorced (2000); Foreign born: 10.9% (2000); Ancestry (includes multiple ancestries): 22.6% Polish, 16.8% German, 14.6% French (except Basque), 12.4% Italian, 11.7% Irish (2000).
Economy: Employment by occupation: 0.0% management, 39.4% professional, 0.0% services, 9.9% sales, 0.0% farming, 31.0% construction, 19.7% production (2000).
Income: Per capita income: $24,868 (2000); Median household income: $40,333 (2000); Poverty rate: 0.0% (2000).
Education: Percent of population age 25 and over with: High school diploma (including GED) or higher: 94.9% (2000); Bachelor's degree or higher: 29.1% (2000).
Housing: Homeownership rate: 83.6% (2000); Median home value: $94,300 (2000); Median rent: $425 per month (2000); Median age of housing: 39 years (2000).
Transportation: Commute to work: 88.2% car, 0.0% public transportation, 0.0% walk, 11.8% work from home (2000); Travel time to work: 3.3% less than 15 minutes, 15.0% 15 to 30 minutes, 46.7% 30 to 45 minutes, 20.0% 45 to 60 minutes, 15.0% 60 minutes or more (2000)

ANNSVILLE (town). Covers a land area of 60.192 square miles and a water area of 0.289 square miles. Located at 43.34° N. Lat.; 75.61° W. Long.
Population: 2,786 (1990); 2,956 (2000); 2,998 (2005); 3,038 (2010 projected); Race: 97.0% White, 2.2% Black, 0.0% Asian, 1.0% Hispanic of any race (2005); Density: 49.8 persons per square mile (2005); Average household size: 2.72 (2005); Median age: 35.6 (2005); Males per 100 females: 109.5 (2005); Marriage status: 21.6% never married, 64.2% now married, 5.3% widowed, 8.9% divorced (2000); Foreign born: 0.7% (2000); Ancestry (includes multiple ancestries): 22.8% Irish, 18.7% German, 12.1% United States or American, 9.8% English, 9.1% Other groups (2000).
Economy: Single-family building permits issued: 0 (2005); Multi-family building permits issued: 0 (2005); Employment by occupation: 8.2% management, 8.5% professional, 16.1% services, 23.0% sales, 0.2% farming, 11.1% construction, 32.8% production (2000).
Income: Per capita income: $18,215 (2005); Median household income: $41,514 (2005); Average household income: $49,419 (2005); Percent of households with income of $100,000 or more: 6.4% (2005); Poverty rate: 12.4% (2000).
Education: Percent of population age 25 and over with: High school diploma (including GED) or higher: 78.9% (2005); Bachelor's degree or higher: 6.4% (2005); Master's degree or higher: 2.4% (2005).
Housing: Homeownership rate: 82.7% (2005); Median home value: $79,744 (2005); Median rent: $375 per month (2000); Median age of housing: 25 years (2000).
Transportation: Commute to work: 93.5% car, 0.4% public transportation, 1.9% walk, 4.3% work from home (2000); Travel time to work: 21.2% less than 15 minutes, 43.0% 15 to 30 minutes, 20.7% 30 to 45 minutes, 9.4% 45 to 60 minutes, 5.7% 60 minutes or more (2000)

AUGUSTA (town). Covers a land area of 27.722 square miles and a water area of 0 square miles. Located at 42.97° N. Lat.; 75.48° W. Long.
Population: 2,070 (1990); 1,966 (2000); 2,035 (2005); 2,099 (2010 projected); Race: 97.5% White, 0.2% Black, 1.2% Asian, 0.8% Hispanic of any race (2005); Density: 73.4 persons per square mile (2005); Average household size: 2.60 (2005); Median age: 37.8 (2005); Males per 100 females: 102.1 (2005); Marriage status: 25.9% never married, 59.0% now married, 7.6% widowed, 7.6% divorced (2000); Foreign born: 1.2% (2000); Ancestry (includes multiple ancestries): 23.2% English, 21.4% German, 17.0% Irish, 7.9% United States or American, 7.4% Polish (2000).
Economy: Single-family building permits issued: 3 (2005); Multi-family building permits issued: 0 (2005); Employment by occupation: 9.2% management, 13.2% professional, 20.1% services, 24.1% sales, 3.5% farming, 13.5% construction, 16.4% production (2000).
Income: Per capita income: $19,350 (2005); Median household income: $39,848 (2005); Average household income: $49,726 (2005); Percent of households with income of $100,000 or more: 8.7% (2005); Poverty rate: 8.6% (2000).
Education: Percent of population age 25 and over with: High school diploma (including GED) or higher: 76.8% (2005); Bachelor's degree or higher: 8.0% (2005); Master's degree or higher: 2.8% (2005).
Housing: Homeownership rate: 77.3% (2005); Median home value: $89,043 (2005); Median rent: $363 per month (2000); Median age of housing: 60+ years (2000).
Transportation: Commute to work: 90.7% car, 0.0% public transportation, 5.5% walk, 3.6% work from home (2000); Travel time to work: 29.2% less than 15 minutes, 46.7% 15 to 30 minutes, 15.5% 30 to 45 minutes, 2.3% 45 to 60 minutes, 6.3% 60 minutes or more (2000)

AVA (town). Covers a land area of 37.663 square miles and a water area of 0.026 square miles. Located at 43.41° N. Lat.; 75.46° W. Long.
Population: 792 (1990); 725 (2000); 712 (2005); 706 (2010 projected); Race: 98.0% White, 1.1% Black, 0.0% Asian, 0.8% Hispanic of any race (2005); Density: 18.9 persons per square mile (2005); Average household size: 2.78 (2005); Median age: 37.4 (2005); Males per 100 females: 107.0 (2005); Marriage status: 26.1% never married, 59.9% now married, 7.5% widowed, 6.5% divorced (2000); Foreign born: 0.7% (2000); Ancestry (includes multiple ancestries): 28.7% German, 19.6% Polish, 17.1% Irish, 11.2% French (except Basque), 11.1% English (2000).
Economy: Single-family building permits issued: 5 (2005); Multi-family building permits issued: 0 (2005); Employment by occupation: 7.5% management, 13.3% professional, 14.3% services, 20.7% sales, 2.0% farming, 11.6% construction, 30.6% production (2000).
Income: Per capita income: $15,994 (2005); Median household income: $35,769 (2005); Average household income: $44,482 (2005); Percent of households with income of $100,000 or more: 7.4% (2005); Poverty rate: 20.1% (2000).
Education: Percent of population age 25 and over with: High school diploma (including GED) or higher: 78.6% (2005); Bachelor's degree or higher: 5.3% (2005); Master's degree or higher: 2.2% (2005).
Housing: Homeownership rate: 88.3% (2005); Median home value: $92,727 (2005); Median rent: $325 per month (2000); Median age of housing: 28 years (2000).
Transportation: Commute to work: 95.2% car, 0.0% public transportation, 3.1% walk, 1.7% work from home (2000); Travel time to work: 18.5% less than 15 minutes, 25.1% 15 to 30 minutes, 25.8% 30 to 45 minutes, 13.2% 45 to 60 minutes, 17.4% 60 minutes or more (2000)

BARNEVELD (village). Aka Trenton. Covers a land area of 0.190 square miles and a water area of 0 square miles. Located at 43.27° N. Lat.; 75.18° W. Long.
History: Nearby, in Steuben Memorial Park, is the reconstructed log cabin and the grave of Baron von Steuben.
Population: 324 (1990); 332 (2000); 351 (2005); 367 (2010 projected); Race: 97.4% White, 0.9% Black, 0.3% Asian, 0.6% Hispanic of any race (2005); Density: 1,849.8 persons per square mile (2005); Average household size: 2.58 (2005); Median age: 38.1 (2005); Males per 100 females: 96.1 (2005); Marriage status: 28.5% never married, 56.2% now married, 6.2% widowed, 9.1% divorced (2000); Foreign born: 0.3% (2000); Ancestry (includes multiple ancestries): 29.5% English, 22.0% Irish, 15.5% German, 12.5% Welsh, 7.7% Polish (2000).
Economy: Light manufacturing. Employment by occupation: 11.8% management, 21.1% professional, 21.7% services, 25.7% sales, 0.0% farming, 6.6% construction, 13.2% production (2000).
Income: Per capita income: $24,366 (2005); Median household income: $48,889 (2005); Average household income: $62,886 (2005); Percent of households with income of $100,000 or more: 16.2% (2005); Poverty rate: 4.8% (2000).
Education: Percent of population age 25 and over with: High school diploma (including GED) or higher: 93.4% (2005); Bachelor's degree or higher: 23.5% (2005); Master's degree or higher: 7.5% (2005).
Housing: Homeownership rate: 60.3% (2005); Median home value: $130,952 (2005); Median rent: $367 per month (2000); Median age of housing: 60+ years (2000).
Transportation: Commute to work: 92.1% car, 0.0% public transportation, 3.3% walk, 3.3% work from home (2000); Travel time to work: 22.6% less than 15 minutes, 50.7% 15 to 30 minutes, 21.9% 30 to 45 minutes, 1.4% 45 to 60 minutes, 3.4% 60 minutes or more (2000)

BLOSSVALE (unincorporated postal area, zip code 13308). Covers a land area of 42.391 square miles and a water area of 0.027 square miles. Located at 43.23° N. Lat.; 75.68° W. Long.
Population: 0 (2000); Race: 97.6% White, 0.3% Black, 0.5% Asian, 0.3% Hispanic of any race (2000); Density: 0.0 persons per square mile (2000); Age: 27.0% under 18, 10.4% over 64 (2000); Marriage status: 25.2% never married, 58.4% now married, 6.9% widowed, 9.4% divorced (2000); Foreign born: 0.6% (2000); Ancestry (includes multiple ancestries): 23.5% German, 19.1% Irish, 12.8% English, 12.6% Italian, 9.9% United States or American (2000).
Economy: Employment by occupation: 9.6% management, 13.1% professional, 17.9% services, 25.3% sales, 0.9% farming, 9.6% construction, 23.6% production (2000).
Income: Per capita income: $16,804 (2000); Median household income: $37,870 (2000); Poverty rate: 7.4% (2000).
Education: Percent of population age 25 and over with: High school diploma (including GED) or higher: 77.9% (2000); Bachelor's degree or higher: 10.7% (2000).
School District(s)
Camden Central School District (PK-12)
    2003-04 Enrollment: 2,845 . . . . (315) 245-4075
Housing: Homeownership rate: 81.8% (2000); Median home value: $74,100 (2000); Median rent: $437 per month (2000); Median age of housing: 36 years (2000).
Transportation: Commute to work: 90.7% car, 0.9% public transportation, 3.3% walk, 4.3% work from home (2000); Travel time to work: 22.9% less than 15 minutes, 40.1% 15 to 30 minutes, 18.4% 30 to 45 minutes, 11.1% 45 to 60 minutes, 7.4% 60 minutes or more (2000)

BOONVILLE (village). Covers a land area of 1.779 square miles and a water area of 0 square miles. Located at 43.48° N. Lat.; 75.33° W. Long. Elevation is 1,146 feet.
Population: 2,220 (1990); 2,138 (2000); 2,108 (2005); 2,096 (2010 projected); Race: 99.4% White, 0.1% Black, 0.0% Asian, 0.2% Hispanic of any race (2005); Density: 1,185.1 persons per square mile (2005); Average household size: 2.39 (2005); Median age: 42.9 (2005); Males per 100 females: 89.1 (2005); Marriage status: 23.4% never married, 50.5% now married, 14.7% widowed, 11.3% divorced (2000); Foreign born: 1.0% (2000); Ancestry (includes multiple ancestries): 26.5% Irish, 22.5% German, 13.3% Polish, 13.3% English, 9.5% French (except Basque) (2000).
Economy: Single-family building permits issued: 0 (2005); Multi-family building permits issued: 0 (2005); Employment by occupation: 7.5% management, 23.5% professional, 25.9% services, 19.9% sales, 0.7% farming, 6.8% construction, 15.8% production (2000).
Income: Per capita income: $19,105 (2005); Median household income: $33,953 (2005); Average household income: $44,154 (2005); Percent of households with income of $100,000 or more: 6.9% (2005); Poverty rate: 12.0% (2000).
Education: Percent of population age 25 and over with: High school diploma (including GED) or higher: 81.5% (2005); Bachelor's degree or higher: 14.1% (2005); Master's degree or higher: 5.9% (2005).
School District(s)
Adirondack Central School District (KG-12)
    2003-04 Enrollment: 1,548 . . . . (315) 942-9200
Housing: Homeownership rate: 60.3% (2005); Median home value: $94,803 (2005); Median rent: $318 per month (2000); Median age of housing: 60+ years (2000).
Safety: Violent crime rate: 28.5 per 10,000 population; Property crime rate: 161.4 per 10,000 population (2004).
Newspapers: Boonville Herald & Adirondack Tourist (General - Circulation 3,400)
Transportation: Commute to work: 89.6% car, 1.3% public transportation, 7.5% walk, 1.3% work from home (2000); Travel time to work: 50.7% less than 15 minutes, 9.4% 15 to 30 minutes, 25.1% 30 to 45 minutes, 8.5% 45 to 60 minutes, 6.3% 60 minutes or more (2000)
Additional Information Contacts
Boonville Chamber of Commerce . . . . (315) 942-5112
    http://www.boonevillechamber.org
Village of Boonville. . . . . (315) 943-2052
    http://village.boonville.ny.us/content

BOONVILLE (town). Covers a land area of 71.908 square miles and a water area of 0.690 square miles. Located at 43.47° N. Lat.; 75.28° W. Long. Elevation is 1,146 feet.
History: Author and critic Walter D. Edmonds born here and lived in nearby Talcottville. Settled c.1791, incorporated 1855.
Population: 4,225 (1990); 4,572 (2000); 4,598 (2005); 4,623 (2010 projected); Race: 99.2% White, 0.1% Black, 0.2% Asian, 0.1% Hispanic of any race (2005); Density: 63.9 persons per square mile (2005); Average household size: 2.52 (2005); Median age: 40.7 (2005); Males per 100 females: 96.2 (2005); Marriage status: 22.7% never married, 57.5% now married, 10.3% widowed, 9.5% divorced (2000); Foreign born: 1.3% (2000); Ancestry (includes multiple ancestries): 23.1% German, 21.2% Irish, 14.3% Polish, 11.9% English, 8.6% French (except Basque) (2000).
Economy: Trade center for dairying region. Manufacturing: dairy products, furniture, lumber, wood products; timber; maple syrup. Single-family building permits issued: 13 (2005); Multi-family building permits issued: 0 (2005); Employment by occupation: 7.8% management, 17.4% professional, 20.3% services, 23.1% sales, 0.6% farming, 10.9% construction, 19.9% production (2000).
Income: Per capita income: $19,320 (2005); Median household income: $41,203 (2005); Average household income: $47,644 (2005); Percent of households with income of $100,000 or more: 7.1% (2005); Poverty rate: 11.0% (2000).
Education: Percent of population age 25 and over with: High school diploma (including GED) or higher: 82.0% (2005); Bachelor's degree or higher: 13.2% (2005); Master's degree or higher: 5.3% (2005).
Housing: Homeownership rate: 73.5% (2005); Median home value: $96,129 (2005); Median rent: $328 per month (2000); Median age of housing: 43 years (2000).
Transportation: Commute to work: 92.3% car, 0.5% public transportation, 3.5% walk, 3.0% work from home (2000); Travel time to work: 39.7% less than 15 minutes, 12.6% 15 to 30 minutes, 27.6% 30 to 45 minutes, 10.5% 45 to 60 minutes, 9.6% 60 minutes or more (2000)

BRIDGEWATER (village). Covers a land area of 0.614 square miles and a water area of 0 square miles. Located at 42.87° N. Lat.; 75.25° W. Long. Elevation is 1,198 feet.
Population: 537 (1990); 579 (2000); 565 (2005); 564 (2010 projected); Race: 98.6% White, 0.5% Black, 0.0% Asian, 2.7% Hispanic of any race (2005); Density: 920.9 persons per square mile (2005); Average household size: 2.81 (2005); Median age: 30.8 (2005); Males per 100 females: 94.2 (2005); Marriage status: 29.5% never married, 55.5% now married, 6.2% widowed, 8.8% divorced (2000); Foreign born: 1.5% (2000); Ancestry (includes multiple ancestries): 19.9% German, 19.5% Irish, 14.1% English, 8.4% French (except Basque), 7.3% Other groups (2000).

Economy: Single-family building permits issued: 1 (2005); Multi-family building permits issued: 0 (2005); Employment by occupation: 2.6% management, 15.8% professional, 23.7% services, 21.1% sales, 1.3% farming, 11.8% construction, 23.7% production (2000).
Income: Per capita income: $13,243 (2005); Median household income: $28,246 (2005); Average household income: $37,226 (2005); Percent of households with income of $100,000 or more: 3.5% (2005); Poverty rate: 12.6% (2000).
Education: Percent of population age 25 and over with: High school diploma (including GED) or higher: 80.8% (2005); Bachelor's degree or higher: 5.0% (2005); Master's degree or higher: 0.0% (2005).
Housing: Homeownership rate: 77.6% (2005); Median home value: $40,690 (2005); Median rent: $338 per month (2000); Median age of housing: 24 years (2000).
Transportation: Commute to work: 90.7% car, 0.0% public transportation, 4.9% walk, 4.4% work from home (2000); Travel time to work: 19.4% less than 15 minutes, 39.8% 15 to 30 minutes, 30.6% 30 to 45 minutes, 3.2% 45 to 60 minutes, 6.9% 60 minutes or more (2000)

BRIDGEWATER (town). Covers a land area of 23.851 square miles and a water area of 0.002 square miles. Located at 42.90° N. Lat.; 75.25° W. Long. Elevation is 1,198 feet.
Population: 1,591 (1990); 1,671 (2000); 1,706 (2005); 1,737 (2010 projected); Race: 97.2% White, 0.6% Black, 0.9% Asian, 1.3% Hispanic of any race (2005); Density: 71.5 persons per square mile (2005); Average household size: 2.77 (2005); Median age: 35.7 (2005); Males per 100 females: 104.1 (2005); Marriage status: 25.9% never married, 60.7% now married, 4.9% widowed, 8.5% divorced (2000); Foreign born: 2.2% (2000); Ancestry (includes multiple ancestries): 19.4% Irish, 16.1% German, 12.2% English, 9.1% Italian, 8.0% French (except Basque) (2000).
Economy: Single-family building permits issued: 2 (2005); Multi-family building permits issued: 0 (2005); Employment by occupation: 6.4% management, 15.5% professional, 18.1% services, 24.5% sales, 1.5% farming, 11.9% construction, 22.0% production (2000).
Income: Per capita income: $15,035 (2005); Median household income: $33,898 (2005); Average household income: $41,640 (2005); Percent of households with income of $100,000 or more: 4.4% (2005); Poverty rate: 10.1% (2000).
Education: Percent of population age 25 and over with: High school diploma (including GED) or higher: 78.4% (2005); Bachelor's degree or higher: 9.1% (2005); Master's degree or higher: 2.5% (2005).
Housing: Homeownership rate: 83.0% (2005); Median home value: $65,800 (2005); Median rent: $345 per month (2000); Median age of housing: 25 years (2000).
Transportation: Commute to work: 92.2% car, 0.0% public transportation, 2.7% walk, 4.4% work from home (2000); Travel time to work: 17.7% less than 15 minutes, 47.7% 15 to 30 minutes, 28.4% 30 to 45 minutes, 3.0% 45 to 60 minutes, 3.1% 60 minutes or more (2000)

CAMDEN (village). Covers a land area of 2.260 square miles and a water area of 0 square miles. Located at 43.33° N. Lat.; 75.74° W. Long. Elevation is 523 feet.
Population: 2,552 (1990); 2,330 (2000); 2,310 (2005); 2,311 (2010 projected); Race: 96.8% White, 0.4% Black, 1.1% Asian, 1.6% Hispanic of any race (2005); Density: 1,022.0 persons per square mile (2005); Average household size: 2.48 (2005); Median age: 39.0 (2005); Males per 100 females: 94.8 (2005); Marriage status: 25.8% never married, 55.5% now married, 7.6% widowed, 11.1% divorced (2000); Foreign born: 1.2% (2000); Ancestry (includes multiple ancestries): 18.5% Irish, 18.3% English, 17.5% German, 8.6% United States or American, 7.4% Other groups (2000).
Economy: Single-family building permits issued: 5 (2005); Multi-family building permits issued: 2 (2005); Employment by occupation: 7.6% management, 17.9% professional, 16.2% services, 30.0% sales, 0.6% farming, 8.1% construction, 19.6% production (2000).
Income: Per capita income: $19,080 (2005); Median household income: $35,573 (2005); Average household income: $46,348 (2005); Percent of households with income of $100,000 or more: 6.4% (2005); Poverty rate: 13.5% (2000).
Education: Percent of population age 25 and over with: High school diploma (including GED) or higher: 82.6% (2005); Bachelor's degree or higher: 11.2% (2005); Master's degree or higher: 5.1% (2005).

School District(s)
Camden Central School District (PK-12)
    2003-04 Enrollment: 2,845 . . . . (315) 245-4075

Housing: Homeownership rate: 58.2% (2005); Median home value: $92,500 (2005); Median rent: $335 per month (2000); Median age of housing: 60+ years (2000).
Safety: Violent crime rate: 34.7 per 10,000 population; Property crime rate: 208.3 per 10,000 population (2004).
Newspapers: Queen Central News (General - Circulation 8,100)
Transportation: Commute to work: 86.1% car, 0.0% public transportation, 10.9% walk, 3.1% work from home (2000); Travel time to work: 48.7% less than 15 minutes, 15.1% 15 to 30 minutes, 19.9% 30 to 45 minutes, 8.0% 45 to 60 minutes, 8.3% 60 minutes or more (2000)

CAMDEN (town). Covers a land area of 54.020 square miles and a water area of 0.124 square miles. Located at 43.34° N. Lat.; 75.76° W. Long. Elevation is 523 feet.
History: Incorporated 1834.
Population: 5,134 (1990); 5,028 (2000); 5,060 (2005); 5,091 (2010 projected); Race: 97.9% White, 0.4% Black, 0.6% Asian, 0.9% Hispanic of any race (2005); Density: 93.7 persons per square mile (2005); Average household size: 2.62 (2005); Median age: 38.6 (2005); Males per 100 females: 100.8 (2005); Marriage status: 24.8% never married, 59.2% now married, 6.6% widowed, 9.4% divorced (2000); Foreign born: 0.7% (2000); Ancestry (includes multiple ancestries): 18.8% Irish, 18.8% German, 18.0% English, 12.1% United States or American, 10.6% French (except Basque) (2000).
Economy: In farming and dairying area. Manufacturing: metal products. Single-family building permits issued: 6 (2005); Multi-family building permits issued: 0 (2005); Employment by occupation: 6.3% management, 18.7% professional, 12.9% services, 28.0% sales, 2.1% farming, 9.0% construction, 22.9% production (2000).
Income: Per capita income: $21,060 (2005); Median household income: $44,893 (2005); Average household income: $54,676 (2005); Percent of households with income of $100,000 or more: 8.9% (2005); Poverty rate: 12.1% (2000).
Education: Percent of population age 25 and over with: High school diploma (including GED) or higher: 81.0% (2005); Bachelor's degree or higher: 13.7% (2005); Master's degree or higher: 7.1% (2005).
Housing: Homeownership rate: 74.0% (2005); Median home value: $100,765 (2005); Median rent: $335 per month (2000); Median age of housing: 51 years (2000).
Transportation: Commute to work: 92.3% car, 0.0% public transportation, 5.8% walk, 2.0% work from home (2000); Travel time to work: 45.8% less than 15 minutes, 20.2% 15 to 30 minutes, 17.7% 30 to 45 minutes, 10.3% 45 to 60 minutes, 6.1% 60 minutes or more (2000)

CASSVILLE (unincorporated postal area, zip code 13318). Aka Richfield Junction. Covers a land area of 24.624 square miles and a water area of 0.094 square miles. Located at 42.93° N. Lat.; 75.24° W. Long. Elevation is 1,210 feet.
Population: 0 (2000); Race: 98.4% White, 0.7% Black, 0.1% Asian, 0.3% Hispanic of any race (2000); Density: 0.0 persons per square mile (2000); Age: 31.2% under 18, 6.2% over 64 (2000); Marriage status: 24.2% never married, 65.4% now married, 3.5% widowed, 6.9% divorced (2000); Foreign born: 1.1% (2000); Ancestry (includes multiple ancestries): 20.5% Irish, 19.2% German, 13.7% English, 12.4% Italian, 8.0% Polish (2000).
Economy: Employment by occupation: 11.0% management, 17.8% professional, 14.3% services, 24.8% sales, 1.2% farming, 11.2% construction, 19.7% production (2000).
Income: Per capita income: $16,299 (2000); Median household income: $41,000 (2000); Poverty rate: 6.2% (2000).
Education: Percent of population age 25 and over with: High school diploma (including GED) or higher: 84.5% (2000); Bachelor's degree or higher: 12.7% (2000).
Housing: Homeownership rate: 85.9% (2000); Median home value: $73,800 (2000); Median rent: $417 per month (2000); Median age of housing: 31 years (2000).
Transportation: Commute to work: 91.4% car, 0.0% public transportation, 2.7% walk, 4.1% work from home (2000); Travel time to work: 19.3% less than 15 minutes, 51.5% 15 to 30 minutes, 23.1% 30 to 45 minutes, 2.6% 45 to 60 minutes, 3.6% 60 minutes or more (2000)

CHADWICKS (unincorporated postal area, zip code 13319). Covers a land area of 1.507 square miles and a water area of 0 square miles. Located at 43.03° N. Lat.; 75.27° W. Long.
Population: 0 (2000); Race: 100.0% White, 0.0% Black, 0.0% Asian, 0.0% Hispanic of any race (2000); Density: 0.0 persons per square mile (2000);

Age: 31.3% under 18, 4.1% over 64 (2000); Marriage status: 23.3% never married, 57.4% now married, 5.4% widowed, 13.8% divorced (2000); Foreign born: 0.8% (2000); Ancestry (includes multiple ancestries): 27.1% Irish, 24.7% English, 20.8% Italian, 17.9% German, 8.6% Welsh (2000).
Economy: Employment by occupation: 10.0% management, 14.5% professional, 22.3% services, 26.3% sales, 0.0% farming, 12.9% construction, 13.9% production (2000).
Income: Per capita income: $16,423 (2000); Median household income: $41,343 (2000); Poverty rate: 6.2% (2000).
Education: Percent of population age 25 and over with: High school diploma (including GED) or higher: 84.8% (2000); Bachelor's degree or higher: 16.1% (2000).
Housing: Homeownership rate: 63.8% (2000); Median home value: $65,200 (2000); Median rent: $371 per month (2000); Median age of housing: 60+ years (2000).
Transportation: Commute to work: 98.8% car, 0.0% public transportation, 1.2% walk, 0.0% work from home (2000); Travel time to work: 36.2% less than 15 minutes, 54.9% 15 to 30 minutes, 4.6% 30 to 45 minutes, 0.0% 45 to 60 minutes, 4.3% 60 minutes or more (2000)

CLARK MILLS (CDP). Covers a land area of 0.928 square miles and a water area of 0.034 square miles. Located at 43.09° N. Lat.; 75.37° W. Long.
Population: 1,303 (1990); 1,424 (2000); 1,330 (2005); 1,221 (2010 projected); Race: 98.3% White, 1.1% Black, 0.0% Asian, 0.2% Hispanic of any race (2005); Density: 1,432.7 persons per square mile (2005); Average household size: 2.22 (2005); Median age: 39.0 (2005); Males per 100 females: 87.1 (2005); Marriage status: 29.8% never married, 50.8% now married, 9.2% widowed, 10.1% divorced (2000); Foreign born: 1.2% (2000); Ancestry (includes multiple ancestries): 19.9% Italian, 19.4% German, 18.6% Irish, 16.1% English, 9.8% Polish (2000).
Economy: Manufacturing: apparel. Employment by occupation: 11.9% management, 13.7% professional, 19.7% services, 32.3% sales, 0.0% farming, 8.4% construction, 14.0% production (2000).
Income: Per capita income: $21,061 (2005); Median household income: $41,210 (2005); Average household income: $46,446 (2005); Percent of households with income of $100,000 or more: 5.0% (2005); Poverty rate: 6.9% (2000).
Education: Percent of population age 25 and over with: High school diploma (including GED) or higher: 85.0% (2005); Bachelor's degree or higher: 11.4% (2005); Master's degree or higher: 3.3% (2005).
Housing: Homeownership rate: 67.3% (2005); Median home value: $54,321 (2005); Median rent: $402 per month (2000); Median age of housing: 35 years (2000).
Transportation: Commute to work: 95.6% car, 0.0% public transportation, 3.0% walk, 0.0% work from home (2000); Travel time to work: 46.9% less than 15 minutes, 44.9% 15 to 30 minutes, 6.6% 30 to 45 minutes, 0.0% 45 to 60 minutes, 1.6% 60 minutes or more (2000)

CLAYVILLE (village). Covers a land area of 0.458 square miles and a water area of 0.012 square miles. Located at 42.97° N. Lat.; 75.25° W. Long.
Population: 463 (1990); 445 (2000); 401 (2005); 383 (2010 projected); Race: 98.5% White, 0.2% Black, 0.0% Asian, 0.0% Hispanic of any race (2005); Density: 874.8 persons per square mile (2005); Average household size: 2.59 (2005); Median age: 35.3 (2005); Males per 100 females: 97.5 (2005); Marriage status: 35.4% never married, 44.4% now married, 6.3% widowed, 13.9% divorced (2000); Foreign born: 3.1% (2000); Ancestry (includes multiple ancestries): 22.7% English, 21.2% Irish, 20.9% German, 18.7% Italian, 10.5% Polish (2000).
Economy: Manufacturing: metal powders, refrigeration and cold storage doors; inert-gas processing. Single-family building permits issued: 0 (2005); Multi-family building permits issued: 0 (2005); Employment by occupation: 7.9% management, 8.7% professional, 19.2% services, 31.9% sales, 0.0% farming, 12.2% construction, 20.1% production (2000).
Income: Per capita income: $15,536 (2005); Median household income: $35,179 (2005); Average household income: $40,194 (2005); Percent of households with income of $100,000 or more: 3.9% (2005); Poverty rate: 12.5% (2000).
Education: Percent of population age 25 and over with: High school diploma (including GED) or higher: 81.6% (2005); Bachelor's degree or higher: 10.5% (2005); Master's degree or higher: 4.3% (2005).
Housing: Homeownership rate: 65.2% (2005); Median home value: $81,364 (2005); Median rent: $353 per month (2000); Median age of housing: 60+ years (2000).

Transportation: Commute to work: 96.1% car, 1.7% public transportation, 0.0% walk, 0.4% work from home (2000); Travel time to work: 25.9% less than 15 minutes, 49.1% 15 to 30 minutes, 14.5% 30 to 45 minutes, 7.0% 45 to 60 minutes, 3.5% 60 minutes or more (2000)

CLINTON (village). Covers a land area of 0.583 square miles and a water area of 0 square miles. Located at 43.04° N. Lat.; 75.38° W. Long. Elevation is 582 feet.
History: Seat of Hamilton College. Elihu Root was born here. Clinton Village Historic District. Incorporated 1843.
Population: 2,238 (1990); 1,952 (2000); 1,917 (2005); 1,905 (2010 projected); Race: 97.8% White, 0.7% Black, 0.9% Asian, 1.7% Hispanic of any race (2005); Density: 3,289.3 persons per square mile (2005); Average household size: 2.06 (2005); Median age: 45.1 (2005); Males per 100 females: 89.8 (2005); Marriage status: 26.4% never married, 55.4% now married, 10.0% widowed, 8.3% divorced (2000); Foreign born: 2.9% (2000); Ancestry (includes multiple ancestries): 25.7% Irish, 19.9% German, 19.4% English, 16.1% Italian, 8.6% Polish (2000).
Economy: Manufacturing: clothing, food products. Single-family building permits issued: 0 (2005); Multi-family building permits issued: 0 (2005); Employment by occupation: 16.8% management, 37.8% professional, 11.5% services, 22.4% sales, 0.0% farming, 5.3% construction, 6.2% production (2000).
Income: Per capita income: $29,082 (2005); Median household income: $46,058 (2005); Average household income: $59,866 (2005); Percent of households with income of $100,000 or more: 17.8% (2005); Poverty rate: 9.7% (2000).
Education: Percent of population age 25 and over with: High school diploma (including GED) or higher: 92.9% (2005); Bachelor's degree or higher: 49.2% (2005); Master's degree or higher: 24.7% (2005).
School District(s)
Clinton Central School District (KG-12)
    2003-04 Enrollment: 1,634 .... (315) 853-5574
Four-year College(s)
Hamilton College
    Fall 2004 Enrollment: 1,792 .... (315) 859-4011
    2005-06 Tuition: In-state $33,350; Out-of-state $33,350
Housing: Homeownership rate: 53.4% (2005); Median home value: $140,714 (2005); Median rent: $428 per month (2000); Median age of housing: 60+ years (2000).
Newspapers: Clinton Courier (General - Circulation 2,200); North Country Paper (General - Circulation 9,309)
Transportation: Commute to work: 87.9% car, 1.5% public transportation, 4.6% walk, 5.5% work from home (2000); Travel time to work: 42.7% less than 15 minutes, 42.7% 15 to 30 minutes, 6.4% 30 to 45 minutes, 3.9% 45 to 60 minutes, 4.3% 60 minutes or more (2000)
Additional Information Contacts
Clinton Chamber of Commerce .... (315) 853-1735
    http://www.clintonnychamber.org
Village of Clinton .... (845) 266-5853
    http://www.townofclinton.com/

DEANSBORO (unincorporated postal area, zip code 13328). Covers a land area of 16.591 square miles and a water area of 0 square miles. Located at 42.98° N. Lat.; 75.42° W. Long.
Population: 0 (2000); Race: 99.0% White, 0.5% Black, 0.2% Asian, 0.3% Hispanic of any race (2000); Density: 0.0 persons per square mile (2000); Age: 30.0% under 18, 10.2% over 64 (2000); Marriage status: 21.3% never married, 61.0% now married, 4.6% widowed, 13.1% divorced (2000); Foreign born: 0.5% (2000); Ancestry (includes multiple ancestries): 23.4% German, 21.3% Irish, 21.1% English, 10.8% Italian, 8.6% Polish (2000).
Economy: Employment by occupation: 19.2% management, 16.6% professional, 11.4% services, 25.6% sales, 0.8% farming, 8.0% construction, 18.5% production (2000).
Income: Per capita income: $19,662 (2000); Median household income: $40,781 (2000); Poverty rate: 16.7% (2000).
Education: Percent of population age 25 and over with: High school diploma (including GED) or higher: 88.4% (2000); Bachelor's degree or higher: 22.0% (2000).
Housing: Homeownership rate: 81.2% (2000); Median home value: $77,000 (2000); Median rent: $408 per month (2000); Median age of housing: 60+ years (2000).
Transportation: Commute to work: 88.8% car, 0.0% public transportation, 3.1% walk, 7.2% work from home (2000); Travel time to work: 28.8% less

than 15 minutes, 47.0% 15 to 30 minutes, 15.4% 30 to 45 minutes, 3.0% 45 to 60 minutes, 5.8% 60 minutes or more (2000)

DEERFIELD (town). Covers a land area of 32.934 square miles and a water area of 0.129 square miles. Located at 43.17° N. Lat.; 75.16° W. Long.
Population: 3,942 (1990); 3,906 (2000); 3,970 (2005); 4,013 (2010 projected); Race: 98.7% White, 0.6% Black, 0.3% Asian, 1.0% Hispanic of any race (2005); Density: 120.5 persons per square mile (2005); Average household size: 2.64 (2005); Median age: 41.7 (2005); Males per 100 females: 99.2 (2005); Marriage status: 21.6% never married, 67.6% now married, 6.2% widowed, 4.6% divorced (2000); Foreign born: 3.4% (2000); Ancestry (includes multiple ancestries): 28.5% Italian, 23.6% Irish, 20.6% Polish, 18.2% German, 8.8% English (2000).
Economy: Single-family building permits issued: 14 (2005); Multi-family building permits issued: 0 (2005); Employment by occupation: 9.5% management, 25.9% professional, 18.1% services, 30.9% sales, 0.0% farming, 8.5% construction, 7.1% production (2000).
Income: Per capita income: $24,235 (2005); Median household income: $54,227 (2005); Average household income: $64,014 (2005); Percent of households with income of $100,000 or more: 12.6% (2005); Poverty rate: 3.8% (2000).
Taxes: Total city taxes per capita: $181 (2004); City property taxes per capita: $143 (2004).
Education: Percent of population age 25 and over with: High school diploma (including GED) or higher: 89.7% (2005); Bachelor's degree or higher: 21.1% (2005); Master's degree or higher: 8.4% (2005).
Housing: Homeownership rate: 93.5% (2005); Median home value: $126,187 (2005); Median rent: $526 per month (2000); Median age of housing: 43 years (2000).
Transportation: Commute to work: 95.0% car, 0.3% public transportation, 1.7% walk, 2.8% work from home (2000); Travel time to work: 37.7% less than 15 minutes, 50.1% 15 to 30 minutes, 8.2% 30 to 45 minutes, 1.9% 45 to 60 minutes, 2.0% 60 minutes or more (2000)

DURHAMVILLE (unincorporated postal area, zip code 13054). Covers a land area of 25.675 square miles and a water area of 0.019 square miles. Located at 43.16° N. Lat.; 75.68° W. Long.
Population: 0 (2000); Race: 97.5% White, 0.0% Black, 0.0% Asian, 0.8% Hispanic of any race (2000); Density: 0.0 persons per square mile (2000); Age: 26.5% under 18, 14.6% over 64 (2000); Marriage status: 23.7% never married, 58.8% now married, 8.5% widowed, 8.9% divorced (2000); Foreign born: 1.1% (2000); Ancestry (includes multiple ancestries): 21.7% German, 13.5% United States or American, 12.2% English, 12.2% Irish, 7.8% Italian (2000).
Economy: Employment by occupation: 8.9% management, 13.6% professional, 16.6% services, 22.6% sales, 0.7% farming, 11.4% construction, 26.2% production (2000).
Income: Per capita income: $16,403 (2000); Median household income: $40,219 (2000); Poverty rate: 7.2% (2000).
Education: Percent of population age 25 and over with: High school diploma (including GED) or higher: 83.3% (2000); Bachelor's degree or higher: 13.4% (2000).

School District(s)
Oneida City School District (KG-12)
    2003-04 Enrollment: 2,550 . . . . (315) 363-2550
Housing: Homeownership rate: 85.4% (2000); Median home value: $74,200 (2000); Median rent: $428 per month (2000); Median age of housing: 49 years (2000).
Transportation: Commute to work: 95.3% car, 3.1% public transportation, 0.0% walk, 0.8% work from home (2000); Travel time to work: 22.2% less than 15 minutes, 37.1% 15 to 30 minutes, 20.5% 30 to 45 minutes, 8.8% 45 to 60 minutes, 11.4% 60 minutes or more (2000)

FLORENCE (town). Covers a land area of 54.964 square miles and a water area of 0.075 square miles. Located at 43.42° N. Lat.; 75.73° W. Long.
Population: 852 (1990); 1,086 (2000); 1,063 (2005); 1,053 (2010 projected); Race: 99.1% White, 0.3% Black, 0.3% Asian, 0.3% Hispanic of any race (2005); Density: 19.3 persons per square mile (2005); Average household size: 2.88 (2005); Median age: 35.8 (2005); Males per 100 females: 107.2 (2005); Marriage status: 26.3% never married, 61.3% now married, 5.7% widowed, 6.7% divorced (2000); Foreign born: 0.3% (2000); Ancestry (includes multiple ancestries): 20.7% United States or American, 16.5% Irish, 13.7% German, 8.6% English, 7.2% French (except Basque) (2000).
Economy: Single-family building permits issued: 7 (2005); Multi-family building permits issued: 0 (2005); Employment by occupation: 6.8% management, 10.2% professional, 9.1% services, 25.3% sales, 1.1% farming, 15.5% construction, 31.9% production (2000).
Income: Per capita income: $15,129 (2005); Median household income: $38,796 (2005); Average household income: $43,584 (2005); Percent of households with income of $100,000 or more: 4.6% (2005); Poverty rate: 9.9% (2000).
Education: Percent of population age 25 and over with: High school diploma (including GED) or higher: 74.8% (2005); Bachelor's degree or higher: 8.2% (2005); Master's degree or higher: 3.1% (2005).
Housing: Homeownership rate: 85.1% (2005); Median home value: $81,613 (2005); Median rent: $402 per month (2000); Median age of housing: 21 years (2000).
Transportation: Commute to work: 95.2% car, 0.6% public transportation, 0.0% walk, 4.1% work from home (2000); Travel time to work: 20.9% less than 15 minutes, 28.8% 15 to 30 minutes, 26.8% 30 to 45 minutes, 15.5% 45 to 60 minutes, 7.9% 60 minutes or more (2000)

FLOYD (town). Covers a land area of 34.598 square miles and a water area of 0.160 square miles. Located at 43.22° N. Lat.; 75.33° W. Long. Elevation is 565 feet.
Population: 3,856 (1990); 3,869 (2000); 3,942 (2005); 4,009 (2010 projected); Race: 97.4% White, 0.3% Black, 0.5% Asian, 1.1% Hispanic of any race (2005); Density: 113.9 persons per square mile (2005); Average household size: 2.72 (2005); Median age: 38.4 (2005); Males per 100 females: 97.0 (2005); Marriage status: 24.1% never married, 61.0% now married, 6.4% widowed, 8.5% divorced (2000); Foreign born: 1.0% (2000); Ancestry (includes multiple ancestries): 19.2% German, 15.5% Irish, 14.7% Italian, 13.6% English, 10.5% Polish (2000).
Economy: Single-family building permits issued: 6 (2005); Multi-family building permits issued: 0 (2005); Employment by occupation: 9.9% management, 18.8% professional, 23.3% services, 22.5% sales, 0.3% farming, 8.3% construction, 17.0% production (2000).
Income: Per capita income: $19,848 (2005); Median household income: $46,890 (2005); Average household income: $53,998 (2005); Percent of households with income of $100,000 or more: 8.6% (2005); Poverty rate: 4.2% (2000).
Education: Percent of population age 25 and over with: High school diploma (including GED) or higher: 87.2% (2005); Bachelor's degree or higher: 12.5% (2005); Master's degree or higher: 3.5% (2005).
Housing: Homeownership rate: 89.6% (2005); Median home value: $102,404 (2005); Median rent: $388 per month (2000); Median age of housing: 30 years (2000).
Transportation: Commute to work: 96.6% car, 0.6% public transportation, 0.0% walk, 1.8% work from home (2000); Travel time to work: 18.1% less than 15 minutes, 54.9% 15 to 30 minutes, 20.0% 30 to 45 minutes, 3.0% 45 to 60 minutes, 4.0% 60 minutes or more (2000)
Additional Information Contacts
Town of Floyd . . . . (315) 865-4256
  http://town.floyd.ny.us/content

FORESTPORT (town). Covers a land area of 77.191 square miles and a water area of 1.776 square miles. Located at 43.47° N. Lat.; 75.16° W. Long.
Population: 1,548 (1990); 1,692 (2000); 1,772 (2005); 1,824 (2010 projected); Race: 98.9% White, 0.2% Black, 0.2% Asian, 0.0% Hispanic of any race (2005); Density: 23.0 persons per square mile (2005); Average household size: 2.26 (2005); Median age: 44.7 (2005); Males per 100 females: 103.2 (2005); Marriage status: 17.6% never married, 66.6% now married, 7.1% widowed, 8.8% divorced (2000); Foreign born: 1.3% (2000); Ancestry (includes multiple ancestries): 25.4% German, 24.4% Irish, 18.0% English, 10.5% French (except Basque), 10.4% Italian (2000).
Economy: Single-family building permits issued: 33 (2005); Multi-family building permits issued: 0 (2005); Employment by occupation: 12.2% management, 14.4% professional, 17.1% services, 27.5% sales, 0.3% farming, 12.3% construction, 16.2% production (2000).
Income: Per capita income: $21,622 (2005); Median household income: $40,733 (2005); Average household income: $48,809 (2005); Percent of households with income of $100,000 or more: 6.4% (2005); Poverty rate: 8.9% (2000).

Education: Percent of population age 25 and over with: High school diploma (including GED) or higher: 81.5% (2005); Bachelor's degree or higher: 15.0% (2005); Master's degree or higher: 4.4% (2005).

School District(s)
Adirondack Central School District (KG-12)
    2003-04 Enrollment: 1,548 . . . . (315) 942-9200

Housing: Homeownership rate: 88.9% (2005); Median home value: $97,778 (2005); Median rent: $408 per month (2000); Median age of housing: 35 years (2000).

Transportation: Commute to work: 94.2% car, 0.3% public transportation, 2.0% walk, 3.0% work from home (2000); Travel time to work: 16.8% less than 15 minutes, 18.7% 15 to 30 minutes, 38.0% 30 to 45 minutes, 17.2% 45 to 60 minutes, 9.2% 60 minutes or more (2000)

HOLLAND PATENT (village). Covers a land area of 0.481 square miles and a water area of 0.005 square miles. Located at 43.24° N. Lat.; 75.25° W. Long. Elevation is 630 feet.

Population: 411 (1990); 461 (2000); 450 (2005); 446 (2010 projected); Race: 98.2% White, 0.0% Black, 0.4% Asian, 0.4% Hispanic of any race (2005); Density: 935.9 persons per square mile (2005); Average household size: 2.25 (2005); Median age: 38.7 (2005); Males per 100 females: 103.6 (2005); Marriage status: 22.4% never married, 64.2% now married, 4.4% widowed, 9.0% divorced (2000); Foreign born: 0.0% (2000); Ancestry (includes multiple ancestries): 29.5% Irish, 20.4% German, 17.0% English, 16.8% Welsh, 11.1% Italian (2000).

Economy: Employment by occupation: 11.5% management, 32.5% professional, 8.5% services, 22.6% sales, 0.9% farming, 7.3% construction, 16.7% production (2000).

Income: Per capita income: $30,411 (2005); Median household income: $54,167 (2005); Average household income: $68,425 (2005); Percent of households with income of $100,000 or more: 19.0% (2005); Poverty rate: 4.1% (2000).

Education: Percent of population age 25 and over with: High school diploma (including GED) or higher: 92.4% (2005); Bachelor's degree or higher: 29.3% (2005); Master's degree or higher: 14.5% (2005).

School District(s)
Holland Patent Central School District (KG-12)
    2003-04 Enrollment: 1,853 . . . . (315) 865-7221

Housing: Homeownership rate: 66.0% (2005); Median home value: $117,188 (2005); Median rent: $374 per month (2000); Median age of housing: 60+ years (2000).

Transportation: Commute to work: 88.6% car, 0.0% public transportation, 4.8% walk, 6.6% work from home (2000); Travel time to work: 28.2% less than 15 minutes, 54.0% 15 to 30 minutes, 6.6% 30 to 45 minutes, 3.8% 45 to 60 minutes, 7.5% 60 minutes or more (2000)

Additional Information Contacts
Village of Holland Patent . . . . (315) 865-4853
    http://village.holland-patent.ny.us/content

KIRKLAND (town). Covers a land area of 33.796 square miles and a water area of 0.073 square miles. Located at 43.04° N. Lat.; 75.38° W. Long.

Population: 10,153 (1990); 10,138 (2000); 10,281 (2005); 10,387 (2010 projected); Race: 95.9% White, 1.2% Black, 1.6% Asian, 1.5% Hispanic of any race (2005); Density: 304.2 persons per square mile (2005); Average household size: 2.93 (2005); Median age: 36.8 (2005); Males per 100 females: 91.0 (2005); Marriage status: 33.2% never married, 52.4% now married, 7.3% widowed, 7.1% divorced (2000); Foreign born: 3.6% (2000); Ancestry (includes multiple ancestries): 23.7% Irish, 20.4% German, 18.1% English, 14.1% Italian, 10.7% Polish (2000).

Economy: Single-family building permits issued: 20 (2005); Multi-family building permits issued: 0 (2005); Employment by occupation: 13.3% management, 31.6% professional, 15.0% services, 26.9% sales, 0.6% farming, 5.1% construction, 7.5% production (2000).

Income: Per capita income: $22,895 (2005); Median household income: $50,519 (2005); Average household income: $64,303 (2005); Percent of households with income of $100,000 or more: 17.2% (2005); Poverty rate: 7.7% (2000).

Education: Percent of population age 25 and over with: High school diploma (including GED) or higher: 90.1% (2005); Bachelor's degree or higher: 37.2% (2005); Master's degree or higher: 19.3% (2005).

Housing: Homeownership rate: 70.7% (2005); Median home value: $132,435 (2005); Median rent: $464 per month (2000); Median age of housing: 45 years (2000).

Safety: Violent crime rate: 2.4 per 10,000 population; Property crime rate: 137.6 per 10,000 population (2004).

Transportation: Commute to work: 81.5% car, 0.3% public transportation, 13.4% walk, 4.3% work from home (2000); Travel time to work: 52.1% less than 15 minutes, 35.1% 15 to 30 minutes, 6.6% 30 to 45 minutes, 2.8% 45 to 60 minutes, 3.4% 60 minutes or more (2000)

LEE (town). Covers a land area of 45.170 square miles and a water area of 0.380 square miles. Located at 43.30° N. Lat.; 75.51° W. Long.

Population: 7,115 (1990); 6,875 (2000); 6,932 (2005); 6,987 (2010 projected); Race: 97.7% White, 0.7% Black, 0.4% Asian, 0.9% Hispanic of any race (2005); Density: 153.5 persons per square mile (2005); Average household size: 2.63 (2005); Median age: 39.8 (2005); Males per 100 females: 99.6 (2005); Marriage status: 21.4% never married, 64.9% now married, 6.9% widowed, 6.9% divorced (2000); Foreign born: 1.9% (2000); Ancestry (includes multiple ancestries): 23.2% German, 18.4% Irish, 16.4% Italian, 12.6% English, 9.0% Polish (2000).

Economy: Single-family building permits issued: 21 (2005); Multi-family building permits issued: 0 (2005); Employment by occupation: 11.8% management, 20.6% professional, 15.8% services, 28.5% sales, 0.9% farming, 5.6% construction, 16.8% production (2000).

Income: Per capita income: $24,368 (2005); Median household income: $54,289 (2005); Average household income: $63,518 (2005); Percent of households with income of $100,000 or more: 15.3% (2005); Poverty rate: 8.1% (2000).

Taxes: Total city taxes per capita: $24 (2004); City property taxes per capita: $3 (2004).

Education: Percent of population age 25 and over with: High school diploma (including GED) or higher: 85.4% (2005); Bachelor's degree or higher: 20.0% (2005); Master's degree or higher: 8.4% (2005).

Housing: Homeownership rate: 85.8% (2005); Median home value: $107,045 (2005); Median rent: $504 per month (2000); Median age of housing: 30 years (2000).

Transportation: Commute to work: 95.3% car, 0.1% public transportation, 1.4% walk, 2.8% work from home (2000); Travel time to work: 22.8% less than 15 minutes, 46.7% 15 to 30 minutes, 17.8% 30 to 45 minutes, 8.5% 45 to 60 minutes, 4.3% 60 minutes or more (2000)

LEE CENTER (unincorporated postal area, zip code 13363). Covers a land area of 21.207 square miles and a water area of 0.037 square miles. Located at 43.31° N. Lat.; 75.50° W. Long.

Population: 0 (2000); Race: 96.7% White, 1.1% Black, 0.3% Asian, 0.1% Hispanic of any race (2000); Density: 0.0 persons per square mile (2000); Age: 30.0% under 18, 14.0% over 64 (2000); Marriage status: 21.1% never married, 63.2% now married, 8.6% widowed, 7.2% divorced (2000); Foreign born: 1.7% (2000); Ancestry (includes multiple ancestries): 24.5% German, 21.9% Irish, 11.3% English, 10.4% Italian, 9.5% Polish (2000).

Economy: Employment by occupation: 12.9% management, 12.7% professional, 15.8% services, 23.2% sales, 0.6% farming, 7.2% construction, 27.4% production (2000).

Income: Per capita income: $16,479 (2000); Median household income: $34,663 (2000); Poverty rate: 14.1% (2000).

Education: Percent of population age 25 and over with: High school diploma (including GED) or higher: 79.6% (2000); Bachelor's degree or higher: 11.4% (2000).

Housing: Homeownership rate: 77.3% (2000); Median home value: $73,300 (2000); Median rent: $533 per month (2000); Median age of housing: 24 years (2000).

Transportation: Commute to work: 95.6% car, 0.0% public transportation, 0.8% walk, 3.6% work from home (2000); Travel time to work: 8.3% less than 15 minutes, 54.4% 15 to 30 minutes, 18.0% 30 to 45 minutes, 14.2% 45 to 60 minutes, 5.1% 60 minutes or more (2000)

MARCY (town). Covers a land area of 32.967 square miles and a water area of 0.447 square miles. Located at 43.17° N. Lat.; 75.27° W. Long.

Population: 8,685 (1990); 9,469 (2000); 9,492 (2005); 9,684 (2010 projected); Race: 62.5% White, 25.3% Black, 0.8% Asian, 18.9% Hispanic of any race (2005); Density: 287.9 persons per square mile (2005); Average household size: 4.60 (2005); Median age: 35.7 (2005); Males per 100 females: 237.4 (2005); Marriage status: 42.0% never married, 49.0% now married, 3.4% widowed, 5.6% divorced (2000); Foreign born: 8.7% (2000); Ancestry (includes multiple ancestries): 13.8% German, 12.9% Italian, 10.3% Irish, 10.1% Polish, 5.1% English (2000).

Economy: Single-family building permits issued: 26 (2005); Multi-family building permits issued: 0 (2005); Employment by occupation: 9.5%

management, 23.2% professional, 16.7% services, 30.1% sales, 0.0% farming, 10.5% construction, 9.9% production (2000).
Income: Per capita income: $18,798 (2005); Median household income: $54,812 (2005); Average household income: $65,297 (2005); Percent of households with income of $100,000 or more: 14.6% (2005); Poverty rate: 5.4% (2000).
Taxes: Total city taxes per capita: $171 (2004); City property taxes per capita: $155 (2004).
Education: Percent of population age 25 and over with: High school diploma (including GED) or higher: 54.2% (2005); Bachelor's degree or higher: 9.7% (2005); Master's degree or higher: 4.0% (2005).

School District(s)

Whitesboro Central School District (KG-12)
    2003-04 Enrollment: 3,863 . . . . (315) 266-3303
Housing: Homeownership rate: 84.8% (2005); Median home value: $126,852 (2005); Median rent: $450 per month (2000); Median age of housing: 37 years (2000).
Transportation: Commute to work: 93.6% car, 0.1% public transportation, 4.0% walk, 2.0% work from home (2000); Travel time to work: 38.2% less than 15 minutes, 52.4% 15 to 30 minutes, 4.0% 30 to 45 minutes, 1.2% 45 to 60 minutes, 4.1% 60 minutes or more (2000)

Additional Information Contacts

Marcy Chamber of Commerce . . . . (315) 865-6144
  http://www.marcychamber.com/

MARSHALL
(town). Covers a land area of 32.811 square miles and a water area of 0 square miles. Located at 42.96° N. Lat.; 75.39° W. Long.
Population: 2,125 (1990); 2,127 (2000); 2,115 (2005); 2,105 (2010 projected); Race: 98.5% White, 0.6% Black, 0.2% Asian, 1.1% Hispanic of any race (2005); Density: 64.5 persons per square mile (2005); Average household size: 2.65 (2005); Median age: 38.5 (2005); Males per 100 females: 97.8 (2005); Marriage status: 26.0% never married, 62.2% now married, 4.3% widowed, 7.6% divorced (2000); Foreign born: 0.8% (2000); Ancestry (includes multiple ancestries): 25.7% Irish, 20.7% English, 19.7% German, 9.6% Italian, 9.1% Polish (2000).
Economy: Single-family building permits issued: 4 (2005); Multi-family building permits issued: 0 (2005); Employment by occupation: 17.2% management, 17.0% professional, 14.5% services, 22.5% sales, 1.7% farming, 10.8% construction, 16.3% production (2000).
Income: Per capita income: $23,545 (2005); Median household income: $48,977 (2005); Average household income: $62,325 (2005); Percent of households with income of $100,000 or more: 12.6% (2005); Poverty rate: 10.1% (2000).
Education: Percent of population age 25 and over with: High school diploma (including GED) or higher: 85.6% (2005); Bachelor's degree or higher: 18.2% (2005); Master's degree or higher: 7.2% (2005).
Housing: Homeownership rate: 79.8% (2005); Median home value: $108,542 (2005); Median rent: $388 per month (2000); Median age of housing: 60+ years (2000).
Transportation: Commute to work: 87.7% car, 0.0% public transportation, 4.1% walk, 7.2% work from home (2000); Travel time to work: 27.2% less than 15 minutes, 44.7% 15 to 30 minutes, 18.1% 30 to 45 minutes, 4.6% 45 to 60 minutes, 5.4% 60 minutes or more (2000)

NEW HARTFORD
(village). Covers a land area of 0.611 square miles and a water area of 0 square miles. Located at 43.06° N. Lat.; 75.28° W. Long. Elevation is 537 feet.
Population: 2,111 (1990); 1,886 (2000); 1,836 (2005); 1,784 (2010 projected); Race: 96.3% White, 0.6% Black, 1.9% Asian, 1.0% Hispanic of any race (2005); Density: 3,005.2 persons per square mile (2005); Average household size: 2.15 (2005); Median age: 42.7 (2005); Males per 100 females: 86.8 (2005); Marriage status: 24.1% never married, 54.8% now married, 13.2% widowed, 7.9% divorced (2000); Foreign born: 2.0% (2000); Ancestry (includes multiple ancestries): 28.3% Irish, 24.3% Italian, 21.8% German, 19.3% English, 9.1% Polish (2000).
Economy: Single-family building permits issued: 0 (2005); Multi-family building permits issued: 0 (2005); Employment by occupation: 15.3% management, 36.0% professional, 14.3% services, 23.2% sales, 0.0% farming, 6.2% construction, 5.0% production (2000).
Income: Per capita income: $26,953 (2005); Median household income: $48,109 (2005); Average household income: $57,917 (2005); Percent of households with income of $100,000 or more: 15.7% (2005); Poverty rate: 5.7% (2000).
Education: Percent of population age 25 and over with: High school diploma (including GED) or higher: 94.9% (2005); Bachelor's degree or higher: 41.3% (2005); Master's degree or higher: 15.4% (2005).

School District(s)

Boces Oneida-Herkimer-Madison (PK-PK)
    2003-04 Enrollment: 308 . . . . (315) 793-8561
New Hartford Central School District (KG-12)
    2003-04 Enrollment: 2,670 . . . . (315) 624-1218
Housing: Homeownership rate: 63.0% (2005); Median home value: $128,372 (2005); Median rent: $449 per month (2000); Median age of housing: 60+ years (2000).
Transportation: Commute to work: 94.2% car, 0.3% public transportation, 1.8% walk, 2.3% work from home (2000); Travel time to work: 61.0% less than 15 minutes, 27.9% 15 to 30 minutes, 6.3% 30 to 45 minutes, 1.3% 45 to 60 minutes, 3.4% 60 minutes or more (2000)

Additional Information Contacts

Village of New Hartford . . . . (315) 733-7500
  http://www.town.new-hartford.ny.us/

NEW HARTFORD
(town). Covers a land area of 25.384 square miles and a water area of 0.098 square miles. Located at 43.06° N. Lat.; 75.28° W. Long. Elevation is 537 feet.
History: Settled c.1787, incorporated 1870.
Population: 21,640 (1990); 21,172 (2000); 21,155 (2005); 21,138 (2010 projected); Race: 95.2% White, 0.8% Black, 3.1% Asian, 0.9% Hispanic of any race (2005); Density: 833.4 persons per square mile (2005); Average household size: 2.41 (2005); Median age: 46.2 (2005); Males per 100 females: 86.3 (2005); Marriage status: 21.5% never married, 58.8% now married, 12.1% widowed, 7.7% divorced (2000); Foreign born: 4.4% (2000); Ancestry (includes multiple ancestries): 27.0% Italian, 20.5% Irish, 16.4% German, 14.1% Polish, 12.0% English (2000).
Economy: Manufacturing: paper products, computer software, consumer goods. Single-family building permits issued: 35 (2005); Multi-family building permits issued: 0 (2005); Employment by occupation: 13.7% management, 30.3% professional, 16.0% services, 26.8% sales, 0.5% farming, 5.6% construction, 7.3% production (2000).
Income: Per capita income: $30,876 (2005); Median household income: $52,210 (2005); Average household income: $73,168 (2005); Percent of households with income of $100,000 or more: 20.7% (2005); Poverty rate: 5.0% (2000).
Taxes: Total city taxes per capita: $208 (2004); City property taxes per capita: $165 (2004).
Education: Percent of population age 25 and over with: High school diploma (including GED) or higher: 86.2% (2005); Bachelor's degree or higher: 32.9% (2005); Master's degree or higher: 14.6% (2005).
Housing: Homeownership rate: 74.5% (2005); Median home value: $127,451 (2005); Median rent: $466 per month (2000); Median age of housing: 41 years (2000).
Transportation: Commute to work: 96.6% car, 0.4% public transportation, 1.1% walk, 1.6% work from home (2000); Travel time to work: 52.8% less than 15 minutes, 37.0% 15 to 30 minutes, 5.0% 30 to 45 minutes, 1.3% 45 to 60 minutes, 3.8% 60 minutes or more (2000)

Additional Information Contacts

Town of New Hartford . . . . (315) 733-7500
  http://www.town.new-hartford.ny.us/

NEW YORK MILLS
(village). Covers a land area of 1.137 square miles and a water area of 0 square miles. Located at 43.10° N. Lat.; 75.29° W. Long.
History: Incorporated 1922.
Population: 3,534 (1990); 3,191 (2000); 3,145 (2005); 3,117 (2010 projected); Race: 98.2% White, 0.3% Black, 0.4% Asian, 1.2% Hispanic of any race (2005); Density: 2,767.1 persons per square mile (2005); Average household size: 2.02 (2005); Median age: 41.7 (2005); Males per 100 females: 83.3 (2005); Marriage status: 26.8% never married, 49.6% now married, 12.4% widowed, 11.2% divorced (2000); Foreign born: 2.3% (2000); Ancestry (includes multiple ancestries): 37.0% Polish, 19.2% Italian, 16.2% German, 15.3% Irish, 9.3% French (except Basque) (2000).
Economy: Manufacturing: machinery, textiles. Single-family building permits issued: 2 (2005); Multi-family building permits issued: 0 (2005); Employment by occupation: 10.4% management, 28.6% professional, 18.1% services, 25.6% sales, 1.5% farming, 7.3% construction, 8.5% production (2000).
Income: Per capita income: $22,363 (2005); Median household income: $35,100 (2005); Average household income: $45,159 (2005); Percent of

households with income of $100,000 or more: 7.2% (2005); Poverty rate: 10.7% (2000).
Education: Percent of population age 25 and over with: High school diploma (including GED) or higher: 80.4% (2005); Bachelor's degree or higher: 15.9% (2005); Master's degree or higher: 5.2% (2005).

School District(s)
New York Mills Union Free School District (KG-12)
   2003-04 Enrollment: 583 . . . . (315) 768-8127
Housing: Homeownership rate: 50.6% (2005); Median home value: $108,589 (2005); Median rent: $400 per month (2000); Median age of housing: 53 years (2000).
Safety: Violent crime rate: 31.6 per 10,000 population; Property crime rate: 221.3 per 10,000 population (2004).
Transportation: Commute to work: 98.0% car, 0.0% public transportation, 1.5% walk, 0.0% work from home (2000); Travel time to work: 55.5% less than 15 minutes, 34.2% 15 to 30 minutes, 4.9% 30 to 45 minutes, 1.7% 45 to 60 minutes, 3.7% 60 minutes or more (2000)

ONEIDA CASTLE (village). Covers a land area of 0.522 square miles and a water area of 0 square miles. Located at 43.07° N. Lat.; 75.63° W. Long.
History: Center of Oneida Territory, site of chief settlement of Oneida people.
Population: 671 (1990); 627 (2000); 604 (2005); 592 (2010 projected); Race: 98.0% White, 0.0% Black, 0.3% Asian, 0.7% Hispanic of any race (2005); Density: 1,157.1 persons per square mile (2005); Average household size: 2.33 (2005); Median age: 42.4 (2005); Males per 100 females: 98.0 (2005); Marriage status: 23.3% never married, 61.3% now married, 8.8% widowed, 6.7% divorced (2000); Foreign born: 3.8% (2000); Ancestry (includes multiple ancestries): 20.3% English, 19.8% German, 18.7% Irish, 17.7% Italian, 7.1% United States or American (2000).
Economy: Single-family building permits issued: 0 (2005); Multi-family building permits issued: 0 (2005); Employment by occupation: 13.8% management, 23.0% professional, 16.6% services, 24.8% sales, 0.0% farming, 6.4% construction, 15.3% production (2000).
Income: Per capita income: $23,365 (2005); Median household income: $45,735 (2005); Average household income: $54,488 (2005); Percent of households with income of $100,000 or more: 12.0% (2005); Poverty rate: 6.8% (2000).
Education: Percent of population age 25 and over with: High school diploma (including GED) or higher: 90.4% (2005); Bachelor's degree or higher: 26.0% (2005); Master's degree or higher: 6.4% (2005).
Housing: Homeownership rate: 70.3% (2005); Median home value: $116,129 (2005); Median rent: $443 per month (2000); Median age of housing: 60+ years (2000).
Transportation: Commute to work: 95.7% car, 0.0% public transportation, 3.1% walk, 1.2% work from home (2000); Travel time to work: 64.1% less than 15 minutes, 11.8% 15 to 30 minutes, 13.9% 30 to 45 minutes, 7.1% 45 to 60 minutes, 3.1% 60 minutes or more (2000)

ORISKANY (village). Covers a land area of 0.830 square miles and a water area of 0 square miles. Located at 43.15° N. Lat.; 75.33° W. Long. Elevation is 423 feet.
History: Obelisk at Oriskany Battlefield (Northwest) marks site of an engagement (Aug. 6, 1777) of the Saratoga campaign, one of the bloodiest battles of the American Revolution. Incorporated 1914.
Population: 1,573 (1990); 1,459 (2000); 1,430 (2005); 1,397 (2010 projected); Race: 98.7% White, 0.3% Black, 0.9% Asian, 0.5% Hispanic of any race (2005); Density: 1,723.0 persons per square mile (2005); Average household size: 2.60 (2005); Median age: 42.3 (2005); Males per 100 females: 81.7 (2005); Marriage status: 22.8% never married, 54.6% now married, 15.6% widowed, 7.0% divorced (2000); Foreign born: 2.1% (2000); Ancestry (includes multiple ancestries): 21.4% German, 21.0% Irish, 17.0% English, 16.4% Italian, 10.6% Polish (2000).
Economy: Manufacturing: transportation equipment, fabricated metal products. Single-family building permits issued: 0 (2005); Multi-family building permits issued: 0 (2005); Employment by occupation: 11.1% management, 20.0% professional, 20.8% services, 25.2% sales, 0.8% farming, 7.3% construction, 14.9% production (2000).
Income: Per capita income: $20,407 (2005); Median household income: $44,040 (2005); Average household income: $52,092 (2005); Percent of households with income of $100,000 or more: 8.9% (2005); Poverty rate: 10.0% (2000).

Education: Percent of population age 25 and over with: High school diploma (including GED) or higher: 86.7% (2005); Bachelor's degree or higher: 14.9% (2005); Master's degree or higher: 5.1% (2005).

School District(s)
Oriskany Central School District (KG-12)
   2003-04 Enrollment: 772 . . . . (315) 768-2058
Housing: Homeownership rate: 71.9% (2005); Median home value: $107,772 (2005); Median rent: $421 per month (2000); Median age of housing: 51 years (2000).
Safety: Violent crime rate: 6.9 per 10,000 population; Property crime rate: 104.1 per 10,000 population (2004).
Transportation: Commute to work: 95.1% car, 0.3% public transportation, 2.5% walk, 1.8% work from home (2000); Travel time to work: 50.1% less than 15 minutes, 41.6% 15 to 30 minutes, 4.1% 30 to 45 minutes, 2.4% 45 to 60 minutes, 1.9% 60 minutes or more (2000)

ORISKANY FALLS (village). Covers a land area of 0.490 square miles and a water area of 0 square miles. Located at 42.93° N. Lat.; 75.46° W. Long.
Population: 795 (1990); 698 (2000); 663 (2005); 649 (2010 projected); Race: 98.2% White, 0.5% Black, 0.5% Asian, 0.6% Hispanic of any race (2005); Density: 1,351.7 persons per square mile (2005); Average household size: 2.33 (2005); Median age: 39.2 (2005); Males per 100 females: 96.2 (2005); Marriage status: 26.8% never married, 49.7% now married, 13.0% widowed, 10.4% divorced (2000); Foreign born: 1.6% (2000); Ancestry (includes multiple ancestries): 25.4% English, 20.0% Irish, 16.1% German, 8.4% United States or American, 7.8% French Canadian (2000).
Economy: Manufacturing of apparel. Single-family building permits issued: 0 (2005); Multi-family building permits issued: 0 (2005); Employment by occupation: 7.3% management, 13.9% professional, 24.7% services, 24.4% sales, 3.1% farming, 10.5% construction, 16.0% production (2000).
Income: Per capita income: $18,457 (2005); Median household income: $31,154 (2005); Average household income: $41,708 (2005); Percent of households with income of $100,000 or more: 6.0% (2005); Poverty rate: 16.5% (2000).
Education: Percent of population age 25 and over with: High school diploma (including GED) or higher: 75.3% (2005); Bachelor's degree or higher: 7.7% (2005); Master's degree or higher: 2.4% (2005).
Housing: Homeownership rate: 57.7% (2005); Median home value: $78,868 (2005); Median rent: $362 per month (2000); Median age of housing: 60+ years (2000).
Transportation: Commute to work: 82.3% car, 0.0% public transportation, 13.4% walk, 3.6% work from home (2000); Travel time to work: 33.3% less than 15 minutes, 43.1% 15 to 30 minutes, 15.0% 30 to 45 minutes, 3.4% 45 to 60 minutes, 5.2% 60 minutes or more (2000)

PARIS (town). Covers a land area of 31.441 square miles and a water area of 0.012 square miles. Located at 42.98° N. Lat.; 75.26° W. Long.
Population: 4,414 (1990); 4,609 (2000); 4,569 (2005); 4,525 (2010 projected); Race: 98.1% White, 0.4% Black, 0.3% Asian, 0.6% Hispanic of any race (2005); Density: 145.3 persons per square mile (2005); Average household size: 2.63 (2005); Median age: 39.6 (2005); Males per 100 females: 96.5 (2005); Marriage status: 24.9% never married, 58.6% now married, 7.4% widowed, 9.1% divorced (2000); Foreign born: 1.1% (2000); Ancestry (includes multiple ancestries): 23.5% Irish, 20.7% German, 19.9% Italian, 16.1% English, 12.1% Polish (2000).
Economy: Single-family building permits issued: 12 (2005); Multi-family building permits issued: 0 (2005); Employment by occupation: 15.6% management, 20.9% professional, 13.4% services, 25.5% sales, 0.8% farming, 11.0% construction, 12.9% production (2000).
Income: Per capita income: $21,083 (2005); Median household income: $46,178 (2005); Average household income: $54,991 (2005); Percent of households with income of $100,000 or more: 11.5% (2005); Poverty rate: 7.3% (2000).
Education: Percent of population age 25 and over with: High school diploma (including GED) or higher: 88.5% (2005); Bachelor's degree or higher: 20.1% (2005); Master's degree or higher: 7.4% (2005).
Housing: Homeownership rate: 81.0% (2005); Median home value: $121,502 (2005); Median rent: $382 per month (2000); Median age of housing: 46 years (2000).
Transportation: Commute to work: 94.7% car, 0.2% public transportation, 2.4% walk, 2.2% work from home (2000); Travel time to work: 26.5% less than 15 minutes, 53.4% 15 to 30 minutes, 11.2% 30 to 45 minutes, 2.8% 45 to 60 minutes, 6.0% 60 minutes or more (2000)

Additional Information Contacts
Town of Paris.................................... (315) 839-5400
  http://town.paris.ny.us/content

PROSPECT
(village). Covers a land area of 0.204 square miles and a water area of 0 square miles. Located at 43.30° N. Lat.; 75.15° W. Long.
Population: 312 (1990); 330 (2000); 349 (2005); 365 (2010 projected); Race: 99.1% White, 0.6% Black, 0.0% Asian, 1.4% Hispanic of any race (2005); Density: 1,714.5 persons per square mile (2005); Average household size: 2.62 (2005); Median age: 36.8 (2005); Males per 100 females: 89.7 (2005); Marriage status: 28.9% never married, 56.6% now married, 5.6% widowed, 8.8% divorced (2000); Foreign born: 0.3% (2000); Ancestry (includes multiple ancestries): 17.6% Polish, 17.6% Irish, 16.4% German, 12.9% English, 12.6% Italian (2000).
Economy: Employment by occupation: 5.3% management, 21.8% professional, 15.3% services, 34.1% sales, 0.0% farming, 10.0% construction, 13.5% production (2000).
Income: Per capita income: $22,428 (2005); Median household income: $56,419 (2005); Average household income: $58,853 (2005); Percent of households with income of $100,000 or more: 12.0% (2005); Poverty rate: 5.4% (2000).
Education: Percent of population age 25 and over with: High school diploma (including GED) or higher: 92.8% (2005); Bachelor's degree or higher: 23.3% (2005); Master's degree or higher: 4.5% (2005).
Housing: Homeownership rate: 78.9% (2005); Median home value: $98,500 (2005); Median rent: $380 per month (2000); Median age of housing: 60+ years (2000).
Transportation: Commute to work: 92.4% car, 1.2% public transportation, 1.2% walk, 4.1% work from home (2000); Travel time to work: 22.7% less than 15 minutes, 41.1% 15 to 30 minutes, 28.2% 30 to 45 minutes, 2.5% 45 to 60 minutes, 5.5% 60 minutes or more (2000)

REMSEN
(village). Covers a land area of 0.371 square miles and a water area of 0 square miles. Located at 43.32° N. Lat.; 75.18° W. Long. Elevation is 1,171 feet.
Population: 518 (1990); 531 (2000); 507 (2005); 499 (2010 projected); Race: 96.4% White, 1.0% Black, 1.2% Asian, 0.0% Hispanic of any race (2005); Density: 1,367.2 persons per square mile (2005); Average household size: 2.59 (2005); Median age: 33.2 (2005); Males per 100 females: 92.0 (2005); Marriage status: 24.3% never married, 61.7% now married, 8.2% widowed, 5.8% divorced (2000); Foreign born: 1.2% (2000); Ancestry (includes multiple ancestries): 20.7% German, 16.8% Welsh, 15.2% Irish, 11.1% French (except Basque), 11.1% English (2000).
Economy: Employment by occupation: 5.0% management, 19.0% professional, 25.8% services, 18.6% sales, 1.8% farming, 11.8% construction, 18.1% production (2000).
Income: Per capita income: $15,917 (2005); Median household income: $33,974 (2005); Average household income: $41,173 (2005); Percent of households with income of $100,000 or more: 3.1% (2005); Poverty rate: 19.0% (2000).
Education: Percent of population age 25 and over with: High school diploma (including GED) or higher: 84.4% (2005); Bachelor's degree or higher: 7.5% (2005); Master's degree or higher: 1.6% (2005).
School District(s)
Remsen Central School District (KG-12)
  2003-04 Enrollment: 617......................... (315) 831-3797
Housing: Homeownership rate: 58.2% (2005); Median home value: $76,296 (2005); Median rent: $318 per month (2000); Median age of housing: 60+ years (2000).
Transportation: Commute to work: 88.1% car, 0.9% public transportation, 5.5% walk, 4.6% work from home (2000); Travel time to work: 33.0% less than 15 minutes, 33.5% 15 to 30 minutes, 25.8% 30 to 45 minutes, 2.4% 45 to 60 minutes, 5.3% 60 minutes or more (2000)

REMSEN
(town). Covers a land area of 35.389 square miles and a water area of 1.488 square miles. Located at 43.36° N. Lat.; 75.15° W. Long. Elevation is 1,171 feet.
History: Reconstructed log cabin of Baron von Steuben, drillmaster to Continental Army, state historic site, 2 miles West.
Population: 1,768 (1990); 1,958 (2000); 1,881 (2005); 1,847 (2010 projected); Race: 97.9% White, 0.4% Black, 0.6% Asian, 0.1% Hispanic of any race (2005); Density: 53.2 persons per square mile (2005); Average household size: 2.58 (2005); Median age: 37.4 (2005); Males per 100 females: 99.9 (2005); Marriage status: 24.8% never married, 59.6% now married, 6.5% widowed, 9.1% divorced (2000); Foreign born: 1.1% (2000); Ancestry (includes multiple ancestries): 20.6% German, 17.0% Welsh, 15.4% Irish, 12.3% English, 11.1% Italian (2000).
Economy: Single-family building permits issued: 8 (2005); Multi-family building permits issued: 0 (2005); Employment by occupation: 10.4% management, 20.5% professional, 19.2% services, 20.0% sales, 1.4% farming, 11.4% construction, 17.1% production (2000).
Income: Per capita income: $19,502 (2005); Median household income: $42,546 (2005); Average household income: $50,079 (2005); Percent of households with income of $100,000 or more: 7.1% (2005); Poverty rate: 11.2% (2000).
Education: Percent of population age 25 and over with: High school diploma (including GED) or higher: 82.9% (2005); Bachelor's degree or higher: 13.5% (2005); Master's degree or higher: 5.2% (2005).
Housing: Homeownership rate: 80.8% (2005); Median home value: $92,340 (2005); Median rent: $329 per month (2000); Median age of housing: 37 years (2000).
Transportation: Commute to work: 94.0% car, 0.7% public transportation, 2.0% walk, 3.1% work from home (2000); Travel time to work: 21.0% less than 15 minutes, 27.2% 15 to 30 minutes, 40.6% 30 to 45 minutes, 6.2% 45 to 60 minutes, 5.0% 60 minutes or more (2000)

ROME
(city). Covers a land area of 74.933 square miles and a water area of 0.747 square miles. Located at 43.21° N. Lat.; 75.46° W. Long. Elevation is 445 feet.
History: Laid out c.1786 on the site of Fort Stanwix. The city was a busy portage point, and had great strategic importance during the French and Indian War and in the American Revolution. The Six Nation Treaty of 1768 was concluded here. Site of the Battle of Oriskany, one of the Revolution's bloodiest battles. Construction on the Erie Canal began (1817) in Rome. Incorporated as a city 1870.
Population: 44,350 (1990); 34,950 (2000); 34,421 (2005); 33,757 (2010 projected); Race: 85.8% White, 9.0% Black, 1.0% Asian, 6.4% Hispanic of any race (2005); Density: 459.4 persons per square mile (2005); Average household size: 2.54 (2005); Median age: 38.9 (2005); Males per 100 females: 107.3 (2005); Marriage status: 30.0% never married, 50.6% now married, 9.3% widowed, 10.1% divorced (2000); Foreign born: 3.8% (2000); Ancestry (includes multiple ancestries): 25.7% Italian, 15.6% Irish, 14.7% German, 9.7% Other groups, 9.5% English (2000).
Economy: Cooking utensils, machine tools and strip steel are among its products. Nearby are realigned Griffiss Air Force Base and Rome Development Center. Unemployment rate: 5.2% (2005); Total civilian labor force: 15,126 (2005); Single-family building permits issued: 17 (2005); Multi-family building permits issued: 0 (2005); Employment by occupation: 11.0% management, 19.6% professional, 21.5% services, 26.2% sales, 0.3% farming, 6.3% construction, 15.2% production (2000).
Income: Per capita income: $20,559 (2005); Median household income: $37,847 (2005); Average household income: $48,187 (2005); Percent of households with income of $100,000 or more: 8.8% (2005); Poverty rate: 15.0% (2000).
Education: Percent of population age 25 and over with: High school diploma (including GED) or higher: 73.7% (2005); Bachelor's degree or higher: 15.7% (2005); Master's degree or higher: 5.7% (2005).
School District(s)
Rome City School District (PK-12)
  2003-04 Enrollment: 6,199 .... (315) 338-6500
Housing: Homeownership rate: 58.2% (2005); Median home value: $87,043 (2005); Median rent: $369 per month (2000); Median age of housing: 50 years (2000).
Hospitals: Central New York Disabilities Services Office (844 beds); Rome Memorial Hospital (129 beds)
Safety: Violent crime rate: 13.9 per 10,000 population; Property crime rate: 203.3 per 10,000 population (2004).
Newspapers: Daily Sentinel (Circulation 14,849); Rome Observer (General - Circulation 11,000)
Transportation: Commute to work: 92.2% car, 1.9% public transportation, 3.6% walk, 1.5% work from home (2000); Travel time to work: 49.2% less than 15 minutes, 32.5% 15 to 30 minutes, 11.8% 30 to 45 minutes, 2.9% 45 to 60 minutes, 3.6% 60 minutes or more (2000); Amtrak: Service available.
Additional Information Contacts
City of Rome .... (315) 336-6000
  http://www.romenewyork.com/
Rome Chamber of Commerce...................... (315) 337-1700
  http://www.romechamber.com

SANGERFIELD (town). Covers a land area of 30.812 square miles and a water area of 0.162 square miles. Located at 42.91° N. Lat.; 75.38° W. Long. Elevation is 1,248 feet.
Population: 2,460 (1990); 2,610 (2000); 2,595 (2005); 2,575 (2010 projected); Race: 98.2% White, 0.3% Black, 0.5% Asian, 0.7% Hispanic of any race (2005); Density: 84.2 persons per square mile (2005); Average household size: 2.73 (2005); Median age: 38.9 (2005); Males per 100 females: 92.2 (2005); Marriage status: 22.0% never married, 59.9% now married, 9.0% widowed, 9.2% divorced (2000); Foreign born: 1.9% (2000); Ancestry (includes multiple ancestries): 21.7% English, 19.4% Irish, 17.7% German, 9.3% Polish, 7.8% French (except Basque) (2000).
Economy: Region of dairy farming; feed mills; mobile homes. Single-family building permits issued: 1 (2005); Multi-family building permits issued: 0 (2005); Employment by occupation: 9.0% management, 21.2% professional, 17.5% services, 26.1% sales, 1.2% farming, 10.3% construction, 14.7% production (2000).
Income: Per capita income: $20,277 (2005); Median household income: $43,206 (2005); Average household income: $55,084 (2005); Percent of households with income of $100,000 or more: 11.4% (2005); Poverty rate: 9.7% (2000).
Education: Percent of population age 25 and over with: High school diploma (including GED) or higher: 83.6% (2005); Bachelor's degree or higher: 18.5% (2005); Master's degree or higher: 6.8% (2005).
Housing: Homeownership rate: 68.2% (2005); Median home value: $107,366 (2005); Median rent: $379 per month (2000); Median age of housing: 60+ years (2000).
Transportation: Commute to work: 89.2% car, 0.7% public transportation, 5.7% walk, 4.3% work from home (2000); Travel time to work: 32.3% less than 15 minutes, 34.9% 15 to 30 minutes, 21.5% 30 to 45 minutes, 3.4% 45 to 60 minutes, 7.9% 60 minutes or more (2000)

SAUQUOIT (unincorporated postal area, zip code 13456). Covers a land area of 25.931 square miles and a water area of 0 square miles. Located at 43.00° N. Lat.; 75.26° W. Long. Elevation is 820 feet.
Population: 0 (2000); Race: 98.7% White, 0.1% Black, 0.3% Asian, 0.5% Hispanic of any race (2000); Density: 0.0 persons per square mile (2000); Age: 26.9% under 18, 13.2% over 64 (2000); Marriage status: 22.5% never married, 60.6% now married, 8.6% widowed, 8.3% divorced (2000); Foreign born: 1.6% (2000); Ancestry (includes multiple ancestries): 23.3% Italian, 21.8% Irish, 18.6% German, 15.7% English, 12.4% Polish (2000).
Economy: Employment by occupation: 17.0% management, 21.7% professional, 13.1% services, 25.7% sales, 1.1% farming, 9.6% construction, 11.8% production (2000).
Income: Per capita income: $19,140 (2000); Median household income: $43,488 (2000); Poverty rate: 5.1% (2000).
Education: Percent of population age 25 and over with: High school diploma (including GED) or higher: 87.4% (2000); Bachelor's degree or higher: 21.2% (2000).
School District(s)
Sauquoit Valley Central School District (KG-12)
   2003-04 Enrollment: 1,293 . . . . (315) 839-6311
Housing: Homeownership rate: 82.6% (2000); Median home value: $90,800 (2000); Median rent: $401 per month (2000); Median age of housing: 41 years (2000).
Transportation: Commute to work: 96.1% car, 0.2% public transportation, 1.5% walk, 2.2% work from home (2000); Travel time to work: 30.9% less than 15 minutes, 53.5% 15 to 30 minutes, 7.6% 30 to 45 minutes, 2.1% 45 to 60 minutes, 5.8% 60 minutes or more (2000)

SHERRILL (city). Covers a land area of 2.024 square miles and a water area of 0 square miles. Located at 43.07° N. Lat.; 75.59° W. Long.
History: Incorporated 1916.
Population: 2,869 (1990); 3,147 (2000); 3,090 (2005); 3,029 (2010 projected); Race: 97.8% White, 0.2% Black, 0.8% Asian, 1.2% Hispanic of any race (2005); Density: 1,526.4 persons per square mile (2005); Average household size: 2.44 (2005); Median age: 41.5 (2005); Males per 100 females: 88.1 (2005); Marriage status: 19.8% never married, 62.9% now married, 9.1% widowed, 8.2% divorced (2000); Foreign born: 2.2% (2000); Ancestry (includes multiple ancestries): 26.8% German, 23.9% English, 23.0% Irish, 14.3% Italian, 5.6% Polish (2000).
Economy: Manufacturing of pumps. Single-family building permits issued: 0 (2005); Multi-family building permits issued: 0 (2005); Employment by occupation: 14.7% management, 20.3% professional, 12.9% services, 32.7% sales, 0.3% farming, 7.6% construction, 11.7% production (2000).
Income: Per capita income: $26,759 (2005); Median household income: $56,747 (2005); Average household income: $64,955 (2005); Percent of households with income of $100,000 or more: 16.5% (2005); Poverty rate: 2.2% (2000).
Education: Percent of population age 25 and over with: High school diploma (including GED) or higher: 89.1% (2005); Bachelor's degree or higher: 24.9% (2005); Master's degree or higher: 8.7% (2005).
School District(s)
Sherrill City School District (PK-12)
   2003-04 Enrollment: 2,425 . . . . (315) 829-2520
Housing: Homeownership rate: 77.5% (2005); Median home value: $126,406 (2005); Median rent: $366 per month (2000); Median age of housing: 47 years (2000).
Safety: Violent crime rate: 6.4 per 10,000 population; Property crime rate: 202.2 per 10,000 population (2004).
Transportation: Commute to work: 93.3% car, 0.3% public transportation, 3.9% walk, 2.0% work from home (2000); Travel time to work: 53.8% less than 15 minutes, 22.2% 15 to 30 minutes, 14.6% 30 to 45 minutes, 6.7% 45 to 60 minutes, 2.7% 60 minutes or more (2000)
Additional Information Contacts
City of Sherrill. . . . . (315) 363-2440
   http://www.sherrillny.org/

STEUBEN (town). Covers a land area of 42.706 square miles and a water area of 0 square miles. Located at 43.33° N. Lat.; 75.24° W. Long. Elevation is 932 feet.
Population: 1,006 (1990); 1,172 (2000); 1,206 (2005); 1,226 (2010 projected); Race: 98.4% White, 0.5% Black, 0.4% Asian, 0.4% Hispanic of any race (2005); Density: 28.2 persons per square mile (2005); Average household size: 2.69 (2005); Median age: 39.4 (2005); Males per 100 females: 91.7 (2005); Marriage status: 23.2% never married, 62.6% now married, 6.5% widowed, 7.7% divorced (2000); Foreign born: 0.2% (2000); Ancestry (includes multiple ancestries): 27.1% German, 16.9% Irish, 13.4% Welsh, 13.0% English, 11.8% Polish (2000).
Economy: Single-family building permits issued: 5 (2005); Multi-family building permits issued: 0 (2005); Employment by occupation: 10.5% management, 20.0% professional, 19.8% services, 21.8% sales, 2.0% farming, 10.3% construction, 15.6% production (2000).
Income: Per capita income: $21,182 (2005); Median household income: $47,079 (2005); Average household income: $56,297 (2005); Percent of households with income of $100,000 or more: 9.6% (2005); Poverty rate: 9.9% (2000).
Education: Percent of population age 25 and over with: High school diploma (including GED) or higher: 85.9% (2005); Bachelor's degree or higher: 14.5% (2005); Master's degree or higher: 6.2% (2005).
Housing: Homeownership rate: 86.0% (2005); Median home value: $109,489 (2005); Median rent: $377 per month (2000); Median age of housing: 24 years (2000).
Transportation: Commute to work: 90.3% car, 0.0% public transportation, 2.0% walk, 5.8% work from home (2000); Travel time to work: 16.3% less than 15 minutes, 38.1% 15 to 30 minutes, 38.4% 30 to 45 minutes, 5.8% 45 to 60 minutes, 1.4% 60 minutes or more (2000)

STITTVILLE (unincorporated postal area, zip code 13469). Covers a land area of 3.755 square miles and a water area of 0.070 square miles. Located at 43.22° N. Lat.; 75.29° W. Long.
Population: 0 (2000); Race: 98.3% White, 0.0% Black, 0.0% Asian, 0.0% Hispanic of any race (2000); Density: 0.0 persons per square mile (2000); Age: 31.3% under 18, 10.1% over 64 (2000); Marriage status: 33.6% never married, 53.8% now married, 4.3% widowed, 8.4% divorced (2000); Foreign born: 0.9% (2000); Ancestry (includes multiple ancestries): 26.8% Irish, 18.2% German, 15.9% Italian, 11.5% Welsh, 8.1% Polish (2000).
Economy: Employment by occupation: 2.2% management, 13.6% professional, 24.8% services, 24.8% sales, 0.0% farming, 17.1% construction, 17.6% production (2000).
Income: Per capita income: $19,017 (2000); Median household income: $44,722 (2000); Poverty rate: 5.4% (2000).
Education: Percent of population age 25 and over with: High school diploma (including GED) or higher: 90.4% (2000); Bachelor's degree or higher: 14.3% (2000).
Housing: Homeownership rate: 80.4% (2000); Median home value: $80,200 (2000); Median rent: $462 per month (2000); Median age of housing: 43 years (2000).
Transportation: Commute to work: 95.2% car, 0.0% public transportation, 0.0% walk, 0.0% work from home (2000); Travel time to work: 25.6% less

than 15 minutes, 53.0% 15 to 30 minutes, 15.3% 30 to 45 minutes, 0.0% 45 to 60 minutes, 6.0% 60 minutes or more (2000)

SYLVAN BEACH (village). Covers a land area of 0.734 square miles and a water area of 0.027 square miles. Located at 43.20° N. Lat.; 75.72° W. Long.
Population: 1,170 (1990); 1,071 (2000); 1,020 (2005); 998 (2010 projected); Race: 97.4% White, 1.0% Black, 0.3% Asian, 0.9% Hispanic of any race (2005); Density: 1,389.0 persons per square mile (2005); Average household size: 2.22 (2005); Median age: 42.5 (2005); Males per 100 females: 104.4 (2005); Marriage status: 25.6% never married, 53.5% now married, 8.5% widowed, 12.4% divorced (2000); Foreign born: 1.0% (2000); Ancestry (includes multiple ancestries): 18.2% German, 18.2% Irish, 15.5% Italian, 12.5% United States or American, 9.1% English (2000).
Economy: Resort village. Single-family building permits issued: 3 (2005); Multi-family building permits issued: 0 (2005); Employment by occupation: 14.3% management, 9.1% professional, 18.4% services, 26.9% sales, 0.0% farming, 6.9% construction, 24.3% production (2000).
Income: Per capita income: $18,495 (2005); Median household income: $32,821 (2005); Average household income: $41,011 (2005); Percent of households with income of $100,000 or more: 4.6% (2005); Poverty rate: 17.0% (2000).
Education: Percent of population age 25 and over with: High school diploma (including GED) or higher: 75.5% (2005); Bachelor's degree or higher: 8.2% (2005); Master's degree or higher: 3.1% (2005).
Housing: Homeownership rate: 73.9% (2005); Median home value: $76,667 (2005); Median rent: $430 per month (2000); Median age of housing: 42 years (2000).
Transportation: Commute to work: 94.0% car, 0.0% public transportation, 5.4% walk, 0.0% work from home (2000); Travel time to work: 25.9% less than 15 minutes, 35.5% 15 to 30 minutes, 23.7% 30 to 45 minutes, 10.3% 45 to 60 minutes, 4.7% 60 minutes or more (2000)

TABERG (unincorporated postal area, zip code 13471). Covers a land area of 81.224 square miles and a water area of 0.186 square miles. Located at 43.34° N. Lat.; 75.60° W. Long.
Population: 0 (2000); Race: 95.6% White, 3.2% Black, 0.1% Asian, 0.2% Hispanic of any race (2000); Density: 0.0 persons per square mile (2000); Age: 31.7% under 18, 8.8% over 64 (2000); Marriage status: 20.9% never married, 65.4% now married, 5.3% widowed, 8.3% divorced (2000); Foreign born: 0.7% (2000); Ancestry (includes multiple ancestries): 21.4% Irish, 18.4% German, 11.4% United States or American, 10.7% English, 9.8% Italian (2000).
Economy: Employment by occupation: 6.9% management, 9.5% professional, 16.1% services, 24.8% sales, 0.6% farming, 11.3% construction, 30.8% production (2000).
Income: Per capita income: $14,674 (2000); Median household income: $36,571 (2000); Poverty rate: 10.8% (2000).
Education: Percent of population age 25 and over with: High school diploma (including GED) or higher: 80.2% (2000); Bachelor's degree or higher: 6.3% (2000).

School District(s)
Camden Central School District (PK-12)
    2003-04 Enrollment: 2,845 . . . . (315) 245-4075

Housing: Homeownership rate: 83.7% (2000); Median home value: $73,700 (2000); Median rent: $338 per month (2000); Median age of housing: 24 years (2000).
Transportation: Commute to work: 94.3% car, 0.3% public transportation, 1.5% walk, 3.9% work from home (2000); Travel time to work: 19.2% less than 15 minutes, 43.0% 15 to 30 minutes, 23.3% 30 to 45 minutes, 8.8% 45 to 60 minutes, 5.6% 60 minutes or more (2000)

TRENTON (town). Aka Barneveld. Covers a land area of 43.316 square miles and a water area of 0.391 square miles. Located at 43.25° N. Lat.; 75.19° W. Long.
Population: 4,682 (1990); 4,670 (2000); 4,729 (2005); 4,785 (2010 projected); Race: 97.7% White, 0.4% Black, 0.8% Asian, 0.4% Hispanic of any race (2005); Density: 109.2 persons per square mile (2005); Average household size: 2.58 (2005); Median age: 40.5 (2005); Males per 100 females: 98.0 (2005); Marriage status: 22.1% never married, 61.8% now married, 4.8% widowed, 11.3% divorced (2000); Foreign born: 1.7% (2000); Ancestry (includes multiple ancestries): 22.3% Irish, 18.3% German, 16.1% Polish, 13.4% English, 13.2% Italian (2000).
Economy: Single-family building permits issued: 12 (2005); Multi-family building permits issued: 0 (2005); Employment by occupation: 13.5% management, 23.9% professional, 14.2% services, 25.5% sales, 0.5% farming, 9.3% construction, 13.1% production (2000).
Income: Per capita income: $28,144 (2005); Median household income: $59,883 (2005); Average household income: $72,350 (2005); Percent of households with income of $100,000 or more: 18.5% (2005); Poverty rate: 5.9% (2000).
Taxes: Total city taxes per capita: $135 (2004); City property taxes per capita: $114 (2004).
Education: Percent of population age 25 and over with: High school diploma (including GED) or higher: 90.8% (2005); Bachelor's degree or higher: 26.0% (2005); Master's degree or higher: 11.0% (2005).
Housing: Homeownership rate: 84.0% (2005); Median home value: $122,983 (2005); Median rent: $398 per month (2000); Median age of housing: 41 years (2000).
Transportation: Commute to work: 95.8% car, 0.1% public transportation, 0.9% walk, 2.7% work from home (2000); Travel time to work: 20.3% less than 15 minutes, 54.4% 15 to 30 minutes, 18.3% 30 to 45 minutes, 3.0% 45 to 60 minutes, 4.1% 60 minutes or more (2000)

UTICA (city). Covers a land area of 16.348 square miles and a water area of 0.261 square miles. Located at 43.09° N. Lat.; 75.23° W. Long. Elevation is 407 feet.
History: The area around Utica was called "Yah-nun-da-da-sis," meaning "around the hill," by the Oneida people, in reference to the way their trails circled the nearby hills. The site was included in Cosby's Manor, a grant of 22,000 acres made by George II to William Cosby, governor of the Province of New York, and others in 1734. In 1758 the British erected Fort Schuyler. It was abandoned in the early 1760's. In 1798 the settlement was incorporated as a village, and the present name was determined by a chance selection from a hatful of paper slips. The Erie Canal brought new prosperity and the city was chartered in 1832. The textile industry, the backbone of Utica's economic structure, began with the opening of the woolen and cotton mills in the mid-1840's.
Population: 68,637 (1990); 60,651 (2000); 59,216 (2005); 57,695 (2010 projected); Race: 77.1% White, 13.8% Black, 3.1% Asian, 7.2% Hispanic of any race (2005); Density: 3,622.2 persons per square mile (2005); Average household size: 2.41 (2005); Median age: 37.8 (2005); Males per 100 females: 89.9 (2005); Marriage status: 34.0% never married, 46.1% now married, 11.2% widowed, 8.7% divorced (2000); Foreign born: 11.9% (2000); Ancestry (includes multiple ancestries): 26.1% Italian, 19.6% Other groups, 12.3% Irish, 10.0% German, 8.6% Polish (2000).
Economy: Unemployment rate: 5.4% (2005); Total civilian labor force: 26,258 (2005); Single-family building permits issued: 6 (2005); Multi-family building permits issued: 3 (2005); Employment by occupation: 9.0% management, 18.1% professional, 21.1% services, 27.9% sales, 0.3% farming, 5.9% construction, 17.7% production (2000).
Income: Per capita income: $16,336 (2005); Median household income: $26,990 (2005); Average household income: $37,403 (2005); Percent of households with income of $100,000 or more: 5.1% (2005); Poverty rate: 24.5% (2000).
Education: Percent of population age 25 and over with: High school diploma (including GED) or higher: 72.9% (2005); Bachelor's degree or higher: 15.5% (2005); Master's degree or higher: 6.3% (2005).

School District(s)
Utica City School District (KG-12)
    2003-04 Enrollment: 9,070 . . . . (315) 792-2222
Whitesboro Central School District (KG-12)
    2003-04 Enrollment: 3,863 . . . . (315) 266-3303

Four-year College(s)
SUNY Institute of Technology at Utica-Rome (Public)
    Fall 2004 Enrollment: 2,432. . . . . (315) 792-7100
    2005-06 Tuition: In-state $5,285; Out-of-state $11,545
Utica College
    Fall 2004 Enrollment: 2,652. . . . . (315) 792-3111
    2005-06 Tuition: In-state $22,030; Out-of-state $22,030

Two-year College(s)
Faxton-St Luke's Healthcare School of Radiologic Technology
    Fall 2004 Enrollment: 30 . . . . (315) 624-6136
    2005-06 Tuition: In-state $5,000; Out-of-state $5,000
Mohawk Valley Community College-Utica Branch (Public)
    Fall 2004 Enrollment: 6,068. . . . . (315) 792-5400
    2005-06 Tuition: In-state $3,294; Out-of-state $6,244

Saint Elizabeth College of Nursing
  Fall 2004 Enrollment: 193 . . . . (315) 798-8144
  2005-06 Tuition: In-state $8,001; Out-of-state $10,325
Saint Elizabeth Medical Center School of Radiography
  Fall 2004 Enrollment: 21 . . . . (315) 798-8258
  2005-06 Tuition: In-state $3,000; Out-of-state $3,000
Utica School of Commerce
  Fall 2004 Enrollment: 355 . . . . (315) 733-2307
  2005-06 Tuition: In-state $10,140; Out-of-state $10,140
Housing: Homeownership rate: 49.2% (2005); Median home value: $75,863 (2005); Median rent: $352 per month (2000); Median age of housing: 60+ years (2000).
Hospitals: Faxton - St. Luke's Healthcare (432 beds); St. Elizabeth Medical Center (201 beds)
Safety: Violent crime rate: 48.2 per 10,000 population; Property crime rate: 420.5 per 10,000 population (2004).
Newspapers: The Observer-Dispatch (Circulation 45,965)
Transportation: Commute to work: 86.2% car, 4.3% public transportation, 6.3% walk, 2.0% work from home (2000); Travel time to work: 49.4% less than 15 minutes, 36.5% 15 to 30 minutes, 8.3% 30 to 45 minutes, 1.8% 45 to 60 minutes, 3.9% 60 minutes or more (2000); Amtrak: Service available.
Additional Information Contacts
City of Utica . . . . (315) 792-0113
  http://www.cityofutica.com/
Mohawk Valley Chamber of Commerce . . . . (315) 724-3151
  http://www.mvchamber.org

VERNON (village). Covers a land area of 0.913 square miles and a water area of 0 square miles. Located at 43.08° N. Lat.; 75.54° W. Long.
Population: 1,288 (1990); 1,155 (2000); 1,177 (2005); 1,201 (2010 projected); Race: 97.6% White, 1.6% Black, 0.1% Asian, 1.4% Hispanic of any race (2005); Density: 1,288.6 persons per square mile (2005); Average household size: 2.26 (2005); Median age: 37.8 (2005); Males per 100 females: 99.5 (2005); Marriage status: 28.8% never married, 50.4% now married, 6.2% widowed, 14.6% divorced (2000); Foreign born: 2.7% (2000); Ancestry (includes multiple ancestries): 19.8% German, 17.4% Irish, 16.2% English, 10.2% Italian, 10.2% Polish (2000).
Economy: Single-family building permits issued: 0 (2005); Multi-family building permits issued: 0 (2005); Employment by occupation: 9.0% management, 21.2% professional, 18.0% services, 22.7% sales, 0.0% farming, 5.9% construction, 23.2% production (2000).
Income: Per capita income: $21,810 (2005); Median household income: $38,618 (2005); Average household income: $48,349 (2005); Percent of households with income of $100,000 or more: 9.4% (2005); Poverty rate: 9.7% (2000).
Education: Percent of population age 25 and over with: High school diploma (including GED) or higher: 85.4% (2005); Bachelor's degree or higher: 20.4% (2005); Master's degree or higher: 5.5% (2005).
School District(s)
Sherrill City School District (PK-12)
  2003-04 Enrollment: 2,425 . . . . (315) 829-2520
Housing: Homeownership rate: 53.6% (2005); Median home value: $98,229 (2005); Median rent: $394 per month (2000); Median age of housing: 59 years (2000).
Safety: Violent crime rate: 0.0 per 10,000 population; Property crime rate: 237.9 per 10,000 population (2004).
Transportation: Commute to work: 94.3% car, 1.1% public transportation, 2.4% walk, 2.2% work from home (2000); Travel time to work: 43.6% less than 15 minutes, 37.5% 15 to 30 minutes, 9.5% 30 to 45 minutes, 4.2% 45 to 60 minutes, 5.3% 60 minutes or more (2000)

VERNON (town). Covers a land area of 38.124 square miles and a water area of 0 square miles. Located at 43.06° N. Lat.; 75.53° W. Long.
Population: 5,333 (1990); 5,335 (2000); 5,439 (2005); 5,533 (2010 projected); Race: 97.8% White, 0.5% Black, 0.4% Asian, 1.0% Hispanic of any race (2005); Density: 142.7 persons per square mile (2005); Average household size: 2.48 (2005); Median age: 39.1 (2005); Males per 100 females: 97.5 (2005); Marriage status: 24.3% never married, 60.9% now married, 5.7% widowed, 9.2% divorced (2000); Foreign born: 2.7% (2000); Ancestry (includes multiple ancestries): 21.2% German, 18.8% English, 16.1% Irish, 11.4% Italian, 8.8% Polish (2000).
Economy: Some manufacturing. Single-family building permits issued: 18 (2005); Multi-family building permits issued: 0 (2005); Employment by occupation: 12.8% management, 19.6% professional, 17.0% services, 22.2% sales, 1.7% farming, 6.7% construction, 19.9% production (2000).
Income: Per capita income: $21,442 (2005); Median household income: $43,445 (2005); Average household income: $52,795 (2005); Percent of households with income of $100,000 or more: 9.6% (2005); Poverty rate: 9.8% (2000).
Education: Percent of population age 25 and over with: High school diploma (including GED) or higher: 85.4% (2005); Bachelor's degree or higher: 17.3% (2005); Master's degree or higher: 4.8% (2005).
Housing: Homeownership rate: 75.5% (2005); Median home value: $103,950 (2005); Median rent: $417 per month (2000); Median age of housing: 44 years (2000).
Transportation: Commute to work: 91.0% car, 1.3% public transportation, 2.1% walk, 4.8% work from home (2000); Travel time to work: 42.0% less than 15 minutes, 33.0% 15 to 30 minutes, 13.9% 30 to 45 minutes, 5.7% 45 to 60 minutes, 5.3% 60 minutes or more (2000)

VERNON CENTER (unincorporated postal area, zip code 13477). Covers a land area of 20.957 square miles and a water area of 0 square miles. Located at 43.03° N. Lat.; 75.50° W. Long. Elevation is 807 feet.
Population: 0 (2000); Race: 98.5% White, 0.1% Black, 0.0% Asian, 1.4% Hispanic of any race (2000); Density: 0.0 persons per square mile (2000); Age: 28.3% under 18, 10.3% over 64 (2000); Marriage status: 25.7% never married, 59.5% now married, 4.8% widowed, 10.0% divorced (2000); Foreign born: 2.1% (2000); Ancestry (includes multiple ancestries): 24.0% German, 21.5% English, 12.4% Irish, 9.7% United States or American, 7.6% Welsh (2000).
Economy: Employment by occupation: 14.7% management, 11.8% professional, 12.6% services, 24.1% sales, 6.7% farming, 7.1% construction, 23.1% production (2000).
Income: Per capita income: $15,385 (2000); Median household income: $37,857 (2000); Poverty rate: 11.3% (2000).
Education: Percent of population age 25 and over with: High school diploma (including GED) or higher: 82.9% (2000); Bachelor's degree or higher: 6.0% (2000).
Housing: Homeownership rate: 82.6% (2000); Median home value: $68,600 (2000); Median rent: $443 per month (2000); Median age of housing: 29 years (2000).
Transportation: Commute to work: 88.0% car, 2.5% public transportation, 2.7% walk, 6.8% work from home (2000); Travel time to work: 32.2% less than 15 minutes, 48.5% 15 to 30 minutes, 11.5% 30 to 45 minutes, 4.0% 45 to 60 minutes, 3.7% 60 minutes or more (2000)

VERONA (town). Covers a land area of 69.288 square miles and a water area of 0.408 square miles. Located at 43.15° N. Lat.; 75.62° W. Long. Elevation is 501 feet.
History: Site of Oneida Nation's Turning Stone Casino (68,000 square foot ; opened in 1990), first legal gambling casino in N.Y. state in over a century. Costing $10 million, it is one of the largest table game operations in the U.S. Owned and operated by the Oneida, one of 70 tribes across the U.S. who are allowed to offer gambling under the Indian Gaming Act of 1988, which was designed to generate wealth on impoverished reservations.
Population: 6,460 (1990); 6,425 (2000); 6,483 (2005); 6,539 (2010 projected); Race: 97.5% White, 0.4% Black, 0.5% Asian, 0.5% Hispanic of any race (2005); Density: 93.6 persons per square mile (2005); Average household size: 2.62 (2005); Median age: 39.2 (2005); Males per 100 females: 102.2 (2005); Marriage status: 23.2% never married, 61.4% now married, 6.3% widowed, 9.1% divorced (2000); Foreign born: 1.4% (2000); Ancestry (includes multiple ancestries): 23.4% German, 15.6% English, 14.3% Irish, 10.4% Italian, 8.2% United States or American (2000).
Economy: Agriculture includes dairy farming, field corn, hay and vegetables. Site of Oneida Nation's Turning Stone Casino. It is one of the largest table game operations in the U.S., with 168 gaming tables. Single-family building permits issued: 45 (2005); Multi-family building permits issued: 28 (2005); Employment by occupation: 6.5% management, 16.0% professional, 17.8% services, 25.7% sales, 0.5% farming, 9.7% construction, 23.9% production (2000).
Income: Per capita income: $20,475 (2005); Median household income: $48,592 (2005); Average household income: $53,238 (2005); Percent of households with income of $100,000 or more: 6.4% (2005); Poverty rate: 5.7% (2000).
Education: Percent of population age 25 and over with: High school diploma (including GED) or higher: 83.7% (2005); Bachelor's degree or higher: 12.8% (2005); Master's degree or higher: 4.7% (2005).

School District(s)
Boces Madison-Oneida (PK-PK)
   2003-04 Enrollment: 343 . . . . (315) 361-5510
Sherrill City School District (PK-12)
   2003-04 Enrollment: 2,425 . . . . (315) 829-2520

Two-year College(s)
Madison Oneida BOCES-Continuing Education (Public)
   Fall 2004 Enrollment: 156 . . . . (315) 361-5800

Housing: Homeownership rate: 84.9% (2005); Median home value: $105,383 (2005); Median rent: $482 per month (2000); Median age of housing: 43 years (2000).
Transportation: Commute to work: 95.1% car, 1.0% public transportation, 1.7% walk, 1.3% work from home (2000); Travel time to work: 35.6% less than 15 minutes, 34.6% 15 to 30 minutes, 15.7% 30 to 45 minutes, 7.6% 45 to 60 minutes, 6.4% 60 minutes or more (2000)

VIENNA (town). Covers a land area of 61.457 square miles and a water area of 33.312 square miles. Located at 43.23° N. Lat.; 75.74° W. Long.
Population: 5,564 (1990); 5,819 (2000); 5,870 (2005); 5,921 (2010 projected); Race: 97.2% White, 0.6% Black, 0.7% Asian, 0.9% Hispanic of any race (2005); Density: 95.5 persons per square mile (2005); Average household size: 2.60 (2005); Median age: 38.4 (2005); Males per 100 females: 100.5 (2005); Marriage status: 21.2% never married, 62.5% now married, 8.3% widowed, 8.0% divorced (2000); Foreign born: 0.7% (2000); Ancestry (includes multiple ancestries): 20.8% German, 19.5% Irish, 16.2% English, 10.5% United States or American, 9.8% Italian (2000).
Economy: Single-family building permits issued: 8 (2005); Multi-family building permits issued: 0 (2005); Employment by occupation: 8.9% management, 13.8% professional, 14.4% services, 26.9% sales, 1.1% farming, 12.1% construction, 22.7% production (2000).
Income: Per capita income: $20,073 (2005); Median household income: $40,665 (2005); Average household income: $52,205 (2005); Percent of households with income of $100,000 or more: 10.2% (2005); Poverty rate: 8.3% (2000).
Education: Percent of population age 25 and over with: High school diploma (including GED) or higher: 78.5% (2005); Bachelor's degree or higher: 11.5% (2005); Master's degree or higher: 5.5% (2005).
Housing: Homeownership rate: 82.5% (2005); Median home value: $96,406 (2005); Median rent: $431 per month (2000); Median age of housing: 34 years (2000).
Transportation: Commute to work: 91.1% car, 0.8% public transportation, 3.0% walk, 4.5% work from home (2000); Travel time to work: 21.3% less than 15 minutes, 30.9% 15 to 30 minutes, 22.7% 30 to 45 minutes, 14.5% 45 to 60 minutes, 10.5% 60 minutes or more (2000)

WATERVILLE (village). Covers a land area of 1.326 square miles and a water area of 0 square miles. Located at 42.93° N. Lat.; 75.37° W. Long. Elevation is 1,237 feet.
History: George Eastman born here. Incorporated 1871.
Population: 1,664 (1990); 1,721 (2000); 1,693 (2005); 1,669 (2010 projected); Race: 97.8% White, 0.4% Black, 0.8% Asian, 1.1% Hispanic of any race (2005); Density: 1,276.7 persons per square mile (2005); Average household size: 2.71 (2005); Median age: 39.2 (2005); Males per 100 females: 81.5 (2005); Marriage status: 24.6% never married, 56.2% now married, 10.9% widowed, 8.3% divorced (2000); Foreign born: 2.2% (2000); Ancestry (includes multiple ancestries): 25.3% Irish, 20.5% English, 17.8% German, 7.8% Italian, 6.3% Polish (2000).
Economy: Manufacturing of plastic injection molding. In dairying and farming area: corn, hay. Single-family building permits issued: 0 (2005); Multi-family building permits issued: 0 (2005); Employment by occupation: 9.7% management, 26.0% professional, 18.6% services, 24.0% sales, 0.5% farming, 10.0% construction, 11.2% production (2000).
Income: Per capita income: $21,447 (2005); Median household income: $42,864 (2005); Average household income: $57,724 (2005); Percent of households with income of $100,000 or more: 12.0% (2005); Poverty rate: 12.3% (2000).
Education: Percent of population age 25 and over with: High school diploma (including GED) or higher: 86.0% (2005); Bachelor's degree or higher: 21.7% (2005); Master's degree or higher: 7.5% (2005).

School District(s)
Waterville Central School District (PK-12)
   2003-04 Enrollment: 1,058 . . . . (315) 841-3900

Housing: Homeownership rate: 60.3% (2005); Median home value: $103,819 (2005); Median rent: $386 per month (2000); Median age of housing: 60+ years (2000).

Newspapers: The Waterville Times (General - Circulation 2,700)
Transportation: Commute to work: 88.3% car, 0.3% public transportation, 8.3% walk, 3.0% work from home (2000); Travel time to work: 33.6% less than 15 minutes, 37.4% 15 to 30 minutes, 17.9% 30 to 45 minutes, 2.9% 45 to 60 minutes, 8.2% 60 minutes or more (2000)

WESTDALE (unincorporated postal area, zip code 13483). Covers a land area of 3.267 square miles and a water area of 0.059 square miles. Located at 43.40° N. Lat.; 75.82° W. Long. Elevation is 550 feet.
Population: 0 (2000); Race: 100.0% White, 0.0% Black, 0.0% Asian, 0.0% Hispanic of any race (2000); Density: 0.0 persons per square mile (2000); Age: 37.0% under 18, 6.3% over 64 (2000); Marriage status: 18.1% never married, 69.8% now married, 8.1% widowed, 4.0% divorced (2000); Foreign born: 0.0% (2000); Ancestry (includes multiple ancestries): 15.9% German, 12.0% Irish, 11.5% United States or American, 11.1% English, 10.6% Other groups (2000).
Economy: Employment by occupation: 4.5% management, 12.4% professional, 6.7% services, 18.0% sales, 0.0% farming, 9.0% construction, 49.4% production (2000).
Income: Per capita income: $13,229 (2000); Median household income: $31,375 (2000); Poverty rate: 6.7% (2000).
Education: Percent of population age 25 and over with: High school diploma (including GED) or higher: 61.2% (2000); Bachelor's degree or higher: 8.5% (2000).
Housing: Homeownership rate: 87.7% (2000); Median home value: $71,700 (2000); Median rent: $238 per month (2000); Median age of housing: 16 years (2000).
Transportation: Commute to work: 82.0% car, 0.0% public transportation, 11.2% walk, 6.7% work from home (2000); Travel time to work: 66.3% less than 15 minutes, 31.3% 15 to 30 minutes, 0.0% 30 to 45 minutes, 0.0% 45 to 60 minutes, 2.4% 60 minutes or more (2000)

WESTERN (town). Covers a land area of 51.365 square miles and a water area of 3.338 square miles. Located at 43.32° N. Lat.; 75.39° W. Long.
Population: 2,057 (1990); 2,029 (2000); 2,103 (2005); 2,166 (2010 projected); Race: 97.2% White, 0.1% Black, 0.9% Asian, 0.7% Hispanic of any race (2005); Density: 40.9 persons per square mile (2005); Average household size: 2.64 (2005); Median age: 39.1 (2005); Males per 100 females: 105.8 (2005); Marriage status: 22.6% never married, 63.4% now married, 6.1% widowed, 7.9% divorced (2000); Foreign born: 2.9% (2000); Ancestry (includes multiple ancestries): 24.0% German, 16.9% Irish, 15.4% English, 11.3% Italian, 10.6% Polish (2000).
Economy: Single-family building permits issued: 8 (2005); Multi-family building permits issued: 0 (2005); Employment by occupation: 15.0% management, 20.3% professional, 18.5% services, 20.5% sales, 3.1% farming, 9.9% construction, 12.7% production (2000).
Income: Per capita income: $23,540 (2005); Median household income: $49,187 (2005); Average household income: $62,192 (2005); Percent of households with income of $100,000 or more: 11.7% (2005); Poverty rate: 8.0% (2000).
Education: Percent of population age 25 and over with: High school diploma (including GED) or higher: 84.0% (2005); Bachelor's degree or higher: 18.0% (2005); Master's degree or higher: 7.9% (2005).
Housing: Homeownership rate: 82.5% (2005); Median home value: $106,505 (2005); Median rent: $376 per month (2000); Median age of housing: 42 years (2000).
Transportation: Commute to work: 90.3% car, 0.4% public transportation, 2.2% walk, 6.0% work from home (2000); Travel time to work: 21.7% less than 15 minutes, 40.7% 15 to 30 minutes, 26.4% 30 to 45 minutes, 5.3% 45 to 60 minutes, 5.9% 60 minutes or more (2000)

WESTERNVILLE (unincorporated postal area, zip code 13486). Covers a land area of 26.854 square miles and a water area of 0 square miles. Located at 43.33° N. Lat.; 75.35° W. Long. Elevation is 562 feet.
Population: 0 (2000); Race: 99.4% White, 0.1% Black, 0.5% Asian, 2.0% Hispanic of any race (2000); Density: 0.0 persons per square mile (2000); Age: 22.9% under 18, 16.4% over 64 (2000); Marriage status: 23.1% never married, 63.9% now married, 6.3% widowed, 6.7% divorced (2000); Foreign born: 0.9% (2000); Ancestry (includes multiple ancestries): 21.8% German, 18.3% English, 14.4% Irish, 12.8% Polish, 10.0% Welsh (2000).
Economy: Employment by occupation: 11.5% management, 21.2% professional, 18.1% services, 20.9% sales, 2.7% farming, 12.6% construction, 12.9% production (2000).

Income: Per capita income: $16,802 (2000); Median household income: $38,125 (2000); Poverty rate: 12.6% (2000).
Education: Percent of population age 25 and over with: High school diploma (including GED) or higher: 83.5% (2000); Bachelor's degree or higher: 12.5% (2000).
Housing: Homeownership rate: 82.7% (2000); Median home value: $70,700 (2000); Median rent: $365 per month (2000); Median age of housing: 60+ years (2000).
Transportation: Commute to work: 90.6% car, 0.0% public transportation, 1.7% walk, 7.8% work from home (2000); Travel time to work: 21.3% less than 15 minutes, 36.6% 15 to 30 minutes, 28.5% 30 to 45 minutes, 6.3% 45 to 60 minutes, 7.2% 60 minutes or more (2000).

WESTMORELAND (town). Covers a land area of 43.133 square miles and a water area of 0.019 square miles. Located at 43.12° N. Lat.; 75.44° W. Long.
Population: 5,737 (1990); 6,207 (2000); 6,332 (2005); 6,454 (2010 projected); Race: 98.1% White, 0.6% Black, 0.3% Asian, 1.1% Hispanic of any race (2005); Density: 146.8 persons per square mile (2005); Average household size: 2.72 (2005); Median age: 39.4 (2005); Males per 100 females: 102.8 (2005); Marriage status: 21.0% never married, 66.3% now married, 6.2% widowed, 6.6% divorced (2000); Foreign born: 2.2% (2000); Ancestry (includes multiple ancestries): 22.0% German, 20.9% Irish, 19.5% English, 13.9% Italian, 13.2% Polish (2000).
Economy: Single-family building permits issued: 19 (2005); Multi-family building permits issued: 0 (2005); Employment by occupation: 12.3% management, 18.8% professional, 19.4% services, 23.9% sales, 1.3% farming, 11.0% construction, 13.2% production (2000).
Income: Per capita income: $21,534 (2005); Median household income: $54,993 (2005); Average household income: $58,375 (2005); Percent of households with income of $100,000 or more: 11.3% (2005); Poverty rate: 5.1% (2000).
Education: Percent of population age 25 and over with: High school diploma (including GED) or higher: 87.7% (2005); Bachelor's degree or higher: 14.9% (2005); Master's degree or higher: 4.2% (2005).

School District(s)
Westmoreland Central School District (KG-12)
    2003-04 Enrollment: 1,155 . . . . (315) 557-2601
Housing: Homeownership rate: 89.2% (2005); Median home value: $107,121 (2005); Median rent: $478 per month (2000); Median age of housing: 32 years (2000).
Transportation: Commute to work: 93.8% car, 0.5% public transportation, 1.3% walk, 3.1% work from home (2000); Travel time to work: 28.2% less than 15 minutes, 54.3% 15 to 30 minutes, 9.3% 30 to 45 minutes, 4.6% 45 to 60 minutes, 3.6% 60 minutes or more (2000).

Additional Information Contacts
Town of Westmoreland . . . . (315) 853-8001
    http://town.westmoreland.ny.us/content

WHITESBORO (village). Covers a land area of 1.073 square miles and a water area of 0 square miles. Located at 43.12° N. Lat.; 75.29° W. Long. Elevation is 434 feet.
History: Settled 1784, incorporated 1813.
Population: 4,195 (1990); 3,943 (2000); 3,845 (2005); 3,745 (2010 projected); Race: 97.8% White, 0.4% Black, 0.3% Asian, 1.9% Hispanic of any race (2005); Density: 3,584.1 persons per square mile (2005); Average household size: 2.17 (2005); Median age: 38.3 (2005); Males per 100 females: 88.2 (2005); Marriage status: 32.8% never married, 42.9% now married, 11.3% widowed, 13.0% divorced (2000); Foreign born: 0.4% (2000); Ancestry (includes multiple ancestries): 25.0% Irish, 20.2% German, 18.7% Italian, 13.8% Polish, 11.7% English (2000).
Economy: Manufacturing of transportation equipment, electronics, caskets. Single-family building permits issued: 0 (2005); Multi-family building permits issued: 0 (2005); Employment by occupation: 7.6% management, 25.1% professional, 15.1% services, 30.6% sales, 0.4% farming, 6.5% construction, 14.7% production (2000).
Income: Per capita income: $19,890 (2005); Median household income: $34,880 (2005); Average household income: $43,151 (2005); Percent of households with income of $100,000 or more: 5.5% (2005); Poverty rate: 13.5% (2000).
Education: Percent of population age 25 and over with: High school diploma (including GED) or higher: 85.4% (2005); Bachelor's degree or higher: 18.3% (2005); Master's degree or higher: 6.4% (2005).

School District(s)
Whitesboro Central School District (KG-12)
    2003-04 Enrollment: 3,863 . . . . (315) 266-3303
Housing: Homeownership rate: 55.1% (2005); Median home value: $89,434 (2005); Median rent: $388 per month (2000); Median age of housing: 56 years (2000).
Safety: Violent crime rate: 18.0 per 10,000 population; Property crime rate: 103.0 per 10,000 population (2004).
Transportation: Commute to work: 98.1% car, 0.5% public transportation, 0.6% walk, 0.9% work from home (2000); Travel time to work: 46.2% less than 15 minutes, 43.1% 15 to 30 minutes, 4.8% 30 to 45 minutes, 3.2% 45 to 60 minutes, 2.7% 60 minutes or more (2000).

Additional Information Contacts
Village of Whitesboro . . . . (315) 736-1613
    http://village.whitesboro.ny.us/content

WHITESTOWN (town). Covers a land area of 27.195 square miles and a water area of 0.005 square miles. Located at 43.12° N. Lat.; 75.30° W. Long.
Population: 18,985 (1990); 18,635 (2000); 18,650 (2005); 18,647 (2010 projected); Race: 97.1% White, 1.1% Black, 0.6% Asian, 1.7% Hispanic of any race (2005); Density: 685.8 persons per square mile (2005); Average household size: 2.43 (2005); Median age: 41.2 (2005); Males per 100 females: 94.1 (2005); Marriage status: 25.0% never married, 56.3% now married, 10.1% widowed, 8.6% divorced (2000); Foreign born: 2.0% (2000); Ancestry (includes multiple ancestries): 21.3% Irish, 21.2% Polish, 20.6% Italian, 19.2% German, 10.5% English (2000).
Economy: Single-family building permits issued: 35 (2005); Multi-family building permits issued: 0 (2005); Employment by occupation: 13.6% management, 23.4% professional, 14.8% services, 29.1% sales, 0.2% farming, 6.7% construction, 12.3% production (2000).
Income: Per capita income: $22,310 (2005); Median household income: $44,490 (2005); Average household income: $53,611 (2005); Percent of households with income of $100,000 or more: 11.3% (2005); Poverty rate: 9.1% (2000).
Education: Percent of population age 25 and over with: High school diploma (including GED) or higher: 86.1% (2005); Bachelor's degree or higher: 21.5% (2005); Master's degree or higher: 8.5% (2005).
Housing: Homeownership rate: 73.1% (2005); Median home value: $111,207 (2005); Median rent: $421 per month (2000); Median age of housing: 46 years (2000).
Transportation: Commute to work: 96.8% car, 0.3% public transportation, 0.7% walk, 1.6% work from home (2000); Travel time to work: 49.4% less than 15 minutes, 40.8% 15 to 30 minutes, 4.4% 30 to 45 minutes, 2.2% 45 to 60 minutes, 3.1% 60 minutes or more (2000).

Additional Information Contacts
Town of Whitestown . . . . (315) 736-1131
    http://town.whitestown.ny.us/content

YORKVILLE (village). Covers a land area of 0.668 square miles and a water area of 0 square miles. Located at 43.11° N. Lat.; 75.27° W. Long.
History: Henry Inman, one of the most prominent and versatile of the first generation of American-trained artists, was born here in 1801.
Population: 3,042 (1990); 2,675 (2000); 2,598 (2005); 2,513 (2010 projected); Race: 97.9% White, 0.6% Black, 0.7% Asian, 1.3% Hispanic of any race (2005); Density: 3,890.4 persons per square mile (2005); Average household size: 2.26 (2005); Median age: 39.7 (2005); Males per 100 females: 89.9 (2005); Marriage status: 29.1% never married, 48.7% now married, 11.0% widowed, 11.2% divorced (2000); Foreign born: 2.2% (2000); Ancestry (includes multiple ancestries): 36.3% Polish, 21.1% Irish, 19.7% Italian, 15.5% German, 11.8% English (2000).
Economy: Manufacturing of pesticides and electric motors. Single-family building permits issued: 1 (2005); Multi-family building permits issued: 0 (2005); Employment by occupation: 8.6% management, 18.5% professional, 17.3% services, 32.3% sales, 0.0% farming, 9.8% construction, 13.5% production (2000).
Income: Per capita income: $19,470 (2005); Median household income: $36,856 (2005); Average household income: $43,693 (2005); Percent of households with income of $100,000 or more: 6.7% (2005); Poverty rate: 12.1% (2000).
Education: Percent of population age 25 and over with: High school diploma (including GED) or higher: 81.3% (2005); Bachelor's degree or higher: 12.5% (2005); Master's degree or higher: 4.1% (2005).
Housing: Homeownership rate: 65.6% (2005); Median home value: $86,667 (2005); Median rent: $417 per month (2000); Median age of housing: 60 years (2000).

Transportation: Commute to work: 94.5% car, 0.6% public transportation, 1.5% walk, 1.8% work from home (2000); Travel time to work: 54.5% less than 15 minutes, 37.3% 15 to 30 minutes, 5.3% 30 to 45 minutes, 0.6% 45 to 60 minutes, 2.2% 60 minutes or more (2000)

Onondaga County

Located in central New York, in the Finger Lakes area; drained by the Seneca and Oswego Rivers; includes Oneida and Skaneateles Lakes. Covers a land area of 780.29 square miles, a water area of 25.40 square miles, and is located in the Eastern Time Zone. The county government was organized in 1794. County seat is Syracuse.

Onondaga County is part of the Syracuse, NY Metropolitan Statistical Area. The entire metro area includes: Madison County, NY; Onondaga County, NY; Oswego County, NY

Weather Station: Syracuse Hancock Int'l Airport   Elevation: 410 feet

	Jan	Feb	Mar	Apr	May	Jun	Jul	Aug	Sep	Oct	Nov	Dec
High	31	33	43	56	69	77	82	80	71	60	48	36
Low	15	16	25	36	47	55	61	59	51	41	33	22
Precip	2.5	2.1	3.0	3.4	3.3	3.7	4.1	3.6	4.2	3.3	3.8	3.2
Snow	33.0	24.0	19.0	4.8	0.2	tr	tr	0.0	tr	0.5	10.7	28.0

High and Low temperatures in degrees Fahrenheit; Precipitation and Snow in inches

Population: 468,973 (1990); 458,336 (2000); 461,915 (2005); 465,353 (2010 projected); Race: 82.7% White, 10.6% Black, 2.7% Asian, 3.2% Hispanic of any race (2005); Density: 592.0 persons per square mile (2005); Average household size: 2.51 (2005); Median age: 37.5 (2005); Males per 100 females: 92.2 (2005).
Religion: Five largest groups: 32.1% Catholic Church, 5.2% The United Methodist Church, 2.0% Jewish Estimate, 1.7% Evangelical Lutheran Church in America, 1.4% Episcopal Church (2000).
Economy: Unemployment rate: 4.6% (2005); Total civilian labor force: 235,184 (2005); Leading industries: 14.9% health care and social assistance; 13.3% retail trade; 12.0% manufacturing (2003); Farms: 725 totaling 156,284 acres (2002); Companies that employ 500 or more persons: 38 (2003); Companies that employ 100 to 499 persons: 280 (2003); Companies that employ less than 100 persons: 11,557 (2003); Black-owned businesses: 612 (2002); Hispanic-owned businesses: 306 (2002); Women-owned businesses: 8,600 (2002); Retail sales per capita: $14,316 (2006). Single-family building permits issued: 1,038 (2005); Multi-family building permits issued: 162 (2005).
Income: Per capita income: $24,307 (2005); Median household income: $45,820 (2005); Average household income: $60,209 (2005); Percent of households with income of $100,000 or more: 15.3% (2005); Poverty rate: 12.1% (2003); Bankruptcy rate: 9.42% (2005).
Taxes: Total county taxes per capita: $676 (2004); County property taxes per capita: $263 (2004).
Education: Percent of population age 25 and over with: High school diploma (including GED) or higher: 85.8% (2005); Bachelor's degree or higher: 28.8% (2005); Master's degree or higher: 12.1% (2005).
Housing: Homeownership rate: 65.3% (2005); Median home value: $117,350 (2005); Median rent: $471 per month (2000); Median age of housing: 42 years (2000).
Health: Birth rate: 124.6 per 10,000 population (2004); Death rate: 88.3 per 10,000 population (2004); Age-adjusted cancer mortality rate: 218.4 deaths per 100,000 population (2002); Air Quality Index: 88.8% good, 10.7% moderate, 0.5% unhealthy for sensitive individuals, 0.0% unhealthy (percent of days in 2005); Number of physicians: 45.4 per 10,000 population (2004); Hospital beds: 39.4 per 10,000 population (2003); Hospital admissions: 1,514.0 per 10,000 population (2003).
Elections: 2004 Presidential election results: 43.8% Bush, 54.2% Kerry, 1.7% Nader, 0.2% Badnarik
National and State Parks: Cicero State Game Management Area; Clark Reservation State Park; Erie Canal State Park; Green Lakes State Park; Three Rivers State Game Management Area
Additional Information Contacts
Onondaga County Government . . . . (315) 435-2070
  http://www.ongov.net/
City of Syracuse . . . . (315) 448-8216
  http://www.syracuse.ny.us/
Town of Camillus . . . . (315) 488-1335
  http://www.townofcamillus.com/
Town of Clay . . . . (315) 652-3800
  http://www.townofclay.org/
Town of Elbridge . . . . (315) 689-9031
  http://www.townofelbridge.com/
Town of Geddes . . . . (315) 468-2528
  http://www.townofgeddes.com/
Town of Lysander . . . . (315) 638-4264
  http://www.townoflysander.org/
Town of Manlius . . . . (315) 637-3521
  http://www.townofmanlius.org/
Town of Marcellus . . . . (315) 673-3269
  http://www.marcellusny.com/
Town of Salina . . . . (315) 457-6661
  http://www.salina.ny.us/
Town of Skaneateles . . . . (315) 685-3473
  http://www.townofskaneateles.com/index.shtml
Town of Van Buren . . . . (315) 635-3009
  http://www.townofvanburen.com/
Village of Elbridge . . . . (315) 689-7851
  http://www.townofelbridge.org/
Village of Liverpool . . . . (315) 457-3441
  http://www.villageofliverpool.org/
Village of Manlius . . . . (315) 682-9171
  http://www.townofmanlius.org/
Village of Marcellus . . . . (315) 673-3112
  http://village.marcellusny.com/
Village of North Syracuse . . . . (315) 458-0900
  http://www.northsyracuse.org/
Village of Skaneateles . . . . (315) 685-3473
  http://www.townofskaneateles.com/index.shtml

Onondaga County Communities

BALDWINSVILLE (village). Covers a land area of 3.078 square miles and a water area of 0.169 square miles. Located at 43.16° N. Lat.; 76.33° W. Long. Elevation is 389 feet.
History: Settled 1796, incorporated 1847.
Population: 6,604 (1990); 7,053 (2000); 7,338 (2005); 7,630 (2010 projected); Race: 96.2% White, 1.0% Black, 1.0% Asian, 1.1% Hispanic of any race (2005); Density: 2,384.3 persons per square mile (2005); Average household size: 2.48 (2005); Median age: 38.3 (2005); Males per 100 females: 89.7 (2005); Marriage status: 23.7% never married, 57.5% now married, 7.9% widowed, 10.9% divorced (2000); Foreign born: 2.0% (2000); Ancestry (includes multiple ancestries): 20.5% Irish, 20.3% German, 18.7% English, 16.2% Italian, 6.6% Polish (2000).
Economy: Resort and shipping center. Manufacturing: consumer goods, paper products, machinery, feed, flour. Timber. Agriculture: potatoes, cabbage. Single-family building permits issued: 14 (2005); Multi-family building permits issued: 0 (2005); Employment by occupation: 12.7% management, 25.4% professional, 13.1% services, 29.4% sales, 0.0% farming, 6.5% construction, 12.9% production (2000).
Income: Per capita income: $23,215 (2005); Median household income: $46,681 (2005); Average household income: $56,131 (2005); Percent of households with income of $100,000 or more: 12.2% (2005); Poverty rate: 8.2% (2000).
Education: Percent of population age 25 and over with: High school diploma (including GED) or higher: 88.4% (2005); Bachelor's degree or higher: 29.5% (2005); Master's degree or higher: 11.4% (2005).
School District(s)
Baldwinsville Central School District (KG-12)
  2003-04 Enrollment: 5,960 . . . . (315) 638-6043
Housing: Homeownership rate: 63.3% (2005); Median home value: $118,000 (2005); Median rent: $429 per month (2000); Median age of housing: 45 years (2000).
Safety: Violent crime rate: 27.8 per 10,000 population; Property crime rate: 269.3 per 10,000 population (2004).
Newspapers: Baldwinsville Messenger (General - Circulation 39,927)
Transportation: Commute to work: 91.7% car, 0.9% public transportation, 3.4% walk, 3.0% work from home (2000); Travel time to work: 21.2% less than 15 minutes, 55.9% 15 to 30 minutes, 18.0% 30 to 45 minutes, 2.2% 45 to 60 minutes, 2.7% 60 minutes or more (2000)
Additional Information Contacts
Baldwinsville Chamber of Commerce . . . . (315) 638-0550
  http://www.baldwinsvillechamber.com

BREWERTON (CDP). Covers a land area of 3.162 square miles and a water area of 0.172 square miles. Located at 43.23° N. Lat.; 76.13° W. Long. Elevation is 385 feet.
History: Here are remains of Fort Brewerton (1759), now in state reservation.
Population: 2,954 (1990); 3,453 (2000); 3,716 (2005); 3,954 (2010 projected); Race: 96.5% White, 0.9% Black, 0.6% Asian, 1.2% Hispanic of any race (2005); Density: 1,175.0 persons per square mile (2005); Average household size: 2.46 (2005); Median age: 35.7 (2005); Males per 100 females: 96.4 (2005); Marriage status: 25.1% never married, 57.2% now married, 6.0% widowed, 11.7% divorced (2000); Foreign born: 2.3% (2000); Ancestry (includes multiple ancestries): 26.3% German, 19.6% Irish, 15.0% Italian, 14.7% English, 9.5% Polish (2000).
Economy: Employment by occupation: 12.1% management, 16.3% professional, 16.6% services, 28.3% sales, 0.0% farming, 9.6% construction, 17.2% production (2000).
Income: Per capita income: $21,844 (2005); Median household income: $49,059 (2005); Average household income: $53,757 (2005); Percent of households with income of $100,000 or more: 9.2% (2005); Poverty rate: 7.5% (2000).
Education: Percent of population age 25 and over with: High school diploma (including GED) or higher: 84.8% (2005); Bachelor's degree or higher: 14.6% (2005); Master's degree or higher: 5.1% (2005).
School District(s)
Central Square Central School District (PK-12)
  2003-04 Enrollment: 5,013 . . . . (315) 668-4220
Housing: Homeownership rate: 68.7% (2005); Median home value: $114,085 (2005); Median rent: $403 per month (2000); Median age of housing: 30 years (2000).
Transportation: Commute to work: 93.8% car, 0.0% public transportation, 3.3% walk, 2.7% work from home (2000); Travel time to work: 26.6% less than 15 minutes, 49.1% 15 to 30 minutes, 19.4% 30 to 45 minutes, 2.2% 45 to 60 minutes, 2.7% 60 minutes or more (2000)

BRIDGEPORT (CDP). Covers a land area of 1.825 square miles and a water area of 0 square miles. Located at 43.15° N. Lat.; 75.97° W. Long.
Population: 1,950 (1990); 1,665 (2000); 1,648 (2005); 1,633 (2010 projected); Race: 96.1% White, 1.1% Black, 0.5% Asian, 0.3% Hispanic of any race (2005); Density: 903.1 persons per square mile (2005); Average household size: 2.55 (2005); Median age: 39.0 (2005); Males per 100 females: 98.1 (2005); Marriage status: 23.8% never married, 57.5% now married, 8.9% widowed, 9.9% divorced (2000); Foreign born: 1.8% (2000); Ancestry (includes multiple ancestries): 18.7% German, 18.5% Irish, 14.6% English, 11.5% French (except Basque), 10.3% Italian (2000).
Economy: Employment by occupation: 3.1% management, 4.7% professional, 19.8% services, 29.8% sales, 0.0% farming, 11.7% construction, 30.8% production (2000).
Income: Per capita income: $16,205 (2005); Median household income: $34,505 (2005); Average household income: $41,269 (2005); Percent of households with income of $100,000 or more: 5.0% (2005); Poverty rate: 12.2% (2000).
Education: Percent of population age 25 and over with: High school diploma (including GED) or higher: 74.5% (2005); Bachelor's degree or higher: 3.8% (2005); Master's degree or higher: 1.0% (2005).
Housing: Homeownership rate: 74.6% (2005); Median home value: $74,528 (2005); Median rent: $350 per month (2000); Median age of housing: 36 years (2000).
Transportation: Commute to work: 95.4% car, 0.0% public transportation, 2.3% walk, 2.3% work from home (2000); Travel time to work: 14.9% less than 15 minutes, 67.4% 15 to 30 minutes, 13.5% 30 to 45 minutes, 1.3% 45 to 60 minutes, 2.9% 60 minutes or more (2000)

CAMILLUS (village). Covers a land area of 0.392 square miles and a water area of 0 square miles. Located at 43.03° N. Lat.; 76.30° W. Long.
Population: 1,264 (1990); 1,249 (2000); 1,223 (2005); 1,200 (2010 projected); Race: 96.9% White, 0.5% Black, 0.4% Asian, 1.2% Hispanic of any race (2005); Density: 3,122.5 persons per square mile (2005); Average household size: 2.15 (2005); Median age: 37.4 (2005); Males per 100 females: 93.8 (2005); Marriage status: 30.0% never married, 47.3% now married, 9.8% widowed, 13.0% divorced (2000); Foreign born: 1.8% (2000); Ancestry (includes multiple ancestries): 26.9% Irish, 21.8% English, 18.7% Italian, 17.3% German, 8.6% Polish (2000).
Economy: Single-family building permits issued: 0 (2005); Multi-family building permits issued: 0 (2005); Employment by occupation: 8.9% management, 19.3% professional, 15.4% services, 33.6% sales, 0.3% farming, 10.9% construction, 11.6% production (2000).
Income: Per capita income: $22,119 (2005); Median household income: $39,420 (2005); Average household income: $47,504 (2005); Percent of households with income of $100,000 or more: 7.6% (2005); Poverty rate: 8.0% (2000).
Education: Percent of population age 25 and over with: High school diploma (including GED) or higher: 87.7% (2005); Bachelor's degree or higher: 20.4% (2005); Master's degree or higher: 6.4% (2005).
School District(s)
West Genesee Central School District (KG-12)
  2003-04 Enrollment: 5,153 . . . . (315) 487-4562
Housing: Homeownership rate: 53.7% (2005); Median home value: $94,672 (2005); Median rent: $440 per month (2000); Median age of housing: 60+ years (2000).
Transportation: Commute to work: 93.8% car, 2.3% public transportation, 3.3% walk, 0.5% work from home (2000); Travel time to work: 26.4% less than 15 minutes, 59.8% 15 to 30 minutes, 7.6% 30 to 45 minutes, 2.0% 45 to 60 minutes, 4.2% 60 minutes or more (2000)

CAMILLUS (town). Covers a land area of 34.459 square miles and a water area of 0 square miles. Located at 43.04° N. Lat.; 76.27° W. Long.
History: Once a major cutlery manufacturing center. Incorporated 1852.
Population: 23,625 (1990); 23,152 (2000); 23,272 (2005); 23,400 (2010 projected); Race: 95.6% White, 1.3% Black, 1.5% Asian, 1.2% Hispanic of any race (2005); Density: 675.3 persons per square mile (2005); Average household size: 2.44 (2005); Median age: 42.0 (2005); Males per 100 females: 91.6 (2005); Marriage status: 21.9% never married, 63.9% now married, 7.3% widowed, 6.8% divorced (2000); Foreign born: 5.4% (2000); Ancestry (includes multiple ancestries): 27.5% Irish, 19.9% Italian, 19.1% German, 16.2% English, 11.3% Polish (2000).
Economy: In dairy and grain area. Single-family building permits issued: 113 (2005); Multi-family building permits issued: 0 (2005); Employment by occupation: 13.6% management, 26.8% professional, 11.8% services, 30.9% sales, 0.2% farming, 7.0% construction, 9.8% production (2000).
Income: Per capita income: $25,920 (2005); Median household income: $54,816 (2005); Average household income: $63,114 (2005); Percent of households with income of $100,000 or more: 15.4% (2005); Poverty rate: 4.3% (2000).
Education: Percent of population age 25 and over with: High school diploma (including GED) or higher: 90.9% (2005); Bachelor's degree or higher: 29.2% (2005); Master's degree or higher: 11.5% (2005).
Housing: Homeownership rate: 80.2% (2005); Median home value: $124,353 (2005); Median rent: $554 per month (2000); Median age of housing: 38 years (2000).
Safety: Violent crime rate: 3.9 per 10,000 population; Property crime rate: 120.5 per 10,000 population (2004).
Transportation: Commute to work: 94.8% car, 1.1% public transportation, 1.1% walk, 2.7% work from home (2000); Travel time to work: 27.7% less than 15 minutes, 57.6% 15 to 30 minutes, 9.9% 30 to 45 minutes, 2.7% 45 to 60 minutes, 2.1% 60 minutes or more (2000)
Additional Information Contacts
Town of Camillus . . . . (315) 488-1335
  http://www.townofcamillus.com/

CICERO (town). Covers a land area of 48.462 square miles and a water area of 0.048 square miles. Located at 43.17° N. Lat.; 76.09° W. Long.
Population: 25,560 (1990); 27,982 (2000); 30,017 (2005); 31,889 (2010 projected); Race: 95.7% White, 1.4% Black, 0.9% Asian, 1.1% Hispanic of any race (2005); Density: 619.4 persons per square mile (2005); Average household size: 2.61 (2005); Median age: 37.5 (2005); Males per 100 females: 96.9 (2005); Marriage status: 22.4% never married, 63.1% now married, 5.6% widowed, 9.0% divorced (2000); Foreign born: 2.4% (2000); Ancestry (includes multiple ancestries): 23.8% Irish, 23.7% German, 22.7% Italian, 13.9% English, 9.6% Polish (2000).
Economy: Limited agriculture: vegetables, grain. Unemployment rate: 4.2% (2005); Total civilian labor force: 16,475 (2005); Single-family building permits issued: 129 (2005); Multi-family building permits issued: 0 (2005); Employment by occupation: 13.1% management, 19.4% professional, 12.4% services, 31.5% sales, 0.2% farming, 8.6% construction, 14.8% production (2000).
Income: Per capita income: $24,662 (2005); Median household income: $56,372 (2005); Average household income: $64,439 (2005); Percent of households with income of $100,000 or more: 15.7% (2005); Poverty rate: 5.1% (2000).

Education: Percent of population age 25 and over with: High school diploma (including GED) or higher: 87.3% (2005); Bachelor's degree or higher: 21.9% (2005); Master's degree or higher: 7.3% (2005).

School District(s)
North Syracuse Central School District (PK-12)
    2003-04 Enrollment: 10,188 . . . . (315) 452-3128

Housing: Homeownership rate: 80.6% (2005); Median home value: $119,459 (2005); Median rent: $494 per month (2000); Median age of housing: 31 years (2000).
Safety: Violent crime rate: 2.6 per 10,000 population; Property crime rate: 184.8 per 10,000 population (2004).
Transportation: Commute to work: 95.2% car, 0.2% public transportation, 1.1% walk, 3.1% work from home (2000); Travel time to work: 27.8% less than 15 minutes, 58.3% 15 to 30 minutes, 9.2% 30 to 45 minutes, 1.7% 45 to 60 minutes, 2.9% 60 minutes or more (2000)

Additional Information Contacts
Cicero Chamber of Commerce . . . . (315) 699-1358
    http://www.cicerochamber.net/

CLAY (town). Covers a land area of 48.006 square miles and a water area of 0.780 square miles. Located at 43.15° N. Lat.; 76.19° W. Long.
Population: 59,749 (1990); 58,805 (2000); 59,482 (2005); 60,104 (2010 projected); Race: 90.7% White, 4.2% Black, 2.5% Asian, 1.8% Hispanic of any race (2005); Density: 1,239.1 persons per square mile (2005); Average household size: 2.60 (2005); Median age: 36.7 (2005); Males per 100 females: 93.2 (2005); Marriage status: 25.5% never married, 60.7% now married, 5.1% widowed, 8.7% divorced (2000); Foreign born: 5.1% (2000); Ancestry (includes multiple ancestries): 22.8% Irish, 22.2% Italian, 21.6% German, 13.5% English, 9.1% Other groups (2000).
Economy: Unemployment rate: 4.1% (2005); Total civilian labor force: 33,905 (2005); Single-family building permits issued: 143 (2005); Multi-family building permits issued: 8 (2005); Employment by occupation: 14.6% management, 22.7% professional, 11.4% services, 32.9% sales, 0.0% farming, 5.9% construction, 12.5% production (2000).
Income: Per capita income: $25,004 (2005); Median household income: $55,616 (2005); Average household income: $64,753 (2005); Percent of households with income of $100,000 or more: 16.4% (2005); Poverty rate: 5.7% (2000).
Taxes: Total city taxes per capita: $242 (2004); City property taxes per capita: $203 (2004).
Education: Percent of population age 25 and over with: High school diploma (including GED) or higher: 90.7% (2005); Bachelor's degree or higher: 27.7% (2005); Master's degree or higher: 9.6% (2005).
Housing: Homeownership rate: 73.3% (2005); Median home value: $116,674 (2005); Median rent: $558 per month (2000); Median age of housing: 27 years (2000).
Safety: Violent crime rate: 3.3 per 10,000 population; Property crime rate: 64.7 per 10,000 population (2004).
Transportation: Commute to work: 95.3% car, 0.8% public transportation, 0.8% walk, 2.4% work from home (2000); Travel time to work: 29.9% less than 15 minutes, 53.6% 15 to 30 minutes, 11.0% 30 to 45 minutes, 2.7% 45 to 60 minutes, 2.8% 60 minutes or more (2000)

Additional Information Contacts
Town of Clay . . . . (315) 652-3800
    http://www.townofclay.org/

DE WITT (town). Covers a land area of 33.855 square miles and a water area of 0.054 square miles. Located at 43.05° N. Lat.; 76.07° W. Long.
Population: 25,366 (1990); 24,071 (2000); 24,406 (2005); 24,685 (2010 projected); Race: 87.3% White, 6.3% Black, 3.7% Asian, 1.9% Hispanic of any race (2005); Density: 720.9 persons per square mile (2005); Average household size: 2.36 (2005); Median age: 42.4 (2005); Males per 100 females: 92.2 (2005); Marriage status: 24.6% never married, 58.0% now married, 8.2% widowed, 9.2% divorced (2000); Foreign born: 8.4% (2000); Ancestry (includes multiple ancestries): 20.7% Irish, 19.4% German, 15.4% Italian, 13.1% English, 11.0% Other groups (2000).
Economy: Residential suburb of Syracuse. Unemployment rate: 3.9% (2005); Total civilian labor force: 12,811 (2005); Single-family building permits issued: 39 (2005); Multi-family building permits issued: 0 (2005); Employment by occupation: 15.4% management, 30.2% professional, 10.8% services, 28.6% sales, 0.1% farming, 4.6% construction, 10.3% production (2000).
Income: Per capita income: $33,658 (2005); Median household income: $53,770 (2005); Average household income: $79,315 (2005); Percent of households with income of $100,000 or more: 24.2% (2005); Poverty rate: 7.2% (2000).
Taxes: Total city taxes per capita: $503 (2004); City property taxes per capita: $448 (2004).
Education: Percent of population age 25 and over with: High school diploma (including GED) or higher: 89.2% (2005); Bachelor's degree or higher: 39.4% (2005); Master's degree or higher: 19.6% (2005).

School District(s)
Jamesville-Dewitt Central School District (KG-12)
    2003-04 Enrollment: 2,717 . . . . (315) 445-8304

Housing: Homeownership rate: 72.3% (2005); Median home value: $133,678 (2005); Median rent: $489 per month (2000); Median age of housing: 41 years (2000).
Safety: Violent crime rate: 11.3 per 10,000 population; Property crime rate: 271.9 per 10,000 population (2004).
Transportation: Commute to work: 91.9% car, 1.5% public transportation, 2.1% walk, 3.6% work from home (2000); Travel time to work: 44.6% less than 15 minutes, 45.4% 15 to 30 minutes, 5.8% 30 to 45 minutes, 1.6% 45 to 60 minutes, 2.6% 60 minutes or more (2000)

EAST SYRACUSE (village). Covers a land area of 1.577 square miles and a water area of 0 square miles. Located at 43.06° N. Lat.; 76.07° W. Long.
Population: 3,343 (1990); 3,178 (2000); 3,091 (2005); 3,005 (2010 projected); Race: 94.1% White, 2.1% Black, 0.2% Asian, 1.7% Hispanic of any race (2005); Density: 1,959.8 persons per square mile (2005); Average household size: 2.24 (2005); Median age: 37.3 (2005); Males per 100 females: 91.5 (2005); Marriage status: 36.6% never married, 38.9% now married, 9.0% widowed, 15.4% divorced (2000); Foreign born: 2.8% (2000); Ancestry (includes multiple ancestries): 22.8% German, 22.0% Irish, 18.5% Italian, 15.2% English, 8.7% Polish (2000).
Economy: Single-family building permits issued: 1 (2005); Multi-family building permits issued: 0 (2005); Employment by occupation: 10.6% management, 12.9% professional, 12.4% services, 34.4% sales, 0.0% farming, 7.6% construction, 22.1% production (2000).
Income: Per capita income: $19,074 (2005); Median household income: $30,526 (2005); Average household income: $42,400 (2005); Percent of households with income of $100,000 or more: 7.2% (2005); Poverty rate: 14.7% (2000).
Education: Percent of population age 25 and over with: High school diploma (including GED) or higher: 74.1% (2005); Bachelor's degree or higher: 11.4% (2005); Master's degree or higher: 3.5% (2005).

School District(s)
East Syracuse-Minoa Central School District (PK-12)
    2003-04 Enrollment: 3,824 . . . . (315) 656-7205

Housing: Homeownership rate: 46.5% (2005); Median home value: $93,981 (2005); Median rent: $409 per month (2000); Median age of housing: 60+ years (2000).
Transportation: Commute to work: 90.1% car, 3.3% public transportation, 5.0% walk, 1.3% work from home (2000); Travel time to work: 52.1% less than 15 minutes, 36.8% 15 to 30 minutes, 7.8% 30 to 45 minutes, 2.0% 45 to 60 minutes, 1.3% 60 minutes or more (2000)

ELBRIDGE (village). Covers a land area of 1.048 square miles and a water area of 0 square miles. Located at 43.03° N. Lat.; 76.44° W. Long.
Population: 1,219 (1990); 1,103 (2000); 1,087 (2005); 1,077 (2010 projected); Race: 96.4% White, 0.2% Black, 1.1% Asian, 2.1% Hispanic of any race (2005); Density: 1,036.9 persons per square mile (2005); Average household size: 2.54 (2005); Median age: 40.8 (2005); Males per 100 females: 99.4 (2005); Marriage status: 17.5% never married, 69.3% now married, 6.9% widowed, 6.2% divorced (2000); Foreign born: 1.9% (2000); Ancestry (includes multiple ancestries): 23.0% English, 20.1% German, 18.6% Irish, 14.0% Italian, 7.0% United States or American (2000).
Economy: Single-family building permits issued: 0 (2005); Multi-family building permits issued: 0 (2005); Employment by occupation: 7.4% management, 23.5% professional, 11.1% services, 30.7% sales, 0.0% farming, 11.5% construction, 15.9% production (2000).
Income: Per capita income: $24,407 (2005); Median household income: $51,111 (2005); Average household income: $61,986 (2005); Percent of households with income of $100,000 or more: 12.9% (2005); Poverty rate: 4.8% (2000).
Education: Percent of population age 25 and over with: High school diploma (including GED) or higher: 91.2% (2005); Bachelor's degree or higher: 21.0% (2005); Master's degree or higher: 9.7% (2005).

School District(s)
Jordan-Elbridge Central School District (KG-12)
    2003-04 Enrollment: 1,703 .... (315) 689-3978
Housing: Homeownership rate: 77.8% (2005); Median home value: $126,493 (2005); Median rent: $433 per month (2000); Median age of housing: 41 years (2000).
Transportation: Commute to work: 91.7% car, 0.6% public transportation, 4.0% walk, 3.8% work from home (2000); Travel time to work: 33.5% less than 15 minutes, 38.0% 15 to 30 minutes, 22.4% 30 to 45 minutes, 3.0% 45 to 60 minutes, 3.1% 60 minutes or more (2000)
Additional Information Contacts
Village of Elbridge .... (315) 689-7851
    http://www.townofelbridge.org/

ELBRIDGE (town). Covers a land area of 37.575 square miles and a water area of 0.713 square miles. Located at 43.05° N. Lat.; 76.45° W. Long.
Population: 6,192 (1990); 6,091 (2000); 6,263 (2005); 6,435 (2010 projected); Race: 97.3% White, 0.6% Black, 0.6% Asian, 1.5% Hispanic of any race (2005); Density: 166.7 persons per square mile (2005); Average household size: 2.57 (2005); Median age: 39.0 (2005); Males per 100 females: 98.3 (2005); Marriage status: 23.4% never married, 60.8% now married, 6.5% widowed, 9.3% divorced (2000); Foreign born: 2.1% (2000); Ancestry (includes multiple ancestries): 23.3% German, 22.4% English, 20.5% Irish, 11.0% Italian, 6.0% Other groups (2000).
Economy: In agricultural area. State rearing station for brown, brook, and rainbow trout. Single-family building permits issued: 12 (2005); Multi-family building permits issued: 0 (2005); Employment by occupation: 9.3% management, 18.8% professional, 15.4% services, 30.1% sales, 1.3% farming, 11.3% construction, 13.9% production (2000).
Income: Per capita income: $22,512 (2005); Median household income: $46,620 (2005); Average household income: $57,634 (2005); Percent of households with income of $100,000 or more: 13.1% (2005); Poverty rate: 6.9% (2000).
Education: Percent of population age 25 and over with: High school diploma (including GED) or higher: 86.5% (2005); Bachelor's degree or higher: 17.9% (2005); Master's degree or higher: 7.3% (2005).
Housing: Homeownership rate: 81.7% (2005); Median home value: $110,408 (2005); Median rent: $393 per month (2000); Median age of housing: 34 years (2000).
Transportation: Commute to work: 92.9% car, 1.9% public transportation, 2.7% walk, 1.9% work from home (2000); Travel time to work: 28.1% less than 15 minutes, 39.7% 15 to 30 minutes, 25.5% 30 to 45 minutes, 3.7% 45 to 60 minutes, 3.0% 60 minutes or more (2000)
Additional Information Contacts
Town of Elbridge .... (315) 689-9031
    http://www.townofelbridge.com/

FABIUS (village). Covers a land area of 0.401 square miles and a water area of 0 square miles. Located at 42.83° N. Lat.; 75.98° W. Long. Elevation is 2,020 feet.
Population: 310 (1990); 355 (2000); 366 (2005); 376 (2010 projected); Race: 97.3% White, 0.0% Black, 0.5% Asian, 3.6% Hispanic of any race (2005); Density: 913.1 persons per square mile (2005); Average household size: 2.79 (2005); Median age: 37.7 (2005); Males per 100 females: 88.7 (2005); Marriage status: 25.9% never married, 64.1% now married, 3.8% widowed, 6.2% divorced (2000); Foreign born: 0.8% (2000); Ancestry (includes multiple ancestries): 25.5% Irish, 23.6% English, 23.1% German, 9.2% Italian, 8.9% United States or American (2000).
Economy: Single-family building permits issued: 0 (2005); Multi-family building permits issued: 0 (2005); Employment by occupation: 13.4% management, 26.3% professional, 12.4% services, 24.2% sales, 0.0% farming, 16.7% construction, 7.0% production (2000).
Income: Per capita income: $21,305 (2005); Median household income: $56,908 (2005); Average household income: $59,523 (2005); Percent of households with income of $100,000 or more: 9.9% (2005); Poverty rate: 5.5% (2000).
Education: Percent of population age 25 and over with: High school diploma (including GED) or higher: 90.0% (2005); Bachelor's degree or higher: 23.8% (2005); Master's degree or higher: 10.4% (2005).
School District(s)
Fabius-Pompey Central School District (KG-12)
    2003-04 Enrollment: 913 .... (315) 683-5301
Housing: Homeownership rate: 74.8% (2005); Median home value: $119,565 (2005); Median rent: $436 per month (2000); Median age of housing: 60+ years (2000).
Transportation: Commute to work: 92.9% car, 0.0% public transportation, 3.3% walk, 3.8% work from home (2000); Travel time to work: 22.2% less than 15 minutes, 44.3% 15 to 30 minutes, 30.1% 30 to 45 minutes, 0.6% 45 to 60 minutes, 2.8% 60 minutes or more (2000)

FABIUS (town). Covers a land area of 46.561 square miles and a water area of 0.235 square miles. Located at 42.82° N. Lat.; 76.00° W. Long. Elevation is 2,020 feet.
Population: 1,760 (1990); 1,974 (2000); 2,040 (2005); 2,105 (2010 projected); Race: 97.0% White, 0.8% Black, 0.3% Asian, 2.4% Hispanic of any race (2005); Density: 43.8 persons per square mile (2005); Average household size: 2.87 (2005); Median age: 37.1 (2005); Males per 100 females: 98.1 (2005); Marriage status: 24.4% never married, 65.0% now married, 4.8% widowed, 5.8% divorced (2000); Foreign born: 1.5% (2000); Ancestry (includes multiple ancestries): 23.7% English, 21.6% German, 21.1% Irish, 8.3% Italian, 7.0% United States or American (2000).
Economy: In dairying area. Ski centers nearby. Single-family building permits issued: 7 (2005); Multi-family building permits issued: 0 (2005); Employment by occupation: 13.6% management, 20.8% professional, 11.9% services, 21.9% sales, 4.6% farming, 16.0% construction, 11.1% production (2000).
Income: Per capita income: $25,201 (2005); Median household income: $58,279 (2005); Average household income: $71,401 (2005); Percent of households with income of $100,000 or more: 18.5% (2005); Poverty rate: 5.7% (2000).
Education: Percent of population age 25 and over with: High school diploma (including GED) or higher: 90.8% (2005); Bachelor's degree or higher: 21.9% (2005); Master's degree or higher: 8.9% (2005).
Housing: Homeownership rate: 81.4% (2005); Median home value: $128,009 (2005); Median rent: $460 per month (2000); Median age of housing: 54 years (2000).
Transportation: Commute to work: 91.6% car, 0.4% public transportation, 2.3% walk, 5.3% work from home (2000); Travel time to work: 22.2% less than 15 minutes, 35.0% 15 to 30 minutes, 31.3% 30 to 45 minutes, 8.1% 45 to 60 minutes, 3.4% 60 minutes or more (2000)

FAIRMOUNT (CDP). Covers a land area of 3.368 square miles and a water area of 0 square miles. Located at 43.04° N. Lat.; 76.24° W. Long.
Population: 11,322 (1990); 10,795 (2000); 11,056 (2005); 11,268 (2010 projected); Race: 94.6% White, 1.8% Black, 1.8% Asian, 1.4% Hispanic of any race (2005); Density: 3,282.4 persons per square mile (2005); Average household size: 2.41 (2005); Median age: 42.7 (2005); Males per 100 females: 90.0 (2005); Marriage status: 21.2% never married, 64.6% now married, 8.0% widowed, 6.2% divorced (2000); Foreign born: 5.5% (2000); Ancestry (includes multiple ancestries): 26.2% Irish, 19.5% Italian, 19.3% German, 15.1% English, 11.5% Polish (2000).
Economy: Considerable retail activity in otherwise residential area. Employment by occupation: 11.7% management, 26.0% professional, 13.4% services, 31.8% sales, 0.1% farming, 6.8% construction, 10.2% production (2000).
Income: Per capita income: $25,072 (2005); Median household income: $53,215 (2005); Average household income: $60,352 (2005); Percent of households with income of $100,000 or more: 13.2% (2005); Poverty rate: 3.7% (2000).
Education: Percent of population age 25 and over with: High school diploma (including GED) or higher: 90.6% (2005); Bachelor's degree or higher: 24.6% (2005); Master's degree or higher: 9.5% (2005).
Housing: Homeownership rate: 79.9% (2005); Median home value: $117,266 (2005); Median rent: $591 per month (2000); Median age of housing: 41 years (2000).
Transportation: Commute to work: 94.4% car, 1.4% public transportation, 1.6% walk, 2.1% work from home (2000); Travel time to work: 28.1% less than 15 minutes, 55.4% 15 to 30 minutes, 11.1% 30 to 45 minutes, 3.1% 45 to 60 minutes, 2.2% 60 minutes or more (2000)

FAYETTEVILLE (village). Covers a land area of 1.729 square miles and a water area of 0 square miles. Located at 43.02° N. Lat.; 76.00° W. Long. Elevation is 531 feet.
History: Incorporated 1844.
Population: 4,340 (1990); 4,190 (2000); 4,216 (2005); 4,256 (2010 projected); Race: 94.7% White, 0.9% Black, 3.2% Asian, 1.6% Hispanic of any race (2005); Density: 2,438.0 persons per square mile (2005); Average

household size: 2.24 (2005); Median age: 41.9 (2005); Males per 100 females: 88.0 (2005); Marriage status: 23.2% never married, 61.4% now married, 6.9% widowed, 8.5% divorced (2000); Foreign born: 5.0% (2000); Ancestry (includes multiple ancestries): 28.1% Irish, 25.6% German, 20.0% English, 9.0% Polish, 8.5% Italian (2000).
Economy: Manufacturing: machinery, paper products. Agriculture: dairy products. Single-family building permits issued: 25 (2005); Multi-family building permits issued: 0 (2005); Employment by occupation: 14.3% management, 41.0% professional, 8.9% services, 23.9% sales, 0.7% farming, 4.5% construction, 6.7% production (2000).
Income: Per capita income: $34,199 (2005); Median household income: $58,660 (2005); Average household income: $76,776 (2005); Percent of households with income of $100,000 or more: 25.6% (2005); Poverty rate: 2.2% (2000).
Education: Percent of population age 25 and over with: High school diploma (including GED) or higher: 96.0% (2005); Bachelor's degree or higher: 55.7% (2005); Master's degree or higher: 29.1% (2005).

School District(s)
Fayetteville-Manlius Central School District (KG-12)
    2003-04 Enrollment: 4,619 . . . . (315) 682-1200
Housing: Homeownership rate: 74.1% (2005); Median home value: $138,671 (2005); Median rent: $507 per month (2000); Median age of housing: 45 years (2000).
Transportation: Commute to work: 92.8% car, 0.4% public transportation, 1.8% walk, 5.0% work from home (2000); Travel time to work: 29.9% less than 15 minutes, 53.6% 15 to 30 minutes, 10.6% 30 to 45 minutes, 3.3% 45 to 60 minutes, 2.7% 60 minutes or more (2000)
Additional Information Contacts
Fayetteville Chamber of Commer . . . . (315) 637-5544
    http://www.fayettevillechamber.org

GALEVILLE (CDP). Covers a land area of 1.141 square miles and a water area of 0 square miles. Located at 43.08° N. Lat.; 76.17° W. Long.
Population: 4,423 (1990); 4,476 (2000); 4,325 (2005); 4,174 (2010 projected); Race: 89.0% White, 5.6% Black, 1.8% Asian, 2.0% Hispanic of any race (2005); Density: 3,790.1 persons per square mile (2005); Average household size: 2.15 (2005); Median age: 44.1 (2005); Males per 100 females: 86.7 (2005); Marriage status: 25.0% never married, 50.8% now married, 14.3% widowed, 9.9% divorced (2000); Foreign born: 6.0% (2000); Ancestry (includes multiple ancestries): 28.9% Italian, 19.1% German, 15.8% Irish, 12.5% English, 9.7% Other groups (2000).
Economy: Employment by occupation: 9.6% management, 18.3% professional, 17.5% services, 29.4% sales, 0.0% farming, 7.3% construction, 17.9% production (2000).
Income: Per capita income: $24,203 (2005); Median household income: $40,363 (2005); Average household income: $50,366 (2005); Percent of households with income of $100,000 or more: 7.4% (2005); Poverty rate: 7.5% (2000).
Education: Percent of population age 25 and over with: High school diploma (including GED) or higher: 79.7% (2005); Bachelor's degree or higher: 15.0% (2005); Master's degree or higher: 4.2% (2005).
Housing: Homeownership rate: 66.9% (2005); Median home value: $91,991 (2005); Median rent: $517 per month (2000); Median age of housing: 44 years (2000).
Transportation: Commute to work: 92.0% car, 2.6% public transportation, 1.3% walk, 2.5% work from home (2000); Travel time to work: 45.8% less than 15 minutes, 43.3% 15 to 30 minutes, 4.4% 30 to 45 minutes, 1.4% 45 to 60 minutes, 5.1% 60 minutes or more (2000)

GEDDES (town). Covers a land area of 9.238 square miles and a water area of 2.956 square miles. Located at 43.05° N. Lat.; 76.21° W. Long.
Population: 17,677 (1990); 17,740 (2000); 17,476 (2005); 17,243 (2010 projected); Race: 96.4% White, 0.7% Black, 0.7% Asian, 1.9% Hispanic of any race (2005); Density: 1,891.7 persons per square mile (2005); Average household size: 2.40 (2005); Median age: 42.7 (2005); Males per 100 females: 87.6 (2005); Marriage status: 24.1% never married, 58.1% now married, 10.4% widowed, 7.4% divorced (2000); Foreign born: 6.2% (2000); Ancestry (includes multiple ancestries): 28.1% Italian, 26.1% Irish, 14.2% German, 14.1% Polish, 10.5% English (2000).
Economy: Single-family building permits issued: 7 (2005); Multi-family building permits issued: 0 (2005); Employment by occupation: 11.3% management, 21.7% professional, 14.8% services, 32.6% sales, 0.4% farming, 7.2% construction, 12.0% production (2000).
Income: Per capita income: $23,813 (2005); Median household income: $46,779 (2005); Average household income: $56,738 (2005); Percent of households with income of $100,000 or more: 13.1% (2005); Poverty rate: 8.2% (2000).
Taxes: Total city taxes per capita: $267 (2004); City property taxes per capita: $241 (2004).
Education: Percent of population age 25 and over with: High school diploma (including GED) or higher: 85.6% (2005); Bachelor's degree or higher: 23.3% (2005); Master's degree or higher: 8.7% (2005).
Housing: Homeownership rate: 76.8% (2005); Median home value: $120,125 (2005); Median rent: $452 per month (2000); Median age of housing: 47 years (2000).
Safety: Violent crime rate: 2.8 per 10,000 population; Property crime rate: 173.3 per 10,000 population (2004).
Transportation: Commute to work: 94.0% car, 1.9% public transportation, 1.4% walk, 2.1% work from home (2000); Travel time to work: 38.7% less than 15 minutes, 50.8% 15 to 30 minutes, 6.5% 30 to 45 minutes, 1.4% 45 to 60 minutes, 2.6% 60 minutes or more (2000)
Additional Information Contacts
Town of Geddes. . . . . (315) 468-2528
    http://www.townofgeddes.com/

JAMESVILLE (unincorporated postal area, zip code 13078). Covers a land area of 40.322 square miles and a water area of 0.384 square miles. Located at 42.97° N. Lat.; 76.07° W. Long. Elevation is 597 feet.
Population: 0 (2000); Race: 92.9% White, 2.8% Black, 1.1% Asian, 0.7% Hispanic of any race (2000); Density: 0.0 persons per square mile (2000); Age: 24.4% under 18, 17.6% over 64 (2000); Marriage status: 22.6% never married, 63.1% now married, 9.4% widowed, 4.8% divorced (2000); Foreign born: 5.7% (2000); Ancestry (includes multiple ancestries): 23.4% Irish, 18.9% German, 14.8% English, 14.2% Italian, 7.5% Other groups (2000).
Economy: Light manufacturing. Employment by occupation: 20.9% management, 33.9% professional, 9.7% services, 20.9% sales, 0.2% farming, 6.9% construction, 7.6% production (2000).
Income: Per capita income: $29,984 (2000); Median household income: $65,917 (2000); Poverty rate: 3.5% (2000).
Education: Percent of population age 25 and over with: High school diploma (including GED) or higher: 89.6% (2000); Bachelor's degree or higher: 41.9% (2000).

School District(s)
Jamesville-Dewitt Central School District (KG-12)
    2003-04 Enrollment: 2,717 . . . . (315) 445-8304
Housing: Homeownership rate: 83.3% (2000); Median home value: $124,500 (2000); Median rent: $608 per month (2000); Median age of housing: 28 years (2000).
Transportation: Commute to work: 93.0% car, 0.0% public transportation, 1.2% walk, 5.8% work from home (2000); Travel time to work: 31.1% less than 15 minutes, 54.3% 15 to 30 minutes, 9.3% 30 to 45 minutes, 1.7% 45 to 60 minutes, 3.5% 60 minutes or more (2000)

JORDAN (village). Covers a land area of 1.156 square miles and a water area of 0 square miles. Located at 43.06° N. Lat.; 76.47° W. Long. Elevation is 395 feet.
History: Incorporated 1835.
Population: 1,439 (1990); 1,314 (2000); 1,368 (2005); 1,429 (2010 projected); Race: 96.8% White, 0.7% Black, 0.7% Asian, 1.5% Hispanic of any race (2005); Density: 1,183.4 persons per square mile (2005); Average household size: 2.56 (2005); Median age: 35.9 (2005); Males per 100 females: 97.1 (2005); Marriage status: 27.5% never married, 51.4% now married, 9.8% widowed, 11.3% divorced (2000); Foreign born: 2.2% (2000); Ancestry (includes multiple ancestries): 24.6% Irish, 24.2% English, 20.3% German, 7.6% Italian, 7.2% Other groups (2000).
Economy: Manufacturing; in dairying area; onions, potatoes, sweet corn, beans. Single-family building permits issued: 0 (2005); Multi-family building permits issued: 0 (2005); Employment by occupation: 11.3% management, 24.1% professional, 15.1% services, 23.9% sales, 0.0% farming, 9.0% construction, 16.5% production (2000).
Income: Per capita income: $18,799 (2005); Median household income: $40,027 (2005); Average household income: $48,070 (2005); Percent of households with income of $100,000 or more: 7.5% (2005); Poverty rate: 8.5% (2000).
Education: Percent of population age 25 and over with: High school diploma (including GED) or higher: 85.0% (2005); Bachelor's degree or higher: 19.0% (2005); Master's degree or higher: 5.5% (2005).

School District(s)
Jordan-Elbridge Central School District (KG-12)
   2003-04 Enrollment: 1,703 . . . . (315) 689-3978
Housing: Homeownership rate: 66.7% (2005); Median home value: $98,300 (2005); Median rent: $387 per month (2000); Median age of housing: 60+ years (2000).
Safety: Violent crime rate: 0.0 per 10,000 population; Property crime rate: 58.4 per 10,000 population (2004).
Transportation: Commute to work: 92.5% car, 0.7% public transportation, 5.1% walk, 1.3% work from home (2000); Travel time to work: 27.3% less than 15 minutes, 29.3% 15 to 30 minutes, 33.4% 30 to 45 minutes, 7.2% 45 to 60 minutes, 2.8% 60 minutes or more (2000)

KIRKVILLE
(unincorporated postal area, zip code 13082). Covers a land area of 24.809 square miles and a water area of 0.242 square miles. Located at 43.10° N. Lat.; 75.96° W. Long.
Population: 0 (2000); Race: 97.3% White, 0.8% Black, 0.1% Asian, 0.3% Hispanic of any race (2000); Density: 0.0 persons per square mile (2000); Age: 25.6% under 18, 12.5% over 64 (2000); Marriage status: 22.7% never married, 62.0% now married, 5.5% widowed, 9.9% divorced (2000); Foreign born: 1.7% (2000); Ancestry (includes multiple ancestries): 23.8% German, 20.1% Irish, 16.1% English, 12.6% Italian, 11.1% French (except Basque) (2000).
Economy: Employment by occupation: 11.9% management, 16.2% professional, 14.4% services, 33.4% sales, 0.8% farming, 11.1% construction, 12.2% production (2000).
Income: Per capita income: $19,607 (2000); Median household income: $42,892 (2000); Poverty rate: 7.8% (2000).
Education: Percent of population age 25 and over with: High school diploma (including GED) or higher: 84.3% (2000); Bachelor's degree or higher: 13.8% (2000).
Housing: Homeownership rate: 85.9% (2000); Median home value: $84,700 (2000); Median rent: $464 per month (2000); Median age of housing: 26 years (2000).
Transportation: Commute to work: 95.2% car, 0.5% public transportation, 2.0% walk, 1.8% work from home (2000); Travel time to work: 21.8% less than 15 minutes, 58.7% 15 to 30 minutes, 16.9% 30 to 45 minutes, 0.5% 45 to 60 minutes, 2.1% 60 minutes or more (2000)

LA FAYETTE
(town). Covers a land area of 39.248 square miles and a water area of 0.349 square miles. Located at 42.91° N. Lat.; 76.10° W. Long.
Population: 4,937 (1990); 4,833 (2000); 4,874 (2005); 4,925 (2010 projected); Race: 95.4% White, 0.3% Black, 0.7% Asian, 0.6% Hispanic of any race (2005); Density: 124.2 persons per square mile (2005); Average household size: 2.59 (2005); Median age: 41.5 (2005); Males per 100 females: 99.2 (2005); Marriage status: 21.8% never married, 64.4% now married, 7.0% widowed, 6.8% divorced (2000); Foreign born: 4.1% (2000); Ancestry (includes multiple ancestries): 20.5% English, 19.4% German, 19.4% Irish, 9.6% Italian, 9.1% United States or American (2000).
Economy: Single-family building permits issued: 23 (2005); Multi-family building permits issued: 0 (2005); Employment by occupation: 15.8% management, 23.9% professional, 12.2% services, 25.2% sales, 1.3% farming, 11.0% construction, 10.7% production (2000).
Income: Per capita income: $29,454 (2005); Median household income: $55,439 (2005); Average household income: $76,191 (2005); Percent of households with income of $100,000 or more: 20.4% (2005); Poverty rate: 5.1% (2000).
Education: Percent of population age 25 and over with: High school diploma (including GED) or higher: 90.1% (2005); Bachelor's degree or higher: 27.6% (2005); Master's degree or higher: 11.4% (2005).
School District(s)
La Fayette Central School District (KG-12)
   2003-04 Enrollment: 1,025 . . . . (315) 677-9728
Housing: Homeownership rate: 83.6% (2005); Median home value: $132,850 (2005); Median rent: $432 per month (2000); Median age of housing: 35 years (2000).
Transportation: Commute to work: 93.6% car, 0.0% public transportation, 2.6% walk, 3.5% work from home (2000); Travel time to work: 23.4% less than 15 minutes, 54.2% 15 to 30 minutes, 14.8% 30 to 45 minutes, 4.9% 45 to 60 minutes, 2.7% 60 minutes or more (2000)

LA FAYETTE
(unincorporated postal area, zip code 13084). Covers a land area of 40.008 square miles and a water area of 0 square miles. Located at 42.88° N. Lat.; 76.11° W. Long.
Population: 0 (2000); Race: 94.2% White, 1.0% Black, 0.0% Asian, 0.6% Hispanic of any race (2000); Density: 0.0 persons per square mile (2000); Age: 28.7% under 18, 12.0% over 64 (2000); Marriage status: 22.5% never married, 63.4% now married, 6.3% widowed, 7.8% divorced (2000); Foreign born: 3.0% (2000); Ancestry (includes multiple ancestries): 19.4% German, 19.3% English, 16.9% Irish, 9.1% United States or American, 7.7% Italian (2000).
Economy: Employment by occupation: 15.3% management, 20.3% professional, 12.6% services, 25.7% sales, 3.4% farming, 11.3% construction, 11.6% production (2000).
Income: Per capita income: $21,826 (2000); Median household income: $46,528 (2000); Poverty rate: 6.9% (2000).
Education: Percent of population age 25 and over with: High school diploma (including GED) or higher: 87.9% (2000); Bachelor's degree or higher: 23.7% (2000).
Housing: Homeownership rate: 79.7% (2000); Median home value: $95,400 (2000); Median rent: $414 per month (2000); Median age of housing: 34 years (2000).
Transportation: Commute to work: 92.2% car, 0.1% public transportation, 4.6% walk, 2.5% work from home (2000); Travel time to work: 23.5% less than 15 minutes, 51.0% 15 to 30 minutes, 19.6% 30 to 45 minutes, 3.1% 45 to 60 minutes, 2.9% 60 minutes or more (2000)

LAKELAND
(CDP). Covers a land area of 1.515 square miles and a water area of 0 square miles. Located at 43.09° N. Lat.; 76.24° W. Long.
Population: 2,822 (1990); 2,852 (2000); 2,896 (2005); 2,927 (2010 projected); Race: 98.1% White, 0.2% Black, 0.9% Asian, 1.3% Hispanic of any race (2005); Density: 1,911.5 persons per square mile (2005); Average household size: 2.60 (2005); Median age: 40.7 (2005); Males per 100 females: 92.2 (2005); Marriage status: 21.6% never married, 66.2% now married, 6.3% widowed, 5.9% divorced (2000); Foreign born: 3.8% (2000); Ancestry (includes multiple ancestries): 30.1% Italian, 24.1% Polish, 14.4% Irish, 12.0% English, 11.7% German (2000).
Economy: Employment by occupation: 6.4% management, 15.0% professional, 14.6% services, 41.4% sales, 0.6% farming, 9.2% construction, 12.8% production (2000).
Income: Per capita income: $23,690 (2005); Median household income: $53,346 (2005); Average household income: $61,584 (2005); Percent of households with income of $100,000 or more: 14.8% (2005); Poverty rate: 4.9% (2000).
Education: Percent of population age 25 and over with: High school diploma (including GED) or higher: 82.9% (2005); Bachelor's degree or higher: 13.5% (2005); Master's degree or higher: 4.0% (2005).
Housing: Homeownership rate: 88.8% (2005); Median home value: $118,904 (2005); Median rent: $504 per month (2000); Median age of housing: 34 years (2000).
Transportation: Commute to work: 96.9% car, 0.0% public transportation, 1.2% walk, 1.4% work from home (2000); Travel time to work: 35.8% less than 15 minutes, 58.3% 15 to 30 minutes, 3.8% 30 to 45 minutes, 0.5% 45 to 60 minutes, 1.7% 60 minutes or more (2000)

LIVERPOOL
(village). Covers a land area of 0.754 square miles and a water area of 0 square miles. Located at 43.10° N. Lat.; 76.21° W. Long. Elevation is 390 feet.
History: Incorporated 1830.
Population: 2,624 (1990); 2,505 (2000); 2,435 (2005); 2,367 (2010 projected); Race: 94.9% White, 1.6% Black, 1.8% Asian, 2.8% Hispanic of any race (2005); Density: 3,229.0 persons per square mile (2005); Average household size: 2.12 (2005); Median age: 40.8 (2005); Males per 100 females: 85.6 (2005); Marriage status: 30.1% never married, 51.9% now married, 10.0% widowed, 7.9% divorced (2000); Foreign born: 4.1% (2000); Ancestry (includes multiple ancestries): 22.6% German, 21.4% Irish, 15.9% Italian, 13.1% English, 10.4% Polish (2000).
Economy: Manufacturing: computers, computer equipment, machinery, corrugated containers, electrical equipment, rubber products. Agriculture: dairy products; poultry. Single-family building permits issued: 2 (2005); Multi-family building permits issued: 0 (2005); Employment by occupation: 14.8% management, 29.4% professional, 12.8% services, 26.7% sales, 0.0% farming, 7.3% construction, 9.0% production (2000).
Income: Per capita income: $25,963 (2005); Median household income: $41,000 (2005); Average household income: $55,105 (2005); Percent of households with income of $100,000 or more: 12.9% (2005); Poverty rate: 11.6% (2000).
Taxes: Total city taxes per capita: $438 (2004); City property taxes per capita: $381 (2004).

Education: Percent of population age 25 and over with: High school diploma (including GED) or higher: 89.9% (2005); Bachelor's degree or higher: 31.0% (2005); Master's degree or higher: 14.8% (2005).

School District(s)
Liverpool Central School District (PK-12)
  2003-04 Enrollment: 8,629 . . . . (315) 453-0225

Two-year College(s)
Bryant and Stratton College-Syracuse North
  Fall 2004 Enrollment: 450 . . . . (315) 652-6500
  2005-06 Tuition: In-state $11,820; Out-of-state $11,820
ITT Technical Institute
  Fall 2004 Enrollment: 393 . . . . (315) 461-8000
  2005-06 Tuition: In-state $14,196; Out-of-state $14,196
National Tractor Trailer School Inc
  Fall 2004 Enrollment: 68 . . . . (315) 451-2430
Onondaga Cortland Madison BOCES
  Fall 2004 Enrollment: 543 . . . . (315) 453-4455

Housing: Homeownership rate: 65.5% (2005); Median home value: $114,327 (2005); Median rent: $499 per month (2000); Median age of housing: 60 years (2000).
Safety: Violent crime rate: 0.0 per 10,000 population; Property crime rate: 190.9 per 10,000 population (2004).
Transportation: Commute to work: 89.0% car, 2.5% public transportation, 3.5% walk, 2.6% work from home (2000); Travel time to work: 38.1% less than 15 minutes, 48.8% 15 to 30 minutes, 9.5% 30 to 45 minutes, 2.2% 45 to 60 minutes, 1.6% 60 minutes or more (2000)

Additional Information Contacts
Liverpool Chamber of Commerce . . . . (315) 457-3895
  http://www.liverpoolchamber.com
Village of Liverpool . . . . (315) 457-3441
  http://www.villageofliverpool.org/

LYNCOURT (CDP). Covers a land area of 1.239 square miles and a water area of 0 square miles. Located at 43.08° N. Lat.; 76.12° W. Long.
Population: 4,696 (1990); 4,268 (2000); 4,194 (2005); 4,168 (2010 projected); Race: 93.1% White, 3.6% Black, 0.5% Asian, 1.1% Hispanic of any race (2005); Density: 3,386.2 persons per square mile (2005); Average household size: 2.18 (2005); Median age: 43.0 (2005); Males per 100 females: 90.7 (2005); Marriage status: 27.0% never married, 50.2% now married, 12.9% widowed, 9.9% divorced (2000); Foreign born: 5.1% (2000); Ancestry (includes multiple ancestries): 41.1% Italian, 23.2% German, 19.7% Irish, 8.2% English, 6.5% Other groups (2000).
Economy: Employment by occupation: 9.0% management, 15.2% professional, 16.4% services, 37.1% sales, 0.0% farming, 7.9% construction, 14.4% production (2000).
Income: Per capita income: $20,872 (2005); Median household income: $35,997 (2005); Average household income: $45,292 (2005); Percent of households with income of $100,000 or more: 5.7% (2005); Poverty rate: 10.0% (2000).
Education: Percent of population age 25 and over with: High school diploma (including GED) or higher: 76.8% (2005); Bachelor's degree or higher: 12.5% (2005); Master's degree or higher: 3.6% (2005).
Housing: Homeownership rate: 70.6% (2005); Median home value: $91,136 (2005); Median rent: $482 per month (2000); Median age of housing: 47 years (2000).
Transportation: Commute to work: 92.5% car, 1.8% public transportation, 3.7% walk, 1.3% work from home (2000); Travel time to work: 49.7% less than 15 minutes, 40.3% 15 to 30 minutes, 7.3% 30 to 45 minutes, 1.3% 45 to 60 minutes, 1.3% 60 minutes or more (2000)

LYSANDER (town). Covers a land area of 61.917 square miles and a water area of 2.702 square miles. Located at 43.17° N. Lat.; 76.35° W. Long. Elevation is 418 feet.
Population: 16,346 (1990); 19,285 (2000); 20,916 (2005); 22,417 (2010 projected); Race: 96.2% White, 0.9% Black, 1.3% Asian, 1.0% Hispanic of any race (2005); Density: 337.8 persons per square mile (2005); Average household size: 2.67 (2005); Median age: 38.9 (2005); Males per 100 females: 97.7 (2005); Marriage status: 20.5% never married, 67.0% now married, 4.7% widowed, 7.8% divorced (2000); Foreign born: 2.6% (2000); Ancestry (includes multiple ancestries): 23.6% Irish, 23.1% German, 19.5% English, 16.1% Italian, 7.2% Polish (2000).
Economy: Created as 1 of many residential, commercial, and industrial projects by N.Y. state's Urban Development Corporation that were meant to accommodate population growth in the area. Despite fears of local residents of increased taxes, the loss of rural character, stifling of industrial competition and the possibility of slums developing due to subsidized low-income housing, the community has been very successful. Single-family building permits issued: 105 (2005); Multi-family building permits issued: 0 (2005); Employment by occupation: 17.2% management, 25.4% professional, 9.3% services, 29.5% sales, 0.0% farming, 6.8% construction, 11.8% production (2000).
Income: Per capita income: $31,340 (2005); Median household income: $69,650 (2005); Average household income: $83,483 (2005); Percent of households with income of $100,000 or more: 29.5% (2005); Poverty rate: 3.8% (2000).
Education: Percent of population age 25 and over with: High school diploma (including GED) or higher: 92.0% (2005); Bachelor's degree or higher: 37.4% (2005); Master's degree or higher: 15.5% (2005).
Housing: Homeownership rate: 81.6% (2005); Median home value: $144,255 (2005); Median rent: $500 per month (2000); Median age of housing: 26 years (2000).
Transportation: Commute to work: 94.3% car, 0.4% public transportation, 0.8% walk, 3.9% work from home (2000); Travel time to work: 21.7% less than 15 minutes, 51.0% 15 to 30 minutes, 21.8% 30 to 45 minutes, 2.5% 45 to 60 minutes, 2.9% 60 minutes or more (2000)

Additional Information Contacts
Town of Lysander . . . . (315) 638-4264
  http://www.townoflysander.org/

MANLIUS (village). Covers a land area of 1.781 square miles and a water area of 0.004 square miles. Located at 43.00° N. Lat.; 75.97° W. Long.
Population: 4,945 (1990); 4,819 (2000); 4,931 (2005); 5,022 (2010 projected); Race: 91.4% White, 1.2% Black, 5.3% Asian, 1.8% Hispanic of any race (2005); Density: 2,768.7 persons per square mile (2005); Average household size: 2.33 (2005); Median age: 40.7 (2005); Males per 100 females: 87.8 (2005); Marriage status: 18.0% never married, 63.3% now married, 11.4% widowed, 7.3% divorced (2000); Foreign born: 10.0% (2000); Ancestry (includes multiple ancestries): 25.2% Irish, 18.4% German, 15.4% English, 14.1% Italian, 10.0% Other groups (2000).
Economy: Single-family building permits issued: 1 (2005); Multi-family building permits issued: 0 (2005); Employment by occupation: 17.8% management, 29.3% professional, 10.3% services, 29.1% sales, 0.2% farming, 4.6% construction, 8.6% production (2000).
Income: Per capita income: $29,362 (2005); Median household income: $53,955 (2005); Average household income: $68,430 (2005); Percent of households with income of $100,000 or more: 22.8% (2005); Poverty rate: 6.4% (2000).
Education: Percent of population age 25 and over with: High school diploma (including GED) or higher: 93.2% (2005); Bachelor's degree or higher: 51.3% (2005); Master's degree or higher: 20.8% (2005).

School District(s)
Fayetteville-Manlius Central School District (KG-12)
  2003-04 Enrollment: 4,619 . . . . (315) 682-1200

Housing: Homeownership rate: 57.8% (2005); Median home value: $159,902 (2005); Median rent: $531 per month (2000); Median age of housing: 33 years (2000).
Transportation: Commute to work: 89.0% car, 1.4% public transportation, 5.4% walk, 3.6% work from home (2000); Travel time to work: 32.3% less than 15 minutes, 48.0% 15 to 30 minutes, 16.3% 30 to 45 minutes, 2.1% 45 to 60 minutes, 1.3% 60 minutes or more (2000)

Additional Information Contacts
Manlius Chamber of Commerce . . . . (315) 682-7400
  http://www.manliuschamber.com/
Village of Manlius . . . . (315) 682-9171
  http://www.townofmanlius.org/

MANLIUS (town). Covers a land area of 49.619 square miles and a water area of 0.344 square miles. Located at 43.03° N. Lat.; 75.99° W. Long.
History: Settled 1789 incorporated 1842,
Population: 30,656 (1990); 31,872 (2000); 32,617 (2005); 33,317 (2010 projected); Race: 93.4% White, 1.1% Black, 3.8% Asian, 1.3% Hispanic of any race (2005); Density: 657.3 persons per square mile (2005); Average household size: 2.50 (2005); Median age: 42.3 (2005); Males per 100 females: 91.4 (2005); Marriage status: 20.3% never married, 65.4% now married, 7.7% widowed, 6.6% divorced (2000); Foreign born: 6.1% (2000); Ancestry (includes multiple ancestries): 23.6% Irish, 21.9% German, 17.3% English, 15.7% Italian, 8.2% Polish (2000).

Economy: Manufacturing: electronic equipment, fabricated metal products, machinery, plastic products. Unemployment rate: 3.6% (2005); Total civilian labor force: 17,065 (2005); Single-family building permits issued: 87 (2005); Multi-family building permits issued: 16 (2005); Employment by occupation: 17.9% management, 31.3% professional, 9.6% services, 28.0% sales, 0.2% farming, 4.9% construction, 8.1% production (2000).
Income: Per capita income: $36,254 (2005); Median household income: $68,305 (2005); Average household income: $90,166 (2005); Percent of households with income of $100,000 or more: 30.3% (2005); Poverty rate: 3.3% (2000).
Education: Percent of population age 25 and over with: High school diploma (including GED) or higher: 93.8% (2005); Bachelor's degree or higher: 47.8% (2005); Master's degree or higher: 22.0% (2005).
Housing: Homeownership rate: 79.5% (2005); Median home value: $146,469 (2005); Median rent: $529 per month (2000); Median age of housing: 33 years (2000).
Safety: Violent crime rate: 8.0 per 10,000 population; Property crime rate: 155.1 per 10,000 population (2004).
Transportation: Commute to work: 93.4% car, 0.8% public transportation, 1.5% walk, 3.8% work from home (2000); Travel time to work: 29.8% less than 15 minutes, 53.3% 15 to 30 minutes, 12.5% 30 to 45 minutes, 2.1% 45 to 60 minutes, 2.3% 60 minutes or more (2000)
Additional Information Contacts
Town of Manlius . . . . (315) 637-3521
http://www.townofmanlius.org/

MARCELLUS (village).
Covers a land area of 0.618 square miles and a water area of 0 square miles. Located at 42.98° N. Lat.; 76.34° W. Long. Elevation is 492 feet.
Population: 1,840 (1990); 1,826 (2000); 1,837 (2005); 1,842 (2010 projected); Race: 97.9% White, 0.4% Black, 0.3% Asian, 1.4% Hispanic of any race (2005); Density: 2,973.0 persons per square mile (2005); Average household size: 2.28 (2005); Median age: 37.4 (2005); Males per 100 females: 89.2 (2005); Marriage status: 25.7% never married, 57.0% now married, 8.1% widowed, 9.1% divorced (2000); Foreign born: 1.6% (2000); Ancestry (includes multiple ancestries): 35.0% Irish, 26.7% German, 21.2% English, 10.6% Italian, 8.1% Polish (2000).
Economy: Single-family building permits issued: 3 (2005); Multi-family building permits issued: 0 (2005); Employment by occupation: 9.0% management, 30.8% professional, 12.3% services, 28.1% sales, 0.3% farming, 9.8% construction, 9.6% production (2000).
Income: Per capita income: $25,397 (2005); Median household income: $49,571 (2005); Average household income: $57,885 (2005); Percent of households with income of $100,000 or more: 11.8% (2005); Poverty rate: 6.3% (2000).
Education: Percent of population age 25 and over with: High school diploma (including GED) or higher: 91.2% (2005); Bachelor's degree or higher: 35.3% (2005); Master's degree or higher: 12.7% (2005).
School District(s)
Marcellus Central School District (KG-12)
  2003-04 Enrollment: 2,147 . . . . (315) 673-0201
Housing: Homeownership rate: 52.5% (2005); Median home value: $132,981 (2005); Median rent: $422 per month (2000); Median age of housing: 50 years (2000).
Transportation: Commute to work: 89.6% car, 1.4% public transportation, 7.8% walk, 1.2% work from home (2000); Travel time to work: 22.0% less than 15 minutes, 47.3% 15 to 30 minutes, 24.2% 30 to 45 minutes, 3.2% 45 to 60 minutes, 3.3% 60 minutes or more (2000)
Additional Information Contacts
Village of Marcellus . . . . (315) 673-3112
http://village.marcellusny.com/

MARCELLUS (town).
Covers a land area of 32.551 square miles and a water area of 0.132 square miles. Located at 42.96° N. Lat.; 76.33° W. Long. Elevation is 492 feet.
History: Incorporated 1846.
Population: 6,465 (1990); 6,319 (2000); 6,347 (2005); 6,388 (2010 projected); Race: 98.0% White, 0.6% Black, 0.2% Asian, 1.2% Hispanic of any race (2005); Density: 195.0 persons per square mile (2005); Average household size: 2.60 (2005); Median age: 39.8 (2005); Males per 100 females: 95.7 (2005); Marriage status: 22.3% never married, 65.8% now married, 5.4% widowed, 6.5% divorced (2000); Foreign born: 1.4% (2000); Ancestry (includes multiple ancestries): 29.1% Irish, 21.1% German, 20.0% English, 10.6% Italian, 7.6% Polish (2000).
Economy: Manufacturing: paper, feed. Agriculture: dairy products. Single-family building permits issued: 10 (2005); Multi-family building permits issued: 0 (2005); Employment by occupation: 14.0% management, 26.2% professional, 12.2% services, 24.4% sales, 0.4% farming, 11.0% construction, 11.7% production (2000).
Income: Per capita income: $28,341 (2005); Median household income: $60,356 (2005); Average household income: $73,812 (2005); Percent of households with income of $100,000 or more: 18.9% (2005); Poverty rate: 3.2% (2000).
Education: Percent of population age 25 and over with: High school diploma (including GED) or higher: 90.9% (2005); Bachelor's degree or higher: 32.6% (2005); Master's degree or higher: 12.7% (2005).
Housing: Homeownership rate: 79.9% (2005); Median home value: $136,555 (2005); Median rent: $428 per month (2000); Median age of housing: 43 years (2000).
Transportation: Commute to work: 90.6% car, 0.7% public transportation, 4.9% walk, 3.6% work from home (2000); Travel time to work: 23.6% less than 15 minutes, 43.9% 15 to 30 minutes, 25.7% 30 to 45 minutes, 2.1% 45 to 60 minutes, 4.7% 60 minutes or more (2000)
Additional Information Contacts
Town of Marcellus . . . . (315) 673-3269
http://www.marcellusny.com/

MARIETTA (unincorporated postal area, zip code 13110).
Covers a land area of 25.919 square miles and a water area of 0.008 square miles. Located at 42.89° N. Lat.; 76.28° W. Long.
Population: 0 (2000); Race: 98.6% White, 0.5% Black, 0.1% Asian, 0.6% Hispanic of any race (2000); Density: 0.0 persons per square mile (2000); Age: 23.8% under 18, 10.9% over 64 (2000); Marriage status: 24.3% never married, 61.0% now married, 5.8% widowed, 9.0% divorced (2000); Foreign born: 2.2% (2000); Ancestry (includes multiple ancestries): 25.2% Irish, 24.0% English, 23.9% German, 5.8% United States or American, 5.7% Italian (2000).
Economy: Employment by occupation: 13.6% management, 15.3% professional, 17.4% services, 30.6% sales, 1.6% farming, 8.2% construction, 13.3% production (2000).
Income: Per capita income: $22,522 (2000); Median household income: $45,164 (2000); Poverty rate: 6.0% (2000).
Education: Percent of population age 25 and over with: High school diploma (including GED) or higher: 91.1% (2000); Bachelor's degree or higher: 25.9% (2000).
Housing: Homeownership rate: 86.6% (2000); Median home value: $88,700 (2000); Median rent: $468 per month (2000); Median age of housing: 40 years (2000).
Transportation: Commute to work: 91.7% car, 0.0% public transportation, 2.4% walk, 5.5% work from home (2000); Travel time to work: 16.7% less than 15 minutes, 32.6% 15 to 30 minutes, 36.4% 30 to 45 minutes, 9.0% 45 to 60 minutes, 5.4% 60 minutes or more (2000)

MATTYDALE (CDP).
Covers a land area of 1.916 square miles and a water area of 0 square miles. Located at 43.09° N. Lat.; 76.14° W. Long.
Population: 6,790 (1990); 6,367 (2000); 6,224 (2005); 6,089 (2010 projected); Race: 92.7% White, 2.4% Black, 1.1% Asian, 3.2% Hispanic of any race (2005); Density: 3,248.7 persons per square mile (2005); Average household size: 2.38 (2005); Median age: 38.5 (2005); Males per 100 females: 92.2 (2005); Marriage status: 29.2% never married, 51.2% now married, 9.1% widowed, 10.5% divorced (2000); Foreign born: 2.9% (2000); Ancestry (includes multiple ancestries): 22.3% German, 22.2% Italian, 21.9% Irish, 12.9% English, 9.0% Other groups (2000).
Economy: Employment by occupation: 10.3% management, 10.9% professional, 16.8% services, 32.4% sales, 0.0% farming, 9.0% construction, 20.6% production (2000).
Income: Per capita income: $21,285 (2005); Median household income: $40,902 (2005); Average household income: $50,566 (2005); Percent of households with income of $100,000 or more: 8.9% (2005); Poverty rate: 9.9% (2000).
Education: Percent of population age 25 and over with: High school diploma (including GED) or higher: 79.8% (2005); Bachelor's degree or higher: 9.1% (2005); Master's degree or higher: 3.0% (2005).
Housing: Homeownership rate: 72.2% (2005); Median home value: $79,767 (2005); Median rent: $558 per month (2000); Median age of housing: 48 years (2000).
Transportation: Commute to work: 92.3% car, 1.4% public transportation, 2.9% walk, 2.2% work from home (2000); Travel time to work: 49.7% less

than 15 minutes, 38.5% 15 to 30 minutes, 7.4% 30 to 45 minutes, 0.8% 45 to 60 minutes, 3.5% 60 minutes or more (2000)

MEMPHIS (unincorporated postal area, zip code 13112). Covers a land area of 20.904 square miles and a water area of 0 square miles. Located at 43.10° N. Lat.; 76.41° W. Long.
Population: 0 (2000); Race: 99.6% White, 0.4% Black, 0.0% Asian, 1.5% Hispanic of any race (2000); Density: 0.0 persons per square mile (2000); Age: 31.8% under 18, 9.5% over 64 (2000); Marriage status: 17.2% never married, 68.9% now married, 6.2% widowed, 7.7% divorced (2000); Foreign born: 1.1% (2000); Ancestry (includes multiple ancestries): 21.7% Irish, 20.7% German, 20.4% English, 14.6% Italian, 9.6% French (except Basque) (2000).
Economy: Employment by occupation: 11.4% management, 14.9% professional, 11.6% services, 29.1% sales, 0.0% farming, 15.0% construction, 17.8% production (2000).
Income: Per capita income: $19,753 (2000); Median household income: $48,922 (2000); Poverty rate: 5.4% (2000).
Education: Percent of population age 25 and over with: High school diploma (including GED) or higher: 88.2% (2000); Bachelor's degree or higher: 18.0% (2000).
Housing: Homeownership rate: 90.7% (2000); Median home value: $90,600 (2000); Median rent: $335 per month (2000); Median age of housing: 36 years (2000).
Transportation: Commute to work: 94.9% car, 0.0% public transportation, 3.0% walk, 2.1% work from home (2000); Travel time to work: 16.7% less than 15 minutes, 46.0% 15 to 30 minutes, 34.0% 30 to 45 minutes, 3.3% 45 to 60 minutes, 0.0% 60 minutes or more (2000)

MINOA (village). Covers a land area of 1.240 square miles and a water area of 0 square miles. Located at 43.07° N. Lat.; 76.00° W. Long.
Population: 3,752 (1990); 3,348 (2000); 3,283 (2005); 3,246 (2010 projected); Race: 96.2% White, 0.7% Black, 1.5% Asian, 0.7% Hispanic of any race (2005); Density: 2,647.8 persons per square mile (2005); Average household size: 2.62 (2005); Median age: 40.3 (2005); Males per 100 females: 88.5 (2005); Marriage status: 21.5% never married, 61.7% now married, 9.5% widowed, 7.3% divorced (2000); Foreign born: 2.5% (2000); Ancestry (includes multiple ancestries): 27.2% German, 26.6% Irish, 20.8% Italian, 15.0% English, 8.8% Polish (2000).
Economy: In dairying area. Single-family building permits issued: 14 (2005); Multi-family building permits issued: 16 (2005); Employment by occupation: 9.3% management, 25.3% professional, 14.8% services, 32.1% sales, 0.0% farming, 5.9% construction, 12.5% production (2000).
Income: Per capita income: $23,153 (2005); Median household income: $53,856 (2005); Average household income: $59,972 (2005); Percent of households with income of $100,000 or more: 13.2% (2005); Poverty rate: 2.0% (2000).
Education: Percent of population age 25 and over with: High school diploma (including GED) or higher: 89.1% (2005); Bachelor's degree or higher: 22.4% (2005); Master's degree or higher: 5.9% (2005).
School District(s)
East Syracuse-Minoa Central School District (PK-12)
 2003-04 Enrollment: 3,824 . . . . (315) 656-7205
Housing: Homeownership rate: 77.1% (2005); Median home value: $106,721 (2005); Median rent: $444 per month (2000); Median age of housing: 31 years (2000).
Transportation: Commute to work: 93.5% car, 2.1% public transportation, 0.8% walk, 3.6% work from home (2000); Travel time to work: 32.3% less than 15 minutes, 54.4% 15 to 30 minutes, 10.8% 30 to 45 minutes, 0.5% 45 to 60 minutes, 1.9% 60 minutes or more (2000)

NEDROW (CDP). Covers a land area of 0.975 square miles and a water area of 0 square miles. Located at 42.97° N. Lat.; 76.14° W. Long. Elevation is 505 feet.
Population: 2,307 (1990); 2,265 (2000); 2,184 (2005); 2,101 (2010 projected); Race: 81.2% White, 9.1% Black, 0.2% Asian, 2.3% Hispanic of any race (2005); Density: 2,239.9 persons per square mile (2005); Average household size: 2.59 (2005); Median age: 39.5 (2005); Males per 100 females: 93.6 (2005); Marriage status: 25.2% never married, 51.0% now married, 12.3% widowed, 11.4% divorced (2000); Foreign born: 2.8% (2000); Ancestry (includes multiple ancestries): 25.3% Irish, 18.2% English, 16.2% Other groups, 15.4% German, 7.9% United States or American (2000).
Economy: Quarrying. Employment by occupation: 8.5% management, 19.8% professional, 19.5% services, 28.1% sales, 0.0% farming, 8.7% construction, 15.4% production (2000).
Income: Per capita income: $20,203 (2005); Median household income: $41,585 (2005); Average household income: $52,402 (2005); Percent of households with income of $100,000 or more: 10.8% (2005); Poverty rate: 4.2% (2000).
Education: Percent of population age 25 and over with: High school diploma (including GED) or higher: 84.2% (2005); Bachelor's degree or higher: 16.2% (2005); Master's degree or higher: 8.6% (2005).
School District(s)
La Fayette Central School District (KG-12)
 2003-04 Enrollment: 1,025 . . . . (315) 677-9728
Onondaga Central School District (PK-12)
 2003-04 Enrollment: 1,048 . . . . (315) 492-1701
Housing: Homeownership rate: 85.2% (2005); Median home value: $82,465 (2005); Median rent: $505 per month (2000); Median age of housing: 50 years (2000).
Transportation: Commute to work: 89.3% car, 6.9% public transportation, 1.8% walk, 1.5% work from home (2000); Travel time to work: 22.3% less than 15 minutes, 64.6% 15 to 30 minutes, 5.0% 30 to 45 minutes, 3.6% 45 to 60 minutes, 4.5% 60 minutes or more (2000)

NORTH SYRACUSE (village). Covers a land area of 1.963 square miles and a water area of 0 square miles. Located at 43.13° N. Lat.; 76.13° W. Long. Elevation is 380 feet.
History: Incorporated 1925.
Population: 7,363 (1990); 6,862 (2000); 6,832 (2005); 6,824 (2010 projected); Race: 93.8% White, 1.8% Black, 1.4% Asian, 1.4% Hispanic of any race (2005); Density: 3,481.0 persons per square mile (2005); Average household size: 2.24 (2005); Median age: 39.4 (2005); Males per 100 females: 91.3 (2005); Marriage status: 26.9% never married, 50.4% now married, 9.6% widowed, 13.1% divorced (2000); Foreign born: 2.4% (2000); Ancestry (includes multiple ancestries): 24.5% Italian, 24.3% Irish, 22.2% German, 14.7% English, 8.0% Polish (2000).
Economy: Hancock International Airport. Single-family building permits issued: 13 (2005); Multi-family building permits issued: 0 (2005); Employment by occupation: 10.5% management, 16.9% professional, 15.3% services, 34.4% sales, 0.0% farming, 7.0% construction, 16.0% production (2000).
Income: Per capita income: $21,489 (2005); Median household income: $41,156 (2005); Average household income: $48,039 (2005); Percent of households with income of $100,000 or more: 6.5% (2005); Poverty rate: 10.2% (2000).
Education: Percent of population age 25 and over with: High school diploma (including GED) or higher: 84.0% (2005); Bachelor's degree or higher: 14.0% (2005); Master's degree or higher: 3.5% (2005).
School District(s)
North Syracuse Central School District (PK-12)
 2003-04 Enrollment: 10,188 . . . . (315) 452-3128
Housing: Homeownership rate: 63.1% (2005); Median home value: $90,193 (2005); Median rent: $532 per month (2000); Median age of housing: 43 years (2000).
Safety: Violent crime rate: 10.2 per 10,000 population; Property crime rate: 171.6 per 10,000 population (2004).
Transportation: Commute to work: 92.2% car, 0.5% public transportation, 2.5% walk, 3.6% work from home (2000); Travel time to work: 37.4% less than 15 minutes, 51.0% 15 to 30 minutes, 7.6% 30 to 45 minutes, 1.7% 45 to 60 minutes, 2.3% 60 minutes or more (2000)
Additional Information Contacts
North Syracuse Chamber of Commerce . . . . (315) 458-4181
 http://www.northsyracuse.org/
Village of North Syracuse . . . . (315) 458-0900
 http://www.northsyracuse.org/

ONONDAGA (town). Aka Onondaga Hill. Covers a land area of 57.727 square miles and a water area of 0.094 square miles. Located at 42.97° N. Lat.; 76.19° W. Long.
Population: 18,396 (1990); 21,063 (2000); 21,486 (2005); 21,947 (2010 projected); Race: 93.3% White, 2.5% Black, 1.5% Asian, 1.5% Hispanic of any race (2005); Density: 372.2 persons per square mile (2005); Average household size: 2.72 (2005); Median age: 41.3 (2005); Males per 100 females: 92.1 (2005); Marriage status: 22.4% never married, 61.1% now married, 9.9% widowed, 6.6% divorced (2000); Foreign born: 5.0% (2000);

Ancestry (includes multiple ancestries): 28.6% Irish, 19.0% German, 17.3% English, 16.3% Italian, 6.8% Other groups (2000).
Economy: Single-family building permits issued: 92 (2005); Multi-family building permits issued: 112 (2005); Employment by occupation: 17.6% management, 28.7% professional, 11.8% services, 25.1% sales, 0.5% farming, 6.6% construction, 9.8% production (2000).
Income: Per capita income: $28,913 (2005); Median household income: $61,642 (2005); Average household income: $77,320 (2005); Percent of households with income of $100,000 or more: 24.1% (2005); Poverty rate: 4.2% (2000).
Education: Percent of population age 25 and over with: High school diploma (including GED) or higher: 90.1% (2005); Bachelor's degree or higher: 35.1% (2005); Master's degree or higher: 13.9% (2005).
Housing: Homeownership rate: 79.4% (2005); Median home value: $144,112 (2005); Median rent: $564 per month (2000); Median age of housing: 34 years (2000).
Transportation: Commute to work: 94.8% car, 1.1% public transportation, 0.7% walk, 3.0% work from home (2000); Travel time to work: 27.0% less than 15 minutes, 56.7% 15 to 30 minutes, 11.0% 30 to 45 minutes, 1.9% 45 to 60 minutes, 3.5% 60 minutes or more (2000)

ONONDAGA RESERVATION (reservation).
Covers a land area of 9.253 square miles and a water area of 0.055 square miles. Located at 42.95° N. Lat.; 76.15° W. Long.
Population: 771 (1990); 1,473 (2000); 1,439 (2005); 1,403 (2010 projected); Race: 35.9% White, 2.8% Black, 0.0% Asian, 0.6% Hispanic of any race (2005); Density: 155.5 persons per square mile (2005); Average household size: 4.96 (2005); Median age: 20.1 (2005); Males per 100 females: 108.2 (2005); Marriage status: 31.8% never married, 56.9% now married, 3.5% widowed, 7.8% divorced (2000); Foreign born: 5.1% (2000); Ancestry (includes multiple ancestries): 1.6% Other groups, 0.5% United States or American, 0.2% German (2000).
Economy: Employment by occupation: 17.9% management, 24.6% professional, 12.5% services, 22.4% sales, 1.7% farming, 11.4% construction, 9.5% production (2000).
Income: Per capita income: $18,110 (2005); Median household income: $78,462 (2005); Average household income: $89,862 (2005); Percent of households with income of $100,000 or more: 30.7% (2005); Poverty rate: 7.6% (2000).
Education: Percent of population age 25 and over with: High school diploma (including GED) or higher: 90.6% (2005); Bachelor's degree or higher: 41.3% (2005); Master's degree or higher: 20.5% (2005).
Housing: Homeownership rate: 90.7% (2005); Median home value: $139,242 (2005); Median rent: $438 per month (2000); Median age of housing: 37 years (2000).
Transportation: Commute to work: 100.0% car, 0.0% public transportation, 0.0% walk, 0.0% work from home (2000); Travel time to work: 26.8% less than 15 minutes, 57.8% 15 to 30 minutes, 0.0% 30 to 45 minutes, 15.3% 45 to 60 minutes, 0.0% 60 minutes or more (2000)

OTISCO (town).
Covers a land area of 29.629 square miles and a water area of 1.540 square miles. Located at 42.86° N. Lat.; 76.23° W. Long. Elevation is 1,474 feet.
Population: 2,255 (1990); 2,561 (2000); 2,616 (2005); 2,673 (2010 projected); Race: 96.6% White, 0.3% Black, 0.9% Asian, 0.7% Hispanic of any race (2005); Density: 88.3 persons per square mile (2005); Average household size: 2.72 (2005); Median age: 37.0 (2005); Males per 100 females: 103.9 (2005); Marriage status: 21.7% never married, 65.3% now married, 4.0% widowed, 9.0% divorced (2000); Foreign born: 1.8% (2000); Ancestry (includes multiple ancestries): 24.9% German, 22.7% Irish, 20.8% English, 6.9% Italian, 5.5% United States or American (2000).
Economy: Single-family building permits issued: 10 (2005); Multi-family building permits issued: 0 (2005); Employment by occupation: 13.7% management, 14.5% professional, 13.6% services, 32.2% sales, 1.7% farming, 11.1% construction, 13.2% production (2000).
Income: Per capita income: $24,776 (2005); Median household income: $50,433 (2005); Average household income: $67,445 (2005); Percent of households with income of $100,000 or more: 15.8% (2005); Poverty rate: 5.7% (2000).
Education: Percent of population age 25 and over with: High school diploma (including GED) or higher: 90.2% (2005); Bachelor's degree or higher: 20.0% (2005); Master's degree or higher: 6.7% (2005).
Housing: Homeownership rate: 82.0% (2005); Median home value: $122,105 (2005); Median rent: $417 per month (2000); Median age of housing: 34 years (2000).

Transportation: Commute to work: 92.7% car, 0.6% public transportation, 1.4% walk, 5.0% work from home (2000); Travel time to work: 19.6% less than 15 minutes, 29.2% 15 to 30 minutes, 38.3% 30 to 45 minutes, 8.3% 45 to 60 minutes, 4.6% 60 minutes or more (2000)

POMPEY (town).
Covers a land area of 66.411 square miles and a water area of 0.060 square miles. Located at 42.93° N. Lat.; 75.98° W. Long. Elevation is 1,673 feet.
Population: 5,267 (1990); 6,159 (2000); 6,538 (2005); 6,889 (2010 projected); Race: 97.1% White, 0.4% Black, 1.1% Asian, 1.1% Hispanic of any race (2005); Density: 98.4 persons per square mile (2005); Average household size: 2.84 (2005); Median age: 40.3 (2005); Males per 100 females: 98.8 (2005); Marriage status: 17.9% never married, 73.4% now married, 4.3% widowed, 4.4% divorced (2000); Foreign born: 4.6% (2000); Ancestry (includes multiple ancestries): 20.4% German, 20.3% English, 18.9% Irish, 10.2% Italian, 6.1% United States or American (2000).
Economy: Single-family building permits issued: 50 (2005); Multi-family building permits issued: 0 (2005); Employment by occupation: 23.2% management, 29.5% professional, 9.0% services, 19.6% sales, 3.0% farming, 8.0% construction, 7.8% production (2000).
Income: Per capita income: $33,289 (2005); Median household income: $69,995 (2005); Average household income: $93,130 (2005); Percent of households with income of $100,000 or more: 30.8% (2005); Poverty rate: 3.9% (2000).
Education: Percent of population age 25 and over with: High school diploma (including GED) or higher: 92.9% (2005); Bachelor's degree or higher: 42.0% (2005); Master's degree or higher: 19.8% (2005).
Housing: Homeownership rate: 91.0% (2005); Median home value: $167,849 (2005); Median rent: $511 per month (2000); Median age of housing: 30 years (2000).
Transportation: Commute to work: 87.7% car, 0.0% public transportation, 3.3% walk, 8.9% work from home (2000); Travel time to work: 19.0% less than 15 minutes, 46.0% 15 to 30 minutes, 26.4% 30 to 45 minutes, 5.4% 45 to 60 minutes, 3.2% 60 minutes or more (2000)

SALINA (town).
Covers a land area of 13.781 square miles and a water area of 1.318 square miles. Located at 43.10° N. Lat.; 76.17° W. Long.
Population: 35,145 (1990); 33,290 (2000); 33,371 (2005); 33,443 (2010 projected); Race: 92.3% White, 2.8% Black, 2.2% Asian, 2.0% Hispanic of any race (2005); Density: 2,421.6 persons per square mile (2005); Average household size: 2.27 (2005); Median age: 40.9 (2005); Males per 100 females: 90.8 (2005); Marriage status: 26.8% never married, 54.7% now married, 9.5% widowed, 8.9% divorced (2000); Foreign born: 5.1% (2000); Ancestry (includes multiple ancestries): 28.1% Italian, 20.9% German, 19.1% Irish, 12.4% English, 7.9% Polish (2000).
Economy: Unemployment rate: 4.5% (2005); Total civilian labor force: 18,287 (2005); Single-family building permits issued: 47 (2005); Multi-family building permits issued: 0 (2005); Employment by occupation: 13.3% management, 20.4% professional, 14.2% services, 30.5% sales, 0.1% farming, 6.7% construction, 14.9% production (2000).
Income: Per capita income: $24,852 (2005); Median household income: $45,193 (2005); Average household income: $56,033 (2005); Percent of households with income of $100,000 or more: 11.4% (2005); Poverty rate: 7.4% (2000).
Education: Percent of population age 25 and over with: High school diploma (including GED) or higher: 85.0% (2005); Bachelor's degree or higher: 21.3% (2005); Master's degree or higher: 7.3% (2005).
Housing: Homeownership rate: 68.7% (2005); Median home value: $96,349 (2005); Median rent: $550 per month (2000); Median age of housing: 42 years (2000).
Transportation: Commute to work: 93.7% car, 1.5% public transportation, 1.9% walk, 2.1% work from home (2000); Travel time to work: 41.0% less than 15 minutes, 48.2% 15 to 30 minutes, 5.8% 30 to 45 minutes, 1.7% 45 to 60 minutes, 3.3% 60 minutes or more (2000)
Additional Information Contacts
Town of Salina . . . . (315) 457-6661
  http://www.salina.ny.us/

SENECA KNOLLS (CDP).
Covers a land area of 1.222 square miles and a water area of 0 square miles. Located at 43.12° N. Lat.; 76.28° W. Long.
Population: 2,383 (1990); 2,138 (2000); 2,133 (2005); 2,049 (2010 projected); Race: 96.2% White, 1.5% Black, 0.2% Asian, 0.8% Hispanic of any race (2005); Density: 1,745.6 persons per square mile (2005); Average household size: 2.51 (2005); Median age: 40.0 (2005); Males per 100

females: 91.3 (2005); Marriage status: 24.7% never married, 56.3% now married, 3.7% widowed, 15.2% divorced (2000); Foreign born: 2.0% (2000); Ancestry (includes multiple ancestries): 27.5% German, 17.1% Irish, 15.7% English, 14.8% Italian, 9.6% French (except Basque) (2000).
Economy: Employment by occupation: 6.3% management, 11.8% professional, 19.7% services, 29.0% sales, 0.0% farming, 9.2% construction, 24.0% production (2000).
Income: Per capita income: $22,155 (2005); Median household income: $43,012 (2005); Average household income: $55,597 (2005); Percent of households with income of $100,000 or more: 10.4% (2005); Poverty rate: 7.2% (2000).
Education: Percent of population age 25 and over with: High school diploma (including GED) or higher: 79.1% (2005); Bachelor's degree or higher: 10.5% (2005); Master's degree or higher: 2.8% (2005).
Housing: Homeownership rate: 87.4% (2005); Median home value: $81,672 (2005); Median rent: $646 per month (2000); Median age of housing: 42 years (2000).
Transportation: Commute to work: 95.8% car, 0.0% public transportation, 0.6% walk, 2.5% work from home (2000); Travel time to work: 30.8% less than 15 minutes, 52.3% 15 to 30 minutes, 6.1% 30 to 45 minutes, 3.9% 45 to 60 minutes, 6.9% 60 minutes or more (2000)

SKANEATELES (village).
Covers a land area of 1.432 square miles and a water area of 0.284 square miles. Located at 42.94° N. Lat.; 76.42° W. Long. Elevation is 865 feet.
Population: 2,809 (1990); 2,616 (2000); 2,644 (2005); 2,633 (2010 projected); Race: 99.0% White, 0.1% Black, 0.3% Asian, 0.3% Hispanic of any race (2005); Density: 1,846.3 persons per square mile (2005); Average household size: 2.33 (2005); Median age: 45.9 (2005); Males per 100 females: 87.5 (2005); Marriage status: 18.4% never married, 65.8% now married, 11.2% widowed, 4.6% divorced (2000); Foreign born: 3.4% (2000); Ancestry (includes multiple ancestries): 30.2% Irish, 23.3% English, 20.4% German, 14.1% Italian, 7.5% Polish (2000).
Economy: Single-family building permits issued: 6 (2005); Multi-family building permits issued: 6 (2005); Employment by occupation: 27.5% management, 32.8% professional, 6.6% services, 23.9% sales, 0.0% farming, 3.3% construction, 6.0% production (2000).
Income: Per capita income: $37,472 (2005); Median household income: $66,360 (2005); Average household income: $86,401 (2005); Percent of households with income of $100,000 or more: 29.9% (2005); Poverty rate: 3.0% (2000).
Education: Percent of population age 25 and over with: High school diploma (including GED) or higher: 94.0% (2005); Bachelor's degree or higher: 59.6% (2005); Master's degree or higher: 24.2% (2005).
School District(s)
Skaneateles Central School District (KG-12)
    2003-04 Enrollment: 1,848 . . . . (315) 291-2221
Housing: Homeownership rate: 71.8% (2005); Median home value: $228,413 (2005); Median rent: $457 per month (2000); Median age of housing: 60+ years (2000).
Safety: Violent crime rate: 7.7 per 10,000 population; Property crime rate: 415.2 per 10,000 population (2004).
Newspapers: Marcellus Observer (General - Circulation 1,300); Skaneateles Press (General - Circulation 2,785)
Transportation: Commute to work: 84.8% car, 1.3% public transportation, 6.1% walk, 6.4% work from home (2000); Travel time to work: 31.3% less than 15 minutes, 26.9% 15 to 30 minutes, 29.0% 30 to 45 minutes, 7.3% 45 to 60 minutes, 5.5% 60 minutes or more (2000)
Additional Information Contacts
Skaneateles Area Chamber of Commerce . . . . (315) 685-0552
    http://www.skaneateles.com
Village of Skaneateles . . . . (315) 685-3473
    http://www.townofskaneateles.com/index.shtml

SKANEATELES (town).
Covers a land area of 42.652 square miles and a water area of 6.098 square miles. Located at 42.94° N. Lat.; 76.41° W. Long. Elevation is 865 feet.
History: Village in a Historic District. Settled before 1800, incorporated 1833.
Population: 7,526 (1990); 7,323 (2000); 7,419 (2005); 7,511 (2010 projected); Race: 98.9% White, 0.1% Black, 0.4% Asian, 0.6% Hispanic of any race (2005); Density: 173.9 persons per square mile (2005); Average household size: 2.50 (2005); Median age: 44.6 (2005); Males per 100 females: 95.8 (2005); Marriage status: 19.8% never married, 65.1% now married, 8.3% widowed, 6.9% divorced (2000); Foreign born: 3.5% (2000);

Ancestry (includes multiple ancestries): 28.9% Irish, 26.0% English, 19.7% German, 11.8% Italian, 8.9% Polish (2000).
Economy: Resort village. Manufacturing: machinery, transportation equipment, consumer goods, wood products, medical instruments. Agriculture includes hay, oats, wheat. Single-family building permits issued: 18 (2005); Multi-family building permits issued: 0 (2005); Employment by occupation: 21.6% management, 28.4% professional, 9.1% services, 24.6% sales, 1.0% farming, 4.8% construction, 10.4% production (2000).
Income: Per capita income: $34,404 (2005); Median household income: $65,803 (2005); Average household income: $85,686 (2005); Percent of households with income of $100,000 or more: 28.0% (2005); Poverty rate: 3.2% (2000).
Taxes: Total city taxes per capita: $367 (2004); City property taxes per capita: $309 (2004).
Education: Percent of population age 25 and over with: High school diploma (including GED) or higher: 91.8% (2005); Bachelor's degree or higher: 46.3% (2005); Master's degree or higher: 17.5% (2005).
Housing: Homeownership rate: 82.2% (2005); Median home value: $195,565 (2005); Median rent: $468 per month (2000); Median age of housing: 49 years (2000).
Transportation: Commute to work: 90.2% car, 0.8% public transportation, 3.3% walk, 5.0% work from home (2000); Travel time to work: 37.0% less than 15 minutes, 28.1% 15 to 30 minutes, 24.2% 30 to 45 minutes, 6.8% 45 to 60 minutes, 3.9% 60 minutes or more (2000)
Additional Information Contacts
Town of Skaneateles . . . . (315) 685-3473
    http://www.townofskaneateles.com/index.shtml

SOLVAY (village).
Covers a land area of 1.644 square miles and a water area of 0 square miles. Located at 43.05° N. Lat.; 76.21° W. Long. Elevation is 503 feet.
History: In the 20th century, after earlier exploited salt springs had lost their deposits, brine wells provided basis for manufacturing of chlorines, caustic soda, and bicarbonate of soda. Former heavy-manufacturing and chemical-manufacturing have disappeared, mainly due to stricter environmental-quality standards. Incorporated 1894.
Population: 6,717 (1990); 6,845 (2000); 6,681 (2005); 6,527 (2010 projected); Race: 94.8% White, 1.0% Black, 0.6% Asian, 3.1% Hispanic of any race (2005); Density: 4,064.8 persons per square mile (2005); Average household size: 2.23 (2005); Median age: 38.8 (2005); Males per 100 females: 87.1 (2005); Marriage status: 30.2% never married, 48.8% now married, 10.4% widowed, 10.5% divorced (2000); Foreign born: 8.9% (2000); Ancestry (includes multiple ancestries): 34.7% Italian, 21.0% Irish, 10.7% Polish, 10.3% English, 9.2% Other groups (2000).
Economy: Major retail shopping centers occupy many former industrial sites. Single-family building permits issued: 1 (2005); Multi-family building permits issued: 4 (2005); Employment by occupation: 10.5% management, 21.0% professional, 15.1% services, 29.2% sales, 0.6% farming, 7.7% construction, 15.9% production (2000).
Income: Per capita income: $21,895 (2005); Median household income: $37,750 (2005); Average household income: $48,657 (2005); Percent of households with income of $100,000 or more: 8.9% (2005); Poverty rate: 12.0% (2000).
Education: Percent of population age 25 and over with: High school diploma (including GED) or higher: 83.4% (2005); Bachelor's degree or higher: 18.5% (2005); Master's degree or higher: 6.6% (2005).
School District(s)
Solvay Union Free School District (KG-12)
    2003-04 Enrollment: 1,747 . . . . (315) 468-1111
Housing: Homeownership rate: 54.4% (2005); Median home value: $105,053 (2005); Median rent: $451 per month (2000); Median age of housing: 59 years (2000).
Safety: Violent crime rate: 22.2 per 10,000 population; Property crime rate: 254.9 per 10,000 population (2004).
Transportation: Commute to work: 93.7% car, 3.2% public transportation, 1.9% walk, 0.2% work from home (2000); Travel time to work: 42.4% less than 15 minutes, 47.5% 15 to 30 minutes, 6.8% 30 to 45 minutes, 1.0% 45 to 60 minutes, 2.3% 60 minutes or more (2000)

SPAFFORD (town).
Covers a land area of 32.830 square miles and a water area of 6.404 square miles. Located at 42.83° N. Lat.; 76.30° W. Long.
Population: 1,675 (1990); 1,661 (2000); 1,694 (2005); 1,727 (2010 projected); Race: 98.8% White, 0.0% Black, 0.2% Asian, 0.6% Hispanic of any race (2005); Density: 51.6 persons per square mile (2005); Average

household size: 2.58 (2005); Median age: 42.3 (2005); Males per 100 females: 104.3 (2005); Marriage status: 22.2% never married, 64.7% now married, 5.2% widowed, 7.9% divorced (2000); Foreign born: 2.1% (2000); Ancestry (includes multiple ancestries): 26.2% English, 23.2% German, 21.5% Irish, 10.0% Italian, 5.6% Dutch (2000).
Economy: Single-family building permits issued: 12 (2005); Multi-family building permits issued: 0 (2005); Employment by occupation: 16.1% management, 28.2% professional, 9.8% services, 22.1% sales, 1.9% farming, 11.3% construction, 10.6% production (2000).
Income: Per capita income: $27,258 (2005); Median household income: $61,055 (2005); Average household income: $70,282 (2005); Percent of households with income of $100,000 or more: 19.8% (2005); Poverty rate: 5.2% (2000).
Education: Percent of population age 25 and over with: High school diploma (including GED) or higher: 90.1% (2005); Bachelor's degree or higher: 39.8% (2005); Master's degree or higher: 16.1% (2005).
Housing: Homeownership rate: 89.5% (2005); Median home value: $146,221 (2005); Median rent: $566 per month (2000); Median age of housing: 37 years (2000).
Transportation: Commute to work: 91.7% car, 0.0% public transportation, 0.6% walk, 7.4% work from home (2000); Travel time to work: 11.0% less than 15 minutes, 27.7% 15 to 30 minutes, 38.5% 30 to 45 minutes, 16.7% 45 to 60 minutes, 6.1% 60 minutes or more (2000)

SYRACUSE
(city). Covers a land area of 25.091 square miles and a water area of 0.551 square miles. Located at 43.04° N. Lat.; 76.14° W. Long. Elevation is 398 feet.
History: The beginnings and early growth of Syracuse are identified with salt. What the French soldiers and Jesuits saw in 1654 was a swamp. The salt springs were discovered by Father Simon LeMoyne. The first settler was Ephraim Webster, who arrived in 1786 and opened a trading station. Syracuse was incorporated as a village in 1825. The name was suggested by John Wilkinson, the first postmaster, who had read a poem describing the ancient Greek city in Sicily, which had also grown around a marsh and salt springs. In 1848, the villages of Syracuse and Salina, together with Lodi, were joined and incorporated as the city of Syracuse in 1881.
Population: 163,860 (1990); 147,306 (2000); 144,232 (2005); 141,416 (2010 projected); Race: 59.0% White, 28.8% Black, 4.4% Asian, 7.0% Hispanic of any race (2005); Density: 5,748.5 persons per square mile (2005); Average household size: 2.48 (2005); Median age: 32.1 (2005); Males per 100 females: 89.7 (2005); Marriage status: 45.4% never married, 37.2% now married, 7.8% widowed, 9.6% divorced (2000); Foreign born: 7.6% (2000); Ancestry (includes multiple ancestries): 32.3% Other groups, 15.9% Irish, 14.1% Italian, 12.2% German, 7.6% English (2000).
Economy: Industrial manufacturing heart of Syracuse region. Diverse light and heavy industries include aluminum castings and molds, industrial electroplating, gears and gear boxes, transmissions, doors and windows, meat packing, glass and wooden containers, tissue paper, gas analysis equipment; machining, screws, steel products, pharmaceuticals. Unemployment rate: 5.7% (2005); Total civilian labor force: 64,785 (2005); Single-family building permits issued: 21 (2005); Multi-family building permits issued: 0 (2005); Employment by occupation: 9.0% management, 23.7% professional, 21.6% services, 25.8% sales, 0.2% farming, 5.3% construction, 14.5% production (2000).
Income: Per capita income: $16,384 (2005); Median household income: $27,037 (2005); Average household income: $39,106 (2005); Percent of households with income of $100,000 or more: 6.4% (2005); Poverty rate: 27.3% (2000).
Taxes: Total city taxes per capita: $202 (2004); City property taxes per capita: $157 (2004).
Education: Percent of population age 25 and over with: High school diploma (including GED) or higher: 76.6% (2005); Bachelor's degree or higher: 24.0% (2005); Master's degree or higher: 11.4% (2005).

School District(s)
Boces Onondaga-Cortland-Madison (PK-PK)
    2003-04 Enrollment: 438 . . . . (315) 433-2602
Central NY Charter School For Math (KG-06)
    2003-04 Enrollment: 585 . . . . (315) 472-5914
Lyncourt Union Free School District (KG-08)
    2003-04 Enrollment: 339 . . . . (315) 455-7571
North Syracuse Central School District (PK-12)
    2003-04 Enrollment: 10,188 . . . . (315) 452-3128
Solvay Union Free School District (KG-12)
    2003-04 Enrollment: 1,747 . . . . (315) 468-1111
Southside Academy Charter School (KG-06)
    2003-04 Enrollment: 252 . . . . (315) 476-3019
Syracuse Acad-Sci Charter School (07-09)
    2003-04 Enrollment: 190 . . . . (315) 443-3564
Syracuse City School District (PK-12)
    2003-04 Enrollment: 22,405 . . . . (315) 435-4161
West Genesee Central School District (KG-12)
    2003-04 Enrollment: 5,153 . . . . (315) 487-4562
Westhill Central School District (KG-12)
    2003-04 Enrollment: 2,049 . . . . (315) 488-6322

Four-year College(s)
Le Moyne College
    Fall 2004 Enrollment: 3,487 . . . . (315) 445-4100
    2005-06 Tuition: In-state $21,280; Out-of-state $21,280
SUNY College of Environmental Science and Forestry (Public)
    Fall 2004 Enrollment: 2,046 . . . . (315) 470-6500
    2005-06 Tuition: In-state $5,032; Out-of-state $11,292
SUNY Health Science Center at Syracuse (Public)
    Fall 2004 Enrollment: 1,194 . . . . (315) 464-4816
Syracuse University
    Fall 2004 Enrollment: 18,247 . . . . (315) 443-1870
    2005-06 Tuition: In-state $28,285; Out-of-state $28,285

Two-year College(s)
Bryant and Stratton College-Main Syracuse
    Fall 2004 Enrollment: 595 . . . . (315) 472-6603
    2005-06 Tuition: In-state $11,820; Out-of-state $11,820
Central Tech Nursing Program (Public)
    Fall 2004 Enrollment: 58 . . . . (315) 435-4150
Crouse Hospital School of Nursing
    Fall 2004 Enrollment: 284 . . . . (315) 470-7481
    2005-06 Tuition: In-state $7,352; Out-of-state $11,568
Onondaga Community College (Public)
    Fall 2004 Enrollment: 8,195 . . . . (315) 498-2622
    2005-06 Tuition: In-state $6,670; Out-of-state $9,850
Phillips Hairstyling Institute
    Fall 2004 Enrollment: 142 . . . . (315) 422-9656
Simmons Institute of Funeral Service Inc
    Fall 2004 Enrollment: 137 . . . . (315) 475-5142
    2005-06 Tuition: In-state $9,800; Out-of-state $9,800
St Joseph's College of Nursing at St Joseph's Hospital Health Center
    Fall 2004 Enrollment: 253 . . . . (315) 448-5040
    2005-06 Tuition: In-state $8,817; Out-of-state $8,817

Housing: Homeownership rate: 40.8% (2005); Median home value: $88,833 (2005); Median rent: $430 per month (2000); Median age of housing: 58 years (2000).
Hospitals: Community General Hospital of Greater Syracuse (356 beds); Crouse Hospital (566 beds); Richard H Hutchings Psychiatric Center (120 beds); SUNY Upstate Medical University (356 beds); St. Joseph's Hospital Health Center (431 beds); Veterans Affairs Medical Center (175 beds)
Safety: Violent crime rate: 89.7 per 10,000 population; Property crime rate: 454.4 per 10,000 population (2004).
Newspapers: Camillus Advocate (General - Circulation 3,783); Cazenovia Republican (General - Circulation 3,744); De Witt Times (General - Circulation 1,984); Fayetteville Eagle Bulletin (General - Circulation 6,010); Liverpool/Salina Review (General - Circulation 4,775); Onondaga Valley News (General - Circulation 7,903); Post-Standard (Circulation 122,055); Solvay-Geddes Express (General - Circulation 10,000); Syracuse New Times (Alternative, General - Circulation 45,500); The Catholic Sun (Catholic - Circulation 32,000); The Star News (General - Circulation 7,200)
Transportation: Commute to work: 79.7% car, 7.0% public transportation, 10.1% walk, 2.0% work from home (2000); Travel time to work: 47.6% less than 15 minutes, 39.5% 15 to 30 minutes, 7.0% 30 to 45 minutes, 2.3% 45 to 60 minutes, 3.7% 60 minutes or more (2000). Amtrak. Service available.
Additional Information Contacts
City of Syracuse . . . . (315) 448-8216
    http://www.syracuse.ny.us/
Syracuse Chamber of Commerce . . . . (315) 470-1800
    http://www.syracusechamber.com

TULLY
(village). Covers a land area of 0.645 square miles and a water area of 0 square miles. Located at 42.79° N. Lat.; 76.10° W. Long. Elevation is 1,252 feet.
Population: 983 (1990); 924 (2000); 924 (2005); 936 (2010 projected); Race: 97.4% White, 0.2% Black, 0.1% Asian, 1.0% Hispanic of any race (2005); Density: 1,432.6 persons per square mile (2005); Average

household size: 2.24 (2005); Median age: 36.5 (2005); Males per 100 females: 90.1 (2005); Marriage status: 26.3% never married, 50.8% now married, 9.4% widowed, 13.4% divorced (2000); Foreign born: 2.2% (2000); Ancestry (includes multiple ancestries): 24.5% Irish, 23.9% German, 18.8% English, 13.0% Italian, 5.9% United States or American (2000).
Economy: Single-family building permits issued: 0 (2005); Multi-family building permits issued: 0 (2005); Employment by occupation: 13.3% management, 26.7% professional, 14.4% services, 25.6% sales, 0.8% farming, 7.5% construction, 11.7% production (2000).
Income: Per capita income: $25,785 (2005); Median household income: $45,890 (2005); Average household income: $57,828 (2005); Percent of households with income of $100,000 or more: 13.1% (2005); Poverty rate: 9.9% (2000).
Education: Percent of population age 25 and over with: High school diploma (including GED) or higher: 93.0% (2005); Bachelor's degree or higher: 29.5% (2005); Master's degree or higher: 14.4% (2005).

School District(s)

Tully Central School District (KG-12)
    2003-04 Enrollment: 1,243 . . . . (315) 696-6204
Housing: Homeownership rate: 49.8% (2005); Median home value: $115,991 (2005); Median rent: $432 per month (2000); Median age of housing: 54 years (2000).
Transportation: Commute to work: 87.0% car, 0.6% public transportation, 7.3% walk, 4.6% work from home (2000); Travel time to work: 34.3% less than 15 minutes, 31.2% 15 to 30 minutes, 30.5% 30 to 45 minutes, 3.1% 45 to 60 minutes, 0.9% 60 minutes or more (2000)

TULLY (town). Covers a land area of 25.862 square miles and a water area of 0.413 square miles. Located at 42.80° N. Lat.; 76.13° W. Long. Elevation is 1,252 feet.
History: One of many former Finger Lake valleys, with rich agricultural soils.
Population: 2,378 (1990); 2,709 (2000); 2,796 (2005); 2,884 (2010 projected); Race: 96.6% White, 0.6% Black, 0.9% Asian, 1.6% Hispanic of any race (2005); Density: 108.1 persons per square mile (2005); Average household size: 2.58 (2005); Median age: 38.3 (2005); Males per 100 females: 91.6 (2005); Marriage status: 22.0% never married, 61.9% now married, 6.4% widowed, 9.7% divorced (2000); Foreign born: 2.1% (2000); Ancestry (includes multiple ancestries): 25.0% Irish, 24.0% German, 21.1% English, 12.8% Italian, 8.1% Other groups (2000).
Economy: Manufacturing of swimming pool chemicals. Agriculture: poultry; potatoes, cabbage, hay. Single-family building permits issued: 6 (2005); Multi-family building permits issued: 0 (2005); Employment by occupation: 15.1% management, 35.3% professional, 10.7% services, 23.4% sales, 0.6% farming, 6.0% construction, 9.0% production (2000).
Income: Per capita income: $30,652 (2005); Median household income: $64,648 (2005); Average household income: $78,942 (2005); Percent of households with income of $100,000 or more: 26.5% (2005); Poverty rate: 6.7% (2000).
Education: Percent of population age 25 and over with: High school diploma (including GED) or higher: 95.3% (2005); Bachelor's degree or higher: 38.7% (2005); Master's degree or higher: 18.4% (2005).
Housing: Homeownership rate: 75.0% (2005); Median home value: $161,170 (2005); Median rent: $440 per month (2000); Median age of housing: 34 years (2000).
Transportation: Commute to work: 87.5% car, 0.2% public transportation, 4.4% walk, 7.0% work from home (2000); Travel time to work: 24.1% less than 15 minutes, 35.5% 15 to 30 minutes, 33.3% 30 to 45 minutes, 3.8% 45 to 60 minutes, 3.3% 60 minutes or more (2000)

VAN BUREN (town). Covers a land area of 35.565 square miles and a water area of 0.553 square miles. Located at 43.12° N. Lat.; 76.34° W. Long.
Population: 13,367 (1990); 12,667 (2000); 12,614 (2005); 12,552 (2010 projected); Race: 96.8% White, 0.8% Black, 0.5% Asian, 0.9% Hispanic of any race (2005); Density: 354.7 persons per square mile (2005); Average household size: 2.35 (2005); Median age: 40.9 (2005); Males per 100 females: 92.0 (2005); Marriage status: 23.3% never married, 56.8% now married, 6.9% widowed, 13.0% divorced (2000); Foreign born: 2.2% (2000); Ancestry (includes multiple ancestries): 21.5% German, 21.0% Irish, 16.7% English, 14.1% Italian, 8.8% French (except Basque) (2000).
Economy: Single-family building permits issued: 27 (2005); Multi-family building permits issued: 0 (2005); Employment by occupation: 10.4% management, 19.6% professional, 15.5% services, 28.6% sales, 0.5% farming, 9.4% construction, 16.0% production (2000).
Income: Per capita income: $23,493 (2005); Median household income: $46,486 (2005); Average household income: $54,906 (2005); Percent of households with income of $100,000 or more: 11.0% (2005); Poverty rate: 6.6% (2000).
Education: Percent of population age 25 and over with: High school diploma (including GED) or higher: 87.4% (2005); Bachelor's degree or higher: 19.2% (2005); Master's degree or higher: 7.1% (2005).
Housing: Homeownership rate: 69.0% (2005); Median home value: $97,910 (2005); Median rent: $512 per month (2000); Median age of housing: 34 years (2000).
Transportation: Commute to work: 94.2% car, 1.1% public transportation, 1.4% walk, 2.7% work from home (2000); Travel time to work: 25.9% less than 15 minutes, 55.7% 15 to 30 minutes, 12.4% 30 to 45 minutes, 2.6% 45 to 60 minutes, 3.4% 60 minutes or more (2000)

Additional Information Contacts
Town of Van Buren . . . . (315) 635-3009
http://www.townofvanburen.com/

VILLAGE GREEN (CDP). Covers a land area of 1.222 square miles and a water area of 0 square miles. Located at 43.13° N. Lat.; 76.30° W. Long.
Population: 4,198 (1990); 3,945 (2000); 3,680 (2005); 3,494 (2010 projected); Race: 96.6% White, 0.8% Black, 1.0% Asian, 1.4% Hispanic of any race (2005); Density: 3,010.8 persons per square mile (2005); Average household size: 2.03 (2005); Median age: 39.9 (2005); Males per 100 females: 89.2 (2005); Marriage status: 23.6% never married, 53.5% now married, 6.7% widowed, 16.3% divorced (2000); Foreign born: 3.2% (2000); Ancestry (includes multiple ancestries): 22.8% German, 20.8% Irish, 16.5% Italian, 15.0% English, 10.1% French (except Basque) (2000).
Economy: Employment by occupation: 11.0% management, 18.9% professional, 14.4% services, 33.9% sales, 1.4% farming, 6.4% construction, 14.0% production (2000).
Income: Per capita income: $25,071 (2005); Median household income: $44,809 (2005); Average household income: $50,861 (2005); Percent of households with income of $100,000 or more: 7.7% (2005); Poverty rate: 6.2% (2000).
Education: Percent of population age 25 and over with: High school diploma (including GED) or higher: 94.8% (2005); Bachelor's degree or higher: 23.1% (2005); Master's degree or higher: 8.7% (2005).
Housing: Homeownership rate: 53.9% (2005); Median home value: $93,486 (2005); Median rent: $569 per month (2000); Median age of housing: 24 years (2000).
Transportation: Commute to work: 94.7% car, 2.9% public transportation, 0.0% walk, 2.0% work from home (2000); Travel time to work: 28.1% less than 15 minutes, 58.7% 15 to 30 minutes, 6.8% 30 to 45 minutes, 2.0% 45 to 60 minutes, 4.4% 60 minutes or more (2000)

WARNERS (unincorporated postal area, zip code 13164). Aka Warner. Covers a land area of 14.271 square miles and a water area of 0.002 square miles. Located at 43.08° N. Lat.; 76.31° W. Long. Elevation is 431 feet.
Population: 0 (2000); Race: 99.4% White, 0.0% Black, 0.4% Asian, 2.3% Hispanic of any race (2000); Density: 0.0 persons per square mile (2000); Age: 23.2% under 18, 16.5% over 64 (2000); Marriage status: 24.8% never married, 63.1% now married, 5.9% widowed, 6.2% divorced (2000); Foreign born: 4.1% (2000); Ancestry (includes multiple ancestries): 30.1% Irish, 24.4% Italian, 16.5% German, 12.9% English, 12.7% Polish (2000).
Economy: Employment by occupation: 12.8% management, 23.8% professional, 16.7% services, 21.9% sales, 0.5% farming, 12.7% construction, 11.5% production (2000).
Income: Per capita income: $21,943 (2000); Median household income: $50,726 (2000); Poverty rate: 3.5% (2000).
Education: Percent of population age 25 and over with: High school diploma (including GED) or higher: 79.7% (2000); Bachelor's degree or higher: 15.9% (2000).
Housing: Homeownership rate: 82.9% (2000); Median home value: $84,600 (2000); Median rent: $477 per month (2000); Median age of housing: 48 years (2000).
Transportation: Commute to work: 94.7% car, 0.6% public transportation, 0.0% walk, 4.7% work from home (2000); Travel time to work: 21.2% less than 15 minutes, 61.4% 15 to 30 minutes, 12.8% 30 to 45 minutes, 3.7% 45 to 60 minutes, 0.9% 60 minutes or more (2000)

WESTVALE (CDP). Covers a land area of 1.348 square miles and a water area of 0 square miles. Located at 43.04° N. Lat.; 76.21° W. Long.
Population: 5,434 (1990); 5,166 (2000); 4,972 (2005); 4,822 (2010 projected); Race: 97.5% White, 0.4% Black, 0.5% Asian, 1.3% Hispanic of any race (2005); Density: 3,689.2 persons per square mile (2005); Average household size: 2.45 (2005); Median age: 45.5 (2005); Males per 100 females: 88.5 (2005); Marriage status: 18.6% never married, 63.0% now married, 12.2% widowed, 6.2% divorced (2000); Foreign born: 3.7% (2000); Ancestry (includes multiple ancestries): 40.5% Irish, 21.0% German, 20.8% Italian, 12.4% Polish, 9.7% English (2000).
Economy: Employment by occupation: 15.8% management, 28.8% professional, 13.9% services, 29.3% sales, 0.2% farming, 4.3% construction, 7.7% production (2000).
Income: Per capita income: $26,832 (2005); Median household income: $58,088 (2005); Average household income: $65,781 (2005); Percent of households with income of $100,000 or more: 19.4% (2005); Poverty rate: 6.0% (2000).
Education: Percent of population age 25 and over with: High school diploma (including GED) or higher: 94.2% (2005); Bachelor's degree or higher: 38.0% (2005); Master's degree or higher: 14.9% (2005).
Housing: Homeownership rate: 96.1% (2005); Median home value: $131,899 (2005); Median rent: $822 per month (2000); Median age of housing: 46 years (2000).
Transportation: Commute to work: 93.5% car, 1.2% public transportation, 0.7% walk, 4.4% work from home (2000); Travel time to work: 34.8% less than 15 minutes, 52.9% 15 to 30 minutes, 8.5% 30 to 45 minutes, 1.2% 45 to 60 minutes, 2.5% 60 minutes or more (2000)

Ontario County

Located in west central New York, in the Finger Lakes area; bounded partly on the east by Seneca Lake; drained by Honeoye, Mud, and Flint Creeks; includes Canandaigua, Honeoye, and Canadice Lakes. Covers a land area of 644.38 square miles, a water area of 18.05 square miles, and is located in the Eastern Time Zone. The county government was organized in 1789. County seat is Canandaigua.

Ontario County is part of the Rochester, NY Metropolitan Statistical Area. The entire metro area includes: Livingston County, NY; Monroe County, NY; Ontario County, NY; Orleans County, NY; Wayne County, NY

Weather Station: Canandaigua 3 S — Elevation: 718 feet

	Jan	Feb	Mar	Apr	May	Jun	Jul	Aug	Sep	Oct	Nov	Dec
High	32	34	42	55	68	77	82	80	72	61	49	38
Low	17	17	25	35	46	56	61	60	53	42	34	24
Precip	1.8	1.7	2.4	3.0	2.9	3.9	3.2	3.2	3.6	3.0	2.9	2.2
Snow	na	na	na	na	0.0	0.0	0.0	0.0	0.0	tr	na	na

High and Low temperatures in degrees Fahrenheit; Precipitation and Snow in inches

Weather Station: Geneva Research Farm — Elevation: 715 feet

	Jan	Feb	Mar	Apr	May	Jun	Jul	Aug	Sep	Oct	Nov	Dec
High	30	32	41	54	67	75	80	78	70	59	47	36
Low	15	16	25	36	47	56	61	59	52	41	32	22
Precip	1.8	1.6	2.2	2.8	3.0	3.7	3.2	3.2	3.6	3.1	3.0	2.3
Snow	15.0	14.6	11.5	3.3	0.1	0.0	0.0	0.0	0.0	0.2	4.5	13.1

High and Low temperatures in degrees Fahrenheit; Precipitation and Snow in inches

Population: 95,101 (1990); 100,224 (2000); 103,446 (2005); 106,762 (2010 projected); Race: 94.2% White, 2.5% Black, 0.9% Asian, 3.0% Hispanic of any race (2005); Density: 160.5 persons per square mile (2005); Average household size: 2.58 (2005); Median age: 39.3 (2005); Males per 100 females: 95.8 (2005).
Religion: Five largest groups: 26.7% Catholic Church, 6.4% The United Methodist Church, 2.5% Presbyterian Church (U.S.A.), 1.7% United Church of Christ, 1.5% Episcopal Church (2000).
Economy: Unemployment rate: 4.5% (2005); Total civilian labor force: 56,121 (2005); Leading industries: 20.9% retail trade; 18.0% manufacturing; 16.4% health care and social assistance (2003); Farms: 896 totaling 194,742 acres (2002); Companies that employ 500 or more persons: 7 (2003); Companies that employ 100 to 499 persons: 56 (2003); Companies that employ less than 100 persons: 2,695 (2003); Black-owned businesses: n/a (2002); Hispanic-owned businesses: n/a (2002); Women-owned businesses: 2,106 (2002); Retail sales per capita: $17,177 (2006). Single-family building permits issued: 384 (2005); Multi-family building permits issued: 45 (2005).
Income: Per capita income: $23,917 (2005); Median household income: $48,875 (2005); Average household income: $61,085 (2005); Percent of households with income of $100,000 or more: 14.2% (2005); Poverty rate: 8.4% (2003); Bankruptcy rate: 4.98% (2005).
Taxes: Total county taxes per capita: $844 (2004); County property taxes per capita: $325 (2004).
Education: Percent of population age 25 and over with: High school diploma (including GED) or higher: 87.4% (2005); Bachelor's degree or higher: 24.9% (2005); Master's degree or higher: 10.2% (2005).
Housing: Homeownership rate: 74.0% (2005); Median home value: $117,505 (2005); Median rent: $476 per month (2000); Median age of housing: 36 years (2000).
Health: Birth rate: 108.2 per 10,000 population (2004); Death rate: 99.7 per 10,000 population (2004); Age-adjusted cancer mortality rate: 218.3 deaths per 100,000 population (2002); Number of physicians: 22.2 per 10,000 population (2004); Hospital beds: 91.1 per 10,000 population (2003); Hospital admissions: 1,279.9 per 10,000 population (2003).
Elections: 2004 Presidential election results: 55.9% Bush, 42.2% Kerry, 1.6% Nader, 0.3% Badnarik

Additional Information Contacts

Ontario County Government	(585) 396-4274
http://www.co.ontario.ny.us/	
City of Canandaigua	(585) 396-5000
http://canandaigua.govoffice.com/	
City of Geneva	(315) 789-2603
http://www.geneva.ny.us/	
Town of Bristol	(585) 229-2400
http://www.townofbristol.org/	
Town of Canandaigua	(585) 394-1120
http://www.townofcanandaigua.org/	
Town of Victor	(585) 742-5020
http://www.victorny.org/	
Village of Bloomfield	(585) 657-7554
http://www.bloomfieldny.org/main.html	
Village of Phelps	(315) 548-3861
http://www.phelpsny.com/village/	

Ontario County Communities

BLOOMFIELD (village). Covers a land area of 1.407 square miles and a water area of 0 square miles. Located at 42.89° N. Lat.; 77.43° W. Long.
Population: 1,452 (1990); 1,267 (2000); 1,269 (2005); 1,286 (2010 projected); Race: 97.8% White, 0.9% Black, 0.0% Asian, 1.4% Hispanic of any race (2005); Density: 901.7 persons per square mile (2005); Average household size: 2.63 (2005); Median age: 37.2 (2005); Males per 100 females: 92.6 (2005); Marriage status: 25.0% never married, 62.4% now married, 5.0% widowed, 7.7% divorced (2000); Foreign born: 1.6% (2000); Ancestry (includes multiple ancestries): 24.7% English, 24.5% German, 22.6% Irish, 9.6% Italian, 6.2% Other groups (2000).
Economy: Single-family building permits issued: 1 (2005); Multi-family building permits issued: 0 (2005); Employment by occupation: 14.5% management, 21.4% professional, 14.5% services, 21.4% sales, 0.9% farming, 11.5% construction, 15.8% production (2000).
Income: Per capita income: $24,860 (2005); Median household income: $52,119 (2005); Average household income: $63,154 (2005); Percent of households with income of $100,000 or more: 14.3% (2005); Poverty rate: 4.1% (2000).
Education: Percent of population age 25 and over with: High school diploma (including GED) or higher: 89.6% (2005); Bachelor's degree or higher: 26.1% (2005); Master's degree or higher: 9.2% (2005).
School District(s)
East Bloomfield Central School District (KG-12)
    2003-04 Enrollment: 1,117 . . . . (585) 657-6121
Housing: Homeownership rate: 66.4% (2005); Median home value: $117,169 (2005); Median rent: $541 per month (2000); Median age of housing: 43 years (2000).
Transportation: Commute to work: 95.9% car, 0.7% public transportation, 0.7% walk, 2.6% work from home (2000); Travel time to work: 24.7% less than 15 minutes, 35.2% 15 to 30 minutes, 29.1% 30 to 45 minutes, 7.8% 45 to 60 minutes, 3.1% 60 minutes or more (2000)
Additional Information Contacts
Village of Bloomfield . . . . (585) 657-7554
    http://www.bloomfieldny.org/main.html

BRISTOL (town). Covers a land area of 36.737 square miles and a water area of 0.016 square miles. Located at 42.82° N. Lat.; 77.42° W. Long. Elevation is 1,169 feet.
Population: 2,071 (1990); 2,421 (2000); 2,432 (2005); 2,452 (2010 projected); Race: 97.7% White, 0.5% Black, 0.5% Asian, 0.5% Hispanic of any race (2005); Density: 66.2 persons per square mile (2005); Average household size: 2.67 (2005); Median age: 40.6 (2005); Males per 100 females: 105.4 (2005); Marriage status: 21.7% never married, 66.4% now married, 3.5% widowed, 8.4% divorced (2000); Foreign born: 1.7% (2000); Ancestry (includes multiple ancestries): 24.6% German, 22.8% English, 21.4% Irish, 12.5% Other groups, 11.7% Italian (2000).
Economy: Single-family building permits issued: 8 (2005); Multi-family building permits issued: 0 (2005); Employment by occupation: 10.8% management, 19.8% professional, 16.1% services, 23.4% sales, 0.9% farming, 16.1% construction, 12.9% production (2000).
Income: Per capita income: $26,830 (2005); Median household income: $59,760 (2005); Average household income: $71,625 (2005); Percent of households with income of $100,000 or more: 18.3% (2005); Poverty rate: 5.5% (2000).
Education: Percent of population age 25 and over with: High school diploma (including GED) or higher: 88.4% (2005); Bachelor's degree or higher: 28.1% (2005); Master's degree or higher: 10.8% (2005).
Housing: Homeownership rate: 90.3% (2005); Median home value: $129,222 (2005); Median rent: $390 per month (2000); Median age of housing: 27 years (2000).
Transportation: Commute to work: 95.2% car, 0.0% public transportation, 1.1% walk, 3.4% work from home (2000); Travel time to work: 15.6% less than 15 minutes, 30.9% 15 to 30 minutes, 27.2% 30 to 45 minutes, 18.9% 45 to 60 minutes, 7.4% 60 minutes or more (2000)
Additional Information Contacts
Town of Bristol . . . . (585) 229-2400
http://www.townofbristol.org/

CANADICE (town). Covers a land area of 30.041 square miles and a water area of 2.411 square miles. Located at 42.71° N. Lat.; 77.55° W. Long.
Population: 1,857 (1990); 1,846 (2000); 1,838 (2005); 1,842 (2010 projected); Race: 97.7% White, 0.5% Black, 0.9% Asian, 1.5% Hispanic of any race (2005); Density: 61.2 persons per square mile (2005); Average household size: 2.34 (2005); Median age: 43.1 (2005); Males per 100 females: 102.9 (2005); Marriage status: 21.5% never married, 61.4% now married, 5.7% widowed, 11.5% divorced (2000); Foreign born: 2.5% (2000); Ancestry (includes multiple ancestries): 30.8% German, 23.2% English, 21.3% Irish, 12.1% Italian, 7.1% Dutch (2000).
Economy: Single-family building permits issued: 4 (2005); Multi-family building permits issued: 0 (2005); Employment by occupation: 13.6% management, 20.6% professional, 11.6% services, 21.7% sales, 0.8% farming, 14.2% construction, 17.4% production (2000).
Income: Per capita income: $24,325 (2005); Median household income: $50,177 (2005); Average household income: $56,811 (2005); Percent of households with income of $100,000 or more: 11.2% (2005); Poverty rate: 6.4% (2000).
Taxes: Total city taxes per capita: $212 (2004); City property taxes per capita: $168 (2004).
Education: Percent of population age 25 and over with: High school diploma (including GED) or higher: 84.5% (2005); Bachelor's degree or higher: 21.0% (2005); Master's degree or higher: 8.8% (2005).
Housing: Homeownership rate: 85.3% (2005); Median home value: $114,875 (2005); Median rent: $334 per month (2000); Median age of housing: 29 years (2000).
Transportation: Commute to work: 94.9% car, 0.8% public transportation, 1.2% walk, 2.8% work from home (2000); Travel time to work: 13.8% less than 15 minutes, 18.8% 15 to 30 minutes, 28.9% 30 to 45 minutes, 26.7% 45 to 60 minutes, 11.7% 60 minutes or more (2000)

CANANDAIGUA (city). Covers a land area of 4.602 square miles and a water area of 0.234 square miles. Located at 42.88° N. Lat.; 77.28° W. Long. Elevation is 767 feet.
Population: 10,725 (1990); 11,264 (2000); 11,323 (2005); 11,420 (2010 projected); Race: 95.1% White, 2.1% Black, 0.9% Asian, 1.4% Hispanic of any race (2005); Density: 2,460.3 persons per square mile (2005); Average household size: 2.34 (2005); Median age: 40.4 (2005); Males per 100 females: 92.7 (2005); Marriage status: 26.3% never married, 50.6% now married, 9.7% widowed, 13.3% divorced (2000); Foreign born: 3.4% (2000); Ancestry (includes multiple ancestries): 21.9% Irish, 20.4% German, 18.9% English, 11.8% Italian, 6.6% Other groups (2000).
Economy: Single-family building permits issued: 25 (2005); Multi-family building permits issued: 6 (2005); Employment by occupation: 11.6% management, 21.6% professional, 19.5% services, 26.7% sales, 0.2% farming, 6.4% construction, 13.9% production (2000).
Income: Per capita income: $21,659 (2005); Median household income: $38,937 (2005); Average household income: $49,067 (2005); Percent of households with income of $100,000 or more: 8.7% (2005); Poverty rate: 9.5% (2000).
Education: Percent of population age 25 and over with: High school diploma (including GED) or higher: 85.0% (2005); Bachelor's degree or higher: 24.6% (2005); Master's degree or higher: 9.6% (2005).
School District(s)
Canandaigua City School District (PK-12)
    2003-04 Enrollment: 4,186 . . . . (585) 396-3700
Two-year College(s)
Finger Lakes Community College (Public)
    Fall 2004 Enrollment: 4,884 . . . . (585) 394-3500
    2005-06 Tuition: In-state $3,160; Out-of-state $6,060
Housing: Homeownership rate: 50.9% (2005); Median home value: $126,032 (2005); Median rent: $501 per month (2000); Median age of housing: 47 years (2000).
Hospitals: FF Thompson Health (113 beds); Veterans Affairs Medical Center (251 beds)
Newspapers: Daily Messenger (Circulation 12,792)
Transportation: Commute to work: 89.0% car, 1.3% public transportation, 6.8% walk, 2.0% work from home (2000); Travel time to work: 49.3% less than 15 minutes, 22.9% 15 to 30 minutes, 15.3% 30 to 45 minutes, 8.9% 45 to 60 minutes, 3.6% 60 minutes or more (2000)
Additional Information Contacts
Canandaigua Chamber of Commerce . . . . (585) 394-4400
    http://www.canandaigua.com/chamber
City of Canandaigua . . . . (585) 396-5000
    http://canandaigua.govoffice.com/

CANANDAIGUA (town). Covers a land area of 56.853 square miles and a water area of 5.655 square miles. Located at 42.85° N. Lat.; 77.30° W. Long. Elevation is 767 feet.
Population: 7,160 (1990); 7,649 (2000); 7,990 (2005); 8,340 (2010 projected); Race: 96.6% White, 0.9% Black, 1.0% Asian, 1.4% Hispanic of any race (2005); Density: 140.5 persons per square mile (2005); Average household size: 2.60 (2005); Median age: 41.3 (2005); Males per 100 females: 97.2 (2005); Marriage status: 22.2% never married, 63.6% now married, 5.8% widowed, 8.4% divorced (2000); Foreign born: 2.8% (2000); Ancestry (includes multiple ancestries): 26.6% German, 19.1% Irish, 18.3% English, 14.5% Italian, 7.0% United States or American (2000).
Economy: Single-family building permits issued: 80 (2005); Multi-family building permits issued: 11 (2005); Employment by occupation: 15.0% management, 27.5% professional, 12.9% services, 22.3% sales, 0.4% farming, 9.7% construction, 12.3% production (2000).
Income: Per capita income: $30,305 (2005); Median household income: $64,130 (2005); Average household income: $78,621 (2005); Percent of households with income of $100,000 or more: 23.3% (2005); Poverty rate: 5.3% (2000).
Education: Percent of population age 25 and over with: High school diploma (including GED) or higher: 92.0% (2005); Bachelor's degree or higher: 33.8% (2005); Master's degree or higher: 16.3% (2005).
Housing: Homeownership rate: 78.2% (2005); Median home value: $146,694 (2005); Median rent: $619 per month (2000); Median age of housing: 23 years (2000).
Transportation: Commute to work: 92.5% car, 0.2% public transportation, 1.5% walk, 5.0% work from home (2000); Travel time to work: 38.9% less than 15 minutes, 25.2% 15 to 30 minutes, 21.2% 30 to 45 minutes, 10.4% 45 to 60 minutes, 4.4% 60 minutes or more (2000)
Additional Information Contacts
Town of Canandaigua . . . . (585) 394-1120
    http://www.townofcanandaigua.org/

CLIFTON SPRINGS (village). Covers a land area of 1.442 square miles and a water area of 0 square miles. Located at 42.96° N. Lat.; 77.13° W. Long. Elevation is 567 feet.
Population: 2,218 (1990); 2,223 (2000); 2,198 (2005); 2,229 (2010 projected); Race: 97.1% White, 1.7% Black, 0.2% Asian, 1.2% Hispanic of any race (2005); Density: 1,524.1 persons per square mile (2005); Average

household size: 2.52 (2005); Median age: 42.1 (2005); Males per 100 females: 86.4 (2005); Marriage status: 25.6% never married, 51.4% now married, 13.3% widowed, 9.7% divorced (2000); Foreign born: 0.8% (2000); Ancestry (includes multiple ancestries): 22.1% German, 20.9% English, 19.4% Dutch, 17.8% Irish, 8.1% Italian (2000).
Economy: Single-family building permits issued: 1 (2005); Multi-family building permits issued: 2 (2005); Employment by occupation: 7.1% management, 27.2% professional, 12.0% services, 24.1% sales, 1.1% farming, 7.8% construction, 20.8% production (2000).
Income: Per capita income: $20,103 (2005); Median household income: $40,250 (2005); Average household income: $48,179 (2005); Percent of households with income of $100,000 or more: 7.1% (2005); Poverty rate: 13.1% (2000).
Education: Percent of population age 25 and over with: High school diploma (including GED) or higher: 85.2% (2005); Bachelor's degree or higher: 20.2% (2005); Master's degree or higher: 6.7% (2005).

School District(s)
Phelps-Clifton Springs Central School District (KG-12)
    2003-04 Enrollment: 2,044 . . . . (315) 548-6420
Housing: Homeownership rate: 57.8% (2005); Median home value: $100,439 (2005); Median rent: $430 per month (2000); Median age of housing: 60+ years (2000).
Hospitals: Clifton Springs Hospital & Clinic (262 beds)
Safety: Violent crime rate: 18.2 per 10,000 population; Property crime rate: 77.3 per 10,000 population (2004).
Transportation: Commute to work: 84.7% car, 0.5% public transportation, 12.6% walk, 1.7% work from home (2000); Travel time to work: 45.1% less than 15 minutes, 31.1% 15 to 30 minutes, 13.9% 30 to 45 minutes, 6.9% 45 to 60 minutes, 3.0% 60 minutes or more (2000)
Additional Information Contacts
Clifton Springs Area Chamber of Commerce. . . . . (315) 462-8200
    http://www.cliftonspringschamber.com

EAST BLOOMFIELD (town). Covers a land area of 33.198 square miles and a water area of 0.138 square miles. Located at 42.89° N. Lat.; 77.42° W. Long. Elevation is 1,017 feet.
Population: 3,258 (1990); 3,361 (2000); 3,381 (2005); 3,442 (2010 projected); Race: 98.5% White, 0.4% Black, 0.2% Asian, 1.0% Hispanic of any race (2005); Density: 101.8 persons per square mile (2005); Average household size: 2.72 (2005); Median age: 38.6 (2005); Males per 100 females: 95.2 (2005); Marriage status: 22.8% never married, 64.2% now married, 4.5% widowed, 8.5% divorced (2000); Foreign born: 2.5% (2000); Ancestry (includes multiple ancestries): 25.6% German, 22.5% English, 21.5% Irish, 8.0% Italian, 7.1% French (except Basque) (2000).
Economy: Single-family building permits issued: 8 (2005); Multi-family building permits issued: 0 (2005); Employment by occupation: 14.6% management, 20.7% professional, 14.3% services, 21.4% sales, 1.8% farming, 10.8% construction, 16.2% production (2000).
Income: Per capita income: $25,459 (2005); Median household income: $57,976 (2005); Average household income: $68,357 (2005); Percent of households with income of $100,000 or more: 20.8% (2005); Poverty rate: 4.1% (2000).
Education: Percent of population age 25 and over with: High school diploma (including GED) or higher: 91.6% (2005); Bachelor's degree or higher: 28.4% (2005); Master's degree or higher: 10.6% (2005).

School District(s)
East Bloomfield Central School District (KG-12)
    2003-04 Enrollment: 1,117 . . . . (585) 657-6121
Housing: Homeownership rate: 79.7% (2005); Median home value: $128,500 (2005); Median rent: $535 per month (2000); Median age of housing: 34 years (2000).
Transportation: Commute to work: 88.5% car, 1.0% public transportation, 1.6% walk, 8.2% work from home (2000); Travel time to work: 17.2% less than 15 minutes, 34.1% 15 to 30 minutes, 32.8% 30 to 45 minutes, 12.0% 45 to 60 minutes, 4.0% 60 minutes or more (2000)

FARMINGTON (town). Covers a land area of 39.449 square miles and a water area of 0 square miles. Located at 42.98° N. Lat.; 77.32° W. Long. Elevation is 600 feet.
Population: 10,381 (1990); 10,585 (2000); 11,044 (2005); 11,512 (2010 projected); Race: 96.1% White, 1.2% Black, 1.1% Asian, 1.6% Hispanic of any race (2005); Density: 280.0 persons per square mile (2005); Average household size: 2.69 (2005); Median age: 36.8 (2005); Males per 100 females: 95.9 (2005); Marriage status: 23.7% never married, 61.4% now married, 4.4% widowed, 10.5% divorced (2000); Foreign born: 2.6% (2000); Ancestry (includes multiple ancestries): 29.7% German, 19.6% Irish, 19.1% English, 15.7% Italian, 6.2% Polish (2000).
Economy: Single-family building permits issued: 45 (2005); Multi-family building permits issued: 0 (2005); Employment by occupation: 12.9% management, 20.1% professional, 13.7% services, 30.1% sales, 0.3% farming, 7.2% construction, 15.6% production (2000).
Income: Per capita income: $22,989 (2005); Median household income: $55,653 (2005); Average household income: $61,728 (2005); Percent of households with income of $100,000 or more: 13.6% (2005); Poverty rate: 5.6% (2000).
Education: Percent of population age 25 and over with: High school diploma (including GED) or higher: 91.6% (2005); Bachelor's degree or higher: 25.2% (2005); Master's degree or higher: 8.2% (2005).
Housing: Homeownership rate: 77.4% (2005); Median home value: $117,973 (2005); Median rent: $596 per month (2000); Median age of housing: 23 years (2000).
Transportation: Commute to work: 95.5% car, 0.4% public transportation, 1.2% walk, 2.3% work from home (2000); Travel time to work: 26.3% less than 15 minutes, 39.6% 15 to 30 minutes, 26.3% 30 to 45 minutes, 5.0% 45 to 60 minutes, 2.8% 60 minutes or more (2000)
Additional Information Contacts
Farmington Chamber of Commerce . . . . (315) 986-8100

GENEVA (city). Covers a land area of 4.256 square miles and a water area of 1.590 square miles. Located at 42.87° N. Lat.; 76.98° W. Long. Elevation is 494 feet.
History: Named for Geneva, Switzerland, by Swiss settlers. The area of the city of Geneva includes the site of the Native American settlement of Kanadesaga. After the Revolution, other settlers began to arrive. Captain Charles Williamson, agent for the Pulteney Estate, recognized the superb advantages of the site and laid out Main Street on the terrace overlooking the lake.
Population: 14,236 (1990); 13,617 (2000); 13,483 (2005); 13,342 (2010 projected); Race: 77.7% White, 12.3% Black, 1.5% Asian, 12.3% Hispanic of any race (2005); Density: 3,168.1 persons per square mile (2005); Average household size: 2.73 (2005); Median age: 32.3 (2005); Males per 100 females: 88.2 (2005); Marriage status: 40.9% never married, 42.5% now married, 8.3% widowed, 8.4% divorced (2000); Foreign born: 3.8% (2000); Ancestry (includes multiple ancestries): 22.9% Italian, 20.8% Irish, 20.4% Other groups, 13.5% German, 11.7% English (2000).
Economy: Single-family building permits issued: 0 (2005); Multi-family building permits issued: 0 (2005); Employment by occupation: 9.4% management, 23.2% professional, 22.2% services, 25.0% sales, 0.4% farming, 5.1% construction, 14.7% production (2000).
Income: Per capita income: $16,532 (2005); Median household income: $33,531 (2005); Average household income: $43,326 (2005); Percent of households with income of $100,000 or more: 6.4% (2005); Poverty rate: 17.5% (2000).
Education: Percent of population age 25 and over with: High school diploma (including GED) or higher: 78.4% (2005); Bachelor's degree or higher: 21.9% (2005); Master's degree or higher: 9.7% (2005).

School District(s)
Geneva City School District (KG-12)
    2003-04 Enrollment: 2,534 . . . . (315) 781-0276

Four-year College(s)
Hobart William Smith Colleges
    Fall 2004 Enrollment: 1,847. . . . . (315) 781-3000
    2005-06 Tuition: In-state $32,737; Out-of-state $32,737

Two-year College(s)
Marion S Whelan School of Nursing of Geneva General Hospital
    Fall 2004 Enrollment: 29 . . . . (315) 787-4005
    2005-06 Tuition: In-state $5,680; Out-of-state $5,680
Housing: Homeownership rate: 53.3% (2005); Median home value: $83,265 (2005); Median rent: $417 per month (2000); Median age of housing: 60+ years (2000).
Hospitals: Geneva General Hospital (136 beds)
Safety: Violent crime rate: 22.9 per 10,000 population; Property crime rate: 268.8 per 10,000 population (2004).
Newspapers: Finger Lakes Times (Circulation 16,794)
Transportation: Commute to work: 80.3% car, 1.9% public transportation, 15.9% walk, 1.4% work from home (2000); Travel time to work: 58.7% less than 15 minutes, 25.5% 15 to 30 minutes, 8.6% 30 to 45 minutes, 3.6% 45 to 60 minutes, 3.5% 60 minutes or more (2000)
Additional Information Contacts

City of Geneva . . . . (315) 789-2603
  http://www.geneva.ny.us/
Geneva Chamber of Commerce . . . . (315) 789-1776
  http://www.genevany.com

GENEVA (town). Covers a land area of 19.105 square miles and a water area of 0.009 square miles. Located at 42.82° N. Lat.; 76.99° W. Long. Elevation is 494 feet.

History: Hobart College and William Smith College are in the city. Settled 1788; Incorporated as village in 1812, as city in 1897.

Population: 2,874 (1990); 3,289 (2000); 3,348 (2005); 3,421 (2010 projected); Race: 91.8% White, 3.1% Black, 2.7% Asian, 2.6% Hispanic of any race (2005); Density: 175.2 persons per square mile (2005); Average household size: 2.28 (2005); Median age: 46.7 (2005); Males per 100 females: 94.8 (2005); Marriage status: 18.8% never married, 62.5% now married, 8.3% widowed, 10.4% divorced (2000); Foreign born: 1.9% (2000); Ancestry (includes multiple ancestries): 25.2% English, 23.2% Irish, 21.5% Italian, 20.2% German, 5.2% Dutch (2000).

Economy: Located in a farm area. Manufacturing of cans and canning machinery, paper containers, metal and optical products and water purification systems. It also has printing plants. Hobart College and William Smith College are in the city. Single-family building permits issued: 6 (2005); Multi-family building permits issued: 0 (2005); Employment by occupation: 13.0% management, 29.4% professional, 17.7% services, 20.4% sales, 0.6% farming, 10.0% construction, 9.0% production (2000).

Income: Per capita income: $25,517 (2005); Median household income: $47,910 (2005); Average household income: $58,195 (2005); Percent of households with income of $100,000 or more: 12.1% (2005); Poverty rate: 3.4% (2000).

Education: Percent of population age 25 and over with: High school diploma (including GED) or higher: 88.5% (2005); Bachelor's degree or higher: 24.1% (2005); Master's degree or higher: 11.4% (2005).

Housing: Homeownership rate: 69.4% (2005); Median home value: $137,670 (2005); Median rent: $509 per month (2000); Median age of housing: 35 years (2000).

Transportation: Commute to work: 95.1% car, 0.8% public transportation, 1.6% walk, 2.1% work from home (2000); Travel time to work: 48.3% less than 15 minutes, 26.9% 15 to 30 minutes, 15.6% 30 to 45 minutes, 3.9% 45 to 60 minutes, 5.3% 60 minutes or more (2000)

GORHAM (town). Covers a land area of 48.903 square miles and a water area of 4.306 square miles. Located at 42.80° N. Lat.; 77.22° W. Long. Elevation is 895 feet.

Population: 3,497 (1990); 3,776 (2000); 3,903 (2005); 4,037 (2010 projected); Race: 98.3% White, 0.5% Black, 0.1% Asian, 0.5% Hispanic of any race (2005); Density: 79.8 persons per square mile (2005); Average household size: 2.66 (2005); Median age: 40.2 (2005); Males per 100 females: 97.0 (2005); Marriage status: 21.3% never married, 60.5% now married, 7.7% widowed, 10.6% divorced (2000); Foreign born: 1.1% (2000); Ancestry (includes multiple ancestries): 21.0% English, 20.0% German, 17.9% Irish, 9.6% United States or American, 9.3% Italian (2000).

Economy: Single-family building permits issued: 43 (2005); Multi-family building permits issued: 0 (2005); Employment by occupation: 13.5% management, 17.1% professional, 16.7% services, 21.0% sales, 0.3% farming, 16.2% construction, 15.0% production (2000).

Income: Per capita income: $23,722 (2005); Median household income: $48,509 (2005); Average household income: $63,055 (2005); Percent of households with income of $100,000 or more: 15.6% (2005); Poverty rate: 7.0% (2000).

Education: Percent of population age 25 and over with: High school diploma (including GED) or higher: 85.7% (2005); Bachelor's degree or higher: 20.8% (2005); Master's degree or higher: 9.7% (2005).

School District(s)
Gorham-Middlesex Central School District (Marcus Whitman) (KG-12)
  2003-04 Enrollment: 1,597 . . . . (585) 554-4848

Housing: Homeownership rate: 84.6% (2005); Median home value: $121,824 (2005); Median rent: $493 per month (2000); Median age of housing: 45 years (2000).

Transportation: Commute to work: 88.3% car, 1.2% public transportation, 1.9% walk, 8.7% work from home (2000); Travel time to work: 22.6% less than 15 minutes, 41.5% 15 to 30 minutes, 18.2% 30 to 45 minutes, 10.6% 45 to 60 minutes, 7.1% 60 minutes or more (2000)

HONEOYE (unincorporated postal area, zip code 14471). Covers a land area of 29.917 square miles and a water area of 0 square miles. Located at 42.76° N. Lat.; 77.50° W. Long. Elevation is 773 feet.

Population: 0 (2000); Race: 99.8% White, 0.0% Black, 0.0% Asian, 0.3% Hispanic of any race (2000); Density: 0.0 persons per square mile (2000); Age: 23.7% under 18, 13.7% over 64 (2000); Marriage status: 24.6% never married, 57.2% now married, 6.0% widowed, 12.3% divorced (2000); Foreign born: 1.9% (2000); Ancestry (includes multiple ancestries): 31.3% German, 20.9% Irish, 16.9% English, 12.6% Italian, 10.8% United States or American (2000).

Economy: Employment by occupation: 13.3% management, 19.8% professional, 9.2% services, 26.2% sales, 0.3% farming, 11.4% construction, 19.9% production (2000).

Income: Per capita income: $24,368 (2000); Median household income: $47,540 (2000); Poverty rate: 5.1% (2000).

Education: Percent of population age 25 and over with: High school diploma (including GED) or higher: 87.1% (2000); Bachelor's degree or higher: 22.3% (2000).

School District(s)
Honeoye Central School District (KG-12)
  2003-04 Enrollment: 1,052 . . . . (585) 229-4125

Housing: Homeownership rate: 83.2% (2000); Median home value: $109,000 (2000); Median rent: $467 per month (2000); Median age of housing: 38 years (2000).

Transportation: Commute to work: 93.9% car, 1.3% public transportation, 1.1% walk, 3.8% work from home (2000); Travel time to work: 22.7% less than 15 minutes, 17.0% 15 to 30 minutes, 19.9% 30 to 45 minutes, 29.7% 45 to 60 minutes, 10.7% 60 minutes or more (2000)

Additional Information Contacts
Honeoye Chamber of Commerce . . . . (716) 229-4564
  http://www.honeoye.com/chambe

HOPEWELL (town). Covers a land area of 35.638 square miles and a water area of 0.023 square miles. Located at 42.89° N. Lat.; 77.19° W. Long.

Population: 3,016 (1990); 3,346 (2000); 3,432 (2005); 3,531 (2010 projected); Race: 97.4% White, 1.0% Black, 0.1% Asian, 3.1% Hispanic of any race (2005); Density: 96.3 persons per square mile (2005); Average household size: 2.64 (2005); Median age: 40.9 (2005); Males per 100 females: 93.6 (2005); Marriage status: 20.1% never married, 62.9% now married, 6.4% widowed, 10.6% divorced (2000); Foreign born: 1.9% (2000); Ancestry (includes multiple ancestries): 26.1% German, 23.5% English, 13.2% Irish, 8.7% Italian, 6.2% Dutch (2000).

Economy: Single-family building permits issued: 11 (2005); Multi-family building permits issued: 0 (2005); Employment by occupation: 10.9% management, 15.7% professional, 12.7% services, 25.2% sales, 1.2% farming, 11.1% construction, 23.2% production (2000).

Income: Per capita income: $18,705 (2005); Median household income: $44,966 (2005); Average household income: $49,123 (2005); Percent of households with income of $100,000 or more: 4.9% (2005); Poverty rate: 7.6% (2000).

Education: Percent of population age 25 and over with: High school diploma (including GED) or higher: 85.7% (2005); Bachelor's degree or higher: 12.3% (2005); Master's degree or higher: 3.6% (2005).

Housing: Homeownership rate: 82.4% (2005); Median home value: $91,814 (2005); Median rent: $424 per month (2000); Median age of housing: 25 years (2000).

Transportation: Commute to work: 94.6% car, 1.3% public transportation, 0.9% walk, 3.3% work from home (2000); Travel time to work: 37.4% less than 15 minutes, 28.0% 15 to 30 minutes, 16.9% 30 to 45 minutes, 11.0% 45 to 60 minutes, 6.7% 60 minutes or more (2000)

IONIA (unincorporated postal area, zip code 14475). Covers a land area of 1.544 square miles and a water area of 0 square miles. Located at 42.93° N. Lat.; 77.49° W. Long.

Population: 0 (2000); Race: 100.0% White, 0.0% Black, 0.0% Asian, 0.0% Hispanic of any race (2000); Density: 0.0 persons per square mile (2000); Age: 32.2% under 18, 4.7% over 64 (2000); Marriage status: 23.3% never married, 67.0% now married, 2.3% widowed, 7.4% divorced (2000); Foreign born: 1.7% (2000); Ancestry (includes multiple ancestries): 28.3% Italian, 27.5% German, 15.9% Dutch, 14.6% English, 13.7% United States or American (2000).

Economy: Employment by occupation: 19.2% management, 16.2% professional, 13.8% services, 26.2% sales, 3.1% farming, 7.7% construction, 13.8% production (2000).
Income: Per capita income: $24,078 (2000); Median household income: $70,625 (2000); Poverty rate: 0.0% (2000).
Education: Percent of population age 25 and over with: High school diploma (including GED) or higher: 94.1% (2000); Bachelor's degree or higher: 40.8% (2000).
Housing: Homeownership rate: 89.6% (2000); Median home value: $166,700 (2000); Median rent: $625 per month (2000); Median age of housing: 30 years (2000).
Transportation: Commute to work: 98.5% car, 0.0% public transportation, 0.0% walk, 1.5% work from home (2000); Travel time to work: 24.2% less than 15 minutes, 39.8% 15 to 30 minutes, 22.7% 30 to 45 minutes, 3.1% 45 to 60 minutes, 10.2% 60 minutes or more (2000)

MANCHESTER (village). Covers a land area of 1.171 square miles and a water area of 0 square miles. Located at 42.96° N. Lat.; 77.22° W. Long.
Population: 1,598 (1990); 1,475 (2000); 1,400 (2005); 1,347 (2010 projected); Race: 97.4% White, 0.5% Black, 0.3% Asian, 1.4% Hispanic of any race (2005); Density: 1,195.7 persons per square mile (2005); Average household size: 2.22 (2005); Median age: 45.1 (2005); Males per 100 females: 97.5 (2005); Marriage status: 23.6% never married, 54.5% now married, 9.0% widowed, 12.8% divorced (2000); Foreign born: 1.2% (2000); Ancestry (includes multiple ancestries): 24.8% German, 22.6% Irish, 21.9% Italian, 21.2% English, 8.9% Dutch (2000).
Economy: Single-family building permits issued: 0 (2005); Multi-family building permits issued: 0 (2005); Employment by occupation: 7.6% management, 19.0% professional, 19.1% services, 22.7% sales, 0.3% farming, 9.9% construction, 21.3% production (2000).
Income: Per capita income: $20,754 (2005); Median household income: $39,478 (2005); Average household income: $46,119 (2005); Percent of households with income of $100,000 or more: 4.6% (2005); Poverty rate: 7.2% (2000).
Education: Percent of population age 25 and over with: High school diploma (including GED) or higher: 84.7% (2005); Bachelor's degree or higher: 13.3% (2005); Master's degree or higher: 5.6% (2005).
Housing: Homeownership rate: 84.8% (2005); Median home value: $71,489 (2005); Median rent: $502 per month (2000); Median age of housing: 42 years (2000).
Transportation: Commute to work: 97.4% car, 0.0% public transportation, 1.6% walk, 0.7% work from home (2000); Travel time to work: 34.0% less than 15 minutes, 41.7% 15 to 30 minutes, 15.9% 30 to 45 minutes, 5.3% 45 to 60 minutes, 3.1% 60 minutes or more (2000)

MANCHESTER (town). Covers a land area of 37.784 square miles and a water area of 0.028 square miles. Located at 42.97° N. Lat.; 77.19° W. Long.
History: Incorporated 1892.
Population: 9,351 (1990); 9,258 (2000); 9,356 (2005); 9,484 (2010 projected); Race: 97.4% White, 0.7% Black, 0.2% Asian, 1.8% Hispanic of any race (2005); Density: 247.6 persons per square mile (2005); Average household size: 2.55 (2005); Median age: 39.9 (2005); Males per 100 females: 96.3 (2005); Marriage status: 23.7% never married, 57.7% now married, 7.7% widowed, 10.9% divorced (2000); Foreign born: 1.6% (2000); Ancestry (includes multiple ancestries): 24.0% German, 20.7% English, 18.2% Irish, 14.5% Dutch, 10.1% Italian (2000).
Economy: Truck freight transfer point. Manufacturing: packaging, fabricated metal products, plastic parts and gears. Agriculture: field and vegetable crops. Single-family building permits issued: 3 (2005); Multi-family building permits issued: 0 (2005); Employment by occupation: 10.5% management, 16.0% professional, 16.8% services, 22.6% sales, 0.7% farming, 10.9% construction, 22.5% production (2000).
Income: Per capita income: $20,468 (2005); Median household income: $43,023 (2005); Average household income: $51,227 (2005); Percent of households with income of $100,000 or more: 6.5% (2005); Poverty rate: 8.4% (2000).
Education: Percent of population age 25 and over with: High school diploma (including GED) or higher: 85.4% (2005); Bachelor's degree or higher: 15.2% (2005); Master's degree or higher: 5.6% (2005).
Housing: Homeownership rate: 79.2% (2005); Median home value: $85,658 (2005); Median rent: $443 per month (2000); Median age of housing: 40 years (2000).
Transportation: Commute to work: 92.9% car, 0.4% public transportation, 4.3% walk, 2.2% work from home (2000); Travel time to work: 36.2% less than 15 minutes, 35.0% 15 to 30 minutes, 18.4% 30 to 45 minutes, 7.2% 45 to 60 minutes, 3.2% 60 minutes or more (2000)

NAPLES (village). Covers a land area of 0.977 square miles and a water area of 0 square miles. Located at 42.61° N. Lat.; 77.40° W. Long. Elevation is 818 feet.
Population: 1,237 (1990); 1,072 (2000); 1,043 (2005); 1,048 (2010 projected); Race: 98.6% White, 0.0% Black, 0.8% Asian, 1.2% Hispanic of any race (2005); Density: 1,067.6 persons per square mile (2005); Average household size: 2.32 (2005); Median age: 40.5 (2005); Males per 100 females: 94.6 (2005); Marriage status: 21.0% never married, 53.7% now married, 10.4% widowed, 14.9% divorced (2000); Foreign born: 3.1% (2000); Ancestry (includes multiple ancestries): 25.8% German, 18.2% English, 17.0% United States or American, 11.9% Irish, 7.8% Dutch (2000).
Economy: Single-family building permits issued: 0 (2005); Multi-family building permits issued: 0 (2005); Employment by occupation: 12.0% management, 22.9% professional, 21.2% services, 19.8% sales, 0.8% farming, 9.8% construction, 13.5% production (2000).
Income: Per capita income: $19,293 (2005); Median household income: $37,378 (2005); Average household income: $44,717 (2005); Percent of households with income of $100,000 or more: 6.4% (2005); Poverty rate: 13.2% (2000).
Education: Percent of population age 25 and over with: High school diploma (including GED) or higher: 83.9% (2005); Bachelor's degree or higher: 21.6% (2005); Master's degree or higher: 8.2% (2005).

School District(s)
Naples Central School District (KG-12)
    2003-04 Enrollment: 980 . . . . (585) 374-7900

Housing: Homeownership rate: 67.1% (2005); Median home value: $94,925 (2005); Median rent: $383 per month (2000); Median age of housing: 60+ years (2000).
Newspapers: The Naples Record (General - Circulation 1,500)
Transportation: Commute to work: 83.2% car, 0.4% public transportation, 10.8% walk, 5.6% work from home (2000); Travel time to work: 41.2% less than 15 minutes, 12.3% 15 to 30 minutes, 22.9% 30 to 45 minutes, 10.8% 45 to 60 minutes, 12.7% 60 minutes or more (2000)

NAPLES (town). Covers a land area of 39.494 square miles and a water area of 0 square miles. Located at 42.62° N. Lat.; 77.42° W. Long. Elevation is 818 feet.
History: Incorporated 1894.
Population: 2,559 (1990); 2,441 (2000); 2,505 (2005); 2,577 (2010 projected); Race: 98.0% White, 0.2% Black, 0.6% Asian, 0.6% Hispanic of any race (2005); Density: 63.4 persons per square mile (2005); Average household size: 2.43 (2005); Median age: 41.4 (2005); Males per 100 females: 92.2 (2005); Marriage status: 18.2% never married, 60.9% now married, 7.5% widowed, 13.4% divorced (2000); Foreign born: 2.2% (2000); Ancestry (includes multiple ancestries): 26.3% German, 20.1% English, 16.0% Irish, 12.3% United States or American, 5.8% Italian (2000).
Economy: In grape-growing Naples valley. Manufacturing: wine, grape juice. Timber. Single-family building permits issued: 8 (2005); Multi-family building permits issued: 0 (2005); Employment by occupation: 13.7% management, 23.3% professional, 16.2% services, 23.6% sales, 1.0% farming, 8.9% construction, 13.3% production (2000).
Income: Per capita income: $20,524 (2005); Median household income: $41,791 (2005); Average household income: $49,755 (2005); Percent of households with income of $100,000 or more: 9.0% (2005); Poverty rate: 10.5% (2000).
Education: Percent of population age 25 and over with: High school diploma (including GED) or higher: 84.7% (2005); Bachelor's degree or higher: 22.7% (2005); Master's degree or higher: 7.0% (2005).
Housing: Homeownership rate: 80.8% (2005); Median home value: $105,263 (2005); Median rent: $382 per month (2000); Median age of housing: 59 years (2000).
Transportation: Commute to work: 88.5% car, 0.4% public transportation, 5.1% walk, 5.6% work from home (2000); Travel time to work: 33.4% less than 15 minutes, 12.1% 15 to 30 minutes, 22.7% 30 to 45 minutes, 15.3% 45 to 60 minutes, 16.4% 60 minutes or more (2000)

PHELPS (village). Covers a land area of 1.169 square miles and a water area of 0 square miles. Located at 42.95° N. Lat.; 77.06° W. Long. Elevation is 601 feet.

Population: 1,978 (1990); 1,969 (2000); 1,946 (2005); 1,991 (2010 projected); Race: 98.4% White, 0.0% Black, 0.1% Asian, 1.9% Hispanic of any race (2005); Density: 1,664.3 persons per square mile (2005); Average household size: 2.44 (2005); Median age: 39.0 (2005); Males per 100 females: 91.0 (2005); Marriage status: 22.0% never married, 58.3% now married, 6.7% widowed, 13.0% divorced (2000); Foreign born: 0.7% (2000); Ancestry (includes multiple ancestries): 24.7% German, 24.4% English, 18.4% Irish, 18.0% Dutch, 8.0% Italian (2000).
Economy: Single-family building permits issued: 0 (2005); Multi-family building permits issued: 4 (2005); Employment by occupation: 10.8% management, 21.3% professional, 14.5% services, 26.4% sales, 0.5% farming, 8.7% construction, 18.0% production (2000).
Income: Per capita income: $21,573 (2005); Median household income: $44,817 (2005); Average household income: $51,990 (2005); Percent of households with income of $100,000 or more: 7.3% (2005); Poverty rate: 6.1% (2000).
Education: Percent of population age 25 and over with: High school diploma (including GED) or higher: 87.7% (2005); Bachelor's degree or higher: 17.3% (2005); Master's degree or higher: 7.4% (2005).

School District(s)
Phelps-Clifton Springs Central School District (KG-12)
    2003-04 Enrollment: 2,044 . . . . (315) 548-6420
Housing: Homeownership rate: 69.6% (2005); Median home value: $93,867 (2005); Median rent: $418 per month (2000); Median age of housing: 60+ years (2000).
Safety: Violent crime rate: 10.3 per 10,000 population; Property crime rate: 25.8 per 10,000 population (2004).
Transportation: Commute to work: 94.6% car, 0.2% public transportation, 2.4% walk, 2.8% work from home (2000); Travel time to work: 32.7% less than 15 minutes, 42.7% 15 to 30 minutes, 16.2% 30 to 45 minutes, 5.1% 45 to 60 minutes, 3.3% 60 minutes or more (2000)
Additional Information Contacts
Phelps Chamber of Commerce . . . . (315) 548-5481
    http://www.phelpsny.com/chamber
Village of Phelps . . . . (315) 548-3861
    http://www.phelpsny.com/village/

PHELPS (town). Covers a land area of 64.978 square miles and a water area of 0.283 square miles. Located at 42.95° N. Lat.; 77.04° W. Long. Elevation is 601 feet.
Population: 6,749 (1990); 7,017 (2000); 7,025 (2005); 7,073 (2010 projected); Race: 97.8% White, 0.2% Black, 0.3% Asian, 1.9% Hispanic of any race (2005); Density: 108.1 persons per square mile (2005); Average household size: 2.59 (2005); Median age: 39.3 (2005); Males per 100 females: 97.8 (2005); Marriage status: 21.5% never married, 61.6% now married, 6.6% widowed, 10.2% divorced (2000); Foreign born: 1.5% (2000); Ancestry (includes multiple ancestries): 24.5% English, 21.6% German, 16.1% Dutch, 15.2% Irish, 9.6% Italian (2000).
Economy: Single-family building permits issued: 7 (2005); Multi-family building permits issued: 0 (2005); Employment by occupation: 10.5% management, 23.0% professional, 14.2% services, 23.7% sales, 1.3% farming, 10.0% construction, 17.3% production (2000).
Income: Per capita income: $23,674 (2005); Median household income: $51,953 (2005); Average household income: $61,051 (2005); Percent of households with income of $100,000 or more: 13.6% (2005); Poverty rate: 4.3% (2000).
Education: Percent of population age 25 and over with: High school diploma (including GED) or higher: 86.6% (2005); Bachelor's degree or higher: 18.6% (2005); Master's degree or higher: 7.8% (2005).
Housing: Homeownership rate: 81.8% (2005); Median home value: $105,302 (2005); Median rent: $419 per month (2000); Median age of housing: 49 years (2000).
Transportation: Commute to work: 92.4% car, 0.6% public transportation, 1.4% walk, 4.9% work from home (2000); Travel time to work: 36.3% less than 15 minutes, 37.6% 15 to 30 minutes, 16.1% 30 to 45 minutes, 6.0% 45 to 60 minutes, 4.0% 60 minutes or more (2000)

RICHMOND (town). Covers a land area of 42.417 square miles and a water area of 1.899 square miles. Located at 42.79° N. Lat.; 77.52° W. Long.
Population: 3,230 (1990); 3,452 (2000); 3,631 (2005); 3,808 (2010 projected); Race: 98.4% White, 0.1% Black, 0.5% Asian, 1.0% Hispanic of any race (2005); Density: 85.6 persons per square mile (2005); Average household size: 2.58 (2005); Median age: 41.6 (2005); Males per 100 females: 101.6 (2005); Marriage status: 22.0% never married, 63.0% now married, 4.7% widowed, 10.2% divorced (2000); Foreign born: 1.5% (2000); Ancestry (includes multiple ancestries): 32.0% German, 19.8% Irish, 17.0% English, 11.0% Italian, 7.8% United States or American (2000).
Economy: Single-family building permits issued: 7 (2005); Multi-family building permits issued: 0 (2005); Employment by occupation: 12.3% management, 22.3% professional, 8.7% services, 23.2% sales, 0.0% farming, 11.1% construction, 22.5% production (2000).
Income: Per capita income: $24,305 (2005); Median household income: $56,163 (2005); Average household income: $62,590 (2005); Percent of households with income of $100,000 or more: 14.5% (2005); Poverty rate: 2.9% (2000).
Education: Percent of population age 25 and over with: High school diploma (including GED) or higher: 90.3% (2005); Bachelor's degree or higher: 21.6% (2005); Master's degree or higher: 7.9% (2005).
Housing: Homeownership rate: 84.0% (2005); Median home value: $131,914 (2005); Median rent: $461 per month (2000); Median age of housing: 36 years (2000).
Transportation: Commute to work: 95.2% car, 0.9% public transportation, 0.9% walk, 2.3% work from home (2000); Travel time to work: 24.1% less than 15 minutes, 19.6% 15 to 30 minutes, 19.8% 30 to 45 minutes, 27.7% 45 to 60 minutes, 8.7% 60 minutes or more (2000)

SENECA (town). Covers a land area of 50.443 square miles and a water area of 0 square miles. Located at 42.83° N. Lat.; 77.07° W. Long.
Population: 2,747 (1990); 2,731 (2000); 2,743 (2005); 2,766 (2010 projected); Race: 97.2% White, 0.5% Black, 0.3% Asian, 2.5% Hispanic of any race (2005); Density: 54.4 persons per square mile (2005); Average household size: 2.79 (2005); Median age: 40.8 (2005); Males per 100 females: 101.2 (2005); Marriage status: 20.1% never married, 68.4% now married, 6.6% widowed, 4.9% divorced (2000); Foreign born: 1.5% (2000); Ancestry (includes multiple ancestries): 25.6% German, 24.4% English, 12.7% Irish, 10.6% Italian, 7.8% Dutch (2000).
Economy: Single-family building permits issued: 6 (2005); Multi-family building permits issued: 0 (2005); Employment by occupation: 11.7% management, 21.7% professional, 10.9% services, 25.8% sales, 3.2% farming, 12.9% construction, 13.8% production (2000).
Income: Per capita income: $19,639 (2005); Median household income: $49,321 (2005); Average household income: $54,698 (2005); Percent of households with income of $100,000 or more: 7.9% (2005); Poverty rate: 3.5% (2000).
Education: Percent of population age 25 and over with: High school diploma (including GED) or higher: 89.3% (2005); Bachelor's degree or higher: 21.1% (2005); Master's degree or higher: 9.5% (2005).
Housing: Homeownership rate: 83.6% (2005); Median home value: $112,466 (2005); Median rent: $433 per month (2000); Median age of housing: 60+ years (2000).
Transportation: Commute to work: 87.2% car, 0.8% public transportation, 4.0% walk, 7.1% work from home (2000); Travel time to work: 37.7% less than 15 minutes, 39.0% 15 to 30 minutes, 12.2% 30 to 45 minutes, 5.5% 45 to 60 minutes, 5.6% 60 minutes or more (2000)

SHORTSVILLE (village). Covers a land area of 0.635 square miles and a water area of 0 square miles. Located at 42.95° N. Lat.; 77.22° W. Long. Elevation is 625 feet.
Population: 1,510 (1990); 1,320 (2000); 1,395 (2005); 1,418 (2010 projected); Race: 98.0% White, 0.1% Black, 0.2% Asian, 1.3% Hispanic of any race (2005); Density: 2,196.6 persons per square mile (2005); Average household size: 2.55 (2005); Median age: 38.8 (2005); Males per 100 females: 94.3 (2005); Marriage status: 23.4% never married, 57.2% now married, 5.9% widowed, 13.5% divorced (2000); Foreign born: 1.4% (2000); Ancestry (includes multiple ancestries): 25.5% German, 23.3% English, 20.0% Irish, 13.6% Italian, 13.0% Dutch (2000).
Economy: Single-family building permits issued: 3 (2005); Multi-family building permits issued: 20 (2005); Employment by occupation: 12.6% management, 17.3% professional, 13.2% services, 24.1% sales, 0.1% farming, 9.1% construction, 23.7% production (2000).
Income: Per capita income: $21,918 (2005); Median household income: $48,367 (2005); Average household income: $55,750 (2005); Percent of households with income of $100,000 or more: 11.5% (2005); Poverty rate: 4.3% (2000).
Education: Percent of population age 25 and over with: High school diploma (including GED) or higher: 90.3% (2005); Bachelor's degree or higher: 17.3% (2005); Master's degree or higher: 6.1% (2005).

School District(s)
Manchester-Shortsville Central School District (Red Jacket) (KG-12)
   2003-04 Enrollment: 929 . . . . (585) 289-3964
Housing: Homeownership rate: 85.6% (2005); Median home value: $92,785 (2005); Median rent: $486 per month (2000); Median age of housing: 60+ years (2000).
Safety: Violent crime rate: 0.0 per 10,000 population; Property crime rate: 7.6 per 10,000 population (2004).
Transportation: Commute to work: 95.0% car, 0.4% public transportation, 2.8% walk, 1.8% work from home (2000); Travel time to work: 38.9% less than 15 minutes, 34.7% 15 to 30 minutes, 18.8% 30 to 45 minutes, 5.0% 45 to 60 minutes, 2.7% 60 minutes or more (2000)

SOUTH BRISTOL (town). Covers a land area of 39.056 square miles and a water area of 2.996 square miles. Located at 42.72° N. Lat.; 77.39° W. Long.
Population: 1,663 (1990); 1,645 (2000); 1,720 (2005); 1,800 (2010 projected); Race: 98.0% White, 0.2% Black, 0.6% Asian, 1.3% Hispanic of any race (2005); Density: 44.0 persons per square mile (2005); Average household size: 2.42 (2005); Median age: 44.1 (2005); Males per 100 females: 104.0 (2005); Marriage status: 21.4% never married, 63.4% now married, 4.3% widowed, 11.0% divorced (2000); Foreign born: 4.0% (2000); Ancestry (includes multiple ancestries): 32.9% German, 21.8% English, 14.8% Irish, 7.1% United States or American, 6.9% Italian (2000).
Economy: Single-family building permits issued: 16 (2005); Multi-family building permits issued: 0 (2005); Employment by occupation: 19.6% management, 22.7% professional, 13.9% services, 20.4% sales, 1.1% farming, 8.0% construction, 14.3% production (2000).
Income: Per capita income: $29,508 (2005); Median household income: $58,310 (2005); Average household income: $71,326 (2005); Percent of households with income of $100,000 or more: 18.6% (2005); Poverty rate: 7.9% (2000).
Taxes: Total city taxes per capita: $258 (2004); City property taxes per capita: $177 (2004).
Education: Percent of population age 25 and over with: High school diploma (including GED) or higher: 92.1% (2005); Bachelor's degree or higher: 34.0% (2005); Master's degree or higher: 12.5% (2005).
Housing: Homeownership rate: 85.9% (2005); Median home value: $138,472 (2005); Median rent: $567 per month (2000); Median age of housing: 26 years (2000).
Transportation: Commute to work: 91.3% car, 0.0% public transportation, 1.6% walk, 6.9% work from home (2000); Travel time to work: 17.9% less than 15 minutes, 24.8% 15 to 30 minutes, 26.7% 30 to 45 minutes, 16.1% 45 to 60 minutes, 14.5% 60 minutes or more (2000)

STANLEY (unincorporated postal area, zip code 14561). Covers a land area of 49.190 square miles and a water area of 0 square miles. Located at 42.81° N. Lat.; 77.13° W. Long. Elevation is 904 feet.
Population: 0 (2000); Race: 97.4% White, 0.6% Black, 0.2% Asian, 2.1% Hispanic of any race (2000); Density: 0.0 persons per square mile (2000); Age: 29.5% under 18, 11.9% over 64 (2000); Marriage status: 19.1% never married, 69.5% now married, 5.3% widowed, 6.0% divorced (2000); Foreign born: 0.9% (2000); Ancestry (includes multiple ancestries): 23.1% English, 21.6% German, 16.5% Irish, 8.4% United States or American, 7.6% Dutch (2000).
Economy: Employment by occupation: 10.9% management, 16.9% professional, 15.7% services, 22.7% sales, 1.3% farming, 14.7% construction, 17.7% production (2000).
Income: Per capita income: $17,737 (2000); Median household income: $43,031 (2000); Poverty rate: 4.8% (2000).
Education: Percent of population age 25 and over with: High school diploma (including GED) or higher: 85.2% (2000); Bachelor's degree or higher: 17.5% (2000).
Housing: Homeownership rate: 84.4% (2000); Median home value: $80,900 (2000); Median rent: $442 per month (2000); Median age of housing: 60+ years (2000).
Transportation: Commute to work: 86.3% car, 1.4% public transportation, 5.6% walk, 5.7% work from home (2000); Travel time to work: 24.6% less than 15 minutes, 42.7% 15 to 30 minutes, 16.2% 30 to 45 minutes, 8.1% 45 to 60 minutes, 8.4% 60 minutes or more (2000)

VICTOR (village). Covers a land area of 1.380 square miles and a water area of 0 square miles. Located at 42.98° N. Lat.; 77.40° W. Long. Elevation is 586 feet.
Population: 2,254 (1990); 2,433 (2000); 2,513 (2005); 2,575 (2010 projected); Race: 96.8% White, 0.6% Black, 1.2% Asian, 2.0% Hispanic of any race (2005); Density: 1,821.4 persons per square mile (2005); Average household size: 2.56 (2005); Median age: 38.6 (2005); Males per 100 females: 99.6 (2005); Marriage status: 23.7% never married, 62.8% now married, 4.5% widowed, 8.9% divorced (2000); Foreign born: 2.6% (2000); Ancestry (includes multiple ancestries): 31.1% German, 27.9% Irish, 19.4% English, 14.1% Italian, 6.1% French (except Basque) (2000).
Economy: Single-family building permits issued: 0 (2005); Multi-family building permits issued: 0 (2005); Employment by occupation: 13.7% management, 27.6% professional, 11.8% services, 27.8% sales, 0.4% farming, 6.8% construction, 11.9% production (2000).
Income: Per capita income: $29,129 (2005); Median household income: $63,697 (2005); Average household income: $74,397 (2005); Percent of households with income of $100,000 or more: 22.1% (2005); Poverty rate: 2.4% (2000).
Education: Percent of population age 25 and over with: High school diploma (including GED) or higher: 94.2% (2005); Bachelor's degree or higher: 38.3% (2005); Master's degree or higher: 15.4% (2005).
School District(s)
Victor Central School District (PK-12)
   2003-04 Enrollment: 3,556 . . . . (585) 924-3252
Housing: Homeownership rate: 74.1% (2005); Median home value: $139,390 (2005); Median rent: $564 per month (2000); Median age of housing: 34 years (2000).
Transportation: Commute to work: 91.2% car, 0.3% public transportation, 3.2% walk, 4.6% work from home (2000); Travel time to work: 33.5% less than 15 minutes, 37.6% 15 to 30 minutes, 24.0% 30 to 45 minutes, 2.2% 45 to 60 minutes, 2.6% 60 minutes or more (2000)
Additional Information Contacts
Victor Chamber of Commerce . . . . (585) 742-1476
   http://www.victorchamber.com

VICTOR (town). Covers a land area of 35.939 square miles and a water area of 0.008 square miles. Located at 42.99° N. Lat.; 77.42° W. Long. Elevation is 586 feet.
History: Incorporated 1879.
Population: 7,191 (1990); 9,977 (2000); 11,544 (2005); 13,000 (2010 projected); Race: 95.3% White, 1.1% Black, 1.7% Asian, 2.5% Hispanic of any race (2005); Density: 321.2 persons per square mile (2005); Average household size: 2.67 (2005); Median age: 39.6 (2005); Males per 100 females: 98.6 (2005); Marriage status: 19.1% never married, 68.0% now married, 5.0% widowed, 7.9% divorced (2000); Foreign born: 4.9% (2000); Ancestry (includes multiple ancestries): 28.6% German, 21.5% Irish, 17.3% English, 15.9% Italian, 5.8% Polish (2000).
Economy: Manufacturing: bearings, materials handling equipment, fiberglass materials, packaging, insulators. Agriculture: grain, beans, sweet corn, peas. Single-family building permits issued: 85 (2005); Multi-family building permits issued: 2 (2005); Employment by occupation: 21.7% management, 27.1% professional, 9.4% services, 26.0% sales, 0.2% farming, 5.8% construction, 9.8% production (2000).
Income: Per capita income: $35,236 (2005); Median household income: $69,199 (2005); Average household income: $93,644 (2005); Percent of households with income of $100,000 or more: 33.0% (2005); Poverty rate: 3.0% (2000).
Taxes: Total city taxes per capita: $306 (2004); City property taxes per capita: $199 (2004).
Education: Percent of population age 25 and over with: High school diploma (including GED) or higher: 92.8% (2005); Bachelor's degree or higher: 40.5% (2005); Master's degree or higher: 18.0% (2005).
Housing: Homeownership rate: 83.8% (2005); Median home value: $170,451 (2005); Median rent: $551 per month (2000); Median age of housing: 19 years (2000).
Transportation: Commute to work: 94.6% car, 0.7% public transportation, 1.1% walk, 3.4% work from home (2000); Travel time to work: 25.6% less than 15 minutes, 42.0% 15 to 30 minutes, 27.2% 30 to 45 minutes, 2.4% 45 to 60 minutes, 2.8% 60 minutes or more (2000)
Additional Information Contacts
Town of Victor . . . . (585) 742-5020
   http://www.victorny.org/

WEST BLOOMFIELD (town). Covers a land area of 25.516 square miles and a water area of 0.037 square miles. Located at 42.91° N. Lat.; 77.52° W. Long. Elevation is 950 feet.
Population: 2,536 (1990); 2,549 (2000); 2,748 (2005); 2,915 (2010 projected); Race: 98.2% White, 0.5% Black, 0.1% Asian, 1.0% Hispanic of any race (2005); Density: 107.7 persons per square mile (2005); Average

household size: 2.47 (2005); Median age: 41.7 (2005); Males per 100 females: 101.5 (2005); Marriage status: 24.0% never married, 60.2% now married, 6.7% widowed, 9.1% divorced (2000); Foreign born: 2.6% (2000); Ancestry (includes multiple ancestries): 28.8% German, 17.6% English, 13.8% Irish, 12.4% Italian, 8.8% United States or American (2000).
Economy: Single-family building permits issued: 8 (2005); Multi-family building permits issued: 0 (2005); Employment by occupation: 13.3% management, 14.5% professional, 16.8% services, 27.6% sales, 2.2% farming, 6.8% construction, 18.8% production (2000).
Income: Per capita income: $22,868 (2005); Median household income: $48,064 (2005); Average household income: $56,564 (2005); Percent of households with income of $100,000 or more: 12.8% (2005); Poverty rate: 3.2% (2000).
Education: Percent of population age 25 and over with: High school diploma (including GED) or higher: 87.3% (2005); Bachelor's degree or higher: 21.0% (2005); Master's degree or higher: 6.5% (2005).
Housing: Homeownership rate: 88.7% (2005); Median home value: $97,800 (2005); Median rent: $440 per month (2000); Median age of housing: 27 years (2000).
Transportation: Commute to work: 92.4% car, 0.3% public transportation, 2.3% walk, 4.7% work from home (2000); Travel time to work: 26.1% less than 15 minutes, 31.8% 15 to 30 minutes, 27.9% 30 to 45 minutes, 11.0% 45 to 60 minutes, 3.2% 60 minutes or more (2000)

Orange County

Located in southeastern New York; bounded on the east by the Hudson River, and on the southwest by the Delaware River and the New Jersey and Pennsylvania borders; includes parts of the Hudson highlands, the Ramapos, and the Shawangunk Range. Covers a land area of 816.34 square miles, a water area of 22.21 square miles, and is located in the Eastern Time Zone. The county government was organized in 1683. County seat is Goshen.

Orange County is part of the Poughkeepsie-Newburgh-Middletown, NY Metropolitan Statistical Area. The entire metro area includes: Dutchess County, NY; Orange County, NY

Weather Station: Middletown 2 NW   Elevation: 698 feet

	Jan	Feb	Mar	Apr	May	Jun	Jul	Aug	Sep	Oct	Nov	Dec
High	35	39	48	61	72	79	84	82	75	64	51	40
Low	18	20	28	39	49	58	63	61	54	43	35	24
Precip	3.0	2.5	3.3	3.9	4.6	4.2	4.0	3.8	4.2	3.6	3.7	3.1
Snow	na	na	na	na	tr	0.0	0.0	0.0	0.0	tr	na	na

High and Low temperatures in degrees Fahrenheit; Precipitation and Snow in inches

Weather Station: Port Jervis   Elevation: 469 feet

	Jan	Feb	Mar	Apr	May	Jun	Jul	Aug	Sep	Oct	Nov	Dec
High	35	39	49	62	73	80	84	82	74	62	51	39
Low	17	19	27	37	47	56	61	60	52	40	32	23
Precip	3.4	3.0	3.3	4.0	4.4	4.1	4.1	3.6	4.4	3.5	3.8	3.4
Snow	12.7	9.6	7.9	1.6	tr	0.0	0.0	0.0	0.0	tr	2.7	7.5

High and Low temperatures in degrees Fahrenheit; Precipitation and Snow in inches

Weather Station: Walden 1 ESE   Elevation: 377 feet

	Jan	Feb	Mar	Apr	May	Jun	Jul	Aug	Sep	Oct	Nov	Dec
High	34	38	47	59	70	78	83	81	73	62	51	39
Low	14	15	25	36	46	55	59	58	49	37	30	20
Precip	3.4	2.4	3.6	3.9	4.5	4.1	4.2	3.6	4.0	3.4	3.8	3.3
Snow	12.2	8.2	7.4	1.4	tr	0.0	0.0	0.0	0.0	tr	1.8	7.0

High and Low temperatures in degrees Fahrenheit; Precipitation and Snow in inches

Weather Station: West Point   Elevation: 318 feet

	Jan	Feb	Mar	Apr	May	Jun	Jul	Aug	Sep	Oct	Nov	Dec
High	36	39	49	62	73	81	86	84	75	63	52	40
Low	20	22	30	40	50	59	64	63	55	44	36	26
Precip	4.0	3.2	4.1	4.2	4.9	4.1	4.3	4.2	4.5	4.2	4.5	3.9
Snow	10.0	8.9	5.7	0.3	0.0	0.0	0.0	0.0	0.0	tr	0.9	4.6

High and Low temperatures in degrees Fahrenheit; Precipitation and Snow in inches

Population: 307,647 (1990); 341,367 (2000); 373,314 (2005); 406,655 (2010 projected); Race: 79.4% White, 9.9% Black, 2.1% Asian, 15.5% Hispanic of any race (2005); Density: 457.3 persons per square mile (2005); Average household size: 2.96 (2005); Median age: 35.4 (2005); Males per 100 females: 100.4 (2005).
Religion: Five largest groups: 46.9% Catholic Church, 4.4% Jewish Estimate, 2.6% The United Methodist Church, 1.7% Presbyterian Church (U.S.A.), 1.1% Episcopal Church (2000).
Economy: Unemployment rate: 4.2% (2005); Total civilian labor force: 178,282 (2005); Leading industries: 20.2% retail trade; 17.4% health care and social assistance; 8.5% wholesale trade (2003); Farms: 706 totaling 107,977 acres (2002); Companies that employ 500 or more persons: 15 (2003); Companies that employ 100 to 499 persons: 141 (2003); Companies that employ less than 100 persons: 8,439 (2003); Black-owned businesses: 1,219 (2002); Hispanic-owned businesses: 1,370 (2002); Women-owned businesses: 7,593 (2002); Retail sales per capita: $14,146 (2006). Single-family building permits issued: 1,301 (2005); Multi-family building permits issued: 529 (2005).
Income: Per capita income: $24,907 (2005); Median household income: $60,025 (2005); Average household income: $72,469 (2005); Percent of households with income of $100,000 or more: 22.6% (2005); Poverty rate: 10.5% (2003); Bankruptcy rate: 4.19% (2005).
Taxes: Total county taxes per capita: $682 (2004); County property taxes per capita: $246 (2004).
Education: Percent of population age 25 and over with: High school diploma (including GED) or higher: 81.5% (2005); Bachelor's degree or higher: 22.3% (2005); Master's degree or higher: 9.1% (2005).
Housing: Homeownership rate: 67.6% (2005); Median home value: $221,551 (2005); Median rent: $631 per month (2000); Median age of housing: 34 years (2000).
Health: Birth rate: 140.6 per 10,000 population (2004); Death rate: 68.3 per 10,000 population (2004); Age-adjusted cancer mortality rate: 223.0 deaths per 100,000 population (2002); Air Quality Index: 74.7% good, 23.1% moderate, 2.2% unhealthy for sensitive individuals, 0.0% unhealthy (percent of days in 2005); Number of physicians: 20.7 per 10,000 population (2004); Hospital beds: 35.8 per 10,000 population (2003); Hospital admissions: 1,133.7 per 10,000 population (2003).
Elections: 2004 Presidential election results: 54.7% Bush, 43.8% Kerry, 1.3% Nader, 0.1% Badnarik
National and State Parks: Hudson Highlands State Park; Storm King State Park

Additional Information Contacts

Orange County Government	(845) 291-4000
http://www.co.orange.ny.us/	
City of Middletown	(845) 586-4566
http://www.ci.middletown.ny.us/	
City of Newburgh	(845) 569-7311
http://www.newburgh-ny.com/	
City of Port Jervis	(845) 858-4014
http://portjervisny.org/	
Town of Cornwall	(845) 534-3770
http://www.cornwallny.com/	
Town of Crawford	(845) 744-2029
http://www.townofcrawford.us/	
Town of Goshen	(845) 294-6996
http://www.townofgoshen.org/	
Town of Hamptonburgh	(845) 427-2424
http://townofhamptonburgh.org/content	
Town of Monroe	(845) 783-1900
http://www.monroeny.org/	
Town of New Windsor	(845) 565-8800
http://town.new-windsor.ny.us/	
Town of Tuxedo	(845) 351-2265
http://www.tuxedogov.org/	
Town of Wallkill	(845) 692-7830
http://www.townofwallkill.com/	
Town of Woodbury	(516) 624-6332
http://www.oysterbaytown.com	
Village of Maybrook	(845) 427-2717
http://www.villageofmaybrook.com/content/	
Village of Monroe	(845) 783-1900
http://www.monroeny.org/	
Village of Otisville	(845) 386-5172
http://www.villageofotisville.com/	
Village of Washingtonville	(845) 496-3221
http://www.washingtonville-ny.org/	

Orange County Communities

BALMVILLE (CDP). Covers a land area of 2.124 square miles and a water area of 0 square miles. Located at 41.52° N. Lat.; 74.02° W. Long.
Population: 2,977 (1990); 3,339 (2000); 3,563 (2005); 3,813 (2010 projected); Race: 70.6% White, 13.6% Black, 4.5% Asian, 14.8% Hispanic of any race (2005); Density: 1,677.8 persons per square mile (2005); Average household size: 2.61 (2005); Median age: 41.2 (2005); Males per 100 females: 91.5 (2005); Marriage status: 18.7% never married, 67.5% now married, 7.2% widowed, 6.5% divorced (2000); Foreign born: 9.6% (2000); Ancestry (includes multiple ancestries): 29.3% Italian, 22.5% Other groups, 20.4% Irish, 12.2% German, 5.5% English (2000).
Economy: Employment by occupation: 14.2% management, 29.5% professional, 13.7% services, 29.0% sales, 0.0% farming, 5.2% construction, 8.3% production (2000).
Income: Per capita income: $33,057 (2005); Median household income: $71,597 (2005); Average household income: $84,762 (2005); Percent of households with income of $100,000 or more: 28.7% (2005); Poverty rate: 2.2% (2000).
Education: Percent of population age 25 and over with: High school diploma (including GED) or higher: 91.3% (2005); Bachelor's degree or higher: 30.8% (2005); Master's degree or higher: 12.4% (2005).
Housing: Homeownership rate: 81.8% (2005); Median home value: $246,191 (2005); Median rent: $731 per month (2000); Median age of housing: 37 years (2000).
Transportation: Commute to work: 95.7% car, 3.4% public transportation, 0.0% walk, 1.0% work from home (2000); Travel time to work: 32.6% less than 15 minutes, 25.5% 15 to 30 minutes, 9.5% 30 to 45 minutes, 8.9% 45 to 60 minutes, 23.5% 60 minutes or more (2000)

BEAVERDAM LAKE-SALISBURY MILLS (CDP). Covers a land area of 2.360 square miles and a water area of 0.260 square miles. Located at 41.43° N. Lat.; 74.11° W. Long.
Population: 2,354 (1990); 2,779 (2000); 2,955 (2005); 3,131 (2010 projected); Race: 90.4% White, 3.5% Black, 1.5% Asian, 7.7% Hispanic of any race (2005); Density: 1,252.2 persons per square mile (2005); Average household size: 3.04 (2005); Median age: 36.8 (2005); Males per 100 females: 98.6 (2005); Marriage status: 26.7% never married, 64.8% now married, 4.2% widowed, 4.3% divorced (2000); Foreign born: 5.8% (2000); Ancestry (includes multiple ancestries): 25.3% Italian, 24.7% Irish, 12.9% Other groups, 12.1% German, 9.8% Polish (2000).
Economy: Employment by occupation: 14.5% management, 24.3% professional, 13.8% services, 28.4% sales, 0.0% farming, 9.6% construction, 9.3% production (2000).
Income: Per capita income: $30,217 (2005); Median household income: $75,475 (2005); Average household income: $90,736 (2005); Percent of households with income of $100,000 or more: 34.1% (2005); Poverty rate: 1.4% (2000).
Education: Percent of population age 25 and over with: High school diploma (including GED) or higher: 91.5% (2005); Bachelor's degree or higher: 26.6% (2005); Master's degree or higher: 12.8% (2005).
Housing: Homeownership rate: 85.2% (2005); Median home value: $254,592 (2005); Median rent: $664 per month (2000); Median age of housing: 32 years (2000).
Transportation: Commute to work: 94.2% car, 1.7% public transportation, 1.0% walk, 2.1% work from home (2000); Travel time to work: 16.5% less than 15 minutes, 37.1% 15 to 30 minutes, 13.7% 30 to 45 minutes, 12.3% 45 to 60 minutes, 20.5% 60 minutes or more (2000)

BLOOMING GROVE (town). Covers a land area of 34.808 square miles and a water area of 0.502 square miles. Located at 41.39° N. Lat.; 74.18° W. Long. Elevation is 360 feet.
Population: 16,651 (1990); 17,351 (2000); 18,534 (2005); 19,838 (2010 projected); Race: 86.9% White, 4.8% Black, 1.9% Asian, 13.1% Hispanic of any race (2005); Density: 532.5 persons per square mile (2005); Average household size: 2.94 (2005); Median age: 37.0 (2005); Males per 100 females: 99.2 (2005); Marriage status: 23.5% never married, 64.8% now married, 5.8% widowed, 5.9% divorced (2000); Foreign born: 6.4% (2000); Ancestry (includes multiple ancestries): 29.8% Irish, 25.8% Italian, 17.3% German, 13.8% Other groups, 6.8% Polish (2000).
Economy: Single-family building permits issued: 65 (2005); Multi-family building permits issued: 0 (2005); Employment by occupation: 13.6% management, 20.9% professional, 16.5% services, 28.5% sales, 0.0% farming, 11.1% construction, 9.4% production (2000).
Income: Per capita income: $29,426 (2005); Median household income: $76,249 (2005); Average household income: $86,146 (2005); Percent of households with income of $100,000 or more: 33.6% (2005); Poverty rate: 3.9% (2000).
Education: Percent of population age 25 and over with: High school diploma (including GED) or higher: 88.3% (2005); Bachelor's degree or higher: 26.7% (2005); Master's degree or higher: 10.7% (2005).
Housing: Homeownership rate: 80.4% (2005); Median home value: $243,944 (2005); Median rent: $673 per month (2000); Median age of housing: 30 years (2000).
Safety: Violent crime rate: 7.5 per 10,000 population; Property crime rate: 98.5 per 10,000 population (2004).
Transportation: Commute to work: 90.6% car, 4.6% public transportation, 1.8% walk, 2.6% work from home (2000); Travel time to work: 17.3% less than 15 minutes, 24.4% 15 to 30 minutes, 16.8% 30 to 45 minutes, 13.3% 45 to 60 minutes, 28.3% 60 minutes or more (2000)

CAMPBELL HALL (unincorporated postal area, zip code 10916). Covers a land area of 21.400 square miles and a water area of 0.042 square miles. Located at 41.45° N. Lat.; 74.24° W. Long.
Population: 0 (2000); Race: 94.9% White, 3.2% Black, 0.6% Asian, 6.4% Hispanic of any race (2000); Density: 0.0 persons per square mile (2000); Age: 28.5% under 18, 12.0% over 64 (2000); Marriage status: 21.9% never married, 68.3% now married, 4.2% widowed, 5.6% divorced (2000); Foreign born: 3.8% (2000); Ancestry (includes multiple ancestries): 30.5% Irish, 29.8% Italian, 19.3% German, 9.7% Polish, 9.2% Other groups (2000).
Economy: Employment by occupation: 14.5% management, 18.5% professional, 16.7% services, 29.4% sales, 0.0% farming, 12.6% construction, 8.3% production (2000).
Income: Per capita income: $27,923 (2000); Median household income: $74,200 (2000); Poverty rate: 1.7% (2000).
Education: Percent of population age 25 and over with: High school diploma (including GED) or higher: 90.1% (2000); Bachelor's degree or higher: 29.3% (2000).
Housing: Homeownership rate: 89.5% (2000); Median home value: $196,100 (2000); Median rent: $615 per month (2000); Median age of housing: 27 years (2000).
Transportation: Commute to work: 90.3% car, 4.5% public transportation, 0.7% walk, 3.5% work from home (2000); Travel time to work: 22.9% less than 15 minutes, 32.1% 15 to 30 minutes, 13.3% 30 to 45 minutes, 9.9% 45 to 60 minutes, 21.8% 60 minutes or more (2000)

CENTRAL VALLEY (CDP). Covers a land area of 2.667 square miles and a water area of 0 square miles. Located at 41.32° N. Lat.; 74.12° W. Long.
Population: 1,929 (1990); 1,857 (2000); 1,877 (2005); 1,953 (2010 projected); Race: 90.7% White, 0.9% Black, 2.0% Asian, 12.3% Hispanic of any race (2005); Density: 703.9 persons per square mile (2005); Average household size: 2.77 (2005); Median age: 38.2 (2005); Males per 100 females: 98.8 (2005); Marriage status: 19.0% never married, 72.6% now married, 4.5% widowed, 3.9% divorced (2000); Foreign born: 7.3% (2000); Ancestry (includes multiple ancestries): 30.9% Irish, 20.5% Italian, 20.2% German, 10.1% Other groups, 9.0% English (2000).
Economy: Location of Woodbury Common, major retail shopping mall, at intersection of N.Y. State Thruway and Route 17. Employment by occupation: 22.1% management, 30.8% professional, 9.1% services, 26.9% sales, 0.0% farming, 6.5% construction, 4.7% production (2000).
Income: Per capita income: $36,650 (2005); Median household income: $79,358 (2005); Average household income: $101,221 (2005); Percent of households with income of $100,000 or more: 36.7% (2005); Poverty rate: 3.2% (2000).
Education: Percent of population age 25 and over with: High school diploma (including GED) or higher: 92.1% (2005); Bachelor's degree or higher: 41.0% (2005); Master's degree or higher: 19.0% (2005).
School District(s)
Monroe-Woodbury Central School District (KG-12)
    2003-04 Enrollment: 7,255 . . . . (845) 928-2321
Housing: Homeownership rate: 68.7% (2005); Median home value: $320,118 (2005); Median rent: $756 per month (2000); Median age of housing: 42 years (2000).
Transportation: Commute to work: 86.6% car, 6.1% public transportation, 2.0% walk, 5.2% work from home (2000); Travel time to work: 24.4% less than 15 minutes, 21.5% 15 to 30 minutes, 21.7% 30 to 45 minutes, 9.8% 45 to 60 minutes, 22.6% 60 minutes or more (2000)

Additional Information Contacts
Central Valley Chamber of Commerce . . . . (845) 928-8082

CHESTER (village).
Covers a land area of 2.116 square miles and a water area of 0 square miles. Located at 41.35° N. Lat.; 74.27° W. Long.
Population: 3,270 (1990); 3,445 (2000); 3,824 (2005); 4,228 (2010 projected); Race: 72.2% White, 14.7% Black, 5.6% Asian, 17.6% Hispanic of any race (2005); Density: 1,807.1 persons per square mile (2005); Average household size: 2.40 (2005); Median age: 36.5 (2005); Males per 100 females: 92.6 (2005); Marriage status: 27.3% never married, 59.2% now married, 5.6% widowed, 8.0% divorced (2000); Foreign born: 6.4% (2000); Ancestry (includes multiple ancestries): 25.7% Irish, 20.9% Italian, 18.7% Other groups, 15.4% German, 8.9% Polish (2000).
Economy: Single-family building permits issued: 9 (2005); Multi-family building permits issued: 0 (2005); Employment by occupation: 13.2% management, 20.5% professional, 15.5% services, 33.4% sales, 0.0% farming, 8.0% construction, 9.4% production (2000).
Income: Per capita income: $29,788 (2005); Median household income: $61,530 (2005); Average household income: $71,278 (2005); Percent of households with income of $100,000 or more: 19.2% (2005); Poverty rate: 6.0% (2000).
Education: Percent of population age 25 and over with: High school diploma (including GED) or higher: 87.0% (2005); Bachelor's degree or higher: 24.1% (2005); Master's degree or higher: 7.7% (2005).
School District(s)
Chester Union Free School District (KG-12)
    2003-04 Enrollment: 979 . . . . (845) 469-5052
Housing: Homeownership rate: 57.1% (2005); Median home value: $175,588 (2005); Median rent: $754 per month (2000); Median age of housing: 25 years (2000).
Safety: Violent crime rate: 22.7 per 10,000 population; Property crime rate: 442.2 per 10,000 population (2004).
Transportation: Commute to work: 92.5% car, 3.1% public transportation, 2.0% walk, 1.0% work from home (2000); Travel time to work: 19.6% less than 15 minutes, 29.9% 15 to 30 minutes, 18.0% 30 to 45 minutes, 10.4% 45 to 60 minutes, 22.1% 60 minutes or more (2000)

CHESTER (town).
Covers a land area of 25.175 square miles and a water area of 0.061 square miles. Located at 41.33° N. Lat.; 74.26° W. Long.
History: Hambletonian, famous trotter, foaled and buried here. Incorporated 1892.
Population: 9,138 (1990); 12,140 (2000); 13,276 (2005); 14,528 (2010 projected); Race: 80.8% White, 10.1% Black, 4.1% Asian, 15.1% Hispanic of any race (2005); Density: 527.4 persons per square mile (2005); Average household size: 3.07 (2005); Median age: 38.2 (2005); Males per 100 females: 110.2 (2005); Marriage status: 25.8% never married, 64.5% now married, 4.1% widowed, 5.6% divorced (2000); Foreign born: 7.0% (2000); Ancestry (includes multiple ancestries): 24.0% Irish, 22.5% Italian, 15.2% German, 14.2% Other groups, 8.7% Polish (2000).
Economy: Agricultural area: dairying; horse breeding. Summer resort. Single-family building permits issued: 48 (2005); Multi-family building permits issued: 0 (2005); Employment by occupation: 15.8% management, 20.5% professional, 15.1% services, 30.5% sales, 0.2% farming, 9.4% construction, 8.5% production (2000).
Income: Per capita income: $31,268 (2005); Median household income: $78,110 (2005); Average household income: $94,163 (2005); Percent of households with income of $100,000 or more: 33.2% (2005); Poverty rate: 7.2% (2000).
Taxes: Total city taxes per capita: $359 (2004); City property taxes per capita: $288 (2004).
Education: Percent of population age 25 and over with: High school diploma (including GED) or higher: 86.2% (2005); Bachelor's degree or higher: 25.8% (2005); Master's degree or higher: 9.1% (2005).
Housing: Homeownership rate: 78.9% (2005); Median home value: $256,810 (2005); Median rent: $741 per month (2000); Median age of housing: 24 years (2000).
Safety: Violent crime rate: 0.0 per 10,000 population; Property crime rate: 36.0 per 10,000 population (2004).
Transportation: Commute to work: 87.5% car, 7.6% public transportation, 0.9% walk, 3.4% work from home (2000); Travel time to work: 16.5% less than 15 minutes, 26.3% 15 to 30 minutes, 16.1% 30 to 45 minutes, 12.4% 45 to 60 minutes, 28.8% 60 minutes or more (2000)

CIRCLEVILLE (unincorporated postal area, zip code 10919).
Aka Firthcliffe. Covers a land area of 3.102 square miles and a water area of 0.005 square miles. Located at 41.52° N. Lat.; 74.37° W. Long.
Population: 0 (2000); Race: 100.0% White, 0.0% Black, 0.0% Asian, 5.7% Hispanic of any race (2000); Density: 0.0 persons per square mile (2000); Age: 32.6% under 18, 8.0% over 64 (2000); Marriage status: 22.4% never married, 58.7% now married, 10.1% widowed, 8.8% divorced (2000); Foreign born: 4.4% (2000); Ancestry (includes multiple ancestries): 30.6% German, 29.2% Irish, 16.7% English, 14.6% Polish, 11.8% Scotch-Irish (2000).
Economy: Employment by occupation: 13.2% management, 24.3% professional, 7.8% services, 20.6% sales, 0.0% farming, 20.6% construction, 13.6% production (2000).
Income: Per capita income: $21,852 (2000); Median household income: $59,583 (2000); Poverty rate: 4.0% (2000).
Education: Percent of population age 25 and over with: High school diploma (including GED) or higher: 96.0% (2000); Bachelor's degree or higher: 27.1% (2000).
School District(s)
Pine Bush Central School District (KG-12)
    2003-04 Enrollment: 6,118 . . . . (845) 744-2031
Housing: Homeownership rate: 87.0% (2000); Median home value: $152,800 (2000); Median rent: $625 per month (2000); Median age of housing: 19 years (2000).
Transportation: Commute to work: 95.5% car, 2.9% public transportation, 0.0% walk, 1.6% work from home (2000); Travel time to work: 15.9% less than 15 minutes, 36.4% 15 to 30 minutes, 32.2% 30 to 45 minutes, 2.9% 45 to 60 minutes, 12.6% 60 minutes or more (2000)

CORNWALL (town).
Aka Cornwall-on-Hudson. Covers a land area of 26.822 square miles and a water area of 1.343 square miles. Located at 41.43° N. Lat.; 74.05° W. Long.
History: Seat of N.Y. Military Academy and private schools. Incorporated 1884.
Population: 11,270 (1990); 12,307 (2000); 12,803 (2005); 13,412 (2010 projected); Race: 92.2% White, 2.0% Black, 1.9% Asian, 8.1% Hispanic of any race (2005); Density: 477.3 persons per square mile (2005); Average household size: 2.63 (2005); Median age: 39.2 (2005); Males per 100 females: 92.0 (2005); Marriage status: 22.0% never married, 64.7% now married, 6.9% widowed, 6.4% divorced (2000); Foreign born: 5.8% (2000); Ancestry (includes multiple ancestries): 27.2% Irish, 23.4% Italian, 17.8% German, 10.9% Other groups, 10.4% English (2000).
Economy: Manufacturing of apparel. Single-family building permits issued: 22 (2005); Multi-family building permits issued: 0 (2005); Employment by occupation: 15.2% management, 28.2% professional, 13.6% services, 25.3% sales, 0.2% farming, 10.1% construction, 7.4% production (2000).
Income: Per capita income: $32,426 (2005); Median household income: $69,902 (2005); Average household income: $84,680 (2005); Percent of households with income of $100,000 or more: 31.2% (2005); Poverty rate: 5.0% (2000).
Taxes: Total city taxes per capita: $438 (2004); City property taxes per capita: $371 (2004).
Education: Percent of population age 25 and over with: High school diploma (including GED) or higher: 90.8% (2005); Bachelor's degree or higher: 35.5% (2005); Master's degree or higher: 17.1% (2005).
School District(s)
Cornwall Central School District (KG-12)
    2003-04 Enrollment: 3,093 . . . . (845) 534-8009
Housing: Homeownership rate: 70.9% (2005); Median home value: $255,011 (2005); Median rent: $647 per month (2000); Median age of housing: 42 years (2000).
Hospitals: Cornwall Hospital (125 beds)
Safety: Violent crime rate: 5.2 per 10,000 population; Property crime rate: 11.5 per 10,000 population (2004).
Newspapers: The Cornwall Local (General - Circulation 3,500)
Transportation: Commute to work: 91.1% car, 3.4% public transportation, 2.5% walk, 2.7% work from home (2000); Travel time to work: 26.7% less than 15 minutes, 30.4% 15 to 30 minutes, 17.5% 30 to 45 minutes, 9.8% 45 to 60 minutes, 15.5% 60 minutes or more (2000)
Additional Information Contacts
Town of Cornwall . . . . (845) 534-3770
    http://www.cornwallny.com/

CORNWALL ON HUDSON (village). Covers a land area of 1.959 square miles and a water area of 0.107 square miles. Located at 41.44° N. Lat.; 74.01° W. Long.
Population: 3,143 (1990); 3,058 (2000); 3,117 (2005); 3,178 (2010 projected); Race: 95.2% White, 0.6% Black, 0.7% Asian, 6.1% Hispanic of any race (2005); Density: 1,591.0 persons per square mile (2005); Average household size: 2.57 (2005); Median age: 40.1 (2005); Males per 100 females: 90.9 (2005); Marriage status: 22.9% never married, 62.6% now married, 7.1% widowed, 7.4% divorced (2000); Foreign born: 4.6% (2000); Ancestry (includes multiple ancestries): 31.2% Irish, 20.0% Italian, 18.8% German, 13.2% English, 9.2% Other groups (2000).
Economy: Single-family building permits issued: 2 (2005); Multi-family building permits issued: 0 (2005); Employment by occupation: 14.0% management, 34.2% professional, 14.1% services, 22.1% sales, 0.3% farming, 9.0% construction, 6.4% production (2000).
Income: Per capita income: $34,559 (2005); Median household income: $72,565 (2005); Average household income: $88,438 (2005); Percent of households with income of $100,000 or more: 33.4% (2005); Poverty rate: 3.9% (2000).
Education: Percent of population age 25 and over with: High school diploma (including GED) or higher: 92.8% (2005); Bachelor's degree or higher: 41.4% (2005); Master's degree or higher: 21.1% (2005).
School District(s)
Cornwall Central School District (KG-12)
    2003-04 Enrollment: 3,093 . . . . (845) 534-8009
Housing: Homeownership rate: 72.7% (2005); Median home value: $252,278 (2005); Median rent: $639 per month (2000); Median age of housing: 52 years (2000).
Safety: Violent crime rate: 0.0 per 10,000 population; Property crime rate: 51.3 per 10,000 population (2004).
Transportation: Commute to work: 85.1% car, 5.2% public transportation, 4.2% walk, 5.3% work from home (2000); Travel time to work: 27.9% less than 15 minutes, 29.5% 15 to 30 minutes, 16.0% 30 to 45 minutes, 11.4% 45 to 60 minutes, 15.2% 60 minutes or more (2000)

CRAWFORD (town). Covers a land area of 40.121 square miles and a water area of 0.036 square miles. Located at 41.57° N. Lat.; 74.31° W. Long.
Population: 6,400 (1990); 7,875 (2000); 9,143 (2005); 10,397 (2010 projected); Race: 93.6% White, 1.6% Black, 1.2% Asian, 7.7% Hispanic of any race (2005); Density: 227.9 persons per square mile (2005); Average household size: 2.86 (2005); Median age: 37.3 (2005); Males per 100 females: 97.6 (2005); Marriage status: 21.5% never married, 65.4% now married, 6.1% widowed, 6.9% divorced (2000); Foreign born: 5.1% (2000); Ancestry (includes multiple ancestries): 22.1% Irish, 21.0% German, 19.6% Italian, 10.5% Polish, 10.0% Other groups (2000).
Economy: Single-family building permits issued: 52 (2005); Multi-family building permits issued: 0 (2005); Employment by occupation: 13.3% management, 22.5% professional, 15.3% services, 26.3% sales, 0.7% farming, 12.2% construction, 9.6% production (2000).
Income: Per capita income: $26,228 (2005); Median household income: $67,352 (2005); Average household income: $74,745 (2005); Percent of households with income of $100,000 or more: 26.0% (2005); Poverty rate: 4.0% (2000).
Education: Percent of population age 25 and over with: High school diploma (including GED) or higher: 84.8% (2005); Bachelor's degree or higher: 23.2% (2005); Master's degree or higher: 9.2% (2005).
Housing: Homeownership rate: 77.5% (2005); Median home value: $231,814 (2005); Median rent: $610 per month (2000); Median age of housing: 25 years (2000).
Safety: Violent crime rate: 39.7 per 10,000 population; Property crime rate: 104.4 per 10,000 population (2004).
Transportation: Commute to work: 92.1% car, 1.4% public transportation, 2.4% walk, 4.1% work from home (2000); Travel time to work: 17.4% less than 15 minutes, 43.7% 15 to 30 minutes, 16.8% 30 to 45 minutes, 6.2% 45 to 60 minutes, 15.9% 60 minutes or more (2000)
Additional Information Contacts
Town of Crawford. . . . . (845) 744-2029
    http://www.townofcrawford.us/

CUDDEBACKVILLE (unincorporated postal area, zip code 12729). Covers a land area of 15.201 square miles and a water area of 0.122 square miles. Located at 41.47° N. Lat.; 74.60° W. Long.
Population: 0 (2000); Race: 92.4% White, 4.1% Black, 0.9% Asian, 5.0% Hispanic of any race (2000); Density: 0.0 persons per square mile (2000); Age: 27.9% under 18, 8.5% over 64 (2000); Marriage status: 18.5% never married, 62.1% now married, 7.6% widowed, 11.9% divorced (2000); Foreign born: 8.9% (2000); Ancestry (includes multiple ancestries): 27.3% German, 13.5% Irish, 10.4% Italian, 9.3% English, 8.7% Other groups (2000).
Economy: Employment by occupation: 9.2% management, 16.4% professional, 18.8% services, 25.8% sales, 0.0% farming, 20.4% construction, 9.5% production (2000).
Income: Per capita income: $18,891 (2000); Median household income: $49,632 (2000); Poverty rate: 8.3% (2000).
Education: Percent of population age 25 and over with: High school diploma (including GED) or higher: 84.5% (2000); Bachelor's degree or higher: 15.8% (2000).
School District(s)
Port Jervis City School District (KG-12)
    2003-04 Enrollment: 3,444 . . . . (845) 858-3175
Housing: Homeownership rate: 76.7% (2000); Median home value: $112,500 (2000); Median rent: $491 per month (2000); Median age of housing: 27 years (2000).
Transportation: Commute to work: 93.3% car, 3.7% public transportation, 1.0% walk, 2.0% work from home (2000); Travel time to work: 10.1% less than 15 minutes, 45.1% 15 to 30 minutes, 22.2% 30 to 45 minutes, 7.1% 45 to 60 minutes, 15.4% 60 minutes or more (2000)

DEERPARK (town). Covers a land area of 66.417 square miles and a water area of 1.446 square miles. Located at 41.42° N. Lat.; 74.65° W. Long.
Population: 7,832 (1990); 7,858 (2000); 8,392 (2005); 8,984 (2010 projected); Race: 94.3% White, 1.8% Black, 0.8% Asian, 5.2% Hispanic of any race (2005); Density: 126.4 persons per square mile (2005); Average household size: 2.64 (2005); Median age: 38.7 (2005); Males per 100 females: 99.6 (2005); Marriage status: 22.6% never married, 59.8% now married, 7.2% widowed, 10.4% divorced (2000); Foreign born: 3.0% (2000); Ancestry (includes multiple ancestries): 24.4% German, 20.9% Irish, 14.6% Italian, 11.1% English, 8.9% Other groups (2000).
Economy: Single-family building permits issued: 44 (2005); Multi-family building permits issued: 0 (2005); Employment by occupation: 6.6% management, 12.8% professional, 20.3% services, 23.9% sales, 0.2% farming, 16.7% construction, 19.5% production (2000).
Income: Per capita income: $20,924 (2005); Median household income: $49,232 (2005); Average household income: $55,216 (2005); Percent of households with income of $100,000 or more: 10.6% (2005); Poverty rate: 9.6% (2000).
Education: Percent of population age 25 and over with: High school diploma (including GED) or higher: 76.8% (2005); Bachelor's degree or higher: 9.4% (2005); Master's degree or higher: 3.6% (2005).
Housing: Homeownership rate: 81.5% (2005); Median home value: $138,961 (2005); Median rent: $542 per month (2000); Median age of housing: 30 years (2000).
Transportation: Commute to work: 93.9% car, 2.5% public transportation, 0.8% walk, 2.2% work from home (2000); Travel time to work: 23.5% less than 15 minutes, 33.3% 15 to 30 minutes, 21.2% 30 to 45 minutes, 8.4% 45 to 60 minutes, 13.5% 60 minutes or more (2000)

FIRTHCLIFFE (CDP). Aka Cornwall. Covers a land area of 3.014 square miles and a water area of 0.025 square miles. Located at 41.44° N. Lat.; 74.03° W. Long.
Population: 4,377 (1990); 4,970 (2000); 5,035 (2005); 5,202 (2010 projected); Race: 91.9% White, 1.5% Black, 1.6% Asian, 10.1% Hispanic of any race (2005); Density: 1,670.6 persons per square mile (2005); Average household size: 2.50 (2005); Median age: 39.6 (2005); Males per 100 females: 87.0 (2005); Marriage status: 22.3% never married, 61.5% now married, 8.6% widowed, 7.6% divorced (2000); Foreign born: 6.8% (2000); Ancestry (includes multiple ancestries): 26.3% Irish, 23.1% Italian, 17.4% German, 12.6% Other groups, 9.0% English (2000).
Economy: Carpet manufacturing. Employment by occupation: 12.8% management, 27.5% professional, 15.6% services, 26.8% sales, 0.3% farming, 8.8% construction, 8.3% production (2000).
Income: Per capita income: $29,493 (2005); Median household income: $61,515 (2005); Average household income: $73,111 (2005); Percent of households with income of $100,000 or more: 23.2% (2005); Poverty rate: 6.7% (2000).

Education: Percent of population age 25 and over with: High school diploma (including GED) or higher: 88.8% (2005); Bachelor's degree or higher: 30.6% (2005); Master's degree or higher: 14.6% (2005).
Housing: Homeownership rate: 60.9% (2005); Median home value: $232,108 (2005); Median rent: $647 per month (2000); Median age of housing: 39 years (2000).
Transportation: Commute to work: 91.6% car, 2.9% public transportation, 3.2% walk, 2.2% work from home (2000); Travel time to work: 30.9% less than 15 minutes, 28.8% 15 to 30 minutes, 14.7% 30 to 45 minutes, 10.8% 45 to 60 minutes, 14.8% 60 minutes or more (2000)

FLORIDA (village). Covers a land area of 1.888 square miles and a water area of 0 square miles. Located at 41.33° N. Lat.; 74.35° W. Long.
History: William H. Seward was born here.
Population: 2,497 (1990); 2,571 (2000); 2,709 (2005); 2,877 (2010 projected); Race: 90.5% White, 3.6% Black, 0.8% Asian, 9.6% Hispanic of any race (2005); Density: 1,434.9 persons per square mile (2005); Average household size: 2.65 (2005); Median age: 38.8 (2005); Males per 100 females: 90.8 (2005); Marriage status: 25.4% never married, 58.5% now married, 7.6% widowed, 8.5% divorced (2000); Foreign born: 4.1% (2000); Ancestry (includes multiple ancestries): 20.4% Polish, 19.7% Italian, 17.1% German, 16.9% Irish, 13.4% Other groups (2000).
Economy: In onion-growing area. Single-family building permits issued: 2 (2005); Multi-family building permits issued: 0 (2005); Employment by occupation: 10.1% management, 26.1% professional, 15.7% services, 28.1% sales, 0.3% farming, 10.1% construction, 9.7% production (2000).
Income: Per capita income: $26,282 (2005); Median household income: $62,815 (2005); Average household income: $69,145 (2005); Percent of households with income of $100,000 or more: 22.3% (2005); Poverty rate: 7.3% (2000).
Education: Percent of population age 25 and over with: High school diploma (including GED) or higher: 86.2% (2005); Bachelor's degree or higher: 24.0% (2005); Master's degree or higher: 8.8% (2005).

School District(s)
Florida Union Free School District (KG-12)
    2003-04 Enrollment: 903 . . . . (845) 651-3095

Housing: Homeownership rate: 81.5% (2005); Median home value: $228,610 (2005); Median rent: $736 per month (2000); Median age of housing: 33 years (2000).
Safety: Violent crime rate: 0.0 per 10,000 population; Property crime rate: 93.7 per 10,000 population (2004).
Transportation: Commute to work: 87.5% car, 5.0% public transportation, 4.9% walk, 2.6% work from home (2000); Travel time to work: 29.1% less than 15 minutes, 25.0% 15 to 30 minutes, 10.0% 30 to 45 minutes, 9.3% 45 to 60 minutes, 26.6% 60 minutes or more (2000)

FORT MONTGOMERY (CDP). Covers a land area of 1.469 square miles and a water area of 0.026 square miles. Located at 41.33° N. Lat.; 73.98° W. Long.
Population: 1,586 (1990); 1,418 (2000); 1,368 (2005); 1,302 (2010 projected); Race: 89.5% White, 2.6% Black, 1.5% Asian, 9.1% Hispanic of any race (2005); Density: 931.0 persons per square mile (2005); Average household size: 2.44 (2005); Median age: 40.0 (2005); Males per 100 females: 99.7 (2005); Marriage status: 28.1% never married, 63.8% now married, 3.4% widowed, 4.7% divorced (2000); Foreign born: 2.9% (2000); Ancestry (includes multiple ancestries): 30.6% Irish, 25.6% Italian, 19.4% German, 17.9% Other groups, 13.7% English (2000).
Economy: Employment by occupation: 11.5% management, 18.4% professional, 22.2% services, 24.4% sales, 0.0% farming, 9.4% construction, 14.1% production (2000).
Income: Per capita income: $32,067 (2005); Median household income: $71,763 (2005); Average household income: $78,335 (2005); Percent of households with income of $100,000 or more: 25.2% (2005); Poverty rate: 2.9% (2000).
Education: Percent of population age 25 and over with: High school diploma (including GED) or higher: 88.5% (2005); Bachelor's degree or higher: 25.1% (2005); Master's degree or higher: 9.0% (2005).

School District(s)
Highland Falls Central School District (KG-12)
    2003-04 Enrollment: 1,209 . . . . (845) 446-9575

Housing: Homeownership rate: 74.5% (2005); Median home value: $201,027 (2005); Median rent: $753 per month (2000); Median age of housing: 43 years (2000).
Transportation: Commute to work: 95.1% car, 3.1% public transportation, 1.8% walk, 0.0% work from home (2000); Travel time to work: 31.4% less than 15 minutes, 29.1% 15 to 30 minutes, 18.2% 30 to 45 minutes, 5.6% 45 to 60 minutes, 15.7% 60 minutes or more (2000)

GARDNERTOWN (CDP). Covers a land area of 4.896 square miles and a water area of 0.008 square miles. Located at 41.52° N. Lat.; 74.05° W. Long.
Population: 4,209 (1990); 4,533 (2000); 4,718 (2005); 4,916 (2010 projected); Race: 77.2% White, 10.2% Black, 2.4% Asian, 15.7% Hispanic of any race (2005); Density: 963.6 persons per square mile (2005); Average household size: 2.76 (2005); Median age: 37.6 (2005); Males per 100 females: 95.2 (2005); Marriage status: 25.8% never married, 57.0% now married, 8.3% widowed, 8.9% divorced (2000); Foreign born: 4.7% (2000); Ancestry (includes multiple ancestries): 23.3% Irish, 22.9% Italian, 18.2% Other groups, 12.5% German, 7.1% English (2000).
Economy: Employment by occupation: 9.7% management, 19.0% professional, 16.3% services, 27.0% sales, 0.3% farming, 13.1% construction, 14.6% production (2000).
Income: Per capita income: $26,578 (2005); Median household income: $64,882 (2005); Average household income: $73,459 (2005); Percent of households with income of $100,000 or more: 22.4% (2005); Poverty rate: 3.2% (2000).
Education: Percent of population age 25 and over with: High school diploma (including GED) or higher: 86.0% (2005); Bachelor's degree or higher: 16.9% (2005); Master's degree or higher: 4.0% (2005).
Housing: Homeownership rate: 81.1% (2005); Median home value: $188,058 (2005); Median rent: $659 per month (2000); Median age of housing: 45 years (2000).
Transportation: Commute to work: 94.3% car, 2.8% public transportation, 0.7% walk, 1.9% work from home (2000); Travel time to work: 34.6% less than 15 minutes, 33.2% 15 to 30 minutes, 13.4% 30 to 45 minutes, 6.0% 45 to 60 minutes, 12.8% 60 minutes or more (2000)

GODEFFROY (unincorporated postal area, zip code 12739). Covers a land area of 3.927 square miles and a water area of 0.051 square miles. Located at 41.43° N. Lat.; 74.60° W. Long.
Population: 0 (2000); Race: 99.3% White, 0.0% Black, 0.0% Asian, 3.0% Hispanic of any race (2000); Density: 0.0 persons per square mile (2000); Age: 21.7% under 18, 14.5% over 64 (2000); Marriage status: 23.9% never married, 53.5% now married, 6.0% widowed, 16.7% divorced (2000); Foreign born: 2.4% (2000); Ancestry (includes multiple ancestries): 31.1% Irish, 29.8% Italian, 15.7% German, 8.4% United States or American, 7.9% Other groups (2000).
Economy: Employment by occupation: 0.0% management, 20.5% professional, 8.5% services, 20.9% sales, 0.8% farming, 28.7% construction, 20.5% production (2000).
Income: Per capita income: $20,159 (2000); Median household income: $42,386 (2000); Poverty rate: 22.6% (2000).
Education: Percent of population age 25 and over with: High school diploma (including GED) or higher: 77.9% (2000); Bachelor's degree or higher: 10.2% (2000).
Housing: Homeownership rate: 76.3% (2000); Median home value: $83,800 (2000); Median rent: $511 per month (2000); Median age of housing: 33 years (2000).
Transportation: Commute to work: 82.2% car, 4.7% public transportation, 5.4% walk, 7.8% work from home (2000); Travel time to work: 24.8% less than 15 minutes, 49.6% 15 to 30 minutes, 2.1% 30 to 45 minutes, 5.0% 45 to 60 minutes, 18.5% 60 minutes or more (2000)

GOSHEN (village). Covers a land area of 3.206 square miles and a water area of 0 square miles. Located at 41.40° N. Lat.; 74.32° W. Long. Elevation is 431 feet.
Population: 5,255 (1990); 5,676 (2000); 5,417 (2005); 5,385 (2010 projected); Race: 83.3% White, 9.7% Black, 2.4% Asian, 11.6% Hispanic of any race (2005); Density: 1,689.7 persons per square mile (2005); Average household size: 2.71 (2005); Median age: 38.1 (2005); Males per 100 females: 105.4 (2005); Marriage status: 22.3% never married, 60.8% now married, 9.2% widowed, 7.7% divorced (2000); Foreign born: 7.7% (2000); Ancestry (includes multiple ancestries): 22.3% Irish, 13.7% German, 13.5% Italian, 9.0% English, 8.9% Other groups (2000).
Economy: Single-family building permits issued: 64 (2005); Multi-family building permits issued: 0 (2005); Employment by occupation: 13.6% management, 25.2% professional, 14.8% services, 26.9% sales, 0.4% farming, 6.4% construction, 12.6% production (2000).
Income: Per capita income: $27,682 (2005); Median household income: $57,061 (2005); Average household income: $72,770 (2005); Percent of

households with income of $100,000 or more: 21.9% (2005); Poverty rate: 4.0% (2000).
Education: Percent of population age 25 and over with: High school diploma (including GED) or higher: 82.8% (2005); Bachelor's degree or higher: 29.8% (2005); Master's degree or higher: 11.7% (2005).

School District(s)
Boces Orange-Ulster (UG-UG)
   2003-04 Enrollment: 925 . . . . (845) 291-0110
Goshen Central School District (KG-12)
   2003-04 Enrollment: 2,921 . . . . (845) 294-2410

Two-year College(s)
Orange Ulster BOCES-School of Practical Nursing (Public)
   Fall 2004 Enrollment: 90 . . . . (845) 291-0100

Housing: Homeownership rate: 52.5% (2005); Median home value: $244,194 (2005); Median rent: $827 per month (2000); Median age of housing: 36 years (2000).
Hospitals: Orange Regional Medical Center Arden Hill Campus (174 beds)
Newspapers: Independent Republican (General - Circulation 3,800)
Transportation: Commute to work: 87.2% car, 3.7% public transportation, 4.1% walk, 4.4% work from home (2000); Travel time to work: 33.3% less than 15 minutes, 31.3% 15 to 30 minutes, 12.4% 30 to 45 minutes, 8.3% 45 to 60 minutes, 14.7% 60 minutes or more (2000)

Additional Information Contacts
Goshen Chamber of Commerce . . . . (845) 294-7741
   http://www.goshennychamber.com
Orange County Chamber of Commerce . . . . (845) 294-8080
   http://www.orangeny.org/

GOSHEN (town).
Covers a land area of 43.846 square miles and a water area of 0.119 square miles. Located at 41.38° N. Lat.; 74.33° W. Long. Elevation is 431 feet.
History: Good Time and Historic (or Harriman) harness-racing tracks are here; and the Hambletonian race is held here. Settled during 18th century; incorporated 1809.
Population: 11,510 (1990); 12,913 (2000); 13,886 (2005); 14,891 (2010 projected); Race: 85.3% White, 8.2% Black, 2.5% Asian, 10.7% Hispanic of any race (2005); Density: 316.7 persons per square mile (2005); Average household size: 3.13 (2005); Median age: 39.3 (2005); Males per 100 females: 102.4 (2005); Marriage status: 22.0% never married, 63.6% now married, 7.5% widowed, 6.9% divorced (2000); Foreign born: 7.9% (2000); Ancestry (includes multiple ancestries): 21.6% Irish, 15.1% Italian, 14.7% German, 11.1% Other groups, 10.1% Polish (2000).
Economy: In dairying and farming area. Manufacturing: veterinary pharmaceuticals, meatpacking. Resort, with lakes nearby. Harness-racing. Single-family building permits issued: 30 (2005); Multi-family building permits issued: 0 (2005); Employment by occupation: 15.5% management, 27.7% professional, 14.1% services, 24.7% sales, 1.3% farming, 7.3% construction, 9.2% production (2000).
Income: Per capita income: $29,424 (2005); Median household income: $69,672 (2005); Average household income: $90,141 (2005); Percent of households with income of $100,000 or more: 29.8% (2005); Poverty rate: 4.5% (2000).
Education: Percent of population age 25 and over with: High school diploma (including GED) or higher: 81.3% (2005); Bachelor's degree or higher: 29.1% (2005); Master's degree or higher: 11.4% (2005).
Housing: Homeownership rate: 68.9% (2005); Median home value: $273,466 (2005); Median rent: $782 per month (2000); Median age of housing: 30 years (2000).
Safety: Violent crime rate: 11.0 per 10,000 population; Property crime rate: 45.2 per 10,000 population (2004).
Transportation: Commute to work: 88.3% car, 2.9% public transportation, 3.2% walk, 4.8% work from home (2000); Travel time to work: 31.1% less than 15 minutes, 29.7% 15 to 30 minutes, 11.2% 30 to 45 minutes, 8.8% 45 to 60 minutes, 19.2% 60 minutes or more (2000)

Additional Information Contacts
Town of Goshen. . . . . (845) 294-6996
   http://www.townofgoshen.org/

GREENVILLE (town).
Covers a land area of 30.264 square miles and a water area of 0.262 square miles. Located at 41.37° N. Lat.; 74.58° W. Long.
Population: 3,145 (1990); 3,800 (2000); 4,437 (2005); 5,056 (2010 projected); Race: 93.4% White, 1.6% Black, 1.5% Asian, 6.2% Hispanic of any race (2005); Density: 146.6 persons per square mile (2005); Average household size: 3.06 (2005); Median age: 37.2 (2005); Males per 100 females: 96.9 (2005); Marriage status: 21.6% never married, 68.3% now married, 5.3% widowed, 4.8% divorced (2000); Foreign born: 5.0% (2000); Ancestry (includes multiple ancestries): 25.6% Irish, 19.1% Italian, 18.7% German, 9.7% Other groups, 9.6% English (2000).
Economy: Single-family building permits issued: 49 (2005); Multi-family building permits issued: 0 (2005); Employment by occupation: 12.6% management, 20.9% professional, 17.2% services, 23.8% sales, 0.3% farming, 13.2% construction, 12.1% production (2000).
Income: Per capita income: $27,505 (2005); Median household income: $70,597 (2005); Average household income: $83,126 (2005); Percent of households with income of $100,000 or more: 27.5% (2005); Poverty rate: 4.3% (2000).
Education: Percent of population age 25 and over with: High school diploma (including GED) or higher: 87.6% (2005); Bachelor's degree or higher: 19.4% (2005); Master's degree or higher: 8.7% (2005).
Housing: Homeownership rate: 87.3% (2005); Median home value: $242,044 (2005); Median rent: $640 per month (2000); Median age of housing: 22 years (2000).
Transportation: Commute to work: 94.8% car, 1.5% public transportation, 1.0% walk, 2.6% work from home (2000); Travel time to work: 15.0% less than 15 minutes, 38.8% 15 to 30 minutes, 18.5% 30 to 45 minutes, 8.7% 45 to 60 minutes, 19.0% 60 minutes or more (2000)

GREENWOOD LAKE (village).
Covers a land area of 2.045 square miles and a water area of 0.416 square miles. Located at 41.22° N. Lat.; 74.29° W. Long. Elevation is 624 feet.
Population: 3,161 (1990); 3,411 (2000); 3,453 (2005); 3,550 (2010 projected); Race: 93.4% White, 1.3% Black, 1.4% Asian, 7.2% Hispanic of any race (2005); Density: 1,688.6 persons per square mile (2005); Average household size: 2.50 (2005); Median age: 38.5 (2005); Males per 100 females: 101.2 (2005); Marriage status: 23.4% never married, 58.0% now married, 7.4% widowed, 11.1% divorced (2000); Foreign born: 5.5% (2000); Ancestry (includes multiple ancestries): 34.4% Irish, 21.9% Italian, 18.9% German, 9.2% English, 9.0% Other groups (2000).
Economy: Single-family building permits issued: 9 (2005); Multi-family building permits issued: 0 (2005); Employment by occupation: 14.1% management, 16.2% professional, 14.5% services, 28.8% sales, 0.0% farming, 14.2% construction, 12.3% production (2000).
Income: Per capita income: $30,175 (2005); Median household income: $65,850 (2005); Average household income: $74,964 (2005); Percent of households with income of $100,000 or more: 22.8% (2005); Poverty rate: 7.0% (2000).
Taxes: Total city taxes per capita: $518 (2004); City property taxes per capita: $443 (2004).
Education: Percent of population age 25 and over with: High school diploma (including GED) or higher: 86.5% (2005); Bachelor's degree or higher: 17.4% (2005); Master's degree or higher: 7.0% (2005).

School District(s)
Greenwood Lake Union Free School District (KG-08)
   2003-04 Enrollment: 694 . . . . (845) 477-7395

Housing: Homeownership rate: 67.2% (2005); Median home value: $182,500 (2005); Median rent: $597 per month (2000); Median age of housing: 46 years (2000).
Safety: Violent crime rate: 40.5 per 10,000 population; Property crime rate: 121.4 per 10,000 population (2004).
Newspapers: Greenwood Lake & West Milford News (General - Circulation 4,000)
Transportation: Commute to work: 87.7% car, 8.6% public transportation, 1.1% walk, 1.5% work from home (2000); Travel time to work: 17.8% less than 15 minutes, 13.4% 15 to 30 minutes, 23.5% 30 to 45 minutes, 16.2% 45 to 60 minutes, 29.2% 60 minutes or more (2000)

Additional Information Contacts
Greenwood Lake Chamber of Commerce . . . . (845) 477-0112
   http://www.greenwoodlakeny.org

HAMPTONBURGH (town).
Covers a land area of 26.780 square miles and a water area of 0.182 square miles. Located at 41.45° N. Lat.; 74.24° W. Long.
Population: 3,922 (1990); 4,686 (2000); 5,610 (2005); 6,511 (2010 projected); Race: 91.2% White, 2.7% Black, 2.2% Asian, 6.4% Hispanic of any race (2005); Density: 209.5 persons per square mile (2005); Average household size: 3.16 (2005); Median age: 39.0 (2005); Males per 100 females: 91.7 (2005); Marriage status: 22.9% never married, 68.6% now married, 3.9% widowed, 4.7% divorced (2000); Foreign born: 5.0% (2000);

Ancestry (includes multiple ancestries): 29.4% Irish, 27.9% Italian, 19.2% German, 8.9% Polish, 8.8% Other groups (2000).
Economy: Single-family building permits issued: 21 (2005); Multi-family building permits issued: 0 (2005); Employment by occupation: 13.9% management, 20.7% professional, 16.2% services, 29.0% sales, 0.0% farming, 12.8% construction, 7.5% production (2000).
Income: Per capita income: $34,205 (2005); Median household income: $87,459 (2005); Average household income: $106,800 (2005); Percent of households with income of $100,000 or more: 41.3% (2005); Poverty rate: 3.0% (2000).
Education: Percent of population age 25 and over with: High school diploma (including GED) or higher: 89.9% (2005); Bachelor's degree or higher: 28.9% (2005); Master's degree or higher: 10.9% (2005).
Housing: Homeownership rate: 88.9% (2005); Median home value: $297,196 (2005); Median rent: $588 per month (2000); Median age of housing: 25 years (2000).
Transportation: Commute to work: 90.8% car, 3.8% public transportation, 0.6% walk, 4.3% work from home (2000); Travel time to work: 23.7% less than 15 minutes, 34.8% 15 to 30 minutes, 12.7% 30 to 45 minutes, 10.8% 45 to 60 minutes, 18.0% 60 minutes or more (2000)
Additional Information Contacts
Town of Hamptonburgh . . . . (845) 427-2424
  http://townofhamptonburgh.org/content

HARRIMAN (village).
Covers a land area of 0.981 square miles and a water area of 0.015 square miles. Located at 41.30° N. Lat.; 74.14° W. Long. Elevation is 542 feet.
Population: 2,288 (1990); 2,252 (2000); 2,245 (2005); 2,259 (2010 projected); Race: 73.1% White, 6.8% Black, 11.5% Asian, 14.5% Hispanic of any race (2005); Density: 2,288.5 persons per square mile (2005); Average household size: 2.40 (2005); Median age: 37.0 (2005); Males per 100 females: 99.0 (2005); Marriage status: 27.5% never married, 57.0% now married, 5.6% widowed, 9.9% divorced (2000); Foreign born: 12.3% (2000); Ancestry (includes multiple ancestries): 26.2% Irish, 24.6% Italian, 19.4% German, 17.6% Other groups, 7.1% English (2000).
Economy: Single-family building permits issued: 2 (2005); Multi-family building permits issued: 0 (2005); Employment by occupation: 15.6% management, 22.4% professional, 16.9% services, 32.4% sales, 0.0% farming, 7.2% construction, 5.4% production (2000).
Income: Per capita income: $32,522 (2005); Median household income: $67,344 (2005); Average household income: $77,409 (2005); Percent of households with income of $100,000 or more: 21.8% (2005); Poverty rate: 2.2% (2000).
Education: Percent of population age 25 and over with: High school diploma (including GED) or higher: 87.7% (2005); Bachelor's degree or higher: 31.1% (2005); Master's degree or higher: 9.8% (2005).
School District(s)
Monroe-Woodbury Central School District (KG-12)
  2003-04 Enrollment: 7,255 . . . . (845) 928-2321
Housing: Homeownership rate: 52.9% (2005); Median home value: $207,949 (2005); Median rent: $870 per month (2000); Median age of housing: 17 years (2000).
Safety: Violent crime rate: 4.4 per 10,000 population; Property crime rate: 196.3 per 10,000 population (2004).
Transportation: Commute to work: 88.7% car, 6.4% public transportation, 2.7% walk, 2.2% work from home (2000); Travel time to work: 27.1% less than 15 minutes, 20.2% 15 to 30 minutes, 23.6% 30 to 45 minutes, 9.3% 45 to 60 minutes, 19.7% 60 minutes or more (2000)

HIGHLAND FALLS (village).
Covers a land area of 1.106 square miles and a water area of 0.011 square miles. Located at 41.36° N. Lat.; 73.96° W. Long.
Population: 3,937 (1990); 3,678 (2000); 3,782 (2005); 3,937 (2010 projected); Race: 69.5% White, 15.9% Black, 3.2% Asian, 15.5% Hispanic of any race (2005); Density: 3,420.5 persons per square mile (2005); Average household size: 2.31 (2005); Median age: 39.2 (2005); Males per 100 females: 95.4 (2005); Marriage status: 24.1% never married, 50.1% now married, 13.0% widowed, 12.8% divorced (2000); Foreign born: 8.6% (2000); Ancestry (includes multiple ancestries): 25.2% Irish, 22.2% Other groups, 15.5% German, 14.3% Italian, 12.1% English (2000).
Economy: Employment by occupation: 15.9% management, 19.5% professional, 21.1% services, 26.3% sales, 0.3% farming, 8.7% construction, 8.2% production (2000).
Income: Per capita income: $26,136 (2005); Median household income: $50,506 (2005); Average household income: $60,346 (2005); Percent of households with income of $100,000 or more: 13.7% (2005); Poverty rate: 4.7% (2000).
Education: Percent of population age 25 and over with: High school diploma (including GED) or higher: 85.2% (2005); Bachelor's degree or higher: 21.2% (2005); Master's degree or higher: 8.8% (2005).
School District(s)
Highland Falls Central School District (KG-12)
  2003-04 Enrollment: 1,209 . . . . (845) 446-9575
Housing: Homeownership rate: 50.5% (2005); Median home value: $202,681 (2005); Median rent: $660 per month (2000); Median age of housing: 49 years (2000).
Safety: Violent crime rate: 18.6 per 10,000 population; Property crime rate: 188.2 per 10,000 population (2004).
Newspapers: News of the Highlands (General - Circulation 2,800)
Transportation: Commute to work: 86.7% car, 4.8% public transportation, 6.8% walk, 1.0% work from home (2000); Travel time to work: 45.7% less than 15 minutes, 18.9% 15 to 30 minutes, 16.8% 30 to 45 minutes, 6.8% 45 to 60 minutes, 11.7% 60 minutes or more (2000)

HIGHLAND MILLS (CDP).
Covers a land area of 1.728 square miles and a water area of 0.005 square miles. Located at 41.35° N. Lat.; 74.12° W. Long.
Population: 2,576 (1990); 3,468 (2000); 4,274 (2005); 5,047 (2010 projected); Race: 79.5% White, 8.5% Black, 4.3% Asian, 14.4% Hispanic of any race (2005); Density: 2,474.0 persons per square mile (2005); Average household size: 2.84 (2005); Median age: 37.3 (2005); Males per 100 females: 91.3 (2005); Marriage status: 22.1% never married, 67.6% now married, 4.5% widowed, 5.8% divorced (2000); Foreign born: 5.2% (2000); Ancestry (includes multiple ancestries): 29.0% Irish, 26.6% Italian, 19.4% Other groups, 17.3% German, 5.3% Polish (2000).
Economy: Employment by occupation: 19.1% management, 23.3% professional, 14.7% services, 27.8% sales, 0.0% farming, 9.1% construction, 6.0% production (2000).
Income: Per capita income: $37,973 (2005); Median household income: $96,952 (2005); Average household income: $107,837 (2005); Percent of households with income of $100,000 or more: 47.7% (2005); Poverty rate: 3.0% (2000).
Education: Percent of population age 25 and over with: High school diploma (including GED) or higher: 90.9% (2005); Bachelor's degree or higher: 37.0% (2005); Master's degree or higher: 13.8% (2005).
Housing: Homeownership rate: 88.2% (2005); Median home value: $250,913 (2005); Median rent: $592 per month (2000); Median age of housing: 18 years (2000).
Transportation: Commute to work: 89.3% car, 9.1% public transportation, 0.3% walk, 1.4% work from home (2000); Travel time to work: 18.6% less than 15 minutes, 15.2% 15 to 30 minutes, 22.2% 30 to 45 minutes, 11.1% 45 to 60 minutes, 33.0% 60 minutes or more (2000)

HIGHLANDS (town).
Covers a land area of 30.898 square miles and a water area of 2.592 square miles. Located at 41.34° N. Lat.; 73.97° W. Long.
Population: 13,667 (1990); 12,484 (2000); 12,880 (2005); 13,351 (2010 projected); Race: 76.4% White, 12.2% Black, 3.6% Asian, 11.0% Hispanic of any race (2005); Density: 416.9 persons per square mile (2005); Average household size: 3.94 (2005); Median age: 23.9 (2005); Males per 100 females: 148.9 (2005); Marriage status: 49.2% never married, 41.3% now married, 4.3% widowed, 5.2% divorced (2000); Foreign born: 5.6% (2000); Ancestry (includes multiple ancestries): 22.4% Other groups, 21.3% Irish, 21.2% German, 12.3% Italian, 10.3% English (2000).
Economy: Single-family building permits issued: 4 (2005); Multi-family building permits issued: 0 (2005); Employment by occupation: 12.8% management, 26.9% professional, 19.1% services, 24.5% sales, 0.4% farming, 7.7% construction, 8.7% production (2000).
Income: Per capita income: $19,723 (2005); Median household income: $61,019 (2005); Average household income: $67,486 (2005); Percent of households with income of $100,000 or more: 17.9% (2005); Poverty rate: 3.6% (2000).
Education: Percent of population age 25 and over with: High school diploma (including GED) or higher: 90.4% (2005); Bachelor's degree or higher: 35.7% (2005); Master's degree or higher: 20.3% (2005).
Housing: Homeownership rate: 40.6% (2005); Median home value: $202,301 (2005); Median rent: $688 per month (2000); Median age of housing: 46 years (2000).
Transportation: Commute to work: 58.0% car, 2.3% public transportation, 35.1% walk, 2.7% work from home (2000); Travel time to work: 68.1% less

than 15 minutes, 13.2% 15 to 30 minutes, 8.6% 30 to 45 minutes, 3.0% 45 to 60 minutes, 7.0% 60 minutes or more (2000)

HUGUENOT (unincorporated postal area, zip code 12746). Covers a land area of 14.410 square miles and a water area of 0.404 square miles. Located at 41.43° N. Lat.; 74.64° W. Long.
Population: 0 (2000); Race: 87.0% White, 0.8% Black, 0.0% Asian, 11.0% Hispanic of any race (2000); Density: 0.0 persons per square mile (2000); Age: 33.6% under 18, 7.5% over 64 (2000); Marriage status: 29.5% never married, 51.3% now married, 7.1% widowed, 12.1% divorced (2000); Foreign born: 1.2% (2000); Ancestry (includes multiple ancestries): 23.5% German, 20.9% Italian, 16.9% Other groups, 15.6% Irish, 14.9% English (2000).
Economy: Employment by occupation: 3.6% management, 14.1% professional, 21.9% services, 23.3% sales, 0.0% farming, 12.2% construction, 24.9% production (2000).
Income: Per capita income: $17,189 (2000); Median household income: $50,263 (2000); Poverty rate: 5.9% (2000).
Education: Percent of population age 25 and over with: High school diploma (including GED) or higher: 69.4% (2000); Bachelor's degree or higher: 10.5% (2000).
Housing: Homeownership rate: 79.6% (2000); Median home value: $105,100 (2000); Median rent: $595 per month (2000); Median age of housing: 29 years (2000).
Transportation: Commute to work: 95.5% car, 2.9% public transportation, 0.0% walk, 1.6% work from home (2000); Travel time to work: 25.3% less than 15 minutes, 30.9% 15 to 30 minutes, 22.4% 30 to 45 minutes, 7.6% 45 to 60 minutes, 13.8% 60 minutes or more (2000)

KIRYAS JOEL (village). Covers a land area of 1.098 square miles and a water area of 0.005 square miles. Located at 41.34° N. Lat.; 74.16° W. Long. Elevation is 842 feet.
History: Founded in 1974 by the Satmar sect of Hasidic Jews to accommodate, in part, their burgeoning population in the Williamsburg section of Brooklyn.
Population: 7,437 (1990); 13,138 (2000); 18,314 (2005); 23,173 (2010 projected); Race: 98.5% White, 0.4% Black, 0.0% Asian, 1.1% Hispanic of any race (2005); Density: 16,675.0 persons per square mile (2005); Average household size: 5.79 (2005); Median age: 17.2 (2005); Males per 100 females: 113.6 (2005); Marriage status: 31.7% never married, 67.0% now married, 1.0% widowed, 0.3% divorced (2000); Foreign born: 8.9% (2000); Ancestry (includes multiple ancestries): 50.7% Other groups, 15.2% Hungarian, 8.0% United States or American, 2.1% Israeli, 1.8% Romanian (2000).
Economy: Single-family building permits issued: 0 (2005); Multi-family building permits issued: 331 (2005); Employment by occupation: 12.3% management, 23.7% professional, 6.5% services, 31.5% sales, 0.3% farming, 7.3% construction, 18.3% production (2000).
Income: Per capita income: $4,590 (2005); Median household income: $17,065 (2005); Average household income: $26,547 (2005); Percent of households with income of $100,000 or more: 2.5% (2005); Poverty rate: 62.2% (2000).
Education: Percent of population age 25 and over with: High school diploma (including GED) or higher: 45.3% (2005); Bachelor's degree or higher: 3.2% (2005); Master's degree or higher: 0.9% (2005).
Housing: Homeownership rate: 30.9% (2005); Median home value: $237,500 (2005); Median rent: $661 per month (2000); Median age of housing: 14 years (2000).
Transportation: Commute to work: 42.4% car, 19.6% public transportation, 29.6% walk, 4.0% work from home (2000); Travel time to work: 44.3% less than 15 minutes, 20.6% 15 to 30 minutes, 12.2% 30 to 45 minutes, 2.2% 45 to 60 minutes, 20.6% 60 minutes or more (2000)

MAYBROOK (village). Covers a land area of 1.337 square miles and a water area of 0 square miles. Located at 41.48° N. Lat.; 74.21° W. Long.
History: Incorporated 1925.
Population: 2,802 (1990); 3,084 (2000); 3,653 (2005); 4,199 (2010 projected); Race: 75.1% White, 12.9% Black, 2.0% Asian, 19.1% Hispanic of any race (2005); Density: 2,731.8 persons per square mile (2005); Average household size: 2.88 (2005); Median age: 32.9 (2005); Males per 100 females: 94.7 (2005); Marriage status: 25.2% never married, 59.3% now married, 6.4% widowed, 9.1% divorced (2000); Foreign born: 6.1% (2000); Ancestry (includes multiple ancestries): 25.4% Italian, 24.0% Irish, 19.7% Other groups, 16.1% German, 8.2% English (2000).
Economy: Manufacturing of textiles and apparel. Single-family building permits issued: 10 (2005); Multi-family building permits issued: 0 (2005); Employment by occupation: 11.2% management, 14.5% professional, 19.6% services, 30.6% sales, 0.0% farming, 9.9% construction, 14.2% production (2000).
Income: Per capita income: $21,683 (2005); Median household income: $57,079 (2005); Average household income: $61,204 (2005); Percent of households with income of $100,000 or more: 11.5% (2005); Poverty rate: 6.1% (2000).
Education: Percent of population age 25 and over with: High school diploma (including GED) or higher: 83.4% (2005); Bachelor's degree or higher: 15.9% (2005); Master's degree or higher: 4.9% (2005).
School District(s)
Valley Central School District (Montgomery) (KG-12)
   2003-04 Enrollment: 5,236 . . . . (845) 457-2400
Housing: Homeownership rate: 59.4% (2005); Median home value: $154,651 (2005); Median rent: $645 per month (2000); Median age of housing: 27 years (2000).
Safety: Violent crime rate: 2.5 per 10,000 population; Property crime rate: 104.7 per 10,000 population (2004).
Transportation: Commute to work: 91.7% car, 3.3% public transportation, 3.1% walk, 2.0% work from home (2000); Travel time to work: 21.8% less than 15 minutes, 33.8% 15 to 30 minutes, 12.6% 30 to 45 minutes, 10.6% 45 to 60 minutes, 21.2% 60 minutes or more (2000)
Additional Information Contacts
Village of Maybrook . . . . (845) 427-2717
   http://www.villageofmaybrook.com/content/

MECHANICSTOWN (CDP). Covers a land area of 3.327 square miles and a water area of 0.071 square miles. Located at 41.45° N. Lat.; 74.39° W. Long.
Population: 5,013 (1990); 6,061 (2000); 6,530 (2005); 7,054 (2010 projected); Race: 63.1% White, 19.3% Black, 3.7% Asian, 27.4% Hispanic of any race (2005); Density: 1,962.9 persons per square mile (2005); Average household size: 2.64 (2005); Median age: 37.3 (2005); Males per 100 females: 87.9 (2005); Marriage status: 25.7% never married, 55.2% now married, 10.0% widowed, 9.2% divorced (2000); Foreign born: 13.9% (2000); Ancestry (includes multiple ancestries): 30.1% Other groups, 19.8% Italian, 13.3% Irish, 12.1% German, 5.2% Polish (2000).
Economy: Employment by occupation: 8.5% management, 16.8% professional, 16.8% services, 34.8% sales, 0.8% farming, 7.6% construction, 14.7% production (2000).
Income: Per capita income: $22,928 (2005); Median household income: $51,468 (2005); Average household income: $59,637 (2005); Percent of households with income of $100,000 or more: 14.3% (2005); Poverty rate: 14.8% (2000).
Education: Percent of population age 25 and over with: High school diploma (including GED) or higher: 75.8% (2005); Bachelor's degree or higher: 13.7% (2005); Master's degree or higher: 5.4% (2005).
Housing: Homeownership rate: 49.0% (2005); Median home value: $144,735 (2005); Median rent: $652 per month (2000); Median age of housing: 25 years (2000).
Transportation: Commute to work: 92.6% car, 3.9% public transportation, 1.5% walk, 2.1% work from home (2000); Travel time to work: 41.0% less than 15 minutes, 24.7% 15 to 30 minutes, 14.9% 30 to 45 minutes, 5.1% 45 to 60 minutes, 14.5% 60 minutes or more (2000)

MIDDLETOWN (city). Covers a land area of 5.140 square miles and a water area of 0.013 square miles. Located at 41.44° N. Lat.; 74.42° W. Long. Elevation is 562 feet.
History: Settled 1756, Incorporated as a city 1888.
Population: 24,224 (1990); 25,388 (2000); 26,184 (2005); 27,210 (2010 projected); Race: 59.1% White, 19.9% Black, 2.2% Asian, 33.7% Hispanic of any race (2005); Density: 5,094.4 persons per square mile (2005); Average household size: 2.67 (2005); Median age: 34.3 (2005); Males per 100 females: 94.3 (2005); Marriage status: 32.6% never married, 48.6% now married, 8.8% widowed, 10.0% divorced (2000); Foreign born: 13.5% (2000); Ancestry (includes multiple ancestries): 35.8% Other groups, 16.9% Irish, 14.8% Italian, 11.1% German, 6.2% English (2000).
Economy: Industrial city. Major regional hub for the region south and east of the Catskills which is also an easy distance away for N.Y. city residents. Summer homes and recreational facilities and activities draw many downstate New Yorkers. Dairying and farming are still viable industries. Diverse manufacturing includes furniture, clothing, electronic, medical instruments, footwear, tools, perfumes, flavors and extracts, pig lead and

alloys and machinery. Unemployment rate: 4.7% (2005); Total civilian labor force: 12,163 (2005); Single-family building permits issued: 52 (2005); Multi-family building permits issued: 0 (2005); Employment by occupation: 8.2% management, 18.5% professional, 21.2% services, 28.5% sales, 1.1% farming, 8.2% construction, 14.3% production (2000).
Income: Per capita income: $20,823 (2005); Median household income: $42,864 (2005); Average household income: $54,338 (2005); Percent of households with income of $100,000 or more: 12.0% (2005); Poverty rate: 17.5% (2000).
Education: Percent of population age 25 and over with: High school diploma (including GED) or higher: 74.2% (2005); Bachelor's degree or higher: 16.9% (2005); Master's degree or higher: 7.4% (2005).

School District(s)
Middletown City School District (PK-12)
   2003-04 Enrollment: 6,577 . . . . (845) 341-5691

Two-year College(s)
Beauty School of Middletown
   Fall 2004 Enrollment: 132 . . . . (845) 343-2171
Orange County Community College (Public)
   Fall 2004 Enrollment: 6,269. . . . . (845) 344-6222
   2005-06 Tuition: In-state $3,218; Out-of-state $6,118

Housing: Homeownership rate: 46.2% (2005); Median home value: $154,211 (2005); Median rent: $604 per month (2000); Median age of housing: 49 years (2000).
Hospitals: Horton Medical Center (286 beds); Middletown Psychiatric Center
Safety: Violent crime rate: 41.3 per 10,000 population; Property crime rate: 260.5 per 10,000 population (2004).
Newspapers: The Times Herald Record (Circulation 87,923)
Transportation: Commute to work: 88.0% car, 5.6% public transportation, 3.7% walk, 1.7% work from home (2000); Travel time to work: 38.2% less than 15 minutes, 30.8% 15 to 30 minutes, 12.5% 30 to 45 minutes, 6.0% 45 to 60 minutes, 12.5% 60 minutes or more (2000)

Additional Information Contacts
City of Middletown . . . . (845) 586-4566
   http://www.ci.middletown.ny.us/

MINISINK (town). Covers a land area of 23.094 square miles and a water area of 0.086 square miles. Located at 41.33° N. Lat.; 74.54° W. Long.
Population: 2,981 (1990); 3,585 (2000); 4,251 (2005); 4,906 (2010 projected); Race: 93.6% White, 2.2% Black, 0.9% Asian, 7.0% Hispanic of any race (2005); Density: 184.1 persons per square mile (2005); Average household size: 3.02 (2005); Median age: 37.7 (2005); Males per 100 females: 96.4 (2005); Marriage status: 23.4% never married, 64.2% now married, 5.0% widowed, 7.5% divorced (2000); Foreign born: 3.1% (2000); Ancestry (includes multiple ancestries): 24.6% Irish, 19.8% German, 17.5% Italian, 15.2% English, 13.2% Polish (2000).
Economy: Single-family building permits issued: 22 (2005); Multi-family building permits issued: 0 (2005); Employment by occupation: 14.3% management, 18.5% professional, 20.0% services, 22.1% sales, 1.3% farming, 11.9% construction, 12.0% production (2000).
Income: Per capita income: $25,433 (2005); Median household income: $65,728 (2005); Average household income: $76,256 (2005); Percent of households with income of $100,000 or more: 24.0% (2005); Poverty rate: 5.8% (2000).
Education: Percent of population age 25 and over with: High school diploma (including GED) or higher: 85.9% (2005); Bachelor's degree or higher: 19.4% (2005); Master's degree or higher: 7.2% (2005).
Housing: Homeownership rate: 82.1% (2005); Median home value: $229,570 (2005); Median rent: $606 per month (2000); Median age of housing: 31 years (2000).
Transportation: Commute to work: 92.8% car, 0.8% public transportation, 1.7% walk, 4.2% work from home (2000); Travel time to work: 12.7% less than 15 minutes, 40.2% 15 to 30 minutes, 22.0% 30 to 45 minutes, 6.4% 45 to 60 minutes, 18.8% 60 minutes or more (2000)

MONROE (village). Covers a land area of 3.428 square miles and a water area of 0.052 square miles. Located at 41.32° N. Lat.; 74.18° W. Long. Elevation is 679 feet.
Population: 6,798 (1990); 7,780 (2000); 8,342 (2005); 8,977 (2010 projected); Race: 86.4% White, 4.2% Black, 3.3% Asian, 13.0% Hispanic of any race (2005); Density: 2,433.6 persons per square mile (2005); Average household size: 3.00 (2005); Median age: 37.4 (2005); Males per 100 females: 98.3 (2005); Marriage status: 22.2% never married, 65.8% now married, 5.1% widowed, 6.8% divorced (2000); Foreign born: 10.3% (2000); Ancestry (includes multiple ancestries): 25.8% Irish, 24.5% Italian, 16.5% Other groups, 11.8% German, 8.9% Polish (2000).
Economy: Single-family building permits issued: 24 (2005); Multi-family building permits issued: 0 (2005); Employment by occupation: 14.5% management, 23.9% professional, 16.1% services, 28.7% sales, 0.0% farming, 6.8% construction, 10.0% production (2000).
Income: Per capita income: $31,679 (2005); Median household income: $84,531 (2005); Average household income: $94,697 (2005); Percent of households with income of $100,000 or more: 38.4% (2005); Poverty rate: 4.8% (2000).
Education: Percent of population age 25 and over with: High school diploma (including GED) or higher: 89.0% (2005); Bachelor's degree or higher: 32.7% (2005); Master's degree or higher: 13.1% (2005).

School District(s)
Kiryas Joel Village Union Free School District (PK-11)
   2003-04 Enrollment: 252 . . . . (845) 782-2300
Monroe-Woodbury Central School District (KG-12)
   2003-04 Enrollment: 7,255 . . . . (845) 928-2321

Four-year College(s)
Uta Mesivta of Kiryas Joel
   Fall 2004 Enrollment: n/a. . . . . (845) 783-9901
   2005-06 Tuition: In-state $5,000; Out-of-state $5,000

Housing: Homeownership rate: 84.1% (2005); Median home value: $263,723 (2005); Median rent: $690 per month (2000); Median age of housing: 28 years (2000).
Safety: Violent crime rate: 37.2 per 10,000 population; Property crime rate: 443.7 per 10,000 population (2004).
Newspapers: The Photo News (General - Circulation 9,000)
Transportation: Commute to work: 85.3% car, 9.2% public transportation, 1.9% walk, 2.6% work from home (2000); Travel time to work: 25.7% less than 15 minutes, 16.9% 15 to 30 minutes, 15.5% 30 to 45 minutes, 10.0% 45 to 60 minutes, 31.9% 60 minutes or more (2000)

Additional Information Contacts
Village of Monroe. . . . . (845) 783-1900
   http://www.monroeny.org/

MONROE (town). Covers a land area of 20.088 square miles and a water area of 1.177 square miles. Located at 41.31° N. Lat.; 74.18° W. Long. Elevation is 679 feet.
History: Incorporated 1894.
Population: 23,035 (1990); 31,407 (2000); 38,174 (2005); 44,652 (2010 projected); Race: 93.1% White, 1.8% Black, 1.8% Asian, 6.7% Hispanic of any race (2005); Density: 1,900.4 persons per square mile (2005); Average household size: 3.95 (2005); Median age: 23.7 (2005); Males per 100 females: 107.6 (2005); Marriage status: 26.1% never married, 65.3% now married, 4.1% widowed, 4.6% divorced (2000); Foreign born: 9.6% (2000); Ancestry (includes multiple ancestries): 31.2% Other groups, 14.6% Irish, 13.0% Italian, 9.0% German, 8.3% Hungarian (2000).
Economy: Summer residential and recreational village. Manufacturing of steel products. Unemployment rate: 3.7% (2005); Total civilian labor force: 13,992 (2005); Single-family building permits issued: 84 (2005); Multi-family building permits issued: 110 (2005); Employment by occupation: 14.1% management, 22.8% professional, 14.0% services, 30.5% sales, 0.1% farming, 8.3% construction, 10.2% production (2000).
Income: Per capita income: $17,980 (2005); Median household income: $54,484 (2005); Average household income: $70,446 (2005); Percent of households with income of $100,000 or more: 25.1% (2005); Poverty rate: 29.1% (2000).
Education: Percent of population age 25 and over with: High school diploma (including GED) or higher: 74.6% (2005); Bachelor's degree or higher: 22.5% (2005); Master's degree or higher: 8.2% (2005).
Housing: Homeownership rate: 64.0% (2005); Median home value: $260,895 (2005); Median rent: $708 per month (2000); Median age of housing: 22 years (2000).
Transportation: Commute to work: 77.6% car, 10.7% public transportation, 6.7% walk, 3.7% work from home (2000); Travel time to work: 29.2% less than 15 minutes, 18.6% 15 to 30 minutes, 16.8% 30 to 45 minutes, 8.0% 45 to 60 minutes, 27.5% 60 minutes or more (2000)

Additional Information Contacts
Town of Monroe. . . . . (845) 783-1900
   http://www.monroeny.org/

MONTGOMERY (village). Covers a land area of 1.390 square miles and a water area of 0.056 square miles. Located at 41.52° N. Lat.; 74.23° W. Long. Elevation is 354 feet.
Population: 2,900 (1990); 3,636 (2000); 4,523 (2005); 5,381 (2010 projected); Race: 84.8% White, 7.2% Black, 1.2% Asian, 12.3% Hispanic of any race (2005); Density: 3,254.7 persons per square mile (2005); Average household size: 2.73 (2005); Median age: 36.3 (2005); Males per 100 females: 94.0 (2005); Marriage status: 25.4% never married, 58.6% now married, 5.2% widowed, 10.8% divorced (2000); Foreign born: 6.8% (2000); Ancestry (includes multiple ancestries): 26.6% Irish, 22.5% Italian, 17.9% German, 13.1% Other groups, 10.9% English (2000).
Economy: Single-family building permits issued: 25 (2005); Multi-family building permits issued: 56 (2005); Employment by occupation: 15.8% management, 24.2% professional, 16.3% services, 25.1% sales, 0.3% farming, 12.2% construction, 6.1% production (2000).
Income: Per capita income: $25,214 (2005); Median household income: $59,680 (2005); Average household income: $67,559 (2005); Percent of households with income of $100,000 or more: 17.7% (2005); Poverty rate: 7.0% (2000).
Education: Percent of population age 25 and over with: High school diploma (including GED) or higher: 87.9% (2005); Bachelor's degree or higher: 26.7% (2005); Master's degree or higher: 11.9% (2005).
School District(s)
Valley Central School District (Montgomery) (KG-12)
    2003-04 Enrollment: 5,236 . . . . (845) 457-2400
Housing: Homeownership rate: 72.6% (2005); Median home value: $195,407 (2005); Median rent: $687 per month (2000); Median age of housing: 25 years (2000).
Transportation: Commute to work: 94.3% car, 3.3% public transportation, 1.4% walk, 1.0% work from home (2000); Travel time to work: 22.3% less than 15 minutes, 37.3% 15 to 30 minutes, 13.5% 30 to 45 minutes, 9.6% 45 to 60 minutes, 17.3% 60 minutes or more (2000)

MONTGOMERY (town). Covers a land area of 50.439 square miles and a water area of 0.640 square miles. Located at 41.54° N. Lat.; 74.20° W. Long. Elevation is 354 feet.
Population: 18,495 (1990); 20,891 (2000); 24,121 (2005); 27,311 (2010 projected); Race: 86.8% White, 5.8% Black, 1.0% Asian, 12.1% Hispanic of any race (2005); Density: 478.2 persons per square mile (2005); Average household size: 2.85 (2005); Median age: 36.3 (2005); Males per 100 females: 95.7 (2005); Marriage status: 24.5% never married, 59.2% now married, 6.9% widowed, 9.4% divorced (2000); Foreign born: 5.1% (2000); Ancestry (includes multiple ancestries): 25.0% Irish, 23.0% Italian, 17.8% German, 12.3% Other groups, 11.3% English (2000).
Economy: Single-family building permits issued: 35 (2005); Multi-family building permits issued: 2 (2005); Employment by occupation: 12.2% management, 18.2% professional, 16.2% services, 27.0% sales, 0.4% farming, 12.2% construction, 13.8% production (2000).
Income: Per capita income: $23,725 (2005); Median household income: $57,329 (2005); Average household income: $66,713 (2005); Percent of households with income of $100,000 or more: 18.4% (2005); Poverty rate: 7.7% (2000).
Taxes: Total city taxes per capita: $191 (2004); City property taxes per capita: $150 (2004).
Education: Percent of population age 25 and over with: High school diploma (including GED) or higher: 82.8% (2005); Bachelor's degree or higher: 19.7% (2005); Master's degree or higher: 7.5% (2005).
Housing: Homeownership rate: 72.2% (2005); Median home value: $187,492 (2005); Median rent: $634 per month (2000); Median age of housing: 35 years (2000).
Transportation: Commute to work: 91.8% car, 2.6% public transportation, 2.8% walk, 2.4% work from home (2000); Travel time to work: 26.6% less than 15 minutes, 37.6% 15 to 30 minutes, 14.5% 30 to 45 minutes, 7.6% 45 to 60 minutes, 13.8% 60 minutes or more (2000)

MOUNT HOPE (town). Covers a land area of 25.193 square miles and a water area of 0.309 square miles. Located at 41.46° N. Lat.; 74.52° W. Long. Elevation is 826 feet.
Population: 5,971 (1990); 6,639 (2000); 7,370 (2005); 8,024 (2010 projected); Race: 72.9% White, 20.5% Black, 2.1% Asian, 18.5% Hispanic of any race (2005); Density: 292.5 persons per square mile (2005); Average household size: 4.17 (2005); Median age: 36.5 (2005); Males per 100 females: 188.6 (2005); Marriage status: 31.2% never married, 58.3% now married, 3.7% widowed, 6.7% divorced (2000); Foreign born: 7.5% (2000); Ancestry (includes multiple ancestries): 16.0% Irish, 15.9% German, 14.7% Italian, 8.1% Other groups, 7.0% English (2000).
Economy: Single-family building permits issued: 30 (2005); Multi-family building permits issued: 0 (2005); Employment by occupation: 10.8% management, 19.8% professional, 16.4% services, 27.2% sales, 0.6% farming, 14.0% construction, 11.1% production (2000).
Income: Per capita income: $20,195 (2005); Median household income: $65,741 (2005); Average household income: $73,049 (2005); Percent of households with income of $100,000 or more: 23.8% (2005); Poverty rate: 5.2% (2000).
Education: Percent of population age 25 and over with: High school diploma (including GED) or higher: 58.2% (2005); Bachelor's degree or higher: 12.7% (2005); Master's degree or higher: 5.1% (2005).
Housing: Homeownership rate: 82.0% (2005); Median home value: $212,394 (2005); Median rent: $601 per month (2000); Median age of housing: 33 years (2000).
Safety: Violent crime rate: 7.0 per 10,000 population; Property crime rate: 36.6 per 10,000 population (2004).
Transportation: Commute to work: 93.9% car, 1.2% public transportation, 1.2% walk, 3.4% work from home (2000); Travel time to work: 18.4% less than 15 minutes, 40.5% 15 to 30 minutes, 16.6% 30 to 45 minutes, 7.8% 45 to 60 minutes, 16.7% 60 minutes or more (2000)

NEW HAMPTON (unincorporated postal area, zip code 10958). Covers a land area of 22.995 square miles and a water area of 0.012 square miles. Located at 41.38° N. Lat.; 74.41° W. Long.
Population: 0 (2000); Race: 86.0% White, 7.1% Black, 1.2% Asian, 8.0% Hispanic of any race (2000); Density: 0.0 persons per square mile (2000); Age: 28.3% under 18, 7.7% over 64; Marriage status: 28.8% never married, 57.9% now married, 4.9% widowed, 8.4% divorced (2000); Foreign born: 6.8% (2000); Ancestry (includes multiple ancestries): 25.5% Irish, 19.9% Italian, 19.4% Polish, 15.4% German, 14.7% Other groups (2000).
Economy: Employment by occupation: 14.2% management, 21.8% professional, 19.1% services, 26.4% sales, 1.6% farming, 9.5% construction, 7.4% production (2000).
Income: Per capita income: $20,316 (2000); Median household income: $61,639 (2000); Poverty rate: 4.2% (2000).
Education: Percent of population age 25 and over with: High school diploma (including GED) or higher: 78.4% (2000); Bachelor's degree or higher: 20.4% (2000).
School District(s)
Goshen Central School District (KG-12)
    2003-04 Enrollment: 2,921 . . . . (845) 294-2410
Housing: Homeownership rate: 83.9% (2000); Median home value: $141,000 (2000); Median rent: $681 per month (2000); Median age of housing: 34 years (2000).
Transportation: Commute to work: 85.5% car, 3.6% public transportation, 5.8% walk, 5.1% work from home (2000); Travel time to work: 30.5% less than 15 minutes, 25.4% 15 to 30 minutes, 14.0% 30 to 45 minutes, 8.1% 45 to 60 minutes, 22.0% 60 minutes or more (2000)

NEW WINDSOR (town). Aka New Windsor Center. Covers a land area of 34.782 square miles and a water area of 2.233 square miles. Located at 41.47° N. Lat.; 74.07° W. Long.
History: Was home of George Clinton. De Witt Clinton was born here.
Population: 22,937 (1990); 22,866 (2000); 24,808 (2005); 26,870 (2010 projected); Race: 78.8% White, 9.3% Black, 2.3% Asian, 16.2% Hispanic of any race (2005); Density: 713.2 persons per square mile (2005); Average household size: 2.71 (2005); Median age: 37.6 (2005); Males per 100 females: 97.7 (2005); Marriage status: 23.8% never married, 60.9% now married, 6.9% widowed, 8.4% divorced (2000); Foreign born: 8.1% (2000); Ancestry (includes multiple ancestries): 26.1% Irish, 23.6% Italian, 18.7% Other groups, 13.2% German, 8.3% English (2000).
Economy: Manufacturing of textiles, furniture. Site of Stewart International Airport, an air force base opened to commercial aircraft in 1990 and now a regional airport. Industrial park located at the airport. Unemployment rate: 4.2% (2005); Total civilian labor force: 12,706 (2005); Single-family building permits issued: 88 (2005); Multi-family building permits issued: 0 (2005); Employment by occupation: 12.8% management, 19.8% professional, 16.4% services, 30.0% sales, 0.1% farming, 10.8% construction, 10.1% production (2000).
Income: Per capita income: $25,631 (2005); Median household income: $57,598 (2005); Average household income: $68,597 (2005); Percent of

households with income of $100,000 or more: 20.0% (2005); Poverty rate: 5.9% (2000).
Taxes: Total city taxes per capita: $491 (2004); City property taxes per capita: $417 (2004).
Education: Percent of population age 25 and over with: High school diploma (including GED) or higher: 85.4% (2005); Bachelor's degree or higher: 21.2% (2005); Master's degree or higher: 8.8% (2005).

School District(s)
Cornwall Central School District (KG-12)
    2003-04 Enrollment: 3,093 .... (845) 534-8009
Newburgh City School District (PK-12)
    2003-04 Enrollment: 13,108 .... (845) 563-3500
Washingtonville Central School District (PK-12)
    2003-04 Enrollment: 5,106 .... (845) 497-2200

Housing: Homeownership rate: 71.8% (2005); Median home value: $209,299 (2005); Median rent: $671 per month (2000); Median age of housing: 31 years (2000).
Safety: Violent crime rate: 33.8 per 10,000 population; Property crime rate: 223.1 per 10,000 population (2004).
Newspapers: The Sentinel (General - Circulation 5,700)
Transportation: Commute to work: 91.7% car, 3.9% public transportation, 1.6% walk, 2.1% work from home (2000); Travel time to work: 30.6% less than 15 minutes, 29.5% 15 to 30 minutes, 13.7% 30 to 45 minutes, 9.0% 45 to 60 minutes, 17.2% 60 minutes or more (2000)

Additional Information Contacts
Town of New Windsor .... (845) 565-8800
    http://town.new-windsor.ny.us/

NEW WINDSOR (CDP).
Covers a land area of 0.541 square miles and a water area of 0 square miles. Located at 39.25° N. Lat.; 90.06° W. Long.
Population: 8,898 (1990); 9,077 (2000); 9,546 (2005); 10,098 (2010 projected); Race: 79.2% White, 8.9% Black, 1.8% Asian, 17.3% Hispanic of any race (2005); Density: 17,645.3 persons per square mile (2005); Average household size: 2.60 (2005); Median age: 38.4 (2005); Males per 100 females: 95.0 (2005); Marriage status: 25.1% never married, 58.4% now married, 8.4% widowed, 8.0% divorced (2000); Foreign born: 7.0% (2000); Ancestry (includes multiple ancestries): 25.4% Irish, 22.9% Italian, 18.3% Other groups, 12.3% German, 8.1% English (2000).
Economy: Employment by occupation: 13.1% management, 18.4% professional, 18.6% services, 30.3% sales, 0.2% farming, 7.8% construction, 11.7% production (2000).
Income: Per capita income: $26,037 (2005); Median household income: $55,272 (2005); Average household income: $67,294 (2005); Percent of households with income of $100,000 or more: 20.1% (2005); Poverty rate: 5.3% (2000).
Education: Percent of population age 25 and over with: High school diploma (including GED) or higher: 83.8% (2005); Bachelor's degree or higher: 21.3% (2005); Master's degree or higher: 7.5% (2005).
Housing: Homeownership rate: 73.3% (2005); Median home value: $196,507 (2005); Median rent: $634 per month (2000); Median age of housing: 36 years (2000).
Transportation: Commute to work: 92.3% car, 2.8% public transportation, 1.3% walk, 2.9% work from home (2000); Travel time to work: 30.9% less than 15 minutes, 30.3% 15 to 30 minutes, 15.7% 30 to 45 minutes, 8.5% 45 to 60 minutes, 14.7% 60 minutes or more (2000)

NEWBURGH (city).
Covers a land area of 3.822 square miles and a water area of 0.959 square miles. Located at 41.50° N. Lat.; 74.02° W. Long. Elevation is 139 feet.
History: Has many old houses, and the streets run sharply to the river. At Hasbrouck House (1750; now a Museum), Washington made his headquarters from April 1782 to Aug. 1783. It was in Newburgh that the Continental Army was disbanded. Mt. St. Mary College is in the city. West Point is located a few miles to the south. Settled 1709 by Palatines; Incorporated 1800.
Population: 26,440 (1990); 28,259 (2000); 28,495 (2005); 29,112 (2010 projected); Race: 36.3% White, 34.9% Black, 1.0% Asian, 43.6% Hispanic of any race (2005); Density: 7,455.4 persons per square mile (2005); Average household size: 3.11 (2005); Median age: 29.6 (2005); Males per 100 females: 90.0 (2005); Marriage status: 41.0% never married, 44.8% now married, 6.1% widowed, 8.0% divorced (2000); Foreign born: 20.3% (2000); Ancestry (includes multiple ancestries): 57.8% Other groups, 9.2% Italian, 8.2% Irish, 5.3% German, 3.0% English (2000).
Economy: The city has become an area wholesale and trucking center that ships fruit and dairy prods. Manufacturing includes transportation equipment, machinery, scientific instruments, apparel, plastic goods and metal products. Unemployment rate: 5.9% (2005); Total civilian labor force: 11,757 (2005); Single-family building permits issued: 5 (2005); Multi-family building permits issued: 2 (2005); Employment by occupation: 5.7% management, 12.4% professional, 22.7% services, 23.8% sales, 0.3% farming, 8.0% construction, 27.2% production (2000).
Income: Per capita income: $14,259 (2005); Median household income: $32,955 (2005); Average household income: $43,181 (2005); Percent of households with income of $100,000 or more: 6.7% (2005); Poverty rate: 25.8% (2000).
Education: Percent of population age 25 and over with: High school diploma (including GED) or higher: 61.8% (2005); Bachelor's degree or higher: 10.9% (2005); Master's degree or higher: 4.5% (2005).

School District(s)
Marlboro Central School District (KG-12)
    2003-04 Enrollment: 2,136 .... (845) 236-5802
Newburgh City School District (PK-12)
    2003-04 Enrollment: 13,108 .... (845) 563-3500
Valley Central School District (Montgomery) (KG-12)
    2003-04 Enrollment: 5,236 .... (845) 457-2400

Four-year College(s)
Mount Saint Mary College
    Fall 2004 Enrollment: 2,621 .... (845) 561-0800
    2005-06 Tuition: In-state $16,930; Out-of-state $16,930

Housing: Homeownership rate: 30.8% (2005); Median home value: $137,362 (2005); Median rent: $549 per month (2000); Median age of housing: 59 years (2000).
Hospitals: St. Luke's Hospital (367 beds)
Safety: Violent crime rate: 127.2 per 10,000 population; Property crime rate: 412.8 per 10,000 population (2004).
Newspapers: Hudson Valley Black Press (Black - Circulation 42,500); Mid Hudson Times (General - Circulation 4,600)
Transportation: Commute to work: 80.5% car, 8.0% public transportation, 7.9% walk, 1.5% work from home (2000); Travel time to work: 39.6% less than 15 minutes, 32.7% 15 to 30 minutes, 16.3% 30 to 45 minutes, 4.0% 45 to 60 minutes, 7.5% 60 minutes or more (2000)

Additional Information Contacts
City of Newburgh .... (845) 569-7311
    http://www.newburgh-ny.com/

NEWBURGH (town).
Covers a land area of 43.692 square miles and a water area of 3.306 square miles. Located at 41.54° N. Lat.; 74.06° W. Long. Elevation is 139 feet.
Population: 24,066 (1990); 27,568 (2000); 30,649 (2005); 33,807 (2010 projected); Race: 78.4% White, 11.1% Black, 3.0% Asian, 14.0% Hispanic of any race (2005); Density: 701.5 persons per square mile (2005); Average household size: 2.80 (2005); Median age: 38.9 (2005); Males per 100 females: 96.0 (2005); Marriage status: 22.0% never married, 64.5% now married, 6.5% widowed, 7.0% divorced (2000); Foreign born: 7.6% (2000); Ancestry (includes multiple ancestries): 26.1% Italian, 22.3% Irish, 19.6% Other groups, 14.4% German, 7.9% English (2000).
Economy: Unemployment rate: 4.0% (2005); Total civilian labor force: 16,316 (2005); Single-family building permits issued: 95 (2005); Multi-family building permits issued: 6 (2005); Employment by occupation: 13.0% management, 23.1% professional, 14.0% services, 26.9% sales, 0.3% farming, 11.0% construction, 11.7% production (2000).
Income: Per capita income: $28,082 (2005); Median household income: $66,715 (2005); Average household income: $77,688 (2005); Percent of households with income of $100,000 or more: 24.1% (2005); Poverty rate: 3.8% (2000).
Taxes: Total city taxes per capita: $441 (2004); City property taxes per capita: $353 (2004).
Education: Percent of population age 25 and over with: High school diploma (including GED) or higher: 86.9% (2005); Bachelor's degree or higher: 23.6% (2005); Master's degree or higher: 9.4% (2005).
Housing: Homeownership rate: 82.3% (2005); Median home value: $228,590 (2005); Median rent: $725 per month (2000); Median age of housing: 34 years (2000).
Safety: Violent crime rate: 9.8 per 10,000 population; Property crime rate: 268.1 per 10,000 population (2004).
Transportation: Commute to work: 94.2% car, 3.0% public transportation, 0.5% walk, 2.0% work from home (2000); Travel time to work: 28.5% less

than 15 minutes, 33.5% 15 to 30 minutes, 13.8% 30 to 45 minutes, 8.2% 45 to 60 minutes, 16.0% 60 minutes or more (2000)

ORANGE LAKE (CDP). Covers a land area of 5.365 square miles and a water area of 0.637 square miles. Located at 41.53° N. Lat.; 74.09° W. Long.
Population: 5,196 (1990); 6,085 (2000); 6,551 (2005); 7,050 (2010 projected); Race: 72.0% White, 18.1% Black, 1.7% Asian, 18.1% Hispanic of any race (2005); Density: 1,221.1 persons per square mile (2005); Average household size: 2.96 (2005); Median age: 40.1 (2005); Males per 100 females: 98.0 (2005); Marriage status: 24.3% never married, 63.4% now married, 7.5% widowed, 4.8% divorced (2000); Foreign born: 7.5% (2000); Ancestry (includes multiple ancestries): 23.3% Irish, 23.1% Other groups, 22.5% Italian, 17.4% German, 10.9% English (2000).
Economy: Employment by occupation: 12.8% management, 22.1% professional, 11.9% services, 28.4% sales, 0.9% farming, 11.3% construction, 12.5% production (2000).
Income: Per capita income: $24,667 (2005); Median household income: $64,451 (2005); Average household income: $70,807 (2005); Percent of households with income of $100,000 or more: 19.5% (2005); Poverty rate: 2.9% (2000).
Education: Percent of population age 25 and over with: High school diploma (including GED) or higher: 84.1% (2005); Bachelor's degree or higher: 24.6% (2005); Master's degree or higher: 8.4% (2005).
Housing: Homeownership rate: 88.9% (2005); Median home value: $222,880 (2005); Median rent: $755 per month (2000); Median age of housing: 32 years (2000).
Transportation: Commute to work: 94.8% car, 2.9% public transportation, 1.0% walk, 1.3% work from home (2000); Travel time to work: 25.7% less than 15 minutes, 37.1% 15 to 30 minutes, 14.1% 30 to 45 minutes, 7.6% 45 to 60 minutes, 15.5% 60 minutes or more (2000)

OTISVILLE (village). Covers a land area of 0.694 square miles and a water area of 0 square miles. Located at 41.47° N. Lat.; 74.53° W. Long. Elevation is 852 feet.
Population: 1,060 (1990); 989 (2000); 1,095 (2005); 1,190 (2010 projected); Race: 84.8% White, 9.4% Black, 0.9% Asian, 11.1% Hispanic of any race (2005); Density: 1,578.7 persons per square mile (2005); Average household size: 2.73 (2005); Median age: 36.6 (2005); Males per 100 females: 90.4 (2005); Marriage status: 28.9% never married, 52.5% now married, 7.0% widowed, 11.6% divorced (2000); Foreign born: 2.2% (2000); Ancestry (includes multiple ancestries): 23.0% German, 22.6% Irish, 20.3% Italian, 16.9% Other groups, 12.4% English (2000).
Economy: Single-family building permits issued: 15 (2005); Multi-family building permits issued: 0 (2005); Employment by occupation: 8.2% management, 19.1% professional, 15.9% services, 26.4% sales, 0.8% farming, 15.5% construction, 14.1% production (2000).
Income: Per capita income: $23,128 (2005); Median household income: $56,636 (2005); Average household income: $63,155 (2005); Percent of households with income of $100,000 or more: 19.7% (2005); Poverty rate: 7.5% (2000).
Education: Percent of population age 25 and over with: High school diploma (including GED) or higher: 81.4% (2005); Bachelor's degree or higher: 12.5% (2005); Master's degree or higher: 6.0% (2005).
School District(s)
Minisink Valley Central School District (KG-12)
    2003-04 Enrollment: 4,543 . . . . (845) 355-5110
Housing: Homeownership rate: 72.8% (2005); Median home value: $163,158 (2005); Median rent: $600 per month (2000); Median age of housing: 57 years (2000).
Transportation: Commute to work: 94.0% car, 0.6% public transportation, 3.2% walk, 1.6% work from home (2000); Travel time to work: 27.3% less than 15 minutes, 32.4% 15 to 30 minutes, 18.8% 30 to 45 minutes, 6.1% 45 to 60 minutes, 15.4% 60 minutes or more (2000)
Additional Information Contacts
Village of Otisville. . . . . (845) 386-5172
  http://www.villageofotisville.com/

PINE BUSH (CDP). Covers a land area of 2.096 square miles and a water area of 0 square miles. Located at 41.60° N. Lat.; 74.29° W. Long. Elevation is 396 feet.
Population: 1,387 (1990); 1,539 (2000); 1,572 (2005); 1,611 (2010 projected); Race: 92.0% White, 1.0% Black, 1.8% Asian, 5.3% Hispanic of any race (2005); Density: 750.2 persons per square mile (2005); Average household size: 2.44 (2005); Median age: 37.4 (2005); Males per 100 females: 86.3 (2005); Marriage status: 26.4% never married, 53.6% now married, 11.9% widowed, 8.1% divorced (2000); Foreign born: 6.4% (2000); Ancestry (includes multiple ancestries): 24.4% Irish, 20.1% Italian, 18.4% German, 14.3% Polish, 10.6% English (2000).
Economy: Manufacturing of textiles. Employment by occupation: 9.7% management, 22.9% professional, 14.8% services, 27.7% sales, 1.0% farming, 14.4% construction, 9.5% production (2000).
Income: Per capita income: $26,062 (2005); Median household income: $54,590 (2005); Average household income: $63,698 (2005); Percent of households with income of $100,000 or more: 17.6% (2005); Poverty rate: 4.5% (2000).
Education: Percent of population age 25 and over with: High school diploma (including GED) or higher: 84.5% (2005); Bachelor's degree or higher: 17.5% (2005); Master's degree or higher: 10.3% (2005).
School District(s)
Pine Bush Central School District (KG-12)
    2003-04 Enrollment: 6,118 . . . . (845) 744-2031
Housing: Homeownership rate: 56.1% (2005); Median home value: $182,914 (2005); Median rent: $528 per month (2000); Median age of housing: 44 years (2000).
Transportation: Commute to work: 89.0% car, 2.4% public transportation, 6.7% walk, 1.8% work from home (2000); Travel time to work: 21.0% less than 15 minutes, 39.1% 15 to 30 minutes, 15.7% 30 to 45 minutes, 9.1% 45 to 60 minutes, 15.1% 60 minutes or more (2000)

PINE ISLAND (unincorporated postal area, zip code 10969). Covers a land area of 10.599 square miles and a water area of 0.016 square miles. Located at 41.29° N. Lat.; 74.48° W. Long. Elevation is 406 feet.
Population: 0 (2000); Race: 98.2% White, 0.6% Black, 1.2% Asian, 9.3% Hispanic of any race (2000); Density: 0.0 persons per square mile (2000); Age: 25.3% under 18, 13.1% over 64 (2000); Marriage status: 24.9% never married, 60.8% now married, 8.9% widowed, 5.3% divorced (2000); Foreign born: 16.0% (2000); Ancestry (includes multiple ancestries): 30.8% Irish, 21.7% Polish, 19.0% Italian, 12.9% Other groups, 7.5% Dutch (2000).
Economy: Employment by occupation: 16.3% management, 18.4% professional, 18.0% services, 29.9% sales, 3.7% farming, 8.7% construction, 5.0% production (2000).
Income: Per capita income: $25,388 (2000); Median household income: $46,083 (2000); Poverty rate: 7.0% (2000).
Education: Percent of population age 25 and over with: High school diploma (including GED) or higher: 74.0% (2000); Bachelor's degree or higher: 15.4% (2000).
School District(s)
Warwick Valley Central School District (KG-12)
    2003-04 Enrollment: 4,682 . . . . (845) 987-3010
Housing: Homeownership rate: 79.3% (2000); Median home value: $144,100 (2000); Median rent: $658 per month (2000); Median age of housing: 38 years (2000).
Transportation: Commute to work: 88.7% car, 0.0% public transportation, 2.0% walk, 5.9% work from home (2000); Travel time to work: 30.6% less than 15 minutes, 25.1% 15 to 30 minutes, 6.7% 30 to 45 minutes, 2.1% 45 to 60 minutes, 35.5% 60 minutes or more (2000)

PORT JERVIS (city). Covers a land area of 2.536 square miles and a water area of 0.178 square miles. Located at 41.37° N. Lat.; 74.68° W. Long. Elevation is 442 feet.
History: Grew after opening (1828) of Delaware and Hudson Canal. It is one of the largest equestrian centers in nation. Settled before 1700, Incorporated 1907.
Population: 9,060 (1990); 8,860 (2000); 9,192 (2005); 9,605 (2010 projected); Race: 84.8% White, 7.2% Black, 0.9% Asian, 11.3% Hispanic of any race (2005); Density: 3,625.0 persons per square mile (2005); Average household size: 2.47 (2005); Median age: 35.6 (2005); Males per 100 females: 91.7 (2005); Marriage status: 31.6% never married, 49.5% now married, 8.0% widowed, 11.0% divorced (2000); Foreign born: 3.0% (2000); Ancestry (includes multiple ancestries): 20.2% German, 19.2% Irish, 14.5% Other groups, 12.0% Italian, 8.4% English (2000).
Economy: Manufacturing of glass, office and school supplies, rubber products, apparel, chemcals, consumer goods and building materials. At the terminus of the Port Jervis Branch of Metro-North commuter railroad. It is one of the largest equestrian centers inthe nation. Single-family building permits issued: 14 (2005); Multi-family building permits issued: 0 (2005); Employment by occupation: 7.2% management, 11.1% professional, 20.9% services, 26.2% sales, 0.7% farming, 12.2% construction, 21.8% production (2000).

Income: Per capita income: $17,734 (2005); Median household income: $32,577 (2005); Average household income: $42,775 (2005); Percent of households with income of $100,000 or more: 5.8% (2005); Poverty rate: 17.5% (2000).
Education: Percent of population age 25 and over with: High school diploma (including GED) or higher: 72.7% (2005); Bachelor's degree or higher: 8.5% (2005); Master's degree or higher: 4.0% (2005).

School District(s)
Port Jervis City School District (KG-12)
   2003-04 Enrollment: 3,444 .... (845) 858-3175
Housing: Homeownership rate: 44.8% (2005); Median home value: $124,438 (2005); Median rent: $516 per month (2000); Median age of housing: 60+ years (2000).
Hospitals: Bon Secours Community Hospital (187 beds)
Safety: Violent crime rate: 23.0 per 10,000 population; Property crime rate: 244.6 per 10,000 population (2004).
Transportation: Commute to work: 86.0% car, 3.2% public transportation, 8.3% walk, 1.1% work from home (2000); Travel time to work: 53.8% less than 15 minutes, 17.5% 15 to 30 minutes, 14.9% 30 to 45 minutes, 4.2% 45 to 60 minutes, 9.6% 60 minutes or more (2000)

Additional Information Contacts
City of Port Jervis............................... (845) 858-4014
   http://portjervisny.org/
Port Jervis Chamber of Commerce .... (845) 856-6694
   http://www.tristatechamber.org

ROCK TAVERN (unincorporated postal area, zip code 12575).
Covers a land area of 15.797 square miles and a water area of 0.030 square miles. Located at 41.47° N. Lat.; 74.15° W. Long.
Population: 0 (2000); Race: 93.1% White, 3.8% Black, 0.7% Asian, 3.9% Hispanic of any race (2000); Density: 0.0 persons per square mile (2000); Age: 31.8% under 18, 6.4% over 64 (2000); Marriage status: 19.2% never married, 69.7% now married, 3.0% widowed, 8.1% divorced (2000); Foreign born: 7.2% (2000); Ancestry (includes multiple ancestries): 37.2% Irish, 20.4% Italian, 16.1% German, 9.9% English, 9.6% Other groups (2000).
Economy: Employment by occupation: 10.8% management, 16.7% professional, 11.0% services, 32.3% sales, 0.0% farming, 22.6% construction, 6.8% production (2000).
Income: Per capita income: $21,803 (2000); Median household income: $59,659 (2000); Poverty rate: 9.4% (2000).
Education: Percent of population age 25 and over with: High school diploma (including GED) or higher: 87.3% (2000); Bachelor's degree or higher: 19.2% (2000).
Housing: Homeownership rate: 84.6% (2000); Median home value: $187,200 (2000); Median rent: $532 per month (2000); Median age of housing: 21 years (2000).
Transportation: Commute to work: 95.5% car, 2.4% public transportation, 0.0% walk, 2.2% work from home (2000); Travel time to work: 23.4% less than 15 minutes, 32.6% 15 to 30 minutes, 14.5% 30 to 45 minutes, 7.4% 45 to 60 minutes, 22.1% 60 minutes or more (2000)

SALISBURY MILLS (unincorporated postal area, zip code 12577).
Covers a land area of 5.298 square miles and a water area of 0 square miles. Located at 41.43° N. Lat.; 74.12° W. Long.
Population: 0 (2000); Race: 91.9% White, 3.1% Black, 1.1% Asian, 14.0% Hispanic of any race (2000); Density: 0.0 persons per square mile (2000); Age: 33.9% under 18, 8.7% over 64 (2000); Marriage status: 24.1% never married, 68.1% now married, 3.9% widowed, 3.8% divorced (2000); Foreign born: 7.7% (2000); Ancestry (includes multiple ancestries): 27.0% Italian, 23.3% Irish, 14.4% German, 13.7% Other groups, 7.4% Polish (2000).
Economy: Employment by occupation: 16.9% management, 27.9% professional, 10.2% services, 25.6% sales, 0.0% farming, 5.4% construction, 14.0% production (2000).
Income: Per capita income: $23,714 (2000); Median household income: $57,012 (2000); Poverty rate: 0.7% (2000).
Education: Percent of population age 25 and over with: High school diploma (including GED) or higher: 93.3% (2000); Bachelor's degree or higher: 28.0% (2000).
Housing: Homeownership rate: 92.3% (2000); Median home value: $167,000 (2000); Median rent: $665 per month (2000); Median age of housing: 31 years (2000).
Transportation: Commute to work: 94.3% car, 4.8% public transportation, 0.0% walk, 0.9% work from home (2000); Travel time to work: 14.5% less than 15 minutes, 29.9% 15 to 30 minutes, 15.8% 30 to 45 minutes, 17.1% 45 to 60 minutes, 22.7% 60 minutes or more (2000)

SCOTCHTOWN (CDP). Covers a land area of 4.234 square miles and a water area of 0 square miles. Located at 41.47° N. Lat.; 74.36° W. Long. Elevation is 725 feet.
Population: 8,765 (1990); 8,954 (2000); 9,186 (2005); 9,523 (2010 projected); Race: 67.6% White, 16.1% Black, 4.8% Asian, 20.2% Hispanic of any race (2005); Density: 2,169.4 persons per square mile (2005); Average household size: 2.73 (2005); Median age: 36.1 (2005); Males per 100 females: 94.5 (2005); Marriage status: 26.5% never married, 58.4% now married, 5.4% widowed, 9.7% divorced (2000); Foreign born: 8.3% (2000); Ancestry (includes multiple ancestries): 25.6% Other groups, 21.6% Italian, 19.7% Irish, 11.4% German, 6.1% Polish (2000).
Economy: Employment by occupation: 11.6% management, 19.4% professional, 13.3% services, 35.8% sales, 0.2% farming, 9.4% construction, 10.2% production (2000).
Income: Per capita income: $25,369 (2005); Median household income: $61,263 (2005); Average household income: $68,634 (2005); Percent of households with income of $100,000 or more: 17.2% (2005); Poverty rate: 5.2% (2000).
Education: Percent of population age 25 and over with: High school diploma (including GED) or higher: 89.4% (2005); Bachelor's degree or higher: 20.4% (2005); Master's degree or higher: 7.6% (2005).
Housing: Homeownership rate: 52.6% (2005); Median home value: $218,973 (2005); Median rent: $704 per month (2000); Median age of housing: 24 years (2000).
Transportation: Commute to work: 89.8% car, 7.6% public transportation, 1.0% walk, 1.6% work from home (2000); Travel time to work: 31.7% less than 15 minutes, 26.7% 15 to 30 minutes, 11.4% 30 to 45 minutes, 8.9% 45 to 60 minutes, 21.4% 60 minutes or more (2000)

SLATE HILL (unincorporated postal area, zip code 10973). Covers a land area of 7.451 square miles and a water area of 0.044 square miles. Located at 41.39° N. Lat.; 74.47° W. Long. Elevation is 505 feet.
Population: 0 (2000); Race: 94.1% White, 0.4% Black, 0.0% Asian, 1.8% Hispanic of any race (2000); Density: 0.0 persons per square mile (2000); Age: 22.0% under 18, 14.4% over 64 (2000); Marriage status: 22.8% never married, 64.5% now married, 5.0% widowed, 7.7% divorced (2000); Foreign born: 5.0% (2000); Ancestry (includes multiple ancestries): 21.9% Italian, 20.1% Irish, 17.0% German, 11.5% English, 6.3% Other groups (2000).
Economy: Employment by occupation: 7.2% management, 21.0% professional, 14.8% services, 23.5% sales, 0.0% farming, 8.9% construction, 24.6% production (2000).
Income: Per capita income: $24,078 (2000); Median household income: $55,729 (2000); Poverty rate: 4.7% (2000).
Education: Percent of population age 25 and over with: High school diploma (including GED) or higher: 83.7% (2000); Bachelor's degree or higher: 17.0% (2000).

School District(s)
Minisink Valley Central School District (KG-12)
   2003-04 Enrollment: 4,543 .... (845) 355-5110
Housing: Homeownership rate: 83.2% (2000); Median home value: $154,800 (2000); Median rent: $488 per month (2000); Median age of housing: 28 years (2000).
Transportation: Commute to work: 92.8% car, 2.7% public transportation, 1.6% walk, 2.9% work from home (2000); Travel time to work: 23.9% less than 15 minutes, 49.0% 15 to 30 minutes, 10.5% 30 to 45 minutes, 5.8% 45 to 60 minutes, 10.9% 60 minutes or more (2000)

SOUTHFIELDS (unincorporated postal area, zip code 10975). Covers a land area of 3.324 square miles and a water area of 0 square miles. Located at 41.24° N. Lat.; 74.17° W. Long. Elevation is 491 feet.
Population: 0 (2000); Race: 100.0% White, 0.0% Black, 0.0% Asian, 4.8% Hispanic of any race (2000); Density: 0.0 persons per square mile (2000); Age: 13.5% under 18, 2.0% over 64 (2000); Marriage status: 45.2% never married, 35.0% now married, 0.0% widowed, 19.8% divorced (2000); Foreign born: 4.8% (2000); Ancestry (includes multiple ancestries): 29.5% Irish, 29.1% German, 20.3% Other groups, 13.9% Italian, 11.2% English (2000).
Economy: Light manufacturing. Bear Mt. recreational area is just East. Employment by occupation: 12.1% management, 6.7% professional, 16.4% services, 41.8% sales, 0.0% farming, 18.8% construction, 4.2% production (2000).

Income: Per capita income: $21,659 (2000); Median household income: $43,482 (2000); Poverty rate: 12.4% (2000).
Education: Percent of population age 25 and over with: High school diploma (including GED) or higher: 87.4% (2000); Bachelor's degree or higher: 30.8% (2000).
Housing: Homeownership rate: 31.1% (2000); Median home value: $n/a (2000); Median rent: $796 per month (2000); Median age of housing: 28 years (2000).
Transportation: Commute to work: 100.0% car, 0.0% public transportation, 0.0% walk, 0.0% work from home (2000); Travel time to work: 9.1% less than 15 minutes, 33.9% 15 to 30 minutes, 44.2% 30 to 45 minutes, 0.0% 45 to 60 minutes, 12.7% 60 minutes or more (2000)

SPARROW BUSH (unincorporated postal area, zip code 12780).
Covers a land area of 28.563 square miles and a water area of 0.540 square miles. Located at 41.42° N. Lat.; 74.72° W. Long.
Population: 0 (2000); Race: 97.1% White, 1.0% Black, 0.0% Asian, 1.7% Hispanic of any race (2000); Density: 0.0 persons per square mile (2000); Age: 27.3% under 18, 11.9% over 64 (2000); Marriage status: 19.0% never married, 64.9% now married, 5.6% widowed, 10.4% divorced (2000); Foreign born: 1.9% (2000); Ancestry (includes multiple ancestries): 25.9% German, 19.1% Irish, 17.0% Italian, 14.2% English, 7.0% Dutch (2000).
Economy: Resort village. Employment by occupation: 9.5% management, 10.3% professional, 17.5% services, 18.4% sales, 0.0% farming, 18.6% construction, 25.8% production (2000).
Income: Per capita income: $17,655 (2000); Median household income: $41,989 (2000); Poverty rate: 13.4% (2000).
Education: Percent of population age 25 and over with: High school diploma (including GED) or higher: 77.2% (2000); Bachelor's degree or higher: 9.6% (2000).
Housing: Homeownership rate: 77.0% (2000); Median home value: $104,300 (2000); Median rent: $636 per month (2000); Median age of housing: 28 years (2000).
Transportation: Commute to work: 95.5% car, 2.0% public transportation, 0.0% walk, 1.7% work from home (2000); Travel time to work: 25.1% less than 15 minutes, 32.7% 15 to 30 minutes, 24.2% 30 to 45 minutes, 8.8% 45 to 60 minutes, 9.2% 60 minutes or more (2000)

THOMPSON RIDGE (unincorporated postal area, zip code 10985).
Covers a land area of 0.246 square miles and a water area of 0 square miles. Located at 41.58° N. Lat.; 74.37° W. Long.
Population: 0 (2000); Race: 100.0% White, 0.0% Black, 0.0% Asian, 0.0% Hispanic of any race (2000); Density: 0.0 persons per square mile (2000); Age: 54.8% under 18, 0.0% over 64 (2000); Marriage status: 28.2% never married, 56.4% now married, 0.0% widowed, 15.4% divorced (2000); Foreign born: 0.0% (2000); Ancestry (includes multiple ancestries): 46.8% Italian, 25.8% German, 9.7% Polish, 9.7% Other groups, 8.1% Irish (2000).
Economy: Employment by occupation: 35.3% management, 29.4% professional, 35.3% services, 0.0% sales, 0.0% farming, 0.0% construction, 0.0% production (2000).
Income: Per capita income: $16,197 (2000); Median household income: $66,250 (2000); Poverty rate: 0.0% (2000).
Education: Percent of population age 25 and over with: High school diploma (including GED) or higher: 78.6% (2000); Bachelor's degree or higher: 0.0% (2000).
Housing: Homeownership rate: 100.0% (2000); Median home value: $143,800 (2000); Median rent: $n/a per month (2000); Median age of housing: 17 years (2000).
Transportation: Commute to work: 100.0% car, 0.0% public transportation, 0.0% walk, 0.0% work from home (2000); Travel time to work: 64.7% less than 15 minutes, 35.3% 15 to 30 minutes, 0.0% 30 to 45 minutes, 0.0% 45 to 60 minutes, 0.0% 60 minutes or more (2000)

TUXEDO (town).
Covers a land area of 47.436 square miles and a water area of 1.920 square miles. Located at 41.22° N. Lat.; 74.18° W. Long.
History: Tuxedo Park colony here, a private residential development begun (1886) by Pierre Lorillard, became known for its sports and social functions. King's College relocated here from Briarcliff Manor.
Population: 3,023 (1990); 3,334 (2000); 3,747 (2005); 4,169 (2010 projected); Race: 88.5% White, 1.9% Black, 5.3% Asian, 6.9% Hispanic of any race (2005); Density: 79.0 persons per square mile (2005); Average household size: 2.46 (2005); Median age: 42.5 (2005); Males per 100 females: 99.2 (2005); Marriage status: 22.4% never married, 63.9% now married, 5.6% widowed, 8.1% divorced (2000); Foreign born: 10.0% (2000); Ancestry (includes multiple ancestries): 23.6% Irish, 23.2% Italian, 15.1% German, 12.2% Other groups, 11.2% English (2000).
Economy: Single-family building permits issued: 14 (2005); Multi-family building permits issued: 0 (2005); Employment by occupation: 20.3% management, 24.3% professional, 12.9% services, 29.0% sales, 0.1% farming, 8.3% construction, 5.2% production (2000).
Income: Per capita income: $46,791 (2005); Median household income: $79,964 (2005); Average household income: $114,518 (2005); Percent of households with income of $100,000 or more: 39.0% (2005); Poverty rate: 3.9% (2000).
Education: Percent of population age 25 and over with: High school diploma (including GED) or higher: 93.1% (2005); Bachelor's degree or higher: 46.6% (2005); Master's degree or higher: 23.0% (2005).
Housing: Homeownership rate: 73.9% (2005); Median home value: $437,166 (2005); Median rent: $754 per month (2000); Median age of housing: 38 years (2000).
Safety: Violent crime rate: 10.2 per 10,000 population; Property crime rate: 81.8 per 10,000 population (2004).
Transportation: Commute to work: 83.4% car, 8.3% public transportation, 2.8% walk, 5.1% work from home (2000); Travel time to work: 18.3% less than 15 minutes, 26.6% 15 to 30 minutes, 20.0% 30 to 45 minutes, 11.5% 45 to 60 minutes, 23.7% 60 minutes or more (2000)
Additional Information Contacts
Town of Tuxedo . . . . (845) 351-2265
  http://www.tuxedogov.org/

TUXEDO PARK (village).
Aka Tuxedo. Covers a land area of 2.679 square miles and a water area of 0.552 square miles. Located at 41.20° N. Lat.; 74.20° W. Long. Elevation is 420 feet.
Population: 706 (1990); 731 (2000); 763 (2005); 796 (2010 projected); Race: 91.5% White, 0.8% Black, 4.2% Asian, 7.9% Hispanic of any race (2005); Density: 284.8 persons per square mile (2005); Average household size: 2.49 (2005); Median age: 45.9 (2005); Males per 100 females: 97.7 (2005); Marriage status: 20.1% never married, 66.7% now married, 4.6% widowed, 8.6% divorced (2000); Foreign born: 15.4% (2000); Ancestry (includes multiple ancestries): 19.4% Other groups, 18.7% Irish, 14.5% Italian, 11.7% English, 10.5% German (2000).
Economy: Single-family building permits issued: 0 (2005); Multi-family building permits issued: 0 (2005); Employment by occupation: 31.2% management, 32.6% professional, 9.7% services, 21.3% sales, 0.6% farming, 2.8% construction, 1.9% production (2000).
Income: Per capita income: $60,704 (2005); Median household income: $89,688 (2005); Average household income: $150,871 (2005); Percent of households with income of $100,000 or more: 44.6% (2005); Poverty rate: 4.4% (2000).
Education: Percent of population age 25 and over with: High school diploma (including GED) or higher: 96.4% (2005); Bachelor's degree or higher: 67.5% (2005); Master's degree or higher: 39.6% (2005).
School District(s)
Tuxedo Union Free School District (KG-12)
  2003-04 Enrollment: 614 . . . . (845) 351-4799
Housing: Homeownership rate: 80.5% (2005); Median home value: $1 million+ (2005); Median rent: $732 per month (2000); Median age of housing: 60+ years (2000).
Transportation: Commute to work: 74.6% car, 16.6% public transportation, 3.9% walk, 4.4% work from home (2000); Travel time to work: 20.2% less than 15 minutes, 15.6% 15 to 30 minutes, 15.0% 30 to 45 minutes, 11.3% 45 to 60 minutes, 37.9% 60 minutes or more (2000)

UNIONVILLE (village).
Covers a land area of 0.250 square miles and a water area of 0 square miles. Located at 41.30° N. Lat.; 74.56° W. Long. Elevation is 1,518 feet.
Population: 548 (1990); 536 (2000); 700 (2005); 865 (2010 projected); Race: 93.0% White, 0.4% Black, 0.0% Asian, 11.4% Hispanic of any race (2005); Density: 2,795.1 persons per square mile (2005); Average household size: 2.70 (2005); Median age: 39.3 (2005); Males per 100 females: 88.7 (2005); Marriage status: 24.7% never married, 52.8% now married, 7.1% widowed, 15.4% divorced (2000); Foreign born: 1.7% (2000); Ancestry (includes multiple ancestries): 27.1% Irish, 19.1% German, 12.7% Other groups, 11.8% English, 8.8% Polish (2000).
Economy: Manufacturing of textiles, rubber goods. Summer resort. Single-family building permits issued: 2 (2005); Multi-family building permits issued: 0 (2005); Employment by occupation: 10.6% management, 17.3% professional, 30.2% services, 15.3% sales, 1.2% farming, 10.6% construction, 14.9% production (2000).

Income: Per capita income: $19,631 (2005); Median household income: $41,955 (2005); Average household income: $51,400 (2005); Percent of households with income of $100,000 or more: 9.7% (2005); Poverty rate: 8.4% (2000).
Education: Percent of population age 25 and over with: High school diploma (including GED) or higher: 74.6% (2005); Bachelor's degree or higher: 12.5% (2005); Master's degree or higher: 4.8% (2005).
Housing: Homeownership rate: 76.1% (2005); Median home value: $150,410 (2005); Median rent: $470 per month (2000); Median age of housing: 60+ years (2000).
Transportation: Commute to work: 93.6% car, 0.0% public transportation, 0.8% walk, 3.2% work from home (2000); Travel time to work: 13.6% less than 15 minutes, 42.1% 15 to 30 minutes, 21.5% 30 to 45 minutes, 9.5% 45 to 60 minutes, 13.2% 60 minutes or more (2000).

VAILS GATE (CDP). Covers a land area of 0.997 square miles and a water area of 0 square miles. Located at 41.45° N. Lat.; 74.05° W. Long.
Population: 3,014 (1990); 3,319 (2000); 3,357 (2005); 3,416 (2010 projected); Race: 60.9% White, 16.5% Black, 6.4% Asian, 27.3% Hispanic of any race (2005); Density: 3,368.6 persons per square mile (2005); Average household size: 2.28 (2005); Median age: 38.4 (2005); Males per 100 females: 92.5 (2005); Marriage status: 23.0% never married, 54.3% now married, 8.5% widowed, 14.2% divorced (2000); Foreign born: 11.0% (2000); Ancestry (includes multiple ancestries): 38.3% Other groups, 19.7% Irish, 16.0% Italian, 9.7% German, 8.4% English (2000).
Economy: Employment by occupation: 11.3% management, 20.5% professional, 19.1% services, 27.3% sales, 0.0% farming, 11.5% construction, 10.3% production (2000).
Income: Per capita income: $23,890 (2005); Median household income: $44,675 (2005); Average household income: $54,445 (2005); Percent of households with income of $100,000 or more: 10.3% (2005); Poverty rate: 10.4% (2000).
Education: Percent of population age 25 and over with: High school diploma (including GED) or higher: 87.5% (2005); Bachelor's degree or higher: 19.4% (2005); Master's degree or higher: 8.9% (2005).
Housing: Homeownership rate: 44.9% (2005); Median home value: $184,946 (2005); Median rent: $692 per month (2000); Median age of housing: 32 years (2000).
Transportation: Commute to work: 88.8% car, 6.2% public transportation, 3.5% walk, 1.5% work from home (2000); Travel time to work: 28.1% less than 15 minutes, 28.9% 15 to 30 minutes, 14.5% 30 to 45 minutes, 13.7% 45 to 60 minutes, 14.9% 60 minutes or more (2000).

WALDEN (village). Covers a land area of 1.970 square miles and a water area of 0.081 square miles. Located at 41.56° N. Lat.; 74.18° W. Long. Elevation is 353 feet.
History: Former factory town. Incorporated 1855.
Population: 5,817 (1990); 6,164 (2000); 6,787 (2005); 7,437 (2010 projected); Race: 85.7% White, 6.4% Black, 0.7% Asian, 14.5% Hispanic of any race (2005); Density: 3,445.9 persons per square mile (2005); Average household size: 2.83 (2005); Median age: 35.1 (2005); Males per 100 females: 92.8 (2005); Marriage status: 28.3% never married, 53.3% now married, 7.0% widowed, 11.5% divorced (2000); Foreign born: 4.5% (2000); Ancestry (includes multiple ancestries): 23.2% Irish, 22.6% Italian, 18.5% German, 14.0% Other groups, 13.1% English (2000).
Economy: Residential village with a few small industries; in dairying and resort area. Single-family building permits issued: 32 (2005); Multi-family building permits issued: 18 (2005); Employment by occupation: 7.1% management, 15.9% professional, 19.0% services, 28.6% sales, 0.5% farming, 10.4% construction, 18.6% production (2000).
Income: Per capita income: $20,805 (2005); Median household income: $49,527 (2005); Average household income: $58,665 (2005); Percent of households with income of $100,000 or more: 15.0% (2005); Poverty rate: 9.8% (2000).
Education: Percent of population age 25 and over with: High school diploma (including GED) or higher: 78.1% (2005); Bachelor's degree or higher: 13.3% (2005); Master's degree or higher: 4.2% (2005).
School District(s)
Valley Central School District (Montgomery) (KG-12)
    2003-04 Enrollment: 5,236 . . . . (845) 457-2400
Housing: Homeownership rate: 65.0% (2005); Median home value: $158,349 (2005); Median rent: $580 per month (2000); Median age of housing: 51 years (2000).
Safety: Violent crime rate: 16.6 per 10,000 population; Property crime rate: 228.1 per 10,000 population (2004).

Newspapers: Wallkill Valley Times (General - Circulation 5,000)
Transportation: Commute to work: 90.0% car, 2.0% public transportation, 5.6% walk, 1.8% work from home (2000); Travel time to work: 30.2% less than 15 minutes, 39.0% 15 to 30 minutes, 14.5% 30 to 45 minutes, 8.1% 45 to 60 minutes, 8.2% 60 minutes or more (2000).

WALLKILL (town). Covers a land area of 62.174 square miles and a water area of 0.582 square miles. Located at 41.47° N. Lat.; 74.39° W. Long.
Population: 23,025 (1990); 24,659 (2000); 26,636 (2005); 28,776 (2010 projected); Race: 73.7% White, 12.9% Black, 3.2% Asian, 18.7% Hispanic of any race (2005); Density: 428.4 persons per square mile (2005); Average household size: 2.72 (2005); Median age: 37.4 (2005); Males per 100 females: 94.3 (2005); Marriage status: 26.7% never married, 56.9% now married, 7.1% widowed, 9.3% divorced (2000); Foreign born: 8.9% (2000); Ancestry (includes multiple ancestries): 22.3% Other groups, 19.7% Italian, 18.7% Irish, 13.6% German, 6.9% English (2000).
Economy: Unemployment rate: 3.9% (2005); Total civilian labor force: 14,309 (2005); Single-family building permits issued: 142 (2005); Multi-family building permits issued: 4 (2005); Employment by occupation: 10.4% management, 18.2% professional, 15.9% services, 32.5% sales, 0.2% farming, 10.4% construction, 12.4% production (2000).
Income: Per capita income: $24,604 (2005); Median household income: $59,362 (2005); Average household income: $66,220 (2005); Percent of households with income of $100,000 or more: 16.7% (2005); Poverty rate: 8.4% (2000).
Taxes: Total city taxes per capita: $356 (2004); City property taxes per capita: $283 (2004).
Education: Percent of population age 25 and over with: High school diploma (including GED) or higher: 83.8% (2005); Bachelor's degree or higher: 17.8% (2005); Master's degree or higher: 6.8% (2005).
School District(s)
Wallkill Central School District (KG-12)
    2003-04 Enrollment: 3,638 . . . . (845) 895-7101
Housing: Homeownership rate: 61.3% (2005); Median home value: $187,884 (2005); Median rent: $679 per month (2000); Median age of housing: 26 years (2000).
Safety: Violent crime rate: 4.6 per 10,000 population; Property crime rate: 101.9 per 10,000 population (2004).
Transportation: Commute to work: 92.1% car, 4.6% public transportation, 1.2% walk, 1.6% work from home (2000); Travel time to work: 33.0% less than 15 minutes, 29.0% 15 to 30 minutes, 13.7% 30 to 45 minutes, 7.0% 45 to 60 minutes, 17.3% 60 minutes or more (2000).
Additional Information Contacts
Town of Wallkill . . . . (845) 692-7830
    http://www.townofwallkill.com/

WALTON PARK (CDP). Covers a land area of 2.370 square miles and a water area of 0.310 square miles. Located at 41.31° N. Lat.; 74.22° W. Long.
Population: 2,231 (1990); 2,330 (2000); 2,618 (2005); 2,917 (2010 projected); Race: 90.6% White, 1.6% Black, 2.0% Asian, 11.2% Hispanic of any race (2005); Density: 1,104.5 persons per square mile (2005); Average household size: 2.98 (2005); Median age: 37.7 (2005); Males per 100 females: 99.8 (2005); Marriage status: 21.5% never married, 70.8% now married, 4.5% widowed, 3.2% divorced (2000); Foreign born: 7.5% (2000); Ancestry (includes multiple ancestries): 29.1% Irish, 21.1% German, 19.6% Italian, 9.5% Polish, 8.5% Other groups (2000).
Economy: Employment by occupation: 13.6% management, 27.7% professional, 14.9% services, 29.5% sales, 0.0% farming, 8.9% construction, 5.5% production (2000).
Income: Per capita income: $33,234 (2005); Median household income: $86,213 (2005); Average household income: $99,097 (2005); Percent of households with income of $100,000 or more: 41.5% (2005); Poverty rate: 2.4% (2000).
Education: Percent of population age 25 and over with: High school diploma (including GED) or higher: 93.4% (2005); Bachelor's degree or higher: 32.4% (2005); Master's degree or higher: 12.2% (2005).
Housing: Homeownership rate: 90.2% (2005); Median home value: $265,848 (2005); Median rent: $729 per month (2000); Median age of housing: 35 years (2000).
Transportation: Commute to work: 86.0% car, 10.1% public transportation, 0.5% walk, 3.4% work from home (2000); Travel time to work: 22.7% less than 15 minutes, 24.3% 15 to 30 minutes, 16.0% 30 to 45 minutes, 7.9% 45 to 60 minutes, 29.1% 60 minutes or more (2000).

WARWICK (village). Covers a land area of 2.234 square miles and a water area of 0 square miles. Located at 41.25° N. Lat.; 74.35° W. Long. Elevation is 538 feet.
Population: 6,107 (1990); 6,412 (2000); 6,591 (2005); 6,855 (2010 projected); Race: 90.3% White, 4.1% Black, 0.8% Asian, 8.3% Hispanic of any race (2005); Density: 2,950.6 persons per square mile (2005); Average household size: 2.49 (2005); Median age: 40.8 (2005); Males per 100 females: 85.0 (2005); Marriage status: 21.5% never married, 63.1% now married, 9.5% widowed, 5.8% divorced (2000); Foreign born: 5.8% (2000); Ancestry (includes multiple ancestries): 26.2% Irish, 21.3% Italian, 15.7% German, 11.2% Other groups, 7.8% English (2000).
Economy: Single-family building permits issued: 44 (2005); Multi-family building permits issued: 0 (2005); Employment by occupation: 20.2% management, 26.2% professional, 17.4% services, 22.5% sales, 0.4% farming, 6.0% construction, 7.4% production (2000).
Income: Per capita income: $29,384 (2005); Median household income: $57,517 (2005); Average household income: $72,737 (2005); Percent of households with income of $100,000 or more: 23.6% (2005); Poverty rate: 4.4% (2000).
Education: Percent of population age 25 and over with: High school diploma (including GED) or higher: 85.8% (2005); Bachelor's degree or higher: 29.0% (2005); Master's degree or higher: 13.7% (2005).
School District(s)
Warwick Valley Central School District (KG-12)
    2003-04 Enrollment: 4,682 . . . . (845) 987-3010
Housing: Homeownership rate: 65.4% (2005); Median home value: $234,532 (2005); Median rent: $651 per month (2000); Median age of housing: 27 years (2000).
Hospitals: St. Anthony Community Hospital (73 beds)
Transportation: Commute to work: 85.1% car, 5.9% public transportation, 4.0% walk, 4.6% work from home (2000); Travel time to work: 33.5% less than 15 minutes, 18.1% 15 to 30 minutes, 11.5% 30 to 45 minutes, 15.4% 45 to 60 minutes, 21.4% 60 minutes or more (2000)
Additional Information Contacts
Warwick Valley Chamber of Commerce . . . . (845) 986-2720
    http://www.warwickcc.org

WARWICK (town). Covers a land area of 101.666 square miles and a water area of 3.193 square miles. Located at 41.26° N. Lat.; 74.35° W. Long. Elevation is 538 feet.
History: Warwick was settled in 1746 by English immigrants from Warwickshire. Warwick Village Historic District. Incorporated in 1867.
Population: 27,174 (1990); 30,764 (2000); 32,755 (2005); 35,051 (2010 projected); Race: 87.8% White, 6.0% Black, 1.3% Asian, 9.1% Hispanic of any race (2005); Density: 322.2 persons per square mile (2005); Average household size: 2.77 (2005); Median age: 39.1 (2005); Males per 100 females: 100.2 (2005); Marriage status: 22.4% never married, 64.8% now married, 6.1% widowed, 6.7% divorced (2000); Foreign born: 5.4% (2000); Ancestry (includes multiple ancestries): 25.6% Irish, 19.6% Italian, 18.4% German, 10.8% Other groups, 10.0% Polish (2000).
Economy: Manufacturing of stop watches, chronographs, rubber gaskets, and rubber goods; in fruit-growing area. State Training School for Boys here. Unemployment rate: 4.0% (2005); Total civilian labor force: 16,606 (2005); Single-family building permits issued: 86 (2005); Multi-family building permits issued: 0 (2005); Employment by occupation: 18.1% management, 22.0% professional, 14.4% services, 26.1% sales, 0.4% farming, 10.4% construction, 8.5% production (2000).
Income: Per capita income: $30,743 (2005); Median household income: $71,063 (2005); Average household income: $84,300 (2005); Percent of households with income of $100,000 or more: 30.5% (2005); Poverty rate: 4.7% (2000).
Education: Percent of population age 25 and over with: High school diploma (including GED) or higher: 86.0% (2005); Bachelor's degree or higher: 26.6% (2005); Master's degree or higher: 11.2% (2005).
Housing: Homeownership rate: 78.6% (2005); Median home value: $250,560 (2005); Median rent: $669 per month (2000); Median age of housing: 34 years (2000).
Transportation: Commute to work: 88.6% car, 4.9% public transportation, 2.4% walk, 3.5% work from home (2000); Travel time to work: 25.8% less than 15 minutes, 18.6% 15 to 30 minutes, 14.3% 30 to 45 minutes, 14.0% 45 to 60 minutes, 27.3% 60 minutes or more (2000)

WASHINGTON HEIGHTS (CDP). Covers a land area of 1.508 square miles and a water area of 0 square miles. Located at 41.46° N. Lat.; 74.41° W. Long.
Population: 1,164 (1990); 1,318 (2000); 1,386 (2005); 1,458 (2010 projected); Race: 75.7% White, 12.7% Black, 2.6% Asian, 17.0% Hispanic of any race (2005); Density: 919.4 persons per square mile (2005); Average household size: 2.62 (2005); Median age: 37.4 (2005); Males per 100 females: 89.6 (2005); Marriage status: 26.7% never married, 47.5% now married, 13.9% widowed, 11.8% divorced (2000); Foreign born: 4.7% (2000); Ancestry (includes multiple ancestries): 23.5% Other groups, 18.5% German, 17.3% Irish, 14.8% Italian, 11.0% English (2000).
Economy: Employment by occupation: 10.6% management, 16.9% professional, 13.7% services, 37.8% sales, 0.0% farming, 6.9% construction, 14.0% production (2000).
Income: Per capita income: $18,267 (2005); Median household income: $44,025 (2005); Average household income: $47,859 (2005); Percent of households with income of $100,000 or more: 6.8% (2005); Poverty rate: 5.3% (2000).
Education: Percent of population age 25 and over with: High school diploma (including GED) or higher: 83.3% (2005); Bachelor's degree or higher: 18.4% (2005); Master's degree or higher: 4.1% (2005).
Housing: Homeownership rate: 77.3% (2005); Median home value: $162,348 (2005); Median rent: $578 per month (2000); Median age of housing: 42 years (2000).
Transportation: Commute to work: 94.4% car, 1.4% public transportation, 4.2% walk, 0.0% work from home (2000); Travel time to work: 40.6% less than 15 minutes, 24.3% 15 to 30 minutes, 23.3% 30 to 45 minutes, 6.7% 45 to 60 minutes, 5.1% 60 minutes or more (2000)

WASHINGTONVILLE (village). Covers a land area of 2.544 square miles and a water area of 0 square miles. Located at 41.43° N. Lat.; 74.15° W. Long.
Population: 4,911 (1990); 5,851 (2000); 6,320 (2005); 6,827 (2010 projected); Race: 83.8% White, 7.5% Black, 1.8% Asian, 16.8% Hispanic of any race (2005); Density: 2,484.6 persons per square mile (2005); Average household size: 2.91 (2005); Median age: 35.9 (2005); Males per 100 females: 96.1 (2005); Marriage status: 23.3% never married, 61.6% now married, 7.7% widowed, 7.4% divorced (2000); Foreign born: 7.0% (2000); Ancestry (includes multiple ancestries): 27.3% Italian, 26.4% Irish, 17.4% German, 14.5% Other groups, 6.4% English (2000).
Economy: Manufacturing of distilled beverages, including wines and brandy spirits; in dairying and resort area. Single-family building permits issued: 0 (2005); Multi-family building permits issued: 0 (2005); Employment by occupation: 13.3% management, 20.3% professional, 17.0% services, 28.9% sales, 0.0% farming, 11.3% construction, 9.1% production (2000).
Income: Per capita income: $28,876 (2005); Median household income: $73,158 (2005); Average household income: $83,797 (2005); Percent of households with income of $100,000 or more: 30.9% (2005); Poverty rate: 3.7% (2000).
Education: Percent of population age 25 and over with: High school diploma (including GED) or higher: 88.8% (2005); Bachelor's degree or higher: 25.4% (2005); Master's degree or higher: 10.7% (2005).
School District(s)
Washingtonville Central School District (PK-12)
    2003-04 Enrollment: 5,106 . . . . (845) 497-2200
Housing: Homeownership rate: 74.9% (2005); Median home value: $225,000 (2005); Median rent: $657 per month (2000); Median age of housing: 17 years (2000).
Safety: Violent crime rate: 0.0 per 10,000 population; Property crime rate: 52.8 per 10,000 population (2004).
Newspapers: Orange County Post (General - Circulation 2,800)
Transportation: Commute to work: 91.6% car, 3.7% public transportation, 2.4% walk, 1.5% work from home (2000); Travel time to work: 17.1% less than 15 minutes, 25.7% 15 to 30 minutes, 14.2% 30 to 45 minutes, 13.7% 45 to 60 minutes, 29.4% 60 minutes or more (2000)
Additional Information Contacts
Village of Washingtonville . . . . (845) 496-3221
    http://www.washingtonville-ny.org/
Washingtonville Chamber of Commerce . . . . (845) 496-3221
    http://www.washingtonville-ny.org

WAWAYANDA (town). Covers a land area of 34.983 square miles and a water area of 0.055 square miles. Located at 41.39° N. Lat.; 74.45° W. Long.
Population: 5,445 (1990); 6,273 (2000); 7,040 (2005); 7,818 (2010 projected); Race: 89.8% White, 2.4% Black, 2.3% Asian, 9.1% Hispanic of any race (2005); Density: 201.2 persons per square mile (2005); Average household size: 2.95 (2005); Median age: 38.0 (2005); Males per 100 females: 99.7 (2005); Marriage status: 23.4% never married, 65.0% now married, 4.4% widowed, 7.2% divorced (2000); Foreign born: 7.2% (2000); Ancestry (includes multiple ancestries): 27.7% Irish, 21.7% Italian, 15.5% German, 11.4% Polish, 10.4% Other groups (2000).
Economy: Single-family building permits issued: 28 (2005); Multi-family building permits issued: 0 (2005); Employment by occupation: 10.8% management, 20.8% professional, 19.3% services, 25.6% sales, 0.6% farming, 10.2% construction, 12.7% production (2000).
Income: Per capita income: $25,935 (2005); Median household income: $68,786 (2005); Average household income: $76,065 (2005); Percent of households with income of $100,000 or more: 24.4% (2005); Poverty rate: 3.7% (2000).
Education: Percent of population age 25 and over with: High school diploma (including GED) or higher: 83.5% (2005); Bachelor's degree or higher: 18.3% (2005); Master's degree or higher: 7.8% (2005).
Housing: Homeownership rate: 85.4% (2005); Median home value: $238,495 (2005); Median rent: $629 per month (2000); Median age of housing: 28 years (2000).
Transportation: Commute to work: 91.5% car, 2.4% public transportation, 2.6% walk, 3.2% work from home (2000); Travel time to work: 27.4% less than 15 minutes, 36.3% 15 to 30 minutes, 12.7% 30 to 45 minutes, 8.4% 45 to 60 minutes, 15.2% 60 minutes or more (2000)

WEST POINT (CDP). Covers a land area of 24.325 square miles and a water area of 0.744 square miles. Located at 41.37° N. Lat.; 74.04° W. Long. Elevation is 161 feet.
History: The site of the United States Military Reservation has been known as West Point since Revolutionary times. In 1802, Congress authorized the establishment of the military academy here. It became a military school of the first order under Major Sylvanus Thayer, superintendent from 1817 to 1833. Many Civil War leaders on both sides were graduates of West Point.
Population: 8,024 (1990); 7,138 (2000); 7,506 (2005); 7,904 (2010 projected); Race: 77.0% White, 12.5% Black, 4.3% Asian, 9.0% Hispanic of any race (2005); Density: 308.6 persons per square mile (2005); Average household size: 7.60 (2005); Median age: 21.6 (2005); Males per 100 females: 207.1 (2005); Marriage status: 66.9% never married, 31.5% now married, 0.2% widowed, 1.5% divorced (2000); Foreign born: 4.7% (2000); Ancestry (includes multiple ancestries): 24.1% German, 23.7% Other groups, 17.8% Irish, 9.0% English, 8.9% Italian (2000).
Economy: Employment by occupation: 9.1% management, 51.2% professional, 12.8% services, 21.2% sales, 0.9% farming, 1.9% construction, 3.0% production (2000).
Income: Per capita income: $13,911 (2005); Median household income: $66,126 (2005); Average household income: $71,971 (2005); Percent of households with income of $100,000 or more: 19.7% (2005); Poverty rate: 2.0% (2000).
Education: Percent of population age 25 and over with: High school diploma (including GED) or higher: 98.2% (2005); Bachelor's degree or higher: 62.5% (2005); Master's degree or higher: 42.0% (2005).

Four-year College(s)
United States Military Academy (Public)
    Fall 2004 Enrollment: 4,183 . . . . (845) 938-4200
Housing: Homeownership rate: 1.3% (2005); Median home value: $1 million+ (2005); Median rent: $969 per month (2000); Median age of housing: 42 years (2000).
Hospitals: Keller Army Community Hospital (35 beds)
Transportation: Commute to work: 34.5% car, 0.8% public transportation, 57.7% walk, 4.2% work from home (2000); Travel time to work: 89.4% less than 15 minutes, 5.3% 15 to 30 minutes, 2.3% 30 to 45 minutes, 0.5% 45 to 60 minutes, 2.6% 60 minutes or more (2000)

WESTTOWN (unincorporated postal area, zip code 10998). Covers a land area of 23.985 square miles and a water area of 0.113 square miles. Located at 41.33° N. Lat.; 74.54° W. Long.
Population: 0 (2000); Race: 95.6% White, 1.7% Black, 0.1% Asian, 4.4% Hispanic of any race (2000); Density: 0.0 persons per square mile (2000); Age: 29.5% under 18, 8.4% over 64 (2000); Marriage status: 23.2% never married, 64.3% now married, 5.0% widowed, 7.5% divorced (2000); Foreign born: 3.1% (2000); Ancestry (includes multiple ancestries): 24.3% Irish, 18.6% German, 16.9% Italian, 15.6% English, 12.7% Polish (2000).
Economy: Employment by occupation: 14.0% management, 19.1% professional, 20.4% services, 21.8% sales, 1.3% farming, 11.8% construction, 11.7% production (2000).
Income: Per capita income: $21,140 (2000); Median household income: $55,638 (2000); Poverty rate: 5.8% (2000).
Education: Percent of population age 25 and over with: High school diploma (including GED) or higher: 86.7% (2000); Bachelor's degree or higher: 19.6% (2000).
Housing: Homeownership rate: 82.4% (2000); Median home value: $144,400 (2000); Median rent: $613 per month (2000); Median age of housing: 30 years (2000).
Transportation: Commute to work: 92.6% car, 0.8% public transportation, 1.7% walk, 4.2% work from home (2000); Travel time to work: 13.2% less than 15 minutes, 40.0% 15 to 30 minutes, 21.9% 30 to 45 minutes, 6.2% 45 to 60 minutes, 18.8% 60 minutes or more (2000)

WOODBURY (town). Covers a land area of 36.164 square miles and a water area of 1.014 square miles. Located at 41.33° N. Lat.; 74.12° W. Long.
Population: 8,236 (1990); 9,460 (2000); 10,931 (2005); 12,376 (2010 projected); Race: 84.8% White, 4.9% Black, 3.8% Asian, 12.5% Hispanic of any race (2005); Density: 302.3 persons per square mile (2005); Average household size: 2.98 (2005); Median age: 36.9 (2005); Males per 100 females: 95.7 (2005); Marriage status: 21.5% never married, 69.4% now married, 4.7% widowed, 4.4% divorced (2000); Foreign born: 5.6% (2000); Ancestry (includes multiple ancestries): 29.6% Irish, 27.6% Italian, 18.0% German, 14.1% Other groups, 6.5% English (2000).
Economy: Single-family building permits issued: 31 (2005); Multi-family building permits issued: 0 (2005); Employment by occupation: 18.2% management, 26.3% professional, 13.0% services, 27.7% sales, 0.4% farming, 8.5% construction, 5.9% production (2000).
Income: Per capita income: $35,108 (2005); Median household income: $92,218 (2005); Average household income: $103,926 (2005); Percent of households with income of $100,000 or more: 43.9% (2005); Poverty rate: 3.3% (2000).
Taxes: Total city taxes per capita: $886 (2004); City property taxes per capita: $754 (2004).
Education: Percent of population age 25 and over with: High school diploma (including GED) or higher: 92.2% (2005); Bachelor's degree or higher: 36.4% (2005); Master's degree or higher: 13.0% (2005).
Housing: Homeownership rate: 82.8% (2005); Median home value: $274,341 (2005); Median rent: $762 per month (2000); Median age of housing: 28 years (2000).
Safety: Violent crime rate: 3.0 per 10,000 population; Property crime rate: 337.8 per 10,000 population (2004).
Transportation: Commute to work: 87.7% car, 7.7% public transportation, 0.8% walk, 3.4% work from home (2000); Travel time to work: 20.0% less than 15 minutes, 19.1% 15 to 30 minutes, 24.0% 30 to 45 minutes, 8.7% 45 to 60 minutes, 28.2% 60 minutes or more (2000)
Additional Information Contacts
Town of Woodbury . . . . (516) 624-6332
  http://www.oysterbaytown.com

Orleans County

Located in western New York; bounded on the north by Lake Ontario; drained by Oak Orchard Creek. Covers a land area of 391.40 square miles, a water area of 426.07 square miles, and is located in the Eastern Time Zone. The county government was organized in 1824. County seat is Albion.

Orleans County is part of the Rochester, NY Metropolitan Statistical Area. The entire metro area includes: Livingston County, NY; Monroe County, NY; Ontario County, NY; Orleans County, NY; Wayne County, NY

Weather Station: Albion 2 NE | | | | | | | | | | | Elevation: 439 feet

	Jan	Feb	Mar	Apr	May	Jun	Jul	Aug	Sep	Oct	Nov	Dec
High	31	34	43	56	69	78	82	80	73	61	48	37
Low	17	18	26	36	47	56	61	60	53	42	33	24
Precip	2.6	2.1	2.8	3.1	2.9	3.5	2.6	3.1	3.8	2.9	3.2	3.2
Snow	19.1	14.9	10.2	2.2	0.3	0.0	0.0	0.0	0.0	tr	5.8	15.1

High and Low temperatures in degrees Fahrenheit; Precipitation and Snow in inches

Population: 41,846 (1990); 44,171 (2000); 43,555 (2005); 42,909 (2010 projected); Race: 89.6% White, 7.0% Black, 0.4% Asian, 3.9% Hispanic of any race (2005); Density: 111.3 persons per square mile (2005); Average household size: 2.86 (2005); Median age: 37.6 (2005); Males per 100 females: 98.5 (2005).
Religion: Five largest groups: 25.1% Catholic Church, 6.8% The United Methodist Church, 2.5% Presbyterian Church (U.S.A.), 2.3% American Baptist Churches in the USA, 1.9% Muslim Estimate (2000).
Economy: Unemployment rate: 5.7% (2005); Total civilian labor force: 20,249 (2005); Leading industries: 24.5% manufacturing; 21.4% health care and social assistance; 17.7% retail trade (2003); Farms: 504 totaling 132,947 acres (2002); Companies that employ 500 or more persons: 0 (2003); Companies that employ 100 to 499 persons: 11 (2003); Companies that employ less than 100 persons: 668 (2003); Black-owned businesses: n/a (2002); Hispanic-owned businesses: n/a (2002); Women-owned businesses: 860 (2002); Retail sales per capita: $7,516 (2006); Single-family building permits issued: 56 (2005); Multi-family building permits issued: 0 (2005).
Income: Per capita income: $18,676 (2005); Median household income: $42,828 (2005); Average household income: $51,357 (2005); Percent of households with income of $100,000 or more: 8.4% (2005); Poverty rate: 12.6% (2003); Bankruptcy rate: 8.25% (2005).
Education: Percent of population age 25 and over with: High school diploma (including GED) or higher: 76.3% (2005); Bachelor's degree or higher: 13.0% (2005); Master's degree or higher: 4.8% (2005).
Housing: Homeownership rate: 76.0% (2005); Median home value: $86,788 (2005); Median rent: $400 per month (2000); Median age of housing: 53 years (2000).
Health: Birth rate: 108.7 per 10,000 population (2004); Death rate: 82.0 per 10,000 population (2004); Age-adjusted cancer mortality rate: 228.8 deaths per 100,000 population (2002); Number of physicians: 7.1 per 10,000 population (2004); Hospital beds: 23.2 per 10,000 population (2003); Hospital admissions: 486.7 per 10,000 population (2003).
Elections: 2004 Presidential election results: 62.3% Bush, 36.0% Kerry, 1.6% Nader, 0.2% Badnarik
National and State Parks: Golden Hill State Park; Lakeside Beach State Park
Additional Information Contacts
Orleans County Government . . . . (585) 589-7053
  http://www.orleansny.com/
Village of Medina . . . . (585) 798-0710
  http://villagemedina.org/content

Orleans County Communities

ALBION (village). Covers a land area of 2.973 square miles and a water area of 0 square miles. Located at 43.24° N. Lat.; 78.19° W. Long. Elevation is 519 feet.
Population: 5,904 (1990); 7,438 (2000); 7,227 (2005); 7,038 (2010 projected); Race: 73.2% White, 17.9% Black, 0.8% Asian, 10.7% Hispanic of any race (2005); Density: 2,430.8 persons per square mile (2005); Average household size: 3.29 (2005); Median age: 33.6 (2005); Males per 100 females: 146.4 (2005); Marriage status: 41.1% never married, 42.2% now married, 7.5% widowed, 9.2% divorced (2000); Foreign born: 5.6% (2000); Ancestry (includes multiple ancestries): 20.2% German, 14.9% English, 14.2% Other groups, 11.3% Irish, 8.5% Italian (2000).
Economy: Single-family building permits issued: 1 (2005); Multi-family building permits issued: 0 (2005); Employment by occupation: 10.5% management, 17.6% professional, 16.3% services, 21.6% sales, 2.0% farming, 9.0% construction, 22.9% production (2000).
Income: Per capita income: $14,160 (2005); Median household income: $31,807 (2005); Average household income: $39,415 (2005); Percent of households with income of $100,000 or more: 3.3% (2005); Poverty rate: 14.9% (2000).
Education: Percent of population age 25 and over with: High school diploma (including GED) or higher: 62.2% (2005); Bachelor's degree or higher: 9.1% (2005); Master's degree or higher: 2.7% (2005).
School District(s)
Albion Central School District (PK-12)
  2003-04 Enrollment: 2,797 . . . . (585) 589-2056
Housing: Homeownership rate: 59.0% (2005); Median home value: $71,095 (2005); Median rent: $407 per month (2000); Median age of housing: 60+ years (2000).
Safety: Violent crime rate: 63.2 per 10,000 population; Property crime rate: 311.1 per 10,000 population (2004).

Transportation: Commute to work: 93.7% car, 0.6% public transportation, 3.7% walk, 1.7% work from home (2000); Travel time to work: 45.5% less than 15 minutes, 21.6% 15 to 30 minutes, 14.5% 30 to 45 minutes, 10.3% 45 to 60 minutes, 8.0% 60 minutes or more (2000)
Additional Information Contacts
Albion Chamber of Commerce . . . . (585) 589-7727
  http://www.orleanschamber.com

ALBION (town). Covers a land area of 25.228 square miles and a water area of 0.118 square miles. Located at 43.24° N. Lat.; 78.20° W. Long. Elevation is 519 feet.
History: Albion was the home of George M. Pullman (1831-1897), originator of the Pullman railroad cars. Pullman was a cabinetmaker here from 1848 to 1855. Disgusted with the dirt, discomfort, and inconvenience of early railroad passenger cars, he conceived the idea of a car with the luxuries of beds and upholstered seats. Incorporated in 1828.
Population: 8,178 (1990); 8,042 (2000); 7,869 (2005); 7,695 (2010 projected); Race: 76.4% White, 15.9% Black, 0.7% Asian, 9.1% Hispanic of any race (2005); Density: 311.9 persons per square mile (2005); Average household size: 3.40 (2005); Median age: 35.0 (2005); Males per 100 females: 142.0 (2005); Marriage status: 38.9% never married, 44.5% now married, 8.0% widowed, 8.6% divorced (2000); Foreign born: 5.1% (2000); Ancestry (includes multiple ancestries): 20.2% German, 15.7% English, 11.2% Other groups, 11.0% Irish, 9.0% Italian (2000).
Economy: Manufactures precision and custom metal fabrication. Stone quarries. Single-family building permits issued: 5 (2005); Multi-family building permits issued: 0 (2005); Employment by occupation: 11.4% management, 20.0% professional, 16.6% services, 20.0% sales, 1.5% farming, 10.4% construction, 20.1% production (2000).
Income: Per capita income: $14,895 (2005); Median household income: $36,529 (2005); Average household income: $42,642 (2005); Percent of households with income of $100,000 or more: 5.2% (2005); Poverty rate: 14.4% (2000).
Education: Percent of population age 25 and over with: High school diploma (including GED) or higher: 64.6% (2005); Bachelor's degree or higher: 11.1% (2005); Master's degree or higher: 4.0% (2005).
Housing: Homeownership rate: 61.8% (2005); Median home value: $85,862 (2005); Median rent: $423 per month (2000); Median age of housing: 60+ years (2000).
Transportation: Commute to work: 92.7% car, 0.5% public transportation, 3.7% walk, 2.7% work from home (2000); Travel time to work: 45.6% less than 15 minutes, 22.2% 15 to 30 minutes, 13.5% 30 to 45 minutes, 10.0% 45 to 60 minutes, 8.7% 60 minutes or more (2000)

BARRE (town). Covers a land area of 55.073 square miles and a water area of 0.012 square miles. Located at 43.18° N. Lat.; 78.20° W. Long.
Population: 2,093 (1990); 2,124 (2000); 1,977 (2005); 1,900 (2010 projected); Race: 98.6% White, 0.4% Black, 0.1% Asian, 0.8% Hispanic of any race (2005); Density: 35.9 persons per square mile (2005); Average household size: 2.84 (2005); Median age: 38.9 (2005); Males per 100 females: 107.0 (2005); Marriage status: 21.1% never married, 65.2% now married, 6.8% widowed, 6.8% divorced (2000); Foreign born: 0.6% (2000); Ancestry (includes multiple ancestries): 28.6% German, 24.2% English, 16.9% Irish, 11.2% United States or American, 9.2% Italian (2000).
Economy: Single-family building permits issued: 5 (2005); Multi-family building permits issued: 0 (2005); Employment by occupation: 9.8% management, 15.2% professional, 13.2% services, 23.3% sales, 3.1% farming, 11.8% construction, 23.6% production (2000).
Income: Per capita income: $20,365 (2005); Median household income: $50,636 (2005); Average household income: $57,932 (2005); Percent of households with income of $100,000 or more: 10.8% (2005); Poverty rate: 6.3% (2000).
Education: Percent of population age 25 and over with: High school diploma (including GED) or higher: 81.6% (2005); Bachelor's degree or higher: 13.0% (2005); Master's degree or higher: 3.6% (2005).
Housing: Homeownership rate: 88.2% (2005); Median home value: $84,773 (2005); Median rent: $492 per month (2000); Median age of housing: 45 years (2000).
Transportation: Commute to work: 92.7% car, 0.0% public transportation, 2.1% walk, 4.0% work from home (2000); Travel time to work: 31.4% less than 15 minutes, 32.0% 15 to 30 minutes, 13.7% 30 to 45 minutes, 15.0% 45 to 60 minutes, 7.9% 60 minutes or more (2000)

CARLTON (town). Covers a land area of 43.708 square miles and a water area of 0.835 square miles. Located at 43.33° N. Lat.; 78.21° W. Long.
Population: 2,808 (1990); 2,960 (2000); 3,046 (2005); 3,112 (2010 projected); Race: 95.8% White, 1.9% Black, 0.1% Asian, 1.1% Hispanic of any race (2005); Density: 69.7 persons per square mile (2005); Average household size: 2.64 (2005); Median age: 40.4 (2005); Males per 100 females: 109.5 (2005); Marriage status: 23.6% never married, 61.5% now married, 4.6% widowed, 10.4% divorced (2000); Foreign born: 1.2% (2000); Ancestry (includes multiple ancestries): 24.8% German, 21.2% English, 13.6% Irish, 12.6% United States or American, 11.0% Italian (2000).
Economy: Single-family building permits issued: 15 (2005); Multi-family building permits issued: 0 (2005); Employment by occupation: 10.7% management, 13.9% professional, 18.0% services, 22.2% sales, 0.6% farming, 14.0% construction, 20.5% production (2000).
Income: Per capita income: $19,797 (2005); Median household income: $44,614 (2005); Average household income: $52,056 (2005); Percent of households with income of $100,000 or more: 8.3% (2005); Poverty rate: 10.3% (2000).
Education: Percent of population age 25 and over with: High school diploma (including GED) or higher: 85.4% (2005); Bachelor's degree or higher: 16.2% (2005); Master's degree or higher: 5.2% (2005).
Housing: Homeownership rate: 82.9% (2005); Median home value: $97,409 (2005); Median rent: $410 per month (2000); Median age of housing: 48 years (2000).
Transportation: Commute to work: 93.2% car, 0.4% public transportation, 1.5% walk, 3.7% work from home (2000); Travel time to work: 18.8% less than 15 minutes, 34.4% 15 to 30 minutes, 21.1% 30 to 45 minutes, 18.7% 45 to 60 minutes, 7.0% 60 minutes or more (2000)

CLARENDON (town). Covers a land area of 35.205 square miles and a water area of 0 square miles. Located at 43.17° N. Lat.; 78.05° W. Long.
Population: 2,705 (1990); 3,392 (2000); 3,557 (2005); 3,659 (2010 projected); Race: 96.8% White, 0.8% Black, 0.4% Asian, 1.4% Hispanic of any race (2005); Density: 101.0 persons per square mile (2005); Average household size: 2.70 (2005); Median age: 38.0 (2005); Males per 100 females: 100.8 (2005); Marriage status: 19.2% never married, 63.8% now married, 7.0% widowed, 10.0% divorced (2000); Foreign born: 0.4% (2000); Ancestry (includes multiple ancestries): 24.0% German, 21.6% Irish, 20.3% English, 13.1% Italian, 6.8% United States or American (2000).
Economy: Single-family building permits issued: 0 (2005); Multi-family building permits issued: 0 (2005); Employment by occupation: 7.3% management, 19.0% professional, 16.3% services, 21.1% sales, 0.0% farming, 10.4% construction, 25.9% production (2000).
Income: Per capita income: $22,050 (2005); Median household income: $51,047 (2005); Average household income: $59,644 (2005); Percent of households with income of $100,000 or more: 10.2% (2005); Poverty rate: 8.1% (2000).
Education: Percent of population age 25 and over with: High school diploma (including GED) or higher: 80.1% (2005); Bachelor's degree or higher: 13.6% (2005); Master's degree or higher: 2.5% (2005).
Housing: Homeownership rate: 90.0% (2005); Median home value: $93,069 (2005); Median rent: $468 per month (2000); Median age of housing: 24 years (2000).
Transportation: Commute to work: 95.1% car, 0.0% public transportation, 0.0% walk, 3.8% work from home (2000); Travel time to work: 20.4% less than 15 minutes, 25.5% 15 to 30 minutes, 36.1% 30 to 45 minutes, 10.4% 45 to 60 minutes, 7.5% 60 minutes or more (2000)

GAINES (town). Covers a land area of 34.390 square miles and a water area of 0.041 square miles. Located at 43.26° N. Lat.; 78.19° W. Long. Elevation is 428 feet.
Population: 3,025 (1990); 3,740 (2000); 3,691 (2005); 3,567 (2010 projected); Race: 94.0% White, 2.8% Black, 0.2% Asian, 3.5% Hispanic of any race (2005); Density: 107.3 persons per square mile (2005); Average household size: 2.52 (2005); Median age: 38.7 (2005); Males per 100 females: 93.2 (2005); Marriage status: 21.2% never married, 60.9% now married, 9.1% widowed, 8.8% divorced (2000); Foreign born: 2.7% (2000); Ancestry (includes multiple ancestries): 24.8% English, 21.5% German, 16.9% Other groups, 15.5% Irish, 10.5% Italian (2000).
Economy: Single-family building permits issued: 1 (2005); Multi-family building permits issued: 0 (2005); Employment by occupation: 10.2% management, 18.9% professional, 18.1% services, 21.4% sales, 0.5% farming, 7.8% construction, 23.2% production (2000).
Income: Per capita income: $18,197 (2005); Median household income: $36,090 (2005); Average household income: $45,940 (2005); Percent of households with income of $100,000 or more: 6.2% (2005); Poverty rate: 10.3% (2000).
Education: Percent of population age 25 and over with: High school diploma (including GED) or higher: 83.9% (2005); Bachelor's degree or higher: 11.3% (2005); Master's degree or higher: 4.6% (2005).
Housing: Homeownership rate: 79.7% (2005); Median home value: $69,133 (2005); Median rent: $321 per month (2000); Median age of housing: 27 years (2000).
Transportation: Commute to work: 96.3% car, 0.0% public transportation, 2.0% walk, 1.4% work from home (2000); Travel time to work: 50.2% less than 15 minutes, 19.3% 15 to 30 minutes, 14.2% 30 to 45 minutes, 9.7% 45 to 60 minutes, 6.6% 60 minutes or more (2000)

HOLLEY (village). Covers a land area of 1.266 square miles and a water area of 0 square miles. Located at 43.22° N. Lat.; 78.02° W. Long. Elevation is 512 feet.
History: Incorporated 1867.
Population: 1,925 (1990); 1,802 (2000); 1,730 (2005); 1,687 (2010 projected); Race: 97.6% White, 0.9% Black, 0.1% Asian, 2.3% Hispanic of any race (2005); Density: 1,366.1 persons per square mile (2005); Average household size: 2.25 (2005); Median age: 36.4 (2005); Males per 100 females: 97.9 (2005); Marriage status: 27.4% never married, 54.3% now married, 5.7% widowed, 12.6% divorced (2000); Foreign born: 1.4% (2000); Ancestry (includes multiple ancestries): 21.5% German, 20.2% Italian, 19.3% Irish, 18.8% English, 7.6% United States or American (2000).
Economy: Manufacturing of pallets and boxes, hardwood lumber, metal fabrications. Agriculture: fruit, grain. Single-family building permits issued: 0 (2005); Multi-family building permits issued: 0 (2005); Employment by occupation: 6.8% management, 14.2% professional, 17.7% services, 28.2% sales, 0.7% farming, 11.7% construction, 20.6% production (2000).
Income: Per capita income: $21,896 (2005); Median household income: $43,784 (2005); Average household income: $49,259 (2005); Percent of households with income of $100,000 or more: 7.5% (2005); Poverty rate: 10.2% (2000).
Education: Percent of population age 25 and over with: High school diploma (including GED) or higher: 84.6% (2005); Bachelor's degree or higher: 16.4% (2005); Master's degree or higher: 5.6% (2005).
School District(s)
Holley Central School District (PK-12)
    2003-04 Enrollment: 1,400 . . . . (585) 638-6316
Housing: Homeownership rate: 54.4% (2005); Median home value: $84,941 (2005); Median rent: $413 per month (2000); Median age of housing: 60+ years (2000).
Transportation: Commute to work: 95.0% car, 0.0% public transportation, 3.9% walk, 1.1% work from home (2000); Travel time to work: 34.9% less than 15 minutes, 23.0% 15 to 30 minutes, 28.0% 30 to 45 minutes, 9.4% 45 to 60 minutes, 4.7% 60 minutes or more (2000)

KENDALL (town). Covers a land area of 32.897 square miles and a water area of 0.077 square miles. Located at 43.33° N. Lat.; 78.04° W. Long. Elevation is 338 feet.
Population: 2,769 (1990); 2,838 (2000); 2,837 (2005); 2,813 (2010 projected); Race: 97.5% White, 0.4% Black, 0.1% Asian, 1.1% Hispanic of any race (2005); Density: 86.2 persons per square mile (2005); Average household size: 2.85 (2005); Median age: 40.6 (2005); Males per 100 females: 105.0 (2005); Marriage status: 21.7% never married, 65.0% now married, 5.0% widowed, 8.3% divorced (2000); Foreign born: 2.2% (2000); Ancestry (includes multiple ancestries): 31.6% German, 18.3% English, 16.8% Irish, 13.1% Italian, 6.9% Polish (2000).
Economy: Single-family building permits issued: 1 (2005); Multi-family building permits issued: 0 (2005); Employment by occupation: 9.0% management, 21.5% professional, 12.3% services, 25.2% sales, 2.2% farming, 12.1% construction, 17.6% production (2000).
Income: Per capita income: $24,885 (2005); Median household income: $58,550 (2005); Average household income: $70,810 (2005); Percent of households with income of $100,000 or more: 18.0% (2005); Poverty rate: 5.0% (2000).
Education: Percent of population age 25 and over with: High school diploma (including GED) or higher: 87.3% (2005); Bachelor's degree or higher: 17.4% (2005); Master's degree or higher: 7.3% (2005).

School District(s)
Kendall Central School District (KG-12)
   2003-04 Enrollment: 1,044 . . . . (585) 659-2741
Housing: Homeownership rate: 89.0% (2005); Median home value: $119,875 (2005); Median rent: $511 per month (2000); Median age of housing: 38 years (2000).
Transportation: Commute to work: 93.2% car, 0.0% public transportation, 2.3% walk, 4.2% work from home (2000); Travel time to work: 18.6% less than 15 minutes, 26.3% 15 to 30 minutes, 28.1% 30 to 45 minutes, 19.0% 45 to 60 minutes, 8.0% 60 minutes or more (2000)

KENT (unincorporated postal area, zip code 14477). Covers a land area of 26.443 square miles and a water area of 0.092 square miles. Located at 43.34° N. Lat.; 78.14° W. Long.
Population: 0 (2000); Race: 93.2% White, 3.4% Black, 1.6% Asian, 0.7% Hispanic of any race (2000); Density: 0.0 persons per square mile (2000); Age: 28.5% under 18, 9.8% over 64 (2000); Marriage status: 25.0% never married, 60.0% now married, 6.7% widowed, 8.3% divorced (2000); Foreign born: 4.5% (2000); Ancestry (includes multiple ancestries): 24.8% German, 16.3% English, 14.0% United States or American, 12.4% Irish, 10.1% Italian (2000).
Economy: Employment by occupation: 8.5% management, 17.1% professional, 17.6% services, 26.9% sales, 0.6% farming, 11.1% construction, 18.3% production (2000).
Income: Per capita income: $19,635 (2000); Median household income: $50,000 (2000); Poverty rate: 5.2% (2000).
Education: Percent of population age 25 and over with: High school diploma (including GED) or higher: 86.0% (2000); Bachelor's degree or higher: 17.6% (2000).
Housing: Homeownership rate: 86.8% (2000); Median home value: $83,800 (2000); Median rent: $390 per month (2000); Median age of housing: 46 years (2000).
Transportation: Commute to work: 95.5% car, 0.6% public transportation, 0.4% walk, 2.4% work from home (2000); Travel time to work: 13.5% less than 15 minutes, 29.4% 15 to 30 minutes, 28.2% 30 to 45 minutes, 23.0% 45 to 60 minutes, 5.9% 60 minutes or more (2000)

LYNDONVILLE (village). Covers a land area of 1.024 square miles and a water area of 0 square miles. Located at 43.32° N. Lat.; 78.38° W. Long. Elevation is 324 feet.
History: Incorporated 1903.
Population: 953 (1990); 862 (2000); 816 (2005); 782 (2010 projected); Race: 98.4% White, 0.0% Black, 0.7% Asian, 1.3% Hispanic of any race (2005); Density: 796.8 persons per square mile (2005); Average household size: 2.62 (2005); Median age: 36.5 (2005); Males per 100 females: 94.7 (2005); Marriage status: 27.0% never married, 55.1% now married, 8.3% widowed, 9.6% divorced (2000); Foreign born: 0.9% (2000); Ancestry (includes multiple ancestries): 27.3% English, 22.6% German, 15.7% Irish, 12.9% United States or American, 10.3% Italian (2000).
Economy: Manufacturing: electronic equipment, apple juice, cider, and vinegar. Agriculture: fruits, grain. Single-family building permits issued: 1 (2005); Multi-family building permits issued: 0 (2005); Employment by occupation: 10.3% management, 18.1% professional, 16.8% services, 22.2% sales, 0.5% farming, 9.0% construction, 23.0% production (2000).
Income: Per capita income: $18,615 (2005); Median household income: $42,500 (2005); Average household income: $48,686 (2005); Percent of households with income of $100,000 or more: 6.7% (2005); Poverty rate: 9.3% (2000).
Education: Percent of population age 25 and over with: High school diploma (including GED) or higher: 85.0% (2005); Bachelor's degree or higher: 18.4% (2005); Master's degree or higher: 9.7% (2005).
School District(s)
Lyndonville Central School District (KG-12)
   2003-04 Enrollment: 788 . . . . (585) 765-3101
Housing: Homeownership rate: 75.6% (2005); Median home value: $84,667 (2005); Median rent: $367 per month (2000); Median age of housing: 60+ years (2000).
Transportation: Commute to work: 91.1% car, 0.8% public transportation, 5.0% walk, 3.1% work from home (2000); Travel time to work: 32.2% less than 15 minutes, 33.3% 15 to 30 minutes, 12.2% 30 to 45 minutes, 12.2% 45 to 60 minutes, 10.0% 60 minutes or more (2000)

MEDINA (village). Covers a land area of 3.269 square miles and a water area of 0.080 square miles. Located at 43.22° N. Lat.; 78.39° W. Long. Elevation is 542 feet.
History: Incorporated 1832.
Population: 6,686 (1990); 6,415 (2000); 6,266 (2005); 6,101 (2010 projected); Race: 89.5% White, 6.3% Black, 0.7% Asian, 3.2% Hispanic of any race (2005); Density: 1,916.6 persons per square mile (2005); Average household size: 2.48 (2005); Median age: 38.1 (2005); Males per 100 females: 85.1 (2005); Marriage status: 28.6% never married, 47.8% now married, 11.6% widowed, 12.0% divorced (2000); Foreign born: 2.4% (2000); Ancestry (includes multiple ancestries): 22.9% German, 19.1% English, 15.9% Other groups, 15.4% Irish, 10.3% Polish (2000).
Economy: Manufacturing of sheet metal, clothing, paper products, consumer goods, metal fabrication, machinery, medical equipment. Agriculture: fruit. Sandstone quarries. Single-family building permits issued: 1 (2005); Multi-family building permits issued: 0 (2005); Employment by occupation: 6.6% management, 16.6% professional, 19.6% services, 19.3% sales, 0.8% farming, 9.4% construction, 27.6% production (2000).
Income: Per capita income: $17,251 (2005); Median household income: $32,049 (2005); Average household income: $40,952 (2005); Percent of households with income of $100,000 or more: 5.0% (2005); Poverty rate: 16.4% (2000).
Education: Percent of population age 25 and over with: High school diploma (including GED) or higher: 75.5% (2005); Bachelor's degree or higher: 13.8% (2005); Master's degree or higher: 5.7% (2005).
School District(s)
Boces Orleans-Niagara (PK-PK)
   2003-04 Enrollment: 159 . . . . (585) 836-7510
Medina Central School District (KG-12)
   2003-04 Enrollment: 1,954 . . . . (585) 798-2700
Housing: Homeownership rate: 59.6% (2005); Median home value: $71,263 (2005); Median rent: $369 per month (2000); Median age of housing: 60+ years (2000).
Hospitals: Medina Memorial Hospital (101 beds)
Newspapers: The Journal-Register (Circulation 4,401)
Transportation: Commute to work: 91.6% car, 0.2% public transportation, 3.9% walk, 2.8% work from home (2000); Travel time to work: 46.2% less than 15 minutes, 22.4% 15 to 30 minutes, 16.5% 30 to 45 minutes, 8.6% 45 to 60 minutes, 6.3% 60 minutes or more (2000)
Additional Information Contacts
Orleans County Chamber of Commerce . . . . (585) 798-4287
   http://www.orleanschamber.com
Village of Medina . . . . (585) 798-0710
   http://villagemedina.org/content

MURRAY (town). Covers a land area of 31.044 square miles and a water area of 0.056 square miles. Located at 43.25° N. Lat.; 78.05° W. Long. Elevation is 419 feet.
Population: 4,921 (1990); 6,259 (2000); 6,134 (2005); 6,058 (2010 projected); Race: 81.5% White, 16.9% Black, 0.1% Asian, 7.0% Hispanic of any race (2005); Density: 197.6 persons per square mile (2005); Average household size: 3.33 (2005); Median age: 36.2 (2005); Males per 100 females: 62.4 (2005); Marriage status: 39.7% never married, 47.7% now married, 3.7% widowed, 8.8% divorced (2000); Foreign born: 3.8% (2000); Ancestry (includes multiple ancestries): 23.7% German, 15.7% Irish, 14.7% Italian, 12.1% English, 5.4% United States or American (2000).
Economy: Single-family building permits issued: 6 (2005); Multi-family building permits issued: 0 (2005); Employment by occupation: 9.1% management, 15.5% professional, 13.5% services, 25.3% sales, 1.9% farming, 14.2% construction, 20.5% production (2000).
Income: Per capita income: $17,259 (2005); Median household income: $47,140 (2005); Average household income: $54,176 (2005); Percent of households with income of $100,000 or more: 9.0% (2005); Poverty rate: 6.9% (2000).
Education: Percent of population age 25 and over with: High school diploma (including GED) or higher: 68.5% (2005); Bachelor's degree or higher: 11.4% (2005); Master's degree or higher: 5.0% (2005).
Housing: Homeownership rate: 74.2% (2005); Median home value: $87,430 (2005); Median rent: $428 per month (2000); Median age of housing: 50 years (2000).
Transportation: Commute to work: 93.8% car, 0.9% public transportation, 2.8% walk, 2.0% work from home (2000); Travel time to work: 25.6% less than 15 minutes, 21.8% 15 to 30 minutes, 33.8% 30 to 45 minutes, 13.0% 45 to 60 minutes, 5.7% 60 minutes or more (2000)

RIDGEWAY (town). Covers a land area of 50.033 square miles and a water area of 0.229 square miles. Located at 43.24° N. Lat.; 78.38° W. Long. Elevation is 420 feet.

Population: 7,341 (1990); 6,886 (2000); 6,737 (2005); 6,575 (2010 projected); Race: 93.0% White, 3.4% Black, 0.7% Asian, 2.0% Hispanic of any race (2005); Density: 134.7 persons per square mile (2005); Average household size: 2.60 (2005); Median age: 37.9 (2005); Males per 100 females: 93.0 (2005); Marriage status: 26.1% never married, 57.9% now married, 6.8% widowed, 9.1% divorced (2000); Foreign born: 1.8% (2000); Ancestry (includes multiple ancestries): 27.4% German, 24.7% English, 14.3% Irish, 12.0% Other groups, 10.8% Polish (2000).
Economy: Single-family building permits issued: 8 (2005); Multi-family building permits issued: 0 (2005); Employment by occupation: 7.8% management, 13.8% professional, 20.9% services, 18.1% sales, 1.5% farming, 12.3% construction, 25.7% production (2000).
Income: Per capita income: $19,197 (2005); Median household income: $38,819 (2005); Average household income: $49,505 (2005); Percent of households with income of $100,000 or more: 8.0% (2005); Poverty rate: 14.4% (2000).
Education: Percent of population age 25 and over with: High school diploma (including GED) or higher: 82.5% (2005); Bachelor's degree or higher: 13.8% (2005); Master's degree or higher: 5.6% (2005).
Housing: Homeownership rate: 71.9% (2005); Median home value: $82,643 (2005); Median rent: $375 per month (2000); Median age of housing: 60+ years (2000).
Transportation: Commute to work: 91.5% car, 0.9% public transportation, 2.4% walk, 4.3% work from home (2000); Travel time to work: 44.3% less than 15 minutes, 26.1% 15 to 30 minutes, 14.2% 30 to 45 minutes, 7.8% 45 to 60 minutes, 7.6% 60 minutes or more (2000).

SHELBY (town). Aka Shelby Center. Covers a land area of 46.344 square miles and a water area of 0.370 square miles. Located at 43.19° N. Lat.; 78.39° W. Long.
Population: 5,509 (1990); 5,420 (2000); 5,338 (2005); 5,257 (2010 projected); Race: 91.5% White, 5.8% Black, 0.4% Asian, 2.7% Hispanic of any race (2005); Density: 115.2 persons per square mile (2005); Average household size: 2.67 (2005); Median age: 39.3 (2005); Males per 100 females: 93.6 (2005); Marriage status: 25.1% never married, 53.7% now married, 11.9% widowed, 9.2% divorced (2000); Foreign born: 2.9% (2000); Ancestry (includes multiple ancestries): 23.4% German, 21.4% English, 14.0% Irish, 11.6% Other groups, 10.6% United States or American (2000).
Economy: Single-family building permits issued: 4 (2005); Multi-family building permits issued: 0 (2005); Employment by occupation: 7.1% management, 18.3% professional, 16.0% services, 20.9% sales, 0.3% farming, 10.8% construction, 26.6% production (2000).
Income: Per capita income: $19,264 (2005); Median household income: $38,143 (2005); Average household income: $49,226 (2005); Percent of households with income of $100,000 or more: 8.3% (2005); Poverty rate: 13.7% (2000).
Education: Percent of population age 25 and over with: High school diploma (including GED) or higher: 72.6% (2005); Bachelor's degree or higher: 13.0% (2005); Master's degree or higher: 4.6% (2005).
Housing: Homeownership rate: 69.5% (2005); Median home value: $77,012 (2005); Median rent: $372 per month (2000); Median age of housing: 60+ years (2000).
Transportation: Commute to work: 93.9% car, 0.1% public transportation, 2.0% walk, 2.2% work from home (2000); Travel time to work: 49.8% less than 15 minutes, 21.9% 15 to 30 minutes, 14.7% 30 to 45 minutes, 7.3% 45 to 60 minutes, 6.3% 60 minutes or more (2000).

WATERPORT (unincorporated postal area, zip code 14571). Covers a land area of 16.194 square miles and a water area of 0.028 square miles. Located at 43.34° N. Lat.; 78.25° W. Long. Elevation is 351 feet.
Population: 0 (2000); Race: 97.6% White, 0.6% Black, 0.0% Asian, 0.0% Hispanic of any race (2000); Density: 0.0 persons per square mile (2000); Age: 27.9% under 18, 10.6% over 64 (2000); Marriage status: 23.3% never married, 61.0% now married, 3.9% widowed, 11.8% divorced (2000); Foreign born: 0.0% (2000); Ancestry (includes multiple ancestries): 24.1% German, 22.4% English, 13.3% Irish, 10.5% Italian, 10.0% United States or American (2000).
Economy: Employment by occupation: 13.8% management, 12.3% professional, 16.4% services, 24.4% sales, 0.7% farming, 14.2% construction, 18.2% production (2000).
Income: Per capita income: $16,876 (2000); Median household income: $40,915 (2000); Poverty rate: 13.9% (2000).

Education: Percent of population age 25 and over with: High school diploma (including GED) or higher: 85.7% (2000); Bachelor's degree or higher: 18.5% (2000).
Housing: Homeownership rate: 82.4% (2000); Median home value: $71,500 (2000); Median rent: $381 per month (2000); Median age of housing: 48 years (2000).
Transportation: Commute to work: 91.8% car, 0.0% public transportation, 3.2% walk, 4.3% work from home (2000); Travel time to work: 26.7% less than 15 minutes, 29.7% 15 to 30 minutes, 17.0% 30 to 45 minutes, 17.9% 45 to 60 minutes, 8.6% 60 minutes or more (2000).

YATES (town). Aka Yates Center. Covers a land area of 37.474 square miles and a water area of 0 square miles. Located at 43.34° N. Lat.; 78.39° W. Long.
Population: 2,497 (1990); 2,510 (2000); 2,369 (2005); 2,273 (2010 projected); Race: 97.6% White, 0.4% Black, 0.4% Asian, 1.1% Hispanic of any race (2005); Density: 63.2 persons per square mile (2005); Average household size: 2.70 (2005); Median age: 38.7 (2005); Males per 100 females: 99.1 (2005); Marriage status: 24.1% never married, 60.6% now married, 6.8% widowed, 8.4% divorced (2000); Foreign born: 0.8% (2000); Ancestry (includes multiple ancestries): 28.3% English, 25.7% German, 13.4% Irish, 9.0% United States or American, 8.3% Polish (2000).
Economy: Single-family building permits issued: 8 (2005); Multi-family building permits issued: 0 (2005); Employment by occupation: 7.3% management, 13.1% professional, 15.4% services, 21.0% sales, 2.5% farming, 13.2% construction, 27.4% production (2000).
Income: Per capita income: $17,492 (2005); Median household income: $41,848 (2005); Average household income: $47,142 (2005); Percent of households with income of $100,000 or more: 5.1% (2005); Poverty rate: 8.3% (2000).
Taxes: Total city taxes per capita: $320 (2004); City property taxes per capita: $300 (2004).
Education: Percent of population age 25 and over with: High school diploma (including GED) or higher: 81.6% (2005); Bachelor's degree or higher: 13.6% (2005); Master's degree or higher: 6.1% (2005).
Housing: Homeownership rate: 83.5% (2005); Median home value: $84,020 (2005); Median rent: $415 per month (2000); Median age of housing: 55 years (2000).
Transportation: Commute to work: 91.6% car, 0.3% public transportation, 2.9% walk, 4.8% work from home (2000); Travel time to work: 27.9% less than 15 minutes, 37.3% 15 to 30 minutes, 10.8% 30 to 45 minutes, 11.2% 45 to 60 minutes, 12.8% 60 minutes or more (2000).

Oswego County

Located in north central New York; bounded on the northwest by Lake Ontario, and on the south by Oneida Lake and the Oneida River; drained by the Oswego and Salmon Rivers. Covers a land area of 953.30 square miles, a water area of 358.88 square miles, and is located in the Eastern Time Zone. The county government was organized in 1816. County seat is Oswego.

Oswego County is part of the Syracuse, NY Metropolitan Statistical Area. The entire metro area includes: Madison County, NY; Onondaga County, NY; Oswego County, NY

Weather Station: Oswego East   Elevation: 347 feet

	Jan	Feb	Mar	Apr	May	Jun	Jul	Aug	Sep	Oct	Nov	Dec
High	30	32	41	53	66	75	80	78	70	59	47	36
Low	16	18	26	36	46	55	62	61	54	43	35	24
Precip	3.8	2.9	3.4	3.3	3.1	3.4	3.0	3.6	4.2	3.8	4.4	3.8
Snow	51.1	35.6	19.5	4.1	tr	0.0	0.0	0.0	tr	0.4	9.1	33.5

High and Low temperatures in degrees Fahrenheit; Precipitation and Snow in inches

Population: 121,771 (1990); 122,377 (2000); 124,311 (2005); 126,257 (2010 projected); Race: 96.9% White, 0.7% Black, 0.5% Asian, 1.7% Hispanic of any race (2005); Density: 130.4 persons per square mile (2005); Average household size: 2.64 (2005); Median age: 36.5 (2005); Males per 100 females: 97.7 (2005).
Religion: Five largest groups: 22.2% Catholic Church, 7.1% The United Methodist Church, 1.2% Evangelical Lutheran Church in America, 1.2% The Wesleyan Church, 0.9% The Christian and Missionary Alliance (2000).
Economy: Unemployment rate: 6.3% (2005); Total civilian labor force: 60,603 (2005); Leading industries: 17.7% retail trade; 16.5% health care and social assistance; 16.3% manufacturing (2003); Farms: 682 totaling 103,156 acres (2002); Companies that employ 500 or more persons: 6

(2003); Companies that employ 100 to 499 persons: 25 (2003); Companies that employ less than 100 persons: 2,050 (2003); Black-owned businesses: n/a (2002); Hispanic-owned businesses: n/a (2002); Women-owned businesses: 1,864 (2002); Retail sales per capita: $10,018 (2006). Single-family building permits issued: 221 (2005); Multi-family building permits issued: 11 (2005).
Income: Per capita income: $19,220 (2005); Median household income: $40,952 (2005); Average household income: $50,180 (2005); Percent of households with income of $100,000 or more: 9.4% (2005); Poverty rate: 13.0% (2003); Bankruptcy rate: 12.17% (2005).
Taxes: Total county taxes per capita: $449 (2004); County property taxes per capita: $262 (2004).
Education: Percent of population age 25 and over with: High school diploma (including GED) or higher: 80.5% (2005); Bachelor's degree or higher: 14.5% (2005); Master's degree or higher: 5.3% (2005).
Housing: Homeownership rate: 73.1% (2005); Median home value: $92,008 (2005); Median rent: $394 per month (2000); Median age of housing: 36 years (2000).
Health: Birth rate: 110.0 per 10,000 population (2004); Death rate: 85.2 per 10,000 population (2004); Age-adjusted cancer mortality rate: 232.1 deaths per 100,000 population (2002); Air Quality Index: 87.2% good, 11.9% moderate, 0.9% unhealthy for sensitive individuals, 0.0% unhealthy (percent of days in 2005); Number of physicians: 8.9 per 10,000 population (2004); Hospital beds: 16.7 per 10,000 population (2003); Hospital admissions: 612.6 per 10,000 population (2003).
Elections: 2004 Presidential election results: 51.0% Bush, 46.8% Kerry, 2.0% Nader, 0.2% Badnarik
National and State Parks: Battle Island State Park; Fort Brewerton State Park; Littlejohn State Game Management Area; Selkirk Shores State Park; Threemile Bay State Game Management Area
Additional Information Contacts
Oswego County Government. . . . . (315) 349-3235
  http://www.co.oswego.ny.us/
City of Fulton . . . . (315) 592-5390
  http://www.cityoffulton.com/
City of Oswego. . . . . (315) 342-8116
  http://www.oswegony.org/
Town of Constantia . . . . (315) 623-7771
  http://townconstantia.org/
Town of Oswego . . . . (315) 343-2424
  http://www.townofoswego.com/
Town of Scriba. . . . . (315) 343-3375
  http://scribany.org/

Oswego County Communities

ALBION (town). Covers a land area of 47.251 square miles and a water area of 0.560 square miles. Located at 43.51° N. Lat.; 76.02° W. Long.
Population: 2,043 (1990); 2,083 (2000); 2,218 (2005); 2,345 (2010 projected); Race: 98.4% White, 0.1% Black, 0.2% Asian, 0.7% Hispanic of any race (2005); Density: 46.9 persons per square mile (2005); Average household size: 2.90 (2005); Median age: 35.0 (2005); Males per 100 females: 98.0 (2005); Marriage status: 25.0% never married, 61.1% now married, 4.5% widowed, 9.4% divorced (2000); Foreign born: 0.3% (2000); Ancestry (includes multiple ancestries): 17.1% English, 15.4% German, 15.1% Irish, 11.3% French (except Basque), 7.0% Other groups (2000).
Economy: Single-family building permits issued: 5 (2005); Multi-family building permits issued: 0 (2005); Employment by occupation: 8.8% management, 11.1% professional, 15.0% services, 23.5% sales, 1.6% farming, 12.2% construction, 27.8% production (2000).
Income: Per capita income: $17,309 (2005); Median household income: $42,792 (2005); Average household income: $50,173 (2005); Percent of households with income of $100,000 or more: 6.9% (2005); Poverty rate: 13.5% (2000).
Education: Percent of population age 25 and over with: High school diploma (including GED) or higher: 79.3% (2005); Bachelor's degree or higher: 8.5% (2005); Master's degree or higher: 3.7% (2005).
Housing: Homeownership rate: 85.9% (2005); Median home value: $75,319 (2005); Median rent: $371 per month (2000); Median age of housing: 26 years (2000).
Transportation: Commute to work: 94.1% car, 0.8% public transportation, 2.4% walk, 2.7% work from home (2000); Travel time to work: 28.0% less than 15 minutes, 21.1% 15 to 30 minutes, 23.1% 30 to 45 minutes, 20.3% 45 to 60 minutes, 7.5% 60 minutes or more (2000)

ALTMAR (village). Covers a land area of 2.160 square miles and a water area of 0.015 square miles. Located at 43.51° N. Lat.; 76.00° W. Long. Elevation is 577 feet.
Population: 336 (1990); 351 (2000); 342 (2005); 336 (2010 projected); Race: 98.0% White, 0.0% Black, 0.0% Asian, 0.0% Hispanic of any race (2005); Density: 158.3 persons per square mile (2005); Average household size: 2.87 (2005); Median age: 33.5 (2005); Males per 100 females: 96.6 (2005); Marriage status: 28.2% never married, 51.7% now married, 6.6% widowed, 13.5% divorced (2000); Foreign born: 0.0% (2000); Ancestry (includes multiple ancestries): 17.3% English, 10.7% United States or American, 8.6% Irish, 8.3% French (except Basque), 5.7% Italian (2000).
Economy: State trout and salmon hatchery for stocking various N United States rivers and streams; prized coho salmon fishing in Salmon River. Single-family building permits issued: 0 (2005); Multi-family building permits issued: 0 (2005); Employment by occupation: 9.5% management, 2.0% professional, 19.6% services, 26.4% sales, 0.7% farming, 12.2% construction, 29.7% production (2000).
Income: Per capita income: $16,428 (2005); Median household income: $36,136 (2005); Average household income: $46,723 (2005); Percent of households with income of $100,000 or more: 3.4% (2005); Poverty rate: 21.4% (2000).
Education: Percent of population age 25 and over with: High school diploma (including GED) or higher: 73.6% (2005); Bachelor's degree or higher: 3.7% (2005); Master's degree or higher: 1.4% (2005).
School District(s)
Altmar-Parish-Williamstown Central School District (KG-12)
  2003-04 Enrollment: 1,647 . . . . (315) 625-5251
Housing: Homeownership rate: 79.0% (2005); Median home value: $65,714 (2005); Median rent: $388 per month (2000); Median age of housing: 37 years (2000).
Transportation: Commute to work: 97.9% car, 0.0% public transportation, 0.7% walk, 1.4% work from home (2000); Travel time to work: 20.0% less than 15 minutes, 29.3% 15 to 30 minutes, 15.0% 30 to 45 minutes, 25.7% 45 to 60 minutes, 10.0% 60 minutes or more (2000)

AMBOY (town). Covers a land area of 37.121 square miles and a water area of 0.607 square miles. Located at 43.37° N. Lat.; 75.92° W. Long.
Population: 1,010 (1990); 1,312 (2000); 1,333 (2005); 1,332 (2010 projected); Race: 96.2% White, 1.5% Black, 0.2% Asian, 1.1% Hispanic of any race (2005); Density: 35.9 persons per square mile (2005); Average household size: 2.75 (2005); Median age: 36.3 (2005); Males per 100 females: 108.3 (2005); Marriage status: 23.7% never married, 60.8% now married, 5.8% widowed, 9.7% divorced (2000); Foreign born: 1.4% (2000); Ancestry (includes multiple ancestries): 16.4% United States or American, 14.2% German, 13.5% English, 12.9% Irish, 10.3% French (except Basque) (2000).
Economy: Single-family building permits issued: 1 (2005); Multi-family building permits issued: 0 (2005); Employment by occupation: 6.6% management, 10.4% professional, 11.4% services, 22.2% sales, 0.4% farming, 23.7% construction, 25.4% production (2000).
Income: Per capita income: $17,322 (2005); Median household income: $37,599 (2005); Average household income: $47,608 (2005); Percent of households with income of $100,000 or more: 6.8% (2005); Poverty rate: 13.5% (2000).
Education: Percent of population age 25 and over with: High school diploma (including GED) or higher: 70.5% (2005); Bachelor's degree or higher: 7.5% (2005); Master's degree or higher: 2.0% (2005).
Housing: Homeownership rate: 83.7% (2005); Median home value: $73,220 (2005); Median rent: $393 per month (2000); Median age of housing: 26 years (2000).
Transportation: Commute to work: 92.9% car, 2.0% public transportation, 0.4% walk, 3.5% work from home (2000); Travel time to work: 10.4% less than 15 minutes, 23.8% 15 to 30 minutes, 27.8% 30 to 45 minutes, 31.5% 45 to 60 minutes, 6.5% 60 minutes or more (2000)

BERNHARDS BAY (unincorporated postal area, zip code 13028). Covers a land area of 19.965 square miles and a water area of 0.361 square miles. Located at 43.27° N. Lat.; 75.93° W. Long.
Population: 0 (2000); Race: 99.4% White, 0.0% Black, 0.0% Asian, 0.9% Hispanic of any race (2000); Density: 0.0 persons per square mile (2000); Age: 27.7% under 18, 9.2% over 64 (2000); Marriage status: 21.1% never married, 64.1% now married, 4.6% widowed, 10.2% divorced (2000); Foreign born: 0.5% (2000); Ancestry (includes multiple ancestries): 30.3%

Irish, 17.1% German, 11.7% Polish, 10.1% English, 8.5% French (except Basque) (2000).
Economy: Resort village on North shore of Oneida Lake. Employment by occupation: 8.8% management, 12.0% professional, 17.1% services, 25.4% sales, 0.0% farming, 17.4% construction, 19.3% production (2000).
Income: Per capita income: $15,781 (2000); Median household income: $41,875 (2000); Poverty rate: 13.9% (2000).
Education: Percent of population age 25 and over with: High school diploma (including GED) or higher: 77.0% (2000); Bachelor's degree or higher: 8.2% (2000).
Housing: Homeownership rate: 83.6% (2000); Median home value: $81,300 (2000); Median rent: $369 per month (2000); Median age of housing: 31 years (2000).
Transportation: Commute to work: 93.4% car, 0.8% public transportation, 1.8% walk, 3.1% work from home (2000); Travel time to work: 12.3% less than 15 minutes, 12.1% 15 to 30 minutes, 37.3% 30 to 45 minutes, 31.4% 45 to 60 minutes, 6.8% 60 minutes or more (2000)

BOYLSTON (town).
Covers a land area of 39.144 square miles and a water area of 0.005 square miles. Located at 43.65° N. Lat.; 75.97° W. Long.
Population: 443 (1990); 505 (2000); 512 (2005); 519 (2010 projected); Race: 97.9% White, 0.0% Black, 0.0% Asian, 3.3% Hispanic of any race (2005); Density: 13.1 persons per square mile (2005); Average household size: 2.56 (2005); Median age: 39.9 (2005); Males per 100 females: 107.3 (2005); Marriage status: 26.8% never married, 59.6% now married, 5.0% widowed, 8.5% divorced (2000); Foreign born: 1.3% (2000); Ancestry (includes multiple ancestries): 21.8% English, 11.7% German, 6.6% Irish, 6.6% United States or American, 6.0% Dutch (2000).
Economy: Single-family building permits issued: 4 (2005); Multi-family building permits issued: 0 (2005); Employment by occupation: 13.9% management, 15.5% professional, 13.1% services, 18.4% sales, 5.3% farming, 22.0% construction, 11.8% production (2000).
Income: Per capita income: $21,484 (2005); Median household income: $45,946 (2005); Average household income: $55,000 (2005); Percent of households with income of $100,000 or more: 12.0% (2005); Poverty rate: 8.3% (2000).
Education: Percent of population age 25 and over with: High school diploma (including GED) or higher: 83.3% (2005); Bachelor's degree or higher: 18.1% (2005); Master's degree or higher: 3.2% (2005).
Housing: Homeownership rate: 86.5% (2005); Median home value: $92,083 (2005); Median rent: $425 per month (2000); Median age of housing: 29 years (2000).
Transportation: Commute to work: 86.4% car, 0.0% public transportation, 0.0% walk, 13.6% work from home (2000); Travel time to work: 18.1% less than 15 minutes, 29.5% 15 to 30 minutes, 17.1% 30 to 45 minutes, 13.8% 45 to 60 minutes, 21.4% 60 minutes or more (2000)

CENTRAL SQUARE (village).
Covers a land area of 1.853 square miles and a water area of 0 square miles. Located at 43.28° N. Lat.; 76.14° W. Long. Elevation is 454 feet.
Population: 1,632 (1990); 1,646 (2000); 1,647 (2005); 1,654 (2010 projected); Race: 97.4% White, 0.9% Black, 1.2% Asian, 1.0% Hispanic of any race (2005); Density: 888.7 persons per square mile (2005); Average household size: 2.15 (2005); Median age: 40.6 (2005); Males per 100 females: 88.0 (2005); Marriage status: 21.6% never married, 54.9% now married, 10.1% widowed, 13.4% divorced (2000); Foreign born: 2.1% (2000); Ancestry (includes multiple ancestries): 25.8% German, 21.8% English, 21.3% Irish, 11.5% Italian, 9.6% French (except Basque) (2000).
Economy: In dairying area. Single-family building permits issued: 5 (2005); Multi-family building permits issued: 0 (2005); Employment by occupation: 10.8% management, 16.9% professional, 12.5% services, 30.2% sales, 0.0% farming, 11.2% construction, 18.3% production (2000).
Income: Per capita income: $22,031 (2005); Median household income: $34,853 (2005); Average household income: $47,308 (2005); Percent of households with income of $100,000 or more: 8.2% (2005); Poverty rate: 12.5% (2000).
Education: Percent of population age 25 and over with: High school diploma (including GED) or higher: 82.8% (2005); Bachelor's degree or higher: 18.2% (2005); Master's degree or higher: 8.2% (2005).
School District(s)
Central Square Central School District (PK-12)
    2003-04 Enrollment: 5,013 . . . . (315) 668-4220
Housing: Homeownership rate: 50.2% (2005); Median home value: $112,969 (2005); Median rent: $421 per month (2000); Median age of housing: 29 years (2000).
Safety: Violent crime rate: 12.1 per 10,000 population; Property crime rate: 326.5 per 10,000 population (2004).
Transportation: Commute to work: 94.2% car, 0.3% public transportation, 3.5% walk, 1.6% work from home (2000); Travel time to work: 29.7% less than 15 minutes, 42.6% 15 to 30 minutes, 24.1% 30 to 45 minutes, 1.6% 45 to 60 minutes, 2.0% 60 minutes or more (2000)
Additional Information Contacts
Fort Brewerton/Greater Oneida Chamber of Commerce . . . (315) 668-3408
   http://www.oneidalakechamber.com

CLEVELAND (village).
Covers a land area of 1.125 square miles and a water area of 0.100 square miles. Located at 43.23° N. Lat.; 75.88° W. Long.
Population: 784 (1990); 758 (2000); 785 (2005); 813 (2010 projected); Race: 99.5% White, 0.3% Black, 0.0% Asian, 0.4% Hispanic of any race (2005); Density: 697.5 persons per square mile (2005); Average household size: 2.69 (2005); Median age: 37.5 (2005); Males per 100 females: 112.2 (2005); Marriage status: 28.1% never married, 53.6% now married, 7.4% widowed, 10.8% divorced (2000); Foreign born: 0.8% (2000); Ancestry (includes multiple ancestries): 23.9% German, 17.2% Irish, 14.9% English, 14.3% United States or American, 8.3% Other groups (2000).
Economy: Agricultural area: dairy products; fruit. Employment by occupation: 7.2% management, 14.7% professional, 21.6% services, 22.4% sales, 0.3% farming, 16.1% construction, 17.8% production (2000).
Income: Per capita income: $16,777 (2005); Median household income: $38,145 (2005); Average household income: $45,103 (2005); Percent of households with income of $100,000 or more: 6.5% (2005); Poverty rate: 12.4% (2000).
Education: Percent of population age 25 and over with: High school diploma (including GED) or higher: 81.8% (2005); Bachelor's degree or higher: 10.3% (2005); Master's degree or higher: 2.9% (2005).
School District(s)
Central Square Central School District (PK-12)
    2003-04 Enrollment: 5,013 . . . . (315) 668-4220
Housing: Homeownership rate: 82.2% (2005); Median home value: $89,143 (2005); Median rent: $397 per month (2000); Median age of housing: 60 years (2000).
Transportation: Commute to work: 93.6% car, 0.0% public transportation, 0.9% walk, 4.1% work from home (2000); Travel time to work: 13.1% less than 15 minutes, 14.3% 15 to 30 minutes, 33.2% 30 to 45 minutes, 31.7% 45 to 60 minutes, 7.6% 60 minutes or more (2000)

CONSTANTIA (town).
Covers a land area of 56.858 square miles and a water area of 42.768 square miles. Located at 43.26° N. Lat.; 75.94° W. Long.
Population: 4,868 (1990); 5,141 (2000); 5,235 (2005); 5,334 (2010 projected); Race: 98.2% White, 0.3% Black, 0.1% Asian, 0.3% Hispanic of any race (2005); Density: 92.1 persons per square mile (2005); Average household size: 2.66 (2005); Median age: 38.9 (2005); Males per 100 females: 106.3 (2005); Marriage status: 20.0% never married, 65.2% now married, 4.5% widowed, 10.3% divorced (2000); Foreign born: 1.6% (2000); Ancestry (includes multiple ancestries): 21.1% Irish, 18.6% German, 13.7% English, 9.2% French (except Basque), 7.7% United States or American (2000).
Economy: State fish hatchery for warm-water fish and walleyes. Single-family building permits issued: 12 (2005); Multi-family building permits issued: 0 (2005); Employment by occupation: 8.1% management, 14.2% professional, 15.1% services, 26.6% sales, 0.3% farming, 16.3% construction, 19.4% production (2000).
Income: Per capita income: $18,057 (2005); Median household income: $43,554 (2005); Average household income: $47,995 (2005); Percent of households with income of $100,000 or more: 6.0% (2005); Poverty rate: 9.5% (2000).
Education: Percent of population age 25 and over with: High school diploma (including GED) or higher: 80.5% (2005); Bachelor's degree or higher: 10.5% (2005); Master's degree or higher: 3.1% (2005).
School District(s)
Central Square Central School District (PK-12)
    2003-04 Enrollment: 5,013 . . . . (315) 668-4220
Housing: Homeownership rate: 85.7% (2005); Median home value: $95,000 (2005); Median rent: $437 per month (2000); Median age of housing: 31 years (2000).

Transportation: Commute to work: 94.0% car, 0.2% public transportation, 0.8% walk, 4.1% work from home (2000); Travel time to work: 11.8% less than 15 minutes, 18.9% 15 to 30 minutes, 38.5% 30 to 45 minutes, 25.0% 45 to 60 minutes, 5.7% 60 minutes or more (2000)
Additional Information Contacts
Town of Constantia . . . . (315) 623-7771
  http://townconstantia.org/

CONSTANTIA (CDP).
Covers a land area of 2.134 square miles and a water area of 0.009 square miles. Located at 43.25° N. Lat.; 76.00° W. Long.
Population: 1,140 (1990); 1,107 (2000); 1,109 (2005); 1,115 (2010 projected); Race: 97.6% White, 0.3% Black, 0.2% Asian, 0.2% Hispanic of any race (2005); Density: 519.8 persons per square mile (2005); Average household size: 2.49 (2005); Median age: 39.6 (2005); Males per 100 females: 102.7 (2005); Marriage status: 18.9% never married, 66.1% now married, 1.3% widowed, 13.7% divorced (2000); Foreign born: 2.4% (2000); Ancestry (includes multiple ancestries): 20.7% English, 16.3% German, 15.0% Irish, 12.1% French (except Basque), 8.7% Scottish (2000).
Economy: Employment by occupation: 11.5% management, 18.5% professional, 9.3% services, 24.4% sales, 0.0% farming, 11.5% construction, 24.6% production (2000).
Income: Per capita income: $19,159 (2005); Median household income: $42,841 (2005); Average household income: $47,640 (2005); Percent of households with income of $100,000 or more: 7.2% (2005); Poverty rate: 8.6% (2000).
Education: Percent of population age 25 and over with: High school diploma (including GED) or higher: 81.2% (2005); Bachelor's degree or higher: 11.5% (2005); Master's degree or higher: 5.1% (2005).
Housing: Homeownership rate: 79.4% (2005); Median home value: $98,750 (2005); Median rent: $441 per month (2000); Median age of housing: 35 years (2000).
Transportation: Commute to work: 96.0% car, 0.0% public transportation, 1.0% walk, 3.0% work from home (2000); Travel time to work: 17.0% less than 15 minutes, 21.1% 15 to 30 minutes, 40.0% 30 to 45 minutes, 19.4% 45 to 60 minutes, 2.5% 60 minutes or more (2000)

FULTON (city).
Covers a land area of 3.821 square miles and a water area of 0.935 square miles. Located at 43.32° N. Lat.; 76.41° W. Long. Elevation is 364 feet.
History: Incorporated as village in 1835, as city in 1902.
Population: 12,929 (1990); 11,855 (2000); 11,572 (2005); 11,314 (2010 projected); Race: 96.3% White, 0.9% Black, 0.4% Asian, 2.5% Hispanic of any race (2005); Density: 3,028.9 persons per square mile (2005); Average household size: 2.37 (2005); Median age: 36.5 (2005); Males per 100 females: 90.2 (2005); Marriage status: 27.4% never married, 53.2% now married, 8.7% widowed, 10.6% divorced (2000); Foreign born: 1.8% (2000); Ancestry (includes multiple ancestries): 17.8% Irish, 17.4% Italian, 15.3% German, 13.9% English, 9.9% French (except Basque) (2000).
Economy: Manufacturing: confectionery, textiles, paper products, firearms, machinery, cutlery, canned foods; sand and gravel. Ships dairy products, fruit, vegetables, poultry. Single-family building permits issued: 3 (2005); Multi-family building permits issued: 0 (2005); Employment by occupation: 5.8% management, 17.1% professional, 18.1% services, 26.4% sales, 0.5% farming, 9.5% construction, 22.6% production (2000).
Income: Per capita income: $17,316 (2005); Median household income: $30,849 (2005); Average household income: $40,521 (2005); Percent of households with income of $100,000 or more: 5.5% (2005); Poverty rate: 19.3% (2000).
Education: Percent of population age 25 and over with: High school diploma (including GED) or higher: 77.3% (2005); Bachelor's degree or higher: 11.8% (2005); Master's degree or higher: 3.2% (2005).
School District(s)
Fulton City School District (KG-12)
  2003-04 Enrollment: 3,875 . . . . (315) 593-5510
Mexico Central School District (KG-12)
  2003-04 Enrollment: 2,682 . . . . (315) 963-8400
Housing: Homeownership rate: 51.8% (2005); Median home value: $82,201 (2005); Median rent: $393 per month (2000); Median age of housing: 60+ years (2000).
Hospitals: Albert Lindley Lee Memorial Hospital (67 beds)
Safety: Violent crime rate: 14.6 per 10,000 population; Property crime rate: 491.4 per 10,000 population (2004).
Newspapers: Fulton Patriot (General - Circulation 6,235); The Valley News (General - Circulation 8,000)
Transportation: Commute to work: 92.5% car, 1.0% public transportation, 4.0% walk, 2.0% work from home (2000); Travel time to work: 43.0% less than 15 minutes, 25.4% 15 to 30 minutes, 22.7% 30 to 45 minutes, 5.4% 45 to 60 minutes, 3.6% 60 minutes or more (2000)
Additional Information Contacts
City of Fulton . . . . (315) 592-5390
  http://www.cityoffulton.com/
Fulton Chamber of Commerce. (315) 598-4231
  http://www.oswegocountychamber.com

GRANBY (town).
Covers a land area of 44.919 square miles and a water area of 1.562 square miles. Located at 43.29° N. Lat.; 76.44° W. Long.
Population: 7,013 (1990); 7,009 (2000); 7,126 (2005); 7,250 (2010 projected); Race: 97.3% White, 0.7% Black, 0.2% Asian, 2.0% Hispanic of any race (2005); Density: 158.6 persons per square mile (2005); Average household size: 2.64 (2005); Median age: 37.0 (2005); Males per 100 females: 98.2 (2005); Marriage status: 24.4% never married, 61.7% now married, 5.7% widowed, 8.2% divorced (2000); Foreign born: 0.7% (2000); Ancestry (includes multiple ancestries): 20.1% German, 17.7% English, 15.9% Irish, 11.0% French (except Basque), 10.9% Italian (2000).
Economy: Single-family building permits issued: 9 (2005); Multi-family building permits issued: 0 (2005); Employment by occupation: 8.4% management, 13.2% professional, 15.9% services, 20.3% sales, 0.7% farming, 11.6% construction, 29.9% production (2000).
Income: Per capita income: $20,315 (2005); Median household income: $42,951 (2005); Average household income: $53,578 (2005); Percent of households with income of $100,000 or more: 10.2% (2005); Poverty rate: 14.2% (2000).
Education: Percent of population age 25 and over with: High school diploma (including GED) or higher: 78.0% (2005); Bachelor's degree or higher: 10.1% (2005); Master's degree or higher: 4.1% (2005).
Housing: Homeownership rate: 82.9% (2005); Median home value: $80,201 (2005); Median rent: $389 per month (2000); Median age of housing: 26 years (2000).
Transportation: Commute to work: 95.4% car, 1.0% public transportation, 0.7% walk, 2.0% work from home (2000); Travel time to work: 35.1% less than 15 minutes, 37.4% 15 to 30 minutes, 18.8% 30 to 45 minutes, 6.2% 45 to 60 minutes, 2.5% 60 minutes or more (2000)

HANNIBAL (village).
Covers a land area of 1.137 square miles and a water area of 0 square miles. Located at 43.32° N. Lat.; 76.57° W. Long. Elevation is 327 feet.
Population: 613 (1990); 542 (2000); 550 (2005); 561 (2010 projected); Race: 98.4% White, 0.9% Black, 0.0% Asian, 0.5% Hispanic of any race (2005); Density: 483.5 persons per square mile (2005); Average household size: 2.50 (2005); Median age: 38.8 (2005); Males per 100 females: 89.7 (2005); Marriage status: 27.2% never married, 51.8% now married, 9.7% widowed, 11.3% divorced (2000); Foreign born: 1.8% (2000); Ancestry (includes multiple ancestries): 24.3% English, 20.5% German, 19.6% Irish, 11.9% Italian, 9.9% United States or American (2000).
Economy: Single-family building permits issued: 1 (2005); Multi-family building permits issued: 0 (2005); Employment by occupation: 7.4% management, 19.1% professional, 14.8% services, 21.0% sales, 1.2% farming, 14.0% construction, 22.6% production (2000).
Income: Per capita income: $20,091 (2005); Median household income: $37,500 (2005); Average household income: $50,227 (2005); Percent of households with income of $100,000 or more: 10.5% (2005); Poverty rate: 13.0% (2000).
Education: Percent of population age 25 and over with: High school diploma (including GED) or higher: 81.5% (2005); Bachelor's degree or higher: 12.1% (2005); Master's degree or higher: 4.3% (2005).
School District(s)
Hannibal Central School District (KG-12)
  2003-04 Enrollment: 1,756 . . . . (315) 564-7902
Housing: Homeownership rate: 72.7% (2005); Median home value: $93,846 (2005); Median rent: $339 per month (2000); Median age of housing: 60+ years (2000).
Transportation: Commute to work: 88.0% car, 2.3% public transportation, 4.6% walk, 4.2% work from home (2000); Travel time to work: 31.0% less than 15 minutes, 31.0% 15 to 30 minutes, 16.1% 30 to 45 minutes, 9.7% 45 to 60 minutes, 12.1% 60 minutes or more (2000)

HANNIBAL (town). Covers a land area of 44.773 square miles and a water area of 0.021 square miles. Located at 43.30° N. Lat.; 76.56° W. Long. Elevation is 327 feet.
Population: 4,616 (1990); 4,957 (2000); 5,045 (2005); 5,137 (2010 projected); Race: 97.9% White, 0.3% Black, 0.1% Asian, 1.2% Hispanic of any race (2005); Density: 112.7 persons per square mile (2005); Average household size: 2.76 (2005); Median age: 35.3 (2005); Males per 100 females: 101.4 (2005); Marriage status: 23.5% never married, 60.0% now married, 5.9% widowed, 10.5% divorced (2000); Foreign born: 1.0% (2000); Ancestry (includes multiple ancestries): 16.5% English, 15.2% Irish, 14.4% German, 10.2% Italian, 9.8% French (except Basque) (2000).
Economy: In dairy and fruit area. Single-family building permits issued: 2 (2005); Multi-family building permits issued: 0 (2005); Employment by occupation: 4.4% management, 12.2% professional, 12.4% services, 20.0% sales, 1.3% farming, 17.1% construction, 32.5% production (2000).
Income: Per capita income: $19,381 (2005); Median household income: $40,072 (2005); Average household income: $53,399 (2005); Percent of households with income of $100,000 or more: 11.4% (2005); Poverty rate: 15.3% (2000).
Education: Percent of population age 25 and over with: High school diploma (including GED) or higher: 74.5% (2005); Bachelor's degree or higher: 7.4% (2005); Master's degree or higher: 2.6% (2005).
Housing: Homeownership rate: 82.0% (2005); Median home value: $80,850 (2005); Median rent: $384 per month (2000); Median age of housing: 23 years (2000).
Transportation: Commute to work: 92.7% car, 0.9% public transportation, 2.8% walk, 3.0% work from home (2000); Travel time to work: 22.4% less than 15 minutes, 32.5% 15 to 30 minutes, 26.1% 30 to 45 minutes, 10.1% 45 to 60 minutes, 8.8% 60 minutes or more (2000)

HASTINGS (town). Covers a land area of 45.771 square miles and a water area of 0.252 square miles. Located at 43.30° N. Lat.; 76.15° W. Long. Elevation is 474 feet.
Population: 8,113 (1990); 8,803 (2000); 9,167 (2005); 9,511 (2010 projected); Race: 97.7% White, 0.4% Black, 0.4% Asian, 0.9% Hispanic of any race (2005); Density: 200.3 persons per square mile (2005); Average household size: 2.57 (2005); Median age: 38.1 (2005); Males per 100 females: 99.0 (2005); Marriage status: 22.7% never married, 61.8% now married, 5.7% widowed, 9.8% divorced (2000); Foreign born: 1.4% (2000); Ancestry (includes multiple ancestries): 20.4% German, 17.9% Irish, 16.0% English, 12.5% French (except Basque), 11.3% Italian (2000).
Economy: Single-family building permits issued: 15 (2005); Multi-family building permits issued: 0 (2005); Employment by occupation: 9.7% management, 14.8% professional, 13.7% services, 27.3% sales, 0.3% farming, 13.0% construction, 21.1% production (2000).
Income: Per capita income: $20,510 (2005); Median household income: $44,729 (2005); Average household income: $52,636 (2005); Percent of households with income of $100,000 or more: 9.4% (2005); Poverty rate: 10.0% (2000).
Education: Percent of population age 25 and over with: High school diploma (including GED) or higher: 81.5% (2005); Bachelor's degree or higher: 11.3% (2005); Master's degree or higher: 4.2% (2005).
Housing: Homeownership rate: 78.9% (2005); Median home value: $100,098 (2005); Median rent: $427 per month (2000); Median age of housing: 25 years (2000).
Transportation: Commute to work: 95.7% car, 0.2% public transportation, 1.5% walk, 2.0% work from home (2000); Travel time to work: 22.0% less than 15 minutes, 37.4% 15 to 30 minutes, 32.4% 30 to 45 minutes, 4.6% 45 to 60 minutes, 3.5% 60 minutes or more (2000)

LACONA (village). Covers a land area of 1.023 square miles and a water area of 0 square miles. Located at 43.64° N. Lat.; 76.06° W. Long. Elevation is 540 feet.
Population: 593 (1990); 590 (2000); 588 (2005); 589 (2010 projected); Race: 98.3% White, 0.3% Black, 0.5% Asian, 1.4% Hispanic of any race (2005); Density: 574.7 persons per square mile (2005); Average household size: 2.37 (2005); Median age: 36.7 (2005); Males per 100 females: 92.2 (2005); Marriage status: 25.9% never married, 52.2% now married, 10.7% widowed, 11.3% divorced (2000); Foreign born: 1.4% (2000); Ancestry (includes multiple ancestries): 23.5% German, 19.4% English, 17.5% Irish, 10.9% United States or American, 9.2% French (except Basque) (2000).
Economy: Manufacturing of wooden architectural fabrications; sand, gravel pits. Single-family building permits issued: 0 (2005); Multi-family building permits issued: 0 (2005); Employment by occupation: 6.1% management, 27.0% professional, 13.5% services, 25.4% sales, 2.0% farming, 8.6% construction, 17.2% production (2000).
Income: Per capita income: $19,520 (2005); Median household income: $38,333 (2005); Average household income: $46,280 (2005); Percent of households with income of $100,000 or more: 10.1% (2005); Poverty rate: 24.6% (2000).
Taxes: Total city taxes per capita: $110 (2004); City property taxes per capita: $81 (2004).
Education: Percent of population age 25 and over with: High school diploma (including GED) or higher: 84.3% (2005); Bachelor's degree or higher: 17.5% (2005); Master's degree or higher: 6.0% (2005).
Housing: Homeownership rate: 62.5% (2005); Median home value: $96,667 (2005); Median rent: $367 per month (2000); Median age of housing: 60+ years (2000).
Transportation: Commute to work: 94.6% car, 0.0% public transportation, 2.1% walk, 3.3% work from home (2000); Travel time to work: 27.5% less than 15 minutes, 17.2% 15 to 30 minutes, 25.8% 30 to 45 minutes, 20.2% 45 to 60 minutes, 9.4% 60 minutes or more (2000)

MEXICO (village). Covers a land area of 2.139 square miles and a water area of 0 square miles. Located at 43.46° N. Lat.; 76.23° W. Long.
Population: 1,555 (1990); 1,572 (2000); 1,645 (2005); 1,717 (2010 projected); Race: 98.2% White, 0.2% Black, 0.3% Asian, 0.8% Hispanic of any race (2005); Density: 769.2 persons per square mile (2005); Average household size: 2.36 (2005); Median age: 37.5 (2005); Males per 100 females: 88.2 (2005); Marriage status: 25.7% never married, 52.7% now married, 8.5% widowed, 13.2% divorced (2000); Foreign born: 0.9% (2000); Ancestry (includes multiple ancestries): 19.4% Irish, 17.6% English, 15.0% German, 13.5% United States or American, 9.8% French (except Basque) (2000).
Economy: Single-family building permits issued: 7 (2005); Multi-family building permits issued: 0 (2005); Employment by occupation: 6.8% management, 28.1% professional, 12.6% services, 24.7% sales, 1.0% farming, 10.8% construction, 16.0% production (2000).
Income: Per capita income: $21,740 (2005); Median household income: $40,444 (2005); Average household income: $51,383 (2005); Percent of households with income of $100,000 or more: 12.1% (2005); Poverty rate: 13.0% (2000).
Education: Percent of population age 25 and over with: High school diploma (including GED) or higher: 88.5% (2005); Bachelor's degree or higher: 22.6% (2005); Master's degree or higher: 8.7% (2005).

School District(s)
Boces Oswego (PK-PK)
    2003-04 Enrollment: 385 . . . . (315) 963-4222
Mexico Central School District (KG-12)
    2003-04 Enrollment: 2,682 . . . . (315) 963-8400

Two-year College(s)
Oswego County BOCES (Public)
    Fall 2004 Enrollment: 76 . . . . (315) 963-4251

Housing: Homeownership rate: 59.3% (2005); Median home value: $90,686 (2005); Median rent: $369 per month (2000); Median age of housing: 60+ years (2000).
Newspapers: Citizen Outlet (General - Circulation 5,500); Mexico Independent Mirror (General - Circulation 3,400); Phoenix Register (General - Circulation 3,100); Pulaski/Salmon River News (General - Circulation 7,500).
Transportation: Commute to work: 89.5% car, 0.4% public transportation, 7.2% walk, 2.7% work from home (2000); Travel time to work: 36.0% less than 15 minutes, 25.8% 15 to 30 minutes, 21.3% 30 to 45 minutes, 12.0% 45 to 60 minutes, 4.8% 60 minutes or more (2000)

Additional Information Contacts
Mexico Chamber of Commerce . . . . (315) 963-1042
    http://www.greatermexicochamber.com

MEXICO (town). Covers a land area of 46.339 square miles and a water area of 0.633 square miles. Located at 43.46° N. Lat.; 76.21° W. Long.
Population: 5,050 (1990); 5,181 (2000); 5,421 (2005); 5,648 (2010 projected); Race: 98.1% White, 0.2% Black, 0.3% Asian, 1.0% Hispanic of any race (2005); Density: 117.0 persons per square mile (2005); Average household size: 2.63 (2005); Median age: 37.7 (2005); Males per 100 females: 99.4 (2005); Marriage status: 22.1% never married, 61.6% now married, 5.9% widowed, 10.4% divorced (2000); Foreign born: 1.0% (2000); Ancestry (includes multiple ancestries): 20.1% English, 17.3% German, 16.5% Irish, 10.6% United States or American, 9.6% French (except Basque) (2000).

Economy: Single-family building permits issued: 14 (2005); Multi-family building permits issued: 0 (2005); Employment by occupation: 6.0% management, 20.4% professional, 11.1% services, 28.8% sales, 0.6% farming, 12.1% construction, 20.9% production (2000).
Income: Per capita income: $20,515 (2005); Median household income: $46,148 (2005); Average household income: $53,809 (2005); Percent of households with income of $100,000 or more: 10.8% (2005); Poverty rate: 11.9% (2000).
Education: Percent of population age 25 and over with: High school diploma (including GED) or higher: 84.6% (2005); Bachelor's degree or higher: 14.7% (2005); Master's degree or higher: 5.1% (2005).
Housing: Homeownership rate: 77.2% (2005); Median home value: $96,243 (2005); Median rent: $385 per month (2000); Median age of housing: 33 years (2000).
Transportation: Commute to work: 93.4% car, 0.1% public transportation, 3.1% walk, 3.0% work from home (2000); Travel time to work: 27.7% less than 15 minutes, 31.5% 15 to 30 minutes, 23.5% 30 to 45 minutes, 11.6% 45 to 60 minutes, 5.7% 60 minutes or more (2000)

MINETTO (town). Covers a land area of 5.792 square miles and a water area of 0.256 square miles. Located at 43.39° N. Lat.; 76.47° W. Long.
Population: 1,822 (1990); 1,663 (2000); 1,669 (2005); 1,680 (2010 projected); Race: 97.4% White, 0.3% Black, 0.8% Asian, 1.6% Hispanic of any race (2005); Density: 288.2 persons per square mile (2005); Average household size: 2.57 (2005); Median age: 43.2 (2005); Males per 100 females: 95.2 (2005); Marriage status: 20.6% never married, 65.8% now married, 5.8% widowed, 7.8% divorced (2000); Foreign born: 2.0% (2000); Ancestry (includes multiple ancestries): 25.0% Irish, 21.2% Italian, 19.0% German, 13.3% English, 9.6% Polish (2000).
Economy: Single-family building permits issued: 8 (2005); Multi-family building permits issued: 0 (2005); Employment by occupation: 7.5% management, 31.5% professional, 14.0% services, 23.9% sales, 0.0% farming, 10.9% construction, 12.2% production (2000).
Income: Per capita income: $25,848 (2005); Median household income: $57,031 (2005); Average household income: $66,369 (2005); Percent of households with income of $100,000 or more: 19.8% (2005); Poverty rate: 5.7% (2000).
Education: Percent of population age 25 and over with: High school diploma (including GED) or higher: 91.2% (2005); Bachelor's degree or higher: 29.6% (2005); Master's degree or higher: 13.7% (2005).

School District(s)
Oswego City School District (KG-12)
    2003-04 Enrollment: 4,809 . . . . (315) 341-5885
Housing: Homeownership rate: 87.4% (2005); Median home value: $125,940 (2005); Median rent: $425 per month (2000); Median age of housing: 38 years (2000).
Transportation: Commute to work: 94.5% car, 0.2% public transportation, 2.2% walk, 2.8% work from home (2000); Travel time to work: 39.2% less than 15 minutes, 43.1% 15 to 30 minutes, 9.9% 30 to 45 minutes, 4.5% 45 to 60 minutes, 3.4% 60 minutes or more (2000)

MINETTO (CDP). Covers a land area of 3.362 square miles and a water area of 0.243 square miles. Located at 43.39° N. Lat.; 76.47° W. Long.
Population: 1,252 (1990); 1,086 (2000); 1,090 (2005); 1,096 (2010 projected); Race: 97.5% White, 0.3% Black, 0.9% Asian, 1.7% Hispanic of any race (2005); Density: 324.2 persons per square mile (2005); Average household size: 2.60 (2005); Median age: 43.5 (2005); Males per 100 females: 91.6 (2005); Marriage status: 20.9% never married, 63.6% now married, 7.4% widowed, 8.1% divorced (2000); Foreign born: 1.3% (2000); Ancestry (includes multiple ancestries): 24.7% Irish, 21.0% Italian, 17.6% German, 14.4% English, 9.4% French (except Basque) (2000).
Economy: Employment by occupation: 5.2% management, 32.2% professional, 13.3% services, 24.4% sales, 0.0% farming, 13.9% construction, 10.9% production (2000).
Income: Per capita income: $25,255 (2005); Median household income: $56,180 (2005); Average household income: $65,542 (2005); Percent of households with income of $100,000 or more: 18.8% (2005); Poverty rate: 6.7% (2000).
Education: Percent of population age 25 and over with: High school diploma (including GED) or higher: 89.7% (2005); Bachelor's degree or higher: 29.4% (2005); Master's degree or higher: 14.4% (2005).

Housing: Homeownership rate: 88.8% (2005); Median home value: $122,076 (2005); Median rent: $428 per month (2000); Median age of housing: 43 years (2000).
Transportation: Commute to work: 93.3% car, 0.4% public transportation, 3.0% walk, 2.8% work from home (2000); Travel time to work: 40.2% less than 15 minutes, 42.6% 15 to 30 minutes, 9.0% 30 to 45 minutes, 5.3% 45 to 60 minutes, 2.9% 60 minutes or more (2000)

NEW HAVEN (town). Covers a land area of 31.175 square miles and a water area of 2.275 square miles. Located at 43.48° N. Lat.; 76.31° W. Long. Elevation is 418 feet.
Population: 2,778 (1990); 2,930 (2000); 3,000 (2005); 3,072 (2010 projected); Race: 98.2% White, 0.2% Black, 0.5% Asian, 1.0% Hispanic of any race (2005); Density: 96.2 persons per square mile (2005); Average household size: 2.70 (2005); Median age: 36.3 (2005); Males per 100 females: 99.9 (2005); Marriage status: 26.7% never married, 60.2% now married, 5.4% widowed, 7.7% divorced (2000); Foreign born: 1.5% (2000); Ancestry (includes multiple ancestries): 17.8% English, 13.3% German, 13.0% Irish, 12.4% United States or American, 9.1% French (except Basque) (2000).
Economy: Single-family building permits issued: 6 (2005); Multi-family building permits issued: 0 (2005); Employment by occupation: 4.4% management, 17.4% professional, 15.3% services, 18.8% sales, 0.6% farming, 15.0% construction, 28.6% production (2000).
Income: Per capita income: $19,913 (2005); Median household income: $43,762 (2005); Average household income: $53,769 (2005); Percent of households with income of $100,000 or more: 10.2% (2005); Poverty rate: 11.3% (2000).
Education: Percent of population age 25 and over with: High school diploma (including GED) or higher: 83.3% (2005); Bachelor's degree or higher: 11.7% (2005); Master's degree or higher: 3.6% (2005).

School District(s)
Mexico Central School District (KG-12)
    2003-04 Enrollment: 2,682 . . . . (315) 963-8400
Housing: Homeownership rate: 83.2% (2005); Median home value: $83,837 (2005); Median rent: $352 per month (2000); Median age of housing: 27 years (2000).
Transportation: Commute to work: 93.2% car, 0.5% public transportation, 1.5% walk, 3.2% work from home (2000); Travel time to work: 25.4% less than 15 minutes, 43.3% 15 to 30 minutes, 15.9% 30 to 45 minutes, 9.1% 45 to 60 minutes, 6.2% 60 minutes or more (2000)

ORWELL (town). Covers a land area of 39.766 square miles and a water area of 1.553 square miles. Located at 43.55° N. Lat.; 75.95° W. Long. Elevation is 808 feet.
Population: 1,171 (1990); 1,254 (2000); 1,251 (2005); 1,255 (2010 projected); Race: 98.6% White, 0.6% Black, 0.1% Asian, 0.5% Hispanic of any race (2005); Density: 31.5 persons per square mile (2005); Average household size: 2.94 (2005); Median age: 39.4 (2005); Males per 100 females: 118.7 (2005); Marriage status: 22.1% never married, 63.5% now married, 7.0% widowed, 7.4% divorced (2000); Foreign born: 1.2% (2000); Ancestry (includes multiple ancestries): 17.9% German, 15.1% English, 11.4% Irish, 6.9% United States or American, 6.7% Italian (2000).
Economy: Single-family building permits issued: 7 (2005); Multi-family building permits issued: 0 (2005); Employment by occupation: 7.1% management, 14.2% professional, 10.6% services, 19.6% sales, 1.3% farming, 21.3% construction, 25.9% production (2000).
Income: Per capita income: $16,680 (2005); Median household income: $39,518 (2005); Average household income: $47,072 (2005); Percent of households with income of $100,000 or more: 7.7% (2005); Poverty rate: 21.5% (2000).
Education: Percent of population age 25 and over with: High school diploma (including GED) or higher: 77.0% (2005); Bachelor's degree or higher: 11.9% (2005); Master's degree or higher: 7.0% (2005).
Housing: Homeownership rate: 80.0% (2005); Median home value: $81,029 (2005); Median rent: $417 per month (2000); Median age of housing: 32 years (2000).
Transportation: Commute to work: 96.3% car, 0.0% public transportation, 0.9% walk, 0.9% work from home (2000); Travel time to work: 21.6% less than 15 minutes, 35.8% 15 to 30 minutes, 18.3% 30 to 45 minutes, 16.8% 45 to 60 minutes, 7.5% 60 minutes or more (2000)

OSWEGO (city). Covers a land area of 7.662 square miles and a water area of 3.575 square miles. Located at 43.45° N. Lat.; 76.50° W. Long. Elevation is 298 feet.

History: The name of Oswego is of Indian origin, meaning "pouring out of waters." The strategic importance of the place led to the erection of a fort in 1722. Soon after military occupation ceased, settlement began. Its commanding position at the terminus of the inland water route made Oswego a busy port.
Population: 19,195 (1990); 17,954 (2000); 18,122 (2005); 18,217 (2010 projected); Race: 94.4% White, 1.3% Black, 1.1% Asian, 3.8% Hispanic of any race (2005); Density: 2,365.3 persons per square mile (2005); Average household size: 2.41 (2005); Median age: 35.8 (2005); Males per 100 females: 88.7 (2005); Marriage status: 34.6% never married, 48.4% now married, 9.1% widowed, 7.9% divorced (2000); Foreign born: 2.7% (2000); Ancestry (includes multiple ancestries): 26.1% Irish, 18.4% Italian, 15.8% German, 12.1% English, 8.7% French (except Basque) (2000).
Economy: Single-family building permits issued: 14 (2005); Multi-family building permits issued: 9 (2005); Employment by occupation: 8.0% management, 20.7% professional, 24.7% services, 23.4% sales, 0.7% farming, 9.1% construction, 13.5% production (2000).
Income: Per capita income: $17,727 (2005); Median household income: $30,081 (2005); Average household income: $41,016 (2005); Percent of households with income of $100,000 or more: 7.1% (2005); Poverty rate: 23.0% (2000).
Education: Percent of population age 25 and over with: High school diploma (including GED) or higher: 79.4% (2005); Bachelor's degree or higher: 21.2% (2005); Master's degree or higher: 9.1% (2005).

School District(s)
Oswego City School District (KG-12)
 2003-04 Enrollment: 4,809 . . . . (315) 341-5885

Four-year College(s)
SUNY College at Oswego (Public)
 Fall 2004 Enrollment: 8,289. (315) 312-2500
 2005-06 Tuition: In-state $5,322; Out-of-state $11,582

Housing: Homeownership rate: 52.6% (2005); Median home value: $92,006 (2005); Median rent: $399 per month (2000); Median age of housing: 60+ years (2000).
Hospitals: Oswego Hospital (74 beds)
Safety: Violent crime rate: 30.7 per 10,000 population; Property crime rate: 357.7 per 10,000 population (2004).
Newspapers: Palladium-Times (Circulation 8,700)
Transportation: Commute to work: 87.8% car, 2.0% public transportation, 7.2% walk, 2.4% work from home (2000); Travel time to work: 61.9% less than 15 minutes, 22.5% 15 to 30 minutes, 6.4% 30 to 45 minutes, 5.4% 45 to 60 minutes, 3.8% 60 minutes or more (2000)
Additional Information Contacts
City of Oswego. . . . . (315) 342-8116
 http://www.oswegony.org/
Oswego Chamber of Commerce . . . . (315) 343-7681
 http://www.oswegochamber.com

OSWEGO (town). Covers a land area of 27.420 square miles and a water area of 1.919 square miles. Located at 43.41° N. Lat.; 76.55° W. Long. Elevation is 298 feet.
History: Trading post established here after the English founded Oswego (1722) became vital to the Albany fur trade. Its strategic location prompted the building of Fort Oswego (1727), Fort George (1755) and Fort Ontario (1755), which were much contested in the colonial wars. Importance as a lake port came with the completion of the Barge Canal (1917) and the St. Lawrence Seaway (1959). Seat of State University College of Arts and Science at Oswego. Founded 1722, Incorporated as a city 1848.
Population: 8,027 (1990); 7,287 (2000); 7,495 (2005); 7,763 (2010 projected); Race: 93.0% White, 2.9% Black, 1.5% Asian, 2.4% Hispanic of any race (2005); Density: 273.3 persons per square mile (2005); Average household size: 4.08 (2005); Median age: 23.1 (2005); Males per 100 females: 92.1 (2005); Marriage status: 33.9% never married, 56.4% now married, 4.0% widowed, 5.6% divorced (2000); Foreign born: 2.6% (2000); Ancestry (includes multiple ancestries): 21.8% Irish, 19.0% German, 14.4% English, 14.4% Italian, 7.6% Polish (2000).
Economy: Largest U.S. port on Lake Ontario, it is a port of entry and a Northern terminus of the Barge Canal. The city's manufacturing includes steel fabrication and rolled aluminum. It is the seat of State University College of Arts and Science at Oswego. Located northeast of Oswego are three nuclear power plants. Single-family building permits issued: 5 (2005); Multi-family building permits issued: 0 (2005); Employment by occupation: 9.8% management, 21.2% professional, 20.1% services, 28.0% sales, 0.4% farming, 9.5% construction, 11.0% production (2000).
Income: Per capita income: $18,221 (2005); Median household income: $57,732 (2005); Average household income: $69,414 (2005); Percent of households with income of $100,000 or more: 20.9% (2005); Poverty rate: 7.8% (2000).
Education: Percent of population age 25 and over with: High school diploma (including GED) or higher: 86.8% (2005); Bachelor's degree or higher: 28.6% (2005); Master's degree or higher: 13.3% (2005).
Housing: Homeownership rate: 84.9% (2005); Median home value: $118,981 (2005); Median rent: $377 per month (2000); Median age of housing: 28 years (2000).
Transportation: Commute to work: 76.1% car, 1.4% public transportation, 18.9% walk, 2.6% work from home (2000); Travel time to work: 53.9% less than 15 minutes, 29.7% 15 to 30 minutes, 7.3% 30 to 45 minutes, 5.5% 45 to 60 minutes, 3.6% 60 minutes or more (2000)
Additional Information Contacts
Town of Oswego . . . . (315) 343-2424
 http://www.townofoswego.com/

PALERMO (town). Covers a land area of 40.601 square miles and a water area of 0.151 square miles. Located at 43.36° N. Lat.; 76.27° W. Long.
Population: 3,582 (1990); 3,686 (2000); 3,762 (2005); 3,839 (2010 projected); Race: 98.0% White, 0.5% Black, 0.2% Asian, 0.6% Hispanic of any race (2005); Density: 92.7 persons per square mile (2005); Average household size: 2.77 (2005); Median age: 36.7 (2005); Males per 100 females: 102.5 (2005); Marriage status: 22.0% never married, 66.3% now married, 3.8% widowed, 8.0% divorced (2000); Foreign born: 0.5% (2000); Ancestry (includes multiple ancestries): 19.1% German, 16.8% English, 11.9% United States or American, 11.2% Irish, 11.0% French (except Basque) (2000).
Economy: Single-family building permits issued: 6 (2005); Multi-family building permits issued: 0 (2005); Employment by occupation: 8.0% management, 12.0% professional, 14.1% services, 26.3% sales, 1.0% farming, 16.9% construction, 21.8% production (2000).
Income: Per capita income: $19,887 (2005); Median household income: $48,072 (2005); Average household income: $55,011 (2005); Percent of households with income of $100,000 or more: 7.5% (2005); Poverty rate: 6.9% (2000).
Education: Percent of population age 25 and over with: High school diploma (including GED) or higher: 79.1% (2005); Bachelor's degree or higher: 9.2% (2005); Master's degree or higher: 3.5% (2005).
Housing: Homeownership rate: 85.6% (2005); Median home value: $95,044 (2005); Median rent: $460 per month (2000); Median age of housing: 24 years (2000).
Transportation: Commute to work: 95.8% car, 0.7% public transportation, 0.0% walk, 2.8% work from home (2000); Travel time to work: 15.5% less than 15 minutes, 30.5% 15 to 30 minutes, 33.9% 30 to 45 minutes, 13.9% 45 to 60 minutes, 6.2% 60 minutes or more (2000)

PARISH (village). Covers a land area of 1.538 square miles and a water area of 0 square miles. Located at 43.40° N. Lat.; 76.12° W. Long. Elevation is 696 feet.
Population: 477 (1990); 512 (2000); 491 (2005); 484 (2010 projected); Race: 99.2% White, 0.0% Black, 0.0% Asian, 0.4% Hispanic of any race (2005); Density: 319.1 persons per square mile (2005); Average household size: 2.63 (2005); Median age: 36.2 (2005); Males per 100 females: 97.2 (2005); Marriage status: 28.5% never married, 57.7% now married, 7.4% widowed, 6.4% divorced (2000); Foreign born: 1.5% (2000); Ancestry (includes multiple ancestries): 21.8% Irish, 15.2% German, 12.5% English, 8.5% French (except Basque), 7.0% Italian (2000).
Economy: Single-family building permits issued: 1 (2005); Multi-family building permits issued: 0 (2005); Employment by occupation: 4.8% management, 19.3% professional, 18.4% services, 20.6% sales, 0.0% farming, 15.8% construction, 21.1% production (2000).
Income: Per capita income: $16,584 (2005); Median household income: $39,306 (2005); Average household income: $43,543 (2005); Percent of households with income of $100,000 or more: 6.4% (2005); Poverty rate: 10.5% (2000).
Education: Percent of population age 25 and over with: High school diploma (including GED) or higher: 87.7% (2005); Bachelor's degree or higher: 12.3% (2005); Master's degree or higher: 3.0% (2005).

School District(s)
Altmar-Parish-Williamstown Central School District (KG-12)
 2003-04 Enrollment: 1,647 . . . . (315) 625-5251

Housing: Homeownership rate: 72.7% (2005); Median home value: $92,432 (2005); Median rent: $390 per month (2000); Median age of housing: 60+ years (2000).
Transportation: Commute to work: 89.4% car, 1.8% public transportation, 4.9% walk, 4.0% work from home (2000); Travel time to work: 25.3% less than 15 minutes, 17.5% 15 to 30 minutes, 29.5% 30 to 45 minutes, 21.7% 45 to 60 minutes, 6.0% 60 minutes or more (2000)

PARISH (town). Covers a land area of 41.777 square miles and a water area of 0.190 square miles. Located at 43.40° N. Lat.; 76.07° W. Long. Elevation is 696 feet.
Population: 2,425 (1990); 2,694 (2000); 2,646 (2005); 2,632 (2010 projected); Race: 98.5% White, 0.5% Black, 0.0% Asian, 0.6% Hispanic of any race (2005); Density: 63.3 persons per square mile (2005); Average household size: 2.76 (2005); Median age: 36.5 (2005); Males per 100 females: 99.5 (2005); Marriage status: 23.9% never married, 62.2% now married, 4.6% widowed, 9.3% divorced (2000); Foreign born: 0.8% (2000); Ancestry (includes multiple ancestries): 17.6% German, 16.9% Irish, 15.1% English, 10.4% French (except Basque), 8.3% Polish (2000).
Economy: Agriculture: dairy products; poultry; vegetables. Single-family building permits issued: 3 (2005); Multi-family building permits issued: 0 (2005); Employment by occupation: 8.1% management, 14.5% professional, 13.7% services, 23.5% sales, 0.0% farming, 15.2% construction, 25.0% production (2000).
Income: Per capita income: $18,328 (2005); Median household income: $42,788 (2005); Average household income: $50,568 (2005); Percent of households with income of $100,000 or more: 8.0% (2005); Poverty rate: 12.7% (2000).
Education: Percent of population age 25 and over with: High school diploma (including GED) or higher: 80.7% (2005); Bachelor's degree or higher: 10.4% (2005); Master's degree or higher: 3.6% (2005).
Housing: Homeownership rate: 85.2% (2005); Median home value: $88,841 (2005); Median rent: $404 per month (2000); Median age of housing: 25 years (2000).
Transportation: Commute to work: 94.0% car, 0.7% public transportation, 2.4% walk, 3.0% work from home (2000); Travel time to work: 20.1% less than 15 minutes, 21.6% 15 to 30 minutes, 39.7% 30 to 45 minutes, 13.3% 45 to 60 minutes, 5.3% 60 minutes or more (2000)

PENNELLVILLE (unincorporated postal area, zip code 13132). Covers a land area of 23.336 square miles and a water area of 0.151 square miles. Located at 43.26° N. Lat.; 76.22° W. Long.
Population: 0 (2000); Race: 97.0% White, 0.7% Black, 0.6% Asian, 0.4% Hispanic of any race (2000); Density: 0.0 persons per square mile (2000); Age: 27.9% under 18, 6.8% over 64 (2000); Marriage status: 24.0% never married, 63.8% now married, 3.2% widowed, 9.0% divorced (2000); Foreign born: 1.7% (2000); Ancestry (includes multiple ancestries): 23.0% German, 16.8% Irish, 16.4% Italian, 14.9% English, 8.2% Polish (2000).
Economy: Employment by occupation: 11.2% management, 23.0% professional, 10.8% services, 23.8% sales, 0.4% farming, 12.8% construction, 18.0% production (2000).
Income: Per capita income: $18,601 (2000); Median household income: $43,929 (2000); Poverty rate: 7.9% (2000).
Education: Percent of population age 25 and over with: High school diploma (including GED) or higher: 85.8% (2000); Bachelor's degree or higher: 21.2% (2000).
Housing: Homeownership rate: 90.5% (2000); Median home value: $85,600 (2000); Median rent: $445 per month (2000); Median age of housing: 23 years (2000).
Transportation: Commute to work: 96.0% car, 1.1% public transportation, 0.4% walk, 1.6% work from home (2000); Travel time to work: 14.3% less than 15 minutes, 44.9% 15 to 30 minutes, 29.1% 30 to 45 minutes, 5.0% 45 to 60 minutes, 6.8% 60 minutes or more (2000)

PHOENIX (village). Covers a land area of 1.145 square miles and a water area of 0.105 square miles. Located at 43.23° N. Lat.; 76.29° W. Long. Elevation is 394 feet.
History: Incorporated 1849.
Population: 2,486 (1990); 2,251 (2000); 2,199 (2005); 2,146 (2010 projected); Race: 98.0% White, 0.4% Black, 0.3% Asian, 1.2% Hispanic of any race (2005); Density: 1,920.8 persons per square mile (2005); Average household size: 2.30 (2005); Median age: 36.9 (2005); Males per 100 females: 88.3 (2005); Marriage status: 26.1% never married, 50.1% now married, 13.0% widowed, 10.7% divorced (2000); Foreign born: 0.8% (2000); Ancestry (includes multiple ancestries): 22.5% Irish, 21.1% German, 16.0% English, 10.5% French (except Basque), 8.8% Italian (2000).
Economy: Manufacturing: consumer goods, hunting and archery bows, conveyor systems, molded thermoplastics, specialized machinery, tools and dies. Agriculture: dairy products; vegetables. Single-family building permits issued: 1 (2005); Multi-family building permits issued: 0 (2005); Employment by occupation: 9.0% management, 11.9% professional, 14.9% services, 29.8% sales, 0.3% farming, 11.2% construction, 22.9% production (2000).
Income: Per capita income: $17,304 (2005); Median household income: $31,522 (2005); Average household income: $39,378 (2005); Percent of households with income of $100,000 or more: 4.1% (2005); Poverty rate: 13.2% (2000).
Education: Percent of population age 25 and over with: High school diploma (including GED) or higher: 78.9% (2005); Bachelor's degree or higher: 13.0% (2005); Master's degree or higher: 4.7% (2005).
School District(s)
Phoenix Central School District (KG-12)
    2003-04 Enrollment: 2,417 . . . . (315) 695-1555
Housing: Homeownership rate: 50.2% (2005); Median home value: $85,000 (2005); Median rent: $401 per month (2000); Median age of housing: 56 years (2000).
Safety: Violent crime rate: 13.5 per 10,000 population; Property crime rate: 189.6 per 10,000 population (2004).
Transportation: Commute to work: 92.2% car, 1.4% public transportation, 2.1% walk, 3.3% work from home (2000); Travel time to work: 25.5% less than 15 minutes, 50.5% 15 to 30 minutes, 20.2% 30 to 45 minutes, 2.4% 45 to 60 minutes, 1.3% 60 minutes or more (2000)
Additional Information Contacts
Phoenix Chamber of Commerce . . . . (315) 695-3599

PULASKI (village). Covers a land area of 3.288 square miles and a water area of 0.141 square miles. Located at 43.56° N. Lat.; 76.12° W. Long.
History: Incorporated 1832.
Population: 2,525 (1990); 2,398 (2000); 2,346 (2005); 2,298 (2010 projected); Race: 97.9% White, 0.3% Black, 0.6% Asian, 1.2% Hispanic of any race (2005); Density: 713.6 persons per square mile (2005); Average household size: 2.29 (2005); Median age: 38.4 (2005); Males per 100 females: 89.0 (2005); Marriage status: 22.1% never married, 50.3% now married, 15.0% widowed, 12.6% divorced (2000); Foreign born: 2.0% (2000); Ancestry (includes multiple ancestries): 19.6% Irish, 19.0% German, 18.9% English, 7.9% French (except Basque), 6.7% United States or American (2000).
Economy: Summer resort. Manufacturing: electronic equipment, paper products. Prized coho salmon fishing in the Salmon River. Trout and salmon hatchery at Altman, 7 miles Southeast. Single-family building permits issued: 1 (2005); Multi-family building permits issued: 0 (2005); Employment by occupation: 7.0% management, 21.2% professional, 22.2% services, 20.5% sales, 0.0% farming, 9.4% construction, 19.7% production (2000).
Income: Per capita income: $17,774 (2005); Median household income: $31,320 (2005); Average household income: $40,329 (2005); Percent of households with income of $100,000 or more: 8.2% (2005); Poverty rate: 15.6% (2000).
Education: Percent of population age 25 and over with: High school diploma (including GED) or higher: 78.6% (2005); Bachelor's degree or higher: 15.3% (2005); Master's degree or higher: 5.0% (2005).
School District(s)
Pulaski Central School District (PK-12)
    2003-04 Enrollment: 1,249 . . . . (315) 298-5188
Housing: Homeownership rate: 48.1% (2005); Median home value: $88,813 (2005); Median rent: $358 per month (2000); Median age of housing: 44 years (2000).
Transportation: Commute to work: 87.9% car, 1.1% public transportation, 7.7% walk, 2.0% work from home (2000); Travel time to work: 37.0% less than 15 minutes, 19.3% 15 to 30 minutes, 26.1% 30 to 45 minutes, 12.9% 45 to 60 minutes, 4.7% 60 minutes or more (2000)
Additional Information Contacts
Pulaski Chamber of Commerce . . . . (315) 298-2213
    http://www.pulaskinychamber.com
Pulaski Eastern Shore Chamber . . . . (315) 298-2213
    http://www.pulaskinychamber.com

REDFIELD (town). Covers a land area of 90.076 square miles and a water area of 3.362 square miles. Located at 43.57° N. Lat.; 75.83° W. Long. Elevation is 951 feet.
Population: 564 (1990); 607 (2000); 624 (2005); 642 (2010 projected); Race: 97.3% White, 1.1% Black, 0.0% Asian, 2.7% Hispanic of any race (2005); Density: 6.9 persons per square mile (2005); Average household size: 2.59 (2005); Median age: 39.4 (2005); Males per 100 females: 94.4 (2005); Marriage status: 20.0% never married, 61.3% now married, 6.3% widowed, 12.4% divorced (2000); Foreign born: 1.4% (2000); Ancestry (includes multiple ancestries): 19.5% German, 17.4% English, 11.8% United States or American, 10.1% Irish, 9.1% French (except Basque) (2000).
Economy: Single-family building permits issued: 15 (2005); Multi-family building permits issued: 0 (2005); Employment by occupation: 6.4% management, 10.2% professional, 15.3% services, 22.0% sales, 0.8% farming, 16.9% construction, 28.4% production (2000).
Income: Per capita income: $15,505 (2005); Median household income: $36,646 (2005); Average household income: $40,145 (2005); Percent of households with income of $100,000 or more: 2.1% (2005); Poverty rate: 12.7% (2000).
Education: Percent of population age 25 and over with: High school diploma (including GED) or higher: 80.0% (2005); Bachelor's degree or higher: 5.5% (2005); Master's degree or higher: 3.9% (2005).
Housing: Homeownership rate: 86.7% (2005); Median home value: $59,796 (2005); Median rent: $265 per month (2000); Median age of housing: 31 years (2000).
Transportation: Commute to work: 91.4% car, 0.9% public transportation, 3.0% walk, 4.7% work from home (2000); Travel time to work: 18.6% less than 15 minutes, 28.1% 15 to 30 minutes, 17.2% 30 to 45 minutes, 15.8% 45 to 60 minutes, 20.4% 60 minutes or more (2000)

RICHLAND (town). Covers a land area of 57.172 square miles and a water area of 2.922 square miles. Located at 43.54° N. Lat.; 76.13° W. Long. Elevation is 529 feet.
Population: 5,917 (1990); 5,824 (2000); 5,806 (2005); 5,798 (2010 projected); Race: 98.0% White, 0.3% Black, 0.5% Asian, 1.0% Hispanic of any race (2005); Density: 101.6 persons per square mile (2005); Average household size: 2.54 (2005); Median age: 37.7 (2005); Males per 100 females: 97.8 (2005); Marriage status: 23.0% never married, 58.4% now married, 8.2% widowed, 10.4% divorced (2000); Foreign born: 1.6% (2000); Ancestry (includes multiple ancestries): 18.6% Irish, 18.1% English, 14.0% German, 8.6% French (except Basque), 7.2% United States or American (2000).
Economy: Single-family building permits issued: 10 (2005); Multi-family building permits issued: 0 (2005); Employment by occupation: 7.5% management, 18.6% professional, 16.5% services, 25.4% sales, 0.4% farming, 11.3% construction, 20.4% production (2000).
Income: Per capita income: $19,482 (2005); Median household income: $40,403 (2005); Average household income: $49,251 (2005); Percent of households with income of $100,000 or more: 10.0% (2005); Poverty rate: 13.4% (2000).
Education: Percent of population age 25 and over with: High school diploma (including GED) or higher: 80.3% (2005); Bachelor's degree or higher: 15.7% (2005); Master's degree or higher: 4.7% (2005).
Housing: Homeownership rate: 67.0% (2005); Median home value: $90,773 (2005); Median rent: $374 per month (2000); Median age of housing: 40 years (2000).
Transportation: Commute to work: 92.9% car, 0.4% public transportation, 4.1% walk, 2.2% work from home (2000); Travel time to work: 38.8% less than 15 minutes, 23.0% 15 to 30 minutes, 20.1% 30 to 45 minutes, 12.7% 45 to 60 minutes, 5.4% 60 minutes or more (2000)

SAND RIDGE (CDP). Covers a land area of 2.416 square miles and a water area of 0.034 square miles. Located at 43.25° N. Lat.; 76.22° W. Long.
Population: 1,312 (1990); 906 (2000); 925 (2005); 945 (2010 projected); Race: 97.0% White, 0.2% Black, 0.8% Asian, 0.6% Hispanic of any race (2005); Density: 382.9 persons per square mile (2005); Average household size: 2.55 (2005); Median age: 37.5 (2005); Males per 100 females: 105.6 (2005); Marriage status: 24.4% never married, 58.5% now married, 2.6% widowed, 14.5% divorced (2000); Foreign born: 0.8% (2000); Ancestry (includes multiple ancestries): 22.0% English, 20.2% Irish, 18.8% German, 18.7% Italian, 7.3% Other groups (2000).
Economy: Employment by occupation: 6.1% management, 11.4% professional, 15.9% services, 30.8% sales, 0.0% farming, 16.9% construction, 18.9% production (2000).
Income: Per capita income: $18,089 (2005); Median household income: $40,036 (2005); Average household income: $46,095 (2005); Percent of households with income of $100,000 or more: 4.1% (2005); Poverty rate: 7.3% (2000).
Education: Percent of population age 25 and over with: High school diploma (including GED) or higher: 83.0% (2005); Bachelor's degree or higher: 7.9% (2005); Master's degree or higher: 1.1% (2005).
Housing: Homeownership rate: 89.5% (2005); Median home value: $59,254 (2005); Median rent: $452 per month (2000); Median age of housing: 23 years (2000).
Transportation: Commute to work: 94.1% car, 1.5% public transportation, 1.7% walk, 0.0% work from home (2000); Travel time to work: 13.2% less than 15 minutes, 51.6% 15 to 30 minutes, 20.0% 30 to 45 minutes, 5.9% 45 to 60 minutes, 9.3% 60 minutes or more (2000)

SANDY CREEK (village). Covers a land area of 1.429 square miles and a water area of 0 square miles. Located at 43.64° N. Lat.; 76.08° W. Long. Elevation is 498 feet.
Population: 793 (1990); 789 (2000); 790 (2005); 793 (2010 projected); Race: 98.9% White, 0.0% Black, 0.0% Asian, 0.3% Hispanic of any race (2005); Density: 552.9 persons per square mile (2005); Average household size: 2.48 (2005); Median age: 38.8 (2005); Males per 100 females: 93.6 (2005); Marriage status: 27.0% never married, 56.9% now married, 7.6% widowed, 8.5% divorced (2000); Foreign born: 2.8% (2000); Ancestry (includes multiple ancestries): 22.4% English, 17.3% German, 13.3% Irish, 12.7% French (except Basque), 7.6% Dutch (2000).
Economy: Single-family building permits issued: 0 (2005); Multi-family building permits issued: 0 (2005); Employment by occupation: 9.9% management, 24.7% professional, 11.4% services, 24.1% sales, 0.6% farming, 9.9% construction, 19.3% production (2000).
Income: Per capita income: $18,823 (2005); Median household income: $37,813 (2005); Average household income: $46,761 (2005); Percent of households with income of $100,000 or more: 7.2% (2005); Poverty rate: 17.5% (2000).
Education: Percent of population age 25 and over with: High school diploma (including GED) or higher: 82.4% (2005); Bachelor's degree or higher: 16.9% (2005); Master's degree or higher: 6.5% (2005).
School District(s)
Sandy Creek Central School District (PK-12)
    2003-04 Enrollment: 1,090 . . . . (315) 387-3445
Housing: Homeownership rate: 66.0% (2005); Median home value: $86,829 (2005); Median rent: $384 per month (2000); Median age of housing: 60+ years (2000).
Transportation: Commute to work: 91.7% car, 1.8% public transportation, 5.0% walk, 1.2% work from home (2000); Travel time to work: 37.6% less than 15 minutes, 20.0% 15 to 30 minutes, 24.5% 30 to 45 minutes, 9.6% 45 to 60 minutes, 8.4% 60 minutes or more (2000)

SANDY CREEK (town). Covers a land area of 42.266 square miles and a water area of 4.271 square miles. Located at 43.64° N. Lat.; 76.11° W. Long. Elevation is 498 feet.
Population: 3,454 (1990); 3,863 (2000); 3,868 (2005); 3,883 (2010 projected); Race: 98.3% White, 0.1% Black, 0.1% Asian, 0.5% Hispanic of any race (2005); Density: 91.5 persons per square mile (2005); Average household size: 2.45 (2005); Median age: 39.4 (2005); Males per 100 females: 100.4 (2005); Marriage status: 21.9% never married, 61.6% now married, 7.2% widowed, 9.4% divorced (2000); Foreign born: 1.1% (2000); Ancestry (includes multiple ancestries): 20.1% English, 20.1% German, 15.0% Irish, 7.9% United States or American, 7.7% French (except Basque) (2000).
Economy: Dairying. Single-family building permits issued: 16 (2005); Multi-family building permits issued: 0 (2005); Employment by occupation: 7.2% management, 18.7% professional, 13.2% services, 24.4% sales, 1.8% farming, 17.4% construction, 17.3% production (2000).
Income: Per capita income: $19,118 (2005); Median household income: $38,578 (2005); Average household income: $46,893 (2005); Percent of households with income of $100,000 or more: 7.7% (2005); Poverty rate: 16.7% (2000).
Education: Percent of population age 25 and over with: High school diploma (including GED) or higher: 78.4% (2005); Bachelor's degree or higher: 12.5% (2005); Master's degree or higher: 4.4% (2005).

Housing: Homeownership rate: 76.3% (2005); Median home value: $93,990 (2005); Median rent: $373 per month (2000); Median age of housing: 37 years (2000).
Transportation: Commute to work: 93.1% car, 0.6% public transportation, 2.3% walk, 3.9% work from home (2000); Travel time to work: 32.7% less than 15 minutes, 16.1% 15 to 30 minutes, 22.6% 30 to 45 minutes, 15.4% 45 to 60 minutes, 13.1% 60 minutes or more (2000)

SCHROEPPEL (town).
Covers a land area of 42.320 square miles and a water area of 0.871 square miles. Located at 43.25° N. Lat.; 76.27° W. Long.
Population: 8,931 (1990); 8,566 (2000); 8,649 (2005); 8,733 (2010 projected); Race: 97.8% White, 0.4% Black, 0.4% Asian, 1.2% Hispanic of any race (2005); Density: 204.4 persons per square mile (2005); Average household size: 2.59 (2005); Median age: 37.9 (2005); Males per 100 females: 99.0 (2005); Marriage status: 22.6% never married, 61.5% now married, 6.7% widowed, 9.2% divorced (2000); Foreign born: 1.2% (2000); Ancestry (includes multiple ancestries): 20.9% German, 20.6% Irish, 14.3% English, 13.8% Italian, 8.5% French (except Basque) (2000).
Economy: Single-family building permits issued: 10 (2005); Multi-family building permits issued: 0 (2005); Employment by occupation: 11.2% management, 18.0% professional, 12.6% services, 24.5% sales, 0.3% farming, 14.1% construction, 19.4% production (2000).
Income: Per capita income: $19,574 (2005); Median household income: $42,500 (2005); Average household income: $50,348 (2005); Percent of households with income of $100,000 or more: 8.4% (2005); Poverty rate: 9.7% (2000).
Education: Percent of population age 25 and over with: High school diploma (including GED) or higher: 81.9% (2005); Bachelor's degree or higher: 16.3% (2005); Master's degree or higher: 5.5% (2005).
Housing: Homeownership rate: 77.5% (2005); Median home value: $95,434 (2005); Median rent: $409 per month (2000); Median age of housing: 29 years (2000).
Transportation: Commute to work: 95.4% car, 1.0% public transportation, 0.7% walk, 2.2% work from home (2000); Travel time to work: 16.8% less than 15 minutes, 46.7% 15 to 30 minutes, 27.8% 30 to 45 minutes, 4.4% 45 to 60 minutes, 4.3% 60 minutes or more (2000)

SCRIBA (town).
Covers a land area of 40.572 square miles and a water area of 3.295 square miles. Located at 43.46° N. Lat.; 76.41° W. Long.
Population: 6,472 (1990); 7,331 (2000); 7,676 (2005); 7,992 (2010 projected); Race: 96.8% White, 0.5% Black, 0.7% Asian, 2.7% Hispanic of any race (2005); Density: 189.2 persons per square mile (2005); Average household size: 2.64 (2005); Median age: 36.2 (2005); Males per 100 females: 105.1 (2005); Marriage status: 27.3% never married, 56.8% now married, 4.0% widowed, 11.9% divorced (2000); Foreign born: 1.5% (2000); Ancestry (includes multiple ancestries): 20.1% Irish, 14.8% Italian, 14.7% English, 13.7% German, 13.1% French (except Basque) (2000).
Economy: Single-family building permits issued: 14 (2005); Multi-family building permits issued: 2 (2005); Employment by occupation: 6.5% management, 16.5% professional, 17.1% services, 22.9% sales, 0.3% farming, 14.6% construction, 22.2% production (2000).
Income: Per capita income: $21,141 (2005); Median household income: $46,046 (2005); Average household income: $55,761 (2005); Percent of households with income of $100,000 or more: 12.5% (2005); Poverty rate: 14.8% (2000).
Education: Percent of population age 25 and over with: High school diploma (including GED) or higher: 81.8% (2005); Bachelor's degree or higher: 12.1% (2005); Master's degree or higher: 4.7% (2005).
Housing: Homeownership rate: 74.9% (2005); Median home value: $107,956 (2005); Median rent: $380 per month (2000); Median age of housing: 23 years (2000).
Transportation: Commute to work: 96.4% car, 0.3% public transportation, 1.8% walk, 1.5% work from home (2000); Travel time to work: 45.5% less than 15 minutes, 36.4% 15 to 30 minutes, 6.5% 30 to 45 minutes, 8.2% 45 to 60 minutes, 3.4% 60 minutes or more (2000)
Additional Information Contacts
Town of Scriba . . . . (315) 343-3375
   http://scribany.org/

VOLNEY (town).
Covers a land area of 48.295 square miles and a water area of 0.854 square miles. Located at 43.34° N. Lat.; 76.39° W. Long.
Population: 5,676 (1990); 6,094 (2000); 6,208 (2005); 6,326 (2010 projected); Race: 98.0% White, 0.3% Black, 0.3% Asian, 0.8% Hispanic of any race (2005); Density: 128.5 persons per square mile (2005); Average household size: 2.73 (2005); Median age: 37.4 (2005); Males per 100 females: 103.4 (2005); Marriage status: 26.1% never married, 60.7% now married, 4.7% widowed, 8.5% divorced (2000); Foreign born: 1.3% (2000); Ancestry (includes multiple ancestries): 19.7% English, 16.7% Irish, 16.0% Italian, 15.5% German, 8.2% French (except Basque) (2000).
Economy: Single-family building permits issued: 11 (2005); Multi-family building permits issued: 0 (2005); Employment by occupation: 11.2% management, 18.3% professional, 10.6% services, 26.3% sales, 0.4% farming, 10.8% construction, 22.3% production (2000).
Income: Per capita income: $22,729 (2005); Median household income: $49,372 (2005); Average household income: $62,050 (2005); Percent of households with income of $100,000 or more: 15.8% (2005); Poverty rate: 6.2% (2000).
Education: Percent of population age 25 and over with: High school diploma (including GED) or higher: 85.0% (2005); Bachelor's degree or higher: 17.4% (2005); Master's degree or higher: 3.5% (2005).
Housing: Homeownership rate: 86.3% (2005); Median home value: $89,054 (2005); Median rent: $415 per month (2000); Median age of housing: 26 years (2000).
Transportation: Commute to work: 93.7% car, 0.7% public transportation, 3.2% walk, 2.1% work from home (2000); Travel time to work: 38.4% less than 15 minutes, 31.9% 15 to 30 minutes, 19.8% 30 to 45 minutes, 6.2% 45 to 60 minutes, 3.8% 60 minutes or more (2000)

WEST MONROE (town).
Covers a land area of 33.721 square miles and a water area of 4.810 square miles. Located at 43.29° N. Lat.; 76.08° W. Long.
Population: 4,393 (1990); 4,428 (2000); 4,519 (2005); 4,613 (2010 projected); Race: 97.3% White, 0.2% Black, 0.5% Asian, 0.4% Hispanic of any race (2005); Density: 134.0 persons per square mile (2005); Average household size: 2.75 (2005); Median age: 37.0 (2005); Males per 100 females: 108.1 (2005); Marriage status: 25.3% never married, 62.1% now married, 2.3% widowed, 10.3% divorced (2000); Foreign born: 2.4% (2000); Ancestry (includes multiple ancestries): 23.9% German, 15.4% Irish, 13.8% French (except Basque), 13.3% English, 13.0% Italian (2000).
Economy: Single-family building permits issued: 15 (2005); Multi-family building permits issued: 0 (2005); Employment by occupation: 9.1% management, 12.5% professional, 14.0% services, 22.7% sales, 0.0% farming, 14.9% construction, 26.8% production (2000).
Income: Per capita income: $19,088 (2005); Median household income: $47,415 (2005); Average household income: $52,502 (2005); Percent of households with income of $100,000 or more: 7.4% (2005); Poverty rate: 11.8% (2000).
Education: Percent of population age 25 and over with: High school diploma (including GED) or higher: 79.7% (2005); Bachelor's degree or higher: 12.4% (2005); Master's degree or higher: 3.6% (2005).
Housing: Homeownership rate: 85.9% (2005); Median home value: $95,469 (2005); Median rent: $434 per month (2000); Median age of housing: 25 years (2000).
Transportation: Commute to work: 95.8% car, 0.0% public transportation, 1.2% walk, 2.5% work from home (2000); Travel time to work: 11.7% less than 15 minutes, 36.9% 15 to 30 minutes, 41.8% 30 to 45 minutes, 7.0% 45 to 60 minutes, 2.6% 60 minutes or more (2000)

WILLIAMSTOWN (town).
Covers a land area of 38.693 square miles and a water area of 0.470 square miles. Located at 43.45° N. Lat.; 75.90° W. Long. Elevation is 613 feet.
Population: 1,279 (1990); 1,350 (2000); 1,387 (2005); 1,422 (2010 projected); Race: 97.7% White, 0.4% Black, 0.6% Asian, 1.7% Hispanic of any race (2005); Density: 35.8 persons per square mile (2005); Average household size: 2.94 (2005); Median age: 31.9 (2005); Males per 100 females: 96.2 (2005); Marriage status: 26.1% never married, 58.9% now married, 5.4% widowed, 9.6% divorced (2000); Foreign born: 0.9% (2000); Ancestry (includes multiple ancestries): 16.3% English, 14.8% German, 13.7% Irish, 11.5% French (except Basque), 10.7% United States or American (2000).
Economy: Lumber and wood products. Single-family building permits issued: 0 (2005); Multi-family building permits issued: 0 (2005); Employment by occupation: 8.4% management, 13.1% professional, 14.0% services, 19.6% sales, 1.1% farming, 13.6% construction, 30.1% production (2000).
Income: Per capita income: $14,079 (2005); Median household income: $35,083 (2005); Average household income: $41,460 (2005); Percent of

households with income of $100,000 or more: 4.5% (2005); Poverty rate: 14.2% (2000).
Education: Percent of population age 25 and over with: High school diploma (including GED) or higher: 76.7% (2005); Bachelor's degree or higher: 7.2% (2005); Master's degree or higher: 2.3% (2005).

School District(s)
Altmar-Parish-Williamstown Central School District (KG-12)
   2003-04 Enrollment: 1,647 . . . . (315) 625-5251
Housing: Homeownership rate: 80.7% (2005); Median home value: $79,753 (2005); Median rent: $382 per month (2000); Median age of housing: 33 years (2000).
Transportation: Commute to work: 93.0% car, 0.8% public transportation, 1.7% walk, 4.2% work from home (2000); Travel time to work: 23.1% less than 15 minutes, 23.7% 15 to 30 minutes, 20.5% 30 to 45 minutes, 23.9% 45 to 60 minutes, 8.9% 60 minutes or more (2000)

Otsego County

Located in central New York; bounded on the west by the Unadilla River; drained by the Susquehanna River; includes Canadarago Lake and other lakes. Covers a land area of 1,002.80 square miles, a water area of 12.31 square miles, and is located in the Eastern Time Zone. The county government was organized in 1791. County seat is Cooperstown.

Otsego County is part of the Oneonta, NY Micropolitan Statistical Area. The entire metro area includes: Otsego County, NY

Weather Station: Cherry Valley 2 NNE   Elevation: 1,358 feet

	Jan	Feb	Mar	Apr	May	Jun	Jul	Aug	Sep	Oct	Nov	Dec
High	28	30	40	53	66	74	78	76	68	57	45	33
Low	11	13	22	33	44	53	58	56	49	38	29	18
Precip	3.0	2.6	3.6	3.8	4.2	4.4	4.4	3.8	4.2	3.6	3.9	3.3
Snow	29.9	19.0	21.7	6.6	0.9	0.0	0.0	0.0	tr	0.8	12.0	25.2

High and Low temperatures in degrees Fahrenheit; Precipitation and Snow in inches

Weather Station: Cooperstown   Elevation: 1,197 feet

	Jan	Feb	Mar	Apr	May	Jun	Jul	Aug	Sep	Oct	Nov	Dec
High	30	34	43	56	68	76	80	78	70	59	47	35
Low	11	13	22	32	43	51	56	55	48	37	29	18
Precip	2.9	2.3	3.3	3.5	3.6	4.2	3.8	3.7	4.0	3.2	3.4	3.0
Snow	23.0	16.5	16.0	5.6	0.8	0.0	0.0	0.0	tr	0.2	7.2	18.2

High and Low temperatures in degrees Fahrenheit; Precipitation and Snow in inches

Population: 60,479 (1990); 61,676 (2000); 62,520 (2005); 63,364 (2010 projected); Race: 95.6% White, 1.9% Black, 0.9% Asian, 2.3% Hispanic of any race (2005); Density: 62.3 persons per square mile (2005); Average household size: 2.61 (2005); Median age: 38.0 (2005); Males per 100 females: 93.3 (2005).
Religion: Five largest groups: 14.9% Catholic Church, 8.5% The United Methodist Church, 2.4% Presbyterian Church (U.S.A.), 2.4% Episcopal Church, 2.1% American Baptist Churches in the USA (2000).
Economy: Unemployment rate: 4.3% (2005); Total civilian labor force: 32,010 (2005); Leading industries: 25.6% health care and social assistance; 18.7% retail trade; 11.5% accommodation and food services (2003); Farms: 1,028 totaling 206,233 acres (2002); Companies that employ 500 or more persons: 4 (2003); Companies that employ 100 to 499 persons: 18 (2003); Companies that employ less than 100 persons: 1,370 (2003); Black-owned businesses: n/a (2002); Hispanic-owned businesses: n/a (2002); Women-owned businesses: 1,317 (2002); Retail sales per capita: $12,646 (2006). Single-family building permits issued: 163 (2005); Multi-family building permits issued: 4 (2005).
Income: Per capita income: $19,277 (2005); Median household income: $37,745 (2005); Average household income: $49,087 (2005); Percent of households with income of $100,000 or more: 8.7% (2005); Poverty rate: 12.6% (2003); Bankruptcy rate: 5.24% (2005).
Education: Percent of population age 25 and over with: High school diploma (including GED) or higher: 82.9% (2005); Bachelor's degree or higher: 21.9% (2005); Master's degree or higher: 9.8% (2005).
Housing: Homeownership rate: 74.0% (2005); Median home value: $112,337 (2005); Median rent: $389 per month (2000); Median age of housing: 51 years (2000).
Health: Birth rate: 89.1 per 10,000 population (2004); Death rate: 101.4 per 10,000 population (2004); Age-adjusted cancer mortality rate: 205.9 deaths per 100,000 population (2002); Number of physicians: 48.5 per 10,000 population (2004); Hospital beds: 66.0 per 10,000 population (2003); Hospital admissions: 2,072.9 per 10,000 population (2003).

Elections: 2004 Presidential election results: 50.1% Bush, 47.7% Kerry, 1.9% Nader, 0.2% Badnarik
National and State Parks: Gilbert Lake State Park
Additional Information Contacts

Otsego County Government	(607) 547-4200
http://www.otsegocounty.com/	
City of Oneonta	(607) 432-6450
http://www.oneonta.ny.us/	
Town of Hartwick	(607) 293-8134
http://www.hartwickny.com/	

Otsego County Communities

BURLINGTON (town). Covers a land area of 44.967 square miles and a water area of 0.059 square miles. Located at 42.72° N. Lat.; 75.14° W. Long. Elevation is 1,542 feet.
Population: 1,036 (1990); 1,085 (2000); 1,129 (2005); 1,166 (2010 projected); Race: 96.9% White, 0.2% Black, 0.5% Asian, 2.1% Hispanic of any race (2005); Density: 25.1 persons per square mile (2005); Average household size: 2.71 (2005); Median age: 38.7 (2005); Males per 100 females: 105.6 (2005); Marriage status: 22.3% never married, 63.9% now married, 5.7% widowed, 8.0% divorced (2000); Foreign born: 1.4% (2000); Ancestry (includes multiple ancestries): 16.5% Irish, 16.3% English, 14.2% German, 9.7% United States or American, 7.9% Other groups (2000).
Economy: Employment by occupation: 18.1% management, 17.7% professional, 12.0% services, 25.2% sales, 1.4% farming, 11.4% construction, 14.1% production (2000).
Income: Per capita income: $17,883 (2005); Median household income: $43,000 (2005); Average household income: $47,933 (2005); Percent of households with income of $100,000 or more: 5.3% (2005); Poverty rate: 11.8% (2000).
Education: Percent of population age 25 and over with: High school diploma (including GED) or higher: 78.9% (2005); Bachelor's degree or higher: 14.8% (2005); Master's degree or higher: 6.9% (2005).
Housing: Homeownership rate: 87.0% (2005); Median home value: $106,132 (2005); Median rent: $328 per month (2000); Median age of housing: 37 years (2000).
Transportation: Commute to work: 85.9% car, 2.3% public transportation, 2.9% walk, 8.6% work from home (2000); Travel time to work: 32.0% less than 15 minutes, 27.4% 15 to 30 minutes, 22.1% 30 to 45 minutes, 8.9% 45 to 60 minutes, 9.7% 60 minutes or more (2000)

BURLINGTON FLATS (unincorporated postal area, zip code 13315). Covers a land area of 51.118 square miles and a water area of 0.055 square miles. Located at 42.72° N. Lat.; 75.14° W. Long. Elevation is 1,282 feet.
Population: 0 (2000); Race: 97.3% White, 0.2% Black, 0.0% Asian, 0.5% Hispanic of any race (2000); Density: 0.0 persons per square mile (2000); Age: 26.2% under 18, 14.7% over 64 (2000); Marriage status: 22.8% never married, 64.1% now married, 6.1% widowed, 7.0% divorced (2000); Foreign born: 1.0% (2000); Ancestry (includes multiple ancestries): 16.6% German, 15.1% Irish, 14.9% English, 9.5% United States or American, 7.2% Dutch (2000).
Economy: Employment by occupation: 13.6% management, 19.0% professional, 13.0% services, 23.4% sales, 3.0% farming, 12.0% construction, 16.0% production (2000).
Income: Per capita income: $15,069 (2000); Median household income: $38,750 (2000); Poverty rate: 11.0% (2000).
Education: Percent of population age 25 and over with: High school diploma (including GED) or higher: 77.5% (2000); Bachelor's degree or higher: 12.5% (2000).
Housing: Homeownership rate: 86.2% (2000); Median home value: $61,600 (2000); Median rent: $345 per month (2000); Median age of housing: 42 years (2000).
Transportation: Commute to work: 87.8% car, 1.9% public transportation, 2.3% walk, 7.8% work from home (2000); Travel time to work: 25.8% less than 15 minutes, 30.2% 15 to 30 minutes, 22.7% 30 to 45 minutes, 11.7% 45 to 60 minutes, 9.6% 60 minutes or more (2000)

BUTTERNUTS (town). Covers a land area of 54.072 square miles and a water area of 0.006 square miles. Located at 42.47° N. Lat.; 75.32° W. Long.
Population: 1,626 (1990); 1,792 (2000); 1,890 (2005); 1,977 (2010 projected); Race: 97.2% White, 1.0% Black, 0.3% Asian, 1.5% Hispanic of any race (2005); Density: 35.0 persons per square mile (2005); Average

household size: 2.46 (2005); Median age: 43.7 (2005); Males per 100 females: 94.2 (2005); Marriage status: 19.4% never married, 65.4% now married, 7.2% widowed, 8.0% divorced (2000); Foreign born: 1.5% (2000); Ancestry (includes multiple ancestries): 19.6% German, 19.0% English, 17.5% Irish, 10.0% Italian, 8.2% Other groups (2000).
Economy: Employment by occupation: 17.2% management, 22.6% professional, 12.1% services, 16.9% sales, 2.0% farming, 9.4% construction, 19.7% production (2000).
Income: Per capita income: $22,527 (2005); Median household income: $46,832 (2005); Average household income: $55,199 (2005); Percent of households with income of $100,000 or more: 11.5% (2005); Poverty rate: 8.6% (2000).
Education: Percent of population age 25 and over with: High school diploma (including GED) or higher: 84.7% (2005); Bachelor's degree or higher: 20.3% (2005); Master's degree or higher: 8.0% (2005).
Housing: Homeownership rate: 84.2% (2005); Median home value: $111,277 (2005); Median rent: $357 per month (2000); Median age of housing: 38 years (2000).
Transportation: Commute to work: 89.8% car, 1.0% public transportation, 2.3% walk, 6.6% work from home (2000); Travel time to work: 19.3% less than 15 minutes, 42.0% 15 to 30 minutes, 22.3% 30 to 45 minutes, 8.2% 45 to 60 minutes, 8.2% 60 minutes or more (2000)

CHERRY VALLEY (village).
Covers a land area of 0.568 square miles and a water area of 0 square miles. Located at 42.80° N. Lat.; 74.75° W. Long. Elevation is 1,326 feet.
Population: 617 (1990); 592 (2000); 639 (2005); 685 (2010 projected); Race: 98.6% White, 0.0% Black, 1.1% Asian, 0.0% Hispanic of any race (2005); Density: 1,124.1 persons per square mile (2005); Average household size: 2.45 (2005); Median age: 41.2 (2005); Males per 100 females: 85.8 (2005); Marriage status: 27.7% never married, 54.4% now married, 10.5% widowed, 7.4% divorced (2000); Foreign born: 4.2% (2000); Ancestry (includes multiple ancestries): 26.5% German, 20.4% Irish, 17.3% English, 12.7% United States or American, 8.2% Italian (2000).
Economy: Employment by occupation: 11.3% management, 30.6% professional, 13.6% services, 26.4% sales, 0.4% farming, 6.8% construction, 10.9% production (2000).
Income: Per capita income: $20,790 (2005); Median household income: $39,688 (2005); Average household income: $50,900 (2005); Percent of households with income of $100,000 or more: 7.7% (2005); Poverty rate: 13.3% (2000).
Education: Percent of population age 25 and over with: High school diploma (including GED) or higher: 81.0% (2005); Bachelor's degree or higher: 20.4% (2005); Master's degree or higher: 8.4% (2005).
School District(s)
Cherry Valley-Springfield Central School District (PK-12)
 2003-04 Enrollment: 700 . . . . (607) 264-9332
Housing: Homeownership rate: 76.2% (2005); Median home value: $108,681 (2005); Median rent: $406 per month (2000); Median age of housing: 60+ years (2000).
Transportation: Commute to work: 84.0% car, 2.3% public transportation, 7.6% walk, 6.1% work from home (2000); Travel time to work: 33.3% less than 15 minutes, 37.4% 15 to 30 minutes, 14.6% 30 to 45 minutes, 8.1% 45 to 60 minutes, 6.5% 60 minutes or more (2000)

CHERRY VALLEY (town).
Covers a land area of 40.062 square miles and a water area of 0 square miles. Located at 42.81° N. Lat.; 74.72° W. Long. Elevation is 1,326 feet.
History: Burned (Nov. 11, 1778) during American Revolution by Native American and Tory forces; over 40 people killed. Settled c.1740.
Population: 1,210 (1990); 1,266 (2000); 1,369 (2005); 1,468 (2010 projected); Race: 98.8% White, 0.0% Black, 0.7% Asian, 0.0% Hispanic of any race (2005); Density: 34.2 persons per square mile (2005); Average household size: 2.58 (2005); Median age: 41.0 (2005); Males per 100 females: 93.9 (2005); Marriage status: 24.1% never married, 61.0% now married, 6.4% widowed, 8.5% divorced (2000); Foreign born: 3.1% (2000); Ancestry (includes multiple ancestries): 23.4% German, 19.7% English, 18.4% Irish, 10.0% United States or American, 7.9% Dutch (2000).
Economy: Employment by occupation: 12.1% management, 26.4% professional, 14.0% services, 22.6% sales, 1.7% farming, 10.9% construction, 12.3% production (2000).
Income: Per capita income: $21,388 (2005); Median household income: $45,575 (2005); Average household income: $55,141 (2005); Percent of households with income of $100,000 or more: 10.4% (2005); Poverty rate: 11.3% (2000).
Education: Percent of population age 25 and over with: High school diploma (including GED) or higher: 84.3% (2005); Bachelor's degree or higher: 22.5% (2005); Master's degree or higher: 9.4% (2005).
Housing: Homeownership rate: 82.3% (2005); Median home value: $119,966 (2005); Median rent: $400 per month (2000); Median age of housing: 60+ years (2000).
Transportation: Commute to work: 86.7% car, 1.2% public transportation, 4.9% walk, 6.2% work from home (2000); Travel time to work: 30.3% less than 15 minutes, 37.7% 15 to 30 minutes, 16.2% 30 to 45 minutes, 7.9% 45 to 60 minutes, 7.9% 60 minutes or more (2000)

COOPERSTOWN (village).
Covers a land area of 1.542 square miles and a water area of 0.039 square miles. Located at 42.69° N. Lat.; 74.92° W. Long. Elevation is 1,264 feet.
History: Founded by William Cooper, who brought his family here in 1787. His son, James Fenimore Cooper, made his home here after returning from abroad in 1833, and the region is described in his Leatherstocking Tales. Fenimore House is the headquarters of N.Y. State Historical Association. Other attractions include Farmers' Museum and the famous National Baseball Hall of Fame and Museum, which commemorates the founding (1839) of baseball here by Abner Doubleday. Incorporated 1807.
Population: 2,180 (1990); 2,032 (2000); 1,797 (2005); 1,755 (2010 projected); Race: 95.2% White, 1.3% Black, 2.4% Asian, 3.3% Hispanic of any race (2005); Density: 1,165.1 persons per square mile (2005); Average household size: 2.18 (2005); Median age: 46.5 (2005); Males per 100 females: 82.4 (2005); Marriage status: 25.0% never married, 53.6% now married, 11.1% widowed, 10.3% divorced (2000); Foreign born: 6.2% (2000); Ancestry (includes multiple ancestries): 21.6% Irish, 19.8% German, 19.1% English, 8.3% Italian, 6.8% Other groups (2000).
Economy: Popular tourist destination. Glimmerglass Opera is here. Employment by occupation: 22.1% management, 33.4% professional, 13.0% services, 23.0% sales, 0.6% farming, 3.5% construction, 4.5% production (2000).
Income: Per capita income: $28,684 (2005); Median household income: $38,653 (2005); Average household income: $60,246 (2005); Percent of households with income of $100,000 or more: 14.9% (2005); Poverty rate: 10.2% (2000).
Education: Percent of population age 25 and over with: High school diploma (including GED) or higher: 89.3% (2005); Bachelor's degree or higher: 41.3% (2005); Master's degree or higher: 21.1% (2005).
School District(s)
Cooperstown Central School District (KG-12)
 2003-04 Enrollment: 1,138 . . . . (607) 547-5364
Housing: Homeownership rate: 53.2% (2005); Median home value: $231,250 (2005); Median rent: $455 per month (2000); Median age of housing: 60+ years (2000).
Hospitals: Bassett Healthcare (180 beds)
Newspapers: Cooperstown Crier (General - Circulation 2,400)
Transportation: Commute to work: 57.1% car, 0.4% public transportation, 34.6% walk, 7.0% work from home (2000); Travel time to work: 69.1% less than 15 minutes, 14.7% 15 to 30 minutes, 10.5% 30 to 45 minutes, 2.0% 45 to 60 minutes, 3.7% 60 minutes or more (2000)
Additional Information Contacts
Cooperstown Chamber of Commerce . . . . (607) 547-9983
 http://www.cooperstownchamber.org

DECATUR (town).
Covers a land area of 20.594 square miles and a water area of 0.177 square miles. Located at 42.67° N. Lat.; 74.70° W. Long.
Population: 356 (1990); 410 (2000); 433 (2005); 451 (2010 projected); Race: 98.6% White, 0.2% Black, 0.2% Asian, 1.4% Hispanic of any race (2005); Density: 21.0 persons per square mile (2005); Average household size: 2.56 (2005); Median age: 45.5 (2005); Males per 100 females: 114.4 (2005); Marriage status: 17.1% never married, 67.3% now married, 7.9% widowed, 7.6% divorced (2000); Foreign born: 3.9% (2000); Ancestry (includes multiple ancestries): 19.6% German, 10.3% Irish, 10.1% United States or American, 10.1% English, 7.5% Italian (2000).
Economy: Employment by occupation: 13.9% management, 16.1% professional, 16.1% services, 21.2% sales, 0.7% farming, 16.8% construction, 15.3% production (2000).
Income: Per capita income: $19,013 (2005); Median household income: $34,545 (2005); Average household income: $48,713 (2005); Percent of

households with income of $100,000 or more: 7.1% (2005); Poverty rate: 4.4% (2000).
Education: Percent of population age 25 and over with: High school diploma (including GED) or higher: 73.7% (2005); Bachelor's degree or higher: 12.4% (2005); Master's degree or higher: 3.5% (2005).
Housing: Homeownership rate: 91.1% (2005); Median home value: $133,036 (2005); Median rent: $400 per month (2000); Median age of housing: 33 years (2000).
Transportation: Commute to work: 88.1% car, 0.0% public transportation, 1.5% walk, 10.4% work from home (2000); Travel time to work: 15.7% less than 15 minutes, 21.5% 15 to 30 minutes, 42.1% 30 to 45 minutes, 5.0% 45 to 60 minutes, 15.7% 60 minutes or more (2000)

EAST SPRINGFIELD (unincorporated postal area, zip code 13333).
Covers a land area of 2.864 square miles and a water area of 0 square miles. Located at 42.84° N. Lat.; 74.80° W. Long. Elevation is 1,325 feet.
Population: 0 (2000); Race: 93.7% White, 0.0% Black, 0.0% Asian, 4.9% Hispanic of any race (2000); Density: 0.0 persons per square mile (2000); Age: 23.9% under 18, 25.4% over 64 (2000); Marriage status: 27.4% never married, 63.2% now married, 9.4% widowed, 0.0% divorced (2000); Foreign born: 4.9% (2000); Ancestry (includes multiple ancestries): 28.2% English, 27.5% German, 16.9% Dutch, 11.3% Other groups, 6.3% Ukrainian (2000).
Economy: Resort village. Employment by occupation: 21.8% management, 27.3% professional, 16.4% services, 16.4% sales, 0.0% farming, 10.9% construction, 7.3% production (2000).
Income: Per capita income: $16,905 (2000); Median household income: $29,464 (2000); Poverty rate: 14.8% (2000).
Education: Percent of population age 25 and over with: High school diploma (including GED) or higher: 73.3% (2000); Bachelor's degree or higher: 24.8% (2000).
Housing: Homeownership rate: 82.0% (2000); Median home value: $68,000 (2000); Median rent: $425 per month (2000); Median age of housing: 60+ years (2000).
Transportation: Commute to work: 92.7% car, 0.0% public transportation, 0.0% walk, 0.0% work from home (2000); Travel time to work: 43.6% less than 15 minutes, 27.3% 15 to 30 minutes, 16.4% 30 to 45 minutes, 0.0% 45 to 60 minutes, 12.7% 60 minutes or more (2000)

EAST WORCESTER (unincorporated postal area, zip code 12064).
Covers a land area of 9.202 square miles and a water area of 0.007 square miles. Located at 42.61° N. Lat.; 74.65° W. Long.
Population: 0 (2000); Race: 96.0% White, 0.0% Black, 0.0% Asian, 4.2% Hispanic of any race (2000); Density: 0.0 persons per square mile (2000); Age: 16.3% under 18, 21.4% over 64 (2000); Marriage status: 17.8% never married, 63.1% now married, 8.4% widowed, 10.8% divorced (2000); Foreign born: 4.4% (2000); Ancestry (includes multiple ancestries): 20.0% German, 19.8% Irish, 15.3% United States or American, 11.6% English, 8.6% Other groups (2000).
Economy: Employment by occupation: 9.6% management, 11.5% professional, 12.0% services, 24.5% sales, 3.8% farming, 8.7% construction, 29.8% production (2000).
Income: Per capita income: $17,852 (2000); Median household income: $31,719 (2000); Poverty rate: 14.2% (2000).
Education: Percent of population age 25 and over with: High school diploma (including GED) or higher: 79.6% (2000); Bachelor's degree or higher: 16.8% (2000).
Housing: Homeownership rate: 91.4% (2000); Median home value: $56,000 (2000); Median rent: $367 per month (2000); Median age of housing: 60+ years (2000).
Transportation: Commute to work: 85.8% car, 0.0% public transportation, 5.4% walk, 8.8% work from home (2000); Travel time to work: 14.5% less than 15 minutes, 21.0% 15 to 30 minutes, 31.2% 30 to 45 minutes, 14.5% 45 to 60 minutes, 18.8% 60 minutes or more (2000)

EDMESTON (town). Covers a land area of 44.552 square miles and a water area of 0.050 square miles. Located at 42.71° N. Lat.; 75.24° W. Long. Elevation is 1,183 feet.
Population: 1,717 (1990); 1,824 (2000); 1,920 (2005); 2,006 (2010 projected); Race: 98.0% White, 0.4% Black, 0.1% Asian, 1.1% Hispanic of any race (2005); Density: 43.1 persons per square mile (2005); Average household size: 2.72 (2005); Median age: 37.7 (2005); Males per 100 females: 99.2 (2005); Marriage status: 24.1% never married, 64.4% now married, 4.5% widowed, 7.0% divorced (2000); Foreign born: 1.6% (2000); Ancestry (includes multiple ancestries): 23.0% English, 16.3% German, 13.7% Irish, 8.0% United States or American, 6.7% Dutch (2000).
Economy: In farming and dairying area; makes artists' paints. Employment by occupation: 17.9% management, 15.0% professional, 15.1% services, 23.8% sales, 1.0% farming, 11.1% construction, 16.2% production (2000).
Income: Per capita income: $20,406 (2005); Median household income: $41,316 (2005); Average household income: $50,758 (2005); Percent of households with income of $100,000 or more: 9.5% (2005); Poverty rate: 13.6% (2000).
Education: Percent of population age 25 and over with: High school diploma (including GED) or higher: 81.9% (2005); Bachelor's degree or higher: 13.3% (2005); Master's degree or higher: 5.3% (2005).

School District(s)
Edmeston Central School District (KG-12)
    2003-04 Enrollment: 567 . . . . (607) 965-8931

Housing: Homeownership rate: 80.6% (2005); Median home value: $93,896 (2005); Median rent: $319 per month (2000); Median age of housing: 52 years (2000).
Transportation: Commute to work: 85.8% car, 2.6% public transportation, 3.9% walk, 7.5% work from home (2000); Travel time to work: 46.3% less than 15 minutes, 17.8% 15 to 30 minutes, 23.3% 30 to 45 minutes, 5.4% 45 to 60 minutes, 7.3% 60 minutes or more (2000)

EXETER (town). Covers a land area of 32.084 square miles and a water area of 0.569 square miles. Located at 42.78° N. Lat.; 75.08° W. Long.
Population: 967 (1990); 954 (2000); 992 (2005); 1,014 (2010 projected); Race: 96.2% White, 1.7% Black, 0.5% Asian, 1.2% Hispanic of any race (2005); Density: 30.9 persons per square mile (2005); Average household size: 2.51 (2005); Median age: 42.5 (2005); Males per 100 females: 101.6 (2005); Marriage status: 22.5% never married, 63.5% now married, 7.6% widowed, 6.4% divorced (2000); Foreign born: 3.5% (2000); Ancestry (includes multiple ancestries): 22.9% German, 13.3% English, 12.2% Irish, 8.9% Dutch, 8.2% Other groups (2000).
Economy: Employment by occupation: 7.2% management, 14.6% professional, 18.7% services, 27.9% sales, 5.0% farming, 12.6% construction, 14.0% production (2000).
Income: Per capita income: $18,735 (2005); Median household income: $40,878 (2005); Average household income: $46,932 (2005); Percent of households with income of $100,000 or more: 6.6% (2005); Poverty rate: 12.3% (2000).
Education: Percent of population age 25 and over with: High school diploma (including GED) or higher: 75.1% (2005); Bachelor's degree or higher: 9.2% (2005); Master's degree or higher: 3.6% (2005).
Housing: Homeownership rate: 85.9% (2005); Median home value: $97,500 (2005); Median rent: $337 per month (2000); Median age of housing: 41 years (2000).
Transportation: Commute to work: 91.8% car, 0.7% public transportation, 1.6% walk, 4.9% work from home (2000); Travel time to work: 17.8% less than 15 minutes, 41.3% 15 to 30 minutes, 18.6% 30 to 45 minutes, 15.6% 45 to 60 minutes, 6.7% 60 minutes or more (2000)

FLY CREEK (unincorporated postal area, zip code 13337). Covers a land area of 19.831 square miles and a water area of 0.010 square miles. Located at 42.74° N. Lat.; 74.98° W. Long.
Population: 0 (2000); Race: 100.0% White, 0.0% Black, 0.0% Asian, 0.0% Hispanic of any race (2000); Density: 0.0 persons per square mile (2000); Age: 33.8% under 18, 10.9% over 64 (2000); Marriage status: 27.8% never married, 55.4% now married, 5.8% widowed, 10.9% divorced (2000); Foreign born: 1.7% (2000); Ancestry (includes multiple ancestries): 34.0% German, 26.4% English, 23.3% Irish, 9.2% United States or American, 6.5% Italian (2000).
Economy: Employment by occupation: 17.5% management, 30.4% professional, 12.0% services, 22.4% sales, 1.7% farming, 13.5% construction, 2.5% production (2000).
Income: Per capita income: $24,613 (2000); Median household income: $48,516 (2000); Poverty rate: 2.8% (2000).
Education: Percent of population age 25 and over with: High school diploma (including GED) or higher: 90.9% (2000); Bachelor's degree or higher: 32.7% (2000).
Housing: Homeownership rate: 82.5% (2000); Median home value: $97,400 (2000); Median rent: $416 per month (2000); Median age of housing: 42 years (2000).
Transportation: Commute to work: 93.1% car, 0.0% public transportation, 0.0% walk, 6.9% work from home (2000); Travel time to work: 37.2% less

than 15 minutes, 39.3% 15 to 30 minutes, 14.5% 30 to 45 minutes, 9.0% 45 to 60 minutes, 0.0% 60 minutes or more (2000)

GARRATTSVILLE (unincorporated postal area, zip code 13342).
Covers a land area of 8.857 square miles and a water area of 0.041 square miles. Located at 42.64° N. Lat.; 75.17° W. Long.
Population: 0 (2000); Race: 100.0% White, 0.0% Black, 0.0% Asian, 0.0% Hispanic of any race (2000); Density: 0.0 persons per square mile (2000); Age: 27.8% under 18, 13.7% over 64 (2000); Marriage status: 24.6% never married, 56.9% now married, 12.6% widowed, 6.0% divorced (2000); Foreign born: 0.0% (2000); Ancestry (includes multiple ancestries): 22.6% German, 20.8% English, 17.5% Irish, 10.8% French (except Basque), 10.4% Dutch (2000).
Economy: Employment by occupation: 17.0% management, 18.1% professional, 10.6% services, 14.9% sales, 4.3% farming, 16.0% construction, 19.1% production (2000).
Income: Per capita income: $15,750 (2000); Median household income: $33,750 (2000); Poverty rate: 20.3% (2000).
Education: Percent of population age 25 and over with: High school diploma (including GED) or higher: 86.0% (2000); Bachelor's degree or higher: 15.4% (2000).
Housing: Homeownership rate: 97.4% (2000); Median home value: $75,000 (2000); Median rent: $325 per month (2000); Median age of housing: 42 years (2000).
Transportation: Commute to work: 92.2% car, 0.0% public transportation, 5.6% walk, 2.2% work from home (2000); Travel time to work: 27.3% less than 15 minutes, 23.9% 15 to 30 minutes, 29.5% 30 to 45 minutes, 9.1% 45 to 60 minutes, 10.2% 60 minutes or more (2000)

GILBERTSVILLE (village).
Covers a land area of 1.003 square miles and a water area of 0 square miles. Located at 42.46° N. Lat.; 75.32° W. Long. Elevation is 1,108 feet.
Population: 388 (1990); 375 (2000); 395 (2005); 415 (2010 projected); Race: 96.5% White, 1.0% Black, 0.3% Asian, 1.5% Hispanic of any race (2005); Density: 393.9 persons per square mile (2005); Average household size: 2.26 (2005); Median age: 45.2 (2005); Males per 100 females: 80.4 (2005); Marriage status: 12.5% never married, 65.4% now married, 13.6% widowed, 8.6% divorced (2000); Foreign born: 3.0% (2000); Ancestry (includes multiple ancestries): 22.8% English, 20.9% German, 20.7% Irish, 9.8% United States or American, 7.9% Italian (2000).
Economy: In dairying and grain-growing area. Single-family building permits issued: 0 (2005); Multi-family building permits issued: 0 (2005); Employment by occupation: 12.1% management, 37.6% professional, 7.6% services, 19.7% sales, 0.0% farming, 7.6% construction, 15.3% production (2000).
Income: Per capita income: $23,294 (2005); Median household income: $45,066 (2005); Average household income: $51,529 (2005); Percent of households with income of $100,000 or more: 10.3% (2005); Poverty rate: 5.8% (2000).
Education: Percent of population age 25 and over with: High school diploma (including GED) or higher: 91.2% (2005); Bachelor's degree or higher: 26.7% (2005); Master's degree or higher: 16.8% (2005).
School District(s)
Gilbertsville-Mount Upton Central School District (KG-12)
    2003-04 Enrollment: 571 . . . . (607) 783-2207
Housing: Homeownership rate: 72.0% (2005); Median home value: $120,930 (2005); Median rent: $298 per month (2000); Median age of housing: 60+ years (2000).
Transportation: Commute to work: 85.7% car, 0.0% public transportation, 5.8% walk, 8.4% work from home (2000); Travel time to work: 25.5% less than 15 minutes, 34.8% 15 to 30 minutes, 25.5% 30 to 45 minutes, 7.1% 45 to 60 minutes, 7.1% 60 minutes or more (2000)

HARTWICK (town).
Covers a land area of 40.158 square miles and a water area of 0.176 square miles. Located at 42.64° N. Lat.; 75.01° W. Long. Elevation is 1,339 feet.
Population: 2,045 (1990); 2,203 (2000); 2,335 (2005); 2,359 (2010 projected); Race: 97.4% White, 0.5% Black, 1.2% Asian, 1.6% Hispanic of any race (2005); Density: 58.1 persons per square mile (2005); Average household size: 2.53 (2005); Median age: 40.7 (2005); Males per 100 females: 97.7 (2005); Marriage status: 23.5% never married, 56.8% now married, 9.6% widowed, 10.2% divorced (2000); Foreign born: 1.1% (2000); Ancestry (includes multiple ancestries): 21.4% English, 20.0% German, 14.3% Irish, 11.7% Other groups, 8.6% United States or American (2000).
Economy: Employment by occupation: 12.1% management, 20.5% professional, 23.7% services, 19.7% sales, 2.0% farming, 12.4% construction, 9.5% production (2000).
Income: Per capita income: $19,789 (2005); Median household income: $33,571 (2005); Average household income: $50,008 (2005); Percent of households with income of $100,000 or more: 8.0% (2005); Poverty rate: 13.9% (2000).
Education: Percent of population age 25 and over with: High school diploma (including GED) or higher: 81.5% (2005); Bachelor's degree or higher: 19.3% (2005); Master's degree or higher: 8.1% (2005).
Housing: Homeownership rate: 82.4% (2005); Median home value: $116,699 (2005); Median rent: $381 per month (2000); Median age of housing: 42 years (2000).
Transportation: Commute to work: 88.7% car, 1.1% public transportation, 2.0% walk, 7.3% work from home (2000); Travel time to work: 38.8% less than 15 minutes, 42.1% 15 to 30 minutes, 15.8% 30 to 45 minutes, 1.3% 45 to 60 minutes, 2.1% 60 minutes or more (2000)
Additional Information Contacts
Town of Hartwick . . . . (607) 293-8134
   http://www.hartwickny.com/

LAURENS (village).
Covers a land area of 0.125 square miles and a water area of 0 square miles. Located at 42.53° N. Lat.; 75.08° W. Long. Elevation is 1,116 feet.
Population: 293 (1990); 277 (2000); 280 (2005); 281 (2010 projected); Race: 98.2% White, 0.0% Black, 0.0% Asian, 1.8% Hispanic of any race (2005); Density: 2,239.8 persons per square mile (2005); Average household size: 2.39 (2005); Median age: 39.9 (2005); Males per 100 females: 94.4 (2005); Marriage status: 27.8% never married, 47.1% now married, 14.8% widowed, 10.3% divorced (2000); Foreign born: 1.4% (2000); Ancestry (includes multiple ancestries): 23.5% Irish, 18.1% English, 17.3% German, 8.7% United States or American, 8.3% Scotch-Irish (2000).
Economy: Employment by occupation: 7.8% management, 12.9% professional, 24.1% services, 30.2% sales, 1.7% farming, 6.9% construction, 16.4% production (2000).
Income: Per capita income: $15,830 (2005); Median household income: $28,542 (2005); Average household income: $37,885 (2005); Percent of households with income of $100,000 or more: 5.1% (2005); Poverty rate: 17.9% (2000).
Education: Percent of population age 25 and over with: High school diploma (including GED) or higher: 86.8% (2005); Bachelor's degree or higher: 14.3% (2005); Master's degree or higher: 5.8% (2005).
School District(s)
Laurens Central School District (KG-12)
    2003-04 Enrollment: 425 . . . . (607) 432-2050
Housing: Homeownership rate: 54.7% (2005); Median home value: $106,522 (2005); Median rent: $359 per month (2000); Median age of housing: 60+ years (2000).
Transportation: Commute to work: 85.3% car, 0.0% public transportation, 6.9% walk, 7.8% work from home (2000); Travel time to work: 33.6% less than 15 minutes, 41.1% 15 to 30 minutes, 18.7% 30 to 45 minutes, 0.0% 45 to 60 minutes, 6.5% 60 minutes or more (2000)

LAURENS (town).
Covers a land area of 42.567 square miles and a water area of 0.104 square miles. Located at 42.53° N. Lat.; 75.11° W. Long. Elevation is 1,116 feet.
Population: 2,349 (1990); 2,402 (2000); 2,429 (2005); 2,439 (2010 projected); Race: 96.9% White, 0.2% Black, 0.1% Asian, 1.7% Hispanic of any race (2005); Density: 57.1 persons per square mile (2005); Average household size: 2.44 (2005); Median age: 40.9 (2005); Males per 100 females: 95.4 (2005); Marriage status: 20.5% never married, 65.6% now married, 4.8% widowed, 9.1% divorced (2000); Foreign born: 2.0% (2000); Ancestry (includes multiple ancestries): 22.0% Irish, 20.2% German, 16.0% English, 10.4% Other groups, 9.2% Italian (2000).
Economy: In dairying area. Employment by occupation: 12.1% management, 19.5% professional, 20.2% services, 21.4% sales, 2.1% farming, 10.1% construction, 14.6% production (2000).
Income: Per capita income: $19,676 (2005); Median household income: $40,340 (2005); Average household income: $48,081 (2005); Percent of households with income of $100,000 or more: 7.7% (2005); Poverty rate: 11.9% (2000).
Education: Percent of population age 25 and over with: High school diploma (including GED) or higher: 85.5% (2005); Bachelor's degree or higher: 19.7% (2005); Master's degree or higher: 9.4% (2005).

Housing: Homeownership rate: 78.6% (2005); Median home value: $114,599 (2005); Median rent: $381 per month (2000); Median age of housing: 41 years (2000).
Transportation: Commute to work: 91.8% car, 1.3% public transportation, 3.5% walk, 2.5% work from home (2000); Travel time to work: 27.0% less than 15 minutes, 54.2% 15 to 30 minutes, 8.6% 30 to 45 minutes, 4.2% 45 to 60 minutes, 6.0% 60 minutes or more (2000)

MARYLAND (town). Covers a land area of 51.751 square miles and a water area of 0.107 square miles. Located at 42.54° N. Lat.; 74.85° W. Long.
Population: 1,716 (1990); 1,920 (2000); 1,914 (2005); 1,908 (2010 projected); Race: 99.2% White, 0.1% Black, 0.1% Asian, 1.2% Hispanic of any race (2005); Density: 37.0 persons per square mile (2005); Average household size: 2.44 (2005); Median age: 41.0 (2005); Males per 100 females: 99.4 (2005); Marriage status: 24.6% never married, 59.4% now married, 9.1% widowed, 6.8% divorced (2000); Foreign born: 2.7% (2000); Ancestry (includes multiple ancestries): 20.5% German, 14.9% Irish, 14.2% English, 10.4% Italian, 8.2% United States or American (2000).
Economy: Employment by occupation: 12.0% management, 17.6% professional, 18.9% services, 21.5% sales, 1.8% farming, 12.1% construction, 16.1% production (2000).
Income: Per capita income: $18,759 (2005); Median household income: $37,802 (2005); Average household income: $45,739 (2005); Percent of households with income of $100,000 or more: 6.8% (2005); Poverty rate: 12.6% (2000).
Education: Percent of population age 25 and over with: High school diploma (including GED) or higher: 82.5% (2005); Bachelor's degree or higher: 15.6% (2005); Master's degree or higher: 5.8% (2005).
Housing: Homeownership rate: 78.0% (2005); Median home value: $99,130 (2005); Median rent: $338 per month (2000); Median age of housing: 48 years (2000).
Transportation: Commute to work: 91.3% car, 1.0% public transportation, 2.2% walk, 5.4% work from home (2000); Travel time to work: 20.9% less than 15 minutes, 48.3% 15 to 30 minutes, 19.1% 30 to 45 minutes, 3.6% 45 to 60 minutes, 8.1% 60 minutes or more (2000)

MIDDLEFIELD (town). Covers a land area of 64.404 square miles and a water area of 1.527 square miles. Located at 42.68° N. Lat.; 74.87° W. Long.
Population: 2,231 (1990); 2,249 (2000); 2,351 (2005); 2,439 (2010 projected); Race: 96.2% White, 1.4% Black, 1.1% Asian, 1.6% Hispanic of any race (2005); Density: 36.5 persons per square mile (2005); Average household size: 2.78 (2005); Median age: 45.7 (2005); Males per 100 females: 96.6 (2005); Marriage status: 19.3% never married, 64.5% now married, 10.8% widowed, 5.4% divorced (2000); Foreign born: 1.9% (2000); Ancestry (includes multiple ancestries): 20.8% German, 19.7% Irish, 17.3% English, 7.4% United States or American, 7.4% Italian (2000).
Economy: Single-family building permits issued: 12 (2005); Multi-family building permits issued: 0 (2005); Employment by occupation: 14.3% management, 34.0% professional, 13.3% services, 18.3% sales, 1.5% farming, 11.8% construction, 6.9% production (2000).
Income: Per capita income: $25,392 (2005); Median household income: $45,667 (2005); Average household income: $66,848 (2005); Percent of households with income of $100,000 or more: 15.7% (2005); Poverty rate: 7.0% (2000).
Education: Percent of population age 25 and over with: High school diploma (including GED) or higher: 81.8% (2005); Bachelor's degree or higher: 28.8% (2005); Master's degree or higher: 14.3% (2005).
Housing: Homeownership rate: 80.5% (2005); Median home value: $158,163 (2005); Median rent: $539 per month (2000); Median age of housing: 35 years (2000).
Transportation: Commute to work: 82.0% car, 1.1% public transportation, 7.1% walk, 9.4% work from home (2000); Travel time to work: 47.4% less than 15 minutes, 28.3% 15 to 30 minutes, 12.7% 30 to 45 minutes, 5.0% 45 to 60 minutes, 6.6% 60 minutes or more (2000)

MILFORD (village). Covers a land area of 0.477 square miles and a water area of 0 square miles. Located at 42.59° N. Lat.; 74.94° W. Long. Elevation is 1,200 feet.
Population: 462 (1990); 511 (2000); 540 (2005); 563 (2010 projected); Race: 96.5% White, 0.2% Black, 1.5% Asian, 3.0% Hispanic of any race (2005); Density: 1,132.0 persons per square mile (2005); Average household size: 2.52 (2005); Median age: 40.4 (2005); Males per 100 females: 92.9 (2005); Marriage status: 26.2% never married, 54.5% now married, 8.8% widowed, 10.5% divorced (2000); Foreign born: 1.6% (2000); Ancestry (includes multiple ancestries): 29.9% English, 21.9% Irish, 18.1% German, 9.6% Italian, 8.1% United States or American (2000).
Economy: Employment by occupation: 7.1% management, 22.4% professional, 24.1% services, 32.0% sales, 0.0% farming, 7.5% construction, 7.1% production (2000).
Income: Per capita income: $22,661 (2005); Median household income: $49,464 (2005); Average household income: $56,974 (2005); Percent of households with income of $100,000 or more: 12.1% (2005); Poverty rate: 7.1% (2000).
Education: Percent of population age 25 and over with: High school diploma (including GED) or higher: 92.3% (2005); Bachelor's degree or higher: 22.4% (2005); Master's degree or higher: 11.5% (2005).

School District(s)
Milford Central School District (KG-12)
    2003-04 Enrollment: 473 . . . . (607) 286-3341
Housing: Homeownership rate: 73.4% (2005); Median home value: $101,230 (2005); Median rent: $359 per month (2000); Median age of housing: 60+ years (2000).
Transportation: Commute to work: 88.6% car, 0.4% public transportation, 6.3% walk, 4.6% work from home (2000); Travel time to work: 31.4% less than 15 minutes, 46.5% 15 to 30 minutes, 15.9% 30 to 45 minutes, 2.7% 45 to 60 minutes, 3.5% 60 minutes or more (2000)

MILFORD (town). Covers a land area of 46.109 square miles and a water area of 1.067 square miles. Located at 42.54° N. Lat.; 74.97° W. Long. Elevation is 1,200 feet.
Population: 2,845 (1990); 2,938 (2000); 2,961 (2005); 2,996 (2010 projected); Race: 97.3% White, 0.9% Black, 0.8% Asian, 2.1% Hispanic of any race (2005); Density: 64.2 persons per square mile (2005); Average household size: 2.38 (2005); Median age: 42.8 (2005); Males per 100 females: 93.3 (2005); Marriage status: 22.0% never married, 60.8% now married, 7.3% widowed, 10.0% divorced (2000); Foreign born: 1.6% (2000); Ancestry (includes multiple ancestries): 19.8% German, 17.9% English, 17.7% Irish, 12.9% Italian, 8.7% United States or American (2000).
Economy: In dairying area. Brewery. Employment by occupation: 12.2% management, 21.2% professional, 15.7% services, 31.4% sales, 1.1% farming, 8.0% construction, 10.4% production (2000).
Income: Per capita income: $21,206 (2005); Median household income: $40,392 (2005); Average household income: $50,012 (2005); Percent of households with income of $100,000 or more: 9.6% (2005); Poverty rate: 13.6% (2000).
Education: Percent of population age 25 and over with: High school diploma (including GED) or higher: 83.0% (2005); Bachelor's degree or higher: 20.8% (2005); Master's degree or higher: 8.2% (2005).
Housing: Homeownership rate: 82.0% (2005); Median home value: $106,232 (2005); Median rent: $357 per month (2000); Median age of housing: 42 years (2000).
Transportation: Commute to work: 90.6% car, 0.4% public transportation, 2.7% walk, 6.1% work from home (2000); Travel time to work: 26.9% less than 15 minutes, 54.9% 15 to 30 minutes, 8.9% 30 to 45 minutes, 4.2% 45 to 60 minutes, 5.0% 60 minutes or more (2000)

MORRIS (village). Covers a land area of 0.729 square miles and a water area of 0.008 square miles. Located at 42.54° N. Lat.; 75.24° W. Long. Elevation is 1,111 feet.
Population: 642 (1990); 591 (2000); 595 (2005); 604 (2010 projected); Race: 96.5% White, 0.3% Black, 0.0% Asian, 3.9% Hispanic of any race (2005); Density: 815.9 persons per square mile (2005); Average household size: 2.22 (2005); Median age: 42.5 (2005); Males per 100 females: 78.7 (2005); Marriage status: 18.5% never married, 55.6% now married, 11.1% widowed, 14.8% divorced (2000); Foreign born: 2.1% (2000); Ancestry (includes multiple ancestries): 23.9% English, 15.5% Irish, 15.0% German, 14.8% Italian, 8.4% Other groups (2000).
Economy: Employment by occupation: 10.0% management, 31.3% professional, 17.8% services, 17.8% sales, 0.0% farming, 10.0% construction, 13.1% production (2000).
Income: Per capita income: $19,916 (2005); Median household income: $37,059 (2005); Average household income: $44,216 (2005); Percent of households with income of $100,000 or more: 7.5% (2005); Poverty rate: 15.3% (2000).
Education: Percent of population age 25 and over with: High school diploma (including GED) or higher: 86.7% (2005); Bachelor's degree or higher: 19.5% (2005); Master's degree or higher: 10.6% (2005).

School District(s)
Morris Central School District (PK-12)
 2003-04 Enrollment: 496 . . . . (607) 263-6100
Housing: Homeownership rate: 66.0% (2005); Median home value: $101,250 (2005); Median rent: $348 per month (2000); Median age of housing: 60+ years (2000).
Transportation: Commute to work: 83.3% car, 0.8% public transportation, 10.1% walk, 5.8% work from home (2000); Travel time to work: 28.9% less than 15 minutes, 43.0% 15 to 30 minutes, 22.3% 30 to 45 minutes, 0.0% 45 to 60 minutes, 5.8% 60 minutes or more (2000)

MORRIS (town). Covers a land area of 39.028 square miles and a water area of 0.087 square miles. Located at 42.53° N. Lat.; 75.25° W. Long. Elevation is 1,111 feet.
Population: 1,787 (1990); 1,867 (2000); 1,881 (2005); 1,901 (2010 projected); Race: 96.4% White, 0.9% Black, 0.3% Asian, 2.2% Hispanic of any race (2005); Density: 48.2 persons per square mile (2005); Average household size: 2.48 (2005); Median age: 39.0 (2005); Males per 100 females: 92.3 (2005); Marriage status: 22.4% never married, 59.2% now married, 7.0% widowed, 11.4% divorced (2000); Foreign born: 2.0% (2000); Ancestry (includes multiple ancestries): 22.9% English, 16.9% German, 14.6% Irish, 9.6% Italian, 7.1% United States or American (2000).
Economy: In dairying area. Manufacturing of veterinary medicines. Otsego county fairground here. Employment by occupation: 13.2% management, 21.1% professional, 13.6% services, 23.7% sales, 1.7% farming, 11.7% construction, 15.0% production (2000).
Income: Per capita income: $19,106 (2005); Median household income: $38,915 (2005); Average household income: $46,744 (2005); Percent of households with income of $100,000 or more: 7.3% (2005); Poverty rate: 12.9% (2000).
Education: Percent of population age 25 and over with: High school diploma (including GED) or higher: 83.5% (2005); Bachelor's degree or higher: 18.2% (2005); Master's degree or higher: 7.0% (2005).
Housing: Homeownership rate: 75.4% (2005); Median home value: $98,972 (2005); Median rent: $354 per month (2000); Median age of housing: 54 years (2000).
Transportation: Commute to work: 89.6% car, 0.2% public transportation, 4.9% walk, 5.3% work from home (2000); Travel time to work: 26.6% less than 15 minutes, 44.7% 15 to 30 minutes, 21.2% 30 to 45 minutes, 3.0% 45 to 60 minutes, 4.5% 60 minutes or more (2000)

MOUNT VISION (unincorporated postal area, zip code 13810). Covers a land area of 39.501 square miles and a water area of 0.101 square miles. Located at 42.61° N. Lat.; 75.09° W. Long. Elevation is 1,169 feet.
Population: 0 (2000); Race: 99.3% White, 0.1% Black, 0.0% Asian, 0.8% Hispanic of any race (2000); Density: 0.0 persons per square mile (2000); Age: 23.8% under 18, 15.3% over 64 (2000); Marriage status: 19.5% never married, 66.0% now married, 5.2% widowed, 9.3% divorced (2000); Foreign born: 1.4% (2000); Ancestry (includes multiple ancestries): 19.4% Irish, 15.7% English, 14.7% German, 11.1% Other groups, 9.1% United States or American (2000).
Economy: Employment by occupation: 11.8% management, 19.3% professional, 19.0% services, 22.8% sales, 3.8% farming, 9.3% construction, 14.1% production (2000).
Income: Per capita income: $16,747 (2000); Median household income: $33,636 (2000); Poverty rate: 14.6% (2000).
Education: Percent of population age 25 and over with: High school diploma (including GED) or higher: 85.3% (2000); Bachelor's degree or higher: 18.6% (2000).
Housing: Homeownership rate: 76.2% (2000); Median home value: $69,000 (2000); Median rent: $374 per month (2000); Median age of housing: 49 years (2000).
Transportation: Commute to work: 88.3% car, 2.7% public transportation, 2.3% walk, 5.1% work from home (2000); Travel time to work: 22.2% less than 15 minutes, 53.6% 15 to 30 minutes, 14.6% 30 to 45 minutes, 4.1% 45 to 60 minutes, 5.4% 60 minutes or more (2000)

NEW LISBON (town). Covers a land area of 44.531 square miles and a water area of 0.142 square miles. Located at 42.63° N. Lat.; 75.14° W. Long. Elevation is 1,234 feet.
Population: 996 (1990); 1,116 (2000); 1,209 (2005); 1,296 (2010 projected); Race: 97.4% White, 1.0% Black, 0.6% Asian, 1.7% Hispanic of any race (2005); Density: 27.1 persons per square mile (2005); Average household size: 2.54 (2005); Median age: 41.5 (2005); Males per 100 females: 95.6 (2005); Marriage status: 21.0% never married, 64.7% now married, 6.5% widowed, 7.8% divorced (2000); Foreign born: 1.2% (2000); Ancestry (includes multiple ancestries): 18.3% German, 16.3% English, 14.2% Irish, 8.2% Dutch, 7.8% United States or American (2000).
Economy: Employment by occupation: 16.1% management, 19.6% professional, 15.3% services, 20.4% sales, 2.3% farming, 11.8% construction, 14.6% production (2000).
Income: Per capita income: $20,424 (2005); Median household income: $40,625 (2005); Average household income: $51,875 (2005); Percent of households with income of $100,000 or more: 9.9% (2005); Poverty rate: 14.5% (2000).
Education: Percent of population age 25 and over with: High school diploma (including GED) or higher: 84.7% (2005); Bachelor's degree or higher: 18.0% (2005); Master's degree or higher: 6.1% (2005).
Housing: Homeownership rate: 88.7% (2005); Median home value: $113,793 (2005); Median rent: $450 per month (2000); Median age of housing: 32 years (2000).
Transportation: Commute to work: 90.1% car, 0.2% public transportation, 2.7% walk, 6.9% work from home (2000); Travel time to work: 16.3% less than 15 minutes, 42.3% 15 to 30 minutes, 26.0% 30 to 45 minutes, 6.1% 45 to 60 minutes, 9.3% 60 minutes or more (2000)

ONEONTA (city). Covers a land area of 4.383 square miles and a water area of 0 square miles. Located at 42.45° N. Lat.; 75.06° W. Long. Elevation is 1,085 feet.
History: Oneonta grew after the coming of the railroad in 1865; however, no vestiges of importance as a railroad center exist today. Brotherhood of Railroad Brakemen founded here in 1883, which was renamed Brotherhood of Railroad Trainmen in 1889. Seat of the State University of N.Y. College at Oneonta and Hartwick College. National Soccer Hall of Fame. Settled c.1780, Incorporated as a city 1909.
Population: 14,051 (1990); 13,292 (2000); 12,725 (2005); 12,149 (2010 projected); Race: 90.5% White, 4.7% Black, 1.9% Asian, 4.5% Hispanic of any race (2005); Density: 2,903.3 persons per square mile (2005); Average household size: 3.21 (2005); Median age: 24.4 (2005); Males per 100 females: 82.6 (2005); Marriage status: 43.5% never married, 43.5% now married, 6.3% widowed, 6.6% divorced (2000); Foreign born: 2.5% (2000); Ancestry (includes multiple ancestries): 19.5% Irish, 14.5% Italian, 14.0% German, 10.6% English, 9.2% Other groups (2000).
Economy: Mobile medical laboratories and clinics, plastic moldings, laboratory apparatus and glass, plasticware and electronic items are produced. In a farm area. Seat of the State University of N.Y. College at Oneonta and Hartwick College. Single-family building permits issued: 0 (2005); Multi-family building permits issued: 0 (2005); Employment by occupation: 8.0% management, 29.2% professional, 23.0% services, 27.1% sales, 0.5% farming, 4.5% construction, 7.7% production (2000).
Income: Per capita income: $13,372 (2005); Median household income: $26,052 (2005); Average household income: $38,770 (2005); Percent of households with income of $100,000 or more: 5.9% (2005); Poverty rate: 30.3% (2000).
Education: Percent of population age 25 and over with: High school diploma (including GED) or higher: 85.8% (2005); Bachelor's degree or higher: 32.6% (2005); Master's degree or higher: 15.2% (2005).
School District(s)
Oneonta City School District (PK-12)
 2003-04 Enrollment: 2,142 . . . . (607) 433-8232
Four-year College(s)
Hartwick College
 Fall 2004 Enrollment: 1,479. . . . . (607) 431-4000
 2005-06 Tuition: In-state $28,885; Out-of-state $28,885
SUNY College at Oneonta (Public)
 Fall 2004 Enrollment: 5,806. . . . . (607) 436-3500
 2005-06 Tuition: In-state $5,362; Out-of-state $11,622
Two-year College(s)
Otsego Area School of Practical Nursing (Public)
 Fall 2004 Enrollment: 38 . . . . (607) 431-2562
 2005-06 Tuition: In-state $14,155; Out-of-state $14,155
Housing: Homeownership rate: 43.3% (2005); Median home value: $106,783 (2005); Median rent: $396 per month (2000); Median age of housing: 60+ years (2000).
Hospitals: AO Fox Memorial Hospital (128 beds)
Safety: Violent crime rate: 40.5 per 10,000 population; Property crime rate: 222.2 per 10,000 population (2004).
Newspapers: The Daily Star (Circulation 17,114)
Transportation: Commute to work: 74.1% car, 3.5% public transportation, 17.4% walk, 3.7% work from home (2000); Travel time to work: 67.7% less

than 15 minutes, 14.6% 15 to 30 minutes, 10.3% 30 to 45 minutes, 2.2% 45 to 60 minutes, 5.2% 60 minutes or more (2000)

Additional Information Contacts
City of Oneonta .... (607) 432-6450
  http://www.oneonta.ny.us/
Otsego County Chamber of Commerce .... (607) 432-4500
  http://www.otsegocountychamber.com

ONEONTA (town). Covers a land area of 33.499 square miles and a water area of 0.141 square miles. Located at 42.47° N. Lat.; 75.07° W. Long. Elevation is 1,085 feet.
Population: 4,828 (1990); 4,994 (2000); 5,068 (2005); 5,169 (2010 projected); Race: 90.7% White, 5.8% Black, 1.2% Asian, 4.0% Hispanic of any race (2005); Density: 151.3 persons per square mile (2005); Average household size: 2.49 (2005); Median age: 41.8 (2005); Males per 100 females: 96.2 (2005); Marriage status: 20.7% never married, 64.5% now married, 6.8% widowed, 8.0% divorced (2000); Foreign born: 1.9% (2000); Ancestry (includes multiple ancestries): 18.1% Irish, 16.8% English, 15.8% Italian, 15.1% German, 5.8% Other groups (2000).
Economy: Single-family building permits issued: 16 (2005); Multi-family building permits issued: 0 (2005); Employment by occupation: 15.8% management, 28.1% professional, 17.6% services, 25.4% sales, 1.1% farming, 6.4% construction, 5.7% production (2000).
Income: Per capita income: $22,407 (2005); Median household income: $42,299 (2005); Average household income: $54,461 (2005); Percent of households with income of $100,000 or more: 11.4% (2005); Poverty rate: 15.2% (2000).
Education: Percent of population age 25 and over with: High school diploma (including GED) or higher: 86.2% (2005); Bachelor's degree or higher: 28.5% (2005); Master's degree or higher: 13.5% (2005).
Housing: Homeownership rate: 77.5% (2005); Median home value: $125,186 (2005); Median rent: $444 per month (2000); Median age of housing: 39 years (2000).
Transportation: Commute to work: 92.5% car, 0.5% public transportation, 2.4% walk, 3.5% work from home (2000); Travel time to work: 60.5% less than 15 minutes, 25.2% 15 to 30 minutes, 8.8% 30 to 45 minutes, 1.5% 45 to 60 minutes, 4.1% 60 minutes or more (2000)

OTEGO (village). Covers a land area of 1.147 square miles and a water area of 0 square miles. Located at 42.39° N. Lat.; 75.17° W. Long.
Population: 1,068 (1990); 1,052 (2000); 1,015 (2005); 1,012 (2010 projected); Race: 96.1% White, 2.4% Black, 0.2% Asian, 2.8% Hispanic of any race (2005); Density: 885.0 persons per square mile (2005); Average household size: 2.69 (2005); Median age: 38.6 (2005); Males per 100 females: 91.5 (2005); Marriage status: 22.0% never married, 63.0% now married, 7.0% widowed, 8.0% divorced (2000); Foreign born: 3.0% (2000); Ancestry (includes multiple ancestries): 17.4% German, 15.6% English, 12.4% Irish, 7.9% Italian, 6.2% Dutch (2000).
Economy: Single-family building permits issued: 4 (2005); Multi-family building permits issued: 0 (2005); Employment by occupation: 12.1% management, 25.6% professional, 13.0% services, 28.8% sales, 0.0% farming, 8.1% construction, 12.4% production (2000).
Income: Per capita income: $19,141 (2005); Median household income: $41,842 (2005); Average household income: $50,152 (2005); Percent of households with income of $100,000 or more: 8.5% (2005); Poverty rate: 11.6% (2000).
Education: Percent of population age 25 and over with: High school diploma (including GED) or higher: 86.3% (2005); Bachelor's degree or higher: 26.9% (2005); Master's degree or higher: 12.7% (2005).

School District(s)
Otego-Unadilla Central School District (KG-12)
  2003-04 Enrollment: 1,259 .... (607) 988-5038
Housing: Homeownership rate: 70.9% (2005); Median home value: $118,966 (2005); Median rent: $406 per month (2000); Median age of housing: 60+ years (2000).
Transportation: Commute to work: 95.9% car, 0.0% public transportation, 0.9% walk, 3.0% work from home (2000); Travel time to work: 28.2% less than 15 minutes, 58.0% 15 to 30 minutes, 6.3% 30 to 45 minutes, 2.8% 45 to 60 minutes, 4.7% 60 minutes or more (2000)

OTEGO (town). Covers a land area of 44.884 square miles and a water area of 0 square miles. Located at 42.41° N. Lat.; 75.18° W. Long.
Population: 3,128 (1990); 3,183 (2000); 3,219 (2005); 3,279 (2010 projected); Race: 97.6% White, 1.0% Black, 0.5% Asian, 1.6% Hispanic of any race (2005); Density: 71.7 persons per square mile (2005); Average household size: 2.53 (2005); Median age: 40.3 (2005); Males per 100 females: 93.9 (2005); Marriage status: 21.6% never married, 60.4% now married, 7.6% widowed, 10.3% divorced (2000); Foreign born: 2.7% (2000); Ancestry (includes multiple ancestries): 18.3% English, 17.8% German, 14.1% Irish, 9.8% United States or American, 9.6% Italian (2000).
Economy: In dairying and grain-growing area. Employment by occupation: 8.0% management, 18.4% professional, 15.6% services, 28.0% sales, 1.0% farming, 13.3% construction, 15.6% production (2000).
Income: Per capita income: $16,252 (2005); Median household income: $33,333 (2005); Average household income: $40,759 (2005); Percent of households with income of $100,000 or more: 5.4% (2005); Poverty rate: 11.4% (2000).
Education: Percent of population age 25 and over with: High school diploma (including GED) or higher: 80.5% (2005); Bachelor's degree or higher: 15.1% (2005); Master's degree or higher: 5.8% (2005).
Housing: Homeownership rate: 79.6% (2005); Median home value: $109,375 (2005); Median rent: $386 per month (2000); Median age of housing: 32 years (2000).
Transportation: Commute to work: 95.5% car, 0.3% public transportation, 1.5% walk, 2.1% work from home (2000); Travel time to work: 25.1% less than 15 minutes, 51.6% 15 to 30 minutes, 13.4% 30 to 45 minutes, 3.8% 45 to 60 minutes, 6.2% 60 minutes or more (2000)

OTSEGO (town). Covers a land area of 54.196 square miles and a water area of 3.572 square miles. Located at 42.73° N. Lat.; 74.95° W. Long.
Population: 3,932 (1990); 3,904 (2000); 3,833 (2005); 3,902 (2010 projected); Race: 97.4% White, 0.8% Black, 1.0% Asian, 2.0% Hispanic of any race (2005); Density: 70.7 persons per square mile (2005); Average household size: 2.25 (2005); Median age: 46.3 (2005); Males per 100 females: 89.8 (2005); Marriage status: 24.0% never married, 58.4% now married, 8.6% widowed, 9.0% divorced (2000); Foreign born: 4.1% (2000); Ancestry (includes multiple ancestries): 22.6% German, 21.2% English, 19.9% Irish, 10.0% Italian, 5.3% Dutch (2000).
Economy: Single-family building permits issued: 8 (2005); Multi-family building permits issued: 2 (2005); Employment by occupation: 19.6% management, 30.7% professional, 13.8% services, 21.6% sales, 1.3% farming, 8.5% construction, 4.5% production (2000).
Income: Per capita income: $28,865 (2005); Median household income: $43,265 (2005); Average household income: $64,003 (2005); Percent of households with income of $100,000 or more: 15.7% (2005); Poverty rate: 7.5% (2000).
Education: Percent of population age 25 and over with: High school diploma (including GED) or higher: 88.6% (2005); Bachelor's degree or higher: 36.1% (2005); Master's degree or higher: 18.4% (2005).
Housing: Homeownership rate: 70.3% (2005); Median home value: $199,338 (2005); Median rent: $442 per month (2000); Median age of housing: 60+ years (2000).
Transportation: Commute to work: 74.3% car, 0.0% public transportation, 17.5% walk, 7.8% work from home (2000); Travel time to work: 55.9% less than 15 minutes, 21.6% 15 to 30 minutes, 11.8% 30 to 45 minutes, 5.2% 45 to 60 minutes, 5.4% 60 minutes or more (2000)

PITTSFIELD (town). Aka Pecktown. Covers a land area of 37.729 square miles and a water area of 0.051 square miles. Located at 42.61° N. Lat.; 75.27° W. Long.
Population: 1,116 (1990); 1,295 (2000); 1,427 (2005); 1,551 (2010 projected); Race: 98.8% White, 0.1% Black, 0.3% Asian, 0.8% Hispanic of any race (2005); Density: 37.8 persons per square mile (2005); Average household size: 2.68 (2005); Median age: 38.9 (2005); Males per 100 females: 104.4 (2005); Marriage status: 20.1% never married, 62.8% now married, 7.3% widowed, 9.8% divorced (2000); Foreign born: 1.5% (2000); Ancestry (includes multiple ancestries): 19.8% English, 16.4% Irish, 14.4% German, 10.1% United States or American, 8.8% Italian (2000).
Economy: Employment by occupation: 10.9% management, 15.9% professional, 15.7% services, 24.9% sales, 3.3% farming, 10.2% construction, 19.2% production (2000).
Income: Per capita income: $18,169 (2005); Median household income: $34,894 (2005); Average household income: $48,736 (2005); Percent of households with income of $100,000 or more: 8.6% (2005); Poverty rate: 17.0% (2000).
Education: Percent of population age 25 and over with: High school diploma (including GED) or higher: 75.3% (2005); Bachelor's degree or higher: 9.9% (2005); Master's degree or higher: 4.0% (2005).

Housing: Homeownership rate: 86.1% (2005); Median home value: $88,500 (2005); Median rent: $338 per month (2000); Median age of housing: 29 years (2000).
Transportation: Commute to work: 88.1% car, 0.5% public transportation, 3.2% walk, 7.1% work from home (2000); Travel time to work: 30.8% less than 15 minutes, 28.6% 15 to 30 minutes, 25.0% 30 to 45 minutes, 11.5% 45 to 60 minutes, 4.0% 60 minutes or more (2000)

PLAINFIELD (town).
Covers a land area of 29.463 square miles and a water area of 0 square miles. Located at 42.82° N. Lat.; 75.19° W. Long.
Population: 850 (1990); 986 (2000); 1,057 (2005); 1,109 (2010 projected); Race: 98.8% White, 0.4% Black, 0.2% Asian, 0.7% Hispanic of any race (2005); Density: 35.9 persons per square mile (2005); Average household size: 2.72 (2005); Median age: 36.2 (2005); Males per 100 females: 102.9 (2005); Marriage status: 21.9% never married, 65.7% now married, 5.2% widowed, 7.2% divorced (2000); Foreign born: 1.4% (2000); Ancestry (includes multiple ancestries): 23.8% English, 22.2% German, 16.1% Irish, 11.4% Polish, 9.2% Italian (2000).
Economy: Employment by occupation: 17.3% management, 16.2% professional, 9.8% services, 22.2% sales, 3.3% farming, 11.8% construction, 19.5% production (2000).
Income: Per capita income: $19,047 (2005); Median household income: $40,411 (2005); Average household income: $51,754 (2005); Percent of households with income of $100,000 or more: 9.5% (2005); Poverty rate: 12.4% (2000).
Education: Percent of population age 25 and over with: High school diploma (including GED) or higher: 82.3% (2005); Bachelor's degree or higher: 13.7% (2005); Master's degree or higher: 5.0% (2005).
Housing: Homeownership rate: 83.5% (2005); Median home value: $101,733 (2005); Median rent: $368 per month (2000); Median age of housing: 30 years (2000).
Transportation: Commute to work: 86.6% car, 1.6% public transportation, 4.3% walk, 7.5% work from home (2000); Travel time to work: 23.3% less than 15 minutes, 24.0% 15 to 30 minutes, 36.0% 30 to 45 minutes, 9.6% 45 to 60 minutes, 7.1% 60 minutes or more (2000)

PORTLANDVILLE (unincorporated postal area, zip code 13834).
Covers a land area of 0.274 square miles and a water area of 0 square miles. Located at 42.53° N. Lat.; 74.96° W. Long.
Population: 0 (2000); Race: 100.0% White, 0.0% Black, 0.0% Asian, 0.0% Hispanic of any race (2000); Density: 0.0 persons per square mile (2000); Age: 34.4% under 18, 15.9% over 64 (2000); Marriage status: 28.3% never married, 43.4% now married, 10.1% widowed, 18.2% divorced (2000); Foreign born: 0.0% (2000); Ancestry (includes multiple ancestries): 34.4% German, 19.9% Italian, 19.9% Irish, 16.6% Other groups, 14.6% Polish (2000).
Economy: Hardwood milling and kiln-drying, and lumber produced in quantity, much for foreign export. Employment by occupation: 15.1% management, 17.0% professional, 13.2% services, 9.4% sales, 0.0% farming, 15.1% construction, 30.2% production (2000).
Income: Per capita income: $12,395 (2000); Median household income: $21,750 (2000); Poverty rate: 39.7% (2000).
Education: Percent of population age 25 and over with: High school diploma (including GED) or higher: 72.2% (2000); Bachelor's degree or higher: 0.0% (2000).
Housing: Homeownership rate: 56.9% (2000); Median home value: $209,400 (2000); Median rent: $300 per month (2000); Median age of housing: 27 years (2000).
Transportation: Commute to work: 100.0% car, 0.0% public transportation, 0.0% walk, 0.0% work from home (2000); Travel time to work: 13.2% less than 15 minutes, 58.5% 15 to 30 minutes, 13.2% 30 to 45 minutes, 0.0% 45 to 60 minutes, 15.1% 60 minutes or more (2000)

RICHFIELD (town). Aka Monticello.
Covers a land area of 30.918 square miles and a water area of 1.526 square miles. Located at 42.85° N. Lat.; 75.01° W. Long.
History: Health resort until mid-20th century; sulphur springs. Incorporated 1934.
Population: 2,711 (1990); 2,423 (2000); 2,395 (2005); 2,401 (2010 projected); Race: 97.6% White, 0.4% Black, 0.6% Asian, 0.5% Hispanic of any race (2005); Density: 77.5 persons per square mile (2005); Average household size: 2.46 (2005); Median age: 43.8 (2005); Males per 100 females: 92.2 (2005); Marriage status: 22.1% never married, 57.1% now married, 9.8% widowed, 11.0% divorced (2000); Foreign born: 2.0% (2000); Ancestry (includes multiple ancestries): 18.7% Irish, 16.4% English, 13.6% German, 8.8% United States or American, 8.6% Polish (2000).
Economy: Manufacturing: fishing tackle, leather sporting goods. In diversified farming area. Employment by occupation: 9.0% management, 18.6% professional, 19.9% services, 22.8% sales, 1.8% farming, 11.9% construction, 15.9% production (2000).
Income: Per capita income: $19,149 (2005); Median household income: $37,514 (2005); Average household income: $46,614 (2005); Percent of households with income of $100,000 or more: 7.0% (2005); Poverty rate: 13.4% (2000).
Education: Percent of population age 25 and over with: High school diploma (including GED) or higher: 75.7% (2005); Bachelor's degree or higher: 15.0% (2005); Master's degree or higher: 8.3% (2005).
Housing: Homeownership rate: 75.1% (2005); Median home value: $105,632 (2005); Median rent: $354 per month (2000); Median age of housing: 59 years (2000).
Transportation: Commute to work: 89.9% car, 1.9% public transportation, 3.0% walk, 5.0% work from home (2000); Travel time to work: 29.6% less than 15 minutes, 32.0% 15 to 30 minutes, 24.5% 30 to 45 minutes, 4.7% 45 to 60 minutes, 9.2% 60 minutes or more (2000)

RICHFIELD SPRINGS (village).
Covers a land area of 0.997 square miles and a water area of 0 square miles. Located at 42.85° N. Lat.; 74.98° W. Long. Elevation is 1,315 feet.
Population: 1,543 (1990); 1,255 (2000); 1,200 (2005); 1,189 (2010 projected); Race: 96.0% White, 0.7% Black, 1.2% Asian, 0.7% Hispanic of any race (2005); Density: 1,204.0 persons per square mile (2005); Average household size: 2.29 (2005); Median age: 47.4 (2005); Males per 100 females: 84.9 (2005); Marriage status: 22.0% never married, 54.9% now married, 12.4% widowed, 10.7% divorced (2000); Foreign born: 2.8% (2000); Ancestry (includes multiple ancestries): 19.9% Irish, 16.2% English, 15.5% German, 9.5% United States or American, 7.7% Polish (2000).
Economy: Employment by occupation: 6.8% management, 19.4% professional, 18.2% services, 27.9% sales, 0.6% farming, 9.4% construction, 17.8% production (2000).
Income: Per capita income: $19,332 (2005); Median household income: $33,580 (2005); Average household income: $43,475 (2005); Percent of households with income of $100,000 or more: 5.9% (2005); Poverty rate: 12.2% (2000).
Education: Percent of population age 25 and over with: High school diploma (including GED) or higher: 74.0% (2005); Bachelor's degree or higher: 15.5% (2005); Master's degree or higher: 7.2% (2005).
School District(s)
Richfield Springs Central School District (KG-12)
    2003-04 Enrollment: 667 . . . . (315) 858-0610
Housing: Homeownership rate: 68.1% (2005); Median home value: $94,203 (2005); Median rent: $340 per month (2000); Median age of housing: 60+ years (2000).
Transportation: Commute to work: 90.5% car, 2.8% public transportation, 4.7% walk, 1.5% work from home (2000); Travel time to work: 28.7% less than 15 minutes, 33.1% 15 to 30 minutes, 21.8% 30 to 45 minutes, 6.4% 45 to 60 minutes, 10.0% 60 minutes or more (2000)
Additional Information Contacts
Richfield Area Chamber of Commerce . . . . (315) 858-2553

ROSEBOOM (town).
Covers a land area of 33.001 square miles and a water area of 0.057 square miles. Located at 42.71° N. Lat.; 74.72° W. Long.
Population: 668 (1990); 684 (2000); 723 (2005); 757 (2010 projected); Race: 97.9% White, 0.1% Black, 1.5% Asian, 1.0% Hispanic of any race (2005); Density: 21.9 persons per square mile (2005); Average household size: 2.51 (2005); Median age: 40.9 (2005); Males per 100 females: 106.0 (2005); Marriage status: 28.3% never married, 55.1% now married, 5.2% widowed, 11.4% divorced (2000); Foreign born: 2.2% (2000); Ancestry (includes multiple ancestries): 29.6% German, 20.0% Irish, 19.5% English, 10.6% Italian, 6.8% United States or American (2000).
Economy: Single-family building permits issued: 2 (2005); Multi-family building permits issued: 0 (2005); Employment by occupation: 13.7% management, 15.6% professional, 19.4% services, 21.8% sales, 0.0% farming, 17.2% construction, 12.4% production (2000).
Income: Per capita income: $21,967 (2005); Median household income: $44,474 (2005); Average household income: $55,148 (2005); Percent of households with income of $100,000 or more: 9.7% (2005); Poverty rate: 10.6% (2000).

Education: Percent of population age 25 and over with: High school diploma (including GED) or higher: 80.2% (2005); Bachelor's degree or higher: 14.1% (2005); Master's degree or higher: 8.7% (2005).
Housing: Homeownership rate: 87.2% (2005); Median home value: $120,055 (2005); Median rent: $408 per month (2000); Median age of housing: 34 years (2000).
Transportation: Commute to work: 90.9% car, 0.0% public transportation, 2.5% walk, 6.3% work from home (2000); Travel time to work: 18.8% less than 15 minutes, 50.6% 15 to 30 minutes, 17.1% 30 to 45 minutes, 4.4% 45 to 60 minutes, 9.1% 60 minutes or more (2000)

SCHENEVUS (unincorporated postal area, zip code 12155). Covers a land area of 59.573 square miles and a water area of 0.110 square miles. Located at 42.60° N. Lat.; 74.82° W. Long. Elevation is 1,266 feet.
Population: 0 (2000); Race: 98.6% White, 0.0% Black, 0.0% Asian, 1.0% Hispanic of any race (2000); Density: 0.0 persons per square mile (2000); Age: 24.2% under 18, 13.0% over 64 (2000); Marriage status: 23.1% never married, 60.0% now married, 9.0% widowed, 7.9% divorced (2000); Foreign born: 2.8% (2000); Ancestry (includes multiple ancestries): 21.9% German, 18.3% Irish, 15.6% English, 11.0% Italian, 8.5% United States or American (2000).
Economy: Employment by occupation: 12.9% management, 16.9% professional, 16.8% services, 21.8% sales, 2.3% farming, 12.2% construction, 17.1% production (2000).
Income: Per capita income: $16,064 (2000); Median household income: $33,533 (2000); Poverty rate: 12.0% (2000).
Education: Percent of population age 25 and over with: High school diploma (including GED) or higher: 82.8% (2000); Bachelor's degree or higher: 15.9% (2000).

School District(s)
Schenevus Central School District (KG-12)
    2003-04 Enrollment: 375 . . . . (607) 638-5530

Housing: Homeownership rate: 78.3% (2000); Median home value: $66,500 (2000); Median rent: $352 per month (2000); Median age of housing: 45 years (2000).
Transportation: Commute to work: 90.0% car, 0.9% public transportation, 3.0% walk, 6.2% work from home (2000); Travel time to work: 15.7% less than 15 minutes, 52.1% 15 to 30 minutes, 19.2% 30 to 45 minutes, 4.6% 45 to 60 minutes, 8.4% 60 minutes or more (2000)

SPRINGFIELD (town). Covers a land area of 42.966 square miles and a water area of 2.482 square miles. Located at 42.83° N. Lat.; 74.86° W. Long.
Population: 1,267 (1990); 1,350 (2000); 1,462 (2005); 1,569 (2010 projected); Race: 98.6% White, 0.1% Black, 0.3% Asian, 1.5% Hispanic of any race (2005); Density: 34.0 persons per square mile (2005); Average household size: 2.54 (2005); Median age: 42.1 (2005); Males per 100 females: 98.9 (2005); Marriage status: 22.5% never married, 62.0% now married, 8.7% widowed, 6.8% divorced (2000); Foreign born: 4.8% (2000); Ancestry (includes multiple ancestries): 22.1% German, 20.7% English, 13.0% Irish, 9.2% Dutch, 7.4% Other groups (2000).
Economy: Employment by occupation: 18.3% management, 21.9% professional, 12.6% services, 20.2% sales, 4.2% farming, 10.8% construction, 12.1% production (2000).
Income: Per capita income: $18,796 (2005); Median household income: $38,269 (2005); Average household income: $47,791 (2005); Percent of households with income of $100,000 or more: 7.1% (2005); Poverty rate: 8.5% (2000).
Education: Percent of population age 25 and over with: High school diploma (including GED) or higher: 86.1% (2005); Bachelor's degree or higher: 21.8% (2005); Master's degree or higher: 8.8% (2005).
Housing: Homeownership rate: 79.7% (2005); Median home value: $118,349 (2005); Median rent: $401 per month (2000); Median age of housing: 60+ years (2000).
Transportation: Commute to work: 79.5% car, 0.0% public transportation, 8.2% walk, 11.0% work from home (2000); Travel time to work: 31.9% less than 15 minutes, 38.1% 15 to 30 minutes, 19.0% 30 to 45 minutes, 3.9% 45 to 60 minutes, 7.2% 60 minutes or more (2000)

SPRINGFIELD CENTER (unincorporated postal area, zip code 13468). Aka Springfield. Covers a land area of 9.378 square miles and a water area of 0.101 square miles. Located at 42.84° N. Lat.; 74.86° W. Long. Elevation is 1,258 feet.
Population: 0 (2000); Race: 97.7% White, 0.0% Black, 0.0% Asian, 4.9% Hispanic of any race (2000); Density: 0.0 persons per square mile (2000); Age: 26.5% under 18, 15.5% over 64 (2000); Marriage status: 25.8% never married, 54.2% now married, 9.2% widowed, 10.8% divorced (2000); Foreign born: 6.8% (2000); Ancestry (includes multiple ancestries): 19.9% German, 17.8% English, 11.2% Irish, 10.4% Other groups, 9.5% Dutch (2000).
Economy: Employment by occupation: 12.8% management, 22.9% professional, 12.3% services, 22.5% sales, 4.4% farming, 9.7% construction, 15.4% production (2000).
Income: Per capita income: $15,919 (2000); Median household income: $30,833 (2000); Poverty rate: 7.3% (2000).
Education: Percent of population age 25 and over with: High school diploma (including GED) or higher: 84.1% (2000); Bachelor's degree or higher: 13.4% (2000).
Housing: Homeownership rate: 75.4% (2000); Median home value: $66,300 (2000); Median rent: $400 per month (2000); Median age of housing: 60+ years (2000).
Transportation: Commute to work: 81.1% car, 0.0% public transportation, 4.0% walk, 15.0% work from home (2000); Travel time to work: 21.2% less than 15 minutes, 42.5% 15 to 30 minutes, 22.3% 30 to 45 minutes, 5.2% 45 to 60 minutes, 8.8% 60 minutes or more (2000)

UNADILLA (village). Covers a land area of 1.078 square miles and a water area of 0 square miles. Located at 42.32° N. Lat.; 75.31° W. Long. Elevation is 1,024 feet.
Population: 1,265 (1990); 1,127 (2000); 1,117 (2005); 1,127 (2010 projected); Race: 97.0% White, 0.6% Black, 0.0% Asian, 1.3% Hispanic of any race (2005); Density: 1,036.0 persons per square mile (2005); Average household size: 2.35 (2005); Median age: 40.4 (2005); Males per 100 females: 93.9 (2005); Marriage status: 27.1% never married, 56.7% now married, 7.0% widowed, 9.2% divorced (2000); Foreign born: 0.7% (2000); Ancestry (includes multiple ancestries): 18.3% Irish, 17.8% English, 15.1% German, 10.7% Other groups, 8.3% United States or American (2000).
Economy: Employment by occupation: 8.0% management, 16.7% professional, 16.0% services, 23.2% sales, 0.7% farming, 11.1% construction, 24.3% production (2000).
Income: Per capita income: $20,376 (2005); Median household income: $39,274 (2005); Average household income: $47,916 (2005); Percent of households with income of $100,000 or more: 8.4% (2005); Poverty rate: 10.8% (2000).
Education: Percent of population age 25 and over with: High school diploma (including GED) or higher: 87.6% (2005); Bachelor's degree or higher: 19.2% (2005); Master's degree or higher: 6.3% (2005).

School District(s)
Otego-Unadilla Central School District (KG-12)
    2003-04 Enrollment: 1,259 . . . . (607) 988-5038

Housing: Homeownership rate: 72.8% (2005); Median home value: $93,800 (2005); Median rent: $339 per month (2000); Median age of housing: 60+ years (2000).
Transportation: Commute to work: 88.5% car, 1.7% public transportation, 4.1% walk, 5.3% work from home (2000); Travel time to work: 41.3% less than 15 minutes, 34.3% 15 to 30 minutes, 12.3% 30 to 45 minutes, 5.4% 45 to 60 minutes, 6.7% 60 minutes or more (2000)

UNADILLA (town). Covers a land area of 46.405 square miles and a water area of 0.235 square miles. Located at 42.35° N. Lat.; 75.32° W. Long. Elevation is 1,024 feet.
History: During the early years of the Revolution, Native American villages in the vicinity of Unadilla were gathering places for Tories bent on destruction of frontier patriot settlements. In 1778, an American force destroyed the villages. The place began to grow with construction of the Catskill Turnpike soon after 1800. Settled in 1790, incorporated in 1827.
Population: 4,343 (1990); 4,548 (2000); 4,555 (2005); 4,573 (2010 projected); Race: 97.4% White, 0.9% Black, 0.2% Asian, 1.6% Hispanic of any race (2005); Density: 98.2 persons per square mile (2005); Average household size: 2.46 (2005); Median age: 39.4 (2005); Males per 100 females: 97.7 (2005); Marriage status: 19.8% never married, 64.0% now married, 6.5% widowed, 9.7% divorced (2000); Foreign born: 1.8% (2000); Ancestry (includes multiple ancestries): 16.6% Irish, 16.5% English, 16.1% German, 9.6% Italian, 7.5% Other groups (2000).
Economy: Manufacturing: machinery, furniture. In farming and dairying area. Employment by occupation: 9.5% management, 16.0% professional, 11.0% services, 23.8% sales, 1.3% farming, 9.8% construction, 28.7% production (2000).
Income: Per capita income: $19,976 (2005); Median household income: $39,259 (2005); Average household income: $49,229 (2005); Percent of

households with income of $100,000 or more: 7.3% (2005); Poverty rate: 12.8% (2000).
Education: Percent of population age 25 and over with: High school diploma (including GED) or higher: 82.7% (2005); Bachelor's degree or higher: 13.8% (2005); Master's degree or higher: 5.4% (2005).
Housing: Homeownership rate: 83.4% (2005); Median home value: $95,794 (2005); Median rent: $330 per month (2000); Median age of housing: 33 years (2000).
Transportation: Commute to work: 92.8% car, 0.8% public transportation, 1.8% walk, 3.9% work from home (2000); Travel time to work: 38.1% less than 15 minutes, 37.5% 15 to 30 minutes, 14.4% 30 to 45 minutes, 4.1% 45 to 60 minutes, 5.9% 60 minutes or more (2000)

WELLS BRIDGE (unincorporated postal area, zip code 13859). Covers a land area of 0.795 square miles and a water area of 0 square miles. Located at 42.36° N. Lat.; 75.24° W. Long. Elevation is 1,047 feet.
Population: 0 (2000); Race: 97.3% White, 2.7% Black, 0.0% Asian, 0.0% Hispanic of any race (2000); Density: 0.0 persons per square mile (2000); Age: 17.9% under 18, 11.7% over 64 (2000); Marriage status: 17.8% never married, 58.9% now married, 7.1% widowed, 16.2% divorced (2000); Foreign born: 4.0% (2000); Ancestry (includes multiple ancestries): 30.0% German, 21.5% English, 14.8% United States or American, 11.2% Irish, 9.0% French (except Basque) (2000).
Economy: Employment by occupation: 21.2% management, 16.8% professional, 3.6% services, 26.3% sales, 0.0% farming, 0.0% construction, 32.1% production (2000).
Income: Per capita income: $20,787 (2000); Median household income: $29,091 (2000); Poverty rate: 2.7% (2000).
Education: Percent of population age 25 and over with: High school diploma (including GED) or higher: 92.0% (2000); Bachelor's degree or higher: 11.5% (2000).
Housing: Homeownership rate: 81.4% (2000); Median home value: $60,000 (2000); Median rent: $400 per month (2000); Median age of housing: 60+ years (2000).
Transportation: Commute to work: 100.0% car, 0.0% public transportation, 0.0% walk, 0.0% work from home (2000); Travel time to work: 29.9% less than 15 minutes, 62.0% 15 to 30 minutes, 0.0% 30 to 45 minutes, 8.0% 45 to 60 minutes, 0.0% 60 minutes or more (2000)

WEST EDMESTON (unincorporated postal area, zip code 13485). Covers a land area of 33.615 square miles and a water area of 0.058 square miles. Located at 42.76° N. Lat.; 75.32° W. Long. Elevation is 1,138 feet.
Population: 0 (2000); Race: 94.5% White, 3.2% Black, 0.5% Asian, 0.5% Hispanic of any race (2000); Density: 0.0 persons per square mile (2000); Age: 33.9% under 18, 8.3% over 64 (2000); Marriage status: 24.9% never married, 63.5% now married, 3.7% widowed, 7.9% divorced (2000); Foreign born: 1.2% (2000); Ancestry (includes multiple ancestries): 19.5% English, 14.4% United States or American, 13.2% Irish, 11.3% Other groups, 10.7% German (2000).
Economy: Employment by occupation: 16.1% management, 11.6% professional, 18.1% services, 23.4% sales, 1.8% farming, 12.9% construction, 16.1% production (2000).
Income: Per capita income: $13,017 (2000); Median household income: $31,618 (2000); Poverty rate: 16.0% (2000).
Education: Percent of population age 25 and over with: High school diploma (including GED) or higher: 75.0% (2000); Bachelor's degree or higher: 8.7% (2000).
Housing: Homeownership rate: 81.3% (2000); Median home value: $53,500 (2000); Median rent: $327 per month (2000); Median age of housing: 49 years (2000).
Transportation: Commute to work: 85.8% car, 0.0% public transportation, 5.2% walk, 9.0% work from home (2000); Travel time to work: 26.0% less than 15 minutes, 24.4% 15 to 30 minutes, 36.9% 30 to 45 minutes, 7.0% 45 to 60 minutes, 5.7% 60 minutes or more (2000)

WEST END (CDP). Covers a land area of 3.775 square miles and a water area of 0 square miles. Located at 42.45° N. Lat.; 75.09° W. Long.
Population: 1,728 (1990); 1,813 (2000); 1,862 (2005); 1,899 (2010 projected); Race: 96.6% White, 0.7% Black, 1.7% Asian, 3.0% Hispanic of any race (2005); Density: 493.2 persons per square mile (2005); Average household size: 2.21 (2005); Median age: 44.2 (2005); Males per 100 females: 92.8 (2005); Marriage status: 26.2% never married, 50.6% now married, 10.7% widowed, 12.4% divorced (2000); Foreign born: 1.9% (2000); Ancestry (includes multiple ancestries): 18.7% Italian, 16.0% Irish, 15.3% German, 15.1% English, 8.6% United States or American (2000).
Economy: Employment by occupation: 9.6% management, 28.3% professional, 19.1% services, 26.3% sales, 0.0% farming, 10.2% construction, 6.5% production (2000).
Income: Per capita income: $17,733 (2005); Median household income: $31,221 (2005); Average household income: $38,321 (2005); Percent of households with income of $100,000 or more: 5.2% (2005); Poverty rate: 14.9% (2000).
Education: Percent of population age 25 and over with: High school diploma (including GED) or higher: 81.3% (2005); Bachelor's degree or higher: 21.4% (2005); Master's degree or higher: 9.8% (2005).
Housing: Homeownership rate: 76.6% (2005); Median home value: $105,048 (2005); Median rent: $428 per month (2000); Median age of housing: 48 years (2000).
Transportation: Commute to work: 91.1% car, 1.0% public transportation, 1.7% walk, 4.2% work from home (2000); Travel time to work: 70.8% less than 15 minutes, 22.2% 15 to 30 minutes, 2.2% 30 to 45 minutes, 0.9% 45 to 60 minutes, 4.0% 60 minutes or more (2000)

WEST ONEONTA (unincorporated postal area, zip code 13861). Covers a land area of 8.683 square miles and a water area of 0.013 square miles. Located at 42.48° N. Lat.; 75.12° W. Long. Elevation is 1,144 feet.
Population: 0 (2000); Race: 98.7% White, 0.0% Black, 0.6% Asian, 0.0% Hispanic of any race (2000); Density: 0.0 persons per square mile (2000); Age: 24.2% under 18, 18.0% over 64 (2000); Marriage status: 22.5% never married, 68.8% now married, 0.7% widowed, 7.9% divorced (2000); Foreign born: 1.3% (2000); Ancestry (includes multiple ancestries): 25.5% English, 25.4% Irish, 23.4% German, 9.8% Italian, 6.2% United States or American (2000).
Economy: Employment by occupation: 14.3% management, 38.8% professional, 11.2% services, 20.8% sales, 2.0% farming, 6.2% construction, 6.7% production (2000).
Income: Per capita income: $18,518 (2000); Median household income: $45,515 (2000); Poverty rate: 5.5% (2000).
Education: Percent of population age 25 and over with: High school diploma (including GED) or higher: 85.7% (2000); Bachelor's degree or higher: 35.8% (2000).
Housing: Homeownership rate: 88.5% (2000); Median home value: $81,900 (2000); Median rent: $438 per month (2000); Median age of housing: 48 years (2000).
Transportation: Commute to work: 95.7% car, 0.0% public transportation, 0.0% walk, 2.8% work from home (2000); Travel time to work: 36.8% less than 15 minutes, 51.2% 15 to 30 minutes, 6.4% 30 to 45 minutes, 5.6% 45 to 60 minutes, 0.0% 60 minutes or more (2000)

WESTFORD (town). Covers a land area of 33.762 square miles and a water area of 0.022 square miles. Located at 42.63° N. Lat.; 74.81° W. Long. Elevation is 1,563 feet.
Population: 634 (1990); 784 (2000); 885 (2005); 981 (2010 projected); Race: 98.4% White, 0.1% Black, 0.2% Asian, 2.7% Hispanic of any race (2005); Density: 26.2 persons per square mile (2005); Average household size: 2.51 (2005); Median age: 40.4 (2005); Males per 100 females: 100.2 (2005); Marriage status: 21.0% never married, 59.9% now married, 10.2% widowed, 8.9% divorced (2000); Foreign born: 2.3% (2000); Ancestry (includes multiple ancestries): 22.4% German, 16.9% Irish, 14.8% English, 11.9% Italian, 9.2% Dutch (2000).
Economy: Employment by occupation: 13.0% management, 14.1% professional, 15.6% services, 23.6% sales, 3.7% farming, 10.4% construction, 19.6% production (2000).
Income: Per capita income: $19,562 (2005); Median household income: $40,122 (2005); Average household income: $49,183 (2005); Percent of households with income of $100,000 or more: 9.9% (2005); Poverty rate: 9.2% (2000).
Education: Percent of population age 25 and over with: High school diploma (including GED) or higher: 80.7% (2005); Bachelor's degree or higher: 16.2% (2005); Master's degree or higher: 5.0% (2005).
Housing: Homeownership rate: 88.1% (2005); Median home value: $100,526 (2005); Median rent: $363 per month (2000); Median age of housing: 28 years (2000).
Transportation: Commute to work: 91.9% car, 0.6% public transportation, 1.7% walk, 5.2% work from home (2000); Travel time to work: 12.0% less than 15 minutes, 48.2% 15 to 30 minutes, 19.6% 30 to 45 minutes, 7.7% 45 to 60 minutes, 12.6% 60 minutes or more (2000)

WORCESTER (town). Covers a land area of 46.710 square miles and a water area of 0.150 square miles. Located at 42.59° N. Lat.; 74.71° W. Long. Elevation is 1,306 feet.
Population: 2,070 (1990); 2,207 (2000); 2,358 (2005); 2,504 (2010 projected); Race: 97.3% White, 0.8% Black, 0.2% Asian, 0.9% Hispanic of any race (2005); Density: 50.5 persons per square mile (2005); Average household size: 2.37 (2005); Median age: 42.3 (2005); Males per 100 females: 93.8 (2005); Marriage status: 21.8% never married, 57.8% now married, 10.8% widowed, 9.6% divorced (2000); Foreign born: 2.4% (2000); Ancestry (includes multiple ancestries): 18.5% German, 17.7% Irish, 11.5% English, 10.6% United States or American, 10.3% Italian (2000).
Economy: Some manufacturing. Employment by occupation: 14.3% management, 20.5% professional, 12.6% services, 20.6% sales, 2.7% farming, 10.6% construction, 18.6% production (2000).
Income: Per capita income: $18,601 (2005); Median household income: $34,465 (2005); Average household income: $43,839 (2005); Percent of households with income of $100,000 or more: 6.5% (2005); Poverty rate: 10.3% (2000).
Education: Percent of population age 25 and over with: High school diploma (including GED) or higher: 75.4% (2005); Bachelor's degree or higher: 17.8% (2005); Master's degree or higher: 7.6% (2005).

School District(s)
Worcester Central School District (KG-12)
   2003-04 Enrollment: 438 . . . . (607) 397-8785

Housing: Homeownership rate: 78.0% (2005); Median home value: $103,017 (2005); Median rent: $351 per month (2000); Median age of housing: 60+ years (2000).
Transportation: Commute to work: 85.2% car, 1.9% public transportation, 4.5% walk, 8.3% work from home (2000); Travel time to work: 25.1% less than 15 minutes, 22.4% 15 to 30 minutes, 27.1% 30 to 45 minutes, 9.3% 45 to 60 minutes, 16.1% 60 minutes or more (2000)

Putnam County

Located in southeastern New York; bounded on the west by the Hudson River, and on the east by Connecticut; includes part of the Taconic Mountains. Covers a land area of 231.28 square miles, a water area of 14.97 square miles, and is located in the Eastern Time Zone. The county government was organized in 1812. County seat is Carmel.

Putnam County is part of the New York-Northern New Jersey-Long Island, NY-NJ-PA Metropolitan Statistical Area. The entire metro area includes: Edison, NJ Metropolitan Division (Middlesex County, NJ; Monmouth County, NJ; Ocean County, NJ; Somerset County, NJ); Nassau-Suffolk, NY Metropolitan Division (Nassau County, NY; Suffolk County, NY); New York-White Plains-Wayne, NY-NJ Metropolitan Division (Bergen County, NJ; Hudson County, NJ; Passaic County, NJ; Bronx County, NY; Kings County, NY; New York County, NY; Putnam County, NY; Queens County, NY; Richmond County, NY; Rockland County, NY; Westchester County, NY); Newark-Union, NJ-PA Metropolitan Division (Essex County, NJ; Hunterdon County, NJ; Morris County, NJ; Sussex County, NJ; Union County, NJ; Pike County, PA)

Population: 83,941 (1990); 95,745 (2000); 101,174 (2005); 106,813 (2010 projected); Race: 91.9% White, 2.2% Black, 1.7% Asian, 9.4% Hispanic of any race (2005); Density: 437.4 persons per square mile (2005); Average household size: 2.90 (2005); Median age: 38.9 (2005); Males per 100 females: 100.2 (2005).
Religion: Five largest groups: 55.9% Catholic Church, 1.4% The United Methodist Church, 1.1% Episcopal Church, 1.0% Jewish Estimate, 1.0% Independent, Non-Charismatic Churches (2000).
Economy: Unemployment rate: 3.7% (2005); Total civilian labor force: 56,243 (2005); Leading industries: 21.4% health care and social assistance; 15.9% retail trade; 10.6% construction (2003); Farms: 52 totaling 6,720 acres (2002); Companies that employ 500 or more persons: 1 (2003); Companies that employ 100 to 499 persons: 23 (2003); Companies that employ less than 100 persons: 2,832 (2003); Black-owned businesses: n/a (2002); Hispanic-owned businesses: n/a (2002); Women-owned businesses: 3,020 (2002); Retail sales per capita: $8,162 (2006). Single-family building permits issued: 141 (2005); Multi-family building permits issued: 0 (2005).
Income: Per capita income: $34,865 (2005); Median household income: $83,109 (2005); Average household income: $100,052 (2005); Percent of households with income of $100,000 or more: 38.8% (2005); Poverty rate: 4.6% (2003); Bankruptcy rate: 3.13% (2005).
Taxes: Total county taxes per capita: $609 (2004); County property taxes per capita: $229 (2004).
Education: Percent of population age 25 and over with: High school diploma (including GED) or higher: 90.2% (2005); Bachelor's degree or higher: 34.0% (2005); Master's degree or higher: 14.2% (2005).
Housing: Homeownership rate: 82.2% (2005); Median home value: $339,358 (2005); Median rent: $813 per month (2000); Median age of housing: 36 years (2000).
Health: Birth rate: 121.1 per 10,000 population (2004); Death rate: 62.7 per 10,000 population (2004); Age-adjusted cancer mortality rate: 231.2 deaths per 100,000 population (2002); Air Quality Index: 92.1% good, 6.0% moderate, 1.6% unhealthy for sensitive individuals, 0.3% unhealthy (percent of days in 2005); Number of physicians: 20.3 per 10,000 population (2004); Hospital beds: 27.3 per 10,000 population (2003); Hospital admissions: 964.5 per 10,000 population (2003).
Elections: 2004 Presidential election results: 56.6% Bush, 42.0% Kerry, 1.2% Nader, 0.0% Badnarik
National and State Parks: Appalachian National Scenic Trail; Clarence Fahnestock Memorial State Park
Additional Information Contacts
Putnam County Government . . . . (845) 225-3641
   http://www.putnamcountyny.com/
Town of Carmel . . . . (845) 628-1500
   http://www.ci.carmel.ny.us/
Town of Kent . . . . (845) 225-3943
   http://www.townofkent.org/
Town of Patterson . . . . (845) 878-6500
   http://www.pattersonny.org/
Town of Putnam Valley . . . . (845) 526-2121
   http://www.putnamvalley.com/
Town of Southeast . . . . (845) 279-4313
   http://www.townofsoutheast-ny.com/Home/

Putnam County Communities

BREWSTER (village). Covers a land area of 0.476 square miles and a water area of 0 square miles. Located at 41.39° N. Lat.; 73.61° W. Long. Elevation is 395 feet.
History: Jurist James Kent born nearby, 1763. Settled 1850, incorporated 1894.
Population: 1,566 (1990); 2,162 (2000); 2,248 (2005); 2,311 (2010 projected); Race: 70.6% White, 7.6% Black, 2.9% Asian, 48.0% Hispanic of any race (2005); Density: 4,724.8 persons per square mile (2005); Average household size: 2.55 (2005); Median age: 34.7 (2005); Males per 100 females: 134.2 (2005); Marriage status: 44.0% never married, 43.2% now married, 5.8% widowed, 7.0% divorced (2000); Foreign born: 32.2% (2000); Ancestry (includes multiple ancestries): 35.2% Other groups, 17.9% Irish, 15.3% Italian, 10.3% German, 6.0% English (2000).
Economy: Trade center for farming, dairying, summer-resort area. Manufacturing: reflective films and papers, high-voltage electronic equipment; plastic assemblies, metal fabrication. Peach Lake resort nearby. Single-family building permits issued: 0 (2005); Multi-family building permits issued: 0 (2005); Employment by occupation: 7.6% management, 14.4% professional, 29.9% services, 19.6% sales, 1.5% farming, 19.2% construction, 7.7% production (2000).
Income: Per capita income: $24,124 (2005); Median household income: $47,023 (2005); Average household income: $60,261 (2005); Percent of households with income of $100,000 or more: 13.0% (2005); Poverty rate: 14.5% (2000).
Education: Percent of population age 25 and over with: High school diploma (including GED) or higher: 70.5% (2005); Bachelor's degree or higher: 18.8% (2005); Master's degree or higher: 6.5% (2005).

School District(s)
Brewster Central School District (KG-12)
   2003-04 Enrollment: 3,726 . . . . (845) 279-8000

Housing: Homeownership rate: 24.8% (2005); Median home value: $272,115 (2005); Median rent: $784 per month (2000); Median age of housing: 57 years (2000).
Transportation: Commute to work: 74.5% car, 15.3% public transportation, 8.3% walk, 0.5% work from home (2000); Travel time to work: 20.5% less than 15 minutes, 31.4% 15 to 30 minutes, 28.2% 30 to 45 minutes, 8.6% 45 to 60 minutes, 11.2% 60 minutes or more (2000)
Additional Information Contacts

Brewster Chamber of Commerce .... (845) 279-2477
http://www.brewsterchamber.com

BREWSTER HILL (CDP). Aka Tonetta Lake Heights. Covers a land area of 0.871 square miles and a water area of 0.110 square miles. Located at 41.42° N. Lat.; 73.60° W. Long.
Population: 2,226 (1990); 2,226 (2000); 2,413 (2005); 2,565 (2010 projected); Race: 95.2% White, 1.2% Black, 2.0% Asian, 5.9% Hispanic of any race (2005); Density: 2,769.6 persons per square mile (2005); Average household size: 2.92 (2005); Median age: 40.5 (2005); Males per 100 females: 98.6 (2005); Marriage status: 24.1% never married, 64.0% now married, 6.2% widowed, 5.6% divorced (2000); Foreign born: 6.9% (2000); Ancestry (includes multiple ancestries): 38.9% Italian, 28.4% Irish, 18.0% German, 9.3% English, 6.7% Other groups (2000).
Economy: Employment by occupation: 11.0% management, 28.9% professional, 10.1% services, 35.3% sales, 0.0% farming, 10.6% construction, 4.1% production (2000).
Income: Per capita income: $27,834 (2005); Median household income: $76,939 (2005); Average household income: $81,409 (2005); Percent of households with income of $100,000 or more: 29.1% (2005); Poverty rate: 0.4% (2000).
Education: Percent of population age 25 and over with: High school diploma (including GED) or higher: 92.9% (2005); Bachelor's degree or higher: 19.7% (2005); Master's degree or higher: 9.5% (2005).
Housing: Homeownership rate: 90.4% (2005); Median home value: $330,601 (2005); Median rent: $1,077 per month (2000); Median age of housing: 41 years (2000).
Transportation: Commute to work: 92.4% car, 7.6% public transportation, 0.0% walk, 0.0% work from home (2000); Travel time to work: 26.9% less than 15 minutes, 24.8% 15 to 30 minutes, 12.4% 30 to 45 minutes, 17.2% 45 to 60 minutes, 18.7% 60 minutes or more (2000)

CARMEL (town). Covers a land area of 36.107 square miles and a water area of 4.578 square miles. Located at 41.38° N. Lat.; 73.72° W. Long. Elevation is 519 feet.
Population: 28,816 (1990); 33,006 (2000); 35,167 (2005); 37,352 (2010 projected); Race: 92.9% White, 1.5% Black, 1.6% Asian, 8.9% Hispanic of any race (2005); Density: 974.0 persons per square mile (2005); Average household size: 3.02 (2005); Median age: 38.5 (2005); Males per 100 females: 99.1 (2005); Marriage status: 23.7% never married, 65.3% now married, 5.6% widowed, 5.4% divorced (2000); Foreign born: 10.0% (2000); Ancestry (includes multiple ancestries): 35.3% Italian, 25.0% Irish, 15.5% German, 9.2% Other groups, 5.5% Polish (2000).
Economy: Trade center for dairying and summer-resort area. Part of Metropolitan N.Y. exurbia. Unemployment rate: 3.6% (2005); Total civilian labor force: 19,347 (2005); Single-family building permits issued: 44 (2005); Multi-family building permits issued: 0 (2005); Employment by occupation: 16.8% management, 23.3% professional, 13.3% services, 26.7% sales, 0.1% farming, 13.0% construction, 6.8% production (2000).
Income: Per capita income: $34,597 (2005); Median household income: $88,402 (2005); Average household income: $104,162 (2005); Percent of households with income of $100,000 or more: 42.2% (2005); Poverty rate: 2.8% (2000).
Taxes: Total city taxes per capita: $544 (2004); City property taxes per capita: $441 (2004).
Education: Percent of population age 25 and over with: High school diploma (including GED) or higher: 90.6% (2005); Bachelor's degree or higher: 33.2% (2005); Master's degree or higher: 13.9% (2005).
School District(s)
Carmel Central School District (KG-12)
    2003-04 Enrollment: 4,857 .... (845) 878-2094
Housing: Homeownership rate: 84.5% (2005); Median home value: $377,010 (2005); Median rent: $829 per month (2000); Median age of housing: 34 years (2000).
Hospitals: Arms Acres (129 beds); Putnam Hospital Center (164 beds)
Safety: Violent crime rate: 5.2 per 10,000 population; Property crime rate: 62.4 per 10,000 population (2004).
Transportation: Commute to work: 90.6% car, 5.4% public transportation, 0.9% walk, 2.5% work from home (2000); Travel time to work: 17.1% less than 15 minutes, 23.9% 15 to 30 minutes, 24.8% 30 to 45 minutes, 16.9% 45 to 60 minutes, 17.3% 60 minutes or more (2000)
Additional Information Contacts
Town of Carmel .... (845) 628-1500
    http://www.ci.carmel.ny.us/

CARMEL HAMLET (CDP). Covers a land area of 8.493 square miles and a water area of 1.960 square miles. Located at 41.42° N. Lat.; 73.67° W. Long.
Population: 4,800 (1990); 5,650 (2000); 6,310 (2005); 6,946 (2010 projected); Race: 91.0% White, 2.1% Black, 1.0% Asian, 12.3% Hispanic of any race (2005); Density: 742.9 persons per square mile (2005); Average household size: 2.81 (2005); Median age: 39.6 (2005); Males per 100 females: 99.9 (2005); Marriage status: 22.8% never married, 62.2% now married, 6.6% widowed, 8.4% divorced (2000); Foreign born: 9.9% (2000); Ancestry (includes multiple ancestries): 31.3% Italian, 26.6% Irish, 19.5% German, 11.7% Other groups, 5.2% English (2000).
Economy: Employment by occupation: 17.6% management, 23.7% professional, 15.2% services, 25.2% sales, 0.0% farming, 11.2% construction, 7.1% production (2000).
Income: Per capita income: $33,679 (2005); Median household income: $77,350 (2005); Average household income: $92,735 (2005); Percent of households with income of $100,000 or more: 35.2% (2005); Poverty rate: 5.1% (2000).
Education: Percent of population age 25 and over with: High school diploma (including GED) or higher: 87.8% (2005); Bachelor's degree or higher: 31.9% (2005); Master's degree or higher: 12.0% (2005).
Housing: Homeownership rate: 77.3% (2005); Median home value: $359,865 (2005); Median rent: $766 per month (2000); Median age of housing: 36 years (2000).
Transportation: Commute to work: 86.9% car, 7.5% public transportation, 2.4% walk, 2.4% work from home (2000); Travel time to work: 22.3% less than 15 minutes, 24.1% 15 to 30 minutes, 20.1% 30 to 45 minutes, 13.8% 45 to 60 minutes, 19.8% 60 minutes or more (2000)

COLD SPRING (village). Covers a land area of 0.606 square miles and a water area of 0.007 square miles. Located at 41.41° N. Lat.; 73.95° W. Long. Elevation is 108 feet.
History: Settled before the American Revolution; incorporated 1846.
Population: 1,998 (1990); 1,983 (2000); 2,016 (2005); 2,063 (2010 projected); Race: 95.4% White, 0.7% Black, 1.7% Asian, 4.2% Hispanic of any race (2005); Density: 3,328.4 persons per square mile (2005); Average household size: 2.15 (2005); Median age: 43.7 (2005); Males per 100 females: 82.6 (2005); Marriage status: 23.2% never married, 55.4% now married, 10.2% widowed, 11.2% divorced (2000); Foreign born: 8.0% (2000); Ancestry (includes multiple ancestries): 30.1% Irish, 24.6% Italian, 14.3% German, 13.5% English, 8.6% Other groups (2000).
Economy: Manufacturing: metal products. In dairying area. Single-family building permits issued: 2 (2005); Multi-family building permits issued: 0 (2005); Employment by occupation: 20.1% management, 30.0% professional, 10.8% services, 22.0% sales, 0.4% farming, 10.4% construction, 6.3% production (2000).
Income: Per capita income: $37,464 (2005); Median household income: $61,438 (2005); Average household income: $80,434 (2005); Percent of households with income of $100,000 or more: 26.5% (2005); Poverty rate: 5.4% (2000).
Education: Percent of population age 25 and over with: High school diploma (including GED) or higher: 92.5% (2005); Bachelor's degree or higher: 39.0% (2005); Master's degree or higher: 15.4% (2005).
School District(s)
Haldane Central School District (KG-12)
    2003-04 Enrollment: 852 .... (845) 265-9254
Housing: Homeownership rate: 61.9% (2005); Median home value: $319,203 (2005); Median rent: $725 per month (2000); Median age of housing: 60+ years (2000).
Newspapers: The Putnam County News & Recorder (General - Circulation 4,200)
Transportation: Commute to work: 67.4% car, 23.6% public transportation, 6.1% walk, 2.8% work from home (2000); Travel time to work: 18.7% less than 15 minutes, 21.4% 15 to 30 minutes, 20.0% 30 to 45 minutes, 4.6% 45 to 60 minutes, 35.2% 60 minutes or more (2000)

GARRISON (unincorporated postal area, zip code 10524). Covers a land area of 19.807 square miles and a water area of 0.157 square miles. Located at 41.36° N. Lat.; 73.92° W. Long. Elevation is 21 feet.
Population: 0 (2000); Race: 96.2% White, 0.6% Black, 2.1% Asian, 3.9% Hispanic of any race (2000); Density: 0.0 persons per square mile (2000); Age: 25.4% under 18, 11.8% over 64 (2000); Marriage status: 22.0% never married, 66.0% now married, 4.5% widowed, 7.5% divorced (2000); Foreign born: 9.4% (2000); Ancestry (includes multiple ancestries): 29.3%

Irish, 28.9% Italian, 17.8% German, 10.8% English, 7.6% Other groups (2000).
Economy: Employment by occupation: 19.9% management, 30.6% professional, 8.4% services, 24.4% sales, 0.2% farming, 10.6% construction, 6.0% production (2000).
Income: Per capita income: $40,276 (2000); Median household income: $83,329 (2000); Poverty rate: 6.1% (2000).
Education: Percent of population age 25 and over with: High school diploma (including GED) or higher: 95.3% (2000); Bachelor's degree or higher: 47.0% (2000).

School District(s)
Garrison Union Free School District (KG-08)
   2003-04 Enrollment: 290 . . . . (845) 424-3689

Housing: Homeownership rate: 86.0% (2000); Median home value: $230,500 (2000); Median rent: $942 per month (2000); Median age of housing: 42 years (2000).
Transportation: Commute to work: 76.4% car, 13.1% public transportation, 1.2% walk, 7.5% work from home (2000); Travel time to work: 21.6% less than 15 minutes, 18.6% 15 to 30 minutes, 18.8% 30 to 45 minutes, 15.2% 45 to 60 minutes, 25.7% 60 minutes or more (2000)

KENT (town).
Covers a land area of 40.628 square miles and a water area of 2.543 square miles. Located at 41.46° N. Lat.; 73.68° W. Long.
Population: 13,183 (1990); 14,009 (2000); 14,551 (2005); 15,137 (2010 projected); Race: 91.8% White, 2.0% Black, 1.7% Asian, 8.4% Hispanic of any race (2005); Density: 358.2 persons per square mile (2005); Average household size: 2.83 (2005); Median age: 39.2 (2005); Males per 100 females: 98.6 (2005); Marriage status: 23.8% never married, 63.7% now married, 5.5% widowed, 7.0% divorced (2000); Foreign born: 6.3% (2000); Ancestry (includes multiple ancestries): 33.8% Irish, 31.3% Italian, 15.2% German, 10.1% Other groups, 7.0% English (2000).
Economy: Single-family building permits issued: 11 (2005); Multi-family building permits issued: 0 (2005); Employment by occupation: 14.7% management, 24.4% professional, 16.1% services, 24.8% sales, 0.4% farming, 11.3% construction, 8.4% production (2000).
Income: Per capita income: $34,493 (2005); Median household income: $81,465 (2005); Average household income: $96,810 (2005); Percent of households with income of $100,000 or more: 37.8% (2005); Poverty rate: 4.1% (2000).
Taxes: Total city taxes per capita: $705 (2004); City property taxes per capita: $635 (2004).
Education: Percent of population age 25 and over with: High school diploma (including GED) or higher: 88.5% (2005); Bachelor's degree or higher: 28.6% (2005); Master's degree or higher: 12.5% (2005).
Housing: Homeownership rate: 83.2% (2005); Median home value: $268,330 (2005); Median rent: $803 per month (2000); Median age of housing: 39 years (2000).
Safety: Violent crime rate: 3.5 per 10,000 population; Property crime rate: 137.1 per 10,000 population (2004).
Transportation: Commute to work: 87.8% car, 6.4% public transportation, 1.2% walk, 4.5% work from home (2000); Travel time to work: 14.1% less than 15 minutes, 25.1% 15 to 30 minutes, 18.6% 30 to 45 minutes, 18.3% 45 to 60 minutes, 23.9% 60 minutes or more (2000)
Additional Information Contacts
Town of Kent . . . . (845) 225-3943
   http://www.townofkent.org/

LAKE CARMEL (CDP).
Covers a land area of 5.163 square miles and a water area of 0.348 square miles. Located at 41.46° N. Lat.; 73.66° W. Long.
Population: 8,482 (1990); 8,663 (2000); 8,985 (2005); 9,326 (2010 projected); Race: 92.0% White, 2.2% Black, 1.2% Asian, 9.1% Hispanic of any race (2005); Density: 1,740.4 persons per square mile (2005); Average household size: 2.82 (2005); Median age: 38.2 (2005); Males per 100 females: 98.5 (2005); Marriage status: 23.3% never married, 64.8% now married, 4.9% widowed, 7.0% divorced (2000); Foreign born: 6.2% (2000); Ancestry (includes multiple ancestries): 35.1% Irish, 33.2% Italian, 14.5% German, 9.6% Other groups, 6.6% English (2000).
Economy: Employment by occupation: 13.6% management, 22.4% professional, 17.4% services, 26.2% sales, 0.2% farming, 11.8% construction, 8.3% production (2000).
Income: Per capita income: $31,911 (2005); Median household income: $78,924 (2005); Average household income: $89,874 (2005); Percent of households with income of $100,000 or more: 35.0% (2005); Poverty rate: 3.8% (2000).
Education: Percent of population age 25 and over with: High school diploma (including GED) or higher: 87.7% (2005); Bachelor's degree or higher: 23.2% (2005); Master's degree or higher: 9.8% (2005).
Housing: Homeownership rate: 84.0% (2005); Median home value: $248,679 (2005); Median rent: $824 per month (2000); Median age of housing: 43 years (2000).
Transportation: Commute to work: 90.6% car, 5.5% public transportation, 0.9% walk, 2.9% work from home (2000); Travel time to work: 15.4% less than 15 minutes, 24.0% 15 to 30 minutes, 18.5% 30 to 45 minutes, 20.1% 45 to 60 minutes, 22.0% 60 minutes or more (2000)

LAKE PEEKSKILL (unincorporated postal area, zip code 10537).
Covers a land area of 2.008 square miles and a water area of 0.098 square miles. Located at 41.33° N. Lat.; 73.88° W. Long.
Population: 0 (2000); Race: 93.5% White, 1.4% Black, 0.0% Asian, 10.0% Hispanic of any race (2000); Density: 0.0 persons per square mile (2000); Age: 22.9% under 18, 9.3% over 64 (2000); Marriage status: 22.5% never married, 59.7% now married, 6.2% widowed, 11.7% divorced (2000); Foreign born: 8.3% (2000); Ancestry (includes multiple ancestries): 27.6% Irish, 22.2% German, 21.5% Italian, 11.7% Other groups, 7.3% English (2000).
Economy: Resort village. Employment by occupation: 14.8% management, 21.6% professional, 16.4% services, 30.7% sales, 1.3% farming, 7.0% construction, 8.3% production (2000).
Income: Per capita income: $28,813 (2000); Median household income: $63,583 (2000); Poverty rate: 2.0% (2000).
Education: Percent of population age 25 and over with: High school diploma (including GED) or higher: 89.7% (2000); Bachelor's degree or higher: 32.6% (2000).
Housing: Homeownership rate: 81.4% (2000); Median home value: $139,700 (2000); Median rent: $865 per month (2000); Median age of housing: 48 years (2000).
Transportation: Commute to work: 89.8% car, 5.4% public transportation, 1.3% walk, 3.5% work from home (2000); Travel time to work: 21.7% less than 15 minutes, 29.8% 15 to 30 minutes, 16.7% 30 to 45 minutes, 11.4% 45 to 60 minutes, 20.4% 60 minutes or more (2000)

MAHOPAC (CDP).
Covers a land area of 5.297 square miles and a water area of 1.135 square miles. Located at 41.37° N. Lat.; 73.73° W. Long. Elevation is 666 feet.
Population: 7,688 (1990); 8,478 (2000); 8,658 (2005); 8,800 (2010 projected); Race: 92.2% White, 1.5% Black, 1.8% Asian, 9.9% Hispanic of any race (2005); Density: 1,634.7 persons per square mile (2005); Average household size: 2.88 (2005); Median age: 38.9 (2005); Males per 100 females: 100.2 (2005); Marriage status: 24.3% never married, 63.1% now married, 7.8% widowed, 4.8% divorced (2000); Foreign born: 12.6% (2000); Ancestry (includes multiple ancestries): 34.0% Italian, 24.5% Irish, 12.0% German, 9.5% Other groups, 6.3% Polish (2000).
Economy: Employment by occupation: 15.3% management, 23.3% professional, 12.1% services, 27.6% sales, 0.2% farming, 14.6% construction, 6.9% production (2000).
Income: Per capita income: $34,287 (2005); Median household income: $80,576 (2005); Average household income: $98,449 (2005); Percent of households with income of $100,000 or more: 35.9% (2005); Poverty rate: 3.8% (2000).
Education: Percent of population age 25 and over with: High school diploma (including GED) or higher: 88.6% (2005); Bachelor's degree or higher: 29.7% (2005); Master's degree or higher: 13.3% (2005).

School District(s)
Mahopac Central School District (KG-12)
   2003-04 Enrollment: 5,289 . . . . (845) 628-3415

Housing: Homeownership rate: 77.8% (2005); Median home value: $365,831 (2005); Median rent: $849 per month (2000); Median age of housing: 37 years (2000).
Newspapers: Beacon Light (General - Circulation 2,700); Brewster Times (General - Circulation 8,200); Carmel Times (General - Circulation 11,800); East Fishkill Record (General - Circulation 3,100); Fishkill Standard (General - Circulation 6,200); La Grange Independent (General - Circulation 2,600); Mahopac Press (General - Circulation 3,200)
Transportation: Commute to work: 90.1% car, 5.7% public transportation, 1.1% walk, 2.7% work from home (2000); Travel time to work: 16.9% less than 15 minutes, 22.5% 15 to 30 minutes, 25.7% 30 to 45 minutes, 17.0% 45 to 60 minutes, 17.9% 60 minutes or more (2000)
Additional Information Contacts

Mahopac Chamber of Commerce .... (845) 628-5553
http://www.mahopacchamber.com/

NELSONVILLE (village).
Covers a land area of 1.043 square miles and a water area of 0.002 square miles. Located at 41.42° N. Lat.; 73.94° W. Long. Elevation is 198 feet.
Population: 585 (1990); 565 (2000); 564 (2005); 568 (2010 projected); Race: 95.0% White, 2.8% Black, 0.2% Asian, 6.0% Hispanic of any race (2005); Density: 540.6 persons per square mile (2005); Average household size: 2.51 (2005); Median age: 41.7 (2005); Males per 100 females: 103.6 (2005); Marriage status: 26.4% never married, 60.0% now married, 5.6% widowed, 8.0% divorced (2000); Foreign born: 7.3% (2000); Ancestry (includes multiple ancestries): 29.3% Italian, 27.7% Irish, 11.2% German, 8.7% Other groups, 8.5% English (2000).
Economy: In dairying area. Single-family building permits issued: 2 (2005); Multi-family building permits issued: 0 (2005); Employment by occupation: 18.8% management, 27.1% professional, 14.7% services, 18.0% sales, 0.0% farming, 14.3% construction, 7.1% production (2000).
Income: Per capita income: $32,048 (2005); Median household income: $65,625 (2005); Average household income: $78,500 (2005); Percent of households with income of $100,000 or more: 25.3% (2005); Poverty rate: 7.7% (2000).
Education: Percent of population age 25 and over with: High school diploma (including GED) or higher: 89.1% (2005); Bachelor's degree or higher: 41.7% (2005); Master's degree or higher: 16.4% (2005).
Housing: Homeownership rate: 65.3% (2005); Median home value: $287,975 (2005); Median rent: $833 per month (2000); Median age of housing: 60+ years (2000).
Transportation: Commute to work: 75.9% car, 21.1% public transportation, 1.1% walk, 1.9% work from home (2000); Travel time to work: 30.7% less than 15 minutes, 15.7% 15 to 30 minutes, 14.9% 30 to 45 minutes, 8.0% 45 to 60 minutes, 30.7% 60 minutes or more (2000)

PATTERSON (town).
Covers a land area of 32.268 square miles and a water area of 0.636 square miles. Located at 41.47° N. Lat.; 73.57° W. Long. Elevation is 450 feet.
History: Patterson is located in a valley which was formerly part of the Patterson Great Swamp. The village, originally named Franklin, was settled about 1770 by Scots discharged from the British army after service in the French and Indian War. The present name was adopted in 1808 when the legislature passed a law abolishing the numerous "Franklins" in the state. The town was then named after Matthew Patterson, an early settler.
Population: 8,679 (1990); 11,306 (2000); 12,114 (2005); 12,951 (2010 projected); Race: 88.0% White, 5.0% Black, 1.9% Asian, 10.9% Hispanic of any race (2005); Density: 375.4 persons per square mile (2005); Average household size: 3.16 (2005); Median age: 36.9 (2005); Males per 100 females: 107.0 (2005); Marriage status: 27.8% never married, 63.1% now married, 3.8% widowed, 5.3% divorced (2000); Foreign born: 5.5% (2000); Ancestry (includes multiple ancestries): 28.7% Italian, 24.6% Irish, 13.9% German, 9.0% Other groups, 6.8% English (2000).
Economy: Single-family building permits issued: 31 (2005); Multi-family building permits issued: 0 (2005); Employment by occupation: 13.2% management, 22.0% professional, 15.7% services, 28.0% sales, 0.0% farming, 12.4% construction, 8.5% production (2000).
Income: Per capita income: $30,007 (2005); Median household income: $77,263 (2005); Average household income: $90,884 (2005); Percent of households with income of $100,000 or more: 33.8% (2005); Poverty rate: 4.9% (2000).
Education: Percent of population age 25 and over with: High school diploma (including GED) or higher: 87.5% (2005); Bachelor's degree or higher: 29.1% (2005); Master's degree or higher: 10.6% (2005).

School District(s)
Carmel Central School District (KG-12)
    2003-04 Enrollment: 4,857 .... (845) 878-2094

Housing: Homeownership rate: 79.9% (2005); Median home value: $284,056 (2005); Median rent: $789 per month (2000); Median age of housing: 33 years (2000).
Transportation: Commute to work: 86.6% car, 5.9% public transportation, 2.9% walk, 3.3% work from home (2000); Travel time to work: 16.7% less than 15 minutes, 24.8% 15 to 30 minutes, 16.0% 30 to 45 minutes, 18.3% 45 to 60 minutes, 24.2% 60 minutes or more (2000)

Additional Information Contacts
Patterson Chamber of Commerce .... (845) 878-4696
http://www.pcofc.org

Town of Patterson .... (845) 878-6500
http://www.pattersonny.org/

PEACH LAKE (CDP).
Covers a land area of 2.699 square miles and a water area of 0.361 square miles. Located at 41.36° N. Lat.; 73.57° W. Long.
Population: 1,499 (1990); 1,671 (2000); 1,769 (2005); 1,863 (2010 projected); Race: 96.3% White, 0.7% Black, 1.1% Asian, 4.2% Hispanic of any race (2005); Density: 655.5 persons per square mile (2005); Average household size: 2.68 (2005); Median age: 40.8 (2005); Males per 100 females: 99.9 (2005); Marriage status: 16.5% never married, 68.5% now married, 7.0% widowed, 8.1% divorced (2000); Foreign born: 7.0% (2000); Ancestry (includes multiple ancestries): 40.7% Irish, 19.7% German, 19.0% Italian, 10.4% English, 7.7% Polish (2000).
Economy: Employment by occupation: 18.0% management, 27.5% professional, 15.7% services, 21.6% sales, 0.0% farming, 10.7% construction, 6.5% production (2000).
Income: Per capita income: $40,493 (2005); Median household income: $87,033 (2005); Average household income: $108,699 (2005); Percent of households with income of $100,000 or more: 41.6% (2005); Poverty rate: 0.0% (2000).
Education: Percent of population age 25 and over with: High school diploma (including GED) or higher: 93.7% (2005); Bachelor's degree or higher: 42.2% (2005); Master's degree or higher: 14.5% (2005).
Housing: Homeownership rate: 90.6% (2005); Median home value: $360,061 (2005); Median rent: $1,075 per month (2000); Median age of housing: 52 years (2000).
Transportation: Commute to work: 91.1% car, 2.6% public transportation, 1.5% walk, 4.7% work from home (2000); Travel time to work: 23.2% less than 15 minutes, 35.4% 15 to 30 minutes, 19.5% 30 to 45 minutes, 13.2% 45 to 60 minutes, 8.7% 60 minutes or more (2000)

PHILIPSTOWN (town).
Covers a land area of 48.828 square miles and a water area of 2.690 square miles. Located at 41.40° N. Lat.; 73.93° W. Long.
Population: 9,242 (1990); 9,422 (2000); 9,933 (2005); 10,472 (2010 projected); Race: 94.6% White, 1.3% Black, 1.5% Asian, 5.4% Hispanic of any race (2005); Density: 203.4 persons per square mile (2005); Average household size: 2.58 (2005); Median age: 42.8 (2005); Males per 100 females: 94.8 (2005); Marriage status: 21.7% never married, 63.9% now married, 5.5% widowed, 8.9% divorced (2000); Foreign born: 9.1% (2000); Ancestry (includes multiple ancestries): 27.9% Irish, 27.3% Italian, 15.8% German, 11.2% English, 7.8% Other groups (2000).
Economy: Single-family building permits issued: 20 (2005); Multi-family building permits issued: 0 (2005); Employment by occupation: 22.2% management, 29.0% professional, 10.5% services, 22.6% sales, 0.2% farming, 10.1% construction, 5.3% production (2000).
Income: Per capita income: $43,389 (2005); Median household income: $83,492 (2005); Average household income: $110,475 (2005); Percent of households with income of $100,000 or more: 40.1% (2005); Poverty rate: 6.0% (2000).
Education: Percent of population age 25 and over with: High school diploma (including GED) or higher: 93.3% (2005); Bachelor's degree or higher: 43.8% (2005); Master's degree or higher: 20.0% (2005).
Housing: Homeownership rate: 77.8% (2005); Median home value: $376,708 (2005); Median rent: $761 per month (2000); Median age of housing: 44 years (2000).
Transportation: Commute to work: 75.2% car, 15.9% public transportation, 2.3% walk, 5.6% work from home (2000); Travel time to work: 20.2% less than 15 minutes, 18.5% 15 to 30 minutes, 18.3% 30 to 45 minutes, 12.6% 45 to 60 minutes, 30.4% 60 minutes or more (2000)

PUTNAM LAKE (CDP).
Covers a land area of 3.867 square miles and a water area of 0.440 square miles. Located at 41.46° N. Lat.; 73.54° W. Long.
Population: 3,459 (1990); 3,855 (2000); 3,908 (2005); 3,991 (2010 projected); Race: 91.1% White, 3.7% Black, 1.4% Asian, 10.4% Hispanic of any race (2005); Density: 1,010.7 persons per square mile (2005); Average household size: 2.88 (2005); Median age: 36.8 (2005); Males per 100 females: 104.0 (2005); Marriage status: 25.3% never married, 62.0% now married, 6.1% widowed, 6.6% divorced (2000); Foreign born: 6.7% (2000); Ancestry (includes multiple ancestries): 31.8% Italian, 28.5% Irish, 15.6% German, 12.4% Other groups, 7.3% English (2000).

Economy: Employment by occupation: 9.7% management, 18.2% professional, 18.4% services, 28.1% sales, 0.0% farming, 14.5% construction, 11.0% production (2000).
Income: Per capita income: $27,797 (2005); Median household income: $68,919 (2005); Average household income: $79,817 (2005); Percent of households with income of $100,000 or more: 27.5% (2005); Poverty rate: 2.0% (2000).
Education: Percent of population age 25 and over with: High school diploma (including GED) or higher: 89.3% (2005); Bachelor's degree or higher: 23.4% (2005); Master's degree or higher: 8.2% (2005).
Housing: Homeownership rate: 86.7% (2005); Median home value: $245,723 (2005); Median rent: $805 per month (2000); Median age of housing: 44 years (2000).
Transportation: Commute to work: 94.5% car, 3.1% public transportation, 0.0% walk, 2.2% work from home (2000); Travel time to work: 11.7% less than 15 minutes, 30.9% 15 to 30 minutes, 12.9% 30 to 45 minutes, 17.1% 45 to 60 minutes, 27.4% 60 minutes or more (2000)

PUTNAM VALLEY (town). Covers a land area of 41.394 square miles and a water area of 1.601 square miles. Located at 41.38° N. Lat.; 73.84° W. Long.
Population: 9,094 (1990); 10,686 (2000); 11,339 (2005); 12,013 (2010 projected); Race: 93.3% White, 2.1% Black, 1.0% Asian, 9.3% Hispanic of any race (2005); Density: 273.9 persons per square mile (2005); Average household size: 2.86 (2005); Median age: 39.3 (2005); Males per 100 females: 99.5 (2005); Marriage status: 22.1% never married, 65.8% now married, 5.6% widowed, 6.5% divorced (2000); Foreign born: 8.9% (2000); Ancestry (includes multiple ancestries): 29.2% Italian, 23.6% Irish, 18.3% German, 9.7% Other groups, 6.8% English (2000).
Economy: Single-family building permits issued: 17 (2005); Multi-family building permits issued: 0 (2005); Employment by occupation: 15.4% management, 28.1% professional, 12.7% services, 26.7% sales, 0.4% farming, 11.7% construction, 5.1% production (2000).
Income: Per capita income: $35,883 (2005); Median household income: $84,513 (2005); Average household income: $101,819 (2005); Percent of households with income of $100,000 or more: 40.5% (2005); Poverty rate: 4.8% (2000).
Education: Percent of population age 25 and over with: High school diploma (including GED) or higher: 91.6% (2005); Bachelor's degree or higher: 38.1% (2005); Master's degree or higher: 16.6% (2005).

School District(s)

Putnam Valley Central School District (KG-12)
 2003-04 Enrollment: 1,934 . . . . (845) 528-8143
Housing: Homeownership rate: 87.5% (2005); Median home value: $329,554 (2005); Median rent: $765 per month (2000); Median age of housing: 39 years (2000).
Transportation: Commute to work: 88.3% car, 5.4% public transportation, 2.1% walk, 3.7% work from home (2000); Travel time to work: 17.9% less than 15 minutes, 24.4% 15 to 30 minutes, 26.9% 30 to 45 minutes, 14.0% 45 to 60 minutes, 16.8% 60 minutes or more (2000)
Additional Information Contacts
Town of Putnam Valley . . . . (845) 526-2121
 http://www.putnamvalley.com/

SOUTHEAST (town). Covers a land area of 32.059 square miles and a water area of 2.920 square miles. Located at 41.40° N. Lat.; 73.60° W. Long.
History: The Tilly Foster Iron Mine (established 1790), located on a 128-acre farm owned by Tilly Foster, was the largest of a number of mines in the area. The town was named after this mine. For a time high-grade iron ore was shipped from here to Pennsylvania. Became open-pit mine in 1889, closed in 1897 after an avalanche.
Population: 14,927 (1990); 17,316 (2000); 18,070 (2005); 18,888 (2010 projected); Race: 90.3% White, 2.5% Black, 2.3% Asian, 12.2% Hispanic of any race (2005); Density: 563.7 persons per square mile (2005); Average household size: 2.79 (2005); Median age: 38.8 (2005); Males per 100 females: 102.5 (2005); Marriage status: 24.1% never married, 63.6% now married, 5.6% widowed, 6.8% divorced (2000); Foreign born: 10.4% (2000); Ancestry (includes multiple ancestries): 31.5% Italian, 28.6% Irish, 16.1% German, 11.7% Other groups, 7.2% English (2000).
Economy: A center of manufacturing: pharmaceuticals, dairy equipment. Single-family building permits issued: 14 (2005); Multi-family building permits issued: 0 (2005); Employment by occupation: 16.8% management, 24.5% professional, 14.3% services, 26.2% sales, 0.4% farming, 11.1% construction, 6.7% production (2000).
Income: Per capita income: $33,617 (2005); Median household income: $77,695 (2005); Average household income: $93,383 (2005); Percent of households with income of $100,000 or more: 34.6% (2005); Poverty rate: 6.1% (2000).
Taxes: Total city taxes per capita: $358 (2004); City property taxes per capita: $261 (2004).
Education: Percent of population age 25 and over with: High school diploma (including GED) or higher: 90.0% (2005); Bachelor's degree or higher: 35.1% (2005); Master's degree or higher: 13.9% (2005).
Housing: Homeownership rate: 77.9% (2005); Median home value: $343,143 (2005); Median rent: $861 per month (2000); Median age of housing: 29 years (2000).
Transportation: Commute to work: 86.9% car, 8.6% public transportation, 1.7% walk, 2.2% work from home (2000); Travel time to work: 20.6% less than 15 minutes, 25.0% 15 to 30 minutes, 21.7% 30 to 45 minutes, 14.1% 45 to 60 minutes, 18.7% 60 minutes or more (2000)
Additional Information Contacts
Town of Southeast . . . . (845) 279-4313
 http://www.townofsoutheast-ny.com/Home/

Queens County and Borough

See New York City

Rensselaer County

Located in eastern New York; bounded on the west by the Hudson River, and on the east by Massachusetts and Vermont; includes part of the Taconic Mountains; drained by the Hoosic River. Covers a land area of 653.96 square miles, a water area of 11.43 square miles, and is located in the Eastern Time Zone. The county government was organized in 1791. County seat is Troy.

Rensselaer County is part of the Albany-Schenectady-Troy, NY Metropolitan Statistical Area. The entire metro area includes: Albany County, NY; Rensselaer County, NY; Saratoga County, NY; Schenectady County, NY; Schoharie County, NY

Weather Station: Grafton   Elevation: 1,558 feet

	Jan	Feb	Mar	Apr	May	Jun	Jul	Aug	Sep	Oct	Nov	Dec
High	28	31	41	54	67	74	78	76	68	57	45	33
Low	12	14	23	34	45	53	58	57	49	39	29	18
Precip	3.0	2.4	3.4	3.8	4.6	4.7	4.3	4.7	4.3	4.1	4.0	2.9
Snow	20.0	15.1	14.2	6.9	0.7	0.0	0.0	0.0	tr	0.9	7.9	15.8

High and Low temperatures in degrees Fahrenheit; Precipitation and Snow in inches

Weather Station: Troy Lock & Dam   Elevation: 22 feet

	Jan	Feb	Mar	Apr	May	Jun	Jul	Aug	Sep	Oct	Nov	Dec
High	31	34	44	57	71	79	84	82	73	61	49	37
Low	13	15	25	37	48	57	63	61	52	40	32	22
Precip	2.2	1.9	2.7	3.2	3.7	3.8	4.0	4.0	3.3	3.4	3.1	2.4
Snow	12.1	9.4	7.2	1.6	tr	0.0	0.0	0.0	0.0	tr	3.4	7.4

High and Low temperatures in degrees Fahrenheit; Precipitation and Snow in inches

Population: 154,429 (1990); 152,538 (2000); 154,951 (2005); 157,380 (2010 projected); Race: 89.0% White, 5.8% Black, 2.3% Asian, 2.9% Hispanic of any race (2005); Density: 236.9 persons per square mile (2005); Average household size: 2.51 (2005); Median age: 38.0 (2005); Males per 100 females: 96.8 (2005).
Religion: Five largest groups: 33.4% Catholic Church, 4.3% The United Methodist Church, 1.8% Evangelical Lutheran Church in America, 1.5% Reformed Church in America, 1.0% Episcopal Church (2000).
Economy: Unemployment rate: 4.2% (2005); Total civilian labor force: 84,047 (2005); Leading industries: 18.7% health care and social assistance; 13.7% retail trade; 12.3% educational services (2003); Farms: 549 totaling 92,344 acres (2002); Companies that employ 500 or more persons: 4 (2003); Companies that employ 100 to 499 persons: 61 (2003); Companies that employ less than 100 persons: 2,760 (2003); Black-owned businesses: n/a (2002); Hispanic-owned businesses: n/a (2002); Women-owned businesses: 2,738 (2002); Retail sales per capita: $9,459 (2006). Single-family building permits issued: 428 (2005); Multi-family building permits issued: 468 (2005).
Income: Per capita income: $24,690 (2005); Median household income: $49,223 (2005); Average household income: $61,001 (2005); Percent of households with income of $100,000 or more: 15.3% (2005); Poverty rate: 9.8% (2003); Bankruptcy rate: 6.99% (2005).

Taxes: Total county taxes per capita: $602 (2004); County property taxes per capita: $224 (2004).
Education: Percent of population age 25 and over with: High school diploma (including GED) or higher: 85.0% (2005); Bachelor's degree or higher: 23.9% (2005); Master's degree or higher: 10.6% (2005).
Housing: Homeownership rate: 65.6% (2005); Median home value: $144,838 (2005); Median rent: $445 per month (2000); Median age of housing: 48 years (2000).
Health: Birth rate: 111.6 per 10,000 population (2004); Death rate: 99.3 per 10,000 population (2004); Age-adjusted cancer mortality rate: 243.3 deaths per 100,000 population (2002); Air Quality Index: 93.4% good, 6.1% moderate, 0.6% unhealthy for sensitive individuals, 0.0% unhealthy (percent of days in 2005); Number of physicians: 17.2 per 10,000 population (2004); Hospital beds: 27.1 per 10,000 population (2003); Hospital admissions: 1,028.7 per 10,000 population (2003).
Elections: 2004 Presidential election results: 47.9% Bush, 49.7% Kerry, 2.1% Nader, 0.2% Badnarik
National and State Parks: State Forest Rensselaer Number 3
Additional Information Contacts
Rensselaer County Government . . . . (518) 270-2900
  http://www.rensco.com/
City of Troy. . . . . (518) 270-4401
  http://www.troyny.gov/
Town of Brunswick. . . . . (518) 279-3461
  http://www.townofbrunswick.org/
Town of East Greenbush . . . . (518) 477-4775
  http://eastgreenbush.org/2005/index.html
Town of Schodack. . . . . (518) 477-7918
  http://www.schodack.org/

Rensselaer County Communities

AVERILL PARK (CDP). Covers a land area of 2.991 square miles and a water area of 0.088 square miles. Located at 42.63° N. Lat.; 73.55° W. Long.
Population: 1,656 (1990); 1,517 (2000); 1,567 (2005); 1,610 (2010 projected); Race: 97.3% White, 0.5% Black, 0.4% Asian, 1.7% Hispanic of any race (2005); Density: 523.9 persons per square mile (2005); Average household size: 2.49 (2005); Median age: 41.0 (2005); Males per 100 females: 95.1 (2005); Marriage status: 23.4% never married, 62.6% now married, 5.0% widowed, 9.0% divorced (2000); Foreign born: 1.6% (2000); Ancestry (includes multiple ancestries): 26.4% German, 23.6% Irish, 13.3% Italian, 11.8% English, 6.3% French (except Basque) (2000).
Economy: Manufacturing: knit goods; fur dressing; wholesale trade. Employment by occupation: 12.8% management, 26.2% professional, 12.5% services, 29.9% sales, 0.0% farming, 8.4% construction, 10.2% production (2000).
Income: Per capita income: $30,990 (2005); Median household income: $63,388 (2005); Average household income: $77,194 (2005); Percent of households with income of $100,000 or more: 25.0% (2005); Poverty rate: 4.8% (2000).
Education: Percent of population age 25 and over with: High school diploma (including GED) or higher: 92.7% (2005); Bachelor's degree or higher: 24.9% (2005); Master's degree or higher: 12.5% (2005).
School District(s)
Averill Park Central School District (KG-12)
  2003-04 Enrollment: 3,546 . . . . (518) 674-7055
Housing: Homeownership rate: 75.4% (2005); Median home value: $179,565 (2005); Median rent: $435 per month (2000); Median age of housing: 42 years (2000).
Transportation: Commute to work: 94.6% car, 0.0% public transportation, 0.7% walk, 2.6% work from home (2000); Travel time to work: 17.1% less than 15 minutes, 36.3% 15 to 30 minutes, 37.5% 30 to 45 minutes, 7.0% 45 to 60 minutes, 2.2% 60 minutes or more (2000)

BERLIN (town). Covers a land area of 59.653 square miles and a water area of 0.274 square miles. Located at 42.66° N. Lat.; 73.38° W. Long. Elevation is 852 feet.
Population: 1,921 (1990); 1,901 (2000); 1,921 (2005); 1,945 (2010 projected); Race: 98.1% White, 0.0% Black, 0.1% Asian, 1.6% Hispanic of any race (2005); Density: 32.2 persons per square mile (2005); Average household size: 2.56 (2005); Median age: 38.7 (2005); Males per 100 females: 100.7 (2005); Marriage status: 22.6% never married, 59.9% now married, 8.7% widowed, 8.7% divorced (2000); Foreign born: 1.9% (2000); Ancestry (includes multiple ancestries): 23.7% German, 19.9% Irish, 15.8% English, 10.3% Italian, 7.9% French (except Basque) (2000).
Economy: Woodworking. Single-family building permits issued: 7 (2005); Multi-family building permits issued: 0 (2005); Employment by occupation: 10.4% management, 13.0% professional, 13.4% services, 26.1% sales, 2.5% farming, 13.5% construction, 21.2% production (2000).
Income: Per capita income: $19,948 (2005); Median household income: $42,838 (2005); Average household income: $51,025 (2005); Percent of households with income of $100,000 or more: 8.5% (2005); Poverty rate: 12.0% (2000).
Education: Percent of population age 25 and over with: High school diploma (including GED) or higher: 77.5% (2005); Bachelor's degree or higher: 16.5% (2005); Master's degree or higher: 7.5% (2005).
School District(s)
Berlin Central School District (KG-12)
  2003-04 Enrollment: 1,040 . . . . (518) 658-2690
Housing: Homeownership rate: 79.8% (2005); Median home value: $118,846 (2005); Median rent: $412 per month (2000); Median age of housing: 43 years (2000).
Transportation: Commute to work: 91.4% car, 1.7% public transportation, 3.1% walk, 2.0% work from home (2000); Travel time to work: 34.7% less than 15 minutes, 15.3% 15 to 30 minutes, 24.6% 30 to 45 minutes, 15.8% 45 to 60 minutes, 9.6% 60 minutes or more (2000)

BRUNSWICK (town). Covers a land area of 44.532 square miles and a water area of 0.111 square miles. Located at 42.74° N. Lat.; 73.61° W. Long. Elevation is 517 feet.
Population: 11,093 (1990); 11,664 (2000); 11,800 (2005); 11,940 (2010 projected); Race: 95.1% White, 1.2% Black, 2.4% Asian, 1.2% Hispanic of any race (2005); Density: 265.0 persons per square mile (2005); Average household size: 2.48 (2005); Median age: 41.6 (2005); Males per 100 females: 97.1 (2005); Marriage status: 23.9% never married, 63.1% now married, 6.4% widowed, 6.6% divorced (2000); Foreign born: 3.4% (2000); Ancestry (includes multiple ancestries): 32.1% Irish, 19.1% German, 14.7% Italian, 11.5% English, 10.6% French (except Basque) (2000).
Economy: Single-family building permits issued: 44 (2005); Multi-family building permits issued: 0 (2005); Employment by occupation: 15.6% management, 27.6% professional, 11.2% services, 28.6% sales, 0.4% farming, 7.5% construction, 9.2% production (2000).
Income: Per capita income: $32,152 (2005); Median household income: $67,120 (2005); Average household income: $78,727 (2005); Percent of households with income of $100,000 or more: 25.6% (2005); Poverty rate: 3.2% (2000).
Education: Percent of population age 25 and over with: High school diploma (including GED) or higher: 91.5% (2005); Bachelor's degree or higher: 36.3% (2005); Master's degree or higher: 17.0% (2005).
Housing: Homeownership rate: 79.9% (2005); Median home value: $173,697 (2005); Median rent: $612 per month (2000); Median age of housing: 38 years (2000).
Transportation: Commute to work: 94.9% car, 0.4% public transportation, 1.2% walk, 2.6% work from home (2000); Travel time to work: 27.3% less than 15 minutes, 44.7% 15 to 30 minutes, 19.7% 30 to 45 minutes, 3.8% 45 to 60 minutes, 4.5% 60 minutes or more (2000)
Additional Information Contacts
Town of Brunswick. . . . . (518) 279-3461
  http://www.townofbrunswick.org/

BUSKIRK (unincorporated postal area, zip code 12028). Covers a land area of 18.252 square miles and a water area of 0.186 square miles. Located at 42.93° N. Lat.; 73.44° W. Long.
Population: 0 (2000); Race: 95.4% White, 1.0% Black, 0.7% Asian, 0.4% Hispanic of any race (2000); Density: 0.0 persons per square mile (2000); Age: 30.6% under 18, 12.0% over 64 (2000); Marriage status: 19.7% never married, 66.2% now married, 5.4% widowed, 8.7% divorced (2000); Foreign born: 1.6% (2000); Ancestry (includes multiple ancestries): 26.5% Irish, 16.5% German, 13.0% English, 12.5% French (except Basque), 9.3% Other groups (2000).
Economy: Employment by occupation: 17.3% management, 16.3% professional, 10.7% services, 15.9% sales, 0.8% farming, 14.9% construction, 24.1% production (2000).
Income: Per capita income: $19,539 (2000); Median household income: $37,100 (2000); Poverty rate: 6.9% (2000).
Education: Percent of population age 25 and over with: High school diploma (including GED) or higher: 81.1% (2000); Bachelor's degree or higher: 19.8% (2000).

Housing: Homeownership rate: 88.0% (2000); Median home value: $82,100 (2000); Median rent: $334 per month (2000); Median age of housing: 34 years (2000).
Transportation: Commute to work: 83.5% car, 2.5% public transportation, 2.1% walk, 11.0% work from home (2000); Travel time to work: 15.2% less than 15 minutes, 46.4% 15 to 30 minutes, 19.0% 30 to 45 minutes, 7.3% 45 to 60 minutes, 12.2% 60 minutes or more (2000)

CASTLETON-ON-HUDSON (village). Aka Castleton on Hudson.
Covers a land area of 0.799 square miles and a water area of <.001 square miles. Located at 42.53° N. Lat.; 73.75° W. Long. Elevation is 21 feet.
History: Settled by the Dutch c.1630; incorporated 1827.
Population: 1,455 (1990); 1,619 (2000); 1,594 (2005); 1,573 (2010 projected); Race: 95.3% White, 2.2% Black, 0.2% Asian, 2.7% Hispanic of any race (2005); Density: 1,994.3 persons per square mile (2005); Average household size: 2.60 (2005); Median age: 39.0 (2005); Males per 100 females: 85.8 (2005); Marriage status: 25.6% never married, 49.6% now married, 14.5% widowed, 10.2% divorced (2000); Foreign born: 0.9% (2000); Ancestry (includes multiple ancestries): 29.5% German, 25.4% Irish, 15.6% Italian, 13.4% English, 8.5% Polish (2000).
Economy: Single-family building permits issued: 0 (2005); Multi-family building permits issued: 0 (2005); Employment by occupation: 16.7% management, 23.9% professional, 10.0% services, 26.5% sales, 0.0% farming, 10.5% construction, 12.4% production (2000).
Income: Per capita income: $22,945 (2005); Median household income: $48,636 (2005); Average household income: $57,708 (2005); Percent of households with income of $100,000 or more: 10.6% (2005); Poverty rate: 8.7% (2000).
Education: Percent of population age 25 and over with: High school diploma (including GED) or higher: 82.4% (2005); Bachelor's degree or higher: 25.6% (2005); Master's degree or higher: 11.8% (2005).
School District(s)
Boces Questar III (R-C-G) (UG-UG)
    2003-04 Enrollment: 305 . . . . (518) 477-8771
East Greenbush Central School District (KG-12)
    2003-04 Enrollment: 4,572 . . . . (518) 477-2755
Schodack Central School District (KG-12)
    2003-04 Enrollment: 1,197 . . . . (518) 732-2297
Housing: Homeownership rate: 60.9% (2005); Median home value: $138,115 (2005); Median rent: $560 per month (2000); Median age of housing: 60+ years (2000).
Transportation: Commute to work: 92.9% car, 0.7% public transportation, 3.2% walk, 2.6% work from home (2000); Travel time to work: 23.9% less than 15 minutes, 52.4% 15 to 30 minutes, 18.6% 30 to 45 minutes, 2.2% 45 to 60 minutes, 2.8% 60 minutes or more (2000)

CROPSEYVILLE (unincorporated postal area, zip code 12052).
Covers a land area of 20.724 square miles and a water area of 0.401 square miles. Located at 42.74° N. Lat.; 73.49° W. Long.
Population: 0 (2000); Race: 99.1% White, 0.0% Black, 0.5% Asian, 0.4% Hispanic of any race (2000); Density: 0.0 persons per square mile (2000); Age: 25.1% under 18, 7.3% over 64 (2000); Marriage status: 19.6% never married, 63.4% now married, 5.4% widowed, 11.6% divorced (2000); Foreign born: 1.5% (2000); Ancestry (includes multiple ancestries): 26.5% Irish, 20.2% German, 14.4% French (except Basque), 13.9% English, 12.4% United States or American (2000).
Economy: Employment by occupation: 10.5% management, 22.4% professional, 10.3% services, 27.9% sales, 0.6% farming, 14.3% construction, 14.0% production (2000).
Income: Per capita income: $21,203 (2000); Median household income: $49,375 (2000); Poverty rate: 7.4% (2000).
Education: Percent of population age 25 and over with: High school diploma (including GED) or higher: 82.6% (2000); Bachelor's degree or higher: 17.1% (2000).
School District(s)
Berlin Central School District (KG-12)
    2003-04 Enrollment: 1,040 . . . . (518) 658-2690
Housing: Homeownership rate: 89.5% (2000); Median home value: $89,000 (2000); Median rent: $575 per month (2000); Median age of housing: 43 years (2000).
Transportation: Commute to work: 93.6% car, 1.3% public transportation, 1.2% walk, 3.9% work from home (2000); Travel time to work: 11.6% less than 15 minutes, 29.5% 15 to 30 minutes, 34.5% 30 to 45 minutes, 17.8% 45 to 60 minutes, 6.6% 60 minutes or more (2000)

EAGLE BRIDGE (unincorporated postal area, zip code 12057).
Covers a land area of 29.215 square miles and a water area of 0.008 square miles. Located at 42.95° N. Lat.; 73.35° W. Long. Elevation is 414 feet.
Population: 0 (2000); Race: 98.4% White, 0.0% Black, 0.0% Asian, 0.4% Hispanic of any race (2000); Density: 0.0 persons per square mile (2000); Age: 27.1% under 18, 14.9% over 64 (2000); Marriage status: 23.9% never married, 67.2% now married, 4.5% widowed, 4.4% divorced (2000); Foreign born: 1.5% (2000); Ancestry (includes multiple ancestries): 26.6% Irish, 23.3% German, 19.8% English, 15.4% United States or American, 7.9% French (except Basque) (2000).
Economy: Employment by occupation: 10.2% management, 19.1% professional, 10.3% services, 21.4% sales, 4.7% farming, 9.2% construction, 25.0% production (2000).
Income: Per capita income: $17,978 (2000); Median household income: $42,684 (2000); Poverty rate: 3.9% (2000).
Education: Percent of population age 25 and over with: High school diploma (including GED) or higher: 87.0% (2000); Bachelor's degree or higher: 21.1% (2000).
Housing: Homeownership rate: 87.9% (2000); Median home value: $91,900 (2000); Median rent: $428 per month (2000); Median age of housing: 40 years (2000).
Transportation: Commute to work: 91.3% car, 0.0% public transportation, 2.8% walk, 5.2% work from home (2000); Travel time to work: 21.5% less than 15 minutes, 31.5% 15 to 30 minutes, 14.9% 30 to 45 minutes, 14.9% 45 to 60 minutes, 17.1% 60 minutes or more (2000)

EAST GREENBUSH (town). Covers a land area of 24.095 square miles and a water area of 0.252 square miles. Located at 42.61° N. Lat.; 73.70° W. Long.
Population: 14,234 (1990); 15,560 (2000); 16,273 (2005); 16,959 (2010 projected); Race: 92.4% White, 3.7% Black, 2.6% Asian, 1.8% Hispanic of any race (2005); Density: 675.4 persons per square mile (2005); Average household size: 2.51 (2005); Median age: 40.8 (2005); Males per 100 females: 90.9 (2005); Marriage status: 23.0% never married, 58.6% now married, 8.4% widowed, 10.0% divorced (2000); Foreign born: 5.0% (2000); Ancestry (includes multiple ancestries): 29.5% Irish, 22.8% German, 22.7% Italian, 13.7% English, 7.7% French (except Basque) (2000).
Economy: Rapidly expanding residential area Southeast of Albany with easy commuter access to center of the capital. Single-family building permits issued: 66 (2005); Multi-family building permits issued: 288 (2005); Employment by occupation: 18.4% management, 27.1% professional, 10.9% services, 29.2% sales, 0.0% farming, 5.3% construction, 9.0% production (2000).
Income: Per capita income: $30,591 (2005); Median household income: $62,518 (2005); Average household income: $75,262 (2005); Percent of households with income of $100,000 or more: 23.4% (2005); Poverty rate: 3.0% (2000).
Taxes: Total city taxes per capita: $443 (2004); City property taxes per capita: $382 (2004).
Education: Percent of population age 25 and over with: High school diploma (including GED) or higher: 90.8% (2005); Bachelor's degree or higher: 34.4% (2005); Master's degree or higher: 15.6% (2005).
School District(s)
East Greenbush Central School District (KG-12)
    2003-04 Enrollment: 4,572 . . . . (518) 477-2755
Housing: Homeownership rate: 75.2% (2005); Median home value: $158,625 (2005); Median rent: $589 per month (2000); Median age of housing: 33 years (2000).
Safety: Violent crime rate: 22.4 per 10,000 population; Property crime rate: 226.8 per 10,000 population (2004).
Transportation: Commute to work: 94.8% car, 1.5% public transportation, 1.3% walk, 2.0% work from home (2000); Travel time to work: 31.0% less than 15 minutes, 53.0% 15 to 30 minutes, 10.2% 30 to 45 minutes, 2.6% 45 to 60 minutes, 3.3% 60 minutes or more (2000)
Additional Information Contacts
Town of East Greenbush . . . . (518) 477-4775
    http://eastgreenbush.org/2005/index.html

EAST GREENBUSH (CDP). Covers a land area of 2.648 square miles and a water area of 0 square miles. Located at 42.59° N. Lat.; 73.70° W. Long.

Population: 3,784 (1990); 4,085 (2000); 4,153 (2005); 4,227 (2010 projected); Race: 90.6% White, 4.1% Black, 3.6% Asian, 1.8% Hispanic of any race (2005); Density: 1,568.1 persons per square mile (2005); Average household size: 2.56 (2005); Median age: 38.4 (2005); Males per 100 females: 92.2 (2005); Marriage status: 23.7% never married, 57.6% now married, 6.7% widowed, 12.0% divorced (2000); Foreign born: 3.4% (2000); Ancestry (includes multiple ancestries): 23.7% German, 23.2% Irish, 22.9% Italian, 16.5% English, 8.2% Polish (2000).
Economy: Employment by occupation: 22.8% management, 27.1% professional, 10.0% services, 26.4% sales, 0.0% farming, 6.2% construction, 7.6% production (2000).
Income: Per capita income: $32,258 (2005); Median household income: $68,881 (2005); Average household income: $81,858 (2005); Percent of households with income of $100,000 or more: 28.2% (2005); Poverty rate: 2.7% (2000).
Education: Percent of population age 25 and over with: High school diploma (including GED) or higher: 95.2% (2005); Bachelor's degree or higher: 43.4% (2005); Master's degree or higher: 20.1% (2005).
Housing: Homeownership rate: 68.2% (2005); Median home value: $189,810 (2005); Median rent: $586 per month (2000); Median age of housing: 29 years (2000).
Transportation: Commute to work: 94.9% car, 1.0% public transportation, 0.8% walk, 2.4% work from home (2000); Travel time to work: 25.9% less than 15 minutes, 52.5% 15 to 30 minutes, 11.8% 30 to 45 minutes, 3.5% 45 to 60 minutes, 6.4% 60 minutes or more (2000)

EAST NASSAU (village).
Covers a land area of 4.899 square miles and a water area of 0.002 square miles. Located at 42.52° N. Lat.; 73.51° W. Long. Elevation is 571 feet.
Population: 587 (1990); 571 (2000); 574 (2005); 579 (2010 projected); Race: 94.8% White, 1.2% Black, 2.8% Asian, 1.2% Hispanic of any race (2005); Density: 117.2 persons per square mile (2005); Average household size: 2.59 (2005); Median age: 39.9 (2005); Males per 100 females: 100.0 (2005); Marriage status: 22.7% never married, 63.7% now married, 4.7% widowed, 8.9% divorced (2000); Foreign born: 3.6% (2000); Ancestry (includes multiple ancestries): 32.9% German, 21.8% Irish, 11.4% Italian, 10.7% English, 8.8% French (except Basque) (2000).
Economy: Single-family building permits issued: 0 (2005); Multi-family building permits issued: 0 (2005); Employment by occupation: 14.0% management, 26.9% professional, 17.5% services, 21.3% sales, 1.0% farming, 4.9% construction, 14.3% production (2000).
Income: Per capita income: $26,307 (2005); Median household income: $49,712 (2005); Average household income: $68,018 (2005); Percent of households with income of $100,000 or more: 16.7% (2005); Poverty rate: 7.9% (2000).
Education: Percent of population age 25 and over with: High school diploma (including GED) or higher: 86.9% (2005); Bachelor's degree or higher: 32.5% (2005); Master's degree or higher: 11.5% (2005).
Housing: Homeownership rate: 82.4% (2005); Median home value: $165,816 (2005); Median rent: $513 per month (2000); Median age of housing: 55 years (2000).
Transportation: Commute to work: 91.6% car, 0.7% public transportation, 1.8% walk, 4.9% work from home (2000); Travel time to work: 5.9% less than 15 minutes, 28.0% 15 to 30 minutes, 50.9% 30 to 45 minutes, 11.4% 45 to 60 minutes, 3.7% 60 minutes or more (2000)

EAST SCHODACK (unincorporated postal area, zip code 12063).
Covers a land area of 0.802 square miles and a water area of 0 square miles. Located at 42.56° N. Lat.; 73.62° W. Long.
Population: 0 (2000); Race: 100.0% White, 0.0% Black, 0.0% Asian, 0.0% Hispanic of any race (2000); Density: 0.0 persons per square mile (2000); Age: 34.3% under 18, 17.4% over 64 (2000); Marriage status: 22.0% never married, 69.5% now married, 8.5% widowed, 0.0% divorced (2000); Foreign born: 3.4% (2000); Ancestry (includes multiple ancestries): 30.3% Irish, 25.3% German, 24.7% Italian, 21.9% Dutch, 12.9% English (2000).
Economy: Employment by occupation: 35.7% management, 6.0% professional, 14.3% services, 15.5% sales, 0.0% farming, 21.4% construction, 7.1% production (2000).
Income: Per capita income: $20,357 (2000); Median household income: $39,375 (2000); Poverty rate: 29.8% (2000).
Education: Percent of population age 25 and over with: High school diploma (including GED) or higher: 82.7% (2000); Bachelor's degree or higher: 32.7% (2000).
Housing: Homeownership rate: 100.0% (2000); Median home value: $112,500 (2000); Median rent: $n/a per month (2000); Median age of housing: 60+ years (2000).
Transportation: Commute to work: 84.5% car, 0.0% public transportation, 0.0% walk, 15.5% work from home (2000); Travel time to work: 9.9% less than 15 minutes, 35.2% 15 to 30 minutes, 54.9% 30 to 45 minutes, 0.0% 45 to 60 minutes, 0.0% 60 minutes or more (2000)

GRAFTON (town).
Covers a land area of 44.889 square miles and a water area of 1.075 square miles. Located at 42.77° N. Lat.; 73.45° W. Long. Elevation is 1,472 feet.
Population: 1,917 (1990); 1,987 (2000); 2,193 (2005); 2,382 (2010 projected); Race: 97.7% White, 0.2% Black, 0.2% Asian, 0.6% Hispanic of any race (2005); Density: 48.9 persons per square mile (2005); Average household size: 2.61 (2005); Median age: 39.7 (2005); Males per 100 females: 102.1 (2005); Marriage status: 23.4% never married, 63.7% now married, 4.7% widowed, 8.1% divorced (2000); Foreign born: 1.7% (2000); Ancestry (includes multiple ancestries): 25.2% Irish, 18.0% German, 13.1% English, 11.5% United States or American, 11.1% Italian (2000).
Economy: Resort village. Single-family building permits issued: 16 (2005); Multi-family building permits issued: 0 (2005); Employment by occupation: 11.5% management, 24.4% professional, 11.7% services, 22.4% sales, 0.8% farming, 13.0% construction, 16.3% production (2000).
Income: Per capita income: $24,685 (2005); Median household income: $55,275 (2005); Average household income: $64,446 (2005); Percent of households with income of $100,000 or more: 15.4% (2005); Poverty rate: 6.0% (2000).
Education: Percent of population age 25 and over with: High school diploma (including GED) or higher: 85.6% (2005); Bachelor's degree or higher: 18.7% (2005); Master's degree or higher: 8.8% (2005).
Housing: Homeownership rate: 89.2% (2005); Median home value: $138,988 (2005); Median rent: $469 per month (2000); Median age of housing: 38 years (2000).
Transportation: Commute to work: 95.7% car, 0.7% public transportation, 1.1% walk, 2.5% work from home (2000); Travel time to work: 10.3% less than 15 minutes, 31.0% 15 to 30 minutes, 31.9% 30 to 45 minutes, 18.3% 45 to 60 minutes, 8.4% 60 minutes or more (2000)

HAMPTON MANOR (CDP).
Covers a land area of 0.631 square miles and a water area of 0.016 square miles. Located at 42.61° N. Lat.; 73.72° W. Long.
Population: 2,655 (1990); 2,525 (2000); 2,516 (2005); 2,499 (2010 projected); Race: 93.6% White, 2.3% Black, 2.8% Asian, 1.0% Hispanic of any race (2005); Density: 3,988.0 persons per square mile (2005); Average household size: 2.38 (2005); Median age: 40.4 (2005); Males per 100 females: 93.7 (2005); Marriage status: 22.2% never married, 54.6% now married, 9.2% widowed, 14.0% divorced (2000); Foreign born: 4.4% (2000); Ancestry (includes multiple ancestries): 32.3% Italian, 30.0% German, 28.9% Irish, 13.0% English, 9.0% French (except Basque) (2000).
Economy: Employment by occupation: 10.2% management, 22.2% professional, 13.5% services, 37.9% sales, 0.0% farming, 5.7% construction, 10.4% production (2000).
Income: Per capita income: $24,762 (2005); Median household income: $48,958 (2005); Average household income: $58,482 (2005); Percent of households with income of $100,000 or more: 10.2% (2005); Poverty rate: 1.3% (2000).
Education: Percent of population age 25 and over with: High school diploma (including GED) or higher: 86.5% (2005); Bachelor's degree or higher: 22.2% (2005); Master's degree or higher: 10.7% (2005).
Housing: Homeownership rate: 76.3% (2005); Median home value: $121,678 (2005); Median rent: $548 per month (2000); Median age of housing: 49 years (2000).
Transportation: Commute to work: 93.8% car, 3.1% public transportation, 3.1% walk, 0.0% work from home (2000); Travel time to work: 32.3% less than 15 minutes, 53.9% 15 to 30 minutes, 12.7% 30 to 45 minutes, 1.0% 45 to 60 minutes, 0.0% 60 minutes or more (2000)

HOOSICK (town).
Covers a land area of 63.021 square miles and a water area of 0.133 square miles. Located at 42.90° N. Lat.; 73.35° W. Long.
History: Bennington Battlefield Park is Northeast. Hoosick Falls Historic District. Incorporated 1827.
Population: 6,696 (1990); 6,759 (2000); 6,774 (2005); 6,794 (2010 projected); Race: 97.5% White, 0.6% Black, 0.5% Asian, 1.1% Hispanic of any race (2005); Density: 107.5 persons per square mile (2005); Average

household size: 2.56 (2005); Median age: 39.6 (2005); Males per 100 females: 92.3 (2005); Marriage status: 24.8% never married, 59.9% now married, 7.7% widowed, 7.5% divorced (2000); Foreign born: 2.3% (2000); Ancestry (includes multiple ancestries): 24.1% Irish, 15.3% German, 10.8% English, 8.7% French (except Basque), 8.0% United States or American (2000).
Economy: In dairying area; diversified manufacturing. Small lakes (resorts) are nearby. Single-family building permits issued: 28 (2005); Multi-family building permits issued: 0 (2005); Employment by occupation: 9.8% management, 19.6% professional, 13.9% services, 22.1% sales, 0.8% farming, 11.8% construction, 22.1% production (2000).
Income: Per capita income: $23,078 (2005); Median household income: $47,870 (2005); Average household income: $59,032 (2005); Percent of households with income of $100,000 or more: 11.5% (2005); Poverty rate: 6.7% (2000).
Education: Percent of population age 25 and over with: High school diploma (including GED) or higher: 83.0% (2005); Bachelor's degree or higher: 18.3% (2005); Master's degree or higher: 8.2% (2005).
Housing: Homeownership rate: 71.4% (2005); Median home value: $130,157 (2005); Median rent: $399 per month (2000); Median age of housing: 60+ years (2000).
Transportation: Commute to work: 89.3% car, 1.2% public transportation, 3.4% walk, 5.9% work from home (2000); Travel time to work: 41.1% less than 15 minutes, 30.2% 15 to 30 minutes, 10.1% 30 to 45 minutes, 10.5% 45 to 60 minutes, 8.2% 60 minutes or more (2000)

HOOSICK FALLS (village). Covers a land area of 1.719 square miles and a water area of 0 square miles. Located at 42.90° N. Lat.; 73.35° W. Long. Elevation is 460 feet.
Population: 3,490 (1990); 3,436 (2000); 3,358 (2005); 3,283 (2010 projected); Race: 97.0% White, 0.7% Black, 0.7% Asian, 1.2% Hispanic of any race (2005); Density: 1,953.4 persons per square mile (2005); Average household size: 2.45 (2005); Median age: 38.4 (2005); Males per 100 females: 91.1 (2005); Marriage status: 26.1% never married, 57.4% now married, 10.7% widowed, 5.7% divorced (2000); Foreign born: 3.5% (2000); Ancestry (includes multiple ancestries): 24.6% Irish, 13.7% German, 9.5% French (except Basque), 9.4% Italian, 9.4% English (2000).
Economy: Single-family building permits issued: 0 (2005); Multi-family building permits issued: 0 (2005); Employment by occupation: 5.5% management, 18.8% professional, 17.3% services, 24.6% sales, 0.0% farming, 10.7% construction, 23.0% production (2000).
Income: Per capita income: $20,126 (2005); Median household income: $42,500 (2005); Average household income: $49,134 (2005); Percent of households with income of $100,000 or more: 7.9% (2005); Poverty rate: 6.6% (2000).
Education: Percent of population age 25 and over with: High school diploma (including GED) or higher: 81.0% (2005); Bachelor's degree or higher: 19.0% (2005); Master's degree or higher: 9.4% (2005).
School District(s)
Hoosick Falls Central School District (KG-12)
    2003-04 Enrollment: 1,249 . . . . (518) 686-7012
Housing: Homeownership rate: 61.0% (2005); Median home value: $119,118 (2005); Median rent: $456 per month (2000); Median age of housing: 60+ years (2000).
Safety: Violent crime rate: 41.3 per 10,000 population; Property crime rate: 165.2 per 10,000 population (2004).
Transportation: Commute to work: 92.7% car, 0.7% public transportation, 3.5% walk, 3.1% work from home (2000); Travel time to work: 47.7% less than 15 minutes, 28.4% 15 to 30 minutes, 9.1% 30 to 45 minutes, 8.7% 45 to 60 minutes, 6.1% 60 minutes or more (2000)

JOHNSONVILLE (unincorporated postal area, zip code 12094). Covers a land area of 27.866 square miles and a water area of 0.061 square miles. Located at 42.89° N. Lat.; 73.49° W. Long. Elevation is 363 feet.
Population: 0 (2000); Race: 94.5% White, 1.7% Black, 0.2% Asian, 1.8% Hispanic of any race (2000); Density: 0.0 persons per square mile (2000); Age: 30.7% under 18, 7.3% over 64 (2000); Marriage status: 28.3% never married, 62.3% now married, 2.9% widowed, 6.5% divorced (2000); Foreign born: 2.2% (2000); Ancestry (includes multiple ancestries): 27.2% Irish, 15.1% German, 13.2% Other groups, 9.5% English, 9.0% French (except Basque) (2000).
Economy: Employment by occupation: 11.3% management, 19.2% professional, 8.7% services, 26.4% sales, 1.2% farming, 15.5% construction, 17.9% production (2000).
Income: Per capita income: $20,116 (2000); Median household income: $50,789 (2000); Poverty rate: 7.9% (2000).
Education: Percent of population age 25 and over with: High school diploma (including GED) or higher: 83.3% (2000); Bachelor's degree or higher: 14.8% (2000).
School District(s)
Brunswick Central School District (Brittonkill) (KG-12)
    2003-04 Enrollment: 1,416 . . . . (518) 279-4600
Housing: Homeownership rate: 85.0% (2005); Median home value: $103,600 (2000); Median rent: $433 per month (2000); Median age of housing: 25 years (2000).
Transportation: Commute to work: 94.6% car, 0.8% public transportation, 0.7% walk, 3.4% work from home (2000); Travel time to work: 14.4% less than 15 minutes, 18.4% 15 to 30 minutes, 38.1% 30 to 45 minutes, 25.9% 45 to 60 minutes, 3.3% 60 minutes or more (2000)

MELROSE (unincorporated postal area, zip code 12121). Covers a land area of 19.538 square miles and a water area of 0.011 square miles. Located at 42.85° N. Lat.; 73.61° W. Long.
Population: 0 (2000); Race: 99.1% White, 0.5% Black, 0.0% Asian, 0.5% Hispanic of any race (2000); Density: 0.0 persons per square mile (2000); Age: 27.1% under 18, 10.2% over 64 (2000); Marriage status: 16.1% never married, 69.8% now married, 5.2% widowed, 8.9% divorced (2000); Foreign born: 2.0% (2000); Ancestry (includes multiple ancestries): 31.1% Irish, 18.0% Italian, 13.4% German, 12.7% French (except Basque), 8.9% English (2000).
Economy: Employment by occupation: 15.3% management, 15.8% professional, 9.5% services, 34.1% sales, 0.8% farming, 8.8% construction, 15.7% production (2000).
Income: Per capita income: $19,611 (2000); Median household income: $54,427 (2000); Poverty rate: 8.1% (2000).
Education: Percent of population age 25 and over with: High school diploma (including GED) or higher: 88.2% (2000); Bachelor's degree or higher: 13.7% (2000).
Housing: Homeownership rate: 91.3% (2000); Median home value: $105,200 (2000); Median rent: $516 per month (2000); Median age of housing: 42 years (2000).
Transportation: Commute to work: 93.7% car, 1.5% public transportation, 0.0% walk, 3.9% work from home (2000); Travel time to work: 19.2% less than 15 minutes, 34.2% 15 to 30 minutes, 34.5% 30 to 45 minutes, 12.1% 45 to 60 minutes, 0.0% 60 minutes or more (2000)

NASSAU (village). Covers a land area of 0.681 square miles and a water area of 0 square miles. Located at 42.51° N. Lat.; 73.61° W. Long. Elevation is 420 feet.
Population: 1,254 (1990); 1,161 (2000); 1,132 (2005); 1,105 (2010 projected); Race: 96.1% White, 1.2% Black, 0.4% Asian, 1.0% Hispanic of any race (2005); Density: 1,662.6 persons per square mile (2005); Average household size: 2.33 (2005); Median age: 40.3 (2005); Males per 100 females: 87.7 (2005); Marriage status: 27.0% never married, 55.7% now married, 8.8% widowed, 8.5% divorced (2000); Foreign born: 1.3% (2000); Ancestry (includes multiple ancestries): 31.1% Irish, 22.5% German, 12.0% English, 10.8% French (except Basque), 10.6% Italian (2000).
Economy: Single-family building permits issued: 2 (2005); Multi-family building permits issued: 0 (2005); Employment by occupation: 9.3% management, 21.1% professional, 13.1% services, 31.3% sales, 0.5% farming, 12.9% construction, 11.8% production (2000).
Income: Per capita income: $20,495 (2005); Median household income: $42,895 (2005); Average household income: $47,737 (2005); Percent of households with income of $100,000 or more: 6.4% (2005); Poverty rate: 7.3% (2000).
Education: Percent of population age 25 and over with: High school diploma (including GED) or higher: 86.1% (2005); Bachelor's degree or higher: 18.4% (2005); Master's degree or higher: 7.6% (2005).
School District(s)
East Greenbush Central School District (KG-12)
    2003-04 Enrollment: 4,572 . . . . (518) 477-2755
Housing: Homeownership rate: 62.3% (2005); Median home value: $135,452 (2005); Median rent: $442 per month (2000); Median age of housing: 54 years (2000).
Safety: Violent crime rate: 26.1 per 10,000 population; Property crime rate: 95.8 per 10,000 population (2004).
Transportation: Commute to work: 93.1% car, 3.2% public transportation, 1.7% walk, 1.8% work from home (2000); Travel time to work: 17.4% less

than 15 minutes, 38.6% 15 to 30 minutes, 32.0% 30 to 45 minutes, 8.4% 45 to 60 minutes, 3.6% 60 minutes or more (2000)

NASSAU (town). Covers a land area of 44.543 square miles and a water area of 0.664 square miles. Located at 42.53° N. Lat.; 73.54° W. Long. Elevation is 420 feet.
Population: 4,989 (1990); 4,818 (2000); 4,831 (2005); 4,853 (2010 projected); Race: 95.8% White, 1.3% Black, 0.8% Asian, 1.3% Hispanic of any race (2005); Density: 108.5 persons per square mile (2005); Average household size: 2.56 (2005); Median age: 39.7 (2005); Males per 100 females: 100.7 (2005); Marriage status: 22.5% never married, 60.7% now married, 6.8% widowed, 10.0% divorced (2000); Foreign born: 1.9% (2000); Ancestry (includes multiple ancestries): 26.6% German, 26.1% Irish, 14.4% English, 10.2% Italian, 8.2% French (except Basque) (2000).
Economy: Manufacturing: textiles, apparel, food and beverages, plastic and wood household furniture. County fairgrounds are here. Single-family building permits issued: 9 (2005); Multi-family building permits issued: 0 (2005); Employment by occupation: 12.7% management, 24.6% professional, 13.8% services, 24.2% sales, 0.4% farming, 11.9% construction, 12.4% production (2000).
Income: Per capita income: $25,881 (2005); Median household income: $55,037 (2005); Average household income: $66,190 (2005); Percent of households with income of $100,000 or more: 16.5% (2005); Poverty rate: 7.7% (2000).
Education: Percent of population age 25 and over with: High school diploma (including GED) or higher: 84.9% (2005); Bachelor's degree or higher: 22.1% (2005); Master's degree or higher: 10.9% (2005).
Housing: Homeownership rate: 76.6% (2005); Median home value: $145,965 (2005); Median rent: $473 per month (2000); Median age of housing: 46 years (2000).
Transportation: Commute to work: 94.2% car, 1.1% public transportation, 1.9% walk, 2.6% work from home (2000); Travel time to work: 15.6% less than 15 minutes, 28.7% 15 to 30 minutes, 40.3% 30 to 45 minutes, 8.8% 45 to 60 minutes, 6.5% 60 minutes or more (2000)

NORTH GREENBUSH (town). Covers a land area of 18.693 square miles and a water area of 0.329 square miles. Located at 42.67° N. Lat.; 73.65° W. Long.
Population: 10,628 (1990); 10,805 (2000); 11,134 (2005); 11,494 (2010 projected); Race: 95.9% White, 1.3% Black, 1.1% Asian, 1.3% Hispanic of any race (2005); Density: 595.6 persons per square mile (2005); Average household size: 2.54 (2005); Median age: 42.8 (2005); Males per 100 females: 91.0 (2005); Marriage status: 22.9% never married, 63.1% now married, 7.9% widowed, 6.1% divorced (2000); Foreign born: 3.1% (2000); Ancestry (includes multiple ancestries): 26.8% Irish, 19.2% German, 18.9% Italian, 9.9% English, 8.6% French (except Basque) (2000).
Economy: Single-family building permits issued: 40 (2005); Multi-family building permits issued: 36 (2005); Employment by occupation: 13.7% management, 25.4% professional, 9.8% services, 30.5% sales, 0.2% farming, 9.5% construction, 11.0% production (2000).
Income: Per capita income: $29,253 (2005); Median household income: $63,935 (2005); Average household income: $73,239 (2005); Percent of households with income of $100,000 or more: 21.9% (2005); Poverty rate: 3.0% (2000).
Education: Percent of population age 25 and over with: High school diploma (including GED) or higher: 90.0% (2005); Bachelor's degree or higher: 26.9% (2005); Master's degree or higher: 12.2% (2005).
Housing: Homeownership rate: 80.3% (2005); Median home value: $169,923 (2005); Median rent: $522 per month (2000); Median age of housing: 39 years (2000).
Safety: Violent crime rate: 18.1 per 10,000 population; Property crime rate: 110.2 per 10,000 population (2004).
Transportation: Commute to work: 94.4% car, 0.6% public transportation, 1.3% walk, 3.4% work from home (2000); Travel time to work: 27.2% less than 15 minutes, 55.3% 15 to 30 minutes, 12.7% 30 to 45 minutes, 2.5% 45 to 60 minutes, 2.3% 60 minutes or more (2000)

PETERSBURGH (town). Covers a land area of 41.604 square miles and a water area of 0 square miles. Located at 42.76° N. Lat.; 73.34° W. Long. Elevation is 684 feet.
Population: 1,469 (1990); 1,563 (2000); 1,648 (2005); 1,730 (2010 projected); Race: 97.5% White, 0.2% Black, 1.4% Asian, 0.7% Hispanic of any race (2005); Density: 39.6 persons per square mile (2005); Average household size: 2.61 (2005); Median age: 40.3 (2005); Males per 100 females: 104.7 (2005); Marriage status: 20.0% never married, 64.3% now married, 7.0% widowed, 8.7% divorced (2000); Foreign born: 2.8% (2000); Ancestry (includes multiple ancestries): 15.4% Irish, 13.8% English, 13.4% German, 10.7% French (except Basque), 9.6% United States or American (2000).
Economy: Single-family building permits issued: 11 (2005); Multi-family building permits issued: 0 (2005); Employment by occupation: 14.8% management, 18.8% professional, 12.7% services, 18.0% sales, 1.6% farming, 14.8% construction, 19.2% production (2000).
Income: Per capita income: $27,118 (2005); Median household income: $58,981 (2005); Average household income: $70,769 (2005); Percent of households with income of $100,000 or more: 21.4% (2005); Poverty rate: 12.3% (2000).
Taxes: Total city taxes per capita: $238 (2004); City property taxes per capita: $217 (2004).
Education: Percent of population age 25 and over with: High school diploma (including GED) or higher: 80.5% (2005); Bachelor's degree or higher: 21.7% (2005); Master's degree or higher: 10.4% (2005).
Housing: Homeownership rate: 85.4% (2005); Median home value: $122,557 (2005); Median rent: $430 per month (2000); Median age of housing: 36 years (2000).
Transportation: Commute to work: 92.2% car, 0.3% public transportation, 1.4% walk, 6.1% work from home (2000); Travel time to work: 20.3% less than 15 minutes, 26.0% 15 to 30 minutes, 22.9% 30 to 45 minutes, 16.5% 45 to 60 minutes, 14.3% 60 minutes or more (2000)

PITTSTOWN (town). Covers a land area of 61.739 square miles and a water area of 3.105 square miles. Located at 42.87° N. Lat.; 73.50° W. Long. Elevation is 578 feet.
Population: 5,468 (1990); 5,644 (2000); 6,140 (2005); 6,596 (2010 projected); Race: 97.3% White, 0.7% Black, 0.4% Asian, 0.9% Hispanic of any race (2005); Density: 99.5 persons per square mile (2005); Average household size: 2.78 (2005); Median age: 36.9 (2005); Males per 100 females: 100.4 (2005); Marriage status: 25.8% never married, 63.1% now married, 3.5% widowed, 7.6% divorced (2000); Foreign born: 1.4% (2000); Ancestry (includes multiple ancestries): 29.0% Irish, 17.3% German, 11.1% English, 11.0% French (except Basque), 9.9% Italian (2000).
Economy: Single-family building permits issued: 25 (2005); Multi-family building permits issued: 6 (2005); Employment by occupation: 12.1% management, 18.5% professional, 10.5% services, 27.8% sales, 0.6% farming, 12.1% construction, 18.4% production (2000).
Income: Per capita income: $22,211 (2005); Median household income: $58,144 (2005); Average household income: $61,764 (2005); Percent of households with income of $100,000 or more: 13.4% (2005); Poverty rate: 6.0% (2000).
Education: Percent of population age 25 and over with: High school diploma (including GED) or higher: 85.6% (2005); Bachelor's degree or higher: 18.6% (2005); Master's degree or higher: 8.1% (2005).
Housing: Homeownership rate: 85.9% (2005); Median home value: $139,742 (2005); Median rent: $433 per month (2000); Median age of housing: 26 years (2000).
Transportation: Commute to work: 94.4% car, 0.9% public transportation, 1.4% walk, 2.6% work from home (2000); Travel time to work: 11.6% less than 15 minutes, 27.0% 15 to 30 minutes, 37.0% 30 to 45 minutes, 18.9% 45 to 60 minutes, 5.6% 60 minutes or more (2000)

POESTENKILL (town). Covers a land area of 32.451 square miles and a water area of 0.136 square miles. Located at 42.68° N. Lat.; 73.55° W. Long. Elevation is 484 feet.
Population: 3,809 (1990); 4,054 (2000); 4,193 (2005); 4,331 (2010 projected); Race: 97.9% White, 0.2% Black, 0.5% Asian, 1.0% Hispanic of any race (2005); Density: 129.2 persons per square mile (2005); Average household size: 2.60 (2005); Median age: 39.5 (2005); Males per 100 females: 103.2 (2005); Marriage status: 23.4% never married, 64.6% now married, 4.9% widowed, 7.2% divorced (2000); Foreign born: 0.6% (2000); Ancestry (includes multiple ancestries): 28.4% Irish, 24.4% German, 13.6% Italian, 12.9% English, 11.2% French (except Basque) (2000).
Economy: Single-family building permits issued: 11 (2005); Multi-family building permits issued: 0 (2005); Employment by occupation: 17.4% management, 17.1% professional, 12.7% services, 28.7% sales, 0.3% farming, 13.5% construction, 10.2% production (2000).
Income: Per capita income: $27,257 (2005); Median household income: $65,308 (2005); Average household income: $70,601 (2005); Percent of households with income of $100,000 or more: 19.6% (2005); Poverty rate: 1.7% (2000).

Taxes: Total city taxes per capita: $230 (2004); City property taxes per capita: $192 (2004).
Education: Percent of population age 25 and over with: High school diploma (including GED) or higher: 89.9% (2005); Bachelor's degree or higher: 20.6% (2005); Master's degree or higher: 7.9% (2005).

School District(s)
Averill Park Central School District (KG-12)
    2003-04 Enrollment: 3,546 . . . . (518) 674-7055

Housing: Homeownership rate: 84.3% (2005); Median home value: $169,208 (2005); Median rent: $474 per month (2000); Median age of housing: 35 years (2000).
Transportation: Commute to work: 94.8% car, 0.3% public transportation, 0.9% walk, 2.5% work from home (2000); Travel time to work: 14.6% less than 15 minutes, 46.4% 15 to 30 minutes, 29.1% 30 to 45 minutes, 8.2% 45 to 60 minutes, 1.6% 60 minutes or more (2000)

POESTENKILL (CDP). Covers a land area of 5.839 square miles and a water area of 0.044 square miles. Located at 42.69° N. Lat.; 73.56° W. Long.
Population: 1,028 (1990); 1,024 (2000); 1,025 (2005); 1,043 (2010 projected); Race: 98.0% White, 0.0% Black, 0.6% Asian, 1.1% Hispanic of any race (2005); Density: 175.5 persons per square mile (2005); Average household size: 2.54 (2005); Median age: 39.8 (2005); Males per 100 females: 97.5 (2005); Marriage status: 19.7% never married, 62.7% now married, 9.4% widowed, 8.3% divorced (2000); Foreign born: 0.5% (2000); Ancestry (includes multiple ancestries): 26.4% German, 26.4% Irish, 19.3% English, 13.9% Dutch, 12.1% Italian (2000).
Economy: Employment by occupation: 18.9% management, 8.0% professional, 5.3% services, 42.9% sales, 1.3% farming, 12.2% construction, 11.4% production (2000).
Income: Per capita income: $24,290 (2005); Median household income: $56,743 (2005); Average household income: $61,780 (2005); Percent of households with income of $100,000 or more: 11.9% (2005); Poverty rate: 1.2% (2000).
Education: Percent of population age 25 and over with: High school diploma (including GED) or higher: 87.3% (2005); Bachelor's degree or higher: 17.4% (2005); Master's degree or higher: 8.3% (2005).
Housing: Homeownership rate: 85.9% (2005); Median home value: $142,969 (2005); Median rent: $550 per month (2000); Median age of housing: 42 years (2000).
Transportation: Commute to work: 92.8% car, 1.4% public transportation, 1.0% walk, 4.8% work from home (2000); Travel time to work: 15.2% less than 15 minutes, 44.9% 15 to 30 minutes, 36.4% 30 to 45 minutes, 3.5% 45 to 60 minutes, 0.0% 60 minutes or more (2000)

RENSSELAER (city). Covers a land area of 3.009 square miles and a water area of 0.323 square miles. Located at 42.64° N. Lat.; 73.73° W. Long. Elevation is 25 feet.
History: The city was formed by the union of several villages within the tract granted to Kiliaen Van Rensselaer by the chartered Dutch West Indies Company. At the 17th-century Fort Crailo, now a museum, the British surgeon Richard Shuckburg is said to have written "Yankee Doodle." Settled 1630 by Dutch, incorporated 1897.
Population: 8,360 (1990); 7,761 (2000); 7,765 (2005); 7,778 (2010 projected); Race: 86.1% White, 9.2% Black, 1.7% Asian, 2.8% Hispanic of any race (2005); Density: 2,580.5 persons per square mile (2005); Average household size: 2.25 (2005); Median age: 37.1 (2005); Males per 100 females: 92.7 (2005); Marriage status: 30.6% never married, 49.4% now married, 8.7% widowed, 11.3% divorced (2000); Foreign born: 4.3% (2000); Ancestry (includes multiple ancestries): 27.8% Irish, 17.4% German, 16.5% Italian, 13.6% Other groups, 9.6% English (2000).
Economy: Chemicals, textiles, leather goods. Single-family building permits issued: 16 (2005); Multi-family building permits issued: 41 (2005); Employment by occupation: 11.4% management, 16.5% professional, 18.6% services, 32.1% sales, 0.1% farming, 9.2% construction, 12.1% production (2000).
Income: Per capita income: $21,820 (2005); Median household income: $39,002 (2005); Average household income: $48,504 (2005); Percent of households with income of $100,000 or more: 8.4% (2005); Poverty rate: 12.8% (2000).
Education: Percent of population age 25 and over with: High school diploma (including GED) or higher: 80.4% (2005); Bachelor's degree or higher: 15.7% (2005); Master's degree or higher: 6.7% (2005).

School District(s)
Albany City School District (PK-12)
    2003-04 Enrollment: 9,919 . . . . (518) 462-7200
East Greenbush Central School District (KG-12)
    2003-04 Enrollment: 4,572 . . . . (518) 477-2755
North Greenbush Common School District (Williams) (KG-01)
    2003-04 Enrollment: 23 . . . . (518) 283-6748
Rensselaer City School District (PK-12)
    2003-04 Enrollment: 1,097 . . . . (518) 465-7509

Housing: Homeownership rate: 51.3% (2005); Median home value: $121,835 (2005); Median rent: $415 per month (2000); Median age of housing: 60+ years (2000).
Safety: Violent crime rate: 30.9 per 10,000 population; Property crime rate: 367.4 per 10,000 population (2004).
Transportation: Commute to work: 87.9% car, 5.6% public transportation, 4.4% walk, 1.7% work from home (2000); Travel time to work: 38.4% less than 15 minutes, 44.8% 15 to 30 minutes, 10.8% 30 to 45 minutes, 2.3% 45 to 60 minutes, 3.7% 60 minutes or more (2000); Amtrak: Service available.

SAND LAKE (town). Covers a land area of 35.201 square miles and a water area of 0.946 square miles. Located at 42.62° N. Lat.; 73.56° W. Long.
Population: 7,642 (1990); 7,987 (2000); 8,221 (2005); 8,457 (2010 projected); Race: 98.0% White, 0.3% Black, 0.5% Asian, 1.1% Hispanic of any race (2005); Density: 233.5 persons per square mile (2005); Average household size: 2.61 (2005); Median age: 40.8 (2005); Males per 100 females: 96.0 (2005); Marriage status: 22.1% never married, 64.9% now married, 4.9% widowed, 8.0% divorced (2000); Foreign born: 1.3% (2000); Ancestry (includes multiple ancestries): 25.2% German, 22.6% Irish, 14.6% English, 13.8% Italian, 8.9% French (except Basque) (2000).
Economy: In fruit-growing area. Single-family building permits issued: 36 (2005); Multi-family building permits issued: 0 (2005); Employment by occupation: 12.6% management, 25.6% professional, 10.1% services, 30.5% sales, 0.0% farming, 9.8% construction, 11.4% production (2000).
Income: Per capita income: $32,566 (2005); Median household income: $67,443 (2005); Average household income: $84,822 (2005); Percent of households with income of $100,000 or more: 26.6% (2005); Poverty rate: 4.7% (2000).
Education: Percent of population age 25 and over with: High school diploma (including GED) or higher: 92.3% (2005); Bachelor's degree or higher: 27.2% (2005); Master's degree or higher: 12.9% (2005).
Housing: Homeownership rate: 81.3% (2005); Median home value: $177,202 (2005); Median rent: $484 per month (2000); Median age of housing: 36 years (2000).
Transportation: Commute to work: 94.9% car, 0.2% public transportation, 0.8% walk, 3.2% work from home (2000); Travel time to work: 14.5% less than 15 minutes, 47.1% 15 to 30 minutes, 30.9% 30 to 45 minutes, 4.7% 45 to 60 minutes, 2.9% 60 minutes or more (2000)

SCHAGHTICOKE (village). Covers a land area of 0.738 square miles and a water area of 0.167 square miles. Located at 42.90° N. Lat.; 73.58° W. Long.
Population: 794 (1990); 676 (2000); 657 (2005); 647 (2010 projected); Race: 95.6% White, 2.3% Black, 0.5% Asian, 0.9% Hispanic of any race (2005); Density: 890.6 persons per square mile (2005); Average household size: 2.46 (2005); Median age: 37.3 (2005); Males per 100 females: 98.5 (2005); Marriage status: 25.9% never married, 55.5% now married, 9.0% widowed, 9.6% divorced (2000); Foreign born: 0.3% (2000); Ancestry (includes multiple ancestries): 25.4% Irish, 21.5% German, 19.0% French (except Basque), 12.3% English, 10.8% Italian (2000).
Economy: Single-family building permits issued: 37 (2005); Multi-family building permits issued: 0 (2005); Employment by occupation: 7.3% management, 11.0% professional, 15.3% services, 38.3% sales, 0.0% farming, 10.3% construction, 17.7% production (2000).
Income: Per capita income: $22,858 (2005); Median household income: $46,346 (2005); Average household income: $56,245 (2005); Percent of households with income of $100,000 or more: 14.2% (2005); Poverty rate: 8.3% (2000).
Education: Percent of population age 25 and over with: High school diploma (including GED) or higher: 87.1% (2005); Bachelor's degree or higher: 10.6% (2005); Master's degree or higher: 2.9% (2005).

School District(s)
Hoosic Valley Central School District (KG-12)
    2003-04 Enrollment: 1,245 . . . . (518) 753-4450

Housing: Homeownership rate: 62.5% (2005); Median home value: $125,000 (2005); Median rent: $397 per month (2000); Median age of housing: 60+ years (2000).
Transportation: Commute to work: 97.9% car, 1.0% public transportation, 0.0% walk, 1.0% work from home (2000); Travel time to work: 7.7% less than 15 minutes, 32.4% 15 to 30 minutes, 30.7% 30 to 45 minutes, 24.0% 45 to 60 minutes, 5.2% 60 minutes or more (2000)

SCHAGHTICOKE (town). Covers a land area of 49.910 square miles and a water area of 1.955 square miles. Located at 42.87° N. Lat.; 73.62° W. Long.
Population: 7,574 (1990); 7,456 (2000); 7,629 (2005); 7,793 (2010 projected); Race: 96.9% White, 1.7% Black, 0.5% Asian, 0.9% Hispanic of any race (2005); Density: 152.9 persons per square mile (2005); Average household size: 2.70 (2005); Median age: 39.7 (2005); Males per 100 females: 98.4 (2005); Marriage status: 22.0% never married, 64.6% now married, 5.9% widowed, 7.5% divorced (2000); Foreign born: 1.3% (2000); Ancestry (includes multiple ancestries): 29.9% Irish, 15.8% Italian, 15.2% German, 12.1% French (except Basque), 9.2% English (2000).
Economy: In dairying area. Employment by occupation: 11.7% management, 18.5% professional, 10.7% services, 32.4% sales, 0.3% farming, 11.1% construction, 15.3% production (2000).
Income: Per capita income: $23,669 (2005); Median household income: $57,267 (2005); Average household income: $63,829 (2005); Percent of households with income of $100,000 or more: 16.4% (2005); Poverty rate: 4.7% (2000).
Education: Percent of population age 25 and over with: High school diploma (including GED) or higher: 88.9% (2005); Bachelor's degree or higher: 15.9% (2005); Master's degree or higher: 6.0% (2005).
Housing: Homeownership rate: 85.3% (2005); Median home value: $146,888 (2005); Median rent: $444 per month (2000); Median age of housing: 42 years (2000).
Transportation: Commute to work: 94.7% car, 1.1% public transportation, 0.8% walk, 3.1% work from home (2000); Travel time to work: 19.2% less than 15 minutes, 32.3% 15 to 30 minutes, 34.4% 30 to 45 minutes, 11.5% 45 to 60 minutes, 2.5% 60 minutes or more (2000)

SCHODACK (town). Covers a land area of 62.228 square miles and a water area of 1.428 square miles. Located at 42.53° N. Lat.; 73.69° W. Long.
Population: 11,839 (1990); 12,536 (2000); 12,854 (2005); 13,175 (2010 projected); Race: 96.8% White, 0.9% Black, 0.7% Asian, 2.1% Hispanic of any race (2005); Density: 206.6 persons per square mile (2005); Average household size: 2.61 (2005); Median age: 40.5 (2005); Males per 100 females: 97.2 (2005); Marriage status: 22.5% never married, 63.7% now married, 6.4% widowed, 7.4% divorced (2000); Foreign born: 2.3% (2000); Ancestry (includes multiple ancestries): 26.8% German, 25.1% Irish, 13.9% Italian, 13.7% English, 8.5% French (except Basque) (2000).
Economy: Single-family building permits issued: 40 (2005); Multi-family building permits issued: 49 (2005); Employment by occupation: 15.7% management, 24.7% professional, 11.9% services, 27.5% sales, 0.1% farming, 10.4% construction, 9.7% production (2000).
Income: Per capita income: $28,874 (2005); Median household income: $62,827 (2005); Average household income: $74,661 (2005); Percent of households with income of $100,000 or more: 22.6% (2005); Poverty rate: 4.3% (2000).
Education: Percent of population age 25 and over with: High school diploma (including GED) or higher: 88.4% (2005); Bachelor's degree or higher: 26.9% (2005); Master's degree or higher: 11.6% (2005).
Housing: Homeownership rate: 81.3% (2005); Median home value: $169,775 (2005); Median rent: $487 per month (2000); Median age of housing: 37 years (2000).
Transportation: Commute to work: 95.1% car, 1.1% public transportation, 1.2% walk, 2.0% work from home (2000); Travel time to work: 19.3% less than 15 minutes, 49.6% 15 to 30 minutes, 23.1% 30 to 45 minutes, 3.4% 45 to 60 minutes, 4.7% 60 minutes or more (2000)
Additional Information Contacts
Town of Schodack . . . . (518) 477-7918
  http://www.schodack.org/

SCHODACK LANDING (unincorporated postal area, zip code 12156). Covers a land area of 16.598 square miles and a water area of 0.006 square miles. Located at 42.48° N. Lat.; 73.73° W. Long.
Population: 0 (2000); Race: 95.3% White, 2.5% Black, 0.0% Asian, 0.0% Hispanic of any race (2000); Density: 0.0 persons per square mile (2000);

Age: 22.8% under 18, 18.2% over 64 (2000); Marriage status: 21.0% never married, 68.1% now married, 4.2% widowed, 6.7% divorced (2000); Foreign born: 1.0% (2000); Ancestry (includes multiple ancestries): 25.3% German, 20.1% Irish, 14.0% English, 11.4% Dutch, 9.0% Italian (2000).
Economy: Employment by occupation: 19.9% management, 9.9% professional, 12.7% services, 23.7% sales, 0.0% farming, 18.2% construction, 15.6% production (2000).
Income: Per capita income: $24,233 (2000); Median household income: $52,550 (2000); Poverty rate: 8.3% (2000).
Education: Percent of population age 25 and over with: High school diploma (including GED) or higher: 89.7% (2000); Bachelor's degree or higher: 19.5% (2000).
Housing: Homeownership rate: 79.0% (2000); Median home value: $95,400 (2000); Median rent: $425 per month (2000); Median age of housing: 60+ years (2000).
Transportation: Commute to work: 92.4% car, 0.0% public transportation, 1.3% walk, 5.7% work from home (2000); Travel time to work: 21.3% less than 15 minutes, 37.7% 15 to 30 minutes, 31.4% 30 to 45 minutes, 5.6% 45 to 60 minutes, 4.0% 60 minutes or more (2000)

STEPHENTOWN (town). Covers a land area of 57.984 square miles and a water area of 0.092 square miles. Located at 42.54° N. Lat.; 73.41° W. Long. Elevation is 878 feet.
Population: 2,521 (1990); 2,873 (2000); 2,973 (2005); 3,072 (2010 projected); Race: 97.8% White, 0.4% Black, 0.2% Asian, 1.7% Hispanic of any race (2005); Density: 51.3 persons per square mile (2005); Average household size: 2.50 (2005); Median age: 39.8 (2005); Males per 100 females: 95.3 (2005); Marriage status: 18.7% never married, 64.4% now married, 5.6% widowed, 11.3% divorced (2000); Foreign born: 1.2% (2000); Ancestry (includes multiple ancestries): 18.4% Irish, 18.1% German, 15.2% English, 9.7% Italian, 9.0% United States or American (2000).
Economy: Single-family building permits issued: 14 (2005); Multi-family building permits issued: 0 (2005); Employment by occupation: 11.1% management, 20.1% professional, 14.9% services, 27.8% sales, 1.4% farming, 12.4% construction, 12.3% production (2000).
Income: Per capita income: $21,030 (2005); Median household income: $46,073 (2005); Average household income: $52,584 (2005); Percent of households with income of $100,000 or more: 7.3% (2005); Poverty rate: 6.6% (2000).
Education: Percent of population age 25 and over with: High school diploma (including GED) or higher: 84.3% (2005); Bachelor's degree or higher: 25.7% (2005); Master's degree or higher: 12.0% (2005).
School District(s)
Berlin Central School District (KG-12)
  2003-04 Enrollment: 1,040 . . . . (518) 658-2690
Housing: Homeownership rate: 82.2% (2005); Median home value: $133,307 (2005); Median rent: $436 per month (2000); Median age of housing: 28 years (2000).
Transportation: Commute to work: 93.0% car, 0.3% public transportation, 1.4% walk, 4.8% work from home (2000); Travel time to work: 16.9% less than 15 minutes, 24.9% 15 to 30 minutes, 33.7% 30 to 45 minutes, 16.2% 45 to 60 minutes, 8.2% 60 minutes or more (2000)

TROY (city). Covers a land area of 10.413 square miles and a water area of 0.603 square miles. Located at 42.73° N. Lat.; 73.68° W. Long. Elevation is 35 feet.
History: The early name of Troy was Pa-an-pa-ack, "field of standing corn." The site was part of the patroonship granted to Kiliaen Van Rensselaer by the Dutch West India Company. For 120 years, it was occupied by Dutch farmers. Some argument took place about the name, but "Troy" was selected in 1789 at a public meeting.
Population: 54,269 (1990); 49,170 (2000); 48,602 (2005); 48,081 (2010 projected); Race: 75.3% White, 14.2% Black, 4.6% Asian, 6.1% Hispanic of any race (2005); Density: 4,667.3 persons per square mile (2005); Average household size: 2.44 (2005); Median age: 33.1 (2005); Males per 100 females: 99.3 (2005); Marriage status: 39.0% never married, 42.8% now married, 8.5% widowed, 9.7% divorced (2000); Foreign born: 5.8% (2000); Ancestry (includes multiple ancestries): 24.3% Irish, 17.5% Other groups, 14.2% Italian, 12.7% German, 9.1% French (except Basque) (2000).
Economy: Unemployment rate: 5.1% (2005); Total civilian labor force: 23,931 (2005); Single-family building permits issued: 25 (2005); Multi-family building permits issued: 48 (2005); Employment by occupation: 10.2% management, 22.2% professional, 19.1% services, 27.2% sales, 0.0% farming, 7.5% construction, 13.8% production (2000).

Income: Per capita income: $18,566 (2005); Median household income: $32,809 (2005); Average household income: $43,415 (2005); Percent of households with income of $100,000 or more: 7.0% (2005); Poverty rate: 19.1% (2000).
Education: Percent of population age 25 and over with: High school diploma (including GED) or higher: 78.0% (2005); Bachelor's degree or higher: 19.7% (2005); Master's degree or higher: 8.4% (2005).

School District(s)
Ark Comm Charter School, The (KG-05)
   2003-04 Enrollment: 97 .... (518) 274-6312
Averill Park Central School District (KG-12)
   2003-04 Enrollment: 3,546 .... (518) 674-7055
Brunswick Central School District (Brittonkill) (KG-12)
   2003-04 Enrollment: 1,416 .... (518) 279-4600
East Greenbush Central School District (KG-12)
   2003-04 Enrollment: 4,572 .... (518) 477-2755
Lansingburgh Central School District (KG-12)
   2003-04 Enrollment: 2,428 .... (518) 233-6850
Troy City School District (PK-12)
   2003-04 Enrollment: 4,857 .... (518) 271-5210

Four-year College(s)
Rensselaer Polytechnic Institute
   Fall 2004 Enrollment: 6,696 .... (518) 276-6000
   2005-06 Tuition: In-state $31,857; Out-of-state $31,857
Russell Sage College
   Fall 2004 Enrollment: 835 .... (518) 244-2000
   2005-06 Tuition: In-state $23,520; Out-of-state $23,520

Two-year College(s)
Hudson Valley Community College (Public)
   Fall 2004 Enrollment: 12,241 .... (518) 629-4822
   2005-06 Tuition: In-state $3,355; Out-of-state $8,755
Rensselaer BOCES-School of Practical Nursing (Public)
   Fall 2004 Enrollment: 74 .... (518) 273-2264
Samaritan Hospital School of Nursing
   Fall 2004 Enrollment: 113 .... (518) 271-3285
   2005-06 Tuition: In-state $6,388; Out-of-state $6,388
Troy School of Beauty Culture
   Fall 2004 Enrollment: 30 .... (518) 273-5144

Housing: Homeownership rate: 40.3% (2005); Median home value: $121,221 (2005); Median rent: $421 per month (2000); Median age of housing: 60+ years (2000).
Hospitals: Samaritan Hospital (238 beds); Seton Health St.Mary's (201 beds)
Safety: Violent crime rate: 61.1 per 10,000 population; Property crime rate: 413.2 per 10,000 population (2004).
Newspapers: The Record (Circulation 19,056)
Transportation: Commute to work: 80.8% car, 6.6% public transportation, 9.7% walk, 2.0% work from home (2000); Travel time to work: 33.4% less than 15 minutes, 45.6% 15 to 30 minutes, 13.1% 30 to 45 minutes, 3.3% 45 to 60 minutes, 4.5% 60 minutes or more (2000)
Additional Information Contacts
City of Troy .... (518) 270-4401
   http://www.troyny.gov/
Rensselaer County Regional Chamber of Commerce ..... (518) 274-7020
   http://www.renscochamber.com

VALLEY FALLS
(village). Covers a land area of 0.439 square miles and a water area of 0.023 square miles. Located at 42.90° N. Lat.; 73.56° W. Long. Elevation is 330 feet.
Population: 527 (1990); 491 (2000); 469 (2005); 463 (2010 projected); Race: 96.4% White, 0.0% Black, 1.1% Asian, 1.1% Hispanic of any race (2005); Density: 1,069.4 persons per square mile (2005); Average household size: 2.70 (2005); Median age: 37.0 (2005); Males per 100 females: 90.7 (2005); Marriage status: 30.6% never married, 51.5% now married, 7.3% widowed, 10.6% divorced (2000); Foreign born: 0.4% (2000); Ancestry (includes multiple ancestries): 31.5% Irish, 17.4% English, 15.7% German, 14.3% Italian, 8.1% French (except Basque) (2000).
Economy: In dairying and grain-growing area. Single-family building permits issued: 1 (2005); Multi-family building permits issued: 0 (2005); Employment by occupation: 11.2% management, 19.7% professional, 15.9% services, 23.6% sales, 1.3% farming, 10.7% construction, 17.6% production (2000).
Income: Per capita income: $25,560 (2005); Median household income: $58,721 (2005); Average household income: $68,894 (2005); Percent of households with income of $100,000 or more: 20.1% (2005); Poverty rate: 4.4% (2000).
Education: Percent of population age 25 and over with: High school diploma (including GED) or higher: 88.5% (2005); Bachelor's degree or higher: 19.0% (2005); Master's degree or higher: 10.5% (2005).
Housing: Homeownership rate: 67.8% (2005); Median home value: $140,698 (2005); Median rent: $407 per month (2000); Median age of housing: 60+ years (2000).
Transportation: Commute to work: 92.5% car, 1.3% public transportation, 3.5% walk, 1.8% work from home (2000); Travel time to work: 17.9% less than 15 minutes, 23.7% 15 to 30 minutes, 36.2% 30 to 45 minutes, 19.2% 45 to 60 minutes, 3.1% 60 minutes or more (2000)

WEST SAND LAKE
(CDP). Covers a land area of 4.744 square miles and a water area of 0.045 square miles. Located at 42.64° N. Lat.; 73.60° W. Long.
Population: 2,145 (1990); 2,439 (2000); 2,559 (2005); 2,701 (2010 projected); Race: 98.7% White, 0.2% Black, 0.6% Asian, 1.1% Hispanic of any race (2005); Density: 539.4 persons per square mile (2005); Average household size: 2.64 (2005); Median age: 40.8 (2005); Males per 100 females: 94.0 (2005); Marriage status: 25.3% never married, 59.2% now married, 5.8% widowed, 9.7% divorced (2000); Foreign born: 2.8% (2000); Ancestry (includes multiple ancestries): 22.7% German, 17.0% Irish, 15.0% English, 11.0% French (except Basque), 10.6% Italian (2000).
Economy: Employment by occupation: 17.1% management, 25.5% professional, 8.6% services, 32.3% sales, 0.0% farming, 8.3% construction, 8.1% production (2000).
Income: Per capita income: $32,097 (2005); Median household income: $65,236 (2005); Average household income: $84,626 (2005); Percent of households with income of $100,000 or more: 25.4% (2005); Poverty rate: 6.8% (2000).
Education: Percent of population age 25 and over with: High school diploma (including GED) or higher: 90.8% (2005); Bachelor's degree or higher: 24.1% (2005); Master's degree or higher: 10.6% (2005).

School District(s)
Averill Park Central School District (KG-12)
   2003-04 Enrollment: 3,546 .... (518) 674-7055

Housing: Homeownership rate: 79.5% (2005); Median home value: $181,573 (2005); Median rent: $475 per month (2000); Median age of housing: 37 years (2000).
Transportation: Commute to work: 94.6% car, 0.6% public transportation, 0.6% walk, 3.5% work from home (2000); Travel time to work: 11.1% less than 15 minutes, 55.7% 15 to 30 minutes, 30.6% 30 to 45 minutes, 1.9% 45 to 60 minutes, 0.7% 60 minutes or more (2000)

WYNANTSKILL
(CDP). Covers a land area of 2.424 square miles and a water area of 0 square miles. Located at 42.69° N. Lat.; 73.64° W. Long.
Population: 3,360 (1990); 3,018 (2000); 3,010 (2005); 3,028 (2010 projected); Race: 97.4% White, 0.6% Black, 0.3% Asian, 0.6% Hispanic of any race (2005); Density: 1,241.8 persons per square mile (2005); Average household size: 2.38 (2005); Median age: 42.9 (2005); Males per 100 females: 93.1 (2005); Marriage status: 24.3% never married, 61.7% now married, 9.2% widowed, 4.9% divorced (2000); Foreign born: 1.9% (2000); Ancestry (includes multiple ancestries): 33.8% Irish, 23.6% Italian, 17.2% German, 13.0% French (except Basque), 9.8% English (2000).
Economy: In dairying area. Employment by occupation: 13.5% management, 23.7% professional, 11.1% services, 29.6% sales, 0.0% farming, 13.0% construction, 9.0% production (2000).
Income: Per capita income: $27,744 (2005); Median household income: $60,079 (2005); Average household income: $65,753 (2005); Percent of households with income of $100,000 or more: 16.9% (2005); Poverty rate: 1.3% (2000).
Education: Percent of population age 25 and over with: High school diploma (including GED) or higher: 87.7% (2005); Bachelor's degree or higher: 20.7% (2005); Master's degree or higher: 8.5% (2005).

School District(s)
Wynantskill Union Free School District (KG-08)
   2003-04 Enrollment: 400 .... (518) 283-4679

Housing: Homeownership rate: 81.8% (2005); Median home value: $149,522 (2005); Median rent: $450 per month (2000); Median age of housing: 45 years (2000).
Transportation: Commute to work: 94.9% car, 1.5% public transportation, 1.9% walk, 1.6% work from home (2000); Travel time to work: 30.4% less

than 15 minutes, 48.0% 15 to 30 minutes, 12.8% 30 to 45 minutes, 3.9% 45 to 60 minutes, 4.9% 60 minutes or more (2000)

Richmond County

See New York City

Rockland County

Located in southeastern New York; bounded on the east by the Hudson River, and on the southwest and south by New Jersey; includes part of the Ramapo Mountains; drained by the Hackensack and Ramapo Rivers. Covers a land area of 174.22 square miles, a water area of 25.12 square miles, and is located in the Eastern Time Zone. The county government was organized in 1798. County seat is New City.

Rockland County is part of the New York-Northern New Jersey-Long Island, NY-NJ-PA Metropolitan Statistical Area. The entire metro area includes: Edison, NJ Metropolitan Division (Middlesex County, NJ; Monmouth County, NJ; Ocean County, NJ; Somerset County, NJ); Nassau-Suffolk, NY Metropolitan Division (Nassau County, NY; Suffolk County, NY); New York-White Plains-Wayne, NY-NJ Metropolitan Division (Bergen County, NJ; Hudson County, NJ; Passaic County, NJ; Bronx County, NY; Kings County, NY; New York County, NY; Putnam County, NY; Queens County, NY; Richmond County, NY; Rockland County, NY; Westchester County, NY); Newark-Union, NJ-PA Metropolitan Division (Essex County, NJ; Hunterdon County, NJ; Morris County, NJ; Sussex County, NJ; Union County, NJ; Pike County, PA)

Population: 265,475 (1990); 286,753 (2000); 295,771 (2005); 305,048 (2010 projected); Race: 73.6% White, 11.7% Black, 6.6% Asian, 12.7% Hispanic of any race (2005); Density: 1,697.7 persons per square mile (2005); Average household size: 3.09 (2005); Median age: 37.2 (2005); Males per 100 females: 96.2 (2005).
Religion: Five largest groups: 44.0% Catholic Church, 31.4% Jewish Estimate, 1.3% Muslim Estimate, 0.9% The United Methodist Church, 0.7% Episcopal Church (2000).
Economy: Unemployment rate: 4.1% (2005); Total civilian labor force: 152,254 (2005); Leading industries: 19.3% health care and social assistance; 14.4% retail trade; 9.5% manufacturing (2003); Farms: 29 totaling n/a acres (2002); Companies that employ 500 or more persons: 15 (2003); Companies that employ 100 to 499 persons: 138 (2003); Companies that employ less than 100 persons: 8,714 (2003); Black-owned businesses: 1,562 (2002); Hispanic-owned businesses: 1,669 (2002); Women-owned businesses: 8,103 (2002); Retail sales per capita: $13,665 (2006). Single-family building permits issued: 308 (2005); Multi-family building permits issued: 168 (2005).
Income: Per capita income: $31,937 (2005); Median household income: $76,836 (2005); Average household income: $97,104 (2005); Percent of households with income of $100,000 or more: 36.7% (2005); Poverty rate: 9.7% (2003); Bankruptcy rate: 2.88% (2005).
Taxes: Total county taxes per capita: $760 (2004); County property taxes per capita: $215 (2004).
Education: Percent of population age 25 and over with: High school diploma (including GED) or higher: 85.1% (2005); Bachelor's degree or higher: 37.2% (2005); Master's degree or higher: 16.1% (2005).
Housing: Homeownership rate: 71.9% (2005); Median home value: $381,396 (2005); Median rent: $811 per month (2000); Median age of housing: 33 years (2000).
Health: Birth rate: 159.3 per 10,000 population (2004); Death rate: 67.9 per 10,000 population (2004); Age-adjusted cancer mortality rate: 195.3 deaths per 100,000 population (2002); Number of physicians: 40.6 per 10,000 population (2004); Hospital beds: 59.5 per 10,000 population (2003); Hospital admissions: 1,209.3 per 10,000 population (2003).
Elections: 2004 Presidential election results: 49.6% Bush, 48.9% Kerry, 1.3% Nader, 0.1% Badnarik
National and State Parks: Bear Mountain State Park; Bear Mountain State Park; Blauvelt State Park; High Tor State Park; Hook Mountain State Park; Palisades State Park; Rockland Lake State Park; Stony Point State Park; Tallman Mountain State Park
Additional Information Contacts
Rockland County Government . . . . (845) 638-5100
  http://www.co.rockland.ny.us/
Town of Clarkstown . . . . (845) 639-2050
  http://www.town.clarkstown.ny.us/
Town of Orangetown . . . . (845) 359-5100
  http://www.orangetown.com/
Town of Ramapo . . . . (845) 357-5100
  http://www.ramapo.org/
Village of Hillburn . . . . (845) 357-2036
  http://www.hillburn.org/
Village of Nyack . . . . (845) 358-0548
  http://www.nyack.org/
Village of Spring Valley . . . . (845) 573-5800
  http://www.villagespringvalley.org/
Village of Suffern . . . . (845) 357-2600
  http://www.suffernvillage.com/

Rockland County Communities

AIRMONT (village). Covers a land area of 4.584 square miles and a water area of 0.002 square miles. Located at 41.09° N. Lat.; 74.10° W. Long. Elevation is 586 feet.
Population: 7,739 (1990); 7,799 (2000); 8,715 (2005); 9,537 (2010 projected); Race: 88.6% White, 4.1% Black, 4.3% Asian, 6.8% Hispanic of any race (2005); Density: 1,901.1 persons per square mile (2005); Average household size: 3.27 (2005); Median age: 40.6 (2005); Males per 100 females: 96.2 (2005); Marriage status: 21.1% never married, 69.4% now married, 4.7% widowed, 4.8% divorced (2000); Foreign born: 9.2% (2000); Ancestry (includes multiple ancestries): 25.5% Italian, 16.4% Irish, 15.5% Other groups, 8.1% Polish, 7.8% German (2000).
Economy: Single-family building permits issued: 4 (2005); Multi-family building permits issued: 0 (2005); Employment by occupation: 24.2% management, 29.3% professional, 8.0% services, 28.1% sales, 0.0% farming, 5.1% construction, 5.4% production (2000).
Income: Per capita income: $34,808 (2005); Median household income: $99,414 (2005); Average household income: $111,875 (2005); Percent of households with income of $100,000 or more: 49.7% (2005); Poverty rate: 3.3% (2000).
Education: Percent of population age 25 and over with: High school diploma (including GED) or higher: 87.6% (2005); Bachelor's degree or higher: 41.3% (2005); Master's degree or higher: 18.7% (2005).
Housing: Homeownership rate: 91.2% (2005); Median home value: $417,166 (2005); Median rent: $509 per month (2000); Median age of housing: 34 years (2000).
Transportation: Commute to work: 84.2% car, 9.8% public transportation, 0.8% walk, 4.8% work from home (2000); Travel time to work: 20.3% less than 15 minutes, 31.3% 15 to 30 minutes, 13.8% 30 to 45 minutes, 11.2% 45 to 60 minutes, 23.5% 60 minutes or more (2000)

BARDONIA (CDP). Covers a land area of 2.562 square miles and a water area of 0.326 square miles. Located at 41.11° N. Lat.; 73.98° W. Long.
Population: 4,473 (1990); 4,367 (2000); 4,421 (2005); 4,479 (2010 projected); Race: 84.5% White, 2.0% Black, 9.6% Asian, 7.0% Hispanic of any race (2005); Density: 1,725.7 persons per square mile (2005); Average household size: 2.95 (2005); Median age: 42.1 (2005); Males per 100 females: 95.1 (2005); Marriage status: 23.9% never married, 65.6% now married, 6.1% widowed, 4.4% divorced (2000); Foreign born: 10.6% (2000); Ancestry (includes multiple ancestries): 30.4% Italian, 16.5% Irish, 14.7% Other groups, 8.8% German, 7.7% Polish (2000).
Economy: Employment by occupation: 19.0% management, 32.8% professional, 11.1% services, 26.4% sales, 0.0% farming, 5.3% construction, 5.5% production (2000).
Income: Per capita income: $42,607 (2005); Median household income: $107,787 (2005); Average household income: $125,733 (2005); Percent of households with income of $100,000 or more: 53.8% (2005); Poverty rate: 1.4% (2000).
Education: Percent of population age 25 and over with: High school diploma (including GED) or higher: 91.1% (2005); Bachelor's degree or higher: 50.0% (2005); Master's degree or higher: 24.3% (2005).
School District(s)
Clarkstown Central School District (KG-12)
  2003-04 Enrollment: 9,350 . . . . (845) 639-6419
Housing: Homeownership rate: 85.3% (2005); Median home value: $481,034 (2005); Median rent: $660 per month (2000); Median age of housing: 29 years (2000).
Transportation: Commute to work: 85.3% car, 9.1% public transportation, 1.9% walk, 3.6% work from home (2000); Travel time to work: 31.2% less

than 15 minutes, 19.0% 15 to 30 minutes, 16.6% 30 to 45 minutes, 11.1% 45 to 60 minutes, 22.1% 60 minutes or more (2000)

BLAUVELT (CDP).
Covers a land area of 4.550 square miles and a water area of 0.067 square miles. Located at 41.06° N. Lat.; 73.95° W. Long. Elevation is 197 feet.
History: Blauvelt section of Palisades Interstate Park is here.
Population: 4,844 (1990); 5,207 (2000); 5,453 (2005); 5,694 (2010 projected); Race: 85.1% White, 2.2% Black, 8.8% Asian, 8.1% Hispanic of any race (2005); Density: 1,198.5 persons per square mile (2005); Average household size: 3.30 (2005); Median age: 38.8 (2005); Males per 100 females: 91.4 (2005); Marriage status: 28.2% never married, 64.1% now married, 4.8% widowed, 2.9% divorced (2000); Foreign born: 12.6% (2000); Ancestry (includes multiple ancestries): 36.0% Irish, 25.9% Italian, 11.7% Other groups, 10.1% German, 6.5% English (2000).
Economy: Employment by occupation: 20.5% management, 24.5% professional, 13.2% services, 28.0% sales, 0.0% farming, 10.2% construction, 3.6% production (2000).
Income: Per capita income: $40,546 (2005); Median household income: $99,060 (2005); Average household income: $129,702 (2005); Percent of households with income of $100,000 or more: 49.4% (2005); Poverty rate: 3.5% (2000).
Education: Percent of population age 25 and over with: High school diploma (including GED) or higher: 91.6% (2005); Bachelor's degree or higher: 40.0% (2005); Master's degree or higher: 15.1% (2005).

School District(s)
South Orangetown Central School District (KG-12)
    2003-04 Enrollment: 3,347 . . . . (845) 680-1050

Housing: Homeownership rate: 94.4% (2005); Median home value: $450,480 (2005); Median rent: $963 per month (2000); Median age of housing: 37 years (2000).
Transportation: Commute to work: 87.7% car, 3.8% public transportation, 2.6% walk, 5.9% work from home (2000); Travel time to work: 36.4% less than 15 minutes, 24.1% 15 to 30 minutes, 11.6% 30 to 45 minutes, 10.1% 45 to 60 minutes, 17.8% 60 minutes or more (2000)

CHESTNUT RIDGE (village).
Covers a land area of 4.941 square miles and a water area of 0.003 square miles. Located at 41.08° N. Lat.; 74.05° W. Long. Elevation is 416 feet.
Population: 7,517 (1990); 7,829 (2000); 7,984 (2005); 8,170 (2010 projected); Race: 66.4% White, 18.1% Black, 8.4% Asian, 10.3% Hispanic of any race (2005); Density: 1,616.0 persons per square mile (2005); Average household size: 3.03 (2005); Median age: 43.1 (2005); Males per 100 females: 95.4 (2005); Marriage status: 18.8% never married, 69.7% now married, 5.1% widowed, 6.4% divorced (2000); Foreign born: 22.5% (2000); Ancestry (includes multiple ancestries): 27.3% Other groups, 14.4% Irish, 13.1% Italian, 11.3% German, 5.8% Polish (2000).
Economy: Manufacturing: computer and electronic equipment. Single-family building permits issued: 18 (2005); Multi-family building permits issued: 0 (2005); Employment by occupation: 21.4% management, 28.6% professional, 9.3% services, 28.0% sales, 0.1% farming, 7.1% construction, 5.6% production (2000).
Income: Per capita income: $35,997 (2005); Median household income: $96,432 (2005); Average household income: $105,411 (2005); Percent of households with income of $100,000 or more: 47.5% (2005); Poverty rate: 3.5% (2000).
Education: Percent of population age 25 and over with: High school diploma (including GED) or higher: 88.5% (2005); Bachelor's degree or higher: 43.4% (2005); Master's degree or higher: 19.2% (2005).

School District(s)
East Ramapo Central School District (Spring Valley) (PK-12)
    2003-04 Enrollment: 9,170 . . . . (845) 577-6011
Edwin Gould Academy-Ramapo Ufsd (08-12)
    2003-04 Enrollment: 168 . . . . (845) 573-5020

Housing: Homeownership rate: 86.4% (2005); Median home value: $375,437 (2005); Median rent: $751 per month (2000); Median age of housing: 34 years (2000).
Transportation: Commute to work: 82.6% car, 11.0% public transportation, 0.5% walk, 5.8% work from home (2000); Travel time to work: 21.2% less than 15 minutes, 24.4% 15 to 30 minutes, 14.1% 30 to 45 minutes, 12.9% 45 to 60 minutes, 27.5% 60 minutes or more (2000)

CLARKSTOWN (town).
Covers a land area of 38.542 square miles and a water area of 8.394 square miles. Located at 41.12° N. Lat.; 73.98° W. Long.
Population: 79,346 (1990); 82,082 (2000); 83,504 (2005); 85,172 (2010 projected); Race: 76.1% White, 8.5% Black, 9.9% Asian, 9.2% Hispanic of any race (2005); Density: 2,166.6 persons per square mile (2005); Average household size: 2.92 (2005); Median age: 40.5 (2005); Males per 100 females: 95.1 (2005); Marriage status: 24.0% never married, 64.7% now married, 6.0% widowed, 5.3% divorced (2000); Foreign born: 16.7% (2000); Ancestry (includes multiple ancestries): 22.7% Italian, 22.2% Other groups, 18.1% Irish, 9.9% German, 6.7% Russian (2000).
Economy: Unemployment rate: 3.8% (2005); Total civilian labor force: 47,315 (2005); Single-family building permits issued: 69 (2005); Multi-family building permits issued: 0 (2005); Employment by occupation: 18.5% management, 31.1% professional, 12.8% services, 25.5% sales, 0.0% farming, 5.9% construction, 6.2% production (2000).
Income: Per capita income: $39,886 (2005); Median household income: $94,008 (2005); Average household income: $115,157 (2005); Percent of households with income of $100,000 or more: 46.3% (2005); Poverty rate: 3.8% (2000).
Taxes: Total city taxes per capita: $929 (2004); City property taxes per capita: $815 (2004).
Education: Percent of population age 25 and over with: High school diploma (including GED) or higher: 89.9% (2005); Bachelor's degree or higher: 44.9% (2005); Master's degree or higher: 20.3% (2005).
Housing: Homeownership rate: 82.1% (2005); Median home value: $405,515 (2005); Median rent: $951 per month (2000); Median age of housing: 31 years (2000).
Safety: Violent crime rate: 16.1 per 10,000 population; Property crime rate: 237.9 per 10,000 population (2004).
Transportation: Commute to work: 87.1% car, 6.9% public transportation, 1.5% walk, 4.1% work from home (2000); Travel time to work: 24.6% less than 15 minutes, 27.4% 15 to 30 minutes, 16.6% 30 to 45 minutes, 11.9% 45 to 60 minutes, 19.5% 60 minutes or more (2000)

Additional Information Contacts
Town of Clarkstown . . . . (845) 639-2050
   http://www.town.clarkstown.ny.us/

CONGERS (CDP).
Covers a land area of 3.150 square miles and a water area of 0.708 square miles. Located at 41.14° N. Lat.; 73.94° W. Long. Elevation is 191 feet.
Population: 7,946 (1990); 8,303 (2000); 8,440 (2005); 8,591 (2010 projected); Race: 81.3% White, 2.2% Black, 10.7% Asian, 10.2% Hispanic of any race (2005); Density: 2,679.3 persons per square mile (2005); Average household size: 3.04 (2005); Median age: 38.8 (2005); Males per 100 females: 96.1 (2005); Marriage status: 23.7% never married, 65.1% now married, 4.9% widowed, 6.3% divorced (2000); Foreign born: 14.5% (2000); Ancestry (includes multiple ancestries): 27.7% Italian, 25.7% Irish, 21.3% Other groups, 13.0% German, 6.6% Polish (2000).
Economy: Employment by occupation: 17.8% management, 27.1% professional, 13.0% services, 26.6% sales, 0.0% farming, 9.3% construction, 6.3% production (2000).
Income: Per capita income: $36,316 (2005); Median household income: $93,392 (2005); Average household income: $109,047 (2005); Percent of households with income of $100,000 or more: 45.8% (2005); Poverty rate: 2.9% (2000).
Education: Percent of population age 25 and over with: High school diploma (including GED) or higher: 89.3% (2005); Bachelor's degree or higher: 36.2% (2005); Master's degree or higher: 15.9% (2005).

School District(s)
Clarkstown Central School District (KG-12)
    2003-04 Enrollment: 9,350 . . . . (845) 639-6419

Housing: Homeownership rate: 85.5% (2005); Median home value: $406,615 (2005); Median rent: $983 per month (2000); Median age of housing: 32 years (2000).
Transportation: Commute to work: 88.3% car, 4.8% public transportation, 2.5% walk, 4.0% work from home (2000); Travel time to work: 22.9% less than 15 minutes, 32.0% 15 to 30 minutes, 15.9% 30 to 45 minutes, 10.0% 45 to 60 minutes, 19.3% 60 minutes or more (2000)

GARNERVILLE (unincorporated postal area, zip code 10923).
Part of the Village of West Haverstraw. Covers a land area of 2.449 square miles and a water area of 0.002 square miles. Located at 41.20° N. Lat.; 74.00° W. Long.
Population: 0 (2000); Race: 74.8% White, 9.2% Black, 3.9% Asian, 24.1% Hispanic of any race (2000); Density: 0.0 persons per square mile (2000); Age: 28.2% under 18, 8.0% over 64 (2000); Marriage status: 28.9% never married, 58.3% now married, 5.0% widowed, 7.8% divorced (2000);

Foreign born: 18.3% (2000); Ancestry (includes multiple ancestries): 30.8% Other groups, 20.7% Italian, 20.6% Irish, 9.8% German, 5.4% United States or American (2000).
Economy: Employment by occupation: 12.7% management, 17.3% professional, 23.3% services, 28.2% sales, 0.0% farming, 9.9% construction, 8.6% production (2000).
Income: Per capita income: $21,818 (2000); Median household income: $57,276 (2000); Poverty rate: 8.0% (2000).
Education: Percent of population age 25 and over with: High school diploma (including GED) or higher: 83.6% (2000); Bachelor's degree or higher: 24.3% (2000).

School District(s)
Haverstraw-Stony Point Central School District (N Rockland) (PK-12)
  2003-04 Enrollment: 8,366 .... (845) 942-3000
Housing: Homeownership rate: 70.6% (2000); Median home value: $200,300 (2000); Median rent: $816 per month (2000); Median age of housing: 33 years (2000).
Transportation: Commute to work: 92.0% car, 4.6% public transportation, 1.8% walk, 1.2% work from home (2000); Travel time to work: 27.6% less than 15 minutes, 29.2% 15 to 30 minutes, 17.5% 30 to 45 minutes, 10.8% 45 to 60 minutes, 14.9% 60 minutes or more (2000)

GRAND VIEW-ON-HUDSON (village). Aka Grand View. Covers a land area of 0.167 square miles and a water area of 0 square miles. Located at 41.06° N. Lat.; 73.92° W. Long. Elevation is 20 feet.
Population: 267 (1990); 284 (2000); 293 (2005); 301 (2010 projected); Race: 92.2% White, 0.0% Black, 5.5% Asian, 1.7% Hispanic of any race (2005); Density: 1,752.9 persons per square mile (2005); Average household size: 2.17 (2005); Median age: 51.3 (2005); Males per 100 females: 90.3 (2005); Marriage status: 12.4% never married, 72.6% now married, 3.7% widowed, 11.2% divorced (2000); Foreign born: 8.5% (2000); Ancestry (includes multiple ancestries): 15.5% German, 15.2% Other groups, 12.4% Irish, 11.7% English, 11.0% Italian (2000).
Economy: Nearby is a section of Palisades Interstate Park. Single-family building permits issued: 0 (2005); Multi-family building permits issued: 0 (2005); Employment by occupation: 28.7% management, 44.6% professional, 0.6% services, 22.3% sales, 0.0% farming, 0.0% construction, 3.8% production (2000).
Income: Per capita income: $93,660 (2005); Median household income: $151,563 (2005); Average household income: $203,278 (2005); Percent of households with income of $100,000 or more: 68.9% (2005); Poverty rate: 1.4% (2000).
Education: Percent of population age 25 and over with: High school diploma (including GED) or higher: 99.2% (2005); Bachelor's degree or higher: 66.9% (2005); Master's degree or higher: 28.8% (2005).
Housing: Homeownership rate: 85.9% (2005); Median home value: $1 million+ (2005); Median rent: $1,200 per month (2000); Median age of housing: 60+ years (2000).
Transportation: Commute to work: 71.1% car, 9.9% public transportation, 0.0% walk, 19.1% work from home (2000); Travel time to work: 12.2% less than 15 minutes, 14.6% 15 to 30 minutes, 12.2% 30 to 45 minutes, 12.2% 45 to 60 minutes, 48.8% 60 minutes or more (2000)

HAVERSTRAW (village). Covers a land area of 1.992 square miles and a water area of 3.076 square miles. Located at 41.19° N. Lat.; 73.96° W. Long. Elevation is 73 feet.
Population: 9,438 (1990); 10,117 (2000); 10,151 (2005); 10,193 (2010 projected); Race: 40.4% White, 12.0% Black, 1.1% Asian, 65.5% Hispanic of any race (2005); Density: 5,095.9 persons per square mile (2005); Average household size: 3.62 (2005); Median age: 33.6 (2005); Males per 100 females: 94.5 (2005); Marriage status: 33.0% never married, 53.1% now married, 7.0% widowed, 7.0% divorced (2000); Foreign born: 36.3% (2000); Ancestry (includes multiple ancestries): 60.0% Other groups, 9.2% Irish, 7.8% Italian, 4.4% German, 3.7% United States or American (2000).
Economy: Single-family building permits issued: 60 (2005); Multi-family building permits issued: 0 (2005); Employment by occupation: 6.1% management, 12.5% professional, 24.2% services, 24.2% sales, 0.2% farming, 11.8% construction, 20.9% production (2000).
Income: Per capita income: $16,567 (2005); Median household income: $47,017 (2005); Average household income: $57,720 (2005); Percent of households with income of $100,000 or more: 16.0% (2005); Poverty rate: 16.9% (2000).
Education: Percent of population age 25 and over with: High school diploma (including GED) or higher: 56.1% (2005); Bachelor's degree or higher: 11.2% (2005); Master's degree or higher: 4.9% (2005).

School District(s)
Haverstraw-Stony Point Central School District (N Rockland) (PK-12)
  2003-04 Enrollment: 8,366 .... (845) 942-3000
Housing: Homeownership rate: 44.5% (2005); Median home value: $244,660 (2005); Median rent: $735 per month (2000); Median age of housing: 46 years (2000).
Safety: Violent crime rate: 45.3 per 10,000 population; Property crime rate: 197.0 per 10,000 population (2004).
Transportation: Commute to work: 80.0% car, 13.5% public transportation, 4.2% walk, 1.4% work from home (2000); Travel time to work: 25.6% less than 15 minutes, 40.7% 15 to 30 minutes, 21.2% 30 to 45 minutes, 5.3% 45 to 60 minutes, 7.2% 60 minutes or more (2000)

HAVERSTRAW (town). Covers a land area of 22.416 square miles and a water area of 5.138 square miles. Located at 41.20° N. Lat.; 74.00° W. Long. Elevation is 73 feet.
History: In Haverstraw, James Wood discovered the modern system of burning brick, and set up brickyards in the town. At its peak, the industry included 40 brickyards.
Population: 32,712 (1990); 33,811 (2000); 35,010 (2005); 36,182 (2010 projected); Race: 60.8% White, 11.4% Black, 3.9% Asian, 37.1% Hispanic of any race (2005); Density: 1,561.8 persons per square mile (2005); Average household size: 3.00 (2005); Median age: 36.9 (2005); Males per 100 females: 94.8 (2005); Marriage status: 28.8% never married, 57.0% now married, 6.4% widowed, 7.8% divorced (2000); Foreign born: 22.7% (2000); Ancestry (includes multiple ancestries): 39.1% Other groups, 18.6% Italian, 15.5% Irish, 7.9% German, 4.4% Polish (2000).
Economy: Manufacturing: furniture, textiles, consumer goods, wire and cable; stone quarrying. Unemployment rate: 5.5% (2005); Total civilian labor force: 18,081 (2005); Single-family building permits issued: 11 (2005); Multi-family building permits issued: 0 (2005); Employment by occupation: 11.0% management, 19.6% professional, 20.2% services, 27.3% sales, 0.1% farming, 9.6% construction, 12.2% production (2000).
Income: Per capita income: $24,925 (2005); Median household income: $60,985 (2005); Average household income: $73,630 (2005); Percent of households with income of $100,000 or more: 24.5% (2005); Poverty rate: 10.6% (2000).
Taxes: Total city taxes per capita: $408 (2004); City property taxes per capita: $355 (2004).
Education: Percent of population age 25 and over with: High school diploma (including GED) or higher: 76.9% (2005); Bachelor's degree or higher: 23.0% (2005); Master's degree or higher: 9.2% (2005).
Housing: Homeownership rate: 63.7% (2005); Median home value: $280,415 (2005); Median rent: $773 per month (2000); Median age of housing: 31 years (2000).
Safety: Violent crime rate: 13.4 per 10,000 population; Property crime rate: 137.1 per 10,000 population (2004).
Transportation: Commute to work: 88.6% car, 6.9% public transportation, 1.9% walk, 2.1% work from home (2000); Travel time to work: 21.8% less than 15 minutes, 34.2% 15 to 30 minutes, 19.4% 30 to 45 minutes, 9.9% 45 to 60 minutes, 14.7% 60 minutes or more (2000)

HILLBURN (village). Covers a land area of 2.228 square miles and a water area of 0.020 square miles. Located at 41.12° N. Lat.; 74.16° W. Long. Elevation is 350 feet.
History: Incorporated 1893.
Population: 892 (1990); 881 (2000); 896 (2005); 915 (2010 projected); Race: 47.0% White, 10.8% Black, 5.8% Asian, 6.6% Hispanic of any race (2005); Density: 402.2 persons per square mile (2005); Average household size: 3.31 (2005); Median age: 36.3 (2005); Males per 100 females: 83.2 (2005); Marriage status: 34.4% never married, 43.5% now married, 8.4% widowed, 13.8% divorced (2000); Foreign born: 4.3% (2000); Ancestry (includes multiple ancestries): 44.3% Other groups, 18.4% Italian, 10.8% German, 8.8% Irish, 4.5% Polish (2000).
Economy: In resort area. Single-family building permits issued: 3 (2005); Multi-family building permits issued: 0 (2005); Employment by occupation: 13.5% management, 12.9% professional, 19.8% services, 27.5% sales, 0.0% farming, 13.2% construction, 13.2% production (2000).
Income: Per capita income: $24,009 (2005); Median household income: $64,261 (2005); Average household income: $79,382 (2005); Percent of households with income of $100,000 or more: 22.5% (2005); Poverty rate: 14.8% (2000).
Education: Percent of population age 25 and over with: High school diploma (including GED) or higher: 78.5% (2005); Bachelor's degree or higher: 16.6% (2005); Master's degree or higher: 5.1% (2005).

Housing: Homeownership rate: 74.9% (2005); Median home value: $261,792 (2005); Median rent: $1,060 per month (2000); Median age of housing: 60+ years (2000).
Transportation: Commute to work: 95.5% car, 4.5% public transportation, 0.0% walk, 0.0% work from home (2000); Travel time to work: 51.1% less than 15 minutes, 23.6% 15 to 30 minutes, 12.8% 30 to 45 minutes, 6.4% 45 to 60 minutes, 6.1% 60 minutes or more (2000)
Additional Information Contacts
Village of Hillburn . . . . (845) 357-2036
   http://www.hillburn.org/

HILLCREST (CDP). Covers a land area of 1.291 square miles and a water area of 0 square miles. Located at 41.13° N. Lat.; 74.03° W. Long. Elevation is 490 feet.
Population: 6,545 (1990); 7,106 (2000); 6,898 (2005); 6,697 (2010 projected); Race: 18.2% White, 57.2% Black, 14.8% Asian, 13.4% Hispanic of any race (2005); Density: 5,344.7 persons per square mile (2005); Average household size: 3.64 (2005); Median age: 38.1 (2005); Males per 100 females: 96.7 (2005); Marriage status: 30.8% never married, 57.8% now married, 6.4% widowed, 5.1% divorced (2000); Foreign born: 37.4% (2000); Ancestry (includes multiple ancestries): 45.9% Other groups, 19.6% Haitian, 5.4% Jamaican, 4.0% United States or American, 3.9% Italian (2000).
Economy: Part of dense cluster of residential commuter communities off Palisades Interstate Parkway at East foot of Ramapo Mts. Employment by occupation: 14.4% management, 23.3% professional, 18.0% services, 26.1% sales, 0.0% farming, 7.2% construction, 11.0% production (2000).
Income: Per capita income: $23,874 (2005); Median household income: $74,613 (2005); Average household income: $84,682 (2005); Percent of households with income of $100,000 or more: 33.9% (2005); Poverty rate: 8.1% (2000).
Education: Percent of population age 25 and over with: High school diploma (including GED) or higher: 76.2% (2005); Bachelor's degree or higher: 28.6% (2005); Master's degree or higher: 9.9% (2005).
Housing: Homeownership rate: 75.2% (2005); Median home value: $288,939 (2005); Median rent: $498 per month (2000); Median age of housing: 35 years (2000).
Transportation: Commute to work: 83.7% car, 11.4% public transportation, 1.4% walk, 2.6% work from home (2000); Travel time to work: 18.0% less than 15 minutes, 30.0% 15 to 30 minutes, 20.4% 30 to 45 minutes, 8.0% 45 to 60 minutes, 23.6% 60 minutes or more (2000)

KASER (village). Covers a land area of 0.171 square miles and a water area of 0 square miles. Located at 41.12° N. Lat.; 74.06° W. Long. Elevation is 550 feet.
Population: 2,661 (1990); 3,316 (2000); 3,409 (2005); 3,496 (2010 projected); Race: 98.1% White, 0.3% Black, 0.6% Asian, 0.8% Hispanic of any race (2005); Density: 19,885.1 persons per square mile (2005); Average household size: 5.07 (2005); Median age: 18.4 (2005); Males per 100 females: 101.2 (2005); Marriage status: 22.4% never married, 74.3% now married, 2.3% widowed, 0.9% divorced (2000); Foreign born: 12.4% (2000); Ancestry (includes multiple ancestries): 41.4% Other groups, 9.6% United States or American, 7.4% Hungarian, 6.6% European, 3.1% Romanian (2000).
Economy: Single-family building permits issued: 0 (2005); Multi-family building permits issued: 25 (2005); Employment by occupation: 8.9% management, 50.7% professional, 4.0% services, 27.3% sales, 0.0% farming, 2.2% construction, 6.9% production (2000).
Income: Per capita income: $5,446 (2005); Median household income: $14,999 (2005); Average household income: $24,137 (2005); Percent of households with income of $100,000 or more: 3.3% (2005); Poverty rate: 66.4% (2000).
Education: Percent of population age 25 and over with: High school diploma (including GED) or higher: 63.6% (2005); Bachelor's degree or higher: 11.8% (2005); Master's degree or higher: 7.0% (2005).
Housing: Homeownership rate: 13.5% (2005); Median home value: $450,000 (2005); Median rent: $528 per month (2000); Median age of housing: 6 years (2000).
Transportation: Commute to work: 45.6% car, 17.4% public transportation, 29.7% walk, 5.5% work from home (2000); Travel time to work: 54.6% less than 15 minutes, 22.9% 15 to 30 minutes, 4.2% 30 to 45 minutes, 3.2% 45 to 60 minutes, 15.1% 60 minutes or more (2000)

MONSEY (CDP). Covers a land area of 2.213 square miles and a water area of 0.020 square miles. Located at 41.11° N. Lat.; 74.06° W. Long. Elevation is 523 feet.
Population: 11,325 (1990); 14,504 (2000); 14,788 (2005); 15,136 (2010 projected); Race: 91.3% White, 4.9% Black, 1.4% Asian, 4.1% Hispanic of any race (2005); Density: 6,682.6 persons per square mile (2005); Average household size: 4.89 (2005); Median age: 20.5 (2005); Males per 100 females: 106.7 (2005); Marriage status: 33.0% never married, 58.9% now married, 4.3% widowed, 3.7% divorced (2000); Foreign born: 16.5% (2000); Ancestry (includes multiple ancestries): 37.6% Other groups, 8.3% United States or American, 5.4% Polish, 5.1% Hungarian, 4.5% European (2000).
Economy: Employment by occupation: 15.1% management, 32.7% professional, 10.3% services, 29.5% sales, 0.0% farming, 4.6% construction, 7.8% production (2000).
Income: Per capita income: $15,549 (2005); Median household income: $45,317 (2005); Average household income: $74,309 (2005); Percent of households with income of $100,000 or more: 21.1% (2005); Poverty rate: 30.6% (2000).
Education: Percent of population age 25 and over with: High school diploma (including GED) or higher: 76.6% (2005); Bachelor's degree or higher: 25.3% (2005); Master's degree or higher: 11.3% (2005).
School District(s)
East Ramapo Central School District (Spring Valley) (PK-12)
   2003-04 Enrollment: 9,170 . . . . (845) 577-6011
Four-year College(s)
Bais Medrash Elyon
   Fall 2004 Enrollment: 41 . . . . (845) 356-7064
   2005-06 Tuition: In-state $7,100; Out-of-state $7,100
Kol Yaakov Torah Center
   Fall 2004 Enrollment: 17 . . . . (845) 425-3863
   2005-06 Tuition: In-state $4,600; Out-of-state $4,600
Ohr Somayach
   Fall 2004 Enrollment: 106 . . . . (845) 425-1370
   2005-06 Tuition: In-state $6,750; Out-of-state $6,750
Rabbinical College Beth Shraga
   Fall 2004 Enrollment: 36 . . . . (845) 356-1980
   2005-06 Tuition: In-state $7,500; Out-of-state $7,500
Yeshiva D'monsey Rabbinical College
   Fall 2004 Enrollment: 99 . . . . (845) 352-5852
   2005-06 Tuition: In-state $3,000; Out-of-state $3,000
Yeshivath Viznitz
   Fall 2004 Enrollment: 418 . . . . (914) 356-1010
   2005-06 Tuition: In-state $4,500; Out-of-state $4,500
Housing: Homeownership rate: 54.3% (2005); Median home value: $406,805 (2005); Median rent: $861 per month (2000); Median age of housing: 33 years (2000).
Transportation: Commute to work: 75.8% car, 9.2% public transportation, 8.3% walk, 4.9% work from home (2000); Travel time to work: 37.0% less than 15 minutes, 22.5% 15 to 30 minutes, 11.9% 30 to 45 minutes, 7.2% 45 to 60 minutes, 21.4% 60 minutes or more (2000)

MONTEBELLO (village). Covers a land area of 4.364 square miles and a water area of 0 square miles. Located at 41.12° N. Lat.; 74.11° W. Long. Elevation is 323 feet.
Population: 3,021 (1990); 3,688 (2000); 4,067 (2005); 4,451 (2010 projected); Race: 92.0% White, 2.5% Black, 3.2% Asian, 3.7% Hispanic of any race (2005); Density: 932.0 persons per square mile (2005); Average household size: 3.17 (2005); Median age: 38.4 (2005); Males per 100 females: 98.4 (2005); Marriage status: 21.2% never married, 72.7% now married, 2.1% widowed, 4.0% divorced (2000); Foreign born: 5.8% (2000); Ancestry (includes multiple ancestries): 24.0% Italian, 18.3% Irish, 10.6% Other groups, 10.4% German, 8.3% Russian (2000).
Economy: Employment by occupation: 28.2% management, 34.3% professional, 6.9% services, 23.1% sales, 0.0% farming, 2.6% construction, 4.9% production (2000).
Income: Per capita income: $54,752 (2005); Median household income: $131,870 (2005); Average household income: $173,143 (2005); Percent of households with income of $100,000 or more: 67.5% (2005); Poverty rate: 3.3% (2000).
Education: Percent of population age 25 and over with: High school diploma (including GED) or higher: 96.2% (2005); Bachelor's degree or higher: 61.2% (2005); Master's degree or higher: 29.5% (2005).

Housing: Homeownership rate: 95.6% (2005); Median home value: $533,128 (2005); Median rent: $705 per month (2000); Median age of housing: 34 years (2000).
Transportation: Commute to work: 81.3% car, 10.2% public transportation, 0.4% walk, 7.8% work from home (2000); Travel time to work: 25.2% less than 15 minutes, 32.0% 15 to 30 minutes, 11.7% 30 to 45 minutes, 13.4% 45 to 60 minutes, 17.6% 60 minutes or more (2000)

MOUNT IVY (CDP).
Covers a land area of 1.467 square miles and a water area of 0.006 square miles. Located at 41.19° N. Lat.; 74.03° W. Long. Elevation is 454 feet.
Population: 6,013 (1990); 6,536 (2000); 7,040 (2005); 7,526 (2010 projected); Race: 72.5% White, 10.7% Black, 5.7% Asian, 18.1% Hispanic of any race (2005); Density: 4,800.4 persons per square mile (2005); Average household size: 2.44 (2005); Median age: 38.5 (2005); Males per 100 females: 91.5 (2005); Marriage status: 28.2% never married, 53.8% now married, 6.8% widowed, 11.2% divorced (2000); Foreign born: 14.5% (2000); Ancestry (includes multiple ancestries): 27.4% Italian, 27.2% Other groups, 16.3% Irish, 8.6% German, 6.8% Polish (2000).
Economy: Employment by occupation: 12.2% management, 22.4% professional, 16.5% services, 29.0% sales, 0.2% farming, 9.5% construction, 10.1% production (2000).
Income: Per capita income: $27,431 (2005); Median household income: $57,678 (2005); Average household income: $66,690 (2005); Percent of households with income of $100,000 or more: 18.5% (2005); Poverty rate: 8.0% (2000).
Education: Percent of population age 25 and over with: High school diploma (including GED) or higher: 88.8% (2005); Bachelor's degree or higher: 30.3% (2005); Master's degree or higher: 11.6% (2005).
Housing: Homeownership rate: 64.7% (2005); Median home value: $195,199 (2005); Median rent: $873 per month (2000); Median age of housing: 25 years (2000).
Transportation: Commute to work: 92.3% car, 4.5% public transportation, 0.8% walk, 1.8% work from home (2000); Travel time to work: 16.1% less than 15 minutes, 34.0% 15 to 30 minutes, 20.4% 30 to 45 minutes, 13.1% 45 to 60 minutes, 16.4% 60 minutes or more (2000)

NANUET (CDP).
Covers a land area of 5.424 square miles and a water area of 0.003 square miles. Located at 41.09° N. Lat.; 74.01° W. Long. Elevation is 284 feet.
History: Named for a local Indian chief. International Shrine of St. Anthony is here.
Population: 14,065 (1990); 16,707 (2000); 17,618 (2005); 18,511 (2010 projected); Race: 67.4% White, 13.9% Black, 12.1% Asian, 10.6% Hispanic of any race (2005); Density: 3,248.2 persons per square mile (2005); Average household size: 2.77 (2005); Median age: 39.2 (2005); Males per 100 females: 92.9 (2005); Marriage status: 26.3% never married, 60.1% now married, 7.1% widowed, 6.5% divorced (2000); Foreign born: 20.6% (2000); Ancestry (includes multiple ancestries): 25.7% Other groups, 22.8% Italian, 16.8% Irish, 8.0% German, 4.2% United States or American (2000).
Economy: Manufacturing of wood products, fabricated metal products, electrical products, machinery. Employment by occupation: 17.6% management, 28.4% professional, 14.3% services, 25.6% sales, 0.0% farming, 5.4% construction, 8.6% production (2000).
Income: Per capita income: $33,335 (2005); Median household income: $79,037 (2005); Average household income: $90,228 (2005); Percent of households with income of $100,000 or more: 36.0% (2005); Poverty rate: 5.2% (2000).
Education: Percent of population age 25 and over with: High school diploma (including GED) or higher: 87.5% (2005); Bachelor's degree or higher: 37.8% (2005); Master's degree or higher: 16.1% (2005).
School District(s)
Nanuet Union Free School District (KG-12)
  2003-04 Enrollment: 2,192 . . . . (845) 627-9888
New York City Public Schools (PK-12)
  2003-04 Enrollment: 1,023,674 . . . . (718) 935-2794
Two-year College(s)
Capri School of Hair Design
  Fall 2004 Enrollment: 75 . . . . (845) 623-6339
Housing: Homeownership rate: 71.0% (2005); Median home value: $355,129 (2005); Median rent: $1,070 per month (2000); Median age of housing: 25 years (2000).
Newspapers: Rockland County Times (General - Circulation 8,000)
Transportation: Commute to work: 85.6% car, 9.3% public transportation, 1.3% walk, 2.9% work from home (2000); Travel time to work: 25.1% less than 15 minutes, 30.0% 15 to 30 minutes, 15.0% 30 to 45 minutes, 12.3% 45 to 60 minutes, 17.7% 60 minutes or more (2000)

NEW CITY (CDP).
Covers a land area of 15.603 square miles and a water area of 0.696 square miles. Located at 41.14° N. Lat.; 73.99° W. Long. Elevation is 163 feet.
Population: 33,745 (1990); 34,038 (2000); 34,363 (2005); 34,857 (2010 projected); Race: 80.9% White, 5.9% Black, 8.8% Asian, 7.8% Hispanic of any race (2005); Density: 2,202.4 persons per square mile (2005); Average household size: 3.04 (2005); Median age: 41.5 (2005); Males per 100 females: 96.4 (2005); Marriage status: 21.6% never married, 68.7% now married, 5.6% widowed, 4.1% divorced (2000); Foreign born: 15.9% (2000); Ancestry (includes multiple ancestries): 21.6% Italian, 19.8% Other groups, 16.8% Irish, 9.9% German, 9.8% Russian (2000).
Economy: Employment by occupation: 20.5% management, 33.9% professional, 10.5% services, 24.5% sales, 0.0% farming, 5.5% construction, 5.1% production (2000).
Income: Per capita income: $44,191 (2005); Median household income: $105,741 (2005); Average household income: $132,794 (2005); Percent of households with income of $100,000 or more: 52.9% (2005); Poverty rate: 2.8% (2000).
Education: Percent of population age 25 and over with: High school diploma (including GED) or higher: 91.1% (2005); Bachelor's degree or higher: 52.5% (2005); Master's degree or higher: 25.1% (2005).
School District(s)
Clarkstown Central School District (KG-12)
  2003-04 Enrollment: 9,350 . . . . (845) 639-6419
East Ramapo Central School District (Spring Valley) (PK-12)
  2003-04 Enrollment: 9,170 . . . . (845) 577-6011
Housing: Homeownership rate: 91.0% (2005); Median home value: $441,759 (2005); Median rent: $856 per month (2000); Median age of housing: 32 years (2000).
Newspapers: The Rockland Jewish Reporter (Jewish - Circulation 22,000)
Transportation: Commute to work: 87.6% car, 6.0% public transportation, 1.1% walk, 4.9% work from home (2000); Travel time to work: 25.0% less than 15 minutes, 23.6% 15 to 30 minutes, 16.4% 30 to 45 minutes, 13.2% 45 to 60 minutes, 21.9% 60 minutes or more (2000)
Additional Information Contacts
New City Chamber of Commerce . . . . (845) 708-7300
  http://www.rockland.org
Rockland County Chamber of Commerce . . . . (845) 708-7300
  http://www.rockland.org

NEW HEMPSTEAD (village). Aka Hempstead.
Covers a land area of 2.840 square miles and a water area of 0.008 square miles. Located at 41.14° N. Lat.; 74.04° W. Long. Elevation is 590 feet.
Population: 4,096 (1990); 4,767 (2000); 5,058 (2005); 5,361 (2010 projected); Race: 60.2% White, 23.2% Black, 9.8% Asian, 13.1% Hispanic of any race (2005); Density: 1,781.2 persons per square mile (2005); Average household size: 3.79 (2005); Median age: 33.7 (2005); Males per 100 females: 99.5 (2005); Marriage status: 24.5% never married, 68.4% now married, 4.4% widowed, 2.7% divorced (2000); Foreign born: 18.1% (2000); Ancestry (includes multiple ancestries): 32.5% Other groups, 8.8% United States or American, 8.1% Russian, 7.7% Polish, 6.5% Italian (2000).
Economy: Single-family building permits issued: 0 (2005); Multi-family building permits issued: 0 (2005); Employment by occupation: 17.1% management, 40.1% professional, 7.3% services, 25.8% sales, 0.0% farming, 5.7% construction, 4.0% production (2000).
Income: Per capita income: $35,197 (2005); Median household income: $105,956 (2005); Average household income: $131,482 (2005); Percent of households with income of $100,000 or more: 53.2% (2005); Poverty rate: 4.2% (2000).
Education: Percent of population age 25 and over with: High school diploma (including GED) or higher: 92.1% (2005); Bachelor's degree or higher: 49.4% (2005); Master's degree or higher: 24.8% (2005).
Housing: Homeownership rate: 95.2% (2005); Median home value: $391,880 (2005); Median rent: $1,375 per month (2000); Median age of housing: 33 years (2000).
Transportation: Commute to work: 85.7% car, 7.2% public transportation, 0.9% walk, 5.0% work from home (2000); Travel time to work: 19.2% less than 15 minutes, 24.5% 15 to 30 minutes, 20.1% 30 to 45 minutes, 14.2% 45 to 60 minutes, 22.1% 60 minutes or more (2000)

NEW SQUARE (village). Covers a land area of 0.361 square miles and a water area of 0 square miles. Located at 41.14° N. Lat.; 74.02° W. Long. Elevation is 540 feet.
History: A community of Orthodox Hasidic Jews of the Skvirer sect lives here.
Population: 2,605 (1990); 4,624 (2000); 6,052 (2005); 7,350 (2010 projected); Race: 95.9% White, 2.2% Black, 1.2% Asian, 0.6% Hispanic of any race (2005); Density: 16,768.3 persons per square mile (2005); Average household size: 5.62 (2005); Median age: 15.5 (2005); Males per 100 females: 105.6 (2005); Marriage status: 25.1% never married, 71.9% now married, 1.9% widowed, 1.1% divorced (2000); Foreign born: 9.6% (2000); Ancestry (includes multiple ancestries): 51.1% Other groups, 8.2% United States or American, 6.7% Hungarian, 3.4% Polish, 1.4% Israeli (2000).
Economy: Single-family building permits issued: 0 (2005); Multi-family building permits issued: 77 (2005); Employment by occupation: 7.1% management, 43.0% professional, 11.7% services, 21.2% sales, 0.0% farming, 5.2% construction, 11.9% production (2000).
Income: Per capita income: $5,382 (2005); Median household income: $14,999 (2005); Average household income: $30,244 (2005); Percent of households with income of $100,000 or more: 5.8% (2005); Poverty rate: 72.5% (2000).
Education: Percent of population age 25 and over with: High school diploma (including GED) or higher: 25.5% (2005); Bachelor's degree or higher: 6.9% (2005); Master's degree or higher: 2.0% (2005).
Housing: Homeownership rate: 17.1% (2005); Median home value: $369,565 (2005); Median rent: $646 per month (2000); Median age of housing: 14 years (2000).
Transportation: Commute to work: 34.5% car, 6.1% public transportation, 54.7% walk, 4.5% work from home (2000); Travel time to work: 65.7% less than 15 minutes, 16.9% 15 to 30 minutes, 5.2% 30 to 45 minutes, 3.1% 45 to 60 minutes, 9.1% 60 minutes or more (2000)

NYACK (village). Covers a land area of 0.770 square miles and a water area of 0.834 square miles. Located at 41.09° N. Lat.; 73.92° W. Long. Elevation is 100 feet.
History: Was a 19th-century health resort, port, and boat-building center. Birthplace of artist Edward Hopper. Settled 1684, incorporated 1833.
Population: 6,558 (1990); 6,737 (2000); 6,707 (2005); 6,729 (2010 projected); Race: 63.8% White, 23.8% Black, 3.0% Asian, 11.6% Hispanic of any race (2005); Density: 8,710.1 persons per square mile (2005); Average household size: 2.07 (2005); Median age: 40.6 (2005); Males per 100 females: 88.3 (2005); Marriage status: 36.1% never married, 43.1% now married, 7.6% widowed, 13.2% divorced (2000); Foreign born: 18.8% (2000); Ancestry (includes multiple ancestries): 26.1% Other groups, 13.6% Irish, 11.7% Italian, 8.7% German, 8.6% Haitian (2000).
Economy: Manufacturing of clothing, leather goods, optical goods. Single-family building permits issued: 1 (2005); Multi-family building permits issued: 11 (2005); Employment by occupation: 15.2% management, 32.4% professional, 17.3% services, 22.4% sales, 0.0% farming, 4.1% construction, 8.6% production (2000).
Income: Per capita income: $38,254 (2005); Median household income: $63,583 (2005); Average household income: $78,954 (2005); Percent of households with income of $100,000 or more: 27.6% (2005); Poverty rate: 6.0% (2000).
Education: Percent of population age 25 and over with: High school diploma (including GED) or higher: 87.8% (2005); Bachelor's degree or higher: 42.5% (2005); Master's degree or higher: 19.0% (2005).

School District(s)
Nyack Union Free School District (KG-12)
    2003-04 Enrollment: 2,858 . . . . (845) 353-7010

Four-year College(s)
Nyack College
    Fall 2004 Enrollment: 2,908. . . . . (845) 358-1710
    2005-06 Tuition: In-state $15,550; Out-of-state $15,550

Housing: Homeownership rate: 35.6% (2005); Median home value: $404,338 (2005); Median rent: $875 per month (2000); Median age of housing: 40 years (2000).
Hospitals: Nyack Hospital (375 beds)
Transportation: Commute to work: 76.2% car, 11.1% public transportation, 7.5% walk, 4.1% work from home (2000); Travel time to work: 25.0% less than 15 minutes, 34.9% 15 to 30 minutes, 16.9% 30 to 45 minutes, 9.0% 45 to 60 minutes, 14.2% 60 minutes or more (2000)
Additional Information Contacts

Nyack Chamber of Commerce. . . . . (845) 353-2221
  http://www.nyack.org/
Village of Nyack . . . . (845) 358-0548
  http://www.nyack.org/

ORANGEBURG (CDP). Covers a land area of 3.106 square miles and a water area of 0 square miles. Located at 41.04° N. Lat.; 73.95° W. Long. Elevation is 67 feet.
Population: 3,583 (1990); 3,388 (2000); 3,689 (2005); 3,979 (2010 projected); Race: 77.2% White, 2.0% Black, 17.2% Asian, 6.7% Hispanic of any race (2005); Density: 1,187.6 persons per square mile (2005); Average household size: 2.51 (2005); Median age: 45.1 (2005); Males per 100 females: 89.1 (2005); Marriage status: 16.6% never married, 65.7% now married, 13.9% widowed, 3.8% divorced (2000); Foreign born: 23.1% (2000); Ancestry (includes multiple ancestries): 25.7% Other groups, 25.0% Irish, 24.4% Italian, 6.3% German, 5.5% Polish (2000).
Economy: Some manufacturing. Site of Rockland Children's Psychiatric Center. Employment by occupation: 11.3% management, 31.5% professional, 15.1% services, 28.0% sales, 0.0% farming, 7.8% construction, 6.3% production (2000).
Income: Per capita income: $35,591 (2005); Median household income: $63,239 (2005); Average household income: $89,070 (2005); Percent of households with income of $100,000 or more: 30.0% (2005); Poverty rate: 5.6% (2000).
Education: Percent of population age 25 and over with: High school diploma (including GED) or higher: 88.9% (2005); Bachelor's degree or higher: 38.3% (2005); Master's degree or higher: 17.6% (2005).

School District(s)
Pearl River Union Free School District (KG-12)
    2003-04 Enrollment: 2,544 . . . . (845) 620-3900
South Orangetown Central School District (KG-12)
    2003-04 Enrollment: 3,347 . . . . (845) 680-1050

Four-year College(s)
Dominican College of Blauvelt
    Fall 2004 Enrollment: 1,414. . . . . (845) 359-7800
    2005-06 Tuition: In-state $17,910; Out-of-state $17,910
Long Island University-Rockland Campus
    Fall 2004 Enrollment: 449 . . . . (845) 359-7200

Housing: Homeownership rate: 70.8% (2005); Median home value: $412,121 (2005); Median rent: $602 per month (2000); Median age of housing: 34 years (2000).
Hospitals: Rockland Childrens Psychiatric Center (54 beds); Rockland Psychiatric Center (550 beds)
Transportation: Commute to work: 81.9% car, 9.6% public transportation, 2.7% walk, 5.9% work from home (2000); Travel time to work: 22.5% less than 15 minutes, 25.1% 15 to 30 minutes, 23.4% 30 to 45 minutes, 11.4% 45 to 60 minutes, 17.5% 60 minutes or more (2000)

ORANGETOWN (town). Covers a land area of 24.180 square miles and a water area of 7.189 square miles. Located at 41.05° N. Lat.; 73.96° W. Long.
Population: 46,742 (1990); 47,711 (2000); 48,722 (2005); 49,833 (2010 projected); Race: 82.1% White, 5.5% Black, 7.6% Asian, 7.7% Hispanic of any race (2005); Density: 2,015.0 persons per square mile (2005); Average household size: 2.73 (2005); Median age: 40.6 (2005); Males per 100 females: 93.8 (2005); Marriage status: 28.1% never married, 58.3% now married, 7.4% widowed, 6.3% divorced (2000); Foreign born: 15.9% (2000); Ancestry (includes multiple ancestries): 30.1% Irish, 20.0% Italian, 17.7% Other groups, 11.9% German, 5.6% English (2000).
Economy: Unemployment rate: 3.9% (2005); Total civilian labor force: 26,939 (2005); Single-family building permits issued: 42 (2005); Multi-family building permits issued: 0 (2005); Employment by occupation: 16.6% management, 29.5% professional, 14.8% services, 25.5% sales, 0.0% farming, 7.1% construction, 6.5% production (2000).
Income: Per capita income: $38,806 (2005); Median household income: $81,258 (2005); Average household income: $103,872 (2005); Percent of households with income of $100,000 or more: 39.6% (2005); Poverty rate: 4.8% (2000).
Taxes: Total city taxes per capita: $760 (2004); City property taxes per capita: $673 (2004).
Education: Percent of population age 25 and over with: High school diploma (including GED) or higher: 90.1% (2005); Bachelor's degree or higher: 43.0% (2005); Master's degree or higher: 18.2% (2005).

Housing: Homeownership rate: 71.4% (2005); Median home value: $432,977 (2005); Median rent: $855 per month (2000); Median age of housing: 40 years (2000).
Safety: Violent crime rate: 13.1 per 10,000 population; Property crime rate: 160.8 per 10,000 population (2004).
Transportation: Commute to work: 83.6% car, 7.9% public transportation, 4.2% walk, 3.9% work from home (2000); Travel time to work: 29.1% less than 15 minutes, 26.3% 15 to 30 minutes, 17.2% 30 to 45 minutes, 10.3% 45 to 60 minutes, 17.2% 60 minutes or more (2000)
Additional Information Contacts
Town of Orangetown .... (845) 359-5100
http://www.orangetown.com/

PALISADES (unincorporated postal area, zip code 10964). Covers a land area of 2.337 square miles and a water area of 0 square miles. Located at 41.01° N. Lat.; 73.92° W. Long. Elevation is 197 feet.
Population: 0 (2000); Race: 91.8% White, 0.9% Black, 6.0% Asian, 3.0% Hispanic of any race (2000); Density: 0.0 persons per square mile (2000); Age: 22.7% under 18, 18.9% over 64 (2000); Marriage status: 24.0% never married, 66.7% now married, 5.3% widowed, 4.0% divorced (2000); Foreign born: 10.8% (2000); Ancestry (includes multiple ancestries): 24.1% Italian, 22.5% Irish, 16.2% German, 15.6% Other groups, 10.0% English (2000).
Economy: Employment by occupation: 27.0% management, 44.5% professional, 8.2% services, 16.6% sales, 0.0% farming, 1.5% construction, 2.1% production (2000).
Income: Per capita income: $56,696 (2000); Median household income: $86,592 (2000); Poverty rate: 4.3% (2000).
Education: Percent of population age 25 and over with: High school diploma (including GED) or higher: 96.5% (2000); Bachelor's degree or higher: 58.2% (2000).
Housing: Homeownership rate: 88.1% (2000); Median home value: $360,200 (2000); Median rent: $950 per month (2000); Median age of housing: 44 years (2000).
Transportation: Commute to work: 85.2% car, 2.4% public transportation, 5.7% walk, 5.9% work from home (2000); Travel time to work: 27.7% less than 15 minutes, 30.1% 15 to 30 minutes, 15.2% 30 to 45 minutes, 15.2% 45 to 60 minutes, 11.8% 60 minutes or more (2000)

PEARL RIVER (CDP). Covers a land area of 6.842 square miles and a water area of 0.352 square miles. Located at 41.06° N. Lat.; 74.01° W. Long. Elevation is 250 feet.
Population: 15,314 (1990); 15,553 (2000); 15,712 (2005); 15,865 (2010 projected); Race: 93.9% White, 0.5% Black, 3.9% Asian, 4.4% Hispanic of any race (2005); Density: 2,296.5 persons per square mile (2005); Average household size: 2.79 (2005); Median age: 40.0 (2005); Males per 100 females: 94.5 (2005); Marriage status: 24.8% never married, 61.9% now married, 9.0% widowed, 4.2% divorced (2000); Foreign born: 10.7% (2000); Ancestry (includes multiple ancestries): 46.6% Irish, 22.5% Italian, 13.6% German, 8.5% Other groups, 4.9% English (2000).
Economy: Residential suburb of New York City. Computer and telecommunications research and development center. Headquarters of Mercedes-Benz of North American. Employment by occupation: 14.6% management, 26.8% professional, 14.6% services, 28.0% sales, 0.0% farming, 8.4% construction, 7.7% production (2000).
Income: Per capita income: $37,331 (2005); Median household income: $87,613 (2005); Average household income: $103,193 (2005); Percent of households with income of $100,000 or more: 43.2% (2005); Poverty rate: 3.4% (2000).
Education: Percent of population age 25 and over with: High school diploma (including GED) or higher: 92.3% (2005); Bachelor's degree or higher: 38.7% (2005); Master's degree or higher: 15.0% (2005).
School District(s)
Pearl River Union Free School District (KG-12)
  2003-04 Enrollment: 2,544 .... (845) 620-3900
Housing: Homeownership rate: 78.3% (2005); Median home value: $414,497 (2005); Median rent: $829 per month (2000); Median age of housing: 43 years (2000).
Transportation: Commute to work: 86.2% car, 8.8% public transportation, 2.3% walk, 2.2% work from home (2000); Travel time to work: 31.0% less than 15 minutes, 22.5% 15 to 30 minutes, 16.8% 30 to 45 minutes, 11.2% 45 to 60 minutes, 18.5% 60 minutes or more (2000)

PIERMONT (village). Covers a land area of 0.672 square miles and a water area of 0.476 square miles. Located at 41.04° N. Lat.; 73.91° W. Long. Elevation is 6 feet.
History: Until the 1980s, manufacturing (paperboard, silk ribbons). Site of Camp Shanks, which was operational during World Wars I and II. Pier (1 mile long) from which village takes its name was used for embarkation of troops. Site where 1983 Woody Allen movie *The Purple Rose of Cairo* was filmed. Incorporated 1847.
Population: 2,163 (1990); 2,607 (2000); 2,622 (2005); 2,653 (2010 projected); Race: 73.4% White, 4.8% Black, 10.5% Asian, 13.2% Hispanic of any race (2005); Density: 3,901.2 persons per square mile (2005); Average household size: 2.15 (2005); Median age: 42.7 (2005); Males per 100 females: 100.9 (2005); Marriage status: 31.3% never married, 50.5% now married, 3.8% widowed, 14.4% divorced (2000); Foreign born: 23.9% (2000); Ancestry (includes multiple ancestries): 29.7% Other groups, 16.1% Irish, 13.3% Italian, 12.8% German, 8.4% United States or American (2000).
Economy: Manufacturing of paperboard and silk ribbons. Single-family building permits issued: 2 (2005); Multi-family building permits issued: 0 (2005); Employment by occupation: 20.5% management, 31.4% professional, 13.1% services, 21.8% sales, 0.0% farming, 6.7% construction, 6.5% production (2000).
Income: Per capita income: $51,532 (2005); Median household income: $74,265 (2005); Average household income: $110,843 (2005); Percent of households with income of $100,000 or more: 36.2% (2005); Poverty rate: 9.0% (2000).
Education: Percent of population age 25 and over with: High school diploma (including GED) or higher: 91.1% (2005); Bachelor's degree or higher: 55.6% (2005); Master's degree or higher: 23.0% (2005).
School District(s)
South Orangetown Central School District (KG-12)
  2003-04 Enrollment: 3,347 .... (845) 680-1050
Housing: Homeownership rate: 59.0% (2005); Median home value: $504,401 (2005); Median rent: $918 per month (2000); Median age of housing: 38 years (2000).
Safety: Violent crime rate: 15.3 per 10,000 population; Property crime rate: 205.9 per 10,000 population (2004).
Transportation: Commute to work: 82.5% car, 7.3% public transportation, 3.4% walk, 6.5% work from home (2000); Travel time to work: 25.8% less than 15 minutes, 31.9% 15 to 30 minutes, 16.8% 30 to 45 minutes, 7.2% 45 to 60 minutes, 18.2% 60 minutes or more (2000)

POMONA (village). Covers a land area of 2.427 square miles and a water area of 0 square miles. Located at 41.18° N. Lat.; 74.05° W. Long.
Population: 2,611 (1990); 2,726 (2000); 2,854 (2005); 3,002 (2010 projected); Race: 71.4% White, 15.0% Black, 8.4% Asian, 8.5% Hispanic of any race (2005); Density: 1,175.7 persons per square mile (2005); Average household size: 2.99 (2005); Median age: 45.1 (2005); Males per 100 females: 99.7 (2005); Marriage status: 21.6% never married, 69.5% now married, 3.5% widowed, 5.4% divorced (2000); Foreign born: 20.6% (2000); Ancestry (includes multiple ancestries): 21.5% Other groups, 18.2% Italian, 11.4% Russian, 11.0% Irish, 7.8% Polish (2000).
Economy: Manufacturing of chemicals. Single-family building permits issued: 15 (2005); Multi-family building permits issued: 0 (2005); Employment by occupation: 18.8% management, 35.1% professional, 10.4% services, 27.6% sales, 0.0% farming, 3.8% construction, 4.3% production (2000).
Income: Per capita income: $47,418 (2005); Median household income: $116,935 (2005); Average household income: $140,037 (2005); Percent of households with income of $100,000 or more: 57.7% (2005); Poverty rate: 2.0% (2000).
Education: Percent of population age 25 and over with: High school diploma (including GED) or higher: 91.6% (2005); Bachelor's degree or higher: 58.9% (2005); Master's degree or higher: 28.0% (2005).
Housing: Homeownership rate: 96.5% (2005); Median home value: $496,380 (2005); Median rent: $1,250 per month (2000); Median age of housing: 27 years (2000).
Hospitals: Summit Park Hospital (57 beds)
Transportation: Commute to work: 84.5% car, 5.7% public transportation, 0.4% walk, 9.0% work from home (2000); Travel time to work: 13.9% less than 15 minutes, 26.8% 15 to 30 minutes, 16.2% 30 to 45 minutes, 12.0% 45 to 60 minutes, 31.1% 60 minutes or more (2000)

RAMAPO (town). Covers a land area of 61.244 square miles and a water area of 0.694 square miles. Located at 41.12° N. Lat.; 74.08° W. Long. Elevation is 314 feet.
Population: 93,861 (1990); 108,905 (2000); 113,463 (2005); 117,975 (2010 projected); Race: 69.6% White, 18.2% Black, 5.2% Asian, 10.5% Hispanic of any race (2005); Density: 1,852.6 persons per square mile (2005); Average household size: 3.48 (2005); Median age: 32.3 (2005); Males per 100 females: 98.2 (2005); Marriage status: 27.8% never married, 61.0% now married, 5.5% widowed, 5.6% divorced (2000); Foreign born: 22.8% (2000); Ancestry (includes multiple ancestries): 31.9% Other groups, 9.2% Italian, 7.9% Irish, 6.9% Haitian, 6.2% United States or American (2000).
Economy: Unemployment rate: 4.0% (2005); Total civilian labor force: 51,820 (2005); Single-family building permits issued: 47 (2005); Multi-family building permits issued: 39 (2005); Employment by occupation: 16.0% management, 28.1% professional, 15.6% services, 25.7% sales, 0.1% farming, 6.3% construction, 8.1% production (2000).
Income: Per capita income: $25,109 (2005); Median household income: $65,717 (2005); Average household income: $85,841 (2005); Percent of households with income of $100,000 or more: 30.7% (2005); Poverty rate: 16.3% (2000).
Taxes: Total city taxes per capita: $385 (2004); City property taxes per capita: $337 (2004).
Education: Percent of population age 25 and over with: High school diploma (including GED) or higher: 81.0% (2005); Bachelor's degree or higher: 34.2% (2005); Master's degree or higher: 14.9% (2005).
Housing: Homeownership rate: 64.2% (2005); Median home value: $358,680 (2005); Median rent: $764 per month (2000); Median age of housing: 33 years (2000).
Transportation: Commute to work: 80.5% car, 10.9% public transportation, 3.9% walk, 3.5% work from home (2000); Travel time to work: 25.8% less than 15 minutes, 31.1% 15 to 30 minutes, 14.7% 30 to 45 minutes, 9.3% 45 to 60 minutes, 19.0% 60 minutes or more (2000)
Additional Information Contacts
Town of Ramapo . . . . (845) 357-5100
  http://www.ramapo.org/

SLOATSBURG (village). Covers a land area of 2.682 square miles and a water area of 0.027 square miles. Located at 41.16° N. Lat.; 74.18° W. Long. Elevation is 343 feet.
History: Settled before 1775, incorporated 1929.
Population: 3,035 (1990); 3,117 (2000); 3,139 (2005); 3,177 (2010 projected); Race: 87.4% White, 5.0% Black, 3.5% Asian, 7.0% Hispanic of any race (2005); Density: 1,170.2 persons per square mile (2005); Average household size: 2.93 (2005); Median age: 38.6 (2005); Males per 100 females: 100.8 (2005); Marriage status: 27.1% never married, 59.6% now married, 7.8% widowed, 5.5% divorced (2000); Foreign born: 7.2% (2000); Ancestry (includes multiple ancestries): 28.0% Irish, 25.4% Italian, 14.6% German, 12.4% English, 11.1% Other groups (2000).
Economy: Single-family building permits issued: 3 (2005); Multi-family building permits issued: 0 (2005); Employment by occupation: 16.6% management, 21.4% professional, 13.7% services, 26.9% sales, 0.0% farming, 10.9% construction, 10.4% production (2000).
Income: Per capita income: $32,982 (2005); Median household income: $83,434 (2005); Average household income: $95,951 (2005); Percent of households with income of $100,000 or more: 39.7% (2005); Poverty rate: 3.0% (2000).
Education: Percent of population age 25 and over with: High school diploma (including GED) or higher: 85.9% (2005); Bachelor's degree or higher: 25.4% (2005); Master's degree or higher: 7.1% (2005).
School District(s)
Ramapo Central School District (Suffern) (KG-12)
  2003-04 Enrollment: 4,596 . . . . (845) 357-7783
Housing: Homeownership rate: 78.5% (2005); Median home value: $295,040 (2005); Median rent: $802 per month (2000); Median age of housing: 48 years (2000).
Transportation: Commute to work: 92.8% car, 2.6% public transportation, 1.1% walk, 3.2% work from home (2000); Travel time to work: 19.1% less than 15 minutes, 36.2% 15 to 30 minutes, 22.7% 30 to 45 minutes, 7.6% 45 to 60 minutes, 14.4% 60 minutes or more (2000)

SOUTH NYACK (village). Covers a land area of 0.613 square miles and a water area of 1.073 square miles. Located at 41.08° N. Lat.; 73.92° W. Long. Elevation is 100 feet.
History: Incorporated 1878.
Population: 3,346 (1990); 3,473 (2000); 3,625 (2005); 3,740 (2010 projected); Race: 69.1% White, 15.2% Black, 6.9% Asian, 9.1% Hispanic of any race (2005); Density: 5,912.9 persons per square mile (2005); Average household size: 2.91 (2005); Median age: 33.3 (2005); Males per 100 females: 96.5 (2005); Marriage status: 36.5% never married, 51.1% now married, 4.9% widowed, 7.5% divorced (2000); Foreign born: 21.1% (2000); Ancestry (includes multiple ancestries): 18.8% Other groups, 16.1% Irish, 14.4% German, 10.8% Italian, 8.9% Haitian (2000).
Economy: Single-family building permits issued: 0 (2005); Multi-family building permits issued: 0 (2005); Employment by occupation: 12.6% management, 34.8% professional, 18.9% services, 23.2% sales, 0.0% farming, 4.0% construction, 6.5% production (2000).
Income: Per capita income: $29,030 (2005); Median household income: $59,854 (2005); Average household income: $79,431 (2005); Percent of households with income of $100,000 or more: 27.7% (2005); Poverty rate: 8.9% (2000).
Education: Percent of population age 25 and over with: High school diploma (including GED) or higher: 87.7% (2005); Bachelor's degree or higher: 51.5% (2005); Master's degree or higher: 24.1% (2005).
School District(s)
Nyack UFSD (KG-12)
  2003-04 Enrollment: 2,858 . . . . (845) 353-7010
Housing: Homeownership rate: 52.4% (2005); Median home value: $438,115 (2005); Median rent: $921 per month (2000); Median age of housing: 60+ years (2000).
Safety: Violent crime rate: 11.1 per 10,000 population; Property crime rate: 105.8 per 10,000 population (2004).
Transportation: Commute to work: 73.5% car, 10.6% public transportation, 11.3% walk, 4.1% work from home (2000); Travel time to work: 36.4% less than 15 minutes, 27.4% 15 to 30 minutes, 14.5% 30 to 45 minutes, 4.7% 45 to 60 minutes, 17.0% 60 minutes or more (2000)

SPARKILL (unincorporated postal area, zip code 10976). Covers a land area of 1.051 square miles and a water area of 0 square miles. Located at 41.02° N. Lat.; 73.92° W. Long. Elevation is 25 feet.
Population: 0 (2000); Race: 86.1% White, 6.2% Black, 2.4% Asian, 9.0% Hispanic of any race (2000); Density: 0.0 persons per square mile (2000); Age: 12.1% under 18, 25.7% over 64 (2000); Marriage status: 44.1% never married, 40.1% now married, 13.5% widowed, 2.2% divorced (2000); Foreign born: 11.1% (2000); Ancestry (includes multiple ancestries): 26.7% Irish, 24.4% Other groups, 19.7% Italian, 9.2% German, 7.0% Polish (2000).
Economy: Lumber; sand, gravel. Employment by occupation: 15.8% management, 22.5% professional, 24.4% services, 24.8% sales, 0.0% farming, 4.2% construction, 8.3% production (2000).
Income: Per capita income: $23,811 (2000); Median household income: $26,875 (2000); Poverty rate: 17.4% (2000).
Education: Percent of population age 25 and over with: High school diploma (including GED) or higher: 82.9% (2000); Bachelor's degree or higher: 41.6% (2000).
Four-year College(s)
Saint Thomas Aquinas College
  Fall 2004 Enrollment: 2,336. . . . . (845) 398-4000
  2005-06 Tuition: In-state $16,600; Out-of-state $16,600
Housing: Homeownership rate: 47.1% (2000); Median home value: $267,800 (2000); Median rent: $373 per month (2000); Median age of housing: 28 years (2000).
Transportation: Commute to work: 82.5% car, 5.2% public transportation, 11.6% walk, 0.7% work from home (2000); Travel time to work: 38.0% less than 15 minutes, 32.8% 15 to 30 minutes, 18.3% 30 to 45 minutes, 3.5% 45 to 60 minutes, 7.4% 60 minutes or more (2000)

SPRING VALLEY (village). Covers a land area of 2.101 square miles and a water area of 0.012 square miles. Located at 41.11° N. Lat.; 74.04° W. Long. Elevation is 450 feet.
History: Named for a spring in the area. Incorporated 1902.
Population: 21,802 (1990); 25,464 (2000); 25,550 (2005); 25,706 (2010 projected); Race: 33.6% White, 45.7% Black, 5.7% Asian, 19.7% Hispanic of any race (2005); Density: 12,163.7 persons per square mile (2005); Average household size: 3.44 (2005); Median age: 31.1 (2005); Males per 100 females: 99.7 (2005); Marriage status: 37.2% never married, 51.3% now married, 5.1% widowed, 6.4% divorced (2000); Foreign born: 43.0% (2000); Ancestry (includes multiple ancestries): 39.3% Other groups,

21.1% Haitian, 5.2% United States or American, 3.8% Jamaican, 3.8% Polish (2000).
Economy: Suburb with office complexes and shopping malls. Single-family building permits issued: 0 (2005); Multi-family building permits issued: 0 (2005); Employment by occupation: 7.8% management, 17.4% professional, 30.3% services, 22.6% sales, 0.3% farming, 8.0% construction, 13.7% production (2000).
Income: Per capita income: $15,115 (2005); Median household income: $43,424 (2005); Average household income: $51,049 (2005); Percent of households with income of $100,000 or more: 9.9% (2005); Poverty rate: 18.7% (2000).
Education: Percent of population age 25 and over with: High school diploma (including GED) or higher: 70.2% (2005); Bachelor's degree or higher: 19.8% (2005); Master's degree or higher: 5.9% (2005).
School District(s)
East Ramapo Central School District (Spring Valley) (PK-12)
    2003-04 Enrollment: 9,170 . . . . (845) 577-6011
Four-year College(s)
Sunbridge College
    Fall 2004 Enrollment: 102 . . . . (845) 425-0055
Housing: Homeownership rate: 31.3% (2005); Median home value: $209,042 (2005); Median rent: $760 per month (2000); Median age of housing: 32 years (2000).
Safety: Violent crime rate: 74.3 per 10,000 population; Property crime rate: 193.3 per 10,000 population (2004).
Transportation: Commute to work: 78.1% car, 15.6% public transportation, 3.7% walk, 1.0% work from home (2000); Travel time to work: 23.3% less than 15 minutes, 42.9% 15 to 30 minutes, 15.5% 30 to 45 minutes, 7.2% 45 to 60 minutes, 11.0% 60 minutes or more (2000)
Additional Information Contacts
Village of Spring Valley . . . . (845) 573-5800
    http://www.villagespringvalley.org/

STONY POINT (town).
Covers a land area of 27.836 square miles and a water area of 3.708 square miles. Located at 41.23° N. Lat.; 74.00° W. Long. Elevation is 116 feet.
History: Named for a local rocky bluff that projects into the Hudson River. Nearby is Stony Point Museum (1936) in battlefield reservation (part of Palisades Interstate Park), commemorating storming of Stony Point by "Mad" Anthony Wayne's Continental forces in July 1779.
Population: 12,814 (1990); 14,244 (2000); 15,072 (2005); 15,886 (2010 projected); Race: 92.5% White, 1.6% Black, 1.8% Asian, 9.2% Hispanic of any race (2005); Density: 541.5 persons per square mile (2005); Average household size: 2.95 (2005); Median age: 39.2 (2005); Males per 100 females: 98.4 (2005); Marriage status: 24.7% never married, 63.2% now married, 5.9% widowed, 6.2% divorced (2000); Foreign born: 7.0% (2000); Ancestry (includes multiple ancestries): 35.8% Irish, 30.7% Italian, 13.8% German, 11.5% Other groups, 6.3% English (2000).
Economy: Single-family building permits issued: 19 (2005); Multi-family building permits issued: 0 (2005); Employment by occupation: 13.4% management, 23.1% professional, 15.5% services, 27.9% sales, 0.1% farming, 11.8% construction, 8.1% production (2000).
Income: Per capita income: $33,386 (2005); Median household income: $84,260 (2005); Average household income: $97,967 (2005); Percent of households with income of $100,000 or more: 38.9% (2005); Poverty rate: 3.7% (2000).
Taxes: Total city taxes per capita: $808 (2004); City property taxes per capita: $681 (2004).
Education: Percent of population age 25 and over with: High school diploma (including GED) or higher: 86.1% (2005); Bachelor's degree or higher: 26.7% (2005); Master's degree or higher: 9.3% (2005).
School District(s)
Haverstraw-Stony Point Central School District (N Rockland) (PK-12)
    2003-04 Enrollment: 8,366 . . . . (845) 942-3000
Housing: Homeownership rate: 84.4% (2005); Median home value: $367,273 (2005); Median rent: $786 per month (2000); Median age of housing: 36 years (2000).
Safety: Violent crime rate: 5.4 per 10,000 population; Property crime rate: 55.9 per 10,000 population (2004).
Transportation: Commute to work: 93.7% car, 2.9% public transportation, 0.2% walk, 2.6% work from home (2000); Travel time to work: 22.6% less than 15 minutes, 32.0% 15 to 30 minutes, 18.2% 30 to 45 minutes, 10.0% 45 to 60 minutes, 17.3% 60 minutes or more (2000)

STONY POINT (CDP).
Covers a land area of 0.313 square miles and a water area of 0 square miles. Located at 39.17° N. Lat.; 90.14° W. Long.
Population: 10,587 (1990); 11,744 (2000); 12,451 (2005); 13,158 (2010 projected); Race: 92.3% White, 1.8% Black, 2.0% Asian, 9.5% Hispanic of any race (2005); Density: 39,730.4 persons per square mile (2005); Average household size: 2.94 (2005); Median age: 39.5 (2005); Males per 100 females: 99.1 (2005); Marriage status: 25.1% never married, 63.4% now married, 5.8% widowed, 5.7% divorced (2000); Foreign born: 7.4% (2000); Ancestry (includes multiple ancestries): 36.8% Irish, 30.9% Italian, 12.7% German, 12.0% Other groups, 5.2% English (2000).
Economy: Employment by occupation: 13.8% management, 21.9% professional, 16.0% services, 29.2% sales, 0.0% farming, 10.9% construction, 8.3% production (2000).
Income: Per capita income: $33,209 (2005); Median household income: $82,705 (2005); Average household income: $97,046 (2005); Percent of households with income of $100,000 or more: 37.8% (2005); Poverty rate: 3.6% (2000).
Education: Percent of population age 25 and over with: High school diploma (including GED) or higher: 85.1% (2005); Bachelor's degree or higher: 25.1% (2005); Master's degree or higher: 8.3% (2005).
Housing: Homeownership rate: 85.0% (2005); Median home value: $355,719 (2005); Median rent: $778 per month (2000); Median age of housing: 36 years (2000).
Transportation: Commute to work: 93.1% car, 3.1% public transportation, 0.3% walk, 2.8% work from home (2000); Travel time to work: 23.9% less than 15 minutes, 32.3% 15 to 30 minutes, 15.8% 30 to 45 minutes, 11.0% 45 to 60 minutes, 17.0% 60 minutes or more (2000)

SUFFERN (village).
Covers a land area of 2.090 square miles and a water area of 0.035 square miles. Located at 41.11° N. Lat.; 74.14° W. Long. Elevation is 313 feet.
History: Named for John Suffern, original member of the first state legislature. Incorporated 1896.
Population: 11,055 (1990); 11,006 (2000); 11,012 (2005); 11,079 (2010 projected); Race: 83.6% White, 3.6% Black, 3.5% Asian, 18.2% Hispanic of any race (2005); Density: 5,268.7 persons per square mile (2005); Average household size: 2.37 (2005); Median age: 40.7 (2005); Males per 100 females: 93.9 (2005); Marriage status: 26.4% never married, 55.2% now married, 7.7% widowed, 10.7% divorced (2000); Foreign born: 18.2% (2000); Ancestry (includes multiple ancestries): 23.7% Other groups, 21.7% Irish, 21.4% Italian, 10.6% German, 6.7% English (2000).
Economy: Trade center. Light manufacturing: cosmetics, toiletries, and pharmaceuticals. Offices. In diversified-farming area. Single-family building permits issued: 3 (2005); Multi-family building permits issued: 16 (2005); Employment by occupation: 16.2% management, 26.8% professional, 16.6% services, 28.6% sales, 0.0% farming, 6.4% construction, 5.4% production (2000).
Income: Per capita income: $32,504 (2005); Median household income: $65,716 (2005); Average household income: $76,921 (2005); Percent of households with income of $100,000 or more: 26.5% (2005); Poverty rate: 5.7% (2000).
Education: Percent of population age 25 and over with: High school diploma (including GED) or higher: 90.5% (2005); Bachelor's degree or higher: 37.1% (2005); Master's degree or higher: 15.4% (2005).
School District(s)
East Ramapo Central School District (Spring Valley) (PK-12)
    2003-04 Enrollment: 9,170 . . . . (845) 577-6011
Ramapo Central School District (Suffern) (KG-12)
    2003-04 Enrollment: 4,596 . . . . (845) 357-7783
Four-year College(s)
Yeshiva Shaarei Torah of Rockland
    Fall 2004 Enrollment: 44 . . . . (845) 352-3431
    2005-06 Tuition: In-state $6,000; Out-of-state $6,000
Two-year College(s)
Rockland Community College (Public)
    Fall 2004 Enrollment: 6,409 . . . . (845) 574-4000
    2005-06 Tuition: In-state $3,050; Out-of-state $5,850
Housing: Homeownership rate: 66.2% (2005); Median home value: $269,674 (2005); Median rent: $861 per month (2000); Median age of housing: 32 years (2000).
Hospitals: Good Samaritan Hospital (370 beds)
Safety: Violent crime rate: 19.9 per 10,000 population; Property crime rate: 123.2 per 10,000 population (2004).

Transportation: Commute to work: 83.3% car, 9.9% public transportation, 2.9% walk, 2.2% work from home (2000); Travel time to work: 30.3% less than 15 minutes, 30.5% 15 to 30 minutes, 13.9% 30 to 45 minutes, 8.7% 45 to 60 minutes, 16.6% 60 minutes or more (2000)

Additional Information Contacts

Suffern Chamber of Commerce . . . . (845) 357-8424
    http://www.suffernchamberofcommerce.org
Village of Suffern . . . . (845) 357-2600
    http://www.suffernvillage.com/

TAPPAN
(CDP). Covers a land area of 2.789 square miles and a water area of 0 square miles. Located at 41.02° N. Lat.; 73.95° W. Long. Elevation is 50 feet.

History: De Wint Mansion was Washington's headquarters in 1780 and 1783. John Andre, British spy in the American Revolution, was tried and hanged here.

Population: 6,867 (1990); 6,757 (2000); 6,770 (2005); 6,832 (2010 projected); Race: 80.1% White, 1.3% Black, 15.1% Asian, 8.0% Hispanic of any race (2005); Density: 2,427.7 persons per square mile (2005); Average household size: 2.94 (2005); Median age: 42.3 (2005); Males per 100 females: 95.4 (2005); Marriage status: 21.8% never married, 68.6% now married, 5.0% widowed, 4.7% divorced (2000); Foreign born: 19.4% (2000); Ancestry (includes multiple ancestries): 24.7% Other groups, 23.8% Irish, 22.8% Italian, 14.1% German, 4.6% Russian (2000).

Economy: Employment by occupation: 18.8% management, 29.0% professional, 12.6% services, 27.2% sales, 0.0% farming, 6.9% construction, 5.5% production (2000).

Income: Per capita income: $39,271 (2005); Median household income: $95,878 (2005); Average household income: $114,984 (2005); Percent of households with income of $100,000 or more: 47.3% (2005); Poverty rate: 3.3% (2000).

Education: Percent of population age 25 and over with: High school diploma (including GED) or higher: 92.6% (2005); Bachelor's degree or higher: 47.0% (2005); Master's degree or higher: 18.7% (2005).

School District(s)
South Orangetown Central School District (KG-12)
    2003-04 Enrollment: 3,347 . . . . (845) 680-1050

Housing: Homeownership rate: 93.1% (2005); Median home value: $442,645 (2005); Median rent: $844 per month (2000); Median age of housing: 37 years (2000).

Transportation: Commute to work: 90.1% car, 4.5% public transportation, 1.5% walk, 3.2% work from home (2000); Travel time to work: 20.5% less than 15 minutes, 24.2% 15 to 30 minutes, 21.0% 30 to 45 minutes, 16.7% 45 to 60 minutes, 17.5% 60 minutes or more (2000)

THIELLS
(CDP). Covers a land area of 1.857 square miles and a water area of 0.015 square miles. Located at 41.20° N. Lat.; 74.00° W. Long. Elevation is 301 feet.

Population: 5,204 (1990); 4,758 (2000); 5,194 (2005); 5,608 (2010 projected); Race: 84.9% White, 4.7% Black, 3.5% Asian, 17.2% Hispanic of any race (2005); Density: 2,796.9 persons per square mile (2005); Average household size: 3.11 (2005); Median age: 39.1 (2005); Males per 100 females: 99.0 (2005); Marriage status: 25.5% never married, 64.3% now married, 5.0% widowed, 5.3% divorced (2000); Foreign born: 10.9% (2000); Ancestry (includes multiple ancestries): 26.3% Italian, 24.6% Irish, 20.1% Other groups, 10.8% German, 7.9% United States or American (2000).

Economy: Employment by occupation: 14.6% management, 25.0% professional, 16.7% services, 30.3% sales, 0.0% farming, 8.3% construction, 5.1% production (2000).

Income: Per capita income: $35,655 (2005); Median household income: $95,189 (2005); Average household income: $110,485 (2005); Percent of households with income of $100,000 or more: 46.9% (2005); Poverty rate: 4.5% (2000).

Education: Percent of population age 25 and over with: High school diploma (including GED) or higher: 90.6% (2005); Bachelor's degree or higher: 32.8% (2005); Master's degree or higher: 11.4% (2005).

School District(s)
Haverstraw-Stony Point Central School District (N Rockland) (PK-12)
    2003-04 Enrollment: 8,366 . . . . (845) 942-3000

Housing: Homeownership rate: 89.2% (2005); Median home value: $364,198 (2005); Median rent: $721 per month (2000); Median age of housing: 27 years (2000).

Transportation: Commute to work: 93.4% car, 4.6% public transportation, 0.2% walk, 1.7% work from home (2000); Travel time to work: 21.4% less than 15 minutes, 30.5% 15 to 30 minutes, 16.2% 30 to 45 minutes, 14.4% 45 to 60 minutes, 17.5% 60 minutes or more (2000)

TOMKINS COVE
(unincorporated postal area, zip code 10986). Covers a land area of 4.731 square miles and a water area of 1.311 square miles. Located at 41.27° N. Lat.; 73.98° W. Long. Elevation is 7 feet.

Population: 0 (2000); Race: 95.9% White, 1.5% Black, 0.7% Asian, 7.6% Hispanic of any race (2000); Density: 0.0 persons per square mile (2000); Age: 25.2% under 18, 10.9% over 64 (2000); Marriage status: 20.8% never married, 59.8% now married, 8.7% widowed, 10.7% divorced (2000); Foreign born: 5.1% (2000); Ancestry (includes multiple ancestries): 32.3% Irish, 25.1% Italian, 18.2% German, 14.2% English, 12.9% Other groups (2000).

Economy: Employment by occupation: 11.0% management, 27.4% professional, 12.2% services, 24.3% sales, 0.9% farming, 16.8% construction, 7.4% production (2000).

Income: Per capita income: $31,443 (2000); Median household income: $76,127 (2000); Poverty rate: 3.3% (2000).

Education: Percent of population age 25 and over with: High school diploma (including GED) or higher: 89.4% (2000); Bachelor's degree or higher: 30.6% (2000).

Housing: Homeownership rate: 82.0% (2000); Median home value: $239,200 (2000); Median rent: $871 per month (2000); Median age of housing: 44 years (2000).

Transportation: Commute to work: 97.6% car, 1.0% public transportation, 0.0% walk, 1.4% work from home (2000); Travel time to work: 16.2% less than 15 minutes, 33.0% 15 to 30 minutes, 24.2% 30 to 45 minutes, 6.0% 45 to 60 minutes, 20.7% 60 minutes or more (2000)

UPPER NYACK
(village). Covers a land area of 1.324 square miles and a water area of 2.904 square miles. Located at 41.10° N. Lat.; 73.92° W. Long. Elevation is 100 feet.

Population: 2,084 (1990); 1,863 (2000); 1,885 (2005); 1,918 (2010 projected); Race: 90.9% White, 3.8% Black, 3.0% Asian, 5.0% Hispanic of any race (2005); Density: 1,423.4 persons per square mile (2005); Average household size: 2.58 (2005); Median age: 46.8 (2005); Males per 100 females: 92.2 (2005); Marriage status: 23.7% never married, 63.8% now married, 5.8% widowed, 6.7% divorced (2000); Foreign born: 8.1% (2000); Ancestry (includes multiple ancestries): 22.6% Irish, 15.4% English, 15.2% German, 13.1% Italian, 11.0% Other groups (2000).

Economy: Single-family building permits issued: 0 (2005); Multi-family building permits issued: 0 (2005); Employment by occupation: 23.0% management, 36.7% professional, 8.1% services, 24.4% sales, 0.0% farming, 5.1% construction, 2.8% production (2000).

Income: Per capita income: $51,607 (2005); Median household income: $103,179 (2005); Average household income: $131,148 (2005); Percent of households with income of $100,000 or more: 51.5% (2005); Poverty rate: 3.4% (2000).

Education: Percent of population age 25 and over with: High school diploma (including GED) or higher: 96.8% (2005); Bachelor's degree or higher: 61.5% (2005); Master's degree or higher: 29.9% (2005).

School District(s)
Nyack Union Free School District (KG-12)
    2003-04 Enrollment: 2,858 . . . . (845) 353-7010

Housing: Homeownership rate: 87.0% (2005); Median home value: $531,832 (2005); Median rent: $921 per month (2000); Median age of housing: 47 years (2000).

Transportation: Commute to work: 79.8% car, 8.2% public transportation, 3.7% walk, 7.9% work from home (2000); Travel time to work: 28.9% less than 15 minutes, 21.3% 15 to 30 minutes, 13.4% 30 to 45 minutes, 11.3% 45 to 60 minutes, 25.2% 60 minutes or more (2000)

VALLEY COTTAGE
(CDP). Covers a land area of 4.274 square miles and a water area of 0 square miles. Located at 41.11° N. Lat.; 73.94° W. Long. Elevation is 126 feet.

Population: 9,006 (1990); 9,269 (2000); 9,187 (2005); 9,073 (2010 projected); Race: 77.8% White, 4.5% Black, 11.9% Asian, 9.0% Hispanic of any race (2005); Density: 2,149.5 persons per square mile (2005); Average household size: 2.74 (2005); Median age: 42.6 (2005); Males per 100 females: 93.0 (2005); Marriage status: 25.4% never married, 61.3% now married, 7.4% widowed, 5.9% divorced (2000); Foreign born: 16.2% (2000); Ancestry (includes multiple ancestries): 25.5% Italian, 23.0% Other groups, 20.1% Irish, 11.1% German, 5.4% Russian (2000).

Economy: Employment by occupation: 15.0% management, 30.2% professional, 14.2% services, 29.2% sales, 0.2% farming, 5.6% construction, 5.7% production (2000).
Income: Per capita income: $39,877 (2005); Median household income: $88,963 (2005); Average household income: $107,929 (2005); Percent of households with income of $100,000 or more: 42.6% (2005); Poverty rate: 2.7% (2000).
Education: Percent of population age 25 and over with: High school diploma (including GED) or higher: 92.2% (2005); Bachelor's degree or higher: 41.2% (2005); Master's degree or higher: 16.8% (2005).

School District(s)
Nyack Union Free School District (KG-12)
    2003-04 Enrollment: 2,858 . . . . (845) 353-7010

Housing: Homeownership rate: 82.4% (2005); Median home value: $339,979 (2005); Median rent: $981 per month (2000); Median age of housing: 29 years (2000).
Transportation: Commute to work: 90.1% car, 5.9% public transportation, 1.2% walk, 2.9% work from home (2000); Travel time to work: 19.9% less than 15 minutes, 34.9% 15 to 30 minutes, 18.0% 30 to 45 minutes, 11.4% 45 to 60 minutes, 15.8% 60 minutes or more (2000)

VIOLA (CDP). Covers a land area of 2.705 square miles and a water area of 0 square miles. Located at 41.12° N. Lat.; 74.08° W. Long. Elevation is 460 feet.
Population: 4,433 (1990); 5,931 (2000); 6,552 (2005); 7,112 (2010 projected); Race: 97.4% White, 0.3% Black, 0.8% Asian, 3.6% Hispanic of any race (2005); Density: 2,421.9 persons per square mile (2005); Average household size: 3.50 (2005); Median age: 27.0 (2005); Males per 100 females: 93.4 (2005); Marriage status: 22.7% never married, 62.5% now married, 11.0% widowed, 3.8% divorced (2000); Foreign born: 13.9% (2000); Ancestry (includes multiple ancestries): 32.7% Other groups, 13.2% Polish, 12.0% Russian, 8.9% United States or American, 5.2% Hungarian (2000).
Economy: Employment by occupation: 23.1% management, 43.8% professional, 4.5% services, 22.5% sales, 0.4% farming, 1.7% construction, 4.0% production (2000).
Income: Per capita income: $29,522 (2005); Median household income: $71,624 (2005); Average household income: $103,215 (2005); Percent of households with income of $100,000 or more: 37.5% (2005); Poverty rate: 6.5% (2000).
Education: Percent of population age 25 and over with: High school diploma (including GED) or higher: 89.6% (2005); Bachelor's degree or higher: 52.0% (2005); Master's degree or higher: 30.1% (2005).
Housing: Homeownership rate: 66.8% (2005); Median home value: $511,710 (2005); Median rent: $643 per month (2000); Median age of housing: 28 years (2000).
Transportation: Commute to work: 76.0% car, 15.4% public transportation, 1.1% walk, 6.7% work from home (2000); Travel time to work: 28.4% less than 15 minutes, 21.0% 15 to 30 minutes, 11.9% 30 to 45 minutes, 9.7% 45 to 60 minutes, 29.0% 60 minutes or more (2000)

WESLEY HILLS (village). Covers a land area of 3.357 square miles and a water area of 0.011 square miles. Located at 41.15° N. Lat.; 74.07° W. Long. Elevation is 534 feet.
Population: 4,305 (1990); 4,848 (2000); 5,118 (2005); 5,336 (2010 projected); Race: 85.1% White, 6.2% Black, 5.8% Asian, 4.7% Hispanic of any race (2005); Density: 1,524.7 persons per square mile (2005); Average household size: 3.42 (2005); Median age: 35.6 (2005); Males per 100 females: 98.7 (2005); Marriage status: 21.8% never married, 73.1% now married, 1.8% widowed, 3.4% divorced (2000); Foreign born: 11.9% (2000); Ancestry (includes multiple ancestries): 21.0% Other groups, 11.4% Russian, 10.7% United States or American, 10.6% Polish, 7.2% German (2000).
Economy: Single-family building permits issued: 9 (2005); Multi-family building permits issued: 0 (2005); Employment by occupation: 19.2% management, 39.1% professional, 8.7% services, 26.4% sales, 0.3% farming, 4.6% construction, 1.7% production (2000).
Income: Per capita income: $33,851 (2005); Median household income: $97,076 (2005); Average household income: $114,371 (2005); Percent of households with income of $100,000 or more: 48.3% (2005); Poverty rate: 7.1% (2000).
Education: Percent of population age 25 and over with: High school diploma (including GED) or higher: 93.6% (2005); Bachelor's degree or higher: 56.0% (2005); Master's degree or higher: 26.2% (2005).

Housing: Homeownership rate: 95.4% (2005); Median home value: $449,235 (2005); Median rent: $1,167 per month (2000); Median age of housing: 33 years (2000).
Transportation: Commute to work: 84.4% car, 10.8% public transportation, 0.9% walk, 3.9% work from home (2000); Travel time to work: 21.0% less than 15 minutes, 30.3% 15 to 30 minutes, 10.2% 30 to 45 minutes, 12.3% 45 to 60 minutes, 26.2% 60 minutes or more (2000)

WEST HAVERSTRAW (village). Covers a land area of 1.543 square miles and a water area of 0.006 square miles. Located at 41.20° N. Lat.; 73.99° W. Long. Elevation is 100 feet.
History: Named, probably, for a variation of the Dutch translation of "oat-straw," or for a Dutch name. Incorporated 1883.
Population: 9,183 (1990); 10,295 (2000); 10,359 (2005); 10,435 (2010 projected); Race: 57.8% White, 14.2% Black, 4.9% Asian, 38.4% Hispanic of any race (2005); Density: 6,711.7 persons per square mile (2005); Average household size: 2.92 (2005); Median age: 36.6 (2005); Males per 100 females: 93.7 (2005); Marriage status: 28.1% never married, 57.0% now married, 6.9% widowed, 7.9% divorced (2000); Foreign born: 21.4% (2000); Ancestry (includes multiple ancestries): 39.1% Other groups, 19.9% Italian, 16.5% Irish, 9.4% German, 3.7% Haitian (2000).
Economy: Manufacturing of synthetic cold-metal solders. State home for crippled children here. Single-family building permits issued: 2 (2005); Multi-family building permits issued: 0 (2005); Employment by occupation: 10.6% management, 16.2% professional, 24.7% services, 27.3% sales, 0.0% farming, 9.6% construction, 11.7% production (2000).
Income: Per capita income: $21,147 (2005); Median household income: $52,563 (2005); Average household income: $60,537 (2005); Percent of households with income of $100,000 or more: 18.5% (2005); Poverty rate: 10.6% (2000).
Education: Percent of population age 25 and over with: High school diploma (including GED) or higher: 78.2% (2005); Bachelor's degree or higher: 16.5% (2005); Master's degree or higher: 6.4% (2005).

School District(s)
Haverstraw-Stony Point Central School District (N Rockland) (PK-12)
    2003-04 Enrollment: 8,366 . . . . (845) 942-3000

Housing: Homeownership rate: 59.1% (2005); Median home value: $258,709 (2005); Median rent: $776 per month (2000); Median age of housing: 34 years (2000).
Hospitals: Helen Hayes Hospital (155 beds)
Transportation: Commute to work: 90.8% car, 4.8% public transportation, 2.4% walk, 1.4% work from home (2000); Travel time to work: 25.7% less than 15 minutes, 32.2% 15 to 30 minutes, 19.4% 30 to 45 minutes, 7.7% 45 to 60 minutes, 15.1% 60 minutes or more (2000)

WEST NYACK (CDP). Covers a land area of 2.915 square miles and a water area of 0 square miles. Located at 41.09° N. Lat.; 73.96° W. Long. Elevation is 65 feet.
Population: 3,437 (1990); 3,282 (2000); 3,465 (2005); 3,665 (2010 projected); Race: 85.7% White, 2.0% Black, 9.4% Asian, 7.1% Hispanic of any race (2005); Density: 1,188.7 persons per square mile (2005); Average household size: 2.92 (2005); Median age: 41.5 (2005); Males per 100 females: 94.2 (2005); Marriage status: 21.7% never married, 66.6% now married, 6.1% widowed, 5.6% divorced (2000); Foreign born: 15.4% (2000); Ancestry (includes multiple ancestries): 26.8% Irish, 24.3% Italian, 17.7% Other groups, 12.3% German, 5.7% English (2000).
Economy: Employment by occupation: 17.3% management, 29.3% professional, 14.3% services, 24.6% sales, 0.0% farming, 7.9% construction, 6.5% production (2000).
Income: Per capita income: $46,750 (2005); Median household income: $116,066 (2005); Average household income: $136,166 (2005); Percent of households with income of $100,000 or more: 58.3% (2005); Poverty rate: 2.6% (2000).
Education: Percent of population age 25 and over with: High school diploma (including GED) or higher: 91.6% (2005); Bachelor's degree or higher: 45.7% (2005); Master's degree or higher: 17.5% (2005).

School District(s)
Boces Rockland (UG-UG)
    2003-04 Enrollment: 594 . . . . (845) 627-4701
Clarkstown Central School District (KG-12)
    2003-04 Enrollment: 9,350 . . . . (845) 639-6419

Two-year College(s)
Rockland County BOCES-Practical Nursing Program (Public)
    Fall 2004 Enrollment: 92 . . . . (845) 627-4770

Housing: Homeownership rate: 88.8% (2005); Median home value: $419,848 (2005); Median rent: $959 per month (2000); Median age of housing: 40 years (2000).
Newspapers: Rockland Review (General - Circulation 26,000)
Transportation: Commute to work: 88.1% car, 6.3% public transportation, 0.0% walk, 5.6% work from home (2000); Travel time to work: 26.7% less than 15 minutes, 23.6% 15 to 30 minutes, 21.7% 30 to 45 minutes, 9.2% 45 to 60 minutes, 18.8% 60 minutes or more (2000)

Saint Lawrence County

Located in northern New York; bounded on the northwest by the St. Lawrence River; drained by the St. Regis, Indian, Grass, Oswegatchie, and Raquette Rivers; plains area, rising to the Adirondacks in the southeast; includes Black and Cranberry Lakes. Covers a land area of 2,685.60 square miles, a water area of 135.88 square miles, and is located in the Eastern Time Zone. The county government was organized in 1802. County seat is Canton.

Weather Station: Canton 4 SE   Elevation: 396 feet

	Jan	Feb	Mar	Apr	May	Jun	Jul	Aug	Sep	Oct	Nov	Dec
High	26	28	38	52	66	74	79	77	69	57	44	32
Low	4	6	18	32	44	53	58	56	47	36	27	13
Precip	2.3	2.0	2.4	2.9	3.0	3.3	3.6	4.0	4.2	3.4	3.4	2.7
Snow	23.8	19.7	15.4	4.5	0.2	0.0	0.0	0.0	tr	0.4	6.9	20.0

High and Low temperatures in degrees Fahrenheit; Precipitation and Snow in inches

Weather Station: Gouverneur 3 NW   Elevation: 419 feet

	Jan	Feb	Mar	Apr	May	Jun	Jul	Aug	Sep	Oct	Nov	Dec
High	27	30	40	55	68	76	81	79	70	58	45	33
Low	6	8	19	32	43	52	56	54	47	36	28	14
Precip	2.5	2.0	2.5	3.0	3.1	3.2	3.1	3.7	4.2	3.5	3.7	2.9
Snow	23.5	17.0	14.7	3.8	0.1	tr	0.0	0.0	tr	0.4	8.1	19.9

High and Low temperatures in degrees Fahrenheit; Precipitation and Snow in inches

Weather Station: Lawrenceville 3 SW   Elevation: 498 feet

	Jan	Feb	Mar	Apr	May	Jun	Jul	Aug	Sep	Oct	Nov	Dec
High	26	29	39	54	68	76	80	78	69	58	44	31
Low	6	9	19	33	45	54	59	57	49	38	28	14
Precip	2.1	1.9	2.2	2.7	2.8	3.7	3.8	4.2	4.0	3.2	3.2	2.6
Snow	17.1	14.2	13.3	4.9	0.4	0.0	0.0	0.0	0.0	0.7	7.2	14.9

High and Low temperatures in degrees Fahrenheit; Precipitation and Snow in inches

Weather Station: Massena Airport   Elevation: 213 feet

	Jan	Feb	Mar	Apr	May	Jun	Jul	Aug	Sep	Oct	Nov	Dec
High	24	27	38	53	68	76	81	79	69	57	43	30
Low	4	7	19	33	45	53	59	56	48	37	28	13
Precip	2.5	2.1	2.4	2.8	2.7	3.3	3.4	3.6	3.9	3.0	3.1	3.0
Snow	17.6	15.7	11.3	4.4	0.1	tr	tr	0.0	tr	0.9	6.3	17.5

High and Low temperatures in degrees Fahrenheit; Precipitation and Snow in inches

Weather Station: Ogdensburg 4 NE   Elevation: 278 feet

	Jan	Feb	Mar	Apr	May	Jun	Jul	Aug	Sep	Oct	Nov	Dec
High	26	29	40	54	68	77	82	80	70	58	45	32
Low	7	10	21	34	46	54	60	57	49	39	30	16
Precip	2.5	2.0	2.2	2.6	2.8	3.1	3.2	3.7	3.9	3.0	3.1	2.7
Snow	na	11.2	9.4	2.4	0.0	0.0	0.0	0.0	0.0	0.2	3.9	na

High and Low temperatures in degrees Fahrenheit; Precipitation and Snow in inches

Weather Station: Wanakena Ranger School   Elevation: 1,509 feet

	Jan	Feb	Mar	Apr	May	Jun	Jul	Aug	Sep	Oct	Nov	Dec
High	26	29	39	51	66	74	78	75	67	55	42	31
Low	3	4	15	29	41	49	54	52	45	34	25	12
Precip	3.0	2.4	2.9	3.0	3.7	3.9	4.6	4.3	4.6	3.8	4.0	3.3
Snow	32.8	24.8	21.2	7.4	1.0	0.0	0.0	0.0	tr	1.2	12.9	26.7

High and Low temperatures in degrees Fahrenheit; Precipitation and Snow in inches

Population: 111,974 (1990); 111,931 (2000); 111,755 (2005); 111,508 (2010 projected); Race: 93.9% White, 2.8% Black, 0.9% Asian, 2.3% Hispanic of any race (2005); Density: 41.6 persons per square mile (2005); Average household size: 2.72 (2005); Median age: 36.4 (2005); Males per 100 females: 102.9 (2005).
Religion: Five largest groups: 31.3% Catholic Church, 5.2% The United Methodist Church, 2.1% Presbyterian Church (U.S.A.), 1.4% Episcopal Church, 0.9% United Church of Christ (2000).
Economy: Unemployment rate: 6.0% (2005); Total civilian labor force: 49,624 (2005); Leading industries: 21.8% health care and social assistance; 16.8% retail trade; 14.4% manufacturing (2003); Farms: 1,451 totaling 403,364 acres (2002); Companies that employ 500 or more persons: 5 (2003); Companies that employ 100 to 499 persons: 36 (2003); Companies that employ less than 100 persons: 2,108 (2003); Black-owned businesses: n/a (2002); Hispanic-owned businesses: n/a (2002); Women-owned businesses: 1,886 (2002); Retail sales per capita: $10,945 (2006). Single-family building permits issued: 233 (2005); Multi-family building permits issued: 2 (2005).
Income: Per capita income: $17,763 (2005); Median household income: $36,043 (2005); Average household income: $45,457 (2005); Percent of households with income of $100,000 or more: 7.1% (2005); Poverty rate: 15.2% (2003); Bankruptcy rate: 5.87% (2005).
Taxes: Total county taxes per capita: $525 (2004); County property taxes per capita: $247 (2004).
Education: Percent of population age 25 and over with: High school diploma (including GED) or higher: 79.3% (2005); Bachelor's degree or higher: 16.6% (2005); Master's degree or higher: 8.1% (2005).
Housing: Homeownership rate: 71.1% (2005); Median home value: $90,022 (2005); Median rent: $359 per month (2000); Median age of housing: 44 years (2000).
Health: Birth rate: 107.9 per 10,000 population (2004); Death rate: 96.5 per 10,000 population (2004); Age-adjusted cancer mortality rate: 234.9 deaths per 100,000 population (2002); Air Quality Index: 87.4% good, 12.6% moderate, 0.0% unhealthy for sensitive individuals, 0.0% unhealthy (percent of days in 2005); Number of physicians: 14.9 per 10,000 population (2004); Hospital beds: 47.1 per 10,000 population (2003); Hospital admissions: 1,210.4 per 10,000 population (2003).
Elections: 2004 Presidential election results: 43.2% Bush, 54.7% Kerry, 1.9% Nader, 0.2% Badnarik
National and State Parks: Adirondack State Park; Cedar Island State Park; Cold Spring Brook State Forest; Degrasse State Forest; Donnerville State Forest; Greenwood Creek State Forest; Higley Flow State Park; Jacques Cartier State Park; Orebed Creek State Forest; Saint Lawrence State Forest; Saint Lawrence State Forest Number 10; Saint Lawrence State Forest Number 12; Saint Lawrence State Forest Number 15; Saint Lawrence State Forest Number 2; Saint Lawrence State Forest Number 23; Saint Lawrence State Forest Number 28; Saint Lawrence State Forest Number 31; Saint Lawrence State Forest Number 6; Saint Lawrence State Forest Number 8; Saint Lawrence State Park; Silver Hill State Forest; Stammer Creek State Forest; Taylor Creek State Forest; Trout Lake State Forest; Whippoorwill Corners State Forest; Wilson Hill State Fish And Game Managemen
Additional Information Contacts

Saint Lawrence County Government	(315) 379-2276
http://www.co.st-lawrence.ny.us/	
City of Ogdensburg	(315) 393-3540
http://www.ogdensburg.org/	
Village of Canton	(315) 386-2871
http://www.village.canton.ny.us/	
Village of Massena	(315) 769-8625
http://village.massena.ny.us/	

Saint Lawrence County Communities

BRASHER (town). Covers a land area of 91.196 square miles and a water area of 0.890 square miles. Located at 44.87° N. Lat.; 74.71° W. Long.
Population: 2,124 (1990); 2,337 (2000); 2,244 (2005); 2,211 (2010 projected); Race: 96.4% White, 0.2% Black, 0.6% Asian, 1.2% Hispanic of any race (2005); Density: 24.6 persons per square mile (2005); Average household size: 2.43 (2005); Median age: 40.1 (2005); Males per 100 females: 95.6 (2005); Marriage status: 25.2% never married, 58.7% now married, 7.8% widowed, 8.3% divorced (2000); Foreign born: 1.7% (2000); Ancestry (includes multiple ancestries): 24.9% French (except Basque), 15.7% Irish, 12.2% United States or American, 9.8% Other groups, 8.2% English (2000).
Economy: Single-family building permits issued: 3 (2005); Multi-family building permits issued: 0 (2005); Employment by occupation: 11.6% management, 15.2% professional, 17.9% services, 23.0% sales, 0.9% farming, 13.9% construction, 17.5% production (2000).
Income: Per capita income: $20,396 (2005); Median household income: $36,220 (2005); Average household income: $49,510 (2005); Percent of households with income of $100,000 or more: 9.2% (2005); Poverty rate: 19.1% (2000).
Taxes: Total city taxes per capita: $194 (2004); City property taxes per capita: $183 (2004).

Education: Percent of population age 25 and over with: High school diploma (including GED) or higher: 75.9% (2005); Bachelor's degree or higher: 9.5% (2005); Master's degree or higher: 4.7% (2005).
Housing: Homeownership rate: 77.7% (2005); Median home value: $75,545 (2005); Median rent: $354 per month (2000); Median age of housing: 33 years (2000).
Transportation: Commute to work: 92.0% car, 0.7% public transportation, 2.8% walk, 4.5% work from home (2000); Travel time to work: 24.2% less than 15 minutes, 50.7% 15 to 30 minutes, 18.7% 30 to 45 minutes, 2.9% 45 to 60 minutes, 3.6% 60 minutes or more (2000)

BRASHER FALLS-WINTHROP (CDP). Covers a land area of 4.458 square miles and a water area of 0.106 square miles. Located at 44.80° N. Lat.; 74.77° W. Long.
Population: 1,271 (1990); 1,140 (2000); 1,110 (2005); 1,105 (2010 projected); Race: 98.2% White, 0.7% Black, 0.1% Asian, 0.5% Hispanic of any race (2005); Density: 249.0 persons per square mile (2005); Average household size: 2.24 (2005); Median age: 42.6 (2005); Males per 100 females: 89.1 (2005); Marriage status: 20.7% never married, 61.0% now married, 12.2% widowed, 6.0% divorced (2000); Foreign born: 3.2% (2000); Ancestry (includes multiple ancestries): 21.6% Irish, 21.1% French (except Basque), 11.7% English, 8.5% Italian, 6.7% United States or American (2000).
Economy: Employment by occupation: 10.4% management, 25.7% professional, 12.3% services, 22.5% sales, 2.2% farming, 16.5% construction, 10.4% production (2000).
Income: Per capita income: $20,133 (2005); Median household income: $34,603 (2005); Average household income: $44,591 (2005); Percent of households with income of $100,000 or more: 9.3% (2005); Poverty rate: 9.3% (2000).
Education: Percent of population age 25 and over with: High school diploma (including GED) or higher: 81.3% (2005); Bachelor's degree or higher: 15.1% (2005); Master's degree or higher: 7.6% (2005).
School District(s)
Brasher Falls Central School District (KG-12)
    2003-04 Enrollment: 1,027 . . . . (315) 389-5131
Housing: Homeownership rate: 65.9% (2005); Median home value: $87,671 (2005); Median rent: $323 per month (2000); Median age of housing: 59 years (2000).
Transportation: Commute to work: 92.3% car, 0.0% public transportation, 5.4% walk, 2.2% work from home (2000); Travel time to work: 32.1% less than 15 minutes, 44.4% 15 to 30 minutes, 19.2% 30 to 45 minutes, 0.5% 45 to 60 minutes, 3.8% 60 minutes or more (2000)

BRIER HILL (unincorporated postal area, zip code 13614). Covers a land area of 8.844 square miles and a water area of 0 square miles. Located at 44.54° N. Lat.; 75.70° W. Long. Elevation is 265 feet.
Population: 0 (2000); Race: 96.2% White, 0.0% Black, 0.0% Asian, 0.0% Hispanic of any race (2000); Density: 0.0 persons per square mile (2000); Age: 25.6% under 18, 18.8% over 64 (2000); Marriage status: 13.2% never married, 68.3% now married, 7.8% widowed, 10.7% divorced (2000); Foreign born: 1.5% (2000); Ancestry (includes multiple ancestries): 14.7% English, 12.0% United States or American, 10.9% Irish, 8.6% French (except Basque), 7.9% Other groups (2000).
Economy: Employment by occupation: 24.5% management, 19.8% professional, 20.8% services, 11.3% sales, 2.8% farming, 4.7% construction, 16.0% production (2000).
Income: Per capita income: $24,933 (2000); Median household income: $33,750 (2000); Poverty rate: 13.9% (2000).
Education: Percent of population age 25 and over with: High school diploma (including GED) or higher: 75.8% (2000); Bachelor's degree or higher: 14.4% (2000).
Housing: Homeownership rate: 78.3% (2000); Median home value: $56,500 (2000); Median rent: $320 per month (2000); Median age of housing: 51 years (2000).
Transportation: Commute to work: 88.7% car, 0.0% public transportation, 2.8% walk, 6.6% work from home (2000); Travel time to work: 29.3% less than 15 minutes, 36.4% 15 to 30 minutes, 19.2% 30 to 45 minutes, 6.1% 45 to 60 minutes, 9.1% 60 minutes or more (2000)

CANTON (village). Covers a land area of 3.236 square miles and a water area of 0.103 square miles. Located at 44.59° N. Lat.; 75.17° W. Long. Elevation is 409 feet.
Population: 6,495 (1990); 5,882 (2000); 5,887 (2005); 5,920 (2010 projected); Race: 90.1% White, 5.6% Black, 1.3% Asian, 2.5% Hispanic of any race (2005); Density: 1,819.5 persons per square mile (2005); Average household size: 3.84 (2005); Median age: 23.2 (2005); Males per 100 females: 99.4 (2005); Marriage status: 46.3% never married, 42.6% now married, 6.7% widowed, 4.4% divorced (2000); Foreign born: 5.1% (2000); Ancestry (includes multiple ancestries): 21.0% Irish, 18.1% English, 12.7% German, 9.5% French (except Basque), 7.9% Other groups (2000).
Economy: Single-family building permits issued: 1 (2005); Multi-family building permits issued: 0 (2005); Employment by occupation: 11.1% management, 35.7% professional, 16.8% services, 22.5% sales, 0.0% farming, 7.6% construction, 6.3% production (2000).
Income: Per capita income: $15,667 (2005); Median household income: $41,468 (2005); Average household income: $52,288 (2005); Percent of households with income of $100,000 or more: 11.9% (2005); Poverty rate: 15.6% (2000).
Education: Percent of population age 25 and over with: High school diploma (including GED) or higher: 90.6% (2005); Bachelor's degree or higher: 44.2% (2005); Master's degree or higher: 25.9% (2005).
School District(s)
Boces St Lawrence-Lewisboces St Lawrence-Lewis (UG-UG)
    2003-04 Enrollment: 527 . . . . (315) 386-4504
Canton Central School District (PK-12)
    2003-04 Enrollment: 1,513 . . . . (315) 386-8561
Four-year College(s)
SUNY College of Technology at Canton (Public)
    Fall 2004 Enrollment: 2,518. . . . . (315) 386-7011
    2005-06 Tuition: In-state $5,380; Out-of-state $8,240
St Lawrence University
    Fall 2004 Enrollment: 2,278. . . . . (315) 229-5011
    2005-06 Tuition: In-state $32,150; Out-of-state $32,150
Two-year College(s)
St Lawrence Lewis County BOCES-Practical Nursing Program (Public)
    Fall 2004 Enrollment: 22 . . . . (315) 353-6693
Housing: Homeownership rate: 47.4% (2005); Median home value: $119,818 (2005); Median rent: $379 per month (2000); Median age of housing: 47 years (2000).
Safety: Violent crime rate: 16.7 per 10,000 population; Property crime rate: 261.2 per 10,000 population (2004).
Newspapers: Saint Lawrence Plaindealer (General - Circulation 3,500)
Transportation: Commute to work: 66.7% car, 0.0% public transportation, 29.3% walk, 3.0% work from home (2000); Travel time to work: 66.2% less than 15 minutes, 19.6% 15 to 30 minutes, 6.5% 30 to 45 minutes, 2.9% 45 to 60 minutes, 4.8% 60 minutes or more (2000)
Additional Information Contacts
Canton Chamber of Commerce . . . . (315) 386-8255
    http://www.cantonnychamber.org
Saint Lawrence County Chamber of Commerce . . . . (315) 386-4000
    http://www.northcountryguide.com/slc-chamber
Village of Canton . . . . (315) 386-2871
    http://www.village.canton.ny.us/

CANTON (town). Covers a land area of 104.802 square miles and a water area of 1.093 square miles. Located at 44.57° N. Lat.; 75.19° W. Long. Elevation is 409 feet.
History: Seat of Saint Lawrence University and the State University of N.Y. College of Technology. Frederic Remington born here. Irving Bacheller born in nearby Pierrepont. Settled 1799, incorporated 1845.
Population: 11,120 (1990); 10,334 (2000); 10,421 (2005); 10,483 (2010 projected); Race: 93.6% White, 3.3% Black, 0.9% Asian, 1.9% Hispanic of any race (2005); Density: 99.4 persons per square mile (2005); Average household size: 3.19 (2005); Median age: 28.3 (2005); Males per 100 females: 98.5 (2005); Marriage status: 36.8% never married, 50.2% now married, 6.9% widowed, 6.0% divorced (2000); Foreign born: 3.2% (2000); Ancestry (includes multiple ancestries): 18.2% Irish, 17.4% English, 11.7% French (except Basque), 10.9% German, 9.2% United States or American (2000).
Economy: Food processing. In agricultural area: dairy products; corn, hay. Single-family building permits issued: 12 (2005); Multi-family building permits issued: 0 (2005); Employment by occupation: 13.2% management, 29.3% professional, 16.3% services, 21.3% sales, 1.2% farming, 8.0% construction, 10.7% production (2000).
Income: Per capita income: $16,496 (2005); Median household income: $39,512 (2005); Average household income: $48,858 (2005); Percent of households with income of $100,000 or more: 9.4% (2005); Poverty rate: 12.4% (2000).

Taxes: Total city taxes per capita: $78 (2004); City property taxes per capita: $69 (2004).
Education: Percent of population age 25 and over with: High school diploma (including GED) or higher: 85.9% (2005); Bachelor's degree or higher: 31.4% (2005); Master's degree or higher: 18.0% (2005).
Housing: Homeownership rate: 65.0% (2005); Median home value: $95,064 (2005); Median rent: $364 per month (2000); Median age of housing: 39 years (2000).
Transportation: Commute to work: 78.2% car, 0.1% public transportation, 17.3% walk, 3.9% work from home (2000); Travel time to work: 54.7% less than 15 minutes, 26.2% 15 to 30 minutes, 9.7% 30 to 45 minutes, 3.9% 45 to 60 minutes, 5.5% 60 minutes or more (2000)

CHASE MILLS (unincorporated postal area, zip code 13621). Covers a land area of 29.567 square miles and a water area of 0.079 square miles. Located at 44.85° N. Lat.; 75.06° W. Long. Elevation is 272 feet.
Population: 0 (2000); Race: 100.0% White, 0.0% Black, 0.0% Asian, 0.8% Hispanic of any race (2000); Density: 0.0 persons per square mile (2000); Age: 29.1% under 18, 10.9% over 64 (2000); Marriage status: 20.6% never married, 58.5% now married, 7.9% widowed, 13.0% divorced (2000); Foreign born: 1.1% (2000); Ancestry (includes multiple ancestries): 18.8% French (except Basque), 12.8% Irish, 11.0% French Canadian, 9.1% Other groups, 8.0% Scottish (2000).
Economy: Employment by occupation: 9.7% management, 20.5% professional, 14.3% services, 24.8% sales, 2.3% farming, 8.9% construction, 19.4% production (2000).
Income: Per capita income: $14,359 (2000); Median household income: $32,750 (2000); Poverty rate: 27.6% (2000).
Education: Percent of population age 25 and over with: High school diploma (including GED) or higher: 83.7% (2000); Bachelor's degree or higher: 16.9% (2000).
Housing: Homeownership rate: 78.5% (2000); Median home value: $46,200 (2000); Median rent: $255 per month (2000); Median age of housing: 37 years (2000).
Transportation: Commute to work: 96.0% car, 0.0% public transportation, 0.0% walk, 4.0% work from home (2000); Travel time to work: 27.5% less than 15 minutes, 37.1% 15 to 30 minutes, 26.7% 30 to 45 minutes, 7.9% 45 to 60 minutes, 0.8% 60 minutes or more (2000)

CHILDWOLD (unincorporated postal area, zip code 12922). Covers a land area of 214.606 square miles and a water area of 6.591 square miles. Located at 44.22° N. Lat.; 74.76° W. Long. Elevation is 1,628 feet.
Population: 0 (2000); Race: 100.0% White, 0.0% Black, 0.0% Asian, 0.0% Hispanic of any race (2000); Density: 0.0 persons per square mile (2000); Age: 9.2% under 18, 33.8% over 64 (2000); Marriage status: 18.6% never married, 61.0% now married, 10.2% widowed, 10.2% divorced (2000); Foreign born: 3.1% (2000); Ancestry (includes multiple ancestries): 23.1% English, 16.9% German, 13.8% Irish, 10.8% Other groups, 9.2% Scottish (2000).
Economy: Employment by occupation: 33.3% management, 6.7% professional, 13.3% services, 33.3% sales, 0.0% farming, 6.7% construction, 6.7% production (2000).
Income: Per capita income: $33,571 (2000); Median household income: $34,000 (2000); Poverty rate: 13.8% (2000).
Education: Percent of population age 25 and over with: High school diploma (including GED) or higher: 81.4% (2000); Bachelor's degree or higher: 27.1% (2000).
Housing: Homeownership rate: 87.9% (2000); Median home value: $65,000 (2000); Median rent: $375 per month (2000); Median age of housing: 37 years (2000).
Transportation: Commute to work: 53.3% car, 0.0% public transportation, 13.3% walk, 33.3% work from home (2000); Travel time to work: 55.0% less than 15 minutes, 25.0% 15 to 30 minutes, 10.0% 30 to 45 minutes, 10.0% 45 to 60 minutes, 0.0% 60 minutes or more (2000)

CLARE (town). Covers a land area of 96.605 square miles and a water area of 0.651 square miles. Located at 44.38° N. Lat.; 74.99° W. Long.
Population: 78 (1990); 112 (2000); 116 (2005); 116 (2010 projected); Race: 94.0% White, 0.0% Black, 0.0% Asian, 0.9% Hispanic of any race (2005); Density: 1.2 persons per square mile (2005); Average household size: 2.42 (2005); Median age: 43.2 (2005); Males per 100 females: 114.8 (2005); Marriage status: 20.0% never married, 64.4% now married, 2.2% widowed, 13.3% divorced (2000); Foreign born: 0.0% (2000); Ancestry (includes multiple ancestries): 21.4% United States or American, 16.2% English, 12.0% Italian, 12.0% German, 10.3% Other groups (2000).
Economy: Single-family building permits issued: 2 (2005); Multi-family building permits issued: 0 (2005); Employment by occupation: 17.5% management, 5.0% professional, 22.5% services, 10.0% sales, 12.5% farming, 20.0% construction, 12.5% production (2000).
Income: Per capita income: $15,129 (2005); Median household income: $31,667 (2005); Average household income: $36,563 (2005); Percent of households with income of $100,000 or more: 4.2% (2005); Poverty rate: 12.8% (2000).
Education: Percent of population age 25 and over with: High school diploma (including GED) or higher: 71.3% (2005); Bachelor's degree or higher: 8.8% (2005); Master's degree or higher: 5.0% (2005).
Housing: Homeownership rate: 79.2% (2005); Median home value: $115,000 (2005); Median rent: $300 per month (2000); Median age of housing: 35 years (2000).
Transportation: Commute to work: 90.0% car, 0.0% public transportation, 0.0% walk, 10.0% work from home (2000); Travel time to work: 22.2% less than 15 minutes, 27.8% 15 to 30 minutes, 38.9% 30 to 45 minutes, 5.6% 45 to 60 minutes, 5.6% 60 minutes or more (2000)

CLIFTON (town). Covers a land area of 135.130 square miles and a water area of 15.227 square miles. Located at 44.21° N. Lat.; 74.94° W. Long.
Population: 917 (1990); 791 (2000); 761 (2005); 747 (2010 projected); Race: 96.5% White, 0.0% Black, 0.0% Asian, 2.1% Hispanic of any race (2005); Density: 5.6 persons per square mile (2005); Average household size: 2.39 (2005); Median age: 44.8 (2005); Males per 100 females: 97.2 (2005); Marriage status: 23.6% never married, 60.2% now married, 12.1% widowed, 4.1% divorced (2000); Foreign born: 1.6% (2000); Ancestry (includes multiple ancestries): 19.7% French (except Basque), 18.6% English, 17.5% Irish, 10.5% United States or American, 9.7% German (2000).
Economy: Single-family building permits issued: 1 (2005); Multi-family building permits issued: 0 (2005); Employment by occupation: 5.1% management, 19.5% professional, 20.6% services, 16.3% sales, 0.0% farming, 10.9% construction, 27.6% production (2000).
Income: Per capita income: $17,896 (2005); Median household income: $37,750 (2005); Average household income: $42,822 (2005); Percent of households with income of $100,000 or more: 4.1% (2005); Poverty rate: 17.4% (2000).
Education: Percent of population age 25 and over with: High school diploma (including GED) or higher: 84.9% (2005); Bachelor's degree or higher: 13.6% (2005); Master's degree or higher: 6.9% (2005).
Housing: Homeownership rate: 83.3% (2005); Median home value: $64,063 (2005); Median rent: $295 per month (2000); Median age of housing: 42 years (2000).
Transportation: Commute to work: 89.9% car, 0.0% public transportation, 7.7% walk, 1.6% work from home (2000); Travel time to work: 41.6% less than 15 minutes, 17.7% 15 to 30 minutes, 7.4% 30 to 45 minutes, 9.9% 45 to 60 minutes, 23.5% 60 minutes or more (2000)

COLTON (town). Covers a land area of 242.093 square miles and a water area of 12.838 square miles. Located at 44.47° N. Lat.; 74.85° W. Long. Elevation is 864 feet.
Population: 1,274 (1990); 1,453 (2000); 1,469 (2005); 1,475 (2010 projected); Race: 99.2% White, 0.0% Black, 0.1% Asian, 1.3% Hispanic of any race (2005); Density: 6.1 persons per square mile (2005); Average household size: 2.35 (2005); Median age: 44.4 (2005); Males per 100 females: 101.0 (2005); Marriage status: 20.7% never married, 61.9% now married, 8.1% widowed, 9.3% divorced (2000); Foreign born: 2.3% (2000); Ancestry (includes multiple ancestries): 25.2% Irish, 18.3% English, 14.5% French (except Basque), 7.9% French Canadian, 7.5% United States or American (2000).
Economy: Single-family building permits issued: 9 (2005); Multi-family building permits issued: 0 (2005); Employment by occupation: 9.8% management, 25.0% professional, 17.3% services, 23.0% sales, 1.3% farming, 12.5% construction, 11.1% production (2000).
Income: Per capita income: $22,939 (2005); Median household income: $42,388 (2005); Average household income: $53,798 (2005); Percent of households with income of $100,000 or more: 9.9% (2005); Poverty rate: 14.7% (2000).
Education: Percent of population age 25 and over with: High school diploma (including GED) or higher: 86.3% (2005); Bachelor's degree or higher: 26.3% (2005); Master's degree or higher: 14.3% (2005).

School District(s)
Colton-Pierrepont Central School District (PK-12)
    2003-04 Enrollment: 408 . . . . (315) 262-2100
Housing: Homeownership rate: 85.1% (2005); Median home value: $117,763 (2005); Median rent: $355 per month (2000); Median age of housing: 35 years (2000).
Transportation: Commute to work: 92.4% car, 0.0% public transportation, 4.1% walk, 2.4% work from home (2000); Travel time to work: 21.6% less than 15 minutes, 37.2% 15 to 30 minutes, 20.8% 30 to 45 minutes, 13.5% 45 to 60 minutes, 6.9% 60 minutes or more (2000)

DE KALB (town). Aka Old De Kalb. Covers a land area of 82.529 square miles and a water area of 0.685 square miles. Located at 44.47° N. Lat.; 75.35° W. Long. Elevation is 441 feet.
Population: 2,153 (1990); 2,213 (2000); 2,310 (2005); 2,341 (2010 projected); Race: 98.3% White, 0.3% Black, 0.0% Asian, 0.4% Hispanic of any race (2005); Density: 28.0 persons per square mile (2005); Average household size: 2.73 (2005); Median age: 35.5 (2005); Males per 100 females: 100.3 (2005); Marriage status: 26.5% never married, 60.1% now married, 5.9% widowed, 7.6% divorced (2000); Foreign born: 1.5% (2000); Ancestry (includes multiple ancestries): 14.8% English, 12.8% United States or American, 11.5% Irish, 10.7% German, 9.8% French (except Basque) (2000).
Economy: Single-family building permits issued: 11 (2005); Multi-family building permits issued: 0 (2005); Employment by occupation: 13.3% management, 18.1% professional, 20.9% services, 19.5% sales, 3.3% farming, 11.3% construction, 13.7% production (2000).
Income: Per capita income: $17,010 (2005); Median household income: $38,062 (2005); Average household income: $46,393 (2005); Percent of households with income of $100,000 or more: 6.2% (2005); Poverty rate: 15.7% (2000).
Education: Percent of population age 25 and over with: High school diploma (including GED) or higher: 78.9% (2005); Bachelor's degree or higher: 11.2% (2005); Master's degree or higher: 6.2% (2005).
Housing: Homeownership rate: 80.1% (2005); Median home value: $73,636 (2005); Median rent: $354 per month (2000); Median age of housing: 60+ years (2000).
Transportation: Commute to work: 89.5% car, 0.0% public transportation, 3.1% walk, 6.5% work from home (2000); Travel time to work: 23.0% less than 15 minutes, 47.0% 15 to 30 minutes, 14.5% 30 to 45 minutes, 7.7% 45 to 60 minutes, 7.7% 60 minutes or more (2000)

DE KALB JUNCTION (unincorporated postal area, zip code 13630). Covers a land area of 49.922 square miles and a water area of 0.027 square miles. Located at 44.49° N. Lat.; 75.29° W. Long.
Population: 0 (2000); Race: 98.4% White, 0.4% Black, 0.0% Asian, 0.6% Hispanic of any race (2000); Density: 0.0 persons per square mile (2000); Age: 28.5% under 18, 13.1% over 64 (2000); Marriage status: 28.2% never married, 56.0% now married, 7.5% widowed, 8.3% divorced (2000); Foreign born: 1.0% (2000); Ancestry (includes multiple ancestries): 14.9% English, 14.2% Irish, 9.9% United States or American, 9.8% German, 9.5% French (except Basque) (2000).
Economy: Employment by occupation: 11.7% management, 20.3% professional, 17.4% services, 21.5% sales, 4.1% farming, 12.4% construction, 12.7% production (2000).
Income: Per capita income: $14,171 (2000); Median household income: $33,603 (2000); Poverty rate: 15.8% (2000).
Education: Percent of population age 25 and over with: High school diploma (including GED) or higher: 77.3% (2000); Bachelor's degree or higher: 14.2% (2000).
School District(s)
Hermon-Dekalb Central School District (PK-12)
    2003-04 Enrollment: 414 . . . . (315) 347-3442
Housing: Homeownership rate: 84.7% (2000); Median home value: $44,400 (2000); Median rent: $352 per month (2000); Median age of housing: 54 years (2000).
Transportation: Commute to work: 91.3% car, 0.0% public transportation, 3.0% walk, 4.9% work from home (2000); Travel time to work: 26.1% less than 15 minutes, 45.6% 15 to 30 minutes, 17.3% 30 to 45 minutes, 5.1% 45 to 60 minutes, 5.8% 60 minutes or more (2000)

DE PEYSTER (town). Covers a land area of 43.063 square miles and a water area of 2.046 square miles. Located at 44.54° N. Lat.; 75.46° W. Long. Elevation is 376 feet.
Population: 913 (1990); 936 (2000); 899 (2005); 865 (2010 projected); Race: 98.2% White, 1.4% Black, 0.0% Asian, 0.6% Hispanic of any race (2005); Density: 20.9 persons per square mile (2005); Average household size: 3.37 (2005); Median age: 29.4 (2005); Males per 100 females: 102.5 (2005); Marriage status: 28.2% never married, 62.3% now married, 4.8% widowed, 4.8% divorced (2000); Foreign born: 1.2% (2000); Ancestry (includes multiple ancestries): 17.5% German, 14.9% French (except Basque), 13.4% Irish, 9.8% English, 9.6% United States or American (2000).
Economy: Single-family building permits issued: 3 (2005); Multi-family building permits issued: 0 (2005); Employment by occupation: 20.7% management, 9.3% professional, 16.7% services, 20.7% sales, 2.5% farming, 10.8% construction, 19.3% production (2000).
Income: Per capita income: $12,781 (2005); Median household income: $33,625 (2005); Average household income: $43,034 (2005); Percent of households with income of $100,000 or more: 6.7% (2005); Poverty rate: 27.2% (2000).
Taxes: Total city taxes per capita: $154 (2004); City property taxes per capita: $150 (2004).
Education: Percent of population age 25 and over with: High school diploma (including GED) or higher: 66.1% (2005); Bachelor's degree or higher: 7.8% (2005); Master's degree or higher: 2.4% (2005).
Housing: Homeownership rate: 85.8% (2005); Median home value: $66,098 (2005); Median rent: $354 per month (2000); Median age of housing: 60+ years (2000).
Transportation: Commute to work: 68.0% car, 0.0% public transportation, 4.3% walk, 23.6% work from home (2000); Travel time to work: 30.9% less than 15 minutes, 43.8% 15 to 30 minutes, 12.1% 30 to 45 minutes, 4.5% 45 to 60 minutes, 8.7% 60 minutes or more (2000)

EDWARDS (village). Covers a land area of 0.974 square miles and a water area of 0.012 square miles. Located at 44.32° N. Lat.; 75.25° W. Long. Elevation is 681 feet.
Population: 487 (1990); 465 (2000); 427 (2005); 413 (2010 projected); Race: 96.5% White, 0.7% Black, 0.0% Asian, 1.9% Hispanic of any race (2005); Density: 438.2 persons per square mile (2005); Average household size: 2.57 (2005); Median age: 38.1 (2005); Males per 100 females: 88.1 (2005); Marriage status: 29.0% never married, 52.1% now married, 10.4% widowed, 8.5% divorced (2000); Foreign born: 0.0% (2000); Ancestry (includes multiple ancestries): 19.6% United States or American, 16.6% Irish, 16.4% French (except Basque), 12.4% Other groups, 12.0% English (2000).
Economy: Single-family building permits issued: 1 (2005); Multi-family building permits issued: 0 (2005); Employment by occupation: 5.9% management, 21.9% professional, 19.5% services, 22.5% sales, 3.6% farming, 16.6% construction, 10.1% production (2000).
Income: Per capita income: $13,776 (2005); Median household income: $34,444 (2005); Average household income: $35,437 (2005); Percent of households with income of $100,000 or more: 1.8% (2005); Poverty rate: 16.8% (2000).
Education: Percent of population age 25 and over with: High school diploma (including GED) or higher: 82.5% (2005); Bachelor's degree or higher: 9.1% (2005); Master's degree or higher: 5.5% (2005).
Housing: Homeownership rate: 69.3% (2005); Median home value: $55,333 (2005); Median rent: $156 per month (2000); Median age of housing: 60+ years (2000).
Transportation: Commute to work: 89.8% car, 0.0% public transportation, 2.4% walk, 6.6% work from home (2000); Travel time to work: 27.7% less than 15 minutes, 29.7% 15 to 30 minutes, 25.2% 30 to 45 minutes, 8.4% 45 to 60 minutes, 9.0% 60 minutes or more (2000)

EDWARDS (town). Covers a land area of 50.741 square miles and a water area of 0.599 square miles. Located at 44.31° N. Lat.; 75.26° W. Long. Elevation is 681 feet.
Population: 1,083 (1990); 1,148 (2000); 1,056 (2005); 1,019 (2010 projected); Race: 97.6% White, 0.6% Black, 0.0% Asian, 1.4% Hispanic of any race (2005); Density: 20.8 persons per square mile (2005); Average household size: 2.62 (2005); Median age: 37.6 (2005); Males per 100 females: 90.6 (2005); Marriage status: 23.2% never married, 61.2% now married, 7.7% widowed, 7.9% divorced (2000); Foreign born: 0.0% (2000); Ancestry (includes multiple ancestries): 21.5% United States or American, 14.9% French (except Basque), 14.4% Irish, 13.4% English, 9.8% Other groups (2000).
Economy: In dairying area. Single-family building permits issued: 5 (2005); Multi-family building permits issued: 0 (2005); Employment by occupation:

7.3% management, 16.1% professional, 16.1% services, 17.8% sales, 7.8% farming, 18.8% construction, 16.1% production (2000).
Income: Per capita income: $16,061 (2005); Median household income: $36,016 (2005); Average household income: $42,084 (2005); Percent of households with income of $100,000 or more: 5.0% (2005); Poverty rate: 19.3% (2000).
Education: Percent of population age 25 and over with: High school diploma (including GED) or higher: 78.2% (2005); Bachelor's degree or higher: 8.1% (2005); Master's degree or higher: 5.4% (2005).
Housing: Homeownership rate: 76.7% (2005); Median home value: $65,156 (2005); Median rent: $275 per month (2000); Median age of housing: 47 years (2000).
Transportation: Commute to work: 89.3% car, 0.0% public transportation, 2.7% walk, 7.5% work from home (2000); Travel time to work: 30.2% less than 15 minutes, 31.0% 15 to 30 minutes, 22.1% 30 to 45 minutes, 7.8% 45 to 60 minutes, 8.9% 60 minutes or more (2000)

FINE (town). Covers a land area of 167.124 square miles and a water area of 2.305 square miles. Located at 44.21° N. Lat.; 75.09° W. Long. Elevation is 960 feet.
Population: 1,813 (1990); 1,622 (2000); 1,585 (2005); 1,545 (2010 projected); Race: 96.9% White, 0.9% Black, 0.5% Asian, 0.4% Hispanic of any race (2005); Density: 9.5 persons per square mile (2005); Average household size: 2.38 (2005); Median age: 44.7 (2005); Males per 100 females: 96.7 (2005); Marriage status: 22.3% never married, 60.1% now married, 9.5% widowed, 8.1% divorced (2000); Foreign born: 1.8% (2000); Ancestry (includes multiple ancestries): 15.4% French (except Basque), 14.0% United States or American, 13.7% Irish, 12.8% English, 11.0% French Canadian (2000).
Economy: Single-family building permits issued: 6 (2005); Multi-family building permits issued: 0 (2005); Employment by occupation: 10.6% management, 17.1% professional, 16.4% services, 22.0% sales, 1.8% farming, 8.9% construction, 23.2% production (2000).
Income: Per capita income: $19,699 (2005); Median household income: $36,512 (2005); Average household income: $46,128 (2005); Percent of households with income of $100,000 or more: 7.2% (2005); Poverty rate: 17.3% (2000).
Education: Percent of population age 25 and over with: High school diploma (including GED) or higher: 75.7% (2005); Bachelor's degree or higher: 10.5% (2005); Master's degree or higher: 3.6% (2005).
Housing: Homeownership rate: 82.4% (2005); Median home value: $65,051 (2005); Median rent: $329 per month (2000); Median age of housing: 46 years (2000).
Transportation: Commute to work: 91.0% car, 0.0% public transportation, 4.1% walk, 3.6% work from home (2000); Travel time to work: 46.8% less than 15 minutes, 19.4% 15 to 30 minutes, 9.5% 30 to 45 minutes, 13.1% 45 to 60 minutes, 11.3% 60 minutes or more (2000)

FOWLER (town). Covers a land area of 59.518 square miles and a water area of 1.182 square miles. Located at 44.28° N. Lat.; 75.41° W. Long. Elevation is 588 feet.
Population: 1,885 (1990); 2,180 (2000); 2,127 (2005); 2,094 (2010 projected); Race: 99.4% White, 0.1% Black, 0.0% Asian, 0.8% Hispanic of any race (2005); Density: 35.7 persons per square mile (2005); Average household size: 2.63 (2005); Median age: 38.2 (2005); Males per 100 females: 99.9 (2005); Marriage status: 22.0% never married, 64.1% now married, 6.7% widowed, 7.2% divorced (2000); Foreign born: 0.5% (2000); Ancestry (includes multiple ancestries): 17.3% United States or American, 13.3% English, 12.6% Irish, 12.3% French (except Basque), 8.8% Other groups (2000).
Economy: Single-family building permits issued: 9 (2005); Multi-family building permits issued: 0 (2005); Employment by occupation: 9.5% management, 12.8% professional, 19.0% services, 26.7% sales, 1.0% farming, 16.1% construction, 14.9% production (2000).
Income: Per capita income: $18,420 (2005); Median household income: $40,447 (2005); Average household income: $48,179 (2005); Percent of households with income of $100,000 or more: 8.0% (2005); Poverty rate: 12.0% (2000).
Education: Percent of population age 25 and over with: High school diploma (including GED) or higher: 77.0% (2005); Bachelor's degree or higher: 7.5% (2005); Master's degree or higher: 3.1% (2005).
Housing: Homeownership rate: 84.8% (2005); Median home value: $97,921 (2005); Median rent: $333 per month (2000); Median age of housing: 29 years (2000).
Transportation: Commute to work: 92.2% car, 0.2% public transportation, 1.0% walk, 6.1% work from home (2000); Travel time to work: 48.0% less than 15 minutes, 25.9% 15 to 30 minutes, 9.9% 30 to 45 minutes, 9.0% 45 to 60 minutes, 7.2% 60 minutes or more (2000)

GOUVERNEUR (village). Covers a land area of 2.127 square miles and a water area of 0.060 square miles. Located at 44.33° N. Lat.; 75.46° W. Long. Elevation is 447 feet.
Population: 4,604 (1990); 4,263 (2000); 4,092 (2005); 3,964 (2010 projected); Race: 93.1% White, 2.4% Black, 0.5% Asian, 4.0% Hispanic of any race (2005); Density: 1,924.0 persons per square mile (2005); Average household size: 2.50 (2005); Median age: 33.7 (2005); Males per 100 females: 90.2 (2005); Marriage status: 22.7% never married, 59.3% now married, 8.9% widowed, 9.1% divorced (2000); Foreign born: 1.2% (2000); Ancestry (includes multiple ancestries): 17.4% United States or American, 12.8% Irish, 11.5% Other groups, 10.9% English, 10.0% French (except Basque) (2000).
Economy: Single-family building permits issued: 0 (2005); Multi-family building permits issued: 0 (2005); Employment by occupation: 6.0% management, 16.3% professional, 23.4% services, 24.7% sales, 1.3% farming, 12.2% construction, 16.0% production (2000).
Income: Per capita income: $13,993 (2005); Median household income: $26,634 (2005); Average household income: $34,438 (2005); Percent of households with income of $100,000 or more: 2.4% (2005); Poverty rate: 18.3% (2000).
Education: Percent of population age 25 and over with: High school diploma (including GED) or higher: 82.6% (2005); Bachelor's degree or higher: 10.1% (2005); Master's degree or higher: 3.7% (2005).
School District(s)
Gouverneur Central School District (KG-12)
    2003-04 Enrollment: 1,743 . . . . (315) 287-4870
Housing: Homeownership rate: 53.0% (2005); Median home value: $68,379 (2005); Median rent: $333 per month (2000); Median age of housing: 60+ years (2000).
Hospitals: EJ Noble Hospital of Gouverneur (87 beds)
Newspapers: Gouverneur Tribune Press (General - Circulation 4,200)
Transportation: Commute to work: 86.0% car, 2.0% public transportation, 9.2% walk, 1.7% work from home (2000); Travel time to work: 54.2% less than 15 minutes, 15.0% 15 to 30 minutes, 15.3% 30 to 45 minutes, 9.8% 45 to 60 minutes, 5.8% 60 minutes or more (2000)
Additional Information Contacts
Gouverneur Chamber of Commerce . . . . (315) 287-0331
   http://www.gouverneurchamber.net

GOUVERNEUR (town). Covers a land area of 71.538 square miles and a water area of 0.902 square miles. Located at 44.34° N. Lat.; 75.47° W. Long. Elevation is 447 feet.
History: Named for Gouverneur Morris, whose mansion still stands. Laid out 1787, Incorporated 1850.
Population: 6,986 (1990); 7,418 (2000); 7,326 (2005); 7,213 (2010 projected); Race: 80.8% White, 12.6% Black, 0.5% Asian, 8.9% Hispanic of any race (2005); Density: 102.4 persons per square mile (2005); Average household size: 2.95 (2005); Median age: 34.5 (2005); Males per 100 females: 125.6 (2005); Marriage status: 31.9% never married, 53.0% now married, 6.8% widowed, 8.4% divorced (2000); Foreign born: 3.0% (2000); Ancestry (includes multiple ancestries): 13.9% United States or American, 11.2% Irish, 10.1% Other groups, 10.0% English, 9.0% French (except Basque) (2000).
Economy: Manufacturing of textiles, clothing, paper, cheese and feed. The mineral sphalerite is extensively mined, yielding zinc, lead and silver in sizable commerical amounts; talc, wollastonite, and limestone quarries; talc mills. Dairying. Employment by occupation: 8.8% management, 17.4% professional, 22.0% services, 21.6% sales, 1.8% farming, 10.9% construction, 17.5% production (2000).
Income: Per capita income: $15,005 (2005); Median household income: $29,373 (2005); Average household income: $35,336 (2005); Percent of households with income of $100,000 or more: 2.1% (2005); Poverty rate: 19.7% (2000).
Education: Percent of population age 25 and over with: High school diploma (including GED) or higher: 69.0% (2005); Bachelor's degree or higher: 8.6% (2005); Master's degree or higher: 3.0% (2005).
Housing: Homeownership rate: 61.7% (2005); Median home value: $71,190 (2005); Median rent: $336 per month (2000); Median age of housing: 50 years (2000).

Transportation: Commute to work: 86.0% car, 1.3% public transportation, 7.9% walk, 4.2% work from home (2000); Travel time to work: 54.3% less than 15 minutes, 14.5% 15 to 30 minutes, 13.9% 30 to 45 minutes, 10.3% 45 to 60 minutes, 7.0% 60 minutes or more (2000)

HAMMOND (village).
Covers a land area of 0.585 square miles and a water area of 0 square miles. Located at 44.44° N. Lat.; 75.69° W. Long. Elevation is 360 feet.
Population: 270 (1990); 302 (2000); 305 (2005); 305 (2010 projected); Race: 98.7% White, 0.0% Black, 0.0% Asian, 0.0% Hispanic of any race (2005); Density: 521.6 persons per square mile (2005); Average household size: 2.35 (2005); Median age: 37.9 (2005); Males per 100 females: 83.7 (2005); Marriage status: 22.1% never married, 62.1% now married, 9.8% widowed, 6.0% divorced (2000); Foreign born: 0.7% (2000); Ancestry (includes multiple ancestries): 15.6% English, 15.0% French (except Basque), 14.6% United States or American, 10.0% German, 9.3% Scottish (2000).
Economy: Single-family building permits issued: 0 (2005); Multi-family building permits issued: 0 (2005); Employment by occupation: 22.9% management, 6.3% professional, 22.9% services, 29.2% sales, 0.0% farming, 10.4% construction, 8.3% production (2000).
Income: Per capita income: $12,705 (2005); Median household income: $22,692 (2005); Average household income: $29,808 (2005); Percent of households with income of $100,000 or more: 3.1% (2005); Poverty rate: 15.0% (2000).
Education: Percent of population age 25 and over with: High school diploma (including GED) or higher: 77.2% (2005); Bachelor's degree or higher: 15.5% (2005); Master's degree or higher: 5.2% (2005).

School District(s)
Hammond Central School District (KG-12)
    2003-04 Enrollment: 329 . . . . (315) 324-5931

Housing: Homeownership rate: 57.7% (2005); Median home value: $60,556 (2005); Median rent: $289 per month (2000); Median age of housing: 60+ years (2000).
Transportation: Commute to work: 71.3% car, 0.0% public transportation, 19.1% walk, 9.6% work from home (2000); Travel time to work: 60.0% less than 15 minutes, 12.9% 15 to 30 minutes, 2.4% 30 to 45 minutes, 11.8% 45 to 60 minutes, 12.9% 60 minutes or more (2000)

Additional Information Contacts
Black Lake Chamber of Commerce . . . . (315) 578-2895
    http://www.blacklakeny.com

HAMMOND (town).
Covers a land area of 62.222 square miles and a water area of 15.685 square miles. Located at 44.43° N. Lat.; 75.73° W. Long. Elevation is 360 feet.
Population: 1,168 (1990); 1,207 (2000); 1,197 (2005); 1,200 (2010 projected); Race: 97.4% White, 0.6% Black, 0.0% Asian, 0.4% Hispanic of any race (2005); Density: 19.2 persons per square mile (2005); Average household size: 2.36 (2005); Median age: 41.8 (2005); Males per 100 females: 98.5 (2005); Marriage status: 23.4% never married, 61.7% now married, 8.5% widowed, 6.5% divorced (2000); Foreign born: 3.3% (2000); Ancestry (includes multiple ancestries): 19.5% English, 13.3% Irish, 12.3% United States or American, 11.6% French (except Basque), 11.2% German (2000).
Economy: Timber. Agriculture: dairying; grain, hay. Single-family building permits issued: 8 (2005); Multi-family building permits issued: 0 (2005); Employment by occupation: 15.5% management, 13.4% professional, 17.0% services, 21.8% sales, 4.1% farming, 12.3% construction, 15.9% production (2000).
Income: Per capita income: $15,971 (2005); Median household income: $28,393 (2005); Average household income: $37,707 (2005); Percent of households with income of $100,000 or more: 5.7% (2005); Poverty rate: 19.0% (2000).
Education: Percent of population age 25 and over with: High school diploma (including GED) or higher: 79.2% (2005); Bachelor's degree or higher: 15.5% (2005); Master's degree or higher: 8.5% (2005).
Housing: Homeownership rate: 75.9% (2005); Median home value: $93,273 (2005); Median rent: $277 per month (2000); Median age of housing: 44 years (2000).
Transportation: Commute to work: 79.1% car, 1.4% public transportation, 7.8% walk, 10.1% work from home (2000); Travel time to work: 42.2% less than 15 minutes, 18.4% 15 to 30 minutes, 19.2% 30 to 45 minutes, 10.2% 45 to 60 minutes, 10.0% 60 minutes or more (2000)

HERMON (village).
Covers a land area of 0.378 square miles and a water area of 0 square miles. Located at 44.46° N. Lat.; 75.22° W. Long. Elevation is 500 feet.
Population: 407 (1990); 402 (2000); 366 (2005); 355 (2010 projected); Race: 97.8% White, 1.9% Black, 0.0% Asian, 0.8% Hispanic of any race (2005); Density: 968.7 persons per square mile (2005); Average household size: 2.60 (2005); Median age: 39.3 (2005); Males per 100 females: 103.3 (2005); Marriage status: 26.5% never married, 57.3% now married, 7.9% widowed, 8.3% divorced (2000); Foreign born: 1.5% (2000); Ancestry (includes multiple ancestries): 20.8% English, 16.8% United States or American, 9.0% French (except Basque), 5.8% German, 5.5% Irish (2000).
Economy: Single-family building permits issued: 0 (2005); Multi-family building permits issued: 0 (2005); Employment by occupation: 5.9% management, 14.5% professional, 28.9% services, 19.1% sales, 2.0% farming, 9.9% construction, 19.7% production (2000).
Income: Per capita income: $16,936 (2005); Median household income: $37,750 (2005); Average household income: $42,624 (2005); Percent of households with income of $100,000 or more: 5.7% (2005); Poverty rate: 21.3% (2000).
Education: Percent of population age 25 and over with: High school diploma (including GED) or higher: 76.9% (2005); Bachelor's degree or higher: 12.7% (2005); Master's degree or higher: 5.6% (2005).
Housing: Homeownership rate: 75.9% (2005); Median home value: $53,696 (2005); Median rent: $313 per month (2000); Median age of housing: 60+ years (2000).
Transportation: Commute to work: 92.6% car, 0.0% public transportation, 4.7% walk, 0.0% work from home (2000); Travel time to work: 20.9% less than 15 minutes, 50.7% 15 to 30 minutes, 20.3% 30 to 45 minutes, 3.4% 45 to 60 minutes, 4.7% 60 minutes or more (2000)

HERMON (town).
Covers a land area of 53.444 square miles and a water area of 0.752 square miles. Located at 44.40° N. Lat.; 75.27° W. Long. Elevation is 500 feet.
Population: 1,041 (1990); 1,069 (2000); 973 (2005); 941 (2010 projected); Race: 97.8% White, 0.9% Black, 1.0% Asian, 0.5% Hispanic of any race (2005); Density: 18.2 persons per square mile (2005); Average household size: 2.62 (2005); Median age: 38.7 (2005); Males per 100 females: 106.6 (2005); Marriage status: 25.2% never married, 57.7% now married, 8.0% widowed, 9.1% divorced (2000); Foreign born: 0.6% (2000); Ancestry (includes multiple ancestries): 18.6% English, 16.5% United States or American, 9.4% Irish, 8.6% French (except Basque), 6.2% Other groups (2000).
Economy: Single-family building permits issued: 9 (2005); Multi-family building permits issued: 0 (2005); Employment by occupation: 8.9% management, 16.5% professional, 22.5% services, 23.4% sales, 1.6% farming, 13.8% construction, 13.3% production (2000).
Income: Per capita income: $16,563 (2005); Median household income: $40,335 (2005); Average household income: $42,931 (2005); Percent of households with income of $100,000 or more: 3.5% (2005); Poverty rate: 19.6% (2000).
Education: Percent of population age 25 and over with: High school diploma (including GED) or higher: 80.0% (2005); Bachelor's degree or higher: 11.9% (2005); Master's degree or higher: 4.3% (2005).
Housing: Homeownership rate: 84.1% (2005); Median home value: $69,231 (2005); Median rent: $310 per month (2000); Median age of housing: 47 years (2000).
Transportation: Commute to work: 92.5% car, 0.0% public transportation, 2.1% walk, 3.8% work from home (2000); Travel time to work: 20.6% less than 15 minutes, 45.1% 15 to 30 minutes, 22.5% 30 to 45 minutes, 5.9% 45 to 60 minutes, 5.9% 60 minutes or more (2000)

HEUVELTON (village).
Covers a land area of 0.771 square miles and a water area of 0.094 square miles. Located at 44.61° N. Lat.; 75.40° W. Long. Elevation is 315 feet.
Population: 771 (1990); 804 (2000); 789 (2005); 789 (2010 projected); Race: 97.6% White, 0.6% Black, 0.1% Asian, 0.5% Hispanic of any race (2005); Density: 1,023.0 persons per square mile (2005); Average household size: 2.51 (2005); Median age: 40.5 (2005); Males per 100 females: 84.8 (2005); Marriage status: 23.3% never married, 56.6% now married, 8.6% widowed, 11.5% divorced (2000); Foreign born: 2.2% (2000); Ancestry (includes multiple ancestries): 20.2% English, 15.8% Irish, 15.1% French (except Basque), 9.2% United States or American, 9.1% French Canadian (2000).

Economy: Single-family building permits issued: 0 (2005); Multi-family building permits issued: 0 (2005); Employment by occupation: 11.2% management, 21.9% professional, 21.9% services, 20.8% sales, 0.3% farming, 5.9% construction, 18.0% production (2000).
Income: Per capita income: $17,755 (2005); Median household income: $35,984 (2005); Average household income: $44,236 (2005); Percent of households with income of $100,000 or more: 5.7% (2005); Poverty rate: 13.7% (2000).
Education: Percent of population age 25 and over with: High school diploma (including GED) or higher: 81.8% (2005); Bachelor's degree or higher: 15.5% (2005); Master's degree or higher: 8.6% (2005).

School District(s)
Heuvelton Central School District (PK-12)
    2003-04 Enrollment: 655 . . . . (315) 344-2414

Housing: Homeownership rate: 68.8% (2005); Median home value: $79,524 (2005); Median rent: $360 per month (2000); Median age of housing: 60+ years (2000).
Transportation: Commute to work: 82.0% car, 0.0% public transportation, 13.7% walk, 3.8% work from home (2000); Travel time to work: 46.2% less than 15 minutes, 38.1% 15 to 30 minutes, 7.3% 30 to 45 minutes, 5.4% 45 to 60 minutes, 3.0% 60 minutes or more (2000)

HOPKINTON (town). Covers a land area of 185.401 square miles and a water area of 1.616 square miles. Located at 44.63° N. Lat.; 74.70° W. Long. Elevation is 795 feet.
Population: 957 (1990); 1,020 (2000); 1,054 (2005); 1,079 (2010 projected); Race: 98.6% White, 0.1% Black, 0.0% Asian, 0.8% Hispanic of any race (2005); Density: 5.7 persons per square mile (2005); Average household size: 2.56 (2005); Median age: 38.4 (2005); Males per 100 females: 102.7 (2005); Marriage status: 20.0% never married, 61.2% now married, 7.4% widowed, 11.4% divorced (2000); Foreign born: 1.2% (2000); Ancestry (includes multiple ancestries): 22.6% French (except Basque), 18.5% English, 13.5% Irish, 11.0% German, 9.8% United States or American (2000).
Economy: Single-family building permits issued: 10 (2005); Multi-family building permits issued: 0 (2005); Employment by occupation: 7.1% management, 17.9% professional, 21.4% services, 20.0% sales, 5.5% farming, 10.8% construction, 17.2% production (2000).
Income: Per capita income: $15,102 (2005); Median household income: $33,774 (2005); Average household income: $38,729 (2005); Percent of households with income of $100,000 or more: 2.2% (2005); Poverty rate: 17.6% (2000).
Education: Percent of population age 25 and over with: High school diploma (including GED) or higher: 80.1% (2005); Bachelor's degree or higher: 12.2% (2005); Master's degree or higher: 5.4% (2005).
Housing: Homeownership rate: 79.8% (2005); Median home value: $73,134 (2005); Median rent: $338 per month (2000); Median age of housing: 37 years (2000).
Transportation: Commute to work: 93.6% car, 0.0% public transportation, 3.3% walk, 3.1% work from home (2000); Travel time to work: 17.7% less than 15 minutes, 33.7% 15 to 30 minutes, 30.3% 30 to 45 minutes, 7.5% 45 to 60 minutes, 10.7% 60 minutes or more (2000)

LAWRENCE (town). Covers a land area of 47.661 square miles and a water area of 0.026 square miles. Located at 44.75° N. Lat.; 74.66° W. Long.
Population: 1,516 (1990); 1,545 (2000); 1,566 (2005); 1,593 (2010 projected); Race: 98.5% White, 0.0% Black, 0.2% Asian, 1.0% Hispanic of any race (2005); Density: 32.9 persons per square mile (2005); Average household size: 2.58 (2005); Median age: 38.4 (2005); Males per 100 females: 99.2 (2005); Marriage status: 23.9% never married, 62.8% now married, 4.6% widowed, 8.6% divorced (2000); Foreign born: 1.9% (2000); Ancestry (includes multiple ancestries): 19.2% French (except Basque), 17.3% Irish, 11.9% English, 8.5% United States or American, 7.8% French Canadian (2000).
Economy: Single-family building permits issued: 7 (2005); Multi-family building permits issued: 0 (2005); Employment by occupation: 11.8% management, 11.6% professional, 21.8% services, 18.8% sales, 3.8% farming, 12.9% construction, 19.3% production (2000).
Income: Per capita income: $15,062 (2005); Median household income: $34,135 (2005); Average household income: $38,923 (2005); Percent of households with income of $100,000 or more: 2.1% (2005); Poverty rate: 16.4% (2000).
Education: Percent of population age 25 and over with: High school diploma (including GED) or higher: 79.7% (2005); Bachelor's degree or higher: 8.9% (2005); Master's degree or higher: 2.1% (2005).
Housing: Homeownership rate: 81.4% (2005); Median home value: $75,732 (2005); Median rent: $307 per month (2000); Median age of housing: 40 years (2000).
Transportation: Commute to work: 88.0% car, 0.0% public transportation, 5.7% walk, 5.7% work from home (2000); Travel time to work: 23.8% less than 15 minutes, 33.4% 15 to 30 minutes, 33.4% 30 to 45 minutes, 4.8% 45 to 60 minutes, 4.6% 60 minutes or more (2000)

LISBON (town). Covers a land area of 108.239 square miles and a water area of 5.431 square miles. Located at 44.70° N. Lat.; 75.32° W. Long. Elevation is 358 feet.
Population: 3,746 (1990); 4,047 (2000); 4,192 (2005); 4,325 (2010 projected); Race: 98.2% White, 0.2% Black, 0.3% Asian, 0.7% Hispanic of any race (2005); Density: 38.7 persons per square mile (2005); Average household size: 2.70 (2005); Median age: 38.4 (2005); Males per 100 females: 99.4 (2005); Marriage status: 22.8% never married, 63.2% now married, 5.7% widowed, 8.2% divorced (2000); Foreign born: 1.9% (2000); Ancestry (includes multiple ancestries): 16.9% French (except Basque), 16.7% Irish, 14.8% English, 13.7% German, 12.7% United States or American (2000).
Economy: Single-family building permits issued: 9 (2005); Multi-family building permits issued: 0 (2005); Employment by occupation: 12.6% management, 18.5% professional, 20.5% services, 20.5% sales, 7.1% farming, 7.4% construction, 13.4% production (2000).
Income: Per capita income: $18,663 (2005); Median household income: $41,804 (2005); Average household income: $50,172 (2005); Percent of households with income of $100,000 or more: 7.5% (2005); Poverty rate: 14.1% (2000).
Education: Percent of population age 25 and over with: High school diploma (including GED) or higher: 83.2% (2005); Bachelor's degree or higher: 15.2% (2005); Master's degree or higher: 5.1% (2005).

School District(s)
Lisbon Central School District (KG-12)
    2003-04 Enrollment: 552 . . . . (315) 393-4951

Housing: Homeownership rate: 84.1% (2005); Median home value: $109,831 (2005); Median rent: $352 per month (2000); Median age of housing: 33 years (2000).
Transportation: Commute to work: 85.5% car, 0.2% public transportation, 4.5% walk, 7.6% work from home (2000); Travel time to work: 43.1% less than 15 minutes, 36.1% 15 to 30 minutes, 12.7% 30 to 45 minutes, 3.8% 45 to 60 minutes, 4.4% 60 minutes or more (2000)

LOUISVILLE (town). Covers a land area of 48.157 square miles and a water area of 15.688 square miles. Located at 44.90° N. Lat.; 75.00° W. Long.
Population: 3,040 (1990); 3,195 (2000); 3,330 (2005); 3,455 (2010 projected); Race: 96.2% White, 0.4% Black, 1.7% Asian, 2.3% Hispanic of any race (2005); Density: 69.1 persons per square mile (2005); Average household size: 2.44 (2005); Median age: 42.5 (2005); Males per 100 females: 101.6 (2005); Marriage status: 21.2% never married, 65.2% now married, 4.4% widowed, 9.2% divorced (2000); Foreign born: 5.8% (2000); Ancestry (includes multiple ancestries): 24.4% French (except Basque), 15.7% Irish, 10.3% United States or American, 10.0% French Canadian, 7.5% English (2000).
Economy: Single-family building permits issued: 10 (2005); Multi-family building permits issued: 0 (2005); Employment by occupation: 10.4% management, 18.0% professional, 16.9% services, 23.5% sales, 0.4% farming, 10.8% construction, 20.0% production (2000).
Income: Per capita income: $22,586 (2005); Median household income: $44,490 (2005); Average household income: $55,222 (2005); Percent of households with income of $100,000 or more: 13.4% (2005); Poverty rate: 11.1% (2000).
Education: Percent of population age 25 and over with: High school diploma (including GED) or higher: 83.1% (2005); Bachelor's degree or higher: 17.2% (2005); Master's degree or higher: 8.8% (2005).
Housing: Homeownership rate: 81.0% (2005); Median home value: $112,318 (2005); Median rent: $451 per month (2000); Median age of housing: 33 years (2000).
Transportation: Commute to work: 94.5% car, 0.0% public transportation, 0.8% walk, 3.8% work from home (2000); Travel time to work: 41.3% less than 15 minutes, 39.3% 15 to 30 minutes, 12.4% 30 to 45 minutes, 4.7% 45 to 60 minutes, 2.3% 60 minutes or more (2000)

MACOMB (town). Covers a land area of 61.229 square miles and a water area of 1.937 square miles. Located at 44.46° N. Lat.; 75.58° W. Long.
Population: 789 (1990); 846 (2000); 901 (2005); 923 (2010 projected); Race: 97.8% White, 0.0% Black, 0.0% Asian, 0.7% Hispanic of any race (2005); Density: 14.7 persons per square mile (2005); Average household size: 2.67 (2005); Median age: 37.6 (2005); Males per 100 females: 105.2 (2005); Marriage status: 27.2% never married, 56.7% now married, 6.7% widowed, 9.4% divorced (2000); Foreign born: 0.9% (2000); Ancestry (includes multiple ancestries): 15.3% Irish, 14.5% English, 11.1% French (except Basque), 8.5% United States or American, 6.1% Other groups (2000).
Economy: Single-family building permits issued: 6 (2005); Multi-family building permits issued: 0 (2005); Employment by occupation: 12.7% management, 14.6% professional, 17.4% services, 18.7% sales, 6.3% farming, 14.6% construction, 15.7% production (2000).
Income: Per capita income: $13,577 (2005); Median household income: $32,586 (2005); Average household income: $36,191 (2005); Percent of households with income of $100,000 or more: 1.5% (2005); Poverty rate: 20.2% (2000).
Education: Percent of population age 25 and over with: High school diploma (including GED) or higher: 78.1% (2005); Bachelor's degree or higher: 11.9% (2005); Master's degree or higher: 5.4% (2005).
Housing: Homeownership rate: 83.7% (2005); Median home value: $81,563 (2005); Median rent: $330 per month (2000); Median age of housing: 38 years (2000).
Transportation: Commute to work: 85.2% car, 0.0% public transportation, 6.5% walk, 5.7% work from home (2000); Travel time to work: 16.6% less than 15 minutes, 34.9% 15 to 30 minutes, 28.0% 30 to 45 minutes, 10.8% 45 to 60 minutes, 9.6% 60 minutes or more (2000)

MADRID (town). Covers a land area of 52.933 square miles and a water area of 0.667 square miles. Located at 44.76° N. Lat.; 75.12° W. Long. Elevation is 310 feet.
Population: 1,568 (1990); 1,828 (2000); 1,907 (2005); 1,980 (2010 projected); Race: 97.3% White, 1.5% Black, 0.1% Asian, 1.3% Hispanic of any race (2005); Density: 36.0 persons per square mile (2005); Average household size: 2.77 (2005); Median age: 40.5 (2005); Males per 100 females: 102.4 (2005); Marriage status: 30.1% never married, 53.1% now married, 6.9% widowed, 9.9% divorced (2000); Foreign born: 1.2% (2000); Ancestry (includes multiple ancestries): 20.4% Irish, 16.7% French (except Basque), 12.7% English, 8.6% Other groups, 7.9% United States or American (2000).
Economy: Single-family building permits issued: 4 (2005); Multi-family building permits issued: 0 (2005); Employment by occupation: 11.1% management, 16.1% professional, 23.7% services, 20.0% sales, 3.8% farming, 13.6% construction, 11.6% production (2000).
Income: Per capita income: $16,544 (2005); Median household income: $37,759 (2005); Average household income: $45,486 (2005); Percent of households with income of $100,000 or more: 5.8% (2005); Poverty rate: 20.2% (2000).
Education: Percent of population age 25 and over with: High school diploma (including GED) or higher: 76.8% (2005); Bachelor's degree or higher: 13.2% (2005); Master's degree or higher: 4.6% (2005).
School District(s)
Madrid-Waddington Central School District (PK-12)
    2003-04 Enrollment: 822 . . . . (315) 322-5746
Housing: Homeownership rate: 78.5% (2005); Median home value: $81,845 (2005); Median rent: $389 per month (2000); Median age of housing: 43 years (2000).
Transportation: Commute to work: 89.2% car, 0.0% public transportation, 2.5% walk, 8.4% work from home (2000); Travel time to work: 23.6% less than 15 minutes, 44.7% 15 to 30 minutes, 24.6% 30 to 45 minutes, 2.8% 45 to 60 minutes, 4.3% 60 minutes or more (2000)

MASSENA (village). Covers a land area of 4.533 square miles and a water area of 0.181 square miles. Located at 44.93° N. Lat.; 74.89° W. Long. Elevation is 237 feet.
Population: 11,846 (1990); 11,209 (2000); 10,955 (2005); 10,713 (2010 projected); Race: 95.1% White, 0.4% Black, 1.0% Asian, 1.6% Hispanic of any race (2005); Density: 2,416.5 persons per square mile (2005); Average household size: 2.29 (2005); Median age: 40.9 (2005); Males per 100 females: 88.6 (2005); Marriage status: 25.8% never married, 55.6% now married, 10.1% widowed, 8.6% divorced (2000); Foreign born: 4.5% (2000); Ancestry (includes multiple ancestries): 25.9% French (except Basque), 18.6% Irish, 10.3% French Canadian, 10.2% English, 8.5% Other groups (2000).
Economy: Single-family building permits issued: 0 (2005); Multi-family building permits issued: 0 (2005); Employment by occupation: 10.0% management, 17.3% professional, 21.0% services, 26.1% sales, 0.2% farming, 9.1% construction, 16.4% production (2000).
Income: Per capita income: $19,278 (2005); Median household income: $33,641 (2005); Average household income: $43,149 (2005); Percent of households with income of $100,000 or more: 6.8% (2005); Poverty rate: 17.6% (2000).
Taxes: Total city taxes per capita: $334 (2004); City property taxes per capita: $308 (2004).
Education: Percent of population age 25 and over with: High school diploma (including GED) or higher: 82.7% (2005); Bachelor's degree or higher: 17.5% (2005); Master's degree or higher: 7.4% (2005).
School District(s)
Massena Central School District (KG-12)
    2003-04 Enrollment: 2,861 . . . . (315) 764-3700
Housing: Homeownership rate: 61.9% (2005); Median home value: $109,536 (2005); Median rent: $374 per month (2000); Median age of housing: 50 years (2000).
Hospitals: Massena Memorial Hospital
Safety: Violent crime rate: 8.2 per 10,000 population; Property crime rate: 273.6 per 10,000 population (2004).
Transportation: Commute to work: 91.4% car, 0.2% public transportation, 5.0% walk, 3.0% work from home (2000); Travel time to work: 63.7% less than 15 minutes, 22.7% 15 to 30 minutes, 7.9% 30 to 45 minutes, 2.6% 45 to 60 minutes, 3.1% 60 minutes or more (2000)
Additional Information Contacts
Massena Chamber of Commerce . . . . (315) 769-3525
    http://www.massenaworks.com/chamber
Village of Massena. . . . . (315) 769-8625
    http://village.massena.ny.us/

MASSENA (town). Covers a land area of 44.672 square miles and a water area of 11.467 square miles. Located at 44.94° N. Lat.; 74.86° W. Long. Elevation is 237 feet.
History: Settled 1792, incorporated 1886.
Population: 13,561 (1990); 13,121 (2000); 12,883 (2005); 12,622 (2010 projected); Race: 94.7% White, 0.3% Black, 0.6% Asian, 1.4% Hispanic of any race (2005); Density: 288.4 persons per square mile (2005); Average household size: 2.34 (2005); Median age: 41.4 (2005); Males per 100 females: 88.8 (2005); Marriage status: 25.3% never married, 55.9% now married, 9.9% widowed, 8.8% divorced (2000); Foreign born: 4.6% (2000); Ancestry (includes multiple ancestries): 25.7% French (except Basque), 18.5% Irish, 10.1% English, 9.6% French Canadian, 9.1% Other groups (2000).
Economy: Aluminum and aluminum products are the chief manufacturing. Two locks and 2 dams of the Saint Lawrence Seaway are nearby. In a summer resort area. An international bridge connects the city with Cornwall, Ontario. Single-family building permits issued: 11 (2005); Multi-family building permits issued: 0 (2005); Employment by occupation: 9.9% management, 15.6% professional, 22.2% services, 24.8% sales, 0.1% farming, 9.9% construction, 17.4% production (2000).
Income: Per capita income: $19,729 (2005); Median household income: $34,542 (2005); Average household income: $44,201 (2005); Percent of households with income of $100,000 or more: 6.8% (2005); Poverty rate: 17.9% (2000).
Taxes: Total city taxes per capita: $124 (2004); City property taxes per capita: $109 (2004).
Education: Percent of population age 25 and over with: High school diploma (including GED) or higher: 82.5% (2005); Bachelor's degree or higher: 16.9% (2005); Master's degree or higher: 6.5% (2005).
Housing: Homeownership rate: 63.2% (2005); Median home value: $110,537 (2005); Median rent: $375 per month (2000); Median age of housing: 49 years (2000).
Transportation: Commute to work: 91.4% car, 0.3% public transportation, 4.7% walk, 3.1% work from home (2000); Travel time to work: 63.1% less than 15 minutes, 22.8% 15 to 30 minutes, 7.8% 30 to 45 minutes, 3.4% 45 to 60 minutes, 2.8% 60 minutes or more (2000)

MORRISTOWN (village). Covers a land area of 0.978 square miles and a water area of 0.046 square miles. Located at 44.58° N. Lat.; 75.64° W. Long. Elevation is 240 feet.

Population: 490 (1990); 456 (2000); 415 (2005); 404 (2010 projected); **Race:** 97.1% White, 1.2% Black, 0.7% Asian, 1.4% Hispanic of any race (2005); **Density:** 424.4 persons per square mile (2005); Average household size: 2.49 (2005); Median age: 37.8 (2005); Males per 100 females: 88.6 (2005); Marriage status: 22.8% never married, 56.2% now married, 9.9% widowed, 11.1% divorced (2000); Foreign born: 2.3% (2000); Ancestry (includes multiple ancestries): 17.4% Irish, 14.4% English, 12.1% French (except Basque), 7.8% United States or American, 7.8% German (2000).
Economy: Single-family building permits issued: 0 (2005); Multi-family building permits issued: 0 (2005); Employment by occupation: 9.6% management, 24.3% professional, 20.9% services, 19.2% sales, 2.3% farming, 6.8% construction, 16.9% production (2000).
Income: Per capita income: $18,145 (2005); Median household income: $31,250 (2005); Average household income: $44,192 (2005); Percent of households with income of $100,000 or more: 6.0% (2005); Poverty rate: 18.9% (2000).
Education: Percent of population age 25 and over with: High school diploma (including GED) or higher: 89.1% (2005); Bachelor's degree or higher: 18.6% (2005); Master's degree or higher: 7.7% (2005).

School District(s)
Morristown Central School District (KG-12)
    2003-04 Enrollment: 416 . . . . (315) 375-8814

Housing: Homeownership rate: 75.4% (2005); Median home value: $72,000 (2005); Median rent: $350 per month (2000); Median age of housing: 60+ years (2000).
Transportation: Commute to work: 88.6% car, 0.0% public transportation, 4.6% walk, 4.6% work from home (2000); Travel time to work: 35.9% less than 15 minutes, 41.9% 15 to 30 minutes, 8.4% 30 to 45 minutes, 4.2% 45 to 60 minutes, 9.6% 60 minutes or more (2000)

MORRISTOWN (town). Covers a land area of 45.874 square miles and a water area of 13.567 square miles. Located at 44.55° N. Lat.; 75.63° W. Long. Elevation is 240 feet.
Population: 2,019 (1990); 2,050 (2000); 1,955 (2005); 1,891 (2010 projected); Race: 97.5% White, 0.5% Black, 0.2% Asian, 1.1% Hispanic of any race (2005); Density: 42.6 persons per square mile (2005); Average household size: 2.45 (2005); Median age: 41.9 (2005); Males per 100 females: 97.7 (2005); Marriage status: 20.0% never married, 62.9% now married, 7.2% widowed, 9.8% divorced (2000); Foreign born: 2.3% (2000); Ancestry (includes multiple ancestries): 16.6% English, 14.9% Irish, 11.8% French (except Basque), 10.3% German, 10.0% United States or American (2000).
Economy: Fishing center; port of entry. Single-family building permits issued: 3 (2005); Multi-family building permits issued: 0 (2005); Employment by occupation: 11.5% management, 20.9% professional, 16.8% services, 21.5% sales, 2.8% farming, 10.4% construction, 16.1% production (2000).
Income: Per capita income: $19,992 (2005); Median household income: $37,514 (2005); Average household income: $48,852 (2005); Percent of households with income of $100,000 or more: 8.3% (2005); Poverty rate: 16.4% (2000).
Education: Percent of population age 25 and over with: High school diploma (including GED) or higher: 85.2% (2005); Bachelor's degree or higher: 15.8% (2005); Master's degree or higher: 7.3% (2005).
Housing: Homeownership rate: 82.3% (2005); Median home value: $91,905 (2005); Median rent: $345 per month (2000); Median age of housing: 42 years (2000).
Transportation: Commute to work: 91.8% car, 0.0% public transportation, 2.4% walk, 5.1% work from home (2000); Travel time to work: 30.2% less than 15 minutes, 44.8% 15 to 30 minutes, 12.8% 30 to 45 minutes, 5.4% 45 to 60 minutes, 6.8% 60 minutes or more (2000)

NICHOLVILLE (unincorporated postal area, zip code 12965). Covers a land area of 10.089 square miles and a water area of 0 square miles. Located at 44.69° N. Lat.; 74.68° W. Long. Elevation is 800 feet.
Population: 0 (2000); Race: 95.2% White, 0.0% Black, 0.0% Asian, 0.4% Hispanic of any race (2000); Density: 0.0 persons per square mile (2000); Age: 28.6% under 18, 12.8% over 64 (2000); Marriage status: 17.8% never married, 62.1% now married, 7.6% widowed, 12.5% divorced (2000); Foreign born: 0.4% (2000); Ancestry (includes multiple ancestries): 19.6% Irish, 19.2% English, 17.4% French (except Basque), 14.5% German, 8.4% Other groups (2000).
Economy: Employment by occupation: 4.9% management, 22.4% professional, 21.3% services, 18.6% sales, 1.6% farming, 12.6% construction, 18.6% production (2000).
Income: Per capita income: $13,917 (2000); Median household income: $31,625 (2000); Poverty rate: 12.6% (2000).
Education: Percent of population age 25 and over with: High school diploma (including GED) or higher: 76.3% (2000); Bachelor's degree or higher: 11.9% (2000).
Housing: Homeownership rate: 75.3% (2000); Median home value: $37,500 (2000); Median rent: $338 per month (2000); Median age of housing: 60+ years (2000).
Transportation: Commute to work: 90.0% car, 0.0% public transportation, 4.4% walk, 5.6% work from home (2000); Travel time to work: 25.9% less than 15 minutes, 30.6% 15 to 30 minutes, 25.9% 30 to 45 minutes, 8.8% 45 to 60 minutes, 8.8% 60 minutes or more (2000)

NORFOLK (town). Aka Norfolk Center. Covers a land area of 56.897 square miles and a water area of 0.846 square miles. Located at 44.82° N. Lat.; 74.96° W. Long. Elevation is 257 feet.
History: Settled in 1809. Amish people moved into the area in the mid-1970s and opened a cheese mill, cheese factories, sawmills, and gristmills; they are no longer here. William P. Rogers, who grew up here, was appointed U.S. Attorney General in 1958.
Population: 4,523 (1990); 4,565 (2000); 4,613 (2005); 4,663 (2010 projected); Race: 96.8% White, 0.5% Black, 0.8% Asian, 0.6% Hispanic of any race (2005); Density: 81.1 persons per square mile (2005); Average household size: 2.47 (2005); Median age: 39.8 (2005); Males per 100 females: 97.3 (2005); Marriage status: 22.1% never married, 59.8% now married, 8.5% widowed, 9.6% divorced (2000); Foreign born: 3.4% (2000); Ancestry (includes multiple ancestries): 22.3% French (except Basque), 12.6% United States or American, 11.9% Irish, 11.9% English, 10.0% French Canadian (2000).
Economy: Single-family building permits issued: 18 (2005); Multi-family building permits issued: 0 (2005); Employment by occupation: 6.6% management, 12.6% professional, 14.9% services, 30.1% sales, 0.5% farming, 15.8% construction, 19.6% production (2000).
Income: Per capita income: $18,736 (2005); Median household income: $36,662 (2005); Average household income: $45,893 (2005); Percent of households with income of $100,000 or more: 6.3% (2005); Poverty rate: 14.7% (2000).
Education: Percent of population age 25 and over with: High school diploma (including GED) or higher: 79.0% (2005); Bachelor's degree or higher: 10.6% (2005); Master's degree or higher: 4.2% (2005).
Housing: Homeownership rate: 76.9% (2005); Median home value: $84,120 (2005); Median rent: $354 per month (2000); Median age of housing: 41 years (2000).
Transportation: Commute to work: 94.0% car, 0.0% public transportation, 1.9% walk, 3.2% work from home (2000); Travel time to work: 29.2% less than 15 minutes, 45.5% 15 to 30 minutes, 17.2% 30 to 45 minutes, 2.7% 45 to 60 minutes, 5.4% 60 minutes or more (2000)

NORTH LAWRENCE (unincorporated postal area, zip code 12967). Covers a land area of 41.575 square miles and a water area of 0.018 square miles. Located at 44.78° N. Lat.; 74.66° W. Long. Elevation is 340 feet.
Population: 0 (2000); Race: 98.7% White, 0.0% Black, 0.0% Asian, 0.6% Hispanic of any race (2000); Density: 0.0 persons per square mile (2000); Age: 26.9% under 18, 10.2% over 64 (2000); Marriage status: 27.4% never married, 59.4% now married, 5.2% widowed, 8.0% divorced (2000); Foreign born: 2.0% (2000); Ancestry (includes multiple ancestries): 21.1% French (except Basque), 17.3% Irish, 13.0% English, 7.9% French Canadian, 7.4% Other groups (2000).
Economy: Employment by occupation: 12.5% management, 12.5% professional, 17.9% services, 21.0% sales, 4.8% farming, 11.4% construction, 19.9% production (2000).
Income: Per capita income: $13,014 (2000); Median household income: $31,815 (2000); Poverty rate: 16.8% (2000).
Education: Percent of population age 25 and over with: High school diploma (including GED) or higher: 77.8% (2000); Bachelor's degree or higher: 9.9% (2000).
Housing: Homeownership rate: 83.0% (2000); Median home value: $53,100 (2000); Median rent: $293 per month (2000); Median age of housing: 48 years (2000).
Transportation: Commute to work: 85.0% car, 0.0% public transportation, 7.3% walk, 6.8% work from home (2000); Travel time to work: 23.1% less than 15 minutes, 35.5% 15 to 30 minutes, 32.4% 30 to 45 minutes, 4.9% 45 to 60 minutes, 4.1% 60 minutes or more (2000)

NORWOOD (village). Covers a land area of 2.070 square miles and a water area of 0.194 square miles. Located at 44.74° N. Lat.; 74.99° W. Long. Elevation is 357 feet.
History: Originally an Adirondack-Saint Lawrence Valley railroad center and industrial village, but now purely a residential community. Incorporated 1871.
Population: 1,841 (1990); 1,685 (2000); 1,617 (2005); 1,546 (2010 projected); Race: 98.3% White, 0.4% Black, 0.7% Asian, 0.7% Hispanic of any race (2005); Density: 781.3 persons per square mile (2005); Average household size: 2.40 (2005); Median age: 40.0 (2005); Males per 100 females: 96.5 (2005); Marriage status: 29.5% never married, 53.3% now married, 7.2% widowed, 10.0% divorced (2000); Foreign born: 1.2% (2000); Ancestry (includes multiple ancestries): 22.0% Irish, 20.2% French (except Basque), 13.5% English, 9.1% German, 8.0% Other groups (2000).
Economy: Single-family building permits issued: 0 (2005); Multi-family building permits issued: 0 (2005); Employment by occupation: 9.1% management, 24.7% professional, 22.2% services, 22.4% sales, 0.3% farming, 8.9% construction, 12.4% production (2000).
Income: Per capita income: $20,573 (2005); Median household income: $41,207 (2005); Average household income: $48,379 (2005); Percent of households with income of $100,000 or more: 7.0% (2005); Poverty rate: 11.6% (2000).
Education: Percent of population age 25 and over with: High school diploma (including GED) or higher: 86.5% (2005); Bachelor's degree or higher: 18.2% (2005); Master's degree or higher: 7.7% (2005).

School District(s)
Norwood-Norfolk Central School District (KG-12)
    2003-04 Enrollment: 1,128 . . . . (315) 353-9951

Housing: Homeownership rate: 71.4% (2005); Median home value: $85,556 (2005); Median rent: $362 per month (2000); Median age of housing: 60+ years (2000).
Safety: Violent crime rate: 0.0 per 10,000 population; Property crime rate: 200.2 per 10,000 population (2004).
Transportation: Commute to work: 94.8% car, 0.0% public transportation, 1.1% walk, 1.7% work from home (2000); Travel time to work: 41.3% less than 15 minutes, 33.6% 15 to 30 minutes, 15.4% 30 to 45 minutes, 3.5% 45 to 60 minutes, 6.2% 60 minutes or more (2000)

OGDENSBURG (city). Covers a land area of 5.067 square miles and a water area of 3.088 square miles. Located at 44.70° N. Lat.; 75.48° W. Long. Elevation is 238 feet.
History: Settled by French missionaries and trappers 1749; was strategically important in the War of 1812. Seat of Mater Dei, and Wadhams Hall Seminary and College and a Museum with works of Frederic Remington, who lived here. Rhoda Fox Graves was the first woman to serve the state's Assembly and Senate. Incorporated as a city 1868.
Population: 13,521 (1990); 12,364 (2000); 11,683 (2005); 11,036 (2010 projected); Race: 83.6% White, 10.8% Black, 0.9% Asian, 7.7% Hispanic of any race (2005); Density: 2,305.6 persons per square mile (2005); Average household size: 2.95 (2005); Median age: 37.2 (2005); Males per 100 females: 132.5 (2005); Marriage status: 37.8% never married, 45.6% now married, 7.3% widowed, 9.3% divorced (2000); Foreign born: 5.2% (2000); Ancestry (includes multiple ancestries): 20.8% French (except Basque), 14.4% Irish, 9.8% English, 8.8% United States or American, 8.1% French Canadian (2000).
Economy: In a resort area. A variety of light industrial products are made here, including shade rollers and blinds. Single-family building permits issued: 1 (2005); Multi-family building permits issued: 0 (2005); Employment by occupation: 7.8% management, 19.4% professional, 26.2% services, 25.8% sales, 0.9% farming, 7.6% construction, 12.3% production (2000).
Income: Per capita income: $17,810 (2005); Median household income: $30,036 (2005); Average household income: $40,643 (2005); Percent of households with income of $100,000 or more: 5.7% (2005); Poverty rate: 18.3% (2000).
Education: Percent of population age 25 and over with: High school diploma (including GED) or higher: 68.1% (2005); Bachelor's degree or higher: 10.2% (2005); Master's degree or higher: 5.1% (2005).

School District(s)
Ogdensburg City School District (PK-12)
    2003-04 Enrollment: 2,018 . . . . (315) 393-0900

Housing: Homeownership rate: 60.0% (2005); Median home value: $74,173 (2005); Median rent: $361 per month (2000); Median age of housing: 60+ years (2000).
Hospitals: Claxton - Hepburn Medical Center (159 beds); St. Lawrence Psychiatric Center (85 beds)
Safety: Violent crime rate: 5.1 per 10,000 population; Property crime rate: 505.3 per 10,000 population (2004).
Newspapers: North Country Catholic (Catholic - Circulation 9,500); Rural News (General - Circulation 10,500); The Journal (Circulation 5,500)
Transportation: Commute to work: 89.0% car, 0.9% public transportation, 6.3% walk, 2.5% work from home (2000); Travel time to work: 71.5% less than 15 minutes, 14.8% 15 to 30 minutes, 6.8% 30 to 45 minutes, 3.4% 45 to 60 minutes, 3.6% 60 minutes or more (2000)

Additional Information Contacts
City of Ogdensburg . . . . (315) 393-3540
    http://www.ogdensburg.org/
Greater Ogdensburg Chamber of Commerce . . . . (315) 393-3620
    http://www.ogdensburgny.com/

OSWEGATCHIE (town). Covers a land area of 65.838 square miles and a water area of 5.537 square miles. Located at 44.62° N. Lat.; 75.46° W. Long. Elevation is 1,372 feet.
Population: 4,036 (1990); 4,370 (2000); 4,383 (2005); 4,441 (2010 projected); Race: 98.7% White, 0.3% Black, 0.3% Asian, 0.3% Hispanic of any race (2005); Density: 66.6 persons per square mile (2005); Average household size: 2.81 (2005); Median age: 39.8 (2005); Males per 100 females: 90.7 (2005); Marriage status: 23.2% never married, 55.7% now married, 11.1% widowed, 10.0% divorced (2000); Foreign born: 1.9% (2000); Ancestry (includes multiple ancestries): 18.4% French (except Basque), 15.7% English, 14.4% Irish, 11.3% United States or American, 7.3% German (2000).
Economy: Single-family building permits issued: 5 (2005); Multi-family building permits issued: 0 (2005); Employment by occupation: 15.6% management, 19.5% professional, 21.3% services, 18.6% sales, 2.1% farming, 9.1% construction, 13.8% production (2000).
Income: Per capita income: $18,786 (2005); Median household income: $41,191 (2005); Average household income: $51,149 (2005); Percent of households with income of $100,000 or more: 8.6% (2005); Poverty rate: 11.6% (2000).
Education: Percent of population age 25 and over with: High school diploma (including GED) or higher: 78.4% (2005); Bachelor's degree or higher: 14.7% (2005); Master's degree or higher: 6.4% (2005).
Housing: Homeownership rate: 82.3% (2005); Median home value: $93,526 (2005); Median rent: $361 per month (2000); Median age of housing: 33 years (2000).
Transportation: Commute to work: 86.6% car, 0.0% public transportation, 4.4% walk, 7.8% work from home (2000); Travel time to work: 52.6% less than 15 minutes, 32.4% 15 to 30 minutes, 7.8% 30 to 45 minutes, 3.8% 45 to 60 minutes, 3.3% 60 minutes or more (2000)

PARISHVILLE (town). Covers a land area of 98.181 square miles and a water area of 3.249 square miles. Located at 44.59° N. Lat.; 74.85° W. Long. Elevation is 903 feet.
Population: 1,901 (1990); 2,049 (2000); 2,028 (2005); 2,034 (2010 projected); Race: 98.8% White, 0.1% Black, 0.3% Asian, 1.0% Hispanic of any race (2005); Density: 20.7 persons per square mile (2005); Average household size: 2.51 (2005); Median age: 38.7 (2005); Males per 100 females: 96.9 (2005); Marriage status: 23.3% never married, 60.6% now married, 6.3% widowed, 9.9% divorced (2000); Foreign born: 0.9% (2000); Ancestry (includes multiple ancestries): 16.6% French (except Basque), 14.2% Irish, 13.4% English, 12.7% United States or American, 10.3% German (2000).
Economy: Single-family building permits issued: 9 (2005); Multi-family building permits issued: 2 (2005); Employment by occupation: 6.9% management, 17.7% professional, 23.1% services, 23.8% sales, 3.0% farming, 14.8% construction, 10.8% production (2000).
Income: Per capita income: $17,776 (2005); Median household income: $37,486 (2005); Average household income: $44,616 (2005); Percent of households with income of $100,000 or more: 5.7% (2005); Poverty rate: 10.7% (2000).
Education: Percent of population age 25 and over with: High school diploma (including GED) or higher: 83.5% (2005); Bachelor's degree or higher: 16.5% (2005); Master's degree or higher: 7.0% (2005).

School District(s)
Parishville-Hopkinton Central School District (KG-12)
    2003-04 Enrollment: 493 . . . . (315) 265-4642
Housing: Homeownership rate: 81.4% (2005); Median home value: $88,478 (2005); Median rent: $315 per month (2000); Median age of housing: 30 years (2000).
Transportation: Commute to work: 94.6% car, 0.2% public transportation, 0.7% walk, 3.8% work from home (2000); Travel time to work: 30.0% less than 15 minutes, 42.2% 15 to 30 minutes, 13.8% 30 to 45 minutes, 8.3% 45 to 60 minutes, 5.8% 60 minutes or more (2000)

PIERCEFIELD (town). Covers a land area of 104.295 square miles and a water area of 6.797 square miles. Located at 44.23° N. Lat.; 74.57° W. Long. Elevation is 1,580 feet.
Population: 285 (1990); 305 (2000); 316 (2005); 317 (2010 projected); Race: 97.2% White, 0.0% Black, 0.9% Asian, 1.3% Hispanic of any race (2005); Density: 3.0 persons per square mile (2005); Average household size: 2.19 (2005); Median age: 48.8 (2005); Males per 100 females: 102.6 (2005); Marriage status: 21.9% never married, 64.8% now married, 9.0% widowed, 4.3% divorced (2000); Foreign born: 0.0% (2000); Ancestry (includes multiple ancestries): 18.8% French Canadian, 18.2% French (except Basque), 16.6% English, 9.6% German, 7.6% Irish (2000).
Economy: Single-family building permits issued: 0 (2005); Multi-family building permits issued: 0 (2005); Employment by occupation: 12.7% management, 14.0% professional, 22.9% services, 29.3% sales, 3.2% farming, 7.0% construction, 10.8% production (2000).
Income: Per capita income: $20,601 (2005); Median household income: $39,853 (2005); Average household income: $45,208 (2005); Percent of households with income of $100,000 or more: 4.2% (2005); Poverty rate: 8.3% (2000).
Education: Percent of population age 25 and over with: High school diploma (including GED) or higher: 81.7% (2005); Bachelor's degree or higher: 12.9% (2005); Master's degree or higher: 2.5% (2005).
Housing: Homeownership rate: 88.9% (2005); Median home value: $76,154 (2005); Median rent: $381 per month (2000); Median age of housing: 43 years (2000).
Transportation: Commute to work: 78.4% car, 0.0% public transportation, 8.5% walk, 13.1% work from home (2000); Travel time to work: 32.3% less than 15 minutes, 46.6% 15 to 30 minutes, 5.3% 30 to 45 minutes, 7.5% 45 to 60 minutes, 8.3% 60 minutes or more (2000)

PIERREPONT (town). Covers a land area of 60.405 square miles and a water area of 0.310 square miles. Located at 44.54° N. Lat.; 75.01° W. Long.
Population: 2,375 (1990); 2,674 (2000); 2,722 (2005); 2,757 (2010 projected); Race: 98.7% White, 0.1% Black, 0.7% Asian, 0.4% Hispanic of any race (2005); Density: 45.1 persons per square mile (2005); Average household size: 2.52 (2005); Median age: 40.3 (2005); Males per 100 females: 104.7 (2005); Marriage status: 21.8% never married, 64.9% now married, 5.2% widowed, 8.1% divorced (2000); Foreign born: 2.5% (2000); Ancestry (includes multiple ancestries): 16.8% Irish, 15.5% English, 13.8% French (except Basque), 8.3% German, 7.6% United States or American (2000).
Economy: Single-family building permits issued: 6 (2005); Multi-family building permits issued: 0 (2005); Employment by occupation: 11.1% management, 24.8% professional, 17.8% services, 23.5% sales, 2.2% farming, 10.5% construction, 10.3% production (2000).
Income: Per capita income: $21,809 (2005); Median household income: $45,763 (2005); Average household income: $55,019 (2005); Percent of households with income of $100,000 or more: 11.2% (2005); Poverty rate: 11.5% (2000).
Education: Percent of population age 25 and over with: High school diploma (including GED) or higher: 86.4% (2005); Bachelor's degree or higher: 21.4% (2005); Master's degree or higher: 9.1% (2005).
Housing: Homeownership rate: 85.2% (2005); Median home value: $111,381 (2005); Median rent: $372 per month (2000); Median age of housing: 26 years (2000).
Transportation: Commute to work: 93.7% car, 0.0% public transportation, 1.3% walk, 3.8% work from home (2000); Travel time to work: 28.1% less than 15 minutes, 48.9% 15 to 30 minutes, 11.1% 30 to 45 minutes, 4.3% 45 to 60 minutes, 7.6% 60 minutes or more (2000)

PITCAIRN (town). Covers a land area of 58.959 square miles and a water area of 0.498 square miles. Located at 44.20° N. Lat.; 75.28° W. Long. Elevation is 782 feet.
Population: 751 (1990); 783 (2000); 834 (2005); 856 (2010 projected); Race: 99.3% White, 0.0% Black, 0.4% Asian, 0.6% Hispanic of any race (2005); Density: 14.1 persons per square mile (2005); Average household size: 2.60 (2005); Median age: 39.6 (2005); Males per 100 females: 112.2 (2005); Marriage status: 21.3% never married, 66.2% now married, 4.9% widowed, 7.5% divorced (2000); Foreign born: 0.6% (2000); Ancestry (includes multiple ancestries): 21.2% United States or American, 18.3% French (except Basque), 13.0% Irish, 8.6% Other groups, 8.2% English (2000).
Economy: Single-family building permits issued: 3 (2005); Multi-family building permits issued: 0 (2005); Employment by occupation: 8.8% management, 18.7% professional, 14.5% services, 15.9% sales, 1.4% farming, 15.9% construction, 24.7% production (2000).
Income: Per capita income: $16,748 (2005); Median household income: $32,946 (2005); Average household income: $43,512 (2005); Percent of households with income of $100,000 or more: 5.9% (2005); Poverty rate: 11.7% (2000).
Education: Percent of population age 25 and over with: High school diploma (including GED) or higher: 72.2% (2005); Bachelor's degree or higher: 8.1% (2005); Master's degree or higher: 3.7% (2005).
Housing: Homeownership rate: 87.9% (2005); Median home value: $59,155 (2005); Median rent: $360 per month (2000); Median age of housing: 27 years (2000).
Transportation: Commute to work: 93.8% car, 0.0% public transportation, 3.3% walk, 2.6% work from home (2000); Travel time to work: 34.2% less than 15 minutes, 21.4% 15 to 30 minutes, 21.1% 30 to 45 minutes, 9.4% 45 to 60 minutes, 13.9% 60 minutes or more (2000)

POTSDAM (village). Covers a land area of 4.387 square miles and a water area of 0.461 square miles. Located at 44.67° N. Lat.; 74.98° W. Long. Elevation is 397 feet.
Population: 10,438 (1990); 9,425 (2000); 9,408 (2005); 9,440 (2010 projected); Race: 90.3% White, 3.2% Black, 4.4% Asian, 2.3% Hispanic of any race (2005); Density: 2,144.3 persons per square mile (2005); Average household size: 3.74 (2005); Median age: 22.3 (2005); Males per 100 females: 109.8 (2005); Marriage status: 69.0% never married, 22.5% now married, 5.2% widowed, 3.3% divorced (2000); Foreign born: 7.5% (2000); Ancestry (includes multiple ancestries): 17.9% Irish, 11.8% German, 10.1% French (except Basque), 10.1% English, 9.8% Italian (2000).
Economy: Single-family building permits issued: 0 (2005); Multi-family building permits issued: 0 (2005); Employment by occupation: 4.5% management, 29.2% professional, 29.4% services, 27.6% sales, 0.4% farming, 3.5% construction, 5.4% production (2000).
Income: Per capita income: $12,090 (2005); Median household income: $23,333 (2005); Average household income: $38,841 (2005); Percent of households with income of $100,000 or more: 8.0% (2005); Poverty rate: 34.0% (2000).
Education: Percent of population age 25 and over with: High school diploma (including GED) or higher: 86.6% (2005); Bachelor's degree or higher: 42.1% (2005); Master's degree or higher: 26.6% (2005).
School District(s)
Potsdam Central School District (PK-12)
    2003-04 Enrollment: 1,415 . . . . (315) 265-2000
Four-year College(s)
Clarkson University
    Fall 2004 Enrollment: 3,123 . . . . (315) 268-6400
    2005-06 Tuition: In-state $25,585; Out-of-state $25,585
SUNY-Potsdam (Public)
    Fall 2004 Enrollment: 4,311 . . . . (315) 267-2000
    2005-06 Tuition: In-state $5,289; Out-of-state $11,549
Housing: Homeownership rate: 32.1% (2005); Median home value: $111,753 (2005); Median rent: $374 per month (2000); Median age of housing: 48 years (2000).
Hospitals: Canton-Potsdam Hospital (94 beds)
Newspapers: Courier-Observer (Circulation 8,000); North Country This Week (General - Circulation 10,600)
Transportation: Commute to work: 62.2% car, 1.2% public transportation, 31.1% walk, 3.5% work from home (2000); Travel time to work: 70.5% less than 15 minutes, 17.1% 15 to 30 minutes, 5.7% 30 to 45 minutes, 2.9% 45 to 60 minutes, 3.8% 60 minutes or more (2000)
Additional Information Contacts
Potsdam Chamber of Commerce . . . . (315) 274-9000
    http://www.potsdam.ny.us/chamber

POTSDAM (town). Covers a land area of 101.461 square miles and a water area of 1.991 square miles. Located at 44.67° N. Lat.; 75.02° W. Long. Elevation is 397 feet.
History: In 1804, William Bullard and others came to Potsdam from Massachusetts, pooled their resources, and purchased a tract of land on which they established the "Union." Property was held in common, an accurate account of labor and materials contributed by each member was kept, and all proceeds were divided pro rata annually. The group prospered for a few years but dissolved in 1810, when the land was evenly divided among the members. In the 19th century, sandstone quarries near Potsdam employed hundreds of workers. Seat of State University of New York College at Potsdam and Clarkson University. Incorporated in 1831.
Population: 16,822 (1990); 15,957 (2000); 16,113 (2005); 16,216 (2010 projected); Race: 93.5% White, 2.0% Black, 2.9% Asian, 1.6% Hispanic of any race (2005); Density: 158.8 persons per square mile (2005); Average household size: 3.12 (2005); Median age: 24.7 (2005); Males per 100 females: 104.5 (2005); Marriage status: 52.7% never married, 36.6% now married, 5.5% widowed, 5.2% divorced (2000); Foreign born: 5.6% (2000); Ancestry (includes multiple ancestries): 16.9% Irish, 12.6% French (except Basque), 11.7% English, 11.4% German, 8.0% Other groups (2000).
Economy: Paper, lumber; kilns. Agriculture: dairy products; corn and hay. Timber. Single-family building permits issued: 10 (2005); Multi-family building permits issued: 0 (2005); Employment by occupation: 6.7% management, 26.8% professional, 24.3% services, 25.5% sales, 0.9% farming, 6.8% construction, 9.0% production (2000).
Income: Per capita income: $15,596 (2005); Median household income: $34,387 (2005); Average household income: $45,362 (2005); Percent of households with income of $100,000 or more: 8.8% (2005); Poverty rate: 23.1% (2000).
Education: Percent of population age 25 and over with: High school diploma (including GED) or higher: 85.0% (2005); Bachelor's degree or higher: 31.6% (2005); Master's degree or higher: 18.6% (2005).
Housing: Homeownership rate: 55.4% (2005); Median home value: $104,272 (2005); Median rent: $370 per month (2000); Median age of housing: 45 years (2000).
Transportation: Commute to work: 76.1% car, 0.8% public transportation, 17.5% walk, 3.7% work from home (2000); Travel time to work: 59.1% less than 15 minutes, 24.2% 15 to 30 minutes, 8.5% 30 to 45 minutes, 3.9% 45 to 60 minutes, 4.3% 60 minutes or more (2000)

RENSSELAER FALLS (village). Covers a land area of 0.294 square miles and a water area of 0.024 square miles. Located at 44.59° N. Lat.; 75.32° W. Long. Elevation is 328 feet.
Population: 323 (1990); 337 (2000); 378 (2005); 418 (2010 projected); Race: 97.4% White, 0.0% Black, 0.5% Asian, 1.1% Hispanic of any race (2005); Density: 1,287.1 persons per square mile (2005); Average household size: 2.64 (2005); Median age: 37.4 (2005); Males per 100 females: 94.8 (2005); Marriage status: 21.5% never married, 53.8% now married, 9.0% widowed, 15.7% divorced (2000); Foreign born: 0.9% (2000); Ancestry (includes multiple ancestries): 16.3% English, 15.4% French (except Basque), 15.4% Irish, 11.4% United States or American, 11.4% French Canadian (2000).
Economy: In dairy and poultry area. Single-family building permits issued: 0 (2005); Multi-family building permits issued: 0 (2005); Employment by occupation: 7.4% management, 17.0% professional, 12.6% services, 31.9% sales, 3.0% farming, 7.4% construction, 20.7% production (2000).
Income: Per capita income: $16,880 (2005); Median household income: $33,676 (2005); Average household income: $44,213 (2005); Percent of households with income of $100,000 or more: 3.5% (2005); Poverty rate: 12.1% (2000).
Education: Percent of population age 25 and over with: High school diploma (including GED) or higher: 88.4% (2005); Bachelor's degree or higher: 13.7% (2005); Master's degree or higher: 5.6% (2005).
Housing: Homeownership rate: 72.0% (2005); Median home value: $69,348 (2005); Median rent: $384 per month (2000); Median age of housing: 60+ years (2000).
Transportation: Commute to work: 93.8% car, 0.0% public transportation, 1.5% walk, 4.6% work from home (2000); Travel time to work: 17.7% less than 15 minutes, 60.5% 15 to 30 minutes, 10.5% 30 to 45 minutes, 3.2% 45 to 60 minutes, 8.1% 60 minutes or more (2000)

RICHVILLE (village). Aka Bigelow. Covers a land area of 0.738 square miles and a water area of 0 square miles. Located at 44.41° N. Lat.; 75.39° W. Long. Elevation is 372 feet.
Population: 311 (1990); 274 (2000); 281 (2005); 282 (2010 projected); Race: 98.2% White, 1.1% Black, 0.0% Asian, 0.0% Hispanic of any race (2005); Density: 380.9 persons per square mile (2005); Average household size: 2.44 (2005); Median age: 38.5 (2005); Males per 100 females: 97.9 (2005); Marriage status: 30.0% never married, 55.1% now married, 7.5% widowed, 7.5% divorced (2000); Foreign born: 3.1% (2000); Ancestry (includes multiple ancestries): 14.8% United States or American, 13.6% Irish, 13.2% French (except Basque), 11.7% English, 9.7% German (2000).
Economy: In dairying area. Single-family building permits issued: 0 (2005); Multi-family building permits issued: 0 (2005); Employment by occupation: 5.9% management, 15.6% professional, 28.9% services, 17.0% sales, 3.0% farming, 10.4% construction, 19.3% production (2000).
Income: Per capita income: $18,301 (2005); Median household income: $40,833 (2005); Average household income: $44,717 (2005); Percent of households with income of $100,000 or more: 2.6% (2005); Poverty rate: 7.4% (2000).
Education: Percent of population age 25 and over with: High school diploma (including GED) or higher: 80.2% (2005); Bachelor's degree or higher: 10.2% (2005); Master's degree or higher: 6.1% (2005).
Housing: Homeownership rate: 74.8% (2005); Median home value: $68,182 (2005); Median rent: $347 per month (2000); Median age of housing: 60+ years (2000).
Transportation: Commute to work: 98.5% car, 0.0% public transportation, 1.5% walk, 0.0% work from home (2000); Travel time to work: 18.5% less than 15 minutes, 40.8% 15 to 30 minutes, 10.0% 30 to 45 minutes, 16.2% 45 to 60 minutes, 14.6% 60 minutes or more (2000)

ROSSIE (town). Covers a land area of 38.076 square miles and a water area of 0.986 square miles. Located at 44.33° N. Lat.; 75.62° W. Long. Elevation is 283 feet.
Population: 770 (1990); 787 (2000); 834 (2005); 866 (2010 projected); Race: 98.1% White, 0.7% Black, 0.1% Asian, 0.2% Hispanic of any race (2005); Density: 21.9 persons per square mile (2005); Average household size: 2.57 (2005); Median age: 37.4 (2005); Males per 100 females: 99.5 (2005); Marriage status: 20.2% never married, 65.4% now married, 6.8% widowed, 7.5% divorced (2000); Foreign born: 1.0% (2000); Ancestry (includes multiple ancestries): 17.7% United States or American, 13.5% English, 11.5% French (except Basque), 9.4% German, 8.9% Irish (2000).
Economy: Single-family building permits issued: 8 (2005); Multi-family building permits issued: 0 (2005); Employment by occupation: 15.5% management, 8.6% professional, 23.4% services, 18.9% sales, 2.4% farming, 13.7% construction, 17.5% production (2000).
Income: Per capita income: $16,097 (2005); Median household income: $30,111 (2005); Average household income: $41,435 (2005); Percent of households with income of $100,000 or more: 5.2% (2005); Poverty rate: 20.6% (2000).
Education: Percent of population age 25 and over with: High school diploma (including GED) or higher: 69.5% (2005); Bachelor's degree or higher: 7.3% (2005); Master's degree or higher: 2.9% (2005).
Housing: Homeownership rate: 76.5% (2005); Median home value: $80,045 (2005); Median rent: $243 per month (2000); Median age of housing: 28 years (2000).
Transportation: Commute to work: 81.7% car, 1.4% public transportation, 4.2% walk, 10.7% work from home (2000); Travel time to work: 22.1% less than 15 minutes, 41.1% 15 to 30 minutes, 18.6% 30 to 45 minutes, 8.5% 45 to 60 minutes, 9.7% 60 minutes or more (2000)

RUSSELL (town). Covers a land area of 96.765 square miles and a water area of 0.534 square miles. Located at 44.40° N. Lat.; 75.14° W. Long. Elevation is 582 feet.
Population: 1,716 (1990); 1,801 (2000); 1,859 (2005); 1,871 (2010 projected); Race: 99.1% White, 0.2% Black, 0.3% Asian, 0.2% Hispanic of any race (2005); Density: 19.2 persons per square mile (2005); Average household size: 2.71 (2005); Median age: 36.1 (2005); Males per 100 females: 98.6 (2005); Marriage status: 23.9% never married, 60.6% now married, 6.3% widowed, 9.2% divorced (2000); Foreign born: 0.7% (2000); Ancestry (includes multiple ancestries): 16.8% United States or American, 14.7% Irish, 13.3% English, 12.7% French (except Basque), 7.3% French Canadian (2000).
Economy: Single-family building permits issued: 6 (2005); Multi-family building permits issued: 0 (2005); Employment by occupation: 6.8% management, 18.4% professional, 23.3% services, 16.5% sales, 2.4% farming, 13.5% construction, 19.1% production (2000).
Income: Per capita income: $17,177 (2005); Median household income: $36,702 (2005); Average household income: $46,401 (2005); Percent of

households with income of $100,000 or more: 6.3% (2005); Poverty rate: 19.2% (2000).
Education: Percent of population age 25 and over with: High school diploma (including GED) or higher: 76.1% (2005); Bachelor's degree or higher: 10.7% (2005); Master's degree or higher: 4.4% (2005).

School District(s)
Edwards-Knox Central School District (PK-12)
    2003-04 Enrollment: 707 . . . . (315) 562-8326
Housing: Homeownership rate: 84.9% (2005); Median home value: $71,727 (2005); Median rent: $325 per month (2000); Median age of housing: 29 years (2000).
Transportation: Commute to work: 95.7% car, 0.0% public transportation, 1.2% walk, 2.1% work from home (2000); Travel time to work: 20.2% less than 15 minutes, 41.0% 15 to 30 minutes, 21.6% 30 to 45 minutes, 7.3% 45 to 60 minutes, 9.9% 60 minutes or more (2000)

SOUTH COLTON (unincorporated postal area, zip code 13687).
Covers a land area of 29.060 square miles and a water area of 0.139 square miles. Located at 44.50° N. Lat.; 74.86° W. Long. Elevation is 927 feet.
Population: 0 (2000); Race: 99.4% White, 0.0% Black, 0.0% Asian, 2.4% Hispanic of any race (2000); Density: 0.0 persons per square mile (2000); Age: 23.5% under 18, 14.9% over 64 (2000); Marriage status: 25.7% never married, 60.9% now married, 6.2% widowed, 7.2% divorced (2000); Foreign born: 4.6% (2000); Ancestry (includes multiple ancestries): 22.9% Irish, 20.1% English, 14.3% French (except Basque), 9.1% French Canadian, 6.4% United States or American (2000).
Economy: Employment by occupation: 8.5% management, 21.3% professional, 17.0% services, 30.5% sales, 1.4% farming, 15.6% construction, 5.7% production (2000).
Income: Per capita income: $17,862 (2000); Median household income: $40,893 (2000); Poverty rate: 17.7% (2000).
Education: Percent of population age 25 and over with: High school diploma (including GED) or higher: 84.6% (2000); Bachelor's degree or higher: 22.8% (2000).
Housing: Homeownership rate: 91.8% (2000); Median home value: $90,500 (2000); Median rent: $331 per month (2000); Median age of housing: 28 years (2000).
Transportation: Commute to work: 97.1% car, 0.0% public transportation, 0.0% walk, 2.9% work from home (2000); Travel time to work: 22.2% less than 15 minutes, 12.6% 15 to 30 minutes, 33.3% 30 to 45 minutes, 16.3% 45 to 60 minutes, 15.6% 60 minutes or more (2000)

STAR LAKE (CDP).
Covers a land area of 4.422 square miles and a water area of 0.388 square miles. Located at 44.16° N. Lat.; 75.03° W. Long. Elevation is 1,480 feet.
Population: 1,092 (1990); 860 (2000); 814 (2005); 791 (2010 projected); Race: 95.6% White, 0.4% Black, 0.7% Asian, 1.2% Hispanic of any race (2005); Density: 184.1 persons per square mile (2005); Average household size: 2.31 (2005); Median age: 43.5 (2005); Males per 100 females: 94.3 (2005); Marriage status: 27.1% never married, 56.8% now married, 8.7% widowed, 7.4% divorced (2000); Foreign born: 3.1% (2000); Ancestry (includes multiple ancestries): 20.9% French (except Basque), 15.7% Irish, 14.7% English, 13.9% Other groups, 13.2% French Canadian (2000).
Economy: Resort village. Employment by occupation: 11.0% management, 21.4% professional, 19.2% services, 17.0% sales, 0.6% farming, 7.5% construction, 23.3% production (2000).
Income: Per capita income: $20,542 (2005); Median household income: $38,261 (2005); Average household income: $47,500 (2005); Percent of households with income of $100,000 or more: 8.2% (2005); Poverty rate: 21.0% (2000).
Education: Percent of population age 25 and over with: High school diploma (including GED) or higher: 78.2% (2005); Bachelor's degree or higher: 13.6% (2005); Master's degree or higher: 6.3% (2005).

School District(s)
Clifton-Fine Central School District (PK-12)
    2003-04 Enrollment: 418 . . . . (315) 848-3335
Housing: Homeownership rate: 75.6% (2005); Median home value: $62,500 (2005); Median rent: $352 per month (2000); Median age of housing: 47 years (2000).
Hospitals: Clifton-Fine Hospital (20 beds)
Transportation: Commute to work: 94.6% car, 0.0% public transportation, 3.0% walk, 1.3% work from home (2000); Travel time to work: 57.8% less than 15 minutes, 10.9% 15 to 30 minutes, 7.1% 30 to 45 minutes, 9.9% 45 to 60 minutes, 14.3% 60 minutes or more (2000)

STOCKHOLM (town).
Covers a land area of 93.936 square miles and a water area of 0.349 square miles. Located at 44.76° N. Lat.; 74.85° W. Long.
Population: 3,533 (1990); 3,592 (2000); 3,862 (2005); 4,061 (2010 projected); Race: 98.2% White, 0.3% Black, 0.2% Asian, 0.7% Hispanic of any race (2005); Density: 41.1 persons per square mile (2005); Average household size: 2.54 (2005); Median age: 37.8 (2005); Males per 100 females: 97.2 (2005); Marriage status: 24.4% never married, 62.4% now married, 6.3% widowed, 6.9% divorced (2000); Foreign born: 3.2% (2000); Ancestry (includes multiple ancestries): 19.7% French (except Basque), 17.8% Irish, 13.4% English, 10.9% United States or American, 9.5% German (2000).
Economy: Single-family building permits issued: 15 (2005); Multi-family building permits issued: 0 (2005); Employment by occupation: 9.1% management, 19.3% professional, 20.3% services, 20.5% sales, 2.9% farming, 11.9% construction, 16.0% production (2000).
Income: Per capita income: $18,060 (2005); Median household income: $35,516 (2005); Average household income: $45,690 (2005); Percent of households with income of $100,000 or more: 7.2% (2005); Poverty rate: 16.0% (2000).
Education: Percent of population age 25 and over with: High school diploma (including GED) or higher: 83.4% (2005); Bachelor's degree or higher: 12.6% (2005); Master's degree or higher: 6.1% (2005).
Housing: Homeownership rate: 80.4% (2005); Median home value: $84,389 (2005); Median rent: $342 per month (2000); Median age of housing: 40 years (2000).
Transportation: Commute to work: 94.1% car, 0.5% public transportation, 0.8% walk, 3.5% work from home (2000); Travel time to work: 28.7% less than 15 minutes, 37.5% 15 to 30 minutes, 28.4% 30 to 45 minutes, 1.8% 45 to 60 minutes, 3.7% 60 minutes or more (2000)

WADDINGTON (village).
Covers a land area of 2.170 square miles and a water area of 0.207 square miles. Located at 44.86° N. Lat.; 75.19° W. Long. Elevation is 273 feet.
Population: 944 (1990); 923 (2000); 911 (2005); 910 (2010 projected); Race: 99.5% White, 0.0% Black, 0.0% Asian, 0.3% Hispanic of any race (2005); Density: 419.7 persons per square mile (2005); Average household size: 2.23 (2005); Median age: 45.9 (2005); Males per 100 females: 92.6 (2005); Marriage status: 20.4% never married, 58.2% now married, 10.2% widowed, 11.1% divorced (2000); Foreign born: 2.2% (2000); Ancestry (includes multiple ancestries): 19.8% Irish, 16.9% French (except Basque), 12.7% English, 8.3% United States or American, 7.6% German (2000).
Economy: Single-family building permits issued: 6 (2005); Multi-family building permits issued: 0 (2005); Employment by occupation: 11.0% management, 18.5% professional, 22.2% services, 23.7% sales, 1.0% farming, 12.5% construction, 11.2% production (2000).
Income: Per capita income: $26,044 (2005); Median household income: $44,205 (2005); Average household income: $57,983 (2005); Percent of households with income of $100,000 or more: 13.2% (2005); Poverty rate: 11.3% (2000).
Education: Percent of population age 25 and over with: High school diploma (including GED) or higher: 85.7% (2005); Bachelor's degree or higher: 17.4% (2005); Master's degree or higher: 10.0% (2005).
Housing: Homeownership rate: 71.1% (2005); Median home value: $102,528 (2005); Median rent: $379 per month (2000); Median age of housing: 47 years (2000).
Transportation: Commute to work: 95.6% car, 0.0% public transportation, 0.5% walk, 2.9% work from home (2000); Travel time to work: 17.6% less than 15 minutes, 53.5% 15 to 30 minutes, 24.6% 30 to 45 minutes, 2.4% 45 to 60 minutes, 1.9% 60 minutes or more (2000)
Additional Information Contacts
Waddington Chamber of Commerce . . . . (315) 388-5576
    http://www.waddingtonny.us./chamber

WADDINGTON (town).
Covers a land area of 51.545 square miles and a water area of 6.445 square miles. Located at 44.84° N. Lat.; 75.20° W. Long. Elevation is 273 feet.
Population: 1,990 (1990); 2,212 (2000); 2,236 (2005); 2,272 (2010 projected); Race: 98.3% White, 0.2% Black, 0.7% Asian, 0.3% Hispanic of any race (2005); Density: 43.4 persons per square mile (2005); Average household size: 2.45 (2005); Median age: 40.3 (2005); Males per 100 females: 95.1 (2005); Marriage status: 19.6% never married, 64.2% now married, 6.6% widowed, 9.6% divorced (2000); Foreign born: 2.3% (2000); Ancestry (includes multiple ancestries): 15.9% Irish, 15.7% French (except

Basque), 11.7% English, 10.8% United States or American, 10.4% German (2000).
Economy: Paper milling. Summer resort; sports fishing. Ferry nearby to Morrisburg, Ontario. Single-family building permits issued: 6 (2005); Multi-family building permits issued: 0 (2005); Employment by occupation: 11.0% management, 17.2% professional, 25.0% services, 20.5% sales, 1.7% farming, 11.2% construction, 13.4% production (2000).
Income: Per capita income: $20,552 (2005); Median household income: $41,208 (2005); Average household income: $50,181 (2005); Percent of households with income of $100,000 or more: 8.1% (2005); Poverty rate: 11.2% (2000).
Education: Percent of population age 25 and over with: High school diploma (including GED) or higher: 82.6% (2005); Bachelor's degree or higher: 15.9% (2005); Master's degree or higher: 7.7% (2005).
Housing: Homeownership rate: 76.3% (2005); Median home value: $97,126 (2005); Median rent: $344 per month (2000); Median age of housing: 39 years (2000).
Transportation: Commute to work: 93.3% car, 0.0% public transportation, 2.7% walk, 3.6% work from home (2000); Travel time to work: 16.1% less than 15 minutes, 47.4% 15 to 30 minutes, 30.6% 30 to 45 minutes, 2.9% 45 to 60 minutes, 3.0% 60 minutes or more (2000)

WINTHROP (unincorporated postal area, zip code 13697). Covers a land area of 64.866 square miles and a water area of 0 square miles. Located at 44.64° N. Lat.; 74.84° W. Long. Elevation is 338 feet.
Population: 0 (2000); Race: 99.0% White, 0.0% Black, 0.0% Asian, 0.0% Hispanic of any race (2000); Density: 0.0 persons per square mile (2000); Age: 23.8% under 18, 14.2% over 64 (2000); Marriage status: 24.4% never married, 61.8% now married, 6.6% widowed, 7.2% divorced (2000); Foreign born: 4.8% (2000); Ancestry (includes multiple ancestries): 18.5% Irish, 16.3% English, 13.9% French (except Basque), 8.3% Italian, 7.7% French Canadian (2000).
Economy: Employment by occupation: 8.2% management, 16.9% professional, 20.8% services, 21.8% sales, 5.0% farming, 14.2% construction, 13.0% production (2000).
Income: Per capita income: $14,932 (2000); Median household income: $29,162 (2000); Poverty rate: 15.0% (2000).
Education: Percent of population age 25 and over with: High school diploma (including GED) or higher: 80.7% (2000); Bachelor's degree or higher: 10.0% (2000).
Housing: Homeownership rate: 78.4% (2000); Median home value: $56,800 (2000); Median rent: $341 per month (2000); Median age of housing: 45 years (2000).
Transportation: Commute to work: 95.5% car, 0.0% public transportation, 1.0% walk, 3.0% work from home (2000); Travel time to work: 20.4% less than 15 minutes, 42.8% 15 to 30 minutes, 30.8% 30 to 45 minutes, 0.9% 45 to 60 minutes, 5.1% 60 minutes or more (2000)

Saratoga County

Located in eastern New York, partly in the Adirondacks; bounded on the east by the Hudson River, and on the south by the Mohawk River; includes Saratoga Lake. Covers a land area of 811.84 square miles, a water area of 31.87 square miles, and is located in the Eastern Time Zone. The county government was organized in 1791. County seat is Ballston Spa.

Saratoga County is part of the Albany-Schenectady-Troy, NY Metropolitan Statistical Area. The entire metro area includes: Albany County, NY; Rensselaer County, NY; Saratoga County, NY; Schenectady County, NY; Schoharie County, NY

Weather Station: Conklingville Dam — Elevation: 807 feet

	Jan	Feb	Mar	Apr	May	Jun	Jul	Aug	Sep	Oct	Nov	Dec
High	29	33	42	54	67	75	79	77	69	58	46	34
Low	8	10	21	33	44	53	58	57	49	38	29	17
Precip	3.8	2.9	4.1	3.8	4.1	4.0	3.9	4.0	4.1	3.6	4.1	3.7
Snow	21.5	14.5	14.8	3.0	0.1	0.0	0.0	0.0	0.0	tr	4.9	17.5

High and Low temperatures in degrees Fahrenheit; Precipitation and Snow in inches

Weather Station: Saratoga Springs 4 SW — Elevation: 308 feet

	Jan	Feb	Mar	Apr	May	Jun	Jul	Aug	Sep	Oct	Nov	Dec
High	31	34	45	59	72	79	84	81	73	61	48	36
Low	10	13	23	34	45	54	59	57	49	37	30	18
Precip	3.3	2.5	3.5	3.5	4.0	3.9	3.7	4.0	3.7	3.5	3.7	3.3
Snow	19.3	12.2	11.5	2.5	tr	0.0	0.0	0.0	tr	tr	4.2	13.5

High and Low temperatures in degrees Fahrenheit; Precipitation and Snow in inches

Population: 181,276 (1990); 200,635 (2000); 213,983 (2005); 227,872 (2010 projected); Race: 94.5% White, 1.8% Black, 1.6% Asian, 2.4% Hispanic of any race (2005); Density: 263.6 persons per square mile (2005); Average household size: 2.52 (2005); Median age: 38.5 (2005); Males per 100 females: 97.3 (2005).
Religion: Five largest groups: 26.8% Catholic Church, 5.2% The United Methodist Church, 1.9% Episcopal Church, 0.9% Evangelical Lutheran Church in America, 0.8% Presbyterian Church (U.S.A.) (2000).
Economy: Unemployment rate: 3.5% (2005); Total civilian labor force: 119,867 (2005); Leading industries: 19.3% retail trade; 11.8% health care and social assistance; 10.9% accommodation and food services (2003); Farms: 592 totaling 74,976 acres (2002); Companies that employ 500 or more persons: 8 (2003); Companies that employ 100 to 499 persons: 69 (2003); Companies that employ less than 100 persons: 4,481 (2003); Black-owned businesses: n/a (2002); Hispanic-owned businesses: 232 (2002); Women-owned businesses: 4,670 (2002); Retail sales per capita: $12,672 (2006). Single-family building permits issued: 980 (2005); Multi-family building permits issued: 399 (2005).
Income: Per capita income: $27,911 (2005); Median household income: $56,222 (2005); Average household income: $69,327 (2005); Percent of households with income of $100,000 or more: 19.2% (2005); Poverty rate: 6.3% (2003); Bankruptcy rate: 6.31% (2005).
Taxes: Total county taxes per capita: $570 (2004); County property taxes per capita: $151 (2004).
Education: Percent of population age 25 and over with: High school diploma (including GED) or higher: 88.2% (2005); Bachelor's degree or higher: 31.1% (2005); Master's degree or higher: 12.5% (2005).
Housing: Homeownership rate: 72.6% (2005); Median home value: $162,937 (2005); Median rent: $535 per month (2000); Median age of housing: 26 years (2000).
Health: Birth rate: 113.5 per 10,000 population (2004); Death rate: 67.4 per 10,000 population (2004); Age-adjusted cancer mortality rate: 214.1 deaths per 100,000 population (2002); Air Quality Index: 92.5% good, 6.5% moderate, 1.0% unhealthy for sensitive individuals, 0.0% unhealthy (percent of days in 2005); Number of physicians: 17.9 per 10,000 population (2004); Hospital beds: 10.0 per 10,000 population (2003); Hospital admissions: 371.7 per 10,000 population (2003).
Elections: 2004 Presidential election results: 52.5% Bush, 45.6% Kerry, 1.6% Nader, 0.2% Badnarik
National and State Parks: Moreau Lake State Park; New York State Game Management Area; Peebles Island State Park; Saratoga National Historical Park; Saratoga Spa State Park
Additional Information Contacts

Saratoga County Government	(518) 885-5388
http://www.co.saratoga.ny.us/	
City of Mechanicville	(518) 664-8331
http://www.mechanicville.com/	
City of Saratoga Springs	(518) 587-3550
http://www.saratoga-springs.org/	
Town of Ballston	(518) 885-8502
http://www.townofballstonny.nycap.rr.com/	
Town of Charlton	(518) 384-0152
http://www.townofcharlton.org/	
Town of Clifton Park	(518) 371-6651
http://www.cliftonpark.org/	
Town of Corinth	(518) 654-9232
http://townofcorinthny.com/	
Town of Edinburg	(518) 863-2034
http://www.edinburgny.com/	
Town of Greenfield	(518) 893-7432
http://www.townofgreenfield.com/	
Town of Hadley	(518) 696-4797
http://www.townofhadley.com/	
Town of Halfmoon	(518) 371-7410
http://www.townofhalfmoon.org/	
Town of Malta	(518) 899-3434
http://www.malta-town.org/	
Town of Milton	(518) 885-9220
http://www.townofmiltonny.org/	
Town of Wilton	(518) 587-1939
http://www.townofwilton.com/	
Village of Round Lake	(518) 899-2800
http://www.roundlakevillage.org/	
Village of Waterford	(518) 235-9898
http://www.waterfordny.org/	

Saratoga County Communities

BALLSTON (town). Covers a land area of 29.611 square miles and a water area of 0.403 square miles. Located at 42.95° N. Lat.; 73.87° W. Long.
Population: 8,078 (1990); 8,729 (2000); 9,041 (2005); 9,440 (2010 projected); Race: 96.3% White, 0.6% Black, 0.8% Asian, 2.4% Hispanic of any race (2005); Density: 305.3 persons per square mile (2005); Average household size: 2.65 (2005); Median age: 41.2 (2005); Males per 100 females: 93.8 (2005); Marriage status: 21.5% never married, 63.9% now married, 7.6% widowed, 7.0% divorced (2000); Foreign born: 2.5% (2000); Ancestry (includes multiple ancestries): 23.4% Irish, 21.7% German, 16.4% English, 13.9% Italian, 9.6% Polish (2000).
Economy: Single-family building permits issued: 57 (2005); Multi-family building permits issued: 2 (2005); Employment by occupation: 13.4% management, 32.6% professional, 11.1% services, 23.5% sales, 0.2% farming, 7.7% construction, 11.5% production (2000).
Income: Per capita income: $27,544 (2005); Median household income: $63,712 (2005); Average household income: $70,943 (2005); Percent of households with income of $100,000 or more: 22.8% (2005); Poverty rate: 4.6% (2000).
Education: Percent of population age 25 and over with: High school diploma (including GED) or higher: 88.7% (2005); Bachelor's degree or higher: 32.2% (2005); Master's degree or higher: 13.6% (2005).
Housing: Homeownership rate: 76.1% (2005); Median home value: $184,654 (2005); Median rent: $505 per month (2000); Median age of housing: 35 years (2000).
Transportation: Commute to work: 92.3% car, 1.1% public transportation, 2.4% walk, 3.9% work from home (2000); Travel time to work: 28.9% less than 15 minutes, 39.0% 15 to 30 minutes, 20.8% 30 to 45 minutes, 8.0% 45 to 60 minutes, 3.3% 60 minutes or more (2000)
Additional Information Contacts
Town of Ballston .... (518) 885-8502
   http://www.townofballstonny.nycap.rr.com/

BALLSTON LAKE (unincorporated postal area, zip code 12019). Covers a land area of 28.962 square miles and a water area of 0.410 square miles. Located at 42.91° N. Lat.; 73.86° W. Long.
Population: 0 (2000); Race: 96.7% White, 0.6% Black, 1.8% Asian, 0.7% Hispanic of any race (2000); Density: 0.0 persons per square mile (2000); Age: 25.8% under 18, 11.2% over 64 (2000); Marriage status: 22.2% never married, 68.2% now married, 3.9% widowed, 5.7% divorced (2000); Foreign born: 4.2% (2000); Ancestry (includes multiple ancestries): 24.7% Irish, 21.6% German, 18.1% Italian, 14.8% English, 9.0% Polish (2000).
Economy: Resort and residential village. Employment by occupation: 17.3% management, 32.2% professional, 10.7% services, 24.8% sales, 0.1% farming, 7.1% construction, 7.8% production (2000).
Income: Per capita income: $28,485 (2000); Median household income: $64,673 (2000); Poverty rate: 1.4% (2000).
Education: Percent of population age 25 and over with: High school diploma (including GED) or higher: 96.0% (2000); Bachelor's degree or higher: 43.9% (2000).
School District(s)
Burnt Hills-Ballston Lake Central School District (KG-12)
   2003-04 Enrollment: 3,447 .... (518) 399-6407
Shenendehowa Central School District (KG-12)
   2003-04 Enrollment: 9,313 .... (518) 881-0610
Housing: Homeownership rate: 75.4% (2000); Median home value: $138,200 (2000); Median rent: $591 per month (2000); Median age of housing: 26 years (2000).
Transportation: Commute to work: 94.0% car, 0.9% public transportation, 0.2% walk, 4.5% work from home (2000); Travel time to work: 21.9% less than 15 minutes, 41.4% 15 to 30 minutes, 27.5% 30 to 45 minutes, 5.6% 45 to 60 minutes, 3.6% 60 minutes or more (2000)

BALLSTON SPA (village). Covers a land area of 1.604 square miles and a water area of 0.007 square miles. Located at 43.00° N. Lat.; 73.85° W. Long. Elevation is 288 feet.
History: Formerly a popular resort. Settled 1771, incorporated 1807.
Population: 4,893 (1990); 5,556 (2000); 5,547 (2005); 5,602 (2010 projected); Race: 94.5% White, 1.8% Black, 0.9% Asian, 3.6% Hispanic of any race (2005); Density: 3,459.2 persons per square mile (2005); Average household size: 2.40 (2005); Median age: 37.7 (2005); Males per 100 females: 89.4 (2005); Marriage status: 28.1% never married, 56.0% now married, 8.8% widowed, 7.1% divorced (2000); Foreign born: 2.0% (2000); Ancestry (includes multiple ancestries): 25.9% Irish, 17.6% German, 16.9% English, 16.9% Italian, 11.1% French (except Basque) (2000).
Economy: Manufacturing: medical equipment, construction materials, paper products, testing and measuring instruments. Mineral springs. Single-family building permits issued: 0 (2005); Multi-family building permits issued: 0 (2005); Employment by occupation: 11.7% management, 26.1% professional, 13.3% services, 26.1% sales, 0.4% farming, 11.4% construction, 11.0% production (2000).
Income: Per capita income: $23,597 (2005); Median household income: $43,425 (2005); Average household income: $54,191 (2005); Percent of households with income of $100,000 or more: 13.0% (2005); Poverty rate: 10.6% (2000).
Education: Percent of population age 25 and over with: High school diploma (including GED) or higher: 80.6% (2005); Bachelor's degree or higher: 25.8% (2005); Master's degree or higher: 11.1% (2005).
School District(s)
Ballston Spa Central School District (KG-12)
   2003-04 Enrollment: 4,521 .... (518) 884-7195
Housing: Homeownership rate: 53.4% (2005); Median home value: $142,084 (2005); Median rent: $438 per month (2000); Median age of housing: 56 years (2000).
Safety: Violent crime rate: 10.8 per 10,000 population; Property crime rate: 252.9 per 10,000 population (2004).
Newspapers: Ballston Journal (General - Circulation 2,300)
Transportation: Commute to work: 89.6% car, 1.3% public transportation, 4.5% walk, 4.4% work from home (2000); Travel time to work: 31.7% less than 15 minutes, 26.3% 15 to 30 minutes, 27.8% 30 to 45 minutes, 9.7% 45 to 60 minutes, 4.6% 60 minutes or more (2000)

BURNT HILLS (unincorporated postal area, zip code 12027). Covers a land area of 9.030 square miles and a water area of 0 square miles. Located at 42.91° N. Lat.; 73.90° W. Long.
Population: 0 (2000); Race: 97.9% White, 0.1% Black, 0.6% Asian, 0.9% Hispanic of any race (2000); Density: 0.0 persons per square mile (2000); Age: 28.0% under 18, 13.3% over 64 (2000); Marriage status: 16.0% never married, 73.6% now married, 4.4% widowed, 6.1% divorced (2000); Foreign born: 3.3% (2000); Ancestry (includes multiple ancestries): 23.9% Irish, 21.1% German, 16.9% English, 15.2% Italian, 11.5% Polish (2000).
Economy: Employment by occupation: 15.1% management, 34.6% professional, 8.9% services, 23.1% sales, 0.4% farming, 7.5% construction, 10.4% production (2000).
Income: Per capita income: $24,437 (2000); Median household income: $62,569 (2000); Poverty rate: 1.5% (2000).
Education: Percent of population age 25 and over with: High school diploma (including GED) or higher: 95.8% (2000); Bachelor's degree or higher: 38.7% (2000).
Housing: Homeownership rate: 87.0% (2000); Median home value: $123,300 (2000); Median rent: $460 per month (2000); Median age of housing: 37 years (2000).
Transportation: Commute to work: 95.1% car, 0.5% public transportation, 1.9% walk, 2.5% work from home (2000); Travel time to work: 28.2% less than 15 minutes, 40.8% 15 to 30 minutes, 17.4% 30 to 45 minutes, 11.1% 45 to 60 minutes, 2.5% 60 minutes or more (2000)

CHARLTON (town). Covers a land area of 32.803 square miles and a water area of 0.020 square miles. Located at 42.95° N. Lat.; 73.99° W. Long. Elevation is 498 feet.
Population: 3,984 (1990); 3,954 (2000); 4,056 (2005); 4,187 (2010 projected); Race: 97.9% White, 0.4% Black, 0.6% Asian, 1.7% Hispanic of any race (2005); Density: 123.6 persons per square mile (2005); Average household size: 2.70 (2005); Median age: 44.8 (2005); Males per 100 females: 95.1 (2005); Marriage status: 17.6% never married, 73.3% now married, 4.5% widowed, 4.6% divorced (2000); Foreign born: 3.4% (2000); Ancestry (includes multiple ancestries): 19.8% German, 17.0% Irish, 15.9% Italian, 15.5% English, 11.9% Polish (2000).
Economy: Single-family building permits issued: 23 (2005); Multi-family building permits issued: 0 (2005); Employment by occupation: 17.7% management, 31.7% professional, 8.9% services, 22.4% sales, 0.4% farming, 7.9% construction, 11.0% production (2000).
Income: Per capita income: $35,611 (2005); Median household income: $77,484 (2005); Average household income: $95,745 (2005); Percent of households with income of $100,000 or more: 31.6% (2005); Poverty rate: 1.2% (2000).

Education: Percent of population age 25 and over with: High school diploma (including GED) or higher: 96.8% (2005); Bachelor's degree or higher: 39.9% (2005); Master's degree or higher: 13.3% (2005).
Housing: Homeownership rate: 95.3% (2005); Median home value: $203,475 (2005); Median rent: $707 per month (2000); Median age of housing: 40 years (2000).
Transportation: Commute to work: 92.2% car, 0.2% public transportation, 0.3% walk, 7.0% work from home (2000); Travel time to work: 18.6% less than 15 minutes, 36.0% 15 to 30 minutes, 29.4% 30 to 45 minutes, 10.3% 45 to 60 minutes, 5.7% 60 minutes or more (2000)
Additional Information Contacts
Town of Charlton . . . . (518) 384-0152
http://www.townofcharlton.org/

CLIFTON PARK (town). Covers a land area of 48.567 square miles and a water area of 1.653 square miles. Located at 42.86° N. Lat.; 73.81° W. Long. Elevation is 321 feet.
Population: 30,117 (1990); 32,995 (2000); 35,919 (2005); 38,871 (2010 projected); Race: 92.8% White, 1.6% Black, 3.8% Asian, 2.5% Hispanic of any race (2005); Density: 739.6 persons per square mile (2005); Average household size: 2.56 (2005); Median age: 40.4 (2005); Males per 100 females: 97.7 (2005); Marriage status: 21.5% never married, 67.8% now married, 4.5% widowed, 6.3% divorced (2000); Foreign born: 5.8% (2000); Ancestry (includes multiple ancestries): 27.9% Irish, 19.5% Italian, 18.9% German, 13.8% English, 8.8% Polish (2000).
Economy: Unemployment rate: 2.7% (2005); Total civilian labor force: 21,354 (2005); Single-family building permits issued: 107 (2005); Multi-family building permits issued: 0 (2005); Employment by occupation: 21.5% management, 35.1% professional, 7.8% services, 25.1% sales, 0.0% farming, 4.2% construction, 6.4% production (2000).
Income: Per capita income: $37,382 (2005); Median household income: $79,518 (2005); Average household income: $94,757 (2005); Percent of households with income of $100,000 or more: 35.8% (2005); Poverty rate: 2.6% (2000).
Taxes: Total city taxes per capita: $240 (2004); City property taxes per capita: $163 (2004).
Education: Percent of population age 25 and over with: High school diploma (including GED) or higher: 95.9% (2005); Bachelor's degree or higher: 52.8% (2005); Master's degree or higher: 22.5% (2005).
School District(s)
Shenendehowa Central School District (KG-12)
    2003-04 Enrollment: 9,313 . . . . (518) 881-0610
Housing: Homeownership rate: 78.7% (2005); Median home value: $206,165 (2005); Median rent: $648 per month (2000); Median age of housing: 22 years (2000).
Newspapers: The Community News (General - Circulation 28,500)
Transportation: Commute to work: 93.9% car, 0.8% public transportation, 0.7% walk, 4.2% work from home (2000); Travel time to work: 19.8% less than 15 minutes, 48.4% 15 to 30 minutes, 25.7% 30 to 45 minutes, 3.7% 45 to 60 minutes, 2.3% 60 minutes or more (2000)
Additional Information Contacts
Southern Saratoga County Chamber of Commerce . . . . . . (518) 371-7748
    http://www.southernsaratoga.com
Town of Clifton Park. . . . . (518) 371-6651
    http://www.cliftonpark.org/

CORINTH (village). Covers a land area of 1.067 square miles and a water area of 0.045 square miles. Located at 43.24° N. Lat.; 73.82° W. Long.
Population: 2,760 (1990); 2,474 (2000); 2,483 (2005); 2,518 (2010 projected); Race: 97.1% White, 0.6% Black, 0.6% Asian, 2.5% Hispanic of any race (2005); Density: 2,327.1 persons per square mile (2005); Average household size: 2.36 (2005); Median age: 38.2 (2005); Males per 100 females: 94.3 (2005); Marriage status: 24.1% never married, 55.3% now married, 9.8% widowed, 10.8% divorced (2000); Foreign born: 1.1% (2000); Ancestry (includes multiple ancestries): 15.2% Irish, 13.8% German, 13.5% Other groups, 12.9% English, 12.0% French (except Basque) (2000).
Economy: Single-family building permits issued: 1 (2005); Multi-family building permits issued: 0 (2005); Employment by occupation: 8.5% management, 15.0% professional, 25.3% services, 22.5% sales, 1.3% farming, 9.8% construction, 17.5% production (2000).
Income: Per capita income: $17,786 (2005); Median household income: $32,711 (2005); Average household income: $41,885 (2005); Percent of households with income of $100,000 or more: 5.7% (2005); Poverty rate: 11.9% (2000).
Education: Percent of population age 25 and over with: High school diploma (including GED) or higher: 80.9% (2005); Bachelor's degree or higher: 10.4% (2005); Master's degree or higher: 4.8% (2005).
School District(s)
Corinth Central School District (KG-12)
    2003-04 Enrollment: 1,254 . . . . (518) 654-2601
Housing: Homeownership rate: 61.3% (2005); Median home value: $101,411 (2005); Median rent: $401 per month (2000); Median age of housing: 54 years (2000).
Safety: Violent crime rate: 44.2 per 10,000 population; Property crime rate: 277.3 per 10,000 population (2004).
Transportation: Commute to work: 88.0% car, 0.0% public transportation, 9.1% walk, 2.5% work from home (2000); Travel time to work: 34.5% less than 15 minutes, 39.1% 15 to 30 minutes, 18.4% 30 to 45 minutes, 3.8% 45 to 60 minutes, 4.2% 60 minutes or more (2000)

CORINTH (town). Covers a land area of 56.801 square miles and a water area of 1.331 square miles. Located at 43.23° N. Lat.; 73.84° W. Long.
History: Incorporated 1886.
Population: 5,923 (1990); 5,985 (2000); 6,109 (2005); 6,284 (2010 projected); Race: 97.7% White, 0.3% Black, 0.3% Asian, 1.4% Hispanic of any race (2005); Density: 107.6 persons per square mile (2005); Average household size: 2.51 (2005); Median age: 38.8 (2005); Males per 100 females: 97.0 (2005); Marriage status: 23.0% never married, 60.1% now married, 7.3% widowed, 9.6% divorced (2000); Foreign born: 1.0% (2000); Ancestry (includes multiple ancestries): 15.9% Irish, 15.9% French (except Basque), 14.2% English, 12.0% Other groups, 11.2% German (2000).
Economy: Manufacturing of metal lockers, gym bleachers; paper milling. Single-family building permits issued: 59 (2005); Multi-family building permits issued: 0 (2005); Employment by occupation: 8.4% management, 13.8% professional, 19.9% services, 25.0% sales, 1.6% farming, 12.1% construction, 19.1% production (2000).
Income: Per capita income: $17,391 (2005); Median household income: $36,902 (2005); Average household income: $43,589 (2005); Percent of households with income of $100,000 or more: 6.0% (2005); Poverty rate: 11.9% (2000).
Education: Percent of population age 25 and over with: High school diploma (including GED) or higher: 76.8% (2005); Bachelor's degree or higher: 10.9% (2005); Master's degree or higher: 4.2% (2005).
Housing: Homeownership rate: 75.4% (2005); Median home value: $109,422 (2005); Median rent: $413 per month (2000); Median age of housing: 38 years (2000).
Transportation: Commute to work: 91.9% car, 0.2% public transportation, 4.5% walk, 3.0% work from home (2000); Travel time to work: 32.2% less than 15 minutes, 36.3% 15 to 30 minutes, 20.1% 30 to 45 minutes, 6.1% 45 to 60 minutes, 5.3% 60 minutes or more (2000)
Additional Information Contacts
Town of Corinth . . . . (518) 654-9232
    http://townofcorinthny.com/

COUNTRY KNOLLS (CDP). Covers a land area of 1.642 square miles and a water area of 0 square miles. Located at 42.91° N. Lat.; 73.81° W. Long.
Population: 2,287 (1990); 2,155 (2000); 2,407 (2005); 2,666 (2010 projected); Race: 94.8% White, 0.8% Black, 3.4% Asian, 0.8% Hispanic of any race (2005); Density: 1,466.1 persons per square mile (2005); Average household size: 2.91 (2005); Median age: 42.2 (2005); Males per 100 females: 101.8 (2005); Marriage status: 18.5% never married, 77.5% now married, 2.0% widowed, 2.0% divorced (2000); Foreign born: 5.2% (2000); Ancestry (includes multiple ancestries): 24.8% Irish, 23.8% German, 19.8% Italian, 14.6% English, 7.5% Polish (2000).
Economy: Employment by occupation: 25.1% management, 35.4% professional, 6.3% services, 25.5% sales, 0.0% farming, 2.6% construction, 5.1% production (2000).
Income: Per capita income: $38,085 (2005); Median household income: $95,073 (2005); Average household income: $110,981 (2005); Percent of households with income of $100,000 or more: 46.7% (2005); Poverty rate: 1.6% (2000).
Education: Percent of population age 25 and over with: High school diploma (including GED) or higher: 97.8% (2005); Bachelor's degree or higher: 59.3% (2005); Master's degree or higher: 25.6% (2005).

Housing: Homeownership rate: 97.3% (2005); Median home value: $217,062 (2005); Median rent: $1,067 per month (2000); Median age of housing: 29 years (2000).
Transportation: Commute to work: 92.4% car, 1.0% public transportation, 0.0% walk, 5.9% work from home (2000); Travel time to work: 23.4% less than 15 minutes, 42.6% 15 to 30 minutes, 28.1% 30 to 45 minutes, 4.7% 45 to 60 minutes, 1.1% 60 minutes or more (2000)

DAY (town). Covers a land area of 64.307 square miles and a water area of 5.245 square miles. Located at 43.30° N. Lat.; 74.01° W. Long.
Population: 746 (1990); 920 (2000); 951 (2005); 989 (2010 projected); Race: 97.6% White, 0.0% Black, 0.4% Asian, 0.8% Hispanic of any race (2005); Density: 14.8 persons per square mile (2005); Average household size: 2.35 (2005); Median age: 45.4 (2005); Males per 100 females: 104.1 (2005); Marriage status: 20.7% never married, 64.5% now married, 9.3% widowed, 5.6% divorced (2000); Foreign born: 1.0% (2000); Ancestry (includes multiple ancestries): 15.5% German, 15.2% United States or American, 13.8% Irish, 11.3% Italian, 9.6% English (2000).
Economy: Single-family building permits issued: 13 (2005); Multi-family building permits issued: 0 (2005); Employment by occupation: 6.9% management, 15.4% professional, 22.0% services, 17.8% sales, 3.0% farming, 14.5% construction, 20.5% production (2000).
Income: Per capita income: $21,937 (2005); Median household income: $41,591 (2005); Average household income: $51,512 (2005); Percent of households with income of $100,000 or more: 12.6% (2005); Poverty rate: 19.1% (2000).
Education: Percent of population age 25 and over with: High school diploma (including GED) or higher: 69.8% (2005); Bachelor's degree or higher: 14.4% (2005); Master's degree or higher: 5.3% (2005).
Housing: Homeownership rate: 90.6% (2005); Median home value: $122,813 (2005); Median rent: $467 per month (2000); Median age of housing: 36 years (2000).
Transportation: Commute to work: 90.6% car, 1.5% public transportation, 2.7% walk, 3.9% work from home (2000); Travel time to work: 18.3% less than 15 minutes, 23.3% 15 to 30 minutes, 19.9% 30 to 45 minutes, 26.5% 45 to 60 minutes, 12.0% 60 minutes or more (2000)

EDINBURG (town). Covers a land area of 60.065 square miles and a water area of 7.013 square miles. Located at 43.22° N. Lat.; 74.09° W. Long.
Population: 1,041 (1990); 1,384 (2000); 1,417 (2005); 1,458 (2010 projected); Race: 98.1% White, 0.2% Black, 0.0% Asian, 1.2% Hispanic of any race (2005); Density: 23.6 persons per square mile (2005); Average household size: 2.26 (2005); Median age: 47.7 (2005); Males per 100 females: 101.0 (2005); Marriage status: 19.9% never married, 62.9% now married, 7.4% widowed, 9.9% divorced (2000); Foreign born: 2.0% (2000); Ancestry (includes multiple ancestries): 17.0% German, 15.8% United States or American, 12.3% Irish, 10.4% English, 8.4% Dutch (2000).
Economy: Single-family building permits issued: 22 (2005); Multi-family building permits issued: 0 (2005); Employment by occupation: 7.8% management, 17.1% professional, 11.8% services, 25.0% sales, 2.2% farming, 14.2% construction, 21.8% production (2000).
Income: Per capita income: $24,580 (2005); Median household income: $45,155 (2005); Average household income: $55,550 (2005); Percent of households with income of $100,000 or more: 11.3% (2005); Poverty rate: 8.3% (2000).
Education: Percent of population age 25 and over with: High school diploma (including GED) or higher: 81.1% (2005); Bachelor's degree or higher: 17.1% (2005); Master's degree or higher: 6.3% (2005).
School District(s)
Edinburg Common School District (KG-06)
    2003-04 Enrollment: 78 . . . . (518) 863-8412
Housing: Homeownership rate: 87.6% (2005); Median home value: $136,565 (2005); Median rent: $353 per month (2000); Median age of housing: 32 years (2000).
Transportation: Commute to work: 94.1% car, 0.3% public transportation, 1.4% walk, 3.4% work from home (2000); Travel time to work: 22.3% less than 15 minutes, 18.9% 15 to 30 minutes, 21.1% 30 to 45 minutes, 19.5% 45 to 60 minutes, 18.2% 60 minutes or more (2000)
Additional Information Contacts
Town of Edinburg. . . . . (518) 863-2034
    http://www.edinburgny.com/

GALWAY (village). Covers a land area of 0.256 square miles and a water area of 0 square miles. Located at 43.01° N. Lat.; 74.03° W. Long.
Population: 151 (1990); 214 (2000); 215 (2005); 218 (2010 projected); Race: 99.5% White, 0.0% Black, 0.0% Asian, 0.0% Hispanic of any race (2005); Density: 838.3 persons per square mile (2005); Average household size: 2.53 (2005); Median age: 38.0 (2005); Males per 100 females: 92.0 (2005); Marriage status: 20.1% never married, 68.9% now married, 6.1% widowed, 4.9% divorced (2000); Foreign born: 1.4% (2000); Ancestry (includes multiple ancestries): 22.5% English, 22.1% German, 15.0% Italian, 13.6% French (except Basque), 11.3% Irish (2000).
Economy: Employment by occupation: 11.4% management, 28.6% professional, 12.4% services, 27.6% sales, 0.0% farming, 14.3% construction, 5.7% production (2000).
Income: Per capita income: $23,221 (2005); Median household income: $42,500 (2005); Average household income: $58,735 (2005); Percent of households with income of $100,000 or more: 11.8% (2005); Poverty rate: 25.4% (2000).
Education: Percent of population age 25 and over with: High school diploma (including GED) or higher: 84.8% (2005); Bachelor's degree or higher: 28.3% (2005); Master's degree or higher: 7.6% (2005).
School District(s)
Galway Central School District (KG-12)
    2003-04 Enrollment: 1,178 . . . . (518) 882-1033
Housing: Homeownership rate: 71.8% (2005); Median home value: $146,591 (2005); Median rent: $350 per month (2000); Median age of housing: 60+ years (2000).
Transportation: Commute to work: 82.9% car, 0.0% public transportation, 7.6% walk, 9.5% work from home (2000); Travel time to work: 33.7% less than 15 minutes, 26.3% 15 to 30 minutes, 24.2% 30 to 45 minutes, 12.6% 45 to 60 minutes, 3.2% 60 minutes or more (2000)

GALWAY (town). Covers a land area of 44.016 square miles and a water area of 0.992 square miles. Located at 43.02° N. Lat.; 74.03° W. Long.
Population: 3,266 (1990); 3,589 (2000); 3,657 (2005); 3,755 (2010 projected); Race: 97.8% White, 0.1% Black, 0.5% Asian, 2.2% Hispanic of any race (2005); Density: 83.1 persons per square mile (2005); Average household size: 2.53 (2005); Median age: 41.8 (2005); Males per 100 females: 100.4 (2005); Marriage status: 19.6% never married, 66.8% now married, 6.0% widowed, 7.7% divorced (2000); Foreign born: 2.6% (2000); Ancestry (includes multiple ancestries): 22.6% Irish, 17.4% English, 17.1% German, 11.3% Italian, 9.1% French (except Basque) (2000).
Economy: In dairying area. Single-family building permits issued: 25 (2005); Multi-family building permits issued: 0 (2005); Employment by occupation: 13.0% management, 22.6% professional, 11.5% services, 24.7% sales, 0.0% farming, 15.0% construction, 13.2% production (2000).
Income: Per capita income: $27,751 (2005); Median household income: $61,148 (2005); Average household income: $69,841 (2005); Percent of households with income of $100,000 or more: 17.2% (2005); Poverty rate: 6.0% (2000).
Education: Percent of population age 25 and over with: High school diploma (including GED) or higher: 92.1% (2005); Bachelor's degree or higher: 23.8% (2005); Master's degree or higher: 11.5% (2005).
Housing: Homeownership rate: 85.5% (2005); Median home value: $170,819 (2005); Median rent: $530 per month (2000); Median age of housing: 37 years (2000).
Transportation: Commute to work: 95.0% car, 0.0% public transportation, 0.8% walk, 4.2% work from home (2000); Travel time to work: 12.1% less than 15 minutes, 34.4% 15 to 30 minutes, 35.0% 30 to 45 minutes, 10.9% 45 to 60 minutes, 7.6% 60 minutes or more (2000)

GANSEVOORT (unincorporated postal area, zip code 12831). Covers a land area of 64.223 square miles and a water area of 0.229 square miles. Located at 43.17° N. Lat.; 73.68° W. Long. Elevation is 249 feet.
Population: 0 (2000); Race: 93.6% White, 3.5% Black, 0.5% Asian, 2.8% Hispanic of any race (2000); Density: 0.0 persons per square mile (2000); Age: 28.1% under 18, 6.6% over 64 (2000); Marriage status: 23.8% never married, 64.6% now married, 3.2% widowed, 8.4% divorced (2000); Foreign born: 2.8% (2000); Ancestry (includes multiple ancestries): 24.2% Irish, 15.6% German, 14.9% English, 13.6% Italian, 10.7% French (except Basque) (2000).
Economy: Employment by occupation: 14.4% management, 23.1% professional, 12.5% services, 26.5% sales, 0.8% farming, 9.3% construction, 13.4% production (2000).
Income: Per capita income: $21,903 (2000); Median household income: $54,138 (2000); Poverty rate: 6.3% (2000).

Education: Percent of population age 25 and over with: High school diploma (including GED) or higher: 85.8% (2000); Bachelor's degree or higher: 27.2% (2000).
Housing: Homeownership rate: 86.5% (2000); Median home value: $120,400 (2000); Median rent: $550 per month (2000); Median age of housing: 15 years (2000).
Transportation: Commute to work: 95.6% car, 0.1% public transportation, 0.4% walk, 3.6% work from home (2000); Travel time to work: 24.0% less than 15 minutes, 42.5% 15 to 30 minutes, 16.0% 30 to 45 minutes, 12.5% 45 to 60 minutes, 5.0% 60 minutes or more (2000)

GREENFIELD

GREENFIELD (town). Covers a land area of 67.409 square miles and a water area of 0.310 square miles. Located at 43.12° N. Lat.; 73.87° W. Long.
Population: 6,338 (1990); 7,362 (2000); 7,875 (2005); 8,410 (2010 projected); Race: 96.7% White, 1.0% Black, 0.4% Asian, 2.1% Hispanic of any race (2005); Density: 116.8 persons per square mile (2005); Average household size: 2.60 (2005); Median age: 37.7 (2005); Males per 100 females: 100.8 (2005); Marriage status: 22.8% never married, 61.3% now married, 6.2% widowed, 9.7% divorced (2000); Foreign born: 1.8% (2000); Ancestry (includes multiple ancestries): 24.7% Irish, 16.4% German, 14.7% English, 11.4% Italian, 9.3% French (except Basque) (2000).
Economy: Single-family building permits issued: 51 (2005); Multi-family building permits issued: 0 (2005); Employment by occupation: 10.5% management, 20.7% professional, 18.1% services, 22.3% sales, 1.6% farming, 11.1% construction, 15.8% production (2000).
Income: Per capita income: $23,221 (2005); Median household income: $48,764 (2005); Average household income: $60,009 (2005); Percent of households with income of $100,000 or more: 13.2% (2005); Poverty rate: 6.1% (2000).
Education: Percent of population age 25 and over with: High school diploma (including GED) or higher: 84.2% (2005); Bachelor's degree or higher: 24.1% (2005); Master's degree or higher: 7.5% (2005).
Housing: Homeownership rate: 82.2% (2005); Median home value: $148,818 (2005); Median rent: $562 per month (2000); Median age of housing: 22 years (2000).
Transportation: Commute to work: 96.7% car, 0.0% public transportation, 0.4% walk, 2.1% work from home (2000); Travel time to work: 25.4% less than 15 minutes, 39.9% 15 to 30 minutes, 13.9% 30 to 45 minutes, 13.3% 45 to 60 minutes, 7.5% 60 minutes or more (2000)
Additional Information Contacts
Town of Greenfield. . . . . (518) 893-7432
http://www.townofgreenfield.com/

GREENFIELD CENTER

GREENFIELD CENTER (unincorporated postal area, zip code 12833). Covers a land area of 38.717 square miles and a water area of 0.154 square miles. Located at 43.12° N. Lat.; 73.85° W. Long.
Population: 0 (2000); Race: 96.9% White, 0.0% Black, 1.5% Asian, 1.2% Hispanic of any race (2000); Density: 0.0 persons per square mile (2000); Age: 27.3% under 18, 9.5% over 64 (2000); Marriage status: 21.9% never married, 62.7% now married, 5.6% widowed, 9.8% divorced (2000); Foreign born: 1.9% (2000); Ancestry (includes multiple ancestries): 20.2% Irish, 15.4% English, 13.7% German, 12.2% Italian, 9.1% United States or American (2000).
Economy: Employment by occupation: 10.1% management, 20.8% professional, 16.3% services, 21.7% sales, 1.6% farming, 12.3% construction, 17.4% production (2000).
Income: Per capita income: $19,194 (2000); Median household income: $44,777 (2000); Poverty rate: 8.2% (2000).
Education: Percent of population age 25 and over with: High school diploma (including GED) or higher: 81.8% (2000); Bachelor's degree or higher: 23.6% (2000).

School District(s)
Saratoga Springs City School District (KG-12)
  2003-04 Enrollment: 6,922 . . . . (518) 583-4708
Housing: Homeownership rate: 85.5% (2000); Median home value: $115,600 (2000); Median rent: $491 per month (2000); Median age of housing: 26 years (2000).
Transportation: Commute to work: 97.5% car, 0.0% public transportation, 0.0% walk, 1.4% work from home (2000); Travel time to work: 25.1% less than 15 minutes, 36.9% 15 to 30 minutes, 14.4% 30 to 45 minutes, 13.9% 45 to 60 minutes, 9.6% 60 minutes or more (2000)

HADLEY

HADLEY (town). Covers a land area of 39.750 square miles and a water area of 1.342 square miles. Located at 43.31° N. Lat.; 73.87° W. Long.
Population: 1,628 (1990); 1,971 (2000); 2,133 (2005); 2,300 (2010 projected); Race: 97.0% White, 1.5% Black, 0.2% Asian, 0.3% Hispanic of any race (2005); Density: 53.7 persons per square mile (2005); Average household size: 2.63 (2005); Median age: 38.3 (2005); Males per 100 females: 98.6 (2005); Marriage status: 24.8% never married, 60.9% now married, 6.6% widowed, 7.8% divorced (2000); Foreign born: 2.4% (2000); Ancestry (includes multiple ancestries): 20.2% Irish, 14.1% French (except Basque), 13.1% English, 12.4% German, 11.1% Other groups (2000).
Economy: Single-family building permits issued: 17 (2005); Multi-family building permits issued: 0 (2005); Employment by occupation: 4.9% management, 15.8% professional, 23.7% services, 23.3% sales, 0.5% farming, 13.9% construction, 17.9% production (2000).
Income: Per capita income: $20,655 (2005); Median household income: $44,216 (2005); Average household income: $54,108 (2005); Percent of households with income of $100,000 or more: 8.1% (2005); Poverty rate: 9.2% (2000).
Education: Percent of population age 25 and over with: High school diploma (including GED) or higher: 80.7% (2005); Bachelor's degree or higher: 11.4% (2005); Master's degree or higher: 3.3% (2005).
Housing: Homeownership rate: 77.0% (2005); Median home value: $120,276 (2005); Median rent: $436 per month (2000); Median age of housing: 28 years (2000).
Transportation: Commute to work: 93.6% car, 0.5% public transportation, 1.5% walk, 2.6% work from home (2000); Travel time to work: 27.5% less than 15 minutes, 24.3% 15 to 30 minutes, 32.1% 30 to 45 minutes, 8.7% 45 to 60 minutes, 7.4% 60 minutes or more (2000)
Additional Information Contacts
Town of Hadley . . . . (518) 696-4797
http://www.townofhadley.com/

HALFMOON

HALFMOON (town). Covers a land area of 32.645 square miles and a water area of 1.013 square miles. Located at 42.85° N. Lat.; 73.74° W. Long.
Population: 13,879 (1990); 18,474 (2000); 19,718 (2005); 21,029 (2010 projected); Race: 92.3% White, 2.0% Black, 3.2% Asian, 3.1% Hispanic of any race (2005); Density: 604.0 persons per square mile (2005); Average household size: 2.33 (2005); Median age: 37.6 (2005); Males per 100 females: 94.8 (2005); Marriage status: 25.4% never married, 58.4% now married, 5.6% widowed, 10.6% divorced (2000); Foreign born: 4.0% (2000); Ancestry (includes multiple ancestries): 24.9% Irish, 17.3% Italian, 16.3% German, 12.4% English, 11.7% French (except Basque) (2000).
Economy: Single-family building permits issued: 109 (2005); Multi-family building permits issued: 0 (2005); Employment by occupation: 17.0% management, 22.0% professional, 12.0% services, 29.5% sales, 0.2% farming, 8.8% construction, 10.5% production (2000).
Income: Per capita income: $27,519 (2005); Median household income: $50,881 (2005); Average household income: $63,505 (2005); Percent of households with income of $100,000 or more: 14.8% (2005); Poverty rate: 4.5% (2000).
Taxes: Total city taxes per capita: $166 (2004); City property taxes per capita: $110 (2004).
Education: Percent of population age 25 and over with: High school diploma (including GED) or higher: 88.7% (2005); Bachelor's degree or higher: 30.7% (2005); Master's degree or higher: 10.5% (2005).
Housing: Homeownership rate: 63.7% (2005); Median home value: $159,395 (2005); Median rent: $596 per month (2000); Median age of housing: 18 years (2000).
Transportation: Commute to work: 94.2% car, 0.6% public transportation, 1.6% walk, 3.0% work from home (2000); Travel time to work: 23.4% less than 15 minutes, 43.4% 15 to 30 minutes, 26.0% 30 to 45 minutes, 3.7% 45 to 60 minutes, 3.5% 60 minutes or more (2000)
Additional Information Contacts
Town of Halfmoon . . . . (518) 371-7410
http://www.townofhalfmoon.org/

MALTA

MALTA (town). Covers a land area of 28.017 square miles and a water area of 3.355 square miles. Located at 42.96° N. Lat.; 73.79° W. Long. Elevation is 342 feet.
Population: 11,709 (1990); 13,005 (2000); 13,725 (2005); 14,508 (2010 projected); Race: 94.8% White, 1.4% Black, 1.7% Asian, 2.3% Hispanic of any race (2005); Density: 489.9 persons per square mile (2005); Average

household size: 2.41 (2005); Median age: 37.3 (2005); Males per 100 females: 100.6 (2005); Marriage status: 22.7% never married, 64.8% now married, 4.1% widowed, 8.3% divorced (2000); Foreign born: 3.2% (2000); Ancestry (includes multiple ancestries): 26.3% Irish, 17.9% German, 17.4% Italian, 15.1% English, 9.3% Polish (2000).
Economy: Single-family building permits issued: 84 (2005); Multi-family building permits issued: 156 (2005); Employment by occupation: 16.3% management, 27.6% professional, 11.1% services, 29.3% sales, 0.2% farming, 6.9% construction, 8.6% production (2000).
Income: Per capita income: $31,237 (2005); Median household income: $65,102 (2005); Average household income: $75,290 (2005); Percent of households with income of $100,000 or more: 22.3% (2005); Poverty rate: 2.4% (2000).
Education: Percent of population age 25 and over with: High school diploma (including GED) or higher: 93.6% (2005); Bachelor's degree or higher: 34.9% (2005); Master's degree or higher: 12.2% (2005).
Housing: Homeownership rate: 68.1% (2005); Median home value: $165,559 (2005); Median rent: $592 per month (2000); Median age of housing: 18 years (2000).
Transportation: Commute to work: 95.2% car, 1.0% public transportation, 0.5% walk, 3.1% work from home (2000); Travel time to work: 22.6% less than 15 minutes, 33.0% 15 to 30 minutes, 32.4% 30 to 45 minutes, 6.0% 45 to 60 minutes, 6.1% 60 minutes or more (2000)
Additional Information Contacts
Town of Malta . . . . (518) 899-3434
http://www.malta-town.org/

MECHANICVILLE (city).
Covers a land area of 0.833 square miles and a water area of 0.076 square miles. Located at 42.90° N. Lat.; 73.69° W. Long. Elevation is 104 feet.
History: Settled before 1700; incorporated as village in 1859, as city in 1915.
Population: 5,249 (1990); 5,019 (2000); 4,986 (2005); 4,993 (2010 projected); Race: 96.6% White, 0.6% Black, 1.2% Asian, 2.0% Hispanic of any race (2005); Density: 5,988.7 persons per square mile (2005); Average household size: 2.23 (2005); Median age: 37.9 (2005); Males per 100 females: 90.2 (2005); Marriage status: 28.2% never married, 51.5% now married, 11.4% widowed, 8.9% divorced (2000); Foreign born: 1.5% (2000); Ancestry (includes multiple ancestries): 38.3% Italian, 26.6% Irish, 14.7% German, 10.6% French (except Basque), 9.0% English (2000).
Economy: Manufacturing of metal goods; railroad shops; in dairying area. Single-family building permits issued: 2 (2005); Multi-family building permits issued: 0 (2005); Employment by occupation: 9.6% management, 14.2% professional, 18.0% services, 33.5% sales, 0.2% farming, 8.8% construction, 15.7% production (2000).
Income: Per capita income: $19,412 (2005); Median household income: $37,537 (2005); Average household income: $43,120 (2005); Percent of households with income of $100,000 or more: 5.4% (2005); Poverty rate: 8.0% (2000).
Education: Percent of population age 25 and over with: High school diploma (including GED) or higher: 79.1% (2005); Bachelor's degree or higher: 14.0% (2005); Master's degree or higher: 5.0% (2005).
School District(s)
Mechanicville City School District (KG-12)
  2003-04 Enrollment: 1,347 . . . . (518) 664-5727
Housing: Homeownership rate: 41.6% (2005); Median home value: $125,573 (2005); Median rent: $421 per month (2000); Median age of housing: 60+ years (2000).
Safety: Violent crime rate: 73.8 per 10,000 population; Property crime rate: 93.8 per 10,000 population (2004).
Newspapers: The Express (General - Circulation 2,650)
Transportation: Commute to work: 89.3% car, 0.9% public transportation, 7.0% walk, 1.6% work from home (2000); Travel time to work: 31.8% less than 15 minutes, 28.7% 15 to 30 minutes, 26.3% 30 to 45 minutes, 9.7% 45 to 60 minutes, 3.6% 60 minutes or more (2000)
Additional Information Contacts
City of Mechanicville . . . . (518) 664-8331
http://www.mechanicville.com/
Mechanicville Area Chamber of Commerce . . . . (518) 664-7791

MIDDLE GROVE (unincorporated postal area, zip code 12850).
Covers a land area of 39.872 square miles and a water area of 0.349 square miles. Located at 43.09° N. Lat.; 73.97° W. Long.
Population: 0 (2000); Race: 95.2% White, 0.7% Black, 2.3% Asian, 1.4% Hispanic of any race (2000); Density: 0.0 persons per square mile (2000);

Age: 24.2% under 18, 10.9% over 64 (2000); Marriage status: 24.9% never married, 59.6% now married, 5.1% widowed, 10.4% divorced (2000); Foreign born: 3.0% (2000); Ancestry (includes multiple ancestries): 21.8% Irish, 20.3% German, 13.1% English, 9.8% Other groups, 8.7% Italian (2000).
Economy: Employment by occupation: 10.6% management, 17.9% professional, 19.8% services, 20.9% sales, 1.8% farming, 13.0% construction, 16.1% production (2000).
Income: Per capita income: $20,531 (2000); Median household income: $42,413 (2000); Poverty rate: 7.6% (2000).
Education: Percent of population age 25 and over with: High school diploma (including GED) or higher: 87.4% (2000); Bachelor's degree or higher: 17.6% (2000).
Housing: Homeownership rate: 82.9% (2000); Median home value: $117,900 (2000); Median rent: $537 per month (2000); Median age of housing: 24 years (2000).
Transportation: Commute to work: 93.7% car, 0.0% public transportation, 0.8% walk, 4.9% work from home (2000); Travel time to work: 11.8% less than 15 minutes, 44.8% 15 to 30 minutes, 25.6% 30 to 45 minutes, 12.7% 45 to 60 minutes, 5.2% 60 minutes or more (2000)

MILTON (town).
Covers a land area of 35.597 square miles and a water area of 0.019 square miles. Located at 43.03° N. Lat.; 73.87° W. Long.
Population: 14,658 (1990); 17,103 (2000); 17,374 (2005); 17,706 (2010 projected); Race: 95.0% White, 1.5% Black, 0.7% Asian, 3.2% Hispanic of any race (2005); Density: 488.1 persons per square mile (2005); Average household size: 2.62 (2005); Median age: 35.4 (2005); Males per 100 females: 100.6 (2005); Marriage status: 25.7% never married, 61.6% now married, 4.3% widowed, 8.4% divorced (2000); Foreign born: 2.2% (2000); Ancestry (includes multiple ancestries): 25.7% Irish, 20.1% German, 16.4% Italian, 15.6% English, 10.5% French (except Basque) (2000).
Economy: Employment by occupation: 13.9% management, 20.4% professional, 16.0% services, 26.8% sales, 0.1% farming, 11.1% construction, 11.8% production (2000).
Income: Per capita income: $23,695 (2005); Median household income: $50,710 (2005); Average household income: $61,333 (2005); Percent of households with income of $100,000 or more: 14.5% (2005); Poverty rate: 6.7% (2000).
Education: Percent of population age 25 and over with: High school diploma (including GED) or higher: 85.4% (2005); Bachelor's degree or higher: 22.6% (2005); Master's degree or higher: 7.7% (2005).
Housing: Homeownership rate: 75.3% (2005); Median home value: $135,202 (2005); Median rent: $466 per month (2000); Median age of housing: 24 years (2000).
Transportation: Commute to work: 93.1% car, 0.9% public transportation, 2.0% walk, 3.6% work from home (2000); Travel time to work: 29.0% less than 15 minutes, 28.7% 15 to 30 minutes, 23.6% 30 to 45 minutes, 13.5% 45 to 60 minutes, 5.1% 60 minutes or more (2000)
Additional Information Contacts
Town of Milton . . . . (518) 885-9220
http://www.townofmiltonny.org/

MILTON (CDP).
Covers a land area of 1.470 square miles and a water area of 0.005 square miles. Located at 43.03° N. Lat.; 73.84° W. Long.
Population: 1,892 (1990); 2,692 (2000); 2,643 (2005); 2,568 (2010 projected); Race: 96.2% White, 1.2% Black, 0.6% Asian, 3.7% Hispanic of any race (2005); Density: 1,798.3 persons per square mile (2005); Average household size: 2.67 (2005); Median age: 36.6 (2005); Males per 100 females: 96.5 (2005); Marriage status: 15.7% never married, 74.0% now married, 4.6% widowed, 5.8% divorced (2000); Foreign born: 5.2% (2000); Ancestry (includes multiple ancestries): 32.0% Irish, 19.3% German, 17.7% English, 14.0% Italian, 9.3% Polish (2000).
Economy: Employment by occupation: 15.9% management, 22.6% professional, 11.8% services, 28.6% sales, 0.0% farming, 12.4% construction, 8.7% production (2000).
Income: Per capita income: $27,401 (2005); Median household income: $65,753 (2005); Average household income: $72,073 (2005); Percent of households with income of $100,000 or more: 20.0% (2005); Poverty rate: 0.3% (2000).
Education: Percent of population age 25 and over with: High school diploma (including GED) or higher: 92.7% (2005); Bachelor's degree or higher: 27.5% (2005); Master's degree or higher: 9.0% (2005).
Housing: Homeownership rate: 90.8% (2005); Median home value: $142,815 (2005); Median rent: $404 per month (2000); Median age of housing: 21 years (2000).

Transportation: Commute to work: 95.7% car, 0.5% public transportation, 1.4% walk, 2.0% work from home (2000); Travel time to work: 23.4% less than 15 minutes, 29.2% 15 to 30 minutes, 26.4% 30 to 45 minutes, 16.2% 45 to 60 minutes, 4.8% 60 minutes or more (2000)

MOREAU (town).
Covers a land area of 42.163 square miles and a water area of 1.447 square miles. Located at 43.27° N. Lat.; 73.64° W. Long.
Population: 13,022 (1990); 13,826 (2000); 14,606 (2005); 15,447 (2010 projected); Race: 92.0% White, 4.7% Black, 0.6% Asian, 3.4% Hispanic of any race (2005); Density: 346.4 persons per square mile (2005); Average household size: 2.64 (2005); Median age: 38.9 (2005); Males per 100 females: 107.4 (2005); Marriage status: 24.3% never married, 59.2% now married, 6.4% widowed, 10.1% divorced (2000); Foreign born: 2.0% (2000); Ancestry (includes multiple ancestries): 22.2% Irish, 16.3% French (except Basque), 14.9% English, 11.6% Italian, 11.0% German (2000).
Economy: Single-family building permits issued: 73 (2005); Multi-family building permits issued: 0 (2005); Employment by occupation: 12.4% management, 16.3% professional, 18.1% services, 25.6% sales, 0.3% farming, 9.7% construction, 17.7% production (2000).
Income: Per capita income: $21,441 (2005); Median household income: $44,114 (2005); Average household income: $53,404 (2005); Percent of households with income of $100,000 or more: 9.9% (2005); Poverty rate: 7.1% (2000).
Taxes: Total city taxes per capita: $199 (2004); City property taxes per capita: $162 (2004).
Education: Percent of population age 25 and over with: High school diploma (including GED) or higher: 82.3% (2005); Bachelor's degree or higher: 14.2% (2005); Master's degree or higher: 5.1% (2005).
Housing: Homeownership rate: 78.7% (2005); Median home value: $125,303 (2005); Median rent: $447 per month (2000); Median age of housing: 31 years (2000).
Transportation: Commute to work: 94.2% car, 0.6% public transportation, 1.8% walk, 3.1% work from home (2000); Travel time to work: 38.2% less than 15 minutes, 40.7% 15 to 30 minutes, 11.9% 30 to 45 minutes, 4.8% 45 to 60 minutes, 4.4% 60 minutes or more (2000)

NORTH BALLSTON SPA (CDP).
Covers a land area of 0.828 square miles and a water area of 0 square miles. Located at 43.01° N. Lat.; 73.85° W. Long.
Population: 1,357 (1990); 1,237 (2000); 1,127 (2005); 1,101 (2010 projected); Race: 95.7% White, 0.0% Black, 0.8% Asian, 4.2% Hispanic of any race (2005); Density: 1,360.9 persons per square mile (2005); Average household size: 2.43 (2005); Median age: 43.6 (2005); Males per 100 females: 95.7 (2005); Marriage status: 25.3% never married, 58.3% now married, 6.7% widowed, 9.7% divorced (2000); Foreign born: 1.8% (2000); Ancestry (includes multiple ancestries): 23.1% Irish, 21.1% English, 19.6% German, 13.5% Italian, 13.5% French (except Basque) (2000).
Economy: Employment by occupation: 12.1% management, 23.8% professional, 17.9% services, 18.8% sales, 0.0% farming, 12.8% construction, 14.6% production (2000).
Income: Per capita income: $25,723 (2005); Median household income: $51,017 (2005); Average household income: $62,235 (2005); Percent of households with income of $100,000 or more: 19.0% (2005); Poverty rate: 6.7% (2000).
Education: Percent of population age 25 and over with: High school diploma (including GED) or higher: 87.0% (2005); Bachelor's degree or higher: 20.6% (2005); Master's degree or higher: 4.7% (2005).
Housing: Homeownership rate: 81.0% (2005); Median home value: $138,908 (2005); Median rent: $350 per month (2000); Median age of housing: 33 years (2000).
Transportation: Commute to work: 91.0% car, 1.0% public transportation, 4.3% walk, 3.6% work from home (2000); Travel time to work: 46.1% less than 15 minutes, 25.5% 15 to 30 minutes, 13.3% 30 to 45 minutes, 12.1% 45 to 60 minutes, 2.9% 60 minutes or more (2000)

NORTHUMBERLAND (town).
Covers a land area of 32.349 square miles and a water area of 0.549 square miles. Located at 43.17° N. Lat.; 73.63° W. Long.
Population: 3,645 (1990); 4,603 (2000); 4,804 (2005); 5,030 (2010 projected); Race: 97.4% White, 0.7% Black, 0.5% Asian, 1.8% Hispanic of any race (2005); Density: 148.5 persons per square mile (2005); Average household size: 2.82 (2005); Median age: 35.4 (2005); Males per 100 females: 101.3 (2005); Marriage status: 21.7% never married, 67.2% now married, 4.2% widowed, 6.9% divorced (2000); Foreign born: 1.0% (2000); Ancestry (includes multiple ancestries): 26.0% Irish, 16.0% German, 15.4% English, 11.2% Italian, 10.5% French (except Basque) (2000).
Economy: Single-family building permits issued: 20 (2005); Multi-family building permits issued: 0 (2005); Employment by occupation: 10.4% management, 19.1% professional, 13.5% services, 27.4% sales, 0.8% farming, 10.7% construction, 18.1% production (2000).
Income: Per capita income: $22,671 (2005); Median household income: $58,396 (2005); Average household income: $63,694 (2005); Percent of households with income of $100,000 or more: 13.4% (2005); Poverty rate: 6.2% (2000).
Education: Percent of population age 25 and over with: High school diploma (including GED) or higher: 86.8% (2005); Bachelor's degree or higher: 19.1% (2005); Master's degree or higher: 6.7% (2005).
Housing: Homeownership rate: 88.5% (2005); Median home value: $138,789 (2005); Median rent: $508 per month (2000); Median age of housing: 17 years (2000).
Transportation: Commute to work: 95.6% car, 0.8% public transportation, 0.8% walk, 2.3% work from home (2000); Travel time to work: 15.8% less than 15 minutes, 38.7% 15 to 30 minutes, 23.4% 30 to 45 minutes, 15.5% 45 to 60 minutes, 6.7% 60 minutes or more (2000)

PORTER CORNERS (unincorporated postal area, zip code 12859).
Covers a land area of 18.427 square miles and a water area of 0.048 square miles. Located at 43.18° N. Lat.; 73.88° W. Long.
Population: 0 (2000); Race: 96.0% White, 0.0% Black, 0.0% Asian, 0.6% Hispanic of any race (2000); Density: 0.0 persons per square mile (2000); Age: 30.8% under 18, 7.0% over 64 (2000); Marriage status: 20.9% never married, 66.1% now married, 4.0% widowed, 9.0% divorced (2000); Foreign born: 1.9% (2000); Ancestry (includes multiple ancestries): 29.4% Irish, 19.2% German, 19.0% English, 13.6% French (except Basque), 8.2% Italian (2000).
Economy: Employment by occupation: 11.2% management, 20.4% professional, 16.9% services, 18.5% sales, 1.9% farming, 12.6% construction, 18.5% production (2000).
Income: Per capita income: $18,285 (2000); Median household income: $49,083 (2000); Poverty rate: 4.0% (2000).
Education: Percent of population age 25 and over with: High school diploma (including GED) or higher: 81.4% (2000); Bachelor's degree or higher: 18.3% (2000).
Housing: Homeownership rate: 94.1% (2000); Median home value: $104,300 (2000); Median rent: $619 per month (2000); Median age of housing: 14 years (2000).
Transportation: Commute to work: 96.7% car, 0.0% public transportation, 1.5% walk, 1.1% work from home (2000); Travel time to work: 16.9% less than 15 minutes, 53.5% 15 to 30 minutes, 11.5% 30 to 45 minutes, 10.8% 45 to 60 minutes, 7.3% 60 minutes or more (2000)

PROVIDENCE (town).
Covers a land area of 44.029 square miles and a water area of 1.064 square miles. Located at 43.10° N. Lat.; 74.05° W. Long.
Population: 1,360 (1990); 1,841 (2000); 1,868 (2005); 1,910 (2010 projected); Race: 97.9% White, 0.7% Black, 0.5% Asian, 2.1% Hispanic of any race (2005); Density: 42.4 persons per square mile (2005); Average household size: 2.70 (2005); Median age: 38.5 (2005); Males per 100 females: 101.9 (2005); Marriage status: 20.4% never married, 67.9% now married, 3.4% widowed, 8.2% divorced (2000); Foreign born: 1.9% (2000); Ancestry (includes multiple ancestries): 19.5% Irish, 18.6% German, 12.2% English, 8.1% Italian, 7.9% Polish (2000).
Economy: Single-family building permits issued: 1 (2005); Multi-family building permits issued: 0 (2005); Employment by occupation: 8.2% management, 16.5% professional, 18.6% services, 21.7% sales, 0.2% farming, 14.5% construction, 20.2% production (2000).
Income: Per capita income: $21,186 (2005); Median household income: $48,654 (2005); Average household income: $57,189 (2005); Percent of households with income of $100,000 or more: 9.5% (2005); Poverty rate: 6.4% (2000).
Education: Percent of population age 25 and over with: High school diploma (including GED) or higher: 83.5% (2005); Bachelor's degree or higher: 12.0% (2005); Master's degree or higher: 3.5% (2005).
Housing: Homeownership rate: 86.4% (2005); Median home value: $127,273 (2005); Median rent: $450 per month (2000); Median age of housing: 22 years (2000).
Transportation: Commute to work: 95.1% car, 0.0% public transportation, 0.6% walk, 4.4% work from home (2000); Travel time to work: 9.2% less

than 15 minutes, 33.4% 15 to 30 minutes, 36.0% 30 to 45 minutes, 16.4% 45 to 60 minutes, 5.0% 60 minutes or more (2000)

REXFORD (unincorporated postal area, zip code 12148). Covers a land area of 14.222 square miles and a water area of 0.170 square miles. Located at 42.84° N. Lat.; 73.86° W. Long.
Population: 0 (2000); Race: 95.9% White, 0.1% Black, 2.0% Asian, 0.3% Hispanic of any race (2000); Density: 0.0 persons per square mile (2000); Age: 23.5% under 18, 16.7% over 64 (2000); Marriage status: 18.2% never married, 68.7% now married, 7.5% widowed, 5.6% divorced (2000); Foreign born: 6.2% (2000); Ancestry (includes multiple ancestries): 26.6% Italian, 23.7% Irish, 18.4% German, 16.8% English, 10.5% Polish (2000).
Economy: Employment by occupation: 23.1% management, 38.9% professional, 7.6% services, 23.6% sales, 0.0% farming, 2.9% construction, 3.8% production (2000).
Income: Per capita income: $31,972 (2000); Median household income: $70,344 (2000); Poverty rate: 4.2% (2000).
Education: Percent of population age 25 and over with: High school diploma (including GED) or higher: 91.9% (2000); Bachelor's degree or higher: 48.5% (2000).

School District(s)
Niskayuna Central School District (KG-12)
    2003-04 Enrollment: 4,258 . . . . (518) 377-4666

Housing: Homeownership rate: 86.1% (2000); Median home value: $168,200 (2000); Median rent: $2,000 per month (2000); Median age of housing: 23 years (2000).
Transportation: Commute to work: 93.5% car, 0.3% public transportation, 0.5% walk, 5.7% work from home (2000); Travel time to work: 17.5% less than 15 minutes, 52.3% 15 to 30 minutes, 21.5% 30 to 45 minutes, 4.1% 45 to 60 minutes, 4.6% 60 minutes or more (2000)

ROCK CITY FALLS (unincorporated postal area, zip code 12863). Covers a land area of 4.657 square miles and a water area of 0 square miles. Located at 43.06° N. Lat.; 73.93° W. Long.
Population: 0 (2000); Race: 98.5% White, 1.5% Black, 0.0% Asian, 1.5% Hispanic of any race (2000); Density: 0.0 persons per square mile (2000); Age: 21.7% under 18, 7.9% over 64 (2000); Marriage status: 18.3% never married, 69.8% now married, 3.5% widowed, 8.4% divorced (2000); Foreign born: 2.2% (2000); Ancestry (includes multiple ancestries): 22.7% Irish, 14.0% German, 10.7% Italian, 8.8% French (except Basque), 7.4% Hungarian (2000).
Economy: Employment by occupation: 20.8% management, 20.4% professional, 13.5% services, 27.7% sales, 0.0% farming, 5.5% construction, 12.0% production (2000).
Income: Per capita income: $24,776 (2000); Median household income: $57,500 (2000); Poverty rate: 2.6% (2000).
Education: Percent of population age 25 and over with: High school diploma (including GED) or higher: 82.4% (2000); Bachelor's degree or higher: 24.1% (2000).
Housing: Homeownership rate: 87.8% (2000); Median home value: $103,300 (2000); Median rent: $621 per month (2000); Median age of housing: 30 years (2000).
Transportation: Commute to work: 98.0% car, 0.0% public transportation, 0.0% walk, 2.0% work from home (2000); Travel time to work: 27.6% less than 15 minutes, 30.3% 15 to 30 minutes, 16.6% 30 to 45 minutes, 17.6% 45 to 60 minutes, 7.9% 60 minutes or more (2000)

ROUND LAKE (village). Covers a land area of 1.081 square miles and a water area of 0.094 square miles. Located at 42.93° N. Lat.; 73.79° W. Long. Elevation is 159 feet.
Population: 765 (1990); 604 (2000); 618 (2005); 623 (2010 projected); Race: 95.3% White, 0.3% Black, 1.8% Asian, 1.6% Hispanic of any race (2005); Density: 571.6 persons per square mile (2005); Average household size: 2.33 (2005); Median age: 39.4 (2005); Males per 100 females: 90.7 (2005); Marriage status: 22.4% never married, 59.1% now married, 6.3% widowed, 12.3% divorced (2000); Foreign born: 2.6% (2000); Ancestry (includes multiple ancestries): 19.8% Irish, 15.7% Italian, 15.5% English, 15.5% French (except Basque), 13.9% German (2000).
Economy: In agricultural area. Single-family building permits issued: 4 (2005); Multi-family building permits issued: 0 (2005); Employment by occupation: 13.1% management, 27.2% professional, 16.2% services, 23.9% sales, 0.6% farming, 8.6% construction, 10.4% production (2000).
Income: Per capita income: $26,036 (2005); Median household income: $48,060 (2005); Average household income: $60,717 (2005); Percent of households with income of $100,000 or more: 17.0% (2005); Poverty rate: 2.6% (2000).
Education: Percent of population age 25 and over with: High school diploma (including GED) or higher: 92.1% (2005); Bachelor's degree or higher: 29.6% (2005); Master's degree or higher: 11.4% (2005).
Housing: Homeownership rate: 82.6% (2005); Median home value: $137,871 (2005); Median rent: $563 per month (2000); Median age of housing: 60+ years (2000).
Transportation: Commute to work: 90.9% car, 0.3% public transportation, 3.1% walk, 5.6% work from home (2000); Travel time to work: 25.8% less than 15 minutes, 42.7% 15 to 30 minutes, 24.5% 30 to 45 minutes, 5.6% 45 to 60 minutes, 1.3% 60 minutes or more (2000)

Additional Information Contacts
Village of Round Lake . . . . (518) 899-2800
   http://www.roundlakevillage.org/

SARATOGA (town). Covers a land area of 40.671 square miles and a water area of 2.239 square miles. Located at 43.07° N. Lat.; 73.62° W. Long.
Population: 5,069 (1990); 5,141 (2000); 5,557 (2005); 5,983 (2010 projected); Race: 97.2% White, 1.2% Black, 0.2% Asian, 2.0% Hispanic of any race (2005); Density: 136.6 persons per square mile (2005); Average household size: 2.48 (2005); Median age: 39.9 (2005); Males per 100 females: 99.5 (2005); Marriage status: 24.9% never married, 58.4% now married, 6.4% widowed, 10.3% divorced (2000); Foreign born: 2.3% (2000); Ancestry (includes multiple ancestries): 20.3% Irish, 13.7% English, 12.8% French (except Basque), 12.8% German, 12.3% Italian (2000).
Economy: Single-family building permits issued: 27 (2005); Multi-family building permits issued: 0 (2005); Employment by occupation: 12.2% management, 22.0% professional, 16.4% services, 22.7% sales, 1.2% farming, 9.5% construction, 16.0% production (2000).
Income: Per capita income: $25,596 (2005); Median household income: $48,558 (2005); Average household income: $62,395 (2005); Percent of households with income of $100,000 or more: 15.8% (2005); Poverty rate: 7.3% (2000).
Education: Percent of population age 25 and over with: High school diploma (including GED) or higher: 83.1% (2005); Bachelor's degree or higher: 21.0% (2005); Master's degree or higher: 10.0% (2005).
Housing: Homeownership rate: 74.2% (2005); Median home value: $138,879 (2005); Median rent: $433 per month (2000); Median age of housing: 46 years (2000).
Transportation: Commute to work: 88.5% car, 0.2% public transportation, 2.9% walk, 8.2% work from home (2000); Travel time to work: 22.7% less than 15 minutes, 41.1% 15 to 30 minutes, 20.7% 30 to 45 minutes, 10.1% 45 to 60 minutes, 5.4% 60 minutes or more (2000)

SARATOGA SPRINGS (city). Covers a land area of 28.428 square miles and a water area of 0.632 square miles. Located at 43.07° N. Lat.; 73.78° W. Long. Elevation is 312 feet.
History: The growth and development of Saratoga Springs has been closely associated with its mineral springs, the waters of which began to be used in 1774. Rumors of the healing powers of the water circulated. In 1789, Gideon Putnam arrived and in 1802 he erected the three-story Union Hall, a hotel for visitors. People were attracted to the spot, and Putnam was ready to sell them lots around his hotel.
Population: 25,001 (1990); 26,186 (2000); 27,879 (2005); 29,620 (2010 projected); Race: 91.6% White, 3.8% Black, 1.6% Asian, 3.1% Hispanic of any race (2005); Density: 980.7 persons per square mile (2005); Average household size: 2.39 (2005); Median age: 37.6 (2005); Males per 100 females: 91.1 (2005); Marriage status: 33.9% never married, 50.3% now married, 7.4% widowed, 8.4% divorced (2000); Foreign born: 3.2% (2000); Ancestry (includes multiple ancestries): 25.6% Irish, 17.8% Italian, 17.1% German, 13.7% English, 9.4% Other groups (2000).
Economy: Unemployment rate: 3.4% (2005); Total civilian labor force: 15,742 (2005); Single-family building permits issued: 104 (2005); Multi-family building permits issued: 205 (2005); Employment by occupation: 14.7% management, 28.5% professional, 17.5% services, 26.7% sales, 0.3% farming, 5.0% construction, 7.3% production (2000).
Income: Per capita income: $30,169 (2005); Median household income: $52,158 (2005); Average household income: $70,205 (2005); Percent of households with income of $100,000 or more: 18.7% (2005); Poverty rate: 8.8% (2000).
Education: Percent of population age 25 and over with: High school diploma (including GED) or higher: 88.9% (2005); Bachelor's degree or higher: 38.7% (2005); Master's degree or higher: 17.8% (2005).

School District(s)
Saratoga Springs City School District (KG-12)
  2003-04 Enrollment: 6,922 . . . . (518) 583-4708
Four-year College(s)
SUNY Empire State College (Public)
  Fall 2004 Enrollment: 9,750. . . . . (518) 587-2100
  2005-06 Tuition: In-state $4,575; Out-of-state $10,835
Skidmore College
  Fall 2004 Enrollment: 2,691. . . . . (518) 580-5000
  2005-06 Tuition: In-state $32,659; Out-of-state $32,659
Two-year College(s)
Washington Saratoga Warren Hamilton Essex BOCES-Practical Nursing (Public)
  Fall 2004 Enrollment: 120 . . . . (518) 581-3670
  2005-06 Tuition: In-state $8,054; Out-of-state $8,054
Housing: Homeownership rate: 56.8% (2005); Median home value: $190,880 (2005); Median rent: $520 per month (2000); Median age of housing: 37 years (2000).
Hospitals: Saratoga Care (243 beds)
Safety: Violent crime rate: 6.9 per 10,000 population; Property crime rate: 159.9 per 10,000 population (2004).
Newspapers: The Saratogian (Circulation 10,605)
Transportation: Commute to work: 84.6% car, 2.0% public transportation, 8.4% walk, 4.1% work from home (2000); Travel time to work: 41.8% less than 15 minutes, 23.2% 15 to 30 minutes, 20.9% 30 to 45 minutes, 9.0% 45 to 60 minutes, 5.0% 60 minutes or more (2000); Amtrak: Service available.
Additional Information Contacts
City of Saratoga Springs . . . . (518) 587-3550
  http://www.saratoga-springs.org/
Saratoga Springs Chamber of Commerce. . . . . (518) 584-3255
  http://www.saratoga.org

SCHUYLERVILLE (village). Covers a land area of 0.529 square miles and a water area of 0.056 square miles. Located at 43.10° N. Lat.; 73.58° W. Long.
Population: 1,366 (1990); 1,197 (2000); 1,349 (2005); 1,502 (2010 projected); Race: 98.3% White, 0.4% Black, 0.0% Asian, 1.9% Hispanic of any race (2005); Density: 2,552.0 persons per square mile (2005); Average household size: 2.19 (2005); Median age: 39.2 (2005); Males per 100 females: 90.3 (2005); Marriage status: 30.1% never married, 47.1% now married, 11.3% widowed, 11.5% divorced (2000); Foreign born: 1.2% (2000); Ancestry (includes multiple ancestries): 25.2% Irish, 15.9% French (except Basque), 14.6% Italian, 11.4% German, 10.9% English (2000).
Economy: Single-family building permits issued: 0 (2005); Multi-family building permits issued: 0 (2005); Employment by occupation: 10.7% management, 20.7% professional, 17.6% services, 25.7% sales, 0.3% farming, 9.2% construction, 15.7% production (2000).
Income: Per capita income: $21,391 (2005); Median household income: $34,157 (2005); Average household income: $44,639 (2005); Percent of households with income of $100,000 or more: 5.8% (2005); Poverty rate: 11.7% (2000).
Education: Percent of population age 25 and over with: High school diploma (including GED) or higher: 82.3% (2005); Bachelor's degree or higher: 17.7% (2005); Master's degree or higher: 4.6% (2005).
School District(s)
Schuylerville Central School District (KG-12)
  2003-04 Enrollment: 1,693 . . . . (518) 695-3255
Housing: Homeownership rate: 50.4% (2005); Median home value: $113,323 (2005); Median rent: $411 per month (2000); Median age of housing: 60+ years (2000).
Transportation: Commute to work: 89.0% car, 0.0% public transportation, 8.3% walk, 2.3% work from home (2000); Travel time to work: 30.0% less than 15 minutes, 35.4% 15 to 30 minutes, 19.3% 30 to 45 minutes, 9.0% 45 to 60 minutes, 6.3% 60 minutes or more (2000)
Additional Information Contacts
Schuylerville Area Chamber of Commerce . . . . (518) 695-5243
  http://www.adirondackchamber.org

SOUTH GLENS FALLS (village). Covers a land area of 1.347 square miles and a water area of 0.141 square miles. Located at 43.29° N. Lat.; 73.63° W. Long. Elevation is 345 feet.
History: Incorporated 1895.
Population: 3,506 (1990); 3,368 (2000); 3,441 (2005); 3,544 (2010 projected); Race: 98.0% White, 1.0% Black, 0.2% Asian, 1.0% Hispanic of any race (2005); Density: 2,554.8 persons per square mile (2005); Average household size: 2.16 (2005); Median age: 39.8 (2005); Males per 100 females: 88.4 (2005); Marriage status: 25.3% never married, 51.7% now married, 9.4% widowed, 13.5% divorced (2000); Foreign born: 1.6% (2000); Ancestry (includes multiple ancestries): 24.1% Irish, 18.5% French (except Basque), 13.7% English, 13.1% Italian, 9.9% German (2000).
Economy: Some manufacturing. Employment by occupation: 15.4% management, 10.1% professional, 17.3% services, 28.1% sales, 0.0% farming, 9.3% construction, 19.9% production (2000).
Income: Per capita income: $18,812 (2005); Median household income: $33,401 (2005); Average household income: $40,212 (2005); Percent of households with income of $100,000 or more: 5.3% (2005); Poverty rate: 10.6% (2000).
Education: Percent of population age 25 and over with: High school diploma (including GED) or higher: 87.1% (2005); Bachelor's degree or higher: 9.1% (2005); Master's degree or higher: 2.3% (2005).
School District(s)
South Glens Falls Central School District (KG-12)
  2003-04 Enrollment: 3,292 . . . . (518) 793-9617
Housing: Homeownership rate: 57.0% (2005); Median home value: $113,086 (2005); Median rent: $420 per month (2000); Median age of housing: 55 years (2000).
Safety: Violent crime rate: 11.7 per 10,000 population; Property crime rate: 306.7 per 10,000 population (2004).
Transportation: Commute to work: 90.5% car, 1.3% public transportation, 4.9% walk, 3.4% work from home (2000); Travel time to work: 53.1% less than 15 minutes, 25.9% 15 to 30 minutes, 13.4% 30 to 45 minutes, 3.8% 45 to 60 minutes, 3.8% 60 minutes or more (2000)

STILLWATER (village). Covers a land area of 1.238 square miles and a water area of 0.194 square miles. Located at 42.94° N. Lat.; 73.65° W. Long.
Population: 1,531 (1990); 1,644 (2000); 1,680 (2005); 1,730 (2010 projected); Race: 96.8% White, 0.5% Black, 1.3% Asian, 1.4% Hispanic of any race (2005); Density: 1,357.2 persons per square mile (2005); Average household size: 2.68 (2005); Median age: 36.8 (2005); Males per 100 females: 91.6 (2005); Marriage status: 24.5% never married, 59.6% now married, 6.8% widowed, 9.1% divorced (2000); Foreign born: 1.5% (2000); Ancestry (includes multiple ancestries): 26.3% Irish, 25.7% Italian, 11.4% German, 11.0% French (except Basque), 10.6% Polish (2000).
Economy: Single-family building permits issued: 7 (2005); Multi-family building permits issued: 0 (2005); Employment by occupation: 9.1% management, 12.5% professional, 13.2% services, 33.0% sales, 0.3% farming, 13.8% construction, 18.1% production (2000).
Income: Per capita income: $20,421 (2005); Median household income: $49,541 (2005); Average household income: $54,804 (2005); Percent of households with income of $100,000 or more: 10.9% (2005); Poverty rate: 10.8% (2000).
Education: Percent of population age 25 and over with: High school diploma (including GED) or higher: 83.7% (2005); Bachelor's degree or higher: 12.4% (2005); Master's degree or higher: 3.8% (2005).
School District(s)
Stillwater Central School District (KG-12)
  2003-04 Enrollment: 1,315 . . . . (518) 373-6100
Housing: Homeownership rate: 66.6% (2005); Median home value: $129,390 (2005); Median rent: $435 per month (2000); Median age of housing: 52 years (2000).
Transportation: Commute to work: 92.7% car, 0.8% public transportation, 1.8% walk, 3.7% work from home (2000); Travel time to work: 25.1% less than 15 minutes, 32.2% 15 to 30 minutes, 26.9% 30 to 45 minutes, 12.5% 45 to 60 minutes, 3.3% 60 minutes or more (2000)

STILLWATER (town). Covers a land area of 41.355 square miles and a water area of 2.210 square miles. Located at 42.95° N. Lat.; 73.67° W. Long.
History: The American Revolutionary battles (Sept. 19, 1777, and Oct. 7, 1777) fought near here are commemorated by Saratoga National Historical Park, 9 miles Southeast of Saratoga Springs.
Population: 7,233 (1990); 7,522 (2000); 8,032 (2005); 8,564 (2010 projected); Race: 97.6% White, 0.6% Black, 0.7% Asian, 0.8% Hispanic of any race (2005); Density: 194.2 persons per square mile (2005); Average household size: 2.65 (2005); Median age: 38.5 (2005); Males per 100 females: 99.7 (2005); Marriage status: 23.9% never married, 61.9% now married, 4.8% widowed, 9.5% divorced (2000); Foreign born: 1.4% (2000);

Ancestry (includes multiple ancestries): 25.2% Irish, 20.9% Italian, 14.1% English, 13.1% German, 12.7% French (except Basque) (2000).
Economy: In dairying area. Single-family building permits issued: 75 (2005); Multi-family building permits issued: 0 (2005); Employment by occupation: 12.3% management, 15.9% professional, 12.3% services, 33.0% sales, 0.6% farming, 11.3% construction, 14.6% production (2000).
Income: Per capita income: $22,873 (2005); Median household income: $54,143 (2005); Average household income: $60,693 (2005); Percent of households with income of $100,000 or more: 13.9% (2005); Poverty rate: 6.7% (2000).
Education: Percent of population age 25 and over with: High school diploma (including GED) or higher: 81.7% (2005); Bachelor's degree or higher: 17.3% (2005); Master's degree or higher: 7.0% (2005).
Housing: Homeownership rate: 83.5% (2005); Median home value: $137,402 (2005); Median rent: $448 per month (2000); Median age of housing: 29 years (2000).
Safety: Violent crime rate: 4.8 per 10,000 population; Property crime rate: 27.3 per 10,000 population (2004).
Transportation: Commute to work: 94.5% car, 0.3% public transportation, 0.9% walk, 4.1% work from home (2000); Travel time to work: 17.2% less than 15 minutes, 32.5% 15 to 30 minutes, 33.1% 30 to 45 minutes, 14.0% 45 to 60 minutes, 3.2% 60 minutes or more (2000)

VICTORY
(village). Aka Victory Mills. Covers a land area of 0.528 square miles and a water area of 0 square miles. Located at 43.08° N. Lat.; 73.59° W. Long.
Population: 598 (1990); 544 (2000); 586 (2005); 626 (2010 projected); Race: 97.1% White, 0.7% Black, 0.0% Asian, 2.9% Hispanic of any race (2005); Density: 1,110.3 persons per square mile (2005); Average household size: 2.82 (2005); Median age: 36.4 (2005); Males per 100 females: 97.3 (2005); Marriage status: 32.4% never married, 51.6% now married, 7.9% widowed, 8.1% divorced (2000); Foreign born: 0.6% (2000); Ancestry (includes multiple ancestries): 20.6% Irish, 9.8% French (except Basque), 8.3% English, 6.9% German, 6.5% Italian (2000).
Economy: Single-family building permits issued: 0 (2005); Multi-family building permits issued: 0 (2005); Employment by occupation: 7.5% management, 18.8% professional, 22.1% services, 18.3% sales, 0.8% farming, 14.2% construction, 18.3% production (2000).
Income: Per capita income: $22,590 (2005); Median household income: $50,018 (2005); Average household income: $63,642 (2005); Percent of households with income of $100,000 or more: 14.4% (2005); Poverty rate: 9.1% (2000).
Education: Percent of population age 25 and over with: High school diploma (including GED) or higher: 76.3% (2005); Bachelor's degree or higher: 11.3% (2005); Master's degree or higher: 5.9% (2005).
Housing: Homeownership rate: 80.3% (2005); Median home value: $116,118 (2005); Median rent: $453 per month (2000); Median age of housing: 54 years (2000).
Transportation: Commute to work: 89.9% car, 2.1% public transportation, 1.7% walk, 4.2% work from home (2000); Travel time to work: 14.5% less than 15 minutes, 48.7% 15 to 30 minutes, 9.6% 30 to 45 minutes, 16.7% 45 to 60 minutes, 10.5% 60 minutes or more (2000)

WATERFORD
(village). Covers a land area of 0.285 square miles and a water area of 0.079 square miles. Located at 42.79° N. Lat.; 73.68° W. Long.
Population: 2,370 (1990); 2,204 (2000); 2,174 (2005); 2,163 (2010 projected); Race: 94.3% White, 1.3% Black, 2.3% Asian, 0.8% Hispanic of any race (2005); Density: 7,626.0 persons per square mile (2005); Average household size: 2.28 (2005); Median age: 36.7 (2005); Males per 100 females: 91.9 (2005); Marriage status: 30.4% never married, 51.6% now married, 7.6% widowed, 10.3% divorced (2000); Foreign born: 2.5% (2000); Ancestry (includes multiple ancestries): 27.0% Irish, 21.8% Italian, 19.9% French (except Basque), 13.2% German, 7.8% English (2000).
Economy: Single-family building permits issued: 2 (2005); Multi-family building permits issued: 0 (2005); Employment by occupation: 9.9% management, 15.3% professional, 18.3% services, 33.2% sales, 0.3% farming, 6.6% construction, 16.4% production (2000).
Income: Per capita income: $20,215 (2005); Median household income: $36,768 (2005); Average household income: $45,887 (2005); Percent of households with income of $100,000 or more: 5.7% (2005); Poverty rate: 12.6% (2000).
Education: Percent of population age 25 and over with: High school diploma (including GED) or higher: 83.5% (2005); Bachelor's degree or higher: 14.2% (2005); Master's degree or higher: 4.0% (2005).

School District(s)
Waterford-Halfmoon Union Free School District (KG-12)
    2003-04 Enrollment: 877 . . . . (518) 237-0800
Housing: Homeownership rate: 45.5% (2005); Median home value: $129,032 (2005); Median rent: $425 per month (2000); Median age of housing: 60+ years (2000).
Transportation: Commute to work: 90.2% car, 3.1% public transportation, 4.9% walk, 1.4% work from home (2000); Travel time to work: 27.4% less than 15 minutes, 52.9% 15 to 30 minutes, 15.0% 30 to 45 minutes, 3.2% 45 to 60 minutes, 1.4% 60 minutes or more (2000)
Additional Information Contacts
Village of Waterford . . . . (518) 235-9898
    http://www.waterfordny.org/

WATERFORD
(town). Covers a land area of 6.554 square miles and a water area of 0.862 square miles. Located at 42.80° N. Lat.; 73.68° W. Long.
History: Incorporated 1794.
Population: 8,695 (1990); 8,515 (2000); 8,714 (2005); 8,973 (2010 projected); Race: 95.5% White, 1.1% Black, 1.8% Asian, 1.8% Hispanic of any race (2005); Density: 1,329.5 persons per square mile (2005); Average household size: 2.38 (2005); Median age: 38.6 (2005); Males per 100 females: 93.0 (2005); Marriage status: 26.6% never married, 58.5% now married, 6.4% widowed, 8.4% divorced (2000); Foreign born: 2.2% (2000); Ancestry (includes multiple ancestries): 28.4% Irish, 20.2% Italian, 19.0% French (except Basque), 16.2% German, 10.2% English (2000).
Economy: Manufacturing of chemicals, non-woven needle-punched products, transportation equipment, computer chips. Single-family building permits issued: 9 (2005); Multi-family building permits issued: 0 (2005); Employment by occupation: 13.9% management, 19.7% professional, 11.3% services, 32.3% sales, 0.1% farming, 8.0% construction, 14.7% production (2000).
Income: Per capita income: $26,064 (2005); Median household income: $51,566 (2005); Average household income: $61,919 (2005); Percent of households with income of $100,000 or more: 13.7% (2005); Poverty rate: 5.7% (2000).
Education: Percent of population age 25 and over with: High school diploma (including GED) or higher: 83.0% (2005); Bachelor's degree or higher: 19.2% (2005); Master's degree or higher: 7.0% (2005).
Housing: Homeownership rate: 59.5% (2005); Median home value: $152,102 (2005); Median rent: $486 per month (2000); Median age of housing: 44 years (2000).
Safety: Violent crime rate: 0.0 per 10,000 population; Property crime rate: 91.2 per 10,000 population (2004).
Transportation: Commute to work: 93.3% car, 1.7% public transportation, 2.8% walk, 2.1% work from home (2000); Travel time to work: 22.4% less than 15 minutes, 53.2% 15 to 30 minutes, 18.1% 30 to 45 minutes, 2.9% 45 to 60 minutes, 3.4% 60 minutes or more (2000)

WILTON
(town). Covers a land area of 35.875 square miles and a water area of 0.093 square miles. Located at 43.14° N. Lat.; 73.73° W. Long.
Population: 10,635 (1990); 12,511 (2000); 15,562 (2005); 18,415 (2010 projected); Race: 96.4% White, 1.2% Black, 0.8% Asian, 1.8% Hispanic of any race (2005); Density: 433.8 persons per square mile (2005); Average household size: 2.69 (2005); Median age: 37.7 (2005); Males per 100 females: 96.6 (2005); Marriage status: 21.2% never married, 65.0% now married, 4.8% widowed, 9.0% divorced (2000); Foreign born: 2.9% (2000); Ancestry (includes multiple ancestries): 24.0% Irish, 15.5% German, 14.7% Italian, 14.6% English, 11.8% French (except Basque) (2000).
Economy: Single-family building permits issued: 88 (2005); Multi-family building permits issued: 36 (2005); Employment by occupation: 15.0% management, 23.2% professional, 13.0% services, 28.7% sales, 0.6% farming, 7.6% construction, 11.9% production (2000).
Income: Per capita income: $26,371 (2005); Median household income: $61,520 (2005); Average household income: $70,754 (2005); Percent of households with income of $100,000 or more: 19.7% (2005); Poverty rate: 5.1% (2000).
Education: Percent of population age 25 and over with: High school diploma (including GED) or higher: 91.0% (2005); Bachelor's degree or higher: 33.9% (2005); Master's degree or higher: 14.4% (2005).
School District(s)
Saratoga Springs City School District (KG-12)
    2003-04 Enrollment: 6,922 . . . . (518) 583-4708
South Glens Falls Central School District (KG-12)
    2003-04 Enrollment: 3,292 . . . . (518) 793-9617

Housing: Homeownership rate: 85.2% (2005); Median home value: $168,569 (2005); Median rent: $505 per month (2000); Median age of housing: 16 years (2000).
Transportation: Commute to work: 95.5% car, 0.4% public transportation, 0.3% walk, 3.0% work from home (2000); Travel time to work: 32.1% less than 15 minutes, 36.3% 15 to 30 minutes, 16.4% 30 to 45 minutes, 10.3% 45 to 60 minutes, 4.9% 60 minutes or more (2000)
Additional Information Contacts
Town of Wilton .... (518) 587-1939
   http://www.townofwilton.com/

Schenectady County

Located in eastern New York; bounded on the north by Schoharie Creek; crossed by the Mohawk River. Covers a land area of 206.10 square miles, a water area of 3.52 square miles, and is located in the Eastern Time Zone. The county government was organized in 1809. County seat is Schenectady.

Schenectady County is part of the Albany-Schenectady-Troy, NY Metropolitan Statistical Area. The entire metro area includes: Albany County, NY; Rensselaer County, NY; Saratoga County, NY; Schenectady County, NY; Schoharie County, NY

Population: 149,285 (1990); 146,555 (2000); 147,914 (2005); 149,239 (2010 projected); Race: 84.8% White, 8.1% Black, 3.0% Asian, 4.3% Hispanic of any race (2005); Density: 717.7 persons per square mile (2005); Average household size: 2.44 (2005); Median age: 39.7 (2005); Males per 100 females: 93.2 (2005).
Religion: Five largest groups: 48.4% Catholic Church, 3.5% Jewish Estimate, 3.4% The United Methodist Church, 3.3% Reformed Church in America, 1.5% Evangelical Lutheran Church in America (2000).
Economy: Unemployment rate: 4.2% (2005); Total civilian labor force: 75,655 (2005); Leading industries: 21.0% health care and social assistance; 15.6% retail trade; 11.2% professional (2003); Farms: 200 totaling 21,727 acres (2002); Companies that employ 500 or more persons: 11 (2003); Companies that employ 100 to 499 persons: 63 (2003); Companies that employ less than 100 persons: 2,925 (2003); Black-owned businesses: 473 (2002); Hispanic-owned businesses: n/a (2002); Women-owned businesses: 3,645 (2002); Retail sales per capita: $11,809 (2006). Single-family building permits issued: 268 (2005); Multi-family building permits issued: 95 (2005).
Income: Per capita income: $25,299 (2005); Median household income: $47,388 (2005); Average household income: $60,616 (2005); Percent of households with income of $100,000 or more: 15.4% (2005); Poverty rate: 11.6% (2003); Bankruptcy rate: 7.25% (2005).
Taxes: Total county taxes per capita: $834 (2004); County property taxes per capita: $360 (2004).
Education: Percent of population age 25 and over with: High school diploma (including GED) or higher: 85.0% (2005); Bachelor's degree or higher: 26.5% (2005); Master's degree or higher: 11.8% (2005).
Housing: Homeownership rate: 66.2% (2005); Median home value: $134,996 (2005); Median rent: $468 per month (2000); Median age of housing: 52 years (2000).
Health: Birth rate: 122.2 per 10,000 population (2004); Death rate: 105.6 per 10,000 population (2004); Age-adjusted cancer mortality rate: 209.2 deaths per 100,000 population (2002); Air Quality Index: 96.7% good, 3.3% moderate, 0.0% unhealthy for sensitive individuals, 0.0% unhealthy (percent of days in 2005); Number of physicians: 32.3 per 10,000 population (2004); Hospital beds: 63.5 per 10,000 population (2003); Hospital admissions: 1,967.3 per 10,000 population (2003).
Elections: 2004 Presidential election results: 46.2% Bush, 51.8% Kerry, 1.7% Nader, 0.3% Badnarik
Additional Information Contacts
Schenectady County Government.................... (518) 388-4220
   http://www.schenectadycounty.com/
Town of Duanesburg................................ (518) 895-8920
   http://www.duanesburg.net/
Town of Glenville................................. (518) 688-1200
   http://www.townofglenville.org/Home/
Town of Niskayuna................................. (518) 386-4500
   http://www.niskayuna.org/Home/

Schenectady County Communities

ALPLAUS (unincorporated postal area, zip code 12008). Part of the Census Designated Place of East Glenville. Covers a land area of 0.830 square miles and a water area of 0 square miles. Located at 42.85° N. Lat.; 73.90° W. Long.
Population: 0 (2000); Race: 96.9% White, 0.0% Black, 2.2% Asian, 1.3% Hispanic of any race (2000); Density: 0.0 persons per square mile (2000); Age: 33.4% under 18, 8.5% over 64 (2000); Marriage status: 12.3% never married, 78.4% now married, 3.7% widowed, 5.6% divorced (2000); Foreign born: 4.3% (2000); Ancestry (includes multiple ancestries): 28.7% Italian, 24.9% Irish, 18.4% German, 13.4% Polish, 7.8% English (2000).
Economy: Employment by occupation: 16.1% management, 29.7% professional, 4.8% services, 28.5% sales, 0.0% farming, 9.6% construction, 11.2% production (2000).
Income: Per capita income: $24,064 (2000); Median household income: $66,908 (2000); Poverty rate: 0.0% (2000).
Education: Percent of population age 25 and over with: High school diploma (including GED) or higher: 85.4% (2000); Bachelor's degree or higher: 30.4% (2000).
Housing: Homeownership rate: 95.4% (2000); Median home value: $113,100 (2000); Median rent: $n/a per month (2000); Median age of housing: 60+ years (2000).
Transportation: Commute to work: 89.8% car, 3.4% public transportation, 1.9% walk, 4.9% work from home (2000); Travel time to work: 25.1% less than 15 minutes, 41.8% 15 to 30 minutes, 28.3% 30 to 45 minutes, 1.6% 45 to 60 minutes, 3.2% 60 minutes or more (2000)

DELANSON (village). Covers a land area of 0.624 square miles and a water area of 0 square miles. Located at 42.74° N. Lat.; 74.18° W. Long.
Population: 361 (1990); 385 (2000); 377 (2005); 374 (2010 projected); Race: 93.4% White, 1.6% Black, 0.0% Asian, 0.3% Hispanic of any race (2005); Density: 603.9 persons per square mile (2005); Average household size: 2.48 (2005); Median age: 39.2 (2005); Males per 100 females: 96.4 (2005); Marriage status: 18.8% never married, 68.4% now married, 5.3% widowed, 7.5% divorced (2000); Foreign born: 2.8% (2000); Ancestry (includes multiple ancestries): 19.2% German, 14.6% Irish, 13.1% English, 9.0% Italian, 8.5% Dutch (2000).
Economy: Single-family building permits issued: 4 (2005); Multi-family building permits issued: 0 (2005); Employment by occupation: 17.8% management, 20.7% professional, 7.7% services, 28.8% sales, 0.0% farming, 11.5% construction, 13.5% production (2000).
Income: Per capita income: $30,877 (2005); Median household income: $67,683 (2005); Average household income: $74,934 (2005); Percent of households with income of $100,000 or more: 20.4% (2005); Poverty rate: 0.5% (2000).
Education: Percent of population age 25 and over with: High school diploma (including GED) or higher: 92.7% (2005); Bachelor's degree or higher: 26.3% (2005); Master's degree or higher: 12.2% (2005).
School District(s)
Duanesburg Central School District (KG-12)
   2003-04 Enrollment: 951 .... (518) 895-2279
Housing: Homeownership rate: 71.7% (2005); Median home value: $138,830 (2005); Median rent: $566 per month (2000); Median age of housing: 60+ years (2000).
Transportation: Commute to work: 98.1% car, 0.0% public transportation, 0.5% walk, 1.4% work from home (2000); Travel time to work: 12.7% less than 15 minutes, 26.8% 15 to 30 minutes, 43.9% 30 to 45 minutes, 13.2% 45 to 60 minutes, 3.4% 60 minutes or more (2000)

DUANE LAKE (CDP). Covers a land area of 2.391 square miles and a water area of 0.179 square miles. Located at 42.75° N. Lat.; 74.11° W. Long.
Population: 358 (1990); 357 (2000); 368 (2005); 376 (2010 projected); Race: 98.6% White, 0.0% Black, 0.0% Asian, 0.3% Hispanic of any race (2005); Density: 153.9 persons per square mile (2005); Average household size: 2.75 (2005); Median age: 43.1 (2005); Males per 100 females: 96.8 (2005); Marriage status: 21.9% never married, 76.7% now married, 0.0% widowed, 1.4% divorced (2000); Foreign born: 0.0% (2000); Ancestry (includes multiple ancestries): 20.0% German, 19.4% Irish, 17.1% English, 13.7% Polish, 12.7% Italian (2000).
Economy: Employment by occupation: 21.1% management, 26.5% professional, 8.1% services, 35.1% sales, 0.0% farming, 4.9% construction, 4.3% production (2000).

Income: Per capita income: $37,323 (2005); Median household income: $103,333 (2005); Average household income: $102,500 (2005); Percent of households with income of $100,000 or more: 53.0% (2005); Poverty rate: 11.1% (2000).
Education: Percent of population age 25 and over with: High school diploma (including GED) or higher: 100.0% (2005); Bachelor's degree or higher: 34.8% (2005); Master's degree or higher: 16.0% (2005).
Housing: Homeownership rate: 93.3% (2005); Median home value: $161,000 (2005); Median rent: $n/a per month (2000); Median age of housing: 41 years (2000).
Transportation: Commute to work: 95.7% car, 0.0% public transportation, 0.0% walk, 4.3% work from home (2000); Travel time to work: 10.2% less than 15 minutes, 40.7% 15 to 30 minutes, 44.1% 30 to 45 minutes, 5.1% 45 to 60 minutes, 0.0% 60 minutes or more (2000)

DUANESBURG (town).
Covers a land area of 71.245 square miles and a water area of 0.890 square miles. Located at 42.78° N. Lat.; 74.17° W. Long. Elevation is 722 feet.
Population: 5,474 (1990); 5,808 (2000); 6,120 (2005); 6,413 (2010 projected); Race: 97.1% White, 0.5% Black, 0.4% Asian, 1.2% Hispanic of any race (2005); Density: 85.9 persons per square mile (2005); Average household size: 2.66 (2005); Median age: 40.0 (2005); Males per 100 females: 100.1 (2005); Marriage status: 18.2% never married, 71.6% now married, 4.3% widowed, 6.0% divorced (2000); Foreign born: 1.9% (2000); Ancestry (includes multiple ancestries): 21.1% German, 18.8% Irish, 16.9% Italian, 16.2% English, 9.2% French (except Basque) (2000).
Economy: Single-family building permits issued: 47 (2005); Multi-family building permits issued: 0 (2005); Employment by occupation: 14.9% management, 24.2% professional, 8.6% services, 26.3% sales, 0.0% farming, 9.9% construction, 16.0% production (2000).
Income: Per capita income: $29,351 (2005); Median household income: $70,817 (2005); Average household income: $77,828 (2005); Percent of households with income of $100,000 or more: 28.3% (2005); Poverty rate: 3.9% (2000).
Education: Percent of population age 25 and over with: High school diploma (including GED) or higher: 90.1% (2005); Bachelor's degree or higher: 23.9% (2005); Master's degree or higher: 10.8% (2005).
Housing: Homeownership rate: 88.0% (2005); Median home value: $160,714 (2005); Median rent: $454 per month (2000); Median age of housing: 35 years (2000).
Transportation: Commute to work: 93.9% car, 0.0% public transportation, 1.1% walk, 4.9% work from home (2000); Travel time to work: 11.4% less than 15 minutes, 35.3% 15 to 30 minutes, 40.1% 30 to 45 minutes, 9.5% 45 to 60 minutes, 3.6% 60 minutes or more (2000)
Additional Information Contacts
Town of Duanesburg . . . . (518) 895-8920
http://www.duanesburg.net/

DUANESBURG (CDP).
Covers a land area of 2.565 square miles and a water area of 0.041 square miles. Located at 42.76° N. Lat.; 74.12° W. Long.
Population: 344 (1990); 339 (2000); 342 (2005); 345 (2010 projected); Race: 97.4% White, 0.0% Black, 0.0% Asian, 5.8% Hispanic of any race (2005); Density: 133.3 persons per square mile (2005); Average household size: 2.16 (2005); Median age: 40.4 (2005); Males per 100 females: 93.2 (2005); Marriage status: 19.7% never married, 60.0% now married, 4.1% widowed, 16.3% divorced (2000); Foreign born: 0.0% (2000); Ancestry (includes multiple ancestries): 26.1% German, 18.6% English, 14.5% Italian, 12.8% Other groups, 10.4% Irish (2000).
Economy: Employment by occupation: 18.0% management, 10.6% professional, 12.7% services, 28.2% sales, 0.0% farming, 13.5% construction, 17.1% production (2000).
Income: Per capita income: $35,789 (2005); Median household income: $68,919 (2005); Average household income: $77,468 (2005); Percent of households with income of $100,000 or more: 28.5% (2005); Poverty rate: 1.7% (2000).
Education: Percent of population age 25 and over with: High school diploma (including GED) or higher: 81.4% (2005); Bachelor's degree or higher: 13.4% (2005); Master's degree or higher: 9.5% (2005).
Housing: Homeownership rate: 69.0% (2005); Median home value: $132,971 (2005); Median rent: $447 per month (2000); Median age of housing: 38 years (2000).
Transportation: Commute to work: 93.0% car, 0.0% public transportation, 7.1% walk, 0.0% work from home (2000); Travel time to work: 7.1% less than 15 minutes, 39.4% 15 to 30 minutes, 44.0% 30 to 45 minutes, 9.5% 45 to 60 minutes, 0.0% 60 minutes or more (2000)

EAST GLENVILLE (CDP).
Covers a land area of 7.267 square miles and a water area of 0.210 square miles. Located at 42.86° N. Lat.; 73.91° W. Long.
Population: 6,518 (1990); 6,064 (2000); 6,293 (2005); 6,529 (2010 projected); Race: 96.4% White, 1.3% Black, 1.4% Asian, 1.6% Hispanic of any race (2005); Density: 866.0 persons per square mile (2005); Average household size: 2.71 (2005); Median age: 45.5 (2005); Males per 100 females: 92.7 (2005); Marriage status: 18.7% never married, 64.2% now married, 10.4% widowed, 6.8% divorced (2000); Foreign born: 2.4% (2000); Ancestry (includes multiple ancestries): 22.5% Irish, 21.5% German, 18.6% Italian, 16.7% English, 12.5% Polish (2000).
Economy: Employment by occupation: 15.3% management, 30.3% professional, 9.6% services, 28.4% sales, 0.0% farming, 7.3% construction, 9.1% production (2000).
Income: Per capita income: $31,237 (2005); Median household income: $69,504 (2005); Average household income: $82,433 (2005); Percent of households with income of $100,000 or more: 25.4% (2005); Poverty rate: 2.0% (2000).
Education: Percent of population age 25 and over with: High school diploma (including GED) or higher: 88.1% (2005); Bachelor's degree or higher: 35.5% (2005); Master's degree or higher: 14.4% (2005).
Housing: Homeownership rate: 85.3% (2005); Median home value: $161,788 (2005); Median rent: $513 per month (2000); Median age of housing: 43 years (2000).
Transportation: Commute to work: 94.2% car, 1.0% public transportation, 1.0% walk, 3.5% work from home (2000); Travel time to work: 27.8% less than 15 minutes, 36.1% 15 to 30 minutes, 27.3% 30 to 45 minutes, 6.0% 45 to 60 minutes, 2.8% 60 minutes or more (2000)

GLENVILLE (town).
Covers a land area of 49.882 square miles and a water area of 0.996 square miles. Located at 42.86° N. Lat.; 73.96° W. Long. Elevation is 303 feet.
Population: 28,771 (1990); 28,183 (2000); 28,481 (2005); 28,761 (2010 projected); Race: 96.7% White, 0.9% Black, 1.2% Asian, 1.7% Hispanic of any race (2005); Density: 571.0 persons per square mile (2005); Average household size: 2.49 (2005); Median age: 43.5 (2005); Males per 100 females: 92.3 (2005); Marriage status: 19.4% never married, 64.0% now married, 9.1% widowed, 7.5% divorced (2000); Foreign born: 2.9% (2000); Ancestry (includes multiple ancestries): 20.9% Irish, 20.5% German, 18.8% Italian, 14.7% English, 10.2% Polish (2000).
Economy: Unemployment rate: 3.5% (2005); Total civilian labor force: 14,862 (2005); Single-family building permits issued: 81 (2005); Multi-family building permits issued: 13 (2005); Employment by occupation: 14.6% management, 26.9% professional, 12.1% services, 27.9% sales, 0.0% farming, 8.0% construction, 10.4% production (2000).
Income: Per capita income: $29,074 (2005); Median household income: $60,874 (2005); Average household income: $71,303 (2005); Percent of households with income of $100,000 or more: 20.9% (2005); Poverty rate: 4.1% (2000).
Taxes: Total city taxes per capita: $251 (2004); City property taxes per capita: $209 (2004).
Education: Percent of population age 25 and over with: High school diploma (including GED) or higher: 90.1% (2005); Bachelor's degree or higher: 31.5% (2005); Master's degree or higher: 13.8% (2005).
Housing: Homeownership rate: 80.5% (2005); Median home value: $144,286 (2005); Median rent: $525 per month (2000); Median age of housing: 46 years (2000).
Hospitals: Conifer Park (225 beds)
Safety: Violent crime rate: 3.4 per 10,000 population; Property crime rate: 89.4 per 10,000 population (2004).
Transportation: Commute to work: 94.2% car, 0.9% public transportation, 1.3% walk, 3.2% work from home (2000); Travel time to work: 31.2% less than 15 minutes, 36.8% 15 to 30 minutes, 22.2% 30 to 45 minutes, 6.3% 45 to 60 minutes, 3.5% 60 minutes or more (2000)
Additional Information Contacts
Town of Glenville . . . . (518) 688-1200
http://www.townofglenville.org/Home/

MARIAVILLE LAKE (CDP).
Covers a land area of 5.654 square miles and a water area of 0.354 square miles. Located at 42.82° N. Lat.; 74.12° W. Long.

Population: 636 (1990); 710 (2000); 789 (2005); 862 (2010 projected); **Race:** 99.1% White, 0.0% Black, 0.4% Asian, 1.8% Hispanic of any race (2005); **Density:** 139.6 persons per square mile (2005); Average household size: 2.69 (2005); Median age: 38.9 (2005); Males per 100 females: 105.5 (2005); Marriage status: 25.6% never married, 66.1% now married, 5.7% widowed, 2.6% divorced (2000); Foreign born: 0.4% (2000); Ancestry (includes multiple ancestries): 21.9% English, 21.9% Italian, 19.9% German, 16.4% French (except Basque), 11.3% Other groups (2000).
Economy: Employment by occupation: 8.9% management, 17.2% professional, 13.8% services, 24.3% sales, 0.0% farming, 23.1% construction, 12.6% production (2000).
Income: Per capita income: $25,095 (2005); Median household income: $58,016 (2005); Average household income: $67,577 (2005); Percent of households with income of $100,000 or more: 12.3% (2005); Poverty rate: 0.0% (2000).
Education: Percent of population age 25 and over with: High school diploma (including GED) or higher: 84.0% (2005); Bachelor's degree or higher: 11.3% (2005); Master's degree or higher: 5.5% (2005).
Housing: Homeownership rate: 87.4% (2005); Median home value: $140,000 (2005); Median rent: $385 per month (2000); Median age of housing: 51 years (2000).
Transportation: Commute to work: 100.0% car, 0.0% public transportation, 0.0% walk, 0.0% work from home (2000); Travel time to work: 5.3% less than 15 minutes, 43.7% 15 to 30 minutes, 46.9% 30 to 45 minutes, 4.1% 45 to 60 minutes, 0.0% 60 minutes or more (2000)

NISKAYUNA (town). Covers a land area of 14.111 square miles and a water area of 0.938 square miles. Located at 42.80° N. Lat.; 73.88° W. Long. Elevation is 196 feet.
Population: 19,048 (1990); 20,295 (2000); 21,406 (2005); 22,432 (2010 projected); **Race:** 87.5% White, 1.8% Black, 8.7% Asian, 2.1% Hispanic of any race (2005); **Density:** 1,517.0 persons per square mile (2005); Average household size: 2.58 (2005); Median age: 43.1 (2005); Males per 100 females: 93.5 (2005); Marriage status: 19.4% never married, 67.7% now married, 6.2% widowed, 6.6% divorced (2000); Foreign born: 9.3% (2000); Ancestry (includes multiple ancestries): 21.0% Irish, 19.7% Italian, 15.2% German, 12.3% English, 11.2% Other groups (2000).
Economy: Single-family building permits issued: 31 (2005); Multi-family building permits issued: 30 (2005); Employment by occupation: 18.1% management, 40.1% professional, 8.2% services, 25.0% sales, 0.2% farming, 3.6% construction, 4.8% production (2000).
Income: Per capita income: $38,700 (2005); Median household income: $81,546 (2005); Average household income: $98,642 (2005); Percent of households with income of $100,000 or more: 35.9% (2005); Poverty rate: 3.2% (2000).
Education: Percent of population age 25 and over with: High school diploma (including GED) or higher: 92.6% (2005); Bachelor's degree or higher: 54.9% (2005); Master's degree or higher: 29.2% (2005).
Housing: Homeownership rate: 82.2% (2005); Median home value: $198,620 (2005); Median rent: $608 per month (2000); Median age of housing: 41 years (2000).
Hospitals: Bellevue Woman's Hospital (40 beds)
Safety: Violent crime rate: 5.2 per 10,000 population; Property crime rate: 230.9 per 10,000 population (2004).
Transportation: Commute to work: 93.2% car, 1.1% public transportation, 1.4% walk, 3.7% work from home (2000); Travel time to work: 33.8% less than 15 minutes, 42.7% 15 to 30 minutes, 18.1% 30 to 45 minutes, 2.7% 45 to 60 minutes, 2.6% 60 minutes or more (2000)
Additional Information Contacts
Town of Niskayuna . . . . (518) 386-4500
    http://www.niskayuna.org/Home/

NISKAYUNA (CDP). Covers a land area of 1.015 square miles and a water area of 0 square miles. Located at 42.81° N. Lat.; 73.89° W. Long.
Population: 4,942 (1990); 4,892 (2000); 4,859 (2005); 4,832 (2010 projected); **Race:** 92.4% White, 1.1% Black, 4.4% Asian, 2.2% Hispanic of any race (2005); **Density:** 4,784.9 persons per square mile (2005); Average household size: 2.50 (2005); Median age: 40.3 (2005); Males per 100 females: 91.1 (2005); Marriage status: 19.3% never married, 66.8% now married, 4.5% widowed, 9.4% divorced (2000); Foreign born: 5.1% (2000); Ancestry (includes multiple ancestries): 25.6% Irish, 19.5% Italian, 16.5% German, 16.3% English, 10.1% Polish (2000).
Economy: Employment by occupation: 16.5% management, 41.9% professional, 8.5% services, 24.2% sales, 0.0% farming, 4.1% construction, 4.9% production (2000).
Income: Per capita income: $34,502 (2005); Median household income: $73,771 (2005); Average household income: $85,671 (2005); Percent of households with income of $100,000 or more: 28.1% (2005); Poverty rate: 1.3% (2000).
Education: Percent of population age 25 and over with: High school diploma (including GED) or higher: 96.9% (2005); Bachelor's degree or higher: 57.0% (2005); Master's degree or higher: 29.8% (2005).
Housing: Homeownership rate: 87.7% (2005); Median home value: $154,873 (2005); Median rent: $579 per month (2000); Median age of housing: 57 years (2000).
Transportation: Commute to work: 93.4% car, 1.3% public transportation, 1.8% walk, 2.9% work from home (2000); Travel time to work: 38.5% less than 15 minutes, 35.1% 15 to 30 minutes, 21.1% 30 to 45 minutes, 2.8% 45 to 60 minutes, 2.5% 60 minutes or more (2000)

PATTERSONVILLE (unincorporated postal area, zip code 12137). Covers a land area of 20.316 square miles and a water area of 0.026 square miles. Located at 42.86° N. Lat.; 74.11° W. Long.
Population: 0 (2000); **Race:** 99.8% White, 0.0% Black, 0.0% Asian, 0.2% Hispanic of any race (2000); **Density:** 0.0 persons per square mile (2000); Age: 23.6% under 18, 10.4% over 64 (2000); Marriage status: 22.5% never married, 65.8% now married, 5.1% widowed, 6.6% divorced (2000); Foreign born: 1.8% (2000); Ancestry (includes multiple ancestries): 22.7% German, 21.1% Italian, 13.8% Irish, 12.9% French (except Basque), 8.8% English (2000).
Economy: Employment by occupation: 7.0% management, 20.4% professional, 16.5% services, 31.5% sales, 0.0% farming, 16.3% construction, 8.3% production (2000).
Income: Per capita income: $20,212 (2000); Median household income: $48,750 (2000); Poverty rate: 3.4% (2000).
Education: Percent of population age 25 and over with: High school diploma (including GED) or higher: 80.5% (2000); Bachelor's degree or higher: 15.3% (2000).

School District(s)
Schalmont Central School District (KG-12)
    2003-04 Enrollment: 2,228 . . . . (518) 355-9200
Housing: Homeownership rate: 88.5% (2000); Median home value: $96,400 (2000); Median rent: $433 per month (2000); Median age of housing: 27 years (2000).
Transportation: Commute to work: 97.3% car, 0.6% public transportation, 0.0% walk, 1.6% work from home (2000); Travel time to work: 7.5% less than 15 minutes, 43.6% 15 to 30 minutes, 35.7% 30 to 45 minutes, 12.4% 45 to 60 minutes, 0.9% 60 minutes or more (2000)

PATTERSONVILLE-ROTTERDAM JUNCTION (CDP). Covers a land area of 1.350 square miles and a water area of 0.161 square miles. Located at 42.87° N. Lat.; 74.05° W. Long.
Population: 768 (1990); 918 (2000); 939 (2005); 957 (2010 projected); **Race:** 98.3% White, 0.3% Black, 0.5% Asian, 1.9% Hispanic of any race (2005); **Density:** 695.5 persons per square mile (2005); Average household size: 2.45 (2005); Median age: 42.3 (2005); Males per 100 females: 95.6 (2005); Marriage status: 27.0% never married, 58.0% now married, 6.3% widowed, 8.7% divorced (2000); Foreign born: 0.6% (2000); Ancestry (includes multiple ancestries): 26.8% German, 26.5% Polish, 19.6% Irish, 17.6% Italian, 10.6% French (except Basque) (2000).
Economy: Employment by occupation: 7.9% management, 20.9% professional, 14.6% services, 33.3% sales, 0.0% farming, 7.6% construction, 15.7% production (2000).
Income: Per capita income: $22,716 (2005); Median household income: $48,971 (2005); Average household income: $55,692 (2005); Percent of households with income of $100,000 or more: 13.8% (2005); Poverty rate: 3.6% (2000).
Education: Percent of population age 25 and over with: High school diploma (including GED) or higher: 94.2% (2005); Bachelor's degree or higher: 15.8% (2005); Master's degree or higher: 7.9% (2005).
Housing: Homeownership rate: 80.4% (2005); Median home value: $146,552 (2005); Median rent: $426 per month (2000); Median age of housing: 47 years (2000).
Transportation: Commute to work: 85.2% car, 0.0% public transportation, 3.7% walk, 6.4% work from home (2000); Travel time to work: 29.2% less than 15 minutes, 34.2% 15 to 30 minutes, 28.0% 30 to 45 minutes, 3.6% 45 to 60 minutes, 5.0% 60 minutes or more (2000)

PRINCETOWN (town). Covers a land area of 24.040 square miles and a water area of 0.043 square miles. Located at 42.80° N. Lat.; 74.07° W. Long.
Population: 2,031 (1990); 2,132 (2000); 2,151 (2005); 2,174 (2010 projected); Race: 98.3% White, 0.2% Black, 0.3% Asian, 0.8% Hispanic of any race (2005); Density: 89.5 persons per square mile (2005); Average household size: 2.62 (2005); Median age: 42.3 (2005); Males per 100 females: 105.2 (2005); Marriage status: 22.8% never married, 64.1% now married, 5.3% widowed, 7.8% divorced (2000); Foreign born: 2.2% (2000); Ancestry (includes multiple ancestries): 22.8% Italian, 19.4% German, 17.9% Irish, 13.6% English, 9.4% French (except Basque) (2000).
Economy: Single-family building permits issued: 6 (2005); Multi-family building permits issued: 0 (2005); Employment by occupation: 13.6% management, 25.1% professional, 12.4% services, 24.6% sales, 0.4% farming, 14.9% construction, 9.1% production (2000).
Income: Per capita income: $30,044 (2005); Median household income: $65,909 (2005); Average household income: $78,811 (2005); Percent of households with income of $100,000 or more: 23.0% (2005); Poverty rate: 3.3% (2000).
Education: Percent of population age 25 and over with: High school diploma (including GED) or higher: 88.9% (2005); Bachelor's degree or higher: 23.8% (2005); Master's degree or higher: 10.8% (2005).
Housing: Homeownership rate: 86.2% (2005); Median home value: $194,088 (2005); Median rent: $562 per month (2000); Median age of housing: 27 years (2000).
Transportation: Commute to work: 95.9% car, 0.5% public transportation, 0.6% walk, 2.8% work from home (2000); Travel time to work: 16.9% less than 15 minutes, 41.3% 15 to 30 minutes, 32.1% 30 to 45 minutes, 5.7% 45 to 60 minutes, 4.0% 60 minutes or more (2000)

ROTTERDAM (town). Aka South Schenectady. Covers a land area of 35.978 square miles and a water area of 0.513 square miles. Located at 42.79° N. Lat.; 73.97° W. Long. Elevation is 340 feet.
History: Settled c.1670, incorporated 1821.
Population: 28,395 (1990); 28,316 (2000); 29,014 (2005); 29,688 (2010 projected); Race: 96.5% White, 1.2% Black, 0.9% Asian, 1.3% Hispanic of any race (2005); Density: 806.4 persons per square mile (2005); Average household size: 2.42 (2005); Median age: 42.2 (2005); Males per 100 females: 93.1 (2005); Marriage status: 21.6% never married, 60.8% now married, 9.0% widowed, 8.6% divorced (2000); Foreign born: 3.2% (2000); Ancestry (includes multiple ancestries): 33.0% Italian, 20.6% Irish, 17.2% German, 13.2% Polish, 9.7% English (2000).
Economy: Unemployment rate: 3.9% (2005); Total civilian labor force: 15,179 (2005); Single-family building permits issued: 44 (2005); Multi-family building permits issued: 52 (2005); Employment by occupation: 12.2% management, 17.1% professional, 14.0% services, 33.7% sales, 0.0% farming, 9.9% construction, 13.0% production (2000).
Income: Per capita income: $24,962 (2005); Median household income: $52,117 (2005); Average household income: $60,272 (2005); Percent of households with income of $100,000 or more: 13.9% (2005); Poverty rate: 4.5% (2000).
Taxes: Total city taxes per capita: $380 (2004); City property taxes per capita: $332 (2004).
Education: Percent of population age 25 and over with: High school diploma (including GED) or higher: 86.7% (2005); Bachelor's degree or higher: 16.3% (2005); Master's degree or higher: 5.5% (2005).
Housing: Homeownership rate: 81.4% (2005); Median home value: $138,536 (2005); Median rent: $490 per month (2000); Median age of housing: 45 years (2000).
Safety: Violent crime rate: 12.2 per 10,000 population; Property crime rate: 297.2 per 10,000 population (2004).
Transportation: Commute to work: 95.1% car, 0.4% public transportation, 1.6% walk, 2.3% work from home (2000); Travel time to work: 33.5% less than 15 minutes, 40.7% 15 to 30 minutes, 19.3% 30 to 45 minutes, 3.7% 45 to 60 minutes, 2.8% 60 minutes or more (2000)

ROTTERDAM (CDP). Covers a land area of 6.930 square miles and a water area of 0 square miles. Located at 42.78° N. Lat.; 73.95° W. Long.
Population: 21,228 (1990); 20,536 (2000); 20,779 (2005); 21,034 (2010 projected); Race: 96.3% White, 1.3% Black, 0.8% Asian, 1.3% Hispanic of any race (2005); Density: 2,998.4 persons per square mile (2005); Average household size: 2.38 (2005); Median age: 42.6 (2005); Males per 100 females: 91.5 (2005); Marriage status: 21.4% never married, 59.9% now married, 10.2% widowed, 8.5% divorced (2000); Foreign born: 3.1% (2000); Ancestry (includes multiple ancestries): 33.0% Italian, 21.1% Irish, 16.0% German, 12.8% Polish, 9.5% French (except Basque) (2000).
Economy: Employment by occupation: 11.2% management, 15.7% professional, 15.1% services, 34.6% sales, 0.1% farming, 10.9% construction, 12.4% production (2000).
Income: Per capita income: $23,728 (2005); Median household income: $48,767 (2005); Average household income: $56,283 (2005); Percent of households with income of $100,000 or more: 11.1% (2005); Poverty rate: 5.2% (2000).
Education: Percent of population age 25 and over with: High school diploma (including GED) or higher: 85.2% (2005); Bachelor's degree or higher: 14.0% (2005); Master's degree or higher: 4.8% (2005).
Housing: Homeownership rate: 82.1% (2005); Median home value: $132,248 (2005); Median rent: $496 per month (2000); Median age of housing: 48 years (2000).
Transportation: Commute to work: 95.4% car, 0.4% public transportation, 1.9% walk, 1.8% work from home (2000); Travel time to work: 35.3% less than 15 minutes, 40.8% 15 to 30 minutes, 17.0% 30 to 45 minutes, 4.2% 45 to 60 minutes, 2.8% 60 minutes or more (2000)

ROTTERDAM JUNCTION (unincorporated postal area, zip code 12150). Covers a land area of 1.170 square miles and a water area of 0.021 square miles. Located at 42.87° N. Lat.; 74.05° W. Long.
Population: 0 (2000); Race: 100.0% White, 0.0% Black, 0.0% Asian, 1.1% Hispanic of any race (2000); Density: 0.0 persons per square mile (2000); Age: 24.4% under 18, 10.9% over 64 (2000); Marriage status: 27.7% never married, 57.8% now married, 5.7% widowed, 8.9% divorced (2000); Foreign born: 0.6% (2000); Ancestry (includes multiple ancestries): 27.3% German, 27.0% Polish, 20.0% Irish, 17.9% Italian, 10.8% French (except Basque) (2000).
Economy: Employment by occupation: 7.9% management, 20.9% professional, 14.6% services, 33.3% sales, 0.0% farming, 7.6% construction, 15.7% production (2000).
Income: Per capita income: $19,165 (2000); Median household income: $46,250 (2000); Poverty rate: 3.7% (2000).
Education: Percent of population age 25 and over with: High school diploma (including GED) or higher: 94.1% (2000); Bachelor's degree or higher: 16.3% (2000).

School District(s)
Schalmont Central School District (KG-12)
    2003-04 Enrollment: 2,228 . . . . (518) 355-9200

Housing: Homeownership rate: 79.2% (2000); Median home value: $109,900 (2000); Median rent: $426 per month (2000); Median age of housing: 46 years (2000).
Transportation: Commute to work: 85.2% car, 0.0% public transportation, 3.7% walk, 6.4% work from home (2000); Travel time to work: 29.2% less than 15 minutes, 34.2% 15 to 30 minutes, 28.0% 30 to 45 minutes, 3.6% 45 to 60 minutes, 5.0% 60 minutes or more (2000)

SCHENECTADY (city). Covers a land area of 10.848 square miles and a water area of 0.140 square miles. Located at 42.80° N. Lat.; 73.92° W. Long. Elevation is 246 feet.
History: The site of Schenectady was called "Schonowe" meaning "big flats" by the Mohawk people. In 1662, Arent Van Curler, with a small group of Dutchmen, emigrated from Albany to the "Groote Vlachte" ("big flats") and purchased land. The first major migration of English into Schenectady began about 1700. In 1848, a locomotive factory was organized that was Schenectady's largest industry for a half century. In 1886, Thomas A. Edison bought two abandoned factory buildings for the Edison Company. In 1892 it was consolidated with the Thompson-Huston Company of Lynn, Massachusetts, to form the General Electric Company. Schenectady became the city that "lights and hauls the world."
Population: 65,566 (1990); 61,821 (2000); 60,742 (2005); 59,771 (2010 projected); Race: 70.9% White, 18.1% Black, 3.1% Asian, 8.2% Hispanic of any race (2005); Density: 5,599.5 persons per square mile (2005); Average household size: 2.35 (2005); Median age: 35.6 (2005); Males per 100 females: 92.5 (2005); Marriage status: 35.5% never married, 44.3% now married, 9.2% widowed, 10.9% divorced (2000); Foreign born: 6.5% (2000); Ancestry (includes multiple ancestries): 21.8% Other groups, 19.7% Italian, 15.8% Irish, 12.2% German, 9.0% Polish (2000).
Economy: Unemployment rate: 5.1% (2005); Total civilian labor force: 29,875 (2005); Single-family building permits issued: 6 (2005); Multi-family building permits issued: 0 (2005); Employment by occupation: 9.1% management, 20.6% professional, 21.8% services, 28.9% sales, 0.1% farming, 6.9% construction, 12.5% production (2000).

Income: Per capita income: $18,391 (2005); Median household income: $32,139 (2005); Average household income: $41,735 (2005); Percent of households with income of $100,000 or more: 5.7% (2005); Poverty rate: 20.8% (2000).
Taxes: Total city taxes per capita: $478 (2004); City property taxes per capita: $423 (2004).
Education: Percent of population age 25 and over with: High school diploma (including GED) or higher: 78.0% (2005); Bachelor's degree or higher: 19.2% (2005); Master's degree or higher: 7.8% (2005).

School District(s)
Intntl Charter School Of Schenectady (KG-05)
   2003-04 Enrollment: 412 . . . . (518) 347-1562
Niskayuna Central School District (KG-12)
   2003-04 Enrollment: 4,258 . . . . (518) 377-4666
Rotterdam-Mohonasen Central School District (KG-12)
   2003-04 Enrollment: 3,340 . . . . (518) 356-8200
Schalmont Central School District (KG-12)
   2003-04 Enrollment: 2,228 . . . . (518) 355-9200
Schenectady City School District (PK-12)
   2003-04 Enrollment: 9,090 . . . . (518) 370-8100
South Colonie Central School District (KG-12)
   2003-04 Enrollment: 5,745 . . . . (518) 869-3576

Four-year College(s)
Graduate College of Union University
   Fall 2004 Enrollment: n/a. . . . . (518) 388-6148
Union College
   Fall 2004 Enrollment: 2,192 . . . . (518) 388-6000

Two-year College(s)
Ellis Hospital School of Nursing
   Fall 2004 Enrollment: 111 . . . . (518) 243-4471
   2005-06 Tuition: In-state $4,876; Out-of-state $4,876
Modern Welding School
   Fall 2004 Enrollment: 76 . . . . (518) 374-1216
Schenectady County Community College (Public)
   Fall 2004 Enrollment: 4,786. . . . . (518) 381-1200
   2005-06 Tuition: In-state $2,868; Out-of-state $5,618

Housing: Homeownership rate: 45.2% (2005); Median home value: $96,272 (2005); Median rent: $444 per month (2000); Median age of housing: 60+ years (2000).
Hospitals: Ellis Hospital (368 beds); St. Clare's Hospital of Schenectady (200 beds); Sunnyview Hospital & Rehabilitation Center (104 beds)
Newspapers: Daily Gazette (Circulation 50,703)
Transportation: Commute to work: 82.6% car, 6.5% public transportation, 6.8% walk, 2.6% work from home (2000); Travel time to work: 37.7% less than 15 minutes, 36.9% 15 to 30 minutes, 17.0% 30 to 45 minutes, 4.2% 45 to 60 minutes, 4.2% 60 minutes or more (2000); Amtrak: Service available.

Additional Information Contacts
Schenectady Chamber of Commerce . . . . (518) 372-5656
   http://www.schenectadychamber.net

SCOTIA (village).
Covers a land area of 1.707 square miles and a water area of 0.076 square miles. Located at 42.83° N. Lat.; 73.96° W. Long. Elevation is 273 feet.

History: Scotia Naval Supply Depot closed. Settled before 1660, incorporated 1904.
Population: 7,417 (1990); 7,957 (2000); 7,816 (2005); 7,690 (2010 projected); Race: 95.9% White, 0.9% Black, 1.5% Asian, 2.5% Hispanic of any race (2005); Density: 4,579.0 persons per square mile (2005); Average household size: 2.44 (2005); Median age: 39.5 (2005); Males per 100 females: 86.2 (2005); Marriage status: 23.5% never married, 56.1% now married, 10.3% widowed, 10.0% divorced (2000); Foreign born: 2.3% (2000); Ancestry (includes multiple ancestries): 23.2% Irish, 19.1% German, 19.0% Italian, 14.2% English, 11.1% French (except Basque) (2000).
Economy: Small industries. Single-family building permits issued: 49 (2005); Multi-family building permits issued: 0 (2005); Employment by occupation: 12.1% management, 23.5% professional, 15.4% services, 30.1% sales, 0.0% farming, 6.9% construction, 12.0% production (2000).
Income: Per capita income: $23,540 (2005); Median household income: $47,854 (2005); Average household income: $55,961 (2005); Percent of households with income of $100,000 or more: 10.4% (2005); Poverty rate: 6.6% (2000).
Education: Percent of population age 25 and over with: High school diploma (including GED) or higher: 87.6% (2005); Bachelor's degree or higher: 24.1% (2005); Master's degree or higher: 10.2% (2005).

School District(s)
Burnt Hills-Ballston Lake Central School District (KG-12)
   2003-04 Enrollment: 3,447 . . . . (518) 399-6407
Scotia-Glenville Central School District (KG-12)
   2003-04 Enrollment: 2,952 . . . . (518) 382-1215

Housing: Homeownership rate: 67.2% (2005); Median home value: $118,432 (2005); Median rent: $504 per month (2000); Median age of housing: 60+ years (2000).
Safety: Violent crime rate: 14.0 per 10,000 population; Property crime rate: 312.5 per 10,000 population (2004).
Transportation: Commute to work: 92.0% car, 2.0% public transportation, 2.8% walk, 2.3% work from home (2000); Travel time to work: 38.1% less than 15 minutes, 32.8% 15 to 30 minutes, 19.0% 30 to 45 minutes, 6.0% 45 to 60 minutes, 4.2% 60 minutes or more (2000)

Schoharie County

Located in east central New York, partly in the Catskills; crossed by The Helderbergs; drained by Schoharie and Catskill Creeks. Covers a land area of 622.02 square miles, a water area of 4.34 square miles, and is located in the Eastern Time Zone. The county government was organized in 1795. County seat is Schoharie.

Schoharie County is part of the Albany-Schenectady-Troy, NY Metropolitan Statistical Area. The entire metro area includes: Albany County, NY; Rensselaer County, NY; Saratoga County, NY; Schenectady County, NY; Schoharie County, NY

Population: 31,876 (1990); 31,582 (2000); 31,730 (2005); 31,863 (2010 projected); Race: 96.5% White, 1.4% Black, 0.4% Asian, 2.3% Hispanic of any race (2005); Density: 51.0 persons per square mile (2005); Average household size: 2.59 (2005); Median age: 39.6 (2005); Males per 100 females: 99.0 (2005).
Religion: Five largest groups: 12.2% Catholic Church, 9.6% The United Methodist Church, 8.1% Evangelical Lutheran Church in America, 2.2% Reformed Church in America, 1.5% Assemblies of God (2000).
Economy: Unemployment rate: 4.8% (2005); Total civilian labor force: 15,854 (2005); Leading industries: 22.5% retail trade; 18.2% health care and social assistance; 14.8% transportation and warehousing (2003); Farms: 579 totaling 112,735 acres (2002); Companies that employ 500 or more persons: 1 (2003); Companies that employ 100 to 499 persons: 6 (2003); Companies that employ less than 100 persons: 583 (2003); Black-owned businesses: n/a (2002); Hispanic-owned businesses: n/a (2002); Women-owned businesses: 635 (2002); Retail sales per capita: $10,153 (2006). Single-family building permits issued: 115 (2005); Multi-family building permits issued: 36 (2005).
Income: Per capita income: $20,695 (2005); Median household income: $41,761 (2005); Average household income: $52,646 (2005); Percent of households with income of $100,000 or more: 10.0% (2005); Poverty rate: 11.6% (2003); Bankruptcy rate: 6.38% (2005).
Education: Percent of population age 25 and over with: High school diploma (including GED) or higher: 81.7% (2005); Bachelor's degree or higher: 17.3% (2005); Master's degree or higher: 8.4% (2005).
Housing: Homeownership rate: 75.4% (2005); Median home value: $122,279 (2005); Median rent: $406 per month (2000); Median age of housing: 36 years (2000).
Health: Birth rate: 96.8 per 10,000 population (2004); Death rate: 87.5 per 10,000 population (2004); Age-adjusted cancer mortality rate: 237.5 deaths per 100,000 population (2002); Number of physicians: 6.6 per 10,000 population (2004); Hospital beds: 12.6 per 10,000 population (2003); Hospital admissions: 354.3 per 10,000 population (2003).
Elections: 2004 Presidential election results: 59.0% Bush, 38.7% Kerry, 2.0% Nader, 0.2% Badnarik
National and State Parks: Max V Shaul State Park

Additional Information Contacts
Schoharie County Government . . . . (518) 295-8383
   http://www.schoharieecounty-ny.gov/
Town of Esperance . . . . (518) 875-6109
   http://townofesperance.org/
Village of Cobleskill . . . . (518) 234-2911
   http://www.schoharieecounty-ny.gov/CountyWebSite/index.jsp

Schoharie County Communities

BLENHEIM (town). Covers a land area of 33.941 square miles and a water area of 0.433 square miles. Located at 42.48° N. Lat.; 74.49° W. Long.
Population: 332 (1990); 330 (2000); 320 (2005); 314 (2010 projected); Race: 96.9% White, 1.9% Black, 0.0% Asian, 3.1% Hispanic of any race (2005); Density: 9.4 persons per square mile (2005); Average household size: 2.16 (2005); Median age: 49.3 (2005); Males per 100 females: 101.3 (2005); Marriage status: 20.8% never married, 59.4% now married, 12.8% widowed, 7.0% divorced (2000); Foreign born: 4.8% (2000); Ancestry (includes multiple ancestries): 24.2% German, 11.2% Irish, 9.7% Dutch, 8.5% English, 6.7% Italian (2000).
Economy: Single-family building permits issued: 1 (2005); Multi-family building permits issued: 0 (2005); Employment by occupation: 18.0% management, 13.5% professional, 22.6% services, 17.3% sales, 0.0% farming, 10.5% construction, 18.0% production (2000).
Income: Per capita income: $25,664 (2005); Median household income: $45,000 (2005); Average household income: $55,490 (2005); Percent of households with income of $100,000 or more: 12.2% (2005); Poverty rate: 8.5% (2000).
Education: Percent of population age 25 and over with: High school diploma (including GED) or higher: 80.5% (2005); Bachelor's degree or higher: 16.3% (2005); Master's degree or higher: 6.5% (2005).
Housing: Homeownership rate: 90.5% (2005); Median home value: $110,606 (2005); Median rent: $225 per month (2000); Median age of housing: 25 years (2000).
Transportation: Commute to work: 78.1% car, 3.9% public transportation, 2.3% walk, 15.6% work from home (2000); Travel time to work: 13.0% less than 15 minutes, 30.6% 15 to 30 minutes, 27.8% 30 to 45 minutes, 15.7% 45 to 60 minutes, 13.0% 60 minutes or more (2000)

BROOME (town). Covers a land area of 47.782 square miles and a water area of 0.283 square miles. Located at 42.50° N. Lat.; 74.30° W. Long.
Population: 949 (1990); 947 (2000); 925 (2005); 909 (2010 projected); Race: 96.3% White, 0.8% Black, 0.1% Asian, 1.9% Hispanic of any race (2005); Density: 19.4 persons per square mile (2005); Average household size: 2.28 (2005); Median age: 45.9 (2005); Males per 100 females: 99.4 (2005); Marriage status: 22.7% never married, 56.5% now married, 9.4% widowed, 11.4% divorced (2000); Foreign born: 2.1% (2000); Ancestry (includes multiple ancestries): 22.7% German, 18.7% Irish, 15.4% Italian, 9.4% United States or American, 6.5% English (2000).
Economy: Employment by occupation: 8.8% management, 16.1% professional, 16.3% services, 22.0% sales, 1.6% farming, 18.4% construction, 16.8% production (2000).
Income: Per capita income: $18,497 (2005); Median household income: $35,714 (2005); Average household income: $42,143 (2005); Percent of households with income of $100,000 or more: 5.2% (2005); Poverty rate: 8.4% (2000).
Education: Percent of population age 25 and over with: High school diploma (including GED) or higher: 81.7% (2005); Bachelor's degree or higher: 11.1% (2005); Master's degree or higher: 5.7% (2005).
Housing: Homeownership rate: 89.9% (2005); Median home value: $100,670 (2005); Median rent: $367 per month (2000); Median age of housing: 30 years (2000).
Transportation: Commute to work: 93.3% car, 1.6% public transportation, 1.4% walk, 3.2% work from home (2000); Travel time to work: 16.7% less than 15 minutes, 34.0% 15 to 30 minutes, 18.6% 30 to 45 minutes, 14.5% 45 to 60 minutes, 16.2% 60 minutes or more (2000)

CARLISLE (town). Covers a land area of 34.167 square miles and a water area of 0.087 square miles. Located at 42.76° N. Lat.; 74.43° W. Long. Elevation is 1,290 feet.
Population: 1,672 (1990); 1,758 (2000); 1,839 (2005); 1,913 (2010 projected); Race: 98.0% White, 0.4% Black, 0.2% Asian, 2.4% Hispanic of any race (2005); Density: 53.8 persons per square mile (2005); Average household size: 2.74 (2005); Median age: 37.0 (2005); Males per 100 females: 98.8 (2005); Marriage status: 24.8% never married, 61.9% now married, 5.9% widowed, 7.5% divorced (2000); Foreign born: 1.8% (2000); Ancestry (includes multiple ancestries): 24.4% German, 18.6% Irish, 14.2% English, 10.0% Dutch, 9.5% Italian (2000).
Economy: Single-family building permits issued: 12 (2005); Multi-family building permits issued: 12 (2005); Employment by occupation: 11.1% management, 18.8% professional, 11.4% services, 27.2% sales, 1.6% farming, 12.5% construction, 17.4% production (2000).
Income: Per capita income: $20,748 (2005); Median household income: $50,679 (2005); Average household income: $56,948 (2005); Percent of households with income of $100,000 or more: 10.0% (2005); Poverty rate: 8.4% (2000).
Education: Percent of population age 25 and over with: High school diploma (including GED) or higher: 86.1% (2005); Bachelor's degree or higher: 16.1% (2005); Master's degree or higher: 7.6% (2005).
Housing: Homeownership rate: 81.5% (2005); Median home value: $124,449 (2005); Median rent: $425 per month (2000); Median age of housing: 29 years (2000).
Transportation: Commute to work: 92.5% car, 0.3% public transportation, 1.9% walk, 5.1% work from home (2000); Travel time to work: 20.7% less than 15 minutes, 29.5% 15 to 30 minutes, 17.0% 30 to 45 minutes, 24.3% 45 to 60 minutes, 8.5% 60 minutes or more (2000)

CENTRAL BRIDGE (unincorporated postal area, zip code 12035). Covers a land area of 13.658 square miles and a water area of 0.038 square miles. Located at 42.72° N. Lat.; 74.35° W. Long. Elevation is 621 feet.
History: George Westinghouse born here.
Population: 0 (2000); Race: 97.4% White, 0.6% Black, 0.0% Asian, 2.0% Hispanic of any race (2000); Density: 0.0 persons per square mile (2000); Age: 25.1% under 18, 10.3% over 64 (2000); Marriage status: 26.3% never married, 57.3% now married, 6.6% widowed, 9.8% divorced (2000); Foreign born: 1.8% (2000); Ancestry (includes multiple ancestries): 21.5% German, 15.7% Irish, 11.4% English, 8.3% United States or American, 7.1% Italian (2000).
Economy: Nearby are the Howe and Secret caverns. Employment by occupation: 9.5% management, 17.1% professional, 14.7% services, 30.0% sales, 2.1% farming, 7.1% construction, 19.5% production (2000).
Income: Per capita income: $16,107 (2000); Median household income: $35,455 (2000); Poverty rate: 7.4% (2000).
Education: Percent of population age 25 and over with: High school diploma (including GED) or higher: 86.4% (2000); Bachelor's degree or higher: 19.3% (2000).
Housing: Homeownership rate: 63.3% (2000); Median home value: $74,500 (2000); Median rent: $396 per month (2000); Median age of housing: 57 years (2000).
Transportation: Commute to work: 93.8% car, 1.1% public transportation, 1.9% walk, 3.2% work from home (2000); Travel time to work: 14.4% less than 15 minutes, 29.5% 15 to 30 minutes, 21.0% 30 to 45 minutes, 23.9% 45 to 60 minutes, 11.2% 60 minutes or more (2000)

CHARLOTTEVILLE (unincorporated postal area, zip code 12036). Covers a land area of 8.976 square miles and a water area of 0.008 square miles. Located at 42.54° N. Lat.; 74.67° W. Long.
Population: 0 (2000); Race: 96.8% White, 0.0% Black, 0.0% Asian, 0.9% Hispanic of any race (2000); Density: 0.0 persons per square mile (2000); Age: 19.8% under 18, 14.9% over 64 (2000); Marriage status: 22.4% never married, 61.2% now married, 7.1% widowed, 9.3% divorced (2000); Foreign born: 2.7% (2000); Ancestry (includes multiple ancestries): 16.2% German, 13.1% Irish, 8.6% Dutch, 7.7% Italian, 6.3% Other groups (2000).
Economy: Employment by occupation: 9.9% management, 12.9% professional, 15.8% services, 26.7% sales, 2.0% farming, 13.9% construction, 18.8% production (2000).
Income: Per capita income: $14,727 (2000); Median household income: $34,167 (2000); Poverty rate: 12.9% (2000).
Education: Percent of population age 25 and over with: High school diploma (including GED) or higher: 71.1% (2000); Bachelor's degree or higher: 9.4% (2000).
Housing: Homeownership rate: 90.0% (2000); Median home value: $52,100 (2000); Median rent: $363 per month (2000); Median age of housing: 42 years (2000).
Transportation: Commute to work: 87.1% car, 2.2% public transportation, 7.5% walk, 3.2% work from home (2000); Travel time to work: 31.1% less than 15 minutes, 22.2% 15 to 30 minutes, 30.0% 30 to 45 minutes, 6.7% 45 to 60 minutes, 10.0% 60 minutes or more (2000)

COBLESKILL (village). Covers a land area of 3.270 square miles and a water area of 0.005 square miles. Located at 42.67° N. Lat.; 74.48° W. Long. Elevation is 932 feet.
Population: 5,256 (1990); 4,533 (2000); 4,421 (2005); 4,387 (2010 projected); Race: 93.3% White, 3.2% Black, 1.4% Asian, 3.1% Hispanic of

any race (2005); Density: 1,352.1 persons per square mile (2005); Average household size: 2.95 (2005); Median age: 29.2 (2005); Males per 100 females: 92.7 (2005); Marriage status: 38.3% never married, 39.4% now married, 14.5% widowed, 7.8% divorced (2000); Foreign born: 2.3% (2000); Ancestry (includes multiple ancestries): 20.4% German, 16.7% Irish, 10.5% Italian, 8.7% Other groups, 6.9% English (2000).
Economy: Single-family building permits issued: 1 (2005); Multi-family building permits issued: 0 (2005); Employment by occupation: 11.3% management, 28.4% professional, 19.1% services, 21.3% sales, 0.5% farming, 4.5% construction, 14.9% production (2000).
Income: Per capita income: $16,462 (2005); Median household income: $29,349 (2005); Average household income: $43,006 (2005); Percent of households with income of $100,000 or more: 8.5% (2005); Poverty rate: 19.8% (2000).
Education: Percent of population age 25 and over with: High school diploma (including GED) or higher: 82.2% (2005); Bachelor's degree or higher: 29.8% (2005); Master's degree or higher: 17.0% (2005).

School District(s)
Cobleskill-Richmondville Central School District (KG-12)
    2003-04 Enrollment: 2,208 . . . . (518) 234-4032

Four-year College(s)
SUNY College of Agriculture and Technology at Cobleskill (Public)
    Fall 2004 Enrollment: 2,514. . . . . (518) 255-5523
    2005-06 Tuition: In-state $5,345; Out-of-state $8,205

Housing: Homeownership rate: 41.1% (2005); Median home value: $141,171 (2005); Median rent: $432 per month (2000); Median age of housing: 48 years (2000).
Hospitals: Bassett Hospital of Schoharie County (40 beds)
Safety: Violent crime rate: 19.8 per 10,000 population; Property crime rate: 367.7 per 10,000 population (2004).
Newspapers: Times-Journal (General - Circulation 6,400)
Transportation: Commute to work: 80.3% car, 0.8% public transportation, 15.8% walk, 3.2% work from home (2000); Travel time to work: 65.7% less than 15 minutes, 14.1% 15 to 30 minutes, 10.1% 30 to 45 minutes, 8.0% 45 to 60 minutes, 2.1% 60 minutes or more (2000)

Additional Information Contacts
Village of Cobleskill . . . . (518) 234-2911
    http://www.schohariecounty-ny.gov/CountyWebSite/index.jsp

COBLESKILL (town).
Covers a land area of 30.619 square miles and a water area of 0.153 square miles. Located at 42.68° N. Lat.; 74.46° W. Long. Elevation is 932 feet.
History: The Borst & Burnhans Plant began in Cobleskill in 1800 as a feed, flour, and grist mill, and became famous for its pancake flour in 1890. The Harder Refrigerator Plant, established in 1859, made threshing machines, silos, manure spreaders, and refrigerators. Seat of State University of N.Y. College of Agriculture and Technology at Cobleskill. Cobleskill Historic District. Settled in 1752, incorporated in 1868.
Population: 7,276 (1990); 6,407 (2000); 6,435 (2005); 6,457 (2010 projected); Race: 94.6% White, 2.5% Black, 1.1% Asian, 2.8% Hispanic of any race (2005); Density: 210.2 persons per square mile (2005); Average household size: 2.79 (2005); Median age: 33.8 (2005); Males per 100 females: 94.4 (2005); Marriage status: 33.0% never married, 46.9% now married, 13.0% widowed, 7.1% divorced (2000); Foreign born: 2.0% (2000); Ancestry (includes multiple ancestries): 21.3% German, 17.6% Irish, 11.4% English, 9.6% Other groups, 9.0% Italian (2000).
Economy: Dairying; manufacturing: construction materials, textiles, molded plastics, metalwork. Howe Caverns at Howes Cave 6 miles East. Single-family building permits issued: 6 (2005); Multi-family building permits issued: 0 (2005); Employment by occupation: 12.4% management, 26.1% professional, 18.6% services, 22.8% sales, 0.8% farming, 4.9% construction, 14.3% production (2000).
Income: Per capita income: $19,011 (2005); Median household income: $35,906 (2005); Average household income: $49,472 (2005); Percent of households with income of $100,000 or more: 10.3% (2005); Poverty rate: 15.3% (2000).
Education: Percent of population age 25 and over with: High school diploma (including GED) or higher: 84.5% (2005); Bachelor's degree or higher: 26.7% (2005); Master's degree or higher: 15.1% (2005).
Housing: Homeownership rate: 55.0% (2005); Median home value: $136,122 (2005); Median rent: $430 per month (2000); Median age of housing: 44 years (2000).
Transportation: Commute to work: 85.5% car, 0.8% public transportation, 10.2% walk, 3.5% work from home (2000); Travel time to work: 55.8% less than 15 minutes, 19.9% 15 to 30 minutes, 11.5% 30 to 45 minutes, 8.8% 45 to 60 minutes, 4.0% 60 minutes or more (2000)

CONESVILLE (town).
Covers a land area of 39.459 square miles and a water area of 0.400 square miles. Located at 42.41° N. Lat.; 74.33° W. Long. Elevation is 1,387 feet.
Population: 684 (1990); 726 (2000); 739 (2005); 742 (2010 projected); Race: 97.6% White, 0.3% Black, 0.0% Asian, 2.4% Hispanic of any race (2005); Density: 18.7 persons per square mile (2005); Average household size: 2.34 (2005); Median age: 46.0 (2005); Males per 100 females: 99.7 (2005); Marriage status: 20.6% never married, 65.1% now married, 6.3% widowed, 7.9% divorced (2000); Foreign born: 3.5% (2000); Ancestry (includes multiple ancestries): 25.2% German, 18.4% Irish, 15.2% Italian, 11.8% English, 10.5% United States or American (2000).
Economy: Single-family building permits issued: 14 (2005); Multi-family building permits issued: 0 (2005); Employment by occupation: 9.1% management, 17.8% professional, 16.7% services, 19.2% sales, 0.7% farming, 17.8% construction, 18.8% production (2000).
Income: Per capita income: $18,870 (2005); Median household income: $35,909 (2005); Average household income: $44,130 (2005); Percent of households with income of $100,000 or more: 5.4% (2005); Poverty rate: 7.4% (2000).
Education: Percent of population age 25 and over with: High school diploma (including GED) or higher: 78.7% (2005); Bachelor's degree or higher: 10.4% (2005); Master's degree or higher: 5.9% (2005).
Housing: Homeownership rate: 88.0% (2005); Median home value: $96,098 (2005); Median rent: $342 per month (2000); Median age of housing: 24 years (2000).
Transportation: Commute to work: 89.9% car, 0.7% public transportation, 4.2% walk, 5.2% work from home (2000); Travel time to work: 26.1% less than 15 minutes, 28.7% 15 to 30 minutes, 14.3% 30 to 45 minutes, 10.3% 45 to 60 minutes, 20.6% 60 minutes or more (2000)

ESPERANCE (village).
Covers a land area of 0.501 square miles and a water area of 0.028 square miles. Located at 42.76° N. Lat.; 74.25° W. Long.
Population: 324 (1990); 380 (2000); 384 (2005); 387 (2010 projected); Race: 96.4% White, 1.8% Black, 1.6% Asian, 0.3% Hispanic of any race (2005); Density: 765.7 persons per square mile (2005); Average household size: 2.51 (2005); Median age: 42.2 (2005); Males per 100 females: 102.1 (2005); Marriage status: 24.7% never married, 56.9% now married, 9.9% widowed, 8.6% divorced (2000); Foreign born: 2.1% (2000); Ancestry (includes multiple ancestries): 16.8% German, 12.7% Other groups, 12.4% United States or American, 10.1% French (except Basque), 10.1% Irish (2000).
Economy: Single-family building permits issued: 2 (2005); Multi-family building permits issued: 0 (2005); Employment by occupation: 5.7% management, 18.4% professional, 10.9% services, 31.0% sales, 0.0% farming, 14.4% construction, 19.5% production (2000).
Income: Per capita income: $20,508 (2005); Median household income: $51,620 (2005); Average household income: $51,471 (2005); Percent of households with income of $100,000 or more: 4.6% (2005); Poverty rate: 3.9% (2000).
Education: Percent of population age 25 and over with: High school diploma (including GED) or higher: 82.8% (2005); Bachelor's degree or higher: 13.4% (2005); Master's degree or higher: 2.6% (2005).
Housing: Homeownership rate: 74.5% (2005); Median home value: $113,265 (2005); Median rent: $425 per month (2000); Median age of housing: 60+ years (2000).
Transportation: Commute to work: 98.8% car, 1.2% public transportation, 0.0% walk, 0.0% work from home (2000); Travel time to work: 4.8% less than 15 minutes, 37.5% 15 to 30 minutes, 32.7% 30 to 45 minutes, 8.3% 45 to 60 minutes, 16.7% 60 minutes or more (2000)

ESPERANCE (town).
Covers a land area of 19.593 square miles and a water area of 0.456 square miles. Located at 42.74° N. Lat.; 74.31° W. Long.
Population: 2,101 (1990); 2,043 (2000); 2,046 (2005); 2,054 (2010 projected); Race: 98.1% White, 0.4% Black, 0.5% Asian, 0.9% Hispanic of any race (2005); Density: 104.4 persons per square mile (2005); Average household size: 2.58 (2005); Median age: 39.7 (2005); Males per 100 females: 104.8 (2005); Marriage status: 22.2% never married, 61.0% now married, 7.0% widowed, 9.8% divorced (2000); Foreign born: 2.2% (2000); Ancestry (includes multiple ancestries): 21.1% German, 12.9% Irish, 9.5% English, 8.9% United States or American, 8.6% Dutch (2000).

Economy: Single-family building permits issued: 7 (2005); Multi-family building permits issued: 0 (2005); Employment by occupation: 10.3% management, 13.8% professional, 16.0% services, 26.7% sales, 0.5% farming, 13.7% construction, 19.1% production (2000).
Income: Per capita income: $21,039 (2005); Median household income: $47,988 (2005); Average household income: $54,350 (2005); Percent of households with income of $100,000 or more: 8.2% (2005); Poverty rate: 7.4% (2000).
Education: Percent of population age 25 and over with: High school diploma (including GED) or higher: 80.9% (2005); Bachelor's degree or higher: 10.8% (2005); Master's degree or higher: 2.8% (2005).
Housing: Homeownership rate: 81.4% (2005); Median home value: $115,761 (2005); Median rent: $417 per month (2000); Median age of housing: 39 years (2000).
Transportation: Commute to work: 93.4% car, 1.2% public transportation, 1.2% walk, 3.9% work from home (2000); Travel time to work: 13.6% less than 15 minutes, 31.8% 15 to 30 minutes, 29.2% 30 to 45 minutes, 15.2% 45 to 60 minutes, 10.2% 60 minutes or more (2000)

Additional Information Contacts
Town of Esperance . . . . (518) 875-6109
  http://townofesperance.org/

FULTON (town). Covers a land area of 64.957 square miles and a water area of 0 square miles. Located at 42.57° N. Lat.; 74.45° W. Long.
Population: 1,514 (1990); 1,495 (2000); 1,456 (2005); 1,442 (2010 projected); Race: 89.5% White, 8.4% Black, 0.1% Asian, 6.2% Hispanic of any race (2005); Density: 22.4 persons per square mile (2005); Average household size: 2.95 (2005); Median age: 36.7 (2005); Males per 100 females: 131.1 (2005); Marriage status: 34.8% never married, 51.6% now married, 5.3% widowed, 8.2% divorced (2000); Foreign born: 3.3% (2000); Ancestry (includes multiple ancestries): 19.5% German, 17.5% Irish, 9.4% Italian, 8.0% English, 7.8% Dutch (2000).
Economy: Employment by occupation: 10.9% management, 16.6% professional, 11.4% services, 23.4% sales, 3.6% farming, 14.5% construction, 19.6% production (2000).
Income: Per capita income: $15,965 (2005); Median household income: $38,962 (2005); Average household income: $45,789 (2005); Percent of households with income of $100,000 or more: 7.3% (2005); Poverty rate: 18.2% (2000).
Education: Percent of population age 25 and over with: High school diploma (including GED) or higher: 66.2% (2005); Bachelor's degree or higher: 11.4% (2005); Master's degree or higher: 5.4% (2005).
Housing: Homeownership rate: 87.4% (2005); Median home value: $124,615 (2005); Median rent: $327 per month (2000); Median age of housing: 39 years (2000).
Transportation: Commute to work: 89.7% car, 2.1% public transportation, 2.1% walk, 4.7% work from home (2000); Travel time to work: 19.6% less than 15 minutes, 29.4% 15 to 30 minutes, 18.7% 30 to 45 minutes, 11.7% 45 to 60 minutes, 20.7% 60 minutes or more (2000)

FULTONHAM (unincorporated postal area, zip code 12071). Covers a land area of 12.743 square miles and a water area of 0 square miles. Located at 42.56° N. Lat.; 74.41° W. Long. Elevation is 706 feet.
Population: 0 (2000); Race: 100.0% White, 0.0% Black, 0.0% Asian, 0.7% Hispanic of any race (2000); Density: 0.0 persons per square mile (2000); Age: 21.2% under 18, 16.0% over 64 (2000); Marriage status: 26.3% never married, 60.8% now married, 5.8% widowed, 7.1% divorced (2000); Foreign born: 3.1% (2000); Ancestry (includes multiple ancestries): 27.4% Irish, 25.3% German, 13.2% English, 12.2% Italian, 9.0% Dutch (2000).
Economy: Employment by occupation: 10.7% management, 27.3% professional, 9.9% services, 24.8% sales, 4.1% farming, 12.4% construction, 10.7% production (2000).
Income: Per capita income: $16,431 (2000); Median household income: $32,917 (2000); Poverty rate: 12.2% (2000).
Education: Percent of population age 25 and over with: High school diploma (including GED) or higher: 73.1% (2000); Bachelor's degree or higher: 16.4% (2000).
Housing: Homeownership rate: 82.0% (2000); Median home value: $80,000 (2000); Median rent: $320 per month (2000); Median age of housing: 60+ years (2000).
Transportation: Commute to work: 95.8% car, 0.0% public transportation, 2.5% walk, 1.7% work from home (2000); Travel time to work: 30.8% less than 15 minutes, 29.1% 15 to 30 minutes, 12.8% 30 to 45 minutes, 9.4% 45 to 60 minutes, 17.9% 60 minutes or more (2000)

GILBOA (town). Covers a land area of 57.763 square miles and a water area of 1.563 square miles. Located at 42.42° N. Lat.; 74.46° W. Long.
Population: 1,207 (1990); 1,215 (2000); 1,197 (2005); 1,180 (2010 projected); Race: 95.8% White, 0.8% Black, 0.8% Asian, 2.6% Hispanic of any race (2005); Density: 20.7 persons per square mile (2005); Average household size: 2.49 (2005); Median age: 45.6 (2005); Males per 100 females: 95.0 (2005); Marriage status: 21.5% never married, 59.9% now married, 10.6% widowed, 8.0% divorced (2000); Foreign born: 4.6% (2000); Ancestry (includes multiple ancestries): 23.7% German, 16.6% Irish, 15.0% Italian, 12.6% English, 7.8% Dutch (2000).
Economy: Single-family building permits issued: 10 (2005); Multi-family building permits issued: 0 (2005); Employment by occupation: 15.6% management, 18.1% professional, 16.6% services, 18.7% sales, 1.9% farming, 16.0% construction, 13.1% production (2000).
Income: Per capita income: $19,639 (2005); Median household income: $36,793 (2005); Average household income: $48,974 (2005); Percent of households with income of $100,000 or more: 9.2% (2005); Poverty rate: 11.9% (2000).
Education: Percent of population age 25 and over with: High school diploma (including GED) or higher: 78.5% (2005); Bachelor's degree or higher: 13.7% (2005); Master's degree or higher: 7.9% (2005).

School District(s)
Gilboa-Conesville Central School District (KG-12)
  2003-04 Enrollment: 396 . . . . (607) 588-7541

Housing: Homeownership rate: 88.8% (2005); Median home value: $126,087 (2005); Median rent: $339 per month (2000); Median age of housing: 27 years (2000).
Transportation: Commute to work: 90.0% car, 3.6% public transportation, 2.5% walk, 3.8% work from home (2000); Travel time to work: 24.2% less than 15 minutes, 30.8% 15 to 30 minutes, 20.5% 30 to 45 minutes, 8.8% 45 to 60 minutes, 15.6% 60 minutes or more (2000)

HOWES CAVE (unincorporated postal area, zip code 12092). Covers a land area of 13.598 square miles and a water area of 0.073 square miles. Located at 42.69° N. Lat.; 74.37° W. Long. Elevation is 801 feet.
Population: 0 (2000); Race: 99.4% White, 0.0% Black, 0.4% Asian, 1.6% Hispanic of any race (2000); Density: 0.0 persons per square mile (2000); Age: 21.2% under 18, 22.0% over 64 (2000); Marriage status: 23.1% never married, 60.7% now married, 8.9% widowed, 7.3% divorced (2000); Foreign born: 2.5% (2000); Ancestry (includes multiple ancestries): 21.4% German, 19.0% Irish, 17.7% English, 6.3% Polish, 5.4% Italian (2000).
Economy: Tourist trade attracted by Howe Caverns, among largest in Northeast U.S., with underground stream and lake. Nearby are Secret Caverns. Employment by occupation: 17.5% management, 9.6% professional, 17.5% services, 25.2% sales, 4.1% farming, 12.5% construction, 13.5% production (2000).
Income: Per capita income: $22,738 (2000); Median household income: $39,038 (2000); Poverty rate: 8.0% (2000).
Education: Percent of population age 25 and over with: High school diploma (including GED) or higher: 79.2% (2000); Bachelor's degree or higher: 15.2% (2000).
Housing: Homeownership rate: 73.7% (2000); Median home value: $76,700 (2000); Median rent: $417 per month (2000); Median age of housing: 60+ years (2000).
Transportation: Commute to work: 88.8% car, 0.0% public transportation, 0.0% walk, 7.6% work from home (2000); Travel time to work: 32.5% less than 15 minutes, 20.3% 15 to 30 minutes, 30.1% 30 to 45 minutes, 13.5% 45 to 60 minutes, 3.7% 60 minutes or more (2000)

JEFFERSON (town). Covers a land area of 43.312 square miles and a water area of 0.119 square miles. Located at 42.49° N. Lat.; 74.60° W. Long. Elevation is 1,873 feet.
Population: 1,190 (1990); 1,285 (2000); 1,300 (2005); 1,292 (2010 projected); Race: 95.8% White, 2.4% Black, 0.0% Asian, 1.6% Hispanic of any race (2005); Density: 30.0 persons per square mile (2005); Average household size: 2.43 (2005); Median age: 46.4 (2005); Males per 100 females: 100.0 (2005); Marriage status: 21.6% never married, 61.7% now married, 7.4% widowed, 9.2% divorced (2000); Foreign born: 3.2% (2000); Ancestry (includes multiple ancestries): 17.7% Irish, 14.5% German, 14.0% Italian, 12.4% United States or American, 10.9% English (2000).
Economy: Employment by occupation: 10.2% management, 23.1% professional, 13.4% services, 25.4% sales, 0.4% farming, 9.8% construction, 17.7% production (2000).

Income: Per capita income: $25,158 (2005); Median household income: $43,242 (2005); Average household income: $61,017 (2005); Percent of households with income of $100,000 or more: 14.9% (2005); Poverty rate: 9.9% (2000).
Education: Percent of population age 25 and over with: High school diploma (including GED) or higher: 81.1% (2005); Bachelor's degree or higher: 18.1% (2005); Master's degree or higher: 9.0% (2005).

School District(s)
Jefferson Central School District (KG-12)
    2003-04 Enrollment: 278 . . . . (607) 652-7821
Housing: Homeownership rate: 83.2% (2005); Median home value: $116,552 (2005); Median rent: $390 per month (2000); Median age of housing: 27 years (2000).
Transportation: Commute to work: 90.3% car, 2.5% public transportation, 2.9% walk, 2.9% work from home (2000); Travel time to work: 24.3% less than 15 minutes, 29.4% 15 to 30 minutes, 25.5% 30 to 45 minutes, 8.2% 45 to 60 minutes, 12.6% 60 minutes or more (2000)

MIDDLEBURGH (village)
Covers a land area of 1.201 square miles and a water area of 0 square miles. Located at 42.59° N. Lat.; 74.33° W. Long.
Population: 1,455 (1990); 1,398 (2000); 1,397 (2005); 1,400 (2010 projected); Race: 96.4% White, 0.2% Black, 0.1% Asian, 4.5% Hispanic of any race (2005); Density: 1,162.8 persons per square mile (2005); Average household size: 2.31 (2005); Median age: 40.9 (2005); Males per 100 females: 89.6 (2005); Marriage status: 23.1% never married, 57.5% now married, 9.2% widowed, 10.1% divorced (2000); Foreign born: 1.8% (2000); Ancestry (includes multiple ancestries): 25.1% German, 24.3% Irish, 16.0% English, 11.9% Dutch, 9.7% Italian (2000).
Economy: Single-family building permits issued: 5 (2005); Multi-family building permits issued: 24 (2005); Employment by occupation: 11.1% management, 19.4% professional, 17.5% services, 23.8% sales, 1.7% farming, 9.8% construction, 16.7% production (2000).
Income: Per capita income: $20,041 (2005); Median household income: $34,474 (2005); Average household income: $45,458 (2005); Percent of households with income of $100,000 or more: 6.9% (2005); Poverty rate: 17.8% (2000).
Education: Percent of population age 25 and over with: High school diploma (including GED) or higher: 81.5% (2005); Bachelor's degree or higher: 19.1% (2005); Master's degree or higher: 6.3% (2005).

School District(s)
Middleburgh Central School District (PK-12)
    2003-04 Enrollment: 1,061 . . . . (518) 827-5567
Housing: Homeownership rate: 60.1% (2005); Median home value: $120,960 (2005); Median rent: $412 per month (2000); Median age of housing: 60+ years (2000).
Transportation: Commute to work: 82.5% car, 2.9% public transportation, 9.7% walk, 4.9% work from home (2000); Travel time to work: 43.4% less than 15 minutes, 18.7% 15 to 30 minutes, 13.3% 30 to 45 minutes, 18.9% 45 to 60 minutes, 5.6% 60 minutes or more (2000)

MIDDLEBURGH (town)
Covers a land area of 49.202 square miles and a water area of 0.076 square miles. Located at 42.60° N. Lat.; 74.32° W. Long.
Population: 3,290 (1990); 3,515 (2000); 3,568 (2005); 3,621 (2010 projected); Race: 97.6% White, 0.4% Black, 0.2% Asian, 2.8% Hispanic of any race (2005); Density: 72.5 persons per square mile (2005); Average household size: 2.50 (2005); Median age: 39.9 (2005); Males per 100 females: 93.9 (2005); Marriage status: 22.4% never married, 58.5% now married, 9.2% widowed, 9.9% divorced (2000); Foreign born: 1.5% (2000); Ancestry (includes multiple ancestries): 24.0% German, 20.4% Irish, 11.8% English, 9.0% Dutch, 8.1% Italian (2000).
Economy: Single-family building permits issued: 10 (2005); Multi-family building permits issued: 0 (2005); Employment by occupation: 9.0% management, 16.3% professional, 17.1% services, 23.0% sales, 2.3% farming, 13.0% construction, 19.4% production (2000).
Income: Per capita income: $20,673 (2005); Median household income: $40,431 (2005); Average household income: $51,055 (2005); Percent of households with income of $100,000 or more: 8.9% (2005); Poverty rate: 15.1% (2000).
Education: Percent of population age 25 and over with: High school diploma (including GED) or higher: 79.3% (2005); Bachelor's degree or higher: 14.6% (2005); Master's degree or higher: 4.6% (2005).

Housing: Homeownership rate: 73.8% (2005); Median home value: $114,905 (2005); Median rent: $412 per month (2000); Median age of housing: 47 years (2000).
Transportation: Commute to work: 90.0% car, 1.4% public transportation, 4.8% walk, 3.8% work from home (2000); Travel time to work: 34.3% less than 15 minutes, 23.6% 15 to 30 minutes, 13.0% 30 to 45 minutes, 18.5% 45 to 60 minutes, 10.6% 60 minutes or more (2000)

NORTH BLENHEIM (unincorporated postal area, zip code 12131)
Covers a land area of 18.106 square miles and a water area of 0.010 square miles. Located at 42.48° N. Lat.; 74.45° W. Long.
Population: 0 (2000); Race: 96.8% White, 3.2% Black, 0.0% Asian, 0.9% Hispanic of any race (2000); Density: 0.0 persons per square mile (2000); Age: 16.3% under 18, 11.8% over 64 (2000); Marriage status: 21.4% never married, 57.7% now married, 10.4% widowed, 10.4% divorced (2000); Foreign born: 6.3% (2000); Ancestry (includes multiple ancestries): 32.1% German, 9.5% Dutch, 9.0% United States or American, 8.6% Irish, 7.2% English (2000).
Economy: Employment by occupation: 19.4% management, 13.6% professional, 23.3% services, 17.5% sales, 0.0% farming, 9.7% construction, 16.5% production (2000).
Income: Per capita income: $21,735 (2000); Median household income: $41,500 (2000); Poverty rate: 8.6% (2000).
Education: Percent of population age 25 and over with: High school diploma (including GED) or higher: 81.8% (2000); Bachelor's degree or higher: 15.9% (2000).
Housing: Homeownership rate: 92.9% (2000); Median home value: $64,000 (2000); Median rent: $225 per month (2000); Median age of housing: 26 years (2000).
Transportation: Commute to work: 81.0% car, 0.0% public transportation, 3.0% walk, 16.0% work from home (2000); Travel time to work: 13.1% less than 15 minutes, 31.0% 15 to 30 minutes, 31.0% 30 to 45 minutes, 16.7% 45 to 60 minutes, 8.3% 60 minutes or more (2000)

RICHMONDVILLE (village)
Covers a land area of 1.814 square miles and a water area of 0 square miles. Located at 42.63° N. Lat.; 74.56° W. Long. Elevation is 1,148 feet.
Population: 843 (1990); 786 (2000); 741 (2005); 730 (2010 projected); Race: 94.7% White, 1.2% Black, 1.1% Asian, 2.8% Hispanic of any race (2005); Density: 408.6 persons per square mile (2005); Average household size: 2.45 (2005); Median age: 35.5 (2005); Males per 100 females: 96.0 (2005); Marriage status: 20.7% never married, 63.0% now married, 6.4% widowed, 9.9% divorced (2000); Foreign born: 2.4% (2000); Ancestry (includes multiple ancestries): 22.0% German, 15.3% Irish, 12.5% United States or American, 9.9% English, 9.2% Italian (2000).
Economy: Single-family building permits issued: 4 (2005); Multi-family building permits issued: 0 (2005); Employment by occupation: 10.5% management, 12.8% professional, 20.2% services, 26.2% sales, 1.1% farming, 8.3% construction, 20.8% production (2000).
Income: Per capita income: $20,047 (2005); Median household income: $40,455 (2005); Average household income: $49,189 (2005); Percent of households with income of $100,000 or more: 9.6% (2005); Poverty rate: 9.0% (2000).
Education: Percent of population age 25 and over with: High school diploma (including GED) or higher: 83.1% (2005); Bachelor's degree or higher: 13.8% (2005); Master's degree or higher: 6.4% (2005).

School District(s)
Cobleskill-Richmondville Central School District (KG-12)
    2003-04 Enrollment: 2,208 . . . . (518) 234-4032
Housing: Homeownership rate: 58.9% (2005); Median home value: $121,233 (2005); Median rent: $377 per month (2000); Median age of housing: 59 years (2000).
Transportation: Commute to work: 93.1% car, 1.1% public transportation, 0.0% walk, 3.7% work from home (2000); Travel time to work: 33.6% less than 15 minutes, 33.9% 15 to 30 minutes, 14.6% 30 to 45 minutes, 9.8% 45 to 60 minutes, 8.0% 60 minutes or more (2000)

RICHMONDVILLE (town)
Covers a land area of 30.200 square miles and a water area of 0.027 square miles. Located at 42.64° N. Lat.; 74.55° W. Long. Elevation is 1,148 feet.
Population: 2,391 (1990); 2,412 (2000); 2,361 (2005); 2,327 (2010 projected); Race: 96.6% White, 0.7% Black, 0.6% Asian, 2.0% Hispanic of any race (2005); Density: 78.2 persons per square mile (2005); Average household size: 2.44 (2005); Median age: 39.2 (2005); Males per 100 females: 101.1 (2005); Marriage status: 22.1% never married, 63.1% now

married, 5.8% widowed, 9.0% divorced (2000); Foreign born: 1.8% (2000); Ancestry (includes multiple ancestries): 21.7% German, 18.2% Irish, 11.2% Italian, 8.9% English, 8.6% United States or American (2000).
Economy: Apparel. Single-family building permits issued: 4 (2005); Multi-family building permits issued: 0 (2005); Employment by occupation: 8.5% management, 15.6% professional, 15.1% services, 24.4% sales, 1.0% farming, 13.2% construction, 22.1% production (2000).
Income: Per capita income: $19,880 (2005); Median household income: $39,300 (2005); Average household income: $48,539 (2005); Percent of households with income of $100,000 or more: 7.9% (2005); Poverty rate: 8.2% (2000).
Education: Percent of population age 25 and over with: High school diploma (including GED) or higher: 79.6% (2005); Bachelor's degree or higher: 14.0% (2005); Master's degree or higher: 6.4% (2005).
Housing: Homeownership rate: 72.6% (2005); Median home value: $116,379 (2005); Median rent: $386 per month (2000); Median age of housing: 31 years (2000).
Transportation: Commute to work: 92.6% car, 1.4% public transportation, 0.0% walk, 3.5% work from home (2000); Travel time to work: 35.5% less than 15 minutes, 31.3% 15 to 30 minutes, 12.3% 30 to 45 minutes, 10.5% 45 to 60 minutes, 10.4% 60 minutes or more (2000)

SCHOHARIE (village).
Covers a land area of 1.651 square miles and a water area of 0 square miles. Located at 42.66° N. Lat.; 74.31° W. Long. Elevation is 611 feet.
Population: 1,045 (1990); 1,030 (2000); 1,029 (2005); 1,034 (2010 projected); Race: 97.4% White, 1.0% Black, 0.2% Asian, 2.1% Hispanic of any race (2005); Density: 623.2 persons per square mile (2005); Average household size: 2.26 (2005); Median age: 44.2 (2005); Males per 100 females: 91.3 (2005); Marriage status: 24.6% never married, 55.5% now married, 10.4% widowed, 9.5% divorced (2000); Foreign born: 1.5% (2000); Ancestry (includes multiple ancestries): 24.6% Irish, 23.4% German, 17.2% English, 11.1% Italian, 10.3% Dutch (2000).
Economy: Single-family building permits issued: 1 (2005); Multi-family building permits issued: 0 (2005); Employment by occupation: 11.5% management, 27.0% professional, 16.7% services, 22.5% sales, 0.9% farming, 8.6% construction, 12.8% production (2000).
Income: Per capita income: $24,492 (2005); Median household income: $38,984 (2005); Average household income: $53,969 (2005); Percent of households with income of $100,000 or more: 14.9% (2005); Poverty rate: 10.7% (2000).
Education: Percent of population age 25 and over with: High school diploma (including GED) or higher: 83.3% (2005); Bachelor's degree or higher: 21.1% (2005); Master's degree or higher: 10.5% (2005).
School District(s)
Schoharie Central School District (KG-12)
    2003-04 Enrollment: 1,148 . . . . (518) 295-8132
Housing: Homeownership rate: 57.2% (2005); Median home value: $144,084 (2005); Median rent: $358 per month (2000); Median age of housing: 60+ years (2000).
Safety: Violent crime rate: 38.9 per 10,000 population; Property crime rate: 126.5 per 10,000 population (2004).
Transportation: Commute to work: 79.5% car, 4.1% public transportation, 9.7% walk, 5.3% work from home (2000); Travel time to work: 33.3% less than 15 minutes, 24.3% 15 to 30 minutes, 20.4% 30 to 45 minutes, 16.3% 45 to 60 minutes, 5.6% 60 minutes or more (2000)
Additional Information Contacts
Schoharie County Chamber of Commerce . . . . (518) 295-7033
    http://www.schohariechamber.com

SCHOHARIE (town).
Covers a land area of 29.796 square miles and a water area of 0.173 square miles. Located at 42.67° N. Lat.; 74.32° W. Long. Elevation is 611 feet.
History: Has 18th-century buildings including Old Stone Fort; 1772, now a museum. Incorporated 1867.
Population: 3,369 (1990); 3,299 (2000); 3,296 (2005); 3,294 (2010 projected); Race: 98.2% White, 0.4% Black, 0.2% Asian, 1.3% Hispanic of any race (2005); Density: 110.6 persons per square mile (2005); Average household size: 2.46 (2005); Median age: 40.8 (2005); Males per 100 females: 92.9 (2005); Marriage status: 23.0% never married, 61.5% now married, 7.5% widowed, 8.0% divorced (2000); Foreign born: 2.5% (2000); Ancestry (includes multiple ancestries): 21.4% German, 17.8% Irish, 13.2% English, 9.9% Italian, 8.0% Polish (2000).
Economy: Trade center in rich farming area; light manufacturing.
Single-family building permits issued: 11 (2005); Multi-family building permits issued: 0 (2005); Employment by occupation: 10.0% management, 19.9% professional, 13.3% services, 28.0% sales, 1.7% farming, 11.2% construction, 15.7% production (2000).
Income: Per capita income: $23,715 (2005); Median household income: $44,747 (2005); Average household income: $57,933 (2005); Percent of households with income of $100,000 or more: 14.7% (2005); Poverty rate: 6.1% (2000).
Education: Percent of population age 25 and over with: High school diploma (including GED) or higher: 86.4% (2005); Bachelor's degree or higher: 19.6% (2005); Master's degree or higher: 11.0% (2005).
Housing: Homeownership rate: 71.2% (2005); Median home value: $138,534 (2005); Median rent: $378 per month (2000); Median age of housing: 45 years (2000).
Transportation: Commute to work: 89.6% car, 1.5% public transportation, 3.5% walk, 4.1% work from home (2000); Travel time to work: 28.2% less than 15 minutes, 24.4% 15 to 30 minutes, 24.0% 30 to 45 minutes, 17.6% 45 to 60 minutes, 5.9% 60 minutes or more (2000)

SEWARD (town).
Covers a land area of 36.384 square miles and a water area of 0.070 square miles. Located at 42.70° N. Lat.; 74.58° W. Long. Elevation is 1,182 feet.
Population: 1,653 (1990); 1,637 (2000); 1,652 (2005); 1,660 (2010 projected); Race: 97.5% White, 0.3% Black, 0.0% Asian, 3.3% Hispanic of any race (2005); Density: 45.4 persons per square mile (2005); Average household size: 2.73 (2005); Median age: 39.5 (2005); Males per 100 females: 101.0 (2005); Marriage status: 21.6% never married, 63.5% now married, 6.9% widowed, 8.0% divorced (2000); Foreign born: 1.8% (2000); Ancestry (includes multiple ancestries): 24.5% German, 15.9% Irish, 11.7% United States or American, 10.4% English, 9.9% Other groups (2000).
Economy: Single-family building permits issued: 10 (2005); Multi-family building permits issued: 0 (2005); Employment by occupation: 12.2% management, 12.5% professional, 14.5% services, 30.0% sales, 2.5% farming, 11.5% construction, 16.8% production (2000).
Income: Per capita income: $22,296 (2005); Median household income: $46,585 (2005); Average household income: $60,880 (2005); Percent of households with income of $100,000 or more: 11.6% (2005); Poverty rate: 8.8% (2000).
Education: Percent of population age 25 and over with: High school diploma (including GED) or higher: 83.4% (2005); Bachelor's degree or higher: 17.6% (2005); Master's degree or higher: 7.3% (2005).
Housing: Homeownership rate: 86.4% (2005); Median home value: $120,685 (2005); Median rent: $389 per month (2000); Median age of housing: 36 years (2000).
Transportation: Commute to work: 91.1% car, 0.6% public transportation, 2.8% walk, 5.0% work from home (2000); Travel time to work: 31.0% less than 15 minutes, 34.0% 15 to 30 minutes, 9.0% 30 to 45 minutes, 11.2% 45 to 60 minutes, 14.9% 60 minutes or more (2000)

SHARON (town).
Covers a land area of 39.083 square miles and a water area of 0.087 square miles. Located at 42.77° N. Lat.; 74.60° W. Long.
History: Former health resort, with sulphur springs.
Population: 1,890 (1990); 1,843 (2000); 1,855 (2005); 1,870 (2010 projected); Race: 98.3% White, 0.5% Black, 0.1% Asian, 1.8% Hispanic of any race (2005); Density: 47.5 persons per square mile (2005); Average household size: 2.67 (2005); Median age: 40.1 (2005); Males per 100 females: 99.9 (2005); Marriage status: 23.4% never married, 58.8% now married, 9.5% widowed, 8.3% divorced (2000); Foreign born: 3.7% (2000); Ancestry (includes multiple ancestries): 21.8% German, 17.5% United States or American, 11.3% Irish, 9.4% English, 8.5% Italian (2000).
Economy: Single-family building permits issued: 6 (2005); Multi-family building permits issued: 0 (2005); Employment by occupation: 15.9% management, 15.1% professional, 13.7% services, 21.4% sales, 1.8% farming, 12.2% construction, 19.8% production (2000).
Income: Per capita income: $21,642 (2005); Median household income: $42,129 (2005); Average household income: $56,225 (2005); Percent of households with income of $100,000 or more: 9.9% (2005); Poverty rate: 15.1% (2000).
Education: Percent of population age 25 and over with: High school diploma (including GED) or higher: 79.5% (2005); Bachelor's degree or higher: 16.3% (2005); Master's degree or higher: 6.7% (2005).
Housing: Homeownership rate: 77.2% (2005); Median home value: $109,203 (2005); Median rent: $390 per month (2000); Median age of housing: 51 years (2000).

Transportation: Commute to work: 84.9% car, 0.0% public transportation, 4.8% walk, 7.7% work from home (2000); Travel time to work: 33.2% less than 15 minutes, 28.9% 15 to 30 minutes, 12.5% 30 to 45 minutes, 10.0% 45 to 60 minutes, 15.3% 60 minutes or more (2000)

SHARON SPRINGS (village).
Covers a land area of 1.826 square miles and a water area of 0 square miles. Located at 42.79° N. Lat.; 74.61° W. Long. Elevation is 1,137 feet.
Population: 591 (1990); 547 (2000); 561 (2005); 573 (2010 projected); Race: 97.9% White, 0.4% Black, 0.0% Asian, 2.7% Hispanic of any race (2005); Density: 307.2 persons per square mile (2005); Average household size: 2.63 (2005); Median age: 45.3 (2005); Males per 100 females: 94.1 (2005); Marriage status: 21.9% never married, 54.0% now married, 14.8% widowed, 9.3% divorced (2000); Foreign born: 9.6% (2000); Ancestry (includes multiple ancestries): 19.6% German, 12.8% English, 10.0% Italian, 9.4% Irish, 7.4% Russian (2000).
Economy: Single-family building permits issued: 0 (2005); Multi-family building permits issued: 0 (2005); Employment by occupation: 18.4% management, 16.5% professional, 12.3% services, 21.2% sales, 0.9% farming, 12.3% construction, 18.4% production (2000).
Income: Per capita income: $23,254 (2005); Median household income: $45,208 (2005); Average household income: $56,491 (2005); Percent of households with income of $100,000 or more: 11.7% (2005); Poverty rate: 12.1% (2000).
Education: Percent of population age 25 and over with: High school diploma (including GED) or higher: 78.6% (2005); Bachelor's degree or higher: 26.2% (2005); Master's degree or higher: 10.6% (2005).
School District(s)
Sharon Springs Central School District (KG-12)
    2003-04 Enrollment: 388 . . . . (518) 284-2266
Housing: Homeownership rate: 62.9% (2005); Median home value: $99,259 (2005); Median rent: $401 per month (2000); Median age of housing: 60+ years (2000).
Transportation: Commute to work: 80.7% car, 0.0% public transportation, 2.8% walk, 10.8% work from home (2000); Travel time to work: 40.7% less than 15 minutes, 27.5% 15 to 30 minutes, 5.3% 30 to 45 minutes, 7.9% 45 to 60 minutes, 18.5% 60 minutes or more (2000)

SLOANSVILLE (unincorporated postal area, zip code 12160).
Covers a land area of 18.937 square miles and a water area of 0.008 square miles. Located at 42.75° N. Lat.; 74.34° W. Long. Elevation is 683 feet.
Population: 0 (2000); Race: 98.7% White, 1.0% Black, 0.0% Asian, 0.7% Hispanic of any race (2000); Density: 0.0 persons per square mile (2000); Age: 26.1% under 18, 10.7% over 64 (2000); Marriage status: 20.8% never married, 63.2% now married, 7.2% widowed, 8.8% divorced (2000); Foreign born: 1.7% (2000); Ancestry (includes multiple ancestries): 23.9% German, 17.5% Irish, 11.8% Dutch, 11.3% English, 9.0% Italian (2000).
Economy: Employment by occupation: 12.9% management, 13.5% professional, 16.0% services, 23.9% sales, 0.0% farming, 13.8% construction, 19.9% production (2000).
Income: Per capita income: $18,596 (2000); Median household income: $45,625 (2000); Poverty rate: 7.4% (2000).
Education: Percent of population age 25 and over with: High school diploma (including GED) or higher: 84.9% (2000); Bachelor's degree or higher: 11.6% (2000).
Housing: Homeownership rate: 81.8% (2000); Median home value: $84,800 (2000); Median rent: $419 per month (2000); Median age of housing: 29 years (2000).
Transportation: Commute to work: 92.6% car, 0.7% public transportation, 0.4% walk, 5.7% work from home (2000); Travel time to work: 17.9% less than 15 minutes, 26.1% 15 to 30 minutes, 26.1% 30 to 45 minutes, 25.0% 45 to 60 minutes, 1.9% 60 minutes or more (2000)

SUMMIT (town).
Covers a land area of 37.132 square miles and a water area of 0.342 square miles. Located at 42.57° N. Lat.; 74.60° W. Long. Elevation is 2,109 feet.
Population: 973 (1990); 1,123 (2000); 1,165 (2005); 1,190 (2010 projected); Race: 97.3% White, 1.2% Black, 0.4% Asian, 1.2% Hispanic of any race (2005); Density: 31.4 persons per square mile (2005); Average household size: 2.40 (2005); Median age: 45.1 (2005); Males per 100 females: 105.1 (2005); Marriage status: 21.6% never married, 60.1% now married, 7.2% widowed, 11.2% divorced (2000); Foreign born: 3.7% (2000); Ancestry (includes multiple ancestries): 21.2% German, 18.1% Irish, 11.9% Italian, 9.6% United States or American, 9.6% English (2000).
Economy: Single-family building permits issued: 9 (2005); Multi-family building permits issued: 0 (2005); Employment by occupation: 11.8% management, 15.5% professional, 14.7% services, 23.9% sales, 2.4% farming, 14.5% construction, 17.1% production (2000).
Income: Per capita income: $20,292 (2005); Median household income: $42,306 (2005); Average household income: $48,742 (2005); Percent of households with income of $100,000 or more: 7.4% (2005); Poverty rate: 15.9% (2000).
Education: Percent of population age 25 and over with: High school diploma (including GED) or higher: 81.4% (2005); Bachelor's degree or higher: 16.8% (2005); Master's degree or higher: 6.5% (2005).
School District(s)
Cobleskill-Richmondville Central School District (KG-12)
    2003-04 Enrollment: 2,208 . . . . (518) 234-4032
Housing: Homeownership rate: 89.3% (2005); Median home value: $104,412 (2005); Median rent: $350 per month (2000); Median age of housing: 31 years (2000).
Transportation: Commute to work: 86.6% car, 2.2% public transportation, 3.3% walk, 6.1% work from home (2000); Travel time to work: 18.8% less than 15 minutes, 33.8% 15 to 30 minutes, 15.8% 30 to 45 minutes, 16.2% 45 to 60 minutes, 15.4% 60 minutes or more (2000)

WARNERVILLE (unincorporated postal area, zip code 12187).
Covers a land area of 19.401 square miles and a water area of 0.009 square miles. Located at 42.62° N. Lat.; 74.46° W. Long. Elevation is 930 feet.
Population: 0 (2000); Race: 94.8% White, 1.2% Black, 0.0% Asian, 1.6% Hispanic of any race (2000); Density: 0.0 persons per square mile (2000); Age: 26.5% under 18, 18.8% over 64 (2000); Marriage status: 21.6% never married, 64.7% now married, 7.1% widowed, 6.6% divorced (2000); Foreign born: 1.3% (2000); Ancestry (includes multiple ancestries): 17.8% Irish, 17.6% German, 10.5% Italian, 9.2% English, 7.6% Other groups (2000).
Economy: Employment by occupation: 11.2% management, 21.2% professional, 10.8% services, 18.6% sales, 0.0% farming, 16.4% construction, 21.9% production (2000).
Income: Per capita income: $15,547 (2000); Median household income: $30,729 (2000); Poverty rate: 14.5% (2000).
Education: Percent of population age 25 and over with: High school diploma (including GED) or higher: 84.7% (2000); Bachelor's degree or higher: 16.2% (2000).
Housing: Homeownership rate: 71.9% (2000); Median home value: $76,800 (2000); Median rent: $400 per month (2000); Median age of housing: 33 years (2000).
Transportation: Commute to work: 89.4% car, 2.3% public transportation, 0.0% walk, 6.1% work from home (2000); Travel time to work: 37.9% less than 15 minutes, 21.4% 15 to 30 minutes, 8.5% 30 to 45 minutes, 12.5% 45 to 60 minutes, 19.8% 60 minutes or more (2000)

WEST FULTON (unincorporated postal area, zip code 12194).
Covers a land area of 13.101 square miles and a water area of 0 square miles. Located at 42.52° N. Lat.; 74.44° W. Long. Elevation is 1,157 feet.
Population: 0 (2000); Race: 100.0% White, 0.0% Black, 0.0% Asian, 0.0% Hispanic of any race (2000); Density: 0.0 persons per square mile (2000); Age: 20.4% under 18, 16.8% over 64 (2000); Marriage status: 30.9% never married, 60.8% now married, 1.0% widowed, 7.2% divorced (2000); Foreign born: 2.7% (2000); Ancestry (includes multiple ancestries): 21.2% Irish, 21.2% German, 15.9% Italian, 9.7% Dutch, 8.0% United States or American (2000).
Economy: Employment by occupation: 9.5% management, 16.7% professional, 10.7% services, 20.2% sales, 9.5% farming, 9.5% construction, 23.8% production (2000).
Income: Per capita income: $16,262 (2000); Median household income: $37,604 (2000); Poverty rate: 20.4% (2000).
Education: Percent of population age 25 and over with: High school diploma (including GED) or higher: 69.2% (2000); Bachelor's degree or higher: 13.7% (2000).
Housing: Homeownership rate: 94.2% (2000); Median home value: $86,500 (2000); Median rent: $358 per month (2000); Median age of housing: 29 years (2000).
Transportation: Commute to work: 97.6% car, 0.0% public transportation, 2.4% walk, 0.0% work from home (2000); Travel time to work: 19.5% less than 15 minutes, 30.5% 15 to 30 minutes, 12.2% 30 to 45 minutes, 0.0% 45 to 60 minutes, 37.8% 60 minutes or more (2000)

WRIGHT (town). Covers a land area of 28.634 square miles and a water area of 0.066 square miles. Located at 42.67° N. Lat.; 74.20° W. Long.
Population: 1,385 (1990); 1,547 (2000); 1,576 (2005); 1,598 (2010 projected); Race: 98.6% White, 0.4% Black, 0.1% Asian, 1.0% Hispanic of any race (2005); Density: 55.0 persons per square mile (2005); Average household size: 2.67 (2005); Median age: 39.2 (2005); Males per 100 females: 101.3 (2005); Marriage status: 21.3% never married, 66.3% now married, 5.5% widowed, 6.9% divorced (2000); Foreign born: 1.4% (2000); Ancestry (includes multiple ancestries): 21.9% German, 15.5% Irish, 13.1% English, 11.1% United States or American, 9.5% Italian (2000).
Economy: Single-family building permits issued: 2 (2005); Multi-family building permits issued: 0 (2005); Employment by occupation: 13.8% management, 18.4% professional, 11.1% services, 27.5% sales, 1.2% farming, 13.1% construction, 14.8% production (2000).
Income: Per capita income: $22,157 (2005); Median household income: $47,667 (2005); Average household income: $59,186 (2005); Percent of households with income of $100,000 or more: 11.4% (2005); Poverty rate: 8.9% (2000).
Education: Percent of population age 25 and over with: High school diploma (including GED) or higher: 87.1% (2005); Bachelor's degree or higher: 17.7% (2005); Master's degree or higher: 9.3% (2005).
Housing: Homeownership rate: 85.3% (2005); Median home value: $131,601 (2005); Median rent: $454 per month (2000); Median age of housing: 37 years (2000).
Transportation: Commute to work: 94.8% car, 0.4% public transportation, 1.4% walk, 3.4% work from home (2000); Travel time to work: 18.4% less than 15 minutes, 22.1% 15 to 30 minutes, 26.7% 30 to 45 minutes, 22.8% 45 to 60 minutes, 10.0% 60 minutes or more (2000)

Schuyler County

Located in west central New York, in the Finger Lakes region; drained by Cayuta and Catherine Creeks; includes Lamoka and Cayuta Lakes and part of Seneca Lake. Covers a land area of 328.71 square miles, a water area of 13.51 square miles, and is located in the Eastern Time Zone. The county government was organized in 1854. County seat is Watkins Glen.
Population: 18,662 (1990); 19,224 (2000); 19,545 (2005); 19,869 (2010 projected); Race: 96.4% White, 1.6% Black, 0.4% Asian, 1.5% Hispanic of any race (2005); Density: 59.5 persons per square mile (2005); Average household size: 2.56 (2005); Median age: 40.1 (2005); Males per 100 females: 100.0 (2005).
Religion: Five largest groups: 46.3% Catholic Church, 9.0% The United Methodist Church, 3.7% American Baptist Churches in the USA, 2.7% Presbyterian Church (U.S.A.), 1.6% The Wesleyan Church (2000).
Economy: Unemployment rate: 5.4% (2005); Total civilian labor force: 9,900 (2005); Leading industries: 28.2% health care and social assistance; 25.6% retail trade; 15.3% manufacturing (2003); Farms: 405 totaling 73,865 acres (2002); Companies that employ 500 or more persons: 0 (2003); Companies that employ 100 to 499 persons: 4 (2003); Companies that employ less than 100 persons: 320 (2003); Black-owned businesses: n/a (2002); Hispanic-owned businesses: n/a (2002); Women-owned businesses: 259 (2002); Retail sales per capita: $10,220 (2006); Single-family building permits issued: 46 (2005); Multi-family building permits issued: 0 (2005).
Income: Per capita income: $19,873 (2005); Median household income: $41,230 (2005); Average household income: $50,281 (2005); Percent of households with income of $100,000 or more: 8.4% (2005); Poverty rate: 11.5% (2003); Bankruptcy rate: 7.13% (2005).
Education: Percent of population age 25 and over with: High school diploma (including GED) or higher: 82.4% (2005); Bachelor's degree or higher: 15.6% (2005); Master's degree or higher: 7.1% (2005).
Housing: Homeownership rate: 77.4% (2005); Median home value: $102,463 (2005); Median rent: $370 per month (2000); Median age of housing: 41 years (2000).
Health: Birth rate: 100.0 per 10,000 population (2004); Death rate: 101.0 per 10,000 population (2004); Age-adjusted cancer mortality rate: 211.2 deaths per 100,000 population (2002); Number of physicians: 7.2 per 10,000 population (2004); Hospital beds: 86.4 per 10,000 population (2003); Hospital admissions: 784.4 per 10,000 population (2003).
Elections: 2004 Presidential election results: 57.7% Bush, 40.1% Kerry, 2.0% Nader, 0.2% Badnarik

National and State Parks: Cliffside State Forest; Connecticut Hill State Game Management Area; Finger Lakes National Forest; Green Mountain National Forest-Hector Ranger District; Watkins Glen State Park
Additional Information Contacts
Schuyler County Government . . . . (607) 535-8100
http://www.lightlink.com/schco

Schuyler County Communities

ALPINE (unincorporated postal area, zip code 14805). Covers a land area of 28.970 square miles and a water area of 0.590 square miles. Located at 42.36° N. Lat.; 76.72° W. Long. Elevation is 1,169 feet.
Population: 0 (2000); Race: 97.3% White, 0.0% Black, 0.3% Asian, 0.6% Hispanic of any race (2000); Density: 0.0 persons per square mile (2000); Age: 30.9% under 18, 9.3% over 64 (2000); Marriage status: 24.1% never married, 56.1% now married, 5.5% widowed, 14.3% divorced (2000); Foreign born: 0.8% (2000); Ancestry (includes multiple ancestries): 24.9% German, 16.3% Irish, 13.2% English, 10.2% United States or American, 8.0% Other groups (2000).
Economy: Employment by occupation: 11.2% management, 17.4% professional, 12.4% services, 24.1% sales, 2.6% farming, 11.2% construction, 21.1% production (2000).
Income: Per capita income: $17,497 (2000); Median household income: $39,028 (2000); Poverty rate: 14.2% (2000).
Education: Percent of population age 25 and over with: High school diploma (including GED) or higher: 87.5% (2000); Bachelor's degree or higher: 14.4% (2000).
Housing: Homeownership rate: 80.6% (2000); Median home value: $65,700 (2000); Median rent: $333 per month (2000); Median age of housing: 37 years (2000).
Transportation: Commute to work: 89.0% car, 2.5% public transportation, 5.1% walk, 3.2% work from home (2000); Travel time to work: 14.4% less than 15 minutes, 37.7% 15 to 30 minutes, 39.1% 30 to 45 minutes, 4.4% 45 to 60 minutes, 4.6% 60 minutes or more (2000)

BEAVER DAMS (unincorporated postal area, zip code 14812). Aka Beaver Dam. Covers a land area of 74.499 square miles and a water area of 0.040 square miles. Located at 42.28° N. Lat.; 76.97° W. Long.
Population: 0 (2000); Race: 93.4% White, 4.3% Black, 0.1% Asian, 2.9% Hispanic of any race (2000); Density: 0.0 persons per square mile (2000); Age: 26.8% under 18, 11.1% over 64 (2000); Marriage status: 25.1% never married, 60.6% now married, 4.9% widowed, 9.5% divorced (2000); Foreign born: 0.6% (2000); Ancestry (includes multiple ancestries): 17.6% German, 16.8% English, 13.8% Irish, 11.2% United States or American, 8.1% Other groups (2000).
Economy: Employment by occupation: 7.5% management, 15.3% professional, 15.9% services, 25.5% sales, 1.2% farming, 12.1% construction, 22.6% production (2000).
Income: Per capita income: $14,537 (2000); Median household income: $36,109 (2000); Poverty rate: 10.8% (2000).
Education: Percent of population age 25 and over with: High school diploma (including GED) or higher: 77.9% (2000); Bachelor's degree or higher: 9.2% (2000).
School District(s)
Watkins Glen Central School District (PK-12)
  2003-04 Enrollment: 1,524 . . . . (607) 535-3219
Housing: Homeownership rate: 86.9% (2000); Median home value: $55,400 (2000); Median rent: $372 per month (2000); Median age of housing: 37 years (2000).
Transportation: Commute to work: 96.0% car, 0.0% public transportation, 1.0% walk, 1.9% work from home (2000); Travel time to work: 12.4% less than 15 minutes, 59.9% 15 to 30 minutes, 20.2% 30 to 45 minutes, 3.8% 45 to 60 minutes, 3.6% 60 minutes or more (2000)

BURDETT (village). Covers a land area of 0.966 square miles and a water area of 0 square miles. Located at 42.41° N. Lat.; 76.84° W. Long. Elevation is 1,003 feet.
Population: 372 (1990); 357 (2000); 372 (2005); 387 (2010 projected); Race: 98.9% White, 0.5% Black, 0.0% Asian, 0.3% Hispanic of any race (2005); Density: 385.0 persons per square mile (2005); Average household size: 2.37 (2005); Median age: 38.6 (2005); Males per 100 females: 89.8 (2005); Marriage status: 22.7% never married, 50.0% now married, 7.8% widowed, 19.5% divorced (2000); Foreign born: 1.1% (2000); Ancestry (includes multiple ancestries): 19.2% Irish, 15.6% Italian, 15.6% English, 13.4% German, 8.1% French (except Basque) (2000).

Economy: In Finger Lakes region. Single-family building permits issued: 0 (2005); Multi-family building permits issued: 0 (2005); Employment by occupation: 8.5% management, 15.1% professional, 19.1% services, 24.6% sales, 2.5% farming, 11.6% construction, 18.6% production (2000).
Income: Per capita income: $18,837 (2005); Median household income: $40,473 (2005); Average household income: $44,634 (2005); Percent of households with income of $100,000 or more: 4.5% (2005); Poverty rate: 8.2% (2000).
Education: Percent of population age 25 and over with: High school diploma (including GED) or higher: 82.9% (2005); Bachelor's degree or higher: 15.2% (2005); Master's degree or higher: 10.5% (2005).
Housing: Homeownership rate: 72.6% (2005); Median home value: $99,091 (2005); Median rent: $345 per month (2000); Median age of housing: 60+ years (2000).
Transportation: Commute to work: 83.5% car, 5.2% public transportation, 2.6% walk, 8.8% work from home (2000); Travel time to work: 23.7% less than 15 minutes, 35.6% 15 to 30 minutes, 23.2% 30 to 45 minutes, 11.9% 45 to 60 minutes, 5.6% 60 minutes or more (2000).

CATHARINE (town). Aka Catherine. Covers a land area of 32.308 square miles and a water area of 0.596 square miles. Located at 42.32° N. Lat.; 76.75° W. Long.
Population: 1,978 (1990); 1,930 (2000); 1,921 (2005); 1,887 (2010 projected); Race: 96.7% White, 0.6% Black, 0.2% Asian, 1.5% Hispanic of any race (2005); Density: 59.5 persons per square mile (2005); Average household size: 2.50 (2005); Median age: 38.3 (2005); Males per 100 females: 98.2 (2005); Marriage status: 22.9% never married, 60.2% now married, 6.5% widowed, 10.4% divorced (2000); Foreign born: 0.7% (2000); Ancestry (includes multiple ancestries): 18.8% German, 18.7% English, 15.3% Irish, 11.2% United States or American, 7.9% Other groups (2000).
Economy: Single-family building permits issued: 4 (2005); Multi-family building permits issued: 0 (2005); Employment by occupation: 12.2% management, 17.3% professional, 14.0% services, 23.5% sales, 1.2% farming, 12.5% construction, 19.4% production (2000).
Income: Per capita income: $19,381 (2005); Median household income: $41,331 (2005); Average household income: $48,298 (2005); Percent of households with income of $100,000 or more: 8.2% (2005); Poverty rate: 11.6% (2000).
Education: Percent of population age 25 and over with: High school diploma (including GED) or higher: 86.8% (2005); Bachelor's degree or higher: 15.9% (2005); Master's degree or higher: 6.3% (2005).
Housing: Homeownership rate: 77.3% (2005); Median home value: $98,491 (2005); Median rent: $365 per month (2000); Median age of housing: 50 years (2000).
Transportation: Commute to work: 88.8% car, 2.6% public transportation, 3.4% walk, 4.9% work from home (2000); Travel time to work: 24.0% less than 15 minutes, 34.0% 15 to 30 minutes, 30.6% 30 to 45 minutes, 8.9% 45 to 60 minutes, 2.5% 60 minutes or more (2000).

CAYUTA (town). Covers a land area of 20.327 square miles and a water area of 0 square miles. Located at 42.27° N. Lat.; 76.66° W. Long. Elevation is 1,107 feet.
Population: 612 (1990); 545 (2000); 536 (2005); 524 (2010 projected); Race: 95.7% White, 1.3% Black, 0.0% Asian, 2.1% Hispanic of any race (2005); Density: 26.4 persons per square mile (2005); Average household size: 2.52 (2005); Median age: 39.2 (2005); Males per 100 females: 104.6 (2005); Marriage status: 24.4% never married, 62.1% now married, 7.1% widowed, 6.4% divorced (2000); Foreign born: 0.0% (2000); Ancestry (includes multiple ancestries): 17.9% German, 16.6% English, 11.8% Irish, 8.2% United States or American, 6.2% Other groups (2000).
Economy: Single-family building permits issued: 0 (2005); Multi-family building permits issued: 0 (2005); Employment by occupation: 9.0% management, 7.7% professional, 9.9% services, 27.5% sales, 2.6% farming, 16.3% construction, 27.0% production (2000).
Income: Per capita income: $18,857 (2005); Median household income: $38,098 (2005); Average household income: $47,453 (2005); Percent of households with income of $100,000 or more: 3.3% (2005); Poverty rate: 6.2% (2000).
Taxes: Total city taxes per capita: $370 (2004); City property taxes per capita: $359 (2004).
Education: Percent of population age 25 and over with: High school diploma (including GED) or higher: 72.7% (2005); Bachelor's degree or higher: 9.0% (2005); Master's degree or higher: 5.2% (2005).

Housing: Homeownership rate: 77.5% (2005); Median home value: $78,718 (2005); Median rent: $348 per month (2000); Median age of housing: 35 years (2000).
Transportation: Commute to work: 95.0% car, 2.3% public transportation, 2.7% walk, 0.0% work from home (2000); Travel time to work: 15.5% less than 15 minutes, 44.3% 15 to 30 minutes, 31.5% 30 to 45 minutes, 2.7% 45 to 60 minutes, 5.9% 60 minutes or more (2000).

DIX (town). Covers a land area of 36.149 square miles and a water area of 0.474 square miles. Located at 42.35° N. Lat.; 76.89° W. Long.
Population: 4,130 (1990); 4,197 (2000); 4,194 (2005); 4,211 (2010 projected); Race: 96.9% White, 0.6% Black, 0.9% Asian, 1.4% Hispanic of any race (2005); Density: 116.0 persons per square mile (2005); Average household size: 2.54 (2005); Median age: 40.3 (2005); Males per 100 females: 90.5 (2005); Marriage status: 20.9% never married, 56.7% now married, 8.8% widowed, 13.6% divorced (2000); Foreign born: 1.8% (2000); Ancestry (includes multiple ancestries): 19.0% German, 16.3% Italian, 15.4% Irish, 15.0% English, 8.4% United States or American (2000).
Economy: Single-family building permits issued: 3 (2005); Multi-family building permits issued: 0 (2005); Employment by occupation: 10.0% management, 14.9% professional, 19.4% services, 23.7% sales, 1.6% farming, 8.9% construction, 21.5% production (2000).
Income: Per capita income: $18,648 (2005); Median household income: $36,907 (2005); Average household income: $46,289 (2005); Percent of households with income of $100,000 or more: 7.3% (2005); Poverty rate: 12.7% (2000).
Education: Percent of population age 25 and over with: High school diploma (including GED) or higher: 81.3% (2005); Bachelor's degree or higher: 15.9% (2005); Master's degree or higher: 7.7% (2005).
Housing: Homeownership rate: 67.4% (2005); Median home value: $98,667 (2005); Median rent: $371 per month (2000); Median age of housing: 52 years (2000).
Transportation: Commute to work: 89.1% car, 0.5% public transportation, 4.5% walk, 5.5% work from home (2000); Travel time to work: 42.8% less than 15 minutes, 27.5% 15 to 30 minutes, 17.4% 30 to 45 minutes, 8.2% 45 to 60 minutes, 4.1% 60 minutes or more (2000).

HECTOR (town). Covers a land area of 102.475 square miles and a water area of 9.985 square miles. Located at 42.47° N. Lat.; 76.79° W. Long.
Population: 4,423 (1990); 4,854 (2000); 5,022 (2005); 5,181 (2010 projected); Race: 97.8% White, 0.6% Black, 0.2% Asian, 0.9% Hispanic of any race (2005); Density: 49.0 persons per square mile (2005); Average household size: 2.54 (2005); Median age: 39.9 (2005); Males per 100 females: 102.2 (2005); Marriage status: 23.1% never married, 61.5% now married, 5.3% widowed, 10.1% divorced (2000); Foreign born: 1.0% (2000); Ancestry (includes multiple ancestries): 21.1% German, 19.0% English, 17.5% Irish, 9.6% Italian, 8.4% United States or American (2000).
Economy: Single-family building permits issued: 22 (2005); Multi-family building permits issued: 0 (2005); Employment by occupation: 14.0% management, 21.7% professional, 18.7% services, 18.7% sales, 3.7% farming, 11.0% construction, 12.3% production (2000).
Income: Per capita income: $23,442 (2005); Median household income: $46,259 (2005); Average household income: $59,266 (2005); Percent of households with income of $100,000 or more: 12.4% (2005); Poverty rate: 11.6% (2000).
Education: Percent of population age 25 and over with: High school diploma (including GED) or higher: 87.0% (2005); Bachelor's degree or higher: 19.4% (2005); Master's degree or higher: 9.0% (2005).
Housing: Homeownership rate: 83.5% (2005); Median home value: $115,229 (2005); Median rent: $387 per month (2000); Median age of housing: 36 years (2000).
Transportation: Commute to work: 88.4% car, 0.6% public transportation, 3.5% walk, 6.5% work from home (2000); Travel time to work: 23.1% less than 15 minutes, 34.7% 15 to 30 minutes, 25.6% 30 to 45 minutes, 11.3% 45 to 60 minutes, 5.4% 60 minutes or more (2000).

MONTOUR (town). Covers a land area of 18.626 square miles and a water area of 0.008 square miles. Located at 42.34° N. Lat.; 76.83° W. Long.
History: Chequaga (or Shequaga) Falls here attract tourists, especially when snowmelt in the spring enhances the awesome spectacle.
Population: 2,528 (1990); 2,446 (2000); 2,509 (2005); 2,607 (2010 projected); Race: 98.0% White, 0.9% Black, 0.2% Asian, 0.4% Hispanic of

any race (2005); Density: 134.7 persons per square mile (2005); Average household size: 2.38 (2005); Median age: 43.9 (2005); Males per 100 females: 86.8 (2005); Marriage status: 20.8% never married, 54.9% now married, 13.6% widowed, 10.7% divorced (2000); Foreign born: 1.3% (2000); Ancestry (includes multiple ancestries): 18.6% English, 18.6% German, 14.7% Irish, 10.5% Italian, 8.2% United States or American (2000).
Economy: Summer resort. Single-family building permits issued: 0 (2005); Multi-family building permits issued: 0 (2005); Employment by occupation: 12.6% management, 15.0% professional, 21.6% services, 29.0% sales, 1.1% farming, 7.3% construction, 13.5% production (2000).
Income: Per capita income: $19,686 (2005); Median household income: $37,143 (2005); Average household income: $45,447 (2005); Percent of households with income of $100,000 or more: 6.7% (2005); Poverty rate: 11.7% (2000).
Taxes: Total city taxes per capita: $174 (2004); City property taxes per capita: $162 (2004).
Education: Percent of population age 25 and over with: High school diploma (including GED) or higher: 78.4% (2005); Bachelor's degree or higher: 15.1% (2005); Master's degree or higher: 5.6% (2005).
Housing: Homeownership rate: 69.7% (2005); Median home value: $99,758 (2005); Median rent: $359 per month (2000); Median age of housing: 46 years (2000).
Transportation: Commute to work: 88.6% car, 2.1% public transportation, 5.9% walk, 2.8% work from home (2000); Travel time to work: 44.7% less than 15 minutes, 22.7% 15 to 30 minutes, 22.0% 30 to 45 minutes, 6.6% 45 to 60 minutes, 4.0% 60 minutes or more (2000)

MONTOUR FALLS (village). Covers a land area of 3.006 square miles and a water area of 0.024 square miles. Located at 42.34° N. Lat.; 76.84° W. Long. Elevation is 457 feet.
Population: 1,845 (1990); 1,797 (2000); 1,836 (2005); 1,890 (2010 projected); Race: 97.5% White, 1.1% Black, 0.3% Asian, 0.5% Hispanic of any race (2005); Density: 610.7 persons per square mile (2005); Average household size: 2.50 (2005); Median age: 46.9 (2005); Males per 100 females: 79.3 (2005); Marriage status: 21.8% never married, 48.0% now married, 19.9% widowed, 10.2% divorced (2000); Foreign born: 1.6% (2000); Ancestry (includes multiple ancestries): 15.4% German, 14.1% English, 10.8% Irish, 10.5% Italian, 10.1% United States or American (2000).
Economy: Single-family building permits issued: 1 (2005); Multi-family building permits issued: 0 (2005); Employment by occupation: 11.2% management, 14.5% professional, 24.4% services, 26.3% sales, 0.3% farming, 5.2% construction, 18.2% production (2000).
Income: Per capita income: $17,118 (2005); Median household income: $31,724 (2005); Average household income: $39,152 (2005); Percent of households with income of $100,000 or more: 4.5% (2005); Poverty rate: 15.3% (2000).
Education: Percent of population age 25 and over with: High school diploma (including GED) or higher: 74.8% (2005); Bachelor's degree or higher: 13.3% (2005); Master's degree or higher: 5.4% (2005).
School District(s)
Odessa-Montour Central School District (KG-12)
    2003-04 Enrollment: 893 . . . . (607) 594-3341
Housing: Homeownership rate: 59.5% (2005); Median home value: $87,195 (2005); Median rent: $355 per month (2000); Median age of housing: 53 years (2000).
Hospitals: Schuyler Hospital (169 beds)
Transportation: Commute to work: 85.5% car, 3.0% public transportation, 8.5% walk, 2.0% work from home (2000); Travel time to work: 50.1% less than 15 minutes, 15.6% 15 to 30 minutes, 22.9% 30 to 45 minutes, 7.1% 45 to 60 minutes, 4.3% 60 minutes or more (2000)

ODESSA (village). Covers a land area of 1.212 square miles and a water area of 0 square miles. Located at 42.33° N. Lat.; 76.78° W. Long. Elevation is 1,050 feet.
Population: 683 (1990); 617 (2000); 622 (2005); 618 (2010 projected); Race: 96.0% White, 1.0% Black, 0.0% Asian, 2.3% Hispanic of any race (2005); Density: 513.3 persons per square mile (2005); Average household size: 2.47 (2005); Median age: 39.2 (2005); Males per 100 females: 87.3 (2005); Marriage status: 24.0% never married, 59.7% now married, 9.4% widowed, 6.9% divorced (2000); Foreign born: 0.0% (2000); Ancestry (includes multiple ancestries): 29.0% English, 13.4% German, 11.7% United States or American, 11.7% Irish, 6.4% Italian (2000).
Economy: Resort village. Single-family building permits issued: 0 (2005); Multi-family building permits issued: 0 (2005); Employment by occupation: 11.6% management, 14.9% professional, 16.6% services, 26.5% sales, 1.0% farming, 10.6% construction, 18.9% production (2000).
Income: Per capita income: $21,063 (2005); Median household income: $46,154 (2005); Average household income: $51,438 (2005); Percent of households with income of $100,000 or more: 10.3% (2005); Poverty rate: 8.9% (2000).
Education: Percent of population age 25 and over with: High school diploma (including GED) or higher: 82.8% (2005); Bachelor's degree or higher: 20.5% (2005); Master's degree or higher: 4.5% (2005).
School District(s)
Odessa-Montour Central School District (KG-12)
    2003-04 Enrollment: 893 . . . . (607) 594-3341
Housing: Homeownership rate: 69.4% (2005); Median home value: $110,061 (2005); Median rent: $385 per month (2000); Median age of housing: 56 years (2000).
Transportation: Commute to work: 85.9% car, 3.1% public transportation, 4.8% walk, 6.2% work from home (2000); Travel time to work: 38.2% less than 15 minutes, 24.6% 15 to 30 minutes, 25.0% 30 to 45 minutes, 8.8% 45 to 60 minutes, 3.3% 60 minutes or more (2000)

ORANGE (town). Covers a land area of 54.099 square miles and a water area of 0.330 square miles. Located at 42.33° N. Lat.; 77.03° W. Long.
Population: 1,561 (1990); 1,752 (2000); 1,762 (2005); 1,752 (2010 projected); Race: 87.7% White, 9.3% Black, 0.6% Asian, 6.4% Hispanic of any race (2005); Density: 32.6 persons per square mile (2005); Average household size: 3.34 (2005); Median age: 29.1 (2005); Males per 100 females: 144.4 (2005); Marriage status: 29.3% never married, 58.2% now married, 5.5% widowed, 7.0% divorced (2000); Foreign born: 0.7% (2000); Ancestry (includes multiple ancestries): 15.0% Irish, 13.1% German, 9.7% English, 8.8% Other groups, 8.0% United States or American (2000).
Economy: Single-family building permits issued: 4 (2005); Multi-family building permits issued: 0 (2005); Employment by occupation: 8.5% management, 18.6% professional, 16.9% services, 22.0% sales, 1.0% farming, 9.8% construction, 23.2% production (2000).
Income: Per capita income: $14,230 (2005); Median household income: $43,304 (2005); Average household income: $45,574 (2005); Percent of households with income of $100,000 or more: 4.6% (2005); Poverty rate: 16.0% (2000).
Education: Percent of population age 25 and over with: High school diploma (including GED) or higher: 77.0% (2005); Bachelor's degree or higher: 7.6% (2005); Master's degree or higher: 3.1% (2005).
Housing: Homeownership rate: 84.6% (2005); Median home value: $87,813 (2005); Median rent: $375 per month (2000); Median age of housing: 27 years (2000).
Transportation: Commute to work: 95.3% car, 0.0% public transportation, 0.9% walk, 3.1% work from home (2000); Travel time to work: 9.5% less than 15 minutes, 41.2% 15 to 30 minutes, 36.2% 30 to 45 minutes, 8.8% 45 to 60 minutes, 4.3% 60 minutes or more (2000)

READING (town). Covers a land area of 27.232 square miles and a water area of 0 square miles. Located at 42.41° N. Lat.; 76.91° W. Long.
Population: 1,810 (1990); 1,786 (2000); 1,808 (2005); 1,831 (2010 projected); Race: 97.2% White, 0.1% Black, 0.6% Asian, 0.6% Hispanic of any race (2005); Density: 66.4 persons per square mile (2005); Average household size: 2.49 (2005); Median age: 43.1 (2005); Males per 100 females: 98.2 (2005); Marriage status: 22.0% never married, 64.3% now married, 7.4% widowed, 6.3% divorced (2000); Foreign born: 1.8% (2000); Ancestry (includes multiple ancestries): 21.1% English, 20.1% German, 19.4% Irish, 11.6% Italian, 9.5% United States or American (2000).
Economy: Single-family building permits issued: 12 (2005); Multi-family building permits issued: 0 (2005); Employment by occupation: 12.9% management, 20.5% professional, 17.9% services, 20.3% sales, 1.3% farming, 9.8% construction, 17.3% production (2000).
Income: Per capita income: $21,422 (2005); Median household income: $45,550 (2005); Average household income: $53,383 (2005); Percent of households with income of $100,000 or more: 8.8% (2005); Poverty rate: 7.7% (2000).
Education: Percent of population age 25 and over with: High school diploma (including GED) or higher: 87.1% (2005); Bachelor's degree or higher: 17.2% (2005); Master's degree or higher: 8.8% (2005).

Housing: Homeownership rate: 84.6% (2005); Median home value: $109,472 (2005); Median rent: $421 per month (2000); Median age of housing: 43 years (2000).
Transportation: Commute to work: 90.3% car, 1.8% public transportation, 1.6% walk, 4.8% work from home (2000); Travel time to work: 35.4% less than 15 minutes, 22.5% 15 to 30 minutes, 23.7% 30 to 45 minutes, 11.9% 45 to 60 minutes, 6.4% 60 minutes or more (2000)

TYRONE (town).
Covers a land area of 37.492 square miles and a water area of 2.114 square miles. Located at 42.43° N. Lat.; 77.06° W. Long.
Population: 1,620 (1990); 1,714 (2000); 1,793 (2005); 1,876 (2010 projected); Race: 96.3% White, 1.4% Black, 0.1% Asian, 1.1% Hispanic of any race (2005); Density: 47.8 persons per square mile (2005); Average household size: 2.53 (2005); Median age: 43.1 (2005); Males per 100 females: 103.8 (2005); Marriage status: 19.6% never married, 67.5% now married, 5.3% widowed, 7.6% divorced (2000); Foreign born: 0.9% (2000); Ancestry (includes multiple ancestries): 19.0% German, 16.3% Irish, 16.0% English, 7.7% Other groups, 7.5% Polish (2000).
Economy: Single-family building permits issued: 0 (2005); Multi-family building permits issued: 0 (2005); Employment by occupation: 12.1% management, 15.8% professional, 17.0% services, 19.0% sales, 3.6% farming, 10.5% construction, 21.9% production (2000).
Income: Per capita income: $17,818 (2005); Median household income: $37,072 (2005); Average household income: $44,996 (2005); Percent of households with income of $100,000 or more: 6.6% (2005); Poverty rate: 13.5% (2000).
Education: Percent of population age 25 and over with: High school diploma (including GED) or higher: 76.1% (2005); Bachelor's degree or higher: 11.0% (2005); Master's degree or higher: 4.8% (2005).
Housing: Homeownership rate: 82.3% (2005); Median home value: $99,556 (2005); Median rent: $339 per month (2000); Median age of housing: 38 years (2000).
Transportation: Commute to work: 92.0% car, 0.0% public transportation, 1.0% walk, 6.4% work from home (2000); Travel time to work: 17.8% less than 15 minutes, 43.1% 15 to 30 minutes, 19.9% 30 to 45 minutes, 11.0% 45 to 60 minutes, 8.3% 60 minutes or more (2000)

WATKINS GLEN (village).
Covers a land area of 1.857 square miles and a water area of 0.388 square miles. Located at 42.38° N. Lat.; 76.87° W. Long. Elevation is 1,008 feet.
History: The resort hotel here is famed for its mineral spring water. An international Grand Prix sports-car race was held here annually until 1981. Incorporated 1842.
Population: 2,230 (1990); 2,149 (2000); 2,116 (2005); 2,115 (2010 projected); Race: 97.8% White, 0.2% Black, 0.9% Asian, 1.7% Hispanic of any race (2005); Density: 1,139.6 persons per square mile (2005); Average household size: 2.27 (2005); Median age: 40.2 (2005); Males per 100 females: 87.6 (2005); Marriage status: 24.6% never married, 50.9% now married, 9.9% widowed, 14.5% divorced (2000); Foreign born: 2.0% (2000); Ancestry (includes multiple ancestries): 23.1% Italian, 20.9% Irish, 19.0% German, 16.6% English, 8.1% United States or American (2000).
Economy: It is in a grape and wine area and has salt mine just north. The resort hotel here is famed for its mineral spring water. Single-family building permits issued: 0 (2005); Multi-family building permits issued: 0 (2005); Employment by occupation: 7.0% management, 19.8% professional, 24.8% services, 25.2% sales, 0.0% farming, 6.2% construction, 17.0% production (2000).
Income: Per capita income: $18,824 (2005); Median household income: $32,414 (2005); Average household income: $42,160 (2005); Percent of households with income of $100,000 or more: 6.3% (2005); Poverty rate: 14.3% (2000)
Education: Percent of population age 25 and over with: High school diploma (including GED) or higher: 87.5% (2005); Bachelor's degree or higher: 19.5% (2005); Master's degree or higher: 9.7% (2005).

School District(s)
Watkins Glen Central School District (PK-12)
    2003-04 Enrollment: 1,524 . . . . (607) 535-3219
Housing: Homeownership rate: 56.4% (2005); Median home value: $108,203 (2005); Median rent: $385 per month (2000); Median age of housing: 60+ years (2000).
Safety: Violent crime rate: 9.4 per 10,000 population; Property crime rate: 717.7 per 10,000 population (2004).

Newspapers: Hi-Lites (General - Circulation 8,500); The Daily News (Circulation 1,500); Watkins Review & Express (General - Circulation 3,200)
Transportation: Commute to work: 83.7% car, 1.5% public transportation, 8.1% walk, 5.4% work from home (2000); Travel time to work: 54.8% less than 15 minutes, 16.7% 15 to 30 minutes, 17.4% 30 to 45 minutes, 6.3% 45 to 60 minutes, 4.8% 60 minutes or more (2000)
Additional Information Contacts
Schuyler County Chamber of Commerce . . . . (607) 535-4300
  http://www.schuylerny.com

Seneca County

Located in west central New York, in the Finger Lakes region; bounded on the east by Cayuga Lake and the Seneca River, and partly on the west by Seneca Lake. Covers a land area of 324.91 square miles, a water area of 65.60 square miles, and is located in the Eastern Time Zone. The county government was organized in 1804. County seat is Waterloo.

Seneca County is part of the Seneca Falls, NY Micropolitan Statistical Area. The entire metro area includes: Seneca County, NY

Population: 33,683 (1990); 33,342 (2000); 35,636 (2005); 38,024 (2010 projected); Race: 90.9% White, 5.7% Black, 0.8% Asian, 3.7% Hispanic of any race (2005); Density: 109.7 persons per square mile (2005); Average household size: 2.59 (2005); Median age: 38.7 (2005); Males per 100 females: 107.1 (2005).
Religion: Five largest groups: 26.4% Catholic Church, 3.8% The United Methodist Church, 2.5% Presbyterian Church (U.S.A.), 1.9% Episcopal Church, 1.2% Reformed Church in America (2000).
Economy: Unemployment rate: 4.7% (2005); Total civilian labor force: 16,834 (2005); Leading industries: 23.3% retail trade; 16.7% health care and social assistance; 14.8% manufacturing (2003); Farms: 466 totaling 127,242 acres (2002); Companies that employ 500 or more persons: 0 (2003); Companies that employ 100 to 499 persons: 8 (2003); Companies that employ less than 100 persons: 665 (2003); Black-owned businesses: n/a (2002); Hispanic-owned businesses: n/a (2002); Women-owned businesses: 713 (2002); Retail sales per capita: $13,420 (2006).
Single-family building permits issued: 36 (2005); Multi-family building permits issued: 2 (2005).
Income: Per capita income: $19,923 (2005); Median household income: $41,239 (2005); Average household income: $50,293 (2005); Percent of households with income of $100,000 or more: 9.0% (2005); Poverty rate: 11.3% (2003); Bankruptcy rate: 6.02% (2005).
Education: Percent of population age 25 and over with: High school diploma (including GED) or higher: 78.8% (2005); Bachelor's degree or higher: 17.3% (2005); Master's degree or higher: 6.9% (2005).
Housing: Homeownership rate: 73.8% (2005); Median home value: $107,804 (2005); Median rent: $416 per month (2000); Median age of housing: 47 years (2000).
Health: Birth rate: 106.3 per 10,000 population (2004); Death rate: 103.2 per 10,000 population (2004); Age-adjusted cancer mortality rate: 223.4 deaths per 100,000 population (2002); Number of physicians: 5.4 per 10,000 population (2004); Hospital beds: 0.0 per 10,000 population (2003); Hospital admissions: 0.0 per 10,000 population (2003).
Elections: 2004 Presidential election results: 52.1% Bush, 45.5% Kerry, 2.1% Nader, 0.3% Badnarik
National and State Parks: Cayuga Lake State Park; Montezuma National Wildlife Refuge; Sampson State Park; Seneca Lake State Park; Womens Rights National Historical Park
Additional Information Contacts
Seneca County Government . . . . (315) 539-1800
  http://www.co.seneca.ny.us/

Seneca County Communities

COVERT (town).
Covers a land area of 31.498 square miles and a water area of 6.141 square miles. Located at 42.59° N. Lat.; 76.70° W. Long. Elevation is 913 feet.
Population: 2,246 (1990); 2,227 (2000); 2,268 (2005); 2,329 (2010 projected); Race: 97.4% White, 1.0% Black, 0.2% Asian, 1.8% Hispanic of any race (2005); Density: 72.0 persons per square mile (2005); Average household size: 2.44 (2005); Median age: 42.7 (2005); Males per 100 females: 101.6 (2005); Marriage status: 21.8% never married, 62.1% now married, 7.5% widowed, 8.6% divorced (2000); Foreign born: 3.2% (2000);

Ancestry (includes multiple ancestries): 17.7% English, 17.6% German, 17.4% Irish, 7.7% Dutch, 7.4% Other groups (2000).
Economy: Employment by occupation: 15.0% management, 32.0% professional, 16.0% services, 21.4% sales, 0.8% farming, 6.6% construction, 8.3% production (2000).
Income: Per capita income: $22,724 (2005); Median household income: $41,903 (2005); Average household income: $55,189 (2005); Percent of households with income of $100,000 or more: 13.7% (2005); Poverty rate: 10.1% (2000).
Education: Percent of population age 25 and over with: High school diploma (including GED) or higher: 86.8% (2005); Bachelor's degree or higher: 29.8% (2005); Master's degree or higher: 15.4% (2005).
Housing: Homeownership rate: 82.1% (2005); Median home value: $113,430 (2005); Median rent: $408 per month (2000); Median age of housing: 49 years (2000).
Transportation: Commute to work: 86.7% car, 2.3% public transportation, 3.1% walk, 7.4% work from home (2000); Travel time to work: 22.2% less than 15 minutes, 29.8% 15 to 30 minutes, 31.3% 30 to 45 minutes, 7.8% 45 to 60 minutes, 8.9% 60 minutes or more (2000)

FAYETTE (town). Covers a land area of 55.190 square miles and a water area of 11.296 square miles. Located at 42.85° N. Lat.; 76.86° W. Long. Elevation is 613 feet.
Population: 3,636 (1990); 3,643 (2000); 3,719 (2005); 3,825 (2010 projected); Race: 96.9% White, 1.4% Black, 0.7% Asian, 1.8% Hispanic of any race (2005); Density: 67.4 persons per square mile (2005); Average household size: 2.62 (2005); Median age: 39.6 (2005); Males per 100 females: 102.6 (2005); Marriage status: 24.6% never married, 61.2% now married, 6.5% widowed, 7.8% divorced (2000); Foreign born: 1.8% (2000); Ancestry (includes multiple ancestries): 26.6% German, 23.8% Irish, 19.8% English, 18.5% Italian, 6.6% French (except Basque) (2000).
Economy: Employment by occupation: 13.0% management, 17.3% professional, 16.1% services, 24.8% sales, 0.8% farming, 10.1% construction, 17.8% production (2000).
Income: Per capita income: $22,316 (2005); Median household income: $49,104 (2005); Average household income: $57,635 (2005); Percent of households with income of $100,000 or more: 12.9% (2005); Poverty rate: 4.3% (2000).
Education: Percent of population age 25 and over with: High school diploma (including GED) or higher: 82.1% (2005); Bachelor's degree or higher: 17.7% (2005); Master's degree or higher: 6.8% (2005).
Housing: Homeownership rate: 83.0% (2005); Median home value: $125,850 (2005); Median rent: $436 per month (2000); Median age of housing: 42 years (2000).
Transportation: Commute to work: 90.4% car, 0.0% public transportation, 3.6% walk, 5.5% work from home (2000); Travel time to work: 39.1% less than 15 minutes, 37.1% 15 to 30 minutes, 13.2% 30 to 45 minutes, 5.0% 45 to 60 minutes, 5.6% 60 minutes or more (2000)

INTERLAKEN (village). Covers a land area of 0.256 square miles and a water area of 0 square miles. Located at 42.61° N. Lat.; 76.72° W. Long. Elevation is 900 feet.
Population: 680 (1990); 674 (2000); 657 (2005); 654 (2010 projected); Race: 96.3% White, 2.0% Black, 0.0% Asian, 2.1% Hispanic of any race (2005); Density: 2,566.3 persons per square mile (2005); Average household size: 2.57 (2005); Median age: 39.1 (2005); Males per 100 females: 88.3 (2005); Marriage status: 25.5% never married, 60.1% now married, 5.1% widowed, 9.3% divorced (2000); Foreign born: 3.8% (2000); Ancestry (includes multiple ancestries): 20.4% English, 14.0% Irish, 13.3% German, 8.6% Other groups, 6.0% Italian (2000).
Economy: Agriculture: sweet corn; field corn; vineyards, wineries. Employment by occupation: 6.9% management, 27.0% professional, 25.6% services, 24.9% sales, 1.4% farming, 6.9% construction, 7.3% production (2000).
Income: Per capita income: $18,666 (2005); Median household income: $36,667 (2005); Average household income: $46,777 (2005); Percent of households with income of $100,000 or more: 7.8% (2005); Poverty rate: 11.5% (2000).
Education: Percent of population age 25 and over with: High school diploma (including GED) or higher: 80.5% (2005); Bachelor's degree or higher: 20.0% (2005); Master's degree or higher: 10.6% (2005).
School District(s)
South Seneca Central School District (PK-12)
    2003-04 Enrollment: 1,040 . . . . (607) 869-9636

Housing: Homeownership rate: 69.5% (2005); Median home value: $93,488 (2005); Median rent: $402 per month (2000); Median age of housing: 60+ years (2000).
Transportation: Commute to work: 84.3% car, 1.0% public transportation, 8.7% walk, 4.2% work from home (2000); Travel time to work: 28.5% less than 15 minutes, 21.9% 15 to 30 minutes, 32.5% 30 to 45 minutes, 4.7% 45 to 60 minutes, 12.4% 60 minutes or more (2000)

JUNIUS (town). Covers a land area of 26.743 square miles and a water area of 0.107 square miles. Located at 42.98° N. Lat.; 76.92° W. Long.
Population: 1,354 (1990); 1,362 (2000); 1,478 (2005); 1,594 (2010 projected); Race: 96.0% White, 1.6% Black, 0.5% Asian, 3.7% Hispanic of any race (2005); Density: 55.3 persons per square mile (2005); Average household size: 2.70 (2005); Median age: 38.2 (2005); Males per 100 females: 103.9 (2005); Marriage status: 24.1% never married, 61.0% now married, 5.6% widowed, 9.3% divorced (2000); Foreign born: 1.2% (2000); Ancestry (includes multiple ancestries): 28.3% German, 17.5% English, 12.4% Irish, 12.0% Italian, 11.2% Other groups (2000).
Economy: Employment by occupation: 9.8% management, 13.8% professional, 17.6% services, 21.1% sales, 2.8% farming, 12.1% construction, 22.9% production (2000).
Income: Per capita income: $19,474 (2005); Median household income: $45,389 (2005); Average household income: $52,619 (2005); Percent of households with income of $100,000 or more: 8.6% (2005); Poverty rate: 7.9% (2000).
Education: Percent of population age 25 and over with: High school diploma (including GED) or higher: 77.5% (2005); Bachelor's degree or higher: 8.7% (2005); Master's degree or higher: 3.6% (2005).
Housing: Homeownership rate: 83.0% (2005); Median home value: $106,818 (2005); Median rent: $381 per month (2000); Median age of housing: 27 years (2000).
Transportation: Commute to work: 91.8% car, 0.3% public transportation, 0.3% walk, 7.3% work from home (2000); Travel time to work: 31.8% less than 15 minutes, 40.3% 15 to 30 minutes, 14.9% 30 to 45 minutes, 7.9% 45 to 60 minutes, 5.1% 60 minutes or more (2000)

LODI (village). Covers a land area of 0.568 square miles and a water area of 0 square miles. Located at 42.61° N. Lat.; 76.82° W. Long.
Population: 364 (1990); 338 (2000); 409 (2005); 471 (2010 projected); Race: 83.9% White, 6.1% Black, 0.0% Asian, 12.7% Hispanic of any race (2005); Density: 720.4 persons per square mile (2005); Average household size: 2.84 (2005); Median age: 36.8 (2005); Males per 100 females: 107.6 (2005); Marriage status: 23.4% never married, 51.5% now married, 10.0% widowed, 15.2% divorced (2000); Foreign born: 0.6% (2000); Ancestry (includes multiple ancestries): 30.0% Irish, 18.0% German, 15.1% Dutch, 14.2% English, 13.6% Other groups (2000).
Economy: Employment by occupation: 4.2% management, 17.6% professional, 32.4% services, 19.7% sales, 0.0% farming, 12.0% construction, 14.1% production (2000).
Income: Per capita income: $16,112 (2005); Median household income: $34,048 (2005); Average household income: $45,764 (2005); Percent of households with income of $100,000 or more: 8.3% (2005); Poverty rate: 30.3% (2000).
Education: Percent of population age 25 and over with: High school diploma (including GED) or higher: 74.7% (2005); Bachelor's degree or higher: 13.2% (2005); Master's degree or higher: 5.1% (2005).
Housing: Homeownership rate: 83.3% (2005); Median home value: $75,000 (2005); Median rent: $325 per month (2000); Median age of housing: 60+ years (2000).
Transportation: Commute to work: 100.0% car, 0.0% public transportation, 0.0% walk, 0.0% work from home (2000); Travel time to work: 24.5% less than 15 minutes, 20.1% 15 to 30 minutes, 26.6% 30 to 45 minutes, 18.0% 45 to 60 minutes, 10.8% 60 minutes or more (2000)

LODI (town). Covers a land area of 34.289 square miles and a water area of 5.471 square miles. Located at 42.59° N. Lat.; 76.84° W. Long.
Population: 1,429 (1990); 1,476 (2000); 1,583 (2005); 1,682 (2010 projected); Race: 91.0% White, 3.3% Black, 0.2% Asian, 6.6% Hispanic of any race (2005); Density: 46.2 persons per square mile (2005); Average household size: 2.63 (2005); Median age: 40.2 (2005); Males per 100 females: 112.8 (2005); Marriage status: 21.4% never married, 62.7% now married, 6.8% widowed, 9.1% divorced (2000); Foreign born: 2.4% (2000); Ancestry (includes multiple ancestries): 17.3% Irish, 17.1% English, 15.7% German, 11.4% Dutch, 9.2% Other groups (2000).

Economy: Employment by occupation: 10.1% management, 16.9% professional, 23.7% services, 17.8% sales, 2.7% farming, 11.0% construction, 17.7% production (2000).
Income: Per capita income: $19,404 (2005); Median household income: $43,214 (2005); Average household income: $50,955 (2005); Percent of households with income of $100,000 or more: 8.5% (2005); Poverty rate: 15.8% (2000).
Education: Percent of population age 25 and over with: High school diploma (including GED) or higher: 81.6% (2005); Bachelor's degree or higher: 17.3% (2005); Master's degree or higher: 7.8% (2005).
Housing: Homeownership rate: 86.2% (2005); Median home value: $99,500 (2005); Median rent: $349 per month (2000); Median age of housing: 44 years (2000).
Transportation: Commute to work: 94.0% car, 0.5% public transportation, 0.8% walk, 3.2% work from home (2000); Travel time to work: 18.7% less than 15 minutes, 24.4% 15 to 30 minutes, 28.8% 30 to 45 minutes, 16.9% 45 to 60 minutes, 11.2% 60 minutes or more (2000).

OVID (village). Covers a land area of 0.419 square miles and a water area of 0 square miles. Located at 42.67° N. Lat.; 76.82° W. Long. Elevation is 703 feet.
Population: 660 (1990); 612 (2000); 684 (2005); 747 (2010 projected); Race: 82.9% White, 6.7% Black, 0.3% Asian, 11.4% Hispanic of any race (2005); Density: 1,632.8 persons per square mile (2005); Average household size: 2.47 (2005); Median age: 35.4 (2005); Males per 100 females: 94.9 (2005); Marriage status: 22.2% never married, 52.5% now married, 14.5% widowed, 10.8% divorced (2000); Foreign born: 0.8% (2000); Ancestry (includes multiple ancestries): 20.9% German, 18.3% English, 15.5% Irish, 8.6% Other groups, 7.1% United States or American (2000).
Economy: Employment by occupation: 8.3% management, 24.0% professional, 13.4% services, 31.1% sales, 0.8% farming, 8.7% construction, 13.8% production (2000).
Income: Per capita income: $17,569 (2005); Median household income: $33,417 (2005); Average household income: $43,384 (2005); Percent of households with income of $100,000 or more: 8.3% (2005); Poverty rate: 12.4% (2000).
Education: Percent of population age 25 and over with: High school diploma (including GED) or higher: 81.8% (2005); Bachelor's degree or higher: 19.8% (2005); Master's degree or higher: 9.2% (2005).

School District(s)
South Seneca Central School District (PK-12)
    2003-04 Enrollment: 1,040 . . . . (607) 869-9636

Housing: Homeownership rate: 59.2% (2005); Median home value: $96,774 (2005); Median rent: $350 per month (2000); Median age of housing: 60+ years (2000).
Newspapers: Reveille Between the Lakes (General - Circulation 2,200); Senior News of the Finger Lakes (Senior Citizen - Circulation 2,500)
Transportation: Commute to work: 90.0% car, 0.8% public transportation, 6.4% walk, 0.8% work from home (2000); Travel time to work: 39.9% less than 15 minutes, 26.2% 15 to 30 minutes, 16.1% 30 to 45 minutes, 8.5% 45 to 60 minutes, 9.3% 60 minutes or more (2000).

OVID (town). Covers a land area of 30.985 square miles and a water area of 7.815 square miles. Located at 42.65° N. Lat.; 76.77° W. Long. Elevation is 703 feet.
Population: 2,306 (1990); 2,757 (2000); 2,751 (2005); 2,810 (2010 projected); Race: 68.5% White, 25.2% Black, 0.1% Asian, 9.2% Hispanic of any race (2005); Density: 88.8 persons per square mile (2005); Average household size: 2.97 (2005); Median age: 35.4 (2005); Males per 100 females: 135.9 (2005); Marriage status: 30.1% never married, 52.0% now married, 7.3% widowed, 10.6% divorced (2000); Foreign born: 1.0% (2000); Ancestry (includes multiple ancestries): 15.3% German, 14.9% English, 11.4% Irish, 9.0% United States or American, 5.2% Other groups (2000).
Economy: In agricultural area: vineyards; fruits, grain; dairy products. Willard Correctional Facility is to West. Employment by occupation: 10.8% management, 24.1% professional, 17.6% services, 22.5% sales, 2.9% farming, 7.1% construction, 15.0% production (2000).
Income: Per capita income: $20,229 (2005); Median household income: $38,662 (2005); Average household income: $53,323 (2005); Percent of households with income of $100,000 or more: 10.4% (2005); Poverty rate: 9.9% (2000).
Education: Percent of population age 25 and over with: High school diploma (including GED) or higher: 72.0% (2005); Bachelor's degree or higher: 19.2% (2005); Master's degree or higher: 7.5% (2005).
Housing: Homeownership rate: 70.6% (2005); Median home value: $109,943 (2005); Median rent: $317 per month (2000); Median age of housing: 45 years (2000).
Transportation: Commute to work: 89.1% car, 0.5% public transportation, 3.4% walk, 5.7% work from home (2000); Travel time to work: 33.8% less than 15 minutes, 20.4% 15 to 30 minutes, 23.2% 30 to 45 minutes, 11.2% 45 to 60 minutes, 11.4% 60 minutes or more (2000).

ROMULUS (town). Covers a land area of 37.802 square miles and a water area of 13.520 square miles. Located at 42.72° N. Lat.; 76.84° W. Long.
Population: 2,532 (1990); 2,036 (2000); 2,555 (2005); 3,003 (2010 projected); Race: 66.2% White, 29.1% Black, 0.6% Asian, 7.2% Hispanic of any race (2005); Density: 67.6 persons per square mile (2005); Average household size: 3.33 (2005); Median age: 35.9 (2005); Males per 100 females: 131.2 (2005); Marriage status: 35.3% never married, 49.6% now married, 7.5% widowed, 7.6% divorced (2000); Foreign born: 1.7% (2000); Ancestry (includes multiple ancestries): 19.5% German, 17.4% English, 13.8% Irish, 8.4% United States or American, 6.4% Italian (2000).
Economy: Rich farming area: vegetables, sweet and field corn, hay and dairying. Employment by occupation: 14.7% management, 21.1% professional, 19.7% services, 18.4% sales, 2.1% farming, 7.2% construction, 16.8% production (2000).
Income: Per capita income: $19,737 (2005); Median household income: $47,358 (2005); Average household income: $59,033 (2005); Percent of households with income of $100,000 or more: 12.8% (2005); Poverty rate: 14.3% (2000).
Education: Percent of population age 25 and over with: High school diploma (including GED) or higher: 63.8% (2005); Bachelor's degree or higher: 16.5% (2005); Master's degree or higher: 6.8% (2005).

School District(s)
Romulus Central School District (PK-12)
    2003-04 Enrollment: 613 . . . . (607) 869-5391

Housing: Homeownership rate: 79.7% (2005); Median home value: $118,519 (2005); Median rent: $435 per month (2000); Median age of housing: 44 years (2000).
Transportation: Commute to work: 86.6% car, 0.6% public transportation, 3.0% walk, 7.7% work from home (2000); Travel time to work: 30.4% less than 15 minutes, 25.7% 15 to 30 minutes, 23.8% 30 to 45 minutes, 9.4% 45 to 60 minutes, 10.8% 60 minutes or more (2000).

SENECA FALLS (village). Covers a land area of 4.426 square miles and a water area of 0.151 square miles. Located at 42.90° N. Lat.; 76.79° W. Long. Elevation is 427 feet.
History: Elizabeth Cady Stanton lived here and helped organize first women's rights convention in U.S., held here in 1848. Women's Rights National Historic Park and Museum, located in the restored Elizabeth Cady Stanton House, and the National Women's Hall of Fame are here. Settled 1787, Incorporated 1831.
Population: 7,448 (1990); 6,861 (2000); 6,882 (2005); 7,008 (2010 projected); Race: 94.7% White, 1.8% Black, 1.7% Asian, 2.3% Hispanic of any race (2005); Density: 1,554.9 persons per square mile (2005); Average household size: 2.35 (2005); Median age: 39.2 (2005); Males per 100 females: 101.6 (2005); Marriage status: 25.7% never married, 56.5% now married, 8.1% widowed, 9.6% divorced (2000); Foreign born: 2.7% (2000); Ancestry (includes multiple ancestries): 30.7% Italian, 19.0% German, 15.9% Irish, 15.7% English, 6.1% Other groups (2000).
Economy: Manufacturing of fabricated metal products, transportation equipment, machinery, electrical equipment and textiles. Employment by occupation: 9.8% management, 21.6% professional, 16.8% services, 26.3% sales, 0.6% farming, 5.6% construction, 19.4% production (2000).
Income: Per capita income: $20,690 (2005); Median household income: $40,557 (2005); Average household income: $48,105 (2005); Percent of households with income of $100,000 or more: 8.2% (2005); Poverty rate: 11.3% (2000).
Education: Percent of population age 25 and over with: High school diploma (including GED) or higher: 85.1% (2005); Bachelor's degree or higher: 22.5% (2005); Master's degree or higher: 7.3% (2005).

School District(s)
Seneca Falls Central School District (KG-12)
    2003-04 Enrollment: 1,499 . . . . (315) 568-5818

Four-year College(s)
New York Chiropractic College
  Fall 2004 Enrollment: 737 . . . . (315) 568-3000
Housing: Homeownership rate: 64.4% (2005); Median home value: $98,352 (2005); Median rent: $456 per month (2000); Median age of housing: 60+ years (2000).
Safety: Violent crime rate: 8.7 per 10,000 population; Property crime rate: 46.3 per 10,000 population (2004).
Transportation: Commute to work: 93.4% car, 0.0% public transportation, 4.5% walk, 1.7% work from home (2000); Travel time to work: 51.0% less than 15 minutes, 27.3% 15 to 30 minutes, 12.3% 30 to 45 minutes, 3.0% 45 to 60 minutes, 6.3% 60 minutes or more (2000)
Additional Information Contacts
Seneca Falls Chamber of Commerce . . . . (315) 568-2906
  http://www.senecachamber.org

SENECA FALLS (town). Covers a land area of 24.239 square miles and a water area of 3.195 square miles. Located at 42.91° N. Lat.; 76.79° W. Long. Elevation is 427 feet.
History: Seneca Falls owes its early industrial development to the 50-foot waterfall which provided power, and its fame to great women who mothered the causes of woman's suffrage, anti-slavery, and temperance. Amelia Jenks Bloomer (1818-1894), wife of the local postmaster, did not invent the bloomers but she introduced them and advocated them as a uniform for women fighting for suffrage. Elizabeth Cady Stanton (1815-1902) moved to Seneca Falls in 1847, and the two called together the first convention of women fighting for suffrage. Susan B. Anthony (1820-1906) also joined the group and was president of the American Women's Suffrage Association until 1900.
Population: 9,384 (1990); 9,347 (2000); 9,446 (2005); 9,636 (2010 projected); Race: 93.7% White, 2.2% Black, 2.0% Asian, 2.6% Hispanic of any race (2005); Density: 389.7 persons per square mile (2005); Average household size: 2.42 (2005); Median age: 38.1 (2005); Males per 100 females: 105.6 (2005); Marriage status: 26.2% never married, 56.8% now married, 7.6% widowed, 9.4% divorced (2000); Foreign born: 3.9% (2000); Ancestry (includes multiple ancestries): 27.9% Italian, 19.2% German, 17.4% Irish, 15.5% English, 6.9% Other groups (2000).
Economy: Employment by occupation: 10.1% management, 20.6% professional, 18.7% services, 25.0% sales, 0.4% farming, 6.1% construction, 19.1% production (2000).
Income: Per capita income: $20,368 (2005); Median household income: $40,292 (2005); Average household income: $48,333 (2005); Percent of households with income of $100,000 or more: 8.5% (2005); Poverty rate: 13.2% (2000).
Education: Percent of population age 25 and over with: High school diploma (including GED) or higher: 84.1% (2005); Bachelor's degree or higher: 22.4% (2005); Master's degree or higher: 7.5% (2005).
Housing: Homeownership rate: 64.3% (2005); Median home value: $107,063 (2005); Median rent: $439 per month (2000); Median age of housing: 55 years (2000).
Transportation: Commute to work: 93.3% car, 0.0% public transportation, 3.8% walk, 1.9% work from home (2000); Travel time to work: 48.8% less than 15 minutes, 29.3% 15 to 30 minutes, 11.9% 30 to 45 minutes, 3.6% 45 to 60 minutes, 6.4% 60 minutes or more (2000)

TYRE (town). Covers a land area of 30.149 square miles and a water area of 2.966 square miles. Located at 42.98° N. Lat.; 76.78° W. Long.
Population: 870 (1990); 899 (2000); 886 (2005); 884 (2010 projected); Race: 95.9% White, 1.1% Black, 0.0% Asian, 2.0% Hispanic of any race (2005); Density: 29.4 persons per square mile (2005); Average household size: 2.64 (2005); Median age: 39.5 (2005); Males per 100 females: 107.5 (2005); Marriage status: 18.6% never married, 67.6% now married, 4.0% widowed, 9.8% divorced (2000); Foreign born: 2.1% (2000); Ancestry (includes multiple ancestries): 25.0% English, 23.4% German, 15.4% Irish, 12.8% Italian, 7.5% Dutch (2000).
Economy: Employment by occupation: 11.9% management, 16.1% professional, 13.9% services, 19.0% sales, 1.6% farming, 15.2% construction, 22.4% production (2000).
Income: Per capita income: $22,370 (2005); Median household income: $49,567 (2005); Average household income: $59,164 (2005); Percent of households with income of $100,000 or more: 10.7% (2005); Poverty rate: 10.2% (2000).
Education: Percent of population age 25 and over with: High school diploma (including GED) or higher: 77.6% (2005); Bachelor's degree or higher: 11.5% (2005); Master's degree or higher: 2.6% (2005).
Housing: Homeownership rate: 83.3% (2005); Median home value: $116,865 (2005); Median rent: $375 per month (2000); Median age of housing: 45 years (2000).
Transportation: Commute to work: 89.8% car, 0.0% public transportation, 2.9% walk, 6.8% work from home (2000); Travel time to work: 32.4% less than 15 minutes, 42.6% 15 to 30 minutes, 11.4% 30 to 45 minutes, 4.8% 45 to 60 minutes, 8.7% 60 minutes or more (2000)

VARICK (town). Covers a land area of 32.286 square miles and a water area of 13.332 square miles. Located at 42.77° N. Lat.; 76.86° W. Long.
Population: 2,161 (1990); 1,729 (2000); 2,071 (2005); 2,403 (2010 projected); Race: 97.2% White, 1.7% Black, 0.0% Asian, 1.4% Hispanic of any race (2005); Density: 64.1 persons per square mile (2005); Average household size: 2.70 (2005); Median age: 38.0 (2005); Males per 100 females: 103.8 (2005); Marriage status: 20.9% never married, 66.8% now married, 4.7% widowed, 7.6% divorced (2000); Foreign born: 1.4% (2000); Ancestry (includes multiple ancestries): 21.5% German, 15.6% Irish, 14.2% English, 12.0% Italian, 8.0% United States or American (2000).
Economy: Employment by occupation: 15.2% management, 20.6% professional, 14.4% services, 22.0% sales, 2.1% farming, 9.5% construction, 16.3% production (2000).
Income: Per capita income: $20,678 (2005); Median household income: $45,142 (2005); Average household income: $55,737 (2005); Percent of households with income of $100,000 or more: 13.4% (2005); Poverty rate: 10.1% (2000).
Education: Percent of population age 25 and over with: High school diploma (including GED) or higher: 78.4% (2005); Bachelor's degree or higher: 19.3% (2005); Master's degree or higher: 8.7% (2005).
Housing: Homeownership rate: 84.9% (2005); Median home value: $140,348 (2005); Median rent: $475 per month (2000); Median age of housing: 42 years (2000).
Transportation: Commute to work: 90.2% car, 0.0% public transportation, 1.7% walk, 7.4% work from home (2000); Travel time to work: 20.3% less than 15 minutes, 53.0% 15 to 30 minutes, 16.8% 30 to 45 minutes, 3.9% 45 to 60 minutes, 5.9% 60 minutes or more (2000)

WATERLOO (village). Covers a land area of 2.095 square miles and a water area of 0.068 square miles. Located at 42.90° N. Lat.; 76.86° W. Long. Elevation is 455 feet.
Population: 5,181 (1990); 5,111 (2000); 5,398 (2005); 5,682 (2010 projected); Race: 96.3% White, 2.0% Black, 0.5% Asian, 2.5% Hispanic of any race (2005); Density: 2,576.3 persons per square mile (2005); Average household size: 2.59 (2005); Median age: 39.8 (2005); Males per 100 females: 92.8 (2005); Marriage status: 23.7% never married, 51.9% now married, 14.0% widowed, 10.4% divorced (2000); Foreign born: 2.3% (2000); Ancestry (includes multiple ancestries): 21.8% German, 19.6% English, 18.4% Irish, 18.1% Italian, 8.7% United States or American (2000).
Economy: Employment by occupation: 11.3% management, 14.3% professional, 17.8% services, 28.9% sales, 0.0% farming, 6.3% construction, 21.3% production (2000).
Income: Per capita income: $17,898 (2005); Median household income: $36,215 (2005); Average household income: $44,904 (2005); Percent of households with income of $100,000 or more: 5.8% (2005); Poverty rate: 12.1% (2000).
Education: Percent of population age 25 and over with: High school diploma (including GED) or higher: 76.5% (2005); Bachelor's degree or higher: 12.9% (2005); Master's degree or higher: 4.9% (2005).
School District(s)
Waterloo Central School District (PK-12)
  2003-04 Enrollment: 2,062 . . . . (315) 539-1500
Housing: Homeownership rate: 70.8% (2005); Median home value: $90,456 (2005); Median rent: $401 per month (2000); Median age of housing: 60+ years (2000).
Safety: Violent crime rate: 11.7 per 10,000 population; Property crime rate: 474.5 per 10,000 population (2004).
Transportation: Commute to work: 92.9% car, 0.4% public transportation, 4.1% walk, 2.2% work from home (2000); Travel time to work: 48.6% less than 15 minutes, 24.7% 15 to 30 minutes, 15.1% 30 to 45 minutes, 5.5% 45 to 60 minutes, 6.2% 60 minutes or more (2000)

WATERLOO (town). Covers a land area of 21.703 square miles and a water area of 0.172 square miles. Located at 42.90° N. Lat.; 76.89° W. Long. Elevation is 455 feet.

History: Official birthplace of the Memorial Day celebaration, May 5, 1866 (celebrated on May 30). Incorporated 1824.
Population: 7,765 (1990); 7,866 (2000); 8,879 (2005); 9,858 (2010 projected); Race: 95.2% White, 2.2% Black, 0.4% Asian, 3.6% Hispanic of any race (2005); Density: 409.1 persons per square mile (2005); Average household size: 2.52 (2005); Median age: 39.6 (2005); Males per 100 females: 98.7 (2005); Marriage status: 24.2% never married, 53.5% now married, 11.1% widowed, 11.2% divorced (2000); Foreign born: 2.0% (2000); Ancestry (includes multiple ancestries): 18.6% German, 18.0% Italian, 17.4% Irish, 15.6% English, 9.5% United States or American (2000).
Economy: Summer recreation. Employment by occupation: 9.7% management, 13.6% professional, 15.6% services, 28.7% sales, 0.1% farming, 10.0% construction, 22.3% production (2000).
Income: Per capita income: $17,437 (2005); Median household income: $34,983 (2005); Average household income: $43,020 (2005); Percent of households with income of $100,000 or more: 4.6% (2005); Poverty rate: 13.4% (2000).
Education: Percent of population age 25 and over with: High school diploma (including GED) or higher: 76.0% (2005); Bachelor's degree or higher: 9.8% (2005); Master's degree or higher: 4.6% (2005).
Housing: Homeownership rate: 71.2% (2005); Median home value: $92,459 (2005); Median rent: $423 per month (2000); Median age of housing: 46 years (2000).
Transportation: Commute to work: 93.5% car, 1.0% public transportation, 3.1% walk, 1.9% work from home (2000); Travel time to work: 49.4% less than 15 minutes, 26.0% 15 to 30 minutes, 12.5% 30 to 45 minutes, 6.7% 45 to 60 minutes, 5.4% 60 minutes or more (2000)

Staten Island Borough

See New York City

Steuben County

Located in southern New York, partly in the Finger Lakes region; bounded on the south by Pennsylvania; drained by the Canisteo, Cohocton, Tioga, and Chemung Rivers; includes part of Keuka Lake. Covers a land area of 1,392.64 square miles, a water area of 11.45 square miles, and is located in the Eastern Time Zone. The county government was organized in 1796. County seat is Bath.

Steuben County is part of the Corning, NY Micropolitan Statistical Area. The entire metro area includes: Steuben County, NY

Weather Station: Bath | | | | | | | | | | | Elevation: 1,118 feet
	Jan	Feb	Mar	Apr	May	Jun	Jul	Aug	Sep	Oct	Nov	Dec
High	32	34	43	56	68	77	81	79	72	60	47	36
Low	13	13	21	32	42	51	55	53	46	36	29	20
Precip	1.8	1.7	2.2	2.7	2.8	3.8	3.2	2.7	3.4	2.6	2.8	2.2
Snow	11.3	10.9	9.2	1.7	tr	tr	0.0	0.0	0.0	tr	3.8	9.8

High and Low temperatures in degrees Fahrenheit; Precipitation and Snow in inches

Population: 99,088 (1990); 98,726 (2000); 98,803 (2005); 98,814 (2010 projected); Race: 95.4% White, 1.8% Black, 1.4% Asian, 1.4% Hispanic of any race (2005); Density: 70.9 persons per square mile (2005); Average household size: 2.49 (2005); Median age: 39.4 (2005); Males per 100 females: 96.0 (2005).
Religion: Five largest groups: 20.5% Catholic Church, 7.0% The United Methodist Church, 3.3% The Wesleyan Church, 2.3% Presbyterian Church (U.S.A.), 2.1% American Baptist Churches in the USA (2000).
Economy: Unemployment rate: 5.8% (2005); Total civilian labor force: 44,880 (2005); Leading industries: 22.8% manufacturing; 19.5% health care and social assistance; 16.1% retail trade (2003); Farms: 1,501 totaling 373,294 acres (2002); Companies that employ 500 or more persons: 10 (2003); Companies that employ 100 to 499 persons: 29 (2003); Companies that employ less than 100 persons: 1,792 (2003); Black-owned businesses: n/a (2002); Hispanic-owned businesses: n/a (2002); Women-owned businesses: 2,048 (2002); Retail sales per capita: $10,162 (2006). Single-family building permits issued: 195 (2005); Multi-family building permits issued: 2 (2005).
Income: Per capita income: $21,357 (2005); Median household income: $40,811 (2005); Average household income: $52,730 (2005); Percent of households with income of $100,000 or more: 10.5% (2005); Poverty rate: 13.6% (2003); Bankruptcy rate: 5.34% (2005).
Taxes: Total county taxes per capita: $622 (2004); County property taxes per capita: $285 (2004).
Education: Percent of population age 25 and over with: High school diploma (including GED) or higher: 82.7% (2005); Bachelor's degree or higher: 18.0% (2005); Master's degree or higher: 7.9% (2005).
Housing: Homeownership rate: 73.5% (2005); Median home value: $96,866 (2005); Median rent: $373 per month (2000); Median age of housing: 45 years (2000).
Health: Birth rate: 114.7 per 10,000 population (2004); Death rate: 104.6 per 10,000 population (2004); Age-adjusted cancer mortality rate: 217.5 deaths per 100,000 population (2002); Air Quality Index: 79.4% good, 20.3% moderate, 0.3% unhealthy for sensitive individuals, 0.0% unhealthy (percent of days in 2005); Number of physicians: 14.3 per 10,000 population (2004); Hospital beds: 100.0 per 10,000 population (2003); Hospital admissions: 1,464.1 per 10,000 population (2003).
Elections: 2004 Presidential election results: 63.8% Bush, 34.3% Kerry, 1.6% Nader, 0.2% Badnarik
National and State Parks: Stony Brook State Park
Additional Information Contacts
Steuben County Government .... (607) 776-9631
http://www.steubencony.org/
City of Hornell .... (607) 324-7421
http://www.cityofhornell.com/
Town of Erwin .... (607) 962-7021
http://www.erwinny.org/

Steuben County Communities

ADDISON (village). Covers a land area of 1.897 square miles and a water area of 0 square miles. Located at 42.10° N. Lat.; 77.23° W. Long. Elevation is 985 feet.
Population: 1,913 (1990); 1,797 (2000); 1,733 (2005); 1,666 (2010 projected); Race: 98.5% White, 0.2% Black, 0.0% Asian, 0.6% Hispanic of any race (2005); Density: 913.4 persons per square mile (2005); Average household size: 2.44 (2005); Median age: 36.3 (2005); Males per 100 females: 90.0 (2005); Marriage status: 25.7% never married, 56.7% now married, 7.8% widowed, 9.8% divorced (2000); Foreign born: 0.4% (2000); Ancestry (includes multiple ancestries): 18.6% United States or American, 15.9% German, 15.0% Irish, 14.7% English, 7.8% Other groups (2000).
Economy: Single-family building permits issued: 2 (2005); Multi-family building permits issued: 0 (2005); Employment by occupation: 8.6% management, 19.2% professional, 18.3% services, 22.3% sales, 1.5% farming, 8.1% construction, 21.9% production (2000).
Income: Per capita income: $18,047 (2005); Median household income: $35,871 (2005); Average household income: $44,111 (2005); Percent of households with income of $100,000 or more: 6.1% (2005); Poverty rate: 17.5% (2000).
Education: Percent of population age 25 and over with: High school diploma (including GED) or higher: 80.7% (2005); Bachelor's degree or higher: 11.9% (2005); Master's degree or higher: 6.5% (2005).
School District(s)
Addison Central School District (PK-12)
    2003-04 Enrollment: 1,336 .... (607) 359-2244
Housing: Homeownership rate: 63.3% (2005); Median home value: $85,529 (2005); Median rent: $344 per month (2000); Median age of housing: 60+ years (2000).
Transportation: Commute to work: 91.4% car, 0.0% public transportation, 3.6% walk, 3.8% work from home (2000); Travel time to work: 30.0% less than 15 minutes, 44.0% 15 to 30 minutes, 16.8% 30 to 45 minutes, 3.4% 45 to 60 minutes, 5.8% 60 minutes or more (2000)

ADDISON (town). Covers a land area of 25.624 square miles and a water area of 0.038 square miles. Located at 42.13° N. Lat.; 77.23° W. Long. Elevation is 985 feet.
History: Incororated 1873.
Population: 2,645 (1990); 2,640 (2000); 2,548 (2005); 2,451 (2010 projected); Race: 98.3% White, 0.4% Black, 0.0% Asian, 0.7% Hispanic of any race (2005); Density: 99.4 persons per square mile (2005); Average household size: 2.53 (2005); Median age: 36.8 (2005); Males per 100 females: 93.2 (2005); Marriage status: 24.4% never married, 58.4% now married, 7.7% widowed, 9.5% divorced (2000); Foreign born: 0.7% (2000); Ancestry (includes multiple ancestries): 17.9% United States or American, 15.3% English, 14.5% German, 13.0% Irish, 7.9% Other groups (2000).
Economy: In dairying region. Single-family building permits issued: 0 (2005); Multi-family building permits issued: 0 (2005); Employment by

occupation: 9.4% management, 18.2% professional, 15.9% services, 22.8% sales, 1.6% farming, 9.8% construction, 22.3% production (2000).
Income: Per capita income: $18,259 (2005); Median household income: $37,563 (2005); Average household income: $46,248 (2005); Percent of households with income of $100,000 or more: 8.0% (2005); Poverty rate: 17.7% (2000).
Taxes: Total city taxes per capita: $121 (2004); City property taxes per capita: $112 (2004).
Education: Percent of population age 25 and over with: High school diploma (including GED) or higher: 78.0% (2005); Bachelor's degree or higher: 13.4% (2005); Master's degree or higher: 6.4% (2005).
Housing: Homeownership rate: 68.4% (2005); Median home value: $87,286 (2005); Median rent: $352 per month (2000); Median age of housing: 52 years (2000).
Safety: Violent crime rate: 22.9 per 10,000 population; Property crime rate: 38.2 per 10,000 population (2004).
Transportation: Commute to work: 92.1% car, 0.0% public transportation, 2.6% walk, 3.7% work from home (2000); Travel time to work: 27.9% less than 15 minutes, 47.2% 15 to 30 minutes, 14.8% 30 to 45 minutes, 5.0% 45 to 60 minutes, 5.2% 60 minutes or more (2000)

ARKPORT (village). Covers a land area of 0.688 square miles and a water area of 0 square miles. Located at 42.39° N. Lat.; 77.69° W. Long. Elevation is 1,194 feet.
Population: 770 (1990); 832 (2000); 818 (2005); 798 (2010 projected); Race: 97.9% White, 0.9% Black, 0.5% Asian, 1.2% Hispanic of any race (2005); Density: 1,189.2 persons per square mile (2005); Average household size: 2.35 (2005); Median age: 41.0 (2005); Males per 100 females: 80.6 (2005); Marriage status: 18.5% never married, 62.2% now married, 9.2% widowed, 10.0% divorced (2000); Foreign born: 0.5% (2000); Ancestry (includes multiple ancestries): 20.1% German, 20.0% Irish, 19.9% English, 8.4% United States or American, 7.8% Italian (2000).
Economy: Manufactures dairy products. Single-family building permits issued: 2 (2005); Multi-family building permits issued: 0 (2005); Employment by occupation: 11.3% management, 24.8% professional, 17.0% services, 19.0% sales, 0.6% farming, 10.0% construction, 17.4% production (2000).
Income: Per capita income: $21,647 (2005); Median household income: $42,909 (2005); Average household income: $50,884 (2005); Percent of households with income of $100,000 or more: 7.8% (2005); Poverty rate: 5.0% (2000).
Education: Percent of population age 25 and over with: High school diploma (including GED) or higher: 85.4% (2005); Bachelor's degree or higher: 17.6% (2005); Master's degree or higher: 9.9% (2005).
School District(s)
Arkport Central School District (KG-12)
    2003-04 Enrollment: 649 . . . . (607) 295-7471
Housing: Homeownership rate: 71.8% (2005); Median home value: $93,208 (2005); Median rent: $331 per month (2000); Median age of housing: 51 years (2000).
Transportation: Commute to work: 87.5% car, 1.3% public transportation, 7.6% walk, 3.0% work from home (2000); Travel time to work: 51.9% less than 15 minutes, 32.5% 15 to 30 minutes, 7.8% 30 to 45 minutes, 1.7% 45 to 60 minutes, 6.1% 60 minutes or more (2000)

ATLANTA (unincorporated postal area, zip code 14808). Covers a land area of 2.778 square miles and a water area of 0 square miles. Located at 42.56° N. Lat.; 77.47° W. Long. Elevation is 1,318 feet.
Population: 0 (2000); Race: 99.5% White, 0.0% Black, 0.0% Asian, 0.0% Hispanic of any race (2000); Density: 0.0 persons per square mile (2000); Age: 27.5% under 18, 14.2% over 64 (2000); Marriage status: 22.5% never married, 61.8% now married, 6.6% widowed, 9.1% divorced (2000); Foreign born: 1.1% (2000); Ancestry (includes multiple ancestries): 38.2% German, 29.5% English, 7.2% United States or American, 6.9% Other groups, 6.6% Irish (2000).
Economy: Employment by occupation: 15.9% management, 11.1% professional, 25.2% services, 11.9% sales, 5.6% farming, 17.0% construction, 13.3% production (2000).
Income: Per capita income: $15,163 (2000); Median household income: $30,000 (2000); Poverty rate: 25.6% (2000).
Education: Percent of population age 25 and over with: High school diploma (including GED) or higher: 78.1% (2000); Bachelor's degree or higher: 8.4% (2000).

Housing: Homeownership rate: 83.8% (2000); Median home value: $58,300 (2000); Median rent: $371 per month (2000); Median age of housing: 60+ years (2000).
Transportation: Commute to work: 90.6% car, 2.2% public transportation, 1.9% walk, 5.2% work from home (2000); Travel time to work: 32.8% less than 15 minutes, 19.4% 15 to 30 minutes, 23.3% 30 to 45 minutes, 8.3% 45 to 60 minutes, 16.2% 60 minutes or more (2000)

AVOCA (village). Covers a land area of 1.179 square miles and a water area of 0 square miles. Located at 42.41° N. Lat.; 77.42° W. Long. Elevation is 1,192 feet.
Population: 1,017 (1990); 1,008 (2000); 1,023 (2005); 1,004 (2010 projected); Race: 97.0% White, 0.9% Black, 0.4% Asian, 2.6% Hispanic of any race (2005); Density: 867.6 persons per square mile (2005); Average household size: 2.73 (2005); Median age: 36.7 (2005); Males per 100 females: 96.0 (2005); Marriage status: 26.4% never married, 56.6% now married, 8.4% widowed, 8.6% divorced (2000); Foreign born: 0.8% (2000); Ancestry (includes multiple ancestries): 23.9% German, 15.2% English, 14.0% Irish, 10.5% United States or American, 7.8% Other groups (2000).
Economy: Single-family building permits issued: 3 (2005); Multi-family building permits issued: 0 (2005); Employment by occupation: 9.0% management, 16.1% professional, 17.6% services, 23.8% sales, 1.0% farming, 7.7% construction, 24.8% production (2000).
Income: Per capita income: $16,289 (2005); Median household income: $37,620 (2005); Average household income: $43,640 (2005); Percent of households with income of $100,000 or more: 4.5% (2005); Poverty rate: 15.4% (2000).
Education: Percent of population age 25 and over with: High school diploma (including GED) or higher: 82.5% (2005); Bachelor's degree or higher: 14.2% (2005); Master's degree or higher: 5.6% (2005).
School District(s)
Avoca Central School District (KG-12)
    2003-04 Enrollment: 657 . . . . (607) 566-2221
Housing: Homeownership rate: 71.2% (2005); Median home value: $76,769 (2005); Median rent: $340 per month (2000); Median age of housing: 60+ years (2000).
Transportation: Commute to work: 95.4% car, 0.0% public transportation, 2.6% walk, 1.3% work from home (2000); Travel time to work: 33.1% less than 15 minutes, 47.9% 15 to 30 minutes, 12.2% 30 to 45 minutes, 2.6% 45 to 60 minutes, 4.2% 60 minutes or more (2000)

AVOCA (town). Covers a land area of 36.292 square miles and a water area of 0.023 square miles. Located at 42.41° N. Lat.; 77.44° W. Long. Elevation is 1,192 feet.
History: Settled 1843, incorporated 1883.
Population: 2,269 (1990); 2,314 (2000); 2,373 (2005); 2,352 (2010 projected); Race: 96.8% White, 1.4% Black, 0.4% Asian, 1.5% Hispanic of any race (2005); Density: 65.4 persons per square mile (2005); Average household size: 2.60 (2005); Median age: 37.6 (2005); Males per 100 females: 103.3 (2005); Marriage status: 21.8% never married, 59.3% now married, 7.1% widowed, 11.7% divorced (2000); Foreign born: 0.6% (2000); Ancestry (includes multiple ancestries): 22.1% German, 16.7% English, 14.0% Irish, 11.9% United States or American, 7.0% Other groups (2000).
Economy: Agricultural area. Single-family building permits issued: 2 (2005); Multi-family building permits issued: 0 (2005); Employment by occupation: 8.1% management, 16.9% professional, 19.3% services, 21.2% sales, 1.4% farming, 10.4% construction, 22.6% production (2000).
Income: Per capita income: $17,122 (2005); Median household income: $36,143 (2005); Average household income: $44,273 (2005); Percent of households with income of $100,000 or more: 4.7% (2005); Poverty rate: 13.6% (2000).
Education: Percent of population age 25 and over with: High school diploma (including GED) or higher: 78.4% (2005); Bachelor's degree or higher: 13.3% (2005); Master's degree or higher: 5.7% (2005).
Housing: Homeownership rate: 76.0% (2005); Median home value: $83,438 (2005); Median rent: $346 per month (2000); Median age of housing: 57 years (2000).
Transportation: Commute to work: 91.0% car, 0.0% public transportation, 2.0% walk, 6.4% work from home (2000); Travel time to work: 27.5% less than 15 minutes, 48.0% 15 to 30 minutes, 16.6% 30 to 45 minutes, 3.4% 45 to 60 minutes, 4.6% 60 minutes or more (2000)

BATH (village). Covers a land area of 2.878 square miles and a water area of 0 square miles. Located at 42.33° N. Lat.; 77.31° W. Long. Elevation is 1,106 feet.
Population: 5,801 (1990); 5,641 (2000); 5,536 (2005); 5,492 (2010 projected); Race: 95.3% White, 1.9% Black, 1.2% Asian, 1.4% Hispanic of any race (2005); Density: 1,923.4 persons per square mile (2005); Average household size: 2.12 (2005); Median age: 43.0 (2005); Males per 100 females: 92.1 (2005); Marriage status: 23.5% never married, 52.7% now married, 9.8% widowed, 14.0% divorced (2000); Foreign born: 1.1% (2000); Ancestry (includes multiple ancestries): 17.5% English, 17.2% Irish, 15.5% German, 10.8% United States or American, 8.0% Italian (2000).
Economy: Single-family building permits issued: 0 (2005); Multi-family building permits issued: 0 (2005); Employment by occupation: 10.6% management, 18.9% professional, 18.5% services, 27.0% sales, 0.2% farming, 8.1% construction, 16.7% production (2000).
Income: Per capita income: $20,325 (2005); Median household income: $31,694 (2005); Average household income: $42,821 (2005); Percent of households with income of $100,000 or more: 7.4% (2005); Poverty rate: 15.5% (2000).
Education: Percent of population age 25 and over with: High school diploma (including GED) or higher: 83.0% (2005); Bachelor's degree or higher: 16.6% (2005); Master's degree or higher: 8.0% (2005).
School District(s)
Bath Central School District (PK-12)
    2003-04 Enrollment: 2,054 . . . . (607) 776-3301
Housing: Homeownership rate: 56.6% (2005); Median home value: $106,171 (2005); Median rent: $363 per month (2000); Median age of housing: 52 years (2000).
Hospitals: Ira Davenport Memorial Hospital (66 beds); Veterans Affairs Medical Center (600 beds)
Safety: Violent crime rate: 23.3 per 10,000 population; Property crime rate: 325.9 per 10,000 population (2004).
Newspapers: Steuben Courier-Advocate (General - Circulation 11,022)
Transportation: Commute to work: 88.0% car, 1.0% public transportation, 6.1% walk, 4.1% work from home (2000); Travel time to work: 57.9% less than 15 minutes, 22.9% 15 to 30 minutes, 12.4% 30 to 45 minutes, 5.3% 45 to 60 minutes, 1.6% 60 minutes or more (2000).

BATH (town). Covers a land area of 95.996 square miles and a water area of 0.308 square miles. Located at 42.32° N. Lat.; 77.30° W. Long. Elevation is 1,106 feet.
History: Bath is the site of the first clearing in Steuben County, made in 1793 by Colonel Charles Williamson (1757-1808), agent for the Pulteney Estate. Williamson chose the site of Bath on the Cohocton River as the location of a future metropolis that was to be the trading, industrial, and distribution center for the entire region. He was too energetic to wait for the normal processes of settlement. His plan was to build the city first, which would then attract settlers. Williamson's overhasty promotions cost his principals more than a million dollars, and he was dismissed from his position in 1801. Incorporated in 1816.
Population: 12,724 (1990); 12,097 (2000); 12,111 (2005); 12,128 (2010 projected); Race: 94.9% White, 2.5% Black, 1.0% Asian, 1.1% Hispanic of any race (2005); Density: 126.2 persons per square mile (2005); Average household size: 2.44 (2005); Median age: 41.8 (2005); Males per 100 females: 101.4 (2005); Marriage status: 22.4% never married, 56.6% now married, 9.1% widowed, 12.0% divorced (2000); Foreign born: 1.1% (2000); Ancestry (includes multiple ancestries): 17.4% English, 15.8% Irish, 14.7% German, 12.3% United States or American, 7.7% Other groups (2000).
Economy: Manufacturing: lighting fixtures; meat packing; aluminum and fiberglass products, building materials, fabricated metal products. In rich agricultural area: dairy products, potatoes; regional tourist center. Single-family building permits issued: 1 (2005); Multi-family building permits issued: 0 (2005); Employment by occupation: 9.7% management, 17.1% professional, 17.2% services, 24.5% sales, 1.2% farming, 10.0% construction, 20.4% production (2000).
Income: Per capita income: $19,547 (2005); Median household income: $37,151 (2005); Average household income: $46,655 (2005); Percent of households with income of $100,000 or more: 8.4% (2005); Poverty rate: 14.5% (2000).
Education: Percent of population age 25 and over with: High school diploma (including GED) or higher: 80.6% (2005); Bachelor's degree or higher: 13.6% (2005); Master's degree or higher: 6.0% (2005).
Housing: Homeownership rate: 67.0% (2005); Median home value: $97,593 (2005); Median rent: $369 per month (2000); Median age of housing: 40 years (2000).
Transportation: Commute to work: 90.0% car, 0.6% public transportation, 4.1% walk, 4.7% work from home (2000); Travel time to work: 49.0% less than 15 minutes, 30.1% 15 to 30 minutes, 13.4% 30 to 45 minutes, 4.2% 45 to 60 minutes, 3.4% 60 minutes or more (2000).

BRADFORD (town). Covers a land area of 24.829 square miles and a water area of 0.037 square miles. Located at 42.33° N. Lat.; 77.13° W. Long.
Population: 699 (1990); 763 (2000); 760 (2005); 760 (2010 projected); Race: 98.8% White, 0.1% Black, 0.3% Asian, 0.3% Hispanic of any race (2005); Density: 30.6 persons per square mile (2005); Average household size: 2.59 (2005); Median age: 38.3 (2005); Males per 100 females: 102.7 (2005); Marriage status: 19.1% never married, 58.0% now married, 8.1% widowed, 14.8% divorced (2000); Foreign born: 0.3% (2000); Ancestry (includes multiple ancestries): 15.3% English, 14.4% German, 14.1% United States or American, 12.1% Irish, 10.0% Polish (2000).
Economy: Single-family building permits issued: 9 (2005); Multi-family building permits issued: 0 (2005); Employment by occupation: 6.1% management, 17.7% professional, 12.5% services, 13.9% sales, 3.2% farming, 13.3% construction, 33.3% production (2000).
Income: Per capita income: $18,568 (2005); Median household income: $41,385 (2005); Average household income: $47,073 (2005); Percent of households with income of $100,000 or more: 6.5% (2005); Poverty rate: 16.4% (2000).
Education: Percent of population age 25 and over with: High school diploma (including GED) or higher: 80.1% (2005); Bachelor's degree or higher: 9.9% (2005); Master's degree or higher: 2.2% (2005).
School District(s)
Bradford Central School District (PK-12)
    2003-04 Enrollment: 327 . . . . (607) 583-4616
Housing: Homeownership rate: 88.7% (2005); Median home value: $76,190 (2005); Median rent: $321 per month (2000); Median age of housing: 25 years (2000).
Transportation: Commute to work: 97.0% car, 0.0% public transportation, 0.6% walk, 2.4% work from home (2000); Travel time to work: 8.9% less than 15 minutes, 41.4% 15 to 30 minutes, 35.3% 30 to 45 minutes, 8.6% 45 to 60 minutes, 5.8% 60 minutes or more (2000).

CAMERON (town). Covers a land area of 46.731 square miles and a water area of 0.021 square miles. Located at 42.19° N. Lat.; 77.39° W. Long. Elevation is 1,051 feet.
Population: 916 (1990); 1,034 (2000); 1,073 (2005); 1,093 (2010 projected); Race: 97.9% White, 0.2% Black, 0.1% Asian, 0.7% Hispanic of any race (2005); Density: 23.0 persons per square mile (2005); Average household size: 2.82 (2005); Median age: 38.1 (2005); Males per 100 females: 111.2 (2005); Marriage status: 24.8% never married, 60.1% now married, 4.4% widowed, 10.7% divorced (2000); Foreign born: 0.2% (2000); Ancestry (includes multiple ancestries): 16.0% United States or American, 12.5% German, 12.0% English, 9.8% Irish, 6.7% Other groups (2000).
Economy: Single-family building permits issued: 4 (2005); Multi-family building permits issued: 0 (2005); Employment by occupation: 8.6% management, 12.4% professional, 19.1% services, 13.4% sales, 2.1% farming, 15.8% construction, 28.6% production (2000).
Income: Per capita income: $17,684 (2005); Median household income: $38,305 (2005); Average household income: $49,934 (2005); Percent of households with income of $100,000 or more: 8.2% (2005); Poverty rate: 21.2% (2000).
Education: Percent of population age 25 and over with: High school diploma (including GED) or higher: 72.0% (2005); Bachelor's degree or higher: 5.6% (2005); Master's degree or higher: 3.2% (2005).
Housing: Homeownership rate: 76.6% (2005); Median home value: $80,263 (2005); Median rent: $340 per month (2000); Median age of housing: 28 years (2000).
Transportation: Commute to work: 94.7% car, 0.5% public transportation, 0.0% walk, 3.9% work from home (2000); Travel time to work: 9.5% less than 15 minutes, 35.9% 15 to 30 minutes, 35.9% 30 to 45 minutes, 8.8% 45 to 60 minutes, 9.8% 60 minutes or more (2000).

CAMERON MILLS (unincorporated postal area, zip code 14820). Covers a land area of 31.198 square miles and a water area of 0 square miles. Located at 42.19° N. Lat.; 77.36° W. Long.

Population: 0 (2000); Race: 93.8% White, 0.8% Black, 0.5% Asian, 1.0% Hispanic of any race (2000); Density: 0.0 persons per square mile (2000); Age: 33.2% under 18, 8.0% over 64 (2000); Marriage status: 24.4% never married, 63.6% now married, 5.7% widowed, 6.3% divorced (2000); Foreign born: 0.5% (2000); Ancestry (includes multiple ancestries): 13.7% United States or American, 12.8% English, 11.4% German, 8.9% Other groups, 8.0% Irish (2000).
Economy: Employment by occupation: 10.8% management, 16.8% professional, 14.7% services, 19.5% sales, 2.4% farming, 12.6% construction, 23.4% production (2000).
Income: Per capita income: $14,591 (2000); Median household income: $39,559 (2000); Poverty rate: 12.7% (2000).
Education: Percent of population age 25 and over with: High school diploma (including GED) or higher: 75.8% (2000); Bachelor's degree or higher: 5.9% (2000).

School District(s)
Addison Central School District (PK-12)
   2003-04 Enrollment: 1,336 . . . . (607) 359-2244
Housing: Homeownership rate: 83.9% (2000); Median home value: $57,500 (2000); Median rent: $367 per month (2000); Median age of housing: 35 years (2000).
Transportation: Commute to work: 94.8% car, 0.0% public transportation, 0.9% walk, 4.3% work from home (2000); Travel time to work: 12.2% less than 15 minutes, 43.6% 15 to 30 minutes, 32.7% 30 to 45 minutes, 4.8% 45 to 60 minutes, 6.7% 60 minutes or more (2000)

CAMPBELL (town). Covers a land area of 40.746 square miles and a water area of 0.032 square miles. Located at 42.23° N. Lat.; 77.16° W. Long.
Population: 3,658 (1990); 3,691 (2000); 3,700 (2005); 3,718 (2010 projected); Race: 98.1% White, 0.8% Black, 0.4% Asian, 0.5% Hispanic of any race (2005); Density: 90.8 persons per square mile (2005); Average household size: 2.56 (2005); Median age: 39.3 (2005); Males per 100 females: 97.0 (2005); Marriage status: 19.1% never married, 62.3% now married, 7.7% widowed, 10.9% divorced (2000); Foreign born: 0.8% (2000); Ancestry (includes multiple ancestries): 17.0% English, 16.7% German, 16.5% Irish, 14.9% United States or American, 5.4% Other groups (2000).
Economy: Single-family building permits issued: 2 (2005); Multi-family building permits issued: 0 (2005); Employment by occupation: 11.0% management, 20.4% professional, 16.2% services, 22.5% sales, 0.5% farming, 12.5% construction, 16.9% production (2000).
Income: Per capita income: $22,596 (2005); Median household income: $46,608 (2005); Average household income: $57,652 (2005); Percent of households with income of $100,000 or more: 12.6% (2005); Poverty rate: 8.2% (2000).
Education: Percent of population age 25 and over with: High school diploma (including GED) or higher: 81.3% (2005); Bachelor's degree or higher: 16.0% (2005); Master's degree or higher: 6.3% (2005).

School District(s)
Campbell-Savona Central School District (PK-12)
   2003-04 Enrollment: 1,218 . . . . (607) 527-4548
Housing: Homeownership rate: 87.4% (2005); Median home value: $100,243 (2005); Median rent: $410 per month (2000); Median age of housing: 31 years (2000).
Transportation: Commute to work: 95.3% car, 0.3% public transportation, 1.0% walk, 3.4% work from home (2000); Travel time to work: 29.3% less than 15 minutes, 47.6% 15 to 30 minutes, 17.1% 30 to 45 minutes, 3.6% 45 to 60 minutes, 2.4% 60 minutes or more (2000)

CANISTEO (village). Covers a land area of 0.967 square miles and a water area of 0 square miles. Located at 42.27° N. Lat.; 77.60° W. Long. Elevation is 1,132 feet.
Population: 2,423 (1990); 2,336 (2000); 2,222 (2005); 2,144 (2010 projected); Race: 97.8% White, 0.3% Black, 0.6% Asian, 2.4% Hispanic of any race (2005); Density: 2,297.2 persons per square mile (2005); Average household size: 2.42 (2005); Median age: 40.3 (2005); Males per 100 females: 89.9 (2005); Marriage status: 23.3% never married, 58.6% now married, 9.7% widowed, 8.4% divorced (2000); Foreign born: 0.4% (2000); Ancestry (includes multiple ancestries): 23.7% German, 17.5% Irish, 15.2% English, 13.5% United States or American, 8.2% Italian (2000).
Economy: Single-family building permits issued: 1 (2005); Multi-family building permits issued: 0 (2005); Employment by occupation: 9.2% management, 21.9% professional, 21.0% services, 20.2% sales, 0.7% farming, 8.7% construction, 18.3% production (2000).
Income: Per capita income: $16,732 (2005); Median household income: $35,609 (2005); Average household income: $40,454 (2005); Percent of households with income of $100,000 or more: 3.2% (2005); Poverty rate: 10.6% (2000).
Education: Percent of population age 25 and over with: High school diploma (including GED) or higher: 85.8% (2005); Bachelor's degree or higher: 17.3% (2005); Master's degree or higher: 5.7% (2005).

School District(s)
Canisteo Central School District (KG-12)
   2003-04 Enrollment: 926 . . . . (607) 698-4225
Housing: Homeownership rate: 70.3% (2005); Median home value: $77,971 (2005); Median rent: $312 per month (2000); Median age of housing: 60+ years (2000).
Safety: Violent crime rate: 43.5 per 10,000 population; Property crime rate: 365.1 per 10,000 population (2004).
Transportation: Commute to work: 84.5% car, 1.7% public transportation, 5.6% walk, 7.0% work from home (2000); Travel time to work: 44.6% less than 15 minutes, 27.8% 15 to 30 minutes, 12.7% 30 to 45 minutes, 3.9% 45 to 60 minutes, 11.0% 60 minutes or more (2000)
Additional Information Contacts
Hornell Area Chamber of Commerce. . . . . (607) 324-0310
   http://www.hornellny.com

CANISTEO (town). Covers a land area of 54.368 square miles and a water area of 0 square miles. Located at 42.25° N. Lat.; 77.58° W. Long. Elevation is 1,132 feet.
History: Settled before 1790, incorporated 1873.
Population: 3,636 (1990); 3,583 (2000); 3,534 (2005); 3,485 (2010 projected); Race: 97.9% White, 0.3% Black, 0.7% Asian, 1.7% Hispanic of any race (2005); Density: 65.0 persons per square mile (2005); Average household size: 2.47 (2005); Median age: 39.6 (2005); Males per 100 females: 94.1 (2005); Marriage status: 23.4% never married, 60.8% now married, 7.5% widowed, 8.3% divorced (2000); Foreign born: 1.1% (2000); Ancestry (includes multiple ancestries): 21.2% German, 15.3% English, 14.8% Irish, 13.1% United States or American, 6.8% Italian (2000).
Economy: Manufacturing: printing, cheese; dairy products, poultry; timber. Single-family building permits issued: 3 (2005); Multi-family building permits issued: 0 (2005); Employment by occupation: 8.5% management, 19.8% professional, 19.9% services, 19.8% sales, 1.7% farming, 12.0% construction, 18.4% production (2000).
Income: Per capita income: $17,399 (2005); Median household income: $39,063 (2005); Average household income: $43,028 (2005); Percent of households with income of $100,000 or more: 4.5% (2005); Poverty rate: 11.6% (2000).
Education: Percent of population age 25 and over with: High school diploma (including GED) or higher: 87.0% (2005); Bachelor's degree or higher: 16.2% (2005); Master's degree or higher: 5.6% (2005).
Housing: Homeownership rate: 75.5% (2005); Median home value: $79,545 (2005); Median rent: $327 per month (2000); Median age of housing: 60+ years (2000).
Transportation: Commute to work: 87.8% car, 1.1% public transportation, 4.8% walk, 5.4% work from home (2000); Travel time to work: 38.4% less than 15 minutes, 29.7% 15 to 30 minutes, 16.9% 30 to 45 minutes, 4.6% 45 to 60 minutes, 10.3% 60 minutes or more (2000)

CATON (town). Covers a land area of 37.793 square miles and a water area of 0.178 square miles. Located at 42.05° N. Lat.; 77.02° W. Long.
Population: 1,888 (1990); 2,097 (2000); 2,101 (2005); 2,128 (2010 projected); Race: 97.7% White, 1.2% Black, 0.1% Asian, 1.0% Hispanic of any race (2005); Density: 55.6 persons per square mile (2005); Average household size: 2.68 (2005); Median age: 39.2 (2005); Males per 100 females: 100.3 (2005); Marriage status: 18.6% never married, 67.0% now married, 4.6% widowed, 9.7% divorced (2000); Foreign born: 0.8% (2000); Ancestry (includes multiple ancestries): 20.9% German, 16.1% English, 12.4% Irish, 11.6% United States or American, 7.3% Italian (2000).
Economy: Single-family building permits issued: 4 (2005); Multi-family building permits issued: 0 (2005); Employment by occupation: 11.9% management, 22.2% professional, 14.8% services, 19.2% sales, 0.8% farming, 10.2% construction, 20.9% production (2000).
Income: Per capita income: $25,693 (2005); Median household income: $55,842 (2005); Average household income: $68,764 (2005); Percent of households with income of $100,000 or more: 15.9% (2005); Poverty rate: 7.5% (2000).

Education: Percent of population age 25 and over with: High school diploma (including GED) or higher: 87.8% (2005); Bachelor's degree or higher: 16.6% (2005); Master's degree or higher: 6.2% (2005).
Housing: Homeownership rate: 92.2% (2005); Median home value: $118,468 (2005); Median rent: $375 per month (2000); Median age of housing: 30 years (2000).
Transportation: Commute to work: 93.9% car, 0.7% public transportation, 0.9% walk, 4.3% work from home (2000); Travel time to work: 12.0% less than 15 minutes, 64.2% 15 to 30 minutes, 17.1% 30 to 45 minutes, 4.2% 45 to 60 minutes, 2.5% 60 minutes or more (2000)

COHOCTON (village). Covers a land area of 1.503 square miles and a water area of 0 square miles. Located at 42.49° N. Lat.; 77.49° W. Long.
Population: 859 (1990); 854 (2000); 962 (2005); 1,037 (2010 projected); Race: 98.4% White, 0.0% Black, 0.0% Asian, 0.2% Hispanic of any race (2005); Density: 640.0 persons per square mile (2005); Average household size: 2.66 (2005); Median age: 36.7 (2005); Males per 100 females: 98.4 (2005); Marriage status: 25.4% never married, 55.4% now married, 7.9% widowed, 11.4% divorced (2000); Foreign born: 0.1% (2000); Ancestry (includes multiple ancestries): 34.5% German, 16.9% English, 11.7% Irish, 11.4% Italian, 6.2% Other groups (2000).
Economy: Single-family building permits issued: 0 (2005); Multi-family building permits issued: 0 (2005); Employment by occupation: 8.9% management, 17.6% professional, 20.7% services, 17.6% sales, 1.7% farming, 12.3% construction, 21.2% production (2000).
Income: Per capita income: $17,448 (2005); Median household income: $40,387 (2005); Average household income: $46,357 (2005); Percent of households with income of $100,000 or more: 7.5% (2005); Poverty rate: 15.3% (2000).
Education: Percent of population age 25 and over with: High school diploma (including GED) or higher: 77.8% (2005); Bachelor's degree or higher: 12.4% (2005); Master's degree or higher: 5.6% (2005).

School District(s)
Wayland-Cohocton Central School District (PK-12)
   2003-04 Enrollment: 1,827 . . . . (585) 728-2211
Housing: Homeownership rate: 78.7% (2005); Median home value: $77,722 (2005); Median rent: $372 per month (2000); Median age of housing: 60+ years (2000).
Transportation: Commute to work: 92.0% car, 0.0% public transportation, 4.3% walk, 3.7% work from home (2000); Travel time to work: 25.6% less than 15 minutes, 36.3% 15 to 30 minutes, 11.3% 30 to 45 minutes, 10.7% 45 to 60 minutes, 16.1% 60 minutes or more (2000)

COHOCTON (town). Covers a land area of 56.070 square miles and a water area of 0 square miles. Located at 42.51° N. Lat.; 77.48° W. Long.
Population: 2,520 (1990); 2,626 (2000); 2,655 (2005); 2,686 (2010 projected); Race: 97.1% White, 0.6% Black, 0.4% Asian, 0.5% Hispanic of any race (2005); Density: 47.4 persons per square mile (2005); Average household size: 2.66 (2005); Median age: 38.2 (2005); Males per 100 females: 98.4 (2005); Marriage status: 21.8% never married, 60.7% now married, 7.1% widowed, 10.5% divorced (2000); Foreign born: 0.6% (2000); Ancestry (includes multiple ancestries): 35.3% German, 22.2% English, 10.9% Irish, 7.5% Other groups, 7.3% Italian (2000).
Economy: In agricultural area; dairy products; sand and gravel. Single-family building permits issued: 6 (2005); Multi-family building permits issued: 0 (2005); Employment by occupation: 13.8% management, 14.7% professional, 15.4% services, 16.1% sales, 2.2% farming, 13.5% construction, 24.4% production (2000).
Income: Per capita income: $17,921 (2005); Median household income: $41,563 (2005); Average household income: $47,578 (2005); Percent of households with income of $100,000 or more: 8.0% (2005); Poverty rate: 17.6% (2000).
Education: Percent of population age 25 and over with: High school diploma (including GED) or higher: 79.6% (2005); Bachelor's degree or higher: 11.3% (2005); Master's degree or higher: 5.0% (2005).
Housing: Homeownership rate: 83.3% (2005); Median home value: $84,521 (2005); Median rent: $380 per month (2000); Median age of housing: 60+ years (2000).
Transportation: Commute to work: 91.1% car, 0.5% public transportation, 2.1% walk, 5.8% work from home (2000); Travel time to work: 28.5% less than 15 minutes, 28.3% 15 to 30 minutes, 21.4% 30 to 45 minutes, 9.7% 45 to 60 minutes, 12.2% 60 minutes or more (2000)

CORNING (city). Covers a land area of 3.107 square miles and a water area of 0.170 square miles. Located at 42.14° N. Lat.; 77.05° W. Long. Elevation is 937 feet.
History: The glass industry, for which the city is famous, began in 1868. Corning glass Museum and the Rockwell Museum, with the largest collection of Western art in the Eastern U.S. and the world's largest collection of Steuben glass, are located in the city. In 1972 the city was heavily damaged by flooding in the wake of Hurricane Agnes. Settled 1788; Incorporated as a city 1890.
Population: 11,938 (1990); 10,842 (2000); 10,503 (2005); 10,156 (2010 projected); Race: 92.1% White, 4.0% Black, 2.1% Asian, 1.3% Hispanic of any race (2005); Density: 3,380.4 persons per square mile (2005); Average household size: 2.14 (2005); Median age: 38.7 (2005); Males per 100 females: 88.2 (2005); Marriage status: 28.8% never married, 50.9% now married, 9.9% widowed, 10.5% divorced (2000); Foreign born: 4.3% (2000); Ancestry (includes multiple ancestries): 17.6% German, 16.3% Irish, 14.0% English, 11.8% Italian, 9.5% Other groups (2000).
Economy: In a dairy and vineyard region. The city is famous for its glass industry. Corning, Inc. has headquarters here. Corning glass products are used in advanced technology industries, such as fiber optics. Single-family building permits issued: 2 (2005); Multi-family building permits issued: 0 (2005); Employment by occupation: 13.9% management, 28.7% professional, 17.3% services, 20.3% sales, 0.2% farming, 6.6% construction, 13.0% production (2000).
Income: Per capita income: $25,515 (2005); Median household income: $37,260 (2005); Average household income: $54,243 (2005); Percent of households with income of $100,000 or more: 12.0% (2005); Poverty rate: 13.0% (2000).
Education: Percent of population age 25 and over with: High school diploma (including GED) or higher: 86.3% (2005); Bachelor's degree or higher: 30.0% (2005); Master's degree or higher: 12.4% (2005).

School District(s)
Corning City School District (PK-12)
   2003-04 Enrollment: 5,833 . . . . (607) 936-3704
Two-year College(s)
Corning Community College (Public)
   Fall 2004 Enrollment: 4,987. . . . . (607) 962-9011
   2005-06 Tuition: In-state $3,480; Out-of-state $6,580
Housing: Homeownership rate: 52.1% (2005); Median home value: $111,499 (2005); Median rent: $414 per month (2000); Median age of housing: 60 years (2000).
Hospitals: Corning Hospital (144 beds)
Safety: Violent crime rate: 31.0 per 10,000 population; Property crime rate: 558.0 per 10,000 population (2004).
Newspapers: The Leader (Circulation 13,086)
Transportation: Commute to work: 87.2% car, 0.8% public transportation, 7.4% walk, 2.9% work from home (2000); Travel time to work: 61.9% less than 15 minutes, 26.3% 15 to 30 minutes, 8.0% 30 to 45 minutes, 1.5% 45 to 60 minutes, 2.3% 60 minutes or more (2000)
Additional Information Contacts
Corning Area Chamber of Commerce . . . . (607) 936-4686
   http://www.corningny.com

CORNING (town). Covers a land area of 36.916 square miles and a water area of 0.404 square miles. Located at 42.14° N. Lat.; 77.03° W. Long. Elevation is 937 feet.
Population: 6,367 (1990); 6,426 (2000); 6,454 (2005); 6,486 (2010 projected); Race: 94.0% White, 3.0% Black, 2.0% Asian, 1.1% Hispanic of any race (2005); Density: 174.8 persons per square mile (2005); Average household size: 2.56 (2005); Median age: 40.7 (2005); Males per 100 females: 97.0 (2005); Marriage status: 19.6% never married, 64.3% now married, 7.3% widowed, 8.8% divorced (2000); Foreign born: 3.4% (2000); Ancestry (includes multiple ancestries): 21.2% German, 15.0% Irish, 14.6% English, 9.8% United States or American, 9.2% Other groups (2000).
Economy: Single-family building permits issued: 7 (2005); Multi-family building permits issued: 0 (2005); Employment by occupation: 13.6% management, 26.3% professional, 15.0% services, 19.7% sales, 0.3% farming, 7.8% construction, 17.4% production (2000).
Income: Per capita income: $26,935 (2005); Median household income: $50,188 (2005); Average household income: $68,741 (2005); Percent of households with income of $100,000 or more: 18.5% (2005); Poverty rate: 8.2% (2000).

Education: Percent of population age 25 and over with: High school diploma (including GED) or higher: 85.0% (2005); Bachelor's degree or higher: 25.0% (2005); Master's degree or higher: 12.0% (2005).
Housing: Homeownership rate: 83.7% (2005); Median home value: $107,597 (2005); Median rent: $463 per month (2000); Median age of housing: 43 years (2000).
Transportation: Commute to work: 94.1% car, 0.2% public transportation, 2.0% walk, 2.7% work from home (2000); Travel time to work: 43.0% less than 15 minutes, 44.1% 15 to 30 minutes, 8.8% 30 to 45 minutes, 1.7% 45 to 60 minutes, 2.5% 60 minutes or more (2000)

DANSVILLE (town).
Covers a land area of 47.993 square miles and a water area of 0.072 square miles. Located at 42.47° N. Lat.; 77.66° W. Long.
Population: 1,811 (1990); 1,977 (2000); 2,008 (2005); 2,036 (2010 projected); Race: 95.6% White, 1.2% Black, 0.2% Asian, 2.5% Hispanic of any race (2005); Density: 41.8 persons per square mile (2005); Average household size: 2.65 (2005); Median age: 38.7 (2005); Males per 100 females: 101.6 (2005); Marriage status: 20.8% never married, 64.1% now married, 5.4% widowed, 9.6% divorced (2000); Foreign born: 0.9% (2000); Ancestry (includes multiple ancestries): 29.5% German, 15.7% English, 15.2% Irish, 9.2% United States or American, 5.8% Other groups (2000).
Economy: Single-family building permits issued: 8 (2005); Multi-family building permits issued: 0 (2005); Employment by occupation: 9.3% management, 12.6% professional, 16.9% services, 25.5% sales, 3.1% farming, 11.9% construction, 20.7% production (2000).
Income: Per capita income: $17,375 (2005); Median household income: $39,111 (2005); Average household income: $45,968 (2005); Percent of households with income of $100,000 or more: 5.1% (2005); Poverty rate: 10.0% (2000).
Education: Percent of population age 25 and over with: High school diploma (including GED) or higher: 83.4% (2005); Bachelor's degree or higher: 9.0% (2005); Master's degree or higher: 3.3% (2005).
Housing: Homeownership rate: 84.7% (2005); Median home value: $96,837 (2005); Median rent: $369 per month (2000); Median age of housing: 27 years (2000).
Transportation: Commute to work: 90.4% car, 0.0% public transportation, 4.0% walk, 5.6% work from home (2000); Travel time to work: 27.4% less than 15 minutes, 37.0% 15 to 30 minutes, 12.1% 30 to 45 minutes, 7.7% 45 to 60 minutes, 15.7% 60 minutes or more (2000)
Additional Information Contacts
Dansville Chamber of Commerce .... (585) 335-6920
http://www.dansvilleny.net

ERWIN (town).
Covers a land area of 38.687 square miles and a water area of 0.463 square miles. Located at 42.15° N. Lat.; 77.12° W. Long.
Population: 6,763 (1990); 7,227 (2000); 7,534 (2005); 7,817 (2010 projected); Race: 88.5% White, 3.0% Black, 7.4% Asian, 2.4% Hispanic of any race (2005); Density: 194.7 persons per square mile (2005); Average household size: 2.39 (2005); Median age: 41.8 (2005); Males per 100 females: 90.6 (2005); Marriage status: 21.5% never married, 59.2% now married, 9.1% widowed, 10.2% divorced (2000); Foreign born: 4.7% (2000); Ancestry (includes multiple ancestries): 21.2% German, 20.7% English, 18.5% Irish, 9.5% Italian, 9.0% Other groups (2000).
Economy: Single-family building permits issued: 17 (2005); Multi-family building permits issued: 0 (2005); Employment by occupation: 17.8% management, 35.5% professional, 11.8% services, 17.3% sales, 0.5% farming, 6.2% construction, 11.0% production (2000).
Income: Per capita income: $32,029 (2005); Median household income: $51,792 (2005); Average household income: $75,554 (2005); Percent of households with income of $100,000 or more: 23.0% (2005); Poverty rate: 6.7% (2000).
Education: Percent of population age 25 and over with: High school diploma (including GED) or higher: 87.8% (2005); Bachelor's degree or higher: 37.5% (2005); Master's degree or higher: 18.1% (2005).
Housing: Homeownership rate: 70.7% (2005); Median home value: $134,736 (2005); Median rent: $382 per month (2000); Median age of housing: 31 years (2000).
Transportation: Commute to work: 95.0% car, 0.3% public transportation, 2.9% walk, 1.5% work from home (2000); Travel time to work: 62.2% less than 15 minutes, 24.2% 15 to 30 minutes, 8.4% 30 to 45 minutes, 2.5% 45 to 60 minutes, 2.6% 60 minutes or more (2000)
Additional Information Contacts
Town of Erwin .... (607) 962-7021
http://www.erwinny.org/

FREMONT (town).
Covers a land area of 32.229 square miles and a water area of 0.130 square miles. Located at 42.39° N. Lat.; 77.60° W. Long.
Population: 912 (1990); 964 (2000); 1,023 (2005); 1,081 (2010 projected); Race: 99.2% White, 0.0% Black, 0.1% Asian, 0.0% Hispanic of any race (2005); Density: 31.7 persons per square mile (2005); Average household size: 2.40 (2005); Median age: 40.6 (2005); Males per 100 females: 101.0 (2005); Marriage status: 21.1% never married, 64.2% now married, 5.3% widowed, 9.4% divorced (2000); Foreign born: 1.3% (2000); Ancestry (includes multiple ancestries): 25.6% German, 15.1% English, 13.4% Irish, 10.3% United States or American, 5.5% French (except Basque) (2000).
Economy: Single-family building permits issued: 5 (2005); Multi-family building permits issued: 0 (2005); Employment by occupation: 9.6% management, 24.6% professional, 10.4% services, 22.7% sales, 2.9% farming, 14.8% construction, 15.0% production (2000).
Income: Per capita income: $20,921 (2005); Median household income: $40,687 (2005); Average household income: $50,123 (2005); Percent of households with income of $100,000 or more: 8.9% (2005); Poverty rate: 13.3% (2000).
Education: Percent of population age 25 and over with: High school diploma (including GED) or higher: 85.5% (2005); Bachelor's degree or higher: 11.0% (2005); Master's degree or higher: 5.0% (2005).
Housing: Homeownership rate: 84.5% (2005); Median home value: $95,976 (2005); Median rent: $298 per month (2000); Median age of housing: 38 years (2000).
Transportation: Commute to work: 92.6% car, 0.0% public transportation, 4.0% walk, 3.4% work from home (2000); Travel time to work: 34.1% less than 15 minutes, 38.9% 15 to 30 minutes, 15.2% 30 to 45 minutes, 5.5% 45 to 60 minutes, 6.4% 60 minutes or more (2000)

GANG MILLS (CDP).
Covers a land area of 6.530 square miles and a water area of 0 square miles. Located at 42.15° N. Lat.; 77.11° W. Long.
Population: 2,699 (1990); 3,304 (2000); 3,608 (2005); 3,764 (2010 projected); Race: 81.9% White, 4.7% Black, 12.0% Asian, 2.5% Hispanic of any race (2005); Density: 552.5 persons per square mile (2005); Average household size: 2.51 (2005); Median age: 39.5 (2005); Males per 100 females: 92.3 (2005); Marriage status: 22.4% never married, 57.8% now married, 9.0% widowed, 10.8% divorced (2000); Foreign born: 6.9% (2000); Ancestry (includes multiple ancestries): 22.2% German, 20.0% English, 20.0% Irish, 13.7% Other groups, 11.3% Italian (2000).
Economy: Employment by occupation: 19.7% management, 42.7% professional, 10.3% services, 15.8% sales, 0.0% farming, 3.5% construction, 8.0% production (2000).
Income: Per capita income: $38,285 (2005); Median household income: $61,277 (2005); Average household income: $93,816 (2005); Percent of households with income of $100,000 or more: 30.4% (2005); Poverty rate: 8.3% (2000).
Education: Percent of population age 25 and over with: High school diploma (including GED) or higher: 88.1% (2005); Bachelor's degree or higher: 45.2% (2005); Master's degree or higher: 22.0% (2005).
Housing: Homeownership rate: 63.1% (2005); Median home value: $164,516 (2005); Median rent: $378 per month (2000); Median age of housing: 25 years (2000).
Transportation: Commute to work: 97.6% car, 0.0% public transportation, 1.1% walk, 1.3% work from home (2000); Travel time to work: 64.8% less than 15 minutes, 20.4% 15 to 30 minutes, 7.5% 30 to 45 minutes, 4.3% 45 to 60 minutes, 3.0% 60 minutes or more (2000)

GREENWOOD (town).
Covers a land area of 41.305 square miles and a water area of 0 square miles. Located at 42.13° N. Lat.; 77.67° W. Long.
Population: 898 (1990); 849 (2000); 853 (2005); 847 (2010 projected); Race: 97.8% White, 0.4% Black, 0.0% Asian, 0.5% Hispanic of any race (2005); Density: 20.7 persons per square mile (2005); Average household size: 2.57 (2005); Median age: 37.5 (2005); Males per 100 females: 103.6 (2005); Marriage status: 25.5% never married, 59.5% now married, 7.6% widowed, 7.3% divorced (2000); Foreign born: 1.5% (2000); Ancestry (includes multiple ancestries): 21.2% Irish, 20.5% German, 20.3% English, 8.7% United States or American, 4.8% Other groups (2000).
Economy: Single-family building permits issued: 4 (2005); Multi-family building permits issued: 0 (2005); Employment by occupation: 12.8% management, 14.2% professional, 13.1% services, 22.0% sales, 4.2% farming, 18.1% construction, 15.7% production (2000).

Income: Per capita income: $16,471 (2005); Median household income: $34,792 (2005); Average household income: $42,319 (2005); Percent of households with income of $100,000 or more: 6.0% (2005); Poverty rate: 19.5% (2000).
Education: Percent of population age 25 and over with: High school diploma (including GED) or higher: 79.1% (2005); Bachelor's degree or higher: 11.2% (2005); Master's degree or higher: 4.1% (2005).

School District(s)
Greenwood Central School District (PK-12)
    2003-04 Enrollment: 177 . . . . (607) 225-4292

Housing: Homeownership rate: 79.2% (2005); Median home value: $68,286 (2005); Median rent: $331 per month (2000); Median age of housing: 59 years (2000).
Transportation: Commute to work: 89.8% car, 0.0% public transportation, 4.3% walk, 5.2% work from home (2000); Travel time to work: 24.7% less than 15 minutes, 33.4% 15 to 30 minutes, 19.2% 30 to 45 minutes, 8.4% 45 to 60 minutes, 14.3% 60 minutes or more (2000)

HAMMONDSPORT (village). Covers a land area of 0.350 square miles and a water area of 0.019 square miles. Located at 42.40° N. Lat.; 77.22° W. Long. Elevation is 743 feet.
History: Birthplace of Glenn Curtiss, who made aviation experiments in the village. Museum. Incorporated 1871.
Population: 929 (1990); 731 (2000); 715 (2005); 697 (2010 projected); Race: 95.7% White, 2.2% Black, 0.3% Asian, 0.3% Hispanic of any race (2005); Density: 2,042.7 persons per square mile (2005); Average household size: 2.16 (2005); Median age: 42.3 (2005); Males per 100 females: 83.8 (2005); Marriage status: 25.3% never married, 56.4% now married, 9.1% widowed, 9.3% divorced (2000); Foreign born: 2.1% (2000); Ancestry (includes multiple ancestries): 27.0% German, 25.4% English, 20.1% Irish, 7.4% United States or American, 6.9% Italian (2000).
Economy: In grape-growing area; wine-making center. Manufacturing of metal products. Summer residential and recreational area. Single-family building permits issued: 0 (2005); Multi-family building permits issued: 0 (2005); Employment by occupation: 14.7% management, 34.7% professional, 13.6% services, 15.0% sales, 1.4% farming, 7.3% construction, 13.3% production (2000).
Income: Per capita income: $22,745 (2005); Median household income: $42,232 (2005); Average household income: $48,912 (2005); Percent of households with income of $100,000 or more: 6.3% (2005); Poverty rate: 5.8% (2000).
Education: Percent of population age 25 and over with: High school diploma (including GED) or higher: 90.6% (2005); Bachelor's degree or higher: 36.1% (2005); Master's degree or higher: 19.0% (2005).

School District(s)
Hammondsport Central School District (KG-12)
    2003-04 Enrollment: 649 . . . . (607) 569-5240

Housing: Homeownership rate: 64.7% (2005); Median home value: $106,410 (2005); Median rent: $381 per month (2000); Median age of housing: 60+ years (2000).
Transportation: Commute to work: 81.9% car, 0.0% public transportation, 11.8% walk, 4.3% work from home (2000); Travel time to work: 50.5% less than 15 minutes, 23.1% 15 to 30 minutes, 15.9% 30 to 45 minutes, 4.5% 45 to 60 minutes, 6.0% 60 minutes or more (2000)

Additional Information Contacts
Hammondsport Chamber of Commerce . . . . (607) 569-2989
http://www.hammondsport.org/

HARTSVILLE (town). Covers a land area of 36.176 square miles and a water area of 0.017 square miles. Located at 42.24° N. Lat.; 77.69° W. Long. Elevation is 1,484 feet.
Population: 546 (1990); 585 (2000); 705 (2005); 815 (2010 projected); Race: 99.4% White, 0.0% Black, 0.0% Asian, 0.3% Hispanic of any race (2005); Density: 19.5 persons per square mile (2005); Average household size: 2.48 (2005); Median age: 41.4 (2005); Males per 100 females: 111.7 (2005); Marriage status: 21.4% never married, 67.4% now married, 6.2% widowed, 4.9% divorced (2000); Foreign born: 1.2% (2000); Ancestry (includes multiple ancestries): 18.5% Irish, 18.4% English, 16.5% German, 14.7% United States or American, 5.7% Italian (2000).
Economy: Single-family building permits issued: 3 (2005); Multi-family building permits issued: 0 (2005); Employment by occupation: 11.3% management, 20.6% professional, 17.0% services, 15.2% sales, 2.8% farming, 14.5% construction, 18.4% production (2000).
Income: Per capita income: $21,798 (2005); Median household income: $47,059 (2005); Average household income: $54,111 (2005); Percent of households with income of $100,000 or more: 6.3% (2005); Poverty rate: 12.3% (2000).
Education: Percent of population age 25 and over with: High school diploma (including GED) or higher: 78.2% (2005); Bachelor's degree or higher: 12.4% (2005); Master's degree or higher: 6.9% (2005).
Housing: Homeownership rate: 90.8% (2005); Median home value: $76,800 (2005); Median rent: $325 per month (2000); Median age of housing: 27 years (2000).
Transportation: Commute to work: 95.4% car, 0.0% public transportation, 2.5% walk, 2.1% work from home (2000); Travel time to work: 27.4% less than 15 minutes, 42.0% 15 to 30 minutes, 12.0% 30 to 45 minutes, 9.5% 45 to 60 minutes, 9.1% 60 minutes or more (2000)

HORNBY (town). Covers a land area of 40.887 square miles and a water area of 0.014 square miles. Located at 42.22° N. Lat.; 77.02° W. Long. Elevation is 1,516 feet.
Population: 1,655 (1990); 1,742 (2000); 1,832 (2005); 1,913 (2010 projected); Race: 96.2% White, 1.1% Black, 1.1% Asian, 0.8% Hispanic of any race (2005); Density: 44.8 persons per square mile (2005); Average household size: 2.81 (2005); Median age: 37.5 (2005); Males per 100 females: 94.1 (2005); Marriage status: 21.8% never married, 63.4% now married, 4.5% widowed, 10.4% divorced (2000); Foreign born: 0.6% (2000); Ancestry (includes multiple ancestries): 15.7% United States or American, 14.3% English, 13.8% German, 13.0% Irish, 9.4% Other groups (2000).
Economy: Single-family building permits issued: 2 (2005); Multi-family building permits issued: 0 (2005); Employment by occupation: 6.6% management, 20.0% professional, 17.1% services, 20.1% sales, 1.1% farming, 12.8% construction, 22.3% production (2000).
Income: Per capita income: $19,657 (2005); Median household income: $41,756 (2005); Average household income: $55,234 (2005); Percent of households with income of $100,000 or more: 11.3% (2005); Poverty rate: 12.3% (2000).
Education: Percent of population age 25 and over with: High school diploma (including GED) or higher: 81.2% (2005); Bachelor's degree or higher: 15.6% (2005); Master's degree or higher: 7.6% (2005).
Housing: Homeownership rate: 89.0% (2005); Median home value: $94,474 (2005); Median rent: $342 per month (2000); Median age of housing: 31 years (2000).
Transportation: Commute to work: 96.3% car, 0.0% public transportation, 0.6% walk, 2.1% work from home (2000); Travel time to work: 27.1% less than 15 minutes, 53.2% 15 to 30 minutes, 14.2% 30 to 45 minutes, 3.0% 45 to 60 minutes, 2.5% 60 minutes or more (2000)

HORNELL (city). Covers a land area of 2.726 square miles and a water area of 0 square miles. Located at 42.32° N. Lat.; 77.66° W. Long. Elevation is 1,164 feet.
History: Settled 1790, incorporated 1906.
Population: 9,877 (1990); 9,019 (2000); 8,708 (2005); 8,380 (2010 projected); Race: 94.4% White, 3.2% Black, 0.8% Asian, 2.4% Hispanic of any race (2005); Density: 3,194.9 persons per square mile (2005); Average household size: 2.49 (2005); Median age: 35.5 (2005); Males per 100 females: 89.2 (2005); Marriage status: 28.2% never married, 50.8% now married, 8.9% widowed, 12.1% divorced (2000); Foreign born: 1.2% (2000); Ancestry (includes multiple ancestries): 23.8% Irish, 20.6% German, 13.9% Italian, 12.2% English, 8.8% United States or American (2000).
Economy: Light manufacturing, including electric equipment and electronics, woven synthetic fabrics. Single-family building permits issued: 4 (2005); Multi-family building permits issued: 0 (2005); Employment by occupation: 9.5% management, 20.3% professional, 22.1% services, 21.9% sales, 0.2% farming, 9.8% construction, 16.2% production (2000).
Income: Per capita income: $16,180 (2005); Median household income: $30,492 (2005); Average household income: $39,091 (2005); Percent of households with income of $100,000 or more: 5.2% (2005); Poverty rate: 21.4% (2000).
Education: Percent of population age 25 and over with: High school diploma (including GED) or higher: 82.6% (2005); Bachelor's degree or higher: 12.8% (2005); Master's degree or higher: 6.4% (2005).

School District(s)
Boces Steuben-Allegany (UG-UG)
    2003-04 Enrollment: 255 . . . . (607) 324-7880
Hornell City School District (KG-12)
    2003-04 Enrollment: 1,884 . . . . (607) 324-1302

Two-year College(s)
St James Mercy Hospital School of Radiologic Science
    Fall 2004 Enrollment: 28 .... (607) 324-8265
    2005-06 Tuition: In-state $4,000; Out-of-state $4,000

Housing: Homeownership rate: 55.6% (2005); Median home value: $74,259 (2005); Median rent: $349 per month (2000); Median age of housing: 60+ years (2000).
Hospitals: St. James Mercy Health System (220 beds)
Safety: Violent crime rate: 61.1 per 10,000 population; Property crime rate: 254.7 per 10,000 population (2004).
Newspapers: The Evening Tribune (Circulation 8,500)
Transportation: Commute to work: 87.2% car, 2.1% public transportation, 7.8% walk, 2.1% work from home (2000); Travel time to work: 58.9% less than 15 minutes, 20.2% 15 to 30 minutes, 10.1% 30 to 45 minutes, 4.3% 45 to 60 minutes, 6.6% 60 minutes or more (2000)

Additional Information Contacts
City of Hornell .... (607) 324-7421
    http://www.cityofhornell.com/
Hornell Area Chamber of Commerce............... (607) 324-0310
    http://www.hornellny.com/

HORNELLSVILLE (town).
Covers a land area of 43.470 square miles and a water area of 0.175 square miles. Located at 42.34° N. Lat.; 77.67° W. Long.
Population: 4,149 (1990); 4,042 (2000); 4,037 (2005); 4,041 (2010 projected); Race: 97.2% White, 0.8% Black, 1.0% Asian, 1.3% Hispanic of any race (2005); Density: 92.9 persons per square mile (2005); Average household size: 2.38 (2005); Median age: 45.6 (2005); Males per 100 females: 89.4 (2005); Marriage status: 17.8% never married, 61.6% now married, 10.3% widowed, 10.3% divorced (2000); Foreign born: 2.6% (2000); Ancestry (includes multiple ancestries): 23.6% German, 21.6% Irish, 17.9% English, 11.1% United States or American, 9.9% Italian (2000).
Economy: Single-family building permits issued: 10 (2005); Multi-family building permits issued: 0 (2005); Employment by occupation: 7.9% management, 24.3% professional, 12.8% services, 27.1% sales, 1.7% farming, 11.3% construction, 14.9% production (2000).
Income: Per capita income: $24,602 (2005); Median household income: $42,758 (2005); Average household income: $57,450 (2005); Percent of households with income of $100,000 or more: 12.7% (2005); Poverty rate: 8.4% (2000).
Education: Percent of population age 25 and over with: High school diploma (including GED) or higher: 85.8% (2005); Bachelor's degree or higher: 18.7% (2005); Master's degree or higher: 9.4% (2005).
Housing: Homeownership rate: 83.8% (2005); Median home value: $95,612 (2005); Median rent: $333 per month (2000); Median age of housing: 37 years (2000).
Transportation: Commute to work: 93.8% car, 0.8% public transportation, 3.4% walk, 2.0% work from home (2000); Travel time to work: 51.4% less than 15 minutes, 27.2% 15 to 30 minutes, 9.1% 30 to 45 minutes, 3.1% 45 to 60 minutes, 9.2% 60 minutes or more (2000)

HOWARD (town).
Covers a land area of 60.639 square miles and a water area of 0.101 square miles. Located at 42.34° N. Lat.; 77.51° W. Long. Elevation is 1,650 feet.
Population: 1,331 (1990); 1,430 (2000); 1,318 (2005); 1,289 (2010 projected); Race: 98.0% White, 0.5% Black, 0.0% Asian, 1.3% Hispanic of any race (2005); Density: 21.7 persons per square mile (2005); Average household size: 2.78 (2005); Median age: 37.4 (2005); Males per 100 females: 98.8 (2005); Marriage status: 23.1% never married, 62.1% now married, 6.1% widowed, 8.7% divorced (2000); Foreign born: 0.4% (2000); Ancestry (includes multiple ancestries): 24.6% English, 23.5% German, 18.4% Irish, 6.6% United States or American, 5.7% Italian (2000).
Economy: Single-family building permits issued: 6 (2005); Multi-family building permits issued: 0 (2005); Employment by occupation: 15.0% management, 16.6% professional, 15.0% services, 19.2% sales, 5.2% farming, 13.3% construction, 15.7% production (2000).
Income: Per capita income: $18,521 (2005); Median household income: $44,878 (2005); Average household income: $50,891 (2005); Percent of households with income of $100,000 or more: 8.9% (2005); Poverty rate: 8.4% (2000).
Education: Percent of population age 25 and over with: High school diploma (including GED) or higher: 85.8% (2005); Bachelor's degree or higher: 13.2% (2005); Master's degree or higher: 6.1% (2005).
Housing: Homeownership rate: 87.3% (2005); Median home value: $95,278 (2005); Median rent: $355 per month (2000); Median age of housing: 30 years (2000).
Transportation: Commute to work: 90.1% car, 0.0% public transportation, 2.9% walk, 7.0% work from home (2000); Travel time to work: 20.8% less than 15 minutes, 55.7% 15 to 30 minutes, 10.5% 30 to 45 minutes, 6.0% 45 to 60 minutes, 7.0% 60 minutes or more (2000)

JASPER (town).
Covers a land area of 52.678 square miles and a water area of 0 square miles. Located at 42.14° N. Lat.; 77.53° W. Long. Elevation is 1,578 feet.
Population: 1,232 (1990); 1,270 (2000); 1,227 (2005); 1,210 (2010 projected); Race: 97.5% White, 0.6% Black, 1.1% Asian, 0.3% Hispanic of any race (2005); Density: 23.3 persons per square mile (2005); Average household size: 3.10 (2005); Median age: 32.0 (2005); Males per 100 females: 102.5 (2005); Marriage status: 27.7% never married, 62.7% now married, 4.1% widowed, 5.5% divorced (2000); Foreign born: 0.2% (2000); Ancestry (includes multiple ancestries): 18.7% German, 14.9% English, 10.6% Irish, 10.3% United States or American, 4.5% Other groups (2000).
Economy: Single-family building permits issued: 24 (2005); Multi-family building permits issued: 0 (2005); Employment by occupation: 14.2% management, 13.6% professional, 9.6% services, 20.0% sales, 5.9% farming, 14.4% construction, 22.3% production (2000).
Income: Per capita income: $15,701 (2005); Median household income: $40,179 (2005); Average household income: $48,649 (2005); Percent of households with income of $100,000 or more: 9.6% (2005); Poverty rate: 20.6% (2000).
Taxes: Total city taxes per capita: $235 (2004); City property taxes per capita: $227 (2004).
Education: Percent of population age 25 and over with: High school diploma (including GED) or higher: 80.9% (2005); Bachelor's degree or higher: 9.4% (2005); Master's degree or higher: 5.6% (2005).

School District(s)
Jasper-Troupsburg Central School District (PK-12)
    2003-04 Enrollment: 664 .... (607) 792-3675

Housing: Homeownership rate: 83.3% (2005); Median home value: $76,098 (2005); Median rent: $307 per month (2000); Median age of housing: 44 years (2000).
Transportation: Commute to work: 80.5% car, 0.8% public transportation, 5.3% walk, 12.3% work from home (2000); Travel time to work: 32.7% less than 15 minutes, 20.7% 15 to 30 minutes, 29.6% 30 to 45 minutes, 9.1% 45 to 60 minutes, 8.0% 60 minutes or more (2000)

LINDLEY (town).
Covers a land area of 37.549 square miles and a water area of 0.342 square miles. Located at 42.04° N. Lat.; 77.14° W. Long. Elevation is 985 feet.
Population: 1,862 (1990); 1,913 (2000); 2,007 (2005); 2,074 (2010 projected); Race: 98.0% White, 0.4% Black, 0.1% Asian, 1.1% Hispanic of any race (2005); Density: 53.5 persons per square mile (2005); Average household size: 2.69 (2005); Median age: 36.8 (2005); Males per 100 females: 101.7 (2005); Marriage status: 19.7% never married, 66.8% now married, 5.6% widowed, 8.0% divorced (2000); Foreign born: 1.2% (2000); Ancestry (includes multiple ancestries): 18.2% English, 17.2% German, 13.0% United States or American, 11.6% Irish, 7.6% Other groups (2000).
Economy: Single-family building permits issued: 3 (2005); Multi-family building permits issued: 0 (2005); Employment by occupation: 9.4% management, 14.3% professional, 14.7% services, 17.5% sales, 0.6% farming, 15.4% construction, 28.1% production (2000).
Income: Per capita income: $18,511 (2005); Median household income: $42,440 (2005); Average household income: $49,869 (2005); Percent of households with income of $100,000 or more: 7.0% (2005); Poverty rate: 15.9% (2000).
Education: Percent of population age 25 and over with: High school diploma (including GED) or higher: 81.4% (2005); Bachelor's degree or higher: 9.2% (2005); Master's degree or higher: 2.9% (2005).
Housing: Homeownership rate: 87.8% (2005); Median home value: $98,378 (2005); Median rent: $358 per month (2000); Median age of housing: 26 years (2000).
Transportation: Commute to work: 93.9% car, 0.2% public transportation, 1.7% walk, 4.1% work from home (2000); Travel time to work: 16.9% less than 15 minutes, 55.1% 15 to 30 minutes, 20.4% 30 to 45 minutes, 5.3% 45 to 60 minutes, 2.3% 60 minutes or more (2000)

NORTH HORNELL (village). Covers a land area of 0.555 square miles and a water area of 0 square miles. Located at 42.34° N. Lat.; 77.66° W. Long.
Population: 822 (1990); 851 (2000); 873 (2005); 874 (2010 projected); Race: 96.4% White, 0.7% Black, 2.3% Asian, 1.6% Hispanic of any race (2005); Density: 1,573.0 persons per square mile (2005); Average household size: 2.76 (2005); Median age: 52.0 (2005); Males per 100 females: 79.6 (2005); Marriage status: 17.9% never married, 63.5% now married, 14.1% widowed, 4.5% divorced (2000); Foreign born: 4.8% (2000); Ancestry (includes multiple ancestries): 28.3% German, 27.3% Irish, 20.4% English, 11.3% Italian, 9.0% Other groups (2000).
Economy: Single-family building permits issued: 3 (2005); Multi-family building permits issued: 0 (2005); Employment by occupation: 10.6% management, 33.0% professional, 12.6% services, 28.7% sales, 1.1% farming, 8.0% construction, 6.0% production (2000).
Income: Per capita income: $28,243 (2005); Median household income: $53,409 (2005); Average household income: $72,318 (2005); Percent of households with income of $100,000 or more: 19.3% (2005); Poverty rate: 6.5% (2000).
Education: Percent of population age 25 and over with: High school diploma (including GED) or higher: 88.3% (2005); Bachelor's degree or higher: 31.1% (2005); Master's degree or higher: 12.7% (2005).
School District(s)
Hornell City School District (KG-12)
    2003-04 Enrollment: 1,884 . . . . (607) 324-1302
Housing: Homeownership rate: 86.1% (2005); Median home value: $115,888 (2005); Median rent: $314 per month (2000); Median age of housing: 54 years (2000).
Transportation: Commute to work: 91.8% car, 2.0% public transportation, 4.7% walk, 1.5% work from home (2000); Travel time to work: 56.7% less than 15 minutes, 21.1% 15 to 30 minutes, 8.6% 30 to 45 minutes, 3.3% 45 to 60 minutes, 10.4% 60 minutes or more (2000)

PAINTED POST (village). Covers a land area of 1.264 square miles and a water area of 0.061 square miles. Located at 42.16° N. Lat.; 77.09° W. Long. Elevation is 948 feet.
History: Settled before 1790; incorporated 1893.
Population: 1,950 (1990); 1,842 (2000); 1,750 (2005); 1,702 (2010 projected); Race: 93.9% White, 1.9% Black, 2.9% Asian, 1.5% Hispanic of any race (2005); Density: 1,384.3 persons per square mile (2005); Average household size: 2.23 (2005); Median age: 42.3 (2005); Males per 100 females: 85.6 (2005); Marriage status: 23.3% never married, 56.7% now married, 11.5% widowed, 8.6% divorced (2000); Foreign born: 3.4% (2000); Ancestry (includes multiple ancestries): 22.8% English, 21.2% Irish, 19.5% German, 11.4% Italian, 5.9% Dutch (2000).
Economy: Some manufacturing. Single-family building permits issued: 0 (2005); Multi-family building permits issued: 0 (2005); Employment by occupation: 13.9% management, 35.9% professional, 11.9% services, 20.2% sales, 0.0% farming, 4.9% construction, 13.3% production (2000).
Income: Per capita income: $27,125 (2005); Median household income: $48,037 (2005); Average household income: $60,137 (2005); Percent of households with income of $100,000 or more: 18.6% (2005); Poverty rate: 5.2% (2000).
Education: Percent of population age 25 and over with: High school diploma (including GED) or higher: 91.0% (2005); Bachelor's degree or higher: 35.1% (2005); Master's degree or higher: 18.0% (2005).
School District(s)
Corning City School District (PK-12)
    2003-04 Enrollment: 5,833 . . . . (607) 936-3704
Two-year College(s)
Steuben-Allegany BOCES-School of Practical Nursing-Coopers (Public)
    Fall 2004 Enrollment: 107 . . . . (607) 324-7880
Housing: Homeownership rate: 62.0% (2005); Median home value: $132,672 (2005); Median rent: $380 per month (2000); Median age of housing: 56 years (2000).
Safety: Violent crime rate: 16.6 per 10,000 population; Property crime rate: 138.4 per 10,000 population (2004).
Transportation: Commute to work: 93.9% car, 0.0% public transportation, 4.7% walk, 1.4% work from home (2000); Travel time to work: 68.1% less than 15 minutes, 20.9% 15 to 30 minutes, 7.9% 30 to 45 minutes, 1.5% 45 to 60 minutes, 1.5% 60 minutes or more (2000)

PRATTSBURGH (town). Covers a land area of 51.718 square miles and a water area of 0.027 square miles. Located at 42.53° N. Lat.; 77.33° W. Long. Elevation is 1,481 feet.
Population: 1,894 (1990); 2,064 (2000); 2,155 (2005); 2,239 (2010 projected); Race: 96.2% White, 1.4% Black, 0.1% Asian, 1.7% Hispanic of any race (2005); Density: 41.7 persons per square mile (2005); Average household size: 2.50 (2005); Median age: 38.6 (2005); Males per 100 females: 99.9 (2005); Marriage status: 23.7% never married, 58.9% now married, 7.4% widowed, 10.0% divorced (2000); Foreign born: 1.6% (2000); Ancestry (includes multiple ancestries): 23.5% German, 18.6% English, 13.4% Irish, 11.9% United States or American, 8.4% Other groups (2000).
Economy: Single-family building permits issued: 3 (2005); Multi-family building permits issued: 0 (2005); Employment by occupation: 11.1% management, 17.1% professional, 18.9% services, 17.6% sales, 1.6% farming, 13.2% construction, 20.6% production (2000).
Income: Per capita income: $17,809 (2005); Median household income: $36,690 (2005); Average household income: $44,573 (2005); Percent of households with income of $100,000 or more: 4.6% (2005); Poverty rate: 17.5% (2000).
Taxes: Total city taxes per capita: $304 (2004); City property taxes per capita: $286 (2004).
Education: Percent of population age 25 and over with: High school diploma (including GED) or higher: 83.5% (2005); Bachelor's degree or higher: 16.5% (2005); Master's degree or higher: 6.4% (2005).
School District(s)
Prattsburgh Central School District (PK-12)
    2003-04 Enrollment: 541 . . . . (607) 522-3795
Housing: Homeownership rate: 81.4% (2005); Median home value: $85,046 (2005); Median rent: $365 per month (2000); Median age of housing: 26 years (2000).
Transportation: Commute to work: 88.4% car, 0.0% public transportation, 6.4% walk, 4.7% work from home (2000); Travel time to work: 26.5% less than 15 minutes, 31.2% 15 to 30 minutes, 19.8% 30 to 45 minutes, 10.8% 45 to 60 minutes, 11.8% 60 minutes or more (2000)

PULTENEY (town). Covers a land area of 33.227 square miles and a water area of 3.193 square miles. Located at 42.53° N. Lat.; 77.18° W. Long. Elevation is 1,049 feet.
Population: 1,417 (1990); 1,405 (2000); 1,383 (2005); 1,361 (2010 projected); Race: 98.4% White, 0.7% Black, 0.0% Asian, 2.3% Hispanic of any race (2005); Density: 41.6 persons per square mile (2005); Average household size: 2.43 (2005); Median age: 44.0 (2005); Males per 100 females: 104.3 (2005); Marriage status: 18.7% never married, 66.3% now married, 7.1% widowed, 7.9% divorced (2000); Foreign born: 1.7% (2000); Ancestry (includes multiple ancestries): 27.4% German, 19.2% English, 14.9% Irish, 8.6% Italian, 6.9% United States or American (2000).
Economy: Single-family building permits issued: 2 (2005); Multi-family building permits issued: 0 (2005); Employment by occupation: 17.8% management, 13.1% professional, 13.6% services, 20.7% sales, 2.4% farming, 11.6% construction, 20.7% production (2000).
Income: Per capita income: $21,417 (2005); Median household income: $41,250 (2005); Average household income: $52,148 (2005); Percent of households with income of $100,000 or more: 7.7% (2005); Poverty rate: 9.7% (2000).
Education: Percent of population age 25 and over with: High school diploma (including GED) or higher: 79.0% (2005); Bachelor's degree or higher: 16.3% (2005); Master's degree or higher: 5.1% (2005).
Housing: Homeownership rate: 88.4% (2005); Median home value: $118,992 (2005); Median rent: $450 per month (2000); Median age of housing: 36 years (2000).
Transportation: Commute to work: 88.8% car, 0.0% public transportation, 2.3% walk, 7.5% work from home (2000); Travel time to work: 22.8% less than 15 minutes, 37.4% 15 to 30 minutes, 20.5% 30 to 45 minutes, 6.2% 45 to 60 minutes, 13.1% 60 minutes or more (2000)

RATHBONE (town). Covers a land area of 36.108 square miles and a water area of 0.006 square miles. Located at 42.14° N. Lat.; 77.35° W. Long.
Population: 892 (1990); 1,080 (2000); 1,122 (2005); 1,144 (2010 projected); Race: 98.1% White, 0.1% Black, 0.0% Asian, 1.1% Hispanic of any race (2005); Density: 31.1 persons per square mile (2005); Average household size: 2.87 (2005); Median age: 37.5 (2005); Males per 100 females: 97.2 (2005); Marriage status: 22.4% never married, 62.7% now

married, 5.4% widowed, 9.5% divorced (2000); Foreign born: 1.0% (2000); Ancestry (includes multiple ancestries): 18.7% United States or American, 13.9% German, 10.0% English, 9.6% Irish, 9.0% Dutch (2000).
Economy: Single-family building permits issued: 0 (2005); Multi-family building permits issued: 0 (2005); Employment by occupation: 10.7% management, 10.5% professional, 15.5% services, 17.6% sales, 0.8% farming, 12.0% construction, 32.8% production (2000).
Income: Per capita income: $16,390 (2005); Median household income: $41,217 (2005); Average household income: $47,033 (2005); Percent of households with income of $100,000 or more: 6.1% (2005); Poverty rate: 20.2% (2000).
Education: Percent of population age 25 and over with: High school diploma (including GED) or higher: 71.0% (2005); Bachelor's degree or higher: 7.5% (2005); Master's degree or higher: 3.1% (2005).
Housing: Homeownership rate: 85.7% (2005); Median home value: $91,356 (2005); Median rent: $347 per month (2000); Median age of housing: 26 years (2000).
Transportation: Commute to work: 89.7% car, 0.0% public transportation, 2.6% walk, 5.6% work from home (2000); Travel time to work: 11.1% less than 15 minutes, 34.5% 15 to 30 minutes, 37.0% 30 to 45 minutes, 10.9% 45 to 60 minutes, 6.6% 60 minutes or more (2000)

REXVILLE (unincorporated postal area, zip code 14877). Covers a land area of 49.739 square miles and a water area of 0.083 square miles. Located at 42.06° N. Lat.; 77.68° W. Long. Elevation is 1,841 feet.
Population: 0 (2000); Race: 99.4% White, 0.0% Black, 0.0% Asian, 0.2% Hispanic of any race (2000); Density: 0.0 persons per square mile (2000); Age: 24.3% under 18, 14.9% over 64 (2000); Marriage status: 25.2% never married, 59.3% now married, 6.0% widowed, 9.5% divorced (2000); Foreign born: 3.1% (2000); Ancestry (includes multiple ancestries): 23.1% German, 18.9% English, 17.7% Irish, 8.3% Other groups, 7.7% Italian (2000).
Economy: Employment by occupation: 17.6% management, 16.6% professional, 10.3% services, 17.6% sales, 2.4% farming, 20.3% construction, 15.2% production (2000).
Income: Per capita income: $14,003 (2000); Median household income: $34,375 (2000); Poverty rate: 17.6% (2000).
Education: Percent of population age 25 and over with: High school diploma (including GED) or higher: 81.1% (2000); Bachelor's degree or higher: 9.6% (2000).
Housing: Homeownership rate: 84.2% (2000); Median home value: $46,500 (2000); Median rent: $319 per month (2000); Median age of housing: 42 years (2000).
Transportation: Commute to work: 83.2% car, 0.0% public transportation, 7.7% walk, 9.1% work from home (2000); Travel time to work: 22.7% less than 15 minutes, 27.3% 15 to 30 minutes, 27.7% 30 to 45 minutes, 10.0% 45 to 60 minutes, 12.3% 60 minutes or more (2000)

RIVERSIDE (village). Covers a land area of 0.283 square miles and a water area of 0.005 square miles. Located at 42.15° N. Lat.; 77.07° W. Long.
Population: 585 (1990); 594 (2000); 565 (2005); 553 (2010 projected); Race: 95.2% White, 1.9% Black, 0.2% Asian, 2.5% Hispanic of any race (2005); Density: 1,993.4 persons per square mile (2005); Average household size: 2.62 (2005); Median age: 38.2 (2005); Males per 100 females: 90.9 (2005); Marriage status: 18.3% never married, 58.9% now married, 10.4% widowed, 12.4% divorced (2000); Foreign born: 2.0% (2000); Ancestry (includes multiple ancestries): 18.8% German, 17.6% Irish, 15.5% English, 8.1% Italian, 7.8% United States or American (2000).
Economy: Single-family building permits issued: 0 (2005); Multi-family building permits issued: 0 (2005); Employment by occupation: 14.1% management, 13.7% professional, 24.8% services, 20.0% sales, 0.0% farming, 3.7% construction, 23.7% production (2000).
Income: Per capita income: $19,566 (2005); Median household income: $39,787 (2005); Average household income: $51,181 (2005); Percent of households with income of $100,000 or more: 8.8% (2005); Poverty rate: 12.0% (2000).
Education: Percent of population age 25 and over with: High school diploma (including GED) or higher: 78.8% (2005); Bachelor's degree or higher: 7.4% (2005); Master's degree or higher: 3.7% (2005).
Housing: Homeownership rate: 74.5% (2005); Median home value: $79,153 (2005); Median rent: $479 per month (2000); Median age of housing: 51 years (2000).
Transportation: Commute to work: 95.0% car, 0.0% public transportation, 3.1% walk, 1.2% work from home (2000); Travel time to work: 54.1% less than 15 minutes, 34.9% 15 to 30 minutes, 6.7% 30 to 45 minutes, 2.4% 45 to 60 minutes, 2.0% 60 minutes or more (2000)

SAVONA (village). Covers a land area of 1.045 square miles and a water area of 0 square miles. Located at 42.28° N. Lat.; 77.21° W. Long.
Population: 974 (1990); 822 (2000); 858 (2005); 883 (2010 projected); Race: 98.4% White, 0.0% Black, 0.2% Asian, 0.9% Hispanic of any race (2005); Density: 821.0 persons per square mile (2005); Average household size: 2.55 (2005); Median age: 37.4 (2005); Males per 100 females: 92.8 (2005); Marriage status: 24.4% never married, 56.2% now married, 8.1% widowed, 11.3% divorced (2000); Foreign born: 0.4% (2000); Ancestry (includes multiple ancestries): 17.1% English, 17.0% German, 14.9% Irish, 13.9% United States or American, 7.9% Other groups (2000).
Economy: Flour, wood products. Single-family building permits issued: 0 (2005); Multi-family building permits issued: 0 (2005); Employment by occupation: 5.7% management, 10.4% professional, 19.3% services, 25.8% sales, 0.0% farming, 14.1% construction, 24.5% production (2000).
Income: Per capita income: $17,736 (2005); Median household income: $38,169 (2005); Average household income: $45,290 (2005); Percent of households with income of $100,000 or more: 5.4% (2005); Poverty rate: 13.9% (2000).
Education: Percent of population age 25 and over with: High school diploma (including GED) or higher: 80.9% (2005); Bachelor's degree or higher: 7.7% (2005); Master's degree or higher: 3.7% (2005).
School District(s)
Campbell-Savona Central School District (PK-12)
    2003-04 Enrollment: 1,218 . . . . (607) 527-4548
Housing: Homeownership rate: 73.2% (2005); Median home value: $86,792 (2005); Median rent: $394 per month (2000); Median age of housing: 60+ years (2000).
Transportation: Commute to work: 93.6% car, 0.0% public transportation, 2.7% walk, 2.4% work from home (2000); Travel time to work: 33.0% less than 15 minutes, 46.2% 15 to 30 minutes, 15.1% 30 to 45 minutes, 4.7% 45 to 60 minutes, 1.1% 60 minutes or more (2000)

SOUTH CORNING (village). Covers a land area of 0.615 square miles and a water area of 0 square miles. Located at 42.12° N. Lat.; 77.03° W. Long.
Population: 1,025 (1990); 1,147 (2000); 1,170 (2005); 1,196 (2010 projected); Race: 88.3% White, 8.9% Black, 1.9% Asian, 1.0% Hispanic of any race (2005); Density: 1,903.7 persons per square mile (2005); Average household size: 2.29 (2005); Median age: 40.5 (2005); Males per 100 females: 91.2 (2005); Marriage status: 27.0% never married, 55.2% now married, 9.0% widowed, 8.7% divorced (2000); Foreign born: 3.6% (2000); Ancestry (includes multiple ancestries): 18.1% German, 15.9% Irish, 15.5% English, 13.3% Other groups, 7.9% Italian (2000).
Economy: Single-family building permits issued: 6 (2005); Multi-family building permits issued: 0 (2005); Employment by occupation: 7.4% management, 25.5% professional, 14.5% services, 24.2% sales, 0.4% farming, 7.4% construction, 20.8% production (2000).
Income: Per capita income: $22,844 (2005); Median household income: $44,653 (2005); Average household income: $52,202 (2005); Percent of households with income of $100,000 or more: 10.0% (2005); Poverty rate: 7.8% (2000).
Education: Percent of population age 25 and over with: High school diploma (including GED) or higher: 85.9% (2005); Bachelor's degree or higher: 25.0% (2005); Master's degree or higher: 10.4% (2005).
Housing: Homeownership rate: 70.3% (2005); Median home value: $97,872 (2005); Median rent: $479 per month (2000); Median age of housing: 47 years (2000).
Transportation: Commute to work: 92.4% car, 0.4% public transportation, 5.9% walk, 0.0% work from home (2000); Travel time to work: 44.5% less than 15 minutes, 45.5% 15 to 30 minutes, 7.0% 30 to 45 minutes, 0.9% 45 to 60 minutes, 2.1% 60 minutes or more (2000)

THURSTON (town). Covers a land area of 36.429 square miles and a water area of 0.092 square miles. Located at 42.22° N. Lat.; 77.27° W. Long.
Population: 1,054 (1990); 1,309 (2000); 1,244 (2005); 1,222 (2010 projected); Race: 97.3% White, 0.9% Black, 0.3% Asian, 1.7% Hispanic of any race (2005); Density: 34.1 persons per square mile (2005); Average household size: 2.78 (2005); Median age: 37.0 (2005); Males per 100 females: 102.3 (2005); Marriage status: 23.7% never married, 60.0% now married, 6.1% widowed, 10.3% divorced (2000); Foreign born: 0.5% (2000); Ancestry (includes multiple ancestries): 14.4% German, 14.3%

Irish, 12.5% English, 10.3% United States or American, 8.9% Other groups (2000).
Economy: Single-family building permits issued: 4 (2005); Multi-family building permits issued: 0 (2005); Employment by occupation: 10.4% management, 12.8% professional, 13.8% services, 21.4% sales, 3.1% farming, 12.1% construction, 26.4% production (2000).
Income: Per capita income: $17,110 (2005); Median household income: $41,983 (2005); Average household income: $47,617 (2005); Percent of households with income of $100,000 or more: 5.8% (2005); Poverty rate: 12.1% (2000).
Education: Percent of population age 25 and over with: High school diploma (including GED) or higher: 78.3% (2005); Bachelor's degree or higher: 7.3% (2005); Master's degree or higher: 1.8% (2005).
Housing: Homeownership rate: 86.4% (2005); Median home value: $96,190 (2005); Median rent: $376 per month (2000); Median age of housing: 27 years (2000).
Transportation: Commute to work: 91.6% car, 0.4% public transportation, 2.1% walk, 5.5% work from home (2000); Travel time to work: 17.7% less than 15 minutes, 48.4% 15 to 30 minutes, 25.4% 30 to 45 minutes, 2.8% 45 to 60 minutes, 5.6% 60 minutes or more (2000)

TROUPSBURG (town). Covers a land area of 61.243 square miles and a water area of 0.014 square miles. Located at 42.05° N. Lat.; 77.54° W. Long.
Population: 1,006 (1990); 1,126 (2000); 1,239 (2005); 1,335 (2010 projected); Race: 96.4% White, 0.2% Black, 1.0% Asian, 2.2% Hispanic of any race (2005); Density: 20.2 persons per square mile (2005); Average household size: 2.93 (2005); Median age: 32.2 (2005); Males per 100 females: 93.0 (2005); Marriage status: 21.8% never married, 64.0% now married, 7.1% widowed, 7.0% divorced (2000); Foreign born: 0.7% (2000); Ancestry (includes multiple ancestries): 22.3% United States or American, 17.3% English, 14.5% German, 10.4% Irish, 4.5% Dutch (2000).
Economy: Single-family building permits issued: 21 (2005); Multi-family building permits issued: 0 (2005); Employment by occupation: 14.8% management, 15.5% professional, 6.4% services, 17.9% sales, 6.9% farming, 11.3% construction, 27.2% production (2000).
Income: Per capita income: $14,621 (2005); Median household income: $36,100 (2005); Average household income: $42,825 (2005); Percent of households with income of $100,000 or more: 4.3% (2005); Poverty rate: 19.7% (2000).
Education: Percent of population age 25 and over with: High school diploma (including GED) or higher: 78.4% (2005); Bachelor's degree or higher: 10.0% (2005); Master's degree or higher: 5.5% (2005).
School District(s)
Jasper-Troupsburg Central School District (PK-12)
    2003-04 Enrollment: 664 . . . . (607) 792-3675
Housing: Homeownership rate: 80.9% (2005); Median home value: $100,006 (2005); Median rent: $317 per month (2000); Median age of housing: 39 years (2000).
Transportation: Commute to work: 75.8% car, 0.0% public transportation, 7.0% walk, 16.6% work from home (2000); Travel time to work: 23.4% less than 15 minutes, 18.3% 15 to 30 minutes, 27.7% 30 to 45 minutes, 15.1% 45 to 60 minutes, 15.6% 60 minutes or more (2000)

TUSCARORA (town). Covers a land area of 37.753 square miles and a water area of 0.028 square miles. Located at 42.05° N. Lat.; 77.25° W. Long.
Population: 1,368 (1990); 1,400 (2000); 1,433 (2005); 1,439 (2010 projected); Race: 98.5% White, 0.1% Black, 0.3% Asian, 0.9% Hispanic of any race (2005); Density: 38.0 persons per square mile (2005); Average household size: 2.75 (2005); Median age: 35.5 (2005); Males per 100 females: 103.6 (2005); Marriage status: 24.5% never married, 62.0% now married, 6.0% widowed, 7.5% divorced (2000); Foreign born: 1.2% (2000); Ancestry (includes multiple ancestries): 21.1% United States or American, 12.2% Irish, 12.2% English, 11.6% German, 6.8% Other groups (2000).
Economy: Single-family building permits issued: 5 (2005); Multi-family building permits issued: 0 (2005); Employment by occupation: 9.0% management, 15.2% professional, 16.6% services, 20.5% sales, 2.3% farming, 14.3% construction, 22.2% production (2000).
Income: Per capita income: $16,678 (2005); Median household income: $36,716 (2005); Average household income: $45,873 (2005); Percent of households with income of $100,000 or more: 7.9% (2005); Poverty rate: 18.1% (2000).

Education: Percent of population age 25 and over with: High school diploma (including GED) or higher: 73.9% (2005); Bachelor's degree or higher: 9.2% (2005); Master's degree or higher: 3.0% (2005).
Housing: Homeownership rate: 82.0% (2005); Median home value: $75,577 (2005); Median rent: $311 per month (2000); Median age of housing: 27 years (2000).
Transportation: Commute to work: 95.5% car, 0.0% public transportation, 0.0% walk, 3.4% work from home (2000); Travel time to work: 20.9% less than 15 minutes, 39.1% 15 to 30 minutes, 24.9% 30 to 45 minutes, 8.6% 45 to 60 minutes, 6.5% 60 minutes or more (2000)

URBANA (town). Covers a land area of 41.113 square miles and a water area of 3.033 square miles. Located at 42.40° N. Lat.; 77.23° W. Long.
Population: 2,807 (1990); 2,546 (2000); 2,492 (2005); 2,434 (2010 projected); Race: 96.8% White, 1.3% Black, 0.7% Asian, 0.5% Hispanic of any race (2005); Density: 60.6 persons per square mile (2005); Average household size: 2.44 (2005); Median age: 46.4 (2005); Males per 100 females: 94.2 (2005); Marriage status: 20.9% never married, 62.9% now married, 6.5% widowed, 9.7% divorced (2000); Foreign born: 1.6% (2000); Ancestry (includes multiple ancestries): 22.1% English, 21.4% German, 17.3% Irish, 9.7% United States or American, 5.9% Other groups (2000).
Economy: Single-family building permits issued: 2 (2005); Multi-family building permits issued: 0 (2005); Employment by occupation: 13.0% management, 23.4% professional, 12.8% services, 20.3% sales, 0.5% farming, 12.5% construction, 17.5% production (2000).
Income: Per capita income: $22,935 (2005); Median household income: $44,057 (2005); Average household income: $54,528 (2005); Percent of households with income of $100,000 or more: 10.5% (2005); Poverty rate: 9.8% (2000).
Taxes: Total city taxes per capita: $536 (2004); City property taxes per capita: $505 (2004).
Education: Percent of population age 25 and over with: High school diploma (including GED) or higher: 83.4% (2005); Bachelor's degree or higher: 22.0% (2005); Master's degree or higher: 10.2% (2005).
Housing: Homeownership rate: 78.6% (2005); Median home value: $109,753 (2005); Median rent: $373 per month (2000); Median age of housing: 60 years (2000).
Transportation: Commute to work: 88.6% car, 0.0% public transportation, 5.7% walk, 5.0% work from home (2000); Travel time to work: 44.9% less than 15 minutes, 28.4% 15 to 30 minutes, 15.5% 30 to 45 minutes, 7.5% 45 to 60 minutes, 3.7% 60 minutes or more (2000)

WAYLAND (village). Covers a land area of 1.034 square miles and a water area of 0 square miles. Located at 42.56° N. Lat.; 77.59° W. Long. Elevation is 1,372 feet.
Population: 1,976 (1990); 1,893 (2000); 1,876 (2005); 1,854 (2010 projected); Race: 97.0% White, 1.2% Black, 0.6% Asian, 2.0% Hispanic of any race (2005); Density: 1,814.9 persons per square mile (2005); Average household size: 2.50 (2005); Median age: 38.3 (2005); Males per 100 females: 93.2 (2005); Marriage status: 21.9% never married, 61.3% now married, 7.6% widowed, 9.2% divorced (2000); Foreign born: 0.4% (2000); Ancestry (includes multiple ancestries): 39.5% German, 21.2% English, 17.7% Irish, 7.9% Italian, 7.3% United States or American (2000).
Economy: Single-family building permits issued: 0 (2005); Multi-family building permits issued: 0 (2005); Employment by occupation: 4.1% management, 19.7% professional, 13.0% services, 28.1% sales, 0.0% farming, 12.6% construction, 22.5% production (2000).
Income: Per capita income: $21,894 (2005); Median household income: $46,492 (2005); Average household income: $54,194 (2005); Percent of households with income of $100,000 or more: 7.3% (2005); Poverty rate: 7.8% (2000).
Taxes: Total city taxes per capita: $171 (2004); City property taxes per capita: $163 (2004).
Education: Percent of population age 25 and over with: High school diploma (including GED) or higher: 81.6% (2005); Bachelor's degree or higher: 14.3% (2005); Master's degree or higher: 5.1% (2005).
School District(s)
Wayland-Cohocton Central School District (PK-12)
    2003-04 Enrollment: 1,827 . . . . (585) 728-2211
Housing: Homeownership rate: 66.7% (2005); Median home value: $101,809 (2005); Median rent: $368 per month (2000); Median age of housing: 60+ years (2000).
Safety: Violent crime rate: 0.0 per 10,000 population; Property crime rate: 64.7 per 10,000 population (2004).

Transportation: Commute to work: 91.0% car, 0.0% public transportation, 5.1% walk, 2.8% work from home (2000); Travel time to work: 45.8% less than 15 minutes, 16.6% 15 to 30 minutes, 14.8% 30 to 45 minutes, 9.9% 45 to 60 minutes, 12.8% 60 minutes or more (2000)

WAYLAND (town).
Covers a land area of 39.032 square miles and a water area of 0.515 square miles. Located at 42.54° N. Lat.; 77.59° W. Long. Elevation is 1,372 feet.
History: Incorporated 1877.
Population: 4,311 (1990); 4,314 (2000); 4,268 (2005); 4,224 (2010 projected); Race: 97.2% White, 1.0% Black, 0.6% Asian, 1.7% Hispanic of any race (2005); Density: 109.3 persons per square mile (2005); Average household size: 2.55 (2005); Median age: 39.1 (2005); Males per 100 females: 96.6 (2005); Marriage status: 22.4% never married, 59.5% now married, 6.4% widowed, 11.7% divorced (2000); Foreign born: 0.6% (2000); Ancestry (includes multiple ancestries): 38.3% German, 22.3% English, 15.2% Irish, 6.7% United States or American, 6.3% Italian (2000).
Economy: Manufacturing of office furniture. Agriculture: dairy products; grain, onions, potatoes. Single-family building permits issued: 1 (2005); Multi-family building permits issued: 0 (2005); Employment by occupation: 7.9% management, 15.0% professional, 15.7% services, 25.6% sales, 2.0% farming, 12.3% construction, 21.4% production (2000).
Income: Per capita income: $21,272 (2005); Median household income: $48,061 (2005); Average household income: $53,806 (2005); Percent of households with income of $100,000 or more: 9.2% (2005); Poverty rate: 11.0% (2000).
Education: Percent of population age 25 and over with: High school diploma (including GED) or higher: 82.8% (2005); Bachelor's degree or higher: 10.5% (2005); Master's degree or higher: 4.0% (2005).
Housing: Homeownership rate: 75.9% (2005); Median home value: $97,321 (2005); Median rent: $368 per month (2000); Median age of housing: 48 years (2000).
Transportation: Commute to work: 94.8% car, 0.3% public transportation, 2.4% walk, 1.5% work from home (2000); Travel time to work: 42.5% less than 15 minutes, 19.3% 15 to 30 minutes, 16.2% 30 to 45 minutes, 8.6% 45 to 60 minutes, 13.4% 60 minutes or more (2000)

WAYNE (town).
Covers a land area of 20.698 square miles and a water area of 1.877 square miles. Located at 42.45° N. Lat.; 77.12° W. Long. Elevation is 1,165 feet.
Population: 1,029 (1990); 1,165 (2000); 1,164 (2005); 1,163 (2010 projected); Race: 97.3% White, 0.0% Black, 1.8% Asian, 0.3% Hispanic of any race (2005); Density: 56.2 persons per square mile (2005); Average household size: 2.32 (2005); Median age: 48.7 (2005); Males per 100 females: 94.6 (2005); Marriage status: 17.0% never married, 68.5% now married, 7.5% widowed, 7.0% divorced (2000); Foreign born: 2.9% (2000); Ancestry (includes multiple ancestries): 20.2% English, 18.7% German, 17.6% Irish, 9.1% Polish, 7.9% United States or American (2000).
Economy: Single-family building permits issued: 0 (2005); Multi-family building permits issued: 0 (2005); Employment by occupation: 16.9% management, 18.8% professional, 10.8% services, 23.7% sales, 1.5% farming, 8.1% construction, 20.2% production (2000).
Income: Per capita income: $25,449 (2005); Median household income: $43,636 (2005); Average household income: $59,009 (2005); Percent of households with income of $100,000 or more: 15.9% (2005); Poverty rate: 8.1% (2000).
Education: Percent of population age 25 and over with: High school diploma (including GED) or higher: 82.5% (2005); Bachelor's degree or higher: 21.8% (2005); Master's degree or higher: 11.2% (2005).
Housing: Homeownership rate: 89.4% (2005); Median home value: $115,708 (2005); Median rent: $405 per month (2000); Median age of housing: 44 years (2000).
Transportation: Commute to work: 94.1% car, 0.0% public transportation, 1.2% walk, 3.5% work from home (2000); Travel time to work: 23.0% less than 15 minutes, 40.3% 15 to 30 minutes, 13.6% 30 to 45 minutes, 10.2% 45 to 60 minutes, 12.8% 60 minutes or more (2000)

WEST UNION (town).
Covers a land area of 41.035 square miles and a water area of 0.083 square miles. Located at 42.05° N. Lat.; 77.69° W. Long.
Population: 412 (1990); 399 (2000); 407 (2005); 409 (2010 projected); Race: 98.0% White, 0.0% Black, 0.0% Asian, 2.0% Hispanic of any race (2005); Density: 9.9 persons per square mile (2005); Average household size: 2.79 (2005); Median age: 41.9 (2005); Males per 100 females: 110.9 (2005); Marriage status: 27.2% never married, 62.6% now married, 3.2% widowed, 7.0% divorced (2000); Foreign born: 2.2% (2000); Ancestry (includes multiple ancestries): 23.3% English, 21.8% German, 17.4% Irish, 11.5% Other groups, 7.1% Italian (2000).
Economy: Single-family building permits issued: 3 (2005); Multi-family building permits issued: 0 (2005); Employment by occupation: 23.0% management, 14.0% professional, 13.0% services, 16.0% sales, 3.5% farming, 16.5% construction, 14.0% production (2000).
Income: Per capita income: $16,720 (2005); Median household income: $44,310 (2005); Average household income: $46,610 (2005); Percent of households with income of $100,000 or more: 7.5% (2005); Poverty rate: 10.8% (2000).
Education: Percent of population age 25 and over with: High school diploma (including GED) or higher: 81.5% (2005); Bachelor's degree or higher: 7.7% (2005); Master's degree or higher: 3.8% (2005).
Housing: Homeownership rate: 81.5% (2005); Median home value: $79,643 (2005); Median rent: $225 per month (2000); Median age of housing: 36 years (2000).
Transportation: Commute to work: 78.9% car, 0.0% public transportation, 10.1% walk, 11.1% work from home (2000); Travel time to work: 20.9% less than 15 minutes, 27.1% 15 to 30 minutes, 29.4% 30 to 45 minutes, 10.7% 45 to 60 minutes, 11.9% 60 minutes or more (2000)

WHEELER (town).
Covers a land area of 46.095 square miles and a water area of 0.037 square miles. Located at 42.44° N. Lat.; 77.33° W. Long.
Population: 1,084 (1990); 1,263 (2000); 1,362 (2005); 1,453 (2010 projected); Race: 95.7% White, 1.1% Black, 0.6% Asian, 2.6% Hispanic of any race (2005); Density: 29.5 persons per square mile (2005); Average household size: 2.83 (2005); Median age: 37.1 (2005); Males per 100 females: 101.8 (2005); Marriage status: 25.5% never married, 59.8% now married, 4.5% widowed, 10.1% divorced (2000); Foreign born: 1.8% (2000); Ancestry (includes multiple ancestries): 19.7% German, 15.9% English, 14.5% Irish, 8.6% Other groups, 7.8% United States or American (2000).
Economy: Single-family building permits issued: 6 (2005); Multi-family building permits issued: 2 (2005); Employment by occupation: 8.6% management, 17.4% professional, 17.7% services, 16.0% sales, 3.2% farming, 13.5% construction, 23.6% production (2000).
Income: Per capita income: $16,594 (2005); Median household income: $40,697 (2005); Average household income: $46,840 (2005); Percent of households with income of $100,000 or more: 6.0% (2005); Poverty rate: 17.9% (2000).
Education: Percent of population age 25 and over with: High school diploma (including GED) or higher: 77.1% (2005); Bachelor's degree or higher: 14.8% (2005); Master's degree or higher: 5.3% (2005).
Housing: Homeownership rate: 83.6% (2005); Median home value: $90,588 (2005); Median rent: $342 per month (2000); Median age of housing: 24 years (2000).
Transportation: Commute to work: 87.3% car, 0.5% public transportation, 2.3% walk, 9.3% work from home (2000); Travel time to work: 28.8% less than 15 minutes, 37.9% 15 to 30 minutes, 17.9% 30 to 45 minutes, 7.4% 45 to 60 minutes, 8.0% 60 minutes or more (2000)

WOODHULL (town).
Covers a land area of 55.379 square miles and a water area of 0.024 square miles. Located at 42.06° N. Lat.; 77.38° W. Long.
Population: 1,518 (1990); 1,524 (2000); 1,470 (2005); 1,445 (2010 projected); Race: 96.1% White, 0.9% Black, 0.4% Asian, 2.0% Hispanic of any race (2005); Density: 26.5 persons per square mile (2005); Average household size: 2.72 (2005); Median age: 35.0 (2005); Males per 100 females: 100.5 (2005); Marriage status: 24.3% never married, 62.6% now married, 5.6% widowed, 7.5% divorced (2000); Foreign born: 0.7% (2000); Ancestry (includes multiple ancestries): 14.6% United States or American, 12.4% German, 12.1% English, 8.2% Irish, 6.5% Dutch (2000).
Economy: Cheese and other dairy products; poultry; grain. Single-family building permits issued: 0 (2005); Multi-family building permits issued: 0 (2005); Employment by occupation: 8.3% management, 17.6% professional, 10.6% services, 22.4% sales, 4.4% farming, 10.7% construction, 25.9% production (2000).
Income: Per capita income: $16,272 (2005); Median household income: $36,684 (2005); Average household income: $44,296 (2005); Percent of households with income of $100,000 or more: 6.5% (2005); Poverty rate: 16.3% (2000).

Education: Percent of population age 25 and over with: High school diploma (including GED) or higher: 77.5% (2005); Bachelor's degree or higher: 7.6% (2005); Master's degree or higher: 3.4% (2005).
Housing: Homeownership rate: 83.7% (2005); Median home value: $84,478 (2005); Median rent: $310 per month (2000); Median age of housing: 39 years (2000).
Transportation: Commute to work: 89.4% car, 0.5% public transportation, 2.8% walk, 6.7% work from home (2000); Travel time to work: 17.0% less than 15 minutes, 23.2% 15 to 30 minutes, 38.7% 30 to 45 minutes, 15.0% 45 to 60 minutes, 6.0% 60 minutes or more (2000)

Suffolk County

Located in southeastern New York; on Long Island, bounded on the south by the Atlantic Ocean, on the east by Block Island Sound, and on the north by Long Island Sound; includes many bays and inlets. Covers a land area of 912.20 square miles, a water area of 1,460.87 square miles, and is located in the Eastern Time Zone. The county government was organized in 1683. County seat is Riverhead.

Suffolk County is part of the New York-Northern New Jersey-Long Island, NY-NJ-PA Metropolitan Statistical Area. The entire metro area includes: Edison, NJ Metropolitan Division (Middlesex County, NJ; Monmouth County, NJ; Ocean County, NJ; Somerset County, NJ); Nassau-Suffolk, NY Metropolitan Division (Nassau County, NY; Suffolk County, NY); New York-White Plains-Wayne, NY-NJ Metropolitan Division (Bergen County, NJ; Hudson County, NJ; Passaic County, NJ; Bronx County, NY; Kings County, NY; New York County, NY; Putnam County, NY; Queens County, NY; Richmond County, NY; Rockland County, NY; Westchester County, NY); Newark-Union, NJ-PA Metropolitan Division (Essex County, NJ; Hunterdon County, NJ; Morris County, NJ; Sussex County, NJ; Union County, NJ; Pike County, PA)

Weather Station: Bridgehampton — Elevation: 59 feet

	Jan	Feb	Mar	Apr	May	Jun	Jul	Aug	Sep	Oct	Nov	Dec
High	38	39	46	56	65	74	81	80	73	63	53	44
Low	23	24	30	39	48	57	64	63	55	44	37	28
Precip	4.6	3.8	4.5	4.3	3.8	3.6	3.1	3.9	3.9	3.7	4.5	4.3
Snow	8.0	7.8	4.4	0.8	tr	0.0	0.0	0.0	0.0	tr	0.8	2.4

High and Low temperatures in degrees Fahrenheit; Precipitation and Snow in inches

Weather Station: Islip Macarthur Airport — Elevation: 82 feet

	Jan	Feb	Mar	Apr	May	Jun	Jul	Aug	Sep	Oct	Nov	Dec
High	na	na	na	na	na	na	na	na	na	na	na	na
Low	na	na	na	na	na	na	na	na	na	na	na	na
Precip	na	na	na	na	na	na	na	na	na	na	na	na
Snow	na	na	na	na	na	na	na	na	na	na	na	na

High and Low temperatures in degrees Fahrenheit; Precipitation and Snow in inches

Weather Station: Patchogue 2 N — Elevation: 52 feet

	Jan	Feb	Mar	Apr	May	Jun	Jul	Aug	Sep	Oct	Nov	Dec
High	39	41	49	59	69	78	83	82	75	65	54	44
Low	22	23	30	38	48	58	64	63	56	44	36	28
Precip	4.3	3.7	4.4	4.4	4.1	4.2	3.4	4.5	3.7	4.0	4.6	4.6
Snow	9.7	9.5	5.1	1.3	tr	0.0	0.0	0.0	0.0	tr	0.8	4.1

High and Low temperatures in degrees Fahrenheit; Precipitation and Snow in inches

Weather Station: Riverhead Research Farm — Elevation: 98 feet

	Jan	Feb	Mar	Apr	May	Jun	Jul	Aug	Sep	Oct	Nov	Dec
High	39	41	48	59	71	79	84	83	75	65	54	44
Low	24	26	32	40	50	59	65	64	58	47	39	30
Precip	4.3	3.5	4.2	4.1	3.8	3.6	3.2	4.1	3.6	3.9	4.3	4.0
Snow	8.8	8.6	4.1	0.7	tr	0.0	0.0	0.0	0.0	tr	0.5	3.0

High and Low temperatures in degrees Fahrenheit; Precipitation and Snow in inches

Weather Station: Setauket Strong — Elevation: 39 feet

	Jan	Feb	Mar	Apr	May	Jun	Jul	Aug	Sep	Oct	Nov	Dec
High	39	41	49	60	70	78	83	82	75	65	55	44
Low	24	25	32	40	50	59	65	64	58	47	39	30
Precip	3.9	3.0	4.1	4.2	3.9	3.7	3.6	3.9	3.6	3.9	3.9	4.0
Snow	4.1	3.8	2.0	0.2	0.0	0.0	0.0	0.0	0.0	0.0	0.1	1.4

High and Low temperatures in degrees Fahrenheit; Precipitation and Snow in inches

Population: 1,321,330 (1990); 1,419,369 (2000); 1,487,601 (2005); 1,558,321 (2010 projected); Race: 81.8% White, 7.8% Black, 3.2% Asian, 13.2% Hispanic of any race (2005); Density: 1,630.8 persons per square mile (2005); Average household size: 3.00 (2005); Median age: 37.9 (2005); Males per 100 females: 96.5 (2005).

Religion: Five largest groups: 51.7% Catholic Church, 7.0% Jewish Estimate, 1.6% The United Methodist Church, 1.4% Evangelical Lutheran Church in America, 1.1% Episcopal Church (2000).
Economy: Unemployment rate: 4.2% (2005); Total civilian labor force: 779,396 (2005); Leading industries: 14.8% health care and social assistance; 14.5% retail trade; 11.6% manufacturing (2003); Farms: 651 totaling 34,127 acres (2002); Companies that employ 500 or more persons: 71 (2003); Companies that employ 100 to 499 persons: 721 (2003); Companies that employ less than 100 persons: 45,311 (2003); Black-owned businesses: 4,432 (2002); Hispanic-owned businesses: 7,111 (2002); Women-owned businesses: 36,422 (2002); Retail sales per capita: $16,051 (2006). Single-family building permits issued: 4,241 (2005); Multi-family building permits issued: 942 (2005).
Income: Per capita income: $30,711 (2005); Median household income: $73,807 (2005); Average household income: $91,310 (2005); Percent of households with income of $100,000 or more: 32.7% (2005); Poverty rate: 7.3% (2003); Bankruptcy rate: 4.38% (2005).
Taxes: Total county taxes per capita: $1,067 (2004); County property taxes per capita: $363 (2004).
Education: Percent of population age 25 and over with: High school diploma (including GED) or higher: 86.1% (2005); Bachelor's degree or higher: 27.3% (2005); Master's degree or higher: 11.8% (2005).
Housing: Homeownership rate: 79.8% (2005); Median home value: $306,575 (2005); Median rent: $861 per month (2000); Median age of housing: 34 years (2000).
Health: Birth rate: 132.8 per 10,000 population (2004); Death rate: 78.1 per 10,000 population (2004); Age-adjusted cancer mortality rate: 217.6 deaths per 100,000 population (2002); Air Quality Index: 81.9% good, 15.3% moderate, 2.7% unhealthy for sensitive individuals, 0.0% unhealthy (percent of days in 2005); Number of physicians: 30.8 per 10,000 population (2004); Hospital beds: 33.2 per 10,000 population (2003); Hospital admissions: 1,044.7 per 10,000 population (2003).
Elections: 2004 Presidential election results: 48.5% Bush, 49.5% Kerry, 1.8% Nader, 0.1% Badnarik
National and State Parks: Belmont Lake State Park; Captree State Park; Caumsett State Park; Fire Island National Seashore; Gilgo State Park; Heckscher State Park; Hither Hills State Park; Middle Island State Game Farm; Morton National Wildlife Refuge; Orient Beach State Park; Robert Moses State Park; Sunken Meadow State Park; Wertheim National Wildlife Refuge; Wildwood State Park
Additional Information Contacts

Suffolk County Government . . . . (631) 852-1400
  http://www.co.suffolk.ny.us/
Town of Babylon . . . . (631) 957-3000
  http://www.townofbabylon.com/
Town of Brookhaven . . . . (631) 451-6955
  http://www.brookhaven.org/
Town of East Hampton . . . . (631) 324-4142
  http://www.town.east-hampton.ny.us/
Town of Huntington . . . . (631) 351-3030
  http://town.huntington.ny.us/
Town of Islip . . . . (631) 224-5691
  http://www.isliptown.org/
Town of Riverhead . . . . (631) 727-3200
  http://www.riverheadli.com/
Town of Smithtown . . . . (631) 360-7600
  http://www.smithtowninfo.com/
Town of Southampton . . . . (631) 283-6000
  http://www.town.southampton.ny.us/
Town of Southold . . . . (631) 765-1800
  http://southoldtown.northfork.net/
Village of Amityville . . . . (631) 264-6000
  http://www.amityville.com/
Village of Bellport . . . . (631) 286-0327
  http://www.bellportvillage.com/
Village of East Hampton . . . . (631) 324-4140
  http://www.town.east-hampton.ny.us/
Village of Lindenhurst . . . . (631) 957-7500
  http://www.villageoflindenhurst.com/
Village of Ocean Beach . . . . (631) 583-5940
  http://www.villageofoceanbeach.org/
Village of Old Field . . . . (631) 941-9412
  http://www.oldfieldny.org/
Village of Patchogue . . . . (631) 475-4300
  http://www.patchoguevillage.org/

Village of Port Jefferson............................ (631) 473-4724
  http://www.portjeff.com/
Village of Saltaire................................. (631) 583-5566
  http://www.saltaire.org/
Village of Southampton............................ (631) 283-6000
  http://www.town.southampton.ny.us/
Village of Westhampton Beach .... (631) 288-1654
  http://www.whbvillage.com/

Suffolk County Communities

AMAGANSETT (CDP). Covers a land area of 6.290 square miles and a water area of 1.755 square miles. Located at 40.98° N. Lat.; 72.12° W. Long. Elevation is 32 feet.
Population: 894 (1990); 1,067 (2000); 1,194 (2005); 1,317 (2010 projected); Race: 94.4% White, 3.0% Black, 0.5% Asian, 6.8% Hispanic of any race (2005); Density: 189.8 persons per square mile (2005); Average household size: 2.22 (2005); Median age: 50.3 (2005); Males per 100 females: 102.4 (2005); Marriage status: 18.6% never married, 60.4% now married, 10.4% widowed, 10.6% divorced (2000); Foreign born: 9.7% (2000); Ancestry (includes multiple ancestries): 25.5% English, 25.3% Irish, 21.6% German, 14.8% Italian, 10.5% Other groups (2000).
Economy: Employment by occupation: 14.1% management, 23.2% professional, 13.5% services, 29.7% sales, 0.4% farming, 12.8% construction, 6.3% production (2000).
Income: Per capita income: $46,292 (2005); Median household income: $69,041 (2005); Average household income: $102,546 (2005); Percent of households with income of $100,000 or more: 32.3% (2005); Poverty rate: 5.3% (2000).
Education: Percent of population age 25 and over with: High school diploma (including GED) or higher: 89.6% (2005); Bachelor's degree or higher: 43.1% (2005); Master's degree or higher: 15.3% (2005).
School District(s)
Amagansett Union Free School District (PK-06)
  2003-04 Enrollment: 125......................... (631) 267-3572
Housing: Homeownership rate: 78.1% (2005); Median home value: $928,763 (2005); Median rent: $864 per month (2000); Median age of housing: 33 years (2000).
Transportation: Commute to work: 68.3% car, 5.4% public transportation, 7.1% walk, 14.0% work from home (2000); Travel time to work: 55.1% less than 15 minutes, 22.6% 15 to 30 minutes, 5.5% 30 to 45 minutes, 2.8% 45 to 60 minutes, 14.0% 60 minutes or more (2000)

AMITYVILLE (village). Covers a land area of 2.094 square miles and a water area of 0.375 square miles. Located at 40.67° N. Lat.; 73.41° W. Long. Elevation is 25 feet.
History: Settled 1780, incorporated 1894.
Population: 9,197 (1990); 9,441 (2000); 9,628 (2005); 9,859 (2010 projected); Race: 80.8% White, 10.2% Black, 1.6% Asian, 12.1% Hispanic of any race (2005); Density: 4,597.7 persons per square mile (2005); Average household size: 2.74 (2005); Median age: 42.2 (2005); Males per 100 females: 90.5 (2005); Marriage status: 24.5% never married, 53.6% now married, 12.4% widowed, 9.5% divorced (2000); Foreign born: 8.7% (2000); Ancestry (includes multiple ancestries): 25.8% Irish, 20.7% Italian, 19.3% German, 16.6% Other groups, 8.0% English (2000).
Economy: Manufacturing: aircraft and aerospace parts, electronic and computer equipment, fiber optical systems, furniture, machinery, food service equipment. Single-family building permits issued: 15 (2005); Multi-family building permits issued: 2 (2005); Employment by occupation: 18.3% management, 21.2% professional, 12.5% services, 29.1% sales, 0.1% farming, 10.0% construction, 8.8% production (2000).
Income: Per capita income: $33,139 (2005); Median household income: $68,342 (2005); Average household income: $88,895 (2005); Percent of households with income of $100,000 or more: 30.6% (2005); Poverty rate: 7.5% (2000).
Education: Percent of population age 25 and over with: High school diploma (including GED) or higher: 85.3% (2005); Bachelor's degree or higher: 26.7% (2005); Master's degree or higher: 11.4% (2005).
School District(s)
Amityville Union Free School District (PK-12)
  2003-04 Enrollment: 3,083....................... (631) 598-6507
Two-year College(s)
Island Drafting and Technical Institute
  Fall 2004 Enrollment: 194....................... (631) 691-8733
  2005-06 Tuition: In-state $11,850; Out-of-state $11,850
Housing: Homeownership rate: 69.5% (2005); Median home value: $339,049 (2005); Median rent: $811 per month (2000); Median age of housing: 45 years (2000).
Hospitals: Brunswick Hospital Center (474 beds); South Oaks Hospital (217 beds)
Safety: Violent crime rate: 7.3 per 10,000 population; Property crime rate: 153.6 per 10,000 population (2004).
Newspapers: Amityville Record (General - Circulation 3,500)
Transportation: Commute to work: 83.1% car, 13.3% public transportation, 0.5% walk, 2.3% work from home (2000); Travel time to work: 28.5% less than 15 minutes, 29.3% 15 to 30 minutes, 15.9% 30 to 45 minutes, 6.6% 45 to 60 minutes, 19.6% 60 minutes or more (2000)
Additional Information Contacts
Amityville Chamber of Commerce..................... (631) 264-6000
  http://www.amityville.com
Village of Amityville................................ (631) 264-6000
  http://www.amityville.com/

AQUEBOGUE (CDP). Covers a land area of 3.838 square miles and a water area of 0.700 square miles. Located at 40.93° N. Lat.; 72.62° W. Long.
Population: 2,072 (1990); 2,254 (2000); 2,279 (2005); 2,284 (2010 projected); Race: 91.8% White, 6.0% Black, 0.3% Asian, 4.9% Hispanic of any race (2005); Density: 593.8 persons per square mile (2005); Average household size: 2.54 (2005); Median age: 42.3 (2005); Males per 100 females: 92.2 (2005); Marriage status: 22.0% never married, 64.2% now married, 7.6% widowed, 6.3% divorced (2000); Foreign born: 5.1% (2000); Ancestry (includes multiple ancestries): 23.8% German, 22.5% Polish, 20.8% Irish, 15.8% Italian, 13.6% Other groups (2000).
Economy: Summer-resort area. Employment by occupation: 15.9% management, 29.9% professional, 12.5% services, 29.4% sales, 1.2% farming, 9.0% construction, 2.0% production (2000).
Income: Per capita income: $30,184 (2005); Median household income: $60,640 (2005); Average household income: $74,769 (2005); Percent of households with income of $100,000 or more: 20.7% (2005); Poverty rate: 10.8% (2000).
Education: Percent of population age 25 and over with: High school diploma (including GED) or higher: 85.5% (2005); Bachelor's degree or higher: 29.2% (2005); Master's degree or higher: 11.7% (2005).
School District(s)
Riverhead Central School District (KG-12)
  2003-04 Enrollment: 4,862....................... (631) 369-6716
Housing: Homeownership rate: 86.6% (2005); Median home value: $289,169 (2005); Median rent: $669 per month (2000); Median age of housing: 23 years (2000).
Transportation: Commute to work: 90.1% car, 1.6% public transportation, 4.4% walk, 3.9% work from home (2000); Travel time to work: 36.7% less than 15 minutes, 31.5% 15 to 30 minutes, 14.8% 30 to 45 minutes, 8.0% 45 to 60 minutes, 9.0% 60 minutes or more (2000)

ASHAROKEN (village). Covers a land area of 1.367 square miles and a water area of 5.129 square miles. Located at 40.93° N. Lat.; 73.38° W. Long. Elevation is 10 feet.
Population: 807 (1990); 625 (2000); 585 (2005); 577 (2010 projected); Race: 95.4% White, 0.2% Black, 3.6% Asian, 2.6% Hispanic of any race (2005); Density: 428.1 persons per square mile (2005); Average household size: 2.42 (2005); Median age: 50.4 (2005); Males per 100 females: 107.4 (2005); Marriage status: 23.1% never married, 61.4% now married, 7.2% widowed, 8.3% divorced (2000); Foreign born: 7.2% (2000); Ancestry (includes multiple ancestries): 29.0% Irish, 23.3% Italian, 19.7% German, 10.6% English, 5.2% Polish (2000).
Economy: Resort village. Single-family building permits issued: 2 (2005); Multi-family building permits issued: 0 (2005); Employment by occupation: 18.1% management, 34.6% professional, 8.0% services, 27.7% sales, 0.8% farming, 7.7% construction, 3.0% production (2000).
Income: Per capita income: $57,262 (2005); Median household income: $114,655 (2005); Average household income: $138,233 (2005); Percent of households with income of $100,000 or more: 57.0% (2005); Poverty rate: 2.6% (2000).
Education: Percent of population age 25 and over with: High school diploma (including GED) or higher: 94.4% (2005); Bachelor's degree or higher: 53.1% (2005); Master's degree or higher: 26.6% (2005).
Housing: Homeownership rate: 87.2% (2005); Median home value: $926,587 (2005); Median rent: $1,344 per month (2000); Median age of housing: 38 years (2000).

Safety: Violent crime rate: 0.0 per 10,000 population; Property crime rate: 46.4 per 10,000 population (2004).
Transportation: Commute to work: 78.1% car, 13.0% public transportation, 2.2% walk, 6.6% work from home (2000); Travel time to work: 16.9% less than 15 minutes, 21.7% 15 to 30 minutes, 21.4% 30 to 45 minutes, 14.5% 45 to 60 minutes, 25.5% 60 minutes or more (2000).

BABYLON (village).
Covers a land area of 2.414 square miles and a water area of 0.345 square miles. Located at 40.69° N. Lat.; 73.32° W. Long. Elevation is 15 feet.
Population: 12,346 (1990); 12,615 (2000); 12,842 (2005); 13,142 (2010 projected); Race: 90.4% White, 3.2% Black, 1.9% Asian, 6.7% Hispanic of any race (2005); Density: 5,320.6 persons per square mile (2005); Average household size: 2.76 (2005); Median age: 39.2 (2005); Males per 100 females: 94.6 (2005); Marriage status: 23.3% never married, 61.8% now married, 7.5% widowed, 7.5% divorced (2000); Foreign born: 6.6% (2000); Ancestry (includes multiple ancestries): 30.7% Irish, 30.1% Italian, 22.8% German, 9.0% Other groups, 7.7% English (2000).
Economy: Single-family building permits issued: 6 (2005); Multi-family building permits issued: 0 (2005); Employment by occupation: 16.4% management, 24.4% professional, 11.2% services, 26.0% sales, 0.2% farming, 11.6% construction, 10.2% production (2000).
Income: Per capita income: $36,734 (2005); Median household income: $81,100 (2005); Average household income: $100,711 (2005); Percent of households with income of $100,000 or more: 37.9% (2005); Poverty rate: 4.1% (2000).
Education: Percent of population age 25 and over with: High school diploma (including GED) or higher: 91.0% (2005); Bachelor's degree or higher: 33.6% (2005); Master's degree or higher: 14.6% (2005).

School District(s)
Babylon Union Free School District (KG-12)
    2003-04 Enrollment: 2,009 . . . . (631) 893-7925

Housing: Homeownership rate: 76.1% (2005); Median home value: $354,995 (2005); Median rent: $905 per month (2000); Median age of housing: 46 years (2000).
Newspapers: The Beacon (General - Circulation 20,000)
Transportation: Commute to work: 82.4% car, 12.3% public transportation, 2.1% walk, 2.6% work from home (2000); Travel time to work: 24.1% less than 15 minutes, 29.9% 15 to 30 minutes, 18.1% 30 to 45 minutes, 6.4% 45 to 60 minutes, 21.6% 60 minutes or more (2000)
Additional Information Contacts
Babylon Chamber of Commerce . . . . (631) 661-7200
   http://www.babylonvillagechamber.org

BABYLON (town).
Covers a land area of 52.294 square miles and a water area of 61.871 square miles. Located at 40.71° N. Lat.; 73.36° W. Long. Elevation is 15 feet.
History: The 1st U.S. wireless station was built here by Marconi. Settled 1689, incorporated as a village 1893.
Population: 202,355 (1990); 211,792 (2000); 218,282 (2005); 225,543 (2010 projected); Race: 73.3% White, 16.5% Black, 2.5% Asian, 13.2% Hispanic of any race (2005); Density: 4,174.2 persons per square mile (2005); Average household size: 3.05 (2005); Median age: 37.5 (2005); Males per 100 females: 93.8 (2005); Marriage status: 27.8% never married, 57.0% now married, 7.9% widowed, 7.3% divorced (2000); Foreign born: 13.1% (2000); Ancestry (includes multiple ancestries): 30.2% Italian, 23.2% Other groups, 20.5% Irish, 15.0% German, 5.4% Polish (2000).
Economy: Unemployment rate: 4.7% (2005); Total civilian labor force: 112,755 (2005); Single-family building permits issued: 127 (2005); Multi-family building permits issued: 0 (2005); Employment by occupation: 12.0% management, 16.9% professional, 16.2% services, 30.4% sales, 0.1% farming, 10.7% construction, 13.7% production (2000).
Income: Per capita income: $26,025 (2005); Median household income: $66,558 (2005); Average household income: $78,644 (2005); Percent of households with income of $100,000 or more: 26.1% (2005); Poverty rate: 6.7% (2000).
Taxes: Total city taxes per capita: $430 (2004); City property taxes per capita: $364 (2004).
Education: Percent of population age 25 and over with: High school diploma (including GED) or higher: 82.1% (2005); Bachelor's degree or higher: 18.6% (2005); Master's degree or higher: 7.0% (2005).
Housing: Homeownership rate: 75.4% (2005); Median home value: $274,978 (2005); Median rent: $869 per month (2000); Median age of housing: 41 years (2000).
Transportation: Commute to work: 86.1% car, 9.6% public transportation, 1.8% walk, 1.7% work from home (2000); Travel time to work: 24.8% less than 15 minutes, 32.9% 15 to 30 minutes, 18.7% 30 to 45 minutes, 7.3% 45 to 60 minutes, 16.4% 60 minutes or more (2000)
Additional Information Contacts
Town of Babylon . . . . (631) 957-3000
   http://www.townofbabylon.com/

BAITING HOLLOW (CDP).
Covers a land area of 3.230 square miles and a water area of 2.203 square miles. Located at 40.96° N. Lat.; 72.74° W. Long. Elevation is 104 feet.
Population: 997 (1990); 1,449 (2000); 2,016 (2005); 2,542 (2010 projected); Race: 95.1% White, 1.9% Black, 0.5% Asian, 5.3% Hispanic of any race (2005); Density: 624.2 persons per square mile (2005); Average household size: 2.38 (2005); Median age: 45.2 (2005); Males per 100 females: 107.8 (2005); Marriage status: 22.6% never married, 67.9% now married, 3.1% widowed, 6.4% divorced (2000); Foreign born: 5.8% (2000); Ancestry (includes multiple ancestries): 24.1% Italian, 24.1% German, 22.7% Irish, 16.3% Polish, 10.8% English (2000).
Economy: Employment by occupation: 8.9% management, 34.6% professional, 9.9% services, 25.1% sales, 0.7% farming, 15.4% construction, 5.4% production (2000).
Income: Per capita income: $46,239 (2005); Median household income: $89,643 (2005); Average household income: $109,460 (2005); Percent of households with income of $100,000 or more: 43.2% (2005); Poverty rate: 4.4% (2000).
Education: Percent of population age 25 and over with: High school diploma (including GED) or higher: 91.6% (2005); Bachelor's degree or higher: 34.4% (2005); Master's degree or higher: 22.1% (2005).
Housing: Homeownership rate: 88.0% (2005); Median home value: $301,705 (2005); Median rent: $1,030 per month (2000); Median age of housing: 18 years (2000).
Transportation: Commute to work: 88.4% car, 6.3% public transportation, 0.0% walk, 5.4% work from home (2000); Travel time to work: 23.1% less than 15 minutes, 27.7% 15 to 30 minutes, 30.2% 30 to 45 minutes, 4.9% 45 to 60 minutes, 14.1% 60 minutes or more (2000)

BAY SHORE (CDP).
Covers a land area of 5.272 square miles and a water area of 0.814 square miles. Located at 40.73° N. Lat.; 73.25° W. Long. Elevation is 215 feet.
History: Named for its location on Great South Bay. Founded 1708.
Population: 21,279 (1990); 23,852 (2000); 24,381 (2005); 25,005 (2010 projected); Race: 61.9% White, 20.7% Black, 3.1% Asian, 25.3% Hispanic of any race (2005); Density: 4,624.8 persons per square mile (2005); Average household size: 2.92 (2005); Median age: 36.5 (2005); Males per 100 females: 97.1 (2005); Marriage status: 30.9% never married, 52.5% now married, 7.3% widowed, 9.3% divorced (2000); Foreign born: 14.2% (2000); Ancestry (includes multiple ancestries): 33.6% Other groups, 20.8% Italian, 19.4% Irish, 12.8% German, 4.3% English (2000).
Economy: It is noted as a fishing and duck-hunting center and has some light manufacturing. Employment by occupation: 10.7% management, 17.2% professional, 15.7% services, 29.2% sales, 0.8% farming, 12.4% construction, 13.9% production (2000).
Income: Per capita income: $25,931 (2005); Median household income: $56,144 (2005); Average household income: $73,094 (2005); Percent of households with income of $100,000 or more: 22.0% (2005); Poverty rate: 12.2% (2000).
Education: Percent of population age 25 and over with: High school diploma (including GED) or higher: 82.2% (2005); Bachelor's degree or higher: 20.7% (2005); Master's degree or higher: 8.4% (2005).

School District(s)
Bay Shore Union Free School District (KG-12)
    2003-04 Enrollment: 5,698 . . . . (631) 968-1117
Brentwood Union Free School District (PK-12)
    2003-04 Enrollment: 16,607 . . . . (631) 434-2325

Housing: Homeownership rate: 59.7% (2005); Median home value: $252,211 (2005); Median rent: $828 per month (2000); Median age of housing: 42 years (2000).
Hospitals: Southside Hospital (371 beds)
Transportation: Commute to work: 86.9% car, 8.7% public transportation, 2.0% walk, 1.6% work from home (2000); Travel time to work: 29.4% less than 15 minutes, 34.9% 15 to 30 minutes, 16.0% 30 to 45 minutes, 5.8% 45 to 60 minutes, 13.8% 60 minutes or more (2000)
Additional Information Contacts

Bay Shore Chamber of Commerce .... (631) 665-7003
http://www.bayshorecommerce.com

BAYPORT (CDP). Covers a land area of 3.713 square miles and a water area of 0.087 square miles. Located at 40.74° N. Lat.; 73.05° W. Long. Elevation is 31 feet.
Population: 7,702 (1990); 8,662 (2000); 9,811 (2005); 10,910 (2010 projected); Race: 95.3% White, 1.1% Black, 1.4% Asian, 5.2% Hispanic of any race (2005); Density: 2,642.2 persons per square mile (2005); Average household size: 2.65 (2005); Median age: 39.3 (2005); Males per 100 females: 92.4 (2005); Marriage status: 21.3% never married, 64.1% now married, 7.7% widowed, 6.9% divorced (2000); Foreign born: 3.8% (2000); Ancestry (includes multiple ancestries): 32.8% Italian, 31.1% Irish, 24.1% German, 9.5% English, 6.9% Other groups (2000).
Economy: In shore-resort area. Employment by occupation: 16.2% management, 25.3% professional, 11.0% services, 29.2% sales, 0.1% farming, 7.8% construction, 10.3% production (2000).
Income: Per capita income: $35,948 (2005); Median household income: $80,760 (2005); Average household income: $94,257 (2005); Percent of households with income of $100,000 or more: 37.3% (2005); Poverty rate: 3.5% (2000).
Education: Percent of population age 25 and over with: High school diploma (including GED) or higher: 90.9% (2005); Bachelor's degree or higher: 32.2% (2005); Master's degree or higher: 14.4% (2005).
School District(s)
Bayport-Blue Point Union Free School District (KG-12)
    2003-04 Enrollment: 2,490 .... (631) 472-7860
Housing: Homeownership rate: 67.7% (2005); Median home value: $369,843 (2005); Median rent: $883 per month (2000); Median age of housing: 34 years (2000).
Transportation: Commute to work: 90.1% car, 5.1% public transportation, 1.3% walk, 3.0% work from home (2000); Travel time to work: 24.2% less than 15 minutes, 34.8% 15 to 30 minutes, 20.6% 30 to 45 minutes, 8.0% 45 to 60 minutes, 12.4% 60 minutes or more (2000)

BAYWOOD (CDP). Covers a land area of 2.246 square miles and a water area of 0 square miles. Located at 40.75° N. Lat.; 73.29° W. Long.
Population: 7,351 (1990); 7,571 (2000); 7,612 (2005); 7,670 (2010 projected); Race: 66.2% White, 13.0% Black, 2.4% Asian, 30.3% Hispanic of any race (2005); Density: 3,389.3 persons per square mile (2005); Average household size: 3.36 (2005); Median age: 36.4 (2005); Males per 100 females: 96.9 (2005); Marriage status: 29.5% never married, 55.2% now married, 6.6% widowed, 8.7% divorced (2000); Foreign born: 13.3% (2000); Ancestry (includes multiple ancestries): 34.9% Other groups, 26.7% Italian, 18.1% Irish, 15.4% German, 4.8% Polish (2000).
Economy: Employment by occupation: 9.8% management, 14.8% professional, 16.4% services, 26.0% sales, 0.3% farming, 10.0% construction, 22.6% production (2000).
Income: Per capita income: $23,141 (2005); Median household income: $67,156 (2005); Average household income: $76,847 (2005); Percent of households with income of $100,000 or more: 24.3% (2005); Poverty rate: 5.5% (2000).
Education: Percent of population age 25 and over with: High school diploma (including GED) or higher: 80.8% (2005); Bachelor's degree or higher: 12.1% (2005); Master's degree or higher: 3.8% (2005).
Housing: Homeownership rate: 84.9% (2005); Median home value: $239,149 (2005); Median rent: $897 per month (2000); Median age of housing: 41 years (2000).
Transportation: Commute to work: 88.5% car, 8.6% public transportation, 0.4% walk, 1.6% work from home (2000); Travel time to work: 26.5% less than 15 minutes, 32.8% 15 to 30 minutes, 17.3% 30 to 45 minutes, 7.9% 45 to 60 minutes, 15.6% 60 minutes or more (2000)

BELLE TERRE (village). Covers a land area of 0.874 square miles and a water area of 0 square miles. Located at 40.95° N. Lat.; 73.06° W. Long. Elevation is 150 feet.
Population: 839 (1990); 832 (2000); 885 (2005); 919 (2010 projected); Race: 91.3% White, 1.2% Black, 4.9% Asian, 2.9% Hispanic of any race (2005); Density: 1,012.9 persons per square mile (2005); Average household size: 2.86 (2005); Median age: 47.0 (2005); Males per 100 females: 99.8 (2005); Marriage status: 21.7% never married, 67.5% now married, 6.3% widowed, 4.5% divorced (2000); Foreign born: 13.1% (2000); Ancestry (includes multiple ancestries): 20.4% Italian, 20.4% Irish, 14.7% German, 13.8% Other groups, 9.8% Russian (2000).
Economy: Summer resort village overlooking Port Jefferson Harbor. Single-family building permits issued: 1 (2005); Multi-family building permits issued: 0 (2005); Employment by occupation: 18.9% management, 49.8% professional, 7.8% services, 19.3% sales, 0.0% farming, 2.1% construction, 2.1% production (2000).
Income: Per capita income: $66,595 (2005); Median household income: $141,797 (2005); Average household income: $188,746 (2005); Percent of households with income of $100,000 or more: 67.3% (2005); Poverty rate: 1.4% (2000).
Education: Percent of population age 25 and over with: High school diploma (including GED) or higher: 98.2% (2005); Bachelor's degree or higher: 65.5% (2005); Master's degree or higher: 43.5% (2005).
Housing: Homeownership rate: 97.1% (2005); Median home value: $745,455 (2005); Median rent: $890 per month (2000); Median age of housing: 35 years (2000).
Transportation: Commute to work: 90.2% car, 3.3% public transportation, 1.2% walk, 5.3% work from home (2000); Travel time to work: 38.5% less than 15 minutes, 21.9% 15 to 30 minutes, 20.7% 30 to 45 minutes, 6.3% 45 to 60 minutes, 12.6% 60 minutes or more (2000)

BELLPORT (village). Covers a land area of 1.459 square miles and a water area of 0.091 square miles. Located at 40.75° N. Lat.; 72.94° W. Long. Elevation is 26 feet.
Population: 2,572 (1990); 2,363 (2000); 2,380 (2005); 2,414 (2010 projected); Race: 93.9% White, 1.5% Black, 2.3% Asian, 2.3% Hispanic of any race (2005); Density: 1,631.3 persons per square mile (2005); Average household size: 2.34 (2005); Median age: 48.2 (2005); Males per 100 females: 91.0 (2005); Marriage status: 21.5% never married, 61.5% now married, 8.2% widowed, 8.8% divorced (2000); Foreign born: 6.5% (2000); Ancestry (includes multiple ancestries): 27.4% Irish, 26.2% Italian, 21.8% German, 16.2% English, 10.2% Other groups (2000).
Economy: Summer resort village. Single-family building permits issued: 3 (2005); Multi-family building permits issued: 0 (2005); Employment by occupation: 12.0% management, 36.5% professional, 7.0% services, 28.4% sales, 0.0% farming, 10.2% construction, 5.9% production (2000).
Income: Per capita income: $44,963 (2005); Median household income: $88,401 (2005); Average household income: $105,194 (2005); Percent of households with income of $100,000 or more: 40.5% (2005); Poverty rate: 1.6% (2000).
Education: Percent of population age 25 and over with: High school diploma (including GED) or higher: 93.7% (2005); Bachelor's degree or higher: 42.6% (2005); Master's degree or higher: 24.9% (2005).
School District(s)
South Country Central School District (PK-12)
    2003-04 Enrollment: 4,758 .... (631) 286-4310
Housing: Homeownership rate: 83.6% (2005); Median home value: $329,293 (2005); Median rent: $746 per month (2000); Median age of housing: 48 years (2000).
Transportation: Commute to work: 86.9% car, 5.3% public transportation, 4.1% walk, 3.4% work from home (2000); Travel time to work: 30.7% less than 15 minutes, 27.8% 15 to 30 minutes, 22.7% 30 to 45 minutes, 6.6% 45 to 60 minutes, 12.1% 60 minutes or more (2000)
Additional Information Contacts
Village of Bellport.................................... (631) 286-0327
    http://www.bellportvillage.com/

BLUE POINT (CDP). Covers a land area of 1.781 square miles and a water area of 0.006 square miles. Located at 40.75° N. Lat.; 73.03° W. Long.
History: Bluepoint oysters take their name from here.
Population: 4,230 (1990); 4,407 (2000); 4,693 (2005); 4,982 (2010 projected); Race: 94.9% White, 1.0% Black, 1.6% Asian, 6.3% Hispanic of any race (2005); Density: 2,635.1 persons per square mile (2005); Average household size: 2.77 (2005); Median age: 39.8 (2005); Males per 100 females: 97.3 (2005); Marriage status: 22.0% never married, 63.4% now married, 6.6% widowed, 8.0% divorced (2000); Foreign born: 4.1% (2000); Ancestry (includes multiple ancestries): 30.0% Irish, 28.9% German, 26.9% Italian, 10.6% English, 8.2% Other groups (2000).
Economy: Building materials. Employment by occupation: 15.0% management, 32.3% professional, 11.4% services, 23.7% sales, 0.6% farming, 8.9% construction, 8.1% production (2000).
Income: Per capita income: $35,085 (2005); Median household income: $83,946 (2005); Average household income: $96,772 (2005); Percent of households with income of $100,000 or more: 38.1% (2005); Poverty rate: 3.6% (2000).

Education: Percent of population age 25 and over with: High school diploma (including GED) or higher: 90.7% (2005); Bachelor's degree or higher: 37.9% (2005); Master's degree or higher: 17.3% (2005).

School District(s)
Bayport-Blue Point Union Free School District (KG-12)
   2003-04 Enrollment: 2,490 . . . . (631) 472-7860

Housing: Homeownership rate: 83.6% (2005); Median home value: $329,371 (2005); Median rent: $858 per month (2000); Median age of housing: 44 years (2000).

Transportation: Commute to work: 90.9% car, 4.5% public transportation, 2.1% walk, 2.5% work from home (2000); Travel time to work: 23.8% less than 15 minutes, 36.7% 15 to 30 minutes, 19.1% 30 to 45 minutes, 7.0% 45 to 60 minutes, 13.4% 60 minutes or more (2000)

BOHEMIA (CDP). Covers a land area of 8.726 square miles and a water area of 0.032 square miles. Located at 40.77° N. Lat.; 73.11° W. Long. Elevation is 65 feet.

Population: 9,556 (1990); 9,871 (2000); 10,916 (2005); 11,926 (2010 projected); Race: 92.7% White, 1.3% Black, 3.2% Asian, 6.1% Hispanic of any race (2005); Density: 1,251.0 persons per square mile (2005); Average household size: 2.95 (2005); Median age: 39.7 (2005); Males per 100 females: 99.1 (2005); Marriage status: 21.7% never married, 63.0% now married, 8.7% widowed, 6.6% divorced (2000); Foreign born: 5.8% (2000); Ancestry (includes multiple ancestries): 38.5% Italian, 28.0% Irish, 22.3% German, 8.5% Other groups, 5.8% Polish (2000).

Economy: Light manufacturing. Employment by occupation: 12.8% management, 21.0% professional, 11.3% services, 31.3% sales, 0.0% farming, 11.2% construction, 12.5% production (2000).

Income: Per capita income: $31,164 (2005); Median household income: $72,585 (2005); Average household income: $89,587 (2005); Percent of households with income of $100,000 or more: 31.9% (2005); Poverty rate: 3.9% (2000).

Education: Percent of population age 25 and over with: High school diploma (including GED) or higher: 84.7% (2005); Bachelor's degree or higher: 20.6% (2005); Master's degree or higher: 8.4% (2005).

School District(s)
Connetquot Central School District (KG-12)
   2003-04 Enrollment: 7,160 . . . . (631) 244-2211

Two-year College(s)
Branford Hall Career Institute-Bohemia Campus
   Fall 2004 Enrollment: 404 . . . . (631) 589-1222

Housing: Homeownership rate: 79.4% (2005); Median home value: $302,029 (2005); Median rent: $926 per month (2000); Median age of housing: 30 years (2000).

Newspapers: Our Place (Holbrook/Holtsville Edition) (General - Circulation 18,900); Our Place (Ronkonkoma Lake Edition) (General - Circulation 32,000)

Transportation: Commute to work: 89.9% car, 6.4% public transportation, 1.2% walk, 1.8% work from home (2000); Travel time to work: 28.8% less than 15 minutes, 29.7% 15 to 30 minutes, 19.5% 30 to 45 minutes, 8.4% 45 to 60 minutes, 13.6% 60 minutes or more (2000)

BRENTWOOD (CDP). Covers a land area of 10.064 square miles and a water area of 0 square miles. Located at 40.78° N. Lat.; 73.24° W. Long. Elevation is 86 feet.

History: Josiah Warren led (1851) an experiment in communal living in Brentwood.

Population: 45,218 (1990); 53,917 (2000); 54,968 (2005); 56,275 (2010 projected); Race: 40.0% White, 20.5% Black, 2.1% Asian, 61.8% Hispanic of any race (2005); Density: 5,461.7 persons per square mile (2005); Average household size: 4.39 (2005); Median age: 32.6 (2005); Males per 100 females: 100.4 (2005); Marriage status: 33.8% never married, 55.0% now married, 4.5% widowed, 6.7% divorced (2000); Foreign born: 34.7% (2000); Ancestry (includes multiple ancestries): 58.4% Other groups, 7.9% Italian, 6.8% Irish, 4.4% German, 2.7% Haitian (2000).

Economy: Mainly residential, with various light industry. In the 1980s, Brentwood built the Heartland Industrial Park, which has spurred the town's growth. Employment by occupation: 7.2% management, 11.3% professional, 19.1% services, 24.5% sales, 0.3% farming, 9.9% construction, 27.9% production (2000).

Income: Per capita income: $16,565 (2005); Median household income: $62,397 (2005); Average household income: $71,208 (2005); Percent of households with income of $100,000 or more: 20.7% (2005); Poverty rate: 11.3% (2000).

Education: Percent of population age 25 and over with: High school diploma (including GED) or higher: 65.8% (2005); Bachelor's degree or higher: 11.2% (2005); Master's degree or higher: 4.3% (2005).

School District(s)
Brentwood Union Free School District (PK-12)
   2003-04 Enrollment: 16,607 . . . . (631) 434-2325

Four-year College(s)
Long Island University-Brentwood
   Fall 2004 Enrollment: 1,065. . . . . (631) 273-5112

Housing: Homeownership rate: 78.5% (2005); Median home value: $239,735 (2005); Median rent: $821 per month (2000); Median age of housing: 36 years (2000).

Transportation: Commute to work: 87.6% car, 7.2% public transportation, 2.1% walk, 1.0% work from home (2000); Travel time to work: 23.4% less than 15 minutes, 39.4% 15 to 30 minutes, 17.7% 30 to 45 minutes, 6.0% 45 to 60 minutes, 13.5% 60 minutes or more (2000)

BRIDGEHAMPTON (CDP). Covers a land area of 9.341 square miles and a water area of 1.835 square miles. Located at 40.93° N. Lat.; 72.30° W. Long. Elevation is 41 feet.

Population: 1,518 (1990); 1,381 (2000); 1,357 (2005); 1,387 (2010 projected); Race: 80.3% White, 15.2% Black, 1.3% Asian, 4.0% Hispanic of any race (2005); Density: 145.3 persons per square mile (2005); Average household size: 2.16 (2005); Median age: 50.4 (2005); Males per 100 females: 94.1 (2005); Marriage status: 22.0% never married, 60.5% now married, 10.5% widowed, 7.0% divorced (2000); Foreign born: 10.2% (2000); Ancestry (includes multiple ancestries): 24.2% Other groups, 19.6% English, 15.7% German, 10.5% Irish, 7.0% Polish (2000).

Economy: In dairying, farming and potato-growing area. Employment by occupation: 10.9% management, 25.3% professional, 15.6% services, 32.4% sales, 0.0% farming, 9.1% construction, 6.7% production (2000).

Income: Per capita income: $53,128 (2005); Median household income: $65,132 (2005); Average household income: $114,618 (2005); Percent of households with income of $100,000 or more: 37.0% (2005); Poverty rate: 8.5% (2000).

Education: Percent of population age 25 and over with: High school diploma (including GED) or higher: 89.7% (2005); Bachelor's degree or higher: 46.7% (2005); Master's degree or higher: 21.1% (2005).

School District(s)
Bridgehampton Union Free School District (PK-12)
   2003-04 Enrollment: 161. . . . . (631) 537-0221

Housing: Homeownership rate: 83.8% (2005); Median home value: $1 million+ (2005); Median rent: $951 per month (2000); Median age of housing: 20 years (2000).

Newspapers: Dan's Papers (General - Circulation 71,000); Montauk Pioneer (General - Circulation 10,000)

Transportation: Commute to work: 74.2% car, 4.2% public transportation, 6.8% walk, 12.1% work from home (2000); Travel time to work: 59.3% less than 15 minutes, 18.2% 15 to 30 minutes, 10.2% 30 to 45 minutes, 0.0% 45 to 60 minutes, 12.4% 60 minutes or more (2000)

BRIGHTWATERS (village). Covers a land area of 0.984 square miles and a water area of 0.043 square miles. Located at 40.72° N. Lat.; 73.26° W. Long. Elevation is 25 feet.

History: Laid out 1907, incorporated 1916.

Population: 3,265 (1990); 3,248 (2000); 3,282 (2005); 3,338 (2010 projected); Race: 93.5% White, 2.2% Black, 1.7% Asian, 5.6% Hispanic of any race (2005); Density: 3,333.8 persons per square mile (2005); Average household size: 2.87 (2005); Median age: 39.7 (2005); Males per 100 females: 94.1 (2005); Marriage status: 20.3% never married, 67.5% now married, 5.3% widowed, 7.0% divorced (2000); Foreign born: 4.1% (2000); Ancestry (includes multiple ancestries): 40.0% Irish, 31.8% Italian, 15.9% German, 11.2% English, 6.4% Other groups (2000).

Economy: Single-family building permits issued: 2 (2005); Multi-family building permits issued: 0 (2005); Employment by occupation: 23.0% management, 32.2% professional, 5.8% services, 29.0% sales, 0.0% farming, 2.5% construction, 7.5% production (2000).

Income: Per capita income: $47,393 (2005); Median household income: $97,041 (2005); Average household income: $136,125 (2005); Percent of households with income of $100,000 or more: 48.2% (2005); Poverty rate: 1.8% (2000).

Education: Percent of population age 25 and over with: High school diploma (including GED) or higher: 96.0% (2005); Bachelor's degree or higher: 53.8% (2005); Master's degree or higher: 22.7% (2005).

Housing: Homeownership rate: 90.8% (2005); Median home value: $410,515 (2005); Median rent: $829 per month (2000); Median age of housing: 51 years (2000).
Transportation: Commute to work: 83.5% car, 11.5% public transportation, 0.3% walk, 4.8% work from home (2000); Travel time to work: 29.4% less than 15 minutes, 24.8% 15 to 30 minutes, 16.7% 30 to 45 minutes, 7.7% 45 to 60 minutes, 21.5% 60 minutes or more (2000)

BROOKHAVEN (town).
Covers a land area of 259.287 square miles and a water area of 272.231 square miles. Located at 40.84° N. Lat.; 72.96° W. Long.
History: Brookhaven was the home of William Floyd (1743-1821), Revolutionary War soldier, statesman, and signer of the Declaration of Independence.
Population: 407,832 (1990); 448,248 (2000); 475,894 (2005); 503,899 (2010 projected); Race: 85.4% White, 5.3% Black, 3.8% Asian, 10.6% Hispanic of any race (2005); Density: 1,835.4 persons per square mile (2005); Average household size: 3.03 (2005); Median age: 36.4 (2005); Males per 100 females: 97.1 (2005); Marriage status: 26.8% never married, 60.0% now married, 6.1% widowed, 7.0% divorced (2000); Foreign born: 8.9% (2000); Ancestry (includes multiple ancestries): 32.8% Italian, 25.1% Irish, 19.5% German, 16.0% Other groups, 6.0% Polish (2000).
Economy: Unemployment rate: 4.2% (2005); Total civilian labor force: 252,744 (2005); Single-family building permits issued: 2,057 (2005); Multi-family building permits issued: 672 (2005); Employment by occupation: 12.7% management, 22.3% professional, 14.3% services, 29.1% sales, 0.2% farming, 11.0% construction, 10.4% production (2000).
Income: Per capita income: $28,560 (2005); Median household income: $72,201 (2005); Average household income: $85,512 (2005); Percent of households with income of $100,000 or more: 30.4% (2005); Poverty rate: 5.9% (2000).
Taxes: Total city taxes per capita: $336 (2004); City property taxes per capita: $240 (2004).
Education: Percent of population age 25 and over with: High school diploma (including GED) or higher: 86.9% (2005); Bachelor's degree or higher: 24.6% (2005); Master's degree or higher: 11.1% (2005).

School District(s)
South Country Central School District (PK-12)
    2003-04 Enrollment: 4,758 . . . . (631) 286-4310

Housing: Homeownership rate: 79.2% (2005); Median home value: $266,725 (2005); Median rent: $851 per month (2000); Median age of housing: 29 years (2000).
Transportation: Commute to work: 90.6% car, 4.6% public transportation, 1.9% walk, 2.2% work from home (2000); Travel time to work: 22.7% less than 15 minutes, 33.0% 15 to 30 minutes, 20.1% 30 to 45 minutes, 8.7% 45 to 60 minutes, 15.4% 60 minutes or more (2000)
Additional Information Contacts
Town of Brookhaven . . . . (631) 451-6955
   http://www.brookhaven.org/

BROOKHAVEN (CDP).
Covers a land area of 6.048 square miles and a water area of 0.133 square miles. Located at 40.77° N. Lat.; 72.91° W. Long.
Population: 3,311 (1990); 3,570 (2000); 3,998 (2005); 4,413 (2010 projected); Race: 80.9% White, 12.9% Black, 0.9% Asian, 9.2% Hispanic of any race (2005); Density: 661.0 persons per square mile (2005); Average household size: 3.18 (2005); Median age: 39.5 (2005); Males per 100 females: 89.0 (2005); Marriage status: 22.5% never married, 62.9% now married, 6.3% widowed, 8.3% divorced (2000); Foreign born: 5.2% (2000); Ancestry (includes multiple ancestries): 25.1% Irish, 21.9% German, 19.6% Italian, 13.1% Other groups, 11.5% English (2000).
Economy: Employment by occupation: 13.0% management, 26.8% professional, 13.1% services, 22.7% sales, 1.3% farming, 10.9% construction, 12.2% production (2000).
Income: Per capita income: $31,605 (2005); Median household income: $81,651 (2005); Average household income: $99,162 (2005); Percent of households with income of $100,000 or more: 37.3% (2005); Poverty rate: 11.5% (2000).
Education: Percent of population age 25 and over with: High school diploma (including GED) or higher: 87.4% (2005); Bachelor's degree or higher: 30.7% (2005); Master's degree or higher: 16.0% (2005).
Housing: Homeownership rate: 83.8% (2005); Median home value: $318,093 (2005); Median rent: $832 per month (2000); Median age of housing: 37 years (2000).
Transportation: Commute to work: 90.5% car, 1.3% public transportation, 1.0% walk, 5.7% work from home (2000); Travel time to work: 35.3% less than 15 minutes, 35.2% 15 to 30 minutes, 14.3% 30 to 45 minutes, 4.3% 45 to 60 minutes, 10.8% 60 minutes or more (2000)

CALVERTON (CDP).
Covers a land area of 28.003 square miles and a water area of 0.515 square miles. Located at 40.92° N. Lat.; 72.73° W. Long.
Population: 4,759 (1990); 5,704 (2000); 6,766 (2005); 7,749 (2010 projected); Race: 83.2% White, 9.5% Black, 1.4% Asian, 8.2% Hispanic of any race (2005); Density: 241.6 persons per square mile (2005); Average household size: 2.21 (2005); Median age: 44.3 (2005); Males per 100 females: 93.5 (2005); Marriage status: 20.3% never married, 55.8% now married, 12.7% widowed, 11.2% divorced (2000); Foreign born: 9.9% (2000); Ancestry (includes multiple ancestries): 23.8% Irish, 22.5% German, 21.6% Italian, 17.4% Other groups, 9.7% Polish (2000).
Economy: Employment by occupation: 9.5% management, 17.1% professional, 23.0% services, 30.1% sales, 0.5% farming, 10.0% construction, 9.9% production (2000).
Income: Per capita income: $26,523 (2005); Median household income: $43,323 (2005); Average household income: $58,502 (2005); Percent of households with income of $100,000 or more: 15.6% (2005); Poverty rate: 10.2% (2000).
Education: Percent of population age 25 and over with: High school diploma (including GED) or higher: 79.6% (2005); Bachelor's degree or higher: 15.9% (2005); Master's degree or higher: 5.8% (2005).

School District(s)
Riverhead Central School District (KG-12)
    2003-04 Enrollment: 4,862 . . . . (631) 369-6716
Riverhead Charter School (KG-05)
    2003-04 Enrollment: 264 . . . . (631) 369-5800

Housing: Homeownership rate: 83.9% (2005); Median home value: $129,861 (2005); Median rent: $825 per month (2000); Median age of housing: 23 years (2000).
Transportation: Commute to work: 91.0% car, 4.1% public transportation, 0.8% walk, 3.1% work from home (2000); Travel time to work: 30.9% less than 15 minutes, 28.2% 15 to 30 minutes, 20.6% 30 to 45 minutes, 9.4% 45 to 60 minutes, 11.0% 60 minutes or more (2000)

CENTER MORICHES (CDP).
Covers a land area of 5.014 square miles and a water area of 0.419 square miles. Located at 40.79° N. Lat.; 72.79° W. Long.
Population: 5,987 (1990); 6,655 (2000); 7,409 (2005); 8,116 (2010 projected); Race: 88.7% White, 5.3% Black, 1.1% Asian, 9.4% Hispanic of any race (2005); Density: 1,477.6 persons per square mile (2005); Average household size: 2.88 (2005); Median age: 37.2 (2005); Males per 100 females: 97.3 (2005); Marriage status: 23.1% never married, 64.4% now married, 5.8% widowed, 6.7% divorced (2000); Foreign born: 5.7% (2000); Ancestry (includes multiple ancestries): 29.8% Italian, 26.8% Irish, 22.9% German, 13.8% Other groups, 10.6% English (2000).
Economy: Employment by occupation: 12.1% management, 25.1% professional, 16.8% services, 24.8% sales, 0.9% farming, 11.7% construction, 8.6% production (2000).
Income: Per capita income: $27,191 (2005); Median household income: $70,099 (2005); Average household income: $77,046 (2005); Percent of households with income of $100,000 or more: 25.2% (2005); Poverty rate: 6.5% (2000).
Education: Percent of population age 25 and over with: High school diploma (including GED) or higher: 84.6% (2005); Bachelor's degree or higher: 23.4% (2005); Master's degree or higher: 10.2% (2005).

School District(s)
Center Moriches Union Free School District (KG-12)
    2003-04 Enrollment: 1,395 . . . . (631) 878-0052
Center Moriches Union Free School District (KG-12)
    2003-04 Enrollment: 1,395 . . . . (631) 878-0052

Housing: Homeownership rate: 79.4% (2005); Median home value: $263,749 (2005); Median rent: $895 per month (2000); Median age of housing: 34 years (2000).
Transportation: Commute to work: 91.7% car, 2.4% public transportation, 2.8% walk, 2.6% work from home (2000); Travel time to work: 22.6% less than 15 minutes, 31.5% 15 to 30 minutes, 22.5% 30 to 45 minutes, 12.0% 45 to 60 minutes, 11.4% 60 minutes or more (2000)

CENTEREACH (CDP). Covers a land area of 7.956 square miles and a water area of 0 square miles. Located at 40.87° N. Lat.; 73.08° W. Long. Elevation is 100 feet.
Population: 26,720 (1990); 27,285 (2000); 28,989 (2005); 30,720 (2010 projected); Race: 89.4% White, 2.4% Black, 4.5% Asian, 9.6% Hispanic of any race (2005); Density: 3,643.5 persons per square mile (2005); Average household size: 3.29 (2005); Median age: 36.8 (2005); Males per 100 females: 98.6 (2005); Marriage status: 26.1% never married, 62.4% now married, 5.2% widowed, 6.3% divorced (2000); Foreign born: 9.2% (2000); Ancestry (includes multiple ancestries): 36.7% Italian, 24.8% Irish, 19.1% German, 14.2% Other groups, 6.6% Polish (2000).
Economy: Employment by occupation: 13.7% management, 19.2% professional, 15.1% services, 31.3% sales, 0.1% farming, 9.7% construction, 10.8% production (2000).
Income: Per capita income: $27,794 (2005); Median household income: $77,964 (2005); Average household income: $89,925 (2005); Percent of households with income of $100,000 or more: 33.4% (2005); Poverty rate: 5.6% (2000).
Education: Percent of population age 25 and over with: High school diploma (including GED) or higher: 87.9% (2005); Bachelor's degree or higher: 22.3% (2005); Master's degree or higher: 8.5% (2005).
School District(s)
Middle Country Central School District (PK-12)
    2003-04 Enrollment: 11,630 . . . . (631) 285-8005
Housing: Homeownership rate: 87.9% (2005); Median home value: $271,042 (2005); Median rent: $869 per month (2000); Median age of housing: 34 years (2000).
Transportation: Commute to work: 91.9% car, 5.1% public transportation, 0.9% walk, 1.9% work from home (2000); Travel time to work: 23.8% less than 15 minutes, 34.4% 15 to 30 minutes, 18.9% 30 to 45 minutes, 7.5% 45 to 60 minutes, 15.4% 60 minutes or more (2000)

CENTERPORT (CDP). Covers a land area of 2.126 square miles and a water area of 1.440 square miles. Located at 40.89° N. Lat.; 73.37° W. Long. Elevation is 50 feet.
Population: 5,333 (1990); 5,446 (2000); 5,670 (2005); 5,912 (2010 projected); Race: 97.0% White, 0.2% Black, 1.6% Asian, 3.0% Hispanic of any race (2005); Density: 2,667.4 persons per square mile (2005); Average household size: 2.68 (2005); Median age: 41.7 (2005); Males per 100 females: 95.0 (2005); Marriage status: 20.3% never married, 67.8% now married, 5.8% widowed, 6.1% divorced (2000); Foreign born: 4.6% (2000); Ancestry (includes multiple ancestries): 29.7% Irish, 25.3% Italian, 22.0% German, 9.5% English, 6.4% Other groups (2000).
Economy: Employment by occupation: 24.4% management, 30.8% professional, 8.7% services, 24.7% sales, 0.0% farming, 7.1% construction, 4.3% production (2000).
Income: Per capita income: $53,385 (2005); Median household income: $112,850 (2005); Average household income: $141,840 (2005); Percent of households with income of $100,000 or more: 56.5% (2005); Poverty rate: 2.9% (2000).
Education: Percent of population age 25 and over with: High school diploma (including GED) or higher: 97.0% (2005); Bachelor's degree or higher: 57.7% (2005); Master's degree or higher: 20.7% (2005).
School District(s)
Harborfields Central School District (KG-12)
    2003-04 Enrollment: 3,560 . . . . (631) 754-5320
Housing: Homeownership rate: 90.8% (2005); Median home value: $549,355 (2005); Median rent: $1,057 per month (2000); Median age of housing: 44 years (2000).
Transportation: Commute to work: 82.8% car, 11.0% public transportation, 1.4% walk, 4.4% work from home (2000); Travel time to work: 19.6% less than 15 minutes, 25.4% 15 to 30 minutes, 20.6% 30 to 45 minutes, 13.6% 45 to 60 minutes, 20.8% 60 minutes or more (2000)

CENTRAL ISLIP (CDP). Covers a land area of 7.264 square miles and a water area of 0 square miles. Located at 40.78° N. Lat.; 73.19° W. Long. Elevation is 88 feet.
Population: 27,789 (1990); 31,950 (2000); 32,723 (2005); 33,605 (2010 projected); Race: 41.5% White, 30.2% Black, 3.8% Asian, 41.3% Hispanic of any race (2005); Density: 4,504.6 persons per square mile (2005); Average household size: 3.67 (2005); Median age: 32.9 (2005); Males per 100 females: 98.1 (2005); Marriage status: 35.2% never married, 52.1% now married, 4.2% widowed, 8.4% divorced (2000); Foreign born: 23.0% (2000); Ancestry (includes multiple ancestries): 50.8% Other groups, 10.0% Italian, 9.8% Irish, 6.5% German, 2.7% Jamaican (2000).
Economy: Employment by occupation: 7.9% management, 13.9% professional, 18.5% services, 29.3% sales, 0.2% farming, 9.7% construction, 20.6% production (2000).
Income: Per capita income: $19,548 (2005); Median household income: $60,763 (2005); Average household income: $70,951 (2005); Percent of households with income of $100,000 or more: 19.5% (2005); Poverty rate: 11.4% (2000).
Education: Percent of population age 25 and over with: High school diploma (including GED) or higher: 74.7% (2005); Bachelor's degree or higher: 15.1% (2005); Master's degree or higher: 5.7% (2005).
School District(s)
Central Islip Union Free School District (PK-12)
    2003-04 Enrollment: 6,741 . . . . (631) 348-5001
Four-year College(s)
New York Institute of Technology-Central Islip
    Fall 2004 Enrollment: 668 . . . . (631) 348-3000
    2005-06 Tuition: In-state $19,236; Out-of-state $19,236
Housing: Homeownership rate: 73.6% (2005); Median home value: $230,226 (2005); Median rent: $832 per month (2000); Median age of housing: 32 years (2000).
Transportation: Commute to work: 87.5% car, 7.3% public transportation, 1.9% walk, 1.1% work from home (2000); Travel time to work: 24.2% less than 15 minutes, 38.7% 15 to 30 minutes, 16.2% 30 to 45 minutes, 5.4% 45 to 60 minutes, 15.5% 60 minutes or more (2000)
Additional Information Contacts
Central Islip-Islandia Chamber. . . . . (631) 435-1658
    http://www.islipchamberofcommerce.com

COLD SPRING HARBOR (CDP). Covers a land area of 3.723 square miles and a water area of 0.188 square miles. Located at 40.86° N. Lat.; 73.44° W. Long. Elevation is 100 feet.
History: Was 19th-century whaling port.
Population: 4,789 (1990); 4,975 (2000); 5,238 (2005); 5,511 (2010 projected); Race: 96.2% White, 0.6% Black, 1.7% Asian, 2.7% Hispanic of any race (2005); Density: 1,406.9 persons per square mile (2005); Average household size: 2.84 (2005); Median age: 41.1 (2005); Males per 100 females: 95.0 (2005); Marriage status: 21.8% never married, 69.2% now married, 5.8% widowed, 3.2% divorced (2000); Foreign born: 5.9% (2000); Ancestry (includes multiple ancestries): 30.6% Irish, 30.5% Italian, 18.5% German, 11.4% English, 6.4% Polish (2000).
Economy: Summer-residence area. Site of Cold Spring Harbor Laboratory (neurobiology genome, plant genetics, and cancer research), DNA Learning Center, world's 1st biotech museum, and Cold Spring Harbor Fish Hatchery and Aquarium. Employment by occupation: 23.2% management, 30.8% professional, 5.6% services, 31.3% sales, 0.0% farming, 5.1% construction, 3.9% production (2000).
Income: Per capita income: $61,541 (2005); Median household income: $116,929 (2005); Average household income: $174,528 (2005); Percent of households with income of $100,000 or more: 56.4% (2005); Poverty rate: 2.2% (2000).
Education: Percent of population age 25 and over with: High school diploma (including GED) or higher: 94.3% (2005); Bachelor's degree or higher: 59.5% (2005); Master's degree or higher: 28.0% (2005).
School District(s)
Cold Spring Harbor Central School District (KG-12)
    2003-04 Enrollment: 2,092 . . . . (631) 692-8036
Housing: Homeownership rate: 89.3% (2005); Median home value: $674,889 (2005); Median rent: $963 per month (2000); Median age of housing: 43 years (2000).
Transportation: Commute to work: 74.1% car, 16.5% public transportation, 2.0% walk, 7.4% work from home (2000); Travel time to work: 20.6% less than 15 minutes, 28.5% 15 to 30 minutes, 18.9% 30 to 45 minutes, 8.6% 45 to 60 minutes, 23.5% 60 minutes or more (2000)

COMMACK (CDP). Covers a land area of 12.062 square miles and a water area of 0 square miles. Located at 40.84° N. Lat.; 73.28° W. Long. Elevation is 150 feet.
Population: 36,124 (1990); 36,367 (2000); 36,912 (2005); 37,549 (2010 projected); Race: 92.9% White, 0.8% Black, 4.9% Asian, 3.7% Hispanic of any race (2005); Density: 3,060.1 persons per square mile (2005); Average household size: 3.07 (2005); Median age: 40.1 (2005); Males per 100 females: 95.5 (2005); Marriage status: 19.2% never married, 69.9% now married, 6.5% widowed, 4.4% divorced (2000); Foreign born: 9.4% (2000);

Ancestry (includes multiple ancestries): 33.4% Italian, 19.4% Irish, 14.1% German, 12.6% Other groups, 7.7% Polish (2000).
Economy: Chiefly residential. Employment by occupation: 18.8% management, 27.1% professional, 10.9% services, 29.7% sales, 0.1% farming, 7.3% construction, 6.1% production (2000).
Income: Per capita income: $36,515 (2005); Median household income: $96,672 (2005); Average household income: $111,252 (2005); Percent of households with income of $100,000 or more: 47.8% (2005); Poverty rate: 2.8% (2000).
Education: Percent of population age 25 and over with: High school diploma (including GED) or higher: 92.6% (2005); Bachelor's degree or higher: 37.4% (2005); Master's degree or higher: 14.9% (2005).

School District(s)
Commack Union Free School District (KG-12)
 2003-04 Enrollment: 7,511 . . . . (631) 912-2010

Two-year College(s)
Long Island Business Institute
 Fall 2004 Enrollment: 917 . . . . (631) 499-7100
 2005-06 Tuition: In-state $9,750; Out-of-state $9,750

Housing: Homeownership rate: 93.3% (2005); Median home value: $423,452 (2005); Median rent: $1,155 per month (2000); Median age of housing: 36 years (2000).
Transportation: Commute to work: 88.1% car, 7.5% public transportation, 0.7% walk, 3.3% work from home (2000); Travel time to work: 22.4% less than 15 minutes, 32.8% 15 to 30 minutes, 17.8% 30 to 45 minutes, 8.1% 45 to 60 minutes, 18.9% 60 minutes or more (2000)

COPIAGUE
(CDP). Covers a land area of 3.190 square miles and a water area of 0.485 square miles. Located at 40.67° N. Lat.; 73.39° W. Long. Elevation is 25 feet.
Population: 20,769 (1990); 21,922 (2000); 22,681 (2005); 23,524 (2010 projected); Race: 76.9% White, 4.9% Black, 2.3% Asian, 27.5% Hispanic of any race (2005); Density: 7,109.3 persons per square mile (2005); Average household size: 3.06 (2005); Median age: 38.1 (2005); Males per 100 females: 100.1 (2005); Marriage status: 27.2% never married, 58.2% now married, 6.1% widowed, 8.4% divorced (2000); Foreign born: 21.7% (2000); Ancestry (includes multiple ancestries): 30.9% Italian, 23.9% Other groups, 19.4% Irish, 14.4% German, 6.4% Polish (2000).
Economy: Residential town on South shore of Long Island. Employment by occupation: 10.8% management, 12.9% professional, 15.6% services, 31.7% sales, 0.1% farming, 12.2% construction, 16.7% production (2000).
Income: Per capita income: $25,653 (2005); Median household income: $64,287 (2005); Average household income: $78,387 (2005); Percent of households with income of $100,000 or more: 25.3% (2005); Poverty rate: 8.0% (2000).
Education: Percent of population age 25 and over with: High school diploma (including GED) or higher: 76.9% (2005); Bachelor's degree or higher: 13.7% (2005); Master's degree or higher: 5.2% (2005).

School District(s)
Copiague Union Free School District (KG-12)
 2003-04 Enrollment: 4,821 . . . . (631) 842-4015

Housing: Homeownership rate: 76.4% (2005); Median home value: $259,635 (2005); Median rent: $872 per month (2000); Median age of housing: 41 years (2000).
Transportation: Commute to work: 84.9% car, 9.5% public transportation, 2.5% walk, 1.8% work from home (2000); Travel time to work: 23.9% less than 15 minutes, 32.2% 15 to 30 minutes, 19.3% 30 to 45 minutes, 8.4% 45 to 60 minutes, 16.2% 60 minutes or more (2000)

Additional Information Contacts
Copiague Chamber of Commerce . . . . (631) 226-2956
 http://copiaguechamber.org/

CORAM
(CDP). Covers a land area of 13.792 square miles and a water area of 0 square miles. Located at 40.89° N. Lat.; 73.01° W. Long. Elevation is 99 feet.
Population: 30,173 (1990); 34,923 (2000); 36,722 (2005); 38,588 (2010 projected); Race: 77.6% White, 10.6% Black, 4.4% Asian, 12.6% Hispanic of any race (2005); Density: 2,662.5 persons per square mile (2005); Average household size: 2.74 (2005); Median age: 36.7 (2005); Males per 100 females: 93.5 (2005); Marriage status: 26.3% never married, 60.1% now married, 5.8% widowed, 7.8% divorced (2000); Foreign born: 10.6% (2000); Ancestry (includes multiple ancestries): 31.7% Italian, 22.7% Other groups, 20.3% Irish, 15.5% German, 6.7% Polish (2000).
Economy: Employment by occupation: 14.8% management, 22.7% professional, 13.3% services, 31.6% sales, 0.2% farming, 9.1% construction, 8.3% production (2000).
Income: Per capita income: $28,773 (2005); Median household income: $69,462 (2005); Average household income: $78,217 (2005); Percent of households with income of $100,000 or more: 27.0% (2005); Poverty rate: 5.6% (2000).
Education: Percent of population age 25 and over with: High school diploma (including GED) or higher: 88.3% (2005); Bachelor's degree or higher: 26.3% (2005); Master's degree or higher: 11.1% (2005).

School District(s)
Longwood Central School District (KG-12)
 2003-04 Enrollment: 9,794 . . . . (631) 345-2172

Housing: Homeownership rate: 68.8% (2005); Median home value: $257,686 (2005); Median rent: $875 per month (2000); Median age of housing: 23 years (2000).
Transportation: Commute to work: 92.0% car, 4.6% public transportation, 0.7% walk, 2.1% work from home (2000); Travel time to work: 17.9% less than 15 minutes, 34.1% 15 to 30 minutes, 20.0% 30 to 45 minutes, 9.7% 45 to 60 minutes, 18.3% 60 minutes or more (2000)

CUTCHOGUE
(CDP). Covers a land area of 8.102 square miles and a water area of 0.422 square miles. Located at 41.01° N. Lat.; 72.47° W. Long.
Population: 2,627 (1990); 2,849 (2000); 2,920 (2005); 3,002 (2010 projected); Race: 92.1% White, 2.6% Black, 0.6% Asian, 8.5% Hispanic of any race (2005); Density: 360.4 persons per square mile (2005); Average household size: 2.53 (2005); Median age: 46.4 (2005); Males per 100 females: 98.5 (2005); Marriage status: 20.4% never married, 66.1% now married, 7.3% widowed, 6.3% divorced (2000); Foreign born: 8.4% (2000); Ancestry (includes multiple ancestries): 28.2% German, 25.4% Irish, 20.5% Polish, 16.1% English, 12.8% Italian (2000).
Economy: Farm, summer resort, and recreation area. Center of a thriving and growing region of vineyards and wineries. Employment by occupation: 21.0% management, 24.2% professional, 11.5% services, 21.0% sales, 3.8% farming, 10.5% construction, 7.9% production (2000).
Income: Per capita income: $39,230 (2005); Median household income: $70,775 (2005); Average household income: $98,257 (2005); Percent of households with income of $100,000 or more: 32.2% (2005); Poverty rate: 5.6% (2000).
Education: Percent of population age 25 and over with: High school diploma (including GED) or higher: 86.0% (2005); Bachelor's degree or higher: 41.1% (2005); Master's degree or higher: 19.4% (2005).

School District(s)
Mattituck-Cutchogue Union Free School District (KG-12)
 2003-04 Enrollment: 1,563 . . . . (631) 298-4242

Housing: Homeownership rate: 87.2% (2005); Median home value: $419,787 (2005); Median rent: $789 per month (2000); Median age of housing: 36 years (2000).
Transportation: Commute to work: 85.8% car, 2.6% public transportation, 4.4% walk, 4.7% work from home (2000); Travel time to work: 38.6% less than 15 minutes, 19.5% 15 to 30 minutes, 16.1% 30 to 45 minutes, 12.4% 45 to 60 minutes, 13.4% 60 minutes or more (2000)

Additional Information Contacts
Cutchogue-New Suffolk Chamber of Commerce . . . . (631) 734-2335
 http://www.cutchoguenewsuffolk.org

DEER PARK
(CDP). Covers a land area of 6.258 square miles and a water area of 0.004 square miles. Located at 40.76° N. Lat.; 73.33° W. Long. Elevation is 74 feet.
Population: 29,019 (1990); 28,316 (2000); 29,027 (2005); 29,810 (2010 projected); Race: 79.0% White, 11.1% Black, 3.9% Asian, 9.8% Hispanic of any race (2005); Density: 4,638.6 persons per square mile (2005); Average household size: 2.94 (2005); Median age: 38.5 (2005); Males per 100 females: 94.9 (2005); Marriage status: 24.7% never married, 61.8% now married, 7.9% widowed, 5.6% divorced (2000); Foreign born: 11.9% (2000); Ancestry (includes multiple ancestries): 42.1% Italian, 20.8% Irish, 16.9% Other groups, 12.2% German, 4.8% Polish (2000).
Economy: Substantial and very diverse manufacturing, much of it derived from supporting aircraft-aerospace industries. Employment by occupation: 13.6% management, 17.2% professional, 15.5% services, 30.2% sales, 0.0% farming, 11.9% construction, 11.6% production (2000).
Income: Per capita income: $27,429 (2005); Median household income: $68,895 (2005); Average household income: $80,051 (2005); Percent of

households with income of $100,000 or more: 27.8% (2005); Poverty rate: 4.7% (2000).
Education: Percent of population age 25 and over with: High school diploma (including GED) or higher: 85.1% (2005); Bachelor's degree or higher: 19.8% (2005); Master's degree or higher: 6.5% (2005).
School District(s)
Deer Park Union Free School District (PK-12)
    2003-04 Enrollment: 4,461 . . . . (631) 274-4010
Housing: Homeownership rate: 81.3% (2005); Median home value: $286,744 (2005); Median rent: $848 per month (2000); Median age of housing: 38 years (2000).
Transportation: Commute to work: 88.1% car, 8.8% public transportation, 1.2% walk, 1.3% work from home (2000); Travel time to work: 22.3% less than 15 minutes, 35.2% 15 to 30 minutes, 17.5% 30 to 45 minutes, 7.6% 45 to 60 minutes, 17.5% 60 minutes or more (2000)

DERING HARBOR (village).
Covers a land area of 0.240 square miles and a water area of 0.014 square miles. Located at 41.09° N. Lat.; 72.34° W. Long.
Population: 28 (1990); 13 (2000); 14 (2005); 15 (2010 projected); Race: 92.9% White, 0.0% Black, 0.0% Asian, 0.0% Hispanic of any race (2005); Density: 58.3 persons per square mile (2005); Average household size: 2.00 (2005); Median age: 48.3 (2005); Males per 100 females: 180.0 (2005); Marriage status: 0.0% never married, 84.6% now married, 0.0% widowed, 15.4% divorced (2000); Foreign born: 0.0% (2000); Ancestry (includes multiple ancestries): 38.5% English, 23.1% Other groups, 23.1% Scottish, 15.4% Polish, 15.4% Russian (2000).
Economy: In summer-resort area. Single-family building permits issued: 0 (2005); Multi-family building permits issued: 0 (2005); Employment by occupation: 100.0% management, 0.0% professional, 0.0% services, 0.0% sales, 0.0% farming, 0.0% construction, 0.0% production (2000).
Income: Per capita income: $35,179 (2005); Median household income: $32,500 (2005); Average household income: $70,357 (2005); Percent of households with income of $100,000 or more: 28.6% (2005); Poverty rate: 0.0% (2000).
Education: Percent of population age 25 and over with: High school diploma (including GED) or higher: 100.0% (2005); Bachelor's degree or higher: 100.0% (2005); Master's degree or higher: 44.4% (2005).
Housing: Homeownership rate: 85.7% (2005); Median home value: $1 million+ (2005); Median rent: $n/a per month (2000); Median age of housing: 60+ years (2000).
Transportation: Commute to work: 40.0% car, 0.0% public transportation, 60.0% walk, 0.0% work from home (2000); Travel time to work: 100.0% less than 15 minutes, 0.0% 15 to 30 minutes, 0.0% 30 to 45 minutes, 0.0% 45 to 60 minutes, 0.0% 60 minutes or more (2000)

DIX HILLS (CDP).
Covers a land area of 15.945 square miles and a water area of 0 square miles. Located at 40.79° N. Lat.; 73.33° W. Long.
Population: 25,849 (1990); 26,024 (2000); 27,083 (2005); 28,202 (2010 projected); Race: 82.6% White, 4.3% Black, 9.7% Asian, 5.1% Hispanic of any race (2005); Density: 1,698.5 persons per square mile (2005); Average household size: 3.22 (2005); Median age: 39.7 (2005); Males per 100 females: 97.8 (2005); Marriage status: 21.1% never married, 71.2% now married, 4.3% widowed, 3.5% divorced (2000); Foreign born: 14.2% (2000); Ancestry (includes multiple ancestries): 28.2% Italian, 20.1% Other groups, 13.7% Irish, 11.1% German, 8.3% Russian (2000).
Economy: Employment by occupation: 20.9% management, 32.8% professional, 7.3% services, 29.7% sales, 0.0% farming, 5.4% construction, 3.7% production (2000).
Income: Per capita income: $47,954 (2005); Median household income: $119,025 (2005); Average household income: $153,781 (2005); Percent of households with income of $100,000 or more: 59.2% (2005); Poverty rate: 2.9% (2000).
Education: Percent of population age 25 and over with: High school diploma (including GED) or higher: 93.5% (2005); Bachelor's degree or higher: 53.0% (2005); Master's degree or higher: 26.3% (2005).
School District(s)
Boces Western Suffolk (Suffolk 3) (UG-UG)
    2003-04 Enrollment: 1,185 . . . . (631) 549-4900
Commack Union Free School District (KG-12)
    2003-04 Enrollment: 7,511 . . . . (631) 912-2010
Half Hollow Hills Central School District (KG-12)
    2003-04 Enrollment: 9,661 . . . . (631) 592-3008

Four-year College(s)
Five Towns College
    Fall 2004 Enrollment: 1,421 . . . . (631) 424-7000
    2005-06 Tuition: In-state $14,100; Out-of-state $14,100
Housing: Homeownership rate: 96.4% (2005); Median home value: $641,955 (2005); Median rent: $1,207 per month (2000); Median age of housing: 31 years (2000).
Hospitals: Sagamore Childrens Psychiatric Center (69 beds)
Transportation: Commute to work: 83.5% car, 10.5% public transportation, 0.7% walk, 5.0% work from home (2000); Travel time to work: 20.7% less than 15 minutes, 33.7% 15 to 30 minutes, 16.7% 30 to 45 minutes, 7.6% 45 to 60 minutes, 21.2% 60 minutes or more (2000)

EAST FARMINGDALE (CDP).
Covers a land area of 5.379 square miles and a water area of 0.025 square miles. Located at 40.72° N. Lat.; 73.42° W. Long.
Population: 4,255 (1990); 5,400 (2000); 5,871 (2005); 6,331 (2010 projected); Race: 69.7% White, 15.3% Black, 5.6% Asian, 16.6% Hispanic of any race (2005); Density: 1,091.4 persons per square mile (2005); Average household size: 3.21 (2005); Median age: 35.8 (2005); Males per 100 females: 102.4 (2005); Marriage status: 28.2% never married, 58.9% now married, 6.0% widowed, 6.9% divorced (2000); Foreign born: 19.8% (2000); Ancestry (includes multiple ancestries): 22.8% Other groups, 22.5% Italian, 20.5% Irish, 13.3% German, 5.3% Polish (2000).
Economy: Employment by occupation: 11.2% management, 20.1% professional, 12.4% services, 34.5% sales, 0.0% farming, 8.2% construction, 13.6% production (2000).
Income: Per capita income: $28,367 (2005); Median household income: $73,870 (2005); Average household income: $88,796 (2005); Percent of households with income of $100,000 or more: 30.6% (2005); Poverty rate: 7.0% (2000).
Education: Percent of population age 25 and over with: High school diploma (including GED) or higher: 80.1% (2005); Bachelor's degree or higher: 21.9% (2005); Master's degree or higher: 8.2% (2005).
Housing: Homeownership rate: 74.0% (2005); Median home value: $299,161 (2005); Median rent: $968 per month (2000); Median age of housing: 43 years (2000).
Transportation: Commute to work: 82.0% car, 11.6% public transportation, 4.7% walk, 0.8% work from home (2000); Travel time to work: 28.4% less than 15 minutes, 31.4% 15 to 30 minutes, 20.1% 30 to 45 minutes, 5.3% 45 to 60 minutes, 14.8% 60 minutes or more (2000)

EAST HAMPTON (village).
Covers a land area of 4.759 square miles and a water area of 0.141 square miles. Located at 40.95° N. Lat.; 72.19° W. Long. Elevation is 36 feet.
Population: 1,403 (1990); 1,334 (2000); 1,314 (2005); 1,320 (2010 projected); Race: 90.8% White, 2.0% Black, 2.5% Asian, 13.3% Hispanic of any race (2005); Density: 276.1 persons per square mile (2005); Average household size: 2.12 (2005); Median age: 52.5 (2005); Males per 100 females: 96.7 (2005); Marriage status: 28.7% never married, 51.5% now married, 11.3% widowed, 8.4% divorced (2000); Foreign born: 17.0% (2000); Ancestry (includes multiple ancestries): 24.4% English, 19.5% Irish, 15.4% Other groups, 13.2% German, 8.6% Italian (2000).
Economy: Single-family building permits issued: 6 (2005); Multi-family building permits issued: 0 (2005); Employment by occupation: 13.6% management, 23.9% professional, 20.6% services, 28.1% sales, 0.8% farming, 9.4% construction, 3.6% production (2000).
Income: Per capita income: $48,334 (2005); Median household income: $62,500 (2005); Average household income: $101,907 (2005); Percent of households with income of $100,000 or more: 29.2% (2005); Poverty rate: 8.2% (2000).
Education: Percent of population age 25 and over with: High school diploma (including GED) or higher: 90.7% (2005); Bachelor's degree or higher: 45.4% (2005); Master's degree or higher: 16.6% (2005).
School District(s)
East Hampton Union Free School District (KG-12)
    2003-04 Enrollment: 1,971 . . . . (631) 329-4104
Springs Union Free School District (PK-08)
    2003-04 Enrollment: 591 . . . . (631) 324-0144
Housing: Homeownership rate: 72.3% (2005); Median home value: $1 million+ (2005); Median rent: $975 per month (2000); Median age of housing: 50 years (2000).
Safety: Violent crime rate: 14.7 per 10,000 population; Property crime rate: 1,201.2 per 10,000 population (2004).

Newspapers: East Hampton Independent (General - Circulation 12,000); The East Hampton Star (General - Circulation 15,516)
Transportation: Commute to work: 67.5% car, 1.5% public transportation, 13.0% walk, 16.3% work from home (2000); Travel time to work: 69.9% less than 15 minutes, 16.1% 15 to 30 minutes, 4.3% 30 to 45 minutes, 2.9% 45 to 60 minutes, 6.8% 60 minutes or more (2000)
Additional Information Contacts
East Hampton Chamber of Commerce . . . . (631) 324-0362
  http://www.easthamptonchamber.com
Village of East Hampton . . . . (631) 324-4140
  http://www.town.east-hampton.ny.us/

EAST HAMPTON (town).
Covers a land area of 74.303 square miles and a water area of 311.608 square miles. Located at 41.00° N. Lat.; 72.12° W. Long. Elevation is 36 feet.
History: Birthplace of John Howard Payne, whose home is now a museum. The village has 3 historic districts containing other significant buildings. Settled 1648, incorporated 1920.
Population: 16,132 (1990); 19,719 (2000); 21,340 (2005); 22,938 (2010 projected); Race: 84.3% White, 3.9% Black, 1.6% Asian, 22.0% Hispanic of any race (2005); Density: 287.2 persons per square mile (2005); Average household size: 2.48 (2005); Median age: 43.4 (2005); Males per 100 females: 99.6 (2005); Marriage status: 26.4% never married, 55.7% now married, 8.1% widowed, 9.7% divorced (2000); Foreign born: 18.2% (2000); Ancestry (includes multiple ancestries): 22.2% Irish, 21.5% Other groups, 16.6% German, 14.8% English, 12.3% Italian (2000).
Economy: Summer homes; diversified farming. Manufacturing of septic systems, jetties, stone revetments; sand and gravel. Fashionable, upper-income area. Single-family building permits issued: 235 (2005); Multi-family building permits issued: 0 (2005); Employment by occupation: 12.2% management, 18.1% professional, 22.3% services, 24.7% sales, 2.3% farming, 15.4% construction, 5.0% production (2000).
Income: Per capita income: $33,539 (2005); Median household income: $57,993 (2005); Average household income: $83,047 (2005); Percent of households with income of $100,000 or more: 25.7% (2005); Poverty rate: 9.0% (2000).
Taxes: Total city taxes per capita: $1,886 (2004); City property taxes per capita: $1,597 (2004).
Education: Percent of population age 25 and over with: High school diploma (including GED) or higher: 86.3% (2005); Bachelor's degree or higher: 35.5% (2005); Master's degree or higher: 14.4% (2005).
Housing: Homeownership rate: 76.2% (2005); Median home value: $491,500 (2005); Median rent: $881 per month (2000); Median age of housing: 25 years (2000).
Transportation: Commute to work: 83.4% car, 2.7% public transportation, 3.1% walk, 8.4% work from home (2000); Travel time to work: 51.3% less than 15 minutes, 27.6% 15 to 30 minutes, 11.1% 30 to 45 minutes, 2.3% 45 to 60 minutes, 7.6% 60 minutes or more (2000)
Additional Information Contacts
Town of East Hampton . . . . (631) 324-4142
  http://www.town.east-hampton.ny.us/

EAST HAMPTON NORTH (CDP).
Covers a land area of 5.578 square miles and a water area of 0 square miles. Located at 40.97° N. Lat.; 72.18° W. Long.
Population: 2,779 (1990); 3,587 (2000); 3,737 (2005); 3,879 (2010 projected); Race: 78.0% White, 7.8% Black, 2.4% Asian, 25.5% Hispanic of any race (2005); Density: 670.0 persons per square mile (2005); Average household size: 2.53 (2005); Median age: 42.3 (2005); Males per 100 females: 93.6 (2005); Marriage status: 24.7% never married, 53.5% now married, 10.4% widowed, 11.4% divorced (2000); Foreign born: 22.0% (2000); Ancestry (includes multiple ancestries): 27.0% Other groups, 21.2% Irish, 16.5% English, 12.8% German, 12.1% Italian (2000).
Economy: Employment by occupation: 10.9% management, 12.6% professional, 27.5% services, 23.2% sales, 2.1% farming, 14.4% construction, 9.2% production (2000).
Income: Per capita income: $31,166 (2005); Median household income: $50,946 (2005); Average household income: $78,893 (2005); Percent of households with income of $100,000 or more: 22.4% (2005); Poverty rate: 12.2% (2000).
Education: Percent of population age 25 and over with: High school diploma (including GED) or higher: 83.5% (2005); Bachelor's degree or higher: 27.8% (2005); Master's degree or higher: 12.9% (2005).

Housing: Homeownership rate: 74.6% (2005); Median home value: $469,048 (2005); Median rent: $783 per month (2000); Median age of housing: 24 years (2000).
Transportation: Commute to work: 89.0% car, 3.3% public transportation, 1.1% walk, 4.0% work from home (2000); Travel time to work: 47.9% less than 15 minutes, 29.9% 15 to 30 minutes, 13.7% 30 to 45 minutes, 1.7% 45 to 60 minutes, 6.8% 60 minutes or more (2000)

EAST ISLIP (CDP).
Covers a land area of 4.106 square miles and a water area of 0.252 square miles. Located at 40.73° N. Lat.; 73.18° W. Long. Elevation is 40 feet.
Population: 13,867 (1990); 14,078 (2000); 14,563 (2005); 15,106 (2010 projected); Race: 95.3% White, 0.8% Black, 1.7% Asian, 5.0% Hispanic of any race (2005); Density: 3,546.6 persons per square mile (2005); Average household size: 3.06 (2005); Median age: 37.9 (2005); Males per 100 females: 95.9 (2005); Marriage status: 22.4% never married, 64.8% now married, 7.0% widowed, 5.8% divorced (2000); Foreign born: 4.8% (2000); Ancestry (includes multiple ancestries): 35.1% Italian, 31.3% Irish, 21.5% German, 6.9% Other groups, 6.1% English (2000).
Economy: In summer resort area. Employment by occupation: 15.1% management, 21.6% professional, 13.3% services, 29.7% sales, 0.2% farming, 9.9% construction, 10.3% production (2000).
Income: Per capita income: $30,872 (2005); Median household income: $81,178 (2005); Average household income: $93,935 (2005); Percent of households with income of $100,000 or more: 36.3% (2005); Poverty rate: 3.7% (2000).
Education: Percent of population age 25 and over with: High school diploma (including GED) or higher: 90.1% (2005); Bachelor's degree or higher: 27.5% (2005); Master's degree or higher: 12.3% (2005).
School District(s)
East Islip Union Free School District (PK-12)
  2003-04 Enrollment: 5,432 . . . . (631) 224-2000
Housing: Homeownership rate: 85.5% (2005); Median home value: $325,424 (2005); Median rent: $834 per month (2000); Median age of housing: 41 years (2000).
Transportation: Commute to work: 88.6% car, 7.1% public transportation, 1.0% walk, 2.7% work from home (2000); Travel time to work: 23.3% less than 15 minutes, 34.8% 15 to 30 minutes, 17.2% 30 to 45 minutes, 7.4% 45 to 60 minutes, 17.3% 60 minutes or more (2000)
Additional Information Contacts
East Islip Chamber of Commerce . . . . (631) 859-5000
  http://www.islplife.com/eastislipchamber/

EAST MARION (CDP).
Covers a land area of 2.097 square miles and a water area of 0.129 square miles. Located at 41.12° N. Lat.; 72.34° W. Long. Elevation is 32 feet.
Population: 717 (1990); 756 (2000); 1,018 (2005); 1,263 (2010 projected); Race: 94.0% White, 1.3% Black, 1.1% Asian, 3.0% Hispanic of any race (2005); Density: 485.5 persons per square mile (2005); Average household size: 2.28 (2005); Median age: 50.8 (2005); Males per 100 females: 97.7 (2005); Marriage status: 18.0% never married, 67.6% now married, 9.3% widowed, 5.2% divorced (2000); Foreign born: 6.4% (2000); Ancestry (includes multiple ancestries): 21.0% Irish, 20.9% German, 15.9% English, 13.9% Polish, 13.9% Italian (2000).
Economy: Employment by occupation: 11.2% management, 15.6% professional, 12.2% services, 33.6% sales, 1.7% farming, 12.9% construction, 12.9% production (2000).
Income: Per capita income: $28,301 (2005); Median household income: $50,291 (2005); Average household income: $64,596 (2005); Percent of households with income of $100,000 or more: 14.1% (2005); Poverty rate: 5.8% (2000).
Education: Percent of population age 25 and over with: High school diploma (including GED) or higher: 88.4% (2005); Bachelor's degree or higher: 28.5% (2005); Master's degree or higher: 11.1% (2005).
Housing: Homeownership rate: 81.6% (2005); Median home value: $349,153 (2005); Median rent: $810 per month (2000); Median age of housing: 38 years (2000).
Transportation: Commute to work: 90.4% car, 5.0% public transportation, 0.0% walk, 4.6% work from home (2000); Travel time to work: 53.9% less than 15 minutes, 21.6% 15 to 30 minutes, 6.3% 30 to 45 minutes, 5.9% 45 to 60 minutes, 12.3% 60 minutes or more (2000)

EAST MORICHES (CDP).
Covers a land area of 5.441 square miles and a water area of 0.148 square miles. Located at 40.80° N. Lat.; 72.75° W. Long. Elevation is 29 feet.

Population: 4,021 (1990); 4,550 (2000); 5,122 (2005); 5,660 (2010 projected); Race: 93.6% White, 1.8% Black, 1.7% Asian, 7.1% Hispanic of any race (2005); Density: 941.4 persons per square mile (2005); Average household size: 2.97 (2005); Median age: 39.8 (2005); Males per 100 females: 97.5 (2005); Marriage status: 22.0% never married, 65.8% now married, 7.4% widowed, 4.7% divorced (2000); Foreign born: 3.5% (2000); Ancestry (includes multiple ancestries): 33.6% Italian, 28.0% Irish, 22.0% German, 12.6% English, 9.6% Other groups (2000).
Economy: In shore-resort area. Employment by occupation: 12.7% management, 22.0% professional, 21.6% services, 26.7% sales, 0.7% farming, 10.8% construction, 5.5% production (2000).
Income: Per capita income: $30,436 (2005); Median household income: $74,496 (2005); Average household income: $89,034 (2005); Percent of households with income of $100,000 or more: 33.9% (2005); Poverty rate: 3.5% (2000).
Education: Percent of population age 25 and over with: High school diploma (including GED) or higher: 87.3% (2005); Bachelor's degree or higher: 26.7% (2005); Master's degree or higher: 12.3% (2005).

School District(s)
East Moriches Union Free School District (KG-08)
    2003-04 Enrollment: 745 . . . . (631) 878-0162

Housing: Homeownership rate: 88.0% (2005); Median home value: $285,559 (2005); Median rent: $771 per month (2000); Median age of housing: 28 years (2000).
Transportation: Commute to work: 94.4% car, 0.5% public transportation, 0.8% walk, 3.5% work from home (2000); Travel time to work: 23.4% less than 15 minutes, 31.2% 15 to 30 minutes, 19.4% 30 to 45 minutes, 11.5% 45 to 60 minutes, 14.6% 60 minutes or more (2000)

EAST NORTHPORT
(CDP). Covers a land area of 5.861 square miles and a water area of 0 square miles. Located at 40.87° N. Lat.; 73.32° W. Long. Elevation is 228 feet.
Population: 20,703 (1990); 20,845 (2000); 21,359 (2005); 21,951 (2010 projected); Race: 93.3% White, 1.2% Black, 3.0% Asian, 5.2% Hispanic of any race (2005); Density: 3,644.2 persons per square mile (2005); Average household size: 2.97 (2005); Median age: 39.6 (2005); Males per 100 females: 98.4 (2005); Marriage status: 21.5% never married, 64.5% now married, 7.3% widowed, 6.7% divorced (2000); Foreign born: 6.6% (2000); Ancestry (includes multiple ancestries): 29.3% Irish, 27.7% Italian, 21.1% German, 9.4% Other groups, 7.6% English (2000).
Economy: Employment by occupation: 15.8% management, 29.0% professional, 12.3% services, 27.6% sales, 0.3% farming, 7.8% construction, 7.1% production (2000).
Income: Per capita income: $33,419 (2005); Median household income: $83,337 (2005); Average household income: $97,263 (2005); Percent of households with income of $100,000 or more: 38.5% (2005); Poverty rate: 4.1% (2000).
Education: Percent of population age 25 and over with: High school diploma (including GED) or higher: 91.8% (2005); Bachelor's degree or higher: 36.7% (2005); Master's degree or higher: 16.2% (2005).

School District(s)
Northport-East Northport Union Free School District (KG-12)
    2003-04 Enrollment: 6,392 . . . . (631) 262-6604

Housing: Homeownership rate: 85.6% (2005); Median home value: $391,702 (2005); Median rent: $903 per month (2000); Median age of housing: 41 years (2000).
Transportation: Commute to work: 85.8% car, 9.2% public transportation, 0.9% walk, 3.5% work from home (2000); Travel time to work: 21.8% less than 15 minutes, 29.2% 15 to 30 minutes, 20.0% 30 to 45 minutes, 9.3% 45 to 60 minutes, 19.7% 60 minutes or more (2000)
Additional Information Contacts
East Northport Chamber of Commerce . . . . (631) 261-3573
    http://www.eastnorthport.com

EAST PATCHOGUE
(CDP). Covers a land area of 8.317 square miles and a water area of 0.156 square miles. Located at 40.76° N. Lat.; 72.98° W. Long. Elevation is 25 feet.
Population: 20,195 (1990); 20,824 (2000); 21,424 (2005); 22,095 (2010 projected); Race: 86.0% White, 4.3% Black, 2.6% Asian, 12.5% Hispanic of any race (2005); Density: 2,576.1 persons per square mile (2005); Average household size: 2.77 (2005); Median age: 39.3 (2005); Males per 100 females: 95.7 (2005); Marriage status: 24.6% never married, 59.9% now married, 8.2% widowed, 7.3% divorced (2000); Foreign born: 9.3% (2000); Ancestry (includes multiple ancestries): 32.9% Italian, 23.8% Irish, 19.7% German, 14.9% Other groups, 7.3% English (2000).
Economy: Employment by occupation: 11.9% management, 19.2% professional, 13.7% services, 29.0% sales, 0.4% farming, 12.7% construction, 13.2% production (2000).
Income: Per capita income: $27,474 (2005); Median household income: $64,521 (2005); Average household income: $75,321 (2005); Percent of households with income of $100,000 or more: 25.7% (2005); Poverty rate: 4.5% (2000).
Education: Percent of population age 25 and over with: High school diploma (including GED) or higher: 83.9% (2005); Bachelor's degree or higher: 19.1% (2005); Master's degree or higher: 8.2% (2005).

School District(s)
South Country Central School District (PK-12)
    2003-04 Enrollment: 4,758 . . . . (631) 286-4310

Housing: Homeownership rate: 67.4% (2005); Median home value: $258,742 (2005); Median rent: $849 per month (2000); Median age of housing: 33 years (2000).
Hospitals: Brookhaven Memorial Hospital Medical Center (321 beds)
Transportation: Commute to work: 91.3% car, 5.5% public transportation, 0.9% walk, 2.1% work from home (2000); Travel time to work: 28.6% less than 15 minutes, 30.1% 15 to 30 minutes, 20.0% 30 to 45 minutes, 5.5% 45 to 60 minutes, 15.8% 60 minutes or more (2000)

EAST QUOGUE
(CDP). Covers a land area of 10.297 square miles and a water area of 1.489 square miles. Located at 40.85° N. Lat.; 72.57° W. Long.
Population: 3,519 (1990); 4,265 (2000); 4,994 (2005); 5,633 (2010 projected); Race: 93.4% White, 0.8% Black, 0.9% Asian, 8.6% Hispanic of any race (2005); Density: 485.0 persons per square mile (2005); Average household size: 2.56 (2005); Median age: 40.5 (2005); Males per 100 females: 99.1 (2005); Marriage status: 22.4% never married, 62.3% now married, 7.4% widowed, 8.0% divorced (2000); Foreign born: 8.5% (2000); Ancestry (includes multiple ancestries): 26.3% Italian, 24.5% Irish, 21.9% German, 8.4% Other groups, 8.3% Polish (2000).
Economy: Employment by occupation: 6.7% management, 22.9% professional, 15.8% services, 31.8% sales, 1.1% farming, 13.6% construction, 8.2% production (2000).
Income: Per capita income: $31,623 (2005); Median household income: $68,253 (2005); Average household income: $80,988 (2005); Percent of households with income of $100,000 or more: 27.3% (2005); Poverty rate: 5.4% (2000).
Education: Percent of population age 25 and over with: High school diploma (including GED) or higher: 92.7% (2005); Bachelor's degree or higher: 28.8% (2005); Master's degree or higher: 11.9% (2005).

School District(s)
East Quogue Union Free School District (KG-06)
    2003-04 Enrollment: 432 . . . . (631) 653-5210

Housing: Homeownership rate: 82.6% (2005); Median home value: $357,280 (2005); Median rent: $848 per month (2000); Median age of housing: 29 years (2000).
Transportation: Commute to work: 92.5% car, 3.7% public transportation, 1.9% walk, 1.4% work from home (2000); Travel time to work: 32.1% less than 15 minutes, 34.8% 15 to 30 minutes, 16.6% 30 to 45 minutes, 3.0% 45 to 60 minutes, 13.6% 60 minutes or more (2000)

EAST SETAUKET
(unincorporated postal area, zip code 11733). Covers a land area of 12.269 square miles and a water area of 0.008 square miles. Located at 40.92° N. Lat.; 72.63° W. Long. Elevation is 63 feet.
Population: 0 (2000); Race: 83.7% White, 3.0% Black, 9.9% Asian, 4.5% Hispanic of any race (2000); Density: 0.0 persons per square mile (2000); Age: 24.1% under 18, 9.5% over 64 (2000); Marriage status: 33.2% never married, 57.9% now married, 4.4% widowed, 4.5% divorced (2000); Foreign born: 14.5% (2000); Ancestry (includes multiple ancestries): 23.7% Italian, 20.7% Irish, 20.0% Other groups, 17.8% German, 7.4% English (2000).
Economy: Employment by occupation: 16.9% management, 38.1% professional, 10.2% services, 24.3% sales, 0.0% farming, 6.1% construction, 4.5% production (2000).
Income: Per capita income: $36,530 (2000); Median household income: $98,056 (2000); Poverty rate: 4.6% (2000).
Education: Percent of population age 25 and over with: High school diploma (including GED) or higher: 94.0% (2000); Bachelor's degree or higher: 54.1% (2000).

School District(s)
Three Village Central School District (KG-12)
    2003-04 Enrollment: 7,986 . . . . (631) 730-4010
Housing: Homeownership rate: 89.8% (2000); Median home value: $281,700 (2000); Median rent: $1,030 per month (2000); Median age of housing: 32 years (2000).
Newspapers: Port Times Record (General - Circulation 5,600); The Village Times (East Setauket) (General - Circulation 21,500); Village Beacon Record (East Setauket) (General - Circulation 8,899)
Transportation: Commute to work: 84.4% car, 4.0% public transportation, 6.6% walk, 3.8% work from home (2000); Travel time to work: 32.7% less than 15 minutes, 27.6% 15 to 30 minutes, 20.2% 30 to 45 minutes, 9.0% 45 to 60 minutes, 10.5% 60 minutes or more (2000)

EAST SHOREHAM (CDP).
Covers a land area of 5.109 square miles and a water area of 0 square miles. Located at 40.95° N. Lat.; 72.88° W. Long.
Population: 5,276 (1990); 5,809 (2000); 6,159 (2005); 6,455 (2010 projected); Race: 94.2% White, 1.6% Black, 1.9% Asian, 5.6% Hispanic of any race (2005); Density: 1,205.6 persons per square mile (2005); Average household size: 3.22 (2005); Median age: 37.6 (2005); Males per 100 females: 99.5 (2005); Marriage status: 21.9% never married, 71.5% now married, 3.2% widowed, 3.4% divorced (2000); Foreign born: 6.9% (2000); Ancestry (includes multiple ancestries): 31.4% Irish, 29.3% Italian, 23.9% German, 7.9% Other groups, 7.3% English (2000).
Economy: Employment by occupation: 14.4% management, 33.1% professional, 14.2% services, 21.8% sales, 0.5% farming, 10.4% construction, 5.6% production (2000).
Income: Per capita income: $35,817 (2005); Median household income: $98,705 (2005); Average household income: $113,990 (2005); Percent of households with income of $100,000 or more: 48.9% (2005); Poverty rate: 4.1% (2000).
Education: Percent of population age 25 and over with: High school diploma (including GED) or higher: 93.3% (2005); Bachelor's degree or higher: 37.2% (2005); Master's degree or higher: 22.3% (2005).
Housing: Homeownership rate: 94.5% (2005); Median home value: $347,623 (2005); Median rent: $1,045 per month (2000); Median age of housing: 27 years (2000).
Transportation: Commute to work: 94.4% car, 1.7% public transportation, 0.7% walk, 2.2% work from home (2000); Travel time to work: 19.1% less than 15 minutes, 30.2% 15 to 30 minutes, 26.9% 30 to 45 minutes, 9.6% 45 to 60 minutes, 14.2% 60 minutes or more (2000)

EASTPORT (CDP).
Covers a land area of 5.493 square miles and a water area of 0.135 square miles. Located at 40.83° N. Lat.; 72.73° W. Long. Elevation is 38 feet.
Population: 1,333 (1990); 1,454 (2000); 1,539 (2005); 1,614 (2010 projected); Race: 90.4% White, 0.8% Black, 1.9% Asian, 14.4% Hispanic of any race (2005); Density: 280.2 persons per square mile (2005); Average household size: 2.63 (2005); Median age: 40.5 (2005); Males per 100 females: 109.1 (2005); Marriage status: 21.9% never married, 61.7% now married, 6.9% widowed, 9.4% divorced (2000); Foreign born: 5.2% (2000); Ancestry (includes multiple ancestries): 23.5% Irish, 20.3% English, 16.1% German, 15.6% Italian, 13.4% Other groups (2000).
Economy: In summer resort area. Employment by occupation: 11.9% management, 20.5% professional, 12.6% services, 25.5% sales, 1.3% farming, 16.8% construction, 11.4% production (2000).
Income: Per capita income: $27,497 (2005); Median household income: $59,882 (2005); Average household income: $71,017 (2005); Percent of households with income of $100,000 or more: 20.9% (2005); Poverty rate: 6.6% (2000).
Education: Percent of population age 25 and over with: High school diploma (including GED) or higher: 84.9% (2005); Bachelor's degree or higher: 25.5% (2005); Master's degree or higher: 11.1% (2005).
School District(s)
Eastport Union Free School District (KG-06)
    2003-04 Enrollment: 1,062 . . . . (631) 878-3782
Housing: Homeownership rate: 74.0% (2005); Median home value: $260,922 (2005); Median rent: $707 per month (2000); Median age of housing: 43 years (2000).
Transportation: Commute to work: 88.1% car, 0.8% public transportation, 6.3% walk, 3.5% work from home (2000); Travel time to work: 30.5% less than 15 minutes, 30.8% 15 to 30 minutes, 18.2% 30 to 45 minutes, 4.6% 45 to 60 minutes, 15.9% 60 minutes or more (2000)

EATONS NECK (CDP).
Covers a land area of 1.007 square miles and a water area of 2.989 square miles. Located at 40.93° N. Lat.; 73.39° W. Long.
Population: 1,499 (1990); 1,388 (2000); 1,402 (2005); 1,391 (2010 projected); Race: 97.8% White, 0.1% Black, 1.4% Asian, 1.3% Hispanic of any race (2005); Density: 1,392.3 persons per square mile (2005); Average household size: 2.67 (2005); Median age: 44.0 (2005); Males per 100 females: 96.1 (2005); Marriage status: 14.6% never married, 75.6% now married, 4.9% widowed, 4.8% divorced (2000); Foreign born: 9.9% (2000); Ancestry (includes multiple ancestries): 23.9% Irish, 23.0% Italian, 22.9% German, 8.4% English, 3.8% Polish (2000).
Economy: Employment by occupation: 31.2% management, 31.3% professional, 9.6% services, 18.8% sales, 0.0% farming, 3.8% construction, 5.3% production (2000).
Income: Per capita income: $51,111 (2005); Median household income: $112,109 (2005); Average household income: $136,231 (2005); Percent of households with income of $100,000 or more: 55.9% (2005); Poverty rate: 2.3% (2000).
Education: Percent of population age 25 and over with: High school diploma (including GED) or higher: 97.4% (2005); Bachelor's degree or higher: 54.2% (2005); Master's degree or higher: 28.1% (2005).
Housing: Homeownership rate: 95.2% (2005); Median home value: $596,393 (2005); Median rent: $1,075 per month (2000); Median age of housing: 35 years (2000).
Transportation: Commute to work: 87.1% car, 7.5% public transportation, 2.8% walk, 2.6% work from home (2000); Travel time to work: 4.2% less than 15 minutes, 19.7% 15 to 30 minutes, 30.1% 30 to 45 minutes, 20.6% 45 to 60 minutes, 25.4% 60 minutes or more (2000)

ELWOOD (CDP).
Covers a land area of 4.825 square miles and a water area of 0 square miles. Located at 40.84° N. Lat.; 73.33° W. Long. Elevation is 220 feet.
Population: 10,916 (1990); 10,916 (2000); 11,243 (2005); 11,647 (2010 projected); Race: 81.4% White, 7.6% Black, 7.4% Asian, 6.8% Hispanic of any race (2005); Density: 2,330.0 persons per square mile (2005); Average household size: 3.16 (2005); Median age: 39.5 (2005); Males per 100 females: 95.8 (2005); Marriage status: 22.3% never married, 66.0% now married, 6.5% widowed, 5.2% divorced (2000); Foreign born: 11.4% (2000); Ancestry (includes multiple ancestries): 29.3% Italian, 19.7% Irish, 17.7% Other groups, 16.0% German, 8.6% Polish (2000).
Economy: Employment by occupation: 18.5% management, 25.0% professional, 11.4% services, 30.1% sales, 0.0% farming, 8.1% construction, 6.9% production (2000).
Income: Per capita income: $40,065 (2005); Median household income: $103,676 (2005); Average household income: $125,630 (2005); Percent of households with income of $100,000 or more: 51.9% (2005); Poverty rate: 2.1% (2000).
Education: Percent of population age 25 and over with: High school diploma (including GED) or higher: 89.8% (2005); Bachelor's degree or higher: 39.9% (2005); Master's degree or higher: 16.1% (2005).
School District(s)
Elwood Union Free School District (KG-12)
    2003-04 Enrollment: 2,512 . . . . (631) 266-5402
Housing: Homeownership rate: 93.6% (2005); Median home value: $427,691 (2005); Median rent: $1,188 per month (2000); Median age of housing: 37 years (2000).
Transportation: Commute to work: 83.1% car, 11.4% public transportation, 0.9% walk, 4.0% work from home (2000); Travel time to work: 20.1% less than 15 minutes, 29.3% 15 to 30 minutes, 18.9% 30 to 45 minutes, 9.2% 45 to 60 minutes, 22.4% 60 minutes or more (2000)

FARMINGVILLE (CDP).
Covers a land area of 4.518 square miles and a water area of 0 square miles. Located at 40.84° N. Lat.; 73.04° W. Long. Elevation is 105 feet.
Population: 14,842 (1990); 16,458 (2000); 17,334 (2005); 18,243 (2010 projected); Race: 91.4% White, 1.7% Black, 2.3% Asian, 10.6% Hispanic of any race (2005); Density: 3,836.7 persons per square mile (2005); Average household size: 3.24 (2005); Median age: 35.6 (2005); Males per 100 females: 101.7 (2005); Marriage status: 28.0% never married, 61.2% now married, 5.2% widowed, 5.6% divorced (2000); Foreign born: 8.8% (2000); Ancestry (includes multiple ancestries): 39.6% Italian, 27.5% Irish, 19.7% German, 12.5% Other groups, 7.2% Polish (2000).

Economy: Employment by occupation: 13.3% management, 17.9% professional, 12.7% services, 30.4% sales, 0.4% farming, 12.9% construction, 12.4% production (2000).
Income: Per capita income: $29,063 (2005); Median household income: $80,698 (2005); Average household income: $93,979 (2005); Percent of households with income of $100,000 or more: 36.6% (2005); Poverty rate: 3.0% (2000).
Education: Percent of population age 25 and over with: High school diploma (including GED) or higher: 87.4% (2005); Bachelor's degree or higher: 21.4% (2005); Master's degree or higher: 6.6% (2005).

School District(s)
Sachem Central School District (KG-12)
    2003-04 Enrollment: 15,378 . . . . (631) 471-1336

Housing: Homeownership rate: 82.5% (2005); Median home value: $270,289 (2005); Median rent: $904 per month (2000); Median age of housing: 30 years (2000).
Transportation: Commute to work: 91.2% car, 5.8% public transportation, 0.9% walk, 1.6% work from home (2000); Travel time to work: 17.6% less than 15 minutes, 38.3% 15 to 30 minutes, 19.8% 30 to 45 minutes, 7.2% 45 to 60 minutes, 17.2% 60 minutes or more (2000)

FIRE ISLAND (CDP). Covers a land area of 8.650 square miles and a water area of 0.004 square miles. Located at 40.65° N. Lat.; 73.12° W. Long.
Population: 250 (1990); 310 (2000); 290 (2005); 296 (2010 projected); Race: 96.2% White, 0.0% Black, 0.7% Asian, 5.2% Hispanic of any race (2005); Density: 33.5 persons per square mile (2005); Average household size: 2.20 (2005); Median age: 43.9 (2005); Males per 100 females: 139.7 (2005); Marriage status: 26.5% never married, 51.9% now married, 3.8% widowed, 17.7% divorced (2000); Foreign born: 1.6% (2000); Ancestry (includes multiple ancestries): 26.2% Irish, 23.3% German, 16.1% Italian, 9.8% English, 9.5% Russian (2000).
Economy: Employment by occupation: 21.1% management, 24.7% professional, 7.2% services, 24.2% sales, 0.0% farming, 22.7% construction, 0.0% production (2000).
Income: Per capita income: $51,662 (2005); Median household income: $75,278 (2005); Average household income: $111,780 (2005); Percent of households with income of $100,000 or more: 43.2% (2005); Poverty rate: 3.1% (2000).
Education: Percent of population age 25 and over with: High school diploma (including GED) or higher: 87.1% (2005); Bachelor's degree or higher: 38.8% (2005); Master's degree or higher: 16.7% (2005).
Housing: Homeownership rate: 79.5% (2005); Median home value: $442,188 (2005); Median rent: $513 per month (2000); Median age of housing: 33 years (2000).
Transportation: Commute to work: 53.4% car, 14.1% public transportation, 11.5% walk, 10.5% work from home (2000); Travel time to work: 46.8% less than 15 minutes, 16.4% 15 to 30 minutes, 7.6% 30 to 45 minutes, 10.5% 45 to 60 minutes, 18.7% 60 minutes or more (2000)

FISHERS ISLAND (CDP). Covers a land area of 4.053 square miles and a water area of 0.151 square miles. Located at 41.26° N. Lat.; 72.00° W. Long.
Population: 329 (1990); 289 (2000); 353 (2005); 412 (2010 projected); Race: 93.2% White, 1.4% Black, 1.7% Asian, 2.3% Hispanic of any race (2005); Density: 87.1 persons per square mile (2005); Average household size: 2.08 (2005); Median age: 45.2 (2005); Males per 100 females: 106.4 (2005); Marriage status: 23.2% never married, 52.7% now married, 8.5% widowed, 15.6% divorced (2000); Foreign born: 4.8% (2000); Ancestry (includes multiple ancestries): 24.9% English, 20.1% Italian, 18.6% Irish, 14.9% German, 10.8% French (except Basque) (2000).
Economy: Employment by occupation: 12.1% management, 13.9% professional, 33.9% services, 19.4% sales, 3.6% farming, 12.7% construction, 4.2% production (2000).
Income: Per capita income: $36,990 (2005); Median household income: $55,625 (2005); Average household income: $76,809 (2005); Percent of households with income of $100,000 or more: 22.4% (2005); Poverty rate: 9.0% (2000).
Education: Percent of population age 25 and over with: High school diploma (including GED) or higher: 95.0% (2005); Bachelor's degree or higher: 40.5% (2005); Master's degree or higher: 19.1% (2005).
Housing: Homeownership rate: 56.5% (2005); Median home value: $454,286 (2005); Median rent: $558 per month (2000); Median age of housing: 60+ years (2000).
Transportation: Commute to work: 70.9% car, 6.7% public transportation, 13.9% walk, 8.5% work from home (2000); Travel time to work: 76.2% less than 15 minutes, 16.6% 15 to 30 minutes, 0.0% 30 to 45 minutes, 2.6% 45 to 60 minutes, 4.6% 60 minutes or more (2000)

FLANDERS (CDP). Covers a land area of 12.270 square miles and a water area of 2.520 square miles. Located at 40.90° N. Lat.; 72.61° W. Long. Elevation is 12 feet.
Population: 3,246 (1990); 3,646 (2000); 3,825 (2005); 4,018 (2010 projected); Race: 65.0% White, 24.1% Black, 0.7% Asian, 20.7% Hispanic of any race (2005); Density: 311.7 persons per square mile (2005); Average household size: 2.95 (2005); Median age: 34.9 (2005); Males per 100 females: 103.1 (2005); Marriage status: 34.7% never married, 47.7% now married, 7.5% widowed, 10.2% divorced (2000); Foreign born: 10.2% (2000); Ancestry (includes multiple ancestries): 33.1% Other groups, 19.8% Italian, 17.0% German, 12.3% Irish, 6.5% Polish (2000).
Economy: Employment by occupation: 7.1% management, 12.0% professional, 18.8% services, 30.1% sales, 2.5% farming, 15.0% construction, 14.5% production (2000).
Income: Per capita income: $21,180 (2005); Median household income: $51,182 (2005); Average household income: $62,377 (2005); Percent of households with income of $100,000 or more: 14.4% (2005); Poverty rate: 13.5% (2000).
Education: Percent of population age 25 and over with: High school diploma (including GED) or higher: 78.2% (2005); Bachelor's degree or higher: 13.1% (2005); Master's degree or higher: 6.3% (2005).
Housing: Homeownership rate: 69.8% (2005); Median home value: $191,151 (2005); Median rent: $785 per month (2000); Median age of housing: 38 years (2000).
Transportation: Commute to work: 87.3% car, 6.0% public transportation, 1.0% walk, 4.6% work from home (2000); Travel time to work: 27.3% less than 15 minutes, 36.0% 15 to 30 minutes, 18.0% 30 to 45 minutes, 7.8% 45 to 60 minutes, 10.9% 60 minutes or more (2000)

FORT SALONGA (CDP). Covers a land area of 9.014 square miles and a water area of 3.799 square miles. Located at 40.90° N. Lat.; 73.30° W. Long. Elevation is 31 feet.
Population: 9,032 (1990); 9,634 (2000); 9,903 (2005); 10,214 (2010 projected); Race: 95.9% White, 0.9% Black, 2.2% Asian, 2.9% Hispanic of any race (2005); Density: 1,098.6 persons per square mile (2005); Average household size: 2.94 (2005); Median age: 41.6 (2005); Males per 100 females: 98.2 (2005); Marriage status: 20.8% never married, 69.4% now married, 4.6% widowed, 5.2% divorced (2000); Foreign born: 5.5% (2000); Ancestry (includes multiple ancestries): 31.7% Italian, 30.3% Irish, 20.5% German, 8.6% English, 6.6% Other groups (2000).
Economy: Employment by occupation: 21.7% management, 35.3% professional, 9.1% services, 24.8% sales, 0.2% farming, 5.3% construction, 3.5% production (2000).
Income: Per capita income: $48,341 (2005); Median household income: $113,690 (2005); Average household income: $141,013 (2005); Percent of households with income of $100,000 or more: 56.2% (2005); Poverty rate: 3.3% (2000).
Education: Percent of population age 25 and over with: High school diploma (including GED) or higher: 96.4% (2005); Bachelor's degree or higher: 51.2% (2005); Master's degree or higher: 25.1% (2005).
Housing: Homeownership rate: 91.9% (2005); Median home value: $613,817 (2005); Median rent: $1,172 per month (2000); Median age of housing: 35 years (2000).
Transportation: Commute to work: 85.6% car, 9.0% public transportation, 0.7% walk, 4.1% work from home (2000); Travel time to work: 21.2% less than 15 minutes, 29.1% 15 to 30 minutes, 23.0% 30 to 45 minutes, 8.5% 45 to 60 minutes, 18.2% 60 minutes or more (2000)

GILGO-OAK BEACH-CAPTREE (CDP). Covers a land area of 2.726 square miles and a water area of 0.921 square miles. Located at 40.64° N. Lat.; 73.27° W. Long.
Population: 305 (1990); 333 (2000); 275 (2005); 266 (2010 projected); Race: 94.9% White, 0.7% Black, 4.4% Asian, 2.9% Hispanic of any race (2005); Density: 100.9 persons per square mile (2005); Average household size: 2.02 (2005); Median age: 51.1 (2005); Males per 100 females: 113.2 (2005); Marriage status: 19.1% never married, 57.6% now married, 12.4% widowed, 11.0% divorced (2000); Foreign born: 2.8% (2000); Ancestry (includes multiple ancestries): 28.8% Irish, 27.2% Italian, 24.8% German, 11.5% English, 6.2% French (except Basque) (2000).

Economy: Employment by occupation: 18.2% management, 23.5% professional, 12.3% services, 27.8% sales, 1.6% farming, 9.6% construction, 7.0% production (2000).
Income: Per capita income: $56,827 (2005); Median household income: $80,556 (2005); Average household income: $114,908 (2005); Percent of households with income of $100,000 or more: 39.7% (2005); Poverty rate: 0.9% (2000).
Education: Percent of population age 25 and over with: High school diploma (including GED) or higher: 93.2% (2005); Bachelor's degree or higher: 43.4% (2005); Master's degree or higher: 17.9% (2005).
Housing: Homeownership rate: 89.0% (2005); Median home value: $604,592 (2005); Median rent: $1,094 per month (2000); Median age of housing: 45 years (2000).
Transportation: Commute to work: 87.2% car, 6.7% public transportation, 1.1% walk, 5.0% work from home (2000); Travel time to work: 15.9% less than 15 minutes, 37.1% 15 to 30 minutes, 12.9% 30 to 45 minutes, 19.4% 45 to 60 minutes, 14.7% 60 minutes or more (2000)

GORDON HEIGHTS (CDP).
Covers a land area of 1.693 square miles and a water area of 0.015 square miles. Located at 40.85° N. Lat.; 72.96° W. Long. Elevation is 157 feet.
Population: 2,200 (1990); 3,094 (2000); 3,361 (2005); 3,623 (2010 projected); Race: 23.1% White, 61.5% Black, 2.6% Asian, 18.5% Hispanic of any race (2005); Density: 1,984.7 persons per square mile (2005); Average household size: 3.69 (2005); Median age: 31.2 (2005); Males per 100 females: 95.9 (2005); Marriage status: 35.3% never married, 49.7% now married, 6.7% widowed, 8.2% divorced (2000); Foreign born: 13.1% (2000); Ancestry (includes multiple ancestries): 56.6% Other groups, 6.6% Italian, 5.6% Jamaican, 4.5% Irish, 3.7% United States or American (2000).
Economy: Employment by occupation: 11.6% management, 14.3% professional, 22.3% services, 31.6% sales, 0.0% farming, 7.7% construction, 12.5% production (2000).
Income: Per capita income: $19,630 (2005); Median household income: $64,405 (2005); Average household income: $71,549 (2005); Percent of households with income of $100,000 or more: 22.1% (2005); Poverty rate: 10.5% (2000).
Education: Percent of population age 25 and over with: High school diploma (including GED) or higher: 80.6% (2005); Bachelor's degree or higher: 18.8% (2005); Master's degree or higher: 6.4% (2005).
Housing: Homeownership rate: 78.7% (2005); Median home value: $236,343 (2005); Median rent: $825 per month (2000); Median age of housing: 19 years (2000).
Transportation: Commute to work: 85.2% car, 10.7% public transportation, 2.0% walk, 0.9% work from home (2000); Travel time to work: 10.2% less than 15 minutes, 36.0% 15 to 30 minutes, 20.1% 30 to 45 minutes, 8.4% 45 to 60 minutes, 25.3% 60 minutes or more (2000)

GREAT RIVER (CDP).
Covers a land area of 4.598 square miles and a water area of 0.451 square miles. Located at 40.72° N. Lat.; 73.16° W. Long.
Population: 1,442 (1990); 1,546 (2000); 1,579 (2005); 1,622 (2010 projected); Race: 98.0% White, 0.0% Black, 0.4% Asian, 2.2% Hispanic of any race (2005); Density: 343.4 persons per square mile (2005); Average household size: 3.01 (2005); Median age: 39.8 (2005); Males per 100 females: 103.5 (2005); Marriage status: 24.5% never married, 62.8% now married, 7.5% widowed, 5.1% divorced (2000); Foreign born: 5.2% (2000); Ancestry (includes multiple ancestries): 25.7% Irish, 24.4% Italian, 17.4% German, 10.7% United States or American, 5.2% Other groups (2000).
Economy: Employment by occupation: 14.8% management, 32.2% professional, 7.1% services, 25.6% sales, 0.0% farming, 13.6% construction, 6.7% production (2000).
Income: Per capita income: $37,199 (2005); Median household income: $90,741 (2005); Average household income: $112,094 (2005); Percent of households with income of $100,000 or more: 44.3% (2005); Poverty rate: 7.9% (2000).
Education: Percent of population age 25 and over with: High school diploma (including GED) or higher: 95.6% (2005); Bachelor's degree or higher: 37.1% (2005); Master's degree or higher: 21.9% (2005).
Housing: Homeownership rate: 89.7% (2005); Median home value: $623,798 (2005); Median rent: $816 per month (2000); Median age of housing: 35 years (2000).
Transportation: Commute to work: 93.0% car, 7.0% public transportation, 0.0% walk, 0.0% work from home (2000); Travel time to work: 17.3% less than 15 minutes, 41.3% 15 to 30 minutes, 14.3% 30 to 45 minutes, 3.7% 45 to 60 minutes, 23.4% 60 minutes or more (2000)

GREENLAWN (CDP).
Covers a land area of 3.670 square miles and a water area of 0.003 square miles. Located at 40.85° N. Lat.; 73.36° W. Long. Elevation is 220 feet.
Population: 13,208 (1990); 13,286 (2000); 13,308 (2005); 13,374 (2010 projected); Race: 74.1% White, 16.7% Black, 3.5% Asian, 8.9% Hispanic of any race (2005); Density: 3,626.0 persons per square mile (2005); Average household size: 2.93 (2005); Median age: 40.2 (2005); Males per 100 females: 89.9 (2005); Marriage status: 25.5% never married, 56.7% now married, 10.9% widowed, 7.0% divorced (2000); Foreign born: 12.7% (2000); Ancestry (includes multiple ancestries): 23.3% Italian, 22.2% Irish, 19.5% Other groups, 16.5% German, 5.5% Polish (2000).
Economy: Employment by occupation: 14.8% management, 25.3% professional, 15.6% services, 26.2% sales, 0.2% farming, 10.0% construction, 7.9% production (2000).
Income: Per capita income: $30,577 (2005); Median household income: $72,060 (2005); Average household income: $88,364 (2005); Percent of households with income of $100,000 or more: 32.6% (2005); Poverty rate: 4.5% (2000).
Education: Percent of population age 25 and over with: High school diploma (including GED) or higher: 87.3% (2005); Bachelor's degree or higher: 33.0% (2005); Master's degree or higher: 14.0% (2005).
School District(s)
Harborfields Central School District (KG-12)
    2003-04 Enrollment: 3,560 . . . . (631) 754-5320
Housing: Homeownership rate: 78.6% (2005); Median home value: $372,746 (2005); Median rent: $622 per month (2000); Median age of housing: 39 years (2000).
Transportation: Commute to work: 84.0% car, 9.9% public transportation, 1.4% walk, 4.0% work from home (2000); Travel time to work: 22.5% less than 15 minutes, 33.5% 15 to 30 minutes, 19.6% 30 to 45 minutes, 6.8% 45 to 60 minutes, 17.6% 60 minutes or more (2000)

GREENPORT (village).
Covers a land area of 0.956 square miles and a water area of 0.251 square miles. Located at 41.10° N. Lat.; 72.36° W. Long. Elevation is 7 feet.
History: By 1840 pursuit of offshore whaling, practiced by both Native Americans and European residents, had turned into a way of industry with ships leaving Cold Springs Harbor, Sag Harbor, and Greenport on 3-year whaling voyages. Greenport Village Historic District. Incorporated 1838.
Population: 1,998 (1990); 2,048 (2000); 2,085 (2005); 2,145 (2010 projected); Race: 71.4% White, 15.6% Black, 0.5% Asian, 25.7% Hispanic of any race (2005); Density: 2,181.4 persons per square mile (2005); Average household size: 2.68 (2005); Median age: 40.6 (2005); Males per 100 females: 89.7 (2005); Marriage status: 35.5% never married, 44.7% now married, 12.0% widowed, 7.8% divorced (2000); Foreign born: 13.4% (2000); Ancestry (includes multiple ancestries): 35.1% Other groups, 15.1% German, 14.4% Irish, 14.3% English, 8.9% Polish (2000).
Economy: Summer recreational village. Manufacturing of textiles; boat repair; fisheries (especially oysters). Single-family building permits issued: 5 (2005); Multi-family building permits issued: 0 (2005); Employment by occupation: 5.8% management, 17.0% professional, 25.5% services, 25.7% sales, 0.5% farming, 13.4% construction, 12.1% production (2000).
Income: Per capita income: $19,122 (2005); Median household income: $34,009 (2005); Average household income: $47,985 (2005); Percent of households with income of $100,000 or more: 9.1% (2005); Poverty rate: 19.7% (2000).
Education: Percent of population age 25 and over with: High school diploma (including GED) or higher: 71.9% (2005); Bachelor's degree or higher: 18.5% (2005); Master's degree or higher: 7.0% (2005).
School District(s)
Greenport Union Free School District (KG-12)
    2003-04 Enrollment: 668 . . . . (631) 477-1950
Housing: Homeownership rate: 55.5% (2005); Median home value: $256,716 (2005); Median rent: $695 per month (2000); Median age of housing: 60+ years (2000).
Hospitals: Eastern Long Island Hospital (80 beds)
Transportation: Commute to work: 75.8% car, 9.6% public transportation, 8.6% walk, 3.6% work from home (2000); Travel time to work: 57.2% less than 15 minutes, 18.5% 15 to 30 minutes, 10.4% 30 to 45 minutes, 5.0% 45 to 60 minutes, 8.9% 60 minutes or more (2000)
Additional Information Contacts
Greenport Chamber of Commerce . . . . (631) 477-1383
   http://www.greenportsouthold.org

GREENPORT WEST (CDP). Covers a land area of 3.323 square miles and a water area of 0.128 square miles. Located at 41.10° N. Lat.; 72.37° W. Long.
Population: 1,678 (1990); 1,679 (2000); 2,147 (2005); 2,582 (2010 projected); Race: 89.8% White, 6.1% Black, 0.4% Asian, 8.8% Hispanic of any race (2005); Density: 646.0 persons per square mile (2005); Average household size: 2.22 (2005); Median age: 49.1 (2005); Males per 100 females: 86.4 (2005); Marriage status: 19.4% never married, 63.4% now married, 11.7% widowed, 5.5% divorced (2000); Foreign born: 8.0% (2000); Ancestry (includes multiple ancestries): 22.6% Irish, 19.2% German, 17.5% English, 17.5% Italian, 16.5% Polish (2000).
Economy: Employment by occupation: 17.0% management, 21.7% professional, 18.9% services, 26.4% sales, 0.3% farming, 9.1% construction, 6.7% production (2000).
Income: Per capita income: $29,839 (2005); Median household income: $51,090 (2005); Average household income: $66,389 (2005); Percent of households with income of $100,000 or more: 16.9% (2005); Poverty rate: 5.7% (2000).
Education: Percent of population age 25 and over with: High school diploma (including GED) or higher: 86.1% (2005); Bachelor's degree or higher: 27.3% (2005); Master's degree or higher: 8.9% (2005).
Housing: Homeownership rate: 76.6% (2005); Median home value: $287,090 (2005); Median rent: $664 per month (2000); Median age of housing: 37 years (2000).
Transportation: Commute to work: 84.9% car, 5.1% public transportation, 3.5% walk, 6.6% work from home (2000); Travel time to work: 53.4% less than 15 minutes, 23.0% 15 to 30 minutes, 5.9% 30 to 45 minutes, 6.7% 45 to 60 minutes, 11.0% 60 minutes or more (2000)

HALESITE (CDP). Covers a land area of 0.863 square miles and a water area of 0.095 square miles. Located at 40.88° N. Lat.; 73.41° W. Long. Elevation is 100 feet.
Population: 2,687 (1990); 2,582 (2000); 2,578 (2005); 2,586 (2010 projected); Race: 93.6% White, 2.2% Black, 1.1% Asian, 4.5% Hispanic of any race (2005); Density: 2,987.3 persons per square mile (2005); Average household size: 2.50 (2005); Median age: 42.4 (2005); Males per 100 females: 98.2 (2005); Marriage status: 25.4% never married, 59.7% now married, 8.9% widowed, 6.0% divorced (2000); Foreign born: 9.5% (2000); Ancestry (includes multiple ancestries): 35.3% Irish, 28.6% Italian, 14.9% German, 10.1% English, 8.7% Other groups (2000).
Economy: In summer recreational and residential area. Employment by occupation: 20.5% management, 30.7% professional, 10.4% services, 31.0% sales, 0.0% farming, 4.4% construction, 3.1% production (2000).
Income: Per capita income: $57,085 (2005); Median household income: $105,721 (2005); Average household income: $142,602 (2005); Percent of households with income of $100,000 or more: 52.2% (2005); Poverty rate: 3.2% (2000).
Education: Percent of population age 25 and over with: High school diploma (including GED) or higher: 94.0% (2005); Bachelor's degree or higher: 52.6% (2005); Master's degree or higher: 19.8% (2005).
Housing: Homeownership rate: 84.3% (2005); Median home value: $527,286 (2005); Median rent: $843 per month (2000); Median age of housing: 47 years (2000).
Transportation: Commute to work: 76.4% car, 17.8% public transportation, 1.3% walk, 4.5% work from home (2000); Travel time to work: 16.8% less than 15 minutes, 25.1% 15 to 30 minutes, 17.9% 30 to 45 minutes, 7.0% 45 to 60 minutes, 33.2% 60 minutes or more (2000)

HAMPTON BAYS (CDP). Covers a land area of 12.043 square miles and a water area of 9.642 square miles. Located at 40.87° N. Lat.; 72.52° W. Long. Elevation is 34 feet.
History: Until 1922 called Good Ground.
Population: 9,348 (1990); 12,236 (2000); 13,062 (2005); 13,885 (2010 projected); Race: 90.2% White, 0.9% Black, 0.9% Asian, 19.7% Hispanic of any race (2005); Density: 1,084.7 persons per square mile (2005); Average household size: 2.57 (2005); Median age: 40.3 (2005); Males per 100 females: 99.4 (2005); Marriage status: 25.1% never married, 56.3% now married, 8.9% widowed, 9.8% divorced (2000); Foreign born: 13.4% (2000); Ancestry (includes multiple ancestries): 25.6% Irish, 21.6% Italian, 17.3% German, 11.6% English, 11.5% Other groups (2000).
Economy: In diversified-farming area; boatyards. Employment by occupation: 11.0% management, 17.1% professional, 16.4% services, 30.3% sales, 0.9% farming, 19.7% construction, 4.6% production (2000).
Income: Per capita income: $27,916 (2005); Median household income: $57,498 (2005); Average household income: $70,914 (2005); Percent of households with income of $100,000 or more: 22.7% (2005); Poverty rate: 10.7% (2000).
Education: Percent of population age 25 and over with: High school diploma (including GED) or higher: 86.4% (2005); Bachelor's degree or higher: 25.8% (2005); Master's degree or higher: 9.8% (2005).
School District(s)
Hampton Bays Union Free School District (KG-12)
    2003-04 Enrollment: 1,769 . . . . (631) 723-2100
Housing: Homeownership rate: 69.9% (2005); Median home value: $293,002 (2005); Median rent: $717 per month (2000); Median age of housing: 29 years (2000).
Transportation: Commute to work: 92.3% car, 2.3% public transportation, 1.9% walk, 3.4% work from home (2000); Travel time to work: 26.4% less than 15 minutes, 36.8% 15 to 30 minutes, 19.0% 30 to 45 minutes, 8.1% 45 to 60 minutes, 9.7% 60 minutes or more (2000)
Additional Information Contacts
Hampton Bays Chamber of Commerce. . . . . (631) 728-2211
   http://www.hamptonbayschamber.com

HAUPPAUGE (CDP). Covers a land area of 10.806 square miles and a water area of 0.150 square miles. Located at 40.81° N. Lat.; 73.20° W. Long. Elevation is 78 feet.
Population: 19,750 (1990); 20,100 (2000); 20,627 (2005); 21,245 (2010 projected); Race: 91.1% White, 1.3% Black, 5.0% Asian, 5.8% Hispanic of any race (2005); Density: 1,908.8 persons per square mile (2005); Average household size: 2.82 (2005); Median age: 40.0 (2005); Males per 100 females: 98.2 (2005); Marriage status: 22.2% never married, 64.4% now married, 5.7% widowed, 7.8% divorced (2000); Foreign born: 8.4% (2000); Ancestry (includes multiple ancestries): 37.5% Italian, 24.2% Irish, 18.8% German, 11.7% Other groups, 6.6% Polish (2000).
Economy: Central Long Island manufacturing-industrial region. Long association with aircraft and aerospace industries has created a technologically sophisticated concentration of electronic, electrical, metals, machinery, and fabrication businesses. Manufacturing of instruments, parts, and supplies; also telecommunications, computers, and software. Employment by occupation: 19.1% management, 25.8% professional, 11.5% services, 29.0% sales, 0.0% farming, 8.2% construction, 6.4% production (2000).
Income: Per capita income: $36,149 (2005); Median household income: $88,566 (2005); Average household income: $101,717 (2005); Percent of households with income of $100,000 or more: 41.8% (2005); Poverty rate: 3.1% (2000).
Education: Percent of population age 25 and over with: High school diploma (including GED) or higher: 92.2% (2005); Bachelor's degree or higher: 37.9% (2005); Master's degree or higher: 15.1% (2005).
School District(s)
Hauppauge Union Free School District (KG-12)
    2003-04 Enrollment: 4,155 . . . . (631) 265-3630
Two-year College(s)
Learning Institute for Beauty Sciences
    Fall 2004 Enrollment: 145 . . . . (631) 724-0440
Housing: Homeownership rate: 82.8% (2005); Median home value: $413,936 (2005); Median rent: $1,088 per month (2000); Median age of housing: 33 years (2000).
Transportation: Commute to work: 91.1% car, 5.8% public transportation, 0.4% walk, 2.3% work from home (2000); Travel time to work: 24.4% less than 15 minutes, 32.2% 15 to 30 minutes, 19.1% 30 to 45 minutes, 8.4% 45 to 60 minutes, 15.8% 60 minutes or more (2000)

HEAD OF THE HARBOR (village). Covers a land area of 2.817 square miles and a water area of 0.228 square miles. Located at 40.89° N. Lat.; 73.16° W. Long. Elevation is 100 feet.
Population: 1,354 (1990); 1,447 (2000); 1,508 (2005); 1,575 (2010 projected); Race: 92.7% White, 1.9% Black, 4.7% Asian, 1.3% Hispanic of any race (2005); Density: 535.3 persons per square mile (2005); Average household size: 2.94 (2005); Median age: 43.4 (2005); Males per 100 females: 101.1 (2005); Marriage status: 19.8% never married, 72.9% now married, 3.9% widowed, 3.4% divorced (2000); Foreign born: 6.8% (2000); Ancestry (includes multiple ancestries): 35.4% Italian, 25.8% Irish, 20.7% German, 12.2% English, 8.6% Other groups (2000).
Economy: In summer-resort area. Single-family building permits issued: 3 (2005); Multi-family building permits issued: 0 (2005); Employment by

occupation: 27.2% management, 36.9% professional, 6.2% services, 20.6% sales, 0.0% farming, 4.1% construction, 4.9% production (2000).
Income: Per capita income: $61,210 (2005); Median household income: $132,267 (2005); Average household income: $179,932 (2005); Percent of households with income of $100,000 or more: 60.8% (2005); Poverty rate: 1.5% (2000).
Education: Percent of population age 25 and over with: High school diploma (including GED) or higher: 96.4% (2005); Bachelor's degree or higher: 58.2% (2005); Master's degree or higher: 28.2% (2005).
Housing: Homeownership rate: 91.2% (2005); Median home value: $874,016 (2005); Median rent: $917 per month (2000); Median age of housing: 33 years (2000).
Transportation: Commute to work: 86.8% car, 5.9% public transportation, 0.3% walk, 7.1% work from home (2000); Travel time to work: 21.5% less than 15 minutes, 30.9% 15 to 30 minutes, 25.0% 30 to 45 minutes, 7.9% 45 to 60 minutes, 14.7% 60 minutes or more (2000)

HOLBROOK (CDP). Covers a land area of 6.823 square miles and a water area of 0 square miles. Located at 40.80° N. Lat.; 73.07° W. Long. Elevation is 118 feet.
Population: 25,273 (1990); 27,512 (2000); 28,841 (2005); 30,235 (2010 projected); Race: 92.7% White, 1.6% Black, 3.6% Asian, 7.4% Hispanic of any race (2005); Density: 4,227.3 persons per square mile (2005); Average household size: 3.00 (2005); Median age: 36.9 (2005); Males per 100 females: 95.1 (2005); Marriage status: 24.3% never married, 63.5% now married, 5.5% widowed, 6.6% divorced (2000); Foreign born: 5.8% (2000); Ancestry (includes multiple ancestries): 39.9% Italian, 27.5% Irish, 18.8% German, 11.3% Other groups, 6.0% Polish (2000).
Economy: Diverse manufacturing: knitted outerwear, welding equipment supplies, plastic molding, auto and industrial fasteners, ironwork, precision machining, corrugated cardboard containers, electronic and electrical products. Employment by occupation: 13.3% management, 20.4% professional, 11.4% services, 33.7% sales, 0.1% farming, 9.4% construction, 11.7% production (2000).
Income: Per capita income: $32,651 (2005); Median household income: $84,988 (2005); Average household income: $97,507 (2005); Percent of households with income of $100,000 or more: 38.3% (2005); Poverty rate: 3.3% (2000).
Education: Percent of population age 25 and over with: High school diploma (including GED) or higher: 90.1% (2005); Bachelor's degree or higher: 22.7% (2005); Master's degree or higher: 7.8% (2005).
School District(s)
Sachem Central School District (KG-12)
    2003-04 Enrollment: 15,378 .... (631) 471-1336
Housing: Homeownership rate: 79.3% (2005); Median home value: $295,156 (2005); Median rent: $996 per month (2000); Median age of housing: 26 years (2000).
Transportation: Commute to work: 91.1% car, 7.0% public transportation, 0.4% walk, 1.3% work from home (2000); Travel time to work: 23.8% less than 15 minutes, 32.2% 15 to 30 minutes, 19.7% 30 to 45 minutes, 6.6% 45 to 60 minutes, 17.7% 60 minutes or more (2000)

HOLTSVILLE (CDP). Covers a land area of 6.957 square miles and a water area of 0 square miles. Located at 40.81° N. Lat.; 73.04° W. Long. Elevation is 116 feet.
Population: 14,972 (1990); 17,006 (2000); 18,847 (2005); 20,618 (2010 projected); Race: 92.6% White, 1.5% Black, 2.3% Asian, 9.4% Hispanic of any race (2005); Density: 2,709.0 persons per square mile (2005); Average household size: 3.14 (2005); Median age: 36.0 (2005); Males per 100 females: 96.3 (2005); Marriage status: 24.3% never married, 65.2% now married, 3.9% widowed, 6.6% divorced (2000); Foreign born: 7.0% (2000); Ancestry (includes multiple ancestries): 40.2% Italian, 29.0% Irish, 20.3% German, 10.2% Other groups, 5.6% Polish (2000).
Economy: Employment by occupation: 13.1% management, 20.2% professional, 14.2% services, 30.7% sales, 0.2% farming, 10.5% construction, 11.2% production (2000).
Income: Per capita income: $29,311 (2005); Median household income: $80,600 (2005); Average household income: $91,455 (2005); Percent of households with income of $100,000 or more: 34.0% (2005); Poverty rate: 3.6% (2000).
Education: Percent of population age 25 and over with: High school diploma (including GED) or higher: 89.3% (2005); Bachelor's degree or higher: 19.8% (2005); Master's degree or higher: 6.2% (2005).
School District(s)
Sachem Central School District (KG-12)
    2003-04 Enrollment: 15,378 .... (631) 471-1336
Housing: Homeownership rate: 85.4% (2005); Median home value: $279,450 (2005); Median rent: $900 per month (2000); Median age of housing: 27 years (2000).
Transportation: Commute to work: 91.4% car, 5.2% public transportation, 0.6% walk, 2.1% work from home (2000); Travel time to work: 24.9% less than 15 minutes, 33.1% 15 to 30 minutes, 18.8% 30 to 45 minutes, 7.4% 45 to 60 minutes, 15.7% 60 minutes or more (2000)
Additional Information Contacts
Farmingville/Holtsville Chamber of Commerce .... (631) 472-1569

HUNTINGTON (town). Covers a land area of 93.962 square miles and a water area of 43.150 square miles. Located at 40.85° N. Lat.; 73.37° W. Long. Elevation is 205 feet.
History: Named for Huntingdon, England, or to mean "hunting town" for its abundance of game. Seat of Immaculate Conception College, World Friends College. Settled 1653.
Population: 191,474 (1990); 195,289 (2000); 200,040 (2005); 205,544 (2010 projected); Race: 85.6% White, 4.8% Black, 4.6% Asian, 8.6% Hispanic of any race (2005); Density: 2,129.0 persons per square mile (2005); Average household size: 2.94 (2005); Median age: 40.0 (2005); Males per 100 females: 96.6 (2005); Marriage status: 23.5% never married, 64.1% now married, 6.7% widowed, 5.8% divorced (2000); Foreign born: 11.2% (2000); Ancestry (includes multiple ancestries): 26.6% Italian, 21.3% Irish, 16.2% German, 16.1% Other groups, 6.4% English (2000).
Economy: Chiefly residential heart of township containing 17 contiguous communities, noted for their precision manufacturing. Numerous harbors and boatyards; major retailing center. Unemployment rate: 3.8% (2005); Total civilian labor force: 105,827 (2005); Single-family building permits issued: 209 (2005); Multi-family building permits issued: 0 (2005); Employment by occupation: 19.3% management, 28.5% professional, 11.2% services, 27.9% sales, 0.1% farming, 7.0% construction, 6.0% production (2000).
Income: Per capita income: $41,995 (2005); Median household income: $94,082 (2005); Average household income: $122,467 (2005); Percent of households with income of $100,000 or more: 46.5% (2005); Poverty rate: 4.6% (2000).
Taxes: Total city taxes per capita: $604 (2004); City property taxes per capita: $479 (2004).
Education: Percent of population age 25 and over with: High school diploma (including GED) or higher: 90.8% (2005); Bachelor's degree or higher: 44.5% (2005); Master's degree or higher: 19.8% (2005).
School District(s)
Cold Spring Harbor Central School District (KG-12)
    2003-04 Enrollment: 2,092 .... (631) 692-8036
Elwood Union Free School District (KG-12)
    2003-04 Enrollment: 2,512 .... (631) 266-5402
Huntington Union Free School District (KG-12)
    2003-04 Enrollment: 4,131 .... (631) 673-2038
South Huntington Union Free School District (KG-12)
    2003-04 Enrollment: 6,111 .... (631) 425-5300
Four-year College(s)
Seminary of the Immaculate Conception
    Fall 2004 Enrollment: 169 .... (631) 423-0483
Housing: Homeownership rate: 85.4% (2005); Median home value: $459,621 (2005); Median rent: $924 per month (2000); Median age of housing: 39 years (2000).
Hospitals: Huntington Hospital (396 beds)
Newspapers: Half Hollow Hills (General - Circulation 15,000); Huntington Record (General - Circulation 6,600); Northport Journal (General - Circulation 1,213); The Long Islander (General - Circulation 7,993)
Transportation: Commute to work: 83.5% car, 10.6% public transportation, 1.3% walk, 4.1% work from home (2000); Travel time to work: 22.1% less than 15 minutes, 30.2% 15 to 30 minutes, 19.6% 30 to 45 minutes, 8.2% 45 to 60 minutes, 19.9% 60 minutes or more (2000)
Additional Information Contacts
Huntington Chamber of Commerce .... (631) 423-5663
    http://www.huntingtonchamber.com
Town of Huntington .... (631) 351-3030
    http://town.huntington.ny.us/

HUNTINGTON (CDP). Covers a land area of 7.534 square miles and a water area of 0.144 square miles. Located at 40.87° N. Lat.; 73.41° W. Long.
Population: 18,217 (1990); 18,403 (2000); 18,817 (2005); 19,348 (2010 projected); Race: 92.4% White, 2.2% Black, 2.2% Asian, 4.8% Hispanic of any race (2005); Density: 2,497.5 persons per square mile (2005); Average household size: 2.59 (2005); Median age: 41.2 (2005); Males per 100 females: 95.3 (2005); Marriage status: 24.1% never married, 62.2% now married, 7.3% widowed, 6.4% divorced (2000); Foreign born: 7.3% (2000); Ancestry (includes multiple ancestries): 25.3% Italian, 25.1% Irish, 18.1% German, 10.8% Other groups, 10.0% English (2000).
Economy: Employment by occupation: 23.6% management, 33.2% professional, 8.6% services, 24.1% sales, 0.2% farming, 5.3% construction, 5.1% production (2000).
Income: Per capita income: $49,614 (2005); Median household income: $96,941 (2005); Average household income: $128,031 (2005); Percent of households with income of $100,000 or more: 48.2% (2005); Poverty rate: 3.8% (2000).
Education: Percent of population age 25 and over with: High school diploma (including GED) or higher: 94.3% (2005); Bachelor's degree or higher: 57.3% (2005); Master's degree or higher: 26.9% (2005).
Housing: Homeownership rate: 81.7% (2005); Median home value: $497,898 (2005); Median rent: $931 per month (2000); Median age of housing: 45 years (2000).
Transportation: Commute to work: 79.4% car, 14.2% public transportation, 1.4% walk, 4.4% work from home (2000); Travel time to work: 22.6% less than 15 minutes, 23.7% 15 to 30 minutes, 21.2% 30 to 45 minutes, 8.3% 45 to 60 minutes, 24.2% 60 minutes or more (2000)

HUNTINGTON BAY (village). Covers a land area of 1.027 square miles and a water area of 1.472 square miles. Located at 40.90° N. Lat.; 73.41° W. Long. Elevation is 60 feet.
History: Site of capture of Nathan Hale by British forces during American Revolution.
Population: 1,521 (1990); 1,496 (2000); 1,558 (2005); 1,609 (2010 projected); Race: 98.1% White, 0.1% Black, 1.1% Asian, 1.6% Hispanic of any race (2005); Density: 1,516.8 persons per square mile (2005); Average household size: 2.73 (2005); Median age: 48.3 (2005); Males per 100 females: 98.7 (2005); Marriage status: 17.5% never married, 69.6% now married, 7.4% widowed, 5.5% divorced (2000); Foreign born: 5.7% (2000); Ancestry (includes multiple ancestries): 26.1% Irish, 21.1% Italian, 20.4% German, 12.0% English, 7.9% Other groups (2000).
Economy: Single-family building permits issued: 2 (2005); Multi-family building permits issued: 0 (2005); Employment by occupation: 32.3% management, 29.5% professional, 4.6% services, 28.1% sales, 0.0% farming, 4.1% construction, 1.4% production (2000).
Income: Per capita income: $79,236 (2005); Median household income: $160,630 (2005); Average household income: $216,200 (2005); Percent of households with income of $100,000 or more: 67.6% (2005); Poverty rate: 2.0% (2000).
Education: Percent of population age 25 and over with: High school diploma (including GED) or higher: 98.0% (2005); Bachelor's degree or higher: 68.1% (2005); Master's degree or higher: 31.0% (2005).
Housing: Homeownership rate: 96.8% (2005); Median home value: $994,243 (2005); Median rent: $1,188 per month (2000); Median age of housing: 52 years (2000).
Safety: Violent crime rate: 0.0 per 10,000 population; Property crime rate: 46.6 per 10,000 population (2004).
Transportation: Commute to work: 73.8% car, 18.6% public transportation, 1.2% walk, 6.4% work from home (2000); Travel time to work: 20.0% less than 15 minutes, 19.5% 15 to 30 minutes, 17.9% 30 to 45 minutes, 9.1% 45 to 60 minutes, 33.4% 60 minutes or more (2000)

HUNTINGTON STATION (CDP). Covers a land area of 5.431 square miles and a water area of 0.004 square miles. Located at 40.84° N. Lat.; 73.40° W. Long. Elevation is 216 feet.
History: Named for Huntingdon, England, or to mean "hunting town". Walt Whitman born here.
Population: 28,247 (1990); 29,910 (2000); 29,729 (2005); 29,740 (2010 projected); Race: 65.8% White, 12.2% Black, 4.0% Asian, 29.9% Hispanic of any race (2005); Density: 5,473.7 persons per square mile (2005); Average household size: 3.11 (2005); Median age: 36.0 (2005); Males per 100 females: 101.1 (2005); Marriage status: 31.9% never married, 54.8% now married, 6.1% widowed, 7.2% divorced (2000); Foreign born: 20.9% (2000); Ancestry (includes multiple ancestries): 32.7% Other groups, 20.3% Italian, 17.3% Irish, 14.0% German, 4.6% Polish (2000).
Economy: Diverse manufacturing base. Popular vacation and fishing area on Long Island's North shore nearby. Employment by occupation: 11.9% management, 20.1% professional, 18.3% services, 28.6% sales, 0.1% farming, 10.1% construction, 10.8% production (2000).
Income: Per capita income: $26,373 (2005); Median household income: $68,312 (2005); Average household income: $81,318 (2005); Percent of households with income of $100,000 or more: 28.1% (2005); Poverty rate: 11.2% (2000).
Education: Percent of population age 25 and over with: High school diploma (including GED) or higher: 79.6% (2005); Bachelor's degree or higher: 27.5% (2005); Master's degree or higher: 10.8% (2005).
School District(s)
Huntington Union Free School District (KG-12)
    2003-04 Enrollment: 4,131 . . . . (631) 673-2038
South Huntington Union Free School District (KG-12)
    2003-04 Enrollment: 6,111 . . . . (631) 425-5300
Housing: Homeownership rate: 70.6% (2005); Median home value: $300,272 (2005); Median rent: $859 per month (2000); Median age of housing: 43 years (2000).
Transportation: Commute to work: 85.2% car, 9.5% public transportation, 2.3% walk, 2.2% work from home (2000); Travel time to work: 27.5% less than 15 minutes, 32.4% 15 to 30 minutes, 20.3% 30 to 45 minutes, 7.0% 45 to 60 minutes, 12.8% 60 minutes or more (2000)

ISLANDIA (village). Covers a land area of 2.232 square miles and a water area of 0 square miles. Located at 40.80° N. Lat.; 73.17° W. Long. Elevation is 68 feet.
Population: 2,769 (1990); 3,057 (2000); 3,171 (2005); 3,295 (2010 projected); Race: 65.6% White, 16.6% Black, 8.3% Asian, 24.8% Hispanic of any race (2005); Density: 1,420.7 persons per square mile (2005); Average household size: 2.99 (2005); Median age: 37.3 (2005); Males per 100 females: 92.3 (2005); Marriage status: 31.1% never married, 53.9% now married, 4.3% widowed, 10.7% divorced (2000); Foreign born: 20.1% (2000); Ancestry (includes multiple ancestries): 36.1% Other groups, 21.1% Italian, 12.9% Irish, 11.4% German, 5.9% Polish (2000).
Economy: Manufacturing. Single-family building permits issued: 0 (2005); Multi-family building permits issued: 0 (2005); Employment by occupation: 13.4% management, 17.6% professional, 12.9% services, 36.9% sales, 0.0% farming, 6.5% construction, 12.8% production (2000).
Income: Per capita income: $29,072 (2005); Median household income: $74,303 (2005); Average household income: $86,969 (2005); Percent of households with income of $100,000 or more: 29.1% (2005); Poverty rate: 5.5% (2000).
Education: Percent of population age 25 and over with: High school diploma (including GED) or higher: 86.4% (2005); Bachelor's degree or higher: 24.4% (2005); Master's degree or higher: 8.6% (2005).
Housing: Homeownership rate: 80.5% (2005); Median home value: $258,895 (2005); Median rent: $970 per month (2000); Median age of housing: 32 years (2000).
Transportation: Commute to work: 86.0% car, 10.4% public transportation, 1.4% walk, 1.7% work from home (2000); Travel time to work: 26.7% less than 15 minutes, 35.7% 15 to 30 minutes, 17.7% 30 to 45 minutes, 5.4% 45 to 60 minutes, 14.3% 60 minutes or more (2000)

ISLIP (town). Covers a land area of 105.275 square miles and a water area of 57.842 square miles. Located at 40.75° N. Lat.; 73.19° W. Long. Elevation is 16 feet.
Population: 299,587 (1990); 322,612 (2000); 333,359 (2005); 345,039 (2010 projected); Race: 73.6% White, 10.3% Black, 2.7% Asian, 23.5% Hispanic of any race (2005); Density: 3,166.6 persons per square mile (2005); Average household size: 3.24 (2005); Median age: 36.4 (2005); Males per 100 females: 97.2 (2005); Marriage status: 27.2% never married, 59.6% now married, 6.0% widowed, 7.2% divorced (2000); Foreign born: 14.6% (2000); Ancestry (includes multiple ancestries): 27.0% Other groups, 25.9% Italian, 21.5% Irish, 14.8% German, 4.5% English (2000).
Economy: Manufacturing includes mixers for food and chemical industries, telecommunications and aerospace instrumentation and aircraft parts. In recreational and duck-farming area. Horticultural crops. Unemployment rate: 4.3% (2005); Total civilian labor force: 175,742 (2005); Single-family building permits issued: 513 (2005); Multi-family building permits issued: 268 (2005); Employment by occupation: 12.1% management, 19.1% professional, 14.5% services, 28.9% sales, 0.2% farming, 10.2% construction, 15.0% production (2000).

Income: Per capita income: $27,195 (2005); Median household income: $73,044 (2005); Average household income: $87,325 (2005); Percent of households with income of $100,000 or more: 30.9% (2005); Poverty rate: 6.6% (2000).
Taxes: Total city taxes per capita: $309 (2004); City property taxes per capita: $235 (2004).
Education: Percent of population age 25 and over with: High school diploma (including GED) or higher: 83.0% (2005); Bachelor's degree or higher: 21.8% (2005); Master's degree or higher: 8.7% (2005).

School District(s)
Islip Union Free School District (KG-12)
   2003-04 Enrollment: 3,636 . . . . (631) 859-2209

Housing: Homeownership rate: 78.6% (2005); Median home value: $283,424 (2005); Median rent: $884 per month (2000); Median age of housing: 35 years (2000).
Transportation: Commute to work: 88.7% car, 7.4% public transportation, 1.2% walk, 1.7% work from home (2000); Travel time to work: 25.8% less than 15 minutes, 34.5% 15 to 30 minutes, 17.4% 30 to 45 minutes, 6.7% 45 to 60 minutes, 15.6% 60 minutes or more (2000)

Additional Information Contacts
Islip Chamber of Commerce . . . . (631) 581-2720
   http://www.islipchamberofcommerce.com/
Town of Islip . . . . (631) 224-5691
   http://www.isliptown.org/

ISLIP (CDP). Covers a land area of 5.402 square miles and a water area of 0.355 square miles. Located at 40.73° N. Lat.; 73.22° W. Long.
Population: 18,924 (1990); 20,575 (2000); 21,154 (2005); 21,813 (2010 projected); Race: 84.1% White, 6.5% Black, 2.8% Asian, 14.1% Hispanic of any race (2005); Density: 3,915.9 persons per square mile (2005); Average household size: 2.97 (2005); Median age: 37.4 (2005); Males per 100 females: 94.9 (2005); Marriage status: 23.4% never married, 60.9% now married, 7.2% widowed, 8.6% divorced (2000); Foreign born: 9.1% (2000); Ancestry (includes multiple ancestries): 29.2% Italian, 25.5% Irish, 17.9% Other groups, 17.7% German, 6.5% English (2000).
Economy: Employment by occupation: 14.4% management, 21.9% professional, 13.2% services, 29.3% sales, 0.2% farming, 10.1% construction, 10.9% production (2000).
Income: Per capita income: $29,967 (2005); Median household income: $74,823 (2005); Average household income: $88,077 (2005); Percent of households with income of $100,000 or more: 31.9% (2005); Poverty rate: 4.1% (2000).
Education: Percent of population age 25 and over with: High school diploma (including GED) or higher: 88.0% (2005); Bachelor's degree or higher: 23.5% (2005); Master's degree or higher: 10.7% (2005).
Housing: Homeownership rate: 73.9% (2005); Median home value: $287,620 (2005); Median rent: $871 per month (2000); Median age of housing: 37 years (2000).
Transportation: Commute to work: 87.0% car, 8.8% public transportation, 1.4% walk, 2.3% work from home (2000); Travel time to work: 26.7% less than 15 minutes, 31.7% 15 to 30 minutes, 17.7% 30 to 45 minutes, 6.4% 45 to 60 minutes, 17.5% 60 minutes or more (2000)

ISLIP TERRACE (CDP). Covers a land area of 1.415 square miles and a water area of 0 square miles. Located at 40.74° N. Lat.; 73.18° W. Long. Elevation is 33 feet.
Population: 5,530 (1990); 5,641 (2000); 5,673 (2005); 5,744 (2010 projected); Race: 94.6% White, 0.7% Black, 2.1% Asian, 9.2% Hispanic of any race (2005); Density: 4,007.9 persons per square mile (2005); Average household size: 3.16 (2005); Median age: 36.4 (2005); Males per 100 females: 96.8 (2005); Marriage status: 24.5% never married, 64.3% now married, 6.9% widowed, 4.3% divorced (2000); Foreign born: 7.1% (2000); Ancestry (includes multiple ancestries): 40.2% Italian, 32.5% Irish, 20.5% German, 11.6% Other groups, 6.2% English (2000).
Economy: Employment by occupation: 12.0% management, 15.7% professional, 16.6% services, 27.7% sales, 0.0% farming, 15.0% construction, 13.1% production (2000).
Income: Per capita income: $27,481 (2005); Median household income: $76,078 (2005); Average household income: $86,136 (2005); Percent of households with income of $100,000 or more: 28.4% (2005); Poverty rate: 2.4% (2000).
Education: Percent of population age 25 and over with: High school diploma (including GED) or higher: 87.7% (2005); Bachelor's degree or higher: 15.2% (2005); Master's degree or higher: 5.5% (2005).

School District(s)
East Islip Union Free School District (PK-12)
   2003-04 Enrollment: 5,432 . . . . (631) 224-2000

Housing: Homeownership rate: 87.6% (2005); Median home value: $286,022 (2005); Median rent: $864 per month (2000); Median age of housing: 39 years (2000).
Transportation: Commute to work: 89.2% car, 7.0% public transportation, 1.3% walk, 1.3% work from home (2000); Travel time to work: 24.1% less than 15 minutes, 40.7% 15 to 30 minutes, 13.9% 30 to 45 minutes, 7.2% 45 to 60 minutes, 14.2% 60 minutes or more (2000)

JAMESPORT (CDP). Covers a land area of 4.422 square miles and a water area of 3.307 square miles. Located at 40.94° N. Lat.; 72.57° W. Long.
Population: 1,520 (1990); 1,526 (2000); 1,701 (2005); 1,854 (2010 projected); Race: 97.5% White, 0.6% Black, 0.6% Asian, 9.2% Hispanic of any race (2005); Density: 384.6 persons per square mile (2005); Average household size: 2.49 (2005); Median age: 44.9 (2005); Males per 100 females: 103.7 (2005); Marriage status: 18.5% never married, 67.5% now married, 8.0% widowed, 6.0% divorced (2000); Foreign born: 8.2% (2000); Ancestry (includes multiple ancestries): 23.3% German, 21.8% Irish, 20.1% Polish, 19.3% Italian, 8.5% English (2000).
Economy: In summer resort area. Employment by occupation: 12.6% management, 26.0% professional, 22.2% services, 23.8% sales, 1.9% farming, 9.0% construction, 4.6% production (2000).
Income: Per capita income: $36,088 (2005); Median household income: $81,034 (2005); Average household income: $88,743 (2005); Percent of households with income of $100,000 or more: 37.1% (2005); Poverty rate: 7.9% (2000).
Education: Percent of population age 25 and over with: High school diploma (including GED) or higher: 89.7% (2005); Bachelor's degree or higher: 31.7% (2005); Master's degree or higher: 16.2% (2005).
Housing: Homeownership rate: 84.6% (2005); Median home value: $334,491 (2005); Median rent: $757 per month (2000); Median age of housing: 36 years (2000).
Transportation: Commute to work: 95.8% car, 0.0% public transportation, 1.9% walk, 0.7% work from home (2000); Travel time to work: 25.6% less than 15 minutes, 33.7% 15 to 30 minutes, 15.4% 30 to 45 minutes, 12.5% 45 to 60 minutes, 12.8% 60 minutes or more (2000)

KINGS PARK (CDP). Covers a land area of 5.892 square miles and a water area of 0.386 square miles. Located at 40.88° N. Lat.; 73.24° W. Long. Elevation is 169 feet.
History: Developed as utopian community in 1872; became farm for insane in 1885. State psychiatric center opened 1892.
Population: 17,655 (1990); 16,146 (2000); 17,012 (2005); 17,913 (2010 projected); Race: 94.4% White, 1.0% Black, 2.4% Asian, 4.4% Hispanic of any race (2005); Density: 2,887.4 persons per square mile (2005); Average household size: 2.92 (2005); Median age: 39.1 (2005); Males per 100 females: 95.7 (2005); Marriage status: 22.8% never married, 62.5% now married, 9.0% widowed, 5.7% divorced (2000); Foreign born: 8.1% (2000); Ancestry (includes multiple ancestries): 36.6% Italian, 30.6% Irish, 20.1% German, 7.3% Other groups, 7.1% Polish (2000).
Economy: Nearby is Sunken Meadow State Park; bathing, hiking, picnicking. Employment by occupation: 14.3% management, 24.5% professional, 16.7% services, 28.0% sales, 0.5% farming, 10.2% construction, 5.9% production (2000).
Income: Per capita income: $32,200 (2005); Median household income: $80,983 (2005); Average household income: $93,045 (2005); Percent of households with income of $100,000 or more: 36.9% (2005); Poverty rate: 3.7% (2000).
Education: Percent of population age 25 and over with: High school diploma (including GED) or higher: 88.3% (2005); Bachelor's degree or higher: 28.1% (2005); Master's degree or higher: 11.2% (2005).

School District(s)
Kings Park Central School District (KG-12)
   2003-04 Enrollment: 4,007 . . . . (631) 269-3210

Housing: Homeownership rate: 79.6% (2005); Median home value: $372,485 (2005); Median rent: $748 per month (2000); Median age of housing: 36 years (2000).
Transportation: Commute to work: 88.0% car, 7.3% public transportation, 1.1% walk, 2.9% work from home (2000); Travel time to work: 23.1% less than 15 minutes, 31.4% 15 to 30 minutes, 16.7% 30 to 45 minutes, 8.4% 45 to 60 minutes, 20.4% 60 minutes or more (2000)

Additional Information Contacts

Kings Park Chamber of Commerce . . . . (631) 269-7678
http://www.kingsparkli.com/

LAKE GROVE (village).
Covers a land area of 2.982 square miles and a water area of 0.001 square miles. Located at 40.85° N. Lat.; 73.11° W. Long. Elevation is 119 feet.
Population: 9,612 (1990); 10,250 (2000); 10,720 (2005); 11,221 (2010 projected); Race: 87.8% White, 1.9% Black, 7.3% Asian, 6.3% Hispanic of any race (2005); Density: 3,594.4 persons per square mile (2005); Average household size: 2.97 (2005); Median age: 36.5 (2005); Males per 100 females: 98.3 (2005); Marriage status: 25.6% never married, 64.5% now married, 6.0% widowed, 3.9% divorced (2000); Foreign born: 8.8% (2000); Ancestry (includes multiple ancestries): 40.7% Italian, 24.6% Irish, 20.3% German, 13.5% Other groups, 5.1% Polish (2000).
Economy: Single-family building permits issued: 28 (2005); Multi-family building permits issued: 0 (2005); Employment by occupation: 15.8% management, 22.2% professional, 11.2% services, 31.2% sales, 0.0% farming, 10.2% construction, 9.4% production (2000).
Income: Per capita income: $33,339 (2005); Median household income: $81,741 (2005); Average household income: $98,613 (2005); Percent of households with income of $100,000 or more: 37.1% (2005); Poverty rate: 5.1% (2000).
Education: Percent of population age 25 and over with: High school diploma (including GED) or higher: 91.1% (2005); Bachelor's degree or higher: 28.2% (2005); Master's degree or higher: 10.2% (2005).
School District(s)
Middle Country Central School District (PK-12)
    2003-04 Enrollment: 11,630 . . . . (631) 285-8005
Sachem Central School District (KG-12)
    2003-04 Enrollment: 15,378 . . . . (631) 471-1336
Housing: Homeownership rate: 78.8% (2005); Median home value: $320,643 (2005); Median rent: $886 per month (2000); Median age of housing: 33 years (2000).
Transportation: Commute to work: 92.3% car, 4.0% public transportation, 0.8% walk, 2.1% work from home (2000); Travel time to work: 18.5% less than 15 minutes, 34.9% 15 to 30 minutes, 20.4% 30 to 45 minutes, 9.3% 45 to 60 minutes, 16.9% 60 minutes or more (2000)

LAKE RONKONKOMA (CDP).
Covers a land area of 4.913 square miles and a water area of 0.003 square miles. Located at 40.83° N. Lat.; 73.11° W. Long. Elevation is 82 feet.
Population: 18,997 (1990); 19,701 (2000); 20,028 (2005); 20,405 (2010 projected); Race: 91.2% White, 1.9% Black, 3.3% Asian, 8.0% Hispanic of any race (2005); Density: 4,076.6 persons per square mile (2005); Average household size: 2.88 (2005); Median age: 38.4 (2005); Males per 100 females: 94.2 (2005); Marriage status: 24.5% never married, 60.6% now married, 8.0% widowed, 6.9% divorced (2000); Foreign born: 7.5% (2000); Ancestry (includes multiple ancestries): 35.9% Italian, 29.2% Irish, 20.5% German, 9.3% Other groups, 6.2% English (2000).
Economy: Employment by occupation: 14.2% management, 18.1% professional, 14.8% services, 32.3% sales, 0.1% farming, 11.5% construction, 9.1% production (2000).
Income: Per capita income: $27,766 (2005); Median household income: $66,694 (2005); Average household income: $78,610 (2005); Percent of households with income of $100,000 or more: 26.5% (2005); Poverty rate: 6.2% (2000).
Education: Percent of population age 25 and over with: High school diploma (including GED) or higher: 85.1% (2005); Bachelor's degree or higher: 22.2% (2005); Master's degree or higher: 6.4% (2005).
School District(s)
Sachem Central School District (KG-12)
    2003-04 Enrollment: 15,378 . . . . (631) 471-1336
Housing: Homeownership rate: 73.1% (2005); Median home value: $280,488 (2005); Median rent: $808 per month (2000); Median age of housing: 33 years (2000).
Transportation: Commute to work: 88.3% car, 7.8% public transportation, 1.1% walk, 1.6% work from home (2000); Travel time to work: 22.9% less than 15 minutes, 36.0% 15 to 30 minutes, 17.3% 30 to 45 minutes, 6.8% 45 to 60 minutes, 17.0% 60 minutes or more (2000)

LAUREL (CDP).
Covers a land area of 3.349 square miles and a water area of 0.078 square miles. Located at 40.97° N. Lat.; 72.55° W. Long. Elevation is 20 feet.
Population: 1,091 (1990); 1,188 (2000); 1,252 (2005); 1,294 (2010 projected); Race: 96.9% White, 1.0% Black, 0.0% Asian, 3.8% Hispanic of any race (2005); Density: 373.8 persons per square mile (2005); Average household size: 2.58 (2005); Median age: 42.6 (2005); Males per 100 females: 102.3 (2005); Marriage status: 20.8% never married, 63.6% now married, 9.8% widowed, 5.8% divorced (2000); Foreign born: 6.1% (2000); Ancestry (includes multiple ancestries): 26.5% Irish, 25.7% Italian, 25.6% German, 20.5% Polish, 14.0% English (2000).
Economy: Employment by occupation: 14.0% management, 25.0% professional, 14.8% services, 24.1% sales, 0.9% farming, 13.9% construction, 7.2% production (2000).
Income: Per capita income: $31,297 (2005); Median household income: $65,179 (2005); Average household income: $80,397 (2005); Percent of households with income of $100,000 or more: 25.8% (2005); Poverty rate: 4.0% (2000).
Education: Percent of population age 25 and over with: High school diploma (including GED) or higher: 91.5% (2005); Bachelor's degree or higher: 31.7% (2005); Master's degree or higher: 15.8% (2005).
Housing: Homeownership rate: 86.0% (2005); Median home value: $355,941 (2005); Median rent: $786 per month (2000); Median age of housing: 35 years (2000).
Transportation: Commute to work: 93.1% car, 1.5% public transportation, 1.1% walk, 3.8% work from home (2000); Travel time to work: 34.5% less than 15 minutes, 31.2% 15 to 30 minutes, 14.7% 30 to 45 minutes, 10.1% 45 to 60 minutes, 9.5% 60 minutes or more (2000)

LINDENHURST (village).
Covers a land area of 3.753 square miles and a water area of 0.060 square miles. Located at 40.68° N. Lat.; 73.37° W. Long. Elevation is 27 feet.
History: Named for Linden, Germany. Incorporated 1923.
Population: 26,879 (1990); 27,819 (2000); 28,907 (2005); 30,087 (2010 projected); Race: 92.2% White, 1.1% Black, 1.9% Asian, 9.0% Hispanic of any race (2005); Density: 7,701.5 persons per square mile (2005); Average household size: 3.06 (2005); Median age: 37.3 (2005); Males per 100 females: 95.2 (2005); Marriage status: 25.8% never married, 60.2% now married, 7.3% widowed, 6.7% divorced (2000); Foreign born: 10.8% (2000); Ancestry (includes multiple ancestries): 38.8% Italian, 26.8% Irish, 20.2% German, 9.6% Other groups, 8.4% Polish (2000).
Economy: Manufacturing: paper, chemicals, electronic equipment. Unemployment rate: 4.9% (2005); Total civilian labor force: 15,185 (2005); Single-family building permits issued: 21 (2005); Multi-family building permits issued: 0 (2005); Employment by occupation: 10.5% management, 16.7% professional, 16.0% services, 31.3% sales, 0.0% farming, 11.1% construction, 14.3% production (2000).
Income: Per capita income: $25,362 (2005); Median household income: $68,596 (2005); Average household income: $77,143 (2005); Percent of households with income of $100,000 or more: 27.0% (2005); Poverty rate: 6.4% (2000).
Education: Percent of population age 25 and over with: High school diploma (including GED) or higher: 83.7% (2005); Bachelor's degree or higher: 16.4% (2005); Master's degree or higher: 5.9% (2005).
School District(s)
Lindenhurst Union Free School District (KG-12)
    2003-04 Enrollment: 7,689 . . . . (631) 226-6511
Housing: Homeownership rate: 80.6% (2005); Median home value: $275,994 (2005); Median rent: $766 per month (2000); Median age of housing: 44 years (2000).
Newspapers: South Bay's Newspaper (General - Circulation 103,000)
Transportation: Commute to work: 86.4% car, 10.3% public transportation, 1.2% walk, 1.3% work from home (2000); Travel time to work: 25.1% less than 15 minutes, 30.8% 15 to 30 minutes, 19.7% 30 to 45 minutes, 7.7% 45 to 60 minutes, 16.8% 60 minutes or more (2000)
Additional Information Contacts
Village of Lindenhurst . . . . (631) 957-7500
http://www.villageoflindenhurst.com/

LLOYD HARBOR (village).
Covers a land area of 9.352 square miles and a water area of 1.285 square miles. Located at 40.91° N. Lat.; 73.45° W. Long. Elevation is 81 feet.
Population: 3,369 (1990); 3,675 (2000); 3,758 (2005); 3,863 (2010 projected); Race: 95.3% White, 0.9% Black, 2.7% Asian, 3.2% Hispanic of any race (2005); Density: 401.8 persons per square mile (2005); Average household size: 3.22 (2005); Median age: 42.1 (2005); Males per 100 females: 97.6 (2005); Marriage status: 18.4% never married, 74.0% now married, 4.3% widowed, 3.3% divorced (2000); Foreign born: 7.4% (2000); Ancestry (includes multiple ancestries): 26.0% Italian, 21.3% Irish, 15.0% English, 12.1% German, 9.4% Other groups (2000).

Economy: Single-family building permits issued: 4 (2005); Multi-family building permits issued: 0 (2005); Employment by occupation: 32.6% management, 33.3% professional, 4.1% services, 26.3% sales, 0.0% farming, 2.0% construction, 1.7% production (2000).
Income: Per capita income: $73,492 (2005); Median household income: $180,000 (2005); Average household income: $236,154 (2005); Percent of households with income of $100,000 or more: 72.0% (2005); Poverty rate: 1.3% (2000).
Education: Percent of population age 25 and over with: High school diploma (including GED) or higher: 97.7% (2005); Bachelor's degree or higher: 71.9% (2005); Master's degree or higher: 37.3% (2005).
Housing: Homeownership rate: 96.1% (2005); Median home value: $1 million+ (2005); Median rent: $667 per month (2000); Median age of housing: 38 years (2000).
Transportation: Commute to work: 79.5% car, 12.0% public transportation, 1.9% walk, 6.5% work from home (2000); Travel time to work: 17.1% less than 15 minutes, 25.6% 15 to 30 minutes, 21.9% 30 to 45 minutes, 10.4% 45 to 60 minutes, 25.1% 60 minutes or more (2000)

MANORVILLE (CDP). Covers a land area of 25.359 square miles and a water area of 0.042 square miles. Located at 40.84° N. Lat.; 72.79° W. Long.
Population: 5,876 (1990); 11,131 (2000); 13,814 (2005); 16,334 (2010 projected); Race: 95.4% White, 1.5% Black, 0.7% Asian, 5.6% Hispanic of any race (2005); Density: 544.7 persons per square mile (2005); Average household size: 2.72 (2005); Median age: 37.9 (2005); Males per 100 females: 98.6 (2005); Marriage status: 19.2% never married, 66.4% now married, 7.1% widowed, 7.4% divorced (2000); Foreign born: 3.2% (2000); Ancestry (includes multiple ancestries): 39.2% Italian, 31.5% Irish, 27.2% German, 7.9% Other groups, 7.8% Polish (2000).
Economy: Employment by occupation: 13.9% management, 24.6% professional, 14.3% services, 25.1% sales, 0.4% farming, 10.2% construction, 11.5% production (2000).
Income: Per capita income: $33,621 (2005); Median household income: $81,270 (2005); Average household income: $91,108 (2005); Percent of households with income of $100,000 or more: 36.3% (2005); Poverty rate: 2.8% (2000).
Education: Percent of population age 25 and over with: High school diploma (including GED) or higher: 90.5% (2005); Bachelor's degree or higher: 25.8% (2005); Master's degree or higher: 10.4% (2005).
School District(s)
Eastport-South Manor Central High School District (07-12)
    2003-04 Enrollment: 1,442 . . . . (631) 878-3782
South Manor Union Free School District (KG-06)
    2003-04 Enrollment: 969 . . . . (631) 878-3782
Housing: Homeownership rate: 80.2% (2005); Median home value: $309,170 (2005); Median rent: $844 per month (2000); Median age of housing: 13 years (2000).
Transportation: Commute to work: 95.3% car, 1.9% public transportation, 0.3% walk, 2.5% work from home (2000); Travel time to work: 16.7% less than 15 minutes, 35.1% 15 to 30 minutes, 22.3% 30 to 45 minutes, 12.0% 45 to 60 minutes, 13.9% 60 minutes or more (2000)

MASTIC (CDP). Covers a land area of 4.481 square miles and a water area of 0.340 square miles. Located at 40.80° N. Lat.; 72.84° W. Long. Elevation is 32 feet.
Population: 13,887 (1990); 15,436 (2000); 16,101 (2005); 16,773 (2010 projected); Race: 80.6% White, 8.6% Black, 1.5% Asian, 16.0% Hispanic of any race (2005); Density: 3,593.5 persons per square mile (2005); Average household size: 3.46 (2005); Median age: 32.1 (2005); Males per 100 females: 99.1 (2005); Marriage status: 28.9% never married, 59.7% now married, 4.4% widowed, 6.9% divorced (2000); Foreign born: 5.1% (2000); Ancestry (includes multiple ancestries): 35.0% Italian, 31.2% Irish, 20.2% German, 18.7% Other groups, 6.2% English (2000).
Economy: Employment by occupation: 7.7% management, 13.5% professional, 17.7% services, 28.6% sales, 0.6% farming, 15.7% construction, 16.2% production (2000).
Income: Per capita income: $20,754 (2005); Median household income: $63,663 (2005); Average household income: $71,320 (2005); Percent of households with income of $100,000 or more: 21.2% (2005); Poverty rate: 13.0% (2000).
Education: Percent of population age 25 and over with: High school diploma (including GED) or higher: 80.4% (2005); Bachelor's degree or higher: 8.6% (2005); Master's degree or higher: 3.2% (2005).
Housing: Homeownership rate: 79.4% (2005); Median home value: $182,993 (2005); Median rent: $921 per month (2000); Median age of housing: 26 years (2000).
Transportation: Commute to work: 93.1% car, 2.6% public transportation, 1.2% walk, 1.7% work from home (2000); Travel time to work: 17.3% less than 15 minutes, 33.0% 15 to 30 minutes, 22.1% 30 to 45 minutes, 10.8% 45 to 60 minutes, 16.8% 60 minutes or more (2000)

MASTIC BEACH (CDP). Covers a land area of 4.232 square miles and a water area of 1.080 square miles. Located at 40.76° N. Lat.; 72.84° W. Long. Elevation is 9 feet.
Population: 10,293 (1990); 11,543 (2000); 12,030 (2005); 12,552 (2010 projected); Race: 83.4% White, 7.5% Black, 1.3% Asian, 14.9% Hispanic of any race (2005); Density: 2,842.9 persons per square mile (2005); Average household size: 3.09 (2005); Median age: 33.0 (2005); Males per 100 females: 100.0 (2005); Marriage status: 29.1% never married, 54.7% now married, 7.0% widowed, 9.2% divorced (2000); Foreign born: 4.9% (2000); Ancestry (includes multiple ancestries): 33.6% Italian, 28.0% Irish, 22.1% German, 17.5% Other groups, 6.2% English (2000).
Economy: Employment by occupation: 6.8% management, 14.7% professional, 19.3% services, 28.2% sales, 0.0% farming, 16.5% construction, 14.5% production (2000).
Income: Per capita income: $19,634 (2005); Median household income: $49,891 (2005); Average household income: $60,470 (2005); Percent of households with income of $100,000 or more: 13.9% (2005); Poverty rate: 11.3% (2000).
Education: Percent of population age 25 and over with: High school diploma (including GED) or higher: 76.1% (2005); Bachelor's degree or higher: 9.9% (2005); Master's degree or higher: 3.5% (2005).
School District(s)
William Floyd Union Free School District (KG-12)
    2003-04 Enrollment: 10,376 . . . . (631) 874-1201
Housing: Homeownership rate: 72.7% (2005); Median home value: $164,672 (2005); Median rent: $811 per month (2000); Median age of housing: 42 years (2000).
Transportation: Commute to work: 91.1% car, 6.5% public transportation, 0.4% walk, 1.3% work from home (2000); Travel time to work: 14.0% less than 15 minutes, 27.5% 15 to 30 minutes, 27.6% 30 to 45 minutes, 10.5% 45 to 60 minutes, 20.5% 60 minutes or more (2000)

MATTITUCK (CDP). Covers a land area of 8.643 square miles and a water area of 1.593 square miles. Located at 40.99° N. Lat.; 72.53° W. Long. Elevation is 16 feet.
Population: 3,905 (1990); 4,198 (2000); 4,095 (2005); 4,049 (2010 projected); Race: 95.8% White, 1.3% Black, 0.6% Asian, 4.2% Hispanic of any race (2005); Density: 473.8 persons per square mile (2005); Average household size: 2.50 (2005); Median age: 44.1 (2005); Males per 100 females: 93.5 (2005); Marriage status: 19.7% never married, 64.5% now married, 8.7% widowed, 7.2% divorced (2000); Foreign born: 4.9% (2000); Ancestry (includes multiple ancestries): 30.5% Irish, 27.1% German, 17.3% Polish, 14.6% Italian, 13.5% English (2000).
Economy: Manufacturing of zinc products for marine industry, machinery. Resort village, popular for summer recreational activities. Employment by occupation: 13.9% management, 22.8% professional, 13.2% services, 28.2% sales, 0.7% farming, 10.6% construction, 10.7% production (2000).
Income: Per capita income: $30,749 (2005); Median household income: $65,356 (2005); Average household income: $76,360 (2005); Percent of households with income of $100,000 or more: 28.7% (2005); Poverty rate: 5.6% (2000).
Education: Percent of population age 25 and over with: High school diploma (including GED) or higher: 91.6% (2005); Bachelor's degree or higher: 34.7% (2005); Master's degree or higher: 17.1% (2005).
School District(s)
Mattituck-Cutchogue Union Free School District (KG-12)
    2003-04 Enrollment: 1,563 . . . . (631) 298-4242
Housing: Homeownership rate: 85.9% (2005); Median home value: $348,588 (2005); Median rent: $737 per month (2000); Median age of housing: 38 years (2000).
Newspapers: Suffolk Times (General - Circulation 15,000); The News-Review (General - Circulation 15,000)
Transportation: Commute to work: 91.8% car, 1.3% public transportation, 2.2% walk, 4.6% work from home (2000); Travel time to work: 35.7% less than 15 minutes, 30.8% 15 to 30 minutes, 9.3% 30 to 45 minutes, 7.7% 45 to 60 minutes, 16.4% 60 minutes or more (2000)
Additional Information Contacts

Mattituck Chamber of Commerce . . . . (631) 298-5757
http://www.mattituckchamber.org/

MEDFORD (CDP).
Covers a land area of 10.527 square miles and a water area of 0 square miles. Located at 40.81° N. Lat.; 72.98° W. Long. Elevation is 101 feet.
Population: 21,070 (1990); 21,985 (2000); 22,738 (2005); 23,579 (2010 projected); Race: 86.4% White, 4.9% Black, 1.7% Asian, 14.0% Hispanic of any race (2005); Density: 2,160.0 persons per square mile (2005); Average household size: 3.19 (2005); Median age: 36.1 (2005); Males per 100 females: 97.2 (2005); Marriage status: 25.9% never married, 62.7% now married, 4.8% widowed, 6.5% divorced (2000); Foreign born: 8.2% (2000); Ancestry (includes multiple ancestries): 32.7% Italian, 23.9% Irish, 20.3% German, 18.5% Other groups, 6.4% English (2000).
Economy: Manufacturing: machinery, cement products, building materials; in farming area. Employment by occupation: 12.2% management, 16.8% professional, 12.3% services, 33.1% sales, 0.1% farming, 13.3% construction, 12.2% production (2000).
Income: Per capita income: $26,842 (2005); Median household income: $76,820 (2005); Average household income: $85,312 (2005); Percent of households with income of $100,000 or more: 31.0% (2005); Poverty rate: 3.3% (2000).
Education: Percent of population age 25 and over with: High school diploma (including GED) or higher: 85.9% (2005); Bachelor's degree or higher: 16.8% (2005); Master's degree or higher: 6.9% (2005).
School District(s)
Patchogue-Medford Union Free School District (PK-12)
    2003-04 Enrollment: 9,101 . . . . (631) 758-1017
Housing: Homeownership rate: 89.3% (2005); Median home value: $246,279 (2005); Median rent: $816 per month (2000); Median age of housing: 26 years (2000).
Transportation: Commute to work: 90.9% car, 5.0% public transportation, 1.3% walk, 2.1% work from home (2000); Travel time to work: 23.4% less than 15 minutes, 34.6% 15 to 30 minutes, 17.4% 30 to 45 minutes, 8.5% 45 to 60 minutes, 16.1% 60 minutes or more (2000)
Additional Information Contacts
Medford Chamber of Commerce . . . . (631) 475-3374

MELVILLE (CDP).
Covers a land area of 11.319 square miles and a water area of 0 square miles. Located at 40.79° N. Lat.; 73.40° W. Long. Elevation is 129 feet.
Population: 12,586 (1990); 14,533 (2000); 15,878 (2005); 17,140 (2010 projected); Race: 87.0% White, 2.6% Black, 7.1% Asian, 4.7% Hispanic of any race (2005); Density: 1,402.8 persons per square mile (2005); Average household size: 2.87 (2005); Median age: 40.3 (2005); Males per 100 females: 95.0 (2005); Marriage status: 20.3% never married, 68.1% now married, 7.1% widowed, 4.6% divorced (2000); Foreign born: 10.4% (2000); Ancestry (includes multiple ancestries): 26.6% Italian, 17.3% Other groups, 10.8% Irish, 10.7% German, 8.2% Russian (2000).
Economy: Employment by occupation: 19.6% management, 30.0% professional, 9.1% services, 33.0% sales, 0.0% farming, 4.6% construction, 3.7% production (2000).
Income: Per capita income: $45,319 (2005); Median household income: $99,192 (2005); Average household income: $129,445 (2005); Percent of households with income of $100,000 or more: 49.6% (2005); Poverty rate: 4.0% (2000).
Education: Percent of population age 25 and over with: High school diploma (including GED) or higher: 92.3% (2005); Bachelor's degree or higher: 48.6% (2005); Master's degree or higher: 23.3% (2005).
School District(s)
Half Hollow Hills Central School District (KG-12)
    2003-04 Enrollment: 9,661 . . . . (631) 592-3008
South Huntington Union Free School District (KG-12)
    2003-04 Enrollment: 6,111 . . . . (631) 425-5300
Two-year College(s)
Katharine Gibbs School-Melville
    Fall 2004 Enrollment: 192 . . . . (631) 370-3300
    2005-06 Tuition: In-state $36,900; Out-of-state $36,900
Housing: Homeownership rate: 84.1% (2005); Median home value: $533,537 (2005); Median rent: $1,691 per month (2000); Median age of housing: 31 years (2000).
Newspapers: Newsday (Circulation 579,351)
Transportation: Commute to work: 85.4% car, 9.4% public transportation, 1.1% walk, 4.0% work from home (2000); Travel time to work: 22.4% less than 15 minutes, 30.5% 15 to 30 minutes, 19.8% 30 to 45 minutes, 6.2% 45 to 60 minutes, 21.1% 60 minutes or more (2000)

MIDDLE ISLAND (CDP).
Covers a land area of 8.251 square miles and a water area of 0.066 square miles. Located at 40.88° N. Lat.; 72.94° W. Long. Elevation is 76 feet.
Population: 7,848 (1990); 9,702 (2000); 11,383 (2005); 12,941 (2010 projected); Race: 81.4% White, 10.0% Black, 3.2% Asian, 8.9% Hispanic of any race (2005); Density: 1,379.7 persons per square mile (2005); Average household size: 2.59 (2005); Median age: 39.1 (2005); Males per 100 females: 92.0 (2005); Marriage status: 25.8% never married, 54.9% now married, 7.4% widowed, 11.9% divorced (2000); Foreign born: 7.4% (2000); Ancestry (includes multiple ancestries): 31.4% Italian, 23.0% Irish, 19.0% German, 15.3% Other groups, 5.8% Polish (2000).
Economy: Employment by occupation: 9.9% management, 17.1% professional, 16.0% services, 36.5% sales, 0.0% farming, 9.6% construction, 10.9% production (2000).
Income: Per capita income: $26,777 (2005); Median household income: $58,117 (2005); Average household income: $68,273 (2005); Percent of households with income of $100,000 or more: 19.7% (2005); Poverty rate: 6.3% (2000).
Education: Percent of population age 25 and over with: High school diploma (including GED) or higher: 86.8% (2005); Bachelor's degree or higher: 18.7% (2005); Master's degree or higher: 8.8% (2005).
School District(s)
Longwood Central School District (KG-12)
    2003-04 Enrollment: 9,794 . . . . (631) 345-2172
Housing: Homeownership rate: 69.3% (2005); Median home value: $224,732 (2005); Median rent: $859 per month (2000); Median age of housing: 21 years (2000).
Transportation: Commute to work: 94.5% car, 2.6% public transportation, 0.6% walk, 1.6% work from home (2000); Travel time to work: 18.5% less than 15 minutes, 35.9% 15 to 30 minutes, 22.6% 30 to 45 minutes, 10.2% 45 to 60 minutes, 12.9% 60 minutes or more (2000)

MILLER PLACE (CDP).
Covers a land area of 7.207 square miles and a water area of 0 square miles. Located at 40.94° N. Lat.; 72.99° W. Long. Elevation is 150 feet.
Population: 9,514 (1990); 10,580 (2000); 12,238 (2005); 13,784 (2010 projected); Race: 96.0% White, 0.4% Black, 1.8% Asian, 4.2% Hispanic of any race (2005); Density: 1,698.1 persons per square mile (2005); Average household size: 3.07 (2005); Median age: 37.1 (2005); Males per 100 females: 98.2 (2005); Marriage status: 22.5% never married, 65.9% now married, 4.2% widowed, 7.4% divorced (2000); Foreign born: 3.6% (2000); Ancestry (includes multiple ancestries): 32.4% Irish, 32.4% Italian, 22.2% German, 7.6% Other groups, 7.1% English (2000).
Economy: Employment by occupation: 17.0% management, 28.8% professional, 13.0% services, 25.0% sales, 0.5% farming, 9.1% construction, 6.5% production (2000).
Income: Per capita income: $32,959 (2005); Median household income: $90,369 (2005); Average household income: $100,494 (2005); Percent of households with income of $100,000 or more: 42.1% (2005); Poverty rate: 2.4% (2000).
Education: Percent of population age 25 and over with: High school diploma (including GED) or higher: 93.9% (2005); Bachelor's degree or higher: 37.5% (2005); Master's degree or higher: 18.6% (2005).
School District(s)
Miller Place Union Free School District (KG-12)
    2003-04 Enrollment: 3,030 . . . . (631) 474-2733
Housing: Homeownership rate: 90.9% (2005); Median home value: $334,935 (2005); Median rent: $838 per month (2000); Median age of housing: 28 years (2000).
Transportation: Commute to work: 92.1% car, 3.8% public transportation, 1.0% walk, 3.0% work from home (2000); Travel time to work: 20.9% less than 15 minutes, 27.1% 15 to 30 minutes, 24.5% 30 to 45 minutes, 9.7% 45 to 60 minutes, 17.9% 60 minutes or more (2000)

MONTAUK (CDP).
Covers a land area of 17.494 square miles and a water area of 2.283 square miles. Located at 41.03° N. Lat.; 71.95° W. Long. Elevation is 9 feet.
History: Name derived from Montauk word for hilly land. Founded on land bought from Montauks in 1686 by settlers from nearby East Hampton to raise cattle. Site of oldest cattle ranch in U.S.
Population: 3,003 (1990); 3,851 (2000); 4,431 (2005); 4,978 (2010 projected); Race: 81.2% White, 0.8% Black, 1.2% Asian, 34.0% Hispanic of

any race (2005); Density: 253.3 persons per square mile (2005); Average household size: 2.47 (2005); Median age: 41.1 (2005); Males per 100 females: 105.9 (2005); Marriage status: 24.9% never married, 57.6% now married, 7.4% widowed, 10.1% divorced (2000); Foreign born: 27.0% (2000); Ancestry (includes multiple ancestries): 28.0% Other groups, 26.5% Irish, 17.3% German, 13.1% Italian, 6.3% English (2000).
Economy: Resort village. East terminus of South Shore line of Long Island Railroad. Commercial- and sport-fishing center. Manufacturing includes electronic components and high-temperature alloys. Prize fishing area, with over 30 world records for marlin, shark and tuna. Yacht harbor. Employment by occupation: 10.3% management, 9.9% professional, 23.3% services, 27.9% sales, 5.8% farming, 19.0% construction, 3.6% production (2000).
Income: Per capita income: $25,839 (2005); Median household income: $47,226 (2005); Average household income: $63,710 (2005); Percent of households with income of $100,000 or more: 17.9% (2005); Poverty rate: 10.6% (2000).
Education: Percent of population age 25 and over with: High school diploma (including GED) or higher: 84.4% (2005); Bachelor's degree or higher: 24.8% (2005); Master's degree or higher: 7.8% (2005).

School District(s)
Montauk Union Free School District (KG-08)
 2003-04 Enrollment: 387 . . . . (631) 668-2474
Housing: Homeownership rate: 66.0% (2005); Median home value: $465,538 (2005); Median rent: $820 per month (2000); Median age of housing: 26 years (2000).
Transportation: Commute to work: 84.4% car, 3.5% public transportation, 6.0% walk, 2.8% work from home (2000); Travel time to work: 53.3% less than 15 minutes, 21.5% 15 to 30 minutes, 13.1% 30 to 45 minutes, 2.8% 45 to 60 minutes, 9.4% 60 minutes or more (2000)
Additional Information Contacts
Montauk Chamber of Commerce. . . . . (631) 668-2428
 http://www.montaukchamber.com

MORICHES (CDP). Covers a land area of 1.948 square miles and a water area of 0.230 square miles. Located at 40.80° N. Lat.; 72.82° W. Long.
Population: 2,067 (1990); 2,319 (2000); 2,734 (2005); 3,147 (2010 projected); Race: 94.6% White, 1.2% Black, 2.2% Asian, 4.6% Hispanic of any race (2005); Density: 1,403.7 persons per square mile (2005); Average household size: 2.09 (2005); Median age: 48.2 (2005); Males per 100 females: 99.9 (2005); Marriage status: 20.5% never married, 63.1% now married, 5.8% widowed, 10.7% divorced (2000); Foreign born: 3.9% (2000); Ancestry (includes multiple ancestries): 33.4% Italian, 33.0% Irish, 19.9% German, 10.8% Polish, 6.1% Other groups (2000).
Economy: Employment by occupation: 17.7% management, 20.1% professional, 16.1% services, 27.4% sales, 1.2% farming, 11.0% construction, 6.5% production (2000).
Income: Per capita income: $41,570 (2005); Median household income: $75,190 (2005); Average household income: $85,887 (2005); Percent of households with income of $100,000 or more: 30.1% (2005); Poverty rate: 5.5% (2000).
Education: Percent of population age 25 and over with: High school diploma (including GED) or higher: 92.5% (2005); Bachelor's degree or higher: 30.6% (2005); Master's degree or higher: 14.0% (2005).

School District(s)
William Floyd Union Free School District (KG-12)
 2003-04 Enrollment: 10,376 . . . . (631) 874-1201
Housing: Homeownership rate: 51.5% (2005); Median home value: $322,321 (2005); Median rent: $916 per month (2000); Median age of housing: 16 years (2000).
Newspapers: South Shore Press (General - Circulation 27,000)
Transportation: Commute to work: 91.0% car, 2.0% public transportation, 2.8% walk, 4.3% work from home (2000); Travel time to work: 20.4% less than 15 minutes, 32.9% 15 to 30 minutes, 25.2% 30 to 45 minutes, 10.9% 45 to 60 minutes, 10.6% 60 minutes or more (2000)

MOUNT SINAI (CDP). Covers a land area of 5.269 square miles and a water area of 0.387 square miles. Located at 40.93° N. Lat.; 73.01° W. Long. Elevation is 102 feet.
Population: 7,762 (1990); 8,734 (2000); 9,497 (2005); 10,257 (2010 projected); Race: 93.9% White, 1.5% Black, 1.8% Asian, 5.4% Hispanic of any race (2005); Density: 1,802.6 persons per square mile (2005); Average household size: 3.22 (2005); Median age: 36.7 (2005); Males per 100 females: 95.9 (2005); Marriage status: 21.4% never married, 69.6% now married, 4.8% widowed, 4.2% divorced (2000); Foreign born: 4.3% (2000); Ancestry (includes multiple ancestries): 38.1% Italian, 27.3% Irish, 19.1% German, 7.7% Other groups, 6.7% Polish (2000).
Economy: Employment by occupation: 20.1% management, 25.8% professional, 12.8% services, 25.9% sales, 0.0% farming, 8.2% construction, 7.3% production (2000).
Income: Per capita income: $38,726 (2005); Median household income: $103,012 (2005); Average household income: $124,588 (2005); Percent of households with income of $100,000 or more: 51.7% (2005); Poverty rate: 3.6% (2000).
Education: Percent of population age 25 and over with: High school diploma (including GED) or higher: 92.8% (2005); Bachelor's degree or higher: 34.2% (2005); Master's degree or higher: 15.6% (2005).

School District(s)
Mount Sinai Union Free School District (KG-12)
 2003-04 Enrollment: 2,417 . . . . (631) 473-1991
Housing: Homeownership rate: 93.2% (2005); Median home value: $381,977 (2005); Median rent: $908 per month (2000); Median age of housing: 24 years (2000).
Transportation: Commute to work: 89.6% car, 6.7% public transportation, 0.4% walk, 2.7% work from home (2000); Travel time to work: 23.6% less than 15 minutes, 27.5% 15 to 30 minutes, 20.2% 30 to 45 minutes, 8.8% 45 to 60 minutes, 19.8% 60 minutes or more (2000)

NAPEAGUE (CDP). Covers a land area of 3.883 square miles and a water area of 6.671 square miles. Located at 40.99° N. Lat.; 72.07° W. Long.
Population: 175 (1990); 223 (2000); 248 (2005); 273 (2010 projected); Race: 96.4% White, 2.0% Black, 0.0% Asian, 10.9% Hispanic of any race (2005); Density: 63.9 persons per square mile (2005); Average household size: 2.19 (2005); Median age: 50.2 (2005); Males per 100 females: 108.4 (2005); Marriage status: 32.8% never married, 45.3% now married, 9.0% widowed, 12.9% divorced (2000); Foreign born: 16.5% (2000); Ancestry (includes multiple ancestries): 24.7% Irish, 22.9% German, 19.5% English, 19.0% Italian, 15.2% Other groups (2000).
Economy: Employment by occupation: 12.1% management, 8.6% professional, 28.4% services, 24.1% sales, 1.7% farming, 13.8% construction, 11.2% production (2000).
Income: Per capita income: $30,655 (2005); Median household income: $54,327 (2005); Average household income: $67,279 (2005); Percent of households with income of $100,000 or more: 21.2% (2005); Poverty rate: 13.3% (2000).
Education: Percent of population age 25 and over with: High school diploma (including GED) or higher: 91.5% (2005); Bachelor's degree or higher: 37.5% (2005); Master's degree or higher: 8.5% (2005).
Housing: Homeownership rate: 82.3% (2005); Median home value: $445,000 (2005); Median rent: $1,063 per month (2000); Median age of housing: 20 years (2000).
Transportation: Commute to work: 95.7% car, 0.0% public transportation, 2.6% walk, 1.7% work from home (2000); Travel time to work: 40.4% less than 15 minutes, 50.9% 15 to 30 minutes, 4.4% 30 to 45 minutes, 0.0% 45 to 60 minutes, 4.4% 60 minutes or more (2000)

NESCONSET (CDP). Covers a land area of 3.827 square miles and a water area of 0.004 square miles. Located at 40.84° N. Lat.; 73.15° W. Long. Elevation is 120 feet.
Population: 10,712 (1990); 11,992 (2000); 13,694 (2005); 15,309 (2010 projected); Race: 92.3% White, 1.3% Black, 4.3% Asian, 4.4% Hispanic of any race (2005); Density: 3,578.3 persons per square mile (2005); Average household size: 2.96 (2005); Median age: 38.4 (2005); Males per 100 females: 96.8 (2005); Marriage status: 22.0% never married, 66.4% now married, 6.6% widowed, 5.1% divorced (2000); Foreign born: 7.0% (2000); Ancestry (includes multiple ancestries): 38.4% Italian, 27.0% Irish, 17.3% German, 9.4% Other groups, 6.8% Polish (2000).
Economy: Manufacturing: transportation equipment, electronic products, plastic products. Employment by occupation: 21.7% management, 26.4% professional, 10.4% services, 29.3% sales, 0.0% farming, 7.6% construction, 4.7% production (2000).
Income: Per capita income: $39,046 (2005); Median household income: $102,955 (2005); Average household income: $114,634 (2005); Percent of households with income of $100,000 or more: 51.7% (2005); Poverty rate: 2.3% (2000).
Education: Percent of population age 25 and over with: High school diploma (including GED) or higher: 93.6% (2005); Bachelor's degree or higher: 38.3% (2005); Master's degree or higher: 17.3% (2005).

School District(s)
Smithtown Central School District (KG-12)
    2003-04 Enrollment: 10,188 . . . . (631) 382-2005
Housing: Homeownership rate: 78.9% (2005); Median home value: $408,077 (2005); Median rent: $983 per month (2000); Median age of housing: 28 years (2000).
Transportation: Commute to work: 90.4% car, 6.6% public transportation, 0.5% walk, 2.1% work from home (2000); Travel time to work: 21.5% less than 15 minutes, 32.7% 15 to 30 minutes, 19.4% 30 to 45 minutes, 9.5% 45 to 60 minutes, 16.8% 60 minutes or more (2000)

NEW SUFFOLK
(CDP). Covers a land area of 0.720 square miles and a water area of 0.048 square miles. Located at 40.99° N. Lat.; 72.47° W. Long.
Population: 374 (1990); 337 (2000); 302 (2005); 298 (2010 projected); Race: 91.4% White, 2.0% Black, 0.3% Asian, 5.6% Hispanic of any race (2005); Density: 419.7 persons per square mile (2005); Average household size: 1.95 (2005); Median age: 53.8 (2005); Males per 100 females: 91.1 (2005); Marriage status: 24.2% never married, 54.6% now married, 12.3% widowed, 8.9% divorced (2000); Foreign born: 11.7% (2000); Ancestry (includes multiple ancestries): 26.4% Irish, 22.7% English, 22.1% German, 7.4% Italian, 7.1% Polish (2000).
Economy: Employment by occupation: 10.6% management, 20.6% professional, 23.3% services, 22.8% sales, 0.0% farming, 14.8% construction, 7.9% production (2000).
Income: Per capita income: $36,772 (2005); Median household income: $61,413 (2005); Average household income: $71,645 (2005); Percent of households with income of $100,000 or more: 26.5% (2005); Poverty rate: 6.1% (2000).
Education: Percent of population age 25 and over with: High school diploma (including GED) or higher: 86.6% (2005); Bachelor's degree or higher: 28.3% (2005); Master's degree or higher: 15.0% (2005).
School District(s)
New Suffolk Common School District (PK-06)
    2003-04 Enrollment: 9 . . . . (631) 734-6940
Housing: Homeownership rate: 78.1% (2005); Median home value: $364,894 (2005); Median rent: $850 per month (2000); Median age of housing: 44 years (2000).
Transportation: Commute to work: 87.0% car, 1.1% public transportation, 3.3% walk, 8.7% work from home (2000); Travel time to work: 47.6% less than 15 minutes, 22.0% 15 to 30 minutes, 10.1% 30 to 45 minutes, 4.2% 45 to 60 minutes, 16.1% 60 minutes or more (2000)

NISSEQUOGUE
(village). Covers a land area of 3.773 square miles and a water area of 0.196 square miles. Located at 40.89° N. Lat.; 73.19° W. Long. Elevation is 106 feet.
Population: 1,620 (1990); 1,543 (2000); 1,595 (2005); 1,653 (2010 projected); Race: 96.7% White, 0.1% Black, 1.2% Asian, 3.4% Hispanic of any race (2005); Density: 422.7 persons per square mile (2005); Average household size: 2.85 (2005); Median age: 43.7 (2005); Males per 100 females: 105.0 (2005); Marriage status: 20.4% never married, 72.6% now married, 3.7% widowed, 3.2% divorced (2000); Foreign born: 5.7% (2000); Ancestry (includes multiple ancestries): 29.2% Italian, 25.0% Irish, 15.3% German, 10.4% English, 9.5% Polish (2000).
Economy: Residential and recreational area. Single-family building permits issued: 1 (2005); Multi-family building permits issued: 0 (2005); Employment by occupation: 31.7% management, 33.2% professional, 6.7% services, 21.9% sales, 0.0% farming, 4.0% construction, 2.5% production (2000).
Income: Per capita income: $67,456 (2005); Median household income: $153,716 (2005); Average household income: $192,473 (2005); Percent of households with income of $100,000 or more: 63.7% (2005); Poverty rate: 2.4% (2000).
Education: Percent of population age 25 and over with: High school diploma (including GED) or higher: 96.0% (2005); Bachelor's degree or higher: 57.3% (2005); Master's degree or higher: 31.4% (2005).
Housing: Homeownership rate: 92.8% (2005); Median home value: $947,240 (2005); Median rent: $956 per month (2000); Median age of housing: 29 years (2000).
Safety: Violent crime rate: 0.0 per 10,000 population; Property crime rate: 75.9 per 10,000 population (2004).
Transportation: Commute to work: 85.2% car, 4.3% public transportation, 0.9% walk, 8.0% work from home (2000); Travel time to work: 18.2% less than 15 minutes, 39.1% 15 to 30 minutes, 20.9% 30 to 45 minutes, 8.8% 45 to 60 minutes, 13.1% 60 minutes or more (2000)

NORTH AMITYVILLE
(CDP). Covers a land area of 2.433 square miles and a water area of 0 square miles. Located at 40.70° N. Lat.; 73.41° W. Long.
Population: 13,775 (1990); 16,572 (2000); 17,127 (2005); 17,747 (2010 projected); Race: 18.0% White, 67.6% Black, 1.2% Asian, 16.6% Hispanic of any race (2005); Density: 7,040.8 persons per square mile (2005); Average household size: 3.28 (2005); Median age: 33.9 (2005); Males per 100 females: 83.9 (2005); Marriage status: 39.0% never married, 42.7% now married, 10.5% widowed, 7.8% divorced (2000); Foreign born: 18.0% (2000); Ancestry (includes multiple ancestries): 61.8% Other groups, 5.9% Jamaican, 4.0% Italian, 3.8% Irish, 3.0% United States or American (2000).
Economy: Employment by occupation: 7.5% management, 15.0% professional, 23.0% services, 27.4% sales, 0.0% farming, 7.6% construction, 19.4% production (2000).
Income: Per capita income: $18,528 (2005); Median household income: $48,228 (2005); Average household income: $58,926 (2005); Percent of households with income of $100,000 or more: 14.5% (2005); Poverty rate: 10.9% (2000).
Education: Percent of population age 25 and over with: High school diploma (including GED) or higher: 74.2% (2005); Bachelor's degree or higher: 14.1% (2005); Master's degree or higher: 5.2% (2005).
Housing: Homeownership rate: 61.5% (2005); Median home value: $219,932 (2005); Median rent: $890 per month (2000); Median age of housing: 34 years (2000).
Transportation: Commute to work: 84.9% car, 10.7% public transportation, 1.4% walk, 1.7% work from home (2000); Travel time to work: 26.2% less than 15 minutes, 37.4% 15 to 30 minutes, 19.6% 30 to 45 minutes, 6.2% 45 to 60 minutes, 10.6% 60 minutes or more (2000)

NORTH BABYLON
(CDP). Covers a land area of 3.367 square miles and a water area of 0.053 square miles. Located at 40.73° N. Lat.; 73.32° W. Long. Elevation is 33 feet.
Population: 17,984 (1990); 17,877 (2000); 18,339 (2005); 18,887 (2010 projected); Race: 89.0% White, 3.0% Black, 2.8% Asian, 10.3% Hispanic of any race (2005); Density: 5,447.1 persons per square mile (2005); Average household size: 2.87 (2005); Median age: 39.1 (2005); Males per 100 females: 93.3 (2005); Marriage status: 25.9% never married, 58.7% now married, 8.3% widowed, 7.2% divorced (2000); Foreign born: 8.1% (2000); Ancestry (includes multiple ancestries): 37.0% Italian, 27.1% Irish, 18.9% German, 12.1% Other groups, 6.9% Polish (2000).
Economy: Employment by occupation: 12.3% management, 18.8% professional, 14.7% services, 32.4% sales, 0.0% farming, 9.4% construction, 12.3% production (2000).
Income: Per capita income: $27,815 (2005); Median household income: $69,835 (2005); Average household income: $79,416 (2005); Percent of households with income of $100,000 or more: 26.3% (2005); Poverty rate: 3.2% (2000).
Education: Percent of population age 25 and over with: High school diploma (including GED) or higher: 85.8% (2005); Bachelor's degree or higher: 21.2% (2005); Master's degree or higher: 7.8% (2005).
School District(s)
North Babylon Union Free School District (KG-12)
    2003-04 Enrollment: 5,220 . . . . (631) 321-3226
Housing: Homeownership rate: 81.1% (2005); Median home value: $282,691 (2005); Median rent: $873 per month (2000); Median age of housing: 42 years (2000).
Transportation: Commute to work: 87.0% car, 8.5% public transportation, 1.7% walk, 1.9% work from home (2000); Travel time to work: 24.5% less than 15 minutes, 31.0% 15 to 30 minutes, 18.7% 30 to 45 minutes, 8.6% 45 to 60 minutes, 17.2% 60 minutes or more (2000)

NORTH BAY SHORE
(CDP). Covers a land area of 2.977 square miles and a water area of 0 square miles. Located at 40.75° N. Lat.; 73.26° W. Long.
Population: 12,799 (1990); 14,992 (2000); 14,691 (2005); 14,452 (2010 projected); Race: 41.5% White, 21.4% Black, 2.5% Asian, 57.3% Hispanic of any race (2005); Density: 4,935.4 persons per square mile (2005); Average household size: 4.02 (2005); Median age: 32.3 (2005); Males per 100 females: 101.6 (2005); Marriage status: 32.1% never married, 56.2% now married, 4.9% widowed, 6.8% divorced (2000); Foreign born: 29.3% (2000); Ancestry (includes multiple ancestries): 58.4% Other groups, 10.1% Italian, 9.3% Irish, 6.9% German, 2.7% United States or American (2000).

Economy: Employment by occupation: 7.0% management, 12.4% professional, 18.8% services, 23.8% sales, 0.2% farming, 10.4% construction, 27.4% production (2000).
Income: Per capita income: $17,064 (2005); Median household income: $59,141 (2005); Average household income: $68,487 (2005); Percent of households with income of $100,000 or more: 17.5% (2005); Poverty rate: 10.4% (2000).
Education: Percent of population age 25 and over with: High school diploma (including GED) or higher: 69.8% (2005); Bachelor's degree or higher: 9.5% (2005); Master's degree or higher: 2.9% (2005).
Housing: Homeownership rate: 75.3% (2005); Median home value: $243,186 (2005); Median rent: $818 per month (2000); Median age of housing: 36 years (2000).
Transportation: Commute to work: 88.9% car, 7.4% public transportation, 1.3% walk, 0.7% work from home (2000); Travel time to work: 25.4% less than 15 minutes, 40.6% 15 to 30 minutes, 14.8% 30 to 45 minutes, 6.8% 45 to 60 minutes, 12.5% 60 minutes or more (2000)

NORTH BELLPORT (CDP).
Covers a land area of 4.648 square miles and a water area of 0 square miles. Located at 40.78° N. Lat.; 72.95° W. Long. Elevation is 49 feet.
Population: 7,989 (1990); 9,007 (2000); 9,840 (2005); 10,655 (2010 projected); Race: 49.5% White, 32.6% Black, 2.3% Asian, 23.5% Hispanic of any race (2005); Density: 2,117.0 persons per square mile (2005); Average household size: 3.75 (2005); Median age: 31.4 (2005); Males per 100 females: 97.1 (2005); Marriage status: 35.5% never married, 52.6% now married, 5.6% widowed, 6.4% divorced (2000); Foreign born: 8.6% (2000); Ancestry (includes multiple ancestries): 46.8% Other groups, 19.9% Italian, 12.2% Irish, 12.1% German, 3.8% English (2000).
Economy: Employment by occupation: 8.5% management, 18.2% professional, 20.0% services, 27.8% sales, 0.2% farming, 10.4% construction, 14.8% production (2000).
Income: Per capita income: $19,998 (2005); Median household income: $63,920 (2005); Average household income: $72,626 (2005); Percent of households with income of $100,000 or more: 22.6% (2005); Poverty rate: 15.5% (2000).
Education: Percent of population age 25 and over with: High school diploma (including GED) or higher: 74.9% (2005); Bachelor's degree or higher: 14.9% (2005); Master's degree or higher: 6.2% (2005).
Housing: Homeownership rate: 75.2% (2005); Median home value: $215,021 (2005); Median rent: $902 per month (2000); Median age of housing: 29 years (2000).
Transportation: Commute to work: 87.9% car, 7.3% public transportation, 1.8% walk, 2.4% work from home (2000); Travel time to work: 24.8% less than 15 minutes, 29.3% 15 to 30 minutes, 19.8% 30 to 45 minutes, 6.7% 45 to 60 minutes, 19.3% 60 minutes or more (2000)

NORTH GREAT RIVER (CDP).
Covers a land area of 2.285 square miles and a water area of 0.025 square miles. Located at 40.76° N. Lat.; 73.17° W. Long.
Population: 3,964 (1990); 3,929 (2000); 3,848 (2005); 3,783 (2010 projected); Race: 92.8% White, 2.4% Black, 1.8% Asian, 8.2% Hispanic of any race (2005); Density: 1,684.4 persons per square mile (2005); Average household size: 3.34 (2005); Median age: 37.2 (2005); Males per 100 females: 98.5 (2005); Marriage status: 23.5% never married, 63.0% now married, 6.2% widowed, 7.2% divorced (2000); Foreign born: 5.4% (2000); Ancestry (includes multiple ancestries): 39.4% Italian, 28.7% Irish, 24.2% German, 10.1% Other groups, 6.9% Polish (2000).
Economy: Employment by occupation: 11.7% management, 15.6% professional, 12.4% services, 37.5% sales, 0.0% farming, 9.5% construction, 13.4% production (2000).
Income: Per capita income: $26,463 (2005); Median household income: $73,588 (2005); Average household income: $88,296 (2005); Percent of households with income of $100,000 or more: 32.9% (2005); Poverty rate: 3.8% (2000).
Education: Percent of population age 25 and over with: High school diploma (including GED) or higher: 86.4% (2005); Bachelor's degree or higher: 15.7% (2005); Master's degree or higher: 5.1% (2005).
Housing: Homeownership rate: 92.2% (2005); Median home value: $294,261 (2005); Median rent: $997 per month (2000); Median age of housing: 36 years (2000).
Transportation: Commute to work: 91.2% car, 7.0% public transportation, 0.2% walk, 0.9% work from home (2000); Travel time to work: 25.4% less than 15 minutes, 36.0% 15 to 30 minutes, 15.4% 30 to 45 minutes, 7.8% 45 to 60 minutes, 15.4% 60 minutes or more (2000)

NORTH HAVEN (village).
Covers a land area of 2.710 square miles and a water area of 0 square miles. Located at 41.02° N. Lat.; 72.31° W. Long.
Population: 713 (1990); 743 (2000); 844 (2005); 944 (2010 projected); Race: 97.6% White, 0.5% Black, 1.2% Asian, 1.8% Hispanic of any race (2005); Density: 311.5 persons per square mile (2005); Average household size: 2.16 (2005); Median age: 51.0 (2005); Males per 100 females: 86.7 (2005); Marriage status: 17.7% never married, 64.3% now married, 10.3% widowed, 7.7% divorced (2000); Foreign born: 8.9% (2000); Ancestry (includes multiple ancestries): 26.1% Irish, 17.7% Italian, 17.5% German, 10.9% English, 9.4% Polish (2000).
Economy: Resort village. Single-family building permits issued: 21 (2005); Multi-family building permits issued: 0 (2005); Employment by occupation: 19.9% management, 30.4% professional, 12.8% services, 25.9% sales, 0.0% farming, 5.1% construction, 6.0% production (2000).
Income: Per capita income: $52,153 (2005); Median household income: $86,250 (2005); Average household income: $112,865 (2005); Percent of households with income of $100,000 or more: 41.5% (2005); Poverty rate: 1.8% (2000).
Education: Percent of population age 25 and over with: High school diploma (including GED) or higher: 92.3% (2005); Bachelor's degree or higher: 46.6% (2005); Master's degree or higher: 23.0% (2005).
Housing: Homeownership rate: 92.1% (2005); Median home value: $734,195 (2005); Median rent: $1,143 per month (2000); Median age of housing: 30 years (2000).
Transportation: Commute to work: 80.7% car, 5.6% public transportation, 0.9% walk, 12.3% work from home (2000); Travel time to work: 16.3% less than 15 minutes, 55.0% 15 to 30 minutes, 6.7% 30 to 45 minutes, 3.7% 45 to 60 minutes, 18.3% 60 minutes or more (2000)

NORTH LINDENHURST (CDP).
Covers a land area of 1.898 square miles and a water area of 0 square miles. Located at 40.70° N. Lat.; 73.38° W. Long.
Population: 10,563 (1990); 11,767 (2000); 12,099 (2005); 12,485 (2010 projected); Race: 84.3% White, 5.1% Black, 2.9% Asian, 16.6% Hispanic of any race (2005); Density: 6,374.0 persons per square mile (2005); Average household size: 3.05 (2005); Median age: 37.5 (2005); Males per 100 females: 97.1 (2005); Marriage status: 26.9% never married, 57.4% now married, 8.0% widowed, 7.7% divorced (2000); Foreign born: 15.7% (2000); Ancestry (includes multiple ancestries): 31.0% Italian, 22.2% Irish, 19.0% German, 18.5% Other groups, 7.9% Polish (2000).
Economy: Employment by occupation: 9.6% management, 12.4% professional, 16.8% services, 31.7% sales, 0.1% farming, 13.0% construction, 16.4% production (2000).
Income: Per capita income: $24,966 (2005); Median household income: $65,304 (2005); Average household income: $75,468 (2005); Percent of households with income of $100,000 or more: 21.6% (2005); Poverty rate: 5.2% (2000).
Education: Percent of population age 25 and over with: High school diploma (including GED) or higher: 82.0% (2005); Bachelor's degree or higher: 13.9% (2005); Master's degree or higher: 5.7% (2005).
Housing: Homeownership rate: 70.4% (2005); Median home value: $256,407 (2005); Median rent: $863 per month (2000); Median age of housing: 42 years (2000).
Transportation: Commute to work: 88.2% car, 8.0% public transportation, 2.2% walk, 1.1% work from home (2000); Travel time to work: 29.4% less than 15 minutes, 29.6% 15 to 30 minutes, 19.7% 30 to 45 minutes, 6.4% 45 to 60 minutes, 14.8% 60 minutes or more (2000)

NORTH PATCHOGUE (CDP).
Covers a land area of 2.132 square miles and a water area of 0.050 square miles. Located at 40.78° N. Lat.; 73.02° W. Long. Elevation is 49 feet.
Population: 7,374 (1990); 7,825 (2000); 7,685 (2005); 7,581 (2010 projected); Race: 90.7% White, 2.2% Black, 1.5% Asian, 12.2% Hispanic of any race (2005); Density: 3,604.0 persons per square mile (2005); Average household size: 2.88 (2005); Median age: 37.1 (2005); Males per 100 females: 99.2 (2005); Marriage status: 25.0% never married, 59.8% now married, 6.8% widowed, 8.5% divorced (2000); Foreign born: 7.1% (2000); Ancestry (includes multiple ancestries): 38.4% Italian, 28.9% Irish, 22.3% German, 11.7% Other groups, 7.4% English (2000).
Economy: Employment by occupation: 12.4% management, 16.2% professional, 12.6% services, 32.4% sales, 0.0% farming, 14.7% construction, 11.7% production (2000).

Income: Per capita income: $27,635 (2005); Median household income: $70,565 (2005); Average household income: $79,238 (2005); Percent of households with income of $100,000 or more: 25.4% (2005); Poverty rate: 3.7% (2000).
Education: Percent of population age 25 and over with: High school diploma (including GED) or higher: 83.7% (2005); Bachelor's degree or higher: 18.4% (2005); Master's degree or higher: 9.0% (2005).
Housing: Homeownership rate: 80.3% (2005); Median home value: $231,401 (2005); Median rent: $778 per month (2000); Median age of housing: 36 years (2000).
Transportation: Commute to work: 91.2% car, 4.2% public transportation, 1.4% walk, 1.7% work from home (2000); Travel time to work: 29.7% less than 15 minutes, 32.7% 15 to 30 minutes, 14.3% 30 to 45 minutes, 8.2% 45 to 60 minutes, 15.1% 60 minutes or more (2000)

NORTH SEA (CDP). Covers a land area of 12.312 square miles and a water area of 1.082 square miles. Located at 40.94° N. Lat.; 72.40° W. Long.
Population: 3,592 (1990); 4,493 (2000); 5,061 (2005); 5,603 (2010 projected); Race: 92.9% White, 1.6% Black, 1.3% Asian, 8.0% Hispanic of any race (2005); Density: 411.0 persons per square mile (2005); Average household size: 2.41 (2005); Median age: 44.6 (2005); Males per 100 females: 97.7 (2005); Marriage status: 22.6% never married, 60.9% now married, 6.3% widowed, 10.2% divorced (2000); Foreign born: 11.0% (2000); Ancestry (includes multiple ancestries): 27.7% Irish, 19.2% Italian, 18.4% German, 12.6% English, 10.7% Polish (2000).
Economy: Employment by occupation: 15.8% management, 26.0% professional, 17.7% services, 21.9% sales, 1.3% farming, 14.7% construction, 2.7% production (2000).
Income: Per capita income: $39,214 (2005); Median household income: $73,912 (2005); Average household income: $94,013 (2005); Percent of households with income of $100,000 or more: 33.3% (2005); Poverty rate: 7.2% (2000).
Education: Percent of population age 25 and over with: High school diploma (including GED) or higher: 90.9% (2005); Bachelor's degree or higher: 35.7% (2005); Master's degree or higher: 16.3% (2005).
Housing: Homeownership rate: 81.5% (2005); Median home value: $492,395 (2005); Median rent: $946 per month (2000); Median age of housing: 31 years (2000).
Transportation: Commute to work: 84.9% car, 3.8% public transportation, 2.5% walk, 6.7% work from home (2000); Travel time to work: 35.8% less than 15 minutes, 33.9% 15 to 30 minutes, 15.3% 30 to 45 minutes, 2.0% 45 to 60 minutes, 13.0% 60 minutes or more (2000)

NORTHAMPTON (CDP). Covers a land area of 9.078 square miles and a water area of 0.102 square miles. Located at 40.88° N. Lat.; 72.69° W. Long.
Population: 397 (1990); 468 (2000); 500 (2005); 533 (2010 projected); Race: 33.4% White, 56.0% Black, 0.8% Asian, 11.8% Hispanic of any race (2005); Density: 55.1 persons per square mile (2005); Average household size: 3.01 (2005); Median age: 34.7 (2005); Males per 100 females: 92.3 (2005); Marriage status: 29.4% never married, 55.8% now married, 3.0% widowed, 11.8% divorced (2000); Foreign born: 8.8% (2000); Ancestry (includes multiple ancestries): 48.5% Other groups, 14.8% German, 10.1% Italian, 9.9% Polish, 7.2% Irish (2000).
Economy: Employment by occupation: 9.9% management, 19.8% professional, 12.8% services, 33.9% sales, 0.8% farming, 9.1% construction, 13.6% production (2000).
Income: Per capita income: $31,985 (2005); Median household income: $56,061 (2005); Average household income: $96,340 (2005); Percent of households with income of $100,000 or more: 25.3% (2005); Poverty rate: 9.0% (2000).
Education: Percent of population age 25 and over with: High school diploma (including GED) or higher: 82.7% (2005); Bachelor's degree or higher: 9.3% (2005); Master's degree or higher: 3.8% (2005).
Housing: Homeownership rate: 68.7% (2005); Median home value: $173,214 (2005); Median rent: $906 per month (2000); Median age of housing: 43 years (2000).
Transportation: Commute to work: 93.8% car, 4.1% public transportation, 0.0% walk, 1.2% work from home (2000); Travel time to work: 48.7% less than 15 minutes, 32.4% 15 to 30 minutes, 10.5% 30 to 45 minutes, 3.4% 45 to 60 minutes, 5.0% 60 minutes or more (2000)

NORTHPORT (village). Aka Old Northport. Covers a land area of 2.314 square miles and a water area of 0.231 square miles. Located at 40.90° N. Lat.; 73.34° W. Long. Elevation is 175 feet.
Population: 7,572 (1990); 7,606 (2000); 7,684 (2005); 7,816 (2010 projected); Race: 96.3% White, 0.7% Black, 1.6% Asian, 2.6% Hispanic of any race (2005); Density: 3,320.7 persons per square mile (2005); Average household size: 2.55 (2005); Median age: 41.9 (2005); Males per 100 females: 95.1 (2005); Marriage status: 22.2% never married, 62.1% now married, 6.4% widowed, 9.3% divorced (2000); Foreign born: 5.8% (2000); Ancestry (includes multiple ancestries): 30.0% Irish, 26.0% Italian, 19.1% German, 10.8% English, 6.5% Other groups (2000).
Economy: Single-family building permits issued: 2 (2005); Multi-family building permits issued: 0 (2005); Employment by occupation: 21.2% management, 35.6% professional, 8.0% services, 24.0% sales, 0.1% farming, 5.8% construction, 5.3% production (2000).
Income: Per capita income: $53,253 (2005); Median household income: $102,829 (2005); Average household income: $135,580 (2005); Percent of households with income of $100,000 or more: 51.2% (2005); Poverty rate: 2.8% (2000).
Education: Percent of population age 25 and over with: High school diploma (including GED) or higher: 95.7% (2005); Bachelor's degree or higher: 53.8% (2005); Master's degree or higher: 24.4% (2005).
School District(s)
Kings Park Central School District (KG-12)
    2003-04 Enrollment: 4,007 . . . . (631) 269-3210
Northport-East Northport Union Free School District (KG-12)
    2003-04 Enrollment: 6,392 . . . . (631) 262-6604
Two-year College(s)
Western Suffolk BOCES (Public)
    Fall 2004 Enrollment: 284 . . . . (631) 667-6000
Housing: Homeownership rate: 76.4% (2005); Median home value: $520,779 (2005); Median rent: $902 per month (2000); Median age of housing: 47 years (2000).
Hospitals: Veterans Affairs Medical Center (524 beds)
Newspapers: The Observer (General - Circulation 9,360)
Transportation: Commute to work: 81.3% car, 8.4% public transportation, 2.3% walk, 6.7% work from home (2000); Travel time to work: 22.3% less than 15 minutes, 25.7% 15 to 30 minutes, 22.4% 30 to 45 minutes, 7.0% 45 to 60 minutes, 22.6% 60 minutes or more (2000)
Additional Information Contacts
Northport Chamber of Commerce . . . . (631) 754-3905
    http://www.northportny.com/chamber_commerce.php

NORTHVILLE (CDP). Covers a land area of 5.223 square miles and a water area of 0.360 square miles. Located at 41.25° N. Lat.; 89.33° W. Long.
Population: 641 (1990); 801 (2000); 926 (2005); 1,038 (2010 projected); Race: 91.9% White, 4.6% Black, 0.1% Asian, 5.1% Hispanic of any race (2005); Density: 177.3 persons per square mile (2005); Average household size: 2.66 (2005); Median age: 42.6 (2005); Males per 100 females: 107.6 (2005); Marriage status: 18.6% never married, 69.2% now married, 11.5% widowed, 0.7% divorced (2000); Foreign born: 8.2% (2000); Ancestry (includes multiple ancestries): 19.6% Irish, 18.0% English, 17.0% German, 14.1% Polish, 14.0% Italian (2000).
Economy: Employment by occupation: 12.0% management, 22.0% professional, 22.0% services, 27.2% sales, 6.0% farming, 6.8% construction, 4.1% production (2000).
Income: Per capita income: $30,650 (2005); Median household income: $67,466 (2005); Average household income: $81,516 (2005); Percent of households with income of $100,000 or more: 26.1% (2005); Poverty rate: 2.6% (2000).
Education: Percent of population age 25 and over with: High school diploma (including GED) or higher: 78.5% (2005); Bachelor's degree or higher: 22.1% (2005); Master's degree or higher: 7.0% (2005).
Housing: Homeownership rate: 90.8% (2005); Median home value: $380,597 (2005); Median rent: $775 per month (2000); Median age of housing: 42 years (2000).
Transportation: Commute to work: 87.3% car, 0.0% public transportation, 7.7% walk, 2.5% work from home (2000); Travel time to work: 42.5% less than 15 minutes, 29.9% 15 to 30 minutes, 11.5% 30 to 45 minutes, 3.1% 45 to 60 minutes, 13.0% 60 minutes or more (2000)

NORTHWEST HARBOR (CDP).
Covers a land area of 14.523 square miles and a water area of 1.579 square miles. Located at 41.00° N. Lat.; 72.21° W. Long.
Population: 2,107 (1990); 3,059 (2000); 3,640 (2005); 4,199 (2010 projected); Race: 88.9% White, 4.0% Black, 1.2% Asian, 13.5% Hispanic of any race (2005); Density: 250.6 persons per square mile (2005); Average household size: 2.62 (2005); Median age: 43.4 (2005); Males per 100 females: 97.3 (2005); Marriage status: 25.7% never married, 60.3% now married, 6.6% widowed, 7.4% divorced (2000); Foreign born: 10.4% (2000); Ancestry (includes multiple ancestries): 20.0% Irish, 19.9% German, 14.2% Other groups, 12.3% English, 11.8% Italian (2000).
Economy: Employment by occupation: 17.9% management, 26.1% professional, 17.4% services, 22.9% sales, 0.7% farming, 12.1% construction, 2.8% production (2000).
Income: Per capita income: $36,788 (2005); Median household income: $70,683 (2005); Average household income: $96,338 (2005); Percent of households with income of $100,000 or more: 33.5% (2005); Poverty rate: 5.3% (2000).
Education: Percent of population age 25 and over with: High school diploma (including GED) or higher: 91.7% (2005); Bachelor's degree or higher: 50.6% (2005); Master's degree or higher: 26.6% (2005).
Housing: Homeownership rate: 85.5% (2005); Median home value: $560,942 (2005); Median rent: $742 per month (2000); Median age of housing: 15 years (2000).
Transportation: Commute to work: 86.6% car, 1.3% public transportation, 0.8% walk, 10.2% work from home (2000); Travel time to work: 58.4% less than 15 minutes, 21.8% 15 to 30 minutes, 9.0% 30 to 45 minutes, 1.7% 45 to 60 minutes, 9.0% 60 minutes or more (2000)

NOYACK (CDP).
Covers a land area of 7.035 square miles and a water area of 0.173 square miles. Located at 40.99° N. Lat.; 72.33° W. Long.
Population: 2,001 (1990); 2,696 (2000); 3,195 (2005); 3,665 (2010 projected); Race: 94.6% White, 1.0% Black, 1.2% Asian, 6.8% Hispanic of any race (2005); Density: 454.1 persons per square mile (2005); Average household size: 2.32 (2005); Median age: 45.1 (2005); Males per 100 females: 97.3 (2005); Marriage status: 24.7% never married, 59.5% now married, 9.7% widowed, 6.0% divorced (2000); Foreign born: 9.5% (2000); Ancestry (includes multiple ancestries): 27.1% Irish, 23.1% German, 15.4% Italian, 14.5% English, 9.3% Other groups (2000).
Economy: Employment by occupation: 16.5% management, 21.0% professional, 19.3% services, 25.3% sales, 0.3% farming, 11.7% construction, 5.8% production (2000).
Income: Per capita income: $36,797 (2005); Median household income: $64,567 (2005); Average household income: $85,194 (2005); Percent of households with income of $100,000 or more: 29.0% (2005); Poverty rate: 3.9% (2000).
Education: Percent of population age 25 and over with: High school diploma (including GED) or higher: 93.2% (2005); Bachelor's degree or higher: 37.8% (2005); Master's degree or higher: 16.3% (2005).
Housing: Homeownership rate: 81.6% (2005); Median home value: $488,764 (2005); Median rent: $874 per month (2000); Median age of housing: 31 years (2000).
Transportation: Commute to work: 88.0% car, 1.8% public transportation, 5.2% walk, 4.3% work from home (2000); Travel time to work: 38.4% less than 15 minutes, 39.6% 15 to 30 minutes, 10.2% 30 to 45 minutes, 4.0% 45 to 60 minutes, 7.8% 60 minutes or more (2000)

OAKDALE (CDP).
Covers a land area of 3.323 square miles and a water area of 0.439 square miles. Located at 40.74° N. Lat.; 73.14° W. Long. Elevation is 17 feet.
History: Seat of Dowling College.
Population: 7,875 (1990); 8,075 (2000); 8,684 (2005); 9,293 (2010 projected); Race: 96.0% White, 2.1% Black, 0.7% Asian, 4.1% Hispanic of any race (2005); Density: 2,613.6 persons per square mile (2005); Average household size: 2.61 (2005); Median age: 40.8 (2005); Males per 100 females: 91.6 (2005); Marriage status: 22.1% never married, 61.1% now married, 8.1% widowed, 8.6% divorced (2000); Foreign born: 4.0% (2000); Ancestry (includes multiple ancestries): 33.9% Italian, 32.7% Irish, 21.0% German, 8.3% English, 7.6% Other groups (2000).
Economy: Employment by occupation: 19.1% management, 26.9% professional, 10.4% services, 29.5% sales, 0.2% farming, 7.6% construction, 6.3% production (2000).
Income: Per capita income: $37,509 (2005); Median household income: $80,525 (2005); Average household income: $97,615 (2005); Percent of households with income of $100,000 or more: 38.3% (2005); Poverty rate: 2.1% (2000).
Education: Percent of population age 25 and over with: High school diploma (including GED) or higher: 92.8% (2005); Bachelor's degree or higher: 33.2% (2005); Master's degree or higher: 14.3% (2005).
School District(s)
Connetquot Central School District (KG-12)
    2003-04 Enrollment: 7,160 . . . . (631) 244-2211
Four-year College(s)
Dowling College
    Fall 2004 Enrollment: 6,092. (631) 244-3000
    2005-06 Tuition: In-state $15,420; Out-of-state $15,420
Housing: Homeownership rate: 78.4% (2005); Median home value: $365,324 (2005); Median rent: $785 per month (2000); Median age of housing: 33 years (2000).
Transportation: Commute to work: 89.9% car, 6.5% public transportation, 0.7% walk, 2.7% work from home (2000); Travel time to work: 21.7% less than 15 minutes, 34.3% 15 to 30 minutes, 20.4% 30 to 45 minutes, 7.3% 45 to 60 minutes, 16.4% 60 minutes or more (2000)

OCEAN BEACH (village).
Covers a land area of 0.143 square miles and a water area of 0 square miles. Located at 40.64° N. Lat.; 73.15° W. Long. Elevation is 12 feet.
Population: 129 (1990); 138 (2000); 113 (2005); 109 (2010 projected); Race: 98.2% White, 0.0% Black, 1.8% Asian, 2.7% Hispanic of any race (2005); Density: 791.9 persons per square mile (2005); Average household size: 2.22 (2005); Median age: 44.8 (2005); Males per 100 females: 130.6 (2005); Marriage status: 7.5% never married, 64.5% now married, 2.2% widowed, 25.8% divorced (2000); Foreign born: 9.2% (2000); Ancestry (includes multiple ancestries): 24.6% Italian, 23.1% German, 16.9% Other groups, 13.1% English, 12.3% Irish (2000).
Economy: Single-family building permits issued: 7 (2005); Multi-family building permits issued: 0 (2005); Employment by occupation: 20.3% management, 10.9% professional, 4.7% services, 28.1% sales, 0.0% farming, 18.8% construction, 17.2% production (2000).
Income: Per capita income: $33,319 (2005); Median household income: $53,125 (2005); Average household income: $73,824 (2005); Percent of households with income of $100,000 or more: 21.6% (2005); Poverty rate: 11.5% (2000).
Education: Percent of population age 25 and over with: High school diploma (including GED) or higher: 82.8% (2005); Bachelor's degree or higher: 28.7% (2005); Master's degree or higher: 12.6% (2005).
School District(s)
Fire Island Union Free School District (PK-06)
    2003-04 Enrollment: 52. . . . . (631) 583-5626
Housing: Homeownership rate: 66.7% (2005); Median home value: $446,154 (2005); Median rent: $630 per month (2000); Median age of housing: 27 years (2000).
Transportation: Commute to work: 29.7% car, 0.0% public transportation, 37.5% walk, 10.9% work from home (2000); Travel time to work: 80.7% less than 15 minutes, 0.0% 15 to 30 minutes, 12.3% 30 to 45 minutes, 0.0% 45 to 60 minutes, 7.0% 60 minutes or more (2000)
Additional Information Contacts
Ocean Beach Chamber of Commerce. . . . . (631) 583-5555
Village of Ocean Beach . . . . (631) 583-5940
    http://www.villageofoceanbeach.org/

OLD FIELD (village).
Covers a land area of 2.063 square miles and a water area of 0.124 square miles. Located at 40.96° N. Lat.; 73.13° W. Long. Elevation is 50 feet.
Population: 765 (1990); 947 (2000); 970 (2005); 993 (2010 projected); Race: 93.9% White, 0.8% Black, 4.0% Asian, 3.5% Hispanic of any race (2005); Density: 470.2 persons per square mile (2005); Average household size: 3.03 (2005); Median age: 42.1 (2005); Males per 100 females: 98.8 (2005); Marriage status: 21.8% never married, 70.2% now married, 4.8% widowed, 3.2% divorced (2000); Foreign born: 9.8% (2000); Ancestry (includes multiple ancestries): 19.7% Italian, 15.1% Irish, 13.3% Other groups, 13.2% German, 8.9% Polish (2000).
Economy: Single-family building permits issued: 2 (2005); Multi-family building permits issued: 0 (2005); Employment by occupation: 17.5% management, 50.9% professional, 12.7% services, 20.6% sales, 0.0% farming, 2.6% construction, 1.2% production (2000).
Income: Per capita income: $80,572 (2005); Median household income: $194,872 (2005); Average household income: $244,234 (2005); Percent of

households with income of $100,000 or more: 76.3% (2005); Poverty rate: 7.4% (2000).
Education: Percent of population age 25 and over with: High school diploma (including GED) or higher: 99.8% (2005); Bachelor's degree or higher: 75.2% (2005); Master's degree or higher: 46.0% (2005).
Housing: Homeownership rate: 92.8% (2005); Median home value: $1 million+ (2005); Median rent: $1,188 per month (2000); Median age of housing: 34 years (2000).
Transportation: Commute to work: 90.2% car, 1.2% public transportation, 1.7% walk, 5.7% work from home (2000); Travel time to work: 25.1% less than 15 minutes, 31.5% 15 to 30 minutes, 18.3% 30 to 45 minutes, 12.2% 45 to 60 minutes, 12.9% 60 minutes or more (2000)
Additional Information Contacts
Village of Old Field . . . . (631) 941-9412
http://www.oldfieldny.org/

ORIENT
ORIENT (CDP). Covers a land area of 5.093 square miles and a water area of 1.026 square miles. Located at 41.14° N. Lat.; 72.28° W. Long.
Population: 817 (1990); 709 (2000); 770 (2005); 819 (2010 projected); Race: 96.0% White, 0.9% Black, 1.4% Asian, 1.4% Hispanic of any race (2005); Density: 151.2 persons per square mile (2005); Average household size: 2.14 (2005); Median age: 56.6 (2005); Males per 100 females: 96.9 (2005); Marriage status: 14.2% never married, 64.2% now married, 11.4% widowed, 10.1% divorced (2000); Foreign born: 7.7% (2000); Ancestry (includes multiple ancestries): 27.3% English, 26.7% German, 22.4% Irish, 13.9% Polish, 8.9% Italian (2000).
Economy: To East are Orient Point resort village, with ferry connections with New London, Connecticut; Orient Point promontory and Orient Beach State Park. Employment by occupation: 14.7% management, 21.6% professional, 9.4% services, 30.6% sales, 0.4% farming, 15.1% construction, 8.2% production (2000).
Income: Per capita income: $33,140 (2005); Median household income: $49,009 (2005); Average household income: $71,038 (2005); Percent of households with income of $100,000 or more: 19.8% (2005); Poverty rate: 4.4% (2000).
Education: Percent of population age 25 and over with: High school diploma (including GED) or higher: 93.8% (2005); Bachelor's degree or higher: 38.8% (2005); Master's degree or higher: 19.2% (2005).
School District(s)
Oysterponds Union Free School District (KG-06)
    2003-04 Enrollment: 106 . . . . (631) 323-2410
Housing: Homeownership rate: 84.4% (2005); Median home value: $466,327 (2005); Median rent: $717 per month (2000); Median age of housing: 43 years (2000).
Transportation: Commute to work: 83.1% car, 3.4% public transportation, 3.0% walk, 8.5% work from home (2000); Travel time to work: 34.3% less than 15 minutes, 24.1% 15 to 30 minutes, 16.2% 30 to 45 minutes, 5.6% 45 to 60 minutes, 19.9% 60 minutes or more (2000)

PATCHOGUE
PATCHOGUE (village). Covers a land area of 2.248 square miles and a water area of 0.270 square miles. Located at 40.76° N. Lat.; 73.01° W. Long. Elevation is 15 feet.
Population: 10,967 (1990); 11,919 (2000); 12,032 (2005); 12,224 (2010 projected); Race: 76.4% White, 5.0% Black, 1.8% Asian, 31.6% Hispanic of any race (2005); Density: 5,351.4 persons per square mile (2005); Average household size: 2.63 (2005); Median age: 36.4 (2005); Males per 100 females: 101.4 (2005); Marriage status: 30.9% never married, 51.3% now married, 6.1% widowed, 11.7% divorced (2000); Foreign born: 17.9% (2000); Ancestry (includes multiple ancestries): 27.6% Other groups, 22.6% Italian, 20.9% Irish, 14.9% German, 7.4% English (2000).
Economy: In shore-resort area. Manufacturing: stamps, tapes, labels, and engraved plates. Single-family building permits issued: 26 (2005); Multi-family building permits issued: 0 (2005). Employment by occupation: 12.0% management, 19.7% professional, 17.0% services, 24.8% sales, 0.6% farming, 10.6% construction, 15.4% production (2000).
Income: Per capita income: $26,796 (2005); Median household income: $55,402 (2005); Average household income: $68,976 (2005); Percent of households with income of $100,000 or more: 21.6% (2005); Poverty rate: 10.7% (2000).
Education: Percent of population age 25 and over with: High school diploma (including GED) or higher: 79.4% (2005); Bachelor's degree or higher: 23.1% (2005); Master's degree or higher: 9.9% (2005).
School District(s)
Boces Eastern Suffolk (Suffolk I) (UG-UG)
    2003-04 Enrollment: 1,908 . . . . (631) 289-2200
Patchogue-Medford Union Free School District (PK-12)
    2003-04 Enrollment: 9,101 . . . . (631) 758-1017
Four-year College(s)
Saint Josephs College-Suffolk Campus
    Fall 2004 Enrollment: 4,005 . . . . (631) 447-3200
    2005-06 Tuition: In-state $12,934; Out-of-state $12,934
Two-year College(s)
Eastern Suffolk BOCES-School of Practical Nursing (Public)
    Fall 2004 Enrollment: 288 . . . . (631) 582-2387
Housing: Homeownership rate: 48.8% (2005); Median home value: $234,059 (2005); Median rent: $776 per month (2000); Median age of housing: 42 years (2000).
Newspapers: Fire Island Tide (General - Circulation 35,000); Long Island Advance (General - Circulation 11,522)
Transportation: Commute to work: 87.1% car, 7.7% public transportation, 2.9% walk, 1.2% work from home (2000); Travel time to work: 23.2% less than 15 minutes, 40.7% 15 to 30 minutes, 21.5% 30 to 45 minutes, 6.2% 45 to 60 minutes, 8.5% 60 minutes or more (2000)
Additional Information Contacts
Greater Patchogue Chamber of Commerce . . . . (631) 475-0121
http://www.patchoguechamber.com
Village of Patchogue . . . . (631) 475-4300
http://www.patchoguevillage.org/

PECONIC
PECONIC (CDP). Covers a land area of 4.831 square miles and a water area of 0.138 square miles. Located at 41.03° N. Lat.; 72.46° W. Long.
Population: 1,100 (1990); 1,081 (2000); 1,133 (2005); 1,171 (2010 projected); Race: 92.5% White, 0.9% Black, 1.3% Asian, 5.2% Hispanic of any race (2005); Density: 234.5 persons per square mile (2005); Average household size: 2.52 (2005); Median age: 46.0 (2005); Males per 100 females: 94.7 (2005); Marriage status: 22.4% never married, 64.1% now married, 7.4% widowed, 6.2% divorced (2000); Foreign born: 3.6% (2000); Ancestry (includes multiple ancestries): 26.3% German, 19.4% Italian, 17.2% Irish, 14.9% English, 13.2% Polish (2000).
Economy: In summer-resort area. Employment by occupation: 20.5% management, 20.3% professional, 21.4% services, 9.9% sales, 3.3% farming, 13.4% construction, 11.2% production (2000).
Income: Per capita income: $29,938 (2005); Median household income: $62,188 (2005); Average household income: $75,546 (2005); Percent of households with income of $100,000 or more: 22.7% (2005); Poverty rate: 3.2% (2000).
Education: Percent of population age 25 and over with: High school diploma (including GED) or higher: 86.1% (2005); Bachelor's degree or higher: 25.7% (2005); Master's degree or higher: 10.5% (2005).
Housing: Homeownership rate: 84.4% (2005); Median home value: $442,143 (2005); Median rent: $821 per month (2000); Median age of housing: 36 years (2000).
Transportation: Commute to work: 84.8% car, 1.8% public transportation, 0.0% walk, 5.1% work from home (2000); Travel time to work: 40.4% less than 15 minutes, 24.1% 15 to 30 minutes, 7.0% 30 to 45 minutes, 4.6% 45 to 60 minutes, 23.9% 60 minutes or more (2000)

POOSPATUCK RESERVATION
POOSPATUCK RESERVATION (reservation). Covers a land area of 0.089 square miles and a water area of 0 square miles. Located at 40.79° N. Lat.; 72.83° W. Long.
Population: 136 (1990); 271 (2000); 337 (2005); 404 (2010 projected); Race: 1.5% White, 19.0% Black, 0.0% Asian, 6.8% Hispanic of any race (2005); Density: 3,781.5 persons per square mile (2005); Average household size: 2.88 (2005); Median age: 28.5 (2005); Males per 100 females: 81.2 (2005); Marriage status: 47.8% never married, 39.6% now married, 9.4% widowed, 3.1% divorced (2000); Foreign born: 0.8% (2000); Ancestry (includes multiple ancestries): 79.9% Other groups, 9.8% United States or American, 2.4% Italian (2000).
Economy: Employment by occupation: 0.0% management, 23.1% professional, 34.6% services, 42.3% sales, 0.0% farming, 0.0% construction, 0.0% production (2000).
Income: Per capita income: $9,629 (2005); Median household income: $16,923 (2005); Average household income: $27,735 (2005); Percent of households with income of $100,000 or more: 1.7% (2005); Poverty rate: 36.6% (2000).
Education: Percent of population age 25 and over with: High school diploma (including GED) or higher: 62.6% (2005); Bachelor's degree or higher: 4.3% (2005); Master's degree or higher: 1.6% (2005).

Housing: Homeownership rate: 87.2% (2005); Median home value: $169,355 (2005); Median rent: $598 per month (2000); Median age of housing: 23 years (2000).
Transportation: Commute to work: 72.7% car, 0.0% public transportation, 27.3% walk, 0.0% work from home (2000); Travel time to work: 27.3% less than 15 minutes, 0.0% 15 to 30 minutes, 36.4% 30 to 45 minutes, 4.5% 45 to 60 minutes, 31.8% 60 minutes or more (2000).

POQUOTT (village).
Covers a land area of 0.437 square miles and a water area of 0.157 square miles. Located at 40.95° N. Lat.; 73.08° W. Long. Elevation is 85 feet.
Population: 770 (1990); 975 (2000); 970 (2005); 974 (2010 projected); Race: 90.1% White, 3.6% Black, 5.1% Asian, 6.1% Hispanic of any race (2005); Density: 2,220.0 persons per square mile (2005); Average household size: 2.80 (2005); Median age: 40.4 (2005); Males per 100 females: 96.8 (2005); Marriage status: 25.4% never married, 63.8% now married, 3.3% widowed, 7.4% divorced (2000); Foreign born: 13.9% (2000); Ancestry (includes multiple ancestries): 26.0% Italian, 19.6% Irish, 17.6% German, 10.3% English, 9.7% Other groups (2000).
Economy: Single-family building permits issued: 0 (2005); Multi-family building permits issued: 0 (2005); Employment by occupation: 17.6% management, 50.2% professional, 5.5% services, 17.6% sales, 0.0% farming, 6.3% construction, 2.9% production (2000).
Income: Per capita income: $62,657 (2005); Median household income: $122,866 (2005); Average household income: $175,151 (2005); Percent of households with income of $100,000 or more: 60.8% (2005); Poverty rate: 3.0% (2000).
Education: Percent of population age 25 and over with: High school diploma (including GED) or higher: 96.6% (2005); Bachelor's degree or higher: 62.8% (2005); Master's degree or higher: 39.0% (2005).
Housing: Homeownership rate: 84.1% (2005); Median home value: $555,556 (2005); Median rent: $1,138 per month (2000); Median age of housing: 43 years (2000).
Transportation: Commute to work: 89.4% car, 2.3% public transportation, 1.0% walk, 5.6% work from home (2000); Travel time to work: 25.3% less than 15 minutes, 27.7% 15 to 30 minutes, 28.1% 30 to 45 minutes, 8.4% 45 to 60 minutes, 10.6% 60 minutes or more (2000)

PORT JEFFERSON (village).
Covers a land area of 3.029 square miles and a water area of 0.026 square miles. Located at 40.94° N. Lat.; 73.06° W. Long. Elevation is 12 feet.
Population: 7,455 (1990); 7,837 (2000); 7,953 (2005); 8,149 (2010 projected); Race: 89.8% White, 2.2% Black, 4.2% Asian, 6.8% Hispanic of any race (2005); Density: 2,625.5 persons per square mile (2005); Average household size: 2.61 (2005); Median age: 42.1 (2005); Males per 100 females: 94.1 (2005); Marriage status: 27.1% never married, 56.8% now married, 6.9% widowed, 9.3% divorced (2000); Foreign born: 13.0% (2000); Ancestry (includes multiple ancestries): 21.8% Irish, 21.8% Italian, 18.9% German, 12.1% Other groups, 10.5% English (2000).
Economy: In orchard and diversified-farming area; sand and gravel; boatyards. Ferry connections with Bridgeport, Connecticut. Port Jefferson Station village, just Southeast, is terminus of North Shore line of Long Island Railroad. Single-family building permits issued: 4 (2005); Multi-family building permits issued: 0 (2005); Employment by occupation: 15.8% management, 44.2% professional, 10.1% services, 17.9% sales, 0.2% farming, 5.7% construction, 6.2% production (2000).
Income: Per capita income: $37,292 (2005); Median household income: $72,577 (2005); Average household income: $95,821 (2005); Percent of households with income of $100,000 or more: 34.2% (2005); Poverty rate: 7.2% (2000).
Education: Percent of population age 25 and over with: High school diploma (including GED) or higher: 92.6% (2005); Bachelor's degree or higher: 53.4% (2005); Master's degree or higher: 32.2% (2005).
School District(s)
Port Jefferson Union Free School District (PK-12)
    2003-04 Enrollment: 1,273 . . . . (631) 476-4404
Housing: Homeownership rate: 71.8% (2005); Median home value: $412,550 (2005); Median rent: $877 per month (2000); Median age of housing: 34 years (2000).
Hospitals: John Mather Memorial Hospital (248 beds)
Transportation: Commute to work: 90.2% car, 4.2% public transportation, 1.3% walk, 4.4% work from home (2000); Travel time to work: 26.7% less than 15 minutes, 31.0% 15 to 30 minutes, 20.3% 30 to 45 minutes, 9.4% 45 to 60 minutes, 12.7% 60 minutes or more (2000)
Additional Information Contacts

Port Jefferson Chamber of Commerce . . . . (631) 473-1414
  http://www.portjeffchamber.com
Village of Port Jefferson. . . . . (631) 473-4724
  http://www.portjeff.com/

PORT JEFFERSON STATION (CDP).
Covers a land area of 2.642 square miles and a water area of 0 square miles. Located at 40.92° N. Lat.; 73.06° W. Long. Elevation is 189 feet.
Population: 7,232 (1990); 7,527 (2000); 7,877 (2005); 8,247 (2010 projected); Race: 84.3% White, 2.8% Black, 5.1% Asian, 12.2% Hispanic of any race (2005); Density: 2,981.6 persons per square mile (2005); Average household size: 2.89 (2005); Median age: 37.3 (2005); Males per 100 females: 95.8 (2005); Marriage status: 27.4% never married, 59.3% now married, 6.7% widowed, 6.6% divorced (2000); Foreign born: 14.0% (2000); Ancestry (includes multiple ancestries): 33.9% Italian, 20.2% Irish, 18.4% German, 14.4% Other groups, 7.2% Polish (2000).
Economy: Manufacturing: aerospace components, prefabricated buildings; publishing. Employment by occupation: 13.9% management, 22.4% professional, 16.0% services, 30.1% sales, 0.0% farming, 8.1% construction, 9.5% production (2000).
Income: Per capita income: $25,626 (2005); Median household income: $64,931 (2005); Average household income: $73,409 (2005); Percent of households with income of $100,000 or more: 26.0% (2005); Poverty rate: 7.6% (2000).
Education: Percent of population age 25 and over with: High school diploma (including GED) or higher: 84.6% (2005); Bachelor's degree or higher: 24.7% (2005); Master's degree or higher: 10.0% (2005).
School District(s)
Brookhaven-Comsewogue Union Free School District (KG-12)
    2003-04 Enrollment: 3,930 . . . . (631) 474-8105
Housing: Homeownership rate: 72.6% (2005); Median home value: $267,627 (2005); Median rent: $853 per month (2000); Median age of housing: 33 years (2000).
Hospitals: St. Charles Hospital and Rehabilitation Center (289 beds)
Transportation: Commute to work: 90.6% car, 5.4% public transportation, 2.3% walk, 1.2% work from home (2000); Travel time to work: 29.2% less than 15 minutes, 27.5% 15 to 30 minutes, 19.9% 30 to 45 minutes, 10.9% 45 to 60 minutes, 12.4% 60 minutes or more (2000)

QUIOQUE (CDP).
Covers a land area of 1.258 square miles and a water area of 0.432 square miles. Located at 40.82° N. Lat.; 72.63° W. Long.
Population: 584 (1990); 800 (2000); 865 (2005); 930 (2010 projected); Race: 72.4% White, 8.3% Black, 2.7% Asian, 21.4% Hispanic of any race (2005); Density: 687.4 persons per square mile (2005); Average household size: 2.42 (2005); Median age: 39.9 (2005); Males per 100 females: 114.1 (2005); Marriage status: 21.5% never married, 56.3% now married, 10.6% widowed, 11.6% divorced (2000); Foreign born: 25.5% (2000); Ancestry (includes multiple ancestries): 29.6% Other groups, 20.6% Irish, 15.5% Italian, 12.5% Polish, 11.1% German (2000).
Economy: Employment by occupation: 14.8% management, 14.8% professional, 24.2% services, 16.6% sales, 0.0% farming, 16.9% construction, 12.7% production (2000).
Income: Per capita income: $34,695 (2005); Median household income: $57,537 (2005); Average household income: $84,048 (2005); Percent of households with income of $100,000 or more: 24.9% (2005); Poverty rate: 5.5% (2000).
Education: Percent of population age 25 and over with: High school diploma (including GED) or higher: 80.5% (2005); Bachelor's degree or higher: 36.9% (2005); Master's degree or higher: 19.5% (2005).
Housing: Homeownership rate: 73.9% (2005); Median home value: $410,526 (2005); Median rent: $637 per month (2000); Median age of housing: 28 years (2000).
Transportation: Commute to work: 78.9% car, 7.1% public transportation, 1.1% walk, 6.1% work from home (2000); Travel time to work: 45.7% less than 15 minutes, 25.5% 15 to 30 minutes, 7.6% 30 to 45 minutes, 8.7% 45 to 60 minutes, 12.6% 60 minutes or more (2000)

QUOGUE (village).
Covers a land area of 4.202 square miles and a water area of 2.444 square miles. Located at 40.82° N. Lat.; 72.60° W. Long.
History: Region originally occupied by Native American tribe of Shinnecocks because of rich hunting and fishing. Nearby Hampton Bays was called Good Ground until 1922. Settled in 1686, when known as Fourth Neck, then Atlanticville, until adoption of present name in 1891.

Population: 898 (1990); 1,018 (2000); 930 (2005); 914 (2010 projected); Race: 93.7% White, 4.0% Black, 0.4% Asian, 3.7% Hispanic of any race (2005); Density: 221.3 persons per square mile (2005); Average household size: 2.24 (2005); Median age: 50.0 (2005); Males per 100 females: 95.8 (2005); Marriage status: 23.8% never married, 59.6% now married, 7.1% widowed, 9.5% divorced (2000); Foreign born: 5.3% (2000); Ancestry (includes multiple ancestries): 21.4% Irish, 21.1% Italian, 19.3% German, 13.5% Other groups, 10.6% English (2000).
Economy: Yachting. Single-family building permits issued: 16 (2005); Multi-family building permits issued: 0 (2005); Employment by occupation: 19.4% management, 27.0% professional, 10.9% services, 24.2% sales, 0.0% farming, 12.7% construction, 5.8% production (2000).
Income: Per capita income: $53,041 (2005); Median household income: $76,993 (2005); Average household income: $118,705 (2005); Percent of households with income of $100,000 or more: 34.7% (2005); Poverty rate: 7.4% (2000).
Education: Percent of population age 25 and over with: High school diploma (including GED) or higher: 90.5% (2005); Bachelor's degree or higher: 44.8% (2005); Master's degree or higher: 21.5% (2005).

School District(s)
Quogue Union Free School District (PK-06)
   2003-04 Enrollment: 126 . . . . (631) 653-4285

Housing: Homeownership rate: 83.4% (2005); Median home value: $863,971 (2005); Median rent: $900 per month (2000); Median age of housing: 26 years (2000).
Safety: Violent crime rate: 18.6 per 10,000 population; Property crime rate: 149.1 per 10,000 population (2004).
Transportation: Commute to work: 77.6% car, 6.4% public transportation, 3.9% walk, 12.0% work from home (2000); Travel time to work: 32.5% less than 15 minutes, 22.2% 15 to 30 minutes, 19.3% 30 to 45 minutes, 7.5% 45 to 60 minutes, 18.4% 60 minutes or more (2000)

REMSENBURG-SPEONK (CDP).
Covers a land area of 5.938 square miles and a water area of 0.089 square miles. Located at 40.82° N. Lat.; 72.70° W. Long.
Population: 1,992 (1990); 2,675 (2000); 2,867 (2005); 3,060 (2010 projected); Race: 94.0% White, 1.6% Black, 0.8% Asian, 7.8% Hispanic of any race (2005); Density: 482.8 persons per square mile (2005); Average household size: 2.86 (2005); Median age: 44.0 (2005); Males per 100 females: 91.8 (2005); Marriage status: 18.8% never married, 66.1% now married, 8.6% widowed, 6.6% divorced (2000); Foreign born: 8.4% (2000); Ancestry (includes multiple ancestries): 25.8% Irish, 22.1% German, 19.5% Italian, 11.5% English, 10.4% Polish (2000).
Economy: Employment by occupation: 16.6% management, 24.7% professional, 16.9% services, 25.7% sales, 0.8% farming, 10.1% construction, 5.2% production (2000).
Income: Per capita income: $38,025 (2005); Median household income: $84,250 (2005); Average household income: $105,708 (2005); Percent of households with income of $100,000 or more: 40.6% (2005); Poverty rate: 4.9% (2000).
Education: Percent of population age 25 and over with: High school diploma (including GED) or higher: 85.6% (2005); Bachelor's degree or higher: 33.1% (2005); Master's degree or higher: 14.6% (2005).
Housing: Homeownership rate: 82.4% (2005); Median home value: $415,517 (2005); Median rent: $863 per month (2000); Median age of housing: 25 years (2000).
Transportation: Commute to work: 89.0% car, 4.3% public transportation, 2.2% walk, 4.0% work from home (2000); Travel time to work: 28.8% less than 15 minutes, 28.8% 15 to 30 minutes, 20.4% 30 to 45 minutes, 7.9% 45 to 60 minutes, 14.0% 60 minutes or more (2000)

RIDGE (CDP).
Covers a land area of 13.466 square miles and a water area of 0.094 square miles. Located at 40.90° N. Lat.; 72.88° W. Long.
Population: 11,972 (1990); 13,380 (2000); 14,482 (2005); 15,568 (2010 projected); Race: 91.2% White, 4.5% Black, 1.0% Asian, 4.6% Hispanic of any race (2005); Density: 1,075.5 persons per square mile (2005); Average household size: 2.42 (2005); Median age: 44.8 (2005); Males per 100 females: 84.1 (2005); Marriage status: 20.6% never married, 58.3% now married, 15.1% widowed, 6.0% divorced (2000); Foreign born: 5.7% (2000); Ancestry (includes multiple ancestries): 33.2% Italian, 28.2% Irish, 21.4% German, 9.3% Other groups, 6.8% English (2000).
Economy: Employment by occupation: 9.4% management, 22.6% professional, 17.5% services, 27.4% sales, 0.5% farming, 13.8% construction, 8.8% production (2000).
Income: Per capita income: $27,097 (2005); Median household income: $50,982 (2005); Average household income: $65,073 (2005); Percent of households with income of $100,000 or more: 20.3% (2005); Poverty rate: 6.5% (2000).
Education: Percent of population age 25 and over with: High school diploma (including GED) or higher: 86.2% (2005); Bachelor's degree or higher: 19.5% (2005); Master's degree or higher: 8.0% (2005).

School District(s)
Longwood Central School District (KG-12)
   2003-04 Enrollment: 9,794 . . . . (631) 345-2172

Housing: Homeownership rate: 87.0% (2005); Median home value: $230,286 (2005); Median rent: $688 per month (2000); Median age of housing: 22 years (2000).
Transportation: Commute to work: 94.3% car, 2.9% public transportation, 0.6% walk, 1.9% work from home (2000); Travel time to work: 18.0% less than 15 minutes, 33.3% 15 to 30 minutes, 23.0% 30 to 45 minutes, 9.4% 45 to 60 minutes, 16.2% 60 minutes or more (2000)

RIVERHEAD (town).
Covers a land area of 67.376 square miles and a water area of 133.906 square miles. Located at 40.93° N. Lat.; 72.70° W. Long. Elevation is 25 feet.
History: Named for its location at the head of the Peconic River. Museum of Suffolk County Historical Society is here.
Population: 22,958 (1990); 27,680 (2000); 33,949 (2005); 39,670 (2010 projected); Race: 83.3% White, 11.2% Black, 1.2% Asian, 8.7% Hispanic of any race (2005); Density: 503.9 persons per square mile (2005); Average household size: 2.55 (2005); Median age: 41.9 (2005); Males per 100 females: 96.4 (2005); Marriage status: 21.8% never married, 60.2% now married, 9.7% widowed, 8.3% divorced (2000); Foreign born: 9.6% (2000); Ancestry (includes multiple ancestries): 22.4% Irish, 20.0% German, 18.8% Italian, 17.3% Other groups, 15.0% Polish (2000).
Economy: Manufacturing: machinery components, capping machines. In resort and farm area: potatoes, sweet corn, cauliflower. Fishing, duck hunting. Unemployment rate: 4.1% (2005); Total civilian labor force: 16,366 (2005); Single-family building permits issued: 168 (2005); Multi-family building permits issued: 0 (2005); Employment by occupation: 10.2% management, 23.8% professional, 17.4% services, 26.4% sales, 1.1% farming, 11.5% construction, 9.5% production (2000).
Income: Per capita income: $27,397 (2005); Median household income: $52,939 (2005); Average household income: $68,895 (2005); Percent of households with income of $100,000 or more: 21.7% (2005); Poverty rate: 8.6% (2000).
Taxes: Total city taxes per capita: $1,127 (2004); City property taxes per capita: $909 (2004).
Education: Percent of population age 25 and over with: High school diploma (including GED) or higher: 81.7% (2005); Bachelor's degree or higher: 21.9% (2005); Master's degree or higher: 10.3% (2005).

School District(s)
Riverhead Central School District (KG-12)
   2003-04 Enrollment: 4,862 . . . . (631) 369-6716

Housing: Homeownership rate: 76.8% (2005); Median home value: $250,581 (2005); Median rent: $729 per month (2000); Median age of housing: 30 years (2000).
Hospitals: Central Suffolk Hospital (214 beds)
Safety: Violent crime rate: 35.3 per 10,000 population; Property crime rate: 362.9 per 10,000 population (2004).
Newspapers: Suffolk Life - Amityville (General - Circulation 17,500); Suffolk Life - Bay Shore (General - Circulation 16,976); Suffolk Life - Bellport/East Patchogue (General - Circulation 11,123); Suffolk Life - Brentwood (General - Circulation 14,305); Suffolk Life - Centereach/Lake Grove (General - Circulation 12,342); Suffolk Life - Central Islip/Hauppauge (General - Circulation 13,957); Suffolk Life - Commack/Kings Park (General - Circulation 17,629); Suffolk Life - Coram/Middle Island (General - Circulation 19,172); Suffolk Life - Deer Park (General - Circulation 19,844); Suffolk Life - Dix Hills/Melville (General - Circulation 13,773); Suffolk Life - East Islip (General - Circulation 13,927); Suffolk Life - Hampton East (General - Circulation 17,165); Suffolk Life - Hampton West (General - Circulation 16,562); Suffolk Life - Holbrook/Bohemia (General - Circulation 14,389); Suffolk Life - Huntington (General - Circulation 18,761); Suffolk Life - Huntington Station (General - Circulation 18,761); Suffolk Life - Lindenhurst (General - Circulation 14,606); Suffolk Life - Mastic/Shirley (General - Circulation 16,394); Suffolk Life - Medford/Holtsville (General - Circulation 13,329); Suffolk Life - Mid-Hampton (General - Circulation 17,244); Suffolk Life - Moriches (General - Circulation 11,529); Suffolk Life - North Fork (General - Circulation 13,976); Suffolk Life - Patchogue

(General - Circulation 12,261); Suffolk Life - Port Jefferson (General - Circulation 14,625); Suffolk Life - Riverhead (General - Circulation 18,186); Suffolk Life - Rocky Point (General - Circulation 15,854); Suffolk Life - Ronkonkoma (General - Circulation 13,416); Suffolk Life - Saint James/Nesconset (General - Circulation 9,652); Suffolk Life - Sayville/Oakdale (General - Circulation 13,294); Suffolk Life - Selden/Farmingville (General - Circulation 12,294); Suffolk Life - Smithtown (General - Circulation 14,622); Suffolk Life - Stony Brook/Setauket (General - Circulation 13,090); Suffolk Life - West Babylon (General - Circulation 19,264); Suffolk Life - West Islip (General - Circulation 8,531)
Transportation: Commute to work: 90.6% car, 2.6% public transportation, 2.4% walk, 3.3% work from home (2000); Travel time to work: 31.4% less than 15 minutes, 28.3% 15 to 30 minutes, 20.9% 30 to 45 minutes, 9.1% 45 to 60 minutes, 10.3% 60 minutes or more (2000)
Additional Information Contacts
Riverhead Chamber of Commerce .... (631) 727-7600
  http://www.riverheadchamber.com
Town of Riverhead................................. (631) 727-3200
  http://www.riverheadli.com/

RIVERHEAD (CDP).
Covers a land area of 15.095 square miles and a water area of 0.355 square miles. Located at 40.92° N. Lat.; 72.66° W. Long.
Population: 8,814 (1990); 10,513 (2000); 13,122 (2005); 15,514 (2010 projected); Race: 67.4% White, 24.8% Black, 1.5% Asian, 13.2% Hispanic of any race (2005); Density: 869.3 persons per square mile (2005); Average household size: 2.70 (2005); Median age: 40.1 (2005); Males per 100 females: 92.8 (2005); Marriage status: 26.0% never married, 53.4% now married, 12.1% widowed, 8.6% divorced (2000); Foreign born: 13.5% (2000); Ancestry (includes multiple ancestries): 30.2% Other groups, 18.1% Polish, 16.2% Irish, 12.7% German, 10.8% Italian (2000).
Economy: Employment by occupation: 5.2% management, 17.6% professional, 18.3% services, 27.1% sales, 1.7% farming, 14.1% construction, 15.9% production (2000).
Income: Per capita income: $19,740 (2005); Median household income: $39,713 (2005); Average household income: $51,866 (2005); Percent of households with income of $100,000 or more: 11.7% (2005); Poverty rate: 13.0% (2000).
Education: Percent of population age 25 and over with: High school diploma (including GED) or higher: 73.6% (2005); Bachelor's degree or higher: 13.8% (2005); Master's degree or higher: 6.6% (2005).
Housing: Homeownership rate: 57.3% (2005); Median home value: $213,434 (2005); Median rent: $685 per month (2000); Median age of housing: 35 years (2000).
Transportation: Commute to work: 88.1% car, 3.1% public transportation, 3.7% walk, 3.1% work from home (2000); Travel time to work: 41.9% less than 15 minutes, 25.0% 15 to 30 minutes, 20.3% 30 to 45 minutes, 6.5% 45 to 60 minutes, 6.2% 60 minutes or more (2000)

RIVERSIDE (CDP).
Covers a land area of 5.103 square miles and a water area of 0.104 square miles. Located at 40.90° N. Lat.; 72.66° W. Long.
Population: 2,389 (1990); 2,875 (2000); 3,028 (2005); 3,180 (2010 projected); Race: 57.9% White, 35.8% Black, 1.0% Asian, 13.1% Hispanic of any race (2005); Density: 593.4 persons per square mile (2005); Average household size: 3.50 (2005); Median age: 37.5 (2005); Males per 100 females: 153.0 (2005); Marriage status: 21.8% never married, 62.8% now married, 8.9% widowed, 6.5% divorced (2000); Foreign born: 7.9% (2000); Ancestry (includes multiple ancestries): 24.5% Other groups, 10.1% Irish, 6.9% German, 5.8% Italian, 5.4% English (2000).
Economy: Employment by occupation: 4.4% management, 7.4% professional, 34.3% services, 30.0% sales, 0.1% farming, 13.2% construction, 10.6% production (2000).
Income: Per capita income: $15,026 (2005); Median household income: $31,124 (2005); Average household income: $38,832 (2005); Percent of households with income of $100,000 or more: 5.1% (2005); Poverty rate: 21.0% (2000).
Education: Percent of population age 25 and over with: High school diploma (including GED) or higher: 60.0% (2005); Bachelor's degree or higher: 6.0% (2005); Master's degree or higher: 2.0% (2005).
Housing: Homeownership rate: 77.6% (2005); Median home value: $81,452 (2005); Median rent: $807 per month (2000); Median age of housing: 27 years (2000).
Transportation: Commute to work: 92.0% car, 3.6% public transportation, 3.9% walk, 0.3% work from home (2000); Travel time to work: 41.7% less than 15 minutes, 26.8% 15 to 30 minutes, 20.8% 30 to 45 minutes, 3.2% 45 to 60 minutes, 7.4% 60 minutes or more (2000)

ROCKY POINT (CDP).
Covers a land area of 10.346 square miles and a water area of 0 square miles. Located at 40.95° N. Lat.; 72.92° W. Long. Elevation is 220 feet.
Population: 8,596 (1990); 10,185 (2000); 11,232 (2005); 12,243 (2010 projected); Race: 94.2% White, 1.0% Black, 1.7% Asian, 6.7% Hispanic of any race (2005); Density: 1,085.6 persons per square mile (2005); Average household size: 2.91 (2005); Median age: 34.8 (2005); Males per 100 females: 100.5 (2005); Marriage status: 23.9% never married, 61.9% now married, 5.3% widowed, 8.9% divorced (2000); Foreign born: 9.0% (2000); Ancestry (includes multiple ancestries): 37.2% Italian, 25.4% Irish, 20.6% German, 11.2% Other groups, 7.7% English (2000).
Economy: In summer resort area. Employment by occupation: 12.1% management, 22.8% professional, 15.5% services, 24.0% sales, 0.4% farming, 14.1% construction, 11.1% production (2000).
Income: Per capita income: $25,263 (2005); Median household income: $62,608 (2005); Average household income: $72,325 (2005); Percent of households with income of $100,000 or more: 22.4% (2005); Poverty rate: 7.7% (2000).
Education: Percent of population age 25 and over with: High school diploma (including GED) or higher: 90.6% (2005); Bachelor's degree or higher: 21.1% (2005); Master's degree or higher: 9.9% (2005).
School District(s)
Rocky Point Union Free School District (KG-12)
  2003-04 Enrollment: 3,594 .... (631) 744-1600
Housing: Homeownership rate: 75.0% (2005); Median home value: $234,446 (2005); Median rent: $760 per month (2000); Median age of housing: 40 years (2000).
Transportation: Commute to work: 93.1% car, 3.6% public transportation, 0.9% walk, 2.2% work from home (2000); Travel time to work: 16.9% less than 15 minutes, 27.1% 15 to 30 minutes, 23.4% 30 to 45 minutes, 12.0% 45 to 60 minutes, 20.6% 60 minutes or more (2000)

RONKONKOMA (CDP).
Covers a land area of 8.174 square miles and a water area of 0.353 square miles. Located at 40.81° N. Lat.; 73.12° W. Long. Elevation is 111 feet.
Population: 20,391 (1990); 20,029 (2000); 20,645 (2005); 21,343 (2010 projected); Race: 92.1% White, 1.3% Black, 3.2% Asian, 8.2% Hispanic of any race (2005); Density: 2,525.7 persons per square mile (2005); Average household size: 3.03 (2005); Median age: 36.9 (2005); Males per 100 females: 98.2 (2005); Marriage status: 24.7% never married, 63.1% now married, 5.7% widowed, 6.5% divorced (2000); Foreign born: 7.8% (2000); Ancestry (includes multiple ancestries): 39.7% Italian, 26.7% Irish, 19.3% German, 11.6% Other groups, 6.8% Polish (2000).
Economy: Residential-manufacturing community. Employment by occupation: 10.7% management, 18.5% professional, 13.7% services, 33.8% sales, 0.0% farming, 12.6% construction, 10.8% production (2000).
Income: Per capita income: $28,597 (2005); Median household income: $77,425 (2005); Average household income: $86,279 (2005); Percent of households with income of $100,000 or more: 31.6% (2005); Poverty rate: 3.7% (2000).
Education: Percent of population age 25 and over with: High school diploma (including GED) or higher: 87.1% (2005); Bachelor's degree or higher: 19.9% (2005); Master's degree or higher: 6.7% (2005).
School District(s)
Connetquot Central School District (KG-12)
  2003-04 Enrollment: 7,160 .... (631) 244-2211
Housing: Homeownership rate: 80.3% (2005); Median home value: $268,082 (2005); Median rent: $940 per month (2000); Median age of housing: 31 years (2000).
Transportation: Commute to work: 90.9% car, 6.4% public transportation, 0.3% walk, 1.8% work from home (2000); Travel time to work: 24.2% less than 15 minutes, 34.5% 15 to 30 minutes, 17.5% 30 to 45 minutes, 6.3% 45 to 60 minutes, 17.5% 60 minutes or more (2000)
Additional Information Contacts
Greater Ronkonkoma Chamber of Commerce .... (631) 471-0302
  http://www.ronkonkomachamber.com

SAG HARBOR (village).
Covers a land area of 1.720 square miles and a water area of 0.748 square miles. Located at 40.99° N. Lat.; 72.29° W. Long.
History: An important 19th-century whaling port. National Historic District. The *Long Island Herald* (1791) was L.I.'s first local paper. The Whalers'

Church and Whalers' Museum, noted for their architecture, are among its historic buildings. Had first customhouse in N.Y., and first post office on L.I., established 1794. Settled 1720-1730, Incorporated 1846.
Population: 2,134 (1990); 2,313 (2000); 2,374 (2005); 2,432 (2010 projected); Race: 83.3% White, 7.8% Black, 1.4% Asian, 11.7% Hispanic of any race (2005); Density: 1,380.6 persons per square mile (2005); Average household size: 2.04 (2005); Median age: 48.7 (2005); Males per 100 females: 92.4 (2005); Marriage status: 27.0% never married, 51.4% now married, 10.4% widowed, 11.2% divorced (2000); Foreign born: 10.3% (2000); Ancestry (includes multiple ancestries): 21.1% Irish, 16.4% Other groups, 15.0% German, 13.7% English, 13.6% Italian (2000).
Economy: Resort village. Single-family building permits issued: 13 (2005); Multi-family building permits issued: 0 (2005); Employment by occupation: 16.1% management, 24.1% professional, 18.7% services, 23.7% sales, 0.0% farming, 13.5% construction, 3.9% production (2000).
Income: Per capita income: $45,132 (2005); Median household income: $62,739 (2005); Average household income: $92,272 (2005); Percent of households with income of $100,000 or more: 25.7% (2005); Poverty rate: 4.2% (2000).
Education: Percent of population age 25 and over with: High school diploma (including GED) or higher: 90.5% (2005); Bachelor's degree or higher: 40.7% (2005); Master's degree or higher: 16.1% (2005).
School District(s)
Sag Harbor Union Free School District (KG-12)
    2003-04 Enrollment: 969 . . . . (631) 725-5300
Housing: Homeownership rate: 70.5% (2005); Median home value: $568,653 (2005); Median rent: $931 per month (2000); Median age of housing: 49 years (2000).
Newspapers: Sag Harbor Express (General - Circulation 3,000)
Transportation: Commute to work: 75.8% car, 2.2% public transportation, 7.2% walk, 14.1% work from home (2000); Travel time to work: 49.7% less than 15 minutes, 30.8% 15 to 30 minutes, 8.4% 30 to 45 minutes, 3.4% 45 to 60 minutes, 7.7% 60 minutes or more (2000)
Additional Information Contacts
Sag Harbor Chamber of Commerce . . . . (631) 725-0011
    http://www.sagharborchamber.com

SAGAPONACK (CDP). Covers a land area of 6.219 square miles and a water area of 1.786 square miles. Located at 40.94° N. Lat.; 72.28° W. Long.
Population: 490 (1990); 582 (2000); 627 (2005); 659 (2010 projected); Race: 90.6% White, 2.7% Black, 3.8% Asian, 4.8% Hispanic of any race (2005); Density: 100.8 persons per square mile (2005); Average household size: 2.30 (2005); Median age: 48.3 (2005); Males per 100 females: 101.6 (2005); Marriage status: 23.6% never married, 60.3% now married, 6.1% widowed, 10.0% divorced (2000); Foreign born: 9.8% (2000); Ancestry (includes multiple ancestries): 29.7% English, 27.9% Irish, 16.6% German, 7.0% Russian, 5.4% Italian (2000).
Economy: Employment by occupation: 19.2% management, 15.8% professional, 19.9% services, 28.3% sales, 1.7% farming, 11.1% construction, 4.0% production (2000).
Income: Per capita income: $52,337 (2005); Median household income: $71,023 (2005); Average household income: $120,201 (2005); Percent of households with income of $100,000 or more: 35.9% (2005); Poverty rate: 1.3% (2000).
Education: Percent of population age 25 and over with: High school diploma (including GED) or higher: 92.0% (2005); Bachelor's degree or higher: 49.5% (2005); Master's degree or higher: 17.6% (2005).
School District(s)
Sagaponack Common School District (01-04)
    2003-04 Enrollment: 16 . . . . (631) 537-0651
Housing: Homeownership rate: 86.1% (2005); Median home value: $1 million+ (2005); Median rent: $1,202 per month (2000); Median age of housing: 20 years (2000).
Transportation: Commute to work: 71.9% car, 4.6% public transportation, 4.6% walk, 18.9% work from home (2000); Travel time to work: 59.7% less than 15 minutes, 23.8% 15 to 30 minutes, 4.8% 30 to 45 minutes, 2.2% 45 to 60 minutes, 9.5% 60 minutes or more (2000)

SAINT JAMES (CDP). Covers a land area of 4.537 square miles and a water area of <.001 square miles. Located at 40.87° N. Lat.; 73.15° W. Long. Elevation is 163 feet.
Population: 12,703 (1990); 13,268 (2000); 13,809 (2005); 14,407 (2010 projected); Race: 96.6% White, 0.3% Black, 1.6% Asian, 4.9% Hispanic of any race (2005); Density: 3,043.8 persons per square mile (2005); Average household size: 2.90 (2005); Median age: 40.6 (2005); Males per 100 females: 89.0 (2005); Marriage status: 19.2% never married, 63.5% now married, 11.6% widowed, 5.7% divorced (2000); Foreign born: 5.2% (2000); Ancestry (includes multiple ancestries): 35.1% Italian, 29.5% Irish, 18.4% German, 6.9% Other groups, 6.2% Polish (2000).
Economy: Employment by occupation: 17.3% management, 25.4% professional, 14.1% services, 26.1% sales, 0.0% farming, 9.3% construction, 7.8% production (2000).
Income: Per capita income: $35,543 (2005); Median household income: $85,263 (2005); Average household income: $101,947 (2005); Percent of households with income of $100,000 or more: 40.5% (2005); Poverty rate: 2.6% (2000).
Education: Percent of population age 25 and over with: High school diploma (including GED) or higher: 90.1% (2005); Bachelor's degree or higher: 31.0% (2005); Master's degree or higher: 14.3% (2005).
School District(s)
Smithtown Central School District (KG-12)
    2003-04 Enrollment: 10,188 . . . . (631) 382-2005
Housing: Homeownership rate: 89.2% (2005); Median home value: $380,409 (2005); Median rent: $855 per month (2000); Median age of housing: 34 years (2000).
Newspapers: Our Town-Saint James (General - Circulation 6,022)
Transportation: Commute to work: 90.2% car, 4.8% public transportation, 0.7% walk, 3.2% work from home (2000); Travel time to work: 23.6% less than 15 minutes, 31.4% 15 to 30 minutes, 20.1% 30 to 45 minutes, 8.6% 45 to 60 minutes, 16.3% 60 minutes or more (2000)
Additional Information Contacts
Holbrook Chamber of Commerce . . . . (631) 471-2725
    http://www.holbrookchamber.com
Saint James Chamber of Commerce. . . . . (631) 862-9000
    http://www.stjamesny.org

SALTAIRE (village). Covers a land area of 0.277 square miles and a water area of 0.051 square miles. Located at 40.63° N. Lat.; 73.19° W. Long. Elevation is 5 feet.
Population: 38 (1990); 43 (2000); 37 (2005); 36 (2010 projected); Race: 64.9% White, 0.0% Black, 13.5% Asian, 0.0% Hispanic of any race (2005); Density: 133.4 persons per square mile (2005); Average household size: 3.08 (2005); Median age: 27.5 (2005); Males per 100 females: 117.6 (2005); Marriage status: 5.4% never married, 75.7% now married, 8.1% widowed, 10.8% divorced (2000); Foreign born: 0.0% (2000); Ancestry (includes multiple ancestries): 75.0% Italian, 25.0% Russian, 17.6% German, 8.8% Irish, 8.8% Swedish (2000).
Economy: Single-family building permits issued: 0 (2005); Multi-family building permits issued: 0 (2005); Employment by occupation: 41.7% management, 8.3% professional, 12.5% services, 25.0% sales, 0.0% farming, 12.5% construction, 0.0% production (2000).
Income: Per capita income: $29,392 (2005); Median household income: $95,833 (2005); Average household income: $90,625 (2005); Percent of households with income of $100,000 or more: 50.0% (2005); Poverty rate: 0.0% (2000).
Education: Percent of population age 25 and over with: High school diploma (including GED) or higher: 100.0% (2005); Bachelor's degree or higher: 42.1% (2005); Master's degree or higher: 31.6% (2005).
Housing: Homeownership rate: 50.0% (2005); Median home value: $1 million+ (2005); Median rent: $525 per month (2000); Median age of housing: 26 years (2000).
Transportation: Commute to work: 16.7% car, 20.8% public transportation, 12.5% walk, 37.5% work from home (2000); Travel time to work: 40.0% less than 15 minutes, 13.3% 15 to 30 minutes, 0.0% 30 to 45 minutes, 26.7% 45 to 60 minutes, 20.0% 60 minutes or more (2000)
Additional Information Contacts
Village of Saltaire. . . . . (631) 583-5566
    http://www.saltaire.org/

SAYVILLE (CDP). Covers a land area of 5.526 square miles and a water area of 0.064 square miles. Located at 40.74° N. Lat.; 73.08° W. Long. Elevation is 28 feet.
Population: 16,550 (1990); 16,735 (2000); 17,418 (2005); 18,133 (2010 projected); Race: 94.4% White, 1.0% Black, 2.7% Asian, 4.1% Hispanic of any race (2005); Density: 3,152.0 persons per square mile (2005); Average household size: 2.97 (2005); Median age: 38.7 (2005); Males per 100 females: 93.4 (2005); Marriage status: 23.2% never married, 63.2% now married, 6.2% widowed, 7.4% divorced (2000); Foreign born: 3.8% (2000);

Ancestry (includes multiple ancestries): 35.6% Irish, 30.8% Italian, 23.4% German, 7.7% English, 6.9% Other groups (2000).
Economy: Yachting center; oysters; flower growing. Manufacturing: waxes and related products, furniture, marble and mica products. Seafront recreational area. Employment by occupation: 15.3% management, 28.5% professional, 11.7% services, 27.1% sales, 0.2% farming, 9.7% construction, 7.5% production (2000).
Income: Per capita income: $34,778 (2005); Median household income: $86,678 (2005); Average household income: $102,452 (2005); Percent of households with income of $100,000 or more: 41.7% (2005); Poverty rate: 4.1% (2000).
Education: Percent of population age 25 and over with: High school diploma (including GED) or higher: 91.8% (2005); Bachelor's degree or higher: 34.9% (2005); Master's degree or higher: 14.8% (2005).

School District(s)
Sayville Union Free School District (KG-12)
    2003-04 Enrollment: 3,593 . . . . (631) 244-6510

Housing: Homeownership rate: 83.4% (2005); Median home value: $356,660 (2005); Median rent: $875 per month (2000); Median age of housing: 39 years (2000).
Newspapers: Islip Bulletin (General - Circulation 6,000); Suffolk County News (General - Circulation 15,000)
Transportation: Commute to work: 89.1% car, 6.1% public transportation, 1.2% walk, 2.5% work from home (2000); Travel time to work: 31.6% less than 15 minutes, 29.0% 15 to 30 minutes, 17.7% 30 to 45 minutes, 6.3% 45 to 60 minutes, 15.4% 60 minutes or more (2000)

Additional Information Contacts
Sayville Chamber of Commerce . . . . (631) 567-5257
    http://www.sayville.com/chamber.html

SELDEN (CDP). Covers a land area of 4.656 square miles and a water area of 0 square miles. Located at 40.87° N. Lat.; 73.04° W. Long. Elevation is 109 feet.
Population: 20,608 (1990); 21,861 (2000); 22,225 (2005); 22,675 (2010 projected); Race: 89.2% White, 2.5% Black, 3.4% Asian, 11.3% Hispanic of any race (2005); Density: 4,773.7 persons per square mile (2005); Average household size: 3.17 (2005); Median age: 35.5 (2005); Males per 100 females: 97.9 (2005); Marriage status: 26.0% never married, 59.6% now married, 6.7% widowed, 7.7% divorced (2000); Foreign born: 7.6% (2000); Ancestry (includes multiple ancestries): 40.1% Italian, 25.8% Irish, 20.9% German, 13.1% Other groups, 5.5% Polish (2000).
Economy: Some manufacturing. Employment by occupation: 11.1% management, 15.3% professional, 15.0% services, 32.3% sales, 0.3% farming, 14.3% construction, 11.7% production (2000).
Income: Per capita income: $23,553 (2005); Median household income: $66,759 (2005); Average household income: $74,405 (2005); Percent of households with income of $100,000 or more: 24.0% (2005); Poverty rate: 5.2% (2000).
Education: Percent of population age 25 and over with: High school diploma (including GED) or higher: 83.7% (2005); Bachelor's degree or higher: 14.1% (2005); Master's degree or higher: 5.0% (2005).

School District(s)
Middle Country Central School District (PK-12)
    2003-04 Enrollment: 11,630 . . . . (631) 285-8005

Two-year College(s)
Suffolk County Community College (Public)
    Fall 2004 Enrollment: 21,117. . . . . (631) 451-4110
    2005-06 Tuition: In-state $3,288; Out-of-state $6,278

Housing: Homeownership rate: 81.2% (2005); Median home value: $250,689 (2005); Median rent: $854 per month (2000); Median age of housing: 33 years (2000).
Transportation: Commute to work: 92.6% car, 4.9% public transportation, 0.8% walk, 1.2% work from home (2000); Travel time to work: 20.5% less than 15 minutes, 36.5% 15 to 30 minutes, 17.5% 30 to 45 minutes, 8.6% 45 to 60 minutes, 16.9% 60 minutes or more (2000)

SETAUKET-EAST SETAUKET (CDP). Covers a land area of 8.464 square miles and a water area of 0.796 square miles. Located at 40.93° N. Lat.; 73.10° W. Long.
Population: 13,634 (1990); 15,931 (2000); 17,415 (2005); 18,839 (2010 projected); Race: 83.4% White, 1.6% Black, 12.5% Asian, 4.6% Hispanic of any race (2005); Density: 2,057.6 persons per square mile (2005); Average household size: 2.85 (2005); Median age: 38.1 (2005); Males per 100 females: 96.9 (2005); Marriage status: 23.4% never married, 66.9% now married, 4.7% widowed, 4.9% divorced (2000); Foreign born: 13.7% (2000); Ancestry (includes multiple ancestries): 24.5% Italian, 22.8% Irish, 19.8% German, 18.5% Other groups, 8.3% English (2000).
Economy: Employment by occupation: 17.4% management, 40.7% professional, 8.8% services, 22.7% sales, 0.0% farming, 6.5% construction, 3.9% production (2000).
Income: Per capita income: $44,745 (2005); Median household income: $99,437 (2005); Average household income: $126,594 (2005); Percent of households with income of $100,000 or more: 49.7% (2005); Poverty rate: 4.0% (2000).
Education: Percent of population age 25 and over with: High school diploma (including GED) or higher: 95.0% (2005); Bachelor's degree or higher: 55.1% (2005); Master's degree or higher: 32.4% (2005).
Housing: Homeownership rate: 83.1% (2005); Median home value: $443,805 (2005); Median rent: $781 per month (2000); Median age of housing: 31 years (2000).
Newspapers: Times of Smithtown St. James and Nesconset (Setauket) (General - Circulation 6,122)
Transportation: Commute to work: 88.6% car, 3.5% public transportation, 3.0% walk, 3.6% work from home (2000); Travel time to work: 31.2% less than 15 minutes, 27.7% 15 to 30 minutes, 21.1% 30 to 45 minutes, 9.6% 45 to 60 minutes, 10.4% 60 minutes or more (2000)

SHELTER ISLAND (town). Covers a land area of 12.135 square miles and a water area of 14.964 square miles. Located at 41.07° N. Lat.; 72.34° W. Long.
Population: 2,263 (1990); 2,228 (2000); 2,443 (2005); 2,653 (2010 projected); Race: 94.9% White, 0.9% Black, 0.7% Asian, 3.2% Hispanic of any race (2005); Density: 201.3 persons per square mile (2005); Average household size: 2.25 (2005); Median age: 51.3 (2005); Males per 100 females: 93.7 (2005); Marriage status: 18.8% never married, 63.7% now married, 10.9% widowed, 6.6% divorced (2000); Foreign born: 7.6% (2000); Ancestry (includes multiple ancestries): 25.4% English, 24.6% German, 23.9% Irish, 13.9% Italian, 7.9% Other groups (2000).
Economy: Single-family building permits issued: 33 (2005); Multi-family building permits issued: 0 (2005); Employment by occupation: 14.1% management, 22.0% professional, 19.9% services, 22.1% sales, 0.6% farming, 12.9% construction, 8.3% production (2000).
Income: Per capita income: $34,575 (2005); Median household income: $56,699 (2005); Average household income: $77,850 (2005); Percent of households with income of $100,000 or more: 21.6% (2005); Poverty rate: 7.7% (2000).
Taxes: Total city taxes per capita: $2,490 (2004); City property taxes per capita: $1,740 (2004).
Education: Percent of population age 25 and over with: High school diploma (including GED) or higher: 93.7% (2005); Bachelor's degree or higher: 42.5% (2005); Master's degree or higher: 18.9% (2005).

School District(s)
Shelter Island Union Free School District (KG-12)
    2003-04 Enrollment: 269 . . . . (631) 749-0302

Housing: Homeownership rate: 83.7% (2005); Median home value: $473,370 (2005); Median rent: $703 per month (2000); Median age of housing: 33 years (2000).
Safety: Violent crime rate: 0.0 per 10,000 population; Property crime rate: 314.1 per 10,000 population (2004).
Newspapers: Shelter Island Reporter (General - Circulation 3,000)
Transportation: Commute to work: 81.4% car, 1.4% public transportation, 4.2% walk, 12.7% work from home (2000); Travel time to work: 62.4% less than 15 minutes, 10.3% 15 to 30 minutes, 15.3% 30 to 45 minutes, 5.1% 45 to 60 minutes, 6.9% 60 minutes or more (2000)

SHELTER ISLAND (CDP). Covers a land area of 6.537 square miles and a water area of 0.144 square miles. Located at 41.06° N. Lat.; 72.32° W. Long.
Population: 1,193 (1990); 1,234 (2000); 1,400 (2005); 1,563 (2010 projected); Race: 93.0% White, 1.4% Black, 0.7% Asian, 4.6% Hispanic of any race (2005); Density: 214.2 persons per square mile (2005); Average household size: 2.34 (2005); Median age: 46.5 (2005); Males per 100 females: 96.6 (2005); Marriage status: 21.0% never married, 59.0% now married, 11.4% widowed, 8.5% divorced (2000); Foreign born: 10.4% (2000); Ancestry (includes multiple ancestries): 28.1% Irish, 23.6% German, 22.9% English, 17.4% Italian, 9.0% Other groups (2000).
Economy: Employment by occupation: 13.5% management, 15.7% professional, 21.0% services, 23.7% sales, 1.0% farming, 16.8% construction, 8.2% production (2000).

Income: Per capita income: $27,105 (2005); Median household income: $47,356 (2005); Average household income: $63,351 (2005); Percent of households with income of $100,000 or more: 15.2% (2005); Poverty rate: 9.0% (2000).
Education: Percent of population age 25 and over with: High school diploma (including GED) or higher: 90.6% (2005); Bachelor's degree or higher: 36.2% (2005); Master's degree or higher: 14.3% (2005).
Housing: Homeownership rate: 78.8% (2005); Median home value: $431,373 (2005); Median rent: $633 per month (2000); Median age of housing: 37 years (2000).
Transportation: Commute to work: 86.8% car, 1.5% public transportation, 3.1% walk, 8.0% work from home (2000); Travel time to work: 68.9% less than 15 minutes, 11.4% 15 to 30 minutes, 14.5% 30 to 45 minutes, 1.1% 45 to 60 minutes, 4.1% 60 minutes or more (2000)

SHELTER ISLAND HEIGHTS (CDP).
Covers a land area of 5.357 square miles and a water area of 0.277 square miles. Located at 41.07° N. Lat.; 72.35° W. Long.
Population: 1,042 (1990); 981 (2000); 1,029 (2005); 1,075 (2010 projected); Race: 97.5% White, 0.4% Black, 0.7% Asian, 1.3% Hispanic of any race (2005); Density: 192.1 persons per square mile (2005); Average household size: 2.15 (2005); Median age: 57.5 (2005); Males per 100 females: 89.2 (2005); Marriage status: 16.3% never married, 69.2% now married, 10.4% widowed, 4.1% divorced (2000); Foreign born: 4.3% (2000); Ancestry (includes multiple ancestries): 28.2% English, 26.1% German, 19.0% Irish, 9.8% Italian, 8.6% Polish (2000).
Economy: Employment by occupation: 13.9% management, 31.1% professional, 18.6% services, 20.2% sales, 0.0% farming, 7.7% construction, 8.6% production (2000).
Income: Per capita income: $44,730 (2005); Median household income: $72,440 (2005); Average household income: $96,091 (2005); Percent of households with income of $100,000 or more: 29.4% (2005); Poverty rate: 6.2% (2000).
Education: Percent of population age 25 and over with: High school diploma (including GED) or higher: 97.5% (2005); Bachelor's degree or higher: 49.8% (2005); Master's degree or higher: 24.4% (2005).
Housing: Homeownership rate: 89.8% (2005); Median home value: $539,130 (2005); Median rent: $860 per month (2000); Median age of housing: 30 years (2000).
Transportation: Commute to work: 74.3% car, 1.2% public transportation, 5.0% walk, 19.5% work from home (2000); Travel time to work: 51.3% less than 15 minutes, 8.7% 15 to 30 minutes, 16.7% 30 to 45 minutes, 11.6% 45 to 60 minutes, 11.6% 60 minutes or more (2000)

SHINNECOCK HILLS (CDP).
Covers a land area of 2.075 square miles and a water area of 0.219 square miles. Located at 40.88° N. Lat.; 72.46° W. Long.
Population: 1,607 (1990); 1,749 (2000); 1,957 (2005); 2,159 (2010 projected); Race: 90.8% White, 2.9% Black, 0.9% Asian, 15.9% Hispanic of any race (2005); Density: 943.2 persons per square mile (2005); Average household size: 3.50 (2005); Median age: 28.2 (2005); Males per 100 females: 83.4 (2005); Marriage status: 50.0% never married, 42.0% now married, 4.3% widowed, 3.7% divorced (2000); Foreign born: 11.1% (2000); Ancestry (includes multiple ancestries): 27.6% German, 20.4% Italian, 17.9% Irish, 14.4% Other groups, 10.3% English (2000).
Economy: Employment by occupation: 11.8% management, 29.1% professional, 15.9% services, 28.5% sales, 0.3% farming, 6.9% construction, 7.5% production (2000).
Income: Per capita income: $34,861 (2005); Median household income: $84,964 (2005); Average household income: $118,144 (2005); Percent of households with income of $100,000 or more: 42.6% (2005); Poverty rate: 13.9% (2000).
Education: Percent of population age 25 and over with: High school diploma (including GED) or higher: 91.4% (2005); Bachelor's degree or higher: 40.1% (2005); Master's degree or higher: 20.3% (2005).
Housing: Homeownership rate: 82.8% (2005); Median home value: $554,228 (2005); Median rent: $841 per month (2000); Median age of housing: 31 years (2000).
Transportation: Commute to work: 68.6% car, 2.8% public transportation, 23.4% walk, 4.4% work from home (2000); Travel time to work: 50.9% less than 15 minutes, 24.0% 15 to 30 minutes, 10.9% 30 to 45 minutes, 3.0% 45 to 60 minutes, 11.3% 60 minutes or more (2000)

SHINNECOCK RESERVATION (reservation).
Covers a land area of 1.307 square miles and a water area of 0 square miles. Located at 40.87° N. Lat.; 72.43° W. Long.
Population: 375 (1990); 504 (2000); 679 (2005); 851 (2010 projected); Race: 12.4% White, 4.3% Black, 0.3% Asian, 11.3% Hispanic of any race (2005); Density: 519.4 persons per square mile (2005); Average household size: 2.89 (2005); Median age: 34.9 (2005); Males per 100 females: 92.9 (2005); Marriage status: 33.4% never married, 27.6% now married, 5.5% widowed, 33.4% divorced (2000); Foreign born: 0.0% (2000); Ancestry (includes multiple ancestries): 61.2% Other groups, 1.3% English, 1.3% Hungarian, 1.3% Italian, 1.3% Irish (2000).
Economy: Employment by occupation: 14.4% management, 8.4% professional, 20.8% services, 56.4% sales, 0.0% farming, 0.0% construction, 0.0% production (2000).
Income: Per capita income: $7,765 (2005); Median household income: $14,999 (2005); Average household income: $22,436 (2005); Percent of households with income of $100,000 or more: 0.0% (2005); Poverty rate: 50.6% (2000).
Education: Percent of population age 25 and over with: High school diploma (including GED) or higher: 93.0% (2005); Bachelor's degree or higher: 61.3% (2005); Master's degree or higher: 0.0% (2005).
Housing: Homeownership rate: 91.9% (2005); Median home value: $289,610 (2005); Median rent: $275 per month (2000); Median age of housing: 25 years (2000).
Transportation: Commute to work: 55.6% car, 0.0% public transportation, 0.0% walk, 44.4% work from home (2000); Travel time to work: 100.0% less than 15 minutes, 0.0% 15 to 30 minutes, 0.0% 30 to 45 minutes, 0.0% 45 to 60 minutes, 0.0% 60 minutes or more (2000)

SHIRLEY (CDP).
Covers a land area of 11.126 square miles and a water area of 0.325 square miles. Located at 40.79° N. Lat.; 72.87° W. Long.
Population: 23,149 (1990); 25,395 (2000); 26,354 (2005); 27,406 (2010 projected); Race: 86.1% White, 4.7% Black, 1.6% Asian, 14.4% Hispanic of any race (2005); Density: 2,368.7 persons per square mile (2005); Average household size: 3.42 (2005); Median age: 33.1 (2005); Males per 100 females: 99.6 (2005); Marriage status: 30.1% never married, 57.3% now married, 5.5% widowed, 7.1% divorced (2000); Foreign born: 8.0% (2000); Ancestry (includes multiple ancestries): 38.6% Italian, 25.4% Irish, 19.0% German, 17.0% Other groups, 6.9% Polish (2000).
Economy: Employment by occupation: 8.8% management, 13.9% professional, 17.8% services, 29.9% sales, 0.0% farming, 13.8% construction, 15.8% production (2000).
Income: Per capita income: $22,067 (2005); Median household income: $65,374 (2005); Average household income: $74,882 (2005); Percent of households with income of $100,000 or more: 23.1% (2005); Poverty rate: 7.8% (2000).
Education: Percent of population age 25 and over with: High school diploma (including GED) or higher: 81.5% (2005); Bachelor's degree or higher: 10.9% (2005); Master's degree or higher: 3.6% (2005).
School District(s)
William Floyd Union Free School District (KG-12)
    2003-04 Enrollment: 10,376 . . . . (631) 874-1201
Housing: Homeownership rate: 83.9% (2005); Median home value: $206,663 (2005); Median rent: $911 per month (2000); Median age of housing: 26 years (2000).
Transportation: Commute to work: 92.9% car, 3.5% public transportation, 1.2% walk, 1.9% work from home (2000); Travel time to work: 19.5% less than 15 minutes, 34.8% 15 to 30 minutes, 22.3% 30 to 45 minutes, 10.1% 45 to 60 minutes, 13.3% 60 minutes or more (2000)
Additional Information Contacts
Mastics and Shirley Chamber of Commerce . . . . (631) 399-2228
   http://www.masticshirleychamber.com

SHOREHAM (village).
Covers a land area of 0.444 square miles and a water area of 0 square miles. Located at 40.95° N. Lat.; 72.90° W. Long.
Population: 540 (1990); 417 (2000); 346 (2005); 342 (2010 projected); Race: 92.8% White, 0.0% Black, 3.2% Asian, 4.6% Hispanic of any race (2005); Density: 778.5 persons per square mile (2005); Average household size: 2.81 (2005); Median age: 46.5 (2005); Males per 100 females: 98.9 (2005); Marriage status: 25.9% never married, 61.0% now married, 8.9% widowed, 4.2% divorced (2000); Foreign born: 12.9% (2000); Ancestry (includes multiple ancestries): 27.3% Italian, 25.4% Irish, 23.0% German, 14.1% Other groups, 13.2% English (2000).

Economy: In summer recreational shore area. Agriculture includes vegetables and poultry. Just North is Shoreham Beach, resort village. Single-family building permits issued: 1 (2005); Multi-family building permits issued: 0 (2005); Employment by occupation: 18.9% management, 36.9% professional, 6.3% services, 25.2% sales, 0.0% farming, 8.6% construction, 4.1% production (2000).
Income: Per capita income: $47,124 (2005); Median household income: $125,833 (2005); Average household income: $132,561 (2005); Percent of households with income of $100,000 or more: 62.6% (2005); Poverty rate: 1.4% (2000).
Education: Percent of population age 25 and over with: High school diploma (including GED) or higher: 95.7% (2005); Bachelor's degree or higher: 64.1% (2005); Master's degree or higher: 46.6% (2005).

School District(s)
Shoreham-Wading River Central School District (KG-12)
    2003-04 Enrollment: 2,677 . . . . (631) 821-8105

Housing: Homeownership rate: 90.2% (2005); Median home value: $487,143 (2005); Median rent: $795 per month (2000); Median age of housing: 38 years (2000).
Transportation: Commute to work: 88.4% car, 1.9% public transportation, 0.9% walk, 8.8% work from home (2000); Travel time to work: 16.8% less than 15 minutes, 39.6% 15 to 30 minutes, 29.4% 30 to 45 minutes, 7.6% 45 to 60 minutes, 6.6% 60 minutes or more (2000)

SMITHTOWN (town). Covers a land area of 53.575 square miles and a water area of 57.801 square miles. Located at 40.86° N. Lat.; 73.21° W. Long. Elevation is 73 feet.
Population: 113,406 (1990); 115,715 (2000); 120,226 (2005); 125,029 (2010 projected); Race: 94.2% White, 0.8% Black, 3.1% Asian, 4.4% Hispanic of any race (2005); Density: 2,244.1 persons per square mile (2005); Average household size: 2.97 (2005); Median age: 39.8 (2005); Males per 100 females: 95.0 (2005); Marriage status: 20.8% never married, 66.5% now married, 7.5% widowed, 5.1% divorced (2000); Foreign born: 7.2% (2000); Ancestry (includes multiple ancestries): 35.3% Italian, 26.0% Irish, 18.7% German, 9.0% Other groups, 6.9% Polish (2000).
Economy: Diversifed light manufacturing includes vinyl products, military and aerospace electronic equipment, chemicals, fabricated metal products, machinery and machinery parts. Unemployment rate: 3.7% (2005); Total civilian labor force: 62,364 (2005); Single-family building permits issued: 96 (2005); Multi-family building permits issued: 0 (2005); Employment by occupation: 18.4% management, 26.6% professional, 12.5% services, 28.4% sales, 0.1% farming, 8.0% construction, 6.0% production (2000).
Income: Per capita income: $37,282 (2005); Median household income: $92,454 (2005); Average household income: $109,784 (2005); Percent of households with income of $100,000 or more: 45.2% (2005); Poverty rate: 3.0% (2000).
Taxes: Total city taxes per capita: $505 (2004); City property taxes per capita: $394 (2004).
Education: Percent of population age 25 and over with: High school diploma (including GED) or higher: 91.5% (2005); Bachelor's degree or higher: 36.4% (2005); Master's degree or higher: 15.9% (2005).

School District(s)
Hauppauge Union Free School District (KG-12)
    2003-04 Enrollment: 4,155 . . . . (631) 265-3630
Smithtown Central School District (KG-12)
    2003-04 Enrollment: 10,188 . . . . (631) 382-2005

Housing: Homeownership rate: 87.2% (2005); Median home value: $417,292 (2005); Median rent: $866 per month (2000); Median age of housing: 34 years (2000).
Hospitals: St Catherine of Siena Medical Center (311 beds)
Newspapers: Brookhaven Review (General - Circulation 1,500); Commack News (General - Circulation 3,862); Huntington News (General - Circulation 4,952); Islip News (General - Circulation 2,043); Ronkonkoma Review (General - Circulation 1,500); Smithtown Messenger (General - Circulation 8,000); The Mid Island News (General - Circulation 2,263); The Smithtown News (General - Circulation 10,426)
Transportation: Commute to work: 89.4% car, 6.1% public transportation, 0.7% walk, 3.2% work from home (2000); Travel time to work: 22.8% less than 15 minutes, 33.1% 15 to 30 minutes, 18.8% 30 to 45 minutes, 8.0% 45 to 60 minutes, 17.3% 60 minutes or more (2000)
Additional Information Contacts
Smithtown Chamber of Commerce . . . . (631) 979-8069
    http://www.smithtownchamber.org
Town of Smithtown . . . . (631) 360-7600
    http://www.smithtowninfo.com/

SMITHTOWN (CDP). Covers a land area of 3.366 square miles and a water area of 0 square miles. Located at 41.42° N. Lat.; 87.98° W. Long.
Population: 25,786 (1990); 26,901 (2000); 27,852 (2005); 28,949 (2010 projected); Race: 95.3% White, 0.9% Black, 2.2% Asian, 4.6% Hispanic of any race (2005); Density: 8,274.3 persons per square mile (2005); Average household size: 3.01 (2005); Median age: 40.2 (2005); Males per 100 females: 93.5 (2005); Marriage status: 20.5% never married, 66.5% now married, 8.2% widowed, 4.8% divorced (2000); Foreign born: 7.4% (2000); Ancestry (includes multiple ancestries): 34.4% Italian, 26.1% Irish, 22.4% German, 8.1% Other groups, 6.6% Polish (2000).
Economy: Employment by occupation: 17.8% management, 28.1% professional, 13.2% services, 27.1% sales, 0.1% farming, 7.4% construction, 6.3% production (2000).
Income: Per capita income: $37,302 (2005); Median household income: $93,145 (2005); Average household income: $111,197 (2005); Percent of households with income of $100,000 or more: 45.8% (2005); Poverty rate: 3.1% (2000).
Education: Percent of population age 25 and over with: High school diploma (including GED) or higher: 90.9% (2005); Bachelor's degree or higher: 37.0% (2005); Master's degree or higher: 17.4% (2005).
Housing: Homeownership rate: 88.3% (2005); Median home value: $433,935 (2005); Median rent: $704 per month (2000); Median age of housing: 35 years (2000).
Transportation: Commute to work: 90.0% car, 5.0% public transportation, 0.9% walk, 3.7% work from home (2000); Travel time to work: 23.1% less than 15 minutes, 36.1% 15 to 30 minutes, 18.1% 30 to 45 minutes, 6.9% 45 to 60 minutes, 15.8% 60 minutes or more (2000)

SOUND BEACH (CDP). Covers a land area of 2.657 square miles and a water area of 0 square miles. Located at 40.95° N. Lat.; 72.97° W. Long. Elevation is 200 feet.
Population: 9,102 (1990); 9,807 (2000); 9,947 (2005); 10,149 (2010 projected); Race: 95.1% White, 0.8% Black, 1.5% Asian, 4.2% Hispanic of any race (2005); Density: 3,743.8 persons per square mile (2005); Average household size: 2.92 (2005); Median age: 35.8 (2005); Males per 100 females: 98.5 (2005); Marriage status: 26.6% never married, 60.2% now married, 5.5% widowed, 7.7% divorced (2000); Foreign born: 7.4% (2000); Ancestry (includes multiple ancestries): 32.9% Irish, 32.6% Italian, 23.3% German, 8.0% Other groups, 6.2% Polish (2000).
Economy: Employment by occupation: 12.5% management, 25.4% professional, 13.2% services, 26.5% sales, 0.5% farming, 12.8% construction, 9.1% production (2000).
Income: Per capita income: $26,069 (2005); Median household income: $67,570 (2005); Average household income: $75,775 (2005); Percent of households with income of $100,000 or more: 24.0% (2005); Poverty rate: 6.9% (2000).
Education: Percent of population age 25 and over with: High school diploma (including GED) or higher: 92.7% (2005); Bachelor's degree or higher: 24.7% (2005); Master's degree or higher: 12.6% (2005).
Housing: Homeownership rate: 80.5% (2005); Median home value: $258,041 (2005); Median rent: $816 per month (2000); Median age of housing: 35 years (2000).
Transportation: Commute to work: 91.0% car, 4.3% public transportation, 0.9% walk, 3.4% work from home (2000); Travel time to work: 18.7% less than 15 minutes, 36.0% 15 to 30 minutes, 20.3% 30 to 45 minutes, 7.7% 45 to 60 minutes, 17.3% 60 minutes or more (2000)

SOUTH HUNTINGTON (CDP). Covers a land area of 3.378 square miles and a water area of 0 square miles. Located at 40.82° N. Lat.; 73.40° W. Long. Elevation is 220 feet.
Population: 9,624 (1990); 9,465 (2000); 9,251 (2005); 9,079 (2010 projected); Race: 91.0% White, 1.2% Black, 5.0% Asian, 5.2% Hispanic of any race (2005); Density: 2,738.7 persons per square mile (2005); Average household size: 2.84 (2005); Median age: 41.6 (2005); Males per 100 females: 94.0 (2005); Marriage status: 23.6% never married, 61.1% now married, 8.6% widowed, 6.6% divorced (2000); Foreign born: 9.7% (2000); Ancestry (includes multiple ancestries): 30.0% Italian, 23.3% Irish, 22.7% German, 10.9% Other groups, 5.8% English (2000).
Economy: Employment by occupation: 20.0% management, 27.0% professional, 10.2% services, 29.5% sales, 0.0% farming, 7.7% construction, 5.7% production (2000).
Income: Per capita income: $39,741 (2005); Median household income: $88,349 (2005); Average household income: $110,885 (2005); Percent of

households with income of $100,000 or more: 43.1% (2005); Poverty rate: 4.4% (2000).
Education: Percent of population age 25 and over with: High school diploma (including GED) or higher: 91.1% (2005); Bachelor's degree or higher: 40.0% (2005); Master's degree or higher: 15.4% (2005).
Housing: Homeownership rate: 86.5% (2005); Median home value: $375,770 (2005); Median rent: $911 per month (2000); Median age of housing: 43 years (2000).
Transportation: Commute to work: 85.6% car, 9.4% public transportation, 1.3% walk, 3.1% work from home (2000); Travel time to work: 21.0% less than 15 minutes, 33.7% 15 to 30 minutes, 18.0% 30 to 45 minutes, 9.7% 45 to 60 minutes, 17.8% 60 minutes or more (2000)

SOUTHAMPTON (village).
Covers a land area of 6.327 square miles and a water area of 0.428 square miles. Located at 40.88° N. Lat.; 72.39° W. Long. Elevation is 45 feet.
Population: 3,980 (1990); 3,965 (2000); 4,117 (2005); 4,282 (2010 projected); Race: 78.0% White, 13.1% Black, 2.1% Asian, 13.3% Hispanic of any race (2005); Density: 650.7 persons per square mile (2005); Average household size: 2.44 (2005); Median age: 44.9 (2005); Males per 100 females: 94.6 (2005); Marriage status: 32.7% never married, 47.9% now married, 10.1% widowed, 9.3% divorced (2000); Foreign born: 14.0% (2000); Ancestry (includes multiple ancestries): 20.3% Other groups, 18.6% Irish, 13.6% Polish, 12.7% Italian, 12.0% German (2000).
Economy: Single-family building permits issued: 14 (2005); Multi-family building permits issued: 0 (2005); Employment by occupation: 13.6% management, 22.3% professional, 21.6% services, 24.5% sales, 0.5% farming, 12.6% construction, 5.0% production (2000).
Income: Per capita income: $39,221 (2005); Median household income: $61,324 (2005); Average household income: $94,864 (2005); Percent of households with income of $100,000 or more: 30.6% (2005); Poverty rate: 6.2% (2000).
Education: Percent of population age 25 and over with: High school diploma (including GED) or higher: 83.6% (2005); Bachelor's degree or higher: 34.8% (2005); Master's degree or higher: 19.4% (2005).

School District(s)
Southampton Union Free School District (PK-12)
    2003-04 Enrollment: 1,769 . . . . (631) 591-4510
Tuckahoe Common School District (PK-08)
    2003-04 Enrollment: 338 . . . . (631) 283-3550

Four-year College(s)
Southampton College of Long Island University
    Fall 2004 Enrollment: 2,727 . . . . (631) 283-4000

Housing: Homeownership rate: 72.6% (2005); Median home value: $689,344 (2005); Median rent: $964 per month (2000); Median age of housing: 45 years (2000).
Hospitals: Southampton Hospital (168 beds)
Safety: Violent crime rate: 22.0 per 10,000 population; Property crime rate: 276.8 per 10,000 population (2004).
Newspapers: The Southampton Press (General - Circulation 40,000)
Transportation: Commute to work: 78.5% car, 4.4% public transportation, 4.9% walk, 9.3% work from home (2000); Travel time to work: 64.4% less than 15 minutes, 19.8% 15 to 30 minutes, 7.9% 30 to 45 minutes, 1.0% 45 to 60 minutes, 6.8% 60 minutes or more (2000)

Additional Information Contacts
Southampton Chamber of Commerce . . . . (631) 283-0402
    http://www.southamptonchamber.com
Village of Southampton . . . . (631) 283-6000
    http://www.town.southampton.ny.us/

SOUTHAMPTON (town).
Covers a land area of 138.879 square miles and a water area of 156.730 square miles. Located at 40.89° N. Lat.; 72.49° W. Long. Elevation is 45 feet.
History: Known for its many fine estates and celebrity residents. Parrish Memorial Art Museum is here, as is Southampton College of Long Island University. Settled 1640 as first English settlement in state, incorporated 1894.
Population: 44,976 (1990); 54,712 (2000); 59,226 (2005); 63,667 (2010 projected); Race: 86.1% White, 6.7% Black, 1.2% Asian, 13.0% Hispanic of any race (2005); Density: 426.5 persons per square mile (2005); Average household size: 2.57 (2005); Median age: 41.8 (2005); Males per 100 females: 100.0 (2005); Marriage status: 25.5% never married, 57.8% now married, 8.0% widowed, 8.7% divorced (2000); Foreign born: 11.2% (2000); Ancestry (includes multiple ancestries): 22.0% Irish, 18.4% Italian, 17.7% German, 14.9% Other groups, 11.2% English (2000).
Economy: Some light manufacturing; in shrinking potato-farming area. Unemployment rate: 4.1% (2005); Total civilian labor force: 30,311 (2005); Single-family building permits issued: 434 (2005); Multi-family building permits issued: 0 (2005); Employment by occupation: 12.6% management, 20.9% professional, 17.5% services, 27.3% sales, 0.8% farming, 14.2% construction, 6.6% production (2000).
Income: Per capita income: $34,481 (2005); Median household income: $63,914 (2005); Average household income: $87,490 (2005); Percent of households with income of $100,000 or more: 28.7% (2005); Poverty rate: 8.3% (2000).
Taxes: Total city taxes per capita: $1,437 (2004); City property taxes per capita: $781 (2004).
Education: Percent of population age 25 and over with: High school diploma (including GED) or higher: 86.3% (2005); Bachelor's degree or higher: 31.2% (2005); Master's degree or higher: 13.8% (2005).
Housing: Homeownership rate: 76.1% (2005); Median home value: $406,927 (2005); Median rent: $811 per month (2000); Median age of housing: 30 years (2000).
Transportation: Commute to work: 85.7% car, 3.7% public transportation, 3.8% walk, 5.6% work from home (2000); Travel time to work: 37.4% less than 15 minutes, 31.3% 15 to 30 minutes, 14.9% 30 to 45 minutes, 5.2% 45 to 60 minutes, 11.3% 60 minutes or more (2000)

Additional Information Contacts
Town of Southampton . . . . (631) 283-6000
    http://www.town.southampton.ny.us/

SOUTHOLD (town).
Covers a land area of 53.717 square miles and a water area of 350.766 square miles. Located at 41.06° N. Lat.; 72.40° W. Long. Elevation is 33 feet.
Population: 19,836 (1990); 20,599 (2000); 21,826 (2005); 23,084 (2010 projected); Race: 92.0% White, 3.2% Black, 0.5% Asian, 7.0% Hispanic of any race (2005); Density: 406.3 persons per square mile (2005); Average household size: 2.42 (2005); Median age: 46.4 (2005); Males per 100 females: 94.2 (2005); Marriage status: 20.2% never married, 63.7% now married, 9.4% widowed, 6.7% divorced (2000); Foreign born: 6.7% (2000); Ancestry (includes multiple ancestries): 24.9% Irish, 24.0% German, 16.2% Italian, 15.3% Polish, 15.2% English (2000).
Economy: Summer resort village. In declining agricultural area: potatoes, vegetables. Boatyards. Single-family building permits issued: 141 (2005); Multi-family building permits issued: 0 (2005); Employment by occupation: 15.1% management, 21.9% professional, 15.5% services, 26.2% sales, 1.9% farming, 11.0% construction, 8.5% production (2000).
Income: Per capita income: $31,322 (2005); Median household income: $57,078 (2005); Average household income: $75,007 (2005); Percent of households with income of $100,000 or more: 24.1% (2005); Poverty rate: 5.8% (2000).
Taxes: Total city taxes per capita: $1,112 (2004); City property taxes per capita: $968 (2004).
Education: Percent of population age 25 and over with: High school diploma (including GED) or higher: 88.2% (2005); Bachelor's degree or higher: 31.5% (2005); Master's degree or higher: 14.2% (2005).

School District(s)
Southold Union Free School District (KG-12)
    2003-04 Enrollment: 1,004 . . . . (631) 765-5400

Housing: Homeownership rate: 80.8% (2005); Median home value: $363,294 (2005); Median rent: $741 per month (2000); Median age of housing: 39 years (2000).
Newspapers: The Traveler Watchman (General - Circulation 21,500)
Transportation: Commute to work: 86.9% car, 3.2% public transportation, 3.6% walk, 4.9% work from home (2000); Travel time to work: 43.5% less than 15 minutes, 23.5% 15 to 30 minutes, 10.5% 30 to 45 minutes, 6.8% 45 to 60 minutes, 15.7% 60 minutes or more (2000)

Additional Information Contacts
Greenport-Southold Chamber . . . . (631) 765-3161
    http://www.greenportsoutholdchamber.org
Town of Southold . . . . (631) 765-1800
    http://southoldtown.northfork.net/

SOUTHOLD (CDP).
Covers a land area of 10.465 square miles and a water area of 0.867 square miles. Located at 41.05° N. Lat.; 72.42° W. Long.
Population: 5,200 (1990); 5,465 (2000); 5,751 (2005); 6,049 (2010 projected); Race: 95.3% White, 1.1% Black, 0.2% Asian, 3.7% Hispanic of any race (2005); Density: 549.5 persons per square mile (2005); Average household size: 2.39 (2005); Median age: 47.6 (2005); Males per 100

females: 94.0 (2005); Marriage status: 15.1% never married, 69.3% now married, 9.4% widowed, 6.1% divorced (2000); Foreign born: 4.9% (2000); Ancestry (includes multiple ancestries): 27.3% Irish, 24.0% German, 21.7% Italian, 13.9% Polish, 13.5% English (2000).
Economy: Employment by occupation: 15.9% management, 23.0% professional, 12.9% services, 30.3% sales, 2.9% farming, 9.1% construction, 5.8% production (2000).
Income: Per capita income: $32,629 (2005); Median household income: $56,229 (2005); Average household income: $76,578 (2005); Percent of households with income of $100,000 or more: 27.4% (2005); Poverty rate: 2.1% (2000).
Education: Percent of population age 25 and over with: High school diploma (including GED) or higher: 91.9% (2005); Bachelor's degree or higher: 30.7% (2005); Master's degree or higher: 14.0% (2005).
Housing: Homeownership rate: 83.5% (2005); Median home value: $369,781 (2005); Median rent: $854 per month (2000); Median age of housing: 33 years (2000).
Transportation: Commute to work: 88.1% car, 2.6% public transportation, 3.5% walk, 4.4% work from home (2000); Travel time to work: 44.3% less than 15 minutes, 20.3% 15 to 30 minutes, 10.5% 30 to 45 minutes, 4.0% 45 to 60 minutes, 21.0% 60 minutes or more (2000)

SPRINGS (CDP). Aka The Springs. Covers a land area of 8.464 square miles and a water area of 0.760 square miles. Located at 41.02° N. Lat.; 72.15° W. Long.
Population: 4,355 (1990); 4,950 (2000); 5,071 (2005); 5,216 (2010 projected); Race: 86.5% White, 1.9% Black, 1.8% Asian, 24.5% Hispanic of any race (2005); Density: 599.1 persons per square mile (2005); Average household size: 2.63 (2005); Median age: 41.5 (2005); Males per 100 females: 102.2 (2005); Marriage status: 29.8% never married, 54.0% now married, 6.5% widowed, 9.6% divorced (2000); Foreign born: 17.9% (2000); Ancestry (includes multiple ancestries): 20.3% Other groups, 20.1% Irish, 17.5% German, 17.5% English, 11.7% Italian (2000).
Economy: Employment by occupation: 9.8% management, 19.4% professional, 22.6% services, 23.1% sales, 2.3% farming, 17.8% construction, 5.1% production (2000).
Income: Per capita income: $31,759 (2005); Median household income: $65,042 (2005); Average household income: $83,411 (2005); Percent of households with income of $100,000 or more: 28.2% (2005); Poverty rate: 8.7% (2000).
Education: Percent of population age 25 and over with: High school diploma (including GED) or higher: 83.1% (2005); Bachelor's degree or higher: 34.5% (2005); Master's degree or higher: 11.1% (2005).
Housing: Homeownership rate: 79.9% (2005); Median home value: $392,283 (2005); Median rent: $1,094 per month (2000); Median age of housing: 23 years (2000).
Transportation: Commute to work: 83.9% car, 2.6% public transportation, 1.0% walk, 9.8% work from home (2000); Travel time to work: 44.8% less than 15 minutes, 35.8% 15 to 30 minutes, 12.3% 30 to 45 minutes, 2.1% 45 to 60 minutes, 5.0% 60 minutes or more (2000)

STONY BROOK (CDP). Covers a land area of 5.742 square miles and a water area of 0.429 square miles. Located at 40.90° N. Lat.; 73.12° W. Long. Elevation is 88 feet.
History: Named for its location, and to promote the town. Restored 1941 to resemble 18th-century village. State University of New York at Stony Brook, one of the university's four graduate centers, and the State University of New York Health Science Center are here.
Population: 13,726 (1990); 13,727 (2000); 14,047 (2005); 14,459 (2010 projected); Race: 89.5% White, 1.5% Black, 7.5% Asian, 3.1% Hispanic of any race (2005); Density: 2,446.2 persons per square mile (2005); Average household size: 2.85 (2005); Median age: 39.8 (2005); Males per 100 females: 95.7 (2005); Marriage status: 20.6% never married, 68.9% now married, 6.0% widowed, 4.5% divorced (2000); Foreign born: 10.7% (2000); Ancestry (includes multiple ancestries): 24.2% Italian, 22.9% Irish, 19.2% German, 13.0% Other groups, 7.5% English (2000).
Economy: Wood products. Employment by occupation: 15.4% management, 41.0% professional, 7.9% services, 26.5% sales, 0.2% farming, 5.2% construction, 3.8% production (2000).
Income: Per capita income: $42,035 (2005); Median household income: $100,118 (2005); Average household income: $119,610 (2005); Percent of households with income of $100,000 or more: 50.1% (2005); Poverty rate: 2.9% (2000).
Education: Percent of population age 25 and over with: High school diploma (including GED) or higher: 95.0% (2005); Bachelor's degree or higher: 54.3% (2005); Master's degree or higher: 30.8% (2005).

School District(s)
Three Village Central School District (KG-12)
    2003-04 Enrollment: 7,986 . . . . (631) 730-4010

Four-year College(s)
Stony Brook University (Public)
    Fall 2004 Enrollment: 21,685. . . . . (631) 632-6000
    2005-06 Tuition: In-state $5,574; Out-of-state $11,834

Housing: Homeownership rate: 92.1% (2005); Median home value: $395,673 (2005); Median rent: $1,246 per month (2000); Median age of housing: 35 years (2000).
Hospitals: Stony Brook University Hospital (504 beds)
Transportation: Commute to work: 89.1% car, 4.3% public transportation, 1.7% walk, 3.8% work from home (2000); Travel time to work: 28.2% less than 15 minutes, 29.2% 15 to 30 minutes, 19.4% 30 to 45 minutes, 10.1% 45 to 60 minutes, 13.0% 60 minutes or more (2000)

TERRYVILLE (CDP). Covers a land area of 3.213 square miles and a water area of 0 square miles. Located at 40.90° N. Lat.; 73.04° W. Long. Elevation is 154 feet.
Population: 10,275 (1990); 10,589 (2000); 11,545 (2005); 12,477 (2010 projected); Race: 89.2% White, 2.0% Black, 2.9% Asian, 13.2% Hispanic of any race (2005); Density: 3,593.2 persons per square mile (2005); Average household size: 3.14 (2005); Median age: 36.2 (2005); Males per 100 females: 98.2 (2005); Marriage status: 25.2% never married, 63.6% now married, 5.6% widowed, 5.6% divorced (2000); Foreign born: 10.0% (2000); Ancestry (includes multiple ancestries): 36.9% Italian, 20.9% Irish, 17.2% German, 13.5% Other groups, 6.7% Polish (2000).
Economy: Employment by occupation: 11.1% management, 23.0% professional, 14.3% services, 32.0% sales, 0.3% farming, 10.4% construction, 8.9% production (2000).
Income: Per capita income: $27,512 (2005); Median household income: $74,085 (2005); Average household income: $85,674 (2005); Percent of households with income of $100,000 or more: 31.1% (2005); Poverty rate: 3.2% (2000).
Education: Percent of population age 25 and over with: High school diploma (including GED) or higher: 87.5% (2005); Bachelor's degree or higher: 22.2% (2005); Master's degree or higher: 8.3% (2005).
Housing: Homeownership rate: 84.8% (2005); Median home value: $277,032 (2005); Median rent: $875 per month (2000); Median age of housing: 31 years (2000).
Transportation: Commute to work: 92.7% car, 3.9% public transportation, 0.1% walk, 2.6% work from home (2000); Travel time to work: 23.9% less than 15 minutes, 31.0% 15 to 30 minutes, 19.3% 30 to 45 minutes, 8.8% 45 to 60 minutes, 17.1% 60 minutes or more (2000)

TUCKAHOE (CDP). Covers a land area of 5.062 square miles and a water area of 0.448 square miles. Located at 40.90° N. Lat.; 72.43° W. Long.
Population: 1,397 (1990); 1,741 (2000); 1,871 (2005); 1,993 (2010 projected); Race: 83.3% White, 5.6% Black, 0.9% Asian, 29.2% Hispanic of any race (2005); Density: 369.6 persons per square mile (2005); Average household size: 2.57 (2005); Median age: 40.5 (2005); Males per 100 females: 97.6 (2005); Marriage status: 22.2% never married, 64.9% now married, 7.2% widowed, 5.7% divorced (2000); Foreign born: 22.6% (2000); Ancestry (includes multiple ancestries): 28.6% Other groups, 16.5% German, 15.5% Irish, 14.3% Italian, 10.3% English (2000).
Economy: Employment by occupation: 11.3% management, 21.0% professional, 21.1% services, 18.8% sales, 1.1% farming, 18.5% construction, 8.2% production (2000).
Income: Per capita income: $34,755 (2005); Median household income: $63,608 (2005); Average household income: $87,723 (2005); Percent of households with income of $100,000 or more: 27.9% (2005); Poverty rate: 8.6% (2000).
Education: Percent of population age 25 and over with: High school diploma (including GED) or higher: 82.1% (2005); Bachelor's degree or higher: 35.4% (2005); Master's degree or higher: 15.4% (2005).
Housing: Homeownership rate: 67.4% (2005); Median home value: $476,882 (2005); Median rent: $717 per month (2000); Median age of housing: 24 years (2000).
Transportation: Commute to work: 91.1% car, 2.6% public transportation, 1.7% walk, 4.0% work from home (2000); Travel time to work: 38.9% less

than 15 minutes, 27.4% 15 to 30 minutes, 20.7% 30 to 45 minutes, 4.9% 45 to 60 minutes, 8.1% 60 minutes or more (2000)

VILLAGE OF THE BRANCH (village). Aka The Branch. Covers a land area of 0.938 square miles and a water area of 0.030 square miles. Located at 40.85° N. Lat.; 73.18° W. Long. Elevation is 63 feet.
Population: 1,642 (1990); 1,895 (2000); 2,035 (2005); 2,163 (2010 projected); Race: 94.6% White, 0.1% Black, 3.1% Asian, 3.7% Hispanic of any race (2005); Density: 2,169.6 persons per square mile (2005); Average household size: 3.10 (2005); Median age: 42.5 (2005); Males per 100 females: 91.1 (2005); Marriage status: 22.2% never married, 64.5% now married, 9.2% widowed, 4.2% divorced (2000); Foreign born: 6.5% (2000); Ancestry (includes multiple ancestries): 32.7% Italian, 23.2% Irish, 21.4% German, 9.1% Other groups, 6.5% English (2000).
Economy: Single-family building permits issued: 0 (2005); Multi-family building permits issued: 0 (2005); Employment by occupation: 18.9% management, 29.5% professional, 8.9% services, 31.2% sales, 0.0% farming, 5.6% construction, 5.9% production (2000).
Income: Per capita income: $36,307 (2005); Median household income: $91,579 (2005); Average household income: $111,018 (2005); Percent of households with income of $100,000 or more: 45.1% (2005); Poverty rate: 4.7% (2000).
Education: Percent of population age 25 and over with: High school diploma (including GED) or higher: 92.1% (2005); Bachelor's degree or higher: 43.5% (2005); Master's degree or higher: 20.2% (2005).
Housing: Homeownership rate: 87.5% (2005); Median home value: $482,313 (2005); Median rent: $1,190 per month (2000); Median age of housing: 34 years (2000).
Transportation: Commute to work: 86.5% car, 6.5% public transportation, 1.9% walk, 4.6% work from home (2000); Travel time to work: 24.4% less than 15 minutes, 30.5% 15 to 30 minutes, 20.1% 30 to 45 minutes, 9.0% 45 to 60 minutes, 15.9% 60 minutes or more (2000)

WADING RIVER (CDP). Covers a land area of 9.798 square miles and a water area of 0.040 square miles. Located at 40.95° N. Lat.; 72.83° W. Long. Elevation is 93 feet.
Population: 5,248 (1990); 6,668 (2000); 8,347 (2005); 9,879 (2010 projected); Race: 93.7% White, 2.3% Black, 1.4% Asian, 5.2% Hispanic of any race (2005); Density: 851.9 persons per square mile (2005); Average household size: 2.76 (2005); Median age: 39.2 (2005); Males per 100 females: 100.3 (2005); Marriage status: 19.8% never married, 67.8% now married, 4.7% widowed, 7.7% divorced (2000); Foreign born: 4.8% (2000); Ancestry (includes multiple ancestries): 31.9% Irish, 28.1% Italian, 26.6% German, 9.6% Polish, 8.2% Other groups (2000).
Economy: Resort village. Employment by occupation: 13.8% management, 30.6% professional, 15.4% services, 23.9% sales, 0.0% farming, 10.2% construction, 6.1% production (2000).
Income: Per capita income: $31,544 (2005); Median household income: $74,978 (2005); Average household income: $86,350 (2005); Percent of households with income of $100,000 or more: 33.5% (2005); Poverty rate: 3.1% (2000).
Education: Percent of population age 25 and over with: High school diploma (including GED) or higher: 91.8% (2005); Bachelor's degree or higher: 32.6% (2005); Master's degree or higher: 15.7% (2005).
School District(s)
Little Flower Union Free School District (03-10)
   2003-04 Enrollment: 97 . . . . (631) 929-4300
Shoreham-Wading River Central School District (KG-12)
   2003-04 Enrollment: 2,677 . . . . (631) 821-8105
Housing: Homeownership rate: 90.2% (2005); Median home value: $308,306 (2005); Median rent: $880 per month (2000); Median age of housing: 32 years (2000).
Newspapers: Community Journal (General - Circulation 7,000)
Transportation: Commute to work: 92.9% car, 1.6% public transportation, 1.1% walk, 3.9% work from home (2000); Travel time to work: 19.2% less than 15 minutes, 31.0% 15 to 30 minutes, 23.0% 30 to 45 minutes, 13.6% 45 to 60 minutes, 13.2% 60 minutes or more (2000)

WAINSCOTT (CDP). Covers a land area of 6.805 square miles and a water area of 0.496 square miles. Located at 40.95° N. Lat.; 72.24° W. Long.
Population: 506 (1990); 628 (2000); 674 (2005); 718 (2010 projected); Race: 88.6% White, 4.6% Black, 0.1% Asian, 10.2% Hispanic of any race (2005); Density: 99.1 persons per square mile (2005); Average household size: 2.44 (2005); Median age: 45.6 (2005); Males per 100 females: 102.4 (2005); Marriage status: 30.8% never married, 52.1% now married, 5.8% widowed, 11.2% divorced (2000); Foreign born: 18.0% (2000); Ancestry (includes multiple ancestries): 26.7% Irish, 22.2% Other groups, 18.9% German, 15.9% Italian, 14.1% English (2000).
Economy: Employment by occupation: 8.7% management, 20.4% professional, 25.2% services, 21.4% sales, 0.6% farming, 19.1% construction, 4.5% production (2000).
Income: Per capita income: $37,951 (2005); Median household income: $54,891 (2005); Average household income: $91,042 (2005); Percent of households with income of $100,000 or more: 23.6% (2005); Poverty rate: 9.6% (2000).
Education: Percent of population age 25 and over with: High school diploma (including GED) or higher: 93.3% (2005); Bachelor's degree or higher: 39.0% (2005); Master's degree or higher: 19.2% (2005).
School District(s)
Child Development Ctr - Hamptons Charter (KG-06)
   2003-04 Enrollment: 69 . . . . (516) 324-3229
Wainscott Common School District (01-03)
   2003-04 Enrollment: 14 . . . . (631) 537-1080
Housing: Homeownership rate: 80.8% (2005); Median home value: $820,946 (2005); Median rent: $1,146 per month (2000); Median age of housing: 17 years (2000).
Transportation: Commute to work: 84.8% car, 1.3% public transportation, 0.0% walk, 11.4% work from home (2000); Travel time to work: 52.1% less than 15 minutes, 24.0% 15 to 30 minutes, 10.6% 30 to 45 minutes, 1.5% 45 to 60 minutes, 11.8% 60 minutes or more (2000)

WATER MILL (unincorporated postal area, zip code 11976). Covers a land area of 11.529 square miles and a water area of 0.320 square miles. Located at 40.92° N. Lat.; 72.34° W. Long. Elevation is 35 feet.
Population: 0 (2000); Race: 97.9% White, 1.7% Black, 0.0% Asian, 3.5% Hispanic of any race (2000); Density: 0.0 persons per square mile (2000); Age: 15.7% under 18, 18.6% over 64 (2000); Marriage status: 23.2% never married, 60.1% now married, 4.3% widowed, 12.4% divorced (2000); Foreign born: 9.2% (2000); Ancestry (includes multiple ancestries): 23.4% German, 22.1% Irish, 19.8% Italian, 19.4% English, 13.0% Polish (2000).
Economy: Resort village. Employment by occupation: 16.5% management, 23.3% professional, 13.7% services, 28.5% sales, 1.9% farming, 9.2% construction, 6.9% production (2000).
Income: Per capita income: $49,346 (2000); Median household income: $81,396 (2000); Poverty rate: 7.5% (2000).
Education: Percent of population age 25 and over with: High school diploma (including GED) or higher: 90.8% (2000); Bachelor's degree or higher: 44.8% (2000).
Housing: Homeownership rate: 89.0% (2000); Median home value: $599,000 (2000); Median rent: $867 per month (2000); Median age of housing: 18 years (2000).
Transportation: Commute to work: 74.4% car, 6.7% public transportation, 4.4% walk, 13.1% work from home (2000); Travel time to work: 51.4% less than 15 minutes, 24.4% 15 to 30 minutes, 11.4% 30 to 45 minutes, 4.4% 45 to 60 minutes, 8.5% 60 minutes or more (2000)

WATERMILL (CDP). Covers a land area of 10.994 square miles and a water area of 1.507 square miles. Located at 40.91° N. Lat.; 72.34° W. Long.
Population: 1,303 (1990); 1,724 (2000); 1,896 (2005); 2,044 (2010 projected); Race: 93.7% White, 3.2% Black, 0.9% Asian, 4.6% Hispanic of any race (2005); Density: 172.5 persons per square mile (2005); Average household size: 2.37 (2005); Median age: 47.6 (2005); Males per 100 females: 102.1 (2005); Marriage status: 23.8% never married, 62.8% now married, 3.8% widowed, 9.7% divorced (2000); Foreign born: 10.2% (2000); Ancestry (includes multiple ancestries): 22.9% Irish, 22.3% German, 20.0% Italian, 18.5% English, 13.3% Polish (2000).
Economy: Employment by occupation: 17.3% management, 21.9% professional, 14.3% services, 26.4% sales, 1.6% farming, 10.6% construction, 7.9% production (2000).
Income: Per capita income: $59,457 (2005); Median household income: $98,246 (2005); Average household income: $140,722 (2005); Percent of households with income of $100,000 or more: 49.0% (2005); Poverty rate: 8.3% (2000).
Education: Percent of population age 25 and over with: High school diploma (including GED) or higher: 89.9% (2005); Bachelor's degree or higher: 42.8% (2005); Master's degree or higher: 22.5% (2005).

Housing: Homeownership rate: 87.9% (2005); Median home value: $1 million+ (2005); Median rent: $867 per month (2000); Median age of housing: 18 years (2000).
Transportation: Commute to work: 72.0% car, 6.8% public transportation, 5.0% walk, 14.5% work from home (2000); Travel time to work: 57.1% less than 15 minutes, 23.0% 15 to 30 minutes, 6.7% 30 to 45 minutes, 4.4% 45 to 60 minutes, 8.9% 60 minutes or more (2000)

WEST BABYLON (CDP).
Covers a land area of 7.706 square miles and a water area of 0.311 square miles. Located at 40.71° N. Lat.; 73.35° W. Long. Elevation is 48 feet.
Population: 42,410 (1990); 43,452 (2000); 44,222 (2005); 45,137 (2010 projected); Race: 81.7% White, 10.6% Black, 2.7% Asian, 10.5% Hispanic of any race (2005); Density: 5,738.8 persons per square mile (2005); Average household size: 3.00 (2005); Median age: 38.0 (2005); Males per 100 females: 92.4 (2005); Marriage status: 26.7% never married, 57.6% now married, 8.1% widowed, 7.7% divorced (2000); Foreign born: 10.8% (2000); Ancestry (includes multiple ancestries): 36.3% Italian, 22.1% Irish, 17.3% German, 17.1% Other groups, 5.5% Polish (2000).
Economy: Employment by occupation: 12.2% management, 16.9% professional, 16.6% services, 30.3% sales, 0.1% farming, 11.3% construction, 12.6% production (2000).
Income: Per capita income: $25,241 (2005); Median household income: $67,348 (2005); Average household income: $75,116 (2005); Percent of households with income of $100,000 or more: 24.9% (2005); Poverty rate: 6.2% (2000).
Education: Percent of population age 25 and over with: High school diploma (including GED) or higher: 82.6% (2005); Bachelor's degree or higher: 17.2% (2005); Master's degree or higher: 6.1% (2005).

School District(s)
West Babylon Union Free School District (KG-12)
    2003-04 Enrollment: 4,940 . . . . (631) 321-3142

Housing: Homeownership rate: 74.7% (2005); Median home value: $269,298 (2005); Median rent: $903 per month (2000); Median age of housing: 40 years (2000).
Transportation: Commute to work: 89.1% car, 7.5% public transportation, 1.2% walk, 1.6% work from home (2000); Travel time to work: 25.1% less than 15 minutes, 33.8% 15 to 30 minutes, 18.7% 30 to 45 minutes, 7.1% 45 to 60 minutes, 15.3% 60 minutes or more (2000)

WEST BAY SHORE (CDP).
Covers a land area of 2.391 square miles and a water area of 0.014 square miles. Located at 40.71° N. Lat.; 73.27° W. Long.
Population: 4,907 (1990); 4,775 (2000); 4,759 (2005); 4,664 (2010 projected); Race: 92.8% White, 1.4% Black, 3.0% Asian, 5.0% Hispanic of any race (2005); Density: 1,990.2 persons per square mile (2005); Average household size: 2.71 (2005); Median age: 43.5 (2005); Males per 100 females: 94.9 (2005); Marriage status: 23.0% never married, 63.7% now married, 8.0% widowed, 5.2% divorced (2000); Foreign born: 6.9% (2000); Ancestry (includes multiple ancestries): 32.5% Italian, 32.0% Irish, 19.3% German, 10.5% Other groups, 7.2% English (2000).
Economy: Employment by occupation: 19.7% management, 30.8% professional, 11.5% services, 25.5% sales, 0.0% farming, 6.5% construction, 6.0% production (2000).
Income: Per capita income: $36,627 (2005); Median household income: $82,241 (2005); Average household income: $98,818 (2005); Percent of households with income of $100,000 or more: 38.3% (2005); Poverty rate: 4.6% (2000).
Education: Percent of population age 25 and over with: High school diploma (including GED) or higher: 91.5% (2005); Bachelor's degree or higher: 33.3% (2005); Master's degree or higher: 16.0% (2005).
Housing: Homeownership rate: 94.7% (2005); Median home value: $320,855 (2005); Median rent: $986 per month (2000); Median age of housing: 41 years (2000).
Transportation: Commute to work: 83.7% car, 11.9% public transportation, 1.1% walk, 3.0% work from home (2000); Travel time to work: 33.0% less than 15 minutes, 28.8% 15 to 30 minutes, 12.6% 30 to 45 minutes, 6.8% 45 to 60 minutes, 18.8% 60 minutes or more (2000)

WEST HAMPTON DUNES (village).
Covers a land area of 0.342 square miles and a water area of 0.521 square miles. Located at 40.77° N. Lat.; 72.71° W. Long. Elevation is 5 feet.
Population: 6 (1990); 11 (2000); 11 (2005); 10 (2010 projected); Race: 90.9% White, 0.0% Black, 9.1% Asian, 0.0% Hispanic of any race (2005); Density: 32.2 persons per square mile (2005); Average household size: 1.57 (2005); Median age: 70.0 (2005); Males per 100 females: 450.0 (2005); Marriage status: 0.0% never married, 100.0% now married, 0.0% widowed, 0.0% divorced (2000); Foreign born: 0.0% (2000); Ancestry (includes multiple ancestries): 75.0% Austrian, 37.5% Irish, 37.5% Polish, 25.0% German, 25.0% Italian (2000).
Economy: Single-family building permits issued: 2 (2005); Multi-family building permits issued: 0 (2005); Employment by occupation: 0.0% management, 40.0% professional, 0.0% services, 0.0% sales, 0.0% farming, 60.0% construction, 0.0% production (2000).
Income: Per capita income: $77,727 (2005); Median household income: $95,833 (2005); Average household income: $122,143 (2005); Percent of households with income of $100,000 or more: 42.9% (2005); Poverty rate: 0.0% (2000).
Education: Percent of population age 25 and over with: High school diploma (including GED) or higher: 100.0% (2005); Bachelor's degree or higher: 36.4% (2005); Master's degree or higher: 0.0% (2005).
Housing: Homeownership rate: 85.7% (2005); Median home value: $1 million+ (2005); Median rent: $n/a per month (2000); Median age of housing: 4 years (2000).
Transportation: Commute to work: 100.0% car, 0.0% public transportation, 0.0% walk, 0.0% work from home (2000); Travel time to work: 60.0% less than 15 minutes, 0.0% 15 to 30 minutes, 0.0% 30 to 45 minutes, 0.0% 45 to 60 minutes, 40.0% 60 minutes or more (2000)

WEST HILLS (CDP).
Covers a land area of 4.954 square miles and a water area of 0 square miles. Located at 40.82° N. Lat.; 73.43° W. Long. Elevation is 340 feet.
Population: 5,849 (1990); 5,607 (2000); 5,691 (2005); 5,811 (2010 projected); Race: 92.9% White, 1.4% Black, 4.1% Asian, 3.4% Hispanic of any race (2005); Density: 1,148.7 persons per square mile (2005); Average household size: 2.79 (2005); Median age: 42.0 (2005); Males per 100 females: 98.5 (2005); Marriage status: 20.7% never married, 69.8% now married, 4.5% widowed, 5.0% divorced (2000); Foreign born: 5.9% (2000); Ancestry (includes multiple ancestries): 33.3% Italian, 19.0% Irish, 16.3% German, 9.8% Other groups, 5.8% English (2000).
Economy: Employment by occupation: 29.1% management, 24.1% professional, 11.5% services, 25.9% sales, 0.2% farming, 6.2% construction, 3.0% production (2000).
Income: Per capita income: $47,489 (2005); Median household income: $102,870 (2005); Average household income: $132,349 (2005); Percent of households with income of $100,000 or more: 51.3% (2005); Poverty rate: 1.8% (2000).
Education: Percent of population age 25 and over with: High school diploma (including GED) or higher: 96.0% (2005); Bachelor's degree or higher: 52.8% (2005); Master's degree or higher: 20.5% (2005).
Housing: Homeownership rate: 94.5% (2005); Median home value: $544,170 (2005); Median rent: $1,169 per month (2000); Median age of housing: 41 years (2000).
Transportation: Commute to work: 81.4% car, 13.6% public transportation, 0.6% walk, 4.3% work from home (2000); Travel time to work: 20.8% less than 15 minutes, 33.6% 15 to 30 minutes, 17.9% 30 to 45 minutes, 5.3% 45 to 60 minutes, 22.3% 60 minutes or more (2000)

WEST ISLIP (CDP).
Covers a land area of 6.196 square miles and a water area of 0.431 square miles. Located at 40.71° N. Lat.; 73.29° W. Long. Elevation is 20 feet.
Population: 28,419 (1990); 28,907 (2000); 30,094 (2005); 31,366 (2010 projected); Race: 96.1% White, 0.6% Black, 1.3% Asian, 4.4% Hispanic of any race (2005); Density: 4,857.3 persons per square mile (2005); Average household size: 3.22 (2005); Median age: 38.2 (2005); Males per 100 females: 96.8 (2005); Marriage status: 22.8% never married, 65.2% now married, 6.7% widowed, 5.3% divorced (2000); Foreign born: 5.4% (2000); Ancestry (includes multiple ancestries): 38.4% Italian, 30.9% Irish, 20.8% German, 7.2% Polish, 7.1% Other groups (2000).
Economy: Employment by occupation: 14.4% management, 21.7% professional, 13.4% services, 28.9% sales, 0.1% farming, 11.7% construction, 9.8% production (2000).
Income: Per capita income: $32,698 (2005); Median household income: $86,821 (2005); Average household income: $105,074 (2005); Percent of households with income of $100,000 or more: 39.7% (2005); Poverty rate: 2.3% (2000).
Education: Percent of population age 25 and over with: High school diploma (including GED) or higher: 90.1% (2005); Bachelor's degree or higher: 26.6% (2005); Master's degree or higher: 10.7% (2005).

School District(s)
West Islip Union Free School District (KG-12)
    2003-04 Enrollment: 5,905 . . . . (631) 893-3200
Housing: Homeownership rate: 93.0% (2005); Median home value: $355,218 (2005); Median rent: $933 per month (2000); Median age of housing: 42 years (2000).
Hospitals: Good Samaritan Hospital Medical Center (431 beds)
Transportation: Commute to work: 88.8% car, 8.6% public transportation, 0.6% walk, 1.6% work from home (2000); Travel time to work: 27.8% less than 15 minutes, 30.6% 15 to 30 minutes, 16.9% 30 to 45 minutes, 8.0% 45 to 60 minutes, 16.6% 60 minutes or more (2000)
Additional Information Contacts
West Islip Chamber of Commerce . . . . (631) 661-3838
    http://www.westislip.com

WEST SAYVILLE (CDP).
Covers a land area of 1.857 square miles and a water area of 0.006 square miles. Located at 40.73° N. Lat.; 73.10° W. Long. Elevation is 20 feet.
Population: 4,680 (1990); 5,003 (2000); 5,142 (2005); 5,307 (2010 projected); Race: 96.3% White, 0.4% Black, 1.8% Asian, 2.6% Hispanic of any race (2005); Density: 2,769.4 persons per square mile (2005); Average household size: 2.84 (2005); Median age: 39.1 (2005); Males per 100 females: 93.2 (2005); Marriage status: 22.0% never married, 62.3% now married, 9.3% widowed, 6.4% divorced (2000); Foreign born: 3.9% (2000); Ancestry (includes multiple ancestries): 31.2% Irish, 31.2% Italian, 19.6% German, 6.3% English, 6.0% Polish (2000).
Economy: Manufacturing of electronic products, foods. In summer resort and recreation area. Employment by occupation: 13.9% management, 25.7% professional, 12.8% services, 27.2% sales, 0.0% farming, 11.6% construction, 8.9% production (2000).
Income: Per capita income: $28,824 (2005); Median household income: $73,172 (2005); Average household income: $81,001 (2005); Percent of households with income of $100,000 or more: 29.6% (2005); Poverty rate: 4.2% (2000).
Education: Percent of population age 25 and over with: High school diploma (including GED) or higher: 87.3% (2005); Bachelor's degree or higher: 25.5% (2005); Master's degree or higher: 11.5% (2005).
School District(s)
Sayville Union Free School District (KG-12)
    2003-04 Enrollment: 3,593 . . . . (631) 244-6510
Housing: Homeownership rate: 82.6% (2005); Median home value: $307,786 (2005); Median rent: $852 per month (2000); Median age of housing: 45 years (2000).
Transportation: Commute to work: 94.6% car, 4.0% public transportation, 0.0% walk, 1.2% work from home (2000); Travel time to work: 25.4% less than 15 minutes, 36.4% 15 to 30 minutes, 14.8% 30 to 45 minutes, 9.4% 45 to 60 minutes, 14.0% 60 minutes or more (2000)

WESTHAMPTON (CDP).
Covers a land area of 8.796 square miles and a water area of 0.075 square miles. Located at 40.82° N. Lat.; 72.66° W. Long. Elevation is 38 feet.
History: Like most of Southern Long Island shore zone, suffering from significant beach erosion due to a succession of mid-1990s Atlantic hurricanes. Part of the original Quogue Purchase of 1666. Westhampton's first summerhouse built by Gen. John A. Dix in 1879; then a three-day journey by stage from Brooklyn until L.I. Railroad extended to Sag Harbor in 1870. By 1920s Westhampton and The Hamptons were the summering place for the rich and famous. Incorporated 1928.
Population: 1,849 (1990); 2,869 (2000); 3,210 (2005); 3,537 (2010 projected); Race: 89.6% White, 4.8% Black, 1.8% Asian, 7.7% Hispanic of any race (2005); Density: 364.9 persons per square mile (2005); Average household size: 2.71 (2005); Median age: 38.0 (2005); Males per 100 females: 101.8 (2005); Marriage status: 22.2% never married, 65.6% now married, 5.0% widowed, 7.2% divorced (2000); Foreign born: 8.5% (2000); Ancestry (includes multiple ancestries): 23.9% Irish, 23.4% Italian, 16.9% German, 12.9% Other groups, 12.8% English (2000).
Economy: Resort village. Just south is Westhampton Beach, shore resort. Employment by occupation: 18.1% management, 22.9% professional, 11.5% services, 30.4% sales, 0.1% farming, 10.4% construction, 6.6% production (2000).
Income: Per capita income: $35,646 (2005); Median household income: $73,972 (2005); Average household income: $95,856 (2005); Percent of households with income of $100,000 or more: 36.4% (2005); Poverty rate: 4.5% (2000).

Education: Percent of population age 25 and over with: High school diploma (including GED) or higher: 90.1% (2005); Bachelor's degree or higher: 40.3% (2005); Master's degree or higher: 15.9% (2005).
Housing: Homeownership rate: 70.4% (2005); Median home value: $459,554 (2005); Median rent: $869 per month (2000); Median age of housing: 31 years (2000).
Transportation: Commute to work: 86.7% car, 6.1% public transportation, 2.5% walk, 3.7% work from home (2000); Travel time to work: 36.2% less than 15 minutes, 26.7% 15 to 30 minutes, 11.5% 30 to 45 minutes, 8.3% 45 to 60 minutes, 17.3% 60 minutes or more (2000)

WESTHAMPTON BEACH (village).
Covers a land area of 2.907 square miles and a water area of 0.072 square miles. Located at 40.80° N. Lat.; 72.64° W. Long.
Population: 1,571 (1990); 1,902 (2000); 1,979 (2005); 2,066 (2010 projected); Race: 86.9% White, 4.5% Black, 1.3% Asian, 11.2% Hispanic of any race (2005); Density: 680.7 persons per square mile (2005); Average household size: 2.40 (2005); Median age: 45.4 (2005); Males per 100 females: 94.8 (2005); Marriage status: 21.8% never married, 60.5% now married, 8.9% widowed, 8.9% divorced (2000); Foreign born: 12.3% (2000); Ancestry (includes multiple ancestries): 27.0% Irish, 16.9% German, 14.9% Other groups, 14.7% English, 14.4% Italian (2000).
Economy: Single-family building permits issued: 21 (2005); Multi-family building permits issued: 0 (2005); Employment by occupation: 12.3% management, 28.3% professional, 13.8% services, 31.7% sales, 0.0% farming, 7.8% construction, 6.1% production (2000).
Income: Per capita income: $40,063 (2005); Median household income: $65,806 (2005); Average household income: $96,279 (2005); Percent of households with income of $100,000 or more: 30.9% (2005); Poverty rate: 9.0% (2000).
Education: Percent of population age 25 and over with: High school diploma (including GED) or higher: 89.7% (2005); Bachelor's degree or higher: 41.3% (2005); Master's degree or higher: 22.7% (2005).
School District(s)
Westhampton Beach Union Free School District (KG-12)
    2003-04 Enrollment: 1,727 . . . . (631) 288-3800
Housing: Homeownership rate: 69.4% (2005); Median home value: $515,523 (2005); Median rent: $819 per month (2000); Median age of housing: 32 years (2000).
Safety: Violent crime rate: 25.6 per 10,000 population; Property crime rate: 184.3 per 10,000 population (2004).
Newspapers: The Southhampton Press-Western Edition (General - Circulation 7,500)
Transportation: Commute to work: 77.3% car, 3.7% public transportation, 7.0% walk, 7.9% work from home (2000); Travel time to work: 45.7% less than 15 minutes, 19.0% 15 to 30 minutes, 13.6% 30 to 45 minutes, 5.8% 45 to 60 minutes, 15.8% 60 minutes or more (2000)
Additional Information Contacts
Village of Westhampton Beach . . . . (631) 288-1654
    http://www.whbvillage.com/
Westhampton Bch Chamber of Commerce . . . . (631) 288-3337
    http://www.whbcc.com

WHEATLEY HEIGHTS (CDP).
Covers a land area of 1.353 square miles and a water area of 0 square miles. Located at 40.76° N. Lat.; 73.36° W. Long.
Population: 5,027 (1990); 5,013 (2000); 5,183 (2005); 5,369 (2010 projected); Race: 30.3% White, 57.0% Black, 3.6% Asian, 14.0% Hispanic of any race (2005); Density: 3,830.3 persons per square mile (2005); Average household size: 3.42 (2005); Median age: 35.9 (2005); Males per 100 females: 95.4 (2005); Marriage status: 28.4% never married, 59.4% now married, 5.8% widowed, 6.4% divorced (2000); Foreign born: 17.9% (2000); Ancestry (includes multiple ancestries): 46.1% Other groups, 10.3% Italian, 8.5% Irish, 6.0% German, 5.4% Haitian (2000).
Economy: Employment by occupation: 18.4% management, 20.7% professional, 14.1% services, 30.9% sales, 0.2% farming, 6.7% construction, 9.0% production (2000).
Income: Per capita income: $31,625 (2005); Median household income: $84,628 (2005); Average household income: $107,706 (2005); Percent of households with income of $100,000 or more: 40.5% (2005); Poverty rate: 4.8% (2000).
Education: Percent of population age 25 and over with: High school diploma (including GED) or higher: 87.2% (2005); Bachelor's degree or higher: 31.3% (2005); Master's degree or higher: 14.2% (2005).

Housing: Homeownership rate: 84.8% (2005); Median home value: $312,729 (2005); Median rent: $791 per month (2000); Median age of housing: 33 years (2000).
Transportation: Commute to work: 82.1% car, 15.3% public transportation, 0.3% walk, 1.8% work from home (2000); Travel time to work: 15.6% less than 15 minutes, 34.4% 15 to 30 minutes, 18.1% 30 to 45 minutes, 8.7% 45 to 60 minutes, 23.1% 60 minutes or more (2000)

WYANDANCH (CDP). Covers a land area of 4.374 square miles and a water area of 0.003 square miles. Located at 40.74° N. Lat.; 73.36° W. Long. Elevation is 56 feet.
Population: 8,771 (1990); 10,546 (2000); 11,258 (2005); 11,977 (2010 projected); Race: 10.4% White, 77.3% Black, 0.7% Asian, 17.5% Hispanic of any race (2005); Density: 2,573.6 persons per square mile (2005); Average household size: 4.25 (2005); Median age: 29.4 (2005); Males per 100 females: 89.7 (2005); Marriage status: 43.1% never married, 42.5% now married, 6.9% widowed, 7.5% divorced (2000); Foreign born: 17.2% (2000); Ancestry (includes multiple ancestries): 75.8% Other groups, 4.6% Haitian, 2.3% African, 2.1% Jamaican, 1.8% United States or American (2000).
Economy: Manufacturing: electrical equipment, transportation equipment, fabricated metal products, telecommunications, fiberglass products, packaging. Employment by occupation: 5.9% management, 11.7% professional, 27.4% services, 27.0% sales, 0.0% farming, 7.0% construction, 20.9% production (2000).
Income: Per capita income: $13,620 (2005); Median household income: $44,081 (2005); Average household income: $56,692 (2005); Percent of households with income of $100,000 or more: 13.9% (2005); Poverty rate: 16.4% (2000).
Education: Percent of population age 25 and over with: High school diploma (including GED) or higher: 65.4% (2005); Bachelor's degree or higher: 7.3% (2005); Master's degree or higher: 2.4% (2005).

School District(s)
Sullivan Charter School
    2003-04 Enrollment: n/a . . . . (631) 841-0841
Wyandanch Union Free School District (PK-12)
    2003-04 Enrollment: 2,280 . . . . (631) 491-1013

Housing: Homeownership rate: 58.2% (2005); Median home value: $208,295 (2005); Median rent: $891 per month (2000); Median age of housing: 36 years (2000).
Transportation: Commute to work: 79.5% car, 11.6% public transportation, 5.6% walk, 1.8% work from home (2000); Travel time to work: 26.0% less than 15 minutes, 39.8% 15 to 30 minutes, 17.3% 30 to 45 minutes, 5.6% 45 to 60 minutes, 11.4% 60 minutes or more (2000)

YAPHANK (CDP). Covers a land area of 13.979 square miles and a water area of 0.114 square miles. Located at 40.83° N. Lat.; 72.92° W. Long.
History: US Camp Upton here was a US Army induction center in World Wars I and II.
Population: 4,841 (1990); 5,025 (2000); 5,388 (2005); 5,743 (2010 projected); Race: 81.9% White, 13.4% Black, 1.5% Asian, 10.2% Hispanic of any race (2005); Density: 385.4 persons per square mile (2005); Average household size: 3.21 (2005); Median age: 38.9 (2005); Males per 100 females: 116.7 (2005); Marriage status: 20.7% never married, 61.0% now married, 7.2% widowed, 11.1% divorced (2000); Foreign born: 6.8% (2000); Ancestry (includes multiple ancestries): 26.3% Irish, 25.6% German, 21.9% Italian, 13.1% Other groups, 6.6% English (2000).
Economy: Employment by occupation: 11.0% management, 25.5% professional, 16.7% services, 23.2% sales, 0.3% farming, 9.4% construction, 13.9% production (2000).
Income: Per capita income: $27,670 (2005); Median household income: $77,328 (2005); Average household income: $82,831 (2005); Percent of households with income of $100,000 or more: 31.1% (2005); Poverty rate: 3.8% (2000).
Education: Percent of population age 25 and over with: High school diploma (including GED) or higher: 83.3% (2005); Bachelor's degree or higher: 20.2% (2005); Master's degree or higher: 9.8% (2005).

School District(s)
Longwood Central School District (KG-12)
    2003-04 Enrollment: 9,794 . . . . (631) 345-2172

Housing: Homeownership rate: 82.7% (2005); Median home value: $238,171 (2005); Median rent: $792 per month (2000); Median age of housing: 26 years (2000).
Transportation: Commute to work: 93.6% car, 3.1% public transportation, 0.3% walk, 2.3% work from home (2000); Travel time to work: 25.3% less than 15 minutes, 29.9% 15 to 30 minutes, 21.9% 30 to 45 minutes, 11.5% 45 to 60 minutes, 11.3% 60 minutes or more (2000)

Sullivan County

Located in southeastern New York; bounded on the west and southwest by the Delaware River and the Pennsylvania border; drained by the Neversink River; includes parts of the Catskills and the Shawangunk Range, and many lakes. Covers a land area of 969.71 square miles, a water area of 27.14 square miles, and is located in the Eastern Time Zone. The county government was organized in 1809. County seat is Monticello.
Population: 69,277 (1990); 73,966 (2000); 75,730 (2005); 77,532 (2010 projected); Race: 83.6% White, 9.3% Black, 1.3% Asian, 11.0% Hispanic of any race (2005); Density: 78.1 persons per square mile (2005); Average household size: 2.64 (2005); Median age: 39.4 (2005); Males per 100 females: 102.7 (2005).
Religion: Five largest groups: 24.9% Catholic Church, 10.0% Jewish Estimate, 4.2% The United Methodist Church, 1.4% Evangelical Lutheran Church in America, 1.1% Presbyterian Church (U.S.A.) (2000).
Economy: Unemployment rate: 4.9% (2005); Total civilian labor force: 35,389 (2005); Leading industries: 24.1% health care and social assistance; 15.1% retail trade; 13.9% accommodation and food services (2003); Farms: 381 totaling 63,614 acres (2002); Companies that employ 500 or more persons: 3 (2003); Companies that employ 100 to 499 persons: 20 (2003); Companies that employ less than 100 persons: 1,983 (2003); Black-owned businesses: n/a (2002); Hispanic-owned businesses: 119 (2002); Women-owned businesses: 1,794 (2002); Retail sales per capita: $11,309 (2006). Single-family building permits issued: 761 (2005); Multi-family building permits issued: 214 (2005).
Income: Per capita income: $21,844 (2005); Median household income: $42,642 (2005); Average household income: $55,435 (2005); Percent of households with income of $100,000 or more: 12.8% (2005); Poverty rate: 13.5% (2003); Bankruptcy rate: 5.94% (2005).
Taxes: Total county taxes per capita: $871 (2004); County property taxes per capita: $493 (2004).
Education: Percent of population age 25 and over with: High school diploma (including GED) or higher: 76.5% (2005); Bachelor's degree or higher: 16.7% (2005); Master's degree or higher: 7.6% (2005).
Housing: Homeownership rate: 68.4% (2005); Median home value: $133,979 (2005); Median rent: $471 per month (2000); Median age of housing: 36 years (2000).
Health: Birth rate: 113.3 per 10,000 population (2004); Death rate: 91.4 per 10,000 population (2004); Age-adjusted cancer mortality rate: 245.7 deaths per 100,000 population (2002); Number of physicians: 14.6 per 10,000 population (2004); Hospital beds: 31.7 per 10,000 population (2003); Hospital admissions: 864.8 per 10,000 population (2003).
Elections: 2004 Presidential election results: 49.5% Bush, 48.6% Kerry, 1.8% Nader, 0.1% Badnarik

Additional Information Contacts
Sullivan County Government . . . . (845) 794-3000
    http://co.sullivan.ny.us/
Town of Bethel . . . . (845) 583-4350
    http://www.town.bethel.ny.us/
Town of Liberty . . . . (845) 292-5111
    http://www.townofliberty.org/
Town of Thompson . . . . (845) 794-2500
    http://www.townofthompson.com/
Village of Monticello. . . . . (845) 794-6130
    http://www.village.monticello.ny.us/

Sullivan County Communities

BARRYVILLE (unincorporated postal area, zip code 12719). Covers a land area of 17.484 square miles and a water area of 0.157 square miles. Located at 41.48° N. Lat.; 74.92° W. Long. Elevation is 620 feet.
Population: 0 (2000); Race: 93.9% White, 5.1% Black, 0.4% Asian, 6.1% Hispanic of any race (2000); Density: 0.0 persons per square mile (2000); Age: 22.6% under 18, 15.5% over 64 (2000); Marriage status: 25.1% never married, 60.4% now married, 9.2% widowed, 5.3% divorced (2000); Foreign born: 5.5% (2000); Ancestry (includes multiple ancestries): 26.6% German, 18.0% Irish, 11.5% Italian, 9.6% Other groups, 9.2% English (2000).

Economy: Employment by occupation: 12.9% management, 21.0% professional, 21.0% services, 18.4% sales, 2.1% farming, 12.9% construction, 11.8% production (2000).
Income: Per capita income: $23,097 (2000); Median household income: $47,750 (2000); Poverty rate: 18.7% (2000).
Education: Percent of population age 25 and over with: High school diploma (including GED) or higher: 78.7% (2000); Bachelor's degree or higher: 22.3% (2000).
Housing: Homeownership rate: 86.1% (2000); Median home value: $109,700 (2000); Median rent: $432 per month (2000); Median age of housing: 34 years (2000).
Transportation: Commute to work: 85.0% car, 4.2% public transportation, 5.0% walk, 1.7% work from home (2000); Travel time to work: 28.9% less than 15 minutes, 20.1% 15 to 30 minutes, 24.9% 30 to 45 minutes, 11.3% 45 to 60 minutes, 14.7% 60 minutes or more (2000)

BETHEL (town).
Covers a land area of 85.407 square miles and a water area of 4.624 square miles. Located at 41.69° N. Lat.; 74.84° W. Long.
History: Site of the 3-day Woodstock rock festival, July 1969.
Population: 3,693 (1990); 4,362 (2000); 4,459 (2005); 4,548 (2010 projected); Race: 88.9% White, 4.9% Black, 0.7% Asian, 14.5% Hispanic of any race (2005); Density: 52.2 persons per square mile (2005); Average household size: 2.62 (2005); Median age: 42.9 (2005); Males per 100 females: 106.8 (2005); Marriage status: 25.7% never married, 54.7% now married, 8.3% widowed, 11.3% divorced (2000); Foreign born: 8.6% (2000); Ancestry (includes multiple ancestries): 19.4% Irish, 18.6% German, 16.2% Other groups, 13.1% Italian, 7.2% United States or American (2000).
Economy: Single-family building permits issued: 84 (2005); Multi-family building permits issued: 0 (2005); Employment by occupation: 14.5% management, 13.9% professional, 18.7% services, 26.6% sales, 1.1% farming, 12.1% construction, 13.1% production (2000).
Income: Per capita income: $26,228 (2005); Median household income: $44,662 (2005); Average household income: $66,424 (2005); Percent of households with income of $100,000 or more: 17.0% (2005); Poverty rate: 14.9% (2000).
Education: Percent of population age 25 and over with: High school diploma (including GED) or higher: 77.6% (2005); Bachelor's degree or higher: 14.0% (2005); Master's degree or higher: 7.6% (2005).
Housing: Homeownership rate: 79.8% (2005); Median home value: $139,457 (2005); Median rent: $503 per month (2000); Median age of housing: 41 years (2000).
Transportation: Commute to work: 84.8% car, 5.9% public transportation, 1.9% walk, 6.0% work from home (2000); Travel time to work: 17.9% less than 15 minutes, 45.7% 15 to 30 minutes, 14.9% 30 to 45 minutes, 5.9% 45 to 60 minutes, 15.6% 60 minutes or more (2000)
Additional Information Contacts
Town of Bethel . . . . (845) 583-4350
  http://www.town.bethel.ny.us/

BLOOMINGBURG (village).
Aka Bloomingburgh. Covers a land area of 0.317 square miles and a water area of 0 square miles. Located at 41.55° N. Lat.; 74.44° W. Long. Elevation is 516 feet.
History: Also spelled Bloomingburgh.
Population: 332 (1990); 353 (2000); 333 (2005); 313 (2010 projected); Race: 91.9% White, 2.4% Black, 3.0% Asian, 11.4% Hispanic of any race (2005); Density: 1,050.6 persons per square mile (2005); Average household size: 2.40 (2005); Median age: 33.8 (2005); Males per 100 females: 88.1 (2005); Marriage status: 27.1% never married, 58.3% now married, 2.8% widowed, 11.7% divorced (2000); Foreign born: 1.0% (2000); Ancestry (includes multiple ancestries): 32.6% Irish, 27.7% German, 14.5% Italian, 8.7% Other groups, 7.7% English (2000).
Economy: In resort area. Single-family building permits issued: 0 (2005); Multi-family building permits issued: 0 (2005); Employment by occupation: 13.2% management, 11.3% professional, 15.9% services, 20.5% sales, 0.0% farming, 12.6% construction, 26.5% production (2000).
Income: Per capita income: $18,453 (2005); Median household income: $39,071 (2005); Average household income: $44,209 (2005); Percent of households with income of $100,000 or more: 2.9% (2005); Poverty rate: 11.1% (2000).
Education: Percent of population age 25 and over with: High school diploma (including GED) or higher: 74.6% (2005); Bachelor's degree or higher: 16.4% (2005); Master's degree or higher: 7.5% (2005).
Housing: Homeownership rate: 57.6% (2005); Median home value: $153,333 (2005); Median rent: $448 per month (2000); Median age of housing: 60+ years (2000).
Transportation: Commute to work: 93.2% car, 0.0% public transportation, 0.7% walk, 2.7% work from home (2000); Travel time to work: 13.2% less than 15 minutes, 52.1% 15 to 30 minutes, 12.5% 30 to 45 minutes, 11.8% 45 to 60 minutes, 10.4% 60 minutes or more (2000)

CALLICOON (town).
Covers a land area of 48.659 square miles and a water area of 0.341 square miles. Located at 41.83° N. Lat.; 74.92° W. Long. Elevation is 781 feet.
History: Seat of St. Joseph Seraphic Seminary.
Population: 3,024 (1990); 3,052 (2000); 3,121 (2005); 3,196 (2010 projected); Race: 94.6% White, 0.9% Black, 0.9% Asian, 6.4% Hispanic of any race (2005); Density: 64.1 persons per square mile (2005); Average household size: 2.48 (2005); Median age: 42.8 (2005); Males per 100 females: 93.9 (2005); Marriage status: 20.6% never married, 61.7% now married, 9.7% widowed, 8.1% divorced (2000); Foreign born: 5.9% (2000); Ancestry (includes multiple ancestries): 33.1% German, 21.5% Irish, 10.1% Italian, 9.5% Other groups, 7.4% English (2000).
Economy: Single-family building permits issued: 23 (2005); Multi-family building permits issued: 0 (2005); Employment by occupation: 10.7% management, 22.5% professional, 20.6% services, 19.2% sales, 0.7% farming, 16.6% construction, 9.8% production (2000).
Income: Per capita income: $23,929 (2005); Median household income: $46,141 (2005); Average household income: $58,919 (2005); Percent of households with income of $100,000 or more: 14.8% (2005); Poverty rate: 10.5% (2000).
Education: Percent of population age 25 and over with: High school diploma (including GED) or higher: 81.4% (2005); Bachelor's degree or higher: 17.1% (2005); Master's degree or higher: 8.3% (2005).
School District(s)
Sullivan West Central School District (KG-12)
  2003-04 Enrollment: 1,568 . . . . (845) 887-5300
Housing: Homeownership rate: 79.6% (2005); Median home value: $143,210 (2005); Median rent: $426 per month (2000); Median age of housing: 43 years (2000).
Newspapers: Sullivan County Democrat (General - Circulation 8,275)
Transportation: Commute to work: 89.4% car, 0.0% public transportation, 4.2% walk, 6.1% work from home (2000); Travel time to work: 30.4% less than 15 minutes, 33.5% 15 to 30 minutes, 19.8% 30 to 45 minutes, 4.8% 45 to 60 minutes, 11.5% 60 minutes or more (2000)

CALLICOON (CDP).
Covers a land area of 0.382 square miles and a water area of 0.081 square miles. Located at 41.76° N. Lat.; 75.05° W. Long.
Population: 222 (1990); 216 (2000); 254 (2005); 291 (2010 projected); Race: 92.5% White, 3.1% Black, 4.3% Asian, 7.9% Hispanic of any race (2005); Density: 664.5 persons per square mile (2005); Average household size: 2.27 (2005); Median age: 43.0 (2005); Males per 100 females: 100.0 (2005); Marriage status: 22.7% never married, 57.7% now married, 7.4% widowed, 12.3% divorced (2000); Foreign born: 12.7% (2000); Ancestry (includes multiple ancestries): 41.4% German, 19.5% Irish, 14.1% Italian, 11.4% Austrian, 6.4% Other groups (2000).
Economy: Employment by occupation: 0.0% management, 8.3% professional, 29.2% services, 20.8% sales, 0.0% farming, 33.3% construction, 8.3% production (2000).
Income: Per capita income: $19,242 (2005); Median household income: $39,167 (2005); Average household income: $43,638 (2005); Percent of households with income of $100,000 or more: 6.3% (2005); Poverty rate: 16.8% (2000).
Education: Percent of population age 25 and over with: High school diploma (including GED) or higher: 76.7% (2005); Bachelor's degree or higher: 12.8% (2005); Master's degree or higher: 5.0% (2005).
Housing: Homeownership rate: 68.8% (2005); Median home value: $115,698 (2005); Median rent: $439 per month (2000); Median age of housing: 60+ years (2000).
Transportation: Commute to work: 91.7% car, 0.0% public transportation, 0.0% walk, 8.3% work from home (2000); Travel time to work: 18.2% less than 15 minutes, 20.5% 15 to 30 minutes, 38.6% 30 to 45 minutes, 15.9% 45 to 60 minutes, 6.8% 60 minutes or more (2000)

CLARYVILLE (unincorporated postal area, zip code 12725).
Covers a land area of 63.248 square miles and a water area of 0.070 square miles. Located at 41.92° N. Lat.; 74.55° W. Long.

Population: 0 (2000); Race: 96.3% White, 0.0% Black, 2.1% Asian, 1.2% Hispanic of any race (2000); Density: 0.0 persons per square mile (2000); Age: 24.5% under 18, 11.6% over 64 (2000); Marriage status: 24.0% never married, 60.0% now married, 3.0% widowed, 13.0% divorced (2000); Foreign born: 2.1% (2000); Ancestry (includes multiple ancestries): 20.7% German, 19.5% English, 19.5% Italian, 19.5% Irish, 12.4% United States or American (2000).
Economy: Employment by occupation: 11.1% management, 28.6% professional, 27.8% services, 19.0% sales, 0.0% farming, 7.9% construction, 5.6% production (2000).
Income: Per capita income: $25,519 (2000); Median household income: $34,844 (2000); Poverty rate: 3.7% (2000).
Education: Percent of population age 25 and over with: High school diploma (including GED) or higher: 87.9% (2000); Bachelor's degree or higher: 22.5% (2000).
Housing: Homeownership rate: 64.8% (2000); Median home value: $86,300 (2000); Median rent: $568 per month (2000); Median age of housing: 40 years (2000).
Transportation: Commute to work: 96.8% car, 0.0% public transportation, 3.2% walk, 0.0% work from home (2000); Travel time to work: 25.8% less than 15 minutes, 35.5% 15 to 30 minutes, 11.3% 30 to 45 minutes, 10.5% 45 to 60 minutes, 16.9% 60 minutes or more (2000)

COCHECTON (town). Covers a land area of 36.653 square miles and a water area of 0.731 square miles. Located at 41.67° N. Lat.; 74.99° W. Long.
Population: 1,318 (1990); 1,328 (2000); 1,377 (2005); 1,428 (2010 projected); Race: 96.2% White, 1.0% Black, 0.7% Asian, 2.4% Hispanic of any race (2005); Density: 37.6 persons per square mile (2005); Average household size: 2.35 (2005); Median age: 44.0 (2005); Males per 100 females: 99.3 (2005); Marriage status: 19.8% never married, 64.0% now married, 7.9% widowed, 8.3% divorced (2000); Foreign born: 4.7% (2000); Ancestry (includes multiple ancestries): 38.6% German, 23.9% Irish, 12.1% Italian, 9.3% United States or American, 7.7% English (2000).
Economy: Single-family building permits issued: 11 (2005); Multi-family building permits issued: 0 (2005); Employment by occupation: 13.6% management, 25.7% professional, 16.6% services, 19.4% sales, 1.3% farming, 12.3% construction, 11.1% production (2000).
Income: Per capita income: $24,669 (2005); Median household income: $47,636 (2005); Average household income: $57,209 (2005); Percent of households with income of $100,000 or more: 13.2% (2005); Poverty rate: 7.2% (2000).
Education: Percent of population age 25 and over with: High school diploma (including GED) or higher: 83.7% (2005); Bachelor's degree or higher: 17.3% (2005); Master's degree or higher: 9.9% (2005).
Housing: Homeownership rate: 82.9% (2005); Median home value: $146,082 (2005); Median rent: $445 per month (2000); Median age of housing: 46 years (2000).
Transportation: Commute to work: 91.0% car, 0.7% public transportation, 2.4% walk, 5.9% work from home (2000); Travel time to work: 22.1% less than 15 minutes, 34.8% 15 to 30 minutes, 25.7% 30 to 45 minutes, 5.9% 45 to 60 minutes, 11.5% 60 minutes or more (2000)

COCHECTON CENTER (unincorporated postal area, zip code 12727). Covers a land area of 0.325 square miles and a water area of 0 square miles. Located at 41.65° N. Lat.; 74.98° W. Long. Elevation is 960 feet.
Population: 0 (2000); Race: 100.0% White, 0.0% Black, 0.0% Asian, 0.0% Hispanic of any race (2000); Density: 0.0 persons per square mile (2000); Age: 0.0% under 18, 16.7% over 64 (2000); Marriage status: 16.7% never married, 66.7% now married, 16.7% widowed, 0.0% divorced (2000); Foreign born: 0.0% (2000); Ancestry (includes multiple ancestries): 66.7% German, 50.0% Norwegian, 16.7% United States or American (2000).
Economy: Employment by occupation: 33.3% management, 0.0% professional, 33.3% services, 0.0% sales, 0.0% farming, 0.0% construction, 33.3% production (2000).
Income: Per capita income: $23,150 (2000); Median household income: $48,750 (2000); Poverty rate: 0.0% (2000).
Education: Percent of population age 25 and over with: High school diploma (including GED) or higher: 100.0% (2000); Bachelor's degree or higher: 0.0% (2000).
Housing: Homeownership rate: 100.0% (2000); Median home value: $112,500 (2000); Median rent: $n/a per month (2000); Median age of housing: 27 years (2000).
Transportation: Commute to work: 100.0% car, 0.0% public transportation, 0.0% walk, 0.0% work from home (2000); Travel time to work: 66.7% less than 15 minutes, 33.3% 15 to 30 minutes, 0.0% 30 to 45 minutes, 0.0% 45 to 60 minutes, 0.0% 60 minutes or more (2000)

DELAWARE (town). Covers a land area of 34.731 square miles and a water area of 0.590 square miles. Located at 41.76° N. Lat.; 75.00° W. Long.
Population: 2,633 (1990); 2,719 (2000); 2,864 (2005); 2,995 (2010 projected); Race: 86.8% White, 10.2% Black, 0.9% Asian, 8.1% Hispanic of any race (2005); Density: 82.5 persons per square mile (2005); Average household size: 2.81 (2005); Median age: 36.6 (2005); Males per 100 females: 101.0 (2005); Marriage status: 27.9% never married, 61.4% now married, 4.6% widowed, 6.1% divorced (2000); Foreign born: 8.6% (2000); Ancestry (includes multiple ancestries): 35.5% German, 19.2% Irish, 14.5% Other groups, 8.4% Italian, 4.6% English (2000).
Economy: Single-family building permits issued: 18 (2005); Multi-family building permits issued: 8 (2005); Employment by occupation: 12.5% management, 20.0% professional, 22.7% services, 20.4% sales, 1.0% farming, 14.4% construction, 8.9% production (2000).
Income: Per capita income: $22,401 (2005); Median household income: $48,633 (2005); Average household income: $62,096 (2005); Percent of households with income of $100,000 or more: 16.1% (2005); Poverty rate: 20.0% (2000).
Education: Percent of population age 25 and over with: High school diploma (including GED) or higher: 85.0% (2005); Bachelor's degree or higher: 17.9% (2005); Master's degree or higher: 6.8% (2005).
Housing: Homeownership rate: 75.9% (2005); Median home value: $139,646 (2005); Median rent: $434 per month (2000); Median age of housing: 45 years (2000).
Transportation: Commute to work: 85.7% car, 1.0% public transportation, 5.7% walk, 7.5% work from home (2000); Travel time to work: 32.7% less than 15 minutes, 30.2% 15 to 30 minutes, 18.0% 30 to 45 minutes, 10.2% 45 to 60 minutes, 9.0% 60 minutes or more (2000)

ELDRED (unincorporated postal area, zip code 12732). Covers a land area of 24.554 square miles and a water area of 0.534 square miles. Located at 41.54° N. Lat.; 74.87° W. Long. Elevation is 1,000 feet.
Population: 0 (2000); Race: 96.9% White, 3.1% Black, 0.0% Asian, 1.5% Hispanic of any race (2000); Density: 0.0 persons per square mile (2000); Age: 22.3% under 18, 20.4% over 64 (2000); Marriage status: 19.2% never married, 62.4% now married, 12.0% widowed, 6.4% divorced (2000); Foreign born: 12.5% (2000); Ancestry (includes multiple ancestries): 31.2% German, 19.3% Irish, 10.1% Italian, 8.9% English, 5.6% United States or American (2000).
Economy: Employment by occupation: 8.6% management, 22.6% professional, 14.8% services, 32.7% sales, 0.0% farming, 11.7% construction, 9.6% production (2000).
Income: Per capita income: $20,409 (2000); Median household income: $38,125 (2000); Poverty rate: 11.7% (2000).
Education: Percent of population age 25 and over with: High school diploma (including GED) or higher: 76.3% (2000); Bachelor's degree or higher: 12.5% (2000).

School District(s)
Eldred Central School District (KG-12)
    2003-04 Enrollment: 733 . . . . (845) 557-6141

Housing: Homeownership rate: 78.9% (2000); Median home value: $103,400 (2000); Median rent: $410 per month (2000); Median age of housing: 31 years (2000).
Transportation: Commute to work: 85.5% car, 4.2% public transportation, 7.1% walk, 3.2% work from home (2000); Travel time to work: 31.0% less than 15 minutes, 25.0% 15 to 30 minutes, 21.5% 30 to 45 minutes, 9.0% 45 to 60 minutes, 13.6% 60 minutes or more (2000)

FALLSBURG (town). Aka Fallsburgh. Covers a land area of 77.620 square miles and a water area of 1.373 square miles. Located at 41.73° N. Lat.; 74.60° W. Long. Elevation is 1,162 feet.
Population: 11,445 (1990); 12,234 (2000); 12,605 (2005); 13,025 (2010 projected); Race: 73.2% White, 16.1% Black, 1.5% Asian, 16.4% Hispanic of any race (2005); Density: 162.4 persons per square mile (2005); Average household size: 3.20 (2005); Median age: 36.9 (2005); Males per 100 females: 131.6 (2005); Marriage status: 36.3% never married, 48.1% now married, 5.9% widowed, 9.7% divorced (2000); Foreign born: 9.8% (2000); Ancestry (includes multiple ancestries): 21.4% Other groups,

11.6% Irish, 10.3% German, 9.8% Italian, 6.1% United States or American (2000).
Economy: Resort village. Single-family building permits issued: 202 (2005); Multi-family building permits issued: 4 (2005); Employment by occupation: 12.6% management, 19.6% professional, 20.7% services, 23.7% sales, 0.5% farming, 9.5% construction, 13.5% production (2000).
Income: Per capita income: $20,018 (2005); Median household income: $40,659 (2005); Average household income: $55,078 (2005); Percent of households with income of $100,000 or more: 13.5% (2005); Poverty rate: 20.5% (2000).
Taxes: Total city taxes per capita: $478 (2004); City property taxes per capita: $450 (2004).
Education: Percent of population age 25 and over with: High school diploma (including GED) or higher: 66.5% (2005); Bachelor's degree or higher: 14.9% (2005); Master's degree or higher: 6.9% (2005).

School District(s)
Fallsburg Central School District (KG-12)
    2003-04 Enrollment: 1,450 . . . . (845) 434-5884
Housing: Homeownership rate: 59.5% (2005); Median home value: $114,849 (2005); Median rent: $468 per month (2000); Median age of housing: 30 years (2000).
Safety: Violent crime rate: 49.8 per 10,000 population; Property crime rate: 64.7 per 10,000 population (2004).
Transportation: Commute to work: 82.9% car, 2.3% public transportation, 9.1% walk, 5.0% work from home (2000); Travel time to work: 38.4% less than 15 minutes, 37.9% 15 to 30 minutes, 8.9% 30 to 45 minutes, 3.9% 45 to 60 minutes, 11.0% 60 minutes or more (2000)

FERNDALE (unincorporated postal area, zip code 12734). Covers a land area of 12.804 square miles and a water area of 0.020 square miles. Located at 41.73° N. Lat.; 74.75° W. Long. Elevation is 1,444 feet.
Population: 0 (2000); Race: 89.1% White, 6.0% Black, 2.4% Asian, 16.4% Hispanic of any race (2000); Density: 0.0 persons per square mile (2000); Age: 16.6% under 18, 18.8% over 64 (2000); Marriage status: 31.6% never married, 60.7% now married, 3.8% widowed, 3.8% divorced (2000); Foreign born: 13.8% (2000); Ancestry (includes multiple ancestries): 34.5% German, 23.5% Other groups, 21.2% Irish, 14.5% English, 13.3% Italian (2000).
Economy: Resort village. Employment by occupation: 1.7% management, 14.5% professional, 22.4% services, 14.8% sales, 16.9% farming, 10.0% construction, 19.7% production (2000).
Income: Per capita income: $17,212 (2000); Median household income: $24,417 (2000); Poverty rate: 16.6% (2000).
Education: Percent of population age 25 and over with: High school diploma (including GED) or higher: 72.4% (2000); Bachelor's degree or higher: 8.0% (2000).
Housing: Homeownership rate: 66.9% (2000); Median home value: $111,300 (2000); Median rent: $506 per month (2000); Median age of housing: 39 years (2000).
Transportation: Commute to work: 87.4% car, 0.0% public transportation, 12.6% walk, 0.0% work from home (2000); Travel time to work: 61.1% less than 15 minutes, 17.9% 15 to 30 minutes, 12.3% 30 to 45 minutes, 1.8% 45 to 60 minutes, 7.0% 60 minutes or more (2000)

FORESTBURGH (town). Covers a land area of 55.204 square miles and a water area of 1.607 square miles. Located at 41.56° N. Lat.; 74.71° W. Long.
Population: 624 (1990); 833 (2000); 924 (2005); 1,013 (2010 projected); Race: 94.2% White, 2.7% Black, 0.0% Asian, 6.3% Hispanic of any race (2005); Density: 16.7 persons per square mile (2005); Average household size: 2.52 (2005); Median age: 44.2 (2005); Males per 100 females: 89.3 (2005); Marriage status: 20.0% never married, 70.0% now married, 3.0% widowed, 7.0% divorced (2000); Foreign born: 5.8% (2000); Ancestry (includes multiple ancestries): 26.2% Irish, 23.8% German, 16.0% Italian, 10.6% Other groups, 10.1% English (2000).
Economy: Single-family building permits issued: 17 (2005); Multi-family building permits issued: 0 (2005); Employment by occupation: 20.1% management, 24.7% professional, 13.3% services, 20.1% sales, 0.0% farming, 13.8% construction, 8.0% production (2000).
Income: Per capita income: $33,636 (2005); Median household income: $65,625 (2005); Average household income: $84,339 (2005); Percent of households with income of $100,000 or more: 23.2% (2005); Poverty rate: 7.0% (2000).
Education: Percent of population age 25 and over with: High school diploma (including GED) or higher: 87.4% (2005); Bachelor's degree or higher: 30.1% (2005); Master's degree or higher: 15.3% (2005).
Housing: Homeownership rate: 82.8% (2005); Median home value: $197,590 (2005); Median rent: $529 per month (2000); Median age of housing: 30 years (2000).
Transportation: Commute to work: 89.5% car, 1.5% public transportation, 3.4% walk, 5.6% work from home (2000); Travel time to work: 27.8% less than 15 minutes, 34.8% 15 to 30 minutes, 16.1% 30 to 45 minutes, 8.8% 45 to 60 minutes, 12.5% 60 minutes or more (2000)

FREMONT (town). Covers a land area of 50.334 square miles and a water area of 0.893 square miles. Located at 41.86° N. Lat.; 75.04° W. Long.
Population: 1,332 (1990); 1,391 (2000); 1,385 (2005); 1,386 (2010 projected); Race: 94.3% White, 1.4% Black, 1.4% Asian, 1.4% Hispanic of any race (2005); Density: 27.5 persons per square mile (2005); Average household size: 2.43 (2005); Median age: 42.2 (2005); Males per 100 females: 99.3 (2005); Marriage status: 21.4% never married, 63.9% now married, 8.7% widowed, 5.9% divorced (2000); Foreign born: 3.3% (2000); Ancestry (includes multiple ancestries): 30.6% German, 22.6% Irish, 10.9% Italian, 9.6% Other groups, 8.3% English (2000).
Economy: Single-family building permits issued: 10 (2005); Multi-family building permits issued: 0 (2005); Employment by occupation: 10.6% management, 24.5% professional, 14.8% services, 22.5% sales, 1.5% farming, 15.1% construction, 11.1% production (2000).
Income: Per capita income: $22,244 (2005); Median household income: $40,536 (2005); Average household income: $54,048 (2005); Percent of households with income of $100,000 or more: 9.6% (2005); Poverty rate: 15.7% (2000).
Education: Percent of population age 25 and over with: High school diploma (including GED) or higher: 81.6% (2005); Bachelor's degree or higher: 15.0% (2005); Master's degree or higher: 5.6% (2005).
Housing: Homeownership rate: 78.6% (2005); Median home value: $135,526 (2005); Median rent: $369 per month (2000); Median age of housing: 44 years (2000).
Transportation: Commute to work: 87.2% car, 1.7% public transportation, 3.4% walk, 7.1% work from home (2000); Travel time to work: 24.2% less than 15 minutes, 25.6% 15 to 30 minutes, 19.6% 30 to 45 minutes, 17.4% 45 to 60 minutes, 13.2% 60 minutes or more (2000)

FREMONT CENTER (unincorporated postal area, zip code 12736). Aka Fremont. Covers a land area of 3.388 square miles and a water area of 0.015 square miles. Located at 41.84° N. Lat.; 75.03° W. Long. Elevation is 1,248 feet.
Population: 0 (2000); Race: 95.3% White, 0.0% Black, 2.0% Asian, 2.0% Hispanic of any race (2000); Density: 0.0 persons per square mile (2000); Age: 27.3% under 18, 12.0% over 64 (2000); Marriage status: 30.6% never married, 45.0% now married, 9.0% widowed, 15.3% divorced (2000); Foreign born: 3.3% (2000); Ancestry (includes multiple ancestries): 35.3% German, 23.3% Irish, 13.3% Italian, 9.3% Other groups, 7.3% English (2000).
Economy: Employment by occupation: 12.2% management, 18.9% professional, 16.2% services, 17.6% sales, 8.1% farming, 12.2% construction, 14.9% production (2000).
Income: Per capita income: $18,336 (2000); Median household income: $32,250 (2000); Poverty rate: 20.7% (2000).
Education: Percent of population age 25 and over with: High school diploma (including GED) or higher: 77.1% (2000); Bachelor's degree or higher: 10.4% (2000).
Housing: Homeownership rate: 61.8% (2000); Median home value: $117,500 (2000); Median rent: $375 per month (2000); Median age of housing: 60+ years (2000).
Transportation: Commute to work: 81.1% car, 0.0% public transportation, 2.7% walk, 16.2% work from home (2000); Travel time to work: 21.0% less than 15 minutes, 29.0% 15 to 30 minutes, 24.2% 30 to 45 minutes, 22.6% 45 to 60 minutes, 3.2% 60 minutes or more (2000)

GLEN SPEY (unincorporated postal area, zip code 12737). Covers a land area of 32.797 square miles and a water area of 1.232 square miles. Located at 41.48° N. Lat.; 74.81° W. Long.
Population: 0 (2000); Race: 94.7% White, 0.9% Black, 0.3% Asian, 4.2% Hispanic of any race (2000); Density: 0.0 persons per square mile (2000); Age: 26.6% under 18, 19.2% over 64 (2000); Marriage status: 18.6% never married, 64.4% now married, 10.2% widowed, 6.9% divorced (2000);

Foreign born: 16.8% (2000); Ancestry (includes multiple ancestries): 25.0% German, 19.6% Irish, 12.7% Ukrainian, 10.4% Italian, 8.3% English (2000).
Economy: Employment by occupation: 14.1% management, 16.9% professional, 20.0% services, 22.9% sales, 0.3% farming, 13.8% construction, 12.0% production (2000).
Income: Per capita income: $18,700 (2000); Median household income: $42,063 (2000); Poverty rate: 12.0% (2000).
Education: Percent of population age 25 and over with: High school diploma (including GED) or higher: 82.5% (2000); Bachelor's degree or higher: 19.1% (2000).

School District(s)
Eldred Central School District (KG-12)
    2003-04 Enrollment: 733 . . . . (845) 557-6141
Housing: Homeownership rate: 84.6% (2000); Median home value: $110,200 (2000); Median rent: $420 per month (2000); Median age of housing: 31 years (2000).
Transportation: Commute to work: 91.8% car, 2.2% public transportation, 2.6% walk, 3.4% work from home (2000); Travel time to work: 15.5% less than 15 minutes, 26.6% 15 to 30 minutes, 21.0% 30 to 45 minutes, 19.8% 45 to 60 minutes, 17.1% 60 minutes or more (2000)

GLEN WILD
(unincorporated postal area, zip code 12738). Covers a land area of 5.754 square miles and a water area of 0.014 square miles. Located at 41.64° N. Lat.; 74.57° W. Long. Elevation is 1,313 feet.
Population: 0 (2000); Race: 90.7% White, 2.2% Black, 0.0% Asian, 6.2% Hispanic of any race (2000); Density: 0.0 persons per square mile (2000); Age: 28.7% under 18, 3.7% over 64 (2000); Marriage status: 8.3% never married, 72.5% now married, 4.4% widowed, 14.8% divorced (2000); Foreign born: 4.7% (2000); Ancestry (includes multiple ancestries): 35.5% Other groups, 11.2% Irish, 10.3% English, 4.4% Armenian, 4.0% Italian (2000).
Economy: Employment by occupation: 12.4% management, 21.5% professional, 14.0% services, 12.9% sales, 0.0% farming, 25.8% construction, 13.4% production (2000).
Income: Per capita income: $20,818 (2000); Median household income: $39,583 (2000); Poverty rate: 18.7% (2000).
Education: Percent of population age 25 and over with: High school diploma (including GED) or higher: 90.5% (2000); Bachelor's degree or higher: 13.2% (2000).
Housing: Homeownership rate: 64.3% (2000); Median home value: $135,300 (2000); Median rent: $498 per month (2000); Median age of housing: 33 years (2000).
Transportation: Commute to work: 93.3% car, 0.0% public transportation, 0.0% walk, 6.7% work from home (2000); Travel time to work: 30.6% less than 15 minutes, 19.4% 15 to 30 minutes, 15.6% 30 to 45 minutes, 16.1% 45 to 60 minutes, 18.3% 60 minutes or more (2000)

GRAHAMSVILLE
(unincorporated postal area, zip code 12740). Covers a land area of 67.238 square miles and a water area of 1.029 square miles. Located at 41.85° N. Lat.; 74.52° W. Long. Elevation is 952 feet.
Population: 0 (2000); Race: 95.9% White, 0.0% Black, 3.4% Asian, 0.0% Hispanic of any race (2000); Density: 0.0 persons per square mile (2000); Age: 26.7% under 18, 14.0% over 64 (2000); Marriage status: 16.7% never married, 70.6% now married, 5.8% widowed, 7.0% divorced (2000); Foreign born: 7.1% (2000); Ancestry (includes multiple ancestries): 16.5% German, 13.8% Irish, 12.9% Italian, 9.3% English, 6.6% Dutch (2000).
Economy: Employment by occupation: 13.5% management, 19.1% professional, 23.1% services, 16.3% sales, 2.0% farming, 14.6% construction, 11.5% production (2000).
Income: Per capita income: $20,964 (2000); Median household income: $45,278 (2000); Poverty rate: 12.2% (2000).
Education: Percent of population age 25 and over with: High school diploma (including GED) or higher: 84.6% (2000); Bachelor's degree or higher: 23.1% (2000).

School District(s)
Tri-Valley Central School District (PK-12)
    2003-04 Enrollment: 1,289 . . . . (845) 985-2296
Housing: Homeownership rate: 82.2% (2000); Median home value: $120,900 (2000); Median rent: $510 per month (2000); Median age of housing: 40 years (2000).
Transportation: Commute to work: 95.2% car, 0.0% public transportation, 0.9% walk, 1.7% work from home (2000); Travel time to work: 33.8% less than 15 minutes, 36.6% 15 to 30 minutes, 11.8% 30 to 45 minutes, 4.1% 45 to 60 minutes, 13.7% 60 minutes or more (2000)

HANKINS
(unincorporated postal area, zip code 12741). Covers a land area of 4.279 square miles and a water area of 0 square miles. Located at 41.83° N. Lat.; 75.08° W. Long. Elevation is 807 feet.
Population: 0 (2000); Race: 90.1% White, 2.4% Black, 2.7% Asian, 1.4% Hispanic of any race (2000); Density: 0.0 persons per square mile (2000); Age: 26.4% under 18, 16.4% over 64 (2000); Marriage status: 23.8% never married, 60.0% now married, 10.2% widowed, 6.0% divorced (2000); Foreign born: 1.4% (2000); Ancestry (includes multiple ancestries): 20.5% German, 19.2% Irish, 16.4% European, 11.3% Polish, 10.6% Other groups (2000).
Economy: Resort village. Employment by occupation: 13.4% management, 24.4% professional, 16.5% services, 19.7% sales, 0.0% farming, 14.2% construction, 11.8% production (2000).
Income: Per capita income: $18,613 (2000); Median household income: $44,500 (2000); Poverty rate: 7.5% (2000).
Education: Percent of population age 25 and over with: High school diploma (including GED) or higher: 87.6% (2000); Bachelor's degree or higher: 22.3% (2000).
Housing: Homeownership rate: 70.6% (2000); Median home value: $77,500 (2000); Median rent: $327 per month (2000); Median age of housing: 49 years (2000).
Transportation: Commute to work: 79.5% car, 8.2% public transportation, 4.9% walk, 7.4% work from home (2000); Travel time to work: 30.1% less than 15 minutes, 15.0% 15 to 30 minutes, 22.1% 30 to 45 minutes, 20.4% 45 to 60 minutes, 12.4% 60 minutes or more (2000)

HARRIS
(unincorporated postal area, zip code 12742). Covers a land area of 1.589 square miles and a water area of 0.003 square miles. Located at 41.72° N. Lat.; 74.72° W. Long.
Population: 0 (2000); Race: 83.8% White, 16.2% Black, 0.0% Asian, 0.0% Hispanic of any race (2000); Density: 0.0 persons per square mile (2000); Age: 32.3% under 18, 16.2% over 64 (2000); Marriage status: 22.8% never married, 58.4% now married, 18.8% widowed, 0.0% divorced (2000); Foreign born: 13.1% (2000); Ancestry (includes multiple ancestries): 43.8% United States or American, 20.8% Greek, 17.7% Italian, 7.7% Russian, 6.2% Other groups (2000).
Economy: Employment by occupation: 32.3% management, 0.0% professional, 38.7% services, 0.0% sales, 0.0% farming, 29.0% construction, 0.0% production (2000).
Income: Per capita income: $16,025 (2000); Median household income: $32,083 (2000); Poverty rate: 30.8% (2000).
Education: Percent of population age 25 and over with: High school diploma (including GED) or higher: 59.1% (2000); Bachelor's degree or higher: 33.0% (2000).
Housing: Homeownership rate: 59.7% (2000); Median home value: $84,400 (2000); Median rent: $422 per month (2000); Median age of housing: 40 years (2000).
Hospitals: Catskill Regional Medical Center (263 beds)
Transportation: Commute to work: 100.0% car, 0.0% public transportation, 0.0% walk, 0.0% work from home (2000); Travel time to work: 38.7% less than 15 minutes, 0.0% 15 to 30 minutes, 32.3% 30 to 45 minutes, 0.0% 45 to 60 minutes, 29.0% 60 minutes or more (2000)

HIGHLAND
(town). Covers a land area of 50.009 square miles and a water area of 1.677 square miles. Located at 41.52° N. Lat.; 74.90° W. Long.
Population: 2,147 (1990); 2,404 (2000); 2,484 (2005); 2,571 (2010 projected); Race: 93.1% White, 3.9% Black, 0.6% Asian, 4.6% Hispanic of any race (2005); Density: 49.7 persons per square mile (2005); Average household size: 2.49 (2005); Median age: 43.7 (2005); Males per 100 females: 99.2 (2005); Marriage status: 23.6% never married, 60.4% now married, 10.1% widowed, 6.0% divorced (2000); Foreign born: 8.6% (2000); Ancestry (includes multiple ancestries): 27.9% German, 21.6% Irish, 11.2% Italian, 8.6% English, 6.9% Other groups (2000).
Economy: Single-family building permits issued: 33 (2005); Multi-family building permits issued: 0 (2005); Employment by occupation: 10.9% management, 19.5% professional, 18.6% services, 26.8% sales, 0.8% farming, 12.2% construction, 11.2% production (2000).
Income: Per capita income: $27,298 (2005); Median household income: $49,452 (2005); Average household income: $67,518 (2005); Percent of households with income of $100,000 or more: 15.2% (2005); Poverty rate: 15.6% (2000).

Education: Percent of population age 25 and over with: High school diploma (including GED) or higher: 78.0% (2005); Bachelor's degree or higher: 17.0% (2005); Master's degree or higher: 6.2% (2005).
Housing: Homeownership rate: 82.8% (2005); Median home value: $154,505 (2005); Median rent: $424 per month (2000); Median age of housing: 34 years (2000).
Transportation: Commute to work: 85.5% car, 4.7% public transportation, 6.2% walk, 2.1% work from home (2000); Travel time to work: 29.9% less than 15 minutes, 20.1% 15 to 30 minutes, 25.7% 30 to 45 minutes, 8.2% 45 to 60 minutes, 16.1% 60 minutes or more (2000)

HIGHLAND LAKE (unincorporated postal area, zip code 12743).
Covers a land area of 15.972 square miles and a water area of 1.205 square miles. Located at 41.53° N. Lat.; 74.84° W. Long.
Population: 0 (2000); Race: 94.4% White, 4.3% Black, 0.0% Asian, 1.2% Hispanic of any race (2000); Density: 0.0 persons per square mile (2000); Age: 27.2% under 18, 14.2% over 64 (2000); Marriage status: 20.1% never married, 59.4% now married, 10.0% widowed, 10.5% divorced (2000); Foreign born: 7.7% (2000); Ancestry (includes multiple ancestries): 30.7% Irish, 26.0% German, 12.1% United States or American, 11.8% Italian, 6.5% Dutch (2000).
Economy: Resort village. Employment by occupation: 18.0% management, 3.3% professional, 20.5% services, 29.5% sales, 0.0% farming, 12.3% construction, 16.4% production (2000).
Income: Per capita income: $21,769 (2000); Median household income: $37,875 (2000); Poverty rate: 20.1% (2000).
Education: Percent of population age 25 and over with: High school diploma (including GED) or higher: 79.8% (2000); Bachelor's degree or higher: 26.0% (2000).
Housing: Homeownership rate: 74.4% (2000); Median home value: $150,700 (2000); Median rent: $475 per month (2000); Median age of housing: 32 years (2000).
Transportation: Commute to work: 88.0% car, 0.0% public transportation, 8.5% walk, 3.4% work from home (2000); Travel time to work: 13.3% less than 15 minutes, 31.9% 15 to 30 minutes, 22.1% 30 to 45 minutes, 12.4% 45 to 60 minutes, 20.4% 60 minutes or more (2000)

HURLEYVILLE (unincorporated postal area, zip code 12747).
Covers a land area of 14.545 square miles and a water area of 0.219 square miles. Located at 41.75° N. Lat.; 74.67° W. Long. Elevation is 1,318 feet.
Population: 0 (2000); Race: 84.7% White, 7.5% Black, 0.4% Asian, 12.3% Hispanic of any race (2000); Density: 0.0 persons per square mile (2000); Age: 19.5% under 18, 15.7% over 64 (2000); Marriage status: 37.8% never married, 43.4% now married, 7.1% widowed, 11.7% divorced (2000); Foreign born: 11.8% (2000); Ancestry (includes multiple ancestries): 24.6% Other groups, 18.3% Irish, 14.3% German, 9.8% English, 8.1% Italian (2000).
Economy: Resort village. Employment by occupation: 19.5% management, 17.0% professional, 26.0% services, 17.7% sales, 0.0% farming, 9.2% construction, 10.6% production (2000).
Income: Per capita income: $15,210 (2000); Median household income: $33,915 (2000); Poverty rate: 19.3% (2000).
Education: Percent of population age 25 and over with: High school diploma (including GED) or higher: 79.2% (2000); Bachelor's degree or higher: 31.4% (2000).
Housing: Homeownership rate: 62.2% (2000); Median home value: $85,500 (2000); Median rent: $478 per month (2000); Median age of housing: 34 years (2000).
Transportation: Commute to work: 70.1% car, 0.7% public transportation, 19.8% walk, 9.4% work from home (2000); Travel time to work: 59.2% less than 15 minutes, 25.8% 15 to 30 minutes, 5.6% 30 to 45 minutes, 0.7% 45 to 60 minutes, 8.6% 60 minutes or more (2000)

JEFFERSONVILLE (village).
Covers a land area of 0.408 square miles and a water area of 0.029 square miles. Located at 41.78° N. Lat.; 74.93° W. Long. Elevation is 1,058 feet.
Population: 484 (1990); 420 (2000); 416 (2005); 416 (2010 projected); Race: 94.5% White, 2.2% Black, 0.0% Asian, 2.6% Hispanic of any race (2005); Density: 1,018.4 persons per square mile (2005); Average household size: 2.62 (2005); Median age: 51.9 (2005); Males per 100 females: 79.3 (2005); Marriage status: 20.3% never married, 58.8% now married, 18.4% widowed, 2.5% divorced (2000); Foreign born: 5.2% (2000); Ancestry (includes multiple ancestries): 26.4% German, 19.2% Irish, 10.5% Polish, 9.7% Italian, 7.8% United States or American (2000).
Economy: Manufacturing: lumber, wood products, and machinery. In resort area. Single-family building permits issued: 0 (2005); Multi-family building permits issued: 0 (2005); Employment by occupation: 11.0% management, 22.8% professional, 24.1% services, 20.0% sales, 0.0% farming, 13.1% construction, 9.0% production (2000).
Income: Per capita income: $20,928 (2005); Median household income: $38,663 (2005); Average household income: $50,487 (2005); Percent of households with income of $100,000 or more: 13.2% (2005); Poverty rate: 6.7% (2000).
Education: Percent of population age 25 and over with: High school diploma (including GED) or higher: 77.2% (2005); Bachelor's degree or higher: 15.4% (2005); Master's degree or higher: 7.7% (2005).
School District(s)
Sullivan West Central School District (KG-12)
  2003-04 Enrollment: 1,568 . . . . (845) 887-5300
Housing: Homeownership rate: 65.4% (2005); Median home value: $128,409 (2005); Median rent: $405 per month (2000); Median age of housing: 60+ years (2000).
Transportation: Commute to work: 78.0% car, 0.0% public transportation, 14.9% walk, 4.3% work from home (2000); Travel time to work: 37.8% less than 15 minutes, 25.9% 15 to 30 minutes, 25.9% 30 to 45 minutes, 5.9% 45 to 60 minutes, 4.4% 60 minutes or more (2000)
Additional Information Contacts
Jeffersonville Chamber of Commerce . . . . (845) 482-5688
  http://www.jeffersonvillechamber.org/

KIAMESHA LAKE (unincorporated postal area, zip code 12751).
Covers a land area of 1.836 square miles and a water area of 0.241 square miles. Located at 41.67° N. Lat.; 74.65° W. Long. Elevation is 1,417 feet.
Population: 0 (2000); Race: 81.1% White, 3.4% Black, 0.0% Asian, 15.8% Hispanic of any race (2000); Density: 0.0 persons per square mile (2000); Age: 24.5% under 18, 18.2% over 64 (2000); Marriage status: 24.9% never married, 52.8% now married, 10.8% widowed, 11.5% divorced (2000); Foreign born: 14.5% (2000); Ancestry (includes multiple ancestries): 30.0% Other groups, 11.9% United States or American, 7.9% Russian, 4.7% Scotch-Irish, 2.9% Ukrainian (2000).
Economy: Employment by occupation: 6.4% management, 29.2% professional, 29.8% services, 21.6% sales, 4.1% farming, 0.0% construction, 8.8% production (2000).
Income: Per capita income: $18,792 (2000); Median household income: $25,804 (2000); Poverty rate: 17.6% (2000).
Education: Percent of population age 25 and over with: High school diploma (including GED) or higher: 77.1% (2000); Bachelor's degree or higher: 31.6% (2000).
Housing: Homeownership rate: 57.5% (2000); Median home value: $55,000 (2000); Median rent: $583 per month (2000); Median age of housing: 24 years (2000).
Transportation: Commute to work: 78.8% car, 0.0% public transportation, 10.3% walk, 0.0% work from home (2000); Travel time to work: 42.4% less than 15 minutes, 42.4% 15 to 30 minutes, 0.0% 30 to 45 minutes, 0.0% 45 to 60 minutes, 15.2% 60 minutes or more (2000)

LAKE HUNTINGTON (unincorporated postal area, zip code 12752).
Covers a land area of 1.234 square miles and a water area of 0.124 square miles. Located at 41.67° N. Lat.; 74.99° W. Long.
Population: 0 (2000); Race: 98.5% White, 0.0% Black, 1.5% Asian, 0.0% Hispanic of any race (2000); Density: 0.0 persons per square mile (2000); Age: 24.1% under 18, 23.4% over 64 (2000); Marriage status: 9.1% never married, 78.2% now married, 7.3% widowed, 5.5% divorced (2000); Foreign born: 2.9% (2000); Ancestry (includes multiple ancestries): 30.7% Irish, 24.8% German, 12.4% Other groups, 10.2% English, 9.5% Russian (2000).
Economy: Resort village. Employment by occupation: 13.5% management, 36.5% professional, 5.8% services, 19.2% sales, 0.0% farming, 19.2% construction, 5.8% production (2000).
Income: Per capita income: $25,615 (2000); Median household income: $53,125 (2000); Poverty rate: 13.1% (2000).
Education: Percent of population age 25 and over with: High school diploma (including GED) or higher: 77.0% (2000); Bachelor's degree or higher: 35.0% (2000).
School District(s)
Sullivan West Central School District (KG-12)
  2003-04 Enrollment: 1,568 . . . . (845) 887-5300

Housing: Homeownership rate: 82.5% (2000); Median home value: $89,400 (2000); Median rent: $294 per month (2000); Median age of housing: 55 years (2000).
Transportation: Commute to work: 88.5% car, 3.8% public transportation, 3.8% walk, 3.8% work from home (2000); Travel time to work: 4.0% less than 15 minutes, 36.0% 15 to 30 minutes, 32.0% 30 to 45 minutes, 14.0% 45 to 60 minutes, 14.0% 60 minutes or more (2000)

LIBERTY (village).
Covers a land area of 2.394 square miles and a water area of 0 square miles. Located at 41.79° N. Lat.; 74.74° W. Long. Elevation is 1,509 feet.
Population: 4,211 (1990); 3,975 (2000); 3,874 (2005); 3,793 (2010 projected); Race: 73.3% White, 15.8% Black, 2.1% Asian, 17.4% Hispanic of any race (2005); Density: 1,618.2 persons per square mile (2005); Average household size: 2.39 (2005); Median age: 40.2 (2005); Males per 100 females: 84.7 (2005); Marriage status: 26.4% never married, 49.0% now married, 13.6% widowed, 10.9% divorced (2000); Foreign born: 10.1% (2000); Ancestry (includes multiple ancestries): 32.3% Other groups, 19.6% German, 12.7% Irish, 9.8% Italian, 6.8% Polish (2000).
Economy: Single-family building permits issued: 4 (2005); Multi-family building permits issued: 68 (2005); Employment by occupation: 6.6% management, 25.8% professional, 20.0% services, 25.2% sales, 0.0% farming, 7.7% construction, 14.7% production (2000).
Income: Per capita income: $21,002 (2005); Median household income: $32,582 (2005); Average household income: $47,213 (2005); Percent of households with income of $100,000 or more: 10.7% (2005); Poverty rate: 15.3% (2000).
Education: Percent of population age 25 and over with: High school diploma (including GED) or higher: 68.3% (2005); Bachelor's degree or higher: 17.6% (2005); Master's degree or higher: 9.1% (2005).

School District(s)
Boces Sullivan (UG-UG)
   2003-04 Enrollment: 267 . . . . (845) 292-0082
Liberty Central School District (PK-12)
   2003-04 Enrollment: 1,882 . . . . (845) 292-6990

Two-year College(s)
Sullivan County BOCES (Public)
   Fall 2004 Enrollment: 59 . . . . (845) 295-4143

Housing: Homeownership rate: 42.2% (2005); Median home value: $110,747 (2005); Median rent: $418 per month (2000); Median age of housing: 46 years (2000).
Safety: Violent crime rate: 45.2 per 10,000 population; Property crime rate: 427.4 per 10,000 population (2004).
Transportation: Commute to work: 84.0% car, 6.3% public transportation, 6.8% walk, 1.8% work from home (2000); Travel time to work: 37.6% less than 15 minutes, 38.7% 15 to 30 minutes, 9.3% 30 to 45 minutes, 3.8% 45 to 60 minutes, 10.6% 60 minutes or more (2000)

Additional Information Contacts
Sullivan County Chamber of Commerce . . . . (845) 292-8500
http://www.catskills.com

LIBERTY (town).
Covers a land area of 79.611 square miles and a water area of 1.101 square miles. Located at 41.80° N. Lat.; 74.76° W. Long. Elevation is 1,509 feet.
History: Settled 1793, incorporated 1870.
Population: 9,825 (1990); 9,632 (2000); 9,643 (2005); 9,644 (2010 projected); Race: 81.5% White, 10.2% Black, 1.6% Asian, 13.5% Hispanic of any race (2005); Density: 121.1 persons per square mile (2005); Average household size: 2.56 (2005); Median age: 40.0 (2005); Males per 100 females: 95.4 (2005); Marriage status: 27.0% never married, 52.3% now married, 11.3% widowed, 9.3% divorced (2000); Foreign born: 8.2% (2000); Ancestry (includes multiple ancestries): 22.3% Other groups, 19.2% German, 15.7% Irish, 11.3% Italian, 8.7% English (2000).
Economy: Summer resort village. Single-family building permits issued: 21 (2005); Multi-family building permits issued: 0 (2005); Employment by occupation: 9.5% management, 18.4% professional, 23.2% services, 24.4% sales, 1.7% farming, 9.0% construction, 13.8% production (2000).
Income: Per capita income: $19,889 (2005); Median household income: $34,525 (2005); Average household income: $47,933 (2005); Percent of households with income of $100,000 or more: 10.0% (2005); Poverty rate: 17.1% (2000).
Education: Percent of population age 25 and over with: High school diploma (including GED) or higher: 71.7% (2005); Bachelor's degree or higher: 15.7% (2005); Master's degree or higher: 7.0% (2005).

Housing: Homeownership rate: 59.6% (2005); Median home value: $123,520 (2005); Median rent: $436 per month (2000); Median age of housing: 41 years (2000).
Transportation: Commute to work: 88.3% car, 3.4% public transportation, 5.4% walk, 2.4% work from home (2000); Travel time to work: 36.8% less than 15 minutes, 38.0% 15 to 30 minutes, 9.7% 30 to 45 minutes, 4.6% 45 to 60 minutes, 11.0% 60 minutes or more (2000)

Additional Information Contacts
Town of Liberty . . . . (845) 292-5111
http://www.townofliberty.org/

LIVINGSTON MANOR (CDP).
Covers a land area of 3.097 square miles and a water area of 0 square miles. Located at 41.89° N. Lat.; 74.82° W. Long. Elevation is 1,433 feet.
Population: 1,482 (1990); 1,355 (2000); 1,365 (2005); 1,386 (2010 projected); Race: 80.9% White, 9.3% Black, 1.5% Asian, 13.1% Hispanic of any race (2005); Density: 440.8 persons per square mile (2005); Average household size: 2.59 (2005); Median age: 33.8 (2005); Males per 100 females: 92.5 (2005); Marriage status: 29.9% never married, 46.5% now married, 11.0% widowed, 12.6% divorced (2000); Foreign born: 3.9% (2000); Ancestry (includes multiple ancestries): 25.1% Other groups, 18.1% German, 17.4% United States or American, 16.4% Irish, 7.5% Italian (2000).
Economy: Manufacturing: corrugated pipe; lumber milling. State brown trout hatchery 7 miles Northeast. Summer and winter skiing resort; heart of Delaware-Sullivan counties trout and fly-fishing region. Employment by occupation: 0.0% management, 16.8% professional, 32.0% services, 20.6% sales, 0.0% farming, 16.6% construction, 14.1% production (2000).
Income: Per capita income: $14,568 (2005); Median household income: $32,143 (2005); Average household income: $37,633 (2005); Percent of households with income of $100,000 or more: 5.3% (2005); Poverty rate: 26.1% (2000).
Education: Percent of population age 25 and over with: High school diploma (including GED) or higher: 67.6% (2005); Bachelor's degree or higher: 8.0% (2005); Master's degree or higher: 2.7% (2005).

School District(s)
Livingston Manor Central School District (PK-12)
   2003-04 Enrollment: 656 . . . . (845) 439-4400

Housing: Homeownership rate: 51.5% (2005); Median home value: $113,063 (2005); Median rent: $458 per month (2000); Median age of housing: 51 years (2000).
Transportation: Commute to work: 92.7% car, 0.0% public transportation, 4.9% walk, 2.4% work from home (2000); Travel time to work: 40.0% less than 15 minutes, 29.3% 15 to 30 minutes, 13.9% 30 to 45 minutes, 1.5% 45 to 60 minutes, 15.4% 60 minutes or more (2000)

LOCH SHELDRAKE (unincorporated postal area, zip code 12759).
Covers a land area of 6.278 square miles and a water area of 0.423 square miles. Located at 41.78° N. Lat.; 74.65° W. Long. Elevation is 1,471 feet.
Population: 0 (2000); Race: 80.5% White, 13.9% Black, 0.0% Asian, 6.0% Hispanic of any race (2000); Density: 0.0 persons per square mile (2000); Age: 32.4% under 18, 13.3% over 64 (2000); Marriage status: 31.1% never married, 53.6% now married, 5.8% widowed, 9.5% divorced (2000); Foreign born: 4.3% (2000); Ancestry (includes multiple ancestries): 23.3% Other groups, 19.4% Irish, 15.8% Italian, 9.2% German, 7.4% Polish (2000).
Economy: Resort village. Employment by occupation: 7.6% management, 17.9% professional, 28.0% services, 22.4% sales, 0.0% farming, 9.4% construction, 14.6% production (2000).
Income: Per capita income: $19,110 (2000); Median household income: $41,098 (2000); Poverty rate: 13.6% (2000).
Education: Percent of population age 25 and over with: High school diploma (including GED) or higher: 86.1% (2000); Bachelor's degree or higher: 15.2% (2000).

Two-year College(s)
Sullivan County Community College (Public)
   Fall 2004 Enrollment: 1,769 . . . . (845) 434-5750
   2005-06 Tuition: In-state $3,306; Out-of-state $6,306

Housing: Homeownership rate: 55.5% (2000); Median home value: $98,600 (2000); Median rent: $464 per month (2000); Median age of housing: 23 years (2000).
Transportation: Commute to work: 92.0% car, 1.8% public transportation, 5.2% walk, 1.0% work from home (2000); Travel time to work: 31.8% less than 15 minutes, 36.0% 15 to 30 minutes, 10.1% 30 to 45 minutes, 3.4% 45 to 60 minutes, 18.8% 60 minutes or more (2000)

LONG EDDY (unincorporated postal area, zip code 12760). Covers a land area of 56.854 square miles and a water area of 0.309 square miles. Located at 41.90° N. Lat.; 75.10° W. Long. Elevation is 847 feet.
Population: 0 (2000); Race: 94.9% White, 1.3% Black, 0.0% Asian, 0.0% Hispanic of any race (2000); Density: 0.0 persons per square mile (2000); Age: 17.4% under 18, 20.7% over 64 (2000); Marriage status: 21.8% never married, 59.2% now married, 12.6% widowed, 6.3% divorced (2000); Foreign born: 4.1% (2000); Ancestry (includes multiple ancestries): 26.0% German, 19.6% Irish, 8.6% United States or American, 8.5% Italian, 8.3% English (2000).
Economy: Employment by occupation: 10.3% management, 21.6% professional, 17.9% services, 20.3% sales, 1.7% farming, 10.7% construction, 17.5% production (2000).
Income: Per capita income: $19,080 (2000); Median household income: $31,111 (2000); Poverty rate: 12.4% (2000).
Education: Percent of population age 25 and over with: High school diploma (including GED) or higher: 71.9% (2000); Bachelor's degree or higher: 11.8% (2000).
Housing: Homeownership rate: 80.7% (2000); Median home value: $62,000 (2000); Median rent: $356 per month (2000); Median age of housing: 36 years (2000).
Transportation: Commute to work: 83.9% car, 1.7% public transportation, 4.9% walk, 9.4% work from home (2000); Travel time to work: 17.8% less than 15 minutes, 30.1% 15 to 30 minutes, 13.5% 30 to 45 minutes, 15.4% 45 to 60 minutes, 23.2% 60 minutes or more (2000)

LUMBERLAND (town). Covers a land area of 47.007 square miles and a water area of 2.630 square miles. Located at 41.48° N. Lat.; 74.81° W. Long.
Population: 1,425 (1990); 1,939 (2000); 1,980 (2005); 2,026 (2010 projected); Race: 96.1% White, 0.3% Black, 1.1% Asian, 2.5% Hispanic of any race (2005); Density: 42.1 persons per square mile (2005); Average household size: 2.50 (2005); Median age: 42.0 (2005); Males per 100 females: 91.9 (2005); Marriage status: 18.5% never married, 63.6% now married, 10.6% widowed, 7.2% divorced (2000); Foreign born: 15.2% (2000); Ancestry (includes multiple ancestries): 24.3% German, 19.0% Irish, 11.3% Ukrainian, 10.0% Italian, 7.9% English (2000).
Economy: Single-family building permits issued: 47 (2005); Multi-family building permits issued: 0 (2005); Employment by occupation: 13.4% management, 17.5% professional, 18.2% services, 23.1% sales, 0.2% farming, 14.0% construction, 13.6% production (2000).
Income: Per capita income: $24,856 (2005); Median household income: $52,755 (2005); Average household income: $62,062 (2005); Percent of households with income of $100,000 or more: 17.9% (2005); Poverty rate: 11.7% (2000).
Education: Percent of population age 25 and over with: High school diploma (including GED) or higher: 84.2% (2005); Bachelor's degree or higher: 20.8% (2005); Master's degree or higher: 9.8% (2005).
Housing: Homeownership rate: 82.7% (2005); Median home value: $162,570 (2005); Median rent: $445 per month (2000); Median age of housing: 30 years (2000).
Transportation: Commute to work: 92.3% car, 2.7% public transportation, 2.2% walk, 2.8% work from home (2000); Travel time to work: 14.8% less than 15 minutes, 26.8% 15 to 30 minutes, 19.8% 30 to 45 minutes, 20.7% 45 to 60 minutes, 17.9% 60 minutes or more (2000)

MAMAKATING (town). Covers a land area of 95.918 square miles and a water area of 2.329 square miles. Located at 41.58° N. Lat.; 74.48° W. Long.
Population: 9,782 (1990); 11,002 (2000); 11,414 (2005); 11,783 (2010 projected); Race: 93.1% White, 2.4% Black, 1.3% Asian, 5.7% Hispanic of any race (2005); Density: 119.0 persons per square mile (2005); Average household size: 2.60 (2005); Median age: 38.1 (2005); Males per 100 females: 100.2 (2005); Marriage status: 23.9% never married, 61.9% now married, 5.3% widowed, 8.9% divorced (2000); Foreign born: 5.4% (2000); Ancestry (includes multiple ancestries): 22.1% Irish, 21.4% German, 19.8% Italian, 12.0% English, 10.4% Other groups (2000).
Economy: Single-family building permits issued: 106 (2005); Multi-family building permits issued: 2 (2005); Employment by occupation: 6.9% management, 22.0% professional, 19.2% services, 25.2% sales, 0.2% farming, 10.2% construction, 16.3% production (2000).
Income: Per capita income: $22,175 (2005); Median household income: $46,292 (2005); Average household income: $57,241 (2005); Percent of households with income of $100,000 or more: 13.2% (2005); Poverty rate: 10.3% (2000).
Education: Percent of population age 25 and over with: High school diploma (including GED) or higher: 83.2% (2005); Bachelor's degree or higher: 17.2% (2005); Master's degree or higher: 8.3% (2005).
Housing: Homeownership rate: 77.8% (2005); Median home value: $134,985 (2005); Median rent: $560 per month (2000); Median age of housing: 39 years (2000).
Transportation: Commute to work: 92.4% car, 2.6% public transportation, 2.4% walk, 2.4% work from home (2000); Travel time to work: 14.4% less than 15 minutes, 37.8% 15 to 30 minutes, 23.4% 30 to 45 minutes, 8.0% 45 to 60 minutes, 16.5% 60 minutes or more (2000)

MONGAUP VALLEY (unincorporated postal area, zip code 12762). Covers a land area of 4.777 square miles and a water area of 0.503 square miles. Located at 41.67° N. Lat.; 74.80° W. Long. Elevation is 1,113 feet.
Population: 0 (2000); Race: 93.1% White, 6.9% Black, 0.0% Asian, 1.4% Hispanic of any race (2000); Density: 0.0 persons per square mile (2000); Age: 18.6% under 18, 5.5% over 64 (2000); Marriage status: 26.6% never married, 48.0% now married, 4.8% widowed, 20.6% divorced (2000); Foreign born: 0.0% (2000); Ancestry (includes multiple ancestries): 32.4% German, 30.3% Italian, 19.7% English, 16.2% Irish, 16.2% Other groups (2000).
Economy: Employment by occupation: 16.1% management, 1.5% professional, 22.1% services, 26.6% sales, 0.0% farming, 15.6% construction, 18.1% production (2000).
Income: Per capita income: $21,586 (2000); Median household income: $35,809 (2000); Poverty rate: 11.4% (2000).
Education: Percent of population age 25 and over with: High school diploma (including GED) or higher: 91.2% (2000); Bachelor's degree or higher: 2.9% (2000).
Housing: Homeownership rate: 71.9% (2000); Median home value: $82,700 (2000); Median rent: $309 per month (2000); Median age of housing: 19 years (2000).
Transportation: Commute to work: 95.5% car, 0.0% public transportation, 0.0% walk, 4.5% work from home (2000); Travel time to work: 41.6% less than 15 minutes, 35.8% 15 to 30 minutes, 22.6% 30 to 45 minutes, 0.0% 45 to 60 minutes, 0.0% 60 minutes or more (2000)

MONTICELLO (village). Covers a land area of 4.066 square miles and a water area of 0.002 square miles. Located at 41.65° N. Lat.; 74.69° W. Long. Elevation is 1,510 feet.
History: Incorporated 1830.
Population: 6,623 (1990); 6,512 (2000); 6,379 (2005); 6,315 (2010 projected); Race: 49.6% White, 33.7% Black, 2.4% Asian, 27.2% Hispanic of any race (2005); Density: 1,568.7 persons per square mile (2005); Average household size: 2.55 (2005); Median age: 35.0 (2005); Males per 100 females: 95.1 (2005); Marriage status: 34.3% never married, 45.3% now married, 7.0% widowed, 13.4% divorced (2000); Foreign born: 13.9% (2000); Ancestry (includes multiple ancestries): 47.5% Other groups, 7.5% United States or American, 6.4% German, 6.0% Irish, 5.3% Italian (2000).
Economy: In timber, dairying, and declining recreational lake area. Manufacturing: furniture, steel fabrication, construction materials. Sand and gravel. Single-family building permits issued: 0 (2005); Multi-family building permits issued: 98 (2005); Employment by occupation: 10.0% management, 19.7% professional, 27.3% services, 30.6% sales, 1.9% farming, 5.5% construction, 5.0% production (2000).
Income: Per capita income: $15,380 (2005); Median household income: $24,233 (2005); Average household income: $36,899 (2005); Percent of households with income of $100,000 or more: 5.4% (2005); Poverty rate: 35.6% (2000).
Education: Percent of population age 25 and over with: High school diploma (including GED) or higher: 65.8% (2005); Bachelor's degree or higher: 14.1% (2005); Master's degree or higher: 6.3% (2005).
School District(s)
Monticello Central School District (KG-12)
    2003-04 Enrollment: 3,523 . . . . (845) 794-7700
Housing: Homeownership rate: 29.2% (2005); Median home value: $106,135 (2005); Median rent: $472 per month (2000); Median age of housing: 37 years (2000).
Safety: Violent crime rate: 78.4 per 10,000 population; Property crime rate: 413.5 per 10,000 population (2004).
Transportation: Commute to work: 86.9% car, 4.8% public transportation, 5.0% walk, 2.7% work from home (2000); Travel time to work: 47.5% less

than 15 minutes, 33.7% 15 to 30 minutes, 7.5% 30 to 45 minutes, 4.3% 45 to 60 minutes, 7.0% 60 minutes or more (2000)

Additional Information Contacts
Village of Monticello.............................. (845) 794-6130
http://www.village.monticello.ny.us/

MOUNTAIN DALE (unincorporated postal area, zip code 12763).
Covers a land area of 10.546 square miles and a water area of 0.141 square miles. Located at 41.69° N. Lat.; 74.52° W. Long.
Population: 0 (2000); Race: 93.6% White, 4.0% Black, 0.0% Asian, 10.0% Hispanic of any race (2000); Density: 0.0 persons per square mile (2000); Age: 19.9% under 18, 14.1% over 64 (2000); Marriage status: 26.5% never married, 58.9% now married, 3.4% widowed, 11.2% divorced (2000); Foreign born: 11.0% (2000); Ancestry (includes multiple ancestries): 24.7% Italian, 14.7% Other groups, 13.4% German, 12.3% Irish, 7.5% English (2000).
Economy: Resort village. Employment by occupation: 8.5% management, 12.7% professional, 21.8% services, 30.0% sales, 0.0% farming, 8.5% construction, 18.6% production (2000).
Income: Per capita income: $18,046 (2000); Median household income: $38,750 (2000); Poverty rate: 16.3% (2000).
Education: Percent of population age 25 and over with: High school diploma (including GED) or higher: 76.6% (2000); Bachelor's degree or higher: 12.4% (2000).
Housing: Homeownership rate: 73.6% (2000); Median home value: $66,600 (2000); Median rent: $437 per month (2000); Median age of housing: 43 years (2000).
Transportation: Commute to work: 89.2% car, 1.6% public transportation, 1.4% walk, 5.7% work from home (2000); Travel time to work: 16.0% less than 15 minutes, 54.7% 15 to 30 minutes, 18.9% 30 to 45 minutes, 7.7% 45 to 60 minutes, 2.6% 60 minutes or more (2000)

NARROWSBURG (CDP).
Covers a land area of 1.377 square miles and a water area of 0.130 square miles. Located at 41.60° N. Lat.; 75.06° W. Long. Elevation is 740 feet.
Population: 402 (1990); 414 (2000); 428 (2005); 440 (2010 projected); Race: 90.4% White, 6.1% Black, 1.2% Asian, 4.4% Hispanic of any race (2005); Density: 310.8 persons per square mile (2005); Average household size: 2.18 (2005); Median age: 44.2 (2005); Males per 100 females: 91.1 (2005); Marriage status: 14.9% never married, 61.5% now married, 17.2% widowed, 6.3% divorced (2000); Foreign born: 4.2% (2000); Ancestry (includes multiple ancestries): 35.7% German, 23.4% Irish, 16.8% Italian, 14.0% Other groups, 13.3% English (2000).
Economy: Resort village. Employment by occupation: 7.3% management, 22.4% professional, 19.8% services, 25.0% sales, 1.0% farming, 13.0% construction, 11.5% production (2000).
Income: Per capita income: $22,004 (2005); Median household income: $39,583 (2005); Average household income: $48,048 (2005); Percent of households with income of $100,000 or more: 6.6% (2005); Poverty rate: 4.7% (2000).
Education: Percent of population age 25 and over with: High school diploma (including GED) or higher: 89.4% (2005); Bachelor's degree or higher: 19.2% (2005); Master's degree or higher: 7.6% (2005).

School District(s)
Sullivan West Central School District (KG-12)
    2003-04 Enrollment: 1,568 .... (845) 887-5300
Housing: Homeownership rate: 75.5% (2005); Median home value: $130,667 (2005); Median rent: $514 per month (2000); Median age of housing: 55 years (2000).
Newspapers: The River Reporter (General - Circulation 3,700)
Transportation: Commute to work: 81.8% car, 1.6% public transportation, 3.7% walk, 12.8% work from home (2000); Travel time to work: 33.1% less than 15 minutes, 16.0% 15 to 30 minutes, 20.2% 30 to 45 minutes, 12.9% 45 to 60 minutes, 17.8% 60 minutes or more (2000)

Additional Information Contacts
Narrowsburg Chamber of Commerce .... (845) 252-7234
http://www.narrowsburg.org

NEVERSINK (town).
Covers a land area of 82.924 square miles and a water area of 3.446 square miles. Located at 41.85° N. Lat.; 74.59° W. Long. Elevation is 1,633 feet.
Population: 2,951 (1990); 3,553 (2000); 3,632 (2005); 3,720 (2010 projected); Race: 96.4% White, 0.7% Black, 0.2% Asian, 2.9% Hispanic of any race (2005); Density: 43.8 persons per square mile (2005); Average household size: 2.61 (2005); Median age: 39.5 (2005); Males per 100 females: 95.3 (2005); Marriage status: 20.4% never married, 66.6% now married, 6.3% widowed, 6.7% divorced (2000); Foreign born: 6.0% (2000); Ancestry (includes multiple ancestries): 19.1% Irish, 15.5% German, 11.6% English, 9.7% Italian, 6.6% Dutch (2000).
Economy: Single-family building permits issued: 21 (2005); Multi-family building permits issued: 0 (2005); Employment by occupation: 10.6% management, 25.4% professional, 24.5% services, 12.0% sales, 1.5% farming, 17.1% construction, 8.9% production (2000).
Income: Per capita income: $19,976 (2005); Median household income: $45,957 (2005); Average household income: $52,196 (2005); Percent of households with income of $100,000 or more: 9.4% (2005); Poverty rate: 11.3% (2000).
Education: Percent of population age 25 and over with: High school diploma (including GED) or higher: 83.5% (2005); Bachelor's degree or higher: 20.5% (2005); Master's degree or higher: 8.0% (2005).
Housing: Homeownership rate: 80.8% (2005); Median home value: $158,082 (2005); Median rent: $519 per month (2000); Median age of housing: 34 years (2000).
Transportation: Commute to work: 95.3% car, 0.0% public transportation, 1.3% walk, 2.4% work from home (2000); Travel time to work: 33.9% less than 15 minutes, 36.4% 15 to 30 minutes, 11.7% 30 to 45 minutes, 3.4% 45 to 60 minutes, 14.5% 60 minutes or more (2000)

NORTH BRANCH (unincorporated postal area, zip code 12766).
Covers a land area of 7.124 square miles and a water area of 0.008 square miles. Located at 41.81° N. Lat.; 74.98° W. Long. Elevation is 1,036 feet.
Population: 0 (2000); Race: 90.3% White, 0.0% Black, 0.0% Asian, 11.6% Hispanic of any race (2000); Density: 0.0 persons per square mile (2000); Age: 25.9% under 18, 12.9% over 64 (2000); Marriage status: 30.1% never married, 58.7% now married, 4.9% widowed, 6.3% divorced (2000); Foreign born: 10.8% (2000); Ancestry (includes multiple ancestries): 45.4% German, 19.4% Irish, 17.5% Other groups, 11.2% Italian, 6.8% English (2000).
Economy: Employment by occupation: 12.4% management, 14.2% professional, 32.1% services, 11.5% sales, 1.8% farming, 17.9% construction, 10.1% production (2000).
Income: Per capita income: $18,733 (2000); Median household income: $35,833 (2000); Poverty rate: 17.5% (2000).
Education: Percent of population age 25 and over with: High school diploma (including GED) or higher: 70.6% (2000); Bachelor's degree or higher: 9.9% (2000).
Housing: Homeownership rate: 66.3% (2000); Median home value: $89,600 (2000); Median rent: $421 per month (2000); Median age of housing: 60+ years (2000).
Transportation: Commute to work: 83.0% car, 0.0% public transportation, 6.4% walk, 10.6% work from home (2000); Travel time to work: 32.8% less than 15 minutes, 34.9% 15 to 30 minutes, 24.6% 30 to 45 minutes, 2.6% 45 to 60 minutes, 5.1% 60 minutes or more (2000)

PARKSVILLE (unincorporated postal area, zip code 12768).
Covers a land area of 34.497 square miles and a water area of 0.432 square miles. Located at 41.86° N. Lat.; 74.73° W. Long. Elevation is 1,673 feet.
Population: 0 (2000); Race: 85.0% White, 13.0% Black, 1.5% Asian, 11.3% Hispanic of any race (2000); Density: 0.0 persons per square mile (2000); Age: 23.0% under 18, 11.1% over 64 (2000); Marriage status: 30.6% never married, 55.4% now married, 3.4% widowed, 10.6% divorced (2000); Foreign born: 8.0% (2000); Ancestry (includes multiple ancestries): 19.9% Other groups, 14.5% Irish, 13.5% German, 13.2% Italian, 9.0% United States or American (2000).
Economy: Resort village. Employment by occupation: 12.7% management, 21.5% professional, 17.7% services, 17.7% sales, 0.0% farming, 19.6% construction, 10.8% production (2000).
Income: Per capita income: $15,686 (2000); Median household income: $38,990 (2000); Poverty rate: 17.6% (2000).
Education: Percent of population age 25 and over with: High school diploma (including GED) or higher: 62.1% (2000); Bachelor's degree or higher: 18.4% (2000).
Housing: Homeownership rate: 80.5% (2000); Median home value: $130,300 (2000); Median rent: $420 per month (2000); Median age of housing: 28 years (2000).
Transportation: Commute to work: 87.7% car, 0.0% public transportation, 5.6% walk, 6.6% work from home (2000); Travel time to work: 26.6% less than 15 minutes, 37.2% 15 to 30 minutes, 10.3% 30 to 45 minutes, 3.5% 45 to 60 minutes, 22.3% 60 minutes or more (2000)

POND EDDY (unincorporated postal area, zip code 12770). Covers a land area of 4.418 square miles and a water area of 0 square miles. Located at 41.44° N. Lat.; 74.84° W. Long. Elevation is 605 feet.
Population: 0 (2000); Race: 98.3% White, 0.0% Black, 0.0% Asian, 0.0% Hispanic of any race (2000); Density: 0.0 persons per square mile (2000); Age: 21.3% under 18, 12.5% over 64 (2000); Marriage status: 21.3% never married, 52.3% now married, 15.2% widowed, 11.2% divorced (2000); Foreign born: 14.2% (2000); Ancestry (includes multiple ancestries): 16.3% German, 15.8% Irish, 9.2% Italian, 8.8% English, 8.8% Other groups (2000).
Economy: Employment by occupation: 7.4% management, 15.7% professional, 14.9% services, 27.3% sales, 0.0% farming, 14.0% construction, 20.7% production (2000).
Income: Per capita income: $20,935 (2000); Median household income: $39,375 (2000); Poverty rate: 17.5% (2000).
Education: Percent of population age 25 and over with: High school diploma (including GED) or higher: 85.3% (2000); Bachelor's degree or higher: 15.9% (2000).
Housing: Homeownership rate: 69.0% (2000); Median home value: $94,400 (2000); Median rent: $613 per month (2000); Median age of housing: 29 years (2000).
Transportation: Commute to work: 97.5% car, 2.5% public transportation, 0.0% walk, 0.0% work from home (2000); Travel time to work: 11.8% less than 15 minutes, 28.6% 15 to 30 minutes, 13.4% 30 to 45 minutes, 25.2% 45 to 60 minutes, 21.0% 60 minutes or more (2000)

ROCK HILL (CDP). Covers a land area of 3.730 square miles and a water area of 0.914 square miles. Located at 41.61° N. Lat.; 74.58° W. Long.
Population: 696 (1990); 1,056 (2000); 1,100 (2005); 1,142 (2010 projected); Race: 93.7% White, 0.5% Black, 2.7% Asian, 4.6% Hispanic of any race (2005); Density: 294.9 persons per square mile (2005); Average household size: 2.38 (2005); Median age: 43.4 (2005); Males per 100 females: 94.7 (2005); Marriage status: 20.5% never married, 71.3% now married, 4.2% widowed, 4.0% divorced (2000); Foreign born: 4.3% (2000); Ancestry (includes multiple ancestries): 16.5% Irish, 12.7% German, 9.9% English, 9.2% Italian, 9.1% Other groups (2000).
Economy: Employment by occupation: 19.8% management, 17.3% professional, 9.6% services, 41.8% sales, 0.0% farming, 4.9% construction, 6.5% production (2000).
Income: Per capita income: $27,932 (2005); Median household income: $56,551 (2005); Average household income: $66,361 (2005); Percent of households with income of $100,000 or more: 11.2% (2005); Poverty rate: 4.0% (2000).
Education: Percent of population age 25 and over with: High school diploma (including GED) or higher: 91.4% (2005); Bachelor's degree or higher: 27.0% (2005); Master's degree or higher: 13.0% (2005).
Housing: Homeownership rate: 82.9% (2005); Median home value: $200,101 (2005); Median rent: $551 per month (2000); Median age of housing: 25 years (2000).
Transportation: Commute to work: 95.4% car, 2.9% public transportation, 0.0% walk, 1.7% work from home (2000); Travel time to work: 38.2% less than 15 minutes, 33.9% 15 to 30 minutes, 9.0% 30 to 45 minutes, 6.8% 45 to 60 minutes, 12.2% 60 minutes or more (2000)

ROCKLAND (town). Covers a land area of 94.290 square miles and a water area of 0.957 square miles. Located at 41.92° N. Lat.; 74.82° W. Long.
Population: 4,096 (1990); 3,913 (2000); 3,972 (2005); 4,040 (2010 projected); Race: 88.8% White, 4.5% Black, 1.3% Asian, 8.5% Hispanic of any race (2005); Density: 42.1 persons per square mile (2005); Average household size: 2.47 (2005); Median age: 40.7 (2005); Males per 100 females: 97.3 (2005); Marriage status: 22.5% never married, 56.9% now married, 10.5% widowed, 10.1% divorced (2000); Foreign born: 4.9% (2000); Ancestry (includes multiple ancestries): 23.1% German, 16.4% Irish, 14.9% Other groups, 13.1% Italian, 9.6% United States or American (2000).
Economy: Single-family building permits issued: 24 (2005); Multi-family building permits issued: 0 (2005); Employment by occupation: 7.2% management, 20.3% professional, 22.7% services, 24.5% sales, 0.4% farming, 14.0% construction, 10.9% production (2000).
Income: Per capita income: $18,836 (2005); Median household income: $36,887 (2005); Average household income: $46,419 (2005); Percent of households with income of $100,000 or more: 8.8% (2005); Poverty rate: 14.0% (2000).
Education: Percent of population age 25 and over with: High school diploma (including GED) or higher: 74.8% (2005); Bachelor's degree or higher: 11.3% (2005); Master's degree or higher: 3.3% (2005).
Housing: Homeownership rate: 69.7% (2005); Median home value: $118,907 (2005); Median rent: $418 per month (2000); Median age of housing: 38 years (2000).
Transportation: Commute to work: 93.0% car, 0.8% public transportation, 3.5% walk, 2.8% work from home (2000); Travel time to work: 35.2% less than 15 minutes, 28.1% 15 to 30 minutes, 21.6% 30 to 45 minutes, 2.8% 45 to 60 minutes, 12.3% 60 minutes or more (2000)

ROSCOE (CDP). Covers a land area of 0.745 square miles and a water area of 0 square miles. Located at 41.93° N. Lat.; 74.91° W. Long. Elevation is 1,280 feet.
Population: 665 (1990); 597 (2000); 593 (2005); 603 (2010 projected); Race: 93.8% White, 1.5% Black, 2.4% Asian, 2.2% Hispanic of any race (2005); Density: 796.3 persons per square mile (2005); Average household size: 2.25 (2005); Median age: 42.1 (2005); Males per 100 females: 92.5 (2005); Marriage status: 20.5% never married, 57.8% now married, 13.7% widowed, 8.1% divorced (2000); Foreign born: 2.9% (2000); Ancestry (includes multiple ancestries): 22.7% German, 21.4% Irish, 14.1% English, 11.4% Italian, 9.0% Other groups (2000).
Economy: Light manufacturing; stone quarrying. Employment by occupation: 8.4% management, 26.6% professional, 11.4% services, 33.0% sales, 0.0% farming, 6.4% construction, 14.1% production (2000).
Income: Per capita income: $21,699 (2005); Median household income: $43,409 (2005); Average household income: $48,926 (2005); Percent of households with income of $100,000 or more: 8.4% (2005); Poverty rate: 4.8% (2000).
Education: Percent of population age 25 and over with: High school diploma (including GED) or higher: 72.7% (2005); Bachelor's degree or higher: 18.0% (2005); Master's degree or higher: 7.7% (2005).
School District(s)
Roscoe Central School District (PK-12)
    2003-04 Enrollment: 295 . . . . (607) 498-4126
Housing: Homeownership rate: 73.0% (2005); Median home value: $118,182 (2005); Median rent: $425 per month (2000); Median age of housing: 58 years (2000).
Transportation: Commute to work: 92.3% car, 0.0% public transportation, 6.6% walk, 1.0% work from home (2000); Travel time to work: 33.9% less than 15 minutes, 19.8% 15 to 30 minutes, 27.6% 30 to 45 minutes, 4.6% 45 to 60 minutes, 14.1% 60 minutes or more (2000)

SMALLWOOD (CDP). Covers a land area of 1.549 square miles and a water area of 0.100 square miles. Located at 41.66° N. Lat.; 74.81° W. Long.
Population: 431 (1990); 566 (2000); 634 (2005); 701 (2010 projected); Race: 96.2% White, 0.8% Black, 0.0% Asian, 3.8% Hispanic of any race (2005); Density: 409.4 persons per square mile (2005); Average household size: 2.16 (2005); Median age: 47.6 (2005); Males per 100 females: 95.7 (2005); Marriage status: 27.2% never married, 52.6% now married, 8.1% widowed, 12.2% divorced (2000); Foreign born: 4.7% (2000); Ancestry (includes multiple ancestries): 35.4% Irish, 20.8% German, 19.4% Italian, 15.3% United States or American, 7.8% English (2000).
Economy: Employment by occupation: 10.9% management, 12.1% professional, 19.9% services, 17.1% sales, 0.0% farming, 19.0% construction, 20.9% production (2000).
Income: Per capita income: $39,407 (2005); Median household income: $62,302 (2005); Average household income: $84,855 (2005); Percent of households with income of $100,000 or more: 25.5% (2005); Poverty rate: 8.9% (2000).
Education: Percent of population age 25 and over with: High school diploma (including GED) or higher: 92.1% (2005); Bachelor's degree or higher: 18.9% (2005); Master's degree or higher: 16.2% (2005).
Housing: Homeownership rate: 85.4% (2005); Median home value: $110,119 (2005); Median rent: $556 per month (2000); Median age of housing: 44 years (2000).
Transportation: Commute to work: 85.7% car, 6.6% public transportation, 0.0% walk, 3.7% work from home (2000); Travel time to work: 27.2% less than 15 minutes, 46.2% 15 to 30 minutes, 9.0% 30 to 45 minutes, 7.9% 45 to 60 minutes, 9.7% 60 minutes or more (2000)

SOUTH FALLSBURG

SOUTH FALLSBURG (CDP). Aka South Fallsburgh. Covers a land area of 5.996 square miles and a water area of 0.141 square miles. Located at 41.71° N. Lat.; 74.63° W. Long.

Population: 2,115 (1990); 2,061 (2000); 1,932 (2005); 1,878 (2010 projected); Race: 72.7% White, 18.2% Black, 1.2% Asian, 16.2% Hispanic of any race (2005); Density: 322.2 persons per square mile (2005); Average household size: 3.09 (2005); Median age: 28.0 (2005); Males per 100 females: 112.1 (2005); Marriage status: 38.0% never married, 47.0% now married, 5.9% widowed, 9.1% divorced (2000); Foreign born: 10.5% (2000); Ancestry (includes multiple ancestries): 30.6% Other groups, 18.7% United States or American, 5.6% German, 4.9% Italian, 4.3% Irish (2000).

Economy: Resort village. Employment by occupation: 12.4% management, 29.5% professional, 15.3% services, 24.7% sales, 0.0% farming, 4.0% construction, 14.0% production (2000).

Income: Per capita income: $16,725 (2005); Median household income: $26,984 (2005); Average household income: $48,276 (2005); Percent of households with income of $100,000 or more: 10.4% (2005); Poverty rate: 26.0% (2000).

Education: Percent of population age 25 and over with: High school diploma (including GED) or higher: 63.5% (2005); Bachelor's degree or higher: 16.2% (2005); Master's degree or higher: 8.8% (2005).

Four-year College(s)

Yeshivath Zichron Moshe
    Fall 2004 Enrollment: 191 . . . . (914) 434-5240
    2005-06 Tuition: In-state $7,200; Out-of-state $7,200

Housing: Homeownership rate: 41.4% (2005); Median home value: $131,195 (2005); Median rent: $491 per month (2000); Median age of housing: 30 years (2000).

Transportation: Commute to work: 76.4% car, 5.8% public transportation, 11.8% walk, 3.2% work from home (2000); Travel time to work: 49.9% less than 15 minutes, 30.0% 15 to 30 minutes, 5.6% 30 to 45 minutes, 2.6% 45 to 60 minutes, 11.9% 60 minutes or more (2000)

SWAN LAKE

SWAN LAKE (unincorporated postal area, zip code 12783). Aka Hurd. Covers a land area of 38.141 square miles and a water area of 0.735 square miles. Located at 41.73° N. Lat.; 74.82° W. Long. Elevation is 1,341 feet.

Population: 0 (2000); Race: 85.2% White, 8.5% Black, 0.2% Asian, 12.9% Hispanic of any race (2000); Density: 0.0 persons per square mile (2000); Age: 18.7% under 18, 16.2% over 64 (2000); Marriage status: 25.9% never married, 57.6% now married, 8.6% widowed, 7.9% divorced (2000); Foreign born: 8.4% (2000); Ancestry (includes multiple ancestries): 17.3% Other groups, 14.2% German, 13.4% Irish, 10.7% Italian, 6.9% Polish (2000).

Economy: Employment by occupation: 17.3% management, 15.8% professional, 17.3% services, 24.2% sales, 2.7% farming, 13.6% construction, 9.1% production (2000).

Income: Per capita income: $24,720 (2000); Median household income: $36,397 (2000); Poverty rate: 10.1% (2000).

Education: Percent of population age 25 and over with: High school diploma (including GED) or higher: 70.3% (2000); Bachelor's degree or higher: 17.1% (2000).

Housing: Homeownership rate: 78.1% (2000); Median home value: $111,800 (2000); Median rent: $466 per month (2000); Median age of housing: 39 years (2000).

Transportation: Commute to work: 86.4% car, 5.0% public transportation, 3.4% walk, 3.8% work from home (2000); Travel time to work: 14.0% less than 15 minutes, 49.3% 15 to 30 minutes, 13.2% 30 to 45 minutes, 6.3% 45 to 60 minutes, 17.2% 60 minutes or more (2000)

THOMPSON

THOMPSON (town). Covers a land area of 84.086 square miles and a water area of 3.295 square miles. Located at 41.65° N. Lat.; 74.67° W. Long.

Population: 13,711 (1990); 14,189 (2000); 14,403 (2005); 14,640 (2010 projected); Race: 70.7% White, 18.9% Black, 2.1% Asian, 16.7% Hispanic of any race (2005); Density: 171.3 persons per square mile (2005); Average household size: 2.54 (2005); Median age: 38.3 (2005); Males per 100 females: 96.5 (2005); Marriage status: 26.6% never married, 55.7% now married, 6.7% widowed, 11.0% divorced (2000); Foreign born: 9.8% (2000); Ancestry (includes multiple ancestries): 30.5% Other groups, 11.5% Irish, 11.0% German, 9.8% Italian, 6.7% United States or American (2000).

Economy: Single-family building permits issued: 107 (2005); Multi-family building permits issued: 32 (2005); Employment by occupation: 12.6% management, 19.3% professional, 21.2% services, 28.9% sales, 1.2% farming, 8.6% construction, 8.1% production (2000).

Income: Per capita income: $21,346 (2005); Median household income: $40,042 (2005); Average household income: $52,759 (2005); Percent of households with income of $100,000 or more: 12.6% (2005); Poverty rate: 23.3% (2000).

Taxes: Total city taxes per capita: $299 (2004); City property taxes per capita: $248 (2004).

Education: Percent of population age 25 and over with: High school diploma (including GED) or higher: 75.2% (2005); Bachelor's degree or higher: 18.2% (2005); Master's degree or higher: 8.4% (2005).

Housing: Homeownership rate: 53.6% (2005); Median home value: $131,883 (2005); Median rent: $483 per month (2000); Median age of housing: 33 years (2000).

Transportation: Commute to work: 91.0% car, 2.6% public transportation, 2.9% walk, 2.7% work from home (2000); Travel time to work: 43.8% less than 15 minutes, 33.4% 15 to 30 minutes, 6.6% 30 to 45 minutes, 4.5% 45 to 60 minutes, 11.8% 60 minutes or more (2000)

Additional Information Contacts
Town of Thompson . . . . (845) 794-2500
    http://www.townofthompson.com/

TUSTEN

TUSTEN (town). Covers a land area of 47.262 square miles and a water area of 1.547 square miles. Located at 41.58° N. Lat.; 74.99° W. Long.

Population: 1,271 (1990); 1,415 (2000); 1,467 (2005); 1,517 (2010 projected); Race: 86.6% White, 8.9% Black, 1.3% Asian, 4.5% Hispanic of any race (2005); Density: 31.0 persons per square mile (2005); Average household size: 2.42 (2005); Median age: 45.5 (2005); Males per 100 females: 101.8 (2005); Marriage status: 18.3% never married, 60.1% now married, 11.7% widowed, 9.8% divorced (2000); Foreign born: 3.9% (2000); Ancestry (includes multiple ancestries): 33.0% German, 24.0% Irish, 11.4% Italian, 11.4% English, 9.1% Other groups (2000).

Economy: Single-family building permits issued: 14 (2005); Multi-family building permits issued: 0 (2005); Employment by occupation: 10.3% management, 18.8% professional, 18.1% services, 28.2% sales, 1.0% farming, 11.7% construction, 11.9% production (2000).

Income: Per capita income: $22,869 (2005); Median household income: $43,271 (2005); Average household income: $51,848 (2005); Percent of households with income of $100,000 or more: 9.7% (2005); Poverty rate: 9.2% (2000).

Education: Percent of population age 25 and over with: High school diploma (including GED) or higher: 83.6% (2005); Bachelor's degree or higher: 19.5% (2005); Master's degree or higher: 9.2% (2005).

Housing: Homeownership rate: 79.2% (2005); Median home value: $137,081 (2005); Median rent: $425 per month (2000); Median age of housing: 36 years (2000).

Transportation: Commute to work: 85.8% car, 2.7% public transportation, 4.3% walk, 7.2% work from home (2000); Travel time to work: 24.1% less than 15 minutes, 21.6% 15 to 30 minutes, 19.3% 30 to 45 minutes, 15.5% 45 to 60 minutes, 19.5% 60 minutes or more (2000)

WHITE LAKE

WHITE LAKE (unincorporated postal area, zip code 12786). Covers a land area of 18.005 square miles and a water area of 2.628 square miles. Located at 41.64° N. Lat.; 74.85° W. Long.

Population: 0 (2000); Race: 88.1% White, 0.4% Black, 1.5% Asian, 19.3% Hispanic of any race (2000); Density: 0.0 persons per square mile (2000); Age: 16.6% under 18, 22.4% over 64 (2000); Marriage status: 18.9% never married, 51.7% now married, 12.5% widowed, 16.8% divorced (2000); Foreign born: 10.1% (2000); Ancestry (includes multiple ancestries): 19.6% Irish, 16.0% Other groups, 14.1% German, 13.1% United States or American, 11.5% Italian (2000).

Economy: Employment by occupation: 32.7% management, 9.2% professional, 9.2% services, 28.1% sales, 1.4% farming, 0.0% construction, 19.4% production (2000).

Income: Per capita income: $37,769 (2000); Median household income: $37,727 (2000); Poverty rate: 28.3% (2000).

Education: Percent of population age 25 and over with: High school diploma (including GED) or higher: 80.3% (2000); Bachelor's degree or higher: 10.6% (2000).

School District(s)

Monticello Central School District (KG-12)
    2003-04 Enrollment: 3,523 . . . . (845) 794-7700

Housing: Homeownership rate: 89.2% (2000); Median home value: $106,900 (2000); Median rent: $431 per month (2000); Median age of housing: 48 years (2000).
Transportation: Commute to work: 72.0% car, 18.8% public transportation, 0.0% walk, 9.2% work from home (2000); Travel time to work: 19.1% less than 15 minutes, 35.1% 15 to 30 minutes, 13.8% 30 to 45 minutes, 13.8% 45 to 60 minutes, 18.1% 60 minutes or more (2000)

WHITE SULPHUR SPRINGS (unincorporated postal area, zip code 12787). Covers a land area of 3.645 square miles and a water area of 0.021 square miles. Located at 41.80° N. Lat.; 74.84° W. Long. Elevation is 1,363 feet.
Population: 0 (2000); Race: 98.7% White, 1.3% Black, 0.0% Asian, 12.2% Hispanic of any race (2000); Density: 0.0 persons per square mile (2000); Age: 37.3% under 18, 12.2% over 64 (2000); Marriage status: 32.9% never married, 51.2% now married, 6.8% widowed, 9.2% divorced (2000); Foreign born: 0.0% (2000); Ancestry (includes multiple ancestries): 33.9% Other groups, 18.5% German, 12.2% United States or American, 11.3% Irish, 10.3% English (2000).
Economy: Employment by occupation: 9.6% management, 9.6% professional, 37.3% services, 34.9% sales, 0.0% farming, 8.4% construction, 0.0% production (2000).
Income: Per capita income: $9,419 (2000); Median household income: $24,938 (2000); Poverty rate: 37.9% (2000).
Education: Percent of population age 25 and over with: High school diploma (including GED) or higher: 58.8% (2000); Bachelor's degree or higher: 10.2% (2000).

School District(s)
Liberty Central School District (PK-12)
    2003-04 Enrollment: 1,882 . . . . (845) 292-6990

Housing: Homeownership rate: 53.3% (2000); Median home value: $87,100 (2000); Median rent: $464 per month (2000); Median age of housing: 27 years (2000).
Transportation: Commute to work: 68.7% car, 0.0% public transportation, 0.0% walk, 31.3% work from home (2000); Travel time to work: 15.8% less than 15 minutes, 70.2% 15 to 30 minutes, 0.0% 30 to 45 minutes, 0.0% 45 to 60 minutes, 14.0% 60 minutes or more (2000)

WOODBOURNE (unincorporated postal area, zip code 12788). Covers a land area of 21.561 square miles and a water area of 0.190 square miles. Located at 41.78° N. Lat.; 74.59° W. Long. Elevation is 1,190 feet.
Population: 0 (2000); Race: 71.9% White, 21.5% Black, 0.0% Asian, 11.4% Hispanic of any race (2000); Density: 0.0 persons per square mile (2000); Age: 19.8% under 18, 8.9% over 64 (2000); Marriage status: 37.5% never married, 46.5% now married, 6.6% widowed, 9.5% divorced (2000); Foreign born: 12.1% (2000); Ancestry (includes multiple ancestries): 10.7% Italian, 10.4% Irish, 10.2% German, 10.0% Other groups, 4.4% English (2000).
Economy: Employment by occupation: 10.2% management, 21.7% professional, 23.0% services, 18.6% sales, 2.3% farming, 15.0% construction, 9.1% production (2000).
Income: Per capita income: $17,171 (2000); Median household income: $32,604 (2000); Poverty rate: 15.8% (2000).
Education: Percent of population age 25 and over with: High school diploma (including GED) or higher: 57.9% (2000); Bachelor's degree or higher: 7.2% (2000).

School District(s)
Fallsburg Central School District (KG-12)
    2003-04 Enrollment: 1,450 . . . . (845) 434-5884

Housing: Homeownership rate: 74.7% (2000); Median home value: $81,800 (2000); Median rent: $478 per month (2000); Median age of housing: 35 years (2000).
Transportation: Commute to work: 94.6% car, 0.0% public transportation, 1.8% walk, 3.6% work from home (2000); Travel time to work: 26.9% less than 15 minutes, 50.3% 15 to 30 minutes, 8.9% 30 to 45 minutes, 4.1% 45 to 60 minutes, 9.7% 60 minutes or more (2000)

WOODRIDGE (village). Covers a land area of 1.545 square miles and a water area of 0.100 square miles. Located at 41.70° N. Lat.; 74.57° W. Long. Elevation is 1,190 feet.
Population: 798 (1990); 902 (2000); 938 (2005); 955 (2010 projected); Race: 70.0% White, 13.2% Black, 1.2% Asian, 28.0% Hispanic of any race (2005); Density: 607.2 persons per square mile (2005); Average household size: 2.52 (2005); Median age: 38.9 (2005); Males per 100 females: 89.5 (2005); Marriage status: 29.0% never married, 55.7% now married, 9.7% widowed, 5.7% divorced (2000); Foreign born: 11.4% (2000); Ancestry (includes multiple ancestries): 37.7% Other groups, 8.2% Italian, 7.8% German, 7.6% Irish, 6.6% United States or American (2000).
Economy: Resort village. Single-family building permits issued: 18 (2005); Multi-family building permits issued: 2 (2005); Employment by occupation: 14.3% management, 18.2% professional, 20.3% services, 22.7% sales, 0.7% farming, 5.6% construction, 18.2% production (2000).
Income: Per capita income: $19,225 (2005); Median household income: $28,250 (2005); Average household income: $47,466 (2005); Percent of households with income of $100,000 or more: 15.1% (2005); Poverty rate: 31.1% (2000).
Education: Percent of population age 25 and over with: High school diploma (including GED) or higher: 68.6% (2005); Bachelor's degree or higher: 17.6% (2005); Master's degree or higher: 7.0% (2005).
Housing: Homeownership rate: 41.1% (2005); Median home value: $126,042 (2005); Median rent: $413 per month (2000); Median age of housing: 42 years (2000).
Safety: Violent crime rate: 41.4 per 10,000 population; Property crime rate: 82.8 per 10,000 population (2004).
Transportation: Commute to work: 76.4% car, 1.8% public transportation, 17.8% walk, 4.0% work from home (2000); Travel time to work: 47.0% less than 15 minutes, 35.6% 15 to 30 minutes, 6.1% 30 to 45 minutes, 4.5% 45 to 60 minutes, 6.8% 60 minutes or more (2000)

WURTSBORO (village). Covers a land area of 1.265 square miles and a water area of 0 square miles. Located at 41.57° N. Lat.; 74.48° W. Long.
Population: 1,048 (1990); 1,234 (2000); 1,309 (2005); 1,315 (2010 projected); Race: 93.0% White, 2.4% Black, 0.9% Asian, 6.1% Hispanic of any race (2005); Density: 1,034.8 persons per square mile (2005); Average household size: 2.54 (2005); Median age: 35.6 (2005); Males per 100 females: 92.5 (2005); Marriage status: 25.5% never married, 58.5% now married, 6.8% widowed, 9.2% divorced (2000); Foreign born: 3.9% (2000); Ancestry (includes multiple ancestries): 23.0% Irish, 20.5% Italian, 17.0% German, 16.4% English, 12.3% Other groups (2000).
Economy: Resort village. Single-family building permits issued: 1 (2005); Multi-family building permits issued: 0 (2005); Employment by occupation: 10.2% management, 15.0% professional, 15.7% services, 31.6% sales, 0.4% farming, 15.2% construction, 12.0% production (2000).
Income: Per capita income: $18,825 (2005); Median household income: $41,103 (2005); Average household income: $47,850 (2005); Percent of households with income of $100,000 or more: 7.2% (2005); Poverty rate: 10.9% (2000).
Education: Percent of population age 25 and over with: High school diploma (including GED) or higher: 83.9% (2005); Bachelor's degree or higher: 13.6% (2005); Master's degree or higher: 6.7% (2005).

School District(s)
Monticello Central School District (KG-12)
    2003-04 Enrollment: 3,523 . . . . (845) 794-7700

Housing: Homeownership rate: 64.1% (2005); Median home value: $130,142 (2005); Median rent: $634 per month (2000); Median age of housing: 36 years (2000).
Transportation: Commute to work: 92.3% car, 1.3% public transportation, 4.0% walk, 2.3% work from home (2000); Travel time to work: 22.0% less than 15 minutes, 37.4% 15 to 30 minutes, 22.6% 30 to 45 minutes, 4.9% 45 to 60 minutes, 13.0% 60 minutes or more (2000)
Additional Information Contacts
Wurtsboro Board of Trade . . . . (845) 888-0330
    http://www.wurtsboro.org

YOUNGSVILLE (unincorporated postal area, zip code 12791). Covers a land area of 3.985 square miles and a water area of 0 square miles. Located at 41.80° N. Lat.; 74.88° W. Long.
Population: 0 (2000); Race: 97.3% White, 0.0% Black, 1.0% Asian, 4.6% Hispanic of any race (2000); Density: 0.0 persons per square mile (2000); Age: 24.7% under 18, 10.0% over 64 (2000); Marriage status: 23.8% never married, 59.0% now married, 5.9% widowed, 11.3% divorced (2000); Foreign born: 2.7% (2000); Ancestry (includes multiple ancestries): 31.1% German, 27.8% Irish, 9.8% Other groups, 8.9% Italian, 8.9% English (2000).
Economy: Dairying. Resort village. Employment by occupation: 8.6% management, 22.6% professional, 15.8% services, 21.7% sales, 0.0% farming, 22.6% construction, 8.6% production (2000).

Income: Per capita income: $20,481 (2000); Median household income: $42,885 (2000); Poverty rate: 8.4% (2000).
Education: Percent of population age 25 and over with: High school diploma (including GED) or higher: 86.8% (2000); Bachelor's degree or higher: 19.1% (2000).
Housing: Homeownership rate: 79.8% (2000); Median home value: $86,100 (2000); Median rent: $413 per month (2000); Median age of housing: 42 years (2000).
Transportation: Commute to work: 92.2% car, 0.0% public transportation, 1.4% walk, 6.5% work from home (2000); Travel time to work: 35.5% less than 15 minutes, 26.6% 15 to 30 minutes, 21.7% 30 to 45 minutes, 3.9% 45 to 60 minutes, 12.3% 60 minutes or more (2000).

YULAN (unincorporated postal area, zip code 12792). Covers a land area of 1.545 square miles and a water area of 0.112 square miles. Located at 41.52° N. Lat.; 74.93° W. Long. Elevation is 1,061 feet.
Population: 0 (2000); Race: 100.0% White, 0.0% Black, 0.0% Asian, 5.3% Hispanic of any race (2000); Density: 0.0 persons per square mile (2000); Age: 16.6% under 18, 10.6% over 64 (2000); Marriage status: 31.5% never married, 60.1% now married, 5.2% widowed, 3.2% divorced (2000); Foreign born: 6.0% (2000); Ancestry (includes multiple ancestries): 24.7% German, 24.4% Irish, 12.0% Italian, 9.5% Other groups, 9.2% English (2000).
Economy: Employment by occupation: 9.8% management, 23.3% professional, 19.0% services, 25.8% sales, 0.0% farming, 10.4% construction, 11.7% production (2000).
Income: Per capita income: $22,984 (2000); Median household income: $51,250 (2000); Poverty rate: 6.4% (2000).
Education: Percent of population age 25 and over with: High school diploma (including GED) or higher: 89.2% (2000); Bachelor's degree or higher: 19.2% (2000).
Housing: Homeownership rate: 88.6% (2000); Median home value: $78,600 (2000); Median rent: $350 per month (2000); Median age of housing: 31 years (2000).
Transportation: Commute to work: 87.7% car, 12.3% public transportation, 0.0% walk, 0.0% work from home (2000); Travel time to work: 31.3% less than 15 minutes, 7.4% 15 to 30 minutes, 34.4% 30 to 45 minutes, 4.9% 45 to 60 minutes, 22.1% 60 minutes or more (2000).

Tioga County

Located in southern New York; bounded on the south by Pennsylvania; crossed by the Susquehanna River. Covers a land area of 518.69 square miles, a water area of 4.21 square miles, and is located in the Eastern Time Zone. The county government was organized in 1791. County seat is Owego.

Tioga County is part of the Binghamton, NY Metropolitan Statistical Area. The entire metro area includes: Broome County, NY; Tioga County, NY

Population: 52,337 (1990); 51,784 (2000); 51,785 (2005); 51,750 (2010 projected); Race: 97.0% White, 0.8% Black, 0.8% Asian, 1.6% Hispanic of any race (2005); Density: 99.8 persons per square mile (2005); Average household size: 2.58 (2005); Median age: 39.5 (2005); Males per 100 females: 97.9 (2005).
Religion: Five largest groups: 12.3% Catholic Church, 12.0% The United Methodist Church, 1.9% American Baptist Churches in the USA, 1.4% Presbyterian Church (U.S.A.), 1.3% Episcopal Church (2000).
Economy: Unemployment rate: 4.8% (2005); Total civilian labor force: 26,333 (2005); Leading industries: 12.5% retail trade; 7.3% health care and social assistance; 7.1% accommodation and food services (2003); Farms: 604 totaling 128,224 acres (2002); Companies that employ 500 or more persons: 2 (2003); Companies that employ 100 to 499 persons: 9 (2003); Companies that employ less than 100 persons: 758 (2003); Black-owned businesses: n/a (2002); Hispanic-owned businesses: n/a (2002); Women-owned businesses: n/a (2002); Retail sales per capita: $6,057 (2006). Single-family building permits issued: 73 (2005); Multi-family building permits issued: 0 (2005).
Income: Per capita income: $21,497 (2005); Median household income: $44,865 (2005); Average household income: $55,049 (2005); Percent of households with income of $100,000 or more: 11.4% (2005); Poverty rate: 9.6% (2003); Bankruptcy rate: 6.26% (2005).
Education: Percent of population age 25 and over with: High school diploma (including GED) or higher: 84.6% (2005); Bachelor's degree or higher: 19.6% (2005); Master's degree or higher: 7.8% (2005).
Housing: Homeownership rate: 77.9% (2005); Median home value: $92,689 (2005); Median rent: $372 per month (2000); Median age of housing: 37 years (2000).
Health: Birth rate: 117.6 per 10,000 population (2004); Death rate: 79.6 per 10,000 population (2004); Age-adjusted cancer mortality rate: 214.9 deaths per 100,000 population (2002); Number of physicians: 7.0 per 10,000 population (2004); Hospital beds: 0.0 per 10,000 population (2003); Hospital admissions: 0.0 per 10,000 population (2003).
Elections: 2004 Presidential election results: 57.6% Bush, 40.6% Kerry, 1.6% Nader, 0.2% Badnarik.
National and State Parks: Fairfield State Forest; Ketchumville State Forest; Oakley Corners State Forest; Robinson Hollow State Forest
Additional Information Contacts
Tioga County Government . . . . (607) 687-8200
  http://www.tiogacountyny.com/
Town of Berkshire . . . . (607) 657-2769
  http://berkshireny.com/

Tioga County Communities

APALACHIN (CDP). Covers a land area of 1.476 square miles and a water area of 0 square miles. Located at 42.07° N. Lat.; 76.15° W. Long. Elevation is 821 feet.
Population: 1,208 (1990); 1,126 (2000); 1,080 (2005); 1,051 (2010 projected); Race: 95.7% White, 1.7% Black, 0.6% Asian, 1.0% Hispanic of any race (2005); Density: 731.9 persons per square mile (2005); Average household size: 2.49 (2005); Median age: 38.0 (2005); Males per 100 females: 97.1 (2005); Marriage status: 31.9% never married, 54.9% now married, 3.5% widowed, 9.8% divorced (2000); Foreign born: 4.4% (2000); Ancestry (includes multiple ancestries): 23.2% English, 20.9% German, 17.0% Other groups, 11.5% Irish, 7.3% Italian (2000).
Economy: Employment by occupation: 11.4% management, 16.5% professional, 15.9% services, 32.2% sales, 0.0% farming, 7.6% construction, 16.4% production (2000).
Income: Per capita income: $18,738 (2005); Median household income: $41,500 (2005); Average household income: $46,236 (2005); Percent of households with income of $100,000 or more: 4.8% (2005); Poverty rate: 11.2% (2000).
Education: Percent of population age 25 and over with: High school diploma (including GED) or higher: 82.9% (2005); Bachelor's degree or higher: 12.0% (2005); Master's degree or higher: 2.5% (2005).
School District(s)
Owego-Apalachin Central School District (PK-12)
  2003-04 Enrollment: 2,337 . . . . (607) 687-6224
Vestal Central School District (KG-12)
  2003-04 Enrollment: 4,266 . . . . (607) 757-2241
Housing: Homeownership rate: 64.0% (2005); Median home value: $85,810 (2005); Median rent: $413 per month (2000); Median age of housing: 42 years (2000).
Transportation: Commute to work: 98.6% car, 0.0% public transportation, 0.0% walk, 1.4% work from home (2000); Travel time to work: 24.2% less than 15 minutes, 68.1% 15 to 30 minutes, 5.2% 30 to 45 minutes, 0.0% 45 to 60 minutes, 2.5% 60 minutes or more (2000)

BARTON (town). Covers a land area of 59.360 square miles and a water area of 0.366 square miles. Located at 42.05° N. Lat.; 76.51° W. Long.
Population: 8,925 (1990); 9,066 (2000); 9,134 (2005); 9,179 (2010 projected); Race: 97.8% White, 0.5% Black, 0.7% Asian, 1.6% Hispanic of any race (2005); Density: 153.9 persons per square mile (2005); Average household size: 2.50 (2005); Median age: 39.5 (2005); Males per 100 females: 92.1 (2005); Marriage status: 22.5% never married, 57.2% now married, 8.7% widowed, 11.7% divorced (2000); Foreign born: 0.9% (2000); Ancestry (includes multiple ancestries): 18.4% German, 16.1% English, 15.3% Irish, 8.2% Italian, 8.0% United States or American (2000).
Economy: Single-family building permits issued: 12 (2005); Multi-family building permits issued: 0 (2005); Employment by occupation: 6.5% management, 21.7% professional, 17.2% services, 22.8% sales, 1.0% farming, 10.1% construction, 20.7% production (2000).
Income: Per capita income: $17,988 (2005); Median household income: $37,762 (2005); Average household income: $44,256 (2005); Percent of households with income of $100,000 or more: 5.0% (2005); Poverty rate: 10.5% (2000).

Education: Percent of population age 25 and over with: High school diploma (including GED) or higher: 79.7% (2005); Bachelor's degree or higher: 12.9% (2005); Master's degree or higher: 6.0% (2005).
Housing: Homeownership rate: 69.4% (2005); Median home value: $85,847 (2005); Median rent: $354 per month (2000); Median age of housing: 51 years (2000).
Transportation: Commute to work: 93.5% car, 0.9% public transportation, 2.3% walk, 1.9% work from home (2000); Travel time to work: 42.3% less than 15 minutes, 28.3% 15 to 30 minutes, 18.5% 30 to 45 minutes, 7.4% 45 to 60 minutes, 3.4% 60 minutes or more (2000).

BERKSHIRE (town). Covers a land area of 30.215 square miles and a water area of 0.007 square miles. Located at 42.30° N. Lat.; 76.18° W. Long. Elevation is 1,056 feet.
Population: 1,303 (1990); 1,366 (2000); 1,393 (2005); 1,398 (2010 projected); Race: 98.6% White, 0.7% Black, 0.1% Asian, 0.7% Hispanic of any race (2005); Density: 46.1 persons per square mile (2005); Average household size: 2.65 (2005); Median age: 38.9 (2005); Males per 100 females: 105.5 (2005); Marriage status: 22.1% never married, 62.7% now married, 5.6% widowed, 9.6% divorced (2000); Foreign born: 1.9% (2000); Ancestry (includes multiple ancestries): 20.0% United States or American, 19.2% English, 15.8% German, 14.2% Irish, 6.9% Dutch (2000).
Economy: Single-family building permits issued: 2 (2005); Multi-family building permits issued: 0 (2005); Employment by occupation: 13.0% management, 13.3% professional, 14.3% services, 22.6% sales, 2.3% farming, 8.7% construction, 25.8% production (2000).
Income: Per capita income: $19,776 (2005); Median household income: $41,743 (2005); Average household income: $52,372 (2005); Percent of households with income of $100,000 or more: 9.3% (2005); Poverty rate: 11.4% (2000).
Taxes: Total city taxes per capita: $233 (2004); City property taxes per capita: $215 (2004).
Education: Percent of population age 25 and over with: High school diploma (including GED) or higher: 82.5% (2005); Bachelor's degree or higher: 14.4% (2005); Master's degree or higher: 3.9% (2005).
Housing: Homeownership rate: 84.2% (2005); Median home value: $78,081 (2005); Median rent: $384 per month (2000); Median age of housing: 37 years (2000).
Transportation: Commute to work: 89.2% car, 2.2% public transportation, 2.5% walk, 6.0% work from home (2000); Travel time to work: 14.4% less than 15 minutes, 20.1% 15 to 30 minutes, 43.2% 30 to 45 minutes, 16.8% 45 to 60 minutes, 5.5% 60 minutes or more (2000).
Additional Information Contacts
Town of Berkshire . . . . (607) 657-2769
http://berkshireny.com/

CANDOR (village). Covers a land area of 0.443 square miles and a water area of 0 square miles. Located at 42.23° N. Lat.; 76.33° W. Long.
Population: 869 (1990); 855 (2000); 832 (2005); 822 (2010 projected); Race: 96.0% White, 0.7% Black, 0.2% Asian, 2.4% Hispanic of any race (2005); Density: 1,879.9 persons per square mile (2005); Average household size: 2.40 (2005); Median age: 35.2 (2005); Males per 100 females: 87.0 (2005); Marriage status: 22.3% never married, 55.8% now married, 9.3% widowed, 12.6% divorced (2000); Foreign born: 0.0% (2000); Ancestry (includes multiple ancestries): 19.1% Irish, 15.4% English, 14.7% German, 14.6% United States or American, 10.0% Other groups (2000).
Economy: Single-family building permits issued: 0 (2005); Multi-family building permits issued: 0 (2005); Employment by occupation: 8.5% management, 18.0% professional, 20.9% services, 27.2% sales, 1.2% farming, 7.0% construction, 17.2% production (2000).
Income: Per capita income: $18,206 (2005); Median household income: $34,052 (2005); Average household income: $43,653 (2005); Percent of households with income of $100,000 or more: 7.5% (2005); Poverty rate: 11.9% (2000).
Education: Percent of population age 25 and over with: High school diploma (including GED) or higher: 83.2% (2005); Bachelor's degree or higher: 14.3% (2005); Master's degree or higher: 7.7% (2005).
School District(s)
Candor Central School District (KG-12)
    2003-04 Enrollment: 928 . . . . (607) 659-5010
Housing: Homeownership rate: 61.4% (2005); Median home value: $77,174 (2005); Median rent: $366 per month (2000); Median age of housing: 60+ years (2000).
Transportation: Commute to work: 87.7% car, 1.0% public transportation, 6.4% walk, 3.2% work from home (2000); Travel time to work: 18.3% less than 15 minutes, 24.4% 15 to 30 minutes, 39.2% 30 to 45 minutes, 12.0% 45 to 60 minutes, 6.1% 60 minutes or more (2000).

CANDOR (town). Covers a land area of 94.530 square miles and a water area of 0.064 square miles. Located at 42.23° N. Lat.; 76.33° W. Long.
Population: 5,310 (1990); 5,317 (2000); 5,296 (2005); 5,283 (2010 projected); Race: 96.7% White, 1.4% Black, 0.3% Asian, 1.4% Hispanic of any race (2005); Density: 56.0 persons per square mile (2005); Average household size: 2.58 (2005); Median age: 37.8 (2005); Males per 100 females: 97.1 (2005); Marriage status: 21.0% never married, 61.4% now married, 5.6% widowed, 12.0% divorced (2000); Foreign born: 1.4% (2000); Ancestry (includes multiple ancestries): 17.3% German, 15.3% English, 13.1% Irish, 8.5% United States or American, 8.4% Other groups (2000).
Economy: Agriculture: dairy products; poultry; grain. Single-family building permits issued: 7 (2005); Multi-family building permits issued: 0 (2005); Employment by occupation: 13.7% management, 17.9% professional, 15.2% services, 21.7% sales, 2.3% farming, 10.1% construction, 19.0% production (2000).
Income: Per capita income: $20,211 (2005); Median household income: $41,406 (2005); Average household income: $52,049 (2005); Percent of households with income of $100,000 or more: 9.3% (2005); Poverty rate: 9.8% (2000).
Taxes: Total city taxes per capita: $185 (2004); City property taxes per capita: $170 (2004).
Education: Percent of population age 25 and over with: High school diploma (including GED) or higher: 82.8% (2005); Bachelor's degree or higher: 12.2% (2005); Master's degree or higher: 2.9% (2005).
Housing: Homeownership rate: 78.1% (2005); Median home value: $82,456 (2005); Median rent: $373 per month (2000); Median age of housing: 31 years (2000).
Transportation: Commute to work: 90.1% car, 0.2% public transportation, 3.1% walk, 6.0% work from home (2000); Travel time to work: 18.4% less than 15 minutes, 36.5% 15 to 30 minutes, 30.2% 30 to 45 minutes, 8.6% 45 to 60 minutes, 6.3% 60 minutes or more (2000).

LOCKWOOD (unincorporated postal area, zip code 14859). Covers a land area of 37.196 square miles and a water area of 0.042 square miles. Located at 42.11° N. Lat.; 76.54° W. Long.
Population: 0 (2000); Race: 99.3% White, 0.0% Black, 0.0% Asian, 0.7% Hispanic of any race (2000); Density: 0.0 persons per square mile (2000); Age: 30.2% under 18, 11.2% over 64 (2000); Marriage status: 14.7% never married, 65.7% now married, 8.1% widowed, 11.5% divorced (2000); Foreign born: 3.0% (2000); Ancestry (includes multiple ancestries): 17.5% Irish, 16.0% German, 9.2% English, 6.7% United States or American, 6.6% Polish (2000).
Economy: Employment by occupation: 8.0% management, 14.1% professional, 14.7% services, 24.0% sales, 0.0% farming, 14.9% construction, 24.2% production (2000).
Income: Per capita income: $14,636 (2000); Median household income: $33,958 (2000); Poverty rate: 8.2% (2000).
Education: Percent of population age 25 and over with: High school diploma (including GED) or higher: 83.3% (2000); Bachelor's degree or higher: 14.6% (2000).
Housing: Homeownership rate: 90.0% (2000); Median home value: $67,500 (2000); Median rent: $412 per month (2000); Median age of housing: 32 years (2000).
Transportation: Commute to work: 94.9% car, 0.0% public transportation, 0.0% walk, 5.1% work from home (2000); Travel time to work: 4.7% less than 15 minutes, 43.8% 15 to 30 minutes, 30.8% 30 to 45 minutes, 14.3% 45 to 60 minutes, 6.5% 60 minutes or more (2000).

NEWARK VALLEY (village). Covers a land area of 0.977 square miles and a water area of 0 square miles. Located at 42.22° N. Lat.; 76.18° W. Long. Elevation is 1,076 feet.
Population: 1,082 (1990); 1,071 (2000); 1,094 (2005); 1,115 (2010 projected); Race: 96.6% White, 1.6% Black, 0.0% Asian, 2.2% Hispanic of any race (2005); Density: 1,120.1 persons per square mile (2005); Average household size: 2.68 (2005); Median age: 36.9 (2005); Males per 100 females: 99.3 (2005); Marriage status: 23.1% never married, 58.1% now married, 9.2% widowed, 9.6% divorced (2000); Foreign born: 1.6% (2000);

Ancestry (includes multiple ancestries): 20.0% German, 19.7% Irish, 17.1% English, 11.0% Italian, 6.5% United States or American (2000).
Economy: Single-family building permits issued: 0 (2005); Multi-family building permits issued: 0 (2005); Employment by occupation: 7.3% management, 25.2% professional, 21.3% services, 20.5% sales, 0.8% farming, 5.5% construction, 19.5% production (2000).
Income: Per capita income: $18,869 (2005); Median household income: $41,947 (2005); Average household income: $49,951 (2005); Percent of households with income of $100,000 or more: 9.1% (2005); Poverty rate: 12.3% (2000).
Education: Percent of population age 25 and over with: High school diploma (including GED) or higher: 86.5% (2005); Bachelor's degree or higher: 23.6% (2005); Master's degree or higher: 8.8% (2005).

School District(s)
Newark Valley Central School District (KG-12)
    2003-04 Enrollment: 1,402 . . . . (607) 642-3221
Housing: Homeownership rate: 72.8% (2005); Median home value: $87,439 (2005); Median rent: $356 per month (2000); Median age of housing: 60+ years (2000).
Transportation: Commute to work: 85.3% car, 1.0% public transportation, 7.5% walk, 5.8% work from home (2000); Travel time to work: 33.6% less than 15 minutes, 35.2% 15 to 30 minutes, 21.3% 30 to 45 minutes, 7.7% 45 to 60 minutes, 2.2% 60 minutes or more (2000)

NEWARK VALLEY (town). Covers a land area of 50.328 square miles and a water area of 0.083 square miles. Located at 42.22° N. Lat.; 76.16° W. Long. Elevation is 1,076 feet.
Population: 4,189 (1990); 4,097 (2000); 4,275 (2005); 4,401 (2010 projected); Race: 97.6% White, 0.7% Black, 0.5% Asian, 1.0% Hispanic of any race (2005); Density: 84.9 persons per square mile (2005); Average household size: 2.70 (2005); Median age: 37.9 (2005); Males per 100 females: 103.2 (2005); Marriage status: 20.0% never married, 66.9% now married, 5.7% widowed, 7.5% divorced (2000); Foreign born: 2.1% (2000); Ancestry (includes multiple ancestries): 20.2% English, 16.3% German, 13.7% Irish, 11.0% Italian, 9.3% United States or American (2000).
Economy: Wood products. Single-family building permits issued: 5 (2005); Multi-family building permits issued: 0 (2005); Employment by occupation: 8.6% management, 23.2% professional, 13.3% services, 19.6% sales, 1.5% farming, 10.8% construction, 23.0% production (2000).
Income: Per capita income: $20,270 (2005); Median household income: $45,756 (2005); Average household income: $54,470 (2005); Percent of households with income of $100,000 or more: 10.2% (2005); Poverty rate: 7.3% (2000).
Education: Percent of population age 25 and over with: High school diploma (including GED) or higher: 85.1% (2005); Bachelor's degree or higher: 19.3% (2005); Master's degree or higher: 6.8% (2005).
Housing: Homeownership rate: 83.5% (2005); Median home value: $88,935 (2005); Median rent: $336 per month (2000); Median age of housing: 35 years (2000).
Transportation: Commute to work: 94.3% car, 0.2% public transportation, 2.1% walk, 2.2% work from home (2000); Travel time to work: 21.1% less than 15 minutes, 36.0% 15 to 30 minutes, 27.6% 30 to 45 minutes, 9.4% 45 to 60 minutes, 6.0% 60 minutes or more (2000)

NICHOLS (village). Covers a land area of 0.511 square miles and a water area of 0 square miles. Located at 42.02° N. Lat.; 76.36° W. Long. Elevation is 789 feet.
Population: 573 (1990); 574 (2000); 548 (2005); 538 (2010 projected); Race: 99.6% White, 0.2% Black, 0.2% Asian, 1.6% Hispanic of any race (2005); Density: 1,073.0 persons per square mile (2005); Average household size: 2.62 (2005); Median age: 36.5 (2005); Males per 100 females: 98.6 (2005); Marriage status: 21.0% never married, 60.4% now married, 9.7% widowed, 8.9% divorced (2000); Foreign born: 0.5% (2000); Ancestry (includes multiple ancestries): 20.3% Irish, 19.0% English, 17.9% United States or American, 14.1% German, 6.4% Other groups (2000).
Economy: Single-family building permits issued: 0 (2005); Multi-family building permits issued: 0 (2005); Employment by occupation: 12.6% management, 21.3% professional, 14.3% services, 17.8% sales, 0.9% farming, 11.3% construction, 21.7% production (2000).
Income: Per capita income: $17,678 (2005); Median household income: $40,802 (2005); Average household income: $46,352 (2005); Percent of households with income of $100,000 or more: 6.7% (2005); Poverty rate: 15.0% (2000).
Education: Percent of population age 25 and over with: High school diploma (including GED) or higher: 83.2% (2005); Bachelor's degree or higher: 14.2% (2005); Master's degree or higher: 6.1% (2005).

School District(s)
Tioga Central School District (KG-12)
    2003-04 Enrollment: 1,164 . . . . (607) 687-8000
Housing: Homeownership rate: 63.2% (2005); Median home value: $80,714 (2005); Median rent: $346 per month (2000); Median age of housing: 60+ years (2000).
Transportation: Commute to work: 94.3% car, 0.0% public transportation, 5.2% walk, 0.4% work from home (2000); Travel time to work: 23.7% less than 15 minutes, 43.9% 15 to 30 minutes, 25.0% 30 to 45 minutes, 4.8% 45 to 60 minutes, 2.6% 60 minutes or more (2000)

NICHOLS (town). Covers a land area of 33.700 square miles and a water area of 0.956 square miles. Located at 42.02° N. Lat.; 76.36° W. Long. Elevation is 789 feet.
Population: 2,525 (1990); 2,584 (2000); 2,576 (2005); 2,606 (2010 projected); Race: 98.7% White, 0.6% Black, 0.3% Asian, 1.4% Hispanic of any race (2005); Density: 76.4 persons per square mile (2005); Average household size: 2.62 (2005); Median age: 39.6 (2005); Males per 100 females: 98.6 (2005); Marriage status: 22.4% never married, 61.5% now married, 8.3% widowed, 7.8% divorced (2000); Foreign born: 1.5% (2000); Ancestry (includes multiple ancestries): 22.0% English, 16.5% German, 15.6% Irish, 11.8% United States or American, 10.0% Other groups (2000).
Economy: Single-family building permits issued: 5 (2005); Multi-family building permits issued: 0 (2005); Employment by occupation: 12.2% management, 17.8% professional, 13.1% services, 22.3% sales, 2.5% farming, 10.4% construction, 21.6% production (2000).
Income: Per capita income: $17,887 (2005); Median household income: $40,402 (2005); Average household income: $46,827 (2005); Percent of households with income of $100,000 or more: 6.6% (2005); Poverty rate: 13.6% (2000).
Education: Percent of population age 25 and over with: High school diploma (including GED) or higher: 82.1% (2005); Bachelor's degree or higher: 13.5% (2005); Master's degree or higher: 5.7% (2005).
Housing: Homeownership rate: 80.1% (2005); Median home value: $82,024 (2005); Median rent: $351 per month (2000); Median age of housing: 45 years (2000).
Transportation: Commute to work: 91.7% car, 0.3% public transportation, 2.8% walk, 4.1% work from home (2000); Travel time to work: 23.3% less than 15 minutes, 42.1% 15 to 30 minutes, 26.9% 30 to 45 minutes, 4.1% 45 to 60 minutes, 3.5% 60 minutes or more (2000)

OWEGO (village). Covers a land area of 2.496 square miles and a water area of 0.219 square miles. Located at 42.10° N. Lat.; 76.26° W. Long. Elevation is 817 feet.
Population: 4,442 (1990); 3,911 (2000); 3,772 (2005); 3,622 (2010 projected); Race: 94.1% White, 1.9% Black, 1.8% Asian, 3.0% Hispanic of any race (2005); Density: 1,511.0 persons per square mile (2005); Average household size: 2.31 (2005); Median age: 39.9 (2005); Males per 100 females: 94.9 (2005); Marriage status: 27.8% never married, 52.6% now married, 9.6% widowed, 10.1% divorced (2000); Foreign born: 3.9% (2000); Ancestry (includes multiple ancestries): 18.2% Irish, 17.5% German, 15.2% English, 10.2% Other groups, 9.3% United States or American (2000).
Economy: Single-family building permits issued: 4 (2005); Multi-family building permits issued: 0 (2005); Employment by occupation: 7.5% management, 19.9% professional, 17.9% services, 30.0% sales, 1.1% farming, 4.3% construction, 19.2% production (2000).
Income: Per capita income: $17,942 (2005); Median household income: $32,863 (2005); Average household income: $40,355 (2005); Percent of households with income of $100,000 or more: 5.8% (2005); Poverty rate: 13.9% (2000).
Education: Percent of population age 25 and over with: High school diploma (including GED) or higher: 80.7% (2005); Bachelor's degree or higher: 22.3% (2005); Master's degree or higher: 9.3% (2005).

School District(s)
Owego-Apalachin Central School District (PK-12)
    2003-04 Enrollment: 2,337 . . . . (607) 687-6224
Housing: Homeownership rate: 50.0% (2005); Median home value: $82,815 (2005); Median rent: $377 per month (2000); Median age of housing: 60+ years (2000).
Safety: Violent crime rate: 26.2 per 10,000 population; Property crime rate: 144.1 per 10,000 population (2004).

Newspapers: Tioga County Courier (General - Circulation 1,340)
Transportation: Commute to work: 84.4% car, 2.2% public transportation, 9.2% walk, 2.0% work from home (2000); Travel time to work: 50.7% less than 15 minutes, 24.0% 15 to 30 minutes, 18.1% 30 to 45 minutes, 2.4% 45 to 60 minutes, 4.9% 60 minutes or more (2000)
Additional Information Contacts
Tioga County Chamber of Commerce . . . . (607) 687-2020
  http://www.tiogachamber.com

OWEGO (town).
Covers a land area of 104.168 square miles and a water area of 1.604 square miles. Located at 42.09° N. Lat.; 76.19° W. Long. Elevation is 817 feet.
History: Owego came into existence as Ah-wah-ga, "where the valley widens." Thomas C. Platt born here. Settled in 1787 and incorporated in 1827 on site of Native American village destroyed (1779) in Sullivan campaign.
Population: 21,279 (1990); 20,365 (2000); 20,161 (2005); 19,919 (2010 projected); Race: 96.0% White, 1.0% Black, 1.5% Asian, 1.8% Hispanic of any race (2005); Density: 193.5 persons per square mile (2005); Average household size: 2.59 (2005); Median age: 40.7 (2005); Males per 100 females: 99.3 (2005); Marriage status: 20.7% never married, 66.1% now married, 5.2% widowed, 8.0% divorced (2000); Foreign born: 2.2% (2000); Ancestry (includes multiple ancestries): 19.7% German, 18.0% Irish, 18.0% English, 10.6% Italian, 7.8% United States or American (2000).
Economy: Railroad junction. Manufacturing: hardwood lumber, computers, railroad items, iron castings. Agriculture: dairy products; poultry. Single-family building permits issued: 25 (2005); Multi-family building permits issued: 0 (2005); Employment by occupation: 12.5% management, 29.0% professional, 12.2% services, 25.2% sales, 0.4% farming, 6.3% construction, 14.4% production (2000).
Income: Per capita income: $25,061 (2005); Median household income: $53,263 (2005); Average household income: $64,330 (2005); Percent of households with income of $100,000 or more: 16.8% (2005); Poverty rate: 6.6% (2000).
Taxes: Total city taxes per capita: $119 (2004); City property taxes per capita: $88 (2004).
Education: Percent of population age 25 and over with: High school diploma (including GED) or higher: 89.6% (2005); Bachelor's degree or higher: 27.7% (2005); Master's degree or higher: 11.2% (2005).
Housing: Homeownership rate: 78.9% (2005); Median home value: $111,125 (2005); Median rent: $390 per month (2000); Median age of housing: 37 years (2000).
Transportation: Commute to work: 93.4% car, 0.7% public transportation, 2.3% walk, 2.6% work from home (2000); Travel time to work: 29.2% less than 15 minutes, 49.6% 15 to 30 minutes, 14.9% 30 to 45 minutes, 2.8% 45 to 60 minutes, 3.3% 60 minutes or more (2000)

RICHFORD (town).
Covers a land area of 38.167 square miles and a water area of 0.021 square miles. Located at 42.36° N. Lat.; 76.18° W. Long.
Population: 1,153 (1990); 1,170 (2000); 1,076 (2005); 1,057 (2010 projected); Race: 99.0% White, 0.1% Black, 0.0% Asian, 1.4% Hispanic of any race (2005); Density: 28.2 persons per square mile (2005); Average household size: 2.61 (2005); Median age: 38.6 (2005); Males per 100 females: 97.8 (2005); Marriage status: 25.5% never married, 56.9% now married, 6.0% widowed, 11.6% divorced (2000); Foreign born: 0.9% (2000); Ancestry (includes multiple ancestries): 21.6% United States or American, 16.9% German, 14.8% English, 10.6% Irish, 9.2% Other groups (2000).
Economy: Single-family building permits issued: 1 (2005); Multi-family building permits issued: 0 (2005); Employment by occupation: 10.6% management, 10.8% professional, 20.1% services, 22.8% sales, 0.4% farming, 11.6% construction, 23.7% production (2000).
Income: Per capita income: $18,532 (2005); Median household income: $42,607 (2005); Average household income: $48,281 (2005); Percent of households with income of $100,000 or more: 6.3% (2005); Poverty rate: 13.8% (2000).
Education: Percent of population age 25 and over with: High school diploma (including GED) or higher: 75.0% (2005); Bachelor's degree or higher: 9.4% (2005); Master's degree or higher: 3.6% (2005).
Housing: Homeownership rate: 82.1% (2005); Median home value: $63,125 (2005); Median rent: $383 per month (2000); Median age of housing: 28 years (2000).
Transportation: Commute to work: 93.0% car, 2.7% public transportation, 1.6% walk, 2.7% work from home (2000); Travel time to work: 8.2% less than 15 minutes, 30.7% 15 to 30 minutes, 42.6% 30 to 45 minutes, 11.4% 45 to 60 minutes, 7.0% 60 minutes or more (2000)

SPENCER (village).
Covers a land area of 1.033 square miles and a water area of 0.012 square miles. Located at 42.21° N. Lat.; 76.49° W. Long. Elevation is 999 feet.
Population: 815 (1990); 731 (2000); 735 (2005); 737 (2010 projected); Race: 97.7% White, 1.0% Black, 0.4% Asian, 0.8% Hispanic of any race (2005); Density: 711.8 persons per square mile (2005); Average household size: 2.42 (2005); Median age: 39.6 (2005); Males per 100 females: 88.5 (2005); Marriage status: 19.4% never married, 60.5% now married, 7.3% widowed, 12.8% divorced (2000); Foreign born: 2.3% (2000); Ancestry (includes multiple ancestries): 16.6% United States or American, 14.6% English, 13.4% German, 10.2% Irish, 9.7% Italian (2000).
Economy: Single-family building permits issued: 0 (2005); Multi-family building permits issued: 0 (2005); Employment by occupation: 9.7% management, 16.5% professional, 19.4% services, 28.8% sales, 0.3% farming, 10.5% construction, 14.8% production (2000).
Income: Per capita income: $16,438 (2005); Median household income: $36,027 (2005); Average household income: $39,449 (2005); Percent of households with income of $100,000 or more: 3.3% (2005); Poverty rate: 14.1% (2000).
Education: Percent of population age 25 and over with: High school diploma (including GED) or higher: 84.8% (2005); Bachelor's degree or higher: 15.2% (2005); Master's degree or higher: 6.5% (2005).
School District(s)
Spencer-Van Etten Central School District (PK-12)
  2003-04 Enrollment: 1,147 . . . . (607) 589-7100
Housing: Homeownership rate: 65.8% (2005); Median home value: $88,824 (2005); Median rent: $379 per month (2000); Median age of housing: 60+ years (2000).
Transportation: Commute to work: 92.8% car, 0.9% public transportation, 1.7% walk, 4.0% work from home (2000); Travel time to work: 18.6% less than 15 minutes, 22.2% 15 to 30 minutes, 42.0% 30 to 45 minutes, 9.3% 45 to 60 minutes, 7.8% 60 minutes or more (2000)

SPENCER (town).
Covers a land area of 49.549 square miles and a water area of 0.335 square miles. Located at 42.21° N. Lat.; 76.48° W. Long. Elevation is 999 feet.
Population: 2,881 (1990); 2,979 (2000); 3,000 (2005); 3,025 (2010 projected); Race: 96.8% White, 0.8% Black, 0.6% Asian, 1.9% Hispanic of any race (2005); Density: 60.5 persons per square mile (2005); Average household size: 2.53 (2005); Median age: 38.3 (2005); Males per 100 females: 97.8 (2005); Marriage status: 20.7% never married, 62.8% now married, 5.7% widowed, 10.8% divorced (2000); Foreign born: 2.2% (2000); Ancestry (includes multiple ancestries): 18.1% German, 16.1% English, 13.9% Irish, 9.8% United States or American, 8.3% Italian (2000).
Economy: In agricultural area: dairy products; poultry; grain. Single-family building permits issued: 3 (2005); Multi-family building permits issued: 0 (2005); Employment by occupation: 11.3% management, 18.8% professional, 14.6% services, 23.1% sales, 2.4% farming, 13.9% construction, 15.9% production (2000).
Income: Per capita income: $18,674 (2005); Median household income: $41,870 (2005); Average household income: $47,200 (2005); Percent of households with income of $100,000 or more: 5.9% (2005); Poverty rate: 8.5% (2000).
Taxes: Total city taxes per capita: $200 (2004); City property taxes per capita: $188 (2004).
Education: Percent of population age 25 and over with: High school diploma (including GED) or higher: 85.8% (2005); Bachelor's degree or higher: 16.5% (2005); Master's degree or higher: 6.4% (2005).
Housing: Homeownership rate: 79.4% (2005); Median home value: $86,686 (2005); Median rent: $378 per month (2000); Median age of housing: 34 years (2000).
Transportation: Commute to work: 92.9% car, 1.4% public transportation, 2.4% walk, 3.1% work from home (2000); Travel time to work: 17.5% less than 15 minutes, 20.0% 15 to 30 minutes, 46.6% 30 to 45 minutes, 10.7% 45 to 60 minutes, 5.1% 60 minutes or more (2000)

TIOGA (town).
Covers a land area of 58.676 square miles and a water area of 0.777 square miles. Located at 42.09° N. Lat.; 76.36° W. Long.
Population: 4,772 (1990); 4,840 (2000); 4,874 (2005); 4,882 (2010 projected); Race: 98.0% White, 0.3% Black, 0.3% Asian, 1.3% Hispanic of any race (2005); Density: 83.1 persons per square mile (2005); Average household size: 2.57 (2005); Median age: 39.1 (2005); Males per 100

females: 97.3 (2005); Marriage status: 20.8% never married, 63.4% now married, 5.7% widowed, 10.1% divorced (2000); Foreign born: 0.6% (2000); Ancestry (includes multiple ancestries): 23.7% German, 20.2% English, 12.6% Irish, 10.6% United States or American, 8.4% Other groups (2000).
Economy: Single-family building permits issued: 9 (2005); Multi-family building permits issued: 0 (2005); Employment by occupation: 8.7% management, 20.3% professional, 13.1% services, 22.7% sales, 0.3% farming, 10.6% construction, 24.4% production (2000).
Income: Per capita income: $20,597 (2005); Median household income: $42,175 (2005); Average household income: $52,865 (2005); Percent of households with income of $100,000 or more: 12.9% (2005); Poverty rate: 6.5% (2000).
Education: Percent of population age 25 and over with: High school diploma (including GED) or higher: 78.2% (2005); Bachelor's degree or higher: 15.2% (2005); Master's degree or higher: 6.5% (2005).
Housing: Homeownership rate: 80.7% (2005); Median home value: $72,622 (2005); Median rent: $371 per month (2000); Median age of housing: 29 years (2000).
Transportation: Commute to work: 93.6% car, 0.3% public transportation, 0.6% walk, 4.6% work from home (2000); Travel time to work: 25.7% less than 15 minutes, 30.5% 15 to 30 minutes, 27.0% 30 to 45 minutes, 10.0% 45 to 60 minutes, 6.8% 60 minutes or more (2000).

WAVERLY
(village). Covers a land area of 2.288 square miles and a water area of 0.050 square miles. Located at 42.00° N. Lat.; 76.53° W. Long. Elevation is 826 feet.
History: Incorporated 1853.
Population: 4,847 (1990); 4,607 (2000); 4,499 (2005); 4,375 (2010 projected); Race: 97.1% White, 0.8% Black, 0.8% Asian, 1.9% Hispanic of any race (2005); Density: 1,966.1 persons per square mile (2005); Average household size: 2.41 (2005); Median age: 40.4 (2005); Males per 100 females: 86.2 (2005); Marriage status: 24.2% never married, 51.6% now married, 12.5% widowed, 11.7% divorced (2000); Foreign born: 1.2% (2000); Ancestry (includes multiple ancestries): 17.6% English, 15.8% Irish, 13.9% German, 8.8% Italian, 8.1% United States or American (2000).
Economy: Manufacturing: feed, commercial beeswax, beekeeping supplies, livestock feed supplements, electric insulating varnishes. Agriculture: dairy products; poultry; bees and honey. Specialized medical facility with neighboring community of Sayre, Pennsylvania. Single-family building permits issued: 0 (2005); Multi-family building permits issued: 0 (2005); Employment by occupation: 6.7% management, 24.7% professional, 17.1% services, 23.0% sales, 0.5% farming, 8.8% construction, 19.2% production (2000).
Income: Per capita income: $17,003 (2005); Median household income: $32,529 (2005); Average household income: $39,671 (2005); Percent of households with income of $100,000 or more: 3.8% (2005); Poverty rate: 13.3% (2000).
Education: Percent of population age 25 and over with: High school diploma (including GED) or higher: 80.2% (2005); Bachelor's degree or higher: 14.9% (2005); Master's degree or higher: 6.8% (2005).

School District(s)
Waverly Central School District (KG-12)
    2003-04 Enrollment: 1,786 . . . . (607) 565-2841

Housing: Homeownership rate: 55.4% (2005); Median home value: $88,108 (2005); Median rent: $361 per month (2000); Median age of housing: 60+ years (2000).
Safety: Violent crime rate: 6.6 per 10,000 population; Property crime rate: 329.4 per 10,000 population (2004).
Transportation: Commute to work: 92.6% car, 1.5% public transportation, 3.5% walk, 0.6% work from home (2000); Travel time to work: 52.4% less than 15 minutes, 21.9% 15 to 30 minutes, 17.7% 30 to 45 minutes, 4.9% 45 to 60 minutes, 3.1% 60 minutes or more (2000).

WILLSEYVILLE
(unincorporated postal area, zip code 13864). Covers a land area of 23.514 square miles and a water area of 0 square miles. Located at 42.29° N. Lat.; 76.38° W. Long.
Population: 0 (2000); Race: 97.3% White, 0.5% Black, 0.0% Asian, 0.0% Hispanic of any race (2000); Density: 0.0 persons per square mile (2000); Age: 20.4% under 18, 13.6% over 64 (2000); Marriage status: 24.0% never married, 59.9% now married, 5.5% widowed, 10.6% divorced (2000); Foreign born: 0.6% (2000); Ancestry (includes multiple ancestries): 21.1% German, 20.4% Irish, 13.4% United States or American, 12.0% Italian, 11.9% Other groups (2000).

Economy: Employment by occupation: 8.3% management, 12.6% professional, 18.5% services, 30.7% sales, 3.1% farming, 16.2% construction, 10.5% production (2000).
Income: Per capita income: $20,168 (2000); Median household income: $41,026 (2000); Poverty rate: 10.2% (2000).
Education: Percent of population age 25 and over with: High school diploma (including GED) or higher: 81.3% (2000); Bachelor's degree or higher: 11.6% (2000).
Housing: Homeownership rate: 83.0% (2000); Median home value: $66,300 (2000); Median rent: $375 per month (2000); Median age of housing: 37 years (2000).
Transportation: Commute to work: 94.4% car, 1.6% public transportation, 0.9% walk, 3.1% work from home (2000); Travel time to work: 2.4% less than 15 minutes, 53.3% 15 to 30 minutes, 36.6% 30 to 45 minutes, 3.0% 45 to 60 minutes, 4.7% 60 minutes or more (2000).

Tompkins County

Located in west central New York; includes part of Cayuga Lake. Covers a land area of 476.05 square miles, a water area of 15.57 square miles, and is located in the Eastern Time Zone. The county government was organized in 1817. County seat is Ithaca.

Tompkins County is part of the Ithaca, NY Metropolitan Statistical Area. The entire metro area includes: Tompkins County, NY

Weather Station: Ithaca Cornell University   Elevation: 958 feet

	Jan	Feb	Mar	Apr	May	Jun	Jul	Aug	Sep	Oct	Nov	Dec
High	30	32	41	54	67	75	80	78	70	59	47	36
Low	14	14	23	34	44	53	57	56	49	38	31	21
Precip	2.1	2.0	2.5	3.2	3.2	3.8	3.7	3.5	3.9	3.3	3.2	2.5
Snow	17.6	14.1	12.2	3.7	0.1	0.0	0.0	0.0	0.0	0.6	5.8	13.8

High and Low temperatures in degrees Fahrenheit; Precipitation and Snow in inches

Population: 94,097 (1990); 96,501 (2000); 103,641 (2005); 111,078 (2010 projected); Race: 82.2% White, 4.0% Black, 9.5% Asian, 3.8% Hispanic of any race (2005); Density: 217.7 persons per square mile (2005); Average household size: 2.59 (2005); Median age: 30.8 (2005); Males per 100 females: 98.9 (2005).
Religion: Five largest groups: 10.5% Catholic Church, 3.7% The United Methodist Church, 2.1% Jewish Estimate, 1.5% United Church of Christ, 1.2% Assemblies of God (2000).
Economy: Unemployment rate: 3.2% (2005); Total civilian labor force: 54,658 (2005); Leading industries: 10.7% retail trade; 10.2% health care and social assistance; 9.1% accommodation and food services (2003); Farms: 563 totaling 100,931 acres (2002); Companies that employ 500 or more persons: 4 (2003); Companies that employ 100 to 499 persons: 37 (2003); Companies that employ less than 100 persons: 2,146 (2003); Black-owned businesses: n/a (2002); Hispanic-owned businesses: n/a (2002); Women-owned businesses: 2,474 (2002); Retail sales per capita: $9,128 (2006). Single-family building permits issued: 224 (2005); Multi-family building permits issued: 116 (2005).
Income: Per capita income: $23,018 (2005); Median household income: $42,359 (2005); Average household income: $58,210 (2005); Percent of households with income of $100,000 or more: 14.2% (2005); Poverty rate: 12.9% (2003); Bankruptcy rate: 3.88% (2005).
Taxes: Total county taxes per capita: $606 (2004); County property taxes per capita: $231 (2004).
Education: Percent of population age 25 and over with: High school diploma (including GED) or higher: 91.5% (2005); Bachelor's degree or higher: 48.8% (2005); Master's degree or higher: 27.5% (2005).
Housing: Homeownership rate: 54.2% (2005); Median home value: $137,812 (2005); Median rent: $529 per month (2000); Median age of housing: 35 years (2000).
Health: Birth rate: 80.3 per 10,000 population (2004); Death rate: 55.0 per 10,000 population (2004); Age-adjusted cancer mortality rate: 198.1 deaths per 100,000 population (2002); Number of physicians: 23.8 per 10,000 population (2004); Hospital beds: 14.9 per 10,000 population (2003); Hospital admissions: 703.7 per 10,000 population (2003).
Elections: 2004 Presidential election results: 33.0% Bush, 64.2% Kerry, 2.2% Nader, 0.5% Badnarik
National and State Parks: Buttermilk Falls State Park; Buttermilk Falls State Park; Danby State Forest; Hammond Hill State Forest; Newfield State Forest; Potato Hill State Forest; Robert H Treman State Park; Shindagin Hollow State Forest; Taughannock Falls State Park; Yellow Barn State Forest

Additional Information Contacts

Tompkins County Government	(607) 274-5434
http://www.co.tompkins.ny.us/	
City of Ithaca	(607) 274-6570
http://www.ci.ithaca.ny.us/	
Town of Dryden	(607) 844-8619
http://www.dryden.ny.us/	
Town of Ithaca	(607) 273-1721
http://www.town.ithaca.ny.us/	
Town of Lansing	(607) 533-8896
http://www.lansingtown.com/	
Town of Ulysses	(607) 387-5767
http://www.trumansburg.ny.us/ulysses/	
Village of Dryden	(607) 844-8622
http://www.dryden-ny.org/	
Village of Lansing	(607) 533-4142
http://people.clarityconnect.com/webpages/vlansing/	
Village of Trumansburg	(607) 387-6501
http://www.trumansburg.ny.us/	

Tompkins County Communities

BROOKTONDALE (unincorporated postal area, zip code 14817). Covers a land area of 45.156 square miles and a water area of 0.053 square miles. Located at 42.36° N. Lat.; 76.35° W. Long.
Population: 0 (2000); Race: 95.3% White, 1.3% Black, 1.8% Asian, 2.4% Hispanic of any race (2000); Density: 0.0 persons per square mile (2000); Age: 27.0% under 18, 10.2% over 64 (2000); Marriage status: 26.9% never married, 51.9% now married, 6.1% widowed, 15.1% divorced (2000); Foreign born: 5.1% (2000); Ancestry (includes multiple ancestries): 21.4% English, 16.0% German, 13.4% United States or American, 12.5% Irish, 7.7% Other groups (2000).
Economy: Employment by occupation: 9.3% management, 30.0% professional, 15.7% services, 21.9% sales, 1.1% farming, 6.9% construction, 15.2% production (2000).
Income: Per capita income: $21,058 (2000); Median household income: $40,823 (2000); Poverty rate: 5.5% (2000).
Education: Percent of population age 25 and over with: High school diploma (including GED) or higher: 87.0% (2000); Bachelor's degree or higher: 31.6% (2000).

School District(s)
Ithaca City School District (PK-12)
    2003-04 Enrollment: 5,751 .... (607) 274-2101

Housing: Homeownership rate: 78.1% (2000); Median home value: $92,000 (2000); Median rent: $442 per month (2000); Median age of housing: 35 years (2000).
Transportation: Commute to work: 87.0% car, 5.5% public transportation, 0.0% walk, 6.9% work from home (2000); Travel time to work: 16.5% less than 15 minutes, 54.8% 15 to 30 minutes, 16.8% 30 to 45 minutes, 3.7% 45 to 60 minutes, 8.1% 60 minutes or more (2000)

CAROLINE (town). Covers a land area of 55.023 square miles and a water area of 0.066 square miles. Located at 42.36° N. Lat.; 76.34° W. Long. Elevation is 1,030 feet.
Population: 3,044 (1990); 2,910 (2000); 3,120 (2005); 3,336 (2010 projected); Race: 91.5% White, 3.7% Black, 1.0% Asian, 3.1% Hispanic of any race (2005); Density: 56.7 persons per square mile (2005); Average household size: 2.45 (2005); Median age: 37.8 (2005); Males per 100 females: 99.1 (2005); Marriage status: 26.1% never married, 55.7% now married, 5.5% widowed, 12.6% divorced (2000); Foreign born: 5.2% (2000); Ancestry (includes multiple ancestries): 20.0% English, 16.2% German, 12.4% United States or American, 11.5% Irish, 9.8% Other groups (2000).
Economy: Single-family building permits issued: 8 (2005); Multi-family building permits issued: 0 (2005); Employment by occupation: 9.5% management, 35.7% professional, 14.1% services, 20.0% sales, 1.5% farming, 7.4% construction, 11.9% production (2000).
Income: Per capita income: $24,155 (2005); Median household income: $49,139 (2005); Average household income: $59,226 (2005); Percent of households with income of $100,000 or more: 15.1% (2005); Poverty rate: 7.4% (2000).
Education: Percent of population age 25 and over with: High school diploma (including GED) or higher: 88.6% (2005); Bachelor's degree or higher: 35.9% (2005); Master's degree or higher: 20.9% (2005).
Housing: Homeownership rate: 71.3% (2005); Median home value: $138,722 (2005); Median rent: $433 per month (2000); Median age of housing: 38 years (2000).
Transportation: Commute to work: 82.9% car, 5.0% public transportation, 1.7% walk, 8.9% work from home (2000); Travel time to work: 21.4% less than 15 minutes, 53.2% 15 to 30 minutes, 15.1% 30 to 45 minutes, 2.9% 45 to 60 minutes, 7.4% 60 minutes or more (2000)

CAYUGA HEIGHTS (village). Covers a land area of 1.768 square miles and a water area of 0 square miles. Located at 42.46° N. Lat.; 76.48° W. Long. Elevation is 800 feet.
Population: 3,457 (1990); 3,273 (2000); 3,742 (2005); 4,262 (2010 projected); Race: 82.5% White, 1.7% Black, 11.7% Asian, 4.7% Hispanic of any race (2005); Density: 2,116.2 persons per square mile (2005); Average household size: 2.14 (2005); Median age: 43.5 (2005); Males per 100 females: 99.5 (2005); Marriage status: 29.1% never married, 59.2% now married, 7.6% widowed, 4.1% divorced (2000); Foreign born: 14.8% (2000); Ancestry (includes multiple ancestries): 21.7% German, 18.2% English, 14.2% Irish, 13.3% Other groups, 7.7% Scottish (2000).
Economy: Residential village in Finger Lakes Region. Single-family building permits issued: 0 (2005); Multi-family building permits issued: 0 (2005); Employment by occupation: 18.5% management, 62.7% professional, 6.0% services, 9.3% sales, 0.0% farming, 2.1% construction, 1.4% production (2000).
Income: Per capita income: $54,478 (2005); Median household income: $89,522 (2005); Average household income: $115,324 (2005); Percent of households with income of $100,000 or more: 46.7% (2005); Poverty rate: 8.7% (2000).
Education: Percent of population age 25 and over with: High school diploma (including GED) or higher: 99.3% (2005); Bachelor's degree or higher: 88.9% (2005); Master's degree or higher: 63.2% (2005).
Housing: Homeownership rate: 52.9% (2005); Median home value: $277,182 (2005); Median rent: $677 per month (2000); Median age of housing: 40 years (2000).
Safety: Violent crime rate: 2.6 per 10,000 population; Property crime rate: 150.7 per 10,000 population (2004).
Transportation: Commute to work: 67.0% car, 9.9% public transportation, 12.0% walk, 7.7% work from home (2000); Travel time to work: 57.6% less than 15 minutes, 28.2% 15 to 30 minutes, 8.7% 30 to 45 minutes, 1.1% 45 to 60 minutes, 4.3% 60 minutes or more (2000)

DANBY (town). Covers a land area of 53.572 square miles and a water area of 0.177 square miles. Located at 42.33° N. Lat.; 76.47° W. Long.
Population: 2,858 (1990); 3,007 (2000); 3,243 (2005); 3,490 (2010 projected); Race: 92.0% White, 3.3% Black, 1.4% Asian, 2.3% Hispanic of any race (2005); Density: 60.5 persons per square mile (2005); Average household size: 2.49 (2005); Median age: 41.0 (2005); Males per 100 females: 103.5 (2005); Marriage status: 23.1% never married, 62.7% now married, 5.1% widowed, 9.0% divorced (2000); Foreign born: 3.3% (2000); Ancestry (includes multiple ancestries): 17.8% German, 17.6% Irish, 12.5% English, 11.7% Italian, 8.9% Other groups (2000).
Economy: Single-family building permits issued: 22 (2005); Multi-family building permits issued: 0 (2005); Employment by occupation: 16.6% management, 29.3% professional, 13.6% services, 19.1% sales, 0.7% farming, 10.8% construction, 9.9% production (2000).
Income: Per capita income: $27,590 (2005); Median household income: $56,769 (2005); Average household income: $68,616 (2005); Percent of households with income of $100,000 or more: 16.8% (2005); Poverty rate: 5.1% (2000).
Education: Percent of population age 25 and over with: High school diploma (including GED) or higher: 90.8% (2005); Bachelor's degree or higher: 37.6% (2005); Master's degree or higher: 18.7% (2005).
Housing: Homeownership rate: 81.1% (2005); Median home value: $137,470 (2005); Median rent: $526 per month (2000); Median age of housing: 28 years (2000).
Transportation: Commute to work: 94.2% car, 0.5% public transportation, 1.3% walk, 4.0% work from home (2000); Travel time to work: 26.1% less than 15 minutes, 49.7% 15 to 30 minutes, 11.3% 30 to 45 minutes, 6.7% 45 to 60 minutes, 6.1% 60 minutes or more (2000)

DRYDEN (village). Covers a land area of 1.658 square miles and a water area of 0 square miles. Located at 42.48° N. Lat.; 76.30° W. Long. Elevation is 1,101 feet.
Population: 1,908 (1990); 1,832 (2000); 1,937 (2005); 2,057 (2010 projected); Race: 95.5% White, 1.6% Black, 0.2% Asian, 1.7% Hispanic of

any race (2005); Density: 1,168.2 persons per square mile (2005); Average household size: 2.32 (2005); Median age: 37.5 (2005); Males per 100 females: 101.8 (2005); Marriage status: 26.3% never married, 59.6% now married, 5.1% widowed, 9.0% divorced (2000); Foreign born: 4.9% (2000); Ancestry (includes multiple ancestries): 21.8% German, 20.5% English, 16.3% Irish, 10.4% Italian, 8.6% Other groups (2000).
Economy: Single-family building permits issued: 1 (2005); Multi-family building permits issued: 0 (2005); Employment by occupation: 14.2% management, 27.3% professional, 14.2% services, 29.6% sales, 0.5% farming, 5.0% construction, 9.3% production (2000).
Income: Per capita income: $22,614 (2005); Median household income: $45,839 (2005); Average household income: $52,458 (2005); Percent of households with income of $100,000 or more: 9.2% (2005); Poverty rate: 9.9% (2000).
Education: Percent of population age 25 and over with: High school diploma (including GED) or higher: 92.8% (2005); Bachelor's degree or higher: 37.3% (2005); Master's degree or higher: 16.1% (2005).

School District(s)
Dryden Central School District (KG-12)
 2003-04 Enrollment: 1,884 . . . . (607) 844-5361

Two-year College(s)
Tompkins-Cortland Community College (Public)
 Fall 2004 Enrollment: 3,201 . . . . (607) 844-8211
 2005-06 Tuition: In-state $3,556; Out-of-state $6,956

Housing: Homeownership rate: 60.6% (2005); Median home value: $127,287 (2005); Median rent: $405 per month (2000); Median age of housing: 39 years (2000).
Safety: Violent crime rate: 0.0 per 10,000 population; Property crime rate: 256.5 per 10,000 population (2004).
Transportation: Commute to work: 86.5% car, 4.5% public transportation, 4.7% walk, 3.4% work from home (2000); Travel time to work: 29.0% less than 15 minutes, 56.0% 15 to 30 minutes, 8.8% 30 to 45 minutes, 3.9% 45 to 60 minutes, 2.3% 60 minutes or more (2000)

Additional Information Contacts
Village of Dryden . . . . (607) 844-8622
 http://www.dryden-ny.org/

DRYDEN
(town). Covers a land area of 93.872 square miles and a water area of 0.289 square miles. Located at 42.48° N. Lat.; 76.35° W. Long. Elevation is 1,101 feet.
Population: 13,251 (1990); 13,532 (2000); 14,599 (2005); 15,732 (2010 projected); Race: 93.8% White, 1.6% Black, 1.8% Asian, 2.0% Hispanic of any race (2005); Density: 155.5 persons per square mile (2005); Average household size: 2.43 (2005); Median age: 36.0 (2005); Males per 100 females: 99.5 (2005); Marriage status: 30.4% never married, 55.7% now married, 4.6% widowed, 9.3% divorced (2000); Foreign born: 5.1% (2000); Ancestry (includes multiple ancestries): 20.1% English, 18.4% German, 16.1% Irish, 10.6% Other groups, 8.9% Italian (2000).
Economy: Manufacturing: copier equipment. Agriculture: fruit; poultry. Residential and retail growth occurring along Dryden-Ithaca axis. Single-family building permits issued: 35 (2005); Multi-family building permits issued: 6 (2005); Employment by occupation: 15.2% management, 32.8% professional, 15.0% services, 21.2% sales, 0.5% farming, 6.6% construction, 8.6% production (2000).
Income: Per capita income: $25,803 (2005); Median household income: $47,011 (2005); Average household income: $62,450 (2005); Percent of households with income of $100,000 or more: 14.3% (2005); Poverty rate: 12.0% (2000).
Education: Percent of population age 25 and over with: High school diploma (including GED) or higher: 90.1% (2005); Bachelor's degree or higher: 40.1% (2005); Master's degree or higher: 20.0% (2005).
Housing: Homeownership rate: 68.0% (2005); Median home value: $133,731 (2005); Median rent: $443 per month (2000); Median age of housing: 28 years (2000).
Transportation: Commute to work: 89.6% car, 2.0% public transportation, 2.8% walk, 4.9% work from home (2000); Travel time to work: 36.9% less than 15 minutes, 47.7% 15 to 30 minutes, 8.1% 30 to 45 minutes, 3.3% 45 to 60 minutes, 4.0% 60 minutes or more (2000)

Additional Information Contacts
Town of Dryden . . . . (607) 844-8619
 http://www.dryden.ny.us/

EAST ITHACA
(CDP). Covers a land area of 1.734 square miles and a water area of 0.037 square miles. Located at 42.42° N. Lat.; 76.45° W. Long.
Population: 2,164 (1990); 2,192 (2000); 2,574 (2005); 2,948 (2010 projected); Race: 69.9% White, 2.8% Black, 23.1% Asian, 3.5% Hispanic of any race (2005); Density: 1,484.5 persons per square mile (2005); Average household size: 2.11 (2005); Median age: 33.3 (2005); Males per 100 females: 108.6 (2005); Marriage status: 46.7% never married, 44.1% now married, 3.1% widowed, 6.1% divorced (2000); Foreign born: 31.0% (2000); Ancestry (includes multiple ancestries): 34.2% Other groups, 13.3% English, 9.9% Irish, 9.9% German, 7.3% Italian (2000).
Economy: Employment by occupation: 10.1% management, 67.7% professional, 9.1% services, 10.8% sales, 0.0% farming, 0.0% construction, 2.3% production (2000).
Income: Per capita income: $28,831 (2005); Median household income: $42,407 (2005); Average household income: $60,778 (2005); Percent of households with income of $100,000 or more: 13.2% (2005); Poverty rate: 15.1% (2000).
Education: Percent of population age 25 and over with: High school diploma (including GED) or higher: 97.5% (2005); Bachelor's degree or higher: 82.2% (2005); Master's degree or higher: 51.4% (2005).
Housing: Homeownership rate: 50.0% (2005); Median home value: $143,005 (2005); Median rent: $600 per month (2000); Median age of housing: 20 years (2000).
Transportation: Commute to work: 61.9% car, 6.4% public transportation, 20.4% walk, 7.6% work from home (2000); Travel time to work: 56.8% less than 15 minutes, 33.2% 15 to 30 minutes, 7.0% 30 to 45 minutes, 1.4% 45 to 60 minutes, 1.6% 60 minutes or more (2000)

ENFIELD
(town). Aka Enfield Center. Covers a land area of 36.884 square miles and a water area of 0.019 square miles. Located at 42.43° N. Lat.; 76.62° W. Long.
Population: 3,054 (1990); 3,369 (2000); 3,689 (2005); 4,013 (2010 projected); Race: 93.4% White, 2.2% Black, 0.7% Asian, 2.2% Hispanic of any race (2005); Density: 100.0 persons per square mile (2005); Average household size: 2.50 (2005); Median age: 36.9 (2005); Males per 100 females: 96.7 (2005); Marriage status: 28.8% never married, 54.2% now married, 4.4% widowed, 12.5% divorced (2000); Foreign born: 3.0% (2000); Ancestry (includes multiple ancestries): 18.8% English, 16.7% Irish, 16.3% German, 10.2% Other groups, 9.1% Italian (2000).
Economy: Single-family building permits issued: 26 (2005); Multi-family building permits issued: 0 (2005); Employment by occupation: 11.8% management, 18.6% professional, 19.2% services, 26.7% sales, 2.7% farming, 8.8% construction, 12.3% production (2000).
Income: Per capita income: $19,329 (2005); Median household income: $39,815 (2005); Average household income: $48,277 (2005); Percent of households with income of $100,000 or more: 6.2% (2005); Poverty rate: 13.5% (2000).
Education: Percent of population age 25 and over with: High school diploma (including GED) or higher: 85.4% (2005); Bachelor's degree or higher: 19.8% (2005); Master's degree or higher: 8.8% (2005).
Housing: Homeownership rate: 74.8% (2005); Median home value: $99,152 (2005); Median rent: $423 per month (2000); Median age of housing: 22 years (2000).
Transportation: Commute to work: 90.4% car, 1.5% public transportation, 1.8% walk, 5.9% work from home (2000); Travel time to work: 22.1% less than 15 minutes, 52.7% 15 to 30 minutes, 17.6% 30 to 45 minutes, 3.9% 45 to 60 minutes, 3.7% 60 minutes or more (2000)

FOREST HOME
(CDP). Covers a land area of 0.262 square miles and a water area of 0.008 square miles. Located at 42.45° N. Lat.; 76.47° W. Long.
Population: 1,125 (1990); 941 (2000); 936 (2005); 934 (2010 projected); Race: 43.1% White, 3.8% Black, 48.1% Asian, 10.1% Hispanic of any race (2005); Density: 3,579.2 persons per square mile (2005); Average household size: 2.18 (2005); Median age: 30.2 (2005); Males per 100 females: 101.3 (2005); Marriage status: 35.8% never married, 60.5% now married, 0.8% widowed, 2.9% divorced (2000); Foreign born: 50.7% (2000); Ancestry (includes multiple ancestries): 45.3% Other groups, 12.2% German, 9.8% Irish, 5.8% Italian, 4.5% English (2000).
Economy: Employment by occupation: 7.3% management, 72.7% professional, 5.0% services, 12.7% sales, 0.0% farming, 1.4% construction, 0.9% production (2000).
Income: Per capita income: $20,574 (2005); Median household income: $23,158 (2005); Average household income: $44,785 (2005); Percent of households with income of $100,000 or more: 12.8% (2005); Poverty rate: 22.0% (2000).

Education: Percent of population age 25 and over with: High school diploma (including GED) or higher: 100.0% (2005); Bachelor's degree or higher: 91.9% (2005); Master's degree or higher: 55.5% (2005).
Housing: Homeownership rate: 17.2% (2005); Median home value: $255,814 (2005); Median rent: $656 per month (2000); Median age of housing: 33 years (2000).
Transportation: Commute to work: 34.8% car, 15.1% public transportation, 39.9% walk, 4.6% work from home (2000); Travel time to work: 40.9% less than 15 minutes, 52.1% 15 to 30 minutes, 2.7% 30 to 45 minutes, 1.5% 45 to 60 minutes, 2.9% 60 minutes or more (2000)

FREEVILLE (village). Covers a land area of 1.080 square miles and a water area of 0.004 square miles. Located at 42.51° N. Lat.; 76.34° W. Long. Elevation is 1,048 feet.
Population: 437 (1990); 505 (2000); 563 (2005); 622 (2010 projected); Race: 97.2% White, 0.4% Black, 0.2% Asian, 1.2% Hispanic of any race (2005); Density: 521.4 persons per square mile (2005); Average household size: 2.35 (2005); Median age: 36.6 (2005); Males per 100 females: 104.0 (2005); Marriage status: 24.9% never married, 52.9% now married, 5.3% widowed, 16.8% divorced (2000); Foreign born: 2.8% (2000); Ancestry (includes multiple ancestries): 21.7% German, 20.7% English, 18.5% Italian, 17.7% Irish, 7.1% French (except Basque) (2000).
Economy: Single-family building permits issued: 1 (2005); Multi-family building permits issued: 0 (2005); Employment by occupation: 17.7% management, 33.1% professional, 12.2% services, 18.5% sales, 0.8% farming, 7.9% construction, 9.8% production (2000).
Income: Per capita income: $20,389 (2005); Median household income: $43,421 (2005); Average household income: $46,875 (2005); Percent of households with income of $100,000 or more: 6.3% (2005); Poverty rate: 9.3% (2000).
Education: Percent of population age 25 and over with: High school diploma (including GED) or higher: 89.3% (2005); Bachelor's degree or higher: 37.1% (2005); Master's degree or higher: 15.1% (2005).

School District(s)
Dryden Central School District (KG-12)
    2003-04 Enrollment: 1,884 . . . . (607) 844-5361
George Junior Republic Union Free School District (07-12)
    2003-04 Enrollment: 159 . . . . (607) 844-6200

Housing: Homeownership rate: 61.3% (2005); Median home value: $128,214 (2005); Median rent: $453 per month (2000); Median age of housing: 60+ years (2000).
Safety: Violent crime rate: 0.0 per 10,000 population; Property crime rate: 270.3 per 10,000 population (2004).
Transportation: Commute to work: 87.1% car, 2.4% public transportation, 3.2% walk, 7.2% work from home (2000); Travel time to work: 32.0% less than 15 minutes, 52.8% 15 to 30 minutes, 7.8% 30 to 45 minutes, 3.5% 45 to 60 minutes, 3.9% 60 minutes or more (2000)

GROTON (village). Covers a land area of 1.731 square miles and a water area of 0 square miles. Located at 42.58° N. Lat.; 76.36° W. Long. Elevation is 995 feet.
Population: 2,452 (1990); 2,470 (2000); 2,445 (2005); 2,486 (2010 projected); Race: 96.8% White, 0.7% Black, 0.0% Asian, 0.4% Hispanic of any race (2005); Density: 1,412.6 persons per square mile (2005); Average household size: 2.51 (2005); Median age: 39.1 (2005); Males per 100 females: 92.1 (2005); Marriage status: 22.2% never married, 57.8% now married, 9.7% widowed, 10.4% divorced (2000); Foreign born: 1.7% (2000); Ancestry (includes multiple ancestries): 17.6% German, 17.3% Irish, 14.1% English, 11.0% United States or American, 9.5% Italian (2000).
Economy: Single-family building permits issued: 0 (2005); Multi-family building permits issued: 0 (2005); Employment by occupation: 9.4% management, 19.4% professional, 23.2% services, 20.1% sales, 0.5% farming, 10.7% construction, 16.6% production (2000).
Income: Per capita income: $20,424 (2005); Median household income: $40,357 (2005); Average household income: $50,546 (2005); Percent of households with income of $100,000 or more: 8.4% (2005); Poverty rate: 5.2% (2000).
Education: Percent of population age 25 and over with: High school diploma (including GED) or higher: 86.9% (2005); Bachelor's degree or higher: 17.4% (2005); Master's degree or higher: 4.0% (2005).

School District(s)
Groton Central School District (PK-12)
    2003-04 Enrollment: 1,131 . . . . (607) 898-5301

Housing: Homeownership rate: 62.8% (2005); Median home value: $98,176 (2005); Median rent: $385 per month (2000); Median age of housing: 60+ years (2000).
Safety: Violent crime rate: 4.0 per 10,000 population; Property crime rate: 195.8 per 10,000 population (2004).
Transportation: Commute to work: 90.5% car, 2.1% public transportation, 4.0% walk, 3.4% work from home (2000); Travel time to work: 21.3% less than 15 minutes, 50.4% 15 to 30 minutes, 19.1% 30 to 45 minutes, 3.5% 45 to 60 minutes, 5.7% 60 minutes or more (2000)

GROTON (town). Covers a land area of 49.549 square miles and a water area of 0.045 square miles. Located at 42.58° N. Lat.; 76.35° W. Long. Elevation is 995 feet.
History: Incorporated 1860.
Population: 5,483 (1990); 5,794 (2000); 6,150 (2005); 6,546 (2010 projected); Race: 96.8% White, 0.8% Black, 0.3% Asian, 1.0% Hispanic of any race (2005); Density: 124.1 persons per square mile (2005); Average household size: 2.62 (2005); Median age: 38.4 (2005); Males per 100 females: 97.3 (2005); Marriage status: 22.5% never married, 62.4% now married, 6.3% widowed, 8.8% divorced (2000); Foreign born: 1.5% (2000); Ancestry (includes multiple ancestries): 21.1% German, 16.4% Irish, 15.6% English, 8.2% Italian, 8.0% United States or American (2000).
Economy: Agriculture: dairy products; field and sweet corn, hay. Single-family building permits issued: 13 (2005); Multi-family building permits issued: 5 (2005); Employment by occupation: 11.0% management, 20.5% professional, 17.7% services, 21.5% sales, 1.3% farming, 10.7% construction, 17.3% production (2000).
Income: Per capita income: $20,881 (2005); Median household income: $47,973 (2005); Average household income: $54,413 (2005); Percent of households with income of $100,000 or more: 9.7% (2005); Poverty rate: 6.0% (2000).
Education: Percent of population age 25 and over with: High school diploma (including GED) or higher: 85.2% (2005); Bachelor's degree or higher: 17.7% (2005); Master's degree or higher: 5.4% (2005).
Housing: Homeownership rate: 76.4% (2005); Median home value: $99,449 (2005); Median rent: $410 per month (2000); Median age of housing: 52 years (2000).
Transportation: Commute to work: 88.5% car, 2.3% public transportation, 2.2% walk, 5.9% work from home (2000); Travel time to work: 20.1% less than 15 minutes, 52.7% 15 to 30 minutes, 19.7% 30 to 45 minutes, 2.9% 45 to 60 minutes, 4.6% 60 minutes or more (2000)

ITHACA (city). Covers a land area of 5.463 square miles and a water area of 0.607 square miles. Located at 42.44° N. Lat.; 76.50° W. Long. Elevation is 814 feet.
History: Detachments of General John Sullivan's expedition crossed the site of Ithaca in 1779. The first settlers came in 1788 and 1789, but when the site was included within the Military Tract and title given to Revolutionary War veterans, these pioneers were obliged to move on. The land was later acquired by Simeon De Witt, surveyor-general of New York State, who gave the place its name. Solid growth began after the opening of Cornell University in 1868. In 1888, Ithaca became a city. For several years beginning in 1914, Ithaca was a center of the motion picture industry.
Population: 29,541 (1990); 29,287 (2000); 30,635 (2005); 32,114 (2010 projected); Race: 68.0% White, 7.4% Black, 18.1% Asian, 6.7% Hispanic of any race (2005); Density: 5,607.6 persons per square mile (2005); Average household size: 2.78 (2005); Median age: 23.9 (2005); Males per 100 females: 104.3 (2005); Marriage status: 65.3% never married, 25.8% now married, 3.1% widowed, 5.7% divorced (2000); Foreign born: 16.0% (2000); Ancestry (includes multiple ancestries): 27.9% Other groups, 13.7% German, 12.5% Irish, 9.8% Italian, 9.3% English (2000).
Economy: Unemployment rate: 3.2% (2005); Total civilian labor force: 15,183 (2005); Single-family building permits issued: 2 (2005); Multi-family building permits issued: 17 (2005); Employment by occupation: 8.8% management, 45.0% professional, 15.5% services, 24.2% sales, 0.5% farming, 2.1% construction, 3.9% production (2000).
Income: Per capita income: $15,389 (2005); Median household income: $24,796 (2005); Average household income: $39,744 (2005); Percent of households with income of $100,000 or more: 8.0% (2005); Poverty rate: 40.2% (2000).
Education: Percent of population age 25 and over with: High school diploma (including GED) or higher: 90.2% (2005); Bachelor's degree or higher: 60.0% (2005); Master's degree or higher: 32.3% (2005).

School District(s)
Boces Tompkins-Seneca-Tioga (UG-UG)
   2003-04 Enrollment: 205 . . . . (607) 257-1551
Ithaca City School District (PK-12)
   2003-04 Enrollment: 5,751 . . . . (607) 274-2101

Four-year College(s)
Cornell University
   Fall 2004 Enrollment: 19,518 . . . . (607) 255-2000
   2005-06 Tuition: In-state $31,467; Out-of-state $31,467
Ithaca College
   Fall 2004 Enrollment: 6,337 . . . . (607) 274-3011
   2005-06 Tuition: In-state $25,194; Out-of-state $25,194

Housing: Homeownership rate: 26.6% (2005); Median home value: $137,554 (2005); Median rent: $515 per month (2000); Median age of housing: 58 years (2000).
Hospitals: Cayuga Medical Center of Ithaca (204 beds)
Newspapers: Ithaca Journal (Circulation 18,938); The Ithaca Times (Alternative, Young Adult - Circulation 24,500)
Transportation: Commute to work: 43.8% car, 7.9% public transportation, 41.2% walk, 4.9% work from home (2000); Travel time to work: 54.5% less than 15 minutes, 37.4% 15 to 30 minutes, 5.8% 30 to 45 minutes, 1.0% 45 to 60 minutes, 1.3% 60 minutes or more (2000)

Additional Information Contacts
City of Ithaca . . . . (607) 274-6570
   http://www.ci.ithaca.ny.us/
Tompkins County/Ithaca Chamber of Commerce . . . . (607) 273-7080
   http://www.tompkinschamber.org

ITHACA (town). Covers a land area of 29.114 square miles and a water area of 1.208 square miles. Located at 42.45° N. Lat.; 76.49° W. Long. Elevation is 814 feet.

History: Settled 1789, Incorporated as a city 1888.
Population: 17,797 (1990); 18,198 (2000); 20,263 (2005); 22,217 (2010 projected); Race: 80.6% White, 3.1% Black, 11.9% Asian, 4.0% Hispanic of any race (2005); Density: 696.0 persons per square mile (2005); Average household size: 2.74 (2005); Median age: 30.6 (2005); Males per 100 females: 92.9 (2005); Marriage status: 43.8% never married, 47.1% now married, 4.7% widowed, 4.3% divorced (2000); Foreign born: 15.4% (2000); Ancestry (includes multiple ancestries): 19.3% Other groups, 16.3% German, 14.7% Irish, 14.6% English, 11.1% Italian (2000).
Economy: It is important chiefly as an educational center, the seat of Cornell University, Ithaca College, and State University of N.Y.'s Cornell campus. Manufacturing includes computer-controlled valves and pumps, logic analyzers and performance-board testers, computer hardware and software, vibration isolators, steel fabrication, precision machining, chains, sprockets and timing belts. Subsurface salt mines and brine wells nearby. Tourism in the Finger Lakes area is important to the city's economy. Single-family building permits issued: 37 (2005); Multi-family building permits issued: 82 (2005); Employment by occupation: 13.0% management, 46.5% professional, 14.6% services, 19.5% sales, 0.5% farming, 2.8% construction, 3.0% production (2000).
Income: Per capita income: $28,510 (2005); Median household income: $51,327 (2005); Average household income: $75,824 (2005); Percent of households with income of $100,000 or more: 24.6% (2005); Poverty rate: 13.2% (2000).
Education: Percent of population age 25 and over with: High school diploma (including GED) or higher: 97.0% (2005); Bachelor's degree or higher: 71.3% (2005); Master's degree or higher: 44.6% (2005).
Housing: Homeownership rate: 52.2% (2005); Median home value: $192,034 (2005); Median rent: $647 per month (2000); Median age of housing: 30 years (2000).
Transportation: Commute to work: 65.5% car, 6.1% public transportation, 21.6% walk, 4.9% work from home (2000); Travel time to work: 59.4% less than 15 minutes, 29.9% 15 to 30 minutes, 5.9% 30 to 45 minutes, 1.9% 45 to 60 minutes, 2.9% 60 minutes or more (2000)

Additional Information Contacts
Town of Ithaca . . . . (607) 273-1721
   http://www.town.ithaca.ny.us/

LANSING (village). Aka South Lansing. Covers a land area of 4.613 square miles and a water area of 0.012 square miles. Located at 42.48° N. Lat.; 76.48° W. Long. Elevation is 418 feet.

Population: 3,242 (1990); 3,417 (2000); 3,793 (2005); 4,252 (2010 projected); Race: 59.8% White, 5.2% Black, 30.5% Asian, 4.2% Hispanic of any race (2005); Density: 822.2 persons per square mile (2005); Average household size: 2.09 (2005); Median age: 33.6 (2005); Males per 100 females: 103.1 (2005); Marriage status: 36.5% never married, 50.2% now married, 7.2% widowed, 6.1% divorced (2000); Foreign born: 32.1% (2000); Ancestry (includes multiple ancestries): 37.2% Other groups, 17.0% English, 11.4% Irish, 11.3% German, 6.6% Italian (2000).
Economy: Single-family building permits issued: 9 (2005); Multi-family building permits issued: 0 (2005); Employment by occupation: 11.6% management, 64.1% professional, 6.1% services, 14.5% sales, 0.4% farming, 1.0% construction, 2.1% production (2000).
Income: Per capita income: $33,784 (2005); Median household income: $44,142 (2005); Average household income: $70,277 (2005); Percent of households with income of $100,000 or more: 18.3% (2005); Poverty rate: 12.3% (2000).
Education: Percent of population age 25 and over with: High school diploma (including GED) or higher: 94.7% (2005); Bachelor's degree or higher: 74.0% (2005); Master's degree or higher: 50.6% (2005).

School District(s)
Lansing Central School District (KG-12)
   2003-04 Enrollment: 1,529 . . . . (607) 533-4294

Housing: Homeownership rate: 28.9% (2005); Median home value: $239,568 (2005); Median rent: $628 per month (2000); Median age of housing: 25 years (2000).
Transportation: Commute to work: 82.0% car, 12.4% public transportation, 0.4% walk, 5.2% work from home (2000); Travel time to work: 51.6% less than 15 minutes, 39.4% 15 to 30 minutes, 6.1% 30 to 45 minutes, 1.1% 45 to 60 minutes, 1.8% 60 minutes or more (2000)

Additional Information Contacts
Village of Lansing . . . . (607) 533-4142
   http://people.clarityconnect.com/webpages/vlansing/

LANSING (town). Aka South Lansing. Covers a land area of 60.716 square miles and a water area of 9.214 square miles. Located at 42.54° N. Lat.; 76.51° W. Long. Elevation is 418 feet.

Population: 9,296 (1990); 10,521 (2000); 11,403 (2005); 12,387 (2010 projected); Race: 79.4% White, 4.9% Black, 12.3% Asian, 3.1% Hispanic of any race (2005); Density: 187.8 persons per square mile (2005); Average household size: 2.37 (2005); Median age: 35.9 (2005); Males per 100 females: 100.9 (2005); Marriage status: 29.6% never married, 58.7% now married, 5.1% widowed, 6.6% divorced (2000); Foreign born: 12.7% (2000); Ancestry (includes multiple ancestries): 17.8% English, 17.4% Other groups, 16.4% German, 12.8% Irish, 7.5% Italian (2000).
Economy: Single-family building permits issued: 32 (2005); Multi-family building permits issued: 0 (2005); Employment by occupation: 13.9% management, 43.2% professional, 7.0% services, 17.9% sales, 0.8% farming, 5.8% construction, 11.5% production (2000).
Income: Per capita income: $30,995 (2005); Median household income: $54,345 (2005); Average household income: $73,111 (2005); Percent of households with income of $100,000 or more: 19.6% (2005); Poverty rate: 6.7% (2000).
Education: Percent of population age 25 and over with: High school diploma (including GED) or higher: 92.9% (2005); Bachelor's degree or higher: 53.7% (2005); Master's degree or higher: 35.0% (2005).
Housing: Homeownership rate: 56.0% (2005); Median home value: $159,988 (2005); Median rent: $590 per month (2000); Median age of housing: 27 years (2000).
Transportation: Commute to work: 89.2% car, 4.7% public transportation, 1.2% walk, 4.7% work from home (2000); Travel time to work: 39.0% less than 15 minutes, 46.6% 15 to 30 minutes, 9.2% 30 to 45 minutes, 2.6% 45 to 60 minutes, 2.6% 60 minutes or more (2000)

Additional Information Contacts
Town of Lansing . . . . (607) 533-8896
   http://www.lansingtown.com/

NEWFIELD (town). Covers a land area of 58.875 square miles and a water area of 0.087 square miles. Located at 42.35° N. Lat.; 76.60° W. Long.

Population: 4,867 (1990); 5,108 (2000); 5,449 (2005); 5,814 (2010 projected); Race: 95.2% White, 1.3% Black, 0.5% Asian, 1.4% Hispanic of any race (2005); Density: 92.6 persons per square mile (2005); Average household size: 2.45 (2005); Median age: 36.3 (2005); Males per 100 females: 94.6 (2005); Marriage status: 20.8% never married, 58.9% now married, 6.1% widowed, 14.2% divorced (2000); Foreign born: 1.6% (2000); Ancestry (includes multiple ancestries): 21.6% German, 17.8% Irish, 17.4% English, 8.4% United States or American, 7.1% Other groups (2000).

Economy: Single-family building permits issued: 14 (2005); Multi-family building permits issued: 0 (2005); Employment by occupation: 10.1% management, 26.5% professional, 16.8% services, 21.1% sales, 0.7% farming, 12.7% construction, 12.2% production (2000).
Income: Per capita income: $19,970 (2005); Median household income: $42,036 (2005); Average household income: $48,928 (2005); Percent of households with income of $100,000 or more: 7.9% (2005); Poverty rate: 9.1% (2000).
Education: Percent of population age 25 and over with: High school diploma (including GED) or higher: 89.5% (2005); Bachelor's degree or higher: 22.5% (2005); Master's degree or higher: 10.3% (2005).

School District(s)
Newfield Central School District (PK-12)
    2003-04 Enrollment: 1,006 . . . . (607) 564-9955

Housing: Homeownership rate: 74.6% (2005); Median home value: $96,626 (2005); Median rent: $404 per month (2000); Median age of housing: 25 years (2000).
Transportation: Commute to work: 91.9% car, 3.2% public transportation, 1.3% walk, 3.5% work from home (2000); Travel time to work: 20.6% less than 15 minutes, 52.7% 15 to 30 minutes, 20.7% 30 to 45 minutes, 4.0% 45 to 60 minutes, 2.0% 60 minutes or more (2000)

NEWFIELD HAMLET
(CDP). Covers a land area of 1.248 square miles and a water area of 0 square miles. Located at 42.36° N. Lat.; 76.59° W. Long.
Population: 692 (1990); 647 (2000); 690 (2005); 738 (2010 projected); Race: 95.2% White, 2.3% Black, 0.0% Asian, 1.7% Hispanic of any race (2005); Density: 552.9 persons per square mile (2005); Average household size: 2.17 (2005); Median age: 40.5 (2005); Males per 100 females: 93.3 (2005); Marriage status: 20.8% never married, 57.0% now married, 8.5% widowed, 13.7% divorced (2000); Foreign born: 5.0% (2000); Ancestry (includes multiple ancestries): 23.8% English, 21.7% Irish, 19.2% United States or American, 18.3% German, 10.0% Italian (2000).
Economy: Employment by occupation: 15.3% management, 28.6% professional, 16.3% services, 11.9% sales, 0.0% farming, 20.7% construction, 7.2% production (2000).
Income: Per capita income: $25,105 (2005); Median household income: $49,762 (2005); Average household income: $54,473 (2005); Percent of households with income of $100,000 or more: 12.3% (2005); Poverty rate: 7.4% (2000).
Education: Percent of population age 25 and over with: High school diploma (including GED) or higher: 92.4% (2005); Bachelor's degree or higher: 28.2% (2005); Master's degree or higher: 14.5% (2005).
Housing: Homeownership rate: 62.6% (2005); Median home value: $108,894 (2005); Median rent: $336 per month (2000); Median age of housing: 53 years (2000).
Transportation: Commute to work: 93.0% car, 4.4% public transportation, 1.9% walk, 0.7% work from home (2000); Travel time to work: 33.3% less than 15 minutes, 42.2% 15 to 30 minutes, 18.4% 30 to 45 minutes, 4.7% 45 to 60 minutes, 1.4% 60 minutes or more (2000)

NORTHEAST ITHACA
(CDP). Covers a land area of 1.455 square miles and a water area of 0.003 square miles. Located at 42.47° N. Lat.; 76.46° W. Long.
Population: 2,533 (1990); 2,655 (2000); 2,752 (2005); 2,825 (2010 projected); Race: 68.2% White, 7.3% Black, 20.2% Asian, 4.8% Hispanic of any race (2005); Density: 1,891.9 persons per square mile (2005); Average household size: 2.44 (2005); Median age: 33.9 (2005); Males per 100 females: 94.8 (2005); Marriage status: 26.8% never married, 64.8% now married, 3.8% widowed, 4.5% divorced (2000); Foreign born: 25.7% (2000); Ancestry (includes multiple ancestries): 28.7% Other groups, 13.6% German, 11.6% Irish, 11.2% English, 9.1% Italian (2000).
Economy: Employment by occupation: 14.5% management, 62.0% professional, 5.4% services, 15.9% sales, 0.0% farming, 0.4% construction, 1.8% production (2000).
Income: Per capita income: $26,587 (2005); Median household income: $50,785 (2005); Average household income: $64,711 (2005); Percent of households with income of $100,000 or more: 20.2% (2005); Poverty rate: 12.1% (2000).
Education: Percent of population age 25 and over with: High school diploma (including GED) or higher: 97.7% (2005); Bachelor's degree or higher: 77.5% (2005); Master's degree or higher: 45.9% (2005).
Housing: Homeownership rate: 48.5% (2005); Median home value: $192,282 (2005); Median rent: $676 per month (2000); Median age of housing: 31 years (2000).
Transportation: Commute to work: 80.1% car, 11.4% public transportation, 3.0% walk, 4.8% work from home (2000); Travel time to work: 54.0% less than 15 minutes, 35.4% 15 to 30 minutes, 7.2% 30 to 45 minutes, 0.8% 45 to 60 minutes, 2.6% 60 minutes or more (2000)

NORTHWEST ITHACA
(CDP). Covers a land area of 2.936 square miles and a water area of 0.644 square miles. Located at 42.46° N. Lat.; 76.53° W. Long.
Population: 1,144 (1990); 1,115 (2000); 1,267 (2005); 1,408 (2010 projected); Race: 91.3% White, 2.7% Black, 2.8% Asian, 2.2% Hispanic of any race (2005); Density: 431.5 persons per square mile (2005); Average household size: 2.32 (2005); Median age: 49.5 (2005); Males per 100 females: 85.8 (2005); Marriage status: 26.7% never married, 54.2% now married, 12.0% widowed, 7.1% divorced (2000); Foreign born: 6.8% (2000); Ancestry (includes multiple ancestries): 21.8% English, 15.3% German, 11.1% Irish, 9.3% Other groups, 8.0% Italian (2000).
Economy: Employment by occupation: 19.9% management, 47.4% professional, 4.4% services, 21.3% sales, 0.0% farming, 5.2% construction, 1.8% production (2000).
Income: Per capita income: $32,707 (2005); Median household income: $53,176 (2005); Average household income: $73,165 (2005); Percent of households with income of $100,000 or more: 21.8% (2005); Poverty rate: 4.9% (2000).
Education: Percent of population age 25 and over with: High school diploma (including GED) or higher: 92.9% (2005); Bachelor's degree or higher: 52.7% (2005); Master's degree or higher: 32.8% (2005).
Housing: Homeownership rate: 58.9% (2005); Median home value: $195,408 (2005); Median rent: $663 per month (2000); Median age of housing: 25 years (2000).
Transportation: Commute to work: 87.2% car, 4.7% public transportation, 0.0% walk, 8.1% work from home (2000); Travel time to work: 28.4% less than 15 minutes, 47.5% 15 to 30 minutes, 10.4% 30 to 45 minutes, 9.3% 45 to 60 minutes, 4.4% 60 minutes or more (2000)

SLATERVILLE SPRINGS
(unincorporated postal area, zip code 14881). Covers a land area of 3.037 square miles and a water area of 0 square miles. Located at 42.39° N. Lat.; 76.35° W. Long. Elevation is 1,120 feet.
Population: 0 (2000); Race: 100.0% White, 0.0% Black, 0.0% Asian, 0.0% Hispanic of any race (2000); Density: 0.0 persons per square mile (2000); Age: 23.9% under 18, 12.8% over 64 (2000); Marriage status: 36.7% never married, 39.2% now married, 14.6% widowed, 9.5% divorced (2000); Foreign born: 0.0% (2000); Ancestry (includes multiple ancestries): 24.4% English, 24.4% German, 17.2% Irish, 16.7% Other groups, 16.7% Italian (2000).
Economy: Employment by occupation: 0.0% management, 50.5% professional, 14.3% services, 28.6% sales, 0.0% farming, 0.0% construction, 6.7% production (2000).
Income: Per capita income: $24,332 (2000); Median household income: $30,536 (2000); Poverty rate: 9.4% (2000).
Education: Percent of population age 25 and over with: High school diploma (including GED) or higher: 88.3% (2000); Bachelor's degree or higher: 46.7% (2000).
Housing: Homeownership rate: 35.5% (2000); Median home value: $103,100 (2000); Median rent: $253 per month (2000); Median age of housing: 47 years (2000).
Transportation: Commute to work: 82.9% car, 0.0% public transportation, 0.0% walk, 17.1% work from home (2000); Travel time to work: 20.7% less than 15 minutes, 60.9% 15 to 30 minutes, 8.0% 30 to 45 minutes, 0.0% 45 to 60 minutes, 10.3% 60 minutes or more (2000)

SOUTH HILL
(CDP). Covers a land area of 5.910 square miles and a water area of 0.089 square miles. Located at 42.41° N. Lat.; 76.49° W. Long.
Population: 5,423 (1990); 6,003 (2000); 6,694 (2005); 7,264 (2010 projected); Race: 89.5% White, 2.5% Black, 2.6% Asian, 3.5% Hispanic of any race (2005); Density: 1,132.6 persons per square mile (2005); Average household size: 5.19 (2005); Median age: 20.6 (2005); Males per 100 females: 84.6 (2005); Marriage status: 66.3% never married, 28.4% now married, 3.1% widowed, 2.3% divorced (2000); Foreign born: 4.5% (2000); Ancestry (includes multiple ancestries): 19.7% Irish, 18.6% German, 17.1% Italian, 13.7% English, 11.2% Other groups (2000).
Economy: Employment by occupation: 8.4% management, 26.8% professional, 27.4% services, 30.0% sales, 0.8% farming, 3.2% construction, 3.3% production (2000).

Income: Per capita income: $15,175 (2005); Median household income: $49,789 (2005); Average household income: $68,732 (2005); Percent of households with income of $100,000 or more: 19.8% (2005); Poverty rate: 23.1% (2000).
Education: Percent of population age 25 and over with: High school diploma (including GED) or higher: 94.8% (2005); Bachelor's degree or higher: 47.7% (2005); Master's degree or higher: 25.7% (2005).
Housing: Homeownership rate: 52.6% (2005); Median home value: $165,661 (2005); Median rent: $784 per month (2000); Median age of housing: 19 years (2000).
Transportation: Commute to work: 52.8% car, 2.3% public transportation, 41.9% walk, 2.0% work from home (2000); Travel time to work: 78.6% less than 15 minutes, 15.2% 15 to 30 minutes, 1.9% 30 to 45 minutes, 1.7% 45 to 60 minutes, 2.6% 60 minutes or more (2000)

TRUMANSBURG (village). Covers a land area of 1.207 square miles and a water area of 0.007 square miles. Located at 42.54° N. Lat.; 76.66° W. Long. Elevation is 876 feet.
History: Settled 1792; incorporated 1865.
Population: 1,611 (1990); 1,581 (2000); 1,697 (2005); 1,824 (2010 projected); Race: 96.1% White, 0.9% Black, 0.8% Asian, 2.7% Hispanic of any race (2005); Density: 1,405.6 persons per square mile (2005); Average household size: 2.27 (2005); Median age: 42.4 (2005); Males per 100 females: 85.1 (2005); Marriage status: 24.5% never married, 57.2% now married, 7.7% widowed, 10.6% divorced (2000); Foreign born: 3.1% (2000); Ancestry (includes multiple ancestries): 21.7% English, 21.0% German, 18.9% Irish, 9.0% Italian, 7.6% United States or American (2000).
Economy: Agriculture: poultry; fruits, grain. Single-family building permits issued: 3 (2005); Multi-family building permits issued: 2 (2005); Employment by occupation: 16.7% management, 31.6% professional, 15.2% services, 22.6% sales, 0.3% farming, 7.0% construction, 6.8% production (2000).
Income: Per capita income: $27,264 (2005); Median household income: $43,778 (2005); Average household income: $61,938 (2005); Percent of households with income of $100,000 or more: 17.9% (2005); Poverty rate: 6.5% (2000).
Education: Percent of population age 25 and over with: High school diploma (including GED) or higher: 92.6% (2005); Bachelor's degree or higher: 45.2% (2005); Master's degree or higher: 22.7% (2005).

School District(s)
Trumansburg Central School District (KG-12)
   2003-04 Enrollment: 1,417 . . . . (607) 387-7551
Housing: Homeownership rate: 61.3% (2005); Median home value: $163,636 (2005); Median rent: $376 per month (2000); Median age of housing: 60+ years (2000).
Newspapers: Candor Chronicle (General - Circulation 600); Interlaken Review (General - Circulation 650); Newfield News (General - Circulation 750); Ovid Gazette (General - Circulation 750); Random Harvest Weekly (General - Circulation 1,200); Trumansburg Free Press (General - Circulation 1,500)
Transportation: Commute to work: 79.1% car, 4.7% public transportation, 8.9% walk, 7.0% work from home (2000); Travel time to work: 31.1% less than 15 minutes, 39.5% 15 to 30 minutes, 21.6% 30 to 45 minutes, 3.6% 45 to 60 minutes, 4.2% 60 minutes or more (2000)
Additional Information Contacts
Trumansburg Area Chamber of Commerce. . . . . (607) 387-9254
   http://www.trumansburgchamber.com
Village of Trumansburg . . . . (607) 387-6501
   http://www.trumansburg.ny.us/

ULYSSES (town). Covers a land area of 32.983 square miles and a water area of 3.862 square miles. Located at 42.51° N. Lat.; 76.61° W. Long.
Population: 4,906 (1990); 4,775 (2000); 5,090 (2005); 5,429 (2010 projected); Race: 96.0% White, 1.3% Black, 0.9% Asian, 1.5% Hispanic of any race (2005); Density: 154.3 persons per square mile (2005); Average household size: 2.35 (2005); Median age: 42.8 (2005); Males per 100 females: 91.7 (2005); Marriage status: 24.0% never married, 60.5% now married, 6.5% widowed, 9.1% divorced (2000); Foreign born: 3.2% (2000); Ancestry (includes multiple ancestries): 19.3% English, 18.6% German, 18.5% Irish, 9.8% Italian, 8.3% United States or American (2000).
Economy: Single-family building permits issued: 16 (2005); Multi-family building permits issued: 4 (2005); Employment by occupation: 15.8% management, 29.3% professional, 16.2% services, 22.4% sales, 0.8% farming, 7.8% construction, 7.6% production (2000).

Income: Per capita income: $26,117 (2005); Median household income: $48,798 (2005); Average household income: $60,807 (2005); Percent of households with income of $100,000 or more: 12.9% (2005); Poverty rate: 7.0% (2000).
Education: Percent of population age 25 and over with: High school diploma (including GED) or higher: 93.4% (2005); Bachelor's degree or higher: 40.9% (2005); Master's degree or higher: 20.4% (2005).
Housing: Homeownership rate: 74.2% (2005); Median home value: $152,150 (2005); Median rent: $424 per month (2000); Median age of housing: 45 years (2000).
Transportation: Commute to work: 84.1% car, 2.5% public transportation, 5.1% walk, 7.4% work from home (2000); Travel time to work: 28.6% less than 15 minutes, 49.4% 15 to 30 minutes, 14.9% 30 to 45 minutes, 2.7% 45 to 60 minutes, 4.4% 60 minutes or more (2000)
Additional Information Contacts
Town of Ulysses. . . . . (607) 387-5767
   http://www.trumansburg.ny.us/ulysses/

Ulster County

Located in southeastern New York, mainly in the Catskills; bounded on the east by the Hudson River; drained by the Wallkill River; includes part of the Shawangunk Range and several small lakes. Covers a land area of 1,126.48 square miles, a water area of 34.28 square miles, and is located in the Eastern Time Zone. The county government was organized in 1683. County seat is Kingston.

Ulster County is part of the Kingston, NY Metropolitan Statistical Area. The entire metro area includes: Ulster County, NY

Weather Station: Mohonk Lake   Elevation: 1,243 feet

	Jan	Feb	Mar	Apr	May	Jun	Jul	Aug	Sep	Oct	Nov	Dec
High	32	35	44	57	68	75	80	78	70	59	47	36
Low	17	19	27	38	49	58	63	62	54	44	34	23
Precip	3.8	3.2	4.3	4.2	5.2	4.2	4.6	4.3	4.7	4.2	4.1	3.8
Snow	15.9	13.4	12.5	3.7	0.5	0.0	0.0	0.0	0.0	0.2	4.0	12.9

High and Low temperatures in degrees Fahrenheit; Precipitation and Snow in inches

Weather Station: Slide Mountain   Elevation: 2,647 feet

	Jan	Feb	Mar	Apr	May	Jun	Jul	Aug	Sep	Oct	Nov	Dec
High	26	29	37	48	61	68	72	70	63	53	42	30
Low	9	10	18	29	41	49	53	52	45	35	26	16
Precip	5.2	4.3	5.5	5.3	6.0	5.3	5.1	4.8	5.4	5.5	6.1	5.1
Snow	23.9	20.1	19.7	7.3	1.4	0.0	0.0	0.0	0.0	0.5	8.6	20.3

High and Low temperatures in degrees Fahrenheit; Precipitation and Snow in inches

Population: 165,310 (1990); 177,749 (2000); 182,812 (2005); 188,008 (2010 projected); Race: 87.6% White, 6.2% Black, 1.5% Asian, 7.3% Hispanic of any race (2005); Density: 162.3 persons per square mile (2005); Average household size: 2.60 (2005); Median age: 39.2 (2005); Males per 100 females: 98.7 (2005).
Religion: Five largest groups: 35.0% Catholic Church, 3.4% Reformed Church in America, 3.4% The United Methodist Church, 3.3% Jewish Estimate, 1.8% Evangelical Lutheran Church in America (2000).
Economy: Unemployment rate: 4.3% (2005); Total civilian labor force: 92,214 (2005); Leading industries: 18.8% retail trade; 17.3% health care and social assistance; 15.4% accommodation and food services (2003); Farms: 532 totaling 83,418 acres (2002); Companies that employ 500 or more persons: 6 (2003); Companies that employ 100 to 499 persons: 71 (2003); Companies that employ less than 100 persons: 4,592 (2003); Black-owned businesses: 287 (2002); Hispanic-owned businesses: 427 (2002); Women-owned businesses: 5,242 (2002); Retail sales per capita: $12,996 (2006); Single-family building permits issued: 767 (2005); Multi-family building permits issued: 143 (2005).
Income: Per capita income: $24,182 (2005); Median household income: $47,919 (2005); Average household income: $60,895 (2005); Percent of households with income of $100,000 or more: 15.4% (2005); Poverty rate: 10.6% (2003); Bankruptcy rate: 5.28% (2005).
Taxes: Total county taxes per capita: $767 (2004); County property taxes per capita: $247 (2004).
Education: Percent of population age 25 and over with: High school diploma (including GED) or higher: 81.8% (2005); Bachelor's degree or higher: 25.0% (2005); Master's degree or higher: 11.2% (2005).
Housing: Homeownership rate: 68.3% (2005); Median home value: $171,576 (2005); Median rent: $542 per month (2000); Median age of housing: 41 years (2000).

Health: Birth rate: 100.7 per 10,000 population (2004); Death rate: 87.1 per 10,000 population (2004); Age-adjusted cancer mortality rate: 227.7 deaths per 100,000 population (2002); Air Quality Index: 93.9% good, 6.1% moderate, 0.0% unhealthy for sensitive individuals, 0.0% unhealthy (percent of days in 2005); Number of physicians: 20.1 per 10,000 population (2004); Hospital beds: 23.8 per 10,000 population (2003); Hospital admissions: 856.4 per 10,000 population (2003).
Elections: 2004 Presidential election results: 43.1% Bush, 54.3% Kerry, 2.3% Nader, 0.3% Badnarik
National and State Parks: Catskill State Park; Home of Franklin D Roosevelt National Historic Site
Additional Information Contacts
Ulster County Government . . . . (845) 340-3900
http://www.co.ulster.ny.us/
City of Kingston . . . . (845) 334-3915
http://www.ci.kingston.ny.us/
Town of Esopus . . . . (845) 331-0676
http://www.esopus.com/
Town of Kingston . . . . (845) 336-8853
http://www.town.kingston.ny.us/
Town of Rosendale . . . . (845) 658-3159
http://www.townofrosendale.com/
Town of Saugerties . . . . (845) 246-2800
http://www.saugerties.ny.us/
Town of Woodstock . . . . (845) 679-2113
http://www.woodstockny.org/
Village of New Paltz . . . . (845) 255-0130
http://www.villageofnewpaltz.org/portal/

Ulster County Communities

ACCORD (CDP). Part of the City of Rochester. Covers a land area of 3.388 square miles and a water area of 0.052 square miles. Located at 41.79° N. Lat.; 74.22° W. Long. Elevation is 249 feet.
Population: 491 (1990); 622 (2000); 641 (2005); 660 (2010 projected); Race: 90.8% White, 2.8% Black, 1.9% Asian, 4.7% Hispanic of any race (2005); Density: 189.2 persons per square mile (2005); Average household size: 2.74 (2005); Median age: 34.3 (2005); Males per 100 females: 94.8 (2005); Marriage status: 27.9% never married, 54.5% now married, 3.5% widowed, 14.1% divorced (2000); Foreign born: 3.8% (2000); Ancestry (includes multiple ancestries): 23.7% Irish, 17.8% German, 11.7% Other groups, 10.7% Dutch, 10.0% Italian (2000).
Economy: Manufacturing focus. Employment by occupation: 7.4% management, 24.5% professional, 13.5% services, 28.1% sales, 0.0% farming, 7.1% construction, 19.4% production (2000).
Income: Per capita income: $26,350 (2005); Median household income: $56,538 (2005); Average household income: $71,848 (2005); Percent of households with income of $100,000 or more: 14.5% (2005); Poverty rate: 4.1% (2000).
Education: Percent of population age 25 and over with: High school diploma (including GED) or higher: 86.5% (2005); Bachelor's degree or higher: 36.7% (2005); Master's degree or higher: 14.3% (2005).
School District(s)
Rondout Valley Central School District (KG-12)
   2003-04 Enrollment: 2,797 . . . . (845) 687-2400
Housing: Homeownership rate: 72.2% (2005); Median home value: $115,909 (2005); Median rent: $622 per month (2000); Median age of housing: 38 years (2000).
Transportation: Commute to work: 91.5% car, 1.6% public transportation, 3.1% walk, 3.9% work from home (2000); Travel time to work: 25.3% less than 15 minutes, 24.5% 15 to 30 minutes, 24.5% 30 to 45 minutes, 15.6% 45 to 60 minutes, 10.2% 60 minutes or more (2000)
Additional Information Contacts
Kerhonkson & Accord Chamber . . . . (845) 626-2616
http://www.ulstertourism.info

BEARSVILLE (unincorporated postal area, zip code 12409). Covers a land area of 9.835 square miles and a water area of 0.214 square miles. Located at 42.06° N. Lat.; 74.16° W. Long.
Population: 0 (2000); Race: 96.4% White, 0.0% Black, 0.0% Asian, 5.2% Hispanic of any race (2000); Density: 0.0 persons per square mile (2000); Age: 15.4% under 18, 18.0% over 64 (2000); Marriage status: 18.7% never married, 59.0% now married, 8.5% widowed, 13.7% divorced (2000); Foreign born: 11.4% (2000); Ancestry (includes multiple ancestries): 30.0% German, 17.5% English, 13.4% Irish, 12.3% Russian, 11.4% Other groups (2000).
Economy: Employment by occupation: 14.3% management, 28.7% professional, 26.2% services, 9.8% sales, 0.0% farming, 12.6% construction, 8.4% production (2000).
Income: Per capita income: $25,992 (2000); Median household income: $37,813 (2000); Poverty rate: 15.4% (2000).
Education: Percent of population age 25 and over with: High school diploma (including GED) or higher: 90.6% (2000); Bachelor's degree or higher: 52.1% (2000).
Housing: Homeownership rate: 78.9% (2000); Median home value: $142,400 (2000); Median rent: $533 per month (2000); Median age of housing: 45 years (2000).
Transportation: Commute to work: 79.7% car, 1.8% public transportation, 2.2% walk, 16.2% work from home (2000); Travel time to work: 26.9% less than 15 minutes, 33.9% 15 to 30 minutes, 18.9% 30 to 45 minutes, 0.0% 45 to 60 minutes, 20.3% 60 minutes or more (2000)

BIG INDIAN (unincorporated postal area, zip code 12410). Covers a land area of 53.114 square miles and a water area of 0.013 square miles. Located at 42.11° N. Lat.; 74.45° W. Long.
Population: 0 (2000); Race: 87.0% White, 0.8% Black, 6.2% Asian, 4.6% Hispanic of any race (2000); Density: 0.0 persons per square mile (2000); Age: 22.9% under 18, 19.3% over 64 (2000); Marriage status: 29.3% never married, 56.5% now married, 7.6% widowed, 6.6% divorced (2000); Foreign born: 13.1% (2000); Ancestry (includes multiple ancestries): 24.9% German, 17.9% English, 16.1% Irish, 13.1% Other groups, 11.2% Dutch (2000).
Economy: Resort village in the Catskill Mountains. Employment by occupation: 8.3% management, 25.2% professional, 16.0% services, 16.9% sales, 0.0% farming, 11.9% construction, 21.6% production (2000).
Income: Per capita income: $19,680 (2000); Median household income: $32,344 (2000); Poverty rate: 14.6% (2000).
Education: Percent of population age 25 and over with: High school diploma (including GED) or higher: 82.4% (2000); Bachelor's degree or higher: 24.5% (2000).
Housing: Homeownership rate: 73.2% (2000); Median home value: $88,800 (2000); Median rent: $377 per month (2000); Median age of housing: 51 years (2000).
Transportation: Commute to work: 77.5% car, 3.8% public transportation, 4.3% walk, 12.6% work from home (2000); Travel time to work: 32.7% less than 15 minutes, 21.1% 15 to 30 minutes, 10.8% 30 to 45 minutes, 20.9% 45 to 60 minutes, 14.4% 60 minutes or more (2000)

BLOOMINGTON (unincorporated postal area, zip code 12411). Covers a land area of 0.456 square miles and a water area of 0 square miles. Located at 41.87° N. Lat.; 74.04° W. Long.
Population: 0 (2000); Race: 95.9% White, 0.0% Black, 0.0% Asian, 0.0% Hispanic of any race (2000); Density: 0.0 persons per square mile (2000); Age: 20.3% under 18, 21.8% over 64 (2000); Marriage status: 13.9% never married, 71.4% now married, 14.7% widowed, 0.0% divorced (2000); Foreign born: 0.0% (2000); Ancestry (includes multiple ancestries): 26.3% German, 22.2% Dutch, 18.0% Italian, 11.4% Irish, 9.5% Other groups (2000).
Economy: Employment by occupation: 13.5% management, 31.4% professional, 14.7% services, 17.9% sales, 0.0% farming, 9.0% construction, 13.5% production (2000).
Income: Per capita income: $20,284 (2000); Median household income: $37,679 (2000); Poverty rate: 6.0% (2000).
Education: Percent of population age 25 and over with: High school diploma (including GED) or higher: 88.5% (2000); Bachelor's degree or higher: 26.6% (2000).
Housing: Homeownership rate: 90.5% (2000); Median home value: $90,700 (2000); Median rent: $296 per month (2000); Median age of housing: 44 years (2000).
Transportation: Commute to work: 95.0% car, 0.0% public transportation, 0.0% walk, 5.0% work from home (2000); Travel time to work: 9.7% less than 15 minutes, 50.0% 15 to 30 minutes, 14.9% 30 to 45 minutes, 25.4% 45 to 60 minutes, 0.0% 60 minutes or more (2000)

BOICEVILLE (unincorporated postal area, zip code 12412). Covers a land area of 12.776 square miles and a water area of 0.027 square miles. Located at 42.00° N. Lat.; 74.26° W. Long.
Population: 0 (2000); Race: 99.5% White, 0.0% Black, 0.0% Asian, 3.1% Hispanic of any race (2000); Density: 0.0 persons per square mile (2000);

Age: 31.3% under 18, 8.6% over 64 (2000); Marriage status: 23.4% never married, 65.0% now married, 5.8% widowed, 5.8% divorced (2000); Foreign born: 5.9% (2000); Ancestry (includes multiple ancestries): 28.5% Italian, 19.5% German, 17.8% Irish, 15.0% English, 7.9% Dutch (2000).
Economy: Summer recreational residences and tourist area. Lumber milling. Employment by occupation: 10.3% management, 32.4% professional, 13.2% services, 15.6% sales, 0.0% farming, 10.7% construction, 17.8% production (2000).
Income: Per capita income: $19,363 (2000); Median household income: $39,948 (2000); Poverty rate: 8.2% (2000).
Education: Percent of population age 25 and over with: High school diploma (including GED) or higher: 83.8% (2000); Bachelor's degree or higher: 34.5% (2000).

School District(s)
Onteora Central School District (KG-12)
   2003-04 Enrollment: 2,172 . . . . (845) 657-6383
Housing: Homeownership rate: 77.3% (2000); Median home value: $107,800 (2000); Median rent: $617 per month (2000); Median age of housing: 33 years (2000).
Transportation: Commute to work: 83.0% car, 3.9% public transportation, 3.9% walk, 9.1% work from home (2000); Travel time to work: 29.2% less than 15 minutes, 30.1% 15 to 30 minutes, 19.9% 30 to 45 minutes, 4.6% 45 to 60 minutes, 16.2% 60 minutes or more (2000)

CHICHESTER
(unincorporated postal area, zip code 12416). Covers a land area of 1.236 square miles and a water area of 0 square miles. Located at 42.10° N. Lat.; 74.29° W. Long.
Population: 0 (2000); Race: 100.0% White, 0.0% Black, 0.0% Asian, 0.0% Hispanic of any race (2000); Density: 0.0 persons per square mile (2000); Age: 31.7% under 18, 12.7% over 64 (2000); Marriage status: 37.7% never married, 47.2% now married, 0.0% widowed, 15.1% divorced (2000); Foreign born: 0.0% (2000); Ancestry (includes multiple ancestries): 44.4% Scottish, 28.6% German, 17.5% Russian, 9.5% English, 7.9% United States or American (2000).
Economy: Skiing nearby. Employment by occupation: 14.7% management, 17.6% professional, 0.0% services, 67.6% sales, 0.0% farming, 0.0% construction, 0.0% production (2000).
Income: Per capita income: $61,771 (2000); Median household income: $40,750 (2000); Poverty rate: 0.0% (2000).
Education: Percent of population age 25 and over with: High school diploma (including GED) or higher: 100.0% (2000); Bachelor's degree or higher: 26.3% (2000).
Housing: Homeownership rate: 58.8% (2000); Median home value: $114,300 (2000); Median rent: $544 per month (2000); Median age of housing: 51 years (2000).
Transportation: Commute to work: 85.3% car, 0.0% public transportation, 0.0% walk, 14.7% work from home (2000); Travel time to work: 0.0% less than 15 minutes, 34.5% 15 to 30 minutes, 17.2% 30 to 45 minutes, 27.6% 45 to 60 minutes, 20.7% 60 minutes or more (2000)

CLINTONDALE
(CDP). Covers a land area of 5.591 square miles and a water area of 0.007 square miles. Located at 41.69° N. Lat.; 74.04° W. Long.
Population: 1,394 (1990); 1,424 (2000); 1,484 (2005); 1,535 (2010 projected); Race: 89.8% White, 4.2% Black, 1.1% Asian, 4.2% Hispanic of any race (2005); Density: 265.4 persons per square mile (2005); Average household size: 2.57 (2005); Median age: 35.8 (2005); Males per 100 females: 93.2 (2005); Marriage status: 31.8% never married, 52.2% now married, 7.8% widowed, 8.3% divorced (2000); Foreign born: 3.4% (2000); Ancestry (includes multiple ancestries): 29.9% Italian, 21.7% Irish, 21.3% German, 10.2% Other groups, 8.4% United States or American (2000).
Economy: In fruit-growing region. Employment by occupation: 18.0% management, 15.2% professional, 18.5% services, 22.0% sales, 0.0% farming, 10.6% construction, 15.6% production (2000).
Income: Per capita income: $21,457 (2005); Median household income: $43,526 (2005); Average household income: $54,554 (2005); Percent of households with income of $100,000 or more: 14.4% (2005); Poverty rate: 12.4% (2000).
Education: Percent of population age 25 and over with: High school diploma (including GED) or higher: 84.1% (2005); Bachelor's degree or higher: 22.9% (2005); Master's degree or higher: 6.2% (2005).
Housing: Homeownership rate: 63.5% (2005); Median home value: $202,574 (2005); Median rent: $533 per month (2000); Median age of housing: 40 years (2000).
Transportation: Commute to work: 88.1% car, 2.1% public transportation, 3.9% walk, 6.0% work from home (2000); Travel time to work: 24.8% less than 15 minutes, 33.5% 15 to 30 minutes, 25.5% 30 to 45 minutes, 8.1% 45 to 60 minutes, 8.1% 60 minutes or more (2000)

COTTEKILL
(unincorporated postal area, zip code 12419). Covers a land area of 1.041 square miles and a water area of 0 square miles. Located at 41.85° N. Lat.; 74.10° W. Long.
Population: 0 (2000); Race: 92.8% White, 0.0% Black, 0.0% Asian, 2.5% Hispanic of any race (2000); Density: 0.0 persons per square mile (2000); Age: 11.8% under 18, 5.5% over 64 (2000); Marriage status: 23.7% never married, 54.0% now married, 6.0% widowed, 16.3% divorced (2000); Foreign born: 3.4% (2000); Ancestry (includes multiple ancestries): 27.4% German, 18.6% English, 15.6% Other groups, 13.9% Irish, 9.7% Polish (2000).
Economy: Employment by occupation: 22.3% management, 29.8% professional, 8.5% services, 29.8% sales, 0.0% farming, 0.0% construction, 9.6% production (2000).
Income: Per capita income: $26,757 (2000); Median household income: $35,893 (2000); Poverty rate: 0.0% (2000).
Education: Percent of population age 25 and over with: High school diploma (including GED) or higher: 91.5% (2000); Bachelor's degree or higher: 45.5% (2000).

School District(s)
Rondout Valley Central School District (KG-12)
   2003-04 Enrollment: 2,797 . . . . (845) 687-2400
Housing: Homeownership rate: 58.6% (2000); Median home value: $120,000 (2000); Median rent: $556 per month (2000); Median age of housing: 40 years (2000).
Transportation: Commute to work: 88.8% car, 3.7% public transportation, 0.0% walk, 3.2% work from home (2000); Travel time to work: 24.2% less than 15 minutes, 32.4% 15 to 30 minutes, 24.7% 30 to 45 minutes, 5.5% 45 to 60 minutes, 13.2% 60 minutes or more (2000)

CRAGSMOOR
(CDP). Covers a land area of 4.370 square miles and a water area of 0 square miles. Located at 41.66° N. Lat.; 74.38° W. Long.
Population: 362 (1990); 474 (2000); 479 (2005); 461 (2010 projected); Race: 93.7% White, 0.0% Black, 0.0% Asian, 4.0% Hispanic of any race (2005); Density: 109.6 persons per square mile (2005); Average household size: 2.47 (2005); Median age: 42.3 (2005); Males per 100 females: 99.6 (2005); Marriage status: 23.7% never married, 57.4% now married, 6.4% widowed, 12.5% divorced (2000); Foreign born: 10.3% (2000); Ancestry (includes multiple ancestries): 23.5% Irish, 19.2% German, 13.7% English, 12.2% Other groups, 11.1% Italian (2000).
Economy: Employment by occupation: 2.5% management, 35.7% professional, 19.5% services, 29.9% sales, 0.0% farming, 12.4% construction, 0.0% production (2000).
Income: Per capita income: $28,398 (2005); Median household income: $69,444 (2005); Average household income: $70,116 (2005); Percent of households with income of $100,000 or more: 20.6% (2005); Poverty rate: 11.1% (2000).
Education: Percent of population age 25 and over with: High school diploma (including GED) or higher: 88.1% (2005); Bachelor's degree or higher: 36.3% (2005); Master's degree or higher: 18.5% (2005).
Housing: Homeownership rate: 86.1% (2005); Median home value: $165,000 (2005); Median rent: $688 per month (2000); Median age of housing: 60+ years (2000).
Transportation: Commute to work: 91.3% car, 0.0% public transportation, 0.0% walk, 8.7% work from home (2000); Travel time to work: 13.2% less than 15 minutes, 34.1% 15 to 30 minutes, 21.8% 30 to 45 minutes, 10.5% 45 to 60 minutes, 20.5% 60 minutes or more (2000)

DENNING
(town). Covers a land area of 105.186 square miles and a water area of 0.070 square miles. Located at 41.94° N. Lat.; 74.48° W. Long.
Population: 524 (1990); 516 (2000); 489 (2005); 462 (2010 projected); Race: 95.7% White, 0.0% Black, 0.2% Asian, 1.6% Hispanic of any race (2005); Density: 4.6 persons per square mile (2005); Average household size: 2.36 (2005); Median age: 44.8 (2005); Males per 100 females: 101.2 (2005); Marriage status: 25.8% never married, 57.4% now married, 7.5% widowed, 9.4% divorced (2000); Foreign born: 1.8% (2000); Ancestry (includes multiple ancestries): 24.3% German, 22.9% Irish, 19.8% English, 13.7% Italian, 10.2% Polish (2000).
Economy: Single-family building permits issued: 4 (2005); Multi-family building permits issued: 0 (2005); Employment by occupation: 11.3%

management, 23.5% professional, 24.3% services, 21.5% sales, 0.0% farming, 6.1% construction, 13.4% production (2000).
Income: Per capita income: $34,663 (2005); Median household income: $49,808 (2005); Average household income: $81,534 (2005); Percent of households with income of $100,000 or more: 17.9% (2005); Poverty rate: 12.0% (2000).
Education: Percent of population age 25 and over with: High school diploma (including GED) or higher: 82.0% (2005); Bachelor's degree or higher: 22.3% (2005); Master's degree or higher: 8.2% (2005).
Housing: Homeownership rate: 81.6% (2005); Median home value: $135,938 (2005); Median rent: $532 per month (2000); Median age of housing: 36 years (2000).
Transportation: Commute to work: 87.2% car, 1.6% public transportation, 6.6% walk, 2.1% work from home (2000); Travel time to work: 17.2% less than 15 minutes, 35.7% 15 to 30 minutes, 19.3% 30 to 45 minutes, 8.0% 45 to 60 minutes, 19.7% 60 minutes or more (2000)

EAST KINGSTON (CDP).
Covers a land area of 0.712 square miles and a water area of 0 square miles. Located at 41.95° N. Lat.; 73.97° W. Long.
Population: 300 (1990); 285 (2000); 291 (2005); 296 (2010 projected); Race: 94.2% White, 5.8% Black, 0.0% Asian, 4.8% Hispanic of any race (2005); Density: 408.7 persons per square mile (2005); Average household size: 2.45 (2005); Median age: 37.7 (2005); Males per 100 females: 107.9 (2005); Marriage status: 42.3% never married, 50.0% now married, 4.0% widowed, 3.6% divorced (2000); Foreign born: 0.0% (2000); Ancestry (includes multiple ancestries): 29.4% Italian, 27.9% Irish, 19.8% German, 9.5% Other groups, 7.6% French (except Basque) (2000).
Economy: Employment by occupation: 2.2% management, 27.5% professional, 10.1% services, 31.2% sales, 0.0% farming, 18.1% construction, 10.9% production (2000).
Income: Per capita income: $23,196 (2005); Median household income: $55,278 (2005); Average household income: $56,723 (2005); Percent of households with income of $100,000 or more: 14.3% (2005); Poverty rate: 15.3% (2000).
Education: Percent of population age 25 and over with: High school diploma (including GED) or higher: 70.3% (2005); Bachelor's degree or higher: 9.9% (2005); Master's degree or higher: 5.2% (2005).
Housing: Homeownership rate: 70.6% (2005); Median home value: $74,545 (2005); Median rent: $485 per month (2000); Median age of housing: 60+ years (2000).
Transportation: Commute to work: 96.5% car, 0.0% public transportation, 0.0% walk, 3.5% work from home (2000); Travel time to work: 43.5% less than 15 minutes, 21.0% 15 to 30 minutes, 17.4% 30 to 45 minutes, 10.9% 45 to 60 minutes, 7.2% 60 minutes or more (2000)

ELLENVILLE (village).
Covers a land area of 8.706 square miles and a water area of 0.062 square miles. Located at 41.71° N. Lat.; 74.38° W. Long. Elevation is 317 feet.
History: Incorporated 1856.
Population: 4,259 (1990); 4,130 (2000); 4,128 (2005); 4,147 (2010 projected); Race: 67.2% White, 12.7% Black, 2.0% Asian, 30.8% Hispanic of any race (2005); Density: 474.1 persons per square mile (2005); Average household size: 2.66 (2005); Median age: 34.0 (2005); Males per 100 females: 88.8 (2005); Marriage status: 32.4% never married, 51.1% now married, 9.1% widowed, 7.4% divorced (2000); Foreign born: 11.1% (2000); Ancestry (includes multiple ancestries): 42.7% Other groups, 10.7% Irish, 9.1% Italian, 8.5% German, 6.7% United States or American (2000).
Economy: Changing lifestyles forced the closing of the large hotels of this resort village. Today it is a popular gathering place for mountaineers and rock climbers tackling the Shawangunk Mts. Area remains a popular recreational destination in summer Employment by occupation: 8.6% management, 16.9% professional, 25.7% services, 23.3% sales, 1.1% farming, 4.9% construction, 19.5% production (2000).
Income: Per capita income: $16,897 (2005); Median household income: $29,965 (2005); Average household income: $44,067 (2005); Percent of households with income of $100,000 or more: 9.5% (2005); Poverty rate: 23.4% (2000).
Education: Percent of population age 25 and over with: High school diploma (including GED) or higher: 68.1% (2005); Bachelor's degree or higher: 13.1% (2005); Master's degree or higher: 5.9% (2005).

School District(s)
Ellenville Central School District (KG-12)
    2003-04 Enrollment: 1,812 . . . . (845) 647-0100

Housing: Homeownership rate: 41.2% (2005); Median home value: $117,232 (2005); Median rent: $508 per month (2000); Median age of housing: 49 years (2000).
Hospitals: Ellenville Regional Hospital (51 beds)
Safety: Violent crime rate: 17.0 per 10,000 population; Property crime rate: 367.0 per 10,000 population (2004).
Newspapers: The Ellenville Press (General - Circulation 2,400)
Transportation: Commute to work: 80.9% car, 3.2% public transportation, 11.5% walk, 2.4% work from home (2000); Travel time to work: 54.5% less than 15 minutes, 16.3% 15 to 30 minutes, 11.3% 30 to 45 minutes, 8.8% 45 to 60 minutes, 9.1% 60 minutes or more (2000)
Additional Information Contacts
Ellenville-Wawarsing Chamber of Commerce . . . . (845) 647-4620
    http://www.ellenvillewawarsingchamberofcommerce.com

ESOPUS (town).
Covers a land area of 37.245 square miles and a water area of 4.643 square miles. Located at 41.85° N. Lat.; 73.99° W. Long.
History: Seat of Mt. St. Alphonsus Theological Seminary. John Burroughs lived near here. Town was formed in 1811, and was partly annexed by Kingston in 1818.
Population: 8,860 (1990); 9,331 (2000); 9,494 (2005); 9,725 (2010 projected); Race: 94.1% White, 2.5% Black, 1.0% Asian, 2.2% Hispanic of any race (2005); Density: 254.9 persons per square mile (2005); Average household size: 2.65 (2005); Median age: 39.8 (2005); Males per 100 females: 93.4 (2005); Marriage status: 28.7% never married, 56.5% now married, 6.7% widowed, 8.2% divorced (2000); Foreign born: 4.6% (2000); Ancestry (includes multiple ancestries): 25.1% Irish, 22.5% German, 18.0% Italian, 9.4% English, 6.4% Other groups (2000).
Economy: In grape-growing and resort area. Single-family building permits issued: 30 (2005); Multi-family building permits issued: 40 (2005); Employment by occupation: 12.0% management, 24.4% professional, 14.2% services, 26.8% sales, 0.2% farming, 10.6% construction, 11.9% production (2000).
Income: Per capita income: $24,821 (2005); Median household income: $52,509 (2005); Average household income: $63,762 (2005); Percent of households with income of $100,000 or more: 15.6% (2005); Poverty rate: 11.7% (2000).
Taxes: Total city taxes per capita: $263 (2004); City property taxes per capita: $222 (2004).
Education: Percent of population age 25 and over with: High school diploma (including GED) or higher: 84.8% (2005); Bachelor's degree or higher: 25.6% (2005); Master's degree or higher: 12.1% (2005).
Housing: Homeownership rate: 73.0% (2005); Median home value: $159,904 (2005); Median rent: $606 per month (2000); Median age of housing: 41 years (2000).
Transportation: Commute to work: 88.7% car, 1.0% public transportation, 2.6% walk, 7.0% work from home (2000); Travel time to work: 24.3% less than 15 minutes, 38.1% 15 to 30 minutes, 22.7% 30 to 45 minutes, 6.8% 45 to 60 minutes, 8.2% 60 minutes or more (2000)
Additional Information Contacts
Town of Esopus . . . . (845) 331-0676
    http://www.esopus.com/

GARDINER (town).
Covers a land area of 44.395 square miles and a water area of 0.549 square miles. Located at 41.69° N. Lat.; 74.18° W. Long. Elevation is 308 feet.
History: A 17th-century gristmill is here.
Population: 4,380 (1990); 5,238 (2000); 5,681 (2005); 6,099 (2010 projected); Race: 94.0% White, 1.8% Black, 0.8% Asian, 5.5% Hispanic of any race (2005); Density: 128.0 persons per square mile (2005); Average household size: 2.58 (2005); Median age: 39.2 (2005); Males per 100 females: 99.3 (2005); Marriage status: 24.2% never married, 62.0% now married, 3.9% widowed, 9.8% divorced (2000); Foreign born: 6.3% (2000); Ancestry (includes multiple ancestries): 25.2% German, 20.7% Irish, 18.7% Italian, 11.9% English, 9.9% Other groups (2000).
Economy: Resort village. Single-family building permits issued: 40 (2005); Multi-family building permits issued: 2 (2005); Employment by occupation: 12.9% management, 27.3% professional, 13.8% services, 22.5% sales, 1.5% farming, 13.5% construction, 8.6% production (2000).
Income: Per capita income: $29,581 (2005); Median household income: $63,061 (2005); Average household income: $75,943 (2005); Percent of households with income of $100,000 or more: 23.9% (2005); Poverty rate: 7.4% (2000).

Education: Percent of population age 25 and over with: High school diploma (including GED) or higher: 89.7% (2005); Bachelor's degree or higher: 34.3% (2005); Master's degree or higher: 16.3% (2005).
Housing: Homeownership rate: 76.4% (2005); Median home value: $250,623 (2005); Median rent: $620 per month (2000); Median age of housing: 26 years (2000).
Transportation: Commute to work: 89.7% car, 1.3% public transportation, 2.4% walk, 6.5% work from home (2000); Travel time to work: 25.5% less than 15 minutes, 25.7% 15 to 30 minutes, 28.7% 30 to 45 minutes, 12.0% 45 to 60 minutes, 8.0% 60 minutes or more (2000)

GARDINER (CDP).
Covers a land area of 3.825 square miles and a water area of 0 square miles. Located at 41.68° N. Lat.; 74.15° W. Long.
Population: 726 (1990); 856 (2000); 957 (2005); 1,056 (2010 projected); Race: 96.6% White, 0.0% Black, 0.4% Asian, 5.3% Hispanic of any race (2005); Density: 250.2 persons per square mile (2005); Average household size: 2.46 (2005); Median age: 39.3 (2005); Males per 100 females: 95.7 (2005); Marriage status: 33.2% never married, 58.2% now married, 3.4% widowed, 5.2% divorced (2000); Foreign born: 6.3% (2000); Ancestry (includes multiple ancestries): 35.0% German, 27.9% Irish, 20.5% Italian, 10.3% English, 8.2% Polish (2000).
Economy: Employment by occupation: 7.8% management, 21.1% professional, 13.9% services, 29.1% sales, 2.3% farming, 16.0% construction, 9.7% production (2000).
Income: Per capita income: $31,600 (2005); Median household income: $64,309 (2005); Average household income: $77,712 (2005); Percent of households with income of $100,000 or more: 28.0% (2005); Poverty rate: 11.7% (2000).
Education: Percent of population age 25 and over with: High school diploma (including GED) or higher: 86.7% (2005); Bachelor's degree or higher: 21.7% (2005); Master's degree or higher: 11.4% (2005).
Housing: Homeownership rate: 71.7% (2005); Median home value: $213,672 (2005); Median rent: $539 per month (2000); Median age of housing: 40 years (2000).
Transportation: Commute to work: 91.5% car, 1.9% public transportation, 2.1% walk, 4.4% work from home (2000); Travel time to work: 31.0% less than 15 minutes, 22.3% 15 to 30 minutes, 29.1% 30 to 45 minutes, 13.6% 45 to 60 minutes, 4.0% 60 minutes or more (2000)

GLASCO (CDP).
Covers a land area of 1.849 square miles and a water area of 0.786 square miles. Located at 42.04° N. Lat.; 73.95° W. Long.
Population: 1,538 (1990); 1,692 (2000); 1,817 (2005); 1,938 (2010 projected); Race: 95.5% White, 1.8% Black, 0.7% Asian, 2.2% Hispanic of any race (2005); Density: 982.6 persons per square mile (2005); Average household size: 2.36 (2005); Median age: 40.0 (2005); Males per 100 females: 90.1 (2005); Marriage status: 22.6% never married, 61.3% now married, 10.1% widowed, 6.0% divorced (2000); Foreign born: 3.0% (2000); Ancestry (includes multiple ancestries): 35.5% Italian, 32.0% German, 23.3% Irish, 9.7% English, 4.6% Dutch (2000).
Economy: Manufacturing: textiles, apparel, construction materials. Employment by occupation: 9.7% management, 15.6% professional, 25.4% services, 26.4% sales, 0.0% farming, 11.0% construction, 11.9% production (2000).
Income: Per capita income: $25,131 (2005); Median household income: $41,386 (2005); Average household income: $58,838 (2005); Percent of households with income of $100,000 or more: 15.8% (2005); Poverty rate: 9.3% (2000).
Education: Percent of population age 25 and over with: High school diploma (including GED) or higher: 82.1% (2005); Bachelor's degree or higher: 16.7% (2005); Master's degree or higher: 7.4% (2005).
School District(s)
Saugerties Central School District (KG-12)
    2003-04 Enrollment: 3,336 . . . . (845) 246-1043
Housing: Homeownership rate: 70.8% (2005); Median home value: $139,239 (2005); Median rent: $568 per month (2000); Median age of housing: 42 years (2000).
Transportation: Commute to work: 96.4% car, 0.0% public transportation, 1.3% walk, 2.3% work from home (2000); Travel time to work: 49.3% less than 15 minutes, 31.0% 15 to 30 minutes, 6.9% 30 to 45 minutes, 9.3% 45 to 60 minutes, 3.5% 60 minutes or more (2000)

GLENFORD (unincorporated postal area, zip code 12433).
Covers a land area of 3.300 square miles and a water area of 0.063 square miles. Located at 42.00° N. Lat.; 74.15° W. Long.
Population: 0 (2000); Race: 96.9% White, 3.1% Black, 0.0% Asian, 0.0% Hispanic of any race (2000); Density: 0.0 persons per square mile (2000); Age: 9.9% under 18, 21.3% over 64 (2000); Marriage status: 25.6% never married, 62.8% now married, 3.2% widowed, 8.5% divorced (2000); Foreign born: 5.1% (2000); Ancestry (includes multiple ancestries): 22.7% Irish, 21.0% English, 17.3% German, 14.5% Italian, 7.7% Dutch (2000).
Economy: Employment by occupation: 11.6% management, 41.3% professional, 9.5% services, 14.8% sales, 0.0% farming, 22.8% construction, 0.0% production (2000).
Income: Per capita income: $26,230 (2000); Median household income: $38,958 (2000); Poverty rate: 3.7% (2000).
Education: Percent of population age 25 and over with: High school diploma (including GED) or higher: 93.4% (2000); Bachelor's degree or higher: 37.5% (2000).
Housing: Homeownership rate: 83.4% (2000); Median home value: $118,800 (2000); Median rent: $600 per month (2000); Median age of housing: 34 years (2000).
Transportation: Commute to work: 91.8% car, 0.0% public transportation, 6.0% walk, 2.2% work from home (2000); Travel time to work: 16.7% less than 15 minutes, 49.4% 15 to 30 minutes, 24.4% 30 to 45 minutes, 3.3% 45 to 60 minutes, 6.1% 60 minutes or more (2000)

GREENFIELD PARK (unincorporated postal area, zip code 12435).
Covers a land area of 7.803 square miles and a water area of 0.027 square miles. Located at 41.72° N. Lat.; 74.52° W. Long.
Population: 0 (2000); Race: 83.2% White, 9.5% Black, 0.0% Asian, 8.8% Hispanic of any race (2000); Density: 0.0 persons per square mile (2000); Age: 24.8% under 18, 11.5% over 64 (2000); Marriage status: 30.0% never married, 59.2% now married, 8.5% widowed, 2.2% divorced (2000); Foreign born: 6.5% (2000); Ancestry (includes multiple ancestries): 52.3% Other groups, 20.6% Irish, 14.5% German, 9.2% English, 5.7% Russian (2000).
Economy: Resort village. Employment by occupation: 0.0% management, 33.3% professional, 28.0% services, 13.6% sales, 0.0% farming, 15.2% construction, 9.8% production (2000).
Income: Per capita income: $17,061 (2000); Median household income: $30,357 (2000); Poverty rate: 18.7% (2000).
Education: Percent of population age 25 and over with: High school diploma (including GED) or higher: 82.1% (2000); Bachelor's degree or higher: 33.9% (2000).
Housing: Homeownership rate: 77.1% (2000); Median home value: $112,500 (2000); Median rent: $600 per month (2000); Median age of housing: 31 years (2000).
Transportation: Commute to work: 100.0% car, 0.0% public transportation, 0.0% walk, 0.0% work from home (2000); Travel time to work: 16.9% less than 15 minutes, 45.6% 15 to 30 minutes, 17.6% 30 to 45 minutes, 5.1% 45 to 60 minutes, 14.7% 60 minutes or more (2000)

HARDENBURGH (town).
Covers a land area of 81.309 square miles and a water area of 0.226 square miles. Located at 42.04° N. Lat.; 74.61° W. Long.
Population: 204 (1990); 208 (2000); 195 (2005); 182 (2010 projected); Race: 94.4% White, 0.5% Black, 3.6% Asian, 1.0% Hispanic of any race (2005); Density: 2.4 persons per square mile (2005); Average household size: 2.17 (2005); Median age: 47.5 (2005); Males per 100 females: 107.4 (2005); Marriage status: 20.6% never married, 58.7% now married, 8.5% widowed, 12.2% divorced (2000); Foreign born: 5.5% (2000); Ancestry (includes multiple ancestries): 27.4% English, 19.6% Irish, 12.8% German, 11.4% Scottish, 8.7% Other groups (2000).
Economy: Single-family building permits issued: 2 (2005); Multi-family building permits issued: 0 (2005); Employment by occupation: 15.4% management, 25.6% professional, 22.2% services, 19.7% sales, 1.7% farming, 10.3% construction, 5.1% production (2000).
Income: Per capita income: $29,816 (2005); Median household income: $44,000 (2005); Average household income: $60,389 (2005); Percent of households with income of $100,000 or more: 11.1% (2005); Poverty rate: 13.2% (2000).
Education: Percent of population age 25 and over with: High school diploma (including GED) or higher: 87.4% (2005); Bachelor's degree or higher: 16.4% (2005); Master's degree or higher: 8.2% (2005).
Housing: Homeownership rate: 74.4% (2005); Median home value: $145,313 (2005); Median rent: $542 per month (2000); Median age of housing: 37 years (2000).
Transportation: Commute to work: 82.1% car, 0.0% public transportation, 4.3% walk, 13.7% work from home (2000); Travel time to work: 25.7% less

than 15 minutes, 31.7% 15 to 30 minutes, 9.9% 30 to 45 minutes, 16.8% 45 to 60 minutes, 15.8% 60 minutes or more (2000)

HIGH FALLS (CDP). Covers a land area of 1.196 square miles and a water area of 0 square miles. Located at 41.82° N. Lat.; 74.12° W. Long.
Population: 661 (1990); 627 (2000); 585 (2005); 580 (2010 projected); Race: 93.8% White, 3.4% Black, 0.5% Asian, 5.3% Hispanic of any race (2005); Density: 489.3 persons per square mile (2005); Average household size: 2.26 (2005); Median age: 44.1 (2005); Males per 100 females: 91.8 (2005); Marriage status: 24.7% never married, 55.1% now married, 14.2% widowed, 6.1% divorced (2000); Foreign born: 4.6% (2000); Ancestry (includes multiple ancestries): 21.3% Irish, 18.2% German, 15.9% Other groups, 8.8% English, 6.3% United States or American (2000).
Economy: In resort and agricultural area. Employment by occupation: 8.8% management, 29.8% professional, 12.6% services, 25.6% sales, 0.0% farming, 16.8% construction, 6.5% production (2000).
Income: Per capita income: $21,543 (2005); Median household income: $44,375 (2005); Average household income: $48,658 (2005); Percent of households with income of $100,000 or more: 6.9% (2005); Poverty rate: 8.4% (2000).
Education: Percent of population age 25 and over with: High school diploma (including GED) or higher: 85.5% (2005); Bachelor's degree or higher: 16.7% (2005); Master's degree or higher: 3.8% (2005).
Housing: Homeownership rate: 72.2% (2005); Median home value: $135,268 (2005); Median rent: $703 per month (2000); Median age of housing: 47 years (2000).
Transportation: Commute to work: 92.4% car, 0.0% public transportation, 0.0% walk, 7.6% work from home (2000); Travel time to work: 11.2% less than 15 minutes, 43.8% 15 to 30 minutes, 18.6% 30 to 45 minutes, 12.8% 45 to 60 minutes, 13.6% 60 minutes or more (2000)

HIGHLAND (CDP). Covers a land area of 4.714 square miles and a water area of 0.354 square miles. Located at 41.71° N. Lat.; 73.96° W. Long. Elevation is 10 feet.
Population: 4,494 (1990); 5,060 (2000); 5,430 (2005); 5,775 (2010 projected); Race: 88.1% White, 5.7% Black, 1.9% Asian, 6.9% Hispanic of any race (2005); Density: 1,151.8 persons per square mile (2005); Average household size: 2.62 (2005); Median age: 40.1 (2005); Males per 100 females: 84.7 (2005); Marriage status: 25.7% never married, 54.4% now married, 11.6% widowed, 8.3% divorced (2000); Foreign born: 5.8% (2000); Ancestry (includes multiple ancestries): 35.2% Italian, 19.0% German, 17.7% Irish, 13.0% Other groups, 8.6% English (2000).
Economy: Summer residential area. Manufacturing: computer equipment, apparel, wine and other beverages, electrical goods. Center of mid-Hudson apple-growing region, largest in state after Wayne county region. Employment by occupation: 11.1% management, 21.5% professional, 16.6% services, 30.4% sales, 0.0% farming, 10.3% construction, 10.1% production (2000).
Income: Per capita income: $23,309 (2005); Median household income: $50,905 (2005); Average household income: $58,136 (2005); Percent of households with income of $100,000 or more: 14.2% (2005); Poverty rate: 6.5% (2000).
Education: Percent of population age 25 and over with: High school diploma (including GED) or higher: 80.6% (2005); Bachelor's degree or higher: 23.6% (2005); Master's degree or higher: 10.0% (2005).
School District(s)
Highland Central School District (KG-12)
    2003-04 Enrollment: 2,075 . . . . (845) 691-1012
Housing: Homeownership rate: 57.5% (2005); Median home value: $162,531 (2005); Median rent: $592 per month (2000); Median age of housing: 41 years (2000).
Newspapers: Highland/Mid-Hudson Post (General - Circulation 1,580); New Paltz Times (General - Circulation 6,083); Southern Ulster Pioneer (General - Circulation 2,422)
Transportation: Commute to work: 91.8% car, 1.7% public transportation, 2.6% walk, 2.7% work from home (2000); Travel time to work: 29.8% less than 15 minutes, 36.0% 15 to 30 minutes, 16.3% 30 to 45 minutes, 7.0% 45 to 60 minutes, 10.9% 60 minutes or more (2000)
Additional Information Contacts
Southern Ulster County Chamber of Commerce . . . . (845) 691-6070
    http://www.southernulsterchamber.org

HILLSIDE (CDP). Covers a land area of 0.841 square miles and a water area of 0 square miles. Located at 41.92° N. Lat.; 74.03° W. Long.
Population: 1,008 (1990); 882 (2000); 852 (2005); 837 (2010 projected); Race: 95.2% White, 1.8% Black, 2.5% Asian, 2.0% Hispanic of any race (2005); Density: 1,013.2 persons per square mile (2005); Average household size: 2.57 (2005); Median age: 46.7 (2005); Males per 100 females: 104.8 (2005); Marriage status: 14.8% never married, 73.9% now married, 4.1% widowed, 7.2% divorced (2000); Foreign born: 4.7% (2000); Ancestry (includes multiple ancestries): 24.3% Irish, 19.2% German, 13.1% United States or American, 10.7% Italian, 8.0% English (2000).
Economy: Employment by occupation: 19.9% management, 37.8% professional, 8.2% services, 25.1% sales, 0.0% farming, 3.2% construction, 5.8% production (2000).
Income: Per capita income: $45,352 (2005); Median household income: $93,598 (2005); Average household income: $116,737 (2005); Percent of households with income of $100,000 or more: 46.8% (2005); Poverty rate: 0.5% (2000).
Education: Percent of population age 25 and over with: High school diploma (including GED) or higher: 95.2% (2005); Bachelor's degree or higher: 52.0% (2005); Master's degree or higher: 26.0% (2005).
Housing: Homeownership rate: 95.2% (2005); Median home value: $265,865 (2005); Median rent: $<$100 per month (2000); Median age of housing: 35 years (2000).
Transportation: Commute to work: 94.6% car, 1.5% public transportation, 0.0% walk, 3.9% work from home (2000); Travel time to work: 49.9% less than 15 minutes, 31.9% 15 to 30 minutes, 8.1% 30 to 45 minutes, 3.8% 45 to 60 minutes, 6.3% 60 minutes or more (2000)

HURLEY (town). Covers a land area of 29.948 square miles and a water area of 6.018 square miles. Located at 41.95° N. Lat.; 74.09° W. Long.
Population: 6,741 (1990); 6,564 (2000); 6,572 (2005); 6,596 (2010 projected); Race: 95.3% White, 1.6% Black, 1.2% Asian, 2.4% Hispanic of any race (2005); Density: 219.4 persons per square mile (2005); Average household size: 2.39 (2005); Median age: 46.5 (2005); Males per 100 females: 94.8 (2005); Marriage status: 21.5% never married, 61.6% now married, 7.3% widowed, 9.5% divorced (2000); Foreign born: 4.6% (2000); Ancestry (includes multiple ancestries): 25.0% German, 21.5% Irish, 14.3% Italian, 14.1% English, 9.0% Polish (2000).
Economy: In agricultural and summer-resort area. Single-family building permits issued: 22 (2005); Multi-family building permits issued: 0 (2005); Employment by occupation: 12.7% management, 29.7% professional, 10.9% services, 25.7% sales, 0.5% farming, 10.3% construction, 10.2% production (2000).
Income: Per capita income: $31,192 (2005); Median household income: $58,333 (2005); Average household income: $73,929 (2005); Percent of households with income of $100,000 or more: 22.3% (2005); Poverty rate: 6.2% (2000).
Education: Percent of population age 25 and over with: High school diploma (including GED) or higher: 89.3% (2005); Bachelor's degree or higher: 33.7% (2005); Master's degree or higher: 16.6% (2005).
School District(s)
Kingston City School District (PK-12)
    2003-04 Enrollment: 8,149 . . . . (845) 339-3000
Housing: Homeownership rate: 86.6% (2005); Median home value: $177,289 (2005); Median rent: $566 per month (2000); Median age of housing: 37 years (2000).
Transportation: Commute to work: 92.3% car, 0.0% public transportation, 1.7% walk, 6.0% work from home (2000); Travel time to work: 25.1% less than 15 minutes, 44.7% 15 to 30 minutes, 11.1% 30 to 45 minutes, 8.7% 45 to 60 minutes, 10.4% 60 minutes or more (2000)

HURLEY (CDP). Covers a land area of 5.503 square miles and a water area of 0.031 square miles. Located at 41.92° N. Lat.; 74.05° W. Long.
Population: 3,771 (1990); 3,561 (2000); 3,712 (2005); 3,847 (2010 projected); Race: 95.5% White, 1.5% Black, 1.4% Asian, 2.8% Hispanic of any race (2005); Density: 674.6 persons per square mile (2005); Average household size: 2.47 (2005); Median age: 45.5 (2005); Males per 100 females: 90.8 (2005); Marriage status: 19.5% never married, 63.8% now married, 8.1% widowed, 8.6% divorced (2000); Foreign born: 5.3% (2000); Ancestry (includes multiple ancestries): 26.2% German, 19.7% Irish, 15.0% Italian, 13.8% English, 10.4% Dutch (2000).
Economy: Employment by occupation: 12.9% management, 31.6% professional, 14.2% services, 23.4% sales, 0.3% farming, 7.0% construction, 10.6% production (2000).
Income: Per capita income: $33,206 (2005); Median household income: $65,987 (2005); Average household income: $81,429 (2005); Percent of

households with income of $100,000 or more: 27.0% (2005); Poverty rate: 2.3% (2000).
Education: Percent of population age 25 and over with: High school diploma (including GED) or higher: 91.9% (2005); Bachelor's degree or higher: 34.9% (2005); Master's degree or higher: 16.0% (2005).
Housing: Homeownership rate: 90.4% (2005); Median home value: $170,621 (2005); Median rent: $549 per month (2000); Median age of housing: 39 years (2000).
Transportation: Commute to work: 93.0% car, 1.3% public transportation, 1.1% walk, 4.6% work from home (2000); Travel time to work: 34.8% less than 15 minutes, 39.8% 15 to 30 minutes, 7.5% 30 to 45 minutes, 11.3% 45 to 60 minutes, 6.6% 60 minutes or more (2000)

KERHONKSON (CDP). Covers a land area of 5.305 square miles and a water area of 0.005 square miles. Located at 41.77° N. Lat.; 74.29° W. Long. Elevation is 264 feet.
Population: 1,640 (1990); 1,732 (2000); 1,704 (2005); 1,664 (2010 projected); Race: 90.1% White, 2.1% Black, 1.5% Asian, 11.9% Hispanic of any race (2005); Density: 321.2 persons per square mile (2005); Average household size: 2.43 (2005); Median age: 39.5 (2005); Males per 100 females: 98.4 (2005); Marriage status: 27.7% never married, 54.8% now married, 7.8% widowed, 9.8% divorced (2000); Foreign born: 10.9% (2000); Ancestry (includes multiple ancestries): 23.5% German, 15.4% Irish, 13.2% Other groups, 12.2% Italian, 9.4% United States or American (2000).
Economy: Popular summer recreational spot. Employment by occupation: 6.9% management, 16.4% professional, 25.1% services, 23.3% sales, 0.0% farming, 8.1% construction, 20.2% production (2000).
Income: Per capita income: $21,495 (2005); Median household income: $41,053 (2005); Average household income: $52,176 (2005); Percent of households with income of $100,000 or more: 12.7% (2005); Poverty rate: 10.2% (2000).
Education: Percent of population age 25 and over with: High school diploma (including GED) or higher: 80.3% (2005); Bachelor's degree or higher: 17.4% (2005); Master's degree or higher: 6.5% (2005).
School District(s)
Rondout Valley Central School District (KG-12)
    2003-04 Enrollment: 2,797 . . . . (845) 687-2400
Housing: Homeownership rate: 66.1% (2005); Median home value: $135,714 (2005); Median rent: $431 per month (2000); Median age of housing: 46 years (2000).
Transportation: Commute to work: 95.5% car, 0.0% public transportation, 1.9% walk, 2.6% work from home (2000); Travel time to work: 31.9% less than 15 minutes, 27.8% 15 to 30 minutes, 26.7% 30 to 45 minutes, 10.3% 45 to 60 minutes, 3.3% 60 minutes or more (2000)

KINGSTON (city). Covers a land area of 7.354 square miles and a water area of 1.298 square miles. Located at 41.92° N. Lat.; 74.00° W. Long. Elevation is 223 feet.
History: In 1615, Dutch traders established a trading post at the present site of Kingston and named it Esopus. A group of Dutch colonists from Albany made the first permanent settlement in 1653. In 1658, Director General Peter Stuyvesant erected a stockade and blockhouse and in 1661 granted a charter to the village, which he called Wiltwyck. In 1669, the English Governor Francis Lovelace gave it its present name in honor of Kingston L'Isle, his family seat in England. Kingston was the site of the New York government during 1777. Boat building and the cement industry both began about 1830.
Population: 23,059 (1990); 23,456 (2000); 23,222 (2005); 23,049 (2010 projected); Race: 77.6% White, 15.0% Black, 1.8% Asian, 8.2% Hispanic of any race (2005); Density: 3,157.7 persons per square mile (2005); Average household size: 2.36 (2005); Median age: 39.0 (2005); Males per 100 females: 89.4 (2005); Marriage status: 32.4% never married, 47.3% now married, 9.7% widowed, 10.6% divorced (2000); Foreign born: 5.1% (2000); Ancestry (includes multiple ancestries): 21.9% Irish, 19.9% Other groups, 18.8% German, 16.1% Italian, 6.1% English (2000).
Economy: Single-family building permits issued: 14 (2005); Multi-family building permits issued: 0 (2005); Employment by occupation: 10.4% management, 22.9% professional, 20.4% services, 26.6% sales, 0.4% farming, 7.1% construction, 12.2% production (2000).
Income: Per capita income: $20,209 (2005); Median household income: $33,888 (2005); Average household income: $46,184 (2005); Percent of households with income of $100,000 or more: 8.5% (2005); Poverty rate: 15.8% (2000).
Education: Percent of population age 25 and over with: High school diploma (including GED) or higher: 78.8% (2005); Bachelor's degree or higher: 20.4% (2005); Master's degree or higher: 8.4% (2005).
School District(s)
Kingston City School District (PK-12)
    2003-04 Enrollment: 8,149 . . . . (845) 339-3000
Housing: Homeownership rate: 47.5% (2005); Median home value: $130,435 (2005); Median rent: $520 per month (2000); Median age of housing: 60 years (2000).
Hospitals: Benedictine Hospital (222 beds); Kingston Hospital (160 beds)
Safety: Violent crime rate: 39.4 per 10,000 population; Property crime rate: 398.5 per 10,000 population (2004).
Newspapers: The Daily Freeman (Circulation 21,313); Woodstock Times (General - Circulation 5,000)
Transportation: Commute to work: 86.7% car, 4.5% public transportation, 4.8% walk, 2.7% work from home (2000); Travel time to work: 52.4% less than 15 minutes, 27.1% 15 to 30 minutes, 8.5% 30 to 45 minutes, 5.9% 45 to 60 minutes, 6.1% 60 minutes or more (2000)
Additional Information Contacts
City of Kingston . . . . (845) 334-3915
   http://www.ci.kingston.ny.us/
Kingston Chamber of Commerce . . . . (845) 338-5100
   http://www.ulsterchamber.org/
Ulster County Chamber of Commerce . . . . (845) 338-5100
   http://www.ulsterchamber.org

KINGSTON (town). Covers a land area of 7.756 square miles and a water area of 0.050 square miles. Located at 41.99° N. Lat.; 74.05° W. Long. Elevation is 223 feet.
History: First permanent settlement (Wiltwyck) was established in 1652. Served as the first capital of New York State until it was burned by the British in Oct. 1777. Many old Dutch stone houses; the Senate house (1676 meeting place of the first state legislature); the old Dutch church (1659) and cemetery (1661); and the burial place of James Clinton. Incorporated as a village 1805, and as a city through the union (1872) of Kingston and Rondout.
Population: 864 (1990); 908 (2000); 881 (2005); 864 (2010 projected); Race: 95.1% White, 2.2% Black, 0.5% Asian, 1.7% Hispanic of any race (2005); Density: 113.6 persons per square mile (2005); Average household size: 2.50 (2005); Median age: 42.4 (2005); Males per 100 females: 108.8 (2005); Marriage status: 23.5% never married, 58.8% now married, 6.2% widowed, 11.6% divorced (2000); Foreign born: 1.1% (2000); Ancestry (includes multiple ancestries): 24.6% Irish, 22.1% German, 18.9% Italian, 9.4% English, 7.6% Dutch (2000).
Economy: A tourist hub for the Catskill-Shawangunk resort area. It has plants that make a variety of manufacturing goods, including data acquisition and control systems, ships, conveyors and separators for sand and gravel, hydraulic systems, electronic and mechanical assemblies, filters and filter systems, machines, boilers and draperies and textiles. The city is also a market for nearby fruit and vegetable farms (especially apples). Single-family building permits issued: 5 (2005); Multi-family building permits issued: 0 (2005); Employment by occupation: 8.7% management, 23.4% professional, 12.8% services, 30.6% sales, 0.0% farming, 11.1% construction, 13.4% production (2000).
Income: Per capita income: $21,586 (2005); Median household income: $48,881 (2005); Average household income: $54,027 (2005); Percent of households with income of $100,000 or more: 9.4% (2005); Poverty rate: 7.6% (2000).
Education: Percent of population age 25 and over with: High school diploma (including GED) or higher: 85.2% (2005); Bachelor's degree or higher: 14.5% (2005); Master's degree or higher: 6.8% (2005).
Housing: Homeownership rate: 86.1% (2005); Median home value: $123,925 (2005); Median rent: $556 per month (2000); Median age of housing: 33 years (2000).
Transportation: Commute to work: 95.4% car, 1.1% public transportation, 1.5% walk, 1.8% work from home (2000); Travel time to work: 27.5% less than 15 minutes, 48.4% 15 to 30 minutes, 7.2% 30 to 45 minutes, 6.8% 45 to 60 minutes, 10.1% 60 minutes or more (2000)
Additional Information Contacts
Town of Kingston . . . . (845) 336-8853
   http://www.town.kingston.ny.us/

LAKE HILL (unincorporated postal area, zip code 12448). Covers a land area of 6.375 square miles and a water area of 0 square miles. Located at 42.07° N. Lat.; 74.18° W. Long.

Population: 0 (2000); Race: 87.9% White, 0.0% Black, 0.0% Asian, 0.0% Hispanic of any race (2000); Density: 0.0 persons per square mile (2000); Age: 8.7% under 18, 22.3% over 64 (2000); Marriage status: 33.5% never married, 56.3% now married, 10.2% widowed, 0.0% divorced (2000); Foreign born: 9.2% (2000); Ancestry (includes multiple ancestries): 35.9% German, 20.4% Irish, 19.9% Italian, 15.0% Russian, 11.7% English (2000).
Economy: Employment by occupation: 23.3% management, 32.8% professional, 9.5% services, 12.9% sales, 0.0% farming, 6.0% construction, 15.5% production (2000).
Income: Per capita income: $60,417 (2000); Median household income: $78,789 (2000); Poverty rate: 3.4% (2000).
Education: Percent of population age 25 and over with: High school diploma (including GED) or higher: 91.0% (2000); Bachelor's degree or higher: 52.7% (2000).
Housing: Homeownership rate: 81.6% (2000); Median home value: $133,000 (2000); Median rent: $905 per month (2000); Median age of housing: 34 years (2000).
Transportation: Commute to work: 78.4% car, 10.3% public transportation, 0.0% walk, 6.9% work from home (2000); Travel time to work: 9.3% less than 15 minutes, 10.2% 15 to 30 minutes, 25.9% 30 to 45 minutes, 10.2% 45 to 60 minutes, 44.4% 60 minutes or more (2000)

LAKE KATRINE (CDP). Covers a land area of 2.210 square miles and a water area of 0.041 square miles. Located at 41.98° N. Lat.; 73.99° W. Long.
Population: 1,998 (1990); 2,396 (2000); 2,393 (2005); 2,396 (2010 projected); Race: 90.8% White, 5.5% Black, 1.5% Asian, 2.4% Hispanic of any race (2005); Density: 1,082.8 persons per square mile (2005); Average household size: 2.87 (2005); Median age: 46.2 (2005); Males per 100 females: 83.4 (2005); Marriage status: 18.5% never married, 63.7% now married, 7.9% widowed, 9.9% divorced (2000); Foreign born: 4.4% (2000); Ancestry (includes multiple ancestries): 18.1% Irish, 14.1% German, 13.8% Italian, 8.3% Other groups, 7.5% United States or American (2000).
Economy: Employment by occupation: 9.6% management, 30.5% professional, 18.7% services, 24.4% sales, 0.0% farming, 5.8% construction, 11.0% production (2000).
Income: Per capita income: $21,767 (2005); Median household income: $44,934 (2005); Average household income: $54,404 (2005); Percent of households with income of $100,000 or more: 12.2% (2005); Poverty rate: 13.2% (2000).
Education: Percent of population age 25 and over with: High school diploma (including GED) or higher: 86.7% (2005); Bachelor's degree or higher: 18.9% (2005); Master's degree or higher: 6.8% (2005).
School District(s)
Kingston City School District (PK-12)
    2003-04 Enrollment: 8,149 . . . . (845) 339-3000
Housing: Homeownership rate: 59.4% (2005); Median home value: $126,835 (2005); Median rent: $621 per month (2000); Median age of housing: 34 years (2000).
Transportation: Commute to work: 94.1% car, 1.2% public transportation, 3.2% walk, 1.5% work from home (2000); Travel time to work: 35.2% less than 15 minutes, 41.0% 15 to 30 minutes, 9.8% 30 to 45 minutes, 10.1% 45 to 60 minutes, 3.9% 60 minutes or more (2000)

LINCOLN PARK (CDP). Covers a land area of 1.361 square miles and a water area of 0.030 square miles. Located at 41.95° N. Lat.; 74.00° W. Long.
Population: 2,481 (1990); 2,337 (2000); 2,502 (2005); 2,669 (2010 projected); Race: 92.4% White, 4.3% Black, 1.5% Asian, 3.3% Hispanic of any race (2005); Density: 1,837.9 persons per square mile (2005); Average household size: 2.18 (2005); Median age: 43.2 (2005); Males per 100 females: 84.4 (2005); Marriage status: 23.9% never married, 53.2% now married, 13.8% widowed, 9.1% divorced (2000); Foreign born: 5.9% (2000); Ancestry (includes multiple ancestries): 23.0% German, 21.8% Irish, 19.2% Italian, 11.0% Other groups, 6.0% Polish (2000).
Economy: Employment by occupation: 16.2% management, 18.3% professional, 16.4% services, 29.5% sales, 1.3% farming, 9.0% construction, 9.3% production (2000).
Income: Per capita income: $21,042 (2005); Median household income: $38,028 (2005); Average household income: $45,316 (2005); Percent of households with income of $100,000 or more: 7.2% (2005); Poverty rate: 12.9% (2000).
Education: Percent of population age 25 and over with: High school diploma (including GED) or higher: 79.4% (2005); Bachelor's degree or higher: 17.8% (2005); Master's degree or higher: 7.1% (2005).

Housing: Homeownership rate: 56.3% (2005); Median home value: $125,199 (2005); Median rent: $488 per month (2000); Median age of housing: 41 years (2000).
Transportation: Commute to work: 91.2% car, 2.9% public transportation, 3.2% walk, 2.0% work from home (2000); Travel time to work: 59.3% less than 15 minutes, 23.4% 15 to 30 minutes, 9.4% 30 to 45 minutes, 2.3% 45 to 60 minutes, 5.7% 60 minutes or more (2000)

LLOYD (town). Covers a land area of 31.731 square miles and a water area of 1.640 square miles. Located at 41.71° N. Lat.; 73.99° W. Long.
Population: 9,275 (1990); 9,941 (2000); 10,476 (2005); 10,989 (2010 projected); Race: 88.5% White, 6.5% Black, 1.5% Asian, 6.2% Hispanic of any race (2005); Density: 330.1 persons per square mile (2005); Average household size: 2.68 (2005); Median age: 39.0 (2005); Males per 100 females: 93.1 (2005); Marriage status: 25.8% never married, 57.8% now married, 8.5% widowed, 7.8% divorced (2000); Foreign born: 5.8% (2000); Ancestry (includes multiple ancestries): 34.3% Italian, 18.9% Irish, 18.6% German, 10.9% Other groups, 8.7% English (2000).
Economy: Single-family building permits issued: 106 (2005); Multi-family building permits issued: 0 (2005); Employment by occupation: 13.7% management, 25.1% professional, 13.7% services, 27.3% sales, 0.6% farming, 9.7% construction, 9.8% production (2000).
Income: Per capita income: $25,749 (2005); Median household income: $58,413 (2005); Average household income: $67,067 (2005); Percent of households with income of $100,000 or more: 19.6% (2005); Poverty rate: 7.3% (2000).
Education: Percent of population age 25 and over with: High school diploma (including GED) or higher: 82.8% (2005); Bachelor's degree or higher: 27.8% (2005); Master's degree or higher: 11.8% (2005).
Housing: Homeownership rate: 65.1% (2005); Median home value: $184,017 (2005); Median rent: $589 per month (2000); Median age of housing: 37 years (2000).
Safety: Violent crime rate: 4.9 per 10,000 population; Property crime rate: 129.5 per 10,000 population (2004).
Transportation: Commute to work: 92.0% car, 2.1% public transportation, 2.2% walk, 3.1% work from home (2000); Travel time to work: 27.2% less than 15 minutes, 37.4% 15 to 30 minutes, 20.0% 30 to 45 minutes, 6.2% 45 to 60 minutes, 9.3% 60 minutes or more (2000)

MALDEN (CDP). Covers a land area of 0.508 square miles and a water area of 0 square miles. Located at 42.09° N. Lat.; 73.93° W. Long.
Population: 376 (1990); 413 (2000); 465 (2005); 498 (2010 projected); Race: 84.1% White, 7.5% Black, 0.4% Asian, 11.4% Hispanic of any race (2005); Density: 915.7 persons per square mile (2005); Average household size: 2.64 (2005); Median age: 34.6 (2005); Males per 100 females: 90.6 (2005); Marriage status: 23.7% never married, 59.3% now married, 6.0% widowed, 11.1% divorced (2000); Foreign born: 5.5% (2000); Ancestry (includes multiple ancestries): 18.4% English, 13.7% German, 13.1% Greek, 11.9% Italian, 10.2% Irish (2000).
Economy: Employment by occupation: 2.1% management, 33.9% professional, 15.3% services, 19.9% sales, 0.0% farming, 17.8% construction, 11.0% production (2000).
Income: Per capita income: $20,962 (2005); Median household income: $45,179 (2005); Average household income: $55,384 (2005); Percent of households with income of $100,000 or more: 6.3% (2005); Poverty rate: 5.5% (2000).
Education: Percent of population age 25 and over with: High school diploma (including GED) or higher: 87.2% (2005); Bachelor's degree or higher: 21.5% (2005); Master's degree or higher: 16.4% (2005).
Housing: Homeownership rate: 72.7% (2005); Median home value: $177,500 (2005); Median rent: $471 per month (2000); Median age of housing: 60+ years (2000).
Transportation: Commute to work: 93.5% car, 0.0% public transportation, 0.0% walk, 6.5% work from home (2000); Travel time to work: 30.9% less than 15 minutes, 19.8% 15 to 30 minutes, 33.2% 30 to 45 minutes, 6.0% 45 to 60 minutes, 10.1% 60 minutes or more (2000)

MARBLETOWN (town). Covers a land area of 54.582 square miles and a water area of 0.608 square miles. Located at 41.85° N. Lat.; 74.15° W. Long.
Population: 5,285 (1990); 5,854 (2000); 6,011 (2005); 6,183 (2010 projected); Race: 94.9% White, 1.7% Black, 0.9% Asian, 2.4% Hispanic of any race (2005); Density: 110.1 persons per square mile (2005); Average household size: 2.40 (2005); Median age: 44.1 (2005); Males per 100 females: 96.6 (2005); Marriage status: 24.6% never married, 58.1% now

married, 7.0% widowed, 10.3% divorced (2000); Foreign born: 2.9% (2000); Ancestry (includes multiple ancestries): 25.7% German, 20.0% Irish, 18.6% Italian, 15.3% English, 8.7% Other groups (2000).
Economy: Single-family building permits issued: 37 (2005); Multi-family building permits issued: 0 (2005); Employment by occupation: 14.5% management, 32.6% professional, 13.5% services, 20.3% sales, 0.5% farming, 9.5% construction, 9.1% production (2000).
Income: Per capita income: $27,275 (2005); Median household income: $52,481 (2005); Average household income: $65,094 (2005); Percent of households with income of $100,000 or more: 17.9% (2005); Poverty rate: 7.3% (2000).
Education: Percent of population age 25 and over with: High school diploma (including GED) or higher: 89.5% (2005); Bachelor's degree or higher: 37.6% (2005); Master's degree or higher: 16.6% (2005).
Housing: Homeownership rate: 79.1% (2005); Median home value: $211,934 (2005); Median rent: $556 per month (2000); Median age of housing: 39 years (2000).
Transportation: Commute to work: 87.1% car, 0.9% public transportation, 2.8% walk, 8.1% work from home (2000); Travel time to work: 23.3% less than 15 minutes, 36.5% 15 to 30 minutes, 19.7% 30 to 45 minutes, 12.2% 45 to 60 minutes, 8.4% 60 minutes or more (2000)

MARLBORO (CDP). Aka Marlborough. Covers a land area of 2.764 square miles and a water area of 0.587 square miles. Located at 41.60° N. Lat.; 73.97° W. Long. Elevation is 11 feet.
History: Also spelled Marlborough.
Population: 2,208 (1990); 2,339 (2000); 2,241 (2005); 2,086 (2010 projected); Race: 94.9% White, 2.1% Black, 0.4% Asian, 6.4% Hispanic of any race (2005); Density: 810.8 persons per square mile (2005); Average household size: 2.48 (2005); Median age: 38.5 (2005); Males per 100 females: 94.4 (2005); Marriage status: 25.6% never married, 55.8% now married, 9.1% widowed, 9.4% divorced (2000); Foreign born: 6.2% (2000); Ancestry (includes multiple ancestries): 33.3% Italian, 28.6% Irish, 11.0% United States or American, 10.5% German, 10.2% English (2000).
Economy: Manufacturing: building materials, dairy and canned foods, beverages. Agriculture: vegetables, grapes, tree fruit. Employment by occupation: 15.4% management, 22.0% professional, 17.2% services, 21.4% sales, 0.6% farming, 9.9% construction, 13.6% production (2000).
Income: Per capita income: $26,601 (2005); Median household income: $52,037 (2005); Average household income: $65,870 (2005); Percent of households with income of $100,000 or more: 19.6% (2005); Poverty rate: 12.0% (2000).
Education: Percent of population age 25 and over with: High school diploma (including GED) or higher: 81.0% (2005); Bachelor's degree or higher: 22.5% (2005); Master's degree or higher: 10.9% (2005).
School District(s)
Marlboro Central School District (KG-12)
    2003-04 Enrollment: 2,136 . . . . (845) 236-5802
Housing: Homeownership rate: 58.0% (2005); Median home value: $205,412 (2005); Median rent: $521 per month (2000); Median age of housing: 47 years (2000).
Transportation: Commute to work: 93.1% car, 2.5% public transportation, 1.8% walk, 2.6% work from home (2000); Travel time to work: 19.9% less than 15 minutes, 36.4% 15 to 30 minutes, 24.3% 30 to 45 minutes, 7.6% 45 to 60 minutes, 11.8% 60 minutes or more (2000)

MARLBOROUGH (town). Covers a land area of 24.828 square miles and a water area of 1.670 square miles. Located at 41.63° N. Lat.; 73.98° W. Long.
Population: 7,430 (1990); 8,263 (2000); 8,390 (2005); 8,504 (2010 projected); Race: 93.6% White, 3.4% Black, 0.4% Asian, 4.9% Hispanic of any race (2005); Density: 337.9 persons per square mile (2005); Average household size: 2.71 (2005); Median age: 38.3 (2005); Males per 100 females: 96.6 (2005); Marriage status: 24.9% never married, 58.9% now married, 7.9% widowed, 8.3% divorced (2000); Foreign born: 6.2% (2000); Ancestry (includes multiple ancestries): 38.2% Italian, 22.3% Irish, 15.6% German, 11.2% English, 9.4% Other groups (2000).
Economy: Single-family building permits issued: 60 (2005); Multi-family building permits issued: 0 (2005); Employment by occupation: 13.9% management, 20.5% professional, 15.1% services, 26.0% sales, 1.6% farming, 12.1% construction, 10.7% production (2000).
Income: Per capita income: $25,840 (2005); Median household income: $58,508 (2005); Average household income: $70,076 (2005); Percent of households with income of $100,000 or more: 21.7% (2005); Poverty rate: 8.2% (2000).

Education: Percent of population age 25 and over with: High school diploma (including GED) or higher: 81.5% (2005); Bachelor's degree or higher: 19.7% (2005); Master's degree or higher: 8.2% (2005).
Housing: Homeownership rate: 69.0% (2005); Median home value: $229,378 (2005); Median rent: $555 per month (2000); Median age of housing: 37 years (2000).
Safety: Violent crime rate: 19.1 per 10,000 population; Property crime rate: 156.6 per 10,000 population (2004).
Transportation: Commute to work: 94.2% car, 2.0% public transportation, 1.4% walk, 2.4% work from home (2000); Travel time to work: 27.2% less than 15 minutes, 37.3% 15 to 30 minutes, 19.0% 30 to 45 minutes, 6.0% 45 to 60 minutes, 10.5% 60 minutes or more (2000)

MILTON (CDP). Covers a land area of 2.841 square miles and a water area of 0.007 square miles. Located at 41.65° N. Lat.; 73.96° W. Long.
Population: 1,308 (1990); 1,251 (2000); 1,121 (2005); 1,044 (2010 projected); Race: 92.1% White, 3.8% Black, 0.5% Asian, 4.5% Hispanic of any race (2005); Density: 394.6 persons per square mile (2005); Average household size: 2.68 (2005); Median age: 38.7 (2005); Males per 100 females: 95.6 (2005); Marriage status: 25.9% never married, 60.2% now married, 7.6% widowed, 6.4% divorced (2000); Foreign born: 4.5% (2000); Ancestry (includes multiple ancestries): 39.8% Italian, 18.2% Irish, 15.4% English, 14.8% German, 9.0% Dutch (2000).
Economy: Agriculture: tree fruit, grapes. Employment by occupation: 18.8% management, 17.0% professional, 13.6% services, 25.3% sales, 1.8% farming, 11.5% construction, 12.0% production (2000).
Income: Per capita income: $28,548 (2005); Median household income: $62,037 (2005); Average household income: $76,561 (2005); Percent of households with income of $100,000 or more: 25.6% (2005); Poverty rate: 5.1% (2000).
Education: Percent of population age 25 and over with: High school diploma (including GED) or higher: 79.6% (2005); Bachelor's degree or higher: 22.0% (2005); Master's degree or higher: 7.1% (2005).
School District(s)
Marlboro Central School District (KG-12)
    2003-04 Enrollment: 2,136 . . . . (845) 236-5802
Housing: Homeownership rate: 69.9% (2005); Median home value: $198,571 (2005); Median rent: $556 per month (2000); Median age of housing: 51 years (2000).
Transportation: Commute to work: 91.6% car, 3.2% public transportation, 2.9% walk, 2.3% work from home (2000); Travel time to work: 37.0% less than 15 minutes, 34.6% 15 to 30 minutes, 14.2% 30 to 45 minutes, 3.4% 45 to 60 minutes, 10.8% 60 minutes or more (2000)

MODENA (unincorporated postal area, zip code 12548). Covers a land area of 6.405 square miles and a water area of 0.017 square miles. Located at 41.66° N. Lat.; 74.11° W. Long. Elevation is 453 feet.
Population: 0 (2000); Race: 94.1% White, 3.4% Black, 0.0% Asian, 4.3% Hispanic of any race (2000); Density: 0.0 persons per square mile (2000); Age: 30.8% under 18, 11.1% over 64 (2000); Marriage status: 23.3% never married, 60.6% now married, 5.9% widowed, 10.2% divorced (2000); Foreign born: 4.4% (2000); Ancestry (includes multiple ancestries): 26.1% Italian, 24.1% Irish, 23.2% German, 9.4% Other groups, 8.9% English (2000).
Economy: Employment by occupation: 8.7% management, 16.9% professional, 19.9% services, 26.2% sales, 0.5% farming, 10.1% construction, 17.8% production (2000).
Income: Per capita income: $19,481 (2000); Median household income: $43,409 (2000); Poverty rate: 12.1% (2000).
Education: Percent of population age 25 and over with: High school diploma (including GED) or higher: 77.9% (2000); Bachelor's degree or higher: 16.3% (2000).
Housing: Homeownership rate: 73.2% (2000); Median home value: $132,100 (2000); Median rent: $580 per month (2000); Median age of housing: 23 years (2000).
Transportation: Commute to work: 91.5% car, 0.8% public transportation, 0.0% walk, 5.9% work from home (2000); Travel time to work: 20.2% less than 15 minutes, 44.1% 15 to 30 minutes, 18.5% 30 to 45 minutes, 7.8% 45 to 60 minutes, 9.4% 60 minutes or more (2000)

MOUNT MARION (unincorporated postal area, zip code 12456). Covers a land area of 0.642 square miles and a water area of 0.026 square miles. Located at 42.03° N. Lat.; 73.99° W. Long. Elevation is 178 feet.
Population: 0 (2000); Race: 96.7% White, 2.1% Black, 1.2% Asian, 0.0% Hispanic of any race (2000); Density: 0.0 persons per square mile (2000);

Age: 20.0% under 18, 18.8% over 64 (2000); Marriage status: 30.8% never married, 54.0% now married, 10.8% widowed, 4.4% divorced (2000); Foreign born: 4.4% (2000); Ancestry (includes multiple ancestries): 34.7% German, 25.4% Irish, 15.9% Italian, 8.3% Other groups, 6.8% English (2000).
Economy: In resort and agricultural area. Employment by occupation: 5.4% management, 8.9% professional, 31.7% services, 19.0% sales, 0.0% farming, 17.1% construction, 17.8% production (2000).
Income: Per capita income: $14,488 (2000); Median household income: $31,739 (2000); Poverty rate: 9.0% (2000).
Education: Percent of population age 25 and over with: High school diploma (including GED) or higher: 79.7% (2000); Bachelor's degree or higher: 3.5% (2000).
Housing: Homeownership rate: 88.0% (2000); Median home value: $67,700 (2000); Median rent: $545 per month (2000); Median age of housing: 44 years (2000).
Transportation: Commute to work: 94.5% car, 3.2% public transportation, 0.0% walk, 2.3% work from home (2000); Travel time to work: 22.1% less than 15 minutes, 51.8% 15 to 30 minutes, 10.2% 30 to 45 minutes, 9.6% 45 to 60 minutes, 6.3% 60 minutes or more (2000)

MOUNT TREMPER (unincorporated postal area, zip code 12457). Aka The Corner. Covers a land area of 18.247 square miles and a water area of 0 square miles. Located at 42.03° N. Lat.; 74.23° W. Long.
Population: 0 (2000); Race: 97.1% White, 0.0% Black, 0.7% Asian, 0.0% Hispanic of any race (2000); Density: 0.0 persons per square mile (2000); Age: 23.6% under 18, 8.4% over 64 (2000); Marriage status: 25.2% never married, 53.6% now married, 4.0% widowed, 17.2% divorced (2000); Foreign born: 4.7% (2000); Ancestry (includes multiple ancestries): 19.4% German, 14.9% Italian, 14.1% Irish, 13.9% Russian, 11.0% Polish (2000).
Economy: Resort village in the Catskills. Employment by occupation: 8.5% management, 36.2% professional, 16.5% services, 16.0% sales, 5.1% farming, 8.9% construction, 8.7% production (2000).
Income: Per capita income: $27,323 (2000); Median household income: $42,026 (2000); Poverty rate: 13.3% (2000).
Education: Percent of population age 25 and over with: High school diploma (including GED) or higher: 93.0% (2000); Bachelor's degree or higher: 44.5% (2000).
Housing: Homeownership rate: 81.2% (2000); Median home value: $119,800 (2000); Median rent: $444 per month (2000); Median age of housing: 45 years (2000).
Transportation: Commute to work: 79.3% car, 3.3% public transportation, 0.0% walk, 16.7% work from home (2000); Travel time to work: 26.9% less than 15 minutes, 35.2% 15 to 30 minutes, 11.7% 30 to 45 minutes, 4.4% 45 to 60 minutes, 21.8% 60 minutes or more (2000)

NAPANOCH (CDP). Covers a land area of 1.196 square miles and a water area of 0.026 square miles. Located at 41.74° N. Lat.; 74.37° W. Long.
Population: 1,068 (1990); 1,168 (2000); 1,084 (2005); 1,036 (2010 projected); Race: 95.3% White, 1.6% Black, 0.8% Asian, 3.1% Hispanic of any race (2005); Density: 906.6 persons per square mile (2005); Average household size: 2.46 (2005); Median age: 39.0 (2005); Males per 100 females: 89.5 (2005); Marriage status: 24.0% never married, 57.9% now married, 10.6% widowed, 7.5% divorced (2000); Foreign born: 4.4% (2000); Ancestry (includes multiple ancestries): 24.5% German, 14.9% English, 14.8% United States or American, 12.3% Irish, 11.1% Dutch (2000).
Economy: Resort village. Employment by occupation: 16.9% management, 18.8% professional, 24.1% services, 21.6% sales, 0.0% farming, 4.5% construction, 14.2% production (2000).
Income: Per capita income: $19,850 (2005); Median household income: $38,824 (2005); Average household income: $48,903 (2005); Percent of households with income of $100,000 or more: 13.2% (2005); Poverty rate: 14.4% (2000).
Education: Percent of population age 25 and over with: High school diploma (including GED) or higher: 75.3% (2005); Bachelor's degree or higher: 11.7% (2005); Master's degree or higher: 4.7% (2005).
School District(s)
Ellenville Central School District (KG-12)
    2003-04 Enrollment: 1,812 . . . . (845) 647-0100
Housing: Homeownership rate: 80.0% (2005); Median home value: $119,444 (2005); Median rent: $508 per month (2000); Median age of housing: 47 years (2000).

Transportation: Commute to work: 91.5% car, 1.4% public transportation, 1.6% walk, 2.7% work from home (2000); Travel time to work: 57.5% less than 15 minutes, 17.2% 15 to 30 minutes, 6.0% 30 to 45 minutes, 7.6% 45 to 60 minutes, 11.8% 60 minutes or more (2000)

NEW PALTZ (village). Covers a land area of 1.733 square miles and a water area of 0.029 square miles. Located at 41.75° N. Lat.; 74.08° W. Long. Elevation is 236 feet.
Population: 5,504 (1990); 6,034 (2000); 6,402 (2005); 6,665 (2010 projected); Race: 69.5% White, 7.7% Black, 9.2% Asian, 13.6% Hispanic of any race (2005); Density: 3,694.9 persons per square mile (2005); Average household size: 3.16 (2005); Median age: 23.3 (2005); Males per 100 females: 80.2 (2005); Marriage status: 65.5% never married, 26.7% now married, 2.9% widowed, 5.0% divorced (2000); Foreign born: 15.5% (2000); Ancestry (includes multiple ancestries): 22.7% Other groups, 22.3% Irish, 15.8% Italian, 14.1% German, 8.0% English (2000).
Economy: Single-family building permits issued: 7 (2005); Multi-family building permits issued: 0 (2005); Employment by occupation: 4.6% management, 28.7% professional, 27.9% services, 29.7% sales, 0.3% farming, 3.5% construction, 5.3% production (2000).
Income: Per capita income: $13,070 (2005); Median household income: $24,550 (2005); Average household income: $37,749 (2005); Percent of households with income of $100,000 or more: 6.9% (2005); Poverty rate: 36.9% (2000).
Education: Percent of population age 25 and over with: High school diploma (including GED) or higher: 93.7% (2005); Bachelor's degree or higher: 54.7% (2005); Master's degree or higher: 25.7% (2005).
School District(s)
Boces Ulster (UG-UG)
    2003-04 Enrollment: 182 . . . . (845) 255-3040
New Paltz Central School District (KG-12)
    2003-04 Enrollment: 2,376 . . . . (845) 256-4020
Four-year College(s)
SUNY College at New Paltz (Public)
    Fall 2004 Enrollment: 7,603. . . . . (845) 257-2121
    2005-06 Tuition: In-state $4,350; Out-of-state $4,350
Two-year College(s)
Hudson Valley School of Advanced Aesthetic Skin Care
    Fall 2004 Enrollment: n/a. . . . . (845) 255-0013
Housing: Homeownership rate: 27.7% (2005); Median home value: $190,052 (2005); Median rent: $591 per month (2000); Median age of housing: 38 years (2000).
Transportation: Commute to work: 67.0% car, 3.5% public transportation, 24.5% walk, 2.7% work from home (2000); Travel time to work: 41.0% less than 15 minutes, 31.2% 15 to 30 minutes, 17.5% 30 to 45 minutes, 4.7% 45 to 60 minutes, 5.6% 60 minutes or more (2000)
Additional Information Contacts
New Paltz Chamber of Commerce . . . . (845) 255-0141
    http://www.newpaltzchamber.org
Village of New Paltz. . . . . (845) 255-0130
    http://www.villageofnewpaltz.org/portal/

NEW PALTZ (town). Covers a land area of 33.903 square miles and a water area of 0.392 square miles. Located at 41.75° N. Lat.; 74.09° W. Long. Elevation is 236 feet.
History: State University of N.Y. College at New Paltz is here. Settled by Huguenots in 1677; incorporated 1887.
Population: 11,286 (1990); 12,830 (2000); 13,756 (2005); 14,510 (2010 projected); Race: 79.7% White, 6.4% Black, 5.2% Asian, 9.3% Hispanic of any race (2005); Density: 405.7 persons per square mile (2005); Average household size: 2.85 (2005); Median age: 28.6 (2005); Males per 100 females: 85.9 (2005); Marriage status: 46.2% never married, 40.9% now married, 4.6% widowed, 8.4% divorced (2000); Foreign born: 11.2% (2000); Ancestry (includes multiple ancestries): 22.7% Irish, 19.2% Italian, 17.6% Other groups, 16.7% German, 7.9% English (2000).
Economy: In agricultural area: dairying; poultry; fruit, vineyards, sweet corn, beans, and tomatoes. Summer recreational area. Single-family building permits issued: 31 (2005); Multi-family building permits issued: 0 (2005); Employment by occupation: 8.9% management, 32.4% professional, 20.8% services, 24.5% sales, 0.5% farming, 5.1% construction, 7.9% production (2000).
Income: Per capita income: $21,447 (2005); Median household income: $44,488 (2005); Average household income: $58,792 (2005); Percent of households with income of $100,000 or more: 16.4% (2005); Poverty rate: 18.6% (2000).

Education: Percent of population age 25 and over with: High school diploma (including GED) or higher: 90.4% (2005); Bachelor's degree or higher: 48.1% (2005); Master's degree or higher: 23.2% (2005).
Housing: Homeownership rate: 54.7% (2005); Median home value: $218,486 (2005); Median rent: $569 per month (2000); Median age of housing: 35 years (2000).
Safety: Violent crime rate: 44.4 per 10,000 population; Property crime rate: 244.7 per 10,000 population (2004).
Transportation: Commute to work: 79.9% car, 2.5% public transportation, 12.7% walk, 3.4% work from home (2000); Travel time to work: 36.8% less than 15 minutes, 28.5% 15 to 30 minutes, 21.1% 30 to 45 minutes, 6.1% 45 to 60 minutes, 7.5% 60 minutes or more (2000)

OLIVE (town). Covers a land area of 58.668 square miles and a water area of 6.470 square miles. Located at 41.95° N. Lat.; 74.25° W. Long.
Population: 4,086 (1990); 4,579 (2000); 4,719 (2005); 4,868 (2010 projected); Race: 96.2% White, 0.8% Black, 1.2% Asian, 2.5% Hispanic of any race (2005); Density: 80.4 persons per square mile (2005); Average household size: 2.40 (2005); Median age: 44.4 (2005); Males per 100 females: 97.9 (2005); Marriage status: 18.4% never married, 64.8% now married, 7.1% widowed, 9.7% divorced (2000); Foreign born: 7.3% (2000); Ancestry (includes multiple ancestries): 27.8% German, 21.2% Irish, 18.7% Italian, 11.3% English, 6.9% Other groups (2000).
Economy: Single-family building permits issued: 26 (2005); Multi-family building permits issued: 0 (2005); Employment by occupation: 11.3% management, 24.9% professional, 12.1% services, 23.8% sales, 0.7% farming, 13.4% construction, 13.9% production (2000).
Income: Per capita income: $25,907 (2005); Median household income: $51,596 (2005); Average household income: $61,781 (2005); Percent of households with income of $100,000 or more: 15.0% (2005); Poverty rate: 5.0% (2000).
Education: Percent of population age 25 and over with: High school diploma (including GED) or higher: 80.0% (2005); Bachelor's degree or higher: 28.1% (2005); Master's degree or higher: 12.5% (2005).
Housing: Homeownership rate: 80.1% (2005); Median home value: $174,278 (2005); Median rent: $523 per month (2000); Median age of housing: 34 years (2000).
Transportation: Commute to work: 87.8% car, 2.4% public transportation, 3.4% walk, 5.5% work from home (2000); Travel time to work: 18.5% less than 15 minutes, 33.3% 15 to 30 minutes, 25.7% 30 to 45 minutes, 8.9% 45 to 60 minutes, 13.6% 60 minutes or more (2000)

OLIVEBRIDGE (unincorporated postal area, zip code 12461). Covers a land area of 31.705 square miles and a water area of 0.015 square miles. Located at 41.91° N. Lat.; 74.24° W. Long. Elevation is 568 feet.
History: Also spelled Olive Bridge.
Population: 0 (2000); Race: 93.6% White, 0.8% Black, 0.4% Asian, 1.4% Hispanic of any race (2000); Density: 0.0 persons per square mile (2000); Age: 20.8% under 18, 15.0% over 64 (2000); Marriage status: 21.5% never married, 62.4% now married, 7.2% widowed, 8.9% divorced (2000); Foreign born: 6.4% (2000); Ancestry (includes multiple ancestries): 29.3% German, 22.6% Irish, 17.8% Italian, 6.8% Other groups, 6.4% Polish (2000).
Economy: Resort village. Employment by occupation: 13.1% management, 19.5% professional, 9.7% services, 26.8% sales, 0.9% farming, 15.0% construction, 14.9% production (2000).
Income: Per capita income: $23,603 (2000); Median household income: $42,400 (2000); Poverty rate: 5.8% (2000).
Education: Percent of population age 25 and over with: High school diploma (including GED) or higher: 77.7% (2000); Bachelor's degree or higher: 26.5% (2000).
Housing: Homeownership rate: 76.1% (2000); Median home value: $114,600 (2000); Median rent: $542 per month (2000); Median age of housing: 35 years (2000).
Transportation: Commute to work: 86.5% car, 4.1% public transportation, 3.3% walk, 4.4% work from home (2000); Travel time to work: 10.0% less than 15 minutes, 29.1% 15 to 30 minutes, 35.5% 30 to 45 minutes, 11.7% 45 to 60 minutes, 13.6% 60 minutes or more (2000)

PHOENICIA (CDP). Covers a land area of 0.463 square miles and a water area of 0 square miles. Located at 42.08° N. Lat.; 74.31° W. Long. Elevation is 840 feet.
Population: 371 (1990); 381 (2000); 379 (2005); 380 (2010 projected); Race: 96.0% White, 0.5% Black, 0.0% Asian, 2.9% Hispanic of any race (2005); Density: 818.8 persons per square mile (2005); Average household size: 1.94 (2005); Median age: 46.8 (2005); Males per 100 females: 93.4 (2005); Marriage status: 22.6% never married, 48.9% now married, 12.1% widowed, 16.4% divorced (2000); Foreign born: 8.5% (2000); Ancestry (includes multiple ancestries): 47.8% German, 40.3% Irish, 9.7% Italian, 8.0% United States or American, 6.0% French (except Basque) (2000).
Economy: Employment by occupation: 11.1% management, 29.2% professional, 15.8% services, 21.1% sales, 0.0% farming, 12.9% construction, 9.9% production (2000).
Income: Per capita income: $21,135 (2005); Median household income: $26,857 (2005); Average household income: $41,077 (2005); Percent of households with income of $100,000 or more: 7.2% (2005); Poverty rate: 13.9% (2000).
Education: Percent of population age 25 and over with: High school diploma (including GED) or higher: 78.3% (2005); Bachelor's degree or higher: 31.7% (2005); Master's degree or higher: 18.6% (2005).

School District(s)
Onteora Central School District (KG-12)
    2003-04 Enrollment: 2,172 . . . . (845) 657-6383

Housing: Homeownership rate: 52.3% (2005); Median home value: $117,647 (2005); Median rent: $394 per month (2000); Median age of housing: 60+ years (2000).
Transportation: Commute to work: 66.7% car, 7.0% public transportation, 11.7% walk, 11.7% work from home (2000); Travel time to work: 47.7% less than 15 minutes, 19.9% 15 to 30 minutes, 17.9% 30 to 45 minutes, 9.3% 45 to 60 minutes, 5.3% 60 minutes or more (2000)

PINE HILL (CDP). Covers a land area of 2.107 square miles and a water area of 0.013 square miles. Located at 42.13° N. Lat.; 74.47° W. Long.
Population: 278 (1990); 308 (2000); 289 (2005); 270 (2010 projected); Race: 87.5% White, 3.1% Black, 5.5% Asian, 5.9% Hispanic of any race (2005); Density: 137.1 persons per square mile (2005); Average household size: 2.19 (2005); Median age: 45.7 (2005); Males per 100 females: 97.9 (2005); Marriage status: 23.9% never married, 64.1% now married, 8.0% widowed, 4.0% divorced (2000); Foreign born: 21.2% (2000); Ancestry (includes multiple ancestries): 20.7% German, 14.7% Other groups, 11.4% United States or American, 9.3% Irish, 8.3% French (except Basque) (2000).
Economy: Resort village. Belle Ayr Mt. (skiing) is nearby. Employment by occupation: 10.2% management, 24.0% professional, 16.8% services, 13.8% sales, 0.0% farming, 6.6% construction, 28.7% production (2000).
Income: Per capita income: $23,596 (2005); Median household income: $40,526 (2005); Average household income: $51,629 (2005); Percent of households with income of $100,000 or more: 8.3% (2005); Poverty rate: 19.4% (2000).
Education: Percent of population age 25 and over with: High school diploma (including GED) or higher: 82.9% (2005); Bachelor's degree or higher: 27.8% (2005); Master's degree or higher: 3.2% (2005).
Housing: Homeownership rate: 63.6% (2005); Median home value: $143,750 (2005); Median rent: $348 per month (2000); Median age of housing: 60+ years (2000).
Transportation: Commute to work: 86.8% car, 0.0% public transportation, 4.2% walk, 9.0% work from home (2000); Travel time to work: 44.7% less than 15 minutes, 9.2% 15 to 30 minutes, 12.5% 30 to 45 minutes, 28.3% 45 to 60 minutes, 5.3% 60 minutes or more (2000)

PLATTEKILL (town). Covers a land area of 35.614 square miles and a water area of 0.082 square miles. Located at 41.65° N. Lat.; 74.07° W. Long. Elevation is 566 feet.
Population: 8,853 (1990); 9,892 (2000); 10,889 (2005); 11,822 (2010 projected); Race: 85.6% White, 5.0% Black, 0.8% Asian, 17.7% Hispanic of any race (2005); Density: 305.8 persons per square mile (2005); Average household size: 2.66 (2005); Median age: 37.2 (2005); Males per 100 females: 97.3 (2005); Marriage status: 26.4% never married, 57.3% now married, 7.0% widowed, 9.3% divorced (2000); Foreign born: 5.2% (2000); Ancestry (includes multiple ancestries): 25.0% Italian, 21.4% Irish, 20.7% Other groups, 16.2% German, 8.1% English (2000).
Economy: Resort village. Single-family building permits issued: 61 (2005); Multi-family building permits issued: 4 (2005); Employment by occupation: 11.3% management, 16.1% professional, 16.3% services, 27.4% sales, 0.3% farming, 13.4% construction, 15.1% production (2000).
Income: Per capita income: $21,993 (2005); Median household income: $46,465 (2005); Average household income: $58,220 (2005); Percent of households with income of $100,000 or more: 12.9% (2005); Poverty rate: 9.6% (2000).

Education: Percent of population age 25 and over with: High school diploma (including GED) or higher: 78.1% (2005); Bachelor's degree or higher: 15.8% (2005); Master's degree or higher: 6.0% (2005).

School District(s)

Wallkill Central School District (KG-12)
    2003-04 Enrollment: 3,638 . . . . (845) 895-7101

Housing: Homeownership rate: 70.1% (2005); Median home value: $174,134 (2005); Median rent: $553 per month (2000); Median age of housing: 26 years (2000).
Safety: Violent crime rate: 0.0 per 10,000 population; Property crime rate: 11.4 per 10,000 population (2004).
Transportation: Commute to work: 92.1% car, 1.7% public transportation, 1.8% walk, 3.5% work from home (2000); Travel time to work: 16.9% less than 15 minutes, 40.2% 15 to 30 minutes, 20.6% 30 to 45 minutes, 7.8% 45 to 60 minutes, 14.5% 60 minutes or more (2000)

PLATTEKILL (CDP). Covers a land area of 5.537 square miles and a water area of 0.576 square miles. Located at 42.38° N. Lat.; 88.23° W. Long.
Population: 906 (1990); 1,050 (2000); 1,127 (2005); 1,196 (2010 projected); Race: 68.2% White, 9.4% Black, 0.9% Asian, 56.4% Hispanic of any race (2005); Density: 203.5 persons per square mile (2005); Average household size: 2.98 (2005); Median age: 34.4 (2005); Males per 100 females: 91.7 (2005); Marriage status: 26.8% never married, 54.1% now married, 4.9% widowed, 14.2% divorced (2000); Foreign born: 10.0% (2000); Ancestry (includes multiple ancestries): 59.3% Other groups, 11.5% Irish, 10.3% German, 9.9% Italian, 6.2% United States or American (2000).
Economy: Employment by occupation: 10.2% management, 9.4% professional, 19.1% services, 26.4% sales, 1.3% farming, 13.1% construction, 20.6% production (2000).
Income: Per capita income: $17,879 (2005); Median household income: $47,750 (2005); Average household income: $53,307 (2005); Percent of households with income of $100,000 or more: 12.4% (2005); Poverty rate: 11.7% (2000).
Education: Percent of population age 25 and over with: High school diploma (including GED) or higher: 78.1% (2005); Bachelor's degree or higher: 10.6% (2005); Master's degree or higher: 5.4% (2005).
Housing: Homeownership rate: 55.6% (2005); Median home value: $202,970 (2005); Median rent: $607 per month (2000); Median age of housing: 33 years (2000).
Transportation: Commute to work: 98.4% car, 1.6% public transportation, 0.0% walk, 0.0% work from home (2000); Travel time to work: 7.5% less than 15 minutes, 47.2% 15 to 30 minutes, 16.4% 30 to 45 minutes, 5.6% 45 to 60 minutes, 23.3% 60 minutes or more (2000)

PORT EWEN (CDP). Covers a land area of 1.955 square miles and a water area of 0.717 square miles. Located at 41.90° N. Lat.; 73.97° W. Long.
Population: 3,444 (1990); 3,650 (2000); 3,651 (2005); 3,669 (2010 projected); Race: 92.5% White, 3.3% Black, 1.4% Asian, 2.3% Hispanic of any race (2005); Density: 1,867.8 persons per square mile (2005); Average household size: 2.42 (2005); Median age: 40.1 (2005); Males per 100 females: 89.4 (2005); Marriage status: 24.5% never married, 59.8% now married, 7.7% widowed, 8.0% divorced (2000); Foreign born: 3.8% (2000); Ancestry (includes multiple ancestries): 31.2% Irish, 24.3% German, 19.4% Italian, 7.6% English, 7.1% Dutch (2000).
Economy: Employment by occupation: 14.1% management, 14.0% professional, 13.3% services, 33.7% sales, 0.0% farming, 10.4% construction, 14.5% production (2000).
Income: Per capita income: $24,292 (2005); Median household income: $45,872 (2005); Average household income: $58,891 (2005); Percent of households with income of $100,000 or more: 14.6% (2005); Poverty rate: 8.0% (2000).
Education: Percent of population age 25 and over with: High school diploma (including GED) or higher: 82.8% (2005); Bachelor's degree or higher: 17.6% (2005); Master's degree or higher: 6.9% (2005).

School District(s)

Kingston City School District (PK-12)
    2003-04 Enrollment: 8,149 . . . . (845) 339-3000

Two-year College(s)

Ulster County BOCES-School of Practical Nursing (Public)
    Fall 2004 Enrollment: 137 . . . . (845) 255-1400

Housing: Homeownership rate: 76.0% (2005); Median home value: $149,438 (2005); Median rent: $609 per month (2000); Median age of housing: 38 years (2000).
Transportation: Commute to work: 90.3% car, 1.2% public transportation, 3.8% walk, 3.7% work from home (2000); Travel time to work: 33.7% less than 15 minutes, 31.9% 15 to 30 minutes, 19.6% 30 to 45 minutes, 5.9% 45 to 60 minutes, 9.0% 60 minutes or more (2000)

RIFTON (CDP). Covers a land area of 1.188 square miles and a water area of 0 square miles. Located at 41.83° N. Lat.; 74.04° W. Long.
Population: 519 (1990); 501 (2000); 517 (2005); 538 (2010 projected); Race: 93.8% White, 1.9% Black, 0.6% Asian, 2.5% Hispanic of any race (2005); Density: 435.4 persons per square mile (2005); Average household size: 2.38 (2005); Median age: 44.3 (2005); Males per 100 females: 90.8 (2005); Marriage status: 25.9% never married, 47.9% now married, 20.8% widowed, 5.4% divorced (2000); Foreign born: 3.2% (2000); Ancestry (includes multiple ancestries): 26.0% Irish, 25.8% German, 20.9% English, 14.2% Italian, 11.4% Polish (2000).
Economy: Employment by occupation: 7.9% management, 27.9% professional, 12.1% services, 7.9% sales, 0.0% farming, 26.8% construction, 17.4% production (2000).
Income: Per capita income: $24,884 (2005); Median household income: $49,392 (2005); Average household income: $59,286 (2005); Percent of households with income of $100,000 or more: 6.0% (2005); Poverty rate: 0.0% (2000).
Education: Percent of population age 25 and over with: High school diploma (including GED) or higher: 88.1% (2005); Bachelor's degree or higher: 16.4% (2005); Master's degree or higher: 7.0% (2005).
Housing: Homeownership rate: 77.4% (2005); Median home value: $136,667 (2005); Median rent: $442 per month (2000); Median age of housing: 45 years (2000).
Transportation: Commute to work: 94.7% car, 0.0% public transportation, 0.0% walk, 2.6% work from home (2000); Travel time to work: 22.2% less than 15 minutes, 37.8% 15 to 30 minutes, 19.5% 30 to 45 minutes, 12.4% 45 to 60 minutes, 8.1% 60 minutes or more (2000)

ROCHESTER (town). Covers a land area of 88.412 square miles and a water area of 0.371 square miles. Located at 41.80° N. Lat.; 74.26° W. Long.
Population: 5,679 (1990); 7,018 (2000); 7,297 (2005); 7,582 (2010 projected); Race: 92.9% White, 2.8% Black, 0.6% Asian, 5.8% Hispanic of any race (2005); Density: 82.5 persons per square mile (2005); Average household size: 2.59 (2005); Median age: 38.9 (2005); Males per 100 females: 101.1 (2005); Marriage status: 27.2% never married, 58.9% now married, 5.3% widowed, 8.7% divorced (2000); Foreign born: 5.7% (2000); Ancestry (includes multiple ancestries): 19.8% Irish, 18.6% German, 11.5% Italian, 11.0% Other groups, 8.3% Dutch (2000).
Economy: Single-family building permits issued: 65 (2005); Multi-family building permits issued: 0 (2005); Employment by occupation: 10.5% management, 21.3% professional, 19.3% services, 23.8% sales, 1.0% farming, 10.8% construction, 13.4% production (2000).
Income: Per capita income: $24,769 (2005); Median household income: $48,800 (2005); Average household income: $64,047 (2005); Percent of households with income of $100,000 or more: 14.2% (2005); Poverty rate: 10.9% (2000).
Education: Percent of population age 25 and over with: High school diploma (including GED) or higher: 82.6% (2005); Bachelor's degree or higher: 23.0% (2005); Master's degree or higher: 11.5% (2005).
Housing: Homeownership rate: 76.4% (2005); Median home value: $164,494 (2005); Median rent: $508 per month (2000); Median age of housing: 31 years (2000).
Transportation: Commute to work: 84.7% car, 4.6% public transportation, 3.7% walk, 6.3% work from home (2000); Travel time to work: 23.0% less than 15 minutes, 28.8% 15 to 30 minutes, 21.7% 30 to 45 minutes, 13.2% 45 to 60 minutes, 13.3% 60 minutes or more (2000)

ROSENDALE (town). Covers a land area of 19.941 square miles and a water area of 0.808 square miles. Located at 41.84° N. Lat.; 74.07° W. Long. Elevation is 187 feet.
History: Incorporated 1890.
Population: 6,220 (1990); 6,352 (2000); 6,385 (2005); 6,449 (2010 projected); Race: 95.4% White, 2.0% Black, 0.5% Asian, 3.1% Hispanic of any race (2005); Density: 320.2 persons per square mile (2005); Average household size: 2.40 (2005); Median age: 39.0 (2005); Males per 100 females: 96.8 (2005); Marriage status: 28.0% never married, 54.0% now

married, 8.0% widowed, 10.0% divorced (2000); Foreign born: 3.8% (2000); Ancestry (includes multiple ancestries): 22.5% Irish, 20.5% German, 18.1% Italian, 11.8% Other groups, 11.5% English (2000).
Economy: Manufacturing: injection-molded thermoformed plastics. Single-family building permits issued: 11 (2005); Multi-family building permits issued: 0 (2005); Employment by occupation: 11.5% management, 27.0% professional, 17.7% services, 22.7% sales, 0.3% farming, 11.6% construction, 9.2% production (2000).
Income: Per capita income: $24,105 (2005); Median household income: $49,450 (2005); Average household income: $57,876 (2005); Percent of households with income of $100,000 or more: 12.2% (2005); Poverty rate: 11.9% (2000).
Education: Percent of population age 25 and over with: High school diploma (including GED) or higher: 86.5% (2005); Bachelor's degree or higher: 28.9% (2005); Master's degree or higher: 12.9% (2005).
Housing: Homeownership rate: 72.7% (2005); Median home value: $142,096 (2005); Median rent: $558 per month (2000); Median age of housing: 48 years (2000).
Safety: Violent crime rate: 0.0 per 10,000 population; Property crime rate: 114.2 per 10,000 population (2004).
Transportation: Commute to work: 88.0% car, 1.8% public transportation, 3.3% walk, 6.6% work from home (2000); Travel time to work: 19.2% less than 15 minutes, 44.2% 15 to 30 minutes, 18.6% 30 to 45 minutes, 9.5% 45 to 60 minutes, 8.5% 60 minutes or more (2000)

Additional Information Contacts
Town of Rosendale . . . . (845) 658-3159
http://www.townofrosendale.com/

ROSENDALE VILLAGE (CDP).
Covers a land area of 1.894 square miles and a water area of 0.071 square miles. Located at 41.84° N. Lat.; 74.07° W. Long.
Population: 1,353 (1990); 1,374 (2000); 1,400 (2005); 1,409 (2010 projected); Race: 94.6% White, 2.4% Black, 0.7% Asian, 4.1% Hispanic of any race (2005); Density: 739.2 persons per square mile (2005); Average household size: 2.24 (2005); Median age: 39.9 (2005); Males per 100 females: 93.6 (2005); Marriage status: 31.0% never married, 48.4% now married, 11.5% widowed, 9.0% divorced (2000); Foreign born: 3.1% (2000); Ancestry (includes multiple ancestries): 26.1% Irish, 23.0% Italian, 22.7% German, 10.6% English, 9.6% Dutch (2000).
Economy: Employment by occupation: 7.5% management, 24.8% professional, 25.0% services, 19.5% sales, 0.0% farming, 8.1% construction, 15.1% production (2000).
Income: Per capita income: $23,283 (2005); Median household income: $42,836 (2005); Average household income: $51,889 (2005); Percent of households with income of $100,000 or more: 9.3% (2005); Poverty rate: 8.2% (2000).
Education: Percent of population age 25 and over with: High school diploma (including GED) or higher: 81.6% (2005); Bachelor's degree or higher: 27.1% (2005); Master's degree or higher: 11.4% (2005).
Housing: Homeownership rate: 61.8% (2005); Median home value: $133,026 (2005); Median rent: $538 per month (2000); Median age of housing: 55 years (2000).
Transportation: Commute to work: 89.2% car, 1.4% public transportation, 4.0% walk, 5.3% work from home (2000); Travel time to work: 23.1% less than 15 minutes, 46.4% 15 to 30 minutes, 17.6% 30 to 45 minutes, 7.6% 45 to 60 minutes, 5.3% 60 minutes or more (2000)

SAUGERTIES (village).
Covers a land area of 1.835 square miles and a water area of 0.441 square miles. Located at 42.07° N. Lat.; 73.95° W. Long. Elevation is 155 feet.
Population: 3,915 (1990); 4,955 (2000); 4,911 (2005); 4,938 (2010 projected); Race: 77.0% White, 14.4% Black, 1.9% Asian, 12.2% Hispanic of any race (2005); Density: 2,675.8 persons per square mile (2005); Average household size: 2.98 (2005); Median age: 35.8 (2005); Males per 100 females: 141.0 (2005); Marriage status: 33.7% never married, 49.4% now married, 6.5% widowed, 10.4% divorced (2000); Foreign born: 5.7% (2000); Ancestry (includes multiple ancestries): 22.1% German, 21.7% Irish, 17.5% Italian, 8.2% English, 7.6% Other groups (2000).
Economy: Single-family building permits issued: 5 (2005); Multi-family building permits issued: 6 (2005); Employment by occupation: 10.4% management, 22.1% professional, 15.5% services, 29.2% sales, 0.0% farming, 6.6% construction, 16.3% production (2000).
Income: Per capita income: $19,937 (2005); Median household income: $39,764 (2005); Average household income: $49,010 (2005); Percent of households with income of $100,000 or more: 8.7% (2005); Poverty rate: 12.2% (2000).
Education: Percent of population age 25 and over with: High school diploma (including GED) or higher: 68.4% (2005); Bachelor's degree or higher: 19.8% (2005); Master's degree or higher: 10.0% (2005).

School District(s)
Saugerties Central School District (KG-12)
    2003-04 Enrollment: 3,336 . . . . (845) 246-1043
Housing: Homeownership rate: 47.1% (2005); Median home value: $139,485 (2005); Median rent: $484 per month (2000); Median age of housing: 60+ years (2000).
Safety: Violent crime rate: 69.0 per 10,000 population; Property crime rate: 133.0 per 10,000 population (2004).
Newspapers: Saugerties Post Star (General - Circulation 2,330); Star Newspaper (General - Circulation 25,000)
Transportation: Commute to work: 90.3% car, 0.5% public transportation, 6.5% walk, 1.9% work from home (2000); Travel time to work: 33.1% less than 15 minutes, 40.1% 15 to 30 minutes, 17.3% 30 to 45 minutes, 6.4% 45 to 60 minutes, 3.0% 60 minutes or more (2000)

SAUGERTIES (town).
Covers a land area of 64.538 square miles and a water area of 3.494 square miles. Located at 42.08° N. Lat.; 73.97° W. Long. Elevation is 155 feet.
History: Former summer resort. Incorporated 1831.
Population: 18,467 (1990); 19,868 (2000); 20,331 (2005); 20,886 (2010 projected); Race: 90.0% White, 5.5% Black, 0.9% Asian, 6.0% Hispanic of any race (2005); Density: 315.0 persons per square mile (2005); Average household size: 2.61 (2005); Median age: 39.2 (2005); Males per 100 females: 104.7 (2005); Marriage status: 26.2% never married, 57.8% now married, 6.5% widowed, 9.5% divorced (2000); Foreign born: 4.1% (2000); Ancestry (includes multiple ancestries): 25.8% German, 23.9% Irish, 19.3% Italian, 9.4% English, 7.6% Dutch (2000).
Economy: Manufacturing: canvas, wire and cable, fire hose fittings and valves, wrapping paper. Limestone, shale quarries. Single-family building permits issued: 97 (2005); Multi-family building permits issued: 87 (2005); Employment by occupation: 9.6% management, 22.8% professional, 14.4% services, 26.6% sales, 0.1% farming, 11.3% construction, 15.2% production (2000).
Income: Per capita income: $23,439 (2005); Median household income: $47,599 (2005); Average household income: $58,889 (2005); Percent of households with income of $100,000 or more: 12.9% (2005); Poverty rate: 8.2% (2000).
Taxes: Total city taxes per capita: $305 (2004); City property taxes per capita: $263 (2004).
Education: Percent of population age 25 and over with: High school diploma (including GED) or higher: 81.9% (2005); Bachelor's degree or higher: 21.0% (2005); Master's degree or higher: 9.8% (2005).
Housing: Homeownership rate: 72.0% (2005); Median home value: $152,049 (2005); Median rent: $507 per month (2000); Median age of housing: 43 years (2000).
Safety: Violent crime rate: 9.2 per 10,000 population; Property crime rate: 170.0 per 10,000 population (2004).
Transportation: Commute to work: 91.8% car, 1.1% public transportation, 2.1% walk, 4.5% work from home (2000); Travel time to work: 28.3% less than 15 minutes, 38.6% 15 to 30 minutes, 18.1% 30 to 45 minutes, 7.2% 45 to 60 minutes, 7.8% 60 minutes or more (2000)

Additional Information Contacts
Town of Saugerties . . . . (845) 246-2800
http://www.saugerties.ny.us/

SAUGERTIES SOUTH (CDP).
Covers a land area of 0.977 square miles and a water area of 0.236 square miles. Located at 42.05° N. Lat.; 73.95° W. Long.
Population: 2,346 (1990); 2,285 (2000); 2,362 (2005); 2,440 (2010 projected); Race: 96.1% White, 1.6% Black, 0.6% Asian, 3.1% Hispanic of any race (2005); Density: 2,418.8 persons per square mile (2005); Average household size: 2.60 (2005); Median age: 41.0 (2005); Males per 100 females: 90.8 (2005); Marriage status: 22.1% never married, 68.1% now married, 6.6% widowed, 3.2% divorced (2000); Foreign born: 2.2% (2000); Ancestry (includes multiple ancestries): 26.5% Irish, 26.4% German, 23.1% Italian, 7.6% Polish, 7.5% English (2000).
Economy: Employment by occupation: 4.9% management, 24.4% professional, 9.9% services, 36.7% sales, 0.0% farming, 8.8% construction, 15.3% production (2000).

Income: Per capita income: $24,579 (2005); Median household income: $58,871 (2005); Average household income: $63,508 (2005); Percent of households with income of $100,000 or more: 12.9% (2005); Poverty rate: 7.0% (2000).
Education: Percent of population age 25 and over with: High school diploma (including GED) or higher: 90.3% (2005); Bachelor's degree or higher: 20.1% (2005); Master's degree or higher: 10.6% (2005).
Housing: Homeownership rate: 77.9% (2005); Median home value: $146,662 (2005); Median rent: $534 per month (2000); Median age of housing: 40 years (2000).
Transportation: Commute to work: 96.2% car, 0.8% public transportation, 0.3% walk, 2.7% work from home (2000); Travel time to work: 33.2% less than 15 minutes, 36.0% 15 to 30 minutes, 17.0% 30 to 45 minutes, 7.8% 45 to 60 minutes, 6.0% 60 minutes or more (2000)

SHANDAKEN (town).
Covers a land area of 119.805 square miles and a water area of 0.023 square miles. Located at 42.11° N. Lat.; 74.38° W. Long.
Population: 3,013 (1990); 3,235 (2000); 3,215 (2005); 3,209 (2010 projected); Race: 93.9% White, 1.5% Black, 1.6% Asian, 3.6% Hispanic of any race (2005); Density: 26.8 persons per square mile (2005); Average household size: 2.18 (2005); Median age: 46.4 (2005); Males per 100 females: 97.6 (2005); Marriage status: 26.2% never married, 53.4% now married, 8.3% widowed, 12.1% divorced (2000); Foreign born: 11.6% (2000); Ancestry (includes multiple ancestries): 25.7% German, 19.6% Irish, 13.5% English, 10.0% Other groups, 10.0% Italian (2000).
Economy: Employment by occupation: 10.2% management, 17.8% professional, 18.3% services, 23.9% sales, 1.3% farming, 15.4% construction, 13.1% production (2000).
Income: Per capita income: $26,049 (2005); Median household income: $38,271 (2005); Average household income: $55,108 (2005); Percent of households with income of $100,000 or more: 13.8% (2005); Poverty rate: 12.3% (2000).
Education: Percent of population age 25 and over with: High school diploma (including GED) or higher: 84.1% (2005); Bachelor's degree or higher: 26.5% (2005); Master's degree or higher: 10.2% (2005).
Housing: Homeownership rate: 72.1% (2005); Median home value: $131,360 (2005); Median rent: $461 per month (2000); Median age of housing: 50 years (2000).
Safety: Violent crime rate: 0.0 per 10,000 population; Property crime rate: 307.9 per 10,000 population (2004).
Transportation: Commute to work: 84.4% car, 3.7% public transportation, 2.1% walk, 8.8% work from home (2000); Travel time to work: 36.8% less than 15 minutes, 23.5% 15 to 30 minutes, 12.4% 30 to 45 minutes, 11.2% 45 to 60 minutes, 16.0% 60 minutes or more (2000)

SHAWANGUNK (town).
Covers a land area of 56.212 square miles and a water area of 0.314 square miles. Located at 41.61° N. Lat.; 74.23° W. Long.
Population: 10,081 (1990); 12,022 (2000); 12,879 (2005); 13,766 (2010 projected); Race: 85.9% White, 8.0% Black, 1.2% Asian, 8.0% Hispanic of any race (2005); Density: 229.1 persons per square mile (2005); Average household size: 3.41 (2005); Median age: 36.8 (2005); Males per 100 females: 131.8 (2005); Marriage status: 27.3% never married, 61.8% now married, 4.6% widowed, 6.4% divorced (2000); Foreign born: 4.4% (2000); Ancestry (includes multiple ancestries): 22.0% Irish, 18.7% German, 15.7% Italian, 10.2% English, 5.1% Other groups (2000).
Economy: Single-family building permits issued: 56 (2005); Multi-family building permits issued: 0 (2005); Employment by occupation: 9.3% management, 19.5% professional, 16.2% services, 25.3% sales, 1.3% farming, 11.7% construction, 16.7% production (2000).
Income: Per capita income: $23,037 (2005); Median household income: $59,994 (2005); Average household income: $71,018 (2005); Percent of households with income of $100,000 or more: 20.0% (2005); Poverty rate: 13.4% (2000).
Education: Percent of population age 25 and over with: High school diploma (including GED) or higher: 74.6% (2005); Bachelor's degree or higher: 14.8% (2005); Master's degree or higher: 5.9% (2005).
Housing: Homeownership rate: 78.9% (2005); Median home value: $215,863 (2005); Median rent: $618 per month (2000); Median age of housing: 34 years (2000).
Safety: Violent crime rate: 4.8 per 10,000 population; Property crime rate: 38.9 per 10,000 population (2004).
Transportation: Commute to work: 89.2% car, 1.6% public transportation, 4.1% walk, 4.9% work from home (2000); Travel time to work: 26.6% less than 15 minutes, 28.8% 15 to 30 minutes, 23.5% 30 to 45 minutes, 9.2% 45 to 60 minutes, 11.9% 60 minutes or more (2000)

SHOKAN (CDP).
Covers a land area of 3.903 square miles and a water area of 0 square miles. Located at 41.97° N. Lat.; 74.21° W. Long.
Population: 1,157 (1990); 1,252 (2000); 1,267 (2005); 1,282 (2010 projected); Race: 95.4% White, 1.3% Black, 2.1% Asian, 2.9% Hispanic of any race (2005); Density: 324.7 persons per square mile (2005); Average household size: 2.47 (2005); Median age: 44.3 (2005); Males per 100 females: 104.0 (2005); Marriage status: 15.9% never married, 63.4% now married, 8.3% widowed, 12.4% divorced (2000); Foreign born: 9.1% (2000); Ancestry (includes multiple ancestries): 29.9% German, 17.8% Irish, 17.4% English, 8.1% Other groups, 7.9% Italian (2000).
Economy: Resort village. Employment by occupation: 12.8% management, 29.3% professional, 8.8% services, 25.3% sales, 1.3% farming, 7.6% construction, 15.0% production (2000).
Income: Per capita income: $26,427 (2005); Median household income: $56,693 (2005); Average household income: $65,396 (2005); Percent of households with income of $100,000 or more: 12.7% (2005); Poverty rate: 5.8% (2000).
Education: Percent of population age 25 and over with: High school diploma (including GED) or higher: 85.5% (2005); Bachelor's degree or higher: 29.9% (2005); Master's degree or higher: 10.5% (2005).
Housing: Homeownership rate: 80.3% (2005); Median home value: $166,401 (2005); Median rent: $483 per month (2000); Median age of housing: 36 years (2000).
Transportation: Commute to work: 92.8% car, 0.0% public transportation, 1.9% walk, 4.0% work from home (2000); Travel time to work: 16.0% less than 15 minutes, 52.6% 15 to 30 minutes, 18.0% 30 to 45 minutes, 3.4% 45 to 60 minutes, 10.1% 60 minutes or more (2000)

STONE RIDGE (CDP).
Covers a land area of 5.213 square miles and a water area of 0.036 square miles. Located at 41.84° N. Lat.; 74.15° W. Long.
Population: 1,000 (1990); 1,173 (2000); 1,179 (2005); 1,192 (2010 projected); Race: 93.0% White, 2.3% Black, 2.6% Asian, 4.3% Hispanic of any race (2005); Density: 226.2 persons per square mile (2005); Average household size: 2.51 (2005); Median age: 45.7 (2005); Males per 100 females: 91.1 (2005); Marriage status: 25.1% never married, 59.1% now married, 9.3% widowed, 6.6% divorced (2000); Foreign born: 1.5% (2000); Ancestry (includes multiple ancestries): 26.3% Irish, 20.4% English, 19.5% German, 16.6% Italian, 13.1% Dutch (2000).
Economy: Employment by occupation: 16.3% management, 27.9% professional, 12.8% services, 29.3% sales, 1.7% farming, 5.2% construction, 6.8% production (2000).
Income: Per capita income: $25,805 (2005); Median household income: $46,140 (2005); Average household income: $64,312 (2005); Percent of households with income of $100,000 or more: 22.4% (2005); Poverty rate: 12.2% (2000).
Education: Percent of population age 25 and over with: High school diploma (including GED) or higher: 87.4% (2005); Bachelor's degree or higher: 28.2% (2005); Master's degree or higher: 10.4% (2005).

School District(s)
Rondout Valley Central School District (KG-12)
   2003-04 Enrollment: 2,797 .... (845) 687-2400

Two-year College(s)
Ulster County Community College (Public)
   Fall 2004 Enrollment: 3,356..................... (845) 687-5000
   2005-06 Tuition: In-state $3,200; Out-of-state $6,400
Housing: Homeownership rate: 83.4% (2005); Median home value: $190,890 (2005); Median rent: $592 per month (2000); Median age of housing: 36 years (2000).
Transportation: Commute to work: 91.4% car, 1.6% public transportation, 0.0% walk, 1.8% work from home (2000); Travel time to work: 41.0% less than 15 minutes, 24.6% 15 to 30 minutes, 14.2% 30 to 45 minutes, 18.5% 45 to 60 minutes, 1.7% 60 minutes or more (2000)
Additional Information Contacts
Marbletown Business Association .... (845) 687-4567
   http://www.marbletown.org/

TILLSON (CDP).
Covers a land area of 2.315 square miles and a water area of 0.031 square miles. Located at 41.83° N. Lat.; 74.07° W. Long. Elevation is 236 feet.
Population: 1,619 (1990); 1,709 (2000); 1,766 (2005); 1,801 (2010 projected); Race: 97.0% White, 1.1% Black, 0.2% Asian, 2.5% Hispanic of

any race (2005); Density: 763.0 persons per square mile (2005); Average household size: 2.66 (2005); Median age: 38.1 (2005); Males per 100 females: 95.8 (2005); Marriage status: 24.1% never married, 60.1% now married, 6.4% widowed, 9.4% divorced (2000); Foreign born: 4.5% (2000); Ancestry (includes multiple ancestries): 24.6% Irish, 18.8% German, 18.6% Italian, 15.4% English, 13.7% Other groups (2000).
Economy: Employment by occupation: 15.9% management, 22.4% professional, 22.2% services, 22.6% sales, 0.0% farming, 9.2% construction, 7.8% production (2000).
Income: Per capita income: $22,504 (2005); Median household income: $51,887 (2005); Average household income: $59,853 (2005); Percent of households with income of $100,000 or more: 15.8% (2005); Poverty rate: 14.5% (2000).
Education: Percent of population age 25 and over with: High school diploma (including GED) or higher: 87.2% (2005); Bachelor's degree or higher: 23.9% (2005); Master's degree or higher: 8.7% (2005).
Housing: Homeownership rate: 86.4% (2005); Median home value: $144,570 (2005); Median rent: $509 per month (2000); Median age of housing: 41 years (2000).
Transportation: Commute to work: 91.1% car, 1.4% public transportation, 0.0% walk, 6.9% work from home (2000); Travel time to work: 15.9% less than 15 minutes, 45.7% 15 to 30 minutes, 22.9% 30 to 45 minutes, 6.6% 45 to 60 minutes, 9.0% 60 minutes or more (2000)

ULSTER (town).
Covers a land area of 26.800 square miles and a water area of 2.081 square miles. Located at 41.96° N. Lat.; 74.01° W. Long.
Population: 12,365 (1990); 12,544 (2000); 12,850 (2005); 13,188 (2010 projected); Race: 93.0% White, 3.6% Black, 1.4% Asian, 3.0% Hispanic of any race (2005); Density: 479.5 persons per square mile (2005); Average household size: 2.55 (2005); Median age: 41.8 (2005); Males per 100 females: 91.4 (2005); Marriage status: 22.9% never married, 59.0% now married, 8.3% widowed, 9.8% divorced (2000); Foreign born: 4.3% (2000); Ancestry (includes multiple ancestries): 21.4% Irish, 20.8% German, 18.9% Italian, 9.0% Other groups, 7.6% English (2000).
Economy: Single-family building permits issued: 36 (2005); Multi-family building permits issued: 0 (2005); Employment by occupation: 12.7% management, 24.0% professional, 17.3% services, 26.8% sales, 0.2% farming, 8.8% construction, 10.1% production (2000).
Income: Per capita income: $25,630 (2005); Median household income: $49,241 (2005); Average household income: $63,366 (2005); Percent of households with income of $100,000 or more: 16.9% (2005); Poverty rate: 9.0% (2000).
Taxes: Total city taxes per capita: $589 (2004); City property taxes per capita: $521 (2004).
Education: Percent of population age 25 and over with: High school diploma (including GED) or higher: 83.3% (2005); Bachelor's degree or higher: 21.5% (2005); Master's degree or higher: 8.9% (2005).
Housing: Homeownership rate: 72.1% (2005); Median home value: $139,599 (2005); Median rent: $568 per month (2000); Median age of housing: 35 years (2000).
Safety: Violent crime rate: 9.4 per 10,000 population; Property crime rate: 181.5 per 10,000 population (2004).
Transportation: Commute to work: 93.5% car, 1.9% public transportation, 2.0% walk, 2.2% work from home (2000); Travel time to work: 42.5% less than 15 minutes, 32.9% 15 to 30 minutes, 10.8% 30 to 45 minutes, 6.8% 45 to 60 minutes, 7.0% 60 minutes or more (2000)

ULSTER PARK (unincorporated postal area, zip code 12487).
Covers a land area of 20.211 square miles and a water area of 0.207 square miles. Located at 41.85° N. Lat.; 73.99° W. Long.
Population: 0 (2000); Race: 95.4% White, 1.7% Black, 0.7% Asian, 1.8% Hispanic of any race (2000); Density: 0.0 persons per square mile (2000); Age: 26.0% under 18, 9.1% over 64 (2000); Marriage status: 29.5% never married, 56.0% now married, 4.9% widowed, 9.6% divorced (2000); Foreign born: 5.6% (2000); Ancestry (includes multiple ancestries): 22.8% Irish, 22.4% German, 19.5% Italian, 10.1% English, 5.4% Dutch (2000).
Economy: Employment by occupation: 11.8% management, 33.3% professional, 12.6% services, 21.1% sales, 0.0% farming, 10.0% construction, 11.3% production (2000).
Income: Per capita income: $20,625 (2000); Median household income: $49,818 (2000); Poverty rate: 9.8% (2000).
Education: Percent of population age 25 and over with: High school diploma (including GED) or higher: 90.1% (2000); Bachelor's degree or higher: 29.9% (2000).

School District(s)
Kingston City School District (PK-12)
   2003-04 Enrollment: 8,149 . . . . (845) 339-3000
Housing: Homeownership rate: 71.7% (2000); Median home value: $112,500 (2000); Median rent: $617 per month (2000); Median age of housing: 43 years (2000).
Transportation: Commute to work: 90.5% car, 0.6% public transportation, 1.3% walk, 7.2% work from home (2000); Travel time to work: 21.6% less than 15 minutes, 40.1% 15 to 30 minutes, 23.7% 30 to 45 minutes, 8.7% 45 to 60 minutes, 5.9% 60 minutes or more (2000)

WALKER VALLEY (CDP).
Covers a land area of 2.068 square miles and a water area of 0.007 square miles. Located at 41.64° N. Lat.; 74.37° W. Long.
Population: 546 (1990); 758 (2000); 862 (2005); 968 (2010 projected); Race: 94.2% White, 2.9% Black, 1.2% Asian, 3.1% Hispanic of any race (2005); Density: 416.8 persons per square mile (2005); Average household size: 2.72 (2005); Median age: 38.3 (2005); Males per 100 females: 109.2 (2005); Marriage status: 25.7% never married, 62.7% now married, 2.8% widowed, 8.8% divorced (2000); Foreign born: 2.8% (2000); Ancestry (includes multiple ancestries): 31.0% German, 27.6% Irish, 22.6% Italian, 13.0% English, 6.6% United States or American (2000).
Economy: Employment by occupation: 11.5% management, 18.5% professional, 13.3% services, 32.0% sales, 0.0% farming, 17.0% construction, 7.8% production (2000).
Income: Per capita income: $26,830 (2005); Median household income: $58,382 (2005); Average household income: $72,957 (2005); Percent of households with income of $100,000 or more: 18.9% (2005); Poverty rate: 6.2% (2000).
Education: Percent of population age 25 and over with: High school diploma (including GED) or higher: 85.8% (2005); Bachelor's degree or higher: 16.0% (2005); Master's degree or higher: 3.4% (2005).
Housing: Homeownership rate: 81.4% (2005); Median home value: $200,018 (2005); Median rent: $817 per month (2000); Median age of housing: 39 years (2000).
Transportation: Commute to work: 92.2% car, 3.9% public transportation, 1.6% walk, 2.3% work from home (2000); Travel time to work: 10.3% less than 15 minutes, 35.7% 15 to 30 minutes, 30.7% 30 to 45 minutes, 15.1% 45 to 60 minutes, 8.2% 60 minutes or more (2000)

WALLKILL (CDP).
Covers a land area of 3.073 square miles and a water area of 0 square miles. Located at 41.60° N. Lat.; 74.17° W. Long. Elevation is 325 feet.
Population: 2,125 (1990); 2,143 (2000); 2,240 (2005); 2,333 (2010 projected); Race: 94.3% White, 2.8% Black, 1.1% Asian, 5.3% Hispanic of any race (2005); Density: 728.9 persons per square mile (2005); Average household size: 2.69 (2005); Median age: 36.2 (2005); Males per 100 females: 97.7 (2005); Marriage status: 24.5% never married, 62.5% now married, 5.3% widowed, 7.7% divorced (2000); Foreign born: 3.8% (2000); Ancestry (includes multiple ancestries): 29.2% Irish, 21.8% German, 20.4% Italian, 10.7% English, 5.9% Polish (2000).
Economy: Manufacturing: transformers, ferrites, electronics components. Summer resort. Employment by occupation: 10.3% management, 17.3% professional, 12.5% services, 34.5% sales, 0.4% farming, 8.7% construction, 16.4% production (2000).
Income: Per capita income: $22,564 (2005); Median household income: $52,905 (2005); Average household income: $60,675 (2005); Percent of households with income of $100,000 or more: 16.6% (2005); Poverty rate: 5.0% (2000).
Education: Percent of population age 25 and over with: High school diploma (including GED) or higher: 84.4% (2005); Bachelor's degree or higher: 20.9% (2005); Master's degree or higher: 6.5% (2005).
Housing: Homeownership rate: 69.4% (2005); Median home value: $190,244 (2005); Median rent: $556 per month (2000); Median age of housing: 41 years (2000).
Transportation: Commute to work: 92.7% car, 1.8% public transportation, 1.9% walk, 3.0% work from home (2000); Travel time to work: 25.3% less than 15 minutes, 28.1% 15 to 30 minutes, 24.7% 30 to 45 minutes, 7.1% 45 to 60 minutes, 14.8% 60 minutes or more (2000)

WAWARSING (town).
Covers a land area of 130.747 square miles and a water area of 3.112 square miles. Located at 41.74° N. Lat.; 74.40° W. Long. Elevation is 288 feet.
Population: 12,348 (1990); 12,889 (2000); 12,833 (2005); 12,807 (2010 projected); Race: 73.0% White, 13.3% Black, 1.3% Asian, 20.3% Hispanic of any race (2005); Density: 98.2 persons per square mile (2005); Average

household size: 2.93 (2005); Median age: 37.4 (2005); Males per 100 females: 117.8 (2005); Marriage status: 32.2% never married, 51.3% now married, 7.3% widowed, 9.2% divorced (2000); Foreign born: 9.9% (2000); Ancestry (includes multiple ancestries): 24.4% Other groups, 13.6% German, 12.5% Irish, 9.5% Italian, 7.0% United States or American (2000).
Economy: Resort village. Single-family building permits issued: 25 (2005); Multi-family building permits issued: 4 (2005); Employment by occupation: 8.9% management, 17.6% professional, 22.7% services, 24.2% sales, 0.8% farming, 8.5% construction, 17.2% production (2000).
Income: Per capita income: $18,609 (2005); Median household income: $39,078 (2005); Average household income: $48,535 (2005); Percent of households with income of $100,000 or more: 10.2% (2005); Poverty rate: 19.1% (2000).
Education: Percent of population age 25 and over with: High school diploma (including GED) or higher: 64.0% (2005); Bachelor's degree or higher: 13.3% (2005); Master's degree or higher: 6.2% (2005).
Housing: Homeownership rate: 62.5% (2005); Median home value: $130,254 (2005); Median rent: $505 per month (2000); Median age of housing: 43 years (2000).
Transportation: Commute to work: 88.6% car, 2.1% public transportation, 5.3% walk, 2.7% work from home (2000); Travel time to work: 45.1% less than 15 minutes, 23.4% 15 to 30 minutes, 12.6% 30 to 45 minutes, 7.8% 45 to 60 minutes, 11.2% 60 minutes or more (2000)

WEST HURLEY (CDP). Covers a land area of 3.778 square miles and a water area of <.001 square miles. Located at 42.00° N. Lat.; 74.10° W. Long.
Population: 2,190 (1990); 2,105 (2000); 2,008 (2005); 1,927 (2010 projected); Race: 93.8% White, 1.7% Black, 1.8% Asian, 2.9% Hispanic of any race (2005); Density: 531.6 persons per square mile (2005); Average household size: 2.38 (2005); Median age: 48.4 (2005); Males per 100 females: 88.5 (2005); Marriage status: 21.1% never married, 62.9% now married, 9.1% widowed, 6.9% divorced (2000); Foreign born: 5.5% (2000); Ancestry (includes multiple ancestries): 22.0% Irish, 22.0% German, 15.0% Italian, 13.8% English, 10.0% Polish (2000).
Economy: In summer-resort and agricultural area. Employment by occupation: 13.1% management, 34.0% professional, 8.1% services, 29.8% sales, 0.0% farming, 6.8% construction, 8.3% production (2000).
Income: Per capita income: $34,324 (2005); Median household income: $61,696 (2005); Average household income: $81,283 (2005); Percent of households with income of $100,000 or more: 28.9% (2005); Poverty rate: 6.5% (2000).
Education: Percent of population age 25 and over with: High school diploma (including GED) or higher: 88.9% (2005); Bachelor's degree or higher: 36.6% (2005); Master's degree or higher: 20.9% (2005).
School District(s)
Onteora Central School District (KG-12)
    2003-04 Enrollment: 2,172 . . . . (845) 657-6383
Housing: Homeownership rate: 86.3% (2005); Median home value: $197,649 (2005); Median rent: $595 per month (2000); Median age of housing: 36 years (2000).
Transportation: Commute to work: 90.2% car, 0.0% public transportation, 1.8% walk, 8.1% work from home (2000); Travel time to work: 20.3% less than 15 minutes, 46.0% 15 to 30 minutes, 10.8% 30 to 45 minutes, 6.6% 45 to 60 minutes, 16.3% 60 minutes or more (2000)

WEST SHOKAN (unincorporated postal area, zip code 12494). Covers a land area of 12.430 square miles and a water area of 0 square miles. Located at 41.96° N. Lat.; 74.27° W. Long.
Population: 0 (2000); Race: 93.1% White, 0.0% Black, 0.0% Asian, 1.0% Hispanic of any race (2000); Density: 0.0 persons per square mile (2000); Age: 22.7% under 18, 15.1% over 64 (2000); Marriage status: 18.2% never married, 63.6% now married, 6.4% widowed, 11.8% divorced (2000); Foreign born: 8.3% (2000); Ancestry (includes multiple ancestries): 26.0% German, 25.2% Italian, 24.5% Irish, 10.0% English, 4.8% Dutch (2000).
Economy: Employment by occupation: 7.5% management, 22.5% professional, 19.0% services, 25.7% sales, 0.0% farming, 20.3% construction, 5.1% production (2000).
Income: Per capita income: $19,698 (2000); Median household income: $48,654 (2000); Poverty rate: 3.6% (2000).
Education: Percent of population age 25 and over with: High school diploma (including GED) or higher: 75.1% (2000); Bachelor's degree or higher: 22.1% (2000).

Housing: Homeownership rate: 89.4% (2000); Median home value: $125,800 (2000); Median rent: $375 per month (2000); Median age of housing: 33 years (2000).
Transportation: Commute to work: 87.4% car, 0.0% public transportation, 4.5% walk, 8.0% work from home (2000); Travel time to work: 25.9% less than 15 minutes, 18.9% 15 to 30 minutes, 20.6% 30 to 45 minutes, 18.0% 45 to 60 minutes, 16.6% 60 minutes or more (2000)

WILLOW (unincorporated postal area, zip code 12495). Covers a land area of 7.344 square miles and a water area of 0 square miles. Located at 42.08° N. Lat.; 74.24° W. Long.
Population: 0 (2000); Race: 94.5% White, 0.0% Black, 0.0% Asian, 0.0% Hispanic of any race (2000); Density: 0.0 persons per square mile (2000); Age: 6.8% under 18, 24.7% over 64 (2000); Marriage status: 18.4% never married, 62.5% now married, 2.9% widowed, 16.2% divorced (2000); Foreign born: 17.8% (2000); Ancestry (includes multiple ancestries): 30.8% English, 21.2% German, 13.0% Danish, 7.5% Dutch, 7.5% Russian (2000).
Economy: Employment by occupation: 13.5% management, 46.1% professional, 6.7% services, 16.9% sales, 0.0% farming, 16.9% construction, 0.0% production (2000).
Income: Per capita income: $42,858 (2000); Median household income: $55,000 (2000); Poverty rate: 4.1% (2000).
Education: Percent of population age 25 and over with: High school diploma (including GED) or higher: 66.9% (2000); Bachelor's degree or higher: 48.5% (2000).
Housing: Homeownership rate: 92.2% (2000); Median home value: $151,100 (2000); Median rent: $425 per month (2000); Median age of housing: 25 years (2000).
Transportation: Commute to work: 65.2% car, 12.4% public transportation, 0.0% walk, 22.5% work from home (2000); Travel time to work: 0.0% less than 15 minutes, 20.3% 15 to 30 minutes, 23.2% 30 to 45 minutes, 29.0% 45 to 60 minutes, 27.5% 60 minutes or more (2000)

WOODSTOCK (town). Covers a land area of 67.501 square miles and a water area of 0.364 square miles. Located at 42.04° N. Lat.; 74.12° W. Long.
History: Best known for its association with the famous 3-day music festival in 1969, Woodstock had a reputation as an artists' colony and progressive retreat long before the 1960s. A tannery center in the 19th century, it became an art colony in 1902. In 1906 the Manhattan-based Arts Student League opened a summer school here, and the adjacent Maverick colony drew social reformers, artists, and performers. To this day the village remains a magnet for tourists, artists, and drifters.
Population: 6,290 (1990); 6,241 (2000); 6,247 (2005); 6,268 (2010 projected); Race: 94.1% White, 1.3% Black, 1.7% Asian, 3.0% Hispanic of any race (2005); Density: 92.5 persons per square mile (2005); Average household size: 2.07 (2005); Median age: 49.8 (2005); Males per 100 females: 94.5 (2005); Marriage status: 24.2% never married, 54.3% now married, 7.8% widowed, 13.7% divorced (2000); Foreign born: 7.1% (2000); Ancestry (includes multiple ancestries): 20.9% German, 16.1% Irish, 15.1% Italian, 12.9% English, 9.8% Polish (2000).
Economy: Single-family building permits issued: 19 (2005); Multi-family building permits issued: 0 (2005); Employment by occupation: 15.1% management, 35.7% professional, 11.2% services, 24.1% sales, 0.4% farming, 6.5% construction, 7.0% production (2000).
Income: Per capita income: $37,444 (2005); Median household income: $56,136 (2005); Average household income: $76,451 (2005); Percent of households with income of $100,000 or more: 23.9% (2005); Poverty rate: 10.2% (2000).
Education: Percent of population age 25 and over with: High school diploma (including GED) or higher: 94.4% (2005); Bachelor's degree or higher: 48.8% (2005); Master's degree or higher: 22.5% (2005).
School District(s)
Kingston City School District (PK-12)
    2003-04 Enrollment: 8,149 . . . . (845) 339-3000
Onteora Central School District (KG-12)
    2003-04 Enrollment: 2,172 . . . . (845) 657-6383
Housing: Homeownership rate: 76.2% (2005); Median home value: $258,671 (2005); Median rent: $630 per month (2000); Median age of housing: 43 years (2000).
Safety: Violent crime rate: 8.0 per 10,000 population; Property crime rate: 205.9 per 10,000 population (2004).
Newspapers: Ulster County Townsman (General - Circulation 5,100)
Transportation: Commute to work: 73.8% car, 3.5% public transportation, 4.3% walk, 17.1% work from home (2000); Travel time to work: 29.0% less

than 15 minutes, 34.5% 15 to 30 minutes, 14.8% 30 to 45 minutes, 7.0% 45 to 60 minutes, 14.6% 60 minutes or more (2000)
Additional Information Contacts
Town of Woodstock . . . . (845) 679-2113
  http://www.woodstockny.org/
Woodstock Chamber of Commerce . . . . (845) 679-6234
  http://www.woodstockchamber.com

WOODSTOCK (CDP). Covers a land area of 0.819 square miles and a water area of 0.043 square miles. Located at 39.65° N. Lat.; 88.02° W. Long.
Population: 2,285 (1990); 2,187 (2000); 2,129 (2005); 2,094 (2010 projected); Race: 92.6% White, 1.7% Black, 2.1% Asian, 4.7% Hispanic of any race (2005); Density: 2,598.9 persons per square mile (2005); Average household size: 1.91 (2005); Median age: 49.7 (2005); Males per 100 females: 90.3 (2005); Marriage status: 29.7% never married, 46.2% now married, 6.3% widowed, 17.7% divorced (2000); Foreign born: 7.1% (2000); Ancestry (includes multiple ancestries): 21.0% German, 20.9% Irish, 13.8% English, 11.8% Italian, 10.5% Other groups (2000).
Economy: Employment by occupation: 16.2% management, 27.0% professional, 14.5% services, 28.1% sales, 0.5% farming, 5.1% construction, 8.7% production (2000).
Income: Per capita income: $32,275 (2005); Median household income: $43,308 (2005); Average household income: $60,233 (2005); Percent of households with income of $100,000 or more: 17.1% (2005); Poverty rate: 11.9% (2000).
Education: Percent of population age 25 and over with: High school diploma (including GED) or higher: 96.5% (2005); Bachelor's degree or higher: 45.2% (2005); Master's degree or higher: 19.9% (2005).
Housing: Homeownership rate: 64.2% (2005); Median home value: $245,652 (2005); Median rent: $580 per month (2000); Median age of housing: 47 years (2000).
Transportation: Commute to work: 71.7% car, 2.4% public transportation, 6.7% walk, 16.4% work from home (2000); Travel time to work: 38.3% less than 15 minutes, 31.6% 15 to 30 minutes, 13.0% 30 to 45 minutes, 7.4% 45 to 60 minutes, 9.7% 60 minutes or more (2000)

ZENA (CDP). Covers a land area of 2.946 square miles and a water area of 0 square miles. Located at 42.02° N. Lat.; 74.08° W. Long.
Population: 1,208 (1990); 1,119 (2000); 1,069 (2005); 1,027 (2010 projected); Race: 94.8% White, 2.0% Black, 1.5% Asian, 1.4% Hispanic of any race (2005); Density: 362.8 persons per square mile (2005); Average household size: 2.45 (2005); Median age: 47.3 (2005); Males per 100 females: 86.2 (2005); Marriage status: 15.0% never married, 63.0% now married, 7.9% widowed, 14.1% divorced (2000); Foreign born: 3.9% (2000); Ancestry (includes multiple ancestries): 26.4% Italian, 21.5% German, 14.3% Irish, 13.5% Polish, 11.6% English (2000).
Economy: Employment by occupation: 13.0% management, 44.0% professional, 4.0% services, 32.6% sales, 0.0% farming, 5.2% construction, 1.2% production (2000).
Income: Per capita income: $34,941 (2005); Median household income: $72,917 (2005); Average household income: $83,245 (2005); Percent of households with income of $100,000 or more: 27.1% (2005); Poverty rate: 5.9% (2000).
Education: Percent of population age 25 and over with: High school diploma (including GED) or higher: 95.6% (2005); Bachelor's degree or higher: 50.8% (2005); Master's degree or higher: 27.5% (2005).
Housing: Homeownership rate: 89.4% (2005); Median home value: $224,848 (2005); Median rent: $646 per month (2000); Median age of housing: 35 years (2000).
Transportation: Commute to work: 85.0% car, 1.4% public transportation, 0.0% walk, 13.6% work from home (2000); Travel time to work: 21.1% less than 15 minutes, 45.1% 15 to 30 minutes, 10.3% 30 to 45 minutes, 6.1% 45 to 60 minutes, 17.4% 60 minutes or more (2000)

Warren County

Located in eastern New York, in the Adirondacks; bounded on the east by Lake George; drained by the Hudson and Schroon Rivers. Covers a land area of 869.29 square miles, a water area of 62.37 square miles, and is located in the Eastern Time Zone. The county government was organized in 1813. County seat is Lake George.

Warren County is part of the Glens Falls, NY Metropolitan Statistical Area. The entire metro area includes: Warren County, NY; Washington County, NY

Weather Station: Glens Falls Airport — Elevation: 318 feet

	Jan	Feb	Mar	Apr	May	Jun	Jul	Aug	Sep	Oct	Nov	Dec
High	28	32	42	56	68	77	82	79	70	58	46	34
Low	7	11	22	34	44	53	58	56	48	36	28	17
Precip	3.0	2.2	3.1	3.0	3.7	3.4	3.5	3.7	3.4	3.1	3.2	2.9
Snow	19.7	12.8	12.7	2.3	tr	0.0	tr	0.0	0.0	tr	4.2	14.2

High and Low temperatures in degrees Fahrenheit; Precipitation and Snow in inches

Weather Station: Glens Falls Farm — Elevation: 501 feet

	Jan	Feb	Mar	Apr	May	Jun	Jul	Aug	Sep	Oct	Nov	Dec
High	30	34	44	58	71	79	83	81	72	61	47	35
Low	9	11	22	33	44	53	58	56	48	37	29	16
Precip	3.4	2.6	3.7	3.7	4.4	4.1	4.1	4.3	4.1	3.6	4.1	3.4
Snow	20.6	12.0	12.6	2.3	tr	0.0	0.0	0.0	0.0	tr	4.2	14.5

High and Low temperatures in degrees Fahrenheit; Precipitation and Snow in inches

Population: 59,209 (1990); 63,303 (2000); 65,513 (2005); 67,791 (2010 projected); Race: 97.1% White, 0.9% Black, 0.7% Asian, 1.7% Hispanic of any race (2005); Density: 75.4 persons per square mile (2005); Average household size: 2.41 (2005); Median age: 40.5 (2005); Males per 100 females: 94.5 (2005).
Religion: Five largest groups: 34.8% Catholic Church, 4.7% The United Methodist Church, 3.1% Presbyterian Church (U.S.A.), 1.8% The Wesleyan Church, 1.4% Episcopal Church (2000).
Economy: Unemployment rate: 4.6% (2005); Total civilian labor force: 35,498 (2005); Leading industries: 17.5% health care and social assistance; 16.1% retail trade; 15.0% manufacturing (2003); Farms: 72 totaling 6,400 acres (2002); Companies that employ 500 or more persons: 8 (2003); Companies that employ 100 to 499 persons: 45 (2003); Companies that employ less than 100 persons: 2,255 (2003); Black-owned businesses: n/a (2002); Hispanic-owned businesses: 128 (2002); Women-owned businesses: 2,653 (2002); Retail sales per capita: $20,839 (2006). Single-family building permits issued: 451 (2005); Multi-family building permits issued: 83 (2005).
Income: Per capita income: $23,664 (2005); Median household income: $43,620 (2005); Average household income: $56,219 (2005); Percent of households with income of $100,000 or more: 11.7% (2005); Poverty rate: 10.0% (2003); Bankruptcy rate: 8.56% (2005).
Taxes: Total county taxes per capita: $967 (2004); County property taxes per capita: $357 (2004).
Education: Percent of population age 25 and over with: High school diploma (including GED) or higher: 84.8% (2005); Bachelor's degree or higher: 23.5% (2005); Master's degree or higher: 9.8% (2005).
Housing: Homeownership rate: 70.5% (2005); Median home value: $139,513 (2005); Median rent: $457 per month (2000); Median age of housing: 34 years (2000).
Health: Birth rate: 101.8 per 10,000 population (2004); Death rate: 87.5 per 10,000 population (2004); Age-adjusted cancer mortality rate: 218.4 deaths per 100,000 population (2002); Number of physicians: 33.8 per 10,000 population (2004); Hospital beds: 52.9 per 10,000 population (2003); Hospital admissions: 2,023.7 per 10,000 population (2003).
Elections: 2004 Presidential election results: 54.6% Bush, 43.2% Kerry, 2.0% Nader, 0.2% Badnarik
National and State Parks: Lake George Beach State Park
Additional Information Contacts
Warren County Government . . . . (518) 761-6535
  http://www.co.warren.ny.us/
City of Glens Falls . . . . (518) 761-3803
  http://www.cityofglensfalls.com/
Town of Queensbury . . . . (518) 761-8200
  http://www.queensbury.net/

Warren County Communities

ADIRONDACK (unincorporated postal area, zip code 12808). Covers a land area of 18.603 square miles and a water area of 0.240 square miles. Located at 43.75° N. Lat.; 73.76° W. Long. Elevation is 842 feet.
Population: 0 (2000); Race: 98.9% White, 0.0% Black, 0.4% Asian, 2.6% Hispanic of any race (2000); Density: 0.0 persons per square mile (2000); Age: 7.8% under 18, 23.1% over 64 (2000); Marriage status: 10.4% never married, 74.7% now married, 5.6% widowed, 9.2% divorced (2000); Foreign born: 3.4% (2000); Ancestry (includes multiple ancestries): 20.1%

German, 13.4% English, 10.8% United States or American, 10.4% Irish, 9.7% Other groups (2000).
Economy: Resort village. Employment by occupation: 12.3% management, 16.2% professional, 10.0% services, 36.9% sales, 0.0% farming, 11.5% construction, 13.1% production (2000).
Income: Per capita income: $28,027 (2000); Median household income: $41,458 (2000); Poverty rate: 6.3% (2000).
Education: Percent of population age 25 and over with: High school diploma (including GED) or higher: 84.5% (2000); Bachelor's degree or higher: 26.5% (2000).
Housing: Homeownership rate: 91.4% (2000); Median home value: $176,800 (2000); Median rent: $400 per month (2000); Median age of housing: 26 years (2000).
Transportation: Commute to work: 94.3% car, 0.0% public transportation, 0.0% walk, 5.7% work from home (2000); Travel time to work: 9.6% less than 15 minutes, 24.3% 15 to 30 minutes, 33.9% 30 to 45 minutes, 14.8% 45 to 60 minutes, 17.4% 60 minutes or more (2000)

ATHOL (unincorporated postal area, zip code 12810). Covers a land area of 47.010 square miles and a water area of 0.407 square miles. Located at 43.48° N. Lat.; 73.89° W. Long.
Population: 0 (2000); Race: 96.6% White, 0.3% Black, 0.4% Asian, 0.6% Hispanic of any race (2000); Density: 0.0 persons per square mile (2000); Age: 23.7% under 18, 14.7% over 64 (2000); Marriage status: 21.7% never married, 66.8% now married, 4.1% widowed, 7.3% divorced (2000); Foreign born: 1.6% (2000); Ancestry (includes multiple ancestries): 17.9% United States or American, 17.5% English, 11.6% German, 11.3% Other groups, 11.0% French (except Basque) (2000).
Economy: Summer resort village in the Adirondack Mountains. Employment by occupation: 7.8% management, 16.5% professional, 21.7% services, 16.5% sales, 1.0% farming, 18.1% construction, 18.4% production (2000).
Income: Per capita income: $15,826 (2000); Median household income: $36,979 (2000); Poverty rate: 12.4% (2000).
Education: Percent of population age 25 and over with: High school diploma (including GED) or higher: 73.8% (2000); Bachelor's degree or higher: 11.8% (2000).
Housing: Homeownership rate: 88.1% (2000); Median home value: $78,600 (2000); Median rent: $300 per month (2000); Median age of housing: 27 years (2000).
Transportation: Commute to work: 93.8% car, 0.0% public transportation, 2.6% walk, 1.3% work from home (2000); Travel time to work: 20.9% less than 15 minutes, 22.6% 15 to 30 minutes, 33.2% 30 to 45 minutes, 13.0% 45 to 60 minutes, 10.3% 60 minutes or more (2000)

BOLTON (town). Covers a land area of 63.397 square miles and a water area of 26.684 square miles. Located at 43.55° N. Lat.; 73.66° W. Long.
Population: 1,855 (1990); 2,117 (2000); 2,145 (2005); 2,183 (2010 projected); Race: 97.4% White, 0.9% Black, 0.7% Asian, 1.1% Hispanic of any race (2005); Density: 33.8 persons per square mile (2005); Average household size: 2.20 (2005); Median age: 48.6 (2005); Males per 100 females: 98.6 (2005); Marriage status: 19.9% never married, 62.7% now married, 8.0% widowed, 9.3% divorced (2000); Foreign born: 3.6% (2000); Ancestry (includes multiple ancestries): 21.4% Irish, 17.3% English, 16.3% German, 12.0% Italian, 9.7% United States or American (2000).
Economy: Employment by occupation: 16.3% management, 20.4% professional, 20.4% services, 25.1% sales, 0.4% farming, 11.3% construction, 6.2% production (2000).
Income: Per capita income: $31,160 (2005); Median household income: $54,302 (2005); Average household income: $68,551 (2005); Percent of households with income of $100,000 or more: 16.6% (2005); Poverty rate: 5.6% (2000).
Taxes: Total city taxes per capita: $497 (2004); City property taxes per capita: $349 (2004).
Education: Percent of population age 25 and over with: High school diploma (including GED) or higher: 89.5% (2005); Bachelor's degree or higher: 30.3% (2005); Master's degree or higher: 13.4% (2005).
Housing: Homeownership rate: 78.5% (2005); Median home value: $219,312 (2005); Median rent: $457 per month (2000); Median age of housing: 34 years (2000).
Safety: Violent crime rate: 9.3 per 10,000 population; Property crime rate: 32.7 per 10,000 population (2004).
Transportation: Commute to work: 85.8% car, 0.0% public transportation, 7.3% walk, 6.5% work from home (2000); Travel time to work: 42.4% less than 15 minutes, 23.1% 15 to 30 minutes, 22.7% 30 to 45 minutes, 6.5% 45 to 60 minutes, 5.4% 60 minutes or more (2000)

BOLTON LANDING (unincorporated postal area, zip code 12814). Covers a land area of 48.195 square miles and a water area of 0.212 square miles. Located at 43.58° N. Lat.; 73.65° W. Long.
Population: 0 (2000); Race: 98.1% White, 0.4% Black, 0.5% Asian, 0.4% Hispanic of any race (2000); Density: 0.0 persons per square mile (2000); Age: 20.5% under 18, 18.7% over 64 (2000); Marriage status: 22.5% never married, 59.8% now married, 8.0% widowed, 9.7% divorced (2000); Foreign born: 3.3% (2000); Ancestry (includes multiple ancestries): 20.3% Irish, 18.3% English, 15.4% German, 11.8% Italian, 9.5% United States or American (2000).
Economy: Resort village. Employment by occupation: 15.3% management, 20.8% professional, 21.3% services, 25.1% sales, 0.3% farming, 10.9% construction, 6.4% production (2000).
Income: Per capita income: $23,812 (2000); Median household income: $45,313 (2000); Poverty rate: 6.2% (2000).
Education: Percent of population age 25 and over with: High school diploma (including GED) or higher: 90.5% (2000); Bachelor's degree or higher: 29.6% (2000).

School District(s)
Bolton Central School District (KG-12)
    2003-04 Enrollment: 295 . . . . (518) 644-2400
Housing: Homeownership rate: 76.7% (2000); Median home value: $140,000 (2000); Median rent: $458 per month (2000); Median age of housing: 35 years (2000).
Transportation: Commute to work: 86.6% car, 0.0% public transportation, 8.2% walk, 5.2% work from home (2000); Travel time to work: 44.4% less than 15 minutes, 22.0% 15 to 30 minutes, 23.1% 30 to 45 minutes, 5.0% 45 to 60 minutes, 5.5% 60 minutes or more (2000)
Additional Information Contacts
Bolton Landing Chamber of Commerce. . . . . (518) 644-3831
    http://www.boltonchamber.com

BRANT LAKE (unincorporated postal area, zip code 12815). Covers a land area of 42.650 square miles and a water area of 2.862 square miles. Located at 43.70° N. Lat.; 73.71° W. Long. Elevation is 800 feet.
History: Sometimes called Horicon.
Population: 0 (2000); Race: 97.1% White, 1.8% Black, 0.0% Asian, 0.4% Hispanic of any race (2000); Density: 0.0 persons per square mile (2000); Age: 25.2% under 18, 20.0% over 64 (2000); Marriage status: 20.8% never married, 63.9% now married, 5.4% widowed, 9.9% divorced (2000); Foreign born: 1.6% (2000); Ancestry (includes multiple ancestries): 16.8% Irish, 15.3% English, 11.8% German, 11.4% United States or American, 10.2% French (except Basque) (2000).
Economy: Employment by occupation: 12.8% management, 9.8% professional, 25.1% services, 24.1% sales, 1.3% farming, 17.3% construction, 9.8% production (2000).
Income: Per capita income: $18,479 (2000); Median household income: $34,917 (2000); Poverty rate: 9.3% (2000).
Education: Percent of population age 25 and over with: High school diploma (including GED) or higher: 80.5% (2000); Bachelor's degree or higher: 14.8% (2000).
Housing: Homeownership rate: 87.8% (2000); Median home value: $89,000 (2000); Median rent: $397 per month (2000); Median age of housing: 33 years (2000).
Transportation: Commute to work: 85.9% car, 0.3% public transportation, 5.5% walk, 7.8% work from home (2000); Travel time to work: 28.8% less than 15 minutes, 34.5% 15 to 30 minutes, 22.6% 30 to 45 minutes, 7.1% 45 to 60 minutes, 7.1% 60 minutes or more (2000)

CHESTER (town). Covers a land area of 84.459 square miles and a water area of 2.644 square miles. Located at 43.67° N. Lat.; 73.84° W. Long.
Population: 3,465 (1990); 3,614 (2000); 3,706 (2005); 3,818 (2010 projected); Race: 97.5% White, 0.2% Black, 0.8% Asian, 1.7% Hispanic of any race (2005); Density: 43.9 persons per square mile (2005); Average household size: 2.76 (2005); Median age: 37.2 (2005); Males per 100 females: 95.6 (2005); Marriage status: 32.4% never married, 53.6% now married, 4.9% widowed, 9.1% divorced (2000); Foreign born: 2.8% (2000); Ancestry (includes multiple ancestries): 19.1% Irish, 16.2% German, 14.4% English, 8.4% French (except Basque), 8.2% Italian (2000).

Economy: Employment by occupation: 8.0% management, 14.8% professional, 25.2% services, 24.7% sales, 1.9% farming, 16.1% construction, 9.3% production (2000).
Income: Per capita income: $20,120 (2005); Median household income: $43,392 (2005); Average household income: $53,038 (2005); Percent of households with income of $100,000 or more: 9.2% (2005); Poverty rate: 12.5% (2000).
Education: Percent of population age 25 and over with: High school diploma (including GED) or higher: 81.7% (2005); Bachelor's degree or higher: 20.6% (2005); Master's degree or higher: 7.9% (2005).
Housing: Homeownership rate: 81.3% (2005); Median home value: $120,786 (2005); Median rent: $367 per month (2000); Median age of housing: 36 years (2000).
Transportation: Commute to work: 88.5% car, 1.1% public transportation, 5.6% walk, 3.7% work from home (2000); Travel time to work: 38.9% less than 15 minutes, 30.4% 15 to 30 minutes, 15.7% 30 to 45 minutes, 7.1% 45 to 60 minutes, 7.9% 60 minutes or more (2000)

CHESTERTOWN (unincorporated postal area, zip code 12817).
Covers a land area of 55.040 square miles and a water area of 2.013 square miles. Located at 43.63° N. Lat.; 73.81° W. Long. Elevation is 827 feet.
Population: 0 (2000); Race: 99.0% White, 0.0% Black, 0.0% Asian, 0.4% Hispanic of any race (2000); Density: 0.0 persons per square mile (2000); Age: 19.5% under 18, 20.2% over 64 (2000); Marriage status: 21.4% never married, 61.4% now married, 6.2% widowed, 11.0% divorced (2000); Foreign born: 2.4% (2000); Ancestry (includes multiple ancestries): 22.9% Irish, 16.9% English, 16.1% German, 8.6% Italian, 7.7% French (except Basque) (2000).
Economy: Manufacturing: log homes. Employment by occupation: 8.8% management, 15.8% professional, 24.1% services, 23.2% sales, 2.3% farming, 17.1% construction, 8.7% production (2000).
Income: Per capita income: $18,502 (2000); Median household income: $36,505 (2000); Poverty rate: 13.5% (2000).
Education: Percent of population age 25 and over with: High school diploma (including GED) or higher: 84.4% (2000); Bachelor's degree or higher: 21.7% (2000).
School District(s)
North Warren Central School District (PK-12)
   2003-04 Enrollment: 640 . . . . (518) 494-3015
Housing: Homeownership rate: 78.9% (2000); Median home value: $93,200 (2000); Median rent: $400 per month (2000); Median age of housing: 33 years (2000).
Transportation: Commute to work: 95.3% car, 0.0% public transportation, 0.8% walk, 3.2% work from home (2000); Travel time to work: 33.1% less than 15 minutes, 30.2% 15 to 30 minutes, 20.5% 30 to 45 minutes, 7.5% 45 to 60 minutes, 8.7% 60 minutes or more (2000)
Additional Information Contacts
North Warren Chamber of Commerce . . . . (518) 494-2722
   http://www.northwarren.com/index/chamber

DIAMOND POINT (unincorporated postal area, zip code 12824).
Covers a land area of 15.405 square miles and a water area of 5.513 square miles. Located at 43.51° N. Lat.; 73.69° W. Long. Elevation is 354 feet.
Population: 0 (2000); Race: 96.2% White, 0.0% Black, 3.1% Asian, 1.7% Hispanic of any race (2000); Density: 0.0 persons per square mile (2000); Age: 17.8% under 18, 19.6% over 64 (2000); Marriage status: 18.3% never married, 65.8% now married, 5.9% widowed, 10.1% divorced (2000); Foreign born: 7.9% (2000); Ancestry (includes multiple ancestries): 24.8% Irish, 21.4% German, 12.5% English, 10.9% Italian, 8.2% Other groups (2000).
Economy: Employment by occupation: 15.1% management, 22.7% professional, 12.9% services, 24.1% sales, 2.5% farming, 18.6% construction, 4.1% production (2000).
Income: Per capita income: $29,755 (2000); Median household income: $53,750 (2000); Poverty rate: 6.6% (2000).
Education: Percent of population age 25 and over with: High school diploma (including GED) or higher: 87.4% (2000); Bachelor's degree or higher: 29.4% (2000).
Housing: Homeownership rate: 84.1% (2000); Median home value: $149,400 (2000); Median rent: $513 per month (2000); Median age of housing: 28 years (2000).
Transportation: Commute to work: 86.6% car, 0.0% public transportation, 5.7% walk, 6.6% work from home (2000); Travel time to work: 35.4% less than 15 minutes, 36.3% 15 to 30 minutes, 14.9% 30 to 45 minutes, 9.8% 45 to 60 minutes, 3.7% 60 minutes or more (2000)

GLENS FALLS (city).
Covers a land area of 3.825 square miles and a water area of 0.103 square miles. Located at 43.31° N. Lat.; 73.64° W. Long. Elevation is 348 feet.
History: The site of Glens Falls was part of the Queensbury Patent, 23,000 acres of land granted in 1759 to 23 men. The water power provided by the 60-foot falls in the Hudson River determined the location of the settlement. During the Revolution the village was destroyed by the British. In 1788, Colonel John Glen of Schenectady acquired land and built mills here. There followed a succession of industrial activities, beginning with lumbering and followed by the manufacture of lime, cement, paper and cellulose.
Population: 15,099 (1990); 14,354 (2000); 14,179 (2005); 14,069 (2010 projected); Race: 95.9% White, 1.7% Black, 0.6% Asian, 2.2% Hispanic of any race (2005); Density: 3,706.4 persons per square mile (2005); Average household size: 2.24 (2005); Median age: 37.1 (2005); Males per 100 females: 93.3 (2005); Marriage status: 30.8% never married, 46.1% now married, 9.5% widowed, 13.6% divorced (2000); Foreign born: 1.7% (2000); Ancestry (includes multiple ancestries): 22.0% Irish, 17.0% French (except Basque), 13.4% English, 12.2% Italian, 11.9% German (2000).
Economy: Single-family building permits issued: 29 (2005); Multi-family building permits issued: 4 (2005); Employment by occupation: 6.8% management, 19.7% professional, 20.1% services, 30.4% sales, 0.2% farming, 6.6% construction, 16.3% production (2000).
Income: Per capita income: $19,877 (2005); Median household income: $32,963 (2005); Average household income: $43,447 (2005); Percent of households with income of $100,000 or more: 6.1% (2005); Poverty rate: 14.8% (2000).
Education: Percent of population age 25 and over with: High school diploma (including GED) or higher: 81.7% (2005); Bachelor's degree or higher: 17.1% (2005); Master's degree or higher: 7.1% (2005).
School District(s)
Glens Falls City School District (KG-12)
   2003-04 Enrollment: 2,522 . . . . (518) 792-1212
Glens Falls Common School District (KG-06)
   2003-04 Enrollment: 161 . . . . (518) 792-3231
Two-year College(s)
Adirondack Beauty School
   Fall 2004 Enrollment: 24 . . . . (518) 745-1646
Housing: Homeownership rate: 48.3% (2005); Median home value: $121,900 (2005); Median rent: $437 per month (2000); Median age of housing: 60+ years (2000).
Hospitals: Glens Falls Hospital (410 beds)
Safety: Violent crime rate: 9.1 per 10,000 population; Property crime rate: 183.3 per 10,000 population (2004).
Newspapers: The Chronicle (General - Circulation 25,000); The Post-Star (Circulation 33,374)
Transportation: Commute to work: 89.2% car, 2.9% public transportation, 5.2% walk, 1.4% work from home (2000); Travel time to work: 59.2% less than 15 minutes, 24.3% 15 to 30 minutes, 8.8% 30 to 45 minutes, 2.2% 45 to 60 minutes, 5.5% 60 minutes or more (2000)
Additional Information Contacts
Adirondack Regional Chambers of Commerce . . . . (518) 798-1761
   http://www.adirondackchamber.org/
City of Glens Falls . . . . (518) 761-3803
   http://www.cityofglensfalls.com/

GLENS FALLS NORTH (CDP).
Covers a land area of 8.090 square miles and a water area of 0.139 square miles. Located at 43.33° N. Lat.; 73.68° W. Long.
Population: 8,139 (1990); 8,061 (2000); 8,087 (2005); 8,162 (2010 projected); Race: 96.3% White, 1.2% Black, 1.2% Asian, 2.3% Hispanic of any race (2005); Density: 999.6 persons per square mile (2005); Average household size: 2.23 (2005); Median age: 42.7 (2005); Males per 100 females: 87.0 (2005); Marriage status: 20.3% never married, 59.3% now married, 9.9% widowed, 10.5% divorced (2000); Foreign born: 4.2% (2000); Ancestry (includes multiple ancestries): 22.9% Irish, 14.7% English, 13.4% French (except Basque), 12.6% German, 12.0% Italian (2000).
Economy: Employment by occupation: 15.8% management, 25.0% professional, 11.9% services, 32.8% sales, 0.2% farming, 6.2% construction, 8.1% production (2000).
Income: Per capita income: $29,888 (2005); Median household income: $47,678 (2005); Average household income: $65,873 (2005); Percent of

households with income of $100,000 or more: 18.9% (2005); Poverty rate: 7.1% (2000).
Education: Percent of population age 25 and over with: High school diploma (including GED) or higher: 90.7% (2005); Bachelor's degree or higher: 35.5% (2005); Master's degree or higher: 16.3% (2005).
Housing: Homeownership rate: 61.5% (2005); Median home value: $171,809 (2005); Median rent: $549 per month (2000); Median age of housing: 25 years (2000).
Transportation: Commute to work: 93.0% car, 0.0% public transportation, 2.3% walk, 4.3% work from home (2000); Travel time to work: 55.5% less than 15 minutes, 24.9% 15 to 30 minutes, 7.9% 30 to 45 minutes, 4.6% 45 to 60 minutes, 7.1% 60 minutes or more (2000).

HAGUE (town). Covers a land area of 64.028 square miles and a water area of 15.588 square miles. Located at 43.73° N. Lat.; 73.52° W. Long. Elevation is 328 feet.
Population: 699 (1990); 854 (2000); 950 (2005); 1,037 (2010 projected); Race: 98.7% White, 0.2% Black, 0.1% Asian, 1.1% Hispanic of any race (2005); Density: 14.8 persons per square mile (2005); Average household size: 2.25 (2005); Median age: 50.8 (2005); Males per 100 females: 95.9 (2005); Marriage status: 14.8% never married, 69.9% now married, 9.4% widowed, 5.9% divorced (2000); Foreign born: 3.2% (2000); Ancestry (includes multiple ancestries): 21.0% Irish, 16.6% English, 14.8% German, 13.5% French (except Basque), 9.3% Other groups (2000).
Economy: Resort village. Employment by occupation: 14.1% management, 17.0% professional, 13.3% services, 26.8% sales, 0.9% farming, 15.6% construction, 12.4% production (2000).
Income: Per capita income: $30,637 (2005); Median household income: $48,043 (2005); Average household income: $68,969 (2005); Percent of households with income of $100,000 or more: 14.9% (2005); Poverty rate: 7.5% (2000).
Education: Percent of population age 25 and over with: High school diploma (including GED) or higher: 84.6% (2005); Bachelor's degree or higher: 26.6% (2005); Master's degree or higher: 12.7% (2005).
Housing: Homeownership rate: 87.7% (2005); Median home value: $154,000 (2005); Median rent: $390 per month (2000); Median age of housing: 37 years (2000).
Transportation: Commute to work: 90.3% car, 0.9% public transportation, 4.1% walk, 4.7% work from home (2000); Travel time to work: 30.7% less than 15 minutes, 36.8% 15 to 30 minutes, 17.0% 30 to 45 minutes, 8.0% 45 to 60 minutes, 7.4% 60 minutes or more (2000).
Additional Information Contacts
Hagye Chamber of Commerce . . . . (518) 543-6353
http://www.hagueticonderoga.com

HORICON (town). Covers a land area of 66.070 square miles and a water area of 5.729 square miles. Located at 43.70° N. Lat.; 73.73° W. Long.
Population: 1,269 (1990); 1,479 (2000); 1,448 (2005); 1,433 (2010 projected); Race: 98.5% White, 0.3% Black, 0.3% Asian, 0.6% Hispanic of any race (2005); Density: 21.9 persons per square mile (2005); Average household size: 2.26 (2005); Median age: 48.2 (2005); Males per 100 females: 100.3 (2005); Marriage status: 19.0% never married, 65.5% now married, 5.9% widowed, 9.6% divorced (2000); Foreign born: 2.1% (2000); Ancestry (includes multiple ancestries): 15.3% English, 14.9% Irish, 13.2% German, 10.7% United States or American, 10.1% French (except Basque) (2000).
Economy: Employment by occupation: 11.8% management, 13.3% professional, 20.8% services, 28.9% sales, 0.8% farming, 14.5% construction, 10.1% production (2000).
Income: Per capita income: $24,475 (2005); Median household income: $42,174 (2005); Average household income: $55,202 (2005); Percent of households with income of $100,000 or more: 9.7% (2005); Poverty rate: 9.7% (2000).
Education: Percent of population age 25 and over with: High school diploma (including GED) or higher: 81.7% (2005); Bachelor's degree or higher: 17.2% (2005); Master's degree or higher: 6.9% (2005).
Housing: Homeownership rate: 87.7% (2005); Median home value: $131,207 (2005); Median rent: $409 per month (2000); Median age of housing: 29 years (2000).
Transportation: Commute to work: 90.3% car, 0.2% public transportation, 3.3% walk, 5.9% work from home (2000); Travel time to work: 28.6% less than 15 minutes, 29.8% 15 to 30 minutes, 24.5% 30 to 45 minutes, 7.8% 45 to 60 minutes, 9.3% 60 minutes or more (2000).

JOHNSBURG (town). Covers a land area of 204.255 square miles and a water area of 2.490 square miles. Located at 43.64° N. Lat.; 74.00° W. Long. Elevation is 1,287 feet.
Population: 2,352 (1990); 2,450 (2000); 2,611 (2005); 2,768 (2010 projected); Race: 98.2% White, 0.3% Black, 0.4% Asian, 0.6% Hispanic of any race (2005); Density: 12.8 persons per square mile (2005); Average household size: 2.40 (2005); Median age: 42.8 (2005); Males per 100 females: 92.1 (2005); Marriage status: 19.8% never married, 60.4% now married, 9.9% widowed, 9.8% divorced (2000); Foreign born: 2.3% (2000); Ancestry (includes multiple ancestries): 19.7% Irish, 16.0% English, 12.4% German, 11.7% United States or American, 9.7% French (except Basque) (2000).
Economy: Resort. Lumbering. Employment by occupation: 10.3% management, 14.4% professional, 20.7% services, 26.2% sales, 1.0% farming, 15.7% construction, 11.7% production (2000).
Income: Per capita income: $18,620 (2005); Median household income: $33,063 (2005); Average household income: $43,210 (2005); Percent of households with income of $100,000 or more: 5.3% (2005); Poverty rate: 17.7% (2000).
Education: Percent of population age 25 and over with: High school diploma (including GED) or higher: 75.1% (2005); Bachelor's degree or higher: 16.0% (2005); Master's degree or higher: 7.2% (2005).
Housing: Homeownership rate: 76.6% (2005); Median home value: $120,161 (2005); Median rent: $347 per month (2000); Median age of housing: 33 years (2000).
Transportation: Commute to work: 87.9% car, 0.3% public transportation, 7.0% walk, 3.6% work from home (2000); Travel time to work: 35.1% less than 15 minutes, 30.5% 15 to 30 minutes, 13.4% 30 to 45 minutes, 9.1% 45 to 60 minutes, 11.9% 60 minutes or more (2000).

KATTSKILL BAY (unincorporated postal area, zip code 12844). Covers a land area of 2.796 square miles and a water area of 0 square miles. Located at 43.49° N. Lat.; 73.63° W. Long.
Population: 0 (2000); Race: 100.0% White, 0.0% Black, 0.0% Asian, 0.0% Hispanic of any race (2000); Density: 0.0 persons per square mile (2000); Age: 19.6% under 18, 15.8% over 64 (2000); Marriage status: 13.3% never married, 69.4% now married, 12.2% widowed, 5.1% divorced (2000); Foreign born: 0.0% (2000); Ancestry (includes multiple ancestries): 27.4% English, 22.1% German, 17.0% Irish, 14.8% Italian, 14.2% United States or American (2000).
Economy: Employment by occupation: 25.8% management, 28.9% professional, 3.1% services, 28.9% sales, 0.0% farming, 8.8% construction, 4.4% production (2000).
Income: Per capita income: $27,472 (2000); Median household income: $42,813 (2000); Poverty rate: 5.7% (2000).
Education: Percent of population age 25 and over with: High school diploma (including GED) or higher: 95.6% (2000); Bachelor's degree or higher: 41.2% (2000).
Housing: Homeownership rate: 86.0% (2000); Median home value: $250,000 (2000); Median rent: $439 per month (2000); Median age of housing: 39 years (2000).
Transportation: Commute to work: 96.2% car, 0.0% public transportation, 3.8% walk, 0.0% work from home (2000); Travel time to work: 15.7% less than 15 minutes, 48.4% 15 to 30 minutes, 19.5% 30 to 45 minutes, 16.4% 45 to 60 minutes, 0.0% 60 minutes or more (2000).

LAKE GEORGE (village). Covers a land area of 0.610 square miles and a water area of 0 square miles. Located at 43.42° N. Lat.; 73.71° W. Long. Elevation is 353 feet.
Population: 969 (1990); 985 (2000); 943 (2005); 930 (2010 projected); Race: 96.5% White, 1.4% Black, 1.0% Asian, 1.0% Hispanic of any race (2005); Density: 1,546.4 persons per square mile (2005); Average household size: 2.14 (2005); Median age: 40.5 (2005); Males per 100 females: 98.1 (2005); Marriage status: 26.3% never married, 48.3% now married, 9.7% widowed, 15.7% divorced (2000); Foreign born: 4.6% (2000); Ancestry (includes multiple ancestries): 28.9% Irish, 19.9% Italian, 18.5% German, 16.0% English, 11.1% French (except Basque) (2000).
Economy: Employment by occupation: 16.6% management, 19.8% professional, 20.2% services, 25.2% sales, 0.4% farming, 9.4% construction, 8.4% production (2000).
Income: Per capita income: $23,161 (2005); Median household income: $35,221 (2005); Average household income: $49,227 (2005); Percent of households with income of $100,000 or more: 9.3% (2005); Poverty rate: 11.1% (2000).

Education: Percent of population age 25 and over with: High school diploma (including GED) or higher: 84.0% (2005); Bachelor's degree or higher: 29.4% (2005); Master's degree or higher: 10.5% (2005).

School District(s)

Lake George Central School District (KG-12)
    2003-04 Enrollment: 1,096 . . . . (518) 668-5456

Housing: Homeownership rate: 48.6% (2005); Median home value: $151,220 (2005); Median rent: $430 per month (2000); Median age of housing: 44 years (2000).

Transportation: Commute to work: 83.3% car, 1.0% public transportation, 6.5% walk, 7.5% work from home (2000); Travel time to work: 37.0% less than 15 minutes, 37.2% 15 to 30 minutes, 13.0% 30 to 45 minutes, 5.5% 45 to 60 minutes, 7.2% 60 minutes or more (2000)

Additional Information Contacts

Lake George Regional Chamber of Commerce. . . . . (518) 668-5755
http://www.lakegeorgechamber.com

LAKE GEORGE (town).
Covers a land area of 30.235 square miles and a water area of 2.453 square miles. Located at 43.43° N. Lat.; 73.71° W. Long. Elevation is 353 feet.

History: Vestiges of Fort William Henry, built by Sir William Johnson, and Fort George are in the village. Incorporated 1903.

Population: 3,211 (1990); 3,578 (2000); 3,606 (2005); 3,656 (2010 projected); Race: 97.3% White, 0.7% Black, 0.8% Asian, 1.4% Hispanic of any race (2005); Density: 119.3 persons per square mile (2005); Average household size: 2.28 (2005); Median age: 44.3 (2005); Males per 100 females: 103.0 (2005); Marriage status: 23.1% never married, 59.8% now married, 5.2% widowed, 12.0% divorced (2000); Foreign born: 3.1% (2000); Ancestry (includes multiple ancestries): 20.6% Irish, 16.9% Italian, 15.5% English, 14.6% German, 11.2% French (except Basque) (2000).

Economy: A year-round tourist and sports center. Employment by occupation: 14.2% management, 26.3% professional, 13.5% services, 25.9% sales, 0.8% farming, 10.9% construction, 8.5% production (2000).

Income: Per capita income: $26,312 (2005); Median household income: $47,532 (2005); Average household income: $59,900 (2005); Percent of households with income of $100,000 or more: 14.0% (2005); Poverty rate: 6.8% (2000).

Taxes: Total city taxes per capita: $562 (2004); City property taxes per capita: $439 (2004).

Education: Percent of population age 25 and over with: High school diploma (including GED) or higher: 87.5% (2005); Bachelor's degree or higher: 31.1% (2005); Master's degree or higher: 13.8% (2005).

Housing: Homeownership rate: 70.8% (2005); Median home value: $168,182 (2005); Median rent: $429 per month (2000); Median age of housing: 32 years (2000).

Transportation: Commute to work: 89.5% car, 1.2% public transportation, 2.4% walk, 5.4% work from home (2000); Travel time to work: 36.6% less than 15 minutes, 41.7% 15 to 30 minutes, 9.1% 30 to 45 minutes, 5.7% 45 to 60 minutes, 6.9% 60 minutes or more (2000)

LAKE LUZERNE (town).
Covers a land area of 52.617 square miles and a water area of 1.441 square miles. Located at 43.31° N. Lat.; 73.82° W. Long.

History: Also called Luzerne.

Population: 2,816 (1990); 3,219 (2000); 3,287 (2005); 3,368 (2010 projected); Race: 97.5% White, 0.4% Black, 0.4% Asian, 1.8% Hispanic of any race (2005); Density: 62.5 persons per square mile (2005); Average household size: 2.49 (2005); Median age: 39.7 (2005); Males per 100 females: 97.5 (2005); Marriage status: 21.8% never married, 60.6% now married, 8.0% widowed, 9.6% divorced (2000); Foreign born: 2.1% (2000); Ancestry (includes multiple ancestries): 21.0% Irish, 15.2% German, 13.5% English, 12.8% French (except Basque), 10.7% Other groups (2000).

Economy: Ski trails nearby. Employment by occupation: 7.8% management, 16.1% professional, 19.7% services, 23.0% sales, 0.9% farming, 14.3% construction, 18.1% production (2000).

Income: Per capita income: $18,016 (2005); Median household income: $38,440 (2005); Average household income: $44,737 (2005); Percent of households with income of $100,000 or more: 4.6% (2005); Poverty rate: 10.3% (2000).

Education: Percent of population age 25 and over with: High school diploma (including GED) or higher: 84.2% (2005); Bachelor's degree or higher: 12.2% (2005); Master's degree or higher: 5.3% (2005).

School District(s)

Hadley-Luzerne Central School District (KG-12)
    2003-04 Enrollment: 1,085 . . . . (518) 696-2112

Housing: Homeownership rate: 82.0% (2005); Median home value: $121,355 (2005); Median rent: $440 per month (2000); Median age of housing: 34 years (2000).

Transportation: Commute to work: 96.1% car, 0.3% public transportation, 2.1% walk, 1.5% work from home (2000); Travel time to work: 23.3% less than 15 minutes, 38.1% 15 to 30 minutes, 22.8% 30 to 45 minutes, 6.5% 45 to 60 minutes, 9.3% 60 minutes or more (2000)

Additional Information Contacts

Lake Luzerne Chamber of Commerce. . . . . (518) 696-3500
http://www.lakeluzernechamber.org

LAKE LUZERNE-HADLEY (CDP).
Covers a land area of 3.763 square miles and a water area of 0.470 square miles. Located at 43.31° N. Lat.; 73.83° W. Long.

Population: 2,066 (1990); 2,240 (2000); 2,336 (2005); 2,445 (2010 projected); Race: 98.3% White, 0.6% Black, 0.1% Asian, 1.0% Hispanic of any race (2005); Density: 620.7 persons per square mile (2005); Average household size: 2.48 (2005); Median age: 39.2 (2005); Males per 100 females: 93.4 (2005); Marriage status: 22.5% never married, 58.7% now married, 8.9% widowed, 9.9% divorced (2000); Foreign born: 1.9% (2000); Ancestry (includes multiple ancestries): 21.0% Irish, 16.8% German, 14.1% English, 13.0% French (except Basque), 12.3% Other groups (2000).

Economy: Employment by occupation: 7.1% management, 11.7% professional, 23.8% services, 23.4% sales, 0.2% farming, 18.1% construction, 15.6% production (2000).

Income: Per capita income: $18,801 (2005); Median household income: $38,973 (2005); Average household income: $46,270 (2005); Percent of households with income of $100,000 or more: 5.0% (2005); Poverty rate: 11.9% (2000).

Education: Percent of population age 25 and over with: High school diploma (including GED) or higher: 81.9% (2005); Bachelor's degree or higher: 10.7% (2005); Master's degree or higher: 2.9% (2005).

Housing: Homeownership rate: 73.6% (2005); Median home value: $110,748 (2005); Median rent: $436 per month (2000); Median age of housing: 38 years (2000).

Transportation: Commute to work: 92.8% car, 0.0% public transportation, 3.3% walk, 3.0% work from home (2000); Travel time to work: 25.3% less than 15 minutes, 31.0% 15 to 30 minutes, 32.4% 30 to 45 minutes, 5.1% 45 to 60 minutes, 6.1% 60 minutes or more (2000)

NORTH CREEK (unincorporated postal area, zip code 12853).
Covers a land area of 117.510 square miles and a water area of 0.846 square miles. Located at 43.68° N. Lat.; 73.97° W. Long. Elevation is 1,028 feet.

Population: 0 (2000); Race: 99.4% White, 0.2% Black, 0.0% Asian, 0.0% Hispanic of any race (2000); Density: 0.0 persons per square mile (2000); Age: 21.1% under 18, 19.8% over 64 (2000); Marriage status: 20.4% never married, 59.1% now married, 10.3% widowed, 10.2% divorced (2000); Foreign born: 2.3% (2000); Ancestry (includes multiple ancestries): 20.7% Irish, 14.9% English, 11.3% French (except Basque), 10.2% German, 9.2% United States or American (2000).

Economy: Wood products; garnet mining. Resort village in the High Peaks section of the Adirondack Mountains. Just Southwest is Gore Mt. skiing center. Employment by occupation: 8.5% management, 12.6% professional, 21.0% services, 27.3% sales, 2.6% farming, 17.5% construction, 10.6% production (2000).

Income: Per capita income: $16,047 (2000); Median household income: $30,357 (2000); Poverty rate: 15.3% (2000).

Education: Percent of population age 25 and over with: High school diploma (including GED) or higher: 73.9% (2000); Bachelor's degree or higher: 14.5% (2000).

School District(s)

Johnsburg Central School District (KG-12)
    2003-04 Enrollment: 441 . . . . (518) 251-2814

Housing: Homeownership rate: 74.0% (2000); Median home value: $81,700 (2000); Median rent: $349 per month (2000); Median age of housing: 36 years (2000).

Newspapers: North Creek News-Enterprise (General - Circulation 1,900)

Transportation: Commute to work: 88.5% car, 0.8% public transportation, 5.8% walk, 3.4% work from home (2000); Travel time to work: 41.0% less than 15 minutes, 30.4% 15 to 30 minutes, 10.8% 30 to 45 minutes, 9.0% 45 to 60 minutes, 8.8% 60 minutes or more (2000)

Additional Information Contacts

Gore Mountain Region Chamber of Commerce . . . . (518) 251-2612
http://www.goremtnregion.org

POTTERSVILLE (unincorporated postal area, zip code 12860). Covers a land area of 16.776 square miles and a water area of 0.115 square miles. Located at 43.72° N. Lat.; 73.81° W. Long. Elevation is 822 feet.
Population: 0 (2000); Race: 94.6% White, 1.0% Black, 1.5% Asian, 3.4% Hispanic of any race (2000); Density: 0.0 persons per square mile (2000); Age: 15.5% under 18, 7.6% over 64 (2000); Marriage status: 58.5% never married, 34.8% now married, 3.5% widowed, 3.1% divorced (2000); Foreign born: 4.7% (2000); Ancestry (includes multiple ancestries): 19.9% German, 15.2% Other groups, 12.9% English, 10.9% Irish, 9.3% French (except Basque) (2000).
Economy: Resort village. Employment by occupation: 8.6% management, 20.0% professional, 25.7% services, 28.1% sales, 0.0% farming, 6.0% construction, 11.7% production (2000).
Income: Per capita income: $12,689 (2000); Median household income: $38,667 (2000); Poverty rate: 14.4% (2000).
Education: Percent of population age 25 and over with: High school diploma (including GED) or higher: 77.0% (2000); Bachelor's degree or higher: 23.2% (2000).
Two-year College(s)
Word of Life Bible Institute
    Fall 2004 Enrollment: 622 . . . . (518) 494-4723
    2005-06 Tuition: In-state $5,350; Out-of-state $5,350
Housing: Homeownership rate: 84.8% (2000); Median home value: $73,900 (2000); Median rent: $367 per month (2000); Median age of housing: 30 years (2000).
Transportation: Commute to work: 73.2% car, 3.3% public transportation, 18.7% walk, 4.8% work from home (2000); Travel time to work: 55.9% less than 15 minutes, 18.6% 15 to 30 minutes, 15.2% 30 to 45 minutes, 4.0% 45 to 60 minutes, 6.4% 60 minutes or more (2000)

QUEENSBURY (town). Covers a land area of 63.011 square miles and a water area of 1.801 square miles. Located at 43.33° N. Lat.; 73.67° W. Long. Elevation is 293 feet.
Population: 22,554 (1990); 25,441 (2000); 27,090 (2005); 28,670 (2010 projected); Race: 97.1% White, 0.8% Black, 0.8% Asian, 1.8% Hispanic of any race (2005); Density: 429.9 persons per square mile (2005); Average household size: 2.50 (2005); Median age: 40.9 (2005); Males per 100 females: 92.9 (2005); Marriage status: 19.7% never married, 64.1% now married, 7.2% widowed, 9.0% divorced (2000); Foreign born: 2.8% (2000); Ancestry (includes multiple ancestries): 22.9% Irish, 17.1% English, 13.8% French (except Basque), 12.7% German, 12.1% Italian (2000).
Economy: Unemployment rate: 3.9% (2005); Total civilian labor force: 14,754 (2005); Single-family building permits issued: 102 (2005); Multi-family building permits issued: 59 (2005); Employment by occupation: 15.1% management, 24.0% professional, 14.1% services, 27.9% sales, 0.2% farming, 8.2% construction, 10.5% production (2000).
Income: Per capita income: $27,466 (2005); Median household income: $53,141 (2005); Average household income: $67,958 (2005); Percent of households with income of $100,000 or more: 17.6% (2005); Poverty rate: 5.0% (2000).
Taxes: Total city taxes per capita: $244 (2004); City property taxes per capita: $178 (2004).
Education: Percent of population age 25 and over with: High school diploma (including GED) or higher: 89.1% (2005); Bachelor's degree or higher: 30.0% (2005); Master's degree or higher: 12.8% (2005).
School District(s)
Queensbury Union Free School District (KG-12)
    2003-04 Enrollment: 3,906 . . . . (518) 742-6000
Two-year College(s)
Adirondack Community College (Public)
    Fall 2004 Enrollment: 3,637 . . . . (518) 743-2200
    2005-06 Tuition: In-state $3,062; Out-of-state $5,932
Housing: Homeownership rate: 76.7% (2005); Median home value: $161,883 (2005); Median rent: $552 per month (2000); Median age of housing: 23 years (2000).
Transportation: Commute to work: 93.9% car, 0.5% public transportation, 1.5% walk, 3.5% work from home (2000); Travel time to work: 46.6% less than 15 minutes, 32.3% 15 to 30 minutes, 10.0% 30 to 45 minutes, 4.4% 45 to 60 minutes, 6.7% 60 minutes or more (2000)
Additional Information Contacts
Town of Queensbury . . . . (518) 761-8200
    http://www.queensbury.net/

SILVER BAY (unincorporated postal area, zip code 12874). Covers a land area of 20.314 square miles and a water area of 0.289 square miles. Located at 43.68° N. Lat.; 73.50° W. Long.
Population: 0 (2000); Race: 96.7% White, 2.0% Black, 1.3% Asian, 0.0% Hispanic of any race (2000); Density: 0.0 persons per square mile (2000); Age: 9.3% under 18, 40.7% over 64 (2000); Marriage status: 11.9% never married, 71.3% now married, 11.9% widowed, 4.9% divorced (2000); Foreign born: 2.7% (2000); Ancestry (includes multiple ancestries): 22.0% German, 19.3% Irish, 17.3% English, 12.7% Scottish, 8.0% Scotch-Irish (2000).
Economy: Resort village. Employment by occupation: 20.3% management, 32.8% professional, 4.7% services, 26.6% sales, 4.7% farming, 10.9% construction, 0.0% production (2000).
Income: Per capita income: $44,347 (2000); Median household income: $54,583 (2000); Poverty rate: 3.3% (2000).
Education: Percent of population age 25 and over with: High school diploma (including GED) or higher: 95.5% (2000); Bachelor's degree or higher: 58.2% (2000).
Housing: Homeownership rate: 87.3% (2000); Median home value: $317,400 (2000); Median rent: $425 per month (2000); Median age of housing: 34 years (2000).
Transportation: Commute to work: 90.2% car, 0.0% public transportation, 0.0% walk, 9.8% work from home (2000); Travel time to work: 41.8% less than 15 minutes, 14.5% 15 to 30 minutes, 12.7% 30 to 45 minutes, 18.2% 45 to 60 minutes, 12.7% 60 minutes or more (2000)

STONY CREEK (town). Covers a land area of 82.368 square miles and a water area of 0.837 square miles. Located at 43.42° N. Lat.; 73.96° W. Long. Elevation is 835 feet.
Population: 670 (1990); 743 (2000); 816 (2005); 886 (2010 projected); Race: 96.9% White, 0.0% Black, 0.6% Asian, 2.3% Hispanic of any race (2005); Density: 9.9 persons per square mile (2005); Average household size: 2.44 (2005); Median age: 42.2 (2005); Males per 100 females: 107.6 (2005); Marriage status: 22.9% never married, 57.7% now married, 8.1% widowed, 11.3% divorced (2000); Foreign born: 1.7% (2000); Ancestry (includes multiple ancestries): 14.8% German, 13.8% English, 13.0% Irish, 11.6% United States or American, 10.9% Italian (2000).
Economy: Resort village. Lakes nearby. Employment by occupation: 7.2% management, 20.5% professional, 14.4% services, 26.9% sales, 3.0% farming, 15.5% construction, 12.5% production (2000).
Income: Per capita income: $16,786 (2005); Median household income: $35,395 (2005); Average household income: $40,823 (2005); Percent of households with income of $100,000 or more: 4.2% (2005); Poverty rate: 16.3% (2000).
Education: Percent of population age 25 and over with: High school diploma (including GED) or higher: 78.0% (2005); Bachelor's degree or higher: 11.1% (2005); Master's degree or higher: 3.4% (2005).
Housing: Homeownership rate: 85.0% (2005); Median home value: $118,605 (2005); Median rent: $388 per month (2000); Median age of housing: 42 years (2000).
Transportation: Commute to work: 95.3% car, 0.8% public transportation, 0.8% walk, 3.1% work from home (2000); Travel time to work: 21.9% less than 15 minutes, 16.2% 15 to 30 minutes, 31.6% 30 to 45 minutes, 15.4% 45 to 60 minutes, 15.0% 60 minutes or more (2000)

THURMAN (town). Covers a land area of 91.309 square miles and a water area of 1.469 square miles. Located at 43.52° N. Lat.; 73.90° W. Long. Elevation is 1,311 feet.
Population: 1,045 (1990); 1,199 (2000); 1,295 (2005); 1,385 (2010 projected); Race: 97.5% White, 0.8% Black, 0.7% Asian, 0.8% Hispanic of any race (2005); Density: 14.2 persons per square mile (2005); Average household size: 2.52 (2005); Median age: 41.0 (2005); Males per 100 females: 105.9 (2005); Marriage status: 22.8% never married, 65.0% now married, 5.1% widowed, 7.1% divorced (2000); Foreign born: 1.9% (2000); Ancestry (includes multiple ancestries): 18.5% English, 14.8% United States or American, 12.7% Irish, 11.7% Other groups, 10.9% German (2000).
Economy: Employment by occupation: 9.0% management, 17.6% professional, 19.9% services, 18.2% sales, 1.7% farming, 16.8% construction, 16.8% production (2000).
Income: Per capita income: $19,388 (2005); Median household income: $40,825 (2005); Average household income: $48,847 (2005); Percent of households with income of $100,000 or more: 8.0% (2005); Poverty rate: 11.9% (2000).

Education: Percent of population age 25 and over with: High school diploma (including GED) or higher: 77.2% (2005); Bachelor's degree or higher: 14.9% (2005); Master's degree or higher: 7.2% (2005).
Housing: Homeownership rate: 87.0% (2005); Median home value: $120,028 (2005); Median rent: $356 per month (2000); Median age of housing: 27 years (2000).
Transportation: Commute to work: 95.0% car, 0.4% public transportation, 1.4% walk, 1.6% work from home (2000); Travel time to work: 17.9% less than 15 minutes, 27.1% 15 to 30 minutes, 32.1% 30 to 45 minutes, 13.7% 45 to 60 minutes, 9.3% 60 minutes or more (2000)

WARRENSBURG (town). Aka Warrenburg Center. Covers a land area of 63.719 square miles and a water area of 1.130 square miles. Located at 43.51° N. Lat.; 73.79° W. Long. Elevation is 749 feet.
Population: 4,174 (1990); 4,255 (2000); 4,380 (2005); 4,518 (2010 projected); Race: 97.9% White, 0.3% Black, 0.6% Asian, 0.7% Hispanic of any race (2005); Density: 68.7 persons per square mile (2005); Average household size: 2.42 (2005); Median age: 39.7 (2005); Males per 100 females: 91.2 (2005); Marriage status: 24.4% never married, 58.4% now married, 6.9% widowed, 10.4% divorced (2000); Foreign born: 2.0% (2000); Ancestry (includes multiple ancestries): 14.6% English, 14.4% Irish, 14.0% German, 10.6% Other groups, 10.5% French (except Basque) (2000).
Economy: Trade center in farm and resort area; lumber, paper milling. Employment by occupation: 6.8% management, 14.6% professional, 21.7% services, 26.4% sales, 1.1% farming, 10.3% construction, 19.1% production (2000).
Income: Per capita income: $17,567 (2005); Median household income: $33,298 (2005); Average household income: $41,582 (2005); Percent of households with income of $100,000 or more: 5.4% (2005); Poverty rate: 16.8% (2000).
Education: Percent of population age 25 and over with: High school diploma (including GED) or higher: 77.4% (2005); Bachelor's degree or higher: 15.4% (2005); Master's degree or higher: 4.3% (2005).

School District(s)
Warrensburg Central School District (KG-12)
2003-04 Enrollment: 961 . . . . (518) 623-2861

Housing: Homeownership rate: 68.9% (2005); Median home value: $114,782 (2005); Median rent: $423 per month (2000); Median age of housing: 31 years (2000).
Newspapers: The Adirondack Journal (General - Circulation 12,600)
Transportation: Commute to work: 90.9% car, 0.3% public transportation, 5.8% walk, 2.4% work from home (2000); Travel time to work: 34.0% less than 15 minutes, 34.6% 15 to 30 minutes, 22.3% 30 to 45 minutes, 4.4% 45 to 60 minutes, 4.7% 60 minutes or more (2000)
Additional Information Contacts
Warrensburg Chamber of Commerce . . . . (518) 623-2161
http://www.warrensburgchamber.com

WARRENSBURG (CDP). Covers a land area of 11.084 square miles and a water area of 0.209 square miles. Located at 43.49° N. Lat.; 73.77° W. Long.
Population: 3,280 (1990); 3,208 (2000); 3,284 (2005); 3,372 (2010 projected); Race: 98.3% White, 0.2% Black, 0.5% Asian, 0.7% Hispanic of any race (2005); Density: 296.3 persons per square mile (2005); Average household size: 2.42 (2005); Median age: 39.8 (2005); Males per 100 females: 89.1 (2005); Marriage status: 22.7% never married, 57.6% now married, 8.2% widowed, 11.4% divorced (2000); Foreign born: 2.1% (2000); Ancestry (includes multiple ancestries): 14.5% English, 12.7% Irish, 12.1% Other groups, 11.8% French (except Basque), 11.5% German (2000).
Economy: Employment by occupation: 7.3% management, 14.4% professional, 20.7% services, 27.0% sales, 1.0% farming, 9.6% construction, 20.0% production (2000).
Income: Per capita income: $17,365 (2005); Median household income: $30,729 (2005); Average household income: $40,696 (2005); Percent of households with income of $100,000 or more: 5.6% (2005); Poverty rate: 17.7% (2000).
Education: Percent of population age 25 and over with: High school diploma (including GED) or higher: 76.0% (2005); Bachelor's degree or higher: 16.1% (2005); Master's degree or higher: 4.1% (2005).
Housing: Homeownership rate: 66.6% (2005); Median home value: $115,938 (2005); Median rent: $410 per month (2000); Median age of housing: 38 years (2000).
Transportation: Commute to work: 88.7% car, 0.4% public transportation, 7.2% walk, 2.9% work from home (2000); Travel time to work: 37.6% less than 15 minutes, 35.3% 15 to 30 minutes, 17.6% 30 to 45 minutes, 5.5% 45 to 60 minutes, 4.0% 60 minutes or more (2000)

WEST GLENS FALLS (CDP). Covers a land area of 4.645 square miles and a water area of 0.106 square miles. Located at 43.30° N. Lat.; 73.68° W. Long.
Population: 5,939 (1990); 6,721 (2000); 6,580 (2005); 6,451 (2010 projected); Race: 97.9% White, 0.5% Black, 0.2% Asian, 1.5% Hispanic of any race (2005); Density: 1,416.6 persons per square mile (2005); Average household size: 2.65 (2005); Median age: 37.8 (2005); Males per 100 females: 92.6 (2005); Marriage status: 21.3% never married, 60.6% now married, 6.7% widowed, 11.4% divorced (2000); Foreign born: 1.5% (2000); Ancestry (includes multiple ancestries): 26.2% Irish, 16.3% French (except Basque), 15.2% English, 9.9% German, 9.6% Italian (2000).
Economy: Employment by occupation: 11.6% management, 18.1% professional, 19.8% services, 25.6% sales, 0.4% farming, 8.3% construction, 16.2% production (2000).
Income: Per capita income: $21,862 (2005); Median household income: $48,543 (2005); Average household income: $56,968 (2005); Percent of households with income of $100,000 or more: 9.8% (2005); Poverty rate: 6.1% (2000).
Education: Percent of population age 25 and over with: High school diploma (including GED) or higher: 81.5% (2005); Bachelor's degree or higher: 16.8% (2005); Master's degree or higher: 6.8% (2005).
Housing: Homeownership rate: 82.3% (2005); Median home value: $120,426 (2005); Median rent: $556 per month (2000); Median age of housing: 19 years (2000).
Transportation: Commute to work: 94.3% car, 1.1% public transportation, 1.5% walk, 2.2% work from home (2000); Travel time to work: 48.6% less than 15 minutes, 32.6% 15 to 30 minutes, 9.6% 30 to 45 minutes, 3.2% 45 to 60 minutes, 6.0% 60 minutes or more (2000)

WEVERTOWN (unincorporated postal area, zip code 12886). Covers a land area of 4.803 square miles and a water area of 0.004 square miles. Located at 43.63° N. Lat.; 73.91° W. Long. Elevation is 1,077 feet.
Population: 0 (2000); Race: 92.3% White, 0.0% Black, 7.7% Asian, 0.0% Hispanic of any race (2000); Density: 0.0 persons per square mile (2000); Age: 24.6% under 18, 4.6% over 64 (2000); Marriage status: 25.0% never married, 44.2% now married, 13.5% widowed, 17.3% divorced (2000); Foreign born: 13.8% (2000); Ancestry (includes multiple ancestries): 24.6% Irish, 20.0% German, 9.2% French (except Basque), 7.7% Other groups, 6.2% Greek (2000).
Economy: Employment by occupation: 39.5% management, 0.0% professional, 34.2% services, 10.5% sales, 0.0% farming, 0.0% construction, 15.8% production (2000).
Income: Per capita income: $15,886 (2000); Median household income: $17,292 (2000); Poverty rate: 9.2% (2000).
Education: Percent of population age 25 and over with: High school diploma (including GED) or higher: 86.7% (2000); Bachelor's degree or higher: 24.4% (2000).
Housing: Homeownership rate: 77.4% (2000); Median home value: $127,800 (2000); Median rent: $n/a per month (2000); Median age of housing: 38 years (2000).
Transportation: Commute to work: 73.7% car, 0.0% public transportation, 26.3% walk, 0.0% work from home (2000); Travel time to work: 52.6% less than 15 minutes, 13.2% 15 to 30 minutes, 18.4% 30 to 45 minutes, 0.0% 45 to 60 minutes, 15.8% 60 minutes or more (2000)

Washington County

Located in eastern New York; bounded on the northwest by Lake George, on the east by Vermont, and on the west by the Hudson River; drained by the Poultney, Mettawee, and Hoosic Rivers; includes part of Lake Champlain. Covers a land area of 835.44 square miles, a water area of 10.40 square miles, and is located in the Eastern Time Zone. The county government was organized in 1772. County seat is Hudson Falls.

Washington County is part of the Glens Falls, NY Metropolitan Statistical Area. The entire metro area includes: Warren County, NY; Washington County, NY

Weather Station: Whitehall   Elevation: 118 feet

	Jan	Feb	Mar	Apr	May	Jun	Jul	Aug	Sep	Oct	Nov	Dec
High	29	33	43	58	72	80	85	81	72	60	47	35
Low	10	12	23	36	47	56	60	59	51	40	31	19
Precip	3.2	2.4	3.1	3.0	3.8	3.3	3.9	4.3	3.9	3.5	3.6	2.8
Snow	18.2	12.0	13.1	2.2	tr	0.0	0.0	0.0	0.0	tr	4.3	14.2

High and Low temperatures in degrees Fahrenheit; Precipitation and Snow in inches

Population: 59,330 (1990); 61,042 (2000); 62,366 (2005); 63,715 (2010 projected); Race: 94.7% White, 3.1% Black, 0.4% Asian, 2.4% Hispanic of any race (2005); Density: 74.7 persons per square mile (2005); Average household size: 2.66 (2005); Median age: 38.9 (2005); Males per 100 females: 105.7 (2005).
Religion: Five largest groups: 22.7% Catholic Church, 6.9% The United Methodist Church, 2.9% Presbyterian Church (U.S.A.), 2.8% American Baptist Churches in the USA, 1.3% Episcopal Church (2000).
Economy: Unemployment rate: 4.4% (2005); Total civilian labor force: 32,210 (2005); Leading industries: 32.8% manufacturing; 18.6% retail trade; 16.3% health care and social assistance (2003); Farms: 887 totaling 206,148 acres (2002); Companies that employ 500 or more persons: 0 (2003); Companies that employ 100 to 499 persons: 17 (2003); Companies that employ less than 100 persons: 1,055 (2003); Black-owned businesses: n/a (2002); Hispanic-owned businesses: n/a (2002); Women-owned businesses: 1,565 (2002); Retail sales per capita: $6,300 (2006); Single-family building permits issued: 257 (2005); Multi-family building permits issued: 391 (2005).
Income: Per capita income: $20,667 (2005); Median household income: $43,387 (2005); Average household income: $53,352 (2005); Percent of households with income of $100,000 or more: 9.9% (2005); Poverty rate: 11.0% (2003); Bankruptcy rate: 8.60% (2005).
Taxes: Total county taxes per capita: $618 (2004); County property taxes per capita: $332 (2004).
Education: Percent of population age 25 and over with: High school diploma (including GED) or higher: 79.4% (2005); Bachelor's degree or higher: 14.3% (2005); Master's degree or higher: 5.6% (2005).
Housing: Homeownership rate: 75.0% (2005); Median home value: $117,911 (2005); Median rent: $410 per month (2000); Median age of housing: 47 years (2000).
Health: Birth rate: 92.5 per 10,000 population (2004); Death rate: 90.3 per 10,000 population (2004); Age-adjusted cancer mortality rate: 233.8 deaths per 100,000 population (2002); Number of physicians: 4.9 per 10,000 population (2004); Hospital beds: 0.0 per 10,000 population (2003); Hospital admissions: 0.0 per 10,000 population (2003).
Elections: 2004 Presidential election results: 55.1% Bush, 42.3% Kerry, 2.3% Nader, 0.3% Badnarik
Additional Information Contacts
Washington County Government . . . . (518) 746-2520
http://www.co.washington.ny.us/

Washington County Communities

ARGYLE (village). Covers a land area of 0.356 square miles and a water area of 0 square miles. Located at 43.23° N. Lat.; 73.49° W. Long.
Population: 295 (1990); 289 (2000); 262 (2005); 259 (2010 projected); Race: 97.3% White, 0.4% Black, 0.0% Asian, 3.1% Hispanic of any race (2005); Density: 735.1 persons per square mile (2005); Average household size: 2.38 (2005); Median age: 39.4 (2005); Males per 100 females: 106.3 (2005); Marriage status: 27.3% never married, 54.6% now married, 10.1% widowed, 7.9% divorced (2000); Foreign born: 1.4% (2000); Ancestry (includes multiple ancestries): 24.0% French (except Basque), 24.0% Irish, 21.2% English, 9.7% Scottish, 8.0% Scotch-Irish (2000).
Economy: Employment by occupation: 3.4% management, 22.1% professional, 24.8% services, 17.2% sales, 1.4% farming, 12.4% construction, 18.6% production (2000).
Income: Per capita income: $23,960 (2005); Median household income: $44,750 (2005); Average household income: $57,068 (2005); Percent of households with income of $100,000 or more: 10.9% (2005); Poverty rate: 10.5% (2000).
Education: Percent of population age 25 and over with: High school diploma (including GED) or higher: 92.2% (2005); Bachelor's degree or higher: 23.3% (2005); Master's degree or higher: 12.2% (2005).
School District(s)
Argyle Central School District (KG-12)
    2003-04 Enrollment: 740 . . . . (518) 638-8243
Housing: Homeownership rate: 69.1% (2005); Median home value: $122,857 (2005); Median rent: $408 per month (2000); Median age of housing: 60+ years (2000).
Transportation: Commute to work: 85.0% car, 2.1% public transportation, 3.6% walk, 9.3% work from home (2000); Travel time to work: 26.0% less than 15 minutes, 35.4% 15 to 30 minutes, 23.6% 30 to 45 minutes, 4.7% 45 to 60 minutes, 10.2% 60 minutes or more (2000)

ARGYLE (town). Covers a land area of 56.692 square miles and a water area of 1.106 square miles. Located at 43.22° N. Lat.; 73.46° W. Long.
Population: 3,031 (1990); 3,688 (2000); 3,741 (2005); 3,796 (2010 projected); Race: 99.0% White, 0.2% Black, 0.0% Asian, 1.4% Hispanic of any race (2005); Density: 66.0 persons per square mile (2005); Average household size: 2.75 (2005); Median age: 40.2 (2005); Males per 100 females: 93.6 (2005); Marriage status: 22.6% never married, 62.4% now married, 6.4% widowed, 8.5% divorced (2000); Foreign born: 1.1% (2000); Ancestry (includes multiple ancestries): 18.3% Irish, 17.6% French (except Basque), 12.1% German, 11.8% English, 8.6% Other groups (2000).
Economy: Dairying area. Employment by occupation: 11.7% management, 12.9% professional, 16.1% services, 23.4% sales, 2.9% farming, 10.9% construction, 22.1% production (2000).
Income: Per capita income: $23,073 (2005); Median household income: $50,160 (2005); Average household income: $62,267 (2005); Percent of households with income of $100,000 or more: 10.7% (2005); Poverty rate: 7.6% (2000).
Education: Percent of population age 25 and over with: High school diploma (including GED) or higher: 81.2% (2005); Bachelor's degree or higher: 12.8% (2005); Master's degree or higher: 3.2% (2005).
Housing: Homeownership rate: 86.3% (2005); Median home value: $124,518 (2005); Median rent: $473 per month (2000); Median age of housing: 27 years (2000).
Transportation: Commute to work: 94.2% car, 0.2% public transportation, 1.2% walk, 4.0% work from home (2000); Travel time to work: 22.1% less than 15 minutes, 44.3% 15 to 30 minutes, 23.1% 30 to 45 minutes, 4.3% 45 to 60 minutes, 6.3% 60 minutes or more (2000)

CAMBRIDGE (village). Covers a land area of 1.672 square miles and a water area of 0 square miles. Located at 43.02° N. Lat.; 73.38° W. Long. Elevation is 496 feet.
Population: 1,967 (1990); 1,925 (2000); 1,852 (2005); 1,835 (2010 projected); Race: 98.2% White, 0.5% Black, 0.3% Asian, 1.9% Hispanic of any race (2005); Density: 1,107.5 persons per square mile (2005); Average household size: 2.50 (2005); Median age: 41.0 (2005); Males per 100 females: 84.3 (2005); Marriage status: 25.2% never married, 52.8% now married, 10.9% widowed, 11.1% divorced (2000); Foreign born: 4.4% (2000); Ancestry (includes multiple ancestries): 18.2% Irish, 16.1% English, 13.2% German, 10.2% Other groups, 10.1% Italian (2000).
Economy: Employment by occupation: 7.4% management, 24.0% professional, 19.4% services, 21.7% sales, 3.8% farming, 10.4% construction, 13.4% production (2000).
Income: Per capita income: $19,197 (2005); Median household income: $36,487 (2005); Average household income: $47,024 (2005); Percent of households with income of $100,000 or more: 9.4% (2005); Poverty rate: 12.5% (2000).
Education: Percent of population age 25 and over with: High school diploma (including GED) or higher: 80.2% (2005); Bachelor's degree or higher: 18.4% (2005); Master's degree or higher: 8.5% (2005).
School District(s)
Cambridge Central School District (KG-12)
    2003-04 Enrollment: 1,096 . . . . (518) 677-2653
Housing: Homeownership rate: 65.7% (2005); Median home value: $119,891 (2005); Median rent: $385 per month (2000); Median age of housing: 60+ years (2000).
Hospitals: Mary McClellan Hospital (25 beds)
Safety: Violent crime rate: 5.2 per 10,000 population; Property crime rate: 219.1 per 10,000 population (2004).
Newspapers: The Eagle (General - Circulation 4,860)
Transportation: Commute to work: 82.7% car, 5.0% public transportation, 8.7% walk, 3.6% work from home (2000); Travel time to work: 43.0% less than 15 minutes, 18.2% 15 to 30 minutes, 15.6% 30 to 45 minutes, 10.5% 45 to 60 minutes, 12.6% 60 minutes or more (2000)

CAMBRIDGE (town). Covers a land area of 36.378 square miles and a water area of 0.120 square miles. Located at 43.01° N. Lat.; 73.44° W. Long. Elevation is 496 feet.
History: Cambridge Historical District within the village. Its weekly, *Washington County Post*, was founded in 1787. Settled c.1761, incorporated 1866.
Population: 1,938 (1990); 2,152 (2000); 2,234 (2005); 2,323 (2010 projected); Race: 97.2% White, 0.9% Black, 0.4% Asian, 1.7% Hispanic of any race (2005); Density: 61.4 persons per square mile (2005); Average household size: 2.63 (2005); Median age: 40.8 (2005); Males per 100 females: 99.3 (2005); Marriage status: 19.5% never married, 65.5% now married, 5.4% widowed, 9.6% divorced (2000); Foreign born: 3.0% (2000); Ancestry (includes multiple ancestries): 20.5% Irish, 18.2% German, 16.6% English, 8.0% Italian, 7.0% French (except Basque) (2000).
Economy: Farm trade center. Single-family building permits issued: 6 (2005); Multi-family building permits issued: 0 (2005); Employment by occupation: 14.4% management, 29.5% professional, 11.3% services, 17.8% sales, 2.0% farming, 9.8% construction, 15.2% production (2000).
Income: Per capita income: $28,236 (2005); Median household income: $57,143 (2005); Average household income: $73,723 (2005); Percent of households with income of $100,000 or more: 19.9% (2005); Poverty rate: 5.9% (2000).
Education: Percent of population age 25 and over with: High school diploma (including GED) or higher: 86.2% (2005); Bachelor's degree or higher: 28.3% (2005); Master's degree or higher: 13.8% (2005).
Housing: Homeownership rate: 80.1% (2005); Median home value: $159,211 (2005); Median rent: $441 per month (2000); Median age of housing: 60+ years (2000).
Transportation: Commute to work: 86.7% car, 0.0% public transportation, 3.6% walk, 9.4% work from home (2000); Travel time to work: 24.5% less than 15 minutes, 26.3% 15 to 30 minutes, 25.1% 30 to 45 minutes, 14.9% 45 to 60 minutes, 9.2% 60 minutes or more (2000)

CLEMONS (unincorporated postal area, zip code 12819). Covers a land area of 42.066 square miles and a water area of 0.195 square miles. Located at 43.58° N. Lat.; 73.47° W. Long.
Population: 0 (2000); Race: 99.5% White, 0.0% Black, 0.0% Asian, 0.0% Hispanic of any race (2000); Density: 0.0 persons per square mile (2000); Age: 28.7% under 18, 14.2% over 64 (2000); Marriage status: 15.2% never married, 68.9% now married, 8.1% widowed, 7.8% divorced (2000); Foreign born: 3.3% (2000); Ancestry (includes multiple ancestries): 15.3% French (except Basque), 14.8% Irish, 14.2% Other groups, 9.8% English, 9.6% United States or American (2000).
Economy: Employment by occupation: 5.1% management, 13.9% professional, 21.5% services, 18.4% sales, 1.3% farming, 19.6% construction, 20.3% production (2000).
Income: Per capita income: $15,704 (2000); Median household income: $28,015 (2000); Poverty rate: 9.8% (2000).
Education: Percent of population age 25 and over with: High school diploma (including GED) or higher: 79.4% (2000); Bachelor's degree or higher: 12.3% (2000).
Housing: Homeownership rate: 76.7% (2000); Median home value: $66,500 (2000); Median rent: $381 per month (2000); Median age of housing: 34 years (2000).
Transportation: Commute to work: 96.1% car, 0.0% public transportation, 1.9% walk, 1.9% work from home (2000); Travel time to work: 25.7% less than 15 minutes, 26.3% 15 to 30 minutes, 24.3% 30 to 45 minutes, 15.8% 45 to 60 minutes, 7.9% 60 minutes or more (2000)

COMSTOCK (unincorporated postal area, zip code 12821). Covers a land area of 10.561 square miles and a water area of 0 square miles. Located at 43.46° N. Lat.; 73.40° W. Long. Elevation is 131 feet.
Population: 0 (2000); Race: 38.3% White, 48.5% Black, 0.5% Asian, 24.0% Hispanic of any race (2000); Density: 0.0 persons per square mile (2000); Age: 4.5% under 18, 1.3% over 64 (2000); Marriage status: 63.4% never married, 32.9% now married, 1.5% widowed, 2.1% divorced (2000); Foreign born: 9.6% (2000); Ancestry (includes multiple ancestries): 3.9% English, 2.8% Irish, 2.2% German, 1.9% French Canadian, 1.3% French (except Basque) (2000).
Economy: Employment by occupation: 1.6% management, 14.2% professional, 35.4% services, 26.0% sales, 1.6% farming, 1.2% construction, 19.9% production (2000).
Income: Per capita income: $10,482 (2000); Median household income: $42,917 (2000); Poverty rate: 6.6% (2000).
Education: Percent of population age 25 and over with: High school diploma (including GED) or higher: 31.2% (2000); Bachelor's degree or higher: 1.4% (2000).

School District(s)
Fort Ann Central School District (PK-12)
    2003-04 Enrollment: 1,076 . . . . (518) 639-5594

Housing: Homeownership rate: 81.9% (2000); Median home value: $83,900 (2000); Median rent: $389 per month (2000); Median age of housing: 21 years (2000).
Transportation: Commute to work: 96.7% car, 0.0% public transportation, 0.0% walk, 3.3% work from home (2000); Travel time to work: 35.3% less than 15 minutes, 18.9% 15 to 30 minutes, 27.3% 30 to 45 minutes, 13.9% 45 to 60 minutes, 4.6% 60 minutes or more (2000)

COSSAYUNA (unincorporated postal area, zip code 12823). Covers a land area of 5.236 square miles and a water area of 0.056 square miles. Located at 43.17° N. Lat.; 73.40° W. Long. Elevation is 474 feet.
Population: 0 (2000); Race: 100.0% White, 0.0% Black, 0.0% Asian, 0.0% Hispanic of any race (2000); Density: 0.0 persons per square mile (2000); Age: 30.2% under 18, 15.7% over 64 (2000); Marriage status: 6.3% never married, 73.4% now married, 4.7% widowed, 15.6% divorced (2000); Foreign born: 0.0% (2000); Ancestry (includes multiple ancestries): 29.7% French (except Basque), 25.0% Irish, 24.4% English, 15.1% Other groups, 13.4% German (2000).
Economy: Employment by occupation: 46.9% management, 0.0% professional, 0.0% services, 30.6% sales, 0.0% farming, 0.0% construction, 22.4% production (2000).
Income: Per capita income: $22,795 (2000); Median household income: $38,125 (2000); Poverty rate: 15.1% (2000).
Education: Percent of population age 25 and over with: High school diploma (including GED) or higher: 67.5% (2000); Bachelor's degree or higher: 19.2% (2000).
Housing: Homeownership rate: 100.0% (2000); Median home value: $86,700 (2000); Median rent: $n/a per month (2000); Median age of housing: 58 years (2000).
Transportation: Commute to work: 69.4% car, 0.0% public transportation, 30.6% walk, 0.0% work from home (2000); Travel time to work: 83.7% less than 15 minutes, 16.3% 15 to 30 minutes, 0.0% 30 to 45 minutes, 0.0% 45 to 60 minutes, 0.0% 60 minutes or more (2000)

DRESDEN (town). Covers a land area of 53.370 square miles and a water area of 1.643 square miles. Located at 43.63° N. Lat.; 73.46° W. Long.
Population: 561 (1990); 677 (2000); 776 (2005); 838 (2010 projected); Race: 99.2% White, 0.4% Black, 0.0% Asian, 0.1% Hispanic of any race (2005); Density: 14.5 persons per square mile (2005); Average household size: 2.41 (2005); Median age: 43.2 (2005); Males per 100 females: 101.6 (2005); Marriage status: 19.3% never married, 65.8% now married, 5.9% widowed, 9.0% divorced (2000); Foreign born: 2.8% (2000); Ancestry (includes multiple ancestries): 20.0% French (except Basque), 14.8% Other groups, 14.0% Irish, 11.3% United States or American, 9.1% Italian (2000).
Economy: Employment by occupation: 7.6% management, 11.0% professional, 17.9% services, 17.2% sales, 2.1% farming, 23.1% construction, 21.0% production (2000).
Income: Per capita income: $21,144 (2005); Median household income: $34,365 (2005); Average household income: $50,955 (2005); Percent of households with income of $100,000 or more: 11.2% (2005); Poverty rate: 9.0% (2000).
Education: Percent of population age 25 and over with: High school diploma (including GED) or higher: 79.7% (2005); Bachelor's degree or higher: 16.0% (2005); Master's degree or higher: 6.1% (2005).
Housing: Homeownership rate: 78.3% (2005); Median home value: $97,447 (2005); Median rent: $407 per month (2000); Median age of housing: 39 years (2000).
Transportation: Commute to work: 89.9% car, 0.7% public transportation, 5.9% walk, 3.5% work from home (2000); Travel time to work: 28.9% less than 15 minutes, 26.4% 15 to 30 minutes, 20.9% 30 to 45 minutes, 15.2% 45 to 60 minutes, 8.7% 60 minutes or more (2000)

EASTON (town). Covers a land area of 62.274 square miles and a water area of 0.910 square miles. Located at 43.03° N. Lat.; 73.53° W. Long.
Population: 2,203 (1990); 2,259 (2000); 2,404 (2005); 2,539 (2010 projected); Race: 98.9% White, 0.5% Black, 0.0% Asian, 1.2% Hispanic of

any race (2005); Density: 38.6 persons per square mile (2005); Average household size: 2.59 (2005); Median age: 40.8 (2005); Males per 100 females: 102.0 (2005); Marriage status: 24.9% never married, 63.8% now married, 5.8% widowed, 5.4% divorced (2000); Foreign born: 0.8% (2000); Ancestry (includes multiple ancestries): 16.9% Irish, 16.3% English, 13.0% German, 12.4% French (except Basque), 10.7% Italian (2000).
Economy: Single-family building permits issued: 16 (2005); Multi-family building permits issued: 0 (2005); Employment by occupation: 15.5% management, 19.0% professional, 11.8% services, 27.2% sales, 2.3% farming, 10.2% construction, 14.1% production (2000).
Income: Per capita income: $23,348 (2005); Median household income: $47,649 (2005); Average household income: $59,957 (2005); Percent of households with income of $100,000 or more: 12.7% (2005); Poverty rate: 6.6% (2000).
Education: Percent of population age 25 and over with: High school diploma (including GED) or higher: 85.6% (2005); Bachelor's degree or higher: 22.9% (2005); Master's degree or higher: 11.3% (2005).
Housing: Homeownership rate: 79.2% (2005); Median home value: $170,000 (2005); Median rent: $479 per month (2000); Median age of housing: 43 years (2000).
Transportation: Commute to work: 87.9% car, 0.4% public transportation, 3.1% walk, 8.4% work from home (2000); Travel time to work: 25.7% less than 15 minutes, 22.6% 15 to 30 minutes, 21.5% 30 to 45 minutes, 18.0% 45 to 60 minutes, 12.1% 60 minutes or more (2000)

FORT ANN (village).
Covers a land area of 0.300 square miles and a water area of 0 square miles. Located at 43.41° N. Lat.; 73.49° W. Long. Elevation is 138 feet.
Population: 419 (1990); 471 (2000); 581 (2005); 692 (2010 projected); Race: 99.1% White, 0.5% Black, 0.0% Asian, 0.7% Hispanic of any race (2005); Density: 1,937.6 persons per square mile (2005); Average household size: 2.46 (2005); Median age: 39.2 (2005); Males per 100 females: 95.0 (2005); Marriage status: 29.0% never married, 55.9% now married, 11.2% widowed, 3.9% divorced (2000); Foreign born: 1.7% (2000); Ancestry (includes multiple ancestries): 15.3% French (except Basque), 13.4% Irish, 12.8% United States or American, 12.8% English, 9.1% Other groups (2000).
Economy: Employment by occupation: 6.2% management, 17.6% professional, 24.3% services, 31.4% sales, 0.0% farming, 4.3% construction, 16.2% production (2000).
Income: Per capita income: $22,289 (2005); Median household income: $46,786 (2005); Average household income: $54,873 (2005); Percent of households with income of $100,000 or more: 8.1% (2005); Poverty rate: 9.1% (2000).
Education: Percent of population age 25 and over with: High school diploma (including GED) or higher: 79.6% (2005); Bachelor's degree or higher: 12.5% (2005); Master's degree or higher: 2.3% (2005).
School District(s)
Fort Ann Central School District (PK-12)
    2003-04 Enrollment: 1,076 . . . . (518) 639-5594
Housing: Homeownership rate: 65.7% (2005); Median home value: $113,438 (2005); Median rent: $410 per month (2000); Median age of housing: 60+ years (2000).
Transportation: Commute to work: 88.0% car, 0.0% public transportation, 4.3% walk, 6.7% work from home (2000); Travel time to work: 39.2% less than 15 minutes, 36.1% 15 to 30 minutes, 16.5% 30 to 45 minutes, 3.1% 45 to 60 minutes, 5.2% 60 minutes or more (2000)

FORT ANN (town).
Covers a land area of 109.471 square miles and a water area of 1.331 square miles. Located at 43.46° N. Lat.; 73.54° W. Long. Elevation is 138 feet.
Population: 6,368 (1990); 6,417 (2000); 6,765 (2005); 7,130 (2010 projected); Race: 67.5% White, 24.1% Black, 0.4% Asian, 14.0% Hispanic of any race (2005); Density: 61.8 persons per square mile (2005); Average household size: 4.42 (2005); Median age: 33.0 (2005); Males per 100 females: 242.4 (2005); Marriage status: 44.3% never married, 47.3% now married, 4.3% widowed, 4.1% divorced (2000); Foreign born: 5.6% (2000); Ancestry (includes multiple ancestries): 10.7% Irish, 9.9% French (except Basque), 8.7% English, 6.0% Italian, 5.4% German (2000).
Economy: Employment by occupation: 9.1% management, 17.7% professional, 18.9% services, 20.8% sales, 3.2% farming, 11.1% construction, 19.3% production (2000).
Income: Per capita income: $16,423 (2005); Median household income: $44,277 (2005); Average household income: $54,663 (2005); Percent of households with income of $100,000 or more: 8.4% (2005); Poverty rate: 6.7% (2000).
Education: Percent of population age 25 and over with: High school diploma (including GED) or higher: 57.4% (2005); Bachelor's degree or higher: 8.5% (2005); Master's degree or higher: 3.1% (2005).
Housing: Homeownership rate: 82.3% (2005); Median home value: $128,888 (2005); Median rent: $421 per month (2000); Median age of housing: 31 years (2000).
Transportation: Commute to work: 92.0% car, 0.0% public transportation, 4.8% walk, 3.1% work from home (2000); Travel time to work: 27.4% less than 15 minutes, 43.8% 15 to 30 minutes, 18.6% 30 to 45 minutes, 4.5% 45 to 60 minutes, 5.7% 60 minutes or more (2000)

FORT EDWARD (village).
Covers a land area of 1.794 square miles and a water area of 0.139 square miles. Located at 43.26° N. Lat.; 73.58° W. Long. Elevation is 144 feet.
Population: 3,564 (1990); 3,141 (2000); 3,123 (2005); 3,103 (2010 projected); Race: 98.6% White, 0.4% Black, 0.4% Asian, 0.2% Hispanic of any race (2005); Density: 1,741.0 persons per square mile (2005); Average household size: 2.46 (2005); Median age: 36.3 (2005); Males per 100 females: 93.5 (2005); Marriage status: 27.3% never married, 55.5% now married, 5.1% widowed, 12.0% divorced (2000); Foreign born: 1.1% (2000); Ancestry (includes multiple ancestries): 22.8% Irish, 22.1% French (except Basque), 15.0% Italian, 13.4% English, 9.6% French Canadian (2000).
Economy: Employment by occupation: 4.6% management, 13.1% professional, 21.5% services, 26.0% sales, 0.0% farming, 10.4% construction, 24.4% production (2000).
Income: Per capita income: $18,300 (2005); Median household income: $35,877 (2005); Average household income: $44,917 (2005); Percent of households with income of $100,000 or more: 6.3% (2005); Poverty rate: 11.2% (2000).
Education: Percent of population age 25 and over with: High school diploma (including GED) or higher: 83.4% (2005); Bachelor's degree or higher: 9.5% (2005); Master's degree or higher: 3.7% (2005).
School District(s)
Fort Edward Union Free School District (PK-12)
    2003-04 Enrollment: 590 . . . . (518) 747-4594
Housing: Homeownership rate: 60.9% (2005); Median home value: $99,609 (2005); Median rent: $377 per month (2000); Median age of housing: 60+ years (2000).
Safety: Violent crime rate: 38.4 per 10,000 population; Property crime rate: 214.7 per 10,000 population (2004).
Transportation: Commute to work: 93.5% car, 1.0% public transportation, 3.2% walk, 2.3% work from home (2000); Travel time to work: 38.0% less than 15 minutes, 42.4% 15 to 30 minutes, 8.1% 30 to 45 minutes, 2.2% 45 to 60 minutes, 9.4% 60 minutes or more (2000); Amtrak: Service available.
Additional Information Contacts
Fort Edward Chamber of Commerce . . . . (518) 747-3000
    http://www.ftedward.com

FORT EDWARD (town).
Covers a land area of 26.797 square miles and a water area of 0.599 square miles. Located at 43.24° N. Lat.; 73.57° W. Long. Elevation is 144 feet.
History: Fort built here in 1755 to protect portage between the Hudson River and Lake Champlain; it was occupied by Burgoyne in 1777. Incorporated 1849.
Population: 6,330 (1990); 5,892 (2000); 5,909 (2005); 5,914 (2010 projected); Race: 98.5% White, 0.4% Black, 0.2% Asian, 0.5% Hispanic of any race (2005); Density: 220.5 persons per square mile (2005); Average household size: 2.58 (2005); Median age: 39.8 (2005); Males per 100 females: 93.8 (2005); Marriage status: 24.3% never married, 57.4% now married, 8.1% widowed, 10.2% divorced (2000); Foreign born: 1.2% (2000); Ancestry (includes multiple ancestries): 21.6% Irish, 19.7% French (except Basque), 13.2% English, 12.9% Italian, 10.0% German (2000).
Economy: Paper milling; light manufacturing. Single-family building permits issued: 2 (2005); Multi-family building permits issued: 0 (2005); Employment by occupation: 8.3% management, 12.4% professional, 17.7% services, 26.5% sales, 0.6% farming, 10.7% construction, 23.8% production (2000).
Income: Per capita income: $19,537 (2005); Median household income: $39,403 (2005); Average household income: $49,024 (2005); Percent of households with income of $100,000 or more: 8.1% (2005); Poverty rate: 9.9% (2000).

Education: Percent of population age 25 and over with: High school diploma (including GED) or higher: 82.4% (2005); Bachelor's degree or higher: 10.6% (2005); Master's degree or higher: 4.2% (2005).
Housing: Homeownership rate: 67.5% (2005); Median home value: $107,342 (2005); Median rent: $388 per month (2000); Median age of housing: 60+ years (2000).
Transportation: Commute to work: 92.8% car, 1.1% public transportation, 2.5% walk, 3.3% work from home (2000); Travel time to work: 39.7% less than 15 minutes, 40.7% 15 to 30 minutes, 9.6% 30 to 45 minutes, 2.1% 45 to 60 minutes, 7.9% 60 minutes or more (2000); Amtrak: Service available.

GRANVILLE (village).
Covers a land area of 1.585 square miles and a water area of 0 square miles. Located at 43.40° N. Lat.; 73.26° W. Long. Elevation is 407 feet.
Population: 2,646 (1990); 2,644 (2000); 2,544 (2005); 2,532 (2010 projected); Race: 97.9% White, 0.2% Black, 0.4% Asian, 0.9% Hispanic of any race (2005); Density: 1,605.4 persons per square mile (2005); Average household size: 2.51 (2005); Median age: 38.5 (2005); Males per 100 females: 88.6 (2005); Marriage status: 25.0% never married, 52.1% now married, 12.3% widowed, 10.7% divorced (2000); Foreign born: 1.4% (2000); Ancestry (includes multiple ancestries): 17.1% Irish, 15.2% French (except Basque), 13.1% English, 9.9% Italian, 9.9% German (2000).
Economy: Single-family building permits issued: 2 (2005); Multi-family building permits issued: 0 (2005); Employment by occupation: 7.4% management, 14.6% professional, 16.4% services, 28.1% sales, 0.6% farming, 10.5% construction, 22.3% production (2000).
Income: Per capita income: $18,009 (2005); Median household income: $33,007 (2005); Average household income: $43,567 (2005); Percent of households with income of $100,000 or more: 5.3% (2005); Poverty rate: 17.2% (2000).
Education: Percent of population age 25 and over with: High school diploma (including GED) or higher: 78.9% (2005); Bachelor's degree or higher: 12.3% (2005); Master's degree or higher: 5.8% (2005).

School District(s)
Granville Central School District (KG-12)
    2003-04 Enrollment: 1,475 . . . . (518) 642-1051

Housing: Homeownership rate: 54.0% (2005); Median home value: $90,230 (2005); Median rent: $392 per month (2000); Median age of housing: 60+ years (2000).
Safety: Violent crime rate: 34.3 per 10,000 population; Property crime rate: 221.0 per 10,000 population (2004).
Newspapers: North Country Free Press (General - Circulation 20,200); Northshire Free Press (General - Circulation 6,500); The Granville Sentinel (General - Circulation 3,300); The Lakes Region Free Press (General - Circulation 8,000); The Whitehall Times (General - Circulation 2,200)
Transportation: Commute to work: 86.9% car, 0.0% public transportation, 7.6% walk, 4.6% work from home (2000); Travel time to work: 61.1% less than 15 minutes, 16.6% 15 to 30 minutes, 14.1% 30 to 45 minutes, 6.1% 45 to 60 minutes, 2.2% 60 minutes or more (2000)

Additional Information Contacts
Granville Chamber of Commerce . . . . (518) 642-2815
   http://www.granvillechamber.com

GRANVILLE (town).
Covers a land area of 56.085 square miles and a water area of 0.033 square miles. Located at 43.42° N. Lat.; 73.30° W. Long. Elevation is 407 feet.
Population: 5,935 (1990); 6,456 (2000); 6,640 (2005); 6,844 (2010 projected); Race: 98.0% White, 0.5% Black, 0.4% Asian, 0.7% Hispanic of any race (2005); Density: 118.4 persons per square mile (2005); Average household size: 2.61 (2005); Median age: 39.4 (2005); Males per 100 females: 96.4 (2005); Marriage status: 23.4% never married, 57.9% now married, 10.0% widowed, 8.7% divorced (2000); Foreign born: 1.1% (2000); Ancestry (includes multiple ancestries): 17.3% Irish, 14.0% French (except Basque), 14.0% English, 8.7% German, 8.4% Other groups (2000).
Economy: Single-family building permits issued: 22 (2005); Multi-family building permits issued: 0 (2005); Employment by occupation: 8.4% management, 14.3% professional, 17.4% services, 26.6% sales, 0.3% farming, 10.7% construction, 22.2% production (2000).
Income: Per capita income: $18,150 (2005); Median household income: $38,956 (2005); Average household income: $46,355 (2005); Percent of households with income of $100,000 or more: 6.5% (2005); Poverty rate: 11.5% (2000).
Education: Percent of population age 25 and over with: High school diploma (including GED) or higher: 79.9% (2005); Bachelor's degree or higher: 12.2% (2005); Master's degree or higher: 4.4% (2005).
Housing: Homeownership rate: 72.8% (2005); Median home value: $96,995 (2005); Median rent: $400 per month (2000); Median age of housing: 50 years (2000).
Transportation: Commute to work: 90.8% car, 0.0% public transportation, 4.0% walk, 3.8% work from home (2000); Travel time to work: 52.1% less than 15 minutes, 18.9% 15 to 30 minutes, 19.3% 30 to 45 minutes, 5.7% 45 to 60 minutes, 4.0% 60 minutes or more (2000)

GREENWICH (village).
Covers a land area of 1.485 square miles and a water area of 0 square miles. Located at 43.09° N. Lat.; 73.49° W. Long. Elevation is 360 feet.
Population: 1,961 (1990); 1,902 (2000); 1,834 (2005); 1,808 (2010 projected); Race: 98.0% White, 0.3% Black, 0.9% Asian, 1.1% Hispanic of any race (2005); Density: 1,234.6 persons per square mile (2005); Average household size: 2.35 (2005); Median age: 37.9 (2005); Males per 100 females: 97.2 (2005); Marriage status: 25.4% never married, 57.6% now married, 8.7% widowed, 8.2% divorced (2000); Foreign born: 1.3% (2000); Ancestry (includes multiple ancestries): 27.3% Irish, 13.3% English, 12.4% German, 10.8% French (except Basque), 6.7% United States or American (2000).
Economy: Employment by occupation: 12.0% management, 18.5% professional, 18.0% services, 26.0% sales, 1.5% farming, 8.0% construction, 16.1% production (2000).
Income: Per capita income: $19,935 (2005); Median household income: $37,464 (2005); Average household income: $46,438 (2005); Percent of households with income of $100,000 or more: 7.6% (2005); Poverty rate: 8.3% (2000).
Education: Percent of population age 25 and over with: High school diploma (including GED) or higher: 81.8% (2005); Bachelor's degree or higher: 21.1% (2005); Master's degree or higher: 8.0% (2005).

School District(s)
Greenwich Central School District (KG-12)
    2003-04 Enrollment: 1,241 . . . . (518) 692-9542

Housing: Homeownership rate: 58.4% (2005); Median home value: $132,748 (2005); Median rent: $404 per month (2000); Median age of housing: 60+ years (2000).
Newspapers: The Journal-Press (General - Circulation 2,900)
Transportation: Commute to work: 87.8% car, 0.2% public transportation, 7.2% walk, 4.0% work from home (2000); Travel time to work: 38.3% less than 15 minutes, 20.5% 15 to 30 minutes, 21.1% 30 to 45 minutes, 10.3% 45 to 60 minutes, 9.9% 60 minutes or more (2000)

Additional Information Contacts
Greenwich Chamber of Commerce . . . . (518) 692-7979
   http://www.greenwichchamber.org

GREENWICH (town).
Covers a land area of 44.001 square miles and a water area of 0.362 square miles. Located at 43.13° N. Lat.; 73.48° W. Long. Elevation is 360 feet.
History: Incorporated 1809.
Population: 4,557 (1990); 4,896 (2000); 4,854 (2005); 4,822 (2010 projected); Race: 97.5% White, 0.4% Black, 1.1% Asian, 0.9% Hispanic of any race (2005); Density: 110.3 persons per square mile (2005); Average household size: 2.48 (2005); Median age: 40.6 (2005); Males per 100 females: 93.5 (2005); Marriage status: 23.3% never married, 61.1% now married, 8.3% widowed, 7.3% divorced (2000); Foreign born: 2.2% (2000); Ancestry (includes multiple ancestries): 24.9% Irish, 17.6% English, 11.4% French (except Basque), 10.3% German, 6.4% United States or American (2000).
Economy: In farming and dairying area. Manufacturing: paper mill, paper products. Employment by occupation: 12.6% management, 18.5% professional, 18.6% services, 24.6% sales, 1.9% farming, 8.3% construction, 15.5% production (2000).
Income: Per capita income: $22,340 (2005); Median household income: $43,931 (2005); Average household income: $55,299 (2005); Percent of households with income of $100,000 or more: 11.0% (2005); Poverty rate: 8.4% (2000).
Education: Percent of population age 25 and over with: High school diploma (including GED) or higher: 83.8% (2005); Bachelor's degree or higher: 19.9% (2005); Master's degree or higher: 7.4% (2005).
Housing: Homeownership rate: 75.1% (2005); Median home value: $135,433 (2005); Median rent: $416 per month (2000); Median age of housing: 60+ years (2000).
Transportation: Commute to work: 90.9% car, 0.1% public transportation, 4.8% walk, 4.1% work from home (2000); Travel time to work: 36.7% less

than 15 minutes, 24.4% 15 to 30 minutes, 20.2% 30 to 45 minutes, 9.1% 45 to 60 minutes, 9.7% 60 minutes or more (2000)

HAMPTON (town). Covers a land area of 22.561 square miles and a water area of 0.077 square miles. Located at 43.55° N. Lat.; 73.29° W. Long. Elevation is 431 feet.
Population: 756 (1990); 871 (2000); 970 (2005); 1,022 (2010 projected); Race: 98.7% White, 0.7% Black, 0.2% Asian, 1.4% Hispanic of any race (2005); Density: 43.0 persons per square mile (2005); Average household size: 2.59 (2005); Median age: 38.1 (2005); Males per 100 females: 98.8 (2005); Marriage status: 19.4% never married, 63.1% now married, 5.9% widowed, 11.6% divorced (2000); Foreign born: 0.7% (2000); Ancestry (includes multiple ancestries): 19.7% United States or American, 14.2% French (except Basque), 9.6% Irish, 7.9% English, 7.0% French Canadian (2000).
Economy: Employment by occupation: 8.0% management, 11.3% professional, 13.1% services, 24.6% sales, 2.0% farming, 14.6% construction, 26.5% production (2000).
Income: Per capita income: $20,320 (2005); Median household income: $44,684 (2005); Average household income: $52,680 (2005); Percent of households with income of $100,000 or more: 10.7% (2005); Poverty rate: 7.1% (2000).
Education: Percent of population age 25 and over with: High school diploma (including GED) or higher: 82.7% (2005); Bachelor's degree or higher: 14.2% (2005); Master's degree or higher: 6.7% (2005).
Housing: Homeownership rate: 82.6% (2005); Median home value: $107,955 (2005); Median rent: $425 per month (2000); Median age of housing: 23 years (2000).
Transportation: Commute to work: 92.8% car, 0.0% public transportation, 2.5% walk, 4.3% work from home (2000); Travel time to work: 36.2% less than 15 minutes, 28.1% 15 to 30 minutes, 18.7% 30 to 45 minutes, 11.6% 45 to 60 minutes, 5.4% 60 minutes or more (2000)

HARTFORD (town). Covers a land area of 43.434 square miles and a water area of 0.036 square miles. Located at 43.35° N. Lat.; 73.40° W. Long. Elevation is 390 feet.
Population: 1,989 (1990); 2,279 (2000); 2,310 (2005); 2,346 (2010 projected); Race: 97.5% White, 0.9% Black, 0.1% Asian, 1.1% Hispanic of any race (2005); Density: 53.2 persons per square mile (2005); Average household size: 2.74 (2005); Median age: 37.3 (2005); Males per 100 females: 102.5 (2005); Marriage status: 23.6% never married, 65.2% now married, 4.8% widowed, 6.4% divorced (2000); Foreign born: 0.8% (2000); Ancestry (includes multiple ancestries): 17.7% Irish, 16.9% French (except Basque), 16.6% English, 11.1% Other groups, 7.8% United States or American (2000).
Economy: Employment by occupation: 8.7% management, 15.9% professional, 14.1% services, 19.3% sales, 2.7% farming, 14.7% construction, 24.8% production (2000).
Income: Per capita income: $20,139 (2005); Median household income: $48,452 (2005); Average household income: $55,118 (2005); Percent of households with income of $100,000 or more: 9.8% (2005); Poverty rate: 4.4% (2000).
Education: Percent of population age 25 and over with: High school diploma (including GED) or higher: 84.0% (2005); Bachelor's degree or higher: 13.9% (2005); Master's degree or higher: 5.4% (2005).
School District(s)
Hartford Central School District (PK-12)
    2003-04 Enrollment: 603 . . . . (518) 632-5931
Housing: Homeownership rate: 82.6% (2005); Median home value: $131,478 (2005); Median rent: $368 per month (2000); Median age of housing: 26 years (2000).
Transportation: Commute to work: 87.4% car, 0.5% public transportation, 3.7% walk, 7.6% work from home (2000); Travel time to work: 26.0% less than 15 minutes, 45.9% 15 to 30 minutes, 17.7% 30 to 45 minutes, 6.0% 45 to 60 minutes, 4.4% 60 minutes or more (2000)

HEBRON (town). Covers a land area of 56.241 square miles and a water area of 0.178 square miles. Located at 43.28° N. Lat.; 73.33° W. Long.
Population: 1,540 (1990); 1,773 (2000); 1,805 (2005); 1,840 (2010 projected); Race: 96.8% White, 0.4% Black, 0.7% Asian, 1.9% Hispanic of any race (2005); Density: 32.1 persons per square mile (2005); Average household size: 2.52 (2005); Median age: 40.2 (2005); Males per 100 females: 101.9 (2005); Marriage status: 22.3% never married, 60.9% now married, 6.8% widowed, 10.0% divorced (2000); Foreign born: 1.4% (2000); Ancestry (includes multiple ancestries): 19.0% Irish, 17.2% English, 11.5% French (except Basque), 9.7% German, 9.0% Other groups (2000).
Economy: Employment by occupation: 11.7% management, 19.5% professional, 13.0% services, 17.4% sales, 2.9% farming, 14.0% construction, 21.5% production (2000).
Income: Per capita income: $21,988 (2005); Median household income: $45,483 (2005); Average household income: $55,119 (2005); Percent of households with income of $100,000 or more: 11.5% (2005); Poverty rate: 9.7% (2000).
Education: Percent of population age 25 and over with: High school diploma (including GED) or higher: 78.3% (2005); Bachelor's degree or higher: 19.0% (2005); Master's degree or higher: 10.1% (2005).
Housing: Homeownership rate: 83.4% (2005); Median home value: $106,677 (2005); Median rent: $425 per month (2000); Median age of housing: 31 years (2000).
Transportation: Commute to work: 90.3% car, 0.1% public transportation, 3.5% walk, 5.8% work from home (2000); Travel time to work: 16.4% less than 15 minutes, 35.5% 15 to 30 minutes, 27.7% 30 to 45 minutes, 11.0% 45 to 60 minutes, 9.4% 60 minutes or more (2000)

HUDSON FALLS (village). Covers a land area of 1.841 square miles and a water area of 0.041 square miles. Located at 43.30° N. Lat.; 73.58° W. Long. Elevation is 294 feet.
History: Settlers arrived in Hudson Falls in the 1760's and built gristmills and sawmills on the river near the 70-foot falls. The Burgoyne campaign delayed development and then the settlement was burned in 1780 by Sir Guy Carleton. In the 19th century, pulpwood, floated down the Hudson River from the Adirondack forests, helped to establish paper manufacturing as the dominant industry.
Population: 7,494 (1990); 6,927 (2000); 6,795 (2005); 6,652 (2010 projected); Race: 97.8% White, 0.6% Black, 0.3% Asian, 0.9% Hispanic of any race (2005); Density: 3,691.8 persons per square mile (2005); Average household size: 2.37 (2005); Median age: 37.4 (2005); Males per 100 females: 90.0 (2005); Marriage status: 25.4% never married, 51.8% now married, 8.7% widowed, 14.1% divorced (2000); Foreign born: 1.2% (2000); Ancestry (includes multiple ancestries): 22.4% French (except Basque), 19.5% Irish, 10.7% Italian, 10.2% Other groups, 9.7% English (2000).
Economy: Single-family building permits issued: 7 (2005); Multi-family building permits issued: 0 (2005); Employment by occupation: 6.4% management, 16.7% professional, 21.6% services, 26.5% sales, 0.4% farming, 8.3% construction, 20.2% production (2000).
Income: Per capita income: $19,136 (2005); Median household income: $35,789 (2005); Average household income: $44,788 (2005); Percent of households with income of $100,000 or more: 5.4% (2005); Poverty rate: 17.2% (2000).
Education: Percent of population age 25 and over with: High school diploma (including GED) or higher: 78.2% (2005); Bachelor's degree or higher: 12.0% (2005); Master's degree or higher: 3.3% (2005).
School District(s)
Boces Washing-Sara-War-Hamltn-Essex (PK-PK)
    2003-04 Enrollment: 514 . . . . (518) 746-3310
Hudson Falls Central School District (KG-12)
    2003-04 Enrollment: 2,418 . . . . (518) 747-2121
Housing: Homeownership rate: 56.5% (2005); Median home value: $104,246 (2005); Median rent: $404 per month (2000); Median age of housing: 60+ years (2000).
Safety: Violent crime rate: 21.8 per 10,000 population; Property crime rate: 177.6 per 10,000 population (2004).
Transportation: Commute to work: 92.2% car, 1.3% public transportation, 2.4% walk, 3.4% work from home (2000); Travel time to work: 42.0% less than 15 minutes, 37.2% 15 to 30 minutes, 10.6% 30 to 45 minutes, 4.2% 45 to 60 minutes, 5.9% 60 minutes or more (2000)
Additional Information Contacts
Hudson Falls Chamber of Commerce . . . . (518) 746-2294

JACKSON (town). Covers a land area of 37.165 square miles and a water area of 0.307 square miles. Located at 43.09° N. Lat.; 73.37° W. Long.
Population: 1,581 (1990); 1,718 (2000); 1,734 (2005); 1,755 (2010 projected); Race: 97.2% White, 0.9% Black, 0.6% Asian, 1.6% Hispanic of any race (2005); Density: 46.7 persons per square mile (2005); Average household size: 2.43 (2005); Median age: 42.0 (2005); Males per 100 females: 98.4 (2005); Marriage status: 20.7% never married, 63.2% now married, 6.5% widowed, 9.6% divorced (2000); Foreign born: 2.4% (2000);

Ancestry (includes multiple ancestries): 18.0% Irish, 14.6% German, 13.7% English, 9.4% French (except Basque), 8.1% Other groups (2000).
Economy: Employment by occupation: 12.2% management, 19.1% professional, 14.4% services, 21.3% sales, 2.9% farming, 8.5% construction, 21.6% production (2000).
Income: Per capita income: $23,785 (2005); Median household income: $47,632 (2005); Average household income: $57,444 (2005); Percent of households with income of $100,000 or more: 11.9% (2005); Poverty rate: 9.6% (2000).
Education: Percent of population age 25 and over with: High school diploma (including GED) or higher: 84.8% (2005); Bachelor's degree or higher: 23.0% (2005); Master's degree or higher: 9.6% (2005).
Housing: Homeownership rate: 81.2% (2005); Median home value: $138,021 (2005); Median rent: $420 per month (2000); Median age of housing: 41 years (2000).
Transportation: Commute to work: 89.7% car, 0.4% public transportation, 2.2% walk, 7.8% work from home (2000); Travel time to work: 28.8% less than 15 minutes, 26.7% 15 to 30 minutes, 20.5% 30 to 45 minutes, 11.3% 45 to 60 minutes, 12.7% 60 minutes or more (2000)

KINGSBURY (town). Covers a land area of 39.866 square miles and a water area of 0.147 square miles. Located at 43.32° N. Lat.; 73.56° W. Long. Elevation is 305 feet.
Population: 11,851 (1990); 11,171 (2000); 11,560 (2005); 11,893 (2010 projected); Race: 98.2% White, 0.4% Black, 0.2% Asian, 0.7% Hispanic of any race (2005); Density: 290.0 persons per square mile (2005); Average household size: 2.45 (2005); Median age: 38.6 (2005); Males per 100 females: 93.5 (2005); Marriage status: 23.7% never married, 55.6% now married, 9.0% widowed, 11.7% divorced (2000); Foreign born: 1.4% (2000); Ancestry (includes multiple ancestries): 20.5% French (except Basque), 18.8% Irish, 11.3% English, 9.5% Italian, 9.2% Other groups (2000).
Economy: Single-family building permits issued: 33 (2005); Multi-family building permits issued: 389 (2005); Employment by occupation: 7.8% management, 14.6% professional, 18.6% services, 27.0% sales, 0.9% farming, 10.0% construction, 21.1% production (2000).
Income: Per capita income: $20,254 (2005); Median household income: $40,486 (2005); Average household income: $49,213 (2005); Percent of households with income of $100,000 or more: 7.9% (2005); Poverty rate: 12.6% (2000).
Education: Percent of population age 25 and over with: High school diploma (including GED) or higher: 79.5% (2005); Bachelor's degree or higher: 11.2% (2005); Master's degree or higher: 4.0% (2005).
Housing: Homeownership rate: 67.4% (2005); Median home value: $110,737 (2005); Median rent: $410 per month (2000); Median age of housing: 52 years (2000).
Transportation: Commute to work: 91.9% car, 1.0% public transportation, 1.9% walk, 3.9% work from home (2000); Travel time to work: 39.9% less than 15 minutes, 39.9% 15 to 30 minutes, 11.0% 30 to 45 minutes, 3.9% 45 to 60 minutes, 5.3% 60 minutes or more (2000)

MIDDLE GRANVILLE (unincorporated postal area, zip code 12849). Covers a land area of 3.126 square miles and a water area of 0.007 square miles. Located at 43.43° N. Lat.; 73.29° W. Long.
Population: 0 (2000); Race: 94.8% White, 0.6% Black, 0.0% Asian, 0.0% Hispanic of any race (2000); Density: 0.0 persons per square mile (2000); Age: 30.2% under 18, 12.7% over 64 (2000); Marriage status: 22.7% never married, 55.2% now married, 6.4% widowed, 15.7% divorced (2000); Foreign born: 3.5% (2000); Ancestry (includes multiple ancestries): 22.7% French (except Basque), 21.4% Irish, 11.2% German, 9.5% English, 5.6% Scotch-Irish (2000).
Economy: In slate-quarrying area. Employment by occupation: 3.1% management, 28.2% professional, 27.5% services, 24.0% sales, 0.0% farming, 9.9% construction, 7.3% production (2000).
Income: Per capita income: $18,756 (2000); Median household income: $44,459 (2000); Poverty rate: 5.9% (2000).
Education: Percent of population age 25 and over with: High school diploma (including GED) or higher: 94.9% (2000); Bachelor's degree or higher: 25.6% (2000).
School District(s)
Granville Central School District (KG-12)
 2003-04 Enrollment: 1,475 . . . . (518) 642-1051
Housing: Homeownership rate: 91.0% (2000); Median home value: $66,100 (2000); Median rent: $575 per month (2000); Median age of housing: 38 years (2000).

Transportation: Commute to work: 95.3% car, 0.0% public transportation, 0.0% walk, 0.0% work from home (2000); Travel time to work: 50.6% less than 15 minutes, 9.9% 15 to 30 minutes, 30.0% 30 to 45 minutes, 7.5% 45 to 60 minutes, 2.0% 60 minutes or more (2000)

PUTNAM (town). Covers a land area of 33.160 square miles and a water area of 2.301 square miles. Located at 43.74° N. Lat.; 73.41° W. Long. Elevation is 339 feet.
Population: 477 (1990); 645 (2000); 740 (2005); 798 (2010 projected); Race: 99.7% White, 0.0% Black, 0.3% Asian, 1.9% Hispanic of any race (2005); Density: 22.3 persons per square mile (2005); Average household size: 2.53 (2005); Median age: 40.7 (2005); Males per 100 females: 103.3 (2005); Marriage status: 18.1% never married, 66.8% now married, 5.8% widowed, 9.3% divorced (2000); Foreign born: 1.1% (2000); Ancestry (includes multiple ancestries): 29.9% Irish, 18.6% French (except Basque), 11.2% United States or American, 11.0% English, 10.0% German (2000).
Economy: Employment by occupation: 8.4% management, 17.4% professional, 18.0% services, 19.3% sales, 1.2% farming, 10.2% construction, 25.5% production (2000).
Income: Per capita income: $26,084 (2005); Median household income: $55,978 (2005); Average household income: $66,104 (2005); Percent of households with income of $100,000 or more: 19.9% (2005); Poverty rate: 5.7% (2000).
Education: Percent of population age 25 and over with: High school diploma (including GED) or higher: 83.4% (2005); Bachelor's degree or higher: 16.6% (2005); Master's degree or higher: 7.7% (2005).
Housing: Homeownership rate: 86.0% (2005); Median home value: $128,963 (2005); Median rent: $363 per month (2000); Median age of housing: 43 years (2000).
Transportation: Commute to work: 93.5% car, 0.0% public transportation, 4.8% walk, 1.6% work from home (2000); Travel time to work: 38.4% less than 15 minutes, 32.1% 15 to 30 minutes, 13.8% 30 to 45 minutes, 4.3% 45 to 60 minutes, 11.5% 60 minutes or more (2000)

SALEM (village). Covers a land area of 2.929 square miles and a water area of 0 square miles. Located at 43.17° N. Lat.; 73.32° W. Long. Elevation is 490 feet.
Population: 958 (1990); 964 (2000); 901 (2005); 894 (2010 projected); Race: 97.2% White, 1.8% Black, 0.0% Asian, 0.6% Hispanic of any race (2005); Density: 307.6 persons per square mile (2005); Average household size: 2.60 (2005); Median age: 38.8 (2005); Males per 100 females: 102.9 (2005); Marriage status: 22.1% never married, 55.6% now married, 9.6% widowed, 12.8% divorced (2000); Foreign born: 0.9% (2000); Ancestry (includes multiple ancestries): 23.0% Irish, 17.6% English, 10.6% German, 9.5% French (except Basque), 6.3% Scotch-Irish (2000).
Economy: Employment by occupation: 7.3% management, 21.4% professional, 19.5% services, 18.4% sales, 3.0% farming, 8.4% construction, 22.1% production (2000).
Income: Per capita income: $21,866 (2005); Median household income: $44,907 (2005); Average household income: $56,311 (2005); Percent of households with income of $100,000 or more: 10.4% (2005); Poverty rate: 4.5% (2000).
Education: Percent of population age 25 and over with: High school diploma (including GED) or higher: 81.7% (2005); Bachelor's degree or higher: 24.9% (2005); Master's degree or higher: 11.1% (2005).
School District(s)
Salem Central School District (KG-12)
 2003-04 Enrollment: 782 . . . . (518) 854-7855
Housing: Homeownership rate: 74.1% (2005); Median home value: $109,750 (2005); Median rent: $388 per month (2000); Median age of housing: 60+ years (2000).
Transportation: Commute to work: 81.8% car, 0.0% public transportation, 12.4% walk, 5.9% work from home (2000); Travel time to work: 39.2% less than 15 minutes, 25.3% 15 to 30 minutes, 18.4% 30 to 45 minutes, 3.5% 45 to 60 minutes, 13.6% 60 minutes or more (2000)

SALEM (town). Covers a land area of 52.467 square miles and a water area of 0.050 square miles. Located at 43.15° N. Lat.; 73.32° W. Long. Elevation is 490 feet.
History: Settled 1764, incorporated 1803.
Population: 2,608 (1990); 2,702 (2000); 2,723 (2005); 2,757 (2010 projected); Race: 97.9% White, 1.2% Black, 0.3% Asian, 0.6% Hispanic of any race (2005); Density: 51.9 persons per square mile (2005); Average household size: 2.48 (2005); Median age: 41.9 (2005); Males per 100 females: 102.8 (2005); Marriage status: 24.6% never married, 58.0% now

married, 7.6% widowed, 9.7% divorced (2000); Foreign born: 1.7% (2000); Ancestry (includes multiple ancestries): 18.4% Irish, 16.6% English, 10.3% German, 9.8% French (except Basque), 7.1% Other groups (2000).
Economy: Manufacturing of apparel, textiles, feed, paper products; lumber milling; slate quarrying. Small lakes (resorts) nearby. Employment by occupation: 11.0% management, 18.5% professional, 13.7% services, 18.7% sales, 5.2% farming, 11.0% construction, 21.9% production (2000).
Income: Per capita income: $24,184 (2005); Median household income: $47,811 (2005); Average household income: $59,566 (2005); Percent of households with income of $100,000 or more: 13.2% (2005); Poverty rate: 8.3% (2000).
Education: Percent of population age 25 and over with: High school diploma (including GED) or higher: 84.7% (2005); Bachelor's degree or higher: 22.1% (2005); Master's degree or higher: 10.3% (2005).
Housing: Homeownership rate: 80.7% (2005); Median home value: $118,598 (2005); Median rent: $398 per month (2000); Median age of housing: 59 years (2000).
Transportation: Commute to work: 85.9% car, 0.6% public transportation, 6.5% walk, 6.2% work from home (2000); Travel time to work: 33.6% less than 15 minutes, 26.7% 15 to 30 minutes, 18.1% 30 to 45 minutes, 8.4% 45 to 60 minutes, 13.1% 60 minutes or more (2000)

SHUSHAN (unincorporated postal area, zip code 12873). Covers a land area of 25.313 square miles and a water area of 0 square miles. Located at 43.11° N. Lat.; 73.31° W. Long.
Population: 0 (2000); Race: 96.7% White, 1.4% Black, 1.1% Asian, 1.3% Hispanic of any race (2000); Density: 0.0 persons per square mile (2000); Age: 21.8% under 18, 19.5% over 64 (2000); Marriage status: 23.0% never married, 58.1% now married, 6.8% widowed, 12.1% divorced (2000); Foreign born: 3.6% (2000); Ancestry (includes multiple ancestries): 19.8% English, 14.9% Irish, 11.2% German, 7.6% United States or American, 6.9% Other groups (2000).
Economy: Employment by occupation: 13.7% management, 21.6% professional, 11.3% services, 20.4% sales, 2.1% farming, 13.9% construction, 17.0% production (2000).
Income: Per capita income: $22,656 (2000); Median household income: $40,500 (2000); Poverty rate: 9.8% (2000).
Education: Percent of population age 25 and over with: High school diploma (including GED) or higher: 89.0% (2000); Bachelor's degree or higher: 26.4% (2000).
Housing: Homeownership rate: 79.6% (2000); Median home value: $78,500 (2000); Median rent: $319 per month (2000); Median age of housing: 60+ years (2000).
Transportation: Commute to work: 87.9% car, 0.0% public transportation, 2.3% walk, 9.8% work from home (2000); Travel time to work: 16.3% less than 15 minutes, 42.6% 15 to 30 minutes, 16.0% 30 to 45 minutes, 8.9% 45 to 60 minutes, 16.3% 60 minutes or more (2000)

WHITE CREEK (town). Covers a land area of 47.864 square miles and a water area of 0.065 square miles. Located at 43.01° N. Lat.; 73.34° W. Long.
Population: 3,196 (1990); 3,411 (2000); 3,435 (2005); 3,458 (2010 projected); Race: 97.2% White, 1.3% Black, 0.6% Asian, 1.5% Hispanic of any race (2005); Density: 71.8 persons per square mile (2005); Average household size: 2.54 (2005); Median age: 40.8 (2005); Males per 100 females: 97.4 (2005); Marriage status: 24.2% never married, 58.9% now married, 8.3% widowed, 8.6% divorced (2000); Foreign born: 2.8% (2000); Ancestry (includes multiple ancestries): 23.9% Irish, 18.8% English, 15.9% German, 10.8% United States or American, 7.9% Other groups (2000).
Economy: Employment by occupation: 9.5% management, 19.1% professional, 16.3% services, 19.6% sales, 5.1% farming, 11.3% construction, 19.1% production (2000).
Income: Per capita income: $19,728 (2005); Median household income: $39,896 (2005); Average household income: $50,026 (2005); Percent of households with income of $100,000 or more: 11.0% (2005); Poverty rate: 6.9% (2000).
Education: Percent of population age 25 and over with: High school diploma (including GED) or higher: 81.9% (2005); Bachelor's degree or higher: 17.9% (2005); Master's degree or higher: 6.4% (2005).
Housing: Homeownership rate: 77.3% (2005); Median home value: $123,495 (2005); Median rent: $388 per month (2000); Median age of housing: 45 years (2000).
Transportation: Commute to work: 86.8% car, 3.2% public transportation, 4.3% walk, 4.9% work from home (2000); Travel time to work: 32.0% less than 15 minutes, 25.9% 15 to 30 minutes, 16.2% 30 to 45 minutes, 11.9% 45 to 60 minutes, 13.9% 60 minutes or more (2000)

WHITEHALL (village). Covers a land area of 4.691 square miles and a water area of 0.132 square miles. Located at 43.55° N. Lat.; 73.40° W. Long. Elevation is 125 feet.
Population: 3,099 (1990); 2,667 (2000); 2,403 (2005); 2,305 (2010 projected); Race: 97.4% White, 0.3% Black, 0.0% Asian, 2.5% Hispanic of any race (2005); Density: 512.3 persons per square mile (2005); Average household size: 2.36 (2005); Median age: 37.9 (2005); Males per 100 females: 90.7 (2005); Marriage status: 26.6% never married, 58.2% now married, 8.6% widowed, 6.6% divorced (2000); Foreign born: 0.5% (2000); Ancestry (includes multiple ancestries): 19.9% French (except Basque), 15.7% Irish, 12.8% Italian, 10.7% United States or American, 9.1% English (2000).
Economy: Employment by occupation: 3.6% management, 4.7% professional, 29.7% services, 25.5% sales, 0.0% farming, 10.7% construction, 25.7% production (2000).
Income: Per capita income: $19,731 (2005); Median household income: $37,069 (2005); Average household income: $46,483 (2005); Percent of households with income of $100,000 or more: 8.5% (2005); Poverty rate: 13.2% (2000).
Education: Percent of population age 25 and over with: High school diploma (including GED) or higher: 81.5% (2005); Bachelor's degree or higher: 8.3% (2005); Master's degree or higher: 3.9% (2005).

School District(s)
Whitehall Central School District (KG-12)
    2003-04 Enrollment: 856 . . . . (518) 499-1772

Housing: Homeownership rate: 59.7% (2005); Median home value: $78,604 (2005); Median rent: $413 per month (2000); Median age of housing: 60+ years (2000).
Safety: Violent crime rate: 11.3 per 10,000 population; Property crime rate: 139.7 per 10,000 population (2004).
Transportation: Commute to work: 87.8% car, 0.0% public transportation, 7.2% walk, 2.0% work from home (2000); Travel time to work: 33.9% less than 15 minutes, 25.5% 15 to 30 minutes, 22.3% 30 to 45 minutes, 9.9% 45 to 60 minutes, 8.3% 60 minutes or more (2000); Amtrak: Service available.

Additional Information Contacts
Whitehall Chamber of Commerce . . . . (518) 499-2292
    http://www.whitehallchamber.com

WHITEHALL (town). Covers a land area of 57.613 square miles and a water area of 1.138 square miles. Located at 43.54° N. Lat.; 73.39° W. Long. Elevation is 125 feet.
History: Settled 1759, incorporated 1806.
Population: 4,409 (1990); 4,035 (2000); 3,766 (2005); 3,640 (2010 projected); Race: 97.5% White, 0.2% Black, 0.3% Asian, 1.7% Hispanic of any race (2005); Density: 65.4 persons per square mile (2005); Average household size: 2.45 (2005); Median age: 39.0 (2005); Males per 100 females: 92.9 (2005); Marriage status: 23.6% never married, 60.3% now married, 8.6% widowed, 7.5% divorced (2000); Foreign born: 0.3% (2000); Ancestry (includes multiple ancestries): 22.7% French (except Basque), 16.7% Irish, 12.4% United States or American, 10.9% Italian, 9.3% English (2000).
Economy: Summer resort. Some manufacturing. Employment by occupation: 4.9% management, 4.9% professional, 26.7% services, 28.3% sales, 0.0% farming, 10.1% construction, 25.1% production (2000).
Income: Per capita income: $20,516 (2005); Median household income: $42,363 (2005); Average household income: $50,237 (2005); Percent of households with income of $100,000 or more: 10.1% (2005); Poverty rate: 12.1% (2000).
Education: Percent of population age 25 and over with: High school diploma (including GED) or higher: 82.0% (2005); Bachelor's degree or higher: 8.0% (2005); Master's degree or higher: 2.9% (2005).
Housing: Homeownership rate: 69.1% (2005); Median home value: $85,294 (2005); Median rent: $416 per month (2000); Median age of housing: 60+ years (2000).
Transportation: Commute to work: 88.2% car, 0.5% public transportation, 5.7% walk, 3.7% work from home (2000); Travel time to work: 30.1% less than 15 minutes, 27.6% 15 to 30 minutes, 20.2% 30 to 45 minutes, 12.0% 45 to 60 minutes, 10.1% 60 minutes or more (2000); Amtrak: Service available.

Wayne County

Located in western New York; bounded on the north by Lake Ontario; drained by the Clyde River. Covers a land area of 604.21 square miles, a water area of 779.93 square miles, and is located in the Eastern Time Zone. The county government was organized in 1823. County seat is Lyons.

Wayne County is part of the Rochester, NY Metropolitan Statistical Area. The entire metro area includes: Livingston County, NY; Monroe County, NY; Ontario County, NY; Orleans County, NY; Wayne County, NY

Weather Station: Sodus Center   Elevation: 419 feet

	Jan	Feb	Mar	Apr	May	Jun	Jul	Aug	Sep	Oct	Nov	Dec
High	32	34	43	56	69	78	82	80	72	61	49	37
Low	17	18	26	36	46	55	61	59	52	42	34	23
Precip	2.5	2.0	2.6	3.1	3.1	3.7	3.2	3.4	4.0	3.9	4.0	2.9
Snow	26.7	17.5	12.6	3.1	tr	0.0	0.0	0.0	0.0	tr	6.7	22.7

High and Low temperatures in degrees Fahrenheit; Precipitation and Snow in inches

Population: 89,123 (1990); 93,765 (2000); 93,730 (2005); 93,629 (2010 projected); Race: 93.3% White, 3.4% Black, 0.7% Asian, 3.2% Hispanic of any race (2005); Density: 155.1 persons per square mile (2005); Average household size: 2.65 (2005); Median age: 38.7 (2005); Males per 100 females: 97.2 (2005).
Religion: Five largest groups: 19.7% Catholic Church, 7.5% The United Methodist Church, 3.3% American Baptist Churches in the USA, 2.9% Presbyterian Church (U.S.A.), 1.7% Reformed Church in America (2000).
Economy: Unemployment rate: 5.0% (2005); Total civilian labor force: 49,022 (2005); Leading industries: 30.5% manufacturing; 16.9% retail trade; 13.4% health care and social assistance (2003); Farms: 904 totaling 165,213 acres (2002); Companies that employ 500 or more persons: 2 (2003); Companies that employ 100 to 499 persons: 28 (2003); Companies that employ less than 100 persons: 1,766 (2003); Black-owned businesses: 104 (2002); Hispanic-owned businesses: n/a (2002); Women-owned businesses: 2,131 (2002); Retail sales per capita: $9,239 (2006); Single-family building permits issued: 212 (2005); Multi-family building permits issued: 82 (2005).
Income: Per capita income: $21,998 (2005); Median household income: $48,768 (2005); Average household income: $57,653 (2005); Percent of households with income of $100,000 or more: 12.4% (2005); Poverty rate: 10.1% (2003); Bankruptcy rate: 5.91% (2005).
Education: Percent of population age 25 and over with: High school diploma (including GED) or higher: 82.3% (2005); Bachelor's degree or higher: 17.1% (2005); Master's degree or higher: 6.3% (2005).
Housing: Homeownership rate: 77.9% (2005); Median home value: $103,505 (2005); Median rent: $414 per month (2000); Median age of housing: 40 years (2000).
Health: Birth rate: 120.0 per 10,000 population (2004); Death rate: 82.9 per 10,000 population (2004); Age-adjusted cancer mortality rate: 225.1 deaths per 100,000 population (2002); Air Quality Index: 97.7% good, 2.3% moderate, 0.0% unhealthy for sensitive individuals, 0.0% unhealthy (percent of days in 2005); Number of physicians: 7.6 per 10,000 population (2004); Hospital beds: 29.3 per 10,000 population (2003); Hospital admissions: 393.9 per 10,000 population (2003).
Elections: 2004 Presidential election results: 60.0% Bush, 38.1% Kerry, 1.6% Nader, 0.2% Badnarik.

Additional Information Contacts
Wayne County Government	(315) 946-5400
http://www.co.wayne.ny.us/	
Town of Palmyra	(315) 597-5521
http://www.palmyrany.com/	
Village of Palmyra	(315) 597-4949
http://www.palmyrany.com/	
Village of Sodus Point	(315) 483-9881
http://www.soduspoint.info/	

Wayne County Communities

ARCADIA (town). Covers a land area of 52.035 square miles and a water area of 0.102 square miles. Located at 43.06° N. Lat.; 77.08° W. Long.
Population: 14,827 (1990); 14,889 (2000); 14,665 (2005); 14,351 (2010 projected); Race: 90.5% White, 4.4% Black, 0.6% Asian, 6.9% Hispanic of any race (2005); Density: 281.8 persons per square mile (2005); Average household size: 2.55 (2005); Median age: 39.8 (2005); Males per 100 females: 91.0 (2005); Marriage status: 24.1% never married, 56.7% now married, 8.8% widowed, 10.4% divorced (2000); Foreign born: 3.1% (2000); Ancestry (includes multiple ancestries): 19.9% German, 17.8% Dutch, 17.7% English, 13.2% Irish, 12.7% Italian (2000).
Economy: Single-family building permits issued: 3 (2005); Multi-family building permits issued: 0 (2005); Employment by occupation: 8.0% management, 19.5% professional, 15.3% services, 22.2% sales, 0.3% farming, 8.5% construction, 26.3% production (2000).
Income: Per capita income: $20,457 (2005); Median household income: $41,298 (2005); Average household income: $50,871 (2005); Percent of households with income of $100,000 or more: 8.2% (2005); Poverty rate: 12.9% (2000).
Education: Percent of population age 25 and over with: High school diploma (including GED) or higher: 77.7% (2005); Bachelor's degree or higher: 15.3% (2005); Master's degree or higher: 6.5% (2005).
Housing: Homeownership rate: 67.2% (2005); Median home value: $88,133 (2005); Median rent: $425 per month (2000); Median age of housing: 47 years (2000).
Transportation: Commute to work: 91.9% car, 0.7% public transportation, 4.3% walk, 1.3% work from home (2000); Travel time to work: 49.7% less than 15 minutes, 25.3% 15 to 30 minutes, 12.5% 30 to 45 minutes, 8.3% 45 to 60 minutes, 4.2% 60 minutes or more (2000)

BUTLER (town). Covers a land area of 37.100 square miles and a water area of 0.060 square miles. Located at 43.18° N. Lat.; 76.77° W. Long.
Population: 2,152 (1990); 2,277 (2000); 2,210 (2005); 2,174 (2010 projected); Race: 89.4% White, 8.1% Black, 0.0% Asian, 5.7% Hispanic of any race (2005); Density: 59.6 persons per square mile (2005); Average household size: 3.04 (2005); Median age: 37.3 (2005); Males per 100 females: 130.7 (2005); Marriage status: 25.0% never married, 60.9% now married, 5.3% widowed, 8.8% divorced (2000); Foreign born: 0.7% (2000); Ancestry (includes multiple ancestries): 18.5% German, 16.4% English, 11.4% Irish, 10.4% Dutch, 7.3% United States or American (2000).
Economy: Single-family building permits issued: 3 (2005); Multi-family building permits issued: 0 (2005); Employment by occupation: 7.1% management, 12.1% professional, 12.4% services, 22.9% sales, 3.6% farming, 15.7% construction, 26.2% production (2000).
Income: Per capita income: $17,579 (2005); Median household income: $42,788 (2005); Average household income: $48,719 (2005); Percent of households with income of $100,000 or more: 5.4% (2005); Poverty rate: 9.8% (2000).
Education: Percent of population age 25 and over with: High school diploma (including GED) or higher: 68.7% (2005); Bachelor's degree or higher: 7.4% (2005); Master's degree or higher: 1.6% (2005).
Housing: Homeownership rate: 81.5% (2005); Median home value: $75,108 (2005); Median rent: $358 per month (2000); Median age of housing: 46 years (2000).
Transportation: Commute to work: 87.5% car, 0.0% public transportation, 5.0% walk, 5.9% work from home (2000); Travel time to work: 34.5% less than 15 minutes, 19.7% 15 to 30 minutes, 23.6% 30 to 45 minutes, 11.5% 45 to 60 minutes, 10.7% 60 minutes or more (2000)

CLYDE (village). Covers a land area of 2.212 square miles and a water area of 0.052 square miles. Located at 43.08° N. Lat.; 76.87° W. Long. Elevation is 400 feet.
History: Incorporated 1835.
Population: 2,409 (1990); 2,269 (2000); 2,203 (2005); 2,132 (2010 projected); Race: 90.8% White, 5.9% Black, 0.0% Asian, 2.5% Hispanic of any race (2005); Density: 995.9 persons per square mile (2005); Average household size: 2.63 (2005); Median age: 37.2 (2005); Males per 100 females: 93.2 (2005); Marriage status: 29.5% never married, 52.4% now married, 9.1% widowed, 9.0% divorced (2000); Foreign born: 2.6% (2000); Ancestry (includes multiple ancestries): 28.8% Italian, 18.2% Irish, 15.2% German, 12.6% Other groups, 9.8% English (2000).
Economy: In dairying and fruit-growing area. Manufacturing: pallets, boxes, and cathode ray tubes. Single-family building permits issued: 0 (2005); Multi-family building permits issued: 0 (2005); Employment by occupation: 9.4% management, 15.3% professional, 12.6% services, 25.9% sales, 0.0% farming, 10.1% construction, 26.7% production (2000).
Income: Per capita income: $18,080 (2005); Median household income: $35,014 (2005); Average household income: $47,154 (2005); Percent of households with income of $100,000 or more: 7.4% (2005); Poverty rate: 10.6% (2000).

Education: Percent of population age 25 and over with: High school diploma (including GED) or higher: 76.4% (2005); Bachelor's degree or higher: 10.2% (2005); Master's degree or higher: 2.9% (2005).

School District(s)
Clyde-Savannah Central School District (PK-12)
    2003-04 Enrollment: 1,090 . . . . (315) 923-7747

Housing: Homeownership rate: 69.0% (2005); Median home value: $69,640 (2005); Median rent: $369 per month (2000); Median age of housing: 60+ years (2000).
Safety: Violent crime rate: 22.5 per 10,000 population; Property crime rate: 413.3 per 10,000 population (2004).
Transportation: Commute to work: 87.2% car, 2.3% public transportation, 6.0% walk, 3.3% work from home (2000); Travel time to work: 39.2% less than 15 minutes, 29.0% 15 to 30 minutes, 16.7% 30 to 45 minutes, 7.6% 45 to 60 minutes, 7.5% 60 minutes or more (2000)

GALEN (town)
Covers a land area of 59.445 square miles and a water area of 0.597 square miles. Located at 43.06° N. Lat.; 76.88° W. Long.
Population: 4,413 (1990); 4,439 (2000); 4,403 (2005); 4,355 (2010 projected); Race: 93.8% White, 3.5% Black, 0.2% Asian, 1.8% Hispanic of any race (2005); Density: 74.1 persons per square mile (2005); Average household size: 2.67 (2005); Median age: 37.8 (2005); Males per 100 females: 96.2 (2005); Marriage status: 24.8% never married, 58.9% now married, 8.0% widowed, 8.3% divorced (2000); Foreign born: 1.8% (2000); Ancestry (includes multiple ancestries): 20.8% German, 18.9% Italian, 16.0% Irish, 14.8% English, 9.5% United States or American (2000).
Economy: Single-family building permits issued: 5 (2005); Multi-family building permits issued: 0 (2005); Employment by occupation: 11.6% management, 12.5% professional, 13.5% services, 22.1% sales, 0.4% farming, 12.6% construction, 27.2% production (2000).
Income: Per capita income: $19,248 (2005); Median household income: $41,185 (2005); Average household income: $51,202 (2005); Percent of households with income of $100,000 or more: 7.9% (2005); Poverty rate: 9.9% (2000).
Education: Percent of population age 25 and over with: High school diploma (including GED) or higher: 77.6% (2005); Bachelor's degree or higher: 9.1% (2005); Master's degree or higher: 2.3% (2005).
Housing: Homeownership rate: 77.6% (2005); Median home value: $76,204 (2005); Median rent: $371 per month (2000); Median age of housing: 60+ years (2000).
Transportation: Commute to work: 89.2% car, 1.1% public transportation, 3.4% walk, 5.7% work from home (2000); Travel time to work: 37.4% less than 15 minutes, 30.2% 15 to 30 minutes, 18.2% 30 to 45 minutes, 7.3% 45 to 60 minutes, 6.9% 60 minutes or more (2000)

HURON (town)
Covers a land area of 39.510 square miles and a water area of 3.686 square miles. Located at 43.24° N. Lat.; 76.89° W. Long.
Population: 2,025 (1990); 2,117 (2000); 2,082 (2005); 2,051 (2010 projected); Race: 92.8% White, 2.6% Black, 0.3% Asian, 4.0% Hispanic of any race (2005); Density: 52.7 persons per square mile (2005); Average household size: 2.57 (2005); Median age: 44.5 (2005); Males per 100 females: 103.1 (2005); Marriage status: 21.1% never married, 63.9% now married, 6.0% widowed, 9.0% divorced (2000); Foreign born: 0.5% (2000); Ancestry (includes multiple ancestries): 22.3% German, 19.1% English, 16.7% Irish, 12.3% Dutch, 11.3% Other groups (2000).
Economy: Single-family building permits issued: 7 (2005); Multi-family building permits issued: 0 (2005); Employment by occupation: 14.7% management, 18.3% professional, 13.6% services, 18.9% sales, 3.3% farming, 10.2% construction, 21.1% production (2000).
Income: Per capita income: $22,812 (2005); Median household income: $46,793 (2005); Average household income: $57,129 (2005); Percent of households with income of $100,000 or more: 15.1% (2005); Poverty rate: 12.6% (2000).
Education: Percent of population age 25 and over with: High school diploma (including GED) or higher: 79.6% (2005); Bachelor's degree or higher: 17.0% (2005); Master's degree or higher: 5.2% (2005).
Housing: Homeownership rate: 80.7% (2005); Median home value: $103,994 (2005); Median rent: $322 per month (2000); Median age of housing: 34 years (2000).
Transportation: Commute to work: 92.0% car, 0.2% public transportation, 1.7% walk, 5.6% work from home (2000); Travel time to work: 29.4% less than 15 minutes, 20.0% 15 to 30 minutes, 18.4% 30 to 45 minutes, 17.6% 45 to 60 minutes, 14.6% 60 minutes or more (2000)

LYONS (village)
Covers a land area of 4.064 square miles and a water area of 0.085 square miles. Located at 43.06° N. Lat.; 76.99° W. Long. Elevation is 438 feet.
Population: 4,280 (1990); 3,695 (2000); 3,544 (2005); 3,385 (2010 projected); Race: 84.6% White, 11.1% Black, 0.8% Asian, 3.9% Hispanic of any race (2005); Density: 872.1 persons per square mile (2005); Average household size: 2.43 (2005); Median age: 39.3 (2005); Males per 100 females: 91.3 (2005); Marriage status: 28.5% never married, 51.9% now married, 7.8% widowed, 11.8% divorced (2000); Foreign born: 2.1% (2000); Ancestry (includes multiple ancestries): 18.9% German, 15.0% Other groups, 14.2% Italian, 14.2% Dutch, 13.6% Irish (2000).
Economy: Single-family building permits issued: 0 (2005); Multi-family building permits issued: 0 (2005); Employment by occupation: 7.0% management, 19.9% professional, 19.1% services, 20.2% sales, 0.8% farming, 8.2% construction, 24.8% production (2000).
Income: Per capita income: $18,203 (2005); Median household income: $38,901 (2005); Average household income: $43,559 (2005); Percent of households with income of $100,000 or more: 4.5% (2005); Poverty rate: 11.9% (2000).
Education: Percent of population age 25 and over with: High school diploma (including GED) or higher: 77.5% (2005); Bachelor's degree or higher: 13.5% (2005); Master's degree or higher: 7.1% (2005).

School District(s)
Lyons Central School District (PK-12)
    2003-04 Enrollment: 1,069 . . . . (315) 946-2200

Housing: Homeownership rate: 59.9% (2005); Median home value: $67,296 (2005); Median rent: $389 per month (2000); Median age of housing: 60+ years (2000).
Safety: Violent crime rate: 66.7 per 10,000 population; Property crime rate: 522.8 per 10,000 population (2004).
Newspapers: Wayne County Star (General - Circulation 7,200)
Transportation: Commute to work: 85.8% car, 2.2% public transportation, 11.6% walk, 0.5% work from home (2000); Travel time to work: 50.1% less than 15 minutes, 26.9% 15 to 30 minutes, 10.1% 30 to 45 minutes, 4.1% 45 to 60 minutes, 8.8% 60 minutes or more (2000)

LYONS (town)
Covers a land area of 37.479 square miles and a water area of 0.123 square miles. Located at 43.07° N. Lat.; 76.99° W. Long. Elevation is 438 feet.
History: Settled 1800; incorporated 1831.
Population: 6,343 (1990); 5,831 (2000); 5,569 (2005); 5,382 (2010 projected); Race: 87.4% White, 9.0% Black, 0.5% Asian, 3.5% Hispanic of any race (2005); Density: 148.6 persons per square mile (2005); Average household size: 2.65 (2005); Median age: 41.0 (2005); Males per 100 females: 94.0 (2005); Marriage status: 25.7% never married, 55.0% now married, 7.9% widowed, 11.5% divorced (2000); Foreign born: 2.3% (2000); Ancestry (includes multiple ancestries): 18.1% German, 13.2% Dutch, 12.3% Irish, 12.1% United States or American, 11.8% Other groups (2000).
Economy: Manufacturing: canned foods, chemicals, condiments, clothing, furniture, silk, brandy. In fruit-growing region. Summer resort. Single-family building permits issued: 8 (2005); Multi-family building permits issued: 0 (2005); Employment by occupation: 10.2% management, 18.7% professional, 16.5% services, 21.1% sales, 0.5% farming, 8.6% construction, 24.4% production (2000).
Income: Per capita income: $19,388 (2005); Median household income: $42,229 (2005); Average household income: $49,680 (2005); Percent of households with income of $100,000 or more: 7.0% (2005); Poverty rate: 9.6% (2000).
Education: Percent of population age 25 and over with: High school diploma (including GED) or higher: 75.6% (2005); Bachelor's degree or higher: 14.6% (2005); Master's degree or higher: 6.6% (2005).
Housing: Homeownership rate: 67.5% (2005); Median home value: $70,048 (2005); Median rent: $391 per month (2000); Median age of housing: 60+ years (2000).
Transportation: Commute to work: 87.5% car, 1.8% public transportation, 8.3% walk, 2.4% work from home (2000); Travel time to work: 44.3% less than 15 minutes, 28.3% 15 to 30 minutes, 12.5% 30 to 45 minutes, 4.9% 45 to 60 minutes, 10.0% 60 minutes or more (2000)

MACEDON (village)
Covers a land area of 1.224 square miles and a water area of 0.006 square miles. Located at 43.06° N. Lat.; 77.30° W. Long. Elevation is 478 feet.

Population: 1,400 (1990); 1,496 (2000); 1,482 (2005); 1,472 (2010 projected); **Race:** 96.6% White, 1.2% Black, 1.3% Asian, 0.4% Hispanic of any race (2005); **Density:** 1,211.2 persons per square mile (2005); Average household size: 2.64 (2005); Median age: 37.9 (2005); Males per 100 females: 97.3 (2005); Marriage status: 21.4% never married, 65.6% now married, 5.2% widowed, 7.8% divorced (2000); Foreign born: 1.8% (2000); Ancestry (includes multiple ancestries): 28.5% German, 20.5% Irish, 16.3% English, 16.3% Italian, 9.5% Dutch (2000).
Economy: Single-family building permits issued: 2 (2005); Multi-family building permits issued: 0 (2005); Employment by occupation: 15.7% management, 22.2% professional, 14.3% services, 23.9% sales, 0.5% farming, 10.0% construction, 13.3% production (2000).
Income: Per capita income: $22,338 (2005); Median household income: $50,763 (2005); Average household income: $58,114 (2005); Percent of households with income of $100,000 or more: 12.5% (2005); Poverty rate: 7.1% (2000).
Education: Percent of population age 25 and over with: High school diploma (including GED) or higher: 88.1% (2005); Bachelor's degree or higher: 20.7% (2005); Master's degree or higher: 7.7% (2005).

School District(s)
Palmyra-Macedon Central School District (KG-12)
   2003-04 Enrollment: 2,222 . . . . (315) 597-3401
Housing: Homeownership rate: 72.2% (2005); Median home value: $115,546 (2005); Median rent: $454 per month (2000); Median age of housing: 34 years (2000).
Transportation: Commute to work: 93.3% car, 0.0% public transportation, 4.3% walk, 1.9% work from home (2000); Travel time to work: 27.8% less than 15 minutes, 40.2% 15 to 30 minutes, 25.6% 30 to 45 minutes, 2.8% 45 to 60 minutes, 3.5% 60 minutes or more (2000)

MACEDON (town). Covers a land area of 38.687 square miles and a water area of 0.170 square miles. Located at 43.07° N. Lat.; 77.30° W. Long. Elevation is 478 feet.
Population: 7,375 (1990); 8,688 (2000); 8,986 (2005); 9,269 (2010 projected); **Race:** 96.5% White, 0.9% Black, 1.0% Asian, 2.0% Hispanic of any race (2005); **Density:** 232.3 persons per square mile (2005); Average household size: 2.64 (2005); Median age: 37.3 (2005); Males per 100 females: 97.4 (2005); Marriage status: 22.7% never married, 64.8% now married, 4.2% widowed, 8.3% divorced (2000); Foreign born: 2.3% (2000); Ancestry (includes multiple ancestries): 25.0% German, 18.8% Irish, 17.1% English, 14.6% Italian, 12.5% Dutch (2000).
Economy: Manufacturing of food flavorings, bases, and syrups. Single-family building permits issued: 35 (2005); Multi-family building permits issued: 2 (2005); Employment by occupation: 12.5% management, 22.9% professional, 11.9% services, 25.7% sales, 0.5% farming, 9.5% construction, 17.0% production (2000).
Income: Per capita income: $23,787 (2005); Median household income: $54,912 (2005); Average household income: $62,738 (2005); Percent of households with income of $100,000 or more: 15.0% (2005); Poverty rate: 6.8% (2000).
Taxes: Total city taxes per capita: $278 (2004); City property taxes per capita: $239 (2004).
Education: Percent of population age 25 and over with: High school diploma (including GED) or higher: 88.8% (2005); Bachelor's degree or higher: 21.5% (2005); Master's degree or higher: 6.6% (2005).
Housing: Homeownership rate: 81.1% (2005); Median home value: $124,621 (2005); Median rent: $511 per month (2000); Median age of housing: 26 years (2000).
Safety: Violent crime rate: 1.1 per 10,000 population; Property crime rate: 87.4 per 10,000 population (2004).
Transportation: Commute to work: 95.7% car, 0.2% public transportation, 1.1% walk, 2.9% work from home (2000); Travel time to work: 21.8% less than 15 minutes, 38.1% 15 to 30 minutes, 29.6% 30 to 45 minutes, 6.7% 45 to 60 minutes, 3.7% 60 minutes or more (2000)

MARION (town). Covers a land area of 29.201 square miles and a water area of 0.067 square miles. Located at 43.15° N. Lat.; 77.18° W. Long. Elevation is 463 feet.
Population: 4,901 (1990); 4,974 (2000); 4,877 (2005); 4,775 (2010 projected); **Race:** 98.0% White, 0.7% Black, 0.2% Asian, 2.0% Hispanic of any race (2005); **Density:** 167.0 persons per square mile (2005); Average household size: 2.79 (2005); Median age: 37.7 (2005); Males per 100 females: 93.0 (2005); Marriage status: 22.1% never married, 62.8% now married, 5.5% widowed, 9.6% divorced (2000); Foreign born: 1.7% (2000); Ancestry (includes multiple ancestries): 23.5% German, 21.3% Dutch, 17.5% English, 13.6% Irish, 8.6% United States or American (2000).
Economy: In fruit-growing region. Single-family building permits issued: 10 (2005); Multi-family building permits issued: 0 (2005); Employment by occupation: 8.1% management, 18.6% professional, 14.3% services, 22.1% sales, 0.9% farming, 12.3% construction, 23.7% production (2000).
Income: Per capita income: $20,866 (2005); Median household income: $52,433 (2005); Average household income: $58,025 (2005); Percent of households with income of $100,000 or more: 11.5% (2005); Poverty rate: 5.4% (2000).
Taxes: Total city taxes per capita: $253 (2004); City property taxes per capita: $225 (2004).
Education: Percent of population age 25 and over with: High school diploma (including GED) or higher: 86.7% (2005); Bachelor's degree or higher: 14.3% (2005); Master's degree or higher: 6.6% (2005).

School District(s)
Marion Central School District (KG-12)
   2003-04 Enrollment: 1,111 . . . . (315) 926-2300
Housing: Homeownership rate: 84.9% (2005); Median home value: $113,779 (2005); Median rent: $434 per month (2000); Median age of housing: 37 years (2000).
Transportation: Commute to work: 94.0% car, 1.0% public transportation, 1.4% walk, 3.6% work from home (2000); Travel time to work: 23.8% less than 15 minutes, 32.7% 15 to 30 minutes, 28.7% 30 to 45 minutes, 9.2% 45 to 60 minutes, 5.6% 60 minutes or more (2000)

NEWARK (village). Covers a land area of 5.383 square miles and a water area of 0.006 square miles. Located at 43.04° N. Lat.; 77.09° W. Long. Elevation is 457 feet.
History: Incorporated 1839.
Population: 9,979 (1990); 9,682 (2000); 9,422 (2005); 9,154 (2010 projected); **Race:** 87.8% White, 5.8% Black, 0.5% Asian, 9.0% Hispanic of any race (2005); **Density:** 1,750.5 persons per square mile (2005); Average household size: 2.49 (2005); Median age: 39.9 (2005); Males per 100 females: 87.8 (2005); Marriage status: 25.2% never married, 53.4% now married, 10.4% widowed, 11.0% divorced (2000); Foreign born: 3.8% (2000); Ancestry (includes multiple ancestries): 18.4% German, 17.2% English, 15.6% Dutch, 15.1% Italian, 14.2% Other groups (2000).
Economy: In agricultural area. Manufacturing: metal products, furniture. Single-family building permits issued: 2 (2005); Multi-family building permits issued: 0 (2005); Employment by occupation: 7.6% management, 19.7% professional, 15.7% services, 23.9% sales, 0.0% farming, 7.4% construction, 25.7% production (2000).
Income: Per capita income: $19,971 (2005); Median household income: $35,656 (2005); Average household income: $47,663 (2005); Percent of households with income of $100,000 or more: 6.8% (2005); Poverty rate: 17.4% (2000).
Education: Percent of population age 25 and over with: High school diploma (including GED) or higher: 75.8% (2005); Bachelor's degree or higher: 15.3% (2005); Master's degree or higher: 7.4% (2005).

School District(s)
Boces Ontar-Senec-Yates-Cayuga-Wayne (UG-UG)
   2003-04 Enrollment: 584 . . . . (315) 322-7284
Newark Central School District (PK-12)
   2003-04 Enrollment: 2,688 . . . . (315) 332-3217

Two-year College(s)
Wayne Finger Lakes BOCES-School of Practical Nursing (Public)
   Fall 2004 Enrollment: 129 . . . . (315) 332-7400
Housing: Homeownership rate: 55.6% (2005); Median home value: $87,527 (2005); Median rent: $431 per month (2000); Median age of housing: 55 years (2000).
Hospitals: ViaHealth of Wayne (305 beds)
Safety: Violent crime rate: 28.3 per 10,000 population; Property crime rate: 380.1 per 10,000 population (2004).
Newspapers: Courier-Gazette (General - Circulation 3,500); Second Section (General - Circulation 31,800).
Transportation: Commute to work: 90.2% car, 0.6% public transportation, 5.9% walk, 0.9% work from home (2000); Travel time to work: 54.8% less than 15 minutes, 21.4% 15 to 30 minutes, 12.6% 30 to 45 minutes, 7.6% 45 to 60 minutes, 3.7% 60 minutes or more (2000)
Additional Information Contacts
Newark Chamber of Commerce . . . . (315) 331-2705

NORTH ROSE (unincorporated postal area, zip code 14516). Covers a land area of 30.398 square miles and a water area of 0.006 square miles. Located at 43.19° N. Lat.; 76.91° W. Long. Elevation is 388 feet.
Population: 0 (2000); Race: 93.9% White, 1.4% Black, 0.1% Asian, 2.5% Hispanic of any race (2000); Density: 0.0 persons per square mile (2000); Age: 24.6% under 18, 14.4% over 64 (2000); Marriage status: 23.6% never married, 62.1% now married, 6.1% widowed, 8.2% divorced (2000); Foreign born: 2.1% (2000); Ancestry (includes multiple ancestries): 23.9% German, 18.4% English, 16.7% Irish, 15.6% Dutch, 11.5% Italian (2000).
Economy: Employment by occupation: 12.3% management, 20.8% professional, 12.2% services, 18.2% sales, 1.4% farming, 10.8% construction, 24.2% production (2000).
Income: Per capita income: $18,938 (2000); Median household income: $38,672 (2000); Poverty rate: 4.7% (2000).
Education: Percent of population age 25 and over with: High school diploma (including GED) or higher: 82.3% (2000); Bachelor's degree or higher: 16.2% (2000).
School District(s)
North Rose-Wolcott Central School District (KG-12)
    2003-04 Enrollment: 1,642 . . . . (315) 594-3141
Housing: Homeownership rate: 79.8% (2000); Median home value: $70,400 (2000); Median rent: $350 per month (2000); Median age of housing: 60+ years (2000).
Transportation: Commute to work: 94.0% car, 0.0% public transportation, 2.5% walk, 3.4% work from home (2000); Travel time to work: 29.0% less than 15 minutes, 23.3% 15 to 30 minutes, 25.7% 30 to 45 minutes, 13.5% 45 to 60 minutes, 8.5% 60 minutes or more (2000)

ONTARIO (town). Covers a land area of 32.217 square miles and a water area of 0.118 square miles. Located at 43.24° N. Lat.; 77.29° W. Long.
Population: 8,560 (1990); 9,778 (2000); 10,149 (2005); 10,499 (2010 projected); Race: 96.1% White, 1.2% Black, 0.9% Asian, 1.7% Hispanic of any race (2005); Density: 315.0 persons per square mile (2005); Average household size: 2.67 (2005); Median age: 38.6 (2005); Males per 100 females: 100.5 (2005); Marriage status: 22.6% never married, 59.8% now married, 6.0% widowed, 11.6% divorced (2000); Foreign born: 1.9% (2000); Ancestry (includes multiple ancestries): 28.8% German, 18.2% English, 16.6% Italian, 15.8% Irish, 9.7% Dutch (2000).
Economy: In agricultural area. Single-family building permits issued: 50 (2005); Multi-family building permits issued: 0 (2005); Employment by occupation: 12.4% management, 22.0% professional, 11.7% services, 26.3% sales, 0.1% farming, 10.5% construction, 17.0% production (2000).
Income: Per capita income: $25,671 (2005); Median household income: $55,277 (2005); Average household income: $68,092 (2005); Percent of households with income of $100,000 or more: 19.8% (2005); Poverty rate: 5.5% (2000).
Taxes: Total city taxes per capita: $302 (2004); City property taxes per capita: $237 (2004).
Education: Percent of population age 25 and over with: High school diploma (including GED) or higher: 87.4% (2005); Bachelor's degree or higher: 20.9% (2005); Master's degree or higher: 7.1% (2005).
Housing: Homeownership rate: 83.0% (2005); Median home value: $131,591 (2005); Median rent: $441 per month (2000); Median age of housing: 27 years (2000).
Transportation: Commute to work: 95.3% car, 0.5% public transportation, 1.4% walk, 2.7% work from home (2000); Travel time to work: 31.5% less than 15 minutes, 34.5% 15 to 30 minutes, 25.5% 30 to 45 minutes, 5.6% 45 to 60 minutes, 2.9% 60 minutes or more (2000)
Additional Information Contacts
Ontario Chamber of Commerce. . . . . (315) 524-5886
  http://www.ontariocountydev.org/

PALMYRA (village). Covers a land area of 1.330 square miles and a water area of 0 square miles. Located at 43.06° N. Lat.; 77.23° W. Long.
Population: 3,621 (1990); 3,490 (2000); 3,430 (2005); 3,376 (2010 projected); Race: 97.2% White, 0.5% Black, 0.4% Asian, 0.8% Hispanic of any race (2005); Density: 2,578.3 persons per square mile (2005); Average household size: 2.31 (2005); Median age: 38.6 (2005); Males per 100 females: 95.3 (2005); Marriage status: 27.4% never married, 52.7% now married, 8.2% widowed, 11.6% divorced (2000); Foreign born: 2.4% (2000); Ancestry (includes multiple ancestries): 30.3% German, 22.6% Irish, 16.1% English, 11.6% Italian, 10.5% Dutch (2000).
Economy: Single-family building permits issued: 7 (2005); Multi-family building permits issued: 40 (2005); Employment by occupation: 8.7% management, 16.1% professional, 16.1% services, 30.0% sales, 0.3% farming, 9.4% construction, 19.4% production (2000).
Income: Per capita income: $21,202 (2005); Median household income: $41,569 (2005); Average household income: $48,930 (2005); Percent of households with income of $100,000 or more: 9.0% (2005); Poverty rate: 6.8% (2000).
Education: Percent of population age 25 and over with: High school diploma (including GED) or higher: 87.2% (2005); Bachelor's degree or higher: 19.6% (2005); Master's degree or higher: 6.8% (2005).
School District(s)
Palmyra-Macedon Central School District (KG-12)
    2003-04 Enrollment: 2,222 . . . . (315) 597-3401
Housing: Homeownership rate: 55.6% (2005); Median home value: $96,419 (2005); Median rent: $436 per month (2000); Median age of housing: 60+ years (2000).
Safety: Violent crime rate: 2.9 per 10,000 population; Property crime rate: 391.6 per 10,000 population (2004).
Newspapers: Courier Journal (General - Circulation 2,600)
Transportation: Commute to work: 93.2% car, 0.9% public transportation, 4.3% walk, 1.2% work from home (2000); Travel time to work: 28.8% less than 15 minutes, 32.0% 15 to 30 minutes, 24.6% 30 to 45 minutes, 10.4% 45 to 60 minutes, 4.3% 60 minutes or more (2000)
Additional Information Contacts
Village of Palmyra . . . . (315) 597-4949
  http://www.palmyrany.com/

PALMYRA (town). Covers a land area of 33.479 square miles and a water area of 0.209 square miles. Located at 43.06° N. Lat.; 77.20° W. Long.
History: Joseph Smith, founder and first president of the Mormon Church, lived and published *The Book of Mormon* here. Hill Cumorah Center pageant held each August atop the glacial drumlin where Smith buried his tablets four miles south of villlage.
Population: 7,690 (1990); 7,672 (2000); 7,781 (2005); 7,878 (2010 projected); Race: 97.1% White, 0.4% Black, 0.7% Asian, 0.9% Hispanic of any race (2005); Density: 232.4 persons per square mile (2005); Average household size: 2.53 (2005); Median age: 39.3 (2005); Males per 100 females: 97.3 (2005); Marriage status: 24.4% never married, 59.9% now married, 5.9% widowed, 9.8% divorced (2000); Foreign born: 2.0% (2000); Ancestry (includes multiple ancestries): 27.2% German, 18.5% Irish, 15.2% Dutch, 14.5% English, 10.4% Italian (2000).
Economy: Manufacturing includes seals, gaskets and packings, machine parts, paper box manufacturing and milling. In fruit-growing area. Agriculture includes dairy products, potatoes and fruit. Single-family building permits issued: 7 (2005); Multi-family building permits issued: 40 (2005); Employment by occupation: 9.5% management, 18.4% professional, 14.4% services, 26.1% sales, 0.4% farming, 12.2% construction, 19.1% production (2000).
Income: Per capita income: $22,774 (2005); Median household income: $50,809 (2005); Average household income: $57,718 (2005); Percent of households with income of $100,000 or more: 12.5% (2005); Poverty rate: 6.4% (2000).
Education: Percent of population age 25 and over with: High school diploma (including GED) or higher: 84.6% (2005); Bachelor's degree or higher: 16.4% (2005); Master's degree or higher: 6.3% (2005).
Housing: Homeownership rate: 72.0% (2005); Median home value: $101,641 (2005); Median rent: $432 per month (2000); Median age of housing: 50 years (2000).
Transportation: Commute to work: 94.5% car, 0.4% public transportation, 2.6% walk, 2.0% work from home (2000); Travel time to work: 27.4% less than 15 minutes, 36.3% 15 to 30 minutes, 21.9% 30 to 45 minutes, 9.6% 45 to 60 minutes, 4.8% 60 minutes or more (2000)
Additional Information Contacts
Town of Palmyra . . . . (315) 597-5521
  http://www.palmyrany.com/

RED CREEK (village). Covers a land area of 0.916 square miles and a water area of 0.023 square miles. Located at 43.24° N. Lat.; 76.72° W. Long.
Population: 566 (1990); 521 (2000); 538 (2005); 527 (2010 projected); Race: 92.6% White, 1.5% Black, 0.6% Asian, 3.7% Hispanic of any race (2005); Density: 587.2 persons per square mile (2005); Average household size: 2.43 (2005); Median age: 35.6 (2005); Males per 100 females: 95.6

(2005); Marriage status: 17.8% never married, 62.9% now married, 5.1% widowed, 14.2% divorced (2000); Foreign born: 1.1% (2000); Ancestry (includes multiple ancestries): 21.8% English, 19.5% German, 14.4% Irish, 10.0% Dutch, 9.3% Other groups (2000).
Economy: Manufacturing: wood flooring, clocks, tanks. Agriculture: fruit. Single-family building permits issued: 0 (2005); Multi-family building permits issued: 0 (2005); Employment by occupation: 6.7% management, 18.8% professional, 14.1% services, 23.5% sales, 0.4% farming, 14.1% construction, 22.4% production (2000).
Income: Per capita income: $18,584 (2005); Median household income: $36,750 (2005); Average household income: $45,034 (2005); Percent of households with income of $100,000 or more: 6.8% (2005); Poverty rate: 18.4% (2000).
Education: Percent of population age 25 and over with: High school diploma (including GED) or higher: 86.8% (2005); Bachelor's degree or higher: 18.9% (2005); Master's degree or higher: 7.8% (2005).

School District(s)
Red Creek Central School District (PK-12)
   2003-04 Enrollment: 1,157 . . . . (315) 754-2010

Housing: Homeownership rate: 73.3% (2005); Median home value: $76,667 (2005); Median rent: $350 per month (2000); Median age of housing: 60+ years (2000).
Newspapers: Post-Herald (General - Circulation 2,400)
Transportation: Commute to work: 88.6% car, 0.0% public transportation, 4.7% walk, 3.9% work from home (2000); Travel time to work: 42.2% less than 15 minutes, 13.1% 15 to 30 minutes, 11.1% 30 to 45 minutes, 19.3% 45 to 60 minutes, 14.3% 60 minutes or more (2000)

ROSE (town). Covers a land area of 33.893 square miles and a water area of 0.006 square miles. Located at 43.16° N. Lat.; 76.88° W. Long. Elevation is 418 feet.
Population: 2,424 (1990); 2,442 (2000); 2,451 (2005); 2,433 (2010 projected); Race: 97.0% White, 0.5% Black, 0.0% Asian, 2.0% Hispanic of any race (2005); Density: 72.3 persons per square mile (2005); Average household size: 2.69 (2005); Median age: 38.7 (2005); Males per 100 females: 92.7 (2005); Marriage status: 23.0% never married, 59.3% now married, 6.5% widowed, 11.1% divorced (2000); Foreign born: 1.6% (2000); Ancestry (includes multiple ancestries): 24.8% German, 18.0% English, 17.9% Irish, 13.3% Dutch, 9.5% United States or American (2000).
Economy: Single-family building permits issued: 6 (2005); Multi-family building permits issued: 0 (2005); Employment by occupation: 8.9% management, 16.0% professional, 12.6% services, 17.6% sales, 2.6% farming, 12.8% construction, 29.6% production (2000).
Income: Per capita income: $19,147 (2005); Median household income: $45,714 (2005); Average household income: $51,354 (2005); Percent of households with income of $100,000 or more: 7.6% (2005); Poverty rate: 5.7% (2000).
Education: Percent of population age 25 and over with: High school diploma (including GED) or higher: 75.4% (2005); Bachelor's degree or higher: 10.0% (2005); Master's degree or higher: 5.0% (2005).
Housing: Homeownership rate: 85.2% (2005); Median home value: $79,389 (2005); Median rent: $365 per month (2000); Median age of housing: 60+ years (2000).
Transportation: Commute to work: 94.0% car, 0.0% public transportation, 1.5% walk, 4.3% work from home (2000); Travel time to work: 24.7% less than 15 minutes, 29.5% 15 to 30 minutes, 25.4% 30 to 45 minutes, 12.1% 45 to 60 minutes, 8.3% 60 minutes or more (2000)

SAVANNAH (town). Covers a land area of 35.982 square miles and a water area of 0.193 square miles. Located at 43.07° N. Lat.; 76.76° W. Long. Elevation is 426 feet.
Population: 1,768 (1990); 1,838 (2000); 1,833 (2005); 1,841 (2010 projected); Race: 95.3% White, 2.1% Black, 0.3% Asian, 1.6% Hispanic of any race (2005); Density: 50.9 persons per square mile (2005); Average household size: 2.72 (2005); Median age: 36.9 (2005); Males per 100 females: 94.2 (2005); Marriage status: 25.9% never married, 57.8% now married, 8.6% widowed, 7.7% divorced (2000); Foreign born: 0.2% (2000); Ancestry (includes multiple ancestries): 24.1% German, 18.0% English, 12.9% Dutch, 11.8% Italian, 11.4% Other groups (2000).
Economy: Potato growing, storage, and shipping center. Single-family building permits issued: 3 (2005); Multi-family building permits issued: 0 (2005); Employment by occupation: 9.5% management, 13.0% professional, 13.5% services, 20.8% sales, 3.0% farming, 10.5% construction, 29.8% production (2000).

Income: Per capita income: $17,398 (2005); Median household income: $41,611 (2005); Average household income: $46,712 (2005); Percent of households with income of $100,000 or more: 7.0% (2005); Poverty rate: 17.1% (2000).
Education: Percent of population age 25 and over with: High school diploma (including GED) or higher: 72.9% (2005); Bachelor's degree or higher: 7.7% (2005); Master's degree or higher: 3.0% (2005).

School District(s)
Clyde-Savannah Central School District (PK-12)
   2003-04 Enrollment: 1,090 . . . . (315) 923-7747

Housing: Homeownership rate: 79.9% (2005); Median home value: $67,207 (2005); Median rent: $341 per month (2000); Median age of housing: 40 years (2000).
Transportation: Commute to work: 91.1% car, 0.3% public transportation, 3.6% walk, 3.7% work from home (2000); Travel time to work: 26.0% less than 15 minutes, 29.8% 15 to 30 minutes, 23.4% 30 to 45 minutes, 9.3% 45 to 60 minutes, 11.5% 60 minutes or more (2000)

SODUS (village). Covers a land area of 0.926 square miles and a water area of 0 square miles. Located at 43.23° N. Lat.; 77.06° W. Long. Elevation is 432 feet.
Population: 1,904 (1990); 1,735 (2000); 1,692 (2005); 1,670 (2010 projected); Race: 78.0% White, 16.3% Black, 0.9% Asian, 5.5% Hispanic of any race (2005); Density: 1,827.2 persons per square mile (2005); Average household size: 2.47 (2005); Median age: 35.6 (2005); Males per 100 females: 81.5 (2005); Marriage status: 25.6% never married, 54.4% now married, 8.3% widowed, 11.7% divorced (2000); Foreign born: 2.2% (2000); Ancestry (includes multiple ancestries): 19.6% Other groups, 19.1% Dutch, 16.9% English, 13.8% German, 10.7% Irish (2000).
Economy: Single-family building permits issued: 1 (2005); Multi-family building permits issued: 0 (2005); Employment by occupation: 6.4% management, 18.1% professional, 19.2% services, 19.8% sales, 1.6% farming, 9.5% construction, 25.4% production (2000).
Income: Per capita income: $17,546 (2005); Median household income: $36,431 (2005); Average household income: $43,321 (2005); Percent of households with income of $100,000 or more: 5.5% (2005); Poverty rate: 15.9% (2000).
Education: Percent of population age 25 and over with: High school diploma (including GED) or higher: 79.9% (2005); Bachelor's degree or higher: 11.3% (2005); Master's degree or higher: 4.8% (2005).

School District(s)
Sodus Central School District (PK-12)
   2003-04 Enrollment: 1,437 . . . . (315) 483-5201

Housing: Homeownership rate: 57.7% (2005); Median home value: $74,929 (2005); Median rent: $383 per month (2000); Median age of housing: 60+ years (2000).
Safety: Violent crime rate: 0.0 per 10,000 population; Property crime rate: 290.1 per 10,000 population (2004).
Transportation: Commute to work: 90.8% car, 1.7% public transportation, 5.7% walk, 1.5% work from home (2000); Travel time to work: 42.0% less than 15 minutes, 27.3% 15 to 30 minutes, 16.2% 30 to 45 minutes, 10.5% 45 to 60 minutes, 4.0% 60 minutes or more (2000)

SODUS (town). Covers a land area of 67.432 square miles and a water area of 1.933 square miles. Located at 43.22° N. Lat.; 77.03° W. Long. Elevation is 432 feet.
History: The raising of silkworms was attempted in Sodus in the 1830s. The attempt failed because mulberry trees could not withstand the severe winters. The lotuses of nearby Sodus Bay are famous. Incorporated in 1918.
Population: 8,877 (1990); 8,949 (2000); 8,898 (2005); 8,836 (2010 projected); Race: 87.3% White, 8.4% Black, 0.7% Asian, 3.6% Hispanic of any race (2005); Density: 132.0 persons per square mile (2005); Average household size: 2.58 (2005); Median age: 40.1 (2005); Males per 100 females: 95.8 (2005); Marriage status: 21.9% never married, 61.2% now married, 6.6% widowed, 10.3% divorced (2000); Foreign born: 2.9% (2000); Ancestry (includes multiple ancestries): 19.3% Dutch, 18.8% German, 14.8% English, 14.3% Other groups, 12.2% Irish (2000).
Economy: Manufacturing of electronic equipment, machinery, foods. Agriculture: fruit. Marinas and summer homes. Single-family building permits issued: 11 (2005); Multi-family building permits issued: 0 (2005); Employment by occupation: 10.1% management, 16.7% professional, 14.1% services, 19.4% sales, 2.2% farming, 10.9% construction, 26.6% production (2000).

Income: Per capita income: $20,814 (2005); Median household income: $43,590 (2005); Average household income: $53,105 (2005); Percent of households with income of $100,000 or more: 10.9% (2005); Poverty rate: 12.2% (2000).
Education: Percent of population age 25 and over with: High school diploma (including GED) or higher: 79.8% (2005); Bachelor's degree or higher: 13.8% (2005); Master's degree or higher: 4.6% (2005).
Housing: Homeownership rate: 78.8% (2005); Median home value: $88,253 (2005); Median rent: $376 per month (2000); Median age of housing: 46 years (2000).
Transportation: Commute to work: 93.5% car, 0.3% public transportation, 2.2% walk, 3.8% work from home (2000); Travel time to work: 30.2% less than 15 minutes, 27.3% 15 to 30 minutes, 23.2% 30 to 45 minutes, 14.9% 45 to 60 minutes, 4.4% 60 minutes or more (2000)

SODUS POINT (village).
Covers a land area of 1.490 square miles and a water area of 0.005 square miles. Located at 43.26° N. Lat.; 76.98° W. Long.
History: Fired upon by British in War of 1812.
Population: 1,190 (1990); 1,160 (2000); 1,071 (2005); 1,010 (2010 projected); Race: 95.9% White, 1.4% Black, 0.1% Asian, 2.4% Hispanic of any race (2005); Density: 718.7 persons per square mile (2005); Average household size: 2.32 (2005); Median age: 42.9 (2005); Males per 100 females: 106.4 (2005); Marriage status: 17.3% never married, 58.4% now married, 9.3% widowed, 14.9% divorced (2000); Foreign born: 2.0% (2000); Ancestry (includes multiple ancestries): 24.7% English, 18.5% German, 16.7% Irish, 16.3% Dutch, 9.4% Italian (2000).
Economy: Resort village. Port of entry. Single-family building permits issued: 3 (2005); Multi-family building permits issued: 0 (2005); Employment by occupation: 8.8% management, 25.4% professional, 17.0% services, 22.0% sales, 0.6% farming, 9.9% construction, 16.3% production (2000).
Income: Per capita income: $25,537 (2005); Median household income: $44,500 (2005); Average household income: $59,199 (2005); Percent of households with income of $100,000 or more: 11.9% (2005); Poverty rate: 13.8% (2000).
Education: Percent of population age 25 and over with: High school diploma (including GED) or higher: 85.0% (2005); Bachelor's degree or higher: 19.1% (2005); Master's degree or higher: 7.0% (2005).
Housing: Homeownership rate: 75.8% (2005); Median home value: $92,615 (2005); Median rent: $462 per month (2000); Median age of housing: 54 years (2000).
Transportation: Commute to work: 92.5% car, 0.0% public transportation, 1.8% walk, 5.3% work from home (2000); Travel time to work: 27.6% less than 15 minutes, 29.9% 15 to 30 minutes, 24.4% 30 to 45 minutes, 14.0% 45 to 60 minutes, 4.2% 60 minutes or more (2000)
Additional Information Contacts
Village of Sodus Point . . . . (315) 483-9881
  http://www.soduspoint.info/

WALWORTH (town).
Covers a land area of 33.825 square miles and a water area of 0.041 square miles. Located at 43.15° N. Lat.; 77.32° W. Long. Elevation is 541 feet.
Population: 6,945 (1990); 8,402 (2000); 8,642 (2005); 8,870 (2010 projected); Race: 96.0% White, 0.9% Black, 1.5% Asian, 2.1% Hispanic of any race (2005); Density: 255.5 persons per square mile (2005); Average household size: 2.91 (2005); Median age: 36.1 (2005); Males per 100 females: 99.5 (2005); Marriage status: 20.6% never married, 69.9% now married, 3.2% widowed, 6.3% divorced (2000); Foreign born: 3.1% (2000); Ancestry (includes multiple ancestries): 29.9% German, 18.3% Italian, 18.2% Irish, 15.0% English, 10.3% Dutch (2000).
Economy: Single-family building permits issued: 36 (2005); Multi-family building permits issued: 0 (2005); Employment by occupation: 14.5% management, 27.4% professional, 11.2% services, 26.8% sales, 0.3% farming, 5.9% construction, 13.9% production (2000).
Income: Per capita income: $26,209 (2005); Median household income: $71,397 (2005); Average household income: $76,080 (2005); Percent of households with income of $100,000 or more: 23.5% (2005); Poverty rate: 2.2% (2000).
Taxes: Total city taxes per capita: $295 (2004); City property taxes per capita: $240 (2004).
Education: Percent of population age 25 and over with: High school diploma (including GED) or higher: 92.6% (2005); Bachelor's degree or higher: 31.8% (2005); Master's degree or higher: 9.8% (2005).

School District(s)
Gananda Central School District (KG-12)
  2003-04 Enrollment: 1,224 . . . . (315) 986-3521
Housing: Homeownership rate: 91.9% (2005); Median home value: $141,081 (2005); Median rent: $515 per month (2000); Median age of housing: 21 years (2000).
Transportation: Commute to work: 96.1% car, 0.2% public transportation, 0.6% walk, 2.7% work from home (2000); Travel time to work: 14.3% less than 15 minutes, 42.8% 15 to 30 minutes, 34.6% 30 to 45 minutes, 6.5% 45 to 60 minutes, 1.9% 60 minutes or more (2000)

WILLIAMSON (town).
Aka Williamson Center. Covers a land area of 34.626 square miles and a water area of 0.025 square miles. Located at 43.24° N. Lat.; 77.19° W. Long. Elevation is 419 feet.
Population: 6,540 (1990); 6,777 (2000); 6,696 (2005); 6,617 (2010 projected); Race: 93.4% White, 3.4% Black, 0.7% Asian, 2.4% Hispanic of any race (2005); Density: 193.4 persons per square mile (2005); Average household size: 2.62 (2005); Median age: 40.1 (2005); Males per 100 females: 96.7 (2005); Marriage status: 21.6% never married, 65.6% now married, 6.3% widowed, 6.6% divorced (2000); Foreign born: 2.9% (2000); Ancestry (includes multiple ancestries): 24.8% German, 20.0% English, 18.9% Dutch, 14.9% Irish, 11.0% Italian (2000).
Economy: Some manufacturing; in fruit-growing region. Single-family building permits issued: 11 (2005); Multi-family building permits issued: 0 (2005); Employment by occupation: 13.9% management, 22.5% professional, 11.8% services, 21.1% sales, 2.5% farming, 9.2% construction, 19.1% production (2000).
Income: Per capita income: $23,684 (2005); Median household income: $55,046 (2005); Average household income: $61,377 (2005); Percent of households with income of $100,000 or more: 12.8% (2005); Poverty rate: 4.7% (2000).
Education: Percent of population age 25 and over with: High school diploma (including GED) or higher: 88.0% (2005); Bachelor's degree or higher: 18.9% (2005); Master's degree or higher: 10.2% (2005).

School District(s)
Williamson Central School District (KG-12)
  2003-04 Enrollment: 1,371 . . . . (315) 589-9661
Housing: Homeownership rate: 81.5% (2005); Median home value: $115,632 (2005); Median rent: $361 per month (2000); Median age of housing: 53 years (2000).
Newspapers: The Sun & Record (General - Circulation 3,100)
Transportation: Commute to work: 92.2% car, 0.2% public transportation, 3.6% walk, 3.4% work from home (2000); Travel time to work: 27.5% less than 15 minutes, 31.1% 15 to 30 minutes, 26.8% 30 to 45 minutes, 13.4% 45 to 60 minutes, 1.2% 60 minutes or more (2000)
Additional Information Contacts
Williamson Chamber of Commerce . . . . (315) 589-8100
  http://www.town.williamson.ny.us

WOLCOTT (village).
Covers a land area of 1.948 square miles and a water area of 0.018 square miles. Located at 43.22° N. Lat.; 76.81° W. Long. Elevation is 378 feet.
Population: 1,544 (1990); 1,712 (2000); 1,597 (2005); 1,532 (2010 projected); Race: 93.2% White, 3.3% Black, 0.1% Asian, 5.9% Hispanic of any race (2005); Density: 819.7 persons per square mile (2005); Average household size: 2.35 (2005); Median age: 37.1 (2005); Males per 100 females: 89.7 (2005); Marriage status: 26.9% never married, 50.9% now married, 9.9% widowed, 12.3% divorced (2000); Foreign born: 2.1% (2000); Ancestry (includes multiple ancestries): 16.4% German, 16.1% English, 13.8% Irish, 13.6% Dutch, 12.4% Other groups (2000).
Economy: Single-family building permits issued: 0 (2005); Multi-family building permits issued: 0 (2005); Employment by occupation: 6.7% management, 15.6% professional, 20.4% services, 17.1% sales, 3.7% farming, 9.9% construction, 26.5% production (2000).
Income: Per capita income: $17,529 (2005); Median household income: $30,808 (2005); Average household income: $41,017 (2005); Percent of households with income of $100,000 or more: 6.0% (2005); Poverty rate: 18.3% (2000).
Education: Percent of population age 25 and over with: High school diploma (including GED) or higher: 71.6% (2005); Bachelor's degree or higher: 10.6% (2005); Master's degree or higher: 3.7% (2005).

School District(s)
North Rose-Wolcott Central School District (KG-12)
  2003-04 Enrollment: 1,642 . . . . (315) 594-3141

Housing: Homeownership rate: 60.5% (2005); Median home value: $70,926 (2005); Median rent: $350 per month (2000); Median age of housing: 60+ years (2000).
Transportation: Commute to work: 90.4% car, 0.9% public transportation, 7.8% walk, 0.3% work from home (2000); Travel time to work: 46.1% less than 15 minutes, 16.1% 15 to 30 minutes, 12.9% 30 to 45 minutes, 14.2% 45 to 60 minutes, 10.7% 60 minutes or more (2000)

WOLCOTT (town). Covers a land area of 39.302 square miles and a water area of 0.859 square miles. Located at 43.25° N. Lat.; 76.77° W. Long. Elevation is 378 feet.
History: Incorporated 1873.
Population: 4,283 (1990); 4,692 (2000); 4,488 (2005); 4,298 (2010 projected); Race: 90.6% White, 5.3% Black, 0.2% Asian, 6.0% Hispanic of any race (2005); Density: 114.2 persons per square mile (2005); Average household size: 2.65 (2005); Median age: 36.7 (2005); Males per 100 females: 106.9 (2005); Marriage status: 25.4% never married, 56.0% now married, 7.5% widowed, 11.1% divorced (2000); Foreign born: 1.8% (2000); Ancestry (includes multiple ancestries): 16.3% English, 15.4% German, 12.6% Irish, 11.8% Dutch, 9.4% United States or American (2000).
Economy: Some manufacturing. Agriculture-shipping point: fruit, dairy products. Summer resort. Single-family building permits issued: 2 (2005); Multi-family building permits issued: 0 (2005); Employment by occupation: 7.0% management, 15.7% professional, 14.7% services, 19.2% sales, 3.4% farming, 10.1% construction, 29.9% production (2000).
Income: Per capita income: $17,926 (2005); Median household income: $38,211 (2005); Average household income: $45,814 (2005); Percent of households with income of $100,000 or more: 6.3% (2005); Poverty rate: 16.7% (2000).
Education: Percent of population age 25 and over with: High school diploma (including GED) or higher: 72.0% (2005); Bachelor's degree or higher: 10.9% (2005); Master's degree or higher: 3.7% (2005).
Housing: Homeownership rate: 74.0% (2005); Median home value: $77,391 (2005); Median rent: $347 per month (2000); Median age of housing: 45 years (2000).
Transportation: Commute to work: 91.0% car, 0.5% public transportation, 4.5% walk, 3.0% work from home (2000); Travel time to work: 35.4% less than 15 minutes, 19.8% 15 to 30 minutes, 15.8% 30 to 45 minutes, 16.2% 45 to 60 minutes, 12.8% 60 minutes or more (2000)

Westchester County

Located in southeastern New York; bounded on the west by the Hudson River, on the southeast by Long Island Sound, and on the east by Connecticut; drained by the Byram, Mianus, and Rippowam Rivers. Covers a land area of 432.82 square miles, a water area of 67.26 square miles, and is located in the Eastern Time Zone. The county government was organized in 1683. County seat is White Plains.

Westchester County is part of the New York-Northern New Jersey-Long Island, NY-NJ-PA Metropolitan Statistical Area. The entire metro area includes: Edison, NJ Metropolitan Division (Middlesex County, NJ; Monmouth County, NJ; Ocean County, NJ; Somerset County, NJ); Nassau-Suffolk, NY Metropolitan Division (Nassau County, NY; Suffolk County, NY); New York-White Plains-Wayne, NY-NJ Metropolitan Division (Bergen County, NJ; Hudson County, NJ; Passaic County, NJ; Bronx County, NY; Kings County, NY; New York County, NY; Putnam County, NY; Queens County, NY; Richmond County, NY; Rockland County, NY; Westchester County, NY); Newark-Union, NJ-PA Metropolitan Division (Essex County, NJ; Hunterdon County, NJ; Morris County, NJ; Sussex County, NJ; Union County, NJ; Pike County, PA)

Weather Station: Dobbs Ferry Ardsley — Elevation: 200 feet

	Jan	Feb	Mar	Apr	May	Jun	Jul	Aug	Sep	Oct	Nov	Dec
High	38	41	50	62	73	80	86	84	76	65	54	43
Low	23	24	32	40	50	59	65	64	56	46	37	28
Precip	4.3	3.5	4.6	4.5	4.9	3.8	4.4	4.3	4.7	4.2	4.6	4.2
Snow	9.7	9.2	6.1	0.9	tr	0.0	0.0	0.0	0.0	tr	0.8	4.5

High and Low temperatures in degrees Fahrenheit; Precipitation and Snow in inches

Weather Station: White Plains Westchester Co Arpt. — Elevation: 396 feet

	Jan	Feb	Mar	Apr	May	Jun	Jul	Aug	Sep	Oct	Nov	Dec
High	35	38	47	58	69	77	82	80	72	61	51	40
Low	21	23	30	40	50	58	64	63	55	44	36	27
Precip	4.5	3.1	4.8	4.4	4.5	3.7	3.6	4.0	4.8	4.2	4.3	4.1
Snow	9.4	8.4	5.4	1.0	tr	0.0	0.0	0.0	0.0	tr	0.4	4.7

High and Low temperatures in degrees Fahrenheit; Precipitation and Snow in inches

Weather Station: Yorktown Heights 1 W — Elevation: 669 feet

	Jan	Feb	Mar	Apr	May	Jun	Jul	Aug	Sep	Oct	Nov	Dec
High	34	37	46	58	69	77	82	81	73	62	51	39
Low	18	20	28	38	49	57	63	61	54	42	34	24
Precip	4.0	3.2	4.2	4.4	4.8	4.1	4.6	4.5	4.8	4.2	4.6	3.8
Snow	10.4	10.0	7.5	2.2	tr	0.0	0.0	0.0	0.0	0.3	1.5	6.1

High and Low temperatures in degrees Fahrenheit; Precipitation and Snow in inches

Population: 874,910 (1990); 923,459 (2000); 945,910 (2005); 968,857 (2010 projected); Race: 68.2% White, 14.7% Black, 5.4% Asian, 18.7% Hispanic of any race (2005); Density: 2,185.4 persons per square mile (2005); Average household size: 2.75 (2005); Median age: 38.8 (2005); Males per 100 females: 92.7 (2005).
Religion: Five largest groups: 50.9% Catholic Church, 10.2% Jewish Estimate, 1.6% Episcopal Church, 1.2% The United Methodist Church, 1.2% Presbyterian Church (U.S.A.) (2000).
Economy: Unemployment rate: 4.1% (2005); Total civilian labor force: 485,012 (2005); Leading industries: 17.3% health care and social assistance; 12.9% retail trade; 8.4% professional (2003); Farms: 129 totaling 9,917 acres (2002); Companies that employ 500 or more persons: 63 (2003); Companies that employ 100 to 499 persons: 517 (2003); Companies that employ less than 100 persons: 30,943 (2003); Black-owned businesses: 7,045 (2002); Hispanic-owned businesses: 8,356 (2002); Women-owned businesses: 31,109 (2002); Retail sales per capita: $16,604 (2006). Single-family building permits issued: 780 (2005); Multi-family building permits issued: 446 (2005).
Income: Per capita income: $40,532 (2005); Median household income: $72,672 (2005); Average household income: $110,344 (2005); Percent of households with income of $100,000 or more: 36.5% (2005); Poverty rate: 8.7% (2003); Bankruptcy rate: 3.41% (2005).
Taxes: Total county taxes per capita: $918 (2004); County property taxes per capita: $555 (2004).
Education: Percent of population age 25 and over with: High school diploma (including GED) or higher: 83.4% (2005); Bachelor's degree or higher: 40.6% (2005); Master's degree or higher: 19.6% (2005).
Housing: Homeownership rate: 60.8% (2005); Median home value: $469,398 (2005); Median rent: $782 per month (2000); Median age of housing: 46 years (2000).
Health: Birth rate: 136.7 per 10,000 population (2004); Death rate: 78.3 per 10,000 population (2004); Age-adjusted cancer mortality rate: 192.6 deaths per 100,000 population (2002); Air Quality Index: 79.7% good, 17.8% moderate, 2.2% unhealthy for sensitive individuals, 0.3% unhealthy (percent of days in 2005); Number of physicians: 70.7 per 10,000 population (2004); Hospital beds: 48.4 per 10,000 population (2003); Hospital admissions: 1,373.5 per 10,000 population (2003).
Elections: 2004 Presidential election results: 40.3% Bush, 58.1% Kerry, 1.4% Nader, 0.2% Badnarik
National and State Parks: Mohansic State Park; Saint Pauls Church National Historic Site

Additional Information Contacts

Westchester County Government	(914) 995-2000
http://www.co.westchester.ny.us/	
City of Mount Vernon	(914) 665-2300
http://www.ci.mount-vernon.ny.us/	
City of New Rochelle	(914) 654-2000
http://www.newrochelleny.com/	
City of Peekskill	(914) 737-3400
http://www.ci.peekskill.ny.us/	
City of Rye	(914) 967-7371
http://www.ryeny.gov/	
City of White Plains	(914) 422-1200
http://www.ci.white-plains.ny.us/	
City of Yonkers	(914) 377-6020
http://www.cityofyonkers.com/	
Town of Bedford	(914) 666-6530
http://www.bedfordny.info/html/home.html	
Town of Cortlandt	(914) 734-1040
http://www.townofcortlandt.com/	

Town of Eastchester	(914) 771-3300
http://www.eastchester.org/	
Town of Greenburgh	(914) 993-1540
http://www.greenburghny.com/	
Town of Harrison	(914) 670-3005
http://www.town.harrison.ny.us/	
Town of Lewisboro	(914) 763-3511
http://www.lewisborogov.com/	
Town of Mamaroneck	(914) 381-7805
http://www.townofmamaroneck.org/	
Town of Mount Pleasant	(914) 742-2300
http://www.mtpleasant.americantowns.com/	
Town of New Castle	(914) 238-4771
http://www.town.new-castle.ny.us/	
Town of North Castle	(914) 273-3321
http://www.northcastleny.com/	
Town of Ossining	(914) 762-6000
http://www.townofossining.com/	
Town of Pelham	(914) 738-1021
http://www.townofpelham.com/home/index.html	
Town of Pound Ridge	(914) 764-5549
http://www.townofpoundridge.com/	
Town of Rye	(914) 939-3075
http://www.townofryeny.com/	
Town of Somers	(914) 277-5366
http://www.somersny.com/	
Town of Yorktown	(914) 962-5722
http://www.yorktownny.org/Home/	
Village of Ardsley	(914) 693-1550
http://www.ardsleyvillage.com/	
Village of Bronxville	(914) 337-6500
http://villageofbronxville.com/	
Village of Buchanan	(914) 737-1033
http://www.villageofbuchanan.org/	
Village of Croton-on-Hudson	(914) 271-4781
http://village.croton-on-hudson.ny.us/Home/	
Village of Dobbs Ferry	(914) 693-2203
http://www.dobbsferry.com/	
Village of Elmsford	(914) 592-6555
http://www.elmsfordny.org/	
Village of Harrison	(914) 670-3030
http://www.town.harrison.ny.us/	
Village of Hastings-on-Hudson	(914) 478-3400
http://www.hastingsgov.org/	
Village of Irvington	(914) 591-7070
http://www.ci.irvington.ny.us/news.asp	
Village of Larchmont	(914) 834-6230
http://www.villageoflarchmont.org/	
Village of Mamaroneck	(914) 777-7722
http://www.village.mamaroneck.ny.us/	
Village of Ossining	(914) 762-8428
http://www.village.ossining.ny.us/	
Village of Pelham	(914) 738-1133
http://www.pelhamny.com/	
Village of Pelham Manor	(914) 738-8820
http://www.pelhammanor.org/	
Village of Pleasantville	(914) 769-1940
http://www.pleasantville.americantowns.com/servlets/WebPage	
Village of Port Chester	(914) 939-2200
http://www.portchesterny.com/	
Village of Rye Brook	(914) 939-1121
http://www.ryebrook.org/	
Village of Scarsdale	(914) 722-1100
http://www.village.scarsdale.ny.us/	
Village of Tuckahoe	(914) 961-3100
http://www.tuckahoe.com/	

Westchester County Communities

AMAWALK (unincorporated postal area, zip code 10501). Covers a land area of 1.165 square miles and a water area of 0 square miles. Located at 41.29° N. Lat.; 73.76° W. Long. Elevation is 384 feet.
Population: 0 (2000); Race: 96.9% White, 0.0% Black, 3.1% Asian, 10.2% Hispanic of any race (2000); Density: 0.0 persons per square mile (2000); Age: 29.4% under 18, 7.5% over 64 (2000); Marriage status: 30.6% never married, 62.9% now married, 2.2% widowed, 4.3% divorced (2000); Foreign born: 16.3% (2000); Ancestry (includes multiple ancestries): 37.8% Italian, 27.8% Irish, 17.5% Other groups, 12.1% German, 5.9% English (2000).
Economy: Employment by occupation: 28.3% management, 34.6% professional, 13.4% services, 21.5% sales, 0.0% farming, 2.2% construction, 0.0% production (2000).
Income: Per capita income: $41,077 (2000); Median household income: $129,692 (2000); Poverty rate: 3.1% (2000).
Education: Percent of population age 25 and over with: High school diploma (including GED) or higher: 97.2% (2000); Bachelor's degree or higher: 58.3% (2000).
Housing: Homeownership rate: 96.6% (2000); Median home value: $365,400 (2000); Median rent: $n/a per month (2000); Median age of housing: 27 years (2000).
Transportation: Commute to work: 79.0% car, 13.4% public transportation, 0.0% walk, 7.6% work from home (2000); Travel time to work: 14.5% less than 15 minutes, 13.0% 15 to 30 minutes, 15.3% 30 to 45 minutes, 31.0% 45 to 60 minutes, 26.3% 60 minutes or more (2000)

ARDSLEY (village). Covers a land area of 1.316 square miles and a water area of 0 square miles. Located at 41.01° N. Lat.; 73.84° W. Long. Elevation is 9 feet.
Population: 4,272 (1990); 4,269 (2000); 5,282 (2005); 6,193 (2010 projected); Race: 80.8% White, 1.8% Black, 15.1% Asian, 5.4% Hispanic of any race (2005); Density: 4,012.4 persons per square mile (2005); Average household size: 2.96 (2005); Median age: 42.9 (2005); Males per 100 females: 96.3 (2005); Marriage status: 18.2% never married, 72.1% now married, 5.3% widowed, 4.4% divorced (2000); Foreign born: 19.0% (2000); Ancestry (includes multiple ancestries): 25.3% Other groups, 21.2% Italian, 15.0% Irish, 8.3% German, 7.5% Polish (2000).
Economy: Manufactures earth-moving equipment, electronics, transportation equipment, medical apparatus. Several major corporations headquarters here. Single-family building permits issued: 3 (2005); Multi-family building permits issued: 0 (2005); Employment by occupation: 23.6% management, 38.1% professional, 7.3% services, 21.9% sales, 0.0% farming, 5.1% construction, 4.0% production (2000).
Income: Per capita income: $55,558 (2005); Median household income: $123,818 (2005); Average household income: $162,329 (2005); Percent of households with income of $100,000 or more: 61.3% (2005); Poverty rate: 1.3% (2000).
Education: Percent of population age 25 and over with: High school diploma (including GED) or higher: 94.7% (2005); Bachelor's degree or higher: 59.1% (2005); Master's degree or higher: 32.7% (2005).

School District(s)
Ardsley Union Free School District (KG-12)
 2003-04 Enrollment: 2,343 . . . . (914) 693-6300
Housing: Homeownership rate: 91.8% (2005); Median home value: $603,299 (2005); Median rent: $1,403 per month (2000); Median age of housing: 44 years (2000).
Safety: Violent crime rate: 6.2 per 10,000 population; Property crime rate: 120.1 per 10,000 population (2004).
Transportation: Commute to work: 78.4% car, 14.2% public transportation, 0.6% walk, 5.6% work from home (2000); Travel time to work: 18.3% less than 15 minutes, 37.0% 15 to 30 minutes, 14.6% 30 to 45 minutes, 9.0% 45 to 60 minutes, 21.0% 60 minutes or more (2000)
Additional Information Contacts
Village of Ardsley . . . . (914) 693-1550
 http://www.ardsleyvillage.com/

ARMONK (CDP). Covers a land area of 6.084 square miles and a water area of 0.035 square miles. Located at 41.12° N. Lat.; 73.70° W. Long. Elevation is 386 feet.
Population: 2,745 (1990); 3,461 (2000); 4,043 (2005); 4,587 (2010 projected); Race: 92.4% White, 0.7% Black, 5.0% Asian, 4.7% Hispanic of any race (2005); Density: 664.6 persons per square mile (2005); Average household size: 2.94 (2005); Median age: 40.0 (2005); Males per 100 females: 90.9 (2005); Marriage status: 18.7% never married, 74.2% now married, 2.6% widowed, 4.5% divorced (2000); Foreign born: 12.5% (2000); Ancestry (includes multiple ancestries): 31.8% Italian, 15.0% Irish, 12.6% Other groups, 12.1% German, 10.6% English (2000).
Economy: Manufacturing: data processing equipment, telecommunications systems, dental products. Suburban community. Former longtime headquarters of IBM Corporation. Employment by

occupation: 26.2% management, 27.1% professional, 8.4% services, 28.6% sales, 0.0% farming, 7.3% construction, 2.4% production (2000).
Income: Per capita income: $66,497 (2005); Median household income: $132,156 (2005); Average household income: $195,236 (2005); Percent of households with income of $100,000 or more: 62.2% (2005); Poverty rate: 1.3% (2000).
Education: Percent of population age 25 and over with: High school diploma (including GED) or higher: 93.0% (2005); Bachelor's degree or higher: 54.8% (2005); Master's degree or higher: 25.8% (2005).

School District(s)
Byram Hills Central School District (KG-12)
    2003-04 Enrollment: 2,707 . . . . (914) 273-4082

Housing: Homeownership rate: 89.3% (2005); Median home value: $903,727 (2005); Median rent: $1,330 per month (2000); Median age of housing: 36 years (2000).
Transportation: Commute to work: 81.0% car, 12.1% public transportation, 1.2% walk, 5.4% work from home (2000); Travel time to work: 27.2% less than 15 minutes, 36.1% 15 to 30 minutes, 11.7% 30 to 45 minutes, 4.3% 45 to 60 minutes, 20.8% 60 minutes or more (2000)

BEDFORD (town). Covers a land area of 37.242 square miles and a water area of 2.106 square miles. Located at 41.22° N. Lat.; 73.67° W. Long. Elevation is 280 feet.
History: Caramoor Art and Music Center. Maximum-security Tacoma Correctional Facility for Women is at nearby Bedford Hills village. Also known as Bedford Village.
Population: 16,906 (1990); 18,133 (2000); 18,969 (2005); 19,749 (2010 projected); Race: 86.8% White, 7.4% Black, 2.5% Asian, 8.6% Hispanic of any race (2005); Density: 509.3 persons per square mile (2005); Average household size: 3.20 (2005); Median age: 38.0 (2005); Males per 100 females: 88.7 (2005); Marriage status: 28.4% never married, 62.1% now married, 4.2% widowed, 5.2% divorced (2000); Foreign born: 12.7% (2000); Ancestry (includes multiple ancestries): 19.1% Italian, 16.7% Irish, 15.1% Other groups, 11.5% German, 11.3% English (2000).
Economy: Single-family building permits issued: 28 (2005); Multi-family building permits issued: 0 (2005); Employment by occupation: 25.6% management, 31.0% professional, 11.0% services, 24.7% sales, 0.1% farming, 4.8% construction, 2.7% production (2000).
Income: Per capita income: $54,175 (2005); Median household income: $115,901 (2005); Average household income: $171,418 (2005); Percent of households with income of $100,000 or more: 55.7% (2005); Poverty rate: 4.9% (2000).
Taxes: Total city taxes per capita: $914 (2004); City property taxes per capita: $779 (2004).
Education: Percent of population age 25 and over with: High school diploma (including GED) or higher: 84.2% (2005); Bachelor's degree or higher: 52.2% (2005); Master's degree or higher: 23.4% (2005).

School District(s)
Bedford Central School District (PK-12)
    2003-04 Enrollment: 4,268 . . . . (914) 241-6010

Housing: Homeownership rate: 74.7% (2005); Median home value: $738,326 (2005); Median rent: $944 per month (2000); Median age of housing: 41 years (2000).
Safety: Violent crime rate: 1.6 per 10,000 population; Property crime rate: 104.8 per 10,000 population (2004).
Transportation: Commute to work: 70.3% car, 18.5% public transportation, 3.2% walk, 7.9% work from home (2000); Travel time to work: 23.1% less than 15 minutes, 26.0% 15 to 30 minutes, 19.1% 30 to 45 minutes, 7.1% 45 to 60 minutes, 24.7% 60 minutes or more (2000)
Additional Information Contacts
Town of Bedford. . . . . (914) 666-6530
    http://www.bedfordny.info/html/home.html

BEDFORD (CDP). Covers a land area of 3.684 square miles and a water area of 0.008 square miles. Located at 41.19° N. Lat.; 73.64° W. Long.
Population: 1,828 (1990); 1,724 (2000); 1,713 (2005); 1,731 (2010 projected); Race: 96.0% White, 0.2% Black, 2.7% Asian, 2.6% Hispanic of any race (2005); Density: 465.0 persons per square mile (2005); Average household size: 3.02 (2005); Median age: 41.4 (2005); Males per 100 females: 99.0 (2005); Marriage status: 25.4% never married, 65.4% now married, 9.0% widowed, 4.2% divorced (2000); Foreign born: 11.5% (2000); Ancestry (includes multiple ancestries): 28.2% Italian, 19.4% English, 18.6% Irish, 10.0% German, 8.8% Other groups (2000).

Economy: Employment by occupation: 29.3% management, 33.1% professional, 9.5% services, 20.0% sales, 0.0% farming, 4.7% construction, 3.4% production (2000).
Income: Per capita income: $57,467 (2005); Median household income: $136,567 (2005); Average household income: $172,707 (2005); Percent of households with income of $100,000 or more: 67.3% (2005); Poverty rate: 2.4% (2000).
Education: Percent of population age 25 and over with: High school diploma (including GED) or higher: 92.7% (2005); Bachelor's degree or higher: 61.4% (2005); Master's degree or higher: 33.1% (2005).
Housing: Homeownership rate: 94.0% (2005); Median home value: $872,449 (2005); Median rent: $2,000+ per month (2000); Median age of housing: 42 years (2000).
Transportation: Commute to work: 71.4% car, 18.5% public transportation, 2.6% walk, 7.6% work from home (2000); Travel time to work: 18.2% less than 15 minutes, 25.1% 15 to 30 minutes, 16.1% 30 to 45 minutes, 17.7% 45 to 60 minutes, 23.0% 60 minutes or more (2000)

BEDFORD HILLS (unincorporated postal area, zip code 10507). Covers a land area of 8.749 square miles and a water area of 0.027 square miles. Located at 41.23° N. Lat.; 73.69° W. Long. Elevation is 350 feet.
Population: 0 (2000); Race: 76.9% White, 13.8% Black, 2.9% Asian, 13.9% Hispanic of any race (2000); Density: 0.0 persons per square mile (2000); Age: 20.1% under 18, 10.1% over 64 (2000); Marriage status: 38.3% never married, 52.4% now married, 4.2% widowed, 5.1% divorced (2000); Foreign born: 16.9% (2000); Ancestry (includes multiple ancestries): 21.4% Other groups, 18.9% Italian, 14.0% Irish, 10.9% German, 7.4% English (2000).
Economy: Employment by occupation: 19.7% management, 27.8% professional, 16.0% services, 26.6% sales, 0.0% farming, 5.3% construction, 4.6% production (2000).
Income: Per capita income: $36,381 (2000); Median household income: $72,568 (2000); Poverty rate: 9.2% (2000).
Education: Percent of population age 25 and over with: High school diploma (including GED) or higher: 70.9% (2000); Bachelor's degree or higher: 34.3% (2000).

School District(s)
Bedford Central School District (PK-12)
    2003-04 Enrollment: 4,268 . . . . (914) 241-6010

Housing: Homeownership rate: 58.5% (2000); Median home value: $348,400 (2000); Median rent: $936 per month (2000); Median age of housing: 38 years (2000).
Newspapers: Bedford/Pound Ridge Record Review (General - Circulation 3,500)
Transportation: Commute to work: 71.9% car, 18.7% public transportation, 5.8% walk, 3.7% work from home (2000); Travel time to work: 25.5% less than 15 minutes, 29.3% 15 to 30 minutes, 17.9% 30 to 45 minutes, 7.1% 45 to 60 minutes, 20.2% 60 minutes or more (2000)

BRIARCLIFF MANOR (village). Covers a land area of 5.925 square miles and a water area of 0.747 square miles. Located at 41.14° N. Lat.; 73.84° W. Long. Elevation is 266 feet.
History: Settled 1896, incorporated 1902.
Population: 7,070 (1990); 7,696 (2000); 8,074 (2005); 8,478 (2010 projected); Race: 89.3% White, 1.8% Black, 6.5% Asian, 3.6% Hispanic of any race (2005); Density: 1,362.7 persons per square mile (2005); Average household size: 3.18 (2005); Median age: 39.6 (2005); Males per 100 females: 87.9 (2005); Marriage status: 20.9% never married, 67.1% now married, 7.3% widowed, 4.8% divorced (2000); Foreign born: 12.2% (2000); Ancestry (includes multiple ancestries): 17.4% Italian, 15.0% Irish, 12.3% Other groups, 9.4% German, 8.6% Russian (2000).
Economy: Single-family building permits issued: 4 (2005); Multi-family building permits issued: 0 (2005); Employment by occupation: 30.4% management, 37.6% professional, 5.5% services, 21.7% sales, 0.2% farming, 2.3% construction, 2.2% production (2000).
Income: Per capita income: $61,587 (2005); Median household income: $143,891 (2005); Average household income: $189,426 (2005); Percent of households with income of $100,000 or more: 65.3% (2005); Poverty rate: 2.5% (2000).
Education: Percent of population age 25 and over with: High school diploma (including GED) or higher: 94.5% (2005); Bachelor's degree or higher: 71.7% (2005); Master's degree or higher: 36.9% (2005).

School District(s)
Briarcliff Manor Union Free School District (KG-12)
    2003-04 Enrollment: 1,717 . . . . (914) 941-8880

Housing: Homeownership rate: 87.1% (2005); Median home value: $706,347 (2005); Median rent: $1,057 per month (2000); Median age of housing: 39 years (2000).
Hospitals: Stony Lodge Hospital (61 beds)
Safety: Violent crime rate: 5.0 per 10,000 population; Property crime rate: 80.8 per 10,000 population (2004).
Transportation: Commute to work: 68.3% car, 21.5% public transportation, 3.2% walk, 6.5% work from home (2000); Travel time to work: 19.7% less than 15 minutes, 25.6% 15 to 30 minutes, 17.3% 30 to 45 minutes, 8.2% 45 to 60 minutes, 29.2% 60 minutes or more (2000)

BRONXVILLE (village).
Covers a land area of 0.952 square miles and a water area of 0 square miles. Located at 40.94° N. Lat.; 73.82° W. Long. Elevation is 109 feet.
History: Seat of Sarah Lawrence College. Settled 1664, incorporated 1898.
Population: 6,028 (1990); 6,543 (2000); 6,491 (2005); 6,484 (2010 projected); Race: 91.0% White, 1.4% Black, 5.1% Asian, 3.4% Hispanic of any race (2005); Density: 6,814.7 persons per square mile (2005); Average household size: 2.88 (2005); Median age: 38.7 (2005); Males per 100 females: 87.3 (2005); Marriage status: 26.4% never married, 63.8% now married, 4.8% widowed, 5.0% divorced (2000); Foreign born: 15.0% (2000); Ancestry (includes multiple ancestries): 26.6% Irish, 14.5% Italian, 14.0% German, 13.3% English, 12.5% Other groups (2000).
Economy: Single-family building permits issued: 0 (2005); Multi-family building permits issued: 0 (2005); Employment by occupation: 35.1% management, 30.4% professional, 7.0% services, 24.5% sales, 0.0% farming, 2.0% construction, 1.0% production (2000).
Income: Per capita income: $80,966 (2005); Median household income: $162,278 (2005); Average household income: $232,602 (2005); Percent of households with income of $100,000 or more: 69.4% (2005); Poverty rate: 2.7% (2000).
Education: Percent of population age 25 and over with: High school diploma (including GED) or higher: 96.6% (2005); Bachelor's degree or higher: 73.6% (2005); Master's degree or higher: 42.8% (2005).
School District(s)
Bronxville Union Free School District (KG-12)
    2003-04 Enrollment: 1,482 . . . . (914) 337-5600
Four-year College(s)
Concordia College
    Fall 2004 Enrollment: 655 . . . . (914) 337-9300
    2005-06 Tuition: In-state $19,800; Out-of-state $19,800
Sarah Lawrence College
    Fall 2004 Enrollment: 1,574. . . . . (914) 337-0700
    2005-06 Tuition: In-state $34,042; Out-of-state $34,042
Housing: Homeownership rate: 76.6% (2005); Median home value: $986,905 (2005); Median rent: $1,818 per month (2000); Median age of housing: 60+ years (2000).
Hospitals: Lawrence Hospital (280 beds)
Safety: Violent crime rate: 4.6 per 10,000 population; Property crime rate: 73.5 per 10,000 population (2004).
Transportation: Commute to work: 36.0% car, 46.2% public transportation, 8.6% walk, 8.0% work from home (2000); Travel time to work: 19.4% less than 15 minutes, 12.5% 15 to 30 minutes, 23.8% 30 to 45 minutes, 22.3% 45 to 60 minutes, 22.0% 60 minutes or more (2000)
Additional Information Contacts
Bronxville Chamber of Commerce. (914) 337-6040
    http://www.bronxvillechamber.com
Village of Bronxville . . . . (914) 337-6500
    http://villageofbronxville.com/

BUCHANAN (village).
Covers a land area of 1.386 square miles and a water area of 0.295 square miles. Located at 41.26° N. Lat.; 73.94° W. Long. Elevation is 40 feet.
History: Incorporated 1928.
Population: 1,970 (1990); 2,189 (2000); 2,231 (2005); 2,280 (2010 projected); Race: 94.8% White, 0.9% Black, 1.6% Asian, 4.7% Hispanic of any race (2005); Density: 1,609.6 persons per square mile (2005); Average household size: 2.70 (2005); Median age: 39.0 (2005); Males per 100 females: 100.4 (2005); Marriage status: 22.9% never married, 62.3% now married, 7.7% widowed, 7.1% divorced (2000); Foreign born: 7.4% (2000); Ancestry (includes multiple ancestries): 32.2% Italian, 29.5% Irish, 12.7% German, 8.2% Other groups, 5.8% United States or American (2000).
Economy: Manufacturing of textiles and apparel. Indian Point nuclear plants are here. Single-family building permits issued: 1 (2005); Multi-family building permits issued: 2 (2005); Employment by occupation: 11.0% management, 20.6% professional, 16.4% services, 28.3% sales, 0.3% farming, 12.6% construction, 10.9% production (2000).
Income: Per capita income: $33,674 (2005); Median household income: $71,438 (2005); Average household income: $90,264 (2005); Percent of households with income of $100,000 or more: 31.5% (2005); Poverty rate: 3.9% (2000).
Education: Percent of population age 25 and over with: High school diploma (including GED) or higher: 87.8% (2005); Bachelor's degree or higher: 25.3% (2005); Master's degree or higher: 10.0% (2005).
School District(s)
Hendrick Hudson Central School District (KG-12)
    2003-04 Enrollment: 2,884 . . . . (914) 736-5200
Housing: Homeownership rate: 71.9% (2005); Median home value: $351,059 (2005); Median rent: $777 per month (2000); Median age of housing: 50 years (2000).
Safety: Violent crime rate: 4.5 per 10,000 population; Property crime rate: 116.7 per 10,000 population (2004).
Transportation: Commute to work: 91.4% car, 6.0% public transportation, 0.0% walk, 2.2% work from home (2000); Travel time to work: 40.2% less than 15 minutes, 21.4% 15 to 30 minutes, 16.6% 30 to 45 minutes, 6.6% 45 to 60 minutes, 15.3% 60 minutes or more (2000)
Additional Information Contacts
Village of Buchanan. . . . . (914) 737-1033
    http://www.villageofbuchanan.org/

CHAPPAQUA (CDP).
Covers a land area of 9.376 square miles and a water area of 0.060 square miles. Located at 41.16° N. Lat.; 73.76° W. Long. Elevation is 496 feet.
History: Originally a Quaker community; later estate area. Horace Greeley lived here.
Population: 8,975 (1990); 9,468 (2000); 9,668 (2005); 9,886 (2010 projected); Race: 90.6% White, 0.9% Black, 6.5% Asian, 2.9% Hispanic of any race (2005); Density: 1,031.1 persons per square mile (2005); Average household size: 3.04 (2005); Median age: 39.6 (2005); Males per 100 females: 97.1 (2005); Marriage status: 15.1% never married, 77.2% now married, 2.5% widowed, 5.3% divorced (2000); Foreign born: 11.0% (2000); Ancestry (includes multiple ancestries): 16.7% Other groups, 14.3% Irish, 14.0% Italian, 13.0% Russian, 8.1% English (2000).
Economy: Manufacturing: photographic equipment and supplies. Employment by occupation: 25.9% management, 42.8% professional, 5.1% services, 22.6% sales, 0.0% farming, 2.6% construction, 1.0% production (2000).
Income: Per capita income: $79,908 (2005); Median household income: $189,651 (2005); Average household income: $242,331 (2005); Percent of households with income of $100,000 or more: 73.9% (2005); Poverty rate: 3.1% (2000).
Education: Percent of population age 25 and over with: High school diploma (including GED) or higher: 97.9% (2005); Bachelor's degree or higher: 79.7% (2005); Master's degree or higher: 48.5% (2005).
School District(s)
Chappaqua Central School District (KG-12)
    2003-04 Enrollment: 4,096 . . . . (914) 238-7200
Housing: Homeownership rate: 92.2% (2005); Median home value: $899,150 (2005); Median rent: $1,419 per month (2000); Median age of housing: 42 years (2000).
Transportation: Commute to work: 62.7% car, 27.7% public transportation, 0.7% walk, 8.0% work from home (2000); Travel time to work: 19.2% less than 15 minutes, 20.4% 15 to 30 minutes, 15.4% 30 to 45 minutes, 8.6% 45 to 60 minutes, 36.4% 60 minutes or more (2000)

CORTLANDT (town).
Covers a land area of 39.671 square miles and a water area of 10.502 square miles. Located at 41.26° N. Lat.; 73.90° W. Long.
Population: 37,357 (1990); 38,467 (2000); 39,894 (2005); 41,345 (2010 projected); Race: 85.8% White, 5.5% Black, 3.2% Asian, 9.8% Hispanic of any race (2005); Density: 1,005.6 persons per square mile (2005); Average household size: 2.86 (2005); Median age: 40.1 (2005); Males per 100 females: 96.5 (2005); Marriage status: 20.7% never married, 65.5% now married, 6.9% widowed, 6.9% divorced (2000); Foreign born: 11.4% (2000); Ancestry (includes multiple ancestries): 26.5% Italian, 23.6% Irish, 14.4% Other groups, 12.6% German, 6.1% English (2000).
Economy: Unemployment rate: 3.7% (2005); Total civilian labor force: 21,485 (2005); Single-family building permits issued: 63 (2005); Multi-family building permits issued: 0 (2005); Employment by occupation:

18.6% management, 29.0% professional, 11.3% services, 26.0% sales, 0.1% farming, 9.0% construction, 6.0% production (2000).
Income: Per capita income: $38,606 (2005); Median household income: $86,242 (2005); Average household income: $108,628 (2005); Percent of households with income of $100,000 or more: 42.0% (2005); Poverty rate: 4.5% (2000).
Taxes: Total city taxes per capita: $485 (2004); City property taxes per capita: $410 (2004).
Education: Percent of population age 25 and over with: High school diploma (including GED) or higher: 90.3% (2005); Bachelor's degree or higher: 41.3% (2005); Master's degree or higher: 19.4% (2005).
Housing: Homeownership rate: 77.9% (2005); Median home value: $381,433 (2005); Median rent: $804 per month (2000); Median age of housing: 42 years (2000).
Transportation: Commute to work: 77.5% car, 14.5% public transportation, 2.1% walk, 5.3% work from home (2000); Travel time to work: 23.3% less than 15 minutes, 18.6% 15 to 30 minutes, 21.8% 30 to 45 minutes, 12.4% 45 to 60 minutes, 23.9% 60 minutes or more (2000)
Additional Information Contacts
Town of Cortlandt. . . . . (914) 734-1040
http://www.townofcortlandt.com/

CORTLANDT MANOR (unincorporated postal area, zip code 10567). Covers a land area of 22.250 square miles and a water area of 0.286 square miles. Located at 41.28° N. Lat.; 73.89° W. Long.
Population: 0 (2000); Race: 86.9% White, 5.7% Black, 2.8% Asian, 8.4% Hispanic of any race (2000); Density: 0.0 persons per square mile (2000); Age: 28.9% under 18, 10.3% over 64 (2000); Marriage status: 20.1% never married, 67.9% now married, 6.2% widowed, 5.8% divorced (2000); Foreign born: 11.8% (2000); Ancestry (includes multiple ancestries): 28.6% Italian, 24.6% Irish, 16.6% Other groups, 11.8% German, 5.8% English (2000).
Economy: Employment by occupation: 18.6% management, 27.9% professional, 12.6% services, 25.7% sales, 0.1% farming, 9.3% construction, 5.9% production (2000).
Income: Per capita income: $31,821 (2000); Median household income: $85,227 (2000); Poverty rate: 3.0% (2000).
Education: Percent of population age 25 and over with: High school diploma (including GED) or higher: 91.4% (2000); Bachelor's degree or higher: 39.9% (2000).
School District(s)
Hendrick Hudson Central School District (KG-12)
    2003-04 Enrollment: 2,884 . . . . (914) 736-5200
Lakeland Central School District (KG-12)
    2003-04 Enrollment: 6,139 . . . . (914) 245-1700
Housing: Homeownership rate: 91.1% (2000); Median home value: $223,400 (2000); Median rent: $894 per month (2000); Median age of housing: 39 years (2000).
Hospitals: Hudson Valley Hospital Center (120 beds); Hudson Valley Hospital Center (128 beds)
Transportation: Commute to work: 82.1% car, 11.9% public transportation, 0.9% walk, 4.7% work from home (2000); Travel time to work: 18.7% less than 15 minutes, 20.3% 15 to 30 minutes, 22.2% 30 to 45 minutes, 14.3% 45 to 60 minutes, 24.5% 60 minutes or more (2000)

CROMPOND (CDP). Covers a land area of 2.486 square miles and a water area of 0.016 square miles. Located at 41.28° N. Lat.; 73.83° W. Long.
Population: 1,895 (1990); 2,050 (2000); 2,197 (2005); 2,329 (2010 projected); Race: 90.5% White, 2.4% Black, 5.5% Asian, 4.8% Hispanic of any race (2005); Density: 883.8 persons per square mile (2005); Average household size: 3.34 (2005); Median age: 42.8 (2005); Males per 100 females: 89.2 (2005); Marriage status: 20.0% never married, 66.6% now married, 9.6% widowed, 3.8% divorced (2000); Foreign born: 13.1% (2000); Ancestry (includes multiple ancestries): 38.0% Italian, 20.2% Irish, 14.7% Other groups, 10.2% German, 5.4% English (2000).
Economy: Employment by occupation: 22.6% management, 26.2% professional, 8.9% services, 27.2% sales, 0.0% farming, 9.0% construction, 6.2% production (2000).
Income: Per capita income: $37,834 (2005); Median household income: $97,476 (2005); Average household income: $120,008 (2005); Percent of households with income of $100,000 or more: 48.4% (2005); Poverty rate: 2.0% (2000).
Education: Percent of population age 25 and over with: High school diploma (including GED) or higher: 87.7% (2005); Bachelor's degree or higher: 41.5% (2005); Master's degree or higher: 21.0% (2005).
School District(s)
Lakeland Central School District (KG-12)
    2003-04 Enrollment: 6,139 . . . . (914) 245-1700
Housing: Homeownership rate: 87.1% (2005); Median home value: $436,493 (2005); Median rent: $963 per month (2000); Median age of housing: 35 years (2000).
Transportation: Commute to work: 88.4% car, 5.6% public transportation, 0.7% walk, 5.2% work from home (2000); Travel time to work: 18.2% less than 15 minutes, 31.5% 15 to 30 minutes, 27.9% 30 to 45 minutes, 6.7% 45 to 60 minutes, 15.7% 60 minutes or more (2000)

CROSS RIVER (unincorporated postal area, zip code 10518). Covers a land area of 4.809 square miles and a water area of 0 square miles. Located at 41.26° N. Lat.; 73.60° W. Long. Elevation is 338 feet.
Population: 0 (2000); Race: 92.0% White, 0.0% Black, 7.2% Asian, 4.9% Hispanic of any race (2000); Density: 0.0 persons per square mile (2000); Age: 33.3% under 18, 6.2% over 64 (2000); Marriage status: 15.8% never married, 71.4% now married, 4.5% widowed, 8.3% divorced (2000); Foreign born: 9.1% (2000); Ancestry (includes multiple ancestries): 18.7% Other groups, 18.4% Irish, 16.3% Italian, 12.1% English, 11.2% German (2000).
Economy: Employment by occupation: 28.6% management, 36.1% professional, 4.2% services, 24.2% sales, 0.0% farming, 3.7% construction, 3.4% production (2000).
Income: Per capita income: $60,782 (2000); Median household income: $156,190 (2000); Poverty rate: 1.1% (2000).
Education: Percent of population age 25 and over with: High school diploma (including GED) or higher: 94.7% (2000); Bachelor's degree or higher: 71.8% (2000).
School District(s)
Katonah-Lewisboro Union Free School District (KG-12)
    2003-04 Enrollment: 4,112 . . . . (914) 763-7001
Housing: Homeownership rate: 95.8% (2000); Median home value: $437,700 (2000); Median rent: $892 per month (2000); Median age of housing: 16 years (2000).
Transportation: Commute to work: 76.2% car, 20.1% public transportation, 0.0% walk, 3.7% work from home (2000); Travel time to work: 12.3% less than 15 minutes, 25.7% 15 to 30 minutes, 29.1% 30 to 45 minutes, 3.3% 45 to 60 minutes, 29.6% 60 minutes or more (2000)

CROTON-ON-HUDSON (village). Aka Croton-Harmon. Covers a land area of 4.749 square miles and a water area of 6.062 square miles. Located at 41.20° N. Lat.; 73.88° W. Long. Elevation is 8 feet.
History: During 1920s, fashionable haven for intellectuals such as Edna St. Vincent Millay, Doris Stevens, Stuart Chase and John Reed. Van Cortlandt Manor, a restored 18th-century Dutch-English manorhouse on 20 acres of what was once 86,000-acre estate is located here. Settled 1609, Incorporated 1898.
Population: 7,018 (1990); 7,606 (2000); 7,912 (2005); 8,235 (2010 projected); Race: 90.1% White, 2.1% Black, 2.2% Asian, 9.3% Hispanic of any race (2005); Density: 1,666.1 persons per square mile (2005); Average household size: 2.71 (2005); Median age: 41.1 (2005); Males per 100 females: 91.4 (2005); Marriage status: 20.0% never married, 67.8% now married, 5.5% widowed, 6.7% divorced (2000); Foreign born: 11.5% (2000); Ancestry (includes multiple ancestries): 20.2% Irish, 18.6% Italian, 13.9% Other groups, 11.6% German, 8.4% English (2000).
Economy: Manufacturing includes machinery, industrial diamonds and metal fabrication. Includes Amtrak and Metro-North railroad yards. Single-family building permits issued: 11 (2005); Multi-family building permits issued: 0 (2005); Employment by occupation: 20.5% management, 35.4% professional, 6.1% services, 26.3% sales, 0.2% farming, 8.0% construction, 3.5% production (2000).
Income: Per capita income: $45,055 (2005); Median household income: $95,507 (2005); Average household income: $121,081 (2005); Percent of households with income of $100,000 or more: 47.7% (2005); Poverty rate: 3.4% (2000).
Education: Percent of population age 25 and over with: High school diploma (including GED) or higher: 92.2% (2005); Bachelor's degree or higher: 54.9% (2005); Master's degree or higher: 30.1% (2005).
School District(s)
Croton-Harmon Union Free School District (KG-12)
    2003-04 Enrollment: 1,549 . . . . (914) 271-4793

Croton-Harmon Union Free School District (KG-12)
  2003-04 Enrollment: 1,549 .... (914) 271-4793
Housing: Homeownership rate: 75.2% (2005); Median home value: $434,386 (2005); Median rent: $859 per month (2000); Median age of housing: 46 years (2000).
Transportation: Commute to work: 63.1% car, 24.5% public transportation, 3.6% walk, 8.7% work from home (2000); Travel time to work: 22.8% less than 15 minutes, 17.6% 15 to 30 minutes, 18.8% 30 to 45 minutes, 9.8% 45 to 60 minutes, 31.0% 60 minutes or more (2000); Amtrak: Service available.
Additional Information Contacts
Village of Croton-on-Hudson .... (914) 271-4781
  http://village.croton-on-hudson.ny.us/Home/

CRUGERS (CDP).
Covers a land area of 0.699 square miles and a water area of 0.557 square miles. Located at 41.23° N. Lat.; 73.92° W. Long.
Population: 1,547 (1990); 1,752 (2000); 1,858 (2005); 1,920 (2010 projected); Race: 90.0% White, 5.1% Black, 1.1% Asian, 5.0% Hispanic of any race (2005); Density: 2,658.0 persons per square mile (2005); Average household size: 2.15 (2005); Median age: 62.5 (2005); Males per 100 females: 73.8 (2005); Marriage status: 12.2% never married, 48.3% now married, 29.3% widowed, 10.3% divorced (2000); Foreign born: 7.1% (2000); Ancestry (includes multiple ancestries): 27.6% Italian, 22.0% Irish, 12.7% German, 7.6% Other groups, 7.0% English (2000).
Economy: Employment by occupation: 17.3% management, 30.8% professional, 16.5% services, 21.3% sales, 0.0% farming, 5.2% construction, 8.8% production (2000).
Income: Per capita income: $36,469 (2005); Median household income: $37,500 (2005); Average household income: $70,991 (2005); Percent of households with income of $100,000 or more: 25.8% (2005); Poverty rate: 5.6% (2000).
Education: Percent of population age 25 and over with: High school diploma (including GED) or higher: 75.5% (2005); Bachelor's degree or higher: 26.2% (2005); Master's degree or higher: 11.6% (2005).
Housing: Homeownership rate: 32.3% (2005); Median home value: $456,111 (2005); Median rent: $663 per month (2000); Median age of housing: 43 years (2000).
Transportation: Commute to work: 79.6% car, 10.3% public transportation, 1.0% walk, 7.9% work from home (2000); Travel time to work: 16.4% less than 15 minutes, 19.0% 15 to 30 minutes, 24.6% 30 to 45 minutes, 18.1% 45 to 60 minutes, 22.0% 60 minutes or more (2000).

DOBBS FERRY (village).
Covers a land area of 2.442 square miles and a water area of 0.727 square miles. Located at 41.01° N. Lat.; 73.86° W. Long. Elevation is 210 feet.
History: Named for Jeremiah Dobbs, who operated a ferry across the Hudson River. Site of Livingston Manor, where George Washington and Marshal Rochambeau of France are said to have planned the Yorktown Campaign. Seat of Mercy College. Incorporated 1873.
Population: 9,940 (1990); 10,622 (2000); 11,233 (2005); 11,798 (2010 projected); Race: 77.5% White, 8.6% Black, 8.8% Asian, 8.8% Hispanic of any race (2005); Density: 4,600.2 persons per square mile (2005); Average household size: 2.82 (2005); Median age: 39.7 (2005); Males per 100 females: 96.2 (2005); Marriage status: 29.4% never married, 55.5% now married, 7.9% widowed, 7.3% divorced (2000); Foreign born: 17.9% (2000); Ancestry (includes multiple ancestries): 21.4% Italian, 20.4% Other groups, 16.5% Irish, 8.3% German, 6.3% Russian (2000).
Economy: Has a chemical research laboratory. Single-family building permits issued: 7 (2005); Multi-family building permits issued: 2 (2005); Employment by occupation: 16.6% management, 35.8% professional, 12.6% services, 27.1% sales, 0.2% farming, 4.1% construction, 3.7% production (2000).
Income: Per capita income: $39,660 (2005); Median household income: $81,161 (2005); Average household income: $111,117 (2005); Percent of households with income of $100,000 or more: 40.7% (2005); Poverty rate: 5.6% (2000).
Education: Percent of population age 25 and over with: High school diploma (including GED) or higher: 87.1% (2005); Bachelor's degree or higher: 50.4% (2005); Master's degree or higher: 25.7% (2005).
School District(s)
Dobbs Ferry Union Free School District (KG-12)
  2003-04 Enrollment: 1,362 .... (914) 693-1506
Greenburgh Eleven Union Free School District (01-12)
  2003-04 Enrollment: 411 .... (914) 693-8500

Four-year College(s)
Mercy College-Main Campus
  Fall 2004 Enrollment: 10,396 .... (914) 693-4500
  2005-06 Tuition: In-state $11,966; Out-of-state $11,966
Housing: Homeownership rate: 59.0% (2005); Median home value: $510,559 (2005); Median rent: $843 per month (2000); Median age of housing: 47 years (2000).
Hospitals: Community Hospital at Dobbs Ferry (50 beds)
Safety: Violent crime rate: 9.0 per 10,000 population; Property crime rate: 104.9 per 10,000 population (2004).
Transportation: Commute to work: 67.3% car, 22.2% public transportation, 6.1% walk, 4.2% work from home (2000); Travel time to work: 24.5% less than 15 minutes, 30.4% 15 to 30 minutes, 16.4% 30 to 45 minutes, 7.5% 45 to 60 minutes, 21.2% 60 minutes or more (2000)
Additional Information Contacts
Village of Dobbs Ferry .... (914) 693-2203
  http://www.dobbsferry.com/

EASTCHESTER (town).
Covers a land area of 4.912 square miles and a water area of 0.096 square miles. Located at 40.95° N. Lat.; 73.81° W. Long. Elevation is 50 feet.
History: Named for the town of Chester in England. Once a township (formed 1788) extending from the present Bronx North to Scarsdale; Mt. Vernon city was separated from it in 1892; the section South of Mt. Vernon was annexed by N.Y. city in 1895.
Population: 30,867 (1990); 31,318 (2000); 31,556 (2005); 31,890 (2010 projected); Race: 86.2% White, 2.8% Black, 7.4% Asian, 5.7% Hispanic of any race (2005); Density: 6,424.8 persons per square mile (2005); Average household size: 2.47 (2005); Median age: 41.1 (2005); Males per 100 females: 88.8 (2005); Marriage status: 24.0% never married, 62.3% now married, 8.3% widowed, 5.4% divorced (2000); Foreign born: 16.7% (2000); Ancestry (includes multiple ancestries): 34.6% Italian, 19.8% Irish, 15.6% Other groups, 9.1% German, 5.8% English (2000).
Economy: Growing Asian community in the area. Unemployment rate: 3.7% (2005); Total civilian labor force: 16,266 (2005); Single-family building permits issued: 4 (2005); Multi-family building permits issued: 0 (2005); Employment by occupation: 25.9% management, 28.7% professional, 10.0% services, 27.0% sales, 0.1% farming, 4.3% construction, 4.1% production (2000).
Income: Per capita income: $54,244 (2005); Median household income: $93,513 (2005); Average household income: $133,813 (2005); Percent of households with income of $100,000 or more: 46.6% (2005); Poverty rate: 4.2% (2000).
Taxes: Total city taxes per capita: $492 (2004); City property taxes per capita: $429 (2004).
Education: Percent of population age 25 and over with: High school diploma (including GED) or higher: 90.8% (2005); Bachelor's degree or higher: 52.0% (2005); Master's degree or higher: 25.1% (2005).
School District(s)
Eastchester Union Free School District (KG-12)
  2003-04 Enrollment: 2,680 .... (914) 793-6130
Tuckahoe Union Free School District (KG-12)
  2003-04 Enrollment: 976 .... (914) 337-5376
Housing: Homeownership rate: 71.2% (2005); Median home value: $530,195 (2005); Median rent: $988 per month (2000); Median age of housing: 51 years (2000).
Transportation: Commute to work: 60.9% car, 30.2% public transportation, 4.0% walk, 4.6% work from home (2000); Travel time to work: 18.7% less than 15 minutes, 26.4% 15 to 30 minutes, 19.1% 30 to 45 minutes, 15.1% 45 to 60 minutes, 20.8% 60 minutes or more (2000)
Additional Information Contacts
Eastchester-Tuckahoe Chamber of Commerce .... (914) 779-7344
Town of Eastchester .... (914) 771-3300
  http://www.eastchester.org/

EASTCHESTER (CDP).
Covers a land area of 3.349 square miles and a water area of 0.096 square miles. Located at 40.95° N. Lat.; 73.80° W. Long.
Population: 18,537 (1990); 18,564 (2000); 18,813 (2005); 19,082 (2010 projected); Race: 88.8% White, 1.2% Black, 7.3% Asian, 4.4% Hispanic of any race (2005); Density: 5,616.7 persons per square mile (2005); Average household size: 2.40 (2005); Median age: 43.0 (2005); Males per 100 females: 88.4 (2005); Marriage status: 21.8% never married, 63.2% now married, 9.8% widowed, 5.2% divorced (2000); Foreign born: 15.9%

(2000); Ancestry (includes multiple ancestries): 42.0% Italian, 19.3% Irish, 12.4% Other groups, 8.0% German, 5.6% Russian (2000).
Economy: Employment by occupation: 24.2% management, 29.7% professional, 10.3% services, 27.1% sales, 0.1% farming, 4.4% construction, 4.2% production (2000).
Income: Per capita income: $50,252 (2005); Median household income: $90,701 (2005); Average household income: $120,538 (2005); Percent of households with income of $100,000 or more: 44.6% (2005); Poverty rate: 3.6% (2000).
Education: Percent of population age 25 and over with: High school diploma (including GED) or higher: 90.6% (2005); Bachelor's degree or higher: 50.6% (2005); Master's degree or higher: 22.8% (2005).
Housing: Homeownership rate: 78.2% (2005); Median home value: $517,718 (2005); Median rent: $961 per month (2000); Median age of housing: 49 years (2000).
Transportation: Commute to work: 68.6% car, 24.9% public transportation, 2.1% walk, 4.2% work from home (2000); Travel time to work: 16.7% less than 15 minutes, 29.9% 15 to 30 minutes, 18.2% 30 to 45 minutes, 13.8% 45 to 60 minutes, 21.5% 60 minutes or more (2000)

ELMSFORD (village).
Covers a land area of 1.096 square miles and a water area of 0 square miles. Located at 41.05° N. Lat.; 73.81° W. Long. Elevation is 173 feet.
History: Incorporated 1910.
Population: 4,114 (1990); 4,676 (2000); 4,716 (2005); 4,775 (2010 projected); Race: 50.3% White, 18.6% Black, 12.4% Asian, 30.1% Hispanic of any race (2005); Density: 4,303.2 persons per square mile (2005); Average household size: 2.82 (2005); Median age: 35.3 (2005); Males per 100 females: 102.9 (2005); Marriage status: 28.8% never married, 57.7% now married, 6.7% widowed, 6.9% divorced (2000); Foreign born: 32.1% (2000); Ancestry (includes multiple ancestries): 43.0% Other groups, 20.5% Italian, 14.3% Irish, 6.5% German, 3.2% United States or American (2000).
Economy: Manufacturing: abrasives, foods, knitting machines, electron tubes, gas detectors, fire-protection equipment, copying and collating machines, umbrellas, batteries, publishing, jewel bearings, wallpapers and fabric, precision-rubber molded products. Single-family building permits issued: 6 (2005); Multi-family building permits issued: 4 (2005); Employment by occupation: 17.0% management, 21.1% professional, 15.4% services, 25.2% sales, 0.0% farming, 10.6% construction, 10.7% production (2000).
Income: Per capita income: $32,792 (2005); Median household income: $72,180 (2005); Average household income: $92,546 (2005); Percent of households with income of $100,000 or more: 33.5% (2005); Poverty rate: 9.3% (2000).
Education: Percent of population age 25 and over with: High school diploma (including GED) or higher: 83.4% (2005); Bachelor's degree or higher: 32.2% (2005); Master's degree or higher: 15.2% (2005).

School District(s)

Ellenville Csd (KG-12)
    2003-04 Enrollment: 1,812 . . . . (845) 647-0100
Elmsford Union Free School District (PK-12)
    2003-04 Enrollment: 965 . . . . (914) 592-8440

Housing: Homeownership rate: 47.8% (2005); Median home value: $390,385 (2005); Median rent: $966 per month (2000); Median age of housing: 42 years (2000).
Safety: Violent crime rate: 23.2 per 10,000 population; Property crime rate: 215.6 per 10,000 population (2004).
Transportation: Commute to work: 80.0% car, 15.4% public transportation, 2.5% walk, 1.0% work from home (2000); Travel time to work: 30.1% less than 15 minutes, 33.6% 15 to 30 minutes, 16.9% 30 to 45 minutes, 7.4% 45 to 60 minutes, 12.0% 60 minutes or more (2000)
Additional Information Contacts
Village of Elmsford . . . . (914) 592-6555
    http://www.elmsfordny.org/

FAIRVIEW (CDP).
Covers a land area of 0.429 square miles and a water area of 0 square miles. Located at 41.04° N. Lat.; 73.79° W. Long.
Population: 2,688 (1990); 2,887 (2000); 2,854 (2005); 2,871 (2010 projected); Race: 12.9% White, 68.8% Black, 3.5% Asian, 17.6% Hispanic of any race (2005); Density: 6,658.2 persons per square mile (2005); Average household size: 3.03 (2005); Median age: 36.5 (2005); Males per 100 females: 89.5 (2005); Marriage status: 38.6% never married, 42.1% now married, 7.7% widowed, 11.5% divorced (2000); Foreign born: 29.2% (2000); Ancestry (includes multiple ancestries): 62.3% Other groups, 7.3% Jamaican, 3.8% Haitian, 2.8% African, 2.0% Barbadian (2000).
Economy: Employment by occupation: 8.4% management, 17.0% professional, 34.4% services, 24.3% sales, 0.6% farming, 7.3% construction, 7.9% production (2000).
Income: Per capita income: $25,190 (2005); Median household income: $57,393 (2005); Average household income: $75,315 (2005); Percent of households with income of $100,000 or more: 25.2% (2005); Poverty rate: 12.0% (2000).
Education: Percent of population age 25 and over with: High school diploma (including GED) or higher: 73.3% (2005); Bachelor's degree or higher: 19.4% (2005); Master's degree or higher: 4.8% (2005).
Housing: Homeownership rate: 43.5% (2005); Median home value: $294,798 (2005); Median rent: $571 per month (2000); Median age of housing: 39 years (2000).
Transportation: Commute to work: 74.7% car, 20.9% public transportation, 1.8% walk, 0.0% work from home (2000); Travel time to work: 28.6% less than 15 minutes, 47.0% 15 to 30 minutes, 13.4% 30 to 45 minutes, 3.5% 45 to 60 minutes, 7.5% 60 minutes or more (2000)

GOLDEN'S BRIDGE (CDP).
Covers a land area of 3.132 square miles and a water area of 0.551 square miles. Located at 41.28° N. Lat.; 73.66° W. Long.
Population: 1,423 (1990); 1,578 (2000); 1,765 (2005); 1,947 (2010 projected); Race: 95.1% White, 1.1% Black, 2.8% Asian, 2.9% Hispanic of any race (2005); Density: 563.5 persons per square mile (2005); Average household size: 2.83 (2005); Median age: 38.0 (2005); Males per 100 females: 92.9 (2005); Marriage status: 13.6% never married, 76.4% now married, 3.6% widowed, 6.4% divorced (2000); Foreign born: 7.4% (2000); Ancestry (includes multiple ancestries): 17.6% Italian, 14.3% Russian, 13.7% Irish, 12.9% German, 7.4% Other groups (2000).
Economy: Employment by occupation: 29.4% management, 38.0% professional, 2.5% services, 20.0% sales, 0.0% farming, 6.3% construction, 3.8% production (2000).
Income: Per capita income: $68,980 (2005); Median household income: $134,091 (2005); Average household income: $195,112 (2005); Percent of households with income of $100,000 or more: 66.8% (2005); Poverty rate: 2.4% (2000).
Education: Percent of population age 25 and over with: High school diploma (including GED) or higher: 99.3% (2005); Bachelor's degree or higher: 68.2% (2005); Master's degree or higher: 29.8% (2005).
Housing: Homeownership rate: 85.6% (2005); Median home value: $572,704 (2005); Median rent: $856 per month (2000); Median age of housing: 31 years (2000).
Transportation: Commute to work: 76.4% car, 20.2% public transportation, 0.0% walk, 3.4% work from home (2000); Travel time to work: 11.5% less than 15 minutes, 33.8% 15 to 30 minutes, 24.0% 30 to 45 minutes, 4.4% 45 to 60 minutes, 26.3% 60 minutes or more (2000)

GRANITE SPRINGS (unincorporated postal area, zip code 10527).
Covers a land area of 2.637 square miles and a water area of 0 square miles. Located at 41.31° N. Lat.; 73.75° W. Long. Elevation is 330 feet.
Population: 0 (2000); Race: 97.6% White, 1.7% Black, 0.7% Asian, 0.0% Hispanic of any race (2000); Density: 0.0 persons per square mile (2000); Age: 24.6% under 18, 10.4% over 64 (2000); Marriage status: 17.2% never married, 75.8% now married, 3.3% widowed, 3.7% divorced (2000); Foreign born: 9.3% (2000); Ancestry (includes multiple ancestries): 29.5% Italian, 21.4% Irish, 19.7% German, 9.4% English, 7.6% Other groups (2000).
Economy: Employment by occupation: 35.7% management, 38.1% professional, 4.8% services, 19.0% sales, 0.0% farming, 1.0% construction, 1.4% production (2000).
Income: Per capita income: $45,701 (2000); Median household income: $114,106 (2000); Poverty rate: 1.9% (2000).
Education: Percent of population age 25 and over with: High school diploma (including GED) or higher: 97.4% (2000); Bachelor's degree or higher: 71.6% (2000).
Housing: Homeownership rate: 95.2% (2000); Median home value: $361,000 (2000); Median rent: $1,500 per month (2000); Median age of housing: 28 years (2000).
Transportation: Commute to work: 78.0% car, 13.0% public transportation, 0.4% walk, 7.1% work from home (2000); Travel time to work: 18.4% less than 15 minutes, 26.8% 15 to 30 minutes, 19.3% 30 to 45 minutes, 11.0% 45 to 60 minutes, 24.6% 60 minutes or more (2000)

GREENBURGH (town). Covers a land area of 30.521 square miles and a water area of 5.659 square miles. Located at 41.03° N. Lat.; 73.83° W. Long.
Population: 83,816 (1990); 86,764 (2000); 91,037 (2005); 95,204 (2010 projected); Race: 69.3% White, 13.5% Black, 10.4% Asian, 11.2% Hispanic of any race (2005); Density: 2,982.7 persons per square mile (2005); Average household size: 2.62 (2005); Median age: 41.0 (2005); Males per 100 females: 91.0 (2005); Marriage status: 24.8% never married, 61.7% now married, 6.8% widowed, 6.8% divorced (2000); Foreign born: 21.0% (2000); Ancestry (includes multiple ancestries): 29.5% Other groups, 17.9% Italian, 13.6% Irish, 7.7% German, 5.7% Russian (2000).
Economy: Unemployment rate: 3.4% (2005); Total civilian labor force: 50,612 (2005); Single-family building permits issued: 14 (2005); Multi-family building permits issued: 0 (2005); Employment by occupation: 22.1% management, 34.0% professional, 10.6% services, 24.0% sales, 0.1% farming, 4.6% construction, 4.7% production (2000).
Income: Per capita income: $49,986 (2005); Median household income: $93,076 (2005); Average household income: $130,034 (2005); Percent of households with income of $100,000 or more: 46.3% (2005); Poverty rate: 3.9% (2000).
Taxes: Total city taxes per capita: $515 (2004); City property taxes per capita: $442 (2004).
Education: Percent of population age 25 and over with: High school diploma (including GED) or higher: 91.0% (2005); Bachelor's degree or higher: 53.8% (2005); Master's degree or higher: 27.5% (2005).
Housing: Homeownership rate: 70.1% (2005); Median home value: $483,311 (2005); Median rent: $940 per month (2000); Median age of housing: 44 years (2000).
Transportation: Commute to work: 70.8% car, 21.6% public transportation, 2.7% walk, 4.3% work from home (2000); Travel time to work: 20.9% less than 15 minutes, 30.4% 15 to 30 minutes, 18.9% 30 to 45 minutes, 9.6% 45 to 60 minutes, 20.1% 60 minutes or more (2000)
Additional Information Contacts
Town of Greenburgh . . . . (914) 993-1540
http://www.greenburghny.com/

GREENVILLE (CDP). Covers a land area of 2.918 square miles and a water area of 0.011 square miles. Located at 40.99° N. Lat.; 73.82° W. Long. Elevation is 300 feet.
Population: 8,983 (1990); 8,648 (2000); 9,260 (2005); 9,840 (2010 projected); Race: 72.9% White, 2.8% Black, 21.9% Asian, 5.2% Hispanic of any race (2005); Density: 3,173.9 persons per square mile (2005); Average household size: 2.58 (2005); Median age: 42.4 (2005); Males per 100 females: 90.2 (2005); Marriage status: 21.3% never married, 66.3% now married, 7.1% widowed, 5.3% divorced (2000); Foreign born: 24.7% (2000); Ancestry (includes multiple ancestries): 28.6% Other groups, 14.0% Italian, 9.8% Russian, 7.8% Polish, 7.7% German (2000).
Economy: Employment by occupation: 28.2% management, 40.0% professional, 5.5% services, 21.4% sales, 0.0% farming, 2.3% construction, 2.6% production (2000).
Income: Per capita income: $71,475 (2005); Median household income: $116,363 (2005); Average household income: $183,502 (2005); Percent of households with income of $100,000 or more: 55.3% (2005); Poverty rate: 2.3% (2000).
Education: Percent of population age 25 and over with: High school diploma (including GED) or higher: 95.6% (2005); Bachelor's degree or higher: 68.3% (2005); Master's degree or higher: 36.8% (2005).
Housing: Homeownership rate: 73.2% (2005); Median home value: $670,918 (2005); Median rent: $1,133 per month (2000); Median age of housing: 42 years (2000).
Transportation: Commute to work: 59.2% car, 33.2% public transportation, 0.9% walk, 6.3% work from home (2000); Travel time to work: 11.0% less than 15 minutes, 25.2% 15 to 30 minutes, 21.6% 30 to 45 minutes, 14.6% 45 to 60 minutes, 27.6% 60 minutes or more (2000)

HARRISON (village). Covers a land area of 16.829 square miles and a water area of 0.560 square miles. Located at 41.00° N. Lat.; 73.71° W. Long. Elevation is 65 feet.
Population: 23,308 (1990); 24,154 (2000); 25,373 (2005); 26,519 (2010 projected); Race: 87.7% White, 1.7% Black, 6.7% Asian, 8.3% Hispanic of any race (2005); Density: 1,507.7 persons per square mile (2005); Average household size: 2.89 (2005); Median age: 38.1 (2005); Males per 100 females: 90.0 (2005); Marriage status: 26.3% never married, 63.3% now married, 5.5% widowed, 4.9% divorced (2000); Foreign born: 18.7% (2000); Ancestry (includes multiple ancestries): 38.0% Italian, 15.9% Irish, 14.1% Other groups, 7.6% German, 4.2% English (2000).
Economy: Manufacturing of industrial vacuums and polishers. Single-family building permits issued: 34 (2005); Multi-family building permits issued: 12 (2005); Employment by occupation: 23.2% management, 25.2% professional, 12.8% services, 27.5% sales, 0.0% farming, 7.0% construction, 4.3% production (2000).
Income: Per capita income: $49,980 (2005); Median household income: $88,670 (2005); Average household income: $142,597 (2005); Percent of households with income of $100,000 or more: 44.6% (2005); Poverty rate: 5.6% (2000).
Education: Percent of population age 25 and over with: High school diploma (including GED) or higher: 87.3% (2005); Bachelor's degree or higher: 45.6% (2005); Master's degree or higher: 20.9% (2005).
School District(s)
Harrison Central School District (KG-12)
    2003-04 Enrollment: 3,382 . . . . (914) 630-3002
Housing: Homeownership rate: 64.6% (2005); Median home value: $819,248 (2005); Median rent: $1,063 per month (2000); Median age of housing: 44 years (2000).
Hospitals: St. Vincent's Hospital-Westchester (133 beds)
Transportation: Commute to work: 70.5% car, 19.9% public transportation, 5.1% walk, 4.0% work from home (2000); Travel time to work: 30.6% less than 15 minutes, 31.2% 15 to 30 minutes, 12.3% 30 to 45 minutes, 10.9% 45 to 60 minutes, 14.9% 60 minutes or more (2000)
Additional Information Contacts
Village of Harrison . . . . (914) 670-3030
http://www.town.harrison.ny.us/

HARRISON (town). Covers a land area of 16.829 square miles and a water area of 0.560 square miles. Located at 41.00° N. Lat.; 73.71° W. Long.
Population: 23,308 (1990); 24,154 (2000); 25,373 (2005); 26,519 (2010 projected); Race: 87.7% White, 1.7% Black, 6.7% Asian, 8.3% Hispanic of any race (2005); Density: 1,507.7 persons per square mile (2005); Average household size: 2.89 (2005); Median age: 38.1 (2005); Males per 100 females: 90.0 (2005); Marriage status: 26.3% never married, 63.3% now married, 5.5% widowed, 4.9% divorced (2000); Foreign born: 18.7% (2000); Ancestry (includes multiple ancestries): 38.0% Italian, 15.9% Irish, 14.1% Other groups, 7.6% German, 4.2% English (2000).
Economy: Employment by occupation: 23.2% management, 25.2% professional, 12.8% services, 27.5% sales, 0.0% farming, 7.0% construction, 4.3% production (2000).
Income: Per capita income: $49,980 (2005); Median household income: $88,670 (2005); Average household income: $142,597 (2005); Percent of households with income of $100,000 or more: 44.6% (2005); Poverty rate: 5.6% (2000).
Taxes: Total city taxes per capita: $1,066 (2004); City property taxes per capita: $940 (2004).
Education: Percent of population age 25 and over with: High school diploma (including GED) or higher: 87.3% (2005); Bachelor's degree or higher: 45.6% (2005); Master's degree or higher: 20.9% (2005).
Housing: Homeownership rate: 64.6% (2005); Median home value: $819,248 (2005); Median rent: $1,063 per month (2000); Median age of housing: 44 years (2000).
Safety: Violent crime rate: 7.1 per 10,000 population; Property crime rate: 134.5 per 10,000 population (2004).
Transportation: Commute to work: 70.5% car, 19.9% public transportation, 5.1% walk, 4.0% work from home (2000); Travel time to work: 30.6% less than 15 minutes, 31.2% 15 to 30 minutes, 12.3% 30 to 45 minutes, 10.9% 45 to 60 minutes, 14.9% 60 minutes or more (2000)
Additional Information Contacts
Town of Harrison . . . . (914) 670-3005
http://www.town.harrison.ny.us/

HARTSDALE (CDP). Covers a land area of 3.204 square miles and a water area of 0 square miles. Located at 41.02° N. Lat.; 73.80° W. Long. Elevation is 182 feet.
Population: 10,052 (1990); 9,830 (2000); 10,144 (2005); 10,462 (2010 projected); Race: 72.3% White, 9.9% Black, 11.8% Asian, 12.5% Hispanic of any race (2005); Density: 3,166.0 persons per square mile (2005); Average household size: 2.24 (2005); Median age: 44.6 (2005); Males per 100 females: 87.4 (2005); Marriage status: 23.2% never married, 62.2% now married, 7.4% widowed, 7.2% divorced (2000); Foreign born: 22.8%

(2000); Ancestry (includes multiple ancestries): 28.3% Other groups, 21.8% Italian, 12.8% Irish, 7.8% German, 5.9% Russian (2000).
Economy: Employment by occupation: 26.2% management, 29.6% professional, 7.0% services, 29.0% sales, 0.0% farming, 3.5% construction, 4.6% production (2000).
Income: Per capita income: $52,953 (2005); Median household income: $91,691 (2005); Average household income: $118,730 (2005); Percent of households with income of $100,000 or more: 45.0% (2005); Poverty rate: 2.6% (2000).
Education: Percent of population age 25 and over with: High school diploma (including GED) or higher: 93.1% (2005); Bachelor's degree or higher: 57.9% (2005); Master's degree or higher: 27.2% (2005).
School District(s)
Greenburgh Central School District (PK-12)
    2003-04 Enrollment: 1,981 . . . . (914) 761-6000
Housing: Homeownership rate: 79.1% (2005); Median home value: $404,711 (2005); Median rent: $985 per month (2000); Median age of housing: 43 years (2000).
Transportation: Commute to work: 65.5% car, 26.5% public transportation, 2.5% walk, 5.0% work from home (2000); Travel time to work: 16.9% less than 15 minutes, 29.6% 15 to 30 minutes, 18.5% 30 to 45 minutes, 9.5% 45 to 60 minutes, 25.4% 60 minutes or more (2000)

HASTINGS-ON-HUDSON (village).
Covers a land area of 1.961 square miles and a water area of 0.946 square miles. Located at 40.99° N. Lat.; 73.87° W. Long. Elevation is 199 feet.
History: Incorporated 1879.
Population: 8,000 (1990); 7,648 (2000); 7,682 (2005); 7,742 (2010 projected); Race: 88.8% White, 2.5% Black, 4.3% Asian, 5.7% Hispanic of any race (2005); Density: 3,917.0 persons per square mile (2005); Average household size: 2.47 (2005); Median age: 44.3 (2005); Males per 100 females: 92.1 (2005); Marriage status: 23.5% never married, 64.7% now married, 6.0% widowed, 5.8% divorced (2000); Foreign born: 12.0% (2000); Ancestry (includes multiple ancestries): 19.0% Irish, 16.7% Italian, 15.1% Other groups, 12.2% German, 9.5% Russian (2000).
Economy: Manufacturing of consumer goods; some light industry. Single-family building permits issued: 0 (2005); Multi-family building permits issued: 25 (2005); Employment by occupation: 20.2% management, 47.9% professional, 6.8% services, 18.6% sales, 0.0% farming, 3.7% construction, 2.8% production (2000).
Income: Per capita income: $55,052 (2005); Median household income: $96,376 (2005); Average household income: $135,710 (2005); Percent of households with income of $100,000 or more: 48.1% (2005); Poverty rate: 3.5% (2000).
Education: Percent of population age 25 and over with: High school diploma (including GED) or higher: 93.4% (2005); Bachelor's degree or higher: 62.4% (2005); Master's degree or higher: 38.8% (2005).
School District(s)
Greenburgh-Graham Union Free School District (02-12)
    2003-04 Enrollment: 297 . . . . (914) 478-1106
Hastings-On-Hudson Union Free School District (KG-12)
    2003-04 Enrollment: 1,670 . . . . (914) 478-6200
Housing: Homeownership rate: 66.2% (2005); Median home value: $624,253 (2005); Median rent: $927 per month (2000); Median age of housing: 60+ years (2000).
Safety: Violent crime rate: 20.5 per 10,000 population; Property crime rate: 133.6 per 10,000 population (2004).
Newspapers: The Rivertowns Enterprise (General - Circulation 6,100)
Transportation: Commute to work: 66.2% car, 25.4% public transportation, 2.2% walk, 6.0% work from home (2000); Travel time to work: 19.2% less than 15 minutes, 24.9% 15 to 30 minutes, 20.8% 30 to 45 minutes, 14.2% 45 to 60 minutes, 20.8% 60 minutes or more (2000)
Additional Information Contacts
Hastings-on-Hudson Chamber of Commerce . . . . (914) 478-0900
    http://www.design-site.net/hastings/
Village of Hastings-on-Hudson . . . . (914) 478-3400
    http://www.hastingsgov.org/

HAWTHORNE (CDP).
Covers a land area of 1.691 square miles and a water area of 0 square miles. Located at 41.10° N. Lat.; 73.79° W. Long. Elevation is 257 feet.
Population: 4,734 (1990); 5,083 (2000); 5,033 (2005); 5,000 (2010 projected); Race: 91.6% White, 4.1% Black, 1.9% Asian, 8.4% Hispanic of any race (2005); Density: 2,976.4 persons per square mile (2005); Average household size: 3.21 (2005); Median age: 39.2 (2005); Males per 100 females: 100.0 (2005); Marriage status: 26.4% never married, 61.5% now married, 7.9% widowed, 4.2% divorced (2000); Foreign born: 12.3% (2000); Ancestry (includes multiple ancestries): 44.1% Italian, 23.9% Irish, 13.5% Other groups, 12.2% German, 3.6% English (2000).
Economy: Manufacturing: jewelry, laboratory equipment, electrical equipment, chemicals, fabricated metal products, ultraviolet absorbers. Employment by occupation: 17.4% management, 24.8% professional, 14.2% services, 30.2% sales, 0.0% farming, 9.5% construction, 3.9% production (2000).
Income: Per capita income: $34,106 (2005); Median household income: $94,323 (2005); Average household income: $107,087 (2005); Percent of households with income of $100,000 or more: 46.7% (2005); Poverty rate: 3.3% (2000).
Education: Percent of population age 25 and over with: High school diploma (including GED) or higher: 87.6% (2005); Bachelor's degree or higher: 33.9% (2005); Master's degree or higher: 12.2% (2005).
School District(s)
Hawthorne-Cedar Knolls Union Free School District (03-12)
    2003-04 Enrollment: 320 . . . . (914) 773-7345
Mount Pleasant Central School District (KG-12)
    2003-04 Enrollment: 1,847 . . . . (914) 769-5500
Housing: Homeownership rate: 88.3% (2005); Median home value: $485,096 (2005); Median rent: $845 per month (2000); Median age of housing: 47 years (2000).
Transportation: Commute to work: 87.0% car, 8.8% public transportation, 1.4% walk, 2.7% work from home (2000); Travel time to work: 31.6% less than 15 minutes, 38.9% 15 to 30 minutes, 11.3% 30 to 45 minutes, 8.2% 45 to 60 minutes, 10.0% 60 minutes or more (2000)

HERITAGE HILLS (CDP).
Covers a land area of 2.315 square miles and a water area of 0 square miles. Located at 41.33° N. Lat.; 73.69° W. Long.
Population: 2,519 (1990); 3,683 (2000); 3,951 (2005); 4,242 (2010 projected); Race: 96.6% White, 1.0% Black, 1.7% Asian, 1.2% Hispanic of any race (2005); Density: 1,706.7 persons per square mile (2005); Average household size: 1.72 (2005); Median age: 66.6 (2005); Males per 100 females: 70.6 (2005); Marriage status: 13.8% never married, 59.8% now married, 17.3% widowed, 9.2% divorced (2000); Foreign born: 13.9% (2000); Ancestry (includes multiple ancestries): 20.1% Italian, 15.6% Irish, 11.3% German, 9.1% Other groups, 8.2% Russian (2000).
Economy: Employment by occupation: 22.5% management, 34.3% professional, 4.2% services, 30.1% sales, 0.6% farming, 2.7% construction, 5.5% production (2000).
Income: Per capita income: $53,020 (2005); Median household income: $69,955 (2005); Average household income: $89,795 (2005); Percent of households with income of $100,000 or more: 32.4% (2005); Poverty rate: 3.3% (2000).
Education: Percent of population age 25 and over with: High school diploma (including GED) or higher: 95.3% (2005); Bachelor's degree or higher: 51.6% (2005); Master's degree or higher: 28.5% (2005).
Housing: Homeownership rate: 92.4% (2005); Median home value: $381,053 (2005); Median rent: $1,385 per month (2000); Median age of housing: 16 years (2000).
Transportation: Commute to work: 85.5% car, 9.9% public transportation, 0.6% walk, 3.5% work from home (2000); Travel time to work: 7.6% less than 15 minutes, 18.6% 15 to 30 minutes, 36.4% 30 to 45 minutes, 12.5% 45 to 60 minutes, 24.8% 60 minutes or more (2000)

IRVINGTON (village).
Covers a land area of 2.789 square miles and a water area of 1.248 square miles. Located at 41.03° N. Lat.; 73.86° W. Long. Elevation is 9 feet.
History: Here at Nevis, once the estate of Alexander Hamilton's son, are a Columbia University arboretum and a children's Museum. Originally called Dearman; renamed (1857) for Washington Irving, who bought the estate Sunnyside (extant) here in 1835. Settled c.1655, Incorporated 1872.
Population: 6,348 (1990); 6,631 (2000); 6,660 (2005); 6,722 (2010 projected); Race: 87.7% White, 1.5% Black, 7.4% Asian, 4.5% Hispanic of any race (2005); Density: 2,387.8 persons per square mile (2005); Average household size: 2.64 (2005); Median age: 40.3 (2005); Males per 100 females: 94.0 (2005); Marriage status: 18.3% never married, 69.7% now married, 5.6% widowed, 6.4% divorced (2000); Foreign born: 15.1% (2000); Ancestry (includes multiple ancestries): 20.1% Irish, 18.2% Italian, 17.9% Other groups, 11.0% German, 8.2% Polish (2000).
Economy: Manufacturing of greenhouses, pool enclosures, elastic webbing for apparel, photographic accessories, adhesives, apparel.

Agriculture includes horticultural crops and vegetables. Single-family building permits issued: 1 (2005); Multi-family building permits issued: 0 (2005); Employment by occupation: 23.9% management, 37.0% professional, 7.4% services, 24.5% sales, 0.0% farming, 3.1% construction, 4.1% production (2000).
Income: Per capita income: $63,227 (2005); Median household income: $112,448 (2005); Average household income: $166,352 (2005); Percent of households with income of $100,000 or more: 54.8% (2005); Poverty rate: 3.1% (2000).
Education: Percent of population age 25 and over with: High school diploma (including GED) or higher: 95.1% (2005); Bachelor's degree or higher: 61.8% (2005); Master's degree or higher: 32.1% (2005).

School District(s)
Abbott Union Free School District (UG-UG)
   2003-04 Enrollment: 85 . . . . (914) 591-7428
Irvington Union Free School District (KG-12)
   2003-04 Enrollment: 1,967 . . . . (914) 591-8501

Housing: Homeownership rate: 74.0% (2005); Median home value: $615,571 (2005); Median rent: $904 per month (2000); Median age of housing: 44 years (2000).
Safety: Violent crime rate: 0.0 per 10,000 population; Property crime rate: 22.5 per 10,000 population (2004).
Transportation: Commute to work: 67.7% car, 22.7% public transportation, 1.4% walk, 7.1% work from home (2000); Travel time to work: 19.8% less than 15 minutes, 26.3% 15 to 30 minutes, 21.2% 30 to 45 minutes, 10.5% 45 to 60 minutes, 22.1% 60 minutes or more (2000)

Additional Information Contacts
Irvington Chamber of Commerce . . . . (914) 591-6208
   http://www.irvingtonnychamber.com/
Village of Irvington . . . . (914) 591-7070
   http://www.ci.irvington.ny.us/news.asp

JEFFERSON VALLEY-YORKTOWN (CDP).
Covers a land area of 6.913 square miles and a water area of 0.080 square miles. Located at 41.31° N. Lat.; 73.80° W. Long.
Population: 14,118 (1990); 14,891 (2000); 15,251 (2005); 15,598 (2010 projected); Race: 90.6% White, 2.7% Black, 4.1% Asian, 6.3% Hispanic of any race (2005); Density: 2,206.3 persons per square mile (2005); Average household size: 2.71 (2005); Median age: 41.7 (2005); Males per 100 females: 90.2 (2005); Marriage status: 17.2% never married, 70.2% now married, 8.8% widowed, 3.7% divorced (2000); Foreign born: 8.6% (2000); Ancestry (includes multiple ancestries): 36.8% Italian, 23.7% Irish, 13.0% German, 12.5% Other groups, 6.2% English (2000).
Economy: Employment by occupation: 19.7% management, 30.1% professional, 9.0% services, 27.5% sales, 0.1% farming, 9.4% construction, 4.2% production (2000).
Income: Per capita income: $42,536 (2005); Median household income: $97,020 (2005); Average household income: $115,041 (2005); Percent of households with income of $100,000 or more: 48.5% (2005); Poverty rate: 2.5% (2000).
Education: Percent of population age 25 and over with: High school diploma (including GED) or higher: 90.6% (2005); Bachelor's degree or higher: 41.4% (2005); Master's degree or higher: 17.6% (2005).
Housing: Homeownership rate: 91.0% (2005); Median home value: $380,262 (2005); Median rent: $823 per month (2000); Median age of housing: 30 years (2000).
Transportation: Commute to work: 88.1% car, 8.6% public transportation, 0.2% walk, 2.9% work from home (2000); Travel time to work: 18.7% less than 15 minutes, 25.1% 15 to 30 minutes, 26.6% 30 to 45 minutes, 12.1% 45 to 60 minutes, 17.5% 60 minutes or more (2000)

KATONAH (unincorporated postal area, zip code 10536).
Covers a land area of 24.499 square miles and a water area of 0.193 square miles. Located at 41.26° N. Lat.; 73.68° W. Long. Elevation is 226 feet.
History: John Jay Homestead State Historic Site. Caramoor Music Festival each summer at Caramoor Center for Music and Arts.
Population: 0 (2000); Race: 93.3% White, 2.6% Black, 1.8% Asian, 2.8% Hispanic of any race (2000); Density: 0.0 persons per square mile (2000); Age: 30.1% under 18, 11.6% over 64 (2000); Marriage status: 21.4% never married, 65.9% now married, 7.3% widowed, 5.5% divorced (2000); Foreign born: 8.8% (2000); Ancestry (includes multiple ancestries): 23.4% Italian, 18.0% Irish, 14.4% German, 10.5% Other groups, 9.9% English (2000).

Economy: Employment by occupation: 26.6% management, 34.5% professional, 7.3% services, 22.6% sales, 0.1% farming, 6.4% construction, 2.4% production (2000).
Income: Per capita income: $50,455 (2000); Median household income: $109,542 (2000); Poverty rate: 2.5% (2000).
Education: Percent of population age 25 and over with: High school diploma (including GED) or higher: 94.7% (2000); Bachelor's degree or higher: 58.5% (2000).

School District(s)
Katonah-Lewisboro Union Free School District (KG-12)
   2003-04 Enrollment: 4,112 . . . . (914) 763-7001

Housing: Homeownership rate: 86.7% (2000); Median home value: $448,600 (2000); Median rent: $965 per month (2000); Median age of housing: 37 years (2000).
Hospitals: Four Winds Hospital (175 beds)
Transportation: Commute to work: 73.6% car, 17.1% public transportation, 1.3% walk, 7.6% work from home (2000); Travel time to work: 19.8% less than 15 minutes, 26.5% 15 to 30 minutes, 24.1% 30 to 45 minutes, 4.8% 45 to 60 minutes, 24.8% 60 minutes or more (2000)

Additional Information Contacts
Katonah Chamber of Commerce . . . . (914) 232-2668
   http://www.katonahchamber.org

LAKE MOHEGAN (CDP).
Covers a land area of 2.905 square miles and a water area of 0.175 square miles. Located at 41.31° N. Lat.; 73.84° W. Long.
Population: 4,831 (1990); 5,979 (2000); 6,137 (2005); 6,288 (2010 projected); Race: 81.4% White, 8.0% Black, 3.9% Asian, 12.6% Hispanic of any race (2005); Density: 2,112.8 persons per square mile (2005); Average household size: 3.01 (2005); Median age: 36.7 (2005); Males per 100 females: 100.4 (2005); Marriage status: 21.9% never married, 63.0% now married, 6.6% widowed, 8.6% divorced (2000); Foreign born: 10.1% (2000); Ancestry (includes multiple ancestries): 33.0% Italian, 20.5% Irish, 20.1% Other groups, 13.3% German, 4.8% Polish (2000).
Economy: Employment by occupation: 18.8% management, 28.1% professional, 10.9% services, 26.5% sales, 0.2% farming, 10.2% construction, 5.3% production (2000).
Income: Per capita income: $34,892 (2005); Median household income: $87,621 (2005); Average household income: $102,826 (2005); Percent of households with income of $100,000 or more: 42.5% (2005); Poverty rate: 4.1% (2000).
Education: Percent of population age 25 and over with: High school diploma (including GED) or higher: 87.3% (2005); Bachelor's degree or higher: 38.2% (2005); Master's degree or higher: 15.3% (2005).
Housing: Homeownership rate: 79.7% (2005); Median home value: $330,108 (2005); Median rent: $1,078 per month (2000); Median age of housing: 32 years (2000).
Transportation: Commute to work: 86.6% car, 10.0% public transportation, 1.0% walk, 2.5% work from home (2000); Travel time to work: 15.5% less than 15 minutes, 19.8% 15 to 30 minutes, 24.2% 30 to 45 minutes, 17.7% 45 to 60 minutes, 22.8% 60 minutes or more (2000)

LARCHMONT (village).
Covers a land area of 1.068 square miles and a water area of 0.004 square miles. Located at 40.92° N. Lat.; 73.75° W. Long. Elevation is 50 feet.
History: Joyce Kilmer lived here. Developed c.1845, incorporated 1891.
Population: 6,181 (1990); 6,485 (2000); 6,549 (2005); 6,640 (2010 projected); Race: 93.7% White, 0.5% Black, 3.2% Asian, 5.0% Hispanic of any race (2005); Density: 6,133.6 persons per square mile (2005); Average household size: 2.66 (2005); Median age: 38.7 (2005); Males per 100 females: 91.9 (2005); Marriage status: 22.2% never married, 66.9% now married, 4.7% widowed, 6.2% divorced (2000); Foreign born: 16.4% (2000); Ancestry (includes multiple ancestries): 19.5% Irish, 14.0% Italian, 13.9% German, 10.1% Other groups, 9.1% French (except Basque) (2000).
Economy: A few small light industries. Yachting center (annual regattas). Single-family building permits issued: 4 (2005); Multi-family building permits issued: 0 (2005); Employment by occupation: 30.2% management, 38.7% professional, 7.3% services, 20.7% sales, 0.0% farming, 1.7% construction, 1.5% production (2000).
Income: Per capita income: $76,565 (2005); Median household income: $139,366 (2005); Average household income: $203,517 (2005); Percent of households with income of $100,000 or more: 61.3% (2005); Poverty rate: 2.3% (2000).

Education: Percent of population age 25 and over with: High school diploma (including GED) or higher: 97.1% (2005); Bachelor's degree or higher: 73.4% (2005); Master's degree or higher: 45.9% (2005).

School District(s)
Mamaroneck Union Free School District (PK-12)
   2003-04 Enrollment: 4,791 .... (914) 220-3005
Housing: Homeownership rate: 71.2% (2005); Median home value: $944,986 (2005); Median rent: $1,013 per month (2000); Median age of housing: 60+ years (2000).
Transportation: Commute to work: 48.2% car, 38.1% public transportation, 3.6% walk, 8.8% work from home (2000); Travel time to work: 15.3% less than 15 minutes, 15.9% 15 to 30 minutes, 20.0% 30 to 45 minutes, 22.2% 45 to 60 minutes, 26.5% 60 minutes or more (2000)
Additional Information Contacts
Village of Larchmont .... (914) 834-6230
   http://www.villageoflarchmont.org/

LEWISBORO (town).
Covers a land area of 27.851 square miles and a water area of 1.270 square miles. Located at 41.26° N. Lat.; 73.58° W. Long. Elevation is 722 feet.
Population: 11,313 (1990); 12,324 (2000); 12,526 (2005); 12,753 (2010 projected); Race: 94.4% White, 1.3% Black, 2.6% Asian, 3.1% Hispanic of any race (2005); Density: 449.8 persons per square mile (2005); Average household size: 2.93 (2005); Median age: 39.2 (2005); Males per 100 females: 95.7 (2005); Marriage status: 16.8% never married, 73.4% now married, 4.0% widowed, 5.8% divorced (2000); Foreign born: 8.1% (2000); Ancestry (includes multiple ancestries): 21.3% Italian, 20.0% Irish, 13.1% German, 11.3% English, 9.3% Other groups (2000).
Economy: Single-family building permits issued: 5 (2005); Multi-family building permits issued: 0 (2005); Employment by occupation: 28.1% management, 34.7% professional, 6.3% services, 23.5% sales, 0.0% farming, 4.3% construction, 3.1% production (2000).
Income: Per capita income: $63,739 (2005); Median household income: $133,145 (2005); Average household income: $186,294 (2005); Percent of households with income of $100,000 or more: 64.4% (2005); Poverty rate: 1.9% (2000).
Education: Percent of population age 25 and over with: High school diploma (including GED) or higher: 96.9% (2005); Bachelor's degree or higher: 65.4% (2005); Master's degree or higher: 30.6% (2005).
Housing: Homeownership rate: 91.1% (2005); Median home value: $661,181 (2005); Median rent: $896 per month (2000); Median age of housing: 27 years (2000).
Safety: Violent crime rate: 2.4 per 10,000 population; Property crime rate: 181.9 per 10,000 population (2004).
Transportation: Commute to work: 78.8% car, 13.5% public transportation, 0.3% walk, 7.2% work from home (2000); Travel time to work: 13.5% less than 15 minutes, 27.3% 15 to 30 minutes, 27.4% 30 to 45 minutes, 7.2% 45 to 60 minutes, 24.6% 60 minutes or more (2000)
Additional Information Contacts
Town of Lewisboro .... (914) 763-3511
   http://www.lewisborogov.com/

LINCOLNDALE (CDP).
Covers a land area of 1.400 square miles and a water area of 0.034 square miles. Located at 41.33° N. Lat.; 73.72° W. Long.
Population: 2,287 (1990); 2,018 (2000); 1,925 (2005); 1,881 (2010 projected); Race: 96.1% White, 0.8% Black, 1.7% Asian, 3.1% Hispanic of any race (2005); Density: 1,374.8 persons per square mile (2005); Average household size: 2.77 (2005); Median age: 38.6 (2005); Males per 100 females: 96.2 (2005); Marriage status: 18.8% never married, 74.6% now married, 2.4% widowed, 4.1% divorced (2000); Foreign born: 9.1% (2000); Ancestry (includes multiple ancestries): 38.4% Italian, 17.3% Irish, 17.3% German, 9.8% Other groups, 9.2% United States or American (2000).
Economy: Employment by occupation: 26.2% management, 23.2% professional, 6.4% services, 27.4% sales, 0.0% farming, 9.7% construction, 7.1% production (2000).
Income: Per capita income: $45,917 (2005); Median household income: $100,621 (2005); Average household income: $127,363 (2005); Percent of households with income of $100,000 or more: 50.3% (2005); Poverty rate: 0.8% (2000).
Education: Percent of population age 25 and over with: High school diploma (including GED) or higher: 94.5% (2005); Bachelor's degree or higher: 47.2% (2005); Master's degree or higher: 19.8% (2005).

School District(s)
Somers Central School District (KG-12)
   2003-04 Enrollment: 3,140 .... (914) 248-7872
Housing: Homeownership rate: 92.4% (2005); Median home value: $409,643 (2005); Median rent: $1,125 per month (2000); Median age of housing: 31 years (2000).
Transportation: Commute to work: 79.9% car, 9.0% public transportation, 0.0% walk, 9.8% work from home (2000); Travel time to work: 17.2% less than 15 minutes, 26.4% 15 to 30 minutes, 27.6% 30 to 45 minutes, 11.8% 45 to 60 minutes, 17.0% 60 minutes or more (2000)

MAMARONECK (village).
Covers a land area of 3.233 square miles and a water area of 3.459 square miles. Located at 40.94° N. Lat.; 73.73° W. Long. Elevation is 47 feet.
Population: 17,325 (1990); 18,752 (2000); 18,750 (2005); 18,794 (2010 projected); Race: 82.5% White, 4.0% Black, 4.1% Asian, 22.6% Hispanic of any race (2005); Density: 5,798.8 persons per square mile (2005); Average household size: 2.66 (2005); Median age: 39.5 (2005); Males per 100 females: 93.2 (2005); Marriage status: 25.0% never married, 60.0% now married, 8.2% widowed, 6.8% divorced (2000); Foreign born: 25.6% (2000); Ancestry (includes multiple ancestries): 28.5% Italian, 26.0% Other groups, 12.5% Irish, 6.9% German, 4.4% United States or American (2000).
Economy: Single-family building permits issued: 3 (2005); Multi-family building permits issued: 0 (2005); Employment by occupation: 19.8% management, 23.2% professional, 13.6% services, 28.2% sales, 0.0% farming, 8.2% construction, 7.0% production (2000).
Income: Per capita income: $39,324 (2005); Median household income: $70,322 (2005); Average household income: $104,110 (2005); Percent of households with income of $100,000 or more: 34.3% (2005); Poverty rate: 6.9% (2000).
Education: Percent of population age 25 and over with: High school diploma (including GED) or higher: 82.9% (2005); Bachelor's degree or higher: 38.3% (2005); Master's degree or higher: 18.5% (2005).

School District(s)
Mamaroneck Union Free School District (PK-12)
   2003-04 Enrollment: 4,791 .... (914) 220-3005
Rye Neck Union Free School District (KG-12)
   2003-04 Enrollment: 1,384 .... (914) 777-5200
Housing: Homeownership rate: 58.8% (2005); Median home value: $528,158 (2005); Median rent: $933 per month (2000); Median age of housing: 50 years (2000).
Safety: Violent crime rate: 9.7 per 10,000 population; Property crime rate: 160.8 per 10,000 population (2004).
Transportation: Commute to work: 70.0% car, 19.7% public transportation, 5.7% walk, 4.0% work from home (2000); Travel time to work: 25.4% less than 15 minutes, 30.7% 15 to 30 minutes, 17.9% 30 to 45 minutes, 8.5% 45 to 60 minutes, 17.5% 60 minutes or more (2000)
Additional Information Contacts
Mamoraneck Chamber of Commerce .... (914) 698-4400
Village of Mamaroneck .... (914) 777-7722
   http://www.village.mamaroneck.ny.us/

MAMARONECK (town).
Covers a land area of 6.617 square miles and a water area of 7.423 square miles. Located at 40.93° N. Lat.; 73.74° W. Long. Elevation is 47 feet.
History: Initially a farming community. Settled 1661, incorporated 1895.
Population: 27,706 (1990); 28,967 (2000); 29,056 (2005); 29,180 (2010 projected); Race: 87.7% White, 2.7% Black, 3.5% Asian, 13.7% Hispanic of any race (2005); Density: 4,390.9 persons per square mile (2005); Average household size: 2.65 (2005); Median age: 39.9 (2005); Males per 100 females: 92.4 (2005); Marriage status: 22.2% never married, 65.6% now married, 6.7% widowed, 5.6% divorced (2000); Foreign born: 21.8% (2000); Ancestry (includes multiple ancestries): 20.3% Other groups, 19.6% Italian, 14.6% Irish, 9.6% German, 7.2% Russian (2000).
Economy: Boating center with an excellent marina. There is some light manufacturing in addition to office and corporate activity. Unemployment rate: 3.2% (2005); Total civilian labor force: 15,203 (2005); Single-family building permits issued: 22 (2005); Multi-family building permits issued: 0 (2005); Employment by occupation: 24.0% management, 31.7% professional, 9.4% services, 25.6% sales, 0.0% farming, 4.6% construction, 4.6% production (2000).
Income: Per capita income: $61,767 (2005); Median household income: $97,451 (2005); Average household income: $163,266 (2005); Percent of

households with income of $100,000 or more: 49.0% (2005); Poverty rate: 4.5% (2000).
Taxes: Total city taxes per capita: $577 (2004); City property taxes per capita: $501 (2004).
Education: Percent of population age 25 and over with: High school diploma (including GED) or higher: 90.6% (2005); Bachelor's degree or higher: 57.3% (2005); Master's degree or higher: 32.1% (2005).
Housing: Homeownership rate: 66.7% (2005); Median home value: $735,214 (2005); Median rent: $978 per month (2000); Median age of housing: 57 years (2000).
Transportation: Commute to work: 56.5% car, 31.4% public transportation, 4.6% walk, 6.7% work from home (2000); Travel time to work: 19.7% less than 15 minutes, 23.1% 15 to 30 minutes, 19.8% 30 to 45 minutes, 14.9% 45 to 60 minutes, 22.4% 60 minutes or more (2000)
Additional Information Contacts
Town of Mamaroneck . . . . (914) 381-7805
  http://www.townofmamaroneck.org/

MILLWOOD (unincorporated postal area, zip code 10546). Covers a land area of 2.367 square miles and a water area of 0.004 square miles. Located at 41.20° N. Lat.; 73.79° W. Long. Elevation is 351 feet.
Population: 0 (2000); Race: 84.3% White, 0.4% Black, 15.0% Asian, 0.3% Hispanic of any race (2000); Density: 0.0 persons per square mile (2000); Age: 28.6% under 18, 3.6% over 64 (2000); Marriage status: 18.1% never married, 74.0% now married, 1.9% widowed, 6.0% divorced (2000); Foreign born: 14.1% (2000); Ancestry (includes multiple ancestries): 19.8% Other groups, 19.5% Irish, 17.7% Italian, 9.4% Russian, 7.0% German (2000).
Economy: Employment by occupation: 25.7% management, 44.8% professional, 9.3% services, 15.9% sales, 0.0% farming, 3.0% construction, 1.1% production (2000).
Income: Per capita income: $49,293 (2000); Median household income: $115,207 (2000); Poverty rate: 1.2% (2000).
Education: Percent of population age 25 and over with: High school diploma (including GED) or higher: 94.7% (2000); Bachelor's degree or higher: 70.9% (2000).
Housing: Homeownership rate: 88.4% (2000); Median home value: $347,100 (2000); Median rent: $1,115 per month (2000); Median age of housing: 24 years (2000).
Transportation: Commute to work: 72.5% car, 22.8% public transportation, 0.0% walk, 4.6% work from home (2000); Travel time to work: 18.2% less than 15 minutes, 26.2% 15 to 30 minutes, 17.6% 30 to 45 minutes, 7.3% 45 to 60 minutes, 30.8% 60 minutes or more (2000)

MOHEGAN LAKE (unincorporated postal area, zip code 10547). Covers a land area of 5.989 square miles and a water area of 0.187 square miles. Located at 41.31° N. Lat.; 73.85° W. Long.
Population: 0 (2000); Race: 83.7% White, 5.4% Black, 3.5% Asian, 11.9% Hispanic of any race (2000); Density: 0.0 persons per square mile (2000); Age: 27.6% under 18, 9.2% over 64 (2000); Marriage status: 23.5% never married, 62.8% now married, 5.7% widowed, 8.0% divorced (2000); Foreign born: 12.4% (2000); Ancestry (includes multiple ancestries): 30.1% Italian, 21.2% Other groups, 19.4% Irish, 12.9% German, 5.7% Polish (2000).
Economy: Employment by occupation: 17.2% management, 25.8% professional, 13.4% services, 27.8% sales, 0.1% farming, 10.4% construction, 5.3% production (2000).
Income: Per capita income: $28,578 (2000); Median household income: $71,875 (2000); Poverty rate: 6.4% (2000).
Education: Percent of population age 25 and over with: High school diploma (including GED) or higher: 86.6% (2000); Bachelor's degree or higher: 37.1% (2000).
School District(s)
Lakeland Central School District (KG-12)
  2003-04 Enrollment: 6,139 . . . . (914) 245-1700
Housing: Homeownership rate: 74.4% (2000); Median home value: $206,400 (2000); Median rent: $938 per month (2000); Median age of housing: 39 years (2000).
Transportation: Commute to work: 86.0% car, 9.2% public transportation, 2.9% walk, 1.7% work from home (2000); Travel time to work: 19.2% less than 15 minutes, 19.3% 15 to 30 minutes, 25.4% 30 to 45 minutes, 16.6% 45 to 60 minutes, 19.5% 60 minutes or more (2000)

MONTROSE (unincorporated postal area, zip code 10548). Covers a land area of 2.933 square miles and a water area of 0.006 square miles. Located at 41.24° N. Lat.; 73.94° W. Long. Elevation is 118 feet.
Population: 0 (2000); Race: 89.9% White, 5.2% Black, 1.6% Asian, 5.6% Hispanic of any race (2000); Density: 0.0 persons per square mile (2000); Age: 23.0% under 18, 14.1% over 64 (2000); Marriage status: 22.8% never married, 61.5% now married, 7.6% widowed, 8.1% divorced (2000); Foreign born: 8.9% (2000); Ancestry (includes multiple ancestries): 32.3% Italian, 31.0% Irish, 14.9% German, 12.7% Other groups, 5.0% English (2000).
Economy: Employment by occupation: 18.0% management, 27.3% professional, 12.2% services, 24.8% sales, 0.0% farming, 9.6% construction, 8.0% production (2000).
Income: Per capita income: $29,004 (2000); Median household income: $65,553 (2000); Poverty rate: 8.3% (2000).
Education: Percent of population age 25 and over with: High school diploma (including GED) or higher: 86.7% (2000); Bachelor's degree or higher: 28.3% (2000).
School District(s)
Hendrick Hudson Central School District (KG-12)
  2003-04 Enrollment: 2,884 . . . . (914) 736-5200
Housing: Homeownership rate: 77.5% (2000); Median home value: $197,200 (2000); Median rent: $796 per month (2000); Median age of housing: 45 years (2000).
Hospitals: Franklin D. Roosevelt Veterans Affairs Hospital (672 beds); Veterans Affairs Hudson Valley Health Care System
Transportation: Commute to work: 82.9% car, 8.2% public transportation, 3.2% walk, 4.0% work from home (2000); Travel time to work: 33.6% less than 15 minutes, 16.2% 15 to 30 minutes, 24.8% 30 to 45 minutes, 8.1% 45 to 60 minutes, 17.3% 60 minutes or more (2000)

MOUNT KISCO (town and village). Covers a land area of 3.126 square miles and a water area of 0 square miles. Located at 41.20° N. Lat.; 73.73° W. Long. Elevation is 289 feet.
History: Incorporated 1874.
Population: 9,108 (1990); 9,983 (2000); 10,022 (2005); 10,075 (2010 projected); Race: 74.0% White, 5.4% Black, 5.3% Asian, 31.7% Hispanic of any race (2005); Density: 3,206.4 persons per square mile (2005); Average household size: 2.55 (2005); Median age: 38.1 (2005); Males per 100 females: 100.2 (2005); Marriage status: 32.1% never married, 53.6% now married, 6.5% widowed, 7.9% divorced (2000); Foreign born: 31.2% (2000); Ancestry (includes multiple ancestries): 32.7% Other groups, 21.2% Italian, 13.7% Irish, 7.7% German, 5.9% English (2000).
Economy: Some light industry: electronics. Single-family building permits issued: 20 (2005); Multi-family building permits issued: 0 (2005); Employment by occupation: 16.6% management, 23.7% professional, 20.8% services, 22.5% sales, 0.0% farming, 9.1% construction, 7.3% production (2000).
Income: Per capita income: $37,775 (2005); Median household income: $64,842 (2005); Average household income: $95,433 (2005); Percent of households with income of $100,000 or more: 29.5% (2005); Poverty rate: 10.5% (2000).
Education: Percent of population age 25 and over with: High school diploma (including GED) or higher: 78.7% (2005); Bachelor's degree or higher: 37.4% (2005); Master's degree or higher: 17.9% (2005).
School District(s)
Bedford Central School District (PK-12)
  2003-04 Enrollment: 4,268 . . . . (914) 241-6010
Four-year College(s)
Yeshiva of Nitra Rabbinical College
  Fall 2004 Enrollment: 206 . . . . (718) 384-5460
  2005-06 Tuition: In-state $5,000; Out-of-state $5,000
Housing: Homeownership rate: 56.2% (2005); Median home value: $397,120 (2005); Median rent: $846 per month (2000); Median age of housing: 37 years (2000).
Hospitals: Northern Westchester Hospital (233 beds)
Safety: Violent crime rate: 21.9 per 10,000 population; Property crime rate: 177.0 per 10,000 population (2004).
Transportation: Commute to work: 70.5% car, 15.5% public transportation, 8.7% walk, 4.0% work from home (2000); Travel time to work: 31.8% less than 15 minutes, 29.6% 15 to 30 minutes, 19.8% 30 to 45 minutes, 5.2% 45 to 60 minutes, 13.6% 60 minutes or more (2000)
Additional Information Contacts

Mount Kisco Chamber of Commerce................... (914) 666-7525
http://www.mtkisco.com/

MOUNT PLEASANT (town). Covers a land area of 27.697 square miles and a water area of 4.994 square miles. Located at 41.11° N. Lat.; 73.79° W. Long. Elevation is 262 feet.
Population: 40,590 (1990); 43,221 (2000); 43,931 (2005); 44,841 (2010 projected); Race: 82.1% White, 5.2% Black, 4.0% Asian, 16.3% Hispanic of any race (2005); Density: 1,586.1 persons per square mile (2005); Average household size: 3.16 (2005); Median age: 37.3 (2005); Males per 100 females: 103.5 (2005); Marriage status: 28.2% never married, 60.7% now married, 6.2% widowed, 4.8% divorced (2000); Foreign born: 18.1% (2000); Ancestry (includes multiple ancestries): 28.8% Italian, 19.5% Other groups, 18.5% Irish, 10.2% German, 5.4% English (2000).
Economy: Unemployment rate: 3.9% (2005); Total civilian labor force: 22,192 (2005); Single-family building permits issued: 24 (2005); Multi-family building permits issued: 0 (2005); Employment by occupation: 20.8% management, 26.5% professional, 13.2% services, 24.3% sales, 0.1% farming, 8.7% construction, 6.3% production (2000).
Income: Per capita income: $41,736 (2005); Median household income: $93,984 (2005); Average household income: $129,339 (2005); Percent of households with income of $100,000 or more: 47.1% (2005); Poverty rate: 4.9% (2000).
Taxes: Total city taxes per capita: $664 (2004); City property taxes per capita: $546 (2004).
Education: Percent of population age 25 and over with: High school diploma (including GED) or higher: 84.5% (2005); Bachelor's degree or higher: 43.6% (2005); Master's degree or higher: 20.4% (2005).
Housing: Homeownership rate: 72.3% (2005); Median home value: $570,496 (2005); Median rent: $872 per month (2000); Median age of housing: 46 years (2000).
Safety: Violent crime rate: 4.1 per 10,000 population; Property crime rate: 68.8 per 10,000 population (2004).
Transportation: Commute to work: 77.2% car, 15.0% public transportation, 3.8% walk, 3.5% work from home (2000); Travel time to work: 27.3% less than 15 minutes, 31.4% 15 to 30 minutes, 16.6% 30 to 45 minutes, 8.3% 45 to 60 minutes, 16.4% 60 minutes or more (2000)
Additional Information Contacts
Town of Mount Pleasant .... (914) 742-2300
http://www.mtpleasant.americantowns.com/

MOUNT VERNON (city). Covers a land area of 4.358 square miles and a water area of 0.019 square miles. Located at 40.91° N. Lat.; 73.83° W. Long. Elevation is 100 feet.
History: Named for George Washington's estate on the Potomac River, which was named for Edward Vernon, British admiral. John Peter Zenger was arrested here for libel in 1733. The city itself was not founded until 1851, when a cooperative group, the Industrial Home Association, bought the land and built a planned community. St. Paul's Church (c.1761), a national historic site, is here. The city, which has a large French-American population, has been the scene of a great deal of controversy over school and housing integration in the 1970s, 1980s, and 1990s.
Population: 67,076 (1990); 68,381 (2000); 68,221 (2005); 68,182 (2010 projected); Race: 24.7% White, 62.0% Black, 2.5% Asian, 12.0% Hispanic of any race (2005); Density: 15,652.6 persons per square mile (2005); Average household size: 2.65 (2005); Median age: 37.4 (2005); Males per 100 females: 83.7 (2005); Marriage status: 36.3% never married, 46.6% now married, 8.5% widowed, 8.5% divorced (2000); Foreign born: 29.1% (2000); Ancestry (includes multiple ancestries): 46.2% Other groups, 12.3% Jamaican, 10.3% Italian, 4.0% Irish, 2.7% United States or American (2000).
Economy: Although primarily a residential suburb of N.Y. city, its manufacturing includes pharmaceuticals and electronic components. Unemployment rate: 5.3% (2005); Total civilian labor force: 34,438 (2005); Single-family building permits issued: 7 (2005); Multi-family building permits issued: 34 (2005); Employment by occupation: 12.0% management, 22.2% professional, 20.3% services, 28.4% sales, 0.0% farming, 8.2% construction, 8.8% production (2000).
Income: Per capita income: $22,819 (2005); Median household income: $44,968 (2005); Average household income: $60,261 (2005); Percent of households with income of $100,000 or more: 16.6% (2005); Poverty rate: 14.2% (2000).
Education: Percent of population age 25 and over with: High school diploma (including GED) or higher: 74.6% (2005); Bachelor's degree or higher: 24.3% (2005); Master's degree or higher: 9.8% (2005).

School District(s)
Mount Vernon City School District (PK-12)
 2003-04 Enrollment: 10,347 .... (914) 665-5201
Two-year College(s)
Dorothea Hopfer School of Nursing-Mt Vernon Hospital
 Fall 2004 Enrollment: 130 .... (914) 664-8000
 2005-06 Tuition: In-state $5,944; Out-of-state $5,944
Westchester School of Beauty Culture
 Fall 2004 Enrollment: 59 .... (914) 699-2344
Housing: Homeownership rate: 37.0% (2005); Median home value: $368,276 (2005); Median rent: $696 per month (2000); Median age of housing: 56 years (2000).
Hospitals: Mount Vernon Hospital (223 beds)
Safety: Violent crime rate: 79.4 per 10,000 population; Property crime rate: 260.6 per 10,000 population (2004).
Transportation: Commute to work: 63.9% car, 27.5% public transportation, 5.5% walk, 2.0% work from home (2000); Travel time to work: 16.3% less than 15 minutes, 33.1% 15 to 30 minutes, 22.6% 30 to 45 minutes, 10.1% 45 to 60 minutes, 18.0% 60 minutes or more (2000)
Additional Information Contacts
City of Mount Vernon.............................. (914) 665-2300
http://www.ci.mount-vernon.ny.us/
Mt Vernon Chamber of Commerce .... (914) 667-7500
http://www.mvnycoc.org

NEW CASTLE (town). Covers a land area of 23.173 square miles and a water area of 0.273 square miles. Located at 41.18° N. Lat.; 73.76° W. Long.
Population: 16,801 (1990); 17,491 (2000); 17,736 (2005); 18,011 (2010 projected); Race: 90.3% White, 1.5% Black, 6.4% Asian, 3.4% Hispanic of any race (2005); Density: 765.4 persons per square mile (2005); Average household size: 3.04 (2005); Median age: 39.9 (2005); Males per 100 females: 97.4 (2005); Marriage status: 17.2% never married, 75.2% now married, 3.0% widowed, 4.6% divorced (2000); Foreign born: 11.3% (2000); Ancestry (includes multiple ancestries): 18.1% Other groups, 14.4% Italian, 12.7% Irish, 11.1% Russian, 8.7% German (2000).
Economy: Single-family building permits issued: 16 (2005); Multi-family building permits issued: 0 (2005); Employment by occupation: 26.6% management, 42.0% professional, 5.8% services, 21.4% sales, 0.0% farming, 3.0% construction, 1.2% production (2000).
Income: Per capita income: $78,162 (2005); Median household income: $185,487 (2005); Average household income: $237,464 (2005); Percent of households with income of $100,000 or more: 74.2% (2005); Poverty rate: 3.5% (2000).
Taxes: Total city taxes per capita: $905 (2004); City property taxes per capita: $742 (2004).
Education: Percent of population age 25 and over with: High school diploma (including GED) or higher: 96.5% (2005); Bachelor's degree or higher: 75.9% (2005); Master's degree or higher: 44.7% (2005).
Housing: Homeownership rate: 91.7% (2005); Median home value: $859,992 (2005); Median rent: $1,279 per month (2000); Median age of housing: 38 years (2000).
Safety: Violent crime rate: 3.4 per 10,000 population; Property crime rate: 55.2 per 10,000 population (2004).
Transportation: Commute to work: 66.4% car, 25.3% public transportation, 0.5% walk, 7.2% work from home (2000); Travel time to work: 17.5% less than 15 minutes, 23.7% 15 to 30 minutes, 16.3% 30 to 45 minutes, 8.0% 45 to 60 minutes, 34.6% 60 minutes or more (2000)
Additional Information Contacts
Town of New Castle............................... (914) 238-4771
http://www.town.new-castle.ny.us/

NEW ROCHELLE (city). Covers a land area of 10.351 square miles and a water area of 2.877 square miles. Located at 40.92° N. Lat.; 73.78° W. Long. Elevation is 94 feet.
History: New Rochelle occupies the site of the villages of the Siwanoy, principal nation of the Wappinger confederacy. In 1689, a group of Huguenot refugees purchased a tract of 6,000 acres and named the settlement for their old home in France, La Rochelle. New Rochelle was incorporated as a village in 1857 and as a city in 1899.
Population: 67,429 (1990); 72,182 (2000); 72,741 (2005); 73,381 (2010 projected); Race: 64.8% White, 20.1% Black, 3.7% Asian, 24.9% Hispanic of any race (2005); Density: 7,027.6 persons per square mile (2005); Average household size: 2.79 (2005); Median age: 38.1 (2005); Males per 100 females: 91.6 (2005); Marriage status: 29.9% never married, 55.1%

now married, 8.2% widowed, 6.8% divorced (2000); Foreign born: 27.3% (2000); Ancestry (includes multiple ancestries): 35.0% Other groups, 20.0% Italian, 8.9% Irish, 5.3% German, 4.4% United States or American (2000).
Economy: Unemployment rate: 4.7% (2005); Total civilian labor force: 37,709 (2005); Single-family building permits issued: 41 (2005); Multi-family building permits issued: 5 (2005); Employment by occupation: 15.5% management, 26.8% professional, 17.0% services, 25.2% sales, 0.1% farming, 8.4% construction, 7.0% production (2000).
Income: Per capita income: $35,274 (2005); Median household income: $64,448 (2005); Average household income: $97,198 (2005); Percent of households with income of $100,000 or more: 31.4% (2005); Poverty rate: 10.5% (2000).
Education: Percent of population age 25 and over with: High school diploma (including GED) or higher: 79.8% (2005); Bachelor's degree or higher: 38.2% (2005); Master's degree or higher: 19.6% (2005).

School District(s)
New Rochelle City School District (PK-12)
    2003-04 Enrollment: 10,464 . . . . (914) 576-4200

Four-year College(s)
Iona College
    Fall 2004 Enrollment: 4,329. . . . . (914) 633-2000
    2005-06 Tuition: In-state $20,980; Out-of-state $20,980
Monroe College-New Rochelle
    Fall 2004 Enrollment: 1,570. . . . . (914) 632-5400
    2005-06 Tuition: In-state $14,650; Out-of-state $14,650
The College of New Rochelle
    Fall 2004 Enrollment: 7,099. . . . . (914) 632-5300
    2005-06 Tuition: In-state $18,300; Out-of-state $18,300

Housing: Homeownership rate: 51.2% (2005); Median home value: $494,846 (2005); Median rent: $801 per month (2000); Median age of housing: 53 years (2000).
Hospitals: Sound Shore Medical Center of Westchester (476 beds)
Safety: Violent crime rate: 31.1 per 10,000 population; Property crime rate: 213.6 per 10,000 population (2004).
Newspapers: Bronx News (General - Circulation 10,000); City News (General - Circulation 17,000); Parkchester News (General - Circulation 12,500); Review Press-Reporter (General - Circulation 3,200); Town and Village (General - Circulation 8,300)
Transportation: Commute to work: 71.8% car, 17.8% public transportation, 6.6% walk, 2.9% work from home (2000); Travel time to work: 22.5% less than 15 minutes, 33.6% 15 to 30 minutes, 21.9% 30 to 45 minutes, 8.1% 45 to 60 minutes, 13.9% 60 minutes or more (2000); Amtrak: Service available.

Additional Information Contacts
City of New Rochelle . . . . (914) 654-2000
    http://www.newrochelleny.com/
New Rochelle Chamber of Commerce . . . . (914) 632-5700
    http://www.newrochellechamber.org/

NORTH CASTLE
NORTH CASTLE (town). Covers a land area of 24.087 square miles and a water area of 2.402 square miles. Located at 41.11° N. Lat.; 73.71° W. Long.
History: Town got its name from a barrier built by the Mohicans to protect themselves from attack.
Population: 10,164 (1990); 10,849 (2000); 11,856 (2005); 12,799 (2010 projected); Race: 91.4% White, 1.8% Black, 4.7% Asian, 5.0% Hispanic of any race (2005); Density: 492.2 persons per square mile (2005); Average household size: 3.03 (2005); Median age: 40.0 (2005); Males per 100 females: 96.9 (2005); Marriage status: 20.1% never married, 71.2% now married, 3.9% widowed, 4.8% divorced (2000); Foreign born: 12.7% (2000); Ancestry (includes multiple ancestries): 26.9% Italian, 15.3% Irish, 14.2% Other groups, 10.2% German, 8.0% English (2000).
Economy: Suburban residential area. Site of IBM's international headquarters. Single-family building permits issued: 23 (2005); Multi-family building permits issued: 0 (2005); Employment by occupation: 26.7% management, 27.1% professional, 9.2% services, 27.3% sales, 0.1% farming, 6.6% construction, 3.0% production (2000).
Income: Per capita income: $66,210 (2005); Median household income: $138,125 (2005); Average household income: $200,271 (2005); Percent of households with income of $100,000 or more: 62.5% (2005); Poverty rate: 3.0% (2000).
Taxes: Total city taxes per capita: $1,281 (2004); City property taxes per capita: $1,054 (2004).
Education: Percent of population age 25 and over with: High school diploma (including GED) or higher: 92.4% (2005); Bachelor's degree or higher: 56.9% (2005); Master's degree or higher: 28.5% (2005).
Housing: Homeownership rate: 87.3% (2005); Median home value: $960,330 (2005); Median rent: $1,033 per month (2000); Median age of housing: 37 years (2000).
Safety: Violent crime rate: 10.3 per 10,000 population; Property crime rate: 120.7 per 10,000 population (2004).
Transportation: Commute to work: 79.5% car, 13.0% public transportation, 2.2% walk, 5.1% work from home (2000); Travel time to work: 23.1% less than 15 minutes, 34.7% 15 to 30 minutes, 16.1% 30 to 45 minutes, 5.9% 45 to 60 minutes, 20.2% 60 minutes or more (2000)

Additional Information Contacts
Town of North Castle . . . . (914) 273-3321
    http://www.northcastleny.com/

NORTH SALEM
NORTH SALEM (town). Covers a land area of 21.420 square miles and a water area of 1.456 square miles. Located at 41.32° N. Lat.; 73.61° W. Long.
History: DeLancey Town Hall, a restored 18th-century Georgian manor, is on the National Register of Historic Places; Museum, Japanese Stroll Garden also here.
Population: 4,725 (1990); 5,173 (2000); 5,269 (2005); 5,396 (2010 projected); Race: 94.5% White, 0.9% Black, 1.1% Asian, 5.0% Hispanic of any race (2005); Density: 246.0 persons per square mile (2005); Average household size: 2.90 (2005); Median age: 41.5 (2005); Males per 100 females: 92.3 (2005); Marriage status: 19.8% never married, 65.1% now married, 8.1% widowed, 7.1% divorced (2000); Foreign born: 10.1% (2000); Ancestry (includes multiple ancestries): 26.8% Irish, 25.1% Italian, 16.3% German, 10.4% Other groups, 8.8% English (2000).
Economy: Raising of horses for hunting and jumping. Single-family building permits issued: 5 (2005); Multi-family building permits issued: 0 (2005); Employment by occupation: 23.8% management, 31.5% professional, 9.7% services, 21.6% sales, 0.0% farming, 9.4% construction, 4.0% production (2000).
Income: Per capita income: $49,402 (2005); Median household income: $117,376 (2005); Average household income: $140,746 (2005); Percent of households with income of $100,000 or more: 59.2% (2005); Poverty rate: 2.0% (2000).
Education: Percent of population age 25 and over with: High school diploma (including GED) or higher: 92.9% (2005); Bachelor's degree or higher: 48.3% (2005); Master's degree or higher: 22.4% (2005).

School District(s)
North Salem Central School District (KG-12)
    2003-04 Enrollment: 1,408 . . . . (914) 669-5414

Housing: Homeownership rate: 86.3% (2005); Median home value: $521,778 (2005); Median rent: $1,000 per month (2000); Median age of housing: 43 years (2000).
Transportation: Commute to work: 81.1% car, 12.3% public transportation, 1.7% walk, 4.6% work from home (2000); Travel time to work: 17.8% less than 15 minutes, 28.0% 15 to 30 minutes, 25.3% 30 to 45 minutes, 7.6% 45 to 60 minutes, 21.3% 60 minutes or more (2000)

OSSINING
OSSINING (village). Covers a land area of 3.216 square miles and a water area of 3.127 square miles. Located at 41.16° N. Lat.; 73.85° W. Long. Elevation is 8 feet.
Population: 22,582 (1990); 24,010 (2000); 24,360 (2005); 24,800 (2010 projected); Race: 54.9% White, 20.9% Black, 5.5% Asian, 34.8% Hispanic of any race (2005); Density: 7,573.6 persons per square mile (2005); Average household size: 2.95 (2005); Median age: 37.0 (2005); Males per 100 females: 118.8 (2005); Marriage status: 34.7% never married, 52.1% now married, 6.1% widowed, 7.1% divorced (2000); Foreign born: 30.4% (2000); Ancestry (includes multiple ancestries): 38.9% Other groups, 14.4% Italian, 9.9% Irish, 6.5% German, 4.3% English (2000).
Economy: Single-family building permits issued: 8 (2005); Multi-family building permits issued: 0 (2005); Employment by occupation: 14.3% management, 23.1% professional, 21.9% services, 21.5% sales, 0.1% farming, 10.6% construction, 8.5% production (2000).
Income: Per capita income: $28,741 (2005); Median household income: $60,424 (2005); Average household income: $82,113 (2005); Percent of households with income of $100,000 or more: 26.6% (2005); Poverty rate: 10.6% (2000).
Education: Percent of population age 25 and over with: High school diploma (including GED) or higher: 69.6% (2005); Bachelor's degree or higher: 28.7% (2005); Master's degree or higher: 12.2% (2005).

School District(s)
Ossining Union Free School District (PK-12)
    2003-04 Enrollment: 4,252 . . . . (914) 941-7700

Four-year College(s)
Kehilath Yakov Rabbinical Seminary
    Fall 2004 Enrollment: 104 . . . . (718) 963-1212
    2005-06 Tuition: In-state $4,600; Out-of-state $4,600

Housing: Homeownership rate: 52.4% (2005); Median home value: $330,411 (2005); Median rent: $810 per month (2000); Median age of housing: 46 years (2000).
Hospitals: Sing Sing Correctional Facility Hospital (29 beds)
Safety: Violent crime rate: 29.2 per 10,000 population; Property crime rate: 109.6 per 10,000 population (2004).
Transportation: Commute to work: 76.1% car, 15.8% public transportation, 3.3% walk, 3.2% work from home (2000); Travel time to work: 22.0% less than 15 minutes, 33.1% 15 to 30 minutes, 21.7% 30 to 45 minutes, 8.3% 45 to 60 minutes, 14.9% 60 minutes or more (2000)

Additional Information Contacts
Greater Ossining Chamber of Commerce . . . . (914) 941-0009
    http://www.ossiningchamber.org
Village of Ossining . . . . (914) 762-8428
    http://www.village.ossining.ny.us/

OSSINING
(town). Covers a land area of 11.698 square miles and a water area of 3.906 square miles. Located at 41.16° N. Lat.; 73.85° W. Long. Elevation is 8 feet.

History: Ossining is the site of Sing Sing state prison (built 1825-1828). This prison was long known for its extreme discipline, but under Thomas Mott Osborne and Lewis Edward Lawes, notable reforms were introduced. By end of 19th century, second-largest industrial center in Westchester. Brickyards produced bricks for Old Croton Aqueduct. Maryknoll, the headquarters of the Catholic Foreign Mission Society, is nearby. Settled c.1750, Incorporated 1813 as Sing Sing, renamed 1901.
Population: 34,124 (1990); 36,534 (2000); 37,415 (2005); 38,369 (2010 projected); Race: 65.9% White, 14.9% Black, 5.9% Asian, 24.9% Hispanic of any race (2005); Density: 3,198.3 persons per square mile (2005); Average household size: 2.98 (2005); Median age: 38.7 (2005); Males per 100 females: 106.8 (2005); Marriage status: 31.1% never married, 56.4% now married, 6.0% widowed, 6.5% divorced (2000); Foreign born: 24.2% (2000); Ancestry (includes multiple ancestries): 30.3% Other groups, 16.2% Italian, 11.9% Irish, 8.1% German, 4.9% English (2000).
Economy: Mainly residential. Some manufacturing including medical instruments and pharmaceuticals. Site of Sing Sing state prison. Unemployment rate: 3.8% (2005); Total civilian labor force: 18,692 (2005); Single-family building permits issued: 5 (2005); Multi-family building permits issued: 0 (2005); Employment by occupation: 18.7% management, 27.5% professional, 17.3% services, 21.5% sales, 0.1% farming, 8.2% construction, 6.8% production (2000).
Income: Per capita income: $38,972 (2005); Median household income: $75,799 (2005); Average household income: $112,463 (2005); Percent of households with income of $100,000 or more: 38.7% (2005); Poverty rate: 8.4% (2000).
Education: Percent of population age 25 and over with: High school diploma (including GED) or higher: 77.7% (2005); Bachelor's degree or higher: 41.0% (2005); Master's degree or higher: 19.8% (2005).
Housing: Homeownership rate: 64.3% (2005); Median home value: $395,701 (2005); Median rent: $821 per month (2000); Median age of housing: 42 years (2000).
Transportation: Commute to work: 75.0% car, 16.9% public transportation, 2.7% walk, 4.1% work from home (2000); Travel time to work: 20.8% less than 15 minutes, 30.9% 15 to 30 minutes, 20.7% 30 to 45 minutes, 8.3% 45 to 60 minutes, 19.3% 60 minutes or more (2000)

Additional Information Contacts
Town of Ossining . . . . (914) 762-6000
    http://www.townofossining.com/

PEEKSKILL
(city). Covers a land area of 4.324 square miles and a water area of 1.152 square miles. Located at 41.28° N. Lat.; 73.92° W. Long. Elevation is 9 feet.

History: Named for Jan Peeck, a Dutch trader from New Amsterdam. In the American Revolution, Peekskill was attacked and burned (1777) by the British; after the war the city became a prominent trade center. In 19th century had foundries based on Putnam County iron deposits. Peter Cooper and Henry Ward Beecher born here. St. Peter's Church, dedicated in 1767, has been restored. Settled 1665. Incorporated as a village 1816, as a city 1940.
Population: 19,536 (1990); 22,441 (2000); 23,906 (2005); 25,320 (2010 projected); Race: 50.1% White, 28.6% Black, 2.7% Asian, 28.5% Hispanic of any race (2005); Density: 5,528.5 persons per square mile (2005); Average household size: 2.60 (2005); Median age: 36.6 (2005); Males per 100 females: 95.5 (2005); Marriage status: 31.4% never married, 49.8% now married, 7.4% widowed, 11.4% divorced (2000); Foreign born: 20.1% (2000); Ancestry (includes multiple ancestries): 43.4% Other groups, 16.3% Italian, 13.4% Irish, 7.1% German, 4.1% United States or American (2000).
Economy: Clothing, leather goods, lighting fixtures and office equipment are made here. Single-family building permits issued: 147 (2005); Multi-family building permits issued: 30 (2005); Employment by occupation: 10.9% management, 18.7% professional, 21.2% services, 26.3% sales, 0.2% farming, 11.5% construction, 11.1% production (2000).
Income: Per capita income: $25,154 (2005); Median household income: $51,650 (2005); Average household income: $64,927 (2005); Percent of households with income of $100,000 or more: 18.8% (2005); Poverty rate: 13.7% (2000).
Education: Percent of population age 25 and over with: High school diploma (including GED) or higher: 75.4% (2005); Bachelor's degree or higher: 21.9% (2005); Master's degree or higher: 9.7% (2005).

School District(s)
Peekskill City School District (PK-12)
    2003-04 Enrollment: 3,055 . . . . (914) 737-3300

Four-year College(s)
Ohr Hameir Theological Seminary
    Fall 2004 Enrollment: 70 . . . . (914) 736-1500
    2005-06 Tuition: In-state $6,700; Out-of-state $6,700

Two-year College(s)
North Westchester School of Hair-Cosmetology
    Fall 2004 Enrollment: 40 . . . . (914) 739-8400

Housing: Homeownership rate: 46.8% (2005); Median home value: $246,455 (2005); Median rent: $742 per month (2000); Median age of housing: 41 years (2000).
Safety: Violent crime rate: 22.6 per 10,000 population; Property crime rate: 115.4 per 10,000 population (2004).
Transportation: Commute to work: 80.5% car, 11.8% public transportation, 5.0% walk, 1.7% work from home (2000); Travel time to work: 24.5% less than 15 minutes, 25.0% 15 to 30 minutes, 24.4% 30 to 45 minutes, 10.4% 45 to 60 minutes, 15.7% 60 minutes or more (2000)

Additional Information Contacts
City of Peekskill . . . . (914) 737-3400
    http://www.ci.peekskill.ny.us/
Hudson Valley Gateway Chamber of Commerce . . . . (914) 737-3600
    http://www.hvgatewaychamber.com/

PELHAM
(village). Covers a land area of 0.822 square miles and a water area of 0.002 square miles. Located at 40.91° N. Lat.; 73.80° W. Long. Elevation is 68 feet.

Population: 6,373 (1990); 6,400 (2000); 6,376 (2005); 6,358 (2010 projected); Race: 81.6% White, 6.3% Black, 6.0% Asian, 9.5% Hispanic of any race (2005); Density: 7,756.3 persons per square mile (2005); Average household size: 2.81 (2005); Median age: 38.1 (2005); Males per 100 females: 92.9 (2005); Marriage status: 28.3% never married, 61.2% now married, 6.4% widowed, 4.1% divorced (2000); Foreign born: 14.9% (2000); Ancestry (includes multiple ancestries): 30.0% Italian, 21.5% Irish, 18.9% Other groups, 10.3% German, 8.6% English (2000).
Economy: Single-family building permits issued: 3 (2005); Multi-family building permits issued: 0 (2005); Employment by occupation: 17.3% management, 38.1% professional, 9.1% services, 27.0% sales, 0.0% farming, 5.0% construction, 3.5% production (2000).
Income: Per capita income: $50,389 (2005); Median household income: $95,180 (2005); Average household income: $141,221 (2005); Percent of households with income of $100,000 or more: 47.3% (2005); Poverty rate: 3.3% (2000).
Education: Percent of population age 25 and over with: High school diploma (including GED) or higher: 90.3% (2005); Bachelor's degree or higher: 56.0% (2005); Master's degree or higher: 28.7% (2005).

School District(s)
Pelham Union Free School District (KG-12)
    2003-04 Enrollment: 2,529 . . . . (914) 738-3434

Housing: Homeownership rate: 66.5% (2005); Median home value: $576,282 (2005); Median rent: $1,001 per month (2000); Median age of housing: 60+ years (2000).
Safety: Violent crime rate: 21.8 per 10,000 population; Property crime rate: 209.0 per 10,000 population (2004).
Newspapers: The Pelham Weekly (General - Circulation 1,600); Westchester Jewish Life (General, Jewish - Circulation 20,000)
Transportation: Commute to work: 59.3% car, 30.2% public transportation, 4.7% walk, 5.6% work from home (2000); Travel time to work: 18.7% less than 15 minutes, 23.8% 15 to 30 minutes, 20.7% 30 to 45 minutes, 17.3% 45 to 60 minutes, 19.4% 60 minutes or more (2000)
Additional Information Contacts
Pelham Chamber of Commerce Inc. . . . . (914) 738-1500
   http://www.pelhamny.com
Village of Pelham . . . . (914) 738-1133
   http://www.pelhamny.com/

PELHAM (town).
Covers a land area of 2.148 square miles and a water area of 0.050 square miles. Located at 40.90° N. Lat.; 73.80° W. Long. Elevation is 68 feet.
History: Settled in 17th century; incorporated 1896.
Population: 11,816 (1990); 11,866 (2000); 11,797 (2005); 11,755 (2010 projected); Race: 85.6% White, 4.7% Black, 4.7% Asian, 7.8% Hispanic of any race (2005); Density: 5,491.3 persons per square mile (2005); Average household size: 2.89 (2005); Median age: 39.0 (2005); Males per 100 females: 94.0 (2005); Marriage status: 24.8% never married, 64.9% now married, 6.1% widowed, 4.3% divorced (2000); Foreign born: 13.3% (2000); Ancestry (includes multiple ancestries): 29.8% Italian, 21.7% Irish, 16.1% Other groups, 11.5% German, 10.0% English (2000).
Economy: Some light manufacturing: kitchen products, map publishing. Employment by occupation: 20.4% management, 37.2% professional, 8.4% services, 25.8% sales, 0.1% farming, 4.4% construction, 3.7% production (2000).
Income: Per capita income: $56,419 (2005); Median household income: $108,229 (2005); Average household income: $162,469 (2005); Percent of households with income of $100,000 or more: 52.9% (2005); Poverty rate: 3.7% (2000).
Taxes: Total city taxes per capita: $166 (2004); City property taxes per capita: $124 (2004).
Education: Percent of population age 25 and over with: High school diploma (including GED) or higher: 91.9% (2005); Bachelor's degree or higher: 59.1% (2005); Master's degree or higher: 30.2% (2005).
Housing: Homeownership rate: 77.0% (2005); Median home value: $666,517 (2005); Median rent: $1,037 per month (2000); Median age of housing: 60+ years (2000).
Transportation: Commute to work: 60.4% car, 29.4% public transportation, 3.4% walk, 6.5% work from home (2000); Travel time to work: 17.8% less than 15 minutes, 23.0% 15 to 30 minutes, 21.7% 30 to 45 minutes, 16.3% 45 to 60 minutes, 21.2% 60 minutes or more (2000)
Additional Information Contacts
Town of Pelham . . . . (914) 738-1021
   http://www.townofpelham.com/home/index.html

PELHAM MANOR (village).
Covers a land area of 1.326 square miles and a water area of 0.048 square miles. Located at 40.89° N. Lat.; 73.80° W. Long. Elevation is 50 feet.
History: Settled in mid-17th century; incorporated 1891.
Population: 5,443 (1990); 5,466 (2000); 5,421 (2005); 5,397 (2010 projected); Race: 90.3% White, 2.9% Black, 3.2% Asian, 5.9% Hispanic of any race (2005); Density: 4,087.3 persons per square mile (2005); Average household size: 2.98 (2005); Median age: 40.2 (2005); Males per 100 females: 95.3 (2005); Marriage status: 20.5% never married, 69.3% now married, 5.7% widowed, 4.5% divorced (2000); Foreign born: 11.6% (2000); Ancestry (includes multiple ancestries): 29.6% Italian, 21.9% Irish, 13.0% German, 12.7% Other groups, 11.6% English (2000).
Economy: Single-family building permits issued: 2 (2005); Multi-family building permits issued: 0 (2005); Employment by occupation: 24.4% management, 35.9% professional, 7.6% services, 24.3% sales, 0.2% farming, 3.7% construction, 3.9% production (2000).
Income: Per capita income: $63,511 (2005); Median household income: $130,842 (2005); Average household income: $189,002 (2005); Percent of households with income of $100,000 or more: 59.9% (2005); Poverty rate: 4.3% (2000).
Education: Percent of population age 25 and over with: High school diploma (including GED) or higher: 93.8% (2005); Bachelor's degree or higher: 62.7% (2005); Master's degree or higher: 32.0% (2005).
Housing: Homeownership rate: 90.2% (2005); Median home value: $745,777 (2005); Median rent: $1,211 per month (2000); Median age of housing: 60+ years (2000).
Safety: Violent crime rate: 20.1 per 10,000 population; Property crime rate: 164.8 per 10,000 population (2004).
Transportation: Commute to work: 61.7% car, 28.4% public transportation, 1.8% walk, 7.6% work from home (2000); Travel time to work: 16.8% less than 15 minutes, 22.0% 15 to 30 minutes, 22.8% 30 to 45 minutes, 15.0% 45 to 60 minutes, 23.4% 60 minutes or more (2000)
Additional Information Contacts
Village of Pelham Manor . . . . (914) 738-8820
   http://www.pelhammanor.org/

PLEASANTVILLE (village).
Covers a land area of 1.819 square miles and a water area of 0 square miles. Located at 41.13° N. Lat.; 73.78° W. Long. Elevation is 304 feet.
Population: 6,592 (1990); 7,172 (2000); 7,165 (2005); 7,202 (2010 projected); Race: 88.3% White, 3.6% Black, 3.1% Asian, 9.8% Hispanic of any race (2005); Density: 3,939.5 persons per square mile (2005); Average household size: 2.73 (2005); Median age: 38.9 (2005); Males per 100 females: 99.2 (2005); Marriage status: 25.2% never married, 62.5% now married, 6.5% widowed, 5.8% divorced (2000); Foreign born: 13.1% (2000); Ancestry (includes multiple ancestries): 27.5% Italian, 26.0% Irish, 13.0% Other groups, 11.4% German, 8.6% English (2000).
Economy: The village has well-known printing and publishing facilities; headquarters of *Reader's Digest* is here. Single-family building permits issued: 1 (2005); Multi-family building permits issued: 0 (2005); Employment by occupation: 23.4% management, 33.1% professional, 10.3% services, 22.7% sales, 0.0% farming, 6.7% construction, 3.8% production (2000).
Income: Per capita income: $48,855 (2005); Median household income: $102,104 (2005); Average household income: $132,387 (2005); Percent of households with income of $100,000 or more: 51.0% (2005); Poverty rate: 4.4% (2000).
Education: Percent of population age 25 and over with: High school diploma (including GED) or higher: 90.9% (2005); Bachelor's degree or higher: 57.0% (2005); Master's degree or higher: 29.3% (2005).
School District(s)
Mount Pleasant-Cottage Union Free School District (03-12)
   2003-04 Enrollment: 349 . . . . (914) 769-0456
Pleasantville Union Free School District (KG-12)
   2003-04 Enrollment: 1,727 . . . . (914) 741-1400
Housing: Homeownership rate: 73.6% (2005); Median home value: $511,976 (2005); Median rent: $916 per month (2000); Median age of housing: 50 years (2000).
Safety: Violent crime rate: 2.8 per 10,000 population; Property crime rate: 9.7 per 10,000 population (2004).
Transportation: Commute to work: 75.2% car, 16.8% public transportation, 2.9% walk, 4.3% work from home (2000); Travel time to work: 23.1% less than 15 minutes, 29.7% 15 to 30 minutes, 16.6% 30 to 45 minutes, 7.3% 45 to 60 minutes, 23.3% 60 minutes or more (2000)
Additional Information Contacts
Village of Pleasantville . . . . (914) 769-1940
   http://www.pleasantville.americantowns.com/servlets/WebPage

PORT CHESTER (village).
Covers a land area of 2.357 square miles and a water area of 0.132 square miles. Located at 41.00° N. Lat.; 73.66° W. Long. Elevation is 34 feet.
History: Named for Chester, England, and for its location as a port on Long Island Sound. Gen. Israel Putnam had his headquarters here 1777-1778. Several Colonial homes remain. Previously called Saw Pits, village was renamed in 1837. Settled after 1660. Incorporated 1868.
Population: 24,728 (1990); 27,867 (2000); 27,955 (2005); 28,093 (2010 projected); Race: 55.0% White, 6.0% Black, 2.4% Asian, 54.0% Hispanic of any race (2005); Density: 11,862.0 persons per square mile (2005); Average household size: 2.97 (2005); Median age: 35.5 (2005); Males per 100 females: 103.5 (2005); Marriage status: 33.1% never married, 52.4% now married, 7.8% widowed, 6.8% divorced (2000); Foreign born: 41.4% (2000); Ancestry (includes multiple ancestries): 48.3% Other groups, 20.7% Italian, 7.5% Irish, 4.2% German, 2.9% United States or American (2000).

Economy: Primarily residential, it produces some household goods. Unemployment rate: 4.3% (2005); Total civilian labor force: 14,826 (2005); Single-family building permits issued: 3 (2005); Multi-family building permits issued: 6 (2005); Employment by occupation: 10.3% management, 15.3% professional, 27.4% services, 23.9% sales, 0.1% farming, 11.6% construction, 11.4% production (2000).
Income: Per capita income: $22,482 (2005); Median household income: $49,606 (2005); Average household income: $66,236 (2005); Percent of households with income of $100,000 or more: 19.1% (2005); Poverty rate: 13.0% (2000).
Education: Percent of population age 25 and over with: High school diploma (including GED) or higher: 68.5% (2005); Bachelor's degree or higher: 20.3% (2005); Master's degree or higher: 8.4% (2005).

School District(s)
Port Chester-Rye Union Free School District (KG-12)
    2003-04 Enrollment: 3,574 . . . . (914) 934-7901

Housing: Homeownership rate: 43.9% (2005); Median home value: $408,630 (2005); Median rent: $854 per month (2000); Median age of housing: 53 years (2000).
Hospitals: New York United Hospital Medical Center (254 beds)
Safety: Violent crime rate: 18.9 per 10,000 population; Property crime rate: 224.2 per 10,000 population (2004).
Newspapers: America Latina (General, Hispanic - Circulation 4,000); Westmore News (General - Circulation 3,500)
Transportation: Commute to work: 74.6% car, 14.3% public transportation, 8.4% walk, 1.8% work from home (2000); Travel time to work: 38.5% less than 15 minutes, 38.2% 15 to 30 minutes, 13.0% 30 to 45 minutes, 3.5% 45 to 60 minutes, 6.9% 60 minutes or more (2000)
Additional Information Contacts
Port Chester-Rye Brook Chamber of Commerce . . . . (914) 939-1900
    http://www.northcountrychamber.com/
Village of Port Chester . . . . (914) 939-2200
    http://www.portchesterny.com/

POUND RIDGE (town). Covers a land area of 22.802 square miles and a water area of 0.676 square miles. Located at 41.20° N. Lat.; 73.58° W. Long. Elevation is 600 feet.
Population: 4,550 (1990); 4,726 (2000); 4,952 (2005); 5,177 (2010 projected); Race: 94.9% White, 1.2% Black, 2.1% Asian, 3.4% Hispanic of any race (2005); Density: 217.2 persons per square mile (2005); Average household size: 2.75 (2005); Median age: 44.1 (2005); Males per 100 females: 95.7 (2005); Marriage status: 17.5% never married, 73.0% now married, 4.4% widowed, 5.1% divorced (2000); Foreign born: 9.6% (2000); Ancestry (includes multiple ancestries): 16.7% Italian, 14.9% Irish, 14.4% English, 12.8% German, 11.4% Russian (2000).
Economy: Single-family building permits issued: 20 (2005); Multi-family building permits issued: 0 (2005); Employment by occupation: 27.5% management, 34.9% professional, 5.8% services, 24.6% sales, 0.0% farming, 3.8% construction, 3.5% production (2000).
Income: Per capita income: $84,375 (2005); Median household income: $172,840 (2005); Average household income: $231,518 (2005); Percent of households with income of $100,000 or more: 73.4% (2005); Poverty rate: 1.7% (2000).
Education: Percent of population age 25 and over with: High school diploma (including GED) or higher: 95.3% (2005); Bachelor's degree or higher: 71.3% (2005); Master's degree or higher: 32.7% (2005).

School District(s)
Bedford Central School District (PK-12)
    2003-04 Enrollment: 4,268 . . . . (914) 241-6010

Housing: Homeownership rate: 93.8% (2005); Median home value: $962,963 (2005); Median rent: $862 per month (2000); Median age of housing: 35 years (2000).
Transportation: Commute to work: 72.4% car, 13.1% public transportation, 5.1% walk, 9.1% work from home (2000); Travel time to work: 15.4% less than 15 minutes, 19.4% 15 to 30 minutes, 27.0% 30 to 45 minutes, 11.5% 45 to 60 minutes, 26.7% 60 minutes or more (2000)
Additional Information Contacts
Town of Pound Ridge . . . . (914) 764-5549
    http://www.townofpoundridge.com/

PURCHASE (unincorporated postal area, zip code 10577). Part of the Village of Harrison. Covers a land area of 6.822 square miles and a water area of 0.007 square miles. Located at 41.03° N. Lat.; 73.71° W. Long. Elevation is 355 feet.
Population: 0 (2000); Race: 85.6% White, 4.1% Black, 4.6% Asian, 6.9% Hispanic of any race (2000); Density: 0.0 persons per square mile (2000); Age: 21.5% under 18, 9.2% over 64 (2000); Marriage status: 48.5% never married, 47.9% now married, 2.4% widowed, 1.2% divorced (2000); Foreign born: 10.8% (2000); Ancestry (includes multiple ancestries): 23.9% Italian, 17.3% Other groups, 16.0% Irish, 12.7% Russian, 8.3% German (2000).
Economy: Employment by occupation: 20.4% management, 27.5% professional, 10.8% services, 37.1% sales, 0.0% farming, 2.1% construction, 2.1% production (2000).
Income: Per capita income: $64,946 (2000); Median household income: $183,686 (2000); Poverty rate: 7.4% (2000).
Education: Percent of population age 25 and over with: High school diploma (including GED) or higher: 94.6% (2000); Bachelor's degree or higher: 69.7% (2000).

School District(s)
Harrison Central School District (KG-12)
    2003-04 Enrollment: 3,382 . . . . (914) 630-3002

Four-year College(s)
Long Island University-Westchester Campus
    Fall 2004 Enrollment: 286 . . . . (914) 251-6510
Manhattanville College
    Fall 2004 Enrollment: 2,628 . . . . (914) 694-2200
    2005-06 Tuition: In-state $25,920; Out-of-state $25,920
SUNY College at Purchase (Public)
    Fall 2004 Enrollment: 3,832 . . . . (914) 251-6000
    2005-06 Tuition: In-state $5,608; Out-of-state $10,610

Housing: Homeownership rate: 87.2% (2000); Median home value: $748,500 (2000); Median rent: $1,671 per month (2000); Median age of housing: 32 years (2000).
Transportation: Commute to work: 48.8% car, 19.7% public transportation, 23.9% walk, 6.7% work from home (2000); Travel time to work: 37.9% less than 15 minutes, 22.9% 15 to 30 minutes, 11.6% 30 to 45 minutes, 10.1% 45 to 60 minutes, 17.4% 60 minutes or more (2000)

PURDYS (unincorporated postal area, zip code 10578). Aka Purdy Station. Covers a land area of 1.985 square miles and a water area of 0.004 square miles. Located at 41.32° N. Lat.; 73.66° W. Long.
Population: 0 (2000); Race: 100.0% White, 0.0% Black, 0.0% Asian, 4.4% Hispanic of any race (2000); Density: 0.0 persons per square mile (2000); Age: 22.6% under 18, 17.7% over 64 (2000); Marriage status: 14.0% never married, 79.2% now married, 4.4% widowed, 2.4% divorced (2000); Foreign born: 4.7% (2000); Ancestry (includes multiple ancestries): 39.6% Irish, 29.1% Italian, 19.1% German, 10.1% Polish, 8.9% Norwegian (2000).
Economy: Employment by occupation: 25.2% management, 23.7% professional, 14.2% services, 26.2% sales, 0.0% farming, 6.2% construction, 4.6% production (2000).
Income: Per capita income: $36,119 (2000); Median household income: $81,605 (2000); Poverty rate: 0.0% (2000).
Education: Percent of population age 25 and over with: High school diploma (including GED) or higher: 90.0% (2000); Bachelor's degree or higher: 40.3% (2000).

School District(s)
Harrison Csd (KG-12)
    2003-04 Enrollment: 3,382 . . . . (914) 630-3002

Housing: Homeownership rate: 100.0% (2000); Median home value: $256,000 (2000); Median rent: $n/a per month (2000); Median age of housing: 44 years (2000).
Transportation: Commute to work: 83.3% car, 12.2% public transportation, 1.6% walk, 2.9% work from home (2000); Travel time to work: 17.2% less than 15 minutes, 18.5% 15 to 30 minutes, 24.8% 30 to 45 minutes, 13.2% 45 to 60 minutes, 26.4% 60 minutes or more (2000)

RYE (city). Covers a land area of 5.777 square miles and a water area of 14.242 square miles. Located at 40.97° N. Lat.; 73.68° W. Long. Elevation is 49 feet.
History: Named for Rye in Sussex, England. In colonial times, Rye was the first stop on the Boston Post Road after N.Y. city. The old Square House, an inn where many Revolutionary notables stayed, is now a museum. Playland, a large county-owned amusement park, is on the beach here. Chief Justice John Jay is buried in Rye. Settled 1660. Incorporated as a city 1942.
Population: 14,936 (1990); 14,955 (2000); 15,059 (2005); 15,188 (2010 projected); Race: 88.7% White, 1.3% Black, 7.2% Asian, 5.5% Hispanic of any race (2005); Density: 2,606.6 persons per square mile (2005); Average

household size: 2.82 (2005); Median age: 38.9 (2005); Males per 100 females: 93.9 (2005); Marriage status: 17.7% never married, 70.7% now married, 6.2% widowed, 5.4% divorced (2000); Foreign born: 21.5% (2000); Ancestry (includes multiple ancestries): 20.6% Irish, 18.1% Italian, 17.2% Other groups, 10.9% English, 10.3% German (2000).
Economy: Cancer-research center, hardware and locks manufacturing company and several corporate offices. Single-family building permits issued: 13 (2005); Multi-family building permits issued: 0 (2005); Employment by occupation: 28.4% management, 29.4% professional, 7.4% services, 29.8% sales, 0.0% farming, 3.5% construction, 1.6% production (2000).
Income: Per capita income: $70,930 (2005); Median household income: $129,966 (2005); Average household income: $198,034 (2005); Percent of households with income of $100,000 or more: 61.4% (2005); Poverty rate: 2.5% (2000).
Education: Percent of population age 25 and over with: High school diploma (including GED) or higher: 94.3% (2005); Bachelor's degree or higher: 68.3% (2005); Master's degree or higher: 34.5% (2005).

School District(s)
Rye City School District (KG-12)
   2003-04 Enrollment: 2,688 . . . . (914) 967-6108

Housing: Homeownership rate: 75.2% (2005); Median home value: $924,279 (2005); Median rent: $1,236 per month (2000); Median age of housing: 50 years (2000).
Hospitals: Rye Hospital Center (34 beds)
Safety: Violent crime rate: 2.6 per 10,000 population; Property crime rate: 180.9 per 10,000 population (2004).
Transportation: Commute to work: 59.0% car, 31.0% public transportation, 2.2% walk, 7.2% work from home (2000); Travel time to work: 26.1% less than 15 minutes, 24.2% 15 to 30 minutes, 11.4% 30 to 45 minutes, 11.5% 45 to 60 minutes, 26.8% 60 minutes or more (2000)
Additional Information Contacts
City of Rye . . . . (914) 967-7371
  http://www.ryeny.gov/

RYE (town).
Covers a land area of 6.967 square miles and a water area of 0.468 square miles. Located at 40.99° N. Lat.; 73.68° W. Long. Elevation is 49 feet.
Population: 39,524 (1990); 43,880 (2000); 44,822 (2005); 45,799 (2010 projected); Race: 67.6% White, 4.4% Black, 3.3% Asian, 37.6% Hispanic of any race (2005); Density: 6,433.7 persons per square mile (2005); Average household size: 2.88 (2005); Median age: 37.4 (2005); Males per 100 females: 99.2 (2005); Marriage status: 29.1% never married, 56.9% now married, 7.7% widowed, 6.4% divorced (2000); Foreign born: 32.5% (2000); Ancestry (includes multiple ancestries): 36.6% Other groups, 24.3% Italian, 9.3% Irish, 5.5% German, 4.0% United States or American (2000).
Economy: Unemployment rate: 3.9% (2005); Total civilian labor force: 23,675 (2005); Employment by occupation: 15.4% management, 19.5% professional, 20.4% services, 25.9% sales, 0.1% farming, 9.6% construction, 9.1% production (2000).
Income: Per capita income: $33,184 (2005); Median household income: $65,381 (2005); Average household income: $94,956 (2005); Percent of households with income of $100,000 or more: 31.1% (2005); Poverty rate: 9.8% (2000).
Taxes: Total city taxes per capita: $59 (2004); City property taxes per capita: $30 (2004).
Education: Percent of population age 25 and over with: High school diploma (including GED) or higher: 75.6% (2005); Bachelor's degree or higher: 30.8% (2005); Master's degree or higher: 14.0% (2005).
Housing: Homeownership rate: 57.4% (2005); Median home value: $494,001 (2005); Median rent: $882 per month (2000); Median age of housing: 49 years (2000).
Transportation: Commute to work: 74.9% car, 15.7% public transportation, 6.3% walk, 2.5% work from home (2000); Travel time to work: 34.2% less than 15 minutes, 35.9% 15 to 30 minutes, 13.6% 30 to 45 minutes, 5.2% 45 to 60 minutes, 11.2% 60 minutes or more (2000)
Additional Information Contacts
Town of Rye. . . . . (914) 939-3075
  http://www.townofryeny.com/

RYE BROOK (village).
Covers a land area of 3.470 square miles and a water area of 0.007 square miles. Located at 41.02° N. Lat.; 73.68° W. Long. Elevation is 250 feet.
Population: 7,765 (1990); 8,602 (2000); 9,455 (2005); 10,254 (2010 projected); Race: 90.9% White, 1.0% Black, 5.0% Asian, 6.2% Hispanic of any race (2005); Density: 2,724.8 persons per square mile (2005); Average household size: 2.73 (2005); Median age: 42.0 (2005); Males per 100 females: 91.2 (2005); Marriage status: 20.0% never married, 67.0% now married, 8.0% widowed, 5.0% divorced (2000); Foreign born: 13.3% (2000); Ancestry (includes multiple ancestries): 26.6% Italian, 14.4% Other groups, 10.1% Irish, 9.9% Russian, 8.0% Polish (2000).
Economy: Single-family building permits issued: 56 (2005); Multi-family building permits issued: 0 (2005); Employment by occupation: 25.1% management, 30.3% professional, 5.7% services, 29.6% sales, 0.0% farming, 4.4% construction, 5.1% production (2000).
Income: Per capita income: $60,028 (2005); Median household income: $115,295 (2005); Average household income: $162,895 (2005); Percent of households with income of $100,000 or more: 56.6% (2005); Poverty rate: 2.9% (2000).
Education: Percent of population age 25 and over with: High school diploma (including GED) or higher: 89.8% (2005); Bachelor's degree or higher: 54.5% (2005); Master's degree or higher: 27.2% (2005).

School District(s)
Blind Brook-Rye Union Free School District (KG-12)
   2003-04 Enrollment: 1,370 . . . . (914) 937-3600
Boces Southern Westchester (UG-UG)
   2003-04 Enrollment: 904 . . . . (914) 937-3820

Housing: Homeownership rate: 87.2% (2005); Median home value: $683,917 (2005); Median rent: $1,115 per month (2000); Median age of housing: 40 years (2000).
Safety: Violent crime rate: 3.2 per 10,000 population; Property crime rate: 110.2 per 10,000 population (2004).
Transportation: Commute to work: 73.6% car, 19.7% public transportation, 1.9% walk, 4.1% work from home (2000); Travel time to work: 27.6% less than 15 minutes, 29.1% 15 to 30 minutes, 12.6% 30 to 45 minutes, 10.0% 45 to 60 minutes, 20.6% 60 minutes or more (2000)
Additional Information Contacts
Village of Rye Brook . . . . (914) 939-1121
  http://www.ryebrook.org/

SCARSDALE (town and village).
Aka Quaker Ridge. Covers a land area of 6.636 square miles and a water area of 0.007 square miles. Located at 40.99° N. Lat.; 73.78° W. Long. Elevation is 240 feet.
History: Named for the Manor of Scarsdale in England, home of early town resident Caleb Heathcote. Settled c.1701, inc. 1915.
Population: 16,987 (1990); 17,823 (2000); 17,904 (2005); 18,014 (2010 projected); Race: 83.0% White, 1.4% Black, 13.7% Asian, 3.2% Hispanic of any race (2005); Density: 2,697.9 persons per square mile (2005); Average household size: 3.16 (2005); Median age: 39.8 (2005); Males per 100 females: 94.4 (2005); Marriage status: 17.0% never married, 76.1% now married, 4.0% widowed, 2.9% divorced (2000); Foreign born: 18.0% (2000); Ancestry (includes multiple ancestries): 22.7% Other groups, 11.6% Russian, 10.7% German, 10.0% Irish, 9.8% Italian (2000).
Economy: Single-family building permits issued: 10 (2005); Multi-family building permits issued: 0 (2005); Employment by occupation: 29.8% management, 42.8% professional, 5.4% services, 19.6% sales, 0.0% farming, 1.2% construction, 1.2% production (2000).
Income: Per capita income: $85,248 (2005); Median household income: $214,175 (2005); Average household income: $268,129 (2005); Percent of households with income of $100,000 or more: 78.3% (2005); Poverty rate: 2.8% (2000).
Taxes: Total city taxes per capita: $1,369 (2004); City property taxes per capita: $1,150 (2004).
Education: Percent of population age 25 and over with: High school diploma (including GED) or higher: 97.1% (2005); Bachelor's degree or higher: 79.8% (2005); Master's degree or higher: 50.4% (2005).

School District(s)
Eastchester Union Free School District (KG-12)
   2003-04 Enrollment: 2,680 . . . . (914) 793-6130
Edgemont Union Free School District (KG-12)
   2003-04 Enrollment: 1,834 . . . . (914) 472-7768
Scarsdale Union Free School District (KG-12)
   2003-04 Enrollment: 4,568 . . . . (914) 721-2410

Housing: Homeownership rate: 90.9% (2005); Median home value: $1 million+ (2005); Median rent: $2,000+ per month (2000); Median age of housing: 60+ years (2000).
Safety: Violent crime rate: 1.7 per 10,000 population; Property crime rate: 136.9 per 10,000 population (2004).

Newspapers: Scarsdale Inquirer (General - Circulation 7,000)
Transportation: Commute to work: 58.1% car, 32.6% public transportation, 0.7% walk, 8.3% work from home (2000); Travel time to work: 16.1% less than 15 minutes, 21.2% 15 to 30 minutes, 15.2% 30 to 45 minutes, 21.3% 45 to 60 minutes, 26.1% 60 minutes or more (2000)

Additional Information Contacts
Scarsdale Chamber of Commerce . . . . (914) 725-1602
  http://www.scarsdalechamber.org
Village of Scarsdale . . . . (914) 722-1100
  http://www.village.scarsdale.ny.us/

SCOTTS CORNERS
(CDP). Covers a land area of 1.774 square miles and a water area of 0 square miles. Located at 41.18° N. Lat.; 73.55° W. Long.
Population: 659 (1990); 624 (2000); 645 (2005); 665 (2010 projected); Race: 95.8% White, 0.5% Black, 2.0% Asian, 3.3% Hispanic of any race (2005); Density: 363.6 persons per square mile (2005); Average household size: 2.71 (2005); Median age: 42.1 (2005); Males per 100 females: 92.5 (2005); Marriage status: 21.9% never married, 69.8% now married, 2.1% widowed, 6.2% divorced (2000); Foreign born: 11.6% (2000); Ancestry (includes multiple ancestries): 14.9% Irish, 14.4% Italian, 13.9% Russian, 10.9% English, 9.9% German (2000).
Economy: Employment by occupation: 28.8% management, 21.8% professional, 3.2% services, 36.9% sales, 0.0% farming, 6.1% construction, 3.2% production (2000).
Income: Per capita income: $79,756 (2005); Median household income: $147,414 (2005); Average household income: $215,714 (2005); Percent of households with income of $100,000 or more: 73.1% (2005); Poverty rate: 1.9% (2000).
Education: Percent of population age 25 and over with: High school diploma (including GED) or higher: 92.0% (2005); Bachelor's degree or higher: 59.0% (2005); Master's degree or higher: 34.3% (2005).
Housing: Homeownership rate: 89.5% (2005); Median home value: $795,673 (2005); Median rent: $850 per month (2000); Median age of housing: 40 years (2000).
Transportation: Commute to work: 81.1% car, 5.8% public transportation, 3.5% walk, 9.6% work from home (2000); Travel time to work: 11.0% less than 15 minutes, 12.4% 15 to 30 minutes, 37.2% 30 to 45 minutes, 12.8% 45 to 60 minutes, 26.6% 60 minutes or more (2000)

SHENOROCK
(CDP). Aka Lake Shenorock. Covers a land area of 0.685 square miles and a water area of 0.035 square miles. Located at 41.33° N. Lat.; 73.73° W. Long.
Population: 1,848 (1990); 1,887 (2000); 2,172 (2005); 2,413 (2010 projected); Race: 95.5% White, 1.2% Black, 1.2% Asian, 6.2% Hispanic of any race (2005); Density: 3,169.4 persons per square mile (2005); Average household size: 2.86 (2005); Median age: 37.6 (2005); Males per 100 females: 93.6 (2005); Marriage status: 25.4% never married, 65.7% now married, 3.7% widowed, 5.3% divorced (2000); Foreign born: 6.9% (2000); Ancestry (includes multiple ancestries): 34.5% Italian, 30.2% Irish, 20.5% German, 10.7% English, 9.7% Other groups (2000).
Economy: Employment by occupation: 14.2% management, 26.4% professional, 15.4% services, 23.4% sales, 0.0% farming, 12.3% construction, 8.3% production (2000).
Income: Per capita income: $30,795 (2005); Median household income: $83,900 (2005); Average household income: $88,126 (2005); Percent of households with income of $100,000 or more: 39.4% (2005); Poverty rate: 2.3% (2000).
Education: Percent of population age 25 and over with: High school diploma (including GED) or higher: 94.1% (2005); Bachelor's degree or higher: 35.1% (2005); Master's degree or higher: 14.5% (2005).
Housing: Homeownership rate: 92.8% (2005); Median home value: $335,152 (2005); Median rent: $1,089 per month (2000); Median age of housing: 50 years (2000).
Transportation: Commute to work: 94.9% car, 1.7% public transportation, 0.0% walk, 2.8% work from home (2000); Travel time to work: 17.7% less than 15 minutes, 26.0% 15 to 30 minutes, 30.7% 30 to 45 minutes, 14.6% 45 to 60 minutes, 11.0% 60 minutes or more (2000)

SHRUB OAK
(CDP). Covers a land area of 1.607 square miles and a water area of 0.024 square miles. Located at 41.33° N. Lat.; 73.83° W. Long.
Population: 1,727 (1990); 1,812 (2000); 1,899 (2005); 2,005 (2010 projected); Race: 91.5% White, 2.4% Black, 1.4% Asian, 11.4% Hispanic of any race (2005); Density: 1,181.5 persons per square mile (2005); Average household size: 2.99 (2005); Median age: 38.0 (2005); Males per 100 females: 96.2 (2005); Marriage status: 22.9% never married, 64.6% now married, 5.4% widowed, 7.1% divorced (2000); Foreign born: 7.4% (2000); Ancestry (includes multiple ancestries): 42.9% Italian, 28.6% Irish, 12.6% German, 10.7% Other groups, 7.4% English (2000).
Economy: Employment by occupation: 14.5% management, 24.4% professional, 16.0% services, 25.7% sales, 0.0% farming, 10.6% construction, 8.8% production (2000).
Income: Per capita income: $34,492 (2005); Median household income: $95,989 (2005); Average household income: $103,150 (2005); Percent of households with income of $100,000 or more: 46.6% (2005); Poverty rate: 2.4% (2000).
Education: Percent of population age 25 and over with: High school diploma (including GED) or higher: 88.6% (2005); Bachelor's degree or higher: 35.0% (2005); Master's degree or higher: 13.3% (2005).

School District(s)
Lakeland Central School District (KG-12)
  2003-04 Enrollment: 6,139 . . . . (914) 245-1700
New York City Public Schools (PK-12)
  2003-04 Enrollment: 1,023,674 . . . . (718) 935-2794
Housing: Homeownership rate: 86.1% (2005); Median home value: $358,769 (2005); Median rent: $661 per month (2000); Median age of housing: 43 years (2000).
Transportation: Commute to work: 89.8% car, 3.2% public transportation, 3.1% walk, 4.0% work from home (2000); Travel time to work: 17.6% less than 15 minutes, 20.4% 15 to 30 minutes, 31.5% 30 to 45 minutes, 16.3% 45 to 60 minutes, 14.2% 60 minutes or more (2000)

SLEEPY HOLLOW
(village). Aka North Tarrytown. Covers a land area of 2.272 square miles and a water area of 2.838 square miles. Located at 41.09° N. Lat.; 73.86° W. Long. Elevation is 75 feet.
Population: 8,152 (1990); 9,212 (2000); 9,274 (2005); 9,378 (2010 projected); Race: 63.4% White, 4.4% Black, 2.4% Asian, 50.7% Hispanic of any race (2005); Density: 4,082.0 persons per square mile (2005); Average household size: 2.94 (2005); Median age: 34.9 (2005); Males per 100 females: 104.1 (2005); Marriage status: 31.9% never married, 57.5% now married, 5.2% widowed, 5.4% divorced (2000); Foreign born: 41.2% (2000); Ancestry (includes multiple ancestries): 46.0% Other groups, 13.3% Italian, 13.1% Irish, 5.8% German, 4.4% English (2000).
Economy: Single-family building permits issued: 1 (2005); Multi-family building permits issued: 33 (2005); Employment by occupation: 16.0% management, 19.1% professional, 25.2% services, 16.4% sales, 0.6% farming, 11.0% construction, 11.7% production (2000).
Income: Per capita income: $32,655 (2005); Median household income: $63,106 (2005); Average household income: $95,524 (2005); Percent of households with income of $100,000 or more: 30.0% (2005); Poverty rate: 7.4% (2000).
Education: Percent of population age 25 and over with: High school diploma (including GED) or higher: 68.4% (2005); Bachelor's degree or higher: 32.4% (2005); Master's degree or higher: 14.8% (2005).

School District(s)
Pocantico Hills Central School District (PK-08)
  2003-04 Enrollment: 363 . . . . (914) 631-2440
Union Free School District Of The Tarrytowns (PK-12)
  2003-04 Enrollment: 2,499 . . . . (914) 631-9404
Housing: Homeownership rate: 37.5% (2005); Median home value: $564,727 (2005); Median rent: $829 per month (2000); Median age of housing: 58 years (2000).
Hospitals: Phelps Memorial Hospital Center (235 beds)
Safety: Violent crime rate: 0.0 per 10,000 population; Property crime rate: 0.0 per 10,000 population (2004).
Transportation: Commute to work: 70.3% car, 18.9% public transportation, 7.9% walk, 2.4% work from home (2000); Travel time to work: 27.9% less than 15 minutes, 32.1% 15 to 30 minutes, 17.2% 30 to 45 minutes, 8.8% 45 to 60 minutes, 14.0% 60 minutes or more (2000)

SOMERS
(town). Covers a land area of 30.042 square miles and a water area of 2.217 square miles. Located at 41.32° N. Lat.; 73.71° W. Long.
History: Formerly a rural, summer lake community. Early Dutch settlement, it was incorporated 1778 as Stephentown. Renamed Somerstown for US naval hero Captain Richard Somers.
Population: 16,216 (1990); 18,346 (2000); 19,740 (2005); 21,090 (2010 projected); Race: 94.3% White, 1.7% Black, 2.1% Asian, 3.8% Hispanic of any race (2005); Density: 657.1 persons per square mile (2005); Average

household size: 2.67 (2005); Median age: 43.8 (2005); Males per 100 females: 91.9 (2005); Marriage status: 19.3% never married, 67.2% now married, 8.6% widowed, 5.0% divorced (2000); Foreign born: 10.5% (2000); Ancestry (includes multiple ancestries): 30.5% Italian, 20.6% Irish, 16.6% German, 10.1% Other groups, 8.1% English (2000).
Economy: Metropolitan New York city exurb. IBM has headquarters here; also beverage and perfume bottling. Has large condominium complex for retirees. Single-family building permits issued: 80 (2005); Multi-family building permits issued: 0 (2005); Employment by occupation: 23.9% management, 30.6% professional, 7.5% services, 26.1% sales, 0.1% farming, 7.3% construction, 4.6% production (2000).
Income: Per capita income: $48,836 (2005); Median household income: $102,287 (2005); Average household income: $129,155 (2005); Percent of households with income of $100,000 or more: 51.1% (2005); Poverty rate: 2.0% (2000).
Education: Percent of population age 25 and over with: High school diploma (including GED) or higher: 94.9% (2005); Bachelor's degree or higher: 50.7% (2005); Master's degree or higher: 23.7% (2005).

School District(s)
Somers Central School District (KG-12)
   2003-04 Enrollment: 3,140 . . . . (914) 248-7872

Housing: Homeownership rate: 93.6% (2005); Median home value: $469,896 (2005); Median rent: $1,207 per month (2000); Median age of housing: 23 years (2000).
Transportation: Commute to work: 83.8% car, 9.4% public transportation, 0.4% walk, 5.8% work from home (2000); Travel time to work: 15.1% less than 15 minutes, 24.0% 15 to 30 minutes, 28.9% 30 to 45 minutes, 12.1% 45 to 60 minutes, 19.9% 60 minutes or more (2000)

Additional Information Contacts
Town of Somers. . . . . (914) 277-5366
   http://www.somersny.com/

SOUTH SALEM
(unincorporated postal area, zip code 10590). Covers a land area of 14.775 square miles and a water area of 0.741 square miles. Located at 41.25° N. Lat.; 73.54° W. Long. Elevation is 550 feet.

Population: 0 (2000); Race: 96.8% White, 0.7% Black, 0.8% Asian, 3.8% Hispanic of any race (2000); Density: 0.0 persons per square mile (2000); Age: 30.6% under 18, 7.7% over 64 (2000); Marriage status: 17.5% never married, 73.7% now married, 3.6% widowed, 5.2% divorced (2000); Foreign born: 8.3% (2000); Ancestry (includes multiple ancestries): 22.3% Italian, 22.0% Irish, 13.4% German, 12.9% English, 8.4% Russian (2000).
Economy: Employment by occupation: 27.4% management, 33.6% professional, 8.3% services, 22.7% sales, 0.0% farming, 4.7% construction, 3.3% production (2000).
Income: Per capita income: $51,017 (2000); Median household income: $101,226 (2000); Poverty rate: 1.6% (2000).
Education: Percent of population age 25 and over with: High school diploma (including GED) or higher: 97.6% (2000); Bachelor's degree or higher: 62.4% (2000).

School District(s)
Katonah-Lewisboro Union Free School District (KG-12)
   2003-04 Enrollment: 4,112 . . . . (914) 763-7001

Housing: Homeownership rate: 91.5% (2000); Median home value: $388,200 (2000); Median rent: $1,072 per month (2000); Median age of housing: 31 years (2000).
Transportation: Commute to work: 80.7% car, 9.3% public transportation, 0.5% walk, 9.3% work from home (2000); Travel time to work: 13.9% less than 15 minutes, 27.0% 15 to 30 minutes, 29.1% 30 to 45 minutes, 9.5% 45 to 60 minutes, 20.5% 60 minutes or more (2000)

TARRYTOWN
(village). Covers a land area of 2.977 square miles and a water area of 2.701 square miles. Located at 41.06° N. Lat.; 73.86° W. Long. Elevation is 7 feet.

History: Named for a variation of the Dutch translation of "wheat". Of interest are Sunnyside, the home of Washington Irving; Sleepy Hollow cemetery, where Irving is buried; Philipsburg Manor, an estate; and Lyndhurst (1838), a Gothic Revival mansion. Philipsburg Manor, an early trading center complex northwest of village center, includes a Dutch farmhouse (c.1683) and a restored operating gristmill. Settled in the 17th century by Dutch. Incorporated 1870.
Population: 10,739 (1990); 11,090 (2000); 11,479 (2005); 11,864 (2010 projected); Race: 73.5% White, 7.6% Black, 8.4% Asian, 18.8% Hispanic of any race (2005); Density: 3,855.4 persons per square mile (2005); Average household size: 2.41 (2005); Median age: 38.6 (2005); Males per 100 females: 83.4 (2005); Marriage status: 29.8% never married, 55.3% now married, 6.9% widowed, 7.9% divorced (2000); Foreign born: 22.3% (2000); Ancestry (includes multiple ancestries): 30.3% Other groups, 19.0% Italian, 18.4% Irish, 7.5% German, 5.8% English (2000).
Economy: Headquarters of several companies. Manufacturing includes motor vehicle assembly, laboratory instruments, food processing, and heating equipment. It is the east terminus of the Tappan Zee Bridge. Seat of Marymount College. Fordham University of N.Y.city maintains a branch campus here. Single-family building permits issued: 2 (2005); Multi-family building permits issued: 0 (2005); Employment by occupation: 23.0% management, 31.2% professional, 14.5% services, 22.8% sales, 0.2% farming, 4.0% construction, 4.3% production (2000).
Income: Per capita income: $45,902 (2005); Median household income: $76,265 (2005); Average household income: $108,723 (2005); Percent of households with income of $100,000 or more: 37.0% (2005); Poverty rate: 4.7% (2000).
Education: Percent of population age 25 and over with: High school diploma (including GED) or higher: 88.2% (2005); Bachelor's degree or higher: 50.6% (2005); Master's degree or higher: 24.3% (2005).

School District(s)
Union Free School District Of The Tarrytowns (PK-12)
   2003-04 Enrollment: 2,499 . . . . (914) 631-9404

Four-year College(s)
Marymount College of Fordham University
   Fall 2004 Enrollment: 1,036. . . . . (914) 631-3200
   2005-06 Tuition: In-state $21,023; Out-of-state $21,023

Housing: Homeownership rate: 52.1% (2005); Median home value: $466,019 (2005); Median rent: $905 per month (2000); Median age of housing: 48 years (2000).
Safety: Violent crime rate: 13.1 per 10,000 population; Property crime rate: 107.6 per 10,000 population (2004).
Transportation: Commute to work: 69.2% car, 19.8% public transportation, 7.2% walk, 3.6% work from home (2000); Travel time to work: 29.2% less than 15 minutes, 25.3% 15 to 30 minutes, 18.8% 30 to 45 minutes, 9.0% 45 to 60 minutes, 17.7% 60 minutes or more (2000)

Additional Information Contacts
Sleepy Hollow Chamber of Commerce . . . . (914) 631-1705
   http://www.sleepyhollowchamber.com

THORNWOOD
(CDP). Covers a land area of 3.396 square miles and a water area of 0 square miles. Located at 41.12° N. Lat.; 73.77° W. Long. Elevation is 360 feet.

Population: 5,635 (1990); 5,980 (2000); 6,246 (2005); 6,512 (2010 projected); Race: 89.1% White, 2.6% Black, 5.2% Asian, 7.9% Hispanic of any race (2005); Density: 1,839.3 persons per square mile (2005); Average household size: 3.15 (2005); Median age: 38.1 (2005); Males per 100 females: 98.5 (2005); Marriage status: 26.6% never married, 62.4% now married, 6.6% widowed, 4.4% divorced (2000); Foreign born: 15.6% (2000); Ancestry (includes multiple ancestries): 41.2% Italian, 17.8% Irish, 13.4% Other groups, 12.3% German, 2.9% United States or American (2000).
Economy: Employment by occupation: 19.2% management, 24.6% professional, 13.0% services, 24.7% sales, 0.0% farming, 12.4% construction, 6.1% production (2000).
Income: Per capita income: $46,147 (2005); Median household income: $105,069 (2005); Average household income: $144,047 (2005); Percent of households with income of $100,000 or more: 52.2% (2005); Poverty rate: 4.0% (2000).
Education: Percent of population age 25 and over with: High school diploma (including GED) or higher: 87.3% (2005); Bachelor's degree or higher: 37.8% (2005); Master's degree or higher: 15.9% (2005).

School District(s)
Mount Pleasant Central School District (KG-12)
   2003-04 Enrollment: 1,847 . . . . (914) 769-5500

Housing: Homeownership rate: 85.7% (2005); Median home value: $584,601 (2005); Median rent: $979 per month (2000); Median age of housing: 42 years (2000).
Transportation: Commute to work: 84.0% car, 11.2% public transportation, 1.6% walk, 1.9% work from home (2000); Travel time to work: 24.2% less than 15 minutes, 36.9% 15 to 30 minutes, 18.7% 30 to 45 minutes, 6.2% 45 to 60 minutes, 14.0% 60 minutes or more (2000)

TUCKAHOE
(village). Covers a land area of 0.610 square miles and a water area of 0 square miles. Located at 40.95° N. Lat.; 73.82° W. Long. Elevation is 107 feet.

History: Settled 1684; incorporated 1903.
Population: 6,302 (1990); 6,211 (2000); 6,252 (2005); 6,324 (2010 projected); Race: 73.4% White, 8.9% Black, 10.1% Asian, 11.9% Hispanic of any race (2005); Density: 10,256.1 persons per square mile (2005); Average household size: 2.33 (2005); Median age: 38.1 (2005); Males per 100 females: 91.8 (2005); Marriage status: 28.1% never married, 58.0% now married, 7.2% widowed, 6.7% divorced (2000); Foreign born: 20.9% (2000); Ancestry (includes multiple ancestries): 33.7% Italian, 28.7% Other groups, 13.9% Irish, 7.4% German, 4.9% Polish (2000).
Economy: Manufacturing of connectors, cable and cable assemblies, bulk pharmaceuticals, grinding machines, tools for electronics assemblies. Single-family building permits issued: 7 (2005); Multi-family building permits issued: 2 (2005); Employment by occupation: 21.5% management, 23.9% professional, 12.3% services, 29.4% sales, 0.0% farming, 6.1% construction, 6.8% production (2000).
Income: Per capita income: $38,514 (2005); Median household income: $71,576 (2005); Average household income: $89,507 (2005); Percent of households with income of $100,000 or more: 33.2% (2005); Poverty rate: 7.2% (2000).
Education: Percent of population age 25 and over with: High school diploma (including GED) or higher: 86.5% (2005); Bachelor's degree or higher: 36.7% (2005); Master's degree or higher: 16.0% (2005).
Housing: Homeownership rate: 46.2% (2005); Median home value: $435,552 (2005); Median rent: $884 per month (2000); Median age of housing: 43 years (2000).
Safety: Violent crime rate: 4.8 per 10,000 population; Property crime rate: 48.0 per 10,000 population (2004).
Transportation: Commute to work: 63.0% car, 29.7% public transportation, 4.7% walk, 2.1% work from home (2000); Travel time to work: 23.8% less than 15 minutes, 29.4% 15 to 30 minutes, 17.2% 30 to 45 minutes, 12.2% 45 to 60 minutes, 17.5% 60 minutes or more (2000)
Additional Information Contacts
Village of Tuckahoe .... (914) 961-3100
  http://www.tuckahoe.com/

VALHALLA (CDP).
Covers a land area of 2.675 square miles and a water area of 0.846 square miles. Located at 41.08° N. Lat.; 73.77° W. Long. Elevation is 222 feet.
Population: 5,167 (1990); 5,379 (2000); 5,394 (2005); 5,407 (2010 projected); Race: 95.0% White, 0.9% Black, 2.7% Asian, 4.6% Hispanic of any race (2005); Density: 2,016.2 persons per square mile (2005); Average household size: 2.87 (2005); Median age: 42.0 (2005); Males per 100 females: 95.3 (2005); Marriage status: 21.6% never married, 65.9% now married, 7.3% widowed, 5.2% divorced (2000); Foreign born: 11.1% (2000); Ancestry (includes multiple ancestries): 39.9% Italian, 25.0% Irish, 12.3% German, 9.6% Other groups, 6.5% English (2000).
Economy: Employment by occupation: 19.9% management, 22.9% professional, 8.9% services, 31.9% sales, 0.0% farming, 8.8% construction, 7.6% production (2000).
Income: Per capita income: $41,260 (2005); Median household income: $91,860 (2005); Average household income: $117,457 (2005); Percent of households with income of $100,000 or more: 44.8% (2005); Poverty rate: 1.7% (2000).
Education: Percent of population age 25 and over with: High school diploma (including GED) or higher: 92.4% (2005); Bachelor's degree or higher: 40.8% (2005); Master's degree or higher: 15.5% (2005).

School District(s)
Greenburgh-North Castle Union Free School District (07-12)
  2003-04 Enrollment: 222 .... (914) 693-4309
Mount Pleasant-Blythedale Union Free School District (UG-UG)
  2003-04 Enrollment: 115 .... (914) 347-1800
Valhalla Union Free School District (KG-12)
  2003-04 Enrollment: 1,438 .... (914) 683-5040

Four-year College(s)
New York Medical College
  Fall 2004 Enrollment: 1,407 .... (914) 594-4000

Two-year College(s)
SUNY Westchester Commmunity College (Public)
  Fall 2004 Enrollment: 11,935 .... (914) 606-6600
  2005-06 Tuition: In-state $3,150; Out-of-state $8,219
Southern Westchester BOCES-Practical Nursing Program (Public)
  Fall 2004 Enrollment: 61 .... (914) 761-3400
Housing: Homeownership rate: 83.9% (2005); Median home value: $551,606 (2005); Median rent: $937 per month (2000); Median age of housing: 45 years (2000).

Hospitals: Blythedale Childrens Hospital (92 beds); Westchester Medical Center (635 beds)
Transportation: Commute to work: 84.4% car, 11.7% public transportation, 0.8% walk, 3.1% work from home (2000); Travel time to work: 27.3% less than 15 minutes, 35.0% 15 to 30 minutes, 17.5% 30 to 45 minutes, 7.1% 45 to 60 minutes, 13.2% 60 minutes or more (2000)

VERPLANCK (CDP).
Covers a land area of 0.693 square miles and a water area of 0.090 square miles. Located at 41.25° N. Lat.; 73.96° W. Long.
Population: 1,088 (1990); 777 (2000); 699 (2005); 646 (2010 projected); Race: 94.4% White, 0.0% Black, 0.1% Asian, 9.7% Hispanic of any race (2005); Density: 1,008.6 persons per square mile (2005); Average household size: 2.57 (2005); Median age: 38.5 (2005); Males per 100 females: 88.9 (2005); Marriage status: 27.6% never married, 43.1% now married, 15.2% widowed, 14.1% divorced (2000); Foreign born: 10.7% (2000); Ancestry (includes multiple ancestries): 40.4% Irish, 33.9% Italian, 15.5% Other groups, 12.1% German, 6.2% English (2000).
Economy: Employment by occupation: 14.0% management, 16.9% professional, 18.8% services, 26.0% sales, 0.0% farming, 11.4% construction, 13.0% production (2000).
Income: Per capita income: $23,080 (2005); Median household income: $47,115 (2005); Average household income: $55,873 (2005); Percent of households with income of $100,000 or more: 20.6% (2005); Poverty rate: 21.9% (2000).
Education: Percent of population age 25 and over with: High school diploma (including GED) or higher: 80.4% (2005); Bachelor's degree or higher: 18.5% (2005); Master's degree or higher: 6.4% (2005).
Housing: Homeownership rate: 64.7% (2005); Median home value: $265,217 (2005); Median rent: $800 per month (2000); Median age of housing: 56 years (2000).
Transportation: Commute to work: 86.7% car, 5.5% public transportation, 0.0% walk, 1.6% work from home (2000); Travel time to work: 33.0% less than 15 minutes, 14.2% 15 to 30 minutes, 29.7% 30 to 45 minutes, 10.9% 45 to 60 minutes, 12.2% 60 minutes or more (2000)

WACCABUC (unincorporated postal area, zip code 10597).
Covers a land area of 1.962 square miles and a water area of 0 square miles. Located at 41.28° N. Lat.; 73.58° W. Long. Elevation is 556 feet.
Population: 0 (2000); Race: 100.0% White, 0.0% Black, 0.0% Asian, 0.0% Hispanic of any race (2000); Density: 0.0 persons per square mile (2000); Age: 26.5% under 18, 2.8% over 64 (2000); Marriage status: 17.3% never married, 76.9% now married, 4.2% widowed, 1.5% divorced (2000); Foreign born: 3.4% (2000); Ancestry (includes multiple ancestries): 26.5% Italian, 22.5% Irish, 22.2% English, 15.7% Russian, 8.6% German (2000).
Economy: Employment by occupation: 25.2% management, 30.9% professional, 5.0% services, 38.8% sales, 0.0% farming, 0.0% construction, 0.0% production (2000).
Income: Per capita income: $66,886 (2000); Median household income: $115,574 (2000); Poverty rate: 0.0% (2000).
Education: Percent of population age 25 and over with: High school diploma (including GED) or higher: 100.0% (2000); Bachelor's degree or higher: 80.9% (2000).
Housing: Homeownership rate: 76.0% (2000); Median home value: $699,100 (2000); Median rent: $850 per month (2000); Median age of housing: 17 years (2000).
Transportation: Commute to work: 77.7% car, 22.3% public transportation, 0.0% walk, 0.0% work from home (2000); Travel time to work: 3.6% less than 15 minutes, 25.2% 15 to 30 minutes, 22.3% 30 to 45 minutes, 12.2% 45 to 60 minutes, 36.7% 60 minutes or more (2000)

WEST HARRISON (unincorporated postal area, zip code 10604).
Covers a land area of 5.102 square miles and a water area of 0.118 square miles. Located at 41.15° N. Lat.; 73.80° W. Long.
Population: 0 (2000); Race: 78.8% White, 9.4% Black, 3.5% Asian, 13.6% Hispanic of any race (2000); Density: 0.0 persons per square mile (2000); Age: 23.0% under 18, 13.7% over 64 (2000); Marriage status: 26.2% never married, 58.0% now married, 7.4% widowed, 8.3% divorced (2000); Foreign born: 23.5% (2000); Ancestry (includes multiple ancestries): 42.4% Italian, 22.4% Other groups, 15.1% Irish, 6.1% German, 3.3% United States or American (2000).
Economy: Employment by occupation: 18.3% management, 22.8% professional, 19.8% services, 24.4% sales, 0.0% farming, 9.1% construction, 5.5% production (2000).

Income: Per capita income: $35,285 (2000); Median household income: $62,553 (2000); Poverty rate: 9.1% (2000).
Education: Percent of population age 25 and over with: High school diploma (including GED) or higher: 80.4% (2000); Bachelor's degree or higher: 35.6% (2000).

School District(s)
Harrison Central School District (KG-12)
    2003-04 Enrollment: 3,382 . . . . (914) 630-3002

Housing: Homeownership rate: 54.7% (2000); Median home value: $365,000 (2000); Median rent: $907 per month (2000); Median age of housing: 43 years (2000).
Transportation: Commute to work: 80.6% car, 14.8% public transportation, 2.1% walk, 2.2% work from home (2000); Travel time to work: 33.9% less than 15 minutes, 33.7% 15 to 30 minutes, 15.4% 30 to 45 minutes, 7.2% 45 to 60 minutes, 9.8% 60 minutes or more (2000).

WHITE PLAINS (city). Covers a land area of 9.801 square miles and a water area of 0.091 square miles. Located at 41.02° N. Lat.; 73.76° W. Long. Elevation is 201 feet.
History: Named for the Weckquaeskeck word "quaropas," meaning "white marshes or plains". Settled by Puritans in 1683. The state convention that ratified the Declaration of Independence met (1776) here. The battle of White Plains (1776), a principal engagement of the American Revolution occurred here. Gen. George Washington briefly made his headquarters here at Elijah Miller House, which still stands. Other buildings from the revolutionary period are also preserved. Incorporated as a village 1866 (originally named Quarrapas by Siwanoy people), as a city 1916.
Population: 48,615 (1990); 53,077 (2000); 57,054 (2005); 60,818 (2010 projected); Race: 61.5% White, 15.0% Black, 5.6% Asian, 28.7% Hispanic of any race (2005); Density: 5,821.3 persons per square mile (2005); Average household size: 2.56 (2005); Median age: 39.6 (2005); Males per 100 females: 91.3 (2005); Marriage status: 31.6% never married, 52.4% now married, 7.6% widowed, 8.4% divorced (2000); Foreign born: 29.3% (2000); Ancestry (includes multiple ancestries): 38.5% Other groups, 15.2% Italian, 11.5% Irish, 6.9% German, 4.1% Russian (2000).
Economy: The city has some very large shopping malls, some light industries, and serves as the headquarters for several corporations and laboratories. Several corporate parks ring the city, and the central business district offers retail stores. Unemployment rate: 3.6% (2005); Total civilian labor force: 30,698 (2005); Single-family building permits issued: 13 (2005); Multi-family building permits issued: 2 (2005); Employment by occupation: 18.7% management, 27.2% professional, 17.2% services, 25.2% sales, 0.1% farming, 5.3% construction, 6.4% production (2000).
Income: Per capita income: $38,535 (2005); Median household income: $65,859 (2005); Average household income: $97,322 (2005); Percent of households with income of $100,000 or more: 31.5% (2005); Poverty rate: 9.8% (2000).
Education: Percent of population age 25 and over with: High school diploma (including GED) or higher: 81.8% (2005); Bachelor's degree or higher: 40.9% (2005); Master's degree or higher: 19.8% (2005).

School District(s)
Greenburgh Central School District (PK-12)
    2003-04 Enrollment: 1,981 . . . . (914) 761-6000
Valhalla Union Free School District (KG-12)
    2003-04 Enrollment: 1,438 . . . . (914) 683-5040
White Plains City School District (PK-12)
    2003-04 Enrollment: 6,844 . . . . (914) 422-2019

Two-year College(s)
Sanford-Brown Institute
    Fall 2004 Enrollment: 399 . . . . (914) 874-2500
The College of Westchester
    Fall 2004 Enrollment: 1,050. (914) 948-4442
    2005-06 Tuition: In-state $17,995; Out-of-state $17,995

Housing: Homeownership rate: 53.2% (2005); Median home value: $443,862 (2005); Median rent: $828 per month (2000); Median age of housing: 46 years (2000).
Hospitals: Burke Rehabilitation Hospital (150 beds); White Plains Hospital Center (307 beds)
Safety: Violent crime rate: 38.0 per 10,000 population; Property crime rate: 256.9 per 10,000 population (2004).
Newspapers: Suburban Street News (General - Circulation 27,000); The Journal News (Circulation 144,001)
Transportation: Commute to work: 69.0% car, 19.7% public transportation, 7.1% walk, 3.5% work from home (2000); Travel time to work: 29.8% less than 15 minutes, 34.7% 15 to 30 minutes, 15.1% 30 to 45 minutes, 7.5% 45 to 60 minutes, 12.9% 60 minutes or more (2000)

Additional Information Contacts
City of White Plains . . . . (914) 422-1200
    http://www.ci.white-plains.ny.us/
White Plains-Business Council of Westchester . . . . (914) 948-2110
    http://www.westchesterny.org

WYKAGYL (unincorporated postal area, zip code 10804). Covers a land area of 4.250 square miles and a water area of 0.166 square miles. Located at 40.95° N. Lat.; 73.78° W. Long.
Population: 0 (2000); Race: 87.5% White, 6.8% Black, 3.5% Asian, 3.1% Hispanic of any race (2000); Density: 0.0 persons per square mile (2000); Age: 27.4% under 18, 17.0% over 64 (2000); Marriage status: 18.6% never married, 70.6% now married, 6.9% widowed, 3.9% divorced (2000); Foreign born: 15.9% (2000); Ancestry (includes multiple ancestries): 18.4% Other groups, 17.7% Italian, 11.5% Irish, 9.0% Russian, 7.8% German (2000).
Economy: Employment by occupation: 24.8% management, 41.9% professional, 3.8% services, 22.5% sales, 0.0% farming, 4.2% construction, 2.7% production (2000).
Income: Per capita income: $57,088 (2000); Median household income: $126,480 (2000); Poverty rate: 2.1% (2000).
Education: Percent of population age 25 and over with: High school diploma (including GED) or higher: 94.5% (2000); Bachelor's degree or higher: 70.0% (2000).
Housing: Homeownership rate: 93.4% (2000); Median home value: $427,200 (2000); Median rent: $1,132 per month (2000); Median age of housing: 50 years (2000).
Transportation: Commute to work: 72.2% car, 20.6% public transportation, 0.8% walk, 5.9% work from home (2000); Travel time to work: 16.2% less than 15 minutes, 30.6% 15 to 30 minutes, 21.6% 30 to 45 minutes, 13.5% 45 to 60 minutes, 18.1% 60 minutes or more (2000)

YONKERS (city). Covers a land area of 18.077 square miles and a water area of 2.239 square miles. Located at 40.94° N. Lat.; 73.86° W. Long. Elevation is 10 feet.
History: Named for Adriaen Van der Donck, whose title was "jonkheer," purchaser of the land. The village of Nappeckamack stood on the site of Yonkers before the Kekeskick Purchase (1639) made by the Dutch West India Company. The city site was included in a grant of land made in 1646 by the company to Adriaen Cornelissen Van der Donck, the first lawyer and first historian of New Netherland. By reason of his wealth and social position, Van der Donck enjoyed the courtesy title of "jonker," the Dutch equivalent of "his young lordship," from which was derived the name of the city.
Population: 188,126 (1990); 196,086 (2000); 197,668 (2005); 199,494 (2010 projected); Race: 54.7% White, 17.9% Black, 6.1% Asian, 30.2% Hispanic of any race (2005); Density: 10,935.0 persons per square mile (2005); Average household size: 2.65 (2005); Median age: 37.4 (2005); Males per 100 females: 89.8 (2005); Marriage status: 32.9% never married, 50.8% now married, 8.5% widowed, 7.8% divorced (2000); Foreign born: 26.4% (2000); Ancestry (includes multiple ancestries): 38.7% Other groups, 18.8% Italian, 12.9% Irish, 4.7% German, 3.3% Polish (2000).
Economy: Unemployment rate: 5.2% (2005); Total civilian labor force: 93,994 (2005); Single-family building permits issued: 38 (2005); Multi-family building permits issued: 127 (2005); Employment by occupation: 13.5% management, 20.7% professional, 17.1% services, 29.9% sales, 0.1% farming, 8.7% construction, 10.1% production (2000).
Income: Per capita income: $25,260 (2005); Median household income: $49,331 (2005); Average household income: $66,307 (2005); Percent of households with income of $100,000 or more: 19.9% (2005); Poverty rate: 15.5% (2000).
Taxes: Total city taxes per capita: $1,346 (2004); City property taxes per capita: $865 (2004).
Education: Percent of population age 25 and over with: High school diploma (including GED) or higher: 76.8% (2005); Bachelor's degree or higher: 24.9% (2005); Master's degree or higher: 10.4% (2005).

School District(s)
Greenburgh-North Castle Union Free School District (07-12)
    2003-04 Enrollment: 222 . . . . (914) 693-4309
Yonkers City School District (PK-12)
    2003-04 Enrollment: 26,201 . . . . (914) 376-8100

Four-year College(s)
Saint Josephs Seminary and College
Fall 2004 Enrollment: 122 . . . . (914) 968-6200
Two-year College(s)
Cochran School of Nursing
Fall 2004 Enrollment: 241 . . . . (914) 964-4296
St Joseph's Medical Center School of Radiography
Fall 2004 Enrollment: 25 . . . . (914) 751-0390

Housing: Homeownership rate: 44.1% (2005); Median home value: $347,203 (2005); Median rent: $683 per month (2000); Median age of housing: 46 years (2000).
Hospitals: St. John's Riverside Hospital (406 beds); St. John's Riverside Hospital (406 beds); St. Joseph's Medical Center (194 beds)
Safety: Violent crime rate: 47.6 per 10,000 population; Property crime rate: 188.7 per 10,000 population (2004).
Newspapers: North Castle News (General - Circulation 3,300); The Eastchester Record (General - Circulation 4,058); The Harrison Independent (General - Circulation 4,300); The Home News and Times (General - Circulation 20,100); The Mount Vernon Independent (General - Circulation 6,000); The Pelham Sun (General - Circulation 3,606); The Rye Chronicle (General - Circulation 3,966); The Sound View News (General - Circulation 6,000)
Transportation: Commute to work: 70.0% car, 23.1% public transportation, 4.2% walk, 2.1% work from home (2000); Travel time to work: 17.9% less than 15 minutes, 34.0% 15 to 30 minutes, 21.7% 30 to 45 minutes, 10.5% 45 to 60 minutes, 15.9% 60 minutes or more (2000); Amtrak: Service available.
Additional Information Contacts
City of Yonkers. . . . . (914) 377-6020
http://www.cityofyonkers.com/
Yonkers Chamber of Commerce . . . . (914) 963-0332
http://www.yonkerschamber.com

YORKTOWN
(town). Covers a land area of 36.698 square miles and a water area of 2.575 square miles. Located at 41.28° N. Lat.; 73.80° W. Long.
History: Nearby, at Crompound (2.5 miles east of Peekskill), is the former anarchist Mohegan colony designed by Lewis Mumford in 1923 and led by American Harry Kelly and Englishmen Joseph Cohen and Leonard Abbott. Also known as the twelve Mohegan Colony and the Modern School Movement, the colony flourished both here and in the Stetton colony in N.J.
Population: 33,314 (1990); 36,318 (2000); 37,406 (2005); 38,508 (2010 projected); Race: 88.7% White, 3.4% Black, 4.4% Asian, 7.6% Hispanic of any race (2005); Density: 1,019.3 persons per square mile (2005); Average household size: 2.86 (2005); Median age: 40.1 (2005); Males per 100 females: 93.6 (2005); Marriage status: 19.6% never married, 67.8% now married, 7.6% widowed, 4.9% divorced (2000); Foreign born: 10.5% (2000); Ancestry (includes multiple ancestries): 34.2% Italian, 22.6% Irish, 14.0% Other groups, 13.0% German, 6.4% English (2000).
Economy: IBM's T.J. Watson Research Center is located here. Unemployment rate: 3.6% (2005); Total civilian labor force: 20,288 (2005); Single-family building permits issued: 25 (2005); Multi-family building permits issued: 162 (2005); Employment by occupation: 19.8% management, 29.2% professional, 9.5% services, 27.0% sales, 0.1% farming, 9.2% construction, 5.1% production (2000).
Income: Per capita income: $40,142 (2005); Median household income: $95,499 (2005); Average household income: $113,635 (2005); Percent of households with income of $100,000 or more: 47.5% (2005); Poverty rate: 2.9% (2000).
Taxes: Total city taxes per capita: $622 (2004); City property taxes per capita: $520 (2004).
Education: Percent of population age 25 and over with: High school diploma (including GED) or higher: 90.4% (2005); Bachelor's degree or higher: 42.9% (2005); Master's degree or higher: 19.5% (2005).
Housing: Homeownership rate: 85.9% (2005); Median home value: $391,719 (2005); Median rent: $835 per month (2000); Median age of housing: 33 years (2000).
Transportation: Commute to work: 86.3% car, 8.4% public transportation, 0.9% walk, 4.1% work from home (2000); Travel time to work: 18.4% less than 15 minutes, 25.3% 15 to 30 minutes, 24.6% 30 to 45 minutes, 12.3% 45 to 60 minutes, 19.5% 60 minutes or more (2000)
Additional Information Contacts
Town of Yorktown . . . . (914) 962-5722
http://www.yorktownny.org/Home/

YORKTOWN HEIGHTS
(CDP). Covers a land area of 5.697 square miles and a water area of 0 square miles. Located at 41.27° N. Lat.; 73.78° W. Long. Elevation is 510 feet.
Population: 7,690 (1990); 7,972 (2000); 8,046 (2005); 8,127 (2010 projected); Race: 89.0% White, 2.5% Black, 5.7% Asian, 7.3% Hispanic of any race (2005); Density: 1,412.3 persons per square mile (2005); Average household size: 3.01 (2005); Median age: 39.9 (2005); Males per 100 females: 96.2 (2005); Marriage status: 21.7% never married, 67.8% now married, 6.8% widowed, 3.7% divorced (2000); Foreign born: 12.4% (2000); Ancestry (includes multiple ancestries): 31.4% Italian, 21.3% Irish, 16.0% Other groups, 13.1% German, 6.7% Polish (2000).
Economy: Employment by occupation: 19.1% management, 28.4% professional, 9.8% services, 27.8% sales, 0.1% farming, 8.7% construction, 6.1% production (2000).
Income: Per capita income: $37,110 (2005); Median household income: $96,798 (2005); Average household income: $109,596 (2005); Percent of households with income of $100,000 or more: 48.2% (2005); Poverty rate: 3.2% (2000).
Education: Percent of population age 25 and over with: High school diploma (including GED) or higher: 90.4% (2005); Bachelor's degree or higher: 44.1% (2005); Master's degree or higher: 23.0% (2005).
School District(s)
Boces Putnam-Northern Westchester (UG-UG)
2003-04 Enrollment: 375 . . . . (845) 248-2300
Lakeland Central School District (KG-12)
2003-04 Enrollment: 6,139 . . . . (914) 245-1700
Yorktown Central School District (KG-12)
2003-04 Enrollment: 4,219 . . . . (914) 243-8001
Two-year College(s)
Putnam-Westchester BOCES Practical Nursing Program (Public)
Fall 2004 Enrollment: 102 . . . . (914) 245-2700

Housing: Homeownership rate: 84.6% (2005); Median home value: $431,017 (2005); Median rent: $517 per month (2000); Median age of housing: 37 years (2000).
Newspapers: North County News (General - Circulation 9,200)
Transportation: Commute to work: 86.1% car, 7.5% public transportation, 1.4% walk, 4.5% work from home (2000); Travel time to work: 21.0% less than 15 minutes, 26.6% 15 to 30 minutes, 20.3% 30 to 45 minutes, 10.7% 45 to 60 minutes, 21.5% 60 minutes or more (2000)
Additional Information Contacts
Yorktown Heights Chamber of Commerce . . . . (914) 245-4599
http://www.yorktownchamber.org

Wyoming County

Located in western New York; drained by the Genesee River. Covers a land area of 592.91 square miles, a water area of 3.53 square miles, and is located in the Eastern Time Zone. The county government was organized in 1841. County seat is Warsaw.

Weather Station: Warsaw 6 SW   Elevation: 1,817 feet

	Jan	Feb	Mar	Apr	May	Jun	Jul	Aug	Sep	Oct	Nov	Dec
High	27	30	39	52	64	73	77	75	68	57	44	33
Low	12	13	20	32	43	52	57	55	48	38	29	19
Precip	3.0	2.3	3.1	3.3	3.7	4.4	4.2	3.8	4.6	3.8	3.8	3.5
Snow	29.8	21.2	17.3	4.9	0.3	0.0	0.0	0.0	0.0	0.6	12.8	23.0

High and Low temperatures in degrees Fahrenheit; Precipitation and Snow in inches

Population: 42,507 (1990); 43,424 (2000); 42,786 (2005); 42,121 (2010 projected); Race: 91.8% White, 5.5% Black, 0.5% Asian, 3.0% Hispanic of any race (2005); Density: 72.2 persons per square mile (2005); Average household size: 2.87 (2005); Median age: 38.4 (2005); Males per 100 females: 118.5 (2005).
Religion: Five largest groups: 29.9% Catholic Church, 4.5% United Church of Christ, 3.9% The United Methodist Church, 2.1% Presbyterian Church (U.S.A.), 1.0% Conservative Baptist Association of America (2000).
Economy: Unemployment rate: 5.4% (2005); Total civilian labor force: 21,616 (2005); Leading industries: 22.9% manufacturing; 16.7% retail trade; 13.8% health care and social assistance (2003); Farms: 767 totaling 215,317 acres (2002); Companies that employ 500 or more persons: 2 (2003); Companies that employ 100 to 499 persons: 8 (2003); Companies that employ less than 100 persons: 819 (2003); Black-owned businesses: n/a (2002); Hispanic-owned businesses: n/a (2002); Women-owned businesses: 702 (2002); Retail sales per capita: $8,802 (2006).

Single-family building permits issued: 72 (2005); Multi-family building permits issued: 24 (2005).
Income: Per capita income: $19,953 (2005); Median household income: $45,059 (2005); Average household income: $53,210 (2005); Percent of households with income of $100,000 or more: 8.6% (2005); Poverty rate: 10.0% (2003); Bankruptcy rate: 5.53% (2005).
Education: Percent of population age 25 and over with: High school diploma (including GED) or higher: 75.4% (2005); Bachelor's degree or higher: 11.4% (2005); Master's degree or higher: 4.4% (2005).
Housing: Homeownership rate: 76.9% (2005); Median home value: $118,008 (2005); Median rent: $379 per month (2000); Median age of housing: 55 years (2000).
Health: Birth rate: 103.3 per 10,000 population (2004); Death rate: 92.6 per 10,000 population (2004); Age-adjusted cancer mortality rate: 227.9 deaths per 100,000 population (2002); Number of physicians: 10.5 per 10,000 population (2004); Hospital beds: 58.9 per 10,000 population (2003); Hospital admissions: 824.3 per 10,000 population (2003).
Elections: 2004 Presidential election results: 64.7% Bush, 33.8% Kerry, 1.3% Nader, 0.2% Badnarik
National and State Parks: Letchworth State Park; Silver Lake State Park
Additional Information Contacts
Wyoming County Government . . . . (716) 786-8800
  http://www.wyomingco.net/
Village of Arcade . . . . (585) 492-1111
  http://www.villageofarcade.org/
Village of Attica . . . . (585) 591-0898
  http://attica.org/
Village of Perry . . . . (585) 237-2216
  http://www.villageofperry.com/

Wyoming County Communities

ARCADE (village). Covers a land area of 2.501 square miles and a water area of 0.004 square miles. Located at 42.53° N. Lat.; 78.42° W. Long. Elevation is 1,455 feet.
Population: 2,148 (1990); 2,026 (2000); 1,913 (2005); 1,850 (2010 projected); Race: 98.8% White, 0.4% Black, 0.4% Asian, 1.3% Hispanic of any race (2005); Density: 764.8 persons per square mile (2005); Average household size: 2.41 (2005); Median age: 37.6 (2005); Males per 100 females: 90.0 (2005); Marriage status: 26.0% never married, 56.5% now married, 8.2% widowed, 9.4% divorced (2000); Foreign born: 1.3% (2000); Ancestry (includes multiple ancestries): 37.3% German, 21.9% English, 18.9% Irish, 9.7% Polish, 5.9% French (except Basque) (2000).
Economy: Employment by occupation: 9.5% management, 18.2% professional, 15.8% services, 24.6% sales, 0.4% farming, 8.4% construction, 23.0% production (2000).
Income: Per capita income: $19,075 (2005); Median household income: $38,239 (2005); Average household income: $45,899 (2005); Percent of households with income of $100,000 or more: 8.1% (2005); Poverty rate: 8.8% (2000).
Education: Percent of population age 25 and over with: High school diploma (including GED) or higher: 84.7% (2005); Bachelor's degree or higher: 13.6% (2005); Master's degree or higher: 4.1% (2005).
School District(s)
Yorkshire-Pioneer Central School District (KG-12)
  2003-04 Enrollment: 2,928 . . . . (716) 492-9304
Housing: Homeownership rate: 61.8% (2005); Median home value: $126,176 (2005); Median rent: $318 per month (2000); Median age of housing: 54 years (2000).
Newspapers: Arcade Herald (General - Circulation 4,900)
Transportation: Commute to work: 90.6% car, 0.7% public transportation, 7.5% walk, 1.3% work from home (2000); Travel time to work: 60.6% less than 15 minutes, 8.9% 15 to 30 minutes, 16.5% 30 to 45 minutes, 8.0% 45 to 60 minutes, 6.0% 60 minutes or more (2000)
Additional Information Contacts
Arcade Area Chamber of Commerce. . . . . (585) 492-2114
  http://www.arcadechamber.org
Village of Arcade . . . . (585) 492-1111
  http://www.villageofarcade.org/

ARCADE (town). Covers a land area of 47.080 square miles and a water area of 0.097 square miles. Located at 42.54° N. Lat.; 78.41° W. Long. Elevation is 1,455 feet.
Population: 3,938 (1990); 4,184 (2000); 4,116 (2005); 4,045 (2010 projected); Race: 98.3% White, 0.2% Black, 0.7% Asian, 0.8% Hispanic of any race (2005); Density: 87.4 persons per square mile (2005); Average household size: 2.45 (2005); Median age: 39.6 (2005); Males per 100 females: 94.2 (2005); Marriage status: 22.9% never married, 58.9% now married, 8.1% widowed, 10.1% divorced (2000); Foreign born: 1.2% (2000); Ancestry (includes multiple ancestries): 37.0% German, 18.8% English, 14.7% Irish, 12.1% Polish, 7.6% Italian (2000).
Economy: Employment by occupation: 10.8% management, 14.5% professional, 17.1% services, 22.1% sales, 1.7% farming, 11.4% construction, 22.4% production (2000).
Income: Per capita income: $19,820 (2005); Median household income: $42,574 (2005); Average household income: $48,617 (2005); Percent of households with income of $100,000 or more: 8.6% (2005); Poverty rate: 7.1% (2000).
Education: Percent of population age 25 and over with: High school diploma (including GED) or higher: 84.1% (2005); Bachelor's degree or higher: 12.4% (2005); Master's degree or higher: 4.0% (2005).
Housing: Homeownership rate: 77.4% (2005); Median home value: $126,634 (2005); Median rent: $339 per month (2000); Median age of housing: 38 years (2000).
Transportation: Commute to work: 91.1% car, 0.6% public transportation, 6.1% walk, 2.3% work from home (2000); Travel time to work: 49.7% less than 15 minutes, 15.5% 15 to 30 minutes, 13.6% 30 to 45 minutes, 12.3% 45 to 60 minutes, 8.9% 60 minutes or more (2000)

ATTICA (village). Covers a land area of 1.683 square miles and a water area of 0 square miles. Located at 42.86° N. Lat.; 78.27° W. Long. Elevation is 998 feet.
Population: 2,630 (1990); 2,597 (2000); 2,444 (2005); 2,283 (2010 projected); Race: 98.9% White, 0.2% Black, 0.2% Asian, 0.6% Hispanic of any race (2005); Density: 1,451.9 persons per square mile (2005); Average household size: 2.38 (2005); Median age: 37.9 (2005); Males per 100 females: 95.1 (2005); Marriage status: 24.1% never married, 58.5% now married, 7.7% widowed, 9.7% divorced (2000); Foreign born: 0.6% (2000); Ancestry (includes multiple ancestries): 41.9% German, 19.8% Irish, 14.7% English, 14.4% Polish, 10.5% Italian (2000).
Economy: Employment by occupation: 7.2% management, 15.7% professional, 30.8% services, 24.2% sales, 1.0% farming, 7.9% construction, 13.1% production (2000).
Income: Per capita income: $21,487 (2005); Median household income: $44,778 (2005); Average household income: $51,085 (2005); Percent of households with income of $100,000 or more: 7.6% (2005); Poverty rate: 9.9% (2000).
Education: Percent of population age 25 and over with: High school diploma (including GED) or higher: 85.6% (2005); Bachelor's degree or higher: 11.0% (2005); Master's degree or higher: 3.1% (2005).
School District(s)
Attica Central School District (KG-12)
  2003-04 Enrollment: 1,840 . . . . (585) 591-0400
Housing: Homeownership rate: 60.4% (2005); Median home value: $116,790 (2005); Median rent: $365 per month (2000); Median age of housing: 60+ years (2000).
Safety: Violent crime rate: 4.0 per 10,000 population; Property crime rate: 154.2 per 10,000 population (2004).
Transportation: Commute to work: 95.2% car, 0.0% public transportation, 3.3% walk, 0.8% work from home (2000); Travel time to work: 42.0% less than 15 minutes, 27.5% 15 to 30 minutes, 15.2% 30 to 45 minutes, 10.6% 45 to 60 minutes, 4.6% 60 minutes or more (2000)
Additional Information Contacts
Village of Attica . . . . (585) 591-0898
  http://attica.org/

ATTICA (town). Covers a land area of 35.709 square miles and a water area of 0.303 square miles. Located at 42.83° N. Lat.; 78.25° W. Long. Elevation is 998 feet.
Population: 7,383 (1990); 6,028 (2000); 5,904 (2005); 5,750 (2010 projected); Race: 77.9% White, 16.8% Black, 0.5% Asian, 7.6% Hispanic of any race (2005); Density: 165.3 persons per square mile (2005); Average household size: 4.11 (2005); Median age: 35.6 (2005); Males per 100 females: 222.3 (2005); Marriage status: 41.7% never married, 46.6% now married, 3.8% widowed, 7.8% divorced (2000); Foreign born: 5.5% (2000); Ancestry (includes multiple ancestries): 28.0% German, 10.5% Irish, 10.2% Polish, 10.0% English, 4.7% Italian (2000).
Economy: Employment by occupation: 9.1% management, 17.0% professional, 25.9% services, 25.9% sales, 1.0% farming, 7.5% construction, 13.7% production (2000).

Income: Per capita income: $19,931 (2005); Median household income: $50,691 (2005); Average household income: $56,477 (2005); Percent of households with income of $100,000 or more: 8.8% (2005); Poverty rate: 6.3% (2000).
Education: Percent of population age 25 and over with: High school diploma (including GED) or higher: 57.7% (2005); Bachelor's degree or higher: 7.9% (2005); Master's degree or higher: 2.4% (2005).
Housing: Homeownership rate: 69.7% (2005); Median home value: $121,389 (2005); Median rent: $364 per month (2000); Median age of housing: 60+ years (2000).
Transportation: Commute to work: 93.0% car, 0.0% public transportation, 3.2% walk, 3.6% work from home (2000); Travel time to work: 37.1% less than 15 minutes, 27.6% 15 to 30 minutes, 16.8% 30 to 45 minutes, 9.6% 45 to 60 minutes, 9.0% 60 minutes or more (2000)

BENNINGTON (town). Covers a land area of 55.048 square miles and a water area of 0.219 square miles. Located at 42.82° N. Lat.; 78.41° W. Long. Elevation is 1,208 feet.
Population: 3,046 (1990); 3,349 (2000); 3,292 (2005); 3,230 (2010 projected); Race: 99.1% White, 0.2% Black, 0.2% Asian, 0.3% Hispanic of any race (2005); Density: 59.8 persons per square mile (2005); Average household size: 2.72 (2005); Median age: 41.7 (2005); Males per 100 females: 104.6 (2005); Marriage status: 22.8% never married, 66.4% now married, 5.0% widowed, 5.8% divorced (2000); Foreign born: 1.3% (2000); Ancestry (includes multiple ancestries): 41.1% German, 21.9% Polish, 13.9% Irish, 12.3% English, 8.0% Italian (2000).
Economy: Employment by occupation: 9.0% management, 19.8% professional, 15.3% services, 21.2% sales, 2.5% farming, 14.1% construction, 18.0% production (2000).
Income: Per capita income: $22,170 (2005); Median household income: $52,721 (2005); Average household income: $60,219 (2005); Percent of households with income of $100,000 or more: 11.4% (2005); Poverty rate: 6.2% (2000).
Taxes: Total city taxes per capita: $256 (2004); City property taxes per capita: $218 (2004).
Education: Percent of population age 25 and over with: High school diploma (including GED) or higher: 81.8% (2005); Bachelor's degree or higher: 14.8% (2005); Master's degree or higher: 8.3% (2005).
Housing: Homeownership rate: 88.9% (2005); Median home value: $147,872 (2005); Median rent: $452 per month (2000); Median age of housing: 38 years (2000).
Transportation: Commute to work: 93.6% car, 0.0% public transportation, 3.1% walk, 3.3% work from home (2000); Travel time to work: 18.1% less than 15 minutes, 35.5% 15 to 30 minutes, 28.0% 30 to 45 minutes, 12.8% 45 to 60 minutes, 5.6% 60 minutes or more (2000)

BLISS (unincorporated postal area, zip code 14024). Covers a land area of 64.684 square miles and a water area of 0.327 square miles. Located at 42.58° N. Lat.; 78.24° W. Long. Elevation is 746 feet.
Population: 0 (2000); Race: 97.0% White, 1.2% Black, 0.4% Asian, 0.2% Hispanic of any race (2000); Density: 0.0 persons per square mile (2000); Age: 32.4% under 18, 8.9% over 64 (2000); Marriage status: 25.3% never married, 60.5% now married, 5.6% widowed, 8.5% divorced (2000); Foreign born: 1.2% (2000); Ancestry (includes multiple ancestries): 33.6% German, 14.7% Irish, 13.3% Polish, 10.7% English, 10.1% United States or American (2000).
Economy: Employment by occupation: 14.2% management, 9.3% professional, 13.8% services, 19.7% sales, 4.8% farming, 15.1% construction, 23.1% production (2000).
Income: Per capita income: $18,193 (2000); Median household income: $36,991 (2000); Poverty rate: 12.0% (2000).
Education: Percent of population age 25 and over with: High school diploma (including GED) or higher: 79.1% (2000); Bachelor's degree or higher: 7.7% (2000).
Housing: Homeownership rate: 81.9% (2000); Median home value: $64,500 (2000); Median rent: $405 per month (2000); Median age of housing: 36 years (2000).
Transportation: Commute to work: 89.8% car, 0.3% public transportation, 2.1% walk, 6.3% work from home (2000); Travel time to work: 22.1% less than 15 minutes, 36.8% 15 to 30 minutes, 14.6% 30 to 45 minutes, 10.7% 45 to 60 minutes, 15.8% 60 minutes or more (2000)

CASTILE (village). Covers a land area of 1.351 square miles and a water area of 0 square miles. Located at 42.63° N. Lat.; 78.05° W. Long. Elevation is 1,397 feet.
Population: 1,078 (1990); 1,051 (2000); 1,030 (2005); 992 (2010 projected); Race: 99.0% White, 0.4% Black, 0.3% Asian, 0.4% Hispanic of any race (2005); Density: 762.2 persons per square mile (2005); Average household size: 2.41 (2005); Median age: 38.1 (2005); Males per 100 females: 95.8 (2005); Marriage status: 28.6% never married, 55.4% now married, 7.0% widowed, 8.9% divorced (2000); Foreign born: 1.3% (2000); Ancestry (includes multiple ancestries): 29.0% German, 19.1% Irish, 17.9% United States or American, 17.8% English, 7.7% Polish (2000).
Economy: Employment by occupation: 7.5% management, 14.3% professional, 19.0% services, 18.4% sales, 2.8% farming, 19.0% construction, 19.0% production (2000).
Income: Per capita income: $19,544 (2005); Median household income: $38,803 (2005); Average household income: $47,033 (2005); Percent of households with income of $100,000 or more: 8.6% (2005); Poverty rate: 9.3% (2000).
Education: Percent of population age 25 and over with: High school diploma (including GED) or higher: 79.7% (2005); Bachelor's degree or higher: 13.5% (2005); Master's degree or higher: 5.7% (2005).
Housing: Homeownership rate: 67.3% (2005); Median home value: $107,200 (2005); Median rent: $327 per month (2000); Median age of housing: 60+ years (2000).
Transportation: Commute to work: 86.9% car, 0.6% public transportation, 4.4% walk, 6.3% work from home (2000); Travel time to work: 42.5% less than 15 minutes, 27.6% 15 to 30 minutes, 11.2% 30 to 45 minutes, 8.6% 45 to 60 minutes, 10.1% 60 minutes or more (2000)

CASTILE (town). Covers a land area of 37.008 square miles and a water area of 1.436 square miles. Located at 42.67° N. Lat.; 78.02° W. Long. Elevation is 1,397 feet.
Population: 3,042 (1990); 2,873 (2000); 2,805 (2005); 2,737 (2010 projected); Race: 98.3% White, 0.5% Black, 0.5% Asian, 0.6% Hispanic of any race (2005); Density: 75.8 persons per square mile (2005); Average household size: 2.50 (2005); Median age: 40.8 (2005); Males per 100 females: 98.1 (2005); Marriage status: 20.7% never married, 63.1% now married, 6.7% widowed, 9.4% divorced (2000); Foreign born: 1.4% (2000); Ancestry (includes multiple ancestries): 28.4% German, 18.4% English, 15.6% Irish, 13.1% United States or American, 9.3% Polish (2000).
Economy: Employment by occupation: 10.5% management, 16.0% professional, 16.1% services, 19.4% sales, 7.4% farming, 14.6% construction, 15.9% production (2000).
Income: Per capita income: $20,044 (2005); Median household income: $40,864 (2005); Average household income: $49,706 (2005); Percent of households with income of $100,000 or more: 7.9% (2005); Poverty rate: 10.7% (2000).
Education: Percent of population age 25 and over with: High school diploma (including GED) or higher: 83.3% (2005); Bachelor's degree or higher: 15.5% (2005); Master's degree or higher: 6.3% (2005).
Housing: Homeownership rate: 74.4% (2005); Median home value: $114,570 (2005); Median rent: $395 per month (2000); Median age of housing: 60+ years (2000).
Transportation: Commute to work: 85.7% car, 0.2% public transportation, 5.4% walk, 8.1% work from home (2000); Travel time to work: 40.9% less than 15 minutes, 28.2% 15 to 30 minutes, 11.4% 30 to 45 minutes, 9.3% 45 to 60 minutes, 10.2% 60 minutes or more (2000)

COVINGTON (town). Covers a land area of 26.134 square miles and a water area of 0 square miles. Located at 42.84° N. Lat.; 78.01° W. Long. Elevation is 1,107 feet.
Population: 1,266 (1990); 1,357 (2000); 1,342 (2005); 1,325 (2010 projected); Race: 97.5% White, 0.1% Black, 0.5% Asian, 0.7% Hispanic of any race (2005); Density: 51.4 persons per square mile (2005); Average household size: 2.82 (2005); Median age: 38.7 (2005); Males per 100 females: 103.6 (2005); Marriage status: 23.1% never married, 64.9% now married, 4.6% widowed, 7.4% divorced (2000); Foreign born: 0.3% (2000); Ancestry (includes multiple ancestries): 30.6% German, 22.4% English, 19.4% Irish, 12.1% United States or American, 4.8% Polish (2000).
Economy: Employment by occupation: 12.0% management, 9.3% professional, 16.1% services, 21.0% sales, 9.9% farming, 12.1% construction, 19.6% production (2000).
Income: Per capita income: $18,737 (2005); Median household income: $46,776 (2005); Average household income: $52,826 (2005); Percent of households with income of $100,000 or more: 7.4% (2005); Poverty rate: 8.1% (2000).

Education: Percent of population age 25 and over with: High school diploma (including GED) or higher: 83.4% (2005); Bachelor's degree or higher: 9.9% (2005); Master's degree or higher: 2.9% (2005).
Housing: Homeownership rate: 88.0% (2005); Median home value: $117,484 (2005); Median rent: $413 per month (2000); Median age of housing: 34 years (2000).
Transportation: Commute to work: 92.0% car, 0.3% public transportation, 4.1% walk, 3.3% work from home (2000); Travel time to work: 33.7% less than 15 minutes, 37.5% 15 to 30 minutes, 13.7% 30 to 45 minutes, 8.8% 45 to 60 minutes, 6.3% 60 minutes or more (2000)

COWLESVILLE (unincorporated postal area, zip code 14037).
Covers a land area of 15.738 square miles and a water area of 0 square miles. Located at 42.81° N. Lat.; 78.46° W. Long. Elevation is 948 feet.
Population: 0 (2000); Race: 98.1% White, 0.9% Black, 0.9% Asian, 1.2% Hispanic of any race (2000); Density: 0.0 persons per square mile (2000); Age: 25.6% under 18, 13.7% over 64 (2000); Marriage status: 23.9% never married, 62.0% now married, 7.8% widowed, 6.3% divorced (2000); Foreign born: 0.9% (2000); Ancestry (includes multiple ancestries): 49.5% German, 22.6% Polish, 13.0% Irish, 12.0% English, 8.5% Italian (2000).
Economy: Employment by occupation: 8.2% management, 21.3% professional, 20.2% services, 19.0% sales, 3.8% farming, 6.7% construction, 20.8% production (2000).
Income: Per capita income: $18,929 (2000); Median household income: $42,000 (2000); Poverty rate: 2.8% (2000).
Education: Percent of population age 25 and over with: High school diploma (including GED) or higher: 83.3% (2000); Bachelor's degree or higher: 20.1% (2000).
Housing: Homeownership rate: 83.1% (2000); Median home value: $88,300 (2000); Median rent: $480 per month (2000); Median age of housing: 49 years (2000).
Transportation: Commute to work: 87.7% car, 0.0% public transportation, 4.3% walk, 8.0% work from home (2000); Travel time to work: 15.9% less than 15 minutes, 29.9% 15 to 30 minutes, 30.1% 30 to 45 minutes, 20.6% 45 to 60 minutes, 3.4% 60 minutes or more (2000)

DALE (unincorporated postal area, zip code 14039).
Covers a land area of 1.480 square miles and a water area of 0 square miles. Located at 42.82° N. Lat.; 78.17° W. Long. Elevation is 1,201 feet.
Population: 0 (2000); Race: 100.0% White, 0.0% Black, 0.0% Asian, 0.0% Hispanic of any race (2000); Density: 0.0 persons per square mile (2000); Age: 20.9% under 18, 2.7% over 64 (2000); Marriage status: 26.4% never married, 59.3% now married, 3.3% widowed, 11.0% divorced (2000); Foreign born: 0.9% (2000); Ancestry (includes multiple ancestries): 49.1% English, 35.5% German, 14.5% Polish, 11.8% Irish, 10.0% French (except Basque) (2000).
Economy: Employment by occupation: 10.0% management, 11.7% professional, 23.3% services, 18.3% sales, 3.3% farming, 18.3% construction, 15.0% production (2000).
Income: Per capita income: $19,911 (2000); Median household income: $54,500 (2000); Poverty rate: 5.5% (2000).
Education: Percent of population age 25 and over with: High school diploma (including GED) or higher: 79.4% (2000); Bachelor's degree or higher: 10.3% (2000).
Housing: Homeownership rate: 71.8% (2000); Median home value: $62,500 (2000); Median rent: $381 per month (2000); Median age of housing: 60+ years (2000).
Transportation: Commute to work: 100.0% car, 0.0% public transportation, 0.0% walk, 0.0% work from home (2000); Travel time to work: 20.0% less than 15 minutes, 40.0% 15 to 30 minutes, 10.0% 30 to 45 minutes, 16.7% 45 to 60 minutes, 13.3% 60 minutes or more (2000)

EAGLE (town)
Covers a land area of 36.383 square miles and a water area of 0.141 square miles. Located at 42.56° N. Lat.; 78.25° W. Long.
Population: 1,155 (1990); 1,194 (2000); 1,175 (2005); 1,157 (2010 projected); Race: 99.1% White, 0.2% Black, 0.2% Asian, 0.2% Hispanic of any race (2005); Density: 32.3 persons per square mile (2005); Average household size: 2.76 (2005); Median age: 38.0 (2005); Males per 100 females: 99.5 (2005); Marriage status: 25.3% never married, 59.1% now married, 5.9% widowed, 9.8% divorced (2000); Foreign born: 1.7% (2000); Ancestry (includes multiple ancestries): 35.0% German, 16.2% Irish, 11.8% Polish, 10.2% English, 9.3% United States or American (2000).
Economy: Employment by occupation: 10.4% management, 9.2% professional, 14.4% services, 20.6% sales, 3.7% farming, 16.5% construction, 25.2% production (2000).
Income: Per capita income: $23,077 (2005); Median household income: $44,574 (2005); Average household income: $63,650 (2005); Percent of households with income of $100,000 or more: 10.3% (2005); Poverty rate: 11.3% (2000).
Education: Percent of population age 25 and over with: High school diploma (including GED) or higher: 78.8% (2005); Bachelor's degree or higher: 9.1% (2005); Master's degree or higher: 1.7% (2005).
Housing: Homeownership rate: 85.2% (2005); Median home value: $100,658 (2005); Median rent: $425 per month (2000); Median age of housing: 39 years (2000).
Transportation: Commute to work: 89.9% car, 0.4% public transportation, 1.6% walk, 6.7% work from home (2000); Travel time to work: 18.5% less than 15 minutes, 37.4% 15 to 30 minutes, 17.4% 30 to 45 minutes, 11.3% 45 to 60 minutes, 15.5% 60 minutes or more (2000)

GAINESVILLE (village).
Covers a land area of 0.852 square miles and a water area of 0 square miles. Located at 42.64° N. Lat.; 78.13° W. Long.
Population: 340 (1990); 304 (2000); 291 (2005); 287 (2010 projected); Race: 99.7% White, 0.0% Black, 0.3% Asian, 0.7% Hispanic of any race (2005); Density: 341.6 persons per square mile (2005); Average household size: 2.62 (2005); Median age: 37.7 (2005); Males per 100 females: 102.1 (2005); Marriage status: 27.5% never married, 59.5% now married, 4.1% widowed, 9.0% divorced (2000); Foreign born: 0.7% (2000); Ancestry (includes multiple ancestries): 25.7% German, 19.3% English, 16.6% United States or American, 13.5% Irish, 9.5% Other groups (2000).
Economy: Employment by occupation: 5.3% management, 12.1% professional, 22.7% services, 25.0% sales, 0.0% farming, 10.6% construction, 24.2% production (2000).
Income: Per capita income: $15,180 (2005); Median household income: $33,793 (2005); Average household income: $39,797 (2005); Percent of households with income of $100,000 or more: 0.0% (2005); Poverty rate: 7.4% (2000).
Education: Percent of population age 25 and over with: High school diploma (including GED) or higher: 78.1% (2005); Bachelor's degree or higher: 9.6% (2005); Master's degree or higher: 4.3% (2005).
School District(s)
Letchworth Central School District (PK-12)
    2003-04 Enrollment: 1,250 . . . . (585) 493-5450
Housing: Homeownership rate: 73.9% (2005); Median home value: $79,231 (2005); Median rent: $383 per month (2000); Median age of housing: 60+ years (2000).
Transportation: Commute to work: 98.4% car, 0.0% public transportation, 1.6% walk, 0.0% work from home (2000); Travel time to work: 24.2% less than 15 minutes, 53.9% 15 to 30 minutes, 8.6% 30 to 45 minutes, 10.2% 45 to 60 minutes, 3.1% 60 minutes or more (2000)

GAINESVILLE (town).
Covers a land area of 35.610 square miles and a water area of 0.111 square miles. Located at 42.66° N. Lat.; 78.11° W. Long.
Population: 2,288 (1990); 2,333 (2000); 2,335 (2005); 2,351 (2010 projected); Race: 98.6% White, 0.1% Black, 0.2% Asian, 0.7% Hispanic of any race (2005); Density: 65.6 persons per square mile (2005); Average household size: 2.62 (2005); Median age: 39.4 (2005); Males per 100 females: 98.7 (2005); Marriage status: 23.6% never married, 60.2% now married, 6.7% widowed, 9.5% divorced (2000); Foreign born: 1.0% (2000); Ancestry (includes multiple ancestries): 31.1% German, 17.7% Irish, 17.6% English, 10.1% Italian, 9.2% United States or American (2000).
Economy: Employment by occupation: 7.3% management, 13.0% professional, 19.9% services, 18.7% sales, 3.5% farming, 11.7% construction, 26.0% production (2000).
Income: Per capita income: $17,784 (2005); Median household income: $41,423 (2005); Average household income: $46,308 (2005); Percent of households with income of $100,000 or more: 5.3% (2005); Poverty rate: 8.0% (2000).
Education: Percent of population age 25 and over with: High school diploma (including GED) or higher: 77.0% (2005); Bachelor's degree or higher: 8.6% (2005); Master's degree or higher: 2.9% (2005).
Housing: Homeownership rate: 79.5% (2005); Median home value: $88,000 (2005); Median rent: $378 per month (2000); Median age of housing: 60+ years (2000).
Transportation: Commute to work: 89.8% car, 0.8% public transportation, 2.2% walk, 5.4% work from home (2000); Travel time to work: 37.6% less than 15 minutes, 32.0% 15 to 30 minutes, 14.3% 30 to 45 minutes, 7.2% 45 to 60 minutes, 8.9% 60 minutes or more (2000)

GENESEE FALLS (town). Covers a land area of 15.537 square miles and a water area of 0.168 square miles. Located at 42.56° N. Lat.; 78.05° W. Long.
Population: 488 (1990); 460 (2000); 475 (2005); 484 (2010 projected); Race: 98.1% White, 0.0% Black, 0.2% Asian, 0.6% Hispanic of any race (2005); Density: 30.6 persons per square mile (2005); Average household size: 2.65 (2005); Median age: 37.8 (2005); Males per 100 females: 96.3 (2005); Marriage status: 28.4% never married, 53.8% now married, 7.8% widowed, 10.0% divorced (2000); Foreign born: 0.5% (2000); Ancestry (includes multiple ancestries): 28.4% German, 21.0% English, 19.8% Irish, 12.4% Italian, 9.8% Dutch (2000).
Economy: Employment by occupation: 12.3% management, 9.5% professional, 12.8% services, 25.1% sales, 6.7% farming, 14.5% construction, 19.0% production (2000).
Income: Per capita income: $17,863 (2005); Median household income: $34,595 (2005); Average household income: $47,402 (2005); Percent of households with income of $100,000 or more: 6.7% (2005); Poverty rate: 20.9% (2000).
Education: Percent of population age 25 and over with: High school diploma (including GED) or higher: 84.2% (2005); Bachelor's degree or higher: 7.7% (2005); Master's degree or higher: 3.9% (2005).
Housing: Homeownership rate: 81.6% (2005); Median home value: $100,909 (2005); Median rent: $345 per month (2000); Median age of housing: 60 years (2000).
Transportation: Commute to work: 83.2% car, 1.1% public transportation, 10.1% walk, 5.6% work from home (2000); Travel time to work: 30.8% less than 15 minutes, 34.3% 15 to 30 minutes, 20.7% 30 to 45 minutes, 4.7% 45 to 60 minutes, 9.5% 60 minutes or more (2000)

JAVA (town). Covers a land area of 47.094 square miles and a water area of 0.218 square miles. Located at 42.65° N. Lat.; 78.37° W. Long.
Population: 2,197 (1990); 2,222 (2000); 2,182 (2005); 2,139 (2010 projected); Race: 99.3% White, 0.1% Black, 0.1% Asian, 0.5% Hispanic of any race (2005); Density: 46.3 persons per square mile (2005); Average household size: 2.70 (2005); Median age: 38.3 (2005); Males per 100 females: 102.2 (2005); Marriage status: 24.9% never married, 65.3% now married, 4.9% widowed, 4.9% divorced (2000); Foreign born: 1.5% (2000); Ancestry (includes multiple ancestries): 42.6% German, 16.4% Irish, 12.8% Polish, 11.9% English, 9.2% United States or American (2000).
Economy: Employment by occupation: 14.3% management, 15.4% professional, 17.2% services, 21.2% sales, 5.7% farming, 11.0% construction, 15.2% production (2000).
Income: Per capita income: $22,786 (2005); Median household income: $52,327 (2005); Average household income: $61,459 (2005); Percent of households with income of $100,000 or more: 14.5% (2005); Poverty rate: 6.3% (2000).
Education: Percent of population age 25 and over with: High school diploma (including GED) or higher: 87.0% (2005); Bachelor's degree or higher: 13.2% (2005); Master's degree or higher: 4.0% (2005).
Housing: Homeownership rate: 83.2% (2005); Median home value: $134,245 (2005); Median rent: $437 per month (2000); Median age of housing: 49 years (2000).
Transportation: Commute to work: 87.1% car, 0.4% public transportation, 5.4% walk, 6.4% work from home (2000); Travel time to work: 27.0% less than 15 minutes, 31.5% 15 to 30 minutes, 22.2% 30 to 45 minutes, 9.7% 45 to 60 minutes, 9.7% 60 minutes or more (2000)

JAVA CENTER (unincorporated postal area, zip code 14082). Aka Java. Covers a land area of 8.450 square miles and a water area of 0.118 square miles. Located at 42.66° N. Lat.; 78.38° W. Long. Elevation is 1,522 feet.
Population: 0 (2000); Race: 99.1% White, 0.0% Black, 0.0% Asian, 0.0% Hispanic of any race (2000); Density: 0.0 persons per square mile (2000); Age: 28.8% under 18, 11.1% over 64 (2000); Marriage status: 25.4% never married, 62.9% now married, 5.6% widowed, 6.1% divorced (2000); Foreign born: 0.0% (2000); Ancestry (includes multiple ancestries): 31.3% German, 16.2% United States or American, 11.1% Polish, 11.1% Irish, 8.1% English (2000).
Economy: Employment by occupation: 12.2% management, 16.0% professional, 18.6% services, 18.6% sales, 8.4% farming, 12.2% construction, 13.9% production (2000).
Income: Per capita income: $19,661 (2000); Median household income: $46,731 (2000); Poverty rate: 7.9% (2000).
Education: Percent of population age 25 and over with: High school diploma (including GED) or higher: 87.1% (2000); Bachelor's degree or higher: 17.8% (2000).
Housing: Homeownership rate: 83.6% (2000); Median home value: $75,900 (2000); Median rent: $463 per month (2000); Median age of housing: 44 years (2000).
Transportation: Commute to work: 88.8% car, 0.0% public transportation, 2.2% walk, 8.9% work from home (2000); Travel time to work: 29.9% less than 15 minutes, 33.8% 15 to 30 minutes, 13.7% 30 to 45 minutes, 12.3% 45 to 60 minutes, 10.3% 60 minutes or more (2000)

JAVA VILLAGE (unincorporated postal area, zip code 14083). Covers a land area of 0.110 square miles and a water area of 0 square miles. Located at 42.67° N. Lat.; 78.44° W. Long.
Population: 0; Race: 100.0% White, 0.0% Black, 0.0% Asian, 0.0% Hispanic of any race (2000); Density: 0.0 persons per square mile (2000); Age: 16.4% under 18, 10.4% over 64 (2000); Marriage status: 32.2% never married, 67.8% now married, 0.0% widowed, 0.0% divorced (2000); Foreign born: 0.0% (2000); Ancestry (includes multiple ancestries): 55.2% German, 44.8% French (except Basque), 14.9% English, 9.0% Irish, 4.5% Polish (2000).
Economy: Employment by occupation: 0.0% management, 11.9% professional, 0.0% services, 50.0% sales, 0.0% farming, 0.0% construction, 38.1% production (2000).
Income: Per capita income: $20,209 (2000); Median household income: $61,250 (2000); Poverty rate: 0.0% (2000).
Education: Percent of population age 25 and over with: High school diploma (including GED) or higher: 90.6% (2000); Bachelor's degree or higher: 0.0% (2000).
Housing: Homeownership rate: 100.0% (2000); Median home value: $74,600 (2000); Median rent: $n/a per month (2000); Median age of housing: 27 years (2000).
Transportation: Commute to work: 100.0% car, 0.0% public transportation, 0.0% walk, 0.0% work from home (2000); Travel time to work: 19.0% less than 15 minutes, 52.4% 15 to 30 minutes, 23.8% 30 to 45 minutes, 4.8% 45 to 60 minutes, 0.0% 60 minutes or more (2000)

MIDDLEBURY (town). Covers a land area of 35.692 square miles and a water area of 0.031 square miles. Located at 42.82° N. Lat.; 78.13° W. Long.
Population: 1,532 (1990); 1,508 (2000); 1,507 (2005); 1,509 (2010 projected); Race: 97.9% White, 0.4% Black, 0.1% Asian, 0.4% Hispanic of any race (2005); Density: 42.2 persons per square mile (2005); Average household size: 2.80 (2005); Median age: 39.1 (2005); Males per 100 females: 100.1 (2005); Marriage status: 22.2% never married, 65.8% now married, 4.8% widowed, 7.2% divorced (2000); Foreign born: 0.9% (2000); Ancestry (includes multiple ancestries): 32.4% German, 29.1% English, 19.2% Irish, 8.4% United States or American, 7.1% Polish (2000).
Economy: Employment by occupation: 12.4% management, 19.1% professional, 13.6% services, 21.0% sales, 5.2% farming, 10.2% construction, 18.5% production (2000).
Income: Per capita income: $19,907 (2005); Median household income: $47,995 (2005); Average household income: $55,250 (2005); Percent of households with income of $100,000 or more: 10.2% (2005); Poverty rate: 5.3% (2000).
Education: Percent of population age 25 and over with: High school diploma (including GED) or higher: 86.9% (2005); Bachelor's degree or higher: 15.3% (2005); Master's degree or higher: 5.6% (2005).
Housing: Homeownership rate: 88.3% (2005); Median home value: $114,796 (2005); Median rent: $425 per month (2000); Median age of housing: 60+ years (2000).
Transportation: Commute to work: 93.7% car, 0.3% public transportation, 1.1% walk, 4.8% work from home (2000); Travel time to work: 29.3% less than 15 minutes, 33.4% 15 to 30 minutes, 15.1% 30 to 45 minutes, 11.4% 45 to 60 minutes, 10.8% 60 minutes or more (2000)

NORTH JAVA (unincorporated postal area, zip code 14113). Covers a land area of 17.718 square miles and a water area of 0.019 square miles. Located at 42.67° N. Lat.; 78.33° W. Long.
Population: 0 (2000); Race: 98.7% White, 0.0% Black, 0.0% Asian, 1.7% Hispanic of any race (2000); Density: 0.0 persons per square mile (2000); Age: 24.4% under 18, 18.5% over 64 (2000); Marriage status: 21.3% never married, 68.4% now married, 7.2% widowed, 3.0% divorced (2000); Foreign born: 2.5% (2000); Ancestry (includes multiple ancestries): 46.1%

German, 18.1% Irish, 9.4% Polish, 7.2% French (except Basque), 6.7% United States or American (2000).
Economy: Employment by occupation: 15.1% management, 15.7% professional, 11.1% services, 22.8% sales, 5.7% farming, 10.3% construction, 19.4% production (2000).
Income: Per capita income: $18,969 (2000); Median household income: $41,750 (2000); Poverty rate: 3.5% (2000).
Education: Percent of population age 25 and over with: High school diploma (including GED) or higher: 84.0% (2000); Bachelor's degree or higher: 12.5% (2000).
Housing: Homeownership rate: 82.4% (2000); Median home value: $85,800 (2000); Median rent: $428 per month (2000); Median age of housing: 58 years (2000).
Transportation: Commute to work: 80.5% car, 1.1% public transportation, 8.9% walk, 9.5% work from home (2000); Travel time to work: 27.9% less than 15 minutes, 26.7% 15 to 30 minutes, 26.3% 30 to 45 minutes, 6.0% 45 to 60 minutes, 13.0% 60 minutes or more (2000)

ORANGEVILLE (town).
Covers a land area of 35.566 square miles and a water area of 0.091 square miles. Located at 42.73° N. Lat.; 78.26° W. Long.
Population: 1,115 (1990); 1,301 (2000); 1,277 (2005); 1,254 (2010 projected); Race: 99.2% White, 0.2% Black, 0.3% Asian, 0.3% Hispanic of any race (2005); Density: 35.9 persons per square mile (2005); Average household size: 2.62 (2005); Median age: 40.3 (2005); Males per 100 females: 97.4 (2005); Marriage status: 22.4% never married, 63.9% now married, 4.6% widowed, 9.1% divorced (2000); Foreign born: 0.7% (2000); Ancestry (includes multiple ancestries): 44.3% German, 17.4% English, 12.2% Irish, 12.1% Polish, 8.1% Italian (2000).
Economy: Employment by occupation: 11.1% management, 16.9% professional, 21.4% services, 19.8% sales, 5.8% farming, 12.2% construction, 12.8% production (2000).
Income: Per capita income: $21,866 (2005); Median household income: $51,598 (2005); Average household income: $57,336 (2005); Percent of households with income of $100,000 or more: 9.9% (2005); Poverty rate: 9.5% (2000).
Education: Percent of population age 25 and over with: High school diploma (including GED) or higher: 86.5% (2005); Bachelor's degree or higher: 11.7% (2005); Master's degree or higher: 4.0% (2005).
Housing: Homeownership rate: 85.2% (2005); Median home value: $138,556 (2005); Median rent: $373 per month (2000); Median age of housing: 29 years (2000).
Transportation: Commute to work: 90.7% car, 0.5% public transportation, 3.2% walk, 4.3% work from home (2000); Travel time to work: 23.6% less than 15 minutes, 33.2% 15 to 30 minutes, 19.7% 30 to 45 minutes, 13.9% 45 to 60 minutes, 9.6% 60 minutes or more (2000)

PERRY (village).
Covers a land area of 2.261 square miles and a water area of 0.112 square miles. Located at 42.71° N. Lat.; 78.00° W. Long. Elevation is 1,363 feet.
Population: 4,219 (1990); 3,945 (2000); 3,771 (2005); 3,643 (2010 projected); Race: 97.2% White, 0.8% Black, 0.5% Asian, 1.8% Hispanic of any race (2005); Density: 1,667.9 persons per square mile (2005); Average household size: 2.48 (2005); Median age: 38.4 (2005); Males per 100 females: 91.3 (2005); Marriage status: 25.7% never married, 55.7% now married, 9.8% widowed, 8.7% divorced (2000); Foreign born: 1.2% (2000); Ancestry (includes multiple ancestries): 24.6% German, 19.4% Irish, 15.6% English, 15.2% Italian, 7.6% Polish (2000).
Economy: Employment by occupation: 8.8% management, 15.0% professional, 16.5% services, 26.1% sales, 1.7% farming, 9.3% construction, 22.5% production (2000).
Income: Per capita income: $18,815 (2005); Median household income: $39,722 (2005); Average household income: $45,880 (2005); Percent of households with income of $100,000 or more: 4.3% (2005); Poverty rate: 8.7% (2000).
Education: Percent of population age 25 and over with: High school diploma (including GED) or higher: 80.1% (2005); Bachelor's degree or higher: 13.5% (2005); Master's degree or higher: 4.2% (2005).
School District(s)
Perry Central School District (PK-12)
    2003-04 Enrollment: 1,094 . . . . (585) 237-0270
Housing: Homeownership rate: 64.7% (2005); Median home value: $91,744 (2005); Median rent: $377 per month (2000); Median age of housing: 60+ years (2000).
Safety: Violent crime rate: 12.9 per 10,000 population; Property crime rate: 273.0 per 10,000 population (2004).
Newspapers: The Perry Herald (General - Circulation 1,150)
Transportation: Commute to work: 92.5% car, 0.3% public transportation, 3.8% walk, 3.4% work from home (2000); Travel time to work: 35.9% less than 15 minutes, 29.2% 15 to 30 minutes, 10.6% 30 to 45 minutes, 14.0% 45 to 60 minutes, 10.3% 60 minutes or more (2000)
Additional Information Contacts
Perry Chamber of Commerce . . . . (585) 237-5040
    http://www.perrychamber.com
Village of Perry. . . . . (585) 237-2216
    http://www.villageofperry.com/
Wyoming County Chamber of Commerce . . . . (800) 951-9774
    http://www.wycochamber.org

PERRY (town).
Covers a land area of 36.374 square miles and a water area of 0.218 square miles. Located at 42.74° N. Lat.; 77.99° W. Long. Elevation is 1,363 feet.
History: In 1833, the Reverend William Arthur became pastor of the First Baptist Church in Perry. His son, Chester Alan Arthur, then four yeas old, was destined to become the 21st President of the United States.
Population: 5,353 (1990); 6,654 (2000); 6,546 (2005); 6,448 (2010 projected); Race: 74.3% White, 19.6% Black, 0.6% Asian, 10.1% Hispanic of any race (2005); Density: 180.0 persons per square mile (2005); Average household size: 3.47 (2005); Median age: 36.0 (2005); Males per 100 females: 172.2 (2005); Marriage status: 39.9% never married, 46.3% now married, 6.0% widowed, 7.8% divorced (2000); Foreign born: 3.9% (2000); Ancestry (includes multiple ancestries): 19.1% German, 14.7% Irish, 13.3% English, 10.0% Italian, 5.5% Polish (2000).
Economy: Employment by occupation: 10.6% management, 15.7% professional, 15.7% services, 25.9% sales, 3.7% farming, 10.2% construction, 18.2% production (2000).
Income: Per capita income: $18,151 (2005); Median household income: $42,994 (2005); Average household income: $52,970 (2005); Percent of households with income of $100,000 or more: 7.1% (2005); Poverty rate: 8.7% (2000).
Education: Percent of population age 25 and over with: High school diploma (including GED) or higher: 59.6% (2005); Bachelor's degree or higher: 9.6% (2005); Master's degree or higher: 3.4% (2005).
Housing: Homeownership rate: 69.2% (2005); Median home value: $97,536 (2005); Median rent: $366 per month (2000); Median age of housing: 60+ years (2000).
Transportation: Commute to work: 91.2% car, 0.3% public transportation, 4.6% walk, 4.0% work from home (2000); Travel time to work: 38.3% less than 15 minutes, 29.3% 15 to 30 minutes, 10.3% 30 to 45 minutes, 11.4% 45 to 60 minutes, 10.7% 60 minutes or more (2000)

PIKE (village).
Covers a land area of 0.982 square miles and a water area of 0.009 square miles. Located at 42.55° N. Lat.; 78.15° W. Long. Elevation is 1,551 feet.
Population: 384 (1990); 382 (2000); 370 (2005); 365 (2010 projected); Race: 95.9% White, 0.0% Black, 1.1% Asian, 0.3% Hispanic of any race (2005); Density: 376.6 persons per square mile (2005); Average household size: 2.91 (2005); Median age: 35.8 (2005); Males per 100 females: 102.2 (2005); Marriage status: 27.9% never married, 56.9% now married, 7.6% widowed, 7.6% divorced (2000); Foreign born: 1.1% (2000); Ancestry (includes multiple ancestries): 34.5% German, 14.9% United States or American, 14.1% Irish, 14.1% English, 10.1% Other groups (2000).
Economy: Employment by occupation: 9.4% management, 10.5% professional, 11.1% services, 21.6% sales, 2.9% farming, 11.7% construction, 32.7% production (2000).
Income: Per capita income: $15,865 (2005); Median household income: $40,938 (2005); Average household income: $46,220 (2005); Percent of households with income of $100,000 or more: 4.7% (2005); Poverty rate: 9.2% (2000).
Education: Percent of population age 25 and over with: High school diploma (including GED) or higher: 82.5% (2005); Bachelor's degree or higher: 5.4% (2005); Master's degree or higher: 2.7% (2005).
Housing: Homeownership rate: 73.2% (2005); Median home value: $77,179 (2005); Median rent: $375 per month (2000); Median age of housing: 60+ years (2000).
Transportation: Commute to work: 89.2% car, 4.2% public transportation, 4.2% walk, 1.2% work from home (2000); Travel time to work: 27.4% less than 15 minutes, 29.3% 15 to 30 minutes, 17.1% 30 to 45 minutes, 14.6% 45 to 60 minutes, 11.6% 60 minutes or more (2000)

PROFILES OF NEW YORK / Wyoming County

PIKE (town). Covers a land area of 31.086 square miles and a water area of 0.129 square miles. Located at 42.56° N. Lat.; 78.14° W. Long. Elevation is 1,551 feet.
Population: 1,081 (1990); 1,086 (2000); 1,075 (2005); 1,069 (2010 projected); Race: 96.5% White, 0.3% Black, 0.4% Asian, 0.7% Hispanic of any race (2005); Density: 34.6 persons per square mile (2005); Average household size: 2.78 (2005); Median age: 38.7 (2005); Males per 100 females: 98.7 (2005); Marriage status: 24.0% never married, 61.7% now married, 5.8% widowed, 8.5% divorced (2000); Foreign born: 0.9% (2000); Ancestry (includes multiple ancestries): 25.8% German, 18.6% English, 11.5% Irish, 9.3% United States or American, 6.5% Italian (2000).
Economy: Employment by occupation: 14.0% management, 10.9% professional, 13.2% services, 20.8% sales, 4.0% farming, 15.8% construction, 21.3% production (2000).
Income: Per capita income: $17,823 (2005); Median household income: $42,575 (2005); Average household income: $49,509 (2005); Percent of households with income of $100,000 or more: 7.2% (2005); Poverty rate: 12.6% (2000).
Education: Percent of population age 25 and over with: High school diploma (including GED) or higher: 81.5% (2005); Bachelor's degree or higher: 7.9% (2005); Master's degree or higher: 3.0% (2005).
Housing: Homeownership rate: 81.7% (2005); Median home value: $88,125 (2005); Median rent: $388 per month (2000); Median age of housing: 60+ years (2000).
Transportation: Commute to work: 91.0% car, 1.3% public transportation, 5.0% walk, 1.7% work from home (2000); Travel time to work: 29.3% less than 15 minutes, 33.9% 15 to 30 minutes, 13.8% 30 to 45 minutes, 7.2% 45 to 60 minutes, 15.9% 60 minutes or more (2000)

PORTAGEVILLE (unincorporated postal area, zip code 14536). Covers a land area of 18.377 square miles and a water area of 0.147 square miles. Located at 42.54° N. Lat.; 78.06° W. Long. Elevation is 1,180 feet.
Population: 0 (2000); Race: 99.1% White, 0.0% Black, 0.3% Asian, 1.4% Hispanic of any race (2000); Density: 0.0 persons per square mile (2000); Age: 27.8% under 18, 12.6% over 64 (2000); Marriage status: 20.8% never married, 61.5% now married, 5.3% widowed, 12.4% divorced (2000); Foreign born: 0.9% (2000); Ancestry (includes multiple ancestries): 27.4% German, 23.5% English, 19.1% Irish, 9.3% United States or American, 6.7% Italian (2000).
Economy: Employment by occupation: 14.3% management, 9.3% professional, 14.0% services, 25.3% sales, 6.0% farming, 13.0% construction, 18.0% production (2000).
Income: Per capita income: $15,247 (2000); Median household income: $33,942 (2000); Poverty rate: 20.8% (2000).
Education: Percent of population age 25 and over with: High school diploma (including GED) or higher: 82.9% (2000); Bachelor's degree or higher: 7.1% (2000).
Housing: Homeownership rate: 82.9% (2000); Median home value: $56,300 (2000); Median rent: $339 per month (2000); Median age of housing: 60+ years (2000).
Transportation: Commute to work: 89.3% car, 0.7% public transportation, 8.0% walk, 1.3% work from home (2000); Travel time to work: 30.4% less than 15 minutes, 34.1% 15 to 30 minutes, 18.9% 30 to 45 minutes, 3.7% 45 to 60 minutes, 12.8% 60 minutes or more (2000)

SHELDON (town). Covers a land area of 47.343 square miles and a water area of 0.029 square miles. Located at 42.72° N. Lat.; 78.37° W. Long. Elevation is 1,512 feet.
Population: 2,487 (1990); 2,561 (2000); 2,541 (2005); 2,517 (2010 projected); Race: 99.5% White, 0.0% Black, 0.1% Asian, 0.2% Hispanic of any race (2005); Density: 53.7 persons per square mile (2005); Average household size: 2.74 (2005); Median age: 38.1 (2005); Males per 100 females: 103.6 (2005); Marriage status: 24.6% never married, 62.9% now married, 5.9% widowed, 6.6% divorced (2000); Foreign born: 0.7% (2000); Ancestry (includes multiple ancestries): 54.1% German, 15.8% Irish, 15.1% Polish, 9.8% French (except Basque), 9.3% English (2000).
Economy: Employment by occupation: 12.0% management, 13.5% professional, 18.2% services, 17.9% sales, 8.0% farming, 11.2% construction, 19.2% production (2000).
Income: Per capita income: $22,472 (2005); Median household income: $50,454 (2005); Average household income: $60,159 (2005); Percent of households with income of $100,000 or more: 10.7% (2005); Poverty rate: 5.8% (2000).
Education: Percent of population age 25 and over with: High school diploma (including GED) or higher: 84.0% (2005); Bachelor's degree or higher: 9.7% (2005); Master's degree or higher: 4.4% (2005).
Housing: Homeownership rate: 83.4% (2005); Median home value: $140,614 (2005); Median rent: $375 per month (2000); Median age of housing: 47 years (2000).
Transportation: Commute to work: 83.2% car, 0.7% public transportation, 8.1% walk, 7.4% work from home (2000); Travel time to work: 28.4% less than 15 minutes, 29.4% 15 to 30 minutes, 24.2% 30 to 45 minutes, 14.2% 45 to 60 minutes, 3.8% 60 minutes or more (2000)

SILVER SPRINGS (village). Covers a land area of 0.946 square miles and a water area of 0.026 square miles. Located at 42.65° N. Lat.; 78.08° W. Long.
Population: 852 (1990); 844 (2000); 843 (2005); 840 (2010 projected); Race: 98.3% White, 0.1% Black, 0.1% Asian, 0.8% Hispanic of any race (2005); Density: 891.2 persons per square mile (2005); Average household size: 2.43 (2005); Median age: 39.9 (2005); Males per 100 females: 89.9 (2005); Marriage status: 23.9% never married, 53.0% now married, 9.6% widowed, 13.6% divorced (2000); Foreign born: 0.6% (2000); Ancestry (includes multiple ancestries): 29.8% German, 17.7% Irish, 11.8% English, 11.5% United States or American, 9.7% Italian (2000).
Economy: Employment by occupation: 5.6% management, 13.6% professional, 25.5% services, 16.8% sales, 3.5% farming, 11.2% construction, 23.8% production (2000).
Income: Per capita income: $18,633 (2005); Median household income: $39,731 (2005); Average household income: $44,503 (2005); Percent of households with income of $100,000 or more: 5.2% (2005); Poverty rate: 8.3% (2000).
Education: Percent of population age 25 and over with: High school diploma (including GED) or higher: 76.1% (2005); Bachelor's degree or higher: 5.2% (2005); Master's degree or higher: 1.9% (2005).
Housing: Homeownership rate: 69.7% (2005); Median home value: $82,593 (2005); Median rent: $364 per month (2000); Median age of housing: 60+ years (2000).
Transportation: Commute to work: 91.2% car, 0.5% public transportation, 3.1% walk, 2.9% work from home (2000); Travel time to work: 37.7% less than 15 minutes, 29.3% 15 to 30 minutes, 14.9% 30 to 45 minutes, 8.1% 45 to 60 minutes, 10.0% 60 minutes or more (2000)

STRYKERSVILLE (unincorporated postal area, zip code 14145). Covers a land area of 28.649 square miles and a water area of 0.034 square miles. Located at 42.72° N. Lat.; 78.43° W. Long. Elevation is 1,083 feet.
Population: 0 (2000); Race: 99.8% White, 0.0% Black, 0.0% Asian, 0.6% Hispanic of any race (2000); Density: 0.0 persons per square mile (2000); Age: 27.6% under 18, 9.8% over 64 (2000); Marriage status: 30.3% never married, 58.4% now married, 4.9% widowed, 6.5% divorced (2000); Foreign born: 0.8% (2000); Ancestry (includes multiple ancestries): 56.2% German, 19.7% Irish, 13.6% French (except Basque), 11.4% Polish, 9.6% English (2000).
Economy: Employment by occupation: 17.0% management, 13.9% professional, 17.6% services, 16.3% sales, 7.6% farming, 11.8% construction, 15.8% production (2000).
Income: Per capita income: $19,105 (2000); Median household income: $45,125 (2000); Poverty rate: 4.1% (2000).
Education: Percent of population age 25 and over with: High school diploma (including GED) or higher: 86.1% (2000); Bachelor's degree or higher: 9.9% (2000).
Housing: Homeownership rate: 84.5% (2000); Median home value: $92,300 (2000); Median rent: $431 per month (2000); Median age of housing: 45 years (2000).
Transportation: Commute to work: 85.4% car, 0.5% public transportation, 5.7% walk, 8.0% work from home (2000); Travel time to work: 26.7% less than 15 minutes, 31.0% 15 to 30 minutes, 25.3% 30 to 45 minutes, 14.0% 45 to 60 minutes, 3.0% 60 minutes or more (2000)

VARYSBURG (unincorporated postal area, zip code 14167). Covers a land area of 33.831 square miles and a water area of 0.008 square miles. Located at 42.75° N. Lat.; 78.32° W. Long. Elevation is 1,157 feet.
Population: 0 (2000); Race: 99.3% White, 0.0% Black, 0.2% Asian, 0.1% Hispanic of any race (2000); Density: 0.0 persons per square mile (2000); Age: 31.6% under 18, 9.4% over 64 (2000); Marriage status: 22.3% never married, 65.7% now married, 4.6% widowed, 7.4% divorced (2000); Foreign born: 0.5% (2000); Ancestry (includes multiple ancestries): 46.9%

German, 18.4% Polish, 11.6% English, 9.7% Irish, 6.7% United States or American (2000).
Economy: Employment by occupation: 7.2% management, 13.1% professional, 24.9% services, 18.7% sales, 6.4% farming, 13.9% construction, 15.8% production (2000).
Income: Per capita income: $17,499 (2000); Median household income: $43,009 (2000); Poverty rate: 9.8% (2000).
Education: Percent of population age 25 and over with: High school diploma (including GED) or higher: 86.7% (2000); Bachelor's degree or higher: 11.2% (2000).

School District(s)
Attica Central School District (KG-12)
    2003-04 Enrollment: 1,840 . . . . (585) 591-0400
Housing: Homeownership rate: 83.8% (2000); Median home value: $81,700 (2000); Median rent: $348 per month (2000); Median age of housing: 36 years (2000).
Transportation: Commute to work: 87.0% car, 0.7% public transportation, 7.8% walk, 3.3% work from home (2000); Travel time to work: 26.6% less than 15 minutes, 33.4% 15 to 30 minutes, 20.9% 30 to 45 minutes, 13.9% 45 to 60 minutes, 5.2% 60 minutes or more (2000)

WARSAW (village).
Covers a land area of 4.124 square miles and a water area of 0 square miles. Located at 42.74° N. Lat.; 78.13° W. Long. Elevation is 1,322 feet.
Population: 3,830 (1990); 3,814 (2000); 3,627 (2005); 3,500 (2010 projected); Race: 96.7% White, 0.6% Black, 1.6% Asian, 0.9% Hispanic of any race (2005); Density: 879.5 persons per square mile (2005); Average household size: 2.53 (2005); Median age: 41.1 (2005); Males per 100 females: 83.5 (2005); Marriage status: 23.1% never married, 55.3% now married, 10.9% widowed, 10.6% divorced (2000); Foreign born: 1.7% (2000); Ancestry (includes multiple ancestries): 31.6% German, 18.6% English, 15.4% Irish, 7.5% United States or American, 7.2% Italian (2000).
Economy: Single-family building permits issued: 0 (2005); Multi-family building permits issued: 24 (2005); Employment by occupation: 9.3% management, 18.0% professional, 20.2% services, 24.7% sales, 0.4% farming, 10.4% construction, 17.0% production (2000).
Income: Per capita income: $19,513 (2005); Median household income: $37,574 (2005); Average household income: $47,322 (2005); Percent of households with income of $100,000 or more: 6.8% (2005); Poverty rate: 11.0% (2000).
Education: Percent of population age 25 and over with: High school diploma (including GED) or higher: 81.0% (2005); Bachelor's degree or higher: 15.6% (2005); Master's degree or higher: 7.3% (2005).

School District(s)
Warsaw Central School District (KG-12)
    2003-04 Enrollment: 1,171 . . . . (585) 786-8000
Housing: Homeownership rate: 57.4% (2005); Median home value: $101,163 (2005); Median rent: $396 per month (2000); Median age of housing: 60+ years (2000).
Hospitals: Wyoming County Community Health System (262 beds)
Safety: Violent crime rate: 2.7 per 10,000 population; Property crime rate: 275.1 per 10,000 population (2004).
Transportation: Commute to work: 88.4% car, 0.4% public transportation, 7.1% walk, 4.1% work from home (2000); Travel time to work: 52.3% less than 15 minutes, 20.3% 15 to 30 minutes, 15.8% 30 to 45 minutes, 4.3% 45 to 60 minutes, 7.4% 60 minutes or more (2000)

WARSAW (town).
Covers a land area of 35.420 square miles and a water area of 0.053 square miles. Located at 42.73° N. Lat.; 78.13° W. Long. Elevation is 1,322 feet.
Population: 5,342 (1990); 5,423 (2000); 5,309 (2005); 5,196 (2010 projected); Race: 97.2% White, 0.4% Black, 1.3% Asian, 0.6% Hispanic of any race (2005); Density: 149.9 persons per square mile (2005); Average household size: 2.52 (2005); Median age: 41.3 (2005); Males per 100 females: 88.1 (2005); Marriage status: 23.7% never married, 57.6% now married, 9.8% widowed, 8.9% divorced (2000); Foreign born: 2.2% (2000); Ancestry (includes multiple ancestries): 32.8% German, 18.5% English, 15.8% Irish, 7.9% Italian, 7.3% United States or American (2000).
Economy: Employment by occupation: 11.0% management, 16.4% professional, 19.2% services, 22.9% sales, 1.4% farming, 11.2% construction, 17.8% production (2000).
Income: Per capita income: $19,592 (2005); Median household income: $39,504 (2005); Average household income: $47,799 (2005); Percent of households with income of $100,000 or more: 6.7% (2005); Poverty rate: 10.6% (2000).
Education: Percent of population age 25 and over with: High school diploma (including GED) or higher: 81.7% (2005); Bachelor's degree or higher: 15.6% (2005); Master's degree or higher: 7.0% (2005).
Housing: Homeownership rate: 65.2% (2005); Median home value: $109,314 (2005); Median rent: $388 per month (2000); Median age of housing: 60+ years (2000).
Transportation: Commute to work: 88.7% car, 1.2% public transportation, 5.9% walk, 3.2% work from home (2000); Travel time to work: 50.6% less than 15 minutes, 21.1% 15 to 30 minutes, 15.2% 30 to 45 minutes, 5.2% 45 to 60 minutes, 7.8% 60 minutes or more (2000)

WETHERSFIELD (town).
Covers a land area of 35.832 square miles and a water area of 0.281 square miles. Located at 42.65° N. Lat.; 78.23° W. Long.
Population: 794 (1990); 891 (2000); 905 (2005); 910 (2010 projected); Race: 96.2% White, 0.9% Black, 1.7% Asian, 1.1% Hispanic of any race (2005); Density: 25.3 persons per square mile (2005); Average household size: 2.70 (2005); Median age: 37.4 (2005); Males per 100 females: 102.9 (2005); Marriage status: 22.5% never married, 65.6% now married, 5.9% widowed, 6.0% divorced (2000); Foreign born: 0.4% (2000); Ancestry (includes multiple ancestries): 35.7% German, 14.1% Polish, 13.4% Irish, 12.0% Italian, 11.7% United States or American (2000).
Economy: Single-family building permits issued: 0 (2005); Multi-family building permits issued: 0 (2005); Employment by occupation: 14.5% management, 10.4% professional, 13.5% services, 19.8% sales, 8.7% farming, 14.0% construction, 19.1% production (2000).
Income: Per capita income: $17,959 (2005); Median household income: $42,110 (2005); Average household income: $48,515 (2005); Percent of households with income of $100,000 or more: 7.8% (2005); Poverty rate: 12.4% (2000).
Taxes: Total city taxes per capita: $306 (2004); City property taxes per capita: $296 (2004).
Education: Percent of population age 25 and over with: High school diploma (including GED) or higher: 77.0% (2005); Bachelor's degree or higher: 6.9% (2005); Master's degree or higher: 1.5% (2005).
Housing: Homeownership rate: 81.8% (2005); Median home value: $100,610 (2005); Median rent: $357 per month (2000); Median age of housing: 39 years (2000).
Transportation: Commute to work: 90.8% car, 0.0% public transportation, 2.4% walk, 4.7% work from home (2000); Travel time to work: 25.8% less than 15 minutes, 38.5% 15 to 30 minutes, 11.5% 30 to 45 minutes, 10.2% 45 to 60 minutes, 14.0% 60 minutes or more (2000)

WYOMING (village).
Covers a land area of 0.672 square miles and a water area of 0 square miles. Located at 42.82° N. Lat.; 78.08° W. Long. Elevation is 991 feet.
Population: 478 (1990); 513 (2000); 538 (2005); 555 (2010 projected); Race: 97.0% White, 0.4% Black, 0.0% Asian, 0.6% Hispanic of any race (2005); Density: 800.4 persons per square mile (2005); Average household size: 2.86 (2005); Median age: 36.3 (2005); Males per 100 females: 92.8 (2005); Marriage status: 24.1% never married, 62.6% now married, 6.0% widowed, 7.3% divorced (2000); Foreign born: 1.2% (2000); Ancestry (includes multiple ancestries): 31.9% English, 23.4% German, 18.5% Irish, 11.9% United States or American, 5.6% Scottish (2000).
Economy: Employment by occupation: 11.7% management, 20.6% professional, 15.9% services, 16.4% sales, 4.2% farming, 12.1% construction, 19.2% production (2000).
Income: Per capita income: $17,996 (2005); Median household income: $44,500 (2005); Average household income: $50,332 (2005); Percent of households with income of $100,000 or more: 9.0% (2005); Poverty rate: 6.0% (2000).
Education: Percent of population age 25 and over with: High school diploma (including GED) or higher: 85.9% (2005); Bachelor's degree or higher: 15.0% (2005); Master's degree or higher: 6.2% (2005).

School District(s)
Wyoming Central School District (KG-08)
    2003-04 Enrollment: 197 . . . . (585) 495-6222
Housing: Homeownership rate: 81.9% (2005); Median home value: $109,286 (2005); Median rent: $428 per month (2000); Median age of housing: 60+ years (2000).
Transportation: Commute to work: 95.0% car, 0.0% public transportation, 1.0% walk, 4.0% work from home (2000); Travel time to work: 33.9% less than 15 minutes, 27.6% 15 to 30 minutes, 19.8% 30 to 45 minutes, 10.9% 45 to 60 minutes, 7.8% 60 minutes or more (2000)

Yates County

Located in west central New York; bounded on the east by Seneca Lake; includes parts of Keuka and Canandaigua Lakes. Covers a land area of 338.24 square miles, a water area of 37.52 square miles, and is located in the Eastern Time Zone. The county government was organized in 1823. County seat is Penn Yan.

Population: 22,810 (1990); 24,621 (2000); 24,885 (2005); 25,145 (2010 projected); Race: 97.7% White, 0.8% Black, 0.3% Asian, 1.4% Hispanic of any race (2005); Density: 73.6 persons per square mile (2005); Average household size: 2.72 (2005); Median age: 38.7 (2005); Males per 100 females: 94.9 (2005).
Religion: Five largest groups: 22.3% Catholic Church, 10.1% The United Methodist Church, 4.7% American Baptist Churches in the USA, 4.0% Old Order Mennonite, 2.6% Presbyterian Church (U.S.A.) (2000).
Economy: Unemployment rate: 4.3% (2005); Total civilian labor force: 13,024 (2005); Leading industries: 21.5% health care and social assistance; 14.7% manufacturing; 12.9% retail trade (2003); Farms: 722 totaling 115,113 acres (2002); Companies that employ 500 or more persons: 1 (2003); Companies that employ 100 to 499 persons: 6 (2003); Companies that employ less than 100 persons: 521 (2003); Black-owned businesses: n/a (2002); Hispanic-owned businesses: n/a (2002); Women-owned businesses: 524 (2002); Retail sales per capita: $7,209 (2006). Single-family building permits issued: 72 (2005); Multi-family building permits issued: 60 (2005).
Income: Per capita income: $18,897 (2005); Median household income: $39,899 (2005); Average household income: $50,084 (2005); Percent of households with income of $100,000 or more: 8.2% (2005); Poverty rate: 12.8% (2003); Bankruptcy rate: 4.60% (2005).
Education: Percent of population age 25 and over with: High school diploma (including GED) or higher: 80.1% (2005); Bachelor's degree or higher: 18.4% (2005); Master's degree or higher: 8.9% (2005).
Housing: Homeownership rate: 77.6% (2005); Median home value: $119,007 (2005); Median rent: $373 per month (2000); Median age of housing: 44 years (2000).
Health: Birth rate: 109.4 per 10,000 population (2004); Death rate: 91.6 per 10,000 population (2004); Age-adjusted cancer mortality rate: 234.8 deaths per 100,000 population (2002); Number of physicians: 11.7 per 10,000 population (2004); Hospital beds: 80.2 per 10,000 population (2003); Hospital admissions: 673.4 per 10,000 population (2003).
Elections: 2004 Presidential election results: 58.9% Bush, 39.3% Kerry, 1.6% Nader, 0.2% Badnarik
Additional Information Contacts
Yates County Government. . . . . (315) 536-5165
http://www.yatescounty.org/

Yates County Communities

BARRINGTON (town). Covers a land area of 35.677 square miles and a water area of 1.371 square miles. Located at 42.53° N. Lat.; 77.06° W. Long.
Population: 1,195 (1990); 1,396 (2000); 1,544 (2005); 1,655 (2010 projected); Race: 99.0% White, 0.3% Black, 0.0% Asian, 0.6% Hispanic of any race (2005); Density: 43.3 persons per square mile (2005); Average household size: 2.87 (2005); Median age: 37.3 (2005); Males per 100 females: 97.7 (2005); Marriage status: 17.0% never married, 71.5% now married, 4.8% widowed, 6.7% divorced (2000); Foreign born: 0.9% (2000); Ancestry (includes multiple ancestries): 18.6% German, 16.2% English, 10.2% Irish, 10.0% United States or American, 5.4% Swiss (2000).
Economy: Single-family building permits issued: 7 (2005); Multi-family building permits issued: 0 (2005); Employment by occupation: 13.8% management, 15.8% professional, 16.2% services, 21.7% sales, 1.3% farming, 13.3% construction, 18.0% production (2000).
Income: Per capita income: $18,130 (2005); Median household income: $41,959 (2005); Average household income: $52,031 (2005); Percent of households with income of $100,000 or more: 8.6% (2005); Poverty rate: 16.9% (2000).
Education: Percent of population age 25 and over with: High school diploma (including GED) or higher: 76.2% (2005); Bachelor's degree or higher: 13.7% (2005); Master's degree or higher: 6.9% (2005).
Housing: Homeownership rate: 92.0% (2005); Median home value: $115,541 (2005); Median rent: $361 per month (2000); Median age of housing: 31 years (2000).
Transportation: Commute to work: 82.4% car, 0.2% public transportation, 2.7% walk, 11.2% work from home (2000); Travel time to work: 30.9% less than 15 minutes, 35.1% 15 to 30 minutes, 13.6% 30 to 45 minutes, 11.8% 45 to 60 minutes, 8.7% 60 minutes or more (2000)

BELLONA (unincorporated postal area, zip code 14415). Aka Gage. Covers a land area of 0.869 square miles and a water area of 0 square miles. Located at 42.75° N. Lat.; 77.02° W. Long.
Population: 0 (2000); Race: 100.0% White, 0.0% Black, 0.0% Asian, 0.0% Hispanic of any race (2000); Density: 0.0 persons per square mile (2000); Age: 0.0% under 18, 29.7% over 64 (2000); Marriage status: 40.5% never married, 48.6% now married, 0.0% widowed, 10.8% divorced (2000); Foreign born: 0.0% (2000); Ancestry (includes multiple ancestries): 32.4% English, 21.6% German, 18.9% Danish, 18.9% United States or American, 8.1% Welsh (2000).
Economy: Employment by occupation: 12.0% management, 0.0% professional, 12.0% services, 16.0% sales, 0.0% farming, 44.0% construction, 16.0% production (2000).
Income: Per capita income: $19,716 (2000); Median household income: $27,500 (2000); Poverty rate: 0.0% (2000).
Education: Percent of population age 25 and over with: High school diploma (including GED) or higher: 90.9% (2000); Bachelor's degree or higher: 0.0% (2000).
Housing: Homeownership rate: 47.8% (2000); Median home value: $55,000 (2000); Median rent: $375 per month (2000); Median age of housing: 60+ years (2000).
Transportation: Commute to work: 81.8% car, 0.0% public transportation, 0.0% walk, 18.2% work from home (2000); Travel time to work: 38.9% less than 15 minutes, 38.9% 15 to 30 minutes, 22.2% 30 to 45 minutes, 0.0% 45 to 60 minutes, 0.0% 60 minutes or more (2000)

BENTON (town). Covers a land area of 41.482 square miles and a water area of 2.956 square miles. Located at 42.72° N. Lat.; 77.04° W. Long.
Population: 2,380 (1990); 2,640 (2000); 2,662 (2005); 2,658 (2010 projected); Race: 98.7% White, 0.6% Black, 0.2% Asian, 0.6% Hispanic of any race (2005); Density: 64.2 persons per square mile (2005); Average household size: 3.06 (2005); Median age: 41.2 (2005); Males per 100 females: 96.3 (2005); Marriage status: 22.7% never married, 62.3% now married, 7.0% widowed, 8.0% divorced (2000); Foreign born: 0.6% (2000); Ancestry (includes multiple ancestries): 26.4% English, 20.5% German, 14.5% Irish, 9.4% Danish, 6.1% United States or American (2000).
Economy: Single-family building permits issued: 7 (2005); Multi-family building permits issued: 0 (2005); Employment by occupation: 18.5% management, 16.4% professional, 15.6% services, 23.6% sales, 3.2% farming, 10.4% construction, 12.3% production (2000).
Income: Per capita income: $17,967 (2005); Median household income: $41,455 (2005); Average household income: $52,693 (2005); Percent of households with income of $100,000 or more: 7.8% (2005); Poverty rate: 13.5% (2000).
Education: Percent of population age 25 and over with: High school diploma (including GED) or higher: 77.5% (2005); Bachelor's degree or higher: 17.5% (2005); Master's degree or higher: 8.5% (2005).
Housing: Homeownership rate: 85.9% (2005); Median home value: $126,240 (2005); Median rent: $435 per month (2000); Median age of housing: 55 years (2000).
Transportation: Commute to work: 84.6% car, 0.8% public transportation, 4.1% walk, 9.4% work from home (2000); Travel time to work: 44.7% less than 15 minutes, 24.3% 15 to 30 minutes, 18.3% 30 to 45 minutes, 4.6% 45 to 60 minutes, 8.2% 60 minutes or more (2000)

BRANCHPORT (unincorporated postal area, zip code 14418). Covers a land area of 40.308 square miles and a water area of 0.035 square miles. Located at 42.60° N. Lat.; 77.20° W. Long. Elevation is 736 feet.
Population: 0 (2000); Race: 96.7% White, 0.0% Black, 1.1% Asian, 1.8% Hispanic of any race (2000); Density: 0.0 persons per square mile (2000); Age: 24.1% under 18, 14.4% over 64 (2000); Marriage status: 22.0% never married, 63.0% now married, 4.6% widowed, 10.4% divorced (2000); Foreign born: 0.7% (2000); Ancestry (includes multiple ancestries): 22.7% German, 18.9% Irish, 18.0% English, 9.9% Italian, 7.6% Other groups (2000).
Economy: Employment by occupation: 13.7% management, 16.8% professional, 21.8% services, 12.4% sales, 2.7% farming, 13.4% construction, 19.3% production (2000).
Income: Per capita income: $15,360 (2000); Median household income: $33,867 (2000); Poverty rate: 10.3% (2000).

Education: Percent of population age 25 and over with: High school diploma (including GED) or higher: 78.5% (2000); Bachelor's degree or higher: 13.1% (2000).

School District(s)
Penn Yan Central School District (PK-12)
    2003-04 Enrollment: 2,035 . . . . (315) 536-3371

Housing: Homeownership rate: 83.5% (2000); Median home value: $71,000 (2000); Median rent: $404 per month (2000); Median age of housing: 31 years (2000).
Transportation: Commute to work: 93.8% car, 0.0% public transportation, 0.9% walk, 3.4% work from home (2000); Travel time to work: 24.3% less than 15 minutes, 37.1% 15 to 30 minutes, 20.2% 30 to 45 minutes, 8.9% 45 to 60 minutes, 9.4% 60 minutes or more (2000).

DRESDEN (village).
Covers a land area of 0.305 square miles and a water area of 0 square miles. Located at 42.68° N. Lat.; 76.95° W. Long.
Population: 339 (1990); 307 (2000); 311 (2005); 313 (2010 projected); Race: 90.4% White, 0.0% Black, 0.0% Asian, 17.0% Hispanic of any race (2005); Density: 1,018.2 persons per square mile (2005); Average household size: 2.61 (2005); Median age: 42.6 (2005); Males per 100 females: 108.7 (2005); Marriage status: 22.4% never married, 58.7% now married, 7.3% widowed, 11.5% divorced (2000); Foreign born: 15.7% (2000); Ancestry (includes multiple ancestries): 24.0% Other groups, 15.4% English, 15.1% Irish, 14.8% German, 9.8% United States or American (2000).
Economy: Single-family building permits issued: 0 (2005); Multi-family building permits issued: 0 (2005); Employment by occupation: 6.9% management, 12.6% professional, 11.4% services, 21.1% sales, 16.0% farming, 10.3% construction, 21.7% production (2000).
Income: Per capita income: $22,212 (2005); Median household income: $48,295 (2005); Average household income: $57,962 (2005); Percent of households with income of $100,000 or more: 10.1% (2005); Poverty rate: 5.7% (2000).
Education: Percent of population age 25 and over with: High school diploma (including GED) or higher: 65.9% (2005); Bachelor's degree or higher: 8.3% (2005); Master's degree or higher: 2.2% (2005).
Housing: Homeownership rate: 73.9% (2005); Median home value: $97,500 (2005); Median rent: $413 per month (2000); Median age of housing: 60+ years (2000).
Transportation: Commute to work: 93.6% car, 1.7% public transportation, 1.2% walk, 1.7% work from home (2000); Travel time to work: 30.2% less than 15 minutes, 36.1% 15 to 30 minutes, 23.7% 30 to 45 minutes, 5.9% 45 to 60 minutes, 4.1% 60 minutes or more (2000).

DUNDEE (village).
Covers a land area of 1.122 square miles and a water area of 0 square miles. Located at 42.52° N. Lat.; 76.97° W. Long. Elevation is 994 feet.
History: Incorporated 1847.
Population: 1,598 (1990); 1,690 (2000); 1,653 (2005); 1,660 (2010 projected); Race: 97.8% White, 1.3% Black, 0.2% Asian, 0.7% Hispanic of any race (2005); Density: 1,473.0 persons per square mile (2005); Average household size: 2.54 (2005); Median age: 39.6 (2005); Males per 100 females: 86.8 (2005); Marriage status: 28.8% never married, 44.9% now married, 12.8% widowed, 13.5% divorced (2000); Foreign born: 1.2% (2000); Ancestry (includes multiple ancestries): 23.0% English, 19.6% German, 9.7% Irish, 8.7% United States or American, 6.3% Dutch (2000).
Economy: In grape-growing area; processing of apple and grape concentrates and juices, canned and bottled vegetables, and snack foods. Single-family building permits issued: 0 (2005); Multi-family building permits issued: 0 (2005); Employment by occupation: 6.5% management, 13.8% professional, 22.2% services, 22.6% sales, 0.4% farming, 8.6% construction, 25.9% production (2000).
Income: Per capita income: $17,017 (2005); Median household income: $29,500 (2005); Average household income: $41,179 (2005); Percent of households with income of $100,000 or more: 5.1% (2005); Poverty rate: 17.0% (2000).
Education: Percent of population age 25 and over with: High school diploma (including GED) or higher: 81.7% (2005); Bachelor's degree or higher: 8.5% (2005); Master's degree or higher: 3.9% (2005).

School District(s)
Dundee Central School District (PK-12)
    2003-04 Enrollment: 959 . . . . (607) 243-5533

Housing: Homeownership rate: 58.1% (2005); Median home value: $89,398 (2005); Median rent: $303 per month (2000); Median age of housing: 60+ years (2000).
Newspapers: Dundee Observer (General - Circulation 3,100)
Transportation: Commute to work: 84.4% car, 0.0% public transportation, 10.2% walk, 2.1% work from home (2000); Travel time to work: 47.5% less than 15 minutes, 31.9% 15 to 30 minutes, 8.4% 30 to 45 minutes, 6.0% 45 to 60 minutes, 6.2% 60 minutes or more (2000)

HIMROD (unincorporated postal area, zip code 14842).
Aka Seneca Lake. Covers a land area of 15.729 square miles and a water area of 0.007 square miles. Located at 42.59° N. Lat.; 76.94° W. Long.
Population: 0 (2000); Race: 99.3% White, 0.0% Black, 0.7% Asian, 0.0% Hispanic of any race (2000); Density: 0.0 persons per square mile (2000); Age: 31.0% under 18, 19.7% over 64 (2000); Marriage status: 11.8% never married, 80.8% now married, 5.4% widowed, 2.0% divorced (2000); Foreign born: 3.1% (2000); Ancestry (includes multiple ancestries): 20.5% United States or American, 13.5% Irish, 12.7% Dutch, 12.3% German, 11.7% English (2000).
Economy: Employment by occupation: 9.4% management, 16.2% professional, 10.4% services, 30.7% sales, 3.9% farming, 19.1% construction, 10.4% production (2000).
Income: Per capita income: $17,496 (2000); Median household income: $42,019 (2000); Poverty rate: 8.5% (2000).
Education: Percent of population age 25 and over with: High school diploma (including GED) or higher: 81.9% (2000); Bachelor's degree or higher: 22.8% (2000).
Housing: Homeownership rate: 93.5% (2000); Median home value: $75,000 (2000); Median rent: $430 per month (2000); Median age of housing: 32 years (2000).
Transportation: Commute to work: 83.1% car, 0.0% public transportation, 0.0% walk, 16.9% work from home (2000); Travel time to work: 34.3% less than 15 minutes, 30.3% 15 to 30 minutes, 11.2% 30 to 45 minutes, 12.4% 45 to 60 minutes, 12.0% 60 minutes or more (2000)

ITALY (town).
Covers a land area of 40.153 square miles and a water area of 0.112 square miles. Located at 42.61° N. Lat.; 77.30° W. Long. Elevation is 1,121 feet.
Population: 1,120 (1990); 1,087 (2000); 1,094 (2005); 1,094 (2010 projected); Race: 98.5% White, 0.1% Black, 0.2% Asian, 0.7% Hispanic of any race (2005); Density: 27.2 persons per square mile (2005); Average household size: 2.54 (2005); Median age: 40.3 (2005); Males per 100 females: 102.6 (2005); Marriage status: 26.5% never married, 60.1% now married, 4.6% widowed, 8.8% divorced (2000); Foreign born: 0.9% (2000); Ancestry (includes multiple ancestries): 25.9% German, 20.6% English, 18.2% Irish, 6.7% Italian, 5.8% Polish (2000).
Economy: Employment by occupation: 6.3% management, 12.1% professional, 22.1% services, 16.9% sales, 2.6% farming, 15.8% construction, 24.3% production (2000).
Income: Per capita income: $18,051 (2005); Median household income: $39,275 (2005); Average household income: $45,818 (2005); Percent of households with income of $100,000 or more: 5.3% (2005); Poverty rate: 12.7% (2000).
Education: Percent of population age 25 and over with: High school diploma (including GED) or higher: 79.8% (2005); Bachelor's degree or higher: 15.2% (2005); Master's degree or higher: 6.4% (2005).
Housing: Homeownership rate: 87.5% (2005); Median home value: $101,699 (2005); Median rent: $372 per month (2000); Median age of housing: 26 years (2000).
Transportation: Commute to work: 94.1% car, 0.6% public transportation, 0.0% walk, 4.6% work from home (2000); Travel time to work: 14.2% less than 15 minutes, 28.8% 15 to 30 minutes, 24.1% 30 to 45 minutes, 14.4% 45 to 60 minutes, 18.5% 60 minutes or more (2000)

JERUSALEM (town).
Covers a land area of 58.881 square miles and a water area of 6.519 square miles. Located at 42.62° N. Lat.; 77.14° W. Long.
Population: 3,784 (1990); 4,525 (2000); 4,556 (2005); 4,548 (2010 projected); Race: 98.2% White, 0.7% Black, 0.3% Asian, 1.1% Hispanic of any race (2005); Density: 77.4 persons per square mile (2005); Average household size: 2.79 (2005); Median age: 39.2 (2005); Males per 100 females: 87.6 (2005); Marriage status: 28.8% never married, 57.7% now married, 5.0% widowed, 8.5% divorced (2000); Foreign born: 3.7% (2000); Ancestry (includes multiple ancestries): 25.7% English, 18.5% German, 15.2% Irish, 8.1% Italian, 6.1% Other groups (2000).
Economy: Single-family building permits issued: 16 (2005); Multi-family building permits issued: 0 (2005); Employment by occupation: 12.7%

management, 24.6% professional, 19.6% services, 19.7% sales, 1.6% farming, 9.5% construction, 12.3% production (2000).
Income: Per capita income: $20,318 (2005); Median household income: $44,324 (2005); Average household income: $55,445 (2005); Percent of households with income of $100,000 or more: 10.8% (2005); Poverty rate: 9.4% (2000).
Education: Percent of population age 25 and over with: High school diploma (including GED) or higher: 87.4% (2005); Bachelor's degree or higher: 26.2% (2005); Master's degree or higher: 14.7% (2005).
Housing: Homeownership rate: 84.6% (2005); Median home value: $141,372 (2005); Median rent: $436 per month (2000); Median age of housing: 36 years (2000).
Transportation: Commute to work: 79.2% car, 0.3% public transportation, 14.4% walk, 4.6% work from home (2000); Travel time to work: 51.1% less than 15 minutes, 24.0% 15 to 30 minutes, 14.1% 30 to 45 minutes, 4.5% 45 to 60 minutes, 6.3% 60 minutes or more (2000)

KEUKA PARK (unincorporated postal area, zip code 14478).
Covers a land area of 12.867 square miles and a water area of 0 square miles. Located at 42.58° N. Lat.; 77.11° W. Long.
History: Seat of Keuka College.
Population: 0 (2000); Race: 96.4% White, 1.1% Black, 0.0% Asian, 0.0% Hispanic of any race (2000); Density: 0.0 persons per square mile (2000); Age: 11.7% under 18, 11.2% over 64 (2000); Marriage status: 43.4% never married, 46.8% now married, 4.6% widowed, 5.1% divorced (2000); Foreign born: 1.7% (2000); Ancestry (includes multiple ancestries): 18.8% English, 17.8% German, 12.3% Irish, 7.2% Dutch, 6.4% Italian (2000).
Economy: Employment by occupation: 8.0% management, 27.6% professional, 26.3% services, 26.8% sales, 1.3% farming, 0.8% construction, 9.2% production (2000).
Income: Per capita income: $15,356 (2000); Median household income: $37,227 (2000); Poverty rate: 12.6% (2000).
Education: Percent of population age 25 and over with: High school diploma (including GED) or higher: 92.1% (2000); Bachelor's degree or higher: 33.6% (2000).
Four-year College(s)
Keuka College
    Fall 2004 Enrollment: 1,206 . . . . (315) 279-5000
    2005-06 Tuition: In-state $18,360; Out-of-state $18,360
Housing: Homeownership rate: 78.6% (2000); Median home value: $107,100 (2000); Median rent: $425 per month (2000); Median age of housing: 38 years (2000).
Transportation: Commute to work: 45.9% car, 1.1% public transportation, 47.3% walk, 5.7% work from home (2000); Travel time to work: 72.7% less than 15 minutes, 14.5% 15 to 30 minutes, 3.8% 30 to 45 minutes, 2.3% 45 to 60 minutes, 6.8% 60 minutes or more (2000)

MIDDLESEX (town).
Covers a land area of 30.865 square miles and a water area of 3.207 square miles. Located at 42.71° N. Lat.; 77.27° W. Long. Elevation is 721 feet.
Population: 1,249 (1990); 1,345 (2000); 1,438 (2005); 1,520 (2010 projected); Race: 98.7% White, 0.5% Black, 0.1% Asian, 0.3% Hispanic of any race (2005); Density: 46.6 persons per square mile (2005); Average household size: 2.54 (2005); Median age: 43.4 (2005); Males per 100 females: 98.9 (2005); Marriage status: 20.1% never married, 62.1% now married, 4.7% widowed, 13.1% divorced (2000); Foreign born: 1.4% (2000); Ancestry (includes multiple ancestries): 28.4% English, 24.6% German, 16.2% Irish, 6.7% United States or American, 5.8% Italian (2000).
Economy: Resort village. In grape-growing region. Single-family building permits issued: 4 (2005); Multi-family building permits issued: 0 (2005); Employment by occupation: 10.0% management, 22.9% professional, 14.9% services, 23.0% sales, 0.6% farming, 11.5% construction, 17.0% production (2000).
Income: Per capita income: $25,195 (2005); Median household income: $48,819 (2005); Average household income: $62,672 (2005); Percent of households with income of $100,000 or more: 14.3% (2005); Poverty rate: 6.6% (2000).
Education: Percent of population age 25 and over with: High school diploma (including GED) or higher: 86.9% (2005); Bachelor's degree or higher: 25.2% (2005); Master's degree or higher: 10.9% (2005).
Housing: Homeownership rate: 89.2% (2005); Median home value: $116,298 (2005); Median rent: $383 per month (2000); Median age of housing: 41 years (2000).
Transportation: Commute to work: 94.2% car, 0.0% public transportation, 2.5% walk, 2.7% work from home (2000); Travel time to work: 19.4% less than 15 minutes, 32.5% 15 to 30 minutes, 22.2% 30 to 45 minutes, 10.9% 45 to 60 minutes, 15.0% 60 minutes or more (2000)

MILO (town).
Covers a land area of 38.376 square miles and a water area of 5.918 square miles. Located at 42.62° N. Lat.; 77.02° W. Long.
Population: 7,023 (1990); 7,026 (2000); 6,941 (2005); 6,957 (2010 projected); Race: 97.3% White, 0.9% Black, 0.3% Asian, 1.3% Hispanic of any race (2005); Density: 180.9 persons per square mile (2005); Average household size: 2.49 (2005); Median age: 38.3 (2005); Males per 100 females: 93.6 (2005); Marriage status: 22.2% never married, 53.9% now married, 11.3% widowed, 12.7% divorced (2000); Foreign born: 2.1% (2000); Ancestry (includes multiple ancestries): 18.9% English, 17.7% German, 13.5% Irish, 8.9% United States or American, 6.1% Danish (2000).
Economy: Single-family building permits issued: 16 (2005); Multi-family building permits issued: 0 (2005); Employment by occupation: 8.1% management, 15.7% professional, 21.0% services, 24.8% sales, 2.0% farming, 8.3% construction, 20.1% production (2000).
Income: Per capita income: $18,111 (2005); Median household income: $34,988 (2005); Average household income: $43,560 (2005); Percent of households with income of $100,000 or more: 6.2% (2005); Poverty rate: 13.8% (2000).
Education: Percent of population age 25 and over with: High school diploma (including GED) or higher: 78.3% (2005); Bachelor's degree or higher: 17.3% (2005); Master's degree or higher: 7.9% (2005).
Housing: Homeownership rate: 65.2% (2005); Median home value: $112,481 (2005); Median rent: $374 per month (2000); Median age of housing: 56 years (2000).
Transportation: Commute to work: 85.7% car, 0.6% public transportation, 7.2% walk, 5.6% work from home (2000); Travel time to work: 48.1% less than 15 minutes, 21.5% 15 to 30 minutes, 15.6% 30 to 45 minutes, 8.7% 45 to 60 minutes, 6.0% 60 minutes or more (2000)

PENN YAN (village).
Covers a land area of 2.269 square miles and a water area of 0.063 square miles. Located at 42.66° N. Lat.; 77.05° W. Long. Elevation is 737 feet.
History: Controversy between the settlers from Pennsylvania and New England over a name for this place was compromised by combining the first syllables of Pennsylvania and Yankee.
Population: 5,294 (1990); 5,219 (2000); 5,046 (2005); 4,990 (2010 projected); Race: 97.2% White, 0.8% Black, 0.3% Asian, 1.4% Hispanic of any race (2005); Density: 2,223.5 persons per square mile (2005); Average household size: 2.44 (2005); Median age: 40.8 (2005); Males per 100 females: 88.1 (2005); Marriage status: 23.3% never married, 49.3% now married, 14.8% widowed, 12.5% divorced (2000); Foreign born: 2.4% (2000); Ancestry (includes multiple ancestries): 19.5% English, 16.8% German, 14.2% Irish, 7.6% United States or American, 6.9% Danish (2000).
Economy: Single-family building permits issued: 3 (2005); Multi-family building permits issued: 60 (2005); Employment by occupation: 7.0% management, 14.5% professional, 25.4% services, 26.6% sales, 1.7% farming, 5.7% construction, 19.2% production (2000).
Income: Per capita income: $17,113 (2005); Median household income: $32,013 (2005); Average household income: $38,764 (2005); Percent of households with income of $100,000 or more: 3.6% (2005); Poverty rate: 13.8% (2000).
Education: Percent of population age 25 and over with: High school diploma (including GED) or higher: 76.0% (2005); Bachelor's degree or higher: 15.0% (2005); Master's degree or higher: 8.0% (2005).
School District(s)
Penn Yan Central School District (PK-12)
    2003-04 Enrollment: 2,035 . . . . (315) 536-3371
Housing: Homeownership rate: 56.7% (2005); Median home value: $109,358 (2005); Median rent: $382 per month (2000); Median age of housing: 60+ years (2000).
Hospitals: Soldiers and Sailors Memorial Hospital (186 beds)
Newspapers: The Chronicle-Express (General - Circulation 4,200)
Transportation: Commute to work: 84.2% car, 0.6% public transportation, 9.3% walk, 4.5% work from home (2000); Travel time to work: 53.7% less than 15 minutes, 19.9% 15 to 30 minutes, 15.2% 30 to 45 minutes, 7.1% 45 to 60 minutes, 4.1% 60 minutes or more (2000)
Additional Information Contacts
Penn Yan Chamber of Commerce . . . . (800) 868-9283
    http://www.yatesny.com

POTTER (town). Covers a land area of 37.247 square miles and a water area of 0 square miles. Located at 42.71° N. Lat.; 77.18° W. Long.
Population: 1,617 (1990); 1,830 (2000); 1,839 (2005); 1,847 (2010 projected); Race: 96.5% White, 0.7% Black, 0.6% Asian, 2.9% Hispanic of any race (2005); Density: 49.4 persons per square mile (2005); Average household size: 3.10 (2005); Median age: 33.9 (2005); Males per 100 females: 103.2 (2005); Marriage status: 25.7% never married, 64.1% now married, 3.7% widowed, 6.5% divorced (2000); Foreign born: 0.9% (2000); Ancestry (includes multiple ancestries): 19.6% German, 19.0% English, 14.0% Irish, 13.2% United States or American, 6.2% Other groups (2000).
Economy: Single-family building permits issued: 4 (2005); Multi-family building permits issued: 0 (2005); Employment by occupation: 12.9% management, 13.7% professional, 15.5% services, 22.3% sales, 4.0% farming, 14.8% construction, 16.7% production (2000).
Income: Per capita income: $19,088 (2005); Median household income: $48,568 (2005); Average household income: $57,841 (2005); Percent of households with income of $100,000 or more: 11.0% (2005); Poverty rate: 9.7% (2000).
Education: Percent of population age 25 and over with: High school diploma (including GED) or higher: 81.5% (2005); Bachelor's degree or higher: 12.4% (2005); Master's degree or higher: 4.9% (2005).
Housing: Homeownership rate: 83.3% (2005); Median home value: $105,696 (2005); Median rent: $453 per month (2000); Median age of housing: 30 years (2000).
Transportation: Commute to work: 87.5% car, 0.2% public transportation, 3.5% walk, 8.1% work from home (2000); Travel time to work: 22.1% less than 15 minutes, 36.9% 15 to 30 minutes, 21.0% 30 to 45 minutes, 8.8% 45 to 60 minutes, 11.2% 60 minutes or more (2000)

ROCK STREAM (unincorporated postal area, zip code 14878). Covers a land area of 15.807 square miles and a water area of 0 square miles. Located at 42.45° N. Lat.; 76.93° W. Long.
Population: 0 (2000); Race: 99.2% White, 0.1% Black, 0.0% Asian, 1.0% Hispanic of any race (2000); Density: 0.0 persons per square mile (2000); Age: 20.6% under 18, 15.6% over 64 (2000); Marriage status: 15.5% never married, 76.9% now married, 3.3% widowed, 4.3% divorced (2000); Foreign born: 2.1% (2000); Ancestry (includes multiple ancestries): 26.6% English, 23.6% German, 19.1% Irish, 12.2% United States or American, 4.5% Dutch (2000).
Economy: Employment by occupation: 12.9% management, 17.1% professional, 13.2% services, 24.6% sales, 1.2% farming, 13.8% construction, 17.4% production (2000).
Income: Per capita income: $18,465 (2000); Median household income: $42,188 (2000); Poverty rate: 4.7% (2000).
Education: Percent of population age 25 and over with: High school diploma (including GED) or higher: 91.4% (2000); Bachelor's degree or higher: 15.7% (2000).
Housing: Homeownership rate: 94.4% (2000); Median home value: $63,800 (2000); Median rent: $263 per month (2000); Median age of housing: 53 years (2000).
Transportation: Commute to work: 86.8% car, 0.6% public transportation, 1.9% walk, 10.1% work from home (2000); Travel time to work: 27.4% less than 15 minutes, 28.4% 15 to 30 minutes, 16.8% 30 to 45 minutes, 19.3% 45 to 60 minutes, 8.1% 60 minutes or more (2000)

RUSHVILLE (village). Covers a land area of 0.638 square miles and a water area of 0 square miles. Located at 42.76° N. Lat.; 77.22° W. Long.
Population: 609 (1990); 621 (2000); 618 (2005); 619 (2010 projected); Race: 94.3% White, 2.4% Black, 0.8% Asian, 2.4% Hispanic of any race (2005); Density: 968.9 persons per square mile (2005); Average household size: 2.73 (2005); Median age: 39.5 (2005); Males per 100 females: 88.4 (2005); Marriage status: 23.9% never married, 59.0% now married, 8.8% widowed, 8.4% divorced (2000); Foreign born: 0.2% (2000); Ancestry (includes multiple ancestries): 25.3% English, 19.5% German, 18.7% Irish, 8.8% United States or American, 6.8% Italian (2000).
Economy: Single-family building permits issued: 0 (2005); Multi-family building permits issued: 0 (2005); Employment by occupation: 7.8% management, 20.4% professional, 20.7% services, 24.3% sales, 0.6% farming, 15.9% construction, 10.4% production (2000).
Income: Per capita income: $19,310 (2005); Median household income: $39,643 (2005); Average household income: $48,805 (2005); Percent of households with income of $100,000 or more: 7.1% (2005); Poverty rate: 9.6% (2000).
Education: Percent of population age 25 and over with: High school diploma (including GED) or higher: 81.3% (2005); Bachelor's degree or higher: 16.0% (2005); Master's degree or higher: 7.6% (2005).
Housing: Homeownership rate: 70.8% (2005); Median home value: $100,090 (2005); Median rent: $242 per month (2000); Median age of housing: 60+ years (2000).
Transportation: Commute to work: 91.1% car, 0.7% public transportation, 1.7% walk, 6.6% work from home (2000); Travel time to work: 26.2% less than 15 minutes, 40.4% 15 to 30 minutes, 18.4% 30 to 45 minutes, 5.3% 45 to 60 minutes, 9.6% 60 minutes or more (2000)

STARKEY (town). Covers a land area of 32.840 square miles and a water area of 6.445 square miles. Located at 42.52° N. Lat.; 76.94° W. Long. Elevation is 809 feet.
Population: 3,173 (1990); 3,465 (2000); 3,501 (2005); 3,560 (2010 projected); Race: 96.4% White, 1.5% Black, 0.6% Asian, 1.8% Hispanic of any race (2005); Density: 106.6 persons per square mile (2005); Average household size: 2.78 (2005); Median age: 37.0 (2005); Males per 100 females: 94.6 (2005); Marriage status: 26.4% never married, 54.0% now married, 9.2% widowed, 10.4% divorced (2000); Foreign born: 3.5% (2000); Ancestry (includes multiple ancestries): 21.3% English, 16.4% German, 10.2% Irish, 9.5% United States or American, 5.8% Other groups (2000).
Economy: Single-family building permits issued: 3 (2005); Multi-family building permits issued: 0 (2005); Employment by occupation: 9.6% management, 12.9% professional, 17.8% services, 22.0% sales, 4.8% farming, 9.2% construction, 23.7% production (2000).
Income: Per capita income: $17,148 (2005); Median household income: $33,474 (2005); Average household income: $46,253 (2005); Percent of households with income of $100,000 or more: 6.2% (2005); Poverty rate: 19.3% (2000).
Education: Percent of population age 25 and over with: High school diploma (including GED) or higher: 77.4% (2005); Bachelor's degree or higher: 16.0% (2005); Master's degree or higher: 7.1% (2005).
Housing: Homeownership rate: 71.3% (2005); Median home value: $114,928 (2005); Median rent: $306 per month (2000); Median age of housing: 50 years (2000).
Transportation: Commute to work: 79.5% car, 0.7% public transportation, 8.7% walk, 8.9% work from home (2000); Travel time to work: 41.6% less than 15 minutes, 26.9% 15 to 30 minutes, 14.6% 30 to 45 minutes, 11.7% 45 to 60 minutes, 5.1% 60 minutes or more (2000)

TORREY (town). Covers a land area of 22.714 square miles and a water area of 10.998 square miles. Located at 42.67° N. Lat.; 76.95° W. Long.
Population: 1,269 (1990); 1,307 (2000); 1,310 (2005); 1,306 (2010 projected); Race: 97.2% White, 0.1% Black, 0.0% Asian, 5.0% Hispanic of any race (2005); Density: 57.7 persons per square mile (2005); Average household size: 2.73 (2005); Median age: 41.9 (2005); Males per 100 females: 102.5 (2005); Marriage status: 23.4% never married, 61.0% now married, 7.7% widowed, 7.9% divorced (2000); Foreign born: 4.2% (2000); Ancestry (includes multiple ancestries): 22.7% German, 18.3% English, 13.8% Irish, 8.3% Other groups, 8.0% United States or American (2000).
Economy: Single-family building permits issued: 10 (2005); Multi-family building permits issued: 0 (2005); Employment by occupation: 13.3% management, 16.3% professional, 14.0% services, 17.5% sales, 8.2% farming, 14.0% construction, 16.8% production (2000).
Income: Per capita income: $19,103 (2005); Median household income: $43,429 (2005); Average household income: $52,223 (2005); Percent of households with income of $100,000 or more: 8.6% (2005); Poverty rate: 12.0% (2000).
Education: Percent of population age 25 and over with: High school diploma (including GED) or higher: 73.3% (2005); Bachelor's degree or higher: 13.6% (2005); Master's degree or higher: 7.0% (2005).
Housing: Homeownership rate: 82.5% (2005); Median home value: $119,175 (2005); Median rent: $402 per month (2000); Median age of housing: 46 years (2000).
Transportation: Commute to work: 85.2% car, 0.5% public transportation, 3.5% walk, 8.5% work from home (2000); Travel time to work: 36.1% less than 15 minutes, 32.1% 15 to 30 minutes, 16.5% 30 to 45 minutes, 7.2% 45 to 60 minutes, 8.0% 60 minutes or more (2000);

PROFILES OF NEW YORK / Alphabetical Place Index

A

Accord CDP (Ulster County), 499
Acra postal area (Greene County), 162
Adams Center CDP (Jefferson County), 183
Adams town (Jefferson County), 183
Adams village (Jefferson County), 183
Addison town (Steuben County), 425
Addison village (Steuben County), 425
Adirondack postal area (Warren County), 514
Afton town (Chenango County), 68
Afton village (Chenango County), 68
Airmont village (Rockland County), 373
Akron village (Erie County), 120
Alabama town (Genesee County), 156
Albany County, 1 - 8
Albany city (Albany County), 1
Albertson CDP (Nassau County), 232
Albion town (Orleans County), 337
Albion town (Oswego County), 341
Albion village (Orleans County), 337
Alden town (Erie County), 121
Alden village (Erie County), 121
Alder Creek postal area (Oneida County), 286
Alexander town (Genesee County), 157
Alexander village (Genesee County), 156
Alexandria Bay village (Jefferson County), 184
Alexandria town (Jefferson County), 184
Alfred Station postal area (Allegany County), 10
Alfred town (Allegany County), 9
Alfred village (Allegany County), 9
Allegany County, 9 - 19
Allegany Reservation reservation (Cattaraugus County), 28
Allegany town (Cattaraugus County), 28
Allegany village (Cattaraugus County), 28
Allen town (Allegany County), 10
Alma town (Allegany County), 10
Almond town (Allegany County), 10
Almond village (Allegany County), 10
Alpine postal area (Schuyler County), 418
Alplaus postal area (Schenectady County), 407
Altamont town (Franklin County), 144
Altamont village (Albany County), 2
Altmar village (Oswego County), 341
Altona CDP (Clinton County), 76
Altona town (Clinton County), 76
Amagansett CDP (Suffolk County), 438
Amawalk postal area (Westchester County), 535
Amboy town (Oswego County), 341
Amenia CDP (Dutchess County), 107
Amenia town (Dutchess County), 107
Ames village (Montgomery County), 226
Amherst town (Erie County), 121
Amity town (Allegany County), 11
Amityville village (Suffolk County), 438
Amsterdam city (Montgomery County), 226
Amsterdam town (Montgomery County), 227
Ancram town (Columbia County), 84
Ancramdale postal area (Columbia County), 84
Andes town (Delaware County), 98
Andes village (Delaware County), 97
Andover town (Allegany County), 11
Andover village (Allegany County), 11
Angelica town (Allegany County), 12
Angelica village (Allegany County), 11
Angola on the Lake CDP (Erie County), 122
Angola village (Erie County), 121
Annsville town (Oneida County), 286
Antwerp town (Jefferson County), 184
Antwerp village (Jefferson County), 184

Apalachin CDP (Tioga County), 488
Appleton postal area (Niagara County), 278
Aquebogue CDP (Suffolk County), 438
Arcade town (Wyoming County), 557
Arcade village (Wyoming County), 557
Arcadia town (Wayne County), 528
Ardsley village (Westchester County), 535
Argyle town (Washington County), 521
Argyle village (Washington County), 521
Arietta town (Hamilton County), 171
Arkport village (Steuben County), 426
Arkville postal area (Delaware County), 98
Arkwright town (Chautauqua County), 50
Arlington CDP (Dutchess County), 107
Armonk CDP (Westchester County), 535
Arverne postal area (Queens County), 272
Asharoken village (Suffolk County), 438
Ashford town (Cattaraugus County), 28
Ashland town (Chemung County), 62
Ashland town (Greene County), 162
Ashville postal area (Chautauqua County), 50
Athens town (Greene County), 162
Athens village (Greene County), 162
Athol postal area (Warren County), 515
Atlanta postal area (Steuben County), 426
Atlantic Beach village (Nassau County), 232
Attica town (Wyoming County), 557
Attica village (Wyoming County), 557
Au Sable Forks CDP (Clinton County), 76
Au Sable town (Clinton County), 76
Auburn city (Cayuga County), 41
Augusta town (Oneida County), 286
Aurelius town (Cayuga County), 41
Aurora town (Erie County), 122
Aurora village (Cayuga County), 41
Austerlitz town (Columbia County), 84
Ava town (Oneida County), 286
Averill Park CDP (Rensselaer County), 365
Avoca town (Steuben County), 426
Avoca village (Steuben County), 426
Avon town (Livingston County), 202
Avon village (Livingston County), 202

B

Babylon town (Suffolk County), 439
Babylon village (Suffolk County), 439
Bainbridge town (Chenango County), 69
Bainbridge village (Chenango County), 68
Baiting Hollow CDP (Suffolk County), 439
Baldwin Harbor CDP (Nassau County), 232
Baldwin CDP (Nassau County), 232
Baldwin town (Chemung County), 62
Baldwinsville village (Onondaga County), 300
Ballston Lake postal area (Saratoga County), 398
Ballston Spa village (Saratoga County), 398
Ballston town (Saratoga County), 398
Balmville CDP (Orange County), 321
Bangor town (Franklin County), 145
Bardonia CDP (Rockland County), 373
Barker town (Broome County), 20
Barker village (Niagara County), 278
Barneveld village (Oneida County), 287
Barnum Island CDP (Nassau County), 233
Barre town (Orleans County), 337
Barrington town (Yates County), 564
Barrytown postal area (Dutchess County), 108
Barryville postal area (Sullivan County), 476
Barton town (Tioga County), 488
Basom postal area (Genesee County), 157
Batavia city (Genesee County), 157
Batavia town (Genesee County), 157
Bath town (Steuben County), 427
Bath village (Steuben County), 427

Baxter Estates village (Nassau County), 233
Bay Park CDP (Nassau County), 233
Bay Shore CDP (Suffolk County), 439
Bayport CDP (Suffolk County), 440
Bayville village (Nassau County), 233
Baywood CDP (Suffolk County), 440
Beacon city (Dutchess County), 108
Bearsville postal area (Ulster County), 499
Beaver Dams postal area (Schuyler County), 418
Beaverdam Lake-Salisbury Mills CDP (Orange County), 321
Bedford Hills postal area (Westchester County), 536
Bedford CDP (Westchester County), 536
Bedford town (Westchester County), 536
Beekman town (Dutchess County), 108
Beekmantown town (Clinton County), 77
Belfast town (Allegany County), 12
Belle Terre village (Suffolk County), 440
Bellerose Terrace CDP (Nassau County), 234
Bellerose village (Nassau County), 234
Bellmont town (Franklin County), 145
Bellmore CDP (Nassau County), 234
Bellona postal area (Yates County), 564
Bellport village (Suffolk County), 440
Belmont village (Allegany County), 12
Bemus Point village (Chautauqua County), 50
Bennington town (Wyoming County), 558
Benson town (Hamilton County), 171
Benton town (Yates County), 564
Bergen town (Genesee County), 158
Bergen village (Genesee County), 158
Berkshire town (Tioga County), 489
Berlin town (Rensselaer County), 365
Berne town (Albany County), 2
Bernhards Bay postal area (Oswego County), 341
Bethany town (Genesee County), 158
Bethel town (Sullivan County), 477
Bethlehem town (Albany County), 2
Bethpage CDP (Nassau County), 234
Big Flats Airport CDP (Chemung County), 63
Big Flats CDP (Chemung County), 62
Big Flats town (Chemung County), 62
Big Indian postal area (Ulster County), 499
Billington Heights CDP (Erie County), 122
Binghamton city (Broome County), 20
Binghamton town (Broome County), 21
Birdsall town (Allegany County), 12
Black Brook town (Clinton County), 77
Black Creek postal area (Allegany County), 12
Black River village (Jefferson County), 184
Blasdell village (Erie County), 122
Blauvelt CDP (Rockland County), 374
Bleecker town (Fulton County), 152
Blenheim town (Schoharie County), 412
Bliss postal area (Wyoming County), 558
Bloomfield village (Ontario County), 313
Blooming Grove town (Orange County), 321
Bloomingburg village (Sullivan County), 477
Bloomingdale postal area (Essex County), 138
Bloomington postal area (Ulster County), 499
Bloomville postal area (Delaware County), 98
Blossvale postal area (Oneida County), 287
Blue Mountain Lake postal area (Hamilton County), 172
Blue Point CDP (Suffolk County), 440
Bohemia CDP (Suffolk County), 441
Boiceville postal area (Ulster County), 499
Bolivar town (Allegany County), 13
Bolivar village (Allegany County), 13

CDP = Census Designated Place

Bolton Landing postal area (Warren County), 515
Bolton town (Warren County), 515
Bombay town (Franklin County), 145
Boonville town (Oneida County), 287
Boonville village (Oneida County), 287
Boston town (Erie County), 123
Bouckville postal area (Madison County), 209
Bovina Center postal area (Delaware County), 98
Bovina town (Delaware County), 98
Bowmansville postal area (Erie County), 123
Boylston town (Oswego County), 342
Bradford town (Steuben County), 427
Branchport postal area (Yates County), 564
Brandon town (Franklin County), 145
Brant Lake postal area (Warren County), 515
Brant town (Erie County), 123
Brasher Falls-Winthrop CDP (Saint Lawrence County), 385
Brasher town (Saint Lawrence County), 384
Breesport postal area (Chemung County), 63
Breezy Point postal area (Queens County), 272
Brentwood CDP (Suffolk County), 441
Brewerton CDP (Onondaga County), 301
Brewster Hill CDP (Putnam County), 361
Brewster village (Putnam County), 360
Briarcliff Manor village (Westchester County), 536
Bridgehampton CDP (Suffolk County), 441
Bridgeport CDP (Onondaga County), 301
Bridgewater town (Oneida County), 288
Bridgewater village (Oneida County), 287
Brier Hill postal area (Saint Lawrence County), 385
Brighton CDP (Monroe County), 217
Brighton town (Franklin County), 145
Brighton town (Monroe County), 217
Brightwaters village (Suffolk County), 441
Brinckerhoff CDP (Dutchess County), 108
Bristol town (Ontario County), 314
Broadalbin town (Fulton County), 153
Broadalbin village (Fulton County), 152
Brockport village (Monroe County), 217
Brocton village (Chautauqua County), 50
Bronx borough (Bronx County), 265
Bronxville village (Westchester County), 537
Brookfield town (Madison County), 209
Brookhaven CDP (Suffolk County), 442
Brookhaven town (Suffolk County), 442
Brooklyn borough (Kings County), 266
Brooktondale postal area (Tompkins County), 493
Brookville village (Nassau County), 235
Broome County, 20 - 26
Broome town (Schoharie County), 412
Brownville town (Jefferson County), 185
Brownville village (Jefferson County), 185
Brunswick town (Rensselaer County), 365
Brushton village (Franklin County), 146
Brutus town (Cayuga County), 42
Buchanan village (Westchester County), 537
Buffalo city (Erie County), 123
Burdett village (Schuyler County), 418
Burke town (Franklin County), 146
Burke village (Franklin County), 146
Burlington Flats postal area (Otsego County), 350
Burlington town (Otsego County), 350
Burns town (Allegany County), 13
Burnt Hills postal area (Saratoga County), 398
Burt postal area (Niagara County), 278
Buskirk postal area (Rensselaer County), 365
Busti town (Chautauqua County), 51

Butler town (Wayne County), 528
Butternuts town (Otsego County), 350
Byron town (Genesee County), 158

C

Cadyville postal area (Clinton County), 77
Cairo CDP (Greene County), 163
Cairo town (Greene County), 163
Calcium CDP (Jefferson County), 185
Caledonia town (Livingston County), 202
Caledonia village (Livingston County), 202
Callicoon CDP (Sullivan County), 477
Callicoon town (Sullivan County), 477
Calverton CDP (Suffolk County), 442
Cambria town (Niagara County), 279
Cambridge town (Washington County), 522
Cambridge village (Washington County), 521
Camden town (Oneida County), 288
Camden village (Oneida County), 288
Cameron Mills postal area (Steuben County), 427
Cameron town (Steuben County), 427
Camillus town (Onondaga County), 301
Camillus village (Onondaga County), 301
Campbell Hall postal area (Orange County), 321
Campbell town (Steuben County), 428
Canaan town (Columbia County), 84
Canadice town (Ontario County), 314
Canajoharie town (Montgomery County), 227
Canajoharie village (Montgomery County), 227
Canandaigua city (Ontario County), 314
Canandaigua town (Ontario County), 314
Canaseraga village (Allegany County), 13
Canastota village (Madison County), 209
Candor town (Tioga County), 489
Candor village (Tioga County), 489
Caneadea town (Allegany County), 14
Canisteo town (Steuben County), 428
Canisteo village (Steuben County), 428
Canton town (Saint Lawrence County), 385
Canton village (Saint Lawrence County), 385
Cape Vincent town (Jefferson County), 186
Cape Vincent village (Jefferson County), 185
Carle Place CDP (Nassau County), 235
Carlisle town (Schoharie County), 412
Carlton town (Orleans County), 338
Carmel Hamlet CDP (Putnam County), 361
Carmel town (Putnam County), 361
Caroga Lake postal area (Fulton County), 153
Caroga town (Fulton County), 153
Caroline town (Tompkins County), 493
Carroll town (Chautauqua County), 51
Carrollton town (Cattaraugus County), 28
Carthage village (Jefferson County), 186
Cassadaga village (Chautauqua County), 51
Cassville postal area (Oneida County), 288
Castile town (Wyoming County), 558
Castile village (Wyoming County), 558
Castle Creek postal area (Broome County), 21
Castleton-on-Hudson village (Rensselaer County), 366
Castorland village (Lewis County), 195
Catharine town (Schuyler County), 419
Catlin town (Chemung County), 63
Cato town (Cayuga County), 42
Cato village (Cayuga County), 42
Caton town (Steuben County), 428
Catskill town (Greene County), 163
Catskill village (Greene County), 163
Cattaraugus County, 27 - 39
Cattaraugus Reservation reservation (Cattaraugus County), 29

Cattaraugus Reservation reservation (Erie County), 124
Cattaraugus village (Cattaraugus County), 29
Cayuga County, 40 - 48
Cayuga Heights village (Tompkins County), 493
Cayuga village (Cayuga County), 42
Cayuta town (Schuyler County), 419
Cazenovia town (Madison County), 210
Cazenovia village (Madison County), 210
Cedarhurst village (Nassau County), 235
Celoron village (Chautauqua County), 51
Center Moriches CDP (Suffolk County), 442
Centereach CDP (Suffolk County), 443
Centerport CDP (Suffolk County), 443
Centerville town (Allegany County), 14
Central Bridge postal area (Schoharie County), 412
Central Islip CDP (Suffolk County), 443
Central Square village (Oswego County), 342
Central Valley CDP (Orange County), 321
Centre Island village (Nassau County), 235
Ceres postal area (Allegany County), 14
Chadwicks postal area (Oneida County), 288
Chaffee postal area (Erie County), 124
Champion town (Jefferson County), 186
Champlain town (Clinton County), 77
Champlain village (Clinton County), 77
Chappaqua CDP (Westchester County), 537
Charleston town (Montgomery County), 227
Charlotte town (Chautauqua County), 52
Charlotteville postal area (Schoharie County), 412
Charlton town (Saratoga County), 398
Chase Mills postal area (Saint Lawrence County), 386
Chateaugay town (Franklin County), 147
Chateaugay village (Franklin County), 146
Chatham town (Columbia County), 85
Chatham village (Columbia County), 85
Chaumont village (Jefferson County), 186
Chautauqua County, 49 - 60
Chautauqua town (Chautauqua County), 52
Chazy town (Clinton County), 78
Cheektowaga CDP (Erie County), 125
Cheektowaga town (Erie County), 124
Chemung County, 61 - 66
Chemung town (Chemung County), 63
Chenango County, 67 - 74
Chenango Forks postal area (Broome County), 21
Chenango town (Broome County), 21
Cherry Creek town (Chautauqua County), 52
Cherry Creek village (Chautauqua County), 52
Cherry Valley town (Otsego County), 351
Cherry Valley village (Otsego County), 351
Chester town (Orange County), 322
Chester town (Warren County), 515
Chester village (Orange County), 322
Chesterfield town (Essex County), 138
Chestertown postal area (Warren County), 516
Chestnut Ridge village (Rockland County), 374
Chichester postal area (Ulster County), 500
Childwold postal area (Saint Lawrence County), 386
Chili town (Monroe County), 217
Chittenango village (Madison County), 210
Churchville village (Monroe County), 218
Churubusco postal area (Clinton County), 78
Cicero town (Onondaga County), 301
Cincinnatus town (Cortland County), 92
Circleville postal area (Orange County), 322
Clare town (Saint Lawrence County), 386

CDP = Census Designated Place

Clarence Center CDP (Erie County), 125
Clarence town (Erie County), 125
Clarendon town (Orleans County), 338
Clark Mills CDP (Oneida County), 289
Clarkson town (Monroe County), 218
Clarkstown town (Rockland County), 374
Clarksville postal area (Albany County), 3
Clarksville town (Allegany County), 14
Claryville postal area (Sullivan County), 477
Claverack town (Columbia County), 85
Claverack-Red Mills CDP (Columbia County), 85
Clay town (Onondaga County), 302
Clayton town (Jefferson County), 187
Clayton village (Jefferson County), 187
Clayville village (Oneida County), 289
Clemons postal area (Washington County), 522
Clermont town (Columbia County), 86
Cleveland village (Oswego County), 342
Clifton Park town (Saratoga County), 399
Clifton Springs village (Ontario County), 314
Clifton town (Saint Lawrence County), 386
Climax postal area (Greene County), 164
Clinton Corners postal area (Dutchess County), 109
Clinton County, 75 - 82
Clinton town (Clinton County), 78
Clinton town (Dutchess County), 109
Clinton village (Oneida County), 289
Clintondale CDP (Ulster County), 500
Clyde village (Wayne County), 528
Clymer town (Chautauqua County), 52
Cobleskill town (Schoharie County), 413
Cobleskill village (Schoharie County), 412
Cochecton Center postal area (Sullivan County), 478
Cochecton town (Sullivan County), 478
Coeymans Hollow postal area (Albany County), 3
Coeymans CDP (Albany County), 3
Coeymans town (Albany County), 3
Cohocton town (Steuben County), 429
Cohocton village (Steuben County), 429
Cohoes city (Albany County), 3
Colchester town (Delaware County), 99
Cold Brook village (Herkimer County), 175
Cold Spring Harbor CDP (Suffolk County), 443
Cold Spring village (Putnam County), 361
Colden town (Erie County), 126
Coldspring town (Cattaraugus County), 29
Colesville town (Broome County), 22
College Point postal area (Queens County), 273
Collins town (Erie County), 126
Colonie town (Albany County), 4
Colonie village (Albany County), 4
Colton town (Saint Lawrence County), 386
Columbia County, 83 - 91
Columbia town (Herkimer County), 175
Columbus town (Chenango County), 69
Commack CDP (Suffolk County), 443
Comstock postal area (Washington County), 522
Concord town (Erie County), 126
Conesus town (Livingston County), 203
Conesville town (Schoharie County), 413
Conewango Valley postal area (Cattaraugus County), 30
Conewango town (Cattaraugus County), 29
Congers CDP (Rockland County), 374
Conklin town (Broome County), 22
Conquest town (Cayuga County), 43
Constable town (Franklin County), 147
Constableville village (Lewis County), 196

Constantia CDP (Oswego County), 343
Constantia town (Oswego County), 342
Cooperstown village (Otsego County), 351
Copake Falls postal area (Columbia County), 86
Copake Lake CDP (Columbia County), 86
Copake town (Columbia County), 86
Copenhagen village (Lewis County), 196
Copiague CDP (Suffolk County), 444
Coram CDP (Suffolk County), 444
Corfu village (Genesee County), 158
Corinth town (Saratoga County), 399
Corinth village (Saratoga County), 399
Corning city (Steuben County), 429
Corning town (Steuben County), 429
Cornwall on Hudson village (Orange County), 323
Cornwall town (Orange County), 322
Cornwallville postal area (Greene County), 164
Corona postal area (Queens County), 273
Cortland County, 92 - 96
Cortland West CDP (Cortland County), 93
Cortland city (Cortland County), 93
Cortlandt Manor postal area (Westchester County), 538
Cortlandt town (Westchester County), 537
Cortlandville town (Cortland County), 93
Cossayuna postal area (Washington County), 522
Cottekill postal area (Ulster County), 500
Country Knolls CDP (Saratoga County), 399
Cove Neck village (Nassau County), 235
Coventry town (Chenango County), 69
Covert town (Seneca County), 421
Covington town (Wyoming County), 558
Cowlesville postal area (Wyoming County), 559
Coxsackie town (Greene County), 164
Coxsackie village (Greene County), 164
Cragsmoor CDP (Ulster County), 500
Craryville postal area (Columbia County), 86
Crawford town (Orange County), 323
Croghan town (Lewis County), 196
Croghan village (Lewis County), 196
Crompond CDP (Westchester County), 538
Cropseyville postal area (Rensselaer County), 366
Cross River postal area (Westchester County), 538
Croton-on-Hudson village (Westchester County), 538
Crown Heights CDP (Dutchess County), 109
Crown Point town (Essex County), 138
Crugers CDP (Westchester County), 539
Cuba town (Allegany County), 15
Cuba village (Allegany County), 14
Cuddebackville postal area (Orange County), 323
Cumberland Head CDP (Clinton County), 78
Cutchogue CDP (Suffolk County), 444
Cuyler town (Cortland County), 93

D

Dale postal area (Wyoming County), 559
Dalton postal area (Livingston County), 203
Danby town (Tompkins County), 493
Dannemora town (Clinton County), 79
Dannemora village (Clinton County), 79
Dansville town (Steuben County), 430
Dansville village (Livingston County), 203
Danube town (Herkimer County), 175
Darien Center postal area (Genesee County), 159
Darien town (Genesee County), 159

Davenport town (Delaware County), 99
Day town (Saratoga County), 400
Dayton town (Cattaraugus County), 30
De Kalb Junction postal area (Saint Lawrence County), 387
De Kalb town (Saint Lawrence County), 387
De Lancey postal area (Delaware County), 99
De Peyster town (Saint Lawrence County), 387
De Ruyter town (Madison County), 211
De Ruyter village (Madison County), 210
De Witt town (Onondaga County), 302
Deansboro postal area (Oneida County), 289
Decatur town (Otsego County), 351
Deer Park CDP (Suffolk County), 444
Deerfield town (Oneida County), 290
Deerpark town (Orange County), 323
Deferiet village (Jefferson County), 187
Delanson village (Schenectady County), 407
Delaware County, 97 - 105
Delaware town (Sullivan County), 478
Delevan village (Cattaraugus County), 30
Delhi town (Delaware County), 99
Delhi village (Delaware County), 99
Delmar CDP (Albany County), 4
Denmark town (Lewis County), 196
Denning town (Ulster County), 500
Denver postal area (Delaware County), 100
Depauville CDP (Jefferson County), 187
Depew village (Erie County), 126
Deposit town (Delaware County), 100
Deposit village (Delaware County), 100
Derby postal area (Erie County), 127
Dering Harbor village (Suffolk County), 445
Dewittville postal area (Chautauqua County), 53
Dexter village (Jefferson County), 187
Diamond Point postal area (Warren County), 516
Diana town (Lewis County), 197
Dickinson Center postal area (Franklin County), 147
Dickinson town (Broome County), 22
Dickinson town (Franklin County), 147
Dix Hills CDP (Suffolk County), 445
Dix town (Schuyler County), 419
Dobbs Ferry village (Westchester County), 539
Dolgeville village (Herkimer County), 175
Dover Plains CDP (Dutchess County), 109
Dover town (Dutchess County), 109
Downsville postal area (Delaware County), 100
Dresden town (Washington County), 522
Dresden village (Yates County), 565
Dryden town (Tompkins County), 494
Dryden village (Tompkins County), 493
Duane Lake CDP (Schenectady County), 407
Duane town (Franklin County), 147
Duanesburg CDP (Schenectady County), 408
Duanesburg town (Schenectady County), 408
Dundee village (Yates County), 565
Dunkirk city (Chautauqua County), 53
Dunkirk town (Chautauqua County), 53
Durham town (Greene County), 165
Durhamville postal area (Oneida County), 290
Dutchess County, 106 - 119

E

Eagle Bay postal area (Herkimer County), 176
Eagle Bridge postal area (Rensselaer County), 366
Eagle town (Wyoming County), 559
Earlton postal area (Greene County), 165

CDP = Census Designated Place

Earlville village (Madison County), 211
East Amherst postal area (Erie County), 127
East Atlantic Beach CDP (Nassau County), 236
East Aurora village (Erie County), 127
East Berne postal area (Albany County), 5
East Bethany postal area (Genesee County), 159
East Bloomfield town (Ontario County), 315
East Branch postal area (Delaware County), 101
East Chatham postal area (Columbia County), 87
East Concord postal area (Erie County), 127
East Durham postal area (Greene County), 165
East Farmingdale CDP (Suffolk County), 445
East Fishkill town (Dutchess County), 110
East Garden City CDP (Nassau County), 236
East Glenville CDP (Schenectady County), 408
East Greenbush CDP (Rensselaer County), 366
East Greenbush town (Rensselaer County), 366
East Hampton North CDP (Suffolk County), 446
East Hampton town (Suffolk County), 446
East Hampton village (Suffolk County), 445
East Hills village (Nassau County), 236
East Islip CDP (Suffolk County), 446
East Ithaca CDP (Tompkins County), 494
East Jewett postal area (Greene County), 165
East Kingston CDP (Ulster County), 501
East Marion CDP (Suffolk County), 446
East Massapequa CDP (Nassau County), 236
East Meadow CDP (Nassau County), 236
East Meredith postal area (Delaware County), 101
East Moriches CDP (Suffolk County), 446
East Nassau village (Rensselaer County), 367
East Northport CDP (Suffolk County), 447
East Norwich CDP (Nassau County), 237
East Otto town (Cattaraugus County), 30
East Patchogue CDP (Suffolk County), 447
East Quogue CDP (Suffolk County), 447
East Randolph village (Cattaraugus County), 30
East Rochester town and village (Monroe County), 218
East Rockaway village (Nassau County), 237
East Schodack postal area (Rensselaer County), 367
East Setauket postal area (Suffolk County), 447
East Shoreham CDP (Suffolk County), 448
East Springfield postal area (Otsego County), 352
East Syracuse village (Onondaga County), 302
East Williston village (Nassau County), 237
East Worcester postal area (Otsego County), 352
Eastchester CDP (Westchester County), 539
Eastchester town (Westchester County), 539
Easton town (Washington County), 522
Eastport CDP (Suffolk County), 448
Eaton town (Madison County), 211
Eatons Neck CDP (Suffolk County), 448
Eden CDP (Erie County), 128
Eden town (Erie County), 127
Edinburg town (Saratoga County), 400
Edmeston town (Otsego County), 352
Edwards town (Saint Lawrence County), 387

Edwards village (Saint Lawrence County), 387
Elba town (Genesee County), 159
Elba village (Genesee County), 159
Elbridge town (Onondaga County), 303
Elbridge village (Onondaga County), 302
Eldred postal area (Sullivan County), 478
Elizabethtown town (Essex County), 138
Elizaville postal area (Columbia County), 87
Elka Park postal area (Greene County), 165
Ellenburg Center postal area (Clinton County), 79
Ellenburg Depot postal area (Clinton County), 79
Ellenburg town (Clinton County), 79
Ellenville village (Ulster County), 501
Ellery town (Chautauqua County), 53
Ellicott town (Chautauqua County), 54
Ellicottville town (Cattaraugus County), 31
Ellicottville village (Cattaraugus County), 31
Ellington town (Chautauqua County), 54
Ellisburg town (Jefferson County), 188
Ellisburg village (Jefferson County), 188
Elma Center CDP (Erie County), 128
Elma town (Erie County), 128
Elmira Heights village (Chemung County), 64
Elmira city (Chemung County), 63
Elmira town (Chemung County), 64
Elmont CDP (Nassau County), 237
Elmsford village (Westchester County), 540
Elwood CDP (Suffolk County), 448
Endicott village (Broome County), 22
Endwell CDP (Broome County), 23
Enfield town (Tompkins County), 494
Ephratah town (Fulton County), 153
Erie County, 120 - 136
Erieville postal area (Madison County), 211
Erin town (Chemung County), 64
Erwin town (Steuben County), 430
Esopus town (Ulster County), 501
Esperance town (Schoharie County), 413
Esperance village (Schoharie County), 413
Essex County, 137 - 143
Essex town (Essex County), 138
Evans Mills village (Jefferson County), 188
Evans town (Erie County), 128
Exeter town (Otsego County), 352

F

Fabius town (Onondaga County), 303
Fabius village (Onondaga County), 303
Fair Haven village (Cayuga County), 43
Fairfield town (Herkimer County), 176
Fairmount CDP (Onondaga County), 303
Fairport village (Monroe County), 218
Fairview CDP (Dutchess County), 110
Fairview CDP (Westchester County), 540
Falconer village (Chautauqua County), 54
Fallsburg town (Sullivan County), 478
Farmersville Station postal area (Cattaraugus County), 31
Farmersville town (Cattaraugus County), 31
Farmingdale village (Nassau County), 238
Farmington town (Ontario County), 315
Farmingville CDP (Suffolk County), 448
Farnham village (Erie County), 129
Fayette town (Seneca County), 422
Fayetteville village (Onondaga County), 303
Felts Mills postal area (Jefferson County), 188
Fenner town (Madison County), 211
Fenton town (Broome County), 23
Ferndale postal area (Sullivan County), 479
Feura Bush postal area (Albany County), 5
Fillmore postal area (Allegany County), 15

Findley Lake postal area (Chautauqua County), 54
Fine town (Saint Lawrence County), 388
Fire Island CDP (Suffolk County), 449
Firthcliffe CDP (Orange County), 323
Fishers Island CDP (Suffolk County), 449
Fishkill town (Dutchess County), 110
Fishkill village (Dutchess County), 110
Flanders CDP (Suffolk County), 449
Fleischmanns village (Delaware County), 101
Fleming town (Cayuga County), 43
Floral Park village (Nassau County), 238
Florence town (Oneida County), 290
Florida town (Montgomery County), 227
Florida village (Orange County), 324
Flower Hill village (Nassau County), 238
Floyd town (Oneida County), 290
Fly Creek postal area (Otsego County), 352
Fonda village (Montgomery County), 228
Forest Hills postal area (Queens County), 273
Forest Home CDP (Tompkins County), 494
Forestburgh town (Sullivan County), 479
Forestport town (Oneida County), 290
Forestville village (Chautauqua County), 54
Fort Ann town (Washington County), 523
Fort Ann village (Washington County), 523
Fort Covington town (Franklin County), 148
Fort Drum CDP (Jefferson County), 188
Fort Edward town (Washington County), 523
Fort Edward village (Washington County), 523
Fort Johnson village (Montgomery County), 228
Fort Montgomery CDP (Orange County), 324
Fort Plain village (Montgomery County), 228
Fort Salonga CDP (Suffolk County), 449
Fowler town (Saint Lawrence County), 388
Frankfort town (Herkimer County), 176
Frankfort village (Herkimer County), 176
Franklin County, 144 - 151
Franklin Square CDP (Nassau County), 238
Franklin town (Delaware County), 101
Franklin town (Franklin County), 148
Franklin village (Delaware County), 101
Franklinville town (Cattaraugus County), 32
Franklinville village (Cattaraugus County), 31
Fredonia village (Chautauqua County), 55
Freedom town (Cattaraugus County), 32
Freehold postal area (Greene County), 165
Freeport village (Nassau County), 239
Freetown town (Cortland County), 93
Freeville village (Tompkins County), 495
Fremont Center postal area (Sullivan County), 479
Fremont town (Steuben County), 430
Fremont town (Sullivan County), 479
French Creek town (Chautauqua County), 55
Frewsburg CDP (Chautauqua County), 55
Friendship CDP (Allegany County), 15
Friendship town (Allegany County), 15
Fulton County, 152 - 155
Fulton city (Oswego County), 343
Fulton town (Schoharie County), 414
Fultonham postal area (Schoharie County), 414
Fultonville village (Montgomery County), 228

G

Gaines town (Orleans County), 338
Gainesville town (Wyoming County), 559
Gainesville village (Wyoming County), 559
Galen town (Wayne County), 529
Galeville CDP (Onondaga County), 304
Gallatin town (Columbia County), 87

CDP = Census Designated Place

Galway town (Saratoga County), 400
Galway village (Saratoga County), 400
Gang Mills CDP (Steuben County), 430
Gansevoort postal area (Saratoga County), 400
Garden City Park CDP (Nassau County), 239
Garden City South CDP (Nassau County), 240
Garden City village (Nassau County), 239
Gardiner CDP (Ulster County), 502
Gardiner town (Ulster County), 501
Gardnertown CDP (Orange County), 324
Garnerville postal area (Rockland County), 374
Garrattsville postal area (Otsego County), 353
Garrison postal area (Putnam County), 361
Gasport CDP (Niagara County), 279
Gates town (Monroe County), 219
Gates-North Gates CDP (Monroe County), 219
Geddes town (Onondaga County), 304
Genesee County, 156 - 160
Genesee Falls town (Wyoming County), 560
Genesee town (Allegany County), 15
Geneseo town (Livingston County), 204
Geneseo village (Livingston County), 203
Geneva city (Ontario County), 315
Geneva town (Ontario County), 316
Genoa town (Cayuga County), 43
Georgetown town (Madison County), 212
German Flatts town (Herkimer County), 176
German town (Chenango County), 69
Germantown CDP (Columbia County), 87
Germantown town (Columbia County), 87
Gerry town (Chautauqua County), 55
Getzville postal area (Erie County), 129
Ghent CDP (Columbia County), 88
Ghent town (Columbia County), 88
Gilbertsville village (Otsego County), 353
Gilboa town (Schoharie County), 414
Gilgo-Oak Beach-Captree CDP (Suffolk County), 449
Glasco CDP (Ulster County), 502
Glen Aubrey postal area (Broome County), 23
Glen Cove city (Nassau County), 240
Glen Head CDP (Nassau County), 240
Glen Park village (Jefferson County), 189
Glen Spey postal area (Sullivan County), 479
Glen Wild postal area (Sullivan County), 480
Glen town (Montgomery County), 229
Glenfield postal area (Lewis County), 197
Glenford postal area (Ulster County), 502
Glenmont postal area (Albany County), 5
Glens Falls North CDP (Warren County), 516
Glens Falls city (Warren County), 516
Glenville town (Schenectady County), 408
Glenwood Landing CDP (Nassau County), 240
Glenwood postal area (Erie County), 129
Gloversville city (Fulton County), 153
Godeffroy postal area (Orange County), 324
Golden's Bridge CDP (Westchester County), 540
Gordon Heights CDP (Suffolk County), 450
Gorham town (Ontario County), 316
Goshen town (Orange County), 325
Goshen village (Orange County), 324
Gouverneur town (Saint Lawrence County), 388
Gouverneur village (Saint Lawrence County), 388
Gowanda village (Cattaraugus County), 32
Grafton town (Rensselaer County), 367
Grahamsville postal area (Sullivan County), 480

Granby town (Oswego County), 343
Grand Gorge postal area (Delaware County), 102
Grand Island town (Erie County), 129
Grand View-on-Hudson village (Rockland County), 375
Granger town (Allegany County), 16
Granite Springs postal area (Westchester County), 540
Granville town (Washington County), 524
Granville village (Washington County), 524
Great Bend CDP (Jefferson County), 189
Great Neck Estates village (Nassau County), 241
Great Neck Gardens CDP (Nassau County), 241
Great Neck Plaza village (Nassau County), 241
Great Neck village (Nassau County), 241
Great River CDP (Suffolk County), 450
Great Valley town (Cattaraugus County), 32
Greece CDP (Monroe County), 219
Greece town (Monroe County), 219
Green Island town and village (Albany County), 5
Greenburgh town (Westchester County), 541
Greene County, 161 - 170
Greene town (Chenango County), 70
Greene village (Chenango County), 69
Greenfield Center postal area (Saratoga County), 401
Greenfield Park postal area (Ulster County), 502
Greenfield town (Saratoga County), 401
Greenlawn CDP (Suffolk County), 450
Greenport West CDP (Suffolk County), 451
Greenport town (Columbia County), 88
Greenport village (Suffolk County), 450
Greenvale CDP (Nassau County), 242
Greenville CDP (Greene County), 166
Greenville CDP (Westchester County), 541
Greenville town (Greene County), 166
Greenville town (Orange County), 325
Greenwich town (Washington County), 524
Greenwich village (Washington County), 524
Greenwood Lake village (Orange County), 325
Greenwood town (Steuben County), 430
Greig town (Lewis County), 197
Groton town (Tompkins County), 495
Groton village (Tompkins County), 495
Grove town (Allegany County), 16
Groveland town (Livingston County), 204
Guilderland town (Albany County), 5
Guilford town (Chenango County), 70

H

Hadley town (Saratoga County), 401
Hagaman village (Montgomery County), 229
Hague town (Warren County), 517
Halcott town (Greene County), 166
Halesite CDP (Suffolk County), 451
Halfmoon town (Saratoga County), 401
Hamburg town (Erie County), 130
Hamburg village (Erie County), 129
Hamden town (Delaware County), 102
Hamilton County, 171 - 173
Hamilton town (Madison County), 212
Hamilton village (Madison County), 212
Hamlin town (Monroe County), 219
Hammond town (Saint Lawrence County), 389
Hammond village (Saint Lawrence County), 389

Hammondsport village (Steuben County), 431
Hampton Bays CDP (Suffolk County), 451
Hampton Manor CDP (Rensselaer County), 367
Hampton town (Washington County), 525
Hamptonburgh town (Orange County), 325
Hancock town (Delaware County), 102
Hancock village (Delaware County), 102
Hankins postal area (Sullivan County), 480
Hannacroix postal area (Greene County), 166
Hannibal town (Oswego County), 344
Hannibal village (Oswego County), 343
Hanover town (Chautauqua County), 56
Harbor Hills CDP (Nassau County), 242
Harbor Isle CDP (Nassau County), 242
Hardenburgh town (Ulster County), 502
Harford town (Cortland County), 94
Harmony town (Chautauqua County), 56
Harpersfield town (Delaware County), 102
Harpursville postal area (Broome County), 23
Harrietstown town (Franklin County), 148
Harriman village (Orange County), 326
Harris Hill CDP (Erie County), 130
Harris postal area (Sullivan County), 480
Harrisburg town (Lewis County), 197
Harrison town (Westchester County), 541
Harrison village (Westchester County), 541
Harrisville village (Lewis County), 197
Hartford town (Washington County), 525
Hartland town (Niagara County), 279
Hartsdale CDP (Westchester County), 541
Hartsville town (Steuben County), 431
Hartwick town (Otsego County), 353
Hastings town (Oswego County), 344
Hastings-on-Hudson village (Westchester County), 542
Hauppauge CDP (Suffolk County), 451
Haverstraw town (Rockland County), 375
Haverstraw village (Rockland County), 375
Haviland CDP (Dutchess County), 110
Hawthorne CDP (Westchester County), 542
Head of the Harbor village (Suffolk County), 451
Hebron town (Washington County), 525
Hector town (Schuyler County), 419
Hemlock postal area (Livingston County), 204
Hempstead town (Nassau County), 243
Hempstead village (Nassau County), 242
Henderson town (Jefferson County), 189
Henrietta town (Monroe County), 220
Hensonville postal area (Greene County), 166
Heritage Hills CDP (Westchester County), 542
Herkimer County, 174 - 181
Herkimer town (Herkimer County), 177
Herkimer village (Herkimer County), 177
Hermon town (Saint Lawrence County), 389
Hermon village (Saint Lawrence County), 389
Herricks CDP (Nassau County), 243
Herrings village (Jefferson County), 189
Heuvelton village (Saint Lawrence County), 389
Hewlett Bay Park village (Nassau County), 243
Hewlett Harbor village (Nassau County), 244
Hewlett Neck village (Nassau County), 244
Hewlett CDP (Nassau County), 243
Hicksville CDP (Nassau County), 244
High Falls CDP (Ulster County), 503
Highland Falls village (Orange County), 326
Highland Lake postal area (Sullivan County), 481
Highland Mills CDP (Orange County), 326
Highland CDP (Ulster County), 503

CDP = Census Designated Place

Highland town (Sullivan County), 480
Highlands town (Orange County), 326
Hillburn village (Rockland County), 375
Hillcrest CDP (Rockland County), 376
Hillsdale town (Columbia County), 88
Hillside Lake CDP (Dutchess County), 111
Hillside CDP (Ulster County), 503
Hilton village (Monroe County), 220
Himrod postal area (Yates County), 565
Hinsdale town (Cattaraugus County), 33
Hobart village (Delaware County), 103
Hoffmeister postal area (Hamilton County), 172
Hogansburg postal area (Franklin County), 148
Holbrook CDP (Suffolk County), 452
Holland Patent village (Oneida County), 291
Holland CDP (Erie County), 130
Holland town (Erie County), 130
Holley village (Orleans County), 338
Hollis postal area (Queens County), 273
Holmes postal area (Dutchess County), 111
Holtsville CDP (Suffolk County), 452
Homer town (Cortland County), 94
Homer village (Cortland County), 94
Honeoye Falls village (Monroe County), 220
Honeoye postal area (Ontario County), 316
Hoosick Falls village (Rensselaer County), 368
Hoosick town (Rensselaer County), 367
Hope town (Hamilton County), 172
Hopewell Junction CDP (Dutchess County), 111
Hopewell town (Ontario County), 316
Hopkinton town (Saint Lawrence County), 390
Horicon town (Warren County), 517
Hornby town (Steuben County), 431
Hornell city (Steuben County), 431
Hornellsville town (Steuben County), 432
Horseheads North CDP (Chemung County), 65
Horseheads town (Chemung County), 65
Horseheads village (Chemung County), 65
Houghton CDP (Allegany County), 16
Hounsfield town (Jefferson County), 190
Howard Beach postal area (Queens County), 273
Howard town (Steuben County), 432
Howes Cave postal area (Schoharie County), 414
Hubbardsville postal area (Madison County), 212
Hudson Falls village (Washington County), 525
Hudson city (Columbia County), 88
Huguenot postal area (Orange County), 327
Hume town (Allegany County), 16
Humphrey town (Cattaraugus County), 33
Hunt postal area (Livingston County), 204
Hunter town (Greene County), 167
Hunter village (Greene County), 167
Huntington Bay village (Suffolk County), 453
Huntington Station CDP (Suffolk County), 453
Huntington CDP (Suffolk County), 453
Huntington town (Suffolk County), 452
Hurley CDP (Ulster County), 503
Hurley town (Ulster County), 503
Hurleyville postal area (Sullivan County), 481
Huron town (Wayne County), 529
Hyde Park town (Dutchess County), 111

I

Ilion village (Herkimer County), 177
Independence town (Allegany County), 16
Indian Lake town (Hamilton County), 172
Inlet town (Hamilton County), 172
Interlaken village (Seneca County), 422
Inwood CDP (Nassau County), 244
Ionia postal area (Ontario County), 316
Ira town (Cayuga County), 44
Irondequoit CDP and town (Monroe County), 220
Irving postal area (Chautauqua County), 56
Irvington village (Westchester County), 542
Ischua town (Cattaraugus County), 33
Island Park village (Nassau County), 245
Islandia village (Suffolk County), 453
Islip Terrace CDP (Suffolk County), 454
Islip CDP (Suffolk County), 454
Islip town (Suffolk County), 453
Italy town (Yates County), 565
Ithaca city (Tompkins County), 495
Ithaca town (Tompkins County), 496

J

Jackson Heights postal area (Queens County), 274
Jackson town (Washington County), 525
Jamesport CDP (Suffolk County), 454
Jamestown West CDP (Chautauqua County), 57
Jamestown city (Chautauqua County), 56
Jamesville postal area (Onondaga County), 304
Jasper town (Steuben County), 432
Java Center postal area (Wyoming County), 560
Java Village postal area (Wyoming County), 560
Java town (Wyoming County), 560
Jay town (Essex County), 139
Jefferson County, 182 - 194
Jefferson Heights CDP (Greene County), 167
Jefferson Valley-Yorktown CDP (Westchester County), 543
Jefferson town (Schoharie County), 414
Jeffersonville village (Sullivan County), 481
Jericho CDP (Nassau County), 245
Jerusalem town (Yates County), 565
Jewett town (Greene County), 167
Johnsburg town (Warren County), 517
Johnson City village (Broome County), 23
Johnsonville postal area (Rensselaer County), 368
Johnstown city (Fulton County), 154
Johnstown town (Fulton County), 154
Jordan village (Onondaga County), 304
Jordanville postal area (Herkimer County), 177
Junius town (Seneca County), 422

K

Kaser village (Rockland County), 376
Katonah postal area (Westchester County), 543
Kattskill Bay postal area (Warren County), 517
Keene Valley postal area (Essex County), 139
Keene town (Essex County), 139
Keeseville village (Clinton County), 80
Kendall town (Orleans County), 338
Kenmore village (Erie County), 131
Kennedy postal area (Chautauqua County), 57
Kensington village (Nassau County), 245
Kent postal area (Orleans County), 339
Kent town (Putnam County), 362
Kerhonkson CDP (Ulster County), 504
Keuka Park postal area (Yates County), 566
Kew Gardens postal area (Queens County), 274
Kiamesha Lake postal area (Sullivan County), 481
Kiantone town (Chautauqua County), 57
Kill Buck postal area (Cattaraugus County), 33
Kinderhook town (Columbia County), 89
Kinderhook village (Columbia County), 89
King Ferry postal area (Cayuga County), 44
Kings County see Brooklyn
Kings Park CDP (Suffolk County), 454
Kings Point village (Nassau County), 245
Kingsbury town (Washington County), 526
Kingston city (Ulster County), 504
Kingston town (Ulster County), 504
Kirkland town (Oneida County), 291
Kirkville postal area (Onondaga County), 305
Kirkwood town (Broome County), 24
Kiryas Joel village (Orange County), 327
Knox town (Albany County), 6
Kortright town (Delaware County), 103

L

La Fargeville CDP (Jefferson County), 190
La Fayette postal area (Onondaga County), 305
La Fayette town (Onondaga County), 305
La Grange town (Dutchess County), 112
Lackawanna city (Erie County), 131
Lacona village (Oswego County), 344
Lagrangeville postal area (Dutchess County), 112
Lake Carmel CDP (Putnam County), 362
Lake Clear postal area (Franklin County), 148
Lake Erie Beach CDP (Erie County), 131
Lake George town (Warren County), 518
Lake George village (Warren County), 517
Lake Grove village (Suffolk County), 455
Lake Hill postal area (Ulster County), 504
Lake Huntington postal area (Sullivan County), 481
Lake Katrine CDP (Ulster County), 505
Lake Luzerne town (Warren County), 518
Lake Luzerne-Hadley CDP (Warren County), 518
Lake Mohegan CDP (Westchester County), 543
Lake Peekskill postal area (Putnam County), 362
Lake Placid village (Essex County), 139
Lake Pleasant town (Hamilton County), 173
Lake Ronkonkoma CDP (Suffolk County), 455
Lake Success village (Nassau County), 246
Lake View postal area (Erie County), 131
Lakeland CDP (Onondaga County), 305
Lakeview CDP (Nassau County), 246
Lakeville postal area (Livingston County), 204
Lakewood village (Chautauqua County), 57
Lancaster town (Erie County), 132
Lancaster village (Erie County), 132
Lanesville postal area (Greene County), 168
Lansing town (Tompkins County), 496
Lansing village (Tompkins County), 496
Lapeer town (Cortland County), 94
Larchmont village (Westchester County), 543
Lattingtown village (Nassau County), 246
Laurel Hollow village (Nassau County), 246
Laurel CDP (Suffolk County), 455
Laurens town (Otsego County), 353
Laurens village (Otsego County), 353
Lawrence town (Saint Lawrence County), 390

CDP = Census Designated Place

Lawrence village (Nassau County), 247
Lawtons postal area (Erie County), 132
Le Ray town (Jefferson County), 190
Le Roy town (Genesee County), 160
Le Roy village (Genesee County), 160
Lebanon town (Madison County), 213
Ledyard town (Cayuga County), 44
Lee Center postal area (Oneida County), 291
Lee town (Oneida County), 291
Leeds CDP (Greene County), 168
Leicester town (Livingston County), 205
Leicester village (Livingston County), 205
Lenox town (Madison County), 213
Leon town (Cattaraugus County), 33
Levittown CDP (Nassau County), 247
Lewis County, 195 - 200
Lewis town (Essex County), 140
Lewis town (Lewis County), 198
Lewisboro town (Westchester County), 544
Lewiston town (Niagara County), 280
Lewiston village (Niagara County), 279
Lexington town (Greene County), 168
Leyden town (Lewis County), 198
Liberty town (Sullivan County), 482
Liberty village (Sullivan County), 482
Lido Beach CDP (Nassau County), 247
Lima town (Livingston County), 205
Lima village (Livingston County), 205
Lime Lake-Machias CDP (Cattaraugus County), 34
Limestone village (Cattaraugus County), 34
Lincklaen town (Chenango County), 70
Lincoln Park CDP (Ulster County), 505
Lincoln town (Madison County), 213
Lincolndale CDP (Westchester County), 544
Lindenhurst village (Suffolk County), 455
Lindley town (Steuben County), 432
Lisbon town (Saint Lawrence County), 390
Lisle town (Broome County), 24
Lisle village (Broome County), 24
Litchfield town (Herkimer County), 178
Little Falls city (Herkimer County), 178
Little Falls town (Herkimer County), 178
Little Genesee postal area (Allegany County), 17
Little Valley town (Cattaraugus County), 34
Little Valley village (Cattaraugus County), 34
Liverpool village (Onondaga County), 305
Livingston County, 201 - 208
Livingston Manor CDP (Sullivan County), 482
Livingston town (Columbia County), 89
Livonia town (Livingston County), 206
Livonia village (Livingston County), 206
Lloyd Harbor village (Suffolk County), 455
Lloyd town (Ulster County), 505
Loch Sheldrake postal area (Sullivan County), 482
Locke town (Cayuga County), 44
Lockport city (Niagara County), 280
Lockport town (Niagara County), 280
Lockwood postal area (Tioga County), 489
Locust Valley CDP (Nassau County), 247
Lodi town (Seneca County), 422
Lodi village (Seneca County), 422
Long Beach city (Nassau County), 248
Long Eddy postal area (Sullivan County), 483
Long Lake town (Hamilton County), 173
Lorenz Park CDP (Columbia County), 89
Lorraine town (Jefferson County), 190
Louisville town (Saint Lawrence County), 390
Lowman postal area (Chemung County), 65
Lowville town (Lewis County), 198
Lowville village (Lewis County), 198
Lumberland town (Sullivan County), 483
Lyme town (Jefferson County), 190

Lynbrook village (Nassau County), 248
Lyncourt CDP (Onondaga County), 306
Lyndon town (Cattaraugus County), 34
Lyndonville village (Orleans County), 339
Lyon Mountain CDP (Clinton County), 80
Lyons Falls village (Lewis County), 199
Lyons town (Wayne County), 529
Lyons village (Wayne County), 529
Lyonsdale town (Lewis County), 199
Lysander town (Onondaga County), 306

M

Macedon town (Wayne County), 530
Macedon village (Wayne County), 529
Machias town (Cattaraugus County), 35
Macomb town (Saint Lawrence County), 391
Madison County, 209 - 215
Madison town (Madison County), 213
Madison village (Madison County), 213
Madrid town (Saint Lawrence County), 391
Mahopac CDP (Putnam County), 362
Maine town (Broome County), 24
Malden Bridge postal area (Columbia County), 90
Malden CDP (Ulster County), 505
Malone town (Franklin County), 149
Malone village (Franklin County), 149
Malta town (Saratoga County), 401
Malverne Park Oaks CDP (Nassau County), 248
Malverne village (Nassau County), 248
Mamakating town (Sullivan County), 483
Mamaroneck town (Westchester County), 544
Mamaroneck village (Westchester County), 544
Manchester town (Ontario County), 317
Manchester village (Ontario County), 317
Manhasset Hills CDP (Nassau County), 249
Manhasset CDP (Nassau County), 249
Manhattan borough (New York County), 268
Manheim town (Herkimer County), 178
Manlius town (Onondaga County), 306
Manlius village (Onondaga County), 306
Mannsville village (Jefferson County), 191
Manorhaven village (Nassau County), 249
Manorville CDP (Suffolk County), 456
Mansfield town (Cattaraugus County), 35
Maplecrest postal area (Greene County), 168
Marathon town (Cortland County), 95
Marathon village (Cortland County), 95
Marbletown town (Ulster County), 505
Marcellus town (Onondaga County), 307
Marcellus village (Onondaga County), 307
Marcy town (Oneida County), 291
Margaretville village (Delaware County), 103
Mariaville Lake CDP (Schenectady County), 408
Marietta postal area (Onondaga County), 307
Marilla town (Erie County), 132
Marion town (Wayne County), 530
Marlboro CDP (Ulster County), 506
Marlborough town (Ulster County), 506
Marshall town (Oneida County), 292
Martinsburg town (Lewis County), 199
Martville postal area (Cayuga County), 44
Maryland town (Otsego County), 354
Masonville town (Delaware County), 103
Maspeth postal area (Queens County), 274
Massapequa Park village (Nassau County), 250
Massapequa CDP (Nassau County), 249
Massena town (Saint Lawrence County), 391
Massena village (Saint Lawrence County), 391
Mastic Beach CDP (Suffolk County), 456

Mastic CDP (Suffolk County), 456
Matinecock village (Nassau County), 250
Mattituck CDP (Suffolk County), 456
Mattydale CDP (Onondaga County), 307
Maybrook village (Orange County), 327
Mayfield town (Fulton County), 155
Mayfield village (Fulton County), 154
Mayville village (Chautauqua County), 57
McDonough town (Chenango County), 70
McGraw village (Cortland County), 95
Mechanicstown CDP (Orange County), 327
Mechanicville city (Saratoga County), 402
Medford CDP (Suffolk County), 457
Medina village (Orleans County), 339
Medusa CDP (Albany County), 6
Melrose Park CDP (Cayuga County), 45
Melrose postal area (Rensselaer County), 368
Melville CDP (Suffolk County), 457
Memphis postal area (Onondaga County), 308
Menands village (Albany County), 6
Mendon town (Monroe County), 221
Mentz town (Cayuga County), 45
Meredith town (Delaware County), 103
Meridian village (Cayuga County), 45
Merrick CDP (Nassau County), 250
Mexico town (Oswego County), 344
Mexico village (Oswego County), 344
Middle Granville postal area (Washington County), 526
Middle Grove postal area (Saratoga County), 402
Middle Island CDP (Suffolk County), 457
Middle Village postal area (Queens County), 274
Middleburgh town (Schoharie County), 415
Middleburgh village (Schoharie County), 415
Middlebury town (Wyoming County), 560
Middlefield town (Otsego County), 354
Middleport village (Niagara County), 280
Middlesex town (Yates County), 566
Middletown city (Orange County), 327
Middletown town (Delaware County), 104
Middleville village (Herkimer County), 179
Milan town (Dutchess County), 112
Milford town (Otsego County), 354
Milford village (Otsego County), 354
Mill Neck village (Nassau County), 250
Millbrook village (Dutchess County), 112
Miller Place CDP (Suffolk County), 457
Millerton village (Dutchess County), 112
Millport village (Chemung County), 65
Millwood postal area (Westchester County), 545
Milo town (Yates County), 566
Milton CDP (Saratoga County), 402
Milton CDP (Ulster County), 506
Milton town (Saratoga County), 402
Mina town (Chautauqua County), 58
Minden town (Montgomery County), 229
Mineola village (Nassau County), 251
Minerva town (Essex County), 140
Minetto CDP (Oswego County), 345
Minetto town (Oswego County), 345
Mineville-Witherbee CDP (Essex County), 140
Minisink town (Orange County), 328
Minoa village (Onondaga County), 308
Modena postal area (Ulster County), 506
Mohawk town (Montgomery County), 229
Mohawk village (Herkimer County), 179
Mohegan Lake postal area (Westchester County), 545
Moira town (Franklin County), 149
Mongaup Valley postal area (Sullivan County), 483

CDP = Census Designated Place

PROFILES OF NEW YORK / Alphabetical Place Index

Monroe County, 216 - 225
Monroe town (Orange County), 328
Monroe village (Orange County), 328
Monsey CDP (Rockland County), 376
Montague town (Lewis County), 199
Montauk CDP (Suffolk County), 457
Montebello village (Rockland County), 376
Montezuma town (Cayuga County), 45
Montgomery County, 226 - 230
Montgomery town (Orange County), 329
Montgomery village (Orange County), 329
Monticello village (Sullivan County), 483
Montour Falls village (Schuyler County), 420
Montour town (Schuyler County), 419
Montrose postal area (Westchester County), 545
Mooers Forks postal area (Clinton County), 80
Mooers CDP (Clinton County), 80
Mooers town (Clinton County), 80
Moravia town (Cayuga County), 46
Moravia village (Cayuga County), 45
Moreau town (Saratoga County), 403
Morehouse town (Hamilton County), 173
Moriah Center postal area (Essex County), 140
Moriah town (Essex County), 140
Moriches CDP (Suffolk County), 458
Morris town (Otsego County), 355
Morris village (Otsego County), 354
Morrisonville CDP (Clinton County), 81
Morristown town (Saint Lawrence County), 392
Morristown village (Saint Lawrence County), 391
Morrisville village (Madison County), 214
Mount Hope town (Orange County), 329
Mount Ivy CDP (Rockland County), 377
Mount Kisco town and village (Westchester County), 545
Mount Marion postal area (Ulster County), 506
Mount Morris town (Livingston County), 206
Mount Morris village (Livingston County), 206
Mount Pleasant town (Westchester County), 546
Mount Sinai CDP (Suffolk County), 458
Mount Tremper postal area (Ulster County), 507
Mount Upton postal area (Chenango County), 70
Mount Vernon city (Westchester County), 546
Mount Vision postal area (Otsego County), 355
Mountain Dale postal area (Sullivan County), 484
Munnsville village (Madison County), 214
Munsey Park village (Nassau County), 251
Munsons Corners CDP (Cortland County), 95
Murray town (Orleans County), 339
Muttontown village (Nassau County), 251
Myers Corner CDP (Dutchess County), 113

N

Nanticoke town (Broome County), 25
Nanuet CDP (Rockland County), 377
Napanoch CDP (Ulster County), 507
Napeague CDP (Suffolk County), 458
Naples town (Ontario County), 317
Naples village (Ontario County), 317
Napoli town (Cattaraugus County), 35
Narrowsburg CDP (Sullivan County), 484
Nassau County, 231 - 264
Nassau town (Rensselaer County), 369
Nassau village (Rensselaer County), 368
Natural Bridge CDP (Jefferson County), 191
Nedrow CDP (Onondaga County), 308
Nelliston village (Montgomery County), 229
Nelson town (Madison County), 214
Nelsonville village (Putnam County), 363
Nesconset CDP (Suffolk County), 458
Neversink town (Sullivan County), 484
New Albion town (Cattaraugus County), 35
New Baltimore town (Greene County), 168
New Berlin town (Chenango County), 71
New Berlin village (Chenango County), 71
New Bremen town (Lewis County), 199
New Cassel CDP (Nassau County), 251
New Castle town (Westchester County), 546
New City CDP (Rockland County), 377
New Hampton postal area (Orange County), 329
New Hartford town (Oneida County), 292
New Hartford village (Oneida County), 292
New Haven town (Oswego County), 345
New Hempstead village (Rockland County), 377
New Hudson town (Allegany County), 17
New Hyde Park village (Nassau County), 252
New Lebanon town (Columbia County), 90
New Lisbon town (Otsego County), 355
New Paltz town (Ulster County), 507
New Paltz village (Ulster County), 507
New Rochelle city (Westchester County), 546
New Russia postal area (Essex County), 141
New Scotland town (Albany County), 6
New Square village (Rockland County), 378
New Suffolk CDP (Suffolk County), 459
New Windsor CDP (Orange County), 330
New Windsor town (Orange County), 329
New Woodstock postal area (Madison County), 214
New York City, 265 - 276
New York Mills village (Oneida County), 292
Newark Valley town (Tioga County), 490
Newark Valley village (Tioga County), 489
Newark village (Wayne County), 530
Newburgh city (Orange County), 330
Newburgh town (Orange County), 330
Newcomb town (Essex County), 141
Newfane CDP (Niagara County), 281
Newfane town (Niagara County), 281
Newfield Hamlet CDP (Tompkins County), 497
Newfield town (Tompkins County), 496
Newport town (Herkimer County), 179
Newport village (Herkimer County), 179
Newstead town (Erie County), 133
Niagara County, 277 - 284
Niagara Falls city (Niagara County), 281
Niagara town (Niagara County), 281
Nichols town (Tioga County), 490
Nichols village (Tioga County), 490
Nicholville postal area (Saint Lawrence County), 392
Niles town (Cayuga County), 46
Nineveh postal area (Broome County), 25
Niskayuna CDP (Schenectady County), 409
Niskayuna town (Schenectady County), 409
Nissequogue village (Suffolk County), 459
Niverville CDP (Columbia County), 90
Norfolk town (Saint Lawrence County), 392
North Amityville CDP (Suffolk County), 459
North Babylon CDP (Suffolk County), 459
North Ballston Spa CDP (Saratoga County), 403
North Bangor postal area (Franklin County), 149
North Bay Shore CDP (Suffolk County), 459
North Bellmore CDP (Nassau County), 252
North Bellport CDP (Suffolk County), 460
North Blenheim postal area (Schoharie County), 415
North Boston CDP (Erie County), 133
North Branch postal area (Sullivan County), 484
North Brookfield postal area (Madison County), 214
North Castle town (Westchester County), 547
North Chili postal area (Monroe County), 221
North Collins town (Erie County), 133
North Collins village (Erie County), 133
North Creek postal area (Warren County), 518
North Dansville town (Livingston County), 206
North East town (Dutchess County), 113
North Elba town (Essex County), 141
North Great River CDP (Suffolk County), 460
North Greenbush town (Rensselaer County), 369
North Harmony town (Chautauqua County), 58
North Haven village (Suffolk County), 460
North Hempstead town (Nassau County), 252
North Hills village (Nassau County), 252
North Hornell village (Steuben County), 433
North Hudson town (Essex County), 141
North Java postal area (Wyoming County), 560
North Lawrence postal area (Saint Lawrence County), 392
North Lindenhurst CDP (Suffolk County), 460
North Lynbrook CDP (Nassau County), 253
North Massapequa CDP (Nassau County), 253
North Merrick CDP (Nassau County), 253
North New Hyde Park CDP (Nassau County), 253
North Norwich town (Chenango County), 71
North Patchogue CDP (Suffolk County), 460
North Pitcher postal area (Chenango County), 71
North Rose postal area (Wayne County), 531
North Salem town (Westchester County), 547
North Sea CDP (Suffolk County), 461
North Syracuse village (Onondaga County), 308
North Tonawanda city (Niagara County), 282
North Valley Stream CDP (Nassau County), 253
North Wantagh CDP (Nassau County), 254
Northampton CDP (Suffolk County), 461
Northampton town (Fulton County), 155
Northeast Ithaca CDP (Tompkins County), 497
Northport village (Suffolk County), 461
Northumberland town (Saratoga County), 403
Northville CDP (Suffolk County), 461
Northville village (Fulton County), 155
Northwest Harbor CDP (Suffolk County), 462
Northwest Ithaca CDP (Tompkins County), 497
Norway town (Herkimer County), 179
Norwich city (Chenango County), 71
Norwich town (Chenango County), 72
Norwood village (Saint Lawrence County), 393
Noyack CDP (Suffolk County), 462
Nunda town (Livingston County), 207
Nunda village (Livingston County), 207
Nyack village (Rockland County), 378

CDP = Census Designated Place

O

Oak Hill postal area (Greene County), 168
Oakdale CDP (Suffolk County), 462
Oakfield town (Genesee County), 160
Oakfield village (Genesee County), 160
Oakland Gardens postal area (Queens County), 274
Ocean Beach village (Suffolk County), 462
Oceanside CDP (Nassau County), 254
Odessa village (Schuyler County), 420
Ogden town (Monroe County), 221
Ogdensburg city (Saint Lawrence County), 393
Ohio town (Herkimer County), 180
Olcott CDP (Niagara County), 282
Old Bethpage CDP (Nassau County), 254
Old Brookville village (Nassau County), 254
Old Chatham postal area (Columbia County), 90
Old Field village (Suffolk County), 462
Old Forge postal area (Herkimer County), 180
Old Westbury village (Nassau County), 254
Olean city (Cattaraugus County), 35
Olean town (Cattaraugus County), 36
Olive town (Ulster County), 508
Olivebridge postal area (Ulster County), 508
Olmstedville postal area (Essex County), 142
Oneida Castle village (Oneida County), 293
Oneida County, 285 - 299
Oneida city (Madison County), 215
Oneonta city (Otsego County), 355
Oneonta town (Otsego County), 356
Onondaga County, 300 - 312
Onondaga Reservation reservation (Onondaga County), 309
Onondaga town (Onondaga County), 308
Ontario County, 313 - 319
Ontario town (Wayne County), 531
Oppenheim town (Fulton County), 155
Orange County, 320 - 335
Orange Lake CDP (Orange County), 331
Orange town (Schuyler County), 420
Orangeburg CDP (Rockland County), 378
Orangetown town (Rockland County), 378
Orangeville town (Wyoming County), 561
Orchard Park town (Erie County), 134
Orchard Park village (Erie County), 133
Orient CDP (Suffolk County), 463
Oriskany Falls village (Oneida County), 293
Oriskany village (Oneida County), 293
Orleans County, 336 - 339
Orleans town (Jefferson County), 191
Orwell town (Oswego County), 345
Osceola town (Lewis County), 200
Ossian town (Livingston County), 207
Ossining town (Westchester County), 548
Ossining village (Westchester County), 547
Oswegatchie town (Saint Lawrence County), 393
Oswego County, 340 - 349
Oswego city (Oswego County), 345
Oswego town (Oswego County), 346
Otego town (Otsego County), 356
Otego village (Otsego County), 356
Otisco town (Onondaga County), 309
Otisville village (Orange County), 331
Otsego County, 350 - 359
Otsego town (Otsego County), 356
Otselic town (Chenango County), 72
Otto town (Cattaraugus County), 36
Ovid town (Seneca County), 423
Ovid village (Seneca County), 423
Owasco town (Cayuga County), 46
Owego town (Tioga County), 491
Owego village (Tioga County), 490
Owls Head postal area (Franklin County), 150
Oxford town (Chenango County), 72
Oxford village (Chenango County), 72
Oyster Bay Cove village (Nassau County), 255
Oyster Bay CDP (Nassau County), 255
Oyster Bay town (Nassau County), 255

P

Painted Post village (Steuben County), 433
Palatine Bridge village (Montgomery County), 230
Palatine town (Montgomery County), 230
Palenville CDP (Greene County), 169
Palermo town (Oswego County), 346
Palisades postal area (Rockland County), 379
Palmyra town (Wayne County), 531
Palmyra village (Wayne County), 531
Pamelia town (Jefferson County), 191
Panama village (Chautauqua County), 58
Paradox postal area (Essex County), 142
Parc CDP (Clinton County), 81
Paris town (Oneida County), 293
Parish town (Oswego County), 347
Parish village (Oswego County), 346
Parishville town (Saint Lawrence County), 393
Parksville postal area (Sullivan County), 484
Parma town (Monroe County), 221
Patchogue village (Suffolk County), 463
Patterson town (Putnam County), 363
Pattersonville postal area (Schenectady County), 409
Pattersonville-Rotterdam Junction CDP (Schenectady County), 409
Paul Smiths postal area (Franklin County), 150
Pavilion town (Genesee County), 161
Pawling town (Dutchess County), 113
Pawling village (Dutchess County), 113
Peach Lake CDP (Putnam County), 363
Pearl River CDP (Rockland County), 379
Peconic CDP (Suffolk County), 463
Peekskill city (Westchester County), 548
Pelham Manor village (Westchester County), 549
Pelham town (Westchester County), 549
Pelham village (Westchester County), 548
Pembroke town (Genesee County), 161
Pendleton town (Niagara County), 282
Penfield town (Monroe County), 222
Penn Yan village (Yates County), 566
Pennellville postal area (Oswego County), 347
Perinton town (Monroe County), 222
Perry town (Wyoming County), 561
Perry village (Wyoming County), 561
Perrysburg town (Cattaraugus County), 37
Perrysburg village (Cattaraugus County), 36
Persia town (Cattaraugus County), 37
Perth town (Fulton County), 155
Peru CDP (Clinton County), 81
Peru town (Clinton County), 81
Petersburgh town (Rensselaer County), 369
Pharsalia town (Chenango County), 73
Phelps town (Ontario County), 318
Phelps village (Ontario County), 317
Philadelphia town (Jefferson County), 192
Philadelphia village (Jefferson County), 191
Philipstown town (Putnam County), 363
Philmont village (Columbia County), 90
Phoenicia CDP (Ulster County), 508
Phoenix village (Oswego County), 347
Piercefield town (Saint Lawrence County), 394
Piermont village (Rockland County), 379
Pierrepont town (Saint Lawrence County), 394
Piffard postal area (Livingston County), 207
Pike town (Wyoming County), 562
Pike village (Wyoming County), 561
Pinckney town (Lewis County), 200
Pine Bush CDP (Orange County), 331
Pine City postal area (Chemung County), 66
Pine Hill CDP (Ulster County), 508
Pine Island postal area (Orange County), 331
Pine Plains CDP (Dutchess County), 114
Pine Plains town (Dutchess County), 114
Pine Valley postal area (Chemung County), 66
Piseco postal area (Hamilton County), 173
Pitcairn town (Saint Lawrence County), 394
Pitcher town (Chenango County), 73
Pittsfield town (Otsego County), 356
Pittsford town (Monroe County), 222
Pittsford village (Monroe County), 222
Pittstown town (Rensselaer County), 369
Plainedge CDP (Nassau County), 256
Plainfield town (Otsego County), 357
Plainview CDP (Nassau County), 256
Plandome Heights village (Nassau County), 256
Plandome Manor village (Nassau County), 256
Plandome village (Nassau County), 256
Plattekill CDP (Ulster County), 509
Plattekill town (Ulster County), 508
Plattsburgh West CDP (Clinton County), 82
Plattsburgh city (Clinton County), 81
Plattsburgh town (Clinton County), 82
Pleasant Valley CDP (Dutchess County), 114
Pleasant Valley town (Dutchess County), 114
Pleasantville village (Westchester County), 549
Plessis postal area (Jefferson County), 192
Plymouth town (Chenango County), 73
Poestenkill CDP (Rensselaer County), 370
Poestenkill town (Rensselaer County), 369
Point Lookout CDP (Nassau County), 257
Poland town (Chautauqua County), 58
Poland village (Herkimer County), 180
Pomfret town (Chautauqua County), 58
Pomona village (Rockland County), 379
Pompey town (Onondaga County), 309
Pond Eddy postal area (Sullivan County), 485
Poospatuck Reservation reservation (Suffolk County), 463
Poquott village (Suffolk County), 464
Port Byron village (Cayuga County), 46
Port Chester village (Westchester County), 549
Port Crane postal area (Broome County), 25
Port Dickinson village (Broome County), 25
Port Ewen CDP (Ulster County), 509
Port Henry village (Essex County), 142
Port Jefferson Station CDP (Suffolk County), 464
Port Jefferson village (Suffolk County), 464
Port Jervis city (Orange County), 331
Port Leyden village (Lewis County), 200
Port Washington North village (Nassau County), 257
Port Washington CDP (Nassau County), 257
Portage town (Livingston County), 207
Portageville postal area (Wyoming County), 562
Porter Corners postal area (Saratoga County), 403
Porter town (Niagara County), 282
Portland town (Chautauqua County), 59

CDP = Census Designated Place

Portlandville postal area (Otsego County), 357
Portville town (Cattaraugus County), 37
Portville village (Cattaraugus County), 37
Potsdam town (Saint Lawrence County), 395
Potsdam village (Saint Lawrence County), 394
Potter town (Yates County), 567
Pottersville postal area (Warren County), 519
Poughkeepsie city (Dutchess County), 115
Poughkeepsie town (Dutchess County), 115
Poughquag postal area (Dutchess County), 115
Pound Ridge town (Westchester County), 550
Prattsburgh town (Steuben County), 433
Prattsville town (Greene County), 169
Preble town (Cortland County), 95
Preston Hollow postal area (Albany County), 7
Preston town (Chenango County), 73
Preston-Potter Hollow CDP (Albany County), 7
Princetown town (Schenectady County), 410
Prospect village (Oneida County), 294
Providence town (Saratoga County), 403
Pulaski village (Oswego County), 347
Pulteney town (Steuben County), 433
Purchase postal area (Westchester County), 550
Purdys postal area (Westchester County), 550
Purling postal area (Greene County), 169
Putnam County, 360 - 363
Putnam Lake CDP (Putnam County), 363
Putnam Valley town (Putnam County), 364
Putnam town (Washington County), 526

Q

Queens borough (Queens County), 271
Queensbury town (Warren County), 519
Quioque CDP (Suffolk County), 464
Quogue village (Suffolk County), 464

R

Ramapo town (Rockland County), 380
Randolph town (Cattaraugus County), 38
Randolph village (Cattaraugus County), 37
Ransomville CDP (Niagara County), 283
Rapids CDP (Niagara County), 283
Raquette Lake postal area (Hamilton County), 173
Rathbone town (Steuben County), 433
Ravena village (Albany County), 7
Reading town (Schuyler County), 420
Red Creek village (Wayne County), 531
Red Hook town (Dutchess County), 116
Red Hook village (Dutchess County), 116
Red House town (Cattaraugus County), 38
Red Oaks Mill CDP (Dutchess County), 116
Redfield town (Oswego County), 348
Redford CDP (Clinton County), 82
Redwood CDP (Jefferson County), 192
Rego Park postal area (Queens County), 275
Remsen town (Oneida County), 294
Remsen village (Oneida County), 294
Remsenburg-Speonk CDP (Suffolk County), 465
Rensselaer County, 364 - 372
Rensselaer Falls village (Saint Lawrence County), 395
Rensselaer city (Rensselaer County), 370
Rensselaerville town (Albany County), 7
Rexford postal area (Saratoga County), 404
Rexville postal area (Steuben County), 434
Rhinebeck town (Dutchess County), 117

Rhinebeck village (Dutchess County), 116
Richburg village (Allegany County), 17
Richfield Springs village (Otsego County), 357
Richfield town (Otsego County), 357
Richford town (Tioga County), 491
Richland town (Oswego County), 348
Richmond County see Staten Island
Richmond Hill postal area (Queens County), 275
Richmond town (Ontario County), 318
Richmondville town (Schoharie County), 415
Richmondville village (Schoharie County), 415
Richville village (Saint Lawrence County), 395
Ridge CDP (Suffolk County), 465
Ridgeway town (Orleans County), 339
Rifton CDP (Ulster County), 509
Riga town (Monroe County), 223
Ripley CDP (Chautauqua County), 59
Ripley town (Chautauqua County), 59
Riverhead CDP (Suffolk County), 466
Riverhead town (Suffolk County), 465
Riverside CDP (Suffolk County), 466
Riverside village (Steuben County), 434
Rochester city (Monroe County), 223
Rochester town (Ulster County), 509
Rock City Falls postal area (Saratoga County), 404
Rock Hill CDP (Sullivan County), 485
Rock Stream postal area (Yates County), 567
Rock Tavern postal area (Orange County), 332
Rockaway Park postal area (Queens County), 275
Rockland County, 373 - 383
Rockland town (Sullivan County), 485
Rockville Centre village (Nassau County), 257
Rocky Point CDP (Suffolk County), 466
Rodman town (Jefferson County), 192
Rome city (Oneida County), 294
Romulus town (Seneca County), 423
Ronkonkoma CDP (Suffolk County), 466
Roosevelt CDP (Nassau County), 258
Root town (Montgomery County), 230
Roscoe CDP (Sullivan County), 485
Rose town (Wayne County), 532
Roseboom town (Otsego County), 357
Rosedale postal area (Queens County), 275
Rosendale Village CDP (Ulster County), 510
Rosendale town (Ulster County), 509
Roslyn Estates village (Nassau County), 258
Roslyn Harbor village (Nassau County), 258
Roslyn Heights CDP (Nassau County), 258
Roslyn village (Nassau County), 258
Rossie town (Saint Lawrence County), 395
Rotterdam Junction postal area (Schenectady County), 410
Rotterdam CDP (Schenectady County), 410
Rotterdam town (Schenectady County), 410
Round Lake village (Saratoga County), 404
Round Top postal area (Greene County), 169
Rouses Point village (Clinton County), 83
Roxbury town (Delaware County), 104
Royalton town (Niagara County), 283
Rush town (Monroe County), 224
Rushford town (Allegany County), 17
Rushville village (Yates County), 567
Russell Gardens village (Nassau County), 259
Russell town (Saint Lawrence County), 395
Russia town (Herkimer County), 180
Rutland town (Jefferson County), 192
Rye Brook village (Westchester County), 551
Rye city (Westchester County), 550

Rye town (Westchester County), 551

S

Sackets Harbor village (Jefferson County), 193
Saddle Rock Estates CDP (Nassau County), 259
Saddle Rock village (Nassau County), 259
Sag Harbor village (Suffolk County), 466
Sagaponack CDP (Suffolk County), 467
Saint Albans postal area (Queens County), 275
Saint Armand town (Essex County), 142
Saint Bonaventure CDP (Cattaraugus County), 38
Saint James CDP (Suffolk County), 467
Saint Johnsville town (Montgomery County), 230
Saint Johnsville village (Montgomery County), 230
Saint Lawrence County, 384 - 396
Saint Regis Falls postal area (Franklin County), 150
Saint Regis Mohawk Reservation reservation (Franklin County), 150
Salamanca city (Cattaraugus County), 38
Salamanca town (Cattaraugus County), 39
Salem town (Washington County), 526
Salem village (Washington County), 526
Salina town (Onondaga County), 309
Salisbury Center postal area (Herkimer County), 181
Salisbury Mills postal area (Orange County), 332
Salisbury CDP (Nassau County), 259
Salisbury town (Herkimer County), 180
Salt Point postal area (Dutchess County), 117
Saltaire village (Suffolk County), 467
Sanborn postal area (Niagara County), 283
Sand Lake town (Rensselaer County), 370
Sand Ridge CDP (Oswego County), 348
Sands Point village (Nassau County), 260
Sandy Creek town (Oswego County), 348
Sandy Creek village (Oswego County), 348
Sanford town (Broome County), 25
Sangerfield town (Oneida County), 295
Santa Clara town (Franklin County), 150
Saranac Lake village (Franklin County), 151
Saranac town (Clinton County), 83
Saratoga County, 397 - 406
Saratoga Springs city (Saratoga County), 404
Saratoga town (Saratoga County), 404
Sardinia town (Erie County), 134
Saugerties South CDP (Ulster County), 510
Saugerties town (Ulster County), 510
Saugerties village (Ulster County), 510
Sauquoit postal area (Oneida County), 295
Savannah town (Wayne County), 532
Savona village (Steuben County), 434
Sayville CDP (Suffolk County), 467
Scarsdale town and village (Westchester County), 551
Schaghticoke town (Rensselaer County), 371
Schaghticoke village (Rensselaer County), 370
Schenectady County, 407 - 410
Schenectady city (Schenectady County), 410
Schenevus postal area (Otsego County), 358
Schodack Landing postal area (Rensselaer County), 371
Schodack town (Rensselaer County), 371
Schoharie County, 411 - 417
Schoharie town (Schoharie County), 416
Schoharie village (Schoharie County), 416
Schroeppel town (Oswego County), 349

CDP = Census Designated Place

PROFILES OF NEW YORK / Alphabetical Place Index

Schroon Lake postal area (Essex County), 143
Schroon town (Essex County), 142
Schuyler County, 418 - 420
Schuyler Falls town (Clinton County), 83
Schuyler town (Herkimer County), 181
Schuylerville village (Saratoga County), 405
Scio town (Allegany County), 18
Scipio Center postal area (Cayuga County), 47
Scipio town (Cayuga County), 47
Scotchtown CDP (Orange County), 332
Scotia village (Schenectady County), 411
Scott town (Cortland County), 96
Scotts Corners CDP (Westchester County), 552
Scottsburg postal area (Livingston County), 208
Scottsville village (Monroe County), 224
Scriba town (Oswego County), 349
Sea Cliff village (Nassau County), 260
Seaford CDP (Nassau County), 260
Searingtown CDP (Nassau County), 260
Selden CDP (Suffolk County), 468
Selkirk postal area (Albany County), 7
Sempronius town (Cayuga County), 47
Seneca County, 421 - 424
Seneca Falls town (Seneca County), 424
Seneca Falls village (Seneca County), 423
Seneca Knolls CDP (Onondaga County), 309
Seneca town (Ontario County), 318
Sennett town (Cayuga County), 47
Setauket-East Setauket CDP (Suffolk County), 468
Seward town (Schoharie County), 416
Shandaken town (Ulster County), 511
Sharon Springs village (Schoharie County), 417
Sharon town (Schoharie County), 416
Shawangunk town (Ulster County), 511
Shelby town (Orleans County), 340
Sheldon town (Wyoming County), 562
Shelter Island Heights CDP (Suffolk County), 469
Shelter Island CDP (Suffolk County), 468
Shelter Island town (Suffolk County), 468
Shenorock CDP (Westchester County), 552
Sherburne town (Chenango County), 74
Sherburne village (Chenango County), 73
Sheridan town (Chautauqua County), 59
Sherman town (Chautauqua County), 60
Sherman village (Chautauqua County), 60
Sherrill city (Oneida County), 295
Shinnecock Hills CDP (Suffolk County), 469
Shinnecock Reservation reservation (Suffolk County), 469
Shirley CDP (Suffolk County), 469
Shokan CDP (Ulster County), 511
Shoreham village (Suffolk County), 469
Shortsville village (Ontario County), 318
Shrub Oak CDP (Westchester County), 552
Shushan postal area (Washington County), 527
Sidney Center postal area (Delaware County), 105
Sidney town (Delaware County), 104
Sidney village (Delaware County), 104
Silver Bay postal area (Warren County), 519
Silver Creek village (Chautauqua County), 60
Silver Springs village (Wyoming County), 562
Sinclairville village (Chautauqua County), 60
Skaneateles town (Onondaga County), 310
Skaneateles village (Onondaga County), 310
Slate Hill postal area (Orange County), 332
Slaterville Springs postal area (Tompkins County), 497

Sleepy Hollow village (Westchester County), 552
Slingerlands postal area (Albany County), 8
Sloan village (Erie County), 134
Sloansville postal area (Schoharie County), 417
Sloatsburg village (Rockland County), 380
Smallwood CDP (Sullivan County), 485
Smithfield town (Madison County), 215
Smithtown CDP (Suffolk County), 470
Smithtown town (Suffolk County), 470
Smithville Flats postal area (Chenango County), 74
Smithville town (Chenango County), 74
Smyrna town (Chenango County), 74
Smyrna village (Chenango County), 74
Sodus Point village (Wayne County), 533
Sodus town (Wayne County), 532
Sodus village (Wayne County), 532
Solon town (Cortland County), 96
Solvay village (Onondaga County), 310
Somers town (Westchester County), 552
Somerset town (Niagara County), 284
Sound Beach CDP (Suffolk County), 470
South Bristol town (Ontario County), 319
South Cairo postal area (Greene County), 169
South Colton postal area (Saint Lawrence County), 396
South Corning village (Steuben County), 434
South Dayton village (Cattaraugus County), 39
South Fallsburg CDP (Sullivan County), 486
South Farmingdale CDP (Nassau County), 260
South Floral Park village (Nassau County), 261
South Glens Falls village (Saratoga County), 405
South Hempstead CDP (Nassau County), 261
South Hill CDP (Tompkins County), 497
South Huntington CDP (Suffolk County), 470
South Kortright postal area (Delaware County), 105
South Lockport CDP (Niagara County), 284
South New Berlin postal area (Chenango County), 75
South Nyack village (Rockland County), 380
South Otselic postal area (Chenango County), 75
South Ozone Park postal area (Queens County), 276
South Plymouth postal area (Chenango County), 75
South Richmond Hill postal area (Queens County), 276
South Salem postal area (Westchester County), 553
South Valley Stream CDP (Nassau County), 261
South Valley town (Cattaraugus County), 39
South Wales postal area (Erie County), 134
Southampton town (Suffolk County), 471
Southampton village (Suffolk County), 471
Southeast town (Putnam County), 364
Southfields postal area (Orange County), 332
Southold CDP (Suffolk County), 471
Southold town (Suffolk County), 471
Southport CDP (Chemung County), 66
Southport town (Chemung County), 66
Spackenkill CDP (Dutchess County), 117
Spafford town (Onondaga County), 310
Sparkill postal area (Rockland County), 380
Sparrow Bush postal area (Orange County), 333

Sparta town (Livingston County), 208
Speculator village (Hamilton County), 174
Spencer town (Tioga County), 491
Spencer village (Tioga County), 491
Spencerport village (Monroe County), 224
Spencertown postal area (Columbia County), 91
Sprakers postal area (Montgomery County), 231
Spring Valley village (Rockland County), 380
Springfield Center postal area (Otsego County), 358
Springfield Gardens postal area (Queens County), 276
Springfield town (Otsego County), 358
Springport town (Cayuga County), 47
Springs CDP (Suffolk County), 472
Springville village (Erie County), 135
Springwater town (Livingston County), 208
Staatsburg CDP (Dutchess County), 117
Stafford town (Genesee County), 161
Stamford town (Delaware County), 105
Stamford village (Delaware County), 105
Stanford town (Dutchess County), 117
Stanfordville postal area (Dutchess County), 118
Stanley postal area (Ontario County), 319
Stannards CDP (Allegany County), 18
Star Lake CDP (Saint Lawrence County), 396
Stark town (Herkimer County), 181
Starkey town (Yates County), 567
Staten Island borough (Richmond County), 277
Stephentown town (Rensselaer County), 371
Sterling town (Cayuga County), 48
Steuben County, 425 - 436
Steuben town (Oneida County), 295
Stewart Manor village (Nassau County), 261
Stillwater town (Saratoga County), 405
Stillwater village (Saratoga County), 405
Stittville postal area (Oneida County), 295
Stockbridge town (Madison County), 215
Stockholm town (Saint Lawrence County), 396
Stockport town (Columbia County), 91
Stockton town (Chautauqua County), 60
Stone Ridge CDP (Ulster County), 511
Stony Brook CDP (Suffolk County), 472
Stony Creek town (Warren County), 519
Stony Point CDP (Rockland County), 381
Stony Point town (Rockland County), 381
Stormville postal area (Dutchess County), 118
Stottville CDP (Columbia County), 91
Stratford town (Fulton County), 156
Strykersville postal area (Wyoming County), 562
Stuyvesant town (Columbia County), 91
Suffern village (Rockland County), 381
Suffolk County, 437 - 475
Sullivan County, 476 - 487
Sullivan town (Madison County), 215
Summerhill town (Cayuga County), 48
Summit town (Schoharie County), 417
Sunnyside postal area (Queens County), 276
Surprise postal area (Greene County), 170
Swain postal area (Allegany County), 18
Swan Lake postal area (Sullivan County), 486
Sweden town (Monroe County), 224
Sylvan Beach village (Oneida County), 296
Syosset CDP (Nassau County), 262
Syracuse city (Onondaga County), 311

T

Taberg postal area (Oneida County), 296

CDP = Census Designated Place

Taghkanic town (Columbia County), 91
Tannersville village (Greene County), 170
Tappan CDP (Rockland County), 382
Tarrytown village (Westchester County), 553
Taylor town (Cortland County), 96
Terryville CDP (Suffolk County), 472
Theresa town (Jefferson County), 193
Theresa village (Jefferson County), 193
Thiells CDP (Rockland County), 382
Thomaston village (Nassau County), 262
Thompson Ridge postal area (Orange County), 333
Thompson town (Sullivan County), 486
Thornwood CDP (Westchester County), 553
Three Mile Bay postal area (Jefferson County), 193
Throop town (Cayuga County), 48
Thurman town (Warren County), 519
Thurston town (Steuben County), 434
Ticonderoga town (Essex County), 143
Tillson CDP (Ulster County), 511
Tioga County, 488 - 491
Tioga town (Tioga County), 491
Tivoli village (Dutchess County), 118
Tomkins Cove postal area (Rockland County), 382
Tompkins County, 492 - 497
Tompkins town (Delaware County), 105
Tonawanda Reservation reservation (Genesee County), 161
Tonawanda CDP (Erie County), 135
Tonawanda city (Erie County), 135
Tonawanda town (Erie County), 135
Torrey town (Yates County), 567
Town Line CDP (Erie County), 136
Treadwell postal area (Delaware County), 106
Trenton town (Oneida County), 296
Triangle town (Broome County), 26
Tribes Hill CDP (Montgomery County), 231
Troupsburg town (Steuben County), 435
Troy city (Rensselaer County), 371
Trumansburg village (Tompkins County), 498
Truxton town (Cortland County), 96
Tuckahoe CDP (Suffolk County), 472
Tuckahoe village (Westchester County), 553
Tully town (Onondaga County), 312
Tully village (Onondaga County), 311
Tupper Lake village (Franklin County), 151
Turin town (Lewis County), 200
Turin village (Lewis County), 200
Tuscarora Reservation reservation (Niagara County), 284
Tuscarora town (Steuben County), 435
Tusten town (Sullivan County), 486
Tuxedo Park village (Orange County), 333
Tuxedo town (Orange County), 333
Tyre town (Seneca County), 424
Tyrone town (Schuyler County), 421

U

Ulster County, 498 - 513
Ulster Park postal area (Ulster County), 512
Ulster town (Ulster County), 512
Ulysses town (Tompkins County), 498
Unadilla town (Otsego County), 358
Unadilla village (Otsego County), 358
Union Springs village (Cayuga County), 48
Union Vale town (Dutchess County), 118
Union town (Broome County), 26
Uniondale CDP (Nassau County), 262
Unionville village (Orange County), 333
University Gardens CDP (Nassau County), 262
Upper Brookville village (Nassau County), 262

Upper Jay postal area (Essex County), 143
Upper Nyack village (Rockland County), 382
Urbana town (Steuben County), 435
Utica city (Oneida County), 296

V

Vails Gate CDP (Orange County), 334
Valatie village (Columbia County), 92
Valhalla CDP (Westchester County), 554
Valley Cottage CDP (Rockland County), 382
Valley Falls village (Rensselaer County), 372
Valley Stream village (Nassau County), 263
Van Buren town (Onondaga County), 312
Van Etten town (Chemung County), 67
Van Etten village (Chemung County), 66
Van Hornesville postal area (Herkimer County), 181
Varick town (Seneca County), 424
Varysburg postal area (Wyoming County), 562
Venice town (Cayuga County), 49
Verbank postal area (Dutchess County), 118
Vermontville postal area (Franklin County), 151
Vernon Center postal area (Oneida County), 297
Vernon town (Oneida County), 297
Vernon village (Oneida County), 297
Verona town (Oneida County), 297
Verplanck CDP (Westchester County), 554
Vestal town (Broome County), 26
Veteran town (Chemung County), 67
Victor town (Ontario County), 319
Victor village (Ontario County), 319
Victory town (Cayuga County), 49
Victory village (Saratoga County), 406
Vienna town (Oneida County), 298
Village Green CDP (Onondaga County), 312
Village of the Branch village (Suffolk County), 473
Villenova town (Chautauqua County), 61
Viola CDP (Rockland County), 383
Virgil town (Cortland County), 97
Volney town (Oswego County), 349
Voorheesville village (Albany County), 8

W

Waccabuc postal area (Westchester County), 554
Waddington town (Saint Lawrence County), 396
Waddington village (Saint Lawrence County), 396
Wading River CDP (Suffolk County), 473
Wainscott CDP (Suffolk County), 473
Walden village (Orange County), 334
Wales town (Erie County), 136
Walker Valley CDP (Ulster County), 512
Wallkill CDP (Ulster County), 512
Wallkill town (Orange County), 334
Walton Park CDP (Orange County), 334
Walton town (Delaware County), 106
Walton village (Delaware County), 106
Walworth town (Wayne County), 533
Wampsville village (Madison County), 216
Wantagh CDP (Nassau County), 263
Wappinger town (Dutchess County), 119
Wappingers Falls village (Dutchess County), 119
Ward town (Allegany County), 18
Warners postal area (Onondaga County), 312
Warnerville postal area (Schoharie County), 417
Warren County, 514 - 519
Warren town (Herkimer County), 181

Warrensburg CDP (Warren County), 520
Warrensburg town (Warren County), 520
Warsaw town (Wyoming County), 563
Warsaw village (Wyoming County), 563
Warwick town (Orange County), 335
Warwick village (Orange County), 335
Washington County, 520 - 527
Washington Heights CDP (Orange County), 335
Washington town (Dutchess County), 119
Washingtonville village (Orange County), 335
Wassaic postal area (Dutchess County), 119
Water Mill postal area (Suffolk County), 473
Waterford town (Saratoga County), 406
Waterford village (Saratoga County), 406
Waterloo town (Seneca County), 424
Waterloo village (Seneca County), 424
Watermill CDP (Suffolk County), 473
Waterport postal area (Orleans County), 340
Watertown city (Jefferson County), 193
Watertown town (Jefferson County), 194
Waterville village (Oneida County), 298
Watervliet city (Albany County), 8
Watkins Glen village (Schuyler County), 421
Watson town (Lewis County), 201
Waverly town (Franklin County), 151
Waverly village (Tioga County), 492
Wawarsing town (Ulster County), 512
Wawayanda town (Orange County), 336
Wayland town (Steuben County), 436
Wayland village (Steuben County), 435
Wayne County, 528 - 533
Wayne town (Steuben County), 436
Webb town (Herkimer County), 182
Webster town (Monroe County), 225
Webster village (Monroe County), 225
Weedsport village (Cayuga County), 49
Wellesley Island postal area (Jefferson County), 194
Wells Bridge postal area (Otsego County), 359
Wells town (Hamilton County), 174
Wellsburg village (Chemung County), 67
Wellsville town (Allegany County), 19
Wellsville village (Allegany County), 18
Wesley Hills village (Rockland County), 383
West Almond town (Allegany County), 19
West Babylon CDP (Suffolk County), 474
West Bay Shore CDP (Suffolk County), 474
West Bloomfield town (Ontario County), 319
West Carthage village (Jefferson County), 194
West Chazy postal area (Clinton County), 83
West Coxsackie postal area (Greene County), 170
West Edmeston postal area (Otsego County), 359
West Elmira CDP (Chemung County), 67
West End CDP (Otsego County), 359
West Falls postal area (Erie County), 136
West Fulton postal area (Schoharie County), 417
West Glens Falls CDP (Warren County), 520
West Hampton Dunes village (Suffolk County), 474
West Harrison postal area (Westchester County), 554
West Haverstraw village (Rockland County), 383
West Hempstead CDP (Nassau County), 263
West Henrietta postal area (Monroe County), 225
West Hills CDP (Suffolk County), 474
West Hurley CDP (Ulster County), 513
West Islip CDP (Suffolk County), 474
West Kill postal area (Greene County), 170

CDP = Census Designated Place

West Leyden postal area (Lewis County), 201
West Monroe town (Oswego County), 349
West Nyack CDP (Rockland County), 383
West Oneonta postal area (Otsego County), 359
West Point CDP (Orange County), 336
West Sand Lake CDP (Rensselaer County), 372
West Sayville CDP (Suffolk County), 475
West Seneca CDP (Erie County), 136
West Seneca town (Erie County), 136
West Shokan postal area (Ulster County), 513
West Sparta town (Livingston County), 208
West Turin town (Lewis County), 201
West Union town (Steuben County), 436
West Valley postal area (Cattaraugus County), 39
West Winfield village (Herkimer County), 182
Westbury village (Nassau County), 264
Westchester County, 534 - 555
Westdale postal area (Oneida County), 298
Westerlo town (Albany County), 8
Western town (Oneida County), 298
Westernville postal area (Oneida County), 298
Westfield town (Chautauqua County), 61
Westfield village (Chautauqua County), 61
Westford town (Otsego County), 359
Westhampton Beach village (Suffolk County), 475
Westhampton CDP (Suffolk County), 475
Westmere CDP (Albany County), 8
Westmoreland town (Oneida County), 299
Weston Mills CDP (Cattaraugus County), 39
Westport town (Essex County), 143
Westtown postal area (Orange County), 336
Westvale CDP (Onondaga County), 313
Westville town (Franklin County), 151
Wethersfield town (Wyoming County), 563
Wevertown postal area (Warren County), 520
Wheatfield town (Niagara County), 284
Wheatland town (Monroe County), 225

Wheatley Heights CDP (Suffolk County), 475
Wheeler town (Steuben County), 436
White Creek town (Washington County), 527
White Lake postal area (Sullivan County), 486
White Plains city (Westchester County), 555
White Sulphur Springs postal area (Sullivan County), 487
Whitehall town (Washington County), 527
Whitehall village (Washington County), 527
Whitesboro village (Oneida County), 299
Whitestone postal area (Queens County), 276
Whitestown town (Oneida County), 299
Whitesville postal area (Allegany County), 19
Whitney Point village (Broome County), 26
Willet town (Cortland County), 97
Williamson town (Wayne County), 533
Williamstown town (Oswego County), 349
Williamsville village (Erie County), 137
Willing town (Allegany County), 19
Williston Park village (Nassau County), 264
Willow postal area (Ulster County), 513
Willsboro town (Essex County), 144
Willseyville postal area (Tioga County), 492
Wilmington town (Essex County), 144
Wilna town (Jefferson County), 195
Wilson town (Niagara County), 285
Wilson village (Niagara County), 284
Wilton town (Saratoga County), 406
Windham CDP (Greene County), 171
Windham town (Greene County), 170
Windsor town (Broome County), 27
Windsor village (Broome County), 27
Winfield town (Herkimer County), 182
Wingdale postal area (Dutchess County), 119
Winthrop postal area (Saint Lawrence County), 397
Wirt town (Allegany County), 19
Wolcott town (Wayne County), 534
Wolcott village (Wayne County), 533
Woodbourne postal area (Sullivan County), 487
Woodbury CDP (Nassau County), 264

Woodbury town (Orange County), 336
Woodhaven postal area (Queens County), 276
Woodhull town (Steuben County), 436
Woodmere CDP (Nassau County), 264
Woodridge village (Sullivan County), 487
Woodsburgh village (Nassau County), 265
Woodside postal area (Queens County), 277
Woodstock CDP (Ulster County), 514
Woodstock town (Ulster County), 513
Worcester town (Otsego County), 360
Worth town (Jefferson County), 195
Wright town (Schoharie County), 418
Wurtsboro village (Sullivan County), 487
Wyandanch CDP (Suffolk County), 476
Wykagyl postal area (Westchester County), 555
Wynantskill CDP (Rensselaer County), 372
Wyoming County, 556 - 563
Wyoming village (Wyoming County), 563

Y

Yaphank CDP (Suffolk County), 476
Yates County, 564 - 567
Yates town (Orleans County), 340
Yonkers city (Westchester County), 555
York town (Livingston County), 208
Yorkshire CDP (Cattaraugus County), 40
Yorkshire town (Cattaraugus County), 40
Yorktown Heights CDP (Westchester County), 556
Yorktown town (Westchester County), 556
Yorkville village (Oneida County), 299
Youngstown village (Niagara County), 285
Youngsville postal area (Sullivan County), 487
Yulan postal area (Sullivan County), 488

Z

Zena CDP (Ulster County), 514

CDP = Census Designated Place

COMPARATIVE STATISTICS

Population

Place	1990	2000	2005 Estimate	2010 Projection
Albany (city)	100,756	95,658	95,781	95,990
Amherst (town)	111,711	116,510	118,014	119,112
Babylon (town)	202,355	211,792	218,282	225,543
Bethlehem (town)	27,552	31,304	32,969	34,583
Binghamton (city)	53,017	47,380	45,839	44,233
Brentwood (CDP)	45,218	53,917	54,968	56,275
Brighton (town)	34,458	35,588	34,859	34,213
Brighton (CDP)	34,455	35,584	34,856	34,210
Brookhaven (town)	407,832	448,248	475,894	503,899
Buffalo (city)	328,123	292,648	282,089	271,548
Carmel (town)	28,816	33,006	35,167	37,352
Centereach (CDP)	26,720	27,285	28,989	30,720
Central Islip (CDP)	27,789	31,950	32,723	33,605
Cheektowaga (town)	99,314	94,019	91,201	88,303
Cheektowaga (CDP)	84,387	79,988	77,745	75,424
Chili (town)	25,178	27,638	28,555	29,429
Cicero (town)	25,560	27,982	30,017	31,889
Clarkstown (town)	79,346	82,082	83,504	85,172
Clay (town)	59,749	58,805	59,482	60,104
Clifton Park (town)	30,117	32,995	35,919	38,871
Colonie (town)	76,536	79,258	81,465	83,696
Commack (CDP)	36,124	36,367	36,912	37,549
Coram (CDP)	30,173	34,923	36,722	38,588
Cortlandt (town)	37,357	38,467	39,894	41,345
Deer Park (CDP)	29,019	28,316	29,027	29,810
East Fishkill (town)	22,101	25,589	28,506	31,320
East Meadow (CDP)	36,909	37,461	38,751	39,936
Eastchester (town)	30,867	31,318	31,556	31,890
Elmira (city)	33,719	30,940	30,115	29,227
Elmont (CDP)	28,612	32,657	32,352	32,031
Franklin Square (CDP)	28,205	29,342	29,772	30,207
Freeport (village)	39,894	43,783	43,710	43,636
Gates (town)	28,583	29,275	28,827	28,358
Greece (town)	90,106	94,141	94,862	95,464
Greenburgh (town)	83,816	86,764	91,037	95,204
Guilderland (town)	28,877	32,688	33,581	34,440
Hamburg (town)	53,735	56,259	56,898	57,407
Haverstraw (town)	32,712	33,811	35,010	36,182
Hempstead (village)	49,435	56,554	56,773	56,985
Hempstead (town)	725,630	755,924	757,215	758,301
Henrietta (town)	36,376	39,028	40,727	42,204
Hicksville (CDP)	40,174	41,260	41,339	41,475
Holbrook (CDP)	25,273	27,512	28,841	30,235
Huntington (town)	191,474	195,289	200,040	205,544
Huntington Station (CDP)	28,247	29,910	29,729	29,740
Irondequoit (CDP/town)	52,371	52,354	51,862	51,388
Islip (town)	299,587	322,612	333,359	345,039
Ithaca (city)	29,541	29,287	30,635	32,114
Jamestown (city)	34,689	31,730	30,261	28,753
Lancaster (town)	32,181	39,019	41,273	43,300

Place	1990	2000	2005 Estimate	2010 Projection
Levittown (CDP)	53,296	53,067	52,983	52,929
Lindenhurst (village)	26,879	27,819	28,907	30,087
Long Beach (city)	33,510	35,462	35,480	35,434
Mamaroneck (town)	27,706	28,967	29,056	29,180
Manlius (town)	30,656	31,872	32,617	33,317
Monroe (town)	23,035	31,407	38,174	44,652
Mount Pleasant (town)	40,590	43,221	43,931	44,841
Mount Vernon (city)	67,076	68,381	68,221	68,182
New City (CDP)	33,745	34,038	34,363	34,857
New Rochelle (city)	67,429	72,182	72,741	73,381
New York (city)	7,322,552	8,008,278	8,113,728	8,219,118
Newburgh (city)	26,440	28,259	28,495	29,112
Newburgh (town)	24,066	27,568	30,649	33,807
Niagara Falls (city)	61,840	55,593	53,415	51,242
North Hempstead (town)	211,355	222,611	224,379	226,048
North Tonawanda (city)	34,989	33,262	31,986	30,712
Oceanside (CDP)	32,423	32,733	33,500	34,218
Orangetown (town)	46,742	47,711	48,722	49,833
Ossining (town)	34,124	36,534	37,415	38,369
Oyster Bay (town)	293,200	293,925	297,388	300,604
Penfield (town)	30,216	34,645	36,106	37,464
Perinton (town)	43,015	46,090	46,600	47,094
Poughkeepsie (town)	40,143	42,777	45,291	47,694
Poughkeepsie (city)	28,844	29,871	30,318	30,934
Ramapo (town)	93,861	108,905	113,463	117,975
Riverhead (town)	22,958	27,680	33,949	39,670
Rochester (city)	231,642	219,773	213,435	207,450
Rome (city)	44,350	34,950	34,421	33,757
Rotterdam (town)	28,395	28,316	29,014	29,688
Rye (town)	39,524	43,880	44,822	45,799
Salina (town)	35,145	33,290	33,371	33,443
Schenectady (city)	65,566	61,821	60,742	59,771
Smithtown (town)	113,406	115,715	120,226	125,029
Southampton (town)	44,976	54,712	59,226	63,667
Syracuse (city)	163,860	147,306	144,232	141,416
Tonawanda (town)	82,464	78,155	75,017	71,903
Tonawanda (CDP)	65,284	61,729	59,323	56,940
Troy (city)	54,269	49,170	48,602	48,081
Union (town)	59,786	56,298	55,318	54,270
Utica (city)	68,637	60,651	59,216	57,695
Valley Stream (village)	33,962	36,368	36,133	35,898
Warwick (town)	27,174	30,764	32,755	35,051
Webster (town)	31,639	37,926	40,571	42,977
West Babylon (CDP)	42,410	43,452	44,222	45,137
West Islip (CDP)	28,419	28,907	30,094	31,366
West Seneca (CDP)	47,866	45,943	44,917	43,859
West Seneca (town)	47,830	45,920	44,892	43,832
White Plains (city)	48,615	53,077	57,054	60,818
Yonkers (city)	188,126	196,086	197,668	199,494
Yorktown (town)	33,314	36,318	37,406	38,508

Physical Characteristics

Place	Density (persons per square mile)	Land Area (square miles)	Water Area (square miles)	Elevation (feet)
Albany (city)	4,480.3	21.38	0.47	127
Amherst (town)	2,216.3	53.25	0.27	600
Babylon (town)	4,174.2	52.29	61.87	15
Bethlehem (town)	675.4	48.81	0.77	n/a
Binghamton (city)	4,391.6	10.44	0.60	863
Brentwood (CDP)	5,461.7	10.06	0.00	86
Brighton (town)	2,255.3	15.46	0.17	458
Brighton (CDP)	2,256.5	15.45	0.17	n/a
Brookhaven (town)	1,835.4	259.29	272.23	n/a
Buffalo (city)	6,945.8	40.61	11.90	583
Carmel (town)	974.0	36.11	4.58	519
Centereach (CDP)	3,643.5	7.96	0.00	100
Central Islip (CDP)	4,504.6	7.26	0.00	88
Cheektowaga (town)	3,088.3	29.53	0.00	659
Cheektowaga (CDP)	3,054.8	25.45	0.00	n/a
Chili (town)	718.4	39.75	0.19	n/a
Cicero (town)	619.4	48.46	0.05	n/a
Clarkstown (town)	2,166.6	38.54	8.39	n/a
Clay (town)	1,239.1	48.01	0.78	n/a
Clifton Park (town)	739.6	48.57	1.65	321
Colonie (town)	1,452.9	56.07	1.80	n/a
Commack (CDP)	3,060.1	12.06	0.00	150
Coram (CDP)	2,662.5	13.79	0.00	99
Cortlandt (town)	1,005.6	39.67	10.50	n/a
Deer Park (CDP)	4,638.6	6.26	0.00	74
East Fishkill (town)	500.9	56.91	0.45	n/a
East Meadow (CDP)	6,160.1	6.29	0.01	40
Eastchester (town)	6,424.8	4.91	0.10	50
Elmira (city)	4,116.7	7.32	0.27	873
Elmont (CDP)	9,500.3	3.41	0.00	43
Franklin Square (CDP)	10,318.2	2.89	0.00	68
Freeport (village)	9,515.4	4.59	0.24	23
Gates (town)	1,892.4	15.23	0.08	n/a
Greece (town)	2,000.3	47.43	3.93	272
Greenburgh (town)	2,982.7	30.52	5.66	n/a
Guilderland (town)	579.7	57.92	0.77	215
Hamburg (town)	1,378.2	41.29	0.02	825
Haverstraw (town)	1,561.8	22.42	5.14	73
Hempstead (village)	15,425.6	3.68	0.00	54
Hempstead (town)	6,312.1	119.96	71.37	54
Henrietta (town)	1,150.2	35.41	0.19	596
Hicksville (CDP)	6,068.8	6.81	0.01	149
Holbrook (CDP)	4,227.3	6.82	0.00	118
Huntington (town)	2,129.0	93.96	43.15	205
Huntington Station (CDP)	5,473.7	5.43	0.00	216
Irondequoit (CDP/town)	3,415.0	15.19	1.63	385
Islip (town)	3,166.6	105.28	57.84	16
Ithaca (city)	5,607.6	5.46	0.61	814
Jamestown (city)	3,370.9	8.98	0.08	1,317
Lancaster (town)	1,090.7	37.84	0.06	696

Place	Density (persons per square mile)	Land Area (square miles)	Water Area (square miles)	Elevation (feet)
Levittown (CDP)	7,705.3	6.88	0.00	75
Lindenhurst (village)	7,701.5	3.75	0.06	27
Long Beach (city)	16,603.4	2.14	1.76	9
Mamaroneck (town)	4,390.9	6.62	7.42	47
Manlius (town)	657.3	49.62	0.34	n/a
Monroe (town)	1,900.4	20.09	1.18	679
Mount Pleasant (town)	1,586.1	27.70	4.99	262
Mount Vernon (city)	15,652.6	4.36	0.02	100
New City (CDP)	2,202.4	15.60	0.70	163
New Rochelle (city)	7,027.6	10.35	2.88	94
New York (city)	26,750.5	303.31	165.56	n/a
Newburgh (city)	7,455.4	3.82	0.96	139
Newburgh (town)	701.5	43.69	3.31	139
Niagara Falls (city)	3,800.7	14.05	2.75	618
North Hempstead (town)	4,187.9	53.58	15.53	n/a
North Tonawanda (city)	3,166.9	10.10	0.84	575
Oceanside (CDP)	6,676.4	5.02	0.40	10
Orangetown (town)	2,015.0	24.18	7.19	n/a
Ossining (town)	3,198.3	11.70	3.91	8
Oyster Bay (town)	2,849.4	104.37	65.13	8
Penfield (town)	962.8	37.50	0.42	n/a
Perinton (town)	1,365.5	34.13	0.31	n/a
Poughkeepsie (town)	1,574.9	28.76	2.43	209
Poughkeepsie (city)	5,893.1	5.14	0.55	209
Ramapo (town)	1,852.6	61.24	0.69	314
Riverhead (town)	503.9	67.38	133.91	25
Rochester (city)	5,956.1	35.83	1.27	513
Rome (city)	459.4	74.93	0.75	445
Rotterdam (town)	806.4	35.98	0.51	340
Rye (town)	6,433.7	6.97	0.47	49
Salina (town)	2,421.6	13.78	1.32	n/a
Schenectady (city)	5,599.5	10.85	0.14	246
Smithtown (town)	2,244.1	53.58	57.80	73
Southampton (town)	426.5	138.88	156.73	45
Syracuse (city)	5,748.5	25.09	0.55	398
Tonawanda (town)	3,989.4	18.80	1.56	572
Tonawanda (CDP)	3,415.7	17.37	1.56	n/a
Troy (city)	4,667.3	10.41	0.60	35
Union (town)	1,572.9	35.17	0.67	n/a
Utica (city)	3,622.2	16.35	0.26	407
Valley Stream (village)	10,501.2	3.44	0.03	18
Warwick (town)	322.2	101.67	3.19	538
Webster (town)	1,191.9	34.04	1.45	408
West Babylon (CDP)	5,738.8	7.71	0.31	48
West Islip (CDP)	4,857.3	6.20	0.43	20
West Seneca (CDP)	2,100.6	21.38	0.02	n/a
West Seneca (town)	2,100.7	21.37	0.02	600
White Plains (city)	5,821.3	9.80	0.09	201
Yonkers (city)	10,935.0	18.08	2.24	10
Yorktown (town)	1,019.3	36.70	2.58	n/a

NOTE: Population Density figures as of 2005; Land Area and Water Area figures as of 2000.

Population by Race/Hispanic Origin

Place	White Alone[1] (%)	Black Alone[1] (%)	Asian Alone[1] (%)	Hispanic[2] (%)
Albany (city)	57.5	31.6	4.5	7.2
Amherst (town)	87.0	4.7	6.6	1.6
Babylon (town)	73.3	16.5	2.5	13.2
Bethlehem (town)	93.4	2.7	2.2	2.4
Binghamton (city)	79.2	10.9	4.0	5.2
Brentwood (CDP)	40.0	20.5	2.1	61.8
Brighton (town)	83.0	4.3	10.2	2.9
Brighton (CDP)	83.0	4.3	10.2	2.9
Brookhaven (town)	85.4	5.3	3.8	10.6
Buffalo (city)	50.7	39.8	1.8	9.1
Carmel (town)	92.9	1.5	1.6	8.9
Centereach (CDP)	89.4	2.4	4.5	9.6
Central Islip (CDP)	41.5	30.2	3.8	41.3
Cheektowaga (town)	93.2	4.0	1.3	1.3
Cheektowaga (CDP)	92.5	4.6	1.5	1.3
Chili (town)	89.5	6.8	1.3	2.1
Cicero (town)	95.7	1.4	0.9	1.1
Clarkstown (town)	76.1	8.5	9.9	9.2
Clay (town)	90.7	4.2	2.5	1.8
Clifton Park (town)	92.8	1.6	3.8	2.5
Colonie (town)	87.8	4.7	5.1	2.4
Commack (CDP)	92.9	0.8	4.9	3.7
Coram (CDP)	77.6	10.6	4.4	12.6
Cortlandt (town)	85.8	5.5	3.2	9.8
Deer Park (CDP)	79.0	11.1	3.9	9.8
East Fishkill (town)	91.6	2.4	3.3	5.2
East Meadow (CDP)	80.3	5.5	9.3	9.6
Eastchester (town)	86.2	2.8	7.4	5.7
Elmira (city)	79.9	14.8	0.7	4.3
Elmont (CDP)	32.8	45.4	9.9	15.6
Franklin Square (CDP)	88.5	1.7	5.4	9.6
Freeport (village)	36.0	36.1	1.6	38.3
Gates (town)	86.0	7.8	2.9	3.8
Greece (town)	92.0	3.5	1.7	3.3
Greenburgh (town)	69.3	13.5	10.4	11.2
Guilderland (town)	89.5	2.8	5.7	2.3
Hamburg (town)	97.5	0.6	0.5	1.8
Haverstraw (town)	60.8	11.4	3.9	37.1
Hempstead (village)	22.1	53.5	1.3	35.6
Hempstead (town)	70.2	16.8	4.6	14.0
Henrietta (town)	81.5	8.0	6.6	3.8
Hicksville (CDP)	78.5	1.9	12.8	12.4
Holbrook (CDP)	92.7	1.6	3.6	7.4
Huntington (town)	85.6	4.8	4.6	8.6
Huntington Station (CDP)	65.8	12.2	4.0	29.9
Irondequoit (CDP/town)	90.8	4.8	1.2	4.1
Islip (town)	73.6	10.3	2.7	23.5
Ithaca (city)	68.0	7.4	18.1	6.7
Jamestown (city)	90.1	3.9	0.7	6.4
Lancaster (town)	97.6	1.0	0.5	0.8

Place	White Alone[1] (%)	Black Alone[1] (%)	Asian Alone[1] (%)	Hispanic[2] (%)
Levittown (CDP)	91.9	0.8	3.9	9.2
Lindenhurst (village)	92.2	1.1	1.9	9.0
Long Beach (city)	81.8	6.4	3.1	15.1
Mamaroneck (town)	87.7	2.7	3.5	13.7
Manlius (town)	93.4	1.1	3.8	1.3
Monroe (town)	93.1	1.8	1.8	6.7
Mount Pleasant (town)	82.1	5.2	4.0	16.3
Mount Vernon (city)	24.7	62.0	2.5	12.0
New City (CDP)	80.9	5.9	8.8	7.8
New Rochelle (city)	64.8	20.1	3.7	24.9
New York (city)	42.7	26.1	10.9	28.6
Newburgh (city)	36.3	34.9	1.0	43.6
Newburgh (town)	78.4	11.1	3.0	14.0
Niagara Falls (city)	73.0	21.2	1.2	2.8
North Hempstead (town)	74.1	6.9	12.2	12.2
North Tonawanda (city)	97.3	0.4	0.8	1.6
Oceanside (CDP)	93.2	0.8	2.4	7.9
Orangetown (town)	82.1	5.5	7.6	7.7
Ossining (town)	65.9	14.9	5.9	24.9
Oyster Bay (town)	87.8	2.0	6.7	6.6
Penfield (town)	92.4	2.5	3.5	1.9
Perinton (town)	92.8	2.0	3.3	1.9
Poughkeepsie (town)	78.9	9.5	7.2	7.1
Poughkeepsie (city)	47.3	38.6	2.1	14.6
Ramapo (town)	69.6	18.2	5.2	10.5
Riverhead (town)	83.3	11.2	1.2	8.7
Rochester (city)	42.7	42.3	2.6	15.1
Rome (city)	85.8	9.0	1.0	6.4
Rotterdam (town)	96.5	1.2	0.9	1.3
Rye (town)	67.6	4.4	3.3	37.6
Salina (town)	92.3	2.8	2.2	2.0
Schenectady (city)	70.9	18.1	3.1	8.2
Smithtown (town)	94.2	0.8	3.1	4.4
Southampton (town)	86.1	6.7	1.2	13.0
Syracuse (city)	59.0	28.8	4.4	7.0
Tonawanda (town)	95.0	1.9	1.5	1.7
Tonawanda (CDP)	94.7	2.0	1.7	1.7
Troy (city)	75.3	14.2	4.6	6.1
Union (town)	91.2	3.2	3.2	1.9
Utica (city)	77.1	13.8	3.1	7.2
Valley Stream (village)	69.7	12.1	9.2	16.8
Warwick (town)	87.8	6.0	1.3	9.1
Webster (town)	94.0	1.9	2.3	2.1
West Babylon (CDP)	81.7	10.6	2.7	10.5
West Islip (CDP)	96.1	0.6	1.3	4.4
West Seneca (CDP)	97.7	0.6	0.7	1.1
West Seneca (town)	97.7	0.6	0.7	1.1
White Plains (city)	61.5	15.0	5.6	28.7
Yonkers (city)	54.7	17.9	6.1	30.2
Yorktown (town)	88.7	3.4	4.4	7.6

NOTE: Data as of 2005; (1) Figures are not in combination with any other race; (2) Persons of Hispanic Origin may be of any race

Average Household Size, Median Age, Male/Female Ratio, and Foreign Born

Place	Average Household Size (persons)	Median Age (years)	Male/Female Ratio (males per 100 females)	Foreign Born (%)
Albany (city)	2.35	33.1	91.4	8.6
Amherst (town)	2.56	40.7	89.8	9.0
Babylon (town)	3.05	37.5	93.8	13.1
Bethlehem (town)	2.56	40.5	91.8	4.8
Binghamton (city)	2.22	37.5	90.9	8.5
Brentwood (CDP)	4.39	32.6	100.4	34.7
Brighton (town)	2.24	41.5	89.4	15.4
Brighton (CDP)	2.24	41.5	89.4	15.4
Brookhaven (town)	3.03	36.4	97.1	8.9
Buffalo (city)	2.38	34.8	89.6	4.4
Carmel (town)	3.02	38.5	99.1	10.0
Centereach (CDP)	3.29	36.8	98.6	9.2
Central Islip (CDP)	3.67	32.9	98.1	23.0
Cheektowaga (town)	2.32	42.6	89.0	4.3
Cheektowaga (CDP)	2.31	42.5	88.6	4.4
Chili (town)	2.68	38.8	94.8	6.6
Cicero (town)	2.61	37.5	96.9	2.4
Clarkstown (town)	2.92	40.5	95.1	16.7
Clay (town)	2.60	36.7	93.2	5.1
Clifton Park (town)	2.56	40.4	97.7	5.8
Colonie (town)	2.53	40.9	93.5	6.8
Commack (CDP)	3.07	40.1	95.5	9.4
Coram (CDP)	2.74	36.7	93.5	10.6
Cortlandt (town)	2.86	40.1	96.5	11.4
Deer Park (CDP)	2.94	38.5	94.9	11.9
East Fishkill (town)	3.06	37.6	98.1	7.1
East Meadow (CDP)	3.03	40.0	99.1	14.5
Eastchester (town)	2.47	41.1	88.8	16.7
Elmira (city)	2.69	33.8	101.8	2.2
Elmont (CDP)	3.37	37.4	91.2	36.9
Franklin Square (CDP)	2.91	41.0	91.0	16.5
Freeport (village)	3.30	36.5	93.5	29.9
Gates (town)	2.46	41.3	92.9	9.4
Greece (town)	2.52	40.3	92.5	6.6
Greenburgh (town)	2.62	41.0	91.0	21.0
Guilderland (town)	2.41	40.4	92.9	6.8
Hamburg (town)	2.52	40.4	91.3	2.9
Haverstraw (town)	3.00	36.9	94.8	22.7
Hempstead (village)	3.83	31.0	92.3	33.2
Hempstead (town)	3.07	39.0	93.1	17.8
Henrietta (town)	3.01	31.5	111.6	8.4
Hicksville (CDP)	3.00	40.5	96.2	18.0
Holbrook (CDP)	3.00	36.9	95.1	5.8
Huntington (town)	2.94	40.0	96.6	11.2
Huntington Station (CDP)	3.11	36.0	101.1	20.9
Irondequoit (CDP/town)	2.32	44.3	86.3	8.1
Islip (town)	3.24	36.4	97.2	14.6
Ithaca (city)	2.78	23.9	104.3	16.0
Jamestown (city)	2.32	36.8	91.5	2.2
Lancaster (town)	2.57	39.5	94.1	2.6

Place	Average Household Size (persons)	Median Age (years)	Male/Female Ratio (males per 100 females)	Foreign Born (%)
Levittown (CDP)	3.06	39.1	95.1	8.5
Lindenhurst (village)	3.06	37.3	95.2	10.8
Long Beach (city)	2.36	42.0	93.7	15.3
Mamaroneck (town)	2.65	39.9	92.4	21.8
Manlius (town)	2.50	42.3	91.4	6.1
Monroe (town)	3.95	23.7	107.6	9.6
Mount Pleasant (town)	3.16	37.3	103.5	18.1
Mount Vernon (city)	2.65	37.4	83.7	29.1
New City (CDP)	3.04	41.5	96.4	15.9
New Rochelle (city)	2.79	38.1	91.6	27.3
New York (city)	2.66	35.8	90.8	35.9
Newburgh (city)	3.11	29.6	90.0	20.3
Newburgh (town)	2.80	38.9	96.0	7.6
Niagara Falls (city)	2.28	39.1	88.7	5.0
North Hempstead (town)	2.91	41.2	93.4	24.9
North Tonawanda (city)	2.40	39.9	95.1	3.6
Oceanside (CDP)	2.90	41.8	94.1	10.6
Orangetown (town)	2.73	40.6	93.8	15.9
Ossining (town)	2.98	38.7	106.8	24.2
Oyster Bay (town)	2.94	41.3	94.7	12.1
Penfield (town)	2.63	42.2	92.3	8.8
Perinton (town)	2.57	41.0	93.2	6.6
Poughkeepsie (town)	2.91	35.5	90.9	10.6
Poughkeepsie (city)	2.49	33.9	92.2	13.9
Ramapo (town)	3.48	32.3	98.2	22.8
Riverhead (town)	2.55	41.9	96.4	9.6
Rochester (city)	2.47	32.6	92.5	7.3
Rome (city)	2.54	38.9	107.3	3.8
Rotterdam (town)	2.42	42.2	93.1	3.2
Rye (town)	2.88	37.4	99.2	32.5
Salina (town)	2.27	40.9	90.8	5.1
Schenectady (city)	2.35	35.6	92.5	6.5
Smithtown (town)	2.97	39.8	95.0	7.2
Southampton (town)	2.57	41.8	100.0	11.2
Syracuse (city)	2.48	32.1	89.7	7.6
Tonawanda (town)	2.31	42.7	88.6	4.5
Tonawanda (CDP)	2.32	43.5	89.1	4.9
Troy (city)	2.44	33.1	99.3	5.8
Union (town)	2.26	40.7	90.9	4.8
Utica (city)	2.41	37.8	89.9	11.9
Valley Stream (village)	2.94	40.4	92.2	19.6
Warwick (town)	2.77	39.1	100.2	5.4
Webster (town)	2.54	40.4	95.0	6.7
West Babylon (CDP)	3.00	38.0	92.4	10.8
West Islip (CDP)	3.22	38.2	96.8	5.4
West Seneca (CDP)	2.47	42.8	91.6	3.1
West Seneca (town)	2.47	42.8	91.6	3.1
White Plains (city)	2.56	39.6	91.3	29.3
Yonkers (city)	2.65	37.4	89.8	26.4
Yorktown (town)	2.86	40.1	93.6	10.5

NOTE: Average Household Size, Median Age, and Male/Female Ratio figures as of 2005. Foreign Born figures as of 2000.

Five Largest Ancestry Groups

Place	Group 1	Group 2	Group 3	Group 4	Group 5
Albany (city)	Other (29.8%)	Irish (18.0%)	Italian (12.4%)	German (10.4%)	English (5.2%)
Amherst (town)	German (25.6%)	Italian (17.8%)	Irish (16.5%)	Polish (13.0%)	Other (10.9%)
Babylon (town)	Italian (30.2%)	Other (23.2%)	Irish (20.5%)	German (15.0%)	Polish (5.4%)
Bethlehem (town)	Irish (24.2%)	German (21.5%)	Italian (16.0%)	English (13.7%)	Other (8.2%)
Binghamton (city)	Irish (19.7%)	Other (16.3%)	Italian (12.8%)	German (12.0%)	English (11.1%)
Brentwood (CDP)	Other (58.4%)	Italian (7.9%)	Irish (6.8%)	German (4.4%)	Haitian (2.7%)
Brighton (town)	Other (18.3%)	German (18.2%)	Irish (16.9%)	English (13.3%)	Italian (11.7%)
Brighton (CDP)	Other (18.3%)	German (18.2%)	Irish (16.9%)	English (13.3%)	Italian (11.7%)
Brookhaven (town)	Italian (32.8%)	Irish (25.1%)	German (19.5%)	Other (16.0%)	Polish (6.0%)
Buffalo (city)	Other (39.5%)	German (13.6%)	Irish (12.2%)	Italian (11.7%)	Polish (11.7%)
Carmel (town)	Italian (35.3%)	Irish (25.0%)	German (15.5%)	Other (9.2%)	Polish (5.5%)
Centereach (CDP)	Italian (36.7%)	Irish (24.8%)	German (19.1%)	Other (14.2%)	Polish (6.6%)
Central Islip (CDP)	Other (50.8%)	Italian (10.0%)	Irish (9.8%)	German (6.5%)	Jamaican (2.7%)
Cheektowaga (town)	Polish (39.9%)	German (29.9%)	Italian (16.0%)	Irish (14.1%)	English (5.8%)
Cheektowaga (CDP)	Polish (39.4%)	German (30.0%)	Italian (15.7%)	Irish (14.0%)	Other (6.0%)
Chili (town)	German (27.2%)	Italian (19.1%)	Irish (18.8%)	English (14.5%)	Other (9.3%)
Cicero (town)	Irish (23.8%)	German (23.7%)	Italian (22.7%)	English (13.9%)	Polish (9.6%)
Clarkstown (town)	Italian (22.7%)	Other (22.2%)	Irish (18.1%)	German (9.9%)	Russian (6.7%)
Clay (town)	Irish (22.8%)	Italian (22.2%)	German (21.6%)	English (13.5%)	Other (9.1%)
Clifton Park (town)	Irish (27.9%)	Italian (19.5%)	German (18.9%)	English (13.8%)	Polish (8.8%)
Colonie (town)	Irish (28.0%)	Italian (20.3%)	German (17.6%)	Other (10.4%)	English (9.7%)
Commack (CDP)	Italian (33.4%)	Irish (19.4%)	German (14.1%)	Other (12.6%)	Polish (7.7%)
Coram (CDP)	Italian (31.7%)	Other (22.7%)	Irish (20.3%)	German (15.5%)	Polish (6.7%)
Cortlandt (town)	Italian (26.5%)	Irish (23.6%)	Other (14.4%)	German (12.6%)	English (6.1%)
Deer Park (CDP)	Italian (42.1%)	Irish (20.8%)	Other (16.9%)	German (12.2%)	Polish (4.8%)
East Fishkill (town)	Italian (30.0%)	Irish (25.9%)	German (19.4%)	Other (10.7%)	English (9.6%)
East Meadow (CDP)	Italian (28.4%)	Other (18.5%)	Irish (17.4%)	German (11.8%)	Polish (8.8%)
Eastchester (town)	Italian (34.6%)	Irish (19.8%)	Other (15.6%)	German (9.1%)	English (5.8%)
Elmira (city)	Irish (17.4%)	German (16.5%)	Other (14.3%)	Italian (11.0%)	English (9.6%)
Elmont (CDP)	Other (33.0%)	Italian (18.4%)	Haitian (10.9%)	German (6.3%)	Jamaican (6.0%)
Franklin Square (CDP)	Italian (47.6%)	Irish (19.1%)	Other (13.9%)	German (13.7%)	Polish (3.8%)
Freeport (village)	Other (52.6%)	Italian (9.1%)	Irish (8.8%)	German (7.5%)	American (3.1%)
Gates (town)	Italian (32.6%)	German (20.1%)	Irish (14.7%)	Other (10.3%)	English (9.6%)
Greece (town)	Italian (27.9%)	German (26.2%)	Irish (18.5%)	English (12.4%)	Other (7.8%)
Greenburgh (town)	Other (29.5%)	Italian (17.9%)	Irish (13.6%)	German (7.7%)	Russian (5.7%)
Guilderland (town)	Irish (24.1%)	Italian (20.5%)	German (20.4%)	English (11.7%)	Other (10.8%)
Hamburg (town)	German (33.9%)	Irish (24.2%)	Polish (22.7%)	Italian (17.9%)	English (10.2%)
Haverstraw (town)	Other (39.1%)	Italian (18.6%)	Irish (15.5%)	German (7.9%)	Polish (4.4%)
Hempstead (village)	Other (61.0%)	Jamaican (5.4%)	Haitian (2.8%)	Italian (2.7%)	Irish (2.4%)
Hempstead (town)	Other (25.5%)	Italian (23.7%)	Irish (17.6%)	German (11.5%)	Polish (5.1%)
Henrietta (town)	German (23.5%)	Irish (17.0%)	Italian (16.2%)	Other (14.8%)	English (13.0%)
Hicksville (CDP)	Italian (28.2%)	Irish (23.4%)	Other (20.1%)	German (16.6%)	Polish (6.2%)
Holbrook (CDP)	Italian (39.9%)	Irish (27.5%)	German (18.8%)	Other (11.3%)	Polish (6.0%)
Huntington (town)	Italian (26.6%)	Irish (21.3%)	German (16.2%)	Other (16.1%)	English (6.4%)
Huntington Station (CDP)	Other (32.7%)	Italian (20.3%)	Irish (17.3%)	German (14.0%)	Polish (4.6%)
Irondequoit (CDP/town)	Italian (28.6%)	German (22.7%)	Irish (18.8%)	English (11.5%)	Other (8.7%)
Islip (town)	Other (27.0%)	Italian (25.9%)	Irish (21.5%)	German (14.8%)	English (4.5%)
Ithaca (city)	Other (27.9%)	German (13.7%)	Irish (12.5%)	Italian (9.8%)	English (9.3%)
Jamestown (city)	Swedish (19.1%)	Italian (18.4%)	German (17.4%)	Irish (14.1%)	English (13.1%)
Lancaster (town)	Polish (35.6%)	German (35.4%)	Italian (18.0%)	Irish (13.9%)	English (7.1%)

Place	Group 1	Group 2	Group 3	Group 4	Group 5
Levittown (CDP)	Italian (34.0%)	Irish (30.4%)	German (18.5%)	Other (12.1%)	Polish (5.5%)
Lindenhurst (village)	Italian (38.8%)	Irish (26.8%)	German (20.2%)	Other (9.6%)	Polish (8.4%)
Long Beach (city)	Other (25.4%)	Irish (20.9%)	Italian (16.3%)	German (9.3%)	Russian (6.7%)
Mamaroneck (town)	Other (20.3%)	Italian (19.6%)	Irish (14.6%)	German (9.6%)	Russian (7.2%)
Manlius (town)	Irish (23.6%)	German (21.9%)	English (17.3%)	Italian (15.7%)	Polish (8.2%)
Monroe (town)	Other (31.2%)	Irish (14.6%)	Italian (13.0%)	German (9.0%)	Hungarian (8.3%)
Mount Pleasant (town)	Italian (28.8%)	Other (19.5%)	Irish (18.5%)	German (10.2%)	English (5.4%)
Mount Vernon (city)	Other (46.2%)	Jamaican (12.3%)	Italian (10.3%)	Irish (4.0%)	American (2.7%)
New City (CDP)	Italian (21.6%)	Other (19.8%)	Irish (16.8%)	German (9.9%)	Russian (9.8%)
New Rochelle (city)	Other (35.0%)	Italian (20.0%)	Irish (8.9%)	German (5.3%)	American (4.4%)
New York (city)	Other (48.1%)	Italian (8.7%)	Irish (5.3%)	German (3.2%)	Russian (3.0%)
Newburgh (city)	Other (57.8%)	Italian (9.2%)	Irish (8.2%)	German (5.3%)	English (3.0%)
Newburgh (town)	Italian (26.1%)	Irish (22.3%)	Other (19.6%)	German (14.4%)	English (7.9%)
Niagara Falls (city)	Italian (23.1%)	Other (20.8%)	German (16.7%)	Irish (13.7%)	Polish (11.0%)
North Hempstead (town)	Other (25.2%)	Italian (17.9%)	Irish (12.9%)	German (8.9%)	Polish (5.9%)
North Tonawanda (city)	German (35.3%)	Polish (20.9%)	Italian (17.0%)	Irish (17.0%)	English (10.2%)
Oceanside (CDP)	Italian (29.0%)	Irish (17.9%)	Other (16.6%)	German (13.2%)	Russian (7.4%)
Orangetown (town)	Irish (30.1%)	Italian (20.0%)	Other (17.7%)	German (11.9%)	English (5.6%)
Ossining (town)	Other (30.3%)	Italian (16.2%)	Irish (11.9%)	German (8.1%)	English (4.9%)
Oyster Bay (town)	Italian (29.9%)	Irish (20.6%)	Other (15.0%)	German (14.5%)	Polish (6.7%)
Penfield (town)	German (24.3%)	Italian (23.5%)	Irish (18.3%)	English (16.2%)	Other (8.0%)
Perinton (town)	German (24.6%)	Irish (20.6%)	Italian (19.6%)	English (16.1%)	Other (7.7%)
Poughkeepsie (town)	Italian (20.5%)	Irish (19.5%)	Other (16.3%)	German (14.3%)	English (10.6%)
Poughkeepsie (city)	Other (39.4%)	Italian (12.4%)	Irish (11.9%)	German (8.6%)	Jamaican (5.1%)
Ramapo (town)	Other (31.9%)	Italian (9.2%)	Irish (7.9%)	Haitian (6.9%)	American (6.2%)
Riverhead (town)	Irish (22.4%)	German (20.0%)	Italian (18.8%)	Other (17.3%)	Polish (15.0%)
Rochester (city)	Other (45.5%)	German (10.9%)	Italian (10.0%)	Irish (9.6%)	English (5.8%)
Rome (city)	Italian (25.7%)	Irish (15.6%)	German (14.7%)	Other (9.7%)	English (9.5%)
Rotterdam (town)	Italian (33.0%)	Irish (20.6%)	German (17.2%)	Polish (13.2%)	English (9.7%)
Rye (town)	Other (36.6%)	Italian (24.3%)	Irish (9.3%)	German (5.5%)	American (4.0%)
Salina (town)	Italian (28.1%)	German (20.9%)	Irish (19.1%)	English (12.4%)	Polish (7.9%)
Schenectady (city)	Other (21.8%)	Italian (19.7%)	Irish (15.8%)	German (12.2%)	Polish (9.0%)
Smithtown (town)	Italian (35.3%)	Irish (26.0%)	German (18.7%)	Other (9.0%)	Polish (6.9%)
Southampton (town)	Irish (22.0%)	Italian (18.4%)	German (17.7%)	Other (14.9%)	English (11.2%)
Syracuse (city)	Other (32.3%)	Irish (15.9%)	Italian (14.1%)	German (12.2%)	English (7.6%)
Tonawanda (town)	German (32.7%)	Italian (24.2%)	Irish (21.5%)	Polish (14.0%)	English (10.6%)
Tonawanda (CDP)	German (33.2%)	Italian (23.5%)	Irish (21.3%)	Polish (14.6%)	English (10.8%)
Troy (city)	Irish (24.3%)	Other (17.5%)	Italian (14.2%)	German (12.7%)	French[1] (9.1%)
Union (town)	Irish (19.1%)	Italian (17.2%)	German (15.0%)	English (14.5%)	Other (9.5%)
Utica (city)	Italian (26.1%)	Other (19.6%)	Irish (12.3%)	German (10.0%)	Polish (8.6%)
Valley Stream (village)	Italian (31.8%)	Other (23.9%)	Irish (17.2%)	German (11.3%)	Polish (4.6%)
Warwick (town)	Irish (25.6%)	Italian (19.6%)	German (18.4%)	Other (10.8%)	Polish (10.0%)
Webster (town)	German (27.0%)	Italian (23.7%)	Irish (18.5%)	English (14.6%)	Polish (7.7%)
West Babylon (CDP)	Italian (36.3%)	Irish (22.1%)	German (17.3%)	Other (17.1%)	Polish (5.5%)
West Islip (CDP)	Italian (38.4%)	Irish (30.9%)	German (20.8%)	Polish (7.2%)	Other (7.1%)
West Seneca (CDP)	German (32.8%)	Polish (30.9%)	Irish (22.9%)	Italian (17.9%)	English (6.7%)
West Seneca (town)	German (32.8%)	Polish (30.9%)	Irish (22.9%)	Italian (17.9%)	English (6.7%)
White Plains (city)	Other (38.5%)	Italian (15.2%)	Irish (11.5%)	German (6.9%)	Russian (4.1%)
Yonkers (city)	Other (38.7%)	Italian (18.8%)	Irish (12.9%)	German (4.7%)	Polish (3.3%)
Yorktown (town)	Italian (34.2%)	Irish (22.6%)	Other (14.0%)	German (13.0%)	English (6.4%)

NOTE: Data as of 2000; (1) except Basque; "Other" includes Hispanic and race groups. Please refer to the Explanation of Data for more information.

Marriage Status

Place	Never Married (%)	Now Married (%)	Widowed (%)	Divorced (%)
Albany (city)	45.5	37.8	8.5	8.2
Amherst (town)	23.6	62.1	7.7	6.6
Babylon (town)	27.8	57.0	7.9	7.3
Bethlehem (town)	19.8	66.0	7.0	7.2
Binghamton (city)	37.0	41.9	9.9	11.3
Brentwood (CDP)	33.8	55.0	4.5	6.7
Brighton (town)	27.1	55.0	9.1	8.7
Brighton (CDP)	27.1	55.0	9.1	8.7
Brookhaven (town)	26.8	60.0	6.1	7.0
Buffalo (city)	40.0	40.5	9.1	10.4
Carmel (town)	23.7	65.3	5.6	5.4
Centereach (CDP)	26.1	62.4	5.2	6.3
Central Islip (CDP)	35.2	52.1	4.2	8.4
Cheektowaga (town)	25.1	55.6	10.9	8.4
Cheektowaga (CDP)	25.3	55.6	10.9	8.2
Chili (town)	25.1	62.7	5.6	6.7
Cicero (town)	22.4	63.1	5.6	9.0
Clarkstown (town)	24.0	64.7	6.0	5.3
Clay (town)	25.5	60.7	5.1	8.7
Clifton Park (town)	21.5	67.8	4.5	6.3
Colonie (town)	26.1	58.7	7.3	7.9
Commack (CDP)	19.2	69.9	6.5	4.4
Coram (CDP)	26.3	60.1	5.8	7.8
Cortlandt (town)	20.7	65.5	6.9	6.9
Deer Park (CDP)	24.7	61.8	7.9	5.6
East Fishkill (town)	20.2	71.0	3.9	4.9
East Meadow (CDP)	21.7	65.2	7.9	5.3
Eastchester (town)	24.0	62.3	8.3	5.4
Elmira (city)	35.8	44.6	7.7	11.9
Elmont (CDP)	29.7	56.2	7.6	6.5
Franklin Square (CDP)	23.5	61.6	9.8	5.1
Freeport (village)	32.9	52.1	7.1	7.9
Gates (town)	23.7	58.5	8.4	9.4
Greece (town)	23.9	59.7	7.7	8.7
Greenburgh (town)	24.8	61.7	6.8	6.8
Guilderland (town)	24.1	60.8	6.6	8.4
Hamburg (town)	23.8	58.9	8.6	8.8
Haverstraw (town)	28.8	57.0	6.4	7.8
Hempstead (village)	45.6	42.4	5.8	6.2
Hempstead (town)	26.8	59.8	7.6	5.7
Henrietta (town)	35.9	52.5	5.1	6.6
Hicksville (CDP)	26.3	60.5	7.9	5.3
Holbrook (CDP)	24.3	63.5	5.5	6.6
Huntington (town)	23.5	64.1	6.7	5.8
Huntington Station (CDP)	31.9	54.8	6.1	7.2
Irondequoit (CDP/town)	22.5	58.4	10.9	8.3
Islip (town)	27.2	59.6	6.0	7.2
Ithaca (city)	65.3	25.8	3.1	5.7
Jamestown (city)	29.3	49.5	8.9	12.3
Lancaster (town)	23.2	61.3	8.3	7.2

Place	Never Married (%)	Now Married (%)	Widowed (%)	Divorced (%)
Levittown (CDP)	24.8	62.0	7.3	5.9
Lindenhurst (village)	25.8	60.2	7.3	6.7
Long Beach (city)	32.7	49.0	8.7	9.5
Mamaroneck (town)	22.2	65.6	6.7	5.6
Manlius (town)	20.3	65.4	7.7	6.6
Monroe (town)	26.1	65.3	4.1	4.6
Mount Pleasant (town)	28.2	60.7	6.2	4.8
Mount Vernon (city)	36.3	46.6	8.5	8.5
New City (CDP)	21.6	68.7	5.6	4.1
New Rochelle (city)	29.9	55.1	8.2	6.8
New York (city)	37.6	47.7	7.0	7.7
Newburgh (city)	41.0	44.8	6.1	8.0
Newburgh (town)	22.0	64.5	6.5	7.0
Niagara Falls (city)	31.7	46.8	10.2	11.4
North Hempstead (town)	24.6	63.0	7.4	5.0
North Tonawanda (city)	26.6	57.2	7.8	8.3
Oceanside (CDP)	22.0	66.1	7.3	4.7
Orangetown (town)	28.1	58.3	7.4	6.3
Ossining (town)	31.1	56.4	6.0	6.5
Oyster Bay (town)	22.7	65.1	7.4	4.8
Penfield (town)	20.4	65.4	6.1	8.1
Perinton (town)	20.0	66.0	6.0	8.1
Poughkeepsie (town)	29.7	57.8	6.2	6.2
Poughkeepsie (city)	40.5	41.5	8.5	9.5
Ramapo (town)	27.8	61.0	5.5	5.6
Riverhead (town)	21.8	60.2	9.7	8.3
Rochester (city)	43.7	38.1	7.0	11.1
Rome (city)	30.0	50.6	9.3	10.1
Rotterdam (town)	21.6	60.8	9.0	8.6
Rye (town)	29.1	56.9	7.7	6.4
Salina (town)	26.8	54.7	9.5	8.9
Schenectady (city)	35.5	44.3	9.2	10.9
Smithtown (town)	20.8	66.5	7.5	5.1
Southampton (town)	25.5	57.8	8.0	8.7
Syracuse (city)	45.4	37.2	7.8	9.6
Tonawanda (town)	25.1	56.4	10.2	8.3
Tonawanda (CDP)	23.9	57.6	10.3	8.2
Troy (city)	39.0	42.8	8.5	9.7
Union (town)	26.6	53.9	9.5	10.1
Utica (city)	34.0	46.1	11.2	8.7
Valley Stream (village)	26.6	58.2	9.0	6.1
Warwick (town)	22.4	64.8	6.1	6.7
Webster (town)	21.8	64.7	6.0	7.6
West Babylon (CDP)	26.7	57.6	8.1	7.7
West Islip (CDP)	22.8	65.2	6.7	5.3
West Seneca (CDP)	24.4	59.3	8.9	7.4
West Seneca (town)	24.4	59.3	8.9	7.4
White Plains (city)	31.6	52.4	7.6	8.4
Yonkers (city)	32.9	50.8	8.5	7.8
Yorktown (town)	19.6	67.8	7.6	4.9

NOTE: Data as of 2000

Employment and Building Permits Issued

Place	Unemployment Rate (%)	Total Civilian Labor Force	Single-Family Building Permits	Multi-Family Building Permits
Albany (city)	4.5	47,692	3	182
Amherst (town)	4.1	61,038	229	234
Babylon (town)	4.7	112,755	127	0
Bethlehem (town)	3.0	17,941	95	0
Binghamton (city)	5.5	20,896	5	2
Brentwood (CDP)	n/a	n/a	n/a	n/a
Brighton (town)	3.5	18,270	24	182
Brighton (CDP)	n/a	n/a	n/a	n/a
Brookhaven (town)	4.2	252,744	2,057	672
Buffalo (city)	6.6	124,741	97	13
Carmel (town)	3.6	19,347	44	0
Centereach (CDP)	n/a	n/a	n/a	n/a
Central Islip (CDP)	n/a	n/a	n/a	n/a
Cheektowaga (town)	5.3	49,421	31	36
Cheektowaga (CDP)	n/a	n/a	n/a	n/a
Chili (town)	4.3	15,608	101	4
Cicero (town)	4.2	16,475	129	0
Clarkstown (town)	3.8	47,315	69	0
Clay (town)	4.1	33,905	143	8
Clifton Park (town)	2.7	21,354	107	0
Colonie (town)	3.5	44,939	94	171
Commack (CDP)	n/a	n/a	n/a	n/a
Coram (CDP)	n/a	n/a	n/a	n/a
Cortlandt (town)	3.7	21,485	63	0
Deer Park (CDP)	n/a	n/a	n/a	n/a
East Fishkill (town)	3.7	15,229	186	0
East Meadow (CDP)	n/a	n/a	n/a	n/a
Eastchester (town)	3.7	16,266	4	0
Elmira (city)	6.1	11,938	6	0
Elmont (CDP)	n/a	n/a	n/a	n/a
Franklin Square (CDP)	n/a	n/a	n/a	n/a
Freeport (village)	5.0	22,717	9	0
Gates (town)	5.1	14,850	40	56
Greece (town)	4.6	50,399	214	10
Greenburgh (town)	3.4	50,612	14	0
Guilderland (town)	2.8	20,201	83	0
Hamburg (town)	4.9	31,567	201	0
Haverstraw (town)	5.5	18,081	11	0
Hempstead (village)	6.2	25,900	34	20
Hempstead (town)	4.3	390,589	638	0
Henrietta (town)	4.1	22,429	171	0
Hicksville (CDP)	n/a	n/a	n/a	n/a
Holbrook (CDP)	n/a	n/a	n/a	n/a
Huntington (town)	3.8	105,827	209	0
Huntington Station (CDP)	n/a	n/a	n/a	n/a
Irondequoit (CDP/town)	4.8	25,676	13	0
Islip (town)	4.3	175,742	513	268
Ithaca (city)	3.2	15,183	7	17
Jamestown (city)	5.3	14,751	5	0
Lancaster (town)	4.4	23,493	110	0

PROFILES OF NEW YORK / Comparative Statistics

Place	Unemployment Rate (%)	Total Civilian Labor Force	Single-Family Building Permits	Multi-Family Building Permits
Levittown (CDP)	n/a	n/a	n/a	n/a
Lindenhurst (village)	4.9	15,185	21	0
Long Beach (city)	4.0	19,748	7	20
Mamaroneck (town)	3.2	15,203	22	0
Manlius (town)	3.6	17,065	87	16
Monroe (town)	3.7	13,992	84	110
Mount Pleasant (town)	3.9	22,192	24	0
Mount Vernon (city)	5.3	34,438	7	34
New City (CDP)	n/a	n/a	n/a	n/a
New Rochelle (city)	4.7	37,709	41	5
New York (city)	5.8	3,733,908	1,300	30,299
Newburgh (city)	5.9	11,757	5	2
Newburgh (town)	4.0	16,316	95	6
Niagara Falls (city)	7.0	24,433	1	0
North Hempstead (town)	3.8	114,315	96	0
North Tonawanda (city)	5.0	17,863	8	0
Oceanside (CDP)	n/a	n/a	n/a	n/a
Orangetown (town)	3.9	26,939	42	0
Ossining (town)	3.8	18,692	5	0
Oyster Bay (town)	3.8	156,452	166	4
Penfield (town)	3.6	19,172	136	0
Perinton (town)	3.4	26,073	66	4
Poughkeepsie (town)	3.8	22,682	43	0
Poughkeepsie (city)	4.7	13,803	18	0
Ramapo (town)	4.0	51,820	47	39
Riverhead (town)	4.1	16,366	168	0
Rochester (city)	6.1	96,446	65	0
Rome (city)	5.2	15,126	17	0
Rotterdam (town)	3.9	15,179	44	52
Rye (town)	3.9	23,675	n/a	n/a
Salina (town)	4.5	18,287	47	0
Schenectady (city)	5.1	29,875	6	0
Smithtown (town)	3.7	62,364	96	0
Southampton (town)	4.1	30,311	434	0
Syracuse (city)	5.7	64,785	21	0
Tonawanda (town)	4.8	40,121	15	0
Tonawanda (CDP)	n/a	n/a	n/a	n/a
Troy (city)	5.1	23,931	25	48
Union (town)	4.6	28,209	38	14
Utica (city)	5.4	26,258	6	3
Valley Stream (village)	4.3	19,154	9	0
Warwick (town)	4.0	16,606	86	0
Webster (town)	3.7	22,063	232	0
West Babylon (CDP)	n/a	n/a	n/a	n/a
West Islip (CDP)	n/a	n/a	n/a	n/a
West Seneca (CDP)	n/a	n/a	n/a	n/a
West Seneca (town)	4.7	24,635	54	0
White Plains (city)	3.6	30,698	13	2
Yonkers (city)	5.2	93,994	38	127
Yorktown (town)	3.6	20,288	25	162

NOTE: Unemployment Rate and Civilian Labor Force are 2005 annual averages; Building permit data covers 2005; n/a not available.

Employment by Occupation

Place	Sales	Professional	Management	Services	Production	Construction
Albany (city)	28.7	28.2	12.8	18.3	7.4	4.6
Amherst (town)	26.7	32.9	19.2	10.7	6.6	3.9
Babylon (town)	30.4	16.9	12.0	16.2	13.7	10.7
Bethlehem (town)	24.3	36.7	18.6	9.9	5.8	4.5
Binghamton (city)	27.0	21.7	9.5	21.1	15.1	5.5
Brentwood (CDP)	24.5	11.3	7.2	19.1	27.9	9.9
Brighton (town)	21.0	45.1	16.0	8.8	5.7	3.4
Brighton (CDP)	21.0	45.1	16.0	8.8	5.7	3.4
Brookhaven (town)	29.1	22.3	12.7	14.3	10.4	11.0
Buffalo (city)	27.0	20.8	8.4	21.1	17.2	5.5
Carmel (town)	26.7	23.3	16.8	13.3	6.8	13.0
Centereach (CDP)	31.3	19.2	13.7	15.1	10.8	9.7
Central Islip (CDP)	29.3	13.9	7.9	18.5	20.6	9.7
Cheektowaga (town)	31.9	16.8	10.5	14.8	18.3	7.5
Cheektowaga (CDP)	32.2	17.3	10.9	14.5	18.0	7.1
Chili (town)	28.4	24.4	13.8	14.1	14.1	5.0
Cicero (town)	31.5	19.4	13.1	12.4	14.8	8.6
Clarkstown (town)	25.5	31.1	18.5	12.8	6.2	5.9
Clay (town)	32.9	22.7	14.6	11.4	12.5	5.9
Clifton Park (town)	25.1	35.1	21.5	7.8	6.4	4.2
Colonie (town)	31.1	24.7	16.4	12.4	8.8	6.5
Commack (CDP)	29.7	27.1	18.8	10.9	6.1	7.3
Coram (CDP)	31.6	22.7	14.8	13.3	8.3	9.1
Cortlandt (town)	26.0	29.0	18.6	11.3	6.0	9.0
Deer Park (CDP)	30.2	17.2	13.6	15.5	11.6	11.9
East Fishkill (town)	26.3	26.6	15.3	10.3	9.7	11.6
East Meadow (CDP)	33.3	24.1	14.8	11.5	7.7	8.6
Eastchester (town)	27.0	28.7	25.9	10.0	4.1	4.3
Elmira (city)	26.2	19.0	8.3	24.3	16.2	5.8
Elmont (CDP)	32.1	18.8	11.5	18.9	10.9	7.5
Franklin Square (CDP)	34.5	17.9	15.4	12.8	8.9	10.4
Freeport (village)	28.0	17.0	10.4	20.6	15.7	8.2
Gates (town)	30.8	17.8	10.1	13.2	21.1	7.0
Greece (town)	29.2	21.5	12.3	13.0	17.5	6.5
Greenburgh (town)	24.0	34.0	22.1	10.6	4.7	4.6
Guilderland (town)	26.3	32.9	20.3	9.1	5.8	5.4
Hamburg (town)	28.6	22.3	12.2	14.8	14.8	7.1
Haverstraw (town)	27.3	19.6	11.0	20.2	12.2	9.6
Hempstead (village)	27.9	14.6	7.3	28.3	14.9	6.7
Hempstead (town)	30.9	22.8	15.3	14.8	8.6	7.5
Henrietta (town)	30.1	27.1	11.5	13.9	11.2	6.2
Hicksville (CDP)	33.3	19.9	13.3	14.8	9.5	8.9
Holbrook (CDP)	33.7	20.4	13.3	11.4	11.7	9.4
Huntington (town)	27.9	28.5	19.3	11.2	6.0	7.0
Huntington Station (CDP)	28.6	20.1	11.9	18.3	10.8	10.1
Irondequoit (CDP/town)	28.0	27.3	14.2	11.7	12.5	6.3
Islip (town)	28.9	19.1	12.1	14.5	15.0	10.2
Ithaca (city)	24.2	45.0	8.8	15.5	3.9	2.1
Jamestown (city)	23.4	18.5	8.2	20.0	23.3	6.5
Lancaster (town)	29.7	19.6	14.0	15.4	13.3	7.9

Place	Sales	Professional	Management	Services	Production	Construction
Levittown (CDP)	34.0	19.7	12.4	15.0	9.0	9.8
Lindenhurst (village)	31.3	16.7	10.5	16.0	14.3	11.1
Long Beach (city)	30.4	26.7	15.6	14.5	6.8	6.0
Mamaroneck (town)	25.6	31.7	24.0	9.4	4.6	4.6
Manlius (town)	28.0	31.3	17.9	9.6	8.1	4.9
Monroe (town)	30.5	22.8	14.1	14.0	10.2	8.3
Mount Pleasant (town)	24.3	26.5	20.8	13.2	6.3	8.7
Mount Vernon (city)	28.4	22.2	12.0	20.3	8.8	8.2
New City (CDP)	24.5	33.9	20.5	10.5	5.1	5.5
New Rochelle (city)	25.2	26.8	15.5	17.0	7.0	8.4
New York (city)	27.4	23.3	13.5	18.6	10.9	6.4
Newburgh (city)	23.8	12.4	5.7	22.7	27.2	8.0
Newburgh (town)	26.9	23.1	13.0	14.0	11.7	11.0
Niagara Falls (city)	29.2	15.1	9.2	20.0	18.7	7.7
North Hempstead (town)	28.4	29.2	19.0	11.4	6.8	5.3
North Tonawanda (city)	28.6	19.4	10.4	14.2	19.8	7.3
Oceanside (CDP)	30.7	26.1	16.7	12.0	6.1	8.3
Orangetown (town)	25.5	29.5	16.6	14.8	6.5	7.1
Ossining (town)	21.5	27.5	18.7	17.3	6.8	8.2
Oyster Bay (town)	30.9	24.7	18.6	11.9	6.7	7.1
Penfield (town)	25.7	30.2	21.1	9.9	8.1	4.8
Perinton (town)	24.8	32.8	22.3	10.0	6.3	3.7
Poughkeepsie (town)	28.1	28.6	11.0	14.8	10.0	7.3
Poughkeepsie (city)	23.7	20.5	9.8	26.9	11.6	7.2
Ramapo (town)	25.7	28.1	16.0	15.6	8.1	6.3
Riverhead (town)	26.4	23.8	10.2	17.4	9.5	11.5
Rochester (city)	23.8	22.1	8.9	21.1	17.7	6.3
Rome (city)	26.2	19.6	11.0	21.5	15.2	6.3
Rotterdam (town)	33.7	17.1	12.2	14.0	13.0	9.9
Rye (town)	25.9	19.5	15.4	20.4	9.1	9.6
Salina (town)	30.5	20.4	13.3	14.2	14.9	6.7
Schenectady (city)	28.9	20.6	9.1	21.8	12.5	6.9
Smithtown (town)	28.4	26.6	18.4	12.5	6.0	8.0
Southampton (town)	27.3	20.9	12.6	17.5	6.6	14.2
Syracuse (city)	25.8	23.7	9.0	21.6	14.5	5.3
Tonawanda (town)	30.6	23.3	11.7	13.5	13.9	6.9
Tonawanda (CDP)	31.2	22.6	11.4	13.4	14.2	7.1
Troy (city)	27.2	22.2	10.2	19.1	13.8	7.5
Union (town)	28.9	23.1	12.2	14.8	14.4	6.4
Utica (city)	27.9	18.1	9.0	21.1	17.7	5.9
Valley Stream (village)	35.6	19.5	14.0	13.9	8.1	8.8
Warwick (town)	26.1	22.0	18.1	14.4	8.5	10.4
Webster (town)	24.4	30.8	17.4	10.5	11.0	5.8
West Babylon (CDP)	30.3	16.9	12.2	16.6	12.6	11.3
West Islip (CDP)	28.9	21.7	14.4	13.4	9.8	11.7
West Seneca (CDP)	30.1	19.5	12.9	15.5	14.4	7.4
West Seneca (town)	30.2	19.5	12.9	15.5	14.4	7.4
White Plains (city)	25.2	27.2	18.7	17.2	6.4	5.3
Yonkers (city)	29.9	20.7	13.5	17.1	10.1	8.7
Yorktown (town)	27.0	29.2	19.8	9.5	5.1	9.2

NOTE: Data as of 2000

Educational Attainment

Place	Percent of Population 25 Years and Over with:		
	High School Diploma including Equivalency	Bachelor's Degree or Higher	Masters's Degree or Higher
Albany (city)	81.3	32.7	15.4
Amherst (town)	91.9	47.5	22.7
Babylon (town)	82.1	18.6	7.0
Bethlehem (town)	93.1	49.8	27.1
Binghamton (city)	77.9	21.3	10.3
Brentwood (CDP)	65.8	11.2	4.3
Brighton (town)	91.4	57.2	30.9
Brighton (CDP)	91.4	57.2	30.9
Brookhaven (town)	86.9	24.6	11.1
Buffalo (city)	75.0	18.8	8.0
Carmel (town)	90.6	33.2	13.9
Centereach (CDP)	87.9	22.3	8.5
Central Islip (CDP)	74.7	15.1	5.7
Cheektowaga (town)	80.5	15.2	4.8
Cheektowaga (CDP)	81.1	16.0	5.2
Chili (town)	89.7	28.8	10.2
Cicero (town)	87.3	21.9	7.3
Clarkstown (town)	89.9	44.9	20.3
Clay (town)	90.7	27.7	9.6
Clifton Park (town)	95.9	52.8	22.5
Colonie (town)	89.1	32.7	14.7
Commack (CDP)	92.6	37.4	14.9
Coram (CDP)	88.3	26.3	11.1
Cortlandt (town)	90.3	41.3	19.4
Deer Park (CDP)	85.1	19.8	6.5
East Fishkill (town)	91.5	35.5	15.5
East Meadow (CDP)	86.2	28.9	12.8
Eastchester (town)	90.8	52.0	25.1
Elmira (city)	74.1	14.3	5.7
Elmont (CDP)	80.0	21.2	8.1
Franklin Square (CDP)	83.1	22.3	8.0
Freeport (village)	72.7	20.3	8.8
Gates (town)	80.8	17.0	5.4
Greece (town)	87.8	23.5	7.7
Greenburgh (town)	91.0	53.8	27.5
Guilderland (town)	92.5	44.9	21.6
Hamburg (town)	87.1	26.2	10.0
Haverstraw (town)	76.9	23.0	9.2
Hempstead (village)	66.3	15.8	6.3
Hempstead (town)	85.3	31.2	13.3
Henrietta (town)	90.4	30.5	11.3
Hicksville (CDP)	86.5	25.8	10.0
Holbrook (CDP)	90.1	22.7	7.8
Huntington (town)	90.8	44.5	19.8
Huntington Station (CDP)	79.6	27.5	10.8
Irondequoit (CDP/town)	84.4	27.9	10.5
Islip (town)	83.0	21.8	8.7
Ithaca (city)	90.2	60.0	32.3
Jamestown (city)	79.3	14.7	6.2
Lancaster (town)	85.8	22.2	7.0

PROFILES OF NEW YORK / Comparative Statistics

Place	Percent of Population 25 Years and Over with:		
	High School Diploma including Equivalency	Bachelor's Degree or Higher	Masters's Degree or Higher
Levittown (CDP)	88.9	22.5	8.4
Lindenhurst (village)	83.7	16.4	5.9
Long Beach (city)	88.7	37.1	14.9
Mamaroneck (town)	90.6	57.3	32.1
Manlius (town)	93.8	47.8	22.0
Monroe (town)	74.6	22.5	8.2
Mount Pleasant (town)	84.5	43.6	20.4
Mount Vernon (city)	74.6	24.3	9.8
New City (CDP)	91.1	52.5	25.1
New Rochelle (city)	79.8	38.2	19.6
New York (city)	72.1	27.2	11.5
Newburgh (city)	61.8	10.9	4.5
Newburgh (town)	86.9	23.6	9.4
Niagara Falls (city)	77.1	12.8	4.9
North Hempstead (town)	86.9	45.5	22.7
North Tonawanda (city)	85.7	19.8	7.2
Oceanside (CDP)	90.2	36.3	17.8
Orangetown (town)	90.1	43.0	18.2
Ossining (town)	77.7	41.0	19.8
Oyster Bay (town)	90.0	38.0	16.0
Penfield (town)	91.4	46.2	19.3
Perinton (town)	94.3	52.0	21.4
Poughkeepsie (town)	87.4	30.8	14.2
Poughkeepsie (city)	72.2	19.3	8.6
Ramapo (town)	81.0	34.2	14.9
Riverhead (town)	81.7	21.9	10.3
Rochester (city)	73.2	20.4	8.1
Rome (city)	73.7	15.7	5.7
Rotterdam (town)	86.7	16.3	5.5
Rye (town)	75.6	30.8	14.0
Salina (town)	85.0	21.3	7.3
Schenectady (city)	78.0	19.2	7.8
Smithtown (town)	91.5	36.4	15.9
Southampton (town)	86.3	31.2	13.8
Syracuse (city)	76.6	24.0	11.4
Tonawanda (town)	87.6	26.9	9.9
Tonawanda (CDP)	87.1	26.3	9.7
Troy (city)	78.0	19.7	8.4
Union (town)	84.9	23.9	10.0
Utica (city)	72.9	15.5	6.3
Valley Stream (village)	86.2	25.0	9.1
Warwick (town)	86.0	26.6	11.2
Webster (town)	91.8	37.4	14.9
West Babylon (CDP)	82.6	17.2	6.1
West Islip (CDP)	90.1	26.6	10.7
West Seneca (CDP)	86.2	20.4	7.2
West Seneca (town)	86.1	20.4	7.2
White Plains (city)	81.8	40.9	19.8
Yonkers (city)	76.8	24.9	10.4
Yorktown (town)	90.4	42.9	19.5

NOTE: Data as of 2005

Income and Poverty

Place	Average Household Income ($)	Median Household Income ($)	Per Capita Income ($)	Households with income of $100,000+ (%)	Poverty Rate[1] (%)
Albany (city)	46,324	33,375	20,375	9.5	21.7
Amherst (town)	80,299	62,294	31,726	25.7	6.4
Babylon (town)	78,644	66,558	26,025	26.1	6.7
Bethlehem (town)	95,264	73,848	37,564	34.2	3.1
Binghamton (city)	40,708	28,299	18,616	6.8	23.7
Brentwood (CDP)	71,208	62,397	16,565	20.7	11.3
Brighton (town)	77,448	58,422	35,237	23.9	6.1
Brighton (CDP)	77,450	58,421	35,239	23.9	6.1
Brookhaven (town)	85,512	72,201	28,560	30.4	5.9
Buffalo (city)	38,195	26,877	16,431	5.6	26.6
Carmel (town)	104,162	88,402	34,597	42.2	2.8
Centereach (CDP)	89,925	77,964	27,794	33.4	5.6
Central Islip (CDP)	70,951	60,763	19,548	19.5	11.4
Cheektowaga (town)	51,364	42,649	22,304	8.9	6.5
Cheektowaga (CDP)	51,534	42,540	22,440	9.1	6.5
Chili (town)	68,859	59,978	25,946	18.4	3.6
Cicero (town)	64,439	56,372	24,662	15.7	5.1
Clarkstown (town)	115,157	94,008	39,886	46.3	3.8
Clay (town)	64,753	55,616	25,004	16.4	5.7
Clifton Park (town)	94,757	79,518	37,382	35.8	2.6
Colonie (town)	74,475	60,079	30,057	21.5	4.7
Commack (CDP)	111,252	96,672	36,515	47.8	2.8
Coram (CDP)	78,217	69,462	28,773	27.0	5.6
Cortlandt (town)	108,628	86,242	38,606	42.0	4.5
Deer Park (CDP)	80,051	68,895	27,429	27.8	4.7
East Fishkill (town)	104,289	91,553	34,237	44.0	2.8
East Meadow (CDP)	91,906	74,633	30,876	33.7	3.8
Eastchester (town)	133,813	93,513	54,244	46.6	4.2
Elmira (city)	38,874	29,897	15,988	5.0	23.1
Elmont (CDP)	82,380	70,056	24,590	28.9	7.5
Franklin Square (CDP)	80,918	69,468	27,874	29.3	5.0
Freeport (village)	75,446	62,490	23,384	25.2	10.6
Gates (town)	58,949	49,982	24,235	12.4	5.6
Greece (town)	63,839	53,210	25,558	15.8	4.8
Greenburgh (town)	130,034	93,076	49,986	46.3	3.9
Guilderland (town)	83,721	67,556	34,979	27.3	4.1
Hamburg (town)	63,844	54,429	25,510	17.2	4.5
Haverstraw (town)	73,630	60,985	24,925	24.5	10.6
Hempstead (village)	60,374	47,936	16,307	16.5	17.7
Hempstead (town)	96,821	77,807	31,749	35.9	5.8
Henrietta (town)	64,818	57,145	22,386	16.2	9.1
Hicksville (CDP)	92,968	77,675	31,270	34.6	3.7
Holbrook (CDP)	97,507	84,988	32,651	38.3	3.3
Huntington (town)	122,467	94,082	41,995	46.5	4.6
Huntington Station (CDP)	81,318	68,312	26,373	28.1	11.2
Irondequoit (CDP/town)	60,177	49,436	26,108	14.2	5.4
Islip (town)	87,325	73,044	27,195	30.9	6.6
Ithaca (city)	39,744	24,796	15,389	8.0	40.2
Jamestown (city)	37,340	27,792	16,474	4.6	19.5
Lancaster (town)	65,101	57,006	25,582	18.2	3.9

PROFILES OF NEW YORK / Comparative Statistics

Place	Average Household Income ($)	Median Household Income ($)	Per Capita Income ($)	Households with income of $100,000+ (%)	Poverty Rate[1] (%)
Levittown (CDP)	89,820	78,405	29,500	33.4	2.9
Lindenhurst (village)	77,143	68,596	25,362	27.0	6.4
Long Beach (city)	84,391	65,002	36,500	28.0	9.4
Mamaroneck (town)	163,266	97,451	61,767	49.0	4.5
Manlius (town)	90,166	68,305	36,254	30.3	3.3
Monroe (town)	70,446	54,484	17,980	25.1	29.1
Mount Pleasant (town)	129,339	93,984	41,736	47.1	4.9
Mount Vernon (city)	60,261	44,968	22,819	16.6	14.2
New City (CDP)	132,794	105,741	44,191	52.9	2.8
New Rochelle (city)	97,198	64,448	35,274	31.4	10.5
New York (city)	65,503	43,515	24,898	17.7	21.2
Newburgh (city)	43,181	32,955	14,259	6.7	25.8
Newburgh (town)	77,688	66,715	28,082	24.1	3.8
Niagara Falls (city)	38,978	29,129	17,236	5.5	19.5
North Hempstead (town)	131,337	92,179	45,366	45.9	4.8
North Tonawanda (city)	53,705	44,619	22,458	11.0	7.2
Oceanside (CDP)	101,946	86,600	35,179	41.9	3.5
Orangetown (town)	103,872	81,258	38,806	39.6	4.8
Ossining (town)	112,463	75,799	38,972	38.7	8.4
Oyster Bay (town)	119,843	90,957	41,176	44.5	3.3
Penfield (town)	90,078	72,184	34,615	32.3	3.7
Perinton (town)	97,041	78,905	37,917	35.1	2.9
Poughkeepsie (town)	75,453	62,694	26,616	23.1	5.7
Poughkeepsie (city)	43,492	30,591	17,792	9.2	22.7
Ramapo (town)	85,841	65,717	25,109	30.7	16.3
Riverhead (town)	68,895	52,939	27,397	21.7	8.6
Rochester (city)	39,569	28,896	16,385	5.9	25.9
Rome (city)	48,187	37,847	20,559	8.8	15.0
Rotterdam (town)	60,272	52,117	24,962	13.9	4.5
Rye (town)	94,956	65,381	33,184	31.1	9.8
Salina (town)	56,033	45,193	24,852	11.4	7.4
Schenectady (city)	41,735	32,139	18,391	5.7	20.8
Smithtown (town)	109,784	92,454	37,282	45.2	3.0
Southampton (town)	87,490	63,914	34,481	28.7	8.3
Syracuse (city)	39,106	27,037	16,384	6.4	27.3
Tonawanda (town)	54,790	45,990	23,870	10.8	6.9
Tonawanda (CDP)	54,311	45,597	23,581	10.5	7.3
Troy (city)	43,415	32,809	18,566	7.0	19.1
Union (town)	49,261	37,214	22,169	9.8	11.3
Utica (city)	37,403	26,990	16,336	5.1	24.5
Valley Stream (village)	85,025	72,102	28,986	31.1	3.5
Warwick (town)	84,300	71,063	30,743	30.5	4.7
Webster (town)	77,623	66,917	30,659	25.5	3.9
West Babylon (CDP)	75,116	67,348	25,241	24.9	6.2
West Islip (CDP)	105,074	86,821	32,698	39.7	2.3
West Seneca (CDP)	58,944	52,067	24,077	12.9	4.6
West Seneca (town)	58,952	52,095	24,081	12.9	4.6
White Plains (city)	97,322	65,859	38,535	31.5	9.8
Yonkers (city)	66,307	49,331	25,260	19.9	15.5
Yorktown (town)	113,635	95,499	40,142	47.5	2.9

NOTE: Data as of 2005 except for Poverty Rate which is from 2000; (1) Percentage of population with income below the poverty level

Taxes

Place	Total City Taxes Per Capita ($)	City Property Taxes Per Capita ($)
Albany (city)	488	419
Amherst (town)	573	520
Babylon (town)	430	364
Bethlehem (town)	360	292
Binghamton (city)	n/a	n/a
Brentwood (CDP)	n/a	n/a
Brighton (town)	371	315
Brighton (CDP)	n/a	n/a
Brookhaven (town)	336	240
Buffalo (city)	533	456
Carmel (town)	544	441
Centereach (CDP)	n/a	n/a
Central Islip (CDP)	n/a	n/a
Cheektowaga (town)	476	445
Cheektowaga (CDP)	n/a	n/a
Chili (town)	n/a	n/a
Cicero (town)	n/a	n/a
Clarkstown (town)	929	815
Clay (town)	242	203
Clifton Park (town)	240	163
Colonie (town)	248	205
Commack (CDP)	n/a	n/a
Coram (CDP)	n/a	n/a
Cortlandt (town)	485	410
Deer Park (CDP)	n/a	n/a
East Fishkill (town)	n/a	n/a
East Meadow (CDP)	n/a	n/a
Eastchester (town)	492	429
Elmira (city)	n/a	n/a
Elmont (CDP)	n/a	n/a
Franklin Square (CDP)	n/a	n/a
Freeport (village)	n/a	n/a
Gates (town)	n/a	n/a
Greece (town)	330	284
Greenburgh (town)	515	442
Guilderland (town)	266	207
Hamburg (town)	423	377
Haverstraw (town)	408	355
Hempstead (village)	n/a	n/a
Hempstead (town)	343	284
Henrietta (town)	128	69
Hicksville (CDP)	n/a	n/a
Holbrook (CDP)	n/a	n/a
Huntington (town)	604	479
Huntington Station (CDP)	n/a	n/a
Irondequoit (CDP/town)	356	314
Islip (town)	309	235
Ithaca (city)	n/a	n/a
Jamestown (city)	n/a	n/a
Lancaster (town)	351	309

Place	Total City Taxes Per Capita ($)	City Property Taxes Per Capita ($)
Levittown (CDP)	n/a	n/a
Lindenhurst (village)	n/a	n/a
Long Beach (city)	n/a	n/a
Mamaroneck (town)	577	501
Manlius (town)	n/a	n/a
Monroe (town)	n/a	n/a
Mount Pleasant (town)	664	546
Mount Vernon (city)	n/a	n/a
New City (CDP)	n/a	n/a
New Rochelle (city)	n/a	n/a
New York (city)	3,548	1,463
Newburgh (city)	n/a	n/a
Newburgh (town)	441	353
Niagara Falls (city)	n/a	n/a
North Hempstead (town)	486	397
North Tonawanda (city)	n/a	n/a
Oceanside (CDP)	n/a	n/a
Orangetown (town)	760	673
Ossining (town)	n/a	n/a
Oyster Bay (town)	503	422
Penfield (town)	236	170
Perinton (town)	n/a	n/a
Poughkeepsie (town)	414	361
Poughkeepsie (city)	n/a	n/a
Ramapo (town)	385	337
Riverhead (town)	1,127	909
Rochester (city)	848	763
Rome (city)	n/a	n/a
Rotterdam (town)	380	332
Rye (town)	59	30
Salina (town)	n/a	n/a
Schenectady (city)	478	423
Smithtown (town)	505	394
Southampton (town)	1,437	781
Syracuse (city)	202	157
Tonawanda (town)	328	294
Tonawanda (CDP)	n/a	n/a
Troy (city)	n/a	n/a
Union (town)	133	117
Utica (city)	n/a	n/a
Valley Stream (village)	n/a	n/a
Warwick (town)	n/a	n/a
Webster (town)	n/a	n/a
West Babylon (CDP)	n/a	n/a
West Islip (CDP)	n/a	n/a
West Seneca (CDP)	n/a	n/a
West Seneca (town)	499	466
White Plains (city)	n/a	n/a
Yonkers (city)	1,346	865
Yorktown (town)	622	520

NOTE: Data as of 2004.

Housing

Place	Homeownership Rate (%)	Median Home Value ($)	Median Age of Housing (years)	Median Rent ($/month)
Albany (city)	38.1	137,999	60	479
Amherst (town)	74.3	142,166	33	598
Babylon (town)	75.4	274,978	41	869
Bethlehem (town)	75.8	204,840	34	653
Binghamton (city)	43.4	84,027	60+	372
Brentwood (CDP)	78.5	239,735	36	821
Brighton (town)	57.7	149,818	39	668
Brighton (CDP)	57.7	149,818	39	668
Brookhaven (town)	79.2	266,725	29	851
Buffalo (city)	43.6	72,589	60+	364
Carmel (town)	84.5	377,010	34	829
Centereach (CDP)	87.9	271,042	34	869
Central Islip (CDP)	73.6	230,226	32	832
Cheektowaga (town)	71.9	100,045	41	468
Cheektowaga (CDP)	71.1	100,421	41	467
Chili (town)	80.1	129,555	30	579
Cicero (town)	80.6	119,459	31	494
Clarkstown (town)	82.1	405,515	31	951
Clay (town)	73.3	116,674	27	558
Clifton Park (town)	78.7	206,165	22	648
Colonie (town)	71.8	172,677	35	596
Commack (CDP)	93.3	423,452	36	1,155
Coram (CDP)	68.8	257,686	23	875
Cortlandt (town)	77.9	381,433	42	804
Deer Park (CDP)	81.3	286,744	38	848
East Fishkill (town)	89.9	309,197	26	639
East Meadow (CDP)	87.1	351,861	45	859
Eastchester (town)	71.2	530,195	51	988
Elmira (city)	48.7	63,687	60+	381
Elmont (CDP)	78.1	326,282	49	791
Franklin Square (CDP)	81.3	378,261	48	821
Freeport (village)	65.4	287,851	46	819
Gates (town)	77.5	109,901	33	561
Greece (town)	75.3	126,032	33	590
Greenburgh (town)	70.1	483,311	44	940
Guilderland (town)	67.0	194,218	27	673
Hamburg (town)	74.5	126,749	38	508
Haverstraw (town)	63.7	280,415	31	773
Hempstead (village)	43.4	268,985	45	788
Hempstead (town)	80.9	370,027	48	847
Henrietta (town)	72.8	126,686	31	643
Hicksville (CDP)	85.7	356,798	46	974
Holbrook (CDP)	79.3	295,156	26	996
Huntington (town)	85.4	459,621	39	924
Huntington Station (CDP)	70.6	300,272	43	859
Irondequoit (CDP/town)	79.7	113,136	46	587
Islip (town)	78.6	283,424	35	884
Ithaca (city)	26.6	137,554	58	515
Jamestown (city)	51.6	75,211	60+	320
Lancaster (town)	77.5	134,217	36	431

Place	Homeownership Rate (%)	Median Home Value ($)	Median Age of Housing (years)	Median Rent ($/month)
Levittown (CDP)	89.7	330,754	50	1,011
Lindenhurst (village)	80.6	275,994	44	766
Long Beach (city)	53.5	357,377	43	962
Mamaroneck (town)	66.7	735,214	57	978
Manlius (town)	79.5	146,469	33	529
Monroe (town)	64.0	260,895	22	708
Mount Pleasant (town)	72.3	570,496	46	872
Mount Vernon (city)	37.0	368,276	56	696
New City (CDP)	91.0	441,759	32	856
New Rochelle (city)	51.2	494,846	53	801
New York (city)	30.2	364,783	51	646
Newburgh (city)	30.8	137,362	59	549
Newburgh (town)	82.3	228,590	34	725
Niagara Falls (city)	58.5	73,110	54	342
North Hempstead (town)	78.4	561,061	48	1,001
North Tonawanda (city)	69.8	99,410	47	431
Oceanside (CDP)	88.5	396,487	44	871
Orangetown (town)	71.4	432,977	40	855
Ossining (town)	64.3	395,701	42	821
Oyster Bay (town)	87.1	439,051	44	973
Penfield (town)	83.3	161,091	27	640
Perinton (town)	80.7	175,695	27	656
Poughkeepsie (town)	69.9	220,331	38	677
Poughkeepsie (city)	37.0	164,051	55	543
Ramapo (town)	64.2	358,680	33	764
Riverhead (town)	76.8	250,581	30	729
Rochester (city)	40.2	73,642	60+	473
Rome (city)	58.2	87,043	50	369
Rotterdam (town)	81.4	138,536	45	490
Rye (town)	57.4	494,001	49	882
Salina (town)	68.7	96,349	42	550
Schenectady (city)	45.2	96,272	60+	444
Smithtown (town)	87.2	417,292	34	866
Southampton (town)	76.1	406,927	30	811
Syracuse (city)	40.8	88,833	58	430
Tonawanda (town)	73.3	108,394	48	467
Tonawanda (CDP)	75.1	110,664	46	476
Troy (city)	40.3	121,221	60+	421
Union (town)	60.5	95,159	48	408
Utica (city)	49.2	75,863	60+	352
Valley Stream (village)	80.5	346,240	52	895
Warwick (town)	78.6	250,560	34	669
Webster (town)	77.8	150,548	27	609
West Babylon (CDP)	74.7	269,298	40	903
West Islip (CDP)	93.0	355,218	42	933
West Seneca (CDP)	78.7	122,645	39	483
West Seneca (town)	78.7	122,671	39	483
White Plains (city)	53.2	443,862	46	828
Yonkers (city)	44.1	347,203	46	683
Yorktown (town)	85.9	391,719	33	835

NOTE: Homeownership Rate and Median Home Value as of 2005; Median Rent and Median Age of Housing as of 2000.

Commute to Work

Place	Automobile (%)	Public Transportation (%)	Walk (%)	Work from Home (%)
Albany (city)	73.0	13.1	10.8	2.4
Amherst (town)	92.6	1.2	2.2	3.5
Babylon (town)	86.1	9.6	1.8	1.7
Bethlehem (town)	92.6	2.0	1.4	3.5
Binghamton (city)	83.1	7.9	5.8	2.0
Brentwood (CDP)	87.6	7.2	2.1	1.0
Brighton (town)	92.0	1.9	1.5	3.9
Brighton (CDP)	91.9	1.9	1.5	3.9
Brookhaven (town)	90.6	4.6	1.9	2.2
Buffalo (city)	79.8	12.3	5.3	1.7
Carmel (town)	90.6	5.4	0.9	2.5
Centereach (CDP)	91.9	5.1	0.9	1.9
Central Islip (CDP)	87.5	7.3	1.9	1.1
Cheektowaga (town)	95.5	1.3	1.4	1.4
Cheektowaga (CDP)	95.3	1.4	1.4	1.5
Chili (town)	94.6	0.7	2.3	1.8
Cicero (town)	95.2	0.2	1.1	3.1
Clarkstown (town)	87.1	6.9	1.5	4.1
Clay (town)	95.3	0.8	0.8	2.4
Clifton Park (town)	93.9	0.8	0.7	4.2
Colonie (town)	92.8	2.6	2.2	2.1
Commack (CDP)	88.1	7.5	0.7	3.3
Coram (CDP)	92.0	4.6	0.7	2.1
Cortlandt (town)	77.5	14.5	2.1	5.3
Deer Park (CDP)	88.1	8.8	1.2	1.3
East Fishkill (town)	91.8	3.9	0.5	3.5
East Meadow (CDP)	86.5	8.4	2.8	2.0
Eastchester (town)	60.9	30.2	4.0	4.6
Elmira (city)	84.1	2.7	9.6	2.3
Elmont (CDP)	78.5	16.4	3.3	1.6
Franklin Square (CDP)	84.2	11.4	1.9	2.0
Freeport (village)	76.2	15.2	4.9	2.2
Gates (town)	95.9	0.8	0.9	1.6
Greece (town)	96.0	0.7	1.1	1.7
Greenburgh (town)	70.8	21.6	2.7	4.3
Guilderland (town)	93.6	1.8	0.9	3.3
Hamburg (town)	94.8	0.5	1.8	2.4
Haverstraw (town)	88.6	6.9	1.9	2.1
Hempstead (village)	63.4	24.3	8.8	1.5
Hempstead (town)	77.7	16.2	2.7	2.6
Henrietta (town)	89.4	1.5	6.3	1.9
Hicksville (CDP)	84.0	12.0	1.9	1.6
Holbrook (CDP)	91.1	7.0	0.4	1.3
Huntington (town)	83.5	10.6	1.3	4.1
Huntington Station (CDP)	85.2	9.5	2.3	2.2
Irondequoit (CDP/town)	94.0	1.6	1.4	2.6
Islip (town)	88.7	7.4	1.2	1.7
Ithaca (city)	43.8	7.9	41.2	4.9
Jamestown (city)	89.0	2.7	5.8	1.3
Lancaster (town)	96.6	0.3	1.0	1.4

Place	Automobile (%)	Public Transportation (%)	Walk (%)	Work from Home (%)
Levittown (CDP)	87.1	9.5	1.2	1.6
Lindenhurst (village)	86.4	10.3	1.2	1.3
Long Beach (city)	71.3	20.7	4.0	2.7
Mamaroneck (town)	56.5	31.4	4.6	6.7
Manlius (town)	93.4	0.8	1.5	3.8
Monroe (town)	77.6	10.7	6.7	3.7
Mount Pleasant (town)	77.2	15.0	3.8	3.5
Mount Vernon (city)	63.9	27.5	5.5	2.0
New City (CDP)	87.6	6.0	1.1	4.9
New Rochelle (city)	71.8	17.8	6.6	2.9
New York (city)	32.9	52.8	10.4	2.9
Newburgh (city)	80.5	8.0	7.9	1.5
Newburgh (town)	94.2	3.0	0.5	2.0
Niagara Falls (city)	89.1	3.1	5.2	1.7
North Hempstead (town)	73.5	18.3	3.6	3.9
North Tonawanda (city)	95.2	0.5	2.2	1.5
Oceanside (CDP)	78.1	16.2	1.6	3.5
Orangetown (town)	83.6	7.9	4.2	3.9
Ossining (town)	75.0	16.9	2.7	4.1
Oyster Bay (town)	82.1	12.7	1.6	3.2
Penfield (town)	94.9	0.3	1.1	3.3
Perinton (town)	93.9	0.3	0.9	4.4
Poughkeepsie (town)	84.8	3.7	8.7	1.9
Poughkeepsie (city)	79.3	9.9	7.0	3.1
Ramapo (town)	80.5	10.9	3.9	3.5
Riverhead (town)	90.6	2.6	2.4	3.3
Rochester (city)	81.7	8.1	6.5	2.3
Rome (city)	92.2	1.9	3.6	1.5
Rotterdam (town)	95.1	0.4	1.6	2.3
Rye (town)	74.9	15.7	6.3	2.5
Salina (town)	93.7	1.5	1.9	2.1
Schenectady (city)	82.6	6.5	6.8	2.6
Smithtown (town)	89.4	6.1	0.7	3.2
Southampton (town)	85.7	3.7	3.8	5.6
Syracuse (city)	79.7	7.0	10.1	2.0
Tonawanda (town)	93.4	2.9	1.7	1.4
Tonawanda (CDP)	93.6	2.6	1.8	1.4
Troy (city)	80.8	6.6	9.7	2.0
Union (town)	89.9	2.4	4.4	2.6
Utica (city)	86.2	4.3	6.3	2.0
Valley Stream (village)	77.3	17.1	3.0	2.0
Warwick (town)	88.6	4.9	2.4	3.5
Webster (town)	94.6	0.6	0.8	3.8
West Babylon (CDP)	89.1	7.5	1.2	1.6
West Islip (CDP)	88.8	8.6	0.6	1.6
West Seneca (CDP)	95.4	1.0	1.8	1.5
West Seneca (town)	95.4	1.0	1.8	1.5
White Plains (city)	69.0	19.7	7.1	3.5
Yonkers (city)	70.0	23.1	4.2	2.1
Yorktown (town)	86.3	8.4	0.9	4.1

NOTE: Data as of 2000

Travel Time to Work

Place	Less than 15 Minutes (%)	15 to 30 Minutes (%)	30 to 45 Minutes (%)	45 to 60 Minutes (%)	60 Minutes or More (%)
Albany (city)	37.7	43.9	12.2	2.5	3.6
Amherst (town)	32.2	48.0	16.0	1.7	2.0
Babylon (town)	24.8	32.9	18.7	7.3	16.4
Bethlehem (town)	28.1	52.5	14.6	1.7	3.1
Binghamton (city)	51.0	37.2	6.3	2.0	3.5
Brentwood (CDP)	23.4	39.4	17.7	6.0	13.5
Brighton (town)	44.5	47.6	5.7	0.9	1.2
Brighton (CDP)	44.5	47.6	5.7	0.9	1.2
Brookhaven (town)	22.7	33.0	20.1	8.7	15.4
Buffalo (city)	32.2	46.4	13.4	3.5	4.6
Carmel (town)	17.1	23.9	24.8	16.9	17.3
Centereach (CDP)	23.8	34.4	18.9	7.5	15.4
Central Islip (CDP)	24.2	38.7	16.2	5.4	15.5
Cheektowaga (town)	32.2	51.7	11.5	2.0	2.7
Cheektowaga (CDP)	31.7	52.0	11.5	2.1	2.8
Chili (town)	28.9	53.9	12.3	2.1	2.9
Cicero (town)	27.8	58.3	9.2	1.7	2.9
Clarkstown (town)	24.6	27.4	16.6	11.9	19.5
Clay (town)	29.9	53.6	11.0	2.7	2.8
Clifton Park (town)	19.8	48.4	25.7	3.7	2.3
Colonie (town)	35.8	49.5	10.4	1.9	2.4
Commack (CDP)	22.4	32.8	17.8	8.1	18.9
Coram (CDP)	17.9	34.1	20.0	9.7	18.3
Cortlandt (town)	23.3	18.6	21.8	12.4	23.9
Deer Park (CDP)	22.3	35.2	17.5	7.6	17.5
East Fishkill (town)	16.5	30.5	18.8	13.8	20.5
East Meadow (CDP)	24.2	32.7	19.7	7.7	15.8
Eastchester (town)	18.7	26.4	19.1	15.1	20.8
Elmira (city)	53.4	31.6	8.4	2.8	3.7
Elmont (CDP)	14.5	27.2	22.8	9.8	25.7
Franklin Square (CDP)	18.7	32.1	23.3	8.8	17.0
Freeport (village)	23.1	32.4	19.1	9.0	16.3
Gates (town)	41.3	47.3	6.7	1.4	3.3
Greece (town)	30.4	53.5	12.3	1.6	2.2
Greenburgh (town)	20.9	30.4	18.9	9.6	20.1
Guilderland (town)	26.4	51.0	16.6	2.3	3.6
Hamburg (town)	31.8	39.6	22.1	3.4	3.1
Haverstraw (town)	21.8	34.2	19.4	9.9	14.7
Hempstead (village)	22.1	29.7	23.9	8.7	15.6
Hempstead (town)	20.7	29.1	20.1	9.4	20.7
Henrietta (town)	38.3	46.8	11.3	1.6	1.9
Hicksville (CDP)	23.4	32.4	18.1	8.6	17.6
Holbrook (CDP)	23.8	32.2	19.7	6.6	17.7
Huntington (town)	22.1	30.2	19.6	8.2	19.9
Huntington Station (CDP)	27.5	32.4	20.3	7.0	12.8
Irondequoit (CDP/town)	32.3	55.0	9.2	1.1	2.4
Islip (town)	25.8	34.5	17.4	6.7	15.6
Ithaca (city)	54.5	37.4	5.8	1.0	1.3
Jamestown (city)	62.7	25.5	5.8	3.1	2.9
Lancaster (town)	27.8	47.4	19.7	2.6	2.5

Place	Less than 15 Minutes (%)	15 to 30 Minutes (%)	30 to 45 Minutes (%)	45 to 60 Minutes (%)	60 Minutes or More (%)
Levittown (CDP)	22.2	35.5	18.6	6.9	16.9
Lindenhurst (village)	25.1	30.8	19.7	7.7	16.8
Long Beach (city)	18.0	23.4	22.2	10.3	26.1
Mamaroneck (town)	19.7	23.1	19.8	14.9	22.4
Manlius (town)	29.8	53.3	12.5	2.1	2.3
Monroe (town)	29.2	18.6	16.8	8.0	27.5
Mount Pleasant (town)	27.3	31.4	16.6	8.3	16.4
Mount Vernon (city)	16.3	33.1	22.6	10.1	18.0
New City (CDP)	25.0	23.6	16.4	13.2	21.9
New Rochelle (city)	22.5	33.6	21.9	8.1	13.9
New York (city)	11.6	22.9	25.3	15.7	24.5
Newburgh (city)	39.6	32.7	16.3	4.0	7.5
Newburgh (town)	28.5	33.5	13.8	8.2	16.0
Niagara Falls (city)	50.0	33.5	12.3	2.3	2.0
North Hempstead (town)	22.6	26.8	18.5	10.0	22.1
North Tonawanda (city)	31.5	49.0	16.1	1.8	1.6
Oceanside (CDP)	20.1	24.2	20.0	11.1	24.5
Orangetown (town)	29.1	26.3	17.2	10.3	17.2
Ossining (town)	20.8	30.9	20.7	8.3	19.3
Oyster Bay (town)	22.8	29.5	18.3	8.1	21.3
Penfield (town)	26.5	57.6	12.3	1.5	2.1
Perinton (town)	27.8	49.3	18.7	2.0	2.2
Poughkeepsie (town)	39.1	32.1	12.4	5.9	10.6
Poughkeepsie (city)	43.5	27.9	15.0	5.0	8.6
Ramapo (town)	25.8	31.1	14.7	9.3	19.0
Riverhead (town)	31.4	28.3	20.9	9.1	10.3
Rochester (city)	36.7	46.3	10.6	2.3	4.0
Rome (city)	49.2	32.5	11.8	2.9	3.6
Rotterdam (town)	33.5	40.7	19.3	3.7	2.8
Rye (town)	34.2	35.9	13.6	5.2	11.2
Salina (town)	41.0	48.2	5.8	1.7	3.3
Schenectady (city)	37.7	36.9	17.0	4.2	4.2
Smithtown (town)	22.8	33.1	18.8	8.0	17.3
Southampton (town)	37.4	31.3	14.9	5.2	11.3
Syracuse (city)	47.6	39.5	7.0	2.3	3.7
Tonawanda (town)	33.1	50.3	12.1	1.9	2.5
Tonawanda (CDP)	34.3	49.3	11.8	1.9	2.7
Troy (city)	33.4	45.6	13.1	3.3	4.5
Union (town)	45.8	43.5	6.3	1.5	3.0
Utica (city)	49.4	36.5	8.3	1.8	3.9
Valley Stream (village)	20.8	28.1	20.3	11.7	19.1
Warwick (town)	25.8	18.6	14.3	14.0	27.3
Webster (town)	31.3	50.6	14.4	1.5	2.1
West Babylon (CDP)	25.1	33.8	18.7	7.1	15.3
West Islip (CDP)	27.8	30.6	16.9	8.0	16.6
West Seneca (CDP)	32.3	46.5	14.8	3.1	3.3
West Seneca (town)	32.3	46.5	14.8	3.1	3.3
White Plains (city)	29.8	34.7	15.1	7.5	12.9
Yonkers (city)	17.9	34.0	21.7	10.5	15.9
Yorktown (town)	18.4	25.3	24.6	12.3	19.5

NOTE: Data as of 2000

Crime

Place	Violent Crime Rate (crimes per 10,000 population)	Property Crime Rate (crimes per 10,000 population)
Albany (city)	120.2	593.6
Amherst (town)	9.9	160.1
Babylon (town)	n/a	n/a
Bethlehem (town)	6.8	155.5
Binghamton (city)	33.4	423.9
Brentwood (CDP)	n/a	n/a
Brighton (town)	11.4	304.4
Brighton (CDP)	n/a	n/a
Brookhaven (town)	n/a	n/a
Buffalo (city)	133.2	569.1
Carmel (town)	5.2	62.4
Centereach (CDP)	n/a	n/a
Central Islip (CDP)	n/a	n/a
Cheektowaga (town)	20.5	327.7
Cheektowaga (CDP)	n/a	n/a
Chili (town)	n/a	n/a
Cicero (town)	2.6	184.8
Clarkstown (town)	16.1	237.9
Clay (town)	3.3	64.7
Clifton Park (town)	n/a	n/a
Colonie (town)	12.0	367.3
Commack (CDP)	n/a	n/a
Coram (CDP)	n/a	n/a
Cortlandt (town)	n/a	n/a
Deer Park (CDP)	n/a	n/a
East Fishkill (town)	30.3	113.4
East Meadow (CDP)	n/a	n/a
Eastchester (town)	n/a	n/a
Elmira (city)	n/a	n/a
Elmont (CDP)	n/a	n/a
Franklin Square (CDP)	n/a	n/a
Freeport (village)	41.3	199.5
Gates (town)	9.3	399.0
Greece (town)	7.9	247.4
Greenburgh (town)	n/a	n/a
Guilderland (town)	9.1	307.0
Hamburg (town)	1.1	79.6
Haverstraw (town)	13.4	137.1
Hempstead (village)	59.9	220.4
Hempstead (town)	n/a	n/a
Henrietta (town)	n/a	n/a
Hicksville (CDP)	n/a	n/a
Holbrook (CDP)	n/a	n/a
Huntington (town)	n/a	n/a
Huntington Station (CDP)	n/a	n/a
Irondequoit (CDP/town)	12.7	383.0
Islip (town)	n/a	n/a
Ithaca (city)	n/a	n/a
Jamestown (city)	54.2	340.8
Lancaster (town)	n/a	n/a

Place	Violent Crime Rate (crimes per 10,000 population)	Property Crime Rate (crimes per 10,000 population)
Levittown (CDP)	n/a	n/a
Lindenhurst (village)	n/a	n/a
Long Beach (city)	29.3	122.0
Mamaroneck (town)	n/a	n/a
Manlius (town)	8.0	155.1
Monroe (town)	n/a	n/a
Mount Pleasant (town)	4.1	68.8
Mount Vernon (city)	79.4	260.6
New City (CDP)	n/a	n/a
New Rochelle (city)	31.1	213.6
New York (city)	68.7	211.3
Newburgh (city)	127.2	412.8
Newburgh (town)	9.8	268.1
Niagara Falls (city)	117.4	549.2
North Hempstead (town)	n/a	n/a
North Tonawanda (city)	10.8	178.0
Oceanside (CDP)	n/a	n/a
Orangetown (town)	13.1	160.8
Ossining (town)	n/a	n/a
Oyster Bay (town)	n/a	n/a
Penfield (town)	n/a	n/a
Perinton (town)	n/a	n/a
Poughkeepsie (town)	18.3	247.0
Poughkeepsie (city)	118.1	398.3
Ramapo (town)	n/a	n/a
Riverhead (town)	35.3	362.9
Rochester (city)	82.7	717.3
Rome (city)	13.9	203.3
Rotterdam (town)	12.2	297.2
Rye (town)	n/a	n/a
Salina (town)	n/a	n/a
Schenectady (city)	n/a	n/a
Smithtown (town)	n/a	n/a
Southampton (town)	n/a	n/a
Syracuse (city)	89.7	454.4
Tonawanda (town)	13.4	169.5
Tonawanda (CDP)	n/a	n/a
Troy (city)	61.1	413.2
Union (town)	n/a	n/a
Utica (city)	48.2	420.5
Valley Stream (village)	n/a	n/a
Warwick (town)	n/a	n/a
Webster (town)	7.0	144.8
West Babylon (CDP)	n/a	n/a
West Islip (CDP)	n/a	n/a
West Seneca (CDP)	n/a	n/a
West Seneca (town)	13.7	230.6
White Plains (city)	38.0	256.9
Yonkers (city)	47.6	188.7
Yorktown (town)	n/a	n/a

NOTE: Data as of 2004.

EDUCATION

New York Public School Educational Profile

Category	Value	Category	Value
Schools *(2003-2004)*	4,531	**Diploma Recipients** *(2002-2003)*	140,096
Instructional Level		White, Non-Hispanic	94,527
Primary	2,524	Black, Non-Hispanic	19,673
Middle	780	Asian/Pacific Islander	9,940
High	804	American Indian/Alaskan Native	455
Other Level	423	Hispanic	15,501
Curriculum		**High School Drop-out Rate** (%) *(2001-2002)*	7.1
Regular	4,238	White, Non-Hispanic	3.3
Special Education	73	Black, Non-Hispanic	12.9
Vocational	25	Asian/Pacific Islander	5.9
Alternative	195	American Indian/Alaskan Native	9.4
Type		Hispanic	14.2
Magnet	31	**Staff** *(2003-2004)*	
Charter	50	Teachers	216,114.6
Title I Eligible	2,820	Average Salary[1] ($)	55,181
School-wide Title I	947	Librarians/Media Specialists	3,317.3
Students *(2003-2004)*	2,882,218	Guidance Counselors	6,440.7
Gender (%)		**Ratios** *(2003-2004)*	
Male	51.4	Student/Teacher Ratio	13.3 to 1
Female	48.6	Student/Librarian Ratio	868.8 to 1
Race/Ethnicity (%)		Student/Counselor Ratio	447.5 to 1
White, Non-Hispanic	53.6	**College Entrance Exam Scores** *(2005)*	
Black, Non-Hispanic	20.0	Scholastic Aptitude Test (SAT)	
Asian/Pacific Islander	6.5	Participation Rate (%)	92
American Indian/Alaskan Native	0.5	Mean SAT Reasoning Test Verbal Score	497
Hispanic	19.4	Mean SAT Reasoning Test Math Score	511
Classification (%)		American College Testing Program (ACT)	
Individual Education Program (IEP)	n/a	Participation Rate (%)	17
Migrant *(2002-2003)*	n/a	Average Composite Score	22.4
English Language Learner (ELL)	n/a	Average English Score	21.3
Eligible for Free Lunch Program	n/a	Average Math Score	22.5
Eligible for Reduced-Price Lunch Program	n/a	Average Reading Score	23.0
Current Spending *($ per student in FY 2003)*	12,398	Average Science Score	22.3
Instruction	8,623		
Support Services	3,483		

Note: For an explanation of data, please refer to the User's Guide in the front of the book; (1) Median

New York NAEP 2005 Test Scores

Reading			Mathematics		
Grade/Category	Value	Rank	Grade/Category	Value	Rank
4th Grade			**4th Grade**		
Average Proficiency	222.7 (1.05)	16/51	Average Proficiency	238.2 (0.85)	30/51
Proficiency by Gender/Race/Ethnicity			Proficiency by Gender/Race/Ethnicity		
Male	220.2 (1.14)	14/51	Male	239.6 (0.96)	29/51
Female	225.2 (1.31)	20/51	Female	236.7 (0.89)	30/51
White, Non-Hispanic	231.8 (0.92)	9/51	White, Non-Hispanic	247.0 (0.78)	16/51
Black, Non-Hispanic	207.4 (1.76)	5/42	Black, Non-Hispanic	221.9 (1.27)	16/42
Asian, Non-Hispanic	236.9 (2.86)	7/27	Asian, Non-Hispanic	254.5 (1.93)	12/25
American Indian, Non-Hispanic	n/a	n/a	American Indian, Non-Hispanic	n/a	n/a
Hispanic	207.9 (1.85)	14/40	Hispanic	225.8 (1.35)	19/41
Proficiency by Class Size			Proficiency by Class Size		
Less than 16 Students	210.1 (5.41)	16/34	Less than 16 Students	224.4 (3.60)	19/35
16 to 18 Students	218.1 (3.68)	15/33	16 to 18 Students	237.9 (2.44)	15/31
19 to 20 Students	227.6 (2.23)	5/38	19 to 20 Students	241.9 (1.90)	12/38
21 to 25 Students	226.3 (1.62)	12/51	21 to 25 Students	240.8 (1.26)	25/51
Greater than 25 Students	220.6 (1.93)	19/36	Greater than 25 Students	236.5 (2.36)	22/33
Percent Attaining Achievement Levels			Percent Attaining Achievement Levels		
Below Basic	31.1 (1.48)	36/51	Below Basic	18.7 (1.04)	25/51
Basic or Above	68.9 (1.48)	16/51	Basic or Above	81.3 (1.04)	27/51
Proficient or Above	33.3 (1.16)	19/51	Proficient or Above	36.1 (1.32)	29/51
Advanced or Above	7.6 (0.64)	15/51	Advanced or Above	4.5 (0.53)	26/51
8th Grade			**8th Grade**		
Average Proficiency	265.1 (0.96)	19/51	Average Proficiency	279.7 (0.90)	28/51
Proficiency by Gender/Race/Ethnicity			Proficiency by Gender/Race/Ethnicity		
Male	260.0 (1.25)	20/51	Male	279.9 (1.01)	30/51
Female	270.2 (1.05)	20/51	Female	279.5 (1.09)	25/51
White, Non-Hispanic	276.2 (0.96)	4/51	White, Non-Hispanic	290.4 (1.23)	15/51
Black, Non-Hispanic	242.5 (2.05)	19/40	Black, Non-Hispanic	258.7 (1.85)	11/41
Asian, Non-Hispanic	273.7 (2.76)	12/24	Asian, Non-Hispanic	297.9 (3.19)	12/23
American Indian, Non-Hispanic	n/a	n/a	American Indian, Non-Hispanic	n/a	n/a
Hispanic	250.5 (1.76)	11/38	Hispanic	262.0 (1.76)	21/38
Proficiency by Parents Highest Level of Ed.			Proficiency by Parents Highest Level of Ed.		
Did Not Finish High School	249.0 (1.88)	13/49	Did Not Finish High School	262.5 (1.92)	24/50
Graduated High School	256.8 (1.52)	17/50	Graduated High School	270.7 (1.36)	20/50
Some Education After High School	267.3 (1.24)	23/50	Some Education After High School	280.1 (1.39)	29/50
Graduated College	274.2 (1.08)	18/50	Graduated College	289.2 (1.25)	29/50
Percent Attaining Achievement Levels			Percent Attaining Achievement Levels		
Below Basic	31.1 (1.48)	36/51	Below Basic	30.0 (1.14)	24/51
Basic or Above	68.9 (1.48)	16/51	Basic or Above	70.0 (1.14)	28/51
Proficient or Above	33.3 (1.16)	19/51	Proficient or Above	30.8 (1.27)	21/51
Advanced or Above	7.6 (0.64)	15/51	Advanced or Above	6.3 (0.51)	16/51

Note: For an explanation of data, please refer to the User's Guide in the front of the book; n/a indicates data not available

Number of Schools

Rank	Number	District Name	City
1	1,225	New York City Public Schools	Brooklyn
2	68	Buffalo City SD	Buffalo
3	62	Rochester City SD	Rochester
4	39	Yonkers City SD	Yonkers
5	35	Syracuse City SD	Syracuse
6	20	Greece Central SD	Rochester
7	18	Brentwood Union Free SD	Brentwood
8	16	Mount Vernon City SD	Mount Vernon
9	15	Albany City SD	Albany
9	15	Elmira City SD	Elmira
9	15	Newburgh City SD	Newburgh
9	15	Rome City SD	Rome
9	15	Sachem Central SD	Holbrook
9	15	Schenectady City SD	Schenectady
9	15	Wappingers Central SD	Wappingers Fls
16	14	Clarkstown Central SD	New City
16	14	Corning City SD	Painted Post
16	14	E Ramapo Central SD (Sprg Val)	Spring Valley
16	14	Kenmore-Tonawanda Union Free SD	Buffalo
16	14	Kingston City SD	Kingston
16	14	Liverpool Central SD	Liverpool
16	14	Middle Country Central SD	Centereach
16	14	West Seneca Central SD	West Seneca
24	13	Half Hollow Hills Central SD	Dix Hills
24	13	Ithaca City SD	Ithaca
24	13	Niagara Falls City SD	Niagara Falls
24	13	Smithtown Central SD	Smithtown
24	13	Utica City SD	Utica
24	13	Williamsville Central SD	East Amherst
30	11	Arlington Central SD	Poughkeepsie
30	11	Auburn City SD	Auburn
30	11	Binghamton City SD	Binghamton
30	11	Levittown Union Free SD	Levittown
30	11	North Syracuse Central SD	N Syracuse
30	11	Patchogue-Medford Union Free SD	Patchogue
30	11	Shenendehowa Central SD	Clifton Park
30	11	Webster Central SD	Webster
38	10	Connetquot Central SD	Bohemia
38	10	Great Neck Union Free SD	Great Neck
38	10	Jamestown City SD	Jamestown
38	10	Lockport City SD	Lockport
38	10	Middletown City SD	Middletown
38	10	New Rochelle City SD	New Rochelle
38	10	Poughkeepsie City SD	Poughkeepsie
38	10	Rush-Henrietta Central SD	Henrietta
38	10	Syosset Central SD	Syosset
38	10	West Irondequoit Central SD	Rochester
38	10	Whitesboro Central SD	Yorkville
49	9	Baldwin Union Free SD	Baldwin
49	9	Bedford Central SD	Mount Kisco
49	9	East Meadow Union Free SD	Westbury
49	9	Haverstraw-Stony Point Cent SD	Garnerville
49	9	Hempstead Union Free SD	Hempstead
49	9	Hicksville Union Free SD	Hicksville
49	9	Lakeland Central SD	Shrub Oak
49	9	Lindenhurst Union Free SD	Lindenhurst
49	9	Massapequa Union Free SD	Massapequa
49	9	North Tonawanda City SD	N Tonawanda
49	9	Northport-East Northport UFSD	Northport
49	9	Oceanside Union Free SD	Oceanside
49	9	Saratoga Springs City SD	Saratoga Spgs
49	9	South Colonie Central SD	Albany
49	9	West Islip Union Free SD	West Islip
64	8	Baldwinsville Central SD	Baldwinsville
64	8	Beacon City SD	Beacon
64	8	Camden Central SD	Camden
64	8	Central Islip Union Free SD	Central Islip
64	8	Central Square Central SD	Central Square
64	8	Commack Union Free SD	E Northport
64	8	Fairport Central SD	Fairport
64	8	Freeport Union Free SD	Freeport
64	8	Huntington Union Free SD	Huntington Stn
64	8	Indian River Central SD	Philadelphia
64	8	Johnstown City SD	Johnstown
64	8	Lancaster Central SD	Lancaster
64	8	Malone Central SD	Malone
64	8	Niskayuna Central SD	Schenectady
64	8	North Colonie Central SD	Latham
64	8	Ogdensburg City SD	Ogdensburg
64	8	Oneida City SD	Oneida
64	8	Pittsford Central SD	Pittsford
64	8	Plainview-Old Bethpage Cent SD	Plainview
64	8	Saranac Lake Central SD	Saranac Lake
64	8	Three Village Central SD	East Setauket
64	8	Troy City SD	Troy
64	8	Uniondale Union Free SD	Uniondale
64	8	Watertown City SD	Watertown
64	8	White Plains City SD	White Plains
64	8	William Floyd Union Free SD	Mastic Beach
90	7	Amsterdam City SD	Amsterdam
90	7	Bay Shore Union Free SD	Bay Shore
90	7	Bethlehem Central SD	Delmar
90	7	East Greenbush Central SD	E Greenbush
90	7	East Islip Union Free SD	Islip Terrace
90	7	East Syracuse-Minoa Central SD	East Syracuse
90	7	Evans-Brant Cent SD (Lake Shore)	Angola
90	7	Garden City Union Free SD	Garden City
90	7	Gates-Chili Central SD	Rochester
90	7	Gloversville City SD	Gloversville
90	7	Guilderland Central SD	Guilderland
90	7	Horseheads Central SD	Horseheads
90	7	Hudson City SD	Hudson
90	7	Hyde Park Central SD	Poughkeepsie
90	7	Lawrence Union Free SD	Lawrence
90	7	Long Beach City SD	Long Beach
90	7	Longwood Central SD	Middle Island
90	7	Lynbrook Union Free SD	Lynbrook
90	7	Mineola Union Free SD	Mineola
90	7	Monroe-Woodbury Central SD	Central Valley
90	7	New York City Geographic Dist 15	Brooklyn
90	7	North Babylon Union Free SD	North Babylon
90	7	Olean City SD	Olean
90	7	Ossining Union Free SD	Ossining
90	7	Oswego City SD	Oswego
90	7	Pearl River Union Free SD	Pearl River
90	7	Peekskill City SD	Peekskill
90	7	Pine Bush Central SD	Pine Bush
90	7	Ramapo Central SD (Suffern)	Hillburn
90	7	Riverhead Central SD	Riverhead
90	7	Rockville Centre Union Free SD	Rockville Ctre
90	7	Saranac Central SD	Dannemora
90	7	Scarsdale Union Free SD	Scarsdale
90	7	South Country Central SD	E Patchogue
90	7	South Glens Falls Central SD	S Glens Falls
90	7	Union-Endicott Central SD	Endicott
90	7	Valley Central SD (Montgomery)	Montgomery
90	7	Vestal Central SD	Vestal
90	7	Warwick Valley Central SD	Warwick
90	7	West Babylon Union Free SD	West Babylon
90	7	West Genesee Central SD	Camillus
131	6	Attica Central SD	Attica
131	6	Averill Park Central SD	Averill Park
131	6	Batavia City SD	Batavia
131	6	Brookhaven-Comsewogue UFSD	Pt Jefferson Stn
131	6	Chappaqua Central SD	Chappaqua
131	6	Churchville-Chili Central SD	Churchville
131	6	Clarence Central SD	Clarence
131	6	Cobleskill-Richmondville CSD	Cobleskill
131	6	Cortland City SD	Cortland
131	6	Coxsackie-Athens Central SD	Coxsackie
131	6	Deer Park Union Free SD	Deer Park
131	6	Dunkirk City SD	Dunkirk
131	6	East Irondequoit Central SD	Rochester
131	6	Elmont Union Free SD	Elmont
131	6	Farmingdale Union Free SD	Farmingdale
131	6	Fayetteville-Manlius Central SD	Manlius
131	6	Frontier Central SD	Hamburg
131	6	Fulton City SD	Fulton
131	6	Glen Cove City SD	Glen Cove
131	6	Glens Falls City SD	Glens Falls
131	6	Goshen Central SD	Goshen
131	6	Greenburgh Central SD	Hartsdale
131	6	Hamburg Central SD	Hamburg
131	6	Harrison Central SD	Harrison
131	6	Iroquois Central SD	Elma
131	6	Katonah-Lewisboro Union Free SD	South Salem
131	6	Mahopac Central SD	Mahopac
131	6	Mamaroneck Union Free SD	Mamaroneck
131	6	Minisink Valley Central SD	Slate Hill
131	6	Monticello Central SD	Monticello
131	6	Niagara-Wheatfield Central SD	Niagara Falls
131	6	North Bellmore Union Free SD	Bellmore
131	6	Oneonta City SD	Oneonta
131	6	Onteora Central SD	Boiceville
131	6	Orchard Park Central SD	Orchard Park
131	6	Pelham Union Free SD	Pelham
131	6	Penfield Central SD	Penfield
131	6	Peru Central SD	Peru
131	6	Port Chester-Rye Union Free SD	Port Chester
131	6	Port Washington Union Free SD	Pt Washington
131	6	Roosevelt Union Free SD	Roosevelt
131	6	Saugerties Central SD	Saugerties
131	6	Scotia-Glenville Central SD	Scotia
131	6	South Huntington Union Free SD	Huntington Stn
131	6	Spencerport Central SD	Spencerport
131	6	Sweet Home Central SD	Amherst
131	6	Tonawanda City SD	Tonawanda
131	6	Wallkill Central SD	Wallkill
131	6	Westbury Union Free SD	Old Westbury
131	6	Yorktown Central SD	Yorktown Hgts
181	5	Adirondack Central SD	Boonville
181	5	Albion Central SD	Albion
181	5	Alden Central SD	Alden
181	5	Altmar-Parish-Williamstown CSD	Parish
181	5	Amityville Union Free SD	Amityville
181	5	Ballston Spa Central SD	Ballston Spa
181	5	Bayport-Blue Point Union Free SD	Bayport
181	5	Bellmore-Merrick Central High SD	North Merrick
181	5	Bethpage Union Free SD	Bethpage
181	5	Brewster Central SD	Brewster
181	5	Brighton Central SD	Rochester
181	5	Broadalbin-Perth Central SD	Broadalbin
181	5	Brockport Central SD	Brockport
181	5	Burnt Hls-Ballston Lake Cent SD	Scotia
181	5	Carmel Central SD	Patterson
181	5	Carthage Central SD	Carthage
181	5	Chittenango Central SD	Chittenango
181	5	Cohoes City SD	Cohoes
181	5	Copiague Union Free SD	Copiague
181	5	Cornwall Central SD	Cornwall-on-Hud
181	5	Dryden Central SD	Dryden
181	5	Eastchester Union Free SD	Eastchester
181	5	Gouverneur Central SD	Gouverneur
181	5	Gowanda Central SD	Gowanda
181	5	Grand Island Central SD	Grand Island
181	5	Hauppauge Union Free SD	Hauppauge
181	5	Hendrick Hudson Central SD	Montrose
181	5	Herricks Union Free SD	New Hyde Park
181	5	Hewlett-Woodmere Union Free SD	Woodmere
181	5	Hilton Central SD	Hilton
181	5	Homer Central SD	Homer
181	5	Hudson Falls Central SD	Hudson Falls
181	5	Islip Union Free SD	Islip
181	5	Jamesville-Dewitt Central SD	Dewitt
181	5	Jericho Union Free SD	Jericho
181	5	Johnson City Central SD	Johnson City
181	5	Kinderhook Central SD	Valatie
181	5	Kings Park Central SD	Kings Park
181	5	Lansing Central SD	Lansing
181	5	Marlboro Central SD	Marlboro
181	5	Massena Central SD	Massena
181	5	Mexico Central SD	Mexico
181	5	New Hartford Central SD	New Hartford
181	5	Newark Central SD	Newark
181	5	Newfane Central SD	Newfane
181	5	North Shore Central SD	Sea Cliff
181	5	Norwich City SD	Norwich
181	5	Nyack Union Free SD	Nyack
181	5	Plainedge Union Free SD	N Massapequa
181	5	Plattsburgh City SD	Plattsburgh
181	5	Port Jervis City SD	Port Jervis
181	5	Red Hook Central SD	Red Hook
181	5	Rondout Valley Central SD	Accord
181	5	Roslyn Union Free SD	Roslyn
181	5	Rye City SD	Rye
181	5	Salamanca City SD	Salamanca
181	5	Sayville Union Free SD	Sayville
181	5	Schalmont Central SD	Schenectady
181	5	Sewanhaka Central High SD	Floral Park
181	5	Sherrill City SD	Verona
181	5	Shoreham-Wading River Central SD	Shoreham
181	5	South Orangetown Central SD	Blauvelt
181	5	Sullivan West Central SD	Callicoon
181	5	Susquehanna Valley Central SD	Conklin
181	5	Union Free SD of the Tarrytowns	Sleepy Hollow
181	5	Victor Central SD	Victor
181	5	Wantagh Union Free SD	Wantagh
181	5	Washingtonville Central SD	Washingtonville
181	5	Waterloo Central SD	Waterloo
181	5	Waverly Central SD	Waverly
181	5	Wayne Central SD	Ontario Center
181	5	West Hempstead Union Free SD	W Hempstead
253	4	Amherst Central SD	Amherst
253	4	Bath Central SD	Bath
253	4	Beekmantown Central SD	West Chazy
253	4	Byram Hills Central SD	Armonk
253	4	Cairo-Durham Central SD	Cairo
253	4	Canandaigua City SD	Canandaigua
253	4	Canastota Central SD	Canastota
253	4	Cheektowaga Central SD	Cheektowaga
253	4	Cheektowaga-Maryvale UFSD	Cheektowaga
253	4	Cheektowaga-Sloan Union Free SD	Sloan
253	4	Chenango Forks Central SD	Binghamton
253	4	Chenango Valley Central SD	Binghamton
253	4	Cold Spring Harbor Central SD	Cold Sprg Harbor
253	4	Dansville Central SD	Dansville
253	4	Dover Union Free SD	Dover Plains
253	4	East Aurora Union Free SD	East Aurora
253	4	Ellenville Central SD	Ellenville
253	4	Elwood Union Free SD	Greenlawn
253	4	Fredonia Central SD	Fredonia
253	4	Geneva City SD	Geneva
253	4	Gorham-Middlesex CSD (M Whitman)	Rushville
253	4	Harborfields Central SD	Greenlawn
253	4	Highland Central SD	Highland

253	4	Holland Patent Central SD	Holland Patent
253	4	Honeoye Falls-Lima Central SD	Honeoye Falls
253	4	Hornell City SD	Hornell
253	4	Irvington Union Free SD	Irvington
253	4	Island Trees Union Free SD	Levittown
253	4	Jordan-Elbridge Central SD	Jordan
253	4	Lackawanna City SD	Lackawanna
253	4	Lansingburgh Central SD	Troy
253	4	Lewiston-Porter Central SD	Youngstown
253	4	Livonia Central SD	Livonia
253	4	Locust Valley Central SD	Locust Valley
253	4	Maine-Endwell Central SD	Endwell
253	4	Malverne Union Free SD	Malverne
253	4	Manhasset Union Free SD	Manhasset
253	4	Medina Central SD	Medina
253	4	Miller Place Union Free SD	Miller Place
253	4	Mount Pleasant Central SD	Thornwood
253	4	Nanuet Union Free SD	Nanuet
253	4	New Hyde Park-Garden City Park	New Hyde Park
253	4	New Paltz Central SD	New Paltz
253	4	North Rose-Wolcott Central SD	Wolcott
253	4	Northeastern Clinton Central SD	Champlain
253	4	Nyc Alternative HS District	New York
253	4	Owego-Apalachin Central SD	Owego
253	4	Palmyra-Macedon Central SD	Palmyra
253	4	Phelps-Clifton Springs Cent SD	Clifton Spgs
253	4	Queensbury Union Free SD	Queensbury
253	4	Ravena-Coeymans-Selkirk CSD	Selkirk
253	4	Rocky Point Union Free SD	Rocky Point
253	4	Rotterdam-Mohonasen Central SD	Schenectady
253	4	Seaford Union Free SD	Seaford
253	4	Skaneateles Central SD	Skaneateles
253	4	Solvay Union Free SD	Solvay
253	4	Somers Central SD	Lincolndale
253	4	South Jefferson Central SD	Adams Center
253	4	Spackenkill Union Free SD	Poughkeepsie
253	4	Springville-Griffith Inst Cent	Springville
253	4	Starpoint Central SD	Lockport
253	4	Taconic Hills Central SD	Craryville
253	4	Valley Stream 13 Union Free SD	Valley Stream
253	4	Valley Stream Central High SD	Valley Stream
253	4	Watkins Glen Central SD	Watkins Glen
253	4	Wayland-Cohocton Central SD	Wayland
253	4	Westhill Central SD	Syracuse
253	4	Whitney Point Central SD	Whitney Point
253	4	Windsor Central SD	Windsor
253	4	Yorkshire-Pioneer Central SD	Yorkshire
323	3	Akron Central SD	Akron
323	3	Ardsley Union Free SD	Ardsley
323	3	Babylon Union Free SD	Babylon
323	3	Briarcliff Manor Union Free SD	Briarcliff Manor
323	3	Canton Central SD	Canton
323	3	Carle Place Union Free SD	Carle Place
323	3	Catskill Central SD	Catskill
323	3	Cazenovia Central SD	Cazenovia
323	3	Chatham Central SD	Chatham
323	3	Cleveland Hill Union Free SD	Cheektowaga
323	3	Clinton Central SD	Clinton
323	3	Croton-Harmon Union Free SD	Croton-On-Hud
323	3	Depew Union Free SD	Depew
323	3	East Hampton Union Free SD	East Hampton
323	3	East Williston Union Free SD	Old Westbury
323	3	Eden Central SD	Eden
323	3	Edgemont Union Free SD	Scarsdale
323	3	Fonda-Fultonville Central SD	Fonda
323	3	Franklin Square Union Free SD	Franklin Square
323	3	General Brown Central SD	Dexter
323	3	Hannibal Central SD	Hannibal
323	3	Hastings-On-Hudson Union Free SD	Hastings-on-Hud
323	3	Ilion Central SD	Ilion
323	3	Liberty Central SD	Liberty
323	3	Marcellus Central SD	Marcellus
323	3	Merrick Union Free SD	Merrick
323	3	Mount Sinai Union Free SD	Mount Sinai
323	3	New York City Geographic Dist 9	Bronx
323	3	Oyster Bay-East Norwich CSD	Oyster Bay
323	3	Penn Yan Central SD	Penn Yan
323	3	Phoenix Central SD	Phoenix
323	3	Pleasantville Union Free SD	Pleasantville
323	3	Putnam Valley Central SD	Putnam Valley
323	3	Royalton-Hartland Central SD	Middleport
323	3	Salmon River Central SD	Ft Covington
323	3	Sherburne-Earlville Central SD	Sherburne
323	3	Southampton Union Free SD	Southampton
323	3	Southwestern Cent SD Jamestown	Jamestown
323	3	Valley Stream 30 Union Free SD	Valley Stream
323	3	Westhampton Beach Union Free SD	Westhampton Bch
323	3	Wilson Central SD	Wilson
323	3	Wyandanch Union Free SD	Wyandanch
365	2	Floral Park-Bellerose UFSD	Floral Park
365	2	Hampton Bays Union Free SD	Hampton Bays
365	2	Mattituck-Cutchogue UFSD	Cutchogue
365	2	Schuylerville Central SD	Schuylerville
369	1	Boces Eastern Suffolk	Patchogue
369	1	Boces Nassau	Garden City

Number of Teachers

Rank	Number	District Name	City
1	70,171	New York City Public Schools	Brooklyn
2	3,022	Buffalo City SD	Buffalo
3	2,833	Rochester City SD	Rochester
4	1,883	Yonkers City SD	Yonkers
5	1,804	Syracuse City SD	Syracuse
6	1,161	Sachem Central SD	Holbrook
7	1,072	Brentwood Union Free SD	Brentwood
8	978	Greece Central SD	Rochester
9	900	Newburgh City SD	Newburgh
10	788	Williamsville Central SD	East Amherst
11	787	Albany City SD	Albany
12	779	Wappingers Central SD	Wappingers Fls
13	746	Middle Country Central SD	Centereach
14	731	Smithtown Central SD	Smithtown
15	720	E Ramapo Central SD (Sprg Val)	Spring Valley
16	711	New Rochelle City SD	New Rochelle
17	706	Half Hollow Hills Central SD	Dix Hills
18	689	Clarkstown Central SD	New City
19	682	Kenmore-Tonawanda Union Free SD	Buffalo
20	673	North Syracuse Central SD	N Syracuse
21	662	Mount Vernon City SD	Mount Vernon
22	658	Schenectady City SD	Schenectady
23	658	Longwood Central SD	Middle Island
24	654	Webster Central SD	Webster
25	636	William Floyd Union Free SD	Mastic Beach
26	635	Shenendehowa Central SD	Clifton Park
27	635	Haverstraw-Stony Point Cent SD	Garnerville
28	631	Arlington Central SD	Poughkeepsie
29	617	Levittown Union Free SD	Levittown
30	611	Massapequa Union Free SD	Massapequa
31	609	East Meadow Union Free SD	Westbury
32	605	Patchogue-Medford Union Free SD	Patchogue
33	604	Utica City SD	Utica
34	604	Syosset Central SD	Syosset
35	599	Three Village Central SD	East Setauket
36	597	Liverpool Central SD	Liverpool
37	593	Boces Eastern Suffolk	Patchogue
38	588	Kingston City SD	Kingston
39	569	Commack Union Free SD	E Northport
40	568	Great Neck Union Free SD	Great Neck
41	566	Elmira City SD	Elmira
42	562	Niagara Falls City SD	Niagara Falls
43	561	White Plains City SD	White Plains
44	557	West Seneca Central SD	West Seneca
45	551	Northport-East Northport UFSD	Northport
46	541	Lindenhurst Union Free SD	Lindenhurst
47	537	Uniondale Union Free SD	Uniondale
48	536	Binghamton City SD	Binghamton
48	536	Boces Nassau	Garden City
50	532	Farmingdale Union Free SD	Farmingdale
51	527	Freeport Union Free SD	Freeport
52	520	Sewanhaka Central High SD	Floral Park
53	518	Connetquot Central SD	Bohemia
54	512	Saratoga Springs City SD	Saratoga Spgs
55	504	Fairport Central SD	Fairport
56	503	Central Islip Union Free SD	Central Islip
57	499	Monroe-Woodbury Central SD	Central Valley
58	498	Rush-Henrietta Central SD	Henrietta
59	481	Rome City SD	Rome
60	478	Ithaca City SD	Ithaca
61	471	Oceanside Union Free SD	Oceanside
62	461	Jamestown City SD	Jamestown
63	458	Pittsford Central SD	Pittsford
64	455	South Huntington Union Free SD	Huntington Stn
65	454	Hempstead Union Free SD	Hempstead
65	454	Lakeland Central SD	Shrub Oak
67	448	Lockport City SD	Lockport
68	447	Middletown City SD	Middletown
69	445	South Colonie Central SD	Albany
70	438	Plainview-Old Bethpage Cent SD	Plainview
71	430	Baldwin Union Free SD	Baldwin
72	429	Bay Shore Union Free SD	Bay Shore
72	429	Frontier Central SD	Hamburg
74	426	West Islip Union Free SD	West Islip
75	426	Guilderland Central SD	Guilderland
76	422	Pine Bush Central SD	Pine Bush
77	417	Corning City SD	Painted Post
78	417	Port Washington Union Free SD	Pt Washington
79	410	Penfield Central SD	Penfield
80	406	Baldwinsville Central SD	Baldwinsville
81	406	Lancaster Central SD	Lancaster
82	402	Mahopac Central SD	Mahopac
83	398	North Colonie Central SD	Latham
84	396	Orchard Park Central SD	Orchard Park
85	388	Hicksville Union Free SD	Hicksville
86	387	Deer Park Union Free SD	Deer Park
87	386	Gates-Chili Central SD	Rochester
88	378	Auburn City SD	Auburn
89	377	East Islip Union Free SD	Islip Terrace
90	376	Valley Central SD (Montgomery)	Montgomery
91	374	Bellmore-Merrick Central High SD	North Merrick
92	372	Scarsdale Union Free SD	Scarsdale
93	371	Mamaroneck Union Free SD	Mamaroneck
94	370	North Babylon Union Free SD	North Babylon
95	367	Ramapo Central SD (Suffern)	Hillburn
96	366	Lawrence Union Free SD	Lawrence
97	363	Huntington Union Free SD	Huntington Stn
98	358	South Country Central SD	E Patchogue
99	356	Poughkeepsie City SD	Poughkeepsie
100	356	Oswego City SD	Oswego
101	355	Troy City SD	Troy
102	354	Chappaqua Central SD	Chappaqua
103	353	Clarence Central SD	Clarence
104	352	Bedford Central SD	Mount Kisco
105	351	Herricks Union Free SD	New Hyde Park
106	349	Long Beach City SD	Long Beach
107	348	Union-Endicott Central SD	Endicott
108	346	Hilton Central SD	Hilton
109	346	West Genesee Central SD	Camillus
110	343	Valley Stream Central High SD	Valley Stream
111	342	Central Square Central SD	Central Square
112	342	Bethlehem Central SD	Delmar
112	342	West Babylon Union Free SD	West Babylon
114	341	Washingtonville Central SD	Washingtonville
115	340	North Tonawanda City SD	N Tonawanda
116	338	East Greenbush Central SD	E Greenbush
117	334	Hamburg Central SD	Hamburg
118	334	Rockville Centre Union Free SD	Rockville Ctre
119	334	Carmel Central SD	Patterson
120	331	Churchville-Chili Central SD	Churchville
121	331	Spencerport Central SD	Spencerport
122	329	Hyde Park Central SD	Poughkeepsie
123	326	Ossining Union Free SD	Ossining
124	326	Fayetteville-Manlius Central SD	Manlius
125	325	Hauppauge Union Free SD	Hauppauge
126	323	Brockport Central SD	Brockport
127	323	Riverhead Central SD	Riverhead
128	322	Canandaigua City SD	Canandaigua
128	322	Vestal Central SD	Vestal
130	320	East Syracuse-Minoa Central SD	East Syracuse
131	317	Yorktown Central SD	Yorktown Hgts
132	316	Jericho Union Free SD	Jericho
133	314	Garden City Union Free SD	Garden City
134	314	Ballston Spa Central SD	Ballston Spa
135	310	Warwick Valley Central SD	Warwick
136	309	Katonah-Lewisboro Union Free SD	South Salem
137	306	Copiague Union Free SD	Copiague
138	305	Sweet Home Central SD	Amherst
139	303	Monticello Central SD	Monticello
140	302	Horseheads Central SD	Horseheads
141	301	Watertown City SD	Watertown
142	301	Harrison Central SD	Harrison
143	300	Niagara-Wheatfield Central SD	Niagara Falls
144	300	Niskayuna Central SD	Schenectady
145	298	Minisink Valley Central SD	Slate Hill
146	297	Amsterdam City SD	Amsterdam
147	295	Indian River Central SD	Philadelphia
148	295	Westbury Union Free SD	Old Westbury
149	293	Whitesboro Central SD	Yorkville
150	290	Fulton City SD	Fulton
151	288	Kings Park Central SD	Kings Park
152	280	Hewlett-Woodmere Union Free SD	Woodmere
153	280	Brighton Central SD	Rochester
154	277	Brewster Central SD	Brewster
155	275	Elmont Union Free SD	Elmont
156	273	Averill Park Central SD	Averill Park
157	272	Brookhaven-Comsewogue UFSD	Pt Jefferson Stn
158	268	Evans-Brant Cent SD (Lake Shore)	Angola
159	268	Mineola Union Free SD	Mineola
160	267	South Orangetown Central SD	Blauvelt
161	263	Roslyn Union Free SD	Roslyn
162	260	Sayville Union Free SD	Sayville
163	260	West Irondequoit Central SD	Rochester
164	259	Wantagh Union Free SD	Wantagh
165	259	Gloversville City SD	Gloversville
166	257	East Irondequoit Central SD	Rochester
166	257	Port Chester-Rye Union Free SD	Port Chester
168	257	Amityville Union Free SD	Amityville
169	255	Lynbrook Union Free SD	Lynbrook
170	255	Queensbury Union Free SD	Queensbury
171	254	Glen Cove City SD	Glen Cove
172	250	Victor Central SD	Victor
173	250	Wallkill Central SD	Wallkill
174	249	Amherst Central SD	Amherst
175	248	Plainedge Union Free SD	N Massapequa
176	248	Roosevelt Union Free SD	Roosevelt
177	247	Harborfields Central SD	Greenlawn
178	246	Beacon City SD	Beacon
179	246	Nyack Union Free SD	Nyack

180	245	South Glens Falls Central SD	S Glens Falls
181	243	Burnt Hls-Ballston Lake Cent SD	Scotia
182	242	Somers Central SD	Lincolndale
183	242	Bethpage Union Free SD	Bethpage
184	239	Manhasset Union Free SD	Manhasset
185	239	Islip Union Free SD	Islip
186	238	North Shore Central SD	Sea Cliff
187	235	Hendrick Hudson Central SD	Montrose
188	234	Peekskill City SD	Peekskill
189	233	Rocky Point Union Free SD	Rocky Point
190	230	Cortland City SD	Cortland
191	228	Grand Island Central SD	Grand Island
192	228	Batavia City SD	Batavia
193	227	Jamesville-Dewitt Central SD	Dewitt
194	225	Yorkshire-Pioneer Central SD	Yorkshire
195	223	Saugerties Central SD	Saugerties
196	222	Port Jervis City SD	Port Jervis
197	222	Geneva City SD	Geneva
198	221	Wayne Central SD	Ontario Center
199	218	Rye City SD	Rye
200	218	Rondout Valley Central SD	Accord
201	217	Rotterdam-Mohonasen Central SD	Schenectady
202	217	Shoreham-Wading River Central SD	Shoreham
203	216	Island Trees Union Free SD	Levittown
204	213	Newark Central SD	Newark
205	213	Eastchester Union Free SD	Eastchester
206	213	Malone Central SD	Malone
207	211	Camden Central SD	Camden
207	211	Carthage Central SD	Carthage
209	210	Goshen Central SD	Goshen
210	209	Scotia-Glenville Central SD	Scotia
211	208	Johnson City Central SD	Johnson City
212	208	Dunkirk City SD	Dunkirk
213	208	Byram Hills Central SD	Armonk
214	206	New Hartford Central SD	New Hartford
215	205	Bayport-Blue Point Union Free SD	Bayport
215	205	Maine-Endwell Central SD	Endwell
217	205	Miller Place Union Free SD	Miller Place
218	204	Seaford Union Free SD	Seaford
219	203	Cornwall Central SD	Cornwall-on-Hud
220	202	Phoenix Central SD	Phoenix
221	202	Massena Central SD	Massena
222	201	Hudson City SD	Hudson
223	201	Locust Valley Central SD	Locust Valley
224	198	Plattsburgh City SD	Plattsburgh
225	198	Pelham Union Free SD	Pelham
226	197	Glens Falls City SD	Glens Falls
227	195	Union Free SD of the Tarrytowns	Sleepy Hollow
228	193	Iroquois Central SD	Elma
229	193	Olean City SD	Olean
230	192	Ravena-Coeymans-Selkirk CSD	Selkirk
231	191	Albion Central SD	Albion
232	191	Norwich City SD	Norwich
233	191	Mexico Central SD	Mexico
234	190	Oneida City SD	Oneida
235	190	Tonawanda City SD	Tonawanda
236	190	Chittenango Central SD	Chittenango
237	190	Beekmantown Central SD	West Chazy
237	190	Honeoye Falls-Lima Central SD	Honeoye Falls
239	190	Homer Central SD	Homer
240	187	Depew Union Free SD	Depew
241	185	Palmyra-Macedon Central SD	Palmyra
242	185	Cheektowaga-Maryvale UFSD	Cheektowaga
243	185	Peru Central SD	Peru
244	184	Ardsley Union Free SD	Ardsley
245	184	Pearl River Union Free SD	Pearl River
246	183	Nanuet Union Free SD	Nanuet
247	182	Lewiston-Porter Central SD	Youngstown
248	182	Susquehanna Valley Central SD	Conklin
249	181	Cobleskill-Richmondville CSD	Cobleskill
250	181	North Bellmore Union Free SD	Bellmore
251	180	West Hempstead Union Free SD	W Hempstead
252	180	Cohoes City SD	Cohoes
253	179	Owego-Apalachin Central SD	Owego
254	179	Lansingburgh Central SD	Troy
255	177	Lackawanna City SD	Lackawanna
256	177	Cheektowaga Central SD	Cheektowaga
257	177	Greenburgh Central SD	Hartsdale
258	177	Starpoint Central SD	Lockport
259	177	Onteora Central SD	Boiceville
260	176	Dryden Central SD	Dryden
261	176	New Paltz Central SD	New Paltz
262	175	Livonia Central SD	Livonia
263	175	Red Hook Central SD	Red Hook
264	174	Sherrill City SD	Verona
265	174	Oneonta City SD	Oneonta
266	173	Southampton Union Free SD	Southampton
267	171	Valley Stream 13 Union Free SD	Valley Stream
268	171	Springville-Griffith Inst Cent	Springville
269	170	Kinderhook Central SD	Valatie
270	170	Penn Yan Central SD	Penn Yan
271	169	Mount Pleasant Central SD	Thornwood
272	168	Hudson Falls Central SD	Hudson Falls
273	168	Schalmont Central SD	Schenectady
274	168	Mount Sinai Union Free SD	Mount Sinai
275	167	Ogdensburg City SD	Ogdensburg
276	167	East Hampton Union Free SD	East Hampton
277	167	Elwood Union Free SD	Greenlawn
278	167	Fredonia Central SD	Fredonia
279	165	Sherburne-Earlville Central SD	Sherburne
280	164	Medina Central SD	Medina
281	163	Westhampton Beach Union Free SD	Westhampton Bch
282	163	Hornell City SD	Hornell
283	161	Marlboro Central SD	Marlboro
284	160	Malverne Union Free SD	Malverne
285	160	Irvington Union Free SD	Irvington
286	159	Phelps-Clifton Springs Cent SD	Clifton Spgs
287	158	Cold Spring Harbor Central SD	Cold Sprg Harbor
288	156	Babylon Union Free SD	Babylon
288	156	Bath Central SD	Bath
290	155	East Williston Union Free SD	Old Westbury
291	154	Waterloo Central SD	Waterloo
292	154	Windsor Central SD	Windsor
293	153	Wyandanch Union Free SD	Wyandanch
294	153	Alden Central SD	Alden
295	152	Wayland-Cohocton Central SD	Wayland
296	152	Whitney Point Central SD	Whitney Point
297	151	Hastings-On-Hudson Union Free SD	Hastings-on-Hud
298	150	Merrick Union Free SD	Merrick
299	150	Newfane Central SD	Newfane
300	150	Spackenkill Union Free SD	Poughkeepsie
301	149	Saranac Central SD	Dannemora
302	148	Chenango Valley Central SD	Binghamton
303	148	Briarcliff Manor Union Free SD	Briarcliff Manor
304	147	Catskill Central SD	Catskill
304	147	North Rose-Wolcott Central SD	Wolcott
306	147	East Aurora Union Free SD	East Aurora
307	146	Westhill Central SD	Syracuse
308	146	Johnstown City SD	Johnstown
309	145	Liberty Central SD	Liberty
310	145	Oyster Bay-East Norwich CSD	Oyster Bay
311	144	Attica Central SD	Attica
312	144	Dansville Central SD	Dansville
313	144	Carle Place Union Free SD	Carle Place
314	143	Taconic Hills Central SD	Craryville
315	143	South Jefferson Central SD	Adams Center
316	142	Skaneateles Central SD	Skaneateles
317	142	Putnam Valley Central SD	Putnam Valley
318	142	Hampton Bays Union Free SD	Hampton Bays
319	142	Chenango Forks Central SD	Binghamton
320	141	Marcellus Central SD	Marcellus
321	139	Edgemont Union Free SD	Scarsdale
321	139	Salmon River Central SD	Ft Covington
323	138	Ellenville Central SD	Ellenville
324	138	Sullivan West Central SD	Callicoon
325	138	Saranac Lake Central SD	Saranac Lake
326	138	Altmar-Parish-Williamstown CSD	Parish
326	138	Mattituck-Cutchogue UFSD	Cutchogue
328	138	Holland Patent Central SD	Holland Patent
329	138	Cazenovia Central SD	Cazenovia
330	137	Jordan-Elbridge Central SD	Jordan
331	137	Adirondack Central SD	Boonville
332	136	Solvay Union Free SD	Solvay
333	134	Broadalbin-Perth Central SD	Broadalbin
334	133	Royalton-Hartland Central SD	Middleport
335	133	Franklin Square Union Free SD	Franklin Square
336	132	Schuylerville Central SD	Schuylerville
337	132	Ilion Central SD	Ilion
338	131	Cairo-Durham Central SD	Cairo
339	129	Coxsackie-Athens Central SD	Coxsackie
340	128	Hannibal Central SD	Hannibal
341	128	Salamanca City SD	Salamanca
342	128	Southwestern Cent SD Jamestown	Jamestown
343	128	Highland Central SD	Highland
344	127	Eden Central SD	Eden
345	127	Pleasantville Union Free SD	Pleasantville
346	126	Gorham-Middlesex CSD (M Whitman)	Rushville
347	125	Waverly Central SD	Waverly
348	125	Clinton Central SD	Clinton
349	124	Northeastern Clinton Central SD	Champlain
350	123	New Hyde Park-Garden City Park	New Hyde Park
351	122	Cleveland Hill Union Free SD	Cheektowaga
351	122	Gowanda Central SD	Gowanda
353	121	Fonda-Fultonville Central SD	Fonda
354	120	Wilson Central SD	Wilson
355	120	Canton Central SD	Canton
356	119	Gouverneur Central SD	Gouverneur
357	117	Valley Stream 30 Union Free SD	Valley Stream
358	117	Lansing Central SD	Lansing
359	116	Croton-Harmon Union Free SD	Croton-On-Hud
360	116	Akron Central SD	Akron
361	115	Dover Union Free SD	Dover Plains
362	114	Cheektowaga-Sloan Union Free SD	Sloan
363	113	Watkins Glen Central SD	Watkins Glen
364	111	Canastota Central SD	Canastota
365	108	Chatham Central SD	Chatham
366	107	General Brown Central SD	Dexter
367	104	Floral Park-Bellerose UFSD	Floral Park
368	n/a	New York City Geographic Dist 9	Bronx
368	n/a	New York City Geographic Dist 15	Brooklyn
368	n/a	Nyc Alternative HS District	New York

Number of Students

Rank	Number	District Name	City
1	1,023,674	New York City Public Schools	Brooklyn
2	41,089	Buffalo City SD	Buffalo
3	34,598	Rochester City SD	Rochester
4	26,201	Yonkers City SD	Yonkers
5	22,405	Syracuse City SD	Syracuse
6	16,607	Brentwood Union Free SD	Brentwood
7	15,378	Sachem Central SD	Holbrook
8	13,799	Greece Central SD	Rochester
9	13,108	Newburgh City SD	Newburgh
10	12,146	Wappingers Central SD	Wappingers Fls
11	11,630	Middle Country Central SD	Centereach
12	10,760	Williamsville Central SD	East Amherst
13	10,464	New Rochelle City SD	New Rochelle
14	10,376	William Floyd Union Free SD	Mastic Beach
15	10,347	Mount Vernon City SD	Mount Vernon
16	10,188	North Syracuse Central SD	N Syracuse
16	10,188	Smithtown Central SD	Smithtown
18	10,102	Arlington Central SD	Poughkeepsie
19	9,919	Albany City SD	Albany
20	9,794	Longwood Central SD	Middle Island
21	9,661	Half Hollow Hills Central SD	Dix Hills
22	9,350	Clarkstown Central SD	New City
23	9,313	Shenendehowa Central SD	Clifton Park
24	9,170	E Ramapo Central SD (Sprg Val)	Spring Valley
25	9,101	Patchogue-Medford Union Free SD	Patchogue
26	9,090	Schenectady City SD	Schenectady
27	9,070	Utica City SD	Utica
28	9,033	Kenmore-Tonawanda Union Free SD	Buffalo
29	8,736	Niagara Falls City SD	Niagara Falls
29	8,736	Webster Central SD	Webster
31	8,629	Liverpool Central SD	Liverpool
32	8,435	Sewanhaka Central High SD	Floral Park
33	8,366	Haverstraw-Stony Point Cent SD	Garnerville
34	8,248	Massapequa Union Free SD	Massapequa
35	8,149	Kingston City SD	Kingston
36	8,094	East Meadow Union Free SD	Westbury
37	8,027	Levittown Union Free SD	Levittown
38	7,986	Three Village Central SD	East Setauket
39	7,697	West Seneca Central SD	West Seneca
40	7,689	Lindenhurst Union Free SD	Lindenhurst
41	7,613	Elmira City SD	Elmira
42	7,511	Commack Union Free SD	E Northport
43	7,255	Monroe-Woodbury Central SD	Central Valley
44	7,160	Connetquot Central SD	Bohemia
45	7,146	Freeport Union Free SD	Freeport
46	7,128	Hempstead Union Free SD	Hempstead
47	7,115	Fairport Central SD	Fairport
48	6,922	Saratoga Springs City SD	Saratoga Spgs
49	6,844	White Plains City SD	White Plains
50	6,741	Central Islip Union Free SD	Central Islip
51	6,623	Syosset Central SD	Syosset
52	6,577	Middletown City SD	Middletown
53	6,472	Farmingdale Union Free SD	Farmingdale
54	6,411	Uniondale Union Free SD	Uniondale
55	6,392	Northport-East Northport UFSD	Northport
56	6,369	Oceanside Union Free SD	Oceanside
57	6,249	Binghamton City SD	Binghamton
58	6,204	Lancaster Central SD	Lancaster
59	6,199	Rome City SD	Rome
60	6,139	Lakeland Central SD	Shrub Oak
61	6,118	Pine Bush Central SD	Pine Bush
62	6,113	Great Neck Union Free SD	Great Neck
63	6,111	South Huntington Union Free SD	Huntington Stn
64	6,022	Pittsford Central SD	Pittsford
65	5,960	Baldwinsville Central SD	Baldwinsville
66	5,905	West Islip Union Free SD	West Islip
67	5,859	Rush-Henrietta Central SD	Henrietta
68	5,833	Corning City SD	Painted Post
69	5,832	Bellmore-Merrick Central High SD	North Merrick
70	5,751	Ithaca City SD	Ithaca
71	5,745	South Colonie Central SD	Albany
72	5,703	Lockport City SD	Lockport
73	5,698	Bay Shore Union Free SD	Bay Shore
74	5,664	Guilderland Central SD	Guilderland
75	5,631	North Colonie Central SD	Latham
76	5,622	Frontier Central SD	Hamburg
77	5,432	East Islip Union Free SD	Islip Terrace
78	5,408	Baldwin Union Free SD	Baldwin
79	5,289	Jamestown City SD	Jamestown
79	5,289	Mahopac Central SD	Mahopac
81	5,266	Hicksville Union Free SD	Hicksville
82	5,236	Valley Central SD (Montgomery)	Montgomery
83	5,220	North Babylon Union Free SD	North Babylon

PROFILES OF NEW YORK / School District Rankings 621

84	5,186	Orchard Park Central SD	Orchard Park
85	5,153	West Genesee Central SD	Camillus
86	5,106	Washingtonville Central SD	Washingtonville
87	5,057	Gates-Chili Central SD	Rochester
88	5,022	Bethlehem Central SD	Delmar
89	5,013	Central Square Central SD	Central Square
90	4,993	Auburn City SD	Auburn
91	4,970	Plainview-Old Bethpage Cent SD	Plainview
92	4,960	Penfield Central SD	Penfield
93	4,940	West Babylon Union Free SD	West Babylon
94	4,920	Clarence Central SD	Clarence
95	4,880	Poughkeepsie City SD	Poughkeepsie
96	4,862	Riverhead Central SD	Riverhead
97	4,857	Carmel Central SD	Patterson
97	4,857	Troy City SD	Troy
99	4,821	Copiague Union Free SD	Copiague
100	4,809	Oswego City SD	Oswego
101	4,791	Mamaroneck Union Free SD	Mamaroneck
102	4,758	South Country Central SD	E Patchogue
103	4,740	Port Washington Union Free SD	Pt Washington
104	4,682	Hyde Park Central SD	Poughkeepsie
104	4,682	Warwick Valley Central SD	Warwick
106	4,643	North Tonawanda City SD	N Tonawanda
107	4,619	Fayetteville-Manlius Central SD	Manlius
108	4,596	Ramapo Central SD (Suffern)	Hillburn
109	4,572	East Greenbush Central SD	E Greenbush
110	4,568	Scarsdale Union Free SD	Scarsdale
111	4,566	Valley Stream Central High SD	Valley Stream
112	4,543	Minisink Valley Central SD	Slate Hill
113	4,536	Union-Endicott Central SD	Endicott
114	4,521	Ballston Spa Central SD	Ballston Spa
115	4,482	Churchville-Chili Central SD	Churchville
116	4,480	Brockport Central SD	Brockport
117	4,461	Deer Park Union Free SD	Deer Park
118	4,458	Long Beach City SD	Long Beach
119	4,441	Hilton Central SD	Hilton
120	4,378	Horseheads Central SD	Horseheads
121	4,350	Spencerport Central SD	Spencerport
122	4,334	Watertown City SD	Watertown
123	4,268	Bedford Central SD	Mount Kisco
124	4,266	Vestal Central SD	Vestal
125	4,258	Niskayuna Central SD	Schenectady
126	4,252	Ossining Union Free SD	Ossining
127	4,248	Elmont Union Free SD	Elmont
128	4,219	Yorktown Central SD	Yorktown Hgts
129	4,186	Canandaigua City SD	Canandaigua
130	4,155	Hauppauge Union Free SD	Hauppauge
131	4,153	Hamburg Central SD	Hamburg
132	4,150	Garden City Union Free SD	Garden City
133	4,131	Huntington Union Free SD	Huntington Stn
134	4,112	Katonah-Lewisboro Union Free SD	South Salem
135	4,096	Chappaqua Central SD	Chappaqua
136	4,060	Niagara-Wheatfield Central SD	Niagara Falls
137	4,036	Westbury Union Free SD	Old Westbury
138	4,007	Kings Park Central SD	Kings Park
139	3,949	West Irondequoit Central SD	Rochester
140	3,939	Herricks Union Free SD	New Hyde Park
141	3,930	Brookhaven-Comsewogue UFSD	Pt Jefferson Stn
142	3,906	Queensbury Union Free SD	Queensbury
143	3,875	Fulton City SD	Fulton
144	3,867	Sweet Home Central SD	Amherst
145	3,863	Whitesboro Central SD	Yorkville
146	3,824	East Syracuse-Minoa Central SD	East Syracuse
147	3,782	Amsterdam City SD	Amsterdam
148	3,726	Brewster Central SD	Brewster
149	3,692	Lawrence Union Free SD	Lawrence
150	3,638	Wallkill Central SD	Wallkill
151	3,636	Islip Union Free SD	Islip
152	3,613	Beacon City SD	Beacon
153	3,606	Plainedge Union Free SD	N Massapequa
153	3,606	Rockville Centre Union Free SD	Rockville Ctre
155	3,594	Rocky Point Union Free SD	Rocky Point
156	3,593	Sayville Union Free SD	Sayville
157	3,582	Brighton Central SD	Rochester
158	3,578	Wantagh Union Free SD	Wantagh
159	3,574	Port Chester-Rye Union Free SD	Port Chester
160	3,560	Harborfields Central SD	Greenlawn
161	3,556	Victor Central SD	Victor
162	3,546	Averill Park Central SD	Averill Park
163	3,523	Monticello Central SD	Monticello
164	3,514	East Irondequoit Central SD	Rochester
165	3,447	Burnt Hls-Ballston Lake Cent SD	Scotia
166	3,444	Port Jervis City SD	Port Jervis
167	3,382	Harrison Central SD	Harrison
168	3,377	Indian River Central SD	Philadelphia
169	3,347	South Orangetown Central SD	Blauvelt
170	3,340	Rotterdam-Mohonasen Central SD	Schenectady
171	3,336	Saugerties Central SD	Saugerties
172	3,327	Hewlett-Woodmere Union Free SD	Woodmere
173	3,292	South Glens Falls Central SD	S Glens Falls
174	3,237	Roslyn Union Free SD	Roslyn
175	3,230	Evans-Brant Cent SD (Lake Shore)	Angola
176	3,226	Gloversville City SD	Gloversville
177	3,210	Jericho Union Free SD	Jericho
178	3,190	Grand Island Central SD	Grand Island
179	3,188	Glen Cove City SD	Glen Cove
180	3,141	Lynbrook Union Free SD	Lynbrook
181	3,140	Somers Central SD	Lincolndale
182	3,125	Amherst Central SD	Amherst
183	3,093	Cornwall Central SD	Cornwall-on-Hud
184	3,083	Amityville Union Free SD	Amityville
185	3,055	Peekskill City SD	Peekskill
186	3,030	Miller Place Union Free SD	Miller Place
187	3,006	Bethpage Union Free SD	Bethpage
188	2,952	Scotia-Glenville Central SD	Scotia
189	2,937	Carthage Central SD	Carthage
190	2,928	Yorkshire-Pioneer Central SD	Yorkshire
191	2,921	Goshen Central SD	Goshen
192	2,905	Iroquois Central SD	Elma
193	2,903	Mineola Union Free SD	Mineola
194	2,884	Hendrick Hudson Central SD	Montrose
195	2,882	Roosevelt Union Free SD	Roosevelt
196	2,861	Massena Central SD	Massena
197	2,858	Nyack Union Free SD	Nyack
198	2,848	Starpoint Central SD	Lockport
199	2,847	Cortland City SD	Cortland
200	2,845	Camden Central SD	Camden
201	2,797	Albion Central SD	Albion
201	2,797	Rondout Valley Central SD	Accord
203	2,795	Island Trees Union Free SD	Levittown
204	2,774	Wayne Central SD	Ontario Center
205	2,717	Jamesville-Dewitt Central SD	Dewitt
206	2,707	Byram Hills Central SD	Armonk
207	2,706	Seaford Union Free SD	Seaford
208	2,700	Manhasset Union Free SD	Manhasset
209	2,688	Newark Central SD	Newark
209	2,688	Rye City SD	Rye
211	2,682	Batavia City SD	Batavia
211	2,682	Mexico Central SD	Mexico
213	2,680	Eastchester Union Free SD	Eastchester
214	2,677	Shoreham-Wading River Central SD	Shoreham
215	2,675	Maine-Endwell Central SD	Endwell
216	2,670	New Hartford Central SD	New Hartford
217	2,652	North Shore Central SD	Sea Cliff
218	2,601	Honeoye Falls-Lima Central SD	Honeoye Falls
219	2,597	Johnson City Central SD	Johnson City
220	2,565	Chittenango Central SD	Chittenango
221	2,550	Oneida City SD	Oneida
222	2,544	Pearl River Union Free SD	Pearl River
223	2,541	Olean City SD	Olean
224	2,534	Geneva City SD	Geneva
225	2,529	Pelham Union Free SD	Pelham
226	2,528	North Bellmore Union Free SD	Bellmore
227	2,522	Glens Falls City SD	Glens Falls
228	2,512	Elwood Union Free SD	Greenlawn
229	2,506	Coxsackie-Athens Central SD	Coxsackie
230	2,499	Malone Central SD	Malone
230	2,499	Union Free SD of the Tarrytowns	Sleepy Hollow
232	2,490	Bayport-Blue Point Union Free SD	Bayport
233	2,478	Cheektowaga-Maryvale UFSD	Cheektowaga
234	2,428	Lansingburgh Central SD	Troy
235	2,425	Sherrill City SD	Verona
236	2,418	Hudson Falls Central SD	Hudson Falls
237	2,417	Hudson City SD	Hudson
237	2,417	Mount Sinai Union Free SD	Mount Sinai
237	2,417	Phoenix Central SD	Phoenix
240	2,416	Cheektowaga Central SD	Cheektowaga
241	2,402	Lewiston-Porter Central SD	Youngstown
242	2,385	Ravena-Coeymans-Selkirk CSD	Selkirk
242	2,385	Springville-Griffith Inst Cent	Springville
244	2,381	Red Hook Central SD	Red Hook
245	2,378	Depew Union Free SD	Depew
246	2,376	New Paltz Central SD	New Paltz
247	2,367	Homer Central SD	Homer
248	2,349	West Hempstead Union Free SD	W Hempstead
249	2,343	Ardsley Union Free SD	Ardsley
249	2,343	Tonawanda City SD	Tonawanda
251	2,337	Owego-Apalachin Central SD	Owego
252	2,303	Peru Central SD	Peru
253	2,285	Kinderhook Central SD	Valatie
254	2,280	Wyandanch Union Free SD	Wyandanch
255	2,275	Locust Valley Central SD	Locust Valley
256	2,247	Norwich City SD	Norwich
257	2,228	Schalmont Central SD	Schenectady
258	2,222	Palmyra-Macedon Central SD	Palmyra
259	2,208	Broadalbin-Perth Central SD	Broadalbin
259	2,208	Cobleskill-Richmondville CSD	Cobleskill
261	2,202	Cohoes City SD	Cohoes
262	2,192	Nanuet Union Free SD	Nanuet
263	2,179	Beekmantown Central SD	West Chazy
264	2,174	Newfane Central SD	Newfane
265	2,172	Onteora Central SD	Boiceville
266	2,168	Johnstown City SD	Johnstown
267	2,147	Marcellus Central SD	Marcellus
268	2,142	Oneonta City SD	Oneonta
269	2,136	Marlboro Central SD	Marlboro
270	2,135	Susquehanna Valley Central SD	Conklin
271	2,132	Livonia Central SD	Livonia
272	2,103	Valley Stream 13 Union Free SD	Valley Stream
273	2,101	Dunkirk City SD	Dunkirk
274	2,092	Cold Spring Harbor Central SD	Cold Sprg Harbor
275	2,091	East Aurora Union Free SD	East Aurora
276	2,075	Highland Central SD	Highland
277	2,072	Alden Central SD	Alden
278	2,062	Waterloo Central SD	Waterloo
279	2,055	Plattsburgh City SD	Plattsburgh
280	2,054	Bath Central SD	Bath
281	2,049	Westhill Central SD	Syracuse
282	2,045	Windsor Central SD	Windsor
283	2,044	Phelps-Clifton Springs Cent SD	Clifton Spgs
283	2,044	South Jefferson Central SD	Adams Center
285	2,041	Lackawanna City SD	Lackawanna
286	2,039	Boces Nassau	Garden City
287	2,035	Penn Yan Central SD	Penn Yan
288	2,032	Chenango Valley Central SD	Binghamton
289	2,018	Ogdensburg City SD	Ogdensburg
290	2,011	New York City Geographic Dist 15	Brooklyn
291	2,009	Babylon Union Free SD	Babylon
292	1,981	Greenburgh Central SD	Hartsdale
293	1,971	East Hampton Union Free SD	East Hampton
294	1,970	Merrick Union Free SD	Merrick
295	1,968	Saranac Central SD	Dannemora
296	1,967	Irvington Union Free SD	Irvington
297	1,954	Medina Central SD	Medina
298	1,942	Franklin Square Union Free SD	Franklin Square
299	1,934	Putnam Valley Central SD	Putnam Valley
300	1,908	Boces Eastern Suffolk	Patchogue
301	1,884	Dryden Central SD	Dryden
301	1,884	Hornell City SD	Hornell
303	1,882	Liberty Central SD	Liberty
304	1,874	Chenango Forks Central SD	Binghamton
305	1,871	Taconic Hills Central SD	Craryville
306	1,858	Whitney Point Central SD	Whitney Point
307	1,857	Fredonia Central SD	Fredonia
308	1,853	Holland Patent Central SD	Holland Patent
309	1,848	Skaneateles Central SD	Skaneateles
310	1,847	Mount Pleasant Central SD	Thornwood
311	1,844	Eden Central SD	Eden
312	1,840	Attica Central SD	Attica
313	1,839	New York City Geographic Dist 9	Bronx
314	1,835	Spackenkill Union Free SD	Poughkeepsie
315	1,834	Edgemont Union Free SD	Scarsdale
316	1,828	Nyc Alternative HS District	New York
317	1,827	Wayland-Cohocton Central SD	Wayland
318	1,826	Malverne Union Free SD	Malverne
319	1,823	New Hyde Park-Garden City Park	New Hyde Park
320	1,817	Catskill Central SD	Catskill
321	1,813	Cairo-Durham Central SD	Cairo
322	1,812	East Williston Union Free SD	Old Westbury
322	1,812	Ellenville Central SD	Ellenville
324	1,804	Cazenovia Central SD	Cazenovia
325	1,794	Ilion Central SD	Ilion
326	1,786	Waverly Central SD	Waverly
327	1,769	Hampton Bays Union Free SD	Hampton Bays
327	1,769	Southampton Union Free SD	Southampton
329	1,758	Sherburne-Earlville Central SD	Sherburne
330	1,757	Dover Union Free SD	Dover Plains
331	1,756	Hannibal Central SD	Hannibal
332	1,752	Southwestern Cent SD Jamestown	Jamestown
333	1,750	Dansville Central SD	Dansville
334	1,747	Solvay Union Free SD	Solvay
335	1,743	Gouverneur Central SD	Gouverneur
336	1,727	Pleasantville Union Free SD	Pleasantville
336	1,727	Westhampton Beach Union Free SD	Westhampton Bch
338	1,717	Briarcliff Manor Union Free SD	Briarcliff Manor
339	1,703	Jordan-Elbridge Central SD	Jordan
340	1,699	Akron Central SD	Akron
341	1,693	Schuylerville Central SD	Schuylerville
342	1,682	Royalton-Hartland Central SD	Middleport
343	1,670	Hastings-On-Hudson Union Free SD	Hastings-on-Hud
344	1,668	Floral Park-Bellerose UFSD	Floral Park
345	1,657	Northeastern Clinton Central SD	Champlain
346	1,647	Altmar-Parish-Williamstown CSD	Parish
347	1,642	North Rose-Wolcott Central SD	Wolcott
348	1,634	Clinton Central SD	Clinton
349	1,625	Saranac Lake Central SD	Saranac Lake
350	1,606	Fonda-Fultonville Central SD	Fonda
351	1,604	Salmon River Central SD	Ft Covington
352	1,597	Gorham-Middlesex CSD (M Whitman)	Rushville
353	1,587	Cleveland Hill Union Free SD	Cheektowaga
354	1,572	General Brown Central SD	Dexter
355	1,569	Oyster Bay-East Norwich CSD	Oyster Bay
356	1,568	Sullivan West Central SD	Callicoon
357	1,563	Mattituck-Cutchogue UFSD	Cutchogue
358	1,549	Croton-Harmon Union Free SD	Croton-On-Hud
359	1,548	Adirondack Central SD	Boonville
360	1,547	Canastota Central SD	Canastota

361	1,532	Gowanda Central SD	Gowanda
362	1,531	Cheektowaga-Sloan Union Free SD	Sloan
363	1,529	Lansing Central SD	Lansing
364	1,524	Watkins Glen Central SD	Watkins Glen
365	1,513	Canton Central SD	Canton
365	1,513	Salamanca City SD	Salamanca
367	1,504	Wilson Central SD	Wilson
368	1,502	Valley Stream 30 Union Free SD	Valley Stream
369	1,501	Chatham Central SD	Chatham
370	1,500	Carle Place Union Free SD	Carle Place

Male Students

Rank	Percent	District Name	City
1	75.8	Boces Nassau	Garden City
2	74.0	Boces Eastern Suffolk	Patchogue
3	68.6	Coxsackie-Athens Central SD	Coxsackie
4	56.3	Broadalbin-Perth Central SD	Broadalbin
5	56.1	Hudson City SD	Hudson
6	55.2	Fonda-Fultonville Central SD	Fonda
7	55.2	Watkins Glen Central SD	Watkins Glen
8	55.1	Lansing Central SD	Lansing
9	54.7	Attica Central SD	Attica
10	54.4	Highland Central SD	Highland
11	53.7	Cleveland Hill Union Free SD	Cheektowaga
12	53.7	Hornell City SD	Hornell
13	53.3	Bath Central SD	Bath
14	53.2	Ossining Union Free SD	Ossining
15	53.2	Edgemont Union Free SD	Scarsdale
16	53.1	Churchville-Chili Central SD	Churchville
17	53.1	Rondout Valley Central SD	Accord
18	53.1	Lackawanna City SD	Lackawanna
19	53.0	Alden Central SD	Alden
20	53.0	East Islip Union Free SD	Islip Terrace
21	53.0	Palmyra-Macedon Central SD	Palmyra
22	53.0	Farmingdale Union Free SD	Farmingdale
23	52.9	Bethlehem Central SD	Delmar
24	52.9	Southwestern Cent SD Jamestown	Jamestown
25	52.8	Phoenix Central SD	Phoenix
26	52.8	Rocky Point Union Free SD	Rocky Point
27	52.8	Niagara-Wheatfield Central SD	Niagara Falls
28	52.8	Pleasantville Union Free SD	Pleasantville
29	52.7	Westhill Central SD	Syracuse
30	52.6	Hampton Bays Union Free SD	Hampton Bays
31	52.6	Deer Park Union Free SD	Deer Park
32	52.6	Wayne Central SD	Ontario Center
33	52.6	Red Hook Central SD	Red Hook
34	52.6	Webster Central SD	Webster
35	52.6	Oswego City SD	Oswego
36	52.6	Brewster Central SD	Brewster
37	52.5	Victor Central SD	Victor
38	52.5	Peru Central SD	Peru
39	52.5	Riverhead Central SD	Riverhead
40	52.5	Eden Central SD	Eden
41	52.5	Valley Stream 13 Union Free SD	Valley Stream
42	52.5	Brentwood Union Free SD	Brentwood
42	52.5	Connetquot Central SD	Bohemia
44	52.4	East Williston Union Free SD	Old Westbury
45	52.4	Homer Central SD	Homer
46	52.4	Longwood Central SD	Middle Island
47	52.4	Glen Cove City SD	Glen Cove
48	52.4	Ogdensburg City SD	Ogdensburg
49	52.3	Roslyn Union Free SD	Roslyn
50	52.3	Wallkill Central SD	Wallkill
51	52.3	Bedford Central SD	Mount Kisco
52	52.3	Chenango Valley Central SD	Binghamton
53	52.3	Ithaca City SD	Ithaca
54	52.2	Greenburgh Central SD	Hartsdale
55	52.2	Washingtonville Central SD	Washingtonville
56	52.2	Ardsley Union Free SD	Ardsley
57	52.2	Vestal Central SD	Vestal
58	52.2	Skaneateles Central SD	Skaneateles
59	52.2	Spencerport Central SD	Spencerport
60	52.2	Warwick Valley Central SD	Warwick
61	52.2	Indian River Central SD	Philadelphia
62	52.2	North Tonawanda City SD	N Tonawanda
63	52.2	North Bellmore Union Free SD	Bellmore
64	52.2	Owego-Apalachin Central SD	Owego
65	52.2	Great Neck Union Free SD	Great Neck
66	52.1	Rye City SD	Rye
67	52.1	Lansingburgh Central SD	Troy
68	52.1	Dansville Central SD	Dansville
69	52.1	Minisink Valley Central SD	Slate Hill
70	52.1	Waverly Central SD	Waverly
71	52.1	Briarcliff Manor Union Free SD	Briarcliff Manor
72	52.1	Amityville Union Free SD	Amityville
73	52.1	Kinderhook Central SD	Valatie
74	52.1	Newark Central SD	Newark
75	52.0	Susquehanna Valley Central SD	Conklin
76	52.0	Whitesboro Central SD	Yorkville
77	52.0	Malverne Union Free SD	Malverne
78	52.0	Hendrick Hudson Central SD	Montrose
79	52.0	Central Square Central SD	Central Square
80	52.0	Clarkstown Central SD	New City
81	52.0	Troy City SD	Troy
82	51.9	New Rochelle City SD	New Rochelle
83	51.9	South Huntington Union Free SD	Huntington Stn
84	51.9	Dover Union Free SD	Dover Plains
85	51.9	Pelham Union Free SD	Pelham
86	51.9	E Ramapo Central SD (Sprg Val)	Spring Valley
87	51.9	New Hartford Central SD	New Hartford
88	51.9	Clarence Central SD	Clarence
89	51.9	Springville-Griffith Inst Cent	Springville
90	51.8	Bethpage Union Free SD	Bethpage
91	51.8	New Hyde Park-Garden City Park	New Hyde Park
92	51.8	Monticello Central SD	Monticello
93	51.8	Newfane Central SD	Newfane
94	51.8	Half Hollow Hills Central SD	Dix Hills
95	51.8	Garden City Union Free SD	Garden City
96	51.8	Lindenhurst Union Free SD	Lindenhurst
97	51.8	Clinton Central SD	Clinton
98	51.8	Gowanda Central SD	Gowanda
99	51.8	William Floyd Union Free SD	Mastic Beach
100	51.8	Port Chester-Rye Union Free SD	Port Chester
101	51.7	Marcellus Central SD	Marcellus
102	51.7	Shenendehowa Central SD	Clifton Park
103	51.7	Island Trees Union Free SD	Levittown
104	51.7	Gloversville City SD	Gloversville
105	51.7	Mahopac Central SD	Mahopac
106	51.7	Wappingers Central SD	Wappingers Fls
107	51.7	Middle Country Central SD	Centereach
108	51.7	Elmira City SD	Elmira
109	51.7	White Plains City SD	White Plains
110	51.6	Cheektowaga Central SD	Cheektowaga
111	51.6	Harborfields Central SD	Greenlawn
112	51.6	Floral Park-Bellerose UFSD	Floral Park
113	51.6	Smithtown Central SD	Smithtown
114	51.6	Saranac Central SD	Dannemora
115	51.6	Union-Endicott Central SD	Endicott
116	51.6	Syosset Central SD	Syosset
117	51.6	South Jefferson Central SD	Adams Center
118	51.6	Wilson Central SD	Wilson
119	51.6	Grand Island Central SD	Grand Island
120	51.6	Chappaqua Central SD	Chappaqua
121	51.6	Nanuet Union Free SD	Nanuet
122	51.6	Yorkshire-Pioneer Central SD	Yorkshire
123	51.6	Glens Falls City SD	Glens Falls
124	51.6	Shoreham-Wading River Central SD	Shoreham
125	51.6	Poughkeepsie City SD	Poughkeepsie
126	51.6	Chenango Forks Central SD	Binghamton
127	51.5	Mount Pleasant Central SD	Thornwood
128	51.5	Rome City SD	Rome
129	51.5	Lewiston-Porter Central SD	Youngstown
130	51.5	West Genesee Central SD	Camillus
131	51.5	Plattsburgh City SD	Plattsburgh
132	51.5	Bay Shore Union Free SD	Bay Shore
133	51.5	Gouverneur Central SD	Gouverneur
134	51.5	Valley Stream Central High SD	Valley Stream
135	51.5	Yonkers City SD	Yonkers
136	51.5	Phelps-Clifton Springs Cent SD	Clifton Spgs
137	51.5	Greece Central SD	Rochester
138	51.4	East Hampton Union Free SD	East Hampton
139	51.4	Hudson Falls Central SD	Hudson Falls
140	51.4	Huntington Union Free SD	Huntington Stn
141	51.4	Beacon City SD	Beacon
142	51.4	Baldwin Union Free SD	Baldwin
143	51.4	Seaford Union Free SD	Seaford
144	51.4	Taconic Hills Central SD	Craryville
145	51.4	Rotterdam-Mohonasen Central SD	Schenectady
146	51.4	Newburgh City SD	Newburgh
147	51.4	Herricks Union Free SD	New Hyde Park
148	51.4	Elmont Union Free SD	Elmont
149	51.4	Eastchester Union Free SD	Eastchester
150	51.4	Valley Central SD (Montgomery)	Montgomery
151	51.4	Scarsdale Union Free SD	Scarsdale
152	51.4	Jordan-Elbridge Central SD	Jordan
153	51.4	Dryden Central SD	Dryden
154	51.4	Baldwinsville Central SD	Baldwinsville
155	51.4	Saugerties Central SD	Saugerties
156	51.3	Ramapo Central SD (Suffern)	Hillburn
157	51.3	Mamaroneck Union Free SD	Mamaroneck
158	51.3	Bellmore-Merrick Central High SD	North Merrick
159	51.3	Manhasset Union Free SD	Manhasset
160	51.3	Starpoint Central SD	Lockport
161	51.3	Scotia-Glenville Central SD	Scotia
162	51.3	Lynbrook Union Free SD	Lynbrook
163	51.3	Orchard Park Central SD	Orchard Park
164	51.3	Kenmore-Tonawanda Union Free SD	Buffalo
165	51.3	Monroe-Woodbury Central SD	Central Valley
166	51.3	Cazenovia Central SD	Cazenovia
167	51.3	Plainview-Old Bethpage Cent SD	Plainview
168	51.3	Long Beach City SD	Long Beach
169	51.3	Saranac Lake Central SD	Saranac Lake
170	51.3	Amsterdam City SD	Amsterdam
171	51.3	North Syracuse Central SD	N Syracuse
172	51.3	Hicksville Union Free SD	Hicksville
173	51.3	Hewlett-Woodmere Union Free SD	Woodmere
174	51.3	Rockville Centre Union Free SD	Rockville Ctre
175	51.2	West Islip Union Free SD	West Islip
176	51.2	Adirondack Central SD	Boonville
177	51.2	Canton Central SD	Canton
178	51.2	Brighton Central SD	Rochester
179	51.2	New York City Public Schools	Brooklyn
180	51.2	Jericho Union Free SD	Jericho
181	51.2	Copiague Union Free SD	Copiague
182	51.2	Miller Place Union Free SD	Miller Place
183	51.2	Niskayuna Central SD	Schenectady
184	51.2	Chatham Central SD	Chatham
185	51.2	Cobleskill-Richmondville CSD	Cobleskill
186	51.2	Liberty Central SD	Liberty
187	51.2	Hempstead Union Free SD	Hempstead
188	51.2	Tonawanda City SD	Tonawanda
189	51.2	Hauppauge Union Free SD	Hauppauge
190	51.2	General Brown Central SD	Dexter
191	51.2	Haverstraw-Stony Point Cent SD	Garnerville
192	51.1	Canandaigua City SD	Canandaigua
193	51.1	Commack Union Free SD	E Northport
194	51.1	Nyack Union Free SD	Nyack
195	51.1	New Paltz Central SD	New Paltz
196	51.1	Medina Central SD	Medina
197	51.1	Liverpool Central SD	Liverpool
198	51.1	Mineola Union Free SD	Mineola
199	51.1	South Colonie Central SD	Albany
200	51.1	Fairport Central SD	Fairport
201	51.1	Guilderland Central SD	Guilderland
202	51.1	Patchogue-Medford Union Free SD	Patchogue
203	51.1	Iroquois Central SD	Elma
204	51.1	Dunkirk City SD	Dunkirk
205	51.1	Solvay Union Free SD	Solvay
206	51.0	West Seneca Central SD	West Seneca
207	51.0	Harrison Central SD	Harrison
208	51.0	Irvington Union Free SD	Irvington
209	51.0	Albany City SD	Albany
210	51.0	Port Jervis City SD	Port Jervis
211	51.0	Cornwall Central SD	Cornwall-on-Hud
212	51.0	Utica City SD	Utica
213	51.0	Rochester City SD	Rochester
214	51.0	Malone Central SD	Malone
215	51.0	Honeoye Falls-Lima Central SD	Honeoye Falls
216	51.0	Central Islip Union Free SD	Central Islip
217	51.0	Buffalo City SD	Buffalo
218	51.0	Jamestown City SD	Jamestown
219	51.0	Niagara Falls City SD	Niagara Falls
220	51.0	Levittown Union Free SD	Levittown
221	51.0	Lawrence Union Free SD	Lawrence
222	50.9	Sweet Home Central SD	Amherst
223	50.9	East Syracuse-Minoa Central SD	East Syracuse
224	50.9	Lockport City SD	Lockport
225	50.9	Roosevelt Union Free SD	Roosevelt
226	50.9	Arlington Central SD	Poughkeepsie
227	50.9	Spackenkill Union Free SD	Poughkeepsie
228	50.9	South Glens Falls Central SD	S Glens Falls
229	50.9	Salmon River Central SD	Ft Covington
230	50.9	Sewanhaka Central High SD	Floral Park
231	50.9	Fayetteville-Manlius Central SD	Manlius
232	50.9	Ballston Spa Central SD	Ballston Spa
233	50.9	Elwood Union Free SD	Greenlawn
234	50.9	Peekskill City SD	Peekskill
235	50.8	Watertown City SD	Watertown
236	50.8	Cheektowaga-Sloan Union Free SD	Sloan
237	50.8	Southampton Union Free SD	Southampton
238	50.8	Katonah-Lewisboro Union Free SD	South Salem
239	50.8	Averill Park Central SD	Averill Park
240	50.8	Goshen Central SD	Goshen
241	50.8	Massapequa Union Free SD	Massapequa
242	50.8	West Hempstead Union Free SD	W Hempstead
243	50.8	Union Free SD of the Tarrytowns	Sleepy Hollow
244	50.8	Cairo-Durham Central SD	Cairo
245	50.8	Hamburg Central SD	Hamburg
246	50.8	Carmel Central SD	Patterson
247	50.8	East Irondequoit Central SD	Rochester
248	50.8	Corning City SD	Painted Post
249	50.8	Port Washington Union Free SD	Pt Washington
250	50.8	Freeport Union Free SD	Freeport
251	50.8	Royalton-Hartland Central SD	Middleport
252	50.8	Somers Central SD	Lincolndale
253	50.8	Salamanca City SD	Salamanca
254	50.8	Camden Central SD	Camden
255	50.8	Babylon Union Free SD	Babylon
256	50.7	Hilton Central SD	Hilton
257	50.7	Mount Vernon City SD	Mount Vernon
258	50.7	West Babylon Union Free SD	West Babylon
259	50.7	Uniondale Union Free SD	Uniondale
260	50.7	North Colonie Central SD	Latham
261	50.7	Three Village Central SD	East Setauket
262	50.7	Pine Bush Central SD	Pine Bush
263	50.7	Auburn City SD	Auburn
264	50.7	Lakeland Central SD	Shrub Oak

PROFILES OF NEW YORK / School District Rankings 623

265	50.7	Sayville Union Free SD	Sayville
266	50.7	Onteora Central SD	Boiceville
267	50.7	Mattituck-Cutchogue UFSD	Cutchogue
268	50.7	Wantagh Union Free SD	Wantagh
269	50.7	Cortland City SD	Cortland
270	50.7	Amherst Central SD	Amherst
271	50.6	Hyde Park Central SD	Poughkeepsie
272	50.6	Massena Central SD	Massena
273	50.6	Williamsville Central SD	East Amherst
274	50.6	Westhampton Beach Union Free SD	Westhampton Bch
275	50.6	Ravena-Coeymans-Selkirk CSD	Selkirk
276	50.6	Queensbury Union Free SD	Queensbury
276	50.6	Rush-Henrietta Central SD	Henrietta
278	50.6	Oneida City SD	Oneida
279	50.6	Albion Central SD	Albion
280	50.6	North Rose-Wolcott Central SD	Wolcott
281	50.6	Oyster Bay-East Norwich CSD	Oyster Bay
282	50.6	Oceanside Union Free SD	Oceanside
283	50.6	Binghamton City SD	Binghamton
284	50.5	East Aurora Union Free SD	East Aurora
285	50.5	Depew Union Free SD	Depew
286	50.5	Middletown City SD	Middletown
287	50.5	Penfield Central SD	Penfield
288	50.5	Sachem Central SD	Holbrook
289	50.5	Schenectady City SD	Schenectady
290	50.5	Whitney Point Central SD	Whitney Point
291	50.5	North Babylon Union Free SD	North Babylon
292	50.5	Waterloo Central SD	Waterloo
293	50.5	Frontier Central SD	Hamburg
293	50.5	Lancaster Central SD	Lancaster
295	50.5	South Country Central SD	E Patchogue
296	50.4	Ellenville Central SD	Ellenville
297	50.4	Livonia Central SD	Livonia
298	50.4	Putnam Valley Central SD	Putnam Valley
299	50.4	Wayland-Cohocton Central SD	Wayland
300	50.4	Merrick Union Free SD	Merrick
301	50.4	Northeastern Clinton Central SD	Champlain
302	50.4	Schuylerville Central SD	Schuylerville
303	50.4	Bayport-Blue Point Union Free SD	Bayport
304	50.4	Cold Spring Harbor Central SD	Cold Spring Harbor
305	50.4	Brookhaven-Comsewogue UFSD	Pt Jefferson Stn
306	50.3	Wyandanch Union Free SD	Wyandanch
307	50.3	Saratoga Springs City SD	Saratoga Spgs
308	50.3	Evans-Brant Cent SD (Lake Shore)	Angola
309	50.3	Kingston City SD	Kingston
310	50.3	New York City Geographic Dist 9	Bronx
311	50.3	Sherrill City SD	Verona
312	50.3	Beekmantown Central SD	West Chazy
313	50.3	Gates-Chili Central SD	Rochester
314	50.3	Franklin Square Union Free SD	Franklin Square
315	50.2	Hastings-On-Hudson Union Free SD	Hastings-on-Hud
316	50.2	Northport-East Northport UFSD	Northport
317	50.2	Byram Hills Central SD	Armonk
318	50.2	Cohoes City SD	Cohoes
319	50.2	Fulton City SD	Fulton
320	50.2	Maine-Endwell Central SD	Endwell
321	50.1	Yorktown Central SD	Yorktown Hgts
322	50.1	Islip Union Free SD	Islip
323	50.1	Syracuse City SD	Syracuse
324	50.1	Kings Park Central SD	Kings Park
325	50.1	Horseheads Central SD	Horseheads
326	50.1	Carthage Central SD	Carthage
327	50.1	Plainedge Union Free SD	N Massapequa
328	50.1	South Orangetown Central SD	Blauvelt
329	50.0	East Meadow Union Free SD	Westbury
330	50.0	Croton-Harmon Union Free SD	Croton-On-Hud
331	50.0	Carle Place Union Free SD	Carle Place
332	49.9	Catskill Central SD	Catskill
333	49.9	Gorham-Middlesex CSD (M Whitman)	Rushville
334	49.9	Mexico Central SD	Mexico
335	49.9	Sullivan West Central SD	Callicoon
336	49.9	Brockport Central SD	Brockport
337	49.9	Windsor Central SD	Windsor
338	49.9	Holland Patent Central SD	Holland Patent
339	49.9	West Irondequoit Central SD	Rochester
340	49.8	East Greenbush Central SD	E Greenbush
341	49.8	Ilion Central SD	Ilion
342	49.8	Fredonia Central SD	Fredonia
343	49.8	Johnson City Central SD	Johnson City
344	49.8	Schalmont Central SD	Schenectady
345	49.7	Burnt Hls-Ballston Lake Cent SD	Scotia
346	49.7	Pittsford Central SD	Pittsford
347	49.7	Valley Stream 30 Union Free SD	Valley Stream
348	49.5	Olean City SD	Olean
349	49.5	North Shore Central SD	Sea Cliff
350	49.4	Chittenango Central SD	Chittenango
351	49.4	Hannibal Central SD	Hannibal
352	49.3	Oneonta City SD	Oneonta
353	49.2	Penn Yan Central SD	Penn Yan
354	49.2	New York City Geographic Dist 15	Brooklyn
355	49.2	Sherburne-Earlville Central SD	Sherburne
356	49.2	Geneva City SD	Geneva
357	49.2	Jamesville-Dewitt Central SD	Dewitt
358	49.1	Batavia City SD	Batavia
359	49.1	Cheektowaga-Maryvale UFSD	Cheektowaga
360	49.1	Locust Valley Central SD	Locust Valley
361	49.1	Westbury Union Free SD	Old Westbury
362	49.0	Pearl River Union Free SD	Pearl River
363	49.0	Norwich City SD	Norwich
364	48.8	Mount Sinai Union Free SD	Mount Sinai
365	48.7	Akron Central SD	Akron
366	48.7	Marlboro Central SD	Marlboro
367	48.6	Canastota Central SD	Canastota
368	48.2	Altmar-Parish-Williamstown CSD	Parish
369	47.6	Johnstown City SD	Johnstown
370	47.0	Nyc Alternative HS District	New York

Female Students

Rank	Percent	District Name	City
1	52.9	Nyc Alternative HS District	New York
2	52.3	Johnstown City SD	Johnstown
3	51.7	Altmar-Parish-Williamstown CSD	Parish
4	51.3	Canastota Central SD	Canastota
5	51.2	Marlboro Central SD	Marlboro
6	51.2	Akron Central SD	Akron
7	51.1	Mount Sinai Union Free SD	Mount Sinai
8	50.9	Norwich City SD	Norwich
9	50.9	Pearl River Union Free SD	Pearl River
10	50.8	Westbury Union Free SD	Old Westbury
11	50.8	Locust Valley Central SD	Locust Valley
12	50.8	Cheektowaga-Maryvale UFSD	Cheektowaga
13	50.8	Batavia City SD	Batavia
14	50.7	Jamesville-Dewitt Central SD	Dewitt
15	50.7	Geneva City SD	Geneva
16	50.7	Sherburne-Earlville Central SD	Sherburne
17	50.7	New York City Geographic Dist 15	Brooklyn
18	50.7	Penn Yan Central SD	Penn Yan
19	50.6	Oneonta City SD	Oneonta
20	50.5	Hannibal Central SD	Hannibal
21	50.5	Chittenango Central SD	Chittenango
22	50.4	North Shore Central SD	Sea Cliff
23	50.4	Olean City SD	Olean
24	50.2	Valley Stream 30 Union Free SD	Valley Stream
25	50.2	Pittsford Central SD	Pittsford
26	50.2	Burnt Hls-Ballston Lake Cent SD	Scotia
27	50.1	Schalmont Central SD	Schenectady
28	50.1	Johnson City Central SD	Johnson City
29	50.1	Fredonia Central SD	Fredonia
30	50.1	Ilion Central SD	Ilion
31	50.1	East Greenbush Central SD	E Greenbush
32	50.0	West Irondequoit Central SD	Rochester
33	50.0	Holland Patent Central SD	Holland Patent
34	50.0	Windsor Central SD	Windsor
35	50.0	Brockport Central SD	Brockport
36	50.0	Sullivan West Central SD	Callicoon
37	50.0	Mexico Central SD	Mexico
38	50.0	Gorham-Middlesex CSD (M Whitman)	Rushville
39	50.0	Catskill Central SD	Catskill
40	50.0	Carle Place Union Free SD	Carle Place
41	49.9	Croton-Harmon Union Free SD	Croton-On-Hud
42	49.9	East Meadow Union Free SD	Westbury
43	49.8	South Orangetown Central SD	Blauvelt
44	49.8	Plainedge Union Free SD	N Massapequa
45	49.8	Carthage Central SD	Carthage
46	49.8	Horseheads Central SD	Horseheads
47	49.8	Kings Park Central SD	Kings Park
48	49.8	Syracuse City SD	Syracuse
49	49.8	Islip Union Free SD	Islip
50	49.8	Yorktown Central SD	Yorktown Hgts
51	49.7	Maine-Endwell Central SD	Endwell
52	49.7	Fulton City SD	Fulton
53	49.7	Cohoes City SD	Cohoes
54	49.7	Byram Hills Central SD	Armonk
55	49.7	Northport-East Northport UFSD	Northport
56	49.7	Hastings-On-Hudson Union Free SD	Hastings-on-Hud
57	49.6	Franklin Square Union Free SD	Franklin Square
58	49.6	Gates-Chili Central SD	Rochester
59	49.6	Beekmantown Central SD	West Chazy
60	49.6	Sherrill City SD	Verona
61	49.6	New York City Geographic Dist 9	Bronx
62	49.6	Kingston City SD	Kingston
63	49.6	Evans-Brant Cent SD (Lake Shore)	Angola
64	49.6	Saratoga Springs City SD	Saratoga Spgs
65	49.6	Wyandanch Union Free SD	Wyandanch
66	49.5	Brookhaven-Comsewogue UFSD	Pt Jefferson Stn
67	49.5	Cold Spring Harbor Central SD	Cold Sprg Harbor
68	49.5	Bayport-Blue Point Union Free SD	Bayport
69	49.5	Schuylerville Central SD	Schuylerville
70	49.5	Northeastern Clinton Central SD	Champlain
71	49.5	Merrick Union Free SD	Merrick
72	49.5	Wayland-Cohocton Central SD	Wayland
73	49.5	Putnam Valley Central SD	Putnam Valley
74	49.5	Livonia Central SD	Livonia
75	49.5	Ellenville Central SD	Ellenville
76	49.4	South Country Central SD	E Patchogue
77	49.4	Frontier Central SD	Hamburg
77	49.4	Lancaster Central SD	Lancaster
79	49.4	Waterloo Central SD	Waterloo
80	49.4	North Babylon Union Free SD	North Babylon
81	49.4	Whitney Point Central SD	Whitney Point
82	49.4	Schenectady City SD	Schenectady
83	49.4	Sachem Central SD	Holbrook
84	49.4	Penfield Central SD	Penfield
85	49.4	Middletown City SD	Middletown
86	49.4	Depew Union Free SD	Depew
87	49.4	East Aurora Union Free SD	East Aurora
88	49.3	Binghamton City SD	Binghamton
89	49.3	Oceanside Union Free SD	Oceanside
90	49.3	Oyster Bay-East Norwich CSD	Oyster Bay
91	49.3	North Rose-Wolcott Central SD	Wolcott
92	49.3	Albion Central SD	Albion
93	49.3	Oneida City SD	Oneida
94	49.3	Queensbury Union Free SD	Queensbury
94	49.3	Rush-Henrietta Central SD	Henrietta
96	49.3	Ravena-Coeymans-Selkirk CSD	Selkirk
97	49.3	Westhampton Beach Union Free SD	Westhampton Bch
98	49.3	Williamsville Central SD	East Amherst
99	49.3	Massena Central SD	Massena
100	49.3	Hyde Park Central SD	Poughkeepsie
101	49.2	Amherst Central SD	Amherst
102	49.2	Cortland City SD	Cortland
103	49.2	Wantagh Union Free SD	Wantagh
104	49.2	Mattituck-Cutchogue UFSD	Cutchogue
105	49.2	Onteora Central SD	Boiceville
106	49.2	Sayville Union Free SD	Sayville
107	49.2	Lakeland Central SD	Shrub Oak
108	49.2	Auburn City SD	Auburn
109	49.2	Pine Bush Central SD	Pine Bush
110	49.2	Three Village Central SD	East Setauket
111	49.2	North Colonie Central SD	Latham
112	49.2	Uniondale Union Free SD	Uniondale
113	49.2	West Babylon Union Free SD	West Babylon
114	49.2	Mount Vernon City SD	Mount Vernon
115	49.2	Hilton Central SD	Hilton
116	49.1	Babylon Union Free SD	Babylon
117	49.1	Camden Central SD	Camden
118	49.1	Salamanca City SD	Salamanca
119	49.1	Somers Central SD	Lincolndale
120	49.1	Royalton-Hartland Central SD	Middleport
121	49.1	Freeport Union Free SD	Freeport
122	49.1	Port Washington Union Free SD	Pt Washington
123	49.1	Corning City SD	Painted Post
124	49.1	East Irondequoit Central SD	Rochester
125	49.1	Carmel Central SD	Patterson
126	49.1	Hamburg Central SD	Hamburg
127	49.1	Cairo-Durham Central SD	Cairo
128	49.1	Union Free SD of the Tarrytowns	Sleepy Hollow
129	49.1	West Hempstead Union Free SD	W Hempstead
130	49.1	Massapequa Union Free SD	Massapequa
131	49.1	Goshen Central SD	Goshen
132	49.1	Averill Park Central SD	Averill Park
133	49.1	Katonah-Lewisboro Union Free SD	South Salem
134	49.1	Southampton Union Free SD	Southampton
135	49.1	Cheektowaga-Sloan Union Free SD	Sloan
136	49.1	Watertown City SD	Watertown
137	49.0	Peekskill City SD	Peekskill
138	49.0	Elwood Union Free SD	Greenlawn
139	49.0	Ballston Spa Central SD	Ballston Spa
140	49.0	Fayetteville-Manlius Central SD	Manlius
141	49.0	Sewanhaka Central High SD	Floral Park
142	49.0	Salmon River Central SD	Ft Covington
143	49.0	South Glens Falls Central SD	S Glens Falls
144	49.0	Spackenkill Union Free SD	Poughkeepsie
145	49.0	Arlington Central SD	Poughkeepsie
146	49.0	Roosevelt Union Free SD	Roosevelt
147	49.0	Lockport City SD	Lockport
148	49.0	East Syracuse-Minoa Central SD	East Syracuse
149	49.0	Sweet Home Central SD	Amherst
150	48.9	Lawrence Union Free SD	Lawrence
151	48.9	Levittown Union Free SD	Levittown
152	48.9	Niagara Falls City SD	Niagara Falls
153	48.9	Jamestown City SD	Jamestown
154	48.9	Buffalo City SD	Buffalo
155	48.9	Central Islip Union Free SD	Central Islip
156	48.9	Honeoye Falls-Lima Central SD	Honeoye Falls
157	48.9	Malone Central SD	Malone
158	48.9	Rochester City SD	Rochester
159	48.9	Utica City SD	Utica
160	48.9	Cornwall Central SD	Cornwall-on-Hud
161	48.9	Port Jervis City SD	Port Jervis
162	48.9	Albany City SD	Albany
163	48.9	Irvington Union Free SD	Irvington
164	48.9	Harrison Central SD	Harrison
165	48.9	West Seneca Central SD	West Seneca
166	48.8	Solvay Union Free SD	Solvay
167	48.8	Dunkirk City SD	Dunkirk
168	48.8	Iroquois Central SD	Elma

169	48.8	Patchogue-Medford Union Free SD	Patchogue
170	48.8	Guilderland Central SD	Guilderland
171	48.8	Fairport Central SD	Fairport
172	48.8	South Colonie Central SD	Albany
173	48.8	Mineola Union Free SD	Mineola
174	48.8	Liverpool Central SD	Liverpool
175	48.8	Medina Central SD	Medina
176	48.8	New Paltz Central SD	New Paltz
177	48.8	Nyack Union Free SD	Nyack
178	48.8	Commack Union Free SD	E Northport
179	48.8	Canandaigua City SD	Canandaigua
180	48.7	Haverstraw-Stony Point Cent SD	Garnerville
181	48.7	General Brown Central SD	Dexter
182	48.7	Hauppauge Union Free SD	Hauppauge
183	48.7	Tonawanda City SD	Tonawanda
184	48.7	Hempstead Union Free SD	Hempstead
185	48.7	Liberty Central SD	Liberty
186	48.7	Cobleskill-Richmondville CSD	Cobleskill
187	48.7	Chatham Central SD	Chatham
188	48.7	Niskayuna Central SD	Schenectady
189	48.7	Miller Place Union Free SD	Miller Place
190	48.7	Copiague Union Free SD	Copiague
191	48.7	Jericho Union Free SD	Jericho
192	48.7	New York City Public Schools	Brooklyn
193	48.7	Brighton Central SD	Rochester
194	48.7	Canton Central SD	Canton
195	48.7	Adirondack Central SD	Boonville
196	48.7	West Islip Union Free SD	West Islip
197	48.6	Rockville Centre Union Free SD	Rockville Ctre
198	48.6	Hewlett-Woodmere Union Free SD	Woodmere
199	48.6	Hicksville Union Free SD	Hicksville
200	48.6	North Syracuse Central SD	N Syracuse
201	48.6	Amsterdam City SD	Amsterdam
202	48.6	Saranac Lake Central SD	Saranac Lake
203	48.6	Long Beach City SD	Long Beach
204	48.6	Plainview-Old Bethpage Cent SD	Plainview
205	48.6	Cazenovia Central SD	Cazenovia
206	48.6	Monroe-Woodbury Central SD	Central Valley
207	48.6	Kenmore-Tonawanda Union Free SD	Buffalo
208	48.6	Orchard Park Central SD	Orchard Park
209	48.6	Lynbrook Union Free SD	Lynbrook
210	48.6	Scotia-Glenville Central SD	Scotia
211	48.6	Starpoint Central SD	Lockport
212	48.6	Manhasset Union Free SD	Manhasset
213	48.6	Bellmore-Merrick Central High SD	North Merrick
214	48.6	Mamaroneck Union Free SD	Mamaroneck
215	48.6	Ramapo Central SD (Suffern)	Hillburn
216	48.5	Saugerties Central SD	Saugerties
217	48.5	Baldwinsville Central SD	Baldwinsville
218	48.5	Dryden Central SD	Dryden
219	48.5	Jordan-Elbridge Central SD	Jordan
220	48.5	Scarsdale Union Free SD	Scarsdale
221	48.5	Valley Central SD (Montgomery)	Montgomery
222	48.5	Eastchester Union Free SD	Eastchester
223	48.5	Elmont Union Free SD	Elmont
224	48.5	Herricks Union Free SD	New Hyde Park
225	48.5	Newburgh City SD	Newburgh
226	48.5	Rotterdam-Mohonasen Central SD	Schenectady
227	48.5	Taconic Hills Central SD	Craryville
228	48.5	Seaford Union Free SD	Seaford
229	48.5	Baldwin Union Free SD	Baldwin
230	48.5	Beacon City SD	Beacon
231	48.5	Huntington Union Free SD	Huntington Stn
232	48.5	Hudson Falls Central SD	Hudson Falls
233	48.5	East Hampton Union Free SD	East Hampton
234	48.4	Greece Central SD	Rochester
235	48.4	Phelps-Clifton Springs Cent SD	Clifton Spgs
236	48.4	Yonkers City SD	Yonkers
237	48.4	Valley Stream Central High SD	Valley Stream
238	48.4	Gouverneur Central SD	Gouverneur
239	48.4	Bay Shore Union Free SD	Bay Shore
240	48.4	Plattsburgh City SD	Plattsburgh
241	48.4	West Genesee Central SD	Camillus
242	48.4	Lewiston-Porter Central SD	Youngstown
243	48.4	Rome City SD	Rome
244	48.4	Mount Pleasant Central SD	Thornwood
245	48.3	Chenango Forks Central SD	Binghamton
246	48.3	Poughkeepsie City SD	Poughkeepsie
247	48.3	Shoreham-Wading River Central SD	Shoreham
248	48.3	Glens Falls City SD	Glens Falls
249	48.3	Yorkshire-Pioneer Central SD	Yorkshire
250	48.3	Nanuet Union Free SD	Nanuet
251	48.3	Chappaqua Central SD	Chappaqua
252	48.3	Grand Island Central SD	Grand Island
253	48.3	Wilson Central SD	Wilson
254	48.3	South Jefferson Central SD	Adams Center
255	48.3	Syosset Central SD	Syosset
256	48.3	Union-Endicott Central SD	Endicott
257	48.3	Saranac Central SD	Dannemora
258	48.3	Smithtown Central SD	Smithtown
259	48.3	Floral Park-Bellerose UFSD	Floral Park
260	48.3	Harborfields Central SD	Greenlawn
261	48.3	Cheektowaga Central SD	Cheektowaga
262	48.2	White Plains City SD	White Plains
263	48.2	Elmira City SD	Elmira
264	48.2	Middle Country Central SD	Centereach
265	48.2	Wappingers Central SD	Wappingers Fls
266	48.2	Mahopac Central SD	Mahopac
267	48.2	Gloversville City SD	Gloversville
268	48.2	Island Trees Union Free SD	Levittown
269	48.2	Shenendehowa Central SD	Clifton Park
270	48.2	Marcellus Central SD	Marcellus
271	48.1	Port Chester-Rye Union Free SD	Port Chester
272	48.1	William Floyd Union Free SD	Mastic Beach
273	48.1	Gowanda Central SD	Gowanda
274	48.1	Clinton Central SD	Clinton
275	48.1	Lindenhurst Union Free SD	Lindenhurst
276	48.1	Garden City Union Free SD	Garden City
277	48.1	Half Hollow Hills Central SD	Dix Hills
278	48.1	Newfane Central SD	Newfane
279	48.1	Monticello Central SD	Monticello
280	48.1	New Hyde Park-Garden City Park	New Hyde Park
281	48.1	Bethpage Union Free SD	Bethpage
282	48.0	Springville-Griffith Inst Cent	Springville
283	48.0	Clarence Central SD	Clarence
284	48.0	New Hartford Central SD	New Hartford
285	48.0	E Ramapo Central SD (Sprg Val)	Spring Valley
286	48.0	Pelham Union Free SD	Pelham
287	48.0	Dover Union Free SD	Dover Plains
288	48.0	South Huntington Union Free SD	Huntington Stn
289	48.0	New Rochelle City SD	New Rochelle
290	47.9	Troy City SD	Troy
291	47.9	Clarkstown Central SD	New City
292	47.9	Central Square Central SD	Central Square
293	47.9	Hendrick Hudson Central SD	Montrose
294	47.9	Malverne Union Free SD	Malverne
295	47.9	Whitesboro Central SD	Yorkville
296	47.9	Susquehanna Valley Central SD	Conklin
297	47.8	Newark Central SD	Newark
298	47.8	Kinderhook Central SD	Valatie
299	47.8	Amityville Union Free SD	Amityville
300	47.8	Briarcliff Manor Union Free SD	Briarcliff Manor
301	47.8	Waverly Central SD	Waverly
302	47.8	Minisink Valley Central SD	Slate Hill
303	47.8	Dansville Central SD	Dansville
304	47.8	Lansingburgh Central SD	Troy
305	47.8	Rye City SD	Rye
306	47.7	Great Neck Union Free SD	Great Neck
307	47.7	Owego-Apalachin Central SD	Owego
308	47.7	North Bellmore Union Free SD	Bellmore
309	47.7	North Tonawanda City SD	N Tonawanda
310	47.7	Indian River Central SD	Philadelphia
311	47.7	Warwick Valley Central SD	Warwick
312	47.7	Spencerport Central SD	Spencerport
313	47.7	Skaneateles Central SD	Skaneateles
314	47.7	Vestal Central SD	Vestal
315	47.7	Ardsley Union Free SD	Ardsley
316	47.7	Washingtonville Central SD	Washingtonville
317	47.7	Greenburgh Central SD	Hartsdale
318	47.6	Ithaca City SD	Ithaca
319	47.6	Chenango Valley Central SD	Binghamton
320	47.6	Bedford Central SD	Mount Kisco
321	47.6	Wallkill Central SD	Wallkill
322	47.6	Roslyn Union Free SD	Roslyn
323	47.5	Ogdensburg City SD	Ogdensburg
324	47.5	Glen Cove City SD	Glen Cove
325	47.5	Longwood Central SD	Middle Island
326	47.5	Homer Central SD	Homer
327	47.5	East Williston Union Free SD	Old Westbury
328	47.4	Brentwood Union Free SD	Brentwood
328	47.4	Connetquot Central SD	Bohemia
330	47.4	Valley Stream 13 Union Free SD	Valley Stream
331	47.4	Eden Central SD	Eden
332	47.4	Riverhead Central SD	Riverhead
333	47.4	Peru Central SD	Peru
334	47.4	Victor Central SD	Victor
335	47.3	Brewster Central SD	Brewster
336	47.3	Oswego City SD	Oswego
337	47.3	Webster Central SD	Webster
338	47.3	Red Hook Central SD	Red Hook
339	47.3	Wayne Central SD	Ontario Center
340	47.3	Deer Park Union Free SD	Deer Park
341	47.3	Hampton Bays Union Free SD	Hampton Bays
342	47.2	Westhill Central SD	Syracuse
343	47.1	Pleasantville Union Free SD	Pleasantville
344	47.1	Niagara-Wheatfield Central SD	Niagara Falls
345	47.1	Rocky Point Union Free SD	Rocky Point
346	47.1	Phoenix Central SD	Phoenix
347	47.0	Southwestern Cent SD Jamestown	Jamestown
348	47.0	Bethlehem Central SD	Delmar
349	46.9	Farmingdale Union Free SD	Farmingdale
350	46.9	Palmyra-Macedon Central SD	Palmyra
351	46.9	East Islip Union Free SD	Islip Terrace
352	46.9	Alden Central SD	Alden
353	46.8	Lackawanna City SD	Lackawanna
354	46.8	Rondout Valley Central SD	Accord
355	46.8	Churchville-Chili Central SD	Churchville
356	46.7	Edgemont Union Free SD	Scarsdale
357	46.7	Ossining Union Free SD	Ossining
358	46.6	Bath Central SD	Bath
359	46.2	Hornell City SD	Hornell
360	46.2	Cleveland Hill Union Free SD	Cheektowaga
361	45.5	Highland Central SD	Highland
362	45.2	Attica Central SD	Attica
363	44.8	Lansing Central SD	Lansing
364	44.7	Watkins Glen Central SD	Watkins Glen
365	44.7	Fonda-Fultonville Central SD	Fonda
366	43.8	Hudson City SD	Hudson
367	43.6	Broadalbin-Perth Central SD	Broadalbin
368	31.3	Coxsackie-Athens Central SD	Coxsackie
369	25.9	Boces Eastern Suffolk	Patchogue
370	24.1	Boces Nassau	Garden City

Individual Education Program Students

Rank	Percent	District Name	City
1	n/a	Adirondack Central SD	Boonville
1	n/a	Akron Central SD	Akron
1	n/a	Albany City SD	Albany
1	n/a	Albion Central SD	Albion
1	n/a	Alden Central SD	Alden
1	n/a	Altmar-Parish-Williamstown CSD	Parish
1	n/a	Amherst Central SD	Amherst
1	n/a	Amityville Union Free SD	Amityville
1	n/a	Amsterdam City SD	Amsterdam
1	n/a	Ardsley Union Free SD	Ardsley
1	n/a	Arlington Central SD	Poughkeepsie
1	n/a	Attica Central SD	Attica
1	n/a	Auburn City SD	Auburn
1	n/a	Averill Park Central SD	Averill Park
1	n/a	Babylon Union Free SD	Babylon
1	n/a	Baldwin Union Free SD	Baldwin
1	n/a	Baldwinsville Central SD	Baldwinsville
1	n/a	Ballston Spa Central SD	Ballston Spa
1	n/a	Batavia City SD	Batavia
1	n/a	Bath Central SD	Bath
1	n/a	Bay Shore Union Free SD	Bay Shore
1	n/a	Bayport-Blue Point Union Free SD	Bayport
1	n/a	Beacon City SD	Beacon
1	n/a	Bedford Central SD	Mount Kisco
1	n/a	Beekmantown Central SD	West Chazy
1	n/a	Bellmore-Merrick Central High SD	North Merrick
1	n/a	Bethlehem Central SD	Delmar
1	n/a	Bethpage Union Free SD	Bethpage
1	n/a	Binghamton City SD	Binghamton
1	n/a	Boces Eastern Suffolk	Patchogue
1	n/a	Boces Nassau	Garden City
1	n/a	Brentwood Union Free SD	Brentwood
1	n/a	Brewster Central SD	Brewster
1	n/a	Briarcliff Manor Union Free SD	Briarcliff Manor
1	n/a	Brighton Central SD	Rochester
1	n/a	Broadalbin-Perth Central SD	Broadalbin
1	n/a	Brockport Central SD	Brockport
1	n/a	Brookhaven-Comsewogue UFSD	Pt Jefferson Stn
1	n/a	Buffalo City SD	Buffalo
1	n/a	Burnt Hls-Ballston Lake Cent SD	Scotia
1	n/a	Byram Hills Central SD	Armonk
1	n/a	Cairo-Durham Central SD	Cairo
1	n/a	Camden Central SD	Camden
1	n/a	Canandaigua City SD	Canandaigua
1	n/a	Canastota Central SD	Canastota
1	n/a	Canton Central SD	Canton
1	n/a	Carle Place Union Free SD	Carle Place
1	n/a	Carmel Central SD	Patterson
1	n/a	Carthage Central SD	Carthage
1	n/a	Catskill Central SD	Catskill
1	n/a	Cazenovia Central SD	Cazenovia
1	n/a	Central Islip Union Free SD	Central Islip
1	n/a	Central Square Central SD	Central Square
1	n/a	Chappaqua Central SD	Chappaqua
1	n/a	Chatham Central SD	Chatham
1	n/a	Cheektowaga Central SD	Cheektowaga
1	n/a	Cheektowaga-Maryvale UFSD	Cheektowaga
1	n/a	Cheektowaga-Sloan Union Free SD	Sloan
1	n/a	Chenango Forks Central SD	Binghamton
1	n/a	Chenango Valley Central SD	Binghamton
1	n/a	Chittenango Central SD	Chittenango
1	n/a	Churchville-Chili Central SD	Churchville
1	n/a	Clarence Central SD	Clarence
1	n/a	Clarkstown Central SD	New City
1	n/a	Cleveland Hill Union Free SD	Cheektowaga
1	n/a	Clinton Central SD	Clinton
1	n/a	Cobleskill-Richmondville CSD	Cobleskill
1	n/a	Cohoes City SD	Cohoes
1	n/a	Cold Spring Harbor Central SD	Cold Sprg Harbor
1	n/a	Commack Union Free SD	E Northport
1	n/a	Connetquot Central SD	Bohemia
1	n/a	Copiague Union Free SD	Copiague

1	n/a	Corning City SD	Painted Post
1	n/a	Cornwall Central SD	Cornwall-on-Hud
1	n/a	Cortland City SD	Cortland
1	n/a	Coxsackie-Athens Central SD	Coxsackie
1	n/a	Croton-Harmon Union Free SD	Croton-On-Hud
1	n/a	Dansville Central SD	Dansville
1	n/a	Deer Park Union Free SD	Deer Park
1	n/a	Depew Union Free SD	Depew
1	n/a	Dover Union Free SD	Dover Plains
1	n/a	Dryden Central SD	Dryden
1	n/a	Dunkirk City SD	Dunkirk
1	n/a	East Aurora Union Free SD	East Aurora
1	n/a	East Greenbush Central SD	E Greenbush
1	n/a	East Hampton Union Free SD	East Hampton
1	n/a	East Irondequoit Central SD	Rochester
1	n/a	East Islip Union Free SD	Islip Terrace
1	n/a	East Meadow Union Free SD	Westbury
1	n/a	E Ramapo Central SD (Sprg Val)	Spring Valley
1	n/a	East Syracuse-Minoa Central SD	East Syracuse
1	n/a	East Williston Union Free SD	Old Westbury
1	n/a	Eastchester Union Free SD	Eastchester
1	n/a	Eden Central SD	Eden
1	n/a	Edgemont Union Free SD	Scarsdale
1	n/a	Ellenville Central SD	Ellenville
1	n/a	Elmira City SD	Elmira
1	n/a	Elmont Union Free SD	Elmont
1	n/a	Elwood Union Free SD	Greenlawn
1	n/a	Evans-Brant Cent SD (Lake Shore)	Angola
1	n/a	Fairport Central SD	Fairport
1	n/a	Farmingdale Union Free SD	Farmingdale
1	n/a	Fayetteville-Manlius Central SD	Manlius
1	n/a	Floral Park-Bellerose UFSD	Floral Park
1	n/a	Fonda-Fultonville Central SD	Fonda
1	n/a	Franklin Square Union Free SD	Franklin Square
1	n/a	Fredonia Central SD	Fredonia
1	n/a	Freeport Union Free SD	Freeport
1	n/a	Frontier Central SD	Hamburg
1	n/a	Fulton City SD	Fulton
1	n/a	Garden City Union Free SD	Garden City
1	n/a	Gates-Chili Central SD	Rochester
1	n/a	General Brown Central SD	Dexter
1	n/a	Geneva City SD	Geneva
1	n/a	Glen Cove City SD	Glen Cove
1	n/a	Glens Falls City SD	Glens Falls
1	n/a	Gloversville City SD	Gloversville
1	n/a	Gorham-Middlesex CSD (M Whitman)	Rushville
1	n/a	Goshen Central SD	Goshen
1	n/a	Gouverneur Central SD	Gouverneur
1	n/a	Gowanda Central SD	Gowanda
1	n/a	Grand Island Central SD	Grand Island
1	n/a	Great Neck Union Free SD	Great Neck
1	n/a	Greece Central SD	Rochester
1	n/a	Greenburgh Central SD	Hartsdale
1	n/a	Guilderland Central SD	Guilderland
1	n/a	Half Hollow Hills Central SD	Dix Hills
1	n/a	Hamburg Central SD	Hamburg
1	n/a	Hampton Bays Union Free SD	Hampton Bays
1	n/a	Hannibal Central SD	Hannibal
1	n/a	Harborfields Central SD	Greenlawn
1	n/a	Harrison Central SD	Harrison
1	n/a	Hastings-On-Hudson Union Free SD	Hastings-on-Hud
1	n/a	Hauppauge Union Free SD	Hauppauge
1	n/a	Haverstraw-Stony Point Cent SD	Garnerville
1	n/a	Hempstead Union Free SD	Hempstead
1	n/a	Hendrick Hudson Central SD	Montrose
1	n/a	Herricks Union Free SD	New Hyde Park
1	n/a	Hewlett-Woodmere Union Free SD	Woodmere
1	n/a	Hicksville Union Free SD	Hicksville
1	n/a	Highland Central SD	Highland
1	n/a	Hilton Central SD	Hilton
1	n/a	Holland Patent Central SD	Holland Patent
1	n/a	Homer Central SD	Homer
1	n/a	Honeoye Falls-Lima Central SD	Honeoye Falls
1	n/a	Hornell City SD	Hornell
1	n/a	Horseheads Central SD	Horseheads
1	n/a	Hudson City SD	Hudson
1	n/a	Hudson Falls Central SD	Hudson Falls
1	n/a	Huntington Union Free SD	Huntington Stn
1	n/a	Hyde Park Central SD	Poughkeepsie
1	n/a	Ilion Central SD	Ilion
1	n/a	Indian River Central SD	Philadelphia
1	n/a	Iroquois Central SD	Elma
1	n/a	Irvington Union Free SD	Irvington
1	n/a	Island Trees Union Free SD	Levittown
1	n/a	Islip Union Free SD	Islip
1	n/a	Ithaca City SD	Ithaca
1	n/a	Jamestown City SD	Jamestown
1	n/a	Jamesville-Dewitt Central SD	Dewitt
1	n/a	Jericho Union Free SD	Jericho
1	n/a	Johnson City Central SD	Johnson City
1	n/a	Johnstown City SD	Johnstown
1	n/a	Jordan-Elbridge Central SD	Jordan
1	n/a	Katonah-Lewisboro Union Free SD	South Salem
1	n/a	Kenmore-Tonawanda Union Free SD	Buffalo
1	n/a	Kinderhook Central SD	Valatie
1	n/a	Kings Park Central SD	Kings Park
1	n/a	Kingston City SD	Kingston
1	n/a	Lackawanna City SD	Lackawanna
1	n/a	Lakeland Central SD	Shrub Oak
1	n/a	Lancaster Central SD	Lancaster
1	n/a	Lansing Central SD	Lansing
1	n/a	Lansingburgh Central SD	Troy
1	n/a	Lawrence Union Free SD	Lawrence
1	n/a	Levittown Union Free SD	Levittown
1	n/a	Lewiston-Porter Central SD	Youngstown
1	n/a	Liberty Central SD	Liberty
1	n/a	Lindenhurst Union Free SD	Lindenhurst
1	n/a	Liverpool Central SD	Liverpool
1	n/a	Livonia Central SD	Livonia
1	n/a	Lockport City SD	Lockport
1	n/a	Locust Valley Central SD	Locust Valley
1	n/a	Long Beach City SD	Long Beach
1	n/a	Longwood Central SD	Middle Island
1	n/a	Lynbrook Union Free SD	Lynbrook
1	n/a	Mahopac Central SD	Mahopac
1	n/a	Maine-Endwell Central SD	Endwell
1	n/a	Malone Central SD	Malone
1	n/a	Malverne Union Free SD	Malverne
1	n/a	Mamaroneck Union Free SD	Mamaroneck
1	n/a	Manhasset Union Free SD	Manhasset
1	n/a	Marcellus Central SD	Marcellus
1	n/a	Marlboro Central SD	Marlboro
1	n/a	Massapequa Union Free SD	Massapequa
1	n/a	Massena Central SD	Massena
1	n/a	Mattituck-Cutchogue UFSD	Cutchogue
1	n/a	Medina Central SD	Medina
1	n/a	Merrick Union Free SD	Merrick
1	n/a	Mexico Central SD	Mexico
1	n/a	Middle Country Central SD	Centereach
1	n/a	Middletown City SD	Middletown
1	n/a	Miller Place Union Free SD	Miller Place
1	n/a	Mineola Union Free SD	Mineola
1	n/a	Minisink Valley Central SD	Slate Hill
1	n/a	Monroe-Woodbury Central SD	Central Valley
1	n/a	Monticello Central SD	Monticello
1	n/a	Mount Pleasant Central SD	Thornwood
1	n/a	Mount Sinai Union Free SD	Mount Sinai
1	n/a	Mount Vernon City SD	Mount Vernon
1	n/a	Nanuet Union Free SD	Nanuet
1	n/a	New Hartford Central SD	New Hartford
1	n/a	New Hyde Park-Garden City Park	New Hyde Park
1	n/a	New Paltz Central SD	New Paltz
1	n/a	New Rochelle City SD	New Rochelle
1	n/a	New York City Geographic Dist 9	Bronx
1	n/a	New York City Geographic Dist 15	Brooklyn
1	n/a	New York City Public Schools	Brooklyn
1	n/a	Newark Central SD	Newark
1	n/a	Newburgh City SD	Newburgh
1	n/a	Newfane Central SD	Newfane
1	n/a	Niagara Falls City SD	Niagara Falls
1	n/a	Niagara-Wheatfield Central SD	Niagara Falls
1	n/a	Niskayuna Central SD	Schenectady
1	n/a	North Babylon Union Free SD	North Babylon
1	n/a	North Bellmore Union Free SD	Bellmore
1	n/a	North Colonie Central SD	Latham
1	n/a	North Rose-Wolcott Central SD	Wolcott
1	n/a	North Shore Central SD	Sea Cliff
1	n/a	North Syracuse Central SD	N Syracuse
1	n/a	North Tonawanda City SD	N Tonawanda
1	n/a	Northeastern Clinton Central SD	Champlain
1	n/a	Northport-East Northport UFSD	Northport
1	n/a	Norwich City SD	Norwich
1	n/a	Nyack Union Free SD	Nyack
1	n/a	Nyc Alternative HS District	New York
1	n/a	Oceanside Union Free SD	Oceanside
1	n/a	Ogdensburg City SD	Ogdensburg
1	n/a	Olean City SD	Olean
1	n/a	Oneida City SD	Oneida
1	n/a	Oneonta City SD	Oneonta
1	n/a	Onteora Central SD	Boiceville
1	n/a	Orchard Park Central SD	Orchard Park
1	n/a	Ossining Union Free SD	Ossining
1	n/a	Oswego City SD	Oswego
1	n/a	Owego-Apalachin Central SD	Owego
1	n/a	Oyster Bay-East Norwich CSD	Oyster Bay
1	n/a	Palmyra-Macedon Central SD	Palmyra
1	n/a	Patchogue-Medford Union Free SD	Patchogue
1	n/a	Pearl River Union Free SD	Pearl River
1	n/a	Peekskill City SD	Peekskill
1	n/a	Pelham Union Free SD	Pelham
1	n/a	Penfield Central SD	Penfield
1	n/a	Penn Yan Central SD	Penn Yan
1	n/a	Peru Central SD	Peru
1	n/a	Phelps-Clifton Springs Cent SD	Clifton Spgs
1	n/a	Phoenix Central SD	Phoenix
1	n/a	Pine Bush Central SD	Pine Bush
1	n/a	Pittsford Central SD	Pittsford
1	n/a	Plainedge Union Free SD	N Massapequa
1	n/a	Plainview-Old Bethpage Cent SD	Plainview
1	n/a	Plattsburgh City SD	Plattsburgh
1	n/a	Pleasantville Union Free SD	Pleasantville
1	n/a	Port Chester-Rye Union Free SD	Port Chester
1	n/a	Port Jervis City SD	Port Jervis
1	n/a	Port Washington Union Free SD	Pt Washington
1	n/a	Poughkeepsie City SD	Poughkeepsie
1	n/a	Putnam Valley Central SD	Putnam Valley
1	n/a	Queensbury Union Free SD	Queensbury
1	n/a	Ramapo Central SD (Suffern)	Hillburn
1	n/a	Ravena-Coeymans-Selkirk CSD	Selkirk
1	n/a	Red Hook Central SD	Red Hook
1	n/a	Riverhead Central SD	Riverhead
1	n/a	Rochester City SD	Rochester
1	n/a	Rockville Centre Union Free SD	Rockville Ctre
1	n/a	Rocky Point Union Free SD	Rocky Point
1	n/a	Rome City SD	Rome
1	n/a	Rondout Valley Central SD	Accord
1	n/a	Roosevelt Union Free SD	Roosevelt
1	n/a	Roslyn Union Free SD	Roslyn
1	n/a	Rotterdam-Mohonasen Central SD	Schenectady
1	n/a	Royalton-Hartland Central SD	Middleport
1	n/a	Rush-Henrietta Central SD	Henrietta
1	n/a	Rye City SD	Rye
1	n/a	Sachem Central SD	Holbrook
1	n/a	Salamanca City SD	Salamanca
1	n/a	Salmon River Central SD	Ft Covington
1	n/a	Saranac Central SD	Dannemora
1	n/a	Saranac Lake Central SD	Saranac Lake
1	n/a	Saratoga Springs City SD	Saratoga Spgs
1	n/a	Saugerties Central SD	Saugerties
1	n/a	Sayville Union Free SD	Sayville
1	n/a	Scarsdale Union Free SD	Scarsdale
1	n/a	Schalmont Central SD	Schenectady
1	n/a	Schenectady City SD	Schenectady
1	n/a	Schuylerville Central SD	Schuylerville
1	n/a	Scotia-Glenville Central SD	Scotia
1	n/a	Seaford Union Free SD	Seaford
1	n/a	Sewanhaka Central High SD	Floral Park
1	n/a	Shenendehowa Central SD	Clifton Park
1	n/a	Sherburne-Earlville Central SD	Sherburne
1	n/a	Sherrill City SD	Verona
1	n/a	Shoreham-Wading River Central SD	Shoreham
1	n/a	Skaneateles Central SD	Skaneateles
1	n/a	Smithtown Central SD	Smithtown
1	n/a	Solvay Union Free SD	Solvay
1	n/a	Somers Central SD	Lincolndale
1	n/a	South Colonie Central SD	Albany
1	n/a	South Country Central SD	E Patchogue
1	n/a	South Glens Falls Central SD	S Glens Falls
1	n/a	South Huntington Union Free SD	Huntington Stn
1	n/a	South Jefferson Central SD	Adams Center
1	n/a	South Orangetown Central SD	Blauvelt
1	n/a	Southampton Union Free SD	Southampton
1	n/a	Southwestern Cent SD Jamestown	Jamestown
1	n/a	Spackenkill Union Free SD	Poughkeepsie
1	n/a	Spencerport Central SD	Spencerport
1	n/a	Springville-Griffith Inst Cent	Springville
1	n/a	Starpoint Central SD	Lockport
1	n/a	Sullivan West Central SD	Callicoon
1	n/a	Susquehanna Valley Central SD	Conklin
1	n/a	Sweet Home Central SD	Amherst
1	n/a	Syosset Central SD	Syosset
1	n/a	Syracuse City SD	Syracuse
1	n/a	Taconic Hills Central SD	Craryville
1	n/a	Three Village Central SD	East Setauket
1	n/a	Tonawanda City SD	Tonawanda
1	n/a	Troy City SD	Troy
1	n/a	Union Free SD of the Tarrytowns	Sleepy Hollow
1	n/a	Union-Endicott Central SD	Endicott
1	n/a	Uniondale Union Free SD	Uniondale
1	n/a	Utica City SD	Utica
1	n/a	Valley Central SD (Montgomery)	Montgomery
1	n/a	Valley Stream 13 Union Free SD	Valley Stream
1	n/a	Valley Stream 30 Union Free SD	Valley Stream
1	n/a	Valley Stream Central High SD	Valley Stream
1	n/a	Vestal Central SD	Vestal
1	n/a	Victor Central SD	Victor
1	n/a	Wallkill Central SD	Wallkill
1	n/a	Wantagh Union Free SD	Wantagh
1	n/a	Wappingers Central SD	Wappingers Fls
1	n/a	Warwick Valley Central SD	Warwick
1	n/a	Washingtonville Central SD	Washingtonville
1	n/a	Waterloo Central SD	Waterloo
1	n/a	Watertown City SD	Watertown
1	n/a	Watkins Glen Central SD	Watkins Glen
1	n/a	Waverly Central SD	Waverly
1	n/a	Wayland-Cohocton Central SD	Wayland
1	n/a	Wayne Central SD	Ontario Center

1	n/a	Webster Central SD	Webster
1	n/a	West Babylon Union Free SD	West Babylon
1	n/a	West Genesee Central SD	Camillus
1	n/a	West Hempstead Union Free SD	W Hempstead
1	n/a	West Irondequoit Central SD	Rochester
1	n/a	West Islip Union Free SD	West Islip
1	n/a	West Seneca Central SD	West Seneca
1	n/a	Westbury Union Free SD	Old Westbury
1	n/a	Westhampton Beach Union Free SD	Westhampton Bch
1	n/a	Westhill Central SD	Syracuse
1	n/a	White Plains City SD	White Plains
1	n/a	Whitesboro Central SD	Yorkville
1	n/a	Whitney Point Central SD	Whitney Point
1	n/a	William Floyd Union Free SD	Mastic Beach
1	n/a	Williamsville Central SD	East Amherst
1	n/a	Wilson Central SD	Wilson
1	n/a	Windsor Central SD	Windsor
1	n/a	Wyandanch Union Free SD	Wyandanch
1	n/a	Yonkers City SD	Yonkers
1	n/a	Yorkshire-Pioneer Central SD	Yorkshire
1	n/a	Yorktown Central SD	Yorktown Hgts

English Language Learner Students

Rank	Percent	District Name	City
1	n/a	Adirondack Central SD	Boonville
1	n/a	Akron Central SD	Akron
1	n/a	Albany City SD	Albany
1	n/a	Albion Central SD	Albion
1	n/a	Alden Central SD	Alden
1	n/a	Altmar-Parish-Williamstown CSD	Parish
1	n/a	Amherst Central SD	Amherst
1	n/a	Amityville Union Free SD	Amityville
1	n/a	Amsterdam City SD	Amsterdam
1	n/a	Ardsley Union Free SD	Ardsley
1	n/a	Arlington Central SD	Poughkeepsie
1	n/a	Attica Central SD	Attica
1	n/a	Auburn City SD	Auburn
1	n/a	Averill Park Central SD	Averill Park
1	n/a	Babylon Union Free SD	Babylon
1	n/a	Baldwin Union Free SD	Baldwin
1	n/a	Baldwinsville Central SD	Baldwinsville
1	n/a	Ballston Spa Central SD	Ballston Spa
1	n/a	Batavia City SD	Batavia
1	n/a	Bath Central SD	Bath
1	n/a	Bay Shore Union Free SD	Bay Shore
1	n/a	Bayport-Blue Point Union Free SD	Bayport
1	n/a	Beacon City SD	Beacon
1	n/a	Bedford Central SD	Mount Kisco
1	n/a	Beekmantown Central SD	West Chazy
1	n/a	Bellmore-Merrick Central High SD	North Merrick
1	n/a	Bethlehem Central SD	Delmar
1	n/a	Bethpage Union Free SD	Bethpage
1	n/a	Binghamton City SD	Binghamton
1	n/a	Boces Eastern Suffolk	Patchogue
1	n/a	Boces Nassau	Garden City
1	n/a	Brentwood Union Free SD	Brentwood
1	n/a	Brewster Central SD	Brewster
1	n/a	Briarcliff Manor Union Free SD	Briarcliff Manor
1	n/a	Brighton Central SD	Rochester
1	n/a	Broadalbin-Perth Central SD	Broadalbin
1	n/a	Brockport Central SD	Brockport
1	n/a	Brookhaven-Comsewogue UFSD	Pt Jefferson Stn
1	n/a	Buffalo City SD	Buffalo
1	n/a	Burnt Hls-Ballston Lake Cent SD	Scotia
1	n/a	Byram Hills Central SD	Armonk
1	n/a	Cairo-Durham Central SD	Cairo
1	n/a	Camden Central SD	Camden
1	n/a	Canandaigua City SD	Canandaigua
1	n/a	Canastota Central SD	Canastota
1	n/a	Canton Central SD	Canton
1	n/a	Carle Place Union Free SD	Carle Place
1	n/a	Carmel Central SD	Patterson
1	n/a	Carthage Central SD	Carthage
1	n/a	Catskill Central SD	Catskill
1	n/a	Cazenovia Central SD	Cazenovia
1	n/a	Central Islip Union Free SD	Central Islip
1	n/a	Central Square Central SD	Central Square
1	n/a	Chappaqua Central SD	Chappaqua
1	n/a	Chatham Central SD	Chatham
1	n/a	Cheektowaga Central SD	Cheektowaga
1	n/a	Cheektowaga-Maryvale UFSD	Cheektowaga
1	n/a	Cheektowaga-Sloan Union Free SD	Sloan
1	n/a	Chenango Forks Central SD	Binghamton
1	n/a	Chenango Valley Central SD	Binghamton
1	n/a	Chittenango Central SD	Chittenango
1	n/a	Churchville-Chili Central SD	Churchville
1	n/a	Clarence Central SD	Clarence
1	n/a	Clarkstown Central SD	New City
1	n/a	Cleveland Hill Union Free SD	Cheektowaga
1	n/a	Clinton Central SD	Clinton
1	n/a	Cobleskill-Richmondville CSD	Cobleskill
1	n/a	Cohoes City SD	Cohoes
1	n/a	Cold Spring Harbor Central SD	Cold Sprg Harbor
1	n/a	Commack Union Free SD	E Northport
1	n/a	Connetquot Central SD	Bohemia
1	n/a	Copiague Union Free SD	Copiague
1	n/a	Corning City SD	Painted Post
1	n/a	Cornwall Central SD	Cornwall-on-Hud
1	n/a	Cortland City SD	Cortland
1	n/a	Coxsackie-Athens Central SD	Coxsackie
1	n/a	Croton-Harmon Union Free SD	Croton-On-Hud
1	n/a	Dansville Central SD	Dansville
1	n/a	Deer Park Union Free SD	Deer Park
1	n/a	Depew Union Free SD	Depew
1	n/a	Dover Union Free SD	Dover Plains
1	n/a	Dryden Central SD	Dryden
1	n/a	Dunkirk City SD	Dunkirk
1	n/a	East Aurora Union Free SD	East Aurora
1	n/a	East Greenbush Central SD	E Greenbush
1	n/a	East Hampton Union Free SD	East Hampton
1	n/a	East Irondequoit Central SD	Rochester
1	n/a	East Islip Union Free SD	Islip Terrace
1	n/a	East Meadow Union Free SD	Westbury
1	n/a	E Ramapo Central SD (Sprg Val)	Spring Valley
1	n/a	East Syracuse-Minoa Central SD	East Syracuse
1	n/a	East Williston Union Free SD	Old Westbury
1	n/a	Eastchester Union Free SD	Eastchester
1	n/a	Eden Central SD	Eden
1	n/a	Edgemont Union Free SD	Scarsdale
1	n/a	Ellenville Central SD	Ellenville
1	n/a	Elmira City SD	Elmira
1	n/a	Elmont Union Free SD	Elmont
1	n/a	Elwood Union Free SD	Greenlawn
1	n/a	Evans-Brant Cent SD (Lake Shore)	Angola
1	n/a	Fairport Central SD	Fairport
1	n/a	Farmingdale Union Free SD	Farmingdale
1	n/a	Fayetteville-Manlius Central SD	Manlius
1	n/a	Floral Park-Bellerose UFSD	Floral Park
1	n/a	Fonda-Fultonville Central SD	Fonda
1	n/a	Franklin Square Union Free SD	Franklin Square
1	n/a	Fredonia Central SD	Fredonia
1	n/a	Freeport Union Free SD	Freeport
1	n/a	Frontier Central SD	Hamburg
1	n/a	Fulton City SD	Fulton
1	n/a	Garden City Union Free SD	Garden City
1	n/a	Gates-Chili Central SD	Rochester
1	n/a	General Brown Central SD	Dexter
1	n/a	Geneva City SD	Geneva
1	n/a	Glen Cove City SD	Glen Cove
1	n/a	Glens Falls City SD	Glens Falls
1	n/a	Gloversville City SD	Gloversville
1	n/a	Gorham-Middlesex CSD (M Whitman)	Rushville
1	n/a	Goshen Central SD	Goshen
1	n/a	Gouverneur Central SD	Gouverneur
1	n/a	Gowanda Central SD	Gowanda
1	n/a	Grand Island Central SD	Grand Island
1	n/a	Great Neck Union Free SD	Great Neck
1	n/a	Greece Central SD	Rochester
1	n/a	Greenburgh Central SD	Hartsdale
1	n/a	Guilderland Central SD	Guilderland
1	n/a	Half Hollow Hills Central SD	Dix Hills
1	n/a	Hamburg Central SD	Hamburg
1	n/a	Hampton Bays Union Free SD	Hampton Bays
1	n/a	Hannibal Central SD	Hannibal
1	n/a	Harborfields Central SD	Greenlawn
1	n/a	Harrison Central SD	Harrison
1	n/a	Hastings-On-Hudson Union Free SD	Hastings-on-Hud
1	n/a	Hauppauge Union Free SD	Hauppauge
1	n/a	Haverstraw-Stony Point Cent SD	Garnerville
1	n/a	Hempstead Union Free SD	Hempstead
1	n/a	Hendrick Hudson Central SD	Montrose
1	n/a	Herricks Union Free SD	New Hyde Park
1	n/a	Hewlett-Woodmere Union Free SD	Woodmere
1	n/a	Hicksville Union Free SD	Hicksville
1	n/a	Highland Central SD	Highland
1	n/a	Hilton Central SD	Hilton
1	n/a	Holland Patent Central SD	Holland Patent
1	n/a	Homer Central SD	Homer
1	n/a	Honeoye Falls-Lima Central SD	Honeoye Falls
1	n/a	Hornell City SD	Hornell
1	n/a	Horseheads Central SD	Horseheads
1	n/a	Hudson City SD	Hudson
1	n/a	Hudson Falls Central SD	Hudson Falls
1	n/a	Huntington Union Free SD	Huntington Stn
1	n/a	Hyde Park Central SD	Poughkeepsie
1	n/a	Ilion Central SD	Ilion
1	n/a	Indian River Central SD	Philadelphia
1	n/a	Iroquois Central SD	Elma
1	n/a	Irvington Union Free SD	Irvington
1	n/a	Island Trees Union Free SD	Levittown
1	n/a	Islip Union Free SD	Islip
1	n/a	Ithaca City SD	Ithaca
1	n/a	Jamestown City SD	Jamestown
1	n/a	Jamesville-Dewitt Central SD	Dewitt
1	n/a	Jericho Union Free SD	Jericho
1	n/a	Johnson City Central SD	Johnson City
1	n/a	Johnstown City SD	Johnstown
1	n/a	Jordan-Elbridge Central SD	Jordan
1	n/a	Katonah-Lewisboro Union Free SD	South Salem
1	n/a	Kenmore-Tonawanda Union Free SD	Buffalo
1	n/a	Kinderhook Central SD	Valatie
1	n/a	Kings Park Central SD	Kings Park
1	n/a	Kingston City SD	Kingston
1	n/a	Lackawanna City SD	Lackawanna
1	n/a	Lakeland Central SD	Shrub Oak
1	n/a	Lancaster Central SD	Lancaster
1	n/a	Lansing Central SD	Lansing
1	n/a	Lansingburgh Central SD	Troy
1	n/a	Lawrence Union Free SD	Lawrence
1	n/a	Levittown Union Free SD	Levittown
1	n/a	Lewiston-Porter Central SD	Youngstown
1	n/a	Liberty Central SD	Liberty
1	n/a	Lindenhurst Union Free SD	Lindenhurst
1	n/a	Liverpool Central SD	Liverpool
1	n/a	Livonia Central SD	Livonia
1	n/a	Lockport City SD	Lockport
1	n/a	Locust Valley Central SD	Locust Valley
1	n/a	Long Beach City SD	Long Beach
1	n/a	Longwood Central SD	Middle Island
1	n/a	Lynbrook Union Free SD	Lynbrook
1	n/a	Mahopac Central SD	Mahopac
1	n/a	Maine-Endwell Central SD	Endwell
1	n/a	Malone Central SD	Malone
1	n/a	Malverne Union Free SD	Malverne
1	n/a	Mamaroneck Union Free SD	Mamaroneck
1	n/a	Manhasset Union Free SD	Manhasset
1	n/a	Marcellus Central SD	Marcellus
1	n/a	Marlboro Central SD	Marlboro
1	n/a	Massapequa Union Free SD	Massapequa
1	n/a	Massena Central SD	Massena
1	n/a	Mattituck-Cutchogue UFSD	Cutchogue
1	n/a	Medina Central SD	Medina
1	n/a	Merrick Union Free SD	Merrick
1	n/a	Mexico Central SD	Mexico
1	n/a	Middle Country Central SD	Centereach
1	n/a	Middletown City SD	Middletown
1	n/a	Miller Place Union Free SD	Miller Place
1	n/a	Mineola Union Free SD	Mineola
1	n/a	Minisink Valley Central SD	Slate Hill
1	n/a	Monroe-Woodbury Central SD	Central Valley
1	n/a	Monticello Central SD	Monticello
1	n/a	Mount Pleasant Central SD	Thornwood
1	n/a	Mount Sinai Union Free SD	Mount Sinai
1	n/a	Mount Vernon City SD	Mount Vernon
1	n/a	Nanuet Union Free SD	Nanuet
1	n/a	New Hartford Central SD	New Hartford
1	n/a	New Hyde Park-Garden City Park	New Hyde Park
1	n/a	New Paltz Central SD	New Paltz
1	n/a	New Rochelle City SD	New Rochelle
1	n/a	New York City Geographic Dist 9	Bronx
1	n/a	New York City Geographic Dist 15	Brooklyn
1	n/a	New York City Public Schools	Brooklyn
1	n/a	Newark Central SD	Newark
1	n/a	Newburgh City SD	Newburgh
1	n/a	Newfane Central SD	Newfane
1	n/a	Niagara Falls City SD	Niagara Falls
1	n/a	Niagara-Wheatfield Central SD	Niagara Falls
1	n/a	Niskayuna Central SD	Schenectady
1	n/a	North Babylon Union Free SD	North Babylon
1	n/a	North Bellmore Union Free SD	Bellmore
1	n/a	North Colonie Central SD	Latham
1	n/a	North Rose-Wolcott Central SD	Wolcott
1	n/a	North Shore Central SD	Sea Cliff
1	n/a	North Syracuse Central SD	N Syracuse
1	n/a	North Tonawanda City SD	N Tonawanda
1	n/a	Northeastern Clinton Central SD	Champlain
1	n/a	Northport-East Northport UFSD	Northport
1	n/a	Norwich City SD	Norwich
1	n/a	Nyack Union Free SD	Nyack
1	n/a	Nyc Alternative HS District	New York
1	n/a	Oceanside Union Free SD	Oceanside
1	n/a	Ogdensburg City SD	Ogdensburg
1	n/a	Olean City SD	Olean
1	n/a	Oneida City SD	Oneida
1	n/a	Oneonta City SD	Oneonta
1	n/a	Onteora Central SD	Boiceville
1	n/a	Orchard Park Central SD	Orchard Park
1	n/a	Ossining Union Free SD	Ossining
1	n/a	Oswego City SD	Oswego
1	n/a	Owego-Apalachin Central SD	Owego
1	n/a	Oyster Bay-East Norwich CSD	Oyster Bay
1	n/a	Palmyra-Macedon Central SD	Palmyra
1	n/a	Patchogue-Medford Union Free SD	Patchogue
1	n/a	Pearl River Union Free SD	Pearl River
1	n/a	Peekskill City SD	Peekskill
1	n/a	Pelham Union Free SD	Pelham
1	n/a	Penfield Central SD	Penfield

PROFILES OF NEW YORK / School District Rankings 627

1	n/a	Penn Yan Central SD	Penn Yan
1	n/a	Peru Central SD	Peru
1	n/a	Phelps-Clifton Springs Cent SD	Clifton Spgs
1	n/a	Phoenix Central SD	Phoenix
1	n/a	Pine Bush Central SD	Pine Bush
1	n/a	Pittsford Central SD	Pittsford
1	n/a	Plainedge Union Free SD	N Massapequa
1	n/a	Plainview-Old Bethpage Cent SD	Plainview
1	n/a	Plattsburgh City SD	Plattsburgh
1	n/a	Pleasantville Union Free SD	Pleasantville
1	n/a	Port Chester-Rye Union Free SD	Port Chester
1	n/a	Port Jervis City SD	Port Jervis
1	n/a	Port Washington Union Free SD	Pt Washington
1	n/a	Poughkeepsie City SD	Poughkeepsie
1	n/a	Putnam Valley Central SD	Putnam Valley
1	n/a	Queensbury Union Free SD	Queensbury
1	n/a	Ramapo Central SD (Suffern)	Hillburn
1	n/a	Ravena-Coeymans-Selkirk CSD	Selkirk
1	n/a	Red Hook Central SD	Red Hook
1	n/a	Riverhead Central SD	Riverhead
1	n/a	Rochester City SD	Rochester
1	n/a	Rockville Centre Union Free SD	Rockville Ctre
1	n/a	Rocky Point Union Free SD	Rocky Point
1	n/a	Rome City SD	Rome
1	n/a	Rondout Valley Central SD	Accord
1	n/a	Roosevelt Union Free SD	Roosevelt
1	n/a	Roslyn Union Free SD	Roslyn
1	n/a	Rotterdam-Mohonasen Central SD	Schenectady
1	n/a	Royalton-Hartland Central SD	Middleport
1	n/a	Rush-Henrietta Central SD	Henrietta
1	n/a	Rye City SD	Rye
1	n/a	Sachem Central SD	Holbrook
1	n/a	Salamanca City SD	Salamanca
1	n/a	Salmon River Central SD	Ft Covington
1	n/a	Saranac Central SD	Dannemora
1	n/a	Saranac Lake Central SD	Saranac Lake
1	n/a	Saratoga Springs City SD	Saratoga Spgs
1	n/a	Saugerties Central SD	Saugerties
1	n/a	Sayville Union Free SD	Sayville
1	n/a	Scarsdale Union Free SD	Scarsdale
1	n/a	Schalmont Central SD	Schenectady
1	n/a	Schenectady City SD	Schenectady
1	n/a	Schuylerville Central SD	Schuylerville
1	n/a	Scotia-Glenville Central SD	Scotia
1	n/a	Seaford Union Free SD	Seaford
1	n/a	Sewanhaka Central High SD	Floral Park
1	n/a	Shenendehowa Central SD	Clifton Park
1	n/a	Sherburne-Earlville Central SD	Sherburne
1	n/a	Sherrill City SD	Verona
1	n/a	Shoreham-Wading River Central SD	Shoreham
1	n/a	Skaneateles Central SD	Skaneateles
1	n/a	Smithtown Central SD	Smithtown
1	n/a	Solvay Union Free SD	Solvay
1	n/a	Somers Central SD	Lincolndale
1	n/a	South Colonie Central SD	Albany
1	n/a	South Country Central SD	E Patchogue
1	n/a	South Glens Falls Central SD	S Glens Falls
1	n/a	South Huntington Union Free SD	Huntington Stn
1	n/a	South Jefferson Central SD	Adams Center
1	n/a	South Orangetown Central SD	Blauvelt
1	n/a	Southampton Union Free SD	Southampton
1	n/a	Southwestern Cent SD Jamestown	Jamestown
1	n/a	Spackenkill Union Free SD	Poughkeepsie
1	n/a	Spencerport Central SD	Spencerport
1	n/a	Springville-Griffith Inst Cent	Springville
1	n/a	Starpoint Central SD	Lockport
1	n/a	Sullivan West Central SD	Callicoon
1	n/a	Susquehanna Valley Central SD	Conklin
1	n/a	Sweet Home Central SD	Amherst
1	n/a	Syosset Central SD	Syosset
1	n/a	Syracuse City SD	Syracuse
1	n/a	Taconic Hills Central SD	Craryville
1	n/a	Three Village Central SD	East Setauket
1	n/a	Tonawanda City SD	Tonawanda
1	n/a	Troy City SD	Troy
1	n/a	Union Free SD of the Tarrytowns	Sleepy Hollow
1	n/a	Union-Endicott Central SD	Endicott
1	n/a	Uniondale Union Free SD	Uniondale
1	n/a	Utica City SD	Utica
1	n/a	Valley Central SD (Montgomery)	Montgomery
1	n/a	Valley Stream 13 Union Free SD	Valley Stream
1	n/a	Valley Stream 30 Union Free SD	Valley Stream
1	n/a	Valley Stream Central High SD	Valley Stream
1	n/a	Vestal Central SD	Vestal
1	n/a	Victor Central SD	Victor
1	n/a	Wallkill Central SD	Wallkill
1	n/a	Wantagh Union Free SD	Wantagh
1	n/a	Wappingers Central SD	Wappingers Fls
1	n/a	Warwick Valley Central SD	Warwick
1	n/a	Washingtonville Central SD	Washingtonville
1	n/a	Waterloo Central SD	Waterloo
1	n/a	Watertown City SD	Watertown
1	n/a	Watkins Glen Central SD	Watkins Glen
1	n/a	Waverly Central SD	Waverly
1	n/a	Wayland-Cohocton Central SD	Wayland
1	n/a	Wayne Central SD	Ontario Center
1	n/a	Webster Central SD	Webster
1	n/a	West Babylon Union Free SD	West Babylon
1	n/a	West Genesee Central SD	Camillus
1	n/a	West Hempstead Union Free SD	W Hempstead
1	n/a	West Irondequoit Central SD	Rochester
1	n/a	West Islip Union Free SD	West Islip
1	n/a	West Seneca Central SD	West Seneca
1	n/a	Westbury Union Free SD	Old Westbury
1	n/a	Westhampton Beach Union Free SD	Westhampton Bch
1	n/a	Westhill Central SD	Syracuse
1	n/a	White Plains City SD	White Plains
1	n/a	Whitesboro Central SD	Yorkville
1	n/a	Whitney Point Central SD	Whitney Point
1	n/a	William Floyd Union Free SD	Mastic Beach
1	n/a	Williamsville Central SD	East Amherst
1	n/a	Wilson Central SD	Wilson
1	n/a	Windsor Central SD	Windsor
1	n/a	Wyandanch Union Free SD	Wyandanch
1	n/a	Yonkers City SD	Yonkers
1	n/a	Yorkshire-Pioneer Central SD	Yorkshire
1	n/a	Yorktown Central SD	Yorktown Hgts

Migrant Students

Rank	Percent	District Name	City
1	n/a	Adirondack Central SD	Boonville
1	n/a	Akron Central SD	Akron
1	n/a	Albany City SD	Albany
1	n/a	Albion Central SD	Albion
1	n/a	Alden Central SD	Alden
1	n/a	Altmar-Parish-Williamstown CSD	Parish
1	n/a	Amherst Central SD	Amherst
1	n/a	Amityville Union Free SD	Amityville
1	n/a	Amsterdam City SD	Amsterdam
1	n/a	Ardsley Union Free SD	Ardsley
1	n/a	Arlington Central SD	Poughkeepsie
1	n/a	Attica Central SD	Attica
1	n/a	Auburn City SD	Auburn
1	n/a	Averill Park Central SD	Averill Park
1	n/a	Babylon Union Free SD	Babylon
1	n/a	Baldwin Union Free SD	Baldwin
1	n/a	Baldwinsville Central SD	Baldwinsville
1	n/a	Ballston Spa Central SD	Ballston Spa
1	n/a	Batavia City SD	Batavia
1	n/a	Bath Central SD	Bath
1	n/a	Bay Shore Union Free SD	Bay Shore
1	n/a	Bayport-Blue Point Union Free SD	Bayport
1	n/a	Beacon City SD	Beacon
1	n/a	Bedford Central SD	Mount Kisco
1	n/a	Beekmantown Central SD	West Chazy
1	n/a	Bellmore-Merrick Central High SD	North Merrick
1	n/a	Bethlehem Central SD	Delmar
1	n/a	Bethpage Union Free SD	Bethpage
1	n/a	Binghamton City SD	Binghamton
1	n/a	Boces Eastern Suffolk	Patchogue
1	n/a	Boces Nassau	Garden City
1	n/a	Brentwood Union Free SD	Brentwood
1	n/a	Brewster Central SD	Brewster
1	n/a	Briarcliff Manor Union Free SD	Briarcliff Manor
1	n/a	Brighton Central SD	Rochester
1	n/a	Broadalbin-Perth Central SD	Broadalbin
1	n/a	Brockport Central SD	Brockport
1	n/a	Brookhaven-Comsewogue UFSD	Pt Jefferson Stn
1	n/a	Buffalo City SD	Buffalo
1	n/a	Burnt Hls-Ballston Lake Cent SD	Scotia
1	n/a	Byram Hills Central SD	Armonk
1	n/a	Cairo-Durham Central SD	Cairo
1	n/a	Camden Central SD	Camden
1	n/a	Canandaigua City SD	Canandaigua
1	n/a	Canastota Central SD	Canastota
1	n/a	Canton Central SD	Canton
1	n/a	Carle Place Union Free SD	Carle Place
1	n/a	Carmel Central SD	Patterson
1	n/a	Carthage Central SD	Carthage
1	n/a	Catskill Central SD	Catskill
1	n/a	Cazenovia Central SD	Cazenovia
1	n/a	Central Islip Union Free SD	Central Islip
1	n/a	Central Square Central SD	Central Square
1	n/a	Chappaqua Central SD	Chappaqua
1	n/a	Chatham Central SD	Chatham
1	n/a	Cheektowaga Central SD	Cheektowaga
1	n/a	Cheektowaga-Maryvale UFSD	Cheektowaga
1	n/a	Cheektowaga-Sloan Union Free SD	Sloan
1	n/a	Chenango Forks Central SD	Binghamton
1	n/a	Chenango Valley Central SD	Binghamton
1	n/a	Chittenango Central SD	Chittenango
1	n/a	Churchville-Chili Central SD	Churchville
1	n/a	Clarence Central SD	Clarence
1	n/a	Clarkstown Central SD	New City
1	n/a	Cleveland Hill Union Free SD	Cheektowaga
1	n/a	Clinton Central SD	Clinton
1	n/a	Cobleskill-Richmondville CSD	Cobleskill
1	n/a	Cohoes City SD	Cohoes
1	n/a	Cold Spring Harbor Central SD	Cold Sprg Harbor
1	n/a	Commack Union Free SD	E Northport
1	n/a	Connetquot Central SD	Bohemia
1	n/a	Copiague Union Free SD	Copiague
1	n/a	Corning City SD	Painted Post
1	n/a	Cornwall Central SD	Cornwall-on-Hud
1	n/a	Cortland City SD	Cortland
1	n/a	Coxsackie-Athens Central SD	Coxsackie
1	n/a	Croton-Harmon Union Free SD	Croton-On-Hud
1	n/a	Dansville Central SD	Dansville
1	n/a	Deer Park Union Free SD	Deer Park
1	n/a	Depew Union Free SD	Depew
1	n/a	Dover Union Free SD	Dover Plains
1	n/a	Dryden Central SD	Dryden
1	n/a	Dunkirk City SD	Dunkirk
1	n/a	East Aurora Union Free SD	East Aurora
1	n/a	East Greenbush Central SD	E Greenbush
1	n/a	East Hampton Union Free SD	East Hampton
1	n/a	East Irondequoit Central SD	Rochester
1	n/a	East Islip Union Free SD	Islip Terrace
1	n/a	East Meadow Union Free SD	Westbury
1	n/a	E Ramapo Central SD (Sprg Val)	Spring Valley
1	n/a	East Syracuse-Minoa Central SD	East Syracuse
1	n/a	East Williston Union Free SD	Old Westbury
1	n/a	Eastchester Union Free SD	Eastchester
1	n/a	Eden Central SD	Eden
1	n/a	Edgemont Union Free SD	Scarsdale
1	n/a	Ellenville Central SD	Ellenville
1	n/a	Elmira City SD	Elmira
1	n/a	Elmont Union Free SD	Elmont
1	n/a	Elwood Union Free SD	Greenlawn
1	n/a	Evans-Brant Cent SD (Lake Shore)	Angola
1	n/a	Fairport Central SD	Fairport
1	n/a	Farmingdale Union Free SD	Farmingdale
1	n/a	Fayetteville-Manlius Central SD	Manlius
1	n/a	Floral Park-Bellerose UFSD	Floral Park
1	n/a	Fonda-Fultonville Central SD	Fonda
1	n/a	Franklin Square Union Free SD	Franklin Square
1	n/a	Fredonia Central SD	Fredonia
1	n/a	Freeport Union Free SD	Freeport
1	n/a	Frontier Central SD	Hamburg
1	n/a	Fulton City SD	Fulton
1	n/a	Garden City Union Free SD	Garden City
1	n/a	Gates-Chili Central SD	Rochester
1	n/a	General Brown Central SD	Dexter
1	n/a	Geneva City SD	Geneva
1	n/a	Glen Cove City SD	Glen Cove
1	n/a	Glens Falls City SD	Glens Falls
1	n/a	Gloversville City SD	Gloversville
1	n/a	Gorham-Middlesex CSD (M Whitman)	Rushville
1	n/a	Goshen Central SD	Goshen
1	n/a	Gouverneur Central SD	Gouverneur
1	n/a	Gowanda Central SD	Gowanda
1	n/a	Grand Island Central SD	Grand Island
1	n/a	Great Neck Union Free SD	Great Neck
1	n/a	Greece Central SD	Rochester
1	n/a	Greenburgh Central SD	Hartsdale
1	n/a	Guilderland Central SD	Guilderland
1	n/a	Half Hollow Hills Central SD	Dix Hills
1	n/a	Hamburg Central SD	Hamburg
1	n/a	Hampton Bays Union Free SD	Hampton Bays
1	n/a	Hannibal Central SD	Hannibal
1	n/a	Harborfields Central SD	Greenlawn
1	n/a	Harrison Central SD	Harrison
1	n/a	Hastings-On-Hudson Union Free SD	Hastings-on-Hud
1	n/a	Hauppauge Union Free SD	Hauppauge
1	n/a	Haverstraw-Stony Point Cent SD	Garnerville
1	n/a	Hempstead Union Free SD	Hempstead
1	n/a	Hendrick Hudson Central SD	Montrose
1	n/a	Herricks Union Free SD	New Hyde Park
1	n/a	Hewlett-Woodmere Union Free SD	Woodmere
1	n/a	Hicksville Union Free SD	Hicksville
1	n/a	Highland Central SD	Highland
1	n/a	Hilton Central SD	Hilton
1	n/a	Holland Patent Central SD	Holland Patent
1	n/a	Homer Central SD	Homer
1	n/a	Honeoye Falls-Lima Central SD	Honeoye Falls
1	n/a	Hornell City SD	Hornell
1	n/a	Horseheads Central SD	Horseheads
1	n/a	Hudson City SD	Hudson
1	n/a	Hudson Falls Central SD	Hudson Falls
1	n/a	Huntington Union Free SD	Huntington Stn
1	n/a	Hyde Park Central SD	Poughkeepsie
1	n/a	Ilion Central SD	Ilion
1	n/a	Indian River Central SD	Philadelphia
1	n/a	Iroquois Central SD	Elma
1	n/a	Irvington Union Free SD	Irvington
1	n/a	Island Trees Union Free SD	Levittown
1	n/a	Islip Union Free SD	Islip

1	n/a	Ithaca City SD	Ithaca
1	n/a	Jamestown City SD	Jamestown
1	n/a	Jamesville-Dewitt Central SD	Dewitt
1	n/a	Jericho Union Free SD	Jericho
1	n/a	Johnson City Central SD	Johnson City
1	n/a	Johnstown City SD	Johnstown
1	n/a	Jordan-Elbridge Central SD	Jordan
1	n/a	Katonah-Lewisboro Union Free SD	South Salem
1	n/a	Kenmore-Tonawanda Union Free SD	Buffalo
1	n/a	Kinderhook Central SD	Valatie
1	n/a	Kings Park Central SD	Kings Park
1	n/a	Kingston City SD	Kingston
1	n/a	Lackawanna City SD	Lackawanna
1	n/a	Lakeland Central SD	Shrub Oak
1	n/a	Lancaster Central SD	Lancaster
1	n/a	Lansing Central SD	Lansing
1	n/a	Lansingburgh Central SD	Troy
1	n/a	Lawrence Union Free SD	Lawrence
1	n/a	Levittown Union Free SD	Levittown
1	n/a	Lewiston-Porter Central SD	Youngstown
1	n/a	Liberty Central SD	Liberty
1	n/a	Lindenhurst Union Free SD	Lindenhurst
1	n/a	Liverpool Central SD	Liverpool
1	n/a	Livonia Central SD	Livonia
1	n/a	Lockport City SD	Lockport
1	n/a	Locust Valley Central SD	Locust Valley
1	n/a	Long Beach City SD	Long Beach
1	n/a	Longwood Central SD	Middle Island
1	n/a	Lynbrook Union Free SD	Lynbrook
1	n/a	Mahopac Central SD	Mahopac
1	n/a	Maine-Endwell Central SD	Endwell
1	n/a	Malone Central SD	Malone
1	n/a	Malverne Union Free SD	Malverne
1	n/a	Mamaroneck Union Free SD	Mamaroneck
1	n/a	Manhasset Union Free SD	Manhasset
1	n/a	Marcellus Central SD	Marcellus
1	n/a	Marlboro Central SD	Marlboro
1	n/a	Massapequa Union Free SD	Massapequa
1	n/a	Massena Central SD	Massena
1	n/a	Mattituck-Cutchogue UFSD	Cutchogue
1	n/a	Medina Central SD	Medina
1	n/a	Merrick Union Free SD	Merrick
1	n/a	Mexico Central SD	Mexico
1	n/a	Middle Country Central SD	Centereach
1	n/a	Middletown City SD	Middletown
1	n/a	Miller Place Union Free SD	Miller Place
1	n/a	Mineola Union Free SD	Mineola
1	n/a	Minisink Valley Central SD	Slate Hill
1	n/a	Monroe-Woodbury Central SD	Central Valley
1	n/a	Monticello Central SD	Monticello
1	n/a	Mount Pleasant Central SD	Thornwood
1	n/a	Mount Sinai Union Free SD	Mount Sinai
1	n/a	Mount Vernon City SD	Mount Vernon
1	n/a	Nanuet Union Free SD	Nanuet
1	n/a	New Hartford Central SD	New Hartford
1	n/a	New Hyde Park-Garden City Park	New Hyde Park
1	n/a	New Paltz Central SD	New Paltz
1	n/a	New Rochelle City SD	New Rochelle
1	n/a	New York City Geographic Dist 9	Bronx
1	n/a	New York City Geographic Dist 15	Brooklyn
1	n/a	New York City Public Schools	Brooklyn
1	n/a	Newark Central SD	Newark
1	n/a	Newburgh City SD	Newburgh
1	n/a	Newfane Central SD	Newfane
1	n/a	Niagara Falls City SD	Niagara Falls
1	n/a	Niagara-Wheatfield Central SD	Niagara Falls
1	n/a	Niskayuna Central SD	Schenectady
1	n/a	North Babylon Union Free SD	North Babylon
1	n/a	North Bellmore Union Free SD	Bellmore
1	n/a	North Colonie Central SD	Latham
1	n/a	North Rose-Wolcott Central SD	Wolcott
1	n/a	North Shore Central SD	Sea Cliff
1	n/a	North Syracuse Central SD	N Syracuse
1	n/a	North Tonawanda City SD	N Tonawanda
1	n/a	Northeastern Clinton Central SD	Champlain
1	n/a	Northport-East Northport UFSD	Northport
1	n/a	Norwich City SD	Norwich
1	n/a	Nyack Union Free SD	Nyack
1	n/a	Nyc Alternative HS District	New York
1	n/a	Oceanside Union Free SD	Oceanside
1	n/a	Ogdensburg City SD	Ogdensburg
1	n/a	Olean City SD	Olean
1	n/a	Oneida City SD	Oneida
1	n/a	Oneonta City SD	Oneonta
1	n/a	Onteora Central SD	Boiceville
1	n/a	Orchard Park Central SD	Orchard Park
1	n/a	Ossining Union Free SD	Ossining
1	n/a	Oswego City SD	Oswego
1	n/a	Owego-Apalachin Central SD	Owego
1	n/a	Oyster Bay-East Norwich CSD	Oyster Bay
1	n/a	Palmyra-Macedon Central SD	Palmyra
1	n/a	Patchogue-Medford Union Free SD	Patchogue
1	n/a	Pearl River Union Free SD	Pearl River
1	n/a	Peekskill City SD	Peekskill
1	n/a	Pelham Union Free SD	Pelham
1	n/a	Penfield Central SD	Penfield
1	n/a	Penn Yan Central SD	Penn Yan
1	n/a	Peru Central SD	Peru
1	n/a	Phelps-Clifton Springs Cent SD	Clifton Spgs
1	n/a	Phoenix Central SD	Phoenix
1	n/a	Pine Bush Central SD	Pine Bush
1	n/a	Pittsford Central SD	Pittsford
1	n/a	Plainedge Union Free SD	N Massapequa
1	n/a	Plainview-Old Bethpage Cent SD	Plainview
1	n/a	Plattsburgh City SD	Plattsburgh
1	n/a	Pleasantville Union Free SD	Pleasantville
1	n/a	Port Chester-Rye Union Free SD	Port Chester
1	n/a	Port Jervis City SD	Port Jervis
1	n/a	Port Washington Union Free SD	Pt Washington
1	n/a	Poughkeepsie City SD	Poughkeepsie
1	n/a	Putnam Valley Central SD	Putnam Valley
1	n/a	Queensbury Union Free SD	Queensbury
1	n/a	Ramapo Central SD (Suffern)	Hillburn
1	n/a	Ravena-Coeymans-Selkirk CSD	Selkirk
1	n/a	Red Hook Central SD	Red Hook
1	n/a	Riverhead Central SD	Riverhead
1	n/a	Rochester City SD	Rochester
1	n/a	Rockville Centre Union Free SD	Rockville Ctre
1	n/a	Rocky Point Union Free SD	Rocky Point
1	n/a	Rome City SD	Rome
1	n/a	Rondout Valley Central SD	Accord
1	n/a	Roosevelt Union Free SD	Roosevelt
1	n/a	Roslyn Union Free SD	Roslyn
1	n/a	Rotterdam-Mohonasen Central SD	Schenectady
1	n/a	Royalton-Hartland Central SD	Middleport
1	n/a	Rush-Henrietta Central SD	Henrietta
1	n/a	Rye City SD	Rye
1	n/a	Sachem Central SD	Holbrook
1	n/a	Salamanca City SD	Salamanca
1	n/a	Salmon River Central SD	Ft Covington
1	n/a	Saranac Central SD	Dannemora
1	n/a	Saranac Lake Central SD	Saranac Lake
1	n/a	Saratoga Springs City SD	Saratoga Spgs
1	n/a	Saugerties Central SD	Saugerties
1	n/a	Sayville Union Free SD	Sayville
1	n/a	Scarsdale Union Free SD	Scarsdale
1	n/a	Schalmont Central SD	Schenectady
1	n/a	Schenectady City SD	Schenectady
1	n/a	Schuylerville Central SD	Schuylerville
1	n/a	Scotia-Glenville Central SD	Scotia
1	n/a	Seaford Union Free SD	Seaford
1	n/a	Sewanhaka Central High SD	Floral Park
1	n/a	Shenendehowa Central SD	Clifton Park
1	n/a	Sherburne-Earlville Central SD	Sherburne
1	n/a	Sherrill City SD	Verona
1	n/a	Shoreham-Wading River Central SD	Shoreham
1	n/a	Skaneateles Central SD	Skaneateles
1	n/a	Smithtown Central SD	Smithtown
1	n/a	Solvay Union Free SD	Solvay
1	n/a	Somers Central SD	Lincolndale
1	n/a	South Colonie Central SD	Albany
1	n/a	South Country Central SD	E Patchogue
1	n/a	South Glens Falls Central SD	S Glens Falls
1	n/a	South Huntington Union Free SD	Huntington Stn
1	n/a	South Jefferson Central SD	Adams Center
1	n/a	South Orangetown Central SD	Blauvelt
1	n/a	Southampton Union Free SD	Southampton
1	n/a	Southwestern Cent SD Jamestown	Jamestown
1	n/a	Spackenkill Union Free SD	Poughkeepsie
1	n/a	Spencerport Central SD	Spencerport
1	n/a	Springville-Griffith Inst Cent	Springville
1	n/a	Starpoint Central SD	Lockport
1	n/a	Sullivan West Central SD	Callicoon
1	n/a	Susquehanna Valley Central SD	Conklin
1	n/a	Sweet Home Central SD	Amherst
1	n/a	Syosset Central SD	Syosset
1	n/a	Syracuse City SD	Syracuse
1	n/a	Taconic Hills Central SD	Craryville
1	n/a	Three Village Central SD	East Setauket
1	n/a	Tonawanda City SD	Tonawanda
1	n/a	Troy City SD	Troy
1	n/a	Union Free SD of the Tarrytowns	Sleepy Hollow
1	n/a	Union-Endicott Central SD	Endicott
1	n/a	Uniondale Union Free SD	Uniondale
1	n/a	Utica City SD	Utica
1	n/a	Valley Central SD (Montgomery)	Montgomery
1	n/a	Valley Stream 13 Union Free SD	Valley Stream
1	n/a	Valley Stream 30 Union Free SD	Valley Stream
1	n/a	Valley Stream Central High SD	Valley Stream
1	n/a	Vestal Central SD	Vestal
1	n/a	Victor Central SD	Victor
1	n/a	Wallkill Central SD	Wallkill
1	n/a	Wantagh Union Free SD	Wantagh
1	n/a	Wappingers Central SD	Wappingers Fls
1	n/a	Warwick Valley Central SD	Warwick
1	n/a	Washingtonville Central SD	Washingtonville
1	n/a	Waterloo Central SD	Waterloo
1	n/a	Watertown City SD	Watertown
1	n/a	Watkins Glen Central SD	Watkins Glen
1	n/a	Waverly Central SD	Waverly
1	n/a	Wayland-Cohocton Central SD	Wayland
1	n/a	Wayne Central SD	Ontario Center
1	n/a	Webster Central SD	Webster
1	n/a	West Babylon Union Free SD	West Babylon
1	n/a	West Genesee Central SD	Camillus
1	n/a	West Hempstead Union Free SD	W Hempstead
1	n/a	West Irondequoit Central SD	Rochester
1	n/a	West Islip Union Free SD	West Islip
1	n/a	West Seneca Central SD	West Seneca
1	n/a	Westbury Union Free SD	Old Westbury
1	n/a	Westhampton Beach Union Free SD	Westhampton Bch
1	n/a	Westhill Central SD	Syracuse
1	n/a	White Plains City SD	White Plains
1	n/a	Whitesboro Central SD	Yorkville
1	n/a	Whitney Point Central SD	Whitney Point
1	n/a	William Floyd Union Free SD	Mastic Beach
1	n/a	Williamsville Central SD	East Amherst
1	n/a	Wilson Central SD	Wilson
1	n/a	Windsor Central SD	Windsor
1	n/a	Wyandanch Union Free SD	Wyandanch
1	n/a	Yonkers City SD	Yonkers
1	n/a	Yorkshire-Pioneer Central SD	Yorkshire
1	n/a	Yorktown Central SD	Yorktown Hgts

Students Eligible for Free Lunch

Rank	Percent	District Name	City
1	n/a	Adirondack Central SD	Boonville
1	n/a	Akron Central SD	Akron
1	n/a	Albany City SD	Albany
1	n/a	Albion Central SD	Albion
1	n/a	Alden Central SD	Alden
1	n/a	Altmar-Parish-Williamstown CSD	Parish
1	n/a	Amherst Central SD	Amherst
1	n/a	Amityville Union Free SD	Amityville
1	n/a	Amsterdam City SD	Amsterdam
1	n/a	Ardsley Union Free SD	Ardsley
1	n/a	Arlington Central SD	Poughkeepsie
1	n/a	Attica Central SD	Attica
1	n/a	Auburn City SD	Auburn
1	n/a	Averill Park Central SD	Averill Park
1	n/a	Babylon Union Free SD	Babylon
1	n/a	Baldwin Union Free SD	Baldwin
1	n/a	Baldwinsville Central SD	Baldwinsville
1	n/a	Ballston Spa Central SD	Ballston Spa
1	n/a	Batavia City SD	Batavia
1	n/a	Bath Central SD	Bath
1	n/a	Bay Shore Union Free SD	Bay Shore
1	n/a	Bayport-Blue Point Union Free SD	Bayport
1	n/a	Beacon City SD	Beacon
1	n/a	Bedford Central SD	Mount Kisco
1	n/a	Beekmantown Central SD	West Chazy
1	n/a	Bellmore-Merrick Central High SD	North Merrick
1	n/a	Bethlehem Central SD	Delmar
1	n/a	Bethpage Union Free SD	Bethpage
1	n/a	Binghamton City SD	Binghamton
1	n/a	Boces Eastern Suffolk	Patchogue
1	n/a	Boces Nassau	Garden City
1	n/a	Brentwood Union Free SD	Brentwood
1	n/a	Brewster Central SD	Brewster
1	n/a	Briarcliff Manor Union Free SD	Briarcliff Manor
1	n/a	Brighton Central SD	Rochester
1	n/a	Broadalbin-Perth Central SD	Broadalbin
1	n/a	Brockport Central SD	Brockport
1	n/a	Brookhaven-Comsewogue UFSD	Pt Jefferson Stn
1	n/a	Buffalo City SD	Buffalo
1	n/a	Burnt Hls-Ballston Lake Cent SD	Scotia
1	n/a	Byram Hills Central SD	Armonk
1	n/a	Cairo-Durham Central SD	Cairo
1	n/a	Camden Central SD	Camden
1	n/a	Canandaigua City SD	Canandaigua
1	n/a	Canastota Central SD	Canastota
1	n/a	Canton Central SD	Canton
1	n/a	Carle Place Union Free SD	Carle Place
1	n/a	Carmel Central SD	Patterson
1	n/a	Carthage Central SD	Carthage
1	n/a	Catskill Central SD	Catskill
1	n/a	Cazenovia Central SD	Cazenovia
1	n/a	Central Islip Union Free SD	Central Islip
1	n/a	Central Square Central SD	Central Square
1	n/a	Chappaqua Central SD	Chappaqua
1	n/a	Chatham Central SD	Chatham
1	n/a	Cheektowaga Central SD	Cheektowaga
1	n/a	Cheektowaga-Maryvale UFSD	Cheektowaga
1	n/a	Cheektowaga-Sloan Union Free SD	Sloan
1	n/a	Chenango Forks Central SD	Binghamton
1	n/a	Chenango Valley Central SD	Binghamton
1	n/a	Chittenango Central SD	Chittenango

1	n/a	Churchville-Chili Central SD	Churchville	1	n/a	Irvington Union Free SD	Irvington	1	n/a	Oyster Bay-East Norwich CSD	Oyster Bay
1	n/a	Clarence Central SD	Clarence	1	n/a	Island Trees Union Free SD	Levittown	1	n/a	Palmyra-Macedon Central SD	Palmyra
1	n/a	Clarkstown Central SD	New City	1	n/a	Islip Union Free SD	Islip	1	n/a	Patchogue-Medford Union Free SD	Patchogue
1	n/a	Cleveland Hill Union Free SD	Cheektowaga	1	n/a	Ithaca City SD	Ithaca	1	n/a	Pearl River Union Free SD	Pearl River
1	n/a	Clinton Central SD	Clinton	1	n/a	Jamestown City SD	Jamestown	1	n/a	Peekskill City SD	Peekskill
1	n/a	Cobleskill-Richmondville CSD	Cobleskill	1	n/a	Jamesville-Dewitt Central SD	Dewitt	1	n/a	Pelham Union Free SD	Pelham
1	n/a	Cohoes City SD	Cohoes	1	n/a	Jericho Union Free SD	Jericho	1	n/a	Penfield Central SD	Penfield
1	n/a	Cold Spring Harbor Central SD	Cold Sprg Harbor	1	n/a	Johnson City Central SD	Johnson City	1	n/a	Penn Yan Central SD	Penn Yan
1	n/a	Commack Union Free SD	E Northport	1	n/a	Johnstown City SD	Johnstown	1	n/a	Peru Central SD	Peru
1	n/a	Connetquot Central SD	Bohemia	1	n/a	Jordan-Elbridge Central SD	Jordan	1	n/a	Phelps-Clifton Springs Cent SD	Clifton Spgs
1	n/a	Copiague Union Free SD	Copiague	1	n/a	Katonah-Lewisboro Union Free SD	South Salem	1	n/a	Phoenix Central SD	Phoenix
1	n/a	Corning City SD	Painted Post	1	n/a	Kenmore-Tonawanda Union Free SD	Buffalo	1	n/a	Pine Bush Central SD	Pine Bush
1	n/a	Cornwall Central SD	Cornwall-on-Hud	1	n/a	Kinderhook Central SD	Valatie	1	n/a	Pittsford Central SD	Pittsford
1	n/a	Cortland City SD	Cortland	1	n/a	Kings Park Central SD	Kings Park	1	n/a	Plainedge Union Free SD	N Massapequa
1	n/a	Coxsackie-Athens Central SD	Coxsackie	1	n/a	Kingston City SD	Kingston	1	n/a	Plainview-Old Bethpage Cent SD	Plainview
1	n/a	Croton-Harmon Union Free SD	Croton-On-Hud	1	n/a	Lackawanna City SD	Lackawanna	1	n/a	Plattsburgh City SD	Plattsburgh
1	n/a	Dansville Central SD	Dansville	1	n/a	Lakeland Central SD	Shrub Oak	1	n/a	Pleasantville Union Free SD	Pleasantville
1	n/a	Deer Park Union Free SD	Deer Park	1	n/a	Lancaster Central SD	Lancaster	1	n/a	Port Chester-Rye Union Free SD	Port Chester
1	n/a	Depew Union Free SD	Depew	1	n/a	Lansing Central SD	Lansing	1	n/a	Port Jervis City SD	Port Jervis
1	n/a	Dover Union Free SD	Dover Plains	1	n/a	Lansingburgh Central SD	Troy	1	n/a	Port Washington Union Free SD	Pt Washington
1	n/a	Dryden Central SD	Dryden	1	n/a	Lawrence Union Free SD	Lawrence	1	n/a	Poughkeepsie City SD	Poughkeepsie
1	n/a	Dunkirk City SD	Dunkirk	1	n/a	Levittown Union Free SD	Levittown	1	n/a	Putnam Valley Central SD	Putnam Valley
1	n/a	East Aurora Union Free SD	East Aurora	1	n/a	Lewiston-Porter Central SD	Youngstown	1	n/a	Queensbury Union Free SD	Queensbury
1	n/a	East Greenbush Central SD	E Greenbush	1	n/a	Liberty Central SD	Liberty	1	n/a	Ramapo Central SD (Suffern)	Hillburn
1	n/a	East Hampton Union Free SD	East Hampton	1	n/a	Lindenhurst Union Free SD	Lindenhurst	1	n/a	Ravena-Coeymans-Selkirk CSD	Selkirk
1	n/a	East Irondequoit Central SD	Rochester	1	n/a	Liverpool Central SD	Liverpool	1	n/a	Red Hook Central SD	Red Hook
1	n/a	East Islip Union Free SD	Islip Terrace	1	n/a	Livonia Central SD	Livonia	1	n/a	Riverhead Central SD	Riverhead
1	n/a	East Meadow Union Free SD	Westbury	1	n/a	Lockport City SD	Lockport	1	n/a	Rochester City SD	Rochester
1	n/a	E Ramapo Central SD (Sprg Val)	Spring Valley	1	n/a	Locust Valley Central SD	Locust Valley	1	n/a	Rockville Centre Union Free SD	Rockville Ctre
1	n/a	East Syracuse-Minoa Central SD	East Syracuse	1	n/a	Long Beach City SD	Long Beach	1	n/a	Rocky Point Union Free SD	Rocky Point
1	n/a	East Williston Union Free SD	Old Westbury	1	n/a	Longwood Central SD	Middle Island	1	n/a	Rome City SD	Rome
1	n/a	Eastchester Union Free SD	Eastchester	1	n/a	Lynbrook Union Free SD	Lynbrook	1	n/a	Rondout Valley Central SD	Accord
1	n/a	Eden Central SD	Eden	1	n/a	Mahopac Central SD	Mahopac	1	n/a	Roosevelt Union Free SD	Roosevelt
1	n/a	Edgemont Union Free SD	Scarsdale	1	n/a	Maine-Endwell Central SD	Endwell	1	n/a	Roslyn Union Free SD	Roslyn
1	n/a	Ellenville Central SD	Ellenville	1	n/a	Malone Central SD	Malone	1	n/a	Rotterdam-Mohonasen Central SD	Schenectady
1	n/a	Elmira City SD	Elmira	1	n/a	Malverne Union Free SD	Malverne	1	n/a	Royalton-Hartland Central SD	Middleport
1	n/a	Elmont Union Free SD	Elmont	1	n/a	Mamaroneck Union Free SD	Mamaroneck	1	n/a	Rush-Henrietta Central SD	Henrietta
1	n/a	Elwood Union Free SD	Greenlawn	1	n/a	Manhasset Union Free SD	Manhasset	1	n/a	Rye City SD	Rye
1	n/a	Evans-Brant Cent SD (Lake Shore)	Angola	1	n/a	Marcellus Central SD	Marcellus	1	n/a	Sachem Central SD	Holbrook
1	n/a	Fairport Central SD	Fairport	1	n/a	Marlboro Central SD	Marlboro	1	n/a	Salamanca City SD	Salamanca
1	n/a	Farmingdale Union Free SD	Farmingdale	1	n/a	Massapequa Union Free SD	Massapequa	1	n/a	Salmon River Central SD	Ft Covington
1	n/a	Fayetteville-Manlius Central SD	Manlius	1	n/a	Massena Central SD	Massena	1	n/a	Saranac Central SD	Dannemora
1	n/a	Floral Park-Bellerose UFSD	Floral Park	1	n/a	Mattituck-Cutchogue UFSD	Cutchogue	1	n/a	Saranac Lake Central SD	Saranac Lake
1	n/a	Fonda-Fultonville Central SD	Fonda	1	n/a	Medina Central SD	Medina	1	n/a	Saratoga Springs City SD	Saratoga Spgs
1	n/a	Franklin Square Union Free SD	Franklin Square	1	n/a	Merrick Union Free SD	Merrick	1	n/a	Saugerties Central SD	Saugerties
1	n/a	Fredonia Central SD	Fredonia	1	n/a	Mexico Central SD	Mexico	1	n/a	Sayville Union Free SD	Sayville
1	n/a	Freeport Union Free SD	Freeport	1	n/a	Middle Country Central SD	Centereach	1	n/a	Scarsdale Union Free SD	Scarsdale
1	n/a	Frontier Central SD	Hamburg	1	n/a	Middletown City SD	Middletown	1	n/a	Schalmont Central SD	Schenectady
1	n/a	Fulton City SD	Fulton	1	n/a	Miller Place Union Free SD	Miller Place	1	n/a	Schenectady City SD	Schenectady
1	n/a	Garden City Union Free SD	Garden City	1	n/a	Mineola Union Free SD	Mineola	1	n/a	Schuylerville Central SD	Schuylerville
1	n/a	Gates-Chili Central SD	Rochester	1	n/a	Minisink Valley Central SD	Slate Hill	1	n/a	Scotia-Glenville Central SD	Scotia
1	n/a	General Brown Central SD	Dexter	1	n/a	Monroe-Woodbury Central SD	Central Valley	1	n/a	Seaford Union Free SD	Seaford
1	n/a	Geneva City SD	Geneva	1	n/a	Monticello Central SD	Monticello	1	n/a	Sewanhaka Central High SD	Floral Park
1	n/a	Glen Cove City SD	Glen Cove	1	n/a	Mount Pleasant Central SD	Thornwood	1	n/a	Shenendehowa Central SD	Clifton Park
1	n/a	Glens Falls City SD	Glens Falls	1	n/a	Mount Sinai Union Free SD	Mount Sinai	1	n/a	Sherburne-Earlville Central SD	Sherburne
1	n/a	Gloversville City SD	Gloversville	1	n/a	Mount Vernon City SD	Mount Vernon	1	n/a	Sherrill City SD	Verona
1	n/a	Gorham-Middlesex CSD (M Whitman)	Rushville	1	n/a	Nanuet Union Free SD	Nanuet	1	n/a	Shoreham-Wading River Central SD	Shoreham
1	n/a	Goshen Central SD	Goshen	1	n/a	New Hartford Central SD	New Hartford	1	n/a	Skaneateles Central SD	Skaneateles
1	n/a	Gouverneur Central SD	Gouverneur	1	n/a	New Hyde Park-Garden City Park	New Hyde Park	1	n/a	Smithtown Central SD	Smithtown
1	n/a	Gowanda Central SD	Gowanda	1	n/a	New Paltz Central SD	New Paltz	1	n/a	Solvay Union Free SD	Solvay
1	n/a	Grand Island Central SD	Grand Island	1	n/a	New Rochelle City SD	New Rochelle	1	n/a	Somers Central SD	Lincolndale
1	n/a	Great Neck Union Free SD	Great Neck	1	n/a	New York City Geographic Dist 9	Bronx	1	n/a	South Colonie Central SD	Albany
1	n/a	Greece Central SD	Rochester	1	n/a	New York City Geographic Dist 15	Brooklyn	1	n/a	South Country Central SD	E Patchogue
1	n/a	Greenburgh Central SD	Hartsdale	1	n/a	New York City Public Schools	Brooklyn	1	n/a	South Glens Falls Central SD	S Glens Falls
1	n/a	Guilderland Central SD	Guilderland	1	n/a	Newark Central SD	Newark	1	n/a	South Huntington Union Free SD	Huntington Stn
1	n/a	Half Hollow Hills Central SD	Dix Hills	1	n/a	Newburgh City SD	Newburgh	1	n/a	South Jefferson Central SD	Adams Center
1	n/a	Hamburg Central SD	Hamburg	1	n/a	Newfane Central SD	Newfane	1	n/a	South Orangetown Central SD	Blauvelt
1	n/a	Hampton Bays Union Free SD	Hampton Bays	1	n/a	Niagara Falls City SD	Niagara Falls	1	n/a	Southampton Union Free SD	Southampton
1	n/a	Hannibal Central SD	Hannibal	1	n/a	Niagara-Wheatfield Central SD	Niagara Falls	1	n/a	Southwestern Cent SD Jamestown	Jamestown
1	n/a	Harborfields Central SD	Greenlawn	1	n/a	Niskayuna Central SD	Schenectady	1	n/a	Spackenkill Union Free SD	Poughkeepsie
1	n/a	Harrison Central SD	Harrison	1	n/a	North Babylon Union Free SD	North Babylon	1	n/a	Spencerport Central SD	Spencerport
1	n/a	Hastings-On-Hudson Union Free SD	Hastings-on-Hud	1	n/a	North Bellmore Union Free SD	Bellmore	1	n/a	Springville-Griffith Inst Cent	Springville
1	n/a	Hauppauge Union Free SD	Hauppauge	1	n/a	North Colonie Central SD	Latham	1	n/a	Starpoint Central SD	Lockport
1	n/a	Haverstraw-Stony Point Cent SD	Garnerville	1	n/a	North Rose-Wolcott Central SD	Wolcott	1	n/a	Sullivan West Central SD	Callicoon
1	n/a	Hempstead Union Free SD	Hempstead	1	n/a	North Shore Central SD	Sea Cliff	1	n/a	Susquehanna Valley Central SD	Conklin
1	n/a	Hendrick Hudson Central SD	Montrose	1	n/a	North Syracuse Central SD	N Syracuse	1	n/a	Sweet Home Central SD	Amherst
1	n/a	Herricks Union Free SD	New Hyde Park	1	n/a	North Tonawanda City SD	N Tonawanda	1	n/a	Syosset Central SD	Syosset
1	n/a	Hewlett-Woodmere Union Free SD	Woodmere	1	n/a	Northeastern Clinton Central SD	Champlain	1	n/a	Syracuse City SD	Syracuse
1	n/a	Hicksville Union Free SD	Hicksville	1	n/a	Northport-East Northport UFSD	Northport	1	n/a	Taconic Hills Central SD	Craryville
1	n/a	Highland Central SD	Highland	1	n/a	Norwich City SD	Norwich	1	n/a	Three Village Central SD	East Setauket
1	n/a	Hilton Central SD	Hilton	1	n/a	Nyack Union Free SD	Nyack	1	n/a	Tonawanda City SD	Tonawanda
1	n/a	Holland Patent Central SD	Holland Patent	1	n/a	Nyc Alternative HS District	New York	1	n/a	Troy City SD	Troy
1	n/a	Homer Central SD	Homer	1	n/a	Oceanside Union Free SD	Oceanside	1	n/a	Union Free SD of the Tarrytowns	Sleepy Hollow
1	n/a	Honeoye Falls-Lima Central SD	Honeoye Falls	1	n/a	Ogdensburg City SD	Ogdensburg	1	n/a	Union-Endicott Central SD	Endicott
1	n/a	Hornell City SD	Hornell	1	n/a	Olean City SD	Olean	1	n/a	Uniondale Union Free SD	Uniondale
1	n/a	Horseheads Central SD	Horseheads	1	n/a	Oneida City SD	Oneida	1	n/a	Utica City SD	Utica
1	n/a	Hudson City SD	Hudson	1	n/a	Oneonta City SD	Oneonta	1	n/a	Valley Central SD (Montgomery)	Montgomery
1	n/a	Hudson Falls Central SD	Hudson Falls	1	n/a	Onteora Central SD	Boiceville	1	n/a	Valley Stream 13 Union Free SD	Valley Stream
1	n/a	Huntington Union Free SD	Huntington Stn	1	n/a	Orchard Park Central SD	Orchard Park	1	n/a	Valley Stream 30 Union Free SD	Valley Stream
1	n/a	Hyde Park Central SD	Poughkeepsie	1	n/a	Ossining Union Free SD	Ossining	1	n/a	Valley Stream Central High SD	Valley Stream
1	n/a	Ilion Central SD	Ilion	1	n/a	Oswego City SD	Oswego	1	n/a	Vestal Central SD	Vestal
1	n/a	Indian River Central SD	Philadelphia	1	n/a	Owego-Apalachin Central SD	Owego	1	n/a	Victor Central SD	Victor
1	n/a	Iroquois Central SD	Elma								

1	n/a	Wallkill Central SD	Wallkill
1	n/a	Wantagh Union Free SD	Wantagh
1	n/a	Wappingers Central SD	Wappingers Fls
1	n/a	Warwick Valley Central SD	Warwick
1	n/a	Washingtonville Central SD	Washingtonville
1	n/a	Waterloo Central SD	Waterloo
1	n/a	Watertown City SD	Watertown
1	n/a	Watkins Glen Central SD	Watkins Glen
1	n/a	Waverly Central SD	Waverly
1	n/a	Wayland-Cohocton Central SD	Wayland
1	n/a	Wayne Central SD	Ontario Center
1	n/a	Webster Central SD	Webster
1	n/a	West Babylon Union Free SD	West Babylon
1	n/a	West Genesee Central SD	Camillus
1	n/a	West Hempstead Union Free SD	W Hempstead
1	n/a	West Irondequoit Central SD	Rochester
1	n/a	West Islip Union Free SD	West Islip
1	n/a	West Seneca Central SD	West Seneca
1	n/a	Westbury Union Free SD	Old Westbury
1	n/a	Westhampton Beach Union Free SD	Westhampton Bch
1	n/a	Westhill Central SD	Syracuse
1	n/a	White Plains City SD	White Plains
1	n/a	Whitesboro Central SD	Yorkville
1	n/a	Whitney Point Central SD	Whitney Point
1	n/a	William Floyd Union Free SD	Mastic Beach
1	n/a	Williamsville Central SD	East Amherst
1	n/a	Wilson Central SD	Wilson
1	n/a	Windsor Central SD	Windsor
1	n/a	Wyandanch Union Free SD	Wyandanch
1	n/a	Yonkers City SD	Yonkers
1	n/a	Yorkshire-Pioneer Central SD	Yorkshire
1	n/a	Yorktown Central SD	Yorktown Hgts

Students Eligible for Reduced-Price Lunch

Rank	Percent	District Name	City
1	n/a	Adirondack Central SD	Boonville
1	n/a	Akron Central SD	Akron
1	n/a	Albany City SD	Albany
1	n/a	Albion Central SD	Albion
1	n/a	Alden Central SD	Alden
1	n/a	Altmar-Parish-Williamstown CSD	Parish
1	n/a	Amherst Central SD	Amherst
1	n/a	Amityville Union Free SD	Amityville
1	n/a	Amsterdam City SD	Amsterdam
1	n/a	Ardsley Union Free SD	Ardsley
1	n/a	Arlington Central SD	Poughkeepsie
1	n/a	Attica Central SD	Attica
1	n/a	Auburn City SD	Auburn
1	n/a	Averill Park Central SD	Averill Park
1	n/a	Babylon Union Free SD	Babylon
1	n/a	Baldwin Union Free SD	Baldwin
1	n/a	Baldwinsville Central SD	Baldwinsville
1	n/a	Ballston Spa Central SD	Ballston Spa
1	n/a	Batavia City SD	Batavia
1	n/a	Bath Central SD	Bath
1	n/a	Bay Shore Union Free SD	Bay Shore
1	n/a	Bayport-Blue Point Union Free SD	Bayport
1	n/a	Beacon City SD	Beacon
1	n/a	Bedford Central SD	Mount Kisco
1	n/a	Beekmantown Central SD	West Chazy
1	n/a	Bellmore-Merrick Central High SD	North Merrick
1	n/a	Bethlehem Central SD	Delmar
1	n/a	Bethpage Union Free SD	Bethpage
1	n/a	Binghamton City SD	Binghamton
1	n/a	Boces Eastern Suffolk	Patchogue
1	n/a	Boces Nassau	Garden City
1	n/a	Brentwood Union Free SD	Brentwood
1	n/a	Brewster Central SD	Brewster
1	n/a	Briarcliff Manor Union Free SD	Briarcliff Manor
1	n/a	Brighton Central SD	Rochester
1	n/a	Broadalbin-Perth Central SD	Broadalbin
1	n/a	Brockport Central SD	Brockport
1	n/a	Brookhaven-Comsewogue UFSD	Pt Jefferson Stn
1	n/a	Buffalo City SD	Buffalo
1	n/a	Burnt Hls-Ballston Lake Cent SD	Scotia
1	n/a	Byram Hills Central SD	Armonk
1	n/a	Cairo-Durham Central SD	Cairo
1	n/a	Camden Central SD	Camden
1	n/a	Canandaigua City SD	Canandaigua
1	n/a	Canastota Central SD	Canastota
1	n/a	Canton Central SD	Canton
1	n/a	Carle Place Union Free SD	Carle Place
1	n/a	Carmel Central SD	Patterson
1	n/a	Carthage Central SD	Carthage
1	n/a	Catskill Central SD	Catskill
1	n/a	Cazenovia Central SD	Cazenovia
1	n/a	Central Islip Union Free SD	Central Islip
1	n/a	Central Square Central SD	Central Square
1	n/a	Chappaqua Central SD	Chappaqua
1	n/a	Chatham Central SD	Chatham
1	n/a	Cheektowaga Central SD	Cheektowaga
1	n/a	Cheektowaga-Maryvale UFSD	Cheektowaga
1	n/a	Cheektowaga-Sloan Union Free SD	Sloan
1	n/a	Chenango Forks Central SD	Binghamton
1	n/a	Chenango Valley Central SD	Binghamton
1	n/a	Chittenango Central SD	Chittenango
1	n/a	Churchville-Chili Central SD	Churchville
1	n/a	Clarence Central SD	Clarence
1	n/a	Clarkstown Central SD	New City
1	n/a	Cleveland Hill Union Free SD	Cheektowaga
1	n/a	Clinton Central SD	Clinton
1	n/a	Cobleskill-Richmondville CSD	Cobleskill
1	n/a	Cohoes City SD	Cohoes
1	n/a	Cold Spring Harbor Central SD	Cold Sprg Harbor
1	n/a	Commack Union Free SD	E Northport
1	n/a	Connetquot Central SD	Bohemia
1	n/a	Copiague Union Free SD	Copiague
1	n/a	Corning City SD	Painted Post
1	n/a	Cornwall Central SD	Cornwall-on-Hud
1	n/a	Cortland City SD	Cortland
1	n/a	Coxsackie-Athens Central SD	Coxsackie
1	n/a	Croton-Harmon Union Free SD	Croton-On-Hud
1	n/a	Dansville Central SD	Dansville
1	n/a	Deer Park Union Free SD	Deer Park
1	n/a	Depew Union Free SD	Depew
1	n/a	Dover Union Free SD	Dover Plains
1	n/a	Dryden Central SD	Dryden
1	n/a	Dunkirk City SD	Dunkirk
1	n/a	East Aurora Union Free SD	East Aurora
1	n/a	East Greenbush Central SD	E Greenbush
1	n/a	East Hampton Union Free SD	East Hampton
1	n/a	East Irondequoit Central SD	Rochester
1	n/a	East Islip Union Free SD	Islip Terrace
1	n/a	East Meadow Union Free SD	Westbury
1	n/a	E Ramapo Central SD (Sprg Val)	Spring Valley
1	n/a	East Syracuse-Minoa Central SD	East Syracuse
1	n/a	East Williston Union Free SD	Old Westbury
1	n/a	Eastchester Union Free SD	Eastchester
1	n/a	Eden Central SD	Eden
1	n/a	Edgemont Union Free SD	Scarsdale
1	n/a	Ellenville Central SD	Ellenville
1	n/a	Elmira City SD	Elmira
1	n/a	Elmont Union Free SD	Elmont
1	n/a	Elwood Union Free SD	Greenlawn
1	n/a	Evans-Brant Cent SD (Lake Shore)	Angola
1	n/a	Fairport Central SD	Fairport
1	n/a	Farmingdale Union Free SD	Farmingdale
1	n/a	Fayetteville-Manlius Central SD	Manlius
1	n/a	Floral Park-Bellerose UFSD	Floral Park
1	n/a	Fonda-Fultonville Central SD	Fonda
1	n/a	Franklin Square Union Free SD	Franklin Square
1	n/a	Fredonia Central SD	Fredonia
1	n/a	Freeport Union Free SD	Freeport
1	n/a	Frontier Central SD	Hamburg
1	n/a	Fulton City SD	Fulton
1	n/a	Garden City Union Free SD	Garden City
1	n/a	Gates-Chili Central SD	Rochester
1	n/a	General Brown Central SD	Dexter
1	n/a	Geneva City SD	Geneva
1	n/a	Glen Cove City SD	Glen Cove
1	n/a	Glens Falls City SD	Glens Falls
1	n/a	Gloversville City SD	Gloversville
1	n/a	Gorham-Middlesex CSD (M Whitman)	Rushville
1	n/a	Goshen Central SD	Goshen
1	n/a	Gouverneur Central SD	Gouverneur
1	n/a	Gowanda Central SD	Gowanda
1	n/a	Grand Island Central SD	Grand Island
1	n/a	Great Neck Union Free SD	Great Neck
1	n/a	Greece Central SD	Rochester
1	n/a	Greenburgh Central SD	Hartsdale
1	n/a	Guilderland Central SD	Guilderland
1	n/a	Half Hollow Hills Central SD	Dix Hills
1	n/a	Hamburg Central SD	Hamburg
1	n/a	Hampton Bays Union Free SD	Hampton Bays
1	n/a	Hannibal Central SD	Hannibal
1	n/a	Harborfields Central SD	Greenlawn
1	n/a	Harrison Central SD	Harrison
1	n/a	Hastings-On-Hudson Union Free SD	Hastings-on-Hud
1	n/a	Hauppauge Union Free SD	Hauppauge
1	n/a	Haverstraw-Stony Point Cent SD	Garnerville
1	n/a	Hempstead Union Free SD	Hempstead
1	n/a	Hendrick Hudson Central SD	Montrose
1	n/a	Herricks Union Free SD	New Hyde Park
1	n/a	Hewlett-Woodmere Union Free SD	Woodmere
1	n/a	Hicksville Union Free SD	Hicksville
1	n/a	Highland Central SD	Highland
1	n/a	Hilton Central SD	Hilton
1	n/a	Holland Patent Central SD	Holland Patent
1	n/a	Homer Central SD	Homer
1	n/a	Honeoye Falls-Lima Central SD	Honeoye Falls
1	n/a	Hornell City SD	Hornell
1	n/a	Horseheads Central SD	Horseheads
1	n/a	Hudson City SD	Hudson
1	n/a	Hudson Falls Central SD	Hudson Falls
1	n/a	Huntington Union Free SD	Huntington Stn
1	n/a	Hyde Park Central SD	Poughkeepsie
1	n/a	Ilion Central SD	Ilion
1	n/a	Indian River Central SD	Philadelphia
1	n/a	Iroquois Central SD	Elma
1	n/a	Irvington Union Free SD	Irvington
1	n/a	Island Trees Union Free SD	Levittown
1	n/a	Islip Union Free SD	Islip
1	n/a	Ithaca City SD	Ithaca
1	n/a	Jamestown City SD	Jamestown
1	n/a	Jamesville-Dewitt Central SD	Dewitt
1	n/a	Jericho Union Free SD	Jericho
1	n/a	Johnson City Central SD	Johnson City
1	n/a	Johnstown City SD	Johnstown
1	n/a	Jordan-Elbridge Central SD	Jordan
1	n/a	Katonah-Lewisboro Union Free SD	South Salem
1	n/a	Kenmore-Tonawanda Union Free SD	Buffalo
1	n/a	Kinderhook Central SD	Valatie
1	n/a	Kings Park Central SD	Kings Park
1	n/a	Kingston City SD	Kingston
1	n/a	Lackawanna City SD	Lackawanna
1	n/a	Lakeland Central SD	Shrub Oak
1	n/a	Lancaster Central SD	Lancaster
1	n/a	Lansing Central SD	Lansing
1	n/a	Lansingburgh Central SD	Troy
1	n/a	Lawrence Union Free SD	Lawrence
1	n/a	Levittown Union Free SD	Levittown
1	n/a	Lewiston-Porter Central SD	Youngstown
1	n/a	Liberty Central SD	Liberty
1	n/a	Lindenhurst Union Free SD	Lindenhurst
1	n/a	Liverpool Central SD	Liverpool
1	n/a	Livonia Central SD	Livonia
1	n/a	Lockport City SD	Lockport
1	n/a	Locust Valley Central SD	Locust Valley
1	n/a	Long Beach City SD	Long Beach
1	n/a	Longwood Central SD	Middle Island
1	n/a	Lynbrook Union Free SD	Lynbrook
1	n/a	Mahopac Central SD	Mahopac
1	n/a	Maine-Endwell Central SD	Endwell
1	n/a	Malone Central SD	Malone
1	n/a	Malverne Union Free SD	Malverne
1	n/a	Mamaroneck Union Free SD	Mamaroneck
1	n/a	Manhasset Union Free SD	Manhasset
1	n/a	Marcellus Central SD	Marcellus
1	n/a	Marlboro Central SD	Marlboro
1	n/a	Massapequa Union Free SD	Massapequa
1	n/a	Massena Central SD	Massena
1	n/a	Mattituck-Cutchogue UFSD	Cutchogue
1	n/a	Medina Central SD	Medina
1	n/a	Merrick Union Free SD	Merrick
1	n/a	Mexico Central SD	Mexico
1	n/a	Middle Country Central SD	Centereach
1	n/a	Middletown City SD	Middletown
1	n/a	Miller Place Union Free SD	Miller Place
1	n/a	Mineola Union Free SD	Mineola
1	n/a	Minisink Valley Central SD	Slate Hill
1	n/a	Monroe-Woodbury Central SD	Central Valley
1	n/a	Monticello Central SD	Monticello
1	n/a	Mount Pleasant Central SD	Thornwood
1	n/a	Mount Sinai Union Free SD	Mount Sinai
1	n/a	Mount Vernon City SD	Mount Vernon
1	n/a	Nanuet Union Free SD	Nanuet
1	n/a	New Hartford Central SD	New Hartford
1	n/a	New Hyde Park-Garden City Park	New Hyde Park
1	n/a	New Paltz Central SD	New Paltz
1	n/a	New Rochelle City SD	New Rochelle
1	n/a	New York City Geographic Dist 9	Bronx
1	n/a	New York City Geographic Dist 15	Brooklyn
1	n/a	New York City Public Schools	Brooklyn
1	n/a	Newark Central SD	Newark
1	n/a	Newburgh City SD	Newburgh
1	n/a	Newfane Central SD	Newfane
1	n/a	Niagara Falls City SD	Niagara Falls
1	n/a	Niagara-Wheatfield Central SD	Niagara Falls
1	n/a	Niskayuna Central SD	Schenectady
1	n/a	North Babylon Union Free SD	North Babylon
1	n/a	North Bellmore Union Free SD	Bellmore
1	n/a	North Colonie Central SD	Latham
1	n/a	North Rose-Wolcott Central SD	Wolcott
1	n/a	North Shore Central SD	Sea Cliff
1	n/a	North Syracuse Central SD	N Syracuse
1	n/a	North Tonawanda City SD	N Tonawanda
1	n/a	Northeastern Clinton Central SD	Champlain
1	n/a	Northport-East Northport UFSD	Northport
1	n/a	Norwich City SD	Norwich
1	n/a	Nyack Union Free SD	Nyack
1	n/a	Nyc Alternative HS District	New York
1	n/a	Oceanside Union Free SD	Oceanside
1	n/a	Ogdensburg City SD	Ogdensburg
1	n/a	Olean City SD	Olean
1	n/a	Oneida City SD	Oneida

1	n/a	Oneonta City SD	Oneonta
1	n/a	Onteora Central SD	Boiceville
1	n/a	Orchard Park Central SD	Orchard Park
1	n/a	Ossining Union Free SD	Ossining
1	n/a	Oswego City SD	Oswego
1	n/a	Owego-Apalachin Central SD	Owego
1	n/a	Oyster Bay-East Norwich CSD	Oyster Bay
1	n/a	Palmyra-Macedon Central SD	Palmyra
1	n/a	Patchogue-Medford Union Free SD	Patchogue
1	n/a	Pearl River Union Free SD	Pearl River
1	n/a	Peekskill City SD	Peekskill
1	n/a	Pelham Union Free SD	Pelham
1	n/a	Penfield Central SD	Penfield
1	n/a	Penn Yan Central SD	Penn Yan
1	n/a	Peru Central SD	Peru
1	n/a	Phelps-Clifton Springs Cent SD	Clifton Spgs
1	n/a	Phoenix Central SD	Phoenix
1	n/a	Pine Bush Central SD	Pine Bush
1	n/a	Pittsford Central SD	Pittsford
1	n/a	Plainedge Union Free SD	N Massapequa
1	n/a	Plainview-Old Bethpage Cent SD	Plainview
1	n/a	Plattsburgh City SD	Plattsburgh
1	n/a	Pleasantville Union Free SD	Pleasantville
1	n/a	Port Chester-Rye Union Free SD	Port Chester
1	n/a	Port Jervis City SD	Port Jervis
1	n/a	Port Washington Union Free SD	Pt Washington
1	n/a	Poughkeepsie City SD	Poughkeepsie
1	n/a	Putnam Valley Central SD	Putnam Valley
1	n/a	Queensbury Union Free SD	Queensbury
1	n/a	Ramapo Central SD (Suffern)	Hillburn
1	n/a	Ravena-Coeymans-Selkirk CSD	Selkirk
1	n/a	Red Hook Central SD	Red Hook
1	n/a	Riverhead Central SD	Riverhead
1	n/a	Rochester City SD	Rochester
1	n/a	Rockville Centre Union Free SD	Rockville Ctre
1	n/a	Rocky Point Union Free SD	Rocky Point
1	n/a	Rome City SD	Rome
1	n/a	Rondout Valley Central SD	Accord
1	n/a	Roosevelt Union Free SD	Roosevelt
1	n/a	Roslyn Union Free SD	Roslyn
1	n/a	Rotterdam-Mohonasen Central SD	Schenectady
1	n/a	Royalton-Hartland Central SD	Middleport
1	n/a	Rush-Henrietta Central SD	Henrietta
1	n/a	Rye City SD	Rye
1	n/a	Sachem Central SD	Holbrook
1	n/a	Salamanca City SD	Salamanca
1	n/a	Salmon River Central SD	Ft Covington
1	n/a	Saranac Central SD	Dannemora
1	n/a	Saranac Lake Central SD	Saranac Lake
1	n/a	Saratoga Springs City SD	Saratoga Spgs
1	n/a	Saugerties Central SD	Saugerties
1	n/a	Sayville Union Free SD	Sayville
1	n/a	Scarsdale Union Free SD	Scarsdale
1	n/a	Schalmont Central SD	Schenectady
1	n/a	Schenectady City SD	Schenectady
1	n/a	Schuylerville Central SD	Schuylerville
1	n/a	Scotia-Glenville Central SD	Scotia
1	n/a	Seaford Union Free SD	Seaford
1	n/a	Sewanhaka Central High SD	Floral Park
1	n/a	Shenendehowa Central SD	Clifton Park
1	n/a	Sherburne-Earlville Central SD	Sherburne
1	n/a	Sherrill City SD	Verona
1	n/a	Shoreham-Wading River Central SD	Shoreham
1	n/a	Skaneateles Central SD	Skaneateles
1	n/a	Smithtown Central SD	Smithtown
1	n/a	Solvay Union Free SD	Solvay
1	n/a	Somers Central SD	Lincolndale
1	n/a	South Colonie Central SD	Albany
1	n/a	South Country Central SD	E Patchogue
1	n/a	South Glens Falls Central SD	S Glens Falls
1	n/a	South Huntington Union Free SD	Huntington Stn
1	n/a	South Jefferson Central SD	Adams Center
1	n/a	South Orangetown Central SD	Blauvelt
1	n/a	Southampton Union Free SD	Southampton
1	n/a	Southwestern Cent SD Jamestown	Jamestown
1	n/a	Spackenkill Union Free SD	Poughkeepsie
1	n/a	Spencerport Central SD	Spencerport
1	n/a	Springville-Griffith Inst Cent	Springville
1	n/a	Starpoint Central SD	Lockport
1	n/a	Sullivan West Central SD	Callicoon
1	n/a	Susquehanna Valley Central SD	Conklin
1	n/a	Sweet Home Central SD	Amherst
1	n/a	Syosset Central SD	Syosset
1	n/a	Syracuse City SD	Syracuse
1	n/a	Taconic Hills Central SD	Craryville
1	n/a	Three Village Central SD	East Setauket
1	n/a	Tonawanda City SD	Tonawanda
1	n/a	Troy City SD	Troy
1	n/a	Union Free SD of the Tarrytowns	Sleepy Hollow
1	n/a	Union-Endicott Central SD	Endicott
1	n/a	Uniondale Union Free SD	Uniondale
1	n/a	Utica City SD	Utica
1	n/a	Valley Central SD (Montgomery)	Montgomery
1	n/a	Valley Stream 13 Union Free SD	Valley Stream
1	n/a	Valley Stream 30 Union Free SD	Valley Stream
1	n/a	Valley Stream Central High SD	Valley Stream
1	n/a	Vestal Central SD	Vestal
1	n/a	Victor Central SD	Victor
1	n/a	Wallkill Central SD	Wallkill
1	n/a	Wantagh Union Free SD	Wantagh
1	n/a	Wappingers Central SD	Wappingers Fls
1	n/a	Warwick Valley Central SD	Warwick
1	n/a	Washingtonville Central SD	Washingtonville
1	n/a	Waterloo Central SD	Waterloo
1	n/a	Watertown City SD	Watertown
1	n/a	Watkins Glen Central SD	Watkins Glen
1	n/a	Waverly Central SD	Waverly
1	n/a	Wayland-Cohocton Central SD	Wayland
1	n/a	Wayne Central SD	Ontario Center
1	n/a	Webster Central SD	Webster
1	n/a	West Babylon Union Free SD	West Babylon
1	n/a	West Genesee Central SD	Camillus
1	n/a	West Hempstead Union Free SD	W Hempstead
1	n/a	West Irondequoit Central SD	Rochester
1	n/a	West Islip Union Free SD	West Islip
1	n/a	West Seneca Central SD	West Seneca
1	n/a	Westbury Union Free SD	Old Westbury
1	n/a	Westhampton Beach Union Free SD	Westhampton Bch
1	n/a	Westhill Central SD	Syracuse
1	n/a	White Plains City SD	White Plains
1	n/a	Whitesboro Central SD	Yorkville
1	n/a	Whitney Point Central SD	Whitney Point
1	n/a	William Floyd Union Free SD	Mastic Beach
1	n/a	Williamsville Central SD	East Amherst
1	n/a	Wilson Central SD	Wilson
1	n/a	Windsor Central SD	Windsor
1	n/a	Wyandanch Union Free SD	Wyandanch
1	n/a	Yonkers City SD	Yonkers
1	n/a	Yorkshire-Pioneer Central SD	Yorkshire
1	n/a	Yorktown Central SD	Yorktown Hgts

Student/Teacher Ratio

Rank	Ratio	District Name	City
1	19.3	Coxsackie-Athens Central SD	Coxsackie
2	16.4	Broadalbin-Perth Central SD	Broadalbin
3	16.3	William Floyd Union Free SD	Mastic Beach
4	16.2	Highland Central SD	Highland
4	16.2	Sewanhaka Central High SD	Floral Park
6	16.1	Starpoint Central SD	Lockport
7	16.0	Arlington Central SD	Poughkeepsie
8	15.9	Floral Park-Bellerose UFSD	Floral Park
9	15.7	Copiague Union Free SD	Copiague
9	15.7	Hempstead Union Free SD	Hempstead
11	15.6	Bellmore-Merrick Central High SD	North Merrick
11	15.6	Middle Country Central SD	Centereach
11	15.6	Mount Vernon City SD	Mount Vernon
11	15.6	Wappingers Central SD	Wappingers Fls
15	15.5	Brentwood Union Free SD	Brentwood
15	15.5	Niagara Falls City SD	Niagara Falls
15	15.5	Port Jervis City SD	Port Jervis
18	15.4	Elmont Union Free SD	Elmont
18	15.4	Rocky Point Union Free SD	Rocky Point
20	15.3	Lancaster Central SD	Lancaster
20	15.3	Queensbury Union Free SD	Queensbury
20	15.3	Rotterdam-Mohonasen Central SD	Schenectady
23	15.2	Cornwall Central SD	Cornwall-on-Hud
23	15.2	Dover Union Free SD	Dover Plains
23	15.2	Islip Union Free SD	Islip
23	15.2	Minisink Valley Central SD	Slate Hill
23	15.2	West Irondequoit Central SD	Rochester
28	15.1	Marcellus Central SD	Marcellus
28	15.1	North Syracuse Central SD	N Syracuse
28	15.1	Warwick Valley Central SD	Warwick
31	15.0	Elwood Union Free SD	Greenlawn
31	15.0	Iroquois Central SD	Elma
31	15.0	Patchogue-Medford Union Free SD	Patchogue
31	15.0	Riverhead Central SD	Riverhead
31	15.0	Saugerties Central SD	Saugerties
31	15.0	Utica City SD	Utica
31	15.0	Washingtonville Central SD	Washingtonville
38	14.9	Longwood Central SD	Middle Island
38	14.9	West Genesee Central SD	Camillus
40	14.8	Johnstown City SD	Johnstown
40	14.8	New Hyde Park-Garden City Park	New Hyde Park
40	14.8	Wyandanch Union Free SD	Wyandanch
43	14.7	Baldwinsville Central SD	Baldwinsville
43	14.7	Bethlehem Central SD	Delmar
43	14.7	Middletown City SD	Middletown
43	14.7	Miller Place Union Free SD	Miller Place
43	14.7	New Rochelle City SD	New Rochelle
43	14.7	Shenendehowa Central SD	Clifton Park
49	14.6	Akron Central SD	Akron
49	14.6	Albion Central SD	Albion
49	14.6	Beacon City SD	Beacon
49	14.6	Central Square Central SD	Central Square
49	14.6	General Brown Central SD	Dexter
49	14.6	New York City Public Schools	Brooklyn
49	14.6	Newburgh City SD	Newburgh
49	14.6	Wallkill Central SD	Wallkill
57	14.5	Carmel Central SD	Patterson
57	14.5	Franklin Square Union Free SD	Franklin Square
57	14.5	Gouverneur Central SD	Gouverneur
57	14.5	Horseheads Central SD	Horseheads
57	14.5	Monroe-Woodbury Central SD	Central Valley
57	14.5	Pine Bush Central SD	Pine Bush
57	14.5	Plainedge Union Free SD	N Massapequa
64	14.4	Ballston Spa Central SD	Ballston Spa
64	14.4	Brookhaven-Comsewogue UFSD	Pt Jefferson Stn
64	14.4	East Islip Union Free SD	Islip Terrace
64	14.4	Eden Central SD	Eden
64	14.4	Harborfields Central SD	Greenlawn
64	14.4	Liverpool Central SD	Liverpool
64	14.4	Mount Sinai Union Free SD	Mount Sinai
64	14.4	Newfane Central SD	Newfane
64	14.4	Watertown City SD	Watertown
64	14.4	West Babylon Union Free SD	West Babylon
74	14.3	Hudson Falls Central SD	Hudson Falls
74	14.3	South Jefferson Central SD	Adams Center
76	14.2	Burnt Hls-Ballston Lake Cent SD	Scotia
76	14.2	East Aurora Union Free SD	East Aurora
76	14.2	Fayetteville-Manlius Central SD	Manlius
76	14.2	Hyde Park Central SD	Poughkeepsie
76	14.2	Lindenhurst Union Free SD	Lindenhurst
76	14.2	Massena Central SD	Massena
76	14.2	Niskayuna Central SD	Schenectady
76	14.2	Victor Central SD	Victor
76	14.2	Waverly Central SD	Waverly
85	14.1	Fairport Central SD	Fairport
85	14.1	Greece Central SD	Rochester
85	14.1	North Babylon Union Free SD	North Babylon
85	14.1	North Colonie Central SD	Latham
85	14.1	Scotia-Glenville Central SD	Scotia
90	14.0	Corning City SD	Painted Post
90	14.0	Mexico Central SD	Mexico
90	14.0	Westhill Central SD	Syracuse
93	13.9	Canastota Central SD	Canastota
93	13.9	Carthage Central SD	Carthage
93	13.9	Clarence Central SD	Clarence
93	13.9	Goshen Central SD	Goshen
93	13.9	Grand Island Central SD	Grand Island
93	13.9	Kings Park Central SD	Kings Park
93	13.9	Kingston City SD	Kingston
93	13.9	North Bellmore Union Free SD	Bellmore
93	13.9	Port Chester-Rye Union Free SD	Port Chester
93	13.9	Sherrill City SD	Verona
93	13.9	Smithtown Central SD	Smithtown
93	13.9	Springville-Griffith Inst Cent	Springville
93	13.9	Valley Central SD (Montgomery)	Montgomery
93	13.9	Yonkers City SD	Yonkers
107	13.8	Brockport Central SD	Brockport
107	13.8	Cairo-Durham Central SD	Cairo
107	13.8	Chatham Central SD	Chatham
107	13.8	Connetquot Central SD	Bohemia
107	13.8	Pearl River Union Free SD	Pearl River
107	13.8	Sayville Union Free SD	Sayville
107	13.8	Schenectady City SD	Schenectady
107	13.8	Wantagh Union Free SD	Wantagh
107	13.8	West Islip Union Free SD	West Islip
107	13.8	West Seneca Central SD	West Seneca
117	13.7	Chenango Valley Central SD	Binghamton
117	13.7	Half Hollow Hills Central SD	Dix Hills
117	13.7	Hannibal Central SD	Hannibal
117	13.7	Honeoye Falls-Lima Central SD	Honeoye Falls
117	13.7	North Tonawanda City SD	N Tonawanda
117	13.7	Poughkeepsie City SD	Poughkeepsie
117	13.7	Troy City SD	Troy
117	13.7	Westbury Union Free SD	Old Westbury
125	13.6	Buffalo City SD	Buffalo
125	13.6	Cheektowaga Central SD	Cheektowaga
125	13.6	Clarkstown Central SD	New City
125	13.6	East Irondequoit Central SD	Rochester
125	13.6	Freeport Union Free SD	Freeport
125	13.6	Hicksville Union Free SD	Hicksville
125	13.6	Ilion Central SD	Ilion
125	13.6	Lansingburgh Central SD	Troy
125	13.6	Putnam Valley Central SD	Putnam Valley
125	13.6	Red Hook Central SD	Red Hook
125	13.6	Southwestern Cent SD Jamestown	Jamestown
125	13.6	Williamsville Central SD	East Amherst
137	13.5	Alden Central SD	Alden
137	13.5	Chittenango Central SD	Chittenango
137	13.5	Churchville-Chili Central SD	Churchville
137	13.5	East Greenbush Central SD	E Greenbush
137	13.5	Lakeland Central SD	Shrub Oak
137	13.5	Massapequa Union Free SD	Massapequa
137	13.5	New Paltz Central SD	New Paltz
137	13.5	Niagara-Wheatfield Central SD	Niagara Falls

137	13.5	Oceanside Union Free SD	Oceanside
137	13.5	Oswego City SD	Oswego
137	13.5	Pleasantville Union Free SD	Pleasantville
137	13.5	Saratoga Springs City SD	Saratoga Spgs
137	13.5	Watkins Glen Central SD	Watkins Glen
150	13.4	Brewster Central SD	Brewster
150	13.4	Camden Central SD	Camden
150	13.4	Central Islip Union Free SD	Central Islip
150	13.4	Cheektowaga-Sloan Union Free SD	Sloan
150	13.4	Elmira City SD	Elmira
150	13.4	Fulton City SD	Fulton
150	13.4	Holland Patent Central SD	Holland Patent
150	13.4	Kinderhook Central SD	Valatie
150	13.4	Oneida City SD	Oneida
150	13.4	South Glens Falls Central SD	S Glens Falls
150	13.4	South Huntington Union Free SD	Huntington Stn
150	13.4	Webster Central SD	Webster
162	13.3	Bay Shore Union Free SD	Bay Shore
162	13.3	Cheektowaga-Maryvale UFSD	Cheektowaga
162	13.3	Croton-Harmon Union Free SD	Croton-On-Hud
162	13.3	East Meadow Union Free SD	Westbury
162	13.3	Fonda-Fultonville Central SD	Fonda
162	13.3	Guilderland Central SD	Guilderland
162	13.3	Katonah-Lewisboro Union Free SD	South Salem
162	13.3	Northeastern Clinton Central SD	Champlain
162	13.3	Seaford Union Free SD	Seaford
162	13.3	South Country Central SD	E Patchogue
162	13.3	Three Village Central SD	East Setauket
162	13.3	Valley Stream Central High SD	Valley Stream
162	13.3	Waterloo Central SD	Waterloo
162	13.3	Windsor Central SD	Windsor
162	13.3	Yorktown Central SD	Yorktown Hgts
177	13.2	Auburn City SD	Auburn
177	13.2	Chenango Forks Central SD	Binghamton
177	13.2	Cold Spring Harbor Central SD	Cold Sprg Harbor
177	13.2	Commack Union Free SD	E Northport
177	13.2	Edgemont Union Free SD	Scarsdale
177	13.2	Garden City Union Free SD	Garden City
177	13.2	Haverstraw-Stony Point Cent SD	Garnerville
177	13.2	Kenmore-Tonawanda Union Free SD	Buffalo
177	13.2	Mahopac Central SD	Mahopac
177	13.2	Marlboro Central SD	Marlboro
177	13.2	Sachem Central SD	Holbrook
177	13.2	Saranac Central SD	Dannemora
177	13.2	Schalmont Central SD	Schenectady
177	13.2	Vestal Central SD	Vestal
177	13.2	Whitesboro Central SD	Yorkville
192	13.1	Bath Central SD	Bath
192	13.1	Cazenovia Central SD	Cazenovia
192	13.1	Frontier Central SD	Hamburg
192	13.1	Gates-Chili Central SD	Rochester
192	13.1	Lewiston-Porter Central SD	Youngstown
192	13.1	Merrick Union Free SD	Merrick
192	13.1	Olean City SD	Olean
192	13.1	Orchard Park Central SD	Orchard Park
192	13.1	Pittsford Central SD	Pittsford
192	13.1	Spencerport Central SD	Spencerport
202	13.0	Averill Park Central SD	Averill Park
202	13.0	Byram Hills Central SD	Armonk
202	13.0	Canandaigua City SD	Canandaigua
202	13.0	Cleveland Hill Union Free SD	Cheektowaga
202	13.0	Clinton Central SD	Clinton
202	13.0	Ellenville Central SD	Ellenville
202	13.0	Lansing Central SD	Lansing
202	13.0	Levittown Union Free SD	Levittown
202	13.0	Maine-Endwell Central SD	Endwell
202	13.0	Ossining Union Free SD	Ossining
202	13.0	Owego-Apalachin Central SD	Owego
202	13.0	Peekskill City SD	Peekskill
202	13.0	Skaneateles Central SD	Skaneateles
202	13.0	Taconic Hills Central SD	Craryville
202	13.0	Union-Endicott Central SD	Endicott
202	13.0	West Hempstead Union Free SD	W Hempstead
202	13.0	Yorkshire-Pioneer Central SD	Yorkshire
219	12.9	Island Trees Union Free SD	Levittown
219	12.9	Liberty Central SD	Liberty
219	12.9	Mamaroneck Union Free SD	Mamaroneck
219	12.9	New Hartford Central SD	New Hartford
219	12.9	Rome City SD	Rome
219	12.9	Somers Central SD	Lincolndale
219	12.9	South Colonie Central SD	Albany
226	12.8	Babylon Union Free SD	Babylon
226	12.8	Brighton Central SD	Rochester
226	12.8	Glens Falls City SD	Glens Falls
226	12.8	Hauppauge Union Free SD	Hauppauge
226	12.8	Hilton Central SD	Hilton
226	12.8	Long Beach City SD	Long Beach
226	12.8	Pelham Union Free SD	Pelham
226	12.8	Phelps-Clifton Springs Cent SD	Clifton Spgs
226	12.8	Rondout Valley Central SD	Accord
226	12.8	Schuylerville Central SD	Schuylerville
226	12.8	Solvay Union Free SD	Solvay
226	12.8	Union Free SD of the Tarrytowns	Sleepy Hollow
238	12.7	Amsterdam City SD	Amsterdam
238	12.7	Ardsley Union Free SD	Ardsley
238	12.7	Attica Central SD	Attica
238	12.7	Depew Union Free SD	Depew
238	12.7	E Ramapo Central SD (Sprg Val)	Spring Valley
238	12.7	Lockport City SD	Lockport
238	12.7	Valley Stream 30 Union Free SD	Valley Stream
245	12.6	Albany City SD	Albany
245	12.6	Baldwin Union Free SD	Baldwin
245	12.6	Canton Central SD	Canton
245	12.6	Gorham-Middlesex CSD (M Whitman)	Rushville
245	12.6	Gowanda Central SD	Gowanda
245	12.6	Newark Central SD	Newark
245	12.6	Royalton-Hartland Central SD	Middleport
245	12.6	Sweet Home Central SD	Amherst
253	12.5	Amherst Central SD	Amherst
253	12.5	Eastchester Union Free SD	Eastchester
253	12.5	Glen Cove City SD	Glen Cove
253	12.5	Homer Central SD	Homer
253	12.5	Ramapo Central SD (Suffern)	Hillburn
253	12.5	South Orangetown Central SD	Blauvelt
253	12.5	Wayne Central SD	Ontario Center
253	12.5	Wilson Central SD	Wilson
261	12.4	Bethpage Union Free SD	Bethpage
261	12.4	Cortland City SD	Cortland
261	12.4	Gloversville City SD	Gloversville
261	12.4	Hamburg Central SD	Hamburg
261	12.4	Hampton Bays Union Free SD	Hampton Bays
261	12.4	Johnson City Central SD	Johnson City
261	12.4	Jordan-Elbridge Central SD	Jordan
261	12.4	Peru Central SD	Peru
261	12.4	Ravena-Coeymans-Selkirk CSD	Selkirk
261	12.4	Syracuse City SD	Syracuse
271	12.3	Catskill Central SD	Catskill
271	12.3	Hendrick Hudson Central SD	Montrose
271	12.3	Irvington Union Free SD	Irvington
271	12.3	Lynbrook Union Free SD	Lynbrook
271	12.3	Oneonta City SD	Oneonta
271	12.3	Onteora Central SD	Boiceville
271	12.3	Roslyn Union Free SD	Roslyn
271	12.3	Rye City SD	Rye
271	12.3	Scarsdale Union Free SD	Scarsdale
271	12.3	Shoreham-Wading River Central SD	Shoreham
271	12.3	Tonawanda City SD	Tonawanda
282	12.2	Cobleskill-Richmondville CSD	Cobleskill
282	12.2	Cohoes City SD	Cohoes
282	12.2	Farmingdale Union Free SD	Farmingdale
282	12.2	Rochester City SD	Rochester
282	12.2	Spackenkill Union Free SD	Poughkeepsie
282	12.2	Valley Stream 13 Union Free SD	Valley Stream
282	12.2	White Plains City SD	White Plains
282	12.2	Whitney Point Central SD	Whitney Point
290	12.1	Bayport-Blue Point Union Free SD	Bayport
290	12.1	Bedford Central SD	Mount Kisco
290	12.1	Dansville Central SD	Dansville
290	12.1	Livonia Central SD	Livonia
290	12.1	Penfield Central SD	Penfield
295	12.0	Amityville Union Free SD	Amityville
295	12.0	Evans-Brant Cent SD (Lake Shore)	Angola
295	12.0	Hudson City SD	Hudson
295	12.0	Ithaca City SD	Ithaca
295	12.0	Jamesville-Dewitt Central SD	Dewitt
295	12.0	Nanuet Union Free SD	Nanuet
295	12.0	Ogdensburg City SD	Ogdensburg
295	12.0	Palmyra-Macedon Central SD	Palmyra
295	12.0	Penn Yan Central SD	Penn Yan
295	12.0	Wayland-Cohocton Central SD	Wayland
305	11.9	Altmar-Parish-Williamstown CSD	Parish
305	11.9	East Syracuse-Minoa Central SD	East Syracuse
305	11.9	Medina Central SD	Medina
305	11.9	Phoenix Central SD	Phoenix
305	11.9	Uniondale Union Free SD	Uniondale
310	11.8	Batavia City SD	Batavia
310	11.8	East Hampton Union Free SD	East Hampton
310	11.8	Hewlett-Woodmere Union Free SD	Woodmere
310	11.8	Norwich City SD	Norwich
310	11.8	Rush-Henrietta Central SD	Henrietta
310	11.8	Salamanca City SD	Salamanca
316	11.7	East Williston Union Free SD	Old Westbury
316	11.7	Malone Central SD	Malone
316	11.7	Saranac Lake Central SD	Saranac Lake
316	11.7	Susquehanna Valley Central SD	Conklin
320	11.6	Binghamton City SD	Binghamton
320	11.6	Briarcliff Manor Union Free SD	Briarcliff Manor
320	11.6	Chappaqua Central SD	Chappaqua
320	11.6	Monticello Central SD	Monticello
320	11.6	Northport-East Northport UFSD	Northport
320	11.6	Nyack Union Free SD	Nyack
320	11.6	Roosevelt Union Free SD	Roosevelt
327	11.5	Beekmantown Central SD	West Chazy
327	11.5	Deer Park Union Free SD	Deer Park
327	11.5	Hornell City SD	Hornell
327	11.5	Jamestown City SD	Jamestown
327	11.5	Lackawanna City SD	Lackawanna
327	11.5	Salmon River Central SD	Ft Covington
333	11.4	Geneva City SD	Geneva
333	11.4	Huntington Union Free SD	Huntington Stn
333	11.4	Indian River Central SD	Philadelphia
333	11.4	Malverne Union Free SD	Malverne
333	11.4	Port Washington Union Free SD	Pt Washington
338	11.3	Adirondack Central SD	Boonville
338	11.3	Locust Valley Central SD	Locust Valley
338	11.3	Manhasset Union Free SD	Manhasset
338	11.3	Mattituck-Cutchogue UFSD	Cutchogue
338	11.3	Plainview-Old Bethpage Cent SD	Plainview
338	11.3	Sullivan West Central SD	Callicoon
344	11.2	Greenburgh Central SD	Hartsdale
344	11.2	Harrison Central SD	Harrison
344	11.2	Herricks Union Free SD	New Hyde Park
347	11.1	Fredonia Central SD	Fredonia
347	11.1	North Rose-Wolcott Central SD	Wolcott
347	11.1	North Shore Central SD	Sea Cliff
350	11.0	Hastings-On-Hudson Union Free SD	Hastings-on-Hud
350	11.0	Syosset Central SD	Syosset
352	10.9	Mount Pleasant Central SD	Thornwood
353	10.8	Mineola Union Free SD	Mineola
353	10.8	Oyster Bay-East Norwich CSD	Oyster Bay
353	10.8	Rockville Centre Union Free SD	Rockville Ctre
356	10.7	Dryden Central SD	Dryden
356	10.7	Great Neck Union Free SD	Great Neck
358	10.6	Sherburne-Earlville Central SD	Sherburne
359	10.5	Westhampton Beach Union Free SD	Westhampton Bch
360	10.4	Carle Place Union Free SD	Carle Place
361	10.3	Plattsburgh City SD	Plattsburgh
362	10.2	Southampton Union Free SD	Southampton
363	10.1	Dunkirk City SD	Dunkirk
363	10.1	Jericho Union Free SD	Jericho
363	10.1	Lawrence Union Free SD	Lawrence
366	3.8	Boces Nassau	Garden City
367	3.2	Boces Eastern Suffolk	Patchogue
368	n/a	New York City Geographic Dist 9	Bronx
368	n/a	New York City Geographic Dist 15	Brooklyn
368	n/a	Nyc Alternative HS District	New York

Student/Librarian Ratio

Rank	Ratio	District Name	City
1	2,644.5	Mahopac Central SD	Mahopac
2	2,075.0	Highland Central SD	Highland
3	1,942.0	Franklin Square Union Free SD	Franklin Square
4	1,934.0	Putnam Valley Central SD	Putnam Valley
5	1,819.0	Wallkill Central SD	Wallkill
6	1,818.0	Islip Union Free SD	Islip
7	1,803.0	Rockville Centre Union Free SD	Rockville Ctre
8	1,794.0	Ilion Central SD	Ilion
9	1,786.0	Waverly Central SD	Waverly
10	1,747.2	Niagara Falls City SD	Niagara Falls
11	1,657.0	Northeastern Clinton Central SD	Champlain
12	1,638.8	Baldwin Union Free SD	Baldwin
13	1,566.8	Troy City SD	Troy
14	1,549.0	Croton-Harmon Union Free SD	Croton-On-Hud
15	1,548.0	Adirondack Central SD	Boonville
16	1,531.0	Cheektowaga-Sloan Union Free SD	Sloan
17	1,504.0	Wilson Central SD	Wilson
18	1,475.5	New York City Public Schools	Brooklyn
19	1,341.0	Mexico Central SD	Mexico
20	1,304.8	Monticello Central SD	Monticello
21	1,283.2	Sayville Union Free SD	Sayville
22	1,264.5	Pelham Union Free SD	Pelham
23	1,256.0	Dryden Central SD	Dryden
24	1,249.5	Union Free SD of the Tarrytowns	Sleepy Hollow
25	1,244.4	White Plains City SD	White Plains
26	1,235.2	William Floyd Union Free SD	Mastic Beach
27	1,209.0	Hudson Falls Central SD	Hudson Falls
28	1,204.3	Beacon City SD	Beacon
29	1,189.5	South Country Central SD	E Patchogue
30	1,166.4	Bellmore-Merrick Central High SD	North Merrick
31	1,156.4	Carmel Central SD	Patterson
32	1,141.5	Valley Stream Central High SD	Valley Stream
33	1,135.8	Minisink Valley Central SD	Slate Hill
34	1,110.3	Hilton Central SD	Hilton
35	1,107.1	Brentwood Union Free SD	Brentwood
36	1,097.3	South Glens Falls Central SD	S Glens Falls
37	1,091.7	Yonkers City SD	Yonkers
38	1,087.6	Elmira City SD	Elmira
39	1,087.0	Newfane Central SD	Newfane
40	1,084.0	Johnstown City SD	Johnstown
41	1,063.0	Ossining Union Free SD	Ossining
42	1,057.3	Middle Country Central SD	Centereach
43	1,056.9	Harrison Central SD	Harrison
44	1,050.5	Dunkirk City SD	Dunkirk
45	1,037.5	Garden City Union Free SD	Garden City
46	1,033.5	Dover Union Free SD	Dover Plains
47	1,027.0	Bath Central SD	Bath
48	1,022.0	South Jefferson Central SD	Adams Center

PROFILES OF NEW YORK / School District Rankings 633

49	1,021.2	Washingtonville Central SD	Washingtonville
50	1,021.1	Port Chester-Rye Union Free SD	Port Chester
51	1,010.0	Miller Place Union Free SD	Miller Place
52	998.6	Auburn City SD	Auburn
53	996.7	Utica City SD	Utica
54	983.5	Irvington Union Free SD	Irvington
55	976.5	Queensbury Union Free SD	Queensbury
56	973.7	Goshen Central SD	Goshen
57	966.4	Cheektowaga Central SD	Cheektowaga
58	963.0	Central Islip Union Free SD	Central Islip
59	960.7	Roosevelt Union Free SD	Roosevelt
60	951.3	New Rochelle City SD	New Rochelle
61	949.3	Starpoint Central SD	Lockport
62	941.0	Liberty Central SD	Liberty
63	939.6	Middletown City SD	Middletown
64	932.3	Albion Central SD	Albion
65	929.6	Mount Sinai Union Free SD	Mount Sinai
66	922.0	Eden Central SD	Eden
67	920.0	Attica Central SD	Attica
68	913.5	Wayland-Cohocton Central SD	Wayland
69	907.0	Buffalo City SD	Buffalo
70	906.5	Cairo-Durham Central SD	Cairo
71	905.3	East Islip Union Free SD	Islip Terrace
72	904.2	Ballston Spa Central SD	Ballston Spa
73	904.0	Newburgh City SD	Newburgh
74	902.0	Seaford Union Free SD	Seaford
75	901.2	Ardsley Union Free SD	Ardsley
76	898.5	Rocky Point Union Free SD	Rocky Point
77	896.5	Waterloo Central SD	Waterloo
78	895.5	Brighton Central SD	Rochester
79	893.3	Eastchester Union Free SD	Eastchester
79	893.3	Freeport Union Free SD	Freeport
81	892.8	Copiague Union Free SD	Copiague
82	890.0	Harborfields Central SD	Greenlawn
82	890.0	Haverstraw-Stony Point Cent SD	Garnerville
84	889.0	Victor Central SD	Victor
85	887.3	Three Village Central SD	East Setauket
85	887.3	Yorkshire-Pioneer Central SD	Yorkshire
87	884.5	Hampton Bays Union Free SD	Hampton Bays
88	878.3	Half Hollow Hills Central SD	Dix Hills
89	876.0	Southwestern Cent SD Jamestown	Jamestown
90	871.5	Gouverneur Central SD	Gouverneur
91	867.0	Honeoye Falls-Lima Central SD	Honeoye Falls
92	866.8	Watertown City SD	Watertown
93	865.7	Johnson City Central SD	Johnson City
93	865.7	Schenectady City SD	Schenectady
95	863.9	Sachem Central SD	Holbrook
96	863.5	Pleasantville Union Free SD	Pleasantville
97	860.7	South Huntington Union Free SD	Huntington Stn
98	854.3	Lindenhurst Union Free SD	Lindenhurst
99	849.5	Akron Central SD	Akron
100	849.0	North Syracuse Central SD	N Syracuse
101	847.0	Olean City SD	Olean
102	846.5	Schuylerville Central SD	Schuylerville
103	845.9	Rochester City SD	Rochester
104	845.3	Brockport Central SD	Brockport
105	841.8	Arlington Central SD	Poughkeepsie
106	841.0	Royalton-Hartland Central SD	Middleport
107	837.2	Canandaigua City SD	Canandaigua
108	835.3	Coxsackie-Athens Central SD	Coxsackie
109	835.0	Rotterdam-Mohonasen Central SD	Schenectady
110	834.0	Floral Park-Bellerose UFSD	Floral Park
111	826.8	Frontier Central SD	Hamburg
112	823.5	Altmar-Parish-Williamstown CSD	Parish
113	821.0	North Rose-Wolcott Central SD	Wolcott
114	820.0	Clarence Central SD	Clarence
115	819.1	Hornell City SD	Hornell
116	817.0	Clinton Central SD	Clinton
117	815.7	Pine Bush Central SD	Pine Bush
118	814.0	Bay Shore Union Free SD	Bay Shore
119	810.3	Riverhead Central SD	Riverhead
120	809.7	Wappingers Central SD	Wappingers Fls
121	809.3	Lansingburgh Central SD	Troy
122	809.0	Williamsville Central SD	East Amherst
123	807.6	Evans Brant Cent SD (Lake Shore)	Angola
124	807.2	Westbury Union Free SD	Old Westbury
125	805.7	Hudson City SD	Hudson
126	805.6	Sweet Home Central SD	Amherst
127	803.0	Fonda-Fultonville Central SD	Fonda
128	801.5	Oswego City SD	Oswego
129	801.4	Kings Park Central SD	Kings Park
130	798.5	Gorham-Middlesex CSD (M Whitman)	Rushville
130	798.5	Mamaroneck Union Free SD	Mamaroneck
132	797.0	Glen Cove City SD	Glen Cove
133	795.8	Sewanhaka Central High SD	Floral Park
134	795.4	Lancaster Central SD	Lancaster
135	795.0	Pearl River Union Free SD	Pearl River
135	795.0	Springville-Griffith Inst Cent	Springville
137	794.2	Webster Central SD	Webster
138	793.5	Cleveland Hill Union Free SD	Cheektowaga
139	792.7	Depew Union Free SD	Depew
140	786.0	General Brown Central SD	Dexter
141	785.0	Somers Central SD	Lincolndale
142	781.3	Amherst Central SD	Amherst
143	780.3	Warwick Valley Central SD	Warwick
144	773.8	North Tonawanda City SD	N Tonawanda
145	773.5	Canastota Central SD	Canastota
146	769.1	Saratoga Springs City SD	Saratoga Spgs
147	768.6	Long Beach City SD	Long Beach
148	767.4	Lakeland Central SD	Shrub Oak
149	766.0	Gowanda Central SD	Gowanda
149	766.0	Ramapo Central SD (Suffern)	Hillburn
151	764.8	Patchogue-Medford Union Free SD	Patchogue
152	760.0	Wyandanch Union Free SD	Wyandanch
153	758.2	Oceanside Union Free SD	Oceanside
154	758.1	East Hampton Union Free SD	East Hampton
155	756.5	Canton Central SD	Canton
156	755.1	Hamburg Central SD	Hamburg
157	753.4	Longwood Central SD	Middle Island
158	747.0	Churchville-Chili Central SD	Churchville
159	745.7	North Babylon Union Free SD	North Babylon
160	745.2	Brewster Central SD	Brewster
161	745.0	Baldwinsville Central SD	Baldwinsville
161	745.0	Shenendehowa Central SD	Clifton Park
163	743.8	South Orangetown Central SD	Blauvelt
164	743.2	Levittown Union Free SD	Levittown
165	742.8	Fredonia Central SD	Fredonia
166	740.7	Palmyra-Macedon Central SD	Palmyra
167	735.5	Island Trees Union Free SD	Levittown
168	734.3	Carthage Central SD	Carthage
169	734.0	Cohoes City SD	Cohoes
170	733.6	Massena Central SD	Massena
171	725.0	Spencerport Central SD	Spencerport
172	724.0	Onteora Central SD	Boiceville
173	721.2	Plainedge Union Free SD	N Massapequa
174	717.5	Port Jervis City SD	Port Jervis
175	716.0	Connetquot Central SD	Bohemia
176	715.7	Marcellus Central SD	Marcellus
177	714.5	Nyack Union Free SD	Nyack
178	714.4	East Greenbush Central SD	E Greenbush
179	711.7	Susquehanna Valley Central SD	Conklin
180	711.3	Monroe-Woodbury Central SD	Central Valley
181	709.2	Averill Park Central SD	Averill Park
182	705.7	West Babylon Union Free SD	West Babylon
183	705.4	E Ramapo Central SD (Sprg Val)	Spring Valley
184	703.2	Yorktown Central SD	Yorktown Hgts
185	700.2	Pittsford Central SD	Pittsford
186	698.1	Valley Central SD (Montgomery)	Montgomery
187	697.0	East Aurora Union Free SD	East Aurora
188	695.8	Hastings-On-Hudson Union Free SD	Hastings-on-Hud
189	693.1	Hewlett-Woodmere Union Free SD	Woodmere
190	692.0	Hempstead Union Free SD	Hempstead
191	689.8	Mount Vernon City SD	Mount Vernon
191	689.8	Whitesboro Central SD	Yorkville
193	681.7	Windsor Central SD	Windsor
194	681.3	Phelps-Clifton Springs Cent SD	Clifton Spgs
195	680.3	Lackawanna City SD	Lackawanna
196	679.4	Albany City SD	Albany
197	679.2	Smithtown Central SD	Smithtown
198	679.1	Kingston City SD	Kingston
199	678.3	Penn Yan Central SD	Penn Yan
200	677.6	Fairport Central SD	Fairport
201	677.3	Chenango Valley Central SD	Binghamton
202	677.1	Port Washington Union Free SD	Pt Washington
203	675.0	Manhasset Union Free SD	Manhasset
204	672.0	Newark Central SD	Newark
205	669.7	Babylon Union Free SD	Babylon
206	668.9	Hyde Park Central SD	Poughkeepsie
207	668.8	Maine-Endwell Central SD	Endwell
207	668.8	Syracuse City SD	Syracuse
209	667.7	Owego-Apalachin Central SD	Owego
210	660.8	Bethlehem Central SD	Delmar
211	659.9	Fayetteville-Manlius Central SD	Manlius
212	658.2	West Irondequoit Central SD	Rochester
213	657.1	Greece Central SD	Rochester
214	656.7	Merrick Union Free SD	Merrick
215	656.5	Herricks Union Free SD	New Hyde Park
216	656.1	West Islip Union Free SD	West Islip
217	656.0	Saranac Central SD	Dannemora
218	655.0	Brookhaven-Comsewogue UFSD	Pt Jefferson Stn
219	652.1	Cheektowaga-Maryvale UFSD	Cheektowaga
220	647.2	Farmingdale Union Free SD	Farmingdale
221	645.8	Fulton City SD	Fulton
222	644.1	Elwood Union Free SD	Greenlawn
222	644.1	West Genesee Central SD	Camillus
224	641.4	West Seneca Central SD	West Seneca
225	639.2	Northport-East Northport UFSD	Northport
226	638.3	South Colonie Central SD	Albany
227	638.0	Grand Island Central SD	Grand Island
228	636.0	Boces Eastern Suffolk	Patchogue
229	634.4	Niagara-Wheatfield Central SD	Niagara Falls
230	633.5	Geneva City SD	Geneva
231	630.5	Glens Falls City SD	Glens Falls
232	629.3	Guilderland Central SD	Guilderland
233	626.6	Central Square Central SD	Central Square
234	625.9	Commack Union Free SD	E Northport
235	624.8	Malone Central SD	Malone
235	624.8	Orchard Park Central SD	Orchard Park
237	624.7	Chenango Forks Central SD	Binghamton
237	624.7	Elmont Union Free SD	Elmont
239	623.7	Taconic Hills Central SD	Craryville
240	623.3	Clarkstown Central SD	New City
241	623.0	Katonah-Lewisboro Union Free SD	South Salem
242	622.6	East Meadow Union Free SD	Westbury
243	622.5	Roslyn Union Free SD	Roslyn
244	620.0	Penfield Central SD	Penfield
245	619.3	Whitney Point Central SD	Whitney Point
246	618.6	Cornwall Central SD	Cornwall-on-Hud
247	617.7	Holland Patent Central SD	Holland Patent
248	616.6	Amityville Union Free SD	Amityville
249	611.7	Spackenkill Union Free SD	Poughkeepsie
250	611.3	Edgemont Union Free SD	Scarsdale
251	611.0	Peekskill City SD	Peekskill
252	610.3	Marlboro Central SD	Marlboro
253	610.0	Poughkeepsie City SD	Poughkeepsie
254	609.6	Watkins Glen Central SD	Watkins Glen
255	605.7	Catskill Central SD	Catskill
256	604.8	Union-Endicott Central SD	Endicott
257	604.3	Phoenix Central SD	Phoenix
258	604.0	East Williston Union Free SD	Old Westbury
258	604.0	Ellenville Central SD	Ellenville
260	602.8	Deer Park Union Free SD	Deer Park
261	602.2	Kenmore-Tonawanda Union Free SD	Buffalo
262	601.3	Cazenovia Central SD	Cazenovia
263	600.5	Lewiston-Porter Central SD	Youngstown
264	600.3	Amsterdam City SD	Amsterdam
265	597.7	Cold Spring Harbor Central SD	Cold Sprg Harbor
266	596.3	Ravena-Coeymans-Selkirk CSD	Selkirk
266	596.3	Wantagh Union Free SD	Wantagh
268	595.3	Red Hook Central SD	Red Hook
269	594.0	New Paltz Central SD	New Paltz
270	593.6	Hauppauge Union Free SD	Hauppauge
271	591.8	Homer Central SD	Homer
272	589.7	Southampton Union Free SD	Southampton
273	588.3	East Syracuse-Minoa Central SD	East Syracuse
274	587.3	West Hempstead Union Free SD	W Hempstead
275	586.0	Sherburne-Earlville Central SD	Sherburne
276	585.7	East Irondequoit Central SD	Rochester
277	585.3	Hannibal Central SD	Hannibal
278	585.1	Chappaqua Central SD	Chappaqua
278	585.1	Hicksville Union Free SD	Hicksville
280	582.2	Indian River Central SD	Philadelphia
281	582.0	Shoreham-Wading River Central SD	Shoreham
282	578.1	Bethpage Union Free SD	Bethpage
283	577.5	Corning City SD	Painted Post
284	576.8	Hendrick Hudson Central SD	Montrose
285	575.9	Syosset Central SD	Syosset
286	575.8	Peru Central SD	Peru
287	575.7	Westhampton Beach Union Free SD	Westhampton Bch
288	572.3	Briarcliff Manor Union Free SD	Briarcliff Manor
289	571.3	Kinderhook Central SD	Valatie
290	570.3	Lockport City SD	Lockport
291	569.0	Camden Central SD	Camden
292	568.1	Binghamton City SD	Binghamton
293	561.9	Gates-Chili Central SD	Rochester
294	561.8	Norwich City SD	Norwich
295	556.0	Burnt Hls-Ballston Lake Cent SD	Scotia
295	556.0	Saugerties Central SD	Saugerties
297	554.8	Wayne Central SD	Ontario Center
298	552.2	Plainview-Old Bethpage Cent SD	Plainview
299	552.0	Broadalbin-Perth Central SD	Broadalbin
299	552.0	Cobleskill-Richmondville CSD	Cobleskill
301	549.9	Massapequa Union Free SD	Massapequa
302	548.4	Rondout Valley Central SD	Accord
303	548.0	Nanuet Union Free SD	Nanuet
304	547.3	Horseheads Central SD	Horseheads
305	544.8	Beekmantown Central SD	West Chazy
306	543.4	Jamesville-Dewitt Central SD	Dewitt
307	540.3	Bedford Central SD	Mount Kisco
308	539.3	Liverpool Central SD	Liverpool
309	539.0	Rome City SD	Rome
310	537.7	Gloversville City SD	Gloversville
311	537.6	Rye City SD	Rye
312	536.4	Batavia City SD	Batavia
313	536.3	North Colonie Central SD	Latham
314	536.2	New Hyde Park-Garden City Park	New Hyde Park
315	535.0	Jericho Union Free SD	Jericho
316	534.7	Salmon River Central SD	Ft Covington
317	534.3	Uniondale Union Free SD	Uniondale
318	534.0	New Hartford Central SD	New Hartford
319	533.3	Vestal Central SD	Vestal
320	533.0	Livonia Central SD	Livonia
321	527.4	Lawrence Union Free SD	Lawrence
322	525.8	Valley Stream 13 Union Free SD	Valley Stream
323	523.5	Lynbrook Union Free SD	Lynbrook
324	523.1	Rush-Henrietta Central SD	Henrietta
325	522.7	Sullivan West Central SD	Callicoon

326	521.0	Mattituck-Cutchogue UFSD	Cutchogue
327	518.1	Schalmont Central SD	Schenectady
328	518.0	Alden Central SD	Alden
329	516.4	Huntington Union Free SD	Huntington Stn
330	513.8	Plattsburgh City SD	Plattsburgh
331	513.0	Chittenango Central SD	Chittenango
332	512.3	Westhill Central SD	Syracuse
333	509.8	Boces Nassau	Garden City
334	509.7	Lansing Central SD	Lansing
335	509.4	Great Neck Union Free SD	Great Neck
336	507.6	Scarsdale Union Free SD	Scarsdale
337	505.6	North Bellmore Union Free SD	Bellmore
338	504.5	Ogdensburg City SD	Ogdensburg
339	504.3	Salamanca City SD	Salamanca
340	500.7	Valley Stream 30 Union Free SD	Valley Stream
341	500.3	Chatham Central SD	Chatham
342	500.0	Carle Place Union Free SD	Carle Place
343	498.0	Bayport-Blue Point Union Free SD	Bayport
344	495.3	Greenburgh Central SD	Hartsdale
345	492.2	Byram Hills Central SD	Armonk
346	492.0	Scotia-Glenville Central SD	Scotia
347	485.0	Sherrill City SD	Verona
348	484.2	Iroquois Central SD	Elma
349	475.5	Oyster Bay-East Norwich CSD	Oyster Bay
350	474.5	Cortland City SD	Cortland
351	465.2	Medina Central SD	Medina
352	462.0	Skaneateles Central SD	Skaneateles
353	457.8	Niskayuna Central SD	Schenectady
354	456.5	Malverne Union Free SD	Malverne
355	442.4	Ithaca City SD	Ithaca
356	442.0	North Shore Central SD	Sea Cliff
357	437.5	Dansville Central SD	Dansville
358	436.8	Solvay Union Free SD	Solvay
359	430.0	Jamestown City SD	Jamestown
360	425.8	Jordan-Elbridge Central SD	Jordan
361	414.7	Mineola Union Free SD	Mineola
362	406.3	Saranac Lake Central SD	Saranac Lake
363	390.5	Tonawanda City SD	Tonawanda
364	379.2	Locust Valley Central SD	Locust Valley
365	364.3	Oneida City SD	Oneida
366	357.0	Oneonta City SD	Oneonta
367	n/a	Mount Pleasant Central SD	Thornwood
367	n/a	New York City Geographic Dist 9	Bronx
367	n/a	New York City Geographic Dist 15	Brooklyn
367	n/a	Nyc Alternative HS District	New York

Student/Counselor Ratio

Rank	Ratio	District Name	City
1	4,248.0	Elmont Union Free SD	Elmont
2	1,104.0	Broadalbin-Perth Central SD	Broadalbin
3	893.0	Waverly Central SD	Waverly
4	835.3	Coxsackie-Athens Central SD	Coxsackie
5	824.5	Utica City SD	Utica
6	810.3	Riverhead Central SD	Riverhead
7	805.7	Hudson City SD	Hudson
8	803.0	Fonda-Fultonville Central SD	Fonda
9	792.0	Hempstead Union Free SD	Hempstead
10	765.5	Cheektowaga-Sloan Union Free SD	Sloan
11	764.5	Lansing Central SD	Lansing
12	722.7	Johnstown City SD	Johnstown
13	709.6	Central Islip Union Free SD	Central Islip
14	693.9	Troy City SD	Troy
15	691.7	Highland Central SD	Highland
16	689.3	Lancaster Central SD	Lancaster
17	684.1	Albany City SD	Albany
18	679.0	East Islip Union Free SD	Islip Terrace
19	658.4	South Glens Falls Central SD	S Glens Falls
20	645.8	Fulton City SD	Fulton
21	645.5	Patchogue-Medford Union Free SD	Patchogue
22	640.8	Lindenhurst Union Free SD	Lindenhurst
23	640.7	Ilion Central SD	Ilion
24	637.5	Oneida City SD	Oneida
25	628.8	William Floyd Union Free SD	Mastic Beach
26	627.1	Hannibal Central SD	Hannibal
27	619.7	Buffalo City SD	Buffalo
28	619.1	Watertown City SD	Watertown
29	617.5	West Babylon Union Free SD	West Babylon
30	613.3	Attica Central SD	Attica
31	612.1	Middle Country Central SD	Centereach
32	611.8	Pine Bush Central SD	Pine Bush
33	607.3	Wappingers Central SD	Wappingers Fls
34	606.4	North Syracuse Central SD	N Syracuse
35	606.3	Sherrill City SD	Verona
36	605.7	Catskill Central SD	Catskill
37	604.5	Hudson Falls Central SD	Hudson Falls
38	604.3	Cairo-Durham Central SD	Cairo
39	602.2	Beacon City SD	Beacon
40	601.1	Oswego City SD	Oswego
41	596.7	Connetquot Central SD	Bohemia
42	595.3	Red Hook Central SD	Red Hook
43	594.8	South Country Central SD	E Patchogue
44	592.1	West Seneca Central SD	West Seneca
45	591.8	Homer Central SD	Homer
46	589.7	Hampton Bays Union Free SD	Hampton Bays
47	587.4	Carthage Central SD	Carthage
48	585.7	Dover Union Free SD	Dover Plains
49	585.3	Hyde Park Central SD	Poughkeepsie
50	585.1	Hicksville Union Free SD	Hicksville
51	580.4	Monroe-Woodbury Central SD	Central Valley
52	580.0	North Babylon Union Free SD	North Babylon
53	576.8	Saratoga Springs City SD	Saratoga Spgs
54	576.6	Rochester City SD	Rochester
55	576.4	Roosevelt Union Free SD	Roosevelt
56	574.0	Port Jervis City SD	Port Jervis
57	571.5	East Greenbush Central SD	E Greenbush
58	569.9	Newburgh City SD	Newburgh
59	567.9	Minisink Valley Central SD	Slate Hill
60	562.0	Kingston City SD	Kingston
61	560.1	Syracuse City SD	Syracuse
62	557.6	Deer Park Union Free SD	Deer Park
63	553.6	Brentwood Union Free SD	Brentwood
64	551.9	Whitesboro Central SD	Yorkville
65	549.9	Massapequa Union Free SD	Massapequa
66	548.2	Amherst Central SD	Amherst
67	547.1	Burnt Hls-Ballston Lake Cent SD	Scotia
68	542.2	Poughkeepsie City SD	Poughkeepsie
69	541.7	Saranac Lake Central SD	Saranac Lake
70	536.4	Mexico Central SD	Mexico
71	535.0	Maine-Endwell Central SD	Endwell
72	534.0	Marlboro Central SD	Marlboro
73	532.3	Gorham-Middlesex CSD (M Whitman)	Rushville
74	531.9	South Colonie Central SD	Albany
75	531.7	Arlington Central SD	Poughkeepsie
75	531.7	Grand Island Central SD	Grand Island
77	528.2	Clarkstown Central SD	New City
78	524.0	Brookhaven-Comsewogue UFSD	Pt Jefferson Stn
78	524.0	General Brown Central SD	Dexter
80	519.7	Wallkill Central SD	Wallkill
81	518.3	Herricks Union Free SD	New Hyde Park
82	518.0	Alden Central SD	Alden
83	517.9	Clarence Central SD	Clarence
84	516.3	Croton-Harmon Union Free SD	Croton-On-Hud
85	516.0	Adirondack Central SD	Boonville
86	515.9	North Tonawanda City SD	N Tonawanda
87	515.7	Canastota Central SD	Canastota
88	515.3	West Genesee Central SD	Camillus
89	515.0	Baldwin Union Free SD	Baldwin
90	514.9	Guilderland Central SD	Guilderland
91	513.8	Ballston Spa Central SD	Ballston Spa
92	513.5	Bath Central SD	Bath
92	513.5	West Islip Union Free SD	West Islip
94	513.4	Rocky Point Union Free SD	Rocky Point
95	513.3	Sayville Union Free SD	Sayville
96	511.6	New York City Public Schools	Brooklyn
97	511.1	Frontier Central SD	Hamburg
98	510.7	Ramapo Central SD (Suffern)	Hillburn
99	510.3	Lackawanna City SD	Lackawanna
100	508.0	Chenango Valley Central SD	Binghamton
100	508.0	Watkins Glen Central SD	Watkins Glen
102	506.8	Geneva City SD	Geneva
103	505.0	Miller Place Union Free SD	Miller Place
103	505.0	Schenectady City SD	Schenectady
105	504.0	Haverstraw-Stony Point Cent SD	Garnerville
105	504.0	Union-Endicott Central SD	Endicott
107	503.3	Monticello Central SD	Monticello
108	502.4	Elwood Union Free SD	Greenlawn
109	501.3	Central Square Central SD	Central Square
110	499.3	Auburn City SD	Auburn
111	496.7	Baldwinsville Central SD	Baldwinsville
112	495.5	Bay Shore Union Free SD	Bay Shore
113	490.7	Fairport Central SD	Fairport
114	488.7	Kings Park Central SD	Kings Park
115	488.5	Medina Central SD	Medina
116	486.8	Goshen Central SD	Goshen
117	486.4	Horseheads Central SD	Horseheads
118	485.6	Lansingburgh Central SD	Troy
119	484.2	Iroquois Central SD	Elma
120	483.5	Putnam Valley Central SD	Putnam Valley
121	483.2	Cheektowaga Central SD	Cheektowaga
122	480.8	Mahopac Central SD	Mahopac
123	480.7	Binghamton City SD	Binghamton
124	477.1	Rotterdam-Mohonasen Central SD	Schenectady
125	476.6	Saugerties Central SD	Saugerties
126	476.0	Valley Central SD (Montgomery)	Montgomery
127	475.8	Elmira City SD	Elmira
128	475.6	New Rochelle City SD	New Rochelle
129	475.2	New Paltz Central SD	New Paltz
130	474.7	Starpoint Central SD	Lockport
131	474.5	Cortland City SD	Cortland
132	474.0	Schalmont Central SD	Schenectady
133	472.2	Levittown Union Free SD	Levittown
134	471.9	Akron Central SD	Akron
135	470.3	Mount Vernon City SD	Mount Vernon
136	469.4	Commack Union Free SD	E Northport
137	468.5	Chenango Forks Central SD	Binghamton
138	468.2	Warwick Valley Central SD	Warwick
139	463.1	Smithtown Central SD	Smithtown
140	461.1	Garden City Union Free SD	Garden City
141	461.0	Eden Central SD	Eden
142	459.9	Lockport City SD	Lockport
143	459.0	Huntington Union Free SD	Huntington Stn
144	458.5	Edgemont Union Free SD	Scarsdale
144	458.5	South Orangetown Central SD	Blauvelt
146	458.2	Carmel Central SD	Patterson
147	457.9	Uniondale Union Free SD	Uniondale
148	457.0	Kinderhook Central SD	Valatie
149	456.5	Malverne Union Free SD	Malverne
150	456.0	Wyandanch Union Free SD	Wyandanch
151	454.6	East Aurora Union Free SD	East Aurora
152	454.5	Islip Union Free SD	Islip
153	454.4	Union Free SD of the Tarrytowns	Sleepy Hollow
154	453.7	Three Village Central SD	East Setauket
155	453.0	Ellenville Central SD	Ellenville
156	451.2	Byram Hills Central SD	Armonk
157	451.1	Niagara-Wheatfield Central SD	Niagara Falls
158	450.8	Plainedge Union Free SD	N Massapequa
159	448.7	Lynbrook Union Free SD	Lynbrook
160	447.3	Wantagh Union Free SD	Wantagh
161	446.8	Port Chester-Rye Union Free SD	Port Chester
162	446.2	Shoreham-Wading River Central SD	Shoreham
163	444.6	Bedford Central SD	Mount Kisco
164	444.5	Victor Central SD	Victor
165	443.3	Averill Park Central SD	Averill Park
166	440.4	Amityville Union Free SD	Amityville
166	440.4	Cohoes City SD	Cohoes
168	439.5	Yorktown Central SD	Yorktown Hgts
169	439.4	Sachem Central SD	Holbrook
170	438.5	Middletown City SD	Middletown
171	438.3	Copiague Union Free SD	Copiague
172	436.7	E Ramapo Central SD (Sprg Val)	Spring Valley
172	436.7	Lewiston-Porter Central SD	Youngstown
174	436.4	Peekskill City SD	Peekskill
175	434.4	Onteora Central SD	Boiceville
176	434.0	Queensbury Union Free SD	Queensbury
177	433.5	Honeoye Falls-Lima Central SD	Honeoye Falls
178	431.5	Farmingdale Union Free SD	Farmingdale
178	431.5	Longwood Central SD	Middle Island
180	430.0	Clinton Central SD	Clinton
181	429.4	Bethpage Union Free SD	Bethpage
181	429.4	Marcellus Central SD	Marcellus
183	427.4	Oceanside Union Free SD	Oceanside
184	427.3	Palmyra-Macedon Central SD	Palmyra
185	427.2	Cheektowaga-Maryvale UFSD	Cheektowaga
186	427.0	Susquehanna Valley Central SD	Conklin
187	426.4	Livonia Central SD	Livonia
188	425.8	Jordan-Elbridge Central SD	Jordan
189	424.9	Owego-Apalachin Central SD	Owego
190	424.3	Yorkshire-Pioneer Central SD	Yorkshire
191	424.0	Pearl River Union Free SD	Pearl River
192	423.3	Schuylerville Central SD	Schuylerville
193	422.9	Ithaca City SD	Ithaca
194	422.8	Harrison Central SD	Harrison
195	421.7	Scotia-Glenville Central SD	Scotia
196	421.5	Pelham Union Free SD	Pelham
197	420.5	Royalton-Hartland Central SD	Middleport
198	419.3	Rockville Centre Union Free SD	Rockville Ctre
199	418.8	Harborfields Central SD	Greenlawn
200	418.4	Cold Spring Harbor Central SD	Cold Sprg Harbor
201	415.5	Hauppauge Union Free SD	Hauppauge
202	415.0	Bayport-Blue Point Union Free SD	Bayport
203	414.0	Brewster Central SD	Brewster
204	413.6	Locust Valley Central SD	Locust Valley
205	412.9	South Huntington Union Free SD	Huntington Stn
206	412.0	Hendrick Hudson Central SD	Montrose
207	411.8	Altmar-Parish-Williamstown CSD	Parish
208	409.8	Westhill Central SD	Syracuse
209	409.3	Lakeland Central SD	Shrub Oak
210	408.8	Phelps-Clifton Springs Cent SD	Clifton Spgs
210	408.8	South Jefferson Central SD	Adams Center
212	408.0	North Shore Central SD	Sea Cliff
213	407.8	Gates-Chili Central SD	Rochester
214	407.5	Churchville-Chili Central SD	Churchville
215	407.3	Rye City SD	Rye
216	406.4	Camden Central SD	Camden
217	404.7	East Meadow Union Free SD	Westbury
218	403.6	Westbury Union Free SD	Old Westbury
219	403.1	Yonkers City SD	Yonkers
220	402.8	Mount Sinai Union Free SD	Mount Sinai
220	402.8	Phoenix Central SD	Phoenix
222	401.8	Babylon Union Free SD	Babylon
223	399.3	Mamaroneck Union Free SD	Mamaroneck
224	398.9	Orchard Park Central SD	Orchard Park
225	398.5	Williamsville Central SD	East Amherst
226	397.5	Springville-Griffith Inst Cent	Springville
227	396.8	Cleveland Hill Union Free SD	Cheektowaga
228	396.2	Greenburgh Central SD	Hartsdale
229	395.3	Newfane Central SD	Newfane

PROFILES OF NEW YORK / School District Rankings 635

230	393.6	Saranac Central SD	Dannemora
231	393.4	Irvington Union Free SD	Irvington
232	392.8	Washingtonville Central SD	Washingtonville
233	392.5	Somers Central SD	Lincolndale
234	392.3	Oyster Bay-East Norwich CSD	Oyster Bay
235	392.0	Sullivan West Central SD	Callicoon
236	390.6	Rush-Henrietta Central SD	Henrietta
237	390.5	Tonawanda City SD	Tonawanda
238	389.6	Syosset Central SD	Syosset
239	388.3	Webster Central SD	Webster
240	386.6	Cornwall Central SD	Cornwall-on-Hud
240	386.6	Seaford Union Free SD	Seaford
242	386.2	East Irondequoit Central SD	Rochester
243	385.7	Manhasset Union Free SD	Manhasset
244	384.0	Newark Central SD	Newark
245	383.3	Greece Central SD	Rochester
246	382.3	Spackenkill Union Free SD	Poughkeepsie
247	381.4	New Hartford Central SD	New Hartford
248	378.2	Amsterdam City SD	Amsterdam
249	377.6	Bethlehem Central SD	Delmar
250	376.4	Kenmore-Tonawanda Union Free SD	Buffalo
251	376.1	Freeport Union Free SD	Freeport
252	375.3	Chatham Central SD	Chatham
253	374.2	Taconic Hills Central SD	Craryville
254	373.3	Brockport Central SD	Brockport
255	371.4	Fredonia Central SD	Fredonia
256	371.0	Johnson City Central SD	Johnson City
257	370.6	Holland Patent Central SD	Holland Patent
258	369.9	White Plains City SD	White Plains
259	369.7	Hewlett-Woodmere Union Free SD	Woodmere
260	369.6	Skaneateles Central SD	Skaneateles
261	367.1	Niskayuna Central SD	Schenectady
262	365.4	Wayland-Cohocton Central SD	Wayland
263	365.3	Nanuet Union Free SD	Nanuet
264	364.6	Corning City SD	Painted Post
265	363.2	Beekmantown Central SD	West Chazy
266	361.1	Hamburg Central SD	Hamburg
267	360.8	Cazenovia Central SD	Cazenovia
268	360.3	Glens Falls City SD	Glens Falls
269	359.7	Roslyn Union Free SD	Roslyn
270	359.6	Great Neck Union Free SD	Great Neck
271	358.0	Liverpool Central SD	Liverpool
272	357.6	Southwestern Cent SD Jamestown	Jamestown
273	357.3	Nyack Union Free SD	Nyack
274	356.7	Jericho Union Free SD	Jericho
275	355.3	Hilton Central SD	Hilton
276	354.3	Ossining Union Free SD	Ossining
277	351.6	Sherburne-Earlville Central SD	Sherburne
278	351.4	Scarsdale Union Free SD	Scarsdale
279	349.6	Albion Central SD	Albion
280	349.4	Solvay Union Free SD	Solvay
281	348.8	Canandaigua City SD	Canandaigua
282	347.6	East Syracuse-Minoa Central SD	East Syracuse
283	345.4	Pleasantville Union Free SD	Pleasantville
284	345.0	Half Hollow Hills Central SD	Dix Hills
285	343.6	Eastchester Union Free SD	Eastchester
286	343.4	Briarcliff Manor Union Free SD	Briarcliff Manor
287	342.0	Chittenango Central SD	Chittenango
288	341.3	North Colonie Central SD	Latham
289	340.7	Ravena-Coeymans-Selkirk CSD	Selkirk
290	339.6	Jamesville-Dewitt Central SD	Dewitt
291	339.2	Penn Yan Central SD	Penn Yan
292	337.7	Indian River Central SD	Philadelphia
293	336.3	Ogdensburg City SD	Ogdensburg
294	336.0	Niagara Falls City SD	Niagara Falls
295	335.9	Vestal Central SD	Vestal
296	335.6	Lawrence Union Free SD	Lawrence
297	334.6	Pittsford Central SD	Pittsford
298	333.0	Evans-Brant Cent SD (Lake Shore)	Angola
299	331.4	Northeastern Clinton Central SD	Champlain
300	331.3	Plainview-Old Bethpage Cent SD	Plainview
301	329.9	Fayetteville-Manlius Central SD	Manlius
302	328.4	North Rose-Wolcott Central SD	Wolcott
303	322.6	Gloversville City SD	Gloversville
304	322.3	Sweet Home Central SD	Amherst
305	321.1	Shenendehowa Central SD	Clifton Park
306	320.8	Salmon River Central SD	Ft Covington
307	318.8	Glen Cove City SD	Glen Cove
308	318.4	Long Beach City SD	Long Beach
309	317.9	Massena Central SD	Massena
310	316.3	Katonah-Lewisboro Union Free SD	South Salem
310	316.3	Rome City SD	Rome
312	315.4	Cobleskill-Richmondville CSD	Cobleskill
313	314.0	Dryden Central SD	Dryden
314	313.7	Liberty Central SD	Liberty
315	312.6	Mattituck-Cutchogue UFSD	Cutchogue
316	312.4	Malone Central SD	Malone
317	311.8	Port Washington Union Free SD	Pt Washington
318	310.7	Spencerport Central SD	Spencerport
319	310.6	Island Trees Union Free SD	Levittown
320	309.7	Whitney Point Central SD	Whitney Point
321	308.8	Mineola Union Free SD	Mineola
322	302.6	Canton Central SD	Canton
323	301.2	Chappaqua Central SD	Chappaqua
324	300.0	Carle Place Union Free SD	Carle Place
325	298.5	Brighton Central SD	Rochester
326	294.6	Waterloo Central SD	Waterloo
327	293.6	Plattsburgh City SD	Plattsburgh
327	293.6	West Hempstead Union Free SD	W Hempstead
329	292.1	Windsor Central SD	Windsor
330	287.9	Peru Central SD	Peru
331	282.1	West Irondequoit Central SD	Rochester
332	278.3	Hastings-On-Hudson Union Free SD	Hastings-on-Hud
333	275.5	Jamestown City SD	Jamestown
334	273.5	Wilson Central SD	Wilson
335	266.4	East Hampton Union Free SD	East Hampton
336	264.2	Depew Union Free SD	Depew
337	263.9	Mount Pleasant Central SD	Thornwood
338	262.6	Dunkirk City SD	Dunkirk
339	260.3	Ardsley Union Free SD	Ardsley
340	258.9	East Williston Union Free SD	Old Westbury
341	256.9	Bellmore-Merrick Central High SD	North Merrick
342	255.3	Gowanda Central SD	Gowanda
343	254.9	Boces Nassau	Garden City
344	254.1	Olean City SD	Olean
345	249.7	Norwich City SD	Norwich
346	249.0	Gouverneur Central SD	Gouverneur
347	248.0	Penfield Central SD	Penfield
348	245.8	Northport-East Northport UFSD	Northport
349	245.4	Rondout Valley Central SD	Accord
350	243.8	Batavia City SD	Batavia
351	241.5	Hornell City SD	Hornell
352	234.2	Valley Stream Central High SD	Valley Stream
353	230.3	Oneonta City SD	Oneonta
354	222.0	Sewanhaka Central High SD	Floral Park
355	221.9	Wayne Central SD	Ontario Center
356	221.1	Southampton Union Free SD	Southampton
357	218.8	Dansville Central SD	Dansville
358	215.9	Westhampton Beach Union Free SD	Westhampton Bch
359	189.1	Salamanca City SD	Salamanca
360	159.0	Boces Eastern Suffolk	Patchogue
361	n/a	Floral Park-Bellerose UFSD	Floral Park
361	n/a	Franklin Square Union Free SD	Franklin Square
361	n/a	Merrick Union Free SD	Merrick
361	n/a	New Hyde Park-Garden City Park	New Hyde Park
361	n/a	New York City Geographic Dist 9	Bronx
361	n/a	New York City Geographic Dist 15	Brooklyn
361	n/a	North Bellmore Union Free SD	Bellmore
361	n/a	Nyc Alternative HS District	New York
361	n/a	Valley Stream 13 Union Free SD	Valley Stream
361	n/a	Valley Stream 30 Union Free SD	Valley Stream

Current Spending per Student in FY2003

Rank	Dollars	District Name	City
1	21,067	Oyster Bay-East Norwich CSD	Oyster Bay
2	20,689	Southampton Union Free SD	Southampton
3	20,639	Manhasset Union Free SD	Manhasset
4	20,305	Mineola Union Free SD	Mineola
5	20,216	Lawrence Union Free SD	Lawrence
6	19,950	Greenburgh Central SD	Hartsdale
7	19,936	Roslyn Union Free SD	Roslyn
8	19,799	Great Neck Union Free SD	Great Neck
9	19,771	Jericho Union Free SD	Jericho
10	19,455	Locust Valley Central SD	Locust Valley
11	19,392	North Shore Central SD	Sea Cliff
12	18,841	East Williston Union Free SD	Old Westbury
13	18,577	Carle Place Union Free SD	Carle Place
14	18,508	Harrison Central SD	Harrison
15	18,418	White Plains City SD	White Plains
16	18,010	Bedford Central SD	Mount Kisco
17	17,822	Briarcliff Manor Union Free SD	Briarcliff Manor
18	17,705	Huntington Union Free SD	Huntington Stn
19	17,527	Hewlett-Woodmere Union Free SD	Woodmere
20	17,511	Port Washington Union Free SD	Pt Washington
21	17,415	Schalmont Central SD	Schenectady
22	17,371	Syosset Central SD	Syosset
23	17,088	Long Beach City SD	Long Beach
24	16,955	Wyandanch Union Free SD	Wyandanch
25	16,867	Scarsdale Union Free SD	Scarsdale
26	16,829	E Ramapo Central SD (Sprg Val)	Spring Valley
27	16,786	Mount Pleasant Central SD	Thornwood
28	16,766	Onteora Central SD	Boiceville
29	16,643	Malverne Union Free SD	Malverne
30	16,562	East Hampton Union Free SD	East Hampton
31	16,514	Nanuet Union Free SD	Nanuet
32	16,487	Plainview-Old Bethpage Cent SD	Plainview
33	16,421	Roosevelt Union Free SD	Roosevelt
34	16,420	Peekskill City SD	Peekskill
35	16,413	Central Islip Union Free SD	Central Islip
36	16,303	Nyack Union Free SD	Nyack
37	16,299	Katonah-Lewisboro Union Free SD	South Salem
38	16,116	Union Free SD of the Tarrytowns	Sleepy Hollow
39	16,093	Rockville Centre Union Free SD	Rockville Ctre
40	16,026	Uniondale Union Free SD	Uniondale
41	15,929	Chappaqua Central SD	Chappaqua
42	15,866	Westhampton Beach Union Free SD	Westhampton Bch
43	15,830	Haverstraw-Stony Point Cent SD	Garnerville
44	15,829	Hempstead Union Free SD	Hempstead
45	15,760	Rye City SD	Rye
46	15,744	Amityville Union Free SD	Amityville
47	15,704	Hendrick Hudson Central SD	Montrose
48	15,505	Herricks Union Free SD	New Hyde Park
49	15,491	Mamaroneck Union Free SD	Mamaroneck
50	15,344	South Orangetown Central SD	Blauvelt
51	15,316	Westbury Union Free SD	Old Westbury
52	15,225	Somers Central SD	Lincolndale
53	15,138	Ellenville Central SD	Ellenville
54	15,125	Glen Cove City SD	Glen Cove
55	15,081	South Country Central SD	E Patchogue
56	15,032	Ossining Union Free SD	Ossining
57	14,973	West Hempstead Union Free SD	W Hempstead
58	14,946	Eastchester Union Free SD	Eastchester
59	14,919	Cold Spring Harbor Central SD	Cold Sprg Harbor
60	14,891	Ramapo Central SD (Suffern)	Hillburn
61	14,889	Irvington Union Free SD	Irvington
62	14,885	Bethpage Union Free SD	Bethpage
63	14,849	Edgemont Union Free SD	Scarsdale
64	14,818	Lackawanna City SD	Lackawanna
65	14,758	Farmingdale Union Free SD	Farmingdale
66	14,750	Croton-Harmon Union Free SD	Croton-On-Hud
67	14,698	Hauppauge Union Free SD	Hauppauge
68	14,668	Bayport-Blue Point Union Free SD	Bayport
69	14,666	Hastings-On-Hudson Union Free SD	Hastings-on-Hud
70	14,642	Garden City Union Free SD	Garden City
71	14,567	Bay Shore Union Free SD	Bay Shore
72	14,524	Sayville Union Free SD	Sayville
73	14,471	Connetquot Central SD	Bohemia
74	14,464	Ardsley Union Free SD	Ardsley
75	14,426	Northport-East Northport UFSD	Northport
76	14,404	Salmon River Central SD	Ft Covington
77	14,364	Levittown Union Free SD	Levittown
78	14,329	Lakeland Central SD	Shrub Oak
79	14,307	Marlboro Central SD	Marlboro
80	14,238	Deer Park Union Free SD	Deer Park
81	14,214	Brewster Central SD	Brewster
82	14,200	Byram Hills Central SD	Armonk
83	14,133	Putnam Valley Central SD	Putnam Valley
84	14,121	Albany City SD	Albany
85	14,107	Yonkers City SD	Yonkers
86	14,102	Sullivan West Central SD	Callicoon
87	14,065	South Huntington Union Free SD	Huntington Stn
88	14,015	Mattituck-Cutchogue UFSD	Cutchogue
89	13,979	New Rochelle City SD	New Rochelle
90	13,935	Lynbrook Union Free SD	Lynbrook
91	13,925	Pleasantville Union Free SD	Pleasantville
92	13,916	Hicksville Union Free SD	Hicksville
93	13,881	Half Hollow Hills Central SD	Dix Hills
94	13,846	Copiague Union Free SD	Copiague
95	13,840	Pearl River Union Free SD	Pearl River
96	13,799	Riverhead Central SD	Riverhead
97	13,794	Longwood Central SD	Middle Island
98	13,745	Freeport Union Free SD	Freeport
99	13,689	Dunkirk City SD	Dunkirk
100	13,647	Smithtown Central SD	Smithtown
101	13,613	Rondout Valley Central SD	Accord
102	13,601	East Meadow Union Free SD	Westbury
103	13,595	Babylon Union Free SD	Babylon
104	13,581	Pelham Union Free SD	Pelham
105	13,546	Baldwin Union Free SD	Baldwin
106	13,511	Liberty Central SD	Liberty
107	13,482	Bellmore-Merrick Central High SD	North Merrick
108	13,427	Valley Stream Central High SD	Valley Stream
109	13,376	Yorktown Central SD	Yorktown Hgts
110	13,366	Mount Sinai Union Free SD	Mount Sinai
111	13,351	North Babylon Union Free SD	North Babylon
112	13,337	Oceanside Union Free SD	Oceanside
113	13,289	Sachem Central SD	Holbrook
114	13,236	Seaford Union Free SD	Seaford
115	13,163	Carmel Central SD	Patterson
116	13,154	Indian River Central SD	Philadelphia
117	13,144	Three Village Central SD	East Setauket
118	13,141	Hudson City SD	Hudson
119	13,052	Depew Union Free SD	Depew
120	13,029	Mahopac Central SD	Mahopac
121	13,019	Shoreham-Wading River Central SD	Shoreham
122	13,001	Poughkeepsie City SD	Poughkeepsie
123	12,986	Brookhaven-Comsewogue UFSD	Pt Jefferson Stn
124	12,913	Massapequa Union Free SD	Massapequa
125	12,899	Commack Union Free SD	E Northport
126	12,879	Buffalo City SD	Buffalo
127	12,836	East Islip Union Free SD	Islip Terrace
128	12,786	Miller Place Union Free SD	Miller Place
129	12,785	Elwood Union Free SD	Greenlawn
130	12,782	Island Trees Union Free SD	Levittown
131	12,753	Plattsburgh City SD	Plattsburgh
132	12,749	Batavia City SD	Batavia
133	12,738	Spackenkill Union Free SD	Poughkeepsie

134	12,723	Monticello Central SD	Monticello
135	12,711	Rochester City SD	Rochester
136	12,643	Johnson City Central SD	Johnson City
137	12,641	Troy City SD	Troy
138	12,634	Port Chester-Rye Union Free SD	Port Chester
139	12,619	Ithaca City SD	Ithaca
140	12,592	Clarkstown Central SD	New City
141	12,591	Hampton Bays Union Free SD	Hampton Bays
142	12,586	Kings Park Central SD	Kings Park
143	12,585	Ravena-Coeymans-Selkirk CSD	Selkirk
144	12,533	William Floyd Union Free SD	Mastic Beach
145	12,505	Plainedge Union Free SD	N Massapequa
146	12,498	West Babylon Union Free SD	West Babylon
147	12,427	Brentwood Union Free SD	Brentwood
148	12,422	Lindenhurst Union Free SD	Lindenhurst
149	12,420	Rush-Henrietta Central SD	Henrietta
150	12,355	New Paltz Central SD	New Paltz
151	12,351	Mount Vernon City SD	Mount Vernon
152	12,349	Islip Union Free SD	Islip
153	12,309	New York City Public Schools	Brooklyn
154	12,283	Patchogue-Medford Union Free SD	Patchogue
155	12,270	Monroe-Woodbury Central SD	Central Valley
156	12,235	Merrick Union Free SD	Merrick
157	12,219	East Syracuse-Minoa Central SD	East Syracuse
157	12,219	Gowanda Central SD	Gowanda
159	12,203	Wantagh Union Free SD	Wantagh
160	12,193	Schuylerville Central SD	Schuylerville
161	12,173	Ogdensburg City SD	Ogdensburg
162	12,166	Lewiston-Porter Central SD	Youngstown
163	12,164	Cohoes City SD	Cohoes
164	12,096	Saranac Lake Central SD	Saranac Lake
165	12,088	Taconic Hills Central SD	Craryville
166	12,077	Middletown City SD	Middletown
167	12,072	North Rose-Wolcott Central SD	Wolcott
168	12,068	Valley Stream 30 Union Free SD	Valley Stream
169	12,044	Niagara Falls City SD	Niagara Falls
170	12,034	Harborfields Central SD	Greenlawn
171	11,989	Gouverneur Central SD	Gouverneur
172	11,909	Kenmore-Tonawanda Union Free SD	Buffalo
173	11,881	Port Jervis City SD	Port Jervis
174	11,848	Syracuse City SD	Syracuse
175	11,829	Gorham-Middlesex CSD (M Whitman)	Rushville
176	11,816	Horseheads Central SD	Horseheads
177	11,794	Cobleskill-Richmondville CSD	Cobleskill
178	11,788	Sewanhaka Central High SD	Floral Park
179	11,766	East Irondequoit Central SD	Rochester
180	11,760	Catskill Central SD	Catskill
181	11,758	Phoenix Central SD	Phoenix
182	11,723	North Bellmore Union Free SD	Bellmore
183	11,722	Brighton Central SD	Rochester
183	11,722	Valley Stream 13 Union Free SD	Valley Stream
185	11,700	Gates-Chili Central SD	Rochester
186	11,695	Watkins Glen Central SD	Watkins Glen
187	11,690	Kingston City SD	Kingston
188	11,687	Fulton City SD	Fulton
189	11,657	West Islip Union Free SD	West Islip
190	11,645	Wilson Central SD	Wilson
191	11,607	Niagara-Wheatfield Central SD	Niagara Falls
192	11,603	Highland Central SD	Highland
193	11,592	Dryden Central SD	Dryden
194	11,569	Fonda-Fultonville Central SD	Fonda
195	11,563	Yorkshire-Pioneer Central SD	Yorkshire
196	11,529	Cheektowaga-Sloan Union Free SD	Sloan
197	11,526	Pittsford Central SD	Pittsford
198	11,510	Sweet Home Central SD	Amherst
199	11,507	Newburgh City SD	Newburgh
200	11,487	Schenectady City SD	Schenectady
201	11,438	Peru Central SD	Peru
202	11,434	Rocky Point Union Free SD	Rocky Point
203	11,426	Jamestown City SD	Jamestown
204	11,416	Goshen Central SD	Goshen
205	11,336	Penfield Central SD	Penfield
206	11,313	Oneonta City SD	Oneonta
207	11,298	Newark Central SD	Newark
208	11,270	Malone Central SD	Malone
209	11,269	Red Hook Central SD	Red Hook
210	11,233	Rome City SD	Rome
211	11,143	Middle Country Central SD	Centereach
212	11,135	Evans-Brant Cent SD (Lake Shore)	Angola
213	11,128	Franklin Square Union Free SD	Franklin Square
214	11,098	Oswego City SD	Oswego
215	11,087	Ballston Spa Central SD	Ballston Spa
216	11,085	Beekmantown Central SD	West Chazy
216	11,085	Cheektowaga-Maryvale UFSD	Cheektowaga
218	11,077	Canton Central SD	Canton
219	11,062	Elmira City SD	Elmira
220	11,040	Northeastern Clinton Central SD	Champlain
221	11,023	Saranac Central SD	Dannemora
222	11,022	Altmar-Parish-Williamstown CSD	Parish
223	11,020	Adirondack Central SD	Boonville
224	11,018	Cortland City SD	Cortland
225	11,013	Sherburne-Earlville Central SD	Sherburne
226	11,012	Geneva City SD	Geneva
227	10,993	Chatham Central SD	Chatham
228	10,987	Liverpool Central SD	Liverpool
229	10,982	Webster Central SD	Webster
230	10,973	Palmyra-Macedon Central SD	Palmyra
231	10,967	Orchard Park Central SD	Orchard Park
232	10,946	Wallkill Central SD	Wallkill
233	10,942	Greece Central SD	Rochester
234	10,924	Wayland-Cohocton Central SD	Wayland
235	10,919	Maine-Endwell Central SD	Endwell
236	10,914	Owego-Apalachin Central SD	Owego
237	10,905	New Hartford Central SD	New Hartford
238	10,897	Hyde Park Central SD	Poughkeepsie
239	10,885	Brockport Central SD	Brockport
239	10,885	South Colonie Central SD	Albany
241	10,882	Utica City SD	Utica
242	10,880	Jamesville-Dewitt Central SD	Dewitt
243	10,867	Chenango Valley Central SD	Binghamton
244	10,838	Pine Bush Central SD	Pine Bush
245	10,831	Penn Yan Central SD	Penn Yan
246	10,819	Medina Central SD	Medina
247	10,812	Union-Endicott Central SD	Endicott
248	10,800	East Greenbush Central SD	E Greenbush
249	10,766	Chenango Forks Central SD	Binghamton
250	10,714	Dansville Central SD	Dansville
251	10,674	Norwich City SD	Norwich
252	10,660	Honeoye Falls-Lima Central SD	Honeoye Falls
253	10,654	Hudson Falls Central SD	Hudson Falls
254	10,637	Warwick Valley Central SD	Warwick
255	10,612	Hornell City SD	Hornell
256	10,603	Springville-Griffith Inst Cent	Springville
257	10,593	Salamanca City SD	Salamanca
258	10,587	Gloversville City SD	Gloversville
259	10,569	Lansingburgh Central SD	Troy
260	10,539	Fairport Central SD	Fairport
261	10,536	Guilderland Central SD	Guilderland
262	10,525	Mexico Central SD	Mexico
263	10,517	Scotia-Glenville Central SD	Scotia
264	10,510	Corning City SD	Painted Post
265	10,508	Akron Central SD	Akron
266	10,505	Susquehanna Valley Central SD	Conklin
267	10,492	Averill Park Central SD	Averill Park
267	10,492	Binghamton City SD	Binghamton
269	10,469	Cornwall Central SD	Cornwall-on-Hud
270	10,451	Holland Patent Central SD	Holland Patent
271	10,433	Canandaigua City SD	Canandaigua
272	10,420	Oneida City SD	Oneida
273	10,405	Hilton Central SD	Hilton
274	10,401	Fredonia Central SD	Fredonia
275	10,390	Carthage Central SD	Carthage
276	10,378	Minisink Valley Central SD	Slate Hill
277	10,375	Shenendehowa Central SD	Clifton Park
278	10,362	Watertown City SD	Watertown
279	10,352	Saugerties Central SD	Saugerties
280	10,310	Cleveland Hill Union Free SD	Cheektowaga
281	10,297	Churchville-Chili Central SD	Churchville
282	10,292	Glens Falls City SD	Glens Falls
283	10,287	Waterloo Central SD	Waterloo
284	10,262	Burnt Hls-Ballston Lake Cent SD	Scotia
285	10,250	Windsor Central SD	Windsor
286	10,246	Niskayuna Central SD	Schenectady
287	10,244	Lansing Central SD	Lansing
288	10,242	New Hyde Park-Garden City Park	New Hyde Park
289	10,233	Floral Park-Bellerose UFSD	Floral Park
290	10,225	Newfane Central SD	Newfane
291	10,217	Elmont Union Free SD	Elmont
292	10,213	Grand Island Central SD	Grand Island
292	10,213	Saratoga Springs City SD	Saratoga Spgs
294	10,192	Phelps-Clifton Springs Cent SD	Clifton Spgs
295	10,171	Royalton-Hartland Central SD	Middleport
296	10,168	Washingtonville Central SD	Washingtonville
297	10,164	Lockport City SD	Lockport
298	10,139	Spencerport Central SD	Spencerport
299	10,107	Hamburg Central SD	Hamburg
300	10,105	North Tonawanda City SD	N Tonawanda
301	10,080	Wappingers Central SD	Wappingers Fls
302	10,077	Southwestern Cent SD Jamestown	Jamestown
303	10,064	Jordan-Elbridge Central SD	Jordan
304	10,052	Bath Central SD	Bath
305	10,049	Victor Central SD	Victor
306	10,044	Cheektowaga Central SD	Cheektowaga
307	10,041	Dover Union Free SD	Dover Plains
308	10,032	Hannibal Central SD	Hannibal
309	10,016	Massena Central SD	Massena
310	10,012	Amherst Central SD	Amherst
311	10,009	Alden Central SD	Alden
312	10,006	West Irondequoit Central SD	Rochester
313	10,002	Clinton Central SD	Clinton
314	9,971	West Seneca Central SD	West Seneca
315	9,967	Whitney Point Central SD	Whitney Point
316	9,962	Williamsville Central SD	East Amherst
317	9,961	Kinderhook Central SD	Valatie
318	9,960	Vestal Central SD	Vestal
319	9,938	Bethlehem Central SD	Delmar
320	9,912	Tonawanda City SD	Tonawanda
321	9,909	Wayne Central SD	Ontario Center
322	9,897	Auburn City SD	Auburn
323	9,874	Beacon City SD	Beacon
324	9,872	Homer Central SD	Homer
325	9,842	Livonia Central SD	Livonia
326	9,830	South Glens Falls Central SD	S Glens Falls
327	9,802	Camden Central SD	Camden
328	9,788	Baldwinsville Central SD	Baldwinsville
329	9,745	Olean City SD	Olean
330	9,736	Westhill Central SD	Syracuse
331	9,733	Cazenovia Central SD	Cazenovia
332	9,710	Canastota Central SD	Canastota
333	9,703	Valley Central SD (Montgomery)	Montgomery
334	9,673	Attica Central SD	Attica
335	9,665	North Colonie Central SD	Latham
336	9,658	Fayetteville-Manlius Central SD	Manlius
337	9,656	Sherrill City SD	Verona
338	9,594	Arlington Central SD	Poughkeepsie
339	9,590	Waverly Central SD	Waverly
340	9,582	Whitesboro Central SD	Yorkville
341	9,577	Amsterdam City SD	Amsterdam
342	9,573	Skaneateles Central SD	Skaneateles
343	9,528	Coxsackie-Athens Central SD	Coxsackie
344	9,499	Chittenango Central SD	Chittenango
345	9,471	Solvay Union Free SD	Solvay
346	9,457	Frontier Central SD	Hamburg
347	9,409	North Syracuse Central SD	N Syracuse
348	9,300	General Brown Central SD	Dexter
349	9,289	South Jefferson Central SD	Adams Center
350	9,213	Iroquois Central SD	Elma
351	9,155	Clarence Central SD	Clarence
352	9,121	Central Square Central SD	Central Square
353	9,078	East Aurora Union Free SD	East Aurora
354	9,073	Cairo-Durham Central SD	Cairo
355	9,065	Johnstown City SD	Johnstown
356	8,966	Starpoint Central SD	Lockport
357	8,939	Lancaster Central SD	Lancaster
358	8,907	Albion Central SD	Albion
359	8,847	West Genesee Central SD	Camillus
360	8,820	Rotterdam-Mohonasen Central SD	Schenectady
361	8,746	Eden Central SD	Eden
362	8,697	Marcellus Central SD	Marcellus
363	8,473	Ilion Central SD	Ilion
364	8,280	Queensbury Union Free SD	Queensbury
365	7,940	Broadalbin-Perth Central SD	Broadalbin
366	n/a	Boces Eastern Suffolk	Patchogue
366	n/a	Boces Nassau	Garden City
366	n/a	New York City Geographic Dist 9	Bronx
366	n/a	New York City Geographic Dist 15	Brooklyn
366	n/a	Nyc Alternative HS District	New York

Number of Diploma Recipients

Rank	Number	District Name	City
1	37,915	New York City Public Schools	Brooklyn
2	1,638	Buffalo City SD	Buffalo
3	1,135	Sewanhaka Central High SD	Floral Park
4	1,021	Rochester City SD	Rochester
5	910	Sachem Central SD	Holbrook
6	901	Greece Central SD	Rochester
7	812	Bellmore-Merrick Central High SD	North Merrick
8	773	Williamsville Central SD	East Amherst
9	761	Wappingers Central SD	Wappingers Fls
10	724	Yonkers City SD	Yonkers
11	681	Clarkstown Central SD	New City
12	670	Middle Country Central SD	Centereach
13	641	Brentwood Union Free SD	Brentwood
14	629	Valley Stream Central High SD	Valley Stream
15	627	Syracuse City SD	Syracuse
16	624	Kenmore-Tonawanda Union Free SD	Buffalo
17	600	Webster Central SD	Webster
18	582	North Syracuse Central SD	N Syracuse
19	580	Shenendehowa Central SD	Clifton Park
20	556	Smithtown Central SD	Smithtown
21	552	West Seneca Central SD	West Seneca
22	543	Half Hollow Hills Central SD	Dix Hills
23	526	E Ramapo Central SD (Sprg Val)	Spring Valley
24	516	Great Neck Union Free SD	Great Neck
24	516	Longwood Central SD	Middle Island
26	512	Liverpool Central SD	Liverpool
27	507	East Meadow Union Free SD	Westbury
28	501	Arlington Central SD	Poughkeepsie
29	496	Massapequa Union Free SD	Massapequa
29	496	Patchogue-Medford Union Free SD	Patchogue
31	489	Fairport Central SD	Fairport
32	485	Kingston City SD	Kingston
33	482	Newburgh City SD	Newburgh
34	479	New Rochelle City SD	New Rochelle
35	472	Lakeland Central SD	Shrub Oak
35	472	Three Village Central SD	East Setauket
37	461	Saratoga Springs City SD	Saratoga Spgs

38	455	Levittown Union Free SD	Levittown
38	455	William Floyd Union Free SD	Mastic Beach
40	454	North Colonie Central SD	Latham
41	445	Syosset Central SD	Syosset
42	443	Pittsford Central SD	Pittsford
43	442	Haverstraw-Stony Point Cent SD	Garnerville
44	419	Lindenhurst Union Free SD	Lindenhurst
45	412	Lancaster Central SD	Lancaster
46	411	Monroe-Woodbury Central SD	Central Valley
47	408	Commack Union Free SD	E Northport
48	406	Orchard Park Central SD	Orchard Park
49	390	West Genesee Central SD	Camillus
50	389	South Colonie Central SD	Albany
51	385	North Babylon Union Free SD	North Babylon
52	382	Albany City SD	Albany
53	380	Oceanside Union Free SD	Oceanside
54	379	Gates-Chili Central SD	Rochester
55	374	Connetquot Central SD	Bohemia
55	374	Guilderland Central SD	Guilderland
57	367	Farmingdale Union Free SD	Farmingdale
58	362	Niagara Falls City SD	Niagara Falls
59	360	White Plains City SD	White Plains
60	358	Corning City SD	Painted Post
60	358	Schenectady City SD	Schenectady
62	357	Bethlehem Central SD	Delmar
63	349	Rush-Henrietta Central SD	Henrietta
64	348	Mahopac Central SD	Mahopac
65	346	Baldwin Union Free SD	Baldwin
66	341	Plainview-Old Bethpage Cent SD	Plainview
66	341	Utica City SD	Utica
68	340	Frontier Central SD	Hamburg
69	339	Clarence Central SD	Clarence
70	337	Mount Vernon City SD	Mount Vernon
71	335	North Tonawanda City SD	N Tonawanda
72	330	Hilton Central SD	Hilton
73	329	Northport-East Northport UFSD	Northport
74	326	Ithaca City SD	Ithaca
75	324	Elmira City SD	Elmira
76	320	Baldwinsville Central SD	Baldwinsville
76	320	Horseheads Central SD	Horseheads
78	319	Hamburg Central SD	Hamburg
79	317	South Huntington Union Free SD	Huntington Stn
80	315	West Irondequoit Central SD	Rochester
81	312	Washingtonville Central SD	Washingtonville
82	311	Fayetteville-Manlius Central SD	Manlius
83	310	Hicksville Union Free SD	Hicksville
84	308	Valley Central SD (Montgomery)	Montgomery
85	307	Uniondale Union Free SD	Uniondale
86	306	Pine Bush Central SD	Pine Bush
87	302	Lockport City SD	Lockport
87	302	Penfield Central SD	Penfield
87	302	West Islip Union Free SD	West Islip
90	300	East Islip Union Free SD	Islip Terrace
91	298	Churchville-Chili Central SD	Churchville
92	296	Vestal Central SD	Vestal
93	292	Spencerport Central SD	Spencerport
94	290	Brockport Central SD	Brockport
95	289	Mamaroneck Union Free SD	Mamaroneck
96	288	Carmel Central SD	Patterson
97	287	Bay Shore Union Free SD	Bay Shore
98	283	South Country Central SD	E Patchogue
99	282	Port Washington Union Free SD	Pt Washington
100	281	East Greenbush Central SD	E Greenbush
100	281	Freeport Union Free SD	Freeport
102	280	Niskayuna Central SD	Schenectady
102	280	West Babylon Union Free SD	West Babylon
104	279	Union-Endicott Central SD	Endicott
105	278	Auburn City SD	Auburn
105	278	Central Islip Union Free SD	Central Islip
105	278	Jamestown City SD	Jamestown
108	277	Ramapo Central SD (Suffern)	Hillburn
109	276	Herricks Union Free SD	New Hyde Park
109	276	Rome City SD	Rome
111	274	East Syracuse-Minoa Central SD	East Syracuse
112	272	Niagara-Wheatfield Central SD	Niagara Falls
113	267	Hewlett-Woodmere Union Free SD	Woodmere
113	267	Scarsdale Union Free SD	Scarsdale
115	264	Middletown City SD	Middletown
116	260	Yorktown Central SD	Yorktown Hgts
117	259	Brighton Central SD	Rochester
117	259	Hauppauge Union Free SD	Hauppauge
119	258	Rockville Centre Union Free SD	Rockville Ctre
120	257	Chappaqua Central SD	Chappaqua
120	257	Warwick Valley Central SD	Warwick
120	257	Whitesboro Central SD	Yorkville
123	253	Binghamton City SD	Binghamton
123	253	Hyde Park Central SD	Poughkeepsie
123	253	Oswego City SD	Oswego
126	249	Central Square Central SD	Central Square
127	247	Bedford Central SD	Mount Kisco
127	247	Kings Park Central SD	Kings Park
129	246	Minisink Valley Central SD	Slate Hill
130	245	Sweet Home Central SD	Amherst
131	244	Canandaigua City SD	Canandaigua
132	241	Lawrence Union Free SD	Lawrence
133	238	Riverhead Central SD	Riverhead
134	234	Long Beach City SD	Long Beach
135	222	Iroquois Central SD	Elma
135	222	New Hartford Central SD	New Hartford
137	219	Averill Park Central SD	Averill Park
137	219	Sayville Union Free SD	Sayville
139	218	Scotia-Glenville Central SD	Scotia
140	215	Ballston Spa Central SD	Ballston Spa
141	214	Garden City Union Free SD	Garden City
141	214	Yorkshire-Pioneer Central SD	Yorkshire
143	213	Burnt Hls-Ballston Lake Cent SD	Scotia
143	213	Fulton City SD	Fulton
143	213	Miller Place Union Free SD	Miller Place
146	212	Amherst Central SD	Amherst
147	211	Queensbury Union Free SD	Queensbury
147	211	Westhampton Beach Union Free SD	Westhampton Bch
149	209	Roslyn Union Free SD	Roslyn
150	208	Katonah-Lewisboro Union Free SD	South Salem
151	205	Copiague Union Free SD	Copiague
151	205	Huntington Union Free SD	Huntington Stn
153	203	Brewster Central SD	Brewster
153	203	East Irondequoit Central SD	Rochester
153	203	Islip Union Free SD	Islip
153	203	Ossining Union Free SD	Ossining
153	203	Plainedge Union Free SD	N Massapequa
153	203	Wallkill Central SD	Wallkill
159	201	Mineola Union Free SD	Mineola
159	201	Rotterdam-Mohonasen Central SD	Schenectady
161	199	Victor Central SD	Victor
162	198	Cornwall Central SD	Cornwall-on-Hud
162	198	Deer Park Union Free SD	Deer Park
164	195	Grand Island Central SD	Grand Island
165	194	West Hempstead Union Free SD	W Hempstead
166	193	Carthage Central SD	Carthage
167	192	Glen Cove City SD	Glen Cove
167	192	Port Jervis City SD	Port Jervis
169	191	Jericho Union Free SD	Jericho
169	191	Rondout Valley Central SD	Accord
169	191	Wantagh Union Free SD	Wantagh
172	190	Port Chester-Rye Union Free SD	Port Chester
172	190	Saugerties Central SD	Saugerties
174	189	Brookhaven-Comsewogue UFSD	Pt Jefferson Stn
174	189	Harborfields Central SD	Greenlawn
176	188	Evans-Brant Cent SD (Lake Shore)	Angola
176	188	Lynbrook Union Free SD	Lynbrook
176	188	Malone Central SD	Malone
179	186	Lewiston-Porter Central SD	Youngstown
180	184	East Hampton Union Free SD	East Hampton
181	180	Bethpage Union Free SD	Bethpage
181	180	Cortland City SD	Cortland
183	179	Jamesville-Dewitt Central SD	Dewitt
184	177	Pearl River Union Free SD	Pearl River
185	176	Goshen Central SD	Goshen
185	176	Hendrick Hudson Central SD	Montrose
185	176	Homer Central SD	Homer
188	175	Sherrill City SD	Verona
189	174	Phoenix Central SD	Phoenix
189	174	Tonawanda City SD	Tonawanda
191	173	Watertown City SD	Watertown
192	171	Somers Central SD	Lincolndale
193	170	Manhasset Union Free SD	Manhasset
194	169	Shoreham-Wading River Central SD	Shoreham
195	167	Massena Central SD	Massena
195	167	Ravena-Coeymans-Selkirk CSD	Selkirk
195	167	Westhill Central SD	Syracuse
198	166	Byram Hills Central SD	Armonk
198	166	Gloversville City SD	Gloversville
198	166	Nyack Union Free SD	Nyack
198	166	Owego-Apalachin Central SD	Owego
198	166	Seaford Union Free SD	Seaford
203	165	Cheektowaga Central SD	Cheektowaga
203	165	Chittenango Central SD	Chittenango
203	165	Newark Central SD	Newark
203	165	South Orangetown Central SD	Blauvelt
207	164	Honeoye Falls-Lima Central SD	Honeoye Falls
208	163	Harrison Central SD	Harrison
208	163	Wayne Central SD	Ontario Center
210	162	Mexico Central SD	Mexico
211	161	Schalmont Central SD	Schenectady
211	161	South Glens Falls Central SD	S Glens Falls
213	160	Cheektowaga-Maryvale UFSD	Cheektowaga
213	160	Rocky Point Union Free SD	Rocky Point
215	159	Camden Central SD	Camden
215	159	Oneida City SD	Oneida
217	157	Westbury Union Free SD	Old Westbury
218	156	Johnson City Central SD	Johnson City
218	156	Newfane Central SD	Newfane
218	156	Springville-Griffith Inst Cent	Springville
221	155	Indian River Central SD	Philadelphia
221	155	Plattsburgh City SD	Plattsburgh
223	154	Hempstead Union Free SD	Hempstead
223	154	Skaneateles Central SD	Skaneateles
223	154	Starpoint Central SD	Lockport
226	153	Poughkeepsie City SD	Poughkeepsie
227	152	Albion Central SD	Albion
227	152	Batavia City SD	Batavia
227	152	Fredonia Central SD	Fredonia
227	152	Penn Yan Central SD	Penn Yan
231	151	Depew Union Free SD	Depew
231	151	Southampton Union Free SD	Southampton
233	150	Alden Central SD	Alden
233	150	East Aurora Union Free SD	East Aurora
235	149	Geneva City SD	Geneva
235	149	Peru Central SD	Peru
237	148	Clinton Central SD	Clinton
237	148	Oneonta City SD	Oneonta
239	147	Glens Falls City SD	Glens Falls
240	146	Amityville Union Free SD	Amityville
240	146	Livonia Central SD	Livonia
242	145	Attica Central SD	Attica
243	144	Beacon City SD	Beacon
244	143	Kinderhook Central SD	Valatie
244	143	Mount Sinai Union Free SD	Mount Sinai
246	141	Babylon Union Free SD	Babylon
246	141	Monticello Central SD	Monticello
246	141	Olean City SD	Olean
246	141	Susquehanna Valley Central SD	Conklin
246	141	Wayland-Cohocton Central SD	Wayland
251	140	Cobleskill-Richmondville CSD	Cobleskill
251	140	Highland Central SD	Highland
251	140	Island Trees Union Free SD	Levittown
251	140	Johnstown City SD	Johnstown
255	139	Maine-Endwell Central SD	Endwell
255	139	Palmyra-Macedon Central SD	Palmyra
257	138	Bayport-Blue Point Union Free SD	Bayport
258	135	Pelham Union Free SD	Pelham
258	135	Phelps-Clifton Springs Cent SD	Clifton Spgs
260	134	Bath Central SD	Bath
261	133	Norwich City SD	Norwich
261	133	Saranac Central SD	Dannemora
263	132	Marcellus Central SD	Marcellus
263	132	North Shore Central SD	Sea Cliff
263	132	Southwestern Cent SD Jamestown	Jamestown
266	131	Elwood Union Free SD	Greenlawn
266	131	Locust Valley Central SD	Locust Valley
268	130	Chenango Valley Central SD	Binghamton
268	130	Peekskill City SD	Peekskill
270	129	Holland Patent Central SD	Holland Patent
271	128	Broadalbin-Perth Central SD	Broadalbin
271	128	Chenango Forks Central SD	Binghamton
271	128	Hudson Falls Central SD	Hudson Falls
274	127	East Williston Union Free SD	Old Westbury
274	127	Ogdensburg City SD	Ogdensburg
276	126	Red Hook Central SD	Red Hook
277	123	Ardsley Union Free SD	Ardsley
277	123	South Jefferson Central SD	Adams Center
279	122	Medina Central SD	Medina
280	121	Cold Spring Harbor Central SD	Cold Sprg Harbor
280	121	Fonda-Fultonville Central SD	Fonda
280	121	General Brown Central SD	Dexter
280	121	Rye City SD	Rye
284	120	Nanuet Union Free SD	Nanuet
285	119	Gouverneur Central SD	Gouverneur
285	119	Sullivan West Central SD	Callicoon
287	118	Mount Pleasant Central SD	Thornwood
287	118	New Paltz Central SD	New Paltz
289	117	Greenburgh Central SD	Hartsdale
289	117	Royalton-Hartland Central SD	Middleport
291	116	Jordan-Elbridge Central SD	Jordan
291	116	Solvay Union Free SD	Solvay
293	114	Ilion Central SD	Ilion
293	114	Schuylerville Central SD	Schuylerville
293	114	Wilson Central SD	Wilson
296	113	Beekmantown Central SD	West Chazy
296	113	Briarcliff Manor Union Free SD	Briarcliff Manor
298	112	Mattituck-Cutchogue UFSD	Cutchogue
298	112	Onteora Central SD	Boiceville
298	112	Saranac Lake Central SD	Saranac Lake
301	111	Adirondack Central SD	Boonville
301	111	Eden Central SD	Eden
301	111	Spackenkill Union Free SD	Poughkeepsie
301	111	Union Free SD of the Tarrytowns	Sleepy Hollow
301	111	Windsor Central SD	Windsor
306	110	Dunkirk City SD	Dunkirk
306	110	Lansing Central SD	Lansing
308	109	Lackawanna City SD	Lackawanna
309	108	Cazenovia Central SD	Cazenovia
309	108	Oyster Bay-East Norwich CSD	Oyster Bay
311	107	Cohoes City SD	Cohoes
311	107	Dansville Central SD	Dansville
311	107	Malverne Union Free SD	Malverne
314	106	Dryden Central SD	Dryden

314	106	Marlboro Central SD	Marlboro
314	106	Pleasantville Union Free SD	Pleasantville
317	105	Canastota Central SD	Canastota
317	105	Eastchester Union Free SD	Eastchester
317	105	Gowanda Central SD	Gowanda
320	104	Cheektowaga-Sloan Union Free SD	Sloan
320	104	Dover Union Free SD	Dover Plains
320	104	Edgemont Union Free SD	Scarsdale
320	104	Hornell City SD	Hornell
320	104	Lansingburgh Central SD	Troy
325	103	Carle Place Union Free SD	Carle Place
325	103	Northeastern Clinton Central SD	Champlain
327	100	Sherburne-Earlville Central SD	Sherburne
327	100	Waterloo Central SD	Waterloo
329	99	Chatham Central SD	Chatham
329	99	Gorham-Middlesex CSD (M Whitman)	Rushville
329	99	Watkins Glen Central SD	Watkins Glen
332	98	Akron Central SD	Akron
332	98	Coxsackie-Athens Central SD	Coxsackie
332	98	Whitney Point Central SD	Whitney Point
335	97	Canton Central SD	Canton
335	97	Troy City SD	Troy
337	95	North Rose-Wolcott Central SD	Wolcott
337	95	Waverly Central SD	Waverly
339	94	Hannibal Central SD	Hannibal
340	92	Irvington Union Free SD	Irvington
341	91	Altmar-Parish-Williamstown CSD	Parish
342	90	Hudson City SD	Hudson
343	88	Salmon River Central SD	Ft Covington
344	86	Roosevelt Union Free SD	Roosevelt
344	86	Taconic Hills Central SD	Craryville
346	79	Catskill Central SD	Catskill
347	78	Cleveland Hill Union Free SD	Cheektowaga
347	78	Ellenville Central SD	Ellenville
349	77	Liberty Central SD	Liberty
350	74	Cairo-Durham Central SD	Cairo
350	74	Hastings-On-Hudson Union Free SD	Hastings-on-Hud
352	73	Croton-Harmon Union Free SD	Croton-On-Hud
353	71	Salamanca City SD	Salamanca
354	66	Wyandanch Union Free SD	Wyandanch
355	0	Amsterdam City SD	Amsterdam
355	0	Hampton Bays Union Free SD	Hampton Bays
357	n/a	New York City Geographic Dist 9	Bronx
357	n/a	New York City Geographic Dist 15	Brooklyn
357	n/a	Nyc Alternative HS District	New York
360	n/a	Boces Eastern Suffolk	Patchogue
360	n/a	Boces Nassau	Garden City
360	n/a	Elmont Union Free SD	Elmont
360	n/a	Floral Park-Bellerose UFSD	Floral Park
360	n/a	Franklin Square Union Free SD	Franklin Square
360	n/a	Merrick Union Free SD	Merrick
360	n/a	New Hyde Park-Garden City Park	New Hyde Park
360	n/a	North Bellmore Union Free SD	Bellmore
360	n/a	Putnam Valley Central SD	Putnam Valley
360	n/a	Valley Stream 13 Union Free SD	Valley Stream
360	n/a	Valley Stream 30 Union Free SD	Valley Stream

High School Drop-out Rate

Rank	Percent	District Name	City
1	31.3	Amityville Union Free SD	Amityville
2	18.4	Schenectady City SD	Schenectady
3	17.5	Roosevelt Union Free SD	Roosevelt
4	14.2	New York City Public Schools	Brooklyn
5	13.0	Rochester City SD	Rochester
6	11.8	Lackawanna City SD	Lackawanna
7	10.7	Poughkeepsie City SD	Poughkeepsie
8	10.2	Batavia City SD	Batavia
9	10.0	Ellenville Central SD	Ellenville
10	9.6	Hempstead Union Free SD	Hempstead
10	9.6	Royalton-Hartland Central SD	Middleport
12	9.5	Niagara Falls City SD	Niagara Falls
13	9.2	Hannibal Central SD	Hannibal
14	8.8	Medina Central SD	Medina
15	8.6	Riverhead Central SD	Riverhead
16	8.4	Bedford Central SD	Mount Kisco
16	8.4	Gouverneur Central SD	Gouverneur
18	8.2	E Ramapo Central SD (Sprg Val)	Spring Valley
19	8.1	Auburn City SD	Auburn
20	7.8	Jamestown City SD	Jamestown
20	7.8	Kingston City SD	Kingston
22	7.7	Monticello Central SD	Monticello
22	7.7	Yonkers City SD	Yonkers
24	7.6	Buffalo City SD	Buffalo
24	7.6	Hornell City SD	Hornell
26	7.5	Elmira City SD	Elmira
27	7.4	North Syracuse Central SD	N Syracuse
28	7.3	Coxsackie-Athens Central SD	Coxsackie
29	7.0	Fulton City SD	Fulton
29	7.0	Lansingburgh Central SD	Troy
31	6.9	Port Jervis City SD	Port Jervis
32	6.8	Yorkshire-Pioneer Central SD	Yorkshire
33	6.6	Central Square Central SD	Central Square
33	6.6	Oneida City SD	Oneida
33	6.6	Port Chester-Rye Union Free SD	Port Chester
33	6.6	Westbury Union Free SD	Old Westbury
37	6.5	Croton-Harmon Union Free SD	Croton-On-Hud
38	6.4	Freeport Union Free SD	Freeport
39	6.3	Catskill Central SD	Catskill
39	6.3	Olean City SD	Olean
41	6.2	Dunkirk City SD	Dunkirk
41	6.2	Plattsburgh City SD	Plattsburgh
43	5.9	Amsterdam City SD	Amsterdam
44	5.8	Camden Central SD	Camden
44	5.8	North Rose-Wolcott Central SD	Wolcott
46	5.7	Gowanda Central SD	Gowanda
46	5.7	Taconic Hills Central SD	Craryville
48	5.5	Beekmantown Central SD	West Chazy
48	5.5	Cleveland Hill Union Free SD	Cheektowaga
48	5.5	Tonawanda City SD	Tonawanda
48	5.5	Watkins Glen Central SD	Watkins Glen
52	5.4	Massena Central SD	Massena
52	5.4	Watertown City SD	Watertown
54	5.2	Evans-Brant Cent SD (Lake Shore)	Angola
54	5.2	Mexico Central SD	Mexico
54	5.2	Spackenkill Union Free SD	Poughkeepsie
57	5.1	Niagara-Wheatfield Central SD	Niagara Falls
58	4.9	Southwestern Cent SD Jamestown	Jamestown
59	4.8	Bellmore-Merrick Central High SD	North Merrick
60	4.7	Albany City SD	Albany
60	4.7	Geneva City SD	Geneva
60	4.7	Rome City SD	Rome
63	4.6	Albion Central SD	Albion
63	4.6	Glen Cove City SD	Glen Cove
63	4.6	Huntington Union Free SD	Huntington Stn
63	4.6	Johnstown City SD	Johnstown
63	4.6	Peru Central SD	Peru
63	4.6	Utica City SD	Utica
69	4.5	Beacon City SD	Beacon
69	4.5	Depew Union Free SD	Depew
69	4.5	Hyde Park Central SD	Poughkeepsie
69	4.5	Mount Vernon City SD	Mount Vernon
73	4.3	Cortland City SD	Cortland
74	4.2	Altmar-Parish-Williamstown CSD	Parish
74	4.2	Sherburne-Earlville Central SD	Sherburne
74	4.2	Springville-Griffith Inst Cent	Springville
77	4.1	Dansville Central SD	Dansville
77	4.1	Frontier Central SD	Hamburg
77	4.1	West Babylon Union Free SD	West Babylon
77	4.1	West Seneca Central SD	West Seneca
81	4.0	Cohoes City SD	Cohoes
81	4.0	Indian River Central SD	Philadelphia
81	4.0	Pine Bush Central SD	Pine Bush
81	4.0	Rondout Valley Central SD	Accord
81	4.0	Salamanca City SD	Salamanca
81	4.0	Waterloo Central SD	Waterloo
81	4.0	West Hempstead Union Free SD	W Hempstead
88	3.9	East Greenbush Central SD	E Greenbush
88	3.9	Johnson City Central SD	Johnson City
88	3.9	Lewiston-Porter Central SD	Youngstown
88	3.9	Newfane Central SD	Newfane
92	3.8	Akron Central SD	Akron
92	3.8	Brookhaven-Comsewogue UFSD	Pt Jefferson Stn
92	3.8	Cairo-Durham Central SD	Cairo
92	3.8	Cheektowaga-Maryvale UFSD	Cheektowaga
92	3.8	Gorham-Middlesex CSD (M Whitman)	Rushville
92	3.8	Livonia Central SD	Livonia
92	3.8	Ossining Union Free SD	Ossining
92	3.8	Saugerties Central SD	Saugerties
92	3.8	South Jefferson Central SD	Adams Center
92	3.8	Syracuse City SD	Syracuse
92	3.8	Whitesboro Central SD	Yorkville
103	3.7	Adirondack Central SD	Boonville
103	3.7	Brentwood Union Free SD	Brentwood
103	3.7	Waverly Central SD	Waverly
106	3.6	Ballston Spa Central SD	Ballston Spa
106	3.6	Chittenango Central SD	Chittenango
106	3.6	Honeoye Falls-Lima Central SD	Honeoye Falls
106	3.6	Ilion Central SD	Ilion
106	3.6	Liverpool Central SD	Liverpool
106	3.6	Lockport City SD	Lockport
106	3.6	Onteora Central SD	Boiceville
106	3.6	Pittsford Central SD	Pittsford
106	3.6	Sweet Home Central SD	Amherst
115	3.5	Averill Park Central SD	Averill Park
115	3.5	Dover Union Free SD	Dover Plains
115	3.5	Lakeland Central SD	Shrub Oak
115	3.5	Queensbury Union Free SD	Queensbury
115	3.5	Three Village Central SD	East Setauket
115	3.5	Windsor Central SD	Windsor
121	3.4	Canandaigua City SD	Canandaigua
121	3.4	Minisink Valley Central SD	Slate Hill
121	3.4	New Paltz Central SD	New Paltz
121	3.4	Wayland-Cohocton Central SD	Wayland
125	3.3	Alden Central SD	Alden
125	3.3	Corning City SD	Painted Post
125	3.3	Islip Union Free SD	Islip
125	3.3	North Tonawanda City SD	N Tonawanda
125	3.3	Red Hook Central SD	Red Hook
125	3.3	Salmon River Central SD	Ft Covington
125	3.3	Union Free SD of the Tarrytowns	Sleepy Hollow
132	3.2	Arlington Central SD	Poughkeepsie
132	3.2	Newark Central SD	Newark
132	3.2	South Orangetown Central SD	Blauvelt
132	3.2	Wappingers Central SD	Wappingers Fls
136	3.1	Baldwin Union Free SD	Baldwin
136	3.1	Cobleskill-Richmondville CSD	Cobleskill
136	3.1	Haverstraw-Stony Point Cent SD	Garnerville
136	3.1	Hicksville Union Free SD	Hicksville
136	3.1	Marcellus Central SD	Marcellus
136	3.1	Rocky Point Union Free SD	Rocky Point
136	3.1	Starpoint Central SD	Lockport
143	3.0	Bay Shore Union Free SD	Bay Shore
143	3.0	East Islip Union Free SD	Islip Terrace
143	3.0	Jordan-Elbridge Central SD	Jordan
143	3.0	Oswego City SD	Oswego
143	3.0	Phoenix Central SD	Phoenix
143	3.0	Wallkill Central SD	Wallkill
149	2.9	Amherst Central SD	Amherst
149	2.9	Holland Patent Central SD	Holland Patent
149	2.9	Victor Central SD	Victor
149	2.9	Wilson Central SD	Wilson
153	2.8	Canton Central SD	Canton
153	2.8	Gates-Chili Central SD	Rochester
153	2.8	Hamburg Central SD	Hamburg
153	2.8	Marlboro Central SD	Marlboro
157	2.7	Eden Central SD	Eden
157	2.7	Hudson Falls Central SD	Hudson Falls
157	2.7	Kenmore-Tonawanda Union Free SD	Buffalo
157	2.7	South Country Central SD	E Patchogue
161	2.6	Connetquot Central SD	Bohemia
161	2.6	Glens Falls City SD	Glens Falls
161	2.6	Longwood Central SD	Middle Island
161	2.6	South Huntington Union Free SD	Huntington Stn
165	2.5	Broadalbin-Perth Central SD	Broadalbin
165	2.5	Carmel Central SD	Patterson
165	2.5	East Syracuse-Minoa Central SD	East Syracuse
165	2.5	Grand Island Central SD	Grand Island
165	2.5	Homer Central SD	Homer
165	2.5	Hudson City SD	Hudson
165	2.5	Oyster Bay-East Norwich CSD	Oyster Bay
165	2.5	Penn Yan Central SD	Penn Yan
165	2.5	Westhampton Beach Union Free SD	Westhampton Bch
174	2.4	Highland Central SD	Highland
174	2.4	Lancaster Central SD	Lancaster
174	2.4	Southampton Union Free SD	Southampton
174	2.4	Sullivan West Central SD	Callicoon
174	2.4	Union-Endicott Central SD	Endicott
174	2.4	Valley Central SD (Montgomery)	Montgomery
174	2.4	West Genesee Central SD	Camillus
181	2.3	Cheektowaga-Sloan Union Free SD	Sloan
181	2.3	Fredonia Central SD	Fredonia
181	2.3	Horseheads Central SD	Horseheads
181	2.3	Long Beach City SD	Long Beach
181	2.3	Newburgh City SD	Newburgh
181	2.3	Ogdensburg City SD	Ogdensburg
181	2.3	White Plains City SD	White Plains
188	2.2	Carthage Central SD	Carthage
188	2.2	East Aurora Union Free SD	East Aurora
188	2.2	Kinderhook Central SD	Valatie
188	2.2	Ramapo Central SD (Suffern)	Hillburn
188	2.2	Rush-Henrietta Central SD	Henrietta
188	2.2	South Glens Falls Central SD	S Glens Falls
194	2.1	Nyack Union Free SD	Nyack
194	2.1	Solvay Union Free SD	Solvay
194	2.1	Susquehanna Valley Central SD	Conklin
194	2.1	Valley Stream Central High SD	Valley Stream
194	2.1	Whitney Point Central SD	Whitney Point
199	2.0	Malone Central SD	Malone
199	2.0	Patchogue-Medford Union Free SD	Patchogue
199	2.0	Ravena-Coeymans-Selkirk CSD	Selkirk
202	1.9	Cazenovia Central SD	Cazenovia
202	1.9	Chenango Forks Central SD	Binghamton
202	1.9	Orchard Park Central SD	Orchard Park
205	1.8	Baldwinsville Central SD	Baldwinsville
205	1.8	Chenango Valley Central SD	Binghamton
205	1.8	Hendrick Hudson Central SD	Montrose
205	1.8	Palmyra-Macedon Central SD	Palmyra
205	1.8	Saranac Lake Central SD	Saranac Lake
205	1.8	Somers Central SD	Lincolndale
211	1.7	Bath Central SD	Bath
211	1.7	Central Islip Union Free SD	Central Islip
211	1.7	Cornwall Central SD	Cornwall-on-Hud
211	1.7	East Irondequoit Central SD	Rochester
211	1.7	Greece Central SD	Rochester
211	1.7	Iroquois Central SD	Elma
211	1.7	Penfield Central SD	Penfield
211	1.7	Spencerport Central SD	Spencerport

Rank	Score	District	Location
219	1.6	Attica Central SD	Attica
219	1.6	Clinton Central SD	Clinton
219	1.6	General Brown Central SD	Dexter
219	1.6	Maine-Endwell Central SD	Endwell
219	1.6	Miller Place Union Free SD	Miller Place
219	1.6	New Hartford Central SD	New Hartford
219	1.6	North Colonie Central SD	Latham
219	1.6	Plainview-Old Bethpage Cent SD	Plainview
227	1.5	Bethlehem Central SD	Delmar
227	1.5	Canastota Central SD	Canastota
227	1.5	Churchville-Chili Central SD	Churchville
227	1.5	Island Trees Union Free SD	Levittown
227	1.5	South Colonie Central SD	Albany
227	1.5	Wayne Central SD	Ontario Center
227	1.5	Williamsville Central SD	East Amherst
234	1.4	Bayport-Blue Point Union Free SD	Bayport
234	1.4	Fairport Central SD	Fairport
234	1.4	Niskayuna Central SD	Schenectady
234	1.4	Saranac Central SD	Dannemora
234	1.4	Uniondale Union Free SD	Uniondale
234	1.4	Webster Central SD	Webster
240	1.3	Greenburgh Central SD	Hartsdale
240	1.3	Hauppauge Union Free SD	Hauppauge
240	1.3	Ithaca City SD	Ithaca
240	1.3	Mamaroneck Union Free SD	Mamaroneck
240	1.3	Northport-East Northport UFSD	Northport
240	1.3	Oneonta City SD	Oneonta
240	1.3	Port Washington Union Free SD	Pt Washington
240	1.3	Troy City SD	Troy
240	1.3	Washingtonville Central SD	Washingtonville
249	1.2	Fayetteville-Manlius Central SD	Manlius
249	1.2	Fonda-Fultonville Central SD	Fonda
249	1.2	Mineola Union Free SD	Mineola
249	1.2	Monroe-Woodbury Central SD	Central Valley
249	1.2	New Rochelle City SD	New Rochelle
249	1.2	Sachem Central SD	Holbrook
249	1.2	Wantagh Union Free SD	Wantagh
256	1.1	Eastchester Union Free SD	Eastchester
256	1.1	Goshen Central SD	Goshen
256	1.1	Jamesville-Dewitt Central SD	Dewitt
256	1.1	Manhasset Union Free SD	Manhasset
256	1.1	Mattituck-Cutchogue UFSD	Cutchogue
256	1.1	Schalmont Central SD	Schenectady
262	1.0	Brockport Central SD	Brockport
262	1.0	Carle Place Union Free SD	Carle Place
262	1.0	Cheektowaga Central SD	Cheektowaga
262	1.0	Harborfields Central SD	Greenlawn
262	1.0	Hewlett-Woodmere Union Free SD	Woodmere
262	1.0	Hilton Central SD	Hilton
262	1.0	Lynbrook Union Free SD	Lynbrook
262	1.0	Mahopac Central SD	Mahopac
262	1.0	Middletown City SD	Middletown
262	1.0	Norwich City SD	Norwich
262	1.0	Sewanhaka Central High SD	Floral Park
262	1.0	Sherrill City SD	Verona
262	1.0	Warwick Valley Central SD	Warwick
262	1.0	Yorktown Central SD	Yorktown Hgts
276	0.9	Bethpage Union Free SD	Bethpage
276	0.9	Binghamton City SD	Binghamton
276	0.9	Clarence Central SD	Clarence
276	0.9	Dryden Central SD	Dryden
276	0.9	Rotterdam-Mohonasen Central SD	Schenectady
276	0.9	Skaneateles Central SD	Skaneateles
276	0.9	Smithtown Central SD	Smithtown
283	0.8	Commack Union Free SD	E Northport
283	0.8	Harrison Central SD	Harrison
283	0.8	Lawrence Union Free SD	Lawrence
283	0.8	Mount Pleasant Central SD	Thornwood
283	0.8	Sayville Union Free SD	Sayville
288	0.7	Clarkstown Central SD	New City
288	0.7	Elwood Union Free SD	Greenlawn
288	0.7	Locust Valley Central SD	Locust Valley
288	0.7	Middle Country Central SD	Centereach
288	0.7	Mount Sinai Union Free SD	Mount Sinai
288	0.7	Northeastern Clinton Central SD	Champlain
288	0.7	Rye City SD	Rye
295	0.6	Brewster Central SD	Brewster
295	0.6	East Meadow Union Free SD	Westbury
295	0.6	Great Neck Union Free SD	Great Neck
295	0.6	Massapequa Union Free SD	Massapequa
295	0.6	North Shore Central SD	Sea Cliff
295	0.6	Pearl River Union Free SD	Pearl River
295	0.6	Pelham Union Free SD	Pelham
295	0.6	Phelps-Clifton Springs Cent SD	Clifton Spgs
295	0.6	Pleasantville Union Free SD	Pleasantville
295	0.6	Saratoga Springs City SD	Saratoga Spgs
295	0.6	Seaford Union Free SD	Seaford
295	0.6	West Irondequoit Central SD	Rochester
295	0.6	William Floyd Union Free SD	Mastic Beach
308	0.5	Brighton Central SD	Rochester
308	0.5	East Hampton Union Free SD	East Hampton
308	0.5	Half Hollow Hills Central SD	Dix Hills
308	0.5	Oceanside Union Free SD	Oceanside
308	0.5	Peekskill City SD	Peekskill
308	0.5	Vestal Central SD	Vestal
314	0.4	Katonah-Lewisboro Union Free SD	South Salem
314	0.4	Kings Park Central SD	Kings Park
314	0.4	Lansing Central SD	Lansing
314	0.4	Plainedge Union Free SD	N Massapequa
314	0.4	Schuylerville Central SD	Schuylerville
314	0.4	West Islip Union Free SD	West Islip
320	0.3	Burnt Hls-Ballston Lake Cent SD	Scotia
320	0.3	Copiague Union Free SD	Copiague
320	0.3	Deer Park Union Free SD	Deer Park
320	0.3	Farmingdale Union Free SD	Farmingdale
324	0.2	Ardsley Union Free SD	Ardsley
324	0.2	Babylon Union Free SD	Babylon
324	0.2	Garden City Union Free SD	Garden City
324	0.2	Gloversville City SD	Gloversville
324	0.2	Guilderland Central SD	Guilderland
324	0.2	Hastings-On-Hudson Union Free SD	Hastings-on-Hud
324	0.2	Herricks Union Free SD	New Hyde Park
324	0.2	Irvington Union Free SD	Irvington
324	0.2	Malverne Union Free SD	Malverne
324	0.2	Nanuet Union Free SD	Nanuet
324	0.2	Scarsdale Union Free SD	Scarsdale
324	0.2	Syosset Central SD	Syosset
324	0.2	Wyandanch Union Free SD	Wyandanch
337	0.1	Jericho Union Free SD	Jericho
337	0.1	Levittown Union Free SD	Levittown
337	0.1	Lindenhurst Union Free SD	Lindenhurst
337	0.1	Owego-Apalachin Central SD	Owego
337	0.1	Rockville Centre Union Free SD	Rockville Ctre
337	0.1	Roslyn Union Free SD	Roslyn
337	0.1	Scotia-Glenville Central SD	Scotia
337	0.1	Shoreham-Wading River Central SD	Shoreham
337	0.1	Westhill Central SD	Syracuse
346	0.0	Briarcliff Manor Union Free SD	Briarcliff Manor
346	0.0	Byram Hills Central SD	Armonk
346	0.0	Chappaqua Central SD	Chappaqua
346	0.0	Chatham Central SD	Chatham
346	0.0	Cold Spring Harbor Central SD	Cold Sprg Harbor
346	0.0	East Williston Union Free SD	Old Westbury
346	0.0	Edgemont Union Free SD	Scarsdale
346	0.0	Hampton Bays Union Free SD	Hampton Bays
346	0.0	Liberty Central SD	Liberty
346	0.0	North Babylon Union Free SD	North Babylon
346	0.0	Putnam Valley Central SD	Putnam Valley
346	0.0	Shenendehowa Central SD	Clifton Park
358	n/a	New York City Geographic Dist 9	Bronx
358	n/a	New York City Geographic Dist 15	Brooklyn
358	n/a	Nyc Alternative HS District	New York
361	n/a	Boces Eastern Suffolk	Patchogue
361	n/a	Boces Nassau	Garden City
361	n/a	Elmont Union Free SD	Elmont
361	n/a	Floral Park-Bellerose UFSD	Floral Park
361	n/a	Franklin Square Union Free SD	Franklin Square
361	n/a	Merrick Union Free SD	Merrick
361	n/a	New Hyde Park-Garden City Park	New Hyde Park
361	n/a	North Bellmore Union Free SD	Bellmore
361	n/a	Valley Stream 13 Union Free SD	Valley Stream
361	n/a	Valley Stream 30 Union Free SD	Valley Stream

2005 New York State NAEP Public School Snapshot
Grade 4 Mathematics

The National Assessment of Educational Progress (NAEP) assesses mathematics in five content areas: number properties and operations; measurement; geometry; data analysis and probability; and algebra. The NAEP mathematics scale ranges from 0 to 500.

Overall Mathematics Results for New York

- In 2005, the average scale score for fourth-grade students in New York was 238. This was not significantly different from[1] their average score in 2003 (236), and was higher than their average score in 1992 (218).
- New York's average score (238) in 2005 was not significantly different from that of the Nation's public schools (237).
- Of the 52 states and other jurisdictions[2] that participated in the 2005 fourth-grade assessment, students' average scale scores in New York were higher than those in 17 jurisdictions, not significantly different from those in 18 jurisdictions, and lower than those in 16 jurisdictions.
- The percentage of students in New York who performed at or above the NAEP *Proficient* level was 36 percent in 2005. This percentage was not significantly different from that in 2003 (33 percent), and was greater than that in 1992 (17 percent).
- The percentage of students in New York who performed at or above the NAEP *Basic* level was 81 percent in 2005. This percentage was not significantly different from that in 2003 (79 percent), and was greater than that in 1992 (57 percent).

Student Percentage at NAEP Achievement Levels

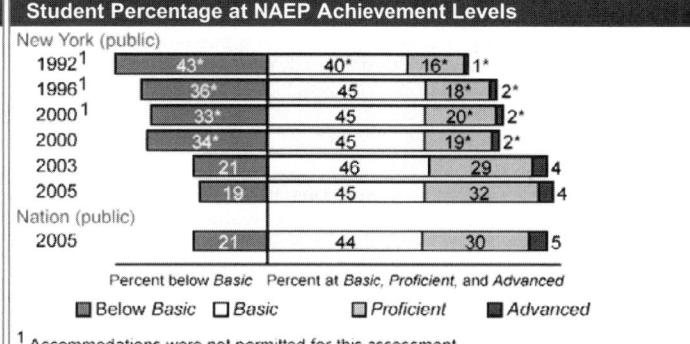

[1] Accommodations were not permitted for this assessment.

NOTE: The NAEP mathematics achievement levels correspond to the following scale points: Below *Basic*, 213 or lower; *Basic*, 214–248; *Proficient*, 249–281; *Advanced*, 282 or above.

Performance of NAEP Reporting Groups in New York

Reporting groups	Percent of students	Average score	Percent below *Basic*	Percent of students at or above *Basic*	Percent of students at or above *Proficient*	Percent *Advanced*
Male	50	240	18	82	39	5
Female	50	237	19	81	33	3
White	53	247	9	91	49	6
Black	21	222	36	64	13	1
Hispanic	19	226	30	70	17	1
Asian/Pacific Islander	7	254	7	93	61	15
American Indian/Alaska Native	1	‡	‡	‡	‡	‡
Eligible for free/reduced-price school lunch	48	228	30	70	21	2
Not eligible for free/reduced-price school lunch	49	248	8	92	50	7

Average Score Gaps Between Selected Groups

- In 2005, male students in New York had an average score that was higher than that of female students by 3 points. In 1992, the average score for male students was higher than that of female students by 7 points.
- In 2005, Black students had an average score that was lower than that of White students by 25 points. In 1992, the average score for Black students was lower than that of White students by 31 points.
- In 2005, Hispanic students had an average score that was lower than that of White students by 21 points. This performance gap was narrower than that of 1992 (32 points).
- In 2005, students who were eligible for free/reduced-price school lunch, an indicator of poverty, had an average score that was lower than that of students who were not eligible for free/reduced-price school lunch by 20 points. This performance gap was narrower than that of 1996 (30 points).
- In 2005, the score gap between students at the 75th percentile and students at the 25th percentile was 37 points. This performance gap was narrower than that of 1992 (43 points).

Mathematics Scale Scores at Selected Percentiles

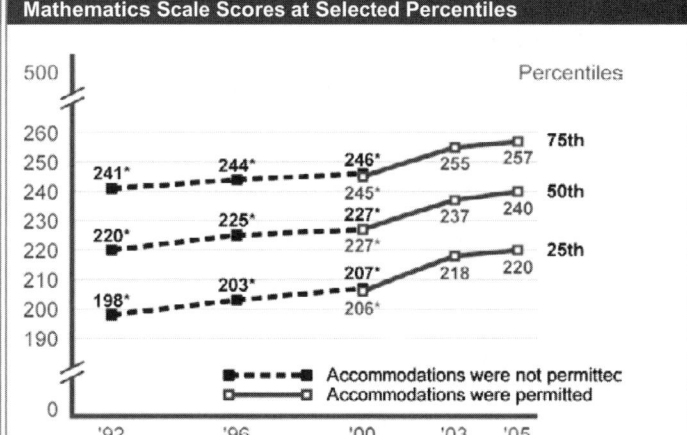

Scores at selected percentiles on the NAEP mathematics scale indicate how well students at lower, middle, and higher levels of the distribution performed.

\# The estimate rounds to zero.   ‡ Reporting standards not met.
* Significantly different from 2005.   ↑ Significantly higher than 2003.   ↓ Significantly lower than 2003.

[1] Comparisons (higher/lower/not different) are based on statistical tests. The .05 level was used for testing statistical significance. Performance comparisons may be affected by differences in exclusion rates across years for students with disabilities (2% nationally in 2005) and English language learners (1% nationally in 2005) in the NAEP samples. Statistical comparisons are calculated on the basis of unrounded scale scores or percentages.
[2] "Other Jurisdictions" refers to the District of Columbia and the Department of Defense Education Activity schools.
NOTE: Detail may not sum to totals because of rounding and because the "Information not available" category for free/reduced-price lunch and the "Unclassifed" category for race/ethnicity are not displayed. Visit http://nces.ed.gov/nationsreportcard/states/ for additional results and detailed information.
SOURCE: U.S. Department of Education, Institute of Education Sciences, National Center for Education Statistics, National Assessment of Educational Progress (NAEP), selected years, 1992–2005 Mathematics Assessments.

2005 New York State NAEP Public School Snapshot
Grade 4 Reading

The National Assessment of Educational Progress (NAEP) assesses reading in two content areas: reading for literary experience and to gain information. The NAEP reading scale ranges from 0 to 500.

Overall Reading Results for New York

- In 2005, the average scale score for fourth-grade students in New York was 223. This was not significantly different from[1] their average score in 2003 (222), and was higher than their average score in 1992 (215).
- New York's average score (223) in 2005 was higher than that of the Nation's public schools (217).
- Of the 52 states and other jurisdictions[2] that participated in the 2005 fourth-grade assessment, students' average scale scores in New York were higher than those in 24 jurisdictions, not significantly different from those in 21 jurisdictions, and lower than those in 6 jurisdictions.
- The percentage of students in New York who performed at or above the NAEP Proficient level was 33 percent in 2005. This percentage was not significantly different from that in 2003 (34 percent), and was greater than that in 1992 (27 percent).
- The percentage of students in New York who performed at or above the NAEP Basic level was 69 percent in 2005. This percentage was not significantly different from that in 2003 (67 percent), and was greater than that in 1992 (61 percent).

Student Percentage at NAEP Achievement Levels

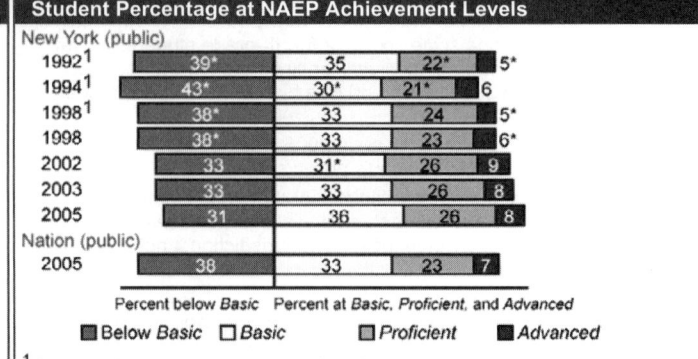

[1] Accommodations were not permitted for this assessment.

NOTE: The NAEP reading achievement levels correspond to the following scale points: Below Basic, 207 or lower; Basic, 208–237; Proficient, 238–267; Advanced 268 or above.

Performance of NAEP Reporting Groups in New York

Reporting groups	Percent of students	Average score	Percent below Basic	Percent of students at or above Basic	Percent of students at or above Proficient	Percent Advanced
Male	50	220	33	67	30	7
Female	50	225	29	71	36	9
White	53	232	20	80	43	10
Black	20	207	50	50	17	2
Hispanic	18	208	48	52	17	3
Asian/Pacific Islander	7	237	19	81	50	16
American Indian/Alaska Native	1	‡	‡	‡	‡	‡
Eligible for free/reduced-price school lunch	49	210	46	54	20	3
Not eligible for free/reduced-price school lunch	48	234	17	83	46	12

Average Score Gaps Between Selected Groups

- In 2005, male students in New York had an average score that was lower than that of female students by 5 points. In 1992, the average score for male students was lower than that of female students by 6 points.
- In 2005, Black students had an average score that was lower than that of White students by 24 points. In 1992, the average score for Black students was lower than that of White students by 27 points.
- In 2005, Hispanic students had an average score that was lower than that of White students by 24 points. This performance gap was narrower than that of 1992 (42 points).
- In 2005, students who were eligible for free/reduced-price school lunch, an indicator of poverty, had an average score that was lower than that of students who were not eligible for free/reduced-price school lunch by 24 points. This performance gap was narrower than that of 1998 (35 points).
- In 2005, the score gap between students at the 75th percentile and students at the 25th percentile was 44 points. In 1992, the score gap between students at the 75th percentile and students at the 25th percentile was 46 points.

Reading Scale Scores at Selected Percentiles

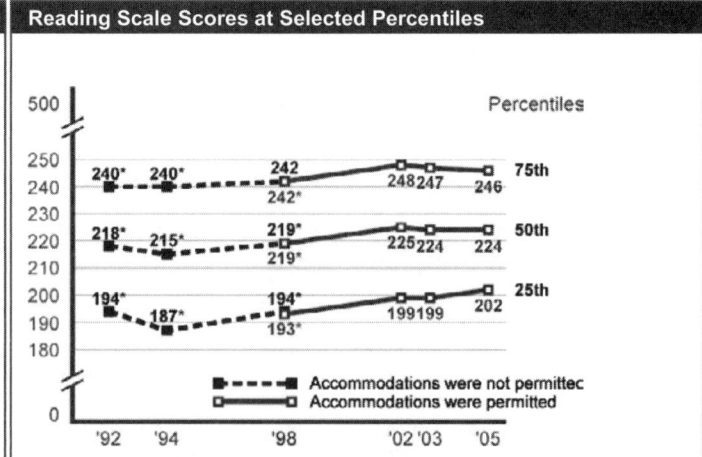

Scores at selected percentiles on the NAEP reading scale indicate how well students at lower, middle, and higher levels of the distribution performed.

\# The estimate rounds to zero.   ‡ Reporting standards not met.
* Significantly different from 2005.   † Significantly higher than 2003. ↓ Significantly lower than 2003.

[1] Comparisons (higher/lower/not different) are based on statistical tests. The .05 level was used for testing statistical significance. Performance comparisons may be affected by differences in exclusion rates across years for students with disabilities (5% nationally in 2005) and English language learners (2% nationally in 2005) in the NAEP samples. Statistical comparisons are calculated on the basis of unrounded scale scores or percentages.
[2] "Other Jurisdictions" refers to the District of Columbia and the Department of Defense Education Activity schools.
NOTE: Detail may not sum to totals because of rounding and because the "Information not available" category for free/reduced-price lunch and the "Unclassifed" category for race/ethnicity are not displayed. Visit http://nces.ed.gov/nationsreportcard/states/ for additional results and detailed information.
SOURCE: U.S. Department of Education, Institute of Education Sciences, National Center for Education Statistics, National Assessment of Educational Progress (NAEP), selected years, 1992–2005 Reading Assessments.

2005 New York State NAEP Public School Snapshot
Grade 4 Writing

The writing assessment of the National Assessment of Educational Progress (NAEP) measures narrative, informative, and persuasive writing–three purposes identified in the NAEP framework. The NAEP writing scale ranges from 0 to 300.

Overall Writing Results for New York

- The average scale score for fourth-grade students in New York was 163.
- New York's average score (163) was higher[1] than that of the nation's public schools (153).
- Students' average scale scores in New York were higher than those in 42 jurisdictions[2], not significantly different from those in 3 jurisdictions, and lower than those in 2 jurisdictions.
- The percentage of students who performed at or above the NAEP *Proficient* level was 37 percent. The percentage of students who performed at or above the *Basic* level was 91 percent.

Student Percentage at Each Achievement Level

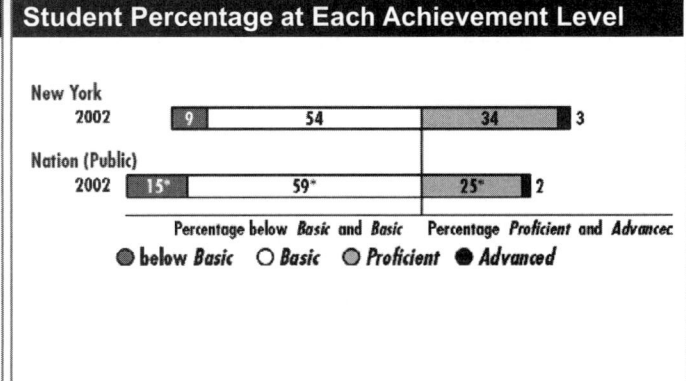

Performance of NAEP Reporting Groups in New York

Reporting groups	Percentage of students	Average Score	Below *Basic*	*Basic*	*Proficient*	*Advanced*
Male	51	156 ↑	12 ↓	58	28 ↑	2
Female	49	170 ↑	6 ↓	50 ↓	40 ↑	4
White	54	172 ↑	4 ↓	49 ↓	42 ↑	4
Black	19	148 ↑	16 ↓	63	20 ↑	1
Hispanic	21	149	16	61	22	1
Asian/Pacific Islander	6	176	4	44	47	5
American Indian/Alaska Native	#	---	---	---	---	---
Free/reduced-priced school lunch						
Eligible	44	150 ↑	16 ↓	61	22 ↑	1
Not eligible	49	172 ↑	4 ↓	49 ↓	43 ↑	4
Information not available	7	175 ↑	5 ↓	43	46 ↑	6

Average Score Gaps Between Selected Groups

- Female students in New York had an average score that was higher than that of male students (14 points). This performance gap was not significantly different from that of the Nation (18 points).
- White students had an average score that was higher than that of Black students (24 points). This performance gap was not significantly different from that of the Nation (20 points).
- White students had an average score that was higher than that of Hispanic students (23 points). This performance gap was not significantly different from that of the Nation (19 points).
- Students who were not eligible for free/reduced-price school lunch had an average score that was higher than that of students who were eligible (22 points). This performance gap was not significantly different from that of the Nation (22 points).

Writing Scale Scores at Selected Percentiles

Scale Score Distribution

	25th Percentile	50th Percentile	75th Percentile
New York	139 ↑	164 ↑	187 ↑
Nation (Public)	128	153	178

An examination of scores at different percentiles on the 0-300 NAEP writing scale at each grade indicates how well students at lower, middle, and higher levels of the distribution performed. For example, the data above shows that 75 percent of students in public schools nationally scored below *178,* while 75 percent of students in New York scored below *187.*

\# Percentage rounds to zero.   --- Reporting standards not met; sample size insufficient to permit a reliable estimate.
* Significantly different from New York.   ↑ Significantly higher than, ↓ lower than appropriate subgroup in the nation (public).
[1] Comparisons (higher/lower/not different) are based on statistical tests. The .05 level was used for testing statistical significance.
[2] "Jurisdictions" includes participating states and other jurisdictions (such as Guam or the District of Columbia).
NOTE: Detail may not sum to totals because of rounding. Score gaps are calculated based on differences between unrounded average scale scores.
Visit http://nces.ed.gov/nationsreportcard/states/ for additional results and detailed information.
SOURCE: U.S. Department of Education, Institute of Education Sciences, National Center for Education Statistics, National Assessment of Educational Progress (NAEP), 2002 Writing Assessment.

2005 New York State NAEP Public School Snapshot
Grade 8 Mathematics

The National Assessment of Educational Progress (NAEP) assesses mathematics in five content areas: number properties and operations; measurement; geometry; data analysis and probability; and algebra. The NAEP mathematics scale ranges from 0 to 500.

Overall Mathematics Results for New York

- In 2005, the average scale score for eighth-grade students in New York was 280. This was not significantly different from[1] their average score in 2003 (280), and was higher than their average score in 1990 (261).
- New York's average score (280) in 2005 was higher than that of the Nation's public schools (278).
- Of the 52 states and other jurisdictions[2] that participated in the 2005 eighth-grade assessment, students' average scale scores in New York were higher than those in 17 jurisdictions, not significantly different from those in 18 jurisdictions, and lower than those in 16 jurisdictions.
- The percentage of students in New York who performed at or above the NAEP *Proficient* level was 31 percent in 2005. This percentage was not significantly different from that in 2003 (32 percent), and was greater than that in 1990 (15 percent).
- The percentage of students in New York who performed at or above the NAEP *Basic* level was 70 percent in 2005. This percentage was not significantly different from that in 2003 (70 percent), and was greater than that in 1990 (50 percent).

Student Percentage at NAEP Achievement Levels

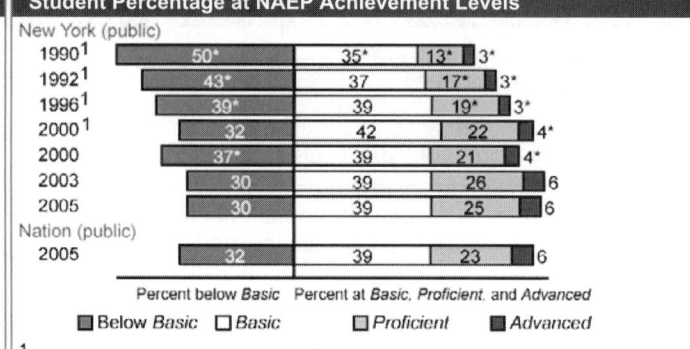

[1] Accommodations were not permitted for this assessment.

NOTE: The NAEP mathematics achievement levels correspond to the following scale points: Below *Basic*, 261 or lower; *Basic*, 262–298; *Proficient*, 299–332; *Advanced*, 333 or above.

Performance of NAEP Reporting Groups in New York

Reporting groups	Percent of students	Average score	Percent below *Basic*	Percent of students at or above *Basic*	Percent of students at or above *Proficient*	Percent *Advanced*
Male	50	280	30	70	31	7
Female	50	280	30	70	30	6
White	55	290	17	83	41	8
Black	19	259	54	46	11	1
Hispanic	18	262	49	51	14	2
Asian/Pacific Islander	7	298	17	83	50	19
American Indian/Alaska Native	#	‡	‡	‡	‡	‡
Eligible for free/reduced-price school lunch	45	267 ↑	44	56	19	3
Not eligible for free/reduced-price school lunch	50	291	17	83	41	9

Average Score Gaps Between Selected Groups

- In 2005, male students in New York had an average score that was not found to be significantly different from that of female students. In 1990, there was no significant difference between the average score of male and female students.
- In 2005, Black students had an average score that was lower than that of White students by 32 points. In 1990, the average score for Black students was lower than that of White students by 39 points.
- In 2005, Hispanic students had an average score that was lower than that of White students by 28 points. In 1990, the average score for Hispanic students was lower than that of White students by 35 points.
- In 2005, students who were eligible for free/reduced-price school lunch, an indicator of poverty, had an average score that was lower than that of students who were not eligible for free/reduced-price school lunch by 24 points. In 1996, the average score for students who were eligible for free/reduced-price school lunch was lower than the score of those not eligible by 29 points.
- In 2005, the score gap between students at the 75th percentile and students at the 25th percentile was 48 points. In 1990, the score gap between students at the 75th percentile and students at the 25th percentile was 50 points.

Mathematics Scale Scores at Selected Percentiles

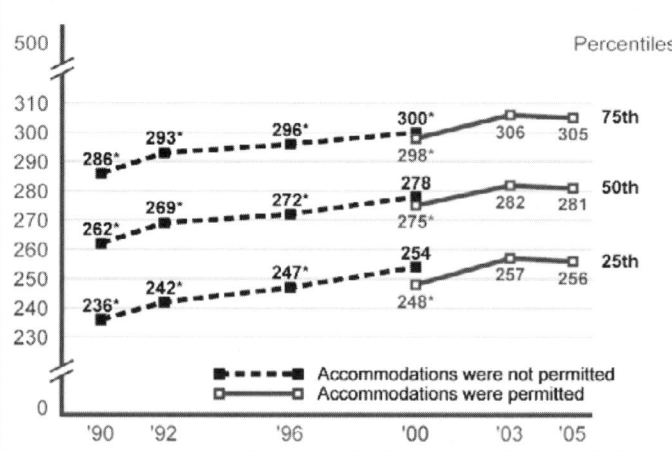

Scores at selected percentiles on the NAEP mathematics scale indicate how well students at lower, middle, and higher levels of the distribution performed.

\# The estimate rounds to zero.   ‡ Reporting standards not met.
* Significantly different from 2005.   ↑ Significantly higher than 2003.   ↓ Significantly lower than 2003.

[1] Comparisons (higher/lower/not different) are based on statistical tests. The .05 level was used for testing statistical significance. Performance comparisons may be affected by differences in exclusion rates across years for students with disabilities (3% nationally in 2005) and English language learners (1% nationally in 2005) in the NAEP samples. Statistical comparisons are calculated on the basis of unrounded scale scores or percentages.
[2] "Other Jurisdictions" refers to the District of Columbia and the Department of Defense Education Activity schools.
NOTE: Detail may not sum to totals because of rounding and because the "Information not available" category for free/reduced-price lunch and the "Unclassifed" category for race/ethnicity are not displayed. Visit http://nces.ed.gov/nationsreportcard/states/ for additional results and detailed information.
SOURCE: U.S. Department of Education, Institute of Education Sciences, National Center for Education Statistics, National Assessment of Educational Progress (NAEP), selected years, 1990–2005 Mathematics Assessments.

2005 New York State NAEP Public School Snapshot
Grade 8 Reading

The National Assessment of Educational Progress (NAEP) assesses reading in three content areas: reading for literary experience, to gain information, and to perform a task. The NAEP reading scale ranges from 0 to 500.

Overall Reading Results for New York

- In 2005, the average scale score for eighth-grade students in New York was 265. This was not significantly different from[1] their average score in 2003 (265), and was not significantly different from their average score in 1998 (265).
- New York's average score (265) in 2005 was higher than that of the Nation's public schools (260).
- Of the 52 states and other jurisdictions[2] that participated in the 2005 eighth-grade assessment, students' average scale scores in New York were higher than those in 24 jurisdictions, not significantly different from those in 17 jurisdictions, and lower than those in 10 jurisdictions.
- The percentage of students in New York who performed at or above the NAEP *Proficient* level was 33 percent in 2005. This percentage was not significantly different from that in 2003 (35 percent), and was not significantly different from that in 1998 (32 percent).
- The percentage of students in New York who performed at or above the NAEP *Basic* level was 75 percent in 2005. This percentage was not significantly different from that in 2003 (75 percent), and was not significantly different from that in 1998 (76 percent).

Student Percentage at NAEP Achievement Levels

Year	Below Basic	Basic	Proficient	Advanced
New York (public)				
1998[1]	22	44	31	2
1998	24	44	30	2
2002	24	44	30	2*
2003	25	40	31	4
2005	25	42	30	3
Nation (public)				
2005	29	42	26	3

Percent below *Basic* Percent at *Basic*, *Proficient*, and *Advanced*
■ Below *Basic* □ *Basic* ▨ *Proficient* ■ *Advanced*

[1] Accommodations were not permitted for this assessment.

NOTE: The NAEP reading achievement levels correspond to the following scale points: Below *Basic*, 242 or lower; *Basic*, 243–280; *Proficient*, 281–322; *Advanced*, 323 or above.

Performance of NAEP Reporting Groups in New York

Reporting groups	Percent of students	Average score	Percent below *Basic*	Percent of students at or above *Basic*	Percent of students at or above *Proficient*	Percent Advanced
Male	50	260	30	70	28	2
Female	50	270	20	80	38	4
White	57	276	13	87	45	5
Black	18	242	49	51	11	#
Hispanic	18	250	39	61	16	1
Asian/Pacific Islander	6	274	18	82	45	6
American Indian/Alaska Native	#	‡	‡	‡	‡	‡
Eligible for free/reduced-price school lunch	45	253	37	63	20	1
Not eligible for free/reduced-price school lunch	50	276	13	87	46	5

Average Score Gaps Between Selected Groups

- In 2005, male students in New York had an average score that was lower than that of female students by 10 points. In 1998, the average score for male students was lower than that of female students by 8 points.
- In 2005, Black students had an average score that was lower than that of White students by 34 points. In 1998, the average score for Black students was lower than that of White students by 28 points.
- In 2005, Hispanic students had an average score that was lower than that of White students by 26 points. In 1998, the average score for Hispanic students was lower than that of White students by 28 points.
- In 2005, students who were eligible for free/reduced-price school lunch, an indicator of poverty, had an average score that was lower than that of students who were not eligible for free/reduced-price school lunch by 24 points. In 1998, the average score for students who were eligible for free/reduced-price school lunch was lower than the score of those not eligible by 25 points.
- In 2005, the score gap between students at the 75th percentile and students at the 25th percentile was 46 points. In 1998, the score gap between students at the 75th percentile and students at the 25th percentile was 43 points.

Reading Scale Scores at Selected Percentiles

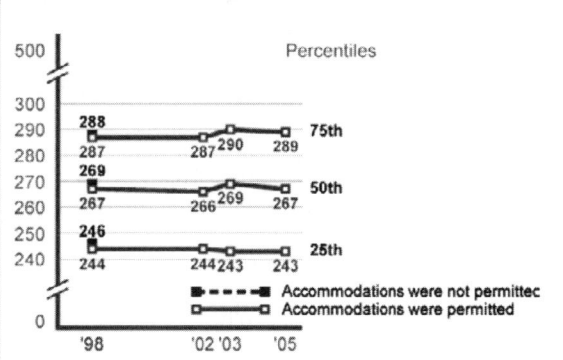

Scores at selected percentiles on the NAEP reading scale indicate how well students at lower, middle, and higher levels of the distribution performed.

\# The estimate rounds to zero.   ‡ Reporting standards not met.
* Significantly different from 2005.   ↑ Significantly higher than 2003. ↓ Significantly lower than 2003.

[1] Comparisons (higher/lower/not different) are based on statistical tests. The .05 level was used for testing statistical significance. Performance comparisons may be affected by differences in exclusion rates across years for students with disabilities (4% nationally in 2005) and English language learners (1% nationally in 2005) in the NAEP samples. Statistical comparisons are calculated on the basis of unrounded scale scores or percentages.
[2] "Other Jurisdictions" refers to the District of Columbia and the Department of Defense Education Activity schools.
NOTE: Detail may not sum to totals because of rounding and because the "Information not available" category for free/reduced-price lunch and the "Unclassifed" category for race/ethnicity are not displayed. Visit http://nces.ed.gov/nationsreportcard/states/ for additional results and detailed information.
SOURCE: U.S. Department of Education, Institute of Education Sciences, National Center for Education Statistics, National Assessment of Educational Progress (NAEP), selected years, 1998–2005 Reading Assessments.

2005 New York State NAEP Public School Snapshot
Grade 8 Writing

The writing assessment of the National Assessment of Educational Progress (NAEP) measures narrative, informative, and persuasive writing–three purposes identified in the NAEP framework. The NAEP writing scale ranges from 0 to 300.

Overall Writing Results for New York

- The average scale score for eighth-grade students in New York was 151. This was higher[1] than the average score (146) in 1998.
- New York's average score (151) was not found to be significantly different from that of the nation's public schools (152).
- Students' average scale scores in New York were higher than those in 17 jurisdictions[2], not significantly different from those in 18 jurisdictions, and lower than those in 11 jurisdictions.
- The percentage of students who performed at or above the NAEP *Proficient* level was 30 percent. This percentage was greater than 1998 (21).

Student Percentage at Each Achievement Level

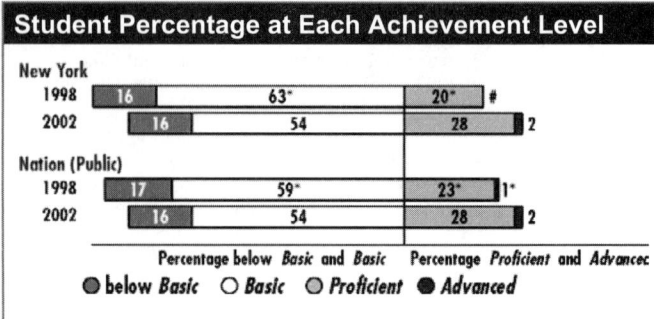

Performance of NAEP Reporting Groups in New York

Reporting groups	Percentage of students	Average Score	Below Basic	Basic	Proficient	Advanced
Male	52	142	22	58 ↓	19 ↑	1
Female	48	162 ↑	10	50 ↓	37 ↑	3 ↑
White	55	163 ↑	8	50 ↓	39 ↑	3 ↑
Black	21	134	27	61	12	#
Hispanic	17	133	29	60	11	#
Asian/Pacific Islander	6	155	14	52	31	3
American Indian/Alaska Native	#	---	---	---	---	---
Free/reduced-priced school lunch						
Eligible	37	134	27	60	13	#
Not eligible	56	165 ↑	8	50 ↓	39 ↑	3 ↑
Information not available	8	136 ↓	30 ↑	53	17	#

Average Score Gaps Between Selected Groups

- Female students in New York had an average score that was higher than that of male students (20 points). This performance gap was not significantly different from that of 1998 (15 points).
- White students had an average score that was higher than that of Black students (30 points). This performance gap was not significantly different from that of 1998 (25 points).
- White students had an average score that was higher than that of Hispanic students (30 points). This performance gap was not significantly different from that of 1998 (31 points).
- Students who were not eligible for free/reduced-price school lunch had an average score that was higher than that of students who were eligible (30 points). This performance gap was not significantly different from that of 1998 (26 points).

Writing Scale Scores at Selected Percentiles

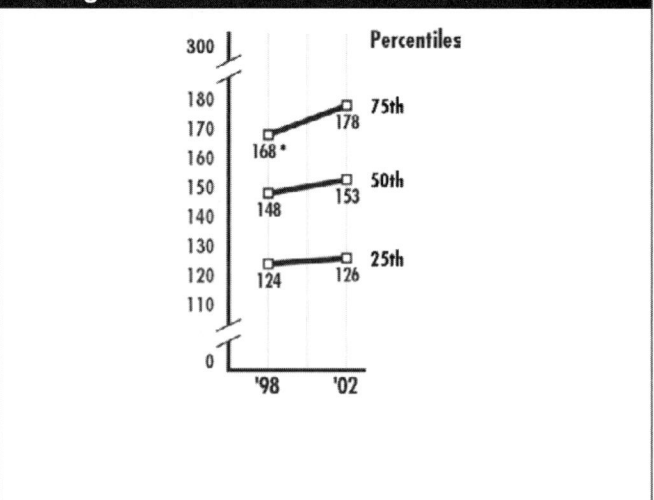

\# Percentage rounds to zero.   --- Reporting standards not met; sample size insufficient to permit a reliable estimate.
* Significantly different from 2002.   ↑ Statistically significantly higher than 1998.   ↓ Statistically significantly lower than 1998.
[1] Comparisons (higher/lower/not different) are based on statistical tests. The .05 level was used for testing statistical significance.
[2] "Jurisdictions" includes participating states and other jurisdictions (such as Guam or the District of Columbia).
NOTE: Detail may not sum to totals because of rounding. Score gaps are calculated based on differences between unrounded average scale scores. Performance changes across years should be interpreted in the context of changes in rates of exclusion of special-needs students, which occurred in some states. See *The Nation's Report Card: Writing 2002* for additional information.
Visit http://nces.ed.gov/nationsreportcard/states/ for additional results and detailed information.
SOURCE: U.S. Department of Education, Institute of Education Sciences, National Center for Education Statistics, National Assessment of Educational Progress (NAEP), 1998 and 2002 Writing Assessments.

Elementary Level
English Language Arts

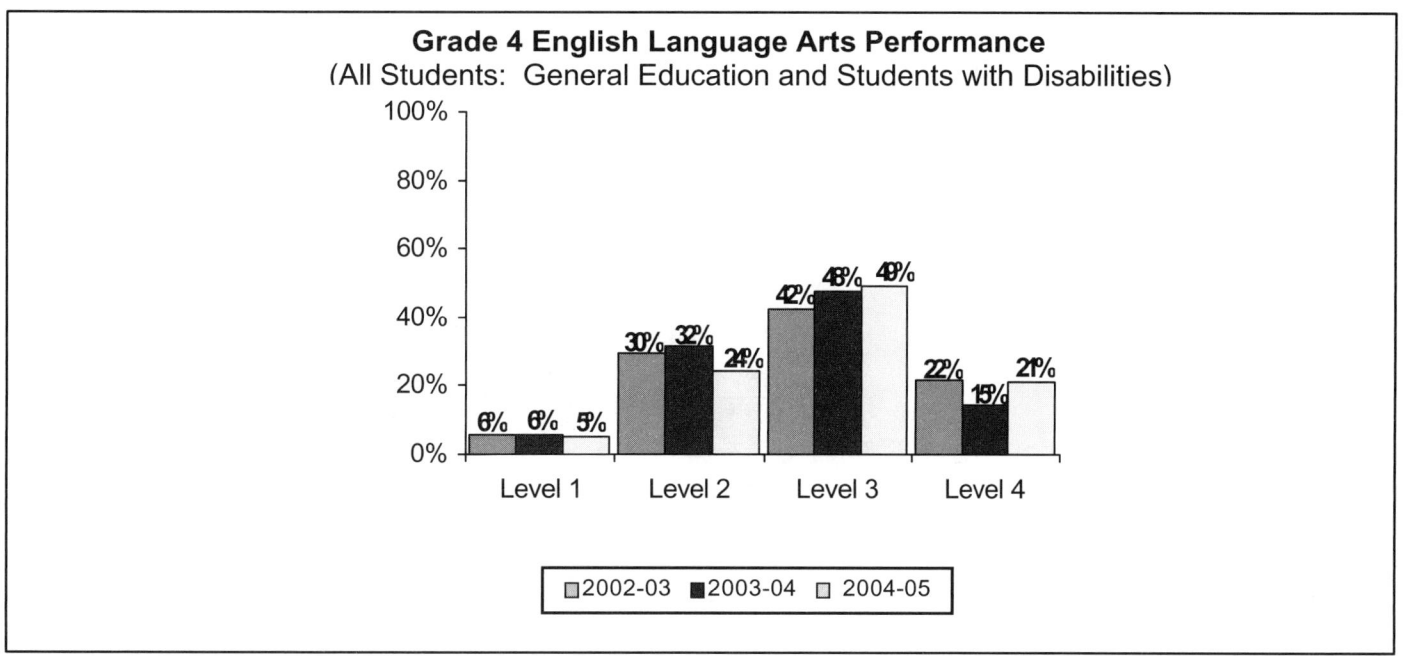

Grade 4 English Language Arts Performance
(All Students: General Education and Students with Disabilities)

Statewide Performance	Counts of Students				Total Tested	Mean Score
	Level 1 455–602	Level 2 603–644	Level 3 645–691	Level 4 692–800		
Feb 2003	12,394	62,455	89,069	45,987	209,905	660
Feb 2004	12,109	65,680	98,097	30,360	206,246	656
Feb 2005	10,588	47,593	96,845	41,455	196,481	665

Elementary-Level English Language Arts Levels — Listening, Reading, and Writing Standards	
Level 4	These students **exceed the standards** and are moving toward high performance on the Regents examination.
Level 3	These students **meet the standards** and, with continued steady growth, should pass the Regents examination.
Level 2	These students **need extra help** to meet the standards and pass the Regents examination.
Level 1	These students have **serious academic deficiencies**.

Performance of Limited English Proficient Students Taking the New York State English as a Second Language Achievement Test (NYSESLAT) as the Measure of English Language Arts Achievement

Grade 4	Level 1	Level 2	Levels 3 & 4	Total Tested
2005	4,128	1,843	5,132	11,103

Performance of Students with Severe Disabilities on the New York State Alternate Assessment (NYSAA) in English

Elementary Level	AA–Level 1	AA–Level 2	AA–Level 3	AA–Level 4	Total Tested
2004–05	23	176	351	1,253	1,803

Elementary Level
Mathematics

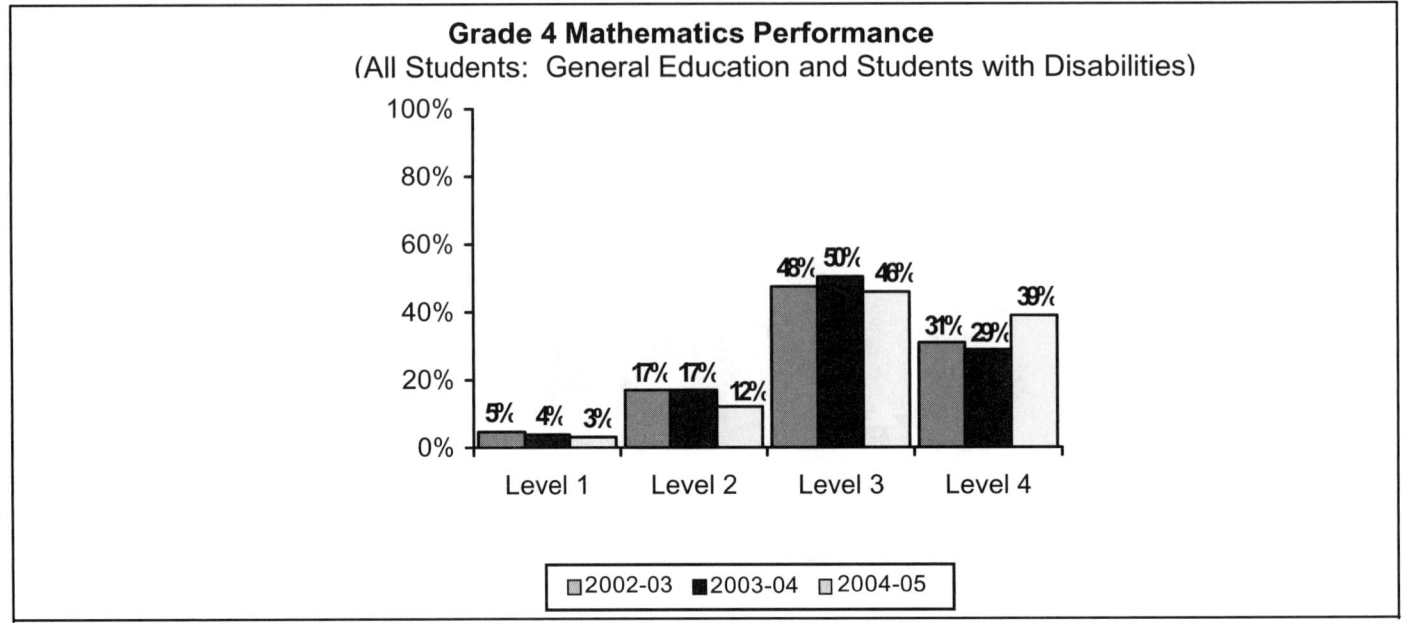

Grade 4 Mathematics Performance
(All Students: General Education and Students with Disabilities)

Statewide Performance	Counts of Students				Total Tested	Mean Score
	Level 1 448–601	Level 2 602–636	Level 3 637–677	Level 4 678–810		
May 2003	10,342	36,918	103,645	67,274	218,179	661
May 2004	8,352	36,455	108,183	61,706	214,696	661
May 2005	6,534	24,969	95,464	80,710	207,677	670

Elementary-Level Mathematics Levels — Knowledge, Reasoning, and Problem-Solving Standards	
Level 4	These students **exceed the standards** and are moving toward high performance on the Regents examination.
Level 3	These students **meet the standards** and, with continued steady growth, should pass the Regents examination.
Level 2	These students **need extra help** to meet the standards and pass the Regents examination.
Level 1	These students have **serious academic deficiencies**.

Performance of Students with Severe Disabilities on the New York State Alternate Assessment (NYSAA) in Mathematics

Elementary Level	AA–Level 1	AA–Level 2	AA–Level 3	AA–Level 4	Total Tested
2004–05	49	184	339	1,181	1,753

Elementary Level
*Science**

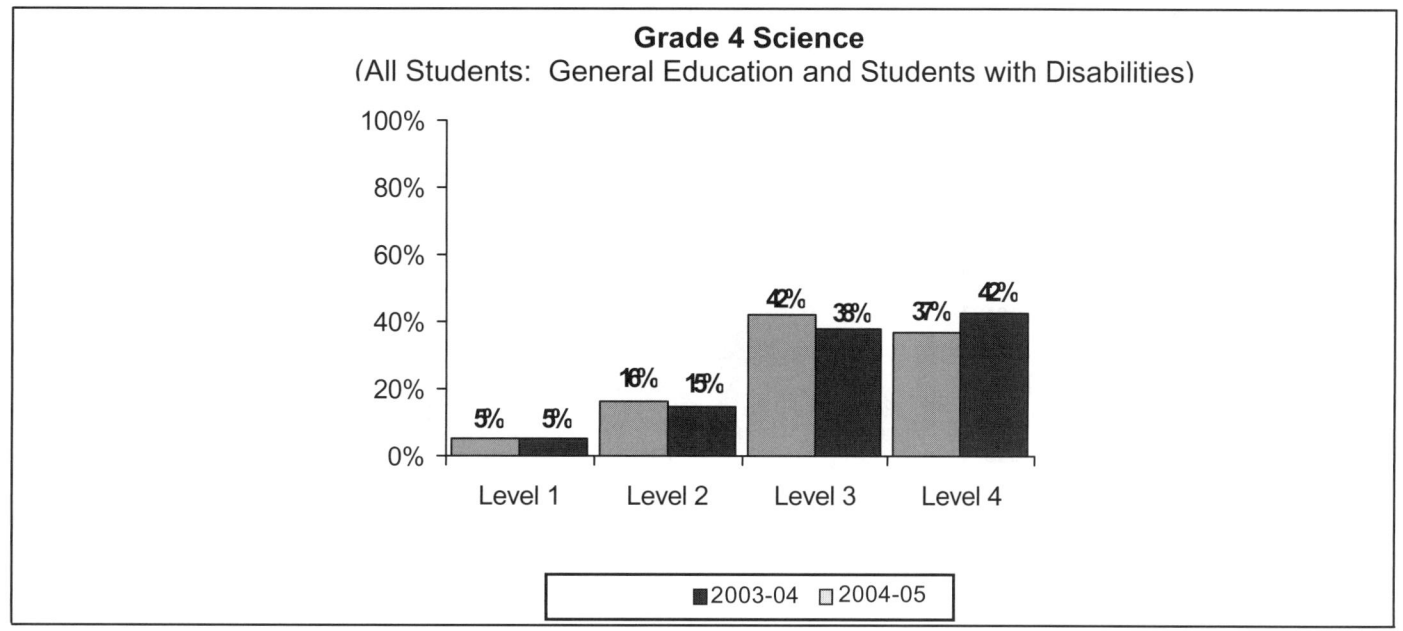

Statewide Performance	Counts of Students				Total Tested	Mean Score
	Level 1 0–44	Level 2 45–64	Level 3 65–84	Level 4 85–100		
May 2004	10,864	34,220	89,088	78,044	212,216	76
May 2005	10,742	29,915	77,410	87,080	205,147	77

Elementary-Level Science Levels — Knowledge, Reasoning, and Problem-Solving Standards	
Level 4	These students **exceed the standards** and are moving toward high performance on the Regents examination.
Level 3	These students **meet the standards** and, with continued steady growth, should pass the Regents examination.
Level 2	These students **need extra help** to meet the standards and pass the Regents examination.
Level 1	These students have **serious academic deficiencies**.

Performance of Students with Severe Disabilities on the New York State Alternate Assessment (NYSAA) in Science

Elementary Level	AA–Level 1	AA–Level 2	AA–Level 3	AA–Level 4	Total Tested
2004–05	52	214	328	1,157	1,751

*Only two years of data are shown because a new assessment in elementary-level science was administered for the first time in 2003–04.

Middle Level
English Language Arts

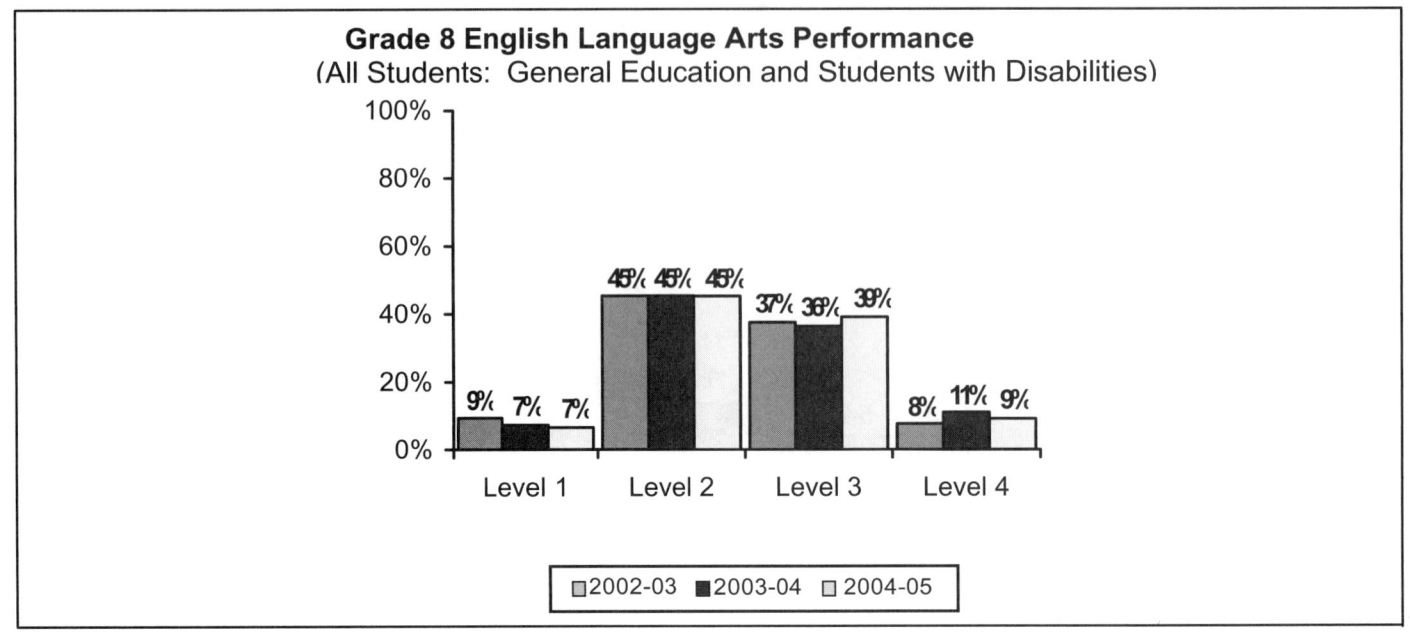

Statewide Performance	Counts of Students				Total Tested	Mean Score
	Level 1 527–657	Level 2 658–696	Level 3 697–736	Level 4 737–830		
January 2003	20,130	96,533	79,747	16,296	212,706	694
January 2004	15,994	98,949	79,256	23,893	218,092	699
January 2005	14,182	97,860	84,352	19,755	216,149	698

Middle-Level English Language Arts Levels — Listening, Reading, and Writing Standards	
Level 4	These students **exceed the standards** and are moving toward high performance on the Regents examination.
Level 3	These students **meet the standards** and, with continued steady growth, should pass the Regents examination.
Level 2	These students **need extra help** to meet the standards and pass the Regents examination.
Level 1	These students have **serious academic deficiencies**.

Performance of Limited English Proficient Students Taking the New York State English as a Second Language Achievement Test (NYSESLAT) as the Measure of English Language Arts Achievement

Grade 8	Level 1	Level 2	Levels 3 & 4	Total Tested
2005	2,031	1,135	4,321	7,487

Performance of Students with Severe Disabilities on the New York State Alternate Assessment (NYSAA) in English

Middle Level	AA–Level 1	AA–Level 2	AA–Level 3	AA–Level 4	Total Tested
2004–05	14	145	342	1,321	1,822

Middle Level
Mathematics

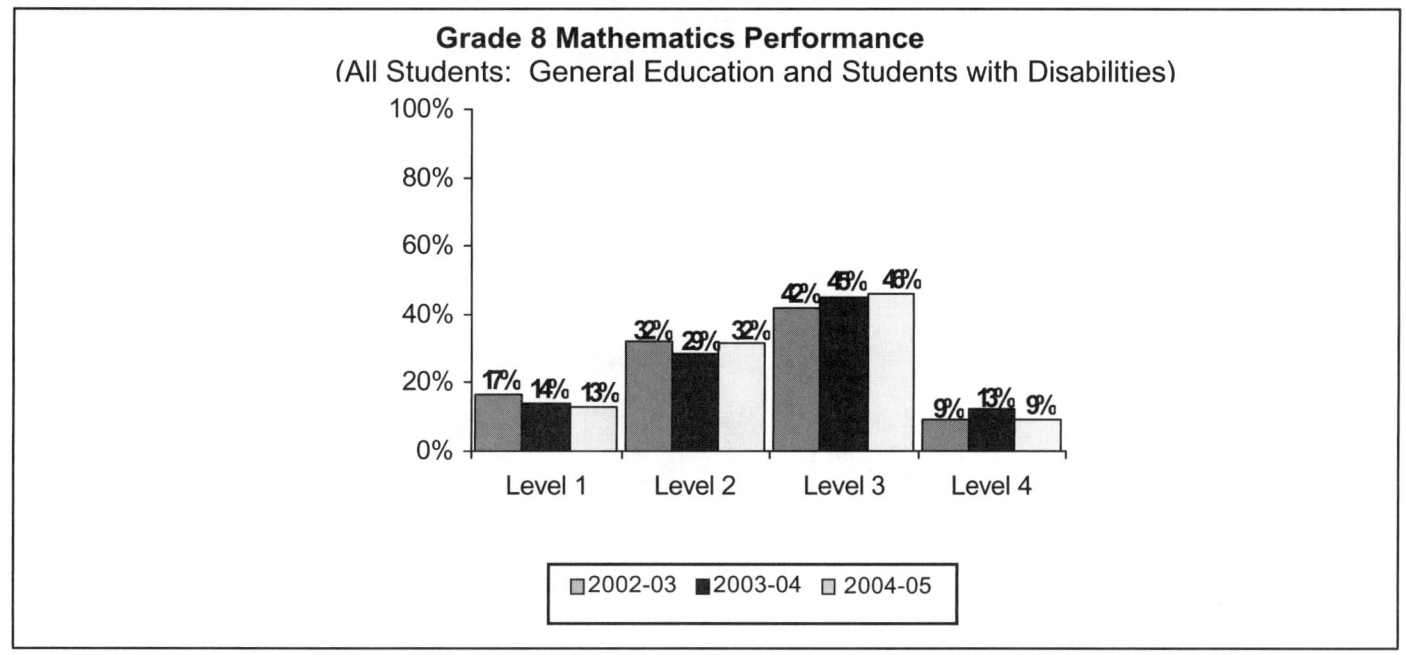

Statewide Performance	Counts of Students					Mean Score
	Level 1 517–680	Level 2 681–715	Level 3 716–759	Level 4 760–882	Total Tested	
May 2003	36,209	70,196	91,864	20,733	219,002	713
May 2004	30,937	63,654	100,371	28,322	223,284	718
May 2005	28,873	69,975	102,061	21,085	221,994	718

Middle-Level Mathematics Levels — Knowledge, Reasoning, and Problem-Solving Standards	
Level 4	These students **exceed the standards** and are moving toward high performance on the Regents examination.
Level 3	These students **meet the standards** and, with continued steady growth, should pass the Regents examination.
Level 2	These students **need extra help** to meet the standards and pass the Regents examination.
Level 1	These students have **serious academic deficiencies**.

Performance of Students with Severe Disabilities on the New York State Alternate Assessment (NYSAA) in Mathematics

Middle Level	AA–Level 1	AA–Level 2	AA–Level 3	AA–Level 4	Total Tested
2004–05	34	185	323	1,251	1,793

Middle Level
*Science**

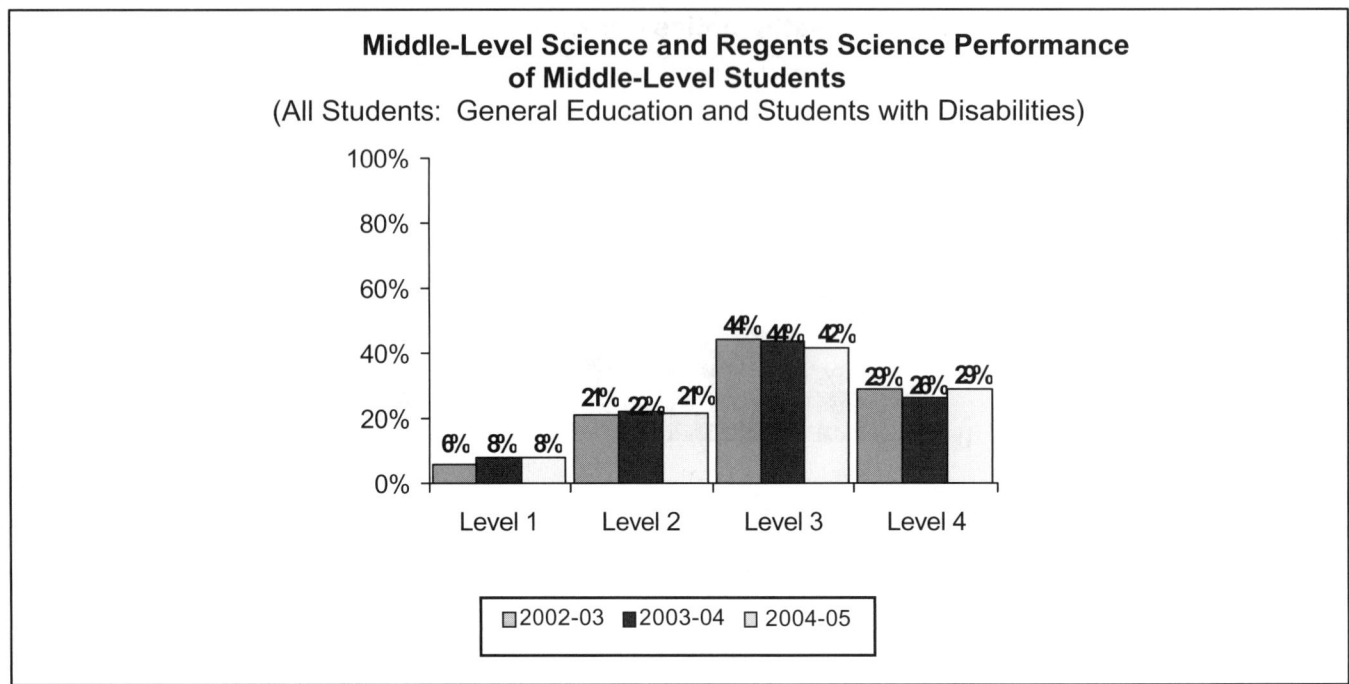

Statewide Performance		Counts of Students					Mean Score
		Level 1	Level 2	Level 3	Level 4	Total Tested	
January/ June 2003	Middle-Level Science	11,097	40,901	84,529	48,950	185,477	73
	Regents Science	53	100	2,676	8,346	11,175	88
January/ June 2004	Middle-Level Science	16,276	46,357	86,921	45,307	194,861	71
	Regents Science	353	398	5,885	10,498	17,134	85
January/ June 2005	Middle-Level Science	16,700	45,205	84,274	49,253	195,432	71
	Regents Science	236	280	4,324	11,712	16,552	87

Middle-Level Science Levels — Knowledge, Reasoning, and Problem-Solving Standards*	
Level 4	These students **exceed the standards** on the middle-level science test and are moving toward high performance on the Regents examinations *or* score 85–100 on a Regents science examination.
Level 3	These students **meet the standards** on the middle-level science test and, with continued steady growth, should pass the Regents examinations *or* score 65–84 on a Regents science examination.
Level 2	These students **need extra help** to meet the standards for middle-level science and to pass the Regents examinations *or* score 55–64 on a Regents science examination.
Level 1	These students have **serious academic deficiencies** as evidenced in the middle-level science test *or* score 0–54 on a Regents science examination.

*Students may demonstrate proficiency in middle-level science by scoring at Level 3 or above on the middle-level science test or by scoring 65 or above on a Regents examination in science.

Performance of Students with Severe Disabilities on the New York State Alternate Assessment (NYSAA) in Science

Middle Level	AA–Level 1	AA–Level 2	AA–Level 3	AA–Level 4	Total Tested
2004–05	34	190	326	1,222	1,772

High School English Achievment after Four Years of Instruction

The graphs and tables below present performance of the 1999, 2000, and 2001 district accountability cohort members, four years after entering grade 9, in meeting the graduation assessment requirement in English. In the graph, students passing approved alternatives to this examination are counted as scoring in the 65 to 84 range. RCT results are not included in the graph. The data in these tables and charts show the performance of the cohorts as of June 30th of the fourth year after first entering grade 9. Data for the cohorts include all students in cohorts in the district's schools, students continuously enrolled in the district who transferred between schools within the district, and students placed outside the district but who are the reporting responsibility of the district.

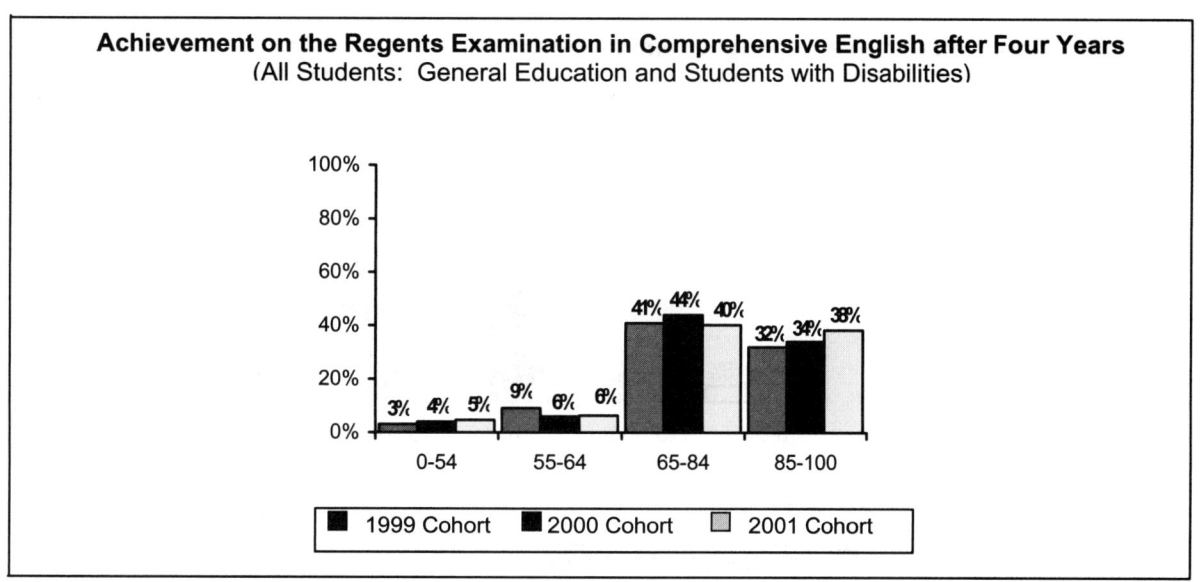

Achievement on the Regents Examination in Comprehensive English after Four Years
(All Students: General Education and Students with Disabilities)

0-54	55-64	65-84	85-100
3%, 4%, 5%	9%, 6%, 6%	41%, 44%, 40%	32%, 34%, 38%

1999 Cohort ■ 2000 Cohort ■ 2001 Cohort ☐

English Graduation Requirement Achievement after Four Years of High School*

	Cohort Members All Students	Highest Score Between 0 and 54	Highest Score Between 55 and 64	Highest Score Between 65 and 84	Highest Score Between 85 and 100	Approved Alternative Credit
1999 Cohort	171,399	5,668	16,143	70,470	55,584	157
2000 Cohort	173,058	6,324	9,698	75,518	58,942	211
2001 Cohort	176,196	8,257	11,109	70,826	67,583	187

*Assessments used to determine counts in this table include the Regents examination in comprehensive English, the component retest in English, and approved alternatives.

Performance of Students Who Took the Regents Competency Tests in Reading and Writing to Meet the Graduation Requirement*

	Passed the RCTs	Failed RCT in Reading and/or Writing
1999 Cohort	2,570	1,776
2000 Cohort	2,423	1,879
2001 Cohort	2,555	2,224

*Includes only students eligible for the safety net who did not score 55 or higher on the Regents examination or an approved alternative. Some students in the "Passed the RCTs" counts are also included in the 0–54 counts in the graph above.

High School Mathematics Achievment after Four Years of Instruction

The graphs and tables below present performance of the 1999, 2000, and 2001 district accountability cohort members, four years after entering grade 9, in meeting the graduation assessment requirement in mathematics. In the graph, students passing approved alternatives to these examinations are counted as scoring in the 65 to 84 range. RCT results are not included in the graph. The data in these tables and charts show the performance of the cohorts as of June 30th of the fourth year after first entering grade 9. Data for the cohorts include all students in cohorts in the district's schools, students continuously enrolled in the district who transferred between schools within the district, and students placed outside the district but who are the reporting responsibility of the district.

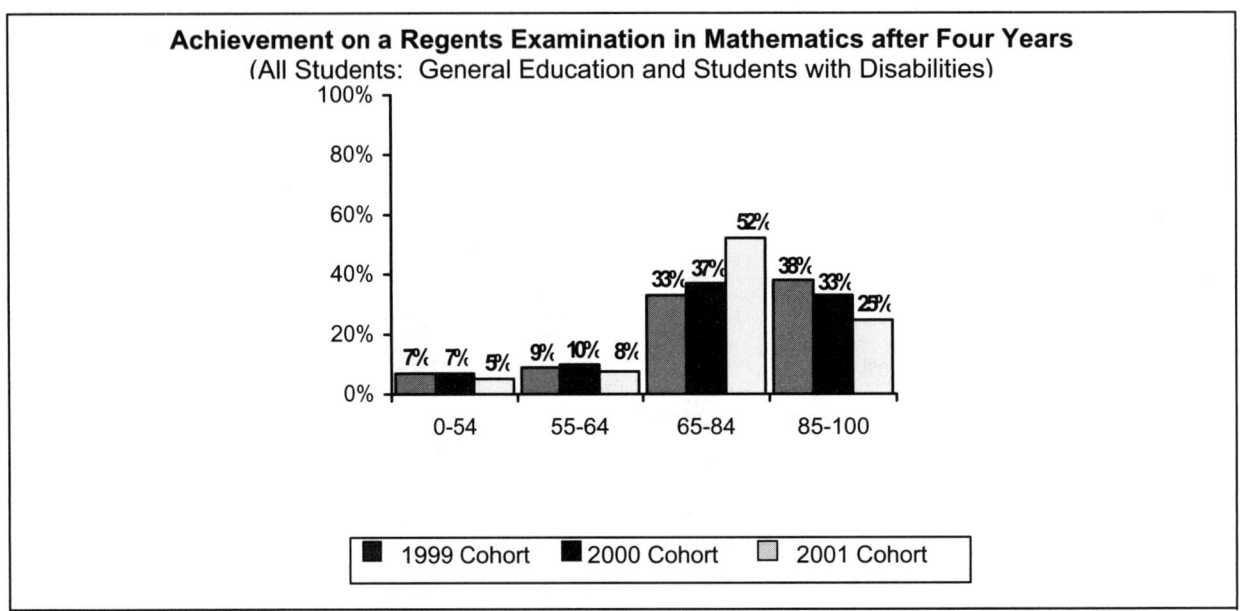

Mathematics Graduation Requirement Achievement after Four Years of High School*						
	Cohort Members All Students	Highest Score Between 0 and 54	Highest Score Between 55 and 64	Highest Score Between 65 and 84	Highest Score Between 85 and 100	Approved Alternative Credit
1999 Cohort	171,399	11,787	16,187	55,808	65,108	32
2000 Cohort	173,058	11,389	17,351	64,599	56,339	30
2001 Cohort	176,196	9,278	13,462	91,908	43,539	14

*Assessments used to determine counts in this table include a Regents examination in mathematics, the component retest in mathematics, and approved alternatives.

Performance of Students Who Took the Regents Competency Test in Mathematics to Meet the Graduation Requirement*		
	Passed the RCT	Failed at Least One RCT
1999 Cohort	4,961	714
2000 Cohort	5,484	660
2001 Cohort	4,715	917

*Includes only students eligible for the safety net who did not score 55 or higher on the Regents examination or an approved alternative. Some students in the "Passed the RCTs" counts are also included in the 0–54 counts in the graph above.

PROFILES OF NEW YORK / Ancestry: Rankings

Acadian/Cajun

Top 10 Places Sorted by Number
Based on all places, regardless of population

Place	Number	%
New York (city) New York City	382	0.00
Lackawanna (city) Erie County	37	0.19
Hempstead (town) Nassau County	36	0.00
Hempstead (village) Nassau County	30	0.05
Wilson (town) Niagara County	17	0.29
Chappaqua (cdp) Westchester County	15	0.16
New Castle (town) Westchester County	15	0.09
Ronkonkoma (cdp) Suffolk County	15	0.07
Islip (town) Suffolk County	15	0.00
Stockton (town) Chautauqua County	14	0.60

Top 10 Places Sorted by Percent
Based on all places, regardless of population

Place	Number	%
Stockton (town) Chautauqua County	14	0.60
Caroline (town) Tompkins County	10	0.35
Northeast Ithaca (cdp) Tompkins County	8	0.30
Wilson (town) Niagara County	17	0.29
West Bloomfield (town) Ontario County	7	0.27
Kinderhook (village) Columbia County	3	0.24
Black River (village) Jefferson County	3	0.23
Painted Post (village) Steuben County	4	0.22
Waddington (village) Saint Lawrence County	2	0.22
Plandome Heights (village) Nassau County	2	0.21

Top 10 Places Sorted by Percent
Based on places with populations of 10,000 or more

Place	Number	%
Lackawanna (city) Erie County	37	0.19
Beekman (town) Dutchess County	13	0.11
New Castle (town) Westchester County	15	0.09
Endicott (village) Broome County	10	0.08
Ronkonkoma (cdp) Suffolk County	15	0.07
Fort Drum (cdp) Jefferson County	8	0.07
Le Ray (town) Jefferson County	11	0.06
Highlands (town) Orange County	8	0.06
Sweden (town) Monroe County	8	0.06
Hempstead (village) Nassau County	30	0.05

Afghan

Top 10 Places Sorted by Number
Based on all places, regardless of population

Place	Number	%
New York (city) New York City	5,446	0.07
Oyster Bay (town) Nassau County	374	0.13
Schenectady (city) Schenectady County	298	0.48
Huntington (town) Suffolk County	285	0.15
Hempstead (town) Nassau County	223	0.03
Hicksville (cdp) Nassau County	213	0.52
Huntington Station (cdp) Suffolk County	181	0.60
Colonie (town) Albany County	148	0.19
Islip (town) Suffolk County	125	0.04
Smithtown (town) Suffolk County	112	0.10

Top 10 Places Sorted by Percent
Based on all places, regardless of population

Place	Number	%
Russell Gardens (village) Nassau County	17	1.58
Menands (village) Albany County	50	1.28
Plainedge (cdp) Nassau County	68	0.74
East Quogue (cdp) Suffolk County	28	0.66
Manhasset Hills (cdp) Nassau County	23	0.63
South Bristol (town) Ontario County	10	0.61
Huntington Station (cdp) Suffolk County	181	0.60
West Haverstraw (village) Rockland County	62	0.60
Kings Park (cdp) Suffolk County	86	0.53
Hicksville (cdp) Nassau County	213	0.52

Top 10 Places Sorted by Percent
Based on places with populations of 10,000 or more

Place	Number	%
Huntington Station (cdp) Suffolk County	181	0.60
West Haverstraw (village) Rockland County	62	0.60
Kings Park (cdp) Suffolk County	86	0.53
Hicksville (cdp) Nassau County	213	0.52
Schenectady (city) Schenectady County	298	0.48
Melville (cdp) Suffolk County	70	0.48
North Babylon (cdp) Suffolk County	44	0.25
North Greenbush (town) Rensselaer County	24	0.22
Plainview (cdp) Nassau County	54	0.21
Holtsville (cdp) Suffolk County	35	0.21

African American/Black

Top 10 Places Sorted by Number
Based on all places, regardless of population

Place	Number	%
New York (city) New York City	2,274,049	28.40
Hempstead (town) Nassau County	118,490	15.67
Buffalo (city) Erie County	112,880	38.57
Rochester (city) Monroe County	89,411	40.68
Mount Vernon (city) Westchester County	42,516	62.18
Syracuse (city) Onondaga County	40,436	27.45
Yonkers (city) Westchester County	35,421	18.06
Babylon (town) Suffolk County	35,262	16.65
Islip (town) Suffolk County	32,429	10.05
Hempstead (village) Nassau County	30,923	54.68

Top 10 Places Sorted by Percent
Based on all places, regardless of population

Place	Number	%
Lakeview (cdp) Nassau County	4,955	88.37
Roosevelt (cdp) Nassau County	12,895	81.34
Wyandanch (cdp) Suffolk County	8,523	80.82
Fairview (cdp) Westchester County	2,224	77.03
North Amityville (cdp) Suffolk County	11,991	72.36
Gordon Heights (cdp) Suffolk County	2,048	66.19
South Floral Park (village) Nassau County	1,042	66.03
Mount Vernon (city) Westchester County	42,516	62.18
Uniondale (cdp) Nassau County	13,411	58.28
East Garden City (cdp) Nassau County	553	56.49

Top 10 Places Sorted by Percent
Based on places with populations of 10,000 or more

Place	Number	%
Roosevelt (cdp) Nassau County	12,895	81.34
Wyandanch (cdp) Suffolk County	8,523	80.82
North Amityville (cdp) Suffolk County	11,991	72.36
Mount Vernon (city) Westchester County	42,516	62.18
Uniondale (cdp) Nassau County	13,411	58.28
Hempstead (village) Nassau County	30,923	54.68
New Cassel (cdp) Nassau County	6,670	50.16
Spring Valley (village) Rockland County	12,294	48.28
Rochester (city) Monroe County	89,411	40.68
North Valley Stream (cdp) Nassau County	6,248	39.57

African American/Black: Not Hispanic

Top 10 Places Sorted by Number
Based on all places, regardless of population

Place	Number	%
New York (city) New York City	2,050,764	25.61
Hempstead (town) Nassau County	113,317	14.99
Buffalo (city) Erie County	110,334	37.70
Rochester (city) Monroe County	85,922	39.10
Mount Vernon (city) Westchester County	41,372	60.50
Syracuse (city) Onondaga County	38,929	26.43
Babylon (town) Suffolk County	33,704	15.91
Yonkers (city) Westchester County	32,131	16.39
Hempstead (village) Nassau County	29,729	52.57
Islip (town) Suffolk County	29,186	9.05

Top 10 Places Sorted by Percent
Based on all places, regardless of population

Place	Number	%
Lakeview (cdp) Nassau County	4,840	86.32
Roosevelt (cdp) Nassau County	12,615	79.57
Wyandanch (cdp) Suffolk County	8,228	78.02
Fairview (cdp) Westchester County	2,186	75.72
North Amityville (cdp) Suffolk County	11,591	69.94
South Floral Park (village) Nassau County	1,017	64.45
Gordon Heights (cdp) Suffolk County	1,941	62.73
Mount Vernon (city) Westchester County	41,372	60.50
Uniondale (cdp) Nassau County	12,907	56.09
East Garden City (cdp) Nassau County	527	53.83

Top 10 Places Sorted by Percent
Based on places with populations of 10,000 or more

Place	Number	%
Roosevelt (cdp) Nassau County	12,615	79.57
Wyandanch (cdp) Suffolk County	8,228	78.02
North Amityville (cdp) Suffolk County	11,591	69.94
Mount Vernon (city) Westchester County	41,372	60.50
Uniondale (cdp) Nassau County	12,907	56.09
Hempstead (village) Nassau County	29,729	52.57
New Cassel (cdp) Nassau County	6,359	47.82
Spring Valley (village) Rockland County	11,930	46.85
Rochester (city) Monroe County	85,922	39.10
North Valley Stream (cdp) Nassau County	6,045	38.29

African American/Black: Hispanic

Top 10 Places Sorted by Number
Based on all places, regardless of population

Place	Number	%
New York (city) New York City	223,285	2.79
Hempstead (town) Nassau County	5,173	0.68
Rochester (city) Monroe County	3,489	1.59
Yonkers (city) Westchester County	3,290	1.68
Islip (town) Suffolk County	3,243	1.01
Buffalo (city) Erie County	2,546	0.87
Brookhaven (town) Suffolk County	1,857	0.41
Babylon (town) Suffolk County	1,558	0.74
Brentwood (cdp) Suffolk County	1,513	2.81
Syracuse (city) Onondaga County	1,507	1.02

Top 10 Places Sorted by Percent
Based on all places, regardless of population

Place	Number	%
Gordon Heights (cdp) Suffolk County	107	3.46
Brentwood (cdp) Suffolk County	1,513	2.81
Wyandanch (cdp) Suffolk County	295	2.80
New York (city) New York City	223,285	2.79
East Garden City (cdp) Nassau County	26	2.66
Monticello (village) Sullivan County	171	2.63
Hillcrest (cdp) Rockland County	186	2.62
Middletown (city) Orange County	647	2.55
Ellenville (village) Ulster County	102	2.47
Haverstraw (village) Rockland County	249	2.46

Top 10 Places Sorted by Percent
Based on places with populations of 10,000 or more

Place	Number	%
Brentwood (cdp) Suffolk County	1,513	2.81
Wyandanch (cdp) Suffolk County	295	2.80
New York (city) New York City	223,285	2.79
Middletown (city) Orange County	647	2.55
Haverstraw (village) Rockland County	249	2.46
North Amityville (cdp) Suffolk County	400	2.41
New Cassel (cdp) Nassau County	311	2.34

Notes: (cdp) census designated place; Refer to the User's Guide in the front of the book for more detailed information.

Place	Number	%
Central Islip (cdp) Suffolk County	715	2.24
Uniondale (cdp) Nassau County	504	2.19
Freeport (village) Nassau County	934	2.13

African, sub-Saharan

Top 10 Places Sorted by Number
Based on all places, regardless of population

Place	Number	%
New York (city) New York City	122,425	1.53
Hempstead (town) Nassau County	5,025	0.66
Rochester (city) Monroe County	4,202	1.91
Buffalo (city) Erie County	3,810	1.30
Yonkers (city) Westchester County	2,228	1.14
Syracuse (city) Onondaga County	2,179	1.48
Albany (city) Albany County	1,810	1.89
Islip (town) Suffolk County	1,421	0.44
Babylon (town) Suffolk County	1,409	0.67
Brookhaven (town) Suffolk County	1,302	0.29

Top 10 Places Sorted by Percent
Based on all places, regardless of population

Place	Number	%
South Floral Park (village) Nassau County	78	4.94
Wyandanch (cdp) Suffolk County	354	3.35
New Cassel (cdp) Nassau County	427	3.21
Fairview (cdp) Westchester County	85	2.84
New Hempstead (village) Rockland County	133	2.77
North Amityville (cdp) Suffolk County	450	2.72
Lakeview (cdp) Nassau County	152	2.71
Elmont (cdp) Nassau County	868	2.66
Hampton Manor (cdp) Rensselaer County	70	2.65
North Valley Stream (cdp) Nassau County	394	2.50

Top 10 Places Sorted by Percent
Based on places with populations of 10,000 or more

Place	Number	%
Wyandanch (cdp) Suffolk County	354	3.35
New Cassel (cdp) Nassau County	427	3.21
North Amityville (cdp) Suffolk County	450	2.72
Elmont (cdp) Nassau County	868	2.66
North Valley Stream (cdp) Nassau County	394	2.50
Hempstead (village) Nassau County	1,300	2.30
Uniondale (cdp) Nassau County	501	2.18
Roosevelt (cdp) Nassau County	314	1.98
Rochester (city) Monroe County	4,202	1.91
Albany (city) Albany County	1,810	1.89

African, Subsaharan: African

Top 10 Places Sorted by Number
Based on all places, regardless of population

Place	Number	%
New York (city) New York City	76,791	0.96
Rochester (city) Monroe County	3,286	1.50
Hempstead (town) Nassau County	3,042	0.40
Buffalo (city) Erie County	2,870	0.98
Syracuse (city) Onondaga County	1,780	1.21
Yonkers (city) Westchester County	1,332	0.68
Albany (city) Albany County	1,188	1.24
Babylon (town) Suffolk County	1,140	0.54
Islip (town) Suffolk County	1,088	0.34
Hempstead (village) Nassau County	1,011	1.79

Top 10 Places Sorted by Percent
Based on all places, regardless of population

Place	Number	%
Fairview (cdp) Westchester County	85	2.84
New Cassel (cdp) Nassau County	366	2.75
Lakeview (cdp) Nassau County	147	2.62
North Amityville (cdp) Suffolk County	422	2.56
Wyandanch (cdp) Suffolk County	248	2.34
South Floral Park (village) Nassau County	35	2.22
Southampton (village) Suffolk County	78	1.97
South Fallsburg (cdp) Sullivan County	43	1.91
Roosevelt (cdp) Nassau County	297	1.87
Hempstead (village) Nassau County	1,011	1.79

Top 10 Places Sorted by Percent
Based on places with populations of 10,000 or more

Place	Number	%
New Cassel (cdp) Nassau County	366	2.75
North Amityville (cdp) Suffolk County	422	2.56
Wyandanch (cdp) Suffolk County	248	2.34
Roosevelt (cdp) Nassau County	297	1.87
Hempstead (village) Nassau County	1,011	1.79
Rochester (city) Monroe County	3,286	1.50
Albany (city) Albany County	1,188	1.24
Syracuse (city) Onondaga County	1,780	1.21
Newburgh (city) Orange County	341	1.21
Uniondale (cdp) Nassau County	275	1.20

African, Subsaharan: Cape Verdean

Top 10 Places Sorted by Number
Based on all places, regardless of population

Place	Number	%
New York (city) New York City	848	0.01
Yonkers (city) Westchester County	137	0.07
Hempstead (town) Nassau County	90	0.01
New Rochelle (city) Westchester County	58	0.08
North Hempstead (town) Nassau County	58	0.03
Freeport (village) Nassau County	39	0.09
Schenectady (city) Schenectady County	36	0.06
Islip (town) Suffolk County	32	0.01
Garden City Park (cdp) Nassau County	28	0.37
Syracuse (city) Onondaga County	28	0.02

Top 10 Places Sorted by Percent
Based on all places, regardless of population

Place	Number	%
Ava (town) Oneida County	5	0.70
Spencer (village) Tioga County	4	0.55
Tupper Lake (village) Franklin County	17	0.43
Garden City Park (cdp) Nassau County	28	0.37
West Winfield (village) Herkimer County	3	0.35
Altamont (town) Franklin County	17	0.28
South Bristol (town) Ontario County	4	0.24
Arlington (cdp) Dutchess County	25	0.20
Baxter Estates (village) Nassau County	2	0.20
North Valley Stream (cdp) Nassau County	25	0.16

Top 10 Places Sorted by Percent
Based on places with populations of 10,000 or more

Place	Number	%
Arlington (cdp) Dutchess County	25	0.20
North Valley Stream (cdp) Nassau County	25	0.16
Westbury (village) Nassau County	21	0.15
Freeport (village) Nassau County	39	0.09
Suffern (village) Rockland County	10	0.09
New Rochelle (city) Westchester County	58	0.08
Yonkers (city) Westchester County	137	0.07
Roosevelt (cdp) Nassau County	11	0.07
Schenectady (city) Schenectady County	36	0.06
Poughkeepsie (town) Dutchess County	25	0.06

African, Subsaharan: Ethiopian

Top 10 Places Sorted by Number
Based on all places, regardless of population

Place	Number	%
New York (city) New York City	1,921	0.02
Rochester (city) Monroe County	383	0.17
Babylon (town) Suffolk County	126	0.06
Wyandanch (cdp) Suffolk County	106	1.00
New Rochelle (city) Westchester County	82	0.11
Troy (city) Rensselaer County	48	0.10
Syracuse (city) Onondaga County	42	0.03
Bay Shore (cdp) Suffolk County	37	0.16
Islip (town) Suffolk County	37	0.01
Ogden (town) Monroe County	34	0.18

Top 10 Places Sorted by Percent
Based on all places, regardless of population

Place	Number	%
Great Bend (cdp) Jefferson County	8	1.03
Wyandanch (cdp) Suffolk County	106	1.00
Liberty (village) Sullivan County	25	0.64
Piermont (village) Rockland County	8	0.31
Liberty (town) Sullivan County	29	0.30
Monroe (village) Orange County	17	0.22
New Paltz (village) Ulster County	13	0.22
Bridgehampton (cdp) Suffolk County	3	0.22
New Square (village) Rockland County	10	0.21
Chester (town) Orange County	23	0.19

Top 10 Places Sorted by Percent
Based on places with populations of 10,000 or more

Place	Number	%
Wyandanch (cdp) Suffolk County	106	1.00
Chester (town) Orange County	23	0.19
Ogden (town) Monroe County	34	0.18
Rochester (city) Monroe County	383	0.17
Bay Shore (cdp) Suffolk County	37	0.16
Lewiston (town) Niagara County	25	0.15
East Greenbush (town) Rensselaer County	23	0.15
Fort Drum (cdp) Jefferson County	18	0.15
North Massapequa (cdp) Nassau County	24	0.13
New Rochelle (city) Westchester County	82	0.11

African, Subsaharan: Ghanian

Top 10 Places Sorted by Number
Based on all places, regardless of population

Place	Number	%
New York (city) New York City	9,921	0.12
Yonkers (city) Westchester County	363	0.19
Albany (city) Albany County	210	0.22
Hempstead (town) Nassau County	193	0.03
Islip (town) Suffolk County	106	0.03
Ramapo (town) Rockland County	87	0.08
Bay Shore (cdp) Suffolk County	78	0.33
Elmont (cdp) Nassau County	61	0.19
Amherst (town) Erie County	48	0.04
Babylon (town) Suffolk County	45	0.02

Top 10 Places Sorted by Percent
Based on all places, regardless of population

Place	Number	%
Northeast Ithaca (cdp) Tompkins County	23	0.85
Newport (village) Herkimer County	4	0.61
New Hempstead (village) Rockland County	24	0.50
Wesley Hills (village) Rockland County	24	0.49
Hamilton (village) Madison County	13	0.37
Greenville (cdp) Westchester County	30	0.35
Bay Shore (cdp) Suffolk County	78	0.33
Inwood (cdp) Nassau County	30	0.32
Wheatley Heights (cdp) Suffolk County	15	0.30
Hamilton (town) Madison County	13	0.23

Top 10 Places Sorted by Percent
Based on places with populations of 10,000 or more

Place	Number	%
Bay Shore (cdp) Suffolk County	78	0.33
Albany (city) Albany County	210	0.22
Yonkers (city) Westchester County	363	0.19

Notes: (cdp) census designated place; Refer to the User's Guide in the front of the book for more detailed information.

PROFILES OF NEW YORK / Ancestry: Rankings

Place	Number	%
Elmont (cdp) Nassau County	61	0.19
Arlington (cdp) Dutchess County	22	0.18
Ithaca (town) Tompkins County	31	0.17
Baldwin (cdp) Nassau County	35	0.15
Mamaroneck (village) Westchester County	28	0.15
North Bay Shore (cdp) Suffolk County	23	0.15
New York (city) New York City	9,921	0.12

African, Subsaharan: Kenyan

Top 10 Places Sorted by Number
Based on all places, regardless of population

Place	Number	%
New York (city) New York City	146	0.00
East Fishkill (town) Dutchess County	63	0.25
Syracuse (city) Onondaga County	60	0.04
Ramapo (town) Rockland County	44	0.04
Arlington (cdp) Dutchess County	41	0.33
Poughkeepsie (town) Dutchess County	41	0.10
Highland Falls (village) Orange County	36	0.98
Highlands (town) Orange County	36	0.29
Ithaca (town) Tompkins County	33	0.18
Spring Valley (village) Rockland County	29	0.11

Top 10 Places Sorted by Percent
Based on all places, regardless of population

Place	Number	%
Forest Home (cdp) Tompkins County	16	1.57
Highland Falls (village) Orange County	36	0.98
Northeast Ithaca (cdp) Tompkins County	17	0.63
Esperance (town) Schoharie County	10	0.49
Upper Nyack (village) Rockland County	7	0.38
Arlington (cdp) Dutchess County	41	0.33
Highlands (town) Orange County	36	0.29
East Fishkill (town) Dutchess County	63	0.25
New Paltz (village) Ulster County	14	0.23
Williamsville (village) Erie County	11	0.20

Top 10 Places Sorted by Percent
Based on places with populations of 10,000 or more

Place	Number	%
Arlington (cdp) Dutchess County	41	0.33
Highlands (town) Orange County	36	0.29
East Fishkill (town) Dutchess County	63	0.25
Ithaca (town) Tompkins County	33	0.18
Spring Valley (village) Rockland County	29	0.11
New Paltz (town) Ulster County	14	0.11
Poughkeepsie (town) Dutchess County	41	0.10
Greenlawn (cdp) Suffolk County	12	0.09
Catskill (town) Greene County	9	0.08
Dix Hills (cdp) Suffolk County	14	0.05

African, Subsaharan: Liberian

Top 10 Places Sorted by Number
Based on all places, regardless of population

Place	Number	%
New York (city) New York City	2,561	0.03
Hempstead (town) Nassau County	218	0.03
Uniondale (cdp) Nassau County	129	0.56
Syracuse (city) Onondaga County	92	0.06
Clay (town) Onondaga County	69	0.12
Hampton Manor (cdp) Rensselaer County	48	1.82
East Greenbush (town) Rensselaer County	48	0.31
North Valley Stream (cdp) Nassau County	42	0.27
Bellmore (cdp) Nassau County	37	0.23
Yonkers (city) Westchester County	33	0.02

Top 10 Places Sorted by Percent
Based on all places, regardless of population

Place	Number	%
Hampton Manor (cdp) Rensselaer County	48	1.82
Uniondale (cdp) Nassau County	129	0.56
East Greenbush (town) Rensselaer County	48	0.31
North Valley Stream (cdp) Nassau County	42	0.27
Bellmore (cdp) Nassau County	37	0.23
New Cassel (cdp) Nassau County	30	0.23
Thiells (cdp) Rockland County	8	0.17
Greenlawn (cdp) Suffolk County	17	0.13
Clay (town) Onondaga County	69	0.12
Poughkeepsie (city) Dutchess County	22	0.07

Top 10 Places Sorted by Percent
Based on places with populations of 10,000 or more

Place	Number	%
Uniondale (cdp) Nassau County	129	0.56
East Greenbush (town) Rensselaer County	48	0.31
North Valley Stream (cdp) Nassau County	42	0.27
Bellmore (cdp) Nassau County	37	0.23
New Cassel (cdp) Nassau County	30	0.23
Greenlawn (cdp) Suffolk County	17	0.13
Clay (town) Onondaga County	69	0.12
Poughkeepsie (city) Dutchess County	22	0.07
Syracuse (city) Onondaga County	92	0.06
Binghamton (city) Broome County	30	0.06

African, Subsaharan: Nigerian

Top 10 Places Sorted by Number
Based on all places, regardless of population

Place	Number	%
New York (city) New York City	17,928	0.22
Hempstead (town) Nassau County	1,196	0.16
Elmont (cdp) Nassau County	383	1.17
New Rochelle (city) Westchester County	310	0.43
Ramapo (town) Rockland County	240	0.22
Greenburgh (town) Westchester County	220	0.25
Hempstead (village) Nassau County	219	0.39
Brookhaven (town) Suffolk County	206	0.05
Mount Vernon (city) Westchester County	165	0.24
North Valley Stream (cdp) Nassau County	146	0.92

Top 10 Places Sorted by Percent
Based on all places, regardless of population

Place	Number	%
South Floral Park (village) Nassau County	43	2.72
New Hempstead (village) Rockland County	99	2.07
Fairview (cdp) Dutchess County	81	1.35
Niverville (cdp) Columbia County	22	1.32
Lansing (village) Tompkins County	37	1.25
Elmont (cdp) Nassau County	383	1.17
North Valley Stream (cdp) Nassau County	146	0.92
Lansing (town) Tompkins County	95	0.92
Hopewell Junction (cdp) Dutchess County	19	0.75
Gordon Heights (cdp) Suffolk County	23	0.74

Top 10 Places Sorted by Percent
Based on places with populations of 10,000 or more

Place	Number	%
Elmont (cdp) Nassau County	383	1.17
North Valley Stream (cdp) Nassau County	146	0.92
Lansing (town) Tompkins County	95	0.92
Westbury (village) Nassau County	98	0.69
Baldwin (cdp) Nassau County	126	0.54
New Rochelle (city) Westchester County	310	0.43
Uniondale (cdp) Nassau County	97	0.42
Hempstead (village) Nassau County	219	0.39
Greenburgh (town) Westchester County	220	0.25
Medford (cdp) Suffolk County	54	0.25

African, Subsaharan: Senegalese

Top 10 Places Sorted by Number
Based on all places, regardless of population

Place	Number	%
New York (city) New York City	2,136	0.03
Yonkers (city) Westchester County	12	0.01
Cayuga Heights (village) Tompkins County	10	0.31
Ithaca (town) Tompkins County	10	0.05
Mount Vernon (city) Westchester County	9	0.01
Aurora (village) Cayuga County	7	0.98
Ledyard (town) Cayuga County	7	0.38
Greenburgh (town) Westchester County	7	0.01
Niagara Falls (city) Niagara County	6	0.01
White Plains (city) Westchester County	5	0.01

Top 10 Places Sorted by Percent
Based on all places, regardless of population

Place	Number	%
Aurora (village) Cayuga County	7	0.98
Ledyard (town) Cayuga County	7	0.38
Cayuga Heights (village) Tompkins County	10	0.31
Ithaca (town) Tompkins County	10	0.05
New York (city) New York City	2,136	0.03
Yonkers (city) Westchester County	12	0.01
Mount Vernon (city) Westchester County	9	0.01
Greenburgh (town) Westchester County	7	0.01
Niagara Falls (city) Niagara County	6	0.01
White Plains (city) Westchester County	5	0.01

Top 10 Places Sorted by Percent
Based on places with populations of 10,000 or more

Place	Number	%
Ithaca (town) Tompkins County	10	0.05
New York (city) New York City	2,136	0.03
Yonkers (city) Westchester County	12	0.01
Mount Vernon (city) Westchester County	9	0.01
Greenburgh (town) Westchester County	7	0.01
Niagara Falls (city) Niagara County	6	0.01
White Plains (city) Westchester County	5	0.01
Troy (city) Rensselaer County	4	0.01

African, Subsaharan: Sierra Leonean

Top 10 Places Sorted by Number
Based on all places, regardless of population

Place	Number	%
New York (city) New York City	798	0.01
Hempstead (town) Nassau County	39	0.01
Yonkers (city) Westchester County	33	0.02
Elmsford (village) Westchester County	29	0.63
Fort Drum (cdp) Jefferson County	29	0.24
Le Ray (town) Jefferson County	29	0.15
Greenburgh (town) Westchester County	29	0.03
Baldwin (cdp) Nassau County	18	0.08
Geneva (town) Ontario County	16	0.49
Ithaca (city) Tompkins County	16	0.06

Top 10 Places Sorted by Percent
Based on all places, regardless of population

Place	Number	%
Elmsford (village) Westchester County	29	0.63
Geneva (town) Ontario County	16	0.49
Fort Drum (cdp) Jefferson County	29	0.24
Putnam Lake (cdp) Putnam County	8	0.21
Fairview (cdp) Dutchess County	11	0.18
Le Ray (town) Jefferson County	29	0.15
Geneseo (village) Livingston County	8	0.11
Stony Brook (cdp) Suffolk County	13	0.10
Baldwin (cdp) Nassau County	18	0.08
Geneseo (town) Livingston County	8	0.08

Notes: (cdp) census designated place; Refer to the User's Guide in the front of the book for more detailed information.

658 PROFILES OF NEW YORK / Ancestry: Rankings

Top 10 Places Sorted by Percent
Based on places with populations of 10,000 or more

Place	Number	%
Fort Drum (cdp) Jefferson County	29	0.24
Le Ray (town) Jefferson County	29	0.15
Stony Brook (cdp) Suffolk County	13	0.10
Baldwin (cdp) Nassau County	18	0.08
North Valley Stream (cdp) Nassau County	11	0.07
Patterson (town) Putnam County	8	0.07
Ithaca (city) Tompkins County	16	0.06
Seaford (cdp) Nassau County	10	0.06
Greenburgh (town) Westchester County	29	0.03
Poughkeepsie (town) Dutchess County	11	0.03

African, Subsaharan: Somalian

Top 10 Places Sorted by Number
Based on all places, regardless of population

Place	Number	%
Buffalo (city) Erie County	457	0.16
New York (city) New York City	247	0.00
Rochester (city) Monroe County	171	0.08
Syracuse (city) Onondaga County	31	0.02
Arlington (cdp) Dutchess County	24	0.19
Poughkeepsie (town) Dutchess County	24	0.06
Geneseo (village) Livingston County	22	0.29
Geneseo (town) Livingston County	22	0.23
Binghamton (city) Broome County	22	0.05
Brighton (town) Monroe County	15	0.04

Top 10 Places Sorted by Percent
Based on all places, regardless of population

Place	Number	%
Geneseo (village) Livingston County	22	0.29
Geneseo (town) Livingston County	22	0.23
Arlington (cdp) Dutchess County	24	0.19
Buffalo (city) Erie County	457	0.16
Rochester (city) Monroe County	171	0.08
Poughkeepsie (town) Dutchess County	24	0.06
Binghamton (city) Broome County	22	0.05
Brighton (town) Monroe County	15	0.04
Syracuse (city) Onondaga County	31	0.02
New York (city) New York City	247	0.00

Top 10 Places Sorted by Percent
Based on places with populations of 10,000 or more

Place	Number	%
Arlington (cdp) Dutchess County	24	0.19
Buffalo (city) Erie County	457	0.16
Rochester (city) Monroe County	171	0.08
Poughkeepsie (town) Dutchess County	24	0.06
Binghamton (city) Broome County	22	0.05
Brighton (town) Monroe County	15	0.04
Syracuse (city) Onondaga County	31	0.02
New York (city) New York City	247	0.00

African, Subsaharan: South African

Top 10 Places Sorted by Number
Based on all places, regardless of population

Place	Number	%
New York (city) New York City	1,399	0.02
North Hempstead (town) Nassau County	145	0.07
Greenburgh (town) Westchester County	107	0.12
Mamaroneck (town) Westchester County	100	0.35
Huntington (town) Suffolk County	67	0.03
Hempstead (town) Nassau County	67	0.01
Rye (city) Westchester County	61	0.41
Elmsford (village) Westchester County	49	1.06
Scarsdale (village) Westchester County	44	0.25
Webster (village) Monroe County	43	0.83

Top 10 Places Sorted by Percent
Based on all places, regardless of population

Place	Number	%
Saddle Rock Estates (cdp) Nassau County	7	1.59
Orient (cdp) Suffolk County	10	1.41
Elmsford (village) Westchester County	49	1.06
Webster (village) Monroe County	43	0.83
Manlius (village) Onondaga County	34	0.70
Lloyd Harbor (village) Suffolk County	25	0.68
Keene (town) Essex County	7	0.66
Saddle Rock (village) Nassau County	5	0.63
Great Neck Gardens (cdp) Nassau County	6	0.54
Adams (village) Jefferson County	8	0.49

Top 10 Places Sorted by Percent
Based on places with populations of 10,000 or more

Place	Number	%
Rye (city) Westchester County	61	0.41
Mamaroneck (town) Westchester County	100	0.35
Scarsdale (village) Westchester County	44	0.25
Goshen (town) Orange County	24	0.19
New Paltz (town) Ulster County	22	0.17
Jericho (cdp) Nassau County	20	0.15
Fort Drum (cdp) Jefferson County	17	0.14
Lansing (town) Tompkins County	14	0.14
Mamaroneck (village) Westchester County	25	0.13
Greenburgh (town) Westchester County	107	0.12

African, Subsaharan: Sudanese

Top 10 Places Sorted by Number
Based on all places, regardless of population

Place	Number	%
New York (city) New York City	859	0.01
Buffalo (city) Erie County	161	0.06
Schenectady (city) Schenectady County	109	0.18
Albany (city) Albany County	105	0.11
Binghamton (city) Broome County	55	0.12
Rochester (city) Monroe County	42	0.02
Chili (town) Monroe County	20	0.07
New Rochelle (city) Westchester County	17	0.02
Cayuga Heights (village) Tompkins County	16	0.50
Ithaca (town) Tompkins County	16	0.09

Top 10 Places Sorted by Percent
Based on all places, regardless of population

Place	Number	%
Cayuga Heights (village) Tompkins County	16	0.50
Schenectady (city) Schenectady County	109	0.18
Bayport (cdp) Suffolk County	12	0.14
Masonville (town) Delaware County	2	0.14
Binghamton (city) Broome County	55	0.12
Albany (city) Albany County	105	0.11
Ithaca (town) Tompkins County	16	0.09
North Valley Stream (cdp) Nassau County	14	0.09
Chili (town) Monroe County	20	0.07
Buffalo (city) Erie County	161	0.06

Top 10 Places Sorted by Percent
Based on places with populations of 10,000 or more

Place	Number	%
Schenectady (city) Schenectady County	109	0.18
Binghamton (city) Broome County	55	0.12
Albany (city) Albany County	105	0.11
Ithaca (town) Tompkins County	16	0.09
North Valley Stream (cdp) Nassau County	14	0.09
Chili (town) Monroe County	20	0.07
Buffalo (city) Erie County	161	0.06
Goshen (town) Orange County	5	0.04
White Plains (city) Westchester County	16	0.03
Troy (city) Rensselaer County	14	0.03

African, Subsaharan: Ugandan

Top 10 Places Sorted by Number
Based on all places, regardless of population

Place	Number	%
New York (city) New York City	104	0.00
Rochester (city) Monroe County	42	0.02
Poughkeepsie (city) Dutchess County	22	0.07
Ithaca (city) Tompkins County	16	0.06
Pittsford (town) Monroe County	14	0.05
Colonie (town) Albany County	14	0.02
Albany (city) Albany County	13	0.01
Spackenkill (cdp) Dutchess County	12	0.26
Poughkeepsie (town) Dutchess County	12	0.03
Niagara Falls (city) Niagara County	11	0.02

Top 10 Places Sorted by Percent
Based on all places, regardless of population

Place	Number	%
Spackenkill (cdp) Dutchess County	12	0.26
Poughkeepsie (city) Dutchess County	22	0.07
Ithaca (city) Tompkins County	16	0.06
Pittsford (town) Monroe County	14	0.05
Highland (cdp) Ulster County	2	0.04
Poughkeepsie (town) Dutchess County	12	0.03
Wappinger (town) Dutchess County	8	0.03
Harrison (village) Westchester County	7	0.03
Rochester (city) Monroe County	42	0.02
Colonie (town) Albany County	14	0.02

Top 10 Places Sorted by Percent
Based on places with populations of 10,000 or more

Place	Number	%
Poughkeepsie (city) Dutchess County	22	0.07
Ithaca (city) Tompkins County	16	0.06
Pittsford (town) Monroe County	14	0.05
Poughkeepsie (town) Dutchess County	12	0.03
Wappinger (town) Dutchess County	8	0.03
Harrison (village) Westchester County	7	0.03
Rochester (city) Monroe County	42	0.02
Colonie (town) Albany County	14	0.02
Niagara Falls (city) Niagara County	11	0.02
Vestal (town) Broome County	5	0.02

African, Subsaharan: Zairian

Top 10 Places Sorted by Number
Based on all places, regardless of population

Place	Number	%
Syracuse (city) Onondaga County	20	0.0
New York (city) New York City	14	0.0

Top 10 Places Sorted by Percent
Based on all places, regardless of population

Place	Number	%
Syracuse (city) Onondaga County	20	0.0
New York (city) New York City	14	0.0

Top 10 Places Sorted by Percent
Based on places with populations of 10,000 or more

Place	Number	%
Syracuse (city) Onondaga County	20	0.0
New York (city) New York City	14	0.0

African, Subsaharan: Zimbabwean

Top 10 Places Sorted by Number
Based on all places, regardless of population

Place	Number
New York (city) New York City	95

PROFILES OF NEW YORK / Ancestry: Rankings

Place	Number	%
righton (town) Monroe County	49	0.14
oram (cdp) Suffolk County	33	0.09
rookhaven (town) Suffolk County	33	0.01
empstead (town) Nassau County	27	0.00
onkers (city) Westchester County	24	0.01
reeport (village) Nassau County	19	0.04
lbany (city) Albany County	18	0.02
oodmere (cdp) Nassau County	8	0.05
arrison (village) Westchester County	8	0.03

Top 10 Places Sorted by Percent
Based on all places, regardless of population

lace	Number	%
iddlesex (town) Yates County	3	0.22
righton (town) Monroe County	49	0.14
hatham (village) Columbia County	2	0.11
oram (cdp) Suffolk County	33	0.09
oodmere (cdp) Nassau County	8	0.05
hatham (town) Columbia County	2	0.05
reeport (village) Nassau County	19	0.04
arrison (village) Westchester County	8	0.03
lbany (city) Albany County	18	0.02
lmira (city) Chemung County	7	0.02

Top 10 Places Sorted by Percent
Based on places with populations of 10,000 or more

lace	Number	%
righton (town) Monroe County	49	0.14
oram (cdp) Suffolk County	33	0.09
oodmere (cdp) Nassau County	8	0.05
reeport (village) Nassau County	19	0.04
arrison (village) Westchester County	8	0.03
lbany (city) Albany County	18	0.02
lmira (city) Chemung County	7	0.02
rookhaven (town) Suffolk County	33	0.01
onkers (city) Westchester County	24	0.01
ew York (city) New York City	95	0.00

African, Subsaharan: Other

Top 10 Places Sorted by Number
Based on all places, regardless of population

lace	Number	%
ew York (city) New York City	6,657	0.08
uffalo (city) Erie County	113	0.04
empstead (town) Nassau County	111	0.01
ount Vernon (city) Westchester County	109	0.16
onkers (city) Westchester County	87	0.04
ew Rochelle (city) Westchester County	86	0.12
lbany (city) Albany County	78	0.08
yracuse (city) Onondaga County	74	0.05
ssining (village) Westchester County	60	0.25
ssining (town) Westchester County	60	0.16

Top 10 Places Sorted by Percent
Based on all places, regardless of population

ace	Number	%
ayuga Heights (village) Tompkins County	44	1.38
alesite (cdp) Suffolk County	32	1.25
outh Nyack (village) Rockland County	26	0.75
enands (village) Albany County	27	0.69
ortheast Ithaca (cdp) Tompkins County	15	0.55
yster Bay Cove (village) Nassau County	11	0.50
oodbury (cdp) Nassau County	35	0.39
uilford (town) Chenango County	11	0.36
haca (town) Tompkins County	59	0.32
legany (village) Cattaraugus County	5	0.27

Top 10 Places Sorted by Percent
Based on places with populations of 10,000 or more

ace	Number	%
haca (town) Tompkins County	59	0.32

Place	Number	%
Ossining (village) Westchester County	60	0.25
New Hartford (town) Oneida County	48	0.23
Port Chester (village) Westchester County	55	0.20
Mount Vernon (city) Westchester County	109	0.16
Ossining (town) Westchester County	60	0.16
Rye (town) Westchester County	55	0.13
New Rochelle (city) Westchester County	86	0.12
Valley Stream (village) Nassau County	34	0.09
New York (city) New York City	6,657	0.08

Alaska Native tribes, specified

Top 10 Places Sorted by Number
Based on all places, regardless of population

Place	Number	%
New York (city) New York City	237	0.00
Hempstead (town) Nassau County	17	0.00
Mechanicstown (cdp) Orange County	10	0.16
Wallkill (town) Orange County	10	0.04
Le Ray (town) Jefferson County	8	0.04
Cicero (town) Onondaga County	8	0.03
Fort Drum (cdp) Jefferson County	7	0.06
Valley Stream (village) Nassau County	7	0.02
Buffalo (city) Erie County	7	0.00
Islip (town) Suffolk County	7	0.00

Top 10 Places Sorted by Percent
Based on all places, regardless of population

Place	Number	%
South Valley (town) Cattaraugus County	2	0.66
Ovid (village) Seneca County	4	0.65
Burdett (village) Schuyler County	2	0.56
Remsen (village) Oneida County	2	0.38
Little Valley (town) Cattaraugus County	6	0.34
Livonia (village) Livingston County	4	0.29
Orleans (town) Jefferson County	5	0.20
Milford (village) Otsego County	1	0.20
Cayuta (town) Schuyler County	1	0.18
Mechanicstown (cdp) Orange County	10	0.16

Top 10 Places Sorted by Percent
Based on places with populations of 10,000 or more

Place	Number	%
Fort Drum (cdp) Jefferson County	7	0.06
Wallkill (town) Orange County	10	0.04
Le Ray (town) Jefferson County	8	0.04
North Valley Stream (cdp) Nassau County	6	0.04
Beacon (city) Dutchess County	5	0.04
Brunswick (town) Rensselaer County	5	0.04
Cicero (town) Onondaga County	8	0.03
Farmington (town) Ontario County	3	0.03
Valley Stream (village) Nassau County	7	0.02
Watertown (city) Jefferson County	6	0.02

Alaska Native: Alaska Athabascan

Top 10 Places Sorted by Number
Based on all places, regardless of population

Place	Number	%
New York (city) New York City	49	0.00
Little Valley (town) Cattaraugus County	6	0.34
Orleans (town) Jefferson County	5	0.20
Livonia (village) Livingston County	4	0.29
Livonia (town) Livingston County	4	0.05
Watertown (city) Jefferson County	4	0.01
North Salem (town) Westchester County	3	0.06
North Valley Stream (cdp) Nassau County	3	0.02
Hempstead (town) Nassau County	3	0.00
Rochester (city) Monroe County	3	0.00

Top 10 Places Sorted by Percent
Based on all places, regardless of population

Place	Number	%
South Valley (town) Cattaraugus County	2	0.66
Little Valley (town) Cattaraugus County	6	0.34
Livonia (village) Livingston County	4	0.29
Orleans (town) Jefferson County	5	0.20
Napoli (town) Cattaraugus County	1	0.09
North Salem (town) Westchester County	3	0.06
Schroon (town) Essex County	1	0.06
Livonia (town) Livingston County	4	0.05
Glen (town) Montgomery County	1	0.05
Lyme (town) Jefferson County	1	0.05

Top 10 Places Sorted by Percent
Based on places with populations of 10,000 or more

Place	Number	%
North Valley Stream (cdp) Nassau County	3	0.02
Watertown (city) Jefferson County	4	0.01
Rotterdam (town) Schenectady County	2	0.01
Gates-North Gates (cdp) Monroe County	1	0.01
Highlands (town) Orange County	1	0.01
Lansing (town) Tompkins County	1	0.01
Mamaroneck (village) Westchester County	1	0.01
Mineola (village) Nassau County	1	0.01
Oneida (city) Madison County	1	0.01
Patterson (town) Putnam County	1	0.01

Alaska Native: Aleut

Top 10 Places Sorted by Number
Based on all places, regardless of population

Place	Number	%
New York (city) New York City	20	0.00
Ovid (village) Seneca County	4	0.65
Ovid (town) Seneca County	4	0.15
Greene (town) Chenango County	4	0.07
Cicero (town) Onondaga County	4	0.01
Stockholm (town) Saint Lawrence County	3	0.08
Waverly (village) Tioga County	3	0.07
Hector (town) Schuyler County	3	0.06
Barton (town) Tioga County	3	0.03
Burdett (village) Schuyler County	2	0.56

Top 10 Places Sorted by Percent
Based on all places, regardless of population

Place	Number	%
Ovid (village) Seneca County	4	0.65
Burdett (village) Schuyler County	2	0.56
Remsen (village) Oneida County	1	0.19
Cayuta (town) Schuyler County	1	0.18
Ovid (town) Seneca County	4	0.15
Sempronius (town) Cayuga County	1	0.11
Remsen (town) Oneida County	2	0.10
Webb (town) Herkimer County	2	0.10
Stockholm (town) Saint Lawrence County	3	0.08
Yates (town) Orleans County	2	0.08

Top 10 Places Sorted by Percent
Based on places with populations of 10,000 or more

Place	Number	%
Cicero (town) Onondaga County	4	0.01
Newburgh (town) Orange County	2	0.01
Corning (city) Steuben County	1	0.01
Cornwall (town) Orange County	1	0.01
Depew (village) Erie County	1	0.01
Elma (town) Erie County	1	0.01
Le Ray (town) Jefferson County	1	0.01
Olean (city) Cattaraugus County	1	0.01
Oneonta (city) Otsego County	1	0.01
Plattsburgh (town) Clinton County	1	0.01

Notes: (cdp) census designated place; Refer to the User's Guide in the front of the book for more detailed information.

Alaska Native: Eskimo

Top 10 Places Sorted by Number
Based on all places, regardless of population

Place	Number	%
New York (city) New York City	65	0.00
Mechanicstown (cdp) Orange County	10	0.16
Wallkill (town) Orange County	10	0.04
Vienna (town) Oneida County	5	0.09
Brunswick (town) Rensselaer County	5	0.04
New Rochelle (city) Westchester County	5	0.01
Fort Drum (cdp) Jefferson County	4	0.03
Le Ray (town) Jefferson County	4	0.02
Syracuse (city) Onondaga County	4	0.00
Guilford (town) Chenango County	3	0.10

Top 10 Places Sorted by Percent
Based on all places, regardless of population

Place	Number	%
Milford (village) Otsego County	1	0.20
Remsen (village) Oneida County	1	0.19
Mechanicstown (cdp) Orange County	10	0.16
Windham (town) Greene County	2	0.12
Great Bend (cdp) Jefferson County	1	0.12
Guilford (town) Chenango County	3	0.10
Vienna (town) Oneida County	5	0.09
Winfield (town) Herkimer County	2	0.09
Rathbone (town) Steuben County	1	0.09
Rodman (town) Jefferson County	1	0.09

Top 10 Places Sorted by Percent
Based on places with populations of 10,000 or more

Place	Number	%
Wallkill (town) Orange County	10	0.04
Brunswick (town) Rensselaer County	5	0.04
Fort Drum (cdp) Jefferson County	4	0.03
Le Ray (town) Jefferson County	4	0.02
Depew (village) Erie County	3	0.02
New Paltz (town) Ulster County	2	0.02
New Rochelle (city) Westchester County	5	0.01
West Islip (cdp) Suffolk County	3	0.01
Cicero (town) Onondaga County	2	0.01
Lockport (town) Niagara County	2	0.01

Alaska Native: Tlingit-Haida

Top 10 Places Sorted by Number
Based on all places, regardless of population

Place	Number	%
New York (city) New York City	77	0.00
Hempstead (town) Nassau County	12	0.00
Valley Stream (village) Nassau County	7	0.02
Beacon (city) Dutchess County	5	0.04
Troy (city) Rensselaer County	4	0.01
Buffalo (city) Erie County	4	0.00
Farmington (town) Ontario County	3	0.03
Fort Drum (cdp) Jefferson County	3	0.02
Le Ray (town) Jefferson County	3	0.02
North Valley Stream (cdp) Nassau County	3	0.02

Top 10 Places Sorted by Percent
Based on all places, regardless of population

Place	Number	%
Tuxedo Park (village) Orange County	1	0.14
Oyster Bay Cove (village) Nassau County	2	0.09
Poestenkill (town) Rensselaer County	2	0.05
Beacon (city) Dutchess County	5	0.04
Lake Success (village) Nassau County	1	0.04
Farmington (town) Ontario County	3	0.03
Avon (town) Livingston County	2	0.03
Avon (village) Livingston County	1	0.03
South Nyack (village) Rockland County	1	0.03

Tuxedo (town) Orange County	1	0.03

Top 10 Places Sorted by Percent
Based on places with populations of 10,000 or more

Place	Number	%
Beacon (city) Dutchess County	5	0.04
Farmington (town) Ontario County	3	0.03
Valley Stream (village) Nassau County	7	0.02
Fort Drum (cdp) Jefferson County	3	0.02
Le Ray (town) Jefferson County	3	0.02
North Valley Stream (cdp) Nassau County	3	0.02
Troy (city) Rensselaer County	4	0.01
Spring Valley (village) Rockland County	2	0.01
Webster (town) Monroe County	2	0.01
Yorktown (town) Westchester County	2	0.01

Alaska Native: All other tribes

Top 10 Places Sorted by Number
Based on all places, regardless of population

Place	Number	%
New York (city) New York City	26	0.00
Freeport (village) Nassau County	1	0.00
Hempstead (town) Nassau County	1	0.00
Ithaca (city) Tompkins County	1	0.00
New Rochelle (city) Westchester County	1	0.00

Top 10 Places Sorted by Percent
Based on all places, regardless of population

Place	Number	%
New York (city) New York City	26	0.00
Freeport (village) Nassau County	1	0.00
Hempstead (town) Nassau County	1	0.00
Ithaca (city) Tompkins County	1	0.00
New Rochelle (city) Westchester County	1	0.00

Top 10 Places Sorted by Percent
Based on places with populations of 10,000 or more

Place	Number	%
New York (city) New York City	26	0.00
Freeport (village) Nassau County	1	0.00
Hempstead (town) Nassau County	1	0.00
Ithaca (city) Tompkins County	1	0.00
New Rochelle (city) Westchester County	1	0.00

Alaska Native tribes, not specified

Top 10 Places Sorted by Number
Based on all places, regardless of population

Place	Number	%
New York (city) New York City	35	0.00
Rochester (city) Monroe County	9	0.00
Warrensburg (town) Warren County	5	0.12
Saratoga Springs (city) Saratoga County	5	0.02
Phelps (town) Ontario County	4	0.06
Carmel (town) Putnam County	4	0.01
Brookhaven (town) Suffolk County	4	0.00
Myers Corner (cdp) Dutchess County	3	0.05
Fort Drum (cdp) Jefferson County	3	0.02
Le Ray (town) Jefferson County	3	0.02

Top 10 Places Sorted by Percent
Based on all places, regardless of population

Place	Number	%
Warrensburg (town) Warren County	5	0.12
Plattsburgh West (cdp) Clinton County	1	0.08
Phelps (town) Ontario County	4	0.06
Myers Corner (cdp) Dutchess County	3	0.05
Penn Yan (village) Yates County	2	0.04
Green Island (village) Albany County	1	0.04
Randolph (town) Cattaraugus County	1	0.04

Milo (town) Yates County	2	0.0
Rhinebeck (village) Dutchess County	1	0.0
Saratoga Springs (city) Saratoga County	5	0.0

Top 10 Places Sorted by Percent
Based on places with populations of 10,000 or more

Place	Number	%
Saratoga Springs (city) Saratoga County	5	0.0
Fort Drum (cdp) Jefferson County	3	0.0
Le Ray (town) Jefferson County	3	0.0
Massena (town) Saint Lawrence County	2	0.0
Carmel (town) Putnam County	4	0.0
Wappinger (town) Dutchess County	3	0.0
Mastic Beach (cdp) Suffolk County	1	0.0
North Babylon (cdp) Suffolk County	1	0.0
Plattsburgh (town) Clinton County	1	0.0
New York (city) New York City	35	0.0

American Indian or Alaska Native, not specified

Top 10 Places Sorted by Number
Based on all places, regardless of population

Place	Number	%
New York (city) New York City	43,524	0.5
Hempstead (town) Nassau County	1,681	0.2
Buffalo (city) Erie County	1,386	0.4
Rochester (city) Monroe County	1,166	0.5
Brookhaven (town) Suffolk County	1,137	0.2
Syracuse (city) Onondaga County	1,081	0.7
Islip (town) Suffolk County	923	0.3
Yonkers (city) Westchester County	900	0.4
Babylon (town) Suffolk County	632	0.3
Albany (city) Albany County	470	0.4

Top 10 Places Sorted by Percent
Based on all places, regardless of population

Place	Number	%
Poospatuck Reservation Suffolk County	24	8.8
Tuscarora Reservation Niagara County	93	8.1
Hillburn (village) Rockland County	41	4.6
Shinnecock Reservation Suffolk County	21	4.1
Herrings (village) Jefferson County	5	3.8
Salamanca (city) Cattaraugus County	181	2.9
Saint Regis Mohawk Reservation Franklin County	80	2.9
Bombay (town) Franklin County	32	2.8
Worth (town) Jefferson County	6	2.5
Newcomb (town) Essex County	12	2.4

Top 10 Places Sorted by Percent
Based on places with populations of 10,000 or more

Place	Number	%
North Amityville (cdp) Suffolk County	146	0.8
Middletown (city) Orange County	218	0.8
North Bay Shore (cdp) Suffolk County	126	0.8
Wyandanch (cdp) Suffolk County	84	0.8
Syracuse (city) Onondaga County	1,081	0.7
Roosevelt (cdp) Nassau County	110	0.6
Niagara Falls (city) Niagara County	375	0.6
Poughkeepsie (city) Dutchess County	190	0.6
Newburgh (city) Orange County	180	0.6
Hempstead (village) Nassau County	355	0.6

Albanian

Top 10 Places Sorted by Number
Based on all places, regardless of population

Place	Number	%
New York (city) New York City	24,577	0.3
Yonkers (city) Westchester County	1,310	0.6
Hempstead (town) Nassau County	488	0.0
Clarkstown (town) Rockland County	257	0.

Notes: (cdp) census designated place; Refer to the User's Guide in the front of the book for more detailed information.

PROFILES OF NEW YORK / Ancestry: Rankings

Place	Number	%
North Hempstead (town) Nassau County	247	0.11
Rochester (city) Monroe County	221	0.10
New City (cdp) Rockland County	171	0.50
Syracuse (city) Onondaga County	170	0.12
White Plains (city) Westchester County	164	0.31
Ossining (town) Westchester County	159	0.44

Top 10 Places Sorted by Percent
Based on all places, regardless of population

Place	Number	%
Leeds (cdp) Greene County	17	5.18
Scotts Corners (cdp) Westchester County	22	3.82
Walker Valley (cdp) Ulster County	26	3.14
Golden's Bridge (cdp) Westchester County	30	1.94
Jamestown West (cdp) Chautauqua County	48	1.91
Bardonia (cdp) Rockland County	78	1.78
Rock Hill (cdp) Sullivan County	17	1.73
Grand View-on-Hudson (village) Rockland County	4	1.41
Highland Mills (cdp) Orange County	46	1.34
Briarcliff Manor (village) Westchester County	94	1.23

Top 10 Places Sorted by Percent
Based on places with populations of 10,000 or more

Place	Number	%
Beekman (town) Dutchess County	114	1.00
Mamakating (town) Sullivan County	110	1.00
Putnam Valley (town) Putnam County	96	0.90
North New Hyde Park (cdp) Nassau County	109	0.75
La Grange (town) Dutchess County	111	0.74
Yonkers (city) Westchester County	1,310	0.67
New City (cdp) Rockland County	171	0.50
Jefferson Valley-Yorktown (cdp) Westchester County	72	0.48
Catskill (town) Greene County	56	0.47
Lewiston (town) Niagara County	75	0.46

Alsatian

Top 10 Places Sorted by Number
Based on all places, regardless of population

Place	Number	%
New York (city) New York City	388	0.00
Hempstead (town) Nassau County	87	0.01
Huntington (town) Suffolk County	55	0.03
Islip (town) Suffolk County	50	0.02
Lowville (village) Lewis County	42	1.20
Lowville (town) Lewis County	42	0.92
Clarence (town) Erie County	39	0.15
Cheektowaga (town) Erie County	38	0.04
Brookhaven (town) Suffolk County	35	0.01
Rockville Centre (village) Nassau County	33	0.13

Top 10 Places Sorted by Percent
Based on all places, regardless of population

Place	Number	%
Lowville (village) Lewis County	42	1.20
Hewlett Neck (village) Nassau County	5	1.01
Lowville (town) Lewis County	42	0.92
Taylor (town) Cortland County	4	0.83
Niverville (cdp) Columbia County	11	0.66
Ellicottville (village) Cattaraugus County	3	0.63
North Great River (cdp) Suffolk County	22	0.56
Houghton (cdp) Allegany County	9	0.52
Dresden (town) Washington County	3	0.45
Caneadea (town) Allegany County	9	0.34

Top 10 Places Sorted by Percent
Based on places with populations of 10,000 or more

Place	Number	%
Clarence (town) Erie County	39	0.15
Rockville Centre (village) Nassau County	33	0.13
New Castle (town) Westchester County	20	0.11

Place	Number	%
Pittsford (town) Monroe County	26	0.10
Hauppauge (cdp) Suffolk County	20	0.10
North Castle (town) Westchester County	11	0.10
Saint James (cdp) Suffolk County	12	0.09
Coram (cdp) Suffolk County	27	0.08
Orchard Park (town) Erie County	22	0.08
Seaford (cdp) Nassau County	12	0.08

American Indian tribes, specified

Top 10 Places Sorted by Number
Based on all places, regardless of population

Place	Number	%
New York (city) New York City	37,382	0.47
Saint Regis Mohawk Reservation Franklin County	2,517	93.26
Buffalo (city) Erie County	2,474	0.85
Syracuse (city) Onondaga County	2,140	1.45
Hempstead (town) Nassau County	1,917	0.25
Brookhaven (town) Suffolk County	1,622	0.36
Rochester (city) Monroe County	1,467	0.67
Islip (town) Suffolk County	1,206	0.37
Niagara Falls (city) Niagara County	903	1.62
Babylon (town) Suffolk County	836	0.39

Top 10 Places Sorted by Percent
Based on all places, regardless of population

Place	Number	%
Saint Regis Mohawk Reservation Franklin County	2,517	93.26
Shinnecock Reservation Suffolk County	435	86.31
Poospatuck Reservation Suffolk County	167	61.62
Allegany Reservation Cattaraugus County	552	50.23
Onondaga Reservation Onondaga County	698	47.39
Tuscarora Reservation Niagara County	169	14.85
Bombay (town) Franklin County	159	13.34
Hillburn (village) Rockland County	113	12.83
Salamanca (city) Cattaraugus County	589	9.66
Dering Harbor (village) Suffolk County	1	7.69

Top 10 Places Sorted by Percent
Based on places with populations of 10,000 or more

Place	Number	%
Massena (town) Saint Lawrence County	421	3.21
Massena (village) Saint Lawrence County	244	2.18
Mastic (cdp) Suffolk County	259	1.68
Niagara Falls (city) Niagara County	903	1.62
North Amityville (cdp) Suffolk County	244	1.47
Syracuse (city) Onondaga County	2,140	1.45
Fort Drum (cdp) Jefferson County	165	1.36
Onondaga (town) Onondaga County	272	1.29
Wyandanch (cdp) Suffolk County	127	1.21
Le Ray (town) Jefferson County	218	1.10

American Indian: Apache

Top 10 Places Sorted by Number
Based on all places, regardless of population

Place	Number	%
New York (city) New York City	342	0.00
Hempstead (town) Nassau County	38	0.01
Brookhaven (town) Suffolk County	37	0.01
Syracuse (city) Onondaga County	29	0.02
Buffalo (city) Erie County	29	0.01
Islip (town) Suffolk County	22	0.01
Rochester (city) Monroe County	19	0.01
Albany (city) Albany County	14	0.01
Le Ray (town) Jefferson County	13	0.07
Yonkers (city) Westchester County	12	0.01

Top 10 Places Sorted by Percent
Based on all places, regardless of population

Place	Number	%
Morehouse (town) Hamilton County	1	0.66
Edwards (village) Saint Lawrence County	3	0.65
Cato (village) Cayuga County	3	0.50
Red Creek (village) Wayne County	2	0.38
North Hudson (town) Essex County	1	0.38
Edwards (town) Saint Lawrence County	3	0.26
Bethany (town) Genesee County	4	0.23
Dryden (village) Tompkins County	4	0.22
Nanticoke (town) Broome County	4	0.22
Conquest (town) Cayuga County	3	0.16

Top 10 Places Sorted by Percent
Based on places with populations of 10,000 or more

Place	Number	%
Mastic Beach (cdp) Suffolk County	10	0.09
Fort Drum (cdp) Jefferson County	10	0.08
Le Ray (town) Jefferson County	13	0.07
Dryden (town) Tompkins County	10	0.07
North Bay Shore (cdp) Suffolk County	9	0.06
Mastic (cdp) Suffolk County	6	0.04
Shawangunk (town) Ulster County	5	0.04
Stony Point (town) Rockland County	5	0.04
Lackawanna (city) Erie County	6	0.03
Lynbrook (village) Nassau County	6	0.03

American Indian: Blackfeet

Top 10 Places Sorted by Number
Based on all places, regardless of population

Place	Number	%
New York (city) New York City	1,454	0.02
Brookhaven (town) Suffolk County	118	0.03
Hempstead (town) Nassau County	112	0.01
Buffalo (city) Erie County	106	0.04
Rochester (city) Monroe County	93	0.04
Syracuse (city) Onondaga County	91	0.06
Islip (town) Suffolk County	83	0.03
Babylon (town) Suffolk County	48	0.02
Albany (city) Albany County	41	0.04
Newburgh (city) Orange County	37	0.13

Top 10 Places Sorted by Percent
Based on all places, regardless of population

Place	Number	%
Gilbertsville (village) Otsego County	4	1.07
Natural Bridge (cdp) Jefferson County	3	0.77
Sand Ridge (cdp) Oswego County	5	0.55
Kortright (town) Delaware County	7	0.43
Crown Point (town) Essex County	9	0.42
Tusten (town) Sullivan County	6	0.42
Norway (town) Herkimer County	3	0.42
Willet (town) Cortland County	4	0.40
Thurston (town) Steuben County	5	0.38
Brandon (town) Franklin County	2	0.37

Top 10 Places Sorted by Percent
Based on places with populations of 10,000 or more

Place	Number	%
Newburgh (city) Orange County	37	0.13
Catskill (town) Greene County	13	0.11
Owego (town) Tioga County	19	0.09
Roosevelt (cdp) Nassau County	15	0.09
North Bay Shore (cdp) Suffolk County	14	0.09
Mastic Beach (cdp) Suffolk County	10	0.09
Wyandanch (cdp) Suffolk County	9	0.09
Binghamton (city) Broome County	37	0.08
Halfmoon (town) Saratoga County	15	0.08
Patterson (town) Putnam County	9	0.08

Notes: (cdp) census designated place; Refer to the User's Guide in the front of the book for more detailed information.

PROFILES OF NEW YORK / Ancestry: Rankings

American Indian: Cherokee

Top 10 Places Sorted by Number
Based on all places, regardless of population

Place	Number	%
New York (city) New York City	6,631	0.08
Hempstead (town) Nassau County	627	0.08
Brookhaven (town) Suffolk County	506	0.11
Rochester (city) Monroe County	377	0.17
Buffalo (city) Erie County	363	0.12
Islip (town) Suffolk County	295	0.09
Babylon (town) Suffolk County	261	0.12
Syracuse (city) Onondaga County	218	0.15
Yonkers (city) Westchester County	211	0.11
Albany (city) Albany County	134	0.14

Top 10 Places Sorted by Percent
Based on all places, regardless of population

Place	Number	%
Poospatuck Reservation Suffolk County	10	3.69
Clare (town) Saint Lawrence County	1	0.89
Hammond (town) Saint Lawrence County	9	0.75
Minerva (town) Essex County	6	0.75
North Bellport (cdp) Suffolk County	66	0.73
Matinecock (village) Nassau County	6	0.72
Hillburn (village) Rockland County	6	0.68
New Hudson (town) Allegany County	5	0.68
Stony Creek (town) Warren County	5	0.67
Riverside (village) Steuben County	4	0.67

Top 10 Places Sorted by Percent
Based on places with populations of 10,000 or more

Place	Number	%
Roosevelt (cdp) Nassau County	69	0.44
Wyandanch (cdp) Suffolk County	43	0.41
North Amityville (cdp) Suffolk County	65	0.39
Fort Drum (cdp) Jefferson County	47	0.39
Mastic Beach (cdp) Suffolk County	37	0.32
Le Ray (town) Jefferson County	56	0.28
Mastic (cdp) Suffolk County	41	0.27
Beacon (city) Dutchess County	33	0.24
Hempstead (village) Nassau County	131	0.23
Bay Shore (cdp) Suffolk County	56	0.23

American Indian: Cheyenne

Top 10 Places Sorted by Number
Based on all places, regardless of population

Place	Number	%
New York (city) New York City	80	0.00
Hempstead (town) Nassau County	8	0.00
Amherst (town) Erie County	7	0.01
Islip (town) Suffolk County	6	0.00
Yonkers (city) Westchester County	6	0.00
Elmira (city) Chemung County	5	0.02
Brookhaven (town) Suffolk County	5	0.00
Syracuse (city) Onondaga County	5	0.00
Halfmoon (town) Saratoga County	4	0.02
Owego (town) Tioga County	4	0.02

Top 10 Places Sorted by Percent
Based on all places, regardless of population

Place	Number	%
Limestone (village) Cattaraugus County	2	0.49
Apalachin (cdp) Tioga County	3	0.27
Carrollton (town) Cattaraugus County	2	0.14
Smyrna (town) Chenango County	2	0.14
Sandy Creek (village) Oswego County	1	0.13
Woodridge (village) Sullivan County	1	0.11
Schoharie (village) Schoharie County	1	0.10
Harriman (village) Orange County	2	0.09
Pike (town) Wyoming County	1	0.09

| **Naples** (town) Ontario County | 2 | 0.08 |

Top 10 Places Sorted by Percent
Based on places with populations of 10,000 or more

Place	Number	%
Elmira (city) Chemung County	5	0.02
Halfmoon (town) Saratoga County	4	0.02
Owego (town) Tioga County	4	0.02
Bath (town) Steuben County	3	0.02
Le Ray (town) Jefferson County	3	0.02
Plattsburgh (city) Clinton County	3	0.02
Fallsburg (town) Sullivan County	2	0.02
Fort Drum (cdp) Jefferson County	2	0.02
North Merrick (cdp) Nassau County	2	0.02
Amherst (town) Erie County	7	0.01

American Indian: Chickasaw

Top 10 Places Sorted by Number
Based on all places, regardless of population

Place	Number	%
New York (city) New York City	85	0.00
Rochester (city) Monroe County	9	0.00
Brookhaven (town) Suffolk County	8	0.00
Penfield (town) Monroe County	5	0.01
West Point (cdp) Orange County	4	0.06
Highlands (town) Orange County	4	0.03
Baldwin (cdp) Nassau County	4	0.02
Shirley (cdp) Suffolk County	4	0.02
Poughkeepsie (town) Dutchess County	4	0.01
Hempstead (town) Nassau County	4	0.00

Top 10 Places Sorted by Percent
Based on all places, regardless of population

Place	Number	%
Brandon (town) Franklin County	1	0.18
Plainfield (town) Otsego County	1	0.10
East Hampton (village) Suffolk County	1	0.07
West Point (cdp) Orange County	4	0.06
Sparta (town) Livingston County	1	0.06
Floyd (town) Oneida County	2	0.05
Savannah (town) Wayne County	1	0.05
Upper Nyack (village) Rockland County	1	0.05
Waddington (town) Saint Lawrence County	1	0.05
West Hurley (cdp) Ulster County	1	0.05

Top 10 Places Sorted by Percent
Based on places with populations of 10,000 or more

Place	Number	%
Highlands (town) Orange County	4	0.03
Tarrytown (village) Westchester County	3	0.03
Baldwin (cdp) Nassau County	4	0.02
Shirley (cdp) Suffolk County	4	0.02
Penfield (town) Monroe County	5	0.01
Poughkeepsie (town) Dutchess County	4	0.01
Medford (cdp) Suffolk County	3	0.01
Bethlehem (town) Albany County	2	0.01
East Hampton (town) Suffolk County	2	0.01
Lindenhurst (village) Suffolk County	2	0.01

American Indian: Chippewa

Top 10 Places Sorted by Number
Based on all places, regardless of population

Place	Number	%
New York (city) New York City	194	0.00
Buffalo (city) Erie County	61	0.02
Niagara Falls (city) Niagara County	33	0.06
Rochester (city) Monroe County	22	0.01
Hempstead (town) Nassau County	21	0.00
Auburn (city) Cayuga County	13	0.05
Schenectady (city) Schenectady County	13	0.02

Syracuse (city) Onondaga County	13	0.01
Brookhaven (town) Suffolk County	12	0.00
Islip (town) Suffolk County	12	0.00

Top 10 Places Sorted by Percent
Based on all places, regardless of population

Place	Number	%
Fleischmanns (village) Delaware County	4	1.14
German (town) Chenango County	2	0.53
Lincklaen (town) Chenango County	2	0.48
Dresden (village) Yates County	1	0.33
Burns (town) Allegany County	4	0.32
Meridian (village) Cayuga County	1	0.29
Byron (town) Genesee County	7	0.28
Palmyra (village) Wayne County	9	0.26
Phoenicia (cdp) Ulster County	1	0.26
Dunkirk (town) Chautauqua County	3	0.22

Top 10 Places Sorted by Percent
Based on places with populations of 10,000 or more

Place	Number	%
Niagara Falls (city) Niagara County	33	0.06
Patterson (town) Putnam County	7	0.06
Auburn (city) Cayuga County	13	0.05
Beacon (city) Dutchess County	5	0.04
North Greenbush (town) Rensselaer County	4	0.04
Montgomery (town) Orange County	6	0.03
Oswego (city) Oswego County	6	0.03
Jefferson Valley-Yorktown (cdp) Westchester County	5	0.03
Fort Drum (cdp) Jefferson County	4	0.03
Seaford (cdp) Nassau County	4	0.03

American Indian: Choctaw

Top 10 Places Sorted by Number
Based on all places, regardless of population

Place	Number	%
New York (city) New York City	255	0.00
Hempstead (town) Nassau County	29	0.00
Buffalo (city) Erie County	22	0.01
Syracuse (city) Onondaga County	18	0.01
Brookhaven (town) Suffolk County	17	0.00
Islip (town) Suffolk County	16	0.00
Babylon (town) Suffolk County	12	0.01
Rochester (city) Monroe County	12	0.01
Huntington (town) Suffolk County	11	0.01
North Hempstead (town) Nassau County	9	0.00

Top 10 Places Sorted by Percent
Based on all places, regardless of population

Place	Number	%
Newcomb (town) Essex County	4	0.83
Sherman (village) Chautauqua County	3	0.42
Athens (village) Greene County	6	0.35
Tuscarora Reservation Niagara County	4	0.35
Otego (village) Otsego County	3	0.29
Arkport (village) Steuben County	2	0.24
Glen Park (village) Jefferson County	1	0.21
Sherman (town) Chautauqua County	3	0.19
Clyde (village) Wayne County	4	0.18
Victory (village) Saratoga County	1	0.18

Top 10 Places Sorted by Percent
Based on places with populations of 10,000 or more

Place	Number	%
Fort Drum (cdp) Jefferson County	7	0.06
Shawangunk (town) Ulster County	7	0.05
Wyandanch (cdp) Suffolk County	5	0.05
Le Ray (town) Jefferson County	8	0.04
Mastic Beach (cdp) Suffolk County	5	0.04
Canandaigua (city) Ontario County	4	0.04
Auburn (city) Cayuga County	8	0.03

Notes: (cdp) census designated place; Refer to the User's Guide in the front of the book for more detailed information.

PROFILES OF NEW YORK / Ancestry: Rankings

Place	Number	%
East Northport (cdp) Suffolk County	6	0.03
West Hempstead (cdp) Nassau County	5	0.03
Catskill (town) Greene County	4	0.03

American Indian: Colville

Top 10 Places Sorted by Number
Based on all places, regardless of population

Place	Number	%
New York (city) New York City	3	0.00
Hector (town) Schuyler County	2	0.04
Rochester (city) Monroe County	2	0.00
Bath (village) Steuben County	1	0.02
Bath (town) Steuben County	1	0.01
Massena (town) Saint Lawrence County	1	0.01
Massena (village) Saint Lawrence County	1	0.01
Poughkeepsie (city) Dutchess County	1	0.00
Ramapo (town) Rockland County	1	0.00
Spring Valley (village) Rockland County	1	0.00

Top 10 Places Sorted by Percent
Based on all places, regardless of population

Place	Number	%
Hector (town) Schuyler County	2	0.04
Bath (village) Steuben County	1	0.02
Bath (town) Steuben County	1	0.01
Massena (town) Saint Lawrence County	1	0.01
Massena (village) Saint Lawrence County	1	0.01
New York (city) New York City	3	0.00
Rochester (city) Monroe County	2	0.00
Poughkeepsie (city) Dutchess County	1	0.00
Ramapo (town) Rockland County	1	0.00
Spring Valley (village) Rockland County	1	0.00

Top 10 Places Sorted by Percent
Based on places with populations of 10,000 or more

Place	Number	%
Bath (town) Steuben County	1	0.01
Massena (town) Saint Lawrence County	1	0.01
Massena (village) Saint Lawrence County	1	0.01
New York (city) New York City	3	0.00
Rochester (city) Monroe County	2	0.00
Poughkeepsie (city) Dutchess County	1	0.00
Ramapo (town) Rockland County	1	0.00
Spring Valley (village) Rockland County	1	0.00

American Indian: Comanche

Top 10 Places Sorted by Number
Based on all places, regardless of population

Place	Number	%
New York (city) New York City	65	0.00
Fort Drum (cdp) Jefferson County	7	0.06
Le Ray (town) Jefferson County	7	0.04
Brookhaven (town) Suffolk County	6	0.00
Hempstead (town) Nassau County	5	0.00
Syracuse (city) Onondaga County	5	0.00
Nedrow (cdp) Onondaga County	4	0.18
Tappan (cdp) Rockland County	4	0.06
Herkimer (village) Herkimer County	4	0.05
Herkimer (town) Herkimer County	4	0.04

Top 10 Places Sorted by Percent
Based on all places, regardless of population

Place	Number	%
Hampton (town) Washington County	2	0.23
Nedrow (cdp) Onondaga County	4	0.18
Thurman (town) Warren County	2	0.17
Claverack-Red Mills (cdp) Columbia County	1	0.09
Waverly (town) Franklin County	1	0.09
Roxbury (town) Delaware County	2	0.08
Hewlett Harbor (village) Nassau County	1	0.08

Place	Number	%
Fort Drum (cdp) Jefferson County	7	0.06
Tappan (cdp) Rockland County	4	0.06
South Bristol (town) Ontario County	1	0.06

Top 10 Places Sorted by Percent
Based on places with populations of 10,000 or more

Place	Number	%
Fort Drum (cdp) Jefferson County	7	0.06
Le Ray (town) Jefferson County	7	0.04
Onondaga (town) Onondaga County	4	0.02
Shirley (cdp) Suffolk County	4	0.02
Lewiston (town) Niagara County	3	0.02
Endicott (village) Broome County	2	0.02
Levittown (cdp) Nassau County	4	0.01
Orangetown (town) Rockland County	4	0.01
Massapequa (cdp) Nassau County	2	0.01
Milton (town) Saratoga County	2	0.01

American Indian: Cree

Top 10 Places Sorted by Number
Based on all places, regardless of population

Place	Number	%
New York (city) New York City	94	0.00
Buffalo (city) Erie County	11	0.00
Islip (town) Suffolk County	7	0.00
Saratoga Springs (city) Saratoga County	6	0.02
Brookhaven (town) Suffolk County	6	0.00
Colonie (town) Albany County	5	0.01
Catskill (town) Greene County	4	0.03
Plattsburgh (city) Clinton County	4	0.02
Guilderland (town) Albany County	4	0.01
Hamburg (town) Erie County	4	0.01

Top 10 Places Sorted by Percent
Based on all places, regardless of population

Place	Number	%
Fleischmanns (village) Delaware County	3	0.85
Birdsall (town) Allegany County	1	0.37
Smallwood (cdp) Sullivan County	2	0.35
Cato (village) Cayuga County	2	0.33
Hammond (village) Saint Lawrence County	1	0.33
Van Etten (village) Chemung County	1	0.17
Accord (cdp) Ulster County	1	0.16
Schaghticoke (village) Rensselaer County	1	0.15
Fultonville (village) Montgomery County	1	0.14
Wells (town) Hamilton County	1	0.14

Top 10 Places Sorted by Percent
Based on places with populations of 10,000 or more

Place	Number	%
Catskill (town) Greene County	4	0.03
Saratoga Springs (city) Saratoga County	6	0.02
Plattsburgh (city) Clinton County	4	0.02
North Bay Shore (cdp) Suffolk County	3	0.02
Chenango (town) Broome County	2	0.02
Mastic Beach (cdp) Suffolk County	2	0.02
Schodack (town) Rensselaer County	2	0.02
Colonie (town) Albany County	5	0.01
Guilderland (town) Albany County	4	0.01
Hamburg (town) Erie County	4	0.01

American Indian: Creek

Top 10 Places Sorted by Number
Based on all places, regardless of population

Place	Number	%
New York (city) New York City	229	0.00
Hempstead (town) Nassau County	21	0.00
Buffalo (city) Erie County	9	0.00
Islip (town) Suffolk County	8	0.00
Rochester (city) Monroe County	8	0.00

Place	Number	%
Fort Drum (cdp) Jefferson County	7	0.06
Le Ray (town) Jefferson County	7	0.04
Brookhaven (town) Suffolk County	7	0.00
Huntington (town) Suffolk County	7	0.00
Gorham (town) Ontario County	6	0.16

Top 10 Places Sorted by Percent
Based on all places, regardless of population

Place	Number	%
Hopewell Junction (cdp) Dutchess County	5	0.19
Gorham (town) Ontario County	6	0.16
Sandy Creek (village) Oswego County	1	0.13
Ischua (town) Cattaraugus County	1	0.11
Woodridge (village) Sullivan County	1	0.11
Otisville (village) Orange County	1	0.10
Calverton (cdp) Suffolk County	5	0.09
Cayuga Heights (village) Tompkins County	3	0.09
Caledonia (village) Livingston County	2	0.09
Tivoli (village) Dutchess County	1	0.09

Top 10 Places Sorted by Percent
Based on places with populations of 10,000 or more

Place	Number	%
Fort Drum (cdp) Jefferson County	7	0.06
Le Ray (town) Jefferson County	7	0.04
Sweden (town) Monroe County	5	0.04
Shawangunk (town) Ulster County	4	0.03
Nesconset (cdp) Suffolk County	3	0.03
Jamestown (city) Chautauqua County	6	0.02
East Fishkill (town) Dutchess County	5	0.02
Riverhead (town) Suffolk County	5	0.02
East Greenbush (town) Rensselaer County	3	0.02
Ithaca (town) Tompkins County	3	0.02

American Indian: Crow

Top 10 Places Sorted by Number
Based on all places, regardless of population

Place	Number	%
New York (city) New York City	44	0.00
Hempstead (town) Nassau County	7	0.00
Freeport (village) Nassau County	6	0.01
Brookhaven (town) Suffolk County	6	0.00
Yonkers (city) Westchester County	6	0.00
Ontario (town) Wayne County	5	0.05
Elmira (city) Chemung County	5	0.02
Mamaroneck (town) Westchester County	5	0.02
Peekskill (city) Westchester County	5	0.02
Buffalo (city) Erie County	5	0.00

Top 10 Places Sorted by Percent
Based on all places, regardless of population

Place	Number	%
Richmondville (village) Schoharie County	1	0.13
Jay (town) Essex County	2	0.09
Apalachin (cdp) Tioga County	2	0.09
Rockland (town) Sullivan County	3	0.08
Lyonsdale (town) Lewis County	1	0.08
Wirt (town) Allegany County	1	0.08
Sodus (village) Wayne County	1	0.06
Ontario (town) Wayne County	5	0.05
Edmeston (town) Otsego County	1	0.05
Hillside Lake (cdp) Dutchess County	1	0.05

Top 10 Places Sorted by Percent
Based on places with populations of 10,000 or more

Place	Number	%
Elmira (city) Chemung County	5	0.02
Mamaroneck (town) Westchester County	5	0.02
Peekskill (city) Westchester County	5	0.02
Fort Drum (cdp) Jefferson County	2	0.02
Oneida (city) Madison County	2	0.02

Notes: (cdp) census designated place; Refer to the User's Guide in the front of the book for more detailed information.

Place	Number	%
Freeport (village) Nassau County	6	0.01
Cortlandt (town) Westchester County	3	0.01
Manlius (town) Onondaga County	3	0.01
Coram (cdp) Suffolk County	2	0.01
De Witt (town) Onondaga County	2	0.01

American Indian: Delaware

Top 10 Places Sorted by Number
Based on all places, regardless of population

Place	Number	%
New York (city) New York City	150	0.00
Ramapo (town) Rockland County	142	0.13
Hillburn (village) Rockland County	104	11.80
Warwick (town) Orange County	38	0.12
Blooming Grove (town) Orange County	33	0.19
Haverstraw (town) Rockland County	29	0.09
Monroe (town) Orange County	21	0.07
Mamakating (town) Sullivan County	20	0.18
Stony Point (town) Rockland County	20	0.14
Wallkill (town) Orange County	18	0.07

Top 10 Places Sorted by Percent
Based on all places, regardless of population

Place	Number	%
Hillburn (village) Rockland County	104	11.80
Nelliston (village) Montgomery County	5	0.80
Otisville (village) Orange County	5	0.51
Cameron (town) Steuben County	5	0.48
Tannersville (village) Greene County	2	0.45
Sloatsburg (village) Rockland County	11	0.35
Saint Johnsville (village) Montgomery County	5	0.30
Kerhonkson (cdp) Ulster County	5	0.29
Apalachin (cdp) Tioga County	3	0.27
Westford (town) Otsego County	2	0.26

Top 10 Places Sorted by Percent
Based on places with populations of 10,000 or more

Place	Number	%
Blooming Grove (town) Orange County	33	0.19
Mamakating (town) Sullivan County	20	0.18
West Haverstraw (village) Rockland County	16	0.16
Stony Point (town) Rockland County	20	0.14
Ramapo (town) Rockland County	142	0.13
Warwick (town) Orange County	38	0.12
Chester (town) Orange County	13	0.11
Haverstraw (town) Rockland County	29	0.09
Wawarsing (town) Ulster County	12	0.09
Haverstraw (village) Rockland County	8	0.08

American Indian: Houma

Top 10 Places Sorted by Number
Based on all places, regardless of population

Place	Number	%
New York (city) New York City	10	0.00
Syracuse (city) Onondaga County	4	0.00
Willing (town) Allegany County	3	0.22
Hanover (town) Chautauqua County	3	0.04
Greenburgh (town) Westchester County	3	0.00
Gouverneur (village) Saint Lawrence County	2	0.05
Albion (village) Orleans County	2	0.03
Gouverneur (town) Saint Lawrence County	2	0.03
Hurley (town) Ulster County	2	0.03
Albion (town) Orleans County	2	0.02

Top 10 Places Sorted by Percent
Based on all places, regardless of population

Place	Number	%
Willing (town) Allegany County	3	0.22
Gouverneur (village) Saint Lawrence County	2	0.05
West Hurley (cdp) Ulster County	1	0.05
Hanover (town) Chautauqua County	3	0.04
Albion (village) Orleans County	2	0.03
Gouverneur (town) Saint Lawrence County	2	0.03
Hurley (town) Ulster County	2	0.03
Fairview (cdp) Westchester County	1	0.03
Albion (town) Orleans County	2	0.02
Manlius (town) Onondaga County	2	0.01

Top 10 Places Sorted by Percent
Based on places with populations of 10,000 or more

Place	Number	%
Manlius (town) Onondaga County	2	0.01
Tarrytown (village) Westchester County	1	0.01
New York (city) New York City	10	0.00
Syracuse (city) Onondaga County	4	0.00
Greenburgh (town) Westchester County	3	0.00
Yonkers (city) Westchester County	2	0.00
Babylon (town) Suffolk County	1	0.00
Cicero (town) Onondaga County	1	0.00
Copiague (cdp) Suffolk County	1	0.00

American Indian: Iroquois

Top 10 Places Sorted by Number
Based on all places, regardless of population

Place	Number	%
Saint Regis Mohawk Reservation Franklin County	2,515	93.18
Buffalo (city) Erie County	1,604	0.55
Syracuse (city) Onondaga County	1,511	1.03
New York (city) New York City	1,069	0.01
Niagara Falls (city) Niagara County	767	1.38
Onondaga Reservation Onondaga County	698	47.39
Rochester (city) Monroe County	631	0.29
Salamanca (city) Cattaraugus County	556	9.12
Allegany Reservation Cattaraugus County	534	48.59
Massena (town) Saint Lawrence County	397	3.03

Top 10 Places Sorted by Percent
Based on all places, regardless of population

Place	Number	%
Saint Regis Mohawk Reservation Franklin County	2,515	93.18
Allegany Reservation Cattaraugus County	534	48.59
Onondaga Reservation Onondaga County	698	47.39
Tuscarora Reservation Niagara County	163	14.32
Bombay (town) Franklin County	157	13.17
Salamanca (city) Cattaraugus County	556	9.12
Nedrow (cdp) Onondaga County	138	6.09
Fort Covington (town) Franklin County	84	5.11
Perrysburg (village) Cattaraugus County	16	3.92
Gowanda (village) Cattaraugus County	91	3.20

Top 10 Places Sorted by Percent
Based on places with populations of 10,000 or more

Place	Number	%
Massena (town) Saint Lawrence County	397	3.03
Massena (village) Saint Lawrence County	223	1.99
Niagara Falls (city) Niagara County	767	1.38
Onondaga (town) Onondaga County	247	1.17
Syracuse (city) Onondaga County	1,511	1.03
Oneida (city) Madison County	86	0.78
Ogdensburg (city) Saint Lawrence County	89	0.72
Geddes (town) Onondaga County	115	0.65
Evans (town) Erie County	109	0.62
Salina (town) Onondaga County	202	0.61

American Indian: Kiowa

Top 10 Places Sorted by Number
Based on all places, regardless of population

Place	Number	%
New York (city) New York City	13	0.00
Carthage (village) Jefferson County	3	0.08
Boonville (town) Oneida County	3	0.07
Wilna (town) Jefferson County	3	0.05
Shinnecock Reservation Suffolk County	2	0.40
Camillus (village) Onondaga County	2	0.16
Colchester (town) Delaware County	2	0.10
Endicott (village) Broome County	2	0.02
Camillus (town) Onondaga County	2	0.01
Henrietta (town) Monroe County	2	0.01

Top 10 Places Sorted by Percent
Based on all places, regardless of population

Place	Number	%
Shinnecock Reservation Suffolk County	2	0.40
Camillus (village) Onondaga County	2	0.16
Colchester (town) Delaware County	2	0.10
Carthage (village) Jefferson County	3	0.08
Lewis (town) Essex County	1	0.08
Boonville (town) Oneida County	3	0.07
Tuscarora (town) Steuben County	1	0.07
Angola on the Lake (cdp) Erie County	1	0.06
Wilna (town) Jefferson County	3	0.05
Hamilton (village) Madison County	1	0.03

Top 10 Places Sorted by Percent
Based on places with populations of 10,000 or more

Place	Number	%
Endicott (village) Broome County	2	0.02
Camillus (town) Onondaga County	2	0.01
Henrietta (town) Monroe County	2	0.01
La Grange (town) Dutchess County	2	0.01
Massapequa (cdp) Nassau County	2	0.01
Chenango (town) Broome County	1	0.01
Elwood (cdp) Suffolk County	1	0.01
Evans (town) Erie County	1	0.01
Farmington (town) Ontario County	1	0.01
Wawarsing (town) Ulster County	1	0.01

American Indian: Latin American Indians

Top 10 Places Sorted by Number
Based on all places, regardless of population

Place	Number	%
New York (city) New York City	22,003	0.27
Hempstead (town) Nassau County	449	0.06
Islip (town) Suffolk County	336	0.10
Yonkers (city) Westchester County	244	0.12
Brentwood (cdp) Suffolk County	213	0.40
Brookhaven (town) Suffolk County	207	0.05
North Hempstead (town) Nassau County	128	0.06
Ramapo (town) Rockland County	108	0.13
Ossining (town) Westchester County	104	0.28
Ossining (village) Westchester County	100	0.42

Top 10 Places Sorted by Percent
Based on all places, regardless of population

Place	Number	%
West Almond (town) Allegany County	3	0.85
West Union (town) Steuben County	3	0.75
Bellerose Terrace (cdp) Nassau County	16	0.74
Piercefield (town) Saint Lawrence County	2	0.66
Shelter Island (town) Suffolk County	11	0.49
Center Moriches (cdp) Suffolk County	32	0.48
Stratford (town) Fulton County	3	0.47
Ossining (village) Westchester County	100	0.42
Eastport (cdp) Suffolk County	6	0.41

Notes: (cdp) census designated place; Refer to the User's Guide in the front of the book for more detailed information.

PROFILES OF NEW YORK / Ancestry: Rankings

Place	Number	%
Wirt (town) Allegany County	5	0.41

Top 10 Places Sorted by Percent
Based on places with populations of 10,000 or more

Place	Number	%
Ossining (village) Westchester County	100	0.42
Brentwood (cdp) Suffolk County	213	0.40
Newburgh (city) Orange County	99	0.35
Suffern (village) Rockland County	32	0.29
Haverstraw (village) Rockland County	29	0.29
Ossining (town) Westchester County	104	0.28
New York (city) New York City	22,003	0.27
Spring Valley (village) Rockland County	62	0.24
Wawarsing (town) Ulster County	28	0.22
Dunkirk (city) Chautauqua County	27	0.21

American Indian: Lumbee

Top 10 Places Sorted by Number
Based on all places, regardless of population

Place	Number	%
New York (city) New York City	87	0.00
Hempstead (town) Nassau County	19	0.00
Hempstead (village) Nassau County	13	0.02
Shrub Oak (cdp) Westchester County	6	0.33
Fulton (city) Oswego County	6	0.05
Yorktown (town) Westchester County	6	0.02
Buffalo (city) Erie County	6	0.00
Huntington (town) Suffolk County	6	0.00
Islip (town) Suffolk County	6	0.00
Ira (town) Cayuga County	5	0.21

Top 10 Places Sorted by Percent
Based on all places, regardless of population

Place	Number	%
Shrub Oak (cdp) Westchester County	6	0.33
Rensselaer Falls (village) Saint Lawrence County	1	0.30
Philadelphia (village) Jefferson County	4	0.26
Ira (town) Cayuga County	5	0.21
Philadelphia (town) Jefferson County	4	0.19
Denning (town) Ulster County	1	0.19
Reading (town) Schuyler County	2	0.11
East Ithaca (cdp) Tompkins County	2	0.09
Hopewell Junction (cdp) Dutchess County	2	0.08
North Ballston Spa (cdp) Saratoga County	1	0.08

Top 10 Places Sorted by Percent
Based on places with populations of 10,000 or more

Place	Number	%
Fulton (city) Oswego County	6	0.05
Le Ray (town) Jefferson County	5	0.03
Canton (town) Saint Lawrence County	3	0.03
Elwood (cdp) Suffolk County	3	0.03
Hempstead (village) Nassau County	13	0.02
Yorktown (town) Westchester County	6	0.02
Riverhead (town) Suffolk County	5	0.02
Bedford (town) Westchester County	4	0.02
Milton (town) Saratoga County	4	0.02
Cornwall (town) Orange County	3	0.02

American Indian: Menominee

Top 10 Places Sorted by Number
Based on all places, regardless of population

Place	Number	%
New York (city) New York City	6	0.00
Fort Drum (cdp) Jefferson County	3	0.02
Le Ray (town) Jefferson County	3	0.02
Hempstead (town) Nassau County	3	0.00
East Meadow (cdp) Nassau County	2	0.01
New Windsor (town) Orange County	2	0.01
Rochester (city) Monroe County	2	0.00
Bennington (town) Wyoming County	1	0.03
Cuba (town) Allegany County	1	0.03
Carmel Hamlet (cdp) Putnam County	1	0.02

Top 10 Places Sorted by Percent
Based on all places, regardless of population

Place	Number	%
Bennington (town) Wyoming County	1	0.03
Cuba (town) Allegany County	1	0.03
Fort Drum (cdp) Jefferson County	3	0.02
Le Ray (town) Jefferson County	3	0.02
Carmel Hamlet (cdp) Putnam County	1	0.02
East Rochester (village) Monroe County	1	0.02
Myers Corner (cdp) Dutchess County	1	0.02
New Paltz (village) Ulster County	1	0.02
East Meadow (cdp) Nassau County	2	0.01
New Windsor (town) Orange County	2	0.01

Top 10 Places Sorted by Percent
Based on places with populations of 10,000 or more

Place	Number	%
Fort Drum (cdp) Jefferson County	3	0.02
Le Ray (town) Jefferson County	3	0.02
East Meadow (cdp) Nassau County	2	0.01
New Windsor (town) Orange County	2	0.01
Lancaster (village) Erie County	1	0.01
New Paltz (town) Ulster County	1	0.01
Plattsburgh (town) Clinton County	1	0.01
New York (city) New York City	6	0.00
Hempstead (town) Nassau County	3	0.00
Rochester (city) Monroe County	2	0.00

American Indian: Navajo

Top 10 Places Sorted by Number
Based on all places, regardless of population

Place	Number	%
New York (city) New York City	187	0.00
Hempstead (town) Nassau County	27	0.00
Le Ray (town) Jefferson County	22	0.11
Rochester (city) Monroe County	21	0.01
Brookhaven (town) Suffolk County	16	0.00
Fort Drum (cdp) Jefferson County	14	0.12
North Valley Stream (cdp) Nassau County	9	0.06
Islip (town) Suffolk County	9	0.00
Calcium (cdp) Jefferson County	8	0.24
Buffalo (city) Erie County	8	0.00

Top 10 Places Sorted by Percent
Based on all places, regardless of population

Place	Number	%
Lyon Mountain (cdp) Clinton County	2	0.44
Shinnecock Reservation Suffolk County	2	0.40
Hamden (town) Delaware County	4	0.31
Altmar (village) Oswego County	1	0.28
Calcium (cdp) Jefferson County	8	0.24
Catlin (town) Chemung County	5	0.19
Denning (town) Ulster County	1	0.19
Fultonville (village) Montgomery County	1	0.14
Charlton (town) Saratoga County	5	0.13
Brasher (town) Saint Lawrence County	3	0.13

Top 10 Places Sorted by Percent
Based on places with populations of 10,000 or more

Place	Number	%
Fort Drum (cdp) Jefferson County	14	0.12
Le Ray (town) Jefferson County	22	0.11
North Valley Stream (cdp) Nassau County	9	0.06
Highlands (town) Orange County	5	0.04
Corning (city) Steuben County	4	0.04
North Massapequa (cdp) Nassau County	5	0.03
Greenlawn (cdp) Suffolk County	4	0.03

Place	Number	%
Ithaca (city) Tompkins County	6	0.02
Milton (town) Saratoga County	4	0.02
Selden (cdp) Suffolk County	4	0.02

American Indian: Osage

Top 10 Places Sorted by Number
Based on all places, regardless of population

Place	Number	%
New York (city) New York City	40	0.00
Freeport (village) Nassau County	4	0.01
Brookhaven (town) Suffolk County	4	0.00
Hempstead (town) Nassau County	4	0.00
Rocky Point (cdp) Suffolk County	3	0.03
Greece (town) Monroe County	3	0.00
New Rochelle (city) Westchester County	3	0.00
Smyrna (town) Chenango County	2	0.14
Philadelphia (village) Jefferson County	2	0.13
Philadelphia (town) Jefferson County	2	0.09

Top 10 Places Sorted by Percent
Based on all places, regardless of population

Place	Number	%
Poospatuck Reservation Suffolk County	1	0.37
Smyrna (town) Chenango County	2	0.14
Philadelphia (village) Jefferson County	2	0.13
Philadelphia (town) Jefferson County	2	0.09
Westport (town) Essex County	1	0.07
Saint Bonaventure (cdp) Cattaraugus County	1	0.05
Carmel Hamlet (cdp) Putnam County	2	0.04
Rocky Point (cdp) Suffolk County	3	0.03
Chester (town) Warren County	1	0.03
Lake Erie Beach (cdp) Erie County	1	0.02

Top 10 Places Sorted by Percent
Based on places with populations of 10,000 or more

Place	Number	%
Rocky Point (cdp) Suffolk County	3	0.03
Freeport (village) Nassau County	4	0.01
Carmel (town) Putnam County	2	0.01
Henrietta (town) Monroe County	2	0.01
Evans (town) Erie County	1	0.01
Hampton Bays (cdp) Suffolk County	1	0.01
Mastic (cdp) Suffolk County	1	0.01
New Paltz (town) Ulster County	1	0.01
Tonawanda (city) Erie County	1	0.01
Wheatfield (town) Niagara County	1	0.01

American Indian: Ottawa

Top 10 Places Sorted by Number
Based on all places, regardless of population

Place	Number	%
New York (city) New York City	13	0.00
Fort Drum (cdp) Jefferson County	5	0.04
Le Ray (town) Jefferson County	5	0.03
Dunkirk (city) Chautauqua County	3	0.02
Rose (town) Wayne County	2	0.08
Oswego (city) Oswego County	2	0.01
Queensbury (town) Warren County	2	0.01
West Seneca (town) Erie County	2	0.00
Walton Park (cdp) Orange County	1	0.04
Shandaken (town) Ulster County	1	0.03

Top 10 Places Sorted by Percent
Based on all places, regardless of population

Place	Number	%
Rose (town) Wayne County	2	0.08
Fort Drum (cdp) Jefferson County	5	0.04
Walton Park (cdp) Orange County	1	0.04
Le Ray (town) Jefferson County	5	0.03
Shandaken (town) Ulster County	1	0.03

Notes: (cdp) census designated place; Refer to the User's Guide in the front of the book for more detailed information.

Place	Number	%
Dunkirk (city) Chautauqua County	3	0.02
Duanesburg (town) Schenectady County	1	0.02
Thornwood (cdp) Westchester County	1	0.02
Oswego (city) Oswego County	2	0.01
Queensbury (town) Warren County	2	0.01

Top 10 Places Sorted by Percent
Based on places with populations of 10,000 or more

Place	Number	%
Fort Drum (cdp) Jefferson County	5	0.04
Le Ray (town) Jefferson County	5	0.03
Dunkirk (city) Chautauqua County	3	0.02
Oswego (city) Oswego County	2	0.01
Queensbury (town) Warren County	2	0.01
Canandaigua (city) Ontario County	1	0.01
Chester (town) Orange County	1	0.01
East Greenbush (town) Rensselaer County	1	0.01
Endicott (village) Broome County	1	0.01
Lewisboro (town) Westchester County	1	0.01

American Indian: Paiute

Top 10 Places Sorted by Number
Based on all places, regardless of population

Place	Number	%
New York (city) New York City	11	0.00
Laurens (town) Otsego County	3	0.12
Charlton (town) Saratoga County	2	0.05
Middletown (city) Orange County	2	0.01
Brookhaven (town) Suffolk County	2	0.00
Hempstead (town) Nassau County	2	0.00
Perrysburg (town) Cattaraugus County	1	0.06
Catharine (town) Schuyler County	1	0.05
Gowanda (village) Cattaraugus County	1	0.04
Minoa (village) Onondaga County	1	0.03

Top 10 Places Sorted by Percent
Based on all places, regardless of population

Place	Number	%
Laurens (town) Otsego County	3	0.12
Perrysburg (town) Cattaraugus County	1	0.06
Charlton (town) Saratoga County	2	0.05
Catharine (town) Schuyler County	1	0.05
Gowanda (village) Cattaraugus County	1	0.04
Minoa (village) Onondaga County	1	0.03
Harrietstown (town) Franklin County	1	0.02
Pompey (town) Onondaga County	1	0.02
Saranac Lake (village) Franklin County	1	0.02
Middletown (city) Orange County	2	0.01

Top 10 Places Sorted by Percent
Based on places with populations of 10,000 or more

Place	Number	%
Middletown (city) Orange County	2	0.01
Batavia (city) Genesee County	1	0.01
Rocky Point (cdp) Suffolk County	1	0.01
Seaford (cdp) Nassau County	1	0.01
New York (city) New York City	11	0.00
Brookhaven (town) Suffolk County	2	0.00
Hempstead (town) Nassau County	2	0.00
Baldwin (cdp) Nassau County	1	0.00
Brentwood (cdp) Suffolk County	1	0.00
Islip (town) Suffolk County	1	0.00

American Indian: Pima

Top 10 Places Sorted by Number
Based on all places, regardless of population

Place	Number	%
Colonie (town) Albany County	7	0.01
New York (city) New York City	5	0.00
Babylon (town) Suffolk County	4	0.00
Amsterdam (town) Montgomery County	3	0.05
Niagara Falls (city) Niagara County	3	0.01
Allen (town) Allegany County	2	0.43
Fort Montgomery (cdp) Orange County	2	0.14
Hilton (village) Monroe County	2	0.03
Highlands (town) Orange County	2	0.02
North Amityville (cdp) Suffolk County	2	0.01

Top 10 Places Sorted by Percent
Based on all places, regardless of population

Place	Number	%
Allen (town) Allegany County	2	0.43
Rushville (village) Yates County	1	0.16
Fort Montgomery (cdp) Orange County	2	0.14
Tusten (town) Sullivan County	1	0.07
Amsterdam (town) Montgomery County	3	0.05
Potter (town) Yates County	1	0.05
Hilton (village) Monroe County	2	0.03
Highlands (town) Orange County	2	0.02
Colonie (town) Albany County	7	0.01
Niagara Falls (city) Niagara County	3	0.01

Top 10 Places Sorted by Percent
Based on places with populations of 10,000 or more

Place	Number	%
Highlands (town) Orange County	2	0.02
Colonie (town) Albany County	7	0.01
Niagara Falls (city) Niagara County	3	0.01
North Amityville (cdp) Suffolk County	2	0.01
Parma (town) Monroe County	2	0.01
New York (city) New York City	5	0.00
Babylon (town) Suffolk County	4	0.00
Rochester (city) Monroe County	2	0.00
De Witt (town) Onondaga County	1	0.00
Deer Park (cdp) Suffolk County	1	0.00

American Indian: Potawatomi

Top 10 Places Sorted by Number
Based on all places, regardless of population

Place	Number	%
New York (city) New York City	27	0.00
Perinton (town) Monroe County	6	0.01
Rochester (city) Monroe County	5	0.00
Dansville (town) Steuben County	4	0.20
Wawayanda (town) Orange County	4	0.06
Oyster Bay (town) Nassau County	4	0.00
Forest Home (cdp) Tompkins County	3	0.32
Lima (village) Livingston County	3	0.12
Lima (town) Livingston County	3	0.07
Milan (town) Dutchess County	3	0.07

Top 10 Places Sorted by Percent
Based on all places, regardless of population

Place	Number	%
Forest Home (cdp) Tompkins County	3	0.32
Dansville (town) Steuben County	4	0.20
Lima (village) Livingston County	3	0.12
Delevan (village) Cattaraugus County	1	0.09
Solon (town) Cortland County	1	0.09
Lima (town) Livingston County	3	0.07
Milan (town) Dutchess County	3	0.07
Seneca (town) Ontario County	2	0.07
Wawayanda (town) Orange County	4	0.06
West Nyack (cdp) Rockland County	2	0.06

Top 10 Places Sorted by Percent
Based on places with populations of 10,000 or more

Place	Number	%
Beekman (town) Dutchess County	3	0.03
Ithaca (town) Tompkins County	3	0.02
Perinton (town) Monroe County	6	0.01
Cortlandt (town) Westchester County	3	0.01
Batavia (city) Genesee County	2	0.01
Chili (town) Monroe County	2	0.01
Glenville (town) Schenectady County	2	0.01
Henrietta (town) Monroe County	2	0.01
Chenango (town) Broome County	1	0.01
Endicott (village) Broome County	1	0.01

American Indian: Pueblo

Top 10 Places Sorted by Number
Based on all places, regardless of population

Place	Number	%
New York (city) New York City	1,162	0.01
Yonkers (city) Westchester County	65	0.03
Islip (town) Suffolk County	34	0.01
Brentwood (cdp) Suffolk County	26	0.05
Hempstead (town) Nassau County	23	0.00
Brookhaven (town) Suffolk County	13	0.00
Roosevelt (cdp) Nassau County	8	0.05
Central Islip (cdp) Suffolk County	8	0.03
Freeport (village) Nassau County	5	0.01
Babylon (town) Suffolk County	5	0.00

Top 10 Places Sorted by Percent
Based on all places, regardless of population

Place	Number	%
Great Bend (cdp) Jefferson County	3	0.37
Litchfield (town) Herkimer County	4	0.26
Pamelia (town) Jefferson County	3	0.10
South Glens Falls (village) Saratoga County	3	0.09
Allegany Reservation Cattaraugus County	1	0.09
Vernon (village) Oneida County	1	0.09
Champion (town) Jefferson County	3	0.07
Gowanda (village) Cattaraugus County	2	0.07
Sackets Harbor (village) Jefferson County	1	0.07
Blauvelt (cdp) Rockland County	3	0.06

Top 10 Places Sorted by Percent
Based on places with populations of 10,000 or more

Place	Number	%
Brentwood (cdp) Suffolk County	26	0.05
Roosevelt (cdp) Nassau County	8	0.05
Yonkers (city) Westchester County	65	0.03
Central Islip (cdp) Suffolk County	8	0.03
Miller Place (cdp) Suffolk County	3	0.03
Geneva (city) Ontario County	3	0.02
Moreau (town) Saratoga County	3	0.02
Haverstraw (village) Rockland County	2	0.02
North Merrick (cdp) Nassau County	2	0.02
Plattsburgh (town) Clinton County	2	0.02

American Indian: Puget Sound Salish

Top 10 Places Sorted by Number
Based on all places, regardless of population

Place	Number	%
New York (city) New York City	7	0.00
Geneva (city) Ontario County	3	0.02
North Bay Shore (cdp) Suffolk County	2	0.01
Islip (town) Suffolk County	2	0.00
Bellport (village) Suffolk County	1	0.04
Kirkwood (town) Broome County	1	0.02
New Paltz (village) Ulster County	1	0.02
Kirkland (town) Oneida County	1	0.01
New Paltz (town) Ulster County	1	0.01
Brookhaven (town) Suffolk County	1	0.00

Top 10 Places Sorted by Percent
Based on all places, regardless of population

Place	Number	%
Bellport (village) Suffolk County	1	0.04

Notes: (cdp) census designated place; Refer to the User's Guide in the front of the book for more detailed information.

PROFILES OF NEW YORK / Ancestry: Rankings

Place	Number	%
Geneva (city) Ontario County	3	0.02
Kirkwood (town) Broome County	1	0.02
New Paltz (village) Ulster County	1	0.02
North Bay Shore (cdp) Suffolk County	2	0.01
Kirkland (town) Oneida County	1	0.01
New Paltz (town) Ulster County	1	0.01
New York (city) New York City	7	0.00
Islip (town) Suffolk County	2	0.00
Brookhaven (town) Suffolk County	1	0.00

Top 10 Places Sorted by Percent
Based on places with populations of 10,000 or more

Place	Number	%
Geneva (city) Ontario County	3	0.02
North Bay Shore (cdp) Suffolk County	2	0.01
Kirkland (town) Oneida County	1	0.01
New Paltz (town) Ulster County	1	0.01
New York (city) New York City	7	0.00
Islip (town) Suffolk County	2	0.00
Brookhaven (town) Suffolk County	1	0.00
Elmira (city) Chemung County	1	0.00
Rome (city) Oneida County	1	0.00

American Indian: Seminole

Top 10 Places Sorted by Number
Based on all places, regardless of population

Place	Number	%
New York (city) New York City	374	0.00
Hempstead (town) Nassau County	37	0.00
Rochester (city) Monroe County	35	0.02
Brookhaven (town) Suffolk County	32	0.01
Buffalo (city) Erie County	22	0.01
Mount Vernon (city) Westchester County	15	0.02
Syracuse (city) Onondaga County	14	0.01
Babylon (town) Suffolk County	12	0.01
Albany (city) Albany County	11	0.01
Islip (town) Suffolk County	11	0.00

Top 10 Places Sorted by Percent
Based on all places, regardless of population

Place	Number	%
Clintondale (cdp) Ulster County	5	0.35
Odessa (village) Schuyler County	2	0.32
Lake Katrine (cdp) Ulster County	5	0.21
Denning (town) Ulster County	1	0.19
Catharine (town) Schuyler County	3	0.16
Mechanicstown (cdp) Orange County	7	0.12
Saranac Lake (village) Franklin County	6	0.12
Old Westbury (village) Nassau County	5	0.12
Lexington (town) Greene County	1	0.12
Ellisburg (town) Jefferson County	4	0.11

Top 10 Places Sorted by Percent
Based on places with populations of 10,000 or more

Place	Number	%
Roosevelt (cdp) Nassau County	10	0.06
Mastic (cdp) Suffolk County	8	0.05
Selden (cdp) Suffolk County	8	0.04
Geneva (city) Ontario County	5	0.04
Ulster (town) Ulster County	5	0.04
Wyandanch (cdp) Suffolk County	4	0.04
Wallkill (town) Orange County	7	0.03
Baldwin (cdp) Nassau County	6	0.03
North Amityville (cdp) Suffolk County	5	0.03
Mastic Beach (cdp) Suffolk County	3	0.03

American Indian: Shoshone

Top 10 Places Sorted by Number
Based on all places, regardless of population

Place	Number	%
New York (city) New York City	24	0.00
Hempstead (town) Nassau County	5	0.00
Syracuse (city) Onondaga County	5	0.00
Salamanca (city) Cattaraugus County	4	0.07
Hampton Bays (cdp) Suffolk County	4	0.03
Elmont (cdp) Nassau County	4	0.01
Guilderland (town) Albany County	4	0.01
Southampton (town) Suffolk County	4	0.01
Brentwood (cdp) Suffolk County	3	0.01
Poughkeepsie (town) Dutchess County	3	0.01

Top 10 Places Sorted by Percent
Based on all places, regardless of population

Place	Number	%
Summit (town) Schoharie County	2	0.18
Kinderhook (village) Columbia County	1	0.08
Salamanca (city) Cattaraugus County	4	0.07
Allegany (village) Cattaraugus County	1	0.05
Bangor (town) Franklin County	1	0.05
Catharine (town) Schuyler County	1	0.05
Pawling (village) Dutchess County	1	0.04
West Sand Lake (cdp) Rensselaer County	1	0.04
Hampton Bays (cdp) Suffolk County	4	0.03
Baldwinsville (village) Onondaga County	2	0.03

Top 10 Places Sorted by Percent
Based on places with populations of 10,000 or more

Place	Number	%
Hampton Bays (cdp) Suffolk County	4	0.03
Elmont (cdp) Nassau County	4	0.01
Guilderland (town) Albany County	4	0.01
Southampton (town) Suffolk County	4	0.01
Brentwood (cdp) Suffolk County	3	0.01
Poughkeepsie (town) Dutchess County	3	0.01
Lysander (town) Onondaga County	2	0.01
Dryden (town) Tompkins County	1	0.01
East Hampton (town) Suffolk County	1	0.01
Horseheads (town) Chemung County	1	0.01

American Indian: Sioux

Top 10 Places Sorted by Number
Based on all places, regardless of population

Place	Number	%
New York (city) New York City	437	0.01
Hempstead (town) Nassau County	61	0.01
Buffalo (city) Erie County	46	0.02
Brookhaven (town) Suffolk County	40	0.01
Rochester (city) Monroe County	37	0.02
Islip (town) Suffolk County	29	0.01
Syracuse (city) Onondaga County	28	0.02
Babylon (town) Suffolk County	20	0.01
Oyster Bay (town) Nassau County	19	0.01
Newburgh (city) Orange County	18	0.06

Top 10 Places Sorted by Percent
Based on all places, regardless of population

Place	Number	%
Corfu (village) Genesee County	5	0.63
Cragsmoor (cdp) Ulster County	3	0.63
Allegany Reservation Cattaraugus County	6	0.55
Danube (town) Herkimer County	5	0.46
Andover (village) Allegany County	4	0.37
Pike (town) Wyoming County	4	0.37
Baxter Estates (village) Nassau County	3	0.30
Dolgeville (village) Herkimer County	6	0.28
Sherman (village) Chautauqua County	2	0.28

Place	Number	%
Unadilla (village) Otsego County	3	0.27

Top 10 Places Sorted by Percent
Based on places with populations of 10,000 or more

Place	Number	%
Fort Drum (cdp) Jefferson County	13	0.11
Le Ray (town) Jefferson County	17	0.09
Geneva (city) Ontario County	10	0.07
Newburgh (city) Orange County	18	0.06
Blooming Grove (town) Orange County	10	0.06
Kent (town) Putnam County	8	0.06
Owego (town) Tioga County	11	0.05
Uniondale (cdp) Nassau County	11	0.05
Beacon (city) Dutchess County	7	0.05
German Flatts (town) Herkimer County	7	0.05

American Indian: Tohono O'Odham

Top 10 Places Sorted by Number
Based on all places, regardless of population

Place	Number	%
New York (city) New York City	43	0.00
Troy (city) Rensselaer County	8	0.02
Huntington (town) Suffolk County	5	0.00
Ramapo (town) Rockland County	5	0.00
Catskill (town) Greene County	4	0.03
Spring Valley (village) Rockland County	3	0.01
Nassau (village) Rensselaer County	2	0.17
Lumberland (town) Sullivan County	2	0.10
Nassau (town) Rensselaer County	2	0.04
Buffalo (city) Erie County	2	0.00

Top 10 Places Sorted by Percent
Based on all places, regardless of population

Place	Number	%
Nassau (village) Rensselaer County	2	0.17
Hillburn (village) Rockland County	1	0.11
Lumberland (town) Sullivan County	2	0.10
Middleport (village) Niagara County	1	0.05
Nassau (town) Rensselaer County	2	0.04
Catskill (town) Greene County	4	0.03
Highland Mills (cdp) Orange County	1	0.03
Westerlo (town) Albany County	1	0.03
Troy (city) Rensselaer County	8	0.02
Newark Valley (town) Tioga County	1	0.02

Top 10 Places Sorted by Percent
Based on places with populations of 10,000 or more

Place	Number	%
Catskill (town) Greene County	4	0.03
Troy (city) Rensselaer County	8	0.02
Spring Valley (village) Rockland County	3	0.01
German Flatts (town) Herkimer County	1	0.01
Haverstraw (village) Rockland County	1	0.01
Lackawanna (city) Erie County	1	0.01
New York (city) New York City	43	0.00
Huntington (town) Suffolk County	5	0.00
Ramapo (town) Rockland County	5	0.00
Buffalo (city) Erie County	2	0.00

American Indian: Ute

Top 10 Places Sorted by Number
Based on all places, regardless of population

Place	Number	%
New York (city) New York City	8	0.00
Brookhaven (town) Suffolk County	4	0.00
Islip (town) Suffolk County	4	0.00
Farmington (town) Ontario County	3	0.03
Mastic (cdp) Suffolk County	3	0.02
Central Islip (cdp) Suffolk County	3	0.01
Port Chester (village) Westchester County	3	0.01

Notes: (cdp) census designated place; Refer to the User's Guide in the front of the book for more detailed information.

PROFILES OF NEW YORK / Ancestry: Rankings

Place	Number	%
Rye (town) Westchester County	3	0.01
Mattydale (cdp) Onondaga County	2	0.03
Fort Drum (cdp) Jefferson County	2	0.02

Top 10 Places Sorted by Percent
Based on all places, regardless of population

Place	Number	%
Lexington (town) Greene County	1	0.12
Farmington (town) Ontario County	3	0.03
Mattydale (cdp) Onondaga County	2	0.03
Mastic (cdp) Suffolk County	3	0.02
Fort Drum (cdp) Jefferson County	2	0.02
Wilton (town) Saratoga County	2	0.02
Amenia (town) Dutchess County	1	0.02
Dansville (village) Livingston County	1	0.02
Hamptonburgh (town) Orange County	1	0.02
North Dansville (town) Livingston County	1	0.02

Top 10 Places Sorted by Percent
Based on places with populations of 10,000 or more

Place	Number	%
Farmington (town) Ontario County	3	0.03
Mastic (cdp) Suffolk County	3	0.02
Fort Drum (cdp) Jefferson County	2	0.02
Wilton (town) Saratoga County	2	0.02
Central Islip (cdp) Suffolk County	3	0.01
Port Chester (village) Westchester County	3	0.01
Rye (town) Westchester County	3	0.01
Le Ray (town) Jefferson County	2	0.01
Salina (town) Onondaga County	2	0.01
Brunswick (town) Rensselaer County	1	0.01

American Indian: Yakama

Top 10 Places Sorted by Number
Based on all places, regardless of population

Place	Number	%
New York (city) New York City	3	0.00
South Corning (village) Steuben County	1	0.09
Austerlitz (town) Columbia County	1	0.07
Gordon Heights (cdp) Suffolk County	1	0.03
Corning (town) Steuben County	1	0.02
Oswego (city) Oswego County	1	0.01
Brookhaven (town) Suffolk County	1	0.00
Manlius (town) Onondaga County	1	0.00
Middletown (city) Orange County	1	0.00
Mount Vernon (city) Westchester County	1	0.00

Top 10 Places Sorted by Percent
Based on all places, regardless of population

Place	Number	%
South Corning (village) Steuben County	1	0.09
Austerlitz (town) Columbia County	1	0.07
Gordon Heights (cdp) Suffolk County	1	0.03
Corning (town) Steuben County	1	0.02
Oswego (city) Oswego County	1	0.01
New York (city) New York City	3	0.00
Brookhaven (town) Suffolk County	1	0.00
Manlius (town) Onondaga County	1	0.00
Middletown (city) Orange County	1	0.00
Mount Vernon (city) Westchester County	1	0.00

Top 10 Places Sorted by Percent
Based on places with populations of 10,000 or more

Place	Number	%
Oswego (city) Oswego County	1	0.01
New York (city) New York City	3	0.00
Brookhaven (town) Suffolk County	1	0.00
Manlius (town) Onondaga County	1	0.00
Middletown (city) Orange County	1	0.00
Mount Vernon (city) Westchester County	1	0.00
Rochester (city) Monroe County	1	0.00

Place	Number	%
Syracuse (city) Onondaga County	1	0.00

American Indian: Yaqui

Top 10 Places Sorted by Number
Based on all places, regardless of population

Place	Number	%
New York (city) New York City	29	0.00
Yonkers (city) Westchester County	7	0.00
Clay (town) Onondaga County	5	0.01
Dansville (town) Steuben County	3	0.15
Buffalo (city) Erie County	3	0.00
Halesite (cdp) Suffolk County	2	0.08
Salamanca (city) Cattaraugus County	2	0.03
Ithaca (city) Tompkins County	2	0.01
Huntington (town) Suffolk County	2	0.00
Rochester (city) Monroe County	2	0.00

Top 10 Places Sorted by Percent
Based on all places, regardless of population

Place	Number	%
Rushville (village) Yates County	1	0.16
Dansville (town) Steuben County	3	0.15
Halesite (cdp) Suffolk County	2	0.08
Grafton (town) Rensselaer County	1	0.05
Potter (town) Yates County	1	0.05
Salamanca (city) Cattaraugus County	2	0.03
Hurley (town) Ulster County	1	0.02
Clay (town) Onondaga County	5	0.01
Ithaca (city) Tompkins County	2	0.01
Canton (town) Saint Lawrence County	1	0.01

Top 10 Places Sorted by Percent
Based on places with populations of 10,000 or more

Place	Number	%
Clay (town) Onondaga County	5	0.01
Ithaca (city) Tompkins County	2	0.01
Canton (town) Saint Lawrence County	1	0.01
Lackawanna (city) Erie County	1	0.01
Port Washington (cdp) Nassau County	1	0.01
South Farmingdale (cdp) Nassau County	1	0.01
New York (city) New York City	29	0.00
Yonkers (city) Westchester County	7	0.00
Buffalo (city) Erie County	3	0.00
Huntington (town) Suffolk County	2	0.00

American Indian: Yuman

Top 10 Places Sorted by Number
Based on all places, regardless of population

Place	Number	%
New York (city) New York City	16	0.00
Hamden (town) Delaware County	3	0.23
Syracuse (city) Onondaga County	2	0.00
Washington Heights (cdp) Orange County	1	0.08
Brasher (town) Saint Lawrence County	1	0.04
Covert (town) Seneca County	1	0.04
Cobleskill (town) Schoharie County	1	0.02
Port Washington (cdp) Nassau County	1	0.01
Sullivan (town) Madison County	1	0.01
Wyandanch (cdp) Suffolk County	1	0.01

Top 10 Places Sorted by Percent
Based on all places, regardless of population

Place	Number	%
Hamden (town) Delaware County	3	0.23
Washington Heights (cdp) Orange County	1	0.08
Brasher (town) Saint Lawrence County	1	0.04
Covert (town) Seneca County	1	0.04
Cobleskill (town) Schoharie County	1	0.02
Port Washington (cdp) Nassau County	1	0.01
Sullivan (town) Madison County	1	0.01

Place	Number	%
Wyandanch (cdp) Suffolk County	1	0.01
New York (city) New York City	16	0.00
Syracuse (city) Onondaga County	2	0.00

Top 10 Places Sorted by Percent
Based on places with populations of 10,000 or more

Place	Number	%
Port Washington (cdp) Nassau County	1	0.01
Sullivan (town) Madison County	1	0.01
Wyandanch (cdp) Suffolk County	1	0.01
New York (city) New York City	16	0.00
Syracuse (city) Onondaga County	2	0.00
Babylon (town) Suffolk County	1	0.00
Greece (town) Monroe County	1	0.00
Hamburg (town) Erie County	1	0.00
North Hempstead (town) Nassau County	1	0.00
Rochester (city) Monroe County	1	0.00

American Indian: All other tribes

Top 10 Places Sorted by Number
Based on all places, regardless of population

Place	Number	%
New York (city) New York City	2,182	0.03
Brookhaven (town) Suffolk County	430	0.10
Shinnecock Reservation Suffolk County	428	84.92
Babylon (town) Suffolk County	292	0.14
Hempstead (town) Nassau County	290	0.04
Islip (town) Suffolk County	238	0.07
Mastic (cdp) Suffolk County	180	1.17
Poospatuck Reservation Suffolk County	153	56.46
North Amityville (cdp) Suffolk County	133	0.80
Syracuse (city) Onondaga County	123	0.08

Top 10 Places Sorted by Percent
Based on all places, regardless of population

Place	Number	%
Shinnecock Reservation Suffolk County	428	84.92
Poospatuck Reservation Suffolk County	153	56.46
Dering Harbor (village) Suffolk County	1	7.69
Mastic (cdp) Suffolk County	180	1.17
Riverside (cdp) Suffolk County	30	1.04
Valley Falls (village) Rensselaer County	5	1.02
Gordon Heights (cdp) Suffolk County	27	0.87
North Amityville (cdp) Suffolk County	133	0.80
German (town) Chenango County	3	0.79
Quiogue (cdp) Suffolk County	6	0.75

Top 10 Places Sorted by Percent
Based on places with populations of 10,000 or more

Place	Number	%
Mastic (cdp) Suffolk County	180	1.17
North Amityville (cdp) Suffolk County	133	0.80
Wyandanch (cdp) Suffolk County	41	0.39
Bay Shore (cdp) Suffolk County	59	0.25
Southampton (town) Suffolk County	113	0.21
Ridge (cdp) Suffolk County	28	0.21
Central Islip (cdp) Suffolk County	65	0.20
Patchogue (village) Suffolk County	23	0.19
Huntington Station (cdp) Suffolk County	51	0.17
Riverhead (town) Suffolk County	47	0.17

American Indian tribes, not specified

Top 10 Places Sorted by Number
Based on all places, regardless of population

Place	Number	%
New York (city) New York City	7,090	0.09
Hempstead (town) Nassau County	360	0.12
Buffalo (city) Erie County	249	0.09
Rochester (city) Monroe County	176	0.08
Islip (town) Suffolk County	169	0.05

Notes: (cdp) census designated place; Refer to the User's Guide in the front of the book for more detailed information.

Place	Number	%
Brookhaven (town) Suffolk County	169	0.04
Yonkers (city) Westchester County	162	0.08
Ramapo (town) Rockland County	141	0.13
Syracuse (city) Onondaga County	130	0.09
Babylon (town) Suffolk County	107	0.05

Top 10 Places Sorted by Percent
Based on all places, regardless of population

Place	Number	%
Poospatuck Reservation Suffolk County	39	14.39
Hillburn (village) Rockland County	104	11.80
Onondaga Reservation Onondaga County	96	6.52
Tuscarora Reservation Niagara County	66	5.80
Allegany Reservation Cattaraugus County	45	4.09
North Collins (village) Erie County	20	1.85
Lodi (village) Seneca County	5	1.48
Saint Regis Mohawk Reservation Franklin County	39	1.44
Brant (town) Erie County	25	1.31
Altmar (village) Oswego County	3	0.85

Top 10 Places Sorted by Percent
Based on places with populations of 10,000 or more

Place	Number	%
Oneida (city) Madison County	49	0.45
Mastic (cdp) Suffolk County	52	0.34
Wyandanch (cdp) Suffolk County	22	0.21
Hempstead (village) Nassau County	99	0.18
Bay Shore (cdp) Suffolk County	33	0.14
North Amityville (cdp) Suffolk County	24	0.14
Ramapo (town) Rockland County	141	0.13
Port Chester (village) Westchester County	35	0.13
Uniondale (cdp) Nassau County	30	0.13
Lake Grove (village) Suffolk County	13	0.13

Arab

Top 10 Places Sorted by Number
Based on all places, regardless of population

Place	Number	%
New York (city) New York City	70,965	0.89
Hempstead (town) Nassau County	3,264	0.43
Yonkers (city) Westchester County	2,697	1.38
North Hempstead (town) Nassau County	1,768	0.79
Buffalo (city) Erie County	1,737	0.59
Brookhaven (town) Suffolk County	1,513	0.34
Utica (city) Oneida County	1,313	2.16
Oyster Bay (town) Nassau County	1,217	0.41
Lackawanna (city) Erie County	1,111	5.83
Syracuse (city) Onondaga County	1,034	0.70

Top 10 Places Sorted by Percent
Based on all places, regardless of population

Place	Number	%
Saddle Rock (village) Nassau County	74	9.36
Lackawanna (city) Erie County	1,111	5.83
Great Neck Gardens (cdp) Nassau County	58	5.19
Clark Mills (cdp) Oneida County	48	3.44
New York Mills (village) Oneida County	109	3.39
Upper Brookville (village) Nassau County	61	3.37
New Hartford (town) Oneida County	688	3.25
Portville (village) Cattaraugus County	34	3.24
Wampsville (village) Madison County	17	3.02
Olean (town) Cattaraugus County	60	2.96

Top 10 Places Sorted by Percent
Based on places with populations of 10,000 or more

Place	Number	%
Lackawanna (city) Erie County	1,111	5.83
New Hartford (town) Oneida County	688	3.25
Olean (city) Cattaraugus County	408	2.66
Utica (city) Oneida County	1,313	2.16
Whitestown (town) Oneida County	358	1.92
Oneida (city) Madison County	183	1.67
Fairmount (cdp) Onondaga County	174	1.61
Grand Island (town) Erie County	285	1.53
Kirkland (town) Oneida County	149	1.47
Yonkers (city) Westchester County	2,697	1.38

Arab: Arab/Arabic

Top 10 Places Sorted by Number
Based on all places, regardless of population

Place	Number	%
New York (city) New York City	14,572	0.18
Yonkers (city) Westchester County	854	0.44
Lackawanna (city) Erie County	617	3.24
Buffalo (city) Erie County	522	0.18
Hempstead (town) Nassau County	460	0.06
Syracuse (city) Onondaga County	370	0.25
Rochester (city) Monroe County	351	0.16
Islip (town) Suffolk County	198	0.06
Clay (town) Onondaga County	185	0.31
Salina (town) Onondaga County	179	0.54

Top 10 Places Sorted by Percent
Based on all places, regardless of population

Place	Number	%
Lackawanna (city) Erie County	617	3.24
Watermill (cdp) Suffolk County	33	1.96
Accord (cdp) Ulster County	13	1.84
Galeville (cdp) Onondaga County	60	1.36
Westvale (cdp) Onondaga County	62	1.20
Amity (town) Allegany County	26	1.17
Manorhaven (village) Nassau County	63	1.03
Lyncourt (cdp) Onondaga County	41	0.94
North Hornell (village) Steuben County	7	0.82
Arlington (cdp) Dutchess County	99	0.80

Top 10 Places Sorted by Percent
Based on places with populations of 10,000 or more

Place	Number	%
Lackawanna (city) Erie County	617	3.24
Arlington (cdp) Dutchess County	99	0.80
Oneida (city) Madison County	67	0.61
Fairmount (cdp) Onondaga County	59	0.55
Salina (town) Onondaga County	179	0.54
Yonkers (city) Westchester County	854	0.44
Suffern (village) Rockland County	44	0.40
De Witt (town) Onondaga County	92	0.38
Geddes (town) Onondaga County	67	0.38
Putnam Valley (town) Putnam County	41	0.38

Arab: Egyptian

Top 10 Places Sorted by Number
Based on all places, regardless of population

Place	Number	%
New York (city) New York City	17,223	0.22
Hempstead (town) Nassau County	965	0.13
Brookhaven (town) Suffolk County	552	0.12
North Hempstead (town) Nassau County	431	0.19
Oyster Bay (town) Nassau County	373	0.13
Islip (town) Suffolk County	318	0.10
Huntington (town) Suffolk County	303	0.16
Valley Stream (village) Nassau County	226	0.62
Yonkers (city) Westchester County	183	0.09
Smithtown (town) Suffolk County	174	0.15

Top 10 Places Sorted by Percent
Based on all places, regardless of population

Place	Number	%
Woodridge (village) Sullivan County	15	1.68
Golden's Bridge (cdp) Westchester County	25	1.61
Islandia (village) Suffolk County	48	1.57
Haviland (cdp) Dutchess County	53	1.42
Montebello (village) Rockland County	38	1.05
Lincoln Park (cdp) Ulster County	23	1.01
Manorhaven (village) Nassau County	58	0.94
Manhasset Hills (cdp) Nassau County	34	0.93
Searingtown (cdp) Nassau County	46	0.91
Melville (cdp) Suffolk County	125	0.86

Top 10 Places Sorted by Percent
Based on places with populations of 10,000 or more

Place	Number	%
Melville (cdp) Suffolk County	125	0.86
Valley Stream (village) Nassau County	226	0.62
Seaford (cdp) Nassau County	90	0.57
Potsdam (town) Saint Lawrence County	77	0.48
Selden (cdp) Suffolk County	90	0.41
Kings Park (cdp) Suffolk County	62	0.38
East Patchogue (cdp) Suffolk County	66	0.32
New City (cdp) Rockland County	106	0.31
Centereach (cdp) Suffolk County	84	0.31
East Massapequa (cdp) Nassau County	61	0.31

Arab: Iraqi

Top 10 Places Sorted by Number
Based on all places, regardless of population

Place	Number	%
New York (city) New York City	957	0.01
North Hempstead (town) Nassau County	334	0.15
Hempstead (town) Nassau County	127	0.02
Olean (city) Cattaraugus County	72	0.47
University Gardens (cdp) Nassau County	71	1.71
Tarrytown (village) Westchester County	62	0.56
Greenburgh (town) Westchester County	62	0.07
Harrison (village) Westchester County	60	0.25
Oyster Bay (town) Nassau County	56	0.02
Cedarhurst (village) Nassau County	46	0.75

Top 10 Places Sorted by Percent
Based on all places, regardless of population

Place	Number	%
Saddle Rock (village) Nassau County	34	4.30
Great Neck Gardens (cdp) Nassau County	30	2.69
Gilgo-Oak Beach-Captree (cdp) Suffolk County	7	2.17
University Gardens (cdp) Nassau County	71	1.71
Saddle Rock Estates (cdp) Nassau County	7	1.59
Searingtown (cdp) Nassau County	39	0.77
Cedarhurst (village) Nassau County	46	0.75
Great Neck Estates (village) Nassau County	20	0.71
Russell Gardens (village) Nassau County	7	0.65
Belle Terre (village) Suffolk County	5	0.60

Top 10 Places Sorted by Percent
Based on places with populations of 10,000 or more

Place	Number	%
Tarrytown (village) Westchester County	62	0.56
Olean (city) Cattaraugus County	72	0.47
Harrison (village) Westchester County	60	0.25
Mineola (village) Nassau County	37	0.19
Rye (city) Westchester County	26	0.17
East Islip (cdp) Suffolk County	22	0.16
North Hempstead (town) Nassau County	334	0.15
Niskayuna (town) Schenectady County	27	0.13
Jericho (cdp) Nassau County	15	0.12
Setauket-East Setauket (cdp) Suffolk County	18	0.11

Arab: Jordanian

Top 10 Places Sorted by Number
Based on all places, regardless of population

Place	Number	%
Yonkers (city) Westchester County	1,093	0.56

Notes: (cdp) census designated place; Refer to the User's Guide in the front of the book for more detailed information.

New York (city) New York City	897	0.01
Hempstead (town) Nassau County	191	0.03
Hyde Park (town) Dutchess County	103	0.49
Oneida (city) Madison County	88	0.80
Brookhaven (town) Suffolk County	69	0.02
Sullivan (town) Madison County	67	0.45
East Fishkill (town) Dutchess County	65	0.25
Poughkeepsie (town) Dutchess County	64	0.15
Lenox (town) Madison County	63	0.73

Top 10 Places Sorted by Percent
Based on all places, regardless of population

Place	Number	%
Wampsville (village) Madison County	16	2.85
Lincoln Park (cdp) Ulster County	38	1.67
Canastota (village) Madison County	47	1.11
Cedarhurst (village) Nassau County	56	0.91
Haviland (cdp) Dutchess County	30	0.81
Oneida (city) Madison County	88	0.80
Crown Heights (cdp) Dutchess County	23	0.77
Lenox (town) Madison County	63	0.73
Marlborough (town) Ulster County	60	0.72
Fair Haven (village) Cayuga County	6	0.68

Top 10 Places Sorted by Percent
Based on places with populations of 10,000 or more

Place	Number	%
Oneida (city) Madison County	88	0.80
Yonkers (city) Westchester County	1,093	0.56
Putnam Valley (town) Putnam County	56	0.52
Hyde Park (town) Dutchess County	103	0.49
Sullivan (town) Madison County	67	0.45
Ulster (town) Ulster County	38	0.30
East Fishkill (town) Dutchess County	65	0.25
Halfmoon (town) Saratoga County	44	0.24
Kent (town) Putnam County	32	0.23
Rye (city) Westchester County	30	0.20

Arab: Lebanese

Top 10 Places Sorted by Number
Based on all places, regardless of population

Place	Number	%
New York (city) New York City	11,419	0.14
Utica (city) Oneida County	945	1.56
Buffalo (city) Erie County	801	0.27
Amherst (town) Erie County	664	0.57
New Hartford (town) Oneida County	554	2.62
Hempstead (town) Nassau County	498	0.07
Niagara Falls (city) Niagara County	388	0.70
Brookhaven (town) Suffolk County	385	0.09
Tonawanda (town) Erie County	341	0.44
Rochester (city) Monroe County	314	0.14

Top 10 Places Sorted by Percent
Based on all places, regardless of population

Place	Number	%
Portville (village) Cattaraugus County	34	3.24
Clark Mills (cdp) Oneida County	44	3.16
Olean (town) Cattaraugus County	60	2.96
New Hartford (village) Oneida County	55	2.92
Upper Brookville (village) Nassau County	48	2.65
New Hartford (town) Oneida County	554	2.62
Deerfield (town) Oneida County	101	2.59
Schuyler (town) Herkimer County	83	2.44
Paris (town) Oneida County	112	2.43
Frankfort (town) Herkimer County	173	2.31

Top 10 Places Sorted by Percent
Based on places with populations of 10,000 or more

Place	Number	%
New Hartford (town) Oneida County	554	2.62

Olean (city) Cattaraugus County	310	2.02
Whitestown (town) Oneida County	301	1.62
Utica (city) Oneida County	945	1.56
Kirkland (town) Oneida County	111	1.09
Grand Island (town) Erie County	185	0.99
North Greenbush (town) Rensselaer County	100	0.93
Terryville (cdp) Suffolk County	79	0.75
Kenmore (village) Erie County	121	0.74
Scarsdale (village) Westchester County	126	0.71

Arab: Moroccan

Top 10 Places Sorted by Number
Based on all places, regardless of population

Place	Number	%
New York (city) New York City	5,116	0.06
Hempstead (town) Nassau County	258	0.03
North Hempstead (town) Nassau County	183	0.08
Huntington (town) Suffolk County	99	0.05
Oyster Bay (town) Nassau County	68	0.02
New Rochelle (city) Westchester County	63	0.09
Babylon (town) Suffolk County	62	0.03
Ramapo (town) Rockland County	56	0.05
South Huntington (cdp) Suffolk County	55	0.58
North New Hyde Park (cdp) Nassau County	54	0.37

Top 10 Places Sorted by Percent
Based on all places, regardless of population

Place	Number	%
Centre Island (village) Nassau County	7	1.57
Saddle Rock (village) Nassau County	10	1.26
Thomaston (village) Nassau County	25	0.96
Roslyn Harbor (village) Nassau County	9	0.90
Pelham Manor (village) Westchester County	48	0.88
Viola (cdp) Rockland County	44	0.74
Schoharie (village) Schoharie County	7	0.68
Hewlett Harbor (village) Nassau County	8	0.63
Shrub Oak (cdp) Westchester County	11	0.60
South Huntington (cdp) Suffolk County	55	0.58

Top 10 Places Sorted by Percent
Based on places with populations of 10,000 or more

Place	Number	%
Pelham (town) Westchester County	48	0.40
North New Hyde Park (cdp) Nassau County	54	0.37
Mineola (village) Nassau County	35	0.18
East Meadow (cdp) Nassau County	51	0.14
Deer Park (cdp) Suffolk County	30	0.11
Plainview (cdp) Nassau County	26	0.10
New Paltz (town) Ulster County	13	0.10
New Rochelle (city) Westchester County	63	0.09
Bellmore (cdp) Nassau County	15	0.09
Woodmere (cdp) Nassau County	14	0.09

Arab: Palestinian

Top 10 Places Sorted by Number
Based on all places, regardless of population

Place	Number	%
New York (city) New York City	3,184	0.04
Yonkers (city) Westchester County	177	0.09
Islip (town) Suffolk County	174	0.05
Hempstead (town) Nassau County	133	0.02
Manlius (town) Onondaga County	117	0.37
Ramapo (town) Rockland County	108	0.10
Camillus (town) Onondaga County	101	0.44
Buffalo (city) Erie County	82	0.03
Greenburgh (town) Westchester County	78	0.09
North Bay Shore (cdp) Suffolk County	77	0.51

Top 10 Places Sorted by Percent
Based on all places, regardless of population

Place	Number	%
Fayetteville (village) Onondaga County	47	1.11
Cherry Valley (village) Otsego County	4	0.65
Fairmount (cdp) Onondaga County	58	0.54
Providence (town) Saratoga County	10	0.54
North Bay Shore (cdp) Suffolk County	77	0.51
Camillus (town) Onondaga County	101	0.44
Monsey (cdp) Rockland County	58	0.39
Manlius (town) Onondaga County	117	0.37
Edinburg (town) Saratoga County	5	0.36
West Hurley (cdp) Ulster County	7	0.33

Top 10 Places Sorted by Percent
Based on places with populations of 10,000 or more

Place	Number	%
Fairmount (cdp) Onondaga County	58	0.54
North Bay Shore (cdp) Suffolk County	77	0.51
Camillus (town) Onondaga County	101	0.44
Monsey (cdp) Rockland County	58	0.39
Manlius (town) Onondaga County	117	0.37
Grand Island (town) Erie County	58	0.31
Niskayuna (town) Schenectady County	46	0.23
Terryville (cdp) Suffolk County	22	0.21
Lake Grove (village) Suffolk County	21	0.20
Putnam Valley (town) Putnam County	17	0.16

Arab: Syrian

Top 10 Places Sorted by Number
Based on all places, regardless of population

Place	Number	%
New York (city) New York City	10,985	0.14
Hempstead (town) Nassau County	424	0.06
Brookhaven (town) Suffolk County	208	0.05
Oyster Bay (town) Nassau County	163	0.06
Huntington (town) Suffolk County	149	0.08
Syracuse (city) Onondaga County	147	0.10
Utica (city) Oneida County	146	0.24
Glens Falls (city) Warren County	131	0.91
Colonie (town) Albany County	131	0.17
New Hartford (town) Oneida County	114	0.54

Top 10 Places Sorted by Percent
Based on all places, regardless of population

Place	Number	%
Manchester (village) Ontario County	29	1.97
Big Flats Airport (cdp) Chemung County	35	1.53
Sands Point (village) Nassau County	38	1.38
Geneva (town) Ontario County	43	1.31
Shortsville (village) Ontario County	17	1.22
Lake George (town) Warren County	39	1.09
Van Etten (village) Chemung County	6	1.07
Louisville (town) Saint Lawrence County	33	1.03
Akron (village) Erie County	31	0.99
Westmoreland (town) Oneida County	60	0.97

Top 10 Places Sorted by Percent
Based on places with populations of 10,000 or more

Place	Number	%
Glens Falls (city) Warren County	131	0.91
New Hartford (town) Oneida County	114	0.54
Geneva (city) Ontario County	67	0.49
Salisbury (cdp) Nassau County	57	0.46
Tonawanda (city) Erie County	73	0.45
New Castle (town) Westchester County	66	0.38
Lansing (town) Tompkins County	39	0.38
Rye (city) Westchester County	49	0.33
Whitestown (town) Oneida County	57	0.31
New City (cdp) Rockland County	96	0.28

Notes: (cdp) census designated place; Refer to the User's Guide in the front of the book for more detailed information.

PROFILES OF NEW YORK / Ancestry: Rankings

Arab: Other

Top 10 Places Sorted by Number
Based on all places, regardless of population

Place	Number	%
New York (city) New York City	6,612	0.08
Lackawanna (city) Erie County	478	2.51
North Hempstead (town) Nassau County	301	0.14
Hempstead (town) Nassau County	208	0.03
Buffalo (city) Erie County	178	0.06
Binghamton (city) Broome County	134	0.28
Clay (town) Onondaga County	106	0.18
Ramapo (town) Rockland County	94	0.09
Huntington (town) Suffolk County	90	0.05
Brookhaven (town) Suffolk County	89	0.02

Top 10 Places Sorted by Percent
Based on all places, regardless of population

Place	Number	%
Hillside (cdp) Ulster County	26	2.83
Lackawanna (city) Erie County	478	2.51
Great Neck Gardens (cdp) Nassau County	28	2.51
Saddle Rock (village) Nassau County	13	1.64
Cedarhurst (village) Nassau County	62	1.01
Roslyn Heights (cdp) Nassau County	47	0.75
Kensington (village) Nassau County	9	0.74
Viola (cdp) Rockland County	43	0.72
Forest Home (cdp) Tompkins County	7	0.69
Asharoken (village) Suffolk County	4	0.62

Top 10 Places Sorted by Percent
Based on places with populations of 10,000 or more

Place	Number	%
Lackawanna (city) Erie County	478	2.51
Binghamton (city) Broome County	134	0.28
Fort Drum (cdp) Jefferson County	33	0.27
Pelham (town) Westchester County	27	0.23
Dobbs Ferry (village) Westchester County	24	0.23
Ulster (town) Ulster County	26	0.21
Clay (town) Onondaga County	106	0.18
Vestal (town) Broome County	47	0.18
Le Ray (town) Jefferson County	33	0.17
Bellmore (cdp) Nassau County	27	0.16

Armenian

Top 10 Places Sorted by Number
Based on all places, regardless of population

Place	Number	%
New York (city) New York City	10,360	0.13
Hempstead (town) Nassau County	1,270	0.17
Oyster Bay (town) Nassau County	877	0.30
North Hempstead (town) Nassau County	717	0.32
Brookhaven (town) Suffolk County	694	0.15
Huntington (town) Suffolk County	621	0.32
Colonie (town) Albany County	398	0.50
Troy (city) Rensselaer County	364	0.74
Islip (town) Suffolk County	329	0.10
Niagara Falls (city) Niagara County	287	0.52

Top 10 Places Sorted by Percent
Based on all places, regardless of population

Place	Number	%
Harbor Hills (cdp) Nassau County	23	4.01
Malverne Park Oaks (cdp) Nassau County	16	3.21
Munsey Park (village) Nassau County	80	3.04
Boylston (town) Oswego County	15	2.74
West Union (town) Steuben County	10	2.45
Plandome Manor (village) Nassau County	20	2.39
Plandome Heights (village) Nassau County	22	2.27
Shinnecock Hills (cdp) Suffolk County	34	1.89
Conesville (town) Schoharie County	12	1.70

| Newfield Hamlet (cdp) Tompkins County | 12 | 1.51 |

Top 10 Places Sorted by Percent
Based on places with populations of 10,000 or more

Place	Number	%
Brunswick (town) Rensselaer County	132	1.13
Garden City (village) Nassau County	186	0.86
Watervliet (city) Albany County	88	0.86
Troy (city) Rensselaer County	364	0.74
North Greenbush (town) Rensselaer County	78	0.73
Miller Place (cdp) Suffolk County	68	0.64
Syosset (cdp) Nassau County	108	0.58
Massapequa Park (village) Nassau County	101	0.58
Highlands (town) Orange County	72	0.58
North New Hyde Park (cdp) Nassau County	77	0.53

Asian

Top 10 Places Sorted by Number
Based on all places, regardless of population

Place	Number	%
New York (city) New York City	889,642	11.11
Hempstead (town) Nassau County	31,057	4.11
North Hempstead (town) Nassau County	22,196	9.97
Oyster Bay (town) Nassau County	15,630	5.32
Brookhaven (town) Suffolk County	15,288	3.41
Yonkers (city) Westchester County	11,006	5.61
Islip (town) Suffolk County	8,817	2.73
Greenburgh (town) Westchester County	8,392	9.67
Huntington (town) Suffolk County	7,887	4.04
Clarkstown (town) Rockland County	6,999	8.53

Top 10 Places Sorted by Percent
Based on all places, regardless of population

Place	Number	%
Forest Home (cdp) Tompkins County	387	41.13
Manhasset Hills (cdp) Nassau County	1,039	28.38
Searingtown (cdp) Nassau County	1,401	27.83
Herricks (cdp) Nassau County	1,028	25.22
Lansing (village) Tompkins County	817	23.91
Garden City Park (cdp) Nassau County	1,645	21.78
Saltaire (village) Suffolk County	9	20.93
Greenville (cdp) Westchester County	1,797	20.78
East Ithaca (cdp) Tompkins County	404	18.43
Muttontown (village) Nassau County	592	17.35

Top 10 Places Sorted by Percent
Based on places with populations of 10,000 or more

Place	Number	%
Ithaca (city) Tompkins County	4,528	15.46
North New Hyde Park (cdp) Nassau County	2,244	15.43
Scarsdale (village) Westchester County	2,431	13.64
Syosset (cdp) Nassau County	2,440	13.16
Jericho (cdp) Nassau County	1,465	11.23
New York (city) New York City	889,642	11.11
North Valley Stream (cdp) Nassau County	1,691	10.71
Elmont (cdp) Nassau County	3,435	10.52
Ithaca (town) Tompkins County	1,909	10.49
Nanuet (cdp) Rockland County	1,745	10.44

Asian: Bangladeshi

Top 10 Places Sorted by Number
Based on all places, regardless of population

Place	Number	%
New York (city) New York City	28,269	0.35
North Hempstead (town) Nassau County	159	0.07
Hempstead (town) Nassau County	150	0.02
Brookhaven (town) Suffolk County	120	0.03
Oyster Bay (town) Nassau County	82	0.03
Islip (town) Suffolk County	78	0.02
Hudson (city) Columbia County	77	1.02
Babylon (town) Suffolk County	76	0.04
Yonkers (city) Westchester County	55	0.03
Hicksville (cdp) Nassau County	40	0.10

Top 10 Places Sorted by Percent
Based on all places, regardless of population

Place	Number	%
Pine Hill (cdp) Ulster County	5	1.62
Hudson (city) Columbia County	77	1.02
Northville (village) Fulton County	6	0.53
Searingtown (cdp) Nassau County	22	0.44
Washington Heights (cdp) Orange County	5	0.38
Bellerose Terrace (cdp) Nassau County	8	0.37
New York (city) New York City	28,269	0.35
North Hills (village) Nassau County	15	0.35
Herricks (cdp) Nassau County	14	0.34
Baxter Estates (village) Nassau County	3	0.30

Top 10 Places Sorted by Percent
Based on places with populations of 10,000 or more

Place	Number	%
New York (city) New York City	28,269	0.35
West Haverstraw (village) Rockland County	18	0.17
Ronkonkoma (cdp) Suffolk County	33	0.16
Copiague (cdp) Suffolk County	26	0.12
Westbury (village) Nassau County	17	0.12
Hicksville (cdp) Nassau County	40	0.10
Deer Park (cdp) Suffolk County	27	0.10
Wappinger (town) Dutchess County	25	0.10
Dix Hills (cdp) Suffolk County	22	0.08
Nanuet (cdp) Rockland County	13	0.08

Asian: Cambodian

Top 10 Places Sorted by Number
Based on all places, regardless of population

Place	Number	%
New York (city) New York City	2,296	0.03
Rochester (city) Monroe County	311	0.14
Syracuse (city) Onondaga County	108	0.07
Ramapo (town) Rockland County	84	0.08
Ithaca (city) Tompkins County	65	0.22
Utica (city) Oneida County	65	0.11
Buffalo (city) Erie County	60	0.02
Haverstraw (town) Rockland County	41	0.12
Hempstead (town) Nassau County	35	0.00
Oyster Bay (town) Nassau County	30	0.01

Top 10 Places Sorted by Percent
Based on all places, regardless of population

Place	Number	%
East Ithaca (cdp) Tompkins County	13	0.59
Pike (village) Wyoming County	2	0.52
Belle Terre (village) Suffolk County	4	0.48
Canisteo (village) Steuben County	10	0.43
Lansing (village) Tompkins County	13	0.38
Mechanicstown (cdp) Orange County	19	0.31
Canisteo (town) Steuben County	11	0.31
Liverpool (village) Onondaga County	7	0.28
Aurora (village) Cayuga County	2	0.28
Lansing (town) Tompkins County	27	0.26

Top 10 Places Sorted by Percent
Based on places with populations of 10,000 or more

Place	Number	%
Lansing (town) Tompkins County	27	0.26
Ithaca (city) Tompkins County	65	0.22
West Haverstraw (village) Rockland County	16	0.16
Rochester (city) Monroe County	311	0.14
Haverstraw (town) Rockland County	41	0.12
Ithaca (town) Tompkins County	22	0.12
Utica (city) Oneida County	65	0.11

Notes: (cdp) census designated place; Refer to the User's Guide in the front of the book for more detailed information.

672 PROFILES OF NEW YORK / Ancestry: Rankings

Place	Number	%
Suffern (village) Rockland County	11	0.10
Spring Valley (village) Rockland County	22	0.09
Ramapo (town) Rockland County	84	0.08

Asian: Chinese, except Taiwanese

Top 10 Places Sorted by Number
Based on all places, regardless of population

Place	Number	%
New York (city) New York City	374,321	4.67
Hempstead (town) Nassau County	6,607	0.87
North Hempstead (town) Nassau County	6,003	2.70
Brookhaven (town) Suffolk County	5,140	1.15
Oyster Bay (town) Nassau County	4,286	1.46
Huntington (town) Suffolk County	2,027	1.04
Amherst (town) Erie County	1,940	1.67
Ithaca (city) Tompkins County	1,700	5.80
Islip (town) Suffolk County	1,548	0.48
Greenburgh (town) Westchester County	1,496	1.72

Top 10 Places Sorted by Percent
Based on all places, regardless of population

Place	Number	%
Forest Home (cdp) Tompkins County	132	14.03
Lansing (village) Tompkins County	309	9.04
Manhasset Hills (cdp) Nassau County	273	7.46
Thomaston (village) Nassau County	183	7.02
Northeast Ithaca (cdp) Tompkins County	185	6.97
Russell Gardens (village) Nassau County	72	6.70
Searingtown (cdp) Nassau County	308	6.12
East Ithaca (cdp) Tompkins County	130	5.93
North Hills (village) Nassau County	252	5.86
University Gardens (cdp) Nassau County	242	5.85

Top 10 Places Sorted by Percent
Based on places with populations of 10,000 or more

Place	Number	%
Ithaca (city) Tompkins County	1,700	5.80
New York (city) New York City	374,321	4.67
North New Hyde Park (cdp) Nassau County	669	4.60
Setauket-East Setauket (cdp) Suffolk County	721	4.53
Syosset (cdp) Nassau County	803	4.33
Lansing (town) Tompkins County	394	3.74
Ithaca (town) Tompkins County	647	3.56
Vestal (town) Broome County	890	3.35
Stony Brook (cdp) Suffolk County	449	3.27
Scarsdale (village) Westchester County	538	3.02

Asian: Filipino

Top 10 Places Sorted by Number
Based on all places, regardless of population

Place	Number	%
New York (city) New York City	62,058	0.77
Hempstead (town) Nassau County	4,712	0.62
Yonkers (city) Westchester County	2,082	1.06
Clarkstown (town) Rockland County	1,856	2.26
Brookhaven (town) Suffolk County	1,723	0.38
Ramapo (town) Rockland County	1,534	1.41
North Hempstead (town) Nassau County	1,479	0.66
Oyster Bay (town) Nassau County	1,372	0.47
Islip (town) Suffolk County	1,155	0.36
Greenburgh (town) Westchester County	742	0.86

Top 10 Places Sorted by Percent
Based on all places, regardless of population

Place	Number	%
Hillcrest (cdp) Rockland County	541	7.61
Orangeburg (cdp) Rockland County	200	5.90
Valley Cottage (cdp) Rockland County	514	5.55
Parc (cdp) Clinton County	2	3.70
New Hempstead (village) Rockland County	135	2.83

Place	Number	%
Hillburn (village) Rockland County	24	2.72
South Valley Stream (cdp) Nassau County	148	2.63
Tappan (cdp) Rockland County	176	2.60
Nanuet (cdp) Rockland County	424	2.54
Poland (village) Herkimer County	11	2.44

Top 10 Places Sorted by Percent
Based on places with populations of 10,000 or more

Place	Number	%
Nanuet (cdp) Rockland County	424	2.54
Clarkstown (town) Rockland County	1,856	2.26
New City (cdp) Rockland County	577	1.70
North Valley Stream (cdp) Nassau County	269	1.70
Salisbury (cdp) Nassau County	193	1.56
Elmont (cdp) Nassau County	491	1.50
Fort Drum (cdp) Jefferson County	182	1.50
Orangetown (town) Rockland County	708	1.48
Valley Stream (village) Nassau County	538	1.48
Ramapo (town) Rockland County	1,534	1.41

Asian: Hmong

Top 10 Places Sorted by Number
Based on all places, regardless of population

Place	Number	%
Syracuse (city) Onondaga County	174	0.12
Clay (town) Onondaga County	27	0.05
New York (city) New York City	26	0.00
Cicero (town) Onondaga County	14	0.05
Augusta (town) Oneida County	9	0.46
Salina (town) Onondaga County	7	0.02
Manlius (town) Onondaga County	6	0.02
Oswego (town) Oswego County	4	0.05
Liverpool (village) Onondaga County	3	0.12
Rochester (city) Monroe County	3	0.00

Top 10 Places Sorted by Percent
Based on all places, regardless of population

Place	Number	%
Augusta (town) Oneida County	9	0.46
Syracuse (city) Onondaga County	174	0.12
Liverpool (village) Onondaga County	3	0.12
Clay (town) Onondaga County	27	0.05
Cicero (town) Onondaga County	14	0.05
Oswego (town) Oswego County	4	0.05
Cazenovia (village) Madison County	1	0.04
South Nyack (village) Rockland County	1	0.03
Salina (town) Onondaga County	7	0.02
Manlius (town) Onondaga County	6	0.02

Top 10 Places Sorted by Percent
Based on places with populations of 10,000 or more

Place	Number	%
Syracuse (city) Onondaga County	174	0.12
Clay (town) Onondaga County	27	0.05
Cicero (town) Onondaga County	14	0.05
Salina (town) Onondaga County	7	0.02
Manlius (town) Onondaga County	6	0.02
Ithaca (city) Tompkins County	2	0.01
Watervliet (city) Albany County	1	0.01
New York (city) New York City	26	0.00
Rochester (city) Monroe County	3	0.00
Albany (city) Albany County	1	0.00

Asian: Indian

Top 10 Places Sorted by Number
Based on all places, regardless of population

Place	Number	%
New York (city) New York City	206,228	2.58
Hempstead (town) Nassau County	11,966	1.58
North Hempstead (town) Nassau County	7,951	3.57

Place	Number	%
Oyster Bay (town) Nassau County	5,415	1.84
Yonkers (city) Westchester County	5,008	2.55
Brookhaven (town) Suffolk County	3,738	0.83
Islip (town) Suffolk County	3,360	1.04
Clarkstown (town) Rockland County	2,596	3.16
Greenburgh (town) Westchester County	2,481	2.86
Ramapo (town) Rockland County	2,157	1.98

Top 10 Places Sorted by Percent
Based on all places, regardless of population

Place	Number	%
Manhasset Hills (cdp) Nassau County	474	12.95
Herricks (cdp) Nassau County	521	12.78
Garden City Park (cdp) Nassau County	941	12.46
Searingtown (cdp) Nassau County	616	12.24
Muttontown (village) Nassau County	365	10.70
Bellerose Terrace (cdp) Nassau County	224	10.38
Albertson (cdp) Nassau County	451	8.67
New Hyde Park (village) Nassau County	739	7.76
North New Hyde Park (cdp) Nassau County	1,122	7.72
Elmont (cdp) Nassau County	2,113	6.47

Top 10 Places Sorted by Percent
Based on places with populations of 10,000 or more

Place	Number	%
North New Hyde Park (cdp) Nassau County	1,122	7.72
Elmont (cdp) Nassau County	2,113	6.47
North Valley Stream (cdp) Nassau County	752	4.76
Hicksville (cdp) Nassau County	1,876	4.55
Nanuet (cdp) Rockland County	639	3.82
North Hempstead (town) Nassau County	7,951	3.57
Salisbury (cdp) Nassau County	439	3.56
Niskayuna (town) Schenectady County	656	3.23
Clarkstown (town) Rockland County	2,596	3.16
Arlington (cdp) Dutchess County	389	3.12

Asian: Indonesian

Top 10 Places Sorted by Number
Based on all places, regardless of population

Place	Number	%
New York (city) New York City	3,017	0.04
Hempstead (town) Nassau County	60	0.01
Oyster Bay (town) Nassau County	49	0.02
Buffalo (city) Erie County	44	0.02
Syracuse (city) Onondaga County	43	0.03
Ithaca (city) Tompkins County	39	0.13
Amherst (town) Erie County	37	0.03
Brookhaven (town) Suffolk County	36	0.01
Islip (town) Suffolk County	32	0.01
Ithaca (town) Tompkins County	28	0.15

Top 10 Places Sorted by Percent
Based on all places, regardless of population

Place	Number	%
Forest Home (cdp) Tompkins County	15	1.59
Cortland West (cdp) Cortland County	4	0.30
Alma (town) Allegany County	2	0.24
Farmingdale (village) Nassau County	19	0.23
Lansing (village) Tompkins County	8	0.23
Naples (town) Ontario County	5	0.20
Northeast Ithaca (cdp) Tompkins County	5	0.19
Cayuga Heights (village) Tompkins County	6	0.18
Allegany Reservation Cattaraugus County	2	0.18
Salamanca (town) Cattaraugus County	1	0.18

Top 10 Places Sorted by Percent
Based on places with populations of 10,000 or more

Place	Number	%
Ithaca (town) Tompkins County	28	0.15
Ithaca (city) Tompkins County	39	0.13
Lansing (town) Tompkins County	9	0.09

Notes: (cdp) census designated place; Refer to the User's Guide in the front of the book for more detailed information.

Place	Number	%
West Haverstraw (village) Rockland County	7	0.07
Niskayuna (town) Schenectady County	13	0.06
Brighton (town) Monroe County	19	0.05
Halfmoon (town) Saratoga County	10	0.05
Sayville (cdp) Suffolk County	9	0.05
Syosset (cdp) Nassau County	9	0.05
Gates-North Gates (cdp) Monroe County	7	0.05

Asian: Japanese

Top 10 Places Sorted by Number
Based on all places, regardless of population

Place	Number	%
New York (city) New York City	26,419	0.33
Greenburgh (town) Westchester County	1,894	2.18
North Hempstead (town) Nassau County	1,130	0.51
Eastchester (town) Westchester County	1,110	3.54
Scarsdale (village) Westchester County	728	4.08
Harrison (village) Westchester County	694	2.87
Greenville (cdp) Westchester County	684	7.91
Hempstead (town) Nassau County	647	0.09
Rye (city) Westchester County	611	4.09
Brookhaven (town) Suffolk County	513	0.11

Top 10 Places Sorted by Percent
Based on all places, regardless of population

Place	Number	%
Greenville (cdp) Westchester County	684	7.91
Forest Home (cdp) Tompkins County	62	6.59
Tuckahoe (village) Westchester County	359	5.78
Manorhaven (village) Nassau County	269	4.38
Rye (city) Westchester County	611	4.09
Scarsdale (village) Westchester County	728	4.08
Eastchester (town) Westchester County	1,110	3.54
Hartsdale (cdp) Westchester County	290	2.95
Harrison (village) Westchester County	694	2.87
Irvington (village) Westchester County	185	2.79

Top 10 Places Sorted by Percent
Based on places with populations of 10,000 or more

Place	Number	%
Rye (city) Westchester County	611	4.09
Scarsdale (village) Westchester County	728	4.08
Eastchester (town) Westchester County	1,110	3.54
Harrison (village) Westchester County	694	2.87
Greenburgh (town) Westchester County	1,894	2.18
Port Washington (cdp) Nassau County	276	1.81
Dobbs Ferry (village) Westchester County	172	1.62
Mamaroneck (village) Westchester County	285	1.52
Tarrytown (village) Westchester County	160	1.44
Mamaroneck (town) Westchester County	314	1.08

Asian: Korean

Top 10 Places Sorted by Number
Based on all places, regardless of population

Place	Number	%
New York (city) New York City	90,208	1.13
North Hempstead (town) Nassau County	3,425	1.54
Hempstead (town) Nassau County	2,559	0.34
Oyster Bay (town) Nassau County	2,505	0.85
Brookhaven (town) Suffolk County	1,689	0.38
Huntington (town) Suffolk County	1,352	0.69
Greenburgh (town) Westchester County	1,196	1.38
Amherst (town) Erie County	1,145	0.98
Yonkers (city) Westchester County	946	0.48
Clarkstown (town) Rockland County	805	0.98

Top 10 Places Sorted by Percent
Based on all places, regardless of population

Place	Number	%
Lake Success (village) Nassau County	204	7.29
Forest Home (cdp) Tompkins County	68	7.23
Lansing (village) Tompkins County	241	7.05
University Gardens (cdp) Nassau County	219	5.29
Searingtown (cdp) Nassau County	256	5.09
Manorhaven (village) Nassau County	290	4.72
Saltaire (village) Suffolk County	2	4.65
Northeast Ithaca (cdp) Tompkins County	111	4.18
Manhasset Hills (cdp) Nassau County	151	4.12
Jericho (cdp) Nassau County	535	4.10

Top 10 Places Sorted by Percent
Based on places with populations of 10,000 or more

Place	Number	%
Jericho (cdp) Nassau County	535	4.10
Syosset (cdp) Nassau County	685	3.69
Lansing (town) Tompkins County	265	2.52
Scarsdale (village) Westchester County	394	2.21
Elwood (cdp) Suffolk County	207	1.90
Ithaca (town) Tompkins County	318	1.75
Ithaca (city) Tompkins County	507	1.73
Vestal (town) Broome County	453	1.71
Dobbs Ferry (village) Westchester County	168	1.58
Orangetown (town) Rockland County	750	1.57

Asian: Laotian

Top 10 Places Sorted by Number
Based on all places, regardless of population

Place	Number	%
Rochester (city) Monroe County	933	0.42
Buffalo (city) Erie County	332	0.11
Union (town) Broome County	316	0.56
New York (city) New York City	316	0.00
Johnson City (village) Broome County	220	1.42
Binghamton (city) Broome County	200	0.42
Syracuse (city) Onondaga County	166	0.11
Perinton (town) Monroe County	118	0.26
Henrietta (town) Monroe County	115	0.29
Greece (town) Monroe County	89	0.09

Top 10 Places Sorted by Percent
Based on all places, regardless of population

Place	Number	%
Johnson City (village) Broome County	220	1.42
Webster (village) Monroe County	43	0.82
Union (town) Broome County	316	0.56
Delevan (village) Cattaraugus County	6	0.55
Rochester (city) Monroe County	933	0.42
Binghamton (city) Broome County	200	0.42
Gates-North Gates (cdp) Monroe County	56	0.37
Arcade (town) Wyoming County	13	0.31
Henrietta (town) Monroe County	115	0.29
Seneca Falls (village) Seneca County	19	0.28

Top 10 Places Sorted by Percent
Based on places with populations of 10,000 or more

Place	Number	%
Johnson City (village) Broome County	220	1.42
Union (town) Broome County	316	0.56
Rochester (city) Monroe County	933	0.42
Binghamton (city) Broome County	200	0.42
Gates-North Gates (cdp) Monroe County	56	0.37
Henrietta (town) Monroe County	115	0.29
Perinton (town) Monroe County	118	0.26
Endicott (village) Broome County	33	0.25
Gates (town) Monroe County	70	0.24
Webster (town) Monroe County	67	0.18

Asian: Malaysian

Top 10 Places Sorted by Number
Based on all places, regardless of population

Place	Number	%
New York (city) New York City	2,287	0.03
Syracuse (city) Onondaga County	32	0.02
Troy (city) Rensselaer County	28	0.06
Ithaca (city) Tompkins County	25	0.09
North Hempstead (town) Nassau County	20	0.01
Amherst (town) Erie County	15	0.01
Hempstead (town) Nassau County	14	0.00
Brookhaven (town) Suffolk County	13	0.00
Greenburgh (town) Westchester County	11	0.01
Huntington (town) Suffolk County	11	0.01

Top 10 Places Sorted by Percent
Based on all places, regardless of population

Place	Number	%
Kerhonkson (cdp) Ulster County	4	0.23
Putnam (town) Washington County	1	0.16
Cold Spring (village) Putnam County	3	0.15
Elmsford (village) Westchester County	5	0.11
Forest Home (cdp) Tompkins County	1	0.11
Albertson (cdp) Nassau County	5	0.10
Plandome Heights (village) Nassau County	1	0.10
Ithaca (city) Tompkins County	25	0.09
Orangeburg (cdp) Rockland County	3	0.09
Great Neck Gardens (cdp) Nassau County	1	0.09

Top 10 Places Sorted by Percent
Based on places with populations of 10,000 or more

Place	Number	%
Ithaca (city) Tompkins County	25	0.09
Hampton Bays (cdp) Suffolk County	8	0.07
Troy (city) Rensselaer County	28	0.06
Nanuet (cdp) Rockland County	7	0.04
North Valley Stream (cdp) Nassau County	6	0.04
Elwood (cdp) Suffolk County	4	0.04
New York (city) New York City	2,287	0.03
Corning (city) Steuben County	3	0.03
Red Hook (town) Dutchess County	3	0.03
Syracuse (city) Onondaga County	32	0.02

Asian: Pakistani

Top 10 Places Sorted by Number
Based on all places, regardless of population

Place	Number	%
New York (city) New York City	34,310	0.43
Hempstead (town) Nassau County	2,039	0.27
Brookhaven (town) Suffolk County	869	0.19
Islip (town) Suffolk County	755	0.23
Huntington (town) Suffolk County	600	0.31
Oyster Bay (town) Nassau County	578	0.20
Yonkers (city) Westchester County	553	0.28
North Hempstead (town) Nassau County	462	0.21
Babylon (town) Suffolk County	387	0.18
Colonie (town) Albany County	309	0.39

Top 10 Places Sorted by Percent
Based on all places, regardless of population

Place	Number	%
Saltaire (village) Suffolk County	7	16.28
Sagaponack (cdp) Suffolk County	10	1.72
Herricks (cdp) Nassau County	45	1.10
Lake Katrine (cdp) Ulster County	24	1.00
North Valley Stream (cdp) Nassau County	151	0.96
South Valley Stream (cdp) Nassau County	48	0.85
Malverne Park Oaks (cdp) Nassau County	4	0.85
Hewlett Bay Park (village) Nassau County	4	0.83
North Bellmore (cdp) Nassau County	164	0.82

Notes: (cdp) census designated place; Refer to the User's Guide in the front of the book for more detailed information.

East Meadow (cdp) Nassau County	302	0.81

Top 10 Places Sorted by Percent
Based on places with populations of 10,000 or more

Place	Number	%
North Valley Stream (cdp) Nassau County	151	0.96
North Bellmore (cdp) Nassau County	164	0.82
East Meadow (cdp) Nassau County	302	0.81
Elmont (cdp) Nassau County	243	0.74
Nesconset (cdp) Suffolk County	85	0.71
Valley Stream (village) Nassau County	248	0.68
Dobbs Ferry (village) Westchester County	58	0.55
Huntington Station (cdp) Suffolk County	153	0.51
Dix Hills (cdp) Suffolk County	132	0.51
Spring Valley (village) Rockland County	125	0.49

Asian: Sri Lankan

Top 10 Places Sorted by Number
Based on all places, regardless of population

Place	Number	%
New York (city) New York City	2,640	0.03
Hempstead (town) Nassau County	64	0.01
Amherst (town) Erie County	54	0.05
New Rochelle (city) Westchester County	43	0.06
Brookhaven (town) Suffolk County	38	0.01
Buffalo (city) Erie County	36	0.01
Ramapo (town) Rockland County	28	0.03
Rochester (city) Monroe County	24	0.01
Penfield (town) Monroe County	22	0.06
Yonkers (city) Westchester County	22	0.01

Top 10 Places Sorted by Percent
Based on all places, regardless of population

Place	Number	%
Coldspring (town) Cattaraugus County	4	0.53
Poquott (village) Suffolk County	3	0.31
Randolph (village) Cattaraugus County	4	0.30
Cassadaga (village) Chautauqua County	2	0.30
Lansing (village) Tompkins County	8	0.23
Randolph (town) Cattaraugus County	4	0.15
Mount Kisco (village) Westchester County	12	0.12
Nyack (village) Rockland County	8	0.12
Orange Lake (cdp) Orange County	7	0.12
Kortright (town) Delaware County	2	0.12

Top 10 Places Sorted by Percent
Based on places with populations of 10,000 or more

Place	Number	%
Scarsdale (village) Westchester County	17	0.10
Lansing (town) Tompkins County	9	0.09
Spring Valley (village) Rockland County	20	0.08
Beacon (city) Dutchess County	9	0.07
Oneida (city) Madison County	8	0.07
New Rochelle (city) Westchester County	43	0.06
Penfield (town) Monroe County	22	0.06
Ithaca (city) Tompkins County	17	0.06
Niskayuna (town) Schenectady County	13	0.06
Monsey (cdp) Rockland County	8	0.06

Asian: Taiwanese

Top 10 Places Sorted by Number
Based on all places, regardless of population

Place	Number	%
New York (city) New York City	5,488	0.07
North Hempstead (town) Nassau County	418	0.19
Hempstead (town) Nassau County	248	0.03
Brookhaven (town) Suffolk County	191	0.04
Oyster Bay (town) Nassau County	161	0.05
Syracuse (city) Onondaga County	155	0.11
Amherst (town) Erie County	125	0.11
Huntington (town) Suffolk County	116	0.06
Ithaca (city) Tompkins County	101	0.34
Ithaca (town) Tompkins County	97	0.53

Top 10 Places Sorted by Percent
Based on all places, regardless of population

Place	Number	%
West Hampton Dunes (village) Suffolk County	1	9.09
Forest Home (cdp) Tompkins County	35	3.72
Old Field (village) Suffolk County	12	1.27
Russell Gardens (village) Nassau County	13	1.21
Greenvale (cdp) Nassau County	24	1.08
North Hills (village) Nassau County	39	0.91
Manhasset Hills (cdp) Nassau County	31	0.85
Thomaston (village) Nassau County	22	0.84
Great Neck Gardens (cdp) Nassau County	9	0.83
Northeast Ithaca (cdp) Tompkins County	20	0.75

Top 10 Places Sorted by Percent
Based on places with populations of 10,000 or more

Place	Number	%
Ithaca (town) Tompkins County	97	0.53
Vestal (town) Broome County	94	0.35
Scarsdale (village) Westchester County	63	0.35
Ithaca (city) Tompkins County	101	0.34
Lansing (town) Tompkins County	29	0.28
Pittsford (town) Monroe County	62	0.23
Setauket-East Setauket (cdp) Suffolk County	36	0.23
Dix Hills (cdp) Suffolk County	53	0.20
Stony Brook (cdp) Suffolk County	27	0.20
North Hempstead (town) Nassau County	418	0.19

Asian: Thai

Top 10 Places Sorted by Number
Based on all places, regardless of population

Place	Number	%
New York (city) New York City	5,002	0.06
Hempstead (town) Nassau County	255	0.03
Yonkers (city) Westchester County	246	0.13
Brookhaven (town) Suffolk County	143	0.03
Islip (town) Suffolk County	110	0.03
Ithaca (city) Tompkins County	109	0.37
Syracuse (city) Onondaga County	103	0.07
North Hempstead (town) Nassau County	93	0.04
Clarkstown (town) Rockland County	75	0.09
Mount Vernon (city) Westchester County	73	0.11

Top 10 Places Sorted by Percent
Based on all places, regardless of population

Place	Number	%
East Ithaca (cdp) Tompkins County	24	1.09
Forest Home (cdp) Tompkins County	6	0.64
Greenvale (cdp) Nassau County	11	0.49
West Nyack (cdp) Rockland County	15	0.46
Malverne Park Oaks (cdp) Nassau County	2	0.43
Ellenburg (town) Clinton County	7	0.39
Black River (village) Jefferson County	5	0.39
Ithaca (city) Tompkins County	109	0.37
South Nyack (village) Rockland County	13	0.37
Baldwin (town) Chemung County	3	0.35

Top 10 Places Sorted by Percent
Based on places with populations of 10,000 or more

Place	Number	%
Ithaca (city) Tompkins County	109	0.37
Ithaca (town) Tompkins County	46	0.25
Scarsdale (village) Westchester County	43	0.24
Pelham (town) Westchester County	25	0.21
Elmont (cdp) Nassau County	52	0.16
Nanuet (cdp) Rockland County	24	0.14
Yonkers (city) Westchester County	246	0.13
Rome (city) Oneida County	46	0.13
Eastchester (town) Westchester County	42	0.13
Salisbury (cdp) Nassau County	15	0.12

Asian: Vietnamese

Top 10 Places Sorted by Number
Based on all places, regardless of population

Place	Number	%
New York (city) New York City	13,010	0.16
Syracuse (city) Onondaga County	1,600	1.09
Buffalo (city) Erie County	1,402	0.48
Rochester (city) Monroe County	1,390	0.63
Utica (city) Oneida County	881	1.45
Hempstead (town) Nassau County	499	0.07
Islip (town) Suffolk County	424	0.13
Binghamton (city) Broome County	395	0.83
Brookhaven (town) Suffolk County	379	0.08
Albany (city) Albany County	353	0.37

Top 10 Places Sorted by Percent
Based on all places, regardless of population

Place	Number	%
Utica (city) Oneida County	881	1.45
Syracuse (city) Onondaga County	1,600	1.09
Gates-North Gates (cdp) Monroe County	144	0.95
Galeville (cdp) Onondaga County	42	0.94
North Collins (village) Erie County	10	0.93
Endicott (village) Broome County	109	0.84
Binghamton (city) Broome County	395	0.83
Gates (town) Monroe County	237	0.81
Springs (cdp) Suffolk County	40	0.81
Hillcrest (cdp) Rockland County	56	0.79

Top 10 Places Sorted by Percent
Based on places with populations of 10,000 or more

Place	Number	%
Utica (city) Oneida County	881	1.45
Syracuse (city) Onondaga County	1,600	1.09
Gates-North Gates (cdp) Monroe County	144	0.95
Endicott (village) Broome County	109	0.84
Binghamton (city) Broome County	395	0.83
Gates (town) Monroe County	237	0.81
Rochester (city) Monroe County	1,390	0.63
Henrietta (town) Monroe County	217	0.56
Salina (town) Onondaga County	182	0.55
Ithaca (city) Tompkins County	143	0.49

Asian: Other Asian, specified

Top 10 Places Sorted by Number
Based on all places, regardless of population

Place	Number	%
New York (city) New York City	3,921	0.05
Hempstead (town) Nassau County	102	0.01
Brookhaven (town) Suffolk County	65	0.01
Buffalo (city) Erie County	59	0.02
Ithaca (city) Tompkins County	52	0.18
Rochester (city) Monroe County	47	0.02
North Hempstead (town) Nassau County	42	0.02
Rensselaer (city) Rensselaer County	39	0.50
Huntington (town) Suffolk County	34	0.02
Islip (town) Suffolk County	34	0.01

Top 10 Places Sorted by Percent
Based on all places, regardless of population

Place	Number	%
Rensselaer (city) Rensselaer County	39	0.50
East Ithaca (cdp) Tompkins County	7	0.32
Wurtsboro (village) Sullivan County	4	0.32
Forest Home (cdp) Tompkins County	3	0.32
Gang Mills (cdp) Steuben County	10	0.30

Notes: (cdp) census designated place; Refer to the User's Guide in the front of the book for more detailed information.

Asian: Other Asian, not specified (continued)

Top 10 Places Sorted by Number
Based on all places, regardless of population

Place	Number	%
Northeast Ithaca (cdp) Tompkins County	8	0.30
New Suffolk (cdp) Suffolk County	1	0.30
Gasport (cdp) Niagara County	3	0.24
Bellerose Terrace (cdp) Nassau County	5	0.23
Great Neck Estates (village) Nassau County	6	0.22

Top 10 Places Sorted by Percent
Based on places with populations of 10,000 or more

Place	Number	%
Ithaca (city) Tompkins County	52	0.18
Ithaca (town) Tompkins County	20	0.11
Scarsdale (village) Westchester County	19	0.11
Dobbs Ferry (village) Westchester County	10	0.09
Brighton (town) Monroe County	28	0.08
Mount Pleasant (town) Westchester County	31	0.07
New Paltz (town) Ulster County	9	0.07
North New Hyde Park (cdp) Nassau County	8	0.06
North Wantagh (cdp) Nassau County	7	0.06
Lake Grove (village) Suffolk County	6	0.06

Asian: Other Asian, not specified

Top 10 Places Sorted by Number
Based on all places, regardless of population

Place	Number	%
New York (city) New York City	29,826	0.37
Hempstead (town) Nassau County	1,091	0.14
North Hempstead (town) Nassau County	837	0.38
Ithaca (city) Tompkins County	620	2.12
Brookhaven (town) Suffolk County	570	0.13
Yonkers (city) Westchester County	513	0.26
Islip (town) Suffolk County	426	0.13
Buffalo (city) Erie County	421	0.14
Oyster Bay (town) Nassau County	389	0.13
Rochester (city) Monroe County	338	0.15

Top 10 Places Sorted by Percent
Based on all places, regardless of population

Place	Number	%
Ithaca (city) Tompkins County	620	2.12
Grand View-on-Hudson (village) Rockland County	5	1.76
Kings Point (village) Nassau County	86	1.69
Saddle Rock Estates (cdp) Nassau County	6	1.42
Searingtown (cdp) Nassau County	65	1.29
Great Neck Gardens (cdp) Nassau County	14	1.29
Great Neck (village) Nassau County	119	1.25
Greenvale (cdp) Nassau County	23	1.03
Benson (town) Hamilton County	2	1.00
Fire Island (cdp) Suffolk County	3	0.97

Top 10 Places Sorted by Percent
Based on places with populations of 10,000 or more

Place	Number	%
Ithaca (city) Tompkins County	620	2.12
North Valley Stream (cdp) Nassau County	92	0.58
Ithaca (town) Tompkins County	80	0.44
Dix Hills (cdp) Suffolk County	111	0.43
North Hempstead (town) Nassau County	837	0.38
Schenectady (city) Schenectady County	232	0.38
New York (city) New York City	29,826	0.37
Binghamton (city) Broome County	158	0.33
Elmont (cdp) Nassau County	109	0.33
Johnson City (village) Broome County	50	0.32

Assyrian/Chaldean/Syriac

Top 10 Places Sorted by Number
Based on all places, regardless of population

Place	Number	%
New York (city) New York City	300	0.00
Yonkers (city) Westchester County	179	0.09
Ossining (town) Westchester County	78	0.21
Cortlandt (town) Westchester County	47	0.12
Greenburgh (town) Westchester County	47	0.05
Mount Pleasant (town) Westchester County	35	0.08
Valhalla (cdp) Westchester County	27	0.51
Pleasant Valley (town) Dutchess County	24	0.26
Kirkland (town) Oneida County	23	0.23
Albany (city) Albany County	23	0.02

Top 10 Places Sorted by Percent
Based on all places, regardless of population

Place	Number	%
Valhalla (cdp) Westchester County	27	0.51
Hamilton (village) Madison County	16	0.46
Brightwaters (village) Suffolk County	10	0.31
Hamilton (town) Madison County	16	0.28
Pleasant Valley (town) Dutchess County	24	0.26
Cooperstown (village) Otsego County	5	0.25
Kirkland (town) Oneida County	23	0.23
Pawling (town) Dutchess County	17	0.23
Old Brookville (village) Nassau County	5	0.23
Ossining (town) Westchester County	78	0.21

Top 10 Places Sorted by Percent
Based on places with populations of 10,000 or more

Place	Number	%
Kirkland (town) Oneida County	23	0.23
Ossining (town) Westchester County	78	0.21
Catskill (town) Greene County	15	0.13
Cortlandt (town) Westchester County	47	0.12
Elwood (cdp) Suffolk County	12	0.11
Yonkers (city) Westchester County	179	0.09
Goshen (town) Orange County	12	0.09
Mount Pleasant (town) Westchester County	35	0.08
Greenburgh (town) Westchester County	47	0.05
Brighton (town) Monroe County	19	0.05

Australian

Top 10 Places Sorted by Number
Based on all places, regardless of population

Place	Number	%
New York (city) New York City	3,155	0.04
Brookhaven (town) Suffolk County	250	0.06
Oyster Bay (town) Nassau County	115	0.04
Mamaroneck (town) Westchester County	88	0.30
Hempstead (town) Nassau County	85	0.01
Yonkers (city) Westchester County	78	0.04
Mastic Beach (cdp) Suffolk County	74	0.64
Cortlandt (town) Westchester County	69	0.18
North Hempstead (town) Nassau County	61	0.03
Croton-on-Hudson (village) Westchester County	59	0.78

Top 10 Places Sorted by Percent
Based on all places, regardless of population

Place	Number	%
Jewett (town) Greene County	15	1.55
Phoenicia (cdp) Ulster County	5	1.24
Munsey Park (village) Nassau County	30	1.14
Upper Brookville (village) Nassau County	17	0.94
Hannibal (village) Oswego County	5	0.91
Larchmont (village) Westchester County	58	0.89
Saugerties South (cdp) Ulster County	19	0.84
Upper Nyack (village) Rockland County	15	0.81
Ovid (village) Seneca County	5	0.81
Greenwood Lake (village) Orange County	27	0.80

Top 10 Places Sorted by Percent
Based on places with populations of 10,000 or more

Place	Number	%
Mastic Beach (cdp) Suffolk County	74	0.64
Potsdam (town) Saint Lawrence County	49	0.31
Mamaroneck (town) Westchester County	88	0.30
Rye (city) Westchester County	43	0.29
New Windsor (town) Orange County	54	0.24
Setauket-East Setauket (cdp) Suffolk County	38	0.24
Pelham (town) Westchester County	25	0.21
Cortlandt (town) Westchester County	69	0.18
Milton (town) Saratoga County	30	0.18
Endicott (village) Broome County	24	0.18

Austrian

Top 10 Places Sorted by Number
Based on all places, regardless of population

Place	Number	%
New York (city) New York City	33,605	0.42
Hempstead (town) Nassau County	6,437	0.85
Oyster Bay (town) Nassau County	3,802	1.29
Brookhaven (town) Suffolk County	3,427	0.76
North Hempstead (town) Nassau County	2,795	1.26
Huntington (town) Suffolk County	2,004	1.03
Islip (town) Suffolk County	1,537	0.48
Greenburgh (town) Westchester County	1,111	1.28
Smithtown (town) Suffolk County	1,088	0.94
Babylon (town) Suffolk County	1,006	0.48

Top 10 Places Sorted by Percent
Based on all places, regardless of population

Place	Number	%
West Hampton Dunes (village) Suffolk County	6	75.00
Palenville (cdp) Greene County	63	5.20
Hewlett Neck (village) Nassau County	23	4.66
Saddle Rock Estates (cdp) Nassau County	20	4.56
Bloomingburg (village) Sullivan County	14	4.52
Great Neck Plaza (village) Nassau County	267	4.21
Cove Neck (village) Nassau County	10	3.82
Harbor Isle (cdp) Nassau County	53	3.75
Russell Gardens (village) Nassau County	40	3.72
Heritage Hills (cdp) Westchester County	127	3.31

Top 10 Places Sorted by Percent
Based on places with populations of 10,000 or more

Place	Number	%
Jericho (cdp) Nassau County	407	3.13
Plainview (cdp) Nassau County	621	2.42
Syosset (cdp) Nassau County	423	2.28
Dobbs Ferry (village) Westchester County	224	2.11
Merrick (cdp) Nassau County	461	2.03
Scarsdale (village) Westchester County	336	1.89
Salisbury (cdp) Nassau County	229	1.86
Somers (town) Westchester County	334	1.82
Mamaroneck (town) Westchester County	508	1.75
Jefferson Valley-Yorktown (cdp) Westchester County	255	1.71

Basque

Top 10 Places Sorted by Number
Based on all places, regardless of population

Place	Number	%
New York (city) New York City	596	0.01
Hempstead (town) Nassau County	91	0.01
Putnam Valley (town) Putnam County	46	0.43
North Hempstead (town) Nassau County	34	0.02
Amherst (town) Erie County	30	0.03
Buffalo (city) Erie County	28	0.01
Mineola (village) Nassau County	25	0.13
Babylon (village) Suffolk County	22	0.17
Albany (city) Albany County	22	0.02
Babylon (town) Suffolk County	22	0.01

Notes: (cdp) census designated place; Refer to the User's Guide in the front of the book for more detailed information.

Top 10 Places Sorted by Percent
Based on all places, regardless of population

Place	Number	%
Bellerose (village) Nassau County	19	1.62
Putnam Valley (town) Putnam County	46	0.43
Spencer (town) Tioga County	12	0.40
Stafford (town) Genesee County	8	0.33
Yorkshire (town) Cattaraugus County	13	0.31
Sherman (village) Chautauqua County	2	0.29
Wellsville (village) Allegany County	12	0.23
Shelter Island (town) Suffolk County	5	0.22
Ardsley (village) Westchester County	9	0.21
Stewart Manor (village) Nassau County	4	0.21

Top 10 Places Sorted by Percent
Based on places with populations of 10,000 or more

Place	Number	%
Putnam Valley (town) Putnam County	46	0.43
Babylon (village) Suffolk County	22	0.17
Mineola (village) Nassau County	25	0.13
East Greenbush (town) Rensselaer County	20	0.13
Garden City (village) Nassau County	21	0.10
Nesconset (cdp) Suffolk County	12	0.10
Arlington (cdp) Dutchess County	9	0.07
Canton (town) Saint Lawrence County	7	0.07
Southeast (town) Putnam County	10	0.06
Scarsdale (village) Westchester County	9	0.05

Belgian

Top 10 Places Sorted by Number
Based on all places, regardless of population

Place	Number	%
New York (city) New York City	3,426	0.04
Brookhaven (town) Suffolk County	415	0.09
Hempstead (town) Nassau County	321	0.04
Irondequoit (cdp) Monroe County	306	0.58
Greece (town) Monroe County	273	0.29
Oyster Bay (town) Nassau County	259	0.09
Huntington (town) Suffolk County	197	0.10
Islip (town) Suffolk County	191	0.06
Greenburgh (town) Westchester County	188	0.22
Rochester (city) Monroe County	161	0.07

Top 10 Places Sorted by Percent
Based on all places, regardless of population

Place	Number	%
Mill Neck (village) Nassau County	15	1.98
Great Neck Gardens (cdp) Nassau County	22	1.97
Wethersfield (town) Wyoming County	12	1.35
Fort Ann (village) Washington County	6	1.28
Harbor Hills (cdp) Nassau County	7	1.22
Sheldon (town) Wyoming County	31	1.21
Walker Valley (cdp) Ulster County	10	1.21
Le Roy (village) Genesee County	51	1.17
Fabius (village) Onondaga County	4	1.05
Java (town) Wyoming County	23	1.04

Top 10 Places Sorted by Percent
Based on places with populations of 10,000 or more

Place	Number	%
Irondequoit (cdp) Monroe County	306	0.58
Pelham (town) Westchester County	59	0.50
Penfield (town) Monroe County	146	0.42
Onondaga (town) Onondaga County	85	0.40
Ogden (town) Monroe County	73	0.40
Parma (town) Monroe County	56	0.38
Mamaroneck (town) Westchester County	105	0.36
Perinton (town) Monroe County	153	0.33
Webster (town) Monroe County	116	0.31
Hyde Park (town) Dutchess County	63	0.30

Brazilian

Top 10 Places Sorted by Number
Based on all places, regardless of population

Place	Number	%
New York (city) New York City	12,176	0.15
Mount Vernon (city) Westchester County	991	1.45
Hempstead (town) Nassau County	581	0.08
New Rochelle (city) Westchester County	384	0.53
Port Chester (village) Westchester County	342	1.23
Rye (town) Westchester County	342	0.78
North Hempstead (town) Nassau County	316	0.14
Mamaroneck (town) Westchester County	257	0.89
Oyster Bay (town) Nassau County	253	0.09
Greenburgh (town) Westchester County	210	0.24

Top 10 Places Sorted by Percent
Based on all places, regardless of population

Place	Number	%
Harbor Hills (cdp) Nassau County	19	3.32
Forest Home (cdp) Tompkins County	24	2.36
Scotts Corners (cdp) Westchester County	13	2.26
Mount Vernon (city) Westchester County	991	1.45
Great River (cdp) Suffolk County	22	1.44
Grand View-on-Hudson (village) Rockland County	4	1.41
Port Chester (village) Westchester County	342	1.23
Shinnecock Hills (cdp) Suffolk County	21	1.17
Heritage Hills (cdp) Westchester County	44	1.15
North Sea (cdp) Suffolk County	48	1.05

Top 10 Places Sorted by Percent
Based on places with populations of 10,000 or more

Place	Number	%
Mount Vernon (city) Westchester County	991	1.45
Port Chester (village) Westchester County	342	1.23
Mamaroneck (town) Westchester County	257	0.89
Rye (town) Westchester County	342	0.78
Scarsdale (village) Westchester County	119	0.67
Mamaroneck (village) Westchester County	107	0.57
Suffern (village) Rockland County	63	0.57
New Rochelle (city) Westchester County	384	0.53
Lansing (town) Tompkins County	49	0.48
Ithaca (town) Tompkins County	81	0.44

British

Top 10 Places Sorted by Number
Based on all places, regardless of population

Place	Number	%
New York (city) New York City	17,030	0.21
Hempstead (town) Nassau County	1,552	0.21
Brookhaven (town) Suffolk County	1,167	0.26
Oyster Bay (town) Nassau County	817	0.28
Huntington (town) Suffolk County	736	0.38
Rochester (city) Monroe County	636	0.29
Amherst (town) Erie County	611	0.52
Syracuse (city) Onondaga County	587	0.40
Islip (town) Suffolk County	568	0.18
North Hempstead (town) Nassau County	542	0.24

Top 10 Places Sorted by Percent
Based on all places, regardless of population

Place	Number	%
Newfield Hamlet (cdp) Tompkins County	51	6.40
Rensselaer Falls (village) Saint Lawrence County	13	4.00
Scotts Corners (cdp) Westchester County	22	3.82
Galway (village) Saratoga County	8	3.76
Houghton (cdp) Allegany County	64	3.70
Centre Island (village) Nassau County	16	3.60
North Hudson (town) Essex County	8	2.99
Rock Hill (cdp) Sullivan County	28	2.85
Copake Lake (cdp) Columbia County	23	2.85
Aurora (village) Cayuga County	20	2.79

Top 10 Places Sorted by Percent
Based on places with populations of 10,000 or more

Place	Number	%
Ithaca (town) Tompkins County	319	1.73
Arlington (cdp) Dutchess County	191	1.54
Ithaca (city) Tompkins County	425	1.47
Rye (city) Westchester County	169	1.13
Lansing (town) Tompkins County	110	1.07
Ogden (town) Monroe County	194	1.05
Dryden (town) Tompkins County	144	1.05
Kirkland (town) Oneida County	103	1.02
Perinton (town) Monroe County	432	0.94
Red Hook (town) Dutchess County	94	0.90

Bulgarian

Top 10 Places Sorted by Number
Based on all places, regardless of population

Place	Number	%
New York (city) New York City	3,826	0.05
Greenburgh (town) Westchester County	147	0.17
Brookhaven (town) Suffolk County	130	0.03
Hartsdale (cdp) Westchester County	104	1.06
Hempstead (town) Nassau County	102	0.01
Rochester (city) Monroe County	81	0.04
Oyster Bay (town) Nassau County	81	0.03
Utica (city) Oneida County	74	0.12
Islip (town) Suffolk County	73	0.02
Tonawanda (town) Erie County	69	0.09

Top 10 Places Sorted by Percent
Based on all places, regardless of population

Place	Number	%
Galway (village) Saratoga County	11	5.16
Fairfield (town) Herkimer County	27	1.64
Hartsdale (cdp) Westchester County	104	1.06
Perrysburg (village) Cattaraugus County	4	1.04
Minetto (town) Oswego County	12	0.72
Batavia (town) Genesee County	35	0.59
Stony Brook (cdp) Suffolk County	65	0.48
Port Jefferson (village) Suffolk County	35	0.45
Whitesboro (village) Oneida County	18	0.45
Perrysburg (town) Cattaraugus County	8	0.45

Top 10 Places Sorted by Percent
Based on places with populations of 10,000 or more

Place	Number	%
Stony Brook (cdp) Suffolk County	65	0.48
North Castle (town) Westchester County	37	0.34
Mamaroneck (village) Westchester County	44	0.23
Kenmore (village) Erie County	35	0.21
Massapequa (cdp) Nassau County	44	0.19
Hauppauge (cdp) Suffolk County	37	0.18
Greenburgh (town) Westchester County	147	0.17
Alden (town) Erie County	18	0.17
Harrison (village) Westchester County	39	0.16
Aurora (town) Erie County	22	0.16

Canadian

Top 10 Places Sorted by Number
Based on all places, regardless of population

Place	Number	%
New York (city) New York City	9,744	0.12
Hempstead (town) Nassau County	1,319	0.17
Brookhaven (town) Suffolk County	1,179	0.26
Amherst (town) Erie County	985	0.85
Buffalo (city) Erie County	753	0.26
Oyster Bay (town) Nassau County	583	0.20
Islip (town) Suffolk County	583	0.18

Notes: (cdp) census designated place; Refer to the User's Guide in the front of the book for more detailed information.

Place	Number	%
Greece (town) Monroe County	516	0.55
Rochester (city) Monroe County	492	0.22
Syracuse (city) Onondaga County	435	0.30

Top 10 Places Sorted by Percent
Based on all places, regardless of population

Place	Number	%
Parc (cdp) Clinton County	11	22.45
Brewster Hill (cdp) Putnam County	121	5.54
La Fargeville (cdp) Jefferson County	32	5.38
Smyrna (village) Chenango County	12	5.11
Mooers (cdp) Clinton County	19	4.73
Newcomb (town) Essex County	22	4.53
Copake Lake (cdp) Columbia County	32	3.96
Morehouse (town) Hamilton County	5	3.91
Redwood (cdp) Jefferson County	24	3.70
Champlain (village) Clinton County	44	3.66

Top 10 Places Sorted by Percent
Based on places with populations of 10,000 or more

Place	Number	%
Lewiston (town) Niagara County	291	1.79
Grand Island (town) Erie County	272	1.46
Ogdensburg (city) Saint Lawrence County	178	1.44
Massena (town) Saint Lawrence County	182	1.39
Massena (village) Saint Lawrence County	146	1.30
Canton (town) Saint Lawrence County	127	1.23
Plattsburgh (town) Clinton County	132	1.19
Watertown (city) Jefferson County	289	1.08
Rye (city) Westchester County	155	1.04
Ogden (town) Monroe County	183	0.99

Carpatho Rusyn

Top 10 Places Sorted by Number
Based on all places, regardless of population

Place	Number	%
New York (city) New York City	138	0.00
Union (town) Broome County	62	0.11
Binghamton (city) Broome County	52	0.11
Owego (town) Tioga County	38	0.19
Johnson City (village) Broome County	30	0.19
New Baltimore (town) Greene County	24	0.71
Chenango (town) Broome County	20	0.17
Endwell (cdp) Broome County	20	0.17
Bardonia (cdp) Rockland County	18	0.41
Clarkstown (town) Rockland County	18	0.02

Top 10 Places Sorted by Percent
Based on all places, regardless of population

Place	Number	%
New Baltimore (town) Greene County	24	0.71
Youngstown (village) Niagara County	9	0.46
Whitney Point (village) Broome County	4	0.42
Bardonia (cdp) Rockland County	18	0.41
Chester (village) Orange County	14	0.39
Skaneateles (village) Onondaga County	7	0.26
Melrose Park (cdp) Cayuga County	5	0.21
Sherburne (village) Chenango County	3	0.21
Owego (town) Tioga County	38	0.19
Johnson City (village) Broome County	30	0.19

Top 10 Places Sorted by Percent
Based on places with populations of 10,000 or more

Place	Number	%
Owego (town) Tioga County	38	0.19
Johnson City (village) Broome County	30	0.19
Chenango (town) Broome County	20	0.17
Endwell (cdp) Broome County	20	0.17
Chester (town) Orange County	14	0.12
Union (town) Broome County	62	0.11
Binghamton (city) Broome County	52	0.11

Place	Number	%
Endicott (village) Broome County	12	0.09
Schodack (town) Rensselaer County	7	0.06
Middletown (city) Orange County	12	0.05

Celtic

Top 10 Places Sorted by Number
Based on all places, regardless of population

Place	Number	%
New York (city) New York City	836	0.01
Syracuse (city) Onondaga County	106	0.07
Brookhaven (town) Suffolk County	98	0.02
Rochester (city) Monroe County	80	0.04
Hempstead (town) Nassau County	78	0.01
Albany (city) Albany County	68	0.07
Buffalo (city) Erie County	65	0.02
Horseheads (town) Chemung County	60	0.31
Islip (town) Suffolk County	60	0.02
Oyster Bay (town) Nassau County	57	0.02

Top 10 Places Sorted by Percent
Based on all places, regardless of population

Place	Number	%
Accord (cdp) Ulster County	22	3.11
Verplanck (cdp) Westchester County	14	1.89
Bellerose (village) Nassau County	22	1.88
Horseheads North (cdp) Chemung County	44	1.52
Montgomery (village) Orange County	48	1.35
Brushton (village) Franklin County	6	1.25
Alexander (village) Genesee County	6	1.24
Wells (town) Hamilton County	8	1.09
Wynantskill (cdp) Rensselaer County	31	0.99
Sand Ridge (cdp) Oswego County	8	0.94

Top 10 Places Sorted by Percent
Based on places with populations of 10,000 or more

Place	Number	%
Horseheads (town) Chemung County	60	0.31
North Greenbush (town) Rensselaer County	31	0.29
Montgomery (town) Orange County	48	0.23
Endicott (village) Broome County	29	0.22
Stony Brook (cdp) Suffolk County	27	0.20
Hauppauge (cdp) Suffolk County	37	0.18
Tarrytown (village) Westchester County	20	0.18
Saint James (cdp) Suffolk County	23	0.17
Corning (city) Steuben County	18	0.17
Cortland (city) Cortland County	30	0.16

Croatian

Top 10 Places Sorted by Number
Based on all places, regardless of population

Place	Number	%
New York (city) New York City	11,948	0.15
Hempstead (town) Nassau County	1,092	0.14
Oyster Bay (town) Nassau County	1,051	0.36
North Hempstead (town) Nassau County	667	0.30
Brookhaven (town) Suffolk County	533	0.12
Hamburg (town) Erie County	458	0.82
Huntington (town) Suffolk County	398	0.20
Buffalo (city) Erie County	363	0.12
Tonawanda (town) Erie County	338	0.43
Lackawanna (city) Erie County	273	1.43

Top 10 Places Sorted by Percent
Based on all places, regardless of population

Place	Number	%
Napeague (cdp) Suffolk County	10	4.33
East Norwich (cdp) Nassau County	68	2.54
North Lynbrook (cdp) Nassau County	14	2.14
Muttontown (village) Nassau County	67	1.98
North Boston (cdp) Erie County	41	1.49

Place	Number	%
Lackawanna (city) Erie County	273	1.43
Manorhaven (village) Nassau County	83	1.35
Sea Cliff (village) Nassau County	65	1.28
Old Westbury (village) Nassau County	51	1.20
Billington Heights (cdp) Erie County	21	1.16

Top 10 Places Sorted by Percent
Based on places with populations of 10,000 or more

Place	Number	%
Lackawanna (city) Erie County	273	1.43
Hamburg (town) Erie County	458	0.82
Floral Park (village) Nassau County	123	0.77
Orchard Park (town) Erie County	205	0.74
Hamburg (village) Erie County	75	0.74
Plainview (cdp) Nassau County	176	0.69
North New Hyde Park (cdp) Nassau County	99	0.68
Tonawanda (city) Erie County	102	0.63
Port Washington (cdp) Nassau County	93	0.61
Pelham (town) Westchester County	71	0.60

Cypriot

Top 10 Places Sorted by Number
Based on all places, regardless of population

Place	Number	%
New York (city) New York City	1,397	0.02
Hempstead (town) Nassau County	203	0.03
Oyster Bay (town) Nassau County	165	0.06
Brookhaven (town) Suffolk County	137	0.03
Huntington (town) Suffolk County	120	0.06
North Hempstead (town) Nassau County	76	0.03
Yonkers (city) Westchester County	73	0.04
Hicksville (cdp) Nassau County	72	0.17
Salisbury (cdp) Nassau County	51	0.41
Greenburgh (town) Westchester County	47	0.05

Top 10 Places Sorted by Percent
Based on all places, regardless of population

Place	Number	%
Rock Hill (cdp) Sullivan County	12	1.22
Southampton (village) Suffolk County	37	0.93
University Gardens (cdp) Nassau County	28	0.68
Atlantic Beach (village) Nassau County	12	0.61
Barnum Island (cdp) Nassau County	11	0.46
Salisbury (cdp) Nassau County	51	0.41
South Hempstead (cdp) Nassau County	12	0.38
Nelsonville (village) Putnam County	2	0.36
Munsey Park (village) Nassau County	9	0.34
West Hills (cdp) Suffolk County	17	0.30

Top 10 Places Sorted by Percent
Based on places with populations of 10,000 or more

Place	Number	%
Salisbury (cdp) Nassau County	51	0.41
Seaford (cdp) Nassau County	39	0.25
Ridge (cdp) Suffolk County	28	0.21
East Rockaway (village) Nassau County	22	0.21
Lake Grove (village) Suffolk County	22	0.21
Holtsville (cdp) Suffolk County	30	0.18
Hicksville (cdp) Nassau County	72	0.17
Thompson (town) Sullivan County	21	0.15
Glen Cove (city) Nassau County	37	0.14
Dix Hills (cdp) Suffolk County	33	0.13

Czech

Top 10 Places Sorted by Number
Based on all places, regardless of population

Place	Number	%
New York (city) New York City	10,659	0.13
Brookhaven (town) Suffolk County	2,115	0.47
Hempstead (town) Nassau County	1,842	0.24

Notes: (cdp) census designated place; Refer to the User's Guide in the front of the book for more detailed information.

PROFILES OF NEW YORK / Ancestry: Rankings

Place	Number	%
Islip (town) Suffolk County	1,662	0.52
Oyster Bay (town) Nassau County	1,287	0.44
Huntington (town) Suffolk County	1,006	0.52
North Hempstead (town) Nassau County	679	0.31
Babylon (town) Suffolk County	609	0.29
Smithtown (town) Suffolk County	593	0.51
Union (town) Broome County	535	0.95

Top 10 Places Sorted by Percent
Based on all places, regardless of population

Place	Number	%
Halcott (town) Greene County	7	3.27
Horseheads North (cdp) Chemung County	90	3.11
Panama (village) Chautauqua County	14	2.86
Alden (village) Erie County	75	2.81
Shokan (cdp) Ulster County	30	2.52
Burlington (town) Otsego County	27	2.48
Walker Valley (cdp) Ulster County	20	2.41
Cold Brook (village) Herkimer County	8	2.29
East Kingston (cdp) Ulster County	6	2.29
Hardenburgh (town) Ulster County	5	2.28

Top 10 Places Sorted by Percent
Based on places with populations of 10,000 or more

Place	Number	%
East Islip (cdp) Suffolk County	191	1.36
Hampton Bays (cdp) Suffolk County	150	1.23
Chenango (town) Broome County	136	1.19
Miller Place (cdp) Suffolk County	125	1.17
Sayville (cdp) Suffolk County	193	1.15
Glenville (town) Schenectady County	316	1.13
Vestal (town) Broome County	274	1.03
Johnson City (village) Broome County	150	0.97
Union (town) Broome County	535	0.95
Horseheads (town) Chemung County	184	0.94

Czechoslovakian

Top 10 Places Sorted by Number
Based on all places, regardless of population

Place	Number	%
New York (city) New York City	8,154	0.10
Hempstead (town) Nassau County	1,549	0.20
Brookhaven (town) Suffolk County	1,281	0.29
Islip (town) Suffolk County	922	0.29
Oyster Bay (town) Nassau County	823	0.28
Union (town) Broome County	709	1.26
Huntington (town) Suffolk County	631	0.32
North Hempstead (town) Nassau County	517	0.23
Babylon (town) Suffolk County	474	0.22
Yonkers (city) Westchester County	453	0.23

Top 10 Places Sorted by Percent
Based on all places, regardless of population

Place	Number	%
Ocean Beach (village) Suffolk County	6	4.62
Stark (town) Herkimer County	15	1.96
Piercefield (town) Saint Lawrence County	6	1.91
Benson (town) Hamilton County	4	1.90
Conklin (town) Broome County	106	1.78
North Collins (village) Erie County	19	1.76
Bleecker (town) Fulton County	10	1.68
Fire Island (cdp) Suffolk County	5	1.64
Rosendale Village (cdp) Ulster County	21	1.60
Sharon Springs (village) Schoharie County	8	1.60

Top 10 Places Sorted by Percent
Based on places with populations of 10,000 or more

Place	Number	%
Endwell (cdp) Broome County	157	1.34
Union (town) Broome County	709	1.26
Johnson City (village) Broome County	182	1.17

Place	Number	%
Chenango (town) Broome County	121	1.06
Endicott (village) Broome County	109	0.84
Stony Brook (cdp) Suffolk County	109	0.80
Vestal (town) Broome County	209	0.79
Milton (town) Saratoga County	130	0.76
Owego (town) Tioga County	152	0.75
Mineola (village) Nassau County	139	0.72

Danish

Top 10 Places Sorted by Number
Based on all places, regardless of population

Place	Number	%
New York (city) New York City	7,460	0.09
Brookhaven (town) Suffolk County	1,660	0.37
Hempstead (town) Nassau County	1,279	0.17
Oyster Bay (town) Nassau County	782	0.27
Islip (town) Suffolk County	623	0.19
Huntington (town) Suffolk County	587	0.30
Babylon (town) Suffolk County	545	0.26
North Hempstead (town) Nassau County	423	0.19
Milo (town) Yates County	421	6.08
Smithtown (town) Suffolk County	394	0.34

Top 10 Places Sorted by Percent
Based on all places, regardless of population

Place	Number	%
Benton (town) Yates County	245	9.35
Torrey (town) Yates County	94	7.19
Penn Yan (village) Yates County	359	6.94
Milo (town) Yates County	421	6.08
Rifton (cdp) Ulster County	28	6.02
Seneca (town) Ontario County	131	4.87
Valley Falls (village) Rensselaer County	21	4.35
High Falls (cdp) Ulster County	26	4.30
Geneva (city) Ontario County	140	4.25
Burdett (village) Schuyler County	15	4.18

Top 10 Places Sorted by Percent
Based on places with populations of 10,000 or more

Place	Number	%
Brunswick (town) Rensselaer County	216	1.84
Hamburg (village) Erie County	121	1.20
Stony Brook (cdp) Suffolk County	159	1.16
Setauket-East Setauket (cdp) Suffolk County	170	1.07
Tarrytown (village) Westchester County	115	1.04
Red Hook (town) Dutchess County	100	0.96
Lake Grove (village) Suffolk County	98	0.94
Glenville (town) Schenectady County	247	0.88
Dryden (town) Tompkins County	117	0.85
Canandaigua (city) Ontario County	95	0.84

Dutch

Top 10 Places Sorted by Number
Based on all places, regardless of population

Place	Number	%
New York (city) New York City	19,402	0.24
Brookhaven (town) Suffolk County	4,271	0.95
Hempstead (town) Nassau County	3,964	0.52
Rochester (city) Monroe County	3,627	1.65
Colonie (town) Albany County	2,859	3.61
Greece (town) Monroe County	2,776	2.95
Arcadia (town) Wayne County	2,672	17.80
Islip (town) Suffolk County	2,588	0.80
Syracuse (city) Onondaga County	2,244	1.52
Schenectady (city) Schenectady County	2,070	3.34

Top 10 Places Sorted by Percent
Based on all places, regardless of population

Place	Number	%
Morehouse (town) Hamilton County	43	33.59

Place	Number	%
Clymer (town) Chautauqua County	390	25.00
Marion (town) Wayne County	1,058	21.26
Clifton Springs (village) Ontario County	424	19.05
Sodus (town) Wayne County	1,729	19.32
Sodus (village) Wayne County	332	19.12
Williamson (town) Wayne County	1,280	18.89
Phelps (village) Ontario County	349	17.96
Arcadia (town) Wayne County	2,672	17.80
Hope (town) Hamilton County	67	17.36

Top 10 Places Sorted by Percent
Based on places with populations of 10,000 or more

Place	Number	%
Arcadia (town) Wayne County	2,672	17.80
Saugerties (town) Ulster County	1,508	7.63
Schodack (town) Rensselaer County	945	7.54
Canandaigua (city) Ontario County	717	6.37
Gloversville (city) Fulton County	930	6.03
Ulster (town) Ulster County	749	5.97
Farmington (town) Ontario County	623	5.89
Catskill (town) Greene County	659	5.56
Rotterdam (town) Schenectady County	1,538	5.42
East Greenbush (town) Rensselaer County	827	5.30

Eastern European

Top 10 Places Sorted by Number
Based on all places, regardless of population

Place	Number	%
New York (city) New York City	30,570	0.38
Hempstead (town) Nassau County	3,765	0.50
North Hempstead (town) Nassau County	2,251	1.01
Oyster Bay (town) Nassau County	2,156	0.73
Greenburgh (town) Westchester County	1,338	1.54
Ramapo (town) Rockland County	1,193	1.10
Huntington (town) Suffolk County	1,175	0.60
Brookhaven (town) Suffolk County	836	0.19
Clarkstown (town) Rockland County	818	1.00
New Rochelle (city) Westchester County	703	0.97

Top 10 Places Sorted by Percent
Based on all places, regardless of population

Place	Number	%
Kensington (village) Nassau County	82	6.75
Sands Point (village) Nassau County	159	5.76
Larchmont (village) Westchester County	330	5.09
Hillside (cdp) Ulster County	42	4.58
Scotts Corners (cdp) Westchester County	26	4.51
Russell Gardens (village) Nassau County	48	4.47
Rye Brook (village) Westchester County	368	4.27
East Hills (village) Nassau County	287	4.18
Hewlett Bay Park (village) Nassau County	20	4.12
New Castle (town) Westchester County	689	3.94

Top 10 Places Sorted by Percent
Based on places with populations of 10,000 or more

Place	Number	%
New Castle (town) Westchester County	689	3.94
Scarsdale (village) Westchester County	647	3.63
Jericho (cdp) Nassau County	377	2.90
Woodmere (cdp) Nassau County	441	2.68
Plainview (cdp) Nassau County	652	2.54
North Castle (town) Westchester County	247	2.28
Lewisboro (town) Westchester County	226	1.83
Mamaroneck (town) Westchester County	527	1.82
New City (cdp) Rockland County	594	1.74
Monsey (cdp) Rockland County	251	1.71

Notes: (cdp) census designated place; Refer to the User's Guide in the front of the book for more detailed information.

PROFILES OF NEW YORK / Ancestry: Rankings

English

Top 10 Places Sorted by Number
Based on all places, regardless of population

Place	Number	%
New York (city) New York City	124,821	1.56
Brookhaven (town) Suffolk County	26,741	5.97
Hempstead (town) Nassau County	23,832	3.15
Islip (town) Suffolk County	14,592	4.52
Oyster Bay (town) Nassau County	13,218	4.50
Rochester (city) Monroe County	12,677	5.77
Huntington (town) Suffolk County	12,454	6.38
Amherst (town) Erie County	11,843	10.16
Buffalo (city) Erie County	11,765	4.02
Greece (town) Monroe County	11,642	12.37

Top 10 Places Sorted by Percent
Based on all places, regardless of population

Place	Number	%
Dering Harbor (village) Suffolk County	5	38.46
Speculator (village) Hamilton County	107	35.08
McGraw (village) Cortland County	317	31.99
Wyoming (village) Wyoming County	158	31.85
Barker (village) Niagara County	173	29.98
Milford (village) Otsego County	152	29.92
Sagaponack (cdp) Suffolk County	161	29.70
Barneveld (village) Oneida County	99	29.46
Lisle (village) Broome County	88	29.24
Middlebury (town) Wyoming County	436	29.12

Top 10 Places Sorted by Percent
Based on places with populations of 10,000 or more

Place	Number	%
Parma (town) Monroe County	3,027	20.40
Dryden (town) Tompkins County	2,752	20.09
Sullivan (town) Madison County	2,979	19.87
Lysander (town) Onondaga County	3,756	19.48
Farmington (town) Ontario County	2,020	19.08
Canandaigua (city) Ontario County	2,131	18.92
Aurora (town) Erie County	2,530	18.08
Kirkland (town) Oneida County	1,833	18.08
Owego (town) Tioga County	3,658	17.96
Lansing (town) Tompkins County	1,836	17.83

Estonian

Top 10 Places Sorted by Number
Based on all places, regardless of population

Place	Number	%
New York (city) New York City	883	0.01
Hempstead (town) Nassau County	203	0.03
Brookhaven (town) Suffolk County	161	0.04
Clarence (town) Erie County	62	0.24
Perinton (town) Monroe County	60	0.13
Amherst (town) Erie County	57	0.05
Oyster Bay (town) Nassau County	56	0.02
North Hempstead (town) Nassau County	49	0.02
Islip (town) Suffolk County	48	0.01
Clarkstown (town) Rockland County	46	0.06

Top 10 Places Sorted by Percent
Based on all places, regardless of population

Place	Number	%
Preston (town) Chenango County	13	1.36
Shelter Island (town) Suffolk County	24	1.08
Greenport West (cdp) Suffolk County	11	0.66
Greenwood Lake (village) Orange County	21	0.63
Shinnecock Hills (cdp) Suffolk County	11	0.61
Somerset (town) Niagara County	16	0.56
Millbrook (village) Dutchess County	8	0.56
Fair Haven (village) Cayuga County	5	0.56
Shelter Island Heights (cdp) Suffolk County	5	0.51

| Tappan (cdp) Rockland County | 32 | 0.48 |

Top 10 Places Sorted by Percent
Based on places with populations of 10,000 or more

Place	Number	%
Brunswick (town) Rensselaer County	36	0.31
Clarence (town) Erie County	62	0.24
Schodack (town) Rensselaer County	29	0.23
Jefferson Valley-Yorktown (cdp) Westchester County	25	0.17
East Hampton (town) Suffolk County	30	0.15
Lynbrook (village) Nassau County	30	0.15
Stony Brook (cdp) Suffolk County	21	0.15
Perinton (town) Monroe County	60	0.13
Bay Shore (cdp) Suffolk County	32	0.13
De Witt (town) Onondaga County	31	0.13

European

Top 10 Places Sorted by Number
Based on all places, regardless of population

Place	Number	%
New York (city) New York City	32,892	0.41
Hempstead (town) Nassau County	3,388	0.45
Oyster Bay (town) Nassau County	1,925	0.65
Ramapo (town) Rockland County	1,745	1.60
North Hempstead (town) Nassau County	1,399	0.63
Brookhaven (town) Suffolk County	1,270	0.28
Huntington (town) Suffolk County	1,178	0.60
Rochester (city) Monroe County	1,007	0.46
Greenburgh (town) Westchester County	756	0.87
Islip (town) Suffolk County	755	0.23

Top 10 Places Sorted by Percent
Based on all places, regardless of population

Place	Number	%
New Hudson (town) Allegany County	62	8.45
Kaser (village) Rockland County	219	6.64
Orwell (town) Oswego County	81	6.42
La Fargeville (cdp) Jefferson County	38	6.39
Danby (town) Tompkins County	190	6.20
Clare (town) Saint Lawrence County	6	5.13
Monsey (cdp) Rockland County	662	4.51
Fremont (town) Sullivan County	60	4.31
New Suffolk (cdp) Suffolk County	14	4.29
Cove Neck (village) Nassau County	11	4.20

Top 10 Places Sorted by Percent
Based on places with populations of 10,000 or more

Place	Number	%
Monsey (cdp) Rockland County	662	4.51
Woodmere (cdp) Nassau County	418	2.54
New Castle (town) Westchester County	404	2.31
Ithaca (city) Tompkins County	630	2.17
Scarsdale (village) Westchester County	350	1.96
Lansing (town) Tompkins County	191	1.85
Plainview (cdp) Nassau County	432	1.69
Dryden (town) Tompkins County	229	1.67
Fulton (city) Oswego County	193	1.63
New Paltz (town) Ulster County	208	1.62

Finnish

Top 10 Places Sorted by Number
Based on all places, regardless of population

Place	Number	%
New York (city) New York City	3,466	0.04
Brookhaven (town) Suffolk County	872	0.19
Hempstead (town) Nassau County	574	0.08
Islip (town) Suffolk County	379	0.12
Huntington (town) Suffolk County	341	0.17
Oyster Bay (town) Nassau County	312	0.11

Smithtown (town) Suffolk County	264	0.23
Ithaca (town) Tompkins County	175	0.95
Babylon (town) Suffolk County	162	0.08
Southampton (town) Suffolk County	154	0.28

Top 10 Places Sorted by Percent
Based on all places, regardless of population

Place	Number	%
Van Etten (village) Chemung County	44	7.69
Van Etten (town) Chemung County	100	6.71
Spencer (village) Tioga County	39	5.32
Ward (town) Allegany County	17	4.10
Spencer (town) Tioga County	113	3.79
Benson (town) Hamilton County	7	3.33
Baldwin (town) Chemung County	27	3.17
Newfield (town) Tompkins County	138	2.75
Danby (town) Tompkins County	83	2.71
Millport (village) Chemung County	7	2.36

Top 10 Places Sorted by Percent
Based on places with populations of 10,000 or more

Place	Number	%
Ithaca (town) Tompkins County	175	0.95
Dryden (town) Tompkins County	114	0.83
Lansing (town) Tompkins County	71	0.69
Stony Brook (cdp) Suffolk County	90	0.66
Van Buren (town) Onondaga County	78	0.62
Bedford (town) Westchester County	92	0.51
East Rockaway (village) Nassau County	51	0.49
Ithaca (city) Tompkins County	136	0.47
Southeast (town) Putnam County	82	0.47
West Islip (cdp) Suffolk County	131	0.45

French, except Basque

Top 10 Places Sorted by Number
Based on all places, regardless of population

Place	Number	%
New York (city) New York City	52,907	0.66
Brookhaven (town) Suffolk County	9,044	2.02
Hempstead (town) Nassau County	8,604	1.14
Syracuse (city) Onondaga County	6,203	4.21
Buffalo (city) Erie County	5,292	1.81
Colonie (town) Albany County	5,256	6.63
Islip (town) Suffolk County	4,982	1.54
Rochester (city) Monroe County	4,561	2.08
Troy (city) Rensselaer County	4,490	9.13
Clay (town) Onondaga County	4,167	7.09

Top 10 Places Sorted by Percent
Based on all places, regardless of population

Place	Number	%
Bellmont (town) Franklin County	783	54.22
Tupper Lake (village) Franklin County	1,962	50.14
Duane (town) Franklin County	65	47.10
Altamont (town) Franklin County	2,789	45.45
Chesterfield (town) Essex County	1,009	41.88
Brandon (town) Franklin County	223	41.68
Waverly (town) Franklin County	456	41.53
Dickinson (town) Franklin County	270	36.19
Brushton (village) Franklin County	171	35.63
Harrisville (village) Lewis County	232	34.99

Top 10 Places Sorted by Percent
Based on places with populations of 10,000 or more

Place	Number	%
Massena (village) Saint Lawrence County	2,901	25.85
Massena (town) Saint Lawrence County	3,373	25.71
Plattsburgh (town) Clinton County	2,705	24.31
Ogdensburg (city) Saint Lawrence County	2,571	20.80
Kingsbury (town) Washington County	2,289	20.49
Plattsburgh (city) Clinton County	3,840	20.48

Notes: (cdp) census designated place; Refer to the User's Guide in the front of the book for more detailed information.

Place	Number	%
Cohoes (city) Albany County	2,984	19.23
Malone (town) Franklin County	2,620	17.49
Glens Falls (city) Warren County	2,450	16.96
Moreau (town) Saratoga County	2,248	16.26

French Canadian

Top 10 Places Sorted by Number
Based on all places, regardless of population

Place	Number	%
New York (city) New York City	10,645	0.13
Brookhaven (town) Suffolk County	2,741	0.61
Syracuse (city) Onondaga County	2,539	1.72
Colonie (town) Albany County	2,452	3.09
Hempstead (town) Nassau County	1,971	0.26
Greece (town) Monroe County	1,640	1.74
Plattsburgh (city) Clinton County	1,622	8.65
Rochester (city) Monroe County	1,568	0.71
Plattsburgh (town) Clinton County	1,554	13.97
Islip (town) Suffolk County	1,534	0.48

Top 10 Places Sorted by Percent
Based on all places, regardless of population

Place	Number	%
Parc (cdp) Clinton County	17	34.69
Mooers (town) Clinton County	718	21.09
Rouses Point (village) Clinton County	484	20.95
Champlain (town) Clinton County	1,135	19.60
Piercefield (town) Saint Lawrence County	59	18.79
Champlain (village) Clinton County	218	18.14
Fort Covington (town) Franklin County	285	17.28
Depauville (cdp) Jefferson County	84	16.97
Clinton (town) Clinton County	124	16.51
Saranac (town) Clinton County	621	14.91

Top 10 Places Sorted by Percent
Based on places with populations of 10,000 or more

Place	Number	%
Plattsburgh (town) Clinton County	1,554	13.97
Massena (village) Saint Lawrence County	1,154	10.28
Massena (town) Saint Lawrence County	1,265	9.64
Plattsburgh (city) Clinton County	1,622	8.65
Malone (town) Franklin County	1,292	8.62
Ogdensburg (city) Saint Lawrence County	996	8.06
Cohoes (city) Albany County	1,177	7.58
Potsdam (town) Saint Lawrence County	920	5.77
Kingsbury (town) Washington County	641	5.74
Watertown (city) Jefferson County	1,365	5.11

German

Top 10 Places Sorted by Number
Based on all places, regardless of population

Place	Number	%
New York (city) New York City	255,536	3.19
Brookhaven (town) Suffolk County	87,375	19.49
Hempstead (town) Nassau County	87,201	11.54
Islip (town) Suffolk County	47,823	14.82
Oyster Bay (town) Nassau County	42,703	14.53
Buffalo (city) Erie County	39,692	13.56
Babylon (town) Suffolk County	31,723	14.98
Huntington (town) Suffolk County	31,620	16.19
Amherst (town) Erie County	29,827	25.60
Cheektowaga (town) Erie County	28,147	29.94

Top 10 Places Sorted by Percent
Based on all places, regardless of population

Place	Number	%
Sheldon (town) Wyoming County	1,385	54.06
Croghan (town) Lewis County	1,669	51.54
New Bremen (town) Lewis County	1,286	48.68
Phoenicia (cdp) Ulster County	192	47.76
Croghan (village) Lewis County	325	46.63
Darien (town) Genesee County	1,400	45.99
Otto (town) Cattaraugus County	376	45.97
Pendleton (town) Niagara County	2,717	44.91
Alabama (town) Genesee County	927	44.72
Alexander (village) Genesee County	216	44.72

Top 10 Places Sorted by Percent
Based on places with populations of 10,000 or more

Place	Number	%
Aurora (town) Erie County	5,502	39.31
Lancaster (village) Erie County	4,285	38.30
Alden (town) Erie County	3,964	37.86
Tonawanda (city) Erie County	6,090	37.74
Wheatfield (town) Niagara County	5,103	36.23
Hamburg (village) Erie County	3,649	36.10
Clarence (town) Erie County	9,289	35.56
Lancaster (town) Erie County	13,820	35.42
North Tonawanda (city) Niagara County	11,748	35.32
Evans (town) Erie County	6,173	35.09

German Russian

Top 10 Places Sorted by Number
Based on all places, regardless of population

Place	Number	%
New York (city) New York City	110	0.00
Horseheads North (cdp) Chemung County	25	0.86
Horseheads (town) Chemung County	25	0.13
Hempstead (village) Nassau County	18	0.03
Hempstead (town) Nassau County	18	0.00
Hillburn (village) Rockland County	15	1.91
Ramapo (town) Rockland County	15	0.01
Albany (city) Albany County	12	0.01
West Haverstraw (village) Rockland County	11	0.11
Haverstraw (town) Rockland County	11	0.03

Top 10 Places Sorted by Percent
Based on all places, regardless of population

Place	Number	%
Hillburn (village) Rockland County	15	1.91
Horseheads North (cdp) Chemung County	25	0.86
Middleburgh (village) Schoharie County	7	0.50
Chester (village) Orange County	10	0.28
Middleburgh (town) Schoharie County	7	0.20
Victory (village) Saratoga County	1	0.19
Wayne (town) Steuben County	2	0.17
Boonville (village) Oneida County	3	0.14
Horseheads (town) Chemung County	25	0.13
West Haverstraw (village) Rockland County	11	0.11

Top 10 Places Sorted by Percent
Based on places with populations of 10,000 or more

Place	Number	%
Horseheads (town) Chemung County	25	0.13
West Haverstraw (village) Rockland County	11	0.11
Chester (town) Orange County	10	0.08
Mastic Beach (cdp) Suffolk County	9	0.08
Beacon (city) Dutchess County	9	0.07
Red Hook (town) Dutchess County	6	0.06
Hempstead (village) Nassau County	18	0.03
Haverstraw (town) Rockland County	11	0.03
Cortlandt (town) Westchester County	10	0.03
White Plains (city) Westchester County	11	0.02

Greek

Top 10 Places Sorted by Number
Based on all places, regardless of population

Place	Number	%
New York (city) New York City	80,145	1.00
Hempstead (town) Nassau County	10,576	1.40
Brookhaven (town) Suffolk County	6,580	1.47
Oyster Bay (town) Nassau County	5,932	2.02
North Hempstead (town) Nassau County	3,529	1.55
Huntington (town) Suffolk County	3,492	1.79
Islip (town) Suffolk County	2,970	0.92
Babylon (town) Suffolk County	2,273	1.07
Smithtown (town) Suffolk County	1,843	1.59
Yonkers (city) Westchester County	1,563	0.80

Top 10 Places Sorted by Percent
Based on all places, regardless of population

Place	Number	%
Malden (cdp) Ulster County	64	13.11
Plandome Manor (village) Nassau County	79	9.43
Halcott (town) Greene County	18	8.41
East Marion (cdp) Suffolk County	52	6.70
Munsey Park (village) Nassau County	171	6.50
Harbor Isle (cdp) Nassau County	79	5.59
Great Neck Gardens (cdp) Nassau County	62	5.55
Upper Brookville (village) Nassau County	94	5.20
Barnum Island (cdp) Nassau County	121	5.02
Tannersville (village) Greene County	22	4.78

Top 10 Places Sorted by Percent
Based on places with populations of 10,000 or more

Place	Number	%
Terryville (cdp) Suffolk County	453	4.28
Bethpage (cdp) Nassau County	573	3.46
Garden City (village) Nassau County	691	3.19
Commack (cdp) Suffolk County	1,083	2.98
Hicksville (cdp) Nassau County	1,103	2.67
North Bellmore (cdp) Nassau County	533	2.65
Miller Place (cdp) Suffolk County	281	2.63
Syosset (cdp) Nassau County	478	2.58
Salisbury (cdp) Nassau County	313	2.54
Rocky Point (cdp) Suffolk County	252	2.46

Guyanese

Top 10 Places Sorted by Number
Based on all places, regardless of population

Place	Number	%
New York (city) New York City	99,537	1.24
Hempstead (town) Nassau County	3,420	0.45
Elmont (cdp) Nassau County	603	1.85
Mount Vernon (city) Westchester County	568	0.83
Islip (town) Suffolk County	553	0.17
Hempstead (village) Nassau County	503	0.89
Babylon (town) Suffolk County	502	0.24
Yonkers (city) Westchester County	426	0.22
Brookhaven (town) Suffolk County	423	0.09
Schenectady (city) Schenectady County	355	0.57

Top 10 Places Sorted by Percent
Based on all places, regardless of population

Place	Number	%
East Garden City (cdp) Nassau County	47	4.72
North Lynbrook (cdp) Nassau County	22	3.36
Bellerose Terrace (cdp) Nassau County	54	2.50
Gordon Heights (cdp) Suffolk County	64	2.07
Elmont (cdp) Nassau County	603	1.85
South Floral Park (village) Nassau County	26	1.65
Bay Park (cdp) Nassau County	37	1.64
South Valley Stream (cdp) Nassau County	90	1.60
North Valley Stream (cdp) Nassau County	236	1.49
South Hempstead (cdp) Nassau County	42	1.32

Top 10 Places Sorted by Percent
Based on places with populations of 10,000 or more

Place	Number	%
Elmont (cdp) Nassau County	603	1.85
North Valley Stream (cdp) Nassau County	236	1.49

Notes: (cdp) census designated place; Refer to the User's Guide in the front of the book for more detailed information.

Place	Number	%
New York (city) New York City	99,537	1.24
Uniondale (cdp) Nassau County	268	1.16
Roosevelt (cdp) Nassau County	156	0.98
Hempstead (village) Nassau County	503	0.89
Mount Vernon (city) Westchester County	568	0.83
Central Islip (cdp) Suffolk County	244	0.77
Freeport (village) Nassau County	326	0.74
North Amityville (cdp) Suffolk County	119	0.72

Hawaii Native/Pacific Islander

Top 10 Places Sorted by Number
Based on all places, regardless of population

Place	Number	%
New York (city) New York City	19,313	0.24
Hempstead (town) Nassau County	792	0.10
Rochester (city) Monroe County	396	0.18
Yonkers (city) Westchester County	384	0.20
Islip (town) Suffolk County	383	0.12
Brookhaven (town) Suffolk County	332	0.07
Buffalo (city) Erie County	289	0.10
White Plains (city) Westchester County	267	0.50
Ramapo (town) Rockland County	254	0.23
North Hempstead (town) Nassau County	216	0.10

Top 10 Places Sorted by Percent
Based on all places, regardless of population

Place	Number	%
Fort Drum (cdp) Jefferson County	143	1.18
South Hill (cdp) Tompkins County	50	0.83
Le Ray (town) Jefferson County	162	0.82
Greenport (village) Suffolk County	16	0.78
Remsenburg-Speonk (cdp) Suffolk County	19	0.71
Spring Valley (village) Rockland County	175	0.69
Hillburn (village) Rockland County	6	0.68
Richfield Springs (village) Otsego County	8	0.64
Cragsmoor (cdp) Ulster County	3	0.63
Lake Placid (village) Essex County	16	0.61

Top 10 Places Sorted by Percent
Based on places with populations of 10,000 or more

Place	Number	%
Fort Drum (cdp) Jefferson County	143	1.18
Le Ray (town) Jefferson County	162	0.82
Spring Valley (village) Rockland County	175	0.69
White Plains (city) Westchester County	267	0.50
Ithaca (city) Tompkins County	135	0.46
Ithaca (town) Tompkins County	77	0.42
Suffern (village) Rockland County	37	0.34
Red Hook (town) Dutchess County	31	0.30
Elmont (cdp) Nassau County	90	0.28
Mount Vernon (city) Westchester County	185	0.27

Hawaii Native/Pacific Islander: Melanesian

Top 10 Places Sorted by Number
Based on all places, regardless of population

Place	Number	%
New York (city) New York City	339	0.00
Port Washington (cdp) Nassau County	5	0.03
White Plains (city) Westchester County	5	0.01
Brookhaven (town) Suffolk County	5	0.00
Hempstead (town) Nassau County	5	0.00
North Hempstead (town) Nassau County	5	0.00
North Valley Stream (cdp) Nassau County	4	0.03
Setauket-East Setauket (cdp) Suffolk County	4	0.03
Hornell (city) Steuben County	3	0.03
Ogden (town) Monroe County	3	0.02

Top 10 Places Sorted by Percent
Based on all places, regardless of population

Place	Number	%
Lansing (village) Tompkins County	2	0.06
Lake Placid (village) Essex County	1	0.04
Northeast Ithaca (cdp) Tompkins County	1	0.04
Salem (town) Washington County	1	0.04
Port Washington (cdp) Nassau County	5	0.03
North Valley Stream (cdp) Nassau County	4	0.03
Setauket-East Setauket (cdp) Suffolk County	4	0.03
Hornell (city) Steuben County	3	0.03
Cayuga Heights (village) Tompkins County	1	0.03
Ogden (town) Monroe County	3	0.02

Top 10 Places Sorted by Percent
Based on places with populations of 10,000 or more

Place	Number	%
Port Washington (cdp) Nassau County	5	0.03
North Valley Stream (cdp) Nassau County	4	0.03
Setauket-East Setauket (cdp) Suffolk County	4	0.03
Ogden (town) Monroe County	3	0.02
Scarsdale (village) Westchester County	3	0.02
Lansing (town) Tompkins County	2	0.02
White Plains (city) Westchester County	5	0.01
Mamaroneck (town) Westchester County	3	0.01
Ithaca (town) Tompkins County	2	0.01
Mamaroneck (village) Westchester County	2	0.01

Hawaii Native/Pacific Islander: Fijian

Top 10 Places Sorted by Number
Based on all places, regardless of population

Place	Number	%
New York (city) New York City	302	0.00
Port Washington (cdp) Nassau County	5	0.03
White Plains (city) Westchester County	5	0.01
North Hempstead (town) Nassau County	5	0.00
Hornell (city) Steuben County	3	0.03
Ogden (town) Monroe County	3	0.02
Mamaroneck (town) Westchester County	3	0.01
Mamaroneck (village) Westchester County	2	0.01
Hempstead (town) Nassau County	2	0.00
Hicksville (cdp) Nassau County	2	0.00

Top 10 Places Sorted by Percent
Based on all places, regardless of population

Place	Number	%
Lake Placid (village) Essex County	1	0.04
Salem (town) Washington County	1	0.04
Port Washington (cdp) Nassau County	5	0.03
Hornell (city) Steuben County	3	0.03
Ogden (town) Monroe County	3	0.02
Larchmont (village) Westchester County	1	0.02
Little Falls (city) Herkimer County	1	0.02
White Plains (city) Westchester County	5	0.01
Mamaroneck (town) Westchester County	3	0.01
Mamaroneck (village) Westchester County	2	0.01

Top 10 Places Sorted by Percent
Based on places with populations of 10,000 or more

Place	Number	%
Port Washington (cdp) Nassau County	5	0.03
Ogden (town) Monroe County	3	0.02
White Plains (city) Westchester County	5	0.01
Mamaroneck (town) Westchester County	3	0.01
Mamaroneck (village) Westchester County	2	0.01
Goshen (town) Orange County	1	0.01
Monsey (cdp) Rockland County	1	0.01
North Amityville (cdp) Suffolk County	1	0.01
North Valley Stream (cdp) Nassau County	1	0.01
Plattsburgh (city) Clinton County	1	0.01

Hawaii Native/Pacific Islander: Other Melanesian

Top 10 Places Sorted by Number
Based on all places, regardless of population

Place	Number	%
New York (city) New York City	37	0.00
Setauket-East Setauket (cdp) Suffolk County	4	0.03
Brookhaven (town) Suffolk County	4	0.00
North Valley Stream (cdp) Nassau County	3	0.02
Hempstead (town) Nassau County	3	0.00
Lansing (village) Tompkins County	2	0.06
Lansing (town) Tompkins County	2	0.02
Ithaca (town) Tompkins County	2	0.01
Scarsdale (village) Westchester County	2	0.01
Northeast Ithaca (cdp) Tompkins County	1	0.04

Top 10 Places Sorted by Percent
Based on all places, regardless of population

Place	Number	%
Lansing (village) Tompkins County	2	0.06
Northeast Ithaca (cdp) Tompkins County	1	0.04
Setauket-East Setauket (cdp) Suffolk County	4	0.03
Cayuga Heights (village) Tompkins County	1	0.03
North Valley Stream (cdp) Nassau County	3	0.02
Lansing (town) Tompkins County	2	0.02
Ticonderoga (town) Essex County	1	0.02
Ithaca (town) Tompkins County	2	0.01
Scarsdale (village) Westchester County	2	0.01
Oswego (city) Oswego County	1	0.01

Top 10 Places Sorted by Percent
Based on places with populations of 10,000 or more

Place	Number	%
Setauket-East Setauket (cdp) Suffolk County	4	0.03
North Valley Stream (cdp) Nassau County	3	0.02
Lansing (town) Tompkins County	2	0.02
Ithaca (town) Tompkins County	2	0.01
Scarsdale (village) Westchester County	2	0.01
Oswego (city) Oswego County	1	0.01
New York (city) New York City	37	0.00
Brookhaven (town) Suffolk County	4	0.00
Hempstead (town) Nassau County	3	0.00
Brighton (town) Monroe County	1	0.00

Hawaii Native/Pacific Islander: Micronesian

Top 10 Places Sorted by Number
Based on all places, regardless of population

Place	Number	%
New York (city) New York City	1,552	0.02
Islip (town) Suffolk County	87	0.03
Hempstead (town) Nassau County	82	0.01
Spring Valley (village) Rockland County	73	0.29
Clarkstown (town) Rockland County	61	0.07
Yonkers (city) Westchester County	51	0.03
Ramapo (town) Rockland County	46	0.04
Le Ray (town) Jefferson County	44	0.22
Fort Drum (cdp) Jefferson County	41	0.34
Buffalo (city) Erie County	36	0.01

Top 10 Places Sorted by Percent
Based on all places, regardless of population

Place	Number	%
Hillburn (village) Rockland County	6	0.68
Remsenburg-Speonk (cdp) Suffolk County	16	0.60
Lake Placid (village) Essex County	14	0.53
Alexander (village) Genesee County	2	0.42
Forestville (village) Chautauqua County	3	0.39
Unionville (village) Orange County	2	0.37
Fabius (town) Onondaga County	7	0.35

Notes: (cdp) census designated place; Refer to the User's Guide in the front of the book for more detailed information.

Place	Number	%
Watson (town) Lewis County	7	0.35
Fort Drum (cdp) Jefferson County	41	0.34
Wethersfield (town) Wyoming County	3	0.34

Top 10 Places Sorted by Percent
Based on places with populations of 10,000 or more

Place	Number	%
Fort Drum (cdp) Jefferson County	41	0.34
Spring Valley (village) Rockland County	73	0.29
Le Ray (town) Jefferson County	44	0.22
Central Islip (cdp) Suffolk County	30	0.09
Dobbs Ferry (village) Westchester County	9	0.08
Clarkstown (town) Rockland County	61	0.07
Highlands (town) Orange County	9	0.07
Brentwood (cdp) Suffolk County	31	0.06
Mamaroneck (town) Westchester County	16	0.06
Watertown (city) Jefferson County	16	0.06

Hawaii Native/Pacific Islander: Guamanian or Chamorro

Top 10 Places Sorted by Number
Based on all places, regardless of population

Place	Number	%
New York (city) New York City	1,486	0.02
Islip (town) Suffolk County	86	0.03
Hempstead (town) Nassau County	76	0.01
Spring Valley (village) Rockland County	73	0.29
Clarkstown (town) Rockland County	61	0.07
Yonkers (city) Westchester County	50	0.03
Ramapo (town) Rockland County	46	0.04
Buffalo (city) Erie County	35	0.01
Brentwood (cdp) Suffolk County	31	0.06
Central Islip (cdp) Suffolk County	30	0.09

Top 10 Places Sorted by Percent
Based on all places, regardless of population

Place	Number	%
Hillburn (village) Rockland County	6	0.68
Remsenburg-Speonk (cdp) Suffolk County	16	0.60
Alexander (village) Genesee County	2	0.42
Forestville (village) Chautauqua County	3	0.39
Lake Placid (village) Essex County	10	0.38
Unionville (village) Orange County	2	0.37
Fabius (town) Onondaga County	7	0.35
Wethersfield (town) Wyoming County	3	0.34
Springwater (town) Livingston County	7	0.30
Spring Valley (village) Rockland County	73	0.29

Top 10 Places Sorted by Percent
Based on places with populations of 10,000 or more

Place	Number	%
Spring Valley (village) Rockland County	73	0.29
Fort Drum (cdp) Jefferson County	25	0.21
Le Ray (town) Jefferson County	28	0.14
Central Islip (cdp) Suffolk County	30	0.09
Dobbs Ferry (village) Westchester County	9	0.08
Clarkstown (town) Rockland County	61	0.07
Brentwood (cdp) Suffolk County	31	0.06
Watertown (city) Jefferson County	16	0.06
Peekskill (city) Westchester County	14	0.06
Mamaroneck (village) Westchester County	11	0.06

Hawaii Native/Pacific Islander: Other Micronesian

Top 10 Places Sorted by Number
Based on all places, regardless of population

Place	Number	%
New York (city) New York City	66	0.00
Fort Drum (cdp) Jefferson County	16	0.13
Le Ray (town) Jefferson County	16	0.08
Binghamton (city) Broome County	12	0.03
Fairview (cdp) Westchester County	9	0.31
Greenburgh (town) Westchester County	9	0.01
Watson (town) Lewis County	7	0.35
East Fishkill (town) Dutchess County	7	0.03
Hempstead (town) Nassau County	6	0.00
Greenwich (town) Washington County	5	0.10

Top 10 Places Sorted by Percent
Based on all places, regardless of population

Place	Number	%
Watson (town) Lewis County	7	0.35
Fairview (cdp) Westchester County	9	0.31
Huron (town) Wayne County	4	0.19
Lake Katrine (cdp) Ulster County	4	0.17
Lake Placid (village) Essex County	4	0.15
Madison (town) Madison County	4	0.14
Fort Drum (cdp) Jefferson County	16	0.13
Waterville (village) Oneida County	2	0.12
Greenwich (town) Washington County	5	0.10
Geneva (town) Ontario County	3	0.09

Top 10 Places Sorted by Percent
Based on places with populations of 10,000 or more

Place	Number	%
Fort Drum (cdp) Jefferson County	16	0.13
Le Ray (town) Jefferson County	16	0.08
Highlands (town) Orange County	5	0.04
Binghamton (city) Broome County	12	0.03
East Fishkill (town) Dutchess County	7	0.03
Arcadia (town) Wayne County	4	0.03
Ulster (town) Ulster County	4	0.03
Mamaroneck (town) Westchester County	5	0.02
Babylon (village) Suffolk County	3	0.02
Goshen (town) Orange County	2	0.02

Hawaii Native/Pacific Islander: Polynesian

Top 10 Places Sorted by Number
Based on all places, regardless of population

Place	Number	%
New York (city) New York City	3,253	0.04
Hempstead (town) Nassau County	163	0.02
Brookhaven (town) Suffolk County	104	0.02
Rochester (city) Monroe County	102	0.05
Syracuse (city) Onondaga County	99	0.07
Le Ray (town) Jefferson County	88	0.44
Islip (town) Suffolk County	85	0.03
Fort Drum (cdp) Jefferson County	77	0.64
Buffalo (city) Erie County	75	0.03
Yonkers (city) Westchester County	70	0.04

Top 10 Places Sorted by Percent
Based on all places, regardless of population

Place	Number	%
Fort Drum (cdp) Jefferson County	77	0.64
Richfield Springs (village) Otsego County	8	0.64
Le Ray (town) Jefferson County	88	0.44
Stark (town) Herkimer County	3	0.39
West Carthage (village) Jefferson County	8	0.38
Westford (town) Otsego County	3	0.38
New Lebanon (town) Columbia County	9	0.37
Birdsall (town) Allegany County	1	0.37
Lumberland (town) Sullivan County	7	0.36
Gouverneur (village) Saint Lawrence County	15	0.35

Top 10 Places Sorted by Percent
Based on places with populations of 10,000 or more

Place	Number	%
Fort Drum (cdp) Jefferson County	77	0.64
Le Ray (town) Jefferson County	88	0.44
Watertown (city) Jefferson County	35	0.13

Place	Number	%
Arlington (cdp) Dutchess County	16	0.13
Oneonta (city) Otsego County	15	0.11
North Bay Shore (cdp) Suffolk County	15	0.10
Dryden (town) Tompkins County	14	0.10
Highlands (town) Orange County	13	0.10
Ithaca (city) Tompkins County	23	0.08
North Babylon (cdp) Suffolk County	14	0.08

Hawaii Native/Pacific Islander: Native Hawaiian

Top 10 Places Sorted by Number
Based on all places, regardless of population

Place	Number	%
New York (city) New York City	1,864	0.02
Hempstead (town) Nassau County	93	0.01
Brookhaven (town) Suffolk County	63	0.01
Syracuse (city) Onondaga County	60	0.04
Islip (town) Suffolk County	59	0.02
Le Ray (town) Jefferson County	56	0.28
Rochester (city) Monroe County	50	0.02
Babylon (town) Suffolk County	49	0.02
Yonkers (city) Westchester County	46	0.02
Fort Drum (cdp) Jefferson County	45	0.37

Top 10 Places Sorted by Percent
Based on all places, regardless of population

Place	Number	%
Richfield Springs (village) Otsego County	5	0.40
Stark (town) Herkimer County	3	0.39
Fort Drum (cdp) Jefferson County	45	0.37
Birdsall (town) Allegany County	1	0.37
Fire Island (cdp) Suffolk County	1	0.32
Lumberland (town) Sullivan County	6	0.31
Calcium (cdp) Jefferson County	10	0.30
Farmersville (town) Cattaraugus County	3	0.29
Le Ray (town) Jefferson County	56	0.28
Eastport (cdp) Suffolk County	4	0.28

Top 10 Places Sorted by Percent
Based on places with populations of 10,000 or more

Place	Number	%
Fort Drum (cdp) Jefferson County	45	0.37
Le Ray (town) Jefferson County	56	0.28
Arlington (cdp) Dutchess County	14	0.11
Watertown (city) Jefferson County	26	0.10
North Bay Shore (cdp) Suffolk County	14	0.09
Middletown (city) Orange County	18	0.07
Gates-North Gates (cdp) Monroe County	11	0.07
Gloversville (city) Fulton County	11	0.07
Putnam Valley (town) Putnam County	7	0.07
Red Hook (town) Dutchess County	7	0.07

Hawaii Native/Pacific Islander: Samoan

Top 10 Places Sorted by Number
Based on all places, regardless of population

Place	Number	%
New York (city) New York City	1,279	0.02
Hempstead (town) Nassau County	53	0.01
Rochester (city) Monroe County	49	0.02
Brookhaven (town) Suffolk County	38	0.01
Syracuse (city) Onondaga County	35	0.02
Fort Drum (cdp) Jefferson County	30	0.25
Le Ray (town) Jefferson County	30	0.15
North Hempstead (town) Nassau County	26	0.01
Buffalo (city) Erie County	25	0.01
Islip (town) Suffolk County	23	0.01

Notes: (cdp) census designated place; Refer to the User's Guide in the front of the book for more detailed information.

PROFILES OF NEW YORK / Ancestry: Rankings

Top 10 Places Sorted by Percent
Based on all places, regardless of population

Place	Number	%
Westford (town) Otsego County	3	0.38
Castorland (village) Lewis County	1	0.33
Gouverneur (village) Saint Lawrence County	12	0.28
Victory (town) Cayuga County	5	0.27
Tuxedo Park (village) Orange County	2	0.27
Fort Drum (cdp) Jefferson County	30	0.25
Inlet (town) Hamilton County	1	0.25
Caroline (town) Tompkins County	7	0.24
Richfield Springs (village) Otsego County	3	0.24
East Moriches (cdp) Suffolk County	9	0.20

Top 10 Places Sorted by Percent
Based on places with populations of 10,000 or more

Place	Number	%
Fort Drum (cdp) Jefferson County	30	0.25
Le Ray (town) Jefferson County	30	0.15
Oneonta (city) Otsego County	11	0.08
Westbury (village) Nassau County	7	0.05
Dryden (town) Tompkins County	5	0.04
Highlands (town) Orange County	5	0.04
New Paltz (town) Ulster County	5	0.04
West Haverstraw (village) Rockland County	4	0.04
Hempstead (village) Nassau County	16	0.03
Long Beach (city) Nassau County	9	0.03

Hawaii Native/Pacific Islander: Tongan

Top 10 Places Sorted by Number
Based on all places, regardless of population

Place	Number	%
New York (city) New York City	26	0.00
Hyde Park (town) Dutchess County	6	0.03
Buffalo (city) Erie County	4	0.00
Staatsburg (cdp) Dutchess County	2	0.22
Fort Drum (cdp) Jefferson County	2	0.02
Glen Cove (city) Nassau County	2	0.01
Ithaca (city) Tompkins County	2	0.01
Le Ray (town) Jefferson County	2	0.01
Niskayuna (town) Schenectady County	2	0.01
Syracuse (city) Onondaga County	2	0.00

Top 10 Places Sorted by Percent
Based on all places, regardless of population

Place	Number	%
Staatsburg (cdp) Dutchess County	2	0.22
Elizabethtown (town) Essex County	1	0.08
Hyde Park (town) Dutchess County	6	0.03
Lansing (village) Tompkins County	1	0.03
Fort Drum (cdp) Jefferson County	2	0.02
Glen Cove (city) Nassau County	2	0.01
Ithaca (city) Tompkins County	2	0.01
Le Ray (town) Jefferson County	2	0.01
Niskayuna (town) Schenectady County	2	0.01
Lansing (town) Tompkins County	1	0.01

Top 10 Places Sorted by Percent
Based on places with populations of 10,000 or more

Place	Number	%
Hyde Park (town) Dutchess County	6	0.03
Fort Drum (cdp) Jefferson County	2	0.02
Glen Cove (city) Nassau County	2	0.01
Ithaca (city) Tompkins County	2	0.01
Le Ray (town) Jefferson County	2	0.01
Niskayuna (town) Schenectady County	2	0.01
Lansing (town) Tompkins County	1	0.01
Pearl River (cdp) Rockland County	1	0.01
New York (city) New York City	26	0.00
Buffalo (city) Erie County	4	0.00

Hawaii Native/Pacific Islander: Other Polynesian

Top 10 Places Sorted by Number
Based on all places, regardless of population

Place	Number	%
New York (city) New York City	84	0.00
Hempstead (town) Nassau County	17	0.00
Schenectady (city) Schenectady County	6	0.01
New Hyde Park (village) Nassau County	5	0.05
Buffalo (city) Erie County	5	0.00
Minoa (village) Onondaga County	4	0.12
Union Vale (town) Dutchess County	4	0.09
Manlius (town) Onondaga County	4	0.01
Point Lookout (cdp) Nassau County	3	0.20
Meredith (town) Delaware County	3	0.19

Top 10 Places Sorted by Percent
Based on all places, regardless of population

Place	Number	%
Point Lookout (cdp) Nassau County	3	0.20
Meredith (town) Delaware County	3	0.19
Minoa (village) Onondaga County	4	0.12
Ira (town) Cayuga County	3	0.12
Lido Beach (cdp) Nassau County	3	0.11
Union Vale (town) Dutchess County	4	0.09
Waddington (town) Saint Lawrence County	2	0.09
Zena (cdp) Ulster County	1	0.09
Highland (town) Sullivan County	2	0.08
Jordan (village) Onondaga County	1	0.08

Top 10 Places Sorted by Percent
Based on places with populations of 10,000 or more

Place	Number	%
North Wantagh (cdp) Nassau County	3	0.02
Ogden (town) Monroe County	3	0.02
Terryville (cdp) Suffolk County	2	0.02
Schenectady (city) Schenectady County	6	0.01
Manlius (town) Onondaga County	4	0.01
Dryden (town) Tompkins County	2	0.01
Mamaroneck (town) Westchester County	2	0.01
Valley Stream (village) Nassau County	2	0.01
Farmington (town) Ontario County	1	0.01
Gloversville (city) Fulton County	1	0.01

Hawaii Native/Pacific Islander: Other Pacific Islander, specified

Top 10 Places Sorted by Number
Based on all places, regardless of population

Place	Number	%
New York (city) New York City	639	0.01
Rochester (city) Monroe County	38	0.02
Hempstead (town) Nassau County	33	0.00
Islip (town) Suffolk County	18	0.01
Brookhaven (town) Suffolk County	18	0.00
Buffalo (city) Erie County	17	0.01
Yonkers (city) Westchester County	15	0.01
New Rochelle (city) Westchester County	13	0.02
Syracuse (city) Onondaga County	11	0.01
Hempstead (village) Nassau County	10	0.02

Top 10 Places Sorted by Percent
Based on all places, regardless of population

Place	Number	%
Peach Lake (cdp) Putnam County	3	0.18
North East (town) Dutchess County	5	0.17
Hewlett Harbor (village) Nassau County	2	0.16
White Creek (town) Washington County	5	0.15
Cortland West (cdp) Cortland County	2	0.15
Gorham (town) Ontario County	5	0.13
Broome (town) Schoharie County	1	0.11
Tyre (town) Seneca County	1	0.11
Portville (town) Cattaraugus County	4	0.10
Niles (town) Cayuga County	1	0.08

Top 10 Places Sorted by Percent
Based on places with populations of 10,000 or more

Place	Number	%
East Rockaway (village) Nassau County	5	0.05
Manorville (cdp) Suffolk County	5	0.04
Port Chester (village) Westchester County	8	0.03
Ronkonkoma (cdp) Suffolk County	6	0.03
Rye (city) Westchester County	5	0.03
Sayville (cdp) Suffolk County	5	0.03
Beacon (city) Dutchess County	4	0.03
Beekman (town) Dutchess County	4	0.03
North Wantagh (cdp) Nassau County	4	0.03
Roosevelt (cdp) Nassau County	4	0.03

Hawaii Native/Pacific Islander: Other Pacific Islander, not specified

Top 10 Places Sorted by Number
Based on all places, regardless of population

Place	Number	%
New York (city) New York City	13,530	0.17
Hempstead (town) Nassau County	509	0.07
Yonkers (city) Westchester County	248	0.13
Rochester (city) Monroe County	237	0.11
White Plains (city) Westchester County	235	0.44
Islip (town) Suffolk County	193	0.06
Brookhaven (town) Suffolk County	178	0.04
Buffalo (city) Erie County	161	0.06
Ramapo (town) Rockland County	157	0.14
North Hempstead (town) Nassau County	149	0.07

Top 10 Places Sorted by Percent
Based on all places, regardless of population

Place	Number	%
South Hill (cdp) Tompkins County	47	0.78
Cragsmoor (cdp) Ulster County	3	0.63
Nissequogue (village) Suffolk County	9	0.58
Greenport (village) Suffolk County	10	0.49
White Plains (city) Westchester County	235	0.44
Greenvale (cdp) Nassau County	9	0.40
South Floral Park (village) Nassau County	6	0.38
Quiogue (cdp) Suffolk County	3	0.38
Red Creek (village) Wayne County	2	0.38
Spring Valley (village) Rockland County	91	0.36

Top 10 Places Sorted by Percent
Based on places with populations of 10,000 or more

Place	Number	%
White Plains (city) Westchester County	235	0.44
Spring Valley (village) Rockland County	91	0.36
Ithaca (city) Tompkins County	103	0.35
Ithaca (town) Tompkins County	62	0.34
Suffern (village) Rockland County	31	0.28
Elmont (cdp) Nassau County	81	0.25
New Cassel (cdp) Nassau County	31	0.23
Haverstraw (village) Rockland County	22	0.22
Mount Vernon (city) Westchester County	144	0.21
Nanuet (cdp) Rockland County	35	0.21

Hispanic or Latino

Top 10 Places Sorted by Number
Based on all places, regardless of population

Place	Number	%
New York (city) New York City	2,160,554	26.98
Hempstead (town) Nassau County	86,657	11.46
Islip (town) Suffolk County	65,031	20.16
Yonkers (city) Westchester County	50,852	25.93

Notes: (cdp) census designated place; Refer to the User's Guide in the front of the book for more detailed information.

PROFILES OF NEW YORK / Ancestry: Rankings

Place	Number	%
Brookhaven (town) Suffolk County	36,041	8.04
Brentwood (cdp) Suffolk County	29,251	54.25
Rochester (city) Monroe County	28,032	12.75
Buffalo (city) Erie County	22,076	7.54
North Hempstead (town) Nassau County	21,872	9.83
Babylon (town) Suffolk County	21,275	10.05

Top 10 Places Sorted by Percent
Based on all places, regardless of population

Place	Number	%
Haverstraw (village) Rockland County	5,998	59.29
Brentwood (cdp) Suffolk County	29,251	54.25
North Bay Shore (cdp) Suffolk County	7,608	50.75
Port Chester (village) Westchester County	12,884	46.23
Sleepy Hollow (village) Westchester County	4,153	45.08
New Cassel (cdp) Nassau County	5,467	41.11
Newburgh (city) Orange County	10,257	36.30
Central Islip (cdp) Suffolk County	11,452	35.84
Freeport (village) Nassau County	14,648	33.46
Rye (town) Westchester County	14,264	32.51

Top 10 Places Sorted by Percent
Based on places with populations of 10,000 or more

Place	Number	%
Haverstraw (village) Rockland County	5,998	59.29
Brentwood (cdp) Suffolk County	29,251	54.25
North Bay Shore (cdp) Suffolk County	7,608	50.75
Port Chester (village) Westchester County	12,884	46.23
New Cassel (cdp) Nassau County	5,467	41.11
Newburgh (city) Orange County	10,257	36.30
Central Islip (cdp) Suffolk County	11,452	35.84
Freeport (village) Nassau County	14,648	33.46
Rye (town) Westchester County	14,264	32.51
Hempstead (village) Nassau County	17,991	31.81

Hispanic: Central American

Top 10 Places Sorted by Number
Based on all places, regardless of population

Place	Number	%
New York (city) New York City	99,099	1.24
Hempstead (town) Nassau County	22,455	2.97
Islip (town) Suffolk County	14,851	4.60
Hempstead (village) Nassau County	8,382	14.82
Brentwood (cdp) Suffolk County	8,221	15.25
North Hempstead (town) Nassau County	6,571	2.95
Freeport (village) Nassau County	4,249	9.70
Huntington (town) Suffolk County	3,623	1.86
Babylon (town) Suffolk County	3,552	1.68
Yonkers (city) Westchester County	3,374	1.72

Top 10 Places Sorted by Percent
Based on all places, regardless of population

Place	Number	%
New Cassel (cdp) Nassau County	2,688	20.21
Brewster (village) Putnam County	360	16.65
Brentwood (cdp) Suffolk County	8,221	15.25
Hempstead (village) Nassau County	8,382	14.82
North Bay Shore (cdp) Suffolk County	2,152	14.35
Inwood (cdp) Nassau County	948	10.17
Freeport (village) Nassau County	4,249	9.70
Huntington Station (cdp) Suffolk County	2,851	9.53
Uniondale (cdp) Nassau County	2,114	9.19
Central Islip (cdp) Suffolk County	2,821	8.83

Top 10 Places Sorted by Percent
Based on places with populations of 10,000 or more

Place	Number	%
New Cassel (cdp) Nassau County	2,688	20.21
Brentwood (cdp) Suffolk County	8,221	15.25
Hempstead (village) Nassau County	8,382	14.82
North Bay Shore (cdp) Suffolk County	2,152	14.35
Freeport (village) Nassau County	4,249	9.70
Huntington Station (cdp) Suffolk County	2,851	9.53
Uniondale (cdp) Nassau County	2,114	9.19
Central Islip (cdp) Suffolk County	2,821	8.83
Roosevelt (cdp) Nassau County	1,290	8.14
Port Chester (village) Westchester County	1,819	6.53

Hispanic: Costa Rican

Top 10 Places Sorted by Number
Based on all places, regardless of population

Place	Number	%
New York (city) New York City	4,939	0.06
Hempstead (town) Nassau County	445	0.06
Southampton (town) Suffolk County	306	0.56
Hampton Bays (cdp) Suffolk County	193	1.58
Islip (town) Suffolk County	187	0.06
East Hampton (town) Suffolk County	178	0.90
Yonkers (city) Westchester County	135	0.07
Amsterdam (city) Montgomery County	128	0.70
North Hempstead (town) Nassau County	99	0.04
Ramapo (town) Rockland County	93	0.09

Top 10 Places Sorted by Percent
Based on all places, regardless of population

Place	Number	%
Springs (cdp) Suffolk County	79	1.60
Hampton Bays (cdp) Suffolk County	193	1.58
East Hampton (village) Suffolk County	21	1.57
East Hampton North (cdp) Suffolk County	33	0.92
East Hampton (town) Suffolk County	178	0.90
Northwest Harbor (cdp) Suffolk County	23	0.75
Bellerose Terrace (cdp) Nassau County	16	0.74
Bridgehampton (cdp) Suffolk County	10	0.72
Amsterdam (city) Montgomery County	128	0.70
Wainscott (cdp) Suffolk County	4	0.64

Top 10 Places Sorted by Percent
Based on places with populations of 10,000 or more

Place	Number	%
Hampton Bays (cdp) Suffolk County	193	1.58
East Hampton (town) Suffolk County	178	0.90
Amsterdam (city) Montgomery County	128	0.70
Southampton (town) Suffolk County	306	0.56
Spring Valley (village) Rockland County	51	0.20
Uniondale (cdp) Nassau County	43	0.19
North Bay Shore (cdp) Suffolk County	27	0.18
Freeport (village) Nassau County	71	0.16
Glen Cove (city) Nassau County	42	0.16
Brentwood (cdp) Suffolk County	72	0.13

Hispanic: Guatemalan

Top 10 Places Sorted by Number
Based on all places, regardless of population

Place	Number	%
New York (city) New York City	15,212	0.19
Hempstead (town) Nassau County	2,094	0.28
Islip (town) Suffolk County	1,347	0.42
Rye (town) Westchester County	1,143	2.60
Ramapo (town) Rockland County	1,116	1.02
Port Chester (village) Westchester County	1,037	3.72
Spring Valley (village) Rockland County	960	3.77
Brentwood (cdp) Suffolk County	710	1.32
Mount Kisco (village) Westchester County	657	6.58
North Hempstead (town) Nassau County	550	0.25

Top 10 Places Sorted by Percent
Based on all places, regardless of population

Place	Number	%
Brewster (village) Putnam County	325	15.03
Mount Kisco (village) Westchester County	657	6.58
Quiogue (cdp) Suffolk County	50	6.25
Jamesport (cdp) Suffolk County	59	3.87
Spring Valley (village) Rockland County	960	3.77
Port Chester (village) Westchester County	1,037	3.72
Flanders (cdp) Suffolk County	107	2.93
Greenport (village) Suffolk County	60	2.93
Mamaroneck (village) Westchester County	544	2.90
Peconic (cdp) Suffolk County	29	2.68

Top 10 Places Sorted by Percent
Based on places with populations of 10,000 or more

Place	Number	%
Spring Valley (village) Rockland County	960	3.77
Port Chester (village) Westchester County	1,037	3.72
Mamaroneck (village) Westchester County	544	2.90
Rye (town) Westchester County	1,143	2.60
Southeast (town) Putnam County	361	2.08
Mamaroneck (town) Westchester County	471	1.63
Brentwood (cdp) Suffolk County	710	1.32
Freeport (village) Nassau County	535	1.22
Peekskill (city) Westchester County	261	1.16
North Bay Shore (cdp) Suffolk County	174	1.16

Hispanic: Honduran

Top 10 Places Sorted by Number
Based on all places, regardless of population

Place	Number	%
New York (city) New York City	25,600	0.32
Hempstead (town) Nassau County	2,452	0.32
Hempstead (village) Nassau County	1,450	2.56
Islip (town) Suffolk County	1,211	0.38
Newburgh (city) Orange County	750	2.65
Yonkers (city) Westchester County	736	0.38
North Hempstead (town) Nassau County	594	0.27
Brentwood (cdp) Suffolk County	546	1.01
Babylon (town) Suffolk County	377	0.18
Huntington (town) Suffolk County	354	0.18

Top 10 Places Sorted by Percent
Based on all places, regardless of population

Place	Number	%
Newburgh (city) Orange County	750	2.65
Hempstead (village) Nassau County	1,450	2.56
New Cassel (cdp) Nassau County	280	2.11
Woodridge (village) Sullivan County	14	1.55
Farmingdale (village) Nassau County	115	1.37
North Bay Shore (cdp) Suffolk County	194	1.29
Liberty (village) Sullivan County	45	1.13
Brentwood (cdp) Suffolk County	546	1.01
Island Park (village) Nassau County	48	1.01
Central Islip (cdp) Suffolk County	300	0.94

Top 10 Places Sorted by Percent
Based on places with populations of 10,000 or more

Place	Number	%
Newburgh (city) Orange County	750	2.65
Hempstead (village) Nassau County	1,450	2.56
New Cassel (cdp) Nassau County	280	2.11
North Bay Shore (cdp) Suffolk County	194	1.29
Brentwood (cdp) Suffolk County	546	1.01
Central Islip (cdp) Suffolk County	300	0.94
Huntington Station (cdp) Suffolk County	252	0.84
Wyandanch (cdp) Suffolk County	80	0.76
Freeport (village) Nassau County	254	0.58
Glen Cove (city) Nassau County	140	0.53

Notes: (cdp) census designated place; Refer to the User's Guide in the front of the book for more detailed information.

Hispanic: Nicaraguan

Top 10 Places Sorted by Number
Based on all places, regardless of population

Place	Number	%
New York (city) New York City	6,451	0.08
Yonkers (city) Westchester County	391	0.20
Hempstead (town) Nassau County	187	0.02
Islip (town) Suffolk County	105	0.03
Brookhaven (town) Suffolk County	55	0.01
Rochester (city) Monroe County	48	0.02
New Rochelle (city) Westchester County	45	0.06
Babylon (town) Suffolk County	35	0.02
Oyster Bay (town) Nassau County	35	0.01
Central Islip (cdp) Suffolk County	33	0.10

Top 10 Places Sorted by Percent
Based on all places, regardless of population

Place	Number	%
Philmont (village) Columbia County	5	0.34
Woodridge (village) Sullivan County	3	0.33
Westhampton (cdp) Suffolk County	7	0.24
Brewster Hill (cdp) Putnam County	5	0.22
Yonkers (city) Westchester County	391	0.20
Cattaraugus (village) Cattaraugus County	2	0.19
Locust Valley (cdp) Nassau County	6	0.17
Chester (village) Orange County	5	0.15
Morrisville (village) Madison County	3	0.14
Inwood (cdp) Nassau County	11	0.12

Top 10 Places Sorted by Percent
Based on places with populations of 10,000 or more

Place	Number	%
Yonkers (city) Westchester County	391	0.20
New Cassel (cdp) Nassau County	14	0.11
West Haverstraw (village) Rockland County	11	0.11
Central Islip (cdp) Suffolk County	33	0.10
Mastic Beach (cdp) Suffolk County	11	0.10
New York (city) New York City	6,451	0.08
Long Beach (city) Nassau County	25	0.07
Woodmere (cdp) Nassau County	12	0.07
North Valley Stream (cdp) Nassau County	11	0.07
Chester (town) Orange County	8	0.07

Hispanic: Panamanian

Top 10 Places Sorted by Number
Based on all places, regardless of population

Place	Number	%
New York (city) New York City	16,847	0.21
Hempstead (town) Nassau County	597	0.08
Islip (town) Suffolk County	298	0.09
Babylon (town) Suffolk County	173	0.08
Brentwood (cdp) Suffolk County	137	0.25
Brookhaven (town) Suffolk County	134	0.03
Hempstead (village) Nassau County	119	0.21
Yonkers (city) Westchester County	115	0.06
Freeport (village) Nassau County	89	0.20
Elmont (cdp) Nassau County	87	0.27

Top 10 Places Sorted by Percent
Based on all places, regardless of population

Place	Number	%
East Garden City (cdp) Nassau County	7	0.72
Lakeview (cdp) Nassau County	31	0.55
Fort Drum (cdp) Jefferson County	57	0.47
Woodridge (village) Sullivan County	4	0.44
West Point (cdp) Orange County	27	0.38
Le Ray (town) Jefferson County	73	0.37
Calcium (cdp) Jefferson County	12	0.36
North Amityville (cdp) Suffolk County	58	0.35
South Floral Park (village) Nassau County	5	0.32
Deferiet (village) Jefferson County	1	0.32

Top 10 Places Sorted by Percent
Based on places with populations of 10,000 or more

Place	Number	%
Fort Drum (cdp) Jefferson County	57	0.47
Le Ray (town) Jefferson County	73	0.37
North Amityville (cdp) Suffolk County	58	0.35
Elmont (cdp) Nassau County	87	0.27
Central Islip (cdp) Suffolk County	85	0.27
Brentwood (cdp) Suffolk County	137	0.25
Middletown (city) Orange County	60	0.24
North Bay Shore (cdp) Suffolk County	36	0.24
Highlands (town) Orange County	29	0.23
New York (city) New York City	16,847	0.21

Hispanic: Salvadoran

Top 10 Places Sorted by Number
Based on all places, regardless of population

Place	Number	%
New York (city) New York City	24,516	0.31
Hempstead (town) Nassau County	15,659	2.07
Islip (town) Suffolk County	11,046	3.42
Brentwood (cdp) Suffolk County	6,387	11.85
Hempstead (village) Nassau County	5,949	10.52
North Hempstead (town) Nassau County	4,993	2.24
Freeport (village) Nassau County	3,094	7.07
Huntington (town) Suffolk County	2,747	1.41
Babylon (town) Suffolk County	2,549	1.20
New Cassel (cdp) Nassau County	2,322	17.46

Top 10 Places Sorted by Percent
Based on all places, regardless of population

Place	Number	%
New Cassel (cdp) Nassau County	2,322	17.46
Brentwood (cdp) Suffolk County	6,387	11.85
North Bay Shore (cdp) Suffolk County	1,630	10.87
Hempstead (village) Nassau County	5,949	10.52
Huntington Station (cdp) Suffolk County	2,304	7.70
Inwood (cdp) Nassau County	670	7.18
Uniondale (cdp) Nassau County	1,648	7.16
Freeport (village) Nassau County	3,094	7.07
Roosevelt (cdp) Nassau County	1,064	6.71
Central Islip (cdp) Suffolk County	1,967	6.16

Top 10 Places Sorted by Percent
Based on places with populations of 10,000 or more

Place	Number	%
New Cassel (cdp) Nassau County	2,322	17.46
Brentwood (cdp) Suffolk County	6,387	11.85
North Bay Shore (cdp) Suffolk County	1,630	10.87
Hempstead (village) Nassau County	5,949	10.52
Huntington Station (cdp) Suffolk County	2,304	7.70
Uniondale (cdp) Nassau County	1,648	7.16
Freeport (village) Nassau County	3,094	7.07
Roosevelt (cdp) Nassau County	1,064	6.71
Central Islip (cdp) Suffolk County	1,967	6.16
Westbury (village) Nassau County	621	4.35

Hispanic: Other Central American

Top 10 Places Sorted by Number
Based on all places, regardless of population

Place	Number	%
New York (city) New York City	5,534	0.07
Hempstead (town) Nassau County	1,021	0.14
Islip (town) Suffolk County	657	0.20
Brentwood (cdp) Suffolk County	337	0.63
Hempstead (village) Nassau County	324	0.57
North Hempstead (town) Nassau County	252	0.11
Freeport (village) Nassau County	180	0.41
Central Islip (cdp) Suffolk County	176	0.55
Uniondale (cdp) Nassau County	136	0.59
Yonkers (city) Westchester County	136	0.07

Top 10 Places Sorted by Percent
Based on all places, regardless of population

Place	Number	%
Greenport (village) Suffolk County	15	0.73
Brentwood (cdp) Suffolk County	337	0.63
Uniondale (cdp) Nassau County	136	0.59
Hempstead (village) Nassau County	324	0.57
Inwood (cdp) Nassau County	53	0.57
North Bay Shore (cdp) Suffolk County	84	0.56
Central Islip (cdp) Suffolk County	176	0.55
Manorhaven (village) Nassau County	33	0.54
Chaumont (village) Jefferson County	3	0.51
Baxter Estates (village) Nassau County	5	0.50

Top 10 Places Sorted by Percent
Based on places with populations of 10,000 or more

Place	Number	%
Brentwood (cdp) Suffolk County	337	0.63
Uniondale (cdp) Nassau County	136	0.59
Hempstead (village) Nassau County	324	0.57
North Bay Shore (cdp) Suffolk County	84	0.56
Central Islip (cdp) Suffolk County	176	0.55
Freeport (village) Nassau County	180	0.41
New Cassel (cdp) Nassau County	43	0.32
Huntington Station (cdp) Suffolk County	87	0.29
Port Chester (village) Westchester County	82	0.29
Port Washington (cdp) Nassau County	41	0.27

Hispanic: Cuban

Top 10 Places Sorted by Number
Based on all places, regardless of population

Place	Number	%
New York (city) New York City	41,123	0.51
Hempstead (town) Nassau County	2,934	0.39
Yonkers (city) Westchester County	1,450	0.74
Rochester (city) Monroe County	1,177	0.54
Brookhaven (town) Suffolk County	1,032	0.23
Islip (town) Suffolk County	929	0.29
Oyster Bay (town) Nassau County	747	0.25
Syracuse (city) Onondaga County	552	0.37
Rye (town) Westchester County	540	1.23
North Hempstead (town) Nassau County	526	0.24

Top 10 Places Sorted by Percent
Based on all places, regardless of population

Place	Number	%
Sleepy Hollow (village) Westchester County	181	1.96
Tarrytown (village) Westchester County	213	1.92
Port Chester (village) Westchester County	465	1.67
Leeds (cdp) Greene County	5	1.36
Bellerose Terrace (cdp) Nassau County	27	1.25
Rye (town) Westchester County	540	1.23
Mount Hope (town) Orange County	80	1.21
Belle Terre (village) Suffolk County	10	1.20
McDonough (town) Chenango County	9	1.03
Hewlett Bay Park (village) Nassau County	5	1.03

Top 10 Places Sorted by Percent
Based on places with populations of 10,000 or more

Place	Number	%
Tarrytown (village) Westchester County	213	1.92
Port Chester (village) Westchester County	465	1.67
Rye (town) Westchester County	540	1.23
Freeport (village) Nassau County	429	0.98
Yonkers (city) Westchester County	1,450	0.74
Rockville Centre (village) Nassau County	152	0.62
Mount Pleasant (town) Westchester County	257	0.59

Notes: (cdp) census designated place; Refer to the User's Guide in the front of the book for more detailed information.

Place	Number	%
Greenburgh (town) Westchester County	501	0.58
White Plains (city) Westchester County	299	0.56
Fallsburg (town) Sullivan County	69	0.56

Hispanic: Dominican Republic

Top 10 Places Sorted by Number
Based on all places, regardless of population

Place	Number	%
New York (city) New York City	406,806	5.08
Hempstead (town) Nassau County	8,433	1.12
Yonkers (city) Westchester County	7,838	4.00
Islip (town) Suffolk County	4,792	1.49
Haverstraw (town) Rockland County	3,764	11.13
Freeport (village) Nassau County	3,226	7.37
Babylon (town) Suffolk County	3,188	1.51
Brentwood (cdp) Suffolk County	2,744	5.09
Haverstraw (village) Rockland County	2,727	26.95
Brookhaven (town) Suffolk County	2,132	0.48

Top 10 Places Sorted by Percent
Based on all places, regardless of population

Place	Number	%
Haverstraw (village) Rockland County	2,727	26.95
Sleepy Hollow (village) Westchester County	1,167	12.67
Haverstraw (town) Rockland County	3,764	11.13
West Haverstraw (village) Rockland County	841	8.17
Freeport (village) Nassau County	3,226	7.37
Copiague (cdp) Suffolk County	1,440	6.57
Brentwood (cdp) Suffolk County	2,744	5.09
New York (city) New York City	406,806	5.08
Yonkers (city) Westchester County	7,838	4.00
North Bay Shore (cdp) Suffolk County	505	3.37

Top 10 Places Sorted by Percent
Based on places with populations of 10,000 or more

Place	Number	%
Haverstraw (village) Rockland County	2,727	26.95
Haverstraw (town) Rockland County	3,764	11.13
West Haverstraw (village) Rockland County	841	8.17
Freeport (village) Nassau County	3,226	7.37
Copiague (cdp) Suffolk County	1,440	6.57
Brentwood (cdp) Suffolk County	2,744	5.09
New York (city) New York City	406,806	5.08
Yonkers (city) Westchester County	7,838	4.00
North Bay Shore (cdp) Suffolk County	505	3.37
Terryville (cdp) Suffolk County	335	3.16

Hispanic: Mexican

Top 10 Places Sorted by Number
Based on all places, regardless of population

Place	Number	%
New York (city) New York City	186,872	2.33
Yonkers (city) Westchester County	7,294	3.72
New Rochelle (city) Westchester County	6,899	9.56
Newburgh (city) Orange County	4,111	14.55
White Plains (city) Westchester County	3,410	6.42
Rye (town) Westchester County	3,253	7.41
Port Chester (village) Westchester County	3,108	11.15
Hempstead (town) Nassau County	2,971	0.39
North Hempstead (town) Nassau County	2,403	1.08
Middletown (city) Orange County	2,038	8.03

Top 10 Places Sorted by Percent
Based on all places, regardless of population

Place	Number	%
Fleischmanns (village) Delaware County	65	18.52
Newburgh (city) Orange County	4,111	14.55
Port Chester (village) Westchester County	3,108	11.15
New Rochelle (city) Westchester County	6,899	9.56
New Cassel (cdp) Nassau County	1,166	8.77
Middletown (city) Orange County	2,038	8.03
Rye (town) Westchester County	3,253	7.41
Dresden (village) Yates County	20	6.51
White Plains (city) Westchester County	3,410	6.42
Greenport (village) Suffolk County	116	5.66

Top 10 Places Sorted by Percent
Based on places with populations of 10,000 or more

Place	Number	%
Newburgh (city) Orange County	4,111	14.55
Port Chester (village) Westchester County	3,108	11.15
New Rochelle (city) Westchester County	6,899	9.56
New Cassel (cdp) Nassau County	1,166	8.77
Middletown (city) Orange County	2,038	8.03
Rye (town) Westchester County	3,253	7.41
White Plains (city) Westchester County	3,410	6.42
Poughkeepsie (city) Dutchess County	1,616	5.41
Suffern (village) Rockland County	595	5.41
Fort Drum (cdp) Jefferson County	563	4.64

Hispanic: Puerto Rican

Top 10 Places Sorted by Number
Based on all places, regardless of population

Place	Number	%
New York (city) New York City	789,172	9.85
Islip (town) Suffolk County	22,298	6.91
Rochester (city) Monroe County	21,897	9.96
Yonkers (city) Westchester County	18,097	9.23
Buffalo (city) Erie County	17,250	5.89
Brookhaven (town) Suffolk County	16,438	3.67
Hempstead (town) Nassau County	15,779	2.09
Brentwood (cdp) Suffolk County	8,254	15.31
Babylon (town) Suffolk County	6,170	2.91
Syracuse (city) Onondaga County	4,885	3.32

Top 10 Places Sorted by Percent
Based on all places, regardless of population

Place	Number	%
Ellenville (village) Ulster County	737	17.85
North Bay Shore (cdp) Suffolk County	2,578	17.20
Dunkirk (city) Chautauqua County	2,238	17.04
Brentwood (cdp) Suffolk County	8,254	15.31
Haverstraw (village) Rockland County	1,494	14.77
West Haverstraw (village) Rockland County	1,464	14.22
Woodridge (village) Sullivan County	123	13.64
Central Islip (cdp) Suffolk County	4,050	12.68
Middletown (city) Orange County	3,066	12.08
Monticello (village) Sullivan County	755	11.59

Top 10 Places Sorted by Percent
Based on places with populations of 10,000 or more

Place	Number	%
North Bay Shore (cdp) Suffolk County	2,578	17.20
Dunkirk (city) Chautauqua County	2,238	17.04
Brentwood (cdp) Suffolk County	8,254	15.31
Haverstraw (village) Rockland County	1,494	14.77
West Haverstraw (village) Rockland County	1,464	14.22
Central Islip (cdp) Suffolk County	4,050	12.68
Middletown (city) Orange County	3,066	12.08
Amsterdam (city) Montgomery County	2,124	11.57
Haverstraw (town) Rockland County	3,812	11.27
Newburgh (city) Orange County	3,069	10.86

Hispanic: South American

Top 10 Places Sorted by Number
Based on all places, regardless of population

Place	Number	%
New York (city) New York City	236,374	2.95
Hempstead (town) Nassau County	11,430	1.51
Islip (town) Suffolk County	7,398	2.29
Brookhaven (town) Suffolk County	4,746	1.0
Yonkers (city) Westchester County	3,944	2.0
Rye (town) Westchester County	3,842	8.7
North Hempstead (town) Nassau County	3,707	1.6
White Plains (city) Westchester County	3,641	6.8
Port Chester (village) Westchester County	3,516	12.6
Brentwood (cdp) Suffolk County	3,139	5.8

Top 10 Places Sorted by Percent
Based on all places, regardless of population

Place	Number	%
Montauk (cdp) Suffolk County	721	18.7
Sleepy Hollow (village) Westchester County	1,321	14.3
Port Chester (village) Westchester County	3,516	12.6
Ossining (village) Westchester County	2,819	11.7
East Hampton North (cdp) Suffolk County	334	9.3
Springs (cdp) Suffolk County	450	9.0
East Hampton (town) Suffolk County	1,757	8.9
Rye (town) Westchester County	3,842	8.7
Patchogue (village) Suffolk County	968	8.1
Ossining (town) Westchester County	2,942	8.0

Top 10 Places Sorted by Percent
Based on places with populations of 10,000 or more

Place	Number	%
Port Chester (village) Westchester County	3,516	12.6
Ossining (village) Westchester County	2,819	11.7
East Hampton (town) Suffolk County	1,757	8.9
Rye (town) Westchester County	3,842	8.7
Patchogue (village) Suffolk County	968	8.1
Ossining (town) Westchester County	2,942	8.0
White Plains (city) Westchester County	3,641	6.8
Peekskill (city) Westchester County	1,314	5.8
Brentwood (cdp) Suffolk County	3,139	5.8
North Bay Shore (cdp) Suffolk County	737	4.9

Hispanic: Argentinean

Top 10 Places Sorted by Number
Based on all places, regardless of population

Place	Number	%
New York (city) New York City	9,578	0.
Hempstead (town) Nassau County	859	0.
Islip (town) Suffolk County	300	0.
North Hempstead (town) Nassau County	297	0.
Brookhaven (town) Suffolk County	265	0.
Oyster Bay (town) Nassau County	242	0.
Yonkers (city) Westchester County	190	0.
Huntington (town) Suffolk County	160	0.
Babylon (town) Suffolk County	149	0.
Greenburgh (town) Westchester County	100	0.

Top 10 Places Sorted by Percent
Based on all places, regardless of population

Place	Number	%
Forest Home (cdp) Tompkins County	11	1.
Russell Gardens (village) Nassau County	7	0.
Malverne Park Oaks (cdp) Nassau County	3	0.
Islandia (village) Suffolk County	19	0.
Millbrook (village) Dutchess County	8	0.
Unionville (village) Orange County	3	0.
Thomaston (village) Nassau County	14	0.
Harbor Hills (cdp) Nassau County	3	0.
Laurel Hollow (village) Nassau County	9	0.
Centre Island (village) Nassau County	2	0.

Top 10 Places Sorted by Percent
Based on places with populations of 10,000 or more

Place	Number	%
Elmont (cdp) Nassau County	86	0.
Mamaroneck (town) Westchester County	71	0.
Mamaroneck (village) Westchester County	47	0.

Notes: (cdp) census designated place; Refer to the User's Guide in the front of the book for more detailed information.

PROFILES OF NEW YORK / Ancestry: Rankings

Place	Number	%
Valley Stream (village) Nassau County	76	0.21
Kiryas Joel (village) Orange County	27	0.21
Newburgh (city) Orange County	57	0.20
Long Beach (city) Nassau County	67	0.19
Central Islip (cdp) Suffolk County	62	0.19
Monroe (town) Orange County	56	0.18
Harrison (village) Westchester County	42	0.17

Hispanic: Bolivian

Top 10 Places Sorted by Number
Based on all places, regardless of population

Place	Number	%
New York (city) New York City	2,942	0.04
Hempstead (town) Nassau County	228	0.03
Rye (town) Westchester County	180	0.41
Port Chester (village) Westchester County	163	0.58
Islip (town) Suffolk County	107	0.03
Brookhaven (town) Suffolk County	67	0.01
Oyster Bay (town) Nassau County	59	0.02
Brentwood (cdp) Suffolk County	51	0.09
White Plains (city) Westchester County	42	0.08
North Hempstead (town) Nassau County	36	0.02

Top 10 Places Sorted by Percent
Based on all places, regardless of population

Place	Number	%
Port Chester (village) Westchester County	163	0.58
Matinecock (village) Nassau County	4	0.48
Rye (town) Westchester County	180	0.41
Inwood (cdp) Nassau County	32	0.34
Westhampton Beach (village) Suffolk County	5	0.26
Mill Neck (village) Nassau County	2	0.24
Islandia (village) Suffolk County	7	0.23
Westhampton (cdp) Suffolk County	6	0.21
East Rockaway (village) Nassau County	20	0.19
Bellerose Terrace (cdp) Nassau County	4	0.19

Top 10 Places Sorted by Percent
Based on places with populations of 10,000 or more

Place	Number	%
Port Chester (village) Westchester County	163	0.58
Rye (town) Westchester County	180	0.41
East Rockaway (village) Nassau County	20	0.19
Salisbury (cdp) Nassau County	19	0.15
Mamaroneck (village) Westchester County	20	0.11
Lynbrook (village) Nassau County	19	0.10
North Wantagh (cdp) Nassau County	12	0.10
Brentwood (cdp) Suffolk County	51	0.09
White Plains (city) Westchester County	42	0.08
Long Beach (city) Nassau County	29	0.08

Hispanic: Chilean

Top 10 Places Sorted by Number
Based on all places, regardless of population

Place	Number	%
New York (city) New York City	5,014	0.06
Hempstead (town) Nassau County	893	0.12
North Hempstead (town) Nassau County	521	0.23
Oyster Bay (town) Nassau County	409	0.14
Islip (town) Suffolk County	249	0.08
Mount Pleasant (town) Westchester County	193	0.45
Sleepy Hollow (village) Westchester County	185	2.01
Brookhaven (town) Suffolk County	168	0.04
Manorhaven (village) Nassau County	164	2.67
Ossining (town) Westchester County	159	0.44

Top 10 Places Sorted by Percent
Based on all places, regardless of population

Place	Number	%
Manorhaven (village) Nassau County	164	2.67
Sleepy Hollow (village) Westchester County	185	2.01
North Lynbrook (cdp) Nassau County	14	1.89
Locust Valley (cdp) Nassau County	56	1.59
Baxter Estates (village) Nassau County	14	1.39
Mill Neck (village) Nassau County	9	1.09
Inwood (cdp) Nassau County	80	0.86
Poquott (village) Suffolk County	8	0.82
Ellenville (village) Ulster County	32	0.77
Port Washington (cdp) Nassau County	106	0.70

Top 10 Places Sorted by Percent
Based on places with populations of 10,000 or more

Place	Number	%
Port Washington (cdp) Nassau County	106	0.70
Ossining (village) Westchester County	152	0.63
Glen Cove (city) Nassau County	132	0.50
Tarrytown (village) Westchester County	54	0.49
Mount Pleasant (town) Westchester County	193	0.45
Ossining (town) Westchester County	159	0.44
Port Chester (village) Westchester County	111	0.40
Wawarsing (town) Ulster County	48	0.37
Elmont (cdp) Nassau County	107	0.33
Rye (town) Westchester County	139	0.32

Hispanic: Colombian

Top 10 Places Sorted by Number
Based on all places, regardless of population

Place	Number	%
New York (city) New York City	77,154	0.96
Hempstead (town) Nassau County	4,403	0.58
Islip (town) Suffolk County	2,951	0.91
White Plains (city) Westchester County	1,458	2.75
Brookhaven (town) Suffolk County	1,400	0.31
Brentwood (cdp) Suffolk County	1,357	2.52
North Hempstead (town) Nassau County	1,219	0.55
New Rochelle (city) Westchester County	1,071	1.48
Babylon (town) Suffolk County	1,071	0.51
Oyster Bay (town) Nassau County	1,066	0.36

Top 10 Places Sorted by Percent
Based on all places, regardless of population

Place	Number	%
Montauk (cdp) Suffolk County	367	9.53
East Hampton North (cdp) Suffolk County	173	4.82
East Hampton (town) Suffolk County	850	4.31
Springs (cdp) Suffolk County	197	3.98
Bellerose Terrace (cdp) Nassau County	60	2.78
White Plains (city) Westchester County	1,458	2.75
Ellenville (village) Ulster County	106	2.57
Brentwood (cdp) Suffolk County	1,357	2.52
Port Chester (village) Westchester County	696	2.50
Mount Kisco (village) Westchester County	226	2.26

Top 10 Places Sorted by Percent
Based on places with populations of 10,000 or more

Place	Number	%
East Hampton (town) Suffolk County	850	4.31
White Plains (city) Westchester County	1,458	2.75
Brentwood (cdp) Suffolk County	1,357	2.52
Port Chester (village) Westchester County	696	2.50
Hampton Bays (cdp) Suffolk County	235	1.92
Ossining (village) Westchester County	456	1.90
North Bay Shore (cdp) Suffolk County	269	1.79
Rye (town) Westchester County	739	1.68
Wawarsing (town) Ulster County	206	1.60
New Rochelle (city) Westchester County	1,071	1.48

Hispanic: Ecuadorian

Top 10 Places Sorted by Number
Based on all places, regardless of population

Place	Number	%
New York (city) New York City	101,005	1.26
Hempstead (town) Nassau County	2,343	0.31
Brookhaven (town) Suffolk County	2,055	0.46
Islip (town) Suffolk County	2,052	0.64
Yonkers (city) Westchester County	1,839	0.94
Ossining (town) Westchester County	1,818	4.98
Ossining (village) Westchester County	1,796	7.48
Rye (town) Westchester County	1,394	3.18
Port Chester (village) Westchester County	1,366	4.90
Mount Pleasant (town) Westchester County	1,119	2.59

Top 10 Places Sorted by Percent
Based on all places, regardless of population

Place	Number	%
Sleepy Hollow (village) Westchester County	991	10.76
Montauk (cdp) Suffolk County	311	8.08
Ossining (village) Westchester County	1,796	7.48
Patchogue (village) Suffolk County	845	7.09
Ossining (town) Westchester County	1,818	4.98
Port Chester (village) Westchester County	1,366	4.90
Springs (cdp) Suffolk County	221	4.46
Peekskill (city) Westchester County	970	4.32
East Hampton (town) Suffolk County	752	3.81
East Hampton North (cdp) Suffolk County	122	3.40

Top 10 Places Sorted by Percent
Based on places with populations of 10,000 or more

Place	Number	%
Ossining (village) Westchester County	1,796	7.48
Patchogue (village) Suffolk County	845	7.09
Ossining (town) Westchester County	1,818	4.98
Port Chester (village) Westchester County	1,366	4.90
Peekskill (city) Westchester County	970	4.32
East Hampton (town) Suffolk County	752	3.81
Rye (town) Westchester County	1,394	3.18
Mount Pleasant (town) Westchester County	1,119	2.59
Tarrytown (village) Westchester County	267	2.41
Spring Valley (village) Rockland County	500	1.96

Hispanic: Paraguayan

Top 10 Places Sorted by Number
Based on all places, regardless of population

Place	Number	%
New York (city) New York City	1,658	0.02
White Plains (city) Westchester County	171	0.32
Harrison (village) Westchester County	94	0.39
Hempstead (town) Nassau County	62	0.01
Mount Vernon (city) Westchester County	61	0.09
Rye (town) Westchester County	51	0.12
North Hempstead (town) Nassau County	48	0.02
Oyster Bay (town) Nassau County	42	0.01
Huntington (town) Suffolk County	40	0.02
Mamaroneck (village) Westchester County	39	0.21

Top 10 Places Sorted by Percent
Based on all places, regardless of population

Place	Number	%
Harrison (village) Westchester County	94	0.39
Shinnecock Hills (cdp) Suffolk County	6	0.34
White Plains (city) Westchester County	171	0.32
Bellerose Terrace (cdp) Nassau County	5	0.23
Mamaroneck (village) Westchester County	39	0.21
Fairview (cdp) Westchester County	6	0.21
Valhalla (cdp) Westchester County	11	0.20
Oxford (village) Chenango County	3	0.19
Scotts Corners (cdp) Westchester County	1	0.16

Notes: (cdp) census designated place; Refer to the User's Guide in the front of the book for more detailed information.

688 PROFILES OF NEW YORK / Ancestry: Rankings

Place	Number	%
Mineola (village) Nassau County	26	0.14

Top 10 Places Sorted by Percent
Based on places with populations of 10,000 or more

Place	Number	%
Harrison (village) Westchester County	94	0.39
White Plains (city) Westchester County	171	0.32
Mamaroneck (village) Westchester County	39	0.21
Mineola (village) Nassau County	26	0.14
Rye (town) Westchester County	51	0.12
Elwood (cdp) Suffolk County	11	0.10
Mount Vernon (city) Westchester County	61	0.09
South Farmingdale (cdp) Nassau County	14	0.09
Greenlawn (cdp) Suffolk County	12	0.09
Bedford (town) Westchester County	15	0.08

Hispanic: Peruvian

Top 10 Places Sorted by Number
Based on all places, regardless of population

Place	Number	%
New York (city) New York City	23,567	0.29
Hempstead (town) Nassau County	1,724	0.23
White Plains (city) Westchester County	1,266	2.39
Islip (town) Suffolk County	1,244	0.39
Rye (town) Westchester County	1,021	2.33
Port Chester (village) Westchester County	919	3.30
New Rochelle (city) Westchester County	791	1.10
Glen Cove (city) Nassau County	659	2.48
Brentwood (cdp) Suffolk County	544	1.01
Oyster Bay (town) Nassau County	538	0.18

Top 10 Places Sorted by Percent
Based on all places, regardless of population

Place	Number	%
Port Chester (village) Westchester County	919	3.30
Glen Cove (city) Nassau County	659	2.48
White Plains (city) Westchester County	1,266	2.39
Rye (town) Westchester County	1,021	2.33
Elmsford (village) Westchester County	105	2.25
Fairview (cdp) Westchester County	50	1.73
Island Park (village) Nassau County	69	1.46
Mamaroneck (village) Westchester County	260	1.39
Bellerose Terrace (cdp) Nassau County	26	1.21
Newburgh (city) Orange County	330	1.17

Top 10 Places Sorted by Percent
Based on places with populations of 10,000 or more

Place	Number	%
Port Chester (village) Westchester County	919	3.30
Glen Cove (city) Nassau County	659	2.48
White Plains (city) Westchester County	1,266	2.39
Rye (town) Westchester County	1,021	2.33
Mamaroneck (village) Westchester County	260	1.39
Newburgh (city) Orange County	330	1.17
North Bay Shore (cdp) Suffolk County	166	1.11
New Rochelle (city) Westchester County	791	1.10
Brentwood (cdp) Suffolk County	544	1.01
Mamaroneck (town) Westchester County	226	0.78

Hispanic: Uruguayan

Top 10 Places Sorted by Number
Based on all places, regardless of population

Place	Number	%
New York (city) New York City	1,907	0.02
Ossining (town) Westchester County	205	0.56
Hempstead (town) Nassau County	185	0.02
Ossining (village) Westchester County	179	0.75
Rye (town) Westchester County	122	0.28
Port Chester (village) Westchester County	95	0.34
Islip (town) Suffolk County	88	0.03
New Rochelle (city) Westchester County	72	0.10
Babylon (town) Suffolk County	50	0.02
Peekskill (city) Westchester County	49	0.22

Top 10 Places Sorted by Percent
Based on all places, regardless of population

Place	Number	%
Ossining (village) Westchester County	179	0.75
Ossining (town) Westchester County	205	0.56
Verplanck (cdp) Westchester County	4	0.51
Plandome Heights (village) Nassau County	4	0.41
Crugers (cdp) Westchester County	7	0.40
Port Chester (village) Westchester County	95	0.34
Otselic (town) Chenango County	3	0.30
Rye (town) Westchester County	122	0.28
Montauk (cdp) Suffolk County	10	0.26
Peekskill (city) Westchester County	49	0.22

Top 10 Places Sorted by Percent
Based on places with populations of 10,000 or more

Place	Number	%
Ossining (village) Westchester County	179	0.75
Ossining (town) Westchester County	205	0.56
Port Chester (village) Westchester County	95	0.34
Rye (town) Westchester County	122	0.28
Peekskill (city) Westchester County	49	0.22
Mamaroneck (village) Westchester County	31	0.17
Putnam Valley (town) Putnam County	13	0.12
Harrison (village) Westchester County	27	0.11
New Rochelle (city) Westchester County	72	0.10
New Castle (town) Westchester County	17	0.10

Hispanic: Venezuelan

Top 10 Places Sorted by Number
Based on all places, regardless of population

Place	Number	%
New York (city) New York City	6,713	0.08
Hempstead (town) Nassau County	235	0.03
Islip (town) Suffolk County	139	0.04
Yonkers (city) Westchester County	126	0.06
Brookhaven (town) Suffolk County	103	0.02
North Hempstead (town) Nassau County	81	0.04
New Rochelle (city) Westchester County	70	0.10
Brentwood (cdp) Suffolk County	65	0.12
Babylon (town) Suffolk County	59	0.03
Oyster Bay (town) Nassau County	54	0.02

Top 10 Places Sorted by Percent
Based on all places, regardless of population

Place	Number	%
Forest Home (cdp) Tompkins County	11	1.17
Halcott (town) Greene County	2	1.04
Cragsmoor (cdp) Ulster County	2	0.42
Fishers Island (cdp) Suffolk County	1	0.35
Kensington (village) Nassau County	4	0.33
Pine Hill (cdp) Ulster County	1	0.32
East Hampton (village) Suffolk County	4	0.30
East Hampton North (cdp) Suffolk County	10	0.28
Great Neck Gardens (cdp) Nassau County	3	0.28
Spackenkill (cdp) Dutchess County	13	0.27

Top 10 Places Sorted by Percent
Based on places with populations of 10,000 or more

Place	Number	%
East Hampton (town) Suffolk County	30	0.15
Glen Cove (city) Nassau County	34	0.13
Mamaroneck (village) Westchester County	25	0.13
Brentwood (cdp) Suffolk County	65	0.12
Mamaroneck (town) Westchester County	32	0.11
West Haverstraw (village) Rockland County	11	0.11
New Rochelle (city) Westchester County	70	0.10
Ithaca (town) Tompkins County	19	0.10
Highlands (town) Orange County	12	0.10
East Rockaway (village) Nassau County	10	0.10

Hispanic: Other South American

Top 10 Places Sorted by Number
Based on all places, regardless of population

Place	Number	%
New York (city) New York City	6,836	0.09
Hempstead (town) Nassau County	498	0.07
Islip (town) Suffolk County	241	0.07
Brookhaven (town) Suffolk County	220	0.05
North Hempstead (town) Nassau County	186	0.08
Oyster Bay (town) Nassau County	159	0.05
Yonkers (city) Westchester County	141	0.07
Rye (town) Westchester County	103	0.23
Brentwood (cdp) Suffolk County	102	0.19
Babylon (town) Suffolk County	100	0.05

Top 10 Places Sorted by Percent
Based on all places, regardless of population

Place	Number	%
Upper Brookville (village) Nassau County	15	0.83
Forest Home (cdp) Tompkins County	7	0.74
High Falls (cdp) Ulster County	4	0.64
Danube (town) Herkimer County	6	0.55
Fairview (cdp) Westchester County	14	0.48
Russell Gardens (village) Nassau County	5	0.47
Bellerose Terrace (cdp) Nassau County	10	0.46
East Garden City (cdp) Nassau County	4	0.41
North Lynbrook (cdp) Nassau County	3	0.40
Quiogue (cdp) Suffolk County	3	0.38

Top 10 Places Sorted by Percent
Based on places with populations of 10,000 or more

Place	Number	%
Patchogue (village) Suffolk County	44	0.37
Port Chester (village) Westchester County	95	0.34
Ossining (village) Westchester County	67	0.28
Mineola (village) Nassau County	46	0.24
Rye (town) Westchester County	103	0.23
Ossining (town) Westchester County	74	0.20
Brentwood (cdp) Suffolk County	102	0.19
North Bay Shore (cdp) Suffolk County	25	0.17
Salisbury (cdp) Nassau County	21	0.17
Kings Park (cdp) Suffolk County	26	0.16

Hispanic: Other

Top 10 Places Sorted by Number
Based on all places, regardless of population

Place	Number	%
New York (city) New York City	401,108	5.01
Hempstead (town) Nassau County	22,655	3.00
Islip (town) Suffolk County	13,353	4.14
Yonkers (city) Westchester County	8,855	4.52
Brookhaven (town) Suffolk County	7,071	1.58
Brentwood (cdp) Suffolk County	6,219	11.53
North Hempstead (town) Nassau County	5,592	2.51
Hempstead (village) Nassau County	5,550	9.81
Babylon (town) Suffolk County	4,608	2.18
Freeport (village) Nassau County	3,815	8.71

Top 10 Places Sorted by Percent
Based on all places, regardless of population

Place	Number	%
Brentwood (cdp) Suffolk County	6,219	11.53
Sleepy Hollow (village) Westchester County	1,004	10.90
Port Chester (village) Westchester County	2,861	10.27
Haverstraw (village) Rockland County	1,037	10.25
North Bay Shore (cdp) Suffolk County	1,476	9.85

Notes: (cdp) census designated place; Refer to the User's Guide in the front of the book for more detailed information.

PROFILES OF NEW YORK / Ancestry: Rankings 689

Place	Number	%
Hempstead (village) Nassau County	5,550	9.81
Freeport (village) Nassau County	3,815	8.71
New Cassel (cdp) Nassau County	1,076	8.09
Rye (town) Westchester County	3,291	7.50
Central Islip (cdp) Suffolk County	2,301	7.20

Top 10 Places Sorted by Percent
Based on places with populations of 10,000 or more

Place	Number	%
Brentwood (cdp) Suffolk County	6,219	11.53
Port Chester (village) Westchester County	2,861	10.27
Haverstraw (village) Rockland County	1,037	10.25
North Bay Shore (cdp) Suffolk County	1,476	9.85
Hempstead (village) Nassau County	5,550	9.81
Freeport (village) Nassau County	3,815	8.71
New Cassel (cdp) Nassau County	1,076	8.09
Rye (town) Westchester County	3,291	7.50
Central Islip (cdp) Suffolk County	2,301	7.20
Uniondale (cdp) Nassau County	1,592	6.92

Hungarian

Top 10 Places Sorted by Number
Based on all places, regardless of population

Place	Number	%
New York (city) New York City	48,879	0.61
Hempstead (town) Nassau County	7,004	0.93
Brookhaven (town) Suffolk County	4,122	0.92
Oyster Bay (town) Nassau County	3,453	1.17
Ramapo (town) Rockland County	2,708	2.49
Monroe (town) Orange County	2,620	8.32
North Hempstead (town) Nassau County	2,470	1.11
Buffalo (city) Erie County	2,190	0.75
Kiryas Joel (village) Orange County	2,010	15.21
Huntington (town) Suffolk County	1,955	1.00

Top 10 Places Sorted by Percent
Based on all places, regardless of population

Place	Number	%
Kiryas Joel (village) Orange County	2,010	15.21
Monroe (town) Orange County	2,620	8.32
Greig (town) Lewis County	102	7.77
Kaser (village) Rockland County	243	7.37
New Square (village) Rockland County	315	6.69
Norfolk (town) Saint Lawrence County	279	6.11
East Kingston (cdp) Ulster County	16	6.11
Kenoza (cdp) Ulster County	56	5.58
Lawrence (village) Nassau County	359	5.50
Viola (cdp) Rockland County	307	5.17

Top 10 Places Sorted by Percent
Based on places with populations of 10,000 or more

Place	Number	%
Kiryas Joel (village) Orange County	2,010	15.21
Monroe (town) Orange County	2,620	8.32
Monsey (cdp) Rockland County	752	5.12
Grand Island (town) Erie County	660	3.54
Tonawanda (city) Erie County	516	3.20
Dobbs Ferry (village) Westchester County	297	2.80
Ramapo (town) Rockland County	2,708	2.49
Woodmere (cdp) Nassau County	399	2.43
Scarsdale (village) Westchester County	417	2.34
Lewisboro (town) Westchester County	277	2.25

Icelander

Top 10 Places Sorted by Number
Based on all places, regardless of population

Place	Number	%
New York (city) New York City	541	0.01
Hempstead (town) Nassau County	97	0.01
Babylon (town) Suffolk County	76	0.04
Brookhaven (town) Suffolk County	63	0.01
Oyster Bay (town) Nassau County	56	0.02
Amityville (village) Suffolk County	46	0.49
Islip (town) Suffolk County	37	0.01
Somers (town) Westchester County	36	0.20
Garden City (village) Nassau County	32	0.15
Brunswick (town) Rensselaer County	30	0.26

Top 10 Places Sorted by Percent
Based on all places, regardless of population

Place	Number	%
Lincolndale (cdp) Westchester County	29	1.53
Homer (village) Cortland County	18	0.54
Ancram (town) Columbia County	8	0.53
Amityville (village) Suffolk County	46	0.49
Keene (town) Essex County	5	0.47
Paris (town) Oneida County	19	0.41
Old Field (village) Suffolk County	4	0.41
Cayuga (village) Cayuga County	2	0.39
Pamelia (town) Jefferson County	11	0.38
Rossie (town) Saint Lawrence County	3	0.38

Top 10 Places Sorted by Percent
Based on places with populations of 10,000 or more

Place	Number	%
West Haverstraw (village) Rockland County	28	0.27
Brunswick (town) Rensselaer County	30	0.26
Somers (town) Westchester County	36	0.20
Rye (city) Westchester County	30	0.20
Garden City (village) Nassau County	32	0.15
Sayville (cdp) Suffolk County	24	0.14
Hauppauge (cdp) Suffolk County	26	0.13
Depew (village) Erie County	20	0.12
Patchogue (village) Suffolk County	13	0.11
Beekman (town) Dutchess County	11	0.10

Iranian

Top 10 Places Sorted by Number
Based on all places, regardless of population

Place	Number	%
New York (city) New York City	8,506	0.11
North Hempstead (town) Nassau County	7,622	3.42
Great Neck (village) Nassau County	2,061	21.60
Kings Point (village) Nassau County	1,486	29.28
Hempstead (town) Nassau County	954	0.13
Oyster Bay (town) Nassau County	751	0.26
Great Neck Plaza (village) Nassau County	580	9.15
Huntington (town) Suffolk County	464	0.24
Flower Hill (village) Nassau County	367	8.14
Brookhaven (town) Suffolk County	325	0.07

Top 10 Places Sorted by Percent
Based on all places, regardless of population

Place	Number	%
Kings Point (village) Nassau County	1,486	29.28
Great Neck (village) Nassau County	2,061	21.60
Harbor Hills (cdp) Nassau County	113	19.72
Saddle Rock (village) Nassau County	123	15.55
Kensington (village) Nassau County	182	14.90
Great Neck Gardens (cdp) Nassau County	147	13.16
Great Neck Estates (village) Nassau County	304	10.76
Great Neck Plaza (village) Nassau County	580	9.15
Flower Hill (village) Nassau County	367	8.14
Thomaston (village) Nassau County	149	5.74

Top 10 Places Sorted by Percent
Based on places with populations of 10,000 or more

Place	Number	%
North Hempstead (town) Nassau County	7,622	3.42
North New Hyde Park (cdp) Nassau County	170	1.17
Mineola (village) Nassau County	179	0.93
North Valley Stream (cdp) Nassau County	131	0.83
Glen Cove (city) Nassau County	179	0.67
Suffern (village) Rockland County	74	0.67
Tarrytown (village) Westchester County	69	0.62
Stony Brook (cdp) Suffolk County	79	0.58
Huntington Station (cdp) Suffolk County	154	0.51
Arlington (cdp) Dutchess County	56	0.45

Irish

Top 10 Places Sorted by Number
Based on all places, regardless of population

Place	Number	%
New York (city) New York City	420,810	5.25
Hempstead (town) Nassau County	133,307	17.63
Brookhaven (town) Suffolk County	112,354	25.06
Islip (town) Suffolk County	69,514	21.55
Oyster Bay (town) Nassau County	60,453	20.57
Babylon (town) Suffolk County	43,411	20.50
Huntington (town) Suffolk County	41,599	21.30
Buffalo (city) Erie County	35,608	12.17
Smithtown (town) Suffolk County	30,091	26.00
North Hempstead (town) Nassau County	28,740	12.91

Top 10 Places Sorted by Percent
Based on all places, regardless of population

Place	Number	%
Pearl River (cdp) Rockland County	7,256	46.60
Point Lookout (cdp) Nassau County	705	46.38
Peach Lake (cdp) Putnam County	694	40.73
Westvale (cdp) Onondaga County	2,082	40.45
Verplanck (cdp) Westchester County	299	40.35
Phoenicia (cdp) Ulster County	162	40.30
Plandome (village) Nassau County	512	40.25
Brightwaters (village) Suffolk County	1,299	39.99
Stewart Manor (village) Nassau County	761	39.23
West Hampton Dunes (village) Suffolk County	3	37.50

Top 10 Places Sorted by Percent
Based on places with populations of 10,000 or more

Place	Number	%
Pearl River (cdp) Rockland County	7,256	46.60
Floral Park (village) Nassau County	5,771	36.10
Stony Point (town) Rockland County	5,104	35.83
Sayville (cdp) Suffolk County	5,967	35.65
Garden City (village) Nassau County	7,627	35.21
Kent (town) Putnam County	4,733	33.79
Rockville Centre (village) Nassau County	8,214	33.43
Miller Place (cdp) Suffolk County	3,459	32.43
Brunswick (town) Rensselaer County	3,757	32.06
Manorville (cdp) Suffolk County	3,515	31.48

Israeli

Top 10 Places Sorted by Number
Based on all places, regardless of population

Place	Number	%
New York (city) New York City	20,946	0.26
Hempstead (town) Nassau County	1,877	0.25
North Hempstead (town) Nassau County	1,348	0.61
Ramapo (town) Rockland County	917	0.84
Oyster Bay (town) Nassau County	821	0.28
Woodmere (cdp) Nassau County	450	2.74
Plainview (cdp) Nassau County	381	1.49
Brookhaven (town) Suffolk County	360	0.08
Monsey (cdp) Rockland County	330	2.25
Monroe (town) Orange County	305	0.97

Top 10 Places Sorted by Percent
Based on all places, regardless of population

Place	Number	%
Kensington (village) Nassau County	78	6.42

Notes: (cdp) census designated place; Refer to the User's Guide in the front of the book for more detailed information.

Place	Number	%
Saddle Rock (village) Nassau County	45	5.69
Great Neck Estates (village) Nassau County	133	4.71
Lawrence (village) Nassau County	248	3.80
Wesley Hills (village) Rockland County	182	3.69
Kaser (village) Rockland County	95	2.88
Woodmere (cdp) Nassau County	450	2.74
Hewlett Bay Park (village) Nassau County	12	2.47
Great Neck (village) Nassau County	224	2.35
Monsey (cdp) Rockland County	330	2.25

Top 10 Places Sorted by Percent
Based on places with populations of 10,000 or more

Place	Number	%
Woodmere (cdp) Nassau County	450	2.74
Monsey (cdp) Rockland County	330	2.25
Kiryas Joel (village) Orange County	274	2.07
Plainview (cdp) Nassau County	381	1.49
Monroe (town) Orange County	305	0.97
Ramapo (town) Rockland County	917	0.84
Melville (cdp) Suffolk County	90	0.62
North Hempstead (town) Nassau County	1,348	0.61
Scarsdale (village) Westchester County	105	0.59
Oceanside (cdp) Nassau County	190	0.58

Italian

Top 10 Places Sorted by Number
Based on all places, regardless of population

Place	Number	%
New York (city) New York City	692,739	8.65
Hempstead (town) Nassau County	179,140	23.70
Brookhaven (town) Suffolk County	147,077	32.81
Oyster Bay (town) Nassau County	87,807	29.87
Islip (town) Suffolk County	83,408	25.85
Babylon (town) Suffolk County	63,967	30.20
Huntington (town) Suffolk County	51,869	26.56
Smithtown (town) Suffolk County	40,891	35.34
North Hempstead (town) Nassau County	39,788	17.87
Yonkers (city) Westchester County	36,907	18.82

Top 10 Places Sorted by Percent
Based on all places, regardless of population

Place	Number	%
Saltaire (village) Suffolk County	51	75.00
Malverne Park Oaks (cdp) Nassau County	259	52.01
Frankfort (village) Herkimer County	1,239	48.93
North Massapequa (cdp) Nassau County	9,368	48.91
Franklin Square (cdp) Nassau County	13,970	47.61
Frankfort (town) Herkimer County	3,349	44.78
Hawthorne (cdp) Westchester County	2,227	44.07
North Lynbrook (cdp) Nassau County	287	43.82
Shrub Oak (cdp) Westchester County	791	42.94
Deer Park (cdp) Suffolk County	11,899	42.10

Top 10 Places Sorted by Percent
Based on places with populations of 10,000 or more

Place	Number	%
North Massapequa (cdp) Nassau County	9,368	48.91
Franklin Square (cdp) Nassau County	13,970	47.61
Deer Park (cdp) Suffolk County	11,899	42.10
Massapequa Park (village) Nassau County	7,169	40.97
Lake Grove (village) Suffolk County	4,236	40.74
Holtsville (cdp) Suffolk County	6,821	40.18
Selden (cdp) Suffolk County	8,748	40.10
Holbrook (cdp) Suffolk County	10,982	39.89
Ronkonkoma (cdp) Suffolk County	7,963	39.73
Farmingville (cdp) Suffolk County	6,530	39.60

Latvian

Top 10 Places Sorted by Number
Based on all places, regardless of population

Place	Number	%
New York (city) New York City	3,777	0.05
Hempstead (town) Nassau County	490	0.06
Oyster Bay (town) Nassau County	275	0.09
Brookhaven (town) Suffolk County	261	0.06
North Hempstead (town) Nassau County	234	0.11
Babylon (town) Suffolk County	170	0.08
Huntington (town) Suffolk County	167	0.09
Buffalo (city) Erie County	144	0.05
De Witt (town) Onondaga County	135	0.56
Islip (town) Suffolk County	135	0.04

Top 10 Places Sorted by Percent
Based on all places, regardless of population

Place	Number	%
New Hudson (town) Allegany County	40	5.45
Lorraine (town) Jefferson County	11	1.20
Tully (village) Onondaga County	11	1.19
Fort Montgomery (cdp) Orange County	16	1.16
Sherman (village) Chautauqua County	8	1.15
Hunter (town) Greene County	29	1.07
Esperance (village) Schoharie County	4	1.04
Argyle (village) Washington County	3	1.04
Caroline (town) Tompkins County	29	1.02
Woodridge (village) Sullivan County	9	1.01

Top 10 Places Sorted by Percent
Based on places with populations of 10,000 or more

Place	Number	%
De Witt (town) Onondaga County	135	0.56
La Grange (town) Dutchess County	78	0.52
Port Washington (cdp) Nassau County	55	0.36
Hampton Bays (cdp) Suffolk County	39	0.32
Mamaroneck (town) Westchester County	80	0.28
Elma (town) Erie County	32	0.28
Saugerties (town) Ulster County	54	0.27
South Farmingdale (cdp) Nassau County	37	0.25
Syosset (cdp) Nassau County	44	0.24
Scarsdale (village) Westchester County	42	0.24

Lithuanian

Top 10 Places Sorted by Number
Based on all places, regardless of population

Place	Number	%
New York (city) New York City	13,847	0.17
Hempstead (town) Nassau County	2,517	0.33
Brookhaven (town) Suffolk County	1,800	0.40
Oyster Bay (town) Nassau County	1,389	0.47
North Hempstead (town) Nassau County	1,128	0.51
Islip (town) Suffolk County	967	0.30
Huntington (town) Suffolk County	962	0.49
Smithtown (town) Suffolk County	583	0.50
Amsterdam (city) Montgomery County	530	2.89
Babylon (town) Suffolk County	505	0.24

Top 10 Places Sorted by Percent
Based on all places, regardless of population

Place	Number	%
Fort Johnson (village) Montgomery County	34	6.81
Hagaman (village) Montgomery County	75	5.57
Saddle Rock Estates (cdp) Nassau County	24	5.47
Amsterdam (town) Montgomery County	240	4.12
East Marion (cdp) Suffolk County	28	3.61
Lyon Mountain (cdp) Clinton County	15	3.11
Thomaston (village) Nassau County	80	3.08
Florida (town) Montgomery County	80	2.93
Amsterdam (city) Montgomery County	530	2.89
Hoosick Falls (village) Rensselaer County	97	2.82

Top 10 Places Sorted by Percent
Based on places with populations of 10,000 or more

Place	Number	%
Amsterdam (city) Montgomery County	530	2.89
Southold (town) Suffolk County	245	1.19
Pittsford (town) Monroe County	284	1.04
Johnson City (village) Broome County	160	1.03
Vestal (town) Broome County	261	0.98
East Greenbush (town) Rensselaer County	152	0.97
East Hampton (town) Suffolk County	189	0.96
Glenville (town) Schenectady County	265	0.94
Watervliet (city) Albany County	92	0.90
Hampton Bays (cdp) Suffolk County	109	0.89

Luxemburger

Top 10 Places Sorted by Number
Based on all places, regardless of population

Place	Number	%
New York (city) New York City	233	0.00
Mamaroneck (town) Westchester County	43	0.15
Larchmont (village) Westchester County	35	0.5
Watertown (city) Jefferson County	28	0.1
Amherst (town) Erie County	28	0.02
Buffalo (city) Erie County	28	0.0
Bethlehem (town) Albany County	26	0.0
Cortlandt (town) Westchester County	25	0.0
Sheldon (town) Wyoming County	23	0.9
Cortland West (cdp) Cortland County	19	1.3

Top 10 Places Sorted by Percent
Based on all places, regardless of population

Place	Number	%
Cortland West (cdp) Cortland County	19	1.3
Laurens (village) Otsego County	3	1.0
Accord (cdp) Ulster County	7	0.9
Sheldon (town) Wyoming County	23	0.9
Hamden (town) Delaware County	11	0.8
Taylor (town) Cortland County	3	0.6
Croghan (village) Lewis County	4	0.5
Larchmont (village) Westchester County	35	0.5
Jamesport (cdp) Suffolk County	8	0.5
Otto (town) Cattaraugus County	3	0.3

Top 10 Places Sorted by Percent
Based on places with populations of 10,000 or more

Place	Number	%
Mamaroneck (town) Westchester County	43	0.1
Watertown (city) Jefferson County	28	0.1
Fallsburg (town) Sullivan County	11	0.0
Bethlehem (town) Albany County	26	0.0
Cortlandt (town) Westchester County	25	0.0
Le Ray (town) Jefferson County	12	0.0
Dunkirk (city) Chautauqua County	8	0.0
Lewisboro (town) Westchester County	7	0.0
Pelham (town) Westchester County	7	0.0
New Hartford (town) Oneida County	10	0.0

Macedonian

Top 10 Places Sorted by Number
Based on all places, regardless of population

Place	Number	%
New York (city) New York City	1,736	0.
Irondequoit (cdp) Monroe County	319	0.6
Chili (town) Monroe County	220	0.8
Clay (town) Onondaga County	215	0.2
Hamburg (town) Erie County	198	0.3
Syracuse (city) Onondaga County	139	0.
West Seneca (town) Erie County	127	0.2

Notes: (cdp) census designated place; Refer to the User's Guide in the front of the book for more detailed information.

Place	Number	%
ackawanna (city) Erie County	113	0.59
Salina (town) Onondaga County	109	0.33
Rochester (city) Monroe County	108	0.05

Top 10 Places Sorted by Percent
Based on all places, regardless of population

Place	Number	%
Elma Center (cdp) Erie County	22	0.90
Blasdell (village) Erie County	24	0.88
North Salem (town) Westchester County	45	0.87
Sloatsburg (village) Rockland County	27	0.87
Galeville (cdp) Onondaga County	36	0.82
Chili (town) Monroe County	220	0.80
Irondequoit (cdp) Monroe County	319	0.61
Lackawanna (city) Erie County	113	0.59
Sodus (town) Wayne County	39	0.44
Boston (town) Erie County	34	0.43

Top 10 Places Sorted by Percent
Based on places with populations of 10,000 or more

Place	Number	%
Chili (town) Monroe County	220	0.80
Irondequoit (cdp) Monroe County	319	0.61
Lackawanna (city) Erie County	113	0.59
Fairmount (cdp) Onondaga County	42	0.39
Clay (town) Onondaga County	215	0.37
Hamburg (town) Erie County	198	0.35
Salina (town) Onondaga County	109	0.33
Onondaga (town) Onondaga County	65	0.31
West Seneca (town) Erie County	127	0.28
Gates (town) Monroe County	71	0.24

Maltese

Top 10 Places Sorted by Number
Based on all places, regardless of population

Place	Number	%
New York (city) New York City	3,082	0.04
Hempstead (town) Nassau County	730	0.10
Brookhaven (town) Suffolk County	587	0.13
Oyster Bay (town) Nassau County	390	0.13
Islip (town) Suffolk County	388	0.12
Babylon (town) Suffolk County	218	0.10
North Hempstead (town) Nassau County	158	0.07
Smithtown (town) Suffolk County	149	0.13
Huntington (town) Suffolk County	140	0.07
Franklin Square (cdp) Nassau County	123	0.42

Top 10 Places Sorted by Percent
Based on all places, regardless of population

Place	Number	%
Lemus Point (village) Chautauqua County	6	1.75
Grand View-on-Hudson (village) Rockland County	3	1.06
Manhasset Hills (cdp) Nassau County	30	0.82
Mastic Beach (cdp) Suffolk County	88	0.76
Farmingdale (village) Nassau County	63	0.75
East Quogue (cdp) Suffolk County	32	0.75
Sandome Manor (village) Nassau County	6	0.72
Walton Park (cdp) Orange County	17	0.71
East Williston (village) Nassau County	17	0.68
Highland Mills (cdp) Orange County	20	0.58

Top 10 Places Sorted by Percent
Based on places with populations of 10,000 or more

Place	Number	%
Mastic Beach (cdp) Suffolk County	88	0.76
Ronkonkoma (cdp) Suffolk County	102	0.51
Franklin Square (cdp) Nassau County	123	0.42
Lake Grove (village) Suffolk County	42	0.40
Rocky Point (cdp) Suffolk County	41	0.40
Shirley (cdp) Suffolk County	84	0.33
Blooming Grove (town) Orange County	58	0.33

Place	Number	%
North Bellmore (cdp) Nassau County	62	0.31
Seaford (cdp) Nassau County	47	0.30
Manorville (cdp) Suffolk County	34	0.30

New Zealander

Top 10 Places Sorted by Number
Based on all places, regardless of population

Place	Number	%
New York (city) New York City	559	0.01
Hempstead (town) Nassau County	86	0.01
Levittown (cdp) Nassau County	56	0.11
Southampton (town) Suffolk County	37	0.07
Yorktown (town) Westchester County	27	0.07
Southampton (village) Suffolk County	26	0.66
Yonkers (city) Westchester County	23	0.01
Northeast Ithaca (cdp) Tompkins County	22	0.81
Ithaca (town) Tompkins County	22	0.12
Nassau (town) Rensselaer County	20	0.42

Top 10 Places Sorted by Percent
Based on all places, regardless of population

Place	Number	%
Sagaponack (cdp) Suffolk County	11	2.03
Northeast Ithaca (cdp) Tompkins County	22	0.81
Southampton (village) Suffolk County	26	0.66
Nassau (town) Rensselaer County	20	0.42
Clinton (village) Oneida County	7	0.36
Waddington (village) Saint Lawrence County	3	0.33
Lake Success (village) Nassau County	7	0.25
New Bremen (town) Lewis County	5	0.19
Otisville (village) Orange County	2	0.19
Woodstock (town) Ulster County	10	0.16

Top 10 Places Sorted by Percent
Based on places with populations of 10,000 or more

Place	Number	%
Rye (city) Westchester County	19	0.13
Ithaca (town) Tompkins County	22	0.12
Levittown (cdp) Nassau County	56	0.11
New Castle (town) Westchester County	19	0.11
Bedford (town) Westchester County	17	0.09
Lewiston (town) Niagara County	14	0.09
New Paltz (town) Ulster County	11	0.09
Southampton (town) Suffolk County	37	0.07
Yorktown (town) Westchester County	27	0.07
Port Washington (cdp) Nassau County	10	0.07

Northern European

Top 10 Places Sorted by Number
Based on all places, regardless of population

Place	Number	%
New York (city) New York City	1,917	0.02
Hempstead (town) Nassau County	156	0.02
Syracuse (city) Onondaga County	107	0.07
Rochester (city) Monroe County	92	0.04
Brookhaven (town) Suffolk County	86	0.02
Huntington (town) Suffolk County	82	0.04
Warwick (town) Orange County	63	0.20
Manlius (town) Onondaga County	61	0.19
Brighton (town) Monroe County	59	0.17
New Rochelle (city) Westchester County	56	0.08

Top 10 Places Sorted by Percent
Based on all places, regardless of population

Place	Number	%
New Suffolk (cdp) Suffolk County	10	3.07
Brandon (town) Franklin County	9	1.68
West Sand Lake (cdp) Rensselaer County	35	1.38
Canaan (town) Columbia County	25	1.37
Aurora (village) Cayuga County	8	1.12

Place	Number	%
Forest Home (cdp) Tompkins County	11	1.08
Hague (town) Warren County	8	0.94
East Hampton (village) Suffolk County	12	0.91
Danube (town) Herkimer County	10	0.91
Churchville (village) Monroe County	17	0.90

Top 10 Places Sorted by Percent
Based on places with populations of 10,000 or more

Place	Number	%
Putnam Valley (town) Putnam County	35	0.33
East Rockaway (village) Nassau County	33	0.32
Fort Drum (cdp) Jefferson County	36	0.30
Schodack (town) Rensselaer County	36	0.29
La Grange (town) Dutchess County	38	0.25
Blooming Grove (town) Orange County	39	0.22
Oneonta (city) Otsego County	28	0.21
Warwick (town) Orange County	63	0.20
Onondaga (town) Onondaga County	43	0.20
East Greenbush (town) Rensselaer County	32	0.20

Norwegian

Top 10 Places Sorted by Number
Based on all places, regardless of population

Place	Number	%
New York (city) New York City	23,849	0.30
Brookhaven (town) Suffolk County	5,636	1.26
Hempstead (town) Nassau County	4,339	0.57
Islip (town) Suffolk County	2,627	0.81
Oyster Bay (town) Nassau County	2,311	0.79
Huntington (town) Suffolk County	1,904	0.97
Babylon (town) Suffolk County	1,678	0.79
Smithtown (town) Suffolk County	1,485	1.28
North Hempstead (town) Nassau County	787	0.35
Buffalo (city) Erie County	627	0.21

Top 10 Places Sorted by Percent
Based on all places, regardless of population

Place	Number	%
Meridian (village) Cayuga County	22	6.40
Rifton (cdp) Ulster County	29	6.24
Smallwood (cdp) Sullivan County	32	4.90
North Haven (village) Suffolk County	36	4.84
Arietta (town) Hamilton County	15	4.60
Gilgo-Oak Beach-Captree (cdp) Suffolk County	14	4.33
Claverack-Red Mills (cdp) Columbia County	43	4.23
Bovina (town) Delaware County	27	4.08
Ashland (town) Greene County	31	4.06
Newfield Hamlet (cdp) Tompkins County	32	4.02

Top 10 Places Sorted by Percent
Based on places with populations of 10,000 or more

Place	Number	%
Saint James (cdp) Suffolk County	347	2.62
Rocky Point (cdp) Suffolk County	263	2.57
Ridge (cdp) Suffolk County	275	2.07
Highlands (town) Orange County	252	2.02
Farmingville (cdp) Suffolk County	331	2.01
Miller Place (cdp) Suffolk County	203	1.90
Saugerties (town) Ulster County	357	1.81
Red Hook (town) Dutchess County	187	1.80
Lansing (town) Tompkins County	182	1.77
Rye (city) Westchester County	260	1.74

Pennsylvania German

Top 10 Places Sorted by Number
Based on all places, regardless of population

Place	Number	%
New York (city) New York City	350	0.00
Binghamton (city) Broome County	223	0.47
Union (town) Broome County	223	0.40

Notes: (cdp) census designated place; Refer to the User's Guide in the front of the book for more detailed information.

Place	Number	%
Elmira (city) Chemung County	203	0.66
Southport (town) Chemung County	189	1.69
Buffalo (city) Erie County	125	0.04
Leon (town) Cattaraugus County	124	8.74
Horseheads (town) Chemung County	102	0.52
Fenton (town) Broome County	99	1.43
Conewango (town) Cattaraugus County	98	5.79

Top 10 Places Sorted by Percent
Based on all places, regardless of population

Place	Number	%
Leon (town) Cattaraugus County	124	8.74
Conewango (town) Cattaraugus County	98	5.79
Napoli (town) Cattaraugus County	57	4.84
Sherman (town) Chautauqua County	43	2.82
Troupsburg (town) Steuben County	26	2.33
Barrington (town) Yates County	32	2.29
Cherry Creek (town) Chautauqua County	25	2.17
Clymer (town) Chautauqua County	32	2.05
Romulus (town) Seneca County	41	2.01
Smallwood (cdp) Sullivan County	13	1.99

Top 10 Places Sorted by Percent
Based on places with populations of 10,000 or more

Place	Number	%
Southport (town) Chemung County	189	1.69
Elmira (city) Chemung County	203	0.66
Endwell (cdp) Broome County	62	0.53
Horseheads (town) Chemung County	102	0.52
Binghamton (city) Broome County	223	0.47
Corning (city) Steuben County	50	0.46
Union (town) Broome County	223	0.40
Johnson City (village) Broome County	60	0.39
Vestal (town) Broome County	96	0.36
Dryden (town) Tompkins County	47	0.34

Polish

Top 10 Places Sorted by Number
Based on all places, regardless of population

Place	Number	%
New York (city) New York City	213,447	2.67
Hempstead (town) Nassau County	38,256	5.06
Cheektowaga (town) Erie County	37,560	39.95
Buffalo (city) Erie County	34,254	11.70
Brookhaven (town) Suffolk County	26,848	5.99
Oyster Bay (town) Nassau County	19,752	6.72
Amherst (town) Erie County	15,136	12.99
West Seneca (town) Erie County	14,236	30.95
Islip (town) Suffolk County	14,034	4.35
Lancaster (town) Erie County	13,903	35.63

Top 10 Places Sorted by Percent
Based on all places, regardless of population

Place	Number	%
Sloan (village) Erie County	2,117	55.84
Depew (village) Erie County	6,687	40.24
Cheektowaga (town) Erie County	37,560	39.95
West Hampton Dunes (village) Suffolk County	3	37.50
New York Mills (village) Oneida County	1,190	37.00
Yorkville (village) Oneida County	973	36.31
Dunkirk (town) Chautauqua County	510	36.27
Lancaster (town) Erie County	13,903	35.63
West Seneca (town) Erie County	14,236	30.95
Lackawanna (city) Erie County	5,656	29.70

Top 10 Places Sorted by Percent
Based on places with populations of 10,000 or more

Place	Number	%
Depew (village) Erie County	6,687	40.24
Cheektowaga (town) Erie County	37,560	39.95
Lancaster (town) Erie County	13,903	35.63
West Seneca (town) Erie County	14,236	30.95
Lackawanna (city) Erie County	5,656	29.70
Lancaster (village) Erie County	3,317	29.65
Elma (town) Erie County	3,284	29.05
Dunkirk (city) Chautauqua County	3,641	27.73
Alden (town) Erie County	2,572	24.57
Hamburg (town) Erie County	12,779	22.74

Portuguese

Top 10 Places Sorted by Number
Based on all places, regardless of population

Place	Number	%
New York (city) New York City	11,307	0.14
North Hempstead (town) Nassau County	3,259	1.46
Brookhaven (town) Suffolk County	2,972	0.66
Yonkers (city) Westchester County	2,558	1.30
Hempstead (town) Nassau County	2,111	0.28
Mineola (village) Nassau County	2,076	10.79
Islip (town) Suffolk County	1,771	0.55
Mount Vernon (city) Westchester County	1,498	2.19
New Rochelle (city) Westchester County	722	1.00
Oyster Bay (town) Nassau County	710	0.24

Top 10 Places Sorted by Percent
Based on all places, regardless of population

Place	Number	%
Mineola (village) Nassau County	2,076	10.79
Williston Park (village) Nassau County	263	3.62
Carle Place (cdp) Nassau County	147	2.80
Sleepy Hollow (village) Westchester County	251	2.72
Andes (village) Delaware County	8	2.54
Pine Bush (village) Orange County	37	2.48
Mahopac (cdp) Putnam County	209	2.44
Ossining (village) Westchester County	528	2.20
Mount Vernon (city) Westchester County	1,498	2.19
Eastport (cdp) Suffolk County	30	2.03

Top 10 Places Sorted by Percent
Based on places with populations of 10,000 or more

Place	Number	%
Mineola (village) Nassau County	2,076	10.79
Ossining (village) Westchester County	528	2.20
Mount Vernon (city) Westchester County	1,498	2.19
Selden (cdp) Suffolk County	421	1.93
Farmingville (cdp) Suffolk County	313	1.90
Ossining (town) Westchester County	615	1.68
Mamaroneck (village) Westchester County	303	1.61
Ronkonkoma (cdp) Suffolk County	295	1.47
North Hempstead (town) Nassau County	3,259	1.46
Yonkers (city) Westchester County	2,558	1.30

Romanian

Top 10 Places Sorted by Number
Based on all places, regardless of population

Place	Number	%
New York (city) New York City	30,360	0.38
Hempstead (town) Nassau County	3,220	0.43
Oyster Bay (town) Nassau County	1,381	0.47
North Hempstead (town) Nassau County	1,317	0.59
Huntington (town) Suffolk County	951	0.49
Brookhaven (town) Suffolk County	919	0.21
Ramapo (town) Rockland County	823	0.76
Clarkstown (town) Rockland County	545	0.66
Yonkers (city) Westchester County	456	0.23
Smithtown (town) Suffolk County	379	0.33

Top 10 Places Sorted by Percent
Based on all places, regardless of population

Place	Number	%
Saddle Rock Estates (cdp) Nassau County	30	6.83
Harbor Hills (cdp) Nassau County	23	4.0
Kaser (village) Rockland County	103	3.
Thomaston (village) Nassau County	73	2.
Sagaponack (cdp) Suffolk County	15	2.
Hewlett Neck (village) Nassau County	13	2.0
Interlaken (village) Seneca County	16	2.
Tuxedo Park (village) Orange County	17	2.
Great Neck Estates (village) Nassau County	65	2.
Lawrence (village) Nassau County	147	2.

Top 10 Places Sorted by Percent
Based on places with populations of 10,000 or more

Place	Number	%
Kiryas Joel (village) Orange County	234	1.
Monsey (cdp) Rockland County	242	1.
Jericho (cdp) Nassau County	171	1.
Plainview (cdp) Nassau County	317	1.
Salisbury (cdp) Nassau County	143	1.
Woodmere (cdp) Nassau County	186	1.
Dix Hills (cdp) Suffolk County	262	1.
Monroe (town) Orange County	311	0.
New Castle (town) Westchester County	174	0.
Syosset (cdp) Nassau County	177	0.

Russian

Top 10 Places Sorted by Number
Based on all places, regardless of population

Place	Number	%
New York (city) New York City	243,015	3.
Hempstead (town) Nassau County	30,246	4.
Oyster Bay (town) Nassau County	14,698	5.
North Hempstead (town) Nassau County	12,446	5.
Brookhaven (town) Suffolk County	10,157	2.
Huntington (town) Suffolk County	8,974	4.
Clarkstown (town) Rockland County	5,482	6.
Islip (town) Suffolk County	5,270	1.
Ramapo (town) Rockland County	4,997	4.
Greenburgh (town) Westchester County	4,988	5.

Top 10 Places Sorted by Percent
Based on all places, regardless of population

Place	Number	%
Hewlett Neck (village) Nassau County	144	29.
Saddle Rock Estates (cdp) Nassau County	112	25.
Saltaire (village) Suffolk County	17	25.
Hewlett Bay Park (village) Nassau County	113	23.
Harbor Hills (cdp) Nassau County	114	19.
Roslyn Estates (village) Nassau County	219	17.
Hewlett Harbor (village) Nassau County	227	17.
Kensington (village) Nassau County	205	16.
East Hills (village) Nassau County	1,147	16.
Jericho (cdp) Nassau County	2,096	16.

Top 10 Places Sorted by Percent
Based on places with populations of 10,000 or more

Place	Number	%
Jericho (cdp) Nassau County	2,096	16.
Woodmere (cdp) Nassau County	2,391	16.
Scarsdale (village) Westchester County	2,075	11.
New Castle (town) Westchester County	1,939	11.
Merrick (cdp) Nassau County	2,502	10.
Plainview (cdp) Nassau County	2,802	10.
New City (cdp) Rockland County	3,352	9.
Lewisboro (town) Westchester County	1,059	8.
Dix Hills (cdp) Suffolk County	2,164	8.
Melville (cdp) Suffolk County	1,195	8.

Notes: (cdp) census designated place; Refer to the User's Guide in the front of the book for more detailed information.

Scandinavian

Top 10 Places Sorted by Number
Based on all places, regardless of population

Place	Number	%
New York (city) New York City	2,129	0.03
Brookhaven (town) Suffolk County	505	0.11
Hempstead (town) Nassau County	317	0.04
Huntington (town) Suffolk County	181	0.09
Oyster Bay (town) Nassau County	176	0.06
Islip (town) Suffolk County	152	0.05
Rochester (city) Monroe County	145	0.07
North Hempstead (town) Nassau County	142	0.06
Babylon (town) Suffolk County	136	0.06
Amherst (town) Erie County	134	0.12

Top 10 Places Sorted by Percent
Based on all places, regardless of population

Place	Number	%
Staatsburg (cdp) Dutchess County	26	2.90
Harrisville (village) Lewis County	16	2.41
Pharsalia (town) Chenango County	12	2.36
Harford (town) Cortland County	21	2.28
Lincolndale (cdp) Westchester County	42	2.21
Westford (town) Otsego County	15	1.95
Hunter (village) Greene County	8	1.69
Eastport (cdp) Suffolk County	23	1.55
Cumberland Head (cdp) Clinton County	23	1.54
Watermill (cdp) Suffolk County	25	1.48

Top 10 Places Sorted by Percent
Based on places with populations of 10,000 or more

Place	Number	%
Somers (town) Westchester County	94	0.51
Greenlawn (cdp) Suffolk County	60	0.45
Southold (town) Suffolk County	85	0.41
East Hampton (town) Suffolk County	77	0.39
Arlington (cdp) Dutchess County	49	0.39
Montgomery (town) Orange County	79	0.38
Rocky Point (cdp) Suffolk County	39	0.38
Stony Brook (cdp) Suffolk County	49	0.36
Red Hook (town) Dutchess County	36	0.35
North Lindenhurst (cdp) Suffolk County	39	0.33

Scotch-Irish

Top 10 Places Sorted by Number
Based on all places, regardless of population

Place	Number	%
New York (city) New York City	21,951	0.27
Hempstead (town) Nassau County	4,687	0.62
Brookhaven (town) Suffolk County	4,402	0.98
Islip (town) Suffolk County	2,406	0.75
Oyster Bay (town) Nassau County	1,919	0.65
Huntington (town) Suffolk County	1,808	0.93
Buffalo (city) Erie County	1,671	0.57
Syracuse (city) Onondaga County	1,669	1.13
Babylon (town) Suffolk County	1,575	0.74
Amherst (town) Erie County	1,500	1.29

Top 10 Places Sorted by Percent
Based on all places, regardless of population

Place	Number	%
Laurens (village) Otsego County	23	8.30
Malverne Park Oaks (cdp) Nassau County	41	8.23
Argyle (village) Washington County	23	7.99
Bovina (town) Delaware County	43	6.50
Salem (village) Washington County	63	6.33
Stone Ridge (cdp) Ulster County	69	5.61
Roscoe (cdp) Sullivan County	38	5.54
Coldspring (town) Cattaraugus County	41	5.37
Interlaken (village) Seneca County	35	5.10
Putnam (town) Washington County	33	5.06

Top 10 Places Sorted by Percent
Based on places with populations of 10,000 or more

Place	Number	%
Lewiston (town) Niagara County	441	2.71
Glenville (town) Schenectady County	707	2.52
Saratoga Springs (city) Saratoga County	647	2.47
Ithaca (town) Tompkins County	454	2.46
Putnam Valley (town) Putnam County	261	2.44
Queensbury (town) Warren County	593	2.34
Babylon (village) Suffolk County	290	2.30
Potsdam (town) Saint Lawrence County	340	2.13
Kingsbury (town) Washington County	238	2.13
Malta (town) Saratoga County	266	2.05

Scottish

Top 10 Places Sorted by Number
Based on all places, regardless of population

Place	Number	%
New York (city) New York City	32,024	0.40
Hempstead (town) Nassau County	5,207	0.69
Brookhaven (town) Suffolk County	4,974	1.11
Islip (town) Suffolk County	2,878	0.89
Buffalo (city) Erie County	2,657	0.91
Rochester (city) Monroe County	2,654	1.21
Oyster Bay (town) Nassau County	2,610	0.89
Amherst (town) Erie County	2,546	2.19
Huntington (town) Suffolk County	2,489	1.27
Syracuse (city) Onondaga County	2,044	1.39

Top 10 Places Sorted by Percent
Based on all places, regardless of population

Place	Number	%
Dering Harbor (village) Suffolk County	3	23.08
Bovina (town) Delaware County	83	12.54
Andes (village) Delaware County	39	12.38
Hardenburgh (town) Ulster County	25	11.42
Leicester (village) Livingston County	47	9.79
Argyle (village) Washington County	28	9.72
Hammond (village) Saint Lawrence County	28	9.30
Hamden (town) Delaware County	109	8.52
Harrisville (village) Lewis County	54	8.14
Youngstown (village) Niagara County	156	7.97

Top 10 Places Sorted by Percent
Based on places with populations of 10,000 or more

Place	Number	%
Massena (village) Saint Lawrence County	525	4.68
Highlands (town) Orange County	560	4.49
Lansing (town) Tompkins County	432	4.19
Ithaca (town) Tompkins County	746	4.04
Canton (town) Saint Lawrence County	401	3.88
Massena (town) Saint Lawrence County	499	3.80
Glenville (town) Schenectady County	1,050	3.74
Canandaigua (city) Ontario County	395	3.51
Chili (town) Monroe County	958	3.47
Grand Island (town) Erie County	637	3.42

Serbian

Top 10 Places Sorted by Number
Based on all places, regardless of population

Place	Number	%
New York (city) New York City	2,652	0.03
Buffalo (city) Erie County	278	0.09
Lackawanna (city) Erie County	151	0.79
Hempstead (town) Nassau County	114	0.02
Grand Island (town) Erie County	84	0.45
Tonawanda (town) Erie County	81	0.10
Orchard Park (town) Erie County	76	0.27
West Seneca (town) Erie County	68	0.15
Brookhaven (town) Suffolk County	61	0.01
Amherst (town) Erie County	58	0.05

Top 10 Places Sorted by Percent
Based on all places, regardless of population

Place	Number	%
Mill Neck (village) Nassau County	8	1.06
Lackawanna (city) Erie County	151	0.79
Clarence Center (cdp) Erie County	12	0.73
Conesville (town) Schoharie County	5	0.71
Perrysburg (town) Cattaraugus County	12	0.68
East Ithaca (cdp) Tompkins County	15	0.65
Halesite (cdp) Suffolk County	16	0.63
Willing (town) Allegany County	8	0.58
Westhampton (cdp) Suffolk County	15	0.53
Dickinson (town) Broome County	28	0.52

Top 10 Places Sorted by Percent
Based on places with populations of 10,000 or more

Place	Number	%
Lackawanna (city) Erie County	151	0.79
Grand Island (town) Erie County	84	0.45
Farmington (town) Ontario County	35	0.33
Orchard Park (town) Erie County	76	0.27
Hamburg (village) Erie County	21	0.21
Niskayuna (town) Schenectady County	35	0.17
New Castle (town) Westchester County	28	0.16
Chester (town) Orange County	19	0.16
West Seneca (town) Erie County	68	0.15
Ithaca (town) Tompkins County	28	0.15

Slavic

Top 10 Places Sorted by Number
Based on all places, regardless of population

Place	Number	%
New York (city) New York City	2,025	0.03
Hempstead (town) Nassau County	263	0.03
Yonkers (city) Westchester County	173	0.09
Buffalo (city) Erie County	165	0.06
Huntington (town) Suffolk County	161	0.08
Oyster Bay (town) Nassau County	139	0.05
Union (town) Broome County	137	0.24
Smithtown (town) Suffolk County	122	0.11
Islip (town) Suffolk County	120	0.04
Walden (village) Orange County	106	1.72

Top 10 Places Sorted by Percent
Based on all places, regardless of population

Place	Number	%
Red House (town) Cattaraugus County	2	4.76
Fort Ann (village) Washington County	13	2.77
Jefferson Heights (cdp) Greene County	24	2.13
Walden (village) Orange County	106	1.72
Northwest Ithaca (cdp) Tompkins County	19	1.72
Allegany (village) Cattaraugus County	30	1.64
Akron (village) Erie County	45	1.44
Peach Lake (cdp) Putnam County	21	1.23
Lincklaen (town) Chenango County	5	1.15
Sloatsburg (village) Rockland County	35	1.12

Top 10 Places Sorted by Percent
Based on places with populations of 10,000 or more

Place	Number	%
Montgomery (town) Orange County	106	0.51
Chenango (town) Broome County	57	0.50
Melville (cdp) Suffolk County	53	0.36
Lansing (town) Tompkins County	34	0.33
Johnson City (village) Broome County	49	0.32
Endicott (village) Broome County	37	0.28
Corning (city) Steuben County	29	0.27

Notes: (cdp) census designated place; Refer to the User's Guide in the front of the book for more detailed information.

694 PROFILES OF NEW YORK / Ancestry: Rankings

Place	Number	%
Catskill (town) Greene County	31	0.26
Malta (town) Saratoga County	32	0.25
Tarrytown (village) Westchester County	28	0.25

Slovak

Top 10 Places Sorted by Number
Based on all places, regardless of population

Place	Number	%
New York (city) New York City	6,459	0.08
Union (town) Broome County	3,039	5.40
Binghamton (city) Broome County	1,704	3.60
Johnson City (village) Broome County	1,044	6.72
Yonkers (city) Westchester County	931	0.47
Hempstead (town) Nassau County	908	0.12
Brookhaven (town) Suffolk County	687	0.15
Endwell (cdp) Broome County	634	5.41
Vestal (town) Broome County	543	2.05
Chenango (town) Broome County	517	4.51

Top 10 Places Sorted by Percent
Based on all places, regardless of population

Place	Number	%
Johnson City (village) Broome County	1,044	6.72
Lisle (village) Broome County	20	6.64
Dickinson (town) Broome County	341	6.39
Maine (town) Broome County	308	5.64
Endwell (cdp) Broome County	634	5.41
Union (town) Broome County	3,039	5.40
Johnstown (city) Fulton County	431	5.07
Binghamton (town) Broome County	244	4.91
Chenango (town) Broome County	517	4.51
Fenton (town) Broome County	299	4.33

Top 10 Places Sorted by Percent
Based on places with populations of 10,000 or more

Place	Number	%
Johnson City (village) Broome County	1,044	6.72
Endwell (cdp) Broome County	634	5.41
Union (town) Broome County	3,039	5.40
Chenango (town) Broome County	517	4.51
Binghamton (city) Broome County	1,704	3.60
Endicott (village) Broome County	457	3.51
Owego (town) Tioga County	516	2.53
Vestal (town) Broome County	543	2.05
Gloversville (city) Fulton County	242	1.57
Tarrytown (village) Westchester County	99	0.89

Slovene

Top 10 Places Sorted by Number
Based on all places, regardless of population

Place	Number	%
New York (city) New York City	1,162	0.01
Hempstead (town) Nassau County	176	0.02
Persia (town) Cattaraugus County	89	3.52
Gowanda (village) Cattaraugus County	85	3.06
Babylon (town) Suffolk County	76	0.04
Little Falls (city) Herkimer County	72	1.40
Worcester (town) Otsego County	71	3.22
Stillwater (town) Saratoga County	66	0.88
Huntington (town) Suffolk County	66	0.03
Manlius (town) Onondaga County	62	0.19

Top 10 Places Sorted by Percent
Based on all places, regardless of population

Place	Number	%
Decatur (town) Otsego County	19	4.90
Persia (town) Cattaraugus County	89	3.52
Worcester (town) Otsego County	71	3.22
Gowanda (village) Cattaraugus County	85	3.06
Little Falls (town) Herkimer County	44	2.86

Place	Number	%
Little Falls (city) Herkimer County	72	1.40
Coldspring (town) Cattaraugus County	10	1.31
Cragsmoor (cdp) Ulster County	6	1.28
Otsego (town) Otsego County	47	1.20
Perrysburg (town) Cattaraugus County	17	0.96

Top 10 Places Sorted by Percent
Based on places with populations of 10,000 or more

Place	Number	%
North Lindenhurst (cdp) Suffolk County	36	0.31
Red Hook (town) Dutchess County	31	0.30
Patterson (town) Putnam County	32	0.28
Milton (town) Saratoga County	44	0.26
Manlius (town) Onondaga County	62	0.19
Floral Park (village) Nassau County	29	0.18
Rye (city) Westchester County	27	0.18
North Wantagh (cdp) Nassau County	21	0.17
Ithaca (town) Tompkins County	29	0.16
Vestal (town) Broome County	40	0.15

Soviet Union

Top 10 Places Sorted by Number
Based on all places, regardless of population

Place	Number	%
New York (city) New York City	550	0.01
Hempstead (town) Nassau County	51	0.01
West Nyack (cdp) Rockland County	45	1.39
Clarkstown (town) Rockland County	45	0.05
Oceanside (cdp) Nassau County	32	0.10
Valley Stream (village) Nassau County	19	0.05
Chester (village) Orange County	9	0.25
Chester (town) Orange County	9	0.07
Ronkonkoma (cdp) Suffolk County	8	0.04
Cortlandt (town) Westchester County	8	0.02

Top 10 Places Sorted by Percent
Based on all places, regardless of population

Place	Number	%
West Nyack (cdp) Rockland County	45	1.39
Chester (village) Orange County	9	0.25
Great Neck Estates (village) Nassau County	5	0.18
Lansing (village) Tompkins County	5	0.17
Kaser (village) Rockland County	5	0.15
Oceanside (cdp) Nassau County	32	0.10
Chester (town) Orange County	9	0.07
Millbrook (village) Dutchess County	1	0.07
Clarkstown (town) Rockland County	45	0.05
Valley Stream (village) Nassau County	19	0.05

Top 10 Places Sorted by Percent
Based on places with populations of 10,000 or more

Place	Number	%
Oceanside (cdp) Nassau County	32	0.10
Chester (town) Orange County	9	0.07
Clarkstown (town) Rockland County	45	0.05
Valley Stream (village) Nassau County	19	0.05
Lansing (town) Tompkins County	5	0.05
Ronkonkoma (cdp) Suffolk County	8	0.04
Peekskill (city) Westchester County	6	0.03
Cortlandt (town) Westchester County	8	0.02
Plainview (cdp) Nassau County	6	0.02
Lewisboro (town) Westchester County	2	0.02

Swedish

Top 10 Places Sorted by Number
Based on all places, regardless of population

Place	Number	%
New York (city) New York City	20,644	0.26
Jamestown (city) Chautauqua County	6,062	19.10
Brookhaven (town) Suffolk County	5,546	1.24
Hempstead (town) Nassau County	4,688	0.62
Islip (town) Suffolk County	2,577	0.80
Oyster Bay (town) Nassau County	2,515	0.86
Huntington (town) Suffolk County	2,447	1.25
Ellicott (town) Chautauqua County	2,039	21.97
Busti (town) Chautauqua County	1,975	25.45
Babylon (town) Suffolk County	1,434	0.68

Top 10 Places Sorted by Percent
Based on all places, regardless of population

Place	Number	%
Bemus Point (village) Chautauqua County	95	27.78
Frewsburg (cdp) Chautauqua County	528	26.82
Carroll (town) Chautauqua County	940	25.82
Busti (town) Chautauqua County	1,975	25.45
Kiantone (town) Chautauqua County	340	24.66
Lakewood (village) Chautauqua County	802	24.56
Ellicott (town) Chautauqua County	2,039	21.97
Jamestown West (cdp) Chautauqua County	542	21.53
Ellery (town) Chautauqua County	985	21.50
Gerry (town) Chautauqua County	426	20.79

Top 10 Places Sorted by Percent
Based on places with populations of 10,000 or more

Place	Number	%
Jamestown (city) Chautauqua County	6,062	19.10
Pomfret (town) Chautauqua County	665	4.53
Fredonia (village) Chautauqua County	429	3.98
Olean (city) Cattaraugus County	525	3.42
Ithaca (town) Tompkins County	410	2.22
Corning (city) Steuben County	240	2.21
Patterson (town) Putnam County	245	2.17
Southold (town) Suffolk County	430	2.09
Canandaigua (city) Ontario County	232	2.06
Saint James (cdp) Suffolk County	272	2.05

Swiss

Top 10 Places Sorted by Number
Based on all places, regardless of population

Place	Number	%
New York (city) New York City	8,108	0.10
Hempstead (town) Nassau County	1,191	0.16
Brookhaven (town) Suffolk County	901	0.20
Oyster Bay (town) Nassau County	630	0.21
Huntington (town) Suffolk County	622	0.32
Islip (town) Suffolk County	550	0.17
Amherst (town) Erie County	459	0.39
North Hempstead (town) Nassau County	439	0.20
Rochester (city) Monroe County	347	0.16
Greenburgh (town) Westchester County	302	0.35

Top 10 Places Sorted by Percent
Based on all places, regardless of population

Place	Number	%
Potter (town) Yates County	104	5.67
Starkey (town) Yates County	200	5.64
Barrington (town) Yates County	76	5.45
Steuben (town) Oneida County	63	5.29
Lewis (town) Lewis County	45	5.07
Osceola (town) Lewis County	14	5.04
Prospect (village) Oneida County	17	4.93
Castorland (village) Lewis County	15	4.98
Constableville (village) Lewis County	14	4.45
Fabius (village) Onondaga County	15	3.94

Top 10 Places Sorted by Percent
Based on places with populations of 10,000 or more

Place	Number	%
North Castle (town) Westchester County	144	1.33
Sullivan (town) Madison County	160	1.07
Rome (city) Oneida County	281	0.81

Notes: (cdp) census designated place; Refer to the User's Guide in the front of the book for more detailed information.

PROFILES OF NEW YORK / Ancestry: Rankings

Place	Number	%
De Witt (town) Onondaga County	181	0.75
Ithaca (town) Tompkins County	136	0.74
Jefferson Valley-Yorktown (cdp) Westchester County	108	0.73
Scarsdale (village) Westchester County	123	0.69
Terryville (cdp) Suffolk County	72	0.68
Yorktown (town) Westchester County	245	0.67
Whitestown (town) Oneida County	125	0.67

Turkish

Top 10 Places Sorted by Number
Based on all places, regardless of population

Place	Number	%
New York (city) New York City	12,221	0.15
Hempstead (town) Nassau County	1,424	0.19
Brookhaven (town) Suffolk County	1,182	0.26
Oyster Bay (town) Nassau County	638	0.22
North Hempstead (town) Nassau County	612	0.27
Rochester (city) Monroe County	593	0.27
Islip (town) Suffolk County	585	0.18
Babylon (town) Suffolk County	544	0.26
Irondequoit (cdp) Monroe County	459	0.88
Huntington (town) Suffolk County	432	0.22

Top 10 Places Sorted by Percent
Based on all places, regardless of population

Place	Number	%
Islandia (village) Suffolk County	86	2.81
East Ithaca (cdp) Tompkins County	46	2.01
Point Lookout (cdp) Nassau County	28	1.84
Golden's Bridge (cdp) Westchester County	26	1.68
Jeffersonville (village) Sullivan County	7	1.66
Fleischmanns (village) Delaware County	5	1.42
Bellerose Terrace (cdp) Nassau County	30	1.39
Herricks (cdp) Nassau County	56	1.37
Angola on the Lake (cdp) Erie County	23	1.33
Peconic (cdp) Suffolk County	14	1.20

Top 10 Places Sorted by Percent
Based on places with populations of 10,000 or more

Place	Number	%
Irondequoit (cdp) Monroe County	459	0.88
East Rockaway (village) Nassau County	88	0.84
North Lindenhurst (cdp) Suffolk County	94	0.80
Rocky Point (cdp) Suffolk County	71	0.69
Commack (cdp) Suffolk County	229	0.63
Medford (cdp) Suffolk County	138	0.63
Long Beach (city) Nassau County	203	0.57
Lynbrook (village) Nassau County	105	0.53
Coram (cdp) Suffolk County	181	0.52
Port Washington (cdp) Nassau County	79	0.52

Ukrainian

Top 10 Places Sorted by Number
Based on all places, regardless of population

Place	Number	%
New York (city) New York City	62,695	0.78
Hempstead (town) Nassau County	4,023	0.53
Brookhaven (town) Suffolk County	2,385	0.53
Rochester (city) Monroe County	2,179	0.99
Yonkers (city) Westchester County	1,975	1.01
Oyster Bay (town) Nassau County	1,917	0.65
Greece (town) Monroe County	1,726	1.83
Irondequoit (cdp) Monroe County	1,643	3.14
Buffalo (city) Erie County	1,439	0.49
Syracuse (city) Onondaga County	1,361	0.92

Top 10 Places Sorted by Percent
Based on all places, regardless of population

Place	Number	%
Lumberland (town) Sullivan County	219	11.29
Kerhonkson (cdp) Ulster County	130	7.25
Warren (town) Herkimer County	76	6.47
Stone Ridge (cdp) Ulster County	76	6.18
Throop (town) Cayuga County	112	6.14
Clayville (village) Oneida County	27	6.01
Fleming (town) Cayuga County	148	5.59
Webster (village) Monroe County	279	5.40
Deerfield (town) Oneida County	203	5.20
Lexington (town) Greene County	41	5.07

Top 10 Places Sorted by Percent
Based on places with populations of 10,000 or more

Place	Number	%
Auburn (city) Cayuga County	1,352	4.73
Fairmount (cdp) Onondaga County	456	4.22
Geddes (town) Onondaga County	735	4.15
Camillus (town) Onondaga County	809	3.49
Cohoes (city) Albany County	522	3.36
Johnson City (village) Broome County	492	3.17
Irondequoit (cdp) Monroe County	1,643	3.14
Watervliet (city) Albany County	284	2.78
Webster (town) Monroe County	958	2.53
Wawarsing (town) Ulster County	279	2.16

United States or American

Top 10 Places Sorted by Number
Based on all places, regardless of population

Place	Number	%
New York (city) New York City	238,385	2.98
Hempstead (town) Nassau County	31,416	4.16
Oyster Bay (town) Nassau County	13,610	4.63
Brookhaven (town) Suffolk County	12,588	2.81
North Hempstead (town) Nassau County	11,272	5.06
Islip (town) Suffolk County	8,893	2.76
Huntington (town) Suffolk County	7,252	3.71
Ramapo (town) Rockland County	6,752	6.20
Babylon (town) Suffolk County	5,586	2.64
Yonkers (city) Westchester County	5,088	2.59

Top 10 Places Sorted by Percent
Based on all places, regardless of population

Place	Number	%
Woodsburgh (village) Nassau County	258	30.64
Deferiet (village) Jefferson County	90	26.09
Plattsburgh West (cdp) Clinton County	316	24.09
Troupsburg (town) Steuben County	249	22.29
Richford (town) Tioga County	248	21.62
Edwards (town) Saint Lawrence County	247	21.46
Red House (town) Cattaraugus County	9	21.43
Clare (town) Saint Lawrence County	25	21.37
Pitcairn (town) Saint Lawrence County	163	21.17
Tuscarora (town) Steuben County	295	21.07

Top 10 Places Sorted by Percent
Based on places with populations of 10,000 or more

Place	Number	%
Bath (town) Steuben County	1,493	12.34
Woodmere (cdp) Nassau County	1,825	11.10
Canton (town) Saint Lawrence County	947	9.16
Plattsburgh (town) Clinton County	1,018	9.15
Ogdensburg (city) Saint Lawrence County	1,083	8.76
Monsey (cdp) Rockland County	1,223	8.32
Fulton (city) Oswego County	984	8.30
Kingsbury (town) Washington County	925	8.28
Merrick (cdp) Nassau County	1,879	8.25
Wilton (town) Saratoga County	1,028	8.22

Welsh

Top 10 Places Sorted by Number
Based on all places, regardless of population

Place	Number	%
New York (city) New York City	8,830	0.11
Union (town) Broome County	1,281	2.28
Utica (city) Oneida County	1,125	1.85
New Hartford (town) Oneida County	1,029	4.86
Brookhaven (town) Suffolk County	1,023	0.23
Hempstead (town) Nassau County	1,013	0.13
Rochester (city) Monroe County	979	0.45
Syracuse (city) Onondaga County	938	0.64
Amherst (town) Erie County	899	0.77
Buffalo (city) Erie County	878	0.30

Top 10 Places Sorted by Percent
Based on all places, regardless of population

Place	Number	%
Remsen (town) Oneida County	329	16.97
Holland Patent (village) Oneida County	74	16.78
Remsen (village) Oneida County	86	16.76
Steuben (town) Oneida County	160	13.43
Barneveld (village) Oneida County	42	12.50
Parc (cdp) Clinton County	6	12.24
Madison (town) Madison County	37	11.67
Montague (town) Lewis County	11	10.89
Duane (town) Franklin County	13	9.42
Russia (town) Herkimer County	218	8.82

Top 10 Places Sorted by Percent
Based on places with populations of 10,000 or more

Place	Number	%
New Hartford (town) Oneida County	1,029	4.86
Kirkland (town) Oneida County	431	4.25
Whitestown (town) Oneida County	781	4.20
German Flatts (town) Herkimer County	472	3.46
Chenango (town) Broome County	388	3.39
Owego (town) Tioga County	635	3.12
Oneida (city) Madison County	341	3.10
Rome (city) Oneida County	868	2.49
Endwell (cdp) Broome County	283	2.42
Lansing (town) Tompkins County	243	2.36

West Indian, excluding Hispanic

Top 10 Places Sorted by Number
Based on all places, regardless of population

Place	Number	%
New York (city) New York City	549,664	6.86
Hempstead (town) Nassau County	36,824	4.87
Mount Vernon (city) Westchester County	11,360	16.61
Ramapo (town) Rockland County	9,716	8.92
Islip (town) Suffolk County	6,903	2.14
Elmont (cdp) Nassau County	6,585	20.16
Spring Valley (village) Rockland County	6,484	25.55
Yonkers (city) Westchester County	6,418	3.27
Hempstead (village) Nassau County	6,264	11.08
Babylon (town) Suffolk County	6,081	2.87

Top 10 Places Sorted by Percent
Based on all places, regardless of population

Place	Number	%
South Floral Park (village) Nassau County	434	27.50
Spring Valley (village) Rockland County	6,484	25.55
Hillcrest (cdp) Rockland County	1,784	25.10
Lakeview (cdp) Nassau County	1,336	23.83
North Valley Stream (cdp) Nassau County	3,709	23.49
Uniondale (cdp) Nassau County	5,030	21.86
Elmont (cdp) Nassau County	6,585	20.16
Mount Vernon (city) Westchester County	11,360	16.61
New Cassel (cdp) Nassau County	2,029	15.26

Notes: (cdp) census designated place; Refer to the User's Guide in the front of the book for more detailed information.

Place	Number	%
Wheatley Heights (cdp) Suffolk County	767	15.24

Top 10 Places Sorted by Percent
Based on places with populations of 10,000 or more

Place	Number	%
Spring Valley (village) Rockland County	6,484	25.55
North Valley Stream (cdp) Nassau County	3,709	23.49
Uniondale (cdp) Nassau County	5,030	21.86
Elmont (cdp) Nassau County	6,585	20.16
Mount Vernon (city) Westchester County	11,360	16.61
New Cassel (cdp) Nassau County	2,029	15.26
Roosevelt (cdp) Nassau County	2,343	14.78
North Amityville (cdp) Suffolk County	1,901	11.51
Hempstead (village) Nassau County	6,264	11.08
Baldwin (cdp) Nassau County	2,578	10.99

West Indian: Bahamian, excluding Hispanic

Top 10 Places Sorted by Number
Based on all places, regardless of population

Place	Number	%
New York (city) New York City	1,658	0.02
Poughkeepsie (city) Dutchess County	55	0.18
Hempstead (town) Nassau County	54	0.01
Yonkers (city) Westchester County	37	0.02
Olean (city) Cattaraugus County	34	0.22
New Rochelle (city) Westchester County	34	0.05
Rochester (city) Monroe County	30	0.01
North Amityville (cdp) Suffolk County	28	0.17
Babylon (town) Suffolk County	28	0.01
Arlington (cdp) Dutchess County	25	0.20

Top 10 Places Sorted by Percent
Based on all places, regardless of population

Place	Number	%
Athens (village) Greene County	4	0.24
Olean (city) Cattaraugus County	34	0.22
Arlington (cdp) Dutchess County	25	0.20
Poughkeepsie (city) Dutchess County	55	0.18
Alfred (village) Allegany County	7	0.18
North Amityville (cdp) Suffolk County	28	0.17
North Valley Stream (cdp) Nassau County	25	0.16
Murray (town) Orleans County	9	0.14
Alfred (town) Allegany County	7	0.14
Chester (town) Warren County	5	0.14

Top 10 Places Sorted by Percent
Based on places with populations of 10,000 or more

Place	Number	%
Olean (city) Cattaraugus County	34	0.22
Arlington (cdp) Dutchess County	25	0.20
Poughkeepsie (city) Dutchess County	55	0.18
North Amityville (cdp) Suffolk County	28	0.17
North Valley Stream (cdp) Nassau County	25	0.16
Lockport (city) Niagara County	19	0.09
East Patchogue (cdp) Suffolk County	17	0.08
East Massapequa (cdp) Nassau County	15	0.08
Batavia (city) Genesee County	11	0.07
Tarrytown (village) Westchester County	8	0.07

West Indian: Barbadian, excluding Hispanic

Top 10 Places Sorted by Number
Based on all places, regardless of population

Place	Number	%
New York (city) New York City	26,816	0.33
Hempstead (town) Nassau County	1,180	0.16
Mount Vernon (city) Westchester County	457	0.67
Elmont (cdp) Nassau County	315	0.96
New Rochelle (city) Westchester County	296	0.41
Islip (town) Suffolk County	270	0.08
Hempstead (village) Nassau County	239	0.42
Freeport (village) Nassau County	186	0.42
Yonkers (city) Westchester County	160	0.08
Rochester (city) Monroe County	155	0.07

Top 10 Places Sorted by Percent
Based on all places, regardless of population

Place	Number	%
Shrub Oak (cdp) Westchester County	40	2.17
Fairview (cdp) Westchester County	60	2.01
Lakeview (cdp) Nassau County	87	1.55
East Garden City (cdp) Nassau County	10	1.01
Elmont (cdp) Nassau County	315	0.96
New Hempstead (village) Rockland County	38	0.79
Gordon Heights (cdp) Suffolk County	23	0.74
Mount Vernon (city) Westchester County	457	0.67
North Valley Stream (cdp) Nassau County	100	0.63
Tuckahoe (village) Westchester County	38	0.61

Top 10 Places Sorted by Percent
Based on places with populations of 10,000 or more

Place	Number	%
Elmont (cdp) Nassau County	315	0.96
Mount Vernon (city) Westchester County	457	0.67
North Valley Stream (cdp) Nassau County	100	0.63
Hempstead (village) Nassau County	239	0.42
Freeport (village) Nassau County	186	0.42
New Rochelle (city) Westchester County	296	0.41
North Amityville (cdp) Suffolk County	62	0.38
New York (city) New York City	26,816	0.33
Uniondale (cdp) Nassau County	74	0.32
Roosevelt (cdp) Nassau County	50	0.32

West Indian: Belizean, excluding Hispanic

Top 10 Places Sorted by Number
Based on all places, regardless of population

Place	Number	%
New York (city) New York City	6,487	0.08
Hempstead (town) Nassau County	209	0.03
Rochester (city) Monroe County	195	0.09
Islip (town) Suffolk County	107	0.03
Elmont (cdp) Nassau County	93	0.28
Central Islip (cdp) Suffolk County	84	0.26
North Hempstead (town) Nassau County	69	0.03
Yonkers (city) Westchester County	64	0.03
Freeport (village) Nassau County	49	0.11
Searingtown (cdp) Nassau County	41	0.81

Top 10 Places Sorted by Percent
Based on all places, regardless of population

Place	Number	%
Searingtown (cdp) Nassau County	41	0.81
Greenvale (cdp) Nassau County	16	0.72
Wheatley Heights (cdp) Suffolk County	28	0.56
Yaphank (cdp) Suffolk County	22	0.43
Munsons Corners (cdp) Cortland County	9	0.37
Brocton (village) Chautauqua County	5	0.32
Elmont (cdp) Nassau County	93	0.28
Central Islip (cdp) Suffolk County	84	0.26
Hamilton (village) Madison County	9	0.26
Kings Point (village) Nassau County	12	0.24

Top 10 Places Sorted by Percent
Based on places with populations of 10,000 or more

Place	Number	%
Elmont (cdp) Nassau County	93	0.28
Central Islip (cdp) Suffolk County	84	0.26
Dryden (town) Tompkins County	30	0.22
Freeport (village) Nassau County	49	0.11
Baldwin (cdp) Nassau County	26	0.11
Rochester (city) Monroe County	195	0.09
Cortlandt (town) Westchester County	34	0.09
New York (city) New York City	6,487	0.08
Hauppauge (cdp) Suffolk County	16	0.08
Fort Drum (cdp) Jefferson County	8	0.07

West Indian: Bermudan, excluding Hispanic

Top 10 Places Sorted by Number
Based on all places, regardless of population

Place	Number	%
New York (city) New York City	608	0.01
Brookhaven (town) Suffolk County	56	0.01
Babylon (town) Suffolk County	34	0.02
Oyster Bay (town) Nassau County	31	0.01
North Bellport (cdp) Suffolk County	27	0.30
Hempstead (town) Nassau County	26	0.00
Old Bethpage (cdp) Nassau County	23	0.43
North Amityville (cdp) Suffolk County	18	0.11
Roosevelt (cdp) Nassau County	18	0.11
Rye (city) Westchester County	16	0.11

Top 10 Places Sorted by Percent
Based on all places, regardless of population

Place	Number	%
Old Bethpage (cdp) Nassau County	23	0.43
Chester (town) Warren County	12	0.33
North Bellport (cdp) Suffolk County	27	0.30
Greenvale (cdp) Nassau County	5	0.23
Eatons Neck (cdp) Suffolk County	2	0.15
Center Moriches (cdp) Suffolk County	9	0.14
North Amityville (cdp) Suffolk County	18	0.11
Roosevelt (cdp) Nassau County	18	0.11
Rye (city) Westchester County	16	0.11
Scotchtown (cdp) Orange County	10	0.11

Top 10 Places Sorted by Percent
Based on places with populations of 10,000 or more

Place	Number	%
North Amityville (cdp) Suffolk County	18	0.11
Roosevelt (cdp) Nassau County	18	0.11
Rye (city) Westchester County	16	0.11
Westbury (village) Nassau County	7	0.05
Red Hook (town) Dutchess County	5	0.05
West Babylon (cdp) Suffolk County	16	0.04
Cortlandt (town) Westchester County	15	0.04
Wallkill (town) Orange County	10	0.04
East Massapequa (cdp) Nassau County	8	0.04
Potsdam (town) Saint Lawrence County	7	0.04

West Indian: British West Indian, excluding Hispanic

Top 10 Places Sorted by Number
Based on all places, regardless of population

Place	Number	%
New York (city) New York City	47,084	0.59
Hempstead (town) Nassau County	1,135	0.15
Mount Vernon (city) Westchester County	365	0.53
Yonkers (city) Westchester County	250	0.13
Hempstead (village) Nassau County	247	0.44
Brookhaven (town) Suffolk County	195	0.04
Islip (town) Suffolk County	190	0.06
North Hempstead (town) Nassau County	170	0.08
Babylon (town) Suffolk County	168	0.08
Greenburgh (town) Westchester County	157	0.18

Top 10 Places Sorted by Percent
Based on all places, regardless of population

Place	Number	%
Shrub Oak (cdp) Westchester County	36	1.95

Notes: (cdp) census designated place; Refer to the User's Guide in the front of the book for more detailed information.

PROFILES OF NEW YORK / Ancestry: Rankings

Place	Number	%
Scotts Corners (cdp) Westchester County	9	1.56
Morrisville (village) Madison County	33	1.52
South Floral Park (village) Nassau County	23	1.46
Gordon Heights (cdp) Suffolk County	34	1.10
Wampsville (village) Madison County	6	1.07
Watermill (cdp) Suffolk County	15	0.89
Manhasset (cdp) Nassau County	72	0.86
Shandaken (town) Ulster County	28	0.85
Eaton (town) Madison County	33	0.68

Top 10 Places Sorted by Percent
Based on places with populations of 10,000 or more

Place	Number	%
New York (city) New York City	47,084	0.59
Mount Vernon (city) Westchester County	365	0.53
North Valley Stream (cdp) Nassau County	84	0.53
Terryville (cdp) Suffolk County	54	0.51
Roosevelt (cdp) Nassau County	78	0.49
Uniondale (cdp) Nassau County	109	0.47
Hempstead (village) Nassau County	247	0.44
Elmont (cdp) Nassau County	145	0.44
North Amityville (cdp) Suffolk County	65	0.39
Freeport (village) Nassau County	139	0.32

West Indian: Dutch West Indian, excluding Hispanic

Top 10 Places Sorted by Number
Based on all places, regardless of population

Place	Number	%
New York (city) New York City	994	0.01
Hempstead (town) Nassau County	53	0.01
Babylon (town) Suffolk County	45	0.02
Greenburgh (town) Westchester County	43	0.05
Yonkers (city) Westchester County	34	0.02
Stony Point (town) Rockland County	26	0.18
Freeport (village) Nassau County	26	0.06
Wheatley Heights (cdp) Suffolk County	24	0.48
West Babylon (cdp) Suffolk County	21	0.05
Brookhaven (town) Suffolk County	20	0.00

Top 10 Places Sorted by Percent
Based on all places, regardless of population

Place	Number	%
Wheatley Heights (cdp) Suffolk County	24	0.48
Spackenkill (cdp) Dutchess County	18	0.39
Pitcairn (town) Saint Lawrence County	2	0.26
Shortsville (village) Ontario County	3	0.22
Lorraine (town) Jefferson County	2	0.22
Stony Point (town) Rockland County	26	0.18
Port Byron (village) Cayuga County	2	0.15
Masonville (town) Delaware County	2	0.14
South Floral Park (village) Nassau County	2	0.13
Marlborough (town) Ulster County	10	0.12

Top 10 Places Sorted by Percent
Based on places with populations of 10,000 or more

Place	Number	%
Stony Point (town) Rockland County	26	0.18
Setauket-East Setauket (cdp) Suffolk County	12	0.08
Freeport (village) Nassau County	26	0.06
Uniondale (cdp) Nassau County	13	0.06
Batavia (city) Genesee County	9	0.06
Greenburgh (town) Westchester County	43	0.05
West Babylon (cdp) Suffolk County	21	0.05
East Fishkill (town) Dutchess County	13	0.05
New Paltz (town) Ulster County	6	0.05
Poughkeepsie (town) Dutchess County	18	0.04

West Indian: Haitian, excluding Hispanic

Top 10 Places Sorted by Number
Based on all places, regardless of population

Place	Number	%
New York (city) New York City	118,769	1.48
Hempstead (town) Nassau County	13,599	1.80
Ramapo (town) Rockland County	7,559	6.94
Spring Valley (village) Rockland County	5,349	21.08
Elmont (cdp) Nassau County	3,572	10.94
Islip (town) Suffolk County	2,487	0.77
North Hempstead (town) Nassau County	2,007	0.90
Uniondale (cdp) Nassau County	1,882	8.18
Babylon (town) Suffolk County	1,819	0.86
North Valley Stream (cdp) Nassau County	1,792	11.35

Top 10 Places Sorted by Percent
Based on all places, regardless of population

Place	Number	%
Spring Valley (village) Rockland County	5,349	21.08
Hillcrest (cdp) Rockland County	1,390	19.56
North Valley Stream (cdp) Nassau County	1,792	11.35
Elmont (cdp) Nassau County	3,572	10.94
New Cassel (cdp) Nassau County	1,257	9.45
South Nyack (village) Rockland County	308	8.87
Nyack (village) Rockland County	576	8.60
Uniondale (cdp) Nassau County	1,882	8.18
Ramapo (town) Rockland County	7,559	6.94
Pomona (village) Rockland County	164	6.00

Top 10 Places Sorted by Percent
Based on places with populations of 10,000 or more

Place	Number	%
Spring Valley (village) Rockland County	5,349	21.08
North Valley Stream (cdp) Nassau County	1,792	11.35
Elmont (cdp) Nassau County	3,572	10.94
New Cassel (cdp) Nassau County	1,257	9.45
Uniondale (cdp) Nassau County	1,882	8.18
Ramapo (town) Rockland County	7,559	6.94
Baldwin (cdp) Nassau County	1,104	4.71
Wyandanch (cdp) Suffolk County	487	4.60
Nanuet (cdp) Rockland County	632	3.78
Roosevelt (cdp) Nassau County	599	3.78

West Indian: Jamaican, excluding Hispanic

Top 10 Places Sorted by Number
Based on all places, regardless of population

Place	Number	%
New York (city) New York City	212,972	2.66
Hempstead (town) Nassau County	15,339	2.03
Mount Vernon (city) Westchester County	8,419	12.31
Yonkers (city) Westchester County	3,822	1.95
Hempstead (village) Nassau County	3,064	5.42
Rochester (city) Monroe County	2,517	1.15
Babylon (town) Suffolk County	2,491	1.18
Uniondale (cdp) Nassau County	2,430	10.56
Islip (town) Suffolk County	2,379	0.74
Elmont (cdp) Nassau County	1,962	6.01

Top 10 Places Sorted by Percent
Based on all places, regardless of population

Place	Number	%
South Floral Park (village) Nassau County	259	16.41
Mount Vernon (city) Westchester County	8,419	12.31
Lakeview (cdp) Nassau County	667	11.90
Uniondale (cdp) Nassau County	2,430	10.56
North Valley Stream (cdp) Nassau County	1,319	8.35
Roosevelt (cdp) Nassau County	1,187	7.49
Fairview (cdp) Westchester County	217	7.26
East Garden City (cdp) Nassau County	70	7.04
Elmont (cdp) Nassau County	1,962	6.01
North Amityville (cdp) Suffolk County	971	5.88

Top 10 Places Sorted by Percent
Based on places with populations of 10,000 or more

Place	Number	%
Mount Vernon (city) Westchester County	8,419	12.31
Uniondale (cdp) Nassau County	2,430	10.56
North Valley Stream (cdp) Nassau County	1,319	8.35
Roosevelt (cdp) Nassau County	1,187	7.49
Elmont (cdp) Nassau County	1,962	6.01
North Amityville (cdp) Suffolk County	971	5.88
Hempstead (village) Nassau County	3,064	5.42
Poughkeepsie (city) Dutchess County	1,524	5.10
New Cassel (cdp) Nassau County	589	4.43
Baldwin (cdp) Nassau County	1,005	4.28

West Indian: Trinidadian and Tobagonian, excluding Hispanic

Top 10 Places Sorted by Number
Based on all places, regardless of population

Place	Number	%
New York (city) New York City	75,584	0.94
Hempstead (town) Nassau County	2,770	0.37
Brookhaven (town) Suffolk County	746	0.17
Islip (town) Suffolk County	733	0.23
Babylon (town) Suffolk County	595	0.28
Hempstead (village) Nassau County	583	1.03
Freeport (village) Nassau County	380	0.87
North Hempstead (town) Nassau County	367	0.16
Yonkers (city) Westchester County	359	0.18
Elmont (cdp) Nassau County	329	1.01

Top 10 Places Sorted by Percent
Based on all places, regardless of population

Place	Number	%
South Floral Park (village) Nassau County	42	2.66
Lakeview (cdp) Nassau County	144	2.57
Roosevelt (cdp) Nassau County	272	1.72
Wheatley Heights (cdp) Suffolk County	65	1.29
Pine Hill (cdp) Ulster County	5	1.29
Quiogue (cdp) Suffolk County	10	1.26
North Amityville (cdp) Suffolk County	207	1.25
Gordon Heights (cdp) Suffolk County	38	1.23
North Valley Stream (cdp) Nassau County	188	1.19
Uniondale (cdp) Nassau County	242	1.05

Top 10 Places Sorted by Percent
Based on places with populations of 10,000 or more

Place	Number	%
Roosevelt (cdp) Nassau County	272	1.72
North Amityville (cdp) Suffolk County	207	1.25
North Valley Stream (cdp) Nassau County	188	1.19
Uniondale (cdp) Nassau County	242	1.05
Hempstead (village) Nassau County	583	1.03
Central Islip (cdp) Suffolk County	326	1.02
Elmont (cdp) Nassau County	329	1.01
New York (city) New York City	75,584	0.94
Freeport (village) Nassau County	380	0.87
Wyandanch (cdp) Suffolk County	70	0.66

West Indian: U.S. Virgin Islander, excluding Hispanic

Top 10 Places Sorted by Number
Based on all places, regardless of population

Place	Number	%
New York (city) New York City	2,790	0.03
Hempstead (town) Nassau County	83	0.01
Port Jefferson (village) Suffolk County	29	0.37
Schenectady (city) Schenectady County	29	0.05

Notes: (cdp) census designated place; Refer to the User's Guide in the front of the book for more detailed information.

PROFILES OF NEW YORK / Ancestry: Rankings

Place	Number	%
Brookhaven (town) Suffolk County	29	0.01
Freeport (village) Nassau County	25	0.06
New Rochelle (city) Westchester County	23	0.03
Rochester (city) Monroe County	23	0.01
North Valley Stream (cdp) Nassau County	22	0.14
Mount Vernon (city) Westchester County	22	0.03

Top 10 Places Sorted by Percent
Based on all places, regardless of population

Place	Number	%
Port Jefferson (village) Suffolk County	29	0.37
Kingston (town) Ulster County	3	0.33
Houghton (cdp) Allegany County	5	0.29
Caneadea (town) Allegany County	5	0.19
North Sea (cdp) Suffolk County	8	0.18
Delaware (town) Sullivan County	5	0.18
Wyandanch (cdp) Suffolk County	17	0.16
New Hempstead (village) Rockland County	7	0.15
Greenport (village) Suffolk County	3	0.15
North Valley Stream (cdp) Nassau County	22	0.14

Top 10 Places Sorted by Percent
Based on places with populations of 10,000 or more

Place	Number	%
Wyandanch (cdp) Suffolk County	17	0.16
North Valley Stream (cdp) Nassau County	22	0.14
Canton (town) Saint Lawrence County	8	0.08
Nanuet (cdp) Rockland County	11	0.07
Fort Drum (cdp) Jefferson County	8	0.07
Freeport (village) Nassau County	25	0.06
Schenectady (city) Schenectady County	29	0.05
Westbury (village) Nassau County	7	0.05
Middletown (city) Orange County	10	0.04
Le Ray (town) Jefferson County	8	0.04

West Indian: West Indian, excluding Hispanic

Top 10 Places Sorted by Number
Based on all places, regardless of population

Place	Number	%
New York (city) New York City	54,585	0.68
Hempstead (town) Nassau County	2,280	0.30
Mount Vernon (city) Westchester County	895	1.31
Yonkers (city) Westchester County	785	0.40
Babylon (town) Suffolk County	741	0.35
Islip (town) Suffolk County	694	0.22
Brookhaven (town) Suffolk County	635	0.14
Hempstead (village) Nassau County	448	0.79
Freeport (village) Nassau County	376	0.86
New Rochelle (city) Westchester County	364	0.50

Top 10 Places Sorted by Percent
Based on all places, regardless of population

Place	Number	%
Lakeview (cdp) Nassau County	127	2.27
Grand View-on-Hudson (village) Rockland County	6	2.12
Wheatley Heights (cdp) Suffolk County	104	2.07
East Hampton North (cdp) Suffolk County	63	1.79
North Amityville (cdp) Suffolk County	247	1.50
Calcium (cdp) Jefferson County	44	1.39
Mount Vernon (city) Westchester County	895	1.31
Uniondale (cdp) Nassau County	270	1.17
South Floral Park (village) Nassau County	18	1.14
North Valley Stream (cdp) Nassau County	167	1.06

Top 10 Places Sorted by Percent
Based on places with populations of 10,000 or more

Place	Number	%
North Amityville (cdp) Suffolk County	247	1.50
Mount Vernon (city) Westchester County	895	1.31
Uniondale (cdp) Nassau County	270	1.17
North Valley Stream (cdp) Nassau County	167	1.06
Baldwin (cdp) Nassau County	232	0.99
Freeport (village) Nassau County	376	0.86
Roosevelt (cdp) Nassau County	136	0.86
Hempstead (village) Nassau County	448	0.79
New York (city) New York City	54,585	0.68
Elwood (cdp) Suffolk County	67	0.62

West Indian: Other, excluding Hispanic

Top 10 Places Sorted by Number
Based on all places, regardless of population

Place	Number	%
New York (city) New York City	1,317	0.02
Hempstead (town) Nassau County	96	0.01
Brookhaven (town) Suffolk County	63	0.01
Mount Vernon (city) Westchester County	43	0.06
Centereach (cdp) Suffolk County	38	0.14
Hempstead (village) Nassau County	35	0.06
Valley Stream (village) Nassau County	28	0.08
Cold Spring (village) Putnam County	17	0.86
Philipstown (town) Putnam County	17	0.18
Coram (cdp) Suffolk County	17	0.05

Top 10 Places Sorted by Percent
Based on all places, regardless of population

Place	Number	%
Cold Spring (village) Putnam County	17	0.86
Philipstown (town) Putnam County	17	0.18
East Norwich (cdp) Nassau County	4	0.15
Centereach (cdp) Suffolk County	38	0.14
West Sayville (cdp) Suffolk County	6	0.12
Mount Kisco (village) Westchester County	10	0.10
Liberty (village) Sullivan County	4	0.10
Valley Stream (village) Nassau County	28	0.08
North Valley Stream (cdp) Nassau County	12	0.08
Putnam Valley (town) Putnam County	7	0.07

Top 10 Places Sorted by Percent
Based on places with populations of 10,000 or more

Place	Number	%
Centereach (cdp) Suffolk County	38	0.14
Valley Stream (village) Nassau County	28	0.08
North Valley Stream (cdp) Nassau County	12	0.08
Putnam Valley (town) Putnam County	7	0.07
Mount Vernon (city) Westchester County	43	0.06
Hempstead (village) Nassau County	35	0.06
North Merrick (cdp) Nassau County	7	0.06
Coram (cdp) Suffolk County	17	0.05
Setauket-East Setauket (cdp) Suffolk County	8	0.05
Ithaca (city) Tompkins County	13	0.04

White

Top 10 Places Sorted by Number
Based on all places, regardless of population

Place	Number	%
New York (city) New York City	3,806,508	47.53
Hempstead (town) Nassau County	575,620	76.15
Brookhaven (town) Suffolk County	402,768	89.85
Oyster Bay (town) Nassau County	269,904	91.83
Islip (town) Suffolk County	255,698	79.26
North Hempstead (town) Nassau County	180,100	80.90
Huntington (town) Suffolk County	174,756	89.49
Babylon (town) Suffolk County	165,170	77.99
Buffalo (city) Erie County	164,588	56.24
Yonkers (city) Westchester County	123,920	63.20

Top 10 Places Sorted by Percent
Based on all places, regardless of population

Place	Number	%
Lorraine (town) Jefferson County	930	100.00
Altmar (village) Oswego County	351	100.00
Constableville (village) Lewis County	305	100.00
Arietta (town) Hamilton County	293	100.00
Laurens (village) Otsego County	277	100.00
Ellisburg (village) Jefferson County	269	100.00
Galway (village) Saratoga County	214	100.00
Benson (town) Hamilton County	201	100.00
Halcott (town) Greene County	193	100.00
Ames (village) Montgomery County	173	100.00

Top 10 Places Sorted by Percent
Based on places with populations of 10,000 or more

Place	Number	%
Elma (town) Erie County	11,253	99.55
Kiryas Joel (village) Orange County	13,076	99.53
Aurora (town) Erie County	13,895	99.28
Lancaster (village) Erie County	11,084	99.07
Hamburg (village) Erie County	10,022	99.07
Kingsbury (town) Washington County	11,061	99.02
Sullivan (town) Madison County	14,827	98.91
German Flatts (town) Herkimer County	13,459	98.78
West Seneca (town) Erie County	45,296	98.64
Evans (town) Erie County	17,342	98.57

White: Not Hispanic

Top 10 Places Sorted by Number
Based on all places, regardless of population

Place	Number	%
New York (city) New York City	2,912,995	36.37
Hempstead (town) Nassau County	526,808	69.69
Brookhaven (town) Suffolk County	378,052	84.34
Oyster Bay (town) Nassau County	259,218	88.19
Islip (town) Suffolk County	220,676	68.41
Huntington (town) Suffolk County	166,630	85.32
North Hempstead (town) Nassau County	165,291	74.25
Buffalo (city) Erie County	155,570	53.16
Babylon (town) Suffolk County	152,316	71.93
Smithtown (town) Suffolk County	108,125	93.4

Top 10 Places Sorted by Percent
Based on all places, regardless of population

Place	Number	%
Altmar (village) Oswego County	351	100.00
Arietta (town) Hamilton County	293	100.00
Galway (village) Saratoga County	214	100.00
Ames (village) Montgomery County	173	100.00
Montague (town) Lewis County	108	100.00
Freetown (town) Cortland County	787	99.74
Essex (town) Essex County	711	99.7
Cold Brook (village) Herkimer County	335	99.70
French Creek (town) Chautauqua County	932	99.68
Constableville (village) Lewis County	304	99.67

Top 10 Places Sorted by Percent
Based on places with populations of 10,000 or more

Place	Number	%
Elma (town) Erie County	11,196	99.0
Aurora (town) Erie County	13,826	98.79
Kiryas Joel (village) Orange County	12,976	98.79
Kingsbury (town) Washington County	11,011	98.57
Sullivan (town) Madison County	14,768	98.57
Hamburg (village) Erie County	9,960	98.46
Lancaster (village) Erie County	11,012	98.4
Depew (village) Erie County	16,292	97.97
West Seneca (town) Erie County	44,969	97.9
Lancaster (town) Erie County	38,206	97.97

Notes: (cdp) census designated place; Refer to the User's Guide in the front of the book for more detailed information.

White: Hispanic

Top 10 Places Sorted by Number
Based on all places, regardless of population

Place	Number	%
New York (city) New York City	893,513	11.16
Hempstead (town) Nassau County	48,812	6.46
Islip (town) Suffolk County	35,022	10.86
Brookhaven (town) Suffolk County	24,716	5.51
Yonkers (city) Westchester County	21,270	10.85
North Hempstead (town) Nassau County	14,809	6.65
Brentwood (cdp) Suffolk County	13,914	25.81
Babylon (town) Suffolk County	12,854	6.07
Oyster Bay (town) Nassau County	10,686	3.64
Rochester (city) Monroe County	10,418	4.74

Top 10 Places Sorted by Percent
Based on all places, regardless of population

Place	Number	%
New Cassel (cdp) Nassau County	3,520	26.47
Brentwood (cdp) Suffolk County	13,914	25.81
North Bay Shore (cdp) Suffolk County	3,791	25.29
Sleepy Hollow (village) Westchester County	2,204	23.93
Port Chester (village) Westchester County	6,293	22.58
Haverstraw (village) Rockland County	2,214	21.88
Brewster (village) Putnam County	438	20.26
Fleischmanns (village) Delaware County	67	19.09
Central Islip (cdp) Suffolk County	5,720	17.90
Rye (town) Westchester County	7,253	16.53

Top 10 Places Sorted by Percent
Based on places with populations of 10,000 or more

Place	Number	%
New Cassel (cdp) Nassau County	3,520	26.47
Brentwood (cdp) Suffolk County	13,914	25.81
North Bay Shore (cdp) Suffolk County	3,791	25.29
Port Chester (village) Westchester County	6,293	22.58
Haverstraw (village) Rockland County	2,214	21.88
Central Islip (cdp) Suffolk County	5,720	17.90
Rye (town) Westchester County	7,253	16.53
Newburgh (city) Orange County	4,530	16.03
West Haverstraw (village) Rockland County	1,650	16.03
Ossining (village) Westchester County	3,739	15.57

Yugoslavian

Top 10 Places Sorted by Number
Based on all places, regardless of population

Place	Number	%
New York (city) New York City	15,273	0.19
Utica (city) Oneida County	2,596	4.28
Hempstead (town) Nassau County	765	0.10
Rochester (city) Monroe County	703	0.32
Syracuse (city) Onondaga County	634	0.43
Oyster Bay (town) Nassau County	518	0.18
Brookhaven (town) Suffolk County	470	0.10
Yonkers (city) Westchester County	358	0.18
Greece (town) Monroe County	354	0.38
Babylon (town) Suffolk County	293	0.14

Top 10 Places Sorted by Percent
Based on all places, regardless of population

Place	Number	%
Utica (city) Oneida County	2,596	4.28
Malden (cdp) Ulster County	9	1.84
Webster (village) Monroe County	87	1.69
Livingston (town) Columbia County	47	1.37
Coldspring (town) Cattaraugus County	10	1.31
Quioque (cdp) Suffolk County	10	1.26
Port Washington North (village) Nassau County	34	1.24
Lake Placid (village) Essex County	32	1.23
Walker Valley (cdp) Ulster County	10	1.21
La Fargeville (cdp) Jefferson County	7	1.18

Top 10 Places Sorted by Percent
Based on places with populations of 10,000 or more

Place	Number	%
Utica (city) Oneida County	2,596	4.28
Lackawanna (city) Erie County	193	1.01
Catskill (town) Greene County	98	0.83
Gloversville (city) Fulton County	90	0.58
Elma (town) Erie County	66	0.58
North Lindenhurst (cdp) Suffolk County	66	0.56
Binghamton (city) Broome County	249	0.53
Syracuse (city) Onondaga County	634	0.43
Penfield (town) Monroe County	147	0.42
Shawangunk (town) Ulster County	51	0.42

Notes: (cdp) census designated place; Refer to the User's Guide in the front of the book for more detailed information.

PROFILES OF NEW YORK / Hispanic: Rankings

Population

Total Population
Top 10 Places Sorted by Number

Place	Number
New York, NY (city)	8,008,278
Hempstead, NY (town) Nassau County	755,924
Brookhaven, NY (town) Suffolk County	448,265
Islip, NY (town) Suffolk County	322,625
Oyster Bay, NY (town) Nassau County	293,925
Buffalo, NY (city) Erie County	292,648
North Hempstead, NY (town) Nassau County	222,611
Rochester, NY (city) Monroe County	219,766
Babylon, NY (town) Suffolk County	211,779
Yonkers, NY (city) Westchester County	196,086

Hispanic
Top 10 Places Sorted by Number

Place	Number
New York, NY (city)	2,161,530
Hempstead, NY (town) Nassau County	86,426
Islip, NY (town) Suffolk County	65,162
Yonkers, NY (city) Westchester County	50,954
Brookhaven, NY (town) Suffolk County	35,859
Brentwood, NY (cdp) Suffolk County	29,367
Rochester, NY (city) Monroe County	27,869
Buffalo, NY (city) Erie County	21,699
North Hempstead, NY (town) Nassau County	21,581
Babylon, NY (town) Suffolk County	21,417

Hispanic
Top 10 Places Sorted by Percent of Total Population

Place	Percent
Haverstraw, NY (village) Rockland County	58.80
Brentwood, NY (cdp) Suffolk County	54.50
North Bay Shore, NY (cdp) Suffolk County	50.73
Port Chester, NY (village) Westchester County	46.48
New Cassel, NY (cdp) Nassau County	41.05
Newburgh, NY (city) Orange County	36.16
Central Islip, NY (cdp) Suffolk County	35.78
Freeport, NY (village) Nassau County	33.59
Rye, NY (town) Westchester County	32.74
Hempstead, NY (village) Nassau County	31.98

Argentinian
Top 10 Places Sorted by Number

Place	Number
New York, NY (city)	10,163
Hempstead, NY (town) Nassau County	970
North Hempstead, NY (town) Nassau County	496

Argentinian
Top 10 Places Sorted by Percent of Hispanic Population

Place	Percent
North Hempstead, NY (town) Nassau County	2.30
Hempstead, NY (town) Nassau County	1.12
New York, NY (city)	0.47

Argentinian
Top 10 Places Sorted by Percent of Total Population

Place	Percent
North Hempstead, NY (town) Nassau County	0.22
Hempstead, NY (town) Nassau County	0.13
New York, NY (city)	0.13

Bolivian
Top 10 Places Sorted by Number

Place	Number
New York, NY (city)	3,341

Bolivian
Top 10 Places Sorted by Percent of Hispanic Population

Place	Percent
New York, NY (city)	0.15

Bolivian
Top 10 Places Sorted by Percent of Total Population

Place	Percent
New York, NY (city)	0.04

Central American
Top 10 Places Sorted by Number

Place	Number
New York, NY (city)	107,991
Hempstead, NY (town) Nassau County	22,826
Islip, NY (town) Suffolk County	15,864
Brentwood, NY (cdp) Suffolk County	9,292
Hempstead, NY (village) Nassau County	8,689
North Hempstead, NY (town) Nassau County	6,964
Freeport, NY (village) Nassau County	4,256
Yonkers, NY (city) Westchester County	4,108
Babylon, NY (town) Suffolk County	3,933
Huntington, NY (town) Suffolk County	3,868

Central American
Top 10 Places Sorted by Percent of Hispanic Population

Place	Percent
Roosevelt, NY (cdp) Nassau County	52.45
Hempstead, NY (village) Nassau County	48.06
Huntington Station, NY (cdp) Suffolk County	44.87
New Cassel, NY (cdp) Nassau County	43.62
Port Washington, NY (cdp) Nassau County	42.55
Uniondale, NY (cdp) Nassau County	41.34
Spring Valley, NY (village) Rockland County	40.30
Westbury, NY (village) Nassau County	37.50
North Hempstead, NY (town) Nassau County	32.27
Southold, NY (town) Suffolk County	31.74

Central American
Top 10 Places Sorted by Percent of Total Population

Place	Percent
New Cassel, NY (cdp) Nassau County	17.90
Brentwood, NY (cdp) Suffolk County	17.24
Hempstead, NY (village) Nassau County	15.37
North Bay Shore, NY (cdp) Suffolk County	15.21
Huntington Station, NY (cdp) Suffolk County	10.06
Freeport, NY (village) Nassau County	9.72
Uniondale, NY (cdp) Nassau County	9.57
Roosevelt, NY (cdp) Nassau County	8.63
Central Islip, NY (cdp) Suffolk County	8.37
Westbury, NY (village) Nassau County	7.21

Chilean
Top 10 Places Sorted by Number

Place	Number
New York, NY (city)	5,725
Hempstead, NY (town) Nassau County	663
North Hempstead, NY (town) Nassau County	645
Oyster Bay, NY (town) Nassau County	395

Chilean
Top 10 Places Sorted by Percent of Hispanic Population

Place	Percent
North Hempstead, NY (town) Nassau County	2.99
Oyster Bay, NY (town) Nassau County	2.60
Hempstead, NY (town) Nassau County	0.77
New York, NY (city)	0.26

Chilean
Top 10 Places Sorted by Percent of Total Population

Place	Percent
North Hempstead, NY (town) Nassau County	0.29
Oyster Bay, NY (town) Nassau County	0.13
Hempstead, NY (town) Nassau County	0.09
New York, NY (city)	0.07

Colombian
Top 10 Places Sorted by Number

Place	Number
New York, NY (city)	81,566
Hempstead, NY (town) Nassau County	4,686
Islip, NY (town) Suffolk County	3,032
Brentwood, NY (cdp) Suffolk County	1,719
White Plains, NY (city) Westchester County	1,298
Brookhaven, NY (town) Suffolk County	1,246
North Hempstead, NY (town) Nassau County	1,238
New Rochelle, NY (city) Westchester County	1,184
Oyster Bay, NY (town) Nassau County	1,178
Yonkers, NY (city) Westchester County	1,165

Colombian
Top 10 Places Sorted by Percent of Hispanic Population

Place	Percent
East Hampton, NY (town) Suffolk County	26.59
Mineola, NY (village) Nassau County	17.00
White Plains, NY (city) Westchester County	10.29
Long Beach, NY (city) Nassau County	9.20
New Rochelle, NY (city) Westchester County	8.23
Oyster Bay, NY (town) Nassau County	7.76
Ossining, NY (village) Westchester County	7.32
Southampton, NY (town) Suffolk County	6.83
Ossining, NY (town) Westchester County	6.77
Greenburgh, NY (town) Westchester County	6.44

Colombian
Top 10 Places Sorted by Percent of Total Population

Place	Percent
East Hampton, NY (town) Suffolk County	3.99
Brentwood, NY (cdp) Suffolk County	3.19
Port Chester, NY (village) Westchester County	2.88
White Plains, NY (city) Westchester County	2.45
Mineola, NY (village) Nassau County	2.22
Ossining, NY (village) Westchester County	2.04
Rye, NY (town) Westchester County	1.94
New Rochelle, NY (city) Westchester County	1.64
Freeport, NY (village) Nassau County	1.37
Ossining, NY (town) Westchester County	1.34

Costa Rican
Top 10 Places Sorted by Number

Place	Number
New York, NY (city)	5,238
Hempstead, NY (town) Nassau County	393

Costa Rican
Top 10 Places Sorted by Percent of Hispanic Population

Place	Percent
Hempstead, NY (town) Nassau County	0.45
New York, NY (city)	0.24

Costa Rican
Top 10 Places Sorted by Percent of Total Population

Place	Percent
New York, NY (city)	0.07
Hempstead, NY (town) Nassau County	0.05

Notes: Please refer to the User's Guide for an explanation of data; tables include places with populations > 9,999 and reflect only those areas that meet Summary File 4 population thresholds, therefore there may be less than 10 places listed

Cuban
Top 10 Places Sorted by Number

Place	Number
New York, NY (city)	41,474
Hempstead, NY (town) Nassau County	3,186
Yonkers, NY (city) Westchester County	1,280
Islip, NY (town) Suffolk County	1,268
Rochester, NY (city) Monroe County	1,151
Brookhaven, NY (town) Suffolk County	1,109
Oyster Bay, NY (town) Nassau County	717
Babylon, NY (town) Suffolk County	671
Rye, NY (town) Westchester County	525
Greenburgh, NY (town) Westchester County	501

Cuban
Top 10 Places Sorted by Percent of Hispanic Population

Place	Percent
Clarks, NY (town) Rockland County	7.00
Greenburgh, NY (town) Westchester County	6.45
Syracuse, NY (city) Onondaga County	5.76
Oyster Bay, NY (town) Nassau County	4.72
Rochester, NY (city) Monroe County	4.13
Hempstead, NY (town) Nassau County	3.69
Rye, NY (town) Westchester County	3.65
Port Chester, NY (village) Westchester County	3.56
Babylon, NY (town) Suffolk County	3.13
Brookhaven, NY (town) Suffolk County	3.09

Cuban
Top 10 Places Sorted by Percent of Total Population

Place	Percent
Port Chester, NY (village) Westchester County	1.65
Rye, NY (town) Westchester County	1.20
Yonkers, NY (city) Westchester County	0.65
Greenburgh, NY (town) Westchester County	0.58
New York, NY (city)	0.52
Rochester, NY (city) Monroe County	0.52
Clarks, NY (town) Rockland County	0.47
Hempstead, NY (town) Nassau County	0.42
Islip, NY (town) Suffolk County	0.39
Babylon, NY (town) Suffolk County	0.32

Dominican
Top 10 Places Sorted by Number

Place	Number
New York, NY (city)	425,739
Hempstead, NY (town) Nassau County	8,534
Yonkers, NY (city) Westchester County	7,846
Islip, NY (town) Suffolk County	4,490
Haverstraw, NY (town) Rockland County	3,747
Freeport, NY (village) Nassau County	3,159
Babylon, NY (town) Suffolk County	2,873
Haverstraw, NY (village) Rockland County	2,610
Brentwood, NY (cdp) Suffolk County	2,298
Brookhaven, NY (town) Suffolk County	2,245

Dominican
Top 10 Places Sorted by Percent of Hispanic Population

Place	Percent
Haverstraw, NY (village) Rockland County	44.27
Rockville Centre, NY (village) Nassau County	41.91
Haverstraw, NY (town) Rockland County	35.10
West Haverstraw, NY (village) Rockland County	30.25
Copiague, NY (cdp) Suffolk County	26.62
Mount Pleasant, NY (town) Westchester County	26.56
Freeport, NY (village) Nassau County	21.48
New York, NY (city)	19.70
Baldwin, NY (cdp) Nassau County	16.79
Yonkers, NY (city) Westchester County	15.40

Dominican
Top 10 Places Sorted by Percent of Total Population

Place	Percent
Haverstraw, NY (village) Rockland County	26.03
Haverstraw, NY (town) Rockland County	11.11
West Haverstraw, NY (village) Rockland County	9.23
Freeport, NY (village) Nassau County	7.22
Copiague, NY (cdp) Suffolk County	5.42
New York, NY (city)	5.32
Brentwood, NY (cdp) Suffolk County	4.26
North Bay Shore, NY (cdp) Suffolk County	4.06
Yonkers, NY (city) Westchester County	4.00
Mount Pleasant, NY (town) Westchester County	3.69

Ecuadorian
Top 10 Places Sorted by Number

Place	Number
New York, NY (city)	106,617
Hempstead, NY (town) Nassau County	2,292
Ossining, NY (town) Westchester County	2,204
Ossining, NY (village) Westchester County	2,204
Brookhaven, NY (town) Suffolk County	1,758
Yonkers, NY (city) Westchester County	1,750
Islip, NY (town) Suffolk County	1,669
Rye, NY (town) Westchester County	1,048
Port Chester, NY (village) Westchester County	1,019
North Hempstead, NY (town) Nassau County	962

Ecuadorian
Top 10 Places Sorted by Percent of Hispanic Population

Place	Percent
Ossining, NY (village) Westchester County	32.92
Ossining, NY (town) Westchester County	30.45
Patchogue, NY (village) Suffolk County	26.23
East Hampton, NY (town) Suffolk County	23.75
Spring Valley, NY (village) Rockland County	19.23
Peekskill, NY (city) Westchester County	14.32
Mount Pleasant, NY (town) Westchester County	12.27
Ramapo, NY (town) Rockland County	8.71
Bay Shore, NY (cdp) Suffolk County	8.47
Port Chester, NY (village) Westchester County	7.87

Ecuadorian
Top 10 Places Sorted by Percent of Total Population

Place	Percent
Ossining, NY (village) Westchester County	9.18
Patchogue, NY (village) Suffolk County	6.28
Ossining, NY (town) Westchester County	6.03
Port Chester, NY (village) Westchester County	3.66
East Hampton, NY (town) Suffolk County	3.56
Peekskill, NY (city) Westchester County	3.10
Spring Valley, NY (village) Rockland County	2.92
Rye, NY (town) Westchester County	2.39
Mount Pleasant, NY (town) Westchester County	1.71
Bay Shore, NY (cdp) Suffolk County	1.68

Guatelmalan
Top 10 Places Sorted by Number

Place	Number
New York, NY (city)	15,986
Hempstead, NY (town) Nassau County	1,867
Ramapo, NY (town) Rockland County	1,493
Rye, NY (town) Westchester County	1,357
Port Chester, NY (village) Westchester County	1,263
Spring Valley, NY (village) Rockland County	1,208
Islip, NY (town) Suffolk County	1,109
North Hempstead, NY (town) Nassau County	729
Brentwood, NY (cdp) Suffolk County	563
Mamaroneck, NY (village) Westchester County	508

Guatelmalan
Top 10 Places Sorted by Percent of Hispanic Population

Place	Percent
Spring Valley, NY (village) Rockland County	31.34
Southeast, NY (town) Putnam County	25.23
Ramapo, NY (town) Rockland County	16.85
Mamaroneck, NY (village) Westchester County	15.35
Mamaroneck, NY (town) Westchester County	12.89
Port Chester, NY (village) Westchester County	9.75
Rye, NY (town) Westchester County	9.44
Southampton, NY (town) Suffolk County	9.29
North Hempstead, NY (town) Nassau County	3.38
Freeport, NY (village) Nassau County	3.33

Guatelmalan
Top 10 Places Sorted by Percent of Total Population

Place	Percent
Spring Valley, NY (village) Rockland County	4.76
Port Chester, NY (village) Westchester County	4.53
Rye, NY (town) Westchester County	3.09
Mamaroneck, NY (village) Westchester County	2.71
Southeast, NY (town) Putnam County	2.05
Mamaroneck, NY (town) Westchester County	1.43
Ramapo, NY (town) Rockland County	1.37
Freeport, NY (village) Nassau County	1.12
Brentwood, NY (cdp) Suffolk County	1.04
Southampton, NY (town) Suffolk County	0.81

Honduran
Top 10 Places Sorted by Number

Place	Number
New York, NY (city)	29,732
Hempstead, NY (town) Nassau County	2,499
Hempstead, NY (village) Nassau County	1,617
Islip, NY (town) Suffolk County	1,216
Yonkers, NY (city) Westchester County	916
Newburgh, NY (city) Orange County	733
North Hempstead, NY (town) Nassau County	732
Brentwood, NY (cdp) Suffolk County	586
Babylon, NY (town) Suffolk County	495
Huntington, NY (town) Suffolk County	462

Honduran
Top 10 Places Sorted by Percent of Hispanic Population

Place	Percent
Hempstead, NY (village) Nassau County	8.94
Newburgh, NY (city) Orange County	7.18
Huntington, NY (town) Suffolk County	3.60
North Hempstead, NY (town) Nassau County	3.39
Hempstead, NY (town) Nassau County	2.89
Babylon, NY (town) Suffolk County	2.31
Brentwood, NY (cdp) Suffolk County	2.00
Islip, NY (town) Suffolk County	1.87
Yonkers, NY (city) Westchester County	1.80
New York, NY (city)	1.38

Honduran
Top 10 Places Sorted by Percent of Total Population

Place	Percent
Hempstead, NY (village) Nassau County	2.86
Newburgh, NY (city) Orange County	2.60
Brentwood, NY (cdp) Suffolk County	1.09
Yonkers, NY (city) Westchester County	0.47
Islip, NY (town) Suffolk County	0.38
New York, NY (city)	0.37
Hempstead, NY (town) Nassau County	0.33
North Hempstead, NY (town) Nassau County	0.33
Huntington, NY (town) Suffolk County	0.24
Babylon, NY (town) Suffolk County	0.23

Notes: Please refer to the User's Guide for an explanation of data; tables include places with populations > 9,999 and reflect only those areas that meet Summary File 4 population thresholds, therefore there may be less than 10 places listed

Mexican
Top 10 Places Sorted by Number

Place	Number
New York, NY (city)	177,527
New Rochelle, NY (city) Westchester County	7,050
Yonkers, NY (city) Westchester County	6,645
Newburgh, NY (city) Orange County	4,569
Rye, NY (town) Westchester County	3,950
Port Chester, NY (village) Westchester County	3,667
White Plains, NY (city) Westchester County	3,251
Hempstead, NY (town) Nassau County	2,706
North Hempstead, NY (town) Nassau County	2,531
Middletown, NY (city) Orange County	1,849

Mexican
Top 10 Places Sorted by Percent of Hispanic Population

Place	Percent
New Rochelle, NY (city) Westchester County	49.03
Newburgh, NY (city) Orange County	44.76
Poughkeepsie, NY (city) Dutchess County	43.43
Fort Drum, NY (cdp) Jefferson County	36.62
Le Ray, NY (town) Jefferson County	32.52
Middletown, NY (city) Orange County	29.14
Port Chester, NY (village) Westchester County	28.31
Rye, NY (town) Westchester County	27.49
New Cassel, NY (cdp) Nassau County	26.40
White Plains, NY (city) Westchester County	25.76

Mexican
Top 10 Places Sorted by Percent of Total Population

Place	Percent
Newburgh, NY (city) Orange County	16.18
Port Chester, NY (village) Westchester County	13.16
New Cassel, NY (cdp) Nassau County	10.84
New Rochelle, NY (city) Westchester County	9.77
Rye, NY (town) Westchester County	9.00
Middletown, NY (city) Orange County	7.30
White Plains, NY (city) Westchester County	6.13
Fort Drum, NY (cdp) Jefferson County	4.91
Poughkeepsie, NY (city) Dutchess County	4.56
Mamaroneck, NY (village) Westchester County	4.16

Nicaraguan
Top 10 Places Sorted by Number

Place	Number
New York, NY (city)	7,412
Yonkers, NY (city) Westchester County	573

Nicaraguan
Top 10 Places Sorted by Percent of Hispanic Population

Place	Percent
Yonkers, NY (city) Westchester County	1.12
New York, NY (city)	0.34

Nicaraguan
Top 10 Places Sorted by Percent of Total Population

Place	Percent
Yonkers, NY (city) Westchester County	0.29
New York, NY (city)	0.09

Panamanian
Top 10 Places Sorted by Number

Place	Number
New York, NY (city)	18,665
Hempstead, NY (town) Nassau County	595
Islip, NY (town) Suffolk County	333

Panamanian
Top 10 Places Sorted by Percent of Hispanic Population

Place	Percent
New York, NY (city)	0.86
Hempstead, NY (town) Nassau County	0.69
Islip, NY (town) Suffolk County	0.51

Panamanian
Top 10 Places Sorted by Percent of Total Population

Place	Percent
New York, NY (city)	0.23
Islip, NY (town) Suffolk County	0.10
Hempstead, NY (town) Nassau County	0.08

Paraguayan
Top 10 Places Sorted by Number

Place	Number
New York, NY (city)	1,551

Paraguayan
Top 10 Places Sorted by Percent of Hispanic Population

Place	Percent
New York, NY (city)	0.07

Paraguayan
Top 10 Places Sorted by Percent of Total Population

Place	Percent
New York, NY (city)	0.02

Peruvian
Top 10 Places Sorted by Number

Place	Number
New York, NY (city)	23,665
Hempstead, NY (town) Nassau County	1,997
White Plains, NY (city) Westchester County	1,480
Islip, NY (town) Suffolk County	1,287
Rye, NY (town) Westchester County	935
Port Chester, NY (village) Westchester County	826
Glen Cove, NY (city) Nassau County	812
New Rochelle, NY (city) Westchester County	704
Oyster Bay, NY (town) Nassau County	642
Brookhaven, NY (town) Suffolk County	581

Peruvian
Top 10 Places Sorted by Percent of Hispanic Population

Place	Percent
Glen Cove, NY (city) Nassau County	15.01
White Plains, NY (city) Westchester County	11.73
Rye, NY (town) Westchester County	6.51
Port Chester, NY (village) Westchester County	6.38
New Rochelle, NY (city) Westchester County	4.90
Oyster Bay, NY (town) Nassau County	4.23
Hempstead, NY (town) Nassau County	2.31
North Hempstead, NY (town) Nassau County	2.25
Islip, NY (town) Suffolk County	1.98
Brentwood, NY (cdp) Suffolk County	1.75

Peruvian
Top 10 Places Sorted by Percent of Total Population

Place	Percent
Glen Cove, NY (city) Nassau County	3.05
Port Chester, NY (village) Westchester County	2.96
White Plains, NY (city) Westchester County	2.79
Rye, NY (town) Westchester County	2.13
New Rochelle, NY (city) Westchester County	0.98
Brentwood, NY (cdp) Suffolk County	0.95
Islip, NY (town) Suffolk County	0.40
New York, NY (city)	0.30
Yonkers, NY (city) Westchester County	0.27
Hempstead, NY (town) Nassau County	0.26

Puerto Rican
Top 10 Places Sorted by Number

Place	Number
New York, NY (city)	784,297
Islip, NY (town) Suffolk County	22,417
Rochester, NY (city) Monroe County	21,755
Yonkers, NY (city) Westchester County	18,429
Brookhaven, NY (town) Suffolk County	17,533
Buffalo, NY (city) Erie County	16,727
Hempstead, NY (town) Nassau County	15,831
Brentwood, NY (cdp) Suffolk County	7,942
Babylon, NY (town) Suffolk County	6,574
Syracuse, NY (city) Onondaga County	4,714

Puerto Rican
Top 10 Places Sorted by Percent of Hispanic Population

Place	Percent
Dunkirk, NY (city) Chautauqua County	88.57
Jamestown, NY (city) Chautauqua County	84.45
Mastic Beach, NY (cdp) Suffolk County	79.98
Utica, NY (city) Oneida County	78.68
Arcadia, NY (town) Wayne County	78.37
Rochester, NY (city) Monroe County	78.06
Buffalo, NY (city) Erie County	77.09
Mastic, NY (cdp) Suffolk County	73.79
Amsterdam, NY (city) Montgomery County	72.54
Chester, NY (town) Orange County	70.73

Puerto Rican
Top 10 Places Sorted by Percent of Total Population

Place	Percent
Dunkirk, NY (city) Chautauqua County	17.70
North Bay Shore, NY (cdp) Suffolk County	17.50
Brentwood, NY (cdp) Suffolk County	14.74
Haverstraw, NY (village) Rockland County	14.26
Central Islip, NY (cdp) Suffolk County	13.79
West Haverstraw, NY (village) Rockland County	13.37
Amsterdam, NY (city) Montgomery County	11.78
Middletown, NY (city) Orange County	11.44
Haverstraw, NY (town) Rockland County	10.79
Wawarsing, NY (town) Ulster County	10.56

Salvadoran
Top 10 Places Sorted by Number

Place	Number
New York, NY (city)	25,266
Hempstead, NY (town) Nassau County	16,356
Islip, NY (town) Suffolk County	12,615
Brentwood, NY (cdp) Suffolk County	7,876
Hempstead, NY (village) Nassau County	6,246
North Hempstead, NY (town) Nassau County	4,936
Freeport, NY (village) Nassau County	3,180
Huntington, NY (town) Suffolk County	2,933
Babylon, NY (town) Suffolk County	2,775
Huntington Station, NY (cdp) Suffolk County	2,480

Salvadoran
Top 10 Places Sorted by Percent of Hispanic Population

Place	Percent
Roosevelt, NY (cdp) Nassau County	41.18
New Cassel, NY (cdp) Nassau County	37.94
Huntington Station, NY (cdp) Suffolk County	36.91
Hempstead, NY (village) Nassau County	34.54
Uniondale, NY (cdp) Nassau County	32.76
Brentwood, NY (cdp) Suffolk County	26.82
Westbury, NY (village) Nassau County	26.02
North Hempstead, NY (town) Nassau County	22.87
Huntington, NY (town) Suffolk County	22.85
Glen Cove, NY (city) Nassau County	22.81

Notes: Please refer to the User's Guide for an explanation of data; tables include places with populations > 9,999 and reflect only those areas that meet Summary File 4 population thresholds, therefore there may be less than 10 places listed

Salvadoran
Top 10 Places Sorted by Percent of Total Population

Place	Percent
New Cassel, NY (cdp) Nassau County	15.57
Brentwood, NY (cdp) Suffolk County	14.62
North Bay Shore, NY (cdp) Suffolk County	11.24
Hempstead, NY (village) Nassau County	11.05
Huntington Station, NY (cdp) Suffolk County	8.28
Uniondale, NY (cdp) Nassau County	7.58
Freeport, NY (village) Nassau County	7.26
Roosevelt, NY (cdp) Nassau County	6.77
Central Islip, NY (cdp) Suffolk County	6.50
Westbury, NY (village) Nassau County	5.01

South American
Top 10 Places Sorted by Number

Place	Number
New York, NY (city)	248,137
Hempstead, NY (town) Nassau County	11,854
Islip, NY (town) Suffolk County	7,434
Brookhaven, NY (town) Suffolk County	4,513
Yonkers, NY (city) Westchester County	4,333
North Hempstead, NY (town) Nassau County	4,238
White Plains, NY (city) Westchester County	3,771
Rye, NY (town) Westchester County	3,498
Oyster Bay, NY (town) Nassau County	3,418
Brentwood, NY (cdp) Suffolk County	3,308

South American
Top 10 Places Sorted by Percent of Hispanic Population

Place	Percent
East Hampton, NY (town) Suffolk County	55.14
Ossining, NY (village) Westchester County	46.08
Ossining, NY (town) Westchester County	43.20
Harrison, NY (village) Westchester County	39.16
Mineola, NY (village) Nassau County	33.49
Patchogue, NY (village) Suffolk County	30.47
White Plains, NY (city) Westchester County	29.88
Glen Cove, NY (city) Nassau County	28.73
Lynbrook, NY (village) Nassau County	27.36
Franklin Square, NY (cdp) Nassau County	26.46

South American
Top 10 Places Sorted by Percent of Total Population

Place	Percent
Ossining, NY (village) Westchester County	12.85
Port Chester, NY (village) Westchester County	11.17
Ossining, NY (town) Westchester County	8.56
East Hampton, NY (town) Suffolk County	8.27
Rye, NY (town) Westchester County	7.97
Patchogue, NY (village) Suffolk County	7.29
White Plains, NY (city) Westchester County	7.10
Brentwood, NY (cdp) Suffolk County	6.14
Glen Cove, NY (city) Nassau County	5.84
Mineola, NY (village) Nassau County	4.38

Spaniard
Top 10 Places Sorted by Number

Place	Number
New York, NY (city)	10,061
Hempstead, NY (town) Nassau County	813
Brookhaven, NY (town) Suffolk County	412

Spaniard
Top 10 Places Sorted by Percent of Hispanic Population

Place	Percent
Brookhaven, NY (town) Suffolk County	1.15
Hempstead, NY (town) Nassau County	0.94
New York, NY (city)	0.47

Spaniard
Top 10 Places Sorted by Percent of Total Population

Place	Percent
New York, NY (city)	0.13
Hempstead, NY (town) Nassau County	0.11
Brookhaven, NY (town) Suffolk County	0.09

Uruguayan
Top 10 Places Sorted by Number

Place	Number
New York, NY (city)	2,049

Uruguayan
Top 10 Places Sorted by Percent of Hispanic Population

Place	Percent
New York, NY (city)	0.09

Uruguayan
Top 10 Places Sorted by Percent of Total Population

Place	Percent
New York, NY (city)	0.03

Venezuelan
Top 10 Places Sorted by Number

Place	Number
New York, NY (city)	7,178

Venezuelan
Top 10 Places Sorted by Percent of Hispanic Population

Place	Percent
New York, NY (city)	0.33

Venezuelan
Top 10 Places Sorted by Percent of Total Population

Place	Percent
New York, NY (city)	0.09

Other Hispanic
Top 10 Places Sorted by Number

Place	Number
New York, NY (city)	366,304
Hempstead, NY (town) Nassau County	20,676
Islip, NY (town) Suffolk County	11,920
Yonkers, NY (city) Westchester County	8,102
Brookhaven, NY (town) Suffolk County	6,304
Brentwood, NY (cdp) Suffolk County	5,658
Hempstead, NY (village) Nassau County	5,262
North Hempstead, NY (town) Nassau County	4,275
Freeport, NY (village) Nassau County	3,820
Babylon, NY (town) Suffolk County	3,754

Other Hispanic
Top 10 Places Sorted by Percent of Hispanic Population

Place	Percent
Peekskill, NY (city) Westchester County	33.09
East Meadow, NY (cdp) Nassau County	32.16
Hempstead, NY (village) Nassau County	29.10
Selden, NY (cdp) Suffolk County	28.41
Long Beach, NY (city) Nassau County	27.47
Centereach, NY (cdp) Suffolk County	26.10
Freeport, NY (village) Nassau County	25.97
Roosevelt, NY (cdp) Nassau County	25.81
North Lindenhurst, NY (cdp) Suffolk County	24.53
Hempstead, NY (town) Nassau County	23.92

Other Hispanic
Top 10 Places Sorted by Percent of Total Population

Place	Percent
Brentwood, NY (cdp) Suffolk County	10.50
Hempstead, NY (village) Nassau County	9.31
North Bay Shore, NY (cdp) Suffolk County	9.18
Haverstraw, NY (village) Rockland County	9.09
Freeport, NY (village) Nassau County	8.72
Port Chester, NY (village) Westchester County	8.48
New Cassel, NY (cdp) Nassau County	8.11
Peekskill, NY (city) Westchester County	7.17
Rye, NY (town) Westchester County	6.17
Central Islip, NY (cdp) Suffolk County	6.04

Median Age

Total Population
Top 10 Places Sorted by Number

Place	Years
Southold, NY (town) Suffolk County	44.3
Irondequoit, NY (cdp) Monroe County	42.7
Somers, NY (town) Westchester County	42.5
Ridge, NY (cdp) Suffolk County	42.2
North New Hyde Park, NY (cdp) Nassau County	42.0
East Hampton, NY (town) Suffolk County	41.8
Jefferson Valley-Yorktown, NY (cdp) Westchester County	41.1
Tonawanda, NY (town) Erie County	41.1
West Seneca, NY (town) Erie County	41.1
De Witt, NY (town) Onondaga County	40.9

Hispanic
Top 10 Places Sorted by Number

Place	Years
Massapequa, NY (cdp) Nassau County	39.0
Dix Hills, NY (cdp) Suffolk County	38.2
Eastchester, NY (town) Westchester County	37.9
North Merrick, NY (cdp) Nassau County	37.4
Chester, NY (town) Orange County	36.8
Kings Park, NY (cdp) Suffolk County	36.7
Somers, NY (town) Westchester County	36.3
Commack, NY (cdp) Suffolk County	36.1
Plainview, NY (cdp) Nassau County	35.9
Massapequa Park, NY (village) Nassau County	35.3

Argentinian
Top 10 Places Sorted by Number

Place	Years
New York, NY (city)	39.0
North Hempstead, NY (town) Nassau County	38.1
Hempstead, NY (town) Nassau County	35.8

Bolivian
Top 10 Places Sorted by Number

Place	Years
New York, NY (city)	33.1

Central American
Top 10 Places Sorted by Number

Place	Years
Long Beach, NY (city) Nassau County	34.3
Mineola, NY (village) Nassau County	33.7
Elmont, NY (cdp) Nassau County	33.6
Levittown, NY (cdp) Nassau County	32.7
Mount Vernon, NY (city) Westchester County	32.1
New York, NY (city)	31.9
Mamaroneck, NY (village) Westchester County	30.9
Mamaroneck, NY (town) Westchester County	30.6
East Hampton, NY (town) Suffolk County	30.5
Port Washington, NY (cdp) Nassau County	30.5

Chilean
Top 10 Places Sorted by Number

Place	Years
Oyster Bay, NY (town) Nassau County	38.6
New York, NY (city)	36.7
Hempstead, NY (town) Nassau County	35.8

Notes: Please refer to the User's Guide for an explanation of data; tables include places with populations > 9,999 and reflect only those areas that meet Summary File 4 population thresholds, therefore there may be less than 10 places listed

Place	Years
North Hempstead, NY (town) Nassau County	31.4

Colombian
Top 10 Places Sorted by Number

Place	Years
Yonkers, NY (city) Westchester County	38.2
White Plains, NY (city) Westchester County	38.1
Mineola, NY (village) Nassau County	37.5
Greenburgh, NY (town) Westchester County	36.4
New York, NY (city)	35.2
North Hempstead, NY (town) Nassau County	34.8
Hempstead, NY (town) Nassau County	34.5
Islip, NY (town) Suffolk County	34.5
East Hampton, NY (town) Suffolk County	34.3
Long Beach, NY (city) Nassau County	33.7

Costa Rican
Top 10 Places Sorted by Number

Place	Years
New York, NY (city)	37.4
Hempstead, NY (town) Nassau County	36.9

Cuban
Top 10 Places Sorted by Number

Place	Years
Port Chester, NY (village) Westchester County	58.1
Rye, NY (town) Westchester County	51.0
New York, NY (city)	45.8
Yonkers, NY (city) Westchester County	43.2
Clarks, NY (town) Rockland County	39.4
Oyster Bay, NY (town) Nassau County	38.7
Brookhaven, NY (town) Suffolk County	38.1
Greenburgh, NY (town) Westchester County	37.7
North Hempstead, NY (town) Nassau County	37.0
Hempstead, NY (town) Nassau County	36.8

Dominican
Top 10 Places Sorted by Number

Place	Years
White Plains, NY (city) Westchester County	34.7
Oyster Bay, NY (town) Nassau County	34.4
Central Islip, NY (cdp) Suffolk County	32.0
Baldwin, NY (cdp) Nassau County	31.8
Brentwood, NY (cdp) Suffolk County	31.8
Port Chester, NY (village) Westchester County	31.7
Uniondale, NY (cdp) Nassau County	31.4
Mount Vernon, NY (city) Westchester County	31.3
West Haverstraw, NY (village) Rockland County	31.3
Islip, NY (town) Suffolk County	31.1

Ecuadorian
Top 10 Places Sorted by Number

Place	Years
Babylon, NY (town) Suffolk County	37.1
Brentwood, NY (cdp) Suffolk County	36.0
Oyster Bay, NY (town) Nassau County	34.8
Hempstead, NY (town) Nassau County	34.7
Central Islip, NY (cdp) Suffolk County	33.1
Yonkers, NY (city) Westchester County	32.9
North Hempstead, NY (town) Nassau County	32.5
New York, NY (city)	31.2
Islip, NY (town) Suffolk County	30.7
Bay Shore, NY (cdp) Suffolk County	30.3

Guatemalan
Top 10 Places Sorted by Number

Place	Years
Babylon, NY (town) Suffolk County	32.6
Huntington, NY (town) Suffolk County	32.1
New York, NY (city)	30.5
Brookhaven, NY (town) Suffolk County	30.4
North Hempstead, NY (town) Nassau County	30.0

Place	Years
Brentwood, NY (cdp) Suffolk County	29.2
Mamaroneck, NY (village) Westchester County	28.8
Rye, NY (town) Westchester County	28.2
Islip, NY (town) Suffolk County	27.7
Port Chester, NY (village) Westchester County	27.7

Honduran
Top 10 Places Sorted by Number

Place	Years
Yonkers, NY (city) Westchester County	30.8
New York, NY (city)	29.7
Hempstead, NY (town) Nassau County	27.7
Hempstead, NY (village) Nassau County	27.0
Huntington, NY (town) Suffolk County	26.8
Brentwood, NY (cdp) Suffolk County	26.6
North Hempstead, NY (town) Nassau County	26.6
Babylon, NY (town) Suffolk County	26.5
Islip, NY (town) Suffolk County	25.4
Newburgh, NY (city) Orange County	24.8

Mexican
Top 10 Places Sorted by Number

Place	Years
Babylon, NY (town) Suffolk County	30.1
Elmont, NY (cdp) Nassau County	29.3
Buffalo, NY (city) Erie County	29.0
Oyster Bay, NY (town) Nassau County	28.1
Greenburgh, NY (town) Westchester County	27.6
Clarks, NY (town) Rockland County	27.3
Brookhaven, NY (town) Suffolk County	26.5
Hempstead, NY (town) Nassau County	26.4
North Hempstead, NY (town) Nassau County	26.3
Mount Vernon, NY (city) Westchester County	26.1

Nicaraguan
Top 10 Places Sorted by Number

Place	Years
New York, NY (city)	33.1
Yonkers, NY (city) Westchester County	30.9

Panamanian
Top 10 Places Sorted by Number

Place	Years
Islip, NY (town) Suffolk County	40.8
New York, NY (city)	38.2
Hempstead, NY (town) Nassau County	36.5

Paraguayan
Top 10 Places Sorted by Number

Place	Years
New York, NY (city)	31.6

Peruvian
Top 10 Places Sorted by Number

Place	Years
North Hempstead, NY (town) Nassau County	40.0
Rye, NY (town) Westchester County	37.6
Port Chester, NY (village) Westchester County	37.5
New York, NY (city)	36.2
Oyster Bay, NY (town) Nassau County	36.1
Yonkers, NY (city) Westchester County	35.1
New Rochelle, NY (city) Westchester County	35.0
Islip, NY (town) Suffolk County	34.4
White Plains, NY (city) Westchester County	33.8
Brentwood, NY (cdp) Suffolk County	33.7

Puerto Rican
Top 10 Places Sorted by Number

Place	Years
East Islip, NY (cdp) Suffolk County	39.1
Dix Hills, NY (cdp) Suffolk County	38.4

Place	Years
Chester, NY (town) Orange County	38.0
Mamaroneck, NY (town) Westchester County	37.8
Franklin Square, NY (cdp) Nassau County	37.3
Jefferson Valley-Yorktown, NY (cdp) Westchester County	37.0
Commack, NY (cdp) Suffolk County	36.8
Hicksville, NY (cdp) Nassau County	36.6
Ogdensburg, NY (city) Saint Lawrence County	36.4
Bedford, NY (town) Westchester County	36.3

Salvadoran
Top 10 Places Sorted by Number

Place	Years
Elmont, NY (cdp) Nassau County	33.4
Mineola, NY (village) Nassau County	33.4
Yonkers, NY (city) Westchester County	30.9
New York, NY (city)	30.3
Hicksville, NY (cdp) Nassau County	29.8
Oyster Bay, NY (town) Nassau County	29.2
Westbury, NY (village) Nassau County	28.8
Rye, NY (town) Westchester County	28.4
Port Chester, NY (village) Westchester County	28.3
Hempstead, NY (village) Nassau County	27.9

South American
Top 10 Places Sorted by Number

Place	Years
Mamaroneck, NY (town) Westchester County	39.2
Mamaroneck, NY (village) Westchester County	38.4
Smith, NY (town) Suffolk County	37.2
East Meadow, NY (cdp) Nassau County	37.0
Mount Vernon, NY (city) Westchester County	36.3
Hicksville, NY (cdp) Nassau County	36.1
Elmont, NY (cdp) Nassau County	35.6
Hempstead, NY (village) Nassau County	35.6
Yonkers, NY (city) Westchester County	35.3
Oyster Bay, NY (town) Nassau County	35.2

Spaniard
Top 10 Places Sorted by Number

Place	Years
Hempstead, NY (town) Nassau County	38.1
New York, NY (city)	36.3
Brookhaven, NY (town) Suffolk County	35.1

Uruguayan
Top 10 Places Sorted by Number

Place	Years
New York, NY (city)	42.8

Venezuelan
Top 10 Places Sorted by Number

Place	Years
New York, NY (city)	28.6

Other Hispanic
Top 10 Places Sorted by Number

Place	Years
Smith, NY (town) Suffolk County	36.2
Holbrook, NY (cdp) Suffolk County	33.7
Warwick, NY (town) Orange County	31.5
Valley Stream, NY (village) Nassau County	30.9
Wallkill, NY (town) Orange County	30.9
New City, NY (cdp) Rockland County	30.4
Thompson, NY (town) Sullivan County	30.0
Southeast, NY (town) Putnam County	29.3
Fishkill, NY (town) Dutchess County	28.6
Selden, NY (cdp) Suffolk County	27.9

Notes: Please refer to the User's Guide for an explanation of data; tables include places with populations > 9,999 and reflect only those areas that meet Summary File 4 population thresholds, therefore there may be less than 10 places listed

Average Household Size

Total Population
Top 10 Places Sorted by Number

Place	Number
New Cassel, NY (cdp) Nassau County	4.50
Brentwood, NY (cdp) Suffolk County	4.24
Wyandanch, NY (cdp) Suffolk County	4.11
North Bay Shore, NY (cdp) Suffolk County	3.94
Roosevelt, NY (cdp) Nassau County	3.87
Monroe, NY (town) Orange County	3.68
Uniondale, NY (cdp) Nassau County	3.65
Central Islip, NY (cdp) Suffolk County	3.54
Mastic, NY (cdp) Suffolk County	3.44
Shirley, NY (cdp) Suffolk County	3.44

Hispanic
Top 10 Places Sorted by Number

Place	Number
New Cassel, NY (cdp) Nassau County	6.54
Roosevelt, NY (cdp) Nassau County	6.25
Lewisboro, NY (town) Westchester County	5.32
Brentwood, NY (cdp) Suffolk County	5.15
Hempstead, NY (village) Nassau County	4.96
Huntington Station, NY (cdp) Suffolk County	4.88
Uniondale, NY (cdp) Nassau County	4.88
Westbury, NY (village) Nassau County	4.85
Copiague, NY (cdp) Suffolk County	4.82
North Bay Shore, NY (cdp) Suffolk County	4.80

Argentinian
Top 10 Places Sorted by Number

Place	Number
North Hempstead, NY (town) Nassau County	3.64
Hempstead, NY (town) Nassau County	3.28
New York, NY (city)	2.54

Bolivian
Top 10 Places Sorted by Number

Place	Number
New York, NY (city)	3.47

Central American
Top 10 Places Sorted by Number

Place	Number
Roosevelt, NY (cdp) Nassau County	7.65
New Cassel, NY (cdp) Nassau County	7.60
Central Islip, NY (cdp) Suffolk County	6.40
Riverhead, NY (town) Suffolk County	6.36
Southold, NY (town) Suffolk County	5.95
Brentwood, NY (cdp) Suffolk County	5.92
Huntington Station, NY (cdp) Suffolk County	5.88
North Bay Shore, NY (cdp) Suffolk County	5.87
Islip, NY (town) Suffolk County	5.85
Westbury, NY (village) Nassau County	5.66

Chilean
Top 10 Places Sorted by Number

Place	Number
North Hempstead, NY (town) Nassau County	3.97
Hempstead, NY (town) Nassau County	3.53
Oyster Bay, NY (town) Nassau County	3.15
New York, NY (city)	2.61

Colombian
Top 10 Places Sorted by Number

Place	Number
Brentwood, NY (cdp) Suffolk County	5.52
Islip, NY (town) Suffolk County	4.74
Huntington, NY (town) Suffolk County	4.08
White Plains, NY (city) Westchester County	4.00
North Hempstead, NY (town) Nassau County	3.87
Hempstead, NY (town) Nassau County	3.81
Brookhaven, NY (town) Suffolk County	3.76
East Hampton, NY (town) Suffolk County	3.74
Mineola, NY (village) Nassau County	3.72
New Rochelle, NY (city) Westchester County	3.65

Costa Rican
Top 10 Places Sorted by Number

Place	Number
Hempstead, NY (town) Nassau County	4.49
New York, NY (city)	2.59

Cuban
Top 10 Places Sorted by Number

Place	Number
Babylon, NY (town) Suffolk County	3.47
Islip, NY (town) Suffolk County	3.42
Clarks, NY (town) Rockland County	3.39
Oyster Bay, NY (town) Nassau County	3.33
Hempstead, NY (town) Nassau County	3.27
Brookhaven, NY (town) Suffolk County	3.06
North Hempstead, NY (town) Nassau County	2.93
Rye, NY (town) Westchester County	2.52
Port Chester, NY (village) Westchester County	2.46
Greenburgh, NY (town) Westchester County	2.42

Dominican
Top 10 Places Sorted by Number

Place	Number
Uniondale, NY (cdp) Nassau County	6.30
Copiague, NY (cdp) Suffolk County	5.86
Babylon, NY (town) Suffolk County	5.56
Brentwood, NY (cdp) Suffolk County	5.47
Valley Stream, NY (village) Nassau County	5.12
Rockville Centre, NY (village) Nassau County	5.08
Freeport, NY (village) Nassau County	5.01
Islip, NY (town) Suffolk County	4.79
Hempstead, NY (town) Nassau County	4.73
Hempstead, NY (village) Nassau County	4.65

Ecuadorian
Top 10 Places Sorted by Number

Place	Number
Spring Valley, NY (village) Rockland County	6.93
Ramapo, NY (town) Rockland County	6.60
Bay Shore, NY (cdp) Suffolk County	6.31
Patchogue, NY (village) Suffolk County	5.76
Islip, NY (town) Suffolk County	4.93
Brentwood, NY (cdp) Suffolk County	4.80
Brookhaven, NY (town) Suffolk County	4.72
Rye, NY (town) Westchester County	4.54
Port Chester, NY (village) Westchester County	4.51
Ossining, NY (town) Westchester County	4.46

Guatelmalan
Top 10 Places Sorted by Number

Place	Number
Brentwood, NY (cdp) Suffolk County	6.14
Islip, NY (town) Suffolk County	5.24
Spring Valley, NY (village) Rockland County	5.10
Port Chester, NY (village) Westchester County	5.03
North Hempstead, NY (town) Nassau County	4.97
Rye, NY (town) Westchester County	4.94
Freeport, NY (village) Nassau County	4.90
Ramapo, NY (town) Rockland County	4.87
Hempstead, NY (village) Nassau County	4.73
Mamaroneck, NY (town) Westchester County	4.72

Honduran
Top 10 Places Sorted by Number

Place	Number
Hempstead, NY (village) Nassau County	5.57
North Hempstead, NY (town) Nassau County	5.54
Islip, NY (town) Suffolk County	5.51
Brentwood, NY (cdp) Suffolk County	5.28
Hempstead, NY (town) Nassau County	4.80
Huntington, NY (town) Suffolk County	4.48
Babylon, NY (town) Suffolk County	4.00
Newburgh, NY (city) Orange County	3.66
New York, NY (city)	3.57
Yonkers, NY (city) Westchester County	3.54

Mexican
Top 10 Places Sorted by Number

Place	Number
New Cassel, NY (cdp) Nassau County	7.57
Brentwood, NY (cdp) Suffolk County	6.68
North Hempstead, NY (town) Nassau County	5.42
Haverstraw, NY (town) Rockland County	5.00
White Plains, NY (city) Westchester County	4.96
Yonkers, NY (city) Westchester County	4.92
Greenburgh, NY (town) Westchester County	4.89
Port Chester, NY (village) Westchester County	4.84
Newburgh, NY (city) Orange County	4.81
Southampton, NY (town) Suffolk County	4.79

Nicaraguan
Top 10 Places Sorted by Number

Place	Number
Yonkers, NY (city) Westchester County	3.99
New York, NY (city)	3.55

Panamanian
Top 10 Places Sorted by Number

Place	Number
Islip, NY (town) Suffolk County	4.11
Hempstead, NY (town) Nassau County	3.26
New York, NY (city)	2.88

Paraguayan
Top 10 Places Sorted by Number

Place	Number
New York, NY (city)	2.82

Peruvian
Top 10 Places Sorted by Number

Place	Number
Babylon, NY (town) Suffolk County	5.56
Brentwood, NY (cdp) Suffolk County	4.46
Rye, NY (town) Westchester County	4.18
Islip, NY (town) Suffolk County	4.16
Port Chester, NY (village) Westchester County	4.10
White Plains, NY (city) Westchester County	4.02
Hempstead, NY (town) Nassau County	4.00
Oyster Bay, NY (town) Nassau County	3.87
Glen Cove, NY (city) Nassau County	3.86
New Rochelle, NY (city) Westchester County	3.64

Puerto Rican
Top 10 Places Sorted by Number

Place	Number
North Babylon, NY (cdp) Suffolk County	5.12
Wyandanch, NY (cdp) Suffolk County	4.64
Chester, NY (town) Orange County	4.42
Ronkonkoma, NY (cdp) Suffolk County	4.26
Brentwood, NY (cdp) Suffolk County	4.24
East Islip, NY (cdp) Suffolk County	4.15
Holtsville, NY (cdp) Suffolk County	4.11
Freeport, NY (village) Nassau County	4.07
Medford, NY (cdp) Suffolk County	4.03

Notes: Please refer to the User's Guide for an explanation of data; tables include places with populations > 9,999 and reflect only those areas that meet Summary File 4 population thresholds, therefore there may be less than 10 places listed

Copiague, NY (cdp) Suffolk County	4.00

Salvadoran
Top 10 Places Sorted by Number

Place	Number
Roosevelt, NY (cdp) Nassau County	8.13
New Cassel, NY (cdp) Nassau County	7.73
Central Islip, NY (cdp) Suffolk County	6.79
Huntington Station, NY (cdp) Suffolk County	6.23
Islip, NY (town) Suffolk County	6.09
North Bay Shore, NY (cdp) Suffolk County	6.04
Brentwood, NY (cdp) Suffolk County	6.02
Huntington, NY (town) Suffolk County	5.92
Babylon, NY (town) Suffolk County	5.90
Hicksville, NY (cdp) Nassau County	5.79

South American
Top 10 Places Sorted by Number

Place	Number
Spring Valley, NY (village) Rockland County	6.06
Patchogue, NY (village) Suffolk County	5.47
Ramapo, NY (town) Rockland County	5.42
Brentwood, NY (cdp) Suffolk County	5.13
Bay Shore, NY (cdp) Suffolk County	5.01
Central Islip, NY (cdp) Suffolk County	4.71
Copiague, NY (cdp) Suffolk County	4.68
Islip, NY (town) Suffolk County	4.65
Huntington Station, NY (cdp) Suffolk County	4.63
Uniondale, NY (cdp) Nassau County	4.61

Spaniard
Top 10 Places Sorted by Number

Place	Number
Hempstead, NY (town) Nassau County	2.76
Brookhaven, NY (town) Suffolk County	2.73
New York, NY (city)	2.38

Uruguayan
Top 10 Places Sorted by Number

Place	Number
New York, NY (city)	2.73

Venezuelan
Top 10 Places Sorted by Number

Place	Number
New York, NY (city)	2.80

Other Hispanic
Top 10 Places Sorted by Number

Place	Number
Roosevelt, NY (cdp) Nassau County	7.43
North Bay Shore, NY (cdp) Suffolk County	6.42
New Cassel, NY (cdp) Nassau County	5.75
Brentwood, NY (cdp) Suffolk County	5.47
Westbury, NY (village) Nassau County	5.39
Huntington Station, NY (cdp) Suffolk County	5.23
Hempstead, NY (village) Nassau County	5.15
Hicksville, NY (cdp) Nassau County	5.03
Carmel, NY (town) Putnam County	5.00
Peekskill, NY (city) Westchester County	4.93

Language Spoken at Home: English Only

Total Populations 5 Years and Over Who Speak English-Only at Home
Top 10 Places Sorted by Number

Place	Number
New York, NY (city)	3,920,797
Hempstead, NY (town) Nassau County	547,956
Brookhaven, NY (town) Suffolk County	357,084
Buffalo, NY (city) Erie County	238,127
Oyster Bay, NY (town) Nassau County	228,112
Islip, NY (town) Suffolk County	227,229
Rochester, NY (city) Monroe County	166,643
Babylon, NY (town) Suffolk County	161,589
Huntington, NY (town) Suffolk County	151,447
North Hempstead, NY (town) Nassau County	141,469

Total Populations 5 Years and Over Who Speak English-Only at Home
Top 10 Places Sorted by Percent

Place	Percent
Southport, NY (town) Chemung County	97.09
Lockport, NY (city) Niagara County	95.74
Elmira, NY (city) Chemung County	95.21
Ogdensburg, NY (city) Saint Lawrence County	94.60
Hamburg, NY (town) Erie County	94.30
Tonawanda, NY (town) Erie County	94.14
Alden, NY (town) Erie County	93.98
Sweden, NY (town) Monroe County	93.86
Manorville, NY (cdp) Suffolk County	93.73
North Tonawanda, NY (city) Niagara County	93.73

Hispanics 5 Years and Over Who Speak English-Only at Home
Top 10 Places Sorted by Number

Place	Number
New York, NY (city)	250,836
Hempstead, NY (town) Nassau County	13,302
Brookhaven, NY (town) Suffolk County	12,000
Islip, NY (town) Suffolk County	10,843
Yonkers, NY (city) Westchester County	6,748
Buffalo, NY (city) Erie County	5,504
Rochester, NY (city) Monroe County	5,364
Babylon, NY (town) Suffolk County	4,575
Oyster Bay, NY (town) Nassau County	3,798
Huntington, NY (town) Suffolk County	2,681

Hispanics 5 Years and Over Who Speak English-Only at Home
Top 10 Places Sorted by Percent

Place	Percent
Southport, NY (town) Chemung County	83.38
Hamburg, NY (town) Erie County	73.41
West Seneca, NY (town) Erie County	73.08
Alden, NY (town) Erie County	72.97
Elmira, NY (city) Chemung County	69.21
Malone, NY (town) Franklin County	67.15
Auburn, NY (city) Cayuga County	65.79
Tonawanda, NY (town) Erie County	65.63
Saugerties, NY (town) Ulster County	65.24
Patterson, NY (town) Putnam County	64.25

Argentinians 5 Years and Over Who Speak English-Only at Home
Top 10 Places Sorted by Number

Place	Number
New York, NY (city)	792
Hempstead, NY (town) Nassau County	187
North Hempstead, NY (town) Nassau County	18

Argentinians 5 Years and Over Who Speak English-Only at Home
Top 10 Places Sorted by Percent

Place	Percent
Hempstead, NY (town) Nassau County	20.04
New York, NY (city)	8.10
North Hempstead, NY (town) Nassau County	3.80

Bolivians 5 Years and Over Who Speak English-Only at Home
Top 10 Places Sorted by Number

Place	Number
New York, NY (city)	281

Bolivians 5 Years and Over Who Speak English-Only at Home
Top 10 Places Sorted by Percent

Place	Percent
New York, NY (city)	8.89

Central Americans 5 Years and Over Who Speak English-Only at Home
Top 10 Places Sorted by Number

Place	Number
New York, NY (city)	10,300
Hempstead, NY (town) Nassau County	981
Islip, NY (town) Suffolk County	908
Brentwood, NY (cdp) Suffolk County	463
Hempstead, NY (village) Nassau County	334
North Hempstead, NY (town) Nassau County	318
Yonkers, NY (city) Westchester County	306
Babylon, NY (town) Suffolk County	242
Brookhaven, NY (town) Suffolk County	207
Huntington, NY (town) Suffolk County	203

Central Americans 5 Years and Over Who Speak English-Only at Home
Top 10 Places Sorted by Percent

Place	Percent
Mount Vernon, NY (city) Westchester County	19.94
Greenburgh, NY (town) Westchester County	17.37
Orange, NY (town) Rockland County	16.91
Middletown, NY (city) Orange County	14.40
Valley Stream, NY (village) Nassau County	13.44
Brookhaven, NY (town) Suffolk County	11.64
Riverhead, NY (town) Suffolk County	11.19
East Hampton, NY (town) Suffolk County	10.85
White Plains, NY (city) Westchester County	10.51
New York, NY (city)	10.21

Chileans 5 Years and Over Who Speak English-Only at Home
Top 10 Places Sorted by Number

Place	Number
New York, NY (city)	602
Hempstead, NY (town) Nassau County	100
North Hempstead, NY (town) Nassau County	70
Oyster Bay, NY (town) Nassau County	62

Chileans 5 Years and Over Who Speak English-Only at Home
Top 10 Places Sorted by Percent

Place	Percent
Oyster Bay, NY (town) Nassau County	16.32
Hempstead, NY (town) Nassau County	15.50
North Hempstead, NY (town) Nassau County	11.65
New York, NY (city)	10.95

Colombians 5 Years and Over Who Speak English-Only at Home
Top 10 Places Sorted by Number

Place	Number
New York, NY (city)	4,377
Hempstead, NY (town) Nassau County	506
Oyster Bay, NY (town) Nassau County	237
Islip, NY (town) Suffolk County	226
Brookhaven, NY (town) Suffolk County	186
North Hempstead, NY (town) Nassau County	142
Babylon, NY (town) Suffolk County	138

Notes: Please refer to the User's Guide for an explanation of data; tables include places with populations > 9,999 and reflect only those areas that meet Summary File 4 population thresholds, therefore there may be less than 10 places listed

Place	
Huntington, NY (town) Suffolk County	94
Yonkers, NY (city) Westchester County	83
White Plains, NY (city) Westchester County	72

Colombians 5 Years and Over Who Speak English-Only at Home
Top 10 Places Sorted by Percent

Place	Percent
Oyster Bay, NY (town) Nassau County	21.33
Huntington, NY (town) Suffolk County	18.76
Brookhaven, NY (town) Suffolk County	15.92
Babylon, NY (town) Suffolk County	13.60
North Hempstead, NY (town) Nassau County	12.31
Hempstead, NY (town) Nassau County	11.59
Ossining, NY (town) Westchester County	10.85
Ossining, NY (village) Westchester County	10.85
Long Beach, NY (city) Nassau County	8.19
Yonkers, NY (city) Westchester County	7.90

Costa Ricans 5 Years and Over Who Speak English-Only at Home
Top 10 Places Sorted by Number

Place	Number
New York, NY (city)	814
Hempstead, NY (town) Nassau County	87

Costa Ricans 5 Years and Over Who Speak English-Only at Home
Top 10 Places Sorted by Percent

Place	Percent
Hempstead, NY (town) Nassau County	23.20
New York, NY (city)	16.21

Cubans 5 Years and Over Who Speak English-Only at Home
Top 10 Places Sorted by Number

Place	Number
New York, NY (city)	7,703
Hempstead, NY (town) Nassau County	1,143
Brookhaven, NY (town) Suffolk County	486
Islip, NY (town) Suffolk County	378
Yonkers, NY (city) Westchester County	292
Oyster Bay, NY (town) Nassau County	279
Babylon, NY (town) Suffolk County	205
North Hempstead, NY (town) Nassau County	198
Rochester, NY (city) Monroe County	186
Greenburgh, NY (town) Westchester County	70

Cubans 5 Years and Over Who Speak English-Only at Home
Top 10 Places Sorted by Percent

Place	Percent
North Hempstead, NY (town) Nassau County	54.85
Brookhaven, NY (town) Suffolk County	47.28
Oyster Bay, NY (town) Nassau County	42.92
Hempstead, NY (town) Nassau County	38.37
Babylon, NY (town) Suffolk County	34.57
Islip, NY (town) Suffolk County	30.86
Yonkers, NY (city) Westchester County	24.50
New York, NY (city)	19.26
Clarks, NY (town) Rockland County	19.01
Syracuse, NY (city) Onondaga County	17.72

Dominicans 5 Years and Over Who Speak English-Only at Home
Top 10 Places Sorted by Number

Place	Number
New York, NY (city)	23,953
Yonkers, NY (city) Westchester County	531
Hempstead, NY (town) Nassau County	496
Islip, NY (town) Suffolk County	299
Brookhaven, NY (town) Suffolk County	265
Babylon, NY (town) Suffolk County	260
Haverstraw, NY (town) Rockland County	216
Haverstraw, NY (village) Rockland County	160
Huntington, NY (town) Suffolk County	155
Oyster Bay, NY (town) Nassau County	149

Dominicans 5 Years and Over Who Speak English-Only at Home
Top 10 Places Sorted by Percent

Place	Percent
Huntington, NY (town) Suffolk County	30.16
Oyster Bay, NY (town) Nassau County	26.65
Ossining, NY (village) Westchester County	20.74
Ossining, NY (town) Westchester County	18.13
Port Chester, NY (village) Westchester County	14.69
Buffalo, NY (city) Erie County	14.67
Valley Stream, NY (village) Nassau County	14.02
Rye, NY (town) Westchester County	13.57
Brookhaven, NY (town) Suffolk County	13.24
North Hempstead, NY (town) Nassau County	11.98

Ecuadorians 5 Years and Over Who Speak English-Only at Home
Top 10 Places Sorted by Number

Place	Number
New York, NY (city)	4,934
Hempstead, NY (town) Nassau County	230
Brookhaven, NY (town) Suffolk County	72
Yonkers, NY (city) Westchester County	69
Oyster Bay, NY (town) Nassau County	67
Islip, NY (town) Suffolk County	65
White Plains, NY (city) Westchester County	57
North Hempstead, NY (town) Nassau County	52
Mount Pleasant, NY (town) Westchester County	44
Central Islip, NY (cdp) Suffolk County	37

Ecuadorians 5 Years and Over Who Speak English-Only at Home
Top 10 Places Sorted by Percent

Place	Percent
Oyster Bay, NY (town) Nassau County	13.67
White Plains, NY (city) Westchester County	13.23
Hempstead, NY (town) Nassau County	10.98
Greenburgh, NY (town) Westchester County	8.55
Central Islip, NY (cdp) Suffolk County	7.51
Mount Pleasant, NY (town) Westchester County	6.37
North Hempstead, NY (town) Nassau County	5.69
New York, NY (city)	4.95
Brookhaven, NY (town) Suffolk County	4.60
Islip, NY (town) Suffolk County	4.27

Guatelmalans 5 Years and Over Who Speak English-Only at Home
Top 10 Places Sorted by Number

Place	Number
New York, NY (city)	952
Islip, NY (town) Suffolk County	109
Hempstead, NY (town) Nassau County	55
Brentwood, NY (cdp) Suffolk County	43
Brookhaven, NY (town) Suffolk County	42
Rye, NY (town) Westchester County	41
New Rochelle, NY (city) Westchester County	35
Port Chester, NY (village) Westchester County	35
North Hempstead, NY (town) Nassau County	27
Hempstead, NY (village) Nassau County	25

Guatelmalans 5 Years and Over Who Speak English-Only at Home
Top 10 Places Sorted by Percent

Place	Percent
Brookhaven, NY (town) Suffolk County	12.46
Islip, NY (town) Suffolk County	10.55
New Rochelle, NY (city) Westchester County	8.93
Brentwood, NY (cdp) Suffolk County	8.04
Huntington, NY (town) Suffolk County	7.94
Hempstead, NY (village) Nassau County	7.79
New York, NY (city)	6.35
Babylon, NY (town) Suffolk County	5.97
Southampton, NY (town) Suffolk County	5.41
North Hempstead, NY (town) Nassau County	4.03

Hondurans 5 Years and Over Who Speak English-Only at Home
Top 10 Places Sorted by Number

Place	Number
New York, NY (city)	2,511
Hempstead, NY (town) Nassau County	127
Yonkers, NY (city) Westchester County	80
Hempstead, NY (village) Nassau County	64
North Hempstead, NY (town) Nassau County	53
Newburgh, NY (city) Orange County	52
Babylon, NY (town) Suffolk County	44
Islip, NY (town) Suffolk County	23
Huntington, NY (town) Suffolk County	6
Brentwood, NY (cdp) Suffolk County	4

Hondurans 5 Years and Over Who Speak English-Only at Home
Top 10 Places Sorted by Percent

Place	Percent
Babylon, NY (town) Suffolk County	10.35
Yonkers, NY (city) Westchester County	9.23
New York, NY (city)	9.14
Newburgh, NY (city) Orange County	8.37
North Hempstead, NY (town) Nassau County	7.76
Hempstead, NY (town) Nassau County	5.47
Hempstead, NY (village) Nassau County	4.29
Islip, NY (town) Suffolk County	2.02
Huntington, NY (town) Suffolk County	1.40
Brentwood, NY (cdp) Suffolk County	0.75

Mexicans 5 Years and Over Who Speak English-Only at Home
Top 10 Places Sorted by Number

Place	Number
New York, NY (city)	15,362
Hempstead, NY (town) Nassau County	802
Buffalo, NY (city) Erie County	800
Brookhaven, NY (town) Suffolk County	635
Yonkers, NY (city) Westchester County	617
Rochester, NY (city) Monroe County	534
Syracuse, NY (city) Onondaga County	417
Islip, NY (town) Suffolk County	402
New Rochelle, NY (city) Westchester County	276
Babylon, NY (town) Suffolk County	243

Mexicans 5 Years and Over Who Speak English-Only at Home
Top 10 Places Sorted by Percent

Place	Percent
Buffalo, NY (city) Erie County	69.69
Syracuse, NY (city) Onondaga County	58.65
Rochester, NY (city) Monroe County	52.15
Brookhaven, NY (town) Suffolk County	40.91
Le Ray, NY (town) Jefferson County	39.00
Fort Drum, NY (cdp) Jefferson County	38.67
Babylon, NY (town) Suffolk County	36.00
Islip, NY (town) Suffolk County	33.14
Hempstead, NY (town) Nassau County	32.30
Oyster Bay, NY (town) Nassau County	26.47

Nicaraguans 5 Years and Over Who Speak English-Only at Home
Top 10 Places Sorted by Number

Place	Number
New York, NY (city)	424

Notes: Please refer to the User's Guide for an explanation of data; tables include places with populations > 9,999 and reflect only those areas that meet Summary File 4 population thresholds, therefore there may be less than 10 places listed

Yonkers, NY (city) Westchester County	21

Nicaraguans 5 Years and Over Who Speak English-Only at Home
Top 10 Places Sorted by Percent

Place	Percent
New York, NY (city)	6.03
Yonkers, NY (city) Westchester County	3.83

Panamanians 5 Years and Over Who Speak English-Only at Home
Top 10 Places Sorted by Number

Place	Number
New York, NY (city)	3,788
Islip, NY (town) Suffolk County	131
Hempstead, NY (town) Nassau County	119

Panamanians 5 Years and Over Who Speak English-Only at Home
Top 10 Places Sorted by Percent

Place	Percent
Islip, NY (town) Suffolk County	39.34
New York, NY (city)	21.19
Hempstead, NY (town) Nassau County	20.70

Paraguayans 5 Years and Over Who Speak English-Only at Home
Top 10 Places Sorted by Number

Place	Number
New York, NY (city)	104

Paraguayans 5 Years and Over Who Speak English-Only at Home
Top 10 Places Sorted by Percent

Place	Percent
New York, NY (city)	7.02

Peruvians 5 Years and Over Who Speak English-Only at Home
Top 10 Places Sorted by Number

Place	Number
New York, NY (city)	1,285
Hempstead, NY (town) Nassau County	207
Islip, NY (town) Suffolk County	99
North Hempstead, NY (town) Nassau County	51
Oyster Bay, NY (town) Nassau County	49
Yonkers, NY (city) Westchester County	48
Glen Cove, NY (city) Nassau County	45
New Rochelle, NY (city) Westchester County	41
Babylon, NY (town) Suffolk County	36
Brookhaven, NY (town) Suffolk County	34

Peruvians 5 Years and Over Who Speak English-Only at Home
Top 10 Places Sorted by Percent

Place	Percent
North Hempstead, NY (town) Nassau County	11.09
Babylon, NY (town) Suffolk County	10.88
Hempstead, NY (town) Nassau County	10.82
Yonkers, NY (city) Westchester County	9.47
Islip, NY (town) Suffolk County	8.13
Oyster Bay, NY (town) Nassau County	7.83
Brookhaven, NY (town) Suffolk County	6.68
New Rochelle, NY (city) Westchester County	6.13
Glen Cove, NY (city) Nassau County	5.97
New York, NY (city)	5.67

Puerto Ricans 5 Years and Over Who Speak English-Only at Home
Top 10 Places Sorted by Number

Place	Number
New York, NY (city)	135,088
Brookhaven, NY (town) Suffolk County	7,493
Islip, NY (town) Suffolk County	6,162
Hempstead, NY (town) Nassau County	5,284
Yonkers, NY (city) Westchester County	3,735
Rochester, NY (city) Monroe County	3,658
Buffalo, NY (city) Erie County	3,510
Babylon, NY (town) Suffolk County	2,472
Oyster Bay, NY (town) Nassau County	1,549
Huntington, NY (town) Suffolk County	1,364

Puerto Ricans 5 Years and Over Who Speak English-Only at Home
Top 10 Places Sorted by Percent

Place	Percent
Saugerties, NY (town) Ulster County	77.97
Malone, NY (town) Franklin County	75.71
Bedford, NY (town) Westchester County	74.47
Ogdensburg, NY (city) Saint Lawrence County	73.67
Shawangunk, NY (town) Ulster County	69.77
Auburn, NY (city) Cayuga County	66.73
Elmira, NY (city) Chemung County	66.67
Tonawanda, NY (town) Erie County	66.60
Riverhead, NY (town) Suffolk County	64.71
Rome, NY (city) Oneida County	63.12

Salvadorans 5 Years and Over Who Speak English-Only at Home
Top 10 Places Sorted by Number

Place	Number
New York, NY (city)	1,423
Islip, NY (town) Suffolk County	562
Hempstead, NY (town) Nassau County	545
Brentwood, NY (cdp) Suffolk County	362
North Hempstead, NY (town) Nassau County	192
Hempstead, NY (village) Nassau County	180
Huntington, NY (town) Suffolk County	152
Babylon, NY (town) Suffolk County	133
Huntington Station, NY (cdp) Suffolk County	133
Yonkers, NY (city) Westchester County	126

Salvadorans 5 Years and Over Who Speak English-Only at Home
Top 10 Places Sorted by Percent

Place	Percent
Orange, NY (town) Rockland County	16.95
Valley Stream, NY (village) Nassau County	9.58
Brookhaven, NY (town) Suffolk County	7.36
Yonkers, NY (city) Westchester County	7.28
Central Islip, NY (cdp) Suffolk County	6.24
New York, NY (city)	6.13
Huntington Station, NY (cdp) Suffolk County	6.06
Huntington, NY (town) Suffolk County	5.80
Babylon, NY (town) Suffolk County	5.32
Brentwood, NY (cdp) Suffolk County	5.16

South Americans 5 Years and Over Who Speak English-Only at Home
Top 10 Places Sorted by Number

Place	Number
New York, NY (city)	14,523
Hempstead, NY (town) Nassau County	1,402
Islip, NY (town) Suffolk County	586
Oyster Bay, NY (town) Nassau County	582
Brookhaven, NY (town) Suffolk County	524
North Hempstead, NY (town) Nassau County	389
Yonkers, NY (city) Westchester County	324
Babylon, NY (town) Suffolk County	282
Huntington, NY (town) Suffolk County	222

Greenburgh, NY (town) Westchester County	185

South Americans 5 Years and Over Who Speak English-Only at Home
Top 10 Places Sorted by Percent

Place	Percent
Oceanside, NY (cdp) Nassau County	24.71
Levittown, NY (cdp) Nassau County	24.06
Franklin Square, NY (cdp) Nassau County	23.20
Rochester, NY (city) Monroe County	23.08
West Babylon, NY (cdp) Suffolk County	22.86
Buffalo, NY (city) Erie County	22.84
Smith, NY (town) Suffolk County	22.59
Baldwin, NY (cdp) Nassau County	21.59
Clarks, NY (town) Rockland County	20.90
Coram, NY (cdp) Suffolk County	19.72

Spaniards 5 Years and Over Who Speak English-Only at Home
Top 10 Places Sorted by Number

Place	Number
New York, NY (city)	1,801
Hempstead, NY (town) Nassau County	289
Brookhaven, NY (town) Suffolk County	253

Spaniards 5 Years and Over Who Speak English-Only at Home
Top 10 Places Sorted by Percent

Place	Percent
Brookhaven, NY (town) Suffolk County	68.01
Hempstead, NY (town) Nassau County	37.05
New York, NY (city)	18.89

Uruguayans 5 Years and Over Who Speak English-Only at Home
Top 10 Places Sorted by Number

Place	Number
New York, NY (city)	71

Uruguayans 5 Years and Over Who Speak English-Only at Home
Top 10 Places Sorted by Percent

Place	Percent
New York, NY (city)	3.54

Venezuelans 5 Years and Over Who Speak English-Only at Home
Top 10 Places Sorted by Number

Place	Number
New York, NY (city)	942

Venezuelans 5 Years and Over Who Speak English-Only at Home
Top 10 Places Sorted by Percent

Place	Percent
New York, NY (city)	13.62

Other Hispanics 5 Years and Over Who Speak English-Only at Home
Top 10 Places Sorted by Number

Place	Number
New York, NY (city)	42,106
Hempstead, NY (town) Nassau County	2,905
Brookhaven, NY (town) Suffolk County	2,137
Islip, NY (town) Suffolk County	1,962
Yonkers, NY (city) Westchester County	868
Oyster Bay, NY (town) Nassau County	820
Babylon, NY (town) Suffolk County	812
Rochester, NY (city) Monroe County	781
Buffalo, NY (city) Erie County	689

Notes: Please refer to the User's Guide for an explanation of data; tables include places with populations > 9,999 and reflect only those areas that meet Summary File 4 population thresholds, therefore there may be less than 10 places listed

PROFILES OF NEW YORK / Hispanic: Rankings

North Hempstead, NY (town) Nassau County   490

Other Hispanics 5 Years and Over Who Speak English-Only at Home
Top 10 Places Sorted by Percent

Place	Percent
Fishkill, NY (town) Dutchess County	79.27
Amherst, NY (town) Erie County	60.88
Schenectady, NY (city) Schenectady County	50.72
Warwick, NY (town) Orange County	48.90
Medford, NY (cdp) Suffolk County	46.48
Albany, NY (city) Albany County	45.19
Syracuse, NY (city) Onondaga County	44.90
Shirley, NY (cdp) Suffolk County	41.94
Clarks, NY (town) Rockland County	40.60
Carmel, NY (town) Putnam County	39.88

Language Spoken at Home: Spanish

Total Populations 5 Years and Over Who Speak Spanish at Home
Top 10 Places Sorted by Number

Place	Number
New York, NY (city)	1,832,402
Hempstead, NY (town) Nassau County	73,660
Islip, NY (town) Suffolk County	51,854
Yonkers, NY (city) Westchester County	41,265
Brentwood, NY (cdp) Suffolk County	24,859
Brookhaven, NY (town) Suffolk County	23,945
Rochester, NY (city) Monroe County	22,336
North Hempstead, NY (town) Nassau County	19,722
Buffalo, NY (city) Erie County	17,478
Babylon, NY (town) Suffolk County	16,830

Total Populations 5 Years and Over Who Speak Spanish at Home
Top 10 Places Sorted by Percent

Place	Percent
Haverstraw, NY (village) Rockland County	55.63
Brentwood, NY (cdp) Suffolk County	50.11
North Bay Shore, NY (cdp) Suffolk County	46.29
Port Chester, NY (village) Westchester County	43.96
New Cassel, NY (cdp) Nassau County	37.63
Newburgh, NY (city) Orange County	32.09
Freeport, NY (village) Nassau County	31.74
Rye, NY (town) Westchester County	31.08
Hempstead, NY (village) Nassau County	30.64
Central Islip, NY (cdp) Suffolk County	29.25

Hispanics 5 Years and Over Who Speak Spanish at Home
Top 10 Places Sorted by Number

Place	Number
New York, NY (city)	1,714,403
Hempstead, NY (town) Nassau County	64,302
Islip, NY (town) Suffolk County	47,972
Yonkers, NY (city) Westchester County	38,871
Brentwood, NY (cdp) Suffolk County	23,999
Brookhaven, NY (town) Suffolk County	19,804
Rochester, NY (city) Monroe County	19,099
North Hempstead, NY (town) Nassau County	16,951
Hempstead, NY (village) Nassau County	14,833
Babylon, NY (town) Suffolk County	14,526

Hispanics 5 Years and Over Who Speak Spanish at Home
Top 10 Places Sorted by Percent

Place	Percent
Tarrytown, NY (village) Westchester County	93.28
Port Chester, NY (village) Westchester County	92.99
East Hampton, NY (town) Suffolk County	92.90
Westbury, NY (village) Nassau County	92.27
Rye, NY (town) Westchester County	92.20
Hempstead, NY (village) Nassau County	92.16
Roosevelt, NY (cdp) Nassau County	91.24
Mineola, NY (village) Nassau County	90.98
White Plains, NY (city) Westchester County	90.82
Glen Cove, NY (city) Nassau County	90.58

Argentinians 5 Years and Over Who Speak Spanish at Home
Top 10 Places Sorted by Number

Place	Number
New York, NY (city)	8,530
Hempstead, NY (town) Nassau County	713
North Hempstead, NY (town) Nassau County	449

Argentinians 5 Years and Over Who Speak Spanish at Home
Top 10 Places Sorted by Percent

Place	Percent
North Hempstead, NY (town) Nassau County	94.73
New York, NY (city)	87.22
Hempstead, NY (town) Nassau County	76.42

Bolivians 5 Years and Over Who Speak Spanish at Home
Top 10 Places Sorted by Number

Place	Number
New York, NY (city)	2,778

Bolivians 5 Years and Over Who Speak Spanish at Home
Top 10 Places Sorted by Percent

Place	Percent
New York, NY (city)	87.86

Central Americans 5 Years and Over Who Speak Spanish at Home
Top 10 Places Sorted by Number

Place	Number
New York, NY (city)	89,497
Hempstead, NY (town) Nassau County	19,765
Islip, NY (town) Suffolk County	13,161
Brentwood, NY (cdp) Suffolk County	7,851
Hempstead, NY (village) Nassau County	7,598
North Hempstead, NY (town) Nassau County	6,127
Freeport, NY (village) Nassau County	3,713
Yonkers, NY (city) Westchester County	3,586
Babylon, NY (town) Suffolk County	3,277
Huntington, NY (town) Suffolk County	3,247

Central Americans 5 Years and Over Who Speak Spanish at Home
Top 10 Places Sorted by Percent

Place	Percent
Wyandanch, NY (cdp) Suffolk County	100.00
Long Beach, NY (city) Nassau County	99.56
Baldwin, NY (cdp) Nassau County	99.13
Mineola, NY (village) Nassau County	98.41
Mamaroneck, NY (town) Westchester County	97.80
Southeast, NY (town) Putnam County	97.74
Hicksville, NY (cdp) Nassau County	97.73
Port Chester, NY (village) Westchester County	97.63
Rye, NY (town) Westchester County	97.45
Glen Cove, NY (city) Nassau County	97.29

Chileans 5 Years and Over Who Speak Spanish at Home
Top 10 Places Sorted by Number

Place	Number
New York, NY (city)	4,724
Hempstead, NY (town) Nassau County	532
North Hempstead, NY (town) Nassau County	531
Oyster Bay, NY (town) Nassau County	307

Chileans 5 Years and Over Who Speak Spanish at Home
Top 10 Places Sorted by Percent

Place	Percent
North Hempstead, NY (town) Nassau County	88.35
New York, NY (city)	85.95
Hempstead, NY (town) Nassau County	82.48
Oyster Bay, NY (town) Nassau County	80.79

Colombians 5 Years and Over Who Speak Spanish at Home
Top 10 Places Sorted by Number

Place	Number
New York, NY (city)	73,065
Hempstead, NY (town) Nassau County	3,838
Islip, NY (town) Suffolk County	2,641
Brentwood, NY (cdp) Suffolk County	1,557
White Plains, NY (city) Westchester County	1,136
New Rochelle, NY (city) Westchester County	1,059
North Hempstead, NY (town) Nassau County	1,010
Brookhaven, NY (town) Suffolk County	966
Yonkers, NY (city) Westchester County	941
Oyster Bay, NY (town) Nassau County	858

Colombians 5 Years and Over Who Speak Spanish at Home
Top 10 Places Sorted by Percent

Place	Percent
Southampton, NY (town) Suffolk County	98.10
Port Chester, NY (village) Westchester County	97.33
East Hampton, NY (town) Suffolk County	96.79
Rye, NY (town) Westchester County	96.62
Greenburgh, NY (town) Westchester County	96.56
New Rochelle, NY (city) Westchester County	96.19
Brentwood, NY (cdp) Suffolk County	95.70
Mineola, NY (village) Nassau County	95.66
White Plains, NY (city) Westchester County	94.04
New York, NY (city)	93.85

Costa Ricans 5 Years and Over Who Speak Spanish at Home
Top 10 Places Sorted by Number

Place	Number
New York, NY (city)	4,204
Hempstead, NY (town) Nassau County	288

Costa Ricans 5 Years and Over Who Speak Spanish at Home
Top 10 Places Sorted by Percent

Place	Percent
New York, NY (city)	83.70
Hempstead, NY (town) Nassau County	76.80

Cubans 5 Years and Over Who Speak Spanish at Home
Top 10 Places Sorted by Number

Place	Number
New York, NY (city)	31,850
Hempstead, NY (town) Nassau County	1,828
Yonkers, NY (city) Westchester County	888
Rochester, NY (city) Monroe County	855
Islip, NY (town) Suffolk County	840
Brookhaven, NY (town) Suffolk County	542
Rye, NY (town) Westchester County	489
Port Chester, NY (village) Westchester County	445
Greenburgh, NY (town) Westchester County	400
Babylon, NY (town) Suffolk County	384

Notes: Please refer to the User's Guide for an explanation of data; tables include places with populations > 9,999 and reflect only those areas that meet Summary File 4 population thresholds, therefore there may be less than 10 places listed

Cubans 5 Years and Over Who Speak Spanish at Home
Top 10 Places Sorted by Percent

Place	Percent
Port Chester, NY (village) Westchester County	96.95
Rye, NY (town) Westchester County	93.50
Greenburgh, NY (town) Westchester County	85.11
Syracuse, NY (city) Onondaga County	82.28
Clarks, NY (town) Rockland County	80.99
Rochester, NY (city) Monroe County	80.06
New York, NY (city)	79.62
Yonkers, NY (city) Westchester County	74.50
Islip, NY (town) Suffolk County	68.57
Babylon, NY (town) Suffolk County	64.76

Dominicans 5 Years and Over Who Speak Spanish at Home
Top 10 Places Sorted by Number

Place	Number
New York, NY (city)	369,363
Hempstead, NY (town) Nassau County	7,357
Yonkers, NY (city) Westchester County	6,678
Islip, NY (town) Suffolk County	3,905
Haverstraw, NY (town) Rockland County	3,245
Freeport, NY (village) Nassau County	2,794
Babylon, NY (town) Suffolk County	2,360
Haverstraw, NY (village) Rockland County	2,219
Brentwood, NY (cdp) Suffolk County	2,123
Brookhaven, NY (town) Suffolk County	1,737

Dominicans 5 Years and Over Who Speak Spanish at Home
Top 10 Places Sorted by Percent

Place	Percent
Uniondale, NY (cdp) Nassau County	100.00
North Bay Shore, NY (cdp) Suffolk County	99.08
Mount Pleasant, NY (town) Westchester County	98.73
Copiague, NY (cdp) Suffolk County	98.46
Rockville Centre, NY (village) Nassau County	98.17
Hempstead, NY (village) Nassau County	98.12
Brentwood, NY (cdp) Suffolk County	96.85
Freeport, NY (village) Nassau County	96.85
White Plains, NY (city) Westchester County	96.12
West Haverstraw, NY (village) Rockland County	94.70

Ecuadorians 5 Years and Over Who Speak Spanish at Home
Top 10 Places Sorted by Number

Place	Number
New York, NY (city)	94,426
Ossining, NY (town) Westchester County	1,983
Ossining, NY (village) Westchester County	1,983
Hempstead, NY (town) Nassau County	1,842
Yonkers, NY (city) Westchester County	1,659
Brookhaven, NY (town) Suffolk County	1,492
Islip, NY (town) Suffolk County	1,450
Rye, NY (town) Westchester County	975
Port Chester, NY (village) Westchester County	946
North Hempstead, NY (town) Nassau County	862

Ecuadorians 5 Years and Over Who Speak Spanish at Home
Top 10 Places Sorted by Percent

Place	Percent
East Hampton, NY (town) Suffolk County	100.00
Patchogue, NY (village) Suffolk County	100.00
Ossining, NY (town) Westchester County	98.56
Ossining, NY (village) Westchester County	98.56
Brentwood, NY (cdp) Suffolk County	98.24
Bay Shore, NY (cdp) Suffolk County	98.05
Rye, NY (town) Westchester County	97.89
Port Chester, NY (village) Westchester County	97.83
Peekskill, NY (city) Westchester County	96.90

Place	
Spring Valley, NY (village) Rockland County	96.73

Guatelmalans 5 Years and Over Who Speak Spanish at Home
Top 10 Places Sorted by Number

Place	Number
New York, NY (city)	13,839
Hempstead, NY (town) Nassau County	1,609
Ramapo, NY (town) Rockland County	1,366
Rye, NY (town) Westchester County	1,188
Port Chester, NY (village) Westchester County	1,103
Spring Valley, NY (village) Rockland County	1,081
Islip, NY (town) Suffolk County	905
North Hempstead, NY (town) Nassau County	643
Brentwood, NY (cdp) Suffolk County	492
Mamaroneck, NY (village) Westchester County	436

Guatelmalans 5 Years and Over Who Speak Spanish at Home
Top 10 Places Sorted by Percent

Place	Percent
Southeast, NY (town) Putnam County	98.86
Ramapo, NY (town) Rockland County	98.06
Freeport, NY (village) Nassau County	98.05
Spring Valley, NY (village) Rockland County	97.56
Port Chester, NY (village) Westchester County	96.92
Mamaroneck, NY (town) Westchester County	96.69
Rye, NY (town) Westchester County	96.66
Hempstead, NY (town) Nassau County	96.23
Mamaroneck, NY (village) Westchester County	96.04
North Hempstead, NY (town) Nassau County	95.97

Hondurans 5 Years and Over Who Speak Spanish at Home
Top 10 Places Sorted by Number

Place	Number
New York, NY (city)	24,611
Hempstead, NY (town) Nassau County	2,183
Hempstead, NY (village) Nassau County	1,417
Islip, NY (town) Suffolk County	1,115
Yonkers, NY (city) Westchester County	787
North Hempstead, NY (town) Nassau County	630
Newburgh, NY (city) Orange County	569
Brentwood, NY (cdp) Suffolk County	532
Huntington, NY (town) Suffolk County	424
Babylon, NY (town) Suffolk County	381

Hondurans 5 Years and Over Who Speak Spanish at Home
Top 10 Places Sorted by Percent

Place	Percent
Brentwood, NY (cdp) Suffolk County	99.25
Huntington, NY (town) Suffolk County	98.60
Islip, NY (town) Suffolk County	97.98
Hempstead, NY (village) Nassau County	95.04
Hempstead, NY (town) Nassau County	94.09
North Hempstead, NY (town) Nassau County	92.24
Newburgh, NY (city) Orange County	91.63
Yonkers, NY (city) Westchester County	90.77
Babylon, NY (town) Suffolk County	89.65
New York, NY (city)	89.55

Mexicans 5 Years and Over Who Speak Spanish at Home
Top 10 Places Sorted by Number

Place	Number
New York, NY (city)	138,913
New Rochelle, NY (city) Westchester County	6,003
Yonkers, NY (city) Westchester County	5,195
Newburgh, NY (city) Orange County	3,645
Rye, NY (town) Westchester County	3,297
Port Chester, NY (village) Westchester County	3,047
White Plains, NY (city) Westchester County	2,730
North Hempstead, NY (town) Nassau County	2,095
Hempstead, NY (town) Nassau County	1,577
Middletown, NY (city) Orange County	1,384

Mexicans 5 Years and Over Who Speak Spanish at Home
Top 10 Places Sorted by Percent

Place	Percent
Mamaroneck, NY (village) Westchester County	99.00
Haverstraw, NY (town) Rockland County	97.30
Mamaroneck, NY (town) Westchester County	95.94
New Cassel, NY (cdp) Nassau County	95.63
New Rochelle, NY (city) Westchester County	95.26
Newburgh, NY (city) Orange County	93.75
Rye, NY (town) Westchester County	93.61
Port Chester, NY (village) Westchester County	93.12
Poughkeepsie, NY (city) Dutchess County	92.90
White Plains, NY (city) Westchester County	91.55

Nicaraguans 5 Years and Over Who Speak Spanish at Home
Top 10 Places Sorted by Number

Place	Number
New York, NY (city)	6,573
Yonkers, NY (city) Westchester County	528

Nicaraguans 5 Years and Over Who Speak Spanish at Home
Top 10 Places Sorted by Percent

Place	Percent
Yonkers, NY (city) Westchester County	96.17
New York, NY (city)	93.46

Panamanians 5 Years and Over Who Speak Spanish at Home
Top 10 Places Sorted by Number

Place	Number
New York, NY (city)	14,009
Hempstead, NY (town) Nassau County	456
Islip, NY (town) Suffolk County	195

Panamanians 5 Years and Over Who Speak Spanish at Home
Top 10 Places Sorted by Percent

Place	Percent
Hempstead, NY (town) Nassau County	79.30
New York, NY (city)	78.35
Islip, NY (town) Suffolk County	58.56

Paraguayans 5 Years and Over Who Speak Spanish at Home
Top 10 Places Sorted by Number

Place	Number
New York, NY (city)	1,288

Paraguayans 5 Years and Over Who Speak Spanish at Home
Top 10 Places Sorted by Percent

Place	Percent
New York, NY (city)	86.91

Peruvians 5 Years and Over Who Speak Spanish at Home
Top 10 Places Sorted by Number

Place	Number
New York, NY (city)	21,172
Hempstead, NY (town) Nassau County	1,703
White Plains, NY (city) Westchester County	1,370
Islip, NY (town) Suffolk County	1,118
Rye, NY (town) Westchester County	821

Notes: Please refer to the User's Guide for an explanation of data; tables include places with populations > 9,999 and reflect only those areas that meet Summary File 4 population thresholds, therefore there may be less than 10 places listed

Place	
Port Chester, NY (village) Westchester County	739
Glen Cove, NY (city) Nassau County	709
New Rochelle, NY (city) Westchester County	628
Oyster Bay, NY (town) Nassau County	566
Brentwood, NY (cdp) Suffolk County	477

Peruvians 5 Years and Over Who Speak Spanish at Home
Top 10 Places Sorted by Percent

Place	Percent
White Plains, NY (city) Westchester County	99.06
Brentwood, NY (cdp) Suffolk County	98.35
Port Chester, NY (village) Westchester County	98.14
Rye, NY (town) Westchester County	96.14
Glen Cove, NY (city) Nassau County	94.03
New Rochelle, NY (city) Westchester County	93.87
New York, NY (city)	93.35
Brookhaven, NY (town) Suffolk County	93.32
Islip, NY (town) Suffolk County	91.87
Oyster Bay, NY (town) Nassau County	90.42

Puerto Ricans 5 Years and Over Who Speak Spanish at Home
Top 10 Places Sorted by Number

Place	Number
New York, NY (city)	585,023
Rochester, NY (city) Monroe County	15,514
Islip, NY (town) Suffolk County	14,453
Yonkers, NY (city) Westchester County	12,560
Buffalo, NY (city) Erie County	11,070
Hempstead, NY (town) Nassau County	9,099
Brookhaven, NY (town) Suffolk County	8,121
Brentwood, NY (cdp) Suffolk County	6,027
Babylon, NY (town) Suffolk County	3,472
Syracuse, NY (city) Onondaga County	3,212

Puerto Ricans 5 Years and Over Who Speak Spanish at Home
Top 10 Places Sorted by Percent

Place	Percent
Wyandanch, NY (cdp) Suffolk County	89.35
North Bay Shore, NY (cdp) Suffolk County	83.54
Brentwood, NY (cdp) Suffolk County	81.57
Haverstraw, NY (village) Rockland County	81.11
New York, NY (city)	80.94
Rochester, NY (city) Monroe County	80.73
Amsterdam, NY (city) Montgomery County	80.30
Utica, NY (city) Oneida County	79.80
Jamestown, NY (city) Chautauqua County	78.37
Glen Cove, NY (city) Nassau County	78.33

Salvadorans 5 Years and Over Who Speak Spanish at Home
Top 10 Places Sorted by Number

Place	Number
New York, NY (city)	21,736
Hempstead, NY (town) Nassau County	14,254
Islip, NY (town) Suffolk County	10,496
Brentwood, NY (cdp) Suffolk County	6,660
Hempstead, NY (village) Nassau County	5,483
North Hempstead, NY (town) Nassau County	4,349
Freeport, NY (village) Nassau County	2,804
Huntington, NY (town) Suffolk County	2,462
Babylon, NY (town) Suffolk County	2,366
Huntington Station, NY (cdp) Suffolk County	2,055

Salvadorans 5 Years and Over Who Speak Spanish at Home
Top 10 Places Sorted by Percent

Place	Percent
Wyandanch, NY (cdp) Suffolk County	100.00
Rye, NY (town) Westchester County	98.71
Port Chester, NY (village) Westchester County	98.63

Westbury, NY (village) Nassau County	98.03
Elmont, NY (cdp) Nassau County	97.97
Mineola, NY (village) Nassau County	97.96
Hicksville, NY (cdp) Nassau County	97.73
Oyster Bay, NY (town) Nassau County	97.16
Glen Cove, NY (city) Nassau County	96.86
Copiague, NY (cdp) Suffolk County	96.77

South Americans 5 Years and Over Who Speak Spanish at Home
Top 10 Places Sorted by Number

Place	Number
New York, NY (city)	218,284
Hempstead, NY (town) Nassau County	9,615
Islip, NY (town) Suffolk County	6,362
Yonkers, NY (city) Westchester County	3,779
North Hempstead, NY (town) Nassau County	3,571
Brookhaven, NY (town) Suffolk County	3,518
White Plains, NY (city) Westchester County	3,379
Rye, NY (town) Westchester County	3,163
Brentwood, NY (cdp) Suffolk County	2,955
Port Chester, NY (village) Westchester County	2,831

South Americans 5 Years and Over Who Speak Spanish at Home
Top 10 Places Sorted by Percent

Place	Percent
Patchogue, NY (village) Suffolk County	100.00
East Hampton, NY (town) Suffolk County	98.18
Port Chester, NY (village) Westchester County	97.42
Mineola, NY (village) Nassau County	97.10
Newburgh, NY (city) Orange County	97.08
Westbury, NY (village) Nassau County	96.90
Ossining, NY (town) Westchester County	96.82
Ossining, NY (village) Westchester County	96.78
North Bay Shore, NY (cdp) Suffolk County	96.64
Rye, NY (town) Westchester County	96.52

Spaniards 5 Years and Over Who Speak Spanish at Home
Top 10 Places Sorted by Number

Place	Number
New York, NY (city)	7,338
Hempstead, NY (town) Nassau County	449
Brookhaven, NY (town) Suffolk County	111

Spaniards 5 Years and Over Who Speak Spanish at Home
Top 10 Places Sorted by Percent

Place	Percent
New York, NY (city)	76.98
Hempstead, NY (town) Nassau County	57.56
Brookhaven, NY (town) Suffolk County	29.84

Uruguayans 5 Years and Over Who Speak Spanish at Home
Top 10 Places Sorted by Number

Place	Number
New York, NY (city)	1,843

Uruguayans 5 Years and Over Who Speak Spanish at Home
Top 10 Places Sorted by Percent

Place	Percent
New York, NY (city)	91.97

Venezuelans 5 Years and Over Who Speak Spanish at Home
Top 10 Places Sorted by Number

Place	Number
New York, NY (city)	5,713

Venezuelans 5 Years and Over Who Speak Spanish at Home
Top 10 Places Sorted by Percent

Place	Percent
New York, NY (city)	82.62

Other Hispanics 5 Years and Over Who Speak Spanish at Home
Top 10 Places Sorted by Number

Place	Number
New York, NY (city)	274,135
Hempstead, NY (town) Nassau County	14,612
Islip, NY (town) Suffolk County	8,335
Yonkers, NY (city) Westchester County	6,058
Brentwood, NY (cdp) Suffolk County	4,360
Hempstead, NY (village) Nassau County	3,917
Brookhaven, NY (town) Suffolk County	3,345
North Hempstead, NY (town) Nassau County	3,090
Freeport, NY (village) Nassau County	2,967
White Plains, NY (city) Westchester County	2,393

Other Hispanics 5 Years and Over Who Speak Spanish at Home
Top 10 Places Sorted by Percent

Place	Percent
Haverstraw, NY (village) Rockland County	95.26
Roosevelt, NY (cdp) Nassau County	93.28
White Plains, NY (city) Westchester County	92.90
Newburgh, NY (city) Orange County	91.56
Hempstead, NY (village) Nassau County	90.94
Brentwood, NY (cdp) Suffolk County	90.72
Mamaroneck, NY (town) Westchester County	89.98
Mineola, NY (village) Nassau County	89.47
Haverstraw, NY (town) Rockland County	89.41
Freeport, NY (village) Nassau County	89.21

Foreign Born

Total Population
Top 10 Places Sorted by Number

Place	Number
New York, NY (city)	2,871,032
Hempstead, NY (town) Nassau County	134,598
North Hempstead, NY (town) Nassau County	55,357
Yonkers, NY (city) Westchester County	51,687
Islip, NY (town) Suffolk County	47,088
Brookhaven, NY (town) Suffolk County	39,730
Oyster Bay, NY (town) Nassau County	35,610
Babylon, NY (town) Suffolk County	27,643
Ramapo, NY (town) Rockland County	24,848
Huntington, NY (town) Suffolk County	21,808

Total Population
Top 10 Places Sorted by Percent

Place	Percent
New Cassel, NY (cdp) Nassau County	45.32
Spring Valley, NY (village) Rockland County	43.04
Port Chester, NY (village) Westchester County	41.39
Elmont, NY (cdp) Nassau County	36.86
Haverstraw, NY (village) Rockland County	36.30
New York, NY (city)	35.85
Brentwood, NY (cdp) Suffolk County	34.74
North Valley Stream, NY (cdp) Nassau County	34.25
Uniondale, NY (cdp) Nassau County	34.05
Hempstead, NY (village) Nassau County	33.19

Hispanic
Top 10 Places Sorted by Number

Place	Number
New York, NY (city)	890,979
Hempstead, NY (town) Nassau County	45,329
Islip, NY (town) Suffolk County	26,849

Notes: Please refer to the User's Guide for an explanation of data; tables include places with populations > 9,999 and reflect only those areas that meet Summary File 4 population thresholds, therefore there may be less than 10 places listed

PROFILES OF NEW YORK / Hispanic: Rankings

Place	
Yonkers, NY (city) Westchester County	20,221
Brentwood, NY (cdp) Suffolk County	14,371
North Hempstead, NY (town) Nassau County	13,546
Hempstead, NY (village) Nassau County	11,974
Rye, NY (town) Westchester County	9,631
Brookhaven, NY (town) Suffolk County	9,294
Freeport, NY (village) Nassau County	9,065

Hispanic
Top 10 Places Sorted by Percent

Place	Percent
East Hampton, NY (town) Suffolk County	80.35
Port Washington, NY (cdp) Nassau County	71.02
Westbury, NY (village) Nassau County	69.42
Spring Valley, NY (village) Rockland County	69.23
New Cassel, NY (cdp) Nassau County	68.36
Port Chester, NY (village) Westchester County	68.23
Rye, NY (town) Westchester County	67.03
Hempstead, NY (village) Nassau County	66.22
White Plains, NY (city) Westchester County	65.99
Suffern, NY (village) Rockland County	65.93

Argentinian
Top 10 Places Sorted by Number

Place	Number
New York, NY (city)	8,137
Hempstead, NY (town) Nassau County	649
North Hempstead, NY (town) Nassau County	415

Argentinian
Top 10 Places Sorted by Percent

Place	Percent
North Hempstead, NY (town) Nassau County	83.67
New York, NY (city)	80.06
Hempstead, NY (town) Nassau County	66.91

Bolivian
Top 10 Places Sorted by Number

Place	Number
New York, NY (city)	2,630

Bolivian
Top 10 Places Sorted by Percent

Place	Percent
New York, NY (city)	78.72

Central American
Top 10 Places Sorted by Number

Place	Number
New York, NY (city)	79,522
Hempstead, NY (town) Nassau County	17,268
Islip, NY (town) Suffolk County	11,385
Hempstead, NY (village) Nassau County	7,090
Brentwood, NY (cdp) Suffolk County	6,822
North Hempstead, NY (town) Nassau County	5,235
Freeport, NY (village) Nassau County	3,178
Yonkers, NY (city) Westchester County	3,109
Huntington, NY (town) Suffolk County	2,960
Babylon, NY (town) Suffolk County	2,839

Central American
Top 10 Places Sorted by Percent

Place	Percent
Southeast, NY (town) Putnam County	96.53
East Hampton, NY (town) Suffolk County	94.12
Southampton, NY (town) Suffolk County	90.22
Long Beach, NY (city) Nassau County	88.66
Ramapo, NY (town) Rockland County	87.09
Orange, NY (town) Rockland County	85.01
Peekskill, NY (city) Westchester County	83.91
Spring Valley, NY (village) Rockland County	83.84

Place	
Mamaroneck, NY (town) Westchester County	82.89
Southold, NY (town) Suffolk County	82.87

Chilean
Top 10 Places Sorted by Number

Place	Number
New York, NY (city)	4,728
Hempstead, NY (town) Nassau County	515
North Hempstead, NY (town) Nassau County	494
Oyster Bay, NY (town) Nassau County	299

Chilean
Top 10 Places Sorted by Percent

Place	Percent
New York, NY (city)	82.59
Hempstead, NY (town) Nassau County	77.68
North Hempstead, NY (town) Nassau County	76.59
Oyster Bay, NY (town) Nassau County	75.70

Colombian
Top 10 Places Sorted by Number

Place	Number
New York, NY (city)	63,228
Hempstead, NY (town) Nassau County	3,349
Islip, NY (town) Suffolk County	2,124
Brentwood, NY (cdp) Suffolk County	1,162
White Plains, NY (city) Westchester County	1,006
Brookhaven, NY (town) Suffolk County	926
North Hempstead, NY (town) Nassau County	922
Yonkers, NY (city) Westchester County	853
New Rochelle, NY (city) Westchester County	852
Babylon, NY (town) Suffolk County	743

Colombian
Top 10 Places Sorted by Percent

Place	Percent
Southampton, NY (town) Suffolk County	90.77
East Hampton, NY (town) Suffolk County	88.04
Ossining, NY (town) Westchester County	85.10
Ossining, NY (village) Westchester County	85.10
Long Beach, NY (city) Nassau County	79.95
New York, NY (city)	77.52
White Plains, NY (city) Westchester County	77.50
Freeport, NY (village) Nassau County	77.30
Port Chester, NY (village) Westchester County	75.47
Greenburgh, NY (town) Westchester County	75.40

Costa Rican
Top 10 Places Sorted by Number

Place	Number
New York, NY (city)	3,795
Hempstead, NY (town) Nassau County	261

Costa Rican
Top 10 Places Sorted by Percent

Place	Percent
New York, NY (city)	72.45
Hempstead, NY (town) Nassau County	66.41

Cuban
Top 10 Places Sorted by Number

Place	Number
New York, NY (city)	25,186
Hempstead, NY (town) Nassau County	1,407
Rochester, NY (city) Monroe County	795
Yonkers, NY (city) Westchester County	788
Islip, NY (town) Suffolk County	583
Brookhaven, NY (town) Suffolk County	422
Rye, NY (town) Westchester County	414
Port Chester, NY (village) Westchester County	388
Oyster Bay, NY (town) Nassau County	333

Place	
Syracuse, NY (city) Onondaga County	291

Cuban
Top 10 Places Sorted by Percent

Place	Percent
Port Chester, NY (village) Westchester County	84.16
Rye, NY (town) Westchester County	78.86
Rochester, NY (city) Monroe County	69.07
Syracuse, NY (city) Onondaga County	66.90
Yonkers, NY (city) Westchester County	61.56
New York, NY (city)	60.73
Greenburgh, NY (town) Westchester County	52.30
Oyster Bay, NY (town) Nassau County	46.44
Islip, NY (town) Suffolk County	45.98
Clarks, NY (town) Rockland County	45.48

Dominican
Top 10 Places Sorted by Number

Place	Number
New York, NY (city)	292,979
Hempstead, NY (town) Nassau County	5,672
Yonkers, NY (city) Westchester County	5,039
Islip, NY (town) Suffolk County	3,067
Haverstraw, NY (town) Rockland County	2,596
Freeport, NY (village) Nassau County	2,289
Babylon, NY (town) Suffolk County	1,961
Haverstraw, NY (village) Rockland County	1,798
Brentwood, NY (cdp) Suffolk County	1,645
Brookhaven, NY (town) Suffolk County	1,187

Dominican
Top 10 Places Sorted by Percent

Place	Percent
Port Chester, NY (village) Westchester County	86.39
Rye, NY (town) Westchester County	85.60
Baldwin, NY (cdp) Nassau County	82.75
Uniondale, NY (cdp) Nassau County	78.09
Copiague, NY (cdp) Suffolk County	73.82
Mount Pleasant, NY (town) Westchester County	73.35
Freeport, NY (village) Nassau County	72.46
Greenburgh, NY (town) Westchester County	71.83
Brentwood, NY (cdp) Suffolk County	71.58
White Plains, NY (city) Westchester County	71.23

Ecuadorian
Top 10 Places Sorted by Number

Place	Number
New York, NY (city)	82,596
Ossining, NY (town) Westchester County	1,929
Ossining, NY (village) Westchester County	1,929
Hempstead, NY (town) Nassau County	1,624
Brookhaven, NY (town) Suffolk County	1,469
Yonkers, NY (city) Westchester County	1,395
Islip, NY (town) Suffolk County	1,251
Rye, NY (town) Westchester County	869
Port Chester, NY (village) Westchester County	856
North Hempstead, NY (town) Nassau County	760

Ecuadorian
Top 10 Places Sorted by Percent

Place	Percent
Spring Valley, NY (village) Rockland County	95.28
Greenburgh, NY (town) Westchester County	94.17
Ramapo, NY (town) Rockland County	93.39
Patchogue, NY (village) Suffolk County	90.64
East Hampton, NY (town) Suffolk County	90.46
Mount Pleasant, NY (town) Westchester County	88.47
Ossining, NY (town) Westchester County	87.52
Ossining, NY (village) Westchester County	87.52
Peekskill, NY (city) Westchester County	86.35
Port Chester, NY (village) Westchester County	84.00

Notes: Please refer to the User's Guide for an explanation of data; tables include places with populations > 9,999 and reflect only those areas that meet Summary File 4 population thresholds, therefore there may be less than 10 places listed

Guatemalan
Top 10 Places Sorted by Number

Place	Number
New York, NY (city)	12,327
Hempstead, NY (town) Nassau County	1,532
Ramapo, NY (town) Rockland County	1,358
Rye, NY (town) Westchester County	1,088
Spring Valley, NY (village) Rockland County	1,073
Port Chester, NY (village) Westchester County	1,014
Islip, NY (town) Suffolk County	788
North Hempstead, NY (town) Nassau County	565
Brentwood, NY (cdp) Suffolk County	463
Freeport, NY (village) Nassau County	439

Guatemalan
Top 10 Places Sorted by Percent

Place	Percent
Southeast, NY (town) Putnam County	96.06
Ramapo, NY (town) Rockland County	90.96
Hempstead, NY (village) Nassau County	90.27
Freeport, NY (village) Nassau County	89.59
Southampton, NY (town) Suffolk County	89.59
Spring Valley, NY (village) Rockland County	88.82
Brentwood, NY (cdp) Suffolk County	82.24
Hempstead, NY (town) Nassau County	82.06
Port Chester, NY (village) Westchester County	80.29
Rye, NY (town) Westchester County	80.18

Honduran
Top 10 Places Sorted by Number

Place	Number
New York, NY (city)	21,249
Hempstead, NY (town) Nassau County	2,158
Hempstead, NY (village) Nassau County	1,452
Islip, NY (town) Suffolk County	971
Yonkers, NY (city) Westchester County	693
North Hempstead, NY (town) Nassau County	589
Newburgh, NY (city) Orange County	507
Brentwood, NY (cdp) Suffolk County	496
Huntington, NY (town) Suffolk County	413
Babylon, NY (town) Suffolk County	377

Honduran
Top 10 Places Sorted by Percent

Place	Percent
Hempstead, NY (village) Nassau County	89.80
Huntington, NY (town) Suffolk County	89.39
Hempstead, NY (town) Nassau County	86.35
Brentwood, NY (cdp) Suffolk County	84.64
North Hempstead, NY (town) Nassau County	80.46
Islip, NY (town) Suffolk County	79.85
Babylon, NY (town) Suffolk County	76.16
Yonkers, NY (city) Westchester County	75.66
New York, NY (city)	71.47
Newburgh, NY (city) Orange County	69.17

Mexican
Top 10 Places Sorted by Number

Place	Number
New York, NY (city)	120,819
New Rochelle, NY (city) Westchester County	5,225
Yonkers, NY (city) Westchester County	4,500
Rye, NY (town) Westchester County	2,953
Newburgh, NY (city) Orange County	2,932
Port Chester, NY (village) Westchester County	2,758
White Plains, NY (city) Westchester County	2,546
North Hempstead, NY (town) Nassau County	1,944
Hempstead, NY (town) Nassau County	1,331
Middletown, NY (city) Orange County	1,203

Mexican
Top 10 Places Sorted by Percent

Place	Percent
Ramapo, NY (town) Rockland County	86.63
Poughkeepsie, NY (city) Dutchess County	83.04
Haverstraw, NY (town) Rockland County	79.84
New Cassel, NY (cdp) Nassau County	79.60
White Plains, NY (city) Westchester County	78.31
North Hempstead, NY (town) Nassau County	76.81
Port Chester, NY (village) Westchester County	75.21
Rye, NY (town) Westchester County	74.76
Mount Vernon, NY (city) Westchester County	74.61
Elmont, NY (cdp) Nassau County	74.45

Nicaraguan
Top 10 Places Sorted by Number

Place	Number
New York, NY (city)	5,641
Yonkers, NY (city) Westchester County	450

Nicaraguan
Top 10 Places Sorted by Percent

Place	Percent
Yonkers, NY (city) Westchester County	78.53
New York, NY (city)	76.11

Panamanian
Top 10 Places Sorted by Number

Place	Number
New York, NY (city)	13,354
Hempstead, NY (town) Nassau County	355
Islip, NY (town) Suffolk County	197

Panamanian
Top 10 Places Sorted by Percent

Place	Percent
New York, NY (city)	71.55
Hempstead, NY (town) Nassau County	59.66
Islip, NY (town) Suffolk County	59.16

Paraguayan
Top 10 Places Sorted by Number

Place	Number
New York, NY (city)	1,233

Paraguayan
Top 10 Places Sorted by Percent

Place	Percent
New York, NY (city)	79.50

Peruvian
Top 10 Places Sorted by Number

Place	Number
New York, NY (city)	19,164
Hempstead, NY (town) Nassau County	1,653
White Plains, NY (city) Westchester County	1,254
Islip, NY (town) Suffolk County	1,046
Rye, NY (town) Westchester County	748
Port Chester, NY (village) Westchester County	668
New Rochelle, NY (city) Westchester County	598
Glen Cove, NY (city) Nassau County	594
Oyster Bay, NY (town) Nassau County	498
Brentwood, NY (cdp) Suffolk County	448

Peruvian
Top 10 Places Sorted by Percent

Place	Percent
Brentwood, NY (cdp) Suffolk County	87.16
North Hempstead, NY (town) Nassau County	86.19
New Rochelle, NY (city) Westchester County	84.94
White Plains, NY (city) Westchester County	84.73
Babylon, NY (town) Suffolk County	83.24
Hempstead, NY (town) Nassau County	82.77
Islip, NY (town) Suffolk County	81.27
New York, NY (city)	80.98
Port Chester, NY (village) Westchester County	80.87
Yonkers, NY (city) Westchester County	80.71

Puerto Rican
Top 10 Places Sorted by Number

Place	Number
New York, NY (city)	10,941
Islip, NY (town) Suffolk County	398
Yonkers, NY (city) Westchester County	321
Brentwood, NY (cdp) Suffolk County	292
Hempstead, NY (town) Nassau County	200
Babylon, NY (town) Suffolk County	175
Rochester, NY (city) Monroe County	153
Wyandanch, NY (cdp) Suffolk County	103
Brookhaven, NY (town) Suffolk County	86
Hempstead, NY (village) Nassau County	67

Puerto Rican
Top 10 Places Sorted by Percent

Place	Percent
Wyandanch, NY (cdp) Suffolk County	17.17
Mamaroneck, NY (town) Westchester County	6.56
Lynbrook, NY (village) Nassau County	6.18
Glen Cove, NY (city) Nassau County	6.07
Oceanside, NY (cdp) Nassau County	4.60
Hempstead, NY (village) Nassau County	4.18
Ossining, NY (village) Westchester County	3.83
Port Chester, NY (village) Westchester County	3.74
Bedford, NY (town) Westchester County	3.72
Brentwood, NY (cdp) Suffolk County	3.68

Salvadoran
Top 10 Places Sorted by Number

Place	Number
New York, NY (city)	19,253
Hempstead, NY (town) Nassau County	12,077
Islip, NY (town) Suffolk County	9,046
Brentwood, NY (cdp) Suffolk County	5,689
Hempstead, NY (village) Nassau County	4,926
North Hempstead, NY (town) Nassau County	3,626
Freeport, NY (village) Nassau County	2,332
Huntington, NY (town) Suffolk County	2,192
Babylon, NY (town) Suffolk County	2,047
Huntington Station, NY (cdp) Suffolk County	1,830

Salvadoran
Top 10 Places Sorted by Percent

Place	Percent
Orange, NY (town) Rockland County	86.92
Elmont, NY (cdp) Nassau County	83.44
Copiague, NY (cdp) Suffolk County	80.54
Mineola, NY (village) Nassau County	80.43
Westbury, NY (village) Nassau County	80.11
Wyandanch, NY (cdp) Suffolk County	79.35
Hempstead, NY (village) Nassau County	78.87
Yonkers, NY (city) Westchester County	76.91
Oyster Bay, NY (town) Nassau County	76.28
New York, NY (city)	76.20

South American
Top 10 Places Sorted by Number

Place	Number
New York, NY (city)	194,268
Hempstead, NY (town) Nassau County	8,696
Islip, NY (town) Suffolk County	5,442
Brookhaven, NY (town) Suffolk County	3,428
Yonkers, NY (city) Westchester County	3,377
North Hempstead, NY (town) Nassau County	3,269

Notes: Please refer to the User's Guide for an explanation of data; tables include places with populations > 9,999 and reflect only those areas that meet Summary File 4 population thresholds, therefore there may be less than 10 places listed

Place	
White Plains, NY (city) Westchester County	3,088
Rye, NY (town) Westchester County	2,760
Ossining, NY (town) Westchester County	2,714
Ossining, NY (village) Westchester County	2,672

South American
Top 10 Places Sorted by Percent

Place	Percent
Spring Valley, NY (village) Rockland County	89.98
East Hampton, NY (town) Suffolk County	89.82
Patchogue, NY (village) Suffolk County	88.49
Westbury, NY (village) Nassau County	88.49
Southampton, NY (town) Suffolk County	87.06
Mamaroneck, NY (town) Westchester County	86.96
Ossining, NY (town) Westchester County	86.79
Ossining, NY (village) Westchester County	86.61
Hempstead, NY (village) Nassau County	86.16
Mount Pleasant, NY (town) Westchester County	85.89

Spaniard
Top 10 Places Sorted by Number

Place	Number
New York, NY (city)	5,914
Hempstead, NY (town) Nassau County	366
Brookhaven, NY (town) Suffolk County	89

Spaniard
Top 10 Places Sorted by Percent

Place	Percent
New York, NY (city)	58.78
Hempstead, NY (town) Nassau County	45.02
Brookhaven, NY (town) Suffolk County	21.60

Uruguayan
Top 10 Places Sorted by Number

Place	Number
New York, NY (city)	1,700

Uruguayan
Top 10 Places Sorted by Percent

Place	Percent
New York, NY (city)	82.97

Venezuelan
Top 10 Places Sorted by Number

Place	Number
New York, NY (city)	6,004

Venezuelan
Top 10 Places Sorted by Percent

Place	Percent
New York, NY (city)	83.64

Other Hispanic
Top 10 Places Sorted by Number

Place	Number
New York, NY (city)	161,350
Hempstead, NY (town) Nassau County	10,389
Islip, NY (town) Suffolk County	5,242
Yonkers, NY (city) Westchester County	3,021
Hempstead, NY (village) Nassau County	2,951
Brentwood, NY (cdp) Suffolk County	2,636
Freeport, NY (village) Nassau County	2,391
North Hempstead, NY (town) Nassau County	2,356
Brookhaven, NY (town) Suffolk County	1,909
White Plains, NY (city) Westchester County	1,698

Other Hispanic
Top 10 Places Sorted by Percent

Place	Percent
Peekskill, NY (city) Westchester County	68.78
Roosevelt, NY (cdp) Nassau County	64.04
Freeport, NY (village) Nassau County	62.59
Ossining, NY (village) Westchester County	61.92
Ossining, NY (town) Westchester County	61.47
White Plains, NY (city) Westchester County	60.32
Westbury, NY (village) Nassau County	59.16
Glen Cove, NY (city) Nassau County	58.90
New Cassel, NY (cdp) Nassau County	58.26
Hicksville, NY (cdp) Nassau County	57.86

Foreign-Born Naturalized Citizens

Total Population
Top 10 Places Sorted by Number

Place	Number
New York, NY (city)	1,278,687
Hempstead, NY (town) Nassau County	73,040
North Hempstead, NY (town) Nassau County	30,865
Oyster Bay, NY (town) Nassau County	22,589
Yonkers, NY (city) Westchester County	22,521
Brookhaven, NY (town) Suffolk County	20,640
Islip, NY (town) Suffolk County	19,295
Babylon, NY (town) Suffolk County	13,644
Huntington, NY (town) Suffolk County	12,618
Ramapo, NY (town) Rockland County	11,707

Total Population
Top 10 Places Sorted by Percent

Place	Percent
North Valley Stream, NY (cdp) Nassau County	21.28
Elmont, NY (cdp) Nassau County	20.82
Uniondale, NY (cdp) Nassau County	17.04
New York, NY (city)	15.97
New Cassel, NY (cdp) Nassau County	14.67
North New Hyde Park, NY (cdp) Nassau County	14.34
North Hempstead, NY (town) Nassau County	13.86
Westbury, NY (village) Nassau County	13.52
Baldwin, NY (cdp) Nassau County	13.41
Spring Valley, NY (village) Rockland County	13.37

Hispanic
Top 10 Places Sorted by Number

Place	Number
New York, NY (city)	300,620
Hempstead, NY (town) Nassau County	14,889
Islip, NY (town) Suffolk County	7,890
Yonkers, NY (city) Westchester County	6,019
North Hempstead, NY (town) Nassau County	3,948
Brentwood, NY (cdp) Suffolk County	3,675
Babylon, NY (town) Suffolk County	3,204
Brookhaven, NY (town) Suffolk County	3,154
Oyster Bay, NY (town) Nassau County	2,674
Freeport, NY (village) Nassau County	2,332

Hispanic
Top 10 Places Sorted by Percent

Place	Percent
East Rockaway, NY (village) Nassau County	27.91
New Castle, NY (town) Westchester County	27.66
North Valley Stream, NY (cdp) Nassau County	27.48
North Merrick, NY (cdp) Nassau County	27.03
Scarsdale, NY (village) Westchester County	25.89
Plainview, NY (cdp) Nassau County	25.61
Dix Hills, NY (cdp) Suffolk County	25.33
North Wantagh, NY (cdp) Nassau County	25.00
Rye, NY (city) Westchester County	24.47
Manlius, NY (town) Onondaga County	24.46

Argentinian
Top 10 Places Sorted by Number

Place	Number
New York, NY (city)	3,710
Hempstead, NY (town) Nassau County	404
North Hempstead, NY (town) Nassau County	155

Argentinian
Top 10 Places Sorted by Percent

Place	Percent
Hempstead, NY (town) Nassau County	41.65
New York, NY (city)	36.50
North Hempstead, NY (town) Nassau County	31.25

Bolivian
Top 10 Places Sorted by Number

Place	Number
New York, NY (city)	890

Bolivian
Top 10 Places Sorted by Percent

Place	Percent
New York, NY (city)	26.64

Central American
Top 10 Places Sorted by Number

Place	Number
New York, NY (city)	30,762
Hempstead, NY (town) Nassau County	3,517
Islip, NY (town) Suffolk County	2,120
Brentwood, NY (cdp) Suffolk County	1,248
North Hempstead, NY (town) Nassau County	1,066
Yonkers, NY (city) Westchester County	948
Hempstead, NY (village) Nassau County	829
Babylon, NY (town) Suffolk County	750
Huntington, NY (town) Suffolk County	572
Freeport, NY (village) Nassau County	570

Central American
Top 10 Places Sorted by Percent

Place	Percent
Levittown, NY (cdp) Nassau County	32.66
New York, NY (city)	28.49
Valley Stream, NY (village) Nassau County	27.02
Elmont, NY (cdp) Nassau County	24.04
West Hempstead, NY (cdp) Nassau County	23.84
Yonkers, NY (city) Westchester County	23.08
Mount Vernon, NY (city) Westchester County	22.25
Clarks, NY (town) Rockland County	20.73
Greenburgh, NY (town) Westchester County	20.69
Baldwin, NY (cdp) Nassau County	20.08

Chilean
Top 10 Places Sorted by Number

Place	Number
New York, NY (city)	1,575
North Hempstead, NY (town) Nassau County	190
Hempstead, NY (town) Nassau County	171
Oyster Bay, NY (town) Nassau County	96

Chilean
Top 10 Places Sorted by Percent

Place	Percent
North Hempstead, NY (town) Nassau County	29.46
New York, NY (city)	27.51
Hempstead, NY (town) Nassau County	25.79
Oyster Bay, NY (town) Nassau County	24.30

Notes: Please refer to the User's Guide for an explanation of data; tables include places with populations > 9,999 and reflect only those areas that meet Summary File 4 population thresholds, therefore there may be less than 10 places listed

PROFILES OF NEW YORK / Hispanic: Rankings

Colombian
Top 10 Places Sorted by Number

Place	Number
New York, NY (city)	25,791
Hempstead, NY (town) Nassau County	1,756
Islip, NY (town) Suffolk County	781
North Hempstead, NY (town) Nassau County	525
Brookhaven, NY (town) Suffolk County	438
Oyster Bay, NY (town) Nassau County	410
Babylon, NY (town) Suffolk County	407
Brentwood, NY (cdp) Suffolk County	341
Yonkers, NY (city) Westchester County	309
White Plains, NY (city) Westchester County	306

Colombian
Top 10 Places Sorted by Percent

Place	Percent
Mineola, NY (village) Nassau County	44.86
North Hempstead, NY (town) Nassau County	42.41
Huntington, NY (town) Suffolk County	40.73
Babylon, NY (town) Suffolk County	37.79
Hempstead, NY (town) Nassau County	37.47
Long Beach, NY (city) Nassau County	37.41
Brookhaven, NY (town) Suffolk County	35.15
Oyster Bay, NY (town) Nassau County	34.80
New York, NY (city)	31.62
Greenburgh, NY (town) Westchester County	30.00

Costa Rican
Top 10 Places Sorted by Number

Place	Number
New York, NY (city)	2,058
Hempstead, NY (town) Nassau County	176

Costa Rican
Top 10 Places Sorted by Percent

Place	Percent
Hempstead, NY (town) Nassau County	44.78
New York, NY (city)	39.29

Cuban
Top 10 Places Sorted by Number

Place	Number
New York, NY (city)	18,100
Hempstead, NY (town) Nassau County	1,114
Yonkers, NY (city) Westchester County	558
Islip, NY (town) Suffolk County	380
Oyster Bay, NY (town) Nassau County	283
Rye, NY (town) Westchester County	282
Brookhaven, NY (town) Suffolk County	270
Port Chester, NY (village) Westchester County	266
Greenburgh, NY (town) Westchester County	248
Rochester, NY (city) Monroe County	217

Cuban
Top 10 Places Sorted by Percent

Place	Percent
Port Chester, NY (village) Westchester County	57.70
Rye, NY (town) Westchester County	53.71
Greenburgh, NY (town) Westchester County	49.50
New York, NY (city)	43.64
Yonkers, NY (city) Westchester County	43.59
Clarks, NY (town) Rockland County	40.57
Oyster Bay, NY (town) Nassau County	39.47
Hempstead, NY (town) Nassau County	34.97
Islip, NY (town) Suffolk County	29.97
North Hempstead, NY (town) Nassau County	29.65

Dominican
Top 10 Places Sorted by Number

Place	Number
New York, NY (city)	105,464
Hempstead, NY (town) Nassau County	2,099
Yonkers, NY (city) Westchester County	1,861
Islip, NY (town) Suffolk County	1,475
Haverstraw, NY (town) Rockland County	891
Brentwood, NY (cdp) Suffolk County	752
Freeport, NY (village) Nassau County	702
Babylon, NY (town) Suffolk County	685
Haverstraw, NY (village) Rockland County	587
Brookhaven, NY (town) Suffolk County	439

Dominican
Top 10 Places Sorted by Percent

Place	Percent
White Plains, NY (city) Westchester County	36.02
Islip, NY (town) Suffolk County	32.85
Brentwood, NY (cdp) Suffolk County	32.72
Baldwin, NY (cdp) Nassau County	31.88
Rye, NY (town) Westchester County	31.28
Central Islip, NY (cdp) Suffolk County	29.41
North Hempstead, NY (town) Nassau County	28.82
Port Chester, NY (village) Westchester County	28.80
Oyster Bay, NY (town) Nassau County	28.77
North Bay Shore, NY (cdp) Suffolk County	27.70

Ecuadorian
Top 10 Places Sorted by Number

Place	Number
New York, NY (city)	24,119
Hempstead, NY (town) Nassau County	831
Yonkers, NY (city) Westchester County	518
Islip, NY (town) Suffolk County	332
Brookhaven, NY (town) Suffolk County	262
North Hempstead, NY (town) Nassau County	258
Ossining, NY (town) Westchester County	238
Ossining, NY (village) Westchester County	238
Babylon, NY (town) Suffolk County	192
Oyster Bay, NY (town) Nassau County	185

Ecuadorian
Top 10 Places Sorted by Percent

Place	Percent
Hempstead, NY (town) Nassau County	36.26
Oyster Bay, NY (town) Nassau County	34.84
Babylon, NY (town) Suffolk County	33.57
Yonkers, NY (city) Westchester County	29.60
North Hempstead, NY (town) Nassau County	26.82
Brentwood, NY (cdp) Suffolk County	24.25
Central Islip, NY (cdp) Suffolk County	23.60
New York, NY (city)	22.62
Greenburgh, NY (town) Westchester County	20.28
Islip, NY (town) Suffolk County	19.89

Guatemalan
Top 10 Places Sorted by Number

Place	Number
New York, NY (city)	3,646
Hempstead, NY (town) Nassau County	449
Islip, NY (town) Suffolk County	234
Rye, NY (town) Westchester County	165
Port Chester, NY (village) Westchester County	159
Brentwood, NY (cdp) Suffolk County	130
North Hempstead, NY (town) Nassau County	87
Babylon, NY (town) Suffolk County	85
Brookhaven, NY (town) Suffolk County	83
Freeport, NY (village) Nassau County	81

Guatemalan
Top 10 Places Sorted by Percent

Place	Percent
Hempstead, NY (town) Nassau County	24.05
Huntington, NY (town) Suffolk County	23.69
Brookhaven, NY (town) Suffolk County	23.51
Brentwood, NY (cdp) Suffolk County	23.09
Babylon, NY (town) Suffolk County	22.85
New York, NY (city)	22.81
Islip, NY (town) Suffolk County	21.10
Freeport, NY (village) Nassau County	16.53
Port Chester, NY (village) Westchester County	12.59
Rye, NY (town) Westchester County	12.16

Honduran
Top 10 Places Sorted by Number

Place	Number
New York, NY (city)	7,279
Yonkers, NY (city) Westchester County	234
Hempstead, NY (town) Nassau County	185
Islip, NY (town) Suffolk County	149
Newburgh, NY (city) Orange County	128
Babylon, NY (town) Suffolk County	114
North Hempstead, NY (town) Nassau County	98
Hempstead, NY (village) Nassau County	94
Brentwood, NY (cdp) Suffolk County	76
Huntington, NY (town) Suffolk County	65

Honduran
Top 10 Places Sorted by Percent

Place	Percent
Yonkers, NY (city) Westchester County	25.55
New York, NY (city)	24.48
Babylon, NY (town) Suffolk County	23.03
Newburgh, NY (city) Orange County	17.46
Huntington, NY (town) Suffolk County	14.07
North Hempstead, NY (town) Nassau County	13.39
Brentwood, NY (cdp) Suffolk County	12.25
Islip, NY (town) Suffolk County	12.25
Hempstead, NY (town) Nassau County	7.40
Hempstead, NY (village) Nassau County	5.81

Mexican
Top 10 Places Sorted by Number

Place	Number
New York, NY (city)	11,508
New Rochelle, NY (city) Westchester County	654
Hempstead, NY (town) Nassau County	399
Yonkers, NY (city) Westchester County	320
Rye, NY (town) Westchester County	283
Newburgh, NY (city) Orange County	277
Port Chester, NY (village) Westchester County	253
Middletown, NY (city) Orange County	198
Mount Vernon, NY (city) Westchester County	192
Brookhaven, NY (town) Suffolk County	180

Mexican
Top 10 Places Sorted by Percent

Place	Percent
Elmont, NY (cdp) Nassau County	24.33
Hempstead, NY (town) Nassau County	14.75
Mount Vernon, NY (city) Westchester County	14.43
Mamaroneck, NY (town) Westchester County	10.76
Mamaroneck, NY (village) Westchester County	10.76
Middletown, NY (city) Orange County	10.71
Hempstead, NY (village) Nassau County	10.21
Brookhaven, NY (town) Suffolk County	10.15
Fort Drum, NY (cdp) Jefferson County	10.08
Le Ray, NY (town) Jefferson County	9.49

Nicaraguan
Top 10 Places Sorted by Number

Place	Number
New York, NY (city)	2,035
Yonkers, NY (city) Westchester County	112

Notes: Please refer to the User's Guide for an explanation of data; tables include places with populations > 9,999 and reflect only those areas that meet Summary File 4 population thresholds, therefore there may be less than 10 places listed

Nicaraguan
Top 10 Places Sorted by Percent

Place	Percent
New York, NY (city)	27.46
Yonkers, NY (city) Westchester County	19.55

Panamanian
Top 10 Places Sorted by Number

Place	Number
New York, NY (city)	8,248
Hempstead, NY (town) Nassau County	281
Islip, NY (town) Suffolk County	128

Panamanian
Top 10 Places Sorted by Percent

Place	Percent
Hempstead, NY (town) Nassau County	47.23
New York, NY (city)	44.19
Islip, NY (town) Suffolk County	38.44

Paraguayan
Top 10 Places Sorted by Number

Place	Number
New York, NY (city)	334

Paraguayan
Top 10 Places Sorted by Percent

Place	Percent
New York, NY (city)	21.53

Peruvian
Top 10 Places Sorted by Number

Place	Number
New York, NY (city)	7,403
Hempstead, NY (town) Nassau County	567
Islip, NY (town) Suffolk County	346
White Plains, NY (city) Westchester County	266
Rye, NY (town) Westchester County	260
Port Chester, NY (village) Westchester County	234
Brookhaven, NY (town) Suffolk County	213
Oyster Bay, NY (town) Nassau County	196
Yonkers, NY (city) Westchester County	176
Glen Cove, NY (city) Nassau County	168

Peruvian
Top 10 Places Sorted by Percent

Place	Percent
Brookhaven, NY (town) Suffolk County	36.66
Yonkers, NY (city) Westchester County	32.65
North Hempstead, NY (town) Nassau County	32.58
New York, NY (city)	31.28
Oyster Bay, NY (town) Nassau County	30.53
Hempstead, NY (town) Nassau County	28.39
Port Chester, NY (village) Westchester County	28.33
Rye, NY (town) Westchester County	27.81
Islip, NY (town) Suffolk County	26.88
Brentwood, NY (cdp) Suffolk County	24.32

Puerto Rican
Top 10 Places Sorted by Number

Place	Number
New York, NY (city)	4,905
Islip, NY (town) Suffolk County	174
Brentwood, NY (cdp) Suffolk County	122
Yonkers, NY (city) Westchester County	99
Rochester, NY (city) Monroe County	57
Hempstead, NY (town) Nassau County	47
Albany, NY (city) Albany County	44
Babylon, NY (town) Suffolk County	43
Brookhaven, NY (town) Suffolk County	41
Mount Vernon, NY (city) Westchester County	40

Puerto Rican
Top 10 Places Sorted by Percent

Place	Percent
Lindenhurst, NY (village) Suffolk County	2.47
East Fishkill, NY (town) Dutchess County	2.41
East Islip, NY (cdp) Suffolk County	2.38
Niagara Falls, NY (city) Niagara County	2.33
Oceanside, NY (cdp) Nassau County	2.30
Haverstraw, NY (village) Rockland County	2.24
Stony Point, NY (town) Rockland County	2.03
Ossining, NY (village) Westchester County	2.00
Long Beach, NY (city) Nassau County	1.97
North Amityville, NY (cdp) Suffolk County	1.93

Salvadoran
Top 10 Places Sorted by Number

Place	Number
New York, NY (city)	5,879
Hempstead, NY (town) Nassau County	2,255
Islip, NY (town) Suffolk County	1,474
Brentwood, NY (cdp) Suffolk County	944
North Hempstead, NY (town) Nassau County	736
Hempstead, NY (village) Nassau County	612
Babylon, NY (town) Suffolk County	457
Yonkers, NY (city) Westchester County	398
Huntington, NY (town) Suffolk County	386
Freeport, NY (village) Nassau County	355

Salvadoran
Top 10 Places Sorted by Percent

Place	Percent
Valley Stream, NY (village) Nassau County	24.83
New York, NY (city)	23.27
Yonkers, NY (city) Westchester County	22.31
Mineola, NY (village) Nassau County	18.97
Babylon, NY (town) Suffolk County	16.47
North Hempstead, NY (town) Nassau County	14.91
Brookhaven, NY (town) Suffolk County	13.85
Hempstead, NY (town) Nassau County	13.79
Uniondale, NY (cdp) Nassau County	13.64
Huntington, NY (town) Suffolk County	13.16

South American
Top 10 Places Sorted by Number

Place	Number
New York, NY (city)	68,444
Hempstead, NY (town) Nassau County	4,144
Islip, NY (town) Suffolk County	1,881
North Hempstead, NY (town) Nassau County	1,447
Yonkers, NY (city) Westchester County	1,227
Brookhaven, NY (town) Suffolk County	1,196
Oyster Bay, NY (town) Nassau County	1,136
Babylon, NY (town) Suffolk County	864
White Plains, NY (city) Westchester County	811
Brentwood, NY (cdp) Suffolk County	724

South American
Top 10 Places Sorted by Percent

Place	Percent
Baldwin, NY (cdp) Nassau County	49.20
East Meadow, NY (cdp) Nassau County	48.45
Smith, NY (town) Suffolk County	42.10
Oceanside, NY (cdp) Nassau County	41.89
Franklin Square, NY (cdp) Nassau County	41.54
Mamaroneck, NY (town) Westchester County	39.37
Valley Stream, NY (village) Nassau County	38.67
Hicksville, NY (cdp) Nassau County	37.41
Coram, NY (cdp) Suffolk County	37.28
Huntington, NY (town) Suffolk County	36.42

Spaniard
Top 10 Places Sorted by Number

Place	Number
New York, NY (city)	1,798
Hempstead, NY (town) Nassau County	162
Brookhaven, NY (town) Suffolk County	25

Spaniard
Top 10 Places Sorted by Percent

Place	Percent
Hempstead, NY (town) Nassau County	19.93
New York, NY (city)	17.87
Brookhaven, NY (town) Suffolk County	6.07

Uruguayan
Top 10 Places Sorted by Number

Place	Number
New York, NY (city)	990

Uruguayan
Top 10 Places Sorted by Percent

Place	Percent
New York, NY (city)	48.32

Venezuelan
Top 10 Places Sorted by Number

Place	Number
New York, NY (city)	1,259

Venezuelan
Top 10 Places Sorted by Percent

Place	Percent
New York, NY (city)	17.54

Other Hispanic
Top 10 Places Sorted by Number

Place	Number
New York, NY (city)	59,639
Hempstead, NY (town) Nassau County	3,407
Islip, NY (town) Suffolk County	1,668
Yonkers, NY (city) Westchester County	964
North Hempstead, NY (town) Nassau County	868
Brentwood, NY (cdp) Suffolk County	732
Brookhaven, NY (town) Suffolk County	651
Babylon, NY (town) Suffolk County	622
Freeport, NY (village) Nassau County	598
Oyster Bay, NY (town) Nassau County	579

Other Hispanic
Top 10 Places Sorted by Percent

Place	Percent
Valley Stream, NY (village) Nassau County	27.12
Cortlandt, NY (town) Westchester County	25.76
Oceanside, NY (cdp) Nassau County	23.13
Uniondale, NY (cdp) Nassau County	22.52
Roosevelt, NY (cdp) Nassau County	22.29
Smith, NY (town) Suffolk County	21.34
Levittown, NY (cdp) Nassau County	20.89
Harrison, NY (village) Westchester County	20.78
North Hempstead, NY (town) Nassau County	20.30
New Rochelle, NY (city) Westchester County	20.16

Notes: Please refer to the User's Guide for an explanation of data; tables include places with populations > 9,999 and reflect only those areas that meet Summary File 4 population thresholds, therefore there may be less than 10 places listed

Educational Attainment: High School Graduates

Total Populations 25 Years and Over Who are High School Graduates
Top 10 Places Sorted by Number

Place	Number
New York, NY (city)	3,814,256
Hempstead, NY (town) Nassau County	431,485
Brookhaven, NY (town) Suffolk County	251,158
Oyster Bay, NY (town) Nassau County	184,305
Islip, NY (town) Suffolk County	173,016
Buffalo, NY (city) Erie County	136,475
North Hempstead, NY (town) Nassau County	133,811
Huntington, NY (town) Suffolk County	122,366
Babylon, NY (town) Suffolk County	115,683
Yonkers, NY (city) Westchester County	101,090

Total Populations 25 Years and Over Who are High School Graduates
Top 10 Places Sorted by Percent

Place	Percent
Scarsdale, NY (village) Westchester County	97.11
Ithaca, NY (town) Tompkins County	97.10
Fort Drum, NY (cdp) Jefferson County	96.90
Lewisboro, NY (town) Westchester County	96.76
Garden City, NY (village) Nassau County	96.69
New Castle, NY (town) Westchester County	96.54
Pittsford, NY (town) Monroe County	96.20
Clifton Park, NY (town) Saratoga County	95.89
Setauket-East Setauket, NY (cdp) Suffolk County	95.06
Somers, NY (town) Westchester County	94.83

Hispanics 25 Years and Over Who are High School Graduates
Top 10 Places Sorted by Number

Place	Number
New York, NY (city)	664,156
Hempstead, NY (town) Nassau County	29,080
Islip, NY (town) Suffolk County	21,318
Yonkers, NY (city) Westchester County	16,075
Brookhaven, NY (town) Suffolk County	13,967
Brentwood, NY (cdp) Suffolk County	8,121
Babylon, NY (town) Suffolk County	7,443
North Hempstead, NY (town) Nassau County	7,357
Oyster Bay, NY (town) Nassau County	6,876
Rochester, NY (city) Monroe County	6,876

Hispanics 25 Years and Over Who are High School Graduates
Top 10 Places Sorted by Percent

Place	Percent
West Seneca, NY (town) Erie County	100.00
Dryden, NY (town) Tompkins County	97.89
De Witt, NY (town) Onondaga County	97.12
Ithaca, NY (town) Tompkins County	97.08
Pittsford, NY (town) Monroe County	95.65
Fort Drum, NY (cdp) Jefferson County	95.34
Le Ray, NY (town) Jefferson County	95.28
Clay, NY (town) Onondaga County	94.37
Jefferson Valley-Yorktown, NY (cdp) Westchester County	93.78
Guilderland, NY (town) Albany County	92.58

Argentinians 25 Years and Over Who are High School Graduates
Top 10 Places Sorted by Number

Place	Number
New York, NY (city)	5,804
Hempstead, NY (town) Nassau County	426
North Hempstead, NY (town) Nassau County	313

Argentinians 25 Years and Over Who are High School Graduates
Top 10 Places Sorted by Percent

Place	Percent
North Hempstead, NY (town) Nassau County	85.52
New York, NY (city)	74.03
Hempstead, NY (town) Nassau County	66.56

Bolivians 25 Years and Over Who are High School Graduates
Top 10 Places Sorted by Number

Place	Number
New York, NY (city)	1,773

Bolivians 25 Years and Over Who are High School Graduates
Top 10 Places Sorted by Percent

Place	Percent
New York, NY (city)	81.97

Central Americans 25 Years and Over Who are High School Graduates
Top 10 Places Sorted by Number

Place	Number
New York, NY (city)	37,555
Hempstead, NY (town) Nassau County	4,852
Islip, NY (town) Suffolk County	3,015
North Hempstead, NY (town) Nassau County	1,649
Brentwood, NY (cdp) Suffolk County	1,541
Hempstead, NY (village) Nassau County	1,359
Yonkers, NY (city) Westchester County	1,148
Babylon, NY (town) Suffolk County	1,049
Huntington, NY (town) Suffolk County	695
Freeport, NY (village) Nassau County	681

Central Americans 25 Years and Over Who are High School Graduates
Top 10 Places Sorted by Percent

Place	Percent
Greenburgh, NY (town) Westchester County	75.63
West Hempstead, NY (cdp) Nassau County	63.69
Valley Stream, NY (village) Nassau County	62.74
Bay Shore, NY (cdp) Suffolk County	61.64
Middletown, NY (city) Orange County	61.24
Baldwin, NY (cdp) Nassau County	60.66
Mount Vernon, NY (city) Westchester County	57.72
Levittown, NY (cdp) Nassau County	56.67
Port Washington, NY (cdp) Nassau County	56.29
Clarks, NY (town) Rockland County	55.14

Chileans 25 Years and Over Who are High School Graduates
Top 10 Places Sorted by Number

Place	Number
New York, NY (city)	3,131
North Hempstead, NY (town) Nassau County	335
Hempstead, NY (town) Nassau County	312
Oyster Bay, NY (town) Nassau County	221

Chileans 25 Years and Over Who are High School Graduates
Top 10 Places Sorted by Percent

Place	Percent
Oyster Bay, NY (town) Nassau County	81.55
North Hempstead, NY (town) Nassau County	79.01
New York, NY (city)	72.90
Hempstead, NY (town) Nassau County	72.22

Colombians 25 Years and Over Who are High School Graduates
Top 10 Places Sorted by Number

Place	Number
New York, NY (city)	37,152
Hempstead, NY (town) Nassau County	2,462
Islip, NY (town) Suffolk County	1,332
Brentwood, NY (cdp) Suffolk County	666
Oyster Bay, NY (town) Nassau County	643
Brookhaven, NY (town) Suffolk County	624
North Hempstead, NY (town) Nassau County	602
Babylon, NY (town) Suffolk County	598
White Plains, NY (city) Westchester County	548
Yonkers, NY (city) Westchester County	513

Colombians 25 Years and Over Who are High School Graduates
Top 10 Places Sorted by Percent

Place	Percent
Oyster Bay, NY (town) Nassau County	84.61
Long Beach, NY (city) Nassau County	83.51
Babylon, NY (town) Suffolk County	80.41
Greenburgh, NY (town) Westchester County	79.32
Hempstead, NY (town) Nassau County	77.37
Brookhaven, NY (town) Suffolk County	76.75
Huntington, NY (town) Suffolk County	74.8
North Hempstead, NY (town) Nassau County	73.9
Mineola, NY (village) Nassau County	73.8
Rye, NY (town) Westchester County	68.7

Costa Ricans 25 Years and Over Who are High School Graduates
Top 10 Places Sorted by Number

Place	Number
New York, NY (city)	2,791
Hempstead, NY (town) Nassau County	15

Costa Ricans 25 Years and Over Who are High School Graduates
Top 10 Places Sorted by Percent

Place	Percent
New York, NY (city)	73.3
Hempstead, NY (town) Nassau County	63.8

Cubans 25 Years and Over Who are High School Graduates
Top 10 Places Sorted by Number

Place	Number
New York, NY (city)	20,89
Hempstead, NY (town) Nassau County	1,72
Brookhaven, NY (town) Suffolk County	66
Islip, NY (town) Suffolk County	63
Yonkers, NY (city) Westchester County	60
Rochester, NY (city) Monroe County	52
Oyster Bay, NY (town) Nassau County	41
Babylon, NY (town) Suffolk County	31
Greenburgh, NY (town) Westchester County	29
Clarks, NY (town) Rockland County	23

Cubans 25 Years and Over Who are High School Graduates
Top 10 Places Sorted by Percent

Place	Percent
North Hempstead, NY (town) Nassau County	95.
Brookhaven, NY (town) Suffolk County	83.6
Oyster Bay, NY (town) Nassau County	83.
Babylon, NY (town) Suffolk County	80.
Hempstead, NY (town) Nassau County	80.
Islip, NY (town) Suffolk County	80.
Clarks, NY (town) Rockland County	79.
Greenburgh, NY (town) Westchester County	78.
Syracuse, NY (city) Onondaga County	74.

Notes: Please refer to the User's Guide for an explanation of data; tables include places with populations > 9,999 and reflect only those areas that meet Summary File 4 population thresholds, therefore there may be less than 10 places listed

PROFILES OF NEW YORK / Hispanic: Rankings

Rochester, NY (city) Monroe County — 65.55

Dominicans 25 Years and Over Who are High School Graduates
Top 10 Places Sorted by Number

Place	Number
New York, NY (city)	114,882
Yonkers, NY (city) Westchester County	2,831
Hempstead, NY (town) Nassau County	2,227
Islip, NY (town) Suffolk County	1,570
Haverstraw, NY (town) Rockland County	958
Brentwood, NY (cdp) Suffolk County	792
Freeport, NY (village) Nassau County	662
Babylon, NY (town) Suffolk County	603
Haverstraw, NY (village) Rockland County	560
Brookhaven, NY (town) Suffolk County	472

Dominicans 25 Years and Over Who are High School Graduates
Top 10 Places Sorted by Percent

Place	Percent
Buffalo, NY (city) Erie County	90.78
Albany, NY (city) Albany County	86.89
Oyster Bay, NY (town) Nassau County	75.52
North Hempstead, NY (town) Nassau County	71.61
Huntington, NY (town) Suffolk County	68.13
Mount Vernon, NY (city) Westchester County	64.64
Yonkers, NY (city) Westchester County	62.07
Central Islip, NY (cdp) Suffolk County	60.87
Islip, NY (town) Suffolk County	59.74
Brentwood, NY (cdp) Suffolk County	58.36

Ecuadorians 25 Years and Over Who are High School Graduates
Top 10 Places Sorted by Number

Place	Number
New York, NY (city)	38,322
Hempstead, NY (town) Nassau County	1,242
Yonkers, NY (city) Westchester County	745
Islip, NY (town) Suffolk County	696
Brookhaven, NY (town) Suffolk County	671
North Hempstead, NY (town) Nassau County	531
Rye, NY (town) Westchester County	327
Port Chester, NY (village) Westchester County	318
Ossining, NY (town) Westchester County	317
Ossining, NY (village) Westchester County	317

Ecuadorians 25 Years and Over Who are High School Graduates
Top 10 Places Sorted by Percent

Place	Percent
Oyster Bay, NY (town) Nassau County	83.38
Hempstead, NY (town) Nassau County	79.77
Brentwood, NY (cdp) Suffolk County	76.07
North Hempstead, NY (town) Nassau County	74.47
Babylon, NY (town) Suffolk County	70.23
Central Islip, NY (cdp) Suffolk County	68.45
Islip, NY (town) Suffolk County	66.86
Greenburgh, NY (town) Westchester County	66.79
Yonkers, NY (city) Westchester County	60.23
Brookhaven, NY (town) Suffolk County	59.38

Guatelmalans 25 Years and Over Who are High School Graduates
Top 10 Places Sorted by Number

Place	Number
New York, NY (city)	4,243
Hempstead, NY (town) Nassau County	580
Islip, NY (town) Suffolk County	313
North Hempstead, NY (town) Nassau County	248
Rye, NY (town) Westchester County	205
Ramapo, NY (town) Rockland County	188
Port Chester, NY (village) Westchester County	163
Babylon, NY (town) Suffolk County	140
Brentwood, NY (cdp) Suffolk County	137
Mamaroneck, NY (village) Westchester County	130

Guatelmalans 25 Years and Over Who are High School Graduates
Top 10 Places Sorted by Percent

Place	Percent
Babylon, NY (town) Suffolk County	61.67
Brookhaven, NY (town) Suffolk County	56.74
Hempstead, NY (town) Nassau County	55.98
North Hempstead, NY (town) Nassau County	54.75
Islip, NY (town) Suffolk County	49.21
Brentwood, NY (cdp) Suffolk County	42.95
New York, NY (city)	42.37
Mamaroneck, NY (village) Westchester County	41.53
Huntington, NY (town) Suffolk County	41.20
Freeport, NY (village) Nassau County	36.86

Hondurans 25 Years and Over Who are High School Graduates
Top 10 Places Sorted by Number

Place	Number
New York, NY (city)	8,525
Hempstead, NY (town) Nassau County	415
Islip, NY (town) Suffolk County	262
Yonkers, NY (city) Westchester County	248
Hempstead, NY (village) Nassau County	213
Babylon, NY (town) Suffolk County	200
Newburgh, NY (city) Orange County	148
North Hempstead, NY (town) Nassau County	127
Brentwood, NY (cdp) Suffolk County	123
Huntington, NY (town) Suffolk County	81

Hondurans 25 Years and Over Who are High School Graduates
Top 10 Places Sorted by Percent

Place	Percent
Babylon, NY (town) Suffolk County	63.49
New York, NY (city)	48.04
Islip, NY (town) Suffolk County	42.19
Newburgh, NY (city) Orange County	40.55
Yonkers, NY (city) Westchester County	39.43
Brentwood, NY (cdp) Suffolk County	38.56
North Hempstead, NY (town) Nassau County	32.07
Huntington, NY (town) Suffolk County	28.83
Hempstead, NY (town) Nassau County	28.31
Hempstead, NY (village) Nassau County	23.30

Mexicans 25 Years and Over Who are High School Graduates
Top 10 Places Sorted by Number

Place	Number
New York, NY (city)	34,207
Yonkers, NY (city) Westchester County	1,094
New Rochelle, NY (city) Westchester County	962
Hempstead, NY (town) Nassau County	894
White Plains, NY (city) Westchester County	678
Brookhaven, NY (town) Suffolk County	645
Rye, NY (town) Westchester County	623
Buffalo, NY (city) Erie County	596
Port Chester, NY (village) Westchester County	585
Newburgh, NY (city) Orange County	575

Mexicans 25 Years and Over Who are High School Graduates
Top 10 Places Sorted by Percent

Place	Percent
Fort Drum, NY (cdp) Jefferson County	100.00
Le Ray, NY (town) Jefferson County	99.49
Buffalo, NY (city) Erie County	78.52
Rochester, NY (city) Monroe County	75.04
Syracuse, NY (city) Onondaga County	71.53
Brookhaven, NY (town) Suffolk County	67.97
Huntington, NY (town) Suffolk County	65.84
Babylon, NY (town) Suffolk County	65.65
Hempstead, NY (town) Nassau County	62.39
Greenburgh, NY (town) Westchester County	57.76

Nicaraguans 25 Years and Over Who are High School Graduates
Top 10 Places Sorted by Number

Place	Number
New York, NY (city)	2,445
Yonkers, NY (city) Westchester County	200

Nicaraguans 25 Years and Over Who are High School Graduates
Top 10 Places Sorted by Percent

Place	Percent
Yonkers, NY (city) Westchester County	55.56
New York, NY (city)	51.10

Panamanians 25 Years and Over Who are High School Graduates
Top 10 Places Sorted by Number

Place	Number
New York, NY (city)	10,649
Hempstead, NY (town) Nassau County	368
Islip, NY (town) Suffolk County	240

Panamanians 25 Years and Over Who are High School Graduates
Top 10 Places Sorted by Percent

Place	Percent
Islip, NY (town) Suffolk County	97.56
Hempstead, NY (town) Nassau County	91.09
New York, NY (city)	78.32

Paraguayans 25 Years and Over Who are High School Graduates
Top 10 Places Sorted by Number

Place	Number
New York, NY (city)	559

Paraguayans 25 Years and Over Who are High School Graduates
Top 10 Places Sorted by Percent

Place	Percent
New York, NY (city)	56.41

Peruvians 25 Years and Over Who are High School Graduates
Top 10 Places Sorted by Number

Place	Number
New York, NY (city)	13,096
Hempstead, NY (town) Nassau County	1,106
Islip, NY (town) Suffolk County	749
White Plains, NY (city) Westchester County	528
Rye, NY (town) Westchester County	451
Glen Cove, NY (city) Nassau County	435
Port Chester, NY (village) Westchester County	399
New Rochelle, NY (city) Westchester County	375
Oyster Bay, NY (town) Nassau County	372
Brookhaven, NY (town) Suffolk County	328

Peruvians 25 Years and Over Who are High School Graduates
Top 10 Places Sorted by Percent

Place	Percent
Islip, NY (town) Suffolk County	87.19
Glen Cove, NY (city) Nassau County	85.13
Hempstead, NY (town) Nassau County	85.01

Notes: Please refer to the User's Guide for an explanation of data; tables include places with populations > 9,999 and reflect only those areas that meet Summary File 4 population thresholds, therefore there may be less than 10 places listed

PROFILES OF NEW YORK / Hispanic: Rankings

Place	Percent
North Hempstead, NY (town) Nassau County	83.97
Brentwood, NY (cdp) Suffolk County	82.56
Brookhaven, NY (town) Suffolk County	81.80
Oyster Bay, NY (town) Nassau County	79.49
New York, NY (city)	77.03
New Rochelle, NY (city) Westchester County	75.45
Yonkers, NY (city) Westchester County	74.08

Puerto Ricans 25 Years and Over Who are High School Graduates
Top 10 Places Sorted by Number

Place	Number
New York, NY (city)	252,164
Islip, NY (town) Suffolk County	8,940
Hempstead, NY (town) Nassau County	7,300
Brookhaven, NY (town) Suffolk County	7,207
Yonkers, NY (city) Westchester County	6,473
Rochester, NY (city) Monroe County	4,974
Buffalo, NY (city) Erie County	4,071
Brentwood, NY (cdp) Suffolk County	2,911
Babylon, NY (town) Suffolk County	2,755
Oyster Bay, NY (town) Nassau County	2,019

Puerto Ricans 25 Years and Over Who are High School Graduates
Top 10 Places Sorted by Percent

Place	Percent
Jefferson Valley-Yorktown, NY (cdp) Westchester County	96.89
North Massapequa, NY (cdp) Nassau County	94.33
Poughkeepsie, NY (town) Dutchess County	94.21
Commack, NY (cdp) Suffolk County	94.04
Holtsville, NY (cdp) Suffolk County	93.92
Stony Point, NY (town) Rockland County	93.82
Holbrook, NY (cdp) Suffolk County	93.33
Eastchester, NY (town) Westchester County	92.40
Dix Hills, NY (cdp) Suffolk County	91.70
York, NY (town) Westchester County	90.57

Salvadorans 25 Years and Over Who are High School Graduates
Top 10 Places Sorted by Number

Place	Number
New York, NY (city)	7,003
Hempstead, NY (town) Nassau County	2,964
Islip, NY (town) Suffolk County	1,931
Brentwood, NY (cdp) Suffolk County	1,153
North Hempstead, NY (town) Nassau County	1,075
Hempstead, NY (village) Nassau County	957
Babylon, NY (town) Suffolk County	518
Yonkers, NY (city) Westchester County	500
Huntington, NY (town) Suffolk County	475
Oyster Bay, NY (town) Nassau County	445

Salvadorans 25 Years and Over Who are High School Graduates
Top 10 Places Sorted by Percent

Place	Percent
Valley Stream, NY (village) Nassau County	57.09
Elmont, NY (cdp) Nassau County	48.89
Mineola, NY (village) Nassau County	47.09
New York, NY (city)	44.59
Yonkers, NY (city) Westchester County	43.33
North Hempstead, NY (town) Nassau County	38.48
Hicksville, NY (cdp) Nassau County	37.37
Oyster Bay, NY (town) Nassau County	35.80
Brookhaven, NY (town) Suffolk County	34.65
Babylon, NY (town) Suffolk County	33.59

South Americans 25 Years and Over Who are High School Graduates
Top 10 Places Sorted by Number

Place	Number
New York, NY (city)	107,193
Hempstead, NY (town) Nassau County	6,194
Islip, NY (town) Suffolk County	3,448
North Hempstead, NY (town) Nassau County	2,262
Brookhaven, NY (town) Suffolk County	2,149
Yonkers, NY (city) Westchester County	1,995
Oyster Bay, NY (town) Nassau County	1,916
White Plains, NY (city) Westchester County	1,568
Rye, NY (town) Westchester County	1,546
Brentwood, NY (cdp) Suffolk County	1,423

South Americans 25 Years and Over Who are High School Graduates
Top 10 Places Sorted by Percent

Place	Percent
Franklin Square, NY (cdp) Nassau County	96.68
Newburgh, NY (city) Orange County	89.55
Rochester, NY (city) Monroe County	88.17
Valley Stream, NY (village) Nassau County	88.02
Smith, NY (town) Suffolk County	87.40
Levittown, NY (cdp) Nassau County	86.08
Oceanside, NY (cdp) Nassau County	83.91
Oyster Bay, NY (town) Nassau County	83.09
Long Beach, NY (city) Nassau County	83.01
Buffalo, NY (city) Erie County	82.41

Spaniards 25 Years and Over Who are High School Graduates
Top 10 Places Sorted by Number

Place	Number
New York, NY (city)	4,876
Hempstead, NY (town) Nassau County	452
Brookhaven, NY (town) Suffolk County	228

Spaniards 25 Years and Over Who are High School Graduates
Top 10 Places Sorted by Percent

Place	Percent
Brookhaven, NY (town) Suffolk County	81.43
Hempstead, NY (town) Nassau County	81.29
New York, NY (city)	67.26

Uruguayans 25 Years and Over Who are High School Graduates
Top 10 Places Sorted by Number

Place	Number
New York, NY (city)	1,087

Uruguayans 25 Years and Over Who are High School Graduates
Top 10 Places Sorted by Percent

Place	Percent
New York, NY (city)	66.12

Venezuelans 25 Years and Over Who are High School Graduates
Top 10 Places Sorted by Number

Place	Number
New York, NY (city)	3,089

Venezuelans 25 Years and Over Who are High School Graduates
Top 10 Places Sorted by Percent

Place	Percent
New York, NY (city)	73.48

Other Hispanics 25 Years and Over Who are High School Graduates
Top 10 Places Sorted by Number

Place	Number
New York, NY (city)	92,381
Hempstead, NY (town) Nassau County	5,437
Islip, NY (town) Suffolk County	3,139
Brookhaven, NY (town) Suffolk County	2,096
Yonkers, NY (city) Westchester County	1,844
Oyster Bay, NY (town) Nassau County	1,248
Brentwood, NY (cdp) Suffolk County	1,209
North Hempstead, NY (town) Nassau County	1,156
Babylon, NY (town) Suffolk County	991
White Plains, NY (city) Westchester County	878

Other Hispanics 25 Years and Over Who are High School Graduates
Top 10 Places Sorted by Percent

Place	Percent
Amherst, NY (town) Erie County	100.00
Carmel, NY (town) Putnam County	95.11
Wallkill, NY (town) Orange County	93.62
Franklin Square, NY (cdp) Nassau County	92.27
Levittown, NY (cdp) Nassau County	84.15
Warwick, NY (town) Orange County	83.90
Cortlandt, NY (town) Westchester County	82.65
Smith, NY (town) Suffolk County	82.23
Holbrook, NY (cdp) Suffolk County	80.52
Medford, NY (cdp) Suffolk County	79.17

Educational Attainment: Four-Year College Graduates

Total Populations 25 Years and Over Who are Four-Year College Graduates
Top 10 Places Sorted by Number

Place	Number
New York, NY (city)	1,446,833
Hempstead, NY (town) Nassau County	158,382
Oyster Bay, NY (town) Nassau County	77,486
Brookhaven, NY (town) Suffolk County	71,086
North Hempstead, NY (town) Nassau County	70,292
Huntington, NY (town) Suffolk County	59,886
Islip, NY (town) Suffolk County	45,456
Amherst, NY (town) Erie County	37,146
Buffalo, NY (city) Erie County	33,436
Greenburgh, NY (town) Westchester County	32,946

Total Populations 25 Years and Over Who are Four-Year College Graduates
Top 10 Places Sorted by Percent

Place	Percent
Scarsdale, NY (village) Westchester County	79.5
New Castle, NY (town) Westchester County	75.9
Ithaca, NY (town) Tompkins County	71.1
Rye, NY (city) Westchester County	68.3
Lewisboro, NY (town) Westchester County	65.6
Pittsford, NY (town) Monroe County	65.3
Garden City, NY (village) Nassau County	61.8
Pelham, NY (town) Westchester County	58.6
Mamaroneck, NY (town) Westchester County	58.3
Ithaca, NY (city) Tompkins County	57.9

Hispanics 25 Years and Over Who are Four-Year College Graduates
Top 10 Places Sorted by Number

Place	Number
New York, NY (city)	130,946
Hempstead, NY (town) Nassau County	7,176
Yonkers, NY (city) Westchester County	3,576
Islip, NY (town) Suffolk County	3,246
Brookhaven, NY (town) Suffolk County	2,746
Oyster Bay, NY (town) Nassau County	2,006
North Hempstead, NY (town) Nassau County	1,966
Greenburgh, NY (town) Westchester County	1,566
Babylon, NY (town) Suffolk County	1,396
Buffalo, NY (city) Erie County	1,396

Notes: Please refer to the User's Guide for an explanation of data; tables include places with populations > 9,999 and reflect only those areas that meet Summary File 4 population thresholds, therefore there may be less than 10 places listed

Hispanics 25 Years and Over Who are Four-Year College Graduates
Top 10 Places Sorted by Percent

Place	Percent
Pittsford, NY (town) Monroe County	70.81
Dryden, NY (town) Tompkins County	68.42
Ithaca, NY (town) Tompkins County	64.94
Ithaca, NY (city) Tompkins County	61.66
Dobbs Ferry, NY (village) Westchester County	59.47
Clifton Park, NY (town) Saratoga County	57.89
Penfield, NY (town) Monroe County	53.58
Scarsdale, NY (village) Westchester County	52.00
Manlius, NY (town) Onondaga County	50.93
Somers, NY (town) Westchester County	50.46

Argentinians 25 Years and Over Who are Four-Year College Graduates
Top 10 Places Sorted by Number

Place	Number
New York, NY (city)	2,334
Hempstead, NY (town) Nassau County	181
North Hempstead, NY (town) Nassau County	176

Argentinians 25 Years and Over Who are Four-Year College Graduates
Top 10 Places Sorted by Percent

Place	Percent
North Hempstead, NY (town) Nassau County	48.09
New York, NY (city)	29.77
Hempstead, NY (town) Nassau County	28.28

Bolivians 25 Years and Over Who are Four-Year College Graduates
Top 10 Places Sorted by Number

Place	Number
New York, NY (city)	430

Bolivians 25 Years and Over Who are Four-Year College Graduates
Top 10 Places Sorted by Percent

Place	Percent
New York, NY (city)	19.88

Central Americans 25 Years and Over Who are Four-Year College Graduates
Top 10 Places Sorted by Number

Place	Number
New York, NY (city)	7,162
Hempstead, NY (town) Nassau County	808
Islip, NY (town) Suffolk County	376
North Hempstead, NY (town) Nassau County	261
Babylon, NY (town) Suffolk County	192
Yonkers, NY (city) Westchester County	188
Hempstead, NY (village) Nassau County	184
Brentwood, NY (cdp) Suffolk County	151
Freeport, NY (village) Nassau County	116
Huntington, NY (town) Suffolk County	104

Central Americans 25 Years and Over Who are Four-Year College Graduates
Top 10 Places Sorted by Percent

Place	Percent
Greenburgh, NY (town) Westchester County	33.50
Mamaroneck, NY (town) Westchester County	17.10
Mineola, NY (village) Nassau County	16.89
Mamaroneck, NY (village) Westchester County	14.36
Bay Shore, NY (cdp) Suffolk County	12.60
White Plains, NY (city) Westchester County	12.57
Mount Vernon, NY (city) Westchester County	11.79
Clarks, NY (town) Rockland County	11.68
Baldwin, NY (cdp) Nassau County	11.48
Levittown, NY (cdp) Nassau County	10.42

Chileans 25 Years and Over Who are Four-Year College Graduates
Top 10 Places Sorted by Number

Place	Number
New York, NY (city)	938
Hempstead, NY (town) Nassau County	100
North Hempstead, NY (town) Nassau County	56
Oyster Bay, NY (town) Nassau County	30

Chileans 25 Years and Over Who are Four-Year College Graduates
Top 10 Places Sorted by Percent

Place	Percent
Hempstead, NY (town) Nassau County	23.15
New York, NY (city)	21.84
North Hempstead, NY (town) Nassau County	13.21
Oyster Bay, NY (town) Nassau County	11.07

Colombians 25 Years and Over Who are Four-Year College Graduates
Top 10 Places Sorted by Number

Place	Number
New York, NY (city)	9,452
Hempstead, NY (town) Nassau County	736
Oyster Bay, NY (town) Nassau County	248
Islip, NY (town) Suffolk County	233
Brookhaven, NY (town) Suffolk County	175
Yonkers, NY (city) Westchester County	158
Babylon, NY (town) Suffolk County	107
North Hempstead, NY (town) Nassau County	107
White Plains, NY (city) Westchester County	102
Brentwood, NY (cdp) Suffolk County	101

Colombians 25 Years and Over Who are Four-Year College Graduates
Top 10 Places Sorted by Percent

Place	Percent
Oyster Bay, NY (town) Nassau County	32.63
Huntington, NY (town) Suffolk County	32.12
Long Beach, NY (city) Nassau County	25.61
Greenburgh, NY (town) Westchester County	24.86
Hempstead, NY (town) Nassau County	23.13
Brookhaven, NY (town) Suffolk County	21.53
Yonkers, NY (city) Westchester County	18.72
New York, NY (city)	16.94
Freeport, NY (village) Nassau County	16.47
Southampton, NY (town) Suffolk County	14.78

Costa Ricans 25 Years and Over Who are Four-Year College Graduates
Top 10 Places Sorted by Number

Place	Number
New York, NY (city)	630
Hempstead, NY (town) Nassau County	37

Costa Ricans 25 Years and Over Who are Four-Year College Graduates
Top 10 Places Sorted by Percent

Place	Percent
New York, NY (city)	16.51
Hempstead, NY (town) Nassau County	15.04

Cubans 25 Years and Over Who are Four-Year College Graduates
Top 10 Places Sorted by Number

Place	Number
New York, NY (city)	7,277
Hempstead, NY (town) Nassau County	525
Brookhaven, NY (town) Suffolk County	271
Yonkers, NY (city) Westchester County	222
Islip, NY (town) Suffolk County	166
Greenburgh, NY (town) Westchester County	164
Rochester, NY (city) Monroe County	161
North Hempstead, NY (town) Nassau County	157
Oyster Bay, NY (town) Nassau County	147
Clarks, NY (town) Rockland County	143

Cubans 25 Years and Over Who are Four-Year College Graduates
Top 10 Places Sorted by Percent

Place	Percent
North Hempstead, NY (town) Nassau County	67.97
Clarks, NY (town) Rockland County	48.47
Greenburgh, NY (town) Westchester County	43.73
Brookhaven, NY (town) Suffolk County	33.92
Syracuse, NY (city) Onondaga County	32.23
Oyster Bay, NY (town) Nassau County	29.40
Hempstead, NY (town) Nassau County	24.56
Yonkers, NY (city) Westchester County	23.57
New York, NY (city)	21.85
Islip, NY (town) Suffolk County	20.99

Dominicans 25 Years and Over Who are Four-Year College Graduates
Top 10 Places Sorted by Number

Place	Number
New York, NY (city)	21,824
Yonkers, NY (city) Westchester County	620
Hempstead, NY (town) Nassau County	538
Islip, NY (town) Suffolk County	223
Haverstraw, NY (town) Rockland County	169
Mount Vernon, NY (city) Westchester County	152
North Hempstead, NY (town) Nassau County	147
Greenburgh, NY (town) Westchester County	131
Brentwood, NY (cdp) Suffolk County	123
Brookhaven, NY (town) Suffolk County	118

Dominicans 25 Years and Over Who are Four-Year College Graduates
Top 10 Places Sorted by Percent

Place	Percent
Albany, NY (city) Albany County	32.79
North Hempstead, NY (town) Nassau County	31.61
Greenburgh, NY (town) Westchester County	31.57
Mount Vernon, NY (city) Westchester County	27.99
Buffalo, NY (city) Erie County	26.70
Huntington, NY (town) Suffolk County	25.00
Ossining, NY (town) Westchester County	24.83
Rye, NY (town) Westchester County	23.92
Port Chester, NY (village) Westchester County	21.53
Valley Stream, NY (village) Nassau County	19.50

Ecuadorians 25 Years and Over Who are Four-Year College Graduates
Top 10 Places Sorted by Number

Place	Number
New York, NY (city)	6,474
Hempstead, NY (town) Nassau County	327
Yonkers, NY (city) Westchester County	175
Oyster Bay, NY (town) Nassau County	117
North Hempstead, NY (town) Nassau County	110
Islip, NY (town) Suffolk County	106
Greenburgh, NY (town) Westchester County	96
Brookhaven, NY (town) Suffolk County	71
Babylon, NY (town) Suffolk County	55
East Hampton, NY (town) Suffolk County	55

Ecuadorians 25 Years and Over Who are Four-Year College Graduates
Top 10 Places Sorted by Percent

Place	Percent
Greenburgh, NY (town) Westchester County	35.04

Notes: Please refer to the User's Guide for an explanation of data; tables include places with populations > 9,999 and reflect only those areas that meet Summary File 4 population thresholds, therefore there may be less than 10 places listed

PROFILES OF NEW YORK / Hispanic: Rankings

Place	
Oyster Bay, NY (town) Nassau County	31.88
Hempstead, NY (town) Nassau County	21.00
North Hempstead, NY (town) Nassau County	15.43
Yonkers, NY (city) Westchester County	14.15
Babylon, NY (town) Suffolk County	13.99
East Hampton, NY (town) Suffolk County	13.35
Central Islip, NY (cdp) Suffolk County	13.25
Brentwood, NY (cdp) Suffolk County	12.88
Peekskill, NY (city) Westchester County	11.47

Guatelmalans 25 Years and Over Who are Four-Year College Graduates
Top 10 Places Sorted by Number

Place	Number
New York, NY (city)	696
Hempstead, NY (town) Nassau County	134
North Hempstead, NY (town) Nassau County	69
Islip, NY (town) Suffolk County	63
Mamaroneck, NY (village) Westchester County	58
Babylon, NY (town) Suffolk County	51
Mamaroneck, NY (town) Westchester County	42
Rye, NY (town) Westchester County	35
Brookhaven, NY (town) Suffolk County	22
Huntington, NY (town) Suffolk County	19

Guatelmalans 25 Years and Over Who are Four-Year College Graduates
Top 10 Places Sorted by Percent

Place	Percent
Babylon, NY (town) Suffolk County	22.47
Mamaroneck, NY (village) Westchester County	18.53
Mamaroneck, NY (town) Westchester County	17.14
North Hempstead, NY (town) Nassau County	15.23
Hempstead, NY (town) Nassau County	12.93
Brookhaven, NY (town) Suffolk County	10.23
Islip, NY (town) Suffolk County	9.91
Huntington, NY (town) Suffolk County	8.80
New York, NY (city)	6.95
Freeport, NY (village) Nassau County	6.20

Hondurans 25 Years and Over Who are Four-Year College Graduates
Top 10 Places Sorted by Number

Place	Number
New York, NY (city)	1,448
Hempstead, NY (town) Nassau County	88
Yonkers, NY (city) Westchester County	58
Islip, NY (town) Suffolk County	35
Hempstead, NY (village) Nassau County	30
Newburgh, NY (city) Orange County	27
Babylon, NY (town) Suffolk County	22
Brentwood, NY (cdp) Suffolk County	19
North Hempstead, NY (town) Nassau County	12
Huntington, NY (town) Suffolk County	9

Hondurans 25 Years and Over Who are Four-Year College Graduates
Top 10 Places Sorted by Percent

Place	Percent
Yonkers, NY (city) Westchester County	9.22
New York, NY (city)	8.16
Newburgh, NY (city) Orange County	7.40
Babylon, NY (town) Suffolk County	6.98
Hempstead, NY (town) Nassau County	6.00
Brentwood, NY (cdp) Suffolk County	5.96
Islip, NY (town) Suffolk County	5.64
Hempstead, NY (village) Nassau County	3.28
Huntington, NY (town) Suffolk County	3.20
North Hempstead, NY (town) Nassau County	3.03

Mexicans 25 Years and Over Who are Four-Year College Graduates
Top 10 Places Sorted by Number

Place	Number
New York, NY (city)	7,693
Hempstead, NY (town) Nassau County	235
Greenburgh, NY (town) Westchester County	201
Yonkers, NY (city) Westchester County	178
New Rochelle, NY (city) Westchester County	175
Brookhaven, NY (town) Suffolk County	172
Rochester, NY (city) Monroe County	162
Buffalo, NY (city) Erie County	154
North Hempstead, NY (town) Nassau County	116
Clarks, NY (town) Rockland County	73

Mexicans 25 Years and Over Who are Four-Year College Graduates
Top 10 Places Sorted by Percent

Place	Percent
Greenburgh, NY (town) Westchester County	31.21
Rochester, NY (city) Monroe County	28.67
Clarks, NY (town) Rockland County	20.86
Buffalo, NY (city) Erie County	20.29
Brookhaven, NY (town) Suffolk County	18.12
Syracuse, NY (city) Onondaga County	17.29
Huntington, NY (town) Suffolk County	16.96
Babylon, NY (town) Suffolk County	16.71
Hempstead, NY (town) Nassau County	16.40
Le Ray, NY (town) Jefferson County	12.24

Nicaraguans 25 Years and Over Who are Four-Year College Graduates
Top 10 Places Sorted by Number

Place	Number
New York, NY (city)	545
Yonkers, NY (city) Westchester County	31

Nicaraguans 25 Years and Over Who are Four-Year College Graduates
Top 10 Places Sorted by Percent

Place	Percent
New York, NY (city)	11.39
Yonkers, NY (city) Westchester County	8.61

Panamanians 25 Years and Over Who are Four-Year College Graduates
Top 10 Places Sorted by Number

Place	Number
New York, NY (city)	2,358
Hempstead, NY (town) Nassau County	157
Islip, NY (town) Suffolk County	60

Panamanians 25 Years and Over Who are Four-Year College Graduates
Top 10 Places Sorted by Percent

Place	Percent
Hempstead, NY (town) Nassau County	38.86
Islip, NY (town) Suffolk County	24.39
New York, NY (city)	17.34

Paraguayans 25 Years and Over Who are Four-Year College Graduates
Top 10 Places Sorted by Number

Place	Number
New York, NY (city)	44

Paraguayans 25 Years and Over Who are Four-Year College Graduates
Top 10 Places Sorted by Percent

Place	Percent
New York, NY (city)	4.44

Peruvians 25 Years and Over Who are Four-Year College Graduates
Top 10 Places Sorted by Number

Place	Number
New York, NY (city)	3,104
Hempstead, NY (town) Nassau County	254
Islip, NY (town) Suffolk County	138
New Rochelle, NY (city) Westchester County	124
White Plains, NY (city) Westchester County	123
Rye, NY (town) Westchester County	106
North Hempstead, NY (town) Nassau County	105
Oyster Bay, NY (town) Nassau County	99
Brookhaven, NY (town) Suffolk County	93
Glen Cove, NY (city) Nassau County	91

Peruvians 25 Years and Over Who are Four-Year College Graduates
Top 10 Places Sorted by Percent

Place	Percent
North Hempstead, NY (town) Nassau County	28.5
New Rochelle, NY (city) Westchester County	24.9
Brookhaven, NY (town) Suffolk County	23.1
Yonkers, NY (city) Westchester County	22.7
Oyster Bay, NY (town) Nassau County	21.1
Hempstead, NY (town) Nassau County	19.5
New York, NY (city)	18.2
Glen Cove, NY (city) Nassau County	17.8
Islip, NY (town) Suffolk County	16.0
Rye, NY (town) Westchester County	15.7

Puerto Ricans 25 Years and Over Who are Four-Year College Graduates
Top 10 Places Sorted by Number

Place	Number
New York, NY (city)	40,30
Hempstead, NY (town) Nassau County	1,67
Yonkers, NY (city) Westchester County	1,34
Islip, NY (town) Suffolk County	1,21
Brookhaven, NY (town) Suffolk County	1,12
Buffalo, NY (city) Erie County	67
Oyster Bay, NY (town) Nassau County	56
Rochester, NY (city) Monroe County	47
Huntington, NY (town) Suffolk County	46
Clarks, NY (town) Rockland County	46

Puerto Ricans 25 Years and Over Who are Four-Year College Graduates
Top 10 Places Sorted by Percent

Place	Percent
Webster, NY (town) Monroe County	39.5
Rockville Centre, NY (village) Nassau County	38.5
Greenburgh, NY (town) Westchester County	37.2
Commack, NY (cdp) Suffolk County	36.7
New City, NY (cdp) Rockland County	36.4
Mount Pleasant, NY (town) Westchester County	35.0
Clarks, NY (town) Rockland County	33.5
East Fishkill, NY (town) Dutchess County	33.4
Mamaroneck, NY (town) Westchester County	33.3
Union, NY (town) Broome County	32.7

Salvadorans 25 Years and Over Who are Four-Year College Graduates
Top 10 Places Sorted by Number

Place	Number
New York, NY (city)	1,1
Hempstead, NY (town) Nassau County	3

Notes: Please refer to the User's Guide for an explanation of data; tables include places with populations > 9,999 and reflect only those areas that meet Summary File 4 population thresholds, therefore there may be less than 10 places listed

PROFILES OF NEW YORK / Hispanic: Rankings

Place	Number
lip, NY (town) Suffolk County	161
orth Hempstead, NY (town) Nassau County	160
empstead, NY (village) Nassau County	137
abylon, NY (town) Suffolk County	78
rentwood, NY (cdp) Suffolk County	74
ineola, NY (village) Nassau County	67
reeport, NY (village) Nassau County	58
untington, NY (town) Suffolk County	54

Salvadorans 25 Years and Over Who are Four-Year College Graduates
Top 10 Places Sorted by Percent

Place	Percent
ineola, NY (village) Nassau County	18.56
alley Stream, NY (village) Nassau County	7.48
ew York, NY (city)	7.28
yandanch, NY (cdp) Suffolk County	5.75
orth Hempstead, NY (town) Nassau County	5.73
cksville, NY (cdp) Nassau County	5.45
ookhaven, NY (town) Suffolk County	5.09
abylon, NY (town) Suffolk County	5.06
en Cove, NY (city) Nassau County	4.47
orth Bay Shore, NY (cdp) Suffolk County	4.08

South Americans 25 Years and Over Who are Four-Year College Graduates
Top 10 Places Sorted by Number

Place	Number
ew York, NY (city)	25,539
mpstead, NY (town) Nassau County	1,819
yster Bay, NY (town) Nassau County	612
rth Hempstead, NY (town) Nassau County	605
nkers, NY (city) Westchester County	587
ip, NY (town) Suffolk County	579
ookhaven, NY (town) Suffolk County	538
eenburgh, NY (town) Westchester County	346
hite Plains, NY (city) Westchester County	328
e, NY (town) Westchester County	319

South Americans 25 Years and Over Who are Four-Year College Graduates
Top 10 Places Sorted by Percent

Place	Percent
ffalo, NY (city) Erie County	61.03
chester, NY (city) Monroe County	48.52
er Park, NY (cdp) Suffolk County	33.33
vittown, NY (cdp) Nassau County	30.93
rrison, NY (village) Westchester County	29.80
eenburgh, NY (town) Westchester County	29.65
ram, NY (cdp) Suffolk County	28.31
maroneck, NY (village) Westchester County	28.30
cksville, NY (cdp) Nassau County	28.11
lley Stream, NY (village) Nassau County	27.95

Spaniards 25 Years and Over Who are Four-Year College Graduates
Top 10 Places Sorted by Number

Place	Number
w York, NY (city)	2,033
mpstead, NY (town) Nassau County	141
ookhaven, NY (town) Suffolk County	66

Spaniards 25 Years and Over Who are Four-Year College Graduates
Top 10 Places Sorted by Percent

Place	Percent
w York, NY (city)	28.05
mpstead, NY (town) Nassau County	25.36
ookhaven, NY (town) Suffolk County	23.57

Uruguayans 25 Years and Over Who are Four-Year College Graduates
Top 10 Places Sorted by Number

Place	Number
New York, NY (city)	331

Uruguayans 25 Years and Over Who are Four-Year College Graduates
Top 10 Places Sorted by Percent

Place	Percent
New York, NY (city)	20.13

Venezuelans 25 Years and Over Who are Four-Year College Graduates
Top 10 Places Sorted by Number

Place	Number
New York, NY (city)	1,424

Venezuelans 25 Years and Over Who are Four-Year College Graduates
Top 10 Places Sorted by Percent

Place	Percent
New York, NY (city)	33.87

Other Hispanics 25 Years and Over Who are Four-Year College Graduates
Top 10 Places Sorted by Number

Place	Number
New York, NY (city)	19,114
Hempstead, NY (town) Nassau County	1,438
Islip, NY (town) Suffolk County	558
Yonkers, NY (city) Westchester County	403
Oyster Bay, NY (town) Nassau County	402
Brookhaven, NY (town) Suffolk County	389
North Hempstead, NY (town) Nassau County	300
Babylon, NY (town) Suffolk County	227
Brentwood, NY (cdp) Suffolk County	205
Greenburgh, NY (town) Westchester County	195

Other Hispanics 25 Years and Over Who are Four-Year College Graduates
Top 10 Places Sorted by Percent

Place	Percent
Amherst, NY (town) Erie County	67.12
Mamaroneck, NY (town) Westchester County	47.93
Albany, NY (city) Albany County	37.27
Franklin Square, NY (cdp) Nassau County	35.36
Cortlandt, NY (town) Westchester County	26.48
Valley Stream, NY (village) Nassau County	25.87
Elmont, NY (cdp) Nassau County	25.16
Smith, NY (town) Suffolk County	24.64
Greenburgh, NY (town) Westchester County	24.50
Oyster Bay, NY (town) Nassau County	24.09

Median Household Income

Total Population
Top 10 Places Sorted by Number

Place	Dollars
Scarsdale, NY (village) Westchester County	182,792
New Castle, NY (town) Westchester County	159,691
North Castle, NY (town) Westchester County	117,815
Lewisboro, NY (town) Westchester County	112,462
Rye, NY (city) Westchester County	110,894
Garden City, NY (village) Nassau County	104,176
Dix Hills, NY (cdp) Suffolk County	104,160
Bedford, NY (town) Westchester County	100,053
Woodmere, NY (cdp) Nassau County	93,212
Merrick, NY (cdp) Nassau County	93,132

Hispanic
Top 10 Places Sorted by Number

Place	Dollars
Lewisboro, NY (town) Westchester County	186,643
Scarsdale, NY (village) Westchester County	154,916
Merrick, NY (cdp) Nassau County	106,276
Somers, NY (town) Westchester County	105,569
Jefferson Valley-Yorktown, NY (cdp) Westchester County	99,802
York, NY (town) Westchester County	96,112
Garden City, NY (village) Nassau County	95,372
Kings Park, NY (cdp) Suffolk County	94,270
Pittsford, NY (town) Monroe County	91,642
Farmingville, NY (cdp) Suffolk County	91,501

Argentinian
Top 10 Places Sorted by Number

Place	Dollars
North Hempstead, NY (town) Nassau County	61,250
Hempstead, NY (town) Nassau County	54,875
New York, NY (city)	43,045

Bolivian
Top 10 Places Sorted by Number

Place	Dollars
New York, NY (city)	40,911

Central American
Top 10 Places Sorted by Number

Place	Dollars
Copiague, NY (cdp) Suffolk County	71,250
New Cassel, NY (cdp) Nassau County	69,188
Greenburgh, NY (town) Westchester County	66,458
Valley Stream, NY (village) Nassau County	65,500
Mineola, NY (village) Nassau County	62,540
Port Washington, NY (cdp) Nassau County	61,635
Levittown, NY (cdp) Nassau County	60,156
Hicksville, NY (cdp) Nassau County	59,063
Central Islip, NY (cdp) Suffolk County	58,804
Brentwood, NY (cdp) Suffolk County	58,295

Chilean
Top 10 Places Sorted by Number

Place	Dollars
North Hempstead, NY (town) Nassau County	50,227
Hempstead, NY (town) Nassau County	49,875
New York, NY (city)	38,262
Oyster Bay, NY (town) Nassau County	36,579

Colombian
Top 10 Places Sorted by Number

Place	Dollars
Huntington, NY (town) Suffolk County	81,577
Oyster Bay, NY (town) Nassau County	67,596
Brentwood, NY (cdp) Suffolk County	65,529
Islip, NY (town) Suffolk County	64,886
Hempstead, NY (town) Nassau County	61,957
Greenburgh, NY (town) Westchester County	59,659
North Hempstead, NY (town) Nassau County	58,125
Brookhaven, NY (town) Suffolk County	57,321
Freeport, NY (village) Nassau County	48,382
Babylon, NY (town) Suffolk County	46,842

Costa Rican
Top 10 Places Sorted by Number

Place	Dollars
Hempstead, NY (town) Nassau County	56,979
New York, NY (city)	32,149

Notes: Please refer to the User's Guide for an explanation of data; tables include places with populations > 9,999 and reflect only those areas that meet Summary File 4 population thresholds, therefore there may be less than 10 places listed

Cuban
Top 10 Places Sorted by Number

Place	Dollars
Oyster Bay, NY (town) Nassau County	93,673
Clarks, NY (town) Rockland County	86,916
North Hempstead, NY (town) Nassau County	86,305
Greenburgh, NY (town) Westchester County	68,917
Brookhaven, NY (town) Suffolk County	68,654
Babylon, NY (town) Suffolk County	68,250
Islip, NY (town) Suffolk County	59,732
Hempstead, NY (town) Nassau County	57,917
Yonkers, NY (city) Westchester County	32,292
New York, NY (city)	31,480

Dominican
Top 10 Places Sorted by Number

Place	Dollars
Huntington, NY (town) Suffolk County	101,706
Oyster Bay, NY (town) Nassau County	100,557
Brentwood, NY (cdp) Suffolk County	60,682
Central Islip, NY (cdp) Suffolk County	59,583
North Hempstead, NY (town) Nassau County	58,214
Copiague, NY (cdp) Suffolk County	57,875
Babylon, NY (town) Suffolk County	56,436
Valley Stream, NY (village) Nassau County	55,313
Brookhaven, NY (town) Suffolk County	51,875
Rye, NY (town) Westchester County	51,595

Ecuadorian
Top 10 Places Sorted by Number

Place	Dollars
Central Islip, NY (cdp) Suffolk County	90,818
Oyster Bay, NY (town) Nassau County	87,336
Patchogue, NY (village) Suffolk County	78,207
Brookhaven, NY (town) Suffolk County	75,685
North Hempstead, NY (town) Nassau County	63,611
Hempstead, NY (town) Nassau County	60,263
Islip, NY (town) Suffolk County	51,394
Bay Shore, NY (cdp) Suffolk County	50,469
Ossining, NY (town) Westchester County	50,212
Ossining, NY (village) Westchester County	50,212

Guatelmalan
Top 10 Places Sorted by Number

Place	Dollars
Brentwood, NY (cdp) Suffolk County	64,000
Babylon, NY (town) Suffolk County	57,656
Freeport, NY (village) Nassau County	53,043
Islip, NY (town) Suffolk County	52,438
Hempstead, NY (town) Nassau County	49,015
Southeast, NY (town) Putnam County	47,404
Huntington, NY (town) Suffolk County	46,528
Spring Valley, NY (village) Rockland County	45,772
Mamaroneck, NY (village) Westchester County	44,113
Ramapo, NY (town) Rockland County	43,750

Honduran
Top 10 Places Sorted by Number

Place	Dollars
Brentwood, NY (cdp) Suffolk County	68,553
Huntington, NY (town) Suffolk County	64,583
Islip, NY (town) Suffolk County	63,462
Hempstead, NY (village) Nassau County	52,917
Babylon, NY (town) Suffolk County	51,058
North Hempstead, NY (town) Nassau County	45,521
Hempstead, NY (town) Nassau County	44,125
Newburgh, NY (city) Orange County	35,903
Yonkers, NY (city) Westchester County	35,529
New York, NY (city)	30,477

Mexican
Top 10 Places Sorted by Number

Place	Dollars
Greenburgh, NY (town) Westchester County	76,909
New Cassel, NY (cdp) Nassau County	60,556
Brentwood, NY (cdp) Suffolk County	55,250
Islip, NY (town) Suffolk County	55,144
Brookhaven, NY (town) Suffolk County	53,542
Clarks, NY (town) Rockland County	52,813
Haverstraw, NY (town) Rockland County	51,932
North Hempstead, NY (town) Nassau County	50,515
Babylon, NY (town) Suffolk County	50,278
Hempstead, NY (town) Nassau County	49,091

Nicaraguan
Top 10 Places Sorted by Number

Place	Dollars
New York, NY (city)	35,152
Yonkers, NY (city) Westchester County	22,734

Panamanian
Top 10 Places Sorted by Number

Place	Dollars
Islip, NY (town) Suffolk County	101,077
Hempstead, NY (town) Nassau County	77,430
New York, NY (city)	33,690

Paraguayan
Top 10 Places Sorted by Number

Place	Dollars
New York, NY (city)	26,910

Peruvian
Top 10 Places Sorted by Number

Place	Dollars
Oyster Bay, NY (town) Nassau County	80,581
Babylon, NY (town) Suffolk County	70,455
Brookhaven, NY (town) Suffolk County	63,125
Islip, NY (town) Suffolk County	59,018
New Rochelle, NY (city) Westchester County	56,750
Port Chester, NY (village) Westchester County	53,182
Rye, NY (town) Westchester County	52,614
Brentwood, NY (cdp) Suffolk County	47,857
Glen Cove, NY (city) Nassau County	46,875
Yonkers, NY (city) Westchester County	45,795

Puerto Rican
Top 10 Places Sorted by Number

Place	Dollars
Jefferson Valley-Yorktown, NY (cdp) Westchester County	121,372
Oceanside, NY (cdp) Nassau County	117,084
York, NY (town) Westchester County	108,618
Farmingville, NY (cdp) Suffolk County	98,791
Commack, NY (cdp) Suffolk County	98,430
Rockville Centre, NY (village) Nassau County	96,318
Carmel, NY (town) Putnam County	92,457
Baldwin, NY (cdp) Nassau County	92,290
North Babylon, NY (cdp) Suffolk County	92,279
Dix Hills, NY (cdp) Suffolk County	92,043

Salvadoran
Top 10 Places Sorted by Number

Place	Dollars
Copiague, NY (cdp) Suffolk County	77,644
New Cassel, NY (cdp) Nassau County	69,188
Valley Stream, NY (village) Nassau County	65,083
Mineola, NY (village) Nassau County	63,077
North Hempstead, NY (town) Nassau County	59,766
Hicksville, NY (cdp) Nassau County	59,233
Oyster Bay, NY (town) Nassau County	57,663
Central Islip, NY (cdp) Suffolk County	57,279
Islip, NY (town) Suffolk County	54,46…
Brentwood, NY (cdp) Suffolk County	53,9…

South American
Top 10 Places Sorted by Number

Place	Dollars
East Meadow, NY (cdp) Nassau County	90,21…
Franklin Square, NY (cdp) Nassau County	80,33…
Levittown, NY (cdp) Nassau County	80,16…
Patchogue, NY (village) Suffolk County	75,78…
Baldwin, NY (cdp) Nassau County	71,25…
Central Islip, NY (cdp) Suffolk County	69,58…
Elmont, NY (cdp) Nassau County	68,51…
Oceanside, NY (cdp) Nassau County	67,69…
Uniondale, NY (cdp) Nassau County	67,60…
Hicksville, NY (cdp) Nassau County	67,38…

Spaniard
Top 10 Places Sorted by Number

Place	Dollars
Brookhaven, NY (town) Suffolk County	71,15…
Hempstead, NY (town) Nassau County	60,37…
New York, NY (city)	40,49…

Uruguayan
Top 10 Places Sorted by Number

Place	Dollars
New York, NY (city)	42,2…

Venezuelan
Top 10 Places Sorted by Number

Place	Dollars
New York, NY (city)	36,5…

Other Hispanic
Top 10 Places Sorted by Number

Place	Dollars
East Meadow, NY (cdp) Nassau County	103,3…
Carmel, NY (town) Putnam County	91,9…
Roosevelt, NY (cdp) Nassau County	88,9…
North Bay Shore, NY (cdp) Suffolk County	80,6…
Uniondale, NY (cdp) Nassau County	75,4…
Shirley, NY (cdp) Suffolk County	65,5…
Medford, NY (cdp) Suffolk County	65,1…
Brentwood, NY (cdp) Suffolk County	64,4…
Amherst, NY (town) Erie County	64,1…
Franklin Square, NY (cdp) Nassau County	62,6…

Per Capita Income

Total Population
Top 10 Places Sorted by Number

Place	Dollars
Scarsdale, NY (village) Westchester County	89,9…
Rye, NY (city) Westchester County	76,5…
New Castle, NY (town) Westchester County	73,8…
North Castle, NY (town) Westchester County	60,6…
Mamaroneck, NY (town) Westchester County	57,8…
Lewisboro, NY (town) Westchester County	54,7…
Garden City, NY (village) Nassau County	53,1…
Bedford, NY (town) Westchester County	53,0…
Pelham, NY (town) Westchester County	51,5…
Eastchester, NY (town) Westchester County	49,9…

Hispanic
Top 10 Places Sorted by Number

Place	Dollars
Rye, NY (city) Westchester County	50,2…
Manlius, NY (town) Onondaga County	41,7…
Scarsdale, NY (village) Westchester County	36,5…
Pittsford, NY (town) Monroe County	36,3…

Notes: Please refer to the User's Guide for an explanation of data; tables include places with populations > 9,999 and reflect only those areas that meet Summary File 4 population thresholds, therefore there may be less than 10 places listed

Pelham, NY (town) Westchester County	34,856
Pearl River, NY (cdp) Rockland County	32,592
Jefferson Valley-Yorktown, NY (cdp) Westchester County	32,380
York, NY (town) Westchester County	29,499
Plainview, NY (cdp) Nassau County	29,064
Levittown, NY (cdp) Nassau County	26,854

Argentinian
Top 10 Places Sorted by Number

Place	Dollars
Hempstead, NY (town) Nassau County	48,996
North Hempstead, NY (town) Nassau County	47,735
New York, NY (city)	27,088

Bolivian
Top 10 Places Sorted by Number

Place	Dollars
New York, NY (city)	17,498

Central American
Top 10 Places Sorted by Number

Place	Dollars
Greenburgh, NY (town) Westchester County	20,397
Southampton, NY (town) Suffolk County	18,728
Valley Stream, NY (village) Nassau County	16,802
Mineola, NY (village) Nassau County	16,732
Levittown, NY (cdp) Nassau County	15,689
Brookhaven, NY (town) Suffolk County	15,582
Long Beach, NY (city) Nassau County	15,502
Elmont, NY (cdp) Nassau County	15,053
Peekskill, NY (city) Westchester County	14,890
Southeast, NY (town) Putnam County	14,700

Chilean
Top 10 Places Sorted by Number

Place	Dollars
North Hempstead, NY (town) Nassau County	22,164
New York, NY (city)	19,184
Oyster Bay, NY (town) Nassau County	18,638
Hempstead, NY (town) Nassau County	14,038

Colombian
Top 10 Places Sorted by Number

Place	Dollars
Greenburgh, NY (town) Westchester County	22,876
Oyster Bay, NY (town) Nassau County	22,679
Long Beach, NY (city) Nassau County	21,221
Hempstead, NY (town) Nassau County	19,947
Huntington, NY (town) Suffolk County	19,632
North Hempstead, NY (town) Nassau County	18,874
Brookhaven, NY (town) Suffolk County	18,217
Mineola, NY (village) Nassau County	17,315
Rye, NY (town) Westchester County	17,095
Babylon, NY (town) Suffolk County	16,338

Costa Rican
Top 10 Places Sorted by Number

Place	Dollars
Hempstead, NY (town) Nassau County	20,530
New York, NY (city)	17,300

Cuban
Top 10 Places Sorted by Number

Place	Dollars
Clarks, NY (town) Rockland County	36,196
Oyster Bay, NY (town) Nassau County	34,271
Greenburgh, NY (town) Westchester County	31,152
Brookhaven, NY (town) Suffolk County	29,528
North Hempstead, NY (town) Nassau County	28,380
Babylon, NY (town) Suffolk County	24,202
New York, NY (city)	23,346
Yonkers, NY (city) Westchester County	21,898
Hempstead, NY (town) Nassau County	21,723
Islip, NY (town) Suffolk County	20,665

Dominican
Top 10 Places Sorted by Number

Place	Dollars
Huntington, NY (town) Suffolk County	29,176
North Hempstead, NY (town) Nassau County	26,968
Oyster Bay, NY (town) Nassau County	22,301
Greenburgh, NY (town) Westchester County	20,168
Rye, NY (town) Westchester County	17,000
Valley Stream, NY (village) Nassau County	16,928
White Plains, NY (city) Westchester County	16,341
Mount Vernon, NY (city) Westchester County	16,095
Port Chester, NY (village) Westchester County	15,800
Baldwin, NY (cdp) Nassau County	14,486

Ecuadorian
Top 10 Places Sorted by Number

Place	Dollars
Greenburgh, NY (town) Westchester County	29,210
Oyster Bay, NY (town) Nassau County	27,287
North Hempstead, NY (town) Nassau County	20,283
Mount Pleasant, NY (town) Westchester County	20,181
Hempstead, NY (town) Nassau County	18,868
White Plains, NY (city) Westchester County	17,180
Brookhaven, NY (town) Suffolk County	16,958
Babylon, NY (town) Suffolk County	15,698
Yonkers, NY (city) Westchester County	15,154
Patchogue, NY (village) Suffolk County	14,308

Guatemalan
Top 10 Places Sorted by Number

Place	Dollars
Brookhaven, NY (town) Suffolk County	21,693
Brentwood, NY (cdp) Suffolk County	16,767
Babylon, NY (town) Suffolk County	15,141
Islip, NY (town) Suffolk County	14,912
Southeast, NY (town) Putnam County	14,638
Southampton, NY (town) Suffolk County	13,384
Huntington, NY (town) Suffolk County	12,832
New York, NY (city)	12,579
Mamaroneck, NY (village) Westchester County	12,428
Hempstead, NY (town) Nassau County	12,072

Honduran
Top 10 Places Sorted by Number

Place	Dollars
Babylon, NY (town) Suffolk County	15,382
Brentwood, NY (cdp) Suffolk County	13,907
Huntington, NY (town) Suffolk County	13,623
Yonkers, NY (city) Westchester County	12,884
Islip, NY (town) Suffolk County	12,479
New York, NY (city)	11,684
North Hempstead, NY (town) Nassau County	11,141
Newburgh, NY (city) Orange County	10,717
Hempstead, NY (town) Nassau County	10,430
Hempstead, NY (village) Nassau County	9,804

Mexican
Top 10 Places Sorted by Number

Place	Dollars
Hempstead, NY (village) Nassau County	22,192
Greenburgh, NY (town) Westchester County	17,398
Hempstead, NY (town) Nassau County	16,850
Buffalo, NY (city) Erie County	16,060
Islip, NY (town) Suffolk County	14,318
Oyster Bay, NY (town) Nassau County	14,288
Babylon, NY (town) Suffolk County	13,512
Brookhaven, NY (town) Suffolk County	13,325
Clarks, NY (town) Rockland County	13,248

Huntington, NY (town) Suffolk County	12,813

Nicaraguan
Top 10 Places Sorted by Number

Place	Dollars
Yonkers, NY (city) Westchester County	12,588
New York, NY (city)	12,419

Panamanian
Top 10 Places Sorted by Number

Place	Dollars
Islip, NY (town) Suffolk County	30,478
Hempstead, NY (town) Nassau County	24,143
New York, NY (city)	19,800

Paraguayan
Top 10 Places Sorted by Number

Place	Dollars
New York, NY (city)	12,653

Peruvian
Top 10 Places Sorted by Number

Place	Dollars
Yonkers, NY (city) Westchester County	34,207
Oyster Bay, NY (town) Nassau County	21,594
Hempstead, NY (town) Nassau County	19,956
Islip, NY (town) Suffolk County	19,036
Brookhaven, NY (town) Suffolk County	17,666
North Hempstead, NY (town) Nassau County	17,652
New York, NY (city)	16,959
New Rochelle, NY (city) Westchester County	16,751
Brentwood, NY (cdp) Suffolk County	16,625
White Plains, NY (city) Westchester County	15,899

Puerto Rican
Top 10 Places Sorted by Number

Place	Dollars
Jefferson Valley-Yorktown, NY (cdp) Westchester County	38,648
York, NY (town) Westchester County	32,455
Oceanside, NY (cdp) Nassau County	31,071
Stony Point, NY (town) Rockland County	28,803
Franklin Square, NY (cdp) Nassau County	28,571
Monroe, NY (town) Orange County	26,415
Greenburgh, NY (town) Westchester County	25,129
Holbrook, NY (cdp) Suffolk County	24,552
Commack, NY (cdp) Suffolk County	24,346
Mamaroneck, NY (town) Westchester County	24,244

Salvadoran
Top 10 Places Sorted by Number

Place	Dollars
Mineola, NY (village) Nassau County	17,283
Valley Stream, NY (village) Nassau County	15,756
Copiague, NY (cdp) Suffolk County	13,283
Yonkers, NY (city) Westchester County	12,682
Brookhaven, NY (town) Suffolk County	12,583
Westbury, NY (village) Nassau County	12,551
New York, NY (city)	12,397
North Hempstead, NY (town) Nassau County	12,397
Wyandanch, NY (cdp) Suffolk County	12,338
Hicksville, NY (cdp) Nassau County	12,283

South American
Top 10 Places Sorted by Number

Place	Dollars
Levittown, NY (cdp) Nassau County	62,849
Elmont, NY (cdp) Nassau County	29,636
Clarks, NY (town) Rockland County	29,383
East Meadow, NY (cdp) Nassau County	26,378
Greenburgh, NY (town) Westchester County	25,300

Notes: Please refer to the User's Guide for an explanation of data; tables include places with populations > 9,999 and reflect only those areas that meet Summary File 4 population thresholds, therefore there may be less than 10 places listed

Place	Dollars
Mamaroneck, NY (village) Westchester County	24,233
Mamaroneck, NY (town) Westchester County	23,743
Franklin Square, NY (cdp) Nassau County	23,200
North Hempstead, NY (town) Nassau County	23,052
Oyster Bay, NY (town) Nassau County	22,678

Spaniard
Top 10 Places Sorted by Number

Place	Dollars
Hempstead, NY (town) Nassau County	26,936
Brookhaven, NY (town) Suffolk County	23,252
New York, NY (city)	22,275

Uruguayan
Top 10 Places Sorted by Number

Place	Dollars
New York, NY (city)	22,884

Venezuelan
Top 10 Places Sorted by Number

Place	Dollars
New York, NY (city)	17,121

Other Hispanic
Top 10 Places Sorted by Number

Place	Dollars
Wallkill, NY (town) Orange County	24,350
Smith, NY (town) Suffolk County	22,993
Mamaroneck, NY (town) Westchester County	22,207
Warwick, NY (town) Orange County	22,197
New Rochelle, NY (city) Westchester County	19,466
Southampton, NY (town) Suffolk County	18,787
Holbrook, NY (cdp) Suffolk County	18,358
Amherst, NY (town) Erie County	18,308
West Babylon, NY (cdp) Suffolk County	17,755
Clarks, NY (town) Rockland County	17,426

Poverty Status

Total Populations with Income Below Poverty Level
Top 10 Places Sorted by Number

Place	Number
New York, NY (city)	1,668,938
Buffalo, NY (city) Erie County	75,120
Rochester, NY (city) Monroe County	54,713
Hempstead, NY (town) Nassau County	42,958
Syracuse, NY (city) Onondaga County	37,485
Yonkers, NY (city) Westchester County	30,089
Brookhaven, NY (town) Suffolk County	25,952
Islip, NY (town) Suffolk County	20,849
Albany, NY (city) Albany County	18,822
Ramapo, NY (town) Rockland County	17,458

Total Populations with Income Below Poverty Level
Top 10 Places Sorted by Percent

Place	Percent
Ithaca, NY (city) Tompkins County	40.24
Oneonta, NY (city) Otsego County	30.28
Monroe, NY (town) Orange County	29.06
Syracuse, NY (city) Onondaga County	27.31
Buffalo, NY (city) Erie County	26.60
Rochester, NY (city) Monroe County	25.90
Newburgh, NY (city) Orange County	25.76
Utica, NY (city) Oneida County	24.50
Binghamton, NY (city) Broome County	23.67
Thompson, NY (town) Sullivan County	23.26

Hispanics with Income Below Poverty Level
Top 10 Places Sorted by Number

Place	Number
New York, NY (city)	654,716
Yonkers, NY (city) Westchester County	13,128
Rochester, NY (city) Monroe County	11,451
Hempstead, NY (town) Nassau County	11,129
Buffalo, NY (city) Erie County	9,578
Islip, NY (town) Suffolk County	7,475
Brookhaven, NY (town) Suffolk County	4,137
Hempstead, NY (village) Nassau County	3,744
Brentwood, NY (cdp) Suffolk County	3,675
Syracuse, NY (city) Onondaga County	3,545

Hispanics with Income Below Poverty Level
Top 10 Places Sorted by Percent

Place	Percent
Oneonta, NY (city) Otsego County	61.32
Utica, NY (city) Oneida County	56.72
Binghamton, NY (city) Broome County	55.88
Elmira, NY (city) Chemung County	53.35
Gloversville, NY (city) Fulton County	51.90
Syracuse, NY (city) Onondaga County	49.73
Dunkirk, NY (city) Chautauqua County	48.39
Cohoes, NY (city) Albany County	44.97
Buffalo, NY (city) Erie County	44.91
Schenectady, NY (city) Schenectady County	44.77

Argentinians with Income Below Poverty Level
Top 10 Places Sorted by Number

Place	Number
New York, NY (city)	1,616
North Hempstead, NY (town) Nassau County	39
Hempstead, NY (town) Nassau County	15

Argentinians with Income Below Poverty Level
Top 10 Places Sorted by Percent

Place	Percent
New York, NY (city)	16.05
North Hempstead, NY (town) Nassau County	8.07
Hempstead, NY (town) Nassau County	1.58

Bolivians with Income Below Poverty Level
Top 10 Places Sorted by Number

Place	Number
New York, NY (city)	539

Bolivians with Income Below Poverty Level
Top 10 Places Sorted by Percent

Place	Percent
New York, NY (city)	16.13

Central Americans with Income Below Poverty Level
Top 10 Places Sorted by Number

Place	Number
New York, NY (city)	26,168
Hempstead, NY (town) Nassau County	4,387
Islip, NY (town) Suffolk County	2,073
Hempstead, NY (village) Nassau County	1,804
Brentwood, NY (cdp) Suffolk County	1,251
Yonkers, NY (city) Westchester County	983
Huntington, NY (town) Suffolk County	981
North Hempstead, NY (town) Nassau County	932
Huntington Station, NY (cdp) Suffolk County	877
Freeport, NY (village) Nassau County	856

Central Americans with Income Below Poverty Level
Top 10 Places Sorted by Percent

Place	Percent
Spring Valley, NY (village) Rockland County	30.42
Huntington Station, NY (cdp) Suffolk County	29.43
Glen Cove, NY (city) Nassau County	29.36
West Hempstead, NY (cdp) Nassau County	28.49
East Hampton, NY (town) Suffolk County	28.47
Uniondale, NY (cdp) Nassau County	26.13

Huntington, NY (town) Suffolk County	25.63
Clarks, NY (town) Rockland County	25.61
Roosevelt, NY (cdp) Nassau County	25.57
Riverhead, NY (town) Suffolk County	24.42

Chileans with Income Below Poverty Level
Top 10 Places Sorted by Number

Place	Number
New York, NY (city)	851
Hempstead, NY (town) Nassau County	120
North Hempstead, NY (town) Nassau County	45
Oyster Bay, NY (town) Nassau County	16

Chileans with Income Below Poverty Level
Top 10 Places Sorted by Percent

Place	Percent
Hempstead, NY (town) Nassau County	18.32
New York, NY (city)	14.94
North Hempstead, NY (town) Nassau County	6.98
Oyster Bay, NY (town) Nassau County	4.05

Colombians with Income Below Poverty Level
Top 10 Places Sorted by Number

Place	Number
New York, NY (city)	14,862
Hempstead, NY (town) Nassau County	456
Islip, NY (town) Suffolk County	383
Yonkers, NY (city) Westchester County	273
Brentwood, NY (cdp) Suffolk County	260
New Rochelle, NY (city) Westchester County	256
White Plains, NY (city) Westchester County	211
East Hampton, NY (town) Suffolk County	180
Rye, NY (town) Westchester County	178
Port Chester, NY (village) Westchester County	171

Colombians with Income Below Poverty Level
Top 10 Places Sorted by Percent

Place	Percent
Ossining, NY (town) Westchester County	35.09
Ossining, NY (village) Westchester County	35.09
Southampton, NY (town) Suffolk County	29.97
Yonkers, NY (city) Westchester County	23.43
East Hampton, NY (town) Suffolk County	23.32
New Rochelle, NY (city) Westchester County	22.09
Port Chester, NY (village) Westchester County	21.30
Rye, NY (town) Westchester County	20.92
New York, NY (city)	18.45
White Plains, NY (city) Westchester County	16.83

Costa Ricans with Income Below Poverty Level
Top 10 Places Sorted by Number

Place	Number
New York, NY (city)	1,194
Hempstead, NY (town) Nassau County	52

Costa Ricans with Income Below Poverty Level
Top 10 Places Sorted by Percent

Place	Percent
New York, NY (city)	22.97
Hempstead, NY (town) Nassau County	14.29

Cubans with Income Below Poverty Level
Top 10 Places Sorted by Number

Place	Number
New York, NY (city)	8,423
Rochester, NY (city) Monroe County	434
Hempstead, NY (town) Nassau County	261
Yonkers, NY (city) Westchester County	244
Syracuse, NY (city) Onondaga County	177
Port Chester, NY (village) Westchester County	77
Rye, NY (town) Westchester County	77

Notes: Please refer to the User's Guide for an explanation of data; tables include places with populations > 9,999 and reflect only those areas that meet Summary File 4 population thresholds, therefore there may be less than 10 places listed

Islip, NY (town) Suffolk County 70
Oyster Bay, NY (town) Nassau County 55
Brookhaven, NY (town) Suffolk County 34

Cubans with Income Below Poverty Level
Top 10 Places Sorted by Percent

Place	Percent
Syracuse, NY (city) Onondaga County	42.65
Rochester, NY (city) Monroe County	38.48
New York, NY (city)	20.67
Yonkers, NY (city) Westchester County	19.54
Port Chester, NY (village) Westchester County	16.70
Rye, NY (town) Westchester County	14.67
Hempstead, NY (town) Nassau County	8.31
North Hempstead, NY (town) Nassau County	7.72
Oyster Bay, NY (town) Nassau County	7.69
Islip, NY (town) Suffolk County	5.77

Dominicans with Income Below Poverty Level
Top 10 Places Sorted by Number

Place	Number
New York, NY (city)	137,756
Yonkers, NY (city) Westchester County	2,029
Hempstead, NY (town) Nassau County	1,366
Haverstraw, NY (town) Rockland County	999
Freeport, NY (village) Nassau County	719
Haverstraw, NY (village) Rockland County	675
Islip, NY (town) Suffolk County	485
Babylon, NY (town) Suffolk County	469
Rochester, NY (city) Monroe County	393
Rockville Centre, NY (village) Nassau County	304

Dominicans with Income Below Poverty Level
Top 10 Places Sorted by Percent

Place	Percent
Rochester, NY (city) Monroe County	47.81
Albany, NY (city) Albany County	44.40
Ossining, NY (village) Westchester County	42.63
Rockville Centre, NY (village) Nassau County	38.24
Buffalo, NY (city) Erie County	36.99
North Bay Shore, NY (cdp) Suffolk County	36.55
Ossining, NY (town) Westchester County	35.32
New York, NY (city)	32.58
West Haverstraw, NY (village) Rockland County	30.91
Haverstraw, NY (town) Rockland County	26.66

Ecuadorians with Income Below Poverty Level
Top 10 Places Sorted by Number

Place	Number
New York, NY (city)	22,350
Ossining, NY (town) Westchester County	460
Ossining, NY (village) Westchester County	460
Yonkers, NY (city) Westchester County	406
Peekskill, NY (city) Westchester County	235
Ramapo, NY (town) Rockland County	228
Spring Valley, NY (village) Rockland County	217
Islip, NY (town) Suffolk County	156
Port Chester, NY (village) Westchester County	141
Rye, NY (town) Westchester County	141

Ecuadorians with Income Below Poverty Level
Top 10 Places Sorted by Percent

Place	Percent
Peekskill, NY (city) Westchester County	33.76
Ramapo, NY (town) Rockland County	29.84
Spring Valley, NY (village) Rockland County	29.60
Yonkers, NY (city) Westchester County	23.20
New York, NY (city)	21.12
Ossining, NY (town) Westchester County	21.12
Ossining, NY (village) Westchester County	21.12
East Hampton, NY (town) Suffolk County	17.66
Greenburgh, NY (town) Westchester County	17.28
Brentwood, NY (cdp) Suffolk County	16.74

Guatemalans with Income Below Poverty Level
Top 10 Places Sorted by Number

Place	Number
New York, NY (city)	3,455
Ramapo, NY (town) Rockland County	399
Hempstead, NY (town) Nassau County	398
Spring Valley, NY (village) Rockland County	334
Rye, NY (town) Westchester County	305
Port Chester, NY (village) Westchester County	302
North Hempstead, NY (town) Nassau County	190
New Rochelle, NY (city) Westchester County	129
Hempstead, NY (village) Nassau County	109
Freeport, NY (village) Nassau County	104

Guatemalans with Income Below Poverty Level
Top 10 Places Sorted by Percent

Place	Percent
Hempstead, NY (village) Nassau County	32.15
New Rochelle, NY (city) Westchester County	29.79
Spring Valley, NY (village) Rockland County	28.94
Brookhaven, NY (town) Suffolk County	27.76
Ramapo, NY (town) Rockland County	27.73
North Hempstead, NY (town) Nassau County	26.06
Huntington, NY (town) Suffolk County	24.62
Port Chester, NY (village) Westchester County	24.03
Rye, NY (town) Westchester County	22.58
New York, NY (city)	21.79

Hondurans with Income Below Poverty Level
Top 10 Places Sorted by Number

Place	Number
New York, NY (city)	8,165
Hempstead, NY (town) Nassau County	519
Hempstead, NY (village) Nassau County	319
North Hempstead, NY (town) Nassau County	158
Yonkers, NY (city) Westchester County	146
Newburgh, NY (city) Orange County	115
Islip, NY (town) Suffolk County	114
Babylon, NY (town) Suffolk County	93
Brentwood, NY (cdp) Suffolk County	71
Huntington, NY (town) Suffolk County	53

Hondurans with Income Below Poverty Level
Top 10 Places Sorted by Percent

Place	Percent
New York, NY (city)	27.65
North Hempstead, NY (town) Nassau County	22.80
Hempstead, NY (town) Nassau County	21.27
Hempstead, NY (village) Nassau County	20.45
Babylon, NY (town) Suffolk County	20.04
Yonkers, NY (city) Westchester County	15.94
Newburgh, NY (city) Orange County	15.69
Brentwood, NY (cdp) Suffolk County	12.48
Huntington, NY (town) Suffolk County	11.47
Islip, NY (town) Suffolk County	9.94

Mexicans with Income Below Poverty Level
Top 10 Places Sorted by Number

Place	Number
New York, NY (city)	57,721
Yonkers, NY (city) Westchester County	2,265
New Rochelle, NY (city) Westchester County	1,628
Newburgh, NY (city) Orange County	1,095
Rye, NY (town) Westchester County	725
Port Chester, NY (village) Westchester County	684
White Plains, NY (city) Westchester County	651
North Hempstead, NY (town) Nassau County	623
Middletown, NY (city) Orange County	605
Poughkeepsie, NY (city) Dutchess County	471

Mexicans with Income Below Poverty Level
Top 10 Places Sorted by Percent

Place	Percent
Syracuse, NY (city) Onondaga County	46.18
Elmont, NY (cdp) Nassau County	37.38
Mamaroneck, NY (town) Westchester County	36.33
Southampton, NY (town) Suffolk County	35.41
Poughkeepsie, NY (city) Dutchess County	34.58
Yonkers, NY (city) Westchester County	34.49
Middletown, NY (city) Orange County	33.22
New York, NY (city)	32.98
Mamaroneck, NY (village) Westchester County	31.37
Buffalo, NY (city) Erie County	29.45

Nicaraguans with Income Below Poverty Level
Top 10 Places Sorted by Number

Place	Number
New York, NY (city)	1,669
Yonkers, NY (city) Westchester County	185

Nicaraguans with Income Below Poverty Level
Top 10 Places Sorted by Percent

Place	Percent
Yonkers, NY (city) Westchester County	32.29
New York, NY (city)	22.74

Panamanians with Income Below Poverty Level
Top 10 Places Sorted by Number

Place	Number
New York, NY (city)	3,921
Hempstead, NY (town) Nassau County	57
Islip, NY (town) Suffolk County	11

Panamanians with Income Below Poverty Level
Top 10 Places Sorted by Percent

Place	Percent
New York, NY (city)	21.09
Hempstead, NY (town) Nassau County	9.84
Islip, NY (town) Suffolk County	3.30

Paraguayans with Income Below Poverty Level
Top 10 Places Sorted by Number

Place	Number
New York, NY (city)	245

Paraguayans with Income Below Poverty Level
Top 10 Places Sorted by Percent

Place	Percent
New York, NY (city)	15.87

Peruvians with Income Below Poverty Level
Top 10 Places Sorted by Number

Place	Number
New York, NY (city)	3,722
Hempstead, NY (town) Nassau County	216
White Plains, NY (city) Westchester County	132
New Rochelle, NY (city) Westchester County	107
Port Chester, NY (village) Westchester County	99
Rye, NY (town) Westchester County	99
Babylon, NY (town) Suffolk County	77
Islip, NY (town) Suffolk County	76
Brookhaven, NY (town) Suffolk County	50
Glen Cove, NY (city) Nassau County	50

Peruvians with Income Below Poverty Level
Top 10 Places Sorted by Percent

Place	Percent
Babylon, NY (town) Suffolk County	23.33
New York, NY (city)	15.82
New Rochelle, NY (city) Westchester County	15.37

Notes: Please refer to the User's Guide for an explanation of data; tables include places with populations > 9,999 and reflect only those areas that meet Summary File 4 population thresholds, therefore there may be less than 10 places listed

728 PROFILES OF NEW YORK / Hispanic: Rankings

Place	Percent
Port Chester, NY (village) Westchester County	11.99
Hempstead, NY (town) Nassau County	10.89
Rye, NY (town) Westchester County	10.59
Brookhaven, NY (town) Suffolk County	9.14
White Plains, NY (city) Westchester County	8.92
Yonkers, NY (city) Westchester County	6.49
Glen Cove, NY (city) Nassau County	6.23

Puerto Ricans with Income Below Poverty Level
Top 10 Places Sorted by Number

Place	Number
New York, NY (city)	268,138
Rochester, NY (city) Monroe County	9,385
Buffalo, NY (city) Erie County	7,801
Yonkers, NY (city) Westchester County	4,787
Islip, NY (town) Suffolk County	2,559
Syracuse, NY (city) Onondaga County	2,331
Brookhaven, NY (town) Suffolk County	2,315
Utica, NY (city) Oneida County	1,623
Dunkirk, NY (city) Chautauqua County	1,133
Newburgh, NY (city) Orange County	1,027

Puerto Ricans with Income Below Poverty Level
Top 10 Places Sorted by Percent

Place	Percent
Elmira, NY (city) Chemung County	77.66
Ogdensburg, NY (city) Saint Lawrence County	66.67
Binghamton, NY (city) Broome County	64.36
Utica, NY (city) Oneida County	60.02
Niagara Falls, NY (city) Niagara County	56.56
Syracuse, NY (city) Onondaga County	51.07
Dunkirk, NY (city) Chautauqua County	48.96
Geneva, NY (city) Ontario County	47.19
Buffalo, NY (city) Erie County	47.15
Schenectady, NY (city) Schenectady County	45.24

Salvadorans with Income Below Poverty Level
Top 10 Places Sorted by Number

Place	Number
New York, NY (city)	6,301
Hempstead, NY (town) Nassau County	3,143
Islip, NY (town) Suffolk County	1,823
Hempstead, NY (village) Nassau County	1,293
Brentwood, NY (cdp) Suffolk County	1,149
Huntington, NY (town) Suffolk County	830
Huntington Station, NY (cdp) Suffolk County	777
Freeport, NY (village) Nassau County	602
North Hempstead, NY (town) Nassau County	537
Uniondale, NY (cdp) Nassau County	529

Salvadorans with Income Below Poverty Level
Top 10 Places Sorted by Percent

Place	Percent
Uniondale, NY (cdp) Nassau County	32.49
Huntington Station, NY (cdp) Suffolk County	31.78
Glen Cove, NY (city) Nassau County	30.25
Huntington, NY (town) Suffolk County	28.69
Elmont, NY (cdp) Nassau County	26.36
Roosevelt, NY (cdp) Nassau County	26.07
Yonkers, NY (city) Westchester County	25.28
New York, NY (city)	25.19
Orange, NY (town) Rockland County	25.14
Brookhaven, NY (town) Suffolk County	22.96

South Americans with Income Below Poverty Level
Top 10 Places Sorted by Number

Place	Number
New York, NY (city)	47,371
Hempstead, NY (town) Nassau County	985
Yonkers, NY (city) Westchester County	836
Islip, NY (town) Suffolk County	738
Ossining, NY (town) Westchester County	663
Ossining, NY (village) Westchester County	652
White Plains, NY (city) Westchester County	478
Brentwood, NY (cdp) Suffolk County	477
Rye, NY (town) Westchester County	443
New Rochelle, NY (city) Westchester County	437

South Americans with Income Below Poverty Level
Top 10 Places Sorted by Percent

Place	Percent
Hempstead, NY (village) Nassau County	29.41
Peekskill, NY (city) Westchester County	29.10
Buffalo, NY (city) Erie County	27.56
Spring Valley, NY (village) Rockland County	25.28
Southampton, NY (town) Suffolk County	22.29
Ossining, NY (town) Westchester County	21.66
Ossining, NY (village) Westchester County	21.60
Cortlandt, NY (town) Westchester County	20.48
Harrison, NY (village) Westchester County	20.00
Ramapo, NY (town) Rockland County	19.53

Spaniards with Income Below Poverty Level
Top 10 Places Sorted by Number

Place	Number
New York, NY (city)	1,781
Hempstead, NY (town) Nassau County	43
Brookhaven, NY (town) Suffolk County	0

Spaniards with Income Below Poverty Level
Top 10 Places Sorted by Percent

Place	Percent
New York, NY (city)	17.91
Hempstead, NY (town) Nassau County	5.32
Brookhaven, NY (town) Suffolk County	0.00

Uruguayans with Income Below Poverty Level
Top 10 Places Sorted by Number

Place	Number
New York, NY (city)	310

Uruguayans with Income Below Poverty Level
Top 10 Places Sorted by Percent

Place	Percent
New York, NY (city)	15.16

Venezuelans with Income Below Poverty Level
Top 10 Places Sorted by Number

Place	Number
New York, NY (city)	1,976

Venezuelans with Income Below Poverty Level
Top 10 Places Sorted by Percent

Place	Percent
New York, NY (city)	27.80

Other Hispanics with Income Below Poverty Level
Top 10 Places Sorted by Number

Place	Number
New York, NY (city)	107,358
Hempstead, NY (town) Nassau County	2,868
Yonkers, NY (city) Westchester County	1,970
Islip, NY (town) Suffolk County	1,406
Hempstead, NY (village) Nassau County	1,116
Rochester, NY (city) Monroe County	885
Buffalo, NY (city) Erie County	817
Brentwood, NY (cdp) Suffolk County	755
Freeport, NY (village) Nassau County	670
Brookhaven, NY (town) Suffolk County	598

Other Hispanics with Income Below Poverty Level
Top 10 Places Sorted by Percent

Place	Percent
Schenectady, NY (city) Schenectady County	53.70
Buffalo, NY (city) Erie County	43.67
Syracuse, NY (city) Onondaga County	43.38
Thompson, NY (town) Sullivan County	39.47
Rochester, NY (city) Monroe County	38.34
Albany, NY (city) Albany County	34.44
New York, NY (city)	30.29
Oceanside, NY (cdp) Nassau County	28.44
West Hempstead, NY (cdp) Nassau County	27.64
Southampton, NY (town) Suffolk County	26.83

Homeownership

Total Populations Who Own Their Own Homes
Top 10 Places Sorted by Number

Place	Number
New York, NY (city)	912,133
Hempstead, NY (town) Nassau County	199,148
Brookhaven, NY (town) Suffolk County	115,894
Oyster Bay, NY (town) Nassau County	86,345
Islip, NY (town) Suffolk County	77,830
North Hempstead, NY (town) Nassau County	60,270
Huntington, NY (town) Suffolk County	56,219
Buffalo, NY (city) Erie County	53,339
Babylon, NY (town) Suffolk County	52,110
Rochester, NY (city) Monroe County	35,777

Total Populations Who Own Their Own Homes
Top 10 Places Sorted by Percent

Place	Percent
Massapequa Park, NY (village) Nassau County	96.60
Dix Hills, NY (cdp) Suffolk County	96.24
Merrick, NY (cdp) Nassau County	94.63
Elwood, NY (cdp) Suffolk County	94.13
Massapequa, NY (cdp) Nassau County	93.93
Somers, NY (town) Westchester County	93.75
Wantagh, NY (cdp) Nassau County	93.74
North New Hyde Park, NY (cdp) Nassau County	93.66
Plainview, NY (cdp) Nassau County	93.40
Garden City, NY (village) Nassau County	93.28

Hispanics Who Own Their Own Homes
Top 10 Places Sorted by Number

Place	Number
New York, NY (city)	91,479
Hempstead, NY (town) Nassau County	9,894
Islip, NY (town) Suffolk County	9,136
Brookhaven, NY (town) Suffolk County	5,142
Brentwood, NY (cdp) Suffolk County	3,970
Babylon, NY (town) Suffolk County	2,851
Yonkers, NY (city) Westchester County	2,769
Oyster Bay, NY (town) Nassau County	2,238
Rochester, NY (city) Monroe County	2,210
Buffalo, NY (city) Erie County	1,789

Hispanics Who Own Their Own Homes
Top 10 Places Sorted by Percent

Place	Percent
Alden, NY (town) Erie County	100.00
Garden City, NY (village) Nassau County	100.00
Massapequa Park, NY (village) Nassau County	100.00
North Merrick, NY (cdp) Nassau County	100.00
North New Hyde Park, NY (cdp) Nassau County	100.00
Scarsdale, NY (village) Westchester County	95.83
Massapequa, NY (cdp) Nassau County	95.68
North Wantagh, NY (cdp) Nassau County	95.31
East Fishkill, NY (town) Dutchess County	93.33
Patterson, NY (town) Putnam County	93.33

Notes: Please refer to the User's Guide for an explanation of data; tables include places with populations > 9,999 and reflect only those areas that meet Summary File 4 population thresholds, therefore there may be less than 10 places listed

Argentinians Who Own Their Own Homes
Top 10 Places Sorted by Number

Place	Number
New York, NY (city)	1,150
Hempstead, NY (town) Nassau County	248
North Hempstead, NY (town) Nassau County	90

Argentinians Who Own Their Own Homes
Top 10 Places Sorted by Percent

Place	Percent
North Hempstead, NY (town) Nassau County	83.33
Hempstead, NY (town) Nassau County	66.49
New York, NY (city)	26.44

Bolivians Who Own Their Own Homes
Top 10 Places Sorted by Number

Place	Number
New York, NY (city)	314

Bolivians Who Own Their Own Homes
Top 10 Places Sorted by Percent

Place	Percent
New York, NY (city)	29.71

Central Americans Who Own Their Own Homes
Top 10 Places Sorted by Number

Place	Number
New York, NY (city)	5,332
Islip, NY (town) Suffolk County	1,723
Hempstead, NY (town) Nassau County	1,636
Brentwood, NY (cdp) Suffolk County	977
Hempstead, NY (village) Nassau County	323
Babylon, NY (town) Suffolk County	306
North Hempstead, NY (town) Nassau County	270
Central Islip, NY (cdp) Suffolk County	262
North Bay Shore, NY (cdp) Suffolk County	255
Freeport, NY (village) Nassau County	250

Central Americans Who Own Their Own Homes
Top 10 Places Sorted by Percent

Place	Percent
Levittown, NY (cdp) Nassau County	70.79
Baldwin, NY (cdp) Nassau County	67.86
North Bay Shore, NY (cdp) Suffolk County	62.50
Valley Stream, NY (village) Nassau County	62.42
Bay Shore, NY (cdp) Suffolk County	62.20
Brentwood, NY (cdp) Suffolk County	61.10
Islip, NY (town) Suffolk County	60.84
Central Islip, NY (cdp) Suffolk County	58.74
Uniondale, NY (cdp) Nassau County	53.05
Copiague, NY (cdp) Suffolk County	52.45

Chileans Who Own Their Own Homes
Top 10 Places Sorted by Number

Place	Number
New York, NY (city)	513
Hempstead, NY (town) Nassau County	89
North Hempstead, NY (town) Nassau County	67
Oyster Bay, NY (town) Nassau County	37

Chileans Who Own Their Own Homes
Top 10 Places Sorted by Percent

Place	Percent
Hempstead, NY (town) Nassau County	49.72
North Hempstead, NY (town) Nassau County	33.17
Oyster Bay, NY (town) Nassau County	33.04
New York, NY (city)	23.39

Colombians Who Own Their Own Homes
Top 10 Places Sorted by Number

Place	Number
New York, NY (city)	5,277
Hempstead, NY (town) Nassau County	727
Islip, NY (town) Suffolk County	485
Brentwood, NY (cdp) Suffolk County	236
Oyster Bay, NY (town) Nassau County	188
North Hempstead, NY (town) Nassau County	170
Brookhaven, NY (town) Suffolk County	167
Babylon, NY (town) Suffolk County	154
White Plains, NY (city) Westchester County	93
Huntington, NY (town) Suffolk County	77

Colombians Who Own Their Own Homes
Top 10 Places Sorted by Percent

Place	Percent
Oyster Bay, NY (town) Nassau County	71.21
Islip, NY (town) Suffolk County	69.78
Brentwood, NY (cdp) Suffolk County	69.21
Huntington, NY (town) Suffolk County	64.17
Hempstead, NY (town) Nassau County	62.08
Babylon, NY (town) Suffolk County	56.83
Brookhaven, NY (town) Suffolk County	54.58
North Hempstead, NY (town) Nassau County	45.33
Long Beach, NY (city) Nassau County	42.97
Greenburgh, NY (town) Westchester County	39.37

Costa Ricans Who Own Their Own Homes
Top 10 Places Sorted by Number

Place	Number
New York, NY (city)	429
Hempstead, NY (town) Nassau County	68

Costa Ricans Who Own Their Own Homes
Top 10 Places Sorted by Percent

Place	Percent
Hempstead, NY (town) Nassau County	57.14
New York, NY (city)	20.54

Cubans Who Own Their Own Homes
Top 10 Places Sorted by Number

Place	Number
New York, NY (city)	4,196
Hempstead, NY (town) Nassau County	597
Brookhaven, NY (town) Suffolk County	286
Islip, NY (town) Suffolk County	220
Oyster Bay, NY (town) Nassau County	195
Yonkers, NY (city) Westchester County	181
Babylon, NY (town) Suffolk County	170
Greenburgh, NY (town) Westchester County	128
Rye, NY (town) Westchester County	124
Clarks, NY (town) Rockland County	115

Cubans Who Own Their Own Homes
Top 10 Places Sorted by Percent

Place	Percent
Clarks, NY (town) Rockland County	100.00
North Hempstead, NY (town) Nassau County	90.00
Oyster Bay, NY (town) Nassau County	85.90
Brookhaven, NY (town) Suffolk County	84.37
Greenburgh, NY (town) Westchester County	77.58
Babylon, NY (town) Suffolk County	73.59
Hempstead, NY (town) Nassau County	72.10
Islip, NY (town) Suffolk County	71.20
Rye, NY (town) Westchester County	50.82
Port Chester, NY (village) Westchester County	48.05

Dominicans Who Own Their Own Homes
Top 10 Places Sorted by Number

Place	Number
New York, NY (city)	11,429
Hempstead, NY (town) Nassau County	786
Islip, NY (town) Suffolk County	646
Yonkers, NY (city) Westchester County	399
Brentwood, NY (cdp) Suffolk County	361
Babylon, NY (town) Suffolk County	355
Haverstraw, NY (town) Rockland County	289
Brookhaven, NY (town) Suffolk County	238
Freeport, NY (village) Nassau County	231
Haverstraw, NY (village) Rockland County	189

Dominicans Who Own Their Own Homes
Top 10 Places Sorted by Percent

Place	Percent
Valley Stream, NY (village) Nassau County	76.04
Brentwood, NY (cdp) Suffolk County	73.98
Oyster Bay, NY (town) Nassau County	69.86
Huntington, NY (town) Suffolk County	67.67
Islip, NY (town) Suffolk County	67.64
Babylon, NY (town) Suffolk County	65.38
Central Islip, NY (cdp) Suffolk County	63.83
Uniondale, NY (cdp) Nassau County	62.65
North Hempstead, NY (town) Nassau County	60.99
North Bay Shore, NY (cdp) Suffolk County	55.03

Ecuadorians Who Own Their Own Homes
Top 10 Places Sorted by Number

Place	Number
New York, NY (city)	4,794
Hempstead, NY (town) Nassau County	393
Islip, NY (town) Suffolk County	240
Brookhaven, NY (town) Suffolk County	168
Brentwood, NY (cdp) Suffolk County	121
Oyster Bay, NY (town) Nassau County	103
Babylon, NY (town) Suffolk County	96
North Hempstead, NY (town) Nassau County	67
Yonkers, NY (city) Westchester County	59
Central Islip, NY (cdp) Suffolk County	57

Ecuadorians Who Own Their Own Homes
Top 10 Places Sorted by Percent

Place	Percent
Oyster Bay, NY (town) Nassau County	100.00
Brentwood, NY (cdp) Suffolk County	82.31
Babylon, NY (town) Suffolk County	67.61
Islip, NY (town) Suffolk County	65.04
Hempstead, NY (town) Nassau County	64.53
Central Islip, NY (cdp) Suffolk County	62.64
Brookhaven, NY (town) Suffolk County	48.84
North Hempstead, NY (town) Nassau County	34.18
Bay Shore, NY (cdp) Suffolk County	30.95
Ramapo, NY (town) Rockland County	21.74

Guatemalans Who Own Their Own Homes
Top 10 Places Sorted by Number

Place	Number
New York, NY (city)	429
Islip, NY (town) Suffolk County	164
Hempstead, NY (town) Nassau County	160
Brentwood, NY (cdp) Suffolk County	90
Freeport, NY (village) Nassau County	36
Brookhaven, NY (town) Suffolk County	28
Hempstead, NY (village) Nassau County	23
Port Chester, NY (village) Westchester County	21
Rye, NY (town) Westchester County	21
Huntington, NY (town) Suffolk County	16

Guatemalans Who Own Their Own Homes
Top 10 Places Sorted by Percent

Place	Percent
Islip, NY (town) Suffolk County	64.57
Brentwood, NY (cdp) Suffolk County	61.64
Freeport, NY (village) Nassau County	37.11
Hempstead, NY (town) Nassau County	34.78

Notes: Please refer to the User's Guide for an explanation of data; tables include places with populations > 9,999 and reflect only those areas that meet Summary File 4 population thresholds, therefore there may be less than 10 places listed

Babylon, NY (town) Suffolk County — Port Chester table

Place	
Babylon, NY (town) Suffolk County	28.30
Brookhaven, NY (town) Suffolk County	24.56
Hempstead, NY (village) Nassau County	24.47
Huntington, NY (town) Suffolk County	17.58
New York, NY (city)	8.64
Port Chester, NY (village) Westchester County	8.14

Hondurans Who Own Their Own Homes
Top 10 Places Sorted by Number

Place	Number
New York, NY (city)	990
Islip, NY (town) Suffolk County	130
Hempstead, NY (town) Nassau County	89
Brentwood, NY (cdp) Suffolk County	60
Babylon, NY (town) Suffolk County	36
Newburgh, NY (city) Orange County	36
Huntington, NY (town) Suffolk County	32
Yonkers, NY (city) Westchester County	20
Hempstead, NY (village) Nassau County	9
North Hempstead, NY (town) Nassau County	7

Hondurans Who Own Their Own Homes
Top 10 Places Sorted by Percent

Place	Percent
Islip, NY (town) Suffolk County	49.06
Brentwood, NY (cdp) Suffolk County	46.15
Huntington, NY (town) Suffolk County	42.67
Babylon, NY (town) Suffolk County	31.03
Newburgh, NY (city) Orange County	19.46
Hempstead, NY (town) Nassau County	17.15
New York, NY (city)	11.36
Yonkers, NY (city) Westchester County	8.85
North Hempstead, NY (town) Nassau County	5.47
Hempstead, NY (village) Nassau County	2.95

Mexicans Who Own Their Own Homes
Top 10 Places Sorted by Number

Place	Number
New York, NY (city)	2,515
Hempstead, NY (town) Nassau County	287
New Rochelle, NY (city) Westchester County	245
Brookhaven, NY (town) Suffolk County	174
Buffalo, NY (city) Erie County	170
Islip, NY (town) Suffolk County	137
Rochester, NY (city) Monroe County	123
Rye, NY (town) Westchester County	110
Newburgh, NY (city) Orange County	108
Yonkers, NY (city) Westchester County	104

Mexicans Who Own Their Own Homes
Top 10 Places Sorted by Percent

Place	Percent
Elmont, NY (cdp) Nassau County	60.20
Brookhaven, NY (town) Suffolk County	57.43
Hempstead, NY (town) Nassau County	53.15
Islip, NY (town) Suffolk County	49.82
Oyster Bay, NY (town) Nassau County	42.06
Rochester, NY (city) Monroe County	40.20
Brentwood, NY (cdp) Suffolk County	40.00
Buffalo, NY (city) Erie County	38.81
Huntington, NY (town) Suffolk County	38.60
Greenburgh, NY (town) Westchester County	37.72

Nicaraguans Who Own Their Own Homes
Top 10 Places Sorted by Number

Place	Number
New York, NY (city)	279
Yonkers, NY (city) Westchester County	53

Nicaraguans Who Own Their Own Homes
Top 10 Places Sorted by Percent

Place	Percent
Yonkers, NY (city) Westchester County	30.46
New York, NY (city)	11.86

Panamanians Who Own Their Own Homes
Top 10 Places Sorted by Number

Place	Number
New York, NY (city)	1,983
Hempstead, NY (town) Nassau County	163
Islip, NY (town) Suffolk County	85

Panamanians Who Own Their Own Homes
Top 10 Places Sorted by Percent

Place	Percent
Islip, NY (town) Suffolk County	94.44
Hempstead, NY (town) Nassau County	77.25
New York, NY (city)	24.61

Paraguayans Who Own Their Own Homes
Top 10 Places Sorted by Number

Place	Number
New York, NY (city)	72

Paraguayans Who Own Their Own Homes
Top 10 Places Sorted by Percent

Place	Percent
New York, NY (city)	16.36

Peruvians Who Own Their Own Homes
Top 10 Places Sorted by Number

Place	Number
New York, NY (city)	1,946
Hempstead, NY (town) Nassau County	240
Islip, NY (town) Suffolk County	234
Brookhaven, NY (town) Suffolk County	87
White Plains, NY (city) Westchester County	82
Oyster Bay, NY (town) Nassau County	80
Port Chester, NY (village) Westchester County	78
Rye, NY (town) Westchester County	78
Brentwood, NY (cdp) Suffolk County	71
North Hempstead, NY (town) Nassau County	45

Peruvians Who Own Their Own Homes
Top 10 Places Sorted by Percent

Place	Percent
Babylon, NY (town) Suffolk County	84.31
Islip, NY (town) Suffolk County	71.56
Brookhaven, NY (town) Suffolk County	71.31
Brentwood, NY (cdp) Suffolk County	59.66
Oyster Bay, NY (town) Nassau County	50.31
Hempstead, NY (town) Nassau County	44.20
North Hempstead, NY (town) Nassau County	41.28
Port Chester, NY (village) Westchester County	35.29
Rye, NY (town) Westchester County	33.33
Yonkers, NY (city) Westchester County	25.33

Puerto Ricans Who Own Their Own Homes
Top 10 Places Sorted by Number

Place	Number
New York, NY (city)	39,245
Islip, NY (town) Suffolk County	3,794
Hempstead, NY (town) Nassau County	2,867
Brookhaven, NY (town) Suffolk County	2,759
Rochester, NY (city) Monroe County	1,694
Brentwood, NY (cdp) Suffolk County	1,429
Yonkers, NY (city) Westchester County	1,295
Buffalo, NY (city) Erie County	1,218
Babylon, NY (town) Suffolk County	981
Central Islip, NY (cdp) Suffolk County	725

Puerto Ricans Who Own Their Own Homes
Top 10 Places Sorted by Percent

Place	Percent
Malone, NY (town) Franklin County	100.0
Shawangunk, NY (town) Ulster County	100.0
West Islip, NY (cdp) Suffolk County	96.7
East Fishkill, NY (town) Dutchess County	95.5
North Babylon, NY (cdp) Suffolk County	94.8
North Valley Stream, NY (cdp) Nassau County	93.9
Oceanside, NY (cdp) Nassau County	93.1
Elmont, NY (cdp) Nassau County	91.6
Medford, NY (cdp) Suffolk County	90.9
New City, NY (cdp) Rockland County	90.1

Salvadorans Who Own Their Own Homes
Top 10 Places Sorted by Number

Place	Number
Islip, NY (town) Suffolk County	1,26…
Hempstead, NY (town) Nassau County	1,06…
New York, NY (city)	87…
Brentwood, NY (cdp) Suffolk County	77…
Hempstead, NY (village) Nassau County	23…
North Hempstead, NY (town) Nassau County	21…
North Bay Shore, NY (cdp) Suffolk County	18…
Babylon, NY (town) Suffolk County	17…
Huntington, NY (town) Suffolk County	17…
Central Islip, NY (cdp) Suffolk County	16…

Salvadorans Who Own Their Own Homes
Top 10 Places Sorted by Percent

Place	Percent
Brentwood, NY (cdp) Suffolk County	61.0
Islip, NY (town) Suffolk County	60.8
North Bay Shore, NY (cdp) Suffolk County	59.2
Central Islip, NY (cdp) Suffolk County	57.4
Copiague, NY (cdp) Suffolk County	56.2
Valley Stream, NY (village) Nassau County	52.4
Uniondale, NY (cdp) Nassau County	50.4
Roosevelt, NY (cdp) Nassau County	40.7
Babylon, NY (town) Suffolk County	39.6
Elmont, NY (cdp) Nassau County	39.5

South Americans Who Own Their Own Homes
Top 10 Places Sorted by Number

Place	Number
New York, NY (city)	15,32…
Hempstead, NY (town) Nassau County	1,88…
Islip, NY (town) Suffolk County	1,22…
Brookhaven, NY (town) Suffolk County	60…
Oyster Bay, NY (town) Nassau County	59…
Brentwood, NY (cdp) Suffolk County	53…
North Hempstead, NY (town) Nassau County	51…
Babylon, NY (town) Suffolk County	45…
Yonkers, NY (city) Westchester County	26…
White Plains, NY (city) Westchester County	25…

South Americans Who Own Their Own Homes
Top 10 Places Sorted by Percent

Place	Percent
Uniondale, NY (cdp) Nassau County	95.…
Levittown, NY (cdp) Nassau County	92.3
Deer Park, NY (cdp) Suffolk County	86.6
Oceanside, NY (cdp) Nassau County	85.0
East Meadow, NY (cdp) Nassau County	83.4
Hicksville, NY (cdp) Nassau County	81.4
Central Islip, NY (cdp) Suffolk County	80.8
Franklin Square, NY (cdp) Nassau County	77.2
Smith, NY (town) Suffolk County	74.6
Brentwood, NY (cdp) Suffolk County	73.…

Notes: Please refer to the User's Guide for an explanation of data; tables include places with populations > 9,999 and reflect only those areas that meet Summary File 4 population thresholds, therefore there may be less than 10 places listed

Spaniards Who Own Their Own Homes
Top 10 Places Sorted by Number

Place	Number
New York, NY (city)	1,347
Hempstead, NY (town) Nassau County	219
Brookhaven, NY (town) Suffolk County	118

Spaniards Who Own Their Own Homes
Top 10 Places Sorted by Percent

Place	Percent
Hempstead, NY (town) Nassau County	86.22
Brookhaven, NY (town) Suffolk County	80.27
New York, NY (city)	34.90

Uruguayans Who Own Their Own Homes
Top 10 Places Sorted by Number

Place	Number
New York, NY (city)	227

Uruguayans Who Own Their Own Homes
Top 10 Places Sorted by Percent

Place	Percent
New York, NY (city)	26.33

Venezuelans Who Own Their Own Homes
Top 10 Places Sorted by Number

Place	Number
New York, NY (city)	445

Venezuelans Who Own Their Own Homes
Top 10 Places Sorted by Percent

Place	Percent
New York, NY (city)	21.29

Other Hispanics Who Own Their Own Homes
Top 10 Places Sorted by Number

Place	Number
New York, NY (city)	12,093
Hempstead, NY (town) Nassau County	1,618
Islip, NY (town) Suffolk County	1,334
Brookhaven, NY (town) Suffolk County	789
Brentwood, NY (cdp) Suffolk County	620
Babylon, NY (town) Suffolk County	521
Oyster Bay, NY (town) Nassau County	394
Yonkers, NY (city) Westchester County	323
North Hempstead, NY (town) Nassau County	273
Central Islip, NY (cdp) Suffolk County	240

Other Hispanics Who Own Their Own Homes
Top 10 Places Sorted by Percent

Place	Percent
Centereach, NY (cdp) Suffolk County	94.19
Warwick, NY (town) Orange County	92.16
Uniondale, NY (cdp) Nassau County	87.95
Medford, NY (cdp) Suffolk County	85.96
West Hempstead, NY (cdp) Nassau County	80.36
Shirley, NY (cdp) Suffolk County	80.00
Copiague, NY (cdp) Suffolk County	79.75
New City, NY (cdp) Rockland County	79.25
Smith, NY (town) Suffolk County	79.05
East Meadow, NY (cdp) Nassau County	78.38

Median Gross Rent

All Specified Renter-Occupied Housing Units
Top 10 Places Sorted by Number

Place	Dollars/Month
Scarsdale, NY (village) Westchester County	2,000+
Melville, NY (cdp) Suffolk County	1,842
Garden City, NY (village) Nassau County	1,604
Somers, NY (town) Westchester County	1,451
New Castle, NY (town) Westchester County	1,375
Dix Hills, NY (cdp) Suffolk County	1,363
Rye, NY (city) Westchester County	1,329
New Cassel, NY (cdp) Nassau County	1,296
Elwood, NY (cdp) Suffolk County	1,292
Commack, NY (cdp) Suffolk County	1,269

Specified Housing Units Rented by Hispanics
Top 10 Places Sorted by Number

Place	Dollars/Month
Lewisboro, NY (town) Westchester County	2,000+
North Wantagh, NY (cdp) Nassau County	1,875
Somers, NY (town) Westchester County	1,875
Merrick, NY (cdp) Nassau County	1,604
Salisbury, NY (cdp) Nassau County	1,500
Commack, NY (cdp) Suffolk County	1,417
New Cassel, NY (cdp) Nassau County	1,398
Melville, NY (cdp) Suffolk County	1,385
North Massapequa, NY (cdp) Nassau County	1,319
Setauket-East Setauket, NY (cdp) Suffolk County	1,302

Specified Housing Units Rented by Argentinians
Top 10 Places Sorted by Number

Place	Dollars/Month
Hempstead, NY (town) Nassau County	985
North Hempstead, NY (town) Nassau County	950
New York, NY (city)	816

Specified Housing Units Rented by Bolivians
Top 10 Places Sorted by Number

Place	Dollars/Month
New York, NY (city)	852

Specified Housing Units Rented by Central Americans
Top 10 Places Sorted by Number

Place	Dollars/Month
Levittown, NY (cdp) Nassau County	1,559
New Cassel, NY (cdp) Nassau County	1,448
Port Washington, NY (cdp) Nassau County	1,254
North Hempstead, NY (town) Nassau County	1,153
Westbury, NY (village) Nassau County	1,136
Port Chester, NY (village) Westchester County	1,129
East Hampton, NY (town) Suffolk County	1,125
Rye, NY (town) Westchester County	1,122
Baldwin, NY (cdp) Nassau County	1,107
Uniondale, NY (cdp) Nassau County	1,086

Specified Housing Units Rented by Chileans
Top 10 Places Sorted by Number

Place	Dollars/Month
Oyster Bay, NY (town) Nassau County	1,135
North Hempstead, NY (town) Nassau County	1,070
Hempstead, NY (town) Nassau County	953
New York, NY (city)	789

Specified Housing Units Rented by Colombians
Top 10 Places Sorted by Number

Place	Dollars/Month
Oyster Bay, NY (town) Nassau County	1,296
Port Chester, NY (village) Westchester County	1,075
Rye, NY (town) Westchester County	1,059
Greenburgh, NY (town) Westchester County	1,010
Babylon, NY (town) Suffolk County	979
Huntington, NY (town) Suffolk County	969
North Hempstead, NY (town) Nassau County	956
Hempstead, NY (town) Nassau County	926
Long Beach, NY (city) Nassau County	905
White Plains, NY (city) Westchester County	902

Specified Housing Units Rented by Costa Ricans
Top 10 Places Sorted by Number

Place	Dollars/Month
Hempstead, NY (town) Nassau County	843
New York, NY (city)	650

Specified Housing Units Rented by Cubans
Top 10 Places Sorted by Number

Place	Dollars/Month
Oyster Bay, NY (town) Nassau County	2,000+
North Hempstead, NY (town) Nassau County	1,050
Brookhaven, NY (town) Suffolk County	950
Hempstead, NY (town) Nassau County	883
Babylon, NY (town) Suffolk County	838
Islip, NY (town) Suffolk County	793
Yonkers, NY (city) Westchester County	695
Greenburgh, NY (town) Westchester County	641
New York, NY (city)	628
Port Chester, NY (village) Westchester County	567

Specified Housing Units Rented by Dominicans
Top 10 Places Sorted by Number

Place	Dollars/Month
Port Chester, NY (village) Westchester County	1,053
Central Islip, NY (cdp) Suffolk County	1,038
Greenburgh, NY (town) Westchester County	1,015
Baldwin, NY (cdp) Nassau County	1,005
Rye, NY (town) Westchester County	992
Uniondale, NY (cdp) Nassau County	965
Babylon, NY (town) Suffolk County	936
Ossining, NY (town) Westchester County	933
Ossining, NY (village) Westchester County	933
Copiague, NY (cdp) Suffolk County	929

Specified Housing Units Rented by Ecuadorians
Top 10 Places Sorted by Number

Place	Dollars/Month
White Plains, NY (city) Westchester County	1,262
Port Chester, NY (village) Westchester County	1,106
Rye, NY (town) Westchester County	1,106
Babylon, NY (town) Suffolk County	1,058
Patchogue, NY (village) Suffolk County	1,045
Brookhaven, NY (town) Suffolk County	1,040
East Hampton, NY (town) Suffolk County	1,029
Peekskill, NY (city) Westchester County	940
Ramapo, NY (town) Rockland County	924
Hempstead, NY (town) Nassau County	922

Specified Housing Units Rented by Guatelmalans
Top 10 Places Sorted by Number

Place	Dollars/Month
North Hempstead, NY (town) Nassau County	1,256
Port Chester, NY (village) Westchester County	1,192
Rye, NY (town) Westchester County	1,171
Huntington, NY (town) Suffolk County	1,101
Mamaroneck, NY (town) Westchester County	1,080
Mamaroneck, NY (village) Westchester County	1,070
Hempstead, NY (village) Nassau County	950
Babylon, NY (town) Suffolk County	933
Southampton, NY (town) Suffolk County	927
Hempstead, NY (town) Nassau County	913

Specified Housing Units Rented by Hondurans
Top 10 Places Sorted by Number

Place	Dollars/Month
North Hempstead, NY (town) Nassau County	1,201
Islip, NY (town) Suffolk County	970
Hempstead, NY (town) Nassau County	934
Hempstead, NY (village) Nassau County	924
Huntington, NY (town) Suffolk County	910
Babylon, NY (town) Suffolk County	867
Brentwood, NY (cdp) Suffolk County	814
Yonkers, NY (city) Westchester County	708

Notes: Please refer to the User's Guide for an explanation of data; tables include places with populations > 9,999 and reflect only those areas that meet Summary File 4 population thresholds, therefore there may be less than 10 places listed

Newburgh, NY (city) Orange County — 706
New York, NY (city) — 623

Specified Housing Units Rented by Mexicans
Top 10 Places Sorted by Number

Place	Dollars/Month
Brentwood, NY (cdp) Suffolk County	1,367
New Cassel, NY (cdp) Nassau County	1,230
Huntington, NY (town) Suffolk County	1,115
North Hempstead, NY (town) Nassau County	1,088
Oyster Bay, NY (town) Nassau County	1,074
White Plains, NY (city) Westchester County	1,058
Clarks, NY (town) Rockland County	1,055
Port Chester, NY (village) Westchester County	1,041
Babylon, NY (town) Suffolk County	1,031
Rye, NY (town) Westchester County	1,028

Specified Housing Units Rented by Nicaraguans
Top 10 Places Sorted by Number

Place	Dollars/Month
Yonkers, NY (city) Westchester County	767
New York, NY (city)	686

Specified Housing Units Rented by Panamanians
Top 10 Places Sorted by Number

Place	Dollars/Month
Islip, NY (town) Suffolk County	950
New York, NY (city)	652
Hempstead, NY (town) Nassau County	600

Specified Housing Units Rented by Paraguayans
Top 10 Places Sorted by Number

Place	Dollars/Month
New York, NY (city)	770

Specified Housing Units Rented by Peruvians
Top 10 Places Sorted by Number

Place	Dollars/Month
Glen Cove, NY (city) Nassau County	1,083
Oyster Bay, NY (town) Nassau County	991
Yonkers, NY (city) Westchester County	983
Port Chester, NY (village) Westchester County	980
Rye, NY (town) Westchester County	974
Brookhaven, NY (town) Suffolk County	964
Hempstead, NY (town) Nassau County	960
New Rochelle, NY (city) Westchester County	958
White Plains, NY (city) Westchester County	923
North Hempstead, NY (town) Nassau County	905

Specified Housing Units Rented by Puerto Ricans
Top 10 Places Sorted by Number

Place	Dollars/Month
Farmingville, NY (cdp) Suffolk County	1,539
Commack, NY (cdp) Suffolk County	1,500
Ronkonkoma, NY (cdp) Suffolk County	1,277
Dix Hills, NY (cdp) Suffolk County	1,203
Hauppauge, NY (cdp) Suffolk County	1,200
Southampton, NY (town) Suffolk County	1,185
Mastic Beach, NY (cdp) Suffolk County	1,183
East Meadow, NY (cdp) Nassau County	1,161
Nanuet, NY (cdp) Rockland County	1,143
Goshen, NY (town) Orange County	1,125

Specified Housing Units Rented by Salvadorans
Top 10 Places Sorted by Number

Place	Dollars/Month
New Cassel, NY (cdp) Nassau County	1,369
Central Islip, NY (cdp) Suffolk County	1,162
Wyandanch, NY (cdp) Suffolk County	1,161
Westbury, NY (village) Nassau County	1,152
North Hempstead, NY (town) Nassau County	1,144

Place	Dollars/Month
Uniondale, NY (cdp) Nassau County	1,116
Hicksville, NY (cdp) Nassau County	1,109
Huntington Station, NY (cdp) Suffolk County	1,103
Rye, NY (town) Westchester County	1,084
Copiague, NY (cdp) Suffolk County	1,077

Specified Housing Units Rented by South Americans
Top 10 Places Sorted by Number

Place	Dollars/Month
Levittown, NY (cdp) Nassau County	1,375
Hicksville, NY (cdp) Nassau County	1,268
Franklin Square, NY (cdp) Nassau County	1,188
Mamaroneck, NY (village) Westchester County	1,130
Deer Park, NY (cdp) Suffolk County	1,125
Mamaroneck, NY (town) Westchester County	1,121
Copiague, NY (cdp) Suffolk County	1,109
Oyster Bay, NY (town) Nassau County	1,109
Smith, NY (town) Suffolk County	1,102
Port Chester, NY (village) Westchester County	1,064

Specified Housing Units Rented by Spaniards
Top 10 Places Sorted by Number

Place	Dollars/Month
Hempstead, NY (town) Nassau County	959
Brookhaven, NY (town) Suffolk County	832
New York, NY (city)	748

Specified Housing Units Rented by Uruguayans
Top 10 Places Sorted by Number

Place	Dollars/Month
New York, NY (city)	797

Specified Housing Units Rented by Venezuelans
Top 10 Places Sorted by Number

Place	Dollars/Month
New York, NY (city)	823

Specified Housing Units Rented by Other Hispanics
Top 10 Places Sorted by Number

Place	Dollars/Month
Roosevelt, NY (cdp) Nassau County	1,750
Medford, NY (cdp) Suffolk County	1,625
New Cassel, NY (cdp) Nassau County	1,587
East Hampton, NY (town) Suffolk County	1,539
Harrison, NY (village) Westchester County	1,360
Westbury, NY (village) Nassau County	1,304
West Hempstead, NY (cdp) Nassau County	1,271
North Bay Shore, NY (cdp) Suffolk County	1,250
Centereach, NY (cdp) Suffolk County	1,125
Holbrook, NY (cdp) Suffolk County	1,125

Median Home Value

All Specified Owner-Occupied Housing Units
Top 10 Places Sorted by Number

Place	Dollars
Scarsdale, NY (village) Westchester County	708,000
Rye, NY (city) Westchester County	635,700
North Castle, NY (town) Westchester County	588,500
Harrison, NY (village) Westchester County	578,700
Mamaroneck, NY (village) Westchester County	553,700
New Castle, NY (town) Westchester County	533,900
Garden City, NY (village) Nassau County	460,000
Bedford, NY (town) Westchester County	447,000
Pelham, NY (town) Westchester County	422,600
Port Washington, NY (cdp) Nassau County	416,100

Specified Housing Units Owned and Occupied by Hispanics
Top 10 Places Sorted by Number

Place	Dollars
Scarsdale, NY (village) Westchester County	633,300
Lewisboro, NY (town) Westchester County	566,700
Harrison, NY (village) Westchester County	423,700
Pelham, NY (town) Westchester County	413,300
Rye, NY (city) Westchester County	385,300
New Castle, NY (town) Westchester County	371,400
Somers, NY (town) Westchester County	356,300
Dobbs Ferry, NY (village) Westchester County	355,900
Garden City, NY (village) Nassau County	347,400
Dix Hills, NY (cdp) Suffolk County	336,400

Specified Housing Units Owned and Occupied by Argentinians
Top 10 Places Sorted by Number

Place	Dollars
North Hempstead, NY (town) Nassau County	392,900
New York, NY (city)	244,100
Hempstead, NY (town) Nassau County	233,500

Specified Housing Units Owned and Occupied by Bolivians
Top 10 Places Sorted by Number

Place	Dollars
New York, NY (city)	224,300

Specified Housing Units Owned and Occupied by Central Americans
Top 10 Places Sorted by Number

Place	Dollars
Port Washington, NY (cdp) Nassau County	300,000
Long Beach, NY (city) Nassau County	269,400
Glen Cove, NY (city) Nassau County	261,700
Clarks, NY (town) Rockland County	260,300
White Plains, NY (city) Westchester County	234,400
Mineola, NY (village) Nassau County	221,200
Oyster Bay, NY (town) Nassau County	219,000
Valley Stream, NY (village) Nassau County	212,900
East Hampton, NY (town) Suffolk County	208,300
Hicksville, NY (cdp) Nassau County	207,800

Specified Housing Units Owned and Occupied by Chileans
Top 10 Places Sorted by Number

Place	Dollars
North Hempstead, NY (town) Nassau County	258,300
Oyster Bay, NY (town) Nassau County	244,600
Hempstead, NY (town) Nassau County	210,500
New York, NY (city)	192,000

Specified Housing Units Owned and Occupied by Colombians
Top 10 Places Sorted by Number

Place	Dollars
Yonkers, NY (city) Westchester County	422,700
White Plains, NY (city) Westchester County	309,500
East Hampton, NY (town) Suffolk County	308,300
Huntington, NY (town) Suffolk County	291,700
Oyster Bay, NY (town) Nassau County	271,400
Mineola, NY (village) Nassau County	271,300
Greenburgh, NY (town) Westchester County	268,100
Port Chester, NY (village) Westchester County	268,100
Rye, NY (town) Westchester County	268,100
North Hempstead, NY (town) Nassau County	259,500

Notes: Please refer to the User's Guide for an explanation of data; tables include places with populations > 9,999 and reflect only those areas that meet Summary File 4 population thresholds, therefore there may be less than 10 places listed

Specified Housing Units Owned and Occupied by Costa Ricans
Top 10 Places Sorted by Number

Place	Dollars
New York, NY (city)	175,700
Hempstead, NY (town) Nassau County	175,000

Specified Housing Units Owned and Occupied by Cubans
Top 10 Places Sorted by Number

Place	Dollars
Greenburgh, NY (town) Westchester County	332,400
Clarks, NY (town) Rockland County	276,900
Yonkers, NY (city) Westchester County	273,100
North Hempstead, NY (town) Nassau County	270,000
Oyster Bay, NY (town) Nassau County	254,500
Rye, NY (town) Westchester County	216,700
New York, NY (city)	215,200
Hempstead, NY (town) Nassau County	209,600
Port Chester, NY (village) Westchester County	193,400
Babylon, NY (town) Suffolk County	159,100

Specified Housing Units Owned and Occupied by Dominicans
Top 10 Places Sorted by Number

Place	Dollars
Rye, NY (town) Westchester County	562,500
Rockville Centre, NY (village) Nassau County	450,000
Mount Vernon, NY (city) Westchester County	418,800
Mount Pleasant, NY (town) Westchester County	275,000
Port Chester, NY (village) Westchester County	275,000
Huntington, NY (town) Suffolk County	258,000
North Hempstead, NY (town) Nassau County	245,400
Oyster Bay, NY (town) Nassau County	238,400
Yonkers, NY (city) Westchester County	232,700
Greenburgh, NY (town) Westchester County	225,000

Specified Housing Units Owned and Occupied by Ecuadorians
Top 10 Places Sorted by Number

Place	Dollars
White Plains, NY (city) Westchester County	410,000
Oyster Bay, NY (town) Nassau County	254,500
Ossining, NY (town) Westchester County	229,500
Ossining, NY (village) Westchester County	229,500
North Hempstead, NY (town) Nassau County	213,600
Yonkers, NY (city) Westchester County	211,800
Ramapo, NY (town) Rockland County	210,500
New York, NY (city)	209,600
Peekskill, NY (city) Westchester County	208,300
Hempstead, NY (town) Nassau County	199,800

Specified Housing Units Owned and Occupied by Guatelmalans
Top 10 Places Sorted by Number

Place	Dollars
New York, NY (city)	205,600
Huntington, NY (town) Suffolk County	204,200
Freeport, NY (village) Nassau County	202,600
Hempstead, NY (town) Nassau County	184,300
Babylon, NY (town) Suffolk County	170,800
Brookhaven, NY (town) Suffolk County	162,500
Islip, NY (town) Suffolk County	147,700
Brentwood, NY (cdp) Suffolk County	142,500
Hempstead, NY (village) Nassau County	112,500
Southampton, NY (town) Suffolk County	112,500

Specified Housing Units Owned and Occupied by Hondurans
Top 10 Places Sorted by Number

Place	Dollars
Yonkers, NY (city) Westchester County	275,000
Hempstead, NY (village) Nassau County	225,000
Hempstead, NY (town) Nassau County	221,600
Babylon, NY (town) Suffolk County	194,400
New York, NY (city)	181,100
Huntington, NY (town) Suffolk County	173,100
Islip, NY (town) Suffolk County	144,100
Brentwood, NY (cdp) Suffolk County	135,400
Newburgh, NY (city) Orange County	97,700
North Hempstead, NY (town) Nassau County	0

Specified Housing Units Owned and Occupied by Mexicans
Top 10 Places Sorted by Number

Place	Dollars
Mamaroneck, NY (town) Westchester County	875,000
Clarks, NY (town) Rockland County	350,000
North Hempstead, NY (town) Nassau County	326,500
Greenburgh, NY (town) Westchester County	284,200
White Plains, NY (city) Westchester County	263,500
Mamaroneck, NY (village) Westchester County	261,100
Mount Vernon, NY (city) Westchester County	260,400
Huntington, NY (town) Suffolk County	231,600
Rye, NY (town) Westchester County	228,600
Port Chester, NY (village) Westchester County	214,300

Specified Housing Units Owned and Occupied by Nicaraguans
Top 10 Places Sorted by Number

Place	Dollars
Yonkers, NY (city) Westchester County	194,800
New York, NY (city)	183,900

Specified Housing Units Owned and Occupied by Panamanians
Top 10 Places Sorted by Number

Place	Dollars
Hempstead, NY (town) Nassau County	192,100
New York, NY (city)	179,700
Islip, NY (town) Suffolk County	161,400

Specified Housing Units Owned and Occupied by Paraguayans
Top 10 Places Sorted by Number

Place	Dollars
New York, NY (city)	198,200

Specified Housing Units Owned and Occupied by Peruvians
Top 10 Places Sorted by Number

Place	Dollars
New Rochelle, NY (city) Westchester County	330,000
Yonkers, NY (city) Westchester County	326,300
White Plains, NY (city) Westchester County	311,400
Glen Cove, NY (city) Nassau County	275,000
Port Chester, NY (village) Westchester County	267,900
Rye, NY (town) Westchester County	267,900
Oyster Bay, NY (town) Nassau County	223,300
New York, NY (city)	221,000
North Hempstead, NY (town) Nassau County	219,200
Hempstead, NY (town) Nassau County	207,500

Specified Housing Units Owned and Occupied by Puerto Ricans
Top 10 Places Sorted by Number

Place	Dollars
Eastchester, NY (town) Westchester County	367,200
Rockville Centre, NY (village) Nassau County	313,900
Dix Hills, NY (cdp) Suffolk County	297,700
Mount Pleasant, NY (town) Westchester County	292,000
New Rochelle, NY (city) Westchester County	282,000
Bedford, NY (town) Westchester County	275,000
North Hempstead, NY (town) Nassau County	274,500
Greenburgh, NY (town) Westchester County	269,200
Jefferson Valley-Yorktown, NY (cdp) Westchester County	262,100
Rye, NY (town) Westchester County	262,000

Specified Housing Units Owned and Occupied by Salvadorans
Top 10 Places Sorted by Number

Place	Dollars
Glen Cove, NY (city) Nassau County	246,900
Mineola, NY (village) Nassau County	234,600
Yonkers, NY (city) Westchester County	229,500
Valley Stream, NY (village) Nassau County	219,700
Oyster Bay, NY (town) Nassau County	207,100
North Hempstead, NY (town) Nassau County	189,000
New York, NY (city)	186,000
New Cassel, NY (cdp) Nassau County	184,800
Westbury, NY (village) Nassau County	183,800
Hempstead, NY (town) Nassau County	173,800

Specified Housing Units Owned and Occupied by South Americans
Top 10 Places Sorted by Number

Place	Dollars
White Plains, NY (city) Westchester County	306,600
Mamaroneck, NY (town) Westchester County	287,500
Mineola, NY (village) Nassau County	280,300
Huntington, NY (town) Suffolk County	266,300
Greenburgh, NY (town) Westchester County	265,600
Rye, NY (town) Westchester County	264,400
North Hempstead, NY (town) Nassau County	263,800
Mamaroneck, NY (village) Westchester County	259,400
Port Chester, NY (village) Westchester County	252,900
Franklin Square, NY (cdp) Nassau County	250,000

Specified Housing Units Owned and Occupied by Spaniards
Top 10 Places Sorted by Number

Place	Dollars
Hempstead, NY (town) Nassau County	233,100
New York, NY (city)	231,700
Brookhaven, NY (town) Suffolk County	152,700

Specified Housing Units Owned and Occupied by Uruguayans
Top 10 Places Sorted by Number

Place	Dollars
New York, NY (city)	256,500

Specified Housing Units Owned and Occupied by Venezuelans
Top 10 Places Sorted by Number

Place	Dollars
New York, NY (city)	203,300

Specified Housing Units Owned and Occupied by Other Hispanics
Top 10 Places Sorted by Number

Place	Dollars
Mamaroneck, NY (town) Westchester County	430,000
Harrison, NY (village) Westchester County	350,000
Port Chester, NY (village) Westchester County	350,000
Rye, NY (town) Westchester County	350,000
Greenburgh, NY (town) Westchester County	327,300
Ossining, NY (town) Westchester County	309,300
Clarks, NY (town) Rockland County	302,900
New Rochelle, NY (city) Westchester County	300,000
White Plains, NY (city) Westchester County	292,500
Mount Pleasant, NY (town) Westchester County	284,000

Notes: Please refer to the User's Guide for an explanation of data; tables include places with populations > 9,999 and reflect only those areas that meet Summary File 4 population thresholds, therefore there may be less than 10 places listed

Population

Total Population
Top 10 Places Sorted by Number

Place	Number
New York, NY	8,008,278
Hempstead, NY (town) Nassau County	755,924
Brookhaven, NY (town) Suffolk County	448,265
Islip, NY (town) Suffolk County	322,625
Oyster Bay, NY (town) Nassau County	293,925
Buffalo, NY (city) Erie County	292,648
North Hempstead, NY (town) Nassau County	222,611
Rochester, NY (city) Monroe County	219,766
Babylon, NY (town) Suffolk County	211,779
Yonkers, NY (city) Westchester County	196,086

Asian
Top 10 Places Sorted by Number

Place	Number
New York, NY	788,110
Hempstead, NY (town) Nassau County	26,248
North Hempstead, NY (town) Nassau County	20,579
Oyster Bay, NY (town) Nassau County	13,857
Brookhaven, NY (town) Suffolk County	13,470
Yonkers, NY (city) Westchester County	9,564
Greenburgh, NY (town) Westchester County	7,818
Huntington, NY (town) Suffolk County	6,823
Clarkstown, NY (town) Rockland County	6,705
Islip, NY (town) Suffolk County	6,279

Asian
Top 10 Places Sorted by Percent of Total Population

Place	Percent
Forest Home, NY (cdp) Tompkins County	35.17
Lansing, NY (village) Tompkins County	26.85
Manhasset Hills, NY (cdp) Nassau County	26.82
Searingtown, NY (cdp) Nassau County	23.29
Garden City Park, NY (cdp) Nassau County	22.84
Herricks, NY (cdp) Nassau County	22.20
East Ithaca, NY (cdp) Tompkins County	20.33
Greenville, NY (cdp) Westchester County	19.30
Muttontown, NY (village) Nassau County	17.05
Northeast Ithaca, NY (cdp) Tompkins County	16.94

Native Hawaiian and Other Pacific Islander
Top 10 Places Sorted by Number

Place	Number
New York, NY	4,870

Native Hawaiian and Other Pacific Islander
Top 10 Places Sorted by Percent of Asian Population

Place	Percent
New York, NY	100.00

Native Hawaiian and Other Pacific Islander
Top 10 Places Sorted by Percent of Total Population

Place	Percent
New York, NY	0.06

Asian Indian
Top 10 Places Sorted by Number

Place	Number
New York, NY	170,182
Hempstead, NY (town) Nassau County	10,199
North Hempstead, NY (town) Nassau County	7,642
Oyster Bay, NY (town) Nassau County	5,141
Yonkers, NY (city) Westchester County	4,689
Brookhaven, NY (town) Suffolk County	3,477
Greenburgh, NY (town) Westchester County	2,586
Islip, NY (town) Suffolk County	2,460
Clarkstown, NY (town) Rockland County	2,394
Huntington, NY (town) Suffolk County	2,025

Asian Indian
Top 10 Places Sorted by Percent of Asian Population

Place	Percent
Muttontown, NY (village) Nassau County	60.21
Elmont, NY (cdp) Nassau County	60.10
Searingtown, NY (cdp) Nassau County	59.69
New Hyde Park, NY (village) Nassau County	56.81
Herricks, NY (cdp) Nassau County	56.13
North New Hyde Park, NY (cdp) Nassau County	55.91
Poughkeepsie, NY (town) Dutchess County	52.70
Spring Valley, NY (village) Rockland County	52.33
Hicksville, NY (cdp) Nassau County	50.26
Mount Vernon, NY (city) Westchester County	49.04

Asian Indian
Top 10 Places Sorted by Percent of Total Population

Place	Percent
Searingtown, NY (cdp) Nassau County	13.90
Herricks, NY (cdp) Nassau County	12.46
Manhasset Hills, NY (cdp) Nassau County	10.90
Garden City Park, NY (cdp) Nassau County	10.75
Muttontown, NY (village) Nassau County	10.27
North New Hyde Park, NY (cdp) Nassau County	8.23
New Hyde Park, NY (village) Nassau County	8.06
Greenville, NY (cdp) Westchester County	6.19
Elmont, NY (cdp) Nassau County	5.85
Hicksville, NY (cdp) Nassau County	4.49

Bangladeshi
Top 10 Places Sorted by Number

Place	Number
New York, NY	19,149

Bangladeshi
Top 10 Places Sorted by Percent of Asian Population

Place	Percent
New York, NY	2.43

Bangladeshi
Top 10 Places Sorted by Percent of Total Population

Place	Percent
New York, NY	0.24

Cambodian
Top 10 Places Sorted by Number

Place	Number
New York, NY	1,619

Cambodian
Top 10 Places Sorted by Percent of Asian Population

Place	Percent
New York, NY	0.21

Cambodian
Top 10 Places Sorted by Percent of Total Population

Place	Percent
New York, NY	0.02

Chinese (except Taiwanese)
Top 10 Places Sorted by Number

Place	Number
New York, NY	357,540
North Hempstead, NY (town) Nassau County	5,598
Hempstead, NY (town) Nassau County	5,339
Brookhaven, NY (town) Suffolk County	4,762
Oyster Bay, NY (town) Nassau County	3,674
Ithaca, NY (city) Tompkins County	1,994
Huntington, NY (town) Suffolk County	1,885
Amherst, NY (town) Erie County	1,683
Greenburgh, NY (town) Westchester County	1,275
Islip, NY (town) Suffolk County	1,162

Chinese (except Taiwanese)
Top 10 Places Sorted by Percent of Asian Population

Place	Percent
Stony Brook, NY (cdp) Suffolk County	52.49
Troy, NY (city) Rensselaer County	51.12
Ithaca, NY (city) Tompkins County	49.37
Fishkill, NY (town) Dutchess County	47.35
Setauket-East Setauket, NY (cdp) Suffolk County	45.77
New York, NY	45.37
Vestal, NY (town) Broome County	40.38
Brookhaven, NY (town) Suffolk County	35.35
North New Hyde Park, NY (cdp) Nassau County	33.63
Syosset, NY (cdp) Nassau County	33.48

Chinese (except Taiwanese)
Top 10 Places Sorted by Percent of Total Population

Place	Percent
Ithaca, NY (city) Tompkins County	6.87
Garden City Park, NY (cdp) Nassau County	5.33
Lake Success, NY (village) Nassau County	5.08
North New Hyde Park, NY (cdp) Nassau County	4.95
New York, NY	4.46
Setauket-East Setauket, NY (cdp) Suffolk County	4.24
Syosset, NY (cdp) Nassau County	4.20
Vestal, NY (town) Broome County	3.20
Stony Brook, NY (cdp) Suffolk County	3.08
North Hempstead, NY (town) Nassau County	2.51

Fijian
Top 10 Places Sorted by Number

Place	Number
No places met population threshold.	

Fijian
Top 10 Places Sorted by Percent of Asian Population

Place	Percent
No places met population threshold.	

Fijian
Top 10 Places Sorted by Percent of Total Population

Place	Percent
No places met population threshold.	

Filipino
Top 10 Places Sorted by Number

Place	Number
New York, NY	58,946
Hempstead, NY (town) Nassau County	4,125
Clarkstown, NY (town) Rockland County	2,182
Yonkers, NY (city) Westchester County	1,817
Brookhaven, NY (town) Suffolk County	1,473
North Hempstead, NY (town) Nassau County	1,357
Ramapo, NY (town) Rockland County	1,356
Oyster Bay, NY (town) Nassau County	1,283
Islip, NY (town) Suffolk County	937
Huntington, NY (town) Suffolk County	758

Filipino
Top 10 Places Sorted by Percent of Asian Population

Place	Percent
Valley Cottage, NY (cdp) Rockland County	71.87
Hillcrest, NY (cdp) Rockland County	51.67
Clarkstown, NY (town) Rockland County	32.54
Ramapo, NY (town) Rockland County	26.43
Valley Stream, NY (village) Nassau County	23.97
Orangetown, NY (town) Rockland County	23.73
New City, NY (cdp) Rockland County	22.84
Levittown, NY (cdp) Nassau County	22.28
Yonkers, NY (city) Westchester County	19.00
Elmont, NY (cdp) Nassau County	17.31

Notes: Please refer to the User's Guide for an explanation of data; tables reflect only those areas that meet Summary File 4 population thresholds, therefore there may be less than 10 places listed

Filipino
Top 10 Places Sorted by Percent of Total Population

Place	Percent
Hillcrest, NY (cdp) Rockland County	7.60
Valley Cottage, NY (cdp) Rockland County	7.22
Clarkstown, NY (town) Rockland County	2.66
New City, NY (cdp) Rockland County	1.73
Elmont, NY (cdp) Nassau County	1.68
Valley Stream, NY (village) Nassau County	1.68
Orangetown, NY (town) Rockland County	1.49
Hicksville, NY (cdp) Nassau County	1.25
Ramapo, NY (town) Rockland County	1.25
East Meadow, NY (cdp) Nassau County	0.93

Guamanian or Chamorro
Top 10 Places Sorted by Number

Place	Number
New York, NY	1,176

Guamanian or Chamorro
Top 10 Places Sorted by Percent of Asian Population

Place	Percent
New York, NY	24.15

Guamanian or Chamorro
Top 10 Places Sorted by Percent of Total Population

Place	Percent
New York, NY	0.01

Hawaiian, Native
Top 10 Places Sorted by Number

Place	Number
New York, NY	776

Hawaiian, Native
Top 10 Places Sorted by Percent of Asian Population

Place	Percent
New York, NY	15.93

Hawaiian, Native
Top 10 Places Sorted by Percent of Total Population

Place	Percent
New York, NY	0.01

Hmong
Top 10 Places Sorted by Number

Place	Number
No places met population threshold.	

Hmong
Top 10 Places Sorted by Percent of Asian Population

Place	Percent
No places met population threshold.	

Hmong
Top 10 Places Sorted by Percent of Total Population

Place	Percent
No places met population threshold.	

Indonesian
Top 10 Places Sorted by Number

Place	Number
New York, NY	1,816

Indonesian
Top 10 Places Sorted by Percent of Asian Population

Place	Percent
New York, NY	0.23

Indonesian
Top 10 Places Sorted by Percent of Total Population

Place	Percent
New York, NY	0.02

Japanese
Top 10 Places Sorted by Number

Place	Number
New York, NY	22,302
Greenburgh, NY (town) Westchester County	1,957
Eastchester, NY (town) Westchester County	1,210
North Hempstead, NY (town) Nassau County	955
Scarsdale, NY (village) Westchester County	784
Harrison, NY (village) Westchester County	693
Rye, NY (city) Westchester County	645
Eastchester, NY (cdp) Westchester County	549
Greenville, NY (cdp) Westchester County	539
Brookhaven, NY (town) Suffolk County	414

Japanese
Top 10 Places Sorted by Percent of Asian Population

Place	Percent
Rye, NY (city) Westchester County	60.00
Eastchester, NY (town) Westchester County	53.42
Harrison, NY (village) Westchester County	51.87
Eastchester, NY (cdp) Westchester County	42.46
Scarsdale, NY (village) Westchester County	35.24
Greenville, NY (cdp) Westchester County	32.61
Greenburgh, NY (town) Westchester County	25.03
North Hempstead, NY (town) Nassau County	4.64
Brookhaven, NY (town) Suffolk County	3.07
New York, NY	2.83

Japanese
Top 10 Places Sorted by Percent of Total Population

Place	Percent
Greenville, NY (cdp) Westchester County	6.29
Scarsdale, NY (village) Westchester County	4.40
Rye, NY (city) Westchester County	4.31
Eastchester, NY (town) Westchester County	3.86
Eastchester, NY (cdp) Westchester County	2.96
Harrison, NY (village) Westchester County	2.87
Greenburgh, NY (town) Westchester County	2.26
North Hempstead, NY (town) Nassau County	0.43
New York, NY	0.28
Oyster Bay, NY (town) Nassau County	0.13

Korean
Top 10 Places Sorted by Number

Place	Number
New York, NY	87,139
North Hempstead, NY (town) Nassau County	3,248
Hempstead, NY (town) Nassau County	2,931
Oyster Bay, NY (town) Nassau County	2,472
Brookhaven, NY (town) Suffolk County	1,434
Yonkers, NY (city) Westchester County	1,063
Greenburgh, NY (town) Westchester County	1,000
Huntington, NY (town) Suffolk County	983
Amherst, NY (town) Erie County	939
Clarkstown, NY (town) Rockland County	721

Korean
Top 10 Places Sorted by Percent of Asian Population

Place	Percent
Lake Success, NY (village) Nassau County	53.17
Jericho, NY (cdp) Nassau County	48.35
Glen Cove, NY (city) Nassau County	37.80
Plainview, NY (cdp) Nassau County	30.96
Commack, NY (cdp) Suffolk County	24.45
Syosset, NY (cdp) Nassau County	24.07
Orangetown, NY (town) Rockland County	18.93
Oyster Bay, NY (town) Nassau County	17.84
Scarsdale, NY (village) Westchester County	17.21
Amherst, NY (town) Erie County	16.89

Korean
Top 10 Places Sorted by Percent of Total Population

Place	Percent
Lake Success, NY (village) Nassau County	8.69
Jericho, NY (cdp) Nassau County	5.52
Syosset, NY (cdp) Nassau County	3.02
Scarsdale, NY (village) Westchester County	2.15
Ithaca, NY (city) Tompkins County	1.64
Plainview, NY (cdp) Nassau County	1.51
Glen Cove, NY (city) Nassau County	1.50
North Hempstead, NY (town) Nassau County	1.46
Orangetown, NY (town) Rockland County	1.19
Greenburgh, NY (town) Westchester County	1.15

Laotian
Top 10 Places Sorted by Number

Place	Number
Rochester, NY (city) Monroe County	805

Laotian
Top 10 Places Sorted by Percent of Asian Population

Place	Percent
Rochester, NY (city) Monroe County	17.15

Laotian
Top 10 Places Sorted by Percent of Total Population

Place	Percent
Rochester, NY (city) Monroe County	0.37

Malaysian
Top 10 Places Sorted by Number

Place	Number
New York, NY	1,197

Malaysian
Top 10 Places Sorted by Percent of Asian Population

Place	Percent
New York, NY	0.15

Malaysian
Top 10 Places Sorted by Percent of Total Population

Place	Percent
New York, NY	0.01

Pakistani
Top 10 Places Sorted by Number

Place	Number
New York, NY	23,855
Hempstead, NY (town) Nassau County	1,407
Brookhaven, NY (town) Suffolk County	738
North Hempstead, NY (town) Nassau County	618
Huntington, NY (town) Suffolk County	437

Pakistani
Top 10 Places Sorted by Percent of Asian Population

Place	Percent
Huntington, NY (town) Suffolk County	6.40
Brookhaven, NY (town) Suffolk County	5.48
Hempstead, NY (town) Nassau County	5.36
New York, NY	3.03
North Hempstead, NY (town) Nassau County	3.00

Pakistani
Top 10 Places Sorted by Percent of Total Population

Place	Percent
New York, NY	0.30
North Hempstead, NY (town) Nassau County	0.28
Huntington, NY (town) Suffolk County	0.22

Notes: Please refer to the User's Guide for an explanation of data; tables reflect only those areas that meet Summary File 4 population thresholds, therefore there may be less than 10 places listed

PROFILES OF NEW YORK / Asian: Rankings

Place	
Hempstead, NY (town) Nassau County	0.19
Brookhaven, NY (town) Suffolk County	0.16

Samoan
Top 10 Places Sorted by Number

Place	Number
New York, NY	729

Samoan
Top 10 Places Sorted by Percent of Asian Population

Place	Percent
New York, NY	14.97

Samoan
Top 10 Places Sorted by Percent of Total Population

Place	Percent
New York, NY	0.01

Sri Lankan
Top 10 Places Sorted by Number

Place	Number
New York, NY	2,004

Sri Lankan
Top 10 Places Sorted by Percent of Asian Population

Place	Percent
New York, NY	0.25

Sri Lankan
Top 10 Places Sorted by Percent of Total Population

Place	Percent
New York, NY	0.03

Taiwanese
Top 10 Places Sorted by Number

Place	Number
New York, NY	4,907
North Hempstead, NY (town) Nassau County	283

Taiwanese
Top 10 Places Sorted by Percent of Asian Population

Place	Percent
North Hempstead, NY (town) Nassau County	1.38
New York, NY	0.62

Taiwanese
Top 10 Places Sorted by Percent of Total Population

Place	Percent
North Hempstead, NY (town) Nassau County	0.13
New York, NY	0.06

Thai
Top 10 Places Sorted by Number

Place	Number
New York, NY	3,823

Thai
Top 10 Places Sorted by Percent of Asian Population

Place	Percent
New York, NY	0.49

Thai
Top 10 Places Sorted by Percent of Total Population

Place	Percent
New York, NY	0.05

Tongan
Top 10 Places Sorted by Number

Place	Number
No places met population threshold.	

Tongan
Top 10 Places Sorted by Percent of Asian Population

Place	Percent
No places met population threshold.	

Tongan
Top 10 Places Sorted by Percent of Total Population

Place	Percent
No places met population threshold.	

Vietnamese
Top 10 Places Sorted by Number

Place	Number
New York, NY	12,310
Syracuse, NY (city) Onondaga County	1,265
Buffalo, NY (city) Erie County	1,177
Rochester, NY (city) Monroe County	1,002
Utica, NY (city) Oneida County	926
Albany, NY (city) Albany County	396
Binghamton, NY (city) Broome County	295

Vietnamese
Top 10 Places Sorted by Percent of Asian Population

Place	Percent
Utica, NY (city) Oneida County	69.52
Buffalo, NY (city) Erie County	30.96
Syracuse, NY (city) Onondaga County	25.78
Rochester, NY (city) Monroe County	21.35
Binghamton, NY (city) Broome County	19.87
Albany, NY (city) Albany County	13.62
New York, NY	1.56

Vietnamese
Top 10 Places Sorted by Percent of Total Population

Place	Percent
Utica, NY (city) Oneida County	1.53
Syracuse, NY (city) Onondaga County	0.86
Binghamton, NY (city) Broome County	0.62
Rochester, NY (city) Monroe County	0.46
Albany, NY (city) Albany County	0.41
Buffalo, NY (city) Erie County	0.40
New York, NY	0.15

Median Age

Total Population
Top 10 Places Sorted by Number

Place	Years
North Hills, NY (village) Nassau County	54.1
Lake Success, NY (village) Nassau County	51.8
Hartsdale, NY (cdp) Westchester County	43.3
Manhasset Hills, NY (cdp) Nassau County	43.3
Thomaston, NY (village) Nassau County	43.2
Roslyn, NY (village) Nassau County	43.1
Woodbury, NY (cdp) Nassau County	43.0
Hastings-on-Hudson, NY (village) Westchester County	42.9
Irondequoit, NY (town) Monroe County	42.7
Flower Hill, NY (village) Nassau County	42.6

Asian
Top 10 Places Sorted by Number

Place	Years
Sands Point, NY (village) Nassau County	48.1
Brookville, NY (village) Nassau County	46.2
Oyster Bay Cove, NY (village) Nassau County	44.1
Thomaston, NY (village) Nassau County	43.7
Baldwin, NY (cdp) Nassau County	42.5
Lake Success, NY (village) Nassau County	41.9
Old Westbury, NY (village) Nassau County	41.3
Monroe, NY (town) Orange County	40.9
West Nyack, NY (cdp) Rockland County	40.5
Laurel Hollow, NY (village) Nassau County	40.3

Native Hawaiian and Other Pacific Islander
Top 10 Places Sorted by Number

Place	Years
New York, NY	27.5

Asian Indian
Top 10 Places Sorted by Number

Place	Years
Pittsford, NY (town) Monroe County	40.2
Clifton Park, NY (town) Saratoga County	38.7
Muttontown, NY (village) Nassau County	38.5
Perinton, NY (town) Monroe County	37.8
New Castle, NY (town) Westchester County	37.2
Salisbury, NY (cdp) Nassau County	37.2
Herricks, NY (cdp) Nassau County	36.1
Scarsdale, NY (village) Westchester County	36.1
Dix Hills, NY (cdp) Suffolk County	35.9
Mount Pleasant, NY (town) Westchester County	35.6

Bangladeshi
Top 10 Places Sorted by Number

Place	Years
New York, NY	29.5

Cambodian
Top 10 Places Sorted by Number

Place	Years
New York, NY	25.8

Chinese (except Taiwanese)
Top 10 Places Sorted by Number

Place	Years
New Castle, NY (town) Westchester County	44.5
Scarsdale, NY (village) Westchester County	42.8
Lake Success, NY (village) Nassau County	42.3
Dix Hills, NY (cdp) Suffolk County	41.4
Yonkers, NY (city) Westchester County	41.2
Huntington, NY (town) Suffolk County	41.1
Plainview, NY (cdp) Nassau County	39.2
Garden City Park, NY (cdp) Nassau County	38.8
Babylon, NY (town) Suffolk County	38.7
Hempstead, NY (town) Nassau County	38.6

Fijian
Top 10 Places Sorted by Number

Place	Years

Filipino
Top 10 Places Sorted by Number

Place	Years
Orangetown, NY (town) Rockland County	47.4
Huntington, NY (town) Suffolk County	40.5
Valley Cottage, NY (cdp) Rockland County	38.4
New York, NY	38.1
Clarkstown, NY (town) Rockland County	37.7
North Hempstead, NY (town) Nassau County	36.9
Ramapo, NY (town) Rockland County	36.4
Babylon, NY (town) Suffolk County	36.3
Greenburgh, NY (town) Westchester County	35.6
Hillcrest, NY (cdp) Rockland County	35.6

Guamanian or Chamorro
Top 10 Places Sorted by Number

Place	Years
New York, NY	24.8

Notes: Please refer to the User's Guide for an explanation of data; tables reflect only those areas that meet Summary File 4 population thresholds, therefore there may be less than 10 places listed

PROFILES OF NEW YORK / Asian: Rankings

Hawaiian, Native
Top 10 Places Sorted by Number

Place	Years
New York, NY	30.6

Hmong
Top 10 Places Sorted by Number

Place	Years

Indonesian
Top 10 Places Sorted by Number

Place	Years
New York, NY	32.2

Japanese
Top 10 Places Sorted by Number

Place	Years
Brookhaven, NY (town) Suffolk County	44.8
Hempstead, NY (town) Nassau County	41.4
Greenville, NY (cdp) Westchester County	37.7
Rye, NY (city) Westchester County	37.5
Oyster Bay, NY (town) Nassau County	37.0
Greenburgh, NY (town) Westchester County	36.4
North Hempstead, NY (town) Nassau County	35.3
Eastchester, NY (cdp) Westchester County	33.3
Harrison, NY (village) Westchester County	33.3
Scarsdale, NY (village) Westchester County	33.2

Korean
Top 10 Places Sorted by Number

Place	Years
Syosset, NY (cdp) Nassau County	42.3
Lake Success, NY (village) Nassau County	41.3
Jericho, NY (cdp) Nassau County	39.2
Glen Cove, NY (city) Nassau County	39.0
Orangetown, NY (town) Rockland County	38.3
Greenburgh, NY (town) Westchester County	38.2
Plainview, NY (cdp) Nassau County	38.1
Scarsdale, NY (village) Westchester County	38.0
Oyster Bay, NY (town) Nassau County	36.4
Clarkstown, NY (town) Rockland County	36.0

Laotian
Top 10 Places Sorted by Number

Place	Years
Rochester, NY (city) Monroe County	26.2

Malaysian
Top 10 Places Sorted by Number

Place	Years
New York, NY	38.0

Pakistani
Top 10 Places Sorted by Number

Place	Years
New York, NY	28.0
Hempstead, NY (town) Nassau County	27.7
Brookhaven, NY (town) Suffolk County	27.2
Huntington, NY (town) Suffolk County	25.5
North Hempstead, NY (town) Nassau County	25.3

Samoan
Top 10 Places Sorted by Number

Place	Years
New York, NY	22.8

Sri Lankan
Top 10 Places Sorted by Number

Place	Years
New York, NY	35.2

Taiwanese
Top 10 Places Sorted by Number

Place	Years
North Hempstead, NY (town) Nassau County	40.8
New York, NY	31.2

Thai
Top 10 Places Sorted by Number

Place	Years
New York, NY	36.1

Tongan
Top 10 Places Sorted by Number

Place	Years

Vietnamese
Top 10 Places Sorted by Number

Place	Years
Rochester, NY (city) Monroe County	30.8
Albany, NY (city) Albany County	30.2
New York, NY	29.8
Utica, NY (city) Oneida County	29.6
Buffalo, NY (city) Erie County	28.6
Binghamton, NY (city) Broome County	28.4
Syracuse, NY (city) Onondaga County	27.8

Average Household Size

Total Population
Top 10 Places Sorted by Number

Place	Number
Brentwood, NY (cdp) Suffolk County	4.24
Monroe, NY (town) Orange County	3.68
Uniondale, NY (cdp) Nassau County	3.65
Central Islip, NY (cdp) Suffolk County	3.54
Hillcrest, NY (cdp) Rockland County	3.49
Brookville, NY (village) Nassau County	3.47
Shirley, NY (cdp) Suffolk County	3.44
Hempstead, NY (village) Nassau County	3.40
Ramapo, NY (town) Rockland County	3.36
Muttontown, NY (village) Nassau County	3.33

Asian
Top 10 Places Sorted by Number

Place	Number
Woodmere, NY (cdp) Nassau County	4.77
Old Brookville, NY (village) Nassau County	4.75
North Valley Stream, NY (cdp) Nassau County	4.56
Copiague, NY (cdp) Suffolk County	4.50
Muttontown, NY (village) Nassau County	4.38
Freeport, NY (village) Nassau County	4.27
New Hyde Park, NY (village) Nassau County	4.27
Congers, NY (cdp) Rockland County	4.26
Hillcrest, NY (cdp) Rockland County	4.26
Selden, NY (cdp) Suffolk County	4.23

Native Hawaiian and Other Pacific Islander
Top 10 Places Sorted by Number

Place	Number
New York, NY	2.97

Asian Indian
Top 10 Places Sorted by Number

Place	Number
Brentwood, NY (cdp) Suffolk County	4.85
North Valley Stream, NY (cdp) Nassau County	4.78
New Hyde Park, NY (village) Nassau County	4.65
Scarsdale, NY (village) Westchester County	4.63
Muttontown, NY (village) Nassau County	4.58
Franklin Square, NY (cdp) Nassau County	4.51
North New Hyde Park, NY (cdp) Nassau County	4.51
Searingtown, NY (cdp) Nassau County	4.34
East Meadow, NY (cdp) Nassau County	4.19
Mount Pleasant, NY (town) Westchester County	4.16

Bangladeshi
Top 10 Places Sorted by Number

Place	Number
New York, NY	4.25

Cambodian
Top 10 Places Sorted by Number

Place	Number
New York, NY	4.01

Chinese (except Taiwanese)
Top 10 Places Sorted by Number

Place	Number
Ramapo, NY (town) Rockland County	4.49
Lake Success, NY (village) Nassau County	4.35
Garden City Park, NY (cdp) Nassau County	4.33
Dix Hills, NY (cdp) Suffolk County	3.73
Orangetown, NY (town) Rockland County	3.72
North New Hyde Park, NY (cdp) Nassau County	3.66
Babylon, NY (town) Suffolk County	3.65
North Hempstead, NY (town) Nassau County	3.64
Valley Stream, NY (village) Nassau County	3.54
Oyster Bay, NY (town) Nassau County	3.42

Fijian
Top 10 Places Sorted by Number

Place	Number

No places met population threshold.

Filipino
Top 10 Places Sorted by Number

Place	Number
Hicksville, NY (cdp) Nassau County	4.50
Levittown, NY (cdp) Nassau County	4.31
Valley Stream, NY (village) Nassau County	4.29
Elmont, NY (cdp) Nassau County	3.93
Hillcrest, NY (cdp) Rockland County	3.93
Valley Cottage, NY (cdp) Rockland County	3.85
Oyster Bay, NY (town) Nassau County	3.83
Clarkstown, NY (town) Rockland County	3.80
Hempstead, NY (town) Nassau County	3.78
New City, NY (cdp) Rockland County	3.78

Guamanian or Chamorro
Top 10 Places Sorted by Number

Place	Number
New York, NY	3.31

Hawaiian, Native
Top 10 Places Sorted by Number

Place	Number
New York, NY	2.65

Hmong
Top 10 Places Sorted by Number

Place	Number

No places met population threshold.

Indonesian
Top 10 Places Sorted by Number

Place	Number
New York, NY	2.82

Notes: Please refer to the User's Guide for an explanation of data; tables reflect only those areas that meet Summary File 4 population thresholds, therefore there may be less than 10 places listed.

PROFILES OF NEW YORK / Asian: Rankings

Japanese
Top 10 Places Sorted by Number

Place	Number
Scarsdale, NY (village) Westchester County	3.83
Harrison, NY (village) Westchester County	3.20
Rye, NY (city) Westchester County	3.18
Eastchester, NY (town) Westchester County	3.07
Greenburgh, NY (town) Westchester County	2.86
Eastchester, NY (cdp) Westchester County	2.76
Hempstead, NY (town) Nassau County	2.45
North Hempstead, NY (town) Nassau County	2.44
Greenville, NY (cdp) Westchester County	2.43
Brookhaven, NY (town) Suffolk County	2.25

Korean
Top 10 Places Sorted by Number

Place	Number
Plainview, NY (cdp) Nassau County	4.16
Scarsdale, NY (village) Westchester County	4.04
Clarkstown, NY (town) Rockland County	3.97
Hempstead, NY (town) Nassau County	3.84
Jericho, NY (cdp) Nassau County	3.73
Oyster Bay, NY (town) Nassau County	3.71
Glen Cove, NY (city) Nassau County	3.68
Commack, NY (cdp) Suffolk County	3.62
North Hempstead, NY (town) Nassau County	3.62
Greenburgh, NY (town) Westchester County	3.54

Laotian
Top 10 Places Sorted by Number

Place	Number
Rochester, NY (city) Monroe County	4.52

Malaysian
Top 10 Places Sorted by Number

Place	Number
New York, NY	2.54

Pakistani
Top 10 Places Sorted by Number

Place	Number
Hempstead, NY (town) Nassau County	5.37
Huntington, NY (town) Suffolk County	4.72
North Hempstead, NY (town) Nassau County	4.52
Brookhaven, NY (town) Suffolk County	4.16
New York, NY	4.09

Samoan
Top 10 Places Sorted by Number

Place	Number
New York, NY	3.41

Sri Lankan
Top 10 Places Sorted by Number

Place	Number
New York, NY	3.23

Taiwanese
Top 10 Places Sorted by Number

Place	Number
North Hempstead, NY (town) Nassau County	3.28
New York, NY	2.52

Thai
Top 10 Places Sorted by Number

Place	Number
New York, NY	2.57

Tongan
Top 10 Places Sorted by Number

Place	Number
No places met population threshold.	

Vietnamese
Top 10 Places Sorted by Number

Place	Number
Rochester, NY (city) Monroe County	3.53
Albany, NY (city) Albany County	3.52
Utica, NY (city) Oneida County	3.51
New York, NY	3.42
Buffalo, NY (city) Erie County	3.40
Syracuse, NY (city) Onondaga County	3.33
Binghamton, NY (city) Broome County	3.32

Language Spoken at Home: English Only

Total Populations 5 Years and Over Who Speak English-Only at Home
Top 10 Places Sorted by Number

Place	Number
New York, NY	3,920,797
Hempstead, NY (town) Nassau County	547,956
Brookhaven, NY (town) Suffolk County	357,084
Buffalo, NY (city) Erie County	238,127
Oyster Bay, NY (town) Nassau County	228,112
Islip, NY (town) Suffolk County	227,229
Rochester, NY (city) Monroe County	166,643
Babylon, NY (town) Suffolk County	161,589
Huntington, NY (town) Suffolk County	151,447
North Hempstead, NY (town) Nassau County	141,469

Total Populations 5 Years and Over Who Speak English-Only at Home
Top 10 Places Sorted by Percent

Place	Percent
Tonawanda, NY (town) Erie County	94.14
Onondaga, NY (town) Onondaga County	93.89
Sayville, NY (cdp) Suffolk County	93.28
Dryden, NY (town) Tompkins County	93.22
Manlius, NY (town) Onondaga County	92.92
Clay, NY (town) Onondaga County	92.73
Clifton Park, NY (town) Saratoga County	92.70
Watertown, NY (city) Jefferson County	92.51
Hyde Park, NY (town) Dutchess County	91.61
Salina, NY (town) Onondaga County	91.44

Asians 5 Years and Over Who Speak English-Only at Home
Top 10 Places Sorted by Number

Place	Number
New York, NY	107,879
Hempstead, NY (town) Nassau County	5,030
North Hempstead, NY (town) Nassau County	3,039
Brookhaven, NY (town) Suffolk County	2,433
Oyster Bay, NY (town) Nassau County	2,136
Yonkers, NY (city) Westchester County	1,396
Huntington, NY (town) Suffolk County	1,339
Islip, NY (town) Suffolk County	1,292
Clarkstown, NY (town) Rockland County	1,231
Greenburgh, NY (town) Westchester County	1,126

Asians 5 Years and Over Who Speak English-Only at Home
Top 10 Places Sorted by Percent

Place	Percent
Cornwall, NY (town) Orange County	46.77
Onondaga, NY (town) Onondaga County	45.25
Long Beach, NY (city) Nassau County	44.07
Le Ray, NY (town) Jefferson County	41.96
Highlands, NY (town) Orange County	40.29
Hempstead, NY (village) Nassau County	39.58
Watertown, NY (city) Jefferson County	39.54
Southampton, NY (town) Suffolk County	38.46
North Castle, NY (town) Westchester County	37.93
Woodbury, NY (town) Orange County	35.32

Native Hawaiian and Other Pacific Islanders 5 Years and Over Who Speak English-Only at Home
Top 10 Places Sorted by Number

Place	Number
New York, NY	2,120

Native Hawaiian and Other Pacific Islanders 5 Years and Over Who Speak English-Only at Home
Top 10 Places Sorted by Percent

Place	Percent
New York, NY	47.55

Asian Indians 5 Years and Over Who Speak English-Only at Home
Top 10 Places Sorted by Number

Place	Number
New York, NY	51,139
Hempstead, NY (town) Nassau County	2,136
North Hempstead, NY (town) Nassau County	1,274
Oyster Bay, NY (town) Nassau County	809
Brookhaven, NY (town) Suffolk County	665
Yonkers, NY (city) Westchester County	625
Clarkstown, NY (town) Rockland County	534
Greenburgh, NY (town) Westchester County	521
Huntington, NY (town) Suffolk County	418
Islip, NY (town) Suffolk County	396

Asian Indians 5 Years and Over Who Speak English-Only at Home
Top 10 Places Sorted by Percent

Place	Percent
Scarsdale, NY (village) Westchester County	47.77
Mount Vernon, NY (city) Westchester County	40.38
Schenectady, NY (city) Schenectady County	40.04
Wappinger, NY (town) Dutchess County	38.18
Cortlandt, NY (town) Westchester County	34.90
New York, NY	32.58
Ithaca, NY (city) Tompkins County	32.07
North Valley Stream, NY (cdp) Nassau County	29.84
Manhasset Hills, NY (cdp) Nassau County	29.07
New City, NY (cdp) Rockland County	28.76

Bangladeshis 5 Years and Over Who Speak English-Only at Home
Top 10 Places Sorted by Number

Place	Number
New York, NY	713

Bangladeshis 5 Years and Over Who Speak English-Only at Home
Top 10 Places Sorted by Percent

Place	Percent
New York, NY	4.07

Cambodians 5 Years and Over Who Speak English-Only at Home
Top 10 Places Sorted by Number

Place	Number
New York, NY	135

Cambodians 5 Years and Over Who Speak English-Only at Home
Top 10 Places Sorted by Percent

Place	Percent
New York, NY	8.69

Notes: Please refer to the User's Guide for an explanation of data; tables reflect only those areas that meet Summary File 4 population thresholds, therefore there may be less than 10 places listed

Chinese (except Taiwanese) 5 Years and Over Who Speak English-Only at Home
Top 10 Places Sorted by Number

Place	Number
New York, NY	26,421
Hempstead, NY (town) Nassau County	1,011
North Hempstead, NY (town) Nassau County	663
Oyster Bay, NY (town) Nassau County	533
Brookhaven, NY (town) Suffolk County	524
Huntington, NY (town) Suffolk County	320
Ithaca, NY (city) Tompkins County	308
Yonkers, NY (city) Westchester County	266
Islip, NY (town) Suffolk County	223
Greenburgh, NY (town) Westchester County	219

Chinese (except Taiwanese) 5 Years and Over Who Speak English-Only at Home
Top 10 Places Sorted by Percent

Place	Percent
Lake Success, NY (village) Nassau County	35.00
Yonkers, NY (city) Westchester County	31.29
New Castle, NY (town) Westchester County	26.90
Poughkeepsie, NY (town) Dutchess County	26.57
Valley Stream, NY (village) Nassau County	23.15
Clarkstown, NY (town) Rockland County	21.59
Islip, NY (town) Suffolk County	20.74
Hempstead, NY (town) Nassau County	20.06
Coram, NY (cdp) Suffolk County	19.75
Babylon, NY (town) Suffolk County	19.59

Fijians 5 Years and Over Who Speak English-Only at Home
Top 10 Places Sorted by Number

Place	Number
No places met population threshold.	

Fijians 5 Years and Over Who Speak English-Only at Home
Top 10 Places Sorted by Percent

Place	Percent
No places met population threshold.	

Filipinos 5 Years and Over Who Speak English-Only at Home
Top 10 Places Sorted by Number

Place	Number
New York, NY	11,331
Hempstead, NY (town) Nassau County	921
Brookhaven, NY (town) Suffolk County	500
Clarkstown, NY (town) Rockland County	428
North Hempstead, NY (town) Nassau County	411
Oyster Bay, NY (town) Nassau County	339
Islip, NY (town) Suffolk County	301
Yonkers, NY (city) Westchester County	287
Huntington, NY (town) Suffolk County	236
Ramapo, NY (town) Rockland County	209

Filipinos 5 Years and Over Who Speak English-Only at Home
Top 10 Places Sorted by Percent

Place	Percent
Brookhaven, NY (town) Suffolk County	35.16
Islip, NY (town) Suffolk County	32.79
North Hempstead, NY (town) Nassau County	31.66
Huntington, NY (town) Suffolk County	31.64
Babylon, NY (town) Suffolk County	30.89
Oyster Bay, NY (town) Nassau County	27.32
Hicksville, NY (cdp) Nassau County	26.08
Orangetown, NY (town) Rockland County	26.02
Hempstead, NY (town) Nassau County	23.83
Elmont, NY (cdp) Nassau County	21.80

Guamanian or Chamorros 5 Years and Over Who Speak English-Only at Home
Top 10 Places Sorted by Number

Place	Number
New York, NY	552

Guamanian or Chamorros 5 Years and Over Who Speak English-Only at Home
Top 10 Places Sorted by Percent

Place	Percent
New York, NY	49.91

Hawaiian, Natives 5 Years and Over Who Speak English-Only at Home
Top 10 Places Sorted by Number

Place	Number
New York, NY	282

Hawaiian, Natives 5 Years and Over Who Speak English-Only at Home
Top 10 Places Sorted by Percent

Place	Percent
New York, NY	40.23

Hmongs 5 Years and Over Who Speak English-Only at Home
Top 10 Places Sorted by Number

Place	Number
No places met population threshold.	

Hmongs 5 Years and Over Who Speak English-Only at Home
Top 10 Places Sorted by Percent

Place	Percent
No places met population threshold.	

Indonesians 5 Years and Over Who Speak English-Only at Home
Top 10 Places Sorted by Number

Place	Number
New York, NY	245

Indonesians 5 Years and Over Who Speak English-Only at Home
Top 10 Places Sorted by Percent

Place	Percent
New York, NY	14.10

Japanese 5 Years and Over Who Speak English-Only at Home
Top 10 Places Sorted by Number

Place	Number
New York, NY	3,914
Brookhaven, NY (town) Suffolk County	122
Hempstead, NY (town) Nassau County	111
Oyster Bay, NY (town) Nassau County	88
Greenburgh, NY (town) Westchester County	80
North Hempstead, NY (town) Nassau County	77
Eastchester, NY (town) Westchester County	60
Eastchester, NY (cdp) Westchester County	48
Greenville, NY (cdp) Westchester County	19
Harrison, NY (village) Westchester County	10

Japanese 5 Years and Over Who Speak English-Only at Home
Top 10 Places Sorted by Percent

Place	Percent
Brookhaven, NY (town) Suffolk County	30.20
Hempstead, NY (town) Nassau County	29.92
Oyster Bay, NY (town) Nassau County	25.36
New York, NY	18.22
Eastchester, NY (cdp) Westchester County	9.60
North Hempstead, NY (town) Nassau County	8.78
Eastchester, NY (town) Westchester County	5.75
Greenburgh, NY (town) Westchester County	4.38
Greenville, NY (cdp) Westchester County	3.82
Harrison, NY (village) Westchester County	1.63

Koreans 5 Years and Over Who Speak English-Only at Home
Top 10 Places Sorted by Number

Place	Number
New York, NY	7,397
Hempstead, NY (town) Nassau County	509
North Hempstead, NY (town) Nassau County	357
Brookhaven, NY (town) Suffolk County	343
Oyster Bay, NY (town) Nassau County	224
Islip, NY (town) Suffolk County	221
Amherst, NY (town) Erie County	189
Huntington, NY (town) Suffolk County	186
Smithtown, NY (town) Suffolk County	143
Rochester, NY (city) Monroe County	135

Koreans 5 Years and Over Who Speak English-Only at Home
Top 10 Places Sorted by Percent

Place	Percent
Islip, NY (town) Suffolk County	39.32
Rochester, NY (city) Monroe County	37.09
Babylon, NY (town) Suffolk County	31.88
Smithtown, NY (town) Suffolk County	31.71
Brookhaven, NY (town) Suffolk County	25.50
Syracuse, NY (city) Onondaga County	22.54
Amherst, NY (town) Erie County	21.82
Huntington, NY (town) Suffolk County	20.00
Hempstead, NY (town) Nassau County	18.16
Orangetown, NY (town) Rockland County	17.76

Laotians 5 Years and Over Who Speak English-Only at Home
Top 10 Places Sorted by Number

Place	Number
Rochester, NY (city) Monroe County	87

Laotians 5 Years and Over Who Speak English-Only at Home
Top 10 Places Sorted by Percent

Place	Percent
Rochester, NY (city) Monroe County	11.65

Malaysians 5 Years and Over Who Speak English-Only at Home
Top 10 Places Sorted by Number

Place	Number
New York, NY	85

Malaysians 5 Years and Over Who Speak English-Only at Home
Top 10 Places Sorted by Percent

Place	Percent
New York, NY	7.25

Pakistanis 5 Years and Over Who Speak English-Only at Home
Top 10 Places Sorted by Number

Place	Number
New York, NY	754
Huntington, NY (town) Suffolk County	55
Hempstead, NY (town) Nassau County	54
Brookhaven, NY (town) Suffolk County	46
North Hempstead, NY (town) Nassau County	32

Notes: Please refer to the User's Guide for an explanation of data; tables reflect only those areas that meet Summary File 4 population thresholds, therefore there may be less than 10 places listed

Pakistanis 5 Years and Over Who Speak English-Only at Home
Top 10 Places Sorted by Percent

Place	Percent
Huntington, NY (town) Suffolk County	14.14
Brookhaven, NY (town) Suffolk County	6.98
North Hempstead, NY (town) Nassau County	5.67
Hempstead, NY (town) Nassau County	4.20
New York, NY	3.49

Samoans 5 Years and Over Who Speak English-Only at Home
Top 10 Places Sorted by Number

Place	Number
New York, NY	289

Samoans 5 Years and Over Who Speak English-Only at Home
Top 10 Places Sorted by Percent

Place	Percent
New York, NY	43.46

Sri Lankans 5 Years and Over Who Speak English-Only at Home
Top 10 Places Sorted by Number

Place	Number
New York, NY	388

Sri Lankans 5 Years and Over Who Speak English-Only at Home
Top 10 Places Sorted by Percent

Place	Percent
New York, NY	20.43

Taiwanese 5 Years and Over Who Speak English-Only at Home
Top 10 Places Sorted by Number

Place	Number
New York, NY	430
North Hempstead, NY (town) Nassau County	21

Taiwanese 5 Years and Over Who Speak English-Only at Home
Top 10 Places Sorted by Percent

Place	Percent
New York, NY	8.97
North Hempstead, NY (town) Nassau County	7.42

Thais 5 Years and Over Who Speak English-Only at Home
Top 10 Places Sorted by Number

Place	Number
New York, NY	330

Thais 5 Years and Over Who Speak English-Only at Home
Top 10 Places Sorted by Percent

Place	Percent
New York, NY	8.81

Tongans 5 Years and Over Who Speak English-Only at Home
Top 10 Places Sorted by Number

Place	Number
No places met population threshold.	

Tongans 5 Years and Over Who Speak English-Only at Home
Top 10 Places Sorted by Percent

Place	Percent
No places met population threshold.	

Vietnamese 5 Years and Over Who Speak English-Only at Home
Top 10 Places Sorted by Number

Place	Number
New York, NY	960
Buffalo, NY (city) Erie County	153
Rochester, NY (city) Monroe County	94
Utica, NY (city) Oneida County	23
Syracuse, NY (city) Onondaga County	21
Albany, NY (city) Albany County	0
Binghamton, NY (city) Broome County	0

Vietnamese 5 Years and Over Who Speak English-Only at Home
Top 10 Places Sorted by Percent

Place	Percent
Buffalo, NY (city) Erie County	15.18
Rochester, NY (city) Monroe County	10.40
New York, NY	8.41
Utica, NY (city) Oneida County	2.79
Syracuse, NY (city) Onondaga County	1.84
Albany, NY (city) Albany County	0.00
Binghamton, NY (city) Broome County	0.00

Foreign Born

Total Population
Top 10 Places Sorted by Number

Place	Number
New York, NY	2,871,032
Hempstead, NY (town) Nassau County	134,598
North Hempstead, NY (town) Nassau County	55,357
Yonkers, NY (city) Westchester County	51,687
Islip, NY (town) Suffolk County	47,088
Brookhaven, NY (town) Suffolk County	39,730
Oyster Bay, NY (town) Nassau County	35,610
Babylon, NY (town) Suffolk County	27,643
Ramapo, NY (town) Rockland County	24,848
Huntington, NY (town) Suffolk County	21,808

Total Population
Top 10 Places Sorted by Percent

Place	Percent
Forest Home, NY (cdp) Tompkins County	50.69
Spring Valley, NY (village) Rockland County	43.04
Port Chester, NY (village) Westchester County	41.39
Hillcrest, NY (cdp) Rockland County	37.44
Elmont, NY (cdp) Nassau County	36.86
New York, NY	35.85
Great Neck, NY (village) Nassau County	35.70
Manorhaven, NY (village) Nassau County	35.63
Brentwood, NY (cdp) Suffolk County	34.74
North Valley Stream, NY (cdp) Nassau County	34.25

Asian
Top 10 Places Sorted by Number

Place	Number
New York, NY	611,328
Hempstead, NY (town) Nassau County	18,314
North Hempstead, NY (town) Nassau County	14,152
Oyster Bay, NY (town) Nassau County	9,676
Brookhaven, NY (town) Suffolk County	9,571
Yonkers, NY (city) Westchester County	7,313
Greenburgh, NY (town) Westchester County	6,042
Islip, NY (town) Suffolk County	4,794
Clarkstown, NY (town) Rockland County	4,665
Huntington, NY (town) Suffolk County	4,656

Asian
Top 10 Places Sorted by Percent

Place	Percent
Hudson, NY (city) Columbia County	89.70
Forest Home, NY (cdp) Tompkins County	89.39
Mamaroneck, NY (town) Westchester County	87.72
East Patchogue, NY (cdp) Suffolk County	86.94
Rockville Centre, NY (village) Nassau County	85.61
Tarrytown, NY (village) Westchester County	84.64
Harrison, NY (village) Westchester County	83.68
Pearl River, NY (cdp) Rockland County	83.50
Cheektowaga, NY (town) Erie County	83.35
Spring Valley, NY (village) Rockland County	82.96

Native Hawaiian and Other Pacific Islander
Top 10 Places Sorted by Number

Place	Number
New York, NY	1,904

Native Hawaiian and Other Pacific Islander
Top 10 Places Sorted by Percent

Place	Percent
New York, NY	39.10

Asian Indian
Top 10 Places Sorted by Number

Place	Number
New York, NY	132,273
Hempstead, NY (town) Nassau County	7,250
North Hempstead, NY (town) Nassau County	5,310
Yonkers, NY (city) Westchester County	3,640
Oyster Bay, NY (town) Nassau County	3,595
Brookhaven, NY (town) Suffolk County	2,492
Islip, NY (town) Suffolk County	2,036
Greenburgh, NY (town) Westchester County	2,002
Clarkstown, NY (town) Rockland County	1,601
Ramapo, NY (town) Rockland County	1,555

Asian Indian
Top 10 Places Sorted by Percent

Place	Percent
Brentwood, NY (cdp) Suffolk County	87.63
Guilderland, NY (town) Albany County	86.96
Brighton, NY (town) Monroe County	84.88
Franklin Square, NY (cdp) Nassau County	84.80
Haverstraw, NY (village) Rockland County	83.69
Islip, NY (town) Suffolk County	82.76
Babylon, NY (town) Suffolk County	82.32
Cheektowaga, NY (town) Erie County	81.45
Cortlandt, NY (town) Westchester County	80.06
Schenectady, NY (city) Schenectady County	80.03

Bangladeshi
Top 10 Places Sorted by Number

Place	Number
New York, NY	16,146

Bangladeshi
Top 10 Places Sorted by Percent

Place	Percent
New York, NY	84.32

Cambodian
Top 10 Places Sorted by Number

Place	Number
New York, NY	1,097

Cambodian
Top 10 Places Sorted by Percent

Place	Percent
New York, NY	67.76

Notes: Please refer to the User's Guide for an explanation of data; tables reflect only those areas that meet Summary File 4 population thresholds, therefore there may be less than 10 places listed.

Chinese (except Taiwanese)
Top 10 Places Sorted by Number

Place	Number
New York, NY	273,113
Brookhaven, NY (town) Suffolk County	3,544
North Hempstead, NY (town) Nassau County	3,538
Hempstead, NY (town) Nassau County	3,291
Oyster Bay, NY (town) Nassau County	2,291
Huntington, NY (town) Suffolk County	1,207
Ithaca, NY (city) Tompkins County	1,175
Amherst, NY (town) Erie County	1,086
Greenburgh, NY (town) Westchester County	913
Syracuse, NY (city) Onondaga County	755

Chinese (except Taiwanese)
Top 10 Places Sorted by Percent

Place	Percent
Setauket-East Setauket, NY (cdp) Suffolk County	84.91
Syracuse, NY (city) Onondaga County	84.83
Buffalo, NY (city) Erie County	80.93
Brighton, NY (town) Monroe County	80.31
New York, NY	76.39
Ramapo, NY (town) Rockland County	74.63
Brookhaven, NY (town) Suffolk County	74.42
Rochester, NY (city) Monroe County	74.40
New Rochelle, NY (city) Westchester County	74.31
Stony Brook, NY (cdp) Suffolk County	73.87

Fijian
Top 10 Places Sorted by Number

Place	Number
No places met population threshold.	

Fijian
Top 10 Places Sorted by Percent

Place	Percent
No places met population threshold.	

Filipino
Top 10 Places Sorted by Number

Place	Number
New York, NY	45,319
Hempstead, NY (town) Nassau County	2,946
Clarkstown, NY (town) Rockland County	1,591
Yonkers, NY (city) Westchester County	1,384
North Hempstead, NY (town) Nassau County	1,002
Oyster Bay, NY (town) Nassau County	974
Ramapo, NY (town) Rockland County	960
Brookhaven, NY (town) Suffolk County	895
Islip, NY (town) Suffolk County	674
Huntington, NY (town) Suffolk County	551

Filipino
Top 10 Places Sorted by Percent

Place	Percent
Babylon, NY (town) Suffolk County	79.37
New York, NY	76.88
Yonkers, NY (city) Westchester County	76.17
East Meadow, NY (cdp) Nassau County	76.15
Oyster Bay, NY (town) Nassau County	75.92
Greenburgh, NY (town) Westchester County	75.65
Orangetown, NY (town) Rockland County	74.02
Hicksville, NY (cdp) Nassau County	73.89
North Hempstead, NY (town) Nassau County	73.84
Valley Stream, NY (village) Nassau County	73.37

Guamanian or Chamorro
Top 10 Places Sorted by Number

Place	Number
New York, NY	371

Guamanian or Chamorro
Top 10 Places Sorted by Percent

Place	Percent
New York, NY	31.55

Hawaiian, Native
Top 10 Places Sorted by Number

Place	Number
New York, NY	226

Hawaiian, Native
Top 10 Places Sorted by Percent

Place	Percent
New York, NY	29.12

Hmong
Top 10 Places Sorted by Number

Place	Number
No places met population threshold.	

Hmong
Top 10 Places Sorted by Percent

Place	Percent
No places met population threshold.	

Indonesian
Top 10 Places Sorted by Number

Place	Number
New York, NY	1,412

Indonesian
Top 10 Places Sorted by Percent

Place	Percent
New York, NY	77.75

Japanese
Top 10 Places Sorted by Number

Place	Number
New York, NY	18,017
Greenburgh, NY (town) Westchester County	1,685
Eastchester, NY (town) Westchester County	1,060
North Hempstead, NY (town) Nassau County	830
Harrison, NY (village) Westchester County	648
Scarsdale, NY (village) Westchester County	637
Rye, NY (city) Westchester County	585
Greenville, NY (cdp) Westchester County	528
Eastchester, NY (cdp) Westchester County	499
Oyster Bay, NY (town) Nassau County	315

Japanese
Top 10 Places Sorted by Percent

Place	Percent
Greenville, NY (cdp) Westchester County	97.96
Harrison, NY (village) Westchester County	93.51
Eastchester, NY (cdp) Westchester County	90.89
Rye, NY (city) Westchester County	90.70
Eastchester, NY (town) Westchester County	87.60
North Hempstead, NY (town) Nassau County	86.91
Greenburgh, NY (town) Westchester County	86.10
Oyster Bay, NY (town) Nassau County	84.22
Scarsdale, NY (village) Westchester County	81.25
New York, NY	80.79

Korean
Top 10 Places Sorted by Number

Place	Number
New York, NY	70,286
North Hempstead, NY (town) Nassau County	2,319
Hempstead, NY (town) Nassau County	2,195
Oyster Bay, NY (town) Nassau County	1,805
Brookhaven, NY (town) Suffolk County	1,136
Yonkers, NY (city) Westchester County	905
Huntington, NY (town) Suffolk County	744
Greenburgh, NY (town) Westchester County	740
Amherst, NY (town) Erie County	671
Clarkstown, NY (town) Rockland County	563

Korean
Top 10 Places Sorted by Percent

Place	Percent
Yonkers, NY (city) Westchester County	85.14
Babylon, NY (town) Suffolk County	85.00
Syracuse, NY (city) Onondaga County	82.62
Islip, NY (town) Suffolk County	81.45
New York, NY	80.66
Ramapo, NY (town) Rockland County	80.52
Brookhaven, NY (town) Suffolk County	79.22
Clarkstown, NY (town) Rockland County	78.09
Glen Cove, NY (city) Nassau County	76.38
Orangetown, NY (town) Rockland County	75.70

Laotian
Top 10 Places Sorted by Number

Place	Number
Rochester, NY (city) Monroe County	606

Laotian
Top 10 Places Sorted by Percent

Place	Percent
Rochester, NY (city) Monroe County	75.28

Malaysian
Top 10 Places Sorted by Number

Place	Number
New York, NY	1,065

Malaysian
Top 10 Places Sorted by Percent

Place	Percent
New York, NY	88.97

Pakistani
Top 10 Places Sorted by Number

Place	Number
New York, NY	19,009
Hempstead, NY (town) Nassau County	1,036
Brookhaven, NY (town) Suffolk County	507
North Hempstead, NY (town) Nassau County	388
Huntington, NY (town) Suffolk County	288

Pakistani
Top 10 Places Sorted by Percent

Place	Percent
New York, NY	79.69
Hempstead, NY (town) Nassau County	73.63
Brookhaven, NY (town) Suffolk County	68.70
Huntington, NY (town) Suffolk County	65.90
North Hempstead, NY (town) Nassau County	62.78

Samoan
Top 10 Places Sorted by Number

Place	Number
New York, NY	159

Samoan
Top 10 Places Sorted by Percent

Place	Percent
New York, NY	21.81

Notes: Please refer to the User's Guide for an explanation of data; tables reflect only those areas that meet Summary File 4 population thresholds, therefore there may be less than 10 places listed

Sri Lankan
Top 10 Places Sorted by Number

Place	Number
New York, NY	1,722

Sri Lankan
Top 10 Places Sorted by Percent

Place	Percent
New York, NY	85.93

Taiwanese
Top 10 Places Sorted by Number

Place	Number
New York, NY	4,003
North Hempstead, NY (town) Nassau County	191

Taiwanese
Top 10 Places Sorted by Percent

Place	Percent
New York, NY	81.58
North Hempstead, NY (town) Nassau County	67.49

Thai
Top 10 Places Sorted by Number

Place	Number
New York, NY	2,847

Thai
Top 10 Places Sorted by Percent

Place	Percent
New York, NY	74.47

Tongan
Top 10 Places Sorted by Number

Place	Number
No places met population threshold.	

Tongan
Top 10 Places Sorted by Percent

Place	Percent
No places met population threshold.	

Vietnamese
Top 10 Places Sorted by Number

Place	Number
New York, NY	9,828
Syracuse, NY (city) Onondaga County	1,083
Buffalo, NY (city) Erie County	976
Rochester, NY (city) Monroe County	757
Utica, NY (city) Oneida County	734
Albany, NY (city) Albany County	315
Binghamton, NY (city) Broome County	272

Vietnamese
Top 10 Places Sorted by Percent

Place	Percent
Binghamton, NY (city) Broome County	92.20
Syracuse, NY (city) Onondaga County	85.61
Buffalo, NY (city) Erie County	82.92
New York, NY	79.84
Albany, NY (city) Albany County	79.55
Utica, NY (city) Oneida County	79.27
Rochester, NY (city) Monroe County	75.55

Foreign-Born Naturalized Citizens

Total Population
Top 10 Places Sorted by Number

Place	Number
New York, NY	1,278,687
Hempstead, NY (town) Nassau County	73,040
North Hempstead, NY (town) Nassau County	30,865
Oyster Bay, NY (town) Nassau County	22,589
Yonkers, NY (city) Westchester County	22,521
Brookhaven, NY (town) Suffolk County	20,640
Islip, NY (town) Suffolk County	19,295
Babylon, NY (town) Suffolk County	13,644
Huntington, NY (town) Suffolk County	12,618
Ramapo, NY (town) Rockland County	11,707

Total Population
Top 10 Places Sorted by Percent

Place	Percent
North Valley Stream, NY (cdp) Nassau County	21.28
Hillcrest, NY (cdp) Rockland County	21.12
Manhasset Hills, NY (cdp) Nassau County	20.87
Elmont, NY (cdp) Nassau County	20.82
Searingtown, NY (cdp) Nassau County	20.57
Great Neck, NY (village) Nassau County	20.37
Lake Success, NY (village) Nassau County	17.88
Garden City Park, NY (cdp) Nassau County	17.04
Uniondale, NY (cdp) Nassau County	17.04
New York, NY	15.97

Asian
Top 10 Places Sorted by Number

Place	Number
New York, NY	263,102
Hempstead, NY (town) Nassau County	10,012
North Hempstead, NY (town) Nassau County	7,690
Oyster Bay, NY (town) Nassau County	5,746
Brookhaven, NY (town) Suffolk County	4,326
Huntington, NY (town) Suffolk County	2,990
Yonkers, NY (city) Westchester County	2,828
Islip, NY (town) Suffolk County	2,447
Clarkstown, NY (town) Rockland County	2,437
Greenburgh, NY (town) Westchester County	2,207

Asian
Top 10 Places Sorted by Percent

Place	Percent
Sands Point, NY (village) Nassau County	58.06
Old Westbury, NY (village) Nassau County	57.99
Cornwall, NY (town) Orange County	55.78
East Northport, NY (cdp) Suffolk County	55.20
Perinton, NY (town) Monroe County	55.05
East Patchogue, NY (cdp) Suffolk County	55.03
West Nyack, NY (cdp) Rockland County	53.94
Briarcliff Manor, NY (village) Westchester County	53.66
Oyster Bay Cove, NY (village) Nassau County	51.80
North Lindenhurst, NY (cdp) Suffolk County	51.60

Native Hawaiian and Other Pacific Islander
Top 10 Places Sorted by Number

Place	Number
New York, NY	819

Native Hawaiian and Other Pacific Islander
Top 10 Places Sorted by Percent

Place	Percent
New York, NY	16.82

Asian Indian
Top 10 Places Sorted by Number

Place	Number
New York, NY	54,421
Hempstead, NY (town) Nassau County	3,958
North Hempstead, NY (town) Nassau County	2,720
Oyster Bay, NY (town) Nassau County	1,991
Brookhaven, NY (town) Suffolk County	1,195
Yonkers, NY (city) Westchester County	1,070
Islip, NY (town) Suffolk County	847
Clarkstown, NY (town) Rockland County	820
Huntington, NY (town) Suffolk County	807
Greenburgh, NY (town) Westchester County	778

Asian Indian
Top 10 Places Sorted by Percent

Place	Percent
Muttontown, NY (village) Nassau County	53.16
Perinton, NY (town) Monroe County	49.65
Smithtown, NY (town) Suffolk County	49.62
Pittsford, NY (town) Monroe County	48.18
Salisbury, NY (cdp) Nassau County	47.88
Colonie, NY (town) Albany County	46.84
Syosset, NY (cdp) Nassau County	45.13
North Valley Stream, NY (cdp) Nassau County	44.71
Franklin Square, NY (cdp) Nassau County	44.05
Clifton Park, NY (town) Saratoga County	43.17

Bangladeshi
Top 10 Places Sorted by Number

Place	Number
New York, NY	4,495

Bangladeshi
Top 10 Places Sorted by Percent

Place	Percent
New York, NY	23.47

Cambodian
Top 10 Places Sorted by Number

Place	Number
New York, NY	524

Cambodian
Top 10 Places Sorted by Percent

Place	Percent
New York, NY	32.37

Chinese (except Taiwanese)
Top 10 Places Sorted by Number

Place	Number
New York, NY	131,495
North Hempstead, NY (town) Nassau County	2,305
Hempstead, NY (town) Nassau County	2,290
Oyster Bay, NY (town) Nassau County	1,670
Brookhaven, NY (town) Suffolk County	1,403
Huntington, NY (town) Suffolk County	799
Greenburgh, NY (town) Westchester County	490
Amherst, NY (town) Erie County	462
Yonkers, NY (city) Westchester County	455
Islip, NY (town) Suffolk County	414

Chinese (except Taiwanese)
Top 10 Places Sorted by Percent

Place	Percent
Hicksville, NY (cdp) Nassau County	55.36
Ramapo, NY (town) Rockland County	53.49
New Castle, NY (town) Westchester County	52.60
Yonkers, NY (city) Westchester County	52.06
Lake Success, NY (village) Nassau County	51.41
Dix Hills, NY (cdp) Suffolk County	50.22
Oyster Bay, NY (town) Nassau County	45.45
Stony Brook, NY (cdp) Suffolk County	44.89
Valley Stream, NY (village) Nassau County	44.22
Colonie, NY (town) Albany County	43.95

Notes: Please refer to the User's Guide for an explanation of data; tables reflect only those areas that meet Summary File 4 population thresholds, therefore there may be less than 10 places listed

PROFILES OF NEW YORK / Asian: Rankings

Fijian
Top 10 Places Sorted by Number

Place	Number
No places met population threshold.	

Fijian
Top 10 Places Sorted by Percent

Place	Percent
No places met population threshold.	

Filipino
Top 10 Places Sorted by Number

Place	Number
New York, NY	23,421
Hempstead, NY (town) Nassau County	1,391
Clarkstown, NY (town) Rockland County	873
Oyster Bay, NY (town) Nassau County	663
North Hempstead, NY (town) Nassau County	649
Yonkers, NY (city) Westchester County	570
Ramapo, NY (town) Rockland County	530
Brookhaven, NY (town) Suffolk County	514
Islip, NY (town) Suffolk County	404
Huntington, NY (town) Suffolk County	394

Filipino
Top 10 Places Sorted by Percent

Place	Percent
Hicksville, NY (cdp) Nassau County	55.71
Babylon, NY (town) Suffolk County	53.78
Huntington, NY (town) Suffolk County	51.98
Oyster Bay, NY (town) Nassau County	51.68
North Hempstead, NY (town) Nassau County	47.83
Greenburgh, NY (town) Westchester County	46.29
Orangetown, NY (town) Rockland County	45.22
Islip, NY (town) Suffolk County	43.12
New City, NY (cdp) Rockland County	40.34
Clarkstown, NY (town) Rockland County	40.01

Guamanian or Chamorro
Top 10 Places Sorted by Number

Place	Number
New York, NY	156

Guamanian or Chamorro
Top 10 Places Sorted by Percent

Place	Percent
New York, NY	13.27

Hawaiian, Native
Top 10 Places Sorted by Number

Place	Number
New York, NY	116

Hawaiian, Native
Top 10 Places Sorted by Percent

Place	Percent
New York, NY	14.95

Hmong
Top 10 Places Sorted by Number

Place	Number
No places met population threshold.	

Hmong
Top 10 Places Sorted by Percent

Place	Percent
No places met population threshold.	

Indonesian
Top 10 Places Sorted by Number

Place	Number
New York, NY	305

Indonesian
Top 10 Places Sorted by Percent

Place	Percent
New York, NY	16.80

Japanese
Top 10 Places Sorted by Number

Place	Number
New York, NY	1,707
Greenburgh, NY (town) Westchester County	117
Brookhaven, NY (town) Suffolk County	62
North Hempstead, NY (town) Nassau County	55
Hempstead, NY (town) Nassau County	43
Scarsdale, NY (village) Westchester County	32
Oyster Bay, NY (town) Nassau County	30
Rye, NY (city) Westchester County	23
Harrison, NY (village) Westchester County	20
Eastchester, NY (town) Westchester County	11

Japanese
Top 10 Places Sorted by Percent

Place	Percent
Brookhaven, NY (town) Suffolk County	14.98
Hempstead, NY (town) Nassau County	11.08
Oyster Bay, NY (town) Nassau County	8.02
New York, NY	7.65
Greenburgh, NY (town) Westchester County	5.98
North Hempstead, NY (town) Nassau County	5.76
Scarsdale, NY (village) Westchester County	4.08
Rye, NY (city) Westchester County	3.57
Harrison, NY (village) Westchester County	2.89
Greenville, NY (cdp) Westchester County	2.04

Korean
Top 10 Places Sorted by Number

Place	Number
New York, NY	24,991
North Hempstead, NY (town) Nassau County	1,259
Hempstead, NY (town) Nassau County	1,226
Oyster Bay, NY (town) Nassau County	994
Brookhaven, NY (town) Suffolk County	555
Huntington, NY (town) Suffolk County	509
Greenburgh, NY (town) Westchester County	421
Yonkers, NY (city) Westchester County	410
Islip, NY (town) Suffolk County	360
Syosset, NY (cdp) Nassau County	254

Korean
Top 10 Places Sorted by Percent

Place	Percent
Islip, NY (town) Suffolk County	60.91
Smithtown, NY (town) Suffolk County	55.48
Huntington, NY (town) Suffolk County	51.78
Lake Success, NY (village) Nassau County	47.74
Syosset, NY (cdp) Nassau County	45.36
Greenburgh, NY (town) Westchester County	42.10
Rochester, NY (city) Monroe County	42.03
Hempstead, NY (town) Nassau County	41.83
Oyster Bay, NY (town) Nassau County	40.21
Ramapo, NY (town) Rockland County	38.78

Laotian
Top 10 Places Sorted by Number

Place	Number
Rochester, NY (city) Monroe County	402

Laotian
Top 10 Places Sorted by Percent

Place	Percent
Rochester, NY (city) Monroe County	49.94

Malaysian
Top 10 Places Sorted by Number

Place	Number
New York, NY	179

Malaysian
Top 10 Places Sorted by Percent

Place	Percent
New York, NY	14.95

Pakistani
Top 10 Places Sorted by Number

Place	Number
New York, NY	6,614
Hempstead, NY (town) Nassau County	392
North Hempstead, NY (town) Nassau County	231
Brookhaven, NY (town) Suffolk County	210
Huntington, NY (town) Suffolk County	170

Pakistani
Top 10 Places Sorted by Percent

Place	Percent
Huntington, NY (town) Suffolk County	38.90
North Hempstead, NY (town) Nassau County	37.38
Brookhaven, NY (town) Suffolk County	28.46
Hempstead, NY (town) Nassau County	27.86
New York, NY	27.73

Samoan
Top 10 Places Sorted by Number

Place	Number
New York, NY	20

Samoan
Top 10 Places Sorted by Percent

Place	Percent
New York, NY	2.74

Sri Lankan
Top 10 Places Sorted by Number

Place	Number
New York, NY	431

Sri Lankan
Top 10 Places Sorted by Percent

Place	Percent
New York, NY	21.51

Taiwanese
Top 10 Places Sorted by Number

Place	Number
New York, NY	2,281
North Hempstead, NY (town) Nassau County	139

Taiwanese
Top 10 Places Sorted by Percent

Place	Percent
North Hempstead, NY (town) Nassau County	49.12
New York, NY	46.4

Notes: Please refer to the User's Guide for an explanation of data; tables reflect only those areas that meet Summary File 4 population thresholds, therefore there may be less than 10 places listed

PROFILES OF NEW YORK / Asian: Rankings

Thai
Top 10 Places Sorted by Number

Place	Number
New York, NY	958

Thai
Top 10 Places Sorted by Percent

Place	Percent
New York, NY	25.06

Tongan
Top 10 Places Sorted by Number

Place	Number
No places met population threshold.	

Tongan
Top 10 Places Sorted by Percent

Place	Percent
No places met population threshold.	

Vietnamese
Top 10 Places Sorted by Number

Place	Number
New York, NY	5,654
Rochester, NY (city) Monroe County	470
Buffalo, NY (city) Erie County	427
Syracuse, NY (city) Onondaga County	378
Utica, NY (city) Oneida County	258
Albany, NY (city) Albany County	231
Binghamton, NY (city) Broome County	155

Vietnamese
Top 10 Places Sorted by Percent

Place	Percent
Albany, NY (city) Albany County	58.33
Binghamton, NY (city) Broome County	52.54
Rochester, NY (city) Monroe County	46.91
New York, NY	45.93
Buffalo, NY (city) Erie County	36.28
Syracuse, NY (city) Onondaga County	29.88
Utica, NY (city) Oneida County	27.86

Educational Attainment: High School Graduates

Total Populations 25 Years and Over Who are High School Graduates
Top 10 Places Sorted by Number

Place	Number
New York, NY	3,814,256
Hempstead, NY (town) Nassau County	431,485
Brookhaven, NY (town) Suffolk County	251,158
Oyster Bay, NY (town) Nassau County	184,305
Islip, NY (town) Suffolk County	173,016
Buffalo, NY (city) Erie County	136,475
North Hempstead, NY (town) Nassau County	133,811
Huntington, NY (town) Suffolk County	122,366
Babylon, NY (town) Suffolk County	115,683
Yonkers, NY (city) Westchester County	101,090

Total Populations 25 Years and Over Who are High School Graduates
Top 10 Places Sorted by Percent

Place	Percent
Forest Home, NY (cdp) Tompkins County	100.00
Munsey Park, NY (village) Nassau County	98.74
Chappaqua, NY (cdp) Westchester County	97.97
Northeast Ithaca, NY (cdp) Tompkins County	97.74
East Hills, NY (village) Nassau County	97.73
East Ithaca, NY (cdp) Tompkins County	97.39
Scarsdale, NY (village) Westchester County	97.11
Sands Point, NY (village) Nassau County	96.97
Garden City, NY (village) Nassau County	96.69
Bronxville, NY (village) Westchester County	96.56

Asians 25 Years and Over Who are High School Graduates
Top 10 Places Sorted by Number

Place	Number
New York, NY	372,377
Hempstead, NY (town) Nassau County	14,362
North Hempstead, NY (town) Nassau County	11,451
Oyster Bay, NY (town) Nassau County	7,886
Brookhaven, NY (town) Suffolk County	6,530
Yonkers, NY (city) Westchester County	5,341
Greenburgh, NY (town) Westchester County	5,057
Huntington, NY (town) Suffolk County	4,167
Clarkstown, NY (town) Rockland County	3,824
Islip, NY (town) Suffolk County	3,393

Asians 25 Years and Over Who are High School Graduates
Top 10 Places Sorted by Percent

Place	Percent
Ardsley, NY (village) Westchester County	100.00
Clifton Park, NY (town) Saratoga County	100.00
East Ithaca, NY (cdp) Tompkins County	100.00
Forest Home, NY (cdp) Tompkins County	100.00
Munsey Park, NY (village) Nassau County	100.00
Northeast Ithaca, NY (cdp) Tompkins County	100.00
Piermont, NY (village) Rockland County	100.00
Somers, NY (town) Westchester County	98.99
Valley Cottage, NY (cdp) Rockland County	98.87
Bronxville, NY (village) Westchester County	98.80

Native Hawaiian and Other Pacific Islanders 25 Years and Over Who are High School Graduates
Top 10 Places Sorted by Number

Place	Number
New York, NY	1,791

Native Hawaiian and Other Pacific Islanders 25 Years and Over Who are High School Graduates
Top 10 Places Sorted by Percent

Place	Percent
New York, NY	66.78

Asian Indians 25 Years and Over Who are High School Graduates
Top 10 Places Sorted by Number

Place	Number
New York, NY	79,753
Hempstead, NY (town) Nassau County	5,513
North Hempstead, NY (town) Nassau County	4,083
Oyster Bay, NY (town) Nassau County	2,829
Yonkers, NY (city) Westchester County	2,292
Brookhaven, NY (town) Suffolk County	1,836
Greenburgh, NY (town) Westchester County	1,628
Clarkstown, NY (town) Rockland County	1,290
Islip, NY (town) Suffolk County	1,262
Huntington, NY (town) Suffolk County	1,256

Asian Indians 25 Years and Over Who are High School Graduates
Top 10 Places Sorted by Percent

Place	Percent
Clifton Park, NY (town) Saratoga County	100.00
Cortlandt, NY (town) Westchester County	100.00
Henrietta, NY (town) Monroe County	100.00
Mineola, NY (village) Nassau County	100.00
Niskayuna, NY (town) Schenectady County	100.00
Dix Hills, NY (cdp) Suffolk County	97.39
Plainview, NY (cdp) Nassau County	96.89
Syosset, NY (cdp) Nassau County	96.67
Huntington, NY (town) Suffolk County	96.54
New Castle, NY (town) Westchester County	96.30

Bangladeshis 25 Years and Over Who are High School Graduates
Top 10 Places Sorted by Number

Place	Number
New York, NY	8,232

Bangladeshis 25 Years and Over Who are High School Graduates
Top 10 Places Sorted by Percent

Place	Percent
New York, NY	72.10

Cambodians 25 Years and Over Who are High School Graduates
Top 10 Places Sorted by Number

Place	Number
New York, NY	398

Cambodians 25 Years and Over Who are High School Graduates
Top 10 Places Sorted by Percent

Place	Percent
New York, NY	48.01

Chinese (except Taiwanese) 25 Years and Over Who are High School Graduates
Top 10 Places Sorted by Number

Place	Number
New York, NY	143,665
Hempstead, NY (town) Nassau County	3,042
North Hempstead, NY (town) Nassau County	3,015
Oyster Bay, NY (town) Nassau County	2,121
Brookhaven, NY (town) Suffolk County	2,034
Huntington, NY (town) Suffolk County	1,145
Greenburgh, NY (town) Westchester County	884
Amherst, NY (town) Erie County	821
Islip, NY (town) Suffolk County	583
Babylon, NY (town) Suffolk County	564

Chinese (except Taiwanese) 25 Years and Over Who are High School Graduates
Top 10 Places Sorted by Percent

Place	Percent
Lake Success, NY (village) Nassau County	98.89
Scarsdale, NY (village) Westchester County	97.98
Setauket-East Setauket, NY (cdp) Suffolk County	97.95
Dix Hills, NY (cdp) Suffolk County	96.31
Poughkeepsie, NY (town) Dutchess County	96.09
Greenburgh, NY (town) Westchester County	95.88
Henrietta, NY (town) Monroe County	95.26
Syosset, NY (cdp) Nassau County	94.95
New Castle, NY (town) Westchester County	94.47
Ithaca, NY (city) Tompkins County	93.65

Fijians 25 Years and Over Who are High School Graduates
Top 10 Places Sorted by Number

Place	Number
No places met population threshold.	

Fijians 25 Years and Over Who are High School Graduates
Top 10 Places Sorted by Percent

Place	Percent
No places met population threshold.	

Notes: Please refer to the User's Guide for an explanation of data; tables reflect only those areas that meet Summary File 4 population thresholds, therefore there may be less than 10 places listed

PROFILES OF NEW YORK / Asian: Rankings

Filipinos 25 Years and Over Who are High School Graduates
Top 10 Places Sorted by Number

Place	Number
New York, NY	39,562
Hempstead, NY (town) Nassau County	2,458
Clarkstown, NY (town) Rockland County	1,399
Yonkers, NY (city) Westchester County	1,152
North Hempstead, NY (town) Nassau County	905
Ramapo, NY (town) Rockland County	828
Oyster Bay, NY (town) Nassau County	819
Brookhaven, NY (town) Suffolk County	803
Islip, NY (town) Suffolk County	666
Huntington, NY (town) Suffolk County	551

Filipinos 25 Years and Over Who are High School Graduates
Top 10 Places Sorted by Percent

Place	Percent
East Meadow, NY (cdp) Nassau County	100.00
Valley Cottage, NY (cdp) Rockland County	100.00
Huntington, NY (town) Suffolk County	99.64
Greenburgh, NY (town) Westchester County	99.27
Clarkstown, NY (town) Rockland County	98.38
New City, NY (cdp) Rockland County	98.27
Babylon, NY (town) Suffolk County	96.82
Orangetown, NY (town) Rockland County	96.24
Hicksville, NY (cdp) Nassau County	95.30
Brookhaven, NY (town) Suffolk County	95.14

Guamanian or Chamorros 25 Years and Over Who are High School Graduates
Top 10 Places Sorted by Number

Place	Number
New York, NY	401

Guamanian or Chamorros 25 Years and Over Who are High School Graduates
Top 10 Places Sorted by Percent

Place	Percent
New York, NY	68.66

Hawaiian, Natives 25 Years and Over Who are High School Graduates
Top 10 Places Sorted by Number

Place	Number
New York, NY	388

Hawaiian, Natives 25 Years and Over Who are High School Graduates
Top 10 Places Sorted by Percent

Place	Percent
New York, NY	72.93

Hmongs 25 Years and Over Who are High School Graduates
Top 10 Places Sorted by Number

Place	Number
No places met population threshold.	

Hmongs 25 Years and Over Who are High School Graduates
Top 10 Places Sorted by Percent

Place	Percent
No places met population threshold.	

Indonesians 25 Years and Over Who are High School Graduates
Top 10 Places Sorted by Number

Place	Number
New York, NY	1,087

Indonesians 25 Years and Over Who are High School Graduates
Top 10 Places Sorted by Percent

Place	Percent
New York, NY	92.12

Japanese 25 Years and Over Who are High School Graduates
Top 10 Places Sorted by Number

Place	Number
New York, NY	17,426
Greenburgh, NY (town) Westchester County	1,279
Eastchester, NY (town) Westchester County	800
North Hempstead, NY (town) Nassau County	750
Harrison, NY (village) Westchester County	406
Rye, NY (city) Westchester County	396
Scarsdale, NY (village) Westchester County	396
Greenville, NY (cdp) Westchester County	375
Eastchester, NY (cdp) Westchester County	350
Brookhaven, NY (town) Suffolk County	299

Japanese 25 Years and Over Who are High School Graduates
Top 10 Places Sorted by Percent

Place	Percent
Eastchester, NY (town) Westchester County	100.00
Eastchester, NY (cdp) Westchester County	100.00
Greenville, NY (cdp) Westchester County	100.00
Harrison, NY (village) Westchester County	100.00
North Hempstead, NY (town) Nassau County	99.73
Rye, NY (city) Westchester County	98.51
Greenburgh, NY (town) Westchester County	98.23
Scarsdale, NY (village) Westchester County	97.06
New York, NY	96.17
Oyster Bay, NY (town) Nassau County	95.76

Koreans 25 Years and Over Who are High School Graduates
Top 10 Places Sorted by Number

Place	Number
New York, NY	51,832
North Hempstead, NY (town) Nassau County	1,780
Hempstead, NY (town) Nassau County	1,599
Oyster Bay, NY (town) Nassau County	1,377
Yonkers, NY (city) Westchester County	695
Brookhaven, NY (town) Suffolk County	679
Greenburgh, NY (town) Westchester County	615
Huntington, NY (town) Suffolk County	570
Jericho, NY (cdp) Nassau County	415
Clarkstown, NY (town) Rockland County	407

Koreans 25 Years and Over Who are High School Graduates
Top 10 Places Sorted by Percent

Place	Percent
Commack, NY (cdp) Suffolk County	100.00
Ithaca, NY (city) Tompkins County	100.00
Huntington, NY (town) Suffolk County	98.45
Jericho, NY (cdp) Nassau County	96.96
Brookhaven, NY (town) Suffolk County	96.59
Orangetown, NY (town) Rockland County	96.15
Smithtown, NY (town) Suffolk County	95.94
Greenburgh, NY (town) Westchester County	95.05
Scarsdale, NY (village) Westchester County	94.17
Lake Success, NY (village) Nassau County	93.82

Laotians 25 Years and Over Who are High School Graduates
Top 10 Places Sorted by Number

Place	Number
Rochester, NY (city) Monroe County	259

Laotians 25 Years and Over Who are High School Graduates
Top 10 Places Sorted by Percent

Place	Percent
Rochester, NY (city) Monroe County	61.37

Malaysians 25 Years and Over Who are High School Graduates
Top 10 Places Sorted by Number

Place	Number
New York, NY	636

Malaysians 25 Years and Over Who are High School Graduates
Top 10 Places Sorted by Percent

Place	Percent
New York, NY	65.16

Pakistanis 25 Years and Over Who are High School Graduates
Top 10 Places Sorted by Number

Place	Number
New York, NY	9,002
Hempstead, NY (town) Nassau County	561
Brookhaven, NY (town) Suffolk County	370
North Hempstead, NY (town) Nassau County	285
Huntington, NY (town) Suffolk County	187

Pakistanis 25 Years and Over Who are High School Graduates
Top 10 Places Sorted by Percent

Place	Percent
North Hempstead, NY (town) Nassau County	91.94
Brookhaven, NY (town) Suffolk County	89.81
Huntington, NY (town) Suffolk County	82.74
Hempstead, NY (town) Nassau County	77.17
New York, NY	68.35

Samoans 25 Years and Over Who are High School Graduates
Top 10 Places Sorted by Number

Place	Number
New York, NY	169

Samoans 25 Years and Over Who are High School Graduates
Top 10 Places Sorted by Percent

Place	Percent
New York, NY	56.52

Sri Lankans 25 Years and Over Who are High School Graduates
Top 10 Places Sorted by Number

Place	Number
New York, NY	950

Sri Lankans 25 Years and Over Who are High School Graduates
Top 10 Places Sorted by Percent

Place	Percent
New York, NY	70.68

Notes: Please refer to the User's Guide for an explanation of data; tables reflect only those areas that meet Summary File 4 population thresholds, therefore there may be less than 10 places listed

PROFILES OF NEW YORK / Asian: Rankings

Taiwanese 25 Years and Over Who are High School Graduates
Top 10 Places Sorted by Number

Place	Number
New York, NY	3,251
North Hempstead, NY (town) Nassau County	167

Taiwanese 25 Years and Over Who are High School Graduates
Top 10 Places Sorted by Percent

Place	Percent
North Hempstead, NY (town) Nassau County	95.43
New York, NY	89.78

Thais 25 Years and Over Who are High School Graduates
Top 10 Places Sorted by Number

Place	Number
New York, NY	2,395

Thais 25 Years and Over Who are High School Graduates
Top 10 Places Sorted by Percent

Place	Percent
New York, NY	86.46

Tongans 25 Years and Over Who are High School Graduates
Top 10 Places Sorted by Number

Place	Number
No places met population threshold.	

Tongans 25 Years and Over Who are High School Graduates
Top 10 Places Sorted by Percent

Place	Percent
No places met population threshold.	

Vietnamese 25 Years and Over Who are High School Graduates
Top 10 Places Sorted by Number

Place	Number
New York, NY	4,482
Buffalo, NY (city) Erie County	402
Rochester, NY (city) Monroe County	361
Syracuse, NY (city) Onondaga County	275
Albany, NY (city) Albany County	172
Utica, NY (city) Oneida County	147
Binghamton, NY (city) Broome County	63

Vietnamese 25 Years and Over Who are High School Graduates
Top 10 Places Sorted by Percent

Place	Percent
Albany, NY (city) Albany County	61.43
New York, NY	57.63
Rochester, NY (city) Monroe County	56.06
Buffalo, NY (city) Erie County	52.76
Binghamton, NY (city) Broome County	40.65
Syracuse, NY (city) Onondaga County	37.01
Utica, NY (city) Oneida County	25.57

Educational Attainment: Four-Year College Graduates

Total Populations 25 Years and Over Who are Four-Year College Graduates
Top 10 Places Sorted by Number

Place	Number
New York, NY	1,446,833
Hempstead, NY (town) Nassau County	158,382
Oyster Bay, NY (town) Nassau County	77,489
Brookhaven, NY (town) Suffolk County	71,089
North Hempstead, NY (town) Nassau County	70,290
Huntington, NY (town) Suffolk County	59,888
Islip, NY (town) Suffolk County	45,456
Amherst, NY (town) Erie County	37,147
Buffalo, NY (city) Erie County	33,435
Greenburgh, NY (town) Westchester County	32,946

Total Populations 25 Years and Over Who are Four-Year College Graduates
Top 10 Places Sorted by Percent

Place	Percent
Forest Home, NY (cdp) Tompkins County	91.76
East Ithaca, NY (cdp) Tompkins County	81.95
Scarsdale, NY (village) Westchester County	79.83
Chappaqua, NY (cdp) Westchester County	79.69
Northeast Ithaca, NY (cdp) Tompkins County	77.84
New Castle, NY (town) Westchester County	75.97
Lansing, NY (village) Tompkins County	74.76
Munsey Park, NY (village) Nassau County	73.93
Bronxville, NY (village) Westchester County	73.56
East Hills, NY (village) Nassau County	73.33

Asians 25 Years and Over Who are Four-Year College Graduates
Top 10 Places Sorted by Number

Place	Number
New York, NY	193,967
Hempstead, NY (town) Nassau County	8,625
North Hempstead, NY (town) Nassau County	7,894
Oyster Bay, NY (town) Nassau County	5,462
Brookhaven, NY (town) Suffolk County	4,654
Greenburgh, NY (town) Westchester County	3,913
Yonkers, NY (city) Westchester County	3,401
Huntington, NY (town) Suffolk County	2,912
Clarkstown, NY (town) Rockland County	2,764
Amherst, NY (town) Erie County	2,595

Asians 25 Years and Over Who are Four-Year College Graduates
Top 10 Places Sorted by Percent

Place	Percent
East Ithaca, NY (cdp) Tompkins County	100.00
Forest Home, NY (cdp) Tompkins County	98.39
Northeast Ithaca, NY (cdp) Tompkins County	97.01
Lansing, NY (village) Tompkins County	95.19
Lansing, NY (town) Tompkins County	92.22
Chappaqua, NY (cdp) Westchester County	91.72
Briarcliff Manor, NY (village) Westchester County	90.07
New Castle, NY (town) Westchester County	90.00
Munsey Park, NY (village) Nassau County	88.64
Dryden, NY (town) Tompkins County	88.51

Native Hawaiian and Other Pacific Islanders 25 Years and Over Who are Four-Year College Graduates
Top 10 Places Sorted by Number

Place	Number
New York, NY	447

Native Hawaiian and Other Pacific Islanders 25 Years and Over Who are Four-Year College Graduates
Top 10 Places Sorted by Percent

Place	Percent
New York, NY	16.67

Asian Indians 25 Years and Over Who are Four-Year College Graduates
Top 10 Places Sorted by Number

Place	Number
New York, NY	41,883
Hempstead, NY (town) Nassau County	3,200
North Hempstead, NY (town) Nassau County	2,863
Oyster Bay, NY (town) Nassau County	2,055
Yonkers, NY (city) Westchester County	1,343
Greenburgh, NY (town) Westchester County	1,322
Brookhaven, NY (town) Suffolk County	1,231
Amherst, NY (town) Erie County	1,022
Huntington, NY (town) Suffolk County	1,021
Islip, NY (town) Suffolk County	926

Asian Indians 25 Years and Over Who are Four-Year College Graduates
Top 10 Places Sorted by Percent

Place	Percent
New Castle, NY (town) Westchester County	94.81
Clifton Park, NY (town) Saratoga County	94.04
Mineola, NY (village) Nassau County	89.08
Scarsdale, NY (village) Westchester County	88.89
Amherst, NY (town) Erie County	88.33
Niskayuna, NY (town) Schenectady County	88.02
Cheektowaga, NY (town) Erie County	87.80
Dix Hills, NY (cdp) Suffolk County	87.69
Manhasset Hills, NY (cdp) Nassau County	87.61
Greenville, NY (cdp) Westchester County	85.97

Bangladeshis 25 Years and Over Who are Four-Year College Graduates
Top 10 Places Sorted by Number

Place	Number
New York, NY	4,366

Bangladeshis 25 Years and Over Who are Four-Year College Graduates
Top 10 Places Sorted by Percent

Place	Percent
New York, NY	38.24

Cambodians 25 Years and Over Who are Four-Year College Graduates
Top 10 Places Sorted by Number

Place	Number
New York, NY	99

Cambodians 25 Years and Over Who are Four-Year College Graduates
Top 10 Places Sorted by Percent

Place	Percent
New York, NY	11.94

Chinese (except Taiwanese) 25 Years and Over Who are Four-Year College Graduates
Top 10 Places Sorted by Number

Place	Number
New York, NY	66,766
North Hempstead, NY (town) Nassau County	1,958
Hempstead, NY (town) Nassau County	1,631
Brookhaven, NY (town) Suffolk County	1,613
Oyster Bay, NY (town) Nassau County	1,474
Huntington, NY (town) Suffolk County	752
Greenburgh, NY (town) Westchester County	713
Amherst, NY (town) Erie County	709
Setauket-East Setauket, NY (cdp) Suffolk County	426
Yonkers, NY (city) Westchester County	402

Chinese (except Taiwanese) 25 Years and Over Who are Four-Year College Graduates
Top 10 Places Sorted by Percent

Place	Percent
Poughkeepsie, NY (town) Dutchess County	91.30
Scarsdale, NY (village) Westchester County	87.85
Setauket-East Setauket, NY (cdp) Suffolk County	87.30
Vestal, NY (town) Broome County	82.61
Ithaca, NY (city) Tompkins County	82.54

Notes: Please refer to the User's Guide for an explanation of data; tables reflect only those areas that meet Summary File 4 population thresholds, therefore there may be less than 10 places listed

Place	
Lake Success, NY (village) Nassau County	81.11
Albany, NY (city) Albany County	80.76
Greenburgh, NY (town) Westchester County	77.33
Stony Brook, NY (cdp) Suffolk County	76.95
Amherst, NY (town) Erie County	76.48

Fijians 25 Years and Over Who are Four-Year College Graduates
Top 10 Places Sorted by Number

Place	Number
No places met population threshold.	

Fijians 25 Years and Over Who are Four-Year College Graduates
Top 10 Places Sorted by Percent

Place	Percent
No places met population threshold.	

Filipinos 25 Years and Over Who are Four-Year College Graduates
Top 10 Places Sorted by Number

Place	Number
New York, NY	27,520
Hempstead, NY (town) Nassau County	1,843
Clarkstown, NY (town) Rockland County	1,112
Yonkers, NY (city) Westchester County	894
North Hempstead, NY (town) Nassau County	691
Ramapo, NY (town) Rockland County	570
Brookhaven, NY (town) Suffolk County	565
Oyster Bay, NY (town) Nassau County	552
Huntington, NY (town) Suffolk County	431
Orangetown, NY (town) Rockland County	383

Filipinos 25 Years and Over Who are Four-Year College Graduates
Top 10 Places Sorted by Percent

Place	Percent
East Meadow, NY (cdp) Nassau County	85.14
New City, NY (cdp) Rockland County	80.06
Greenburgh, NY (town) Westchester County	78.78
Clarkstown, NY (town) Rockland County	78.20
Huntington, NY (town) Suffolk County	77.94
Valley Cottage, NY (cdp) Rockland County	77.68
Elmont, NY (cdp) Nassau County	76.88
Orangetown, NY (town) Rockland County	75.84
Yonkers, NY (city) Westchester County	73.52
North Hempstead, NY (town) Nassau County	71.68

Guamanian or Chamorros 25 Years and Over Who are Four-Year College Graduates
Top 10 Places Sorted by Number

Place	Number
New York, NY	41

Guamanian or Chamorros 25 Years and Over Who are Four-Year College Graduates
Top 10 Places Sorted by Percent

Place	Percent
New York, NY	7.02

Hawaiian, Natives 25 Years and Over Who are Four-Year College Graduates
Top 10 Places Sorted by Number

Place	Number
New York, NY	125

Hawaiian, Natives 25 Years and Over Who are Four-Year College Graduates
Top 10 Places Sorted by Percent

Place	Percent
New York, NY	23.50

Hmongs 25 Years and Over Who are Four-Year College Graduates
Top 10 Places Sorted by Number

Place	Number
No places met population threshold.	

Hmongs 25 Years and Over Who are Four-Year College Graduates
Top 10 Places Sorted by Percent

Place	Percent
No places met population threshold.	

Indonesians 25 Years and Over Who are Four-Year College Graduates
Top 10 Places Sorted by Number

Place	Number
New York, NY	461

Indonesians 25 Years and Over Who are Four-Year College Graduates
Top 10 Places Sorted by Percent

Place	Percent
New York, NY	39.07

Japanese 25 Years and Over Who are Four-Year College Graduates
Top 10 Places Sorted by Number

Place	Number
New York, NY	11,154
Greenburgh, NY (town) Westchester County	926
Eastchester, NY (town) Westchester County	533
North Hempstead, NY (town) Nassau County	460
Rye, NY (city) Westchester County	296
Scarsdale, NY (village) Westchester County	286
Greenville, NY (cdp) Westchester County	283
Eastchester, NY (cdp) Westchester County	279
Harrison, NY (village) Westchester County	278
Oyster Bay, NY (town) Nassau County	170

Japanese 25 Years and Over Who are Four-Year College Graduates
Top 10 Places Sorted by Percent

Place	Percent
Eastchester, NY (cdp) Westchester County	79.71
Greenville, NY (cdp) Westchester County	75.47
Rye, NY (city) Westchester County	73.63
Greenburgh, NY (town) Westchester County	71.12
Scarsdale, NY (village) Westchester County	70.10
Harrison, NY (village) Westchester County	68.47
Eastchester, NY (town) Westchester County	66.63
New York, NY	61.56
North Hempstead, NY (town) Nassau County	61.17
Oyster Bay, NY (town) Nassau County	60.07

Koreans 25 Years and Over Who are Four-Year College Graduates
Top 10 Places Sorted by Number

Place	Number
New York, NY	25,875
North Hempstead, NY (town) Nassau County	1,251
Oyster Bay, NY (town) Nassau County	921
Hempstead, NY (town) Nassau County	905
Brookhaven, NY (town) Suffolk County	538
Greenburgh, NY (town) Westchester County	456
Amherst, NY (town) Erie County	387
Yonkers, NY (city) Westchester County	386
Huntington, NY (town) Suffolk County	360
Clarkstown, NY (town) Rockland County	321

Koreans 25 Years and Over Who are Four-Year College Graduates
Top 10 Places Sorted by Percent

Place	Percent
Ithaca, NY (city) Tompkins County	96.10
Amherst, NY (town) Erie County	85.24
Syracuse, NY (city) Onondaga County	81.35
Brookhaven, NY (town) Suffolk County	76.53
Lake Success, NY (village) Nassau County	73.03
Clarkstown, NY (town) Rockland County	72.30
Greenburgh, NY (town) Westchester County	70.48
Jericho, NY (cdp) Nassau County	68.22
North Hempstead, NY (town) Nassau County	64.89
Huntington, NY (town) Suffolk County	62.18

Laotians 25 Years and Over Who are Four-Year College Graduates
Top 10 Places Sorted by Number

Place	Number
Rochester, NY (city) Monroe County	50

Laotians 25 Years and Over Who are Four-Year College Graduates
Top 10 Places Sorted by Percent

Place	Percent
Rochester, NY (city) Monroe County	11.85

Malaysians 25 Years and Over Who are Four-Year College Graduates
Top 10 Places Sorted by Number

Place	Number
New York, NY	202

Malaysians 25 Years and Over Who are Four-Year College Graduates
Top 10 Places Sorted by Percent

Place	Percent
New York, NY	20.70

Pakistanis 25 Years and Over Who are Four-Year College Graduates
Top 10 Places Sorted by Number

Place	Number
New York, NY	4,826
Hempstead, NY (town) Nassau County	357
Brookhaven, NY (town) Suffolk County	254
North Hempstead, NY (town) Nassau County	223
Huntington, NY (town) Suffolk County	108

Pakistanis 25 Years and Over Who are Four-Year College Graduates
Top 10 Places Sorted by Percent

Place	Percent
North Hempstead, NY (town) Nassau County	71.94
Brookhaven, NY (town) Suffolk County	61.65
Hempstead, NY (town) Nassau County	49.11
Huntington, NY (town) Suffolk County	47.79
New York, NY	36.64

Samoans 25 Years and Over Who are Four-Year College Graduates
Top 10 Places Sorted by Number

Place	Number
New York, NY	35

Samoans 25 Years and Over Who are Four-Year College Graduates
Top 10 Places Sorted by Percent

Place	Percent
New York, NY	11.71

Notes: Please refer to the User's Guide for an explanation of data; tables reflect only those areas that meet Summary File 4 population thresholds, therefore there may be less than 10 places listed

Sri Lankans 25 Years and Over Who are Four-Year College Graduates
Top 10 Places Sorted by Number

Place	Number
New York, NY	447

Sri Lankans 25 Years and Over Who are Four-Year College Graduates
Top 10 Places Sorted by Percent

Place	Percent
New York, NY	33.26

Taiwanese 25 Years and Over Who are Four-Year College Graduates
Top 10 Places Sorted by Number

Place	Number
New York, NY	2,288
North Hempstead, NY (town) Nassau County	138

Taiwanese 25 Years and Over Who are Four-Year College Graduates
Top 10 Places Sorted by Percent

Place	Percent
North Hempstead, NY (town) Nassau County	78.86
New York, NY	63.19

Thais 25 Years and Over Who are Four-Year College Graduates
Top 10 Places Sorted by Number

Place	Number
New York, NY	1,189

Thais 25 Years and Over Who are Four-Year College Graduates
Top 10 Places Sorted by Percent

Place	Percent
New York, NY	42.92

Tongans 25 Years and Over Who are Four-Year College Graduates
Top 10 Places Sorted by Number

Place	Number

No places met population threshold.

Tongans 25 Years and Over Who are Four-Year College Graduates
Top 10 Places Sorted by Percent

Place	Percent

No places met population threshold.

Vietnamese 25 Years and Over Who are Four-Year College Graduates
Top 10 Places Sorted by Number

Place	Number
New York, NY	1,980
Buffalo, NY (city) Erie County	125
Syracuse, NY (city) Onondaga County	95
Albany, NY (city) Albany County	81
Rochester, NY (city) Monroe County	71
Utica, NY (city) Oneida County	9
Binghamton, NY (city) Broome County	5

Vietnamese 25 Years and Over Who are Four-Year College Graduates
Top 10 Places Sorted by Percent

Place	Percent
Albany, NY (city) Albany County	28.93
New York, NY	25.46
Buffalo, NY (city) Erie County	16.40

Syracuse, NY (city) Onondaga County	12.79
Rochester, NY (city) Monroe County	11.02
Binghamton, NY (city) Broome County	3.23
Utica, NY (city) Oneida County	1.57

Median Household Income

Total Population
Top 10 Places Sorted by Number

Place	Dollars
Brookville, NY (village) Nassau County	200,001
Laurel Hollow, NY (village) Nassau County	200,001
Oyster Bay Cove, NY (village) Nassau County	200,001
Sands Point, NY (village) Nassau County	200,001
Muttontown, NY (village) Nassau County	184,386
Scarsdale, NY (village) Westchester County	182,792
Chappaqua, NY (cdp) Westchester County	163,201
New Castle, NY (town) Westchester County	159,691
Old Westbury, NY (village) Nassau County	155,749
East Hills, NY (village) Nassau County	149,726

Asian
Top 10 Places Sorted by Number

Place	Dollars
Muttontown, NY (village) Nassau County	200,001
Oyster Bay Cove, NY (village) Nassau County	200,001
Sands Point, NY (village) Nassau County	200,001
Laurel Hollow, NY (village) Nassau County	192,979
Briarcliff Manor, NY (village) Westchester County	187,303
Munsey Park, NY (village) Nassau County	184,324
North Hills, NY (village) Nassau County	171,052
Cornwall, NY (town) Orange County	166,639
Rye, NY (city) Westchester County	165,155
New Castle, NY (town) Westchester County	162,255

Native Hawaiian and Other Pacific Islander
Top 10 Places Sorted by Number

Place	Dollars
New York, NY	27,143

Asian Indian
Top 10 Places Sorted by Number

Place	Dollars
Muttontown, NY (village) Nassau County	200,001
New Castle, NY (town) Westchester County	200,001
Scarsdale, NY (village) Westchester County	200,001
Searingtown, NY (cdp) Nassau County	171,148
Manhasset Hills, NY (cdp) Nassau County	159,057
Port Washington, NY (cdp) Nassau County	142,846
Cortlandt, NY (town) Westchester County	130,655
Pittsford, NY (town) Monroe County	129,814
Plainview, NY (cdp) Nassau County	126,123
Mount Pleasant, NY (town) Westchester County	119,072

Bangladeshi
Top 10 Places Sorted by Number

Place	Dollars
New York, NY	33,071

Cambodian
Top 10 Places Sorted by Number

Place	Dollars
New York, NY	37,422

Chinese (except Taiwanese)
Top 10 Places Sorted by Number

Place	Dollars
Scarsdale, NY (village) Westchester County	127,232
New Castle, NY (town) Westchester County	124,081
Lake Success, NY (village) Nassau County	115,043
Greenburgh, NY (town) Westchester County	113,220
Dix Hills, NY (cdp) Suffolk County	103,986

North New Hyde Park, NY (cdp) Nassau County	103,622
Syosset, NY (cdp) Nassau County	102,288
Clarkstown, NY (town) Rockland County	92,970
North Hempstead, NY (town) Nassau County	92,438
Colonie, NY (town) Albany County	91,601

Fijian
Top 10 Places Sorted by Number

Place	Dollars

No places met population threshold.

Filipino
Top 10 Places Sorted by Number

Place	Dollars
Orangetown, NY (town) Rockland County	124,458
Hicksville, NY (cdp) Nassau County	117,280
Levittown, NY (cdp) Nassau County	107,066
New City, NY (cdp) Rockland County	102,806
North Hempstead, NY (town) Nassau County	102,601
Hillcrest, NY (cdp) Rockland County	102,026
Babylon, NY (town) Suffolk County	101,850
Valley Cottage, NY (cdp) Rockland County	101,523
Clarkstown, NY (town) Rockland County	101,218
Oyster Bay, NY (town) Nassau County	100,529

Guamanian or Chamorro
Top 10 Places Sorted by Number

Place	Dollars
New York, NY	22,708

Hawaiian, Native
Top 10 Places Sorted by Number

Place	Dollars
New York, NY	34,432

Hmong
Top 10 Places Sorted by Number

Place	Dollars

No places met population threshold.

Indonesian
Top 10 Places Sorted by Number

Place	Dollars
New York, NY	39,338

Japanese
Top 10 Places Sorted by Number

Place	Dollars
Rye, NY (city) Westchester County	172,971
Harrison, NY (village) Westchester County	152,015
Scarsdale, NY (village) Westchester County	121,839
Eastchester, NY (town) Westchester County	110,772
Eastchester, NY (cdp) Westchester County	108,728
Greenville, NY (cdp) Westchester County	101,071
Greenburgh, NY (town) Westchester County	91,717
North Hempstead, NY (town) Nassau County	83,201
Oyster Bay, NY (town) Nassau County	78,685
Brookhaven, NY (town) Suffolk County	63,900

Korean
Top 10 Places Sorted by Number

Place	Dollars
Scarsdale, NY (village) Westchester County	170,098
Lake Success, NY (village) Nassau County	108,819
Greenburgh, NY (town) Westchester County	105,965
North Hempstead, NY (town) Nassau County	86,969
Plainview, NY (cdp) Nassau County	78,077
Oyster Bay, NY (town) Nassau County	73,194
Islip, NY (town) Suffolk County	72,740
Syosset, NY (cdp) Nassau County	72,250
Jericho, NY (cdp) Nassau County	67,692

Notes: Please refer to the User's Guide for an explanation of data; tables reflect only those areas that meet Summary File 4 population thresholds, therefore there may be less than 10 places listed.

Clarkstown, NY (town) Rockland County	63,375

Laotian
Top 10 Places Sorted by Number

Place	Dollars
Rochester, NY (city) Monroe County	37,841

Malaysian
Top 10 Places Sorted by Number

Place	Dollars
New York, NY	33,929

Pakistani
Top 10 Places Sorted by Number

Place	Dollars
North Hempstead, NY (town) Nassau County	76,005
Hempstead, NY (town) Nassau County	73,750
Huntington, NY (town) Suffolk County	58,542
Brookhaven, NY (town) Suffolk County	46,458
New York, NY	37,093

Samoan
Top 10 Places Sorted by Number

Place	Dollars
New York, NY	35,313

Sri Lankan
Top 10 Places Sorted by Number

Place	Dollars
New York, NY	42,069

Taiwanese
Top 10 Places Sorted by Number

Place	Dollars
North Hempstead, NY (town) Nassau County	73,333
New York, NY	52,123

Thai
Top 10 Places Sorted by Number

Place	Dollars
New York, NY	46,897

Tongan
Top 10 Places Sorted by Number

Place	Dollars

No places met population threshold.

Vietnamese
Top 10 Places Sorted by Number

Place	Dollars
Rochester, NY (city) Monroe County	39,444
New York, NY	37,393
Syracuse, NY (city) Onondaga County	31,493
Utica, NY (city) Oneida County	29,219
Binghamton, NY (city) Broome County	27,188
Buffalo, NY (city) Erie County	27,059
Albany, NY (city) Albany County	22,396

Per Capita Income

Total Population
Top 10 Places Sorted by Number

Place	Dollars
Oyster Bay Cove, NY (village) Nassau County	103,203
North Hills, NY (village) Nassau County	100,093
Sands Point, NY (village) Nassau County	95,647
Scarsdale, NY (village) Westchester County	89,907
Bronxville, NY (village) Westchester County	89,483
Muttontown, NY (village) Nassau County	88,020
Brookville, NY (village) Nassau County	84,375
Laurel Hollow, NY (village) Nassau County	83,366
Old Brookville, NY (village) Nassau County	77,874
Chappaqua, NY (cdp) Westchester County	77,835

Asian
Top 10 Places Sorted by Number

Place	Dollars
Oyster Bay Cove, NY (village) Nassau County	104,543
Muttontown, NY (village) Nassau County	88,928
Sands Point, NY (village) Nassau County	83,122
Old Westbury, NY (village) Nassau County	77,912
Briarcliff Manor, NY (village) Westchester County	76,275
Laurel Hollow, NY (village) Nassau County	72,351
Rye, NY (city) Westchester County	69,806
North Hills, NY (village) Nassau County	65,050
Munsey Park, NY (village) Nassau County	59,410
Flower Hill, NY (village) Nassau County	58,316

Native Hawaiian and Other Pacific Islander
Top 10 Places Sorted by Number

Place	Dollars
New York, NY	13,118

Asian Indian
Top 10 Places Sorted by Number

Place	Dollars
Muttontown, NY (village) Nassau County	110,041
Scarsdale, NY (village) Westchester County	89,444
New Castle, NY (town) Westchester County	71,684
Port Washington, NY (cdp) Nassau County	58,821
Searingtown, NY (cdp) Nassau County	56,329
Manhasset Hills, NY (cdp) Nassau County	54,926
Pittsford, NY (town) Monroe County	52,366
Greenville, NY (cdp) Westchester County	50,360
Ossining, NY (town) Westchester County	46,263
Cortlandt, NY (town) Westchester County	45,687

Bangladeshi
Top 10 Places Sorted by Number

Place	Dollars
New York, NY	10,364

Cambodian
Top 10 Places Sorted by Number

Place	Dollars
New York, NY	13,582

Chinese (except Taiwanese)
Top 10 Places Sorted by Number

Place	Dollars
Poughkeepsie, NY (town) Dutchess County	60,914
Scarsdale, NY (village) Westchester County	55,691
Plainview, NY (cdp) Nassau County	47,866
Lake Success, NY (village) Nassau County	44,156
Greenburgh, NY (town) Westchester County	40,941
New Castle, NY (town) Westchester County	39,683
Syosset, NY (cdp) Nassau County	36,392
Oyster Bay, NY (town) Nassau County	34,004
North Hempstead, NY (town) Nassau County	33,651
Valley Stream, NY (village) Nassau County	33,168

Fijian
Top 10 Places Sorted by Number

Place	Dollars

No places met population threshold.

Filipino
Top 10 Places Sorted by Number

Place	Dollars
Huntington, NY (town) Suffolk County	52,453

New City, NY (cdp) Rockland County	42,877
North Hempstead, NY (town) Nassau County	38,800
Orangetown, NY (town) Rockland County	37,602
Greenburgh, NY (town) Westchester County	35,692
Clarkstown, NY (town) Rockland County	32,491
Babylon, NY (town) Suffolk County	32,182
Valley Cottage, NY (cdp) Rockland County	29,467
East Meadow, NY (cdp) Nassau County	28,873
Islip, NY (town) Suffolk County	28,214

Guamanian or Chamorro
Top 10 Places Sorted by Number

Place	Dollars
New York, NY	11,529

Hawaiian, Native
Top 10 Places Sorted by Number

Place	Dollars
New York, NY	17,095

Hmong
Top 10 Places Sorted by Number

Place	Dollars

No places met population threshold.

Indonesian
Top 10 Places Sorted by Number

Place	Dollars
New York, NY	17,028

Japanese
Top 10 Places Sorted by Number

Place	Dollars
Oyster Bay, NY (town) Nassau County	66,261
Rye, NY (city) Westchester County	57,629
Greenburgh, NY (town) Westchester County	50,784
Greenville, NY (cdp) Westchester County	50,331
North Hempstead, NY (town) Nassau County	44,889
Eastchester, NY (cdp) Westchester County	44,199
Eastchester, NY (town) Westchester County	40,102
New York, NY	38,572
Harrison, NY (village) Westchester County	37,554
Scarsdale, NY (village) Westchester County	36,925

Korean
Top 10 Places Sorted by Number

Place	Dollars
Scarsdale, NY (village) Westchester County	48,602
Lake Success, NY (village) Nassau County	42,903
Greenburgh, NY (town) Westchester County	39,625
North Hempstead, NY (town) Nassau County	27,269
Commack, NY (cdp) Suffolk County	24,785
Oyster Bay, NY (town) Nassau County	23,257
Ramapo, NY (town) Rockland County	23,049
Smithtown, NY (town) Suffolk County	22,434
Syosset, NY (cdp) Nassau County	22,256
Islip, NY (town) Suffolk County	21,073

Laotian
Top 10 Places Sorted by Number

Place	Dollars
Rochester, NY (city) Monroe County	11,127

Malaysian
Top 10 Places Sorted by Number

Place	Dollars
New York, NY	16,548

Notes: Please refer to the User's Guide for an explanation of data; tables reflect only those areas that meet Summary File 4 population thresholds, therefore there may be less than 10 places listed

PROFILES OF NEW YORK / Asian: Rankings

Pakistani
Top 10 Places Sorted by Number

Place	Dollars
North Hempstead, NY (town) Nassau County	24,302
Huntington, NY (town) Suffolk County	21,819
Hempstead, NY (town) Nassau County	19,393
Brookhaven, NY (town) Suffolk County	15,627
New York, NY	12,108

Samoan
Top 10 Places Sorted by Number

Place	Dollars
New York, NY	13,721

Sri Lankan
Top 10 Places Sorted by Number

Place	Dollars
New York, NY	21,876

Taiwanese
Top 10 Places Sorted by Number

Place	Dollars
New York, NY	30,329
North Hempstead, NY (town) Nassau County	27,918

Thai
Top 10 Places Sorted by Number

Place	Dollars
New York, NY	22,566

Tongan
Top 10 Places Sorted by Number

Place	Dollars
No places met population threshold.	

Vietnamese
Top 10 Places Sorted by Number

Place	Dollars
Binghamton, NY (city) Broome County	35,330
New York, NY	16,043
Buffalo, NY (city) Erie County	12,974
Albany, NY (city) Albany County	12,468
Rochester, NY (city) Monroe County	12,423
Syracuse, NY (city) Onondaga County	10,636
Utica, NY (city) Oneida County	9,739

Poverty Status

Total Populations with Income Below Poverty Level
Top 10 Places Sorted by Number

Place	Number
New York, NY	1,668,938
Buffalo, NY (city) Erie County	75,120
Rochester, NY (city) Monroe County	54,713
Hempstead, NY (town) Nassau County	42,958
Syracuse, NY (city) Onondaga County	37,485
Yonkers, NY (city) Westchester County	30,089
Brookhaven, NY (town) Suffolk County	25,952
Islip, NY (town) Suffolk County	20,849
Albany, NY (city) Albany County	18,822
Ramapo, NY (town) Rockland County	17,458

Total Populations with Income Below Poverty Level
Top 10 Places Sorted by Percent

Place	Percent
Ithaca, NY (city) Tompkins County	40.24
New Paltz, NY (village) Ulster County	36.93
Monroe, NY (town) Orange County	29.06
Syracuse, NY (city) Onondaga County	27.31
Buffalo, NY (city) Erie County	26.60
Rochester, NY (city) Monroe County	25.90
Hudson, NY (city) Columbia County	25.56
Utica, NY (city) Oneida County	24.50
Binghamton, NY (city) Broome County	23.67
Poughkeepsie, NY (city) Dutchess County	22.73

Asians with Income Below Poverty Level
Top 10 Places Sorted by Number

Place	Number
New York, NY	152,674
Ithaca, NY (city) Tompkins County	1,564
Syracuse, NY (city) Onondaga County	1,474
Hempstead, NY (town) Nassau County	1,343
Buffalo, NY (city) Erie County	1,330
Amherst, NY (town) Erie County	976
Brookhaven, NY (town) Suffolk County	945
North Hempstead, NY (town) Nassau County	875
Rochester, NY (city) Monroe County	840
Yonkers, NY (city) Westchester County	788

Asians with Income Below Poverty Level
Top 10 Places Sorted by Percent

Place	Percent
New Paltz, NY (village) Ulster County	62.85
Ithaca, NY (city) Tompkins County	62.34
Binghamton, NY (city) Broome County	47.38
New Paltz, NY (town) Ulster County	44.13
Troy, NY (city) Rensselaer County	42.01
Red Hook, NY (town) Dutchess County	36.71
Buffalo, NY (city) Erie County	36.02
Hudson, NY (city) Columbia County	35.22
Northeast Ithaca, NY (cdp) Tompkins County	32.75
Forest Home, NY (cdp) Tompkins County	32.40

Native Hawaiian and Other Pacific Islanders with Income Below Poverty Level
Top 10 Places Sorted by Number

Place	Number
New York, NY	1,231

Native Hawaiian and Other Pacific Islanders with Income Below Poverty Level
Top 10 Places Sorted by Percent

Place	Percent
New York, NY	26.31

Asian Indians with Income Below Poverty Level
Top 10 Places Sorted by Number

Place	Number
New York, NY	28,751
Hempstead, NY (town) Nassau County	469
Islip, NY (town) Suffolk County	372
Yonkers, NY (city) Westchester County	353
North Hempstead, NY (town) Nassau County	241
Clarkstown, NY (town) Rockland County	233
New City, NY (cdp) Rockland County	215
Buffalo, NY (city) Erie County	198
Brookhaven, NY (town) Suffolk County	188
Syracuse, NY (city) Onondaga County	184

Asian Indians with Income Below Poverty Level
Top 10 Places Sorted by Percent

Place	Percent
Ithaca, NY (city) Tompkins County	45.62
Brentwood, NY (cdp) Suffolk County	38.39
Henrietta, NY (town) Monroe County	37.00
Buffalo, NY (city) Erie County	34.32
Syracuse, NY (city) Onondaga County	28.48
Albany, NY (city) Albany County	27.89
Herricks, NY (cdp) Nassau County	22.64
New City, NY (cdp) Rockland County	20.15
Glen Cove, NY (city) Nassau County	18.77
Rochester, NY (city) Monroe County	17.19

Bangladeshis with Income Below Poverty Level
Top 10 Places Sorted by Number

Place	Number
New York, NY	5,447

Bangladeshis with Income Below Poverty Level
Top 10 Places Sorted by Percent

Place	Percent
New York, NY	28.60

Cambodians with Income Below Poverty Level
Top 10 Places Sorted by Number

Place	Number
New York, NY	495

Cambodians with Income Below Poverty Level
Top 10 Places Sorted by Percent

Place	Percent
New York, NY	30.82

Chinese (except Taiwanese) with Income Below Poverty Level
Top 10 Places Sorted by Number

Place	Number
New York, NY	78,628
Ithaca, NY (city) Tompkins County	748
Brookhaven, NY (town) Suffolk County	480
North Hempstead, NY (town) Nassau County	404
Buffalo, NY (city) Erie County	399
Hempstead, NY (town) Nassau County	389
Troy, NY (city) Rensselaer County	384
Syracuse, NY (city) Onondaga County	362
Amherst, NY (town) Erie County	311
Rochester, NY (city) Monroe County	250

Chinese (except Taiwanese) with Income Below Poverty Level
Top 10 Places Sorted by Percent

Place	Percent
Ithaca, NY (city) Tompkins County	66.02
Troy, NY (city) Rensselaer County	55.73
Buffalo, NY (city) Erie County	51.75
Syracuse, NY (city) Onondaga County	46.11
Henrietta, NY (town) Monroe County	42.86
Albany, NY (city) Albany County	31.62
Rochester, NY (city) Monroe County	29.98
Vestal, NY (town) Broome County	27.27
New York, NY	22.14
Amherst, NY (town) Erie County	21.73

Fijians with Income Below Poverty Level
Top 10 Places Sorted by Number

Place	Number
No places met population threshold.	

Fijians with Income Below Poverty Level
Top 10 Places Sorted by Percent

Place	Percent
No places met population threshold.	

Filipinos with Income Below Poverty Level
Top 10 Places Sorted by Number

Place	Number
New York, NY	3,207
Hempstead, NY (town) Nassau County	104
Yonkers, NY (city) Westchester County	85
Brookhaven, NY (town) Suffolk County	77
Clarkstown, NY (town) Rockland County	57
Oyster Bay, NY (town) Nassau County	46
Elmont, NY (cdp) Nassau County	26
Ramapo, NY (town) Rockland County	24

Notes: Please refer to the User's Guide for an explanation of data; tables reflect only those areas that meet Summary File 4 population thresholds, therefore there may be less than 10 places listed

PROFILES OF NEW YORK / Asian: Rankings

Place	
Islip, NY (town) Suffolk County	21
North Hempstead, NY (town) Nassau County	18

Filipinos with Income Below Poverty Level
Top 10 Places Sorted by Percent

Place	Percent
Brookhaven, NY (town) Suffolk County	5.90
New York, NY	5.48
Elmont, NY (cdp) Nassau County	4.73
Yonkers, NY (city) Westchester County	4.71
Oyster Bay, NY (town) Nassau County	3.59
New City, NY (cdp) Rockland County	2.71
Clarkstown, NY (town) Rockland County	2.61
Hempstead, NY (town) Nassau County	2.52
Islip, NY (town) Suffolk County	2.24
Ramapo, NY (town) Rockland County	1.78

Guamanian or Chamorros with Income Below Poverty Level
Top 10 Places Sorted by Number

Place	Number
New York, NY	209

Guamanian or Chamorros with Income Below Poverty Level
Top 10 Places Sorted by Percent

Place	Percent
New York, NY	18.37

Hawaiian, Natives with Income Below Poverty Level
Top 10 Places Sorted by Number

Place	Number
New York, NY	180

Hawaiian, Natives with Income Below Poverty Level
Top 10 Places Sorted by Percent

Place	Percent
New York, NY	24.93

Hmongs with Income Below Poverty Level
Top 10 Places Sorted by Number

Place	Number
No places met population threshold.	

Hmongs with Income Below Poverty Level
Top 10 Places Sorted by Percent

Place	Percent
No places met population threshold.	

Indonesians with Income Below Poverty Level
Top 10 Places Sorted by Number

Place	Number
New York, NY	366

Indonesians with Income Below Poverty Level
Top 10 Places Sorted by Percent

Place	Percent
New York, NY	20.24

Japanese with Income Below Poverty Level
Top 10 Places Sorted by Number

Place	Number
New York, NY	5,155
Eastchester, NY (town) Westchester County	111
Eastchester, NY (cdp) Westchester County	111
Greenburgh, NY (town) Westchester County	98
Hempstead, NY (town) Nassau County	96
Scarsdale, NY (village) Westchester County	93
Harrison, NY (village) Westchester County	56
North Hempstead, NY (town) Nassau County	30
Rye, NY (city) Westchester County	27
Oyster Bay, NY (town) Nassau County	14

Japanese with Income Below Poverty Level
Top 10 Places Sorted by Percent

Place	Percent
Hempstead, NY (town) Nassau County	25.74
New York, NY	23.59
Eastchester, NY (cdp) Westchester County	20.22
Scarsdale, NY (village) Westchester County	11.86
Eastchester, NY (town) Westchester County	9.26
Harrison, NY (village) Westchester County	8.28
Greenburgh, NY (town) Westchester County	5.12
Rye, NY (city) Westchester County	4.19
Oyster Bay, NY (town) Nassau County	3.74
North Hempstead, NY (town) Nassau County	3.25

Koreans with Income Below Poverty Level
Top 10 Places Sorted by Number

Place	Number
New York, NY	14,593
Syracuse, NY (city) Onondaga County	263
Amherst, NY (town) Erie County	260
Oyster Bay, NY (town) Nassau County	245
Ithaca, NY (city) Tompkins County	166
Hempstead, NY (town) Nassau County	155
Jericho, NY (cdp) Nassau County	111
North Hempstead, NY (town) Nassau County	105
Yonkers, NY (city) Westchester County	104
Clarkstown, NY (town) Rockland County	91

Koreans with Income Below Poverty Level
Top 10 Places Sorted by Percent

Place	Percent
Ithaca, NY (city) Tompkins County	68.60
Syracuse, NY (city) Onondaga County	52.29
Amherst, NY (town) Erie County	34.39
Rochester, NY (city) Monroe County	23.36
Glen Cove, NY (city) Nassau County	22.86
Babylon, NY (town) Suffolk County	22.00
New York, NY	17.03
Jericho, NY (cdp) Nassau County	15.48
Clarkstown, NY (town) Rockland County	12.62
Ramapo, NY (town) Rockland County	12.43

Laotians with Income Below Poverty Level
Top 10 Places Sorted by Number

Place	Number
Rochester, NY (city) Monroe County	77

Laotians with Income Below Poverty Level
Top 10 Places Sorted by Percent

Place	Percent
Rochester, NY (city) Monroe County	9.57

Malaysians with Income Below Poverty Level
Top 10 Places Sorted by Number

Place	Number
New York, NY	238

Malaysians with Income Below Poverty Level
Top 10 Places Sorted by Percent

Place	Percent
New York, NY	19.88

Pakistanis with Income Below Poverty Level
Top 10 Places Sorted by Number

Place	Number
New York, NY	6,332
Brookhaven, NY (town) Suffolk County	64
North Hempstead, NY (town) Nassau County	36
Huntington, NY (town) Suffolk County	24
Hempstead, NY (town) Nassau County	9

Pakistanis with Income Below Poverty Level
Top 10 Places Sorted by Percent

Place	Percent
New York, NY	26.59
Brookhaven, NY (town) Suffolk County	8.94
North Hempstead, NY (town) Nassau County	5.83
Huntington, NY (town) Suffolk County	5.49
Hempstead, NY (town) Nassau County	0.64

Samoans with Income Below Poverty Level
Top 10 Places Sorted by Number

Place	Number
New York, NY	236

Samoans with Income Below Poverty Level
Top 10 Places Sorted by Percent

Place	Percent
New York, NY	33.15

Sri Lankans with Income Below Poverty Level
Top 10 Places Sorted by Number

Place	Number
New York, NY	444

Sri Lankans with Income Below Poverty Level
Top 10 Places Sorted by Percent

Place	Percent
New York, NY	22.16

Taiwanese with Income Below Poverty Level
Top 10 Places Sorted by Number

Place	Number
New York, NY	761
North Hempstead, NY (town) Nassau County	23

Taiwanese with Income Below Poverty Level
Top 10 Places Sorted by Percent

Place	Percent
New York, NY	15.79
North Hempstead, NY (town) Nassau County	8.52

Thais with Income Below Poverty Level
Top 10 Places Sorted by Number

Place	Number
New York, NY	367

Thais with Income Below Poverty Level
Top 10 Places Sorted by Percent

Place	Percent
New York, NY	9.60

Tongans with Income Below Poverty Level
Top 10 Places Sorted by Number

Place	Number
No places met population threshold.	

Tongans with Income Below Poverty Level
Top 10 Places Sorted by Percent

Place	Percent
No places met population threshold.	

Notes: Please refer to the User's Guide for an explanation of data; tables reflect only those areas that meet Summary File 4 population thresholds, therefore there may be less than 10 places listed.

Vietnamese with Income Below Poverty Level
Top 10 Places Sorted by Number

Place	Number
New York, NY	3,335
Buffalo, NY (city) Erie County	263
Syracuse, NY (city) Onondaga County	235
Utica, NY (city) Oneida County	208
Rochester, NY (city) Monroe County	200
Albany, NY (city) Albany County	97
Binghamton, NY (city) Broome County	34

Vietnamese with Income Below Poverty Level
Top 10 Places Sorted by Percent

Place	Percent
New York, NY	27.81
Albany, NY (city) Albany County	24.49
Utica, NY (city) Oneida County	22.46
Buffalo, NY (city) Erie County	22.44
Rochester, NY (city) Monroe County	20.30
Syracuse, NY (city) Onondaga County	18.82
Binghamton, NY (city) Broome County	11.76

Homeownership

Total Populations Who Own Their Own Homes
Top 10 Places Sorted by Number

Place	Number
New York, NY	912,133
Hempstead, NY (town) Nassau County	199,148
Brookhaven, NY (town) Suffolk County	115,894
Oyster Bay, NY (town) Nassau County	86,345
Islip, NY (town) Suffolk County	77,830
North Hempstead, NY (town) Nassau County	60,270
Huntington, NY (town) Suffolk County	56,219
Buffalo, NY (city) Erie County	53,339
Babylon, NY (town) Suffolk County	52,110
Rochester, NY (city) Monroe County	35,777

Total Populations Who Own Their Own Homes
Top 10 Places Sorted by Percent

Place	Percent
Manhasset Hills, NY (cdp) Nassau County	98.37
Searingtown, NY (cdp) Nassau County	97.60
Lake Success, NY (village) Nassau County	97.24
East Hills, NY (village) Nassau County	97.07
Sands Point, NY (village) Nassau County	96.74
Dix Hills, NY (cdp) Suffolk County	96.24
Herricks, NY (cdp) Nassau County	95.70
Muttontown, NY (village) Nassau County	95.23
North Hills, NY (village) Nassau County	95.13
Munsey Park, NY (village) Nassau County	95.10

Asians Who Own Their Own Homes
Top 10 Places Sorted by Number

Place	Number
New York, NY	85,118
Hempstead, NY (town) Nassau County	5,235
North Hempstead, NY (town) Nassau County	4,321
Oyster Bay, NY (town) Nassau County	2,902
Brookhaven, NY (town) Suffolk County	1,750
Huntington, NY (town) Suffolk County	1,487
Clarkstown, NY (town) Rockland County	1,394
Greenburgh, NY (town) Westchester County	1,356
Yonkers, NY (city) Westchester County	1,311
Islip, NY (town) Suffolk County	1,081

Asians Who Own Their Own Homes
Top 10 Places Sorted by Percent

Place	Percent
East Hills, NY (village) Nassau County	100.00
Elwood, NY (cdp) Suffolk County	100.00
Old Brookville, NY (village) Nassau County	100.00
Old Westbury, NY (village) Nassau County	100.00
Sands Point, NY (village) Nassau County	100.00
Dix Hills, NY (cdp) Suffolk County	98.14
Searingtown, NY (cdp) Nassau County	97.53
East Fishkill, NY (town) Dutchess County	97.40
Manhasset Hills, NY (cdp) Nassau County	96.42
Lake Success, NY (village) Nassau County	95.93

Native Hawaiian and Other Pacific Islanders Who Own Their Own Homes
Top 10 Places Sorted by Number

Place	Number
New York, NY	300

Native Hawaiian and Other Pacific Islanders Who Own Their Own Homes
Top 10 Places Sorted by Percent

Place	Percent
New York, NY	23.55

Asian Indians Who Own Their Own Homes
Top 10 Places Sorted by Number

Place	Number
New York, NY	17,284
Hempstead, NY (town) Nassau County	2,063
North Hempstead, NY (town) Nassau County	1,606
Oyster Bay, NY (town) Nassau County	1,087
Yonkers, NY (city) Westchester County	585
Brookhaven, NY (town) Suffolk County	557
Greenburgh, NY (town) Westchester County	496
Clarkstown, NY (town) Rockland County	476
Huntington, NY (town) Suffolk County	476
Elmont, NY (cdp) Nassau County	398

Asian Indians Who Own Their Own Homes
Top 10 Places Sorted by Percent

Place	Percent
Dix Hills, NY (cdp) Suffolk County	100.00
Herricks, NY (cdp) Nassau County	100.00
Manhasset Hills, NY (cdp) Nassau County	100.00
North Valley Stream, NY (cdp) Nassau County	100.00
Salisbury, NY (cdp) Nassau County	100.00
Scarsdale, NY (village) Westchester County	100.00
Searingtown, NY (cdp) Nassau County	100.00
Franklin Square, NY (cdp) Nassau County	97.92
Nanuet, NY (cdp) Rockland County	95.04
North New Hyde Park, NY (cdp) Nassau County	94.62

Bangladeshis Who Own Their Own Homes
Top 10 Places Sorted by Number

Place	Number
New York, NY	739

Bangladeshis Who Own Their Own Homes
Top 10 Places Sorted by Percent

Place	Percent
New York, NY	17.03

Cambodians Who Own Their Own Homes
Top 10 Places Sorted by Number

Place	Number
New York, NY	80

Cambodians Who Own Their Own Homes
Top 10 Places Sorted by Percent

Place	Percent
New York, NY	19.95

Chinese (except Taiwanese) Who Own Their Own Homes
Top 10 Places Sorted by Number

Place	Number
New York, NY	46,358
Hempstead, NY (town) Nassau County	1,417
North Hempstead, NY (town) Nassau County	1,388
Oyster Bay, NY (town) Nassau County	928
Brookhaven, NY (town) Suffolk County	549
Huntington, NY (town) Suffolk County	433
Greenburgh, NY (town) Westchester County	306
Islip, NY (town) Suffolk County	269
Amherst, NY (town) Erie County	235
Syosset, NY (cdp) Nassau County	215

Chinese (except Taiwanese) Who Own Their Own Homes
Top 10 Places Sorted by Percent

Place	Percent
Dix Hills, NY (cdp) Suffolk County	100.00
Garden City Park, NY (cdp) Nassau County	100.00
Syosset, NY (cdp) Nassau County	100.00
Valley Stream, NY (village) Nassau County	100.00
Scarsdale, NY (village) Westchester County	95.56
North New Hyde Park, NY (cdp) Nassau County	91.92
Lake Success, NY (village) Nassau County	91.18
Oyster Bay, NY (town) Nassau County	90.10
Hempstead, NY (town) Nassau County	89.68
North Hempstead, NY (town) Nassau County	89.38

Fijians Who Own Their Own Homes
Top 10 Places Sorted by Number

Place	Number
No places met population threshold.	

Fijians Who Own Their Own Homes
Top 10 Places Sorted by Percent

Place	Percent
No places met population threshold.	

Filipinos Who Own Their Own Homes
Top 10 Places Sorted by Number

Place	Number
New York, NY	7,304
Hempstead, NY (town) Nassau County	811
Clarkstown, NY (town) Rockland County	453
Yonkers, NY (city) Westchester County	293
North Hempstead, NY (town) Nassau County	286
Ramapo, NY (town) Rockland County	270
Oyster Bay, NY (town) Nassau County	236
Islip, NY (town) Suffolk County	199
Brookhaven, NY (town) Suffolk County	198
Huntington, NY (town) Suffolk County	179

Filipinos Who Own Their Own Homes
Top 10 Places Sorted by Percent

Place	Percent
Elmont, NY (cdp) Nassau County	95.65
New City, NY (cdp) Rockland County	95.21
Valley Stream, NY (village) Nassau County	95.00
East Meadow, NY (cdp) Nassau County	94.83
Levittown, NY (cdp) Nassau County	93.62
Huntington, NY (town) Suffolk County	90.40
Babylon, NY (town) Suffolk County	90.14
Valley Cottage, NY (cdp) Rockland County	89.74
Hicksville, NY (cdp) Nassau County	87.29
Hempstead, NY (town) Nassau County	85.28

Notes: Please refer to the User's Guide for an explanation of data; tables reflect only those areas that meet Summary File 4 population thresholds, therefore there may be less than 10 places listed

PROFILES OF NEW YORK / Asian: Rankings

Guamanian or Chamorros Who Own Their Own Homes
Top 10 Places Sorted by Number

Place	Number
New York, NY	37

Guamanian or Chamorros Who Own Their Own Homes
Top 10 Places Sorted by Percent

Place	Percent
New York, NY	14.23

Hawaiian, Natives Who Own Their Own Homes
Top 10 Places Sorted by Number

Place	Number
New York, NY	65

Hawaiian, Natives Who Own Their Own Homes
Top 10 Places Sorted by Percent

Place	Percent
New York, NY	29.02

Hmongs Who Own Their Own Homes
Top 10 Places Sorted by Number

Place	Number
No places met population threshold.	

Hmongs Who Own Their Own Homes
Top 10 Places Sorted by Percent

Place	Percent
No places met population threshold.	

Indonesians Who Own Their Own Homes
Top 10 Places Sorted by Number

Place	Number
New York, NY	84

Indonesians Who Own Their Own Homes
Top 10 Places Sorted by Percent

Place	Percent
New York, NY	12.28

Japanese Who Own Their Own Homes
Top 10 Places Sorted by Number

Place	Number
New York, NY	2,082
Greenburgh, NY (town) Westchester County	160
North Hempstead, NY (town) Nassau County	141
Eastchester, NY (town) Westchester County	86
Brookhaven, NY (town) Suffolk County	85
Hempstead, NY (town) Nassau County	70
Oyster Bay, NY (town) Nassau County	60
Rye, NY (city) Westchester County	55
Scarsdale, NY (village) Westchester County	38
Eastchester, NY (cdp) Westchester County	37

Japanese Who Own Their Own Homes
Top 10 Places Sorted by Percent

Place	Percent
Brookhaven, NY (town) Suffolk County	66.93
Hempstead, NY (town) Nassau County	47.30
Oyster Bay, NY (town) Nassau County	44.78
North Hempstead, NY (town) Nassau County	38.42
Greenburgh, NY (town) Westchester County	27.07
Rye, NY (city) Westchester County	26.07
Eastchester, NY (cdp) Westchester County	20.90
Eastchester, NY (town) Westchester County	20.87
Greenville, NY (cdp) Westchester County	19.34
New York, NY	17.42

Koreans Who Own Their Own Homes
Top 10 Places Sorted by Number

Place	Number
New York, NY	6,003
North Hempstead, NY (town) Nassau County	543
Oyster Bay, NY (town) Nassau County	406
Hempstead, NY (town) Nassau County	369
Greenburgh, NY (town) Westchester County	197
Brookhaven, NY (town) Suffolk County	172
Huntington, NY (town) Suffolk County	161
Clarkstown, NY (town) Rockland County	158
Orangetown, NY (town) Rockland County	121
Yonkers, NY (city) Westchester County	116

Koreans Who Own Their Own Homes
Top 10 Places Sorted by Percent

Place	Percent
Lake Success, NY (village) Nassau County	97.10
Plainview, NY (cdp) Nassau County	83.12
Syosset, NY (cdp) Nassau County	81.75
Clarkstown, NY (town) Rockland County	73.83
Smithtown, NY (town) Suffolk County	73.21
Orangetown, NY (town) Rockland County	71.60
Greenburgh, NY (town) Westchester County	69.61
Oyster Bay, NY (town) Nassau County	68.93
Huntington, NY (town) Suffolk County	68.51
Scarsdale, NY (village) Westchester County	67.00

Laotians Who Own Their Own Homes
Top 10 Places Sorted by Number

Place	Number
Rochester, NY (city) Monroe County	122

Laotians Who Own Their Own Homes
Top 10 Places Sorted by Percent

Place	Percent
Rochester, NY (city) Monroe County	64.21

Malaysians Who Own Their Own Homes
Top 10 Places Sorted by Number

Place	Number
New York, NY	86

Malaysians Who Own Their Own Homes
Top 10 Places Sorted by Percent

Place	Percent
New York, NY	18.45

Pakistanis Who Own Their Own Homes
Top 10 Places Sorted by Number

Place	Number
New York, NY	1,095
Hempstead, NY (town) Nassau County	219
North Hempstead, NY (town) Nassau County	124
Brookhaven, NY (town) Suffolk County	75
Huntington, NY (town) Suffolk County	71

Pakistanis Who Own Their Own Homes
Top 10 Places Sorted by Percent

Place	Percent
North Hempstead, NY (town) Nassau County	79.49
Huntington, NY (town) Suffolk County	76.34
Hempstead, NY (town) Nassau County	75.78
Brookhaven, NY (town) Suffolk County	49.67
New York, NY	18.29

Samoans Who Own Their Own Homes
Top 10 Places Sorted by Number

Place	Number
New York, NY	28

Samoans Who Own Their Own Homes
Top 10 Places Sorted by Percent

Place	Percent
New York, NY	16.87

Sri Lankans Who Own Their Own Homes
Top 10 Places Sorted by Number

Place	Number
New York, NY	209

Sri Lankans Who Own Their Own Homes
Top 10 Places Sorted by Percent

Place	Percent
New York, NY	32.48

Taiwanese Who Own Their Own Homes
Top 10 Places Sorted by Number

Place	Number
New York, NY	94
North Hempstead, NY (town) Nassau County	7

Taiwanese Who Own Their Own Homes
Top 10 Places Sorted by Percent

Place	Percent
North Hempstead, NY (town) Nassau County	97.3
New York, NY	48.6

Thais Who Own Their Own Homes
Top 10 Places Sorted by Number

Place	Number
New York, NY	48

Thais Who Own Their Own Homes
Top 10 Places Sorted by Percent

Place	Percent
New York, NY	34.2

Tongans Who Own Their Own Homes
Top 10 Places Sorted by Number

Place	Number
No places met population threshold.	

Tongans Who Own Their Own Homes
Top 10 Places Sorted by Percent

Place	Percent
No places met population threshold.	

Vietnamese Who Own Their Own Homes
Top 10 Places Sorted by Number

Place	Number
New York, NY	8
Rochester, NY (city) Monroe County	1
Buffalo, NY (city) Erie County	1
Syracuse, NY (city) Onondaga County	
Utica, NY (city) Oneida County	
Albany, NY (city) Albany County	
Binghamton, NY (city) Broome County	

Vietnamese Who Own Their Own Homes
Top 10 Places Sorted by Percent

Place	Percent
Rochester, NY (city) Monroe County	58
Buffalo, NY (city) Erie County	42
Albany, NY (city) Albany County	37
Binghamton, NY (city) Broome County	28
Syracuse, NY (city) Onondaga County	23
New York, NY	23
Utica, NY (city) Oneida County	20

Notes: Please refer to the User's Guide for an explanation of data; tables reflect only those areas that meet Summary File 4 population thresholds, therefore there may be less than 10 places listed

PROFILES OF NEW YORK / Asian: Rankings

Median Gross Rent

All Specified Renter-Occupied Housing Units
Top 10 Places Sorted by Number

Place	Dollars/Month
Lake Success, NY (village) Nassau County	2,000+
Manhasset Hills, NY (cdp) Nassau County	2,000+
Munsey Park, NY (village) Nassau County	2,000+
North Hills, NY (village) Nassau County	2,000+
Scarsdale, NY (village) Westchester County	2,000+
Bronxville, NY (village) Westchester County	1,899
Melville, NY (cdp) Suffolk County	1,842
Ardsley, NY (village) Westchester County	1,736
Merricks, NY (cdp) Nassau County	1,729
Old Westbury, NY (village) Nassau County	1,642

Specified Housing Units Rented by Asians
Top 10 Places Sorted by Number

Place	Dollars/Month
Ardsley, NY (village) Westchester County	2,000+
Briarcliff Manor, NY (village) Westchester County	2,000+
Bronxville, NY (village) Westchester County	2,000+
Chappaqua, NY (cdp) Westchester County	2,000+
Dix Hills, NY (cdp) Suffolk County	2,000+
Eastchester, NY (cdp) Westchester County	2,000+
Eastchester, NY (town) Westchester County	2,000+
Garden City, NY (village) Nassau County	2,000+
Lake Success, NY (village) Nassau County	2,000+
Manhasset Hills, NY (cdp) Nassau County	2,000+

Specified Housing Units Rented by Native Hawaiian and Other Pacific Islanders
Top 10 Places Sorted by Number

Place	Dollars/Month
New York, NY	689

Specified Housing Units Rented by Asian Indians
Top 10 Places Sorted by Number

Place	Dollars/Month
Muttontown, NY (village) Nassau County	2,000+
New Castle, NY (town) Westchester County	2,000+
Smithtown, NY (town) Suffolk County	1,521
Plainview, NY (cdp) Nassau County	1,446
North New Hyde Park, NY (cdp) Nassau County	1,444
Commack, NY (cdp) Suffolk County	1,375
Nanuet, NY (cdp) Rockland County	1,375
Huntington, NY (town) Suffolk County	1,259
West Hempstead, NY (cdp) Nassau County	1,214
North Hempstead, NY (town) Nassau County	1,201

Specified Housing Units Rented by Bangladeshis
Top 10 Places Sorted by Number

Place	Dollars/Month
New York, NY	773

Specified Housing Units Rented by Cambodians
Top 10 Places Sorted by Number

Place	Dollars/Month
New York, NY	724

Specified Housing Units Rented by Chinese (except Taiwanese)
Top 10 Places Sorted by Number

Place	Dollars/Month
Lake Success, NY (village) Nassau County	2,000+
New Castle, NY (town) Westchester County	2,000+
Scarsdale, NY (village) Westchester County	2,000+
Stony Brook, NY (cdp) Suffolk County	2,000+
Clarkstown, NY (town) Rockland County	1,636
Greenburgh, NY (town) Westchester County	1,386
Ramapo, NY (town) Rockland County	1,352
North Hempstead, NY (town) Nassau County	1,104
Orangetown, NY (town) Rockland County	1,038
Babylon, NY (town) Suffolk County	1,033

Specified Housing Units Rented by Fijians
Top 10 Places Sorted by Number

Place	Dollars/Month
No places met population threshold.	

Specified Housing Units Rented by Filipinos
Top 10 Places Sorted by Number

Place	Dollars/Month
Babylon, NY (town) Suffolk County	2,000+
Huntington, NY (town) Suffolk County	2,000+
Levittown, NY (cdp) Nassau County	1,625
Hillcrest, NY (cdp) Rockland County	1,508
Hicksville, NY (cdp) Nassau County	1,458
North Hempstead, NY (town) Nassau County	1,213
Clarkstown, NY (town) Rockland County	1,208
Oyster Bay, NY (town) Nassau County	1,138
Valley Stream, NY (village) Nassau County	1,125
Brookhaven, NY (town) Suffolk County	953

Specified Housing Units Rented by Guamanian or Chamorros
Top 10 Places Sorted by Number

Place	Dollars/Month
New York, NY	725

Specified Housing Units Rented by Hawaiian, Natives
Top 10 Places Sorted by Number

Place	Dollars/Month
New York, NY	630

Specified Housing Units Rented by Hmongs
Top 10 Places Sorted by Number

Place	Dollars/Month
No places met population threshold.	

Specified Housing Units Rented by Indonesians
Top 10 Places Sorted by Number

Place	Dollars/Month
New York, NY	859

Specified Housing Units Rented by Japanese
Top 10 Places Sorted by Number

Place	Dollars/Month
Eastchester, NY (town) Westchester County	2,000+
Eastchester, NY (cdp) Westchester County	2,000+
Greenburgh, NY (town) Westchester County	2,000+
Greenville, NY (cdp) Westchester County	2,000+
Harrison, NY (village) Westchester County	2,000+
Oyster Bay, NY (town) Nassau County	2,000+
Rye, NY (city) Westchester County	2,000+
Scarsdale, NY (village) Westchester County	2,000+
North Hempstead, NY (town) Nassau County	1,863
Brookhaven, NY (town) Suffolk County	1,292

Specified Housing Units Rented by Koreans
Top 10 Places Sorted by Number

Place	Dollars/Month
Lake Success, NY (village) Nassau County	2,000+
Scarsdale, NY (village) Westchester County	2,000+
Plainview, NY (cdp) Nassau County	1,797
Smithtown, NY (town) Suffolk County	1,625
Syosset, NY (cdp) Nassau County	1,602
Jericho, NY (cdp) Nassau County	1,537
North Hempstead, NY (town) Nassau County	1,462
Commack, NY (cdp) Suffolk County	1,448
Huntington, NY (town) Suffolk County	1,429
Glen Cove, NY (city) Nassau County	1,413

Specified Housing Units Rented by Laotians
Top 10 Places Sorted by Number

Place	Dollars/Month
Rochester, NY (city) Monroe County	550

Specified Housing Units Rented by Malaysians
Top 10 Places Sorted by Number

Place	Dollars/Month
New York, NY	803

Specified Housing Units Rented by Pakistanis
Top 10 Places Sorted by Number

Place	Dollars/Month
North Hempstead, NY (town) Nassau County	1,278
Hempstead, NY (town) Nassau County	1,250
Brookhaven, NY (town) Suffolk County	1,051
Huntington, NY (town) Suffolk County	950
New York, NY	789

Specified Housing Units Rented by Samoans
Top 10 Places Sorted by Number

Place	Dollars/Month
New York, NY	580

Specified Housing Units Rented by Sri Lankans
Top 10 Places Sorted by Number

Place	Dollars/Month
New York, NY	899

Specified Housing Units Rented by Taiwanese
Top 10 Places Sorted by Number

Place	Dollars/Month
North Hempstead, NY (town) Nassau County	1,125
New York, NY	996

Specified Housing Units Rented by Thais
Top 10 Places Sorted by Number

Place	Dollars/Month
New York, NY	783

Specified Housing Units Rented by Tongans
Top 10 Places Sorted by Number

Place	Dollars/Month
No places met population threshold.	

Specified Housing Units Rented by Vietnamese
Top 10 Places Sorted by Number

Place	Dollars/Month
New York, NY	743
Albany, NY (city) Albany County	588
Buffalo, NY (city) Erie County	540
Rochester, NY (city) Monroe County	532
Syracuse, NY (city) Onondaga County	448
Utica, NY (city) Oneida County	421
Binghamton, NY (city) Broome County	419

Median Home Value

All Specified Owner-Occupied Housing Units
Top 10 Places Sorted by Number

Place	Dollars
Brookville, NY (village) Nassau County	1,000,000+
Old Westbury, NY (village) Nassau County	1,000,000+
Sands Point, NY (village) Nassau County	1,000,000+
Oyster Bay Cove, NY (village) Nassau County	974,900
Old Brookville, NY (village) Nassau County	972,100
Bronxville, NY (village) Westchester County	959,600
Laurel Hollow, NY (village) Nassau County	897,200
Muttontown, NY (village) Nassau County	831,100

Notes: Please refer to the User's Guide for an explanation of data; tables reflect only those areas that meet Summary File 4 population thresholds, therefore there may be less than 10 places listed

Scarsdale, NY (village) Westchester County	708,000
Munsey Park, NY (village) Nassau County	702,300

Specified Housing Units Owned and Occupied by Asians
Top 10 Places Sorted by Number

Place	Dollars
Old Brookville, NY (village) Nassau County	1,000,000+
Oyster Bay Cove, NY (village) Nassau County	1,000,000+
Sands Point, NY (village) Nassau County	1,000,000+
Brookville, NY (village) Nassau County	916,700
Laurel Hollow, NY (village) Nassau County	886,400
North Hills, NY (village) Nassau County	868,800
Munsey Park, NY (village) Nassau County	791,700
Harrison, NY (village) Westchester County	726,000
Scarsdale, NY (village) Westchester County	684,600
Muttontown, NY (village) Nassau County	679,400

Specified Housing Units Owned and Occupied by Native Hawaiian and Other Pacific Islanders
Top 10 Places Sorted by Number

Place	Dollars
New York, NY	189,400

Specified Housing Units Owned and Occupied by Asian Indians
Top 10 Places Sorted by Number

Place	Dollars
Muttontown, NY (village) Nassau County	772,100
Scarsdale, NY (village) Westchester County	738,900
New Castle, NY (town) Westchester County	668,600
Greenville, NY (cdp) Westchester County	616,100
Mount Pleasant, NY (town) Westchester County	548,600
Searingtown, NY (cdp) Nassau County	535,900
Port Washington, NY (cdp) Nassau County	506,900
Manhasset Hills, NY (cdp) Nassau County	490,800
Dix Hills, NY (cdp) Suffolk County	434,900
White Plains, NY (city) Westchester County	385,700

Specified Housing Units Owned and Occupied by Bangladeshis
Top 10 Places Sorted by Number

Place	Dollars
New York, NY	253,000

Specified Housing Units Owned and Occupied by Cambodians
Top 10 Places Sorted by Number

Place	Dollars
New York, NY	50,700

Specified Housing Units Owned and Occupied by Chinese (except Taiwanese)
Top 10 Places Sorted by Number

Place	Dollars
Lake Success, NY (village) Nassau County	616,100
Scarsdale, NY (village) Westchester County	613,600
White Plains, NY (city) Westchester County	408,300
Dix Hills, NY (cdp) Suffolk County	381,600
North Hempstead, NY (town) Nassau County	376,500
Greenburgh, NY (town) Westchester County	342,200
Syosset, NY (cdp) Nassau County	328,000
New Castle, NY (town) Westchester County	316,700
Garden City Park, NY (cdp) Nassau County	301,200
Plainview, NY (cdp) Nassau County	294,300

Specified Housing Units Owned and Occupied by Fijians
Top 10 Places Sorted by Number

Place	Dollars

No places met population threshold.

Specified Housing Units Owned and Occupied by Filipinos
Top 10 Places Sorted by Number

Place	Dollars
Huntington, NY (town) Suffolk County	335,200
Greenburgh, NY (town) Westchester County	305,000
North Hempstead, NY (town) Nassau County	276,800
Orangetown, NY (town) Rockland County	267,300
New City, NY (cdp) Rockland County	245,200
East Meadow, NY (cdp) Nassau County	238,700
Oyster Bay, NY (town) Nassau County	235,600
Yonkers, NY (city) Westchester County	234,600
Clarkstown, NY (town) Rockland County	231,100
Hicksville, NY (cdp) Nassau County	221,300

Specified Housing Units Owned and Occupied by Guamanian or Chamorros
Top 10 Places Sorted by Number

Place	Dollars
New York, NY	406,700

Specified Housing Units Owned and Occupied by Hawaiian, Natives
Top 10 Places Sorted by Number

Place	Dollars
New York, NY	177,100

Specified Housing Units Owned and Occupied by Hmongs
Top 10 Places Sorted by Number

Place	Dollars

No places met population threshold.

Specified Housing Units Owned and Occupied by Indonesians
Top 10 Places Sorted by Number

Place	Dollars
New York, NY	255,800

Specified Housing Units Owned and Occupied by Japanese
Top 10 Places Sorted by Number

Place	Dollars
Greenville, NY (cdp) Westchester County	625,000
Rye, NY (city) Westchester County	548,600
Eastchester, NY (town) Westchester County	425,000
Scarsdale, NY (village) Westchester County	400,000
North Hempstead, NY (town) Nassau County	386,000
Eastchester, NY (cdp) Westchester County	381,600
Greenburgh, NY (town) Westchester County	364,100
Oyster Bay, NY (town) Nassau County	271,400
Brookhaven, NY (town) Suffolk County	251,700
New York, NY	247,500

Specified Housing Units Owned and Occupied by Koreans
Top 10 Places Sorted by Number

Place	Dollars
Scarsdale, NY (village) Westchester County	712,000
Lake Success, NY (village) Nassau County	652,300
Greenburgh, NY (town) Westchester County	445,300
North Hempstead, NY (town) Nassau County	430,400
Yonkers, NY (city) Westchester County	379,200
Jericho, NY (cdp) Nassau County	346,200
Oyster Bay, NY (town) Nassau County	328,900
Smithtown, NY (town) Suffolk County	297,700
Huntington, NY (town) Suffolk County	290,500
Clarkstown, NY (town) Rockland County	290,000

Specified Housing Units Owned and Occupied by Laotians
Top 10 Places Sorted by Number

Place	Dollars
Rochester, NY (city) Monroe County	51,400

Specified Housing Units Owned and Occupied by Malaysians
Top 10 Places Sorted by Number

Place	Dollars
New York, NY	227,900

Specified Housing Units Owned and Occupied by Pakistanis
Top 10 Places Sorted by Number

Place	Dollars
North Hempstead, NY (town) Nassau County	273,700
Hempstead, NY (town) Nassau County	263,600
New York, NY	250,900
Huntington, NY (town) Suffolk County	246,100
Brookhaven, NY (town) Suffolk County	171,600

Specified Housing Units Owned and Occupied by Samoans
Top 10 Places Sorted by Number

Place	Dollars
New York, NY	137,500

Specified Housing Units Owned and Occupied by Sri Lankans
Top 10 Places Sorted by Number

Place	Dollars
New York, NY	217,300

Specified Housing Units Owned and Occupied by Taiwanese
Top 10 Places Sorted by Number

Place	Dollars
North Hempstead, NY (town) Nassau County	375,000
New York, NY	256,300

Specified Housing Units Owned and Occupied by Thais
Top 10 Places Sorted by Number

Place	Dollars
New York, NY	197,900

Specified Housing Units Owned and Occupied by Tongans
Top 10 Places Sorted by Number

Place	Dollars

No places met population threshold.

Specified Housing Units Owned and Occupied by Vietnamese
Top 10 Places Sorted by Number

Place	Dollars
New York, NY	218,400
Albany, NY (city) Albany County	83,300
Rochester, NY (city) Monroe County	62,600
Utica, NY (city) Oneida County	53,100
Binghamton, NY (city) Broome County	45,000
Syracuse, NY (city) Onondaga County	37,100
Buffalo, NY (city) Erie County	32,500

Notes: Please refer to the User's Guide for an explanation of data; tables reflect only those areas that meet Summary File 4 population thresholds, therefore there may be less than 10 places listed

NEW YORK

PHYSICAL FEATURES. New York State contains 49,576 square miles, inclusive of 1,637 square miles of inland water, but exclusive of the boundary-water areas of Long Island Sound, New York Harbor, Lake Ontario, and Lake Erie. The major portion of the State lies generally between latitudes 42° and 45° N. and between longitudes 73° 30' and 79° 45' W. However, in the extreme southeast, a triangular portion extends southward to about latitude 40° 30' N., while Long Island lies eastward to about longitude 72° W.

The principal highland regions of the State are the Adirondacks in the northeast and the Appalachian Plateau (Southern Plateau) in the south. A minor highland region occurs in southeastern New York where the Hudson River has cut a valley between the Palisades on the west, near the New Jersey border, and the Taconic Mountains on the east, along the Connecticut and Massachusetts border. Just west of the Adirondacks and the upper Black River Valley in Lewis County is another minor highland known as Tug Hill. Much of the eastern border of the State consists of a long, narrow lowland region which is occupied by Lake Champlain, Lake George, and the middle and lower portions of the Hudson Valley.

Approximately 40 percent of New York State has an elevation of more than 1,000 feet above sea level. In northwestern Essex County are a number of peaks with an elevation of between 4,000 to 5,000 feet. The highest point, Mount Marcy, reaches a height of 5,344 feet above sea level. The Appalachian Plateau merges variously into the Great Lakes Plain of western New York with gradual- to steep-sloping terrain. This Plateau is penetrated by the valleys of the Finger Lakes which extend southward from the Great Lakes Plain. Other prominent lakes plus innumerable smaller lakes and ponds dot the landscape, with more than 1,500 in the Adirondack region alone.

GENERAL CLIMATE. The climate of New York State is broadly representative of the humid continental type which prevails in the Northeastern United States, but its diversity is not usually encountered within an area of comparable size. The geographical position of the State and the usual course of air masses, governed by the large-scale patterns of atmospheric circulation, provide general climatic controls. Differences in latitude, character of the topography, and proximity to large bodies of water have pronounced effects on the climate.

Lengthy periods of either abnormally cold or warm weather result from the movement of great high pressure (anticyclonic) systems into and through the Eastern United States. Cold winter temperatures prevail over New York whenever Arctic air masses, under high barometric pressure, flow southward from central Canada or from Hudson Bay. High pressure systems often move just off the Atlantic coast, become more or less stagnant for several days, and then a persistent air flow from the southwest or south affects the State. This circulation brings the very warm, often humid weather of the summer season and the mild, more pleasant temperatures during the fall, winter, and spring seasons.

TEMPERATURE. Many atmospheric and physiographic controls on the climate result in a considerable variation of temperature conditions over New York State. The average annual mean temperature ranges from about 40°F. in the Adirondacks to near 55°F. in the New York City area. The winters are long and cold in the Plateau Divisions of the State. Winter temperatures are moderated considerably in the Great Lakes Plain of western New York. The moderating influence of Lakes Erie and Ontario is comparable to that produced by the Atlantic Ocean in the southern portion of the Hudson Valley.

The summer climate is cool in the Adirondacks, Catskills, and higher elevations of the Southern Plateau. The New York City area and lower portions of the Hudson Valley have rather warm summers by comparison, with some periods of high, uncomfortable humidity. The remainder of New York State enjoys pleasantly warm summers, marred by only occasional, brief intervals of sultry conditions. Summer daytime temperatures usually range from the upper 70s to mid-80s over much of the State. The moderating effect of Lakes Erie and Ontario on temperatures assumes practical importance during the spring and fall seasons. The lake waters warm slowly in the spring, the effect of which is to reduce the warming of the atmosphere over adjacent land areas. In the fall season, the lake waters cool more slowly than the land areas and thus serve as a heat source.

PRECIPITATION. Moisture for precipitation in New York State is transported primarily from the Gulf of Mexico and Atlantic Ocean through circulation patterns and storm systems of the atmosphere. Distribution of precipitation within the State is greatly influenced by topography and proximity to the

Great Lakes or Atlantic Ocean. Average annual amounts in excess of 50 inches occur in the western Adirondacks, Tug Hill area, and the Catskills, while slightly less than that amount is noted in the higher elevations of the Western Plateau southeast of Lake Erie. Areas of least rainfall, with average accumulations of about 30 inches, occur near Lake Ontario in the extreme western counties, in the lower half of the Genesee River Valley, and in the vicinity of Lake Champlain.

New York State has a fairly uniform distribution of precipitation during the year. There are no distinctly dry or wet seasons which are regularly repeated on an annual basis. Minimum precipitation occurs in the winter season. Maximum amounts are noted in the summer season throughout the State except along the Great Lakes where slight peaks of similar magnitude occur in both the spring and fall seasons.

SNOWFALL. The climate of New York State is marked by abundant snowfall. With the exception of the Coastal Division, the State receives an average seasonal amount of 40 inches or more. The average snowfall is greater than 70 inches over some 60 percent of New York's area. The moderating influence of the Atlantic Ocean reduces the snow accumulation to 25 to 35 inches in the New York City area and on Long Island. About one-third of the winter season precipitation in the Coastal Division occurs from storms which also yield at least one inch of snow. The great bulk of the winter precipitation in upstate New York comes as snow.

A durable snow cover generally begins to develop in the Adirondacks and northern lowlands by late November and remains on the ground until various times in April, depending upon late winter snowfall and early spring temperatures. The Southern Plateau, Great Lakes Plain in southern portions of western upstate New York, and the Hudson Valley experience a continuous snow cover from about mid-December to mid-March, with maximum depths usually occurring in February. Bare ground may occur briefly in the lower elevations of these regions during some winters. From late December or early January through February, the Atlantic coastal region of the State experiences alternating periods of measurable snow cover and bare ground.

FLOODS. Although major floods are relatively infrequent, the greatest potential and frequency for floods occur in the early spring when substantial rains combine with rapid snowmelting to produce a heavy runoff. Damaging floods are caused at other times of the year by prolonged periods of heavy rainfall.

WINDS AND STORMS. The prevailing wind is generally from the west in New York State. A southwest component becomes evident in winds during the warmer months while a northwest component is characteristic of the colder one-half of the year. Thunderstorms occur on an average of about 30 days in a year throughout the State. Destructive winds and lightning strikes in local areas are common with the more vigorous warm-season thunderstorms. Locally, hail occurs with more severe thunderstorms. Tornadoes are not common. About 3 or 4 of these storms strike limited, localized areas of New York State in most years. Tornadoes occur generally between late May and late August. Storms of freezing rain occur on one or more occasions during the winter season and often affect a wide area of the State in any one incident. Such storms are usually limited to a thin but dangerous coating of ice on exposed surfaces. Hurricanes and tropical storms periodically cause serious and heavy losses in the vicinity of Long Island and southeastern upstate New York. The greatest storm hazard in terms of area affected is heavy snow. Coastal northeaster storms occur with some frequency in most winters. Blizzard conditions of heavy snow, high winds, and rapidly falling temperature occur occasionally, but are much less characteristic of New York's climate than in the plains of Midwestern United States.

OTHER CLIMATIC ELEMENTS. The climate of the State features much cloudy weather during the months of November, December, and January in upstate New York. From June through September, however, about 60 to 70 percent of the possible sunshine hours is received. In the Atlantic coastal region, the sunshine hours increases from 50 percent of possible in the winter to about 65 percent of possible in the summer. The occurrence of heavy dense fog is variable over the State. The valleys and ridges of the Southern Plateau are most subject to periods of fog, with occurrences averaging about 50 days in a year. In the Great Lakes Plain and northern valleys, the frequency decreases to only 10 to 20 days annually. In those portions of the State with greater maritime influence, the frequency of dense fog in a year ranges from about 35 days on the south shore of Long Island to 25 days in the Hudson Valley.

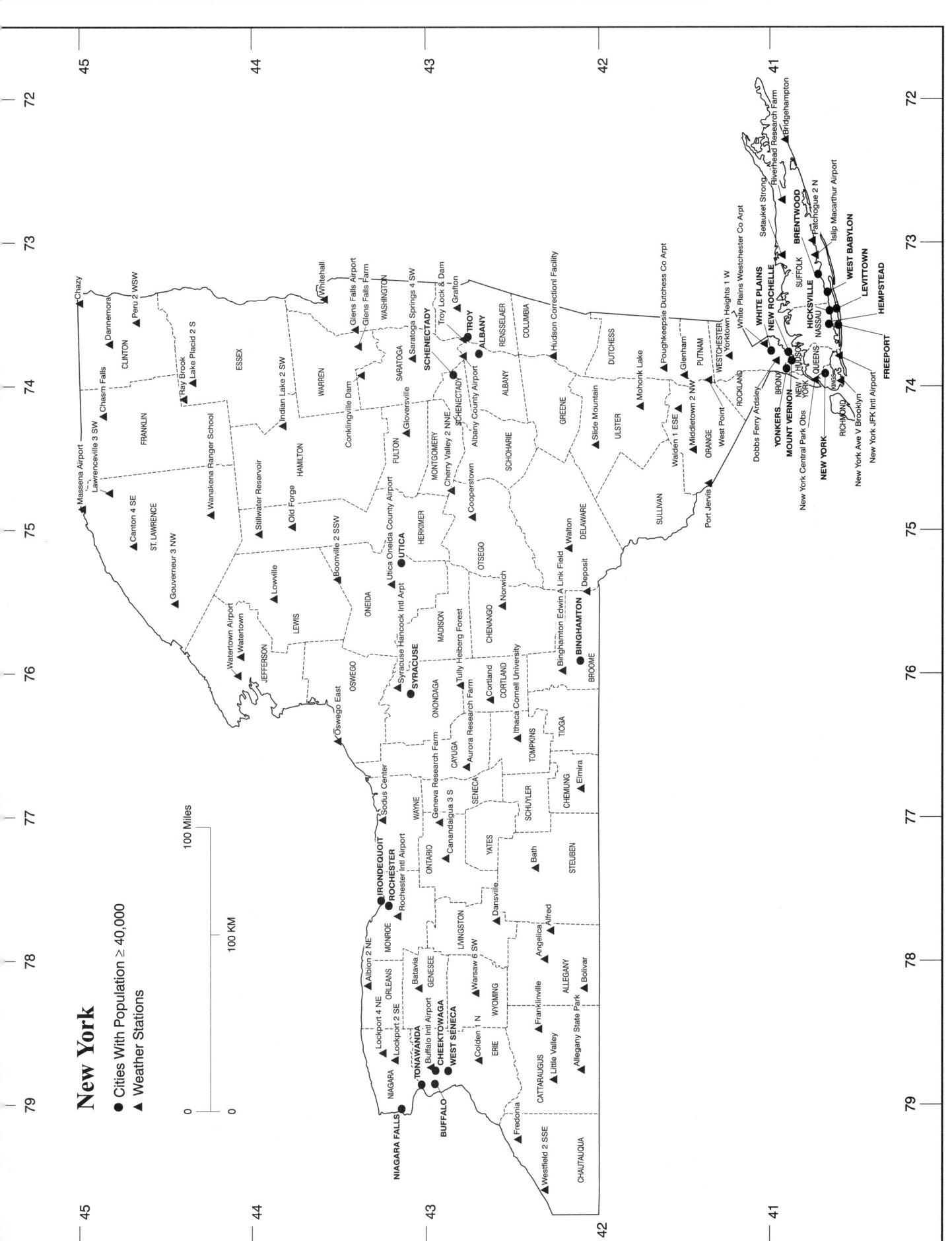

New York Weather Stations by County

County	Station Name
Albany	Albany County Airport
Allegany	Alfred
	Angelica
	Bolivar
Broome	Binghamton Edwin A. Link Field
Cattaraugus	Allegany State Park
	Franklinville
	Little Valley
Cayuga	Aurora Research Farm
Chautauqua	Fredonia
	Westfield 2 SSE
Chemung	Elmira
Chenango	Norwich
Clinton	Chazy
	Dannemora
	Peru 2 WSW
Columbia	Hudson Correctionl Facility
Cortland	Cortland
	Tully Heiberg Forest
Delaware	Deposit
	Walton
Dutchess	Glenham
	Poughkeepsie Dutchess Co. Arpt.
Erie	Buffalo Int'l Airport
	Colden 1 N
Essex	Lake Placid 2 S
	Ray Brook
Franklin	Chasm Falls
Fulton	Gloversville
Genesee	Batavia
Hamilton	Indian Lake 2 SW
Herkimer	Old Forge
	Stillwater Reservoir
Jefferson	Watertown
	Watertown Airport
Kings	New York Avenue V Brooklyn
Lewis	Lowville
Livingston	Dansville
Monroe	Rochester Int'l Airport
New York	New York Central Park Observatory
Niagara	Lockport 2 SE
	Lockport 4 NE
Oneida	Boonville 2 SSW
	Utica Oneida County Airport
Onondaga	Syracuse Hancock Int'l Airport
Ontario	Canandaigua 3 S
	Geneva Research Farm
Orange	Middletown 2 NW
	Port Jervis
	Walden 1 ESE
	West Point
Orleans	Albion 2 NE
Oswego	Oswego East
Otsego	Cherry Valley 2 NNE
	Cooperstown
Queens	New York JFK Int'l Airport
	New York Laguardia Airport
Rensselaer	Grafton
	Troy Lock & Dam
Saratoga	Conklingville Dam
	Saratoga Springs 4 SW
St. Lawrence	Canton 4 SE
	Gouverneur 3 NW
	Lawrenceville 3 SW
	Massena Airport
	Ogdensburg 4 NE
	Wanakena Ranger School
Steuben	Bath
Suffolk	Bridgehampton
	Islip Macarthur Airport
	Patchogue 2 N
	Riverhead Research Farm
	Setauket Strong
Tompkins	Ithaca Cornell University
Ulster	Mohonk Lake
	Slide Mountain
Warren	Glens Falls Airport
	Glens Falls Farm
Washington	Whitehall
Wayne	Sodus Center
Westchester	Dobbs Ferry Ardsley
	White Plains Westchester Co. Arpt.
	Yorktown Heights 1 W
Wyoming	Warsaw 6 SW

New York Weather Stations by City

City	Station Name	Miles
Albany	Albany County Airport	6
	Grafton	18
	Troy Lock & Dam	8
Binghamton	Binghamton Edwin A. Link Field	8
	Montrose, PA	17
Brentwood	Patchogue 2 N	13
	Setauket Strong	15
	Islip Macarthur Airport	8
Buffalo	Buffalo Int'l Airport	6
	Colden 1 N	19
	Lockport 2 SE	17
Cheektowaga	Buffalo Int'l Airport	2
	Colden 1 N	17
	Lockport 2 SE	16
Freeport	New York JFK Int'l Airport	11
	New York Laguardia Airport	18
Hempstead	New York Central Park Observatory	19
	New York JFK Int'l Airport	10
	New York Laguardia Airport	15
Hicksville	New York JFK Int'l Airport	16
	New York Laguardia Airport	19
Irondequoit	Rochester Int'l Airport	8
Levittown	New York JFK Int'l Airport	16
	New York Laguardia Airport	20
Mount Vernon	Dobbs Ferry Ardsley	6
	New York Central Park Observatory	11
	New York JFK Int'l Airport	18
	New York Laguardia Airport	9
	White Plains Westchester Co. Arpt.	12
New Rochelle	Stamford 5 N, CT	18
	Dobbs Ferry Ardsley	6
	New York Central Park Observatory	13
	New York JFK Int'l Airport	19
	New York Laguardia Airport	11
	White Plains Westchester Co. Arpt.	11
New York	Little Falls, NJ	20
	Newark Int'l Airport, NJ	14
	Dobbs Ferry Ardsley	20
	New York Avenue V Brooklyn	9
	New York Central Park Observatory	5
	New York JFK Int'l Airport	8
	New York Laguardia Airport	4
Niagara Falls	Buffalo Int'l Airport	18
	Lockport 2 SE	17
Rochester	Rochester Int'l Airport	5
Schenectady	Albany County Airport	8
	Saratoga Springs 4 SW	17
	Troy Lock & Dam	13
Syracuse (cont.)	Syracuse Hancock Int'l Airport	6
	Tully Heiberg Forest	19
Tonawanda	Buffalo Int'l Airport	7
	Lockport 2 SE	13
	Lockport 4 NE	19
Troy	Albany County Airport	6
	Grafton	11
	Troy Lock & Dam	1
Utica	Utica Oneida County Airport	8
West Babylon	Patchogue 2 N	20
	Islip Macarthur Airport	14
West Seneca	Buffalo Int'l Airport	7
	Colden 1 N	12
White Plains	Stamford 5 N, CT	13
	Dobbs Ferry Ardsley	4
	New York Central Park Observatory	20
	New York Laguardia Airport	18
	White Plains Westchester Co. Arpt.	4
	Yorktown Heights 1 W	17
Yonkers	Little Falls, NJ	19
	Dobbs Ferry Ardsley	5
	New York Central Park Observatory	12
	New York Laguardia Airport	11
	White Plains Westchester Co. Arpt.	12

Note: Miles is the distance between the geographic center of the city and the weather station.

New York Weather Stations by Elevation

Feet	Station Name
2,647	Slide Mountain
1,938	Lake Placid 2 S
1,896	Tully Heiberg Forest
1,817	Warsaw 6 SW
1,768	Alfred
1,719	Old Forge
1,689	Stillwater Reservoir
1,660	Indian Lake 2 SW
1,624	Little Valley
1,617	Ray Brook
1,597	Binghamton Edwin A. Link Field
1,578	Bolivar
1,578	Boonville 2 SSW
1,558	Grafton
1,548	Franklinville
1,509	Wanakena Ranger School
1,499	Allegany State Park
1,443	Angelica
1,358	Cherry Valley 2 NNE
1,338	Dannemora
1,243	Mohonk Lake
1,240	Walton
1,197	Cooperstown
1,128	Cortland
1,118	Bath
1,059	Chasm Falls
1,023	Colden 1 N
1,017	Norwich
997	Deposit
958	Ithaca Cornell University
898	Batavia
898	Gloversville
859	Lowville
843	Elmira
830	Aurora Research Farm
807	Conklingville Dam
757	Fredonia
718	Canandaigua 3 S
715	Geneva Research Farm
711	Utica Oneida County Airport
705	Westfield 2 SSE
702	Buffalo Int'l Airport
698	Middletown 2 NW
669	Yorktown Heights 1 W
659	Dansville
603	Lockport 2 SE
597	Rochester Int'l Airport
508	Peru 2 WSW
501	Glens Falls Farm
498	Lawrenceville 3 SW
495	Watertown
469	Port Jervis
439	Albion 2 NE
439	Lockport 4 NE
419	Gouverneur 3 NW
419	Sodus Center
410	Syracuse Hancock Int'l Airport
396	Canton 4 SE
396	White Plains Westchester Co. Arpt.
377	Walden 1 ESE
347	Oswego East
318	Glens Falls Airport
318	West Point
314	Watertown Airport
308	Saratoga Springs 4 SW
278	Ogdensburg 4 NE
272	Albany County Airport
272	Glenham
213	Massena Airport
200	Dobbs Ferry Ardsley
167	Chazy
154	Poughkeepsie Dutchess Co. Arpt.
131	New York Central Park Observatory
118	Whitehall
98	Riverhead Research Farm
82	Islip Macarthur Airport
59	Bridgehampton
59	Hudson Correctionl Facility
52	Patchogue 2 N
39	Setauket Strong
22	Troy Lock & Dam
19	New York Avenue V Brooklyn
13	New York JFK Int'l Airport
9	New York Laguardia Airport

Albany County Airport

Albany is located on the west bank of the Hudson River some 150 miles north of New York City, and 8 miles south of the confluence of the Mohawk and Hudson Rivers. The river-front portion of the city is only a few feet above sea level, and there is a tidal effect upstream to Troy. Eleven miles west of Albany the Helderberg hill range rises to 1,800 feet. Between it and the Hudson River the valley floor is gently rolling, ranging some 200 to 500 feet above sea level. East of the city there is more rugged terrain 5 or 6 miles wide with elevations of 300 to 600 feet. Farther to the east the terrain rises more sharply. It reaches a north-south range of hills 12 miles east of Albany with elevations ranging to 2,000 feet.

The climate at Albany is primarily continental in character, but is subjected to some modification by the Atlantic Ocean. The moderating effect on temperatures is more pronounced during the warmer months than in winter when outbursts of cold air sweep down from Canada. In the warmer seasons, temperatures rise rapidly in the daytime. However, temperatures also fall rapidly after sunset so that the nights are relatively cool. Occasionally there are extended periods of oppressive heat up to a week or more in duration.

Winters are usually cold and sometimes fairly severe. Maximum temperatures during the colder winters are often below freezing and nighttime lows are frequently below 10 degrees. Sub-zero readings occur about 12 times a year. Snowfall throughout the area is quite variable and snow flurries are quite frequent during the winter. Precipitation is sufficient to serve the economy of the region in most years, and only occasionally do periods of drought exist. Most of the rainfall in the summer is from thunderstorms. Tornadoes are quite rare and hail is not usually of any consequence.

Wind velocities are moderate. The north-south Hudson River Valley has a marked effect on the lighter winds and in the warm months, average wind direction is usually southerly. Destructive winds rarely occur.

The area enjoys one of the highest percentages of sunshine in the entire state. Seldom does the area experience long periods of cloudy days and long periods of smog are rare.

Based on the 1951-1980 period, the average first occurrence of 32 degrees Fahrenheit in the fall is September 29 and the average last occurrence in the spring is May 7.

Albany County Airport *Albany County*   Elevation: 272 ft.   Latitude: 42° 45' N   Longitude: 73° 48' W

	JAN	FEB	MAR	APR	MAY	JUN	JUL	AUG	SEP	OCT	NOV	DEC	YEAR
Mean Maximum Temp. (°F)	30.7	34.2	44.3	57.7	70.0	77.7	82.7	80.3	72.0	60.3	48.0	36.0	57.8
Mean Temp. (°F)	21.7	24.8	34.7	46.8	58.2	66.3	71.4	69.3	61.0	49.6	39.4	28.0	47.6
Mean Minimum Temp. (°F)	12.7	15.3	25.0	35.8	46.5	54.9	60.0	58.2	50.0	38.8	30.8	19.9	37.3
Extreme Maximum Temp. (°F)	65	68	89	92	94	96	99	97	93	86	81	71	99
Extreme Minimum Temp. (°F)	-28	-21	-6	13	28	36	40	34	28	17	5	-20	-28
Days Maximum Temp. ≥ 90°F	0	0	0	0	0	1	4	2	0	0	0	0	7
Days Maximum Temp. ≤ 32°F	17	12	4	0	0	0	0	0	0	0	1	10	44
Days Minimum Temp. ≤ 32°F	29	26	24	12	1	0	0	0	1	8	18	27	146
Days Minimum Temp. ≤ 0°F	6	4	0	0	0	0	0	0	0	0	0	2	12
Heating Degree Days (base 65°F)	1,336	1,130	933	544	231	60	8	24	161	474	762	1,141	6,804
Cooling Degree Days (base 65°F)	0	0	0	3	28	108	220	169	49	3	0	0	581
Mean Precipitation (in.)	2.63	2.24	3.14	3.21	3.56	3.62	3.42	3.63	3.33	3.23	3.29	2.75	38.05
Maximum Precipitation (in.)	6.4	5.0	5.9	7.9	9.0	7.4	7.0	7.3	7.9	8.8	8.1	6.7	47.2
Minimum Precipitation (in.)	0.4	0.2	0.3	1.1	1.0	0.6	0.5	0.7	0.4	0.2	0.6	0.6	21.5
Maximum 24-hr. Precipitation (in.)	1.8	1.6	2.0	2.0	2.2	3.5	2.7	4.1	3.5	2.8	2.2	3.2	4.1
Days With ≥ 0.1" Precipitation	6	5	6	7	8	7	6	7	7	6	7	7	79
Days With ≥ 1.0" Precipitation	0	0	1	1	1	1	1	1	1	1	1	0	9
Mean Snowfall (in.)	17.2	12.5	11.1	2.5	trace	trace	trace	0.0	trace	0.2	5.0	13.6	62.1
Maximum Snowfall (in.)	48	35	35	18	2	0	0	0	0	7	25	58	107
Maximum 24-hr. Snowfall (in.)	13	17	22	17	2	0	0	0	0	7	22	14	22
Days With ≥ 1.0" Snow Depth	20	17	8	1	0	0	0	0	0	0	3	13	62
Thunderstorm Days	< 1	< 1	1	1	3	5	6	5	2	1	< 1	< 1	24
Foggy Days	10	9	11	9	12	13	14	17	17	15	13	12	152
Predominant Sky Cover	OVR	OVR	OVR	OVR	OVR	OVR	OVR	OVR	OVR	OVR	OVR	OVR	OVR
Mean Relative Humidity 7am (%)	77	77	76	72	74	77	80	85	88	86	82	80	80
Mean Relative Humidity 4pm (%)	64	59	54	48	50	53	53	55	57	56	64	67	57
Mean Dewpoint (°F)	14	15	23	33	45	55	60	59	52	41	31	20	38
Prevailing Wind Direction	WNW	WNW	WNW	WNW	S	S	S	S	S	S	WNW	WNW	S
Prevailing Wind Speed (mph)	15	15	15	15	10	9	8	8	9	9	14	14	12
Maximum Wind Gust (mph)	62	67	61	58	67	59	77	62	64	60	67	63	77

Binghamton Edwin A. Link Field

Binghamton, in south central New York lies in a comparatively narrow valley at the confluence of the Susquehanna and Chenango Rivers. Within a radius of 5 miles, hills rise to elevations of 1,400-1,600 feet above mean sea level. In the spring, melting snow, sometimes supplemented by rainfall, occasionally causes flooding in the city and along the streams.

The climate of Binghamton is representative of the humid area of the north-eastern United States and is primarily continental in type. The area, being adjacent to the so-called St. Lawrence Valley storm track, and also subject to cold air masses approaching from the west and north, has a variable climate, characterized by frequent and rapid changes. Furthermore, diurnal and seasonal changes assist in the production of an invigorating climate. As a rule, the temperature rises rapidly to moderate daytime levels with readings of 90 degrees or above only a few days in any month summer nights provide favorable sleeping conditions.

Winters are usually cold, but not commonly severe. Highest daytime temperatures average in the high 20s to low 30s, while the lowest nighttime readings average from the mid-teens to low 20s. Ordinarily a few sub-zero readings may be expected in January and February, with a lesser number in November, December, and March. The transitional seasons, spring and autumn, are the most variable of the year.

Most of the precipitation in the Binghamton area derives from moisture laden air transported from the Gulf of Mexico and cyclonic systems moving northward along the Atlantic coast. The annual rainfall is rather evenly distributed over the year. However, the greatest average monthly amounts occur during the growing season, April through September. As a rule, rainfall is ample for good crop growth and comes mostly in the form of thunderstorms. Annual snowfall is around 50 inches in Binghamton and above 85 inches at Edwin A. Link Field, some 10 miles to the NNW, and about 700 feet higher in elevation. Most of the snow falls during the normal winter months. However, heavy snows can occur as early as November and as late as April. Being adjacent to the track of storms that move through the St. Lawrence Valley, and being under the influence of winds that sweep across Lakes Erie and Ontario to the interior of the state, the area is subject to much cloudiness and winter snow flurries.

For the most part, the winds at Binghamton have northerly and westerly components. Tornadoes, although rare, have struck in the Binghamton area.

Based on the 1951-1980 period, the growing season averages 150 to 160 days. Usually the last spring frost occurs during early May, and the first frost in autumn during early October.

Binghamton Edwin A. Link Field *Broome Co.*   Elevation: 1,597 ft.   Latitude: 42° 12' N   Longitude: 75° 59' W

	JAN	FEB	MAR	APR	MAY	JUN	JUL	AUG	SEP	OCT	NOV	DEC	YEAR
Mean Maximum Temp. (°F)	28.8	31.5	40.8	53.7	66.1	73.9	78.8	76.6	68.4	57.1	44.8	33.9	54.5
Mean Temp. (°F)	21.9	24.1	32.8	44.6	56.4	64.4	69.4	67.3	59.5	48.6	38.0	27.5	46.2
Mean Minimum Temp. (°F)	15.0	16.6	24.6	35.4	46.6	54.8	59.9	58.0	50.5	40.1	31.2	21.1	37.8
Extreme Maximum Temp. (°F)	63	63	82	88	89	92	98	94	91	81	77	65	98
Extreme Minimum Temp. (°F)	-15	-15	-7	9	25	33	43	38	25	17	3	-18	-18
Days Maximum Temp. ≥ 90°F	0	0	0	0	0	0	1	0	0	0	0	0	1
Days Maximum Temp. ≤ 32°F	20	15	8	1	0	0	0	0	0	0	4	14	62
Days Minimum Temp. ≤ 32°F	29	26	24	12	1	0	0	0	0	6	18	27	143
Days Minimum Temp. ≤ 0°F	4	2	0	0	0	0	0	0	0	0	0	1	7
Heating Degree Days (base 65°F)	1,329	1,148	994	610	284	87	20	40	194	504	804	1,155	7,169
Cooling Degree Days (base 65°F)	0	0	1	3	23	79	164	122	37	2	0	0	431
Mean Precipitation (in.)	2.51	2.42	2.94	3.39	3.42	3.68	3.52	3.40	3.64	2.95	3.34	3.08	38.29
Maximum Precipitation (in.)	6.4	4.4	6.0	8.6	6.5	9.5	7.4	7.5	9.7	9.4	7.5	6.1	48.0
Minimum Precipitation (in.)	0.8	0.4	0.7	1.0	0.8	1.0	0.8	0.6	0.6	0.3	1.0	0.9	29.9
Maximum 24-hr. Precipitation (in.)	1.5	2.2	1.6	2.9	2.9	3.1	3.2	2.6	3.5	3.5	2.6	2.7	3.5
Days With ≥ 0.1" Precipitation	6	6	7	7	8	8	7	7	7	7	8	7	85
Days With ≥ 1.0" Precipitation	0	0	0	1	0	1	1	1	1	1	0	0	6
Mean Snowfall (in.)	19.8	15.7	14.5	4.5	0.2	trace	0.0	0.0	trace	0.8	7.8	17.5	80.8
Maximum Snowfall (in.)	44	44	38	23	3	0	0	0	trace	12	29	60	138
Maximum 24-hr. Snowfall (in.)	18	21	19	12	3	0	0	0	trace	7	11	14	21
Days With ≥ 1.0" Snow Depth	24	21	14	2	0	0	0	0	0	0	6	16	83
Thunderstorm Days	< 1	< 1	1	2	4	6	7	5	3	1	< 1	< 1	29
Foggy Days	11	10	13	12	14	15	16	19	17	15	14	13	169
Predominant Sky Cover	OVR	OVR	OVR	OVR	OVR	OVR	OVR	OVR	OVR	OVR	OVR	OVR	OVR
Mean Relative Humidity 7am (%)	80	79	79	76	78	83	85	89	90	85	82	82	82
Mean Relative Humidity 4pm (%)	69	65	60	54	54	57	57	59	62	60	68	72	61
Mean Dewpoint (°F)	15	16	23	32	44	54	59	58	51	40	31	20	37
Prevailing Wind Direction	WNW	NW	NW	NW	NW	SW	SW	SW	SW	S	SW	WNW	NW
Prevailing Wind Speed (mph)	14	14	14	13	12	9	8	8	9	9	10	14	12
Maximum Wind Gust (mph)	61	56	58	64	54	60	74	63	48	51	58	54	74

Buffalo Int'l Airport

The country surrounding Buffalo is comparatively low and level to the west. To the east and south the land is gently rolling, rising to pronounced hills within 12 to 18 miles, and to 1,000 feet above the level of Lake Erie about 35 miles south-southeast of the city. A steep slope of 50 to 100 feet lies east-west one and a half miles to the north. The eastern end of Lake Erie is nine miles to the west-southwest, while Lake Ontario lies 25 miles to the north, the two being connected by the Niagara River, which flows north-northwestward from the end of Lake Erie.

Buffalo is located near the mean position of the polar front. Its weather is varied and changeable, characteristic of the latitude. Wide seasonal swings of temperature from hot to cold are tempered appreciably by the proximity of Lakes Erie and Ontario. Lake Erie lies to the southwest, the direction of the prevailing wind. Wind flow throughout the year is somewhat higher due to this exposure. The vigorous interplay of warm and cold air masses during the winter and early spring months causes one or more windstorms. Precipitation is moderate and fairly evenly divided throughout the twelve months.

The spring season is more cloudy and cooler than points not affected by the cold lake. Spring growth of vegetation is retarded, protecting it from late spring frosts. With heavy winter ice accumulations in the lake, typical spring conditions are delayed until late May or early June.

Summer comes suddenly in mid-June. Lake breezes temper the extreme heat of the summer season. Temperatures of 90 degrees and above are infrequent. There is more summer sunshine here than in any other section of the state. Due to the stabilizing effects of Lake Erie, thunderstorms are relatively infrequent. Most of them are caused by frontal action. To the north and south of the city thunderstorms occur more often.

Autumn has long, dry periods and is frost free usually until mid-October. Cloudiness increases in November, continuing mostly cloudy throughout the winter and early spring. Snow flurries off the lake begin in mid-November or early December. Outbreaks of Arctic air in December and throughout the winter months produce locally heavy snowfalls from the lake. At the same time, temperatures of well below zero over Canada and the midwest are raised 10 to 30 degrees in crossing the lakes. Only on rare occasions do polar air masses drop southward from eastern Hudson Bay across Lake Ontario without appreciable warming.

Buffalo Int'l Airport *Erie County*   Elevation: 702 ft.   Latitude: 42° 56' N   Longitude: 78° 44' W

	JAN	FEB	MAR	APR	MAY	JUN	JUL	AUG	SEP	OCT	NOV	DEC	YEAR
Mean Maximum Temp. (°F)	30.9	32.8	41.9	54.4	66.8	75.4	80.3	78.4	70.6	59.3	47.1	36.4	56.2
Mean Temp. (°F)	24.3	25.6	33.9	45.4	57.3	66.2	71.3	69.5	61.8	51.0	40.5	30.1	48.1
Mean Minimum Temp. (°F)	17.6	18.4	25.8	36.4	47.6	56.9	62.2	60.5	53.0	42.7	33.9	23.8	39.9
Extreme Maximum Temp. (°F)	67	70	79	94	90	96	97	96	90	82	73	74	97
Extreme Minimum Temp. (°F)	-16	-18	-7	12	28	36	47	38	32	22	9	-10	-18
Days Maximum Temp. ≥ 90°F	0	0	0	0	0	0	2	1	0	0	0	0	3
Days Maximum Temp. ≤ 32°F	17	14	7	1	0	0	0	0	0	0	2	11	52
Days Minimum Temp. ≤ 32°F	28	25	24	10	0	0	0	0	0	3	14	25	129
Days Minimum Temp. ≤ 0°F	2	1	0	0	0	0	0	0	0	0	0	1	4
Heating Degree Days (base 65°F)	1,256	1,105	957	585	262	62	7	19	142	431	729	1,076	6,631
Cooling Degree Days (base 65°F)	0	0	0	4	28	105	218	169	54	4	0	0	582
Mean Precipitation (in.)	3.14	2.42	2.98	2.99	3.30	3.69	3.18	3.83	3.86	3.29	3.83	3.79	40.30
Maximum Precipitation (in.)	6.9	5.9	6.0	5.9	7.2	8.4	8.9	10.7	9.0	9.1	9.8	8.7	53.5
Minimum Precipitation (in.)	1.0	0.8	1.2	1.3	1.2	0.1	0.9	1.1	0.8	0.3	1.5	1.7	28.5
Maximum 24-hr. Precipitation (in.)	1.8	2.1	2.0	1.7	3.4	5.0	3.4	3.9	4.9	2.5	2.1	1.7	5.0
Days With ≥ 0.1" Precipitation	9	7	8	8	7	7	6	7	7	8	9	10	93
Days With ≥ 1.0" Precipitation	0	0	0	0	1	1	1	1	1	0	1	0	6
Mean Snowfall (in.)	26.7	18.0	12.5	3.5	0.3	trace	trace	trace	trace	0.3	9.6	24.8	95.7
Maximum Snowfall (in.)	68	54	29	15	8	0	0	0	trace	3	31	68	176
Maximum 24-hr. Snowfall (in.)	18	18	15	6	8	0	0	0	trace	3	19	34	34
Days With ≥ 1.0" Snow Depth	21	20	10	2	0	0	0	0	0	0	4	15	72
Thunderstorm Days	< 1	< 1	1	2	3	5	6	6	4	2	1	< 1	30
Foggy Days	12	12	14	13	14	13	13	15	13	13	13	13	158
Predominant Sky Cover	OVR	OVR	OVR	OVR	OVR	OVR	SCT	OVR	OVR	OVR	OVR	OVR	OVR
Mean Relative Humidity 7am (%)	79	80	80	77	76	77	79	83	83	81	80	80	79
Mean Relative Humidity 4pm (%)	73	70	65	57	55	54	54	56	59	60	69	73	62
Mean Dewpoint (°F)	18	18	25	34	44	54	59	59	52	42	33	23	39
Prevailing Wind Direction	WSW	WSW	SW	SW	SW	SW	SW	SW	SW	SW	W	W	SW
Prevailing Wind Speed (mph)	18	17	16	15	14	14	13	13	13	15	15	15	15
Maximum Wind Gust (mph)	71	82	73	74	64	79	59	81	62	63	73	69	82

Islip Macarthur Airport

Long Island is the terminal moraine marking the southernmost advance of the ice sheet along the Atlantic Coast during the last ice age. The terrain is generally flat, with only a gradual rise in elevation from Long Island Sound on the northern shore and from the Atlantic Ocean on the southern shore toward the middle of the island. Islip is located about half-way out Long Island on the southern coast. The airport is located about seven miles to the northeast of the city. Islip is protected from flooding during periods of high tides by Fire Island, a natural barrier located about three miles offshore. Most of the air masses affecting Islip are continental in origin, however the ocean has a pronounced influence on the climate of the area.

A cool sea breeze blowing off the ocean during the summer months helps to alleviate the afternoon heat. There are an average of 7 days between June and September when the afternoon temperature exceeds 90 degrees, while farther inland there are 10 to 15 such days.

It is uncommon for the eye of a tropical storm to pass directly over Long Island. Tropical weather systems moving along the Atlantic Coast, however, are capable of producing episodes of heavy rain and strong winds in the late summer or fall.

The winter season is relatively mild. Below zero temperatures are reported on only one or two days in about half the winters. Temperatures of 10 degrees below zero or colder are extremely rare. The seasonal snowfall averages about 29 inches. Almost all of this snow falls between December and March. Coastal low pressure systems, Northeasters, are the principle source of this snow. These weather systems will occasionally produce a heavy snowfall. There are usually extended periods during the winter when the ground is bare of snow.

Based on the 1951-1980 period, the average date of the last spring temperature of 32 degrees is April 27 and the average first fall occurrence is October 21. Inland locations would expect a shorter freeze-free season.

Islip Macarthur Airport *Suffolk County*   Elevation: 82 ft.   Latitude: 40° 47' N   Longitude: 73° 06' W

	JAN	FEB	MAR	APR	MAY	JUN	JUL	AUG	SEP	OCT	NOV	DEC	YEAR
Mean Maximum Temp. (°F)	na	na	na	na	na	na	na	na	na	na	na	na	na
Mean Temp. (°F)	na	na	na	na	na	na	na	na	na	na	na	na	na
Mean Minimum Temp. (°F)	na	na	na	na	na	na	na	na	na	na	na	na	na
Extreme Maximum Temp. (°F)	na	na	na	na	na	na	na	na	na	na	na	na	na
Extreme Minimum Temp. (°F)	na	na	na	na	na	na	na	na	na	na	na	na	na
Days Maximum Temp. ≥ 90°F	na	na	na	na	na	na	na	na	na	na	na	na	na
Days Maximum Temp. ≤ 32°F	na	na	na	na	na	na	na	na	na	na	na	na	na
Days Minimum Temp. ≤ 32°F	na	na	na	na	na	na	na	na	na	na	na	na	na
Days Minimum Temp. ≤ 0°F	na	na	na	na	na	na	na	na	na	na	na	na	na
Heating Degree Days (base 65°F)	na	na	na	na	na	na	na	na	na	na	na	na	na
Cooling Degree Days (base 65°F)	na	na	na	na	na	na	na	na	na	11	na	na	na
Mean Precipitation (in.)	na	na	na	na	na	na	na	na	na	na	na	na	na
Maximum Precipitation (in.)	6.3	5.5	5.5	5.1	10.1	7.9	8.4	13.8	5.1	8.7	8.0	6.1	65.3
Minimum Precipitation (in.)	1.3	1.1	1.3	1.3	0.7	0.6	1.2	0.5	0.8	0.3	1.3	0.9	34.4
Maximum 24-hr. Precipitation (in.)	1.6	2.3	2.5	1.8	4.0	3.5	2.7	6.7	2.2	3.9	2.6	2.6	6.7
Days With ≥ 0.1" Precipitation	na	na	na	na	na	na	na	na	na	na	na	na	na
Days With ≥ 1.0" Precipitation	na	na	na	na	na	na	na	na	na	na	na	na	na
Mean Snowfall (in.)	na	na	na	na	na	na	na	na	na	na	na	na	na
Maximum Snowfall (in.)	14	20	13	3	0	0	0	0	0	0	8	10	34
Maximum 24-hr. Snowfall (in.)	6	7	8	3	0	0	0	0	0	0	8	9	9
Days With ≥ 1.0" Snow Depth	na	na	na	na	na	na	na	na	na	na	na	na	na
Thunderstorm Days	< 1	< 1	1	2	3	5	6	4	2	1	1	< 1	25
Foggy Days	15	14	16	16	18	16	22	19	17	15	14	14	196
Predominant Sky Cover	OVR	OVR	OVR	OVR	OVR	SCT	OVR	SCT	OVR	CLR	OVR	OVR	OVR
Mean Relative Humidity 7am (%)	76	76	77	76	76	77	81	84	85	85	80	76	79
Mean Relative Humidity 4pm (%)	62	59	57	58	59	59	63	63	63	62	62	60	61
Mean Dewpoint (°F)	22	22	28	38	48	58	65	64	57	46	36	26	43
Prevailing Wind Direction	WNW	NW	NW	SW	SW	SW	SW	SW	SW	SW	SW	WNW	SW
Prevailing Wind Speed (mph)	13	13	13	10	10	10	10	9	10	10	10	12	12
Maximum Wind Gust (mph)	na	na	na	na	na	na	na	na	na	na	na	na	na

New York Central Park Observatory

New York City, in area exceeding 300 square miles, is located on the Atlantic coastal plain at the mouth of the Hudson River. The terrain is laced with numerous waterways, all but one of the five boroughs in the city are situated on islands. Elevations range from less than 50 feet over most of Manhattan, Brooklyn, and Queens to almost 300 feet in northern Manhattan and the Bronx, and over 400 feet in Staten Island.

The New York Metropolitan area is close to the path of most storm and frontal systems which move across the North American continent. Therefore, weather conditions affecting the city most often approach from a westerly direction, resulting in higher temperatures in summer and lower ones in winter than would otherwise be expected in a coastal area. However, the frequent passage of weather systems often helps reduce the length of extremes.

Although continental influence predominates, oceanic influence is by no means absent. During the summer local sea breezes, winds blowing onshore from the cool water surface, often moderate the afternoon heat. The effect of the sea breeze diminishes inland. On winter mornings, ocean temperatures which are warm relative to the land reinforce the effect of the city heat island and low temperatures are often 10-20 degrees lower in the inland suburbs than in the central city. The relatively warm water temperatures also delay the advent of winter snows. Conversely, the lag in warming of water temperatures keeps spring temperatures relatively cool.

Precipitation is moderate and distributed fairly evenly throughout the year. Most of the rainfall from May through October comes from thunderstorms, usually of brief duration and sometimes intense. Heavy rains of long duration associated with tropical storms occur infrequently in late summer or fall. For the other seasons precipitation is associated with widespread storm areas, producing day-long rain or snow. Coastal storms, occurring most often in the fall and winter months, produce on occasion considerable amounts of precipitation, record rains, snows, and high winds.

The average annual precipitation is reasonably uniform within the city but higher in the suburbs and less on eastern Long Island. Annual snowfall totals also show a consistent increase to the north and west of the city with lesser amounts along the south shores and the eastern end of Long Island.

Local Climatological Data is published for three locations in New York City, Central Park, La Guardia Airport, and John°F. Kennedy International Airport.

Based on the 1951-1980 period, the average first occurrence of 32 degrees Fahrenheit in the fall is November 11 and the average last occurrence in the spring is April 1.

New York Central Park Observatory *New York County* Elevation: 131 ft. Latitude: 40° 47' N Longitude: 73° 58' W

	JAN	FEB	MAR	APR	MAY	JUN	JUL	AUG	SEP	OCT	NOV	DEC	YEAR
Mean Maximum Temp. (°F)	38.5	41.3	50.2	61.6	71.8	79.9	85.5	83.9	76.1	64.7	54.1	43.7	62.6
Mean Temp. (°F)	32.2	34.6	42.6	52.9	63.0	71.6	77.2	75.8	68.3	57.2	47.7	37.8	55.1
Mean Minimum Temp. (°F)	26.0	27.7	34.9	44.2	54.1	63.2	68.9	67.8	60.5	49.6	41.1	31.8	47.5
Extreme Maximum Temp. (°F)	66	75	86	96	97	98	104	99	99	88	81	75	104
Extreme Minimum Temp. (°F)	-2	0	10	21	36	46	53	50	43	29	17	-1	-2
Days Maximum Temp. ≥ 90°F	0	0	0	0	1	3	8	5	1	0	0	0	18
Days Maximum Temp. ≤ 32°F	9	5	1	0	0	0	0	0	0	0	0	4	19
Days Minimum Temp. ≤ 32°F	22	19	11	1	0	0	0	0	0	0	4	15	72
Days Minimum Temp. ≤ 0°F	0	0	0	0	0	0	0	0	0	0	0	0	0
Heating Degree Days (base 65°F)	1,009	853	691	367	121	14	1	1	40	253	516	836	4,702
Cooling Degree Days (base 65°F)	0	0	3	8	68	228	393	341	144	19	2	0	1,206
Mean Precipitation (in.)	4.07	3.30	4.27	4.06	4.62	3.75	4.52	4.22	4.15	3.91	4.35	3.94	49.16
Maximum Precipitation (in.)	10.5	6.0	10.4	8.3	10.2	9.3	11.8	12.4	9.3	7.8	12.4	10.0	67.0
Minimum Precipitation (in.)	0.6	0.5	0.9	1.3	0.6	1.2	1.3	0.2	1.3	0.1	0.3	0.6	26.1
Maximum 24-hr. Precipitation (in.)	3.4	3.0	3.4	3.4	4.0	3.1	3.5	4.6	5.5	4.1	7.4	2.5	7.4
Days With ≥ 0.1" Precipitation	7	6	7	7	8	7	7	6	6	6	6	7	80
Days With ≥ 1.0" Precipitation	1	1	1	1	1	1	1	1	1	1	1	1	12
Mean Snowfall (in.)	7.3	7.5	3.4	0.4	trace	0.0	trace	0.0	0.0	trace	0.4	2.2	21.2
Maximum Snowfall (in.)	20	26	17	10	trace	0	0	0	0	trace	5	12	53
Maximum 24-hr. Snowfall (in.)	12	16	10	10	trace	0	0	0	0	trace	4	7	16
Days With ≥ 1.0" Snow Depth	9	8	2	0	0	0	0	0	0	0	0	2	21
Thunderstorm Days	< 1	< 1	1	1	3	4	5	4	1	1	< 1	< 1	20
Foggy Days	0	0	0	0	0	0	0	0	0	0	1	< 1	1
Predominant Sky Cover	OVR	OVR	OVR	OVR	OVR	SCT	SCT	SCT	OVR	CLR	OVR	OVR	OVR
Mean Relative Humidity 7am (%)	67	67	66	64	72	74	74	76	78	75	72	69	71
Mean Relative Humidity 4pm (%)	55	53	50	45	52	55	53	54	56	55	58	59	54
Mean Dewpoint (°F)	18	19	26	34	47	57	62	62	56	44	34	25	40
Prevailing Wind Direction	NW	NW	NW	NW	NE	SW	SW	SW	SW	W	W	NW	NW
Prevailing Wind Speed (mph)	12	12	13	12	10	8	8	8	8	8	9	12	10
Maximum Wind Gust (mph)	52	51	63	46	44	41	46	43	52	46	58	64	64

New York JFK Int'l Airport

New York City, in area exceeding 300 square miles, is located on the Atlantic coastal plain at the mouth of the Hudson River. The terrain is laced with numerous waterways, all but one of the five boroughs in the city are situated on islands. Elevations range from less than 50 feet over most of Manhattan, Brooklyn, and Queens to almost 300 feet in northern Manhattan and the Bronx, and over 400 feet in Staten Island.

The New York Metropolitan area is close to the path of most storm and frontal systems which move across the North American continent. Therefore, weather conditions affecting the city most often approach from a westerly direction, resulting in higher temperatures in summer and lower ones in winter than would otherwise be expected in a coastal area. However, the frequent passage of weather systems often helps reduce the length of extremes.

Although continental influence predominates, oceanic influence is by no means absent. During the summer local sea breezes, winds blowing onshore from the cool water surface, often moderate the afternoon heat. The effect of the sea breeze diminishes inland. On winter mornings, ocean temperatures which are warm relative to the land reinforce the effect of the city heat island and low temperatures are often 10-20 degrees lower in the inland suburbs than in the central city. The relatively warm water temperatures also delay the advent of winter snows. Conversely, the lag in warming of water temperatures keeps spring temperatures relatively cool.

Precipitation is moderate and distributed fairly evenly throughout the year. Most of the rainfall from May through October comes from thunderstorms, usually of brief duration and sometimes intense. Heavy rains of long duration associated with tropical storms occur infrequently in late summer or fall. For the other seasons precipitation is associated with widespread storm areas, producing day-long rain or snow. Coastal storms, occurring most often in the fall and winter months, produce on occasion considerable amounts of precipitation, record rains, snows, and high winds.

The average annual precipitation is reasonably uniform within the city but higher in the suburbs and less on eastern Long Island. Annual snowfall totals also show a consistent increase to the north and west of the city with lesser amounts along the south shores and the eastern end of Long Island.

Local Climatological Data is published for three locations in New York City, Central Park, La Guardia Airport, and John°F. Kennedy International Airport.

Based on the 1951-1980 period, the average first occurrence of 32 degrees Fahrenheit in the fall is November 11 and the average last occurrence in the spring is April 1.

New York JFK Int'l Airport Queens County Elevation: 13 ft. Latitude: 40° 39' N Longitude: 73° 48' W

	JAN	FEB	MAR	APR	MAY	JUN	JUL	AUG	SEP	OCT	NOV	DEC	YEAR
Mean Maximum Temp. (°F)	38.7	40.9	48.6	58.7	68.3	77.3	83.0	82.1	75.1	64.3	54.0	44.1	61.2
Mean Temp. (°F)	32.4	34.3	41.6	51.0	60.7	69.8	75.8	74.9	67.9	57.0	47.4	37.9	54.2
Mean Minimum Temp. (°F)	26.0	27.6	34.5	43.4	53.0	62.3	68.6	67.7	60.6	49.6	40.7	31.7	47.1
Extreme Maximum Temp. (°F)	65	71	85	90	95	98	102	100	98	88	77	75	102
Extreme Minimum Temp. (°F)	-2	2	8	20	37	48	55	50	41	30	19	2	-2
Days Maximum Temp. ≥ 90°F	0	0	0	0	0	2	4	3	1	0	0	0	10
Days Maximum Temp. ≤ 32°F	8	5	1	0	0	0	0	0	0	0	0	3	17
Days Minimum Temp. ≤ 32°F	23	19	11	1	0	0	0	0	0	0	4	16	74
Days Minimum Temp. ≤ 0°F	0	0	0	0	0	0	0	0	0	0	0	0	0
Heating Degree Days (base 65°F)	1,005	862	720	414	160	17	0	2	39	256	524	834	4,833
Cooling Degree Days (base 65°F)	0	0	0	1	36	178	351	313	133	15	0	0	1,027
Mean Precipitation (in.)	3.55	2.75	3.78	3.72	4.07	3.57	3.76	3.62	3.41	3.08	3.46	3.30	42.07
Maximum Precipitation (in.)	8.3	4.9	8.2	9.5	10.7	8.1	8.5	8.3	9.6	6.6	9.5	6.7	59.1
Minimum Precipitation (in.)	0.5	1.0	0.9	1.4	0.6	trace	0.5	0.2	1.0	0.9	0.3	0.6	25.4
Maximum 24-hr. Precipitation (in.)	2.6	2.5	2.4	3.1	2.9	2.8	3.2	3.8	4.5	3.2	3.9	2.5	4.5
Days With ≥ 0.1" Precipitation	7	6	7	6	7	6	6	6	6	5	6	6	74
Days With ≥ 1.0" Precipitation	1	1	1	1	1	1	1	1	1	1	1	1	12
Mean Snowfall (in.)	6.8	7.1	3.4	0.6	trace	0.0	trace	0.0	0.0	trace	0.3	2.3	20.5
Maximum Snowfall (in.)	20	25	16	8	0	0	0	0	0	trace	4	22	49
Maximum 24-hr. Snowfall (in.)	13	20	9	8	0	0	0	0	0	trace	3	18	20
Days With ≥ 1.0" Snow Depth	6	5	2	0	0	0	0	0	0	0	0	2	15
Thunderstorm Days	< 1	< 1	1	2	3	4	5	5	2	1	1	< 1	24
Foggy Days	10	9	11	11	13	12	13	12	11	10	11	10	133
Predominant Sky Cover	OVR	OVR	OVR	OVR	OVR	OVR	SCT	SCT	OVR	CLR	OVR	OVR	OVR
Mean Relative Humidity 7am (%)	71	71	71	70	73	74	75	78	79	78	76	73	74
Mean Relative Humidity 4pm (%)	61	59	57	58	61	63	63	63	62	60	61	62	61
Mean Dewpoint (°F)	21	22	28	37	48	58	64	63	57	46	36	26	42
Prevailing Wind Direction	NW	NW	NW	S	S	S	S	S	S	WSW	NW	NW	S
Prevailing Wind Speed (mph)	16	17	17	13	13	12	12	12	12	10	15	16	14
Maximum Wind Gust (mph)	59	60	68	61	71	56	54	68	60	62	67	61	71

New York Laguardia Airport

New York City, in area exceeding 300 square miles, is located on the Atlantic coastal plain at the mouth of the Hudson River. The terrain is laced with numerous waterways, all but one of the five boroughs in the city are situated on islands. Elevations range from less than 50 feet over most of Manhattan, Brooklyn, and Queens to almost 300 feet in northern Manhattan and the Bronx, and over 400 feet in Staten Island.

The New York Metropolitan area is close to the path of most storm and frontal systems which move across the North American continent. Therefore, weather conditions affecting the city most often approach from a westerly direction, resulting in higher temperatures in summer and lower ones in winter than would otherwise be expected in a coastal area. However, the frequent passage of weather systems often helps reduce the length of extremes.

Although continental influence predominates, oceanic influence is by no means absent. During the summer local sea breezes, winds blowing onshore from the cool water surface, often moderate the afternoon heat. The effect of the sea breeze diminishes inland. On winter mornings, ocean temperatures which are warm relative to the land reinforce the effect of the city heat island and low temperatures are often 10-20 degrees lower in the inland suburbs than in the central city. The relatively warm water temperatures also delay the advent of winter snows. Conversely, the lag in warming of water temperatures keeps spring temperatures relatively cool.

Precipitation is moderate and distributed fairly evenly throughout the year. Most of the rainfall from May through October comes from thunderstorms, usually of brief duration and sometimes intense. Heavy rains of long duration associated with tropical storms occur infrequently in late summer or fall. For the other seasons precipitation is associated with widespread storm areas, producing day-long rain or snow. Coastal storms, occurring most often in the fall and winter months, produce on occasion considerable amounts of precipitation, record rains, snows, and high winds.

The average annual precipitation is reasonably uniform within the city but higher in the suburbs and less on eastern Long Island. Annual snowfall totals also show a consistent increase to the north and west of the city with lesser amounts along the south shores and the eastern end of Long Island.

Local Climatological Data is published for three locations in New York City, Central Park, La Guardia Airport, and John°F. Kennedy International Airport.

Based on the 1951-1980 period, the average first occurrence of 32 degrees Fahrenheit in the fall is November 11 and the average last occurrence in the spring is April 1.

New York Laguardia Airport Queens County   Elevation: 9 ft.   Latitude: 40° 47' N   Longitude: 73° 53' W

	JAN	FEB	MAR	APR	MAY	JUN	JUL	AUG	SEP	OCT	NOV	DEC	YEAR
Mean Maximum Temp. (°F)	38.2	40.8	49.0	59.9	70.5	79.2	84.7	82.9	75.3	64.3	53.7	43.7	61.8
Mean Temp. (°F)	32.3	34.5	41.9	52.1	62.4	71.5	77.2	75.9	68.5	57.6	47.7	38.0	55.0
Mean Minimum Temp. (°F)	26.3	28.1	34.8	44.4	54.3	63.7	69.6	68.8	61.6	50.9	41.7	32.2	48.0
Extreme Maximum Temp. (°F)	66	73	83	91	97	99	103	99	96	87	80	75	103
Extreme Minimum Temp. (°F)	-3	0	8	22	38	46	56	51	44	32	18	-1	-3
Days Maximum Temp. ≥ 90°F	0	0	0	0	1	3	6	4	1	0	0	0	15
Days Maximum Temp. ≤ 32°F	9	6	1	0	0	0	0	0	0	0	0	4	20
Days Minimum Temp. ≤ 32°F	22	18	10	1	0	0	0	0	0	0	3	14	68
Days Minimum Temp. ≤ 0°F	0	0	0	0	0	0	0	0	0	0	0	0	0
Heating Degree Days (base 65°F)	1,007	855	710	386	130	14	1	1	37	241	514	830	4,726
Cooling Degree Days (base 65°F)	0	0	1	4	63	231	399	352	156	21	1	0	1,228
Mean Precipitation (in.)	3.49	2.81	3.93	3.64	4.08	3.50	4.24	4.04	3.67	3.29	3.72	3.45	43.86
Maximum Precipitation (in.)	8.7	5.7	8.7	11.5	9.3	8.1	12.3	16.0	9.6	7.3	9.9	7.7	60.8
Minimum Precipitation (in.)	0.5	0.7	0.9	1.0	0.4	trace	0.7	0.1	1.0	0.1	0.3	0.3	22.2
Maximum 24-hr. Precipitation (in.)	3.1	2.2	3.1	2.8	2.8	4.0	3.5	6.4	3.6	3.4	4.4	2.7	6.4
Days With ≥ 0.1" Precipitation	7	6	7	6	7	6	6	6	6	5	6	7	75
Days With ≥ 1.0" Precipitation	1	1	1	1	1	1	1	1	1	1	1	1	12
Mean Snowfall (in.)	7.4	7.9	3.8	0.4	trace	0.0	trace	0.0	0.0	trace	0.4	2.7	22.6
Maximum Snowfall (in.)	18	26	19	8	trace	0	0	0	0	1	6	22	60
Maximum 24-hr. Snowfall (in.)	11	17	14	8	trace	0	0	0	0	1	6	16	17
Days With ≥ 1.0" Snow Depth	8	6	2	0	0	0	0	0	0	0	0	2	18
Thunderstorm Days	< 1	< 1	1	2	3	4	5	5	2	1	< 1	< 1	23
Foggy Days	10	9	10	10	11	9	8	8	8	8	9	10	110
Predominant Sky Cover	OVR	OVR	OVR	OVR	OVR	OVR	SCT	SCT	OVR	OVR	OVR	OVR	OVR
Mean Relative Humidity 7am (%)	67	67	67	67	71	71	73	75	76	74	71	68	71
Mean Relative Humidity 4pm (%)	57	55	52	51	53	53	54	56	56	55	57	59	55
Mean Dewpoint (°F)	20	21	27	36	48	57	63	62	56	45	35	25	41
Prevailing Wind Direction	NW	WNW	NW	NW	S	S	S	S	S	SW	WNW	WNW	NW
Prevailing Wind Speed (mph)	17	17	17	16	12	12	12	12	10	12	15	16	14
Maximum Wind Gust (mph)	61	67	71	63	56	56	59	73	64	71	76	77	77

Rochester Int'l Airport

Rochester is located at the mouth of the Genesee River at about the mid point of the south shore of Lake Ontario. The river flows northward from northwest Pennsylvania and empties into Lake Ontario. The land slopes from a lakeshore elevation of 246 feet to over 1,000 feet some 20 miles south. The airport is located just south of the city.

Lake Ontario plays a major role in the Rochester weather. In the summer its cooling effect inhibits the temperature from rising much above the low to mid 90s. In the winter the modifying temperature effect prevents temperatures from falling below -15 degrees most of the time, although temperatures at locations more than 15 miles inland do drop below -30 degrees.

The lake plays a major role in winter snowfall distribution. Well inland from the lake and toward the airport, the seasonal snowfall is usually less than in the area north of the airport and toward the lakeshore where wide variations occur. This is due to what is called the lake effect. Snowfalls of one to two feet or more in 24 hours are common near the lake in winter due the lake effect alone. The lake rarely freezes over because of its depth. The area is also prone to other heavy snowstorms and blizzards because of its proximity to the paths of low pressure systems coming up the east coast, out of the Ohio Valley.

Precipitation is rather evenly distributed throughout the year. Excessive rains occur infrequently but may be caused by slowly moving thunderstorms, slowly moving or stalled major low pressure systems, or by hurricanes and tropical storms that move inland. Hail occurs occasionally and heavy fog is rare.

The growing season averages 150 to 180 days. The years first frost usually occurs in late September and the last frost typically occurs in mid-May.

Rochester Int'l Airport Monroe County   Elevation: 597 ft.   Latitude: 43° 07' N   Longitude: 77° 41' W

	JAN	FEB	MAR	APR	MAY	JUN	JUL	AUG	SEP	OCT	NOV	DEC	YEAR
Mean Maximum Temp. (°F)	31.3	33.3	42.6	55.8	68.4	77.3	82.1	79.7	71.7	60.2	47.7	36.6	57.2
Mean Temp. (°F)	24.1	25.4	34.0	45.9	57.6	66.5	71.5	69.5	61.7	50.9	40.4	29.9	48.1
Mean Minimum Temp. (°F)	16.8	17.5	25.4	36.0	46.7	55.7	60.9	59.2	51.7	41.5	33.0	23.1	39.0
Extreme Maximum Temp. (°F)	68	73	83	93	94	95	98	95	95	86	79	72	98
Extreme Minimum Temp. (°F)	-17	-19	-7	13	26	36	45	38	30	20	5	-12	-19
Days Maximum Temp. ≥ 90°F	0	0	0	0	0	1	4	2	0	0	0	0	7
Days Maximum Temp. ≤ 32°F	17	14	6	1	0	0	0	0	0	0	2	10	50
Days Minimum Temp. ≤ 32°F	28	25	23	11	1	0	0	0	0	4	15	25	132
Days Minimum Temp. ≤ 0°F	3	2	0	0	0	0	0	0	0	0	0	1	6
Heating Degree Days (base 65°F)	1,263	1,111	954	572	258	62	9	22	148	437	732	1,081	6,649
Cooling Degree Days (base 65°F)	0	0	1	4	31	106	211	164	52	4	0	0	573
Mean Precipitation (in.)	2.30	2.05	2.56	2.69	2.77	3.34	2.97	3.53	3.41	2.69	2.88	2.79	33.98
Maximum Precipitation (in.)	5.8	5.1	5.0	4.1	6.6	6.8	6.0	6.0	6.3	7.8	7.0	4.6	40.5
Minimum Precipitation (in.)	0.7	0.7	0.5	1.2	0.4	0.2	0.6	0.8	0.3	0.2	0.4	0.6	22.4
Maximum 24-hr. Precipitation (in.)	1.3	1.8	1.5	1.8	3.4	2.6	3.3	2.3	3.5	2.9	2.0	1.5	3.5
Days With ≥ 0.1" Precipitation	7	6	7	7	7	7	6	7	7	6	7	8	82
Days With ≥ 1.0" Precipitation	0	0	0	0	0	1	1	1	1	0	0	0	4
Mean Snowfall (in.)	25.7	22.1	16.3	4.9	0.5	trace	trace	0.0	trace	0.1	8.0	21.9	99.5
Maximum Snowfall (in.)	60	65	40	20	11	0	0	0	trace	3	23	46	152
Maximum 24-hr. Snowfall (in.)	18	18	18	10	11	0	0	0	trace	3	12	18	18
Days With ≥ 1.0" Snow Depth	22	21	13	2	0	0	0	0	0	0	4	15	77
Thunderstorm Days	< 1	< 1	1	2	3	5	6	6	3	1	< 1	< 1	27
Foggy Days	8	9	10	10	10	10	11	13	12	11	11	10	125
Predominant Sky Cover	OVR	OVR	OVR	OVR	OVR	OVR	SCT	OVR	OVR	OVR	OVR	OVR	OVR
Mean Relative Humidity 7am (%)	79	80	80	78	77	79	82	86	88	85	82	81	81
Mean Relative Humidity 4pm (%)	71	69	63	56	53	53	52	55	59	60	69	73	61
Mean Dewpoint (°F)	18	18	25	35	45	55	60	59	53	42	33	23	39
Prevailing Wind Direction	WSW	WSW	WSW	WSW	WSW	WSW	SW	SW	SW	WSW	WSW	WSW	WSW
Prevailing Wind Speed (mph)	16	15	15	14	13	12	8	8	8	12	14	14	13
Maximum Wind Gust (mph)	63	70	68	71	64	52	56	62	51	60	67	55	71

Syracuse Hancock Int'l Airport

Syracuse is located approximately at the geographical center of the state. Gently rolling terrain stretches northward for about 30 miles to the eastern end of Lake Ontario. Oneida Lake is about 8 miles northeast of Syracuse. Approximately five miles south of the city, hills rise to 1,500 feet. Immediately to the west, the terrain is gently rolling with elevations 500 to 800 feet above sea level.

The climate of Syracuse is primarily continental in character and comparatively humid. Nearly all cyclonic systems moving from the interior of the country through the St. Lawrence Valley will affect the Syracuse area. Seasonal and diurnal changes are marked and produce an invigorating climate.

In the summer and in portions of the transitional seasons, temperatures usually rise rapidly during the daytime to moderate levels and as a rule fall rapidly after sunset. The nights are relatively cool and comfortable. There are only a few days in a year when atmospheric humidity causes great personal discomfort.

Winters are usually cold and are sometimes severe in part. Daytime temperatures average in the low 30s with nighttime lows in the teens. Low winter temperatures below -25 degrees have been recorded. The autumn, winter, and spring seasons display marked variability.

Based on the 1951-1980 period, the average first occurrence of 32 degrees Fahrenheit in the fall is October 16 and the average last occurrence in the spring is April 28.

Precipitation in the Syracuse area is derived principally from cyclonic storms which pass from the interior of the country through the St. Lawrence Valley. Lake Ontario provides the source of significant winter precipitation. The lake is quite deep and never freezes so cold air flowing over the lake is quickly saturated and produces the cloudiness and snow squalls which are a well-known feature of winter weather in the Syracuse area.

The precipitation is uncommonly well distributed, averaging about 3 inches per month throughout the year. Snowfall is moderately heavy with an average just over 100 inches. There are about 30 days per year with thunderstorms.

Wind velocities are moderate, but during the winter months there are numerous days with sufficient winds to cause blowing and drifting snow.

During December, January, and February there is much cloudiness. Syracuse receives only about one-third of possible sunshine during winter months. Approximately two-thirds of possible sunshine is received during the warm months.

Syracuse Hancock Int'l Airport *Onondaga Co.*   Elevation: 410 ft.   Latitude: 43° 07' N   Longitude: 76° 06' W

	JAN	FEB	MAR	APR	MAY	JUN	JUL	AUG	SEP	OCT	NOV	DEC	YEAR
Mean Maximum Temp. (°F)	31.1	33.4	42.9	56.3	68.9	77.2	81.9	79.6	71.3	59.8	47.6	36.4	57.2
Mean Temp. (°F)	23.1	25.0	34.0	46.1	57.8	66.2	71.2	69.3	61.4	50.4	40.2	29.2	47.8
Mean Minimum Temp. (°F)	15.0	16.4	25.1	35.9	46.5	55.1	60.5	58.9	51.3	40.9	32.7	21.9	38.4
Extreme Maximum Temp. (°F)	69	69	87	92	96	97	97	97	93	84	76	70	97
Extreme Minimum Temp. (°F)	-25	-26	-15	9	27	36	45	42	28	19	5	-22	-26
Days Maximum Temp. ≥ 90°F	0	0	0	0	0	2	4	2	0	0	0	0	8
Days Maximum Temp. ≤ 32°F	17	13	6	0	0	0	0	0	0	0	2	10	48
Days Minimum Temp. ≤ 32°F	28	25	24	11	1	0	0	0	0	5	15	26	135
Days Minimum Temp. ≤ 0°F	4	3	1	0	0	0	0	0	0	0	0	1	9
Heating Degree Days (base 65°F)	1,294	1,124	954	564	248	65	8	23	153	450	739	1,104	6,726
Cooling Degree Days (base 65°F)	0	0	1	4	29	109	215	167	50	3	0	0	578
Mean Precipitation (in.)	2.54	2.10	3.02	3.37	3.33	3.66	4.07	3.61	4.19	3.26	3.79	3.15	40.09
Maximum Precipitation (in.)	5.8	5.4	6.8	8.1	7.4	12.3	9.5	8.4	8.8	8.3	6.8	5.5	57.9
Minimum Precipitation (in.)	1.0	0.6	1.0	1.2	0.8	1.0	0.9	1.3	0.8	0.2	1.3	0.8	27.1
Maximum 24-hr. Precipitation (in.)	1.4	1.9	1.3	2.4	2.4	3.6	3.9	3.0	2.5	3.5	2.1	1.8	3.9
Days With ≥ 0.1" Precipitation	7	6	8	8	8	8	7	7	8	8	9	9	93
Days With ≥ 1.0" Precipitation	0	0	0	1	0	1	1	1	1	1	0	0	6
Mean Snowfall (in.)	33.0	24.0	19.0	4.8	0.2	trace	trace	0.0	trace	0.5	10.7	28.0	120.2
Maximum Snowfall (in.)	72	73	54	16	2	0	0	trace	trace	6	34	65	208
Maximum 24-hr. Snowfall (in.)	22	21	22	7	2	0	0	trace	trace	3	12	16	22
Days With ≥ 1.0" Snow Depth	24	21	14	2	0	0	0	0	0	0	5	16	82
Thunderstorm Days	< 1	< 1	1	2	3	5	6	5	3	1	1	< 1	27
Foggy Days	10	9	11	10	11	11	12	13	14	12	12	11	136
Predominant Sky Cover	OVR	OVR	OVR	OVR	OVR	OVR	OVR	OVR	OVR	OVR	OVR	OVR	OVR
Mean Relative Humidity 7am (%)	77	78	78	76	76	77	79	85	86	84	80	79	80
Mean Relative Humidity 4pm (%)	69	67	60	52	53	54	54	57	60	60	68	72	60
Mean Dewpoint (°F)	16	17	24	34	45	55	60	59	53	42	32	22	38
Prevailing Wind Direction	WSW	WSW	WNW	WNW	WNW	WNW	WSW	WSW	WSW	WSW	WSW	WSW	WSW
Prevailing Wind Speed (mph)	15	14	14	14	12	12	9	9	9	10	13	14	12
Maximum Wind Gust (mph)	58	56	61	63	76	67	66	49	48	60	58	63	76

PROFILES OF NEW YORK / Weather: Cooperative Stations

Albion 2 NE *Orleans County*   Elevation: 439 ft.   Latitude: 43° 17' N   Longitude: 78° 10' W

	JAN	FEB	MAR	APR	MAY	JUN	JUL	AUG	SEP	OCT	NOV	DEC	YEAR
Mean Maximum Temp. (°F)	31.2	33.6	42.9	56.0	68.8	77.9	82.5	80.3	72.6	60.8	47.8	37.0	57.6
Mean Temp. (°F)	24.2	25.9	34.3	46.1	57.7	67.0	71.8	70.0	62.8	51.5	40.5	30.3	48.5
Mean Minimum Temp. (°F)	17.0	18.2	25.6	36.0	46.6	55.9	61.1	59.6	52.9	42.0	33.2	23.6	39.3
Extreme Maximum Temp. (°F)	67	74	80	90	91	96	101	97	92	84	74	75	101
Extreme Minimum Temp. (°F)	-15	-20	-5	9	28	35	45	39	32	22	8	-10	-20
Days Maximum Temp. ≥ 90°F	0	0	0	0	0	1	4	2	0	0	0	0	7
Days Maximum Temp. ≤ 32°F	17	13	6	1	0	0	0	0	0	0	2	9	48
Days Minimum Temp. ≤ 32°F	29	25	24	11	1	0	0	0	0	4	15	25	134
Days Minimum Temp. ≤ 0°F	2	2	0	0	0	0	0	0	0	0	0	0	4
Heating Degree Days (base 65°F)	1,260	1,097	945	567	252	57	7	18	126	418	730	1,069	6,546
Cooling Degree Days (base 65°F)	0	0	1	4	34	126	236	187	68	5	0	0	661
Mean Precipitation (in.)	2.63	2.07	2.78	3.06	2.94	3.54	2.59	3.08	3.75	2.88	3.23	3.16	35.71
Days With ≥ 0.1" Precipitation	7	6	7	8	7	7	6	7	7	7	9	9	87
Days With ≥ 1.0" Precipitation	0	0	0	0	0	1	0	1	1	0	0	0	3
Mean Snowfall (in.)	19.1	14.9	10.2	2.2	0.3	0.0	0.0	0.0	0.0	trace	5.8	15.1	67.6
Days With ≥ 1.0" Snow Depth	16	13	7	1	0	0	0	0	0	0	4	11	52

Alfred *Allegany County*   Elevation: 1,768 ft.   Latitude: 42° 16' N   Longitude: 77° 47' W

	JAN	FEB	MAR	APR	MAY	JUN	JUL	AUG	SEP	OCT	NOV	DEC	YEAR
Mean Maximum Temp. (°F)	30.6	33.9	43.5	55.8	68.0	75.7	79.6	77.8	70.3	59.4	46.4	36.1	56.4
Mean Temp. (°F)	21.2	23.4	32.2	43.5	54.7	62.9	67.1	65.5	58.5	47.7	37.3	27.5	45.1
Mean Minimum Temp. (°F)	11.8	12.9	21.1	31.1	41.4	50.0	54.6	53.1	46.6	35.9	28.2	19.0	33.8
Extreme Maximum Temp. (°F)	63	66	83	91	93	93	96	93	91	81	75	68	96
Extreme Minimum Temp. (°F)	-25	-26	-16	5	18	28	37	27	20	15	2	-21	-26
Days Maximum Temp. ≥ 90°F	0	0	0	0	0	1	1	0	0	0	0	0	2
Days Maximum Temp. ≤ 32°F	17	13	5	1	0	0	0	0	0	0	2	11	49
Days Minimum Temp. ≤ 32°F	29	27	26	17	6	0	0	0	2	11	21	28	167
Days Minimum Temp. ≤ 0°F	6	6	2	0	0	0	0	0	0	0	0	2	16
Heating Degree Days (base 65°F)	1,351	1,169	1,009	642	327	113	38	59	215	531	823	1,155	7,432
Cooling Degree Days (base 65°F)	0	0	0	1	14	57	110	76	23	0	0	0	281
Mean Precipitation (in.)	2.14	1.97	2.66	2.98	3.42	4.46	3.71	3.28	3.98	3.33	3.30	2.79	38.02
Days With ≥ 0.1" Precipitation	6	6	7	8	8	8	8	7	8	7	8	8	89
Days With ≥ 1.0" Precipitation	0	0	0	0	0	1	1	1	1	1	0	0	5
Mean Snowfall (in.)	20.2	16.7	14.5	4.2	0.4	0.0	0.0	0.0	0.0	0.5	8.6	18.3	83.4
Days With ≥ 1.0" Snow Depth	25	22	15	2	0	0	0	0	0	0	5	17	86

Allegany State Park *Cattaraugus County*   Elevation: 1,499 ft.   Latitude: 42° 06' N   Longitude: 78° 45' W

	JAN	FEB	MAR	APR	MAY	JUN	JUL	AUG	SEP	OCT	NOV	DEC	YEAR
Mean Maximum Temp. (°F)	30.1	32.7	41.7	54.5	66.6	74.8	78.5	76.7	69.0	58.1	45.6	34.9	55.3
Mean Temp. (°F)	21.3	22.8	31.1	42.8	53.5	62.0	66.1	64.7	57.6	47.1	37.3	27.2	44.5
Mean Minimum Temp. (°F)	12.4	12.9	20.4	31.0	40.4	49.2	53.7	52.7	46.1	36.0	28.9	19.5	33.6
Extreme Maximum Temp. (°F)	63	68	80	89	90	92	97	93	89	82	74	70	97
Extreme Minimum Temp. (°F)	-22	-25	-17	9	19	24	29	31	23	14	-1	-16	-25
Days Maximum Temp. ≥ 90°F	0	0	0	0	0	0	1	0	0	0	0	0	1
Days Maximum Temp. ≤ 32°F	18	15	7	1	0	0	0	0	0	0	3	12	56
Days Minimum Temp. ≤ 32°F	30	27	27	19	7	1	0	0	2	11	21	28	173
Days Minimum Temp. ≤ 0°F	5	5	2	0	0	0	0	0	0	0	0	2	14
Heating Degree Days (base 65°F)	1,349	1,185	1,045	662	360	131	53	72	238	548	825	1,165	7,633
Cooling Degree Days (base 65°F)	0	0	0	1	12	48	96	70	21	1	0	0	249
Mean Precipitation (in.)	3.03	2.48	3.29	3.47	3.88	4.88	4.31	4.13	4.50	3.81	4.06	3.67	45.51
Days With ≥ 0.1" Precipitation	9	8	9	9	9	10	8	8	9	10	10	11	110
Days With ≥ 1.0" Precipitation	0	0	0	0	1	1	1	1	1	1	0	0	6
Mean Snowfall (in.)	na	na	na	na	trace	0.0	0.0	0.0	0.0	0.1	na	na	na
Days With ≥ 1.0" Snow Depth	27	25	18	2	0	0	0	0	0	0	7	19	98

Angelica *Allegany County*   Elevation: 1,443 ft.   Latitude: 42° 18' N   Longitude: 77° 59' W

	JAN	FEB	MAR	APR	MAY	JUN	JUL	AUG	SEP	OCT	NOV	DEC	YEAR
Mean Maximum Temp. (°F)	31.2	33.8	43.1	55.8	68.0	75.5	79.6	77.5	70.5	59.7	46.8	36.2	56.5
Mean Temp. (°F)	22.0	23.3	32.0	43.3	54.3	62.4	66.8	65.2	58.4	47.8	37.9	27.8	45.1
Mean Minimum Temp. (°F)	12.7	12.8	20.7	30.8	40.5	49.3	54.0	52.8	46.3	35.9	29.0	19.4	33.7
Extreme Maximum Temp. (°F)	63	67	82	89	91	93	97	94	90	82	77	70	97
Extreme Minimum Temp. (°F)	-33	-30	-20	9	19	28	36	30	21	14	0	-20	-33
Days Maximum Temp. ≥ 90°F	0	0	0	0	0	1	1	0	0	0	0	0	2
Days Maximum Temp. ≤ 32°F	17	13	6	1	0	0	0	0	0	0	2	11	50
Days Minimum Temp. ≤ 32°F	29	26	26	18	8	1	0	0	2	12	20	28	170
Days Minimum Temp. ≤ 0°F	6	6	2	0	0	0	0	0	0	0	0	2	16
Heating Degree Days (base 65°F)	1,329	1,171	1,019	647	337	125	44	64	216	528	808	1,147	7,435
Cooling Degree Days (base 65°F)	0	0	0	1	10	48	98	69	22	1	0	0	249
Mean Precipitation (in.)	2.01	2.00	2.43	2.90	3.18	4.60	3.73	3.82	3.76	3.16	3.00	2.49	37.08
Days With ≥ 0.1" Precipitation	6	6	7	7	8	9	8	8	8	8	8	7	90
Days With ≥ 1.0" Precipitation	0	0	0	0	0	1	1	1	1	1	0	0	5
Mean Snowfall (in.)	15.1	11.3	10.1	3.0	0.2	0.0	0.0	0.0	0.0	0.3	5.7	13.4	59.1
Days With ≥ 1.0" Snow Depth	24	21	13	2	0	0	0	0	0	0	5	16	81

PROFILES OF NEW YORK / Weather: Cooperative Stations

Aurora Research Farm *Cayuga County* Elevation: 830 ft. Latitude: 42° 44' N Longitude: 76° 39' W

	JAN	FEB	MAR	APR	MAY	JUN	JUL	AUG	SEP	OCT	NOV	DEC	YEAR
Mean Maximum Temp. (°F)	31.0	33.0	41.9	54.9	67.5	76.2	81.2	79.5	71.7	59.8	47.5	36.7	56.7
Mean Temp. (°F)	23.3	24.9	33.3	45.3	57.0	65.9	70.7	69.0	61.6	50.4	40.1	29.6	47.6
Mean Minimum Temp. (°F)	15.6	16.6	24.8	35.6	46.4	55.6	60.1	58.5	51.4	40.9	32.6	22.5	38.4
Extreme Maximum Temp. (°F)	67	67	85	93	94	96	101	97	98	85	81	69	101
Extreme Minimum Temp. (°F)	-21	-19	-11	10	25	34	43	40	27	20	5	-15	-21
Days Maximum Temp. ≥ 90°F	0	0	0	0	1	1	4	2	1	0	0	0	9
Days Maximum Temp. ≤ 32°F	17	13	7	1	0	0	0	0	0	0	2	10	50
Days Minimum Temp. ≤ 32°F	29	26	24	12	1	0	0	0	0	5	15	26	138
Days Minimum Temp. ≤ 0°F	3	2	0	0	0	0	0	0	0	0	0	1	6
Heating Degree Days (base 65°F)	1,285	1,128	975	591	277	76	18	30	152	451	740	1,090	6,813
Cooling Degree Days (base 65°F)	0	0	1	6	35	115	210	168	61	5	0	0	601
Mean Precipitation (in.)	1.87	1.87	2.50	3.22	3.20	4.16	3.40	3.65	4.25	3.26	3.43	2.52	37.33
Days With ≥ 0.1" Precipitation	5	5	7	8	8	8	8	7	8	7	8	6	85
Days With ≥ 1.0" Precipitation	0	0	0	0	1	0	1	1	1	0	0	0	4
Mean Snowfall (in.)	14.0	12.1	11.3	4.3	0.4	0.0	0.0	0.0	0.0	0.4	5.9	13.4	61.8
Days With ≥ 1.0" Snow Depth	23	21	13	3	0	0	0	0	0	0	0	5	15	80

Batavia *Genesee County* Elevation: 898 ft. Latitude: 43° 00' N Longitude: 78° 11' W

	JAN	FEB	MAR	APR	MAY	JUN	JUL	AUG	SEP	OCT	NOV	DEC	YEAR
Mean Maximum Temp. (°F)	31.7	34.0	43.7	56.6	68.9	77.7	81.7	79.5	72.2	61.2	48.2	36.8	57.7
Mean Temp. (°F)	23.9	25.3	34.3	46.1	57.8	66.7	71.1	69.1	62.0	51.2	40.3	29.5	48.1
Mean Minimum Temp. (°F)	16.0	16.5	24.8	35.5	46.6	55.7	60.5	58.6	51.8	41.1	32.5	22.2	38.5
Extreme Maximum Temp. (°F)	64	72	81	92	92	95	96	95	93	83	76	73	96
Extreme Minimum Temp. (°F)	-22	-25	-15	6	24	32	45	33	29	20	2	-18	-25
Days Maximum Temp. ≥ 90°F	0	0	0	0	0	1	2	1	0	0	0	0	4
Days Maximum Temp. ≤ 32°F	16	13	6	0	0	0	0	0	0	0	2	10	47
Days Minimum Temp. ≤ 32°F	29	26	24	12	1	0	0	0	0	5	16	26	139
Days Minimum Temp. ≤ 0°F	3	3	1	0	0	0	0	0	0	0	0	1	8
Heating Degree Days (base 65°F)	1,270	1,115	946	566	250	59	9	25	140	427	733	1,092	6,632
Cooling Degree Days (base 65°F)	0	0	1	5	32	118	211	158	56	5	0	0	586
Mean Precipitation (in.)	1.92	1.88	2.30	3.01	3.31	3.90	3.31	3.60	4.01	3.10	2.80	2.41	35.55
Days With ≥ 0.1" Precipitation	5	5	6	7	8	8	6	7	8	8	7	7	82
Days With ≥ 1.0" Precipitation	0	0	0	0	0	1	1	1	1	1	0	0	5
Mean Snowfall (in.)	21.3	17.1	12.6	3.9	0.4	0.0	0.0	0.0	0.0	0.2	6.8	20.0	82.3
Days With ≥ 1.0" Snow Depth	20	17	9	2	0	0	0	0	0	0	3	15	66

Bath *Steuben County* Elevation: 1,118 ft. Latitude: 42° 21' N Longitude: 77° 21' W

	JAN	FEB	MAR	APR	MAY	JUN	JUL	AUG	SEP	OCT	NOV	DEC	YEAR
Mean Maximum Temp. (°F)	32.1	34.0	42.7	55.9	68.1	76.5	81.0	79.2	71.8	60.1	46.8	36.4	57.0
Mean Temp. (°F)	22.7	23.6	32.0	44.0	54.9	63.5	68.1	66.3	59.1	48.1	38.0	28.0	45.7
Mean Minimum Temp. (°F)	12.9	13.1	21.2	32.1	41.7	50.5	55.2	53.4	46.5	35.9	29.0	19.5	34.2
Extreme Maximum Temp. (°F)	64	69	84	90	94	93	101	96	92	85	77	70	101
Extreme Minimum Temp. (°F)	-24	-25	-18	8	23	28	39	28	24	15	1	-16	-25
Days Maximum Temp. ≥ 90°F	0	0	0	0	0	1	3	1	0	0	0	0	5
Days Maximum Temp. ≤ 32°F	16	13	6	0	0	0	0	0	0	0	2	10	47
Days Minimum Temp. ≤ 32°F	29	27	26	17	5	0	0	0	2	12	20	28	166
Days Minimum Temp. ≤ 0°F	5	5	1	0	0	0	0	0	0	0	0	2	13
Heating Degree Days (base 65°F)	1,297	1,163	1,016	624	318	105	33	52	203	518	805	1,142	7,276
Cooling Degree Days (base 65°F)	0	0	0	2	14	68	137	95	29	1	0	0	346
Mean Precipitation (in.)	1.77	1.67	2.22	2.72	2.80	3.78	3.24	2.68	3.44	2.64	2.84	2.16	31.96
Days With ≥ 0.1" Precipitation	4	4	6	7	7	7	7	6	7	6	7	5	73
Days With ≥ 1.0" Precipitation	0	0	0	0	0	1	1	1	1	1	0	0	5
Mean Snowfall (in.)	11.3	10.9	9.2	1.7	trace	trace	0.0	0.0	0.0	trace	3.8	9.8	46.7
Days With ≥ 1.0" Snow Depth	21	21	12	2	0	0	0	0	0	0	4	14	74

Bolivar *Allegany County* Elevation: 1,578 ft. Latitude: 42° 05' N Longitude: 78° 11' W

	JAN	FEB	MAR	APR	MAY	JUN	JUL	AUG	SEP	OCT	NOV	DEC	YEAR
Mean Maximum Temp. (°F)	30.4	33.4	42.5	55.0	66.9	74.6	78.6	77.0	69.4	58.8	46.0	35.3	55.7
Mean Temp. (°F)	20.6	22.5	31.6	43.0	53.7	61.8	66.2	64.8	57.5	46.7	37.0	26.7	44.3
Mean Minimum Temp. (°F)	10.7	11.6	20.7	31.0	40.5	48.9	53.7	52.6	45.7	34.5	28.0	18.0	33.0
Extreme Maximum Temp. (°F)	62	65	82	88	92	91	97	93	88	82	76	68	97
Extreme Minimum Temp. (°F)	-34	-32	-20	8	19	26	35	31	23	12	0	-25	-34
Days Maximum Temp. ≥ 90°F	0	0	0	0	0	0	1	1	0	0	0	0	2
Days Maximum Temp. ≤ 32°F	18	14	6	1	0	0	0	0	0	0	3	12	54
Days Minimum Temp. ≤ 32°F	30	27	27	18	8	1	0	0	2	14	22	28	177
Days Minimum Temp. ≤ 0°F	7	6	2	0	0	0	0	0	0	0	0	3	18
Heating Degree Days (base 65°F)	1,370	1,193	1,029	654	356	138	55	70	237	562	833	1,181	7,678
Cooling Degree Days (base 65°F)	0	0	0	0	12	52	104	75	18	1	0	0	263
Mean Precipitation (in.)	2.27	1.87	2.73	3.07	3.37	4.95	4.41	3.77	4.15	3.20	3.23	2.82	39.84
Days With ≥ 0.1" Precipitation	6	6	8	8	8	9	9	8	8	8	8	8	94
Days With ≥ 1.0" Precipitation	0	0	0	0	1	1	1	1	1	1	0	0	6
Mean Snowfall (in.)	19.3	14.7	12.4	2.9	0.2	trace	0.0	0.0	0.0	0.5	7.5	18.9	76.4
Days With ≥ 1.0" Snow Depth	26	24	16	3	0	0	0	0	0	0	7	20	96

PROFILES OF NEW YORK / Weather: Cooperative Stations

Boonville 2 SSW Oneida County   Elevation: 1,578 ft.   Latitude: 43° 27' N   Longitude: 75° 21' W

	JAN	FEB	MAR	APR	MAY	JUN	JUL	AUG	SEP	OCT	NOV	DEC	YEAR
Mean Maximum Temp. (°F)	24.4	27.3	36.1	49.8	63.6	71.5	75.9	74.1	65.6	54.2	41.1	29.7	51.1
Mean Temp. (°F)	16.0	18.5	27.7	40.6	53.5	61.6	66.2	64.5	56.4	45.4	34.1	22.3	42.2
Mean Minimum Temp. (°F)	7.6	9.7	19.2	31.4	43.3	51.5	56.4	55.0	47.2	36.6	27.1	14.9	33.3
Extreme Maximum Temp. (°F)	57	55	77	85	87	89	94	93	89	79	69	62	94
Extreme Minimum Temp. (°F)	-31	-24	-18	-1	22	29	33	35	25	14	1	-33	-33
Days Maximum Temp. ≥ 90°F	0	0	0	0	0	0	0	0	0	0	0	0	0
Days Maximum Temp. ≤ 32°F	24	19	12	2	0	0	0	0	0	0	6	19	82
Days Minimum Temp. ≤ 32°F	30	27	28	18	3	0	0	0	1	11	22	29	169
Days Minimum Temp. ≤ 0°F	10	8	2	0	0	0	0	0	0	0	0	4	24
Heating Degree Days (base 65°F)	1,513	1,307	1,151	725	362	141	50	76	269	601	919	1,318	8,432
Cooling Degree Days (base 65°F)	0	0	0	1	10	43	93	67	15	0	0	0	229
Mean Precipitation (in.)	5.68	4.37	5.00	4.56	4.38	4.77	4.06	4.58	5.98	4.78	5.82	5.85	59.83
Days With ≥ 0.1" Precipitation	13	10	11	9	9	9	8	8	9	10	12	13	121
Days With ≥ 1.0" Precipitation	1	1	1	1	1	1	1	1	2	1	1	1	13
Mean Snowfall (in.)	59.3	42.8	34.7	10.2	0.9	trace	0.0	0.0	trace	2.2	21.2	47.3	218.6
Days With ≥ 1.0" Snow Depth	30	28	30	14	1	0	0	0	0	1	13	27	144

Bridgehampton Suffolk County   Elevation: 59 ft.   Latitude: 40° 57' N   Longitude: 72° 18' W

	JAN	FEB	MAR	APR	MAY	JUN	JUL	AUG	SEP	OCT	NOV	DEC	YEAR
Mean Maximum Temp. (°F)	38.4	39.4	46.4	55.6	65.4	74.4	80.7	79.7	72.9	62.9	53.1	43.7	59.4
Mean Temp. (°F)	30.6	31.9	38.5	47.1	56.7	65.8	72.1	71.2	64.1	53.7	44.9	35.9	51.1
Mean Minimum Temp. (°F)	22.9	24.4	30.5	38.6	47.8	57.2	63.5	62.7	55.3	44.5	36.7	28.1	42.7
Extreme Maximum Temp. (°F)	62	63	79	85	93	95	102	98	93	83	73	70	102
Extreme Minimum Temp. (°F)	-11	-5	6	14	29	39	48	41	35	24	10	-5	-11
Days Maximum Temp. ≥ 90°F	0	0	0	0	0	0	2	1	0	0	0	0	3
Days Maximum Temp. ≤ 32°F	8	6	1	0	0	0	0	0	0	0	0	3	18
Days Minimum Temp. ≤ 32°F	26	22	19	6	0	0	0	0	0	3	11	21	108
Days Minimum Temp. ≤ 0°F	0	0	0	0	0	0	0	0	0	0	0	0	0
Heating Degree Days (base 65°F)	1,058	928	816	530	262	53	4	8	87	348	597	895	5,586
Cooling Degree Days (base 65°F)	0	0	0	0	11	91	237	198	65	6	0	0	608
Mean Precipitation (in.)	4.56	3.82	4.50	4.27	3.76	3.61	3.07	3.93	3.87	3.73	4.45	4.31	47.88
Days With ≥ 0.1" Precipitation	7	6	8	7	7	6	5	5	5	6	7	8	77
Days With ≥ 1.0" Precipitation	1	1	1	1	1	1	1	1	1	1	1	1	12
Mean Snowfall (in.)	8.0	7.8	4.4	0.8	trace	0.0	0.0	0.0	0.0	trace	0.8	2.4	24.2
Days With ≥ 1.0" Snow Depth	9	7	3	0	0	0	0	0	0	0	0	2	21

Canandaigua 3 S Ontario County   Elevation: 718 ft.   Latitude: 42° 51' N   Longitude: 77° 17' W

	JAN	FEB	MAR	APR	MAY	JUN	JUL	AUG	SEP	OCT	NOV	DEC	YEAR
Mean Maximum Temp. (°F)	32.4	34.3	42.5	55.0	67.7	76.7	81.7	79.6	71.9	60.6	48.6	37.9	57.4
Mean Temp. (°F)	24.5	25.8	33.8	45.2	57.0	66.3	71.5	69.7	62.4	51.3	41.1	30.8	48.3
Mean Minimum Temp. (°F)	16.5	17.2	25.0	35.4	46.3	55.9	61.3	59.8	52.8	42.0	33.6	23.6	39.1
Extreme Maximum Temp. (°F)	66	67	85	88	93	94	98	96	95	85	80	71	98
Extreme Minimum Temp. (°F)	-14	-17	-4	12	27	37	45	42	33	23	9	-12	-17
Days Maximum Temp. ≥ 90°F	0	0	0	0	0	1	3	2	0	0	0	0	6
Days Maximum Temp. ≤ 32°F	16	13	6	1	0	0	0	0	0	0	2	9	47
Days Minimum Temp. ≤ 32°F	28	26	24	11	1	0	0	0	0	3	14	25	132
Days Minimum Temp. ≤ 0°F	2	2	0	0	0	0	0	0	0	0	0	0	4
Heating Degree Days (base 65°F)	1,250	1,100	961	589	270	65	10	23	134	422	710	1,055	6,589
Cooling Degree Days (base 65°F)	0	0	0	2	30	113	227	175	63	6	0	0	616
Mean Precipitation (in.)	1.76	1.65	2.37	3.01	2.87	3.92	3.15	3.18	3.56	2.96	2.90	2.24	33.57
Days With ≥ 0.1" Precipitation	5	5	6	7	8	8	7	7	7	7	7	6	80
Days With ≥ 1.0" Precipitation	0	0	0	0	0	1	0	1	1	0	0	0	3
Mean Snowfall (in.)	na	na	na	na	0.0	0.0	0.0	0.0	0.0	trace	na	na	na
Days With ≥ 1.0" Snow Depth	na	na	na	na	0	0	0	0	0	0	na	na	na

Canton 4 SE St. Lawrence County   Elevation: 396 ft.   Latitude: 44° 35' N   Longitude: 75° 07' W

	JAN	FEB	MAR	APR	MAY	JUN	JUL	AUG	SEP	OCT	NOV	DEC	YEAR
Mean Maximum Temp. (°F)	25.6	28.3	38.4	52.4	66.0	74.3	79.3	77.1	68.6	56.8	44.3	31.6	53.6
Mean Temp. (°F)	14.8	17.3	28.3	42.1	55.1	63.6	68.6	66.3	58.0	46.4	35.9	22.1	43.2
Mean Minimum Temp. (°F)	3.9	6.3	18.1	31.8	44.1	52.9	57.8	55.5	47.3	35.9	27.4	12.7	32.8
Extreme Maximum Temp. (°F)	66	65	92	89	90	92	93	97	91	82	77	68	97
Extreme Minimum Temp. (°F)	-40	-40	-26	-8	21	29	35	32	22	13	-4	-37	-40
Days Maximum Temp. ≥ 90°F	0	0	0	0	0	0	1	0	0	0	0	0	1
Days Maximum Temp. ≤ 32°F	21	17	10	1	0	0	0	0	0	0	4	15	68
Days Minimum Temp. ≤ 32°F	30	27	27	17	3	0	0	0	2	12	21	29	168
Days Minimum Temp. ≤ 0°F	13	11	3	0	0	0	0	0	0	0	0	7	34
Heating Degree Days (base 65°F)	1,552	1,342	1,131	682	321	109	36	67	236	572	868	1,323	8,239
Cooling Degree Days (base 65°F)	0	0	0	2	18	75	155	112	30	2	0	0	394
Mean Precipitation (in.)	2.34	2.01	2.40	2.89	2.98	3.28	3.56	3.99	4.19	3.35	3.43	2.73	37.15
Days With ≥ 0.1" Precipitation	6	5	6	7	8	7	7	8	9	8	8	7	86
Days With ≥ 1.0" Precipitation	0	0	0	0	0	1	1	1	1	1	1	0	6
Mean Snowfall (in.)	23.8	19.7	15.4	4.5	0.2	0.0	0.0	0.0	trace	0.4	6.9	20.0	90.9
Days With ≥ 1.0" Snow Depth	27	24	19	4	0	0	0	0	0	0	7	20	101

PROFILES OF NEW YORK / Weather: Cooperative Stations

Chasm Falls *Franklin County* Elevation: 1,059 ft. Latitude: 44° 45' N Longitude: 74° 13' W

	JAN	FEB	MAR	APR	MAY	JUN	JUL	AUG	SEP	OCT	NOV	DEC	YEAR
Mean Maximum Temp. (°F)	25.7	28.5	38.9	52.3	66.9	74.6	78.8	75.9	67.2	56.2	43.2	30.4	53.2
Mean Temp. (°F)	15.3	17.4	28.2	41.2	54.2	62.4	67.0	64.6	56.5	45.9	34.9	21.1	42.4
Mean Minimum Temp. (°F)	4.7	6.3	17.5	30.1	41.5	50.2	55.2	53.3	45.8	35.6	26.4	11.9	31.5
Extreme Maximum Temp. (°F)	61	64	75	87	90	93	95	95	88	81	72	64	95
Extreme Minimum Temp. (°F)	-36	-42	-24	-5	20	27	35	31	23	12	-5	-30	-42
Days Maximum Temp. ≥ 90°F	0	0	0	0	0	0	1	0	0	0	0	0	1
Days Maximum Temp. ≤ 32°F	21	18	9	1	0	0	0	0	0	0	5	17	71
Days Minimum Temp. ≤ 32°F	30	27	28	19	5	0	0	0	2	13	23	29	176
Days Minimum Temp. ≤ 0°F	12	11	4	0	0	0	0	0	0	0	0	7	34
Heating Degree Days (base 65°F)	1,536	1,338	1,134	710	342	127	45	83	266	585	898	1,352	8,416
Cooling Degree Days (base 65°F)	0	0	0	0	10	48	108	70	14	0	na	0	na
Mean Precipitation (in.)	2.69	2.54	2.85	2.97	3.32	4.04	4.28	5.55	4.38	3.55	3.79	3.47	43.43
Days With ≥ 0.1" Precipitation	9	7	9	9	9	9	9	10	9	9	10	9	108
Days With ≥ 1.0" Precipitation	0	0	0	0	0	1	1	1	1	1	1	0	6
Mean Snowfall (in.)	27.3	26.1	20.3	8.3	0.4	trace	0.0	0.0	0.0	0.8	11.9	26.1	121.2
Days With ≥ 1.0" Snow Depth	30	28	29	12	0	0	0	0	0	1	11	25	136

Chazy *Clinton County* Elevation: 167 ft. Latitude: 44° 53' N Longitude: 73° 26' W

	JAN	FEB	MAR	APR	MAY	JUN	JUL	AUG	SEP	OCT	NOV	DEC	YEAR
Mean Maximum Temp. (°F)	26.7	29.6	39.6	54.5	68.2	76.3	80.7	78.4	68.9	57.0	44.5	32.3	54.7
Mean Temp. (°F)	16.4	19.1	29.7	43.8	56.3	64.9	69.5	67.2	58.3	47.2	36.3	23.3	44.3
Mean Minimum Temp. (°F)	6.0	8.6	19.7	33.0	44.4	53.5	58.3	56.0	47.7	37.5	28.1	14.4	33.9
Extreme Maximum Temp. (°F)	61	60	79	90	94	97	97	100	93	85	74	66	100
Extreme Minimum Temp. (°F)	-44	-41	-22	6	25	30	38	32	22	14	-2	-28	-44
Days Maximum Temp. ≥ 90°F	0	0	0	0	0	1	2	1	0	0	0	0	4
Days Maximum Temp. ≤ 32°F	20	16	8	0	0	0	0	0	0	0	3	15	62
Days Minimum Temp. ≤ 32°F	30	27	26	15	2	0	0	0	1	10	20	28	159
Days Minimum Temp. ≤ 0°F	12	9	3	0	0	0	0	0	0	0	0	6	30
Heating Degree Days (base 65°F)	1,502	1,290	1,088	631	280	75	18	44	219	545	854	1,286	7,832
Cooling Degree Days (base 65°F)	0	0	0	2	14	80	165	117	26	1	0	0	405
Mean Precipitation (in.)	1.15	na	1.37	2.38	2.92	3.15	3.56	3.90	3.46	3.04	2.58	1.51	na
Days With ≥ 0.1" Precipitation	na	na	na	na	7	7	8	7	7	7	na	na	na
Days With ≥ 1.0" Precipitation	0	na	0	0	0	0	1	1	1	1	0	na	na
Mean Snowfall (in.)	14.0	11.0	9.1	2.9	0.1	0.0	0.0	0.0	0.0	0.3	5.8	12.8	56.0
Days With ≥ 1.0" Snow Depth	24	22	15	2	0	0	0	0	0	0	4	19	86

Cherry Valley 2 NNE *Otsego County* Elevation: 1,358 ft. Latitude: 42° 49' N Longitude: 74° 44' W

	JAN	FEB	MAR	APR	MAY	JUN	JUL	AUG	SEP	OCT	NOV	DEC	YEAR
Mean Maximum Temp. (°F)	27.7	30.4	39.9	53.3	66.3	74.0	78.2	76.1	68.1	57.0	44.6	32.9	54.0
Mean Temp. (°F)	19.3	21.7	30.8	43.1	55.2	63.4	68.0	66.1	58.6	47.7	37.0	25.3	44.7
Mean Minimum Temp. (°F)	10.9	12.8	21.7	33.0	44.2	52.7	57.6	56.1	49.0	38.3	29.4	17.7	35.3
Extreme Maximum Temp. (°F)	65	62	80	85	87	89	93	92	87	81	76	66	93
Extreme Minimum Temp. (°F)	-23	-26	-14	7	20	32	38	35	25	15	3	-25	-26
Days Maximum Temp. ≥ 90°F	0	0	0	0	0	0	0	0	0	0	0	0	0
Days Maximum Temp. ≤ 32°F	20	16	8	1	0	0	0	0	0	0	4	15	64
Days Minimum Temp. ≤ 32°F	30	27	27	16	2	0	0	0	1	9	19	29	160
Days Minimum Temp. ≤ 0°F	7	5	1	0	0	0	0	0	0	0	0	3	16
Heating Degree Days (base 65°F)	1,410	1,218	1,053	651	312	104	30	55	215	532	833	1,223	7,636
Cooling Degree Days (base 65°F)	0	0	0	1	14	60	129	93	28	1	0	0	326
Mean Precipitation (in.)	2.97	2.59	3.64	3.82	4.20	4.37	4.37	3.82	4.15	3.56	3.90	3.28	44.67
Days With ≥ 0.1" Precipitation	8	6	8	8	9	9	8	7	8	8	9	8	96
Days With ≥ 1.0" Precipitation	0	1	1	1	1	1	1	1	1	1	1	0	10
Mean Snowfall (in.)	29.9	19.0	21.7	6.6	0.9	0.0	0.0	0.0	trace	0.8	12.0	25.2	116.1
Days With ≥ 1.0" Snow Depth	22	21	15	4	0	0	0	0	0	0	6	17	85

Colden 1 N *Erie County* Elevation: 1,023 ft. Latitude: 42° 40' N Longitude: 78° 41' W

	JAN	FEB	MAR	APR	MAY	JUN	JUL	AUG	SEP	OCT	NOV	DEC	YEAR
Mean Maximum Temp. (°F)	30.0	32.5	41.4	54.3	66.9	75.1	79.1	77.3	69.9	58.9	46.4	35.4	55.6
Mean Temp. (°F)	21.5	22.8	31.3	43.3	54.6	63.2	67.5	66.1	58.9	48.3	38.3	28.0	45.3
Mean Minimum Temp. (°F)	13.0	13.1	21.1	32.2	42.2	51.3	56.0	54.7	47.9	37.6	30.1	20.6	35.0
Extreme Maximum Temp. (°F)	64	70	80	91	88	91	96	95	92	84	75	72	96
Extreme Minimum Temp. (°F)	-24	-30	-18	4	21	28	39	30	27	15	-3	-25	-30
Days Maximum Temp. ≥ 90°F	0	0	0	0	0	0	1	0	0	0	0	0	1
Days Maximum Temp. ≤ 32°F	18	14	8	1	0	0	0	0	0	0	3	12	56
Days Minimum Temp. ≤ 32°F	30	27	26	17	5	0	0	0	1	9	20	28	163
Days Minimum Temp. ≤ 0°F	6	5	2	0	0	0	0	0	0	0	0	2	15
Heating Degree Days (base 65°F)	1,342	1,185	1,038	648	333	112	35	54	208	513	794	1,141	7,403
Cooling Degree Days (base 65°F)	0	0	0	2	15	62	119	91	29	1	0	0	319
Mean Precipitation (in.)	3.73	2.80	3.55	3.73	3.60	4.22	4.13	4.20	4.92	4.00	4.81	4.51	48.20
Days With ≥ 0.1" Precipitation	11	9	10	9	9	8	8	8	9	10	11	12	114
Days With ≥ 1.0" Precipitation	0	0	0	1	0	1	1	1	1	1	1	1	8
Mean Snowfall (in.)	47.2	28.6	18.7	6.3	0.3	0.0	0.0	0.0	0.0	0.7	17.8	37.9	157.5
Days With ≥ 1.0" Snow Depth	28	25	19	3	0	0	0	0	0	0	7	21	103

Conklingville Dam *Saratoga County*   Elevation: 807 ft.   Latitude: 43° 19' N   Longitude: 73° 56' W

	JAN	FEB	MAR	APR	MAY	JUN	JUL	AUG	SEP	OCT	NOV	DEC	YEAR
Mean Maximum Temp. (°F)	29.0	32.7	41.6	54.3	66.9	74.5	79.0	76.8	68.8	57.6	45.8	33.6	55.0
Mean Temp. (°F)	18.7	21.6	31.3	43.6	55.7	63.9	68.6	66.8	58.8	47.6	37.5	25.1	44.9
Mean Minimum Temp. (°F)	8.3	10.4	20.9	32.9	44.4	53.2	58.2	56.7	48.7	37.6	29.3	16.5	34.8
Extreme Maximum Temp. (°F)	60	61	80	86	90	92	95	90	87	82	75	67	95
Extreme Minimum Temp. (°F)	-29	-30	-13	7	27	30	43	35	28	17	4	-22	-30
Days Maximum Temp. ≥ 90°F	0	0	0	0	0	0	1	0	0	0	0	0	1
Days Maximum Temp. ≤ 32°F	19	13	5	0	0	0	0	0	0	0	1	12	50
Days Minimum Temp. ≤ 32°F	30	27	27	15	2	0	0	0	0	8	20	29	158
Days Minimum Temp. ≤ 0°F	9	7	2	0	0	0	0	0	0	0	0	3	21
Heating Degree Days (base 65°F)	1,431	1,221	1,039	635	299	91	20	42	202	533	817	1,232	7,562
Cooling Degree Days (base 65°F)	0	0	0	0	14	64	141	105	23	1	0	0	348
Mean Precipitation (in.)	3.75	2.87	4.05	3.84	4.11	4.00	3.89	3.95	4.08	3.63	4.08	3.70	45.95
Days With ≥ 0.1" Precipitation	7	6	8	8	8	8	7	7	7	7	8	8	89
Days With ≥ 1.0" Precipitation	1	1	1	1	1	1	1	1	1	1	1	1	12
Mean Snowfall (in.)	21.5	14.5	14.8	3.0	0.1	0.0	0.0	0.0	0.0	trace	4.9	17.5	76.3
Days With ≥ 1.0" Snow Depth	26	26	22	3	0	0	0	0	0	0	4	20	101

Cooperstown *Otsego County*   Elevation: 1,197 ft.   Latitude: 42° 42' N   Longitude: 74° 55' W

	JAN	FEB	MAR	APR	MAY	JUN	JUL	AUG	SEP	OCT	NOV	DEC	YEAR
Mean Maximum Temp. (°F)	30.4	33.5	42.7	55.7	68.3	75.6	79.8	77.8	69.9	59.2	46.6	35.3	56.2
Mean Temp. (°F)	20.9	23.0	32.2	43.8	55.4	63.5	67.9	66.4	58.8	48.2	37.8	26.8	45.4
Mean Minimum Temp. (°F)	11.5	12.5	21.6	31.8	42.5	51.3	56.0	55.0	47.7	37.1	29.0	18.3	34.5
Extreme Maximum Temp. (°F)	64	64	87	90	90	92	97	92	90	83	79	66	97
Extreme Minimum Temp. (°F)	-29	-30	-18	6	22	30	37	33	25	12	2	-24	-30
Days Maximum Temp. ≥ 90°F	0	0	0	0	0	0	1	0	0	0	0	0	1
Days Maximum Temp. ≤ 32°F	18	13	5	0	0	0	0	0	0	0	3	12	51
Days Minimum Temp. ≤ 32°F	30	27	26	17	5	0	0	0	2	10	20	28	165
Days Minimum Temp. ≤ 0°F	7	6	2	0	0	0	0	0	0	0	0	3	18
Heating Degree Days (base 65°F)	1,360	1,179	1,011	631	303	100	30	47	208	516	810	1,178	7,373
Cooling Degree Days (base 65°F)	0	0	0	1	11	61	128	97	27	1	0	0	326
Mean Precipitation (in.)	2.89	2.27	3.29	3.53	3.59	4.24	3.84	3.69	4.00	3.22	3.43	3.03	41.02
Days With ≥ 0.1" Precipitation	7	6	8	8	8	8	7	7	8	8	8	8	91
Days With ≥ 1.0" Precipitation	0	0	1	1	1	1	1	1	1	1	1	0	9
Mean Snowfall (in.)	23.0	16.5	16.0	5.6	0.8	0.0	0.0	0.0	trace	0.2	7.2	18.2	87.5
Days With ≥ 1.0" Snow Depth	27	26	19	4	0	0	0	0	0	0	6	20	102

Cortland *Cortland County*   Elevation: 1,128 ft.   Latitude: 42° 36' N   Longitude: 76° 11' W

	JAN	FEB	MAR	APR	MAY	JUN	JUL	AUG	SEP	OCT	NOV	DEC	YEAR
Mean Maximum Temp. (°F)	30.2	32.5	41.3	54.1	67.4	76.0	80.7	79.1	70.3	58.9	46.0	35.2	56.0
Mean Temp. (°F)	22.6	24.0	32.6	44.3	56.4	65.1	69.8	68.0	59.8	49.2	38.8	28.5	46.6
Mean Minimum Temp. (°F)	15.0	15.5	23.8	34.4	45.3	54.1	58.9	56.9	49.2	39.5	31.6	21.7	37.2
Extreme Maximum Temp. (°F)	64	65	85	90	93	96	100	98	92	85	79	68	100
Extreme Minimum Temp. (°F)	-18	-18	-13	11	24	33	45	39	28	18	7	-17	-18
Days Maximum Temp. ≥ 90°F	0	0	0	0	1	1	3	2	0	0	0	0	7
Days Maximum Temp. ≤ 32°F	18	14	8	1	0	0	0	0	0	0	3	12	56
Days Minimum Temp. ≤ 32°F	29	25	24	14	2	0	0	0	0	7	16	26	143
Days Minimum Temp. ≤ 0°F	4	4	1	0	0	0	0	0	0	0	0	1	10
Heating Degree Days (base 65°F)	1,306	1,151	998	619	287	85	20	38	188	484	779	1,125	7,080
Cooling Degree Days (base 65°F)	0	0	1	3	26	103	190	144	40	2	0	0	509
Mean Precipitation (in.)	2.66	2.53	3.11	3.23	3.18	4.03	3.51	3.03	3.97	3.22	3.49	3.50	39.46
Days With ≥ 0.1" Precipitation	7	6	7	7	8	8	7	6	7	8	8	9	88
Days With ≥ 1.0" Precipitation	0	0	0	0	0	1	1	1	1	1	0	0	5
Mean Snowfall (in.)	22.4	19.1	15.1	4.0	trace	0.0	0.0	0.0	0.0	0.4	8.3	22.0	91.3
Days With ≥ 1.0" Snow Depth	26	24	16	3	0	0	0	0	0	0	6	18	93

Dannemora *Clinton County*   Elevation: 1,338 ft.   Latitude: 44° 43' N   Longitude: 73° 43' W

	JAN	FEB	MAR	APR	MAY	JUN	JUL	AUG	SEP	OCT	NOV	DEC	YEAR
Mean Maximum Temp. (°F)	25.8	29.1	38.7	52.0	66.3	74.5	79.0	76.4	67.7	56.0	42.1	30.8	53.2
Mean Temp. (°F)	16.6	19.8	29.5	42.4	55.5	64.0	68.8	66.4	57.8	46.8	34.7	22.6	43.7
Mean Minimum Temp. (°F)	7.4	10.5	20.3	32.8	44.6	53.5	58.5	56.3	47.9	37.6	27.4	14.3	34.3
Extreme Maximum Temp. (°F)	64	62	77	86	90	94	98	97	90	82	72	63	98
Extreme Minimum Temp. (°F)	-34	-25	-22	2	18	32	42	33	25	15	0	-28	-34
Days Maximum Temp. ≥ 90°F	0	0	0	0	0	1	1	0	0	0	0	0	2
Days Maximum Temp. ≤ 32°F	22	17	9	1	0	0	0	0	0	0	6	17	72
Days Minimum Temp. ≤ 32°F	30	27	27	15	2	0	0	0	1	10	21	29	162
Days Minimum Temp. ≤ 0°F	10	7	2	0	0	0	0	0	0	0	0	5	24
Heating Degree Days (base 65°F)	1,496	1,271	1,094	674	309	95	23	52	233	558	901	1,309	8,015
Cooling Degree Days (base 65°F)	0	0	0	2	16	71	140	93	22	1	0	0	345
Mean Precipitation (in.)	2.33	1.95	2.31	2.91	3.17	3.62	3.82	4.37	3.95	3.36	3.33	2.84	37.96
Days With ≥ 0.1" Precipitation	6	5	6	7	8	8	8	8	8	8	8	7	87
Days With ≥ 1.0" Precipitation	0	0	0	0	0	1	1	1	1	1	1	0	6
Mean Snowfall (in.)	na	na	na	3.6	trace	0.0	0.0	0.0	trace	0.2	na	na	na
Days With ≥ 1.0" Snow Depth	na	na	na	na	0	0	0	0	0	0	na	na	na

PROFILES OF NEW YORK / Weather: Cooperative Stations

Dansville Livingston County   Elevation: 659 ft.   Latitude: 42° 34' N   Longitude: 77° 43' W

	JAN	FEB	MAR	APR	MAY	JUN	JUL	AUG	SEP	OCT	NOV	DEC	YEAR
Mean Maximum Temp. (°F)	32.8	35.3	44.3	56.7	69.5	78.3	82.7	80.8	73.0	61.7	48.9	38.2	58.5
Mean Temp. (°F)	24.2	25.9	34.1	45.4	57.0	65.9	70.5	68.7	61.3	50.4	40.3	30.3	47.8
Mean Minimum Temp. (°F)	15.6	16.4	24.0	34.1	44.5	53.4	58.3	56.5	49.4	39.1	31.7	22.4	37.1
Extreme Maximum Temp. (°F)	68	71	85	91	94	95	100	96	94	85	80	73	100
Extreme Minimum Temp. (°F)	-22	-18	-8	12	22	30	41	33	28	16	7	-17	-22
Days Maximum Temp. ≥ 90°F	0	0	0	0	1	2	5	3	1	0	0	0	12
Days Maximum Temp. ≤ 32°F	16	12	5	1	0	0	0	0	0	0	1	9	44
Days Minimum Temp. ≤ 32°F	29	26	24	15	3	0	0	0	1	7	17	26	148
Days Minimum Temp. ≤ 0°F	4	3	1	0	0	0	0	0	0	0	0	1	9
Heating Degree Days (base 65°F)	1,257	1,097	950	587	272	76	17	33	161	449	733	1,067	6,699
Cooling Degree Days (base 65°F)	0	0	1	4	28	110	198	151	54	3	0	0	549
Mean Precipitation (in.)	1.50	1.34	1.85	2.57	2.91	3.66	3.21	3.36	3.56	2.78	2.62	2.04	31.40
Days With ≥ 0.1" Precipitation	4	4	5	7	8	8	7	7	7	7	6	6	76
Days With ≥ 1.0" Precipitation	0	0	0	0	0	1	1	1	1	1	0	0	5
Mean Snowfall (in.)	12.6	10.4	7.4	2.5	0.2	0.0	0.0	0.0	0.0	trace	3.6	10.5	47.2
Days With ≥ 1.0" Snow Depth	16	14	5	1	0	0	0	0	0	0	2	8	46

Deposit Delaware County   Elevation: 997 ft.   Latitude: 42° 04' N   Longitude: 75° 26' W

	JAN	FEB	MAR	APR	MAY	JUN	JUL	AUG	SEP	OCT	NOV	DEC	YEAR
Mean Maximum Temp. (°F)	31.5	35.2	44.8	58.3	70.3	77.0	80.7	79.2	71.1	60.5	47.7	36.0	57.7
Mean Temp. (°F)	22.2	24.8	33.9	45.7	56.8	64.7	68.9	67.7	60.2	49.2	38.9	27.8	46.7
Mean Minimum Temp. (°F)	12.9	14.3	23.0	33.0	43.3	52.3	57.1	56.1	49.3	37.9	30.0	19.6	35.7
Extreme Maximum Temp. (°F)	63	67	85	90	92	92	98	92	92	84	80	68	98
Extreme Minimum Temp. (°F)	-31	-25	-14	11	22	29	37	34	27	14	2	-19	-31
Days Maximum Temp. ≥ 90°F	0	0	0	0	0	1	2	1	0	0	0	0	4
Days Maximum Temp. ≤ 32°F	16	11	4	0	0	0	0	0	0	0	1	10	42
Days Minimum Temp. ≤ 32°F	29	26	25	15	4	0	0	0	1	10	19	28	157
Days Minimum Temp. ≤ 0°F	6	5	1	0	0	0	0	0	0	0	0	2	14
Heating Degree Days (base 65°F)	1,322	1,130	958	574	265	78	22	33	174	484	778	1,147	6,965
Cooling Degree Days (base 65°F)	0	0	0	1	15	72	151	117	35	2	0	0	393
Mean Precipitation (in.)	2.88	2.65	3.36	3.82	3.91	3.93	3.99	4.06	3.78	3.56	4.04	3.35	43.33
Days With ≥ 0.1" Precipitation	7	7	8	8	9	9	8	7	7	7	8	7	92
Days With ≥ 1.0" Precipitation	0	0	0	1	1	1	1	1	1	1	1	1	9
Mean Snowfall (in.)	17.0	11.4	na	3.2	trace	0.0	0.0	0.0	0.0	trace	4.2	na	na
Days With ≥ 1.0" Snow Depth	18	na	na	1	0	0	0	0	0	0	3	na	na

Dobbs Ferry Ardsley Westchester County   Elevation: 200 ft.   Latitude: 41° 00' N   Longitude: 73° 50' W

	JAN	FEB	MAR	APR	MAY	JUN	JUL	AUG	SEP	OCT	NOV	DEC	YEAR
Mean Maximum Temp. (°F)	37.9	41.2	50.1	61.9	72.6	80.4	85.6	83.6	75.8	64.6	53.7	42.8	62.5
Mean Temp. (°F)	30.4	32.9	40.9	51.2	61.5	69.9	75.3	73.8	66.2	55.1	45.5	35.6	53.2
Mean Minimum Temp. (°F)	22.9	24.4	31.5	40.5	50.5	59.3	64.9	63.8	56.5	45.6	37.3	28.3	43.8
Extreme Maximum Temp. (°F)	65	75	86	96	97	98	104	97	98	85	80	77	104
Extreme Minimum Temp. (°F)	-10	-3	4	17	29	40	49	44	34	27	12	-4	-10
Days Maximum Temp. ≥ 90°F	0	0	0	0	1	3	7	5	1	0	0	0	17
Days Maximum Temp. ≤ 32°F	10	6	1	0	0	0	0	0	0	0	0	4	21
Days Minimum Temp. ≤ 32°F	26	22	17	4	0	0	0	0	0	2	9	21	101
Days Minimum Temp. ≤ 0°F	1	0	0	0	0	0	0	0	0	0	0	0	1
Heating Degree Days (base 65°F)	1,066	901	742	413	149	22	1	3	66	310	580	906	5,159
Cooling Degree Days (base 65°F)	0	0	1	4	47	174	324	271	106	11	1	0	939
Mean Precipitation (in.)	4.30	3.45	4.55	4.50	4.85	3.81	4.38	4.25	4.68	4.16	4.58	4.23	51.74
Days With ≥ 0.1" Precipitation	7	6	7	7	8	7	7	6	6	6	7	8	82
Days With ≥ 1.0" Precipitation	1	1	1	1	1	1	1	1	1	1	1	1	12
Mean Snowfall (in.)	9.7	9.2	6.1	0.9	trace	0.0	0.0	0.0	0.0	trace	0.8	4.5	31.2
Days With ≥ 1.0" Snow Depth	14	12	4	0	0	0	0	0	0	0	1	5	36

Elmira Chemung County   Elevation: 843 ft.   Latitude: 42° 06' N   Longitude: 76° 48' W

	JAN	FEB	MAR	APR	MAY	JUN	JUL	AUG	SEP	OCT	NOV	DEC	YEAR
Mean Maximum Temp. (°F)	32.5	35.2	44.0	57.0	69.6	78.1	82.6	80.7	72.7	60.9	48.5	37.5	58.3
Mean Temp. (°F)	23.7	25.4	33.6	45.3	56.7	65.3	70.1	68.3	60.7	49.2	39.6	29.5	47.3
Mean Minimum Temp. (°F)	14.8	15.5	23.3	33.6	43.6	52.6	57.7	55.9	48.6	37.6	30.6	21.5	36.3
Extreme Maximum Temp. (°F)	66	69	86	92	96	97	102	97	95	87	78	69	102
Extreme Minimum Temp. (°F)	-19	-21	-9	9	24	32	40	31	28	15	3	-16	-21
Days Maximum Temp. ≥ 90°F	0	0	0	0	1	2	4	3	1	0	0	0	11
Days Maximum Temp. ≤ 32°F	15	12	5	0	0	0	0	0	0	0	1	9	42
Days Minimum Temp. ≤ 32°F	29	26	25	15	3	0	0	0	1	9	18	27	153
Days Minimum Temp. ≤ 0°F	4	3	0	0	0	0	0	0	0	0	0	1	8
Heating Degree Days (base 65°F)	1,275	1,112	966	587	277	79	17	33	168	483	756	1,094	6,847
Cooling Degree Days (base 65°F)	0	0	0	3	27	108	200	152	49	2	0	0	541
Mean Precipitation (in.)	1.88	1.99	2.64	2.86	2.96	3.82	3.50	3.33	3.52	2.86	3.06	2.38	34.80
Days With ≥ 0.1" Precipitation	5	5	6	7	8	8	7	6	7	6	7	6	78
Days With ≥ 1.0" Precipitation	0	0	1	0	0	1	1	1	1	1	1	0	7
Mean Snowfall (in.)	10.2	9.9	8.8	1.7	0.1	0.0	0.0	0.0	0.0	0.2	2.9	8.9	42.7
Days With ≥ 1.0" Snow Depth	18	16	8	1	0	0	0	0	0	0	2	10	55

PROFILES OF NEW YORK / Weather: Cooperative Stations

Franklinville Cattaraugus County   Elevation: 1,548 ft.   Latitude: 42° 20' N   Longitude: 78° 28' W

	JAN	FEB	MAR	APR	MAY	JUN	JUL	AUG	SEP	OCT	NOV	DEC	YEAR
Mean Maximum Temp. (°F)	29.0	31.5	40.4	52.9	65.7	73.9	78.1	76.1	68.8	57.8	45.0	34.3	54.5
Mean Temp. (°F)	19.7	21.1	29.5	41.5	52.6	61.5	65.7	64.0	57.1	46.4	36.5	26.2	43.5
Mean Minimum Temp. (°F)	10.3	10.7	18.6	30.0	39.5	48.8	53.3	51.9	45.4	35.0	27.9	18.1	32.4
Extreme Maximum Temp. (°F)	62	67	80	87	90	92	97	95	89	80	74	71	97
Extreme Minimum Temp. (°F)	-28	-36	-23	2	20	26	35	28	23	14	-3	-28	-36
Days Maximum Temp. ≥ 90°F	0	0	0	0	0	0	1	0	0	0	0	0	1
Days Maximum Temp. ≤ 32°F	19	15	8	1	0	0	0	0	0	0	4	13	60
Days Minimum Temp. ≤ 32°F	30	27	28	19	9	0	0	0	2	13	21	28	177
Days Minimum Temp. ≤ 0°F	8	7	3	0	0	0	0	0	0	0	0	3	21
Heating Degree Days (base 65°F)	1,400	1,233	1,094	699	387	143	60	83	249	569	848	1,196	7,961
Cooling Degree Days (base 65°F)	0	0	0	1	10	46	90	61	18	0	0	0	226
Mean Precipitation (in.)	2.51	2.01	2.81	3.16	3.60	4.33	3.99	3.81	4.30	3.66	3.56	3.07	40.81
Days With ≥ 0.1" Precipitation	8	6	8	8	8	9	8	8	9	9	9	9	99
Days With ≥ 1.0" Precipitation	0	0	0	0	0	1	1	1	1	1	0	0	5
Mean Snowfall (in.)	28.0	16.5	14.6	4.2	0.2	0.0	0.0	0.0	0.0	0.6	11.5	25.5	101.1
Days With ≥ 1.0" Snow Depth	25	22	15	3	0	0	0	0	0	0	7	20	92

Fredonia Chautauqua County   Elevation: 757 ft.   Latitude: 42° 27' N   Longitude: 79° 14' W

	JAN	FEB	MAR	APR	MAY	JUN	JUL	AUG	SEP	OCT	NOV	DEC	YEAR
Mean Maximum Temp. (°F)	32.4	34.7	44.0	56.1	68.0	76.5	80.4	78.7	72.4	61.4	49.1	38.1	57.6
Mean Temp. (°F)	25.7	26.9	35.3	46.5	57.9	66.8	71.2	69.7	63.4	52.8	42.3	31.9	49.2
Mean Minimum Temp. (°F)	18.9	19.0	26.6	36.9	47.7	57.1	61.9	60.6	54.3	44.2	35.5	25.7	40.7
Extreme Maximum Temp. (°F)	66	71	82	91	90	93	95	93	90	83	75	74	95
Extreme Minimum Temp. (°F)	-17	-17	-10	10	27	35	47	37	34	22	8	-8	-17
Days Maximum Temp. ≥ 90°F	0	0	0	0	0	0	1	1	0	0	0	0	2
Days Maximum Temp. ≤ 32°F	15	13	6	0	0	0	0	0	0	0	1	9	44
Days Minimum Temp. ≤ 32°F	28	25	23	10	1	0	0	0	0	2	12	24	125
Days Minimum Temp. ≤ 0°F	2	2	0	0	0	0	0	0	0	0	0	0	4
Heating Degree Days (base 65°F)	1,212	1,070	914	554	247	60	8	17	112	377	674	1,019	6,264
Cooling Degree Days (base 65°F)	0	0	2	5	33	122	208	173	72	7	0	0	622
Mean Precipitation (in.)	2.59	2.13	2.73	3.22	3.28	3.94	3.85	3.82	4.98	4.12	4.20	3.38	42.24
Days With ≥ 0.1" Precipitation	8	7	7	8	7	7	7	7	9	9	10	10	96
Days With ≥ 1.0" Precipitation	0	0	0	0	0	1	1	1	1	1	1	0	6
Mean Snowfall (in.)	27.0	16.6	10.5	2.5	0.3	0.0	0.0	0.0	0.0	0.3	7.6	21.2	86.0
Days With ≥ 1.0" Snow Depth	24	20	10	1	0	0	0	0	0	0	4	15	74

Geneva Research Farm Ontario County   Elevation: 715 ft.   Latitude: 42° 53' N   Longitude: 77° 02' W

	JAN	FEB	MAR	APR	MAY	JUN	JUL	AUG	SEP	OCT	NOV	DEC	YEAR
Mean Maximum Temp. (°F)	29.8	32.0	40.7	53.8	66.6	75.4	80.1	78.3	70.4	58.6	46.6	35.8	55.7
Mean Temp. (°F)	22.3	24.1	32.7	44.8	56.7	65.7	70.5	68.7	61.1	49.8	39.5	28.9	47.0
Mean Minimum Temp. (°F)	14.7	16.2	24.6	35.8	46.7	55.9	60.8	59.1	51.6	40.9	32.3	22.0	38.4
Extreme Maximum Temp. (°F)	67	69	84	85	92	95	97	95	92	83	77	70	97
Extreme Minimum Temp. (°F)	-15	-16	-7	10	27	36	46	40	30	22	6	-12	-16
Days Maximum Temp. ≥ 90°F	0	0	0	0	0	1	2	1	0	0	0	0	4
Days Maximum Temp. ≤ 32°F	18	15	8	1	0	0	0	0	0	0	2	11	55
Days Minimum Temp. ≤ 32°F	29	26	25	11	1	0	0	0	0	4	16	27	139
Days Minimum Temp. ≤ 0°F	3	3	0	0	0	0	0	0	0	0	0	1	7
Heating Degree Days (base 65°F)	1,318	1,149	996	603	280	74	14	30	159	468	761	1,112	6,964
Cooling Degree Days (base 65°F)	0	0	1	4	27	103	196	149	46	3	0	0	529
Mean Precipitation (in.)	1.76	1.63	2.24	2.81	2.97	3.67	3.15	3.18	3.59	3.09	3.00	2.34	33.43
Days With ≥ 0.1" Precipitation	5	5	6	7	8	8	7	7	7	7	7	6	80
Days With ≥ 1.0" Precipitation	0	0	0	0	0	1	1	1	1	1	0	0	5
Mean Snowfall (in.)	15.0	14.6	11.5	3.3	0.1	0.0	0.0	0.0	0.0	0.2	4.5	13.1	62.3
Days With ≥ 1.0" Snow Depth	22	20	12	2	0	0	0	0	0	0	4	14	74

Glenham Dutchess County   Elevation: 272 ft.   Latitude: 41° 31' N   Longitude: 73° 56' W

	JAN	FEB	MAR	APR	MAY	JUN	JUL	AUG	SEP	OCT	NOV	DEC	YEAR
Mean Maximum Temp. (°F)	35.7	38.9	48.4	60.2	72.3	80.6	85.7	84.2	76.1	64.5	52.5	40.4	61.6
Mean Temp. (°F)	25.9	28.7	38.3	49.7	60.8	69.5	74.6	73.0	64.8	53.2	43.0	31.6	51.1
Mean Minimum Temp. (°F)	16.2	18.5	28.1	39.0	49.4	58.2	63.4	61.7	53.4	41.9	33.4	22.8	40.5
Extreme Maximum Temp. (°F)	66	75	84	96	98	100	103	99	100	90	82	73	103
Extreme Minimum Temp. (°F)	-16	-11	-2	16	30	38	45	39	31	20	11	-10	-16
Days Maximum Temp. ≥ 90°F	0	0	0	0	2	3	8	6	2	0	0	0	21
Days Maximum Temp. ≤ 32°F	12	8	2	0	0	0	0	0	0	0	0	6	28
Days Minimum Temp. ≤ 32°F	29	25	21	7	0	0	0	0	0	5	15	26	128
Days Minimum Temp. ≤ 0°F	3	1	0	0	0	0	0	0	0	0	0	0	4
Heating Degree Days (base 65°F)	1,204	1,019	823	463	176	32	3	9	95	367	653	1,028	5,872
Cooling Degree Days (base 65°F)	0	0	1	7	56	178	320	267	97	10	1	0	937
Mean Precipitation (in.)	3.28	2.91	3.41	3.97	4.44	4.09	4.76	4.00	3.99	3.74	3.82	3.33	45.74
Days With ≥ 0.1" Precipitation	6	6	7	7	8	7	7	6	6	6	6	6	78
Days With ≥ 1.0" Precipitation	1	1	1	1	1	1	1	1	1	1	1	1	12
Mean Snowfall (in.)	11.7	9.5	5.8	1.1	trace	0.0	0.0	0.0	0.0	0.1	1.9	6.6	36.7
Days With ≥ 1.0" Snow Depth	15	12	5	1	0	0	0	0	0	0	1	7	41

PROFILES OF NEW YORK / Weather: Cooperative Stations

Glens Falls Airport *Warren County*   Elevation: 318 ft.   Latitude: 43° 21' N   Longitude: 73° 37' W

	JAN	FEB	MAR	APR	MAY	JUN	JUL	AUG	SEP	OCT	NOV	DEC	YEAR
Mean Maximum Temp. (°F)	28.0	31.9	42.1	56.1	68.4	76.9	81.6	79.1	70.2	58.2	45.8	33.8	56.0
Mean Temp. (°F)	17.8	21.3	32.1	44.9	56.5	65.0	70.0	67.8	58.9	47.3	37.1	25.2	45.3
Mean Minimum Temp. (°F)	7.4	10.6	22.1	33.7	44.5	53.1	58.3	56.4	47.6	36.4	28.4	16.6	34.6
Extreme Maximum Temp. (°F)	64	65	86	90	93	97	100	96	95	82	78	69	100
Extreme Minimum Temp. (°F)	-35	-30	-16	9	24	34	40	31	25	16	1	-29	-35
Days Maximum Temp. ≥ 90°F	0	0	0	0	0	1	3	1	0	0	0	0	5
Days Maximum Temp. ≤ 32°F	19	14	5	0	0	0	0	0	0	0	2	13	53
Days Minimum Temp. ≤ 32°F	29	27	26	14	2	0	0	0	1	11	21	28	159
Days Minimum Temp. ≤ 0°F	10	7	1	0	0	0	0	0	0	0	0	4	22
Heating Degree Days (base 65°F)	1,459	1,228	1,013	597	275	74	15	37	207	542	830	1,227	7,504
Cooling Degree Days (base 65°F)	0	0	0	1	16	81	179	130	30	1	0	0	438
Mean Precipitation (in.)	2.95	2.16	3.10	3.01	3.72	3.39	3.50	3.70	3.40	3.09	3.19	2.87	38.08
Days With ≥ 0.1" Precipitation	6	5	7	7	8	7	7	7	7	6	7	6	80
Days With ≥ 1.0" Precipitation	1	0	1	1	1	0	1	1	1	1	0	1	9
Mean Snowfall (in.)	19.7	12.8	12.7	2.3	trace	0.0	trace	0.0	0.0	trace	4.2	14.2	65.9
Days With ≥ 1.0" Snow Depth	25	23	14	1	0	0	0	0	0	0	3	17	83

Glens Falls Farm *Warren County*   Elevation: 501 ft.   Latitude: 43° 20' N   Longitude: 73° 44' W

	JAN	FEB	MAR	APR	MAY	JUN	JUL	AUG	SEP	OCT	NOV	DEC	YEAR
Mean Maximum Temp. (°F)	30.3	34.4	44.1	58.1	70.8	78.8	83.0	80.5	72.0	60.7	46.9	35.0	57.9
Mean Temp. (°F)	19.6	22.9	32.8	45.6	57.5	65.7	70.4	68.1	60.0	48.7	37.7	25.7	46.2
Mean Minimum Temp. (°F)	8.8	11.4	21.5	33.0	44.2	52.5	57.6	55.7	47.8	36.8	28.5	16.5	34.5
Extreme Maximum Temp. (°F)	63	65	86	90	92	97	98	96	92	83	75	65	98
Extreme Minimum Temp. (°F)	-34	-26	-13	0	19	31	40	32	23	9	-2	-25	-34
Days Maximum Temp. ≥ 90°F	0	0	0	0	0	2	4	2	0	0	0	0	8
Days Maximum Temp. ≤ 32°F	17	11	3	0	0	0	0	0	0	0	1	11	43
Days Minimum Temp. ≤ 32°F	30	27	27	15	2	0	0	0	1	11	20	29	162
Days Minimum Temp. ≤ 0°F	9	7	1	0	0	0	0	0	0	0	0	4	21
Heating Degree Days (base 65°F)	1,402	1,182	991	580	247	65	11	31	181	499	812	1,211	7,212
Cooling Degree Days (base 65°F)	0	0	0	2	22	101	197	147	40	2	0	0	511
Mean Precipitation (in.)	3.35	2.56	3.68	3.66	4.38	4.12	4.07	4.31	4.12	3.61	4.07	3.40	45.33
Days With ≥ 0.1" Precipitation	7	5	7	7	8	8	7	7	7	7	8	7	85
Days With ≥ 1.0" Precipitation	1	0	1	1	1	1	1	1	1	1	1	1	11
Mean Snowfall (in.)	20.6	12.0	12.6	2.3	trace	0.0	0.0	0.0	0.0	trace	4.2	14.5	66.2
Days With ≥ 1.0" Snow Depth	28	26	19	3	0	0	0	0	0	0	4	20	100

Gloversville *Fulton County*   Elevation: 898 ft.   Latitude: 43° 04' N   Longitude: 74° 20' W

	JAN	FEB	MAR	APR	MAY	JUN	JUL	AUG	SEP	OCT	NOV	DEC	YEAR
Mean Maximum Temp. (°F)	28.1	31.5	41.3	55.5	68.5	76.1	80.5	78.5	70.1	58.5	45.2	33.2	55.6
Mean Temp. (°F)	19.2	21.7	31.5	44.4	56.6	65.0	69.6	67.6	59.6	47.9	37.3	25.3	45.5
Mean Minimum Temp. (°F)	10.2	11.8	21.6	33.2	44.8	53.7	58.6	56.6	49.0	37.2	29.3	17.5	35.3
Extreme Maximum Temp. (°F)	60	62	83	89	90	94	94	95	91	83	76	60	95
Extreme Minimum Temp. (°F)	-29	-26	-14	9	27	36	44	38	27	17	5	-23	-29
Days Maximum Temp. ≥ 90°F	0	0	0	0	0	1	2	1	0	0	0	0	4
Days Maximum Temp. ≤ 32°F	20	15	6	0	0	0	0	0	0	0	2	13	56
Days Minimum Temp. ≤ 32°F	30	27	27	15	2	0	0	0	1	10	19	29	160
Days Minimum Temp. ≤ 0°F	8	6	1	0	0	0	0	0	0	0	0	3	18
Heating Degree Days (base 65°F)	1,414	1,217	1,032	612	272	75	17	35	187	524	826	1,222	7,433
Cooling Degree Days (base 65°F)	0	0	0	1	17	83	164	116	30	1	0	0	412
Mean Precipitation (in.)	3.07	2.74	3.53	3.69	4.01	4.23	3.98	4.05	4.13	3.60	3.77	3.48	44.28
Days With ≥ 0.1" Precipitation	7	6	7	7	8	8	7	7	8	7	8	8	88
Days With ≥ 1.0" Precipitation	1	0	1	1	1	1	1	1	1	1	1	0	10
Mean Snowfall (in.)	20.9	15.6	14.1	3.0	trace	0.0	0.0	0.0	0.0	trace	5.1	17.5	76.2
Days With ≥ 1.0" Snow Depth	27	27	23	4	0	0	0	0	0	0	5	22	108

Gouverneur 3 NW *St. Lawrence County*   Elevation: 419 ft.   Latitude: 44° 21' N   Longitude: 75° 31' W

	JAN	FEB	MAR	APR	MAY	JUN	JUL	AUG	SEP	OCT	NOV	DEC	YEAR
Mean Maximum Temp. (°F)	27.0	30.1	40.3	54.6	68.0	76.1	80.9	78.8	70.2	58.3	44.9	32.6	55.1
Mean Temp. (°F)	16.3	19.2	29.6	43.3	55.4	64.0	68.7	66.6	58.4	47.3	36.4	23.4	44.0
Mean Minimum Temp. (°F)	5.5	8.3	18.8	31.9	42.7	51.8	56.4	54.4	46.6	36.3	28.0	14.1	32.9
Extreme Maximum Temp. (°F)	65	64	81	87	90	96	95	98	94	81	78	69	98
Extreme Minimum Temp. (°F)	-45	-37	-27	-2	20	29	36	32	22	14	-3	-37	-45
Days Maximum Temp. ≥ 90°F	0	0	0	0	0	2	1	0	0	0	0	0	3
Days Maximum Temp. ≤ 32°F	20	16	8	0	0	0	0	0	0	0	3	14	61
Days Minimum Temp. ≤ 32°F	30	27	26	17	3	0	0	0	2	11	20	28	164
Days Minimum Temp. ≤ 0°F	12	9	4	0	0	0	0	0	0	0	0	6	31
Heating Degree Days (base 65°F)	1,506	1,287	1,091	648	305	95	26	54	219	543	851	1,285	7,910
Cooling Degree Days (base 65°F)	0	0	0	2	10	68	144	106	26	1	0	0	357
Mean Precipitation (in.)	2.49	2.04	2.52	3.02	3.09	3.19	3.14	3.73	4.20	3.45	3.66	2.93	37.46
Days With ≥ 0.1" Precipitation	7	5	7	7	8	7	7	7	8	8	9	7	87
Days With ≥ 1.0" Precipitation	0	0	0	0	0	0	1	1	1	1	1	0	5
Mean Snowfall (in.)	23.5	17.0	14.7	3.8	0.1	trace	0.0	0.0	trace	0.4	8.1	19.9	87.5
Days With ≥ 1.0" Snow Depth	28	25	19	3	0	0	0	0	0	0	6	21	102

PROFILES OF NEW YORK / Weather: Cooperative Stations

Grafton *Rensselaer County*   Elevation: 1,558 ft.   Latitude: 42° 47' N   Longitude: 73° 28' W

	JAN	FEB	MAR	APR	MAY	JUN	JUL	AUG	SEP	OCT	NOV	DEC	YEAR
Mean Maximum Temp. (°F)	28.5	31.5	40.8	54.0	66.7	73.8	78.4	75.8	67.7	57.0	44.5	33.4	54.3
Mean Temp. (°F)	20.1	22.7	31.7	43.9	56.0	63.7	68.3	66.3	58.6	48.1	37.0	25.8	45.2
Mean Minimum Temp. (°F)	11.6	13.9	22.5	33.7	45.2	53.5	58.2	56.7	49.4	39.2	29.5	18.2	36.0
Extreme Maximum Temp. (°F)	61	62	83	87	88	90	93	91	89	81	76	62	93
Extreme Minimum Temp. (°F)	-26	-23	-11	5	23	32	41	32	27	15	3	-23	-26
Days Maximum Temp. ≥ 90°F	0	0	0	0	0	0	0	0	0	0	0	0	0
Days Maximum Temp. ≤ 32°F	20	15	7	1	0	0	0	0	0	0	4	15	62
Days Minimum Temp. ≤ 32°F	30	27	26	15	2	0	0	0	1	8	19	28	156
Days Minimum Temp. ≤ 0°F	6	5	1	0	0	0	0	0	0	0	0	3	15
Heating Degree Days (base 65°F)	1,387	1,189	1,027	629	290	97	24	50	214	518	833	1,208	7,466
Cooling Degree Days (base 65°F)	0	0	0	2	14	62	135	95	26	1	0	0	335
Mean Precipitation (in.)	3.00	2.43	3.38	3.81	4.57	4.66	4.34	4.72	4.28	4.07	3.97	2.94	46.17
Days With ≥ 0.1" Precipitation	7	6	8	9	9	9	8	8	8	8	9	8	97
Days With ≥ 1.0" Precipitation	1	0	1	1	1	1	1	1	1	1	1	0	10
Mean Snowfall (in.)	20.0	15.1	14.2	6.9	0.7	0.0	0.0	0.0	trace	0.9	7.9	15.8	81.5
Days With ≥ 1.0" Snow Depth	25	24	18	4	0	0	0	0	0	0	5	19	95

Hudson Correctionl Facility *Columbia County*   Elevation: 59 ft.   Latitude: 42° 15' N   Longitude: 73° 48' W

	JAN	FEB	MAR	APR	MAY	JUN	JUL	AUG	SEP	OCT	NOV	DEC	YEAR
Mean Maximum Temp. (°F)	33.6	37.1	47.3	61.3	73.0	80.5	84.8	82.3	73.7	62.6	50.2	38.4	60.4
Mean Temp. (°F)	24.2	27.1	36.6	48.6	59.9	68.1	72.6	70.7	62.7	51.5	41.2	30.4	49.5
Mean Minimum Temp. (°F)	14.8	17.1	25.9	35.8	46.7	55.7	60.5	59.1	51.7	40.5	32.1	22.3	38.5
Extreme Maximum Temp. (°F)	66	72	91	94	95	100	101	100	96	85	82	71	101
Extreme Minimum Temp. (°F)	-26	-18	-8	12	24	34	40	37	28	18	5	-15	-26
Days Maximum Temp. ≥ 90°F	0	0	0	0	1	3	6	3	1	0	0	0	14
Days Maximum Temp. ≤ 32°F	13	9	2	0	0	0	0	0	0	0	1	7	32
Days Minimum Temp. ≤ 32°F	29	25	23	12	1	0	0	0	0	6	17	27	140
Days Minimum Temp. ≤ 0°F	5	3	0	0	0	0	0	0	0	0	0	1	9
Heating Degree Days (base 65°F)	1,259	1,062	874	491	188	36	4	13	124	414	708	1,066	6,239
Cooling Degree Days (base 65°F)	0	0	1	3	35	138	244	196	62	4	0	0	683
Mean Precipitation (in.)	3.00	2.48	3.24	3.58	4.32	3.63	3.79	3.81	3.87	3.53	3.35	2.95	41.55
Days With ≥ 0.1" Precipitation	6	5	6	7	8	7	6	6	7	6	6	6	76
Days With ≥ 1.0" Precipitation	1	0	1	1	1	1	1	1	1	1	1	1	11
Mean Snowfall (in.)	na	na	4.4	1.5	0.0	0.0	0.0	0.0	0.0	0.1	1.1	na	na
Days With ≥ 1.0" Snow Depth	17	14	6	0	0	0	0	0	0	0	1	9	47

Indian Lake 2 SW *Hamilton County*   Elevation: 1,660 ft.   Latitude: 43° 45' N   Longitude: 74° 17' W

	JAN	FEB	MAR	APR	MAY	JUN	JUL	AUG	SEP	OCT	NOV	DEC	YEAR
Mean Maximum Temp. (°F)	25.4	28.2	36.8	49.2	63.2	71.1	75.3	73.4	65.1	54.0	41.2	30.3	51.1
Mean Temp. (°F)	14.2	16.3	25.6	38.3	50.9	59.4	63.9	62.2	54.3	43.3	33.0	20.9	40.2
Mean Minimum Temp. (°F)	3.1	4.3	14.3	27.2	38.5	47.6	52.5	51.0	43.5	32.6	24.6	11.4	29.2
Extreme Maximum Temp. (°F)	55	56	74	85	87	90	93	94	88	77	68	64	94
Extreme Minimum Temp. (°F)	-35	-36	-25	-2	20	27	34	29	23	9	-9	-29	-36
Days Maximum Temp. ≥ 90°F	0	0	0	0	0	0	0	0	0	0	0	0	0
Days Maximum Temp. ≤ 32°F	23	18	10	1	0	0	0	0	0	0	6	18	76
Days Minimum Temp. ≤ 32°F	30	28	29	22	9	1	0	0	3	17	24	30	193
Days Minimum Temp. ≤ 0°F	14	12	5	0	0	0	0	0	0	0	0	6	37
Heating Degree Days (base 65°F)	1,569	1,372	1,215	795	436	187	87	119	321	666	954	1,361	9,082
Cooling Degree Days (base 65°F)	0	0	0	0	4	24	60	38	8	0	0	0	134
Mean Precipitation (in.)	3.05	2.29	3.08	2.79	3.49	3.71	3.54	3.86	4.28	3.75	3.51	2.70	40.05
Days With ≥ 0.1" Precipitation	7	5	7	7	8	9	8	8	8	8	7	7	89
Days With ≥ 1.0" Precipitation	0	0	1	0	0	1	1	1	1	1	1	0	7
Mean Snowfall (in.)	na	na	na	na	0.0	0.0	0.0	0.0	0.0	0.2	na	na	na
Days With ≥ 1.0" Snow Depth	na	na	na	na	0	0	0	0	0	0	0	na	na

Ithaca Cornell University *Tompkins County*   Elevation: 958 ft.   Latitude: 42° 27' N   Longitude: 76° 27' W

	JAN	FEB	MAR	APR	MAY	JUN	JUL	AUG	SEP	OCT	NOV	DEC	YEAR
Mean Maximum Temp. (°F)	30.5	32.5	41.2	54.0	66.6	74.8	79.6	78.1	70.3	58.7	46.6	35.8	55.7
Mean Temp. (°F)	22.1	23.4	32.3	43.9	55.3	63.9	68.5	67.2	59.7	48.6	38.9	28.4	46.0
Mean Minimum Temp. (°F)	13.6	14.4	23.2	33.7	43.9	52.9	57.5	56.2	49.0	38.5	31.2	21.0	36.3
Extreme Maximum Temp. (°F)	66	67	85	89	93	93	98	93	92	84	78	69	98
Extreme Minimum Temp. (°F)	-24	-23	-17	11	22	31	40	34	24	17	-4	-19	-24
Days Maximum Temp. ≥ 90°F	0	0	0	0	0	0	2	1	0	0	0	0	3
Days Maximum Temp. ≤ 32°F	18	14	7	1	0	0	0	0	0	0	2	11	53
Days Minimum Temp. ≤ 32°F	29	26	25	15	3	0	0	0	1	9	17	27	152
Days Minimum Temp. ≤ 0°F	5	5	1	0	0	0	0	0	0	0	0	2	13
Heating Degree Days (base 65°F)	1,325	1,167	1,009	631	315	105	34	49	193	504	776	1,127	7,235
Cooling Degree Days (base 65°F)	0	0	1	2	20	77	153	126	41	2	0	0	422
Mean Precipitation (in.)	2.05	2.04	2.54	3.19	3.22	3.82	3.67	3.48	3.88	3.26	3.17	2.53	36.85
Days With ≥ 0.1" Precipitation	6	5	6	8	8	8	8	7	7	7	7	6	83
Days With ≥ 1.0" Precipitation	0	0	0	0	0	1	1	1	1	1	0	0	5
Mean Snowfall (in.)	17.6	14.1	12.2	3.7	0.1	0.0	0.0	0.0	0.0	0.6	5.8	13.8	67.9
Days With ≥ 1.0" Snow Depth	22	21	12	2	0	0	0	0	0	0	5	14	76

Lake Placid 2 S *Essex County*   Elevation: 1,938 ft.   Latitude: 44° 15' N   Longitude: 73° 59' W

	JAN	FEB	MAR	APR	MAY	JUN	JUL	AUG	SEP	OCT	NOV	DEC	YEAR
Mean Maximum Temp. (°F)	25.8	29.4	38.5	50.9	64.6	72.6	76.6	74.1	66.0	55.1	42.2	30.9	52.2
Mean Temp. (°F)	14.9	18.0	27.1	39.3	51.7	60.0	64.5	62.4	54.8	44.3	33.1	20.9	40.9
Mean Minimum Temp. (°F)	4.1	6.2	15.6	27.6	38.7	47.5	52.4	50.6	43.3	33.4	24.0	10.9	29.5
Extreme Maximum Temp. (°F)	60	62	78	86	87	92	94	92	92	79	68	62	94
Extreme Minimum Temp. (°F)	-32	-37	-30	-5	19	25	31	27	20	11	-8	-31	-37
Days Maximum Temp. ≥ 90°F	0	0	0	0	0	0	0	0	0	0	0	0	0
Days Maximum Temp. ≤ 32°F	22	18	10	1	0	0	0	0	0	0	6	17	74
Days Minimum Temp. ≤ 32°F	30	27	29	21	9	1	0	0	4	16	25	30	192
Days Minimum Temp. ≤ 0°F	13	10	5	0	0	0	0	0	0	0	1	8	37
Heating Degree Days (base 65°F)	1,549	1,325	1,168	765	413	176	77	117	311	636	949	1,362	8,848
Cooling Degree Days (base 65°F)	0	0	0	0	5	32	70	45	9	0	0	0	161
Mean Precipitation (in.)	2.62	1.98	2.70	2.70	3.19	3.96	4.00	4.29	4.32	3.58	3.35	2.62	39.31
Days With ≥ 0.1" Precipitation	7	5	7	7	9	9	9	9	9	8	8	7	94
Days With ≥ 1.0" Precipitation	0	0	0	0	0	1	1	1	1	1	1	0	6
Mean Snowfall (in.)	na	na	na	na	0.3	0.0	0.0	0.0	trace	1.1	na	na	na
Days With ≥ 1.0" Snow Depth	na	na	na	na	0	0	0	0	0	1	na	na	na

Lawrenceville 3 SW *St. Lawrence County*   Elevation: 498 ft.   Latitude: 44° 43' N   Longitude: 74° 45' W

	JAN	FEB	MAR	APR	MAY	JUN	JUL	AUG	SEP	OCT	NOV	DEC	YEAR
Mean Maximum Temp. (°F)	25.5	29.0	39.3	53.8	67.9	75.9	80.2	77.8	69.2	57.5	44.1	31.2	54.3
Mean Temp. (°F)	16.0	19.1	29.4	43.5	56.3	64.9	69.7	67.5	59.2	47.9	36.2	22.6	44.4
Mean Minimum Temp. (°F)	6.4	9.2	19.4	32.8	44.7	54.0	59.2	57.1	49.1	38.2	28.3	14.0	34.4
Extreme Maximum Temp. (°F)	67	64	80	86	90	94	93	97	92	82	75	68	97
Extreme Minimum Temp. (°F)	-34	-31	-21	3	22	30	35	36	24	17	0	-29	-34
Days Maximum Temp. ≥ 90°F	0	0	0	0	0	1	1	0	0	0	0	0	2
Days Maximum Temp. ≤ 32°F	21	17	9	1	0	0	0	0	0	0	5	17	70
Days Minimum Temp. ≤ 32°F	30	27	27	16	3	0	0	0	1	9	21	29	163
Days Minimum Temp. ≤ 0°F	11	8	3	0	0	0	0	0	0	0	0	6	28
Heating Degree Days (base 65°F)	1,515	1,290	1,096	642	287	87	20	46	203	526	858	1,310	7,880
Cooling Degree Days (base 65°F)	0	0	0	2	22	95	179	133	35	3	0	0	469
Mean Precipitation (in.)	2.14	1.92	2.22	2.73	2.83	3.69	3.75	4.16	3.95	3.23	3.20	2.58	36.40
Days With ≥ 0.1" Precipitation	7	6	7	8	7	8	8	8	8	7	9	8	91
Days With ≥ 1.0" Precipitation	0	0	0	0	0	1	1	1	1	0	0	0	4
Mean Snowfall (in.)	17.1	14.2	13.3	4.9	0.4	0.0	0.0	0.0	0.0	0.7	7.2	14.9	72.7
Days With ≥ 1.0" Snow Depth	27	24	19	4	0	0	0	0	0	0	7	20	101

Little Valley *Cattaraugus County*   Elevation: 1,624 ft.   Latitude: 42° 15' N   Longitude: 78° 49' W

	JAN	FEB	MAR	APR	MAY	JUN	JUL	AUG	SEP	OCT	NOV	DEC	YEAR
Mean Maximum Temp. (°F)	29.7	32.1	41.0	53.6	66.2	74.5	78.8	76.9	69.2	58.0	45.6	34.7	55.0
Mean Temp. (°F)	21.1	22.4	30.7	42.4	53.6	62.3	66.8	65.3	58.2	47.5	37.5	27.3	44.6
Mean Minimum Temp. (°F)	12.4	12.7	20.4	31.3	40.9	50.1	54.7	53.6	47.1	37.0	29.5	19.8	34.1
Extreme Maximum Temp. (°F)	62	67	80	88	89	92	96	94	90	81	75	71	96
Extreme Minimum Temp. (°F)	-26	-28	-16	6	20	29	36	31	26	15	-5	-22	-28
Days Maximum Temp. ≥ 90°F	0	0	0	0	0	1	0	0	0	0	0	0	1
Days Maximum Temp. ≤ 32°F	19	15	8	1	0	0	0	0	0	0	4	13	60
Days Minimum Temp. ≤ 32°F	30	27	26	18	7	0	0	0	1	10	20	28	167
Days Minimum Temp. ≤ 0°F	6	6	2	0	0	0	0	0	0	0	0	2	16
Heating Degree Days (base 65°F)	1,356	1,195	1,056	671	362	127	46	63	224	536	817	1,161	7,614
Cooling Degree Days (base 65°F)	0	0	0	1	12	52	110	78	24	1	0	0	278
Mean Precipitation (in.)	3.69	3.01	3.57	3.63	3.83	4.75	4.29	4.37	4.85	4.15	4.78	4.33	49.25
Days With ≥ 0.1" Precipitation	12	9	10	10	9	10	9	9	10	10	12	13	123
Days With ≥ 1.0" Precipitation	0	0	0	0	0	1	1	1	1	1	1	0	6
Mean Snowfall (in.)	31.5	22.3	18.1	6.3	0.4	0.0	0.0	0.0	0.0	1.0	14.9	33.4	127.9
Days With ≥ 1.0" Snow Depth	26	23	15	3	0	0	0	0	0	0	8	19	94

Lockport 2 SE *Niagara County*   Elevation: 603 ft.   Latitude: 43° 08' N   Longitude: 78° 41' W

	JAN	FEB	MAR	APR	MAY	JUN	JUL	AUG	SEP	OCT	NOV	DEC	YEAR
Mean Maximum Temp. (°F)	31.6	33.9	43.2	56.5	69.2	77.2	81.5	79.4	71.4	60.0	47.5	36.6	57.3
Mean Temp. (°F)	24.1	25.8	34.0	46.0	58.1	66.4	71.3	69.5	61.8	51.0	40.0	29.6	48.1
Mean Minimum Temp. (°F)	16.6	17.6	24.8	35.5	46.8	55.4	61.0	59.6	52.1	41.9	32.5	22.6	38.9
Extreme Maximum Temp. (°F)	66	65	81	89	91	93	100	95	94	84	76	73	100
Extreme Minimum Temp. (°F)	-15	-19	-7	7	26	33	46	38	30	19	6	-12	-19
Days Maximum Temp. ≥ 90°F	0	0	0	0	0	1	2	1	0	0	0	0	4
Days Maximum Temp. ≤ 32°F	16	13	5	0	0	0	0	0	0	0	2	10	46
Days Minimum Temp. ≤ 32°F	29	26	25	12	1	0	0	0	0	4	16	27	140
Days Minimum Temp. ≤ 0°F	2	2	0	0	0	0	0	0	0	0	0	1	5
Heating Degree Days (base 65°F)	1,261	1,102	953	566	241	61	8	20	144	431	742	1,090	6,619
Cooling Degree Days (base 65°F)	0	0	0	4	32	109	217	171	56	4	0	0	593
Mean Precipitation (in.)	2.53	2.24	2.77	3.12	3.03	3.56	3.05	3.42	3.72	3.06	3.47	3.25	37.22
Days With ≥ 0.1" Precipitation	8	7	7	8	6	7	5	6	7	7	9	9	86
Days With ≥ 1.0" Precipitation	0	0	0	0	1	1	1	0	1	0	0	0	5
Mean Snowfall (in.)	24.3	18.5	12.1	4.2	0.4	trace	0.0	0.0	trace	trace	7.5	19.1	86.1
Days With ≥ 1.0" Snow Depth	23	21	12	1	0	0	0	0	0	0	4	16	77

PROFILES OF NEW YORK / Weather: Cooperative Stations

Lockport 4 NE *Niagara County*   Elevation: 439 ft.   Latitude: 43° 12' N   Longitude: 78° 38' W

	JAN	FEB	MAR	APR	MAY	JUN	JUL	AUG	SEP	OCT	NOV	DEC	YEAR
Mean Maximum Temp. (°F)	30.7	32.3	41.5	54.4	67.2	75.9	80.9	79.1	71.4	59.6	47.8	36.1	56.4
Mean Temp. (°F)	23.6	24.7	33.3	45.2	56.7	65.5	70.7	69.0	61.4	50.3	40.5	29.4	47.5
Mean Minimum Temp. (°F)	16.4	17.1	25.0	35.9	46.2	55.1	60.4	58.8	51.4	41.0	33.1	22.6	38.6
Extreme Maximum Temp. (°F)	61	62	80	86	90	93	99	96	94	85	75	74	99
Extreme Minimum Temp. (°F)	-14	-16	-7	11	28	36	46	40	31	22	9	-12	-16
Days Maximum Temp. ≥ 90°F	0	0	0	0	0	0	2	1	0	0	0	0	3
Days Maximum Temp. ≤ 32°F	17	15	7	1	0	0	0	0	0	0	2	10	52
Days Minimum Temp. ≤ 32°F	29	26	24	12	1	0	0	0	0	4	15	26	137
Days Minimum Temp. ≤ 0°F	2	1	0	0	0	0	0	0	0	0	0	0	3
Heating Degree Days (base 65°F)	1,279	1,131	978	592	281	77	13	27	155	453	730	1,097	6,813
Cooling Degree Days (base 65°F)	0	0	0	5	29	97	208	163	56	4	na	0	na
Mean Precipitation (in.)	2.08	2.24	2.75	3.24	2.92	3.56	3.09	3.59	3.86	2.94	3.23	3.34	36.84
Days With ≥ 0.1" Precipitation	7	6	7	8	7	8	6	7	7	8	9	8	88
Days With ≥ 1.0" Precipitation	0	0	0	0	0	1	1	1	1	0	0	0	4
Mean Snowfall (in.)	15.2	15.6	8.8	2.9	0.3	0.0	0.0	0.0	0.0	trace	4.0	16.1	62.9
Days With ≥ 1.0" Snow Depth	22	22	12	2	0	0	0	0	0	0	4	16	78

Lowville *Lewis County*   Elevation: 859 ft.   Latitude: 43° 48' N   Longitude: 75° 29' W

	JAN	FEB	MAR	APR	MAY	JUN	JUL	AUG	SEP	OCT	NOV	DEC	YEAR
Mean Maximum Temp. (°F)	26.1	29.0	38.1	52.2	65.9	74.4	79.0	76.9	68.0	56.2	43.6	31.6	53.4
Mean Temp. (°F)	16.4	19.0	28.8	42.2	54.5	63.1	67.7	65.7	57.2	46.3	35.8	23.2	43.3
Mean Minimum Temp. (°F)	6.6	8.9	19.5	32.2	43.1	51.8	56.3	54.5	46.3	36.4	28.0	14.8	33.2
Extreme Maximum Temp. (°F)	58	59	80	87	89	97	94	94	92	81	70	65	97
Extreme Minimum Temp. (°F)	-35	-32	-25	5	23	28	39	32	24	17	0	-29	-35
Days Maximum Temp. ≥ 90°F	0	0	0	0	0	0	1	1	0	0	0	0	2
Days Maximum Temp. ≤ 32°F	21	17	9	1	0	0	0	0	0	0	4	15	67
Days Minimum Temp. ≤ 32°F	30	27	27	17	3	0	0	0	2	11	21	29	167
Days Minimum Temp. ≤ 0°F	11	9	3	0	0	0	0	0	0	0	0	5	28
Heating Degree Days (base 65°F)	1,502	1,292	1,115	679	333	114	36	64	250	573	870	1,289	8,117
Cooling Degree Days (base 65°F)	0	0	0	1	11	58	121	89	22	1	0	0	303
Mean Precipitation (in.)	3.57	2.50	3.03	3.12	3.08	3.39	3.58	3.52	4.11	3.53	4.11	3.62	41.16
Days With ≥ 0.1" Precipitation	9	6	7	7	8	7	7	7	8	8	9	9	92
Days With ≥ 1.0" Precipitation	0	0	0	0	0	0	1	1	1	1	1	1	6
Mean Snowfall (in.)	37.9	22.7	17.5	5.0	0.3	0.0	0.0	0.0	trace	0.7	10.3	30.7	125.1
Days With ≥ 1.0" Snow Depth	29	26	21	5	0	0	0	0	0	0	8	24	113

Massena Airport *St. Lawrence County*   Elevation: 213 ft.   Latitude: 44° 56' N   Longitude: 74° 51' W

	JAN	FEB	MAR	APR	MAY	JUN	JUL	AUG	SEP	OCT	NOV	DEC	YEAR
Mean Maximum Temp. (°F)	24.2	27.4	38.0	53.4	68.0	76.3	81.2	78.5	69.1	56.9	43.3	30.2	53.9
Mean Temp. (°F)	14.2	17.4	28.6	43.3	56.5	64.9	69.9	67.4	58.5	47.0	35.6	21.6	43.7
Mean Minimum Temp. (°F)	4.0	7.4	19.1	33.1	45.0	53.5	58.6	56.2	47.8	37.0	27.8	13.0	33.5
Extreme Maximum Temp. (°F)	66	63	84	89	95	97	96	100	95	85	74	65	100
Extreme Minimum Temp. (°F)	-38	-38	-26	7	20	31	38	36	26	15	-5	-33	-38
Days Maximum Temp. ≥ 90°F	0	0	0	0	0	1	3	1	0	0	0	0	5
Days Maximum Temp. ≤ 32°F	22	18	10	1	0	0	0	0	0	0	5	17	73
Days Minimum Temp. ≤ 32°F	30	27	27	15	2	0	0	0	1	11	20	29	162
Days Minimum Temp. ≤ 0°F	12	10	3	0	0	0	0	0	0	0	0	7	32
Heating Degree Days (base 65°F)	1,572	1,338	1,123	647	279	82	18	46	219	555	875	1,338	8,092
Cooling Degree Days (base 65°F)	0	0	0	1	20	88	181	123	29	2	0	0	444
Mean Precipitation (in.)	2.54	2.11	2.43	2.84	2.68	3.27	3.39	3.55	3.86	2.99	3.05	3.00	35.71
Days With ≥ 0.1" Precipitation	8	6	7	7	7	7	7	7	7	7	8	8	86
Days With ≥ 1.0" Precipitation	0	0	0	0	0	1	1	1	1	0	0	0	4
Mean Snowfall (in.)	17.6	15.7	11.3	4.4	0.1	trace	trace	0.0	trace	0.9	6.3	17.5	73.8
Days With ≥ 1.0" Snow Depth	27	24	18	3	0	0	0	0	0	0	5	20	97

Middletown 2 NW *Orange County*   Elevation: 698 ft.   Latitude: 41° 28' N   Longitude: 74° 27' W

	JAN	FEB	MAR	APR	MAY	JUN	JUL	AUG	SEP	OCT	NOV	DEC	YEAR
Mean Maximum Temp. (°F)	34.8	38.6	48.2	60.8	72.0	79.4	83.9	82.2	74.6	63.7	51.1	39.6	60.7
Mean Temp. (°F)	26.4	29.2	38.2	49.8	60.7	68.7	73.5	71.8	64.4	53.5	42.8	32.1	50.9
Mean Minimum Temp. (°F)	17.9	19.8	28.1	38.9	49.4	58.0	63.0	61.4	54.2	43.2	34.6	24.4	41.1
Extreme Maximum Temp. (°F)	64	71	85	92	92	93	101	96	94	87	78	71	101
Extreme Minimum Temp. (°F)	-23	-13	-3	18	32	40	45	41	27	23	12	-10	-23
Days Maximum Temp. ≥ 90°F	0	0	0	0	0	2	4	2	1	0	0	0	9
Days Maximum Temp. ≤ 32°F	13	8	2	0	0	0	0	0	0	0	0	7	30
Days Minimum Temp. ≤ 32°F	28	25	21	6	0	0	0	0	0	3	13	25	121
Days Minimum Temp. ≤ 0°F	2	1	0	0	0	0	0	0	0	0	0	0	3
Heating Degree Days (base 65°F)	1,191	1,003	825	454	167	27	2	7	93	356	659	1,014	5,798
Cooling Degree Days (base 65°F)	0	0	1	5	42	152	279	225	83	7	0	0	794
Mean Precipitation (in.)	3.02	2.52	3.29	3.94	4.56	4.18	4.04	3.79	4.18	3.63	3.68	3.11	43.94
Days With ≥ 0.1" Precipitation	6	5	7	7	8	8	7	6	6	6	6	6	78
Days With ≥ 1.0" Precipitation	1	0	1	1	1	1	1	1	1	1	1	1	11
Mean Snowfall (in.)	na	na	na	na	trace	0.0	0.0	0.0	0.0	trace	na	na	na
Days With ≥ 1.0" Snow Depth	na	na	na	na	0	0	0	0	0	0	na	na	na

Mohonk Lake *Ulster County*   Elevation: 1,243 ft.   Latitude: 41° 46' N   Longitude: 74° 09' W

	JAN	FEB	MAR	APR	MAY	JUN	JUL	AUG	SEP	OCT	NOV	DEC	YEAR
Mean Maximum Temp. (°F)	31.5	35.0	44.3	57.3	68.3	75.4	80.0	77.9	70.1	59.3	47.3	36.2	56.9
Mean Temp. (°F)	24.2	26.9	35.5	47.4	58.7	66.6	71.5	69.8	62.2	51.5	40.5	29.7	48.7
Mean Minimum Temp. (°F)	16.9	18.7	26.6	37.5	49.0	57.7	63.0	61.7	54.2	43.7	33.7	23.1	40.5
Extreme Maximum Temp. (°F)	59	70	84	91	90	94	98	96	92	82	76	67	98
Extreme Minimum Temp. (°F)	-19	-13	-3	10	28	37	46	43	33	21	9	-9	-19
Days Maximum Temp. ≥ 90°F	0	0	0	0	0	1	2	1	0	0	0	0	4
Days Maximum Temp. ≤ 32°F	17	12	4	0	0	0	0	0	0	0	2	11	46
Days Minimum Temp. ≤ 32°F	29	25	23	9	0	0	0	0	0	3	14	26	129
Days Minimum Temp. ≤ 0°F	3	1	0	0	0	0	0	0	0	0	0	0	4
Heating Degree Days (base 65°F)	1,257	1,071	909	525	221	52	7	16	131	414	728	1,088	6,419
Cooling Degree Days (base 65°F)	0	0	1	3	33	120	230	178	58	4	0	0	627
Mean Precipitation (in.)	3.76	3.15	4.27	4.20	5.20	4.18	4.56	4.32	4.72	4.17	4.14	3.84	50.51
Days With ≥ 0.1" Precipitation	7	6	8	7	8	7	7	7	7	6	7	7	84
Days With ≥ 1.0" Precipitation	1	1	1	1	1	1	1	1	2	1	1	1	13
Mean Snowfall (in.)	15.9	13.4	12.5	3.7	0.5	0.0	0.0	0.0	0.0	0.2	4.0	12.9	63.1
Days With ≥ 1.0" Snow Depth	24	22	16	2	0	0	0	0	0	0	0	3	14	81

New York Avenue V Brooklyn *Kings County*   Elevation: 19 ft.   Latitude: 40° 36' N   Longitude: 73° 59' W

	JAN	FEB	MAR	APR	MAY	JUN	JUL	AUG	SEP	OCT	NOV	DEC	YEAR
Mean Maximum Temp. (°F)	38.8	41.8	49.6	60.2	70.7	79.3	84.8	83.3	76.1	65.0	54.2	43.6	62.3
Mean Temp. (°F)	32.5	34.9	42.2	52.2	62.5	71.5	77.2	76.0	68.7	57.6	47.7	37.6	55.1
Mean Minimum Temp. (°F)	26.1	28.0	34.8	44.0	54.2	63.6	69.6	68.5	61.3	50.2	41.1	31.6	47.8
Extreme Maximum Temp. (°F)	65	73	83	89	96	97	103	101	98	86	80	75	103
Extreme Minimum Temp. (°F)	-4	1	10	19	38	46	54	51	44	30	17	-1	-4
Days Maximum Temp. ≥ 90°F	0	0	0	0	1	3	6	4	1	0	0	0	15
Days Maximum Temp. ≤ 32°F	8	5	1	0	0	0	0	0	0	0	0	4	18
Days Minimum Temp. ≤ 32°F	22	18	11	1	0	0	0	0	0	0	4	15	71
Days Minimum Temp. ≤ 0°F	0	0	0	0	0	0	0	0	0	0	0	0	0
Heating Degree Days (base 65°F)	1,000	843	699	384	127	12	0	1	32	239	514	842	4,693
Cooling Degree Days (base 65°F)	0	0	0	4	57	218	391	342	150	17	1	0	1,180
Mean Precipitation (in.)	3.85	3.02	4.06	3.94	4.32	3.51	4.29	4.14	3.92	3.43	3.90	3.55	45.93
Days With ≥ 0.1" Precipitation	7	6	7	6	7	7	6	6	6	5	6	6	75
Days With ≥ 1.0" Precipitation	1	1	1	1	1	1	1	1	1	1	1	1	12
Mean Snowfall (in.)	7.2	7.8	3.6	0.4	trace	0.0	0.0	0.0	0.0	trace	0.4	2.1	21.5
Days With ≥ 1.0" Snow Depth	8	7	3	0	0	0	0	0	0	0	0	1	19

Norwich *Chenango County*   Elevation: 1,017 ft.   Latitude: 42° 32' N   Longitude: 75° 32' W

	JAN	FEB	MAR	APR	MAY	JUN	JUL	AUG	SEP	OCT	NOV	DEC	YEAR
Mean Maximum Temp. (°F)	31.2	34.0	43.6	56.3	68.9	76.5	80.8	79.0	71.0	59.9	47.0	35.6	57.0
Mean Temp. (°F)	21.5	23.2	32.6	44.3	55.8	64.0	68.5	66.9	59.2	48.2	37.9	27.4	45.8
Mean Minimum Temp. (°F)	11.7	12.5	21.6	32.3	42.7	51.4	56.1	54.7	47.3	36.4	28.7	19.1	34.5
Extreme Maximum Temp. (°F)	62	65	86	89	91	93	96	96	93	84	79	66	96
Extreme Minimum Temp. (°F)	-27	-25	-15	9	20	30	38	32	22	11	3	-22	-27
Days Maximum Temp. ≥ 90°F	0	0	0	0	0	1	2	1	0	0	0	0	4
Days Maximum Temp. ≤ 32°F	17	13	5	0	0	0	0	0	0	0	2	11	48
Days Minimum Temp. ≤ 32°F	30	26	26	16	4	0	0	0	2	11	21	28	164
Days Minimum Temp. ≤ 0°F	7	6	1	0	0	0	0	0	0	0	0	2	16
Heating Degree Days (base 65°F)	1,342	1,173	997	615	295	95	26	44	201	515	807	1,159	7,269
Cooling Degree Days (base 65°F)	0	0	0	2	16	76	153	117	34	1	0	0	399
Mean Precipitation (in.)	2.77	2.35	3.02	3.40	3.72	4.09	3.57	3.45	4.22	3.27	3.73	3.34	40.93
Days With ≥ 0.1" Precipitation	7	6	7	8	9	8	7	7	8	7	8	8	90
Days With ≥ 1.0" Precipitation	0	0	0	0	1	1	1	1	1	1	1	0	7
Mean Snowfall (in.)	18.0	14.0	11.4	3.3	0.1	0.0	0.0	0.0	0.0	0.3	6.0	15.8	68.9
Days With ≥ 1.0" Snow Depth	26	25	16	2	0	0	0	0	0	0	5	16	90

Ogdensburg 4 NE *St. Lawrence County*   Elevation: 278 ft.   Latitude: 44° 44' N   Longitude: 75° 27' W

	JAN	FEB	MAR	APR	MAY	JUN	JUL	AUG	SEP	OCT	NOV	DEC	YEAR
Mean Maximum Temp. (°F)	26.0	29.4	40.0	53.9	67.7	76.7	81.6	79.6	70.2	58.1	45.1	31.8	55.0
Mean Temp. (°F)	16.8	19.7	30.6	43.8	56.6	65.5	70.8	68.4	59.5	48.6	37.6	23.7	45.1
Mean Minimum Temp. (°F)	7.4	10.1	21.0	33.7	45.5	54.2	59.9	57.3	49.0	39.0	29.8	15.6	35.2
Extreme Maximum Temp. (°F)	66	60	81	83	89	96	94	99	92	82	75	65	99
Extreme Minimum Temp. (°F)	-31	-31	-22	3	20	33	42	35	25	14	-1	-26	-31
Days Maximum Temp. ≥ 90°F	0	0	0	0	0	1	2	1	0	0	0	0	4
Days Maximum Temp. ≤ 32°F	20	16	7	0	0	0	0	0	0	0	3	14	60
Days Minimum Temp. ≤ 32°F	28	26	26	14	1	0	0	0	1	7	18	26	147
Days Minimum Temp. ≤ 0°F	11	7	2	0	0	0	0	0	0	0	0	5	25
Heating Degree Days (base 65°F)	1,491	1,272	1,061	630	272	70	9	30	185	505	817	1,272	7,614
Cooling Degree Days (base 65°F)	0	0	0	1	19	95	207	148	23	2	0	0	495
Mean Precipitation (in.)	2.48	2.02	2.17	2.63	2.75	3.10	3.23	3.67	3.88	2.99	3.14	2.74	34.80
Days With ≥ 0.1" Precipitation	6	6	6	7	7	7	7	7	7	7	7	6	80
Days With ≥ 1.0" Precipitation	0	0	0	0	0	0	1	1	1	0	0	0	3
Mean Snowfall (in.)	na	11.2	9.4	2.4	0.0	0.0	0.0	0.0	0.0	0.2	3.9	na	na
Days With ≥ 1.0" Snow Depth	25	24	20	2	0	0	0	0	0	0	4	18	93

PROFILES OF NEW YORK / Weather: Cooperative Stations

Old Forge *Herkimer County*   Elevation: 1,719 ft.   Latitude: 43° 42' N   Longitude: 74° 59' W

	JAN	FEB	MAR	APR	MAY	JUN	JUL	AUG	SEP	OCT	NOV	DEC	YEAR
Mean Maximum Temp. (°F)	24.5	28.3	37.1	49.8	64.2	71.8	75.9	73.7	65.3	54.2	41.0	29.8	51.3
Mean Temp. (°F)	13.1	15.9	25.4	37.9	51.2	59.5	63.8	62.1	54.2	43.3	32.2	20.0	39.9
Mean Minimum Temp. (°F)	1.4	3.4	13.6	26.0	38.1	47.2	51.7	50.4	43.1	32.3	23.4	10.0	28.4
Extreme Maximum Temp. (°F)	59	58	76	86	87	89	90	91	87	78	69	60	91
Extreme Minimum Temp. (°F)	-43	-52	-36	-10	16	24	30	23	19	3	-10	-38	-52
Days Maximum Temp. ≥ 90°F	0	0	0	0	0	0	0	0	0	0	0	0	0
Days Maximum Temp. ≤ 32°F	24	18	11	2	0	0	0	0	0	0	7	19	81
Days Minimum Temp. ≤ 32°F	31	28	29	23	9	1	0	0	4	17	25	30	197
Days Minimum Temp. ≤ 0°F	15	12	6	0	0	0	0	0	0	0	1	8	42
Heating Degree Days (base 65°F)	1,607	1,381	1,223	807	426	184	85	119	325	667	976	1,391	9,191
Cooling Degree Days (base 65°F)	0	0	0	1	5	30	61	39	8	0	0	0	144
Mean Precipitation (in.)	4.15	2.90	3.73	3.65	4.04	4.23	4.45	4.43	5.28	4.46	4.85	4.30	50.47
Days With ≥ 0.1" Precipitation	12	8	9	9	9	9	9	9	9	10	11	11	115
Days With ≥ 1.0" Precipitation	0	0	0	1	0	1	1	1	1	1	1	1	8
Mean Snowfall (in.)	58.9	39.1	38.1	13.4	2.2	trace	0.0	0.0	trace	3.4	24.5	47.1	226.7
Days With ≥ 1.0" Snow Depth	30	26	27	13	1	0	0	0	0	1	14	27	139

Oswego East *Oswego County*   Elevation: 347 ft.   Latitude: 43° 28' N   Longitude: 76° 30' W

	JAN	FEB	MAR	APR	MAY	JUN	JUL	AUG	SEP	OCT	NOV	DEC	YEAR
Mean Maximum Temp. (°F)	30.2	32.3	41.0	53.3	65.7	75.2	80.2	78.4	70.5	58.9	46.9	35.8	55.7
Mean Temp. (°F)	23.3	25.2	33.6	44.9	56.0	65.4	71.0	69.6	62.1	51.2	40.8	29.8	47.7
Mean Minimum Temp. (°F)	16.4	18.0	26.2	36.4	46.3	55.5	61.7	60.7	53.7	43.4	34.7	23.7	39.7
Extreme Maximum Temp. (°F)	65	63	83	90	91	94	94	95	90	85	74	69	95
Extreme Minimum Temp. (°F)	-15	-20	-7	13	28	36	47	43	30	21	11	-16	-20
Days Maximum Temp. ≥ 90°F	0	0	0	0	0	0	2	1	0	0	0	0	3
Days Maximum Temp. ≤ 32°F	18	15	7	0	0	0	0	0	0	0	1	11	52
Days Minimum Temp. ≤ 32°F	29	25	24	10	1	0	0	0	0	3	12	25	129
Days Minimum Temp. ≤ 0°F	3	2	0	0	0	0	0	0	0	0	0	1	6
Heating Degree Days (base 65°F)	1,285	1,118	967	600	292	77	8	15	132	425	720	1,086	6,725
Cooling Degree Days (base 65°F)	0	0	1	2	19	95	205	169	52	4	0	0	547
Mean Precipitation (in.)	3.78	2.87	3.36	3.25	3.14	3.40	3.01	3.64	4.20	3.80	4.44	3.81	42.70
Days With ≥ 0.1" Precipitation	10	8	9	8	8	8	6	7	8	8	11	10	101
Days With ≥ 1.0" Precipitation	0	0	0	0	0	0	1	1	1	1	0	0	4
Mean Snowfall (in.)	51.1	35.6	19.5	4.1	trace	0.0	0.0	0.0	trace	0.4	9.1	33.5	153.3
Days With ≥ 1.0" Snow Depth	27	25	17	2	0	0	0	0	0	0	5	18	94

Patchogue 2 N *Suffolk County*   Elevation: 52 ft.   Latitude: 40° 48' N   Longitude: 73° 00' W

	JAN	FEB	MAR	APR	MAY	JUN	JUL	AUG	SEP	OCT	NOV	DEC	YEAR
Mean Maximum Temp. (°F)	39.1	41.2	49.2	59.4	69.5	78.3	83.4	82.4	75.4	64.8	54.3	44.2	61.8
Mean Temp. (°F)	30.3	32.2	39.6	48.8	58.8	68.0	73.7	72.7	65.5	54.6	45.3	35.9	52.1
Mean Minimum Temp. (°F)	21.5	23.1	30.0	38.1	48.0	57.6	63.9	62.9	55.6	44.3	36.2	27.5	42.4
Extreme Maximum Temp. (°F)	62	68	83	90	97	96	98	102	97	84	77	68	102
Extreme Minimum Temp. (°F)	-13	-6	5	12	28	36	46	40	34	20	10	0	-13
Days Maximum Temp. ≥ 90°F	0	0	0	0	0	1	4	3	1	0	0	0	9
Days Maximum Temp. ≤ 32°F	8	5	1	0	0	0	0	0	0	0	0	3	17
Days Minimum Temp. ≤ 32°F	26	23	19	7	1	0	0	0	0	3	12	22	113
Days Minimum Temp. ≤ 0°F	1	1	0	0	0	0	0	0	0	0	0	0	2
Heating Degree Days (base 65°F)	1,068	921	780	481	209	33	2	5	71	324	585	896	5,375
Cooling Degree Days (base 65°F)	0	0	0	1	25	144	291	248	93	10	0	0	812
Mean Precipitation (in.)	4.25	3.66	4.39	4.44	4.06	4.20	3.44	4.54	3.74	3.98	4.61	4.59	49.90
Days With ≥ 0.1" Precipitation	8	7	8	8	8	7	6	6	6	6	8	9	87
Days With ≥ 1.0" Precipitation	1	1	1	1	1	1	1	1	1	1	1	1	12
Mean Snowfall (in.)	9.7	9.5	5.1	1.3	trace	0.0	0.0	0.0	0.0	trace	0.8	4.1	30.5
Days With ≥ 1.0" Snow Depth	10	7	2	0	0	0	0	0	0	0	0	3	22

Peru 2 WSW *Clinton County*   Elevation: 508 ft.   Latitude: 44° 34' N   Longitude: 73° 34' W

	JAN	FEB	MAR	APR	MAY	JUN	JUL	AUG	SEP	OCT	NOV	DEC	YEAR
Mean Maximum Temp. (°F)	27.7	31.0	41.1	54.5	68.6	76.9	81.8	78.9	69.8	58.0	45.0	32.9	55.5
Mean Temp. (°F)	17.8	20.9	31.1	43.7	56.4	65.3	70.2	67.5	58.9	47.7	36.8	24.3	45.0
Mean Minimum Temp. (°F)	7.9	10.8	21.0	32.8	44.2	53.5	58.6	56.0	47.9	37.3	28.5	15.6	34.5
Extreme Maximum Temp. (°F)	64	63	83	90	93	98	100	100	90	84	74	69	100
Extreme Minimum Temp. (°F)	-34	-30	-17	5	24	29	40	36	24	16	1	-26	-34
Days Maximum Temp. ≥ 90°F	0	0	0	0	0	1	3	2	0	0	0	0	6
Days Maximum Temp. ≤ 32°F	20	15	7	0	0	0	0	0	0	0	3	14	59
Days Minimum Temp. ≤ 32°F	30	27	26	16	2	0	0	0	1	10	20	28	160
Days Minimum Temp. ≤ 0°F	10	7	2	0	0	0	0	0	0	0	0	4	23
Heating Degree Days (base 65°F)	1,457	1,239	1,045	635	282	74	14	42	206	532	840	1,256	7,622
Cooling Degree Days (base 65°F)	0	0	0	2	22	92	190	126	30	2	0	0	464
Mean Precipitation (in.)	1.58	1.54	1.84	2.58	2.61	3.34	3.38	3.42	3.10	2.76	2.67	2.02	30.84
Days With ≥ 0.1" Precipitation	4	4	5	6	7	7	7	7	6	6	6	4	69
Days With ≥ 1.0" Precipitation	0	0	0	0	0	1	1	1	1	1	1	0	6
Mean Snowfall (in.)	13.5	12.1	11.1	4.0	0.0	0.0	0.0	0.0	0.0	0.5	4.3	12.9	58.4
Days With ≥ 1.0" Snow Depth	na	na	na	1	0	0	0	0	0	0	1	na	na

PROFILES OF NEW YORK / Weather: Cooperative Stations

Port Jervis *Orange County*   Elevation: 469 ft.   Latitude: 41° 23' N   Longitude: 74° 41' W

	JAN	FEB	MAR	APR	MAY	JUN	JUL	AUG	SEP	OCT	NOV	DEC	YEAR
Mean Maximum Temp. (°F)	34.7	38.8	48.9	62.1	73.1	80.1	84.5	82.0	73.5	62.1	50.6	39.2	60.8
Mean Temp. (°F)	25.9	28.9	38.0	49.4	60.2	68.0	72.8	70.9	63.0	51.3	41.5	31.1	50.1
Mean Minimum Temp. (°F)	17.1	19.0	26.9	36.6	47.2	55.9	61.0	59.7	52.4	40.4	32.4	23.0	39.3
Extreme Maximum Temp. (°F)	66	74	87	96	96	96	100	97	94	84	79	73	100
Extreme Minimum Temp. (°F)	-19	-14	-3	11	26	35	40	38	28	18	9	-13	-19
Days Maximum Temp. ≥ 90°F	0	0	0	0	1	2	6	3	1	0	0	0	13
Days Maximum Temp. ≤ 32°F	12	7	2	0	0	0	0	0	0	0	1	7	29
Days Minimum Temp. ≤ 32°F	28	25	23	11	1	0	0	0	0	7	17	27	139
Days Minimum Temp. ≤ 0°F	3	2	0	0	0	0	0	0	0	0	0	1	6
Heating Degree Days (base 65°F)	1,206	1,011	832	467	181	36	3	11	121	421	699	1,043	6,031
Cooling Degree Days (base 65°F)	0	0	1	5	39	137	264	206	70	4	0	0	726
Mean Precipitation (in.)	3.41	2.98	3.85	4.01	4.42	4.12	4.10	3.64	4.44	3.47	3.79	3.44	45.67
Days With ≥ 0.1" Precipitation	7	6	7	8	8	7	7	6	6	6	6	7	81
Days With ≥ 1.0" Precipitation	1	1	1	1	1	1	1	1	1	1	1	1	12
Mean Snowfall (in.)	12.7	9.6	7.9	1.6	trace	0.0	0.0	0.0	0.0	trace	2.7	7.5	42.0
Days With ≥ 1.0" Snow Depth	21	17	9	0	0	0	0	0	0	0	0	2	10	59

Poughkeepsie Dutchess Co. Arpt. *Dutchess Co.*   Elevation: 154 ft.   Latitude: 41° 38' N   Longitude: 73° 53' W

	JAN	FEB	MAR	APR	MAY	JUN	JUL	AUG	SEP	OCT	NOV	DEC	YEAR
Mean Maximum Temp. (°F)	34.1	38.1	47.5	59.5	70.5	78.8	83.8	82.0	74.0	62.4	50.8	39.3	60.1
Mean Temp. (°F)	24.7	28.1	37.1	47.9	58.7	67.2	72.4	70.8	62.6	50.8	41.1	30.6	49.3
Mean Minimum Temp. (°F)	15.2	17.9	26.6	36.2	46.8	55.6	60.9	59.6	51.1	39.2	31.3	21.9	38.5
Extreme Maximum Temp. (°F)	64	73	86	94	95	96	103	98	97	85	80	72	103
Extreme Minimum Temp. (°F)	-20	-15	-3	16	28	35	43	38	30	18	3	-14	-20
Days Maximum Temp. ≥ 90°F	0	0	0	0	0	2	6	3	1	0	0	0	12
Days Maximum Temp. ≤ 32°F	13	8	2	0	0	0	0	0	0	0	1	7	31
Days Minimum Temp. ≤ 32°F	29	25	23	11	1	0	0	0	0	8	18	27	142
Days Minimum Temp. ≤ 0°F	4	2	0	0	0	0	0	0	0	0	0	1	7
Heating Degree Days (base 65°F)	1,241	1,037	858	510	218	46	6	14	130	436	712	1,059	6,267
Cooling Degree Days (base 65°F)	0	0	0	3	29	111	240	195	64	3	0	0	645
Mean Precipitation (in.)	3.02	2.61	3.48	3.80	4.80	3.65	4.79	3.87	3.55	3.56	3.54	3.14	43.81
Days With ≥ 0.1" Precipitation	6	6	7	6	8	7	7	6	6	6	6	7	78
Days With ≥ 1.0" Precipitation	0	0	1	1	1	1	1	1	1	1	1	1	10
Mean Snowfall (in.)	10.6	8.2	5.5	1.6	0.0	0.0	0.0	0.0	0.0	trace	2.2	6.4	34.5
Days With ≥ 1.0" Snow Depth	17	12	5	1	0	0	0	0	0	0	1	8	44

Ray Brook *Essex County*   Elevation: 1,617 ft.   Latitude: 44° 18' N   Longitude: 74° 06' W

	JAN	FEB	MAR	APR	MAY	JUN	JUL	AUG	SEP	OCT	NOV	DEC	YEAR
Mean Maximum Temp. (°F)	25.6	28.9	37.8	50.3	64.4	72.5	77.0	75.1	66.6	54.6	41.4	30.2	52.0
Mean Temp. (°F)	14.8	16.9	25.9	38.9	51.5	60.2	64.7	62.8	54.7	43.7	32.8	20.8	40.7
Mean Minimum Temp. (°F)	4.0	4.8	13.9	27.4	38.6	47.8	52.4	50.4	42.8	32.9	24.2	11.4	29.2
Extreme Maximum Temp. (°F)	61	60	79	89	89	93	93	96	93	79	69	61	96
Extreme Minimum Temp. (°F)	-35	-34	-25	-5	18	26	33	28	22	9	-5	-31	-35
Days Maximum Temp. ≥ 90°F	0	0	0	0	0	0	1	0	0	0	0	0	1
Days Maximum Temp. ≤ 32°F	22	18	10	2	0	0	0	0	0	0	7	18	77
Days Minimum Temp. ≤ 32°F	30	27	29	22	9	1	0	0	5	16	25	30	194
Days Minimum Temp. ≤ 0°F	13	13	6	0	0	0	0	0	0	0	0	7	39
Heating Degree Days (base 65°F)	1,552	1,355	1,206	777	418	174	78	115	314	653	959	1,365	8,966
Cooling Degree Days (base 65°F)	0	0	0	1	6	37	80	56	12	0	0	0	192
Mean Precipitation (in.)	2.67	2.08	2.73	2.87	3.16	3.89	3.91	4.18	4.17	3.47	3.57	2.97	39.67
Days With ≥ 0.1" Precipitation	8	6	7	8	9	8	8	9	8	8	9	8	96
Days With ≥ 1.0" Precipitation	0	0	0	0	0	1	1	1	1	1	0	0	5
Mean Snowfall (in.)	27.7	21.6	21.3	11.0	1.2	trace	0.0	trace	trace	2.0	14.8	24.9	124.5
Days With ≥ 1.0" Snow Depth	na	na	na	na	0	0	0	0	0	0	na	na	na

Riverhead Research Farm *Suffolk County*   Elevation: 98 ft.   Latitude: 40° 58' N   Longitude: 72° 43' W

	JAN	FEB	MAR	APR	MAY	JUN	JUL	AUG	SEP	OCT	NOV	DEC	YEAR
Mean Maximum Temp. (°F)	39.1	40.6	48.4	59.2	70.6	79.1	84.2	82.5	75.5	64.7	54.1	44.3	61.9
Mean Temp. (°F)	31.7	33.1	40.3	49.6	60.2	69.1	74.6	73.3	66.6	55.9	46.4	37.1	53.2
Mean Minimum Temp. (°F)	24.2	25.6	32.1	39.9	49.8	59.1	64.9	64.0	57.6	47.1	38.7	29.9	44.4
Extreme Maximum Temp. (°F)	68	68	80	92	96	97	100	96	97	84	78	76	100
Extreme Minimum Temp. (°F)	-8	-1	9	18	32	40	47	45	37	28	17	0	-8
Days Maximum Temp. ≥ 90°F	0	0	0	0	1	2	5	3	1	0	0	0	12
Days Maximum Temp. ≤ 32°F	8	5	1	0	0	0	0	0	0	0	0	3	17
Days Minimum Temp. ≤ 32°F	25	22	17	3	0	0	0	0	0	1	7	19	94
Days Minimum Temp. ≤ 0°F	0	0	0	0	0	0	0	0	0	0	0	0	0
Heating Degree Days (base 65°F)	1,026	894	760	459	174	24	1	2	51	283	551	857	5,082
Cooling Degree Days (base 65°F)	0	0	0	1	35	167	319	265	106	10	0	0	903
Mean Precipitation (in.)	4.30	3.50	4.22	4.10	3.76	3.64	3.16	4.10	3.61	3.87	4.32	4.04	46.62
Days With ≥ 0.1" Precipitation	7	6	7	7	7	6	5	6	5	6	7	7	76
Days With ≥ 1.0" Precipitation	1	1	1	1	1	1	1	1	1	1	1	1	12
Mean Snowfall (in.)	8.8	8.6	4.1	0.7	trace	0.0	0.0	0.0	0.0	trace	0.5	3.0	25.7
Days With ≥ 1.0" Snow Depth	9	7	2	0	0	0	0	0	0	0	0	2	20

PROFILES OF NEW YORK / Weather: Cooperative Stations

Saratoga Springs 4 SW *Saratoga County*   Elevation: 308 ft.   Latitude: 43° 02' N   Longitude: 73° 49' W

	JAN	FEB	MAR	APR	MAY	JUN	JUL	AUG	SEP	OCT	NOV	DEC	YEAR
Mean Maximum Temp. (°F)	30.7	34.3	44.8	58.9	71.9	79.4	84.0	81.5	72.9	61.1	47.9	35.8	58.6
Mean Temp. (°F)	20.5	23.4	33.9	46.5	58.6	66.7	71.5	69.3	60.7	49.3	38.7	26.9	47.2
Mean Minimum Temp. (°F)	10.3	12.5	23.0	34.0	45.2	53.9	59.0	57.0	48.6	37.5	29.6	18.0	35.7
Extreme Maximum Temp. (°F)	63	64	88	92	92	96	97	96	94	85	82	67	97
Extreme Minimum Temp. (°F)	-33	-29	-13	10	25	33	40	37	24	15	5	-22	-33
Days Maximum Temp. ≥ 90°F	0	0	0	0	1	2	5	2	1	0	0	0	11
Days Maximum Temp. ≤ 32°F	17	11	3	0	0	0	0	0	0	0	1	10	42
Days Minimum Temp. ≤ 32°F	30	26	25	14	2	0	0	0	1	11	19	28	156
Days Minimum Temp. ≤ 0°F	8	6	1	0	0	0	0	0	0	0	0	3	18
Heating Degree Days (base 65°F)	1,373	1,169	957	552	223	54	7	23	169	483	783	1,174	6,967
Cooling Degree Days (base 65°F)	0	0	0	3	30	118	227	171	50	3	0	0	602
Mean Precipitation (in.)	3.28	2.49	3.53	3.52	3.97	3.93	3.69	3.98	3.70	3.54	3.73	3.33	42.69
Days With ≥ 0.1" Precipitation	7	5	7	7	8	7	6	6	7	7	7	7	81
Days With ≥ 1.0" Precipitation	1	0	1	1	1	1	1	1	1	1	1	1	11
Mean Snowfall (in.)	19.3	12.2	11.5	2.5	trace	0.0	0.0	0.0	trace	trace	4.2	13.5	63.2
Days With ≥ 1.0" Snow Depth	26	25	16	2	0	0	0	0	0	0	3	19	91

Setauket Strong *Suffolk County*   Elevation: 39 ft.   Latitude: 40° 58' N   Longitude: 73° 06' W

	JAN	FEB	MAR	APR	MAY	JUN	JUL	AUG	SEP	OCT	NOV	DEC	YEAR
Mean Maximum Temp. (°F)	39.0	41.0	49.3	60.2	70.1	78.3	83.3	81.7	74.8	64.6	54.6	44.3	61.8
Mean Temp. (°F)	31.7	33.1	40.4	50.3	60.0	68.8	74.2	73.0	66.4	56.1	46.9	37.1	53.2
Mean Minimum Temp. (°F)	24.4	25.2	31.8	40.4	49.8	59.1	65.1	64.1	58.0	47.5	38.9	29.8	44.5
Extreme Maximum Temp. (°F)	67	69	81	92	95	96	99	95	96	83	77	75	99
Extreme Minimum Temp. (°F)	-4	-1	7	17	30	41	48	45	39	29	17	-2	-4
Days Maximum Temp. ≥ 90°F	0	0	0	0	0	2	4	2	1	0	0	0	9
Days Maximum Temp. ≤ 32°F	8	4	1	0	0	0	0	0	0	0	0	3	16
Days Minimum Temp. ≤ 32°F	25	22	16	4	0	0	0	0	0	0	6	19	92
Days Minimum Temp. ≤ 0°F	0	0	0	0	0	0	0	0	0	0	0	0	0
Heating Degree Days (base 65°F)	1,026	893	755	436	182	28	1	3	53	278	541	858	5,054
Cooling Degree Days (base 65°F)	0	0	0	2	39	154	301	250	101	9	0	0	856
Mean Precipitation (in.)	3.85	3.04	4.11	4.18	3.86	3.71	3.55	3.92	3.61	3.91	3.91	3.95	45.60
Days With ≥ 0.1" Precipitation	6	6	6	7	7	6	6	5	6	6	6	7	74
Days With ≥ 1.0" Precipitation	1	1	1	1	1	1	1	1	1	1	1	1	12
Mean Snowfall (in.)	4.1	3.8	2.0	0.2	0.0	0.0	0.0	0.0	0.0	0.0	0.1	1.4	11.6
Days With ≥ 1.0" Snow Depth	na	na	1	0	0	0	0	0	0	0	0	0	na

Slide Mountain *Ulster County*   Elevation: 2,647 ft.   Latitude: 42° 01' N   Longitude: 74° 25' W

	JAN	FEB	MAR	APR	MAY	JUN	JUL	AUG	SEP	OCT	NOV	DEC	YEAR
Mean Maximum Temp. (°F)	26.4	28.8	36.7	48.4	60.9	67.6	71.8	70.4	63.1	53.4	41.6	30.4	50.0
Mean Temp. (°F)	17.9	19.6	27.5	38.9	50.7	58.1	62.6	61.3	54.3	44.1	34.0	23.0	41.0
Mean Minimum Temp. (°F)	9.4	10.4	18.3	29.3	40.5	48.6	53.3	52.2	45.3	34.7	26.3	15.6	32.0
Extreme Maximum Temp. (°F)	57	57	76	85	85	85	88	85	83	77	72	58	88
Extreme Minimum Temp. (°F)	-23	-20	-13	2	21	30	39	35	26	14	0	-22	-23
Days Maximum Temp. ≥ 90°F	0	0	0	0	0	0	0	0	0	0	0	0	0
Days Maximum Temp. ≤ 32°F	22	17	11	2	0	0	0	0	0	0	7	18	77
Days Minimum Temp. ≤ 32°F	30	27	28	20	6	0	0	0	2	13	23	30	179
Days Minimum Temp. ≤ 0°F	8	6	2	0	0	0	0	0	0	0	0	3	19
Heating Degree Days (base 65°F)	1,454	1,276	1,155	777	439	213	106	131	323	642	924	1,295	8,735
Cooling Degree Days (base 65°F)	0	0	0	0	4	15	42	26	7	0	0	0	94
Mean Precipitation (in.)	5.21	4.32	5.52	5.25	5.96	5.33	5.08	4.84	5.40	5.49	6.08	5.13	63.61
Days With ≥ 0.1" Precipitation	8	7	9	8	10	9	9	8	8	7	9	9	101
Days With ≥ 1.0" Precipitation	1	1	1	2	1	1	1	1	1	2	2	1	15
Mean Snowfall (in.)	23.9	20.1	19.7	7.3	1.4	0.0	0.0	0.0	0.0	0.5	8.6	20.3	101.8
Days With ≥ 1.0" Snow Depth	28	27	25	9	0	0	0	0	0	0	9	23	121

Sodus Center *Wayne County*   Elevation: 419 ft.   Latitude: 43° 12' N   Longitude: 77° 01' W

	JAN	FEB	MAR	APR	MAY	JUN	JUL	AUG	SEP	OCT	NOV	DEC	YEAR
Mean Maximum Temp. (°F)	32.0	34.3	43.3	55.8	68.7	77.6	81.9	80.0	72.4	60.7	48.5	37.0	57.7
Mean Temp. (°F)	24.5	26.0	34.5	46.1	57.5	66.4	71.3	69.6	62.4	51.2	41.1	30.2	48.4
Mean Minimum Temp. (°F)	16.9	17.6	25.7	36.3	46.3	55.2	60.5	59.1	52.4	41.7	33.5	23.3	39.1
Extreme Maximum Temp. (°F)	68	67	85	92	92	95	99	97	94	85	76	70	99
Extreme Minimum Temp. (°F)	-15	-24	-6	13	26	35	45	40	28	21	10	-9	-24
Days Maximum Temp. ≥ 90°F	0	0	0	0	0	2	4	2	1	0	0	0	9
Days Maximum Temp. ≤ 32°F	16	13	5	0	0	0	0	0	0	0	1	9	44
Days Minimum Temp. ≤ 32°F	28	25	24	10	1	0	0	0	0	4	14	26	132
Days Minimum Temp. ≤ 0°F	3	2	0	0	0	0	0	0	0	0	0	1	6
Heating Degree Days (base 65°F)	1,249	1,096	939	569	254	63	9	21	132	425	713	1,073	6,543
Cooling Degree Days (base 65°F)	0	0	1	4	27	109	209	167	57	4	0	0	578
Mean Precipitation (in.)	2.48	2.04	2.57	3.13	3.11	3.65	3.18	3.37	4.00	3.87	3.96	2.89	38.25
Days With ≥ 0.1" Precipitation	7	6	7	8	7	7	7	7	8	9	10	8	91
Days With ≥ 1.0" Precipitation	0	0	0	1	1	1	1	1	1	1	0	0	5
Mean Snowfall (in.)	26.7	17.5	12.6	3.1	trace	0.0	0.0	0.0	0.0	trace	6.7	22.7	89.3
Days With ≥ 1.0" Snow Depth	24	23	13	1	0	0	0	0	0	0	4	16	81

Stillwater Reservoir *Herkimer County* Elevation: 1,689 ft. Latitude: 43° 53' N Longitude: 75° 02' W

	JAN	FEB	MAR	APR	MAY	JUN	JUL	AUG	SEP	OCT	NOV	DEC	YEAR
Mean Maximum Temp. (°F)	24.5	27.5	36.4	48.9	63.3	70.6	75.1	73.2	65.1	54.3	41.1	29.6	50.8
Mean Temp. (°F)	13.1	15.3	25.0	38.5	52.2	60.5	65.1	63.6	55.7	44.6	33.5	20.4	40.6
Mean Minimum Temp. (°F)	1.5	3.0	13.5	28.1	41.0	50.3	55.1	53.9	46.1	34.9	25.8	11.2	30.4
Extreme Maximum Temp. (°F)	59	58	75	84	88	88	89	90	88	80	71	61	90
Extreme Minimum Temp. (°F)	-40	-44	-34	-12	19	30	38	31	26	12	-6	-33	-44
Days Maximum Temp. ≥ 90°F	0	0	0	0	0	0	0	0	0	0	0	0	0
Days Maximum Temp. ≤ 32°F	24	19	11	2	0	0	0	0	0	0	7	19	82
Days Minimum Temp. ≤ 32°F	30	27	29	21	5	0	0	0	1	14	23	29	179
Days Minimum Temp. ≤ 0°F	15	13	7	0	0	0	0	0	0	0	0	7	42
Heating Degree Days (base 65°F)	1,607	1,399	1,234	789	398	163	66	91	286	625	938	1,376	8,972
Cooling Degree Days (base 65°F)	0	0	0	0	6	33	75	53	11	0	0	0	178
Mean Precipitation (in.)	3.65	2.70	3.31	3.61	3.92	4.28	4.62	4.79	5.08	4.20	4.64	4.21	49.01
Days With ≥ 0.1" Precipitation	11	8	10	9	9	9	9	9	9	10	11	11	115
Days With ≥ 1.0" Precipitation	0	0	0	0	1	1	1	1	1	1	1	0	6
Mean Snowfall (in.)	51.7	35.4	29.8	10.4	1.1	0.0	0.0	0.0	trace	2.2	19.1	41.1	190.8
Days With ≥ 1.0" Snow Depth	31	28	29	9	0	0	0	0	0	1	13	28	139

Troy Lock & Dam *Rensselaer County* Elevation: 22 ft. Latitude: 42° 45' N Longitude: 73° 41' W

	JAN	FEB	MAR	APR	MAY	JUN	JUL	AUG	SEP	OCT	NOV	DEC	YEAR
Mean Maximum Temp. (°F)	31.4	34.4	44.1	57.4	70.5	78.7	83.9	82.0	73.5	61.4	49.0	36.9	58.6
Mean Temp. (°F)	22.4	24.9	34.8	47.2	59.4	68.1	73.3	71.3	62.7	50.9	40.8	29.2	48.8
Mean Minimum Temp. (°F)	13.3	15.4	25.4	37.0	48.3	57.5	62.6	60.5	52.0	40.4	32.4	21.5	38.9
Extreme Maximum Temp. (°F)	65	67	86	89	92	96	101	96	96	86	83	69	101
Extreme Minimum Temp. (°F)	-23	-17	-3	15	30	39	47	40	30	21	10	-15	-23
Days Maximum Temp. ≥ 90°F	0	0	0	0	1	2	6	3	1	0	0	0	13
Days Maximum Temp. ≤ 32°F	16	11	4	0	0	0	0	0	0	0	1	9	41
Days Minimum Temp. ≤ 32°F	29	26	24	9	0	0	0	0	0	5	16	26	135
Days Minimum Temp. ≤ 0°F	5	3	0	0	0	0	0	0	0	0	0	1	9
Heating Degree Days (base 65°F)	1,314	1,125	929	531	200	41	4	13	126	432	721	1,102	6,538
Cooling Degree Days (base 65°F)	0	0	0	3	32	140	270	217	67	3	1	0	733
Mean Precipitation (in.)	2.21	1.93	2.71	3.22	3.68	3.75	3.97	4.02	3.30	3.35	3.08	2.36	37.58
Days With ≥ 0.1" Precipitation	5	5	6	7	8	7	7	7	7	6	7	6	78
Days With ≥ 1.0" Precipitation	0	0	1	1	1	1	1	1	1	1	0	0	8
Mean Snowfall (in.)	12.1	9.4	7.2	1.6	trace	0.0	0.0	0.0	0.0	trace	3.4	7.4	41.1
Days With ≥ 1.0" Snow Depth	21	17	8	1	0	0	0	0	0	0	2	11	60

Tully Heiberg Forest *Cortland County* Elevation: 1,896 ft. Latitude: 42° 46' N Longitude: 76° 05' W

	JAN	FEB	MAR	APR	MAY	JUN	JUL	AUG	SEP	OCT	NOV	DEC	YEAR
Mean Maximum Temp. (°F)	26.5	28.8	37.3	50.3	63.2	71.3	76.0	74.3	66.2	55.0	42.7	31.5	51.9
Mean Temp. (°F)	18.7	20.6	29.0	41.1	53.2	61.6	66.3	64.8	57.1	46.2	35.5	24.6	43.2
Mean Minimum Temp. (°F)	10.9	12.3	20.6	31.9	43.1	51.9	56.6	55.3	47.8	37.4	28.3	17.6	34.5
Extreme Maximum Temp. (°F)	61	58	80	85	88	89	93	90	89	80	74	65	93
Extreme Minimum Temp. (°F)	-20	-22	-11	5	17	30	37	33	22	14	1	-29	-29
Days Maximum Temp. ≥ 90°F	0	0	0	0	0	0	0	0	0	0	0	0	0
Days Maximum Temp. ≤ 32°F	22	18	11	2	0	0	0	0	0	0	6	17	76
Days Minimum Temp. ≤ 32°F	30	27	27	16	4	0	0	0	1	10	21	29	165
Days Minimum Temp. ≤ 0°F	7	5	1	0	0	0	0	0	0	0	0	2	15
Heating Degree Days (base 65°F)	1,429	1,249	1,111	713	371	141	52	74	253	576	877	1,247	8,093
Cooling Degree Days (base 65°F)	0	0	0	2	10	49	102	74	21	1	0	0	259
Mean Precipitation (in.)	2.91	2.87	3.40	3.84	3.95	4.61	4.02	3.79	4.91	3.78	3.86	3.63	45.57
Days With ≥ 0.1" Precipitation	9	8	9	9	9	9	7	8	9	9	9	10	105
Days With ≥ 1.0" Precipitation	0	0	0	1	1	1	1	1	1	1	1	0	8
Mean Snowfall (in.)	27.5	24.4	22.8	8.7	0.7	trace	0.0	0.0	trace	1.6	12.5	27.0	125.2
Days With ≥ 1.0" Snow Depth	28	27	26	9	0	0	0	0	0	1	11	24	126

Utica Oneida County Airport *Oneida County* Elevation: 711 ft. Latitude: 43° 09' N Longitude: 75° 23' W

	JAN	FEB	MAR	APR	MAY	JUN	JUL	AUG	SEP	OCT	NOV	DEC	YEAR
Mean Maximum Temp. (°F)	28.7	31.2	40.6	54.3	67.5	75.9	80.5	78.4	69.9	57.9	45.4	34.0	55.4
Mean Temp. (°F)	21.1	23.3	32.5	44.9	57.0	65.5	70.4	68.6	60.4	49.1	38.5	27.2	46.5
Mean Minimum Temp. (°F)	13.6	15.4	24.3	35.5	46.4	55.1	60.2	58.7	50.8	40.2	31.5	20.3	37.7
Extreme Maximum Temp. (°F)	65	64	85	91	91	95	96	95	94	83	79	69	96
Extreme Minimum Temp. (°F)	-27	-21	-12	9	25	33	44	40	25	19	6	-23	-27
Days Maximum Temp. ≥ 90°F	0	0	0	0	0	1	3	1	0	0	0	0	5
Days Maximum Temp. ≤ 32°F	19	15	7	0	0	0	0	0	0	0	3	13	57
Days Minimum Temp. ≤ 32°F	28	26	24	11	1	0	0	0	0	6	16	27	139
Days Minimum Temp. ≤ 0°F	5	4	1	0	0	0	0	0	0	0	0	2	12
Heating Degree Days (base 65°F)	1,351	1,171	1,002	598	265	76	13	30	176	489	789	1,165	7,125
Cooling Degree Days (base 65°F)	0	0	1	2	23	94	188	142	43	2	0	0	495
Mean Precipitation (in.)	3.47	2.99	3.66	3.55	3.73	4.08	3.69	3.57	4.48	3.36	4.04	4.03	44.65
Days With ≥ 0.1" Precipitation	10	8	9	8	9	8	6	7	8	8	10	10	101
Days With ≥ 1.0" Precipitation	0	0	1	1	1	0	1	1	1	1	1	0	8
Mean Snowfall (in.)	26.4	19.0	17.1	3.7	trace	0.0	trace	trace	trace	0.6	9.8	21.9	98.5
Days With ≥ 1.0" Snow Depth	26	23	16	3	0	0	0	0	0	0	6	18	92

PROFILES OF NEW YORK / Weather: Cooperative Stations

Walden 1 ESE *Orange County* Elevation: 377 ft. Latitude: 41° 33' N Longitude: 74° 10' W

	JAN	FEB	MAR	APR	MAY	JUN	JUL	AUG	SEP	OCT	NOV	DEC	YEAR
Mean Maximum Temp. (°F)	34.4	37.6	46.9	58.9	70.2	78.4	83.2	81.4	73.4	62.3	51.0	38.9	59.7
Mean Temp. (°F)	24.2	26.5	36.2	47.5	58.0	66.5	71.4	69.6	61.1	49.5	40.4	29.7	48.4
Mean Minimum Temp. (°F)	13.9	15.4	25.5	36.0	45.7	54.6	59.5	57.7	48.7	36.6	29.8	20.4	37.0
Extreme Maximum Temp. (°F)	69	70	86	95	94	94	100	96	96	89	80	73	100
Extreme Minimum Temp. (°F)	-27	-18	-7	12	27	33	41	35	27	16	4	-14	-27
Days Maximum Temp. ≥ 90°F	0	0	0	0	0	2	5	3	1	0	0	0	11
Days Maximum Temp. ≤ 32°F	13	9	3	0	0	0	0	0	0	0	1	7	33
Days Minimum Temp. ≤ 32°F	29	26	24	11	2	0	0	0	1	11	20	28	152
Days Minimum Temp. ≤ 0°F	5	3	0	0	0	0	0	0	0	0	0	1	9
Heating Degree Days (base 65°F)	1,259	1,080	886	524	239	60	10	22	159	476	731	1,089	6,535
Cooling Degree Days (base 65°F)	0	0	1	4	27	110	218	170	48	3	0	0	581
Mean Precipitation (in.)	3.37	2.41	3.59	3.86	4.49	4.11	4.22	3.56	3.99	3.39	3.75	3.28	44.02
Days With ≥ 0.1" Precipitation	7	6	7	7	8	7	7	6	7	6	6	7	81
Days With ≥ 1.0" Precipitation	1	0	1	1	1	1	1	1	1	1	1	1	11
Mean Snowfall (in.)	12.2	8.2	7.4	1.4	trace	0.0	0.0	0.0	0.0	trace	1.8	7.0	38.0
Days With ≥ 1.0" Snow Depth	20	16	8	1	0	0	0	0	0	0	1	10	56

Walton *Delaware County* Elevation: 1,240 ft. Latitude: 42° 10' N Longitude: 75° 08' W

	JAN	FEB	MAR	APR	MAY	JUN	JUL	AUG	SEP	OCT	NOV	DEC	YEAR
Mean Maximum Temp. (°F)	31.1	34.3	43.9	56.9	69.5	76.8	81.3	79.3	70.8	60.1	47.0	35.4	57.2
Mean Temp. (°F)	21.5	23.8	33.4	44.8	56.1	64.0	68.5	67.1	59.4	48.6	38.1	27.1	46.0
Mean Minimum Temp. (°F)	11.8	13.3	22.7	32.7	42.6	51.0	55.7	54.8	47.9	37.1	29.2	18.8	34.8
Extreme Maximum Temp. (°F)	61	67	83	89	92	92	98	94	92	85	80	66	98
Extreme Minimum Temp. (°F)	-33	-26	-17	7	21	29	36	31	24	11	0	-22	-33
Days Maximum Temp. ≥ 90°F	0	0	0	0	0	1	2	1	0	0	0	0	4
Days Maximum Temp. ≤ 32°F	17	13	5	0	0	0	0	0	0	0	3	12	50
Days Minimum Temp. ≤ 32°F	29	26	25	15	5	0	0	0	2	11	20	28	161
Days Minimum Temp. ≤ 0°F	7	6	2	0	0	0	0	0	0	0	0	3	18
Heating Degree Days (base 65°F)	1,343	1,157	974	600	287	92	26	41	196	504	800	1,168	7,188
Cooling Degree Days (base 65°F)	0	0	0	1	14	67	144	108	32	2	0	0	368
Mean Precipitation (in.)	3.02	2.82	3.58	3.96	4.25	4.16	4.45	4.12	3.98	4.02	4.32	3.67	46.35
Days With ≥ 0.1" Precipitation	7	7	8	9	9	9	9	7	8	7	8	8	96
Days With ≥ 1.0" Precipitation	0	0	1	1	1	1	1	1	1	1	1	1	10
Mean Snowfall (in.)	23.4	19.0	16.9	6.4	0.4	trace	0.0	0.0	trace	0.5	9.0	20.3	95.9
Days With ≥ 1.0" Snow Depth	26	24	17	4	0	0	0	0	0	0	7	20	98

Wanakena Ranger School *St. Lawrence County* Elevation: 1,509 ft. Latitude: 44° 09' N Longitude: 74° 54' W

	JAN	FEB	MAR	APR	MAY	JUN	JUL	AUG	SEP	OCT	NOV	DEC	YEAR
Mean Maximum Temp. (°F)	26.2	29.1	38.6	51.3	66.0	73.6	77.7	75.4	66.8	55.3	42.0	31.1	52.8
Mean Temp. (°F)	14.7	16.7	26.7	40.0	53.3	61.5	65.9	63.9	55.7	44.8	33.5	21.5	41.5
Mean Minimum Temp. (°F)	3.2	4.3	14.8	28.5	40.6	49.5	54.1	52.3	44.6	34.3	25.0	11.8	30.3
Extreme Maximum Temp. (°F)	62	59	74	83	88	93	94	95	90	79	71	62	95
Extreme Minimum Temp. (°F)	-41	-41	-31	-10	19	27	35	30	22	10	-12	-35	-41
Days Maximum Temp. ≥ 90°F	0	0	0	0	0	0	0	0	0	0	0	0	0
Days Maximum Temp. ≤ 32°F	22	17	9	1	0	0	0	0	0	0	6	16	71
Days Minimum Temp. ≤ 32°F	30	27	28	21	7	1	0	0	3	15	24	29	185
Days Minimum Temp. ≤ 0°F	13	12	5	0	0	0	0	0	0	0	1	7	38
Heating Degree Days (base 65°F)	1,553	1,360	1,180	745	366	143	57	90	285	621	937	1,337	8,674
Cooling Degree Days (base 65°F)	0	0	0	1	9	47	94	63	13	0	0	0	227
Mean Precipitation (in.)	3.03	2.38	2.91	3.03	3.73	3.93	4.59	4.25	4.60	3.83	3.96	3.25	43.49
Days With ≥ 0.1" Precipitation	10	7	8	8	9	9	9	8	9	8	10	9	104
Days With ≥ 1.0" Precipitation	0	0	0	0	1	1	1	1	1	1	0	0	6
Mean Snowfall (in.)	32.8	24.8	21.2	7.4	1.0	0.0	0.0	0.0	trace	1.2	12.9	26.7	128.0
Days With ≥ 1.0" Snow Depth	30	28	28	9	0	0	0	0	0	1	11	25	132

Warsaw 6 SW *Wyoming County* Elevation: 1,817 ft. Latitude: 42° 41' N Longitude: 78° 13' W

	JAN	FEB	MAR	APR	MAY	JUN	JUL	AUG	SEP	OCT	NOV	DEC	YEAR
Mean Maximum Temp. (°F)	27.4	30.0	38.8	51.9	64.4	73.0	77.4	75.2	68.0	56.9	43.8	32.9	53.3
Mean Temp. (°F)	19.6	21.4	29.8	42.2	53.7	62.7	67.0	65.1	58.0	47.5	36.3	25.8	44.1
Mean Minimum Temp. (°F)	11.6	12.8	20.5	32.4	43.1	52.3	56.5	54.9	48.1	38.0	28.8	18.6	34.8
Extreme Maximum Temp. (°F)	61	66	80	86	88	88	99	91	91	82	72	70	99
Extreme Minimum Temp. (°F)	-22	-28	-15	8	22	30	40	32	26	16	-4	-23	-28
Days Maximum Temp. ≥ 90°F	0	0	0	0	0	0	1	0	0	0	0	0	1
Days Maximum Temp. ≤ 32°F	21	17	11	1	0	0	0	0	0	0	5	15	70
Days Minimum Temp. ≤ 32°F	30	27	27	17	4	0	0	0	1	9	21	28	164
Days Minimum Temp. ≤ 0°F	6	5	1	0	0	0	0	0	0	0	0	2	14
Heating Degree Days (base 65°F)	1,403	1,224	1,084	679	357	122	44	70	230	537	854	1,211	7,815
Cooling Degree Days (base 65°F)	0	0	1	2	16	56	113	78	22	1	0	0	289
Mean Precipitation (in.)	2.99	2.30	3.07	3.32	3.65	4.41	4.18	3.81	4.60	3.79	3.82	3.47	43.41
Days With ≥ 0.1" Precipitation	10	8	9	9	9	9	8	8	10	9	10	11	110
Days With ≥ 1.0" Precipitation	0	0	0	0	1	1	1	1	1	1	0	0	6
Mean Snowfall (in.)	29.8	21.2	17.3	4.9	0.3	0.0	0.0	0.0	0.0	0.6	12.8	23.0	109.9
Days With ≥ 1.0" Snow Depth	27	23	18	4	0	0	0	0	0	0	8	21	101

Annual Extreme Maximum Temperature

Highest

Rank	Station Name	°F
1	Dobbs Ferry Ardsley	104
1	New York Central Park Obs	104
3	Glenham	103
3	New York Avenue V Brooklyn	103
3	New York Laguardia Airport	103
3	Poughkeepsie Dutchess Co. Arpt.	103
7	Bridgehampton	102
7	Elmira	102
7	New York JFK Int'l Airport	102
7	Patchogue 2 N	102
7	West Point	102
12	Albion 2 NE	101
12	Aurora Research Farm	101
12	Bath	101
12	Hudson Correctionl Facility	101
12	Middletown 2 NW	101
12	Troy Lock & Dam	101
18	Chazy	100
18	Cortland	100
18	Dansville	100
18	Glens Falls Airport	100
18	Lockport 2 SE	100
18	Massena Airport	100
18	Peru 2 WSW	100
18	Port Jervis	100

Lowest

Rank	Station Name	°F
1	Slide Mountain	88
2	Stillwater Reservoir	90
3	Old Forge	91
4	Cherry Valley 2 NNE	93
4	Grafton	93
4	Tully Heiberg Forest	93
7	Boonville 2 SSW	94
7	Indian Lake 2 SW	94
7	Lake Placid 2 S	94
10	Chasm Falls	95
10	Conklingville Dam	95
10	Fredonia	95
10	Gloversville	95
10	Oswego East	95
10	Wanakena Ranger School	95
10	Watertown Airport	95
17	Alfred	96
17	Batavia	96
17	Colden 1 N	96
17	Little Valley	96
17	Norwich	96
17	Ray Brook	96
17	Utica Oneida County Airport	96
24	Allegany State Park	97
24	Angelica	97

Annual Mean Maximum Temperature

Highest

Rank	Station Name	°F
1	New York Central Park Obs	62.6
2	Dobbs Ferry Ardsley	62.5
3	New York Avenue V Brooklyn	62.3
4	Riverhead Research Farm	61.9
5	New York Laguardia Airport	61.8
5	Patchogue 2 N	61.8
5	Setauket Strong	61.8
8	West Point	61.7
9	Glenham	61.6
10	New York JFK Int'l Airport	61.2
11	Port Jervis	60.8
12	Middletown 2 NW	60.7
13	Hudson Correctionl Facility	60.4
14	Poughkeepsie Dutchess Co. Arpt.	60.1
15	Walden 1 ESE	59.7
16	Bridgehampton	59.4
16	White Plains Westchester Co Arpt.	59.4
18	Yorktown Heights 1 W	59.2
19	Saratoga Springs 4 SW	58.6
19	Troy Lock & Dam	58.6
21	Dansville	58.5
22	Elmira	58.3
23	Whitehall	58.0
24	Glens Falls Farm	57.9
25	Albany County Airport	57.8

Lowest

Rank	Station Name	°F
1	Slide Mountain	50.0
2	Stillwater Reservoir	50.8
3	Boonville 2 SSW	51.1
3	Indian Lake 2 SW	51.1
5	Old Forge	51.3
6	Tully Heiberg Forest	51.9
7	Ray Brook	52.0
8	Lake Placid 2 S	52.2
9	Wanakena Ranger School	52.8
10	Chasm Falls	53.2
10	Dannemora	53.2
12	Warsaw 6 SW	53.3
13	Lowville	53.4
14	Canton 4 SE	53.6
15	Massena Airport	53.9
16	Cherry Valley 2 NNE	54.0
17	Grafton	54.3
17	Lawrenceville 3 SW	54.3
19	Binghamton Edwin A. Link Field	54.5
19	Franklinville	54.5
21	Chazy	54.7
22	Watertown	54.9
22	Watertown Airport	54.9
24	Conklingville Dam	55.0
24	Little Valley	55.0

Annual Mean Temperature

Highest

Rank	Station Name	°F
1	New York Avenue V Brooklyn	55.1
1	New York Central Park Obs	55.1
3	New York Laguardia Airport	55.0
4	New York JFK Int'l Airport	54.2
5	Dobbs Ferry Ardsley	53.2
5	Riverhead Research Farm	53.2
5	Setauket Strong	53.2
8	Patchogue 2 N	52.1
9	West Point	52.0
10	Bridgehampton	51.1
10	Glenham	51.1
12	White Plains Westchester Co Arpt.	51.0
13	Middletown 2 NW	50.9
14	Port Jervis	50.1
15	Yorktown Heights 1 W	50.0
16	Hudson Correctionl Facility	49.5
17	Poughkeepsie Dutchess Co. Arpt.	49.3
18	Fredonia	49.2
19	Troy Lock & Dam	48.8
20	Mohonk Lake	48.7
20	Westfield 2 SSE	48.7
22	Albion 2 NE	48.5
23	Sodus Center	48.4
23	Walden 1 ESE	48.4
25	Canandaigua 3 S	48.3

Lowest

Rank	Station Name	°F
1	Old Forge	39.9
2	Indian Lake 2 SW	40.2
3	Stillwater Reservoir	40.6
4	Ray Brook	40.7
5	Lake Placid 2 S	40.9
6	Slide Mountain	41.0
7	Wanakena Ranger School	41.5
8	Boonville 2 SSW	42.2
9	Chasm Falls	42.4
10	Canton 4 SE	43.2
10	Tully Heiberg Forest	43.2
12	Lowville	43.3
13	Franklinville	43.5
14	Dannemora	43.7
14	Massena Airport	43.7
16	Gouverneur 3 NW	44.0
17	Warsaw 6 SW	44.1
18	Bolivar	44.3
18	Chazy	44.3
20	Lawrenceville 3 SW	44.4
21	Allegany State Park	44.5
22	Little Valley	44.6
23	Cherry Valley 2 NNE	44.7
24	Conklingville Dam	44.9
24	Watertown Airport	44.9

Annual Mean Minimum Temperature

Highest

Rank	Station Name	°F
1	New York Laguardia Airport	48.0
2	New York Avenue V Brooklyn	47.8
3	New York Central Park Obs	47.5
4	New York JFK Int'l Airport	47.1
5	Setauket Strong	44.5
6	Riverhead Research Farm	44.4
7	Dobbs Ferry Ardsley	43.8
8	Bridgehampton	42.7
9	White Plains Westchester Co Arpt.	42.6
10	Patchogue 2 N	42.4
11	West Point	42.3
12	Middletown 2 NW	41.1
12	Westfield 2 SSE	41.1
14	Yorktown Heights 1 W	40.8
15	Fredonia	40.7
16	Glenham	40.5
16	Mohonk Lake	40.5
18	Buffalo Int'l Airport	39.9
19	Oswego East	39.7
20	Albion 2 NE	39.3
20	Port Jervis	39.3
22	Canandaigua 3 S	39.1
22	Sodus Center	39.1
24	Rochester Int'l Airport	39.0
25	Lockport 2 SE	38.9

Lowest

Rank	Station Name	°F
1	Old Forge	28.4
2	Indian Lake 2 SW	29.2
2	Ray Brook	29.2
4	Lake Placid 2 S	29.5
5	Wanakena Ranger School	30.3
6	Stillwater Reservoir	30.4
7	Chasm Falls	31.5
8	Slide Mountain	32.0
9	Franklinville	32.4
10	Canton 4 SE	32.8
11	Gouverneur 3 NW	32.9
12	Bolivar	33.0
13	Lowville	33.2
14	Boonville 2 SSW	33.3
15	Massena Airport	33.5
16	Allegany State Park	33.6
17	Angelica	33.7
18	Alfred	33.8
19	Chazy	33.9
20	Little Valley	34.1
21	Bath	34.2
22	Dannemora	34.3
23	Lawrenceville 3 SW	34.4
24	Cooperstown	34.5
24	Glens Falls Farm	34.5

Annual Extreme Minimum Temperature

Highest

Rank	Station Name	°F
1	New York Central Park Obs	-2
1	New York JFK Int'l Airport	-2
3	New York Laguardia Airport	-3
4	New York Avenue V Brooklyn	-4
4	Setauket Strong	-4
6	Riverhead Research Farm	-8
7	Dobbs Ferry Ardsley	-10
7	White Plains Westchester Co Arpt.	-10
9	Bridgehampton	-11
10	Patchogue 2 N	-13
11	West Point	-15
11	Yorktown Heights 1 W	-15
13	Geneva Research Farm	-16
13	Glenham	-16
13	Lockport 4 NE	-16
16	Canandaigua 3 S	-17
16	Fredonia	-17
18	Binghamton Edwin A. Link Field	-18
18	Buffalo Int'l Airport	-18
18	Cortland	-18
21	Lockport 2 SE	-19
21	Mohonk Lake	-19
21	Port Jervis	-19
21	Rochester Int'l Airport	-19
21	Westfield 2 SSE	-19

Lowest

Rank	Station Name	°F
1	Old Forge	-52
2	Gouverneur 3 NW	-45
3	Chazy	-44
3	Stillwater Reservoir	-44
5	Watertown Airport	-43
6	Chasm Falls	-42
7	Wanakena Ranger School	-41
8	Canton 4 SE	-40
9	Massena Airport	-38
9	Whitehall	-38
11	Lake Placid 2 S	-37
12	Franklinville	-36
12	Indian Lake 2 SW	-36
14	Glens Falls Airport	-35
14	Lowville	-35
14	Ray Brook	-35
17	Bolivar	-34
17	Dannemora	-34
17	Glens Falls Farm	-34
17	Lawrenceville 3 SW	-34
17	Peru 2 WSW	-34
17	Watertown	-34
23	Angelica	-33
23	Boonville 2 SSW	-33
23	Saratoga Springs 4 SW	-33

July Mean Maximum Temperature

Highest

Rank	Station Name	°F
1	West Point	86.1
2	Glenham	85.7
3	Dobbs Ferry Ardsley	85.6
4	New York Central Park Obs	85.5
5	Hudson Correctionl Facility	84.8
5	New York Avenue V Brooklyn	84.8
7	New York Laguardia Airport	84.7
7	Whitehall	84.7
9	Port Jervis	84.5
10	Riverhead Research Farm	84.2
11	Saratoga Springs 4 SW	84.0
12	Middletown 2 NW	83.9
12	Troy Lock & Dam	83.9
14	Poughkeepsie Dutchess Co. Arpt.	83.8
15	Patchogue 2 N	83.4
16	Setauket Strong	83.3
17	Walden 1 ESE	83.2
18	Glens Falls Farm	83.0
18	New York JFK Int'l Airport	83.0
20	Albany County Airport	82.7
20	Dansville	82.7
22	Elmira	82.6
23	Albion 2 NE	82.5
24	White Plains Westchester Co Arpt.	82.4
25	Yorktown Heights 1 W	82.2

Lowest

Rank	Station Name	°F
1	Slide Mountain	71.8
2	Stillwater Reservoir	75.1
3	Indian Lake 2 SW	75.3
4	Boonville 2 SSW	75.9
4	Old Forge	75.9
6	Tully Heiberg Forest	76.0
7	Lake Placid 2 S	76.6
8	Ray Brook	77.0
9	Warsaw 6 SW	77.4
10	Wanakena Ranger School	77.7
11	Franklinville	78.1
12	Cherry Valley 2 NNE	78.2
13	Grafton	78.4
14	Allegany State Park	78.5
15	Bolivar	78.6
16	Binghamton Edwin A. Link Field	78.8
16	Chasm Falls	78.8
16	Little Valley	78.8
19	Conklingville Dam	79.0
19	Dannemora	79.0
19	Lowville	79.0
22	Colden 1 N	79.1
23	Canton 4 SE	79.3
24	Watertown Airport	79.4
25	Alfred	79.6

PROFILES OF NEW YORK / Weather: Station Rankings

January Mean Minimum Temperature

Highest

Rank	Station Name	°F
1	New York Laguardia Airport	26.3
2	New York Avenue V Brooklyn	26.1
3	New York Central Park Obs	26.0
3	New York JFK Int'l Airport	26.0
5	Setauket Strong	24.4
6	Riverhead Research Farm	24.2
7	Bridgehampton	22.9
7	Dobbs Ferry Ardsley	22.9
9	Patchogue 2 N	21.5
10	White Plains Westchester Co Arpt.	21.0
11	West Point	20.0
12	Fredonia	18.9
13	Westfield 2 SSE	18.4
14	Yorktown Heights 1 W	18.0
15	Middletown 2 NW	17.9
16	Buffalo Int'l Airport	17.6
17	Port Jervis	17.1
18	Albion 2 NE	17.0
19	Mohonk Lake	16.9
19	Sodus Center	16.9
21	Rochester Int'l Airport	16.8
22	Lockport 2 SE	16.6
23	Canandaigua 3 S	16.5
24	Lockport 4 NE	16.4
24	Oswego East	16.4

Lowest

Rank	Station Name	°F
1	Old Forge	1.4
2	Stillwater Reservoir	1.5
3	Indian Lake 2 SW	3.1
4	Wanakena Ranger School	3.2
5	Canton 4 SE	3.9
6	Massena Airport	4.0
6	Ray Brook	4.0
8	Lake Placid 2 S	4.1
9	Chasm Falls	4.7
10	Gouverneur 3 NW	5.5
11	Chazy	6.0
12	Lawrenceville 3 SW	6.4
13	Lowville	6.6
14	Dannemora	7.4
14	Glens Falls Airport	7.4
14	Ogdensburg 4 NE	7.4
17	Boonville 2 SSW	7.6
18	Peru 2 WSW	7.9
19	Conklingville Dam	8.3
20	Glens Falls Farm	8.8
21	Watertown	9.0
22	Watertown Airport	9.3
23	Slide Mountain	9.4
24	Whitehall	9.9
25	Gloversville	10.2

Number of Annual Heating Degree Days

Highest

Rank	Station Name	Num.
1	Old Forge	9,191
2	Indian Lake 2 SW	9,082
3	Stillwater Reservoir	8,972
4	Ray Brook	8,966
5	Lake Placid 2 S	8,848
6	Slide Mountain	8,735
7	Wanakena Ranger School	8,674
8	Boonville 2 SSW	8,432
9	Chasm Falls	8,416
10	Canton 4 SE	8,239
11	Lowville	8,117
12	Tully Heiberg Forest	8,093
13	Massena Airport	8,092
14	Dannemora	8,015
15	Franklinville	7,961
16	Gouverneur 3 NW	7,910
17	Lawrenceville 3 SW	7,880
18	Chazy	7,832
19	Warsaw 6 SW	7,815
20	Bolivar	7,678
21	Cherry Valley 2 NNE	7,636
22	Allegany State Park	7,633
23	Peru 2 WSW	7,622
24	Watertown Airport	7,616
25	Little Valley	7,614

Lowest

Rank	Station Name	Num.
1	New York Avenue V Brooklyn	4,693
2	New York Central Park Obs	4,702
3	New York Laguardia Airport	4,726
4	New York JFK Int'l Airport	4,833
5	Setauket Strong	5,054
6	Riverhead Research Farm	5,082
7	Dobbs Ferry Ardsley	5,159
8	Patchogue 2 N	5,375
9	West Point	5,523
10	Bridgehampton	5,586
11	White Plains Westchester Co Arpt.	5,719
12	Middletown 2 NW	5,798
13	Glenham	5,872
14	Port Jervis	6,031
15	Yorktown Heights 1 W	6,033
16	Hudson Correctionl Facility	6,239
17	Fredonia	6,264
18	Poughkeepsie Dutchess Co. Arpt.	6,267
19	Mohonk Lake	6,419
20	Westfield 2 SSE	6,430
21	Walden 1 ESE	6,535
22	Troy Lock & Dam	6,538
23	Sodus Center	6,543
24	Albion 2 NE	6,546
25	Canandaigua 3 S	6,589

Number of Annual Cooling Degree Days

Highest

Rank	Station Name	Num.
1	New York Laguardia Airport	1,228
2	New York Central Park Obs	1,206
3	New York Avenue V Brooklyn	1,180
4	New York JFK Int'l Airport	1,027
5	Dobbs Ferry Ardsley	939
6	Glenham	937
7	Riverhead Research Farm	903
8	West Point	895
9	Setauket Strong	856
10	Patchogue 2 N	812
11	Middletown 2 NW	794
12	White Plains Westchester Co Arpt.	776
13	Troy Lock & Dam	733
14	Port Jervis	726
15	Yorktown Heights 1 W	696
16	Hudson Correctionl Facility	683
17	Albion 2 NE	661
17	Whitehall	661
19	Poughkeepsie Dutchess Co. Arpt.	645
20	Westfield 2 SSE	637
21	Mohonk Lake	627
22	Fredonia	622
23	Canandaigua 3 S	616
24	Bridgehampton	608
25	Saratoga Springs 4 SW	602

Lowest

Rank	Station Name	Num.
1	Slide Mountain	94
2	Indian Lake 2 SW	134
3	Old Forge	144
4	Lake Placid 2 S	161
5	Stillwater Reservoir	178
6	Ray Brook	192
7	Franklinville	226
8	Wanakena Ranger School	227
9	Boonville 2 SSW	229
10	Allegany State Park	249
10	Angelica	249
12	Tully Heiberg Forest	259
13	Bolivar	263
14	Little Valley	278
15	Alfred	281
16	Warsaw 6 SW	289
17	Lowville	303
18	Colden 1 N	319
19	Cherry Valley 2 NNE	326
19	Cooperstown	326
21	Grafton	335
22	Dannemora	345
23	Bath	346
24	Conklingville Dam	348
25	Gouverneur 3 NW	357

Annual Precipitation

Highest

Rank	Station Name	Inches
1	Slide Mountain	63.61
2	Boonville 2 SSW	59.83
3	Dobbs Ferry Ardsley	51.74
4	Yorktown Heights 1 W	50.96
5	Mohonk Lake	50.51
6	Old Forge	50.47
7	West Point	50.03
8	White Plains Westchester Co Arpt.	49.95
9	Patchogue 2 N	49.90
10	Little Valley	49.25
11	New York Central Park Obs	49.16
12	Stillwater Reservoir	49.01
13	Colden 1 N	48.20
14	Bridgehampton	47.88
15	Riverhead Research Farm	46.62
16	Walton	46.35
17	Westfield 2 SSE	46.23
18	Grafton	46.17
19	Conklingville Dam	45.95
20	New York Avenue V Brooklyn	45.93
21	Glenham	45.74
22	Port Jervis	45.67
23	Setauket Strong	45.60
24	Tully Heiberg Forest	45.57
25	Allegany State Park	45.51

Lowest

Rank	Station Name	Inches
1	Peru 2 WSW	30.84
2	Dansville	31.40
3	Bath	31.96
4	Geneva Research Farm	33.43
5	Canandaigua 3 S	33.57
6	Rochester Int'l Airport	33.98
7	Watertown Airport	34.25
8	Elmira	34.80
8	Ogdensburg 4 NE	34.80
10	Batavia	35.55
11	Albion 2 NE	35.71
11	Massena Airport	35.71
13	Lawrenceville 3 SW	36.40
14	Lockport 4 NE	36.84
15	Ithaca Cornell University	36.85
16	Angelica	37.08
17	Canton 4 SE	37.15
18	Lockport 2 SE	37.22
19	Aurora Research Farm	37.33
20	Gouverneur 3 NW	37.46
21	Troy Lock & Dam	37.58
22	Dannemora	37.96
23	Alfred	38.02
24	Albany County Airport	38.05
25	Glens Falls Airport	38.08

Number of Days Annually With Greater Than or Equal to 0.1" Precipitation

Highest

Rank	Station Name	Days
1	Little Valley	123
2	Boonville 2 SSW	121
3	Old Forge	115
3	Stillwater Reservoir	115
5	Colden 1 N	114
6	Allegany State Park	110
6	Warsaw 6 SW	110
8	Chasm Falls	108
9	Tully Heiberg Forest	105
10	Wanakena Ranger School	104
11	Oswego East	101
11	Slide Mountain	101
11	Utica Oneida County Airport	101
14	Franklinville	99
15	Grafton	97
15	Watertown	97
15	Westfield 2 SSE	97
18	Cherry Valley 2 NNE	96
18	Fredonia	96
18	Ray Brook	96
18	Walton	96
22	Bolivar	94
22	Lake Placid 2 S	94
24	Buffalo Int'l Airport	93
24	Syracuse Hancock Int'l Airport	93

Lowest

Rank	Station Name	Days
1	Peru 2 WSW	69
2	Bath	73
3	New York JFK Int'l Airport	74
3	Setauket Strong	74
5	New York Avenue V Brooklyn	75
5	New York Laguardia Airport	75
7	Dansville	76
7	Hudson Correctionl Facility	76
7	Riverhead Research Farm	76
10	Bridgehampton	77
11	Elmira	78
11	Glenham	78
11	Middletown 2 NW	78
11	Poughkeepsie Dutchess Co. Arpt.	78
11	Troy Lock & Dam	78
11	White Plains Westchester Co Arpt.	78
17	Albany County Airport	79
18	Canandaigua 3 S	80
18	Geneva Research Farm	80
18	Glens Falls Airport	80
18	New York Central Park Obs	80
18	Ogdensburg 4 NE	80
23	Port Jervis	81
23	Saratoga Springs 4 SW	81
23	Walden 1 ESE	81

Number of Days Annually With Greater Than or Equal to 1.0" Precipitation

Highest

Rank	Station Name	Days
1	Slide Mountain	15
1	Yorktown Heights 1 W	15
3	Boonville 2 SSW	13
3	Mohonk Lake	13
3	White Plains Westchester Co Arpt.	13
6	Bridgehampton	12
6	Conklingville Dam	12
6	Dobbs Ferry Ardsley	12
6	Glenham	12
6	New York Avenue V Brooklyn	12
6	New York Central Park Obs	12
6	New York JFK Int'l Airport	12
6	New York Laguardia Airport	12
6	Patchogue 2 N	12
6	Port Jervis	12
6	Riverhead Research Farm	12
6	Setauket Strong	12
6	West Point	12
19	Glens Falls Farm	11
19	Hudson Correctionl Facility	11
19	Middletown 2 NW	11
19	Saratoga Springs 4 SW	11
19	Walden 1 ESE	11
24	Cherry Valley 2 NNE	10
24	Gloversville	10

Lowest

Rank	Station Name	Days
1	Watertown Airport	2
2	Albion 2 NE	3
2	Canandaigua 3 S	3
2	Ogdensburg 4 NE	3
5	Aurora Research Farm	4
5	Lawrenceville 3 SW	4
5	Lockport 4 NE	4
5	Massena Airport	4
5	Oswego East	4
5	Rochester Int'l Airport	4
11	Alfred	5
11	Angelica	5
11	Batavia	5
11	Bath	5
11	Cortland	5
11	Dansville	5
11	Franklinville	5
11	Geneva Research Farm	5
11	Gouverneur 3 NW	5
11	Ithaca Cornell University	5
11	Lockport 2 SE	5
11	Ray Brook	5
11	Sodus Center	5
24	Allegany State Park	6
24	Binghamton Edwin A. Link Field	6

Annual Snowfall

Highest

Rank	Station Name	Inches
1	Old Forge	226.7
2	Boonville 2 SSW	218.6
3	Stillwater Reservoir	190.8
4	Colden 1 N	157.5
5	Oswego East	153.3
6	Wanakena Ranger School	128.0
7	Little Valley	127.9
8	Tully Heiberg Forest	125.2
9	Lowville	125.1
10	Ray Brook	124.5
11	Chasm Falls	121.2
12	Syracuse Hancock Int'l Airport	120.2
13	Cherry Valley 2 NNE	116.1
14	Watertown	110.8
15	Warsaw 6 SW	109.9
16	Slide Mountain	101.8
17	Franklinville	101.1
18	Rochester Int'l Airport	99.5
19	Utica Oneida County Airport	98.5
20	Walton	95.9
21	Buffalo Int'l Airport	95.7
22	Cortland	91.3
23	Watertown Airport	91.1
24	Canton 4 SE	90.9
25	Sodus Center	89.3

Lowest

Rank	Station Name	Inches
1	Setauket Strong	11.6
2	New York JFK Int'l Airport	20.5
3	New York Central Park Obs	21.2
4	New York Avenue V Brooklyn	21.5
5	New York Laguardia Airport	22.6
6	Bridgehampton	24.2
7	Riverhead Research Farm	25.7
8	White Plains Westchester Co Arpt.	29.3
9	West Point	30.4
10	Patchogue 2 N	30.5
11	Dobbs Ferry Ardsley	31.2
12	Poughkeepsie Dutchess Co. Arpt.	34.5
13	Glenham	36.7
14	Walden 1 ESE	38.0
14	Yorktown Heights 1 W	38.0
16	Troy Lock & Dam	41.1
17	Port Jervis	42.0
18	Elmira	42.7
19	Bath	46.7
20	Dansville	47.2
21	Chazy	56.0
22	Peru 2 WSW	58.4
23	Angelica	59.1
24	Aurora Research Farm	61.8
25	Albany County Airport	62.1

Note: See User's Guide for explanation of data.

Deadliest Storm Events in New York State: April 1996 - April 2006

Rank	Location or County	Date	Storm Event	Fatalities	Injuries	Property Damage ($mil.)	Crop Damage ($mil.)
1	New York City/Long Island	7/4/1999	Excessive Heat	33	0	0.0	0.0
2	Doraville	6/13/2003	Flash Flood	5	0	0.1	0.0
3	New York City/Long Island	3/6/1997	High Wind (64 kts.)	5	9	0.0	0.0
4	New York City/Long Island	8/8/2001	Excessive Heat	4	1	0.0	0.0
5	Nassau County	6/15/2002	Rough Seas	4	0	0.0	0.0
6	New York City/Long Island	1/17/2000	Extreme Windchill	3	0	0.0	0.0
7	Southern Suffolk County	1/27/2005	Extreme Cold/wind Chill	3	0	0.0	0.0
8	Rockaway Beach	7/23/2001	Rip Currents	3	0	0.0	0.0
9	New York City/Long Island	10/19/1996	High Wind (80 kts.)	3	0	0.0	0.0
10	Baldwinsville	9/7/1998	Thunderstorm Wind	3	7	90.0	0.0
11	SW Suffolk County	5/18/2003	Heavy Surf/High Surf	3	0	0.0	0.0
12	Delaware County	10/29/2003	Flood	2	1	0.1	0.0
13	Queens County	6/3/1996	Urban/Small Stream Flooding	2	21	0.0	0.0
14	Montauk	8/10/2002	Rip Currents	2	0	0.0	0.0
15	Erie, Genesee, Wyoming, and Livingston Counties	7/8/1998	Flood	2	0	1.7	0.1
16	Queens Village	7/18/1997	Thunderstorm Wind (50 kts.)	2	16	0.0	0.0
17	College Point	8/11/2004	Flash Flood	2	0	0.0	0.0
18	Point Lookout	10/1/2001	Rough Seas	2	0	0.0	0.0
19	Brooklyn	6/5/2005	Rip Current	2	0	0.0	0.0
20	Broome County	4/2/2005	Flash Flood	2	0	1.0	0.0

Most Destructive Storm Events in New York State: April 1996 - April 2006

Rank	Location or County	Date	Storm Event	Fatalities	Injuries	Property Damage ($mil.)	Crop Damage ($mil.)
1	Baldwinsville	9/7/1998	Thunderstorm Wind	3	7	90.0	0.0
2	Saratoga County	5/31/1998	Tornado (F3)	0	68	60.0	0.0
3	Western New York State	11/20/2000	Heavy Snow	0	0	46.5	0.0
4	Genesee Valley, Finger Lakes, and North Country	4/4/2003	Ice Storm	1	0	28.6	8.6
5	Onondaga, Cayuga, Chenango, Oneida, and Yates Counties	4/4/2003	Ice Storm	0	0	28.5	0.0
6	Clinton County	11/9/1996	Flash Flood	0	0	23.0	0.0
7	Rochester Airport	9/6/1998	Thunderstorm Wind (78 kts.)	0	1	20.0	2.0
8	West Brookville	8/30/2004	Flash Flood	0	0	20.0	0.0
9	Montezuma	9/7/1998	Thunderstorm Wind	0	3	20.0	0.0
10	New York City/Long Island	2/17/2003	Heavy Snow	0	0	20.0	0.0
11	Westchester, Orange, Putnam, and Rockland Counties	4/2/2005	Flood	0	0	17.0	0.0
12	Sullivan County	9/18/2004	Flash Flood	0	0	15.0	0.0
13	Steuben County	11/8/1996	Flash Flood	0	0	14.4	0.0
14	Genesee, Niagara, Northern Erie, and Wyoming Counties	12/24/2001	Heavy Snow	0	0	14.3	0.0
15	Jefferson and Lewis Counties	1/8/1998	Ice Storm	0	0	12.0	0.0
16	Delaware County	9/18/2004	Flash Flood	0	0	12.0	0.0
17	Cortland County	4/1/2005	Flood	0	0	12.0	0.0
18	New York City/Long Island	10/19/1996	Coastal Flood	0	0	11.5	0.0
19	Champlain Valley/Northern New York	1/6/1998	Ice Storm	1	0	11.0	0.0
20	Nassau County	10/14/2005	Flash Flood	0	0	11.0	0.0
21	Suffolk County	10/14/2005	Flash Flood	0	0	11.0	0.0
22	Verona	9/7/1998	Thunderstorm Wind	0	0	10.0	0.0
23	Sullivan County	4/2/2005	Flash Flood	0	0	10.0	0.0
24	Rensselaer County	5/31/1998	Tornado (F2)	0	0	10.0	0.2
25	Broome County	9/17/2004	Flash Flood	0	0	10.0	0.0
26	Nunda	8/9/2003	Flash Flood	0	0	10.0	0.0

Grey House Publishing
Business Directories

New York State Directory, 2006/07

The *New York State Directory*, published annually since 1983, is a comprehensive and easy-to-use guide to accessing public officials and private sector organizations and individuals who influence public policy in the state of New York. *The New York State Directory* includes important information on all New York state legislators and congressional representatives, including biographies and key committee assignments. It also includes staff rosters for all branches of New York state government and for federal agencies and departments that impact the state policy process. Following the state government section are 25 chapters covering policy areas from agriculture through veterans' affairs. Each chapter identifies the state, local and federal agencies and officials that formulate or implement policy. In addition, each chapter contains a roster of private sector experts and advocates who influence the policy process. The directory also offers appendices that include statewide party officials; chambers of commerce; lobbying organizations; public and private universities and colleges; television, radio and print media; and local government agencies and officials.

New York State Directory - 800 pages; Softcover ISBN 1-59237-145-0; $145.00
New York State Directory with Profiles of New York – 2 volumes; 1,600 pages; Softcover ISBN 1-59237-162-0; $225

Profiles of New York ♦ Profiles of Florida ♦ Profiles of Texas ♦ Profiles of Illinois ♦ Profiles of Michigan ♦ Profiles of Ohio

Packed with over 50 pieces of data that make up a complete, user-friendly profile of each state, these directories go even further by then pulling selected data and providing it in ranking list form for even easier comparisons between the 100 largest towns and cities! The careful layout gives the user an easy-to-read snapshot of every single place and county in the state, from the biggest metropolis to the smallest unincorporated hamlet. The richness of each place or county profile is astounding in its depth, from history to weather, all packed in an easy-to-navigate, compact format. No need for piles of multiple sources with this volume on your desk. Here is a look at just a few of the data sets you'll find in each profile: History, Geography, Climate, Population, Vital Statistics, Economy, Income, Taxes, Education, Housing, Health & Environment, Public Safety, Newspapers, Transportation, Presidential Election Results, Information Contacts and Chambers of Commerce. As an added bonus, there is a section on Selected Statistics, where data from the 100 largest towns and cities is arranged into easy-to-use charts. Each of 22 different data points has its own two-page spread with the cities listed in alpha order so researchers can easily compare and rank cities. A remarkable compilation that offers overviews and insights into each corner of the state, *Profiles of New York*, *Profiles of Florida* and *Profiles of Texas* go beyond Census statistics, beyond metro area coverage, beyond the 100 best places to live. Drawn from official census information, other government statistics and original research, you will have at your fingertips data that's available nowhere else in one single source. Data will be published on additional states in 2006 and 2007.

Profiles of New York: 800 pages; Softcover ISBN 1-59237-161-2; $149.00 ♦ Profiles of Florida: 800 pages; Softcover ISBN 1-59237-160-8; $149.00 ♦ Profiles of Texas: 800 pages; Softcover ISBN 1-59237-111-6; $149.00 ♦ Profiles of Illinois: 800 pages; Softcover ISBN 1-59237-148-5; $149.00 ♦ Profiles of Michigan: 800 pages; Softcover ISBN 1-59237-149-3; $149.00 ♦ Profiles of Ohio: 800 pages; Softcover ISBN 1-59237-175-2; $149.00

The Directory of Business Information Resources, 2007

With 100% verification, over 1,000 new listings and more than 12,000 updates, this 2007 edition of *The Directory of Business Information Resources* is the most up-to-date source for contacts in over 98 business areas – from advertising and agriculture to utilities and wholesalers. This carefully researched volume details: the Associations representing each industry; the Newsletters that keep members current; the Magazines and Journals - with their "Special Issues" - that are important to the trade, the Conventions that are "must attends," Databases, Directories and Industry Web Sites that provide access to must-have marketing resources. Includes contact names, phone & fax numbers, web sites and e-mail addresses. This one-volume resource is a gold mine of information and would be a welcome addition to any reference collection.

"This is a most useful and easy-to-use addition to any researcher's library." –The Information Professionals Institute

800 pages; Softcover ISBN 1-59237-146-9, $195.00 ♦ Online Database $495.00

To preview any of our Directories Risk-Free for 30 days, call (800) 562-2139 or fax to (518) 789-0556

Nations of the World, 2006 A Political, Economic and Business Handbook

This completely revised edition covers all the nations of the world in an easy-to-use, single volume. Each nation is profiled in a single chapter that includes Key Facts, Political & Economic Issues, a Country Profile and Business Information. In this fast-changing world it is extremely important to make sure that the most up-to-date information is included in your reference collection. This edition is ju the answer. Each of the 200+ country chapters have been carefully reviewed by a political expert to make sure that the text reflects th most current information on Politics, Travel Advisories, Economics and more. You'll find such vital information as a Country Map, Population Characteristics, Inflation, Agricultural Production, Foreign Debt, Political History, Foreign Policy, Regional Insecurity, Economics, Trade & Tourism, Historical Profile, Political Systems, Ethnicity, Languages, Media, Climate, Hotels, Chambers of Commerce, Banking, Travel Information and more. Five Regional Chapters follow the main text and include a Regional Map, an Introductory Article, Key Indicators and Currencies for the Region. As an added bonus, an all-inclusive CD-ROM is available as a companion to the printed text. Noted for its sophisticated, up-to-date and reliable compilation of political, economic and business information, this brand new edition will be an important acquisition to any public, academic or special library reference collection.

"A useful addition to both general reference collections and business collections." —RUS

1,700 pages; Print Version Only Softcover ISBN 1-59237-0079-9, $155.00

The Directory of Venture Capital & Private Equity Firms, 2006

This edition has been extensively updated and broadly expanded to offer direct access to over 2,800 Domestic and International Venture Capital Firms, including address, phone & fax numbers, e-mail addresses and web sites for both primary and branch locations Entries include details on the firm's Mission Statement, Industry Group Preferences, Geographic Preferences, Average and Minimum Investments and Investment Criteria. You'll also find details that are available nowhere else, including the Firm's Portfolio Companie and extensive information on each of the firm's Managing Partners, such as Education, Professional Background and Directorships held, along with the Partner's E-mail Address. *The Directory of Venture Capital & Private Equity Firms* offers five important indexes: Geographic Index, Executive Name Index, Portfolio Company Index, Industry Preference Index and College & University Index. With its comprehensive coverage and detailed, extensive information on each company, *The Directory of Venture Capital & Private Equi Firms* is an important addition to any finance collection.

"The sheer number of listings, the descriptive information provided and the outstanding indexing make this directory a better value than its princi competitor, Pratt's Guide to Venture Capital Sources. Recommended for business collections in large public, academic and business libraries." —Cho

1,300 pages; Softcover ISBN 1-59237-102-7, $450.00 ♦ Online Database (includes a free copy of the directory) $889.00

The Directory of Mail Order Catalogs, 2006

Published since 1981, this updated edition features 100% verification of data and is the premier source of information on the mail orde catalog industry. Details over 12,000 consumer catalog companies with 44 different product chapters from Animals to Toys & Games Contains detailed contact information including e-mail addresses and web sites along with important business details such as employe size, years in business, sales volume, catalog size, number of catalogs mailed and more. Four indexes provide quick access to information: Catalog & Company Name Index, Geographic Index, Product Index and Web Sites Index.

"This is a godsend for those looking for information." —Reference Book Rev

1,700 pages; Softcover ISBN 1-59237-103-5 $250.00 ♦ Online Database (includes a free copy of the directory) $495.00

The Directory of Business to Business Catalogs, 2006

The completely updated *Directory of Business to Business Catalogs,* provides details on over 6,000 suppliers of everything from computer to laboratory supplies... office products to office design... marketing resources to safety equipment... landscaping to maintenance suppliers... building construction and much more. Detailed entries offer mailing address, phone & fax numbers, e-mail addresses, wel sites, key contacts, sales volume, employee size, catalog printing information and more. Jut about every kind of product a business needs in its day-to-day operations is covered in this carefully-researched volume. Three indexes are provided for at-a-glance access to information: Catalog & Company Name Index, Geographic Index and Web Sites Index.

"An excellent choice for libraries... wishing to supplement their business supplier resources." —Bookt

800 pages; Softcover ISBN 1-59237-105-1, $165.00 ♦ Online Database (includes a free copy of the directory) $325.00

To preview any of our Directories Risk-Free for 30 days, call (800) 562-2139 or fax to (518) 789-055

Sports Market Place Directory, 2006

For over 20 years, this comprehensive, up-to-date directory has offered direct access to the Who, What, When & Where of the Sports Industry. With over 20,000 updates and enhancements, the *Sports Market Place Directory* is the most detailed, comprehensive and current sports business reference source available. In 1,800 information-packed pages, *Sports Market Place Directory* profiles contact information and key executives for: Single Sport Organizations, Professional Leagues, Multi-Sport Organizations, Disabled Sports, High School & Youth Sports, Military Sports, Olympic Organizations, Media, Sponsors, Sponsorship & Marketing Event Agencies, Event & Meeting Calendars, Professional Services, College Sports, Manufacturers & Retailers, Facilities and much more. *The Sports Market Place Directory* provides organization's contact information with detailed descriptions including: Key Contacts, physical, mailing, email and web addresses plus phone and fax numbers. Plus, nine important indexes make sure that you can find the information you're looking for quickly and easily: Entry Index, Single Sport Index, Media Index, Sponsor Index, Agency Index, Manufacturers Index, Brand Name Index, Facilities Index and Executive/Geographic Index. For over twenty years, *The Sports Market Place Directory* has assisted thousands of individuals in their pursuit of a career in the sports industry. Why not use "THE SOURCE" that top recruiters, headhunters and career placement centers use to find information on or about sports organizations and key hiring contacts.

1800 pages; Softcover ISBN 1-59237-139-6, $225.00 ◆ Online Database $479.00

Thomas Food and Beverage Market Place, 2006

Thomas Food and Beverage Market Place is bigger and better than ever with thousands of new companies, thousands of updates to existing companies and two revised and enhanced product category indexes. This comprehensive directory profiles over 18,000 Food & Beverage Manufacturers, 12,000 Equipment & Supply Companies, 2,200 Transportation & Warehouse Companies, 2,000 Brokers & Wholesalers, 8,000 Importers & Exporters, 900 Industry Resources and hundreds of Mail Order Catalogs. Listings include detailed contact Information, Sales Volumes, Key Contacts, Brand & Product Information, Packaging Details and much more. *Thomas Food and Beverage Market Place* is available as a three-volume printed set, a subscription-based Online Database via the Internet, on CD-ROM, as well as mailing lists and a licensable database.

"An essential purchase for those in the food industry but will also be useful in public libraries where needed. Much of the information will be difficult and time consuming to locate without this handy three-volume ready-reference source." –ARBA

3000 pages, 3 Volume Set; Softcover ISBN 1-59237-096-9, $495.00 ◆ CD-ROM $695.00 ◆ CD-ROM & 3 Volume Set Combo $895.00 ◆ Online Database $695.00 ◆ Online Database & 3 Volume Set Combo, $895.00

The Grey House Homeland Security Directory, 2006

This updated edition features the latest contact information for government and private organizations involved with Homeland Security along with the latest product information and provides detailed profiles of nearly 1,000 Federal & State Organizations & Agencies and over 3,000 Officials and Key Executives involved with Homeland Security. These listings are incredibly detailed and include Mailing Address, Phone & Fax Numbers, Email Addresses & Web Sites, a complete Description of the Agency and a complete list of the Officials and Key Executives associated with the Agency. Next, *The Grey House Homeland Security Directory* provides the go-to source for Homeland Security Products & Services. This section features over 2,000 Companies that provide Consulting, Products or Services. With this Buyer's Guide at their fingertips, users can locate suppliers of everything from Training Materials to Access Controls, from Perimeter Security to BioTerrorism Countermeasures and everything in between – complete with contact information and product descriptions. A handy Product Locator Index is provided to quickly and easily locate suppliers of a particular product. Lastly, an Information Resources Section provides immediate access to contact information for hundreds of Associations, Newsletters, Magazines, Trade Shows, Databases and Directories that focus on Homeland Security. This comprehensive, information-packed resource will be a welcome tool for any company or agency that is in need of Homeland Security information and will be a necessary acquisition for the reference collection of all public libraries and large school districts.

"Compiles this information in one place and is discerning in content. A useful purchase for public and academic libraries." –Booklist

pages; Softcover ISBN 1-59237-084-5, $195.00 ◆ Online Database (includes a free copy of the directory) $385.00

The Grey House Transportation Security Directory & Handbook

This brand new title is the only reference of its kind that brings together current data on Transportation Security. With information on everything from Regulatory Authorities to Security Equipment, this top-flight database brings together the relevant information necessary for creating and maintaining a security plan for a wide range of transportation facilities. With this current, comprehensive directory at the ready you'll have immediate access to: Regulatory Authorities & Legislation; Information Resources; Sample Security Plans & Checklists; Contact Data for Major Airports, Seaports, Railroads, Trucking Companies and Oil Pipelines; Security Service Providers; Recommended Equipment & Product Information and more. Using the *Grey House Transportation Security Directory & Handbook*, managers will be able to quickly and easily assess their current security plans; develop contacts to create and maintain new security procedures; and source the products and services necessary to adequately maintain a secure environment. This valuable resource is a must for all Security Managers at Airports, Seaports, Railroads, Trucking Companies and Oil Pipelines.

pages; Softcover ISBN 1-59237-075-6, $195

To preview any of our Directories Risk-Free for 30 days, call (800) 562-2139 or fax to (518) 789-0556

The Grey House Safety & Security Directory, 2006

The Grey House Safety & Security Directory is the most comprehensive reference tool and buyer's guide for the safety and security industry. Arranged by safety topic, each chapter begins with OSHA regulations for the topic, followed by Training Articles written by top professionals in the field and Self-Inspection Checklists. Next, each topic contains Buyer's Guide sections that feature related products and services. Topics include Administration, Insurance, Loss Control & Consulting, Protective Equipment & Apparel, Noise Vibration, Facilities Monitoring & Maintenance, Employee Health Maintenance & Ergonomics, Retail Food Services, Machine Guard Process Guidelines & Tool Handling, Ordinary Materials Handling, Hazardous Materials Handling, Workplace Preparation & Maintenance, Electrical Lighting & Safety, Fire & Rescue and Security. The Buyer's Guide sections are carefully indexed within each topic area to ensure that you can find the supplies needed to meet OSHA's regulations. Six important indexes make finding information and product manufacturers quick and easy: Geographical Index of Manufacturers and Distributors, Company Profile Index, Brand Name Index, Product Index, Index of Web Sites and Index of Advertisers. This comprehensive, up-to-date reference will provide every tool necessary to make sure a business is in compliance with OSHA regulations and locate the products and services needed to meet those regulations.

"Presents industrial safety information for engineers, plant managers, risk managers, and construction site supervisors..." –Ch

1,500 pages, 2 Volume Set; Softcover ISBN 1-59237-104-3, $225.00

The Grey House Biometric Information Directory, 2006

The Biometric Information Directory is the only comprehensive source for current biometric industry information. This 2006 edition is the first published by Grey House. With 100% updated information, this latest edition offers a complete, current look, in both print and online form, of biometric companies and products – one of the fastest growing industries in today's economy. Detailed profiles of manufacturers of the latest biometric technology, including Finger, Voice, Face, Hand, Signature, Iris, Vein and Palm Identification systems. Data on the companies include key executives, company size and a detailed, indexed description of their product line. Plus, the Directory also includes valuable business resources, and current editorial make this edition the easiest way for the business community and consumers alike to access the largest, most current compilation of biometric industry information available on the market today. The new edition boasts increased numbers of companies, contact names and company data, with over 700 manufacturers and service providers. Information in the directory includes: Editorial on Advancements in Biometrics; Profiles of 700+ companies listed with contact information; Organizations, Trade & Educational Associations, Publications, Conferences, Trade Shows and Expositions Worldwide; Web Site Index; Biometric & Vendors Services Index by Types of Biometrics; and a Glossary of Biometric Terms. This resource will be an important source for anyone who is considering the use of a biometric product, investing in the development of biometric technology, support existing marketing and sales efforts and will be an important acquisition for the business reference collection for large public and business libraries.

800 pages; Softcover ISBN 1-59237-121-3, $225

The Grey House Performing Arts Directory, 2007

The Grey House Performing Arts Directory is the most comprehensive resource covering the Performing Arts. This important directory provides current information on over 8,500 Dance Companies, Instrumental Music Programs, Opera Companies, Choral Groups, Theater Companies, Performing Arts Series and Performing Arts Facilities. Plus, this edition now contains a brand new section on Artist Management Groups. In addition to mailing address, phone & fax numbers, e-mail addresses and web sites, dozens of other fields of available information include mission statement, key contacts, facilities, seating capacity, season, attendance and more. This directory also provides an important Information Resources section that covers hundreds of Performing Arts Associations, Magazines Newsletters, Trade Shows, Directories, Databases and Industry Web Sites. Five indexes provide immediate access to this wealth of information: Entry Name, Executive Name, Performance Facilities, Geographic and Information Resources. *The Grey House Performing Arts Directory* pulls together thousands of Performing Arts Organizations, Facilities and Information Resources into an easy-to-use source – this kind of comprehensiveness and extensive detail is not available in any resource on the market place today.

"Immensely useful and user-friendly ... recommended for public, academic and certain special library reference collections." –Boo

1,500 pages; Softcover ISBN 1-59237-138-8, $185.00 ◆ Online Database $335.00

To preview any of our Directories Risk-Free for 30 days, call (800) 562-2139 or fax to (518) 789-055

The Rauch Guide to the US Adhesives & Sealants, Cosmetics & Toiletries, Ink, Paint, Plastics, Pulp & Paper and Rubber Industries

The Rauch Guides are known worldwide for their comprehensive marketing information. Acquired by Grey House Publishing in 2005, new updated and revised editions will be published throughout 2005 and 2006. Each Guide provides market facts and figures in a highly organized format, ideal for today's busy personnel, serving as ready-references for top executives as well as the industry newcomer. *The Rauch Guides* save time and money by organizing widely scattered information and providing estimates for important business decisions, some of which are available nowhere else. Each Guide is organized into several information-packed chapters. After a brief introduction, the ECONOMICS section provides data on industry shipments; long-term growth and forecasts; prices; company performance; employment, expenditures, and productivity; transportation and geographical patterns; packaging; foreign trade; and government regulations. Next, TECHNOLOGY & RAW MATERIALS provide market, technical, and raw material information for chemicals, equipment and related materials, including market size and leading suppliers, prices, end uses, and trends. PRODUCTS & MARKETS provide information for each major industry product, including market size and historical trends, leading suppliers, five-year forecasts, industry structure, and major end uses. For easy access, each *Guide* contains a chapter on INDUSTRY ACTIVITIES, ORGANIZATIONS & SOURCES OF INFORMATION with detailed information on meetings, exhibits, and trade shows, sources of statistical information, trade associations, technical and professional societies, and trade and technical periodicals. Next, the COMPANY DIRECTORY profiles major industry companies, both public and private. Generally several hundred companies are analyzed. Information includes complete contact information, web address, estimated total and domestic sales, product description, and recent mergers and acquisitions. Each Guide also contains several APPENDICES that provide a cross-reference of suppliers, subsidiaries and divisions. The Rauch Guides will prove to be an invaluable source of market information, company data, trends and forecasts that anyone in these fast-paced industries.

The Rauch Guide to the U.S. Paint Industry Softcover ISBN 1-59237-127-2 $595 ♦ The Rauch Guide to the U.S. Plastics Industry Softcover ISBN 1-59237-128-0 $595 ♦ The Rauch Guide to the U.S. Adhesives and Sealants Industry Softcover ISBN 1-59237-129-9 $595 ♦ The Rauch Guide to the U.S. Ink Industry Softcover ISBN 1-59237-126-4 $595 ♦ The Rauch Guide to the U.S. Rubber Industry Softcover ISBN 1-59237-130-2 $595 ♦ The Rauch Guide to the U.S. Pulp and Paper Industry Softcover ISBN 1-59237-131-0 $595 ♦ The Rauch Guide to the U.S. Cosmetic and Toiletries Industry Softcover ISBN 1-59237-132-9 $895

Research Services Directory: Commercial & Corporate Research Centers

This Ninth Edition provides access to well over 8,000 independent Commercial Research Firms, Corporate Research Centers and Laboratories offering contract services for hands-on, basic or applied research. *Research Services Directory* covers the thousands of types of research companies, including Biotechnology & Pharmaceutical Developers, Consumer Product Research, Defense Contractors, Electronics & Software Engineers, Think Tanks, Forensic Investigators, Independent Commercial Laboratories, Information Brokers, Market & Survey Research Companies, Medical Diagnostic Facilities, Product Research & Development Firms and more. Each entry provides the company's name, mailing address, phone & fax numbers, key contacts, web site, e-mail address, as well as a company description and research and technical fields served. Four indexes provide immediate access to this wealth of information: Research Firms Index, Geographic Index, Personnel Name Index and Subject Index.

"An important source for organizations in need of information about laboratories, individuals and other facilities." –ARBA

1400 pages; Softcover ISBN 1-59237-003-9, $395.00 ♦ Online Database (includes a free copy of the directory) $850.00

International Business and Trade Directories

Completely updated, the Third Edition of *International Business and Trade Directories* now contains more than 10,000 entries, over 2,000 more than the last edition, making this directory the most comprehensive resource of the worlds business and trade directories. Entries include content descriptions, price, publisher's name and address, web site and e-mail addresses, phone and fax numbers and editorial staff. Organized by industry group, and then by region, this resource puts over 10,000 industry-specific business and trade directories at the reader's fingertips. Three indexes are included for quick access to information: Geographic Index, Publisher Index and Title Index. Public, college and corporate libraries, as well as individuals and corporations seeking critical market information will want to add this directory to their marketing collection.

"Reasonably priced for a work of this type, this directory should appeal to larger academic, public and corporate libraries with an international focus." –Library Journal

1800 pages; Softcover ISBN 1-930956-63-0, $225.00 ♦ Online Database (includes a free copy of the directory) $450.00

To preview any of our Directories Risk-Free for 30 days, call (800) 562-2139 or fax to (518) 789-0556

Universal Reference Publications
Statistical & Demographic Reference Books

America's Top-Rated Cities, 2006
America's Top-Rated Cities provides current, comprehensive statistical information and other essential data in one easy-to-use source on the 100 "top" cities that have been cited as the best for business and living in the U.S. This handbook allows readers to see, at a glance, a concise social, business, economic, demographic and environmental profile of each city, including brief evaluative comments. In addition to detailed data on Cost of Living, Finances, Real Estate, Education, Major Employers, Media, Crime and Climate, city reports now include Housing Vacancies, Tax Audits, Bankruptcy, Presidential Election Results and more. This outstanding source of information will be widely used in any reference collection.

"The only source of its kind that brings together all of this information into on easy-to-use source. It will be beneficial to many business and public libraries." –ARB

2,500 pages, 4 Volume Set; Softcover ISBN 1-59237-076-4, $195.00

America's Top-Rated Smaller Cities, 2006/07
A perfect companion to *America's Top-Rated Cities*, *America's Top-Rated Smaller Cities* provides current, comprehensive business and living profiles of smaller cities (population 25,000-99,999) that have been cited as the best for business and living in the United States. Sixty cities make up this 2004 edition of *America's Top-Rated Smaller Cities*, all are top-ranked by Population Growth, Median Income, Unemployment Rate and Crime Rate. City reports reflect the most current data available on a wide-range of statistics, including Employment & Earnings, Household Income, Unemployment Rate, Population Characteristics, Taxes, Cost of Living, Education, Health Care, Public Safety, Recreation, Media, Air & Water Quality and much more. Plus, each city report contains a Background of the City, and an Overview of the State Finances. *America's Top-Rated Smaller Cities* offers a reliable, one-stop source for statistical data that, before now, could only be found scattered in hundreds of sources. This volume is designed for a wide range of readers: individual considering relocating a residence or business; professionals considering expanding their business or changing careers; general and market researchers; real estate consultants; human resource personnel; urban planners and investors.

"Provides current, comprehensive statistical information in one easy-to-use source... Recommended for public and academic libraries and specialized collections." –Library Journ

1,100 pages; Softcover ISBN 1-59237-135-3, $160.00

Profiles of America: Facts, Figures & Statistics for Every Populated Place in the United States
Profiles of America is the only source that pulls together, in one place, statistical, historical and descriptive information about every plac in the United States in an easy-to-use format. This award winning reference set, now in its second edition, compiles statistics and data from over 20 different sources – the latest census information has been included along with more than nine brand new statistical topics This Four-Volume Set details over 40,000 places, from the biggest metropolis to the smallest unincorporated hamlet, and provides statistical details and information on over 50 different topics including Geography, Climate, Population, Vital Statistics, Economy, Income, Taxes, Education, Housing, Health & Environment, Public Safety, Newspapers, Transportation, Presidential Election Results and Information Contacts or Chambers of Commerce. Profiles are arranged, for ease-of-use, by state and then by county. Each count begins with a County-Wide Overview and is followed by information for each Community in that particular county. The Community Profiles within the county are arranged alphabetically. *Profiles of America* is a virtual snapshot of America at your fingertips and a unique compilation of information that will be widely used in any reference collection.

A Library Journal Best Reference Book "An outstanding compilation." –Library Jour

10,000 pages; Four Volume Set; Softcover ISBN 1-891482-80-7, $595.00

The Comparative Guide to American Suburbs, 2005
The Comparative Guide to American Suburbs is a one-stop source for Statistics on the 2,000+ suburban communities surrounding the 50 largest metropolitan areas – their population characteristics, income levels, economy, school system and important data on how they compare to one another. Organized into 50 Metropolitan Area chapters, each chapter contains an overview of the Metropolitan Area, detailed Map followed by a comprehensive Statistical Profile of each Suburban Community, including Contact Information, Physical Characteristics, Population Characteristics, Income, Economy, Unemployment Rate, Cost of Living, Education, Chambers of Commer and more. Next, statistical data is sorted into Ranking Tables that rank the suburbs by twenty different criteria, including Population Per Capita Income, Unemployment Rate, Crime Rate, Cost of Living and more. *The Comparative Guide to American Suburbs* is the best source for locating data on suburbs. Those looking to relocate, as well as those doing preliminary market research, will find this an invaluable timesaving resource.

"Public and academic libraries will find this compilation useful... The work draws togeth figures from many sources and will be especially helpful for job relocation decisions." – Bookli

1,700 pages; Softcover ISBN 1-59237-004-7, $130.00

To preview any of our Directories Risk-Free for 30 days, call (800) 562-2139 or fax to (518) 789-0556

The Asian Databook: Statistics for all US Counties & Cities with Over 10,000 Population

This is the first-ever resource that compiles statistics and rankings on the US Asian population. *The Asian Databook* presents over 20 statistical data points for each city and county, arranged alphabetically by state, then alphabetically by place name. Data reported for each place includes Population, Languages Spoken at Home, Foreign-Born, Educational Attainment, Income Figures, Poverty Status, Homeownership, Home Values & Rent, and more. Next, in the Rankings Section, the top 75 places are listed for each data element. These easy-to-access ranking tables allow the user to quickly determine trends and population characteristics. This kind of comparative data can not be found elsewhere, in print or on the web, in a format that's as easy-to-use or more concise. A useful resource for those searching for demographics data, career search and relocation information and also for market research. With data ranging from Ancestry to Education, *The Asian Databook* presents a useful compilation of information that will be a much-needed resource in the reference collection of any public or academic library along with the marketing collection of any company whose primary focus in on the Asian population.

000 pages; Softcover ISBN 1-59237-044-6 $150.00

The Hispanic Databook: Statistics for all US Counties & Cities with Over 10,000 Population

Previously published by Toucan Valley Publications, this second edition has been completely updated with figures from the latest census and has been broadly expanded to include dozens of new data elements and a brand new Rankings section. The Hispanic population in the United States has increased over 42% in the last 10 years and accounts for 12.5% of the total US population. For ease-of-use, *The Hispanic Databook* presents over 20 statistical data points for each city and county, arranged alphabetically by state, then alphabetically by place name. Data reported for each place includes Population, Languages Spoken at Home, Foreign-Born, Educational Attainment, Income Figures, Poverty Status, Homeownership, Home Values & Rent, and more. Next, in the Rankings Section, the top places are listed for each data element. These easy-to-access ranking tables allow the user to quickly determine trends and population characteristics. This kind of comparative data can not be found elsewhere, in print or on the web, in a format that's as easy-to-use or more concise. A useful resource for those searching for demographics data, career search and relocation information and also for market research. With data ranging from Ancestry to Education, *The Hispanic Databook* presents a useful compilation of information that will be a much-needed resource in the reference collection of any public or academic library along with the marketing collection of any company whose primary focus in on the Hispanic population.

"This accurate, clearly presented volume of selected Hispanic demographics is recommended for large public libraries and research collections." -Library Journal

000 pages; Softcover ISBN 1-59237-008-X, $150.00

Ancestry in America: A Comparative Guide to Over 200 Ethnic Backgrounds

This brand new reference work pulls together thousands of comparative statistics on the Ethnic Backgrounds of all populated places in the United States with populations over 10,000. Never before has this kind of information been reported in a single volume. Section One, Statistics by Place, is made up of a list of over 200 ancestry and race categories arranged alphabetically by each of the 5,000 different places with populations over 10,000. The population number of the ancestry group in that city or town is provided along with the percent that group represents of the total population. This informative city-by-city section allows the user to quickly and easily explore the ethnic makeup of all major population bases in the United States. Section Two, Comparative Rankings, contains three tables for each ethnicity and race. In the first table, the top 150 populated places are ranked by population number for that particular ancestry group, regardless of population. In the second table, the top 150 populated places are ranked by the percent of the total population for that ancestry group. In the third table, those top 150 populated places with 10,000 population are ranked by population number for each ancestry group. These easy-to-navigate tables allow users to see ancestry population patterns and make city-by-city comparisons as well. Plus, as an added bonus with the purchase of *Ancestry in America*, a free companion CD-ROM is available that lists statistics and rankings for all of the 35,000 populated places in the United States. This brand new, information-packed resource will serve a wide range or research requests for demographics, population characteristics, relocation information and much more. *Ancestry in America: A Comparative Guide to Over 200 Ethnic Backgrounds* will be an important acquisition to all reference collections.

"This compilation will serve a wide range of research requests for population characteristics … it offers much more detail than other sources." –Booklist

500 pages; Softcover ISBN 1-59237-029-2, $225.00

To preview any of our Directories Risk-Free for 30 days, call (800) 562-2139 or fax to (518) 789-0556

The American Tally: Statistics & Comparative Rankings for U.S. Cities with Populations over 10,000

This important statistical handbook compiles, all in one place, comparative statistics on all U.S. cities and towns with a 10,000+ population. *The American Tally* provides statistical details on over 4,000 cities and towns and profiles how they compare with one another in Population Characteristics, Education, Language & Immigration, Income & Employment and Housing. Each section begins with an alphabetical listing of cities by state, allowing for quick access to both the statistics and relative rankings of any city. Next, the highest and lowest cities are listed in each statistic. These important, informative lists provide quick reference to which cities are at both extremes of the spectrum for each statistic. Unlike any other reference, *The American Tally* provides quick, easy access to comparative statistics – a must-have for any reference collection.

"A solid library reference." -Bookwat

500 pages; Softcover ISBN 1-930956-29-0, $125.00

The Grey House Handbook on Alternative Energy, 2006

This is the first ever resource to pull together information, resources and statistics for all types of Alternative Energy, including Hydro Wind, Solar, Coal, Natural Gas and Atomic Energy sources. The Handbook begins with an informative Introduction to Alternative Energy Resources, including editorial on the history of energy, the necessity of using alternative energy, conservation and the economics of using alternative energy sources. Plus, handy charts are also included that cover uses of energy sources today; forecasts energy sources and the availability of energy sources in the future. Next, readers will find chapters on each Type of Energy Source. Chapters begin with an Introduction to the specific energy source, History, Strengths & Drawbacks, Industrial & Residential Use and Trends. Several articles are also included for each energy source, followed by Resources, including Associations, Magazines, Trade Shows and Vendors. The Grey House Handbook on Alternative Energy also contains a informative, useful section on Statistics. These charts allow for easy location of very specific data. A handy Glossary and section on Public Energy Companies is also included for eas reference. Three indexes, Product Index, Subject Index and Entry Name Index allow the user to locate specific resources quickly and easily. As the need for alternative energy sources continues to grow, having access to these resources will become more and more important. This first edition will prove useful to the reference collections public and academic libraries.

800 pages; Softcover ISBN 1-59237-134-5; $165.00

The Environmental Resource Handbook, 2005/06

The Environmental Resource Handbook is the most up-to-date and comprehensive source for Environmental Resources and Statistics. Section I: Resources provides detailed contact information for thousands of information sources, including Associations & Organizations, Awards & Honors, Conferences, Foundations & Grants, Environmental Health, Government Agencies, National Parks & Wildlife Refuges, Publications, Research Centers, Educational Programs, Green Product Catalogs, Consultants and much more. Section II: Statistics, provides statistics and rankings on hundreds of important topics, including Children's Environmental Index, Municipal Finances, Toxic Chemicals, Recycling, Climate, Air & Water Quality and more. This kind of up-to-date environmental data all in one place, is not available anywhere else on the market place today. This vast compilation of resources and statistics is a must-have for all public and academic libraries as well as any organization with a primary focus on the environment.

"…the intrinsic value of the information make it worth consideration by libraries wi environmental collections and environmentally concerned users." –Booki

1,000 pages; Softcover ISBN 1-59237-090-X, $155.00 ♦ Online Database $300.00

Weather America, A Thirty-Year Summary of Statistical Weather Data and Rankings

This valuable resource provides extensive climatological data for over 4,000 National and Cooperative Weather Stations throughout the United States. *Weather America* begins with a new Major Storms section that details major storm events of the nation and a National Rankings section that details rankings for several data elements, such as Maximum Temperature and Precipitation. The ma body of *Weather America* is organized into 50 state sections. Each section provides a Data Table on each Weather Station, organized alphabetically, that provides statistics on Maximum and Minimum Temperatures, Precipitation, Snowfall, Extreme Temperatures, Foggy Days, Humidity and more. State sections contain two brand new features in this edition – a City Index and a narrative Description of the climatic conditions of the state. Each section also includes a revised Map of the State that includes not only weathe stations, but cities and towns.

"Best Reference Book of the Year." –Library Journ

2,013 pages; Softcover ISBN 1-891482-29-7, $175.00

To preview any of our Directories Risk-Free for 30 days, call (800) 562-2139 or fax to (518) 789-0556

Mackenzie & Harris
General Reference Titles

The Value of a Dollar 1600-1859, The Colonial Era to The Civil War

Following the format of the widely acclaimed, T*he Value of a Dollar, 1860-2004*, *The Value of a Dollar 1600-1859, The Colonial Era to The Civil War* records the actual prices of thousands of items that consumers purchased from the Colonial Era to the Civil War. Our editorial department had been flooded with requests from users of our Value of a Dollar for the same type of information, just from an earlier time period. This new volume is just the answer – with pricing data from 1600 to 1859. Arranged into five-year chapters, each 5-year chapter includes a Historical Snapshot, Consumer Expenditures, Investments, Selected Income, Income/Standard Jobs, Food Basket, Standard Prices and Miscellany. There is also a section on Trends. This informative section charts the change in price over time and provides added detail on the reasons prices changed within the time period, including industry developments, changes in consumer attitudes and important historical facts. This fascinating survey will serve a wide range of research needs and will be useful in any high school, public and academic library reference collections.

pages; Hardcover ISBN 1-59237-094-2, $135.00

The Value of a Dollar 1860-2004, Third Edition

A guide to practical economy, *The Value of a Dollar* records the actual prices of thousands of items that consumers purchased from the Civil War to the present, along with facts about investment options and income opportunities. This brand new Third Edition boasts a brand new addition to each five-year chapter, a section on Trends. This informative section charts the change in price over time and provides added detail on the reasons prices changed within the time period, including industry developments, changes in consumer attitudes and important historical facts. Plus, a brand new chapter for 2000-2004 has been added. Each 5-year chapter includes a Historical Snapshot, Consumer Expenditures, Investments, Selected Income, Income/Standard Jobs, Food Basket, Standard Prices and Miscellany. This interesting and useful publication will be widely used in any reference collection.

"Recommended for high school, college and public libraries." –ARBA

pages; Hardcover ISBN 1-59237-074-8, $135.00

Working Americans 1880-1999
Volume I: The Working Class, Volume II: The Middle Class, Volume III: The Upper Class

Each of the volumes in the *Working Americans 1880-1999* series focuses on a particular class of Americans, The Working Class, The Middle Class and The Upper Class over the last 120 years. Chapters in each volume focus on one decade and profile three to five families. Family Profiles include real data on Income & Job Descriptions, Selected Prices of the Times, Annual Income, Annual Budgets, Family Finances, Life at Work, Life at Home, Life in the Community, Working Conditions, Cost of Living, Amusements and much more. Each chapter also contains an Economic Profile with Average Wages of other Professions, a selection of Typical Pricing, Key Events & Inventions, News Profiles, Articles from Local Media and Illustrations. The *Working Americans* series captures the lifestyles of each of the classes from the last twelve decades, covers a vast array of occupations and ethnic backgrounds and travels the entire nation. These interesting and useful compilations of portraits of the American Working, Middle and Upper Classes during the last 120 years will be an important addition to any high school, public or academic library reference collection.

"These interesting, unique compilations of economic and social facts, figures and graphs will support multiple research needs. They will engage and enlighten patrons in high school, public and academic library collections." –Booklist

Volume I: The Working Class ◆ 558 pages; Hardcover ISBN 1-891482-81-5, $145.00
Volume II: The Middle Class ◆ 591 pages; Hardcover ISBN 1-891482-72-6; $145.00
Volume III: The Upper Class ◆ 567 pages; Hardcover ISBN 1-930956-38-X, $145.00

Working Americans 1880-1999 Volume IV: Their Children

This Fourth Volume in the highly successful *Working Americans 1880-1999* series focuses on American children, decade by decade from 1880 to 1999. This interesting and useful volume introduces the reader to three children in each decade, one from each of the Working, Middle and Upper classes. Like the first three volumes in the series, the individual profiles are created from interviews, diaries, statistical studies, biographies and news reports. Profiles cover a broad range of ethnic backgrounds, geographic area and lifestyles – everything from an orphan in Memphis in 1882, following the Yellow Fever epidemic of 1878 to an eleven-year-old nephew of a beer baron and owner of the New York Yankees in New York City in 1921. Chapters also contain important supplementary materials including News Features as well as information on everything from Schools to Parks, Infectious Diseases to Childhood Fears along with Entertainment, Family Life and much more to provide an informative overview of the lifestyles of children from each decade. This interesting account of what life was like for Children in the Working, Middle and Upper Classes will be a welcome addition to the reference collection of any high school, public or academic library.

pages; Hardcover ISBN 1-930956-35-5, $145.00

To preview any of our Directories Risk-Free for 30 days, call (800) 562-2139 or fax to (518) 789-0556

Working Americans 1880-2003 Volume V: Americans At War

Working Americans 1880-2003 Volume V: Americans At War is divided into 11 chapters, each covering a decade from 1880-2003 and examines the lives of Americans during the time of war, including declared conflicts, one-time military actions, protests, and preparations for war. Each decade includes several personal profiles, whether on the battlefield or on the homefront, that tell the stor of civilians, soldiers, and officers during the decade. The profiles examine: Life at Home; Life at Work; and Life in the Community. Each decade also includes an Economic Profile with statistical comparisons, a Historical Snapshot, News Profiles, local News Articles and Illustrations that provide a solid historical background to the decade being examined. Profiles range widely not only geographically, but also emotionally, from that of a girl whose leg was torn off in a blast during WWI, to the boredom of being stationed in the Dakotas as the Indian Wars were drawing to a close. As in previous volumes of the *Working Americans* series, information is presented in narrative form, but hard facts and real-life situations back up each story. The basis of the profiles come fro diaries, private print books, personal interviews, family histories, estate documents and magazine articles. For easy reference, *Workin Americans 1880-2003 Volume V: Americans At War* includes an in-depth Subject Index. The *Working Americans* series has become an important reference for public libraries, academic libraries and high school libraries. This fifth volume will be a welcome addition to a of these types of reference collections.

600 pages; Hardcover ISBN 1-59237-024-1; $145.00
Five Volume Set (Volumes I-V), Hardcover ISBN 1-59237-034-9, $675.00

Working Americans 1880-2005 Volume VI: Women at Work

Unlike any other volume in the *Working Americans* series, this Sixth Volume, is the first to focus on a particular gender of Americans. *Volume VI: Women at Work*, traces what life was like for working women from the 1860's to the present time. Beginning with the life of a maid in 1890 and a store clerk in 1900 and ending with the life and times of the modern working women, this text captures the struggle, strengths and changing perception of the American woman at work. Each chapter focuses on one decade and profiles three to five wome with real data on Income & Job Descriptions, Selected Prices of the Times, Annual Income, Annual Budgets, Family Finances, Life at Work, Life at Home, Life in the Community, Working Conditions, Cost of Living, Amusements and much more. For even broader acces to the events, economics and attitude towards women throughout the past 130 years, each chapter is supplemented with News Profiles, Articles from Local Media, Illustrations, Economic Profiles, Typical Pricing, Key Events, Inventions and more. This important volume illustrates what life was like for working women over time and allows the reader to develop an understanding of the changing role of women at work. These interesting and useful compilations of portraits of women at work will be an important addition to any high scho public or academic library reference collection.

600 pages; Hardcover ISBN 1-59237-063-2; $145.00

Working Americans 1880-2005 Volume VII: Social Movements

The newest addition to the widely-successful *Working Americans* series, *Volume VII: Social Movements* explores how Americans sought and fought for change from the 1880s to the present time. Following the format of previous volumes in the Working Americans series, the t examines the lives of 34 individuals who have worked — often behind the scenes — to bring about change. Issues include topics as diver as the Anti-smoking movement of 1901 to efforts by Native Americans to reassert their long lost rights. Along the way, the book will profile individuals brave enough to demand suffrage for Kansas women in 1912 or demand an end to lynching during a March on Washington in 1923. Each profile is enriched with real data on Income & Job Descriptions, Selected Prices of the Times, Annual Income & Budgets, Life at Work, Life at Home, Life in the Community, along with News Features, Key Events, and Illustrations. The depth of information contained in each profile allow the user to explore the private, financial and public lives of these subjects, deepening our understanding of how calls for change took place in our society. A must-purchase for the reference collections of high school libraries, public libraries and academic libraries.

600 pages; Hardcover ISBN 1-59237-101-9; $145.00
Seven Volume Set (Volumes I-VII), Hardcover ISBN 1-59237-133-7, $945.00

The Encyclopedia of Warrior Peoples & Fighting Groups

Many military groups throughout the world have excelled in their craft either by fortuitous circumstances, outstanding leadership, o intense training. This new second edition of The Encyclopedia of Warrior Peoples and Fighting Groups explores the origins and leadership of these outstanding combat forces, chronicles their conquests and accomplishments, examines the circumstances surrounding their decline or disbanding, and assesses their influence on the groups and methods of warfare that followed. This editic has been completely updated with information through 2005 and contains over 20 new entries. Readers will encounter ferocious trib charismatic leaders, and daring militias, from ancient times to the present, including Amazons, Buffalo Soldiers, Green Berets, Iron Brigade, Kamikazes, Peoples of the Sea, Polish Winged Hussars, Sacred Band of Thebes, Teutonic Knights, and Texas Rangers. Wit over 100 alphabetical entries, numerous cross-references and illustrations, a comprehensive bibliography, and index, the Encyclopedi of Warrior Peoples and Fighting Groups is a valuable resource for readers seeking insight into the bold history of distinguished fighting forces.

"This work is especially useful for high school students, undergraduates, and gen readers with an interest in military history." –Library Jou

Pub. Date: May 2006; Hardcover ISBN 1-59237-116-7; $135.00

To preview any of our Directories Risk-Free for 30 days, call (800) 562-2139 or fax to (518) 789-055

The Encyclopedia of Invasions & Conquests, From the Ancient Times to the Present

Throughout history, invasions and conquests have played a remarkable role in shaping our world and defining our boundaries, both physically and culturally. This second edition of the popular Encyclopedia of Invasions & Conquests, a comprehensive guide to over [ ]0 invasions, conquests, battles and occupations from ancient times to the present, takes readers on a journey that includes the Roman [co]nquest of Britain, the Portuguese colonization of Brazil, and the Iraqi invasion of Kuwait, to name a few. New articles will explore [th]e late 20th and 21st centuries, with a specific focus on recent conflicts in Afghanistan, Kuwait, Iraq, Yugoslavia, Grenada and [Ch]echnya. Categories of entries include countries, invasions and conquests, and individuals. In addition to covering the military [asp]ects of invasions and conquests, entries cover some of the political, economic, and cultural aspects, for example, the effects of a [co]nquest on the invade country's political and monetary system and in its language and religion. The entries on leaders – among them [Sar]gon, Alexander the Great, William the Conqueror, and Adolf Hitler – deal with the people who sought to gain control, expand [po]wer, or exert religious or political influence over others through military means. Revised and updated for this second edition, entries [are] arranged alphabetically within historical periods. Each chapter provides a map to help readers locate key areas and geographical [fea]tures, and bibliographical references appear at the end of each entry. Other useful features include cross-references, a cumulative [bib]liography and a comprehensive subject index. This authoritative, well-organized, lucidly written volume will prove invaluable for a [var]iety of readers, including high school students, military historians, members of the armed forces, history buffs and hobbyists.

"Engaging writing, sensible organization, nice illustrations, interesting and obscure facts, and useful maps make this book a pleasure to read." –ARBA

Pub. Date: March 2006; Hardcover ISBN 1-59237-114-0; $135.00

Encyclopedia of Prisoners of War & Internment

This authoritative second edition provides a valuable overview of the history of prisoners of war and interned civilians, from earliest times to the present. Written by an international team of experts in the field of POW studies, this fascinating and thought-provoking volume includes entries on a wide range of subjects including the Crusades, Plains Indian Warfare, concentration camps, the two world wars, and famous POWs throughout history, as well as atrocities, escapes, and much more. Written in a clear and easily understandable style, this informative reference details over 350 entries, 30% larger than the first edition, that survey the history of prisoners of war and interned civilians from the earliest times to the present, with emphasis on the 19th and 20th centuries. Medical conditions, international law, exchanges of prisoners, organizations working on behalf of POWs, and trials associated with the treatment of captives are just some of the themes explored. Entries range from the Ardeatine Caves Massacre to Kurt Vonnegut. Entries are arranged alphabetically, plus illustrations and maps are provided for easy reference. The text also includes an introduction, bibliography, appendix of selected documents, and end-of-entry reading suggestions. This one-of-a-kind reference will be a helpful addition to the reference collections of all public libraries, high schools, and university libraries and will prove invaluable to historians and military enthusiasts.

"Thorough and detailed yet accessible to the lay reader. Of special interest to subject specialists and historians; recommended for public and academic libraries." - Library Journal

Pub. Date: March 2006; Hardcover ISBN 1-59237-120-5; $135.00

The Religious Right, A Reference Handbook

Timely and unbiased, this third edition updates and expands its examination of the religious right and its influence on our government, citizens, society, and politics. From the fight to outlaw the teaching of Darwin's theory of evolution to the struggle to outlaw abortion, the religious right is continually exerting an influence on public policy. This text explores the influence of religion on legislation and society, while examining the alignment of the religious right with the political right. A historical survey of the movement highlights [the] shift to "hands-on" approach to politics and the struggle to present a unified front. The coverage offers a critical historical survey of [the] religious right movement, focusing on its increased involvement in the political arena, attempts to forge coalitions, and notable successes and failures. The text offers complete coverage of biographies of the men and women who have advanced the cause and an up[-to-]date chronology illuminate the movement's goals, including their accomplishments and failures. This edition offers an extensive update to all sections along with several brand new entries. Two new sections complement this third edition, a chapter on legal issues [and] court decisions and a chapter on demographic statistics and electoral patterns. To aid in further research, The Religious Right, [offe]rs an entire section of annotated listings of print and non-print resources, as well as of organizations affiliated with the religious [righ]t, and those opposing it. Comprehensive in its scope, this work offers easy-to-read, pertinent information for those seeking to [und]erstand the religious right and its evolving role in American society. A must for libraries of all sizes, university religion [dep]artments, activists, high schools and for those interested in the evolving role of the religious right.

" Recommended for all public and academic libraries." - Library Journal

Pub. Date: November 2006; Hardcover ISBN 1-59237-113-2; $135.00

To preview any of our Directories Risk-Free for 30 days, call (800) 562-2139 or fax to (518) 789-0556

From Suffrage to the Senate, An Encyclopedia of American Women in Politics

From Suffrage to the Senate is a comprehensive and valuable compendium of biographies of leading women in U.S. politics, past and present, and an examination of the wide range of women's movements. Up to date through 2006, this dynamically illustrated reference work explores American women's path to political power and social equality from the struggle for the right to vote and the abolition of slavery to the first African American woman in the U.S. Senate and beyond. This new edition includes over 150 new entries and a brand new section on trends and demographics of women in politics. The in-depth coverage also traces the political heritage of the abolition, labor, suffrage, temperance, and reproductive rights movements. The alphabetically arranged entries include biographies of every woman from across the political spectrum who has served in the U.S. House and Senate, along with women in the Judiciary and the U.S. Cabinet and, new to this edition, biographies of activists and political consultants. Bibliographical references follow each entry. For easy reference, a handy chronology is provided detailing 150 years of women's history. This up-to-date reference will be a must-purchase for women's studies departments, high schools and public libraries and will be a handy resource for those researching the key players in women's politics, past and present.

"An engaging tool that would be useful in high school, public, and academic library looking for an overview of the political history of women in the US." –Book

Pub. Date: October 2006; Two Volume Set; Hardcover ISBN 1-59237-117-5; $195.00

An African Biographical Dictionary

This landmark second edition is the only biographical dictionary to bring together, in one volume, cultural, social and political leaders both historical and contemporary – of the sub-Saharan region. Over 800 biographical sketches of prominent Africans, as well as foreigners who have affected the continent's history, are featured, 150 more than the previous edition. The wide spectrum of leaders includes religious figures, writers, politicians, scientists, entertainers, sports personalities and more. Access to these fascinating individuals is provided in a user-friendly format. The biographies are arranged alphabetically, cross-referenced and indexed. Entries include the country or countries in which the person was significant and the commonly accepted dates of birth and death. Each biographical sketch is chronologically written; entries for cultural personalities add an evaluation of their work. This information is followed by a selection of references often found in university and public libraries, including autobiographies and principal biographic works. Appendixes list each individual by country and by field of accomplishment – rulers, musicians, explorers, missionaries, businessmen, physicists – nearly thirty categories in all. Another convenient appendix lists heads of state since independence by country. Up-to-date and representative of African societies as a whole, An African Biographical Dictionary provides a wealth of vital information for students of African culture and is an indispensable reference guide for anyone interested in African affairs.

"An unquestionable convenience to have these concise, informative biographies gathered in one source, indexed, and analyzed by appendixes listing entrants by nation and occupational field." –Wilson Library Bull

Pub. Date: July 2006; Hardcover ISBN 1-59237-112-4; $125.00

American Environmental Leaders, From Colonial Times to the Present

A comprehensive and diverse award winning collection of biographies of the most important figures in American environmentalism. Few subjects arouse the passions the way the environment does. How will we feed an ever-increasing population and how can that food be made safe for consumption? Who decides how land is developed? How can environmental policies be made fair for everyone, including multiethnic groups, women, children, and the poor? American Environmental Leaders presents more than 350 biographies of men and women who have devoted their lives to studying, debating, and organizing these and other controversial issues over the last 200 years. In addition to the scientists who have analyzed how human actions affect nature, we are introduced to poets, landscape architects, presidents, painters, activists, even sanitation engineers, and others who have forever altered how we think about the environment. The easy to use A–Z format provides instant access to these fascinating individuals, and frequent cross references indicate others with whom individuals worked (and sometimes clashed). End of entry references provide users with a starting point for further research.

"Highly recommended for high school, academic, and public libraries needing environmental biographical information." –Library Journal/Starred Review

Two Volume Set; Hardcover ISBN 1-57607-385-8 $175.00

World Cultural Leaders of the Twentieth Century

An expansive two volume set that covers 450 worldwide cultural icons, World Cultural Leaders of the Twentieth Century includes each person's works, achievements, and professional careers in a thorough essay. Who was the originator of the term "documentary"? Which poet married the daughter of the famed novelist Thomas Mann in order to help her escape Nazi Germany? Which British writer served as an agent in Russia against the Bolsheviks before the 1917 revolution? These and many more questions are answered in this illuminating text. A handy two volume set that makes it easy to look up 450 worldwide cultural icons: novelists, poets, playwrights, painters, sculptors, architects, dancers, choreographers, actors, directors, filmmakers, singers, composers, and musicians. World Cultural Leaders of the Twentieth Century provides entries (many of them illustrated) covering the person's works, achievements, and professional career in a thorough essay and offers interesting facts and statistics. Entries are fully cross-referenced so that readers can learn how various individuals influenced others. A thorough general index completes the coverage.

"Fills a need for handy, concise information on a wide array of international cultural figures."-AL

Two Volume Set; Hardcover ISBN 1-57607-038-7 $175.00

To preview any of our Directories Risk-Free for 30 days, call (800) 562-2139 or fax to (518) 789-055

Sedgwick Press
Health Directories

The Complete Directory for People with Disabilities, 2006

A wealth of information, now in one comprehensive sourcebook. Completely updated, this edition contains more information than ever before, including thousands of new entries and enhancements to existing entries and thousands of additional web sites and e-mail addresses. This up-to-date directory is the most comprehensive resource available for people with disabilities, detailing Independent Living Centers, Rehabilitation Facilities, State & Federal Agencies, Associations, Support Groups, Periodicals & Books, Assistive Devices, Employment & Education Programs, Camps and Travel Groups. Each year, more libraries, schools, colleges, hospitals, rehabilitation centers and individuals add *The Complete Directory for People with Disabilities* to their collections, making sure that this information is readily available to the families, individuals and professionals who can benefit most from the amazing wealth of resources cataloged here.

"No other reference tool exists to meet the special needs of the disabled in one convenient resource for information." –Library Journal

1200 pages; Softcover ISBN 1-59237-083-7, $165.00 ♦ Online Database $215.00 ♦ Online Database & Directory Combo $300.00

The Complete Directory for People with Chronic Illness, 2005/06

Thousands of hours of research have gone into this completely updated 2005/06 edition – several new chapters have been added along with thousands of new entries and enhancements to existing entries. Plus, each chronic illness chapter has been reviewed by an medical expert in the field. This widely-hailed directory is structured around the 90 most prevalent chronic illnesses – from Asthma to Cancer to Wilson's Disease – and provides a comprehensive overview of the support services and information resources available for people diagnosed with a chronic illness. Each chronic illness has its own chapter and contains a brief description in layman's language, followed by important resources for National & Local Organizations, State Agencies, Newsletters, Books & Periodicals, Libraries & Research Centers, Support Groups & Hotlines, Web Sites and much more. This directory is an important resource for health care professionals, the collections of hospital and health care libraries, as well as an invaluable tool for people with a chronic illness and their support network.

"A must purchase for all hospital and health care libraries and is strongly recommended for all public library reference departments." –ARBA

1200 pages; Softcover ISBN 1-59237-081-0, $165.00 ♦ Online Database $215.00 ♦ Online Database & Directory Combo $300.00

The Complete Learning Disabilities Directory, 2005

The Complete Learning Disabilities Directory is the most comprehensive database of Programs, Services, Curriculum Materials, Professional Meetings & Resources, Camps, Newsletters and Support Groups for teachers, students and families concerned with learning disabilities. This information-packed directory includes information about Associations & Organizations, Schools, Colleges & Testing Materials, Government Agencies, Legal Resources and much more. For quick, easy access to information, this directory contains four indexes: Entry Name Index, Subject Index and Geographic Index. With every passing year, the field of learning disabilities attracts more attention and the network of caring, committed and knowledgeable professionals grows every day. This directory is an invaluable research tool for these parents, students and professionals.

"Due to its wealth and depth of coverage, parents, teachers and others… should find this an invaluable resource." -Booklist

900 pages; Softcover ISBN 1-59237-092-6, $145.00 ♦ Online Database $195.00 ♦ Online Database & Directory Combo $280.00

The Complete Mental Health Directory, 2006

This is the most comprehensive resource covering the field of behavioral health, with critical information for both the layman and the mental health professional. For the layman, this directory offers understandable descriptions of 25 Mental Health Disorders as well as detailed information on Associations, Media, Support Groups and Mental Health Facilities. For the professional, *The Complete Mental Health Directory* offers critical and comprehensive information on Managed Care Organizations, Information Systems, Government Agencies and Provider Organizations. This comprehensive volume of needed information will be widely used in any reference collection.

"… the strength of this directory is that it consolidates widely dispersed information into a single volume." –Booklist

600 pages; Softcover ISBN 1-59237-124-8, $165.00 ♦ Online Database $215.00 ♦ Online & Directory Combo $300.00

Older Americans Information Directory, 2006/07

Completely updated for 2006/07, this sixth edition has been completely revised and now contains 1,000 new listings, over 8,000 updates to existing listings and over 3,000 brand new e-mail addresses and web sites. You'll find important resources for Older Americans including National, Regional, State & Local Organizations, Government Agencies, Research Centers, Libraries &

To preview any of our Directories Risk-Free for 30 days, call (800) 562-2139 or fax to (518) 789-0556

Information Centers, Legal Resources, Discount Travel Information, Continuing Education Programs, Disability Aids & Assistive Devices, Health, Print Media and Electronic Media. Three indexes: Entry Index, Subject Index and Geographic Index make it easy to find just the right source of information. This comprehensive guide to resources for Older Americans will be a welcome addition to an reference collection.

"Highly recommended for academic, public, health science and consumer libraries..." –Cho

1,200 pages; Softcover ISBN 1-59237-136-1, $165.00 ♦ Online Database $215.00 ♦ Online Database & Directory Combo $300.00

The Complete Directory for Pediatric Disorders, 2005

This important directory provides parents and caregivers with information about Pediatric Conditions, Disorders, Diseases and Disabilities, including Blood Disorders, Bone & Spinal Disorders, Brain Defects & Abnormalities, Chromosomal Disorders, Congenital Heart Defects, Movement Disorders, Neuromuscular Disorders and Pediatric Tumors & Cancers. This carefully written directory offers: understandable Descriptions of 15 major bodily systems; Descriptions of more than 200 Disorders and a Resources Section, detailing National Agencies & Associations, State Associations, Online Services, Libraries & Resource Centers, Research Centers, Support Groups & Hotlines, Camps, Books and Periodicals. This resource will provide immediate access to information crucial to families and caregivers when coping with children's illnesses.

"Recommended for public and consumer health libraries." –Library Jour

1,200 pages; Softcover ISBN 1-59237-045-4, $165.00 ♦ Online Database $215.00 ♦ Online Database & Directory Combo $300.00

The Complete Directory for People with Rare Disorders, 2006/07

This outstanding reference provides comprehensive and needed access to important information on over 1,000 rare disorders, includin Cancers and Muscular, Genetic and Blood Disorders. An informative Disorder Description is provided for each of the 1,100 disorders (rare Cancers and Muscular, Genetic and Blood Disorders) followed by information on National and State Organizations dealing with particular disorder, Umbrella Organizations that cover a wide range of disorders, the Publications that can be useful when researching disorder and the Government Agencies to contact. Detailed and up-to-date listings contain mailing address, phone and fax numbers, web sites and e-mail addresses along with a description. For quick, easy access to information, this directory contains two indexes: Entry Name Index and Acronym/Keyword Index along with an informative Guide for Rare Disorder Advocates. *The Complete Directo for People with Rare Disorders* will be an invaluable tool for the thousands of families that have been struck with a rare or "orphan" disease, who feel that they have no place to turn and will be a much-used addition to the reference collection of any public or academic library.

"Quick access to information... public libraries and hospital patient libraries will find this a usef resource in directing users to support groups or agencies dealing with a rare disorder." –Book

800 pages; Softcover ISBN 1-59237-123-X, $165.00

The Directory of Drug & Alcohol Residential Rehabilitation Facilities

This brand new directory is the first-ever resource to bring together, all in one place, data on the thousands of drug and alcohol residential rehabilitation facilities in the United States. *The Directory of Drug & Alcohol Residential Rehabilitation Facilities* covers over 1,000 facilities, with detailed contact information for each one, including mailing address, phone and fax numbers, email addresses and web sites, mission statement, type of treatment programs, cost, average length of stay, numbers of residents and counselors, accreditation, insurance plans accepted, type of environment, religious affiliation, education components and much more. It also contains a helpful chapter on General Resources that provides contact information for Associations, Print & Electronic Media, Suppor Groups and Conferences. Multiple indexes allow the user to pinpoint the facilities that meet very specific criteria. This time-saving tool is what so many counselors, parents and medical professionals have been asking for. *The Directory of Drug & Alcohol Residential Rehabilitation Facilities* will be a helpful tool in locating the right source for treatment for a wide range of individuals. This comprehensive directory will be an important acquisition for all reference collections: public and academic libraries, case managers, social workers, state agencies and many more.

"This is an excellent, much needed directory that fills an important gap..." –Book

300 pages; Softcover ISBN 1-59237-031-4, $135.00

To preview any of our Directories Risk-Free for 30 days, call (800) 562-2139 or fax to (518) 789-055

Sedgwick Press
Education Directories

The Comparative Guide to American Elementary & Secondary Schools, 2006

The only guide of its kind, this award winning compilation offers a snapshot profile of every public school district in the United States serving 1,500 or more students – more than 5,900 districts are covered. Organized alphabetically by district within state, each chapter begins with a Statistical Overview of the state. Each district listing includes contact information (name, address, phone number and web site) plus Grades Served, the Numbers of Students and Teachers and the Number of Regular, Special Education, Alternative and Vocational Schools in the district along with statistics on Student/Classroom Teacher Ratios, Drop Out Rates, Ethnicity, the Numbers of Librarians and Guidance Counselors and District Expenditures per student. As an added bonus, *The Comparative Guide to American Elementary and Secondary Schools* provides important ranking tables, both by state and nationally, for each data element. For easy navigation through this wealth of information, this handbook contains a useful City Index that lists all districts that operate schools within a city. These important comparative statistics are necessary for anyone considering relocation or doing comparative research on their own district and would be a perfect acquisition for any public library or school district library.

"This straightforward guide is an easy way to find general information. Valuable for academic and large public library collections." –ARBA

400 pages; Softcover ISBN 1-59237-137-X, $125.00

Educators Resource Directory, 2005/06

Educators Resource Directory is a comprehensive resource that provides the educational professional with thousands of resources and statistical data for professional development. This directory saves hours of research time by providing immediate access to Associations, Organizations, Conferences & Trade Shows, Educational Research Centers, Employment Opportunities & Teaching Abroad, School Library Services, Scholarships, Financial Resources, Professional Consultants, Computer Software & Testing Resources and much more. Plus, this comprehensive directory also includes a section on Statistics and Rankings with over 100 tables, including statistics on Average Teacher Salaries, SAT/ACT scores, Revenues & Expenditures and more. These important statistics will allow the user to see how their school rates among others, make relocation decisions and so much more. For quick access to information, this directory contains four indexes: Entry & Publisher Index, Geographic Index, a Subject & Grade Index and Web Sites Index. *Educators Resource Directory* will be a well-used addition to the reference collection of any school district, education department or public library.

"Recommended for all collections that serve elementary and secondary school professionals." –Choice

500 pages; Softcover ISBN 1-59237-080-2, $145.00 ♦ Online Database $195.00 ♦ Online Database & Directory Combo $280.00

Sedgwick Press
Hospital & Health Plan Directories

The Comparative Guide to American Hospitals

This brand new title is the first ever resource to compare all of the nation's hospitals by 17 measures of quality in the treatment of heart attack, heart failure and pneumonia. This data is based on the recently announced Hospital Compare, produced by Medicare, and is available in print and in a unique and user-friendly format from Grey House Publishing, along with extra contact information from Grey House's *Directory of Hospital Personnel*. *The Comparative Guide to American Hospitals* provides a snapshot profile of each of the nations 6,000 hospitals. These informative profiles illustrate how the hospital rates in 17 important areas: Heart Attack Care (% who receive Aspirin at Arrival, Aspirin at Discharge, ACE Inhibitor for LVSD, Beta Blocker at Arrival, Beta Blocker at Discharge, Thrombolytic Agent Received, PTCA Received and Adult Smoking Cessation Advice); Heart Failure (% who receive LVF Assessment, ACE Inhibitor for LVSD, Discharge Instructions, Adult Smoking Cessation Advice); and Pneumonia (% who receive Initial Antibiotic Timing, Pneumococcal Vaccination, Oxygenation Assessment, Blood Culture Performed and Adult Smoking Cessation Advice). Each profile includes the raw percentage for that hospital, the state average, the US average and data on the top hospital. For easy access to contact information, each profile includes the hospitals address, phone and fax numbers, email and web addresses, type and accreditation along with 5 top key administrations. These profiles will allow the user to quickly identify the quality of the hospital and have the necessary information at their fingertips to make contact with that hospital. Most importantly, *The Comparative Guide to American Hospitals* provides an easy-to-use Ranking Table for each of the data elements to allow the user to quickly locate the hospitals with the best level of service. This brand new title will be a must for the reference collection at all public, medical and academic libraries.

500 pages; Softcover ISBN 1-59237-109-4 $175.00

To preview any of our Directories Risk-Free for 30 days, call (800) 562-2139 or fax to (518) 789-0556

The Directory of Hospital Personnel, 2006

The Directory of Hospital Personnel is the best resource you can have at your fingertips when researching or marketing a product or service to the hospital market. A "Who's Who" of the hospital universe, this directory puts you in touch with over 150,000 key decision-makers. With 100% verification of data you can rest assured that you will reach the right person with just one call. Every hospital in the U.S. is profiled, listed alphabetically by city within state. Plus, three easy-to-use, cross-referenced indexes put the facts at your fingertips faster and more easily than any other directory: Hospital Name Index, Bed Size Index and Personnel Index. *The Directory of Hospital Personnel* is the only complete source for key hospital decision-makers by name. Whether you want to define or restructure sales territories… locate hospitals with the purchasing power to accept your proposals… keep track of important contacts or colleagues… or find information on which insurance plans are accepted, *The Directory of Hospital Personnel* gives you the information you need – easily, efficiently, effectively and accurately.

"Recommended for college, university and medical libraries." -ARL

2,500 pages; Softcover ISBN 1-59237-107-8 $275.00 ♦ Online Database $545.00 ♦ Online Database & Directory Combo, $650.00

The Directory of Health Care Group Purchasing Organizations, 2006

This comprehensive directory provides the important data you need to get in touch with over 800 Group Purchasing Organizations. By providing in-depth information on this growing market and its members, *The Directory of Health Care Group Purchasing Organizatio* fills a major need for the most accurate and comprehensive information on over 800 GPOs – Mailing Address, Phone & Fax Numbers, E-mail Addresses, Key Contacts, Purchasing Agents, Group Descriptions, Membership Categorization, Standard Vendor Proposal Requirements, Membership Fees & Terms, Expanded Services, Total Member Beds & Outpatient Visits represented and more. Five Indexes provide a number of ways to locate the right GPO: Alphabetical Index, Expanded Services Index, Organization Type Index, Geographic Index and Member Institution Index. With its comprehensive and detailed information on each purchasing organization, *The Directory of Health Care Group Purchasing Organizations* is the go-to source for anyone looking to target this market.

"The information is clearly arranged and easy to access…recommended for those needing this very specialized information." –ARL

1,000 pages; Softcover ISBN 1-59237-0091-8, $325.00 ♦ Online Database, $650.00 ♦ Online Database & Directory Combo, $750.00

The HMO/PPO Directory, 2006

The HMO/PPO Directory is a comprehensive source that provides detailed information about Health Maintenance Organizations and Preferred Provider Organizations nationwide. This comprehensive directory details more information about more managed health ca organizations than ever before. Over 1,100 HMOs, PPOs and affiliated companies are listed, arranged alphabetically by state. Detaile listings include Key Contact Information, Prescription Drug Benefits, Enrollment, Geographical Areas served, Affiliated Physicians & Hospitals, Federal Qualifications, Status, Year Founded, Managed Care Partners, Employer References, Fees & Payment Information and more. Plus, five years of historical information is included related to Revenues, Net Income, Medical Loss Ratios, Membership Enrollment and Number of Patient Complaints. Five easy-to-use, cross-referenced indexes will put this vast array of information at your fingertips immediately: HMO Index, PPO Index, Other Providers Index, Personnel Index and Enrollment Index. *The HMO/PPO Directory* provides the most comprehensive information on the most companies available on the market place today.

"Helpful to individuals requesting certain HMO/PPO issues such as co-payment costs, subscription costs and patient complaint Individuals concerned (or those with questions) about their insurance may find this text to be of use to them." -AR

600 pages; Softcover ISBN 1-59237-100-0, $275.00 ♦ Online Database, $495.00 ♦ Online Database & Directory Combo, $600.00

The Directory of Independent Ambulatory Care Centers

This first edition of *The Directory of Independent Ambulatory Care Centers* provides access to detailed information that, before now, could only be found scattered in hundreds of different sources. This comprehensive and up-to-date directory pulls together a vast array of contact information for over 7,200 Ambulatory Surgery Centers, Ambulatory General and Urgent Care Clinics, and Diagnostic Imaging Centers that are not affiliated with a hospital or major medical center. Detailed listings include Mailing Address, Phone & F Numbers, E-mail and Web Site addresses, Contact Name and Phone Numbers of the Medical Director and other Key Executives and Purchasing Agents, Specialties & Services Offered, Year Founded, Numbers of Employees and Surgeons, Number of Operating Room Number of Cases seen per year, Overnight Options, Contracted Services and much more. Listings are arranged by State, by Center Category and then alphabetically by Organization Name. Two indexes provide quick and easy access to this wealth of information: Entry Name Index and Specialty/Service Index. *The Directory of Independent Ambulatory Care Centers* is a must-have resource for anyo marketing a product or service to this important industry and will be an invaluable tool for those searching for a local care center tha will meet their specific needs.

"Among the numerous hospital directories, no other provides information on independent ambulatory cente A handy, well-organized resource that would be useful in medical center libraries and public libraries." –Ch

986 pages; Softcover ISBN 1-930956-90-8, $185.00 ♦ Online Database, $365.00 ♦ Online Database & Directory Combo, $450.00

To preview any of our Directories Risk-Free for 30 days, call (800) 562-2139 or fax to (518) 789-055

MAPS

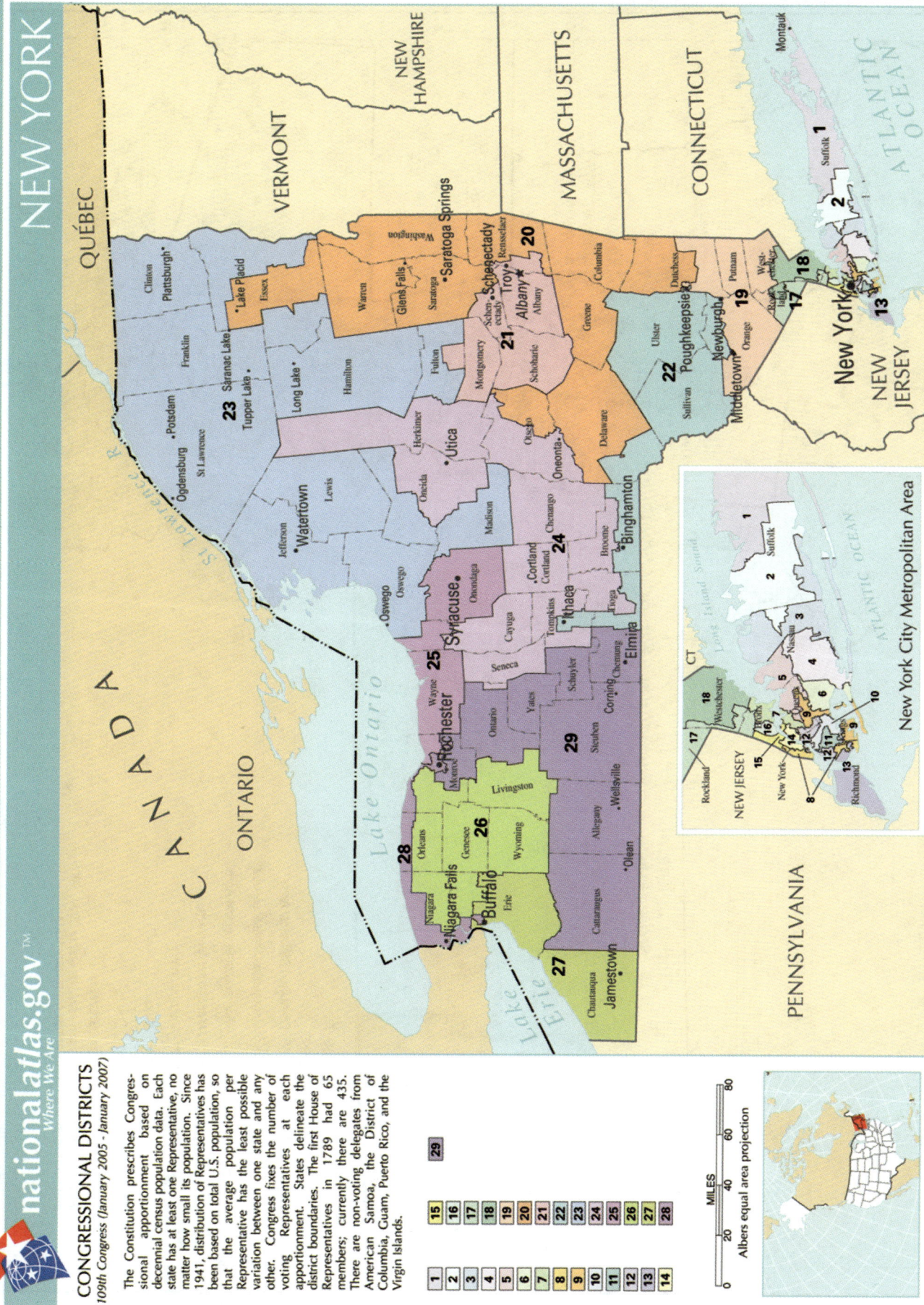

NEW YORK - Core Based Statistical Areas and Counties

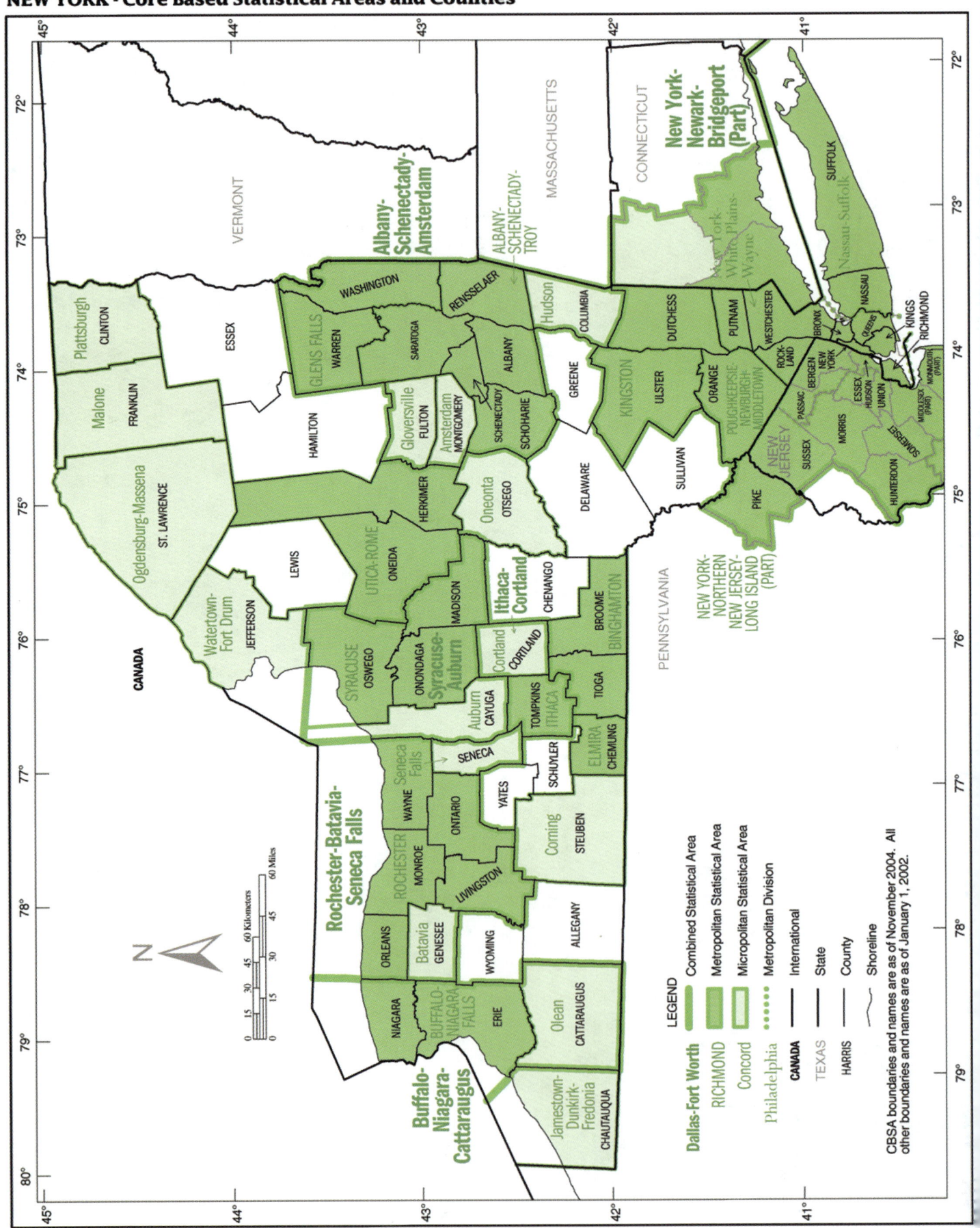

Population (2005)

Legend
- 250,000 and Over
- 100,000 to 249,999
- 50,000 to 99,999
- 25,000 to 49,999
- 0 to 24,999

Note: Copyright © 1988-2003 Microsoft Corp. and/or its suppliers. All rights reserved. © Copyright 2002 by Geographic Data Technology, Inc. All rights reserved. © 2002 Navigation Technologies. All rights reserved.

Percent White Alone (2005)

Legend
- 95.0 and Over
- 90.0 to 94.9
- 85.0 to 89.9
- 80.0 to 84.9
- 0 to 79.9

Note: Copyright © 1988-2003 Microsoft Corp. and/or its suppliers. All rights reserved. © Copyright 2002 by Geographic Data Technology, Inc. All rights reserved. © 2002 Navigation Technologies. All rights reserved.

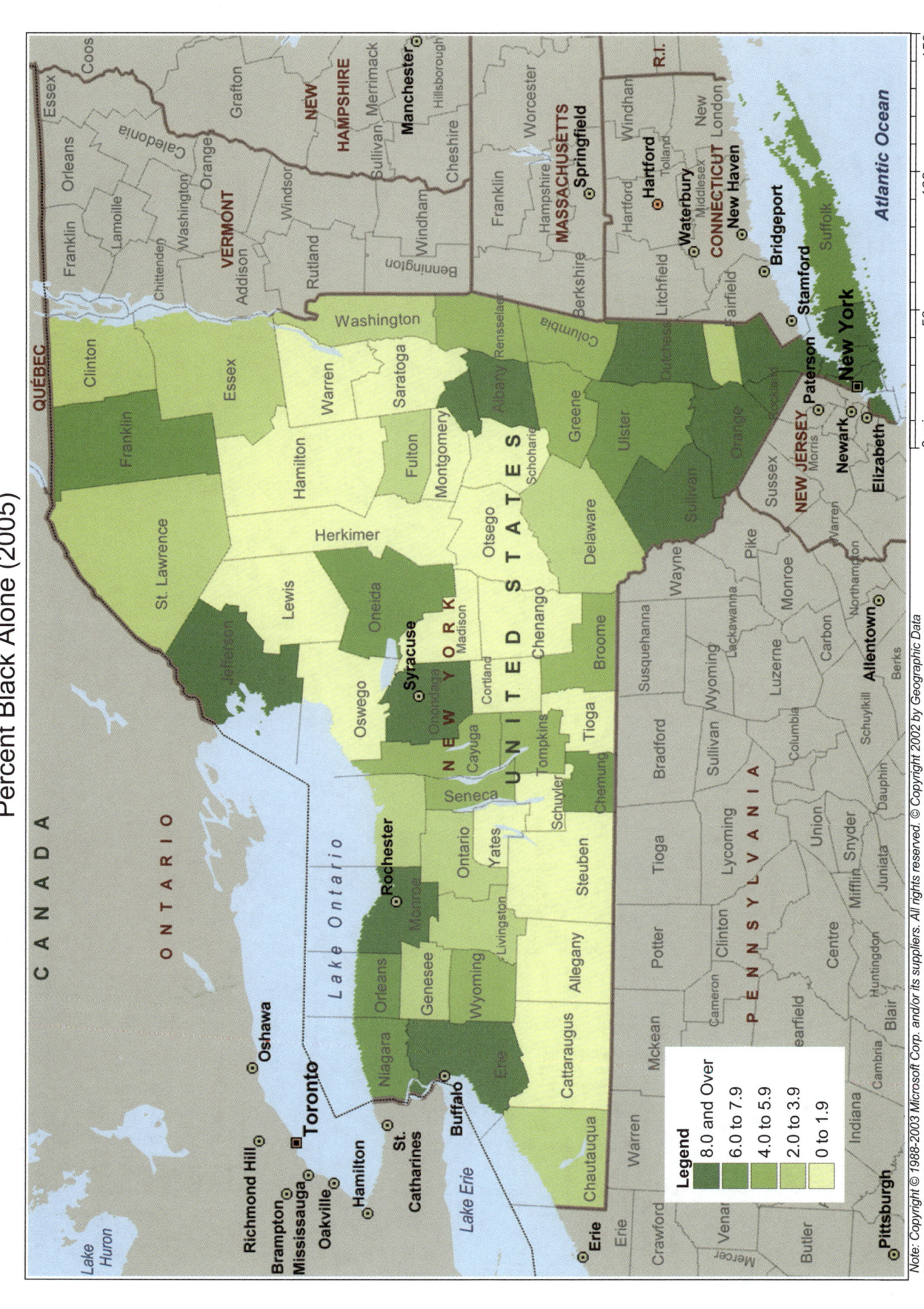

Percent Asian Alone (2005)

Legend
- 3.0 and Over
- 2.0 to 2.9
- 1.0 to 1.9
- 0.5 to 0.9
- 0 to 0.4

Note: Copyright © 1988-2003 Microsoft Corp. and/or its suppliers. All rights reserved. © Copyright 2002 by Geographic Data Technology, Inc. All rights reserved. © 2002 Navigation Technologies. All rights reserved.

Percent Hispanic (2005)

Legend
- 8.0 and Over
- 6.0 to 7.9
- 4.0 to 5.9
- 2.0 to 3.9
- 0 to 1.9

Note: Copyright © 1988-2003 Microsoft Corp. and/or its suppliers. All rights reserved. © Copyright 2002 by Geographic Data Technology, Inc. All rights reserved. © 2002 Navigation Technologies. All rights reserved.

Average Household Size (2005)

Legend
- 2.80 to 3.09
- 2.70 to 2.79
- 2.60 to 2.69
- 2.50 to 2.59
- 2.08 to 2.49

Note: Copyright © 1988-2003 Microsoft Corp. and/or its suppliers. All rights reserved. © Copyright 2002 by Geographic Data Technology, Inc. © 2002 Navigation Technologies. All rights reserved.

Median Age (2005)

Legend
- 40.0 to 46.6
- 39.0 to 39.9
- 38.0 to 38.9
- 37.0 to 37.9
- 30.8 to 36.9

Note: Copyright © 1988-2003 Microsoft Corp. and/or its suppliers. All rights reserved. © Copyright 2002 by Geographic Data Technology, Inc. All rights reserved. © 2002 Navigation Technologies. All rights reserved.

Median Household Income (2005)

Legend
- 50,000 to 83,109
- 46,000 to 49,999
- 42,000 to 45,999
- 38,000 to 41,999
- 31,202 to 37,999

Note: Copyright © 1988-2003 Microsoft Corp. and/or its suppliers. All rights reserved. © Copyright 2002 by Geographic Data Technology, Inc. All rights reserved. © 2002 Navigation Technologies. All rights reserved.

Percent of Population Living in Poverty (2003)

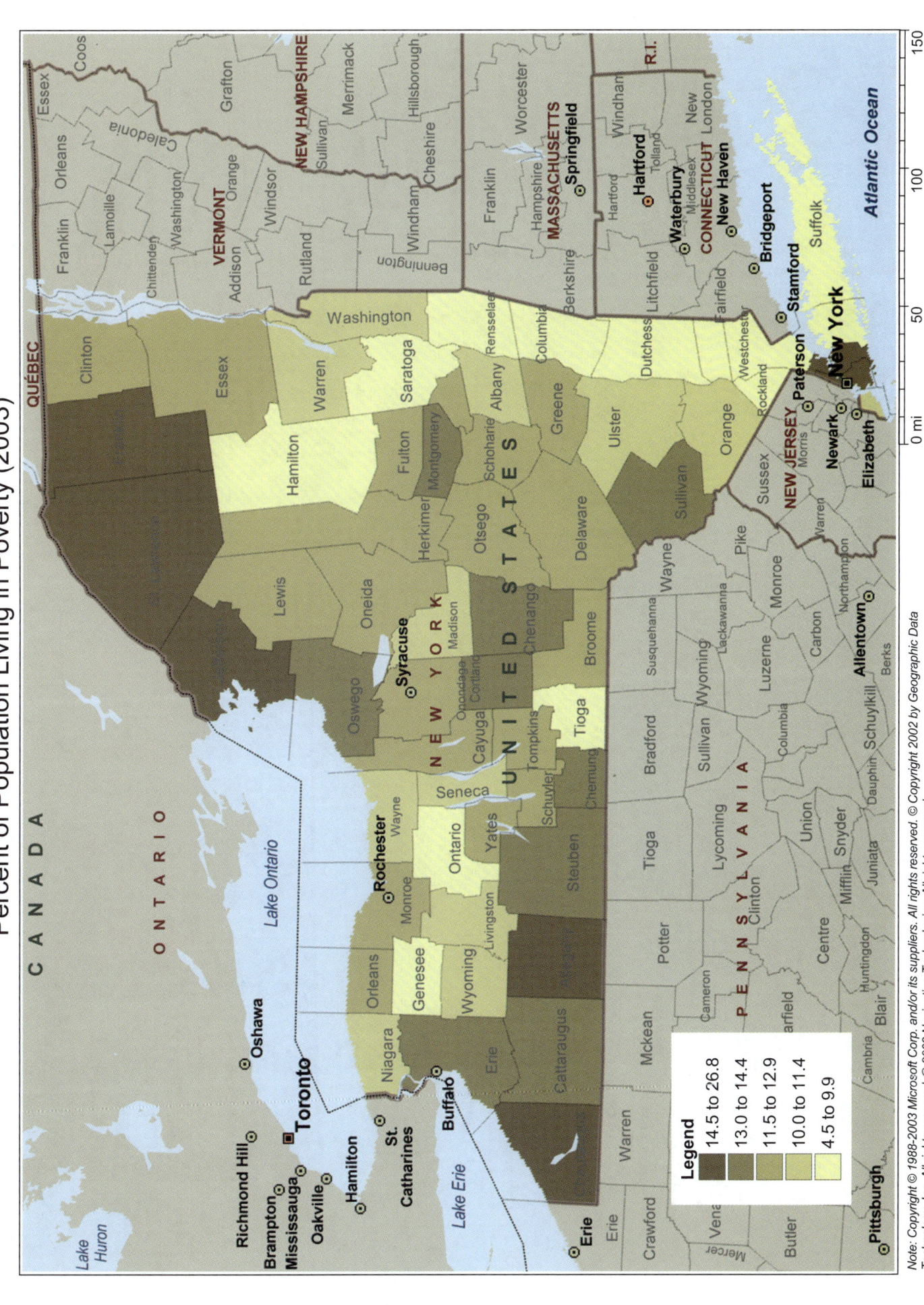

Median Home Value (2005)

Legend
- 200,000 to 628,900
- 155,000 to 199,999
- 135,000 to 154,999
- 115,000 to 134,999
- 95,000 to 114,999
- 78,200 to 94,999

Note: Copyright © 1988-2003 Microsoft Corp. and/or its suppliers. All rights reserved. © Copyright 2002 by Geographic Data Technology, Inc. All rights reserved. © 2002 Navigation Technologies. All rights reserved.

Percent of Population Who Own Their Own Homes (2005)

Legend
- 76.0 to 82.2
- 73.5 to 75.9
- 70.0 to 73.4
- 65.5 to 69.9
- 19.6 to 65.4

Note: Copyright © 1988-2003 Microsoft Corp. and/or its suppliers. All rights reserved. © Copyright 2002 by Geographic Data Technology, Inc. All rights reserved. © 2002 Navigation Technologies. All rights reserved.

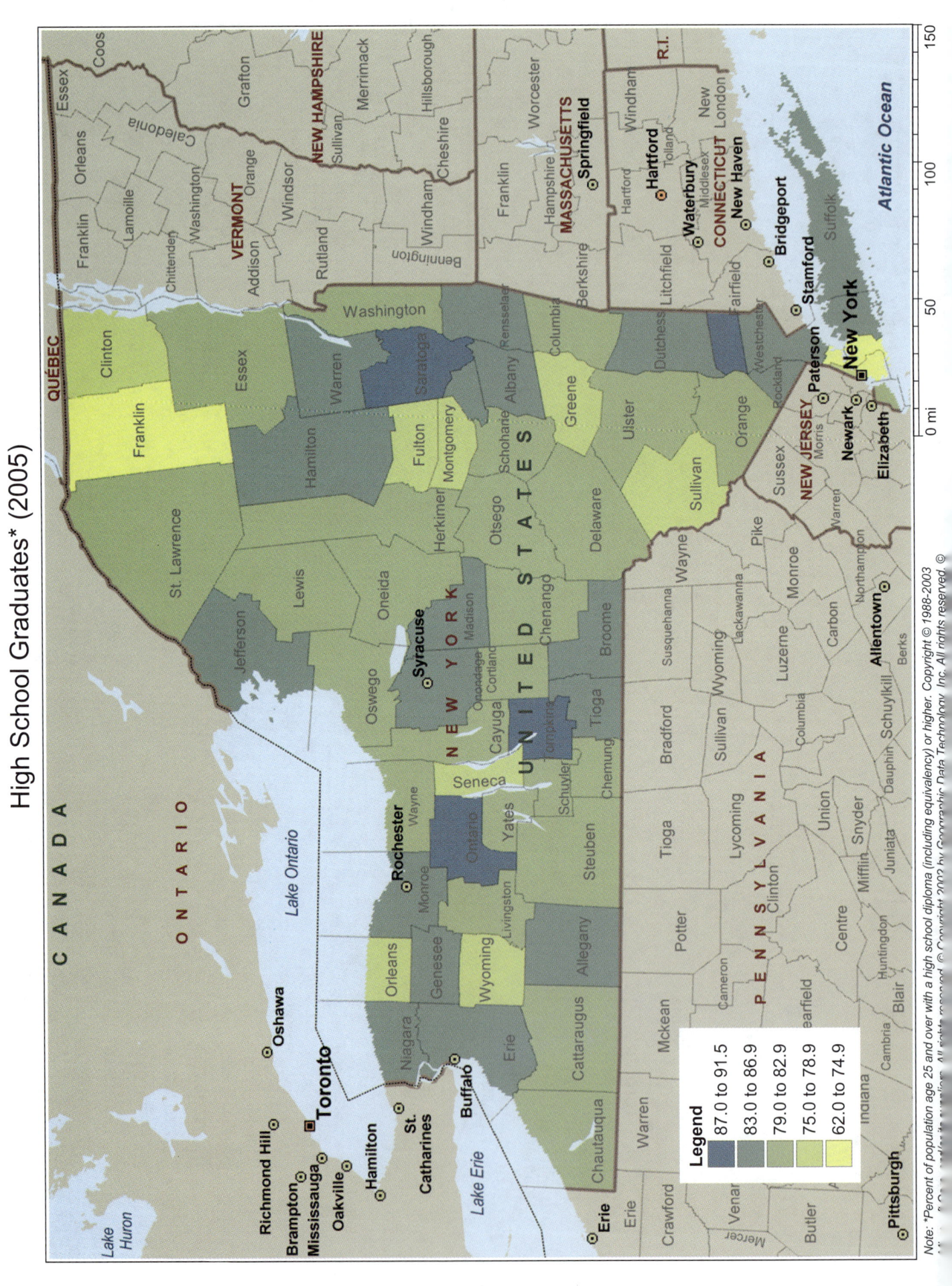

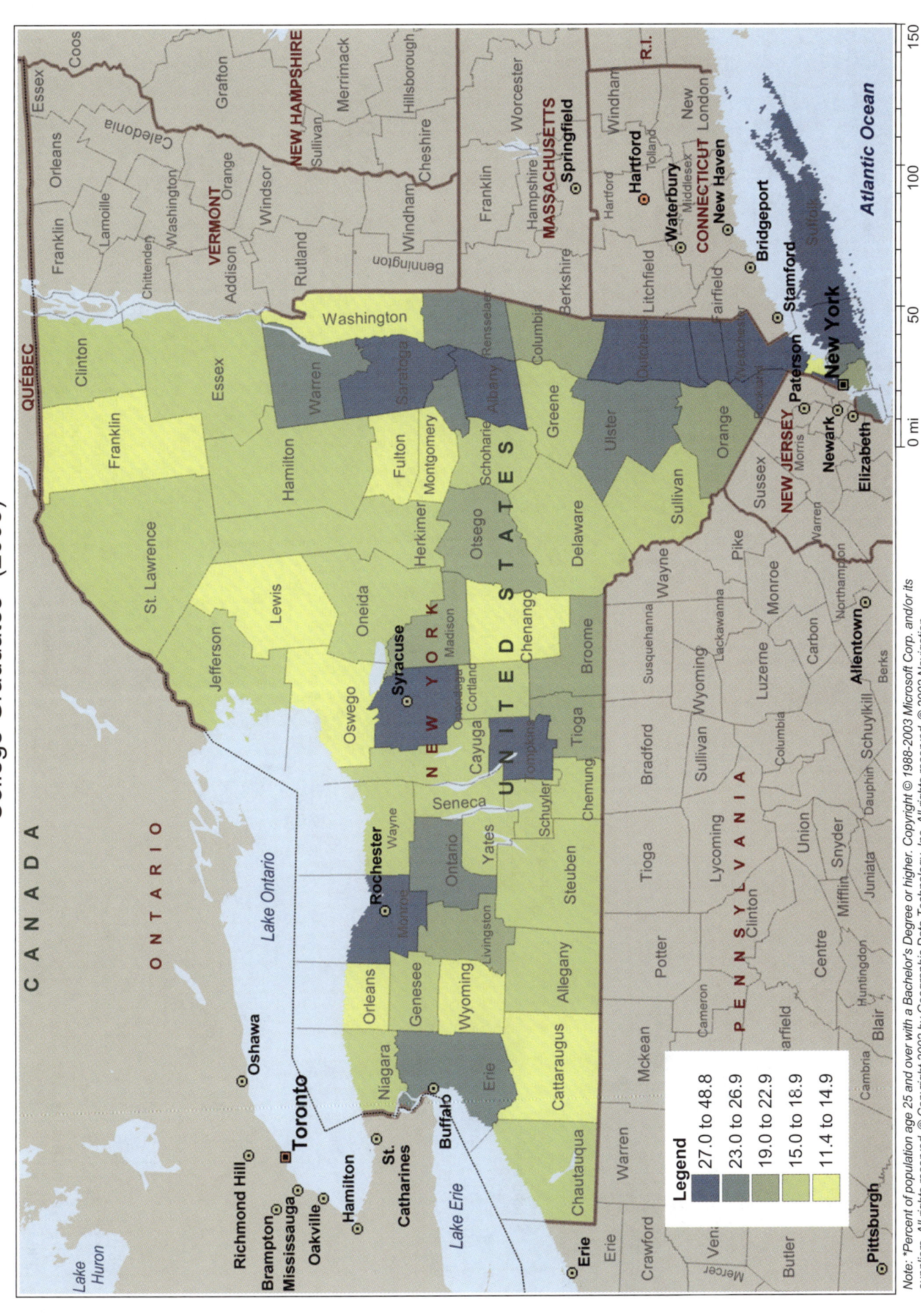

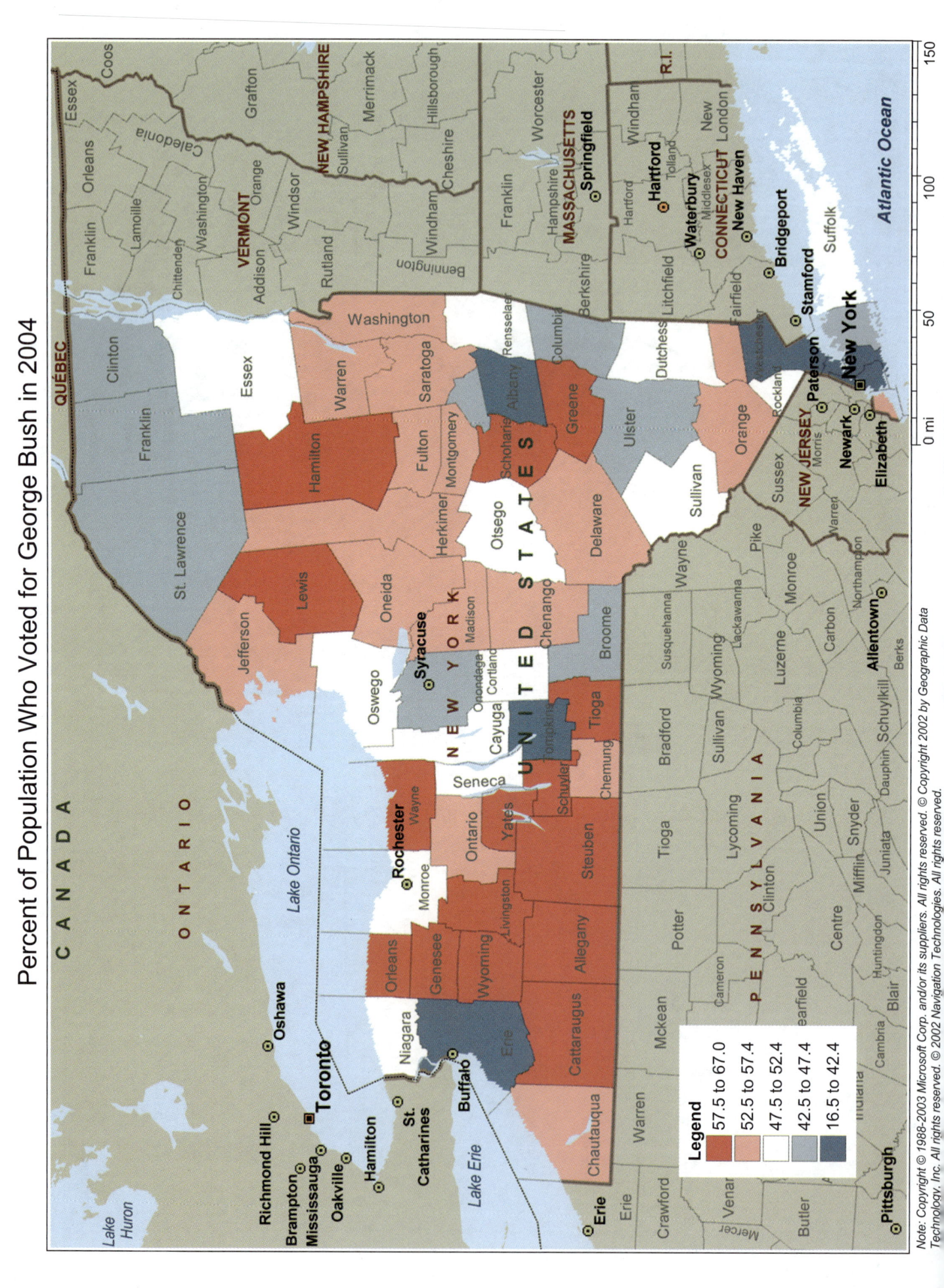